21st EDITION

THE GOOD SCHOOLS GUIDE

www.goodschoolsguide.co.uk

21st Edition published 2017 by Lucas Publishing Ltd
10 Greycoat Place, London SW1P 1SB

www.goodschoolsguide.co.uk

ISBN 978-1-909963-11-5 The Good Schools Guide 21st Edition

A CIP catalogue record for this book is available from the British Library

Typeset by Theresa Hare, Optima Information Design
Printed by BeamReach

A CIP catalogue record for this book is available from the British Library.

Design: David Preston, Harriet Plyler

Editorial review by Beth Noakes and team: Janita Clamp, Charlotte Phillips, Emma Lee-Potter, Kathryn Berger, Amanda Perkins, Helen Croston

Advertising sales by Charlotte Hollingshead and Jo Dodds, Publishing Matters

Project management: Katja Lips

Everything held together by: Shari Lord

Cover photos:

FRONT COVER

Eaton Square School, Whitgift School, Wellington College, King's Bruton, Loretto School, Parliament Hill School

BACK COVER

St Helen's School, Forest School

Acknowledgements
We should also like to thank the countless friends, pupils, parents, staff, moles – they know who they are but we're not telling – who contribute invaluably and to whom we are deeply indebted. Please keep the information coming.

Writers:
Ali Barrett
Ali Hutchinson
Alison Cooper
Alison Pope
Amanda Lynch
Anna Colclough
Anne Hadley
Anne Prendergast
Ashley Cavers
Bernadette Henniker
Bernadette John
Beth Noakes
Bethan Hutton
Carolyn Murphy
Carolyn Thomas
Catriona Prest
Charles Cowling
Charlotte Obolensky
Charlotte Phillips
Charlotte Simpson
Christine Jefferson
Claire Kingston
David Hargreaves
Deidre Shields
Elizabeth Coatman
Elizabeth Moody-Stuart
Elsa Booth
Emma Jones
Emma Lee-Potter
Emma Vickers
Faye Monserrat
Godfrey Bishop
Grace Moody-Stuart
Guy Canning
Hazel Davies
Jackie Lixenburg
Jane Devoy
Janet Breeze
Janette Wallis
Janita Clamp
Jill Kastner
Judith French
Juliet Austin
Kalantha Brewis
Karen Fitzpatrick
Kate Hilpern
Kate Symington
Linda Tanner
Lisa Freedman
Lucy Heywood
Mary Bremner
Mary Langford
Mary Pegler
Mary-Ann Smillie
Melanie Bloxham
Melanie Sanderson
Nicky Adams
Patrea More Nisbett
Paul Grahamslaw
Phoebe Bentinck
Ralph Lucas
Reena Shaughnessy
Richard Field
Rosemary Taylor
Sally McKeown
Sandra Hutchinson
Sara Dewar
Sara Freakley
Sarah Evans
Sharon Cowling
Sophie Irwin
Stewart Binns
Sue Fieldman
Susan Bailes
Susan Hamlyn
Suzanne Everest

Contents

A LEVEL RESULTS 2016
QE COLLEGE
Overall pass rate 100%
A*/A - A level results - 87%
A*/B - A level results - 98%
QE FACULTY
Overall pass rate 100%
A*/A - A level results - 84%
A*/B - A level results - 96%

"We were looking for our children to change schools. However in the independent sector this has financial implications. Our problems in this regard were solved by the offer of Day or Boarding Awards (our choice) for both children. They moved, are now happy, and doing very well. QE is growing in size because it is run in a refreshing, modern and much better way. There are plenty of day children."

Enjoy a 6th Form education at QE and pay no fees!....

Day Award up to £25,000, Boarding Award up to £65,000

If your child's GCSE grades are predicted

10 Grade A star GCSE's worth up to 100% of the fees

9 A star and 1 A Grade GCSE's worth up to 80% of the fees

8 A star and 2 A Grade GCSE's worth up to 60% of the fees

7 A star and 3 A Grade GCSE's worth up to 40% of the fees

Queen Ethelburga's Collegiate

Independent Education Girls & Boys 3 to 19 years Day & Boarding
Thorpe Underwood, Yorkshire. Phone: 01423 333 330
Email: info@QE.org Web: www.QE.org

Are we all about academics?

No, but were you aware the Daily Telegraph and The Times both rank QE College as the top most academically successful day and boarding school in the North for A*/ A grades at A Level and equivalent results and our Faculty of Queen Ethelburga's, the second most academically successful co-educational day and boarding school in the North for A*/ A grades at A Level and equivalent results?

Are we all about Sport?

No independent school in the North has the equivalent of our £30m Sports Village. A parent said we are now in a league above the rest. See: www.qesportsvillage.org

Are we all about superb facilities?

No, but we have invested over £80m in superb new teaching facilities and resources in the last 8 years - way more than any other independent school in the North.

Are we all about boarding?

No, but no one comes close to the quality of our boarding accommodation. The best in the UK. All bedrooms have private bathroom, air-con, TV, phone & mini-kitchen.

Are we all about day pupils?

No, but it is interesting to note our day fees are, on average, over 14% less cost than other local independent schools and our bus service covers a very big local area.

Is it all about Scholarships and Awards?

No, but then again who else offers over £3m in Scholarships and Awards every year? Even without any form of Scholarship or Award, sending your child to QE could save you between £3,000 and £7,000 in day fees a year, compared to elsewhere.

All of the above are perhaps the reasons why appreciably more parents have chosen QE this year than last year.

QE £30m Sports Village

Elite Sports Academy Awards worth upto £7,000

Day or boarding, upto 100%. Membership costs of Elite Sports Academies for: Athletics, Basketball, Cricket, Football, Netball, Rugby, Swimming.

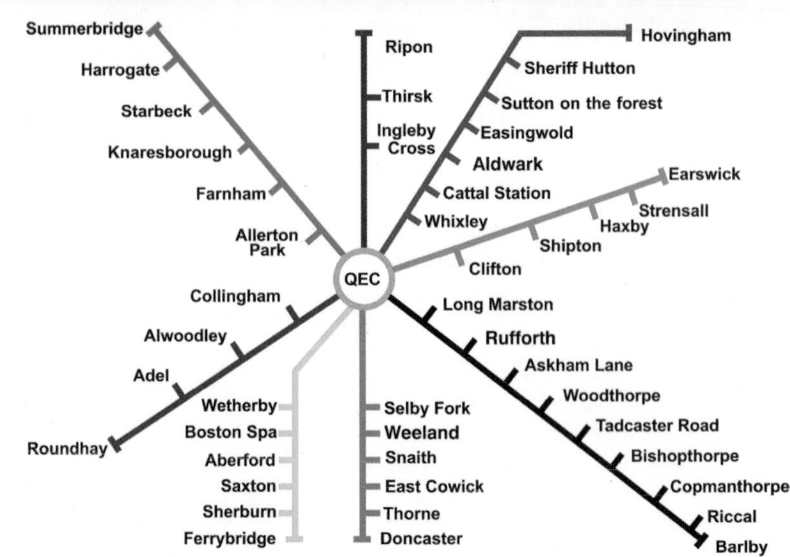

Key to symbols

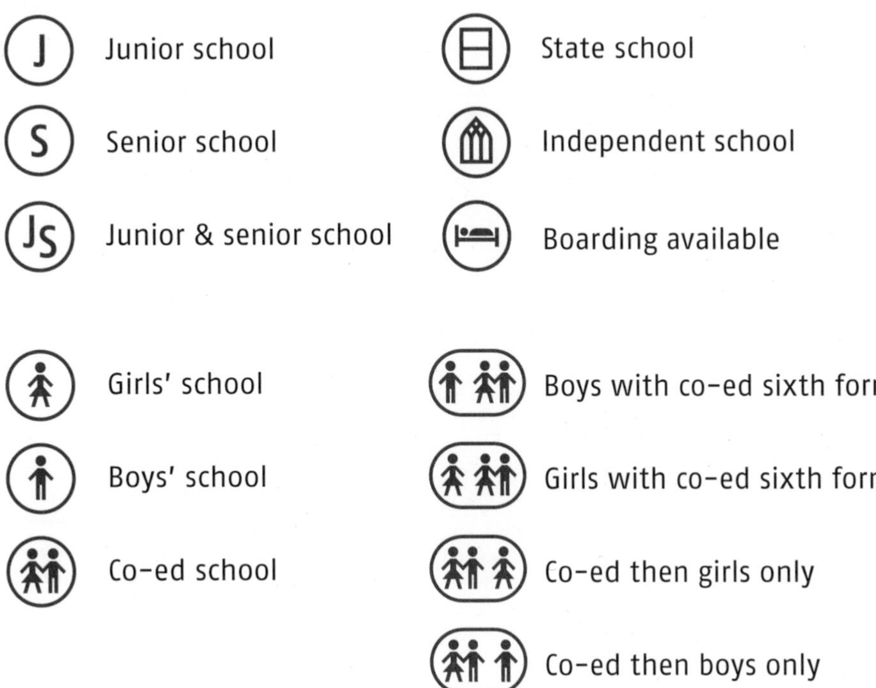

Map pin (reference number indicates school's position on the map at the front of the section)

Map of The Good Schools Guide regions

For UK-wide map of schools for special educational needs see p. 1855

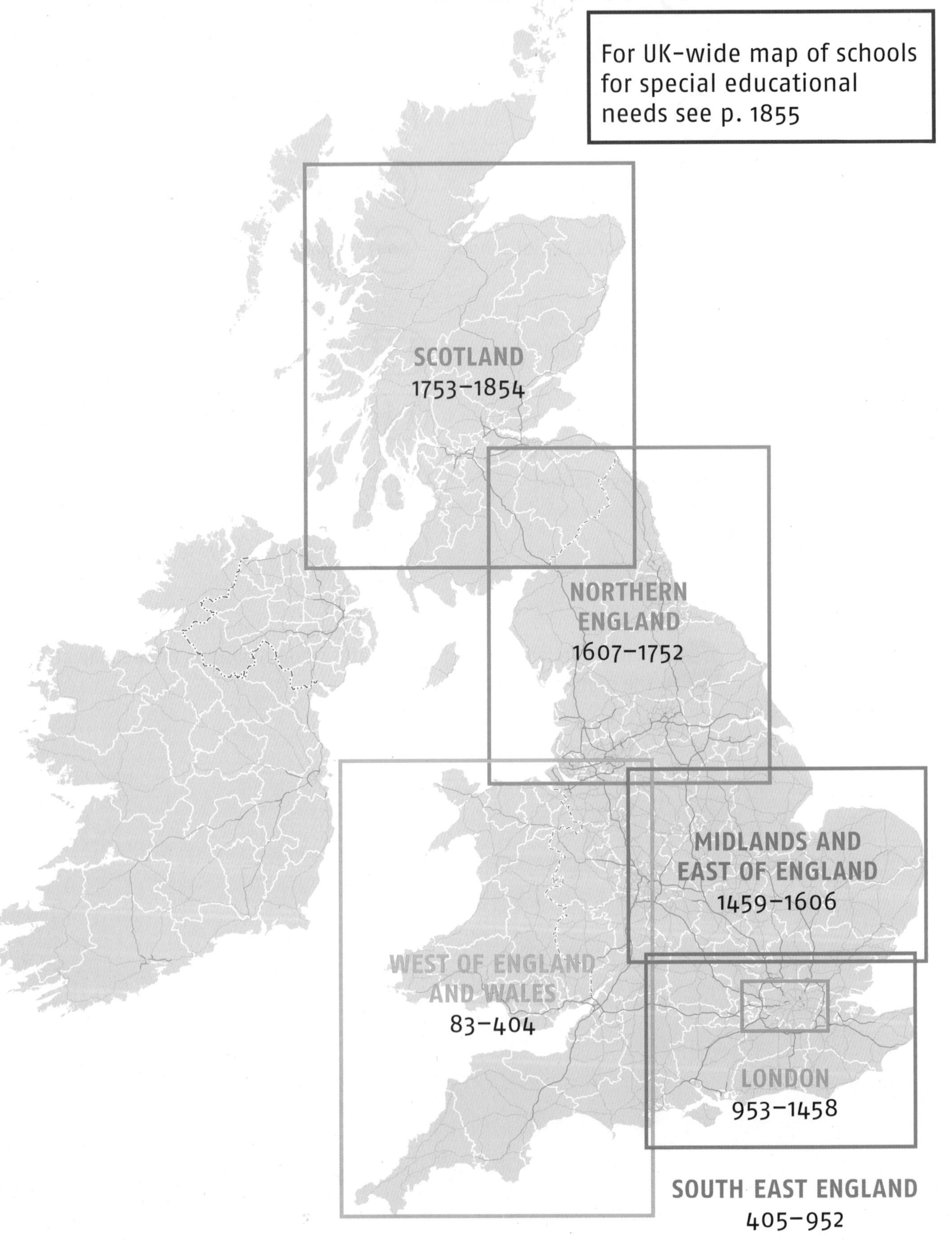

The Good Schools Guide charter

We take our independence very seriously and the separation of commercial and editorial content is absolute. No school can pay to be included in (or choose to be excluded from) The Good Schools Guide, and we do not charge schools for reviews.

In recent years we have helped to defray our costs by selling advertising space and licensing schools to reprint their own reviews for a fee. We make these offers only to schools that are already in the Guide on merit. Whether or not they choose to advertise has no bearing on their inclusion in the Guide nor on the content of their review. Schools we have not chosen for inclusion in the Guide are not allowed to advertise.

Our printed guides and website offer advice on a vast range of education matters. We also have a fee paying, personal consultancy service for parents (Good Schools Guide Education Consultants). We receive no commission nor any other payment from any school for these services. If you have any questions or concerns about our commercial policy, please contact **editor@goodschoolsguide.co.uk.**

Introduction

Welcome to The Good Schools Guide, founded 32 years ago by parents determined to find out what schools were really like, and which would suit their children best. That's still us. The schools in the Guide are here because parents tell us that they should be – and because parents come in a bewildering variety of flavours, so do the schools.

The Good Schools Guide reviews are as much about capturing the spirit and ethos of a school as they are about bus routes, uniform and facilities. Our writers visit every school and talk to heads, parents, teachers and pupils to build up a picture of the kind of place it is and what kind of child it would – or would not – suit. Browsing through the Guide is the best way we know to make a manageable shortlist, and to discover schools that you had never heard of but could be just right for your children. If you think we have missed a great school, please tell us. If despite deep study of the Guide you remain undecided, please ask: even a book of this size cannot accommodate the full breadth and depth of our educational know-how.

The weight of this book is testament to the number of fine schools in the UK, and to the quality of education they provide. Sadly, when we turn to the future things are looking considerably less positive. We think that state schools will find it difficult to continue the recent trend of improvement. They are facing real-term funding cuts of some £3 billion by 2020, from a combination of increasing but unfunded staff costs and a funding freeze despite inflation and rising pupil numbers. The 'fair funding' exercise will redistribute funding from schools in London and other urban areas to more rural districts. Sixth forms, whose funding has already been cut over several years, face an even bleaker future. Schools are cutting support staff, axing less popular sixth form subjects and asking parents for cash to make up the deficit. Some are replacing experienced teachers with cheaper young, newly qualified staff. Chronically underfunded FE colleges – historically always the poorest relation – are in no condition to take up the slack.

Funding cuts are also biting when it comes to providing support for children with additional needs. Following the legislation which introduced Education, Health and Care Plans (EHCP) in 2014, fewer children are classed as having SEN. The proportion has dropped from 20 per cent to 15 per cent, so many fewer children now have an automatic right to support. Schools are supposed to provide for children with milder needs out of their overall budget, but when that is being sliced every which way ... Meanwhile parents of the children with more severe needs, who should qualify for an EHCP, are finding it far too difficult to get one. Local authorities are failing to meet statutory deadlines for EHCP assessments, and we've seen plenty of anecdotal evidence (plus an in-depth BBC analysis) suggesting that councils are deliberately refusing EHCPs on first request, and subsequently, as a way of buying time and/or saving money.

Independent schools are facing, or at least ought to be facing, a self-imposed squeeze. A four-fold increase in fees in the last 20 years or so – often funding lavish boarding accommodation or super sports halls – has seen schools priced well beyond the reach of their once core clientele. Many of the accountants, doctors and country solicitors who would once have sent their children to private school now tend to aim at grammar schools or successful comprehensives. There is talk of fee-freezes in the head teachers' councils – and we can think of lots of ways that costs might be cut – but we will leave off believing it until we see it.

Financial pressure on families is shown in falling rolls at some northern and western independent schools in particular, resulting in mergers, closures and conversions to free schools. Meanwhile, the top London independents are experiencing ever-increasing numbers of applicants, as international families compete with locals for places. Several prep schools are expanding their age range or opening separate senior schools, and we will watch these with interest.

There is a welcome drive among independent schools to increase the number of bursaries they offer – we keep a close eye on this for our bursaries advice service. The Independent Schools Council has even suggested that the government should co-fund 10,000 new bursaries a year: Mrs May has yet to put her hand up for this idea, perhaps she's too busy with another hot potato of her own making – plans for more grammar schools.

On the brighter side, we continue to visit schools that delight us with their resourcefulness and resilience, their eccentricities, and their determination to provide a good, well-rounded education for all the children in their care regardless of DfE fads.

Speaking of which, the Gove reform tsunami has now reached the parental shore. Those comforting 'levels' have been swept away, GCSEs are no longer A* to G but 9 to 1, and it's all change on the syllabuses. Grab a firm hold of the Good Schools Guide life-raft.

State and private schools

The vast majority of children in the UK will attend their local primary and secondary schools. Around seven per cent of children are educated privately with some parents mixing and matching state and private provision.

The state system

State primary

Primary schools start at 3 (if they have a nursery class) or 4 and most run through to 11, though there are some infants' schools (3-7) and junior schools (7-11), often but not always linked with automatic entry from one to the other. Increasing numbers of senior schools are opening linked primary schools, and will eventually become all-through schools.

The cut-off date by age is 31 August in both state and private schools in England (though some private schools may be more flexible). This means that if your child's birthday is on 31 August they will start in the reception class when just 4, whilst a child with a 1 September birthday will actually be just 5 when they start.

> *If you are aiming at a selective secondary school you may have to rope in a tutor*

Virtually all British state primary schools are co-ed and non-selective academically, though faith schools mostly select by church attendance.

State primary schools may not have the specialist teachers, small class sizes or facilities enjoyed by private prep schools but the quality of teaching shouldn't be inferior. If you're lucky enough to live close to a good primary school and have a good state comprehensive down the road then your children's education is sorted. However, state primaries don't prepare children for 11+ entrance exams, so if you are aiming at a selective secondary school you will probably have to rope in a tutor in year 5 or so (see Tutors and Tutoring, page xx).

State secondary

There is a much greater variety of state secondary schools: single sex and co-ed, selective and non-selective, plus those that select a proportion of students on the basis of, for instance, academic, music or dance prowess.

The vast majority of secondary schools are non-selective. A few academically selective grammar schools remain in areas such as Buckinghamshire, Kent and Lincolnshire, and the government has plans to open many more. The BRIT school in south London for 14-19 year olds is the only state performing arts school in the

country with entry by audition. University technical colleges or UTCs, also for 14-19 year olds, specialise in vocational areas such as computing and engineering and have links with local employers. Studio schools are small schools for the same age group that include plenty of work experience alongside academia and vocational courses. Nearly all other secondary schools are for 11-16 or 11-18 year olds.

Some students move on after GCSEs to a sixth form colleges for 16-18 year olds. These tend to offer a wide range of subjects and to have an atmosphere more akin to a college than a school.

Academies and free schools

Increasing numbers of state schools – particularly secondary schools – are becoming academies. These are state funded but often run by academy chains, and the current government's aim is for all schools to become academies over the next few years.

Free schools were originally intended to be set up by groups of parents and some of the early ones were, though many were set up by religious groups, and now most have academy chain backers. UTCs and studio schools are both types of free school.

Both academies and free schools are outside local authority control, can decide on their own admissions criteria (though they should abide by the national code), do not have to teach the national curriculum and may employ unqualified teachers.

The private system

What's in a name?

Private school; independent school; public school. All three of these seemingly contradictory terms mean essentially the same thing: school fees.

Private schools charge for the education and facilities they provide. They do not have to follow the national curriculum which means that children at many prep (junior) schools do not take Sats. Senior school pupils do take GCSEs, A levels, Pre-U or IB examinations although many private schools favour the IGCSE (the 'I' stands for international) course which is regarded as somewhat more demanding. Private schools are not inspected by Ofsted although boarding facilities are subject to government inspection. The body that inspects private schools is the ISI (Independent Schools Inspectorate).

Pre-prep and prep schools

Private junior schools (boys', girls' and co-ed) usually take children from the age of 3 or 4 until they are 11 or 13. Some, called pre-preps, run from 3-7, and are often linked to preps that run from 7-13. These are likely to have small classes, specialist teachers and a relatively biddable intake. Don't assume the teaching will be better than at a state school – both sectors include those who would be better off in a different profession.

As the name suggests, prep schools prepare your child for entrance exams to secondary schools and advise on which are likely to be most suitable. A prep school is judged at least partly by its leavers' destinations, so it will do its best to ensure your child moves on to a decent secondary school, even if the head has to dampen down your expectations.

Senior schools

Independent senior schools range from the ferociously selective to those that provide a gentle haven from hothousing or social integration – with admissions policies to match. A glance at the league tables will give a clue as to the degree of selection they operate.

Historically, girls' independent secondaries have started at 11 and boys' at 13, but increasing numbers – especially boys only schools that have turned co-ed – are switching their main intake to 11, with shrinking numbers of 13+ places. Thirteen plus schools with linked junior schools will often offer 11+ places in their junior schools with guaranteed transfer to the senior school, mostly aimed at state school pupils and those whose prep school finishes at 11.

All of these seemingly contradictory terms mean the same thing: school fees

Some independent schools go all the way through from 3 or 4 to 18, which can provide welcome continuity and freedom from 11+ or 13+ selection tests. However, few guarantee that a child who is struggling academically will be able to stay on with their peers, and teenagers may well decide at 16 (particularly if they have been in the same single-sex school since 4) that the grass looks greener elsewhere.

Independent sixth form colleges

Independent sixth form colleges, sometimes called crammers, were originally set up to prepare students for university entrance, particularly Oxbridge. They still specialise in this field, generally offering a variety of routes that include full two year A levels and shorter courses for those who need to improve on past grades. Classes are small, the focus is on exam practice and extracurricular options are limited.

Choosing a school

What is a good school? Put simply, a good school is a school that is right for your child; a place where they will be happy and enthused about learning. Unfortunately for prospective parents, battling through the whirlwind of information, hype and conflicting opinions that swirls around any school makes choice far from simple. Here are some factors to consider.

Results

Schools tend to be judged by their results – for a state primary, that will be key stage 2 Sats, the maths and English tests children take in year 6. Plus the Ofsted grade – with an Outstanding rating the Holy Grail. These two are often interlinked, with Ofsted caring more about data progression in maths and literacy than whether it is a happy school with an enriching curriculum. Or, for that matter, whether it is doing a fantastic job in difficult circumstances.

For a private prep school, the 'results' are the secondary school destinations, and these, of course, depend on how selective the entry is at 3+, 4+ or 7+. But just because a prep has good links with a top public school and sends a large proportion of pupils there it doesn't necessarily follow that your child will be amongst them – or that it would be an appropriate destination. A middle-of-the-road child is liable to lose confidence rapidly if they find themselves bumping along in the bottom sets of a highly academic school. If you notice that your child is showing signs of finding learning difficult, do talk to the SENCo about how and whether the school can help.

Are children encouraged to find their voice, to sing and play instruments, to act and dance?

At secondary level, there is a plethora of data to ponder, including GCSE and A level/IB/Pre-U results and university destinations. Again, these will depend to a large extent on the level of 11+ or 13+ selection – or, in a state comprehensive school, to the affluence of the intake. And again, other children's results won't tell you how well your child will do at a particular school.

Logistics

If you have boys and girls, how important is it that they all go to the same school(s)? Co-ed schools, and particular those with a sibling policy, will make life and logistics easier. State primary schools, of course, are more-or-less all co-ed and give siblings priority. The more competitive preps may look askance at a less academic younger sibling. All-through schools may offer a seamless transition from 4-18, but bear in mind that most will renegotiate at some stage if your child is really struggling to keep up.

Unless you are prepared to be a long-term chauffeur, ensure that the school is easily accessible – whether by walking, cycling, public transport or school bus. It will be much less stressful for all concerned, and it makes for a much easier and happier life if friends are nearby.

If you are choosing a boarding school, bear in mind that there will be school concerts and matches, parents' evenings and quiz nights. Experienced boarding parents advise that 90 minutes is probably the maximum realistic travelling time from home.

Environment

If your child is a gentle soul who needs lots of encouragement, will they flourish in an overtly competitive environment – particularly if they are amongst the less able cohort in a highly selective school? Alternatively, a child who likes to be top may get frustrated in a laid-back school that refrains from rankings or competition.

If you are a family with bohemian leanings, you may not feel at home with a boater-and-blazer type of school where everyone leaps to their feet when the head appears. Similarly, those with traditional leanings may find a no-uniform, first-names only environment too unstructured.

However good the results, your child is unlikely to thrive in a school where a blind eye is turned to bullying and they have no-one to turn to. All schools have pastoral care policies, but how confident are you that these are put into practice?

Enrichment

A town school is unlikely to have green acres of playing fields on the doorstep, but does the school make the best of what is available, perhaps going off to a nearby park or sports centre for regular games or playtimes? Are children encouraged to find their voice, to sing and play instruments, to act and dance? Is their artwork proudly displayed?

There may be plenty of extracurricular activities listed in the prospectus or on the website, but do they actually happen? If Japanese or polo or orienteering are important to your child, check that the relevant staff member hasn't just gone off on sabbatical to New Zealand. If your child loves sport but is athletically-challenged, are there teams for all? Are the grade 1 recorder players given a chance of the spotlight, or just the music scholars?

Staff

The head may not be a brilliant public speaker, but you should feel they are steering the ship in the right direction. Do the children shrink away as they pass, or run up to share news? When you have a problem – and there are bound to be some – do you feel you could approach the head without awkwardness and be confident of a fair hearing?

Do staff seem friendly – to you and to each other? Is there a good mix of ages? A large proportion of very young staff can inject vigour and enthusiasm, but may signal that the school isn't willing to pay for experience and qualifications.

Feeling at home

It's vital to visit several schools, if only to compare and contrast. You'll know soon after walking in if the school is at least a possibility. Many independent schools have invested heavily in state-of-the-art facilities, but don't be swayed by glitz, unless this is indeed important to you. Does this feel like a place where you would happily drop off your child for years to come, confident not that it is the most fashionable local school, but the one where they are most likely to thrive?

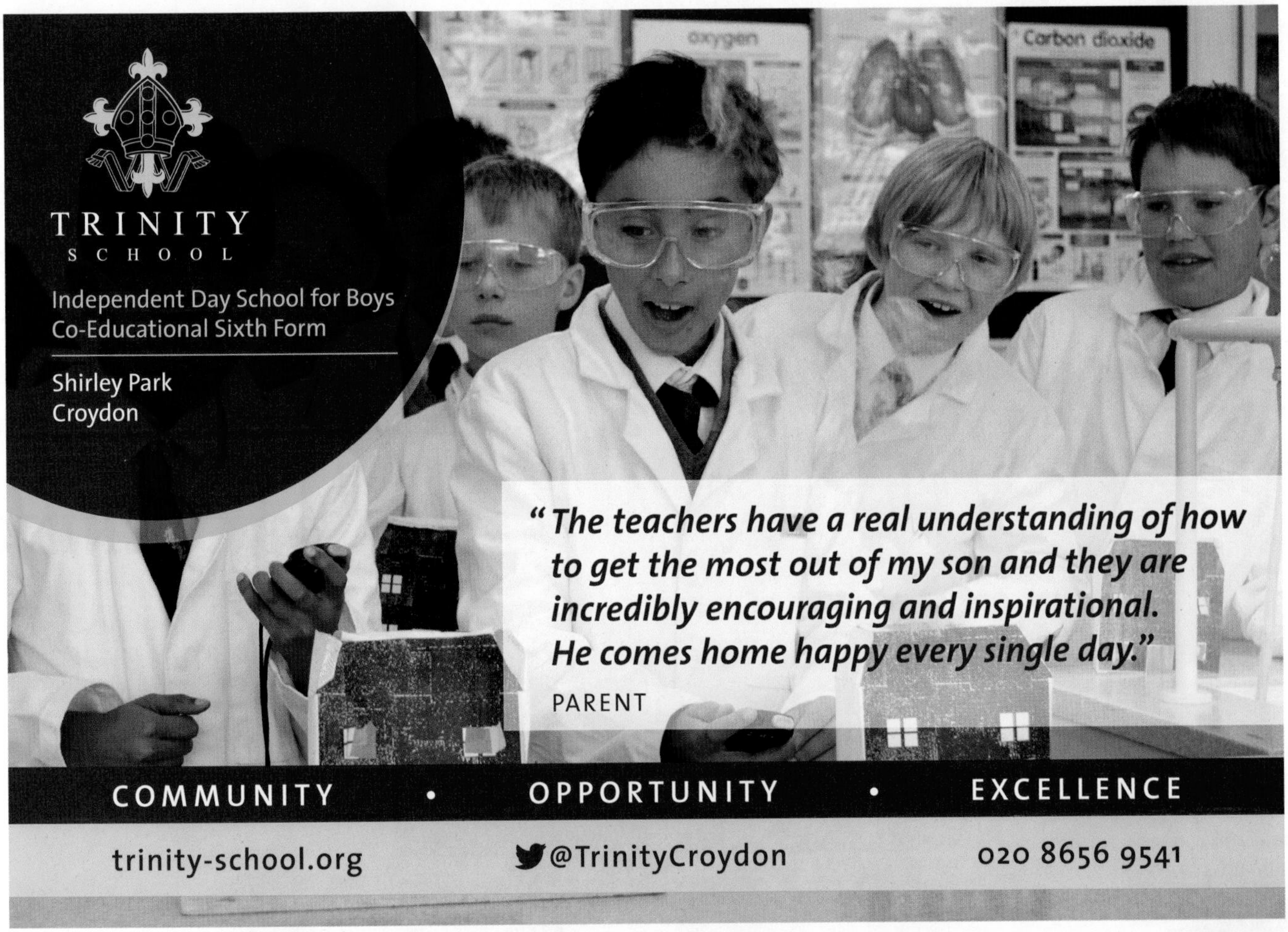
TRINITY
SCHOOL
Independent Day School for Boys
Co-Educational Sixth Form
Shirley Park
Croydon
"The teachers have a real understanding of how to get the most out of my son and they are incredibly encouraging and inspirational. He comes home happy every single day."
PARENT
COMMUNITY • OPPORTUNITY • EXCELLENCE
trinity-school.org
@TrinityCroydon
020 8656 9541

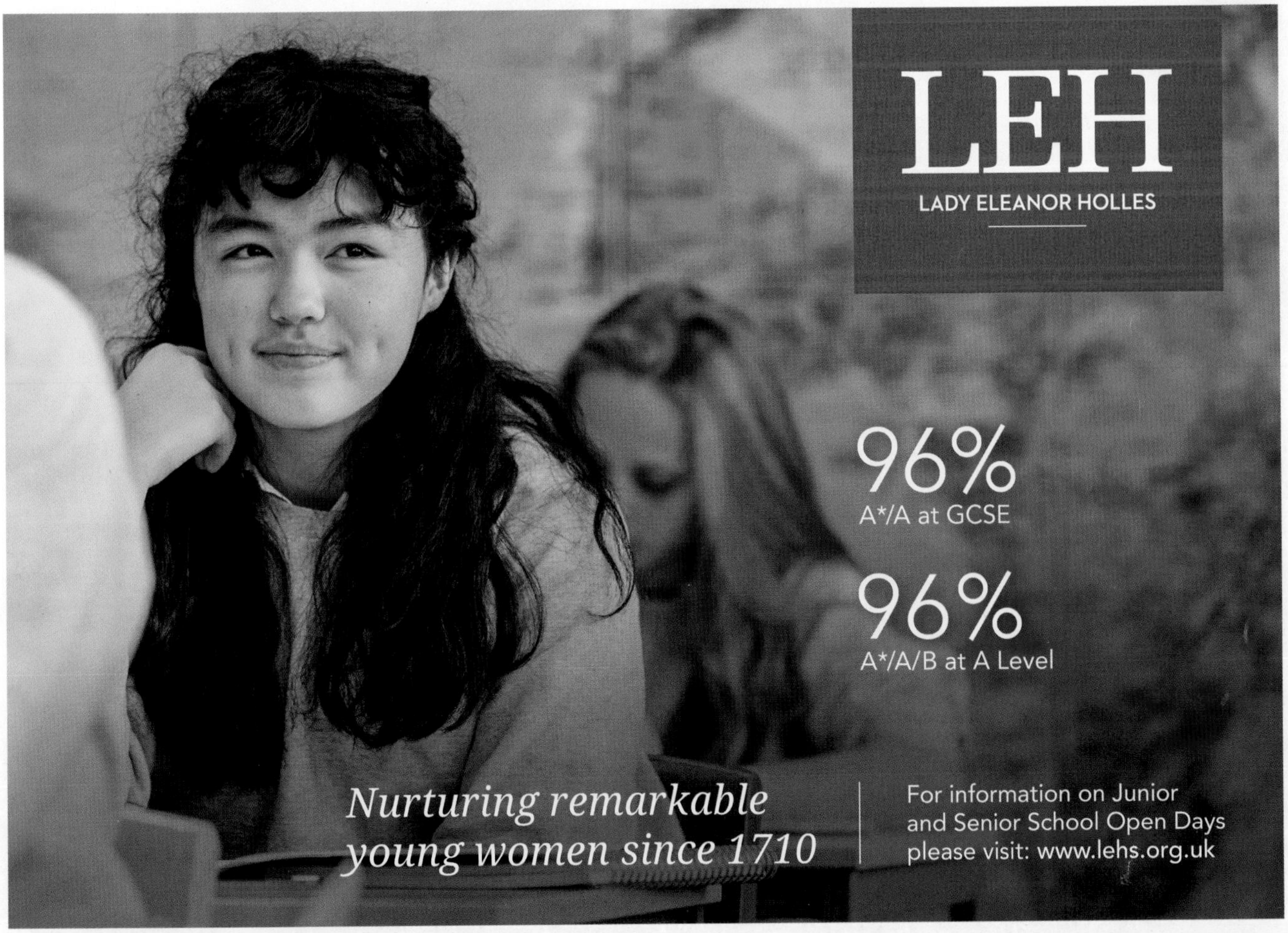
LEH
LADY ELEANOR HOLLES
96%
A*/A at GCSE
96%
A*/A/B at A Level
Nurturing remarkable young women since 1710
For information on Junior and Senior School Open Days please visit: www.lehs.org.uk

Applying to a state school

Choosing where you would like your child to take their first steps into school or spend their teenage years can be a nerve-wracking experience. For state schools, especially primary schools, where you live will be a deciding factor.

Location, location

The primary schools you are considering are likely to be very local. The main admissions criteria for non-faith schools are generally siblings and then distance – which can be less than a few hundred metres for the popular ones. Secondary schools are far more varied in their character and in their admissions criteria. These may also include academic selection and/or auditions for performing arts aptitude. You may be able to apply under more than one of these.

Timing

Applications are made through your local authority in the autumn of the year before your child starts school or moves on to secondary school. The cut-off date for secondary admissions is 31 October of year 6. For primary schools it is 15 January before the September start date.

If the primary school has a nursery class for 3 year olds you apply direct to the school when your child is 2; however, you will still need to reapply for a reception (4 year old) place via the local authority.

Academically selective grammar schools, and some that partially select by aptitude for eg music, now do their admissions tests/auditions in the summer term of year 5 or the September of year 6, so that they can give out initial results before the October closing date for applications. This will usually involve registering with the school during the year 5 summer term – so check dates carefully.

How do state schools offer places?

There are some general rules that most schools adhere to:

- Statement of special education need or Education, Health and Care Plan naming the school. These children come first in line and must be given a place.
- Looked after/previously looked after children. These generally come next.
- Siblings. These often, but not always, come third. Check carefully before you move miles away after your first-born has got a place.
- Exceptional medical or social need. This generally involves a letter from a doctor or social worker explaining why the school in question is the only

one that will cope with your child's needs. Very few children get a place by this route.

- Distance. Generally as the crow flies, but sometimes by the shortest walking route, Sometimes faith schools designate parishes, and other schools may designate particular areas as their catchment. Some secondaries have feeder primary schools. Grammar schools are increasingly limiting the distance applicants may travel to school. Your local authority should have information on how close you probably have to live to any individual school (except faith schools) to be in with a chance of a place.

Grammar schools

These are academically selective by entrance exam (usually some combination of maths, English and reasoning tests). Increasing numbers give preference to children who live relatively locally; some also prioritise students on pupil premium. You will be told if your child has reached the qualifying standard before the closing date for applications, but not if he will actually be offered a place.

Aptitude

Some schools select part of their intake by aptitude for eg music, dance, technology or languages.

Fair banding

An increasing number of non-selective schools use fair banding to divide applicants into ability bands, taking an equal number from each band.

Faith schools

These may demand that you baptised your child before she was 6 months old and have attended a specific church weekly for the past five years. They are no longer allowed to give points for eg brass polishing and flower arranging, felt to advantage middle class applicants.

Free schools and academies

These may set their own entrance criteria, though they should abide by the national admissions code. They, like most faith schools, also decide which applicants to accept (local authorities make that decision for community schools) and thus are vulnerable to accusations of cherry-picking easy-to-teach pupils.

Filling in the form

You can list of up six choices of schools, depending on area, and it's vital to include at least one where you are more-or-less sure of getting a place – even if it isn't your first choice. If you don't, you may only be offered an undersubscribed school some distance away. For faith schools, you will probably have to fill in a supplementary application form and get it signed by your religious leader. If a new free school is opening in your area, you will quite likely in its first year be able to apply direct to the school in addition to your six other choices.

NB Put your school choices in order of preference – if you qualify for places at more than one, you will only be offered the school highest on your list. The schools don't know where else you have applied, and don't know if you have put them first or last – only the local authority knows that.

Moving to the UK

As long as you have a right of abode in England, you can apply for a state school place here. However, you can't apply till you have an address in the country and are living here (except for Forces/diplomatic families and those applying to state boarding schools).

If you are applying for a school place not at normal admissions times – ie reception or year 7 – admissions will probably be handled by individual schools, though you will have to complete the in-year admissions form. Your local authority should be able to give your information on which schools have spaces, but it's worth contacting schools direct too.

Don't want the school you are offered?

You can appeal for a place at a school you prefer, but do it quickly. In the meantime, accept the school you have been offered (otherwise the local authority is under no obligation to find you a school at all). Ensure you are on the waiting list for any schools you would be happy with. And do visit the school you have been offered: you may find that contrary to local reputation, it is up and coming and will suit your child very well.

Applying to a private school

If you think a school might be a good fit for your child, request a private visit and make sure it includes time to see the head and watch the school at work. Each school will have its own entrance procedure but nearly all charge a non-refundable registration fee.

Preps and pre-preps

As their name suggests, the main aim of 'preparatory schools', or prep schools, is to prepare children for entry to fee-paying senior schools at 11 or 13. Traditionally, pre-preps take children from 3 or 4 and prepare them for moving on to preps at 7 or 8. There are fewer stand-alone pre-preps than there used to be as their main market, the boarding prep, has declined in numbers. Today, many pre-preps and preps are linked, with a more-or-less seamless transition between them and sometimes their senior school too. In London, with fierce competition for 7+ places at top prep schools, quite a few stand-alone pre-preps survive. Their raison d'être is preparing children for these competitive exams, which can mean the pressure starts in year 1 with regular practice papers.

Preps tend to stand or fall by their senior school destinations. Parents, whether they are aiming to get their 3 or 4 year old into the pre-prep of a chosen all-through school, or their 8 year old into a prep that sends many of its pupils to the top day or boarding schools, are generally looking ahead. Yet all-through selective schools rarely guarantee that children they take in at 3 or 4 or even 7 will have a seamless transfer upwards. If your child is felt to be struggling, you may well be advised to look elsewhere. Equally, a child who fails to gain a place at the pre-prep stage may well have developed sufficiently to sail in there or elsewhere later on. As ever, a school that helps your child to become a happy and confident learner is the best investment.

All-through selective schools rarely guarantee a seamless transfer upwards

Try to get a balanced view of the school – chat to pupils, staff, other parents and don't allow the marketing manager to dominate your visit. Before (and after), browse the website, prospectus and marketing literature – they'll all be glossy with happy, smiley faces, but do you like the tone and the events they put centre stage? Same old faces, same old names or a good smattering of faces, across the ages? Some preps are very traditional – blazers and boaters are often a clue; others more relaxed – sweatshirts could be a signal. You can probably tell, even without visiting, whether or not your family ethos is likely to be a good fit.

Entry requirements at age 3 or 4 vary considerably from 'first-come, first-served'

(this could in fact mean name down at birth, or depend on whether or not the head likes the look of you) to mini-assessment days complete with interview and observations to see just how well Harriet integrates with her peers and playmates. Few will expect children to read and write on entry but such is the pressure for places at favoured schools that, to the dismay of may heads, parents have been known to enlist the help of tutors for their 3-year-olds. In general the play and learning that goes on at home or nursery school should be adequate preparation. At age 7 or 8, nearly every prep school operates a formal assessment process.

Senior schools

If your child is already at a prep school then the process of selecting and applying to the 'right' senior school should mainly be taken care of – it's a large part of what you're paying them to do.

It used to be the case that parents rarely challenged a prep's advice about which senior school would best suit their son or daughter, but heads tell us that 'managing parental expectations' is now a significant part of their job. A prep school's reputation stands or falls on the destinations of its pupils at 11 and/or 13; prep school heads spend a large part of their time visiting senior schools and getting to know their pupil profiles. Experienced heads can spot which children should be aiming for which senior schools fairly early on and if this conflicts with parental ambitions then he or she will advise accordingly. No school will 'under sell' an able child, so if you disagree with the advice you have been given you should be able to have a frank discussion about the reasons behind it. The decision about which senior school to apply for should be at least as much about where a child would fit in and be happy as it is about academic ability.

Parents have been known to enlist the help of tutors for their 3-year-olds

State primary to independent senior

Plenty of children from state primary schools do move on to independent secondaries, often with scholarships or bursaries. It is not the state primary school's job to prepare children for independent school entrance exams, so most parents take on a tutor for a year or so to ensure their children are used to, say, writing a story in half an hour, and timing their answers. Neither can you expect a primary school head to advise on likely senior schools, so you will need to make your own judgement on which schools are likely to be suitable for your child.

Applying from abroad

The first step is often an online UKiset test which measures academic English language skills. Most schools will also ask overseas applicants to sit their own entrance test, and are generally happy to send tests abroad, though they may ask applicants to attend interviews in person.

Pre-tests

An increasing number of senior schools offer provisional places based on the results of 'pre-tests' taken in year 6 or 7 (age 10 or 11). Senior schools use these tests as a filter and to give an early indication of demand for places. Many prep school heads are concerned that pre-tests don't suit late developers (often boys) who may not come into their own academically this early.

Pre-tests are age-standardised and include multiple-choice tests in maths, English, verbal and non-verbal reasoning. If your son or daughter is offered a place after completing these tests, he or she will normally still be required to sit the common entrance examinations in year 8.

11+ and 13+ tests

The 11+ test is taken in year 6 and comprises papers in English, maths and sometimes reasoning. Some schools set their own papers, others are part of consortiums that set common exams and share results.

The 13+ common entrance is a test taken in year 8 for entry to many independent schools. Core subjects are English, maths and science and candidates may also sit papers in history, geography, modern foreign languages, , ancient Greek and Latin. Tests are taken at the candidate's own school and are marked by the school to which they are applying.

Most independent girls' and co-ed day schools accept pupils from age 11. There are still some traditional boys' schools such as Westminster and St Paul's and boarding schools such as Eton and Harrow that start at 13+. Thirteen plus schools with linked junior schools will often offer 11+ places in their junior schools with guaranteed transfer to the senior school, mostly aimed at state school pupils and those whose prep school finishes at 11.

Interviews

While state schools are prohibited from interviewing any but potential sixth form (or boarding) students, the interview is an integral part of nearly every private school admissions process, and tends to send the applicant's parents, rather than the actual applicant, into a spin. Parents feel considerably more responsible for their child's social presentation than for his or her ability to do long division or conjugate French verbs. And, while a school may breezily describe the interview as 'just a chance to get to know the child better', this hardly quells fears about sending young Daniel or Daniella into the lion's den.

Oversubscribed selective schools will often only meet the child after a written exam (generally used as a first edit), and the interview itself will probably contain a significant component of maths, comprehension or reasoning. The aim here is to probe intellectual strengths and weaknesses in order to select from the central bulk of candidates or to pick scholarship material. Finding out a little about a child's character is only of secondary importance.

Even the most academic schools, however, are not necessarily just looking for those guaranteed to deliver a stream of A*s. Some use interviews as an opportunity to create as balanced a community as possible:

Personality, of course, will always be the most variable aspect of any interview and all interviewers have a personal bias. They may hate boastful children, or those who say their favourite leisure activity is computer games; they may prefer Arsenal fans to Tottenham supporters; but some schools do make a strenuous attempt to counteract the sense of one adult sitting in judgement on one child. One senior school sees candidates individually before sending them off to a lesson where they can be observed by another teacher as they work in a group.

The best interviewers can and do overcome the limitations both of the written examination and of the child. 'Children, even very shy ones, like to talk about themselves, their friends, their families and their pets. I get them to describe what they did on Sunday, or I turn my back and ask them to describe something in the room. Sometimes I even get a child to sing or dance. I am looking for sparkly eyes and interest. If a child just sits there like a pudding, you usually don't take them.' Some schools get over the 'what to talk about' dilemma by asking children to bring along a favourite object. If, however, the child pitches up with a copy of Proust or boasts a collection of Roman ceramics, parents shouldn't be surprised if the interviewer is somewhat sceptical.

This hardly quells fears about sending young Daniel or Daniella into the lion's den

Although most heads are honest in their report about a child – after all, their reputation depends on it – the interview can also benefit them. 'Occasionally, a prep school head knows perfectly well that a child is not suited to our school, but the parents just won't listen. Coming from us it doesn't sour the relationship with the school.'

Parents, stand back!

Concerned parents often do their best to control the outcome of the interview, but professional preparation is seen as a waste of time, both by those who interview and by teachers. 'I always tell parents if they're paying to coach 3-year-olds, they might as well burn £20 notes,' said a junior school head who has the daunting task of selecting 40 4-year-olds from 200 applicants in a two-tier interview. 'The only useful preparation is to talk to them, play with them and read them stories.'

The head of a west London pre-prep does her best to relax the 7-year-olds she sends to prep school interviews by providing them with as much factual information as she can beforehand. 'I try to prepare them for what they'll find. I usually describe the head – because I'm a smallish woman they might expect all heads to be like me – and I'll tell them what the school looks like. Beyond that I just say, "Look them in the eye, answer carefully and be honest." Children sell themselves.'

Some pre-preps and prep schools provide mock interviews, some will carefully guide children on what books or hobbies that might show to best advantage, but most interviewers say they always know when a child has been coached, and honesty – at least in theory – is the quality they're looking for. 'I tell children,' says one private tutor who prepares children for 11 plus, 'to say what's in their heart, not what their teacher told them to say.'

Parents, step forward

Although the school interview is nominally about the child, the school is also interviewing parents and it's they who may need a little preparation while their child can happily be him or herself. A balance between supportive, respectful (schools are ever keen to avoid the pushy parent from hell) and interesting (but nor do they like dull ones) is best.

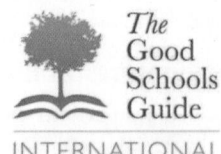

Catholic Day and Boarding School for girls aged 11 to 18

- Experience teaching the **IB Diploma** for over 35 years
- Exclusive pre-IB Middle Years Programme
- Nurture and support: girls gain excellent results
- Places achieved at top Universities worldwide
- Scholarships and bursaries available
- Multilingualism: up to 9 languages taught
- Internationalism: over 40 nationalities, yet one shared mission
- All faiths welcome

Please contact: admissions@marymountlondon.com www.marymountlondon.com Tel: 020 8949 0571
George Road, Kingston upon Thames, Surrey KT2 7PE.

Truly Independent

St Christopher School

LETCHWORTH GARDEN CITY

- Day and Boarding for girls and boys, aged 3 to 18
- Forward-thinking, creative and supportive environment
- Excellent teaching, successful pupils and fantastic facilities – all a short train ride from North London and Cambridge

01462 650947 admissions@stchris.co.uk www.stchris.co.uk

Boarding schools

It's fair to say that no other educational topic inspires such vehement and polarised opinions as boarding schools. But while the clichés of Dickensian cruelty remain deadlocked against those of St Trinian's and Hogwarts in the court of public opinion, a quiet revolution has taken place.

Boarding 21st century style

Boarding schools have changed beyond measure in the last 50 years, not least because all schools, and society, have done so too. Traditional full boarding schools remain, albeit in much reduced numbers, but for many children 'boarding' just means staying at school a couple of nights a week.

Boarding school heads tell us that the boarding family profile is much more varied than it used to be. These days it's likely that both parents are working – sometimes abroad or a long commute away. While boarding is still a tradition in some families, others come to it for the first time for a variety of reasons. Maybe your child has a particular aptitude – specialist boarding schools have the facilities and specialist staff on hand to develop sporting or musical talents. Families with several children may opt for flexi or weekly boarding because it's preferable to hours in the car on multiple school runs. Sixth form boarding is particularly popular and a great preparation for university – although some may find university accommodation less salubrious than their school's. In other circumstances a small, nurturing boarding school can provide stability and a haven for a child with special educational needs or an unhappy home life.

One thing that hasn't changed for the better is the cost of sending a child to boarding school, now running at £30,000+ a year. While this does not discourage applications from wealthy international families, there are real concerns that the middle class British parents, who for years have just managed to afford private education by scrimping, saving and remortgaging, are being priced out of the market. A few years ago, possibly because of the economic downturn, the boarding demographic in some schools was not well managed. While this may have secured short-term benefits, bursars quickly realised that parents – whether they come from Beijing or Bognor – want their children to be part of a diverse and well-integrated boarding community.

The clichés of Dickensian cruelty remain deadlocked against those of Hogwarts

Boarding, 21st century style, is flourishing. The number of families choosing boarding schools for their children is increasing and the decision to board is, as often as not, made by children themselves. This latest edition of The Good Schools

Guide contains reviews of over 300 boarding schools, from small country preps to some of education's most famous names.

What age to start boarding?

Most children start boarding at the age of 11 or 13. At this age children themselves tend to have a say in the matter. Indeed, Good Schools Guide writers report that children often ask their parents to let them board – rather than the other way round. Some prep schools admit boarders under 10 and make special provision for them with bedrooms that look much closer to how things are at home (rather than dorms) and, because numbers will be small, an evening regime that is flexible. At Horris Hill, for example, where they have a few boarders under the age of 10, 'if it's hot they can have a swim, if everyone's exhausted they go to bed early.'

The sixth form is another entry point for first time boarders. We visit many schools where there are more boarders in the sixth form than lower down the school – largely because 16 to 18-year-olds are keen to concentrate on their studies, socialise with their friends in their spare time and get a taste of living away from home prior to university. Sixth form boarders will generally have their own study bedrooms in separate accommodation with well-equipped kitchens (Ocado will deliver to boarding schools!), washing machines, even yoga studios. At Westonbirt school where over three-quarters of sixth formers board, one girl told us, 'there aren't so many distractions, it helps us stay focused on our studies.'

'We do not want to be a finishing school for the titled'

Today's boarding schools pride themselves on helping students become more independent before university. At Heathfield, an all-girls' boarding school in Ascot, Berkshire, girls in the upper sixth live in their own bungalow on site while Burford School, a co-ed state boarding school in Oxfordshire, has created a flat within the boarding house for a group of sixth form girls – to get them ready for the university years. At Rendcomb school in Gloucestershire groups of sixth formers take turns to stay for five days in the school flat in the nearby village. They are given housekeeping money and (apart from lunch at school) must manage this and the chores. Apparently sometimes it runs like clockwork, sometimes 'mummies deliver food parcels and help clean up at the end.'

What type of boarding? Full, weekly or flexi?

Once you've decided you'd like your son or daughter to board it's important to choose the arrangement that best suits your child. Unlike the old days, when families packed their little darlings off to school at the age of 7 or 8 and didn't clap eyes on them till the end of term, today's parents have a plethora of options – full boarding, weekly boarding and flexi boarding.

Whichever option you go for, there's no doubt that boarding schools are more skilled than ever at helping their charges settle in and feel at home. They run taster weekends, get new pupils to start before the rest of the school arrives and appoint buddies and mentors to guide them through the first few weeks and beyond. Pupils are encouraged to keep in regular touch with their parents – and it's not just a handwritten letter hastily scribbled before church on Sunday mornings either. Children can email, Skype and – if mobile phones are allowed – text or phone home when they wish.

Full boarding

Full boarding schools are in the minority these days but if you're looking for a school where everyone boards and there isn't a mass exodus at weekends, you still have quite a few options.

Boys' full boarding schools

These include many of the most famous names in British education such as Eton, Winchester, Radley and Harrow. Historically boys from upper class families were sent here to be educated as future leaders, statesmen, bishops and military commanders. Today boys compete for places from all over the world. The former head of Eton, Anthony Little, feels schools like his should be 'needs blind'. He told the Good Schools Guide, 'We do not want to be a finishing school for the titled and rich.' Noble sentiments and ones that wealthy schools such as his are trying to live up to with scholarships and 100 per cent bursaries.

At these schools all pupils board and may go home only for exeats, usually two per term, Saturday pm to Sunday pm. However, parents are more involved with school life than formerly; those who live close enough attend matches, concerts and plays. Technology enables much closer contact over long distances too, although boys whose families live abroad must still have guardians, either relatives or else professional guardians to act in loco parentis. Boys at these senior schools may well have attended full boarding boys' preps such as Cothill House and Horris Hill, or preps where boarding is compulsory for all in the last two years (6 and 7) such as Caldicott and Papplewick.

The boys are running around in the sunshine, surrounded by their friends

'I know that full boarding numbers across the country are declining, but I am certain that there will always be a place for schools like Cothill,' says headmaster Duncan Bailey. 'On summer evenings, when the boys are running around in the sunshine, surrounded by their friends, or building camps on the edge of the woods, there are few better places for any active boy to be – whatever their age.'

Girls' full boarding schools

Benenden is among the very few few exclusively full boarding schools for girls left.

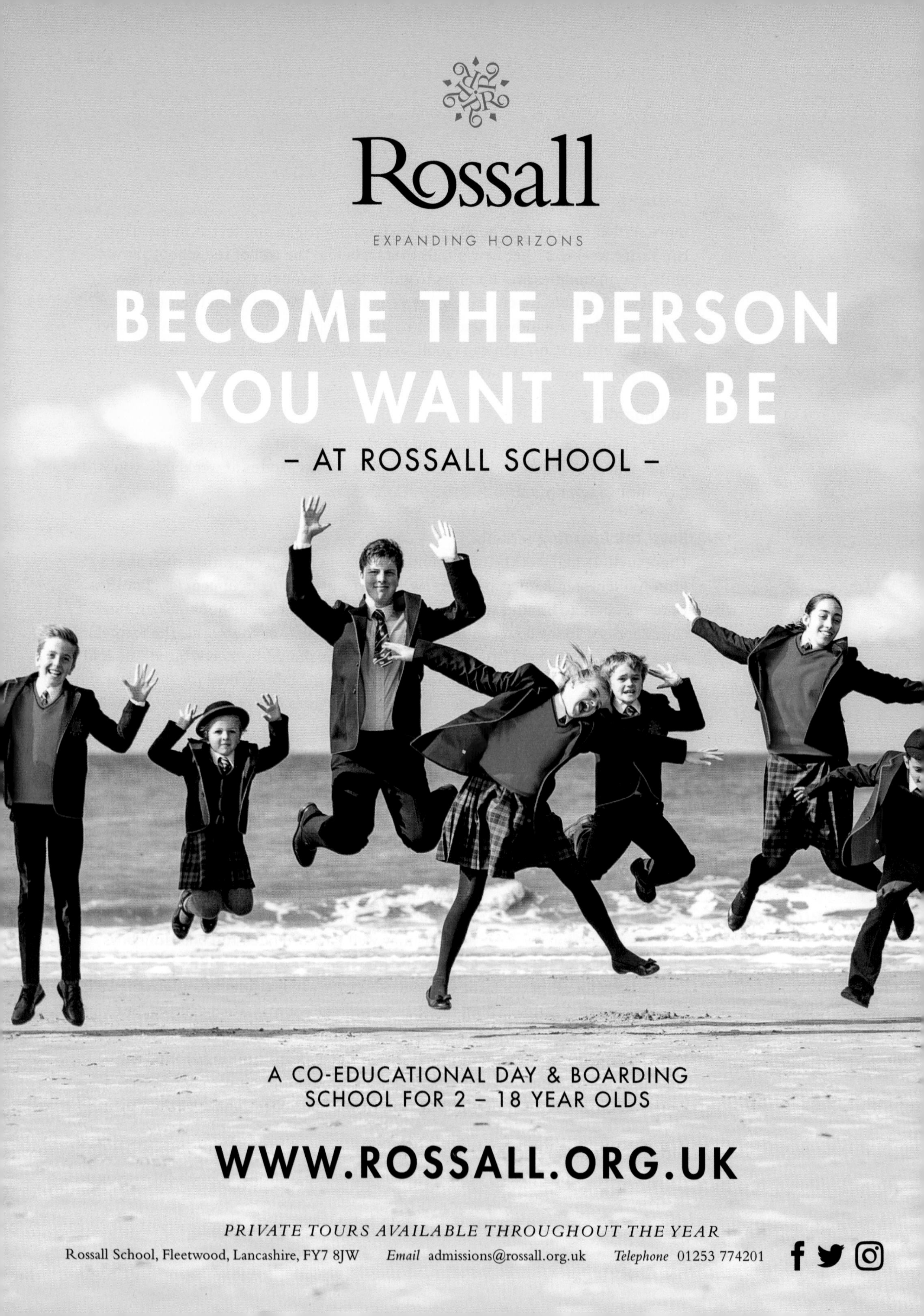

Downne House, Wycombe Abbey, Sherborne Girls and Tudor Hall are essentially full boarding (no flexi/weekly) but also take a few local day pupils. Hanford School in Dorset is one of a tiny handful of girls boarding preps.

The best known girls' boarding schools such as Roedean, Badminton and The Cheltenham Ladies' College were established in the mid- to late 19th century by formidable pioneers of women's education. This makes them relative newcomers compared to the likes of Winchester College, believed to be Britain's oldest school, which was founded in 1382. It also explains why most girls' schools lack the extensive property portfolios and endowments held by their brothers.

Co-ed full boarding schools

If you want your sons and daughters to attend a full boarding school together there are quite a few co-ed choices including Ampleforth, Milton Abbey, Uppingham and Marlborough College. Because of its proximity to London, Wellington College is de facto weekly boarding since so many pupils go home for Saturday night, nevertheless all boarders must spend two Saturday nights in school per term. All these schools also take a small number of day pupils but don't offer weekly or flexi boarding options. Girls and boys live in separate boarding accommodation with clear rules about what is out of bounds to visitors of the opposite sex. Some schools have co-ed sixth form boarding houses but boundaries are in place.

One prep school headmaster describes it as 'like glorified hotel management'

Weekly boarding

Weekly boarding is growing in popularity, particularly for children who live too far away to be day pupils or whose parents work long hours and/or frequently travel abroad for work. Weekly boarders either go home on Friday evenings or Saturday afternoons and return to school on Sunday evenings or Monday mornings. For many children, this offers the best of both worlds: they can enjoy school during the week, work hard and spend lots of time with their friends, then relax at home with their parents on Saturdays and Sundays.

Parents are keen on weekly boarding too. They like the fact that they don't have to nag about homework or getting up on time in the morning and feel that home time is 'quality time.' Many opt for boarding schools within an hour or so's drive so they can still turn up for sports matches, concerts and drama productions during the term. The mother of a year 7 boarder who drops her son off at Sexey's School (a state boarding school in Somerset) on Monday mornings and picks him up on Friday afternoons says her family gets 'the best of both worlds,' adding that with no Saturday school 'we get a proper family weekend.'

Flexi boarding

Flexi boarding gets a mixed press; parents are generally in favour but for some schools it's a step too far. One prep headmaster describes it as 'a bit of a nightmare, like glorified hotel management.' Unlike full and weekly boarding, one school's definition of 'flexi' may not be the same as another's. It's certainly never going to be bed and breakfast at the drop of a hat. Most schools require parents to book boarding nights at the beginning of each term, with Thursdays and Fridays being the most popular. Not surprising if it means parents can enjoy a night out without having to find a babysitter (and not have to get up for the Saturday morning school run).

While it can be complicated for schools to manage, flexi boarding could be just the ticket if your child has to stay at school late for sport, music or drama one or two nights a week, or if you want to dip your toe in the water and see if boarding suits your family. Schools that offer flexi boarding will inevitably have some spare beds and many told us that they will always do their best to accommodate a pupil at short notice if there's a family emergency.

Applying to a boarding school from abroad

British boarding schools have never enjoyed a higher international standing; each year thousands of pupils from all over the world come to the UK for a taste of boarding life. We're delighted to say that the experience for all boarding pupils, including those from overseas, is much better than it used to be.

Major rethinks on how pupils are cared for and substantial investment in facilities (much of it compulsory following the imposition of new regulations) have seen the best traditions retained but some of the less attractive aspects banished for ever.

Pastoral care is now given as much prominence as academic standards. Newly refurbished accommodation is bordering on luxurious (but don't expect many en-suite bathrooms) and the transformation of school food is nothing short of miraculous, though fish and chips and custard – separately, of course – remain culinary fixtures.

But before completing the registration form and committing your sizeable deposit, it's worth double checking that you know exactly what you are buying and whether it will suit your family.

English language support

The vast majority of international pupils follow a mainstream curriculum and work towards standard 16 and 18 plus qualifications. For those whose English isn't yet quite good enough or whose previous education puts them behind others of the same age, extra support from teachers who specialise in EAL (English as an Additional Language) may be needed.

Some schools run separate classes in key subjects, structured to allow more time for the language component so that maths and science students, for example, have sufficient understanding to decode word-based problems. These classes may be charged as an extra cost so check what's included in the fees.

A growing number of independent schools run international study centres aimed at preparing overseas pupils who are not yet fluent in English for mainstream schools. Alongside intensive English language tuition, many offer GCSEs or IGCSEs. If you are considering one, find out about their leavers' destinations. If most don't move into the mainstream school, where do they go, and how much help do they get?

Check also how much interaction the study centre pupils have with their mainstream peers. Do they share sports, clubs, outings, accommodation? Who is around to socialise with during evenings and weekends?

Social life

While the academic side of boarding is undoubtedly important, the social dimension is just as vital. An isolated child is rarely a very successful one. Schools with substantial numbers of international pupils will invariably portray themselves as a glorious melting pot where nation speaks unto nation and pupils leave with their ideals intact, their horizons and tolerance vastly expanded and a lifetime of reunions all over the world to look forward to. In many cases, when a school selects a blend of nationalities, such as at UWC Atlantic College, this is exactly what happens. Good Schools Guide reviewers regularly hear of enduring friendships that span religious or cultural divides, or of lessons enriched by pupils on opposite sides of wars, sanctions or economic policy.

It works less well when a school operates a monoculture policy. A large number of pupils from one nation in a single year group may help fend off homesickness but can also reduce the motivation for pupils to immerse themselves in their host country's language and way of life – an opportunity lost rather than gained. It's okay to ask admissions staff for numbers if you're at all concerned. Similarly, a school where the number of overseas pupils is so small that they are swamped by the prevailing culture can also lead to a miserable experience – particularly if they are the only full boarders in the place at weekends while everyone else goes home. Immersion is one thing, invisibility quite another – so it's also essential to find out just how many pupils of your child's age are around over the weekend. Many schools start off with a packed house for Saturday morning lessons or matches but empty out seconds after the final whistle (or bell) sounds.

Pupils can form enduring friendships that span religious or cultural divides

Exporting education – big names abroad

Finally, for those happy to ditch some of the trimmings, it's increasingly possible to get the ethos, results and teaching quality of a traditional British education without travelling anywhere near the UK. Over the past few years, some of the most famous names in education have opened offshoots overseas. You can get a Harrow education in Bangkok, Beijing or Hong Kong, become a Haileybury pupil in Kazakhstan and or sign up for Cranleigh or Brighton College in Abu Dhabi. Ethos and teaching standards are recognisably the same even if the facilities (sport is often air-conditioned and inside, for example) aren't.

Be careful when employing agents

There are many agents, 'consultants' or educational firms who will offer to find your child a place in a UK school. If their service is free of charge to you, the agent may well be getting a commission from schools; this means that you will be guided to apply only to those schools the agent represents, whether or not they are right for your child. Similarly, firms or individuals charging a fee for securing your child a 'guaranteed' school place should also sound alarm bells. Reputable schools do not give agents (or anyone else) 'guaranteed' places. Speak to the schools yourself.

Remember ...

- Big names are attractive but famous isn't always best. A school may be trading on past glories rather than future brilliance, so check whether you're being sold the up to date version.
- Look past fabulous exam results. Top schools do well because they select top pupils. What it proves is that parents of the brightest children send them here. It doesn't necessarily tell you how well it teaches them.
- Do visit any school you are interested in, and bring your child if possible. No prospectus, however glossy, beats experiencing a school in the flesh.
- Check how EAL provision (if required) is organised. Ideally, ask to sit in on some lessons to give you an idea of the standards/commitment and enthusiasm you'll be getting – and try to talk to similar pupils.
- Consider applying for scholarships if your child is outstanding (academic, musical and sporting excellence are the norms) and ensure that your idea of excellence is the same as the school's but...
- Don't be won over by worthless scholarships, sometimes offered as an incentive by schools to seal the deal.
- The key entry points into UK schools are at age 11, 13 or 16. Many schools will look at potential pupils outside these times, but bear in mind that it's often on a one in, one out basis – places become available only if another family leaves.
- Check how often a child won't be boarding. Half terms, bank holidays and occasional weekend exeats all add up to a considerable chunk of time when pupils aren't in school and will need somewhere else to stay. A guardian – or local friends or relatives – is essential but you may also want to ensure family visits coincide with these dates.

SHIPLAKE COLLEGE
HENLEY-ON-THAMES

Boys (11-18) and girls (16-18)

Beautiful riverside site near Henley-on-Thames

Easy access to M4 and M40; 30 minutes from Heathrow

Early assessments available for Year 9 boarders

'Excellent' across all nine ISI inspection categories

www.shiplake.org.uk

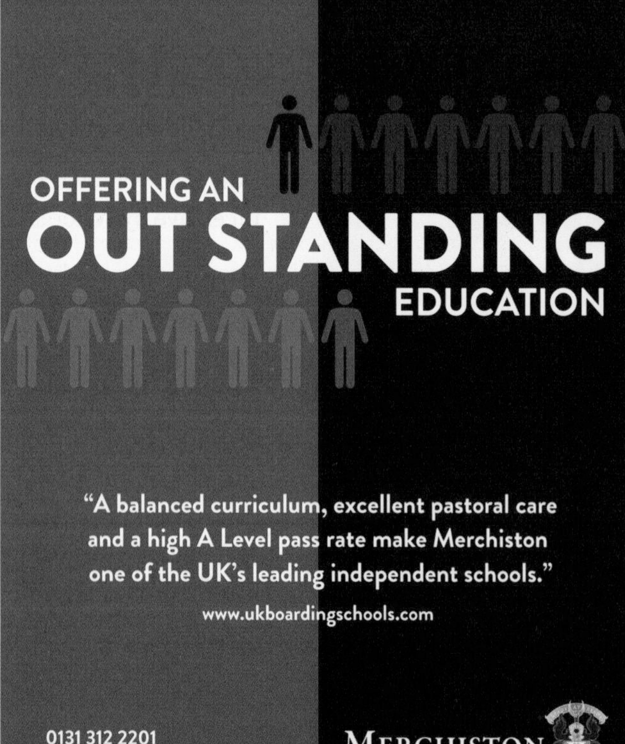

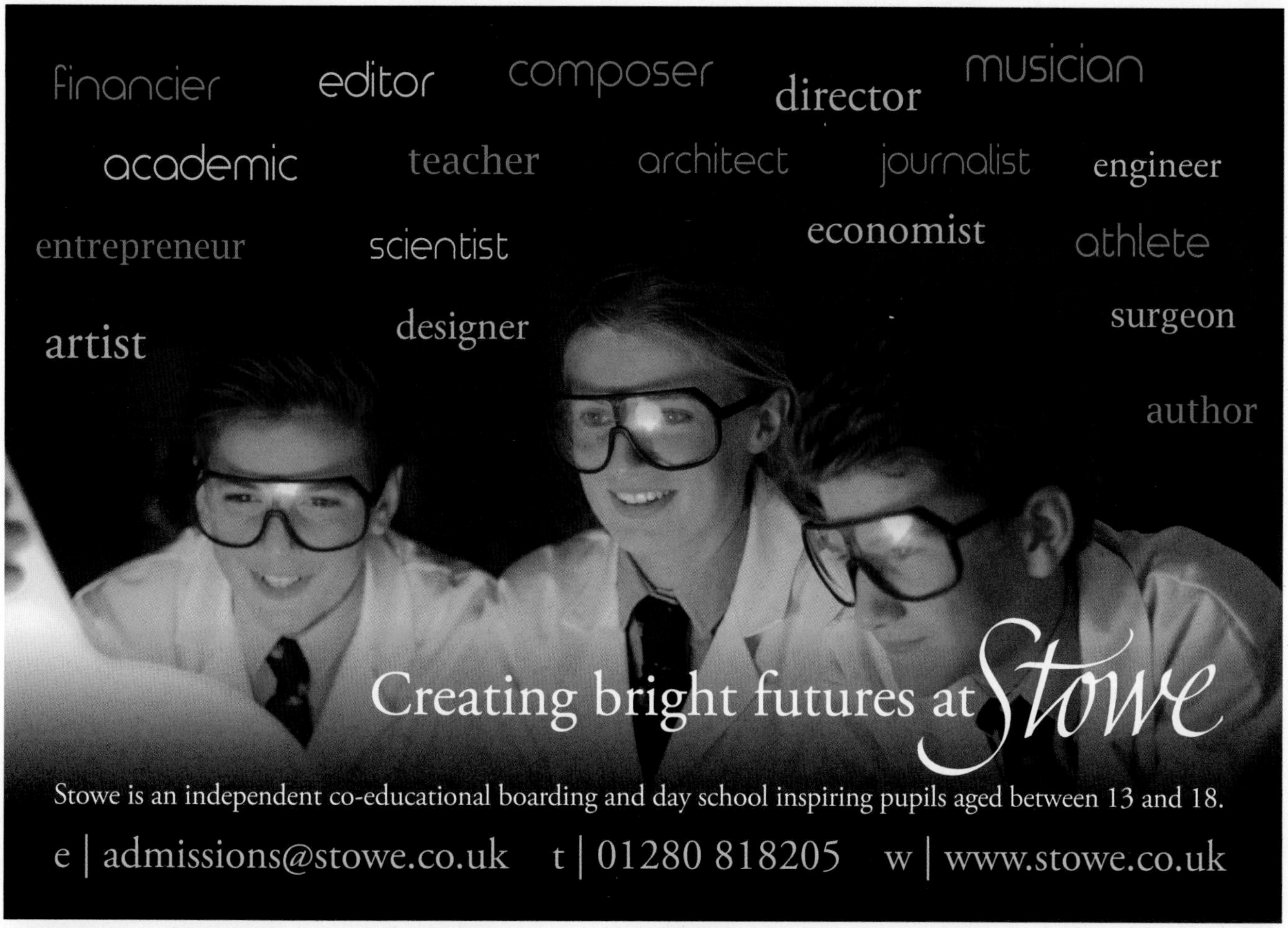
financier
editor
composer
director
musician
academic
teacher
architect
journalist
engineer
entrepreneur
scientist
economist
athlete
artist
designer
surgeon
author
Creating bright futures at Stowe
Stowe is an independent co-educational boarding and day school inspiring pupils aged between 13 and 18.
e | admissions@stowe.co.uk t | 01280 818205 w | www.stowe.co.uk

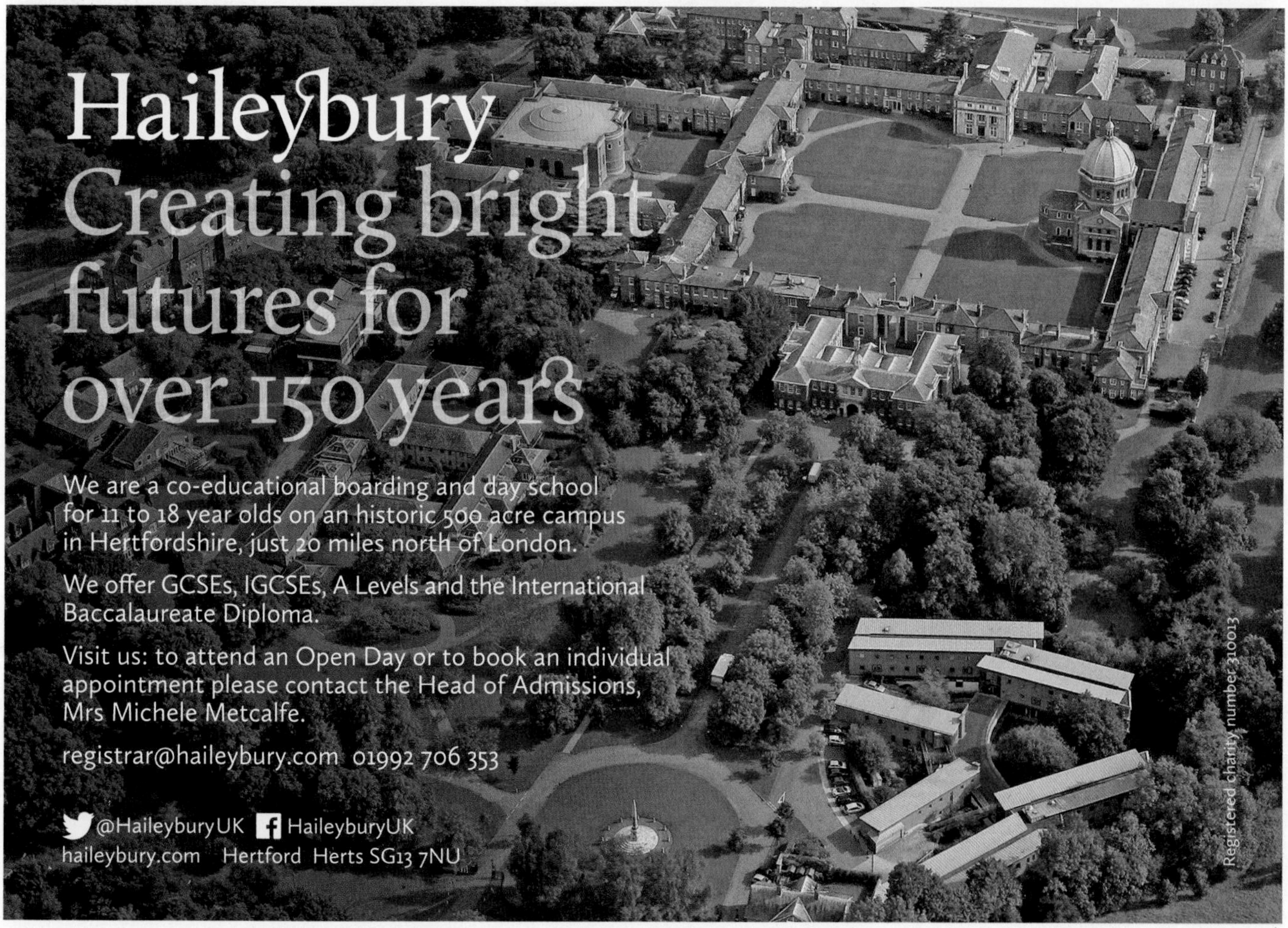
Haileybury
Creating bright futures for over 150 years
We are a co-educational boarding and day school for 11 to 18 year olds on an historic 500 acre campus in Hertfordshire, just 20 miles north of London.
We offer GCSEs, IGCSEs, A Levels and the International Baccalaureate Diploma.
Visit us: to attend an Open Day or to book an individual appointment please contact the Head of Admissions, Mrs Michele Metcalfe.
registrar@haileybury.com 01992 706 353
@HaileyburyUK HaileyburyUK
haileybury.com Hertford Herts SG13 7NU
Registered charity number 310013

Tutors and tutoring

Tutoring is endemic in the UK these days; in London the top agencies have parents queuing up to pay £80+ an hour to buy their child an advantage. They'd have you believe that without a tutor your toddler will miss the academic boat, but keep your head – there's still plenty of time.

Two is too early

Seriously, there are folks out there offering to tutor children as young as 2, but don't be taken in. Spend the money at a wonderful bookshop and read to your child instead. What pre-school-age children need is not tutoring and angst, but time and love from the grown-ups who care for them. If you're reading this article, you are by default an educated, thinking parent who wants the best for your child, so give her the treasures of your mind, your vocabulary, your tastes; they will far out-class anything a tutor can provide.

A clear reason

When do you need a tutor? Put simply, when there is a clear and specific reason for using one. Your child may need help with the 11+ or 13+ entry to an academically selective senior school. Or perhaps he's struggling with a particular GCSE/A level subject. Or she may be falling behind at school. Or he may have missed school through illness or some other crisis. Where there is a known goal to work towards, or a genuine problem to address, tutoring comes into its own.

For a shy child who's under-performing, a friendly tutor can be a godsend. Free from the distractions of the classroom and other pupils, he or she can sit quietly with your child and concentrate solely on whatever's confusing her, filling in gaps in her knowledge and building up her confidence. Grades start to improve, and the child becomes a happier learner, keener to put her hand up in class and more relaxed about going to school. For a teenager who's struggling with maths, demoralised by always coming last in his set and stressed about approaching exams, quality one-to-one teaching from someone with no preconceptions about him can make the difference between failure and success; between giving up and keeping on.

Spend the money at a wonderful bookshop and read to your child instead

Or it could be that you're putting your child through the state system to begin with while you save up for the independent senior school you hope he'll attend. But an over-stretched primary school teacher, with 30 children to get ready for their Sats, will have no interest in helping Harry prepare for independent school entrance, and even mention of the local grammar school is unlikely to get a sympathetic response. After all, from her perspective, selective education isn't what school's about. No matter how bright your child is, he'll be up against other children who have been intensively coached so tutoring is pretty much essential unless you are confident about your ability to fill in gaps.

A real need

Perhaps you feel your child needs a tutor even though he's already at a good preparatory school. Well, maybe. Be very sure, though, that the need is real. Parents of privately educated children are already paying for their child's education twice, once through their taxes and once through the school fees. Do you really want to make it three times? Depending on where he is, a year's tutoring in the run-up to common entrance may make sense, if only because it'll bring you peace of mind. But to have your tutored 7-year-old win a place at a high-achieving prep and then immediately start having him tutored some more just because everyone else is doing it, will only exhaust him and your bank account. Wave him off to St Brainiac's with a proud smile, and let the school do its work.

They don't choose to spread it around that their child struggles at school

On the other hand, if you've just relocated to the UK from overseas, using a tutor is an excellent way to get your kids up to speed with the English system and help them to feel more assured and comfortable in lessons. This in turn will help them to make friends, and the whole settling-in process will be smoother. For a child in a new country, confidence is key.

Where to look

If you want a tutor for your child, how do you find one? The best way should be word of mouth, of course. However, tutoring is one of those things parents usually do in secret, either because they don't choose to spread it around that their child struggles at school, or because they've no wish to increase the opposition's chances in the race for places. Try asking a friend with an older child, who won't begrudge your using what they no longer need. If this doesn't bring results, don't worry.

Tutor companies

The first of these is to approach a tutor company – we review many of the best of these on the Good Schools Guide website. A reputable agency will be skilled at matching your child to the right person, and will give you redress if you're not happy. The work of looking will be taken off your hands, and, since the tutors usually come to you, the whole process becomes very straightforward. Most are London based however, and this is the most expensive way of employing a tutor.

Almost all companies will charge you a registration fee, which can be anything from a few quid to a hair-raising £180, and the hourly rate for tuition will be high (be prepared for at least £45), because the company will take a cut before paying the teacher.

Some of the really big tutorial companies cover too wide a geographical area to interview all their tutors in person, but they will have interviewed them by phone, and checked their references and DBS record.

Online search

A cheaper option is finding a tutor online. Tutors often advertise their services via websites which usually charge around £20 to put you in touch with someone who seems suitable. The website companies run checks to ascertain whether the tutor advertising is who they claim to be, but otherwise it's down to you to judge people's suitability. Use your common sense. If a person's replies to your messages are semi-literate, don't engage them as an English tutor. Tuition rates vary from around £16 ph – probably an undergraduate trying to earn a bit of extra cash – to £45+ ph for an experienced and qualified teacher.

Do your homework

Whether you're paying top whack for Kensington's finest hand-picked Oxbridge scholars, or searching through the online jungle with only your five wits to guide you, there are some measures it's sensible to take. After all, this is your child. Self-employed individuals are unlikely to be DBS-checked, because the law prevents them from running a check on themselves, so ask to see references or to speak to previous clients. In fact, do this even if they are DBS-checked. Interview the tutor on the phone before fixing a first date, and don't feel pressured into accepting someone who doesn't sound right. Don't be afraid to sit in on the first lesson, and afterwards ask your child what she thought. If the tutor is travelling to you, check that they can get there easily. Lastly – and this wisdom comes from years of weary experience – insist on punctuality. A tutor who is routinely late will soon drive you up the wall.

If a person's replies are semi-literate, don't engage them as an English tutor

In short, if you do your homework your child's tutoring experiences should be happy, productive and affordable. Good luck.

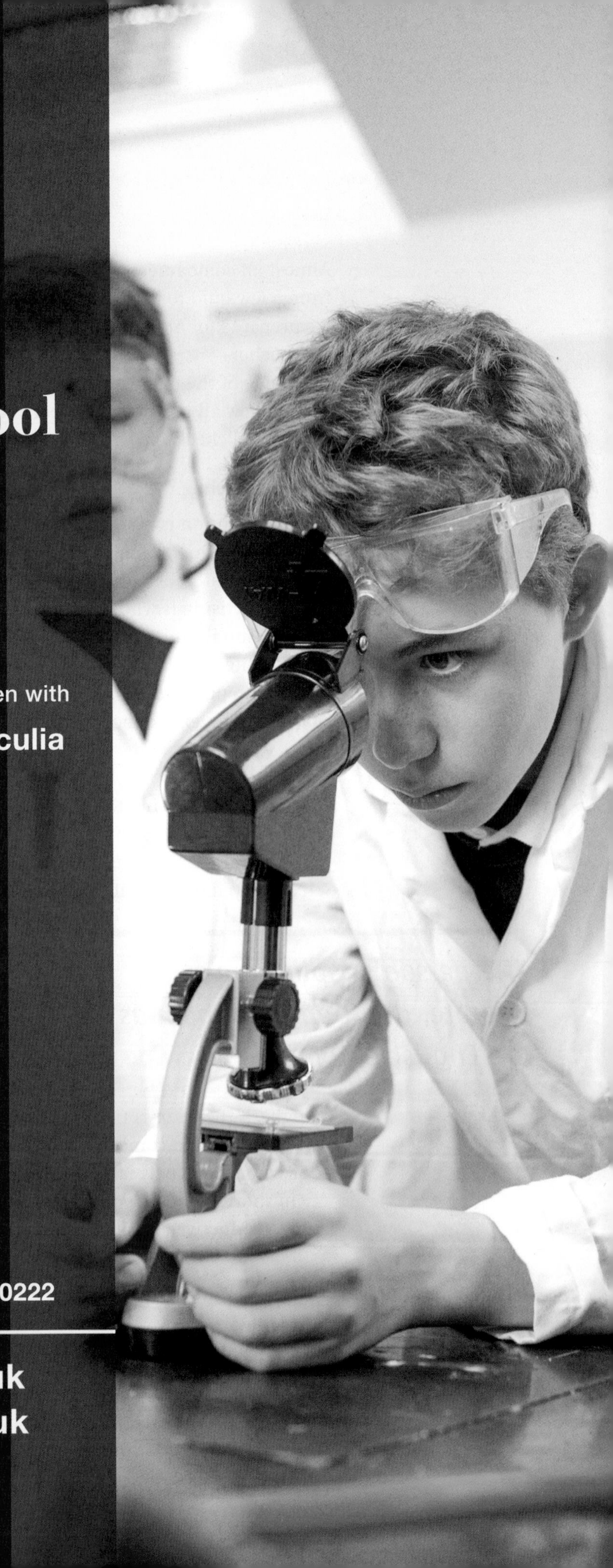

Children with special needs

The scramble for school places has an extra layer of complexity when your child has additional needs. It's not just the decision between state and independent, but also between mainstream and specialist. While mainstream schools will all talk the talk about inclusive education, finding those that truly do well by special needs children is another matter.

How do I know whether my child has special needs?

If your child has a difficulty that makes learning harder for them than most children of the same age, then they may have a special need. Sometimes the difficulties are apparent from early childhood, but other conditions such as mild autism spectrum disorders, auditory processing difficulties or dyslexia may not become clear until well into their schooling. And other factors outside of any disability can affect a child's ability to learn and can be counted as a special educational need – such as mental health disorders, or the after-effects of early trauma in adopted children.

Signs of an undiagnosed special need include poor school performance which does not tally with the child's general ability; frequent reports of misbehaviour or failing to pay attention in class; a dislike of going to school, or onsets of headaches/tummy aches when it is time to go to school; refusal to put pen to paper, even though articulate; regular clashes over homework; poor handwriting, presentation and pencil grip; difficulties in understanding the nuance in language, social expectations, or making friends; clumsiness or lack of spatial awareness; and feelings of frustration or anxiety which may manifest as angry outbursts.

Specialist school places are expensive, so you may have to fight for state funding

If your child needs extra help at school he will be far from alone. Between 15 and 20 per cent (depending on whose statistics you believe) of all children have some form of additional need. Around three per cent have more significant needs, and this is the group that qualifies for an Education, Health and Care Plan (EHCP), which can provide the funding for a special school place or additional help within a mainstream school, and the ability to take priority in school admissions. Those who do not qualify for an EHCP receive support from the school's own resources under a system known as SEN Support, and they are subject to the same admissions criteria as other children.

Where do I go for help?

For a young child, your GP or health visitor can advise on specialist assessments, for example from a speech therapist where there are possible issues with speech and language, or an occupational therapist for concerns over co-ordination. Be warned that waiting times to see NHS therapists are lengthy, and if you can possibly afford it, it will be worth organising one privately.

For a school age child, your first port of call should be the class teacher or the school's special educational needs co-ordinator (SENCo). They may suggest an assessment by an educational psychologist which will be able to identify any difficulties. Once again there can be a lengthy wait to see a local authority one, and if you want to get things moving quickly (or you feel the school are not taking your concerns seriously) you can commission one privately.

State or independent?

You have a right to name any state school for your child with special needs (although for a selective school, they would still need to pass the entrance exam). All are required by law to make any necessary adjustments, or to supply extra provision, that your child may need. The only grounds on which they can refuse a place to your child is where this would interfere with the efficient education of other children, or would not be an efficient use of resources. The schools' application of this premise varies hugely, from those who just toe the legal line, to those where the head truly embraces the idea of inclusive education, and is supported by a well-qualified and enthusiastic SENCo. Winkling out these gems is no easy task, and schools that aren't welcoming will use subtle ploys such as having no SENCo available at an open day, or generally making you feel so unwelcome that you won't bother applying.

Schools that aren't welcoming will use subtle ploys such as having no SENCo available

Independent schools have more freedom to select pupils. If they don't want to accept your child there is little you can do – even if you have grounds to challenge this decision under equality law, you are likely to be disinclined to do so when a school has taken this attitude. A few are genuinely welcoming to children with special needs, but they tend to have a quota on how many they admit in order not to overwhelm the special needs staff. Others will look at each child on merit, but the reality is there is little chance of a place for anything beyond mild needs.

It is possible, but rarely achieved, to get state funding for an independent school for a child with SEN. Parents have successfully argued for this on grounds of school size/class size/or peer group.

Mainstream or special school?

Most parents start with an inbuilt reluctance to contemplate a special school; but equally they can feel a huge sense of relief when their child has been placed in a specialist setting.

The right option for your child will depend very much on his/her individual circumstances. The biggest misconception is that a special school will somehow quash any potential – in fact the reverse can be true, and a child who has floundered in mainstream can suddenly make huge leaps when the teaching is properly tailored to his needs, or when his self-esteem is restored. And behavioural problems can disappear overnight when a child finds himself in a setting which understands his frustration and has the means to break through. It is possible to take a full range of GCSEs in a special school; they will always make provision for a pupil to work to the best of his ability.

Any additional therapies needed will be more readily available in a specialist school, and it can make all the difference that staff at these schools have specifically opted for special needs teaching. The downside is that these places are more costly, so you need to ready yourself for a fight with the local authority, and you will sometimes need to take a case to Tribunal in order to compel the local authority to pay for this.

Conversely some children with milder or transient needs will be better placed within the academic expectations and peer group available in a mainstream school. But the quality of support available can be extremely variable, so it is important to do your homework about exactly what provision there will be for your child, and how inclusive it will be. At primary school in particular, inclusion can mean quite the opposite when the child spends her days working separately in the corner with a teaching assistant. Therapy provision will be delivered by external agencies and it can be patchy, and it will be an add-on, instead of infused through every part of the day as in a specialist school.

A child who has floundered in mainstream can suddenly make great leaps

Be sure to have an individual meeting with the head and SENCo – are these people you will be able to deal with readily if there is an issue? Are they enthusiastic about the idea of taking your child, do they have knowledge and experience of his/her condition? Look for evidence of understanding across all teaching and support staff, rather than an attitude that this is a matter for the learning support department. And beware the well-meaning but inexperienced – it can become wearing when you have to keep close tabs on everything.

Where do I start?

Trying to organise schooling for a special needs child is bewildering and stressful. The Good Schools Guide online has informative features covering the various types of special needs, your legal rights, how to get an EHCP, family issues, and much more. This book contains a small selection of our special school reviews, but the website features more than 100 special schools across the country.

If you need individual help to identify the right school for your child, our team of expert SEN consultants can help.

goodschoolsguide.co.uk

Child protection

If you are preparing to entrust your child to a school – whether day or boarding – you will most likely assume that your child will be safe and that all members of the school's staff will take the greatest care to ensure that this is always the case.

The chances are that your expectations will be fulfilled. Unfortunately, in a sad minority of cases that is not what happens. We have all read news reports of bullying and abuse and may have shuddered at the thought that those very people who smilingly welcome our children into their care may be the last people to whom we would entrust them, if we knew all.

A flood of historical allegations against schools, court cases, mobile phones, flexi-boarding, more parental involvement, the internet, sex education and heightened awareness have together helped usher in some sunlight and fresh air. Schools are now a less than perfect setting for paedophiles and bullies. Child protection policies, found on every school website, usefully make plain the possibility of abuse at schools – something rarely contemplated a generation ago.

Abuse can occur at any school, anywhere. Fame is no protection, and nor is obscurity. Some kinds of school, though, need to take particular care – and that they do should be obvious to you when you visit. International schools have transient pupil populations, and teachers whose histories may be overseas and hard to research. Specialist music teaching necessarily involves a good deal of physical contact with the teacher and the pupil alone in a closed room. Religious schools can have a system of authority that keeps abuse concealed. Boarding schools can become very closed worlds. Special schools may have to deal with a large range of communication and emotional difficulties.

What matters is that passing on concerns is a routine thing and is welcomed by the school

What can you do?

Parents do well to warn their children – gently but seriously – of the dangers, however remote these may be, so they feel that it is easy to speak to you should they meet them. It is worth pointing out that abuse can come from anyone – including a teacher or an adult they know well, or from another child at the school.

Raise your own antennae at any school you may be considering. You can inquire about the steps taken to safeguard children in the same way you might ask about bullying or learning support. As always, much can be gleaned from the head's attitude when questions about child protection are asked. Is he or she ill at ease? Defensive? Or happy to engage, and proud of the steps their school has taken? Openness is what you're looking for.

How easy is it for a child, or a parent for that matter, to report an incident? Schools make this possible in a variety of ways; what matters is that passing on concerns is a routine thing (children and parents do it about lots of things all the time), and is welcomed by the school, and is low-stakes: the person registering the concern knows that they are not putting their relationships within the school at risk, let alone threatening someone's place in the school. That may seem an odd thing to say, but if you fear to report, say, careless management of a museum trip because it will harm an otherwise much-loved teacher, you probably choose to stay mum. Your concerns have to cross a high threshold before you communicate them, so you never pass on those troubling observations that may be the outward indication of serious problems. To be safe, schools need to hear the little voices, not just the shouting.

Do not think less of a school because a case of abuse has been brought to light there. Tabloid coverage can be the price the school has to pay for handling a case of abuse or bullying openly. It is inevitable that abuse will occur somewhere. What matters is how well the school deals with it, how well it performs in bringing the abuse to light and how open it is on the subject with current and future parents.

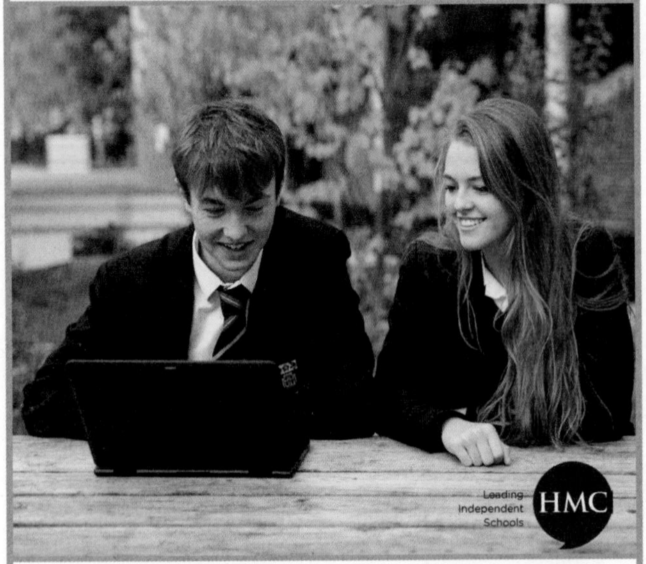

Leading Independent Schools
HMC

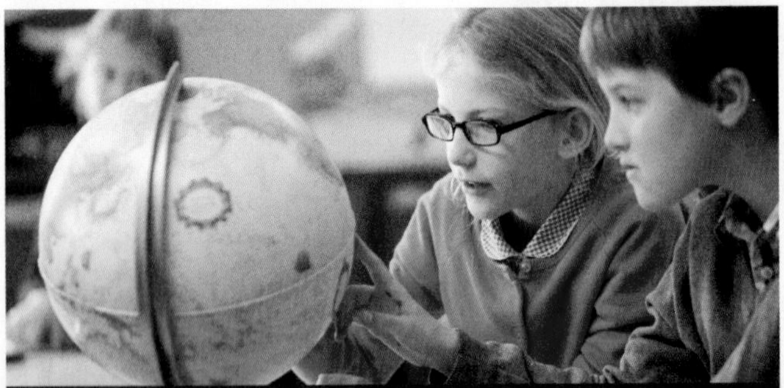

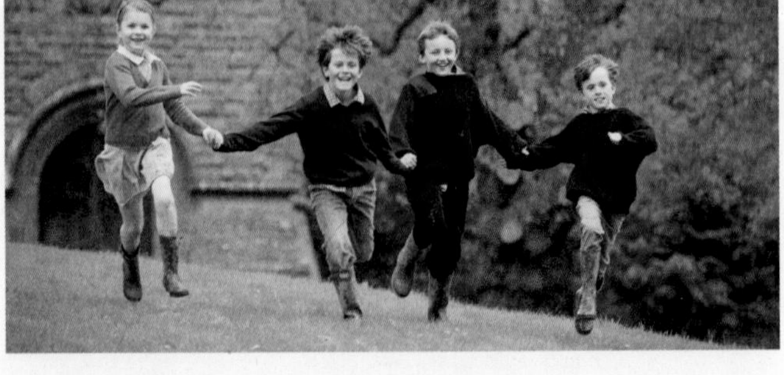

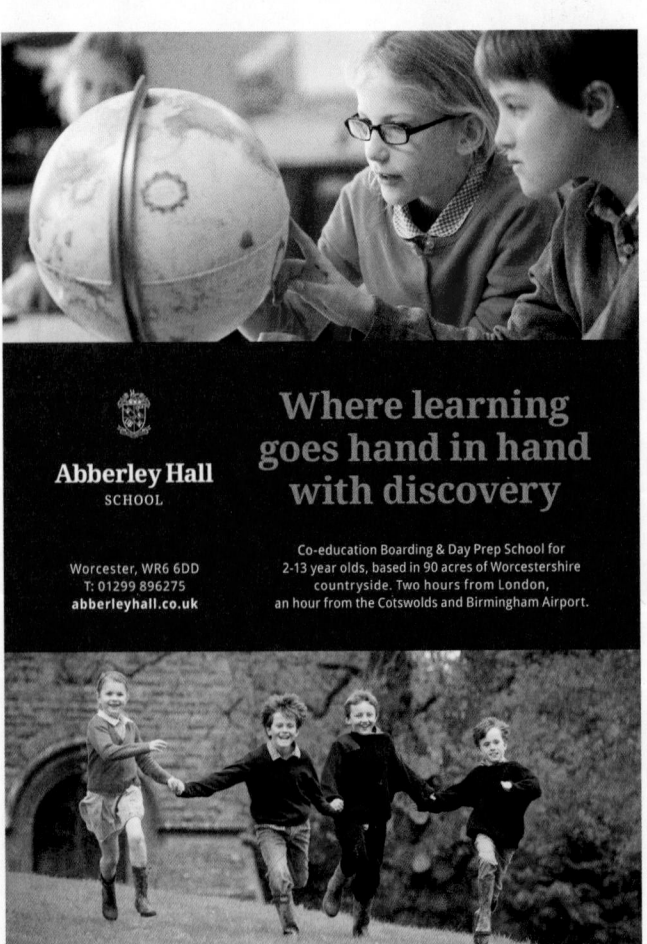

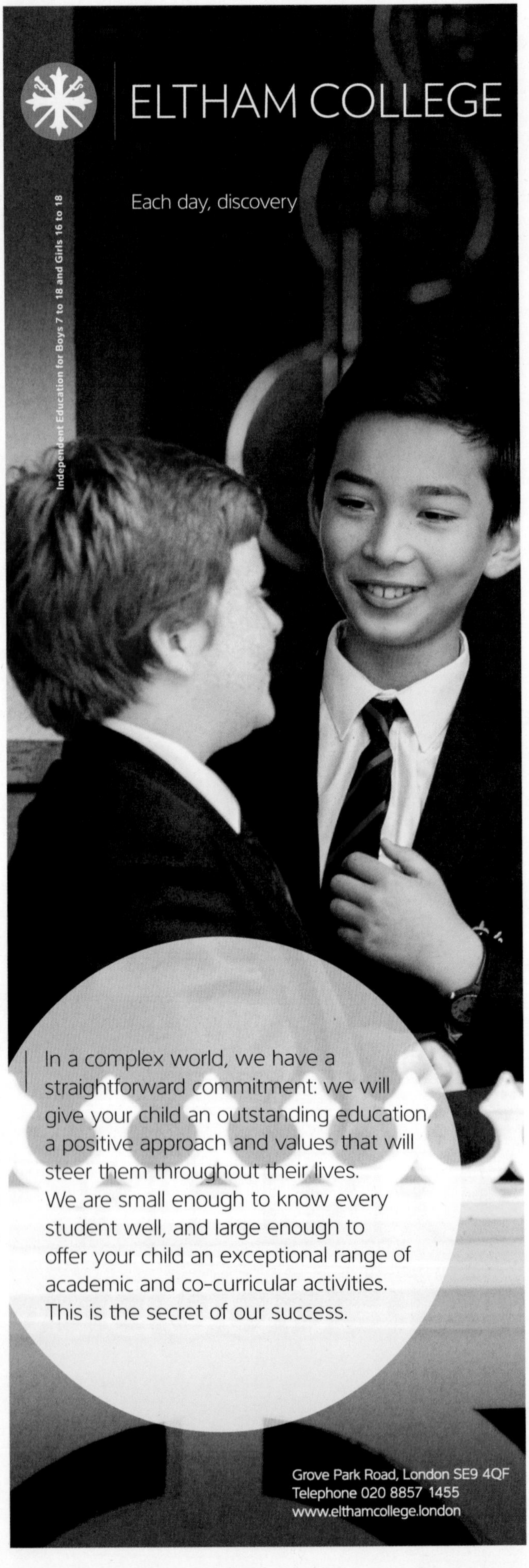

ELTHAM COLLEGE
Independent Education for Boys 7 to 18 and Girls 16 to 18
Each day, discovery
In a complex world, we have a straightforward commitment: we will give your child an outstanding education, a positive approach and values that will steer them throughout their lives.
We are small enough to know every student well, and large enough to offer your child an exceptional range of academic and co-curricular activities.
This is the secret of our success.
Grove Park Road, London SE9 4QF
Telephone 020 8857 1455
www.elthamcollege.london

DISCOVERING
INSPIRING
UNDERSTANDING
EXPLORING
QUESTIONING
INTERPRETING
PERFORMING
CHALLENGING
IMAGINING
Going beyond what the eyes can see.
OPEN MORNINGS
3rd February and 12th May 2017
Independent co-educational preparatory day, flexi and full-time boarding school, ages 2-13. Lymington, Hampshire SO41 5ZG. Please contact the School Registrar on 01590 613 303 or email registrar@walhampton.com
www.walhampton.com
Registered Charity No. 307330
Walhampton

the most inspiring classroom in the country
VINCIT QUI SE VINCIT
WINDERMERE
SCHOOL
+44 (0) 15394 46164
www.windermereschool.co.uk
admissions@windermereschool.co.uk

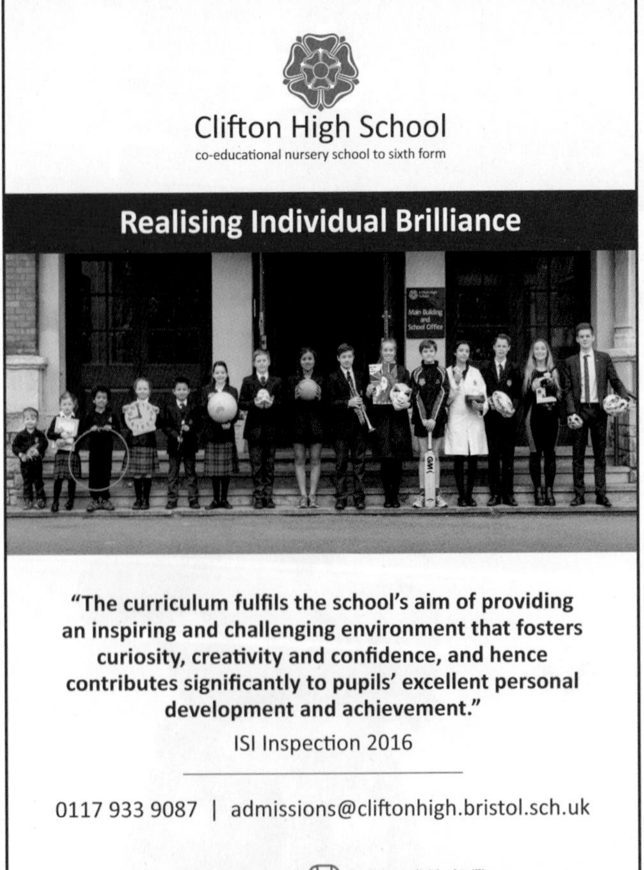

Clifton High School
co-educational nursery school to sixth form
Realising Individual Brilliance
"The curriculum fulfils the school's aim of providing an inspiring and challenging environment that fosters curiosity, creativity and confidence, and hence contributes significantly to pupils' excellent personal development and achievement."
ISI Inspection 2016
0117 933 9087 | admissions@cliftonhigh.bristol.sch.uk
The Diamond Edge Model
Realising Individual Brilliance

Be a Mount Girl
The UK's only Quaker school for girls
THE MOUNT
INDEPENDENT.THINKING.

Good Schools Guide Education Consultants

Our vast experience, coupled with the data, inside information and expertise of the entire team, is available to parents who need assistance with any aspect of their child's education. We are sympathetic and will help in whatever way we can to set you and your child on the right track. It is this individual attention which gives us our unique reputation.

Expert advice

Good Schools Guide Education Consultants (GSGEC) is a personal service for individual families covering every aspect of schools and education. Our consultants are our most experienced and knowledgeable writers. Many are based in or near London but we have experts in all aspects of education, all over the UK. They have visited countless schools, quizzed innumerable parents, children, teachers and heads. Most importantly, all our consultants take as much care over their clients' children – their schooling, happiness and well-being – as they would over their own.

Consultancy built around your needs

Most clients come to us because they need expert help to find schools for their children, but we can help in countless other ways and we flex our services to meet your requirements. All the information you give us is treated in the strictest confidence.

Our main consultancy services are outlined below. Our website contains full details about these, including the costs; you can also read profiles of our consultants with details of their professional expertise.

London Service

Our London service is designed to meet the needs of families new to London who need guidance, not just on schools but on residential areas, commuting, nurseries, playgroups, tutors and much more.

State School Service

This service, run by our expert in state education, is for parents who are interested in state schools only. It can give advice on matter such as admissions criteria, catchment areas and grammar schools.

Special Educational Needs

Our team of SEN experts is unique. We have specialists in eg dyslexia, autism, speech and language problems and we have extensive knowledge of both mainstream and special schools which cater for children with these difficulties.

Academic Assessments

If you are not sure what academic level your child is at, particularly if you are coming from overseas, we can arrange academic assessments.

Scholarships and Bursaries

We have amassed information on scholarships and bursaries to create a unique central resource, with information on the fee assistance available at more than 700 independent schools.

Contact us

Phone us on +44 (0)203 286 6824 or send a brief email to: consultants@goodschoolsguide.co.uk outlining what you need. Tell us the age of your child and where you live plus your contact details. We will respond within 48 hours, discuss how best to help you and ensure we match you with the right consultant. Consultations can be by phone, email or face to face, and we can find a consultant to speak to you within an hour if necessary.

How much?

Ours is one of the most competitively priced tailor-made consultancy services in the UK. Check our website for current fees.

goodschoolsguide.co.uk

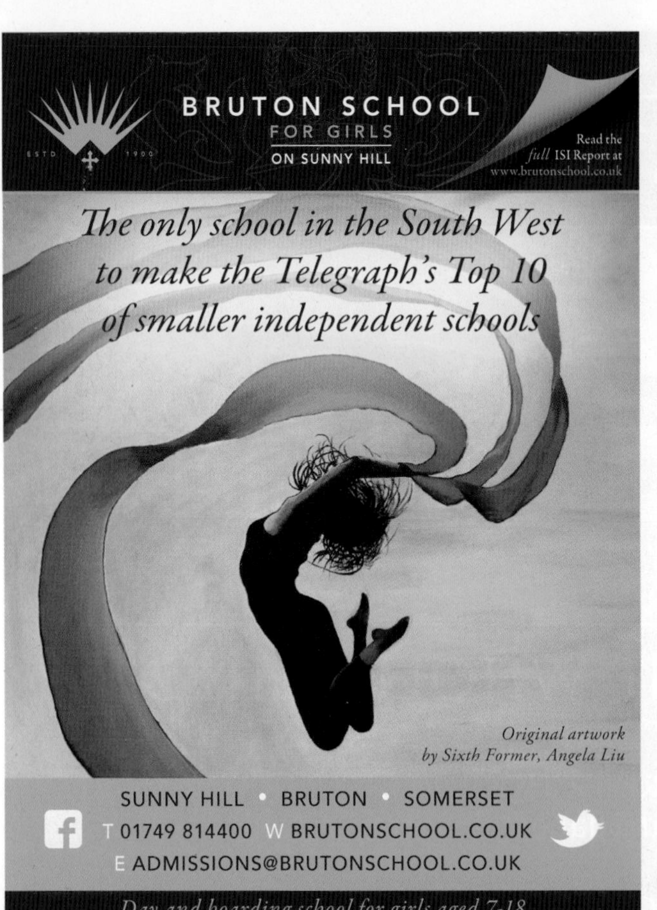

BRUTON SCHOOL
FOR GIRLS
ON SUNNY HILL
ESTD 1900
Read the *full* ISI Report at www.brutonschool.co.uk
The only school in the South West to make the Telegraph's Top 10 of smaller independent schools
Original artwork by Sixth Former, Angela Liu
SUNNY HILL • BRUTON • SOMERSET
T 01749 814400 W BRUTONSCHOOL.CO.UK
E ADMISSIONS@BRUTONSCHOOL.CO.UK
Day and boarding school for girls aged 7-18
Day school for girls and boys aged 3-7

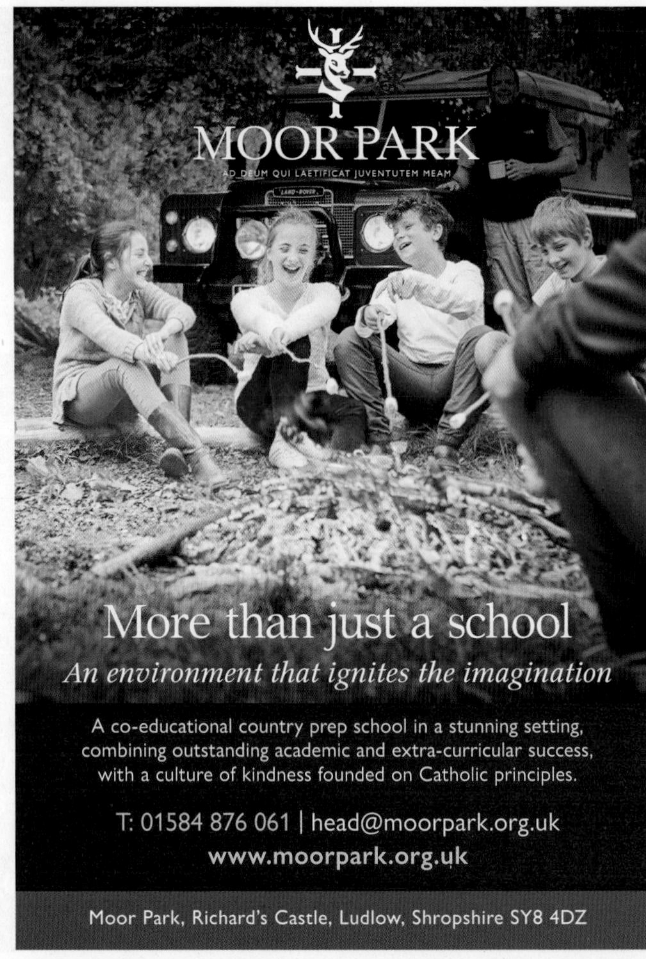

MOOR PARK
AD DEUM QUI LAETIFICAT JUVENTUTEM MEAM
More than just a school
An environment that ignites the imagination
A co-educational country prep school in a stunning setting, combining outstanding academic and extra-curricular success, with a culture of kindness founded on Catholic principles.
T: 01584 876 061 | head@moorpark.org.uk
www.moorpark.org.uk
Moor Park, Richard's Castle, Ludlow, Shropshire SY8 4DZ

HAZLEGROVE
...making the most of childhood
"it's the school of choice for many families making the big move out of London"
Good Schools Guide
BONJOUR
• Innovative & inspiring education for boys & girls aged 2 1/2 to 13
• Prep school boarding at its very best - available from 7 years
• Do arrange to visit - you will be assured of a warm welcome
To visit, call Sarah-Jane on 01963 442606
Hazlegrove, Sparkford, Somerset BA22 7JA

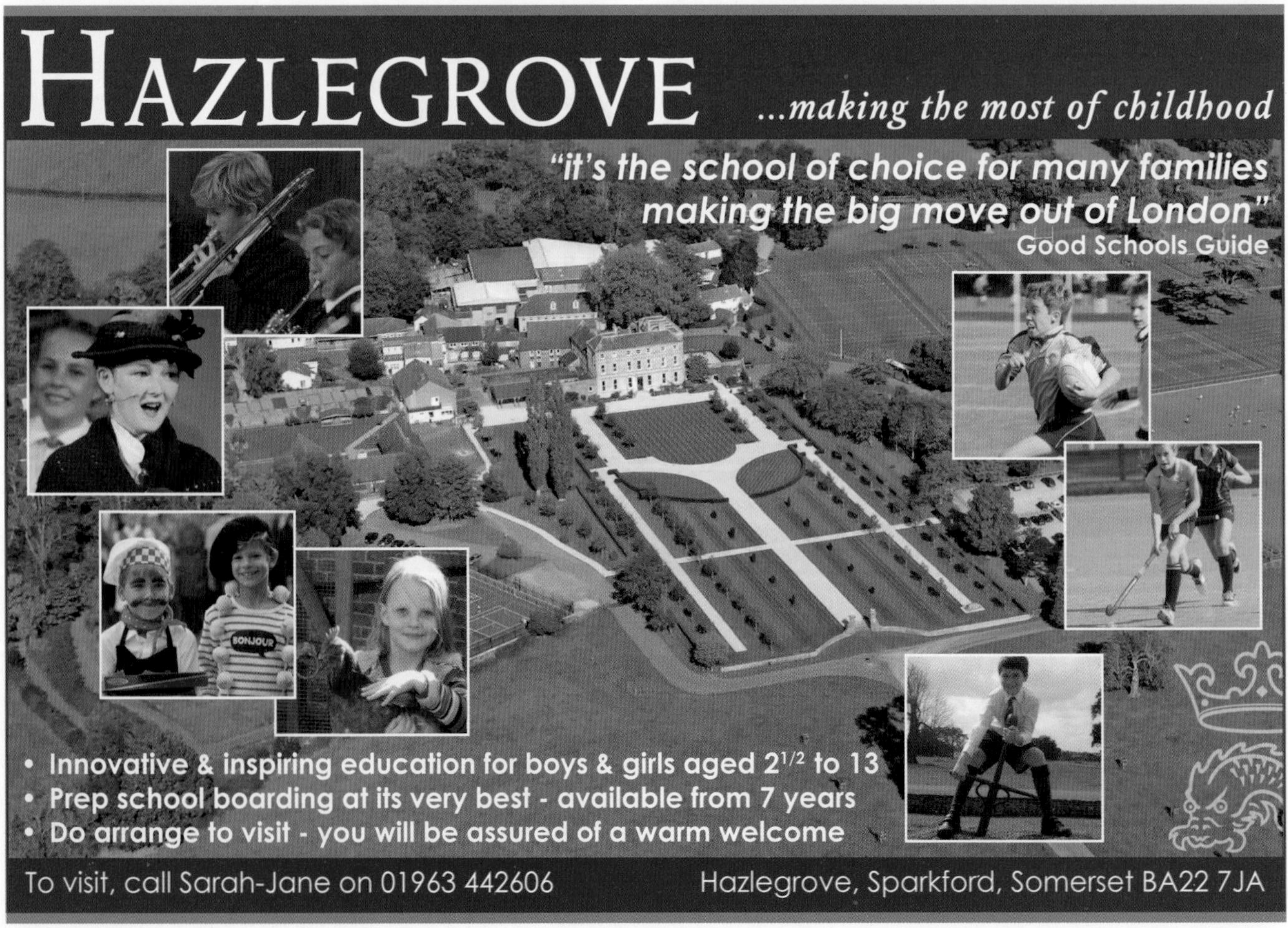

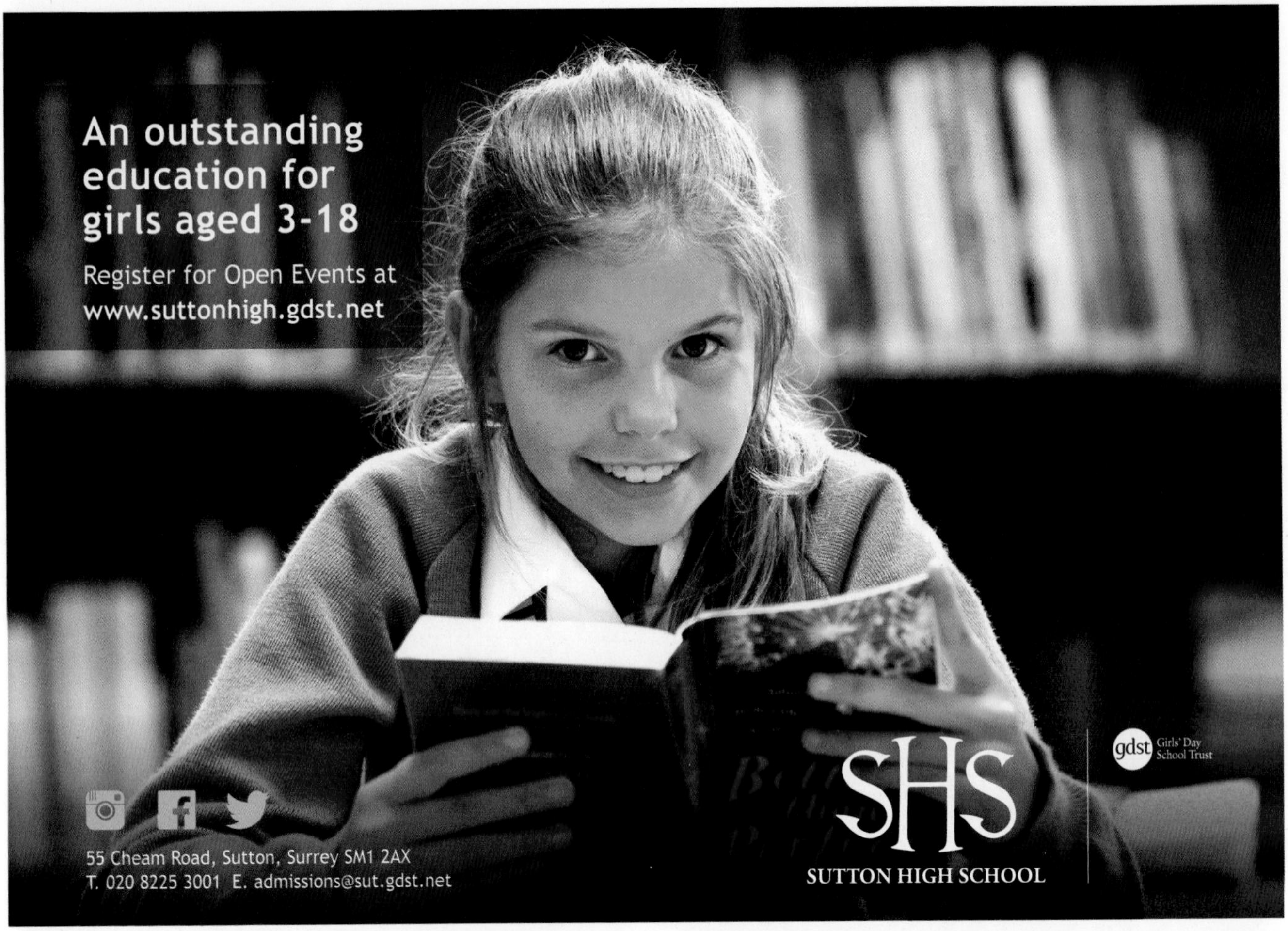

"What we learn with pleasure we never forget"
Alfred Mercier
Open Days every November, or to arrange an individual tour throughout the year please call 0161 224 1077
Withington GIRLS' SCHOOL
wgs.org
Means -tested bursaries now available from Year 5 upwards
To arrange a tour call 0161 224 1077
Wellington Road, Fallowfield, Manchester M14 6BL

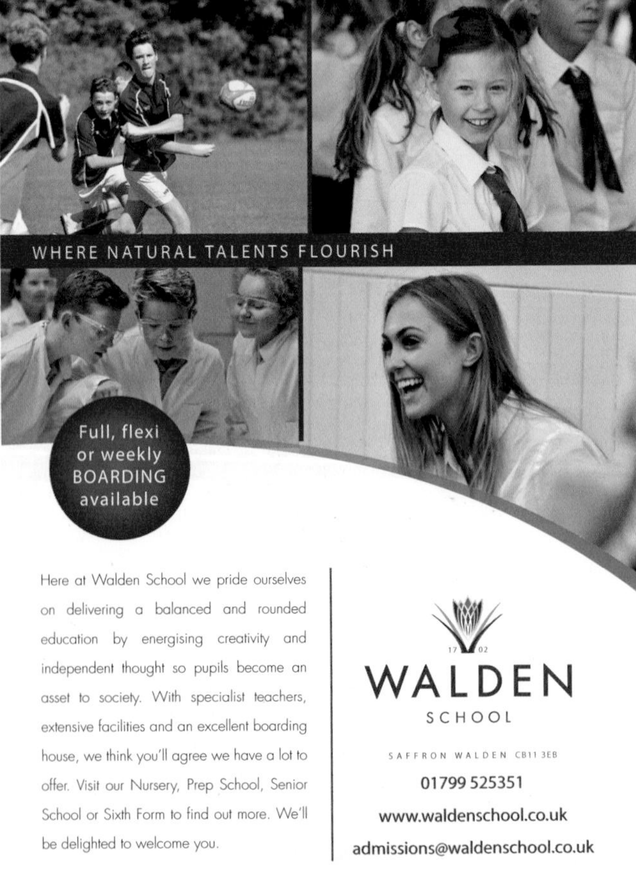

WHERE NATURAL TALENTS FLOURISH
Full, flexi or weekly BOARDING available
Here at Walden School we pride ourselves on delivering a balanced and rounded education by energising creativity and independent thought so pupils become an asset to society. With specialist teachers, extensive facilities and an excellent boarding house, we think you'll agree we have a lot to offer. Visit our Nursery, Prep School, Senior School or Sixth Form to find out more. We'll be delighted to welcome you.
17 02
WALDEN SCHOOL
SAFFRON WALDEN CB11 3EB
01799 525351
www.waldenschool.co.uk
admissions@waldenschool.co.uk
An independent day and boarding school for boys and girls aged 3 to 18

The Good Schools Guide International

goodschoolsguide.co.uk/international

The Good Schools Guide International does for international schools what The Good Schools Guide does for UK schools – visits and reviews the best ones for children 3-18, state or independent, wherever they are.

Written for parents, the GSGI covers top British, IB, American and international schools catering to English-speaking expats in over 55 cities worldwide. All schools reviewed have been visited by GSGI editors. We take no solicitations or money from schools – they're in (or out) whether they like it or not.

Reviews are completely independent, forthright and we stand behind every word. Overviews and articles give the inside scoop on everything from headmasters, sports, school runs and local traffic to life on the ground for expats.

For corporate rates or international consultants, call +44(0) 203 286 6824.

Uni in the USA

goodschoolsguide.co.uk/universities

The British guide to great universities from Harvard to Hong Kong. We tell you how to choose, how to apply and how to pay

Q: How many Stanford students does it take to change a light bulb?
A: One, dude.

Written by funny, sharp-eyed British students and co-authored by Anthony Nemecek, former Director of the Fulbright US Education Service, our popular British students' guide to US universities is available in paperback and online.

The down-to-earth, often hilarious, reviews of selected American colleges and international universities could only have been written by students interviewing students. One reviewer couch-surfed across the US by Greyhound bus, interviewing hundreds of students as he wrote his spot-on reviews, then legged it across Europe as still more intrepid souls — all students — took on universities in Asia and Australia.

All told, they reviewed over 100 universities in 12 countries, reporting on getting in, money matters, fellow students, life on campus and life outside. In short, what it's really like to be there.

To subscribe online or buy the paperback, go to **goodschoolsguide.co.uk/universities**. For university consultancies abroad or in the UK, contact **consultants@goodschoolsguide.co.uk** or call us on +44(0) 203 286 6824.

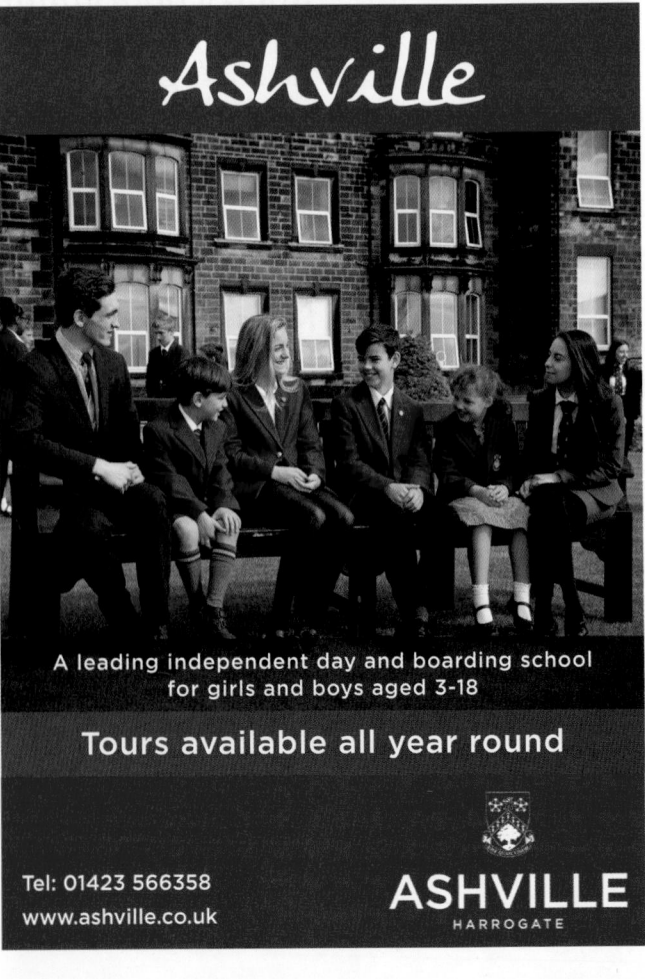

Additional publications from The Good Schools Guide

The Good Schools Guide: **Boarding Schools**

Reviews 350+ boarding schools across Britain, independent and state, with advice on when to start boarding, applying from abroad, sex and drugs and homesickness, boarding for a child with SEN.

The Good Schools Guide: **London North**

Candid reviews of state and private schools north of the Thames. Packed with local north London knowledge. Also explains how the English school system works, state and independent school admissions and much more.

The Good Schools Guide: **London South**

Invaluable guide to state and private schools south of the Thames. Includes pen portraits all the boroughs, your guide to navigating the English schooling system, how admissions work and much more.

The Good Schools Guide **online subscription**

All the latest reviews plus details of every school in Britain, with exam data, catchment maps, university entrance information. Advice on choosing a school, SEN, tutors, talented children and much more.

Uni in the USA

Written by students who have been through the US system, features in-depth descriptions of 70 US universities, plus the inside track on getting in and preparing for life across the pond.

Uni in the USA...and Beyond **online subscription**

Includes student reviews of universities across Canada, Europe and the Far East, from Alberta to Abu Dhabi, and advice from SATs to visas.

The Good Schools Guide International **online subscription**

The one-stop educational shop for expats. Reviews of the best state and independent schools round the globe, plus insider knowledge on life overseas.

All available via goodschoolsguide.co.uk

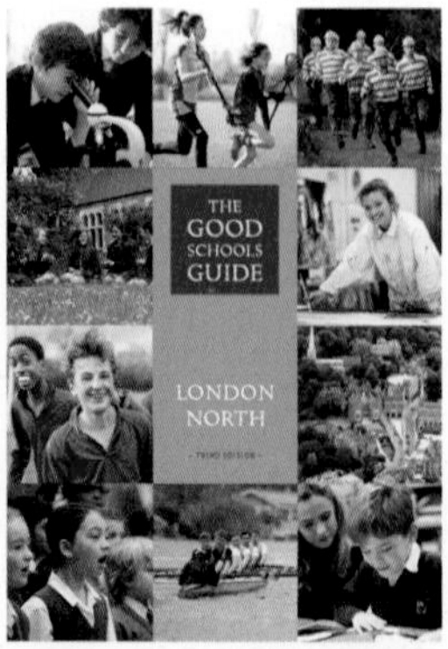

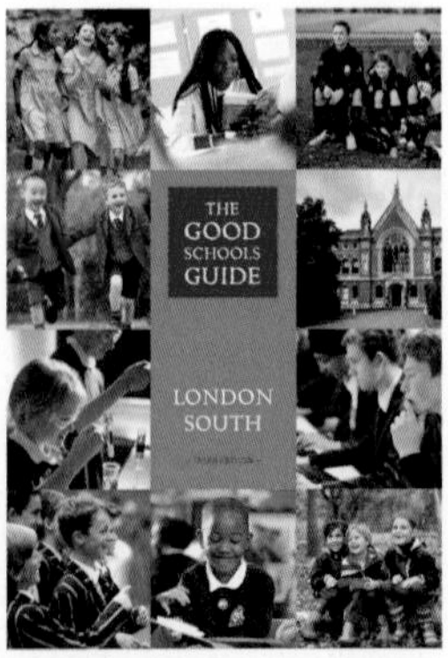

West of England and Wales

City of Bristol
Cheshire
Clwyd
Cornwall
Devon
Dorset
Glamorgan
Gloucestershire
Herefordshire
Monmouthshire
Powys
Shropshire
Somerset
Staffordshire
Wiltshire
Worcestershire

Junior Schools
Senior Schools
Junior & Senior Schools
Anglesey
Caernarfon Bay
GWYNEDD
CONWY
DENBIGHSHIRE
Liverpool
Birkenhead
Warrington
Oldham
Sheffield
Chester
CHESHIRE
Stoke-on-trent
DERBYSHIRE
Derby
STAFFORDSHIRE
Leicester
Wolverhampton
West Bromwich
Birmingham
BIRMINGHAM
Coventry
SHROPSHIRE
POWYS
CEREDIGION
Redditch
Worcester
WARWICKSHIRE
WALES
CARMARTHENSHIRE
Gloucester
Cheltenham
OXFORDSHIRE
Oxford
MONMOUTHSHIRE
NEATH PORT TALBOT
SWANSEA
Swansea
Swindon
Cardiff
Bristol
Bath
WEST BERKSHIRE
Channel
Barnstaple Bay
SOMERSET
Basingstoke
DEVON
Exeter
Bournemouth
DORSET
Lyme Bay
CORNWALL
TORBAY
Plymouth
Truro
English

WEST OF ENGLAND AND WALES

Abberley Hall

Worcester WR6 6DD

Pupils: 273; 60 boys, 24 girls full, 38 part boarders • Ages: 2–13 (boarding from year 3) • C of E

Fees: Day £8,475 – £18,030; Boarding £19,655 – £22,635 pa

Tel: 01299 896275
Email: louise.brook@abberleyhall.co.uk
Website: www.abberleyhall.co.uk

Headmaster: Since 2014, Will Lockett, previously classics teacher and housemaster at Bryanston. One of a small number of prep school heads who have moved from senior schools. In Will's case, the move was quite simply because he loves Abberley. An old boy of the school, he is revelling in the move to this age group. 'They are so refreshingly enthusiastic about everything', he says. He has a classics degree from Manchester, still teaches some and relishes it, no doubt contributing to the status the subject has with the children. A great believer in the value of routines, he says children respond to the structure of boarding and he has even introduced half an hour silent reading in bed before lights out. Everyone likes it. Will's style is brisk and vigorous. He knows exactly what is going on and children and staff are keen to keep it that way. 'He has respect without fear from the children,' a parent told us.

His wife, Beth, is fully involved, overseeing junior boarding and doing some teaching. A headmaster's wife to die for is the verdict of parents, who say she is very maternal and nurturing in her approach to the children. There are three Lockett children, the youngest at Abberley and the older two at Shewsbury. Will is spending his first few years at the school consolidating all the strengths and bringing new challenges in terms of independent learning and outdoor education.

Entrance: Non-selective. Children are assessed either before arrival or when they arrive to ensure there is clarity about educational needs and, with older children, to help determine which academic sets are appropriate.

Exit: The vast majority stay to the end of year 8. This is a school that is a serious player in the CE stakes. In 2016, 32 scholarships amidst the 45 year 8s and they are a range – academic, sport, art, drama, DT. The head says parents are very keen to seek advice on senior schools, which they recognise as objective and in the child's best interests, and school prides itself on pointing parents in the right direction. Offers are typically from both the big names – Winchester, Eton, Radley, Harrow, Cheltenham Ladies' College, Cheltenham College – and the best of the Midlands schools – Rugby, Shrewsbury, Moreton Hall, Stowe, Malvern College, Malvern St James, King's Worcester.

Remarks: Ninety acres of park and woodland surround Abberley Hall, a 19th century edifice of some significance. The bluebells were out along the drive on our visit to add to the idyllic rural setting in which the children grow up. The buildings are on a slope and the gentle Worcestershire hills frame the school site. Inside, the first impressions are of a grand but comfortable past. While we talk to the headmaster, a glorious peacock pecks at the window as if he wants to join us. Many of the original features of the old house remain – large oil paintings on the impressive staircase, wonderful great wood framed doors, a family theatre now converted into a girls' dormitory with its original pastoral murals. The headmaster's study is the old library, apparently untouched since an era of leisurely scholarship.

But there is nothing leisurely about the scholarship at Abberley today. It is a high-powered prep school that prepares children with great success for the top senior schools in the country. It offers a traditional academic curriculum. The older children have 30 hours of lessons a week. 'It would be nice to have a few less lessons,' one or two year 8s said to us plaintively. Languages are a huge strength – Greek is taught from year 6, there are three hours of French a week and two and a half of Latin. It pays off in terms of scholarship examinations, the head tells us. From year 3, the children have twice yearly exams. It is low key to start with but it means the children are getting used to tests. Science, maths, design and manufacture have a practical, cross-curricular emphasis that is impressive. When the children learn about pressure in science, they look at saturation diving in design and manufacture. It keeps the children fully engaged with the more theoretical aspects, the head of design and manufacture tells us.

The workshops are open at lunch time and after school for children to work on their own design projects – about a third of the school is engaged on one of these. Art is striking with a practising artist running workshops twice a week – 'It has been a huge help for the children preparing for scholarships', the head of art tells us. There are textiles, ceramics, print-making, painting onto canvas and use of different media. The head is keen to develop even further the profile and challenge of the creative arts.

The older children told us that the high academic standards were what made the school stand out. 'We can get help from teachers whenever we want,' they say, 'and we can sign up for extra academic coaching sessions'. The school is preparing the children for senior schools where they will need to take the initiative in planning and shaping their own learning and there is no doubt that the older ones get this. Parents are enthusiastic about the quality of the teaching. 'They go the extra mile,' was how one described staff. Once year 8s have completed all their exams, there is a challenging leavers' programme of events for them. The head says that feedback from senior schools is that Abberley children are notably good at grasping opportunities.

Because the school is non-selective, learning support is taken seriously. Class size is kept to 15 maximum, allowing for much individual support within the classroom. Then there is dyslexia screening in years 1 and 2 and careful scrutiny of ongoing assessments. Where a need is identified, the head of learning support will step in. The school may do its own further assessment or advise an educational psychologist's report to help tailor future learning. What happens next depends on the level of need and is very much individually determined. It may be two half hour support lessons a week, a teaching assistant helping within a class, curriculum adjustments, special exam access arrangements. Parents say that the children take needing extra help as a matter of course – there is absolutely no stigma attached.

The head says it is not what happens in lessons that distinguishes the outstanding boarding school, but what happens at weekends. Abberley Hall is committed to full boarding. There is no flexi-boarding but there is part boarding, where parents commit to specific days a week a term in advance. One weekend in three is full boarding, one is optional and the third is an exeat, so the most a child would be continuously at school is likely to be three weeks, which we think is right for children at this age and a good preparation for senior boarding schools. Many of the weekend activities, which the children tell us they adore and are keenly anticipated, are open to parents. Just before we visited there had been the annual fun run where everyone dressed up to complete various length runs around the grounds. The grounds are fully used. The children have built an outdoor pizza oven, there are outdoor classrooms and mini Duke of Edinburgh style award activities outdoors one afternoon a week. There are clear rules about where in the grounds children can explore but plenty of space for climbing trees and building dams. The head is keen to introduce even more challenge to the outdoor education programmes.

Extracurricular life is teeming – every teacher offers two activities a week. Music is highly valued and a big part of the school. Not only lessons but practices are timetabled for the children which, with 200 instrumental lessons going on, must take some doing. There is a lunchtime concert series and, as with other extracurricular activities, the emphasis is on everyone getting a chance to perform at some stage. Many take RSM exams and do very well and there are regular music scholarships awarded. A group goes each week to the CBSO Children's Choir in Birmingham, which opens up huge opportunities for music-making. There are lots of instrumental ensembles and choirs. The senior chapel choir is invited to sing around the area, regularly performing at Worcester Cathedral. Parents describe the music as 'sensational' and are delighted by the high expectations from staff. There is a 'phenomenally ambitious' annual musical. 'The staff are not just wanting performance but perfection', one parent told us approvingly.

The school is considered to punch well above its weight in sport, which happens every day with matches on Wednesdays and Saturdays and sports tours. Facilities are brilliant. Rugby coaching is exceptional even by standards outside the prep school world. Girls' cricket is taken as seriously as boys' cricket. Lots of the children said sport is a great thing about the school, but even those who admitted to not being particularly keen appreciate the choice they have and the chance to be outside.

There is drama and bee-keeping, run by the headmaster, fishing and film making, spy club and electronics; the list goes on. Children can bring their horses from home and ride round the grounds on their bikes. It is a day packed full of intellectual and outdoor activities – 'Gumboots and Greek' is the school's current strapline and it is a good reflection of what life is like. Parents like the lack of hierarchy in school activities. There is no sense that the rugby players are any more valued or respected than the grade 1 flautist. The school is also noted for its enthusiasm for discovering new talents – children are not labelled as 'a sportsperson' and that is that. All this does mean the days are long and, particularly for parents considering boarding, it is important to ensure their child is ready for this degree of activity.

Abberley has its own chalet in the French Alps and all year 5s and 7s have a couple of weeks out there each year to immerse themselves in a different culture and pick up a bit more French, which they are learning alongside Spanish, Latin and Greek. A Chinese school exchange is also planned.

The children we spoke to enthused about boarding. The accommodation is very un-institutional, using the variety of spaces in the old buildings. Pastoral support is strong and the turnover of staff small. Head has introduced a new tutor system for the older children so years 6, 7 and 8 have their own personal tutor for three years, who acts as a single point of contact for parents and with whom the children have a weekly individual meeting. We think this is an excellent model to ensure no one slips through the pastoral net.

'We are not big on punishment', says the head and indeed the discipline issues with which staff are dealing are low key. The focus is on getting children to think about their own behaviour and how it impacts on others. Parents say that the school's attitude to problems has always been to leave it to school and not encourage parents to be very much involved. The new head seems to be changing this a bit, but everyone we spoke to seemed very confident in the school's ability to sort things out quickly and humanely and follow through on issues. The school is keen on giving the children responsibilities and has created new roles in the last couple of years to ensure the opportunities are there to learn about leadership. There is a visiting CofE chaplain and a traditional chapel service four times a week, with family services some Sundays.

Family backgrounds range from landowners and farming families to professionals and business people, and they are highly supportive of the school, generally living close enough to attend matches, concerts, Sunday chapel and the many other events. They had just helped organise a long distance walk to raise money to take out to a community in South Africa when the sports teams go on a tour. There are some children whose family connections with Abberley go back several generations. Parents and staff value the range of children – not just in terms of background but also in terms of their educational needs.

The children are strikingly open and unaffected, living witness to the head's belief that prep school children retain their innocence longer. They are unselfconscious, gutsy and ready to talk to adults appropriately. They are being prepared for a work hard, play hard culture. They love the outdoor freedom and they also know life is a serious and competitive business, which they are up for. The school is in its centenary year. It has much to be proud of in its past and everything to suggest the future is golden for the children lucky enough to come here.

Adams' Grammar School

High Street, Newport, Shropshire TF10 7BD

Pupils: 890; 95 boarders • Ages: 11–18 • Sixth form: 315 (84 girls)

Fees: Day free; Boarding: £10,965 – £12,540 pa

Tel: 01952 386300
Email: TAW705Enquiries@taw.org.uk
Website: www.adamsgs.org.uk

Headmaster: Since January 2015, Gary Hickey, previously deputy head. Degree in music and drama from Manchester Met and a PGCE from Birmingham City, and has been awarded a Teacher Fellowship by Cambridge University. Gary is a man of many talents: he scooped a special commendation for 'extraordinary work in drama' in the 2000 National Teaching Awards, and lectures globally on raising the achievement of boys. He is also an award-winning theatre director and a professional musician. He joined Adams in 2009, understands it through and through and knows just what potential he has been handed.

Academic matters: Strong results, as you would expect in a selective school boosted by girls coming into the sixth form. A levels were 80 per cent A*-B grades in 2016 and 49 per cent A*/A. GCSEs were 60 per cent A*/A grades. Value added is great too. There is a real ethos of hard work from the word go. Staff know students well enough to stop the sort of coasting you can often find with boys after the first year or so. Form teachers are known to email parents after just one late homework and parents find that reassuring. Chemistry and physics results are particularly good – but so is English. Class sizes up to 30 at the lower end of the school but much smaller groups in the sixth form.

Curriculum is a traditional grammar school one – except there is no classics other than Latin, which is offered along with Mandarin and Polish as an after-school or lunchtime class. Though music and art are encouraged, the numbers taking them at A level are small. One or two slightly unusual A levels such as geology, government and politics and PE. DT popular; has just embraced a

Life Bike Design project where the boys are enthusiastically rising to the challenge of building their own bikes.

Very few statemented children and a small number with milder learning difficulties, all of which are broadly dealt with in the classroom, though a part time SENCo has just started. Students testify to plenty of support from staff if things get tough. There is peer support and sixth form mentoring for younger boys.

Games, options, the arts: A long-serving member of staff told us that the school used to be known as the rugby school that did maths and science very well. Things move on. The science is still excellent and rugby is thriving, but you are as likely to find the students throwing themselves into music and drama as much as into games. Sport itself has expanded, and although we heard one request for girls' rugby, the sporting offer is considered wide enough to suit most tastes. The swimming pool has been covered and even football has controversially been introduced, and students say they love their sport, whatever the weather. House sports competitions include cross-country in the beautiful grounds of the junior boarding house, to get even the less athletically inclined involved, and the emphasis is on inclusion, not solely on the gifted few. But those with the expertise are encouraged to play at regional and national level as well as for the school. Biannual rugby, hockey and netball tours abroad for senior teams.

Performing arts, which also blossomed under the previous head, looks set to continue to grow under the current one, with his degree in music and drama. The tremendously popular house drama and music events draw the whole school into the arts. There are opportunities for the very best actors, actresses and singers in the big school productions – The Crucible, Les Mis, Romeo and Juliet and Grease in recent years. A refurbished art space, although not enormous, stimulates some pretty sensational artwork that is seen around the school.

CCF is very strong and many ex-students join Sandhurst, the Royal Air Force College or Royal Naval College. There are plenty of Easter and summer camps on offer, and boys can join the CCF marching band. There is a good range of clubs and societies. A poet in residence brings in the culture that is not as readily available in the heart of Shropshire as it would be in a big city.

Boarding: The senior boarding house is one of a group of Georgian town houses along the Newport High Street; parts of it are decidedly tatty. Junior boarding is idyllically housed about a mile away in a gorgeous Georgian mansion. 'Grade 2 listed buildings cost'; school has clearly spent money on the interior here. There are 100 acres of land attached to the house, used by the whole school for various sporting activities. Boys are bussed to and from the main school. The number of boarders about at weekends varies but there are always full boarders there. Activities centre round games, with some visits and other offerings depending on numbers and popularity. Day boarding – an optional extra for years 7-9 – includes tea, after-school activities and supervised prep, with a 7.30pm pick up.

Background and atmosphere: The school dates back to 1656 – it was founded by haberdasher William Adams – and is one of the Haberdashers' group of schools. Behind the senior boarding house is a series of more modern and imaginatively refurbished specialist teaching areas; the new music block is in a converted coach house. The new areas such as the sixth form centre are impressive but there is further to go on refurbishment.

Everyone talks about the house system. The school has managed to generate house energy and vitality without losing a basic allegiance to the school. 'It's not nasty competitiveness', said one boy, 'it's nice tribalism', and we heard about one excellent dancer teaching those in rival houses how to move. The various house competitions encourage everyone to try new areas and the strong narrative is that everyone has a contribution to make. 'It is a great day whoever wins,' one boy told us. 'You have the freedom to choose whether to take part, but everyone wants to because you would be letting the house down if you don't.' There are school and house traditions that apparently take a bit of getting used to but are much loved.

It is unusual to find a predominantly boys' school tackle headlong and consistently the prejudices that can plague all male institutions, so Adams' very active and visible commitment to celebrating diversity is hugely refreshing. What used to be casually swept aside as male 'banter' is now no longer acceptable and is rigorously scrutinised for racist, sexist or homophobic overtones by the boys themselves. One of the heads of house who pioneered the work told us that initially there was a raised eyebrow or two amongst colleagues, but soon everyone was behind the work. Relevant news articles are routinely circulated, there is a dedicated school noticeboard and dedicated tutor time. The governors have had a presentation and such matters are the standard fare in school assemblies. Girls coming into the sixth form still report a certain amount of 'laddishness' at first, but 'we roll our eyes, get on with our work and they soon get over it.' Students spoke easily about such matters as respect, community and equality, and see a major strength of the school as encouraging everyone to be themselves.

Staff say it's a lovely place and all want their children to come. 'Every year someone's child doesn't get through the exam and it is a real sadness for everyone'. Parents say it is warm and friendly and has the intimate feel of a small school. Pupils spontaneously want to share not only personal news but also what they have been reading or hearing. There is an informality about the relationships and a sense of mutual respect. The occasional child who doesn't flourish is probably the one who doesn't talk to staff or take opportunities.

Pastoral care, well-being and discipline: The school rightly prides itself on its pastoral care and we got a strong sense that not only were all the staff alert to individual needs but the students looked out for each other. There is close communication between the boarding house staff and those running the whole school house system, where pastoral responsibility securely sits. Misdemeanours are dealt with very promptly using a traditional range of sanctions. We were pleased to note frontline staff reported full support from parents. 'We know they will back the school to the hilt when it comes to having to punish someone'. None of the 'my child right or wrong' attitude increasingly common in fee-paying schools. Counsellors attend regularly and the school is very well staffed in non-lesson time.

There is a zero tolerance approach to drugs, parents told us. Other offences are firmly stamped on and the boys know from the start that the school will take any deviation from their high standards very seriously. However, the nurturing goes hand in hand with this and the comment from all the parents we spoke to was that discipline and pastoral care were spot on.

Pupils and parents: The boys are unselfconscious and articulate. They look smart, and the accolade of having won a place at Adams' acts as a real boost to the less confident. The majority of day boys come from a 20 mile radius of the school, which includes Wolverhampton and Telford, so there is more racial and social diversity than you would expect from a school that draws on the Shrewsbury set and is in deep Shropshire countryside. The school does some work with local primaries to try to widen access, but the overall impression is that most students come from middle class professional backgrounds.

Boarders come from across the country and the world (some eight per cent from overseas). If parents are looking for budget boarding with excellent exam results, this is hard to beat. Adams' is one of only a very few academically selective state UK boarding schools.

A

The school has taken girls into the sixth form since 1993. They are still in the minority, about 70 in a sixth form of 300, which means, according to one girl, that they form a very close community. The type of girl who does well (and, probably, who applies in the first place) is likely to be feisty and willing to speak her mind – 'just like the women who work here,' said one male teacher somewhat ruefully.

The only kind of child who might not thrive here, one parent speculated, is the one who has been heavily coached for the entrance exam. 'The boys put themselves under pressure: they are all very ambitious and only one can be top,' another parent said.

Old boys include Blue Peter presenter Radzi Chinyanganya, disc jockey Simon Bates, Labour leader Jeremy Corbyn and England rugby player Graham Kitchener.

Entrance: About four or five applicants for every place. The exam is one used by other selective state Midlands schools and is administered centrally, away from the school. It aims to be something which it's hard to coach for and includes reading comprehension, maths and non-verbal reasoning. For sixth form entry there is an expectation of at least five Bs at GCSE, but most have much higher results.

For boarding places, after looked after children, places go to those performing highly in the entrance tests, with Forces children and then boarding need the next in priority order.

Exit: At the end of year 11 a few go to sixth forms that have a wider range of subjects. Vast majority of sixth formers to university – 12 to Oxbridge and 10 medics in 2016; Birmingham and Cardiff currently the most popular destinations.

Money matters: Tuition is free. The only charge is for boarding, with an optional day boarder fee. Lots of flexibility.

Remarks: Amazing value for money as far as boarding is concerned – exam results, academic rigour combined with the community boarding ethos. But this being a state school you are exposed to the vagaries of the political climate and funding constraints of a particular government.

As good as it gets for boys in a single sex school in its determination to prepare them for a world where white patriarchy is no longer the default model. It is a particular type of girl who blossoms in a predominantly male environment – those who do, no doubt have brilliant advantage when they move on.

There is a charm about Adams' that is part to do with its rural catchment, part with an unaffected enthusiasm and part a thoughtfulness – not a combination that is easy to find.

Alderley Edge School for Girls

Wilmslow Road, Alderley Edge, Cheshire SK9 7QE

Pupils: 506 • Ages: 2–18 • Sixth form: 64

Fees: £7,470 – £11,448 pa

Tel: 01625 583028
Email: admissions@aesg.co.uk
Website: www.aesg.info

Headmistress: Since September 2016, Helen Jeys, previously deputy head at Manchester High School for Girls. Theology degree from Durham and PGCE from Cambridge; has taught religion and philosophy at Manchester Grammar, Malvern Girls' College and Hulme Grammar School for Boys. She has written on philosophy and pastoral care, and enjoys playing the cello and piano.

Head of junior school: Since 2013, Bridget Howard BEd (50s), previously deputy head. Educated at St Albans High, then Rolle College Exeter; returned to St Albans to teach in the prep, then a stint in Sydney, before coming back to teach at Manchester High Prep and Bolton School Girls Junior.

Academic matters: Large 'learning enhancement unit' with SENCo's office in junior school, mainly helping dyslexic pupils. Class size average is 15, maximum 22 herre. Maths sets from year 4, reading age and spelling assessed yearly and summer tests.

Senior school no longer just embracing arms under those who slip through other nets at 11+. In 2016, 39 per cent A*/A at A level/Pre-U, 70 per cent A*/B; 45 per cent A*/A at GCSE. Cambridge Pre-U can be taken alongside A levels. The ability profile is above average, but recent ISI inspection also described the educational experience here as outstanding and the curriculum as excellent.

Three classes to each year with a maximum promise of 25, and when year 9 classes overfilled they were divided to form additional group. Some sixth form teaching sets are tiny. From year 7, girls conduct self-evaluation and review their own progress. No shortage of computers or study areas, with four ICT suites, a library and designated sixth form computer and study rooms under an apex roof with girders and skylights. Setting for maths from year 7, science from year 9, 'with plenty of chances to change groups if you do well'. Maths clinic every lunchtime, other subjects on various days and girls say, 'The teachers here teach because it's their passion and not just their job'. Pupils are helped with learning difficulties and the head has re-launched gifted and talented scheme.

Games, options, the arts: Three all-weather pitches, two large gyms, a verdant sports field and a modern drama and dance studio with mirrored wall. On sports corridor walls motivational quotes undergird photos of the girls playing sport and a photo-wall of fame celebrates diverse individual successes, some at national level, from horse riding and ice skating to dance, squash and tae kwon do. Netball, hockey and cross-country popular, swimming at Wilmslow leisure centre. Teams play in Cheshire leagues with netball particularly strong, regularly reaching NW finals, and a keen football team includes a Manchester City youth player.

Girls say, 'Music here is massive,' with several bands, orchestra and choirs. Keyboard suite, lots of girls take singing lessons. Music exams, success at renowned Alderley Edge Music Festival, celebrated at prizegiving in Manchester's Bridgewater Hall. Art displayed everywhere with particularly exciting 3D models outside main art rooms. The head of art, here nearly 30 years, clearly loves the place, 'and the girls we turn out are so well rounded'. Separate sixth form art room where each girl has own space. Lots of after school clubs, 'best thing about school,' say some girls, trips and exchanges, Comenius European links, D of E, Mock Trial, charity fundraising and links with Kenyan school and women's project.

Background and atmosphere: Founded in 1999 from the merging of Mount Carmel RC convent school on the present site and the Anglican St Hilary's run by the Woodard Corporation from the south end of the village. Now describes itself as an ecumenical unified Christian school with the motto line, 'Aspire not to have more, but to be more'. Prep school on same site and shares some facilities. Compulsory monthly Eucharist is 'boring' in some girls' books, and they're not afraid to say so, but most accept it happily. Four houses named after saints Emilie, Francis, Joan and Hilary, three chaplains, visiting clergy and rallying assemblies; 'We're not turning them all into nuns, but it sets a moral framework and builds positive self-image, esteem and worth,' says school.

Fabulous poster-sized professional photos of the girls at work, rest and play lining every corridor do much the same thing and detract from the uninspiring hotchpotch of red-brick buildings once you pass the modern front façade. Girls seem happy and relaxed, corridor manners more hurly burly than stuffy. Happy eager girls cosseted in lower years, gradually blossoming and integrating with seniors for seamless integration at 11. Girls share senior hall, dining room, ICT suite, sports facilities and, as they advance up the years, a stairwell, the new dance studio and the senior library.

Breakfast available free from 8am and the dining room is a sociable place where younger girls dine first and staff cluster chatting too. Bread and pastries at break for a nominal charge. Sixth form privileges include not queuing for lunch, 'handy on Friday chip day', a wider range of muffins and buns from their own all day coffee bar and a new 'chill out' common room in which to enjoy them and a natter. An annual highlight for pupils and staff is the house entertainment afternoon, organised by the captains, where everyone performs or contributes backstage.

Pastoral care, well-being and discipline: From the 'golden rules' corridor junior girls selected 'Do be honest, do not cover up the truth' as most important. Friendship Council encourages girls to be friendly and work things through. 'It was the anti-bullying council, but there wasn't any bullying, so we didn't have anything to do and it was changed to the friendship council,' say girls, who describe the way they're treated as 'firm but fair' and say, 'It's a fun community'. Much emphasis on rewarding good behaviour and effort with certificates, letters home and even chocolate. Merit system includes personal and house points. Referral cards for work related and behavioural lapses – 'We have high expectations and don't stand any nonsense'. Big sister scheme teams sixth formers with year 7s while they settle in. Girls describe friendship and 'knowing everyone' as the best thing about AESG – as one sixth former said, 'We genuinely don't want to leave; this is a school where everybody knows your name'. They're not quickly forgotten, as a leavers' destination board carries large photos of smiling girls (no pouting here) and inspiriting news of where they are now. Parents agree: 'The pastoral care is great – you can ring them at any time'; 'My daughter's extremely happy there – all the girls are so nice'.

Pupils and parents: Overwhelmingly white and middle class, although 20 or so with English as second language. Not all regular churchgoers, even small minority from other faiths – 'I've not noticed the Christian stuff,' one parent told us. Neat navy uniforms introduced as a new colour when the two schools merged and girls don't seem to push the boundaries – instead they look unspoilt and innocently young, with minimal make up and jewellery. Girls come from as far as central Manchester and Stoke on Trent. Most, however, hail from rural local areas, so Cheshire set strongly represented, though as one mum put it, 'There are lots of fat cars in the car park, but I'm not the only one who sacrifices to send my daughter here'. Good bus network and near train station; traffic congestion at pick up time.

Entrance: Open to any who are sympathetic to school's ecumenical ethos. No assessment for entry to nursery (now taking from 2 years, minimum two days or three half days from 3 plus) or infant school. Places in junior years offered after a taster day in school, not sitting papers as such but including some reading, writing and numeracy during a normal school day. Looking for 'behaviour, attitude and a focused work ethic' from the bright to middle ability ranges, 'girls who're likely to get into the seniors', but keen to protect happy atmosphere – 'We have absolutely no disruptive elements in our classes'. Spaces in some years.

To senior school by maths, English and verbal reasoning exams, interview and reference, looking for a broad band of ability, girls who'll fit in. Has catch-all reputation of not setting bar over dauntingly high, although school says it regularly turns away girls 'due to their academic profile not being sufficiently high to cope with our academic curriculum'. Entry higher up school includes science and language papers. Half year 7 straight from prep, at home here from the off. Taster day for prospective year 6 girls to really see what it's like.

Exit: Almost all junior girls move on up to the senior school. A few move to high flying Manchester High, Withington or elsewhere. Some 35-50 per cent leave post-GCSE (53 per cent in 2016) – mostly to vocational courses and/or state sector and a further 10 per cent at end of year 12. Most sixth formers straight to university with Durham, Leeds, Sheffield and Nottingham all popular (London usually features as well). Occasional Oxbridge success (two in 2016). Mix of courses from mechanomics with robotics, pharmacy, medicine (four places in 2016), history and psychology to childhood studies. The others leave for gap years, which includes a welcome back at school for post A level university applications, or to post A level apprenticeships at eg Bentley Motors and Bank of New York.

Money matters: Some reduction for siblings. Some automatic academic scholarships, others by application for music, sport and art; a few means-tested bursaries and academic 13+ and sixth form scholarships.

Remarks: Charming girls' school just beyond the very southernmost outstretched fingertip of Manchester's conurbation. A new vigour of academic purpose mingles with the strong Christian ethos that so celebrates and values each girl here, urging her on to be all that she can be.

Altrincham Grammar School for Boys

4

Marlborough Road, Bowdon, Altrincham, Cheshire WA14 2RS

Pupils: 1,250 • Ages: 11–18 • Sixth form: 250

Tel: 01619 280858
Email: trichardson@agsb.co.uk
Website: www.agsb.co.uk

Headmaster: Since 2003, Mr Tim Gartside, 50s, born in Rochdale, married with three children. Formerly deputy head at Westcliffe High School for Boys and an old boy of Oldham Hulme Grammar. Studied history at Edinburgh, teaches occasionally to cover for absent colleagues, has been an Ofsted inspector since 2013. Says he'll be here until he retires, but no complacency even in this high-achieving school, constantly moving forward and always something still to do. Time out for him is catching up with the family, reading (mainly current affairs and history) and supporting Rochdale FC. Quietly spoken with a measured approach, he is warm and welcoming

A

and displays a reassuring balance of academic and commercial nous, keenly aware of the need to balance the books with shrinking budgets whilst pushing forward and developing the school, no lack of ambition here. He's a busy man, very much involved with structural change as the school evolves as part of a multi-academy trust with Mr Gartside as executive head.

Academic matters: When they have the capacity they'll take 210 each year but currently they can only manage an annual intake of around 180 selected from over a 1,000 hopeful applicants. Highly selective, it's no surprise that results are excellent but it's also outstanding for value-added at A level, clear evidence of some very good work going on. A strong and wide GCSE curriculum means that most boys take 12 GCSEs; it's a heavy load but the thinking behind it is to deter boys from dropping subjects too early, thereby allowing them then to consider the widest possible range of options for A level. The head hints that the downside of this approach is that they probably lose out on a percentage of As and A*s as a result of extending the GCSE workload, but with 35 per cent A* grades in 2016 grades, it's probably a moot point. The system clearly works because at A level in 2016 an impressive 58 per cent of grades were A*/A. The range of options at A level is narrower, with a keen focus on trad subjects.

There are five dedicated IT suites with additional help on hand from undergraduates from Manchester University. Maths seems to dominate thinking, it's a third of the entrance exam and there are even maths prefects here – the wiz kids willing and able to assist with any tough assignments ('or even long division,' chipped in a younger boy) as and when necessary; strong in science, as evidenced by exam results with triple science for all the norm; history, geography and geology are also very popular. No shortage of linguists either, beginning with two languages in year 7, choosing from French, German and Spanish; these then continue into year 8 though one can be dropped in favour of either Latin or Chinese. MFL exchanges take place annually with partner schools in France, Germany and Spain; immersion courses in China, Russia and the Middle East have taken intrepid boys and staff to far flung destinations, as have the school's links with the Apeejay schools in Delhi, India. For boys who are super-keen or super-able when it comes to languages there are after school classes in Mandarin Chinese, Spanish, Italian, Japanese and Arabic, and if you're a parent or simply someone who lives locally, then you too can join these classes. The school's own prospectus offers up a masterclass in persuading boys to take up languages: 'If have you've ever scoffed at Ronaldo's grasp of English, Joey Barton's French or felt puzzled over Messi's Spanish..' Brilliant.

Heartfelt praise from the boys for the school SENCo who works alongside enthusiastic and knowledgeable teaching assistants. Boys tell us they are supported not only in their learning but also in managing and supporting the occasional health issue such as diabetes.

Games, options, the arts: Sporting facilities are superb, and couple that with some of the most enthusiastic PE teachers we've ever met, this is now rated the fifth best state school in the country for competitive sporting achievement by School Sport magazine. Facilities include a sand-based hockey/football Astroturf, two cricket wickets (one Astro, one grass), three grass rugby pitches, two grass football pitches, a large multi-functional sports hall (four badminton courts, short tennis, basketball with electronic score board, two cricket nets, volleyball, five-a-side football and indoor hockey goals), a fitness/dance studio, 12 table tennis tables, 10 changing rooms and a very modern and well equipped fitness suite. There's even a coffee shop. It's very refreshing to hear staff elucidating on their healthy sport-for-all approach: it's all about breadth and finding something that works for everyone and they can proudly boast of top results in minority sports such as table tennis and badminton – you don't have to play for the first XV rugby team to be a hero here. The boys are proud of their sporting prowess; when asked who are the toughest schools to play against they claim: "We can pretty much take on anyone in football and rugby; the only ones who might threaten us are a few random, obscure private schools where the players are all steak-heads...' – a veiled hint for more protein in school lunches, perhaps? The extracurricular sport, including yoga, widens the range even further, and if Ultimate Frisbee is your thing, then this may just be the school for you. A fiercely contested rowing competition – that's rowing machines, we're not on the Thames here – brought out the heroes amongst staff and pupils alike.

It's cool to be good at music here; everyone in years 7/8 learns a musical instrument and many continue throughout their school career. A dedicated music IT suite contains 19 iMacs with professional sequencing and publishing software; there's also a well-equipped keyboard suite; six practice rooms each with a piano and amplifier with MP3 connectivity and a large rehearsal area containing enough percussion instruments to make a serious amount of noise. A range of ensembles include choirs, orchestras, wind, jazz and swing bands and it would be a challenge to find an instrument not taught by visiting peripatetic teachers. There's even a barber shop choir and a staff choir. One of the pupils runs a guitar club and there are music mentors for those who are serious about the subject.

Superb artwork on display around the school, much talent in evidence; design technology is impressive with all the necessary kit, including laser cutters, to boost jeopardy and excite and challenge the boys with some real hands-on skills and learning.

There's not much drama on offer in lower school, much to the chagrin of some of the younger boys who have happy memories of their primary school productions, but staff are aware and it may happen, though they might struggle to fit it in to their extremely busy timetable. A number of the older boys are working on LAMDA qualifications and they take the lead roles in the school's annual drama production, with expert training from a TV and film actress in aspects of voice and movement.

Societies and clubs are plentiful; take your pick from Amnesty International, Christian society, Duke of Edinburgh Award, Hindu society, ICT, Islamic society, public speaking & debating, robotic club, scheme film club, science club, website design and Young Enterprise. The school chess club dates back to 1912.

Background and atmosphere: The Altrincham County High School for Boys, as it was originally known, was founded in 1912. It opened with only 57 pupils and three staff (a head master, a deputy and one other) housed in the distinctively decorated red-brick building which still forms the central block of the school. The south wing and the assembly hall were added in 1938 and a science block in 1964; from the mid 1990s there has been considerable further development including the Stamford Hall (large dining hall), new classrooms, laboratories and a sixth form centre. 2008 saw a major redevelopment of sports facilities, and the most recent addition is an imposing physics centre opened by Professor Brian Cox in 2014.

Located just outside the town centre, the school is bang on the railway line with Hale station just 400 metres away and half a mile to the Altrincham tram stop. No need for school buses here, public transport is excellent and, helpfully, comes from all directions. Too many boarded up shops in the town centre, which seems at odds with the large expensive properties on the school's doorstep; what a difference a mile makes. Bags of history telling the story of this long-established school, and the Old Altrinchamanians Society meets annually to regale success stories. Parts of the old building feel a little austere with its wood panelling and tiled walls, but the boys genuinely don't notice or feel it and the younger ones remark on the 'friendly feel' and seem to thrive in this competitive, rigorous environment. There are two old boys on the staff but the profile has changed over the years, currently slightly more female than male and the average age has fallen. Staff turnover is low and parents value that stability.

The cover of the latest annual school review depicts a striking cartoon of a schoolboy ripping open his shirt to reveal a superhero vest bearing the school logo and inside the cover are the names of the heroes of the year, both in and out of school. Definitely a school for boys, it's written right through the place like Blackpool through a stick of rock, exuding masculinity from every pore..there's lots of wood and tiling in the original building alongside portraits of war heroes – old boys and former masters are decorated with poppies for remembrance. It's a place that recognises and remembers its heroes..

Pastoral care, well-being and discipline: 'I've always been a friendly, outgoing chap,' says the head boy who, along with his fellow prefects, plays a central role in the day-to-day running of the school. They, along with staff, are visible around the school site at breaktimes and lunchtimes, keeping an eye on the well-being of pupils. 'Bullying is rare,' they tell us, as is fighting, the older boys appearing supportive of the younger ones and keen to keep the peace. Pupil mentors from year 10 upwards work with younger pupils advising on academic or pastoral matters. Pupils' work is closely and regularly monitored and reported upon; there's nowhere to hide here. Parents receive termly updates on progress with grades on effort and attainment in each subject. Pupils whose attainment or effort is not up to expectations will be monitored more closely – 'there's a big difference in the level of support for those who are struggling with their work and those who simply can't be bothered,' the boys tell us. A yellow card system keeps everyone in check and sanctions are tangible, with litter-picking being one option for those who fail to toe the line. Plenty of recognition and commendations for excellent work and/or effort with praise through postcards home to parents. Usual rules re phones – you can carry it but it has to be off, and disrespecting teachers is, say the boys, 'a big no-no'. They acknowledge the presence of a small number of smokers amongst the older boys who disappear from the premises at lunchtime to head for a nearby alley (the teachers are apparently in a different alley); they know they're there but they keep an eye. Typically very conscious of sticking to the rule book, for the boys it's all about fairness and a sense of justice; they know where they stand and they prefer it that way. The head, they tell us is 'very friendly,' but 'we wouldn't want to push it'. Clearly there is a line, they know where it is and have no wish to cross it.

Food, they tell us, is 'authentic, nutritious and ethically sourced', just a shame about the small portions.. 'bring your own if you have a big appetite,' say the boys. They would also like 'more space in the dining hall please', though year 10 and 11s have their own space in the sports hall coffee shop and sixth formers have the option of eating in the sixth form centre, which has a coffee bar with leather sofas and the lingering aroma of toast.

Pupils and parents: The school has undoubtedly changed over the years, particularly in respect of its ethnic mix, reflective of a wider area demographic. A third come from beyond the local area, bringing a good school mix from Cheshire and central Manchester. 'Don't use tutors to help your son pass the entrance exam,' say parents, adding, 'if they are able they will pass, if not, it could be a miserable experience for them.' The view is very much that both boys and parents need to value academic excellence in order to thrive here. One parent of a clearly bright boy chose this school because 'he needed to be pushed' and commented on the fact that the school is especially 'well-organised when it comes to supporting/preparing for exams'.

Pupils are a bright, articulate and enormously likeable bunch – no arrogance but plenty of ambition. Very happy to chat and they clearly feel lucky to be here, countering our suggestion that 'the perfect school doesn't exist' with a polite but firm 'I beg to differ – this school is perfect for me'. They are well turned-out too, no long hair, no facial hair, no piercings, shirts in, ties tied, all they need is a smidgen of shoe polish and they'd rival Sandhurst. For sixth formers it's a business wear dress code; most wear suits.

Entrance: Up to 70 feeder schools, Altrincham Prep probably the largest, followed by Bowden C of E, Stamford Park, Altrincham C of E and The Bollin. Priority for catchment is WA13, 14 and 15, then Trafford LA addresses in M33. Entrance exam on the second Saturday in September for places in year 7, with application made directly to the school by late July of year 5. There are a small number of places available for sixth form applicants each year; entrance requires 48 GCSE points including three grade As or better.

Exit: A very small number leave post GCSE to join co-ed or sixth forms offering less trad subjects; by far the majority stay put. Good number to Oxbridge each year, nine in 2016, plus three medics; most to Russell Group universities, a few with gap years and/or work placements. Former pupils include Graham Brady MP, two members of the Stone Roses band, cricketer Paul Allot and educationalist Dylan Wiliam.

Remarks: An article in the Sunday Times on the best places to live in Britain described Altrincham as the number one place for schools – and AGSB is one of the reasons why. The school motto translates as Work Conquers All and it's as though these boys are on a mission to prove that. They seem super-competitive in all things, yet it appears friendly and good-humoured with plenty of banter. They've got the message, they're here to work and play hard, and they do.

Altrincham Grammar School for Girls

Cavendish Road, Bowdon, Altrincham, Cheshire WA14 2NL

Pupils: 1,320 • Ages: 11–18 • Sixth form: 340

Tel: 01619 125912
Email: admin@aggs.bfet.uk
Website: www.aggs.trafford.sch.uk

Executive Headteacher: Since 2014, Ms Stephanie Gill, 40s, born here in the north west, has two daughters. Formerly deputy head at West Kirby Grammar on the Wirral where she was previously a pupil; has experience of both state and independent school sectors. Read natural sciences at Cambridge, though describes herself as a mathematician. Had a spell working in the civil service 'just to check' before moving into education, and relaxes with Argentinean tango and salsa dancing. Bright, blonde and bold, she exudes a quiet yet determined ambition for the girls in her care; she has a lot of high expectations to manage here, but seems unfazed by the challenge. Describing her staff as 'able and committed', there is nowhere to hide with plenty of school-led high quality professional development going on in this dynamic school.

Academic matters: Some 1,000 apply for 174 places each year so yes, it is very selective, having a large pond from which to fish. The expectation is nine GCSEs, which is the 'right' number they tell us, followed by a choice of 20 A levels from which most will choose four in year 12. In 2016, 80 per cent graded A*-A at GCSE; results are equally impressive at A level with 90 per cent of grades at A*/B and 66 per cent A*/A. Plenty of rigour here; the girls drive themselves and each other quite hard, foot to the floor most of the time. There is no setting in any subject anywhere. Maths is important here, as is science, with half taking separate sciences at GCSE and biology, chemistry and maths leading the field at A level. While independent study is encouraged and supported, school also acknowledges many girls prefer a cooperative learning style – hence plenty of group work too.

A choice of two languages from French, German and Spanish at key stage 3 before then opting for one language as core and one other as optional in key stage 4. The school has recently been awarded the British Council's prestigious International School Award for 2015-18 and they are proud of their links with other schools and institutions across five continents. There is a busy and flourishing English department with a year 7 and 8 creative café writing club, literary film club, KS3 blog, mentoring clubs, the sixth form reading group, English Society and Oxbridge preparation. Regular visits to the theatre are also encouraged and there's a stimulating programme of visits from outside speakers including young fiction writers and lecturers from prestigious universities to deliver workshops for sixth formers. The range of subjects is very traditional, with the possible exception of psychology, which is proving a popular choice at A level. The Extended Project Qualification (EPQ) is optional in year 13 but most see it as useful preparation for university or even a valid add-on if entering straight into a career.

Few with learning difficulties/disabilities – mostly mild dyslexia. In-class support for statemented disabilities; mild physical disabilities can be accommodated. The gifted and talented blog is fascinating for those who wish to take their thinking a little further and deeper – consider Japanese fashion using maths: 'Do you realise you are wearing a MATHS equation at this very moment in time....?' is the opener, or try rapping and learning numbers in Japanese, apparently a great way to get tired muscles moving on cold frosty mornings. Then when the music died down, the girls got to work putting their new-found knowledge to work on a Japanese book marker (with a bit of macrame thrown in); or even combining science and Japanese in the building of bee-houses (yes, we were intrigued as well...). If Elizabethan English is more your thing, try the mouth-watering Shakespeare takeaway: 'I'll have a stuffed pig's bladder with onions and a side order of...gooseberry foole please, and make it snappy!' And all this before the school day even starts...

Games, options, the arts: While there are heaps of sport on offer, a new sports hall remains high on the wish list for both girls and parents. PE specialists lead national innovative pilots and as Youth Sport Trust members school believes that 'health and exercise go hand in hand with academic achievement'. Netball and hockey seem to dominate; there are six netball courts and two Astroturf hockey pitches with matches for A and B teams on Saturdays. The range on offer is wide, on and off curriculum, and includes badminton (at Altrincham Leisure Centre), dance, athletics, tennis, rounders, cross-country running, cricket, rugby, taekwondo and football, so hopefully something for (almost) everyone. Plenty of sporting success locally, regionally and nationally.

Music is strong and plays a very powerful role here with numerous concerts each term, some in school and others held in the local church. On alternate years there is a music tour at the end of the summer term; destinations have included the Rhine, Spain, France, Germany, Italy, China and Salisbury and Durham cathedrals. Eighteen ensembles and choirs meet weekly and include a number of student-led groups – try Quakapella for something different...Art, design and textiles are all evident around school, hugely impressive work, standards are very high with some inspirational teaching going on. There is abundant high quality drama, both on and off curriculum here with ample theatre visits, lots to inspire aspiring drama queens.

The extracurricular range on offer is vast; some of the more unusual activities to tempt you include the youth action group, politics society, street dance crew, Indian dance club, worldwide quiz, Japanese, Chinese, Italian, Latin, jewellery club, medical society, LGBT alliance, pro-share investor challenge and, for Harry Potter aficionados, Quidditch. Add to those D of E and all the usual clubs and societies you might expect and it's a wonder they ever make it home.

Trips and excursions are many and varied, but no lightweight jollies; it's all about learning, enrichment and 'opportunities to develop'. Take, for example, the keen scientists who went to CERN in Geneva and the Florida Space Centre and linguists actively involved in Comenius projects. We spoke to one parent whose daughter spent a month in Ecuador helping in a local village project, which included a short stay in the Ecuadorian jungle. For sporty types there are netball and hockey trips to Barcelona and ski trips to California.

Background and atmosphere: You'll find the impressive gateway to the school in the upmarket, leafy residential area of Bowdon. Don't even bother trying to park on site; you'll be lucky to find a parking place and ticked off if you try to park illicitly in places reserved for staff. The school reception is very smart, light, bright and chrome with an almost corporate feel, echoed in the school's conference and training facility. But it's a smorgasbord of buildings that are now home to the biggest girls' grammar school in England. It being a split site, one parent originally wished for a footbridge over the road until her daughter pointed out to her the fact that crossing this road 'afforded the girls the opportunity to become safer road-users'. The daughter was quite right, of course, and it's not an especially busy road; there is a crossing, and the girls (and staff) all look out for one another.

It all began in the late 19th century when Cheshire County Education Authority acquired Bowdon Lodge, a substantial but derelict local landmark. The plan to turn it into a school met much opposition as it was thought that the 'tone' of the neighbourhood would suffer as a result. In 1910 the building finally opened its doors to 60 boys and girls under the care of eight members of staff. The Education Act of 1944 saw the school become selective and 30 years later it became Altrincham Grammar School for Girls. In 2011, AGGS was one of the first schools to be awarded national teaching school status and during that year the new Breeze Hill facility was opened by the then education secretary, Michael Gove. The building incorporates an ICT suite, more classrooms and a teacher training facility. Also in 2011 AGGS became the lead sponsor school within The Bright Futures Educational Trust, a new multi-academy educational trust with Dana Ross-Wawrzynski as CEO of the trust and executive principal of the school. However, the trust has since been served a financial notice to improve or face closure.

Pastoral care, well-being and discipline: They take their anti-bullying policy seriously with anti-bullying ambassadors (who have their own blog and Twitter account) for those who feel they need some extra power to their elbow. 'It's not a major problem,' say the girls, whilst admitting that kids in general 'can be cruel to each other sometimes'. Detentions serve as effective sanctions for those who don't play the game, but most do and they wear their much-decorated school blazers with pride – lots of lapel badges in evidence for academic and sporting success as well as for additional leadership roles in school. The head tells us that 'it's fine to be different here – ok, in fact, to be geeky'. The school has adopted mindfulness as an approach to managing stress and pressure and there are clear targets based around resilience. Plenty of discussion around school on pastoral care, support and well-being, acknowledging the 'ups and downs of teenage girls'.

Pupils and parents: There are a good few appeals each year, unsurprising considering the competition for places and school expects an increase in the number of pupil premium students in 2017. Technically it is an eight mile catchment area, but realistically probably more like 5.5 miles in most years. School reflects the ethnically diverse population of this very popular local authority with around 39 per cent ethnic minority on roll. The academic success of the school is well-documented but the 'cultural diversity and spirit of tolerance' are also high on parents' priorities here, as is the 'mutual respect between staff and pupils'. Parents mostly live locally and feel the pressure at entrance exam time: 'it was nerve-wracking for parents'; they also advise that prospective parents: 'think carefully about their child's ability to thrive in a strongly academic school'. Most parents are delighted with the level and frequency of communication from school, for a small few it's a little heavy on the inbox.

Pupils are polite, articulate and hardworking; there's always a target to hit, a challenge to take on. Displaying a gritty northern determination to succeed, they are aware of high expectations, from both home and school, and the need to manage and keep up with the rigour. They are quite a political bunch, encouraged to share their views with mock referendums and a presence on the youth parliament. Uniform is navy, green and yellow, short skirts, long jumpers and blazers, with business attire for sixth form. Former pupils include Helen Czerski, physicist, oceanographer and broadcaster.

Entrance: Entrance exam (verbal and non-verbal reasoning plus maths) held in September each year; apply to the school between April and June of year 5 for a place in year 7. Now offer 10 priority places for students attracting pupil premium. Up to 50 feeder schools including Bowdon Prep, Withington and Manchester High plus a large number of maintained primaries. High entry requirements for sixth form, under old system was four As and two Bs with minimum B in English and maths – now converting to new GCSE 1-9 system.

Exit: Nearly all stay on for sixth form – 86 per cent in 2016. Vast majority to Russell Group (northern universities particularly popular), around 15 to Oxbridge each year (18 in 2016) and good number of medics (16 in 2016). Handful to high level apprenticeships or art foundation courses.

Remarks: The Latin motto translates as 'bravely, faithfully, cheerfully'. It may not be the most accurate description of your average teenage girl, but at least AGGS know what their school motto is and try their best to go with it. It's no walk in the park here but it certainly appears to be a happy and busy place, with bright, ambitious girls challenged and supported in equal measure by a very strong team of staff.

Altrincham Preparatory School

6

Marlborough Road, Bowdon, Altrincham, Cheshire WA14 2RR

Pupils: 320 • Ages: 2-11

Fees: £6,030 – £8,055 pa

Tel: 01619 283366
Email: admin@altprep.co.uk
Website: www.altprep.co.uk

Head Master: Since 2000, Mr Andrew Potts BSc PGCE, married with five grown up children, formerly secondary deputy head at the British School of Paris. He's a zoologist by training (note the animal skulls in his office) but doesn't currently teach. He is however very involved in the teaching in that he works with the staff to develop their skills, especially with reference to teaching boys. Male role models are important here, and alongside competence in the classroom he asks that all his staff have a 'passion for learning that they want to share with the boys'. He has travelled widely and has a wide range of interests, music being a key love of his life and, fittingly, he's keen for the school to become a choral school. Hugely likeable if somewhat avuncular and slightly old school in his approach, views IT as an important life skill but others, such as being able to converse coherently and interact graciously, are non-negotiables and possibly valued even more. Exhibiting a bright and breezy persona, he knows everyone and is enormously proud of his school and the boys' achievements here. Says it's all about 'the development of a personable young lad who is confident, but not cocky and who is able to express himself so that he can stand up for himself'; and with four sons of his own, he should know a thing or two about raising boys.

Entrance: Not selective at 3+ and 4+; higher up, prospective candidates spend a day at the school.

Exit: The majority to Altrincham Grammar Schools for Boys, a representative sample to local independent grammars, most notably The Manchester Grammar School and an occasional boy to an independent boarding school out of area.

Remarks: Although the school isn't selective, it is carefully and deliberately selected by parents who put their sons here for a reason. Yes, they buy into the ethos but they are also here, crucially, as a major and proven entry point to the school right across the road – Altrincham Grammar School for Boys. The big brother over the road, although no direct relation (they are very distinct and separate entities) offers what parents consider to be a welcome fee break in the sandwich between prep and uni. It is a credit to this school that, despite not being selective on entry, they still manage to get these boys through the rigour of the 11+ exam into an excellent and highly over-subscribed state grammar school.

The school is a limited company; governors are both shareholders and directors, with strong family links back to the 1936 founders. Split between two sites – one for the younger boys (nursery to year 2) set in two older refurbished buildings, and one for the older boys (years 3 to 6) in an open, spacious site in very impressive brick-built modern buildings. Both sites offer attractive, well-managed areas for learning and playing in an upmarket residential area of Altrincham, a short drive from the town centre, the wealthy, leafy suburbs of Bowdon and Hale

B

close by. The younger ones enjoy a delightful spacious play area, mainly grassed plus soft surface play space, and the continuous provision across indoor and outdoor space means that good use is made of the whole setting.

There are currently 29 pre-schoolers who, at the time of our visit, were enjoying the toys and bikes in the sunny gardens. 'Lots of nurturing,' say parents, with a teaching assistant 'never too far away to offer a few words of encouragement and a little hug if needed'. Maroon and grey uniforms for all with slight age-appropriate variations in style and oodles of sports kit for the older ones.

This boy-centric school exudes energy and enthusiasm – plenty of competition in everything from sport to reading and times tables. The youngest learn phonics with actions (no sitting still here), and whilst admittedly the boys gravitate to non-fiction as their default choice for reading books, fiction choices are carefully selected to include dungeons and dragons, the macabre and ghost stories a-plenty. An engagement with fiction is a must according to the head as a tool in 'promoting civilised behaviour' from which they can learn a great deal about self and others. Yes, your writing can be about sport if you so wish, but no gender excuses for bad handwriting – some fabulous examples on display and from an early age too. Maths is very strong here, the boys are super-keen, but in maths, as in all other subjects, there is no setting, no streaming, no pigeonholing and likewise no limited expectations. Desks for the older boys, tables for the younger ones and plenty of interaction between the boys and their teachers. Currently two parallel classes per year group, form teachers have a pastoral role alongside the teaching of the core curriculum; specialist staff for French, music, art, design technology and sport. School houses (names after World War II heroes) add extra fizz and competition to school events, house points are gained and guarded by the boys with real fervour. Minus points, far less popular and, to be fair, far less prevalent, are doled out for bad behaviour, shouting out in class and for 'failing to put your name on your homework or test papers,' according to the boys. The boys, typically, have a keen sense of fairness; they value their role on the school council, assessing areas of school life from school rules to the improvement of school lunches ('we're currently working on the chicken nuggets'). The school has its own chef and the food is good; 'chips could be better,' say the boys, presumably noting that they aren't yet triple-cooked here. They bring their own healthy snacks for break time.

Classrooms are bright, well-equipped and attractive. Generous specialist teaching areas for non-core subjects and terrific sports facilities include all-weather hockey pitches (off-site) and football, rugby, cricket and tennis on-site. It would be hard to find a primary or even prep school that could match their sporting facilities, so no surprise that they are leading the IAPS field nationally at hockey and reaching the finals in a range of other sports. Of course this high sporting achievement may come at a slight cost, with one or two mutters from parents about those with plenty of enthusiasm but less ability 'frequently being left out', though this appears to contradict the school's philosophy that all boys will represent the school at some point during their time at APS. There are adventure playgrounds on both school sites for fun and games during breaks. Music is very strong here, no surprise with the personal interest taken by the head; everyone plays the recorder, there are senior and junior choirs, an orchestra, guitar, brass and string groups and peripatetics working alongside to offer individual tuition in a wide range of other instruments. There are various plays, musicals and concerts throughout the year for proud parents. As a non-denominational school with an ethnic mix (as befits the local demographic), there is no proselytising but the school is comfortable enough in its own skin to mix the singing of hymns in assembly with the teaching and appreciation of all other faiths. SEN support is offered where necessary, though school shies away from diagnoses and labelling, adopting an approach of teaching strategies to cope rather than 'allowing labels to become excuses'. School trips, home and away, are popular, the Lake District and France being favourites.

Apart from the occasional grumble about homework, the boys are a happy bunch. They describe the teachers as 'friendly' and whilst they are undoubtedly kept very busy, that's exactly the way they like it. They know the rules and mostly play by them, proud of their blazer lapel badges in recognition of sporting and academic achievements. They also note that working hard and 'even holding doors open for people' is noticed and appreciated, which gives everyone, regardless of ability, a shot at public praise and appreciation. They are well-mannered, happy to chat (about anything) and yet businesslike in their approach to getting the job done in terms of working towards the next step on their educational ladder. No phones allowed, though if you walk to and from school you can bring a phone, but it's left in the school office for the day.

Parents describe 'an amazingly calm and welcoming atmosphere; it was a bit like house-hunting when you walk into a property and you know it's "the one" – we walked down the school drive..turned to each other and said "yes", this is the school for our son".' The advice from current parents is to join in with Parent Society activities – they are 'great fun and a fantastic way to meet other parents.'

Staff are a mix of long-standing individuals and newer blood. Much praise for staff from parents, including admin, support staff and the 'great PTA'. The school is very much serving the local population: parents are predominantly professionals; medics, accountant, company directors and lawyers much in evidence and, as ever, the school gate committee is strong. They like this suburban school that 'feels as though it is in a village', and whilst parking at the site for younger children can be a little problematic, they value the improved space, systems and facilities offered by the newer site as their sons grow, literally, into the bigger school. Staggered start and finish times and before and after-school care mean that parents can easily manage the drop-off and pick-up for younger and older sons at both sites. Attracted by the fact that 'it feels so male', one family recalls their initial visit when they noted menus from medieval times on the display boards featured eyeball soup – 'you wouldn't get that in a girls' school,' they add, smiling.

'I could write a whole essay on why APS is a fantastic school,' said one parent. 'We have watched our son develop into a fine, confident, caring and intelligent young man from being a shy and timid 3 year old. He has always been happy at APS and they have prepared him well for the next big step to grammar school.'

Backwell School

Station Road, Backwell, Bristol BS48 3BX

Pupils: 1,783 • Ages: 11–18 • Sixth form: 382

Tel: 01275 463371
Email: mailbox@backwellschool.net
Website: www.backwellschool.net

Interim Headteacher: Jon Nunes, deputy head, is holding the reins until the end of the 2018 academic year.

Academic matters: Fifty-nine per cent A*-B grades at A level in 2016 and 33 per cent A*/A; regular Oxbridge places (four in 2016).

Boys outshine girls in maths and physics whilst girls perform better overall. In 2016, 74 per cent got 5+ A*-C grades at GCSE; 28 per cent A*/A grades, with majority of pupils taking 10 subjects, including six options drawn from creative areas, languages and humanities. Half achieve English Baccalaureate annually. Strong in core subjects, especially science and maths, and majority takes at least one modern foreign language to GCSE. A Teaching School with innovative courses for experienced staff as well as new teacher induction and graduate training programmes.

Wider than usual choice at A2. Critical thinking encouraged as an additional AS option in year 13. BTec in leisure and tourism and creative and media diploma in sixth form, but more demand for academic subjects. In year 7, mixed-ability teaching operates across half the age group with setting in maths from the outset, and in modern languages, science and geography from year 8. Setting by ability increases further up the school. Enrichment programme styled Xtra Bytes runs twilight GCSE lessons in Latin, plus fast-track music. Strong PSHE course with lots of careers guidance. Plenty of computer suites but not OTT, plus Apple Macs for graphic work. Lots of buzz in DT and loads of original designs.

Has a well-earned reputation for special needs including its gifted and talented programme. 'Having the right attitude towards special needs has helped raise expectations of pupils across the ability range,' says head. Puts its money where its mouth is by providing priority accommodation for special needs on ground floor of stunning new building; lift provides wheelchair access to maths classrooms above. All children screened on entry for dyslexia with about 160 currently receiving individualised support. SENCo manages specialist staff including 16 LSAs.

Games, options, the arts: Range of sports (including swimming in years 7 and 8) offered as part of core PE provision, also timetabled in sixth form. Plenty available during extended lunchtime and after school; free late bus for those staying for activities. Pupils use adjacent leisure centre as well as school's sports hall and eight floodlit all-weather tennis courts. No Astroturf but extensive playing fields, which provide room to breathe at lunch-time during drier months. House competitions and some inter-school matches with teams practising and playing after school. Steady flow of representative players at county level. Community sports leadership award is a popular addition for some.

1950s theatre seating 400, and studio theatre for smaller productions in sixth form centre. Outreach work in primaries and participation in local festivals. Full orchestra and range of bands, choirs and ensembles. About 20 per cent of pupils have instrumental lessons and school holds regular concerts at St George's in Bristol.

Lots of trips within curriculum (art department were at Tate Modern when we visited). Sixth form leavers go on World Challenge expeditions biennially.

Background and atmosphere: Opened in 1954 as a secondary modern; reorganised in 1969 as a comprehensive, with its own sixth form since 1979. In recent years has expanded rapidly and built reputation over a wide area for good discipline and academic success. Carefully concealed but close to village centre. New canopied entrance leads to a modern reception area and spacious foyer, where displays include plenty of art plus evidence of recent school successes. New buildings for special needs and maths (with a multi-coloured roof) and new visual arts studios with vibrant, student-designed art on external cladding. Library is at heart of school life and includes a separate fiction classroom with 7,000 titles, all supervised by a doubly qualified teacher/librarian; equipped with laptops for online quiet study by sixth formers; identikit fingerprint technology used successfully for checking out loans. New-ish sixth form building houses common room, lecture theatre, dance studio and classrooms.

Pastoral care, well-being and discipline: Commonsense prevails – mobile phones are allowed for emergency use but confiscated if used otherwise during working day. Pastoral system a strength – parents and pupils emphasise how supportive and helpful they find the teachers. One mother described how she received a 'prompt and effective response' when her daughter was subjected to some 'low level irritation' from another year 7 pupil. The large numbers are broken down into manageable units – maintains a separate dining facility for year 7; years 8-11 share two kitchens between their four houses. Sixth formers have their own centre, so GCSE pupils are interviewed regularly by head of house to gauge progress, and sixth formers have lots of support too.

House areas double up as social and teaching areas with little evidence of fabric suffering as a consequence. House assemblies in own areas but year assemblies held in theatre. Trained school nurse also monitors attendance and 'uses some discretion' before contacting parents. Nice balance between long-term, experienced staff and younger teachers who move for promotion elsewhere. School council plays part in shaping policies and includes representatives from all age groups, with meetings attended by a governor and clerked by school bursar. Part-time adult mentors help with management of behaviour and learning programmes for relatively small number of disaffected.

Pupils and parents: Predominantly well-behaved, motivated pupils from affluent rural suburbs eight miles south-west of Bristol. Parents expect school to deliver a rounded, orderly, academic education and generally seem pleased with results. Years 7-11 look comfortable and smart in navy sweatshirts over white polo shirts trimmed with house colours. Sixth formers lack 'attitude' and generally wear sensible gear. Presence of a large sixth form helps to 'foster strong work ethic'. 'Some teachers don't believe in homework,' reported younger pupils, but plenty for exam candidates. One girl who was repeatedly 'picked on' at a rival comprehensive said she'd never had a moment's bother here. Active parents' association with fundraising and donations to school's coffers. Former pupils include film director, Kirk Jones, plus loads of media types, academics and sportspeople.

Entrance: LA manages admissions to year 7 – those from catchment area will get a place but heavy demand from elsewhere. Places siblings in same house and takes care to avoid pupils from one feeder school dominating any tutor group. Handles entries into other year groups and sixth form; the latter attracts some from Bristol independent schools.

Exit: Around a third go to FE colleges at 16, much less than from most comprehensives in the LA. A few go directly into employment, but the majority remain in the sixth form. Most year 13 leavers proceed to higher education across a wide a range of courses and universities. Four to Oxbridge and five medics in 2016.

Money matters: Parents contribute to school fund to assist with societies and expeditions – financial support available in cases of hardship in accordance with school's comprehensive ethos.

Remarks: Much friendlier than you would expect, given its size. House system ensures pupils in years 7 to 11 have a strong sense of identity. Hugely successful sixth form. Lots of younger, enthusiastic and committed teachers. Positive and reassuring buzz through busy working day confirms how well this place justifies parents' description of it as 'a really good all-round sc hool'.

B

Badminton School

Westbury Road, Westbury-on-Trym, Bristol BS9 3BA

Pupils: 440; 175 full, 16 weekly/flexi boarders • Ages: 3-18 (boarding from age 9) • Sixth form: 105

Fees: Day £9,600 – £17,850; Boarding £21,300 – £35,250 pa

Tel: 01179 055271
Email: admissions@badmintonschool.co.uk
Website: www.badmintonschool.co.uk

Headmistress: Since 2012, Mrs Rebecca Tear (40s) BSc MA PGCE. Her degree in chemistry from Exeter preceded a career in teaching science almost exclusively to girls, and which included other significant responsibilities eg head of sixth form and deputy head at Wycombe Abbey, taking in a masters in leadership in education along the way. An unequivocal believer in single sex education from her early teaching practice, where she saw how the less confident girls needed bringing out in lessons, she says, 'Teaching girls by themselves breaks down any preconceptions, barriers or stereotyping; when subjects don't acquire masculine or feminine connotations, girls tend to make more realistic personal choices.'

Somewhat jolly hockey sticks in manner – she strode across the drawing room, extending a hand and introducing herself as 'Bex' – we warmed to her no-nonsense and open personality; staff describe her as a real hit with the girls. For her part, Mrs Tear has made strenuous efforts to bring parents and guardians into school more: new ventures like the summer fair and fireworks night have been welcomed. 'I don't want the first time I meet a parent to be in a bad news situation', she says.

Married to another chemistry teacher, she has two young sons who doubtless counterbalance all those girls. Passions include outdoorsy things like running, ski-ing and cycling with her family, and she is a keen cook – though at home she regrets the lack of a lab technician to wash up for her.

Head of junior school: Since 2010, Ms Emma Davies BA PGCE (40s). Brought up and educated in Wales (where she still lives) and maintaining her Welsh lilt to this day, Mrs Davies has taught in a variety of prep schools including one in Malaysia, most recently as deputy head at the junior part of Bristol Grammar. Her first degree is in English, but she admits to a love of history and runs the history club at school. Ms Davies exemplifies the lifelong learning the school aims to instil: she is doing a distance MEd in educational leadership and writing a children's book 'very slowly'. Interests outside work centre mainly on her family – she has two daughters at the school – and include indulging her love of history at museums and National Trust properties. Whilst she is clearly warm and very approachable, some parents expressed frustration with a slow and unsatisfactory response to pressing concerns, such as SEN provision within school, and feel that considerably more should be done to make the school fully inclusive to all who attend it.

Academic matters: Whilst it is non-selective before year 3, academic expectations are set out early: '..some misspelt words will inevitably occur in written work. Great store is however set by accurate spelling which does not come naturally to many,' says the handbook. As well as high rates of entry to the senior school, Sats results at the end of year 6 tell a remarkable story: against a nationally expected level 4, these girls are all achieving high level 5s and some level 6s in maths, partly as a result of very small classes, and perhaps partly from learning their times tables to the funkiest rap we have ever heard. French is taught from the off, and from years 3-6 girls also try out Spanish, German and Latin in rotation.

Younger girls are taught by their class teachers and expected to practice reading at home, but from year 3, subject teachers take over and there is formal prep every night. Moving between classes and having the right books and equipment demands much of these 7-8 year olds, and some parents we spoke to were very critical of the lack of support given to the less organised or mature. In fact we picked up considerable dissatisfaction from some about SEN provision generally: an unwillingness on the school's part to acknowledge that 'drip-fed support little and often in school' would enable girls needing a bit of a boost with writing or organisation to access the curriculum so much better than being packed off for a weekly session at the Bristol Dyslexia Centre a taxi ride away. Our latest intelligence tells us that the appointment of a SEN specialist is under serious consideration.

Selection at senior school entry, rigorous exam preparation and small classes (averaging 14 until GCSE) all the way through the school make for stunning results, and a reputation as Bristol's most academic school. A level results in 2016 saw 68 per cent A*/A (90 per cent A*-B) grades, with the majority of girls taking four subjects. At GCSE, 76 per cent A*/A in 2016. Options are (unusually) not blocked, so virtually any subject combination is possible. SAT training also provided for those hoping to go to American universities, plus the first ever opportunities fair, which featured a talk on world class university applications. Girls greatly encouraged to take on all manner of academic challenges outside school; two girls were recently invited to go to a UK Mathematical Trust Olympiad training camp, out of only 22 youngsters in the country, and external essay prizes are frequently awarded. Everyone does English Speaking Board exams, which, for the year 8 class we visited, involved learning, reciting and discussing chunks of poetry – a Shakespeare sonnet in one case. Years 8 and 9 are also offered a 10 week STEM experience with engineering or manufacturing companies with Go4SET. 'They push them, but not in any way too much,' said one mother, who also appreciated the way teachers go over work with individuals when they find it difficult. EPQ added to sixth form enrichment programme.

SEN provision is modest – not much call for it here – and mostly delivered by 'flexible in-house support'. Weekly sessions at Bristol Dyslexia Centre to improve skills in English and maths are laid on for more severe cases: whilst some parents accept this, others resent the extra time expended, and the stigma associated with leaving the school by taxi, and feel that daily intervention would be a darn sight more use. More emphasis is given to extending the gifted and talented – a term the school avoids. EAL is also offered in school to support overseas girls.

Games, options, the arts: Junior school offers the broad curriculum and facilities which parents opting for an independent education expect, with some kind of sport, PE or swimming every day, and timetabled drama and music. Girls try out a range of three musical instruments early on; bizarrely, the cello is the most popular choice for private lessons – about a third of girls take these – which take place in the school day at the senior school. (We heard a heartrending account of one little girl in tears because she could not remember the door code to the music school, so missed half her lesson and was in trouble all round). Self-confidence is built by performing in concerts, plays and by the English Speaking Board exams, where poetry is learnt, delivered and discussed. Sport and exercise loom large – hurrah – but apparently only the best players are selected for teams, which tends to demotivate less skilled players.

Games and sports are well catered for in the senior school (Astro, tennis courts, netball courts and a 25m pool, with construction soon to start on a new sports hall) on the school's site, unlike so many of Bristol's schools, whose playing fields are a bus ride away across the suspension bridge. Hockey, netball, tennis and swimming are the main sports, but an innovative range of activities including kick-boxing and water polo means that no-one has an excuse to be idle. Badminton's riders enjoy considerable success: one was selected for the Prince Philip cup – the height of mounted athleticism. Hockey and netball players are regularly selected for the county. One parent was unhappy that only top players were ever picked for teams, and that mediocre participants barely got a game; also that the (beautiful) pool was used very little by the girls 'because it was always being hired out'. The absence of swimming teams or even a swimming club is an oddity.

Artistic life flourishes too, with top notch music, drama and art. Much is rightly made of high calibre musicians (one to the Royal College on Saturdays, two to the National Children's Orchestra, several playing in city orchestras, a recent leaver in training for The Sixteen) and school is fortunate to perform in St George's Bristol, a national concert venue. Most girls learn one instrument if not two, and school is proud of the number and scope of ensembles it lays on for musicians of all standards and persuasions. New music building has enabled school to bring all of its music teaching and practice activities to a single location and created a new focus for the department. The building includes teaching and practice rooms, a new music library and a generous classroom for curricular music lessons. Drama reasonably prominent too, with six productions a year plus a staff pantomime, as well as collaborations with outside initiatives at local innovative theatre the Tobacco Factory and Garden Opera, recently as a chorus of urchins in Carmen. Several notable actresses are OBs: Clare Bloom, Phyllida Law and Rosamunde Pike.

Art is housed in a most appealing setting, where mannequins dressed in creations fit for a Milan catwalk grace the entrance. Textiles, ceramics, painting, digital media (aka photography) and all types of artistic endeavour go on here. Badminton girls gain places at prestigious colleges such as Central St Martins.

Boarding: From age 9 although there's only a handful of junior boarders. Boarders accommodated in three houses grouped by age – interestingly, Bartlett houses girls from years 5-8, spanning both junior and senior schools. Sanderson is the newest build for the middle girls; sixth formers are separate. One parent reported a tendency to cliques among the girls, which she felt the school did little to address, and that it 'feels like a boarding school which day girls attend'; another felt that integration was fine.

Weekends fairly relaxed for those who stay in school: girls might be involved in sports or drama, off on a surfing trip, going out for a meal or to the theatre. As elsewhere boarders from abroad are required to have a guardian, but here they do so much more than that rather dry word suggests and are more like surrogate mums – we applaud this.

Background and atmosphere: Founded over 150 years ago, Badminton is older than most girls' schools of its type and was set up to provide the same educational opportunities for girls as their brothers enjoyed. That sense of academic seriousness, courage, confidence and an international outlook still prevail – girls here tackle any academic challenge head-on. Originally sited in Badminton House in nearby Clifton, it moved to its present premises on the edge of the downs in Bristol, arguably the greenest and most desirable part of the city. Main building is Georgian and gracious (we were ushered in to a warm and luxuriously carpeted drawing room, where Classic FM played discreetly); over the years the site has been filled in with all sorts of additions of varying degrees of beauty, making the school compact, rather than crowded. Nestling on the edge of the Badminton site, the junior school is certainly the senior school's little sister and firmly under its wing.

Groups of girls scurry purposefully about the place in their practical uniform of blue shirts, sweaters and checked skirts. 'Why no trousers?' asked one mum. Sixth form dress is much less restricted than in some schools: torn jeans and strappy tops are out, otherwise more or less anything goes. Overseas girls are welcome here and come in droves, mostly from Hong Kong but a good few from Russia and Nigeria; a sprinkling from the rest of the world. Bristol's own ethnic and religious mix well represented and catered for too: any dish containing pork was firmly labelled at lunch. Old Badmintonians include Indira Ghandi and Princess Haya Bint Al Hussein of Jordan.

Male company is provided mostly by QEH, Bristol's only remaining boys' school (albeit one that will admit sixth form girls from 2017) – academic and social interactions, we gather, which include a shared minibus from Chepstow.

Pastoral care, well-being and discipline: Discipline, in as much as it is needed in this high-achieving environment, works on girls' general desire to please, and dislike of letting people down, so the head might well say, 'I am rather disappointed that I have to speak to you, Jemima', on the rare occasions that girls come before her. Smoking, alcohol and drugs will lead sinners straight to her study. Achievement of all kinds is recognised, but interestingly there is no honours board, and school's annual open day is as much about displays, demonstrations, music, drama and food than interminable speechifying; the only prize awarded is the Iris Murdoch (another OB) prize for creative writing.

Pastoral care reads as well as one would expect for a school like this, with a tutor assigned to each girl, a vertical house system and peer mentoring, but one mother told us her daughter's confidence had been undermined by too great an emphasis on academics, and too little on making supportive friendships.

We loved the way the bigger girls supported the littler ones: at the end of our visit, they were snuggled up on beanbags looking at books with year 6s. One little dot could not stop yawning at the end of her busy day; another could hardly be torn away from her riveting story to talk to us. Vertical tutor groups lie at the heart of these close relationships and are a feature of the school.

Pupils and parents: Quite mixed socially and ethnically, but united by high academic expectations and aspirations. We found the girls friendly, unpretentious and open-minded – and were pleased to see some tucking into the sponge pudding we are probably no longer allowed to call spotted dick. 'The school does not turn out a mass product,' said one mother with several years' knowledge

Entrance: Non-selective until year 3, though all are informally assessed during a taster day, partly to judge social skills and 'readiness to learn'. From year 3, more formal assessments in English, maths and non-verbal reasoning.

Most senior school girls arrive in year 7, but everyone below sixth form is required to sit papers in English (English as a foreign language for those who have been at school in the UK for less than two years) and maths and to do an online reasoning test. The transition from the junior school is not automatic and girls do exactly the same assessments as those coming from elsewhere (in practice, the vast majority are accepted). Sixth form hopefuls must sit papers in two of the subjects they intend studying at A level, plus a general paper. All applicants are interviewed, via Skype when necessary.

B

Exit: Ninety per cent of juniors to the senior school via exactly the same entrance exams as external candidates will sit. These appear to hold no terrors, as girls have been well prepared throughout their time at the school; end of year assessments (aka exams) take place from year 3.

Some fall-out after GCSEs (around 20 per cent) from day girls wanting pastures new, and perhaps boys in particular. Those who stay go not only to our most prestigious universities, but also to top notch international ones in Asia and the US. London is the most popular destination, followed by Durham, and a good handful to Oxbridge each year (three in 2016). Wide choice of degree courses, more sciences than arts; two medics and two dentists in 2016.

Money matters: Fees are much in line with comparable schools, though boarders from outside the EU pay over £2000 more per year to cover the cost of escorted journeys to UK international airports – and of the boarding travel co-ordinator. Scholarships are awarded to a maximum of 20 per cent of fees; bursaries are means tested. New-ish regional award for girls 'who will bring something special to Badminton'; the school intends this as a way to recognise wider achievement and potential than the range of scholarships currently on offer.

Remarks: Undoubtedly a distinguished Bristol institution, yet its size, compact site, high proportion of boarders and fearsome academic reputation (which frightens some off) mean it enjoys a lower profile than it should in the city. The head describes it as a hidden gem, so her mission, should she choose to accept it, is perhaps to polish up all its facets so it shines a brighter local light. Badminton Junior is a great choice for bright, organised and confident girls, where they will receive excellent opportunities in the classroom, on the pitch and on the platform. The diffident, disorganised, dyslexic, dyspraxic or ditsy should look elsewhere.

Balcarras School

East End Road, Charlton Kings, Cheltenham, Gloucestershire GL53 8QF

Pupils: 1,400 • Ages: 11–18 • Sixth form: 400

Tel: 01242 515881
Email: admin@balcarras.gloucs.sch.uk
Website: www.balcarras.gloucs.sch.uk

Headteacher: Since September 2016, Dominic Burke, previously deputy head. Degree from York, master's from Sheffield and teacher training qualification from Leeds. First teaching post in Evesham; joined Balcarras in 2007 as head of history. Two young sons; enjoys golf and running and supports Leeds United.

Academic matters: The school's strategy is to set high expectations for its pupils and then give them the support they need to achieve those expectations. It's one that is clearly working. Sixty-three per cent of grades were A*-B at A level in 2016, making it one of the best performing state secondaries in the south west. Over 30 subjects on offer – maths is the most popular (further maths also available) and the psychology department has just had to expand to accommodate demand. The sixth form is bearing the brunt of recent funding cuts (with a £300k smaller pot than the previous year) but facilities are impressive nonetheless. The purpose-built sixth form centre has two large study areas alongside well-equipped science labs and IT and business suites.

At GCSE, 78 per cent of students achieved 5+ A*-C with English and maths in 2016, with 37 per cent of those grades A*-A. The school used to be a technology college and is still strong on design and ICT, with seven specialist DT rooms including a wide range of CAD/CAM equipment, a laser cutter and a 3D printer. Product design students recently enjoyed a visit to the Ducati and Ferrari factories in Italy.

The school prides itself on being inclusive. It has around 140 children on the special needs register (24 on full statements/ EHC plans) and strong support is in evidence, with two full-time SEN specialists and good disabled access (including lifts) available throughout the school. One father of a child with a statement told us he 'could not speak highly enough' of the SEN department and was impressed with the regular feedback and opportunities to meet with staff.

Games, options, the arts: Balcarras has 3.5 acres of playing fields, with four rugby pitches, a cricket field and a large, floodlit Astro pitch. An indoor sports centre is open for community use on week day evenings and weekends, providing a valuable additional revenue source for the school. The school punches well above its weight against the local grammars and private schools and recently won the County Plate in hockey.

An active cycling club offers the chance for pupils to take part in mountain biking and road cycling and the school recently opened its own cycle speedway track. Balcarras encourages all pupils to take part in sports outside lessons – archery, badminton and dance are all popular choices and a number of pupils have represented the school at county and national events. One former pupil made it to the pentathlon event at the 2012 Olympics.

The week before we visited was the annual house music event, an X-Factor style competition between the four school houses, each performing a 45 minute show. Highly competitive and involving a huge amount of work and energy, it was still the talk of the school as we took our tour. Parents describe the music and drama provision as 'very impressive'. The school is well represented at the local Cheltenham Music Festival and the chamber choir recently won a national Music for Youth award. It has two high-spec drama studios, and music facilities recently expanded.

The list of school trips is impressive for a state secondary, perhaps reflective of the relatively affluent local demographic. Borneo and Malawi have been among the more exotic recent expedition destinations, while the biennial music tours have included Venice and Barcelona. Duke of Edinburgh is very popular and the school was a recent competitor in the European finals for Young Enterprise.

Background and atmosphere: History on this site stretches back to 1958, when the co-ed Charlton Kings County Secondary School moved here. Balcarras was formed in 1986 as a result of a shake-up in the local education system which scrapped single sex schools.

Cheery, bright and modern, the school has made the most of its functional appearance. Big classrooms are flooded with natural light and large open views create a healthy sense of space. Primary colours abound (even floors and furniture are painted red) and walls are crammed with examples of work – an impressive display of pop art adorned the reception area when we visited. Rows of team photos and certificates all add to the sense of pride and celebration in the school's many achievements.

The school canteen has had a recent facelift and a varied menu promotes healthy eating (pupils are only allowed one cake). A new café has also been opened for sixth formers, 'to stop them going to the Chinese in town'.

Teachers are very visible in the corridors and playgrounds, not just supervising but chatting and interacting with pupils. A lack of formality – one teacher has displayed his loyalty to Cardiff FC by plastering stickers all over his classroom door – does not compromise a pervasive sense of calm authority and well-maintained discipline.

Pastoral care, well-being and discipline: Staff credit this balance between discipline and fun to the mantra of 'A,B,C and the three E's'. (Attendance, Behaviour and Curriculum – Extracurricula / Enjoyment /Environment). A strong house system also helps control behaviour issues, as does attention to detail. 'Being strict on the small things, such as manners and uniform, helps with the big behaviour', explained one teacher. Parents also commented on the good manners of children both inside and outside of the school, which is located in a very residential area of Cheltenham. Pupils might moan good-humouredly that teachers 'are always nagging about the uniform', but it's an approach that works. The school topped the county for attendance recently and school says permanent exclusions are 'very rare', despite having welcomed 'more than our fair share' of excluded children from other schools.

Parents did report cases of emotional bullying (nothing unusual there), but all felt that incidents had been handled effectively by the school. The school has implemented a Bring your Own Device programme and all staff are trained in how to manage any cases of online bullying or social media abuse. Anonymous questionnaires help monitor the emotional health of pupils and as one pupil commented, teachers 'work very hard to get to know you'. Paired reading between sixth formers and year 7s is just one indicator of the caring environment evident throughout the school.

Pupils and parents: As one parent remarked, 'Cheltenham is arguably the most middle class town in England', and social mix reflects this, with less than 10 per cent of children receiving the pupil premium. Worth noting, however, that the percentage of pupil premium students achieving 5+ A*/C including English and maths at Balcarras is more than double the national average. Pupils talk with pride about 'ridiculously high' reputation of the school and are clearly chuffed at being able to give the local grammars and independents a run for their money. Parents, too, are aware of how lucky they are to have Balcarras on their doorstep. All those we spoke to praised the 'excellent' teaching, observing how staff are quick to encourage and motivate their children. Communication channels are clear and effective. One dad described how after expressing concerns about his son being in the wrong set, his class teacher established clear goals that resulted in his son being moved up the following term.

Entrance: Balcarras has 194 places, but applications treble this number. Admission criteria serves the immediate area, but at sixth form pupils travel from further afield (one sixth former we spoke to has a three hour daily round trip on the bus). Minimum requirement for entry to sixth form is two Bs and three Cs at GCSE including English and maths.

Exit: Around 30 per cent leaves after GCSEs. Plenty of tailored support to help pupils through exams and 'Futures' lessons to prepare for life beyond school. Up to half to Russell Group, including one to Oxbridge in 2016, plus one medic and two vets.

Remarks: Strong leadership and dedicated staff make this a school worth queuing up for.

Beaudesert Park School

Minchinhampton, Gloucestershire GL6 9AF

Pupils: 450; 13 weekly, 59 flexi boarders • Ages: 4-13 (boarding from 8)

Fees: Day £8,496 – £16,488; Boarding £21,426 pa

Tel: 01453 832072
Email: office@bps.school
Website: www.beaudesert.gloucs.sch.uk

Headmaster: Since 1997, James Womersley (50s). Educated at The Dragon and St Edward's Oxford, studied economics, history 'and rugby' at Durham, PGCE from Oxford. Came to Beaudesert after Eagle House, Emanuel London and nine years at his old prep school. He cites this time at the Dragon, where he became a housemaster, as a formative influence.

Mr W and his wife, Fiona, make a prep school power couple. Parents can be assured that whatever (or whoever) comes their way, the Womersleys have probably seen it before. Mrs W comes from a prep school family, although she claims it was the 'last thing I thought I'd find myself doing'. Nothing daunted, she takes care of marketing, catering, pastoral and safeguarding – and somehow manages to look groomed and elegant at the same time. The Womersleys are a great advert for the youth-enhancing properties of prep school life – fizzing with energy and joie de vivre. Certainly not ready for retirement, 'not while we're still enjoying it'. Their three sons all went to Beaudesert and St Edward's Oxford.

The Womersleys' job satisfaction must be infectious; they've created a school with a strong sense of identity and 'real soul', as one parent put it. The atmosphere is professional and collaborative, everyone we met was relaxed and friendly (well, it was near the end of term...). Mr W speaks of his teaching staff with pride – several current heads and deputy heads cut their teeth at Beaudesert.

He describes Beaudesert as 'virtually independent', by which he means that paths to schools such as Marlborough and Cheltenham College are well maintained – after all, it's the reason many families choose this prep. Nonetheless, parents can be confident that advice about senior schools is unbiased by anything apart from their child's best interests.

Although Mr W no longer teaches he does take cover lessons. And what job would he do if he hadn't become a prep school head? He ponders – perhaps he never thought of doing anything else. 'An art historian' he says finally.

You might think that the indefatigable Womersleys spend their leisure time having a well-earned sit down, but you'd be wrong. They play golf and tennis and enjoy skiing. Phew.

Entrance: While not fiercely selective, Mr W says Beaudesert attracts a 'generally high level' and 'families with bright children'. Pupils come from local nurseries or, since 2012, the school's own. Transfer from pre-prep generally straightforward.

Exit: Majority in roughly equal numbers to Cheltenham College and Marlborough, then St Mary's Calne, Badminton, Cheltenham Ladies' College, Downe House (girls) and Eton, Radley, Winchester, Sherborne (boys). Also Bradfield, Malvern College, Stowe and St Edward's Oxford. Good spread of scholarships every year too (12 in 2016).

Remarks: Beaudesert Park School was founded in Warwickshire in 1908, moving to its mock Tudor Cotswold folly 10 years later. That folly has been joined over the years by buildings in a variety of architectural styles, the latest being a superb performing arts centre. Any deficit in architectural coherence is more than made up for by character – round every corner is a different view, whether it's terraced lawns and playing fields or the free-range cattle on Minchinhampton Common, who look as though they could wander into the car park (they can't, thanks to a grid). Towers, curved walls, covered outside staircases and walkways – it all looks rather like an animated Escher drawing as pupils go busily up and down between lessons.

Although Mr Womersley regrets the dominance of exams in schools today, he's a champion of CE and believes it gives children a worthwhile goal. 'They work hard and get the joy of success', he says. But as several parents told us, at Beaudesert the balance between academic work and the myriad other activities on offer is skilfully maintained. Those who have moved their children from London preps really notice the difference and value the unpressurised environment – even more so when their children go on to gain places at top senior schools. 'They challenge the children academically by keeping them engaged,' said one. Homework is sensible too, certainly not hours every night. Nursery and pre-prep have their own mini-school with all the facilities including a hall and stage.

Pupils setted for maths, English and languages (French, Latin from year 6, optional Greek for scholars). No separate scholarship stream. Well-equipped labs where legendary 'screaming jelly baby' and other spectacular experiments are staged – obviously science is not impervious to Mr W's performing arts campaign. Old-fashioned values do not extend to technology and there's a full complement of whiteboards, iPads and the like. Delightful, bright art studios with separate ceramics room and proper kiln. SEN provision received mixed reviews. Pupils told us the help they'd received was 'brilliant', but parents raised concerns. Several thought that a school with a relatively unselective intake should have wider in-house experience to identify specific learning needs early on.

Part of the charm of Beaudesert, according to parents, is that it's a proper 'outdoors' school: 'It's a real country school', 'a proper all-round education', 'the children are connected to their surroundings.' Several made the distinction between country preps that are 'sporty' and Beaudesert, where, in addition to plenty of sport, there's free range tree climbing, den building, night camps, forest school for the little ones and bushcraft ('It's mainly about knives', a Just William character told us).

Main sports arranged along pretty traditional lines, rugby, football and cricket for the chaps, netball and rounders for the girls. Both do hockey (girls very successfully) and there's some overlap with cricket coaching. Athletics for all in the summer, plus tennis and cross-country. We didn't hear any grumbles about teams and matches, most parents thought the arrangements were fair enough and that pupils in the B and C teams enjoyed their games just as much as those in the As. Swimming is a real strength – all Beaudesert pupils learn to swim and indoor and outdoor pools mean year round training. The school regularly qualifies for IAPS national finals and swimmers compete in local and national teams. This being Gloucestershire, there's a fair amount of equestrian activity – school team recently won national junior polo championships. Golf, fly fishing and mountain biking also on offer. Pupils can bring their own bikes and learn cycle safety and maintenance.

In defiance of Noel Coward's advice, Mr W believes that everybody's daughter or son benefits from taking to the stage. Even before the opening of the new performing arts centre, music and drama were enthusiastically pursued by the majority. Minutes after the builders left preparations were under way for the inaugural concert, featuring school choirs, orchestra, ensembles and soloists. This glass and Cotswold stone building sits, appropriately enough, at the centre of the school and hosts plays, concerts, assemblies, parents' evenings, music and drama lessons and exhibitions. The exterior features distinctive cedar planks, rather like xylophone keys, positioned to deflect the light.

Pupils can board from year 4 and most will have some experience of boarding by the time they leave. Options are flexi or weekly – everyone goes home after Saturday school (lessons until 12.30pm) or matches. Boarders up to year 6 can work towards bronze, silver and gold Beaudesert Badges – activities include first aid, cookery, gardening, outdoor skills and charity work.

One boarding house with boys' and girls' sections up different staircases. Jolly kitchens and comfortable shared areas for 'TV and talking'. Brightly decorated boys' dorms run into each other (no doors), girls have separate (shared) rooms. Everything clean and homely. 'I love boarding, you get to sleep over with all your friends,' said one of our guides. Houseparents plus matrons, nurses and gappies oversee proceedings. 'There's always someone to talk to,' we were told. Food gets a big thumbs up, especially pulled pork buns and good old treacle sponge.

Year 8 girls informed us proudly of the small privileges of seniority – white shirts in winter, benches in assembly, 'senior snacks' (cereal and squash at 8pm on a Friday) and, best of all, 'senior supper' with the Womersleys – none typical 12 year olds' aspirations. Advocates of the 'real world' undoubtedly educate their children elsewhere and even its biggest fans concede that there is a Beaudesert bubble, but how many parents would wish their children to grow up more quickly?

Houses, we were told, are 'no big deal', thus rather suiting their prosaic names: A, B, C and D. No head boys and girls, instead all year 8s have duties and responsibilities. Newish school council has achieved victories including modifications to the year 8 uniform. 'Boys can choose their own socks, but they mustn't be luminous or white.' What else would improve their school, we asked? Modest proposals included golf buggies to transport pupils to games fields over the common, flattening the bump in the Astro, compelling teachers to sit their own exams, and 'unlimited ice cream'.

According to Mr W, the parent profile has changed in the 19 years he has been at the helm of Beaudesert – these days both parents are probably working, often weekly commuting to London. He welcomes the fact that parents are 'in a lot more' and encourages their involvement. Families all fairly local – few alternatives in the immediate area and weekly boarding only see to that. No PTA but active Friends of Beaudesert who organise fundraisers and socials. No class reps either – they don't really feature in the boarding model – but most parents happy with home-school communications, prompt replies to enquiries and general delightfulness of front of house staff. High praise, too, for pastoral care and teachers' 'genuine concern' for pupils, 'Nothing's too much trouble. You can't fault it', we were told.

Beaudesert and its lucky pupils continue to thrive under the expert custodianship of the Womersleys. Mr W has no need of educational jargon; his philosophy is a simple one: healthy, happy children learn best. Happiness isn't a subject to be taught, it should be the founding principle of any school – it certainly is at Beaudesert.

Beechen Cliff School

Alexandra Park, Bath, Somerset BA2 4RE

Pupils: 1,300; 32 boarders (boys only) • Ages: 11-18 • Sixth form: 352 (110 girls)

Fees: Boarding: £10,800 pa. Day pupils free

Tel: 01225 480466
Email: headmaster@beechencliff.org.uk
Website: www.beechencliff.org.uk

Headmaster: Since 2005, Mr Andrew Davies (40s), history graduate of University of Sussex. Married to Anne, an assistant head, with two teenage children, one at his school, one at local girls' independent. Career has followed normal trajectory (teaching, head of dept, head of humanities, deputy head) in five local authorities, plus a spell in the commercial sector as principal of Kings International College in Surrey. Has worked in the most and least desirable bits of SW England, so no airs and graces. Direct, engaging and warm, he is passionate about providing his flock with all manner of opportunity to extend and test themselves.

Refreshingly liberated, too, from some spectres of state education: 'We are not slaves to Ofsted', he says, but with a major success story on his hands, he can afford not to be. Still teaches – he offers GCSE in humanities to year 9 boys in their own time: take-up and results are good. Keen shot, cricketer (coaches both) and general outdoor type who involves himself in school endeavours, such as the Centurion Challenge, 100 mile slog in 48 hours as a Roman foot soldier. Proud of his school, and encourages his pupils to be the same. Well liked and respected by parents, who reckon he's 'good at dragging the goods out of the non-academic' as well as the academic.

Academic matters: Completely non-selective on entry but tends to get more able boys by default. All year 7s assessed with cognitive ability tests on entry to enable better setting than Sats scores provide. Results at GCSE and A level have crept up over last few years and academic aspiration encouraged. In 2016, 82 per cent got at least five grades A*-C at GCSE including maths and English (35 per cent of grades A*/A) with 30 per cent A*/A at A level.

Has specialist technology college status and is a founder member of Bath Educational Trust set up in 2009, a collaboration between Hayesfield School (sister school), Bath University, City of Bath College and global engineering firm Rotork, headquartered in Bath, which aims to 'to provide a better experience for children'. In fact it provides a lot of good practical stuff too, such as far more options post-16, resources and economies of scale in terms of buying power, as well as a smart minibus to shuttle pupils between sites. BET will evaluate its efforts by tracking pupils' early careers until the age of 25.

Thriving and oversubscribed sixth form where IB was offered since 2009 jointly with Hayesfield: those who teach and learn unequivocal in their praise, however suspended for the moment because of modest take-up. However, EPQ offered.

A level choices still extensive at 27 subjects, with the possibility of more at Hayesfield or Bath College. Others can choose Route 2, where they spend a year doing more vocational things at Bath College, along with retakes of English and/or maths GCSE.

Enthusiastic and proactive head of sixth form has gone down well with pupils and their parents. The academically precocious are encouraged to push on and take GCSEs early or AS in year 11; maths and further maths are taught within the same timetable. Most pupils start a second foreign language in year 8 (German, Spanish, Italian) and classics on offer after school. Clearly the message is that pupils will be given extra chances to get ahead, but the onus rests firmly on them. Nonetheless, a few parents worry that a good work ethic is not sufficiently instilled in the boys, and that to be labelled a 'keener' is social death; it is fair to add that the school comes down hard on this. Less able pupils taught in smaller sets and emphasis placed on extracurricular opportunities and successes for those in the bottom set for everything.

Busy SEN department caters for most needs one would expect to find in mainstream, the difference perhaps being that, in tune with the school's general ethos, pupils are expected to take responsibility for their own learning – 'I can't be doing with this excuse culture in education,' states the head. Lessons seem a good blend of purpose and fun, with lots of participation, and hi tech infrastructure to support them. Significant amounts of homework from year 7 compensate for short day – school ends at 3.40pm.

Games, options, the arts: Simply masses on offer, particularly for a state school, due in part to the all-hours culture where so much happens after the school day and at weekends; indeed it is the only comprehensive in Bath to take on the independents at Saturday fixtures. Impressive array of sporting successes in rugby, football, hockey, cricket and shooting borne out by the honours board in the entrance hall, where Amy Williams (GB's only gold medallist in the 2010 winter Olympics) appears, along with fellow Olympian Jason Gardener – and Roger Bannister. Competitive sport taken pretty seriously and winning is encouraged; some parents feel that the school's rugby and cricket coaches select more top players from city clubs than those outside Bath, but the school strenuously asserts that team selection done strictly on merit. Amazing results emanate from facilities which recently received massive investment, including the all-important all-weather pitch. Tennis and athletics in summer. Super sports hall has exterior climbing wall on one end, funded through parental gift aid. Strong links with top notch facilities (such as a 50m pool) and expertise at nearby Bath University too. Enough choice for sixth form girls, including rugby, but they say they are not compelled to do anything in the sporting line.

Art and DT have their own well-equipped if dilapidated block – and a committed following producing high quality work. Provision in photography hugely enhanced by the arrival of an industrial printer, bid for by the head of art, who has other grand plans (eg gallery space), if only funds would permit. Music, now housed in a splendid new block with a recording studio alongside more traditional teaching and practice rooms, attracts fewer takers, despite avoiding the trap of being a girls' preserve below sixth form, but there's a good range from brass to folk, and they do compete and succeed in the Mid-Somerset Festival, and tour Europe. School recently held its first internal young musician competition. Some plays done in collaboration with the (all female) Royal High; choices like Tartuffe and A Midsummer Night's Dream suggest no lack of ambition. Beechen Cliff also makes its mark locally at Model UN and debating with other schools. Much 'boys' own' stuff goes on in terms of outdoor activities aside from team games: Ten Tors race, Centurion Challenge, D of E and all the opportunities offered at Tir-y-Cwm, the school's cottage in the Brecons, a gem of an asset. All of year 7 go for a weekend's bonding near the start of their first term; thence participation in orienteering, climbing and caving is voluntary. Trips on offer compare well with far better resourced schools, and go beyond the confines of Europe, to Africa for charity work and Canada for skiing.

Boarding: Since 2013, 26 boarding places on offer for boys whose family circumstances mean they would benefit from the stability of a boarding education, or for whom proximity to Bath University's facilities and coaching programmes would enable them to exploit their sporting gifts and potential fully. Accommodation is more Travelodge than Sheraton: rooms are neat, clean, all en-suite and wireless.

Background and atmosphere: Feels and looks like a boys' grammar (which of course it was). It became a comprehensive in 1972, after amalgamating with the then boys' secondary modern, and takes its name from the hill on which its 1930s buildings stand. Its future was touch-and-go in 1990, but its head and governors mounted a huge campaign ending in the High Court to get it grant maintained status, and keep it open. Beechen remains prominent on the Bath scene in every way, and in recent years has upgraded its infrastructure to give its sixth formers, sportsmen and musicians what they deserve. One parent left a recent open evening wondering why he had shelled out so much money on independent education for his children, when he could have had so much of it for free at Beechen. Definitely a sense of tradition about the place (boys are addressed as 'gentlemen', 'gents' or 'chaps'), but it's not oppressive: all seem to absorb the values of discipline, courtesy, academic confidence and pride the school promotes, not least in its year book, The Gryphon. Loyalty and considerable affection from its old boys/girls (Old Sulians), and former members of staff come in to teach extra sessions – for love.

The head has beefed up the house system, renaming them after illustrious authors, after whom local roads are also named (this part of Bath is known as poets' corner); introducing a house tie and vertical tutor groups within houses to engender a spot of house loyalty. He's hot on uniform too: boys are picked up on untucked shirts and half-mast ties even outside school, no trainers or wild hair either. Some feel, however, that sixth form girls get away with murder as far as dress is concerned. Food is terrific too: Beechen's departed award-winning chef leaves much broader gastronomic horizons and a take-up for school meals much higher than average behind him – a new kitchen and dining hall are on the horizon. There's a real effort to source food locally – indeed, some of the salad and veg are grown on site by students. Popular snack bar forms part of a gorgeous new sixth form centre, with views over Bath and a sunny terrace with café tables. Some parents worry that they are given too much leeway by being allowed off site in free periods – 'they are still at school after all' – and that staff do not crack the whip sufficiently over punctuality or wasting time in free periods.

Pastoral care, well-being and discipline: Undoubted reward culture for all achievement is balanced by traditional sanctions for those who play fast and loose with expected standards, academic or otherwise. Anyone re-interpreting the uniform can expect to receive 250 lines on the vice of scruffiness, slackers get academic detentions on Saturdays. 'Pupils need to see consequences for their actions', as the head says. Parents report good relationships within school and quick response times from staff; the school takes concerns seriously. Sixth formers provide pastoral input to junior boys within tutor groups, in class on occasion and as directors in music and drama. Expectations of them are laid out in the sixth form code they sign before entry. No-one mentioned smoking, drink or drugs – possibly because they are strictly extracurricular?

Pupils and parents: 'Middle class and aspirant, reflecting Bath as a whole', according to the head, who woos newcomers, parents that is, with Pimms and lemonade. Mostly white and very local: the catchment area is strictly drawn. Some 20 per cent of boarders from overseas. Much emphasis put on the partnership between parents and the school, and it is the sense of shared values, rather than class or money, which unites them. The vast majority are totally supportive – 'it really wouldn't suit non-conformists or anyone with authority issues,' said one mother. Strong family connections too. Active PTA runs a gift-aid scheme, whose funds are doled out to successful bidders from amongst the staff or pupils for extras that wealthier schools would take for granted – a climbing wall and better stage lighting, for example. Old Sulians include several sporting greats (see above), as well as Arnold Ridley (Private Godfrey in Dad's Army), Andrew Lincoln (Drop the Dead Donkey, This Life, Love Actually), Curt Smith (Tears for Fears), research scientist, Nobel prize winner and generous benefactor Sir Richard Roberts and the current head of MI6, Sir John Sawers.

Entrance: There are 192 places on offer at 11, 'without reference to ability or aptitude', to boys living within the Greater Bath Consortium. When it's oversubscribed, precedence is given to normal state sector criteria of boys in care, followed by siblings. Applications taken in October for the following September. Admissions policy below sixth form is rigid – worth scrutinising the local authority website, especially as they prefer applications online. In practice, boys come from nearly 20 different primary schools – and the odd prep. Sixth form entry – boys and girls – by interview, but conditional on five GCSE passes, ideally with B or above for subjects chosen for A level. At least 20 places for outsiders at this stage.

Exit: A third or so leave after GCSEs. Some 50-60 per cent of upper sixth leavers to universities all over the country to pursue a diversity of courses. Seven to Oxbridge in 2016, including a medic; Exeter popular recently; also eg Cardiff, Southampton and Sheffield; subjects range from Abrahamic religions to aeronautics and astronautics. Plaudits from work experience placements indicate that those who start work straight from school are well equipped to do so.

Money matters: Well-supported by fundraising and parental contributions, which are, shall we say, greatly encouraged by the school, and bring in some £90K per annum. Less advantaged pupils are able to take part in trips and music lessons by means of a special school fund. Staff keep a sharp eye out for opportunities to bid for or win equipment there is no school budget for; an entrepreneurial culture prevails. Boarding fees are met by parents and are roughly a third cheaper than the boarding component of independent school fees.

Remarks: A Bath institution and good counterweight to local independents, in that it manages to offer much of what they do for free, but for boys only below sixth form. An outstanding non-selective choice for almost any boy, or sixth form girl, now with 26 boarding places for boys.

Bishop Wordsworth's Grammar School

11 The Close, Salisbury, Wiltshire SP1 2ED

Pupils: 928 • Ages: 11–18 • Sixth form: 292 • C of E

Tel: 01722 333851
Email: admin@bws.wilts.sch.uk
Website: www.bws.wilts.sch.uk

Head Master: Since 2002, Dr Stuart Smallwood BSc PhD PGCE NPQH (50s), formerly deputy head. Brought up in Kent and a product of a grammar school like the one he now heads, Dr

Smallwood graduated in geology from Leeds and got his doctorate from Cambridge. A brush with the civil service preceded his move into teaching; he has taught in only two schools, though his career follows a conventional path to his current post as head of one of the best state schools in the country. As such, he can press on in pursuit of even greater academic glory without the burden of having to fill fee-paying places; Bishop's offers places only to one in three applicants. 'I only ever wanted to work in this type of school', he told us from his modest, darkly panelled office, where a sheaf of commendations awaited signing on his desk, 'and my aim is to build on this school's particular character and location to create a regional entity'. Somewhat uncompromising in manner, Dr Smallwood is respected by the boys, who describe him variously as 'authoritative', 'dedicated' and 'ambitious for the school'. Married to Charlotte, who teaches English at the girls' equivalent, South Wilts, with a daughter at university and two sons in the school, Dr Smallwood might be found bird-watching, star-gazing or tinkering with his model railway in his spare time; sadly, his failing knees mean no more running

Academic matters: The raison d'être of this top performing school: it's not all that matters here, but nearly. 'Academic excellence for starters,' said the head, when asked about his priorities for the school. Results reflect the high academic bar at entry: in 2016, 69 per cent A*/A grades at GCSE, with particular strengths in maths and all three sciences. Oddly, for a specialist language college, language results lag a little behind, despite the requirement to study two languages to the end of year 9, then to take at least one at GCSE. We liked the quadrilingual notices around the school – bon effort! Many GCSE courses start in year 9, and some (maths and statistics often) are taken a year early.

At A level, 32 subjects are offered, half of which are taught in collaboration with South Wilts; theatre studies is a new offering. Again, stunning results, with 36 per cent A*/A and 70 per cent A*/B in 2016. Star subjects at A level are maths, sciences, geography and geology both in take-up and results, again fewer languages including English. EPQ now offered and increased take up. Boys talked about the calibre of teaching staff and academic respect, working both ways between them and their teachers: 'They beg you to take their subject for A level,' said one, whilst others praised the amount of support given. 'They fall over themselves to help you,' said another, hot from a one-to-one session on mechanics. We were struck by the keen attention paid to rainfall graphs by a large geography class we dropped in on, but a group of younger boys in a German class were fidgety. One mother reckoned the language teaching is too dry, and inclined to miss the point that language is primarily a means for communication. Some reservations about the science teaching also reached us – a bit old-fashioned and not always right for boys who find it hard.

Standards are kept up by close and supportive relationships between teachers and the boys, and 'by just the right amount of homework, though it might be sacrilege to say it', opined one year 7 lad. The transfer to sixth form is 'an achievement, not a given'; as well as a minimum of six GCSEs at B or above, including Bs for English and maths, there is also a chat with each hopeful about subject choices and possible careers. The head is not above booting boys out if their AS results are not up to snuff (most will do three linear A levels plus EPQ from 2017) but he would do so only if a boy was clearly not suited to post-16 study – 'very rare,' said he – and despite the best efforts of the mentor each boy is assigned. SEN provision caters for the usual range of dyslexia, dyspraxia and Asperger's, and helps boys with difficulties in getting organised, having liaised with feeder primary schools – but it's pretty low profile at this school, we sense.

Games, options, the arts: There is life beyond rugby and cross-country, if you look hard, but both these sports are taken with incredible seriousness: 'loyalty verging on the psychopathic and the coach is terrifying', said one mother whose son was proud to play in the 1st XV. The fixture list includes the gamut of schools more closely associated with the game: Sherborne, Bryanston, Millfield, Marlborough and other local titans, and top teams get to play at prestigious venues such as Rosslyn Park. Passions run exceedingly high on the touchline, say parents. Cross-country also has a massive following and produces successes at county level. All the playing fields are a brisk trot away – the school is truly shoehorned into a confined space behind the cathedral close – but the boys grumble less about this than they do about the lack of space in the yard to play football at lunchtime. Some parents think the school is 'myopic about other sports' and bemoan the lack of tennis courts, for example, but basketball enjoys a strong following. At least sport-phobes are allowed to hate it in peace and, in sixth form, to spend their Wednesday afternoons in other profitable ways like hospital volunteering; everyone we spoke to confirmed that there will be a group of like-minded boys to hang out with, whether that be geeks, nerds, jocks or eccentrics, which we found reassuring and refreshing. Slackers and rebels won't find too many kindred spirits, however.

Music also very strong at Bishops, as befits a school overlooked by Salisbury Cathedral, the finest, most unified example of early English architecture in the world, with a distinguished choral tradition. Choir sings at school functions in the cathedral and tours regularly, as well as the odd national event like the schools' prom in the Albert Hall, and accompanying the LSO. About 10 per cent learns a musical instrument, taught by a small army of peripatetics. Two orchestras, string groups, wind bands and other ensembles cater for players of all abilities (and possibly none).

Art and drama less important at this somewhat two-dimensional school: many more creative pursuits take place outside the timetable as part of the 40 clubs on offer, and it would not be the right choice for an artistic and delicate flower, reckon parents.

An ambitious range of trips is laid on – as well as destinations one might expect for the linguists, classicists, musicians and (art) historians, rugby teams travel the world. Two ski trips, junior mountain-biking in Croatia or Morocco and a biennial trip to the developing world (Himalayas, Vietnam) add to the offer.

Background and atmosphere: Named after its founder in 1890, who set it up entirely out of his own pocket, and true to its founding principles, the school still delivers an education 'within the context of Christian belief and practice', but this perhaps plays out more in the relationships forged in school than in overt religious observance. It looks and feels like the city grammar school it is proud to be, occupying a very central site accessed through two unmarked entrances. Reception is housed in an ancient coach-house, whose cobbles still deter anyone unwise enough to wear heels. Just as well it's a boys' school, though it was co-ed till 1928. Inside its confines, a remarkable amount of ancient and modern has been crammed, including the chapel, sports hall, a gorgeous new teaching block and – amazingly – some green space. Everyone mentioned the lack of space as the school's only real limitation (new block under construction to house the increased year 7 intake from 2017); we visited on a Wednesday when the place was eerily empty, the boys being occupied on the rugby pitches. But we did spot the lines painted in the yard, presumably to control lunch queues.

A discernible air of academic seriousness pervades – 'the boys have to work,' said one mother approvingly – and do substantial amounts at home, particularly in the case of keen sportsmen. Expectations are pitched high – many top universities were

B

represented at a recent careers evening, which included a lecture from a Cambridge admissions tutor. The boys we spoke to unquestionably feel lucky to be there. Parents also appreciate the efforts the school makes to turn them into good citizens, and are generally happy with the quality of reports and parents' evenings. It all feels jolly conventional – and no bad thing, in our view. The boys looked much tidier than many we meet and we did not see any adventurous hair, tattoos or piercings. When asked about drink, drugs and other extracurricular pursuits, one brave soul cited one incidence of drugs he knew about, which he felt had been dealt with the right degree of severity. Not cool in this school, evidently.

Pastoral care, well-being and discipline: Boys rate pastoral care highly and reckon there is always someone to talk to when times are hard; heads of lower and middle school came in for particular praise, as did sixth form mentors. The view from parents was mixed: 'I think it's good, but not all of us would agree,' said one. When we brought up the dreaded subject of bullying, the boys looked a bit blank, and confirmed they felt school was 'a safe place to be'. Academic discipline is tight, and a falling off in performance will swiftly be gripped; parents and boys both felt that such rigour would not suit everyone. Commendations for absolute and relative achievement provide a good balance, especially when incentivised with chocolate.

Pupils and parents: Almost exclusively white and middle class, very few pupils in receipt of free school meals: something the head is not entirely comfortable with and wants to address – as far as this is possible in Salisbury and its prosperous environs. Everyone involved in Bishops appears to share a palpable sense of aspiration, whether in academic, musical or sporting pursuits; 'It suits those who come from families with traditional values,' said a parent. The edgy or unconventional might not feel Bishops was a natural home. Most parents are in professional occupations of some kind

Entrance: Tough, tough, tough. Huge competition for 160 places in year 7 (reflects increase to five form entry) from about 50 local primary schools and some independents. Eleven plus (school's own test in English, maths and verbal reasoning) is taken with utmost seriousness: 'I've been crammed since I was 4', said one boy with a wink. 'There was no way I wasn't getting in.' The formal process starts in year 5 when the prospectus is sent out to all primary schools within the 'designated area', roughly a five mile radius around the city. Applications are made via Wiltshire council, and the exam is taken in September of year 6. Priority, amongst those who have passed the exam, to looked after children and those on free school meals. School runs coaching sessions as part of its commercial activity (free for those on state benefits), and we imagine that local tutors make a mint. Over 50 arrive at sixth form, with a clutch of good GCSEs at B or (mostly) above.

Exit: University applications receive top priority, with the school hosting a university fair attracting all the top names. Also very clued up on summer schools, chances to study abroad and all sorts of ways to enhance applications. One aspiring medic told us his personal statement had gone through 10 drafts before submission. Most jump through the UCAS hoops in their last year, but we were assured that the school continues to support boys who opt to apply post A level (around 20 per cent take gap years). In 2016, a disappointing five to Oxbridge, six medics and 43 per cent overall to top universities. Bishops has recently become a SAT centre for entry to American universities; the head has a commendably global outlook. Very few boys thin out after GCSE (under 10 per cent) and those that do are generally seeking more freedom and possibly girls eg at sixth form college. Distinguished old boys include Ralph Fiennes, Lord MacDonald (ex DPP), Hamish Milne (concert pianist), international rugby players Richard Hill and David Egerton, hockey international John Shaw. William Golding taught at Bishops for 17 years.

Money matters: The school became an academy in 2011, which, after an initial injection of funds, heralds faintly anxious times ahead; its commercial activities include adult non-examined language classes (with a terrific take-up) and lettings such as a non-residential summer school. Interestingly, the boys we spoke to alluded to the careful use of school resources – 'the school does well with what it has', said one. Parents are asked for a termly voluntary contribution to fund extras, gift-aided where possible; 'We're just grateful to escape the burden of school fees!' admitted one.

Remarks: Bishops occupies some interesting territory between the independent and state sectors, and is a member of HMC. As its founder said, 'I should like to found a school which shall be equal to the greatest and best of our public schools' – it seems in many ways he has done exactly that. 'Even if I had had the money for an independent school, I would still have sent my son to Bishops,' said a parent – sums it up, really.

The Blue School

Kennion Road, Wells, Somerset BA5 2NR

Pupils: 1,646 • Ages: 11–18 • Sixth form: 330 • C of E

Tel: 01749 678799
Email: office@blue.somerset.sch.uk
Website: www.theblueschoolwells.co.uk

Head: Since 1999, Mr Steve Jackson (40s); joined as deputy head in 1989, so has seen it all. Used to teach design technology and PE. Married to a deputy head; three children. Insists on showing new parents and visitors around the school himself. Except us, who were asked not to visit what is already a chronically oversubscribed school. 'A good front man,' said a parent, but 'not engaged in the day-to-day life of the school'. Publicity, website, school profile etc seemingly low on the agenda.

Academic matters: A genuinely comprehensive school. Standards are high at GCSE (65 per cent 5+ A*-C including maths and English in 2016) and consistently good in the core subjects of English, maths and science. Concerns about provision for the less academic at GCSE have been addressed with entry level history and French, and four science pathways to cater for all abilities. Links with Strode College for the more vocationally-minded. At A level (38 per cent A*/A grades in 2016, 87 per cent A*-C) there is a broad selection of subjects on offer, though – as ever – take-up for modern languages low. Seventy-four per cent of BTecs were D or higher in 2016. Has specialist school status in science and mathematics. Outstanding work in design technology and PE. Much use of ICT within the classroom and brilliant ICT provision throughout. The staff seem genuinely keen to embrace the new technology; they feel ahead of the game due to local company support.

On arrival in year 7, boys and girls are taught together and in mixed ability groups, apart from English and maths where they are setted. At GCSE almost all subjects are setted. Generally little staff movement, and a considerable proportion has been at the school for longer than 10 years, perhaps why one parent said he thought the school was resting on its laurels and that a few teachers were merely going through the motions. A strong belief that if a child is well-motivated then they can do very well here, less so if not. Some think the school should instil a better work ethic early on so children deal better with GCSE pressures.

SEN provision appears to be good, with close liaison between departments and the SENCo and a flexible approach. Pupils struggling with literacy are helped within class or withdrawn for small group work at behest of subject teachers; SENCo runs assessments on request, esp from parents who suspect difficulties. Maths dept more autonomous, with its own specialist TA who sets up in-class/individual/small group sessions according to need. General assessments done in class, which means first week of new academic year can be 'a bit chaotic', until all five sets are sorted out. Bottom sets might number only eight pupils. Pretty well all behavioural issues are catered for, as befits an inclusive school. SENCo says that the school 'does not hunt out children with emotional or behavioural difficulties but tries to support them in their education. However, [parents of] kids on the autistic spectrum hunt us out, even transferring into the area to attend "The Blue".'

Games, options, the arts: Walking into the design technology block feels like entering an art school department – fabulous work and ambitious projects. Regularly wins design awards eg Arkwright Scholarships etc and has established close working links with local businesses for funding and work placements. Bench seating in the historic Palace Fields gardens in Wells was designed by A level pupils at the school. The presence of the sports development centre means that there is a huge choice available in addition to the traditional – including caving and rock climbing actively pursued in nearby Mendips – and the school produces a smattering of county players every year. Music is prominent with orchestra, wind band, jazz band, choir and guitar group – so plenty of opportunity to get involved. Drama a strength with regular productions, and not frightened of tackling ambitious works eg Peer Gynt. Several trips abroad each year, often exotic – witness two World Challenge expeditions, to Africa and the Himalayas, in two years.

Background and atmosphere: Dates back to 1641 when it was established as a charitable foundation via the legacy of local churchman Ezekiel Barkham. The name was adopted over time owing to the blue dyed uniforms provided for the original pupils. A big school plonked in a spacious 33 acres. Slightly elevated position means a fantastic view. Three gyms, a school hall and three dining areas. £2m science block opened by the Princess Royal incorporating six laboratories, prep rooms and a large state-of-the-art ICT facility for use by own students and those from partner primary schools. The 'Blue' theme is carried throughout the décor – blue carpets, chairs, blinds, lino, walls, though 'it all looks a bit tired', said one parent. Work is in hand to make the school more environmentally sustainable, with the lead coming from the unusual 250-person school council, hailed nationally as an example of best practice. Twenty-five council teams raise awareness and funds for what really matters to them, eg Fairtrade, buddying, fitness, cuisine. A great way to demonstrate passion and commitment amongst the young. Dining facilities have won healthy eating awards; in fact 'The Blue' is first school to be awarded FEAST status, by Raymond Blanc no less, which conferred swish catering training facilities for use inside and outside education. Locally-obtained fresh meat and vegetables are used and free chilled water is provided in each of the main buildings. Students also grow some of their own produce.

Pastoral care, well-being and discipline: Although a church school, no overt signs of Christianity. An assembly every morning with hymn singing and reading from appropriate texts; however the format is guided by 'worthship' rather than worship. Achievement is valued – every opportunity is taken to publicise (bulletins, posters around the school and regular contributions to local press) and praise. A firm but realistic attitude towards all matters of discipline. Smoking within the building results in a one-day exclusion, as does swearing. The headteacher holds half-termly Saturday morning detentions for students who need redirection.

Pupils and parents: Serves an area of generally advantaged, white, British, English-speaking households; the strong PTA reflects this and raises considerable sums for major purchases, eg a new minibus. Liaison with parents is good, with regular newsletters, meaningful reports and parents' evenings and a recent initiative 'Parent Pay' (how true..) where payment for school meals, trips etc can be made online.

Entrance: Around 250 a year from local primary schools – mainly from within the city of Wells and surrounding villages. Oversubscribed and estate agents don't help this problem. Worth getting a map of the catchment area from the school.

Exit: Over 50 per cent stay on to do A levels at sixth form (though weaker A level candidates encouraged to bail out if year 12 results disappoint) and, of those, about 80 per cent move on to higher or further education. Six to Oxbridge in 2016.

Remarks: Solid state option sailing serenely on within a sea of local independents. The emphasis is on motivation and enthusiasm, amply demonstrated by the range of subjects and activities on offer.

Blundell's School

14

Blundell's Road, Tiverton, Devon EX16 4DN

Pupils: 802 • Ages: 3–18 (boarding from 8) • Sixth form: 205 • C of E

Fees: Day £6,495 – £21,105; Boarding £19,590 – £32,865 pa

Tel: 01884 252543
Email: registrars@blundells.org
Website: www.blundells.org

Head: Since 2013, Mrs Nicola Huggett (40s) MA PGCE (Oxon). Educated at St Gabriel's and Marlborough, she read PPE at Oxford before embarking on a brief career in advertising with J Walter Thompson – brief because she soon realised it was not for her. 'Why did no-one tell me about teaching before?' she says of her experience shadowing a teacher in a comprehensive near her home. Since then her career has taken her via Haileybury, ultimately as head of boarding, during a time when the school went fully co-ed and introduced IB, and Downe House as deputy head, before being made the first female head of Blundell's since its inception in 1604. Only moderate harrumphing greeted her appointment, and those foolish enough to do so must now be eating their words, such has been the wave of approval from all quarters. 'A wow appointment,' declared one mother. Mrs Huggett is clearly superwoman – as well as running a school, where she still teaches four lessons a week, she also runs marathons, rides – oh, and raises four children of her own, all at Blundell's. Husband Spencer runs a car dealership in Barnstaple and has always moved around with

B

her. 'Blundell's appealed to me because there's an honest and unpretentious feel about the place – and I'm a country girl,' she says. 'Though when I saw the sign that said Headmaster's Visitors, I said "That'll be the first thing to go!".'

Head of prep: Since 2011, Mr Andrew Southgate BA Ed (30s). Raised in Maidstone, but ventured westwards for his degree in physical education and history at St Luke's, Exeter. He spent the first 13 years of his career at Moulsford Prep, ending up as deputy head. Impossibly youthful, he came bounding out of his office to meet us, and his enthusiasm for Blundell's, Devon, prep schools, children and life in general is infectious. Though he denies it – 'I talk quite a good game of rugby' he says – he looks pretty fit: there is talk of introducing a veterans' rugby team for keen dads, and he still coaches and referees. Married to Sarah, with two children in the school, Mr Southgate has gone down very well with parents, who appreciate the aspirations and pride he has injected into 'what was a somewhat complacent offering', according to one. We also heard 'passion, energy and buzz, yet willing to take criticism'. Praise indeed.

Academic matters: 'The children who come here are a broad church,' says the prep school head, 'and our challenge is to accommodate them all; we're not an academic hothouse'. The last few years have seen significant changes to SEN provision (not least its renaming as Learning Success), increased hours for the SEN specialist, targeted reading groups every morning of the week (no extra charge) as well as handwriting club and a TA in all lower sets.

Traditionally not the brightest star in the firmament of south west schools, but there's a determination on the senior school head's part to make the school as academic as it is sporty. ('She'll have her work cut out for her,' remarked one parent.) To that end she has made some key appointments since she arrived, such as a head of learning support, who is an ed psych, and a switched-on academic deputy from Wycombe Abbey, as well as introducing a proper tutor system, which has gone down well with parents. A level results are sound, with 67 per cent graded A*/B and 41 per cent A*/A in 2016; sciences, geography and maths – good take-up of further maths too – are most popular, languages lamentably not, though it is impressive to note that the school has run Spanish, Russian and Latin for sole takers. Parents reckon that student aspirations are being raised under the newish regime; many already take EPQ in sixth form alongside A levels. The brightest sparks are invited to join the scholars' club, which 'offers stimulation for rapid progress' in the dry language beloved of inspectors. At GCSE, 51 per cent graded A*/A in 2016. DT enjoys a big take-up: we would have been happy to give house-room to many of the items of small wooden furniture we saw. Students with a wide range of intellectual gifts are catered for: at GCSE science for example, school offers choice between IGCSE or less demanding boards. Everyone does French and Latin from the start with the choice of German and Spanish in year 9. Just over a fifth of students receive SEN support, including plenty of help for those whose first language is not English.

Games, options, the arts: Make no mistake, this is a very sporty school, and might not be the place for a pale aesthete. That said, there is masses on offer for those with little or no eye for a ball, as well as the usual fare of rugby, hockey (both huge here) netball and cricket (for girls too, plus football, tennis, squash and fives): CCF, D of E, Ten Tors and the Devizes to Westminster canoe race keenly pursued. In the spring, the whole school participates in the (frankly bonkers) Russell – named for the eponymous Jack (of terrier fame and an OB) – a hotly contested cross-country race for which local landowners open their land. We had never seen quite such cheerfully muddy girls as the ones we met just back from a practice. General heartiness extends to an outdoor pool only – 'reassuringly heated,' says school – though an indoor one is on everyone's wish list, and keen swimmers can use the indoor facilities in Tiverton. Riding strong here too – Blundell's riders regularly compete at events in the south west and recently won the National Schools Jumping-with-style contest – but it's not the kind of school where turning up with a horsebox is de rigueur; no equines on site.

Activities range from aerobics to yoga; everyone is expected to sign up for a minimum of two. Boarders are offered an adventure and leadership programme over eight weekends comprising gorge-walking and survival training along with other feats of derring-do. But Blundell's isn't just good at the strenuous stuff: a long tradition of debating both in school and beyond was crowned by winning the ESU national final recently. Artists in all media compete and show their work far beyond the school, with success at the Tate, in the Saatchi Art Prize for Schools (online but also, more excitingly, in the Kings Road) and more locally in Tiverton and Exeter. We were gutted that an art scholar's rendition of the Mona Lisa in peanut butter and chocolate spread had (presumably) been eaten before our visit. Music facilities have just been brought bang up to date with an editing suite and composition/technology studio, but there has long been masses of music both sung and played: concerts and recitals, plus recently Grease, Cabaret and open mic night on the lighter side. In the last couple of years groups have been to Prague, Brittany and Venice, as well as prestigious venues nearer home. Drama takes places in the Ondaatje Hall, named for its generous donor, the notable philanthropist, brother of the author and an OB; plenty of backstage and technical experience on offer as well as acting, plus visits and workshops from French and Spanish theatre groups – a great initiative which other schools would do well to emulate. A long tradition of house and year group plays means there are opportunities for all budding thespians.

Boarding: Relationships between staff and students seem extremely good, with house staff coming in for particular praise – some email parents with photos of boarders' activities and high jinks just about the moment they happen. The seven houses accommodate a mix of all kinds of boarders (full, weekly, flexi) and day pupils, divided into two co-ed at the beginning and end of a student's time at Blundell's, two girls' and three boys'; all are known by their initials – NC, SH etc. The latter, School House, for years 7 and 8, was one of the first matters the head tackled on arrival as a result of considerable parental dissatisfaction: all now report huge improvements.

Twice as many boys as girls are full boarders and parents of full boarders rather wish more kids stayed in at weekends, and that the food was, on occasion, more girl-friendly. Some of their accommodation could do with a bit of tlc too. The crowning glory of boarding has to be Westlake, the co-ed sixth form house where students get as close a feeling of university life as possible before they get there, yet where girls and boys respectively can retreat from the hurly-burly to their own part of the house.

Background and atmosphere: Four-square Victorian red-brick buildings face more modern additions across Blundells Road in Tiverton – such is the importance of the school to the town that it has a road named after it – set off by gracious green spaces and a distinctive clock tower; though the school was founded by the generous legacy of one of England's wealthiest cloth merchants, Peter Blundell, over 200 hundred years earlier, it moved to its permanent home only in the 1880s. The values of that time persist in some measure today with the school's emphasis on 'distinguished performance in those games which the Victorians [had] developed to replace the rude sports of earlier centuries'. No more cock-fighting then. Definitely a traditional feel about the place, with a bewildering number of ties, though certainly not fuddy-duddy, with boys below sixth form wearing tawny tweed jackets, the colour of autumn bracken on Dartmoor, and girls red ones. Even the sixth form wear uniform; their jackets are navy blue, striped for those who have been awarded full colours – given not only for sports, but all manner of accomplishment.

What in other schools might be called assembly takes place in Big School and is called Latin prayer, concluding as it does with the Lord's prayer in Latin; chapel on other mornings in the school's own beautiful chapel. The first girls arrived in 1975 and the school went fully co-ed in 1992. We are delighted that the last head girl exercised her right to keep a pig at school for her final term, something conferred on the head boy from the start.

Prep is Sited next to the senior school, so able to use some of its facilities, but separately run and administered. Attractive semi-rural setting in 12 acres on the edge of Tiverton, where outdoor learning is top of the pops, complete with pond and wetland area. Old red-brick house has been beautifully extended and adapted to create light and airy spaces, where art is effectively displayed. We particularly liked the science lab and the fabulous and well-equipped food technology room, where sessions for everyone are timetabled and keen young Blumenthals knock up delicious fare for parents and any other lucky diners. School lunch looked and smelled pretty good too.

Parents love the friendly and inclusive feel of the place, the lack of arrogance among the students and the resilience the school instils in them. 'Absolutely non-stop programme of extracurricular activities means my children are absolutely exhausted by the time they come home – perhaps they need more soothing down-time at weekends to recover,' observed one mother of boarders. Great affection and loyalty for the school from past and present students and staff – one finally took retirement after 30 years' service; terrific and longstanding network of events for OBs, not just the 'winter lunches' in Devon, but all over the world.

Pastoral care, well-being and discipline: Valuing the individual child is top priority at the prep, as is the nurturing environment: 'After all they are still little at that age', say parents. Discipline appears to be kept with a lightish touch – parents of drinkers and smokers can expect 'to be invited in to discuss a way forward', according to the head. Drugs weren't even mentioned, and bullying gets zero tolerance. 'There's a sexting issue every year in year 9,' said one mother phlegmatically, 'but the school just deals with it'.

Pupils and parents: Mostly local but a good handful (about 15 per cent) from abroad, giving the school a more cosmopolitan feel than mid Devon might otherwise manage. Among the farmers, local professionals and the military, there are boarders from Cornwall, where there is little on offer, and of course refugees from London in search of a better life; some first time buyers of independent schooling too, one of whom said, 'My son is having the kind of education that I work for and dream of him having'. Pupils are as grounded and unpretentious as any you will find at a UK boarding school, the kind who will have a go and take a risk; we suspect that the rebellious, the precious and the show-off would not thrive here.

Entrance: Prospective prep school pupils spend a taster day in school, during which an assessment in English and maths is carried out. To the senior school mostly at 11, by means of papers in English, maths and non-verbal reasoning in the January preceding entry; at 13+ via common entrance or the school's own entrance test in English and maths in June. At sixth form, hopefuls have to satisfy relatively undemanding entrance requirements of a minimum of five GCSEs at a C or above with at least a B in subjects to be taken to A2, plus interview

Exit: Vast majority from the prep move on to the senior school at 11+ by means of entrance tests in English, maths and non-verbal reasoning. 'No-one is looking anywhere else now,' remarked one mother, but those who might are equally well prepared for entrance tests elsewhere.

Up to 20 per cent leave after GCSEs. The vast majority to university and traditional ones at that, up and down the country. 'No-one goes to Exeter – too close to home,' sixth formers informed us. Recent Oxbridge successes (two in 2016 plus two medics) may well boost applications in that direction. Popular universities include Durham, Imperial College, Warwick, Reading, Bristol, Leeds and Manchester. Degree choices again tend towards the conventional and/or vocational, such as medicine, geography, economics, biochemistry, law and business management.

After that, Old Blundellians fan out across the globe, to the extent that there are OB gatherings in South Africa, Japan, Germany and Hong Kong. An extremely busy development office ensures strong links with the old school tie. Famous OBs include RD Blackmore, (the hero of whose chef d'oeuvre Lorna Doone was a fictional pupil), 40s actor Gerald Hamer and his director son Robert (Kind Hearts and Coronets), defence correspondent and author Robert Fox, organist Peter Hurford, TV journalist Claire Marshall and the drummer of The Vamps, Tristan Evans.

Money matters: For the first 300 years of its existence, Blundell's was maintained by the profits from its properties in Tiverton and estate in south Devon, but these days fees charged are in line with comparable schools. Decent range of scholarships for sport, music, art, drama, all-round as well as academic; only music and academic at 11+. Peter Blundell Foundation bursaries are awarded in cases of financial need where 'Governors wish to reflect the spirit of Peter Blundell's vision'. The school is innovative in attracting an array of corporate sponsors to fund events.

Remarks: Ancient and distinguished Devon institution preserving traditional values and feel, yet turning out considerate and balanced young people all set for careers across the globe. Not perhaps for those seeking exclusively to scale the heights of academia or social cachet, but deserves far higher prominence than the lowish profile ('Not in the west country!' protests school) it currently assumes. Over to you, Mrs Huggett.

Bournemouth School

15

East Way, Bournemouth BH8 9PY

Pupils: 1,060 • Ages: 11–18 • Sixth form: 320 (including girls)

Tel: 01202 512609
Email: office@bournemouth-school.org
Website: www.bournemouth-school.org

Headmaster: Since 2009, Dr Dorian Lewis (40s), previously deputy head at mixed comprehensive, Queen Elizabeth, Wimborne, notching up experience managing curriculum, doing the National Qualification for Head Teachers. A chemistry graduate from Southampton (did his PhD there too), originating from Wales, taught at Thomas Hardye school in Dorchester until appointed to head of science at Wimborne.

Married with three children in local schools, he relishes his teaching, taking extra chemistry for exam years and thriving on personal contact with staff, pupils and parents. A smiling and reassuringly cuddly demeanour conceals iron determination to get the very best for his boys and a razor sharp awareness of what needs doing. His biggest shock as when he took over was the amount of time spent in 'fruitless' meetings, so he immediately set about reorganising the management to produce more 'fruit'.

Feeling the 'good' standards reported in a 2008 inspection left room for improvement, he saw his first year as a 'quiet revolution' – 'Last year a complete development plan for staffing and curriculum, this year the same for buildings'. 'Continuous cohesive management' is his term for galvanising everyone on his 'very talented and capable staff', from the cleaners to the super-efficient business manager, in his own 'velvet revolution'. Indeed, the latest Ofsted report in 2011 judged the school 'outstanding'.

Academic matters: In 2016, 61 per cent A*/A grades at GCSE; 35 per cent A*/A at A level – lowish such a selective school, with maths making up the vast majority of the A* grades (as well as being by far the most popular A level subject). Dr Lewis agrees with the inspectors that the teaching, though successful, is pretty traditional – lots of chalk, talk and write; all fine, but needing a little 'oomph', which he is rapidly providing – interactive whiteboards, classroom technology etc – and latest report talks about 'strong collaboration between skilled teachers and enthusiastic boys'. Boys at all levels were clearly engaged with their work and most talked ardently about it.

Classes in first three years study the basics plus art, music and technology, with Latin (but no Greek) and French, plus another language chosen from German, Spanish, Italian, and Mandarin Chinese. All take at least 12 GCSEs, with 'fast track' being phased out in favour of the biggest possible bunch of the very best grades ('It's what the unis want').

The 22 plus mainstream subjects on offer at A level include a raft of technologies, government and politics, further maths, psychology and sports science. Results, as mentioned, disappointing this year and, for a specialist language school, the take-up of languages is regrettably low (Dr Lewis has already homed in on this and is 'holding the line' on a compulsory GCSE language for all). Sixth formers can add the Extended Project Qualification (EPQ).

The individual learning needs service is focused mainly on the potential problems of the very bright, coping with a higher than average percentage of Asperger's or similar. Four teaching assistants give in-class and individual support. Lots of personal supervision by designated teacher for children who need 'looking after', and a gifted and talented co-ordinator ensures exceptional students get enough curriculum enrichment and acceleration to keep them on task.

Games, options, the arts: Unashamedly an academic hothouse (some parents would like to see it a bit 'more rounded'), but a vast range of sports, activities and hobbies, all pursued with a determination generated by 1,100 plus highly intelligent and competitive boys (and girls in the sixth form). Dr Lewis protests that actually too much rather than too little, but is immensely proud of sporting successes, giving a ball-by-ball account of the final matches of the Glanvill and Aegon team tennis cups (they were runners up in both).

Music is on a grand (and loud) scale, featuring big and concert bands with 50 plus players apiece, lots of brass and much singing. Most years a distinguished performer or two goes on to music college. Choirs and singers abound, as to be expected from the school which produced Gareth Malone. The enormous Javanese Gamelan (takes up a whole room), which has highlighted the identity of the music department, is departing for a museum, so perhaps Gareth could come back and identify another area of musical excellence to keep the side up.

Smashing portraiture on show in the music department and a stunning front hall display of one versatile student's work. Art department bristles with artists in residence and has ongoing links with the Bournemouth Arts University College.

Terrific sports centre and all-weather pitches. Football teams in every year group scooped up prizes in local and county competitions, as did the first rugby team. Athletics etc and oodles of cricket. Duke of Edinburgh is pretty new, with Prince Edward visiting to give it a boost. Mammoth CCF with masses of activities for all three services and (another) band with a female bandmaster. Sea Scouts take pride of place in a list of other extracurricular bursting with technological activities (a group built and raced a car) and cultural/arty enterprise (links and visits to Japan/China etc). Loads of chess, films etc etc and a current student won Tesco's junior Masterchef, perhaps spurred on by the shiny cookery kitchens in place for lower school lessons and a pre-uni cooking class.

Background and atmosphere: Born the day Queen Victoria died in 1901, the school moved to its current hallowed portals as WW2 erupted. Only staff and prefects can use the echoing front hall and staircase, where walls groan under notices of awards and achievements. Spectacular for sheer length and solidity and the outsize central clock tower, the buildings are otherwise unremarkable, having been consistently modernised in strict rotation (ie a lab one year means an arts classroom the next), with the result that nothing is really out of date but nothing stands out. Functional new maths block, 'managed in house, which saved thousands', and all mod cons everywhere: wireless computer networks eat money, though don't look spectacular, but all technology is bang up to date. Extensive wooded grounds, including the copse much loved by Gareth Malone, freely available to roam in, since 'Bournemouth boys can be trusted'.

Only the best is good enough here and boys appear to thrive on cut-throat competition. Not for the fainthearted, but the feeling is friendly, and boys respond to Dr Lewis's mantra of 'hard work, discipline, smart appearance and respect' by showing real interest – even junior mathematicians seemed enthralled. Most were reasonably tidy, happy to converse and making responsible use of the facilities left open to them at downtimes.

Sixth form (now taking girls) area buzzes with music/TV/conversation/work all going on at once. A helpful sixth form pastoral assistant is on duty at all times to give support on UCAS etc. Masses of older boys at work in the library, with a quiet academic hum and comfortable feel conducive to intellectual conversation or the odd game of chess. It is generously staffed and light and airy, at the top of a newish building with lecture hall and small classrooms, which make it ripe for development into a self-contained sixth form and adult education area.

Sixth formers have freedom to come and go as they please, so their bicycles litter the inner courtyard, chained to any available railings, unlike lower school bikes which are stowed neatly underneath it. Courses such as sociology and drama are taken in the girls' school and the pinstriped sixth form boys socialise freely with their less formally clad female counterparts. Spaces between buildings are nicely got up for sitting in summer and one courtyard has a horticultural feel, though the veg was struggling a bit.

Pastoral care, well-being and discipline: A competitive house system complete with tutor groups 'helps you to make friends', as well as providing a forum for informal monitoring of progress and social issues. Uniform is pretty neat, with quite well-cut grey suits (no one looked baggy-kneed) and own choice suits in sixth form, where long hair is a not much used privilege. Prefects on duty in the dining room – Dr Lewis says they virtually run the school.

Discipline, when needed, is firm, based mainly on temporary exclusion, though Dr Lewis has not shrunk from permanent exclusion when absolutely necessary, and the school is successfully draconian about bullying in any form. Parents can get immediate access to the head if he is there (in a curiously unadorned meeting room, since he has opted for a tiny working office). Any whisper of drugs results in parental involvement and appropriate 'severe sanctions'.

Pupils and parents: A broader academic mix than might be expected, especially at sixth form, where entry to courses may be less demanding than some less academic schools. Some ethnic diversity but, being Bournemouth, Anglo-Saxons predominate. Flourishing parents' association and a star-spangled list of OBs including '60s comedian Benny Hill, Sir David English of The Daily Mail, Blur guitarist Alix James, educationalist Mike Tomlinson and news reader Mark Austin.

Entrance: No specific catchment, but those outside Bournemouth have to apply via their own LA. Boys admitted by exam process, which starts with an application or 'expression of interest' in September. Testing is year 7 maths, English and verbal reasoning – takes the top 150. Later years admitted by assessment, if a vacancy comes up, but not open to those who failed at 11. Sixth form has extra 70 places and is by GCSE results: six or more A*-B including maths and English.

Exit: Majority to university, including four to Oxbridge and five medics in 2016; general scattering of blue chip and others.

Remarks: Solid as the rock of Gibraltar and nearly as traditional, though Dr Lewis is bringing in some innovative teaching and ideas. His breath of fresh air approach has transformed the prospectus, made major organisational changes and set some even more ambitious targets. Definitely for the intellectually tough. A school to be reckoned with.

Bournemouth School for Girls

Castle Gate Close, Castle Lane West, Bournemouth BH8 9UJ

Pupils: 1,155 • Ages: 11–18 • Sixth form: 315

Tel: 01202 526289
Email: office@bsg.bournemouth.sch.uk
Website: www.bsg.bournemouth.sch.uk

Headteacher: Since 2004, Alistair Brien, married with three children, both of whose daughters attended Bournemouth School for Girls (BSG). Deputy at BSG from 1998, and previously director of sixth form studies at Arnewood School, housemaster at Keswick School and teacher at Aylesbury Grammar. Degree in German from Exeter, author of several German textbooks, and Ofsted inspector.

Most likely to say 'this is not an exam factory' (once you've passed the one to get in); and 'he is true to his word', said a parent. 'Warm and approachable', said another. 'He is very involved with the school', she added, and came to her daughter's final presentation for her EPQ at lunchtime to be supportive.

Pupils like him and clearly think he's game – 'he drinks all the cocktails in the cocktail challenge' (20+ concoctions – a challenge in itself). A tendency to do magic tricks in assembly – much appreciated by pupils.

Academic matters: Pupils at BSG, the highest performing state school in the area, are selected for their high ability and aptitude, and 'it is a pressurised environment', says the head, 'but from the girls and their parents, not me'. The head's view is: 'Do your best: your best is good enough'. There are some very competitive groups, say pupils, who always ask each other their grades, but equally some that are less so: girls cleave towards their natural community. Pupils generally take work seriously – 'everyone here wants to get good grades and works hard', said one; another, that 'being amongst your intellectual equals makes you work harder'. ['Pupils] all had to work hard to get in', said a parent, 'so both they and their parents are quite motivated. I'm not saying there're not any shenanigans', she added. Thank goodness for that.

Good exam results are expected by both girls and parents, and excellence is generally achieved – 66 per cent A*/A at GCSE, 40 per cent A*/A at A level in 2016. At GCSE pupils take a core of English literature, English language, maths, three sciences, RS, and four choices, totalling 11. Pupils are strongly encouraged to include a language, and history and/or geography (most do). The school might encourage a pupil struggling with 11 to drop a subject to take the pressure off. There's plenty of one-to-one support from form tutors and heads of house, and attainment and progress are regularly monitored, so any problems are picked up early. Pupils say that teachers are very supportive of problems, and many sixth formers become study buddies to help younger pupils. There's also the head's secret weapon: his learning centre, staffed by TAs, where students can benefit from one-to-one support: for those with SEN, or anyone in need of a bit of extra help; someone who has been off sick long term might come here to catch up.

There are not many pupils with SEN (currently 35), who need to excel in the entrance exam to get here, just like everyone else (although special provision made as necessary to sit the test). But once you're in, the support is 'amazing,' said a parent. It is provided both in and out of lessons, a parent of an autistic child saying how carefully assistance had been designed to cater specifically for her daughter's needs: 'Going to BSG has transformed her life. She wouldn't be in the same place without it...it has really levelled the playing field for her, and helped her perform to the best of her capabilities'. A pupil with Asperger's went to Cambridge recently, and another pupil with special needs has received an offer from Cambridge last year.

At GCSE there are seven teaching groups with 24 per class, with bigger classes lower down the school (not currently exceeding 29).The school will try to run A level courses however small the number of interested pupils, so some classes have just two pupils (they will have one fewer lessons a week than better populated subjects).

'Teachers range from good to inspirational', said a parent, who also appreciated the good mix of female and male teachers. Psychology is consistently amongst the most popular A levels – the teachers 'capture and ignite imaginations', said a parent, this class also benefiting from regular visits from a tortoiseshell cat, curled up asleep on a chair when we visited. Biology, history, maths, English literature and maths are also popular A levels. Sixth formers are expected to be proactive in their learning, with teachers happily marking any extra work done. 'Lessons go at a fast and furious pace', said a parent, often surprising those joining the school in the sixth form.

The careers department has recently transformed -'it's very outward looking now', say the girls. There's no longer an assumption that pupils will be going to university, and it offers advice about work, colleges and apprenticeships. One-to-one career interviews are available to all, with university interview practice for anyone who needs it: of a speed dating format for those applying for medicine, and specially tailored for Oxbridge candidates. The head described the advantages of a year in industry for a pupil who was initially rejected by Cambridge, but accepted after a year out: there's no lack of enterprise here, and understanding the world of work is quite a focus. The careers department will help pupils to find to find work placements if needed, employers visit to talk about jobs, the school runs a business breakfast with local employers and there's plenty of enterprise competition, not least the famous cocktail challenge, which has whiffs of The Apprentice in the challenge to construct a (non-alcoholic) cocktail, design the packing and do a marketing presentation.

Games, options, the arts: The head says 'academic excellence is important but so is being a well-rounded person who makes a difference – and finding an area where you can shine'. And this could be anything – recently a pupil achieved dog obedience champion at Crufts. 'Finding a passion gives a child that all-important self confidence', claims the head.

Sport is one of many activities here, and despite the limited and rather tired facilities (a new sports hall is a priority when funds are available), they do very well. All the usual teams, excelling at national or county level at football, cricket, table tennis, badminton, athletics, rounders and netball. The school finished second in the National Schools Badminton Championships – 'even though they're just playing in the hall or the gym, where all the markings have worn away', said a bemused but happy parent.

Public speaking, debating and quizzes are extremely popular here, and must partly account for the great articulacy of the pupils. Plenty of clubs: Amnesty is well attended, as are knitting and jewellery making; many clubs are run by sixth formers for younger pupils, and most take place at lunchtime (school buses mean the after-school slot is tricky). CCF is very popular: they join and outnumber the grammar boys next door for this, and enthuse about the super trips: the RAF to Gibraltar, the navy section 'on actual boats'. Lots do D of E, with a growing number gaining gold.

A splendid new art block, art also being displayed neatly around the school, and some lovely textiles including a gorgeous Swan Lake dress, and light up ball dress (the batteries are stored in a pack on a strap underneath – not perhaps for vigorous dancers). Art and textiles are not as popular as more academic subjects here, but the work is exciting and imaginative, and nearly all those taking these subjects excel in exams.

The music room was full of year 7s and a cheerful cacophony of noise – flute, keyboards, other instruments and chatter. In a side room, some girls were trying to add chords to their compositions. 'It's difficult', said one, 'but easier if...' she gestured at the keyboard, note names scrawled on keys. Most girls learn an instrument, and if their parents can't afford lessons, the school will help. Pupils audition for the chamber choir (performing with the Bournemouth Symphony Orchestra as part of its concert season); all comers to the Big Heart and Soul choir. Drama also very popular, most of the school playing some part in the annual production, usually with the boys' grammar, with whom they take it in turns to host; though the recent Daisy Pulls It Off was very much an all girls affair.

Background and atmosphere: Considering the ferocious competition to get into this school, the atmosphere is surprisingly relaxed and friendly. One parent chose BSG because of this, but also said they were 'shocked' by the confidence of the girls who showed them around, compared to other grammar schools.

Doesn't feel like a theatrical production (as many fee-paying schools). A parent, whose daughters had both attended a local private school, said the atmosphere of the grammar is more 'real'. The overwhelming impression is of an efficient and focused school. It feels unlikely that anything would get left out or be out of place, or that a well-organised session would not take place at its allotted time. Girls here know they are fortunate (having battled in through the 11+) and are generally studious, the lessons concentrated.

Girls are delighted to be without boys: 'disruptive and loud,' said one, evidently remembering with some horror her primary school; though pupils hastened to add that they have plenty to do with boys, joining the boys' grammar next door in a political society, debating (they regularly flatten the boys) and CCF. Boys from the Bishop Winchester Academy (which the school sponsors), also come in for economic and finance lessons.

Communication is good, parents being kept put to date by email, and the parent portal, where parents can pay for lunches and trips. Tutors and head of house respond promptly to emails, and the head is available to parents on a drop in basis every morning.

Smart blue and white uniform with a snowdrop badge (the only flower out when the school opened in 1918, and chosen as a symbol of hope). 'It's nice when it's not rolled up at the waist', said a parent, who chuckles at the head's annual reminder to parents that 'skirts grown out of need replacing'. Another said 'sizing is all crazy', and the design is 'a bit boring...' but the girls seem happy with it. Casual dress for sixth formers, required to be 'modest' but actually they wear pretty much what they want to. No blue jeans allowed, but no shortage of short skirts – modest apparently draws the line at bare tummies. 'Now we can paint our nails, no one wants to...'

Buildings were state of the art in the early 1960s. They're not beautiful, but largely well kept, and the two new centres were built in complementary style. School is full to capacity at 1180, says the head, but doesn't feel full to bursting. Peaceful well stocked library.

A school with a social conscience which has been recognised nationally by Prince Charles's Step Up to Serve campaign. All the usual charity work, but it's not just buying donuts from Asda and flogging them at exorbitant prices. Pupils are strongly encouraged to get involved with the local community, and many take part in the National Citizen Service programme and the Lions club service awards.

School council, two reps from each class, whose purpose is to take school forward, not whinge. Pupils will report back on new staff, who have to teach a trial lesson, and may even be involved in the interview process.

Delicious food, with a good array of options. Sixth formers also have Heidi and her food bar constantly available in their common room (a lovely sixth form perk – their common room is a very happy place).

A house system was introduced a few years ago to encourage a sense of community across age groups, charity fundraising and friendly competition – and the girls are keen participants in house events. 'They're all involved', says the head, 'not just the crack squad'.

Pastoral care, well-being and discipline: The support offered to pupils by this school is described by one parent as the best thing about it, citing their knowledge of individual pupils, and flexibility in their approach to them. One parent described the extra care given to her children when one of the family was about to have an operation; another said it was noticed when one of her children lost a lot of weight, and gently raised with her by a teacher, who was concerned it might be due to the stress of GCSEs.

When pupils join in year 7, the school works hard on promoting healthy friendships as the best way of preventing bullying – 'I give you permission to make lots of friends', says the head, trying to dilute small established cliques. Friendship continues as a PSE topic, and if bullying occurs, they will try and bring pupils together but, failing this, re-work form groupings.

A parent described how one her daughters experienced name calling in year 7: the whole class were called in and told in no uncertain terms it must stop now; it made a big impression on the girls. She also said that lunchtime clubs were a salvation for her shy daughter when she started the school in year 7, meaning she didn't have to brave the playground.

The rarely-needed school counsellor is no more, but they now have more hours from the school nurse, which is working better (and who also has a direct link to local authority services). A parent told us how helpful the nurse had been to a child having problems sleeping at night, suffering from separation anxiety before a school trip away. Upper school can self-refer, and stressed or anxious pupils may well end up in her care, though it is usual to go through the tutor and head of house first.

Sixth formers are allocated classes to visit and listen to in an attempt to pick up any problems, and there are plenty of adults girls could go to with a problem – form tutors and heads of house, and many said they would go one of the deputy heads: 'always helpful, but doesn't overstep the mark'.

School policies contain a detailed code of conduct for misbehaviour, which rather belies the enlightened approach to discipline here. Rules on jewellery and make up are flexibly enforced, one parent describing her daughter receiving a 'polite reminder' when discrete make up got a bit much, and ruminating that 'a certain amount of tolerance means less abuse'. Girls are dealt with gently, on the basis that exaggerated rules are more likely to lead to rebellion; and this is reflected in the head's encouragement to staff to praise good behaviour and let the others conform in response. Effort and good behaviour are incentivised through the sticker system, certificates and pens. None excluded in the last year, although the usual hard offences would result in exclusion.

Pupils and parents: All walks of life, said a parent. There are families with a lot of money, said another, but not all are from privileged backgrounds. 'Not particularly middle class', said another. Parents are often 'very focused,' said one carefully, some of them anticipating their child's grades, university and career trajectory with extraordinary certainty.

Entrance: Oversubscribed, with some 450 going for 166 places. Of those who pass the exams in English, maths and verbal reasoning, places allocated firstly to those with an education, health and care plan, next to those who scored highest in the test, then to those who are resident in the borough of Bournemouth, and finally to others out of catchment. The strong preference for Bournemouth residents is likely to increase but was under consultation at time of writing.

'Prepare (as you would for any exam) but don't coach', says the head. Seventy places for pupils from other schools in the sixth form, allocated on the basis of GCSE results.

Exit: About a quarter leave after GCSEs. Most to sixth formers university, around half to Russell Group; six to Oxbridge in 2016, plus seven medics and three vets. A scattering to foundation art, employment, apprenticeships and gap years.

Money matters: Bursary fund available for sixth formers.

Remarks: The head says it wouldn't suit someone who failed to take advantages of all the opportunities the girls have here, with pupils saying something similar: competitive entry perhaps results in pupils who are particularly aware of their good fortune and determined to take advantage of it. Not for those who aren't academic, say parents; although views vary about those who just make it in by the skin of their teeth: in a competitive school where pupils regularly compare grades, this may damage those with fragile self-esteem; on the other hand, the value added to those who just scrape in is excellent.

A fast paced academic school, which manages to offer the girls a wealth of opportunities on a limited budget, and which has a more lively social conscience than many wealthier schools. Produces relaxed and confident girls who feel well set up for life.

Bristol Grammar School

University Road, Bristol BS8 1SR

Pupils: 1,329 • Ages: 4–18 • Sixth form: 295

Fees: £7,770 – £13,860 pa

Tel: 01179 736006
Email: recruitment@bgs.bristol.sch.uk
Website: www.bristolgrammarschool.co.uk

Headmaster: Since 2008, Roderick MacKinnon Bsc PGCE (50s). Educated at Aylesbury Grammar School before reading engineering at Leicester University. Became a captain in the Royal Artillery. Science teacher at the Minster School, Southwell; head of physics at Tiffin Girls'; deputy head at Colchester Royal Grammar School. Head for 13 years at Bexley Grammar School before making switch to the independent sector at BGS. Has just seen his first year 7 cohort off to university, so 'no longer new head in eyes of parents'. Families admire his deep interest in, and commitment to, children's lives.

Having 'inherited a great school' with a long history, he has respected and fostered traditions while bringing in innovations, especially in the use of technology. He has strong and thoughtful views on education and approves of the new linear A levels, rather than modular system, which is 'an exam treadmill that takes time out of the cycle of learning'. He thinks national exams at 16 may be an anachronism. Determined to ensure that history, RE, dance, drama and music are not squeezed out of the national curriculum. Most of all, he believes in developing the craft of teaching as the best route to great learning.

Head of junior school: Since 2011, Peter Huckle BA, MEd, PGCE. Educated at Monks Park School, Bristol; Birmingham University and Bristol University. Taught geography at Patchway High School for two years before joining BGS in 1980. Has held various teaching roles in 35 years at BGS including head of house, head of years 7 and 8 and deputy head, but describes current role as 'the best job in the school'. Soft-spoken and smiling, his passion for education is clearly as strong as ever. Believes the introduction of the infant school in 2010 has brought fresh energy to the school as a whole. A member of the RFU Elite Refereeing Unit, his interests include reading and theatre.

Academic matters: Children start at age 4 in two reception classes in one of the school's several houses on Elton Road. Free-flow over two floors, including three play spaces, and an outdoor area with Astroturf, ride on toys, a covered area for outdoor learning, shelters – all the requirements for early learning. The school may be anything but purpose-built, but it makes imaginative use of its restricted space. Wipe-clean parent information boards outside classrooms at pick-up times outlining 'What we did today' are a nice touch, complemented by up-to-date communication with parents, sharing children's learning through an online learning journey programme using a secure log-in. Parent portal will be next step. 'Partnership with parents very important right from the outset.' Comprehensive weekly newsletters too. 'There's almost too much communication – it can be overwhelming,' one parent said.

Vibrant learning on show in the year 1 and 2 classrooms. Teachers make use of Bristol's heritage – eg Brunel's SS Great Britain and Clifton Suspension Bridge – and assets such as the central library and the aquarium to plan exciting lessons in a topic-based curriculum. Volunteer parent help in school is valued and encouraged.

Infant children have regular forest school sessions in the school's own woodland at its sports centre at Failand, overseen by BGS's director of outdoor education. It's magical. On our visit, year 2 children gathered in a purpose-built 'Hobbit hut' to be given their challenge: to capture spring by taking a photograph of a raindrop on a leaf using an iPad. Reception children go there for one full day every fortnight and years 1/2 for a morning a week. Years 3/4 alternate forest school with PE and swimming.

Transition from infants to juniors in year 3 is gentle, with cosy areas, a reading corner, and a teaching assistant in each class. Subject specialists teach their subject across years 3 to 6 in the junior school and sometimes senior school staff are invited to share their expertise too. Children are set by ability for maths from year 3. English curriculum includes Talk for Writing and Shakespeare in Schools. Teachers supported by specialist teaching assistants for maths, English, arts and PE. Older children make use of senior school sports, science, languages and DT facilities.

In-class support for individual junior pupils with specific learning needs, overseen by assistant head. Whole school approach, supported by two specialist TA and a part-time literacy teacher for one-to-one. Additional support for pupils with exceptional ability and EAL too.

Proportion of students achieving highest grades in GCSE, IGCSE and A level continues to increase. In 2016, 60 per cent of grades were A*/A at A level, 71 per cent at GCSE. Excellent outcomes are result of improved teaching, according to head.

Broad curriculum is reviewed regularly to ensure it meets changing needs and demands. Sciences taught separately from year 8. French and Spanish taught in year 7; option to drop one MFL in favour of German or Russian in year 9. 'Personalised curriculum' in year 9 is proving popular: students choose nine subjects from a range of 20 to study alongside English, maths, biology, chemistry and physics. Students usually reduce to five options plus core subjects in years 10 and 11, with most sitting 11 GCSEs. Classes are split into two groups of 12 in year 11.

Large sixth form means excellent range of A level subjects on offer. Maths very strong – about half year group doing A level, with 30 studying further maths too. English literature follows Cambridge Pre-U course. English language and creative writing are A level options. One parent praised 'phenomenal support for girls in engineering and science'. Science labs have been refurbished to a high standard – some parents may lament the loss of the old wooden benches, but there's no such sentiment from the students. Being close to University of Bristol and its ChemLabS state of the art facilities is a big plus. Lots of opportunities for fieldwork and work outside the classroom. EPQ on offer to all, plus a scholars' programme for the most talented students; also a BGS Leadership Diploma.

Level of homework gradually increases from year 7 and end-of-term exams are held for all. Students and parents see them as positive – 'it helps to keep things in your brain' – and they praise the interactive lessons and the standards of teaching. 'This school prepares you to deal with the wider world,' said one student. One parent who has seen three students through the school said the process was well managed. 'Exams every year makes them feel comfortable with it by the time they come to GCSE and A level. There is plenty of time for exam practice and revision. My sons were pushed without feeling they were under too much pressure or fear of failure.'

Parents also generally happy with the standard of information and reports on achievement and progress. Much sharing of data and tracking online. 'The traditional school report is often six weeks out of date by the time it has been written, collated, checked and posted,' head pointed out. 'Nowadays it is about "working with" children and families, not "doing to" children and families. Young staff are very comfortable with this.'

Prolific use of iPads by children in year 8 and year 9, especially for languages teaching. 'We won't have textbooks in 10 years' time.' Teachers all have iPads and laptops and make use of interactive whiteboards. Timetable has been altered to give longer lessons and travel time between classes, and an unusually long lunch break – 90 minutes. This allows time to eat and 50 minutes to attend one of the many clubs. One parent said her son had found this difficult at first, struggling to concentrate for four one-hour lessons, but overall staff and students like the arrangement.

A pivotal change, according to staff and head, is in being open to learning from one another and sharing good practice. 'There's been a real push to let people in to classrooms, hold learning walks, get everyone involved. Teachers are approaching lessons more like artisan makers.'

Significant number of pupils with dyslexia and a few with dyspraxia, ADD, hearing impairment, physical disabilities. Whole school support for SEN overseen by an assistant head, supported by a part-time SENco and part-time dyslexia teacher. Additional support for pupils with exceptional ability and EAL too.

Games, options, the arts: Staff, students and parents are unanimous: BGS is a very busy school. 'There's no end to the variety of opportunities for students in and out of school hours,' said one parent. 'It's almost impossible to keep track of all the stuff that's going on,' said another. A teacher acknowledged: 'Students can be challenging – they are always looking to extend their knowledge. They want us to provide as much as possible – fixtures, activities, trips.'

School has a long and proud sporting history, especially for hockey and rugby. Recent tours to South Africa and New Zealand were 'brilliantly run,' one dad reported. More than 20 sports on offer, including track cycling, yoga, street dance and fencing. Synchronised swimming star Anastasija Bates is a recent alumna. Fabulous on-site sports centre includes a gym and a climbing wall as well as sports hall and squash courts. Facilities at the sports ground at Failand include impressive pitches overlooked from a superb pavilion. There's also a low ropes course and woodland for forest school activities. Junior boys play rugby, hockey, tennis and cricket; girls do hockey, netball, tennis and rounders. One parent complained that there was less emphasis on girls' sport than boys – fewer matches.

BGS has a director of outdoor learning and three staff trained as outdoor leaders. Many staff, not just PE teachers, involved in sports and other extracurricular provision. It's accepted by them that taking part in activities after school and on Saturday morning is all part of what makes BGS work. 'Engagement and commitment is more than just what happens 9-4 on weekdays.' Being taught geography by the person who took cricket practice 'creates a definite dynamic', building relationships that benefit all. Also, allowing teachers to follow their passions inspires and encourages students. 'You can't salami-slice children – you have to care for the whole child, building their confidence and making them feel safe and secure,' as head put it. Parents agree with him that these informal conversations on the touchline – and, equally, after rehearsals and performances – help reinforce shared values and bonding.

'About a third of students and staff are involved on any one Saturday, and not always the same third,' we were told.

Very strong emphasis on music, arts, dance and drama. New performing arts centre in 2016, incorporating a 240-seat theatre, 180-seat auditorium, music classrooms and a dance studio. Head is passionate about maximising opportunities for performing and creative arts both in and outside the curriculum. Believes it is crucial in helping prepare for adult life in 21st century by fostering skills in communication, collaboration and presentation.

Very strong emphasis on building confidence in junior school through opportunities for performance: a MADD (Music, Art, Dance and Drama) evening, teatime concerts, a performing arts day and productions. Also creativity – participating in Arts Award scheme and developing skills. Opportunities for individual musical instrument tuition (everyone learns violin from age 5) and speech and drama classes.

Every Friday afternoon, there's a wide-ranging activities programme for juniors, some with professional instructors. Staff – including some from senior school – run many clubs, often following their own passions, whether for Irish dancing or chess. BGS hosted semi-finals of English primary schools' chess championships, with 500 entrants from around the country. Children love the activities and trips – dry ski slope a particular favourite. Ukulele, blogging, coding and Mandarin just some of what's on offer. 'Children could do something every five minutes of the day if they wanted to,' said one teacher. 'Children like to be busy. They like to be fully occupied and challenged,' said another. 'My kids love it; they come out buzzing,' said a parent.

Definite move away from 'macho' image in recent years; for example, all boys do dance in senior school. 'Softer' activities are encouraged for boys and girls, with clubs such as textiles, beekeeping and Bake Off. This adds to a quirky feel around the school site, with yarnbombing in the trees, beehives on the science block roof and kayaks parked under the cherry blossom.

Facilities for creative arts – housed in one of Elton Road houses, complete with garden studios – and design technology, in a superb underground workshop, are outstanding. BGS regularly excels in the Greenpower build-a-car competition. The school stages its own annual Wildlife Photographer of the Year competition and the stunning winning entries are on display around the campus.

Music is currently taught in one of the houses in Elton Road and many students also learn instruments – you'll find up to 40 having lessons at any one time. Lots of opportunities to perform in choirs, bands and choirs, in prestigious venues and on tour as well as for school events. House singing competition a highlight of the year. New centre will mean music technology courses can be introduced. Food and nutrition is an increasingly popular subject, taught in well-equipped kitchens. Pupils split into smaller classes – maximum 14 – for DT, art and music.

Trips and expeditions are on offer for all age groups. Morocco trek for Year 9 epitomises BGS's aims – life-changing, learning, friendships and adventure. Wild camping in the Atlas Mountains 'creates the magic and allows time for proper conversations', according to staff. 'It is is quite nice not having to worry "where's my phone?"' a student commented. Duke of Edinburgh Award scheme also popular.

Sixth formers value their wide-ranging lecture programme – from hypnotism to James Bond. They also follow a Back Yourself programme to develop confidence in social situations.

Appropriately for a school that has Allen Lane, founder of Penguin Books, among its alumni, BGS is famed for its literary events – more than 200 author visits in 15 years – and for its library, which houses more than 34,000 titles and has a generous budget for replenishment.

The wood-panelled Great Hall is used for all manner of activities, from daily lunch for 1,500 to grand occasions. One memorable event in 2015 was a 15-hour whole-school reading of Homer's Odyssey (in English) involving students of all ages, teachers, ex-students, support staff, parents, university staff and undergraduates.

Guidance on future choices is provided by two careers staff, who are supported well by returning alumni.

Background and atmosphere: Friendly and welcoming. Location alongside the University of Bristol is a great advantage, providing a harmonious academic setting. BGS was founded in 1532 and has been at Tyndall's Park site since 1879. Whole school population now takes part in Charter Day procession down Park Street to Bristol Cathedral. 'We celebrate our identity as a school at the heart of the city, where we began. We are reminded of our legacy and the achievements of our predecessors,' head explained.

Staff, students and parents speak of 'tremendous ethos of achievement in the school' and are glad that 'achievement in any field is celebrated'. Teachers seen as cheerful, positive, busy, enthusiastic, with some described as 'extraordinary,' 'fabulous' and 'inspiring'. Parents in awe of way school is organised. 'I've not heard of anything poorly run or poorly delivered.'

One said: 'Rod MacKinnon has dragged the school into the 21st century. He's made it highly competitive with other schools in Bristol – less stuffy.'

Paradoxically, since the introduction of infant school classes in 2010, a stronger 'whole school' ethos has developed across BGS. Staff, students and parents value the all-through, 4-18 mix. All ages share the same breakfast club; sixth formers help infants with reading; year 2s sing in the BGS assembly. The head, who has been around long enough to remember the introduction of girls to the senior school in 1980, says it's great. 'Everyone is valued equally.'

Pastoral care, well-being and discipline: House system in junior school – four houses, not linked to those in the senior school – supports pastoral care and personal development. It gives children contact with a different group from their peers and provides opportunities for competition and rewards, such as star of the day and house captains. It's also important for charity activities, a priority for the head. Fairy cake Friday is just one popular example.

'Bucket filling' is a principle introduced in year 1. The idea is that if we are kind and help others we make them feel good, ie 'fill up their bucket', while the opposite also applies. A side effect of being considerate is that we make ourselves feel good too. 'Year 1 children regularly note examples of filling each other's buckets and have gone into house assemblies in the senior school to explain the concept to 11-18 year-olds. The feedback from these assemblies has been excellent. Senior pupils love the concept and are amazed by how articulate and confident 5 and 6 year-olds can be,' head explains.

Nurturing and supportive culture extends to staff, who appreciate the chance to build relationships with children and welcome opportunities for professional development. Peer observations between the infant, junior and senior school are seen as beneficial to all. One long-serving staff member observed that the increase in support staff and the feeling that everyone is part of one team was very different to the more regimented style of decades past. Parents praise easy access to staff and swift action on any concerns. Some staff are perhaps a touch too accommodating – answering emails from demanding mums and dads at 7am.

Senior house system has been strengthened in recent years, with head of house as pastoral leader. Six houses, each with its own colour. Trips, parties, social and competitive activities as well as personal support and a family atmosphere. 'Classic boarding school model,' says head. 'House is like a school within a school,' says a staff member. Peer mentoring is a strong feature of pastoral care too.

A student help desk is staffed all day to answer any enquiries. There's also a full-time nurse and a counsellor three days a week. One parent praised 'immediate and appropriate response

B

after a family bereavement – it was nice to know the school knew and understood'.

Strong investment in transition, as children come into year 7 from many different primary schools. One mum said: 'Coming from a small primary, I was worried my daughter would struggle in a big secondary, but she is relishing the different characters, has made friends and is enjoying lessons. She has discovered climbing and is absolutely obsessed with it.'

Emphasis on positive reinforcement and encouragement of expected behaviour. Parents appreciate the many cards, postcards, and letters commending their children. Some are less keen on the necessary communications about infringements; one parent said being texted because his son was late for school was 'a bit nanny statish'.

Pupils and parents: BGS became independent in 1979 following abolition of direct grant system and went co-ed a year later. Steady increase in proportion of girls. One long-serving staff members said there was 'no doubt this had benefited the school enormously; it has created a more amiable atmosphere'. Males still in majority but most students, staff and parents agree 'it has never felt an overly boys' school'. Nature of the school changed again with the move to bursaries from assisted places scheme. Majority of students come from north west Bristol. Not many from excessively wealthy backgrounds; bias towards professionals. Phenomenal number of staff send their own children to BGS because 'it offers so many opportunities. Something for everyone to fit into'. Several recent leavers have returned as teachers.

Entrance: Infants usually join in reception at age 4, following an informal assessment and a report from the child's current nursery. Entrants to junior school, mostly at year 3, sit tests in English and verbal and non-verbal reasoning. Expanded entry at start of year 5.

Most students join senior school in year 7, about half from the juniors and the rest from up to 40 primaries in Bristol and beyond. External candidates sit January entrance exam tests in verbal and non-verbal reasoning and English and also attend an interview. Reference from the primary school and Sats predictions where applicable also required. Additional tests for entrants to years 8, 9 and 10.

More than 90 per cent of year 11s stay on for sixth form. Admission to lower sixth from elsewhere is dependent on interviews in proposed subjects and reference from head of current school. Offers usually conditional on good grades at GCSE or equivalent.

Exit: Children who joined the school at the beginning of year 5 or earlier no longer have to sit entrance exam for the senior school but transfer on the recommendation of the junior school head. Around 98 per cent go through. Small percentage leave at 16 to go to state or other sixth forms. Most leavers at 18 go to higher education; eight students made it to Oxbridge in 2016.

Money matters: Some financial assistance for highly academic junior school pupils from low-income families through the Peloquin Award scholarships. Academic scholarships, creative and performing arts scholarships, and sport scholarships, available in years 7 and 9. Two Pople Trust Awards (for outstanding maths, physics, chemistry and biology students) on offer in year 10. Means-tested School Assisted Places Scheme available to excellent candidates from low-income backgrounds.

Remarks: Mutual respect goes a long way in ensuring that the shared commitment to enabling young people to leave BGS as well-rounded individuals, equipped for life in the fast-changing world of the 21st century, is fulfilled.

Bristol Steiner School

Redland Hill House, Redland Hill, Bristol BS6 6UX

Pupils: 235 • Ages: 3–16

Fees: £7,2075 – £7,512 pa

Tel: 01179 339990
Email: admissions@bristolsteinerschool.org
Website: www.bristolsteinerschool.org

College of Teachers: As in other Steiner schools, a 'college of teachers' replaces the headteacher. The school's management group comprises trustees and staff representatives.

Academic matters: Teaching here is very different from most schools, a fact acknowledged even by the inspectorate, which produces a different kind of report with separate criteria for Steiner schools. Though not aimed at exam qualifications children can and do take GCSE, normally in English, maths, history and science, with French, art, German and additional science also available. Groups are vey small – anything between six and 14, with smaller groups for some exam subjects, which are mostly taught by specialists. Day to day teaching, however, consists of a two hour main lesson which is topic-based with topics lasting about three weeks and ranging from ancient history and study of art to organic chemistry, embryology, mathematics and ethics. These topics balance over a year to provide experience of the full curriculum, and each year has an over-arching theme such as Polarity and the Way Things Work. There is great emphasis on presentation, including illustration and embellishment of work, as well as plenty of time given to practical subjects. Teachers are impressive, and the sophistication and freedom of discussion in lessons is notable, as is the standard of much of the work produced. Topic lessons have a formalised start and finish, which emphases the 'spiritual' (not necessarily Christian) significance of daily activity (NB do read up on Steiner's philosophy of anthroposophy). Compulsory field trips or exhibition visits form the basis of some topics, with plenty of freedom for pupils to follow up their own areas of interest, though when nearing exam years the teachers guide them towards the essential skills. The level of interest and engagement is impressive. Presentation is integral to all studies and we saw some outstanding examples.

Exam lessons are 40 minutes, with doubles where necessary, and pupils sit AQA and OCR exams. Several of the students we spoke to came from academic families whose parents confidently expected them to go on to university and other courses. In the past, students from Bristol Steiner have ended up at Oxford (maths) and other 'good' unis. Not all, however, achieve this, and there is quite a high proportion of those for whom Steiner is a refuge from the stress of mainstream schooling. Pupils seem to take fewer GCSEs than than in mainstream schools as they also follow a Steiner curriculum. Results indicate that bright pupils can do really well – between 15 and 30 per cent A*/A grades, and the majority getting B/C, with a few Ds and below. With very small groups it is difficult to identify exceptional trends, and over the last few years all subjects have had a few really good grades. The school offers some learning support, but the vital help is the patient and sympathetic teaching and excellent relationship between staff and pupils in very small classes, which gives strong support to all pupils. In addition, a qualified SENCo coordinates the special needs programme. Currently no statemented children, but a number require support. Pupils are screened for dyslexia at class 2 and 4 stages. Children are withdrawn either individually or up to three at a time. The building and site are unsuitable for physically-challenged pupils.

No Sats here: academic results not seen as 'be all and end all' by parents; staff seek to instil genuine thirst for knowledge and feel that too many children are 'damaged' in assessment-driven mainstream schools. Steiner viewed childhood as integrating the developing personality in three successive seven-year stages. Bristol Steiner typically places creativity and emotional security ahead of early intellectual achievement. We spoke to parents whose children had been 'late starters' in reading but who had gone on to shine in GCSEs. Kindergarten, on a separate site, is firmly committed to education through play and activity (such as baking, craft, music) as a foundation for learning and eschews formal teaching. Children here spend about an hour a day at 'play' outside in what looks much like an adventure playground on a sloping garden behind the school. Even the main lesson includes periods outside: letting off steam or learning maths through movement such as 'tag', finger clicking or skipping. TV/VCR/DVD and computers are all eschewed as being counter-creative for young children

Games, options, the arts: Huge emphasis on arts and crafts. Pupils enthusiastically showed us woodwork, beautifully carved bowls and boxes and some impressive chairs. Music, drama and a full craft programme including photography, printing, sculpture, needlework and even ironwork. The work we actually saw was of a high standard, though there is not quite as much on display as in many schools – perhaps because students are encouraged to see a practical value in their creations and take them home. Much of the art was extremely detailed and, though imaginative, almost photographic in its observation – though there was some really exciting photo-collage work in a classroom. Equally, woodwork seemed to emphasize skill in working to a pattern rather than creativity. Art here also includes recitation and drama as well as painting, plus modelling in beeswax and clay, as the traditional divisions between subjects are constantly blurred. The Steiner ethos means games are not really competitive, but the games teacher is very happy to get a game of football going on a cold day. Gym and games are taught separately, and an outside area close to the school is used for a variety of informal sports

Background and atmosphere: This is one of many Steiner schools, all of which place creativity and emotional security ahead of early intellectual achievement. Run on a shoestring since 1973 in a handsome, rambling, red-brick mansion on the edge of Bristol, the school may seem quirky to some, but there was no doubt that some of the pupils we met were focussed on academic progress and utterly supportive of their school. Less cooperative pupils were managed sympathetically by staff and by contemporaries. On four floors, with numerous passages and stone staircases decorated with rag-rolled paint, leading to rather small classrooms, (class sizes are pretty small) all of which surprise the visitor with an elaborate chalk picture on the blackboard (no whiteboards here). A back garden allows for some play space on site.

French and other subjects take place in 'the bean can', a circular room like an agricultural silo, which provides surprisingly good teaching accommodation. Pupils would like another for the art department.

Central to Steiner philosophy is compulsory Eurythmy sessions, which to the uninitiated look like dancing. This is taken seriously by pupils, who regard it as 'relaxing' or 'soothing', though they are not above the occasional giggle when a movement goes wrong. Complicated formations to music of their choice (Bach when we saw it) teach them awareness of self and others and sensitivity to the spirit of the music as well as training memory and developing both sides of the brain. Though some of Steiner's theories now seem off beat to say the least, the reality seen in practice here is gentle, creative and effective. One parent said 'curative' Eurythmy (used on a one-to-one basis with younger children) had 'worked wonders' for her 'withdrawn' daughter, but had no idea why or how.

Pastoral care, well-being and discipline: The school divides into four sections: the kindergarten, Rowan Tree, for under-6s on a separate site, while the main building houses the lower (6-11), middle (11-14) and upper (14-16) schools. Class guardians for each year group form strong relationships with pupils, and accompany their charges up through the year groups. There does not appear to be a formal structure beyond this, but classes are encouraged to consider the needs of the school. Currently they are suggesting a new 'bean can' room for the art department. No uniform, and first names for everybody. Most pupils are exceptionally communicative and open, and mix freely with other Bristol schoolchildren. Very good at getting intelligent interest from unusual or disaffected children, and our observation was that motivated pupils learn from this as well.

Pupils and parents: Parents from all walks of life and immensely supportive. There seems to be a distinct sense of extended school family. Parents not only fundraise but form working parties to improve facilities and (after suitable DBS checks) assist the trips and expeditions integral to some taught topics.

Entrance: Fewer than hoped for have gone on from kindergarten into the main school recently, but the upper school has grown. Under some pressure from the new Bristol Steiner Academy (free school) which has taken over the Old St Matthias teacher training site in Fishponds.

Exit: Now that the school takes pupils up to GCSE, most stay up to 16 and then go on to local sixth form colleges etc; some, thence to uni, including a recent Oxbridge entrant.

Money matters: Fees are modest in comparison with most. Run on a shoestring.

Remarks: Steiner principles are controversial, but for any parent in Bristol looking for a broader, deeper philosophy of education we would recommend investigating this Steiner alternative. If you value a real respect and love for learning over smart facilities and technical one-upmanship, it is definitely worth considering. Equally, children here seem to learn to deal with each other very well – a life skill worth having.

Bromsgrove School

Worcester Road, Bromsgrove, Worcestershire B61 7DU

Pupils: 976; 441 full and weekly boarders • Ages: 13–18 • Sixth form: 441 • C of E

Fees: Day £7,170 – £15,420; Boarding: £16,200 – £33,855 pa

Tel: 01527 579679
Email: admissions@bromsgrove-school.co.uk
Website: www.bromsgrove-school.co.uk

Headmaster: Since 2014, Peter Clague, previously principal of Kristin School in Auckland, New Zealand. He grew up in South

Auckland, spent his first teaching years there and was at Kristin School for 15 years. He has a BA from Auckland University and an MBA from Massey University.

Academic matters: Small classes, outstanding teachers and high expectations produce some very impressive results. Prides itself on value added – not least because it competes for pupils with the King Edward VI foundation schools in Birmingham. Not highly selective on intake but makes a very good showing at GCSE – 64 per cent A*/A grades in 2016.

Facilities for all subjects are very good, in many subjects outstanding. An impressive library, careers and IT complex with lots of well-lit desks and plenty of natural light and space. Range of modern foreign languages available, including Italian and Russian. Latin and classics on offer. All pupils take IGCSEs in English, maths and sciences. Most take 11 subjects at GCSE.

Of the 900+ pupils, over 400 are in the sixth form. Offers both A levels and the IB. A level results are excellent across the board with 86 per cent A*-B grades and 60 per cent A*/A in 2016, and particularly strong results in economics, maths, languages and biology. A wide range of subjects available, including politics, drama and design technology. The IB is a relatively recent introduction (the first cohort completed it in 2011) and the head and staff are passionate about it. At present about 20 per cent of the sixth form take the IB. Initial results were somewhat disappointing, but the 2016 cohort averaged an impressive 38 points. Whether parents will catch the enthusiasm of the staff remains to be seen.

While not by any means a hothouse, pupils need to be up to the mark and ready to push themselves to make the most of what it offers. Possibly not a school for the very timid, children battling with dyslexia or those with other less 'mainstream' learning profiles.

Games, options, the arts: Outstanding standard and range of sports. For a start it has fantastic facilities – 25m swimming pool, two Astroturfs, dance studios, gym, new sports arena and lots of playing fields, netball and tennis courts. It also has excellent coaching – recent coaches have included the England under-18 rugby coach, and an international hockey player. Three Bromsgrovians in current England rugby squad. Cricket has had its share of caps; also a large number of students who play representative sport in hockey (Bromsgrovians represented Great Britain and Germany at the 2012 Olympics), netball, swimming, fencing and show jumping. Plays to win. That said, you don't have to be a sporting demigod to represent the school – A to D teams for most sports and development squads, so enthusiasm and application all it takes to get stuck in.

A wide range of activities on offer from jewellery making to RADA classes, film club and debating. The CCF is strong – a proud history of achievement in the Services (five VCs are commemorated in the school chapel). D of E Award is very popular and other forms of community service are strongly encouraged.

Unique Saturday morning programme – optional for most pupils (compulsory for staff). Offers a vast array of intellectual, cultural and physical activities, from Oxbridge extension lessons to ethics, first aid and table tennis. According to pupils, 'Everyone comes in,' and staff reckon take up of even fairly esoteric activities is very high.

After some time in the shadows, music is now coming on in leaps and bounds – more than 30 a year now take it at GCSE. Lots of opportunities to play in orchestras, informal concerts, chamber and chapel choirs, pop, and jazz ensemble etc. The school choir has recently performed in St Paul's Cathedral and St John the Divine in New York. A new music block is next on the wish list.

Gorgeous DT/art block with excellent woodwork and metalwork facilities, beautiful light studios. Great textile work and paintings on display.

Boarding: One mixed, two girls' and three boys' boarding houses, each with own parents' association. Staffed by resident houseparents (all academic teachers), resident assistant houseparent and team of tutors who share day and evening duties. Sixth form boarders can eat in at Housman Hall in the evening but it's communal meals otherwise.

Activities range from theatre trips to London and Stratford and concerts to paintballing and go-karting (aim, says school is to 'inform, entertain and, occasionally, thrill'). Enough full boarders (there are no exeats) to avoid ghost town atmosphere. School 'nourishes boarders without forcefeeding'.

Background and atmosphere: Founded as a charity school in the 15th century, re-founded in the reign of Edward VI and substantially reinvigorated in the 17th century (some lovely original buildings still extant). The 100-acre campus is situated in the centre of Bromsgrove but has no feel of a town centre school – very spacious, landscaped and looked after with great care. Despite the enormous building activity (including the current construction of a new performing arts centre, with separate concert halls for music and drama) and the very significant increase in pupil numbers in recent years, does not feel overcrowded. The house system seems to prevent pupils from feeling swamped.

Very happy buzz, well ordered, with polite and focused pupils. Puts great emphasis on pupils being themselves and not trying to fit into a particular Bromsgrove 'shape'. Whether the passion is for sport, aviation, engineering or music, pupils are encouraged to be their best and given the resources they need to try out their ideas. 'We do what we think is right for the pupils regardless,' say staff. The school tradition is middle-of-the-road Anglican – twice weekly chapel is compulsory but with the emphasis on ethos not denomination. All faiths and none are welcomed.

No bells between lessons and although the atmosphere is relaxed, uniforms and bedrooms have to be kept neat and tidy – spot checks carried out. Staff wear gowns to chapel and detentions are held in a panelled 17th century hall, where wrongdoers have to explain themselves to staff in front of the head boy and girl, so in some respects quite a traditional feel. Day and boarding pupils pretty equally split – good balance between the two. Day pupils participate enthusiastically in weekend activities.

Pastoral care, well-being and discipline: All pupils are divided into houses – houseparents and their tutor teams (roughly one tutor to 10 pupils) provide daily input, support and oversight. 'We can tell from the way they walk in whether they're looking forward to the day or not,' say staff. Houses are furnished and designed with great attention to detail, have a home from home feel and very good boarding facilities.

School has team of trained student listeners and pupil-led anti bullying policy. Pupils say bullying not an issue, all staff are approachable and that any issue would be 'picked up straight away'. Parents praise the school for its 'positive input and affirmation of the children', excellent communications and ethos. 'It's about creativity, not ego,' one told us. 'The school delivers good citizens. No one gets pushed into a mould.'

No second chances for pupils who break the rules on sex or drugs – very few do. 'We have an ethos of responsibility and good behaviour,' say staff. 'The pupils are very good at self policing.'

Pupils and parents: Pupils are a delight – happy, enthusiastic, unpretentious and genuinely keen to take on responsibilities and contribute to the school and the wider community. Optional Saturday classes are full, huge enthusiasm for the vast array of extracurricular activities. A large local catchment from Worcestershire, Shropshire, Warwickshire and Birmingham, and boarders from all over – Italy, Germany, Russia and China. Most UK parents are professionals, middle class and Midlands-based. A significant number of Forces families. Staff say parents are very collaborative and supportive. Not many landed gentry – and this is not a school where a title would cut much ice.

Entrance: For the senior school entry is via the school's own test or CE. The largest cohort come from Bromsgrove's own large prep (700 strong), whose pupils are assessed informally and most of whom progress to the senior school, and which has now merged with Winterfold House Prep (Winterfold has kept its name, uniform and identity as an RC prep school). Entry to the sixth form is massively oversubscribed – GCSEs at B or above essential.

Exit: Few leave after GCSEs. Virtually all sixth formers to university, with three-quarters gaining places at top universities – Cardiff, Bath, Bristol, UCL, LSE and Exeter particularly popular. Five to Oxbridge in 2016 and seven medics.

Money matters: Scholarships, though available, are nominal and carry kudos, not cash. However bursaries, strictly means-tested and worth up to 100 per cent of fees, are available to the right candidates. Serious about enabling access for those who would benefit from what it has to offer.

Remarks: A remarkably impressive and exciting school. Produces engaged, friendly, unstuffy and highly successful pupils who thrive within an excellent academic and pastoral environment, with national standard sports. 'We are free to do what we think best because we're under the radar,' says the school. We don't think they will stay under the radar for long.

Bruton School for Girls

Sunny Hill, Bruton, Somerset BA10 0NT

Pupils: 276; 63 full, 9 weekly boarders • Ages: Girls 2–18, boys 2–7 (boarding from year 4) • Sixth form: 47

Fees: Day £5,700 – £15,900; Boarding £18,855 – £29,085 pa

Tel: 01749 814400
Email: admissions@brutonschool.co.uk
Website: www.brutonschool.co.uk

Headmistress: Since 2012, Mrs Nicola (Nicky) Botterill BSc MA NPQH FRGS FRSA (late 40s). A geographer by academic discipline, with a first degree from Middlesex Poly and a master's from the Institute of Education, Mrs Botterill has taught in girls' schools for her entire career, except for one stint in a mixed state school, ascending through the hierarchy as far as the deputy headship of St Mary's Calne, from where she was appointed head of BSG.

'I felt immediately at home here and found the girls grounded and unstuffy', she says. Early exposure to travel and living abroad as a child imbued her with a love of adventure and foreign climes; the fact that she took a mid-career gap year has done it no harm at all.

Bruton is small girls' school in a part of south west England that is richly populated with good schools. Mrs Botterill was brought in to increase numbers but has achieved rather more than that since her arrival – her work supporting newly qualified teachers within the Girls' Schools Association was recognised by their award for 'an outstanding contribution from a recently appointed head' in 2014 – and has garnered approval from all quarters. 'She did not grab the reins, but took the time to get to know people'; 'But you know she's in charge,' say parents. In her trademark fuchsia jacket and pashmina, we found her engagingly warm, frank, chatty, approachable – all reiterated by parents and girls. Any free time she might have could be spent doing arts and crafts, such as pottery and stained glass, even DIY on occasion.

Head of Sunny Hill Prep: Since 2010, Mrs Helen Snow BEd (50s), previously deputy head. A breadth of teaching experience preceding her arrival at Sunny Hill (elementary teaching in the US, secondary in the UK, a stint in Berlin – some occasioned by her husband's job moves) means she truly knows that primary is where her heart lies. 'I've taken the best bits of the national curriculum and left the rubbish', she says: outdoor learning and bushcraft are big here and the school is a forest school (there's a nature reserve on site in a former railway cutting), leading on naturally to the rigours of D of E in the senior school.

Warm and cuddly (we imagine), one father described her as 'everything you would want in a prep school headmistress', with the sort of compassion and vision which led her to set up an office in the school for a father whose child had broken her leg, but who wanted to be in school. A lover of the outdoors, Mrs Snow has two black labradors (and a teenage daughter); she is currently learning to ski – 'It reminds me of how it feels to learn something from scratch,' she says. She also enjoys less hearty delights such as gastronomy and theatre and possibly (though not necessarily) her current training to be an ISI inspector.

Academic matters: Non-selective it may be – very strong value-added: the prep school is in the top 12 per cent nationally – but there is no shortage of scope or range (or fun) in the academic offering, which caters equally well for the brightest little sparks. We loved the wall frieze of This Little Piggy captioned by the Latin club – 'Vii vii vii usque domum'. 'Whatever the ability of the girl, we'll do jolly well by her', as the head says.

Senior school scores highly on value-added. Sixty-eight per cent of GCSEs were graded A*/A in 2016; 44 per cent of A levels taken came in at A*/A. Before GCSE, the curriculum includes compulsory classics (including Greek and Latin), DT and 'home technology'. In sixth form, Leith's certificate in food and wine is popular – we would happily have stayed in any ski chalet catered by BSG students, judging by what was being made in the kitchen. Typically, girls take nine or 10 subjects at GCSE, to include separate sciences, but no language, ancient or modern, is compulsory; a choice of French, German, Spanish or Latin is offered. Flexible and enlightened enough to allow girls to take certain GCSEs (eg French and maths) two or three years early, in exceptional cases. Twenty-one subjects to choose from in sixth form.

Small class sizes, averaging under 10, hard work and the 'enthusiastic, effective teachers – the kind you get in a grammar school,' according to one parent, contribute to the school's academic success and high praise is given to SEN diagnosis and support: 'My daughter's in-house plan is tailored to her', said another, whose daughter had fled the local comprehensive. The wide ability range 'has meant my girls have learnt to tolerate all levels of ability, which is much more like real life,' commented one thoughtful mother of clearly bright girls. Stand-out subjects are English, drama, art and biology; some report that maths is currently in flux. Our impression was of interesting subject matter (West Side Story being used to demonstrate the realities of immigration for Hispanics, capital punishment v the safety and protection of prisoners) being delivered with IT as support rather than as a substitute for honest-to-goodness teaching, to a very compliant, quiescent flock – just for our benefit?

B

Games, options, the arts: Hockey and netball the main games here, with no fewer than 17 netball teams. An impressive fixture list where BSG looks more like David up against local Goliaths Sherborne Girls and King Edwards Bath. Several netball courts doubling up for tennis, a delightfully sunny Astro where strenuous hockey practice was taking place when we visited, plus an athletics track behind the main group of buildings. At present the swimming pool is an outdoors, solar-heated, summer only affair; the five swimming teams use opponents' indoor facilities for matches at less clement times of year. An indoor pool is top of the parental wish list. Although there is a riding team, this is not the kind of place where girls bring their own steeds, and the ability to pilot a horsebox is not a requirement for entry. Sporty activities include quidditch and tchoukball (truly – we wished we'd seen either).

Music comes in for high praise – deservedly so, judging by the singing practice for the director of music's own composition that we heard, the recital at assembly and admissions to national and county youth choir and orchestra. A school orchestra, smaller ensembles for brass and strings inter alia, a Baroque group, theory classes for those taking grades and plenty of opportunities to play beyond the school gates make for a rich musical offering: we enjoyed the CD (and cookies) we were given on departure very much.

Drama takes place in the Hobhouse theatre: although it is a popular option, outside the devised and scripted requirements of public exams – when we witnessed genuine belly laughs and dramatic talent in the GCSE piece we saw – the scope seems limited to one musical per year, but 'Please please don't make us play boys again,' beg the girls. The art department is truly vibrant – a crammed creative space where girls seem to be able to pursue any artistic fancy: the series of photographs resulting from one girl persuading an obliging friend to immerse herself in milk in a variety of poses was memorable. Good links with the arty town of Bruton enrich the life of the school – the installation by a local artist of felt poppies suspended on threads to commemorate the First World War was innovative and moving. Plenty of trips to local and not so local theatre, concerts and galleries complement the lively arts scene within school.

Plenty on offer after school too: 'My daughter would stay until 5.30pm every day in some club or other,' said one prep school mother 'Folk club, netball, judo, viola...' Wrap around care from 7.45am-6pm.

Boarding: Boarding (officially from year 4, but occasionally younger in the case of one small girl we met whose elder sisters all board and who was determined not to miss out) takes place in the cosy old vicarage where all junior boarders (just a handful from the prep) up to year 9 are housed. Day girls are free to join in with weekend activities and intermittent sleep-overs. Two other boarding houses for senior school boarders. Accommodation is homely and not obsessively tidy: a couple of sixth form girls had transformed their room into a Christmas grotto, complete with glitter and a snow scene, without attracting the wrath of the domestic staff. Intra-school allegiance, which might attach to houses with full vertical boarding in a bigger school, is created by assigning each girl (day and boarding) to one of four halls named for local stately homes.

Background and atmosphere: One of a disproportionate number of schools in Bruton (owing to the beneficence of Hugh Sexey, an auditor of the Exchequer in the early 1600s), a small charming Somerset market town of golden stone, BSG sits on Sunny Hill, certainly so the day we visited, with distant hazy views of Glastonbury Tor. Established in 1900 and known originally as Sunny Hill School (the name retained by the prep), it has mostly been independent but spent 30 years in the maintained sector early in the last century. It is possibly this which gives the school a delightful lack of pretension and snobbery, 'a place where the teachers don't parade like cockerels, but where they get a remarkable amount out of the girls,' in the words of one mother. 'It's slightly Enid Blyton with cocoa and biscuits at break,' said another. We liked the fresh air and heartiness about the place – the gaps between buildings necessarily mean a breather between lessons, through the beautifully tended grounds and eccentric pop-up garden, with its giant chessmen.

Sunny by name and sunny by nature, the prep school sits at the top of the Bruton School site, a short walk from the senior school. Though very small, it benefits from the facilities and specialist languages and games staff of its big sister, whilst retaining its own cosy atmosphere. 'In and of itself, the prep school is none too impressive, but its alliance with the senior school makes up for a lot,' was the cool appraisal of one father – but even he would surely have been impressed with the dissection of a cow's heart (from an obliging local butcher) we saw in a year 6 biology lesson. (The squeamish were taught from a 3D model by a kindly TA.)

Proud and unapologetic to be a girls' school, where both the girls and their parents choose to be: 'My daughter was offered the chance to move at sixth form and declined,' one parent told us, another recounted a story of her daughter taking refuge from the local state offering and finding sanctuary at BSG. 'We landed on our feet here', said yet another satisfied customer. The school's size means that girls form friendships across year groups, and we felt a genuine sense of community over a delicious lunch of steak pie and fresh veg. 'Friendly' kept popping up as the most common adjective used to describe the school: 'My daughter took all of two days to settle in,' reported one happy mother.

Pastoral care, well-being and discipline: The pastoral side and the immense care the school takes over every girl in it are hugely appreciated by parents. 'The staff really get to know the children and don't just tell you the things you want to hear, they tell it how it is', said a prep school mother, who had no notes of criticism whatsoever. Hot on friendship issues, a perennial subtext in girls' schools. 'Bruton stood out over other local schools,' in one parent's view, 'and the school is not afraid to tackle issues head on, yet sensitively'. Tutor groups are mixed age until sixth form (these meet daily), and between tutors and heads of halls, no-one appears to fall through the net. Relationships between staff and students and between the students themselves are sound and supportive, 'but we do teach them resilience and that things going wrong isn't necessarily a problem,' adds the head. 'Honourables' are awarded for exceptional work, 'hallmarks' for acts of courtesy and community-mindedness, colours for sporting prowess. Discipline is not a matter which seems to rear its ugly head very often: rudeness, lateness and wilder interpretations of uniform do not go unremarked; smokers and drinkers can expect a sliding scale of punishment, whilst druggies and persistent offenders face exclusion. 'Fluffy and lenient we are not,' states the head.

Pupils and parents: 'Confident without being arrogant' – that overworked phrase to which every school aspires – is echoed by parents. We found the girls, who arrive in anything from helicopters to old bangers, cheerful, unpretentious and very happy to be at this school. 'This isn't the place for hair-flicking city types, but for well-grounded families, wanting the best for their girls', says Mrs Snow. 'Our parents aren't flashy but aren't without aspiration either'. A welcoming parent community helps to reassure first time buyers that they have made a wise choice. About one fifth of girls is from overseas.

Famous old girls include Clarissa Farr, (soon to be ex-)High Mistress of St Paul's Girls' School and journalists Viv Groskop, Imogen Sellars and Catherine Davies.

Entrance: Non-selective from nursery upwards; meeting with head and maths and English assessments for entry into prep. To senior school via online verbal and non-verbal reasoning tests to assess potential, plus interview. At sixth form the bar is higher, at five GCSEs at grade C or above, with Bs at subjects to be taken at A level. Termly open days and visits by arrangement. Main feeders at year 7 are the prep and local primary schools, at year 9 local preps. Several buses serve surrounding area within 20 mile radius.

Exit: Boys leave after year 2; the majority of girls to the senior school by means of verbal and non-verbal reasoning tests, for diagnostic purposes only. Sixth formers to a wide range of universities and an equal variety of courses. Most girls get to their first choice: everything from veterinary medicine at Cambridge to Arabic and Islamic studies at SOAS to retail management at De Montfort.

Money matters: As independent education goes, good value for money, at about 25 per cent cheaper than its most expensive competitors. 'Bruton offers everything academic and holistic a parent could ask from a 21st century girls' school, without charging the ridiculous fees that most other schools charge', so said one mother. Scholarships, awarded for the usual range of talents, are nominal, but governors' exhibitions are awarded in cases of means-tested need to a maximum value of 40 per cent of fees.

Remarks: 'It's just not very BSG to promote itself,' one father remarked, but if we were expecting an apologetic little school lurking in rural Somerset, we did not find it. Hidden gem is more like it – a place of unpretentious endeavour where girls can be girls and achieve as much as they are capable of. 'Follow the gleam,' may be the school motto, but in our view it could be time for a spotlight.

Bryanston School

Bryanston, Blandford Forum, Dorset DT11 0PX

Pupils: 685; 600 boarders • Ages: 13–18 • Sixth form: 285 • C of E

Fees: Day £29,229; Boarding £35,646 pa

Tel: 01258 452411
Email: admissions@bryanston.co.uk
Website: www.bryanston.co.uk

Head: Since 2005, Ms Sarah Thomas (50s). A GDST girl hailing from Birkenhead and proud of it, Ms Thomas read Lit Hum (classics – the proper kind with Greek) at Oxford, before becoming an articled clerk to a notary public. Both her parents taught, but their entreaties not to follow in their footsteps clearly fell on deaf ears, for she left the law to do her PGCE at King's College London, before longish stints at Sevenoaks and Uppingham. All that formative experience of co-ed boarding has equipped her admirably for Bryanston. 'A female head is just a part of who we are, and the best part of my job is recruiting outstanding staff', she says. We found her a (charming) force to be reckoned with, whom we can imagine causing stuffier members of HMC to choke on their sherry. 'Splendid', say parents, '100 per cent approachable, with fine powers of judgment'. Ms Thomas makes a point of keeping her hand in at the chalk-face – everybody has to do Latin in the first year, and a fair few take it on to GCSE; a brainy minority do Greek as well.

Ms Thomas' husband teaches at nearby Hanford and writes children's books and plays; they have two daughters at university. In her precious time off? 'Reading – for its peaceful aspects and the opportunity to lose myself in other worlds', she says, plus walking her dog and cooking.

Academic matters: Not desperately selective, with an expectation of 50 per cent for each subject at CE – but what marks this school out is the way academic life is structured. The timetable contains assignment periods for each subject alongside lessons, where prep, further study or one-to-one sessions with the subject teacher take place – the latter ominously named 'correction periods'. In the first three years, assignment periods are supervised by the subject teacher, providing access and extra help outside lessons. Academic progress is tracked more tightly here than in any school this editor had seen: weekly assessments are provided by each subject teacher and entered on the e-chart, the online mark-sheet to which parents also have access. All assignments (prep) are set to be handed in a week later, so being organised and learning to manage a workload is a skill learnt early. 'The tutorial system ensures success,' says the school: each student is allocated a tutor for the duration of his/her time at the school – so far, so conventional – but these individuals do so very much more than that somewhat over-used term suggests. 'We tutors deal with the academic, spiritual, moral and act as a kind of PA', said one. Parents greatly value this and tutors' accessibility both to students and parents. SEN provision supports what goes on in class: each department appoints a staff member to liaise with learning support. One-to-one tuition is available; all help offered is discreet and without stigma. School claims to 'deliver for every child we admit.'

So does it pay off? At GCSE in 2016, 51 per cent A*/A grades and in some years, school is on a par with local independents such as the Sherborne schools, where entry requirements are higher. 'My daughter got results beyond our wildest dreams', raved one mother, who also reckoned that Bryanston had been perfect for all three of her children, with differing abilities and interests. Visual arts of all kind very popular and successful, as is Latin and Greek; results suggest as much enthusiasm as aptitude for Latin, but it is heart-warming to see such a resurgence in classical languages. School keeps a Greek theatre tucked away in its extensive grounds, and the JACT summer school in Greek – of formidable repute – for all-comers is held here. At A level, 73 per cent graded A*/B and 38.7 per cent A*/A in 2016, but value-added shows up strongly against comparable schools. Business studies and English are the most popular choices, sciences hot on their heels, followed by art and design in its various forms. History and geography have a moderate following; modern languages surprisingly little, along with music and drama. First IB results in 2014, with an average of 35 points and one pupil achieving the maximum of 45.

Games, options, the arts: The scope is amazing – clearly something for the most idle couch potato. All the sports and facilities one would expect in a school of this type feature (rugby, hockey, netball, cricket, tennis, rowing) and both hockey and lacrosse are on offer in consecutive terms. Luscious grounds stretch down to the river Stour, where rowing of increasing seriousness takes place out of a beautiful new boathouse designed by an OB and keen oarsman (sadly we weren't shown this). New arrivals learn navigation skills and how to survive a night in the open – useful for those times when they get lost in the grounds. A carousel of adventurous options takes place in the second year, comprising (amongst other things) falconry, canoeing and rock-climbing. Riding might seem quite mundane; we were bemused not even to be shown the stabling, indoor and all-weather schools, or cross-country course on our visit. Keen riders can bring their own steeds. Sailing in the school's own fleet of Lasers in Poole harbour. School is notable local and national player in a variety of sports. OBs include Phil de Glanville.

The art at Bryanston hits you between the eyes as you walk in. Enormous canvasses adorn the long walls of each of the central corridors in the main building: the scope of the department and amount of available hanging space, plus the skills and dedication of teachers and students, mean the most ambitious projects can be executed. The art department is divided into 2D and 3D; both aspects enjoy a passionate following and are fabulously resourced. Best work of both past and present pupils has twice been showcased in Cork St (no less). School's reputation for a creative curriculum is well deserved, and fulfils the aspiration for 'the joy of the abundant life' which an early headmaster articulated.

Music and drama (both excellent and ambitious in scope) tend to be avidly pursued for the love of them, rather than chasing yet another GCSE. The 600 seat Coade Hall measures up as well as any school theatre facility, indeed visiting theatre companies stage performances here. Usual musicals (Cabaret, Guys and Dolls in recent years) sometimes include a showing for prep schools – canny marketing! Annual play for each year group (eg The Crucible, Pride and Prejudice in a specially adapted version). Much student-led drama, and our guides enthused about house drama, where even the most reluctant performers tread the boards. New Tom Wheare Music School (named after retired head) includes stunning 300 seat concert hall with huge stage designed to hold a large-scale symphony orchestra, plus, inter alia, large numbers of practice rooms, recital rooms, recording studios, soundproofed band rooms and courtyard area for outdoor performances (plans for performances and masterclasses from renowned musicians). Let's hope they are generous with it. Again, any musical whim can probably be accommodated – if not here, then where? Over a fifth of students sing in a group or choir: we heard the first rehearsal of one of mixed age and mixed ability during the lunch hour, and tuneful and enthusiastic it was too. Musicians perform all over the place, including London and abroad – the dance band to Paris, the chamber choir and orchestra to Florence. All students have to learn a musical instrument in the first year, which may be where the enthusiasm and lung capacity to play the bagpipes starts – there is even a pipe band. 'What the musicians did in the hols' was an interesting little aside in the school's extensive literature; one boy's attendance at a course at Berklee College in Boston helped him gain a place on its coveted degree programme.

Extracurricular activities are taken seriously here in pursuit of the abundant life – there is everything from Accessorise (jewellery) to yoga, and a choice of four out of more than 100 is compulsory in the first two years.

Boarding: Three boarding houses are contained within the main building, the rest scattered over the grounds immediately around the main building. Accommodation is comfortable rather than de luxe. Everybody eats centrally in the delightfully refurbished dining hall, and the food is all it's cracked up to be: we sampled the excellent salad bar but the hot choices and puddings all smelt and looked scrummy too. Rather cool café in lieu of tuck shop sells smoothies, cookies, pizza and other appealing fare; houses also have kitchens for making snacks and drinks. When we asked about the long walk into Blandford, students looked slightly blank – why would they need to do that when everything is at school?

On whole school weekends, all pupils stay in school and work together towards a common goal, eg a charity fundraising event, pupil-led arts festival, sponsored walk etc, but on open weekends they may go home after Saturday morning lessons/ any match commitments.

Background and atmosphere: Exceedingly long drive through woods leads eventually to a baby château perched on a rise overlooking the river Stour. Modelled on Menars in the Loire valley by Norman Shaw, the house had to be sold to meet the death duties of Viscount Portman after the family had lived there for just 30 years. In 1928 a young Australian school master bought it and founded the school on traditional and modern principles – et nova et vetera, as the motto says. Going co-ed in the early 70s was well ahead of the trend, and Bryanston has kept its reputation for blazing a trail – 'Just don't call us progressive,' said the head, with a visible shudder.

Acres (400) of grounds and beautiful bold modern additions surround the house, which aside from the diggers and heavy plant constructing the new music school, make a harmonious whole. Inside, two long parquet-floored corridors dotted with sofas in the main house give the continuing impression of being fortunate residents of a mansion, though everyone looks more purposeful. Even the staff and visitors' loos were contained in a spacious cloakroom with leather armchairs in which to retreat from the fray.. Teaching spaces are high spec, particularly the science labs, with their wet and dry areas in the newish Sanger building, named after a double laureate biochemist and OB.

Pastoral care, well-being and discipline: Exceptionally good care is taken of all students. Newbies meet their tutors on arrival at school, and the team formed between him/her and the housemaster or mistress (known as a hsm, to rhyme with bosom) is a tight one. It seems as though it would be hard for any unhappiness or falling off in performance or morale to go unnoticed. Each house has a distinct character and students are placed in them according to a process 'akin to Hogwarts' sorting hat', according to the head. Boys spend a year in one of two junior houses; girls go straight into the house in which they will spend their whole time at the school.

We liked the understated but definite sense of a spiritual life at Bryanston, led by the chaplain. As well as the church in the grounds, there is a dear little chapel in the vaults of the main house which acts as a calm retreat from the hurly burly of life going on outside its open doors. One parent told us her son had 'quietly gone off and got himself confirmed', slightly to her surprise (but pleasure).

The persistent reputation for unchecked behaviour and general licence, drugs in particular, has been slow to die, but one parent briskly dismissed it as 'quite unmerited'. According to the school and the parents we spoke to, any involvement would result in immediate expulsion – and the kids know it. A civilised and age-appropriate view is taken of alcohol for sixth formers, 'carefully monitored under adult supervision,' says school. Any misdemeanours are 'harshly dealt with,' a mother confirmed. The school rules and regs fit on one side of paper and are unequivocal and up to date, eg 'Computers/iPods/MP3s must not be used to watch films, play games, listen to music in lessons, prep and after lights out'. For a school with a dress code rather than uniform below sixth form, we found the students tidier than at many other schools: the drill is a coloured polo shirt with a sweater with black or navy trousers or skirts; more leeway for sixth form.

Pupils and parents: When asked if she could sum up a Bryanston pupil, the head said no she couldn't, though one hallmark would be 'someone comfortable in their own skin', who would enjoy being a part of things. We were actually allowed to meet very few, just the head boy and girl who showed us around, who were of course charming and very much on-message. As for the parents, quite a range professionally from doctors to financiers to creative types, but they struck us as exceptionally thoughtful about their children's education. The geographical spread, in common with many schools, has contracted so that Bryanston is really a south west school, though with a significant minority coming from London and the south east, and a handful from the furthest reaches of the UK. A few from overseas.

Notable OBs include Lucian Freud, all the Conran boys, Mark Elder, John Eliot Gardiner (who sent his daughter too), Ben Fogle and Emilia Fox.

Entrance: There are 130 places at 13+ via CE (50 per cent expected in all papers) or by Bryanston's own papers from an amazing number of prep schools. Close links forged with preps and prospective parents; instead of open days with a cast of thousands, the school arranges group visits for 12 or so families, as well as individual visits. Registered pupils are also invited to various events in the two years before they arrive. Between 25-30 new students arrive at sixth form for which 50 points at GCSE are required, after a day of tests (maths, English and abilities) and interviews at the school. Existing pupils also have to meet the points requirement, waived only in very exceptional cases.

Exit: Three per cent left after GCSEs in 2016. Nearly half of upper sixth leavers apply to university once they have their results. The head of sixth form is all for this, and has tweaked the school's UCAS process to accommodate it. University strategy starts with tutors early in lower sixth and the vast majority of students do go on, whenever they apply. 'Less formal relationships between staff and students mean they are confident enough to bounce up to them and ask for what they need,' he says of the application process. About half take gap years.

Degree courses, interestingly, tend to be conventional choices (business in various forms, engineering, architecture, history and English – but classics too – hurrah!) in conventional places: Bristol, Leeds, Oxford Brookes and UWE. A sprinkling of medics, linguist and politicians too, plus around 10 per cent to art foundation courses.An average of five to Oxbridge each year.

A few gripes about careers and higher education guidance at AS level from parents; while they like the rather unpressured approach to UCAS, they feel alternatives should be more clearly spelt out. Newish head of sixth form appointment is grounds for optimism, however.

Money matters: Fees in line with comparable schools but some items (stationery, art and DT materials) appear on the bill as extras. Scholarships across a range of disciplines including DT and ICT to a maximum of 25 per cent of fees. Bursaries on application.

Remarks: Stunning school with unrivalled facilities and a great deal of latitude and encouragement for students to explore any aspect of academic, sporting and artistic life which takes their fancy. Too much too young? Possibly. A great deal more traditional than its reputation would suggest, but myths can take a long time to break down. We could not find any detractors, try as we might!

Brymore Academy

Cannington, Bridgwater, Somerset TA5 2NB

Pupils: 262; 150 boarders • Ages: 11-17 • Sixth form: 3, boarding only (tuition at Bridgewater College)

Fees: Boarding £9,9700 pa; Day pupils free

Tel: 01278 652369
Email: office@brymore.somerset.sch.uk
Website: www.brymoreacademy.co.uk

Head: Since 2011, Mr Mark Thomas (acting head since September 2010). Originally from Cornwall, Mr Thomas came to Brymore from Courtfields School, Wellington where he had been deputy and acting head. Previously deputy head at Brittons Academy in Rainham, his early teaching career was mainly in London. Down to earth, no-nonsense and determined, he is married with one young son – 'too young to think about Brymore yet!' – and his wife teaches locally. He spends several nights each week in his school house in the grounds. Sport is both his subject and his hobby though he says, cheerfully, that he hasn't had time for anything except Brymore since his appointment. Determined to 'keep the unique identity and nature of Brymore but create a truly secure atmosphere while raising academic expectations and achievement'. The pride of boys and teachers in their achievements, their interest in academic as well as practical work, as well as the national 'Raise Online' statistics, give strong witness to how much he has achieved in four years. Parents were a little apprehensive about changes, particularly the number of new staff and higher academic expectations, but now feel 'it has all come together'.

Academic matters: Since Mr Thomas' appointment there have been huge changes, with nearly three-quarters of current teaching staff appointed since 2011. Five of these are Brymore alumni, so tradition has certainly not gone out with the bathwater.

The farm and gardens are the heart of learning at Brymore. Practical hands-on farm work: tractor driving (from 13), milking, winter and summer feeding of cattle, pigs and poultry, calving and lambing, cultivation of vegetables and maintenance of the grounds. Getting up at 6am, come rain, come shine, come snow and ice, for seven days a week, making and maintaining heavy equipment, means learning to keep yourself fit and disciplined enough to do it all. If, in the past, the academic curriculum has taken second place, this balance is being altered in a major curriculum overhaul.

From year 10 up boys are now in sets (so a boy may be in a fast set for one subject and a more supportive group for another according to individual need) and years 7 to 9 are three streamed groups. A six day timetable gives 30 one hour lessons (doubles for practical subjects). Much more flexible options now with horticulture and agriculture compulsory for first three years but for not for exam years (10 and 11). This makes room for choice and art, modern foreign languages, history and geography, though there is still huge and successful take up in practical land-based subjects. Sadly for Brymore, these subject results won't register in the new league tables, though Mr Thomas is fighting the cause! Modern foreign languages haven't worked though to results yet, but there is a big take up of French in the lower school. Engineering can be taken to 'Industry standard' and DT is a core subject. Academic

B

expectations are high. One boy aiming at an engineering career told us he hoped to go on to grammar school to study maths, higher maths and economics A Level, while another, readily admitting to struggling with English, relished his reading and was an exceptionally articulate living proof of success. In 2016, 48 per cent got 5+ A*-C GCSE grades including maths and English; 10 per cent A*/A grades.

Classes average 16, though there are much smaller groups for boys needing more help and every boy has an individual learning plan. Mentors regularly discuss progress, both academic and personal, and help boys to set and achieve appropriate targets. Very comprehensive learning support is managed by a SENCo with a team of 10 full time, qualified learning support assistants. Most are subject specialists working in their subject area, and the others plug gaps. Resourceful staff are dedicated to improving achievement, and initiatives such as reading nights – just being read to – for younger boys, house points for reading journals, triple input marking, which encourages boys to correct and learn from their own and others' work, are clearly having an impact. Statistics for improvement in maths are not quite as impressive as in English, where the school is in the top three per cent in national stats for improvement, but are OK, and the maths department is still developing new strategies.

Games, options, the arts: Brymore is a sporty school with good rugby, doing respectably at district level – no mean achievement with year groups of under 30 in competition with year groups bigger than the whole Brymore population. Hockey, mountain biking, with an exciting new track and bikes sponsored by Sport England, daily training on the MUGA (multi usage games area), a small Astroturf area, and above all, the Chad Hill daily run: three and a half miles of cross-country which is all but compulsory ('expected' is official terminology).

Sport and activities are partly in curriculum, partly after school, but central to everything is the agricultural and horticultural practice and theory. Taught elements are in the teaching day but in addition every boy has to take his turn in the routine of the farm, boarding for a seven day week in order to be up 6am and be permanently on hand for emergencies. DT and engineering centres round farming. One boy explained that a few days fencing showed him the need for an efficient trailer for fencing materials. Brymore's metal and wood workshops, including smithy and foundry, enable really professional work, from handy little metal hammers made by beginners to roadworthy trailers and specialist tractor accessories – things with real practical value on the farm.

There is a farm manager and a head groundsman, but all the work on the farm and maintaining the grounds and gardens is done by boys. There is nothing to make you understand better why people shouldn't trample across a perfect lawn than mowing it yourself! Horticultural minded boys can have personal plots in the walled garden and use of the potting and tool sheds to grow their own crops – Brymore's kitchens happily buy salad, potatoes and veg from them. Art and music are newly available as options. Languages and other options may be taught outside the main school day.

Boarding: Since a major refurbish, boarding is comfortable and clean, the slightly institutional layout softened by posters of giant tractors, 'great big combine harvesters', animals and sport and no institutional smell. Bins outside the doors of the two newish boarding houses take muddy farm clothes and sports gear. Dorms sleep four, except in the main house, where it's up to six. Very tidy – a few unwashed coffee mugs in the boys' kitchen sink confirmed that it is actually lived in. Each house has its own houseparents and relief team for continuity.

Background and atmosphere: Brymore was founded as a School of Rural Technology in 1952 for sons of Somerset farmers on an impressive 60-acre farm on the edge of Cannington, between the Quantocks and Bristol Channel. Half a mile of tree-lined drive ends in a cluster of farm buildings which surround the original 13th century house, much added to over the centuries, and once owned by the Cromwell's financier John Pym. Exceptionally loyal ex-pupils meet and encourage the current generation at the annual, misleadingly named, Pym's Night. Boys really seem to value the traditional standards of Brymore and are proud of taking part in the local church festivals – harvest especially – and of their reputation among local farmers: Brymore boys are useful on the farm. Shoes are miraculously clean despite farmyard mud, smart black uniform sports the Brymore spur and motto Diligentia et Labore on the pocket. It is also emblazoned on the walls in each boarding house, as the boys' chosen decoration. Parents and staff praise Brymore as 'feeling more like an independent school'. 'The noise of 180 boys singing out at full volume nearly knocks you out,' a proud parent commented after her first carol service.

Pastoral care, well-being and discipline: Brymore had a reputation as a pretty tough place in the past, but its toughness now focuses on the personal resilience and responsibility of the boys rather than rough and tumble rivalries. 'Resilience, Responsibility and Resourcefulness' is used as a strap-line by staff and pupils alike and there is no doubt constant reference to it has rubbed off on the boys' approach to academic and farm work. Day and boarding pupils mix in the three houses (not to be confused with the boarding houses), with house masters and tutors, who meet them weekly. Vertical tutor groups means the oldest mentor the year 7s and get to know all age groups. Year 11 boys take the usual prefect duties (hotly contested) and supervise younger ones for milking and feeding duties. Currently, they are very keen on creating an anti-bullying atmosphere, and are super-watchful over the newly-admitted first years. Down to earth matron on duty all day and liked by boys. Food said to be 'better than it was' but still a cause of some contention.

Pupils and parents: The farming community both local and much further flung (boarders from Hong Kong, France, Norway and midlands) definitely dominates, but boys and parents are beginning to demand a wider outlook and academic curriculum. Past pupils visit frequently and are still part of school life. One, teaching blacksmithing at Brymore alongside his own small business, makes an excellent role model. Others include MEP Neil Parish, Mark Irish, England U21 rugby player, Alex Wright, British race walking champion, and Robert Watts, Brymore's head of boarding. Both alumni and parents fundraise enthusiastically.

Entrance: About 50 pupils, 28 boarders and 22 day boys, admitted to year 7. Currently there is a similar intake to year 9, though this will inevitably diminish once the early years are full. Now oversubscribed. Day places on the usual Somerset criteria, a combination of first come first served and distance from the school. Boarding places also now oversubscribed, open to any boy qualifying for UK schooling and 'suitability for boarding'. Brymore is good with boys who haven't thrived in mainstream, but increased demand has meant that the academic profile of the school is now higher that previously.

Exit: A few boarders stay on to year 12 but attend all courses at Bridgewater College. A large contingent to agricultural colleges, Kingston Maurward, Duchy College Cornwall, Bridgwater College (Cannington Centre) and all over the country. 'Brymore boys often get fast tracked at college,' said one farmer dad. A significant interest in engineering, and some boys go on to do A levels with a view to uni places. Lack of modern foreign language teaching has been a bit of a barrier with local sixth form college, so it's as well it's now on offer. Many to apprenticeships and a significant number end up running their own businesses.

Money matters: Fees only for boarding, not tuition, so miles cheaper than the independent sector, despite recent fee rises. Some pupils obtain educational grants from home LAs. All day boys, known as 'out boarders', have to board and pay for the weeks they are on farm duties, though some have found educational grants for this.

Remarks: There are still too few schools like Brymore and, though more are being established, it will be hard to rival its atmosphere and achievement. Articulate, friendly boys are not afraid of the pressures and daily grind of farm work. If this is what hands on experience and responsibility gives to children, schools could do with more of it. No hayseeds at Brymore – more business aware agriculturalists who understand the need to supply food and respect the land that grows it. Parents appreciate that every member of staff is there to give the very best possible education to their children.

Canford School

23

Wimborne, Dorset BH21 3AD

Pupils: 640; 450 full boarders • Ages: 13–18 • Sixth form: 260 • C of E

Fees: Day £25,509; Boarding £33,513 pa.

Tel: 01202 847207
Email: admissions@canford.com
Website: www.canford.com

Headmaster: Since 2013, Ben Vessey BA MA MBA (40s). Educated at Magdalen College School, Oxford, then read history at Southampton. Intended to join the army but after tearing both knee ligaments playing rugby worked as an oil and gas broker for five years in the City and on placement in Texas. 'But when I came back from the US I realised that it wasn't what I wanted to do,' he says. Applied to Dauntsey's, who snapped him up to teach history. Became head of history and housemaster there, followed by four and a half years as head of history, politics and law at Millfield. Spent six years as senior deputy head at Christ's Hospital – 'it was a great apprenticeship for headship,' he says. Along the way he did an MA in history, a PGCE and an MBA in education management.

Loves teaching and teaches five periods a fortnight to a year 9 history set. 'I write reports and do parents' meetings and it keeps me in touch with the rhythms of teachers' busy routines,' he says. Much in evidence around the school and makes a point of dropping in on lessons to see colleagues in action in the classroom. Has lunch with pupils and staff as often as possible and supper with them twice a week. 'I leave them alone at breakfast,' he jokes.

Energetic, enthusiastic and impressively focused, he lives and breathes the school. He loves Sounds of Canford (the school's informal concert series), watches as many concerts, plays and sports matches as he can and catches up with Year of Genius, an innovative enrichment project launched by the school, as he cycles on his spin bike. Lives in a house on-site with his wife Harriet, their three sons (the eldest of whom started as a day boy at Canford at the same time as his dad) and two black labradors. In his spare time he plays golf, cycles and reads (he's a fan of Bernard Cornwell's Sharpe novels and other historical fiction). Winston Churchill is his hero and a bronze miniature of the legendary PM left to the school by old boy Terrence Cobden Pike has pride of place in his study. Churchill was a relation of the Guest family who owned Canford before it became a school and apparently he spent many summer holidays there.

C

Academic matters: Results are easily as good as other co-ed schools with illustrious names. In 2016, 53 per cent A*/A at A level and 82 per cent A*-B (figures include Pre-U for art and languages). At GCSE, 68 per cent A*/A. Considering the breadth of intake this speaks volumes for the first-rate teaching. Maths and chemistry are the most popular A level subjects but many pupils do a mix of sciences, arts and humanities subjects. EPQ on offer too. Sixth formers we spoke to were full of praise for the support in the run-up to A levels and the study skills workshops on offer. Study leave is awarded on an individual basis but most sixth formers opt to stay in school, keen to make the most of timetabled lessons, past papers and one-to-one help. 'Everyone works hard here,' a sixth former told us while another said: 'The teachers want you to do well and they really support you.'

All year 9s do French and Latin, as well as German or Spanish. Most take 10 subjects at GCSE, including at least one language and two sciences. Pupils are set for maths and languages from the word go. Computer science has been introduced throughout the school and is increasingly popular – 16 taking it at GCSE when we visited, 11 at AS and three at A2. 'Prep schools should be trying to embed computer science in the curriculum, rather than just IT,' we were told. Good provision for those with learning difficulties, mostly dyslexia, mild dyspraxia and language attention difficulties. Learning support housed in the Lovell Building, along with the humanities department. Year 9 pupils who need additional support can take extra English instead of Latin, while in years 10 and 11 learning skills are offered for a number of pupils instead of one GCSE subject, with focus on developing study skills. One-to-one tuition available when the need arises. Average class size is 15 in years 9 to 11, nine in the lower sixth and eight in the upper sixth.

Facilities throughout the school are second to none. Glorious library (complete with oak panelling, chandeliers and 18,000 books, DVDs and audio CDs, plus thousands of virtual resources). Excellent science labs. We liked the fact that every classroom and office has an inspiring and appropriate moniker – Roddick (after Body Shop founder Anita Roddick) for economics and business and Olympus for classics are just two examples. Even the book cupboard in the classics department gets its own name – Hades, of course.

Pro-active careers department organises advice on GCSE and A level subjects, annual careers symposium and interview experience. Work experience isn't compulsory but a growing number of students are applying for internships and work placements. In 2015, sixth formers gained places on two of the UK's top corporate career programmes.

Games, options, the arts: Sport is a big deal here and Canford teams score notable successes at every level. Main sports are rugby, hockey and cricket for boys, hockey, netball and tennis for girls and athletics and rowing for both. Rowing VIII were Henley finalists recently. Acres of pitches, floodlit AstroTurf, real tennis court (there aren't many of those around), fitness suite and a 25m indoor swimming pool. In years 9 to 11, four teams regularly fielded per year group so everyone gets the chance to represent the school. Other options include cross country, sailing, dance, basketball, golf, squash, badminton, canoeing and fitness. Sports facilities and pool are used by local

C

community at allotted times. When we visited a keep fit class for the elderly was in full swing in the sports hall.

Art is stunning – and in many cases highly original and ambitious. We were particularly taken with a vast oil painting (3.5m x 1.5m) of a turtle family. Canford pupils have achieved the highest Pre-U grades for art for two years running and up to eight students a year go on to do art foundation courses. Music is terrific, with a large number of choirs, orchestras, strings groups and jazz band. Around half of pupils take individual music lessons. Two major concerts a year, one at Canford, the other at the Lighthouse in Poole, home of the Bournemouth Symphony Orchestra. Lots of drama, with opportunities on stage, backstage and in technical roles. Several pupils have won National Youth Theatre places in recent years. Productions, house plays and an annual school musical take place in the Layard Theatre, opened by film and theatre director Sir Richard Eyre in 1999. Theatre used by professional companies too.

CCF isn't compulsory but is very popular. In 2015 nine cadets from the Royal Marine section beat the likes of Harrow, Winchester and Shrewsbury to win the Pringle Trophy, the premier inter-schools' cadet competition. Others opt for D of E, adventure training and/or community service programme. Seniors work in local primary schools and with disabled groups, run drama workshops and coach sport while juniors work as conservation volunteers. School is the lead sponsor of The Bourne Academy, a secondary school in Bournemouth. Canford pupils act as teaching assistants for languages, computing and science and sign up for book clubs and quizzes.

School is full of bright ideas – everything from Radio Canford to Connections, a general studies programme that challenges pupils to think beyond the curriculum and links different academic disciplines. Another innovation that caught our eye was Yellow Hour, an hour set aside twice a term for pupils and staff to perform in front of an informal audience. Recent highlights included the director of studies performing a maths equation and the head reading a short story he'd written. Year 9s do a carousel of activities every Wednesday – sculling, mixed lacrosse, bell ringing, even etiquette. A plethora of academic, sporting and cultural trips abroad as well as community projects in Argentina, Ghana and India. The Canford Partnership was set up following the discovery (and sale) of a £7 million Assyrian Frieze in the school tuck shop in 1994 and supports worthwhile community projects in the UK and Third World.

Boarding: Full boarding only, no weekly boarding. Flexible exeat system means pupils can spend several Saturday nights a term at home if they want but on average two-thirds of boarders stay in school at weekends. Seven boarding houses – four for boys and three for girls (plus three mixed day houses). Each house has a married houseparent, three tutors and at least one matron (described by one teacher as 'the heart and soul of the boarding house'). Houses are modern and well equipped. In Beaufort, one of the girls' houses, youngest girls are in dorms of four, year 10s and 11s in twos and sixth formers get singles. When pupils arrive at 13 they are assigned a mentor from the year above and are so busy that they settle in quickly – weekend activities programme includes an assault course, pizza nights and trips to the beach. Beaufort housemistress has two cats and two dogs – 'they're brilliant therapy for anyone who feels homesick,' she says.

Most boarding houses are close to the main school buildings but Court and Franklin, two of the boys' houses, are a scenic seven-minute walk from the main school. Boys told us they enjoy the stroll and some bike or skateboard back and forth. Youngest pupils hand their mobile phones in at night but a housemaster we spoke to says pupils are so busy that electronic devices aren't generally a problem. Boys in his house prefer to play Connect Four and chess than stare at screens in their spare time. Very refreshing to hear.

Background and atmosphere: Canford is one of the most beautiful schools in the country. Located in 250 acres of parkland beside the River Stour, it even has its own Victorian arboretum, complete with 350 tree species and one of the largest sweet chestnut trees in the UK. A building of some sort has stood on the Canford site since the Domesday Book. The oldest parts are a pretty Norman church, used for services but too small to take the whole school, and the early 15th century John O'Gaunt's kitchen, used for debates, meetings and receptions. The stunning 19th century main building, originally known as Canford Manor and designed by Edward Blore and later Sir Charles Barry (architect of the Houses of Parliament), is Grade I listed. Lord Wimborne sold the manor in 1923 and the school was founded the same year. It first admitted girls into the sixth form in 1969, went fully co-ed in 1995 and is now 60 per cent boys, 40 per cent girls.

School is a mix of grand, historic buildings and ultra-modern, but stylish additions. Dining hall, known as the Great Hall, where Edward, Prince of Wales danced in 1890 following a ritual slaughter of birds at a shooting party, is particularly magnificent. These days a modern cafeteria system is in place. Food is cooked in-house and gets the firm thumbs-up from pupils. All meals eaten in the Great Hall but there are kitchens with tea and toast-making facilities in every house, plus a tuck shop known as the Grubber.

The whole place fizzes with activity from dawn till dusk. Youngsters we spoke to said there's so much going on that it can be 'a bit overwhelming' at first but they quickly learn time management skills. Day pupils must be in school by 8.15am and leave at 6pm, although many stay on later. All look smart – blue jumpers and tartan skirts for girls up to year 11, tweed jackets and ties for boys, sixth form girls in navy. Everyone has to be presentable, we were told. No heavy eyeliner for girls – the look is 'healthy and glowing.'

Pastoral care, well-being and discipline: Parents told us that there's plenty of support via the tutor system. Doctors' surgeries held every weekday and confidential counselling services available on site. Pupils describe the chaplain, known as 'Rev Jack,' as 'really charismatic' and praise him for the way 'he involves everyone.' Midweek chapel for all, plus compulsory service for boarders on Sundays.

Zero tolerance on drugs. If pupils are caught smoking outdoors they get detention and parents are informed. If caught smoking indoors they are suspended. School aims to educate pupils about 'sensible, social drinking under controlled conditions' and sixth formers are allowed to have maximum of two drinks (wine and beer) with food at Saturday evening socials in the sixth form centre. 'It is very closely monitored,' we were told by a group of upper sixths.

Pupils and parents: Most pupils live within a 90-minute drive of the school. A sizeable chunk come from Dorset, Hampshire, Sussex, Surrey and Wiltshire and a smattering from London and further afield. Around three per cent of boarders are international students – from places like Hong Kong, Poland and Bulgaria. Quite a few sons and daughters of Old Canfordians and lots of siblings and cousins. Day pupils come from all directions. School puts on 50-seater coach from Bournemouth and Poole, plus minibuses from Dorchester, Blandford and Wool to the west and Christchurch, Ringwood and Fordingbridge to the east.

The pupils we met said personalities of all types thrive at Canford. 'If you are a quiet sort of person the teachers will help you gain confidence,' one girl told us. Those we met were enthusiastic, full of appreciation for the quality of teaching and delightfully unpretentious. Parents (who include lots of medics) praised the place for its academic results, good communication and down-to-earth atmosphere. 'It's not stuffy at all,' one said.

Their only criticism was that no building is big enough to hold the whole school for the Remembrance Day service.

Entrance: Pre-assessment in year 7 (literacy, numeracy and reasoning, plus interview, group activities and prep head's report), with offers made to more than 60 per cent for conditional 13+ places. Registrar suggests that parents should register children for pre-assessment by the end of year 6 and says school is looking to identify 'attitude and a have a go mentality as much as raw ability.' If you don't register by then, 'the door isn't closed.' A few places usually come up in year 8. CE benchmark is 55 per cent, although vast majority achieve higher. Candidates who haven't attended prep schools take entrance exam in year 8 (this aims to spot academic potential rather than test knowledge). Around 125 places for year 9 cohort (known as Shells), including 30 to 35 scholarships. Pupils come from around 100 prep schools. Large numbers of boarders from Twyford, Port Regis, Highfield, Chafyn Grove, Walhampton, Westbourne House and Forres Sandle Manor. Day pupils often from nearby Castle Court and Dumpton.

Twenty-five to 30 join in the sixth form – assessment test in November the year before plus minimum of 42 points on students' best seven GCSEs (A* equates to eight, A to seven, B to six etc). A grades expected in subjects to be studied at AS level and at least Bs in English and maths. Highly competitive at this stage – around four applicants (slightly more girls than boys) for every place.

Exit: Around 10 to 15 a year leave after GCSE (12 per cent in 2016) – for academic or personal reasons or for a change of scene. After A level, more than 95 per cent to university. Bristol, Cardiff, Durham, Exeter and Manchester perennially popular, with courses ranging from biochemical sciences and medicine to history and business. Six per cent to Oxbridge in 2016. Interest in US universities is growing and school has its own international university adviser.

Money matters: A range of 13+ and 16+ scholarships, plus means-tested bursaries worth up to 100 per cent of fees.

Remarks: As we said last time, a very special school and one that can easily hold its own with the most popular in the country. With its first-rate teaching, stunning setting and innovative ideas, Canford is definitely at the top of its game.

Cardiff Sixth Form College

1-3 Trinity Court, 21 – 27 Newport Road, Cardiff CF24 0AA

Pupils: 324; 298 boarders • Ages: 16-18

Fees: Day £15,000; Boarding £36,000 – £39,725 pa

Tel: 02920 493121
Email: enquiries@ccoex.com
Website: www.ccoex.com/

Founder: Yasmin Sarwar. Something of a legend in her field. She came over from Malaysia to study for A levels. She had excellent results and progressed to university. Once she had graduated she began to help struggling students, and her success spread to such an extent that the house from which she worked proved too small. In 2011 she moved into what had been a large office block in Trinity Road. It is now the sixth form college from where her reputation has continued to spread. It is largely her personal drive and energy which has driven successes on to triumphs, with the college becoming not only the largest in Wales but, in the last four years, top of the independent schools A level results as published by The Times and The Telegraph. The college A level students have never scored beneath 93 per cent A*/A grades.

Mrs Sarwar is much admired by pupils and staff, though mixed with that admiration is a healthy dose of respect, awe and even a little fear. 'I'm always five minutes away from dismissal,' a teacher told us with a lopsided grin. There was much joking along those lines – an exaggerated joking like nervous soldiers preparing to go over the top – but fundamentally those teachers clearly recognise her strengths: the long hours she works and the astonishing amount of time she gives to individual pupils and groups. They recognise that Mrs Sawar works every bit as hard as they do; in fact she 'keeps hours that would exhaust me,' one senior member of staff told us. There seem to be no limits to her energy and we heard stories of late night take-aways being delivered to her office to sustain groups of students she was helping as they battled with their UCAS applications. In 2011 she won Pearson's Science Tutor of the Year and the school's prospectus has a picture of a rather tight-lipped Mr Cameron signing her award at 10 Downing Street.

She, it is clear, cares deeply for her students – 'and not just because they earn the best A levels in the country', she says. 'I love the pupils.' No wonder she refers to herself as the Tiger Mother. It is tough love: she admires resilience and determination; after all, she has shown plenty of that herself.

Anyone conjuring up a vision of an old grey-haired teacher – a sort of Miss Trinian figure – is way off target: Mrs Sawar is a snappy dresser, with a fine array of very trendy high heeled shoes, making her look elegant as well as purposeful. She listens intently and, when required, argues her corner vigorously. To criticise her is to flirt in the mouth of the tiger. 'What can be wrong with the school?' she asks. 'We have the best A level results in the country.' So there it is.

Academic matters: The recent BBC programme entitled Britain's Brainiest School did not encourage everyone. Although we were sent a CD of the programme we did not watch it before we visited, but people who had watched it insisted on telling us what they thought. Some were impressed by the professionalism of the approach, the overall success of the pupils and the astonishing A level results 'that would help pupils get into any university.' For those who like statistics, 93 per cent of A levels were A*/A and 99 per cent A*-B in 2016. That's one side of it. 'But they must get an awful grinding,' others said. By the time we arrived we had been dragooned into expecting a hothouse atmosphere of gritted teeth, furrowed brow and clenched fists.

In fact from the moment we set off on our tour, during break, we met with something else. We came across pupils and staff lolling around in passageways, talking and laughing with all the ease of natural friendship. The leading actors in The Lion King were effortlessly discussing the play with the producer, who happened to be head of maths. We were generously drawn into the animated and entertaining conversation and invited to watch the extracts being performed during the Evening of Culture later in the week. We met a student who was reading Milton for English A level and who discussed it with zest and perception; other students were involved in critical thinking, politics, business studies, economics et al. Of course maths, further maths, chemistry, physics, biology – the usual suspects – were there. Best of all we were almost literally locked into a small room with about five mathematicians. The conversation was lively, witty and enjoyable. These were highly experienced and committed maths teachers who were blissfully happy because they no longer taught in schools where they had distracting responsibilities. Instead they were teaching/sharing the subject they loved, and to such bright and enthusiastic pupils. Later, during our visit to the Cultural Evening, we saw those Einsteins appear in a song and dance routine. The chorus went something like 'the more Maths you do, the better looking you become'. These teachers were a wonderful demonstration of scholarship and fun.

Games, options, the arts: Pupils looking to play competitive rugby or football, cricket or golf will find it difficult, though it is possible. 'Physical well-being,' as the school calls it, is more practical and utilitarian: health and leisure facilities are the centre of physical activities and 'students will be provided with custom-made fitness plans based on their individual needs......' It's all there in the prospectus: a balance to the more cerebral side of their time studying. All carefully and sensibly worked out and supported by a professional medical team who come on a regular basis. There are numerous sports clubs including football, netball, swimming and tennis. But not in the school's grounds.

Boarding: The term 'boarding' is not quite what people familiar with boarding schools in the UK might expect. Boarding here means literally sleeping in rooms which offer modern furniture and excellent facilities for working in – as good if not better than many universities. There isn't a specific houseparent dealing exclusively with boys or girls in their houses, but there are always adults around checking the students in and out and qualified counsellors who lend an expert ear to anyone who needs some TLC. The delightful person who showed us round seemed to know everyone's names. The atmosphere is calm, friendly and inviting and the building, which is over a coffee shop, is just over the road from the teaching block. Clean, comfortable and safe.

Background and atmosphere: The school is very much the brain child of the co-founder. She is realistically fixed on her pupils achieving top grades in any subject they attempt and she knows the school will not necessarily suit everyone. It is, as she said, 'a question of horses for courses. You have to be right for the place.'

For a start, this is a multi-cultural atmosphere with students from 40 different nationalities. One of the students told us, 'Internationals, while mixing with other nationalities, of course, keep their nationality. There's no compulsion but we appreciate the freedom to express ourselves. We are different and we rejoice in that. One of the obvious expressions lies in the different costume worn with pride and dignity on special occasions.' We witnessed this during the Cultural Evening and very exciting it was. The atmosphere was one of open friendliness between pupils and staff, a friendliness which was most generously extended to this ancient interloper. Overall it seemed a happy place. We met some Welsh students, all of whom were obviously clever – they'd been given very generous scholarships – but they are very much in the minority. One of them, in particular, is a very promising rugby player, who replied in response to our questions, 'I love the opportunity of meeting so many people from around the world.' He's global as they all are. It was very good to see so many alumni coming back for the evening and being cheered in.

Pastoral care, well-being and discipline: Students have tutors to support and advise and told us that staff overall were very friendly and understanding. Certainly the atmosphere is cheerful as well as purposeful. There is a tremendous amount of preparation for entry into universities including much interview practice and many tutor-led societies exploring eg critical thinking, extended learning, various competitions such as senior maths, debating, Model United Nations, study skills – on and on it goes. No wonder the entrance level into universities is so high. As for discipline there are groups, called houses and given classical names. Apparently they are looked after by individual masters but there was no mention of that during our visit. Perhaps it's all done so well that it's taken for granted. Certainly the students were courteous and well behaved in a natural, friendly manner.

Pupils and parents: Parents mostly come from far away, but we met one delightful, happy parent who had made the journey from the far East especially to discuss the possibility of another of her children joining the school. 'They all keep us in touch,' she said, and, 'Skype is wonderful, though when my daughter first left home I was very sad.' At the Culture Evening we met many, many parents who were thrilled to be there and part of the whole occasion, enjoying the food and the dancing. We heard nothing but praise and appreciation, including from those (few) parents who live in Wales.

Entrance: Everyone takes entrance tests and are interviewed (by Skype if necessary). International students may be accepted purely on these results, as long as they have a high level of English fluency (IELTS 6.5), or if they already have at least six A*s at I/GCSE including their proposed A level subjects. Day students must obtain at least six A* grades at GCSE (those applying for scholarships must get at least nine A*s), plus passing the entrance test and interview.

Exit: In 2016, 21 to Cambridge, with 45 off to the London colleges, plus many to top universities round the country to study courses including medicine, law, engineering, economics and PPE. Large numbers of medics generally include some going to universities in Hong Kong, Australia and Ireland.

Money matters: There are generous scholarships for locals – up 100 per cent for those with all A*s at GCSE – and those we met seemed very happy. Scholarships of up to 50 per cent for overseas applicants.

At time of writing college was under investigation by South Wales Police for alleged historical financial irregularities.

Remarks: People who spoke to us before we visited expressed suspicion. 'It must be very tough, very restrictive, utterly humourless. Think force-feeding: the embodiment of Brave New World; robotic machines.' Such were the comments we heard from people who had not visited. This ageing GSG scribbler came away impressed by what was being achieved. There is, of course, a difference between education and the achievement of excellent grades. One might be seen as infusion for life; the other might be seen as stamp collecting. But what we saw was youth working hard to achieve results worthy of their talents and for which they deserved credit. The teaching is excellent and, most important, morale seems high with delightful relationships between staff and pupils.

That wonderful evening of music and dance, energy and liveliness with bags of skill, humour and well-tuned banter revealed the synthesis of this society. The Tiger Mother was a superb compère, effortlessly weaving in the ideas, images and ambitions she wanted her audience of parents and other visitors to imbue. Her son, almost as decorous in his special togs as his mother, made a small speech and bowed to an appreciative audience. National dress, a variety of hats and music. What a colourful evening of creativity, happiness, joy and delight. One member of staff sitting next to us leaned over and whispered, 'and this is the collection of young who are described by critics as ground down, overworked and harassed. Remember!' We will remember, and with much pleasure.

Castle Court

Knoll Lane, Corfe Mullen, Wimborne, Dorset BH21 3RF

Pupils: 370 • Ages: 2–13 • C of E

Fees: £8,325 (reception to year 2); £14,985 (year 3 to year 6)

Tel: 01202 694438
Email: admissions@castlecourt.com
Website: www.castlecourt.com

Headmaster: Since 2010, Mr Richard Stevenson BA PGCE (40s). Educated at Castle Court, King's Bruton and Poole Grammar, followed by the University of Portsmouth, where he read politics, economics and philosophy. Always wanted to teach and did his teacher training at Southampton. Spent his early career at Edinburgh House in New Milton (now Ballard School) and Holmwood House in Colchester. Prior to taking the helm at Castle Court he was head of Kelly College Prep in Tavistock for seven years.

School numbers have grown by 45 per cent under his leadership (he's only the fourth head in the school's history). Dynamic and approachable, with a sense of fun, he firmly believes that children should be allowed to be children and not grow up too quickly. Hence no mobile phones, iPods or PSPs in school (parents approve). Proud of the fact that pupils are allowed to climb trees (up to three times their height) and play conkers (he's not averse to a game himself although a year 7 boy beat him in a match last year). Doesn't teach these days but observes teachers' lessons on a regular basis. Highly visible around the school, greeting children as they arrive in the mornings and sitting down to lunch with them most days. At lunch he encourages pupils to chat and be sociable, throwing out general knowledge questions – 'What's the name of the foreign secretary?' and 'What's the capital of Iceland?' – as he serves lunch on his table. 'It's not just a time to eat,' he explains. 'It's about getting to know them.' School prides itself on being academic but the head says it's all about 'character' too. 'Children are allowed to be themselves here,' he says. 'We want them to be comfortable in their own skin.'

Lives in a house on site with his wife Lucy, who is a year 2 teaching assistant and very involved in school life. They have four children – one at Cardiff University, one at Canford and two at Clayesmore (the three youngest all attended Castle Court). Enjoys sailing and walking their two dogs in his spare time.

Entrance: Children visit with their parents prior to starting but no interviews or formal testing. The most common entry points are nursery, reception and year 3 (where there's a three-form entry) but it's worth trying in other years too. Some year groups are full so places further up the school may be harder to come by. Scholarships offered, plus some means-tested bursaries.

Exit: At 13, around a third head to Canford (just down the road), 20 per cent to Clayesmore and the rest to Bryanston, Millfield, Sherborne, Sherborne Girls, Winchester and the like. Most to co-ed schools and a third choose boarding. An impressive array of scholarships and exhibitions (20 in 2016). Up to ten pupils a year leave at 11 for the four local grammars. School runs grammar school preparation sessions for boys applying to Poole Grammar and Bournemouth School and for girls applying to Parkstone Grammar and Bournemouth School for Girls.

Remarks: Delightfully rural, yet accessible too, just a few miles from the coastal towns of Bournemouth and Poole. Founded in 1948 and moved to its present site in 1968. The rambling country house at the heart of the school is tucked away in 50 acres on the outskirts of Corfe Mullen and the site boasts everything a child could wish for – 17 acres of woodland to play in, two adventure playgrounds, a 17-ft tepee and a menagerie of guinea pigs, chickens and four pigs. The place has a Famous Five feel to it (indeed Enid Blyton's famous novels were inspired by her holidays at nearby Studland), with children encouraged to enjoy the great outdoors, pond-dipping, badger watching and making camps in the woods. Girls were admitted for the first time in the 1970s and the school has appointed a female teacher as 'head of girls'.

Children seem to have a whale of a time here, while achieving impressive results. Older pupils taught by subject specialists. Maths set by ability from year 1, English from year 3 and Latin, languages and science from year 6. French taught from reception, Spanish from year 3 and most do Latin from year 5. Teaching is exciting and forward thinking. Maximum class sizes of 16 in reception and 18 after that. Each child has a form tutor (who may or may not teach them) and tutor groups meet every morning. 'The children know that their form tutor is the first person they go to if they've got a problem,' says the head. 'We believe that if they are happy they will learn.' Pupils' progress carefully tracked, although new director of studies points out that while data is important, it's simply 'a tool'. 'We don't reduce the children to a number,' she says. Year 3 pupils and up are given iPads (no 3G though). Children take them to every lesson but aren't allowed to use them at break-times or on the bus. Year 3 and 4 pupils leave them in smart red lockers at the end of the day but older children are allowed to take them home (not at half-term or in the holidays).

All pupils screened for dyslexia from year 2 onwards. Learning development department is housed in three rooms – ten per cent of pupils receive support for dyslexia, dyspraxia and mild or moderate communication, emotional or behavioural needs, either one to one or in small groups. A healthy mix of experienced and more recently qualified teachers (during our visit we met a geography teacher who was about to celebrate his 100th term at the school). 'We want people with experience and longevity and people with fresh ideas,' says the head.

School is very sporty. Boys play football, rugby, cricket, tennis and athletics and girls do hockey, netball, rounders, cricket, tennis and athletics. Facilities are excellent, including a full-size Astroturf, eight games pitches, five tennis courts and a 22-metre swimming pool. New sports hall will be ready in 2017. Old-fashioned virtues of shaking hands after matches and entertaining away teams are held in high regard (the school's homemade Battenberg is much admired too). Tennis and swimming academies are popular and older children get the chance to try other sports, like rowing, sailing and golf. 'It's about getting to know what suits them,' says the head. Year 3 children camp in the woods each summer, year 4 camps off-site, year 5 goes to Normandy and year 6 heads to the Dorset coast, where they try their hands at kayaking and coasteering.

Music is excellent, with 70 per cent taking instrument lessons, mostly from year 3. A plethora of music groups to join, including junior and senior orchestras, rock bands ('an Ed Sheeran number had all the mums in tears,' says the head), a guitar group, string ensemble, clarinet ensemble, even a samba group. Art and DT are impressive. The first thing visitors see when they walk into the school is a stunning sculpture of multicoloured birds in a papier-mâché tree. We admired the pop art skateboards created by year 8 pupils too. Drama galore – 'we get them up on stage as much as possible,' say staff. Every pupil gets their moment in the spotlight – a year 3 performance of Alice in Wonderland featured 13 Alices. In the same vein, every child is invited on to the stage on speech day to receive a book.

Nursery and pre-prep children are housed in the main school so they're very much part of things. Bright, welcoming classrooms buzzing with activity, plus a forest school. Nursery and pre-prep head says 'small children like to be active and busy' – and they certainly are here. They venture outside in all weathers, kitted out in wellies and jazzy red and blue splash-suits. When we visited we saw a reception class enjoying a 'Smartie maths' lesson, where the children were enthusiastically counting different coloured Smarties and recording them on a graph. No eating allowed – but teachers promised they could take the sweets home for half-term.

Food is cooked on-site and the whole school sits down to lunch together, younger children with their year groups, older ones with their houses. No cafeteria system – teachers sit at each table and serve out the lunch. Pupils stay on the same table for a term, then move round. Grace said at the start. When we visited the pupils happily tucked into homemade pizza, potatoes and salad, followed by rice krispie cakes and chocolate sauce. 'The food's good here,' said one boy appreciatively. 'Especially the Eton mess.' They take it in turns to stack the plates and clear away.

Breakfast club opens from 7.45am for children from year 1 (younger ones by special arrangement) – a boon for working parents. School day finishes at 4.15pm but there's a host of after-school activities, everything from film making and 'pig patrol' to cross country and mountain biking. Children can do their homework at school but the head prefers them to take it home – so they learn to be organised and parents get an idea of what they are doing.

Year 7s and 8s get the opportunity to be prefects – 'everyone has a chance,' says the head – but there's no head boy or head girl. Pupils' uniform looks very smart. Ties for boys and girls and chic stripy blazers that fashion-conscious parents reckon bear a distinct resemblance to a recent Mulberry collection. We heard a few quibbles about the price but apart from that everyone seems to love them.

Pupils are sparky and enthusiastic but ultra-polite, standing up when visitors enter the classroom. Good communication between school and parents – teachers' email addresses available to all, plus parents' evenings in the autumn and spring terms and a written report in the summer. Pre-prep children's red diaries go back and forth between school and home each day, keeping parents up to date with pupils' progress. School also provides a very civilised sitting room, where parents can sit and have a coffee. Pupils come from all over – lots from Poole, Bournemouth and Wimborne and others from Ringwood, Blandford, Swanage, Wareham, Dorchester and Weymouth. Fourteen minibuses ferry children to and from school in the mornings and afternoons. Parents include quite a few old Castellans and some who have relocated from London. No open days. As the head says: 'Every day is an open day here.'

Chafyn Grove School

26

Bourne Avenue, Salisbury, Wiltshire SP1 1LR

Pupils: 270; 43 boarders • Ages: 3–13 • C of E

Fees: Day £6,750 – £16,290; Boarding +£6,210 pa

Tel: 01722 333423
Email: office@chafyngrove.co.uk
Website: www.chafyngrove.co.uk

Headmaster: Since September 2016, Simon Head, previously headmaster of Moreton Hall School in Suffolk. He held a short service limited commission with the Royal Green Jackets before studying classics at Cambridge, where he also acquired his PGCE. He has taught at Dulwich College Prep and Pembroke House in Kenya, and was then deputy head at St John's Beaumont in Windsor before becoming head of Moreton Hall. He is married to Sarah, also a teacher, and they have two young sons.

Entrance: Children join at all ages and stages and from all over the area. Entry is non-selective. After registration, places are offered two terms before joining and children are invited to spend a day at the school the term before they begin. Scholarships of up to 15 per cent are available in years 2 (academic and all-rounder), 4 (add music and sport) and 6 (add drama and art). Forces discounts of 10 per cent (day) and 15 per cent (boarding) and sibling discounts from five to 15 per cent are also offered. Means-tested bursaries typically range between 10 and 40 per cent of the combined tuition and boarding fee.

Exit: Canford, Dauntsey's and Millfield top the list of 'next schools', followed by other relatively local choices, eg Bryanston, Clayesmore, Marlborough and Winchester. Otherwise pupils disperse to a range of schools, eg Charterhouse, Clifton College, Godolphin, Hampshire Collegiate and Monkton Coombe. Sports and all-rounder awards dominate the scholarship lists, but academic awards are on the up with a scattering of art, DT and music scholarships and exhibitions. Around 10 leave at 11 each year for the Salisbury grammar schools and independents.

Remarks: A 1914 school photograph shows just 17 boys and three members of staff sitting in the grounds of a large Victorian building. Today, that solemn handful of Edwardian scholars would be very surprised to find nearly 300 pupils at Chafyn Grove, including over 100 girls.

Founded in 1876 as Salisbury School and changed its name in 1916 following an endowment by Lady Chafyn Grove. Although it caters for a wide ability range, there is a work ethic firmly in place. Has taken the unusual step of dropping history, geography and RS from the common entrance syllabus to focus on maths, English, science, French and Latin. This doesn't mean that pupils don't study these subjects, just that teachers can be more flexible in their approach, eg lessons on early history topics such as the Crusades and medieval life and geography lessons on South America. French is taught from year 1, Spanish in years 4 and 5 and Latin from year 6. Latin is strong and some pupils get to near GCSE standard. The odd truly hopeless linguist is allowed to drop languages rather than self-destruct in CE. Maths is set for everyone from year 3, top sets are streamed for all subjects from year 5 and lower sets in the last two years. Scholars aiming for the likes of Eton are educated separately, with extra lessons and lots of practice papers. This is certainly a change from times past, when 'Eton, Winchester and Harrow were not Chafyn's remit.'

Sessions in thinking, presentation, research and current affairs freshen up the timetable. Year 8 also studies business skills, involving Dragon's Den-style pitches and advertising campaigns to create and market a product for sale at the end of the year. Teaching body is very stable, with several married couples and long-standing staff members. 'You only realise how well they're being taught when they get to the next school.' At the time of our visit, there were 42 pupils on the SEN register. Taught by five members of staff in two dedicated rooms, there is a broad sphere of activity which includes study skills, spelling and learning support alongside help for dyslexia, dyspraxia, EAL etc. One-to-one sessions once or twice a week are free and school is honest about which conditions it can support.

School has the strongest sport in Salisbury and its reputation gives the opposition food for thought before walking out against Chafyn Grove. Everyone plays in a team and with so many – up to 20 on match days – school can send its top teams further afield to other seriously sporty schools, eg Sandroyd and Port Regis, whilst B and C teams play elsewhere. All the usual sports on offer; boys and girls can also take part in archery, riding, sailing, cross-country and steeplechase. There is an equestrian and a sailing team, both of which compete successfully. Outdoor swimming pool used in summer. In addition to the regular tally of match wins by all teams throughout the year, all four first hockey teams reached the national final recently, which school promptly won. Lots of individual success in athletics, eg U13 Hurdles National Prep Schools Champion. A team of coaches fosters everyone's talent (not just the superstars) on school's pitches and Astroturf, which spread out behind the school up to (distant) railway embankment at edge of school grounds. There's enough space for a gym, squash and tennis courts. Phone app keeps parents abreast of sports fixtures. 'I try to tone down sport a bit as the children do win a lot – they have to get used to the fact that it isn't all about winning,' said a parent. Saturday school (from year 4) is often taken up with matches.

Art department is roomy and light, with plenty of quality work on display including some excellent papier mâché creations. We noticed a good reference library for art and DT. Drama has long been of a high standard and parents rave about the quality of the annual spring production. 'The singing is always very good in these.' Years 3 and 4 put on their own play in the summer term. In music, we'd award a merit. One third of pupils were learning an instrument at the time of our visit and school teaches up to ABRSM grade VI. Some parents feel this isn't enough, although we feel that given the excellent sport and academics, school does a pretty decent job since many serious musicians are likely to head for the Cathedral School. Singing is very popular and there are three choirs, as well as a school orchestra, training orchestra and Jazz Band. Large performance hall has good acoustics, a grand piano and an organ. Practice rooms are small but masses of space for storing instruments and music. Instrumental lessons rotate through the timetable and practice sessions are scheduled for boarders.

Lots of trips, including the usual, eg Normandy, London, the theatre and skiing, and the less usual – a visit to a Sikh temple. Activities during the last two periods on Monday and Thursday are intended to 'give children room to breathe' and include gardening, cookery, golf and Mandarin. In a nod to childhoods of yesteryear, year 4s go on annual Pioneer Camp and learn to put up tents, tie knots and stalk. Bushcraft weekends for seniors involve building shelters and campfires, as well as catching, gutting and cooking their own fish.

Boarding accommodation is comfortable and homely; parents speak very highly of boarding houseparents and matrons. 'They are totally on top of who, where, what and why.' Rooms are shared (6-8 per room) and boarding life is well organised, with shower rotas and different items of clothing collected daily for laundering. Year 8 girls have an ensuite shower room which, though clean, is crying out for new tiles. Boarders' sitting room and green room where children can Skype parents. Mobiles are allowed in free time but must be handed in at night. At the time of our visit, there were 26 full boarders, 20 boarding three nights a week and 40 casual boarders, averaging 40 to 50 per night. One third stay in on weekends and there is a full programme of activities, eg bowling, shopping, cycle rides in the woods and trips to London and the beach.

The original Victorian building is still home for the boarders, but most of the teaching takes place in modern buildings which seem to flow into one another on school's compact site. Children were engaged and interested in academic lessons; traditional classroom seating with everyone facing forwards. 'Children like their teachers and don't want to disappoint them.' However, atmosphere is neither old fashioned nor very strict (no standing for visitors). Our two student guides were polite, confident and very honest in their answers to our questions. 'It's a great school if your child is confident and outgoing and knows who they are,' said a parent.

Pupils feel comfortable about reporting any problems to teachers, who do their best to resolve unkind behaviour. 'They name names and know exactly who is doing what.' Likewise parents feel that they can turn to the staff. 'They are very likeable and approachable and they're always in the playground at pick-up times.' School will summon parents and children and rap heads together if a situation appears to be escalating. There is a seven-point system to discourage bullying and extra mentoring sessions in place for girls in years 5 and 6. Every pupil belongs to an Eight (house) with appealing names – Wasps, Frogs, Birds and Knights. Food is prepared in the school kitchen by the chef and served cafeteria style; meal times are informal and children sit where they like. Lunch was good on the day we visited with plenty of fruit and veg. Day children can arrive at 8am if parents work and stay on for supervised prep until 7pm.

Lovely modern pre-prep with bright, spacious classrooms, own hall and play area. Reception starts small, after which numbers gradually increase. Children in pre-prep can stay until 5:30pm and have their own after-school club and activities including paper craft, football, netball and hockey.

Like most Salisbury schools, there is a mix of local professionals, Forces, business and London commuters. Only a handful from abroad, mostly Spain and a few English with parents working overseas. 'We can't distinguish parents' wealth and professions.' Parents confirm that atmosphere is 'not snooty or overpowering'. A quick snoop along Bourne Avenue at pick-up time confirms that cars are mostly common or garden.

A busy, happy and academically sound school which still retains a friendly, family atmosphere. Will suit confident children who are happy in their own skin. Needless to say, sporty children are in their element here, although parents of the very talented might need to keep small feet firmly planted on the ground. Is, without a doubt, the go-to school for sport in Salisbury.

Cheadle Hulme School

C

Claremont Road, Cheadle Hulme, Cheadle, Cheshire SK8 6EF

Pupils: 1,411 • Ages: 4–18 • Sixth form: 267

Fees: £8,244 – £11,412 pa

Tel: 0161 488 3345
Email: admissions@chschool.co.uk
Website: www.cheadlehulmeschool.co.uk

Head: Since 2010, Ms Lucy Pearson BA (40s). Educated at Keble College, Oxford, where she read English literature and language, followed by an Open University teaching degree. Previously deputy head at Wellington College in Berkshire. She opened the bowling for the England women's cricket team from 1996 to 2005, consistently a lead wicket-taking fast bowler and player of the year in 2000 and 2003. Not surprisingly, she still coaches cricket at Cheadle Hulme.

Charismatic and dynamic, a huge champion of co-education – 'There are so many lessons to learn for boys and girls being educated together,' she says. 'Many children just don't fit the mould in single sex schools. Our function isn't to prepare just one type of child. There is a robustness about co-education. It teaches children about human interaction.' Clearly very ambitious for the school, she says that it has 'the potential to be outstanding at everything. We can be more forward thinking, more modern, more exciting'.

A father told us that 'she's really energised the place,' and pupils reckon she is 'friendly and chatty' and 'fun, but not a pushover'. One boy remarked: 'She's at everything, even Saturday sporting fixtures. I was on a battlefields trip in France and she even turned up there.'

A former member of the National Youth Choir, she loves reading and walking her dog, Frankie.

Head of junior school: Since 2009, Mrs Barbara Bottoms, BSc (50s). Married with two grown up children. Educated at Liverpool University, where she studied chemistry and maths. Previously head at Bury Grammar School for Girls' junior department. Overjoyed to have returned to co-education. 'When I look into the playground I see a normal society where we are all learning about each other,' she told us. 'It's been like coming home.'

Parents praise the positive changes she's made. 'She's not the sort of head who has huge presence,' said one. 'She's not there at the school gates, but all the teachers are being made to teach new year groups and she's brought in specialist teachers. She is accessible if you need her but she likes to get on with things quietly. No big fanfare.'

Head is a keen theatre-goer in her spare time, and loves watching any sport.

Academic matters: Class sizes in the junior school are bigger than other independent schools in the area and this causes some parents to grumble. Two form entry throughout, with 20 in a class in the infants, 24 in years 3 and 4 and 26 in years 5 and 6. However, classes are split for many lessons. Netbooks are used in years 4 and 5 and there are plans to introduce them throughout school. French is taught all the way through the infants and then rotated with Spanish and German in the juniors.

Children we spoke to were delighted that Wednesday is 'no homework night.' Some parents complained, however, that a lot of homework has to be done on a computer via the school's virtual online environment. This seems to cause problems for families with multiple children all trying to use the home computer at once.

Continues to have good exam results – nearly 70 per cent A*/A grades at GCSE in 2016 and 44 per cent at A level (78 per cent A*/B). However, although exam results are ultimately the paymaster, the head says that 'there must be fun in education. Hard work must be balanced with support'. Pupils appreciate the wide range of teaching styles the school employs and comment that teachers are very approachable. All subject areas hold weekly clinics – pupils can drop in if they need assistance and regular revision classes are held for those taking exams.

Regular effort grades have been introduced to ensure no child slips through the net. All pupils in the upper sixth take extension classes to gain depth in subjects unrelated to their A level work. IGCSEs and Extended Project Qualification (EPQ) available in some subjects and the Pre-U offered in philosophy, business studies and economics.

The school has seen a rise in popularity recently and prep schools are reporting more pupils turning down places at other prestigious independents to take up places here. As a result, an extra form introduced to cope with increased demand. Although head denies any desire to keep climbing the league tables or for the school to become more selective (it currently has a broader intake than some of its competitors), does seem to be a move to broaden and enrich academic opportunities available to pupils.

Full time head of learning support can cope with mild to moderate SEN, as long as pupils can cope with the curriculum. Pupils assessed on an individual basis.

Games, options, the arts: Drama is very popular and has its own studios. Many performances take place in the atmospheric, but slightly cramped, Holden Hall. Music is outstanding, with many orchestras, choirs, a cappella group, concert band, ensembles, samba and rock bands, to name but a few.

Lots of sport in the juniors, including cricket, hockey, football, cross country and netball. Plenty of extracurricular activities, from bird watching to string ball. 'Every child can find something they love,' one dad told us, 'whether it's music, drama, sport or a hobby. This place does it all. My daughter loves the fact that the head takes tennis after school every week.' Successful sporting teams in the seniors, but still plenty of opportunity to get involved if you don't make the teams. Many pupils represent their sport at club, county and country levels.

Vast array of extracurricular activities on offer, including school's own radio station, film club, table tennis and a charities committee.

Background and atmosphere: Established in 1855 as a co-educational school for 'orphans and necessitous children of warehouse men and clerks'. Expansive, leafy grounds have a collegiate feel. Pupils look very at home but seem purposefully busy. The main stately Victorian building sits comfortably next to their modern counterparts with their spacious, airy classrooms. Year 7 has own block to ease the transition from little to big school. Sixth formers have their own common rooms and butty bar, but the few we spoke to grumbled that their facilities could do with a revamp. Smart bottle green and black uniform, changing to navy blue in the sixth form.

Food gets a big thumbs-up. Plenty of good quality options to choose from in the canteen (which boasts stained glass windows and high tech finger print recognition system). 'Grab and go' lunch bags available for pupils too busy to queue.

Light, modern junior school buildings with music, art, IT and science rooms. Ovens for baking are regularly used and we saw a group of little ones making cookies, or 'yummies,' as one boy called them. Big TV screen in the entrance runs a good news feed celebrating pupils' achievements and keeping everyone up to date with what's going on in school.

Pastoral care, well-being and discipline: Junior school a lively place that manages to have a relaxed feel and where children seem genuinely happy. 'When they leave here,' says the head, 'they are confident, responsible children who have learned from failure and experienced success.'

Parents can't praise the pastoral system highly enough. One mother, whose son found adjusting to senior school life very difficult, said that staff were fantastic, often taking the time to ring her in the evening.

Sixth formers act as peer mentors to new year 7s, to help them settle and give them someone to talk to. 'It was brilliant,' one boy told us. 'I could ask him lots of questions that I felt silly asking a teacher.'

Pupils and parents: Mainly from south Manchester, Cheshire and Derbyshire. Parents are mostly professional and from a cross-section of backgrounds. Now starting to pick up more Asian families, who have in the past tended to choose the Manchester independents. Extensive bus routes, plus a pick up and drop off service from the local station.

Notable former pupils include MEP Chris Davies, BBC political editor Nick Robinson, political correspondent Lucy Ward, BBC broadcaster Katie Derham, political correspondent Stephen Day, soprano Susan Bullock, Labour peer Lord Dubs and actor Daniel Rigby.

Entrance: Assessment for reception takes place in the autumn term of the year prior to entry. Places are offered in December, earlier than other schools. 'It's play-based in small groups,' the head told us. 'We want children we can engage and interest – they need to be excited to learn.' The school take another four to six children in year 3, and then four more in year 5. Assessment at this stage is formal, in English, maths and reasoning. School is over-subscribed so early birds get the worm here.

Competitive entrance exam at 11 in English, maths and verbal reasoning, followed by separate interviews with pupils and parents.

Exit: Most (around 90 per cent) of juniors progress to the senior school after sitting entrance exam along with external candidates, although a few are lost to the single sex schools in Manchester. Head meets all year 4 parents individually to discuss progress, so there is plenty of time to look at other possibilities if your child won't make it. 'We'd feel like we'd let them down if they didn't go up,' says the head.

Some 20-25 per cent leaves after GCSEs. Two to Oxbridge in 2016 and three medics; others to eg Sheffield, Newcastle, Leeds, Nottingham and Liverpool.

Money matters: Substantial bursary fund makes a Cheadle Hulme education a reality for many families. No academic scholarships, but sports and music scholarships offered for year 7 entry, plus music scholarship also offered for sixth form.

Remarks: A vibrant, action-packed school that is rapidly increasing in popularity. Pupils are bright, well supported and gently cared for to achieve their best.

Cheltenham College Preparatory School

Linked with Cheltenham College

Thirlestaine Road, Cheltenham GL53 7AB

Pupils: 391; 70 boarders • Ages: 3-13 • C of E

Fees: Day £7,680 – £17,250; Boarding £17,175 – £22,410 pa

Tel: 01242 522697
Email: theprep@cheltenhamcollege.org
Website: www.cheltenhamcollege.org

Headmaster: Since 2013, Mr Jonathan Whybrow BEd (50s). Educated at St Paul's School and 'loved every minute.' Joined the Royal Marines and then studied for a BEd in physical education and geography at Exeter. Much of his early career was spent at schools in or near London including Latymer Upper, Emanuel School, Devonshire House Prep (where he was deputy head). Previous headships at City of London Freemen's School, Ashtead and then Beachborough School, Northamptonshire. Married with two daughters, one at the school.

The headship of Cheltenham College Prep has been through a rather uneasy time but, cross everything, Mr W is a keeper. He set his sights on the school as early as 1999 when he attended a conference here and 'fell in love.' He says that he knew there and then that he 'wanted to be part of one of England's great schools.' The stars didn't align in his and the school's favour until 2013, but now he's arrived and does he ever mean business. His mantra comes courtesy of the Royal Marines: Don't be late; don't ask your troops to do what you wouldn't do yourself; concurrent activity (aka multitasking).

Parents we spoke to were very, very happy. Several were in awe not only of his energy but also his mysterious capacity to be all places at once. 'He's everywhere,' said one, 'and he sorts things out straight away. We're so lucky.' Pupils equally impressed, 'He knew everybody's names by the end of the first week,' we were told.

When he's not being omnipresent at school Mr W enjoys golf, skiing, supporting West Ham and holidays in his house in France. He proudly showed us the 'burnt orange' 1977 MG tucked away in a garage – a recent acquisition and one he hadn't quite got round to telling his family about. (He has now.)

Entrance: Taster day for entrance to nursery and up to year 3. For years 4-6 it's a taster day and entry assessments in maths, English and non-verbal reasoning. More choosy later on to ensure pupils are up to CE at 13. Discount available for third and subsequent siblings. Generous discounts for Forces families; means-tested bursaries available. A further 20 or so children arrive at 11+ and at this age scholarships of up to 30 per cent of fees in a variety of areas may be awarded. These are valid throughout Cheltenham College.

Exit: 'Four or five' leave at age 11 for local grammars or girls' schools. Majority stay on until 13 and then move over the road to senior school. Those who don't stay go on to (recently) Eton, Harrow, Marlborough, Radley, Wellington and Cheltenham Ladies'.

C

Remarks: School has been on present site – friendly jumble of Edwardian red-brick and newer additions in extensive grounds just across the road from senior school – since 1908. It was founded in 1863 as the 'College Juvenile Department' and spent a couple of years squashed into a corner of the big school. Parents might be interested to learn that boarding fees in 1865 were 50 guineas (£52.50) a year and it was an extra £1 for a seat in the chapel. Smart rebranding has seen the name change from Cheltenham College Junior School to Preparatory School, with typography emphasising the 'Preparatory School' part of the name. 'It's about trust,' says Mr Whybrow, 'parents must be confident that we will do the same job as a stand-alone prep. If Cheltenham College is not the right senior school for your child then we'll say so.' Understandably, he would prefer pupils to remain until age 13, but the local education market is a competitive one and realpolitik extends to what Mr W calls 'help' for children applying to grammar schools. He's not quite so generous when it comes to the occasional cheeky bit of poaching by a certain nearby girls' school, crisply describing his relationship with The Cheltenham Ladies' College as 'businesslike'.

This has always been a popular prep but parents' loyalty has been tested in recent times by the drift that inevitably results from a rapid turnover of leadership. It's not often that we hear a pupil describe their headmaster as 'the best we've had.' Mr Whybrow is candid about the effect that time of 'uncertainty' had on the morale of pupils, parents and staff. Bringing with him a wealth of experience from leading stand-alone and linked preps, he implemented some changes straight away that were visible on the first day of term – new signage, a general freshening up – small things that make a big difference. In consultation with parents he has re-instated French classes for the youngest children, brought back 'proper' prize-giving (we saw the new trophies in his study), revived the very popular school musical which had 'got lost' and appointed a director of co-curricular activities to beef up this aspect of provision. Longer-term plans involve material improvements to facilities and organisation that will benefit everyone.

High-ceilinged classrooms, old wooden desks and iPads – teaching and learning at Cheltenham College Prep is a creative mix of the best of traditional methods and the latest technology. Small classes, subject specialist teaching and plenty of individual attention enable pupils to progress at their own rate – something parents really appreciate. 'The teachers are very encouraging, it's made such a difference to my child's confidence' and, 'they make time to follow a child's interest in a subject and take teaching beyond the curriculum.'

Pupils learn French as soon as they start in the Kingfishers and between years 6 and 8 pupils can opt for French or Spanish. Most are expected to take Latin – the class we saw looked like so much fun we wanted to stay and decline a verb or two – and there's also the option of 'off timetable' Greek. There are currently lessons on a Saturday morning but Mr W says that this is 'under discussion.'

Learning support has its cheerful offices in the Coach House, there are two full-time members of staff plus a team of part-time assistants. All children are screened and extra support is mostly given in small groups or parent funded one to one sessions. EAL is also based here; Cheltenham may not strike the observer as excessively multicultural but the headquarters of ARRC (NATO Allied Rapid Reaction Corps) is close by.

Pre-prep, known as Kingfishers, occupies low-rise chalet, not an architectural gem but more than compensated for by the fresh air facilities, including forest school. Information boards outside let parents know what their children have been doing each day – great for conversations on the way home. During our visit Mr W reduced a class of 3-year-olds, their elegant ballet mistress and this reviewer to hysterical laughter by his attempts at 'naughty toes' and 'good toes'. We're sure he wouldn't mind us observing that he is not built for the ballet.

Whether it's sport, music or drama, 'inclusion' is the starting point – there are teams from A to E and bands and choirs 'for all'. Every child has the opportunity to play in a competitive sports team from year 3. Lively house competitions – not just the usual sport but creative stuff too such as poetry, photography and music. Plenty of matches, pupils claimed that the win/lose rate with nearest rivals is pretty even. National winners in schools' rugby recently; finalists in national comps for hockey, netball and also skiing.

Everyone is enjoying the extended range of after-school clubs – 30 or so options including polo, equestrian, archery, chess, street dance and the enticingly named 'Grow your own money.' In addition to termly calendars the school now produces a what's on of events for the whole year – much appreciated by busy parents – with dates for everything from school photos to 'try boarding' nights and theatre visits.

As we walked through the grounds in golden autumnal sunshine, Mr W (who in another life would be a farmer) stops at a muddy pen to scratch the backs of the Gloucester Old Spots, two of which would be attending bonfire night in sausage form. He's keen to extend the forest school provision to include more animals: lambs are next and also chickens who will take up residence on an island in the lake – we hope Gloucestershire foxes can't swim.

Improvements to the school's rather convoluted layout are next on Mr W's to do list – he wants to consolidate teaching into departments. A consequence of this has been a sad farewell to the atmospheric DT room with its parquet floor, wooden cupboards and historic sawdust from thousands of bird boxes – the new DT block opened in 2016. Outside in the corridor are glass cases displaying beautiful model boats made by a former teacher (they used to be sailed on the lake) and a drop-down model railway track. Art room similarly characterful but will be spared the same fate, not being located in the path of progress. The music department has a rather grand home, Lake House, with baronial fire places and wood-panelled walls. Nearly all pupils learn at least once instrument and there are plenty of opportunities to play or sing – whether it's chapel choir, jazz band, guitar group or, as on our visit, to compose and perform at a polyphone (surprisingly tuneful blue plastic tubes) workshop.

Mr W is a great believer in what he calls 'prep school world', in other words junior pupils should be self-sufficient when it comes to facilities. Fortunately this prep occupies a large site and any sharing is by choice rather than necessity. A new science block, full size rugby pitches, Astros and a sports hall that's about to get a £7m makeover are all at the disposal of the juniors.

One parent told us that 'children are encouraged to express their own opinions,' so we put this to the test and asked a few what they thought about their school. 'There are loads of new activities', 'We have a proper roast on Sunday, everyone sits down and is served at the table.' 'Mr Whybrow is amazing.' Yes, yes, but how about some constructive criticism? 'I wish they hadn't stopped us playing football in the car park. There's not enough time at lunch to change into a tracksuit and go out on to the field.'

One central boarding house on two floors (girls below, boys above, shared common room) and dorms divided into rather charming old style curtained cubicles with notice boards and cabin beds – those we saw were not over tidy, just comfortable, with soft toys, photos and the ubiquitous bunting. All freshly painted and carpeted, new bathrooms too. Lots of staff on hand – house parents, a matron and five gappies. After activities in the evening there's 'properly supervised' prep – overseen by the head or deputy head. School is aware that even very young children are under increased pressure these days and the head and teachers are vigilant to ensure that pupils keep things in perspective. 'School can be pretty full on, we need to be sure there's a good balance', says Mr W.

Boarding reasonably flexible but school can no longer accommodate 'drop of the hat' requests, especially at the end of the week. At around £35 a night we're not surprised it's so popular – the majority of prep parents are both working (medics, GCHQ, Forces, not so many farming families these days) and this certainly helps.

A few unsteady years would dent the confidence of any school so it's testament to staff and parents' faith in Cheltenham Prep that they've come out of the experience bigger, brighter and bolder. It's heartening to see this historic school under dynamic new leadership facing the future with energy and optimism.

Cheltenham College

Linked with Cheltenham College Preparatory School

Bath Road, Cheltenham, Gloucestershire GL53 7LD

Pupils: 660; 530 boarders • Ages: 13–18 • Sixth form: 280 • C of E

Fees: Day £25,980 – £26,925; Boarding £34,650 – £35,595 pa

Tel: 01242 265600
Email: registrar@cheltenhamcollege.org
Website: www.cheltenhamcollege.org

Headmaster: Since 2010, Dr Alex Peterken BA MA DEd (30s). Five children, one at the college and two at the prep; he enjoys choral singing (bass) and walking in the Cotswolds. Dr Peterken was educated at The Prebendal School, Chichester where he was head boy and head chorister, thence to Eton College as a Music Exhibitioner. BA in theology from Durham, MA in educational management from London and a doctorate in education from Surrey. After 11 years at Charterhouse where he was head of higher education and careers and latterly housemaster of Saunderites, he joined the College in 2008 as deputy head and still teaches religious studies.

Referred to admiringly as 'the man with the plan,' he fearlessly embarked on a programme of significant changes when he took up the headship, building for the future on the school's traditional strengths. Has he succeeded? 'It's the same but better,' we were told over and over again, so that's a yes. Genial, youthful (was one of the youngest HMC heads) and delightfully unstuffy, he teaches half a term of RS to all the first years and sits in on lessons, 'not at the back; I sit next to the pupils and ask questions.' Pupils can visit Dr Peterken, without an appointment, before chapel each morning; he wants to know what's going on, what's exercising his charges. While there may not be queues at his door at 8 in the morning, all the pupils we spoke to said that they 'felt listened to'.

Academic matters: In 2016, 70 per cent A*/A at GCSE. IGCSEs are offered in maths, English literature and science and were recently introduced for history and geography. Maths, English, DT, music, history and science results are particularly impressive. At A level in 2016, 46 per cent A*/A grades and 74 per cent A*/B. Dr Peterken has no time for the excuse 'you can't do all things well', and while there are no plans to become more selective or chase league table rankings, there is a strong drive to enrich the academic opportunities for all students via a broader approach to the curriculum and programmes that enable pupils to learn more effectively.

Lessons are 35 minutes long and the new two-week timetable is, apparently, much less confusing than its eight-day predecessor. We saw thoughtful group work (boys and girls at separate tables) in Latin and a biology class where all but one were learning to love leaf mould and get to know its inhabitants.

The sixth form has received considerable attention with the introduction of an independent learning project for the lower sixth designed to extend and deepen subject knowledge (offered in addition to the EPQ). The college is also the first UK independent school to run an innovative accredited leadership and life skills course in the sixth form based on Sean Covey's book 'The 7 Habits of Highly Effective Teenagers'. Pupils can choose from 24 A level subjects including textiles, theatre studies, history of art and Latin and Greek. Critical thinking can be taken as an AS.

One of the assurances Dr Peterken and his team gives is that no pupil is allowed to 'slip under the radar'; academic problems are tackled promptly via an 'academic support plan' drawn up with the pupil, parents, housemaster, tutor and subject teachers. The head is also very keen for pupils to learn from each other: disorganised pupils are assigned a buddy to help them on the path to order; older and wiser pupils give talks along the lines of 'Things we wished we'd known ...'

EAL pupils attend an induction programme prior to the start of the academic year and are supported by two EAL specialists. Learning support department caters not only for those with mild dyslexia, dyspraxia, ADHD etc but also ensures the gifted and talented are suitably challenged. The role of this department extends to the whole school, overseeing initiatives to develop the learning potential of all pupils.

Main school library has just been completely revamped, its wonderful tiers of gothic windows pour light onto new shelves and lounging readers. Banished with the old furniture is conversation; a kind of un-modernisation which, according to our guides, has been welcomed by all. Even more enticing than golden silence are the iPads mounted on black metal plinths that pupils can use to search the library catalogue which does not, we are told, extend to Angry Birds.

Games, options, the arts: Dr Edward Wilson the Antarctic explorer was educated here and no fewer than three intrepid members of staff (one of whom is director of activities) have climbed Everest – surely some kind of a record. While the hills and fields of Gloucestershire offer little to challenge explorers or mountaineers, pretty much everything else is available to fortunate Cheltonians. The first ever inter-school rugby match was played on the school's splendid pitch in 1844, overlooked no doubt by the confection of a pavilion that resembles a miniature Brunel railway station. In the summer this perfect pitch, which won the College's groundsman Groundsman of the Year award, plays host to the venerable Cheltenham cricket festival.

County and national triumphs in rugby, hockey, cricket, tennis, rowing and polo; coaching for all abilities is now 'much more professional' and even third and fourth team matches are keenly contested and enthusiastically supported. Rackets (a forerunner of squash) is one of the more arcane sports on offer and the college has won the national championships three times and is consistently in the top four. Golf, swimming, water polo, dance and fitness are part of the exhaustive (and exhausting) sports programme as is yoga, a surprising hit with the boys; apparently it is very effective for rugby injuries.

CCF, Young Enterprise and D of E are all enthusiastically tackled, the latter being offered in its less common cycling, horseback and ski-touring options in addition to the usual walking challenge. Service activities take place every Wednesday and volunteers give their time locally at schools and residential homes. Longstanding links with Kenya see college pupils working on projects there, often carrying this on into gap years.

Art, music and modern language teaching takes place in the rather grand neo-classical surroundings of Thirlestaine House, a former gentleman's residence. Its original features – huge mirrors, chandeliers, ornate cornices and radiator covers – have survived generations of school children (just) and create a suitably bohemian home for the creative chaos of art and pottery studios. The long gallery is venue for exhibitions, lectures and public events. Two students have gained places at RADA for costume design and backstage training courtesy of the outstanding DT department while another gained a place for acting.

Nearly half of pupils learn a musical instrument, a lower uptake than comparable schools but the figure is increasing. Chapel and chamber choirs plus orchestras, bands and ensembles must keep that 40 per cent pretty busy. Performing arts centre complete with dance studio, green room and, less predictably, a plaster frieze of the Parthenon uncovered during refurbishment. School and house plays and reviews are hugely popular, everyone is encouraged to get involved either performing or backstage.

The College also plays its part in Cheltenham's cultural life, participating in the annual festival fest. The combined choirs of the college and Dean Close opened a recent music festival. Harmony with nearby Dean Close and the Ladies' College is described as 'cooperative' with pragmatic sharing of visiting speakers, careers events and collaboration between international students' societies. Pupils are more forthright, acknowledging and enjoying the rivalry.

Boarding: Houses are in residential roads just outside the campus perimeter – separating 'home' and school is considered very important: the head encourages pupils to adopt a professional attitude to school, 'it's a place of work', whereas houses are a home from home, informal and a place for relaxation. Parents are encouraged to join in with weekend or social events and are pretty much in agreement with Ofsted's conclusion that boarding provision at the college is 'outstanding.'

In addition to a matron, each house has a resident tutor who hosts academic 'clinics' outside school hours. Christowe, one of the original Victorian boys' boarding houses, has been beautifully decorated by the current housemaster and his wife (an interior designer) and there's not a whiff of the institutional in the first floor family rooms. As with all the boys' houses, 60 or so boys live here, sharing for the younger and single rooms for sixth formers. The common room and library are full of house memorabilia (house names a constant in the college); fascinating archive photos and a mini museum all foster a sense of continuity and house identity. Wonderful cushions decorated with the piratical house insignia of skull and crossbones were a gift from a parent. Clubby red-painted snooker and games room much admired. Ashmead, one of the girls' houses, was built round a garden quad with secure key pad entry system, lovely light bedrooms and civilised socialising areas. Boys are allowed to visit for film evenings and the like – apparently rom-coms are rather favoured. The housemistress heads off cliques by splitting up prep school groups and changing room-mates each year. All residents meet twice a day – a practical system that also enables staff to observe shifting dynamics. House staff and prefects alert to meal skipping and similar warning signs when 'faddy could tip into eating disorder.'

Background and atmosphere: Beautiful mellow Victorian gothic buildings along Cheltenham's busy Bath Road undergoing final stages of major re-vamp – grade 1 listed status an expensive headache but good news for Gloucestershire's stone masons and other master craftsmen. It's easy to see why visiting Americans (NATO base nearby) get a touch of the vapours; it's every inch the English public school. Public areas certainly getting the five star treatment though classrooms remain workaday and well used (all have requisite IT and smart boards). Stonework not the only area revamped: Dr Peterken has installed a duo of deputies, one pastoral, one academic, a director of learning, a new head of sixth form and 30 new members of teaching staff. Numbers, like results, are rising and a modest increase in places (about 40) is planned, as is another girls' boarding house. Students and parents tell us that much has changed for the better, not change's sake. Singled out for mention were improved home school communication and relations between teachers and pupils. Interestingly, members of staff said that they thought this had always been one of the strengths of the college but our sixth form guides were very certain that things were different and teachers were 'much more involved and friendly'. The staff we met lived up to their billing and were indeed friendly, funny, charmingly young fogeyish in a few cases, and clearly enjoying both the teaching and strong sense of community at the College.

Pastoral care, well-being and discipline: Pupils start each day in the glorious chapel, no doubt energised for study by the famously enthusiastic hymn singing. This is such a feature of college life that a recent group of upper sixth leavers asked if they could record themselves in the chapel singing favourite hymns as a parting memento. The house system is everything here, for boarders and day pupils alike; each is a community within a community and fiercely competitive. Every house has its own character and distinguishing traditions such as prefect blazers and boaters (worn with pride apparently).

Housemasters/mistresses first in line for problems whether academic or social and liaise very closely with teaching staff to ensure 'joined up' care. Older pupils train for peer mentoring responsibilities and can often pick up on wobbles before they become serious. Mobile phones (aka 'the biggest headache') only allowed in houses and, along with laptops, must be handed in before bed. If a housemaster overhears parents being berated or harangued – not uncommon in a school population that is totally teenage – he will challenge (hooray!). The writing of proper thank you letters (to former prep schools, weekend hosts and the like) is another courtesy expected of pupils. While most pupils come from similar backgrounds, staff are alert to potentially insensitive displays of conspicuous consumerism – affording one the unexpected chance to ask a parent to 'take back the mink'.

Some pupils disgruntled about tightening up on trips into Cheltenham town centre – now only Sundays unless there's a legitimate need. Head has responded to parents' view that since the school offers so many activities, 'hanging around in town' need not be a supplementary option. Bath Road still in bounds for banks, supermarkets and cafés, not that the last should be necessary – food is plentiful with lots of choice: salad bar, curries, carvery and good puds served in the former chapel and 'legendary' bacon rolls and snacks dispensed by the very friendly ladies in the tuck shop. This is a town school and necessarily takes firm line on drugs, drink and similar misdemeanours. Sixth form privileges are realistic – at 17 pupils can go out for a meal at an 'approved' restaurant; at 18 they may visit a similarly endorsed pub. The sixth form social room in the main school has a café/bar; 'we have to prepare them for life beyond school', one housemaster told us.

Pupils and parents: Good mix of first time buyers, second generation Cheltonians, Forces and international. Around 18 per cent from outside UK – 30 countries represented. Not snobby or excessively label conscious. Many boarders are from local area or within a few hours of Cheltenham. Children don't have to grow up too fast here; they're down-to-earth, polite and confident without being arrogant. 'It's not a London school', one parent said approvingly. Uniform of navy and cerise plus usual complexity of ties generally adhered to, all pupils wear own choice of pastel shirts; boys' individuality expressed mainly via hair.

OCs include Rageh Omar, journalist; Tim Bevan, film producer; General Sir Michael Rose; Nigel and Jack Davenport, actors; James Whitaker, royal correspondent; James Stout, world rackets champion; Sir Alan Haselhurst MP, The Right Hon Lord Anthony Colwyn CB and the Norfolk coroner, William Morris. Several events marked the centenary of Dr Edward Wilson who died with Scott in the Antarctic in 1912.

Entrance: Increasingly competitive. Most via common entrance, 40 per cent from own prep school, others from plethora of localish preps including Beaudesert Park, Abberley Hall, Pinewood, St Hugh's, Hatherop Castle, The Dragon, Bilton Grange, Moor Park and St John's on the Hill. Entrants from state schools take exam (papers in English, maths and, where appropriate, French); sixth form candidates require at least five B grades at GCSE and must sit papers in subjects to be studied.

Exit: Around ten per cent leaves after GCSEs. Almost all sixth formers to higher education. Handful to Oxbridge (six in 2016), most to top universities, huge range from Bath to Manchester to UCL. Most popular subject choices: biological sciences, psychology, economics and management, history, engineering.

Money matters: Scholarships (up to 25 per cent) and exhibitions (10 per cent) offered at 13+ and 16+ in academic, art, DT (13+ only), drama, music and sport. All-round award may be made at college's discretion. Additional means-tested bursaries also available.

Remarks: Radical modernisation does not always fit easily with old traditions, whether architecturally or educationally, but Cheltenham College has emerged refreshed and ready for a new era. This school is a happy, spirited community inspiring real affection and loyalty in its members.

Cheltenham Ladies' College

Bayshill Road, Cheltenham, Gloucestershire GL50 3EP

Pupils: 850; 669 boarders • Ages: 11–18 • Sixth form: 350

Fees: Day £23,040 – £26,220; Boarding £34,320 – £38,670 pa

Tel: 01242 520691
Email: enquiries@cheltladiescollege.org
Website: www.cheltladiescollege.org

Principal: Since 2011, Eve Jardine-Young MA (30s). Educated in Malawi, won a sixth form scholarship to the school she now leads, a place she credits with 'changing her life profoundly.' After graduating in engineering from Cambridge she worked for Ove Arup (structural engineers) before moving into teaching. Taught economics at Radley, moved to Epsom College where she was housemistress and head of sixth form, thence to Blundell's as director of studies. Married, her husband also works in education. Hobbies include reading, music (she is, apparently, rather a good pianist), gardening and a talkative cockatoo.

Her appointment surprised some, but the CLC Council has a record of selecting left field candidates although they've only had to choose 11 since the school was founded in 1853. Ms Jardine-Young described the protracted recruitment process as: 'Extraordinary, the Council are very involved and take their responsibility extremely seriously.' Ms Jardine-Young lives up to her name and looks scarcely old enough for such a heavy mantle (or such big shoes, albeit worn with the previous owner's blessing). When asked if she felt the weight of history on her shoulders she said she saw her responsibility as 'stewardship, not of buildings but of tradition and future potential.'

So far Ms Jardine-Young has wisely kept her head down, watching and learning the ropes of the mighty ship CLC and we don't expect her to turn up in the press any time soon banging the drum for girls' schools. Her experience in both single sex and co-ed establishments keeps her diplomatic on this subject, 'at their best, both systems work very well'. The words most often used by parents and girls to describe the principal are 'friendly,' 'approachable' and 'sincere' and indeed she is; talkative she may be but she is not a loose cannon, so we wondered why a marketing person sat in on our interview. Apparently it was for 'training purposes.'

Ms Jardine-Young is her own woman and, in the best possible way, has not yet developed a headish persona. She isn't fixed, she likes exploring ideas and thinking aloud, but don't be fooled, she brings a formidable intellect to her alma mater. Nostalgic talk of a Proustian flashback courtesy of the smell of varnish is followed by discussion of the school's institutional 'meta language'...'while we rightly praise girls who achieve, do we give enough thought to what it means to be a winner? Do we articulate other values frequently enough?' She brims with excitement and vigour and her commitment to and passion for the school shine through. She says she has plans. We can't wait.

Academic matters: League tables may come and go but CLC's academic record remains mighty. In 2016, 90 per cent A*/A at GCSE. At A level an impressive 68 per cent of passes were at A* or A, 90 per cent A*-B. Sciences, maths, economics, history and English by far the most favoured subjects but there are plenty of options and small numbers take Japanese, physical education, theatre studies, classical Greek and history of art. New engineering, enterprise and technology department. It's early days but so far the IB results are extremely strong: points average of 40 (out of 45) in 2016. Recent golds in chemistry and biology Olympiads and finalists in the national maths team challenge. It must be said that, as in similar schools, pupils from the Far East raise the bar considerably in subjects such as maths and music. We have also heard from several sources that for some a popular summer holiday activity is subject extension classes in Hong Kong. The principal says, 'We're not producing clones, the model of exam grades at any cost leads to mental brittleness.' Try telling that to the tiger mothers.

The year 7 music lesson we observed was pretty serious, girls working at a high level, keen to answer questions, otherwise quiet and diligent. IB French – a debate on the uses of philosophy – was a bit livelier. The science labs looked like those in a university, girls in white coats utterly engrossed in their experiments. Parents tell us that while the prevailing mood is indeed serious there are 'inspirational' teachers and the girls enjoy their lessons. Average class size is 16 (seven in the sixth form), progress is monitored closely and girls move up or down through sets as necessary. The brightest may take one or two subjects early but most do 10 or so GCSEs at the normal time and in their stride. Parents impressed by proactive way in which teachers identify any problems and put solutions (extra lessons etc) in place swiftly. Pupils must learn to manage their time from day one – not only do they have to get to and from house to school promptly but they also have free periods for music lessons/practice and homework.

Small numbers with EAL or SpLD, mainly dyslexia. Specialist support for girls who need help with study skills, literacy and mathematics, but clearly CLC is not the place for those with significant problems and the school is frank about this. Most areas of school fully accessible by wheelchair but distance of houses precludes all but a day pupil in these circumstances.

Games, options, the arts: Full programme of music and drama – size of school means there are opportunities for all who wish to perform; impressive results in LAMDA and music exams. Up to 50 music scholars (abandon hope if you're not grade 8 or diploma at 11) must delight the ears at concerts and lunchtime recitals. College's jewel in the crown is the new arts centre, the Parabola (it's in Parabola Road). Just across from main school, it has a 300-seat theatre, dance rehearsal rooms and small gallery primarily for school use but also hosts public shows and exhibitions. It's carving out a niche as a venue for new writing and experimental theatre, the type of thing that attracts a bijou audience, in Cheltenham at least. The town's many festivals also provide plenty of opportunities for cultural enrichment.

Impressive plate glass and metal arts building, school often has artists and writers in residence too, most but not all, women. Super textiles dept (school produced designers Katharine Hamnett and Amanda Wakeley) sadly Marie Celesteish with only three or so girls taking it beyond GCSE. Cornucopia of extracurricular options as one would expect but school is explicit in warning girls that academics must come first. Strong tradition of charitable doings: prefects nominate three UK and three international causes to fundraise for each year. Pupils also volunteer to work at St Hilda's East, the charity established in 1889 by the 'Guild' (alumni association, now 10,000 strong) in London's East End. 'What,' we asked naively, 'is Hilda patron saint of?' Answer came there none but a few red faces and a Google later we discovered that she is saint in charge of learning. Old girls who work at City law firms also do pro bono work for the charity. We doubt Miss Beale would recognise today's East Enders but the area served by the charity is still very deprived and there remains much for the Cheltenham Ladies to do. Closer to home there is a well established community links programme and girls from year 11 upwards are to be found all over the locality helping out at homeless shelters, animal sanctuaries, primary schools and retirement homes.

Sports acreage and facilities (partly open to public) are pretty good and about to get even better when the sports hall extension is completed. This will enable sports such as hockey, tennis and lacrosse to be played all year round. Notable individual achievements in athletics, tennis, skiing, riding; team sport triumphs more frequently at county level although recently CLC has got through to national finals in hockey, tennis and dry slope skiing. Most agree that sport not in premier league with few opportunities for the C,D,E team players to turn out (given size of school there must be a fair number of these). Some physical activity compulsory all the way through with zumba and pilates for the less sporty from year 5, but the sixth formers we saw were hardly rushing to the gymnasium. On the other hand we hear of considerable efforts made to find something for the keen but not so able to participate in. The school is most successful at national level in equestrian sports, with a girl in the GB under 16 team and talented riders competing for India and Australia. Not sure the school can take direct credit for this – Gloucestershire with its links to the European riding scene may have been a deciding factor. There's no stabling at the school but girls may keep their mounts 20 minutes away in Leckhampton. Polo is played at Birdlip.

Boarding: Younger girls' dorms spacious and very jolly with home duvets, under-bed storage and lots of photos and personalisation. At the foot of every bed was a brightly coloured tuck box. Single rooms for older girls are small but characterful, many with inspiring views. A place in one of the old-fashioned 'cubs,' dorms where beds have a curtain around them, highly coveted.

Parents full of praise for pastoral care whether for boarders or day girls – house mistresses in particular singled out for responding to email/telephone calls by return. Incidents – friendship issues or bullying – nipped in bud equally promptly, we hear. Girls bring their own laptops but internet use is heavily monitored. Boarders may use social networking sites from year 3 up out of school hours. The sixth form house we visited was originally the indefatigable Miss Beale's teacher training college. With its elegant library (plus wireless of course), it is intended to be a 'halfway house to university.' Girls may come and go with more freedom but the academic tutors and house mistresses liaise to minimise girls pushing themselves too hard and staff on each floor listen out for late night working.

Background and atmosphere: Miss Dorothea Beale led the school (including a nursery and a teacher training college) from 1858. She was a suffragette who pioneered women's education at a time when biology had to be code-named 'human geography' to stop irate fathers taking their girls home, because to learn about such things would make them unmarriageable. Not content with revolutionising women's school education, the astonishing Miss Beale also founded St Hilda's College, Oxford. What would she make of today's Cheltenham Ladies as they sweep all before them, outperforming most boys and becoming leaders in their chosen careers? Ms Jardine-Young says that the college has become 'more open, less introspective,' since she was a pupil there. Her aim is to take that forward and enable girls to 'become more adventurous learners, prepared to succeed but resilient enough to cope with failure.'

The main entrance to the college is on one of Cheltenham's wide boulevards. If it weren't for girls in PE kit massing on the steps it could be mistaken for a corporate HQ and, with 800+ pupils and over 600 employees, in one sense that's what it is. Behind lies a glorious quad, three parts Victorian gothic creeper-clad grandeur, one part grim 1970s concrete modernism. Miss Beale wanted her girls to learn in surroundings as beautiful as those boys had been favoured with for hundreds of years. The original fabric of the college, with its wonderful chequerboard marble corridor, grand library, mullion windows and arts and crafts frescoes, was thus as much a political statement as a seat of learning. The teaching rooms we saw were in the main functional and surprisingly anonymous. You couldn't tell you were at such a legendary school unless you happened to be daydreaming and looked out of the window (and we're sure that never happens).

On the day of our visit there had been something of a non-story in the national press about 'draconian guidelines' issued to ensure that 'mufti' (or home clothes) were sufficiently modest. School rather twitchy about this and we never did get the chance to ask girls what their opinion was. Parents say they resented the tone of the letter rather than its content (some outraged by both). Many admitted that they were pleased to deflect responsibility for discouraging tiny shorts etc onto school. Uniform is pretty dreary though – the most enthusiasm we could elicit from parents was that 'it does the job.' The good people of Cheltenham may have nicknamed the girls 'greenflies' but something a little less evolved, 'algae', perhaps, would more precisely describe the shade of the green skirts and jumpers. Sixth formers may wear navy pin-stripe trousers although to this reviewer the effect of these with regulation shirt and jumper is a curious half-bank worker, half-schoolgirl centaur. But away with such frivolous concerns; we feel the disapproving shade of Miss Beale urging us to look at the bigger picture. She's right, of course.

Pastoral care, well-being and discipline: This is a big school and the house system works well by breaking it down into manageable units – roughly 60 girls per house. Whole school meets every day in the Princess Hall for prayers, notices etc. Houses, most substantial and Victorian, but pleasingly not too unsympathetically subdivided, are scattered in nearby leafy residential roads and strings of Ladies' College girls walking to and fro are one of Cheltenham's perennial sights (hence, perhaps, worries about unsuitable attire on mufti days). Some houses are quite a hike away, conveniently making sensible footwear a must. Fair bit of road crossing necessary and this concerns new parents as girls travel in unaccompanied groups. Girls eat all meals in their house, a buffet lunch is available in the main school for those taking exams or with commitments that use up travelling time. Each house has its own chefs but meals are planned centrally – economies of scale no doubt, also cuts down on lunch envy – girls get to choose favourite menus. Eating environment and food seemed pleasant enough in the houses we visited. Significant boarding refurbishment project planned and to enable this a new junior boarding house has been acquired into which each house will 'decant' in turn; also new sixth form house.

Pupils and parents: So sorry to undermine a popular cliché but we encountered no braying Henriettas or snooty aristos, just normal girls – friendly, unaffected and full of fun. Our year 9 lunch companions were sweetly excited about how much they 'loved going to Waitrose' (store has wisely established itself as the nearest supermarket) and triumphant that they had persuaded the local ice cream van to call at their house. Some observe (as did we) that nationalities tend to stick together both in and out of lessons – inevitable perhaps – and a look at the results lists in the excellent school magazine tells its own, by now familiar, story of the formidable Chinese work ethic.

We hear whispers on the GSG grapevine that the school is not quite as fashionable with metropolitan parents as once it was, but London is still the home city of boarding majority. In the main, parents are the usual spectrum of by no means rich professionals who choose the college because of the opportunities it offers their bright daughters. Several mentioned that they valued the school's relative conservatism and high expectations in a world of declining standards. All said that the pace is fast; too fast for a few.

Entrance: Entrance exam at 11+ (English, maths, VR). 'Please don't coach,' the school begs parents. 'We can spot the child who has been coached.' We imagine most parents have their hands over their ears and are singing loudly. At 13+ exams in maths, English, science, VR and French (if previously studied). For entry to the sixth form girls must sit exams in the subjects they wish to study.

So what exactly, we quizzed the head of admissions, does CLC look for? All girls take the same exam, thus candidates from outside the UK must have a very high standard of English. Every admission is considered on an individual basis; a girl's extracurricular interests are an important factor. The message from parents is, if you think it will suit your daughter, have a go. One told us, 'my daughter wasn't top in her prep school but she got a place and is loving it.' CLC wants girls who 'accept that they are joining a community.' Families are strongly encouraged to visit several times so that they know 'what they are getting.' Indeed families are under nearly as much scrutiny as girls themselves. Great importance is attached to what the school calls 'generosity of spirit' – interpret that as you wish. Roughly 25 per cent from outside the UK (expats as well as foreign nationals), many from the Far East, and the IB programme attracts strong candidates from Europe and South Africa. The 200 day girls keep school's Gloucestershire roots strong.

Exit: A few leave post-GCSE but most stay on and benefit hugely from the higher education and careers advice provided by the school's Professional Guidance Centre. Support includes subject mentors to aid with further reading and personal statements, interview training and the opportunity to talk with Guild members about university and career choices.

In 2016, 19 Oxbridge places. Rest to top universities at home (eg Edinburgh, Durham, UCL, Bristol) or abroad. US increasingly popular with offers in 2016 from Berkeley, NYU and Minerva among others. Careers of old girls give a flavour of what Cheltenham ladies do next: heaps of lawyers, MPs, medics and scientists. They include Nicola Horlick (financier), Cheryl Gillan (Conservative MP), Rachel Lomax (first woman Deputy Governor of the Bank of England), Dame Mary Archer (scientist), Lisa Jardine (historian) and Rosie Boycott (journalist).

Money matters: Plenty of 'merit based awards' and scholarships for eg academics, art, sport and music. 'Limited amount' of funding for means-tested bursaries and some help for families of current pupils in financial difficulties. Bursaries intended to widen access to college are 'carefully awarded' to girls who would benefit from a college education. Principal very keen to extend opportunities in this area.

Remarks: A top flight school with strong traditional values and a clear sense of purpose. For the bright and energetic all rounder this school offers an exceptional education that is both broad and deep, with endless opportunities for fun and enrichment along the way.

Chew Valley School

Chew Lane, Chew Magna, Bristol BS40 8QB

Pupils: 1,135 • Ages: 11–18 • Sixth form: 185

Tel: 01275 332272
Email: enquiries@chewvalleyschool.co.uk
Website: www.chewvalleyschool.co.uk

Head: Since September 2016, Gareth Beynon, previously head of Clevedon School. Geography degree from Manchester and masters in educational management from Institute of Education. Taught in Surrey before moving to leadership position in Clevedon. Keen rugby player (previously) and supporter (currently). Married with one daughter.

Academic matters: Success across the board, particularly impressive for a non-selective school. Everyone does either French or Spanish in year 7, star performers are identified, fast-tracked and encouraged to take up German in year 8. Maths setted from the start, science in broad ability bands, everything else mixed ability groups. GCSE results have risen steadily over the past few years – in 2016, 70 per cent got five plus A*-C including English and maths, 20 per cent A*/A grades. The study camp, run in the Easter holidays, must help. Not flattered by government value added measures due to the trad profile of the exams taken here.

A level results are good too, with 49 per cent A*-B grades in 2016 and 20 per cent A*/A. Strongest subjects seem to be maths (including further maths) and sciences, sociology, psychology and drama. Twenty-nine subjects offered at A level. Academics are taken seriously here: Oxbridge hopefuls are

C

assigned external mentors from amongst the governors or local businesses; the AQA baccalaureate (A levels, AS critical thinking and EPQ) is offered and pupils present their EPQ submissions at a special evening. But the school does not want 'Oxbridge to be the achievement we shout loudest about': it's as much about making sure that the more vocationally bound get the courses they want too. Around 25 per cent of the GCSE cohort take an applied route. The G&T register records prowess in all sorts of areas, not just brainpower.

Parents largely content with academic offering, though one mentioned frustration with just five minutes laid on with each subject teacher per year, and felt that there could be more precision for individuals, eg 'What does my child have to do to get an A*, rather than an A?' SEN provision universally praised: totally free of stigma, and housed in a series of rooms which act as a safe haven for those who find the hurly-burly and unstructured nature of break-times difficult, or for those who want a quiet place to knock off coursework. (The library isn't always as quiet as pupils would like, they told us.) School has 12 per cent recorded as SEN; out of 100 or so, 18 have statements. Some vexation that disruptive kids without statements cannot be given the help/means/resources to bring about better classroom behaviour – a common complaint in tightly-resourced state schools.

We found lessons lively and engaging, particularly a Spanish one, where pupils were building complex sentences with towers of books. A sixth form PHSE class engaged pupils in a discussion of student finances. Marked work was displayed on the walls, showing off both pupils' and teachers' expertise.

Games, options, the arts: Stacks on offer, appreciated by everyone. Chew Valley's rural location and 30 acre site mean masses of pitches, tennis courts, an Astro and gardens. All usual sports feature, plus girls' rugby and sailing on nearby Chew Valley Lake. Pupils enjoy busy fixture list with local schools plus links with community clubs and Bath University for facilities (eg 50m pool) and specialist sports teaching. Team performance is impressive, yet still some parents grumble that the 'sports just don't compare with independent schools'. Extracurricular outdoorsy stuff also offered by committed staff, such as Ten Tors and D of E. Gym and sports centre on site shared with general public, which reduces cost. Certainly enough sport beyond traditional games to keep everyone happy, including a committed and successful cheerleading group – we could hardly squeeze into the PE office for pompoms.

School has had performing arts status since 2003. Terrific debating, public speaking and plays. Music described as 'amazing' by one mum (around a quarter of pupils take extra music lessons and achieve grade 8 in some cases). Ensembles range from orchestra, flute group, to brass, folk and all the way to rock band; singers can choose from several choirs and less formal set-ups. Dance dept (which caters for boys too) puts on own festival which attracts the twinkle-toed from primaries, secondaries and even universities on occasion. Regular prizes from annual Mid-Somerset Festival.

Visual arts appear as rather a poor relation to its all-singing-all-dancing siblings. Both art and DT facilities looked well-loved and used, and school has in the past curated the LA's schools' art exhibition, yet all that unadorned breeze block inside the school was crying out for some vibrant canvasses. More on show please!

No poverty of ambitions in terms of expeditions, however: Chew Valley pupils have recently been to India, to Lesotho and to Honduras, where two new bird species were identified.

Background and atmosphere: Looks like the 50 year old secondary modern it once was, with a clutch of undistinguished low level buildings – with the exception of the stunning new sixth form block overlooking the lake. Chew Valley has enjoyed a well-deserved reputation for excellence for many years and now has a building to reflect it, with teaching space, seminar rooms and a café, where students were hard at work when we visited. School is fortunate to have so much green space, enough to grow veg and to keep chickens, who reside at Cluckingham Palace.

It all feels buzzy and purposeful, in fact we were practically trampled by chattering kids en route to various destinations – no flattening themselves against the wall as the head sweeps by. This lack of undue deference meant lively and stimulating conversation with pupils who identified clearly what they love about the school (range of stuff on offer, encouragement to start clubs or activities, great relationships with staff, school grounds and their use as outdoor classrooms), and what's on their wish-list (proper performance space which does not double as dining hall, better stocked library). Lunchtimes are very busy with clubs and the Learning to Lead programme – a very upswept version of a school council, with over 100 pupils 'working in teams with real power and responsibility'. The wind turbine in the grounds which supplies some of the school's power, the healthy meals in the canteen and the residents of Cluck House are evidence of their work. So significant has this been that team members have been to two national conferences to talk about how it's done. Parents like it – as long as there are enough willing volunteers to run all these teams. Charities extremely well supported through various team-based initiatives also.

Bad behaviour is dealt with by the behaviour support teacher: 'We will not have our lessons disrupted,' states the school. Time after time we were told about the family atmosphere and the tremendous loyalty ex-pupils feel; parents value the fact that the school provides the climate and opportunity to try things out: 'My child has found a real delight in drama which has had a knock-on effect in English,' said one mother, 'they really do blossom in all sorts of ways'.

Uniform is practical, cheap and standards are enforced. Sixth formers wear whatever they like.

Pastoral care, well-being and discipline: Generally judged to be exceptional, and not just by Ofsted. School has had designated home/school liaison officer for the last 10 years, who dragged herself in from her sickbed to talk to us, and who acts as a point of contact for parents; matters raised are then referred on to the right person – medical, academic or pastoral. She can also refer troubled pupils to external sources of support, as well as advising parents in crisis. Some services eg counselling are brought into school because of its rural location and provided from Lake View, an unobtrusive building in the school grounds designated for small group teaching.

Parents and pupils appreciate clarity on the perennial irritants of fags and booze, and the more insidious matter of drugs; school says none of it presents a great problem, but won't stop short of exclusions – fixed term or permanent – for those who transgress.

No-one mentioned bullying, but all parents we talked to praised the speed and quality of the school's response to any issues they raised. The prevailing climate seems to be one of praise, far and above blame.

Pupils and parents: Predominantly local – school serves the 120 square miles of the Chew Valley and is a key feature of the community. Wide-ish economic mix of families of modest means – 'There's rural poverty even in Chew Valley,' says school – all the way to Bristol professionals who choose to live south of the city, and who may well do so on account of the school. A few refugees from south Bristol schools, most of which are 'well rough'. One young man told us he had gone off the idea of his local school when someone threw a chair out of the window during a lesson the day he visited. Not exactly ethnically diverse – this was about the only note of criticism Ofsted could muster.

We found everyone we met bright, articulate and positive. Parents actively encouraged to be part of school life – there's an enthusiastic School Society which raises funds and puts on events – but some felt that even greater use could be made of parental expertise in applying for grants etc. All report good communication, and appear genuinely committed to and grateful for the education Chew Valley lays on. Former pupils include John Garden (keyboards in The Scissor Sisters); recording flautist Nicola Woodward and professional percussionist Justin Woodward.

Entrance: At year 7, 196 places and demand outstrips supply. Majority of intake will live within 'school's area of prime responsibility', but some places will go to out of area applicants. Check LA (Bath and NE Somerset) criteria with care. School sits (awkwardly) on the borders of two other LAs, South Bristol and North Somerset. At sixth form, a minimum of five GCSE grades A*-C to include English and maths is required.

Exit: Some fall-out post GCSE to employment or to sixth form colleges. By that stage the urban temptations of Bristol (St Brendan's, City of Bristol) or even Norton Radstock college exert a pull – and they put on huge range of courses.

Of those who stay on, a handful start work, another handful take gap years and the majority go to the university of their first choice, covering a great range: eg Cardiff and Plymouth popular; one to Cambridge (architecture) in 2016 and one medic. UCAS preparation is thorough. Degree choices are many and various – from accounting to tourism, via Chinese studies and a notable attraction to earth sciences.

Remarks: A model of comprehensive education, this school truly serves all the interested parties in its community. 'A private school without fees', 'If I had my time again, I would definitely choose Chew Valley' say parents. About as good as it gets – worth moving for.

Christ College, Brecon

Brecon, Powys LD3 8AF

Pupils: 400; 178 full, 21 flexi, 201 day boarders • Ages: 7-18 (boarding from year 5) • Sixth form: 145

Fees: Day £8,628 – £17,463; Boarding £16,299 – £26,982 pa

Tel: 01874 615440
Email: enquiries@christcollegebrecon.com
Website: www.christcollegebrecon.com

Head: Since 2007, Mrs Emma Taylor MA. Exhibitioner at New College Oxford where she read PPE. In the best possible way, it shows. Some years ago when she was a housemistress at Canford, following a spell of teaching philosophy, religious studies and economics at Stowe, a perceptive Good Schools Guide scribbler described her as 'formidable and wonderful.' Coincidentally she then moved on to Dean Close where she was deputy head before arriving at Brecon. This current scribbler marvels at such perception and is happy to employ the same words. Both words are appropriate, but the word 'formidable' needs some explanation. This head is not a pompous, bombastic dictator. She is, as one member of staff told us, 'warm, perceptive and sensitive to ideas and innovations.' It is said that the lot of the girls has improved since her arrival, though no-one has suggested that she's a fire eating feminist. 'She's too level headed for that,' one distinguished granny told us. She knows everyone and seems to remember everything. 'That can be a bit scary but she has a good sense of humour and she does care about us,' one young pupil told us. She is held in much affection by staff, pupils and parents. What makes her so formidable is an inner strength and refusal to give in to anything that she sees as foolish, dangerous, dishonest or just plain wrong. Formidable. Her decision over rugby fixtures is a fine example, something which will become apparent later. She is generally acknowledged as being right about most things. Right but never smug.

She is greatly respected in the world of education. Serendipity led us to discover a wide range of people who have known and admired her in various stages of her career. She has broadcast on radio and television on education and political issues, eg on BBC Radio Wales as a member of the 'Manifesto Corner' team.

Academic matters: One of the really tedious pictorial clichés published by so many schools in August is of groups of pupils leaping up into the air clutching their A level results – or so it is to be assumed. It's a silly picture because it's so obviously lacking in any spontaneity and you feel the leavers have been treated like performing fleas. 'One, two three, now jump into the air as high as you can,' encourages the photographer absurdly. The pictures are enforced as useful advertising for the school. Humbug!

Christ College, Brecon does not go in for that sort of silliness though, naturally, they are happy to share their delight. After all, they have a lot to celebrate. They have always had their bright pupils moving on to Oxbridge and top medical schools but overall results have improved, and in the recent A level results CCB came in the top 100 schools in the Daily Telegraph league tables. In 2016, 43 per cent A*/A grades. The most obvious way of showing academic prowess is through endless grid systems. Statistics. Statistical junkies can get a fix here, of course, but the celebration and relief that accompanies success here is more human than most. This school is less about numbers, it's about human beings and their deserved achievements. A recent publication contains a wonderful account of two boys, great friends, and the academic rivalry which they shared for most of their time in the school. The writing is superb, like a short story. In fact there is genuine suspense as we read on, wondering who has indeed performed better overall. It's typical of this wonderful school that they should invest statistics with such human interest.

Having said all that the overall statistics are impressive and not to be ignored. They should be celebrated, but above all they should be put into perspective against the background of superb teaching, mutual respect and, yes, friendship between staff and pupils. Classes are small and that helps, though not as much as is frequently claimed. After all, small classes with lousy teaching will produce lousy results. We witnessed some absolutely tremendous teaching. The facilities and classrooms are generously laid out and the pupils respond fearlessly. They spoke to us unashamedly of the exciting quality of the teachers, the energy and fun they injected and the extra time teachers were prepared to offer for catch up and clarification. We saw sparky language teaching, lively music and drama, history, sciences, maths, biology: all demanding subjects – no raffia dolly-making here – and all warmly appreciated by pupils. It pays dividends. Medicine, science and engineering courses are the most popular. GCSE results were excellent, demonstrating the popularity and success of technical and creative subjects. In 2016, 44 per cent A*/A grades. The overall academic standards of the school have improved without the aggressive insistence on the importance of grades adopted by so many schools. Here the grades are merely the boxes: it's the contents that matter and the way those contents are treated.

And what about those people with SEN? There aren't many at CCB who have SEN and those who do have been described as 'moderate mostly'. But it's almost worth cultivating some SEN in order to be closeted with the highly qualified, approachable teacher who presides in her classroom ever ready to help anyone who drops in. A previous GSG scribbler referred to those visits as pit stops and that's how the SEN guru likes it to be. She perceives her visitors as engaged in learning to overcome weaknesses, developing a sense of belonging and togetherness, of readiness and enhanced expectations. Let them stop by when they want to. She is full of wisdom and compassion. Every Thursday afternoon is tea party time: often, we were told, pretty lively. The parents we spoke to about her 'couldn't find the words to do her justice.' One final joy: most schools charge for help with SEN. At CCB pupils and parents pay with heartfelt gratitude and affection.

Games, options, the arts: Rugby is regarded by many as the number one sport at CCB. However, there is a strong move gathering impetus in the medical world and parts of the media to ban tackling throughout inter-school rugby. Oblivious to that, some ailing schools have turned themselves into something like rugby academies with much emphasis on wooing the biggest and the fastest players. The head, who enjoys watching rugby, spotted the potential dangers of such one-sided games and decided that the fixture list should change to ensure safety and competitiveness. It was a sane and sensible decision but initially brought her considerable flack from those who felt that boys should learn to deal with hard knocks and a broken bone or two. However, she stood her ground formidably before eventually winning her point. Rugby is still extremely popular with continued investment in the sport and its coaching with a former rugby professional appointed as director of rugby in recent years.

Lest anyone assume the head sees little but mindless biffing and banging in rugby, let them get hold of a copy of The Herald, Michaelmas 2015, the college news. There the head writes movingly and elegantly about what can be learned from the New Zealand rugby team, listing as ideal qualities 'humility, pride in the team, commitment to one another and diligent determination to make incremental improvements in performance.' Of course this isn't just about rugby: it's about living, about conduct, about integrity and it's very good stuff. Arnold would have recognised the message.

But rugby is by no means the only game. There is some football played, a lot of hockey – the school has a number of international hockey players, past and present, boys and girls. The boys as well as girls have been recent Welsh champions at U18s, U14s and U12s and there are outstanding netball teams. Lots of cricket, including a 20:20 Festival involving players from the UK and abroad. There's masses to do and much to be admired. Most pupils enjoy getting involved with a variety of sports and activities. Just as well. One pupil told us that he had been selected for five different sports 'and I'm not much good at any of them. But it was terrific fun and we didn't lose them all.'

Brecon is the HQ of the army in Wales, as a trip to the nearby cathedral with its regimental chapel confirms. The CCF is enormously popular, and when you've met the man who runs it you're half way towards understanding why. When we met him he was busy polishing up a trophy to return. Internet news suggests it's back in CCB, along with two silver medals won by what sounds a formidably tough, determined and clear-headed cadet. CCF is compulsory in yrs 9 and 10; girls as well and female staff.

Drama is driven by a dynamic head of department who enthuses not just the pupils but all members of the school community to tread the boards and join in. With an annual community project to rope such amateur thespians in, as well as an ambitious school production for the different age groups, it really does produce some of the highest quality productions. Their Les Mis was 'jaw-dropping', according to one West End fan we met who had seen the Christ College version.

Music is terrific. We were shown round by the director of music and met some delightful and talented pupils practising for a concert at the end of the week in the recently enlarged music building. It wasn't difficult to persuade us to return two days later for a concert at the Royal Welsh College of Music and Drama, part of the school's celebrations of the 475th anniversary of its foundation by royal charter. It was a thrilling concert full of energy and skill, sensitivity and passion, from the youngest to the most senior. Choral singing that might have been written for Polly Garter, for as the Reverend Eli Jenkins murmured, and many of the audience might have done that evening, 'thank the Lord we're a musical nation'. Orchestras of all or most ages playing together; a delightful pupil making an excellent debut on the drums; from the youngest – who were wonderful – to the oldest instrumentalists who played with such skill, the evening was moving and exciting. Eli Jenkins was right.

We met a lot of parents at the school concert and no, they were not selected for their unique loyalty. They had come to support their children and the staff and what they all said in reply to our questions about academics was that it was 'cool to work'. One parent volunteered the notion that the pupils worked hard 'out of inspired interest and loyalty.' That seemed to sum up everything. Another phrase that remains is about the school, overall: 'Whatever they do, they do well.' The results of a recent survey would suggest that fewer than five per cent of parents would disagree with that.

Boarding: Boarding is convenient, of course, that's part of it all, but it ignores the fact that for many boys and girls, boarding is fun. The rooms are designed and built to be attractive. One or two of the students, who had older siblings at university, recognised that the rooms in which they lived were much nicer than they would get at most universities. They're nicer than many homes: snooker table, luxurious, comfortable sofas, large screen televisions, efficient showers and always friends to talk to. But they have responsibilities, and many to whom we spoke talked of the satisfaction they feel in being given positions of authority and so opportunities to pay back the treatment they had received. How ominous that would have sounded 100 years ago. Nowadays it's part of the rhythmic pattern of the school; the feeling of continuity and progress: history in the making. All staff are involved in boarding.

The six day and boarding houses include Alway House, where year 5 and 6 pupils from St Nicholas House junior school can weekly board with the year 7 and 8s.

Background and atmosphere: Founded in 1541 by Henry VIII on the site of the sacked and wracked Black Friars' church, victim of the Dissolution. Students are touchingly proud of this ancientness, as of the crowned 'h' tag, which is the school's logo, and of the fact that the chapel where they meet every morning has been worshipped in continuously since around 1250.

Wonderful new junior school: the St Nicholas House for boys and girls aged 7-11 (opened in September 2014) and Alway House (boys and girls aged 11-13) which is, unbelievably, over 50 years old. A joyous building and full of intelligently conceived fittings and decorations, an area for sleeping, playing inside and out, ICT for researching particular topics and always kind, creative helpers from all walks of the school and not just walks, because on Fridays they go for a country run. Delightful, challenging climbing frames guiding young adventurers to the distance, where always and for ever the hills beckon and invite.

How lucky those very young are and how appreciative everyone seems, from the youngest to the lower sixth volunteers.

Numerically this is a small school, though it has grown in numbers since the head's arrival. It is amongst the happiest we have ever visited. From the genuinely warm welcome with which we were greeted at reception – something commented on by many parents – and thence throughout the whole tour (with a thoughtful and entertaining mixture of guides) we were treated with courtesy and spontaneous good will. Lunch with delicious food in the wonderful ancient refectory in the company of delightful sixth formers was a real pleasure. Our hosts were confident and entertaining without a hint of arrogance or self-consciousness; informative in their effortless appreciation of the school and generous minded about each other and the staff.

Pastoral care, well-being and discipline: The happiness is palpable and high spirited and that says much about the discipline. Pupils and staff walk around greeting, smiling and chatting and, when they see visitors approaching, focus the eyes and smile inclusively. At some schools visitors are greeted with pasted smiles and glazed eyes: well-trained but fundamentally indifferent. Staff and pupils clearly get on well with each other. Discipline is based on common sense and mutual consideration, and that is presumably what is meant by well-being. We were told stories of incidents in which anxieties and problems were spotted and addressed not only by the head, though she seems to be always in the know, but by teachers, class assistants, senior pupils and ground staff. Everyone is everyone's responsibility. In reply to our question about the school's tangible happiness, one sixth form girl told us: 'It's like a jigsaw: everyone seems to fit in.'

The head of school and deputy (one boy and one girl – this year the head of school is a girl) are selected by the head following nominations from staff and pupils, and there are 15 prefects. Duties? 'Not arduous,' said one. 'People are pretty reasonable.' 'Cowed?' Certainly not. 'Comfortably co-ed' – no difference of opportunities.

Pupils and parents: Most pupils come from a radius of, say, 50 miles or so, the sons and daughters of army officers, farmers, businesspeople. The usual suspects but, in our experience, considerably more loyal to the school than blasé parents in the home counties. 'Fewer demanding expectations,' we were told by parents with experience of both areas. Most boarding schools these days have a number of students from abroad and CCB is no exception. But here you do not get the impression, as with some schools, that they have been imported in lorry loads simply to boost grades in the sixth form. In the nicest possible way, those 17 per cent or so of pupils from China, Hong Kong, Japan, Nepal – there's a strong contingent of Gurkhas in Brecon – and Germans in the sixth form are almost invisible at first visit. The school seems much better at fully integrating pupils from abroad so that many get stuck in to rugby, cricket and choir singing. Those pupils from aboard whom we met were genuinely happy and involved.

Entrance: Into year 3 for St Nicholas House via an entry morning with 'a range of academic and creative activities', plus small group meetings with the college head and the head of St Nicholas House. Into years 7 and 9 by English and maths assessments and IQ test, plus interview and school reports. Sixth form entry by GCSE predictions, IQ test, school report and interview.

Exit: About 10 (on average) leave after GCSEs. Not because they're unhappy, we were assured by prefects and senior pupils, but often for sporting reasons or simply for a change – occasionally geographical. We did not detect any specific grumblings or rumblings of discontent. Of those who stay, most go on to university and to a wide range of subjects. The very helpful literature potential parents and pupils receive in reply to expressing an interest will clarify that. That literature is, incidentally, amongst the best of its kind we have ever seen and read: informative without being chest thumping, elegantly expressed and genuinely interesting. You could read it in bed without falling asleep and that's not true of all prospectuses. These ones would sit easily at the Hay Literary Festival.

Sixth form leavers to eg Cardiff, Exeter, Sheffield, UWE to study subjects such as architecture, medicine (three medics/pharmacists in 2016), music and engineering. One off to Oxford to study chemistry in 2016.

Money matters: There are scholarships and bursaries available for the able and needy. Don't be afraid to ask. Incidentally there are no inescapable extras – in fact The Good Schools Guide recently voted CCB in the Top Ten Value for Money Boarding Schools in the UK. We do not have shares in the school.

Remarks: When you step back from GCSEs and A level grades; from rugby results and hockey triumphs; from CCF marches and medals; when you pause to marvel at the hills around, enfolding the school and beckoning; when you listen to the wonderful singing in the chapel founded nearly 800 years ago and restored by Gilbert Scott about 600 years later; when you consider that at the time the English Bible was being hammered out by that group of scholars and fanatics presided over by James 1, the Scottish King, Christ College Brecon had already been in existence for nearly 100 years, it is not difficult to feel that much has been absorbed from history and the world around. Perhaps it is not too fanciful to think that the extraordinary atmosphere of friendship, mutual loyalty and academic endeavour has emanated from the variety and insistence of the past. Like many schools of ancient foundation CCB hasn't always been in a good place, but it certainly is now. What's more there is history in the making. Ask about the expansion into the Far East. Great things are being delivered, even more is promised and this is a school that warrants admiration, loyalty and, above all, trust. Go and see for yourselves.

Churston Ferrers Grammar School

Greenway Road, Churston Ferrers, Brixham, Devon TQ5 0LN

Pupils: 996 • Ages: 11–18 • Sixth form: 288

Tel: 01803 842289
Email: secretary@churston.torbay.sch.uk
Website: www.churstongrammar.com

Headteacher: Since 2007, Mr Robert Owers BA PGCE CFES NPQH (in his 40s), originally from Upminster, educated at Warwick University. He taught at two large co-ed comprehensives in Essex before becoming deputy head at Chelmsford County High School for Girls.

A family man, he lives just round the corner and the school is home from home. His wife teaches drama at Churston and both his son and daughter are pupils there. Chatty and approachable, he's a keen sportsman, particularly football and cricket, but jokes that any spare time these days is spent being the 'dad taxi'.

Keen to emphasise that although the school is a grammar school, it's not elitist and does not 'aspire to the single-sex public school ethos'. No blazers, no Latin, no old school traditions. Sensitive to the different social backgrounds of the children and families, he tries to ensure everyone is comfortable and not intimidated – Churston is a school 'for the most able local students irrespective of social background.'

Parents say, 'The school is clearly very well led by a charismatic and outstanding head and team; the general feeling is that whilst the academic aspects and outcome are key, they also want their students to experience many different things, be brave and join clubs, try sports they might never have thought about, fundraise, help out, be open to new things and the school will support them.'

Academic matters: Grades fluctuate. In 2016, 30 per cent A*/A and 65 per cent A*-B at A level. Top results in biology, history, maths and psychology. Interestingly, these subjects also have the highest number of pupils taking them. Lower grades in the arts, particularly English language. At GCSE, 55 per cent A*/A, slightly higher than the previous year. Lowest grades in the arts again, particularly music and drama.

One parent said, 'Academically Churston Ferrers teaches some subjects extremely well with teachers that enthuse students. Those subjects include languages, maths, history, economics. English and some sciences less popular.' The school offers 23 subjects at A level and has recently decided that pupils will only take nine GCSEs instead of the 10 previously offered. There has been no resistance to this change from parents or pupils.

The school takes great pride in its links to other schools around the world and the valuable lessons are learnt from these collaborations. One such project is Comenius, a European Union educational project which has helped them set up partnerships with schools in Hungary, Italy (Sicily), Norway, France and Germany. Not only do the students get the opportunity to learn about other European cultures, but it also helps their personal development. It's a very popular project and one that the school intends to continue even if it has to provide the funding.

There's an impressive DT lab; DT includes food technology to GCSE and textiles. After GCSE, there is a strong split between girls taking textiles, and boys taking design. This is a real shame and was disappointedly written off as stereotypical. There's around 600 computers in the whole school but much of this equipment will be gradually phased out as more and more Chromebooks are rolled out.

Learning support is looked after by the student services team and SENCo along with a LSA. The student services area is currently under reconstruction, but once finished there will be a full-time counsellor and literacy support co-ordinator there at all times. There are currently 12 special needs pupils and four are statemented. Action plans for individual or group work are set up according to needs, and screening is ongoing. The literacy groups are for any pupils who may not be reaching their full potential for some reason or other. The school provides them with extra help but they have to forego learning a second language.

Games, options, the arts: There are great sports facilities at Churston; the playing fields outside the new sports hall are pretty inspiring, with a view down the valley to the sea. Just round the corner, on the other side of the steam rail track, there are more playing fields plus a pavilion. The old sports hall is still in use, plus there's a gym for older pupils, new Astroturf and cage for basketball and netball, four tennis courts, three football pitches and a very small heated outdoor swimming pool for summer use only. The school has had some outstanding success in certain areas: the basketball team, led by two ex-England coaches, is renowned Devon champion, and has been national champion twice in the last 15 years. Quite a few pupils play at county or national level in a wide variety of sports, and this is very much encouraged by the school. One parent said, 'Our request for our son to tour South Africa with Devon cricket board was well received and supported. '

'The academic emphasis can mean the arts are underinvested,' said one parent, but this is being addressed with the construction of the new drama studio and a new art and music block. The lack of a studio hasn't stopped the productions, though, and a recent one, The Lion, the Witch and the Wardrobe, involved 80 students of all ages. Other productions have included Blue Remembered Hills and Born To Dance.

There's impressive artwork on display in the art rooms and corridors, but this is another department that has been earmarked for improvement and development. One recent art project that we particularly liked the sound of involved year 11 pupils plus some ex-students who were driving a car to Croatia to raise money for Rowcroft Hospice. They had to decorate an old Mercedes in a day with a unique and eye-catching design. A great project on many levels.

'Over the last five years, music in the school has improved dramatically, with some great school concerts,' say parents. Around 25 per cent of pupils learn an instrument, but the department really is tiny. The pupils we saw were squeezed into the main room (boys on drums and girls on flutes and violins) and were very keen to express their desperation for more space. The school is hoping that the next phase of funding will enable them to extend both the music and the art departments, and indeed the new music and art block which opened in 2016 has fantastic space for the students.

There's the usual array of lunchtime and after-school clubs in sport, music, drama, science and debating, plus Sustainable Futures and Food For Life groups. A new addition is a Quidditch Club that pupils set up themselves with school funding – they have, however, paid it all back through fundraising. Other extracurrricular activities include Duke of Edinburgh awards, for which Churston has the largest commitment in the area. Parents enthuse, 'The extracurricular trips abroad that the school organises are superb, with trips to visit WW1 battlefields, to sing in Italy, language exchange trips, adventure trips to France, as well as opportunities to travel to China, South Africa and Peru. The commitment from staff to organise these and commit their own time is outstanding.'

The school helps families plan these trips with a programme called 'Seven years at Churston'. It kicks off with a residential trip in year 7, foreign exchanges in years 8 and 9 plus the battlefields trip. From year 10 onwards the trips fall into three different categories. Firstly, and the most talked about, is the social enterprise trip. This is to Peru, where the school has built up a strong relationship with local schools over the years. One parent commented, 'He relished the month spent in Peru this summer, where a group of 20 students and three teachers undertook a mixture of helping local primary schools [build shade canopies from old sails] and exploring the culture and history of Peru. He matured a great deal in that month.' As well as planning the next trip, the school is also adding another strand to this project by setting up a mentoring project with the business studies students. The other categories include cultural trips, most recently to China and South Africa, and a sports tour, which most recently saw netball, football and basketball teams touring Holland.

Background and atmosphere: Originally Dartmouth Grammar School, Churston Ferrers is one of 42 co-educational grammar schools in the country. Set amongst the rolling hills of Devon in a picturesque seaside location, the school immediately gives an impression of calm and tranquility. It's been extensively modernised since 1957 and the modern entrance with sliding doors and reception is more like a business building. However, the displayed trophies, wooden plaques for heads of houses and photo galleries make this very much a school. A particularly nice touch is the screen at the entrance that gives live updates to visitors and pupils alike.

The school is modern with wide corridors and windows looking onto adjoining classrooms. It doesn't feel like a traditional grammar or public school, no signs of old school traditions here; it feels and looks much more like a modern comprehensive. There's a small beep to indicate end and start of lessons but there's no mad rush to get to the next class as the lessons here are longer, on average 75 minutes, and they are all followed by a short 10/15 minute break for drink, snack or breather. This is all rather civilized and pupils seem relaxed.

The Cube is a newer building, built in 2008 as a learning and resources centre. It's open from 8am to 5pm and is a library and a work area with both reference books and Chromebooks available. There's also a teacher on hand. Pupils there were getting homework done before home time, giving them time for after-school clubs, other activities and a home life.

The recently built sixth form centre is across a large courtyard scattered with seating and table tennis tables and surrounded by allotments. Approximately 300 students are catered for here; they have their own snack kitchen and a large, comfy common room. Upstairs are classrooms and a large computer room with 60 computers. Part of the computer room is sectioned off as a supervised study area – that's detention room to you and me. Unsurprisingly, this is mainly frequented by boys.

Most of the staff here are relatively new and have been appointed by the current head over the last seven years. A third are under 30 years old and around two-thirds are female. The head has recently appointed two female physics teachers in the hope that they can encourage more girls to take the subject and start putting these stereotypes to bed. They still have a long way to go with persuading any boys to take textiles or join a dance group, but the girls are taking note and getting involved in maths as well as physics.

The pupils are split into five houses led by year 11 students. There are regular house assemblies, inter-house competitions, charity fundraising, growing and selling of allotment produce, recycling, drama productions and much more that bring together pupils of all ages and encourage them to work as a community. There's also a new mentor website for younger pupils where they can ask sixth form ambassadors for help – mostly used for maths homework, we hear.

Pastoral care, well-being and discipline: The one thing every parent agreed on is the school's 'outstanding pastoral care', saying, 'We feel the school is very well run with a truly human hand'. There's a large student services team that ensures there's always someone available. The pupils here are from all walks of life and the school is keen to make sure they support them in any way needed. The head considers this to be the most important part of the school, believing that happiness is more important than grades. Quirkiness and individuality allowed. Kindness promoted. Relationships respected.

'The school manages the balance between approachability and discipline in a careful manner, resulting in a positive culture and ethos in the school,' say parents. 'We have seen very little evidence of bullying within the school'. Incidents seem to be 'handled appropriately and sensitively, and resolved in a timely manner. Was very impressed with the skill of the team involved.' One parent said of their experience: 'Our son did not lose his confidence as a result of this incident but retained his self- esteem about it...He felt safe and supported...and there have not been any problems since. He also received a huge amount of support from all years in the wider school community.'

There are lunchtime detentions for failure to complete work, usually applying to around 10 students. Five detentions leads to an after-school detention. Friday night detentions are for repeated detentions or more serious issues like smoking or bad behaviour. Second offences lead to suspension. Zero tolerance to drugs, immediate expulsion.

Pupils and parents: Mainly from Torbay, most families are local, Brixham, Paignton, but some from as far as Totnes. As with all grammar schools, there are pupils from varied backgrounds; parents are solicitors, directors, nurses, PAs. There is a strong sense of family at the school, and most of the parents we spoke to had all their children at Churston. One said, 'Churston was all our first choice, for its academic achievement, positive attitudes towards learning and family friendliness. Churston is a comparatively small secondary school, so the staff and students (and parents too if they join the PTA) get to know each other well.'

Parents feel communication is good, are also invited, along with their children, to complete surveys – a useful tool for letting pupils in particular have their say. They recently requested more drama, hence a new drama studio. Cardigans can now be worn instead of the unflattering sweatshirts and boys (and girls) can wear earrings from year 10 onwards. Another request, undoubtedly from parents, was the installation of a salad bar plus a new catering manager to address the nutritional concerns. And a change championed by parents and pupils alike was the reduction of homework to one hour a night for years 7 and 8, increasing to two hours higher up. However, a voluntary homework scheme has also been set to keep some keen pupils and mainly parents happy. One said, 'He has been given appropriate extension work in subjects he is particularly good at and encouraged to reach his potential.'

Entrance: The three grammar schools in Torbay operate a co-ordinated entrance examination with all pupils taking the same tests on the same days. Tests include English, maths and verbal, numerical and non-verbal reasoning. No practice material but familiarisation booklets provided. Approximately 140 out of 300 applicants are successful, usually split as 75 girls and 65 boys.

Induction days and events have been very successful in the past. Parents said, 'All of them settled very quickly – the transition was handled very smoothly with meetings and events in the summer term before they started and lots of information. Another added, 'There were several events organised to help integrate us as families and these were extremely helpful.... we did a Lego exercise, to show team-building, and how they work with the children to help them come out of their shells, or stand back for a while if they are natural leaders. This was fascinating, and incredibly exciting to think that they were considering the whole child in this way.'

On average 40-55 pupils join the sixth form from other schools or colleges, mainly Brixham and Dartmouth Community Colleges. Students must have at least six GCSEs at A*-B, plus grade C or above in mathematics and grade B in English. They also need to meet the individual subject requirements.

Exit: The majority (some 75 per cent) of students stay on for sixth form, and most of these go onto university. Three to Oxbridge in 2016 (medicine, law and chemistry). Most popular universities are the more local ones, Plymouth, Cardiff, Exeter, Swansea, though several to London unis. Any famous leavers? Andy Parsons, the comedian. No comment.

One parent reflected that there was room for improvement. 'Given that the school is a grammar school in an area of low wealth and low expectations, it is disappointing that the school does not do more to lift the ambitions and aspirations of its students leaving school. Given the academic potential of its students, it perhaps should be sending more students each year than it does to Russell Group or equivalent universities. However, that is as much a reflection of the geographical area and the families here as it is of the school.' Interesting.

Money matters: The school ringfences some pupil premium funding to help disadvantaged pupils participate in the range of enrichment opportunities and school trips. This gives families the chance to plan ahead, and it all ties in with the Seven Years at Churston programme of school trips. Funds can also be used to help with revision books, laptops, uniforms, sports or music activities. There is a separate bursary fund 16-19 available for sixth formers.

Remarks: If you live in Torbay, there are three grammar schools to choose from, one for the girls, one for the boys and Churston for those in favour of a co-educational school life. It's a small, family-orientated school that is academic but not exceptional. The biggest difference with Churston is that it's much more relaxed than your average grammar school, maybe because it's co-ed or maybe it's because they aren't stuck in the past tying themselves to traditions. The head and his team work hard to keep the school open to new challenges, fully adaptable for change and in tune with the rest of the world, not just the rolling hills of Devon.

Cirencester Deer Park School

Stroud Road, Cirencester, Gloucestershire GL7 1XB

Pupils: 965 • Ages: 11–16

Tel: 01285 653447
Email: enquiries@deerparkschool.net
Website: www.deerparkschool.net

Head: Since 2003, Ms Chiquita Henson. Read English at Sheffield, PGCE at Bristol. Has taught at Deer Park since 1989 and was deputy head from 1994. Friendly, open and very professional, she was described by a pupil as 'not scary but she gets respect'. Just managing the school's awards and status changes must be a full-time job, but she teaches the occasional lesson and goes on a weekly 'learning walk' where, unannounced, she observes teaching and learning in a particular year group and 'feeds back to staff'. Beyond school she is involved in consultancy, initial teacher training and is trustee of a local educational charity. When asked what makes a good teacher she opts for 'vocation and inspiration, people who give their knowledge but also a little bit of themselves'. Seems to give Deer Park considerably more than a little of herself – parents praise the school's strong leadership team, though a few felt that the head was sometimes 'not so visible'. Free time is for family, catching up with reading and travel.

Academic matters: The head describes the school's successful application for academy status as a 'challenging journey', motivated by a vision that went 'beyond money'. She states that 'greater autonomy will ensure the school maintains its broad curriculum and personalised learning (highly valued by parents and Ofsted)'. At a time when less fortunate schools are having to narrow their focus, academy status allows Deer Park to keep as many qualification options open as necessary.

In 2016 GCSEs, 66 per cent of pupils achieved five or more A*-C including English and maths, with 27 per cent A*/A grades. Students for whom this route is not suitable may opt for BTec First Certificate (continuous assessment, equivalent to two GCSEs) in practical subjects such as applied science, art and design, sport, performing arts and business. Other vocational subjects such as hair and beauty, motor vehicles and childcare are currently offered. Whatever their qualifications are called, when they leave at 16, the school's aim is that pupils will have become 'independent learners and creative thinkers'.

Five lessons of 60 minutes per day are arranged into a two-week timetable. Occasional 'standstill days' when year groups go off timetable and focus on one topic such as slavery – organisations who work in the field run creative activities and the children work collaboratively. The aim is to encourage the pupils to see how different subjects link together and to 'build learning power'.

Lunches are staggered to give lower years plenty of outside time and avoid competing football matches. Pupils are setted by ability in year 7 for maths and for languages and science in year 8, but this is flexible. Year 11 pupils are given targeted revision lessons according to predicted grades. About 20 per cent choose to do triple science, with the rest following the dual award or BTec route. Modern languages on offer are French, German and Spanish.

Big focus on applied and independent learning: we saw a drama lesson where pupils were being gently prompted to evaluate and improve their own performance. In a science lesson pupils were using computers for research, learning about reliable sources – 'We're taught that books are often the most reliable,' said our guide. Pupil teacher relations are respectful and relaxed, and in classes we visited pupils were not distracted from their work by visitors. Two parents' evenings a year, one with the child's tutor, the other with subject teachers; a few grumble that it's not always possible to meet all teachers at the latter, but agree that staff respond very promptly to emails or phone calls.

Parents very positive about the way in which the school organises personalised learning. Individual targets are agreed, these are monitored and if a pupil falls below, help is arranged straight away to get them back on track; the most able children are also stretched and given extension tasks – no coasting allowed. Others appreciate the way that 'resources are shared equally' – in other words, every child gets attention, not just those at the extremes.

Learning support team base is next door to the art rooms. They work with some 13 statemented pupils, another 140 or so are on school action programmes. Provision in place for those with visual or hearing impairment or mobility problems. Highly regarded and successful LIFT (Learning in the Fast Track) scheme is an intensive programme that uses synthetic phonics to improve literacy skills of children who join with low reading ages.

Games, options, the arts: Lots of the above via timetabled lessons, lunchtime and after-school clubs. Choir, orchestra, jazz and steel bands perform locally and abroad. All encouraged to take up an instrument (though our fine year 10 guides had managed to resist). Rehearsals were under way for a summer concert and our visit was accompanied by some very tuneful musicianship. Major whole school production every two years.

Wide programme of inter-school sports fixtures with success at town and county level. Year 11 students can become games captains and take a course to develop leadership skills that they put into practice running clubs and teams. Our year 10 guide seemed to do every sport on offer and had enjoyed umpiring cricket matches at nearby primary schools. Huge sports hall supplements outdoor space. Colours for sports displayed in trophy cabinet.

Resistant materials GCSE class was boys only (apparently two girls taking it in the year above) and girls outnumbering boys in graphics, but lower down the school all get a chance to try out art, DT, food technology, textiles etc. All must take one creative subject at GCSE – the parent of one boy who would not 'naturally have chosen anything arty' is now very enthusiastic about GCSE catering. Students' photographs, paintings and ceramics displayed everywhere, with no danger of being overshadowed by sixth form talents.

Background and atmosphere: Take a deep breath (the information on the school's website is pretty thorough), and click the link to 'history'. This school is a fascinating palimpsest of every change of government and educational dogma since the 1960s. The head has been here long enough to greet direct grant schools coming back in the 21st century as academies – granted academy status in 2011. Also displayed on the website and in the reception area are more badges than on Baden-Powell's sleeve – logos for local, national and international initiatives (no wonder graphic design is such a popular GCSE option). Became a technology college in the early 1990s – a smart move resulting in generous provision of PCs in dedicated 'faculty' IT suites, supplemented by iMacs for music technology. Has also been awarded Schools of Creativity status and a Sportsmark. So, does all this result in an identity crisis? The head is pragmatic. 'Specialisms enable the school to develop a curriculum that is as broad as possible, going beyond core subjects'.

In place of a motto has a rather gnomic phrase beneath its name: 'More than a visible curriculum'. It may not be catchy, but the key words here are 'more than' – the head is determined to grasp every opportunity that's going to broaden and widen the educational experience of local children. Not culturally diverse – the head feels that the award of International School is particularly important: trips abroad are made available to pupils who wouldn't normally get such opportunities.

Mainly 60s buildings with later more or less appealing additions, surrounded by trees and an enviable acreage of playing fields, tennis and netball courts, plus an Astroturf pitch that keeps games going all winter. It's a shame that on the day we visited the path to reception was decorated with discarded wrappers – the school does everything it can with plenty of bins and litter patrols, but on this occasion the packaging seemed to be winning. Head observes wryly that the children are passionate about global environmental issues, but dolphins and rainforests are clearly more engaging than boring old tidiness closer to home. Multi-purpose main hall serves as theatre, venue for whole school assemblies, dining room and occasional gym. Newer Atrium is a light modern space used for exhibitions and socialising at break. Kiosk selling sandwiches, drinks etc probably source of litter – nowhere else to run to at lunchtime (unless you want to visit the Royal Agricultural College over the road).

Uniform is smart navy blue polo shirts with school badge and black trousers or skirts, but revamp in the pipeline at time of our visit. Parents we spoke to not convinced that this will put an end to girls customising skirts à la mode when 'girls from all the other schools do it too'.

All classrooms display yellow posters with the school's 'golden rules' about behaviour and attitude in lessons; also prominent in teaching rooms and on the website are the 'four Rs': resilience, resourcefulness, reflectivity and reciprocity. The head says that these 'form the core aims of teaching and learning'. They're fine words, and we think we know what she means.

Pastoral care, well-being and discipline: Strong belief in 'harnessing the student voice' – collaboration with pupils has resulted in refurbishment of lavatories and even the move of a whole department. Students felt that the languages faculty was a little isolated, so it was relocated closer to the centre of the school; the result was an increased take up of modern languages. No rules as such – instead the whole school has put together 10 'standards', which are regularly reviewed. Transgression results in traditional sanctions, ie detentions for late homework or low-level disruption. Where possible fixed term exclusions (they send the wrong message) are replaced by an 'alternative to exclusion'. Has an inclusion centre for children who need to be out of lessons or for hospital educated children and others who require a gradual supported entry into mainstream lessons.

Discipline doesn't seem to be a major problem – although on our visit we saw a couple of disgruntled pupils standing outside classroom doors, the prevailing atmosphere was studious calm. Our guide said that although this is a large school, she had felt 'recognised as an individual' from day one. Another pupil said that when she came to Deer Park she didn't think she was good at anything, but with the help of her teachers she has discovered that she is.

Pupils and parents: Mixed, as one might expect. Plenty of middle class parents with 'high expectations', who chose Deer Park because it is truly comprehensive (nearby Stroud and Cheltenham operate grammar school system). One such said that the choice of Deer Park over a grammar for her children had 'never felt like a compromise'. Pupils also drawn from less privileged pockets of Cirencester and beyond, but below national average for free school meals. Slight fall in roll (demographics the culprit here) means parents can apply from out of catchment and pupils travel in from as far as Painswick, Stroud and Cricklade – school and public bus services deliver.

Former pupils include Olympic rower Peter Reed and Joe Harris, 18, youngest elected councillor in the country.

Entrance: Approx 33 primaries feed CDPS, but some of the smaller village schools will only be sending one or two per year. Our guides said that most joined the school knowing at least a few other pupils – plenty of partnership work with local primaries promotes smooth transition.

Exit: Nearly all stay in education; many move to next door Cirencester College and some to school sixth forms in Stroud or Cheltenham.

Remarks: Education reforms come and go, and Ms Henson and her team have played a long and successful game on behalf of the children of Cirencester to ensure that their school remains at the forefront of comprehensive excellence. Academy status brings new challenges, but Ms Henson is determined to keep the broadest possible curriculum. Resilience is one of the school's 'four Rs' – Deer Park works hard in order that pupils leave prepared to tackle whatever the future may hold with optimism and confidence. Apply now, before the birthrate rises.

Clayesmore School

Iwerne Minster, Blandford Forum, Dorset DT11 8LL

Pupils: 726; 251 full boarders • Ages: 3–18 • Sixth form: 181 • C of E

Fees: Day £7,350 – 25,020; Boarding £16,860 – £34,110 pa

Tel: 01747 812122
Email: mmccafferty@clayesmore.com
Website: www.clayesmore.com

Head: Since September 2016, Joanne Thomson, previously senior deputy head at Christ's Hospital School. Degree from Warwick, where she captained the 1st XI hockey for three years; masters from Keele. Has been head of English and head of girls' games at Foremarke Hall, ran a boarding house and held various senior posts at Aiglon College in Switzerland. A keen skier, she and her husband Frank (also a teacher and former deputy head) have two teenage children.

Head of prep: Since September 2014, William Dunlop, previously head of first year at Kingston Grammar School. He is a former pupil at Clayesmore Pre-Prep. English degree from Liverpool, then did officer training at Sandhurst and joined the army. Married to Celia, also a teacher; they have two young children at the school.

Academic matters: Years 3 and 4 are taught by form teachers (two sets in year 4 with setting in maths and English). From year 5 children are taught increasingly by subject specialists with 30 minute single or hour long doubles. Lots of practical work (DT and cookery were obviously favourites), geographers go out and about locally: eg locating source of river Iwerne. French is specialist from year 3 (songs and games in pre-prep), separate sciences are taught from year 7 and also Latin to higher sets. Two pre-university and four postgraduate teaching assistants provide support in classrooms and boarding areas. ICT geared to encouraging individualised learning and games are restricted. Personal tutors hold regular tutor group meetings, are responsible for PSHE and stay in charge for two years at a time.

'Not in business of boosting league table positions,' says school, though both GCSE and A level results exceed admission level expectations. In 2016, 29 per cent A*/A at A level; 46 per cent A*/A at GCSE. Year groups of around 100, six sets in core subjects. Interesting variation in English (not met elsewhere) where both top GCSE sets in English are co-ed but lower sets are single sex: 'works really well,' we were told by HOD. Pupils setted in French, science and maths (some entered for IGCSE). Spinney Centre has classrooms for geography, history, business studies and careers, all bristling with the latest computer technology. Welcome flexibility in A level choices and new subjects being added (psychology the newest arrival). Now also offers EPQ and BTecs in IT, hospitality and sport.

Gracious library is well stocked and boarders can study there until 9pm. Adjacent ICT room gleams with Apple hardware in constant use. Launch of VLE facility will give every pupil own screen on school network. DT facilities are good (large workshop with CAD-CAM router and separate graphics studio). Various examples of recent projects on display including a 'storage tyre on wheels' design used in pre-prep. DT students get to try their hand in real world outside (eg with local craftsman David Bowerman). We saw (and smelled) yummy nosh being prepared in food science area: pupils working towards BTec award. HOD runs valued activity (usually as part of CCF programme) for autistic pupils from nearby Forum School. Good take up for languages (French, Spanish and German all available to A level) and Latin also on menu. Language teaching facilities include a digital lab; foreign visits and exchanges are well established. Geographers go to Iceland for fieldwork, scientists have been to CERN, Geneva.

New business centre replicates a trading environment and gives a further boost to success of business studies and economics. BTec qualifications in ICT, hospitality, sport plus travel and tourism keep less academic on board for sixth. Small classes and switched-on teaching account for upward drift. Sixth form essay society and evening lectures broaden horizons; careers teaching includes HE visits.

By no means a specialist SpLD school but provides outstanding learning support for children with slight to moderate learning difficulties: 14 staff (all fully qualified), superb learning support centre (LSC) atop Jubilee Building which includes a lecture hall and IT hub as well as individual teaching rooms. School proud of getting dyslexics into top universities: 'My son has flown since joining Clayesmore and has overcome his dyslexia,' chirped a very satisfied mother. All children are assessed, by an educational psychologist if needed. About 35 per cent of pupils have some form of support, and a 'tiny number' have serious needs. 'Children don't have to have a label,' said SENCo. Progressively more group lessons which are a fraction of cost for one-to-one help. Pupils generally come out of language classes, extra sessions can be timetabled if necessary, everything and anything to help. Good communication between LSC staff and subject teachers: 'have moved to software that supports every teacher in every classroom.' Support for most able too though labels such as 'gifted and talented' are seen as divisive. CReSTeD specialist unit category: listing essential for Forces children, who will be deprived of 'unlimited help indefinitely' otherwise. Strong EAL too, with up to six hours a week, either individual or in pairs. Extra charge for both based on level of need. Academic staff hold frequent meetings to assess pupils' performance and communicate any steps taken quickly to parents.

Games, options, the arts: Sports facilities are superb; prep school has inclusive approach (over 90 per cent play in six or more matches) which doesn't detract from success. County level representation in cricket, rugby, hockey and football. Cross-country, swimming (boarders get a 45 minute slot after prep), tennis and squash (coaching in both) and athletics also on menu. Autumn term split between soccer and rugby for boys. Wide range of sporting activities includes horse-riding and sailing (pupils compete at prep schools regatta). House system provides basis for keen competition (including music) in many areas of school life culminating in annual sports day.

All senior school pupils do sport three times a week and have access to great facilities. Year 9 pupils are expected to try out in major sports. As pupils move up through school there is greater flexibility: non team players generally find their niche by year 11. Impressive fixture lists with some notable successes against bigger schools. A sprinkling of county players, some individuals reaching national levels eg in athletics, and cross-country plus nationally successful orienteering team. Locals share impressive leisure complex: indoor pool, gym, squash courts and modern fitness suite. Sixth formers get free membership for out-of-school sessions. Open swimming in evenings is popular. A few élite swimmers train daily from silly o'clock. Floodlit Astroturf for hockey, tennis and netball. Expeditions on Dartmoor and more ambitiously to Everest base camp, Borneo and Malawi. Regular sports tours abroad (one in pipeline to India). CCF facility includes a rifle range, army and RAF sections for pupils in years 10, 11 and sixth form. Many opt for D of E: high medal haul including golds. Sailing at Ringwood and horse-riding also part of sports programme.

'It's cool to be a musician,' say prep school pupils, most of whom have individual lessons: best reach grade 6/7 level as well as national children's orchestras. Lots of performance opportunities for budding musicians, chapel choir has toured widely. Recent finalists in Pro-Corda competition. Picnic in park welcomes other preps and is school's annual jazz bash in grounds. Exciting senior music happens in purpose-built department run by committed director, assistant and 14 peripatetics. Pupils have scored 100 per cent success in music exams up to diploma level over last 15 years (including 24 at grade 8 in last three years). Concert band has raised staggering £50K for charity over last six years. Regular music tours with singers and instrumentalists: choir has sung at St Mark's, Venice. Next stop for musicians: Helsinki and Tallinn. School welcomes visiting artists: latterly David Owen Norris. Sophisticated electronic keyboards and recording studio useful for A level music technology. Regular representation in national youth choirs and orchestras. Composition master class in Salisbury, loads of internal concerts, ensembles for strings and woodwind, brass group, flute choir. Recent performances have included Marriage of Figaro and Dido and Aeneas.

Drama brings creative arts together in prep school for four major annual productions in senior theatre and 20+ children have LAMDA lessons with good results. Four senior staff currently involved in teaching drama including dynamic HOD whose youthful appearance belies his age. A level theatre studies and three major school productions a year part of varied and inventive menu. Many pupils get involved on technical side; costumes department particularly professional and is overseen by ex-Star Wars wardrobe mistress. Auditioning for Hairspray when we visited and puppets hanging up in green room were for enacting Russian folk tales – quite a skill manipulating puppets. Dance based in social centre and drumming in band room nearby. Masses of tripettes: Bristol, the Old Vic, London. 'Reading plays' give access to more pupils: can perform in costume with script in hand. Mystery plays at Christmas.

Mexican trees of life and Quentin Blake style illustrations competed for wall space in prep art room where lunchtime and after-school activities include pottery, banner art, model making and photography. Outstanding senior art department focuses on championing individuality and creative thinking. Separate village location in former primary school increases the counter-cultural feel: pottery, painting and drawing and sculpture all have discrete spaces.Lively HOD and a real sense of bustle and fun. Sixth formers have a dedicated work space. Latest addition is iMac suite for digital art. We liked the displays of art around the school and admired some senior students' work. End of year exhibition gains universal plaudits. Regular trips to galleries in London and Paris. New DT facility has workshops and design labs.

Keen Greenpower group of pupils won prize for best engineered vehicle at Goodwood meet for electric cars. Recyclers aplenty: eco committee run by geography department.

Prep pupils get out and about: whether it is theatre visits, year 5 pupils experiencing living history in period homes or reception class down at the farm to meet the animals. Popular arts/science week runs at the end of the summer term. Other highlights are ski trips, post common entrance visit to France or Spain for rafting, climbing etc and year 7 trip to Normandy. Year 8 prefects, school and boarding councils ensure pupils' opinions are heard. We liked the annual magazine and the pic filled weekly e-letter (one of the better ones we've seen).Huge range of extra activities four afternoons a week in senior school and all staff expected to run at least one. Pupils can do anything from fencing and yoga to textiles and pottery.

Boarding: Prep boarding full (60 or so) when we visited, day children may stay for a minimum of two nights a week all term if space available. Experienced houseparents (husband teaches by day and is on duty five nights a week, wife provides 'lifeline to parents' by phone) live on site and are supported by assistants, matrons and 'the sisters' (qualified nurses who act as 'super mums'); parents are informed if children in sickbay overnight. Dormitories kept up to mark with reward system which includes extra muck; children are allowed back after working day. Largest dormitories for youngest and thereafter boarders thin out into smaller units. Mobile phones permitted for boarders (overseas boarders also have access to Skype) but have to be handed back to staff before lights out. Relaxed atmosphere at weekends with 40+ children on site: 'we're never bored,' said pupils: late rise on Sundays and lots of 'amazing' trips (we were told about power boat rides). Boarders' Council involved in selecting next batch of assistants.

No dip in senior boarding (60 per cent of pupils) over last eight years. Experienced married houseparents lend distinctive flavour to each of the boarding houses (three boys' and three girls') – all on site except for Devine in former village rectory (where sixth form head of house had cooked a roast lunch for 32 boys the Sunday prior to our visit). Five boys live in a separate house nearby known as 'number four' under the supervision of an adjacent tutor. All round boarding facilities for boys and girls warrant inspectors' recent praise. No separate day houses: works well in school which is majority boarding. Medical centre provides 24 hour cover with permanent nursing staff.

Variety of boarding spaces – most year 9 rooms are five or six bedders, older ones get threes and fours and sixth form either share study bedrooms or get their own. The Capital is sixth form social area with a café (open from 10.30am for paninis, milk shakes etc) down in the London underground-themed basement of main house. 'Watching TV after games a favourite form of relaxation,' sixth formers told us. No alcohol served during week though prefects are granted pub leave on Friday nights. Social centre cum tuck shop for years 9-11 is next to music school and opens up after prep; stages open mic nights etc. Great efforts made to have fun weekends for boarders, including discos, talent contests and popular sixth form parties – houses take turns to organise. Saturday shopping trips organised to gentrified Blandford or Shaftesbury. Southampton shopping mall is most popular destination (for staff too). Duty staff organise Sunday excursions after chapel to local places of interest such as Bath. Boarders may go home on Saturdays after their match commitments – generally mid afternoon – returning by 9pm on Sundays.

Background and atmosphere: Vaguely reminiscent of his gothic revivalist Natural History Museum, the main house (completed in 1878) was designed by Alfred Waterhouse and built for 2nd Baron Wolverton as his country seat. Founded in 1896 by Alexander Devine, school moved to 'Clayesmore's promised land' in 1933 after earlier incarnations in Middlesex, Berkshire and Hampshire. Set in idyllic 62 acre site of well-maintained grounds including a lake (complete with kingfishers and swans) in rural Dorset north of Blandford Forum in the lee of ancient Hambledon Hill.

Sharing senior school site, main prep school building forms a two storey cruciform shape. Proximity of dormitories and classrooms seen as a major advantage. Impressive Everett building provides four classrooms for years 3 and 4, a geography room, two science laboratories and residential accommodation on top floor. Previously based in Charlton Marshall, school was founded in 1929 by Dick Everett, succeeded in 1963 by Lt Col Ivor Edwards-Stewart who, when he retired in 1974, 'funded a school of a most modern design' on the senior school campus. Dedicated play area where pupils have 'muck' (drink and snack) at breaks. Adjacent former gym has been refurbished as drama studio plus social area for year 8 pupils. Surprisingly successful blend of the makeshift (eg creative art department flourishing in somewhat dated prefab) and the purpose built. Former stately squash court houses music department for both prep and senior schools with plenty of practice rooms, separate classrooms, joint ensemble room and a music technology suite. New adventure playground and play facilities include improved ball-park. Joint use also made of sports facilities, senior school dining room (three minute trail to meals even on short legs), chapel and leisure centre.

Pre-prep of 60+ children housed in purpose-built, timber-clad classrooms: delightful sylvan setting with bird watching and pond dipping in Zen garden. Nursery area interconnects with reception class: bugs theme well in evidence (including mobiles) when we visited. All-in-one waterproofs at the ready to help make most of safe outside play and veggie growing areas. Nursery vouchers are accepted. Phonic approach to reading with liking for Read Write Inc. SENCo gives support from outset (all children are assessed aged 5) and one-to-one help where necessary. One mother we spoke to was thrilled by how regular 'Mr Tongue' activity sessions with his teacher had helped her son's speech problem. Regular 'coffee and catch-up' gatherings after drop-off provide opportunity to explain anything of importance and open door policy allows for daily contact between staff and parents. Much use made of circle time to improve children's social and communication skills. Before and after-school clubs and wide range of activities (including swimming) are included in fees.

C

Overriding impression is of a self-contained and happy extended family. Prep children and seniors (often elder siblings) co-exist happily cheek-by-jowl in these beautiful surroundings. Recent additions include Jubilee Building (nine science labs, ICT and learning support) and the even newer Spinney Centre. We were surprised at the lack of a zebra crossing (not for lack of trying on school's part) to get across busy A350 to reach picture postcard village of Iwerne (pronounced Euan) Minster where Devine house (for boys) and the quirky art department can be found. Pleasantly airy dining-hall serves wholesome nosh with copious salad and vegetarian options Good cross-cultural influences include a celebration meal for Chinese New Year. Lovely chapel not quite large enough for increased size of school: one house drops out weekly for Friday service, trad Sunday morning service for boarders. 'School is radically different from five years ago,' claimed deputy head (formerly head of English at Cheltenham Ladies') who pointed to a 'growth mindset' amongst staff.

Pastoral care, well-being and discipline: Prep school parents emphasise good pastoral care and importance given to individual child. 'School wants children to be happy and settled,' we were told. Elder siblings at senior school can be met regularly and are invited to prep for birthday parties.

Senior school reputedly keeps a tight lid on discipline, led by head, deputies and pastoral staff. Rare suspensions for more serious behaviour problems but general ethos one of carrot rather than stick. Tutors (sixth formers choose their own) meet pupils weekly. Christian tradition important (school has Anglican chaplain) but not overbearing.

Pupils and parents: Has become a serious contender on local circuit: we met pupils who had preferred Clayesmore's more intimate atmosphere to impressive facilities elsewhere. Good mix socially: unpretentious lot with some brainboxes but mainly honest citizens who work hard and tend to outperform expectations. A recent sixth former gained selection for Global Young Leaders Conference in Washington as well as a place at Oxford. School minibus service covers all points of the compass within a 25 mile radius with some parents ferrying to and from pick-up points from further afield. Can sometimes stay over if late night activities, weekly boarding OK (casual boarding if space available). Senior pupils can bring their own cars. About five per cent are London refugees, a good sprinkling of expat children (Forces, diplomatic etc) plus a small number of foreign students – eg Russia and Germany. No great green wellie influence. Still predominantly Anglo-Saxon, prep school has won British Council award for international education. Involvement in Comenius programme and global partnerships with Portugal, Gambia and Bangladesh (visiting Bangladeshi teachers were 'bowled over by openness of Clayesmore'). Refugees from state schools and academic hothouses equally at home. Staff-parent meetings timed to coincide with start of two-night exeats. Friends of Clayesmore raise funds for all manner of projects and needs. Clayesmore Society promotes 'The Clayesmore Season', a year-round extravaganza of wider social and cultural activities for family and friends. Electronic reports and newsletters keep parents well informed. Interesting list of former pupils includes former Beatles manager, Brian Epstein; Stephen Joseph (pioneer of theatre in the round); TV artist, Tony Hart; Queen's orthopaedic surgeon, Sir Rodney Sweetnam.

Entrance: Taster day, report from previous school and informal assessment (educational psychologist's report sometimes required) for prep school entrance. Like the senior school, a mainstream school, with a cracking learning support team: 'will take any child we can develop educationally'. Highly praised by CReSTed for its success with dyslexic children. Admissions ramp up dramatically at year 7 (mainly transfers from local primaries). Nursery takes from rising 3s upwards and majority continue through school.

'Ring Margaret' to arrange initial senior school visit (you'll be assured of a tour with pupils and a chat with head). Common entrance at 13+ (places not conditional once offered) for those from prep schools, interview with the head. Flexibility over admissions: school likes to take whole range of academic ability. Sibling friendly: 'if Frank can come so can Phyllis,' we were told. 'Willing all-rounders' and 'kind and thoughtful people' are particularly welcome. Just under half come from own prep with rest from 20 or so local (and some not so local) prep schools: Forres Sandle Manor, Walhampton, Highfield, Durlston Court, Port Regis, Dumpton, Sherborne Prep and Castle Court figure large plus a few from maintained schools. Academic, music and art scholarships, several species of all-rounder awards made each year. Sixth form entrants (from a variety of state and independent schools) need five A/C passes at GCSE.

Exit: More or less seamless transfer from prep to senior school: 90 per cent go on (prep provides half senior school entry). Others to senior schools including Cheltenham College, Dean Close, Oundle, Radley, Rugby, Tudor Hall.

A quarter or so leave after GCSEs for state alternatives. Sixth form leavers head mainly to higher education: a surprisingly steady trickle to Oxbridge (two in 2016), more to Russell Group and then a host of other university destinations eg UCL, Bath, Exeter, Edinburgh, Leeds, Central St Martins, Southampton, Oxford Brookes. Some Forces, some vocational courses. School turns out vets, medics (six in 2016) plus strong art, drama and music stream.

Money matters: Not bargain basement but oodles of scholarships to compensate and help shallower pockets – sixth form up to eight, with a minimum of four reserved for those not presently in the school, others for local candidates (means-tested), plus internal, and music (string players preferred). Scholarships, exhibitions and bursarial help for academics, music and art for entry into senior school at 13 (continuity awards operate from 11 to A level) and more means-tested awards. Closed bursaries for serving members of the Forces.

Remarks: Likely to impress from the moment the prospectus (like no other) drops through the letterbox. Lives up to its marketing image surprisingly well and possibly exceeds it in human terms. Probably what a boarding school should be: not oversize, caring, happy and successful across all ability levels. Ten out of 10 for effort.

Clifton College

32 College Road, Clifton, Bristol BS8 3JH

Pupils: 1,013; 350 boarders • Ages: 2–18 (boarding from year 4) • Sixth form: 336 • C of E

Fees: Day £12,465 – £24,330; Boarding £15,465 – £36,780 pa

Tel: 0117 315 7000
Email: admissions@cliftoncollege.com
Website: www.cliftoncollege.com

Head: Since 2016, Dr Tim Greene MA DPhil (Oxon), who was interim head during the spring term before being appointed head in March 2016. He came to Clifton as head of chemistry in 2006, becoming deputy head (academic) in 2013. He read chemistry, took his DPhil and subsequently became a senior research fellow in inorganic chemistry at Oxford. In 2001, he joined the chemistry department at Exeter University, moving into secondary education at Queen's College, Taunton, in 2005 as head of chemistry. He is married to Lydia Massiah and they have three sons.

Head of prep: Since 2008, John Milne (40s). Educated at Montrose Academy and Dartmouth College, an Ivy League university in the US, where he studied British history; played professional football for Aberdeen before doing PGCE at Bristol University. Met his wife Helen when he started working at Clifton in 1994 (she was a housemistress). The couple ran the British School in Manila until they were persuaded to return with their family. Has piloted the school through a period of significant change, raising its academic profile and leading a merger of the nursery and pre-prep (Butcombe) with Clifton Prep to create one of England's largest prep schools. Parents welcome his strong personality, direct and approachable nature and visibility around the school, firmly setting ethos and values. Jo Newman, formerly at Yateley Manor School in Hampshire, headmistress of the pre-prep, also said to be 'a breath of fresh air'.

Academic matters: Very strong EYFS provision with nursery and reception in own building, fabulously equipped for child-led learning. Messy room was a beach when we visited – one child had insisted on bringing her swimsuit. Children love the smart table, with age-appropriate games and apps, which encourage collaboration. Wonderful early years library. Lovely outdoor area with willow tunnel, fake grass, sandpits, spider frame. Three reception classes. Forest school – every week – an integral part of the curriculum. Lots of feedback for parents – interactive learning diaries, including video and audio, with mums and dads encouraged to add photos and information from home.

Y1 and Y2 follow a topic-based curriculum, with plenty of innovative and imaginative activities to suit all types of learners. Children use iPads increasingly. Four Y3 classes, learning mainly with their class teachers. Y4 has science lessons with specialist teachers; more specialist teaching in various subjects as children move up the school. Scholarship class for high fliers in Y8. Standards and expectations high, but parents and staff adamant that school is not a hothouse. One parent said she specifically chose the school because she felt it would not 'push them to hard too quickly academically' and would develop the whole child. One-to-one support from specialist teachers where needed for children in pre-prep found to have dyslexia, dyscalculia or dyspraxia or other specific learning needs. Prep school has its own specialist learning centre, the Coach House, where short and long term needs are addressed 'as part of the school, not an added extra.' Parents feel that communication has improved. 'Previously reports were a bit vague. A really positive change is that we can access achievement points online through the parent portal. It means I can give my children immediate praise and feedback.'

Academic profile of the school has sharpened, resulting in dramatic improvements in GCSE and A level results, though something of a dip in 2016. 'We have established a new benchmark in terms of expectations,' said head. In 2016, 80 per cent A*-B, 50 per cent A*/A at A level. At I/GCSE, 69 per cent A*/A grades. Success attributed to tougher entrance requirements at all levels and recruitment of very high calibre teachers, including an Oxford don and a research fellow. 'We have some fantastic young subject specialists among our staff. This is a competitive neck of the woods – we have to be on our mettle.' As well as keeping up with Bristol day schools, Clifton now feels it can match many of the top independent schools. Science has always been strong – several Nobel Prizewinners among alumni. Excellent facilities over three floors of the school science building, including the Stone Library, with more than 5,000 science titles. Classics also enjoying a resurgence.

English has been something of a poor relation, but changes expected since the opening in 2015 of a new centre for the subject and for modern foreign languages. Aim is for it to have a university atmosphere, with seminar rooms and a cafeteria. Broad range of subjects on offer in third form (Y9) and fourth and fifth forms (Y10-11). Thirty A level subjects as well as a range of supplementary subjects (sector E) to further develop strengths and interests. Sixth form growing rapidly – now makes up half the school. EAL lessons are provided where needed and additional classes can be purchased. Individual support for students with dyslexia and other specific learning needs is provided to improve literacy and numeracy and exam skills. Independent learning department, with its own head, is in a separate building to ease stress.

Games, options, the arts: 'There's a breathless hush in the Close to-night, Ten to make and the match to win' – lines written by Clifton headmaster Henry Newbolt in 1881 about the beautiful Clifton cricket pitch. Seven years later, AEJ Collins scored 628 not out there in a house match, and WG Grace also played on the turf. No wonder cricket is still a major draw: 'Watching my son play cricket on the Close is just incredible,' said one father. 'He is so proud to wear the kit.' Four ex-county cricketers on the staff providing high-standard coaching for boys and girls, and school has firm links with Gloucestershire CCC. School is the site of the the oldest English inter-school contest in the game of rugby, Clifton College vs Marlborough, the Governor's Cup. Clifton won the 150th anniversary contest recently; trophy presented by Old Cliftonian John Inverdale. It was noted that the rules of the game might have changed since the original 20-a-side fixture, but the rivalry had not. Swimming pool, gym and other sporting facilities on site but most of the games provision is over the Clifton suspension bridge at the school's 90-acre Beggar's Bush grounds. These include a water-based hockey pitch, 3G rugby pitch and a netball and tennis dome. Hockey for girls and boys also of high standard; Lily Owsley won first full international cap while still at the school and was part of the gold medal-winning GB team at the Rio Olympics. Real tennis, racquets, fives, water polo, chess, fencing ... the list goes on. Lots of outdoor pursuits, CCF, trips, expeditions 'developing the whole child'.

Pupils have swimming lessons in the college pool from reception onwards. A host of other sports both on site and at the college's sports ground at Beggar's Bush, including rugby, hockey and football. 'My boys absolutely love the sport, even though they are not A-team kids,' said one mum. Saturday school from year 4 now sports activities only, no lessons. Years 7 and 8 have two lessons followed by matches.

Music is also integral – 'It's in the fabric of the school, embedded, starting in the Pre (prep school). We have an absolutely brilliant music department. Music is seen as a cool thing to do.' Outstanding facilities for recording and practice in the Joseph Cooper Music School. More than half of pupils take instrumental lessons, and they have a wide range of opportunities to perform – chapel, recital hall, theatre – in classical, jazz, blues and many other styles, both solo and in orchestras and ensembles. Alumnus violinist Julia Hwang, BBC Young Musician of the Year finalist, won a scholarship to Cambridge and recently two students won organ scholarships to Oxford. Singing prominent too; chamber choir one of many opportunities. Links with Bristol Old Vic Theatre School provide opportunities for students, as does the Redgrave Theatre, named after former pupil Sir Michael Redgrave. Annual college musical and Shakespeare play are highlights of the school year. New dance studio with sprung floor. Students have talents in art too; Clifton has won the annual Bristol schools' art competition for six years out of nine. DT has been transformed and is now 'more girl-friendly, linked to art rather than a subset of engineering', including graphic design, CAD-CAM and resistant materials. Photography (school has its own darkroom), sculpture and ceramics also popular.

As the prep head points out, 'it's not every school that has a zoo in its back garden.' A firm link has now been established with Bristol Zoo education centre. Positive relationships with state primaries too, and not just in the middle-class area near the school. Music projects and teacher exchanges have been set up with inner-city schools and those on deprived estates and there are aspirations for more local schools to be able to make use of the Beggar's Bush facilities.

Boarding: The school offers day, flexi and full boarding, with the latest trend towards full boarding, often even for those whose family homes are nearby. A total of 11 day and boarding houses for the upper school – with more girls' houses now because of increasing demand. There's a continual programme to upgrade the boarding houses, with the girls and boys often given a say over décor and furnishings. Even parents get involved, helping to upgrade a garden area, for example. Spacious communal facilities, with lots of games and activities. House singing competitions and plays keep them all pretty busy. 'It's full on; you never get bored,' a pupil told us. Some pupils complained to inspectors that there were too many evening and weekend activities, but it was judged that there were 'appropriate facilities to be alone or to mix informally with friends should they so wish'.

There's a day house and a combined day/boarding house each for girls and boys in the prep. Children join the houses from Y4; Y3s have a common room where they can start to feel more independent. Families value the pastoral support from matrons, houseparents and their teams. 'I feel like they are surrounded by people who care. There is always someone to talk to.' 'It is a very nurturing environment.' 'So many people get to know your child, each from a different perspective.' Houses, mostly in Victorian buildings, are well maintained and continually upgraded. A major investment in recent years saw the £3.5 million development of 1 The Avenue, which contains a girls' and boys' day house and a dance studio.

Most full boarders in the prep are Y7 and Y8, although some are younger. British boarders largely from Forces families. 'School is 24/7 even for day pupils,' says head. Weekly boarding and flexi-boarding options popular with busy local families, as are early start and late pick-up wraparound care. Sleepovers for day pupils popular. 'Still a critical mass of boarders around at weekends.' Recognition that children (and adults) get tired and possibly tearful from busy school day and need TLC. Emphasis on supporting families – 'one stop shop, we take care of everything'.

Staff are very sensitive to individual needs and provide a listening ear, and the pupils support one another. 'It's like an extended family, with sisterly relationships.' Houseparents also celebrate personal achievements as well as academic – one has initiated a 'Good Egg' honours board. The dorms are equipped with robust, good quality furniture that can also be used to provide some personal space. Younger pupils are in rooms of up to six, while GCSE students are in threes and sixth-formers in twins or singles. Children swap rooms every term. The houses include kitchen and laundry areas and pupils are encouraged to be increasingly independent.

Background and atmosphere: Describes itself as a traditional British public school with modern teaching values. Founded in 1862 as a 'public school for the people of Bristol' and housed in imposing Victorian buildings. German and Russian families particularly attracted by the 'English boarding school experience package – and we certainly tick the Hogwarts box'. Each day begins in the impressive chapel with a hymn and an assembly led by a different department. Although robustly Anglican, there's also a synagogue as part of the school's Jewish heritage and students of all faiths or none are accommodated. You can wander the cloisters and see team sheets posted on carved wooden boards – though, crucially, the information is also available online. There's a sixth form common room in the Crypt – and how many schools have their own Armoury? The Percival Library is the highlight – 15,000 books on carved wooden shelves, some adorned with fairy lights. A whole wall of titles about or by Old Cliftonians from John Cleese to Earl Haig. During our visit there was a wonderful Alice in Wonderland theme, including a curtain of playing cards, but the 21st century is represented too, with a 3D printer in the library and some excellent DT creations on display in modern cabinets. Dictionaries in many languages are a necessity. Three full-time professional librarians manage physical and digital stock and periodicals and run activities including film clubs, book clubs, creative writing clubs, competitions and events. Lessons still take place on Saturdays, followed by matches. Saturday brunch, a recent innovation, has gone down well with pupils. All food is tasty and ample and the catering operation is impressive.

Prep school restructured from three separate schools – nursery, pre-prep and prep school (popularly known as the Pre) – to an all-through school, aligned with the upper school, allowing for a more seamless curriculum and learning experience for children and for families. Head admits it has been hard for staff – 'not without its issues' – but everyone realised it was being done for the right reasons. 'Some were initially territorial but are now seeing tangible benefits.' In the transition, seven staff with a total of 198 years' experience left. Those who remain are 'reinvigorated', enjoying the challenge of being responsible for curriculum progression from Y1-Y8.

Children benefit from being taught by specialists for music, science, technology, languages, and from access to improved facilities for art and IT. 'There can't be many pre-prep schools that have these kind of facilities at their disposal. We have found subtle ways to keep the best bits and give each part of the school its distinct identity. We were braced for a reaction but parents have embraced it. They were confident the merger would work. They now feel part of one college, not a piece of a big jigsaw. They buy into the Clifton lifestyle and ethos.' Term dates and exeats aligned too. One parent confirmed: 'There was a lot of difference academically between Butcombe (the pre-prep) and the Pre – that's not the case now.' Parents are impressed that the school has sought their views and acted upon them. 'There has been a real willingness to listen.' 'It's a sign of a school that wants to move forward.'

'There is a perception of Clifton as "the toffs on the hill" and I think we have softened that image,' said Mr Milne. He is determined to continue to break down barriers and ensure his pupils realise how fortunate they are and how important it is to care for others. 'We are very much changed, more engaging and more accessible. We can't afford to follow what we did 50 or 70 years ago. The thing I am most proud of is the way social impact has taken off in the prep school,' he said. 'We have always been charity minded but we are taking a step further than cake sales.' As well as working with organisations such as Fairbridge and Prince's Trust, the school runs a unique project called 'Colour My Life' in which staff, parents and some children redecorate and refurbish a home for an underprivileged family, Changing Rooms-style. 'It is one of the most meaningful things we have done. It changes children's outlooks dramatically.'

Pastoral care, well-being and discipline: House masters and mistresses are the lynchpins, leading a team of tutors, matrons and support staff. Pupils of all ages know exactly where to go if they need help or advice and are hugely appreciative of the way they are looked after at school. The school has its own medical centre too. Parents seem happy with the systems in place to let them know what's happening. A comprehensive handbook outlines rules, sanctions and guidelines for so many eventualities. To an outside observer, it's a fascinating mix of ancient and modern: rustication, exeats and removing hands from pockets when passing through the Memorial Arch through to policies on the use of 'legal highs' and dietary supplements. Changes in ICT require all schools to be constantly on the alert; while Skyping mum and dad from the other side of the world is an obvious boon, the use of Wifi enabled devices also presents many challenges.

And, sadly, it's nothing new. Clifton was rocked by the arrest in 2014 of a housemaster who had been downloading indecent images. He was jailed and the school described his actions as an 'unforgivable breach of trust' and an 'affront to our values'. Specialist education lawyers were appointed to ensure best practice over safeguarding and child protection, partly in response to an unannounced ISI inspection in July 2015 that found some written procedures were not up to date, but a reinspection in January 2016 gave it the thumbs up. Parents we spoke to all said they were satisfied with the way college had responded to the matter. 'I think they've handled it well – changes are visible but not obtrusive,' said one.

Pupils and parents: More than 40 nationalities in the school. No one overseas group is dominant. China is the biggest – not Russia, as sometimes perceived. The Russians that do come are from wealthy but not oligarchical backgrounds. Hong Kong has always been strong, these days from both expat Brit and Chinese families. Biggest growth is in children from Western Europe – often with parents working at Airbus in Bristol or EDF in Somerset. Reputation of Bristol as a lively European city, with a wide mix of entrepreneurs and innovators, is a draw. Proximity of the airport makes the school accessible from around the globe. Very able students from countries such as Ukraine are being drawn to Clifton by word of mouth: 'It's a quality rather than a quantity argument for us. Our brand recognition is higher in some countries than in the UK, maybe because we are not inside the M25.'

As one pupil said, having native MFL and Mandarin speakers is a great help when it comes to homework and practising for oral exams. 'We have friends from all over the world.' one pupil observed. This is seen as an asset by many Bristol parents, including doctors, lawyers and other professionals. Proportion of girls in the school continues to increase – now around 40 per cent.

Sixth form has mushroomed; big demand for places, especially for girls. Parents see it as a conduit to the top universities. British families love the life-enriching experience of mixing with brilliant young people from around the world and gaining a global address book. 'The education is excellent, but it is the contacts and opportunities the children are getting that make Clifton stand out,' said one father. Students from some countries struggle a bit with cricket, but football proves a lingua franca and there is a multinational team. 'Our international dimension is one of the great strengths of the school.' Diverse, eclectic. Broader mix of social and economic backgrounds than in some similar schools, thanks to 100 per cent bursaries, which enable sons and daughters of taxi drivers to mingle happily with wealthy offspring of Old Cliftonians. Day and boarding is about a 50/50 split. This, coupled with the position within walking distance of the city centre, enables the school and its staff and pupils to be closely linked with the community.

Alumni include John Cleese, Simon Russell Beale, W G Grace and Sir Arthur Thomas Quiller-Couch.

Entrance: Informal assessment in literacy and maths for Y1, Y2, Y3 (none in EYFS). Entrance tests in English, maths and general ability for Y4-8, Minimum requirement usually appropriate national curriculum Sats level for age group.

Most join the senior school from the prep school, after taking an entrance exam of the same standard as common entrance. Some bring scholarships awarded at 11+. Additional scholarships available at 13+. External candidates take common entrance or common scholarship at age 13. Entry to the sixth form usually conditional on achieving three A grades and three B grades at GCSE, plus an English language paper for overseas students.

Exit: Majority at the prep take scholarship exam and move on to upper school. Some sit common entrance for other major public schools such as Wellington, Marlborough, Kings Bruton.

Around 10-15 per cent leave after GCSEs and others join. Eight Oxbridge places in 2016 and 11 medics/dentists. Other destinations include UCL, Imperial, LSE. But not only academia; high achievers in the arts go to higher education at the London School of Fashion, Central St Martins and the Vienna Conservatoire.

Money matters: Academic, art, music, organ and sport scholarships and awards for up to 25 per cent of fees are offered on merit at 13+ and for sixth form and means-tested bursaries up to 100 per cent of fees are available.

Remarks: Visiting Clifton on a sunny day, the setting is almost too perfect. Among Bristol residents, the college is often viewed as full of rich, rugby kids with little grasp on the realities of life. But these stereotypes go nowhere near telling the story of the school. Whatever their backgrounds, the students are aware that the privileges they enjoy go way beyond the material. They are courteous and respectful – and modest about their frequently incredible achievements. Many of them are fluent in two or three languages. We met a brilliant young Somali boy from a disadvantaged area of Bristol who loves astronomy, intends to become an inventor and has settled in wonderfully to the school. Excellent prospectus gives a flavour – but explore the extensive website to get the widest perspective on life at Clifton College in the second decade of the 21st century.

Clifton High School

College Road, Bristol BS8 3JD

Pupils: 570 • Ages: 3-18 • Sixth form: 65

Fees: £8,340 – £14,160 pa

Tel: 01179 730201
Email: schooloffice@cliftonhigh.bristol.sch.uk
Website: www.cliftonhigh.bristol.sch.uk

Head of School: Since 2008, Dr Alison Neill (50s) PhD BSc PGCE. At Clifton High School for 30 years, progressing from biology teacher to head of sixth form, deputy head, then head of school. Universally (and deservedly) admired by students, staff and parents for not only securing the school's future after what its own literature understates as 'a period of uncertainty at the start of the 21st century' but transforming it. Excellent ratings across the board in 2016 ISI report validate her action in developing a genuine all-through school and turning it co-ed throughout, with a diamond edge model where boys and girls are taught separately for some subjects in years 7- 9. 'It was the right thing to do,' she says. 'We have found our niche.'

Her trademark red hair and colourful clothes mirror Dr Neill's undiminished passion and enthusiasm for inspiring and supporting young people. She delights in seeing old girls return with their own children and takes a keen interest in all current pupils, reading every report from nursery through to sixth form and spending one-to-one time with university applicants as they prepare personal statements.

'Honest' and 'truthful' crop up often in her description of the school's recent history – and its future. Flash new facilities aren't an option. Instead, careful research is carried out before any changes are introduced. Systems and structures have been streamlined and updated to ensure consistency of policy and process. Astute recruitment of younger staff has added dynamism and a sharper edge. Very outward-looking – support from Society of Heads is valued and actively contributes to work on safeguarding, CPD and leadership and management. Strong believer in strategic direction and distributed leadership.

Academic matters: Realising Individual Brilliance is the school's tagline and this emphasis on bringing out the best in every child is valued by parents. Some pupils achieve straight As, but the achievement of everyone who achieves better than expected results is celebrated. Small sixth form cohort causes fluctuating A level headline figures and quite a dip in 2016 with 26 per cent A*/A grades. School says these were in line with ALIS predictions and the value added was the same as in 2015. Fifty per cent A*/A at GCSE. Culture of high expectations and attention to detail. Some parents think brightest pupils used not to be pushed enough but say this has changed recently.

Diamond edge model and all-through might be the USPs but are not principal reasons cited for choosing the school. In a survey, parents of children aged 3 to 18 unanimously said top priority was the 'safe and friendly environment'. This starts in nursery and reception, where there is emphasis on learning through play, led by trained teachers and following the early years foundation stage framework, with perhaps a stronger leaning towards mark-making and introducing letters and words than in some settings. Cursive writing taught from reception. Tapestry online communication system used to share learning journeys with parents. Syllabus based on national curriculum but adapted to needs of pupils – 'we handpick what suits our children'. On-site weekly forest school provision for early years children; off-site for years 1 and 2.

A feature of the all-through school is the use of specialist teachers right from nursery, where children receive input for music and reading. By the time they reach year 6, children have lessons from specialists in eight subjects in the senior school building. 'It gives them a new view of the world,' a parent said. Junior art room, science lab, computer room. Aim is for seamless progression, avoiding dips at transition points. New head of mathematics, with deputy heads and head of school, is leading a drive for excellence. School is investing in staff CPD and development of middle leaders.

Science and modern languages are strengths. Separate sciences are taught from year 7. Children study a rotation of French, German and Spanish in year 7, dropping to two languages in year 8. Latin taught in years 7 and 8 and optional thereafter. Tech rotation in years 7 and 8 too, encompassing music tech, design and innovation, food, creative technology and textiles. Boys and girls are taught separately in years 7-9 for English, maths, biology, physics, chemistry, computing and IT, PE and games and in mixed classes for everything else. From year 10, all classes are mixed. Clifton High was first school in south west to introduce diamond edge, citing 'persuasive arguments' that the model suited the different learning styles of young people of that age. Staff say system is now embedded and enables stretch and challenge. ISI endorsed it, saying 'pupils benefit greatly from the way teaching is adapted to meet the differing needs of boys and girls'. Parents generally happy with it, although one wondered whether putting brightest students of both genders together would be more beneficial. Another said her son liked diamond as it meant he was with more of his friends for more lessons. Students barely seem to notice; they are split into groups for various activities anyway so this is just one more.

Students usually encouraged to sit nine GCSE subjects and three A levels. Nineteen subjects on offer at A level as well as EPQ. HLPQ recently introduced for younger students. Clifton High is also only school outside London to offer specialist teaching of the French curriculum set up by CNED (Centre National d'Enseignement à Distance). It is integrated into each child's timetable, enabling them to learn alongside their peers in England but be able to return to schooling in France at any stage.

Children with SEN are looked after by the enhanced learning department, which also provides for the most able pupils and those with EAL. Some children have additional learning needs including dyslexia, dyspraxia, dyscalculia and ADHD. One-to-one, small group and in-class support by five specialist teachers as needed. Two-week induction for EAL students, followed by individual support. Bespoke provision for pupils with exceptional ability, for example, a maths prodigy in year 4 is already doing GCSE course.

Games, options, the arts: Remarkable number of clubs in proportion to number of pupils – more than 90 across juniors and seniors. Before and after school and at lunchtimes, with senior sports fixtures on Saturdays. One parent suggested pruning for 'quality rather than quantity' but others, and children, value the range. 'More clubs than anyone can fit in a day. Suits my rather quirky boys,' said a mum. Everything from water polo to dissection; circus skills to robotics; debating to singing. Serious about enriching experience for children. Scores of trips too, at least two a week – geography field trips, foreign language visits, World Challenge, ski-ing, sports tours, theatre outings, a planned volunteering venture in The Gambia. Curriculum trips included in fees, which is appreciated by families.

Swimming pool on site; lessons from year 1, supported by sixth formers. Synchronised swimming club and partnership with Bristol Henleaze Swimming Club and University of Bristol swim coaches to train elite squad swimmers from years 4 to 13.

PE lessons and some games at on-site school gymnasium and MUGA but most team games at the school's pitches at Coombe Dingle, shared with the university. Traditional options – rugby, football and cricket for boys and hockey and netball for girls. Tennis and badminton popular with those less keen on team games. School not just for 'softer' boys though; parents insist that rugby and football are strong and smaller numbers can be an advantage: 'if you want to be in the team, you're in!' High number of fixtures also welcomed. Students would like a fitness gym on site.

Music, art and drama all have many outlets too – school production during annual Marquee Week is a highlight. Large scale art installation in stairwell planned to mark 140th anniversary. Private speech and drama lessons and instrumental lessons on offer.

Strong commitment to eco issues. First all-through in south west to gain Eco Schools Green Flag. Grounds, used as extension to classrooms, include a pond, an insect hotel known as Bugingham Palace, beehives, bird boxes, compost areas and a wildflower meadow.

Background and atmosphere: 'It's more like a community than a school,' said a student. All-through ethos much more than lip service. Deputy heads have cross-phase responsibilities; one for up to year 2 and KS3 and the other for KS2 and KS4. Lots of opportunities for pupils of different ages to work together. One mum tells how her son was so impressed in reception by his head boy buddy, a historian, that eight years on he still aspires to emulate him. Years 3 to 13 have joint assemblies – or 'squashy prayers' as the younger children call them. It's becoming a bit crowded as pupil numbers grow. Maximum class size is 20, with two forms of entry up to Year 6, moving to three forms of entry from year 7. Girl/boy numbers now nearly equal.

Students hugely appreciative of teachers' efforts on their behalf. 'Great support, both in their subjects and pastorally. They actually care.' Staff know pupils extremely well and delight in celebrating their talents. Parents, pupils and staff say everyone wants to do well and top academic performers are not considered geeks or nerds – nor are boys who like cooking or singing.

'Culture of Safety' is central to the strategic plan for Clifton High, which is explicit in its expectations of children, staff, parents and visitors – a sensible child protection and safeguarding leaflet is issued to the latter on arrival. There's even a 'no photography' notice in the staff loo.

Communication is another priority. Website and printed marketing information is very clear and of a high standard. Parents happy with levels of information they receive about children's progress and find staff very approachable, face to face or on the phone for younger pupils and email for older. 'We have an email address for every teacher and if there are any issues they are dealt with quickly.' Dr Neill is adamant, though, that staff will not answer emails after 6pm, to protect teachers' well-being. Pupils say internal communication could be better- often short notice of events and activities.

Gradual programme of refurbishment; a new food room had been added before our visit as well as a welcome room for prospective parents. Science next on list for an update, but leaders won't rush into change for sake of it. Wifi being installed and upgraded – not an easy task in Victorian buildings – so school can consider options for using technology to aid teaching and learning. No rush for iPads. Aim is for future-proofing. Continued use of lovely grounds as an asset – an outdoor classroom is latest addition. Parents are realistic: 'They don't have the facilities that other schools have. It's the quality of the teaching staff that keeps us here, their passion and enthusiasm, and also the pastoral care.'

Pastoral care, well-being and discipline: Pastoral matters are top of the agenda at every staff meeting at Clifton High. Providing the best care for every individual is paramount. Dr Neill is acutely aware of increasing pressures on young people, especially from social media, and potential effect on mental health and emotional well-being. She believes becoming co-ed throughout has helped the atmosphere in the school: 'Even a handful of boys dissipates the angst among women and girls.' Male head of pastoral care insists all staff have a pastoral commitment, as well as pupils and parents, and must develop emotional intelligence. 'We're all in it together.' Two tutors for every class of 20. Where possible, one man and one woman per class. Timetabled fortnightly one-to-one tutorials, covering personal issues and life outside school as well as academic matters. All backed up with extensive online records. There's a school nurse and two school counsellors. Sensitive handling – their offices are deliberately sited so that children can visit without anyone knowing where they are going and why and there's a text appointment system – though ultimate aim is to remove stigma over asking for help. Strong peer support programme, with appropriate training, valued by pupils and parents. Year 7 bonding trip also highly successful.

Emphasis on developing pupils' sense of responsibility, rather than too many strict rules. For example, no ban on mobile phones, just expectation that they will be used sensibly. Clear 'what to do if' information in pupil planners. Broad PSHCE programme. 'Respect other people's decisions, opinions, individuality and differences,' says pupil charter.

Very big on rewards at all key stages: house points, brilliance points, emerald envelopes, merit certificates etc etc. Positive reinforcement. Clear ladder of consequences for misdemeanours.

Oddly restrictive on sixth-formers, who are expected to remain on site all day and work in the library during all free periods. Extensive Futures and Skills programme to prepare sixth-formers for adult life.

Early birds club, after-school activities club and a homework room accommodate the need for children to be at school out of hours.

Boarding with host families is offered to some sixth form international students. ISI described this provision as 'exceptional'. No boarders at the time of our visit, but facility to use host families when necessary is viewed as invaluable.

Pupils and parents: The school's vision is to 'develop and attract pupils of above average ability'. There's a recognition that children have talents other than passing exams. Dr Neill also keen to honour loyalty of parents. Most pupils come from professional and business families in Bristol. More than 50 children are French – a reflection of international local employers including Airbus and EDF – with quotas per year group to ensure balance.

Entrance: Nursery, non selective; reception and years 1 and 2, informal assessment by class teacher; years 3-6, formal assessment in English, maths and reading, school report; year 7, entrance exams in English, maths, verbal and non-verbal reasoning for external candidates, meeting for child and parents with head or deputy; similar for years 8 and 9 plus school report; sixth form, school report, actual or predicted exam results, interview, possible subject-specific exams. International students must sit English and maths exams and achieve IELT score of more than 5.5.

Exit: Typically between a fifth and a third leaves after year 6, usually for bigger schools rather than for single sex. Similar proportion leaves after year 11 for bigger independents or state sixth forms that offer wider range of subjects. No pupil has been asked to leave in the last two years. Three-quarters of sixth formers to Russell Group unis in 2016.

Money matters: Scholarships, including for music and sport, and school assisted places bring reductions of up to 50 per cent. Foundation aims eventually to offer 100 per cent scholarships for academically able from disadvantaged backgrounds.

Remarks: 'Everybody knows everybody else.' This was the remarkably consistent message we received during our visits, with parents, children, staff, leaders and governors all agreeing that it was what made Clifton High special. Although the school is growing, it remains small enough for each individual to matter. 'It's very nurturing,' said one parent. 'The atmosphere is quite lovely. It makes me feel I've come home.'

Colyton Grammar School

Whitwell Lane, Colyford, Colyton, Devon EX24 6HN

Pupils: 824 • Ages: 11–18 • Sixth form: 216

Tel: 01297 552327
Email: admin@colytongrammar.devon.sch.uk
Website: www.colytongrammar.devon.sch.uk

Head Teacher: Since September 2016, Tim Harris, previously deputy head of Reading School. History degree from Newcastle and PGCE from Sussex; has previously held a range of posts in non-selective schools in the Berkshire area. He is married with a young son.

Academic matters: Unusual, even revolutionary, in that pupils currently do two years at key stage 3 and two at GCSE, which leaves them with three for A level – but this is changing from 2017. Most do four plus general studies; in 2016, 69 per cent of all entries got A*/A. Despite the accelerated curriculum, GCSE results are fairly impressive – 73 per cent A*/A grades in 2016. Results are generally spectacular considering that, though selective, this is not one of the super selective warhorses. Everyone takes GCSE maths, English lang and lit, three separate sciences, French and RS, plus at least three others.

A level is enriched by the Baccalaureate, which means that pupils also do a personal research paper, critical thinking AS level and programme of community service and awareness, which is integral to their studies. While, as a qualification, this does not increase their chances of a good university place, it gives them a head start in writing their UCAS applications and makes them independent learners – and they seem to enjoy it.

German offered as a second lang, though not a big take up, and Spanish only as a non-exam activity together with Japanese and Latin (though some do take them to GCSE). DT, product design (fantastic DT facilities, though the school doesn't reckon it's one of its strongest subjects), sport, psychology, drama and business studies available, but no economics or engineering, though enterprising pupils have been known to teach themselves subjects such as scientific engineering, with successful results.

Everything is superbly equipped. A rolling modernisation programme has kept everything pretty well up to date, with oodles of computers for class use and in study areas (including some smashing Macs in the music department courtesy of performing arts) and a further IT infrastructure on the way. New labs, music, technology have been added to the site and recently a food technology lab, plus major refurbishment of other technical facilities. Friendly library with librarian or helpful parents on hand and a really efficient lending system, which nonetheless considers books being read more important than books being back on shelves. Cosy corner has subject based academic journals for specialist to browse – and they use it.

Not a huge amount of SEN, though school will provide for pupils with specific needs (eg deafness).

Games, options, the arts: Definitely a school for the all rounder. Huge value attached to extracurricular, which none the less happens mainly in the long lunch hour, because of the scattered catchment (travel difficulties) with only sport, some music and film club regularly after school. Lots of good sports facilities, tennis, hockey, netball and other all weather surfaces all fully occupied at our visit time, and a state-of-the-art sports hall shared with the community who have access during the school day as well as evenings etc. Beautiful sprung floored studio, impressive main hall with everything from cricket nets to TV playback for analysis of performance (PA again), all maintained and cared for by pupils and community users alike. Masses of success in all sports: teams and individuals have an impressive record in east Devon, in netball, tennis, athletics, rugby, badminton, football (girls and boys) and cricket, and also feature regularly at national level in tennis, netball, rugby sevens etc. Lots of outdoor stuff, with a regular crop of D of E golds, as well as Ten Tors. Colyton pupils have starred in every thing from British maths and science Olympiads and poetry competitions to cycle building and mock trial teams, in all of which the school's entries have hit the jackpot.

Music pretty strong and much loved by pupils with three or four big choirs, orchestra and smaller groups set up as interests change. Fantastic new music block equipped with all singing and dancing Mac computers for composing and music quizzes and well as a recording studio, lashings of instruments including smashing new Yamaha Grand pianos provided by the Parents' Association. Lots of adventurous choral stuff on a grand scale with composers Alexander Lestrange and Will Todds conducting own works as well as major trad items like Messiah and Mozart. Though there is a very big take up of instrumental teaching and GCSE music, not many take A level, presumably because of the pressure to do career subjects rather than for lack of enthusiasm. Drama is in the old school hall, now equipped with proper, raked seating, and there are annual productions, recently featuring Shakespeare musicals based on Winter's Tale, Comedy of Errors (taking advantage of some conveniently gifted twins), as well as more serious productions. Modern, airy and impressive art department filled to the brim with work in all media: fascinating pottery sculpture outside the door, some very accomplished painting and portraiture and recently the school has been 'excited and privileged' to have its own sheep and lamb, in the style of German architect Friedensreich Hundertwasser, included in the multi-coloured flock 'grazing' outside Exeter cathedral.

There's not much you can't do at Colyton because anyone with an interest can set up a group, so astronomy, Christian Union, Carnegie (book reviews) etc vie with the usual suspects: Young Enterprise, chess, dance et al, not to forget the extremely enterprising Green Society, which was one of the first tranche of green flags winners and keeps it end up by organising house energy saving contests and building a bug hotel called the Crawl Inn in the field behind the school. Trips abound, music and art doing alternate UK and foreign visits, while a recent initiative is inspecting English vineyard ecology with a view to doing the same in France and Germany under Exeter University's 'Life in the Vines' scheme. The expected range of foreign exchanges. history/geog fieldwork, ski trips and theatre visits.

Background and atmosphere: From the outside, unremarkable, except for the difficulty of actually finding it, hidden as it is among fields and woods along extremely narrow lanes, the school is a pleasant collection of low pink brick buildings. The pretty front façade and cloistered original buildings date from the 30s when the school moved from Colyton town, where it had originally occupied the church porch. It was started in 1546 by the 'feoffees' of Colyton for the benefit of boys of the town, when Henry VIII allowed them to keep the land he had seized from them on condition it was used for the benefit of all.

Once inside the main school, rooms are roomy though low (seagulls tap dance on the flat roofs), and different sections of the school are separated by grassy areas edged with flowers though which one eventually reaches the main campus. This is extremely attractive and beautifully planted with lavender, roses and shrubs in raised beds with outdoor seating areas for the canteen, called Take Five! The huge Cotrill hall, originally a barn, on one edge, provides an assembly space, big enough for the whole school, which meets thrice weekly as well as a concert and exam hall. Whole school assemblies typify the family feel of the school. Pupils have a sense of being grounded in the community, emphasised by the war memorial, which they honour annually, and by the presence of local people and parents in the sports hall and libraries, as well as by the close knit house system and schemes for prefects mentoring younger pupils.

Plenty of new buildings with spanking new labs (the very latest for food technology) technical department and language labs, all situated, like the two sixth form houses, in domestic looking buildings surrounded by gardens, which enhance the villagy feel of Colyton. It also feels very calm despite the masses of activity in all areas.

The sixth form common rooms, though jam-packed at break times, were buzzing gently, not noisy, and the only litter evident in the entire visit was a postage stamp size scrap of paper under a table crowded with chatting youngsters. From one of the English rooms in the upper sixth house (year 12 and 13 are together, while year 11 has its own transitional house), there is a glimpse of the sea over the hill, as well as swathes of maize, pasture, trees and hedges.

Pastoral care, well-being and discipline: Pastoral care is extensive and provided by the school houses: Ash, Beech, Cedar and Oak. In lower school each of the four forms in each year constitutes a house tutor group, though from GCSE onward the form ceases to be a teaching unit. In the three 'sixth form years' the groups are mixed for pastoral supervision, though house loyalties and responsibilities remain. A school counsellor to provides help and supports and trains sixth formers to mentor the rest. Pupils and parents say (and the inspection report endorses) that the atmosphere of trust in the school is such that any problems between pupils are quickly shared with staff, so the bullying policy and code of sanctions are rarely needed. No culture of 'don't tell on your mates' means that bullying hardly happens and any 'name calling or that sort of thing' is dealt with at once. Sanctions are mainly detention with the ultimate for serious crime being 'head's detention' on a Saturday with the threat of exclusion to enforce it. Lots of time spent training new pupils to respect the facilities evidently works very well. Minimum supervision 'because it's not needed in IT rooms, break times' etc. Pupils teachers, ground and canteen staff all seem to function like one big, and happy, family.

Pupils and parents: Pupils come from all over East Devon as far as Exeter one way and Bridport and Chard the other. No school transport but a combination of public and private transport provides a pretty comprehensive network. Pitifully minimal free buses only to those further than three miles for whom it is the nearest school. Very British on the whole though a few enthusiastic families have moved into the area, one even from China. Uniform, strictly adhered to for years 7-10, is black trousers/skirts, white shirt, school blazer and tie. Years 11-13 have choice of black, navy (or dark grey trousers for boys) and jackets, cardigans with blue and white striped shirts worn with quite informal interpretation of the rules in the handbook – school is allowing a fitted shirt for girls to be worn outside skirts. Canteen is open for breakfast but not after school and pupils can stay till 5pm or for matches or the occasional after-school activity, but most rely on the post-school buses. Dividing the school day into only four periods timetabled over a two weeks means that less time wasted, so more than an hour is free for lunchtime extracurricular and tutor time. Small body of supportive parents (with its own excellent website) does masses of fundraising (£30,000 for a new minibus) and a range of services in library etc. Parents commend the school's initiative and openness and think that, if choice is limited by the school's size, it's more than made up for by flexibility and support. Singularly few carps and those mainly about food, uniform and contacting teachers. There is a simple but evidently effective school home agreement, an annual full report and a termly summary of achievement and commitment grades.

Entrance: At 11: not limited to a catchment area but strictly by exam in order of merit for those who qualify by passing the NFER verbal reasoning plus NFER maths and/or school's own English paper (register by early September of year 6). Oversubscribed by about three to one and about half who qualify get in. Apply initially via local authority but parents also have to apply direct to Colyton for the familiarisation/ practice test day. School advises that it's useful to do a few trial tests to see how they work but insists coaching doesn't help. No sixth form admissions in 2017, when the school is changing from a three year to two year sixth form.

Exit: A few may drift off to sixth form college, where they currently have to repeat a year. Impressive tranche to Oxbridge – 14 in 2016 – with two-thirds to top universities (Cardiff, Bath, Birmingham, Durham and Exeter popular); bags of doctors and vets (12 in 2016) and lawyers along with the odd theologian, neuroscientist or astrophysicist, plus a few to art or music.

Money matters: Lots of extras, trips etc and no support for transport.

Remarks: A gem of a school! Truly academic because pupils are interested, happy because everyone trusts each other, unpressurised because of excellent organisation and fun because it combines pleasant surrounding with adventurous activities. Lucky East Devon..

Concord College

39

Acton Burnell Hall, Shrewsbury, Shropshire SY5 7PF

Pupils: 550; 468 full boarders • Ages: 13–18 • Sixth form: 361

Fees: Day £13,500; Boarding £36,000 pa

Tel: 01694 731631
Email: admissions@concordcollege.org.uk
Website: www.concordcollegeuk.com

Principal: Since 2005, Mr Neil Hawkins MA (40s). An experienced schoolmaster, whose former jobs include head of history at Sevenoaks, where he also coached cricket. Immediately before joining Concord he was director of studies at The Leys School, Cambridge. A graduate of the university there, he read history and, even more importantly, 'saw this lovely lady during the first lecture I attended and invited her back to my rooms for tea afterwards'. The lovely lady, Vanessa, now Mrs Hawkins, keeps an eye on the girls' welfare and teaches geography. Students we spoke to described her in the same words as her husband had used.

Engaging, warm and welcoming, with a bubbling sense of humour and an air of inner calm, Mr Hawkins clearly delights in being at Concord – 'As a historian, it is wonderful. Look out there. Over to the right the castle and to the left the Parliamentary Barn'. As principal, he talks with infectious enthusiasm about the students, the staff and the whole set up, cheerfully and convincingly dealing with common misconceptions of the college.

'He really cares about us,' said a student. 'He knows our names, comes into lunch every day and asks us how we're getting on and he listens to our answers. That is why so many student-led initiatives are implemented.' 'He certainly has his finger on the pulse,' said one parent. The right man for the job, and during his reign the college has gone from strength to strength.

Academic matters: The very smart coffee table prospectus – brochure might be a better word – has eye-watering pictures of the beauty of the setting, the excellent facilities and, prominently, masses of statistics. So, too, does the website, so rather than make this entry read like a company report, we highlight unique features. The impressive statistics are freely available elsewhere.

To an extent the school owes its continuing success to statistics. It is, after all, an international school. Parents and children living abroad and searching for the 'best schools' are bound to look closely at league tables and take note. Older, more distinguished, schools may rely on their historical reputation and the perceived social advantages that go with them, but affluent parents from abroad – and 85 per cent of the students are from overseas – are pragmatic in their approach and will go for what appears in those ghastly league tables. Above all, they want to see results, and where better than in those league tables? Concord, not surprisingly, trumpets theirs. In terms of results they are hugely successful, regularly up in the top five of co-educational schools, out-punching many public schools in Shropshire and beyond. 'But,' says the principal, 'I always tell prospective parents and pupils we're not a crammer. We offer so much more.'

And here's the interesting thing about Concord's success compared with so many traditional schools jostling for position in the market place. It uses its results (78 per cent A*/A grades at A level in 2016, and 81 per cent A*/A at GCSE) as an initial attraction and then displays its full range of wares; many other schools display their wares first and then speak quietly, sometimes rather defensively, about their results. Both approaches can stimulate doubts. Visitors to Concord may have them allayed.

In the sixth form students choose to study either three or four subjects to A level. Unsurprisingly, maths and sciences are the most popular subjects, but the principal has been keen to broaden the academic scope to include European languages, history and geography. He cites two Oxford PPE students and a Cambridge historian in recent years, along with other Oxbridge successes. Clearly such possibilities exist, though the humanities at A level are unlikely outstrip maths and the sciences.

The lower school has expanded to over 150 pupils, including a number of local day pupils, some of them from nearby prep schools. The parent of a local girl, who had turned down the offer of a scholarship from a nearby public school, told us that her daughter was ecstatically happy and had grown immeasurably in confidence. 'The best thing we ever did was to send our daughter to Concord, the first school she has ever attended where she has been really happy.' One prep school head we spoke to was full of the praise for Concord's 'delightful' pupils and the amazing facilities.

We had a fascinating series of tours into specific areas of the school, all conducted by different groups of students from the junior to those in their last years. So we were able to talk in depth with some 16 students. They were uniformly open and fresh in their enthusiasm for talking about their school and clearly immensely happy. Not the faintest whiff of arrogance, cynicism or world weariness. Impossible to winkle out a serious complaint and no, the principal had not bribed them. What emerged, with a strength which might surprise some, is that it is 'cool to be clever and to work hard'. Nothing conceited about this, no smugness about recognising they had academic talents, no hint of intellectual superciliousness. They just seemed to delight in their talents and the opportunities to exercise them.

Just as well – academic study is unashamedly and vigorously promoted as the most important aspect of the college. Every Saturday morning students in year 10 and above sit internal tests to give them as much preparation as possible for the public examinations. Some may gasp in horror, muttering 'crammer, crammer', but it does not seem to the students to be force-feeding. One very impressive girl told us it was just to ensure they were 'conceptually sound' – a memorable phrase. This was the same girl, incidentally, who told us, 'I chose to come to Concord because my school in Singapore was too relentlessly academic.' We asked about the pressure to perform well in these and the public exams. 'The pressure does not come so much from the teachers', we were told. 'We are disappointed with ourselves if we do badly.' So is it self-imposed pressure? The boy we asked just chuckled – it was obviously a silly question.

It is sometimes suggested, and some league tables seem to confirm it, that confronted with bright, dedicated girls, boys tend to shrug their shoulders and switch off. Not so here, it would seem. The boys we met and witnessed were perfectly happy to admit how keen they were to do well. It is interesting to note that the boys sometimes outperform the girls.

Games, options, the arts: One of the frequently repeated criticisms that circulate in Shropshire and beyond is that Concord has impressive facilities for sport but no-one uses them. The few football teams perform reasonably well in local leagues; rugby is on the decline. Sport is offered as a recreation, not a religion. That's not to say no interest. One boy told us that when a football match is on the television in the senior school common room (the West End), a visitor might think that Concord was a girls' school – not a boy to be seen (all watching the game). Squash and basketball flourish – we were shown the results of a three-figure thrashing the latter team dished out to a famous local public school; archery, badminton, tennis, athletics, water-polo, fencing, riding, climbing and mountain biking are on offer, with some county players. A huge and impressive sports hall, but really enthusiastic games players should look elsewhere. Lower sixth form students must now attend some physical fitness sessions – mens sana in corpore sano is not completely ignored.

Over the years the school has spread out to include some or much of the village of Acton Burnell, and there in the attractive village is one of the jewels in the Concord crown: the art building. This has no architectural merit at all beyond being functional – the jewels are kept inside, where we saw some inspirational work completed and in progress. Evidence of much imaginative and creative work in textiles, ceramics, photography, painting and graphics. Art is increasingly popular, partly because 'It uses another part of your brain and needs a different sort of concentration', partly because an increasing number of students want to go on to study architecture and, every bit as popular a reason, because it is fun.

Wonderful, wonderful music school, with as good a concert hall as any we have seen. Now well over 100 students take music lessons and more than 60 sing in the choir. A student recently won the Shropshire Concerto competition and for the last two years over 200 students have been involved in charitable fundraising concerts. We were lucky enough to attend an evening concert, which was memorable not just for the high standard of the singing and playing (by all ages), but also for the obvious enjoyment shared by participants and audience alike. A short and entertaining play followed, written and produced by a student. We've seen slicker productions, but it was performed with huge intelligence and zest.

The philosophy club is hugely popular, as are Scrabble, bridge, international societies, charity club, Outreach (voluntary work) and the choir. One Eastern European boy told us, 'In my country, if something is voluntary we run out of the door and into the street. Here I am interested and I go, perhaps because it is voluntary.'

Boarding: The 17 boarding houses, some in the village just beyond the school gates, are comfortable and well laid out; the houseparents are warmly appreciated. The superbly roomy and comfortable common room, the West End, is a popular rendezvous, encouraging school rather than cliquey house friendships and contributing to the sense of community. The food is astonishingly good and in generous proportions and variety – we know of no other school where the dining room is thickly carpeted.

A unique feature of the school is that overseas pupils can – and up to 250 do – stay on during part of the Christmas and all of the Easter holidays, as well as half term holidays, at no extra expense.

Background and atmosphere: As the principal observed, he has a beautiful view from the window of his study in the handsome 18th century building at the heart of the school campus. It is also of historical significance, since the 13th century ruined barn housed what is often referred to as the first meeting of a parliament where the Commons was seriously represented, summoned by Edward I. It gave the principal the opportunity to write that the Princess Royal in 2010 may have been the first member of the royal family to visit since 1283. T S Eliot would have delighted in the Elizabethan tomb in the parish church erected, to Sir Richard Lee, an ancestor of Robert E Lee – here, the intersection of the timeless moment.

The main house, which appears magically out of nowhere as you approach through the lanes of very rural Shropshire, was built in 1814 by a prominent Catholic family who, during the Napoleonic war, gave sanctuary to the Benedictine monks who later went on to found Ampleforth, Downside and Stoneyhurst.

Do the students know about all this history? Well, clearly they know some. Telling us about the excitement and beauty of the fireworks display on the recent 5 November, one of them pointed to the ruined walls of the Parliament Barn and said, 'We succeeded this year.' Others volunteered how much they liked the beauty of the surroundings and the elegance of the main building – 'It does make a difference'.

Over the years, a village of new buildings has grown up around the campus, nearly all of them in keeping with their surroundings. The overall effect is aesthetically pleasing, blending in with the glorious wooded hills that back on to the house – no battle here between beauty and utility. The new, bright, fascinatingly-designed library is a necessary enlargement to the wonderful early 19th century gothic chapel which used to house the books, but now offers comfortable chairs and computers in its new role as a common room. In a room off the chapel (firmly locked) we were told there was a ghost – that is unconfirmed

The school was founded in Sussex in 1949. Nearly 25 years later it moved to its present site and four years later the college accepted girls for the first time. In 1983 it became a charitable trust with a board of trustees, and in order to attract the most able students a substantial scholarship programme was introduced. So nothing hasty about the way in which the school has evolved – no shoring up, no swift changes of direction, just steady building, in every sense.

It is an obviously happy school. Staff and students greet one with a smile of welcome and reveal themselves as friendly, easy conversationalists. Like puppies, if the analogy may be excused, they seem to know no fear but greet with an open freshness, expecting the same in return. This is clearly the result of mutual respect and affection between students and staff, where an impressive mixture of long-serving teachers and young risers. Students obviously cherish the strong sense of community. They had touching stories to tell about the warmth of the welcome they experienced on arrival for the first time – 'I was very anxious as the taxi drew up, but everyone was so kind when I went inside the building that after 10 minutes I suddenly remembered my parents were still in the car'. Another younger girl felt that their shared learning of English drew together students from varied backgrounds and languages.

They showed mutual physical respect – no jostling and shoving, no groups of no-good boyos huddling in the corner planning their next escapade, no boisterous calls, but plenty of vivacity and liveliness, natural courtesy without enforced restriction, boys and girls walking freely together.

Pastoral care, well-being and discipline: The high profile staff involvement is benign rather than military, with a lack of silly idiosyncratic school rules. None of the 20 or so students we asked could come up with any obvious bone of contention. They feel they are listened to and, in return, accept what has been arrived at, often through mutual consent. Trust is at the heart of it all. Smoking and drinking can lead to rustication and eventually expulsion; involvement with drugs leads to instant dismissal.

Pupils and parents: Past pupils remain deeply loyal to their school and frequently send their children to follow in their footsteps. Around 84 per cent of boarders are from overseas. Asians predominate, but a strong African contingent and a burgeoning number from Eastern Europe – in fact about 40 nationalities. A number of local day pupils from a variety of backgrounds has further increased the diversity.

Entrance: Day and boarding applications welcome for year 9, year 10 or year 12. The school is unashamedly selective, especially for year 12 candidates.

Exit: An impressive array of top universities. In 2016, 25 to Oxbridge, and 29 medics; the London universities next along the list, alongside Warwick, Durham, Bristol and York.

Money matters: The school is generous, though not profligate, with scholarships. Details on the website.

Remarks: Those who prefer the chapel and team games approach of the traditional public school won't wish to consider Concord, as in many ways it is the antithesis. Students who seek an excellent academic grounding particularly, but not quite exclusively, in the sciences might be attracted. Those who see the future as global rather than merely western should be interested: international friendships are there for the making. A school where intellect and academia are celebrated, but not at the expense of personal happiness. It really is more than an exam factory – it could be the start of a great adventure.

C

Cotham School

Cotham Lawn Road, Cotham, Bristol BS6 6DT

Pupils: 1,532 • Ages: 11–18 • Sixth form: 860 (joint sixth form with Redland Green School, North Bristol Post-16 Centre)

Tel: 01179 198000
Email: info@cotham.bristol.sch.uk
Website: www.cotham.bristol.sch.uk

Head: Since September 2015, Ms Jo Butler, previously associate head at Preston Manor School in London. Fine art degree from Hull; NPQH, MA leadership from Institute of Education, London. Two teenage daughters.

Academic matters: Results are good for the broadly average ability intake: in 2016, 67 per cent five plus GCSEs including English and maths at A*-C, 24 per cent A*/A grades; at A level, 53 per cent A*-B and 26 per cent A*/A grades.

The sixth form – North Bristol Post 16 Centre – has been a joint operation with nearby Redland Green School since the latter opened in 2007. Sixth form options cover the full academic range, apart from classics. Music, dance, drama and performing arts are popular, but biggest subjects are maths and English.

Most classes are mixed ability up to GCSE, but maths is setted from part-way through year 7, and pull-out groups for those needing more support in core subjects. About a third of year 11 take separate science GCSEs rather than core science, and a handful of BTec courses are offered in business, sports, art and ICT.

Half assigned to do French and the other half German from year 7, and the majority continue to GCSE; Spanish is the optional second language. Latin not offered in the main timetable, but twilight classes are available for those who are interested.

Enrichment schemes for the brightest ones include participation in local and national maths challenges, where Cotham holds its own against many of the local independent schools. Maths was an official specialism, along with ICT.

A specialist, nine-person inclusion/SEN team with its own suite of rooms looks after the 150 or so pupils with special needs, most of them minor.

Games, options, the arts: Dance is the big thing here – specialist school for the performing arts, with a particular strength in dance, so everyone dances for at least the first couple of years. Lots of performances, some to a very high standard, and a fair number take it as far as GCSE or further. Drama in and out of school hours is popular and inclusive.

Music also good – not many schools can boast a complete gamelan orchestra set-up, on top of the more conventional facilities. About 10 per cent of students take private music lessons at school, and practice rooms are available for use at lunchtimes.

Not the sportiest of schools, but plenty going on for the keen. The gym is large and modern; space for outdoor games on site is limited, and more of it was eaten up in the recent redevelopment, but everyone gets a chance at team sports at shared sports fields a coach ride away. The school's performance in less mainstream sports – badminton, basketball, athletics – is respectable, and occasional successes in rugby and netball.

Outdoor pursuits are a strength, despite the inner-city location. Good take up of the Duke of Edinburgh award and a high standard achieved. Also a good track record in the Ten Tors challenge.

Background and atmosphere: Started as Cotham Grammar School in the 1930s but was on a downward slide in reputation and results even before it turned comprehensive in 2001. Under the current head, Ofsted ratings have moved up from satisfactory to good to outstanding, and the school's reputation has soared, making it one of the most oversubscribed in the city. Converted to academy status in 2011, despite some parental opposition.

Shifts in admissions policies and catchment areas have changed the school's character over the years, and the glut of independent schools within a mile or two means some of the brighter potential recruits are skimmed off before entry. The improving reputation may be changing that, although two former independent schools turned academies are also attracting students from the core catchment area. Responding to demand by adding an extra year 7 class every year since 2011, so school will eventually expand to around 1600.

A massive rebuilding and refurbishment programme just squeaked in before the Building Schools for the Future initiative was abolished, so well-designed new buildings with modern labs and art rooms, and the original 1930s building (housing mainly maths and languages) is looking refreshed and more user-friendly. Next on the wish-list is a larger capacity hall, as the one in the main building cannot hold the whole school. Flexible performance spaces get plenty of use for school shows as well as by community groups. The library is large, well-stocked and well-used.

Cotham's half of the shared sixth form is based in a Victorian house along the road from the main school, although A level teaching is scattered over the whole site, and for some classes involves a 15-minute walk to Redland Green. The timetable allows for a steady stream of teenagers walking back and forth between the two at break times.

The site is a bit cramped for the expanding school population, but well-planned, with covered outdoor areas for eating and conversation, as well as areas of grass and tarmac. School food – all 'fairly traded' – is 'pretty good', but the dining room is tiny for the pupil numbers, so many bring packed lunches. No one is allowed off site at lunch time until the sixth form.

Pastoral care, well-being and discipline: A big school – and getting bigger – so a few parents mutter about children getting lost in the crowd, and what they can get up to unsupervised in hidden corners of the site at break times. The head is seen as aiming for a tough but fair stance on discipline and generally as succeeding, with a robust bullying policy and low tolerance for disruption. Uniform – logo sweatshirts and black skirts or trousers – can come across as a bit scruffy.

Form tutors are the first stop for pastoral issues, but a school counsellor to help with problems arising at home as well as in school, and anyone can use weekly drop-in sessions with the counsellor, nurse or outside agencies specialising in drugs, alcohol and sexual health.

Does its best to make transition from primary school easy and has close contacts with feeder schools. Most year 7s will already have spent time at Cotham getting involved in dance programmes while still at primary school, and they get a 'bonding' outdoor activity trip early in the year.

Pupils and parents: As wide a range as you would expect from a school with a catchment stretching down to edgy inner-city areas on one side and over to the arty Georgian terraces of Clifton on the other. Students speak 27 different languages – a broad ethnic mix. Lots of academic, medical and media parents (the school is close to the University of Bristol, the Bristol Royal Infirmary and the BBC). Some parents say the Clifton kids tend to stick in one group, the Somali kids in another and so on, but others report more mixing as time goes on.

Entrance: No changes planned under academy status: non-selective intake, applications through the local authority, and priority depends mainly on distance from the school, with a mapped area of first responsibility.

Exit: About four-fifths stay on for joint sixth entitled North Bristol Post-16 Centre. Lose around 10 per cent at end of year 12. Around a third go on to Russell Group universities, including a few to Oxbridge (eight in 2016) and some medics (12 in 2016).

Remarks: A thriving comprehensive with an arty urban atmosphere, dealing well with local and national challenges, but the pace of the last few years' improvements could be hard to maintain, even with the academy status.

The Cotswold Academy

The Avenue, Bourton-on-the-Water, Cheltenham, Gloucestershire GL54 2BD

Pupils: 1,300 • Ages: 11–18 • Sixth form: 250

Tel: 01451 820554
Email: admin@thecotswoldschool.co.uk
Website: www.cotswold.gloucs.sch.uk

Principal: Since 2011, Will Morgan BSc (Econ) NPQH and Ofsted inspector. Born in Wales, the lilt lingers. Born to teach, too, something that strikes you at once, in his case vocation being not so much innate as congenital, for his father was a teacher also. Has been at The Cotswold since 1997. Promoted from the ranks to head of sixth form in 2002, from thence to the top, quite an achievement since fortune rarely favours the internal candidate and everyone was after this job. Fizzing with physical energy, the possessor of a mind 100 per cent present in the moment, he gives you his complete attention. He's the sort – you can see this at first sight – who gets things done and makes things happen, but he's not one of these kickass super-heads drafted in to turn a school around – because The Cotswold has been riding high for years; the way they do things now is deep in the school's DNA. His job, perhaps rather more invidious, is to keep it where it is. At the top. That's not a recipe for resting on laurels, of course; schools are like sharks: stop swimming and you die.

He evidently loves this place and, though charismatic (and engaging and funny), is not in any way a 'l'ecole c'est moi' sort of head. On the contrary, he is quick to spread the credit: 'I'm only the captain of the side, I am very well supported.' He is, too, by staff and parents, and also by his governors. He has a strong sense of humour and he does a disarming line in self-deprecation: 'My successor as head of sixth form is doing a much better job than I ever did.' So he is comfortable in his position and unquestionably in charge. He's not the ruthless sort but he's resolute – 'unrelenting,' says Ofsted – because he is filled with a sense of mission. School represents the best start a child can get; nothing must stand in the way of that. By all accounts Mr Morgan is an effective manager, but he's not the type who blathers stats slathered with jargon. Okay, 'we're very tight on the data,' not so that the school can look good on paper but so that any student on the blink can be rapidly and precisely supported – as also any underperforming teacher. Underpinning all this is the school's bottom-line belief that the model of a comprehensive school is capable of serving all the needs of every single one of its students, regardless of ability or background: 'Ours is the ethos of a comprehensive school translated to the new environment of competition.' A string of rave inspection reports would seem to endorse this idealistic, egalitarian vision. As, also, the number of students beating a path from local independent schools, something Mr Morgan relishes. 'Cobwebby' is his word for them.

The regulatory architecture and administrative systems of the school are state of the art, but how does it all actually work at the human level? Here is perhaps Mr Morgan's strongest suit. He's a great believer in relationships – interconnectedness. His understanding of the students is impressively insightful. We watched the rapport. He knows them. They all know him. 'He really does care about them,' said a parent. He has a very good students'-eye view of his school as also, we discovered, do the teachers.

Initial first-hand accounts of the school we received were so glowing that we felt impelled to dig deep to uncover the discrepancies between amplification and actuality. Toil as we might, we unearthed nothing but golden nuggets. Truly, there is something special going on here.

Academic matters: Subjects studied are exclusively mainstream, traditional and academic. The school set this course when it started, resisted fads and fashions along the way and finds itself, rightly and happily, on the right side of educational history with nothing to learn from the present government's reform agenda, and nothing to jettison. Results over recent years have been consistent with only minor, inevitable fluctuations.

The 2016 GCSE results were typical. The percentage scoring 5+ grades at A*-C including English and maths was 82, way above the national average and consistent with scores over the preceding few years. Fifty-two per cent achieved their EBacc, twice the national average. Thirty-three per cent of all GCSE entries were at the top A* and A grades. Value-added scores were excellent at all ability levels, especially – this is the really significant bit – among the lower attainers. What's more, progress made by disadvantaged students was at a very similar rate to that of all the others. So the school is unquestionably bringing out the best in all of its students, not just those who are going to look good in the shop window. Around 70 per cent of students proceed to the sixth form; the rest go on to vocational courses at FE colleges or begin apprenticeships.

2016 A level results were also typical. Sixty-eight per cent of grades were A*-B; and 36 per cent were A* or A. Maths and sciences especially strong, as are business studies, geography and history. French, Italian and Spanish on the menu. The school does not cull less able students in order to protect its statistical bottom line. Value-added scores respectable, reflective of the distance covered up to GCSE. In the aftermath of cuts in the post-16 budget, it is encouraging to see the sixth form expanding to 250, which ought to enable the school to fund a good range of subjects.

The sprinters are exceptionally well catered for, no doubt about it: 'I don't believe any other school could have helped my daughter get such good results,' said one parent. But what about the strugglers? Most schools are good at one or the other, not both. We found that students with special needs are exceptionally carefully provided for, as evidenced by the school's Pupil Premium Award in 2016. Support specialists address the full span, from a little light dyslexia to significant learning difficulties and physical disabilities. Provision does not happen in therapeutic isolation but, instead, blurs imperceptibly into pastoral care because all the teachers here spend a good deal of time talking and thinking about the well-being of all their students and constantly share insights with each other and the SEN team. Yes, the aspiration of a 'level playing field for every single student' is not just wishful thinking in a policy document or a bit of eyewash in a vision statement, it really is borne out and made real at the front line. Any prudent scepticism we might have had was blown away by the testimony of parents: 'This school really does have a very big heart'. There was the Asperger's lad with 4s in his Sats on entry who left with straight As in his A levels. He was the recipient of an impressively multi-agency regime which included gap year students hired in to help him with his social skills. 'This was the only school that was positive,' said his mother. 'We still can't believe how well he did. They even picked his classes around him, teachers and students.' Her daughter won a place at a local grammar school but unhesitatingly opted for The Cotswold instead. The mother of a boy with learning difficulties said, 'I can't praise them enough' and is still marvelling that he left with a GCSE in art. "He made lots of friends – we never had any problems with him being picked on."

The school is able to attract excellent teachers not only because of its reputation as a great place to work but also because they can find affordable housing in Cheltenham and Gloucester before rising up the pay scale and moving into one of the villages.

Games, options, the arts: With ample grounds and plenty of outdoorsy students, sport thrives here. Weekly fixtures with local schools for rugby, football, cricket, netball, hockey. Inter-house competitions. Other sports on offer range from cross-country to horsemanship. Yes, there is an equestrian team, for this is racehorse country and at Festival time, in the classroom, minds must be lured back from the Gold Cup. There's a temptingly rich range of extracurricular clubs on offer at lunchtime and after school – 'something for absolutely everyone, indoors and out,' a parent told us. There's Duke of Edinburgh, there's an annual fashion show. There's plenty of music, which is on the up – choir to Gloucester cathedral annually, jazz group to Cheltenham Jazz Festival, tours abroad, inter-house comp, concerts by professional players. Drama is really going places with a brilliant new head of dept. Art is longstandingly stunning.

The school has British Council International status and sponsors trips to faraway places – big point of pride and some big name destinations: Nicaragua, New York, Iceland. There are language exchanges, sports, art and IT trips to Europe. When we visited, the physicists were very fired up about their upcoming trip to CERN. These students certainly get to discover that there's life outside Bourton.

Background and atmosphere: The present school is the offspring of the forced marriage in 1988 of the local secondary mod and Westwood's Grammar School (founded 1589). Wouldn't be where it is today without 16 years' outstanding leadership until 2011 by the redoubtable Mrs Holland, for she it was who set the course – core subjects for all until age 16 – so there's been no frantic pulling up of socks post EBacc. The Cotswold remains a school that very much looks to itself and whose inspiration comes from the values it has set itself, making it not a 'better than' but, rather, a 'best we can be' sort of place. Accolades when they have come have come unlooked for – to their slightly surprised gratification.

Technically The Cotswold is an academy (one of the first wave in 2010) but in Mr Morgan's analysis it is 'a grammar school within a comprehensive'. True up to a point, but no grammar school vanities here and the sixth formers are in any case more reminiscent of sixth form college students in their general grown-upness and pre-university demeanour. When we burst into their common room unannounced... sssh, everyone was beavering away in an amazingly purposeful way. You don't often see that.

Set in all of 32 green acres on the outer fringes of Bourton. Some handsome new buildings. Good new maths block (2014). Overall, better than yer average. Classy sports hall with swimming pool, gym and steam room spa used by the whole community. Bright displays in the classrooms. Lively, cheerful, roomy. Panoramic views of the glorious Gloucestershire landscape from classroom windows – the students sit with their backs to them – so, a country feel. Expansion is constrained by an archaeological preservation order on most of the grounds and also by self-denying ordinance: they feel that to grow is to risk losing something so they do so only circumspectly.

The school is upping its presence in the community and beyond. There's a marketing and development manager – an uncommon appointment – whose role is to improve links with local schools and businesses. There's one-to-one careers guidance, as you would expect, plus a programme of guest speakers from universities and vocational colleges. Local employers come in to talk about apprenticeships. Strong links with the Rotary and a strong showing in Rotary competitions.

They're a charitable lot. They've sent coats to Syria, and every year at Christmas time the year 11 students lay on an afternoon of festivities for local senior citizens.

Former students include jockeys Sam and Willy Twiston-Davies, motor racing ace Alice Powell and stammerer Richard Whincup (Google him) whose speech day adventures say so much about this place.

Pastoral care, well-being and discipline: The first thing that strikes you when you arrive, along with the cheery greeting from the receptionist (makes such a difference) is the marvellous calm of the place. It's an impression confirmed when you tour the school – purposeful students, fired-up teachers, all of them going places. Too good to be true? Sure, occasional evidence of fleeting teenage world-weariness behind some desks, but on the whole exactly as you'd like it. Significantly, teachers don't break stride when the principal walks in, neither do the students.

Parents rate the pastoral care highly. Support systems are actively interventionist – and some of these students need a lot of support. All feeder schools are visited in the year before a child comes so that strategies can be created for those with issues of any kind, from special needs to chaotic home life, where efforts are made also to get parents onside. The school wants, said a parent, 'everyone to be busy, to try new things, never to miss out', especially the less confident and those from deprived homes, who are equipped with refurbed laptops so they don't feel different. Teachers play an active part in monitoring the morale of all their students. They really are an impressively extra-mile lot. There are even 'invisible tutors' unknown to their charges, making sure they're happy having a go. How good is that?

Pastoral care systems reactively pick up on and address discipline issues, nipping bad things in the bud at the talk-it-through stage if possible. Everyone agrees that good conduct is an expectation exerted with rigour – 'they can come down hard,' said one parent, 'but they're fair' – and the code has plenty of student buy-in. One parent whose Asperger's son lashed out on the school bus feared the worst, but the head sat the two lads down, they talked it through and now they're great friends. Mr Morgan says that young people are kinder today. Has human nature really changed that much? We think he should credit himself and his team for a culture in which diversity of personality is celebrated. Is this a safe space for the bookish, the nerdy and the eccentric? One mother was reassured when her daughters were about to start here: 'There is a friend for everyone at The Cotswold.' Sounds a bit cheesy? Well, the best schools are. Exclusion is rare. One capital crime is affecting the work and happiness of other students. Another is a one-off act of violence. They're hot on bullying and actively discourage Facebook. School uniform is worn exactly as prescribed, shirts adrift instantly denounced. Dress code for sixth formers smart casual, with the scales tipping towards casual. Parents praise response times when problems arise: 'They really do care if something's not right'. There is a thriving PTA.

Pupils and parents: The complete Cotswold spectrum, socially, from the landed to the dispossessed. Bourton, self-styled Venice of the Cotswolds, is a never-never land English idyll – the old part, that is, twee as can be, frozen in time, mossed cottages, babbling brook, golden stone, the full monty – the sort of place where tourists daily overwhelm the inhabitants and possibly trample them underfoot. All this make believe quickly dissipates at the periphery of the village, where mundane contemporary realities and associated dowdy domestic architecture reassert themselves. The same is true of surrounding villages where well-heeled prosperity and rural deprivation live cheek by jowl. Does this lead to stratification at school? Cliques? No, say the students, but we didn't take no for an answer and drilled down. And, d'you know, they're right. It turns out that the school really is what it sets out to be: socially, a level playing field. One student said 'It's funny, you get invited to someone's house and when you arrive it's, like, really big and you think wow, I never knew'. One prominently posh student assured us she'd had 'no problems at all' transferring from an independent school. The experience had certainly not impaired her vowels. The mix here is majority white and 'working class'.

The recent decline in rating of another local school has left The Cotswold pre-eminent. It was Sunday Times Comprehensive of the Year 2015-16 and is listed by Tatler. Its resultant popularity means that the area from which it recruits outside its catchment area is shrinking year on year, but not significantly on account of middle-class colonisation.

Entrance: Priority to looked after children, siblings, those living in the catchment area then by distance. Five A*-Cs at GCSE for sixth form, mostly with top grades for chosen A levels. Accepts new students at all ages if there's room.

Exit: In 2016, four to Oxbridge and around half to Russell Group universities. Those with a vocational bent urged to stay to the end of year 11 and get some decent GCSEs under their belts. Big focus presently on post-16 education pathways.

Remarks: Difficult to land a glove on, try as we might. Here is a school which has been marching to the beat of its own drum for decades, propelled by its idea of an education and making good on its commitment to providing a level playing for all, regardless of ability, disability or social background. For parents who can afford an independent education it offers a compelling alternative; for those who can't it offers a best-chance saloon.

Dauntsey's School

West Lavington, Devizes, Wiltshire SN10 4HE

Pupils: 833; 295 full boarders • Ages: 11–18 • Sixth form: 273

Fees: Day £17,940; Boarding £29,700 – £34,290 pa

Tel: 01380 814500
Email: info@dauntseys.org
Website: www.dauntseys.org

Head Master: Since 2012, Mr Mark Lascelles (40s), previously lower master, and temporary acting head of King's School Canterbury – something of a rough ride. He was educated at Shrewsbury School and Durham, where he read geography and was keen and proficient in cricket and football to county level and beyond. Now he only plays social cricket – frustrating, as he is very competitive. Back at Shrewsbury for a further 17 years, he became a housemaster and coached many of the Shrewsbury teams before joining King's School in 2009. He is married to Amber, a teacher and graduate of Durham, who was a national level canoeist. They have three young daughters.

Mr Lascelles is stunned by 'the quality of pupils' at Dauntsey's, not just their academic level but their genuine niceness and the energy injected by having an intake at 11: something he had 'missed out on before'. He sees Dauntsey's as a collegiate school, for families who understand about good education, and are not blinded by fashionable pretension.

So far both the curriculum and the classrooms are quite traditional (he promised not to make changes early) but the stunningly high level of pupil satisfaction registered in the recent ISI inspection bears witness to the excellence of the teaching. Parents like him and say he is accessible, listens and takes a personal interest in all pupils, meeting the school bus every morning and being a friendly presence at most activities. He had a hard act to follow and is very different to his predecessor, 'but has finally mastered the art of feeding biscuits to paddling canoeists as they pass in the Devizes to Westminster race!' Out of school he enjoys travel, skiing, reading and theatre – and is rapidly developing a taste for musicals, which is just as well as at the time of our visit Dauntsey's was about to put on Sondheim's Into the Woods followed by Mamma Mia.

Academic matters: Over the last few years Dauntsey's has come up quite a few pegs in the academic stakes and has a pretty impressive record for a 'not overly selective' school – though of course success breeds demand which ups the ante. In 2016, 46 per cent A*/A grades at A level and 78 per cent at GCSE – mostly IGCSEs which, pupils say, 'prepare better for A level'.

Big Cheeses of the school world locally should look to their laurels or Dauntsey's might pip them at the post. Curriculum includes a four language carousel of French, German, Latin, and Spanish for the first year from which two or three languages may be chosen. Other languages – Mandarin, Russian, Japanese, Greek, Arabic etc – are done in extracurricular time. Native speakers are encouraged to take exams in their own languages.

Three science IGCSEs for two-thirds of the year group; the rest do dual award science (three sciences taken as two GCSEs). Spanking new science labs full of GCSE groups practising practicals. A spectacular full-size skeleton monoplane hangs in the hallway and the charming courtyard with super bosky pond has raised beds crammed with Japanese anemones.

No limits on choices at A level. Pupils can now take three plus an additional AS, the EPQ, sport or Dauntsey's own leadership qualification. DT (resistant materials), in a whizzy new class room, with new courses in psychology, history of art and English language starting. Outstanding in maths and further maths and more than sound across a very wide board including theatre studies, music technology and class civ as well as the mainstream stuff.

Class size around 16 in GCSE years. Busy SEN department with three full-time staff providing help, within the timetable but at extra cost. Mainly helps mild dyslexia and offers a safety net for the organisationally challenged but, 'If pupils pass the entrance exam,' says the head, 'it is rare for us to say we can't cope with their special needs'. Impressively wheelchair friendly (even disabled wet-room showers) for a school with no current need for it. Thirty or so need and get EFL tuition, which is thrown in as part of the special enhanced international fees. Efficient IT taken for granted, having virtually reached IT saturation point, though pupils are pretty impressed that free standing printers at convenient points access and print from their personal files activated by thumbprint. Pupils register by thumbprint too for afternoon school, but house staff like to lay eyes on everyone in the morning.

Games, options, the arts: Sport is definitely big and timetabled three times a week. Boys' and girls' hockey, rugby and cricket doing pretty well at county and regional level. Football played in senior years, tennis, for all, and netball, for girls, all tackled competitively. A smart-looking rugby pavilion graces the grassy expanse in front of the main school and a new pavilion with lecture facilities was recently completed.

Girls regularly send a hockey team to South Africa to match the triennial rugby tour of the Australia, and there is no shortage of opportunity. The recently acquired Mercers' field has extensive pitches, 'levelled by computer,' pupils say. Archery happens there but was elusive on our visit, though we spotted the coach's van. A huge range of 'strenuous pursuits' available in the 'long break'.

Situation alone gives Dauntsey's a whiff of bracing contact with the great outdoors, focussed, during our visit, on the whole school cross-county race. The delightful lower school guides, when asked what happened to non-sporty people, didn't think there were any. Some parents feel that the less talented enthusiasts need more chances to play in teams, even against each other. Masses of expeditions like the Brecons Challenge and a long distance canoe race from Devizes to Westminster. Moonrakers, a third year programme, offers all sorts of outdoor adventure challenges (at no extra cost), and the more ambitious Dauntsey's Mountaineering and Expedition Society travels to the orphanage they have adopted in Romania or visits their contacts in Bhutan. Lots do D of E though they skip silver because of exam pressure.

Solid rather than spectacular facilities – indoor swimming pool, two handsome Astros, sports hall, new dance studio, athletics track a hike away – a source of grumbles for a few; macho fitness area with scary weights and levers has had a facelift and a bit more space. Too unusual to omit is the sailing club. No Optimists or Fireflies on a pond for Dauntsey's, instead school has bought a 100 year old tall ship, the Jolie Brise. Pupils have competed in the Fastnet (she actually won the first in 1925); they also cruise more lazily off the Isle of Wight. Everyone gets a go in mixed teams of eight and parents are envious.

What the music department lacks in size it makes up in enthusiasm – multitudinous groups of every genre happily play away, certainly more than 20 groups timetabled – choirs, orchestras bands. It needs a bit more space. A good take up of instrumental tuition on every instrument ever invented makes for plentiful concerts with some mature and accomplished performance. Practice sessions timetabled for junior boarders.

There is serious drama – King Lear is probably as serious as it gets – when enthusiastic performers can be weaned away from everyone's first love, the many enormous school musicals and 'extraordinary performances' which sometimes even make it to London theatres. Smashing A level results in theatre studies. The multi-function 'memorial' school hall has really good lighting and equipment thanks links with the West End. Plans are a foot to refurbish it with better seating (sinking into the floor) though it would be a pity to end such bizarre juxtapositions as the stately school altar, sanctuary and organ at one end and a stunning full size white puppet cow at the other. Annabel's, the well-equipped drama studio, has everything needed to launch careers via the Edinburgh fringe and such venues. Good and popular dance studios too – it's in the curriculum – with a few boys taking part.

Across the playing field, the chimneyed art block has a deceptively arts and crafts look but is full of all the relevant IT and pottery things. It's about to get an upgrade to make more space and dark room for photography planned for A level. Head of art keen on observational drawing. Bags of school trips – modern languages to Spain and France, geography to Iceland, RS to India, Adventurers to Bhutan, skiing in Italy

There's not much you can't do at Dauntsey's, which is probably just as well for 300 or so boarders residing in a leafy backwater.

Boarding: One advantage of being almost at the back of beyond is that Dauntsey's has plenty of room to spread itself – a seven hole golf course at the Manor House (co-ed boarding for juniors) who undoubtedly get the prettiest building. Some choose to ramble home through a lovely mile of so of woodland path, from which their Victorian mock Tudor mansion welcomes them at 4.30pm into a spacious galleried hall with inviting sofas round blazing fire in winter, to take tea and delicious looking scones and cake. It's a spick and span version of Hogwarts, with its long oak tables and panelled common rooms smelling of furniture polish rather than 60 small boys and girls. Dormitories are functional but spacious with lovely views, weekends full of well planned, child friendly activity, mostly on the spot.

Boarding houses (single sex), both old and new are exceptionally spacious, some with en-suite facilities and all have kitchens, workspace and proper recreation area. A sixth former described it as 'certainly better than adequate but not quite luxury'. Day houses get everything the boarders have except the bedrooms and the juniors have their own similar on-site day centre.

Background and atmosphere: Founded in West Lavington in 1542 on the deathbed largesse of William Dauntsey, master of the Worshipful Company of Mercers, the school opened in 1895. Mercers' Company still provides six governors, occasional generous financial help and annual knees-up for its associated schools which include an unlikely spread from St Paul's Schools in London – both boys' and girls' versions – to Peter Symonds College (state sixth form in Winchester), two new academies and The Royal Ballet School.

Lawns and trees enhance the setting of the handsome main school building, and the recently redesigned reception area is reminiscent of a five star hotel with its glass topped tables, comfortable furniture and well lit pictures changed regularly by the art department – and it is nice to see the artist's names. Other facilities are more functional, but very well maintained. Perhaps a bit countrified for some hardened Londoners – until 1930 the school was known as Dauntsey's Agricultural School.

Dauntsey's has mushroomed, to the extent that buildings jostle haphazardly with an increasing number of lawned and planted milling-about spaces between buildings, so the brightly coloured maps at every corner are necessity not decoration. A young pupil claimed to have taken only a week to find his way about. What impresses is that it has absolutely every facility a school should have but nothing extravagant.

The most spectacular feature is a superb bright and airy new library – which must say something about academic priorities. Some exposed desks/computers down the centre of the building may not be everyone's cup of tea (where do they hide the sweet packet?) but more sheltered study space is available upstairs plus round tables and comfy chairs for a good read. Fooling around can be done in the cyber café or in the tuckshop. Lessons finish at 4pm and it is technically possible for day pupils to creep off then, but most stay on for prep or take part in clubs or sports until the mass bus exodus at 5.30pm. Boarders have two hours of prep in the evenings, one just before and one after supper.

Uniform is as expensive but not more than most. Girls have a rather limp blue check skirt with blue blouse and pullover. Boys in blue shirt and grey-blue jacket. No uniform in sixth form but smart-ish dress required (suits or chinos, tie and jacket for boys and at least a nod towards formality for girls) – quite widely interpreted. The reversible black and white rugby shirts are just being phased out for smart though less popular mainly white ones which wash better but get smelly very quickly. The busy school shop has an endless supply to lend to those who forget games things. The san is modern and inviting with quiet places to sit and suffer and comfortable looking bedrooms. Pupils definitely value the care given there, including counselling.

Pastoral care, well-being and discipline: Much less privilege orientated than many schools, so apart from the 17 Club, which is the hub of sixth form social life, and biscuits at morning break, sixth form and prefects live and work alongside the upper school and take a full part in house life. Relationships between year groups are definitely flexible. The pastoral system functions through the houses, in which the house staff and at least four assistants act as tutors to about 60 pupils. Parents say problems are handled successfully and with great sensitivity.

Breakfast provided for all-comers in the pleasant dining hall. Boarders have to be there by 8.15am. Buffet service with spectacular and popular 'live cook' every day and all meals in on the fees though not compulsory. Staggered sittings to manage flow of hungry diners but a few choose to use the house kitchens if the dining room is full.

Responsibilities taken seriously by prefects and captains of houses, who are selected by head and staff. Drugs get immediate expulsion and pupils know it. Apart from that, 'rules are', pupils say, 'a matter of common sense', though a new rule book is issued each year. The comments they made on 'how far into the opposite sex house' they are allowed showed they had a pretty shrewd idea of what is and is not acceptable. They also emphasised the trust between pupils and staff.

Pupils and parents: Not toffs on the whole, more local families, farmers and small businesses, with quite a number from state primaries or first time buyers. Lots of professional families with two parents working to earn the fees. Being just over an hour from London, Bristol and Southampton makes boarding pretty accessible from UK or abroad. International intake widening from Hong Kong and Russia to a wide spread of countries: Europe and beyond. Fifteen bus routes from Salisbury (south), Swindon (north), west to Frome and east to Hungerford and Andover, which puts them into competition with a number of good grammar schools as well as some top independents.

Entrance: At 11+, from state schools and a few preps, entry is by Dauntsey's own exam (maths, English, VR and optional music auditions). Selective in that they accept about the same standard of candidates as Salisbury Grammar, according to the head. At 13+ they take mainly boarders from prep school and some from abroad via 13+ CE or scholarship exams, with very few day places at this stage, adding an extra two forms. Feeders include Chafyn Grove, St Francis (Pewsey) and St Margaret's (Calne), All Hallows and Thorngrove plus many local state primaries. Everyone sitting an exam at 11+ is automatically considered for a scholarship and around 15 pupils out of 80 admitted get some sort of award.

Some 50 pupils join the school for sixth form, around a third from abroad – a minimum of three A and three B grades at GCSE is required from UK pupils, plus interview.

Exit: A trickle – some 10 per cent – leave after GCSEs, mainly for local sixth from colleges. Good proportion to solid science, medicine, languages etc courses at uni (Exeter, Bristol, Birmingham and Cardiff popular recently) and a respectable number to Oxbridge (four in 2016 plus five medics).

Money matters: Much more aware than many schools that parents' resources are not infinite. The vibe from parents is that day fees here particularly good value for money. A few nice touches: music lessons cost the full whack for first instrument but less for second and subsequent ones; a 10 per cent reduction for siblings who are boarding at the same time (a very sibling-friendly school). Mercers' connection is a help when it comes to funding building projects but not a bottomless pit.

Remarks: It's in there competing with the heavies but still unpretentious, with feet firmly on the ground. Parents value its special atmosphere, rooted in being reasonably non-selective, both academically and socially. Steadily improving results and facilities are putting Dauntsey's among the front-runners in the area. Its friendliness, breezy campus and outdoorsy image belie a focussed academic purpose, which encompasses arts and sciences, though it doesn't inhibit the pupils from having a pretty good time. Dauntsey's is fab.

D

Dean Close School

Shelburne Road, Cheltenham, Gloucestershire GL51 6HE

Pupils: 899 pupils; 240 full, 30 flexi boarders • Ages: 2–18 • Sixth form: 182

Fees: Day £10,765 – £23,316; Boarding £18,882 – £35,316 pa

Tel: 01242 258044
Email: registrar@deanclose.org.uk
Website: www.deanclose.org.uk

Headmaster: Since 2015, Bradley Salisbury MEd PGCE, deputy head at the school since 2009 and a successful acting headmaster. After studying at University of Leeds (completed part time masters at Bristol), taught religious studies at Gordano School before moving first to Bristol Cathedral School as head of department and head of years ten and 11 and then to Wells Cathedral School where he was head of religious studies and a housemaster.

Head of prep: Since September 2015, Paddy Moss, who was previously head of St Andrew's Prep School, Turi, in Kenya. He attended the school himself in the 1970s and was head of the prep between 2006 and 2015. His wife, Julie, is also a teacher and they have three daughters.

Pre-prep, fondly known as The Squirrels, headed since 2011 by Dr Carolyn Shelley.

Academic matters: Early years' focus on developing children's senses, to prepare them for learning in prep and beyond. Plenty of hands-on activities, positive reinforcement and encouragement for achievement of all kinds, not just academic. These Squirrels are fortunate enough to have their own forest school in the extensive grounds – regular visits allow them to experience the changing seasons, go on expeditions and meet small invertebrates. Back indoors, facilities are just as appealing: great library and ICT suite – all designed for this age group – plus ground floor classrooms linked by creative areas.

The school aims to 'fire the imagination and enthusiasm of every pupil', and children here benefit from subject specialist teachers, increasingly as they move towards common entrance. Setting from year 6 onwards based on individual learning plans. Subject knowledge boosted by frequent trips and plenty of hands-on activities – the emphasis is still on fun and teamwork. Those with mild dyslexia, numeracy or specific curriculum needs are supported in groups or one-to-one by specialist SEN staff; EFL also offered.

Solid results for all at GCSE and A level and though year groups vary, the trend is upwards. The head says that the school looks for 'attitude as well as aptitude', a statement that demonstrates his confidence in the school's proven ability to develop and boost its pupils.

In 2016, GCSE/IGCSE: 58 per cent A*/A. Twenty-two subjects offered, with most taking 10 or 11, smallish numbers for classics, Latin and Greek. Separate sciences, excellent maths and physics results. At A level, 67 per cent A*-B, 41 per cent A*/A. Once again the mathematicians are light years ahead with A*/As – whatever it is they put in the water in the maths department should be bottled.

Classes are small, between 15 and 20 (12 in the sixth form) and teachers, according to one parent 'work with each child's individual abilities', and, according to another, 'achieve miracles'. Mild SEN (dyslexia, dyspraxia) catered for and EAL is taught in individual lessons or groups.

The head is proud of the extension programme for sixth formers designed to help them develop critical thinking skills, engage with different ideas and 'confront non-standard stuff'. A critical essay competition open to the whole school is judged by an external adjudicator and keenly contested.

Games, options, the arts: Dean Close is the Schola Cantorum for Tewkesbury Abbey, educating the boy choristers who sing there (four evensongs and Sunday services). Several other choirs, orchestras, ensembles and bands give ample opportunities for young players and singers to perform in house and at public events such as the Cheltenham festival of performing arts. Speech and drama thriving, with both timetabled and extracurricular sessions – great for confidence building. The list of clubs, many set up by the children themselves, runs from the predictable Warhammer to the gloriously unexpected Norman Wisdom film club, and takes in Fun with Wool, Start Greek, gymnastics and riding along the way.

Prep is separated by playing fields from big school but with use of seniors' specialist sports facilities, such as dance studio and pool, in addition to their own considerable outdoor and indoor provision. At least four sessions of timetabled sport a week plus the option to join clubs and try out shooting, climbing, dance and golf. The floodlit, covered play area is a great asset, a huge space for pupils to race about, kick balls and even roller blade in, no matter what the West Country weather throws at them.

Hockey is the game here for senior boys and girls, with seemingly every team vanquishing all comers, including the likes of Millfield, to become county champions and national finalists. One of our guides was a rugby fanatic but realistic about his school's performance against the big names: 'We're probably not near the top'. Emphasis is on everyone getting a game – at least three and up to five teams for every year group. A pool, gym, rifle range, dance studio and climbing wall and, in addition to acres of playing fields, a large covered pitch so the younger children can play outside whatever the weather.

Equestrian sport is an increasingly popular option – this being Gloucestershire, a handy polo club in nearby Birdlip where riders can learn this sport from scratch. Teams take part in schools show jumping, cross-country, eventing and dressage competitions, with individuals competing at national and international level in all disciplines. No stabling, though, so you'll have to leave the pony at home.

Music here was described by one parent as 'second to none' – all are encouraged to take up an instrument or sing. Practice sessions are not timetabled but schedules are agreed with music tutors, which apparently results in more productive practice. The music school houses teaching and practice rooms and the Prince Michael Hall, used for concerts and public speaking. Hosts of chamber ensembles, rock bands, choirs and orchestras and musicians perform locally and nationally. Regular tours have taken them to Paris, Venice and New York. A strong tradition of Oxbridge organ and choral awards; the boy choristers from Tewkesbury Abbey's Schola Cantorum (stars of many a CD) are educated here. In residence is the new head of strings, the celebrated Carducci Quartet.

Art, too, has its own purpose built 'school' and exhibition space. Results at GCSE and A level are strong, a good proportion go on to continue their artistic education in some of the country's most acclaimed art colleges, including Central St Martin's, Chelsea, Camberwell and The Slade, and further afield such as the Charles Cecil Studios in Florence. Sixth form artists have allocated spaces where they can leave out works in progress. The art school's BonBernard Gallery is used to display both pupils' and professionals' work.

In addition to a studio theatre and a large amphitheatre in the grounds, fortunate thespians can also tread the boards of the Bacon Theatre, a 550 seat venue that wouldn't look out of place in small town. Named after former headmaster, Christopher Bacon, it hosts at least eight school plays a year, a major musical such as Les Misérables or Guys and Dolls every two years, as well as numerous professional productions; lecturing luminaries including Judi Dench, Samuel West and Peter Hall. In addition to GCSE and A level theatre studies, pupils are prepared for the RADA and LAMDA examinations up to diploma level. The school theatre company, Close Up Theatre, has performed sell-out plays at the Edinburgh Fringe for several years.

Add to the above a huge choice of clubs and societies, CCF training, D of E and a community action programme where pupils work on projects locally and abroad (building a school in Uganda) – it's no wonder boarding (or 'day' boarding, two nights a week) is so popular with local pupils: they don't want to miss out.

Boarding: Approximately a third of prep school pupils board – the vast majority are full boarders, meaning plenty of company after school and at weekends. In addition a very few places for 'day' boarders, who stay up to three nights a week. Of course many structured activities and outings, but equally important is free time to play outside and explore the extensive grounds, woods and brook. Three boarding houses: one for boys, one for girls and Wilton, a mixed house for the youngest; each is presided over by houseparents – a married couple with children, resident matron, two tutors and non-resident staff. Common rooms with televisions (weekends only), Wii, games consoles etc, plus table tennis, craft and model making areas, baking, a graffiti wall and milk shake nights are just some of the temptations on offer.

No chance for backsliding in instrument practice – one of the tutors in each boarding house is a musical (grade 8 minimum) gappie whose job is to oversee scales, accompany on the piano and encourage young singers and players. Boarders' rooms are bright and full of home comforts; we liked the customised carrels in the girls' prep room – all feathers and glitter. Children can speak to family via Skype and text, but no personal laptops allowed. Parents receive a Friday evening email from housemaster telling them what's been going on, so they can chat knowledgably with their offspring – a boon for those with uncommunicative young.

The senior girls' boarding house we visited was light and modern with glass brick floors in the corridors. Rooms were reassuringly untidy (inspections on Sundays), customised with posters, photos and plenty of home from home clutter. 'Keep calm and carry on' seems to be the motto de choix on many walls. Sixth formers have single rooms with linked ensuites and plenty of Cath Kidson bunting. Fourth form prep is done in separate study areas and monitored by sixth formers. Downstairs are squashy sofas with bright red cushions, board games, puzzles, a Wii, DVDs and music. Saturday night is film night. Boys' boarding similar standard but less bunting, and sofas evidenced rougher treatment.

Background and atmosphere: One parent described the atmosphere at Dean Close as 'relaxed yet achieving' and that just about sums it up, rather more succinctly in fact than the colour printing fest of promotional literature – considerably more quality photography, paper and gloss than other schools we've visited and needing its own Dean Close carrier bag. School mags, The Decanian and Young Decanian, are similarly shiny and flawless and perhaps just a little corporate. The school is more humane and down to earth than its brochures let on; the pupils we met were charming and grounded – one said that the best thing about school life was being part of a 'community of individuals'.

Occupying 50 green acres just beyond the centre of Cheltenham, it could be quite a daunting place but somehow keeps the protective ethos of a small school on its big site. The main school is a familiar mix of Victorian and later additions – although it is by no means short of the latest smartboards and ICT equipment, we were delighted to see a well-stocked library like an upturned boat and a wonderful high ceilinged history classroom with piles of books, walls covered in posters and a makeshift display of shells (exploding variety) and a tin helmet. And was that chalk dust floating in the shaft of sunlight coming from the tall windows? Probably not. The head has plans for a major redevelopment in the heart of the school, 'a radical approach to teaching space' (plus a new swimming pool) – we hope the history classroom's days aren't numbered.

The dining hall serves hearty home-cooked food with plenty of choice, pupils and staff eat at refectory tables with a fine view of the grounds. Boys and girls we spoke to were generally positive about the meals – several said they thought the food had improved while they had been there. Boarders can supplement with toast, hot chocolate and other snacks they prepare in the kitchenettes.

The prep school has opened a newish £4.5 million building which includes a reception area, theatre, music suite, hall for drama, concerts, assemblies and exams, plus IT suite, drama rooms and classrooms. The new classrooms are arranged to aid cross-curricular work. Prep-prep facilities are just as appealing: great library and ICT suite – all designed for this age group – plus ground floor classrooms linked by creative areas.

Pastoral care, well-being and discipline: The principles of Christianity form the moral heart of the school and for some this is a deciding factor, but 'no pressure' to get involved beyond cultural Christianity. One parent, not a churchgoer, was positively evangelical about what he identified as the 'spirit and energy' of the school. Our guide, who was very involved in this aspect of school life, said, 'It's not uncool to be a Christian here.' A whole school evensong in the chapel every Friday and voluntary communion and Bible studies plus a pupil-run Christian Union. The popular female chaplain organises various programmes to develop pupils' spiritual awareness.

No significant behaviour problems – main challenge, according to the head, is day pupils, who very occasionally get into trouble 'off-site' at Cheltenham's seedy dives. (Are there any?) Testing for any suspected of substance abuse; immediate dismissal for dealing. School takes a 'cultural approach' to bullying and staff vigilant for anything, even if it's just chit-chat, that may make a child feel isolated. Head very hot on challenging what he feels is a contemporary fashion for sexist put-downs. Prefects trained to look out for anyone feeling wobbly. Parents we spoke to describe pastoral care as 'fantastic', 'The staff genuinely care about the children'. A few grumbles from parents of day pupils, who wanted more opportunities to discuss their child's progress than the termly meetings with staff, but all agreed teachers were approachable and quick to respond to queries.

Seems to have the balance just right, providing a secure, caring environment in which pupils receive a first class academic grounding and explore their own talents and interests. As one prep school parent put it, 'The school doesn't expect them to grow up too fast – it lets them enjoy just being children.' In senior prep (years 7 and 8), pupils are given more responsibilities in order to develop independence and leadership skills, ready for senior school. All take part in community action projects and trips are further afield – Snowdon, camping in Devon and fencing in France, for example.

Pupils and parents: A good number of boarding parents are first-time buyers – the lack of old boy snobbery is a big draw. Significant numbers of Forces and diplomatic families are delighted to find a school where all their children can be educated together. School keen to stress its 'local' character, but even pupils whose parents live within bus distance elect to board when they get older (both our guides fell into this category). Mix of established families and London defectors has energised population in recent years. Roughly 15 per cent from overseas but no dominant nationality.

Famous Old Decanians include Tom Johnson and Pete Brown, rugby players; Hugh Quarshie, actor; George Adamson, author of Born Free; Francis Bacon, artist; Lord Bernard Ribeiro, former president of Royal College of Surgeons.

Entrance: To pre-prep via taster day including informal assessment. Own exam for prep school entrance (English, maths, VR) plus interview and school report. Year 3s mostly from own pre-prep, but roughly a third more come into year 7 from local preps and primaries. School makes the test as unthreatening as possible – on our visit we saw one girl enjoying chocolate and having a fuss made of her in the office, having finished her paper. Choristers (boys only) auditioned between 7-11 years.

'Quite accessible,' according to the senior school head, but two applications for every place; he adds that one of the qualities Dean Close looks for is curiosity, children who will 'have a go' and embrace every opportunity the school offers. Pupils enter at 13 from the school's own prep and after common entrance from others such as Pinewood, Beaudesert Park, Hatherop Castle, Prior Park, St John's-on-the-Hill. Sixth form entrants are accepted on the basis of three subject-based papers with VR or EAL.

Exit: Nearly all move up from the prep to the senior school. Some five per cent go on to a mixture of other schools – Malvern, Eton, Marlborough. Over 60 per cent to Russell Group, handful every year to Oxbridge (three in 2016), plus a few to art college, drama school and music conservatoire. Popular subjects: engineering, economics (no surprise there, given calibre of mathematicians) and classics; favoured institutions currently Bristol, Bath, Durham and Exeter.

Money matters: Described by more than one parent as 'value for money'. Scholarships and exhibitions for 13+ and 16+ entry awarded for excellence in academics, music, sport, art, drama, DT, plus a few for 'all rounders'. Small number of 100 per cent bursaries for those who 'could benefit from a Dean Close education'.

Remarks: Dean Close is a warm and welcoming school, aspirational without being snobby and secure in its strong moral and social values. As one of our guides said, 'You don't have to be a type to fit in here – you just have to be keen to give everything a try.'

Devonport High School for Boys

Paradise Road, Stoke, Plymouth PL1 5QP

D

Pupils: 1,150 • Ages: 11–18 • Sixth form: 240 (40 girls)

Tel: 01752 208787
Email: headteacher@dhsb.org
Website: www.dhsb.org

Headmaster: Since 2015, Dan Roberts (30s). Originally from Manchester, Dan studied a degree in marine biology at Plymouth University before completing his PGCE at University of St Mark and St John. His first teaching jobs, as science teacher, were at Tamarside Community College, now Marine Academy Plymouth, and later at saltash.net school, as head of science. For a complete change of scene he then jetted off to the Seychelles to be head of an international school for two years before returning to Plymouth as deputy at DHSB (moving up to the role of head two years later). Dan has not only won national and international teaching awards, most recently the TES ICT Visionary in Education, he also has a worldwide reputation for IT and consultancy. He still teaches IT and is able to pull on his extensive network to share knowledge and provide pupils with unique insights into the world of technology. Recently a class studying future homes and smart technology were treated to a personal workshop via Skype with the inventor of Smart Rings.

Father of two young boys, he's made a good impression on parents so far; 'I find the head teacher extremely amiable and approachable,' we were told. After our visit, we agree. Popular with pupils too; 'a lot of the boys were very pleased when Dan Roberts was selected for the job.' With his passion and expertise for technology (he even runs his own blog posting on learning, technology and leadership), he is guiding the school to the next level, making it more than just a traditional boys' grammar school. Parents are pleased with this new direction. 'The school is constantly evolving and embraces technology which I see as extremely positive, leaving the boys both socially and academically ready to move on to the next stage of their lives.'

Academic matters: In 2016, at A level, 63 per cent A*-B and 36 per cent A*/A grades. At GCSE, 43 per cent A*/A grades. Consistently in top 200 schools for A level total point score. Some girls join the sixth form and 26 A level subjects are offered, with more available from local schools in the consortium (Notre Dame, St Boniface and Eggbuckland). One language is compulsory at GCSE after an opportunity to try them all (French, Spanish, German, Mandarin and Latin) in year 7. All three science subjects are also compulsory at GCSE. Everyone takes non-exam courses in RS and PSHE.

Science and maths are the strongest subjects and the school's reputation for this is well known locally. And nationally, they have been in the finals of the Big Bang science and engineering competition for the last two years. Prospective sixth form pupils hoping to specialise in these subjects make a beeline for DHSB. Other popular subjects with equally impressive results are engineering and business studies. Psychology also growing in popularity.

The learning support department is housed in a small cottage on the school campus that provides a suitably calm environment for anyone needing extra help. The school can support pupils with dyslexia and dyscalculia plus those diagnosed with autism spectrum disorders. All teaching staff are given ongoing training plus there is a SENCo, a counsellor and six teaching assistants in the learning support department. Also available at the school but provided by the LA is a communication interaction team, an educational psychology service and a sensory service for children with visual or hearing needs. The school has a new SEND webpage with a whole range of resources and information for parents and pupils, and one parent told us, 'I particularly like the openness of the school to support different areas of children's development. The transparency of available sources ensures that there is no stigma in asking for help.'

Games, options, the arts: Good reputation for sport and plenty of options so there really is something for everyone. Football, rugby, athletics, cricket, fencing, rowing, cross-country, badminton, swimming. table-tennis, gymnastics and even American football. Basketball is particularly popular and successful; some pupils play for the Plymouth Raiders. Ultimate frisbee is another top sport and they are currently the national champions. In rugby, DHSB are the Devon Cup winners, and in football they are the Devon Wednesday League champions. In both sports, some pupils have gone on to play at national levels. Other recent success stories include a European U17 hurdles champion and a 2012 Olympic swimmer. For a city school there's plenty of space and facilities; rugby fields, a cricket pitch, a cross-country route, hard courts, Astroturf, a new sports hall and a fully equipped gym.

For the arty types, there's a newly decorated drama studio, brighter now; apparently the old blackened version was 'scary'. Regular productions are performed in the excellent theatre with tiered seating for 300. In the last few years the school has produced Macbeth and Romeo and Juliet plus musical performances of Joseph and the Amazing Technicolour Dreamcoat, The Wizard of Oz, Bugsy Malone and Guys and Dolls. These large productions are often run in collaboration with girls from partner schools. There are also three termly musical concerts and plenty of after-school activities including school orchestra, swing band, choir and rock club. Music is based in a small cottage on site, which includes a classroom with Apple Macs, a recording studio and individual practice rooms. Art is in the main building and standards on display were good; interesting collages of local landmarks as well as some portraits. Good DT facilities, 3D printer, lathes, CAD, plus engineering software and product design equipment.

Extracurricular clubs are run during lunchtimes as many pupils have long bus journeys home. Boys can choose from a great variety of activities including table tennis, circus skills, philosophy, photography, bands, investor challenge, trampolining, street surfing, Chinese and Young Enterprise club. Lots of engineering activities including one dedicated to remote controlled 4x4 vehicles. The Ten Tors challenge and D of E awards are increasingly popular and the school has strong links with the local air training corps.

Plenty of trips too. Year 7 get started straight away with a week of bushcraft, camping and survival, plus every year has an enrichment week in the summer and a challenge week in the winter. Boys can go surfing and camping in Cornwall, on residentials in France or paddle boarding, caving, canoeing; the list is endless and adventurous. There's also an annual ski trip, sports tours and language exchanges (the Mandarin class is off to China next year). One parent commented, 'DHSB offers many opportunities so that different subject areas and outside interests can be explored. In year 7 my son took part in the Christmas show and the band performance. This year he is going on a school trip to Italy to visit, amongst other things, the Lamborghini museum.'

Background and atmosphere: Founded in 1896, DHSB moved to its present site in 1945. The main building is a huge grey stone grade 2 listed building, which served as a prison during the Napoleonic wars and as a hospital during WWII. At the back of the school runs the colonnade (46 archways in total, we were told) overlooking the Astroturf, hard courts and playing fields below. On the second floor, classrooms open out onto a wide walkway balcony above the colonnade. Inside, it's spacious; high ceilings and wide corridors. And grey with a hefty amount of blue paint everywhere else. Basic and functional, no soft touches, very much a boys' school.

However, the new library (the learning commons) was a pleasant surprise; colourful and modern. There are workstations and study benches made of whiteboard wipeable tops ('the best bit', boys told us). All have orange USB ports or Mac chrome books. The reading area is sectioned off with bookshelves and covered in fake grass and beanbags. Upstairs is a quiet study area, all fitted out in same modern style, with a small canteen on hand next door.

Sixth formers have their own area, pretty basic when we visited but due to be renovated over the summer, all in the same style and design as the library. They already have their own canteen. All the canteens on site are called Refuel and the pupils we spoke to were very happy with the food. Parents are not so pleased: they believe the long queues for the popular food is steering their boys towards the more unhealthy fast-food options. Possibly.

Pastoral care, well-being and discipline: 'The pupils' polite and courteous behaviour is very impressive,' parents said. The boys we met were well mannered and proud of their school. The head has had a recent overhaul of the rules and has made things a little stricter. The focus has been on very low level disruption which had never been monitored before. Level 1 disruption is perhaps being told to be quiet, and level 3 is being asked to leave the classroom. The new system requires teachers to report all level 1s and after three offences, it's detention. Although this has seemed a little harsh or unfair to some, it has cut the number of higher-level incidents to almost zero. However, one parent suggested, 'I wonder if better communication about discipline might help parents and boys so the perceived disparity is minimised?' Good idea.

The head is keen to give pupils plenty of leadership opportunities. Sixth form girls are encouraged to challenge boys and give the younger boys female role models too. There are more than just sixth form leaders, there are peer mentors from year 9, subject ambassadors, prefects, house leaders, digital leaders and eco-leaders, to name but a few. There has also been a huge rise in the number of pupils taking part in the D of E awards; 25 bronze awards last year, 109 this year. Plus the completion rate has gone from 20 per cent to 60 per cent and still rising. One parent told us, 'I can see both my boys developing into more confident young men with each day that passes.'

Pastoral care is good and pupils have access to a counsellor in the learning support department plus the school nurse. As well as tutors, teachers, mentors and peers for support, pupils have information, advice and guidance lessons led by tutors and external speakers. There is also a dedicated family support adviser and a support link page on the website for families and pupils.

Pupils and parents: Pupils travel from within a 750 square mile catchment area. A local bus company is used by all three Plymouth grammars to ferry them to and fro. Some pupils come from as far as Okehampton, Truro or Beesands, others are local city boys. The large majority of parents keep up with news on Twitter and the head's blog is hugely popular. Parents told us, 'I find the communication at the school excellent. We are constantly kept in the loop with text, email and Twitter.' To improve the communication further, the school has recently added more events for parents in the form of educational workshops. Recent topics have been 'How a teenage brain works' and 'How the boys use Google apps.' Parents have also been offered training on the new homework platform. The platform has been designed and built by the head and the head of IT so all updates and suggestions for improvements are welcome, making it truly bespoke and fit for purpose.

Entrance: Boys come from 80 feeder primary schools. DHSB takes up to 12 per cent of Plymouth's boys. There are open days and the familiarisation sessions. These are free and candidates sit an English paper and a maths paper, both set by the school. Papers are taken home and mark schemes given to parents. The actual DHSB admission tests include multiple choice English and maths papers plus an internally set DHSB English paper (testing composition skills).

Once accepted, pupils are given transition projects to work on at home and then in groups on the induction days. One parent told us, 'The boys thoroughly enjoyed the induction days and came home extremely excited at the prospect of joining the school.' Another added, 'The year 7 bushcraft week away is also a great way for the boys to bond.'

Sixth form entry requires a minimum average of 48 points in at least eight subjects, and at least a C grade in both English language and maths. Approximately 20 students from other schools join at sixth form, around 15 per cent of the intake. Around 40 girls are currently in the sixth form. Girls are recommended to apply in the first instance to DHSB partner girls' or coeducational schools.

Exit: The majority stays on for A levels. Around 85 per cent of sixth formers go straight on to university, with four Oxbridge places in 2016 and nine medics. DHSB continues to support gap year students in their applications the year after they leave. South west universities are popular – Exeter, Plymouth, Bristol, UWE, Bath. Generous sponsorship from Engineers' Employers' Federation and BAE Systems results in large number heading into engineering and science courses.

Money matters: Families can speak to the family support advisor to find out about help with any costs.

Remarks: Built on traditional foundations, this boys' city grammar school has a great reputation for science and engineering. With his own passion for science, and expertise in IT, the new head has already started building on this. There are now so many more opportunities for the boys; by the time they leave they are not just academically wise, but worldly too.

Devonport High School for Girls

Lyndhurst Road, Peverell, Plymouth PL2 3DL

Pupils: 805 • Ages: 11–18 • Sixth form: 230

Tel: 01752 705024
Email: dhsg@devonportgirls.plymouth.sch.uk
Website: https://www.dhsg.co.uk

Head Teacher: Since 2009, Mrs Anita Hemsi BSc MA (Ed) PGCE NPQH.

Academic matters: High standards – 60 per cent A*/A at GCSE in 2016 and 34 per cent at A level. Choice of 20 A level subjects, further options including politics, psychology, sports studies and media studies – part of a consortium, the Link Partnership, which allows more timetable flexibility. English, the sciences and maths are particularly popular A level choices and students often sit additional Institute of Biology British Olympiad exam. French, Latin, Spanish, Mandarin and German available at GCSE and French, German and Spanish offered at A level. Budding engineers invented collapsible mobile platform to lift equipment on and off ships, which has been adopted by the Royal Navy. Weaker achievers or students with SEN receive ample support.

Games, options, the arts: Dance taught in main school hall. Sporting stars have made national squads in hockey, netball, rugby, swimming, diving and athletics, and improved sporting facilities are likely to further boost success. Music is a strength, with more than a third of girls playing an instrument and many achieving grade 7 or 8 by year 10. Orchestra, music groups and choir perform a carol concert in the city church each year. Drama group from key stages 3, 4 and 5 perform to parents at least once a year with one main school production in the summer term. Active Christian Union. DHSG is a self-certificating Duke of Edinburgh Centre and runs its own unit. Students have the opportunity to take part in Enterprise Days where local business people visit school to set challenges and judge outcomes. Students gain experience of designing business models, managing budgets and meeting strict deadlines.

Background and atmosphere: Founded in 1911, moved to its present purpose-built site in 1937. The red-brick building is off a busy road opposite parkland. No great views and access by car is somewhat puzzling. Originally built for three forms of entry but since expanded to four – in recent years a new language & business, mathematics and psychology block has been built to replace huts. Low turnover of staff – teachers almost seem relieved to be here, 'Pupils listen and like to learn'. Sixth form has own centre with kitchen and study. Every girl has access to internet and own email.

Pastoral care, well-being and discipline: Good level of care and support; discipline is a 'quiet word in their ear'. Students are well cared for by a dedicated pastoral support team. Four houses: Edgcumbe, Flete, Hartland and Kitley. The form tutors support students on a daily basis through years 7–11; heads of house monitor their progress and welfare, celebrates their achievements and provides additional support when required. Pastoral support begins with transitional visits to students' primary schools and an induction day in year 6. Year 8 transition mentors help new year 7s settle in; specially trained sixth form academic and pastoral mentors are also available. Teambuilding activity at Escot Park in September of year 7. School nurse and youth counsellor from Youth Enquiry Service run weekly drop-in sessions. School council instead of prefect system – each form elects a member. Girls have been sent home for minor incidents but few exclusions. Sixth formers expected to dress smartly. Everyone in school is 'expected' to contribute to school's chosen annual charity. Good attendance record and extremely positive attitudes.

Pupils and parents: Attracts girls from some 50 feeder schools in Plymouth, west Devon and south-east Cornwall. Many professional parents from doctors and nurses to lawyers and scientists.

Entrance: Plymouth exam: multiple choice and written English. Pupils admitted in the order of their exam score until the maximum intake of 120 is reached. Sixth form entry is open on interview to students who have achieved at least five GCSEs at grades A*-C, with B grades in subjects (or equivalent) they wish to pursue at A level – 46 average point score.

Exit: Some 85 to 90 per cent migrate into sixth form, others move away or choose vocational courses. A few go into modern apprenticeships. Most continue to further education, although gap years popular. Usually several to Oxbridge; others to eg Cardiff, Exeter, Bristol, Southampton and London universities.

Remarks: Currently preferred choice for parents wanting single-sex selective education for girls. Students seem well prepared not just for academic success but also for life after school.

The Downs Malvern

Linked with Malvern College

Brockhill Road, Colwall, Malvern, Worcestershire WR13 6EY

Pupils: 223 (two-thirds boys); 43 boarders • Ages: 2–13 (boarders from year 3) • C of E

Fees: Day £6,753 – £16,221; Boarding £12,237 – £21,471 pa

Tel: 01684 544100
Email: registrar@thedowns.malcol.org
Website: www.thedownsmalvern.org.uk

Head: Since 2009, Alastair (known to everyone as Sam) Cook. Previously head of Pembroke House in Gilgil, Kenya, he is a graduate from Westminster College, Oxford. There is something of the gentleman's club about his study. The comfortable chairs, old school photos and stirring mountain landscapes speak of a man and school at ease with the world. Alastair Cook certainly is that and much more. He has energetically meshed three schools (The Downs merged with Malvern College Prep in 2008) together into a now seamless unit, worked on relationships with Malvern College to mutual benefit and made himself much respected and loved by parents and the children whom he places firmly at the centre of everything. He teaches, does sport with the pre-preps and runs a swimming club. 'He is always around when the children arrive, there with his dog, at matches, just all the time', said one parent. He knows all the children, even those who have just arrived. 'You would never worry about approaching him over anything', said a mother.

Entrance: Entrance is non-selective – can support all but those with serious learning difficulties. Informal observations and interviews on taster days, combined with discussions with parents, lead to offers. Depending on the age of the child, may also request information from the current school.

Exit: More or less all take the common entrance and about 90 per cent go onto Malvern College – there is a strong flow through in curriculum terms. A smattering goes to other local schools or further flung public schools. If there is a problem academically, parents are told at an early stage and alternative plans discussed.

Remarks: The Downs has the feel of a much-loved school with the bucket-loads of unspoilt charm that you find in the very best rural preps. It spreads over the Malvern Hills and the only downside we could see were the narrow roads and precipitous bends on the way there. There is a flexibility and breadth about everything. Pick-up times are to suit parents not the school, boarding can be when families need it – it is all about individuals growing up in a community that cares, and for which families too care and show respect. The curriculum has all the academic rigour combined with creativity that you would hope for – strong science in suitably equipped labs ('We get to use proper chemicals,' one 10 year old was bursting to tell us), French is all the way through with Spanish or German in years 7 and 8, Latin from year 6, art has its own kiln and there is masses of music.

All of this spills out of the classroom into the rich extracurricular programme that runs at lunchtimes, after school and on Saturday mornings (not compulsory but much loved by parents). There is sport galore (including girls' soccer), gardening, chess, Chinese, pottery, cookery, world history, computer coding, current affairs, science in the news, touch-typing, debating, Scrabble, endless drama and music and so it goes on. Perhaps what best sums up the timeless charm is the little steam train that runs through the school grounds. The oldest miniature light railway in the world, this is a serious educational tool. The children learn to drive and maintain it. The wholesome environment too is fully utilised – the children are outside as much as possible, soaking in subliminally, we would like to think, the awe-inspiring rolling landscape, but also using it for serious geographical and scientific measurements and as inspiration for their artwork, which is of a seriously high standard.

There are plenty of links with the world outside the school. Its own first rate facilities are supplemented by some use of Malvern College – its theatre, chapel, swimming pool, for instance. The choir sings locally and the school hosts national music and art events for other schools. About three-quarters of the boarders are from overseas (11 different countries when we visited) and parents commented on how well the school integrates the day pupils and the boarders. The school offers excellent preparation to overseas boarders wanting to brush up their English and understand British values ready for senior school. There are fun and cosily low key events organised at weekends for boarders – a visit to the circus, theme parks, ice skating, Christmas shopping. The flexi-boarding is popular with parents who want to give their children a taste of boarding before the full immersion as they move on to Malvern College. The boarding accommodation is in The Warren – rightly named as it rambles round the centre of the original school buildings, not smart but very homely.

Parents say the teachers are very quick to pick up on any individual needs and that they take huge pride in the children's small achievements. 'Go to Friday assemblies', parents urged us. 'Everyone is invited and we really get a sense of how much the school praises the children, how the discipline works in practice, the clear moral message the school is getting across, and we can see the opportunities all the children get for developing confidence through public speaking.'

The head told us, 'Care comes first and then education'. Parents and children praised the flexibility and common sense – no rigid rules that stunt children. Fairness is the basis of the approach to discipline. Teachers want to find out what the situation actually is by spending time talking to children involved in any difficulties – and then it is a quiet word and a real attempt to equip the children with the skills to move forward.

'So what do you give school out of 10?', we asked one boy. 'Ten+++', he said with a big grin.

The Downs School

Charlton House, Wraxall, Bristol BS48 1PF

Pupils: 281 • Ages: 4–13

Fees: £10,260 – £15,555 pa

Tel: 01275 852008
Email: office@thedownsschool.co.uk
Website: www.thedownsschool.co.uk

Headmaster: Since 2001, Marcus Gunn MA (Ed) PGCE BA IAPS. Originally from Yorkshire, studied history at Liverpool, and qualified as a teacher almost a decade later. During that time, as well as windsurfing whenever possible, he taught history and games for five years, taking on such a wide range of duties that he now sees the whole experience as an apprenticeship. Studied a masters in education and leadership at 40. Now lives in the school grounds with wife Valerie, the 'glue that holds it all together.' As well as matron duties she hosts events for parents, even taking them out for a coffee and chat if needed. All three children have flown the nest. As a couple, they have transformed The Downs School from a failing boarding school to a leading prep. It is obvious that they live and breathe the place, even out of hours; Marcus is 'weekend zoo-keeper' for pets' corner, very busy since the bunnies multiplied overnight.

Parents have nothing but praise for Marcus. One told us, 'he clearly likes children,' another agreed, saying, 'He wants them to do well and he certainly wants them all to be happy.' Others said, 'I think Marcus Gunn is a very kind man.' And, 'He is definitely in control, but interacts well with the children.' '[He is] not afraid to get his hands dirty and to reach the children on their level'. Even in our brief meeting it was clear he cares for the children here.

Working closely with Marcus is the new head of pre-prep, Heather Fulton. Originally from New Zealand, her previous post was head of kindergarten at DUCKS, Dulwich College. Like Marcus, she is also an independent schools inspector.

Entrance: The Downs School is the only independent prep school in the area. Around 15 children a year come from Charlton nursery. One parent said, 'Our eldest had started at Charlton Nursery at the top of the drive. We asked what went on down there and were told there was a very special school at the bottom. We duly drove on and before we reached the end we knew our son had to come here. It really was as simple as that.'

Admission by application and informal assessment. Inclusive, but restricted by numbers, and at least one or two children per year won't be accepted if needs cannot be met by learning support. Scholarships available at year 4 entry, mainly for academic potential, and can equate up to 25 per cent of the day pupil fee. Means-tested bursaries also available.

On entry, each child is allocated a guide to help them settle in. 'Children at the Downs are really proud to be chosen as guides and do take the role seriously,' said one parent. Another told us, 'In reception the settling in process is smooth and anxiety free. Cleverly the school invites new mums to coffee on the first morning straight after drop off.... the children are quickly distracted by cheerful classrooms, pet guinea pigs and smiley teachers.'

Exit: Almost all stay on until 13, at most one pupil a year leaves at 11. 'By staying until 13 the children have the opportunity to mature emotionally and become comfortable in their own skin. They are prepared for the rigours of year 9 both academically and emotionally, and as a parent, that is something I am hugely grateful for.' On our visit, our year 8 guides showed us a 'secret' door under the oak paneled stairs. Stone steps lead down to a cellar and their very own common room equipped with sofas, TV, music system, mini pool table and a toaster. 'They have enjoyed being top of the pile and having privileges like the year 8 common room and just generally being treated slightly differently by the staff.'

Only school in the area that follows the common entrance syllabus. This year there are pupils entering for Eton, Winchester and Marlborough. Most pupils gain scholarships to senior schools including Clifton College, Winchester College, Badminton, Blundell's, Bryanston, Cheltenham College, Clifton College, King's Taunton, Malvern College, Queen Elizabeth's Hospital, Marlborough, Millfield, Monmouth and Sherborne. 'Our eldest son left The Downs with a top academic scholarship to his next school, something we would never have expected, our next child received a sports scholarship,' one mother told us. The Downs School helps pupils choose the right school, so it is rare that pupils do not get accepted by their first choice.

Remarks: The long drive to the school, the stunning setting, the grand entrance with huge fireplace and oak paneled walls (even more amazing with Christmas decorations); it's easy to see why parents are bowled over immediately. This is a family-run prep school that makes the most of the outdoors too – overalls and wellies for outside play, and lessons in the forest school. 'Our children are happy there, and safe, and cared for, and challenged.' Parents love this school and they are all very much involved in life here, 'The Downs School is a haven in which all of my very different children are thriving and learning and playing in a culture of freedom and inclusivity that we as a family are delighted to be a part of.'

It is situated in Charlton House, a magnificent Victorian mansion surrounded by 60 acres of idyllic parkland, just five miles from Bristol. Marcus says the school is 'traditional' but 'progressive.' They have old fashioned-expectations; standing when an adult enters the room, shaking teachers' hands at the end of the day, good eye contact. One parent told us, 'The Downs has helped them to develop social graces eg meet and greet opposition or visitors to the school.' They encourage old-fashioned play; building dens, playing with skipping ropes, making daisy chains. Parents confirmed, saying, 'Mr Gunn once told me that if the year 8 children didn't still want to go outside and build dens then he wasn't doing his job properly. Children are encouraged to be children.' In fact his latest building project is a treehouse, designed as a witch's hat with a bridge, that is used as an outdoor classroom – a magical place to learn. So how is the school progressive? Marcus says they are 'brave enough to be independent and go off curriculum.' In addition to the curriculum, they teach theory of music, history of art, etiquette and even accountancy. Life and leadership skills are taught on the school camping trips.

Over the last year, well-being has been the top priority. With this in mind the school has reviewed their very full curriculum. The school was a boarding school up until 2004 and has been run like one in many ways ever since; long days and sports every Saturday. Breakfast is available from 7.30am (around 40 children daily), and the day finishes at 5pm with clubs until 6pm (5pm for pre-prep). Supper is available until 7pm. To ease the pressure and allow the children to enjoy their home-life, homework has been reduced for younger pupils who now have prep time at school. The number of sports fixtures on Wednesdays have also been reduced. One parent told us, 'I would emphasise that choosing the Downs is a lifestyle choice, particularly if you have several children, as from year 3 they will be joining in Saturday sports, which can be at any time of day.... If you are a family that likes to go away at weekends, The Downs will not fit that lifestyle. '

Academically, the pupils do very well. There are two classes in each year group and class sizes currently average 15. Science is popular and practical. Other subjects like history also use this tack – each year group has a history day, Vikings or Normans, for example. Pupils dress up, make weapons, re-enact battles. French is taught from reception, Spanish from year 6, and Latin is available to those hoping to go to Winchester College. Parents say, 'Some of the teaching is excellent (biology and chemistry, humanities, English, in particular), some is not so excellent but none of it is poor. All the teachers are very approachable, and as it is such a small school all teachers know all of the children (all the children know each other too – it's like a big family).'

Classrooms are in Charlton House, and also in the recently built new block. 'Much warmer!' pupils told us. There are interactive whiteboards in all classrooms, and two ICT suites with touchscreen computers. The head told us, 'We have the infrastructure to embrace whatever technology we wish.' Although tablets are available in several departments, they have decided against taking the next step, for the moment. IT is taught from reception. The school has a strict no mobile phone policy. One parent felt that technology could help some areas: 'The school has been slow in embracing new technology that can help children with learning differences (laptop and iPad usage is hit and miss, depending largely on the individual teacher.) I'm not sure that all the teachers accept that children have different learning styles – it's getting better, but I am continuously in contact with the learning support department.'

Around 22 children need extra support from the learning support team, mainly for dyslexia, dyscalculia and dyspraxia. 'The learning support department is lovely, very kind and supportive. Help with maths is superb,' one parent told us. The head of the department used to be head of learning support at Clifton College. Her team members are all specialist trained; there is an in-house speech therapist and an occupational therapist. As well as one-to-one therapy, they also provide group therapy in the form of social interaction role-play sessions. These are informal sessions and aimed at children that may be having some behavioural management issues. One parent told us their story: '[My son] is a very intelligent child with very complex learning difficulties who felt he was useless....Within one term [he] had transformed into a confident child who began to love school.' The school also offers talented children, or scholars as they are known, a real challenge – they do well here; results are impressive all round.

Sport is a big part of life here. Great facilities. Two Astroturf pitches, rugby, cricket and rounders pitches, sports hall with cricket nets, an outdoor heated swimming pool, two netball courts and nine tennis courts. Remarkable success for such a small school; one parent told us about her daughter: 'Her year at school had only seven girls but made it to the netball nationals in years 6 and 8, and hockey nationals in year 6, an amazing achievement with only seven girls.' Rugby and hockey are the main players here and there was a recent tour to Edinburgh. Many of the sports are played at national level, including athletics. All pupils from year 3 play in a team. Girls can play rugby and cricket if they want to. 'Parents are very, very actively supportive of the sports teams. Always the Downs will have a big crowd of parents watching matches (home and away, and for all the teams – all levels).' For some parents, the sport has been too much in the past. 'We used to find the status that sport held amongst the school community was too high and that the sporty children were put on a pedestal by everyone, often to the detriment of other children. However, Marcus Gunn and his team have been working hard to find an equilibrium between the academic, sport and performing arts balance, not to mention the myriad of other activities available on tap all hours of the day.' For non-sporty children there is

The Downs Award Scheme, offering alternatives like caving, climbing or orienteering. However, pupils are still given the option to play team sports as well. This gives them the best of both worlds and means nobody is excluded.

Good art facilities including a pottery and textiles room. The parents' association sponsors an annual arts week for the school, inviting artists in for workshops. The Christmas pre-prep production of the Nutcracker Nativity was in full flight on our visit, and year 8s were busy preparing for the talent show auditions. Other recent productions include Bugsy Malone and Porridge, a 'nursery-noir' by year 6, 'Goldie Lox and friends do organised crime.' Every year group performs a production annually. All productions take place in the school's theatre. Dance is on offer: jazz, tap and ballet tuition, plus Bollywood and street dance after-school clubs. Some 85 per cent play a musical instrument. In year 3, pupils have specialist instruction for one term in the violin, ukhele and clarinet. In year 4, trumpet, violin and fife. Years 4 and 6 all study the theory of music, taking Associated Board exams. Choir is compulsory. There are four choirs: 'My daughter in year 7 has sung at St George's Chapel Windsor Castle; the chamber choir which she is in has got to the final of the Barnardo's Choir of the Year last year.' The chamber choir has just qualified for this final again – at the Royal Festival Hall in February. There are formal and informal concerts so everybody can 'have their moment of glory.' There is even a soul band which includes all ages, grown-ups too.

As expected of any traditional school, there is a house system, and each regularly raises money for charity. The eco-committee has made a big impact recently with its 'switch-off fortnight' and is planning a 'waste week' and a 'water week.' The school council is busy 'making small changes that make a big difference'; pre-prep would like mangos and strawberries in fruit snacks, and the preps would like a pot in each classroom with spare ink cartridges. Parents told us, 'What the school does is allow each of them to explore within and without their comfort zones, always encouraging adventurous decisions and offering praise when due.' Annual exchange trips to France and Spain, geography trips, camping trips and the usual local visits to museums and galleries.

Definitely no complaints about the pastoral care. Matrons, led by a qualified nurse, 'are absolutely fantastic. [the nurse] knows all the children well and is happy to give plenty of hugs and TLC whenever required. My children all adore her.' Another told us, 'Our eldest son has a severe nut allergy.... The school was brilliant; it wasn't a problem for them at all.' Pastoral care is stretched to give parents support too. Heather, head of pre-prep, encourages parents to engage by setting up coffee mornings, and the school organises seminars. Most recently, a clinical psychologist spoke about the teenage brain and underachieving boys, plus another talk e-safety. Baroness Floella Benjamin (Play School) is confirmed for next term. The school is aware of the pressure of secondary school admissions, and has an open door policy for parents and pupils alike.

There is so much on offer at The Downs School it's hard to see how they fit it all in. But they do, and the children thrive on it; 'They loved the longer days, the more varied education, eg match teas and socialising with opposition after sports matches, the vast music opportunities, informal and formal concerts, and the clubs available. They have thrived from day one.' The Downs is a school where tradition is important, but not to the point where outdated thinking holds back development. It's a school that challenges academically, but never loses sight of the fact that children need to play, and enjoy to learn. And where the parents love school life as much as the pupils.

Downside School

Stratton-on-the-Fosse, Bath, Somerset BA3 4RJ

Pupils: 370; 285 boarders • Ages: 11-18 • Sixth form: 153 • RC

Fees: Boarding £23,562 – £31,608 pa. Day £14,940 – £17,712 pa

Tel: 01761 235103
Email: admissions@downside.co.uk
Website: www.downside.co.uk

Head Master: Since 2014, Dr James Whitehead MA MPhil PhD (40s). Previously second master at Worth. Educated at Stonyhurst and Oxford. After an MA in English at Oxford and MPhil in modern poetry at University of Stirling, he worked in the civil service and as a bookseller in his early 20s, then did his PhD (on Thomas Hardy's poetry) at the University of Manchester. Studying for his doctorate 'ignited my love of teaching' and when he spotted an ad for a post at Radley he decided to apply. He spent four years there, as an English teacher, sub-tutor (assistant housemaster) and rugby coach, before moving to Downside as head of English (and later director of studies). 'It was a time of rapid change and development at Downside,' he says. 'We were the most improved school in the country in the league tables.' During this period he introduced new appraisal, reporting and rewards systems – things that are commonplace in schools now but weren't then.

He spent seven years at Worth before taking up the headship at Downside. 'It was a historic opportunity to become the first lay head here,' he says. Since his arrival he has focused on the school's academic delivery, staff development and looking after pupils' well-being, as well as overseeing a substantial development programme. 'I think we're really motoring,' he says. 'There is a very joyful atmosphere here – which is how a school should be.' He's proud of the way Downside nurtures 'a real sense of intellectual enquiry' and does his bit by delivering sixth form lectures on subjects like Dante in half an hour, celebrity worship syndrome and faith and modern poetry. He makes time to referee rugby matches too.

Cerebral, forward-thinking and experienced at getting 'the nuts and bolts' of schools right, he is a fellow of the Royal Society of Arts and is passionate about literature and sport. His actress wife Nicola does some LAMDA teaching at Downside and they have two young daughters, both pupils at All Hallows Prep. In his spare time he enjoys walking the family's two labradors, golf and reading.

Academic matters: Results have come on leaps and bounds in recent years. In 2016, 46 per cent A*/A and 70 per cent A*/B at A level and 50 per cent A*/A at GCSE. Usual subjects at A level, plus business studies, economics, history of art, PE, photography and psychology. History department offers the Pre-U – head of history says the qualification involves 'good, old-fashioned essay writing' and enables youngsters to study topics such as monasticism in the 9th century and the Gregorian reforms of the 11th century as well as more recent fare.

Most pupils take 11 GCSEs. English, maths and RS are compulsory and all are encouraged to take at least one language, a humanity and a creative subject. French, German and Spanish are the main languages, but Italian, Mandarin, Russian, Polish, Chinese, Portuguese and Arabic can be arranged. Most pupils do three separate sciences. Director of studies says the school believes in setting 'ambitious realistic targets' and tracks

D

and monitors pupils' progress throughout. School's intake is 'selective, but broadly mixed ability' and its value added scores are particularly impressive. Maximum class sizes of 20 up to GCSE and 16 in the sixth form but classes are often smaller than this. Pupils are set in maths and science up to GCSE. A variety of academic societies, including the Knowles, where Oxbridge candidates present their own research papers.

Head has brought learning support department into the heart of the school (it used to be housed in a separate block). Support given to 30 pupils, either one-to-one or in small groups, but department also offers drop-in sessions for anyone needing additional help. EAL is also available.

Games, options, the arts: With 500 acres of grounds to run around in, fresh air and exercise are an integral part of Downside life. As well as rugby, hockey, football and cricket for the boys and hockey, netball, tennis and rounders for the girls, there's a wealth of other sports on offer, including aerobics, athletics, badminton, cross-country, fencing, squash and swimming. Pupils have three games sessions during the week, plus matches on Saturday afternoons, but many do far more than this. Sixth formers get just as much sport as their younger counterparts – everything from boxercise to circuit training. When we visited, a group of older girls were in the middle of an energetic zumba class, music blasting across the courtyard. Sports facilities include an indoor pool (donated by a family whose son tragically died in a Naples swimming accident in 1925 and refurbished in 2010), rugby pitches galore, football pitches, cricket squares, Astroturf, a glorious 1930s sports pavilion and a sports centre with a weights room and fitness suite.

Parents report that the music is outstanding. Half the pupils have instrumental lessons and there's a multitude of orchestras, chamber ensembles and choirs (the Schola Cantorum is the oldest Roman Catholic school choir in the UK), along with jazz ensembles, a barbershop ensemble, pipe band, brass band, even an open-mic night. Art department has been refurbished and is equipped with Macs, photographic studio, 3D printers and glass making facilities. Printmaking, textiles, oil painting, landscapes, portraits, graphic illustration, photography, fused glass – you name it, Downside does it. 'I'm a firm believer that everybody is creative in some shape or form,' the dynamic head of art told us. School has strong links with Hauser & Wirth Somerset, the contemporary art gallery in nearby Bruton. Busy drama department. School puts on a whole school play and musical every year, plus a host of other performances in refurbished 500-seat theatre. New performing arts centre and brand new music school.

All year 9s are expected to do CCF for at least part of the year. Many carry on while others opt for D of E and Ten Tors expeditions across Dartmoor. Action-packed co-curricular programme includes chess, astronomy, Model United Nations, Young Enterprise, sewing, contemporary dance and fly fishing.

Boarding: Most pupils board – boarding is 'part of our USP,' says the head. Four boys' houses and two girls' houses. All junior boys (years 7, 8 and 9) start in Powell, a boarding house located in the main school, with open plan dorms and bunk beds for the youngest and a homely kitchen where boys get to cook (and eat) cookies, crumbles and pizza. A parent said some of the boys' dorms could do with a bit of updating but her children think they are fine as they are. Junior girls go straight into Isabella or Caverel, the two girls' boarding houses.

House staff are adept at helping children to settle in. 'No one gets lost here,' we were told. A housemother reckons that Ovaltine, warm wheat bags (the modern answer to hot water bottles) and talking helps to stave off homesickness. Pupils are kept occupied at weekends with lots of trips and inter-house competitions. Up until the sixth form pupils hand in their mobile phones at night so they get a good night's sleep and aren't distracted by Facebook, Snapchat and the like. Parents thoroughly approve.

Although technically doesn't offer weekly boarding, boarders can go home on any bar four of the weekends each term. These are 'closed' weekends, the ones immediately after or just before holidays or half terms. Otherwise, pupils are welcome to go home after they have completed their sports involvement on a Saturday afternoon, which is some time between 3:30pm and 5:30pm, on other weekends. They then return to school for the Sunday evening.

Background and atmosphere: The magnificent Downside Abbey adjoins the school and is visible for miles across the rolling Somerset landscape. The school has been on its present site in the village of Stratton-on-the-Fosse since 1814 but dates back more than 400 years. The Benedictine community of St Gregory the Great was founded in France in 1606 by English and Welsh monks living in exile because of the penal laws in England against Catholics. By 1617 English Catholics were sending their boys across the Channel to be educated there. When it became safe in the early 19th century for Catholics to provide education once more the school moved to England. Downside's monastic community (currently 12 monks, some of whom teach) has been in residence for 200 years. Members of an apostolic community from Chile – the Manquehue Apostolic Movement – have a base at Downside too. The school went co-ed in 2005 and the boy/girl ratio is now 60:40.

Downside has a rich cultural heritage. The abbey's Monastic Library, housed in a 1970s building, is one of the largest private libraries in the UK and has a collection of more than 400,000 books and papers, many of them very rare. 'It's like having an Oxford college library on the campus,' says the head. The school's atmosphere and setting are traditional, with historic corridors (the science corridor is lined with pictures of old boys who died in the First and Second World Wars), parquet floors and pupils hurrying to classes in their eye-catching uniform. Worn by all (including the sixth form), the uniform comprises mid-length kilts and red or black jumpers for the girls and black jackets and pinstriped trousers for the boys. The pupils' maroon and gold game kit is particularly jazzy – good for spotting players on the games pitch.

School food much improved following the appointment of new caterers (manager formerly worked for River Cottage Canteen Bristol, part of Hugh Fearnley-Whittingstall's culinary empire). A stylish café serves cappuccinos, cookies and toasties during breaks and evenings. Fifty per cent of teaching staff live on site or in Stratton-on-the-Fosse.

Pastoral care, well-being and discipline: A strong sense of spirituality pervades the school. Around 80 per cent of pupils are Catholic but children from other Christian denominations are welcome. School has a distinctively Catholic and Benedictine character and incorporates the eight aspects of a Benedictine education – welcome, listening, reverence and humility, teaching and learning, personal discipline, concern for the individual, building communion and stewardship of gifts.

School's most recent inspection report commented that 'pupils of all faiths and none possess an inner confidence, and a strong sense of their own identity.' Everyone is expected to participate in the school's spiritual life. Sunday mass in the abbey is compulsory, as is hymn practice on Friday afternoon. While Downside's monastic community prays formally six times a day, each boarding house has prayers in the morning and evening. School chaplains visit each house at least once a week and the school chapel is always open for those who want to go and pray. A third of the school takes part in voluntary prayer groups but it's very much up to individuals. A father with two children at Downside emphasised that religion isn't forced on the pupils – 'it's a gentle, subtle part of what is there,' he said. A mother we spoke to praised the school's ethos. 'There's an emphasis on the whole person,' she said. 'Everyone is made to feel welcome.'

Excellent pastoral care and tolerance for the individual produces happy children. Each pupil has a tutor to oversee academic matters and there's a raft of people to talk to if they encounter problems – tutors, housemasters and housemistresses, housemothers, the chaplaincy team, health centre staff and a school counsellor who visits twice a week. Pupils generally well behaved. Policies on smoking, alcohol and drugs are very clearly spelled out. Smokers are enrolled on a smoking cessation programme in the health centre. 'Responsible' drinking permitted at the sixth form bar.

Sixth form has its own study centre (very quiet and studious when we visited). UCAS coordinator guides pupils through their university entrance. Pupils are prepared well for life after school via spiritual, moral, social and cultural education (SMSC) – topics covered include how to set up a bank account, relationships, even mortgages. School also runs themed weeks on issues like e-safety, alcohol and drugs.

Pupils and parents: Boarders (28 per cent international students) come from all over. At the beginning and end of term school buses ferry pupils to London, airports and local stations. Day pupils tend to live within a 30-minure drive – places like Shepton Mallet, Frome, Bruton and the Chew Valley.

Head says that while some of the pupils are from very privileged backgrounds no one is materialistic or showy. A parent with three boys at the school concurred. 'A lot of schools are quite flash these days,' she said. 'Downside isn't like that at all. The pupils are very well mannered and the school gives them really good values. They know what is right and what is wrong.' An old boy with two children at the school told us that while his daughter was 'almost surgically attached' to her mobile phone before moving to Downside she hardly uses it these days. 'The school is very good at keeping them busy,' he says. 'In my day Sunday was a quiet day but now there are coaches going off all over the place.'

Alumni (known as Old Gregorians) include writer and journalist Auberon Waugh, hotelier Rocco Forte, scriptwriter Peter Morgan and interior designer David Mlinaric. You can spot an Old Gregorian at a dinner party, we were told, because they will always offer to do the washing up afterwards. 'It's that blend of good manners and service,' explained the director of pastoral care.

Entrance: Pupils must be able to cope with the school's 'traditional academic curriculum.' At 11+ and 12+ entrance is via the Downside Junior Assessment Test (English and maths), plus reports and references from pupil's current school. At 13+ most applicants take CE (required mark of 50 per cent but the average is 65 per cent). At 16+ pupils sit tests in subjects they are planning to take at A level. B grades at GCSE required (As for maths and the sciences if they are planning to study these at A level).

Exit: A handful leave after GCSE, usually for day schools or to study vocational subjects. At 18 the vast majority head to university (gap years not so popular these days). One to Oxford in 2016, others to eg UCL, Exeter, Manchester, King's College London, Reading, Leeds,

York, Edinburgh, Newcastle, Birmingham, Cardiff, SOAS and the Royal Academy of Music.

Money matters: A 'substantial number' of scholarships and exhibitions are available (the number and size are at the discretion of the head). Means-tested bursaries, discounts of 2.5 per cent for children of Old Gregorians and 10 per cent for siblings.

Remarks: A boarding school with a strong moral compass. Downside is a great choice for Catholics and those seeking strong spiritual direction in a school. Its unpretentiousness, happy atmosphere and keen academic focus give pupils the chance to concentrate on acquiring their own intellectual and spiritual toolkit and to grow up in their own time.

D

Dumpton School

Deans Grove House, Deans Grove, Wimborne, Dorset BH21 7AF

Pupils: 347 • Ages: 2–13

Fees: £8,265– £14,808 pa

Tel: 01202 883818
Email: secretary@dumpton.com
Website: www.dumpton.com

Headmaster: Since 2005, Mr Andrew Browning BSc PGCE MA CChem MRSC (50s). Educated at Farnborough Grammar, read chemistry at Southampton University, followed by PGCE and masters in education at the Open University, the latter whilst teaching at Canford. He spent 22 years there, progressing to head of chemistry, housemaster and finally registrar – 'useful experience in advising parents on choice of secondary,' he says. Along the way he won the prestigious Salter's Prize for the teaching of chemistry. He still relishes teaching the subject at Dumpton (he spends about a third of the week teaching), as well as coaching CE and scholarship pupils and running the school's beekeeping club.

Inherited a fine school from his revered predecessor, with a strong staff and loyal following. Now he's had time to make his mark, parents report that he has maintained both, while giving the school a new impetus and professionalism. He lives and breathes Dumpton. He and his family live in the school's main building. His wife Jo, an experienced teacher with eight years at Castle Court under her belt, runs the mothers' and toddlers' group, acts as child protection officer, sorts out pastoral niggles and sometimes steps in as a supply teacher. Their two children are pupils at the school.

Entrance: Most join Dumpton nursery, often via toddlers' group, but pupils can come at any time, provided space – though usually not much. No test, but academic criteria apply after pre-prep and a good record is expected. Pupils are mainly local, but such is the school's reputation that local can mean as far as Hampshire or north Dorset and Wiltshire.

Exit: Canford is currently top of the pops, followed by Bryanston, then Talbot Health, Clayesmore and Poole grammars, plus a smattering of the big names. A minority opt for boarding or single sex schools. Many parents are reluctant to let children miss 'that special last year' at 13 and the dazzling record of scholarships (academic, sport, art and music) to top independent schools. Annual scholarships often reach 20 or more – the record is 36.

Remarks: School moved from Kent (where they were at Dumpton House) to Dorset during the Second World War, and then had a peripatetic trip round local stately homes, arriving at Dean's Grove (previously the headquarters of the Dalgety piggery) from Gaunt's House in 1986. The grounds and buildings are much nicer than the prospectus and website show. Red-brick classrooms, labs, barn-like art room (at the top of a spectacular outdoor spiral staircase), new DT and food tech dept and sports hall (not in its first youth) cluster round the pleasant and spacious main house in a series of courtyards.

A parent of three told us that the teaching staff are 'brilliant, really committed and inspiring', and the curriculum is demanding enough for plenty of pupils to sweep up spectacular scholarships. French is taught from the beginning of the pre-prep – by fully qualified native speakers, Latin but no Greek, proper science – taken for granted in a school run by a chemist – and plenty of technology, music and art, all backed up with theory as well as practice. Everywhere bristling with technology – several computer rooms now and interactive whiteboards et al everywhere. Some streaming, especially in scholarship years. Lessons are evidently enjoyed as well as taken seriously. Pupils have traffic light coloured pages in their homework diaries and leaving a red page open on the desk indicates to the teacher that you have not understood – a system which seems to work. No Sats but masses of careful tracking and assessment pick up anyone struggling. Lots of unobtrusive help for special needs, with a team of three to provide it.

No boarders now – every scrap of former boarding space is in use for teaching. The long school day (from 8.20am to 5.45pm for the prep section, though the younger ones do less) means that no one needs to take work home apart from some reading or at scholarship time. Prep is done after tea, except on Wednesdays, which are games afternoons – so comparatively little games at weekends. Loads of activities packed in as well as prep after tea and at lunchtime. Head is an eco enthusiast, so an enchanting eco trail, complete with dipping ponds, pontoons, plentiful but tasteful information points and a BBQ and camping site for summer sleepovers. Lots of awards for this project mean real scientists work with pupils, encouraged by input from the Ecology and Hydrology Centre at Winfrith. Splendid all weather pitches, fantastic play areas with tempting climbing structures, a real small boat, a run for the family/school dog and multiple seating and shelter areas (enjoyed in summer outdoor classes and by waiting mums). The newly covered pool is not quite so ecological but justified by a footprint less than that of frequent bus trips to Wimborne.

The bursar plays an unusually pivotal role in this family orientated community. He followed head from Canford, where he had run the catering, and has since become not only a planner and designer of facilities but also a sports coach.

One of only three negative school rules forbids crossing the road without an adult – the others forbid swearing and making others unhappy. The attraction over the road is a huge cricket pitch and athletics track with a stunningly picturesque oak in the centre; has recently bought two more acres of adjoining land which will become another sports area. Sports facilities are so good that Dumpton hosts festivals in netball, rugby etc, thus upping its impressive sporty record. Every child from year 3 up was in a match somewhere the day after our visit and the pupils sweep the board in most sports locally and beyond. As one parent commented: 'Dumpton's the perfect size, small enough to have a real family atmosphere and big enough to have proper teams, plays and music.'

Music is now vibrant, since the recent restructuring of the music department. Masses of instrumental and choral work emanate from the music school and a separate hut takes the steel band (so popular that staff have one too). The comfy school hall –'just big enough to take the prep or pre-prep all together, so we can't get any bigger' – has a seriously well-equipped stage lighting system, courtesy of the Friends of Dumpton. An extension has created a multi-purpose performing arts venue with Arts Courtyard. With all this going for it, Dumpton is generous with its support of the local community schools and clubs. Parents are welcomed into school and given chances to sample the delicious nut-free lunches and watch the children in the re-vamped dining area. Free choice of meals for older children and staff sit with pupils.

Tinies progress from Ducklings to Robins and Woodpeckers in the nursery (phonics from year dot) and thence to pre-prep. Boys in shorts for summer until 11 and grey trousers for winter. Girls in blue tartan skirts and all older pupils in snazzy gingham shirts or white blouses with dark blue edging. Buses to major surrounding towns. It feels like a traditional prep school but everything is bang up to date. We can't fault it.

The Elms School

Colwall, Malvern, Worcestershire WR13 6EF

Pupils: 156; 42 full, 84 flexi boarders • Ages: 3–13 (boarders from 8) • C of E

Fees: Day £8,805 – £19,650; Boarding £22,950 pa

Tel: 01684 540344
Email: office@elmsschool.co.uk
Website: www.elmsschool.co.uk

Head: Since 2010, Mr Alastair J L Thomas (30s). Mr Thomas is married with two daughters, the eldest of whom is at the school. A degree in French from King's College, London was followed by a brief stint at John Lewis before he joined Kingshott Prep School, where he became head of French. Moved to The Downs School nearby as head of French and Latin before becoming deputy head at Lambrook in Ascot.

A very social animal, approachable and full of energy, very keen on sports and music, eager to update the facilities of the school while retaining its ethos of fresh air, muddy knees, and plenty of independence. Staff say he is 'making things happen' and in particular cite his improvements in the profile of drama and music. He says the perception of the school is that the academics need to be strengthened – something he feels is unjustified, although he accepts that facilities need to be modernised. Teaches study skills and eats breakfast and lunch in hall with the children.

Wife, Hannah, throws herself into the life at the school – especially the gardens, which she has transformed.

Entrance: Entrance into pre-prep as early as 3, regular intake at 7 and 8. Most children from Herefordshire, Gloucestershire, Worcestershire, Monmouthshire and Powys. A few Forces families and a handful from overseas. Entry is by assessment rather than selection, and children who are intending to board can stay the night to test the waters. No scholarships but means-tested bursaries of up to 100 per cent for those 'who could benefit from what we offer'. 'We can and do get our children into leading public schools but we also support children who struggle'.

Exit: A few girls still leave at 11 but most stay on to 13. On exit the children go to a variety of schools: Malvern College, Cheltenham College, Bryanston, Radley, Heathfield, Eton, Rugby, Winchester, Wellington, Harrow, Milton Abbey, Oundle, lots to Shrewsbury. The school achieves a good collection of scholarships including a number for art and sport. A bright child could do very well here but it is not primarily an academic school.

Remarks: The oldest prep school in England, founded by Humphry Walwyn in 1614. Facing away from what passes for the main road in the village of Colwall, near Malvern, it opens out onto a site of 150 acres full of lovely green spaces and beautiful gardens. The school itself has rather the feeling of a collection of period houses that have grown together, sometimes in a slightly idiosyncratic manner. However, the school is much more than its academic buildings. For a start it has enviable sports facilities – including Astroturf, games field, swimming pool, a large sports hall, a stables of about 15-20 ponies (boarders can also bring their own) and a new outdoor riding arena. Sport obviously important – riding and shooting particularly so; the school has its own pistol and rifle shooting clubs. Then there is the school farm – rural studies compulsory up to and including year 7– which boasts a prize Hereford bull as well as Gloucester Old Spots, walked by the children round the grounds, a large flock of hens and a rather lovely vegetable garden. Each year group has a plot in which it is expected to grow its own vegetables. The children clearly love their involvement in the farm and take pleasure and pride in it. And they all speak very highly of the food – beef, pork and eggs come from the farm when available.

Boarding and teaching accommodation require some modernisation. The boarding facilities are a little overcrowded, although homely and tidy. Every child in the prep school (not pre-prep) has a designated bed; there are rest periods after lunch every day. This means that day children can board when they want. Newly completed science block.

The children are genuinely charming – friendly, respectful but responsive, confident and very happy indeed; well motivated and thoroughly self disciplined – we saw groups working on their art, music and sports during break, all purposeful, focussed and notably unsupervised, teachers within range if needed but leaving them to their own devices if not. There is an impressive new auditorium/theatre with some good music practice spaces, a beautiful new grand piano, and good sized music classroom attached at the back. A good art room too – full of innovative, varied and careful work. Parents say their children are very happy and they are keen on the head, whom they perceive as raising the academic standard of the school while retaining its ethos.They appreciate the variety of activities offered and the freedom of each child to 'be a little bit eccentric' if they want to.

Relatively high fees fund a staff:pupil ratio of about 1:7. Academically sound with many long-serving staff who say relationships with children are excellent, respectful but friendly and that parents are extremely supportive. Two ICT rooms, a pleasant library, not much prep as Saturday school is compulsory, and most reinforcement/prep style work is done within the classroom. Traditional curriculum includes a strong classics department. Follows a policy of moving children through classes as the need appears – the school calls this the ladder system – which can mean that the brighter sparks might spend the last two years in the top class. However, it is clear that the school is sensitive to parental concerns and in reality the majority of pupils are taught within a cohort of their own age. Groups are very small and no class is larger than 13; the smallest we saw was seven. The teaching model seems to work well and certainly destinations on exit don't point to any major hiccups.

On the whole a very traditional feel – there is something of the flavour of the Famous Five about the place – which may raise the hackles of some potential parents. Boys wear cord shorts and tweed blazers, girls wear kilts and jumpers, the children go out for a walk before breakfast and have outdoor activities every afternoon. There are no mobile phones, no cash, no sweets and no straying out of the school grounds. Chapel four times a week with visits from the local vicar and Catholic pupils taken to mass once a week. There are proper napkins at mealtimes, and grace is said. Some staff keep dogs in their classrooms and there is a 'pet palace' for the children's own rabbits and other small animals. Some parents may think it too sheltered by far, others will breathe a sigh of relief when they find it.

Weekend activities range from The Elms Tetrathlon to bugboarding to Nerf Gun War. Children might also go off geocaching in the Malvern Hills, paintballing or ice skating, or on a shopping trip to Cheltenham.

A school which wears its differences from the mainstream with pride but which is now also taking seriously the need for some changes. With its farm, fields and outdoor ethos this is a glorious place to get muddy while you learn – and somehow it manages to preserve childhood while fostering independence.

E

Exeter Cathedral School

The Chantry, Palace Gate, Exeter EX1 1HX

Pupils: 303; 6 full, 12 weekly, many flexi boarders • Ages: 3–13 (boarding from 8)

Fees: Day £6,714 – £11,199; Boarding + £6,990

Tel: 01392 255298
Email: registrar@exetercs.org
Website: www.exetercs.org

Headmaster: Since January 2016, James Featherstone (30s). Previously head of lower school at the Perse School in Cambridge. Studied French and Spanish at Durham, then did a PGCE there, and was a choral scholar at Durham Cathedral. He later joined the choir of Jesus College, Cambridge and became part of the professional quintet at St-John-at-Hampstead, London.

James and his family live in Hall House, the pre-prep school, and have embraced life in the southwest, making the most of nearby moors and beaches. Julia, his wife, was previously assistant director of music at the Stephen Perse Foundation and now teaches music part-time at ECS. Both are well-suited to this lifestyle; James is son of a headmaster so grew up living in boarding schools, and Julia spent her childhood living in vicarages.

To date, James has made significant improvements at ECS with his ambitious makeover plans, plus he has appointed new staff and repositioned older ones. Parents have been kept up to date with his newsletter and are so far impressed. 'I think he has exactly the right attitude for ECS,' one told us; 'a breath of fresh air,' said another. One added that he 'is dynamic, accessible, enthusiastic and ambitious for the school with a passion for nurturing the best in all his pupils and ensuring that they understand that success is not just based on grades but being a good person too.'

Entrance: Taster days with informal assessment, plus interview with headmaster. Voice trials for choristers (boys and girls). All special needs considered, although the school only supports mild needs currently. Children will only be turned away if their behaviour is not up to scratch on taster day (most are given a second chance). If a child doesn't fully meet academic standards, school may offer places as long as a learning support plan is agreed. Choristers must be above the baseline academically. Choristerships worth 25 per cent off tuition fee; there are currently 36 choristers at the school.

As well as taster days there are 'Come and be a chorister for a day' and 'Taste of boarding' sleepovers for prospective and current pupils alike. The entrance process and settling in is seamless. The school has a tea party for all new children and their teachers in Hall House just before term starts. Parents said, 'We were impressed with the staff, and the general warmth of the place.' Several told us that they chose ECS as it was the most natural step on from a small village primary school so suited their children best. Another parent told us, 'It was very much what the school could offer them, rather than whether the [children] would assist their results. Very refreshing compared to some of the other schools!'

Exit: Majority stay on to 13. In 2016, all year 8s gained places at their first choice school, some with scholarships, several with multiple offers. The head has recently appointed a head of scholarships, to guide pupils and parents through the process. Destinations include Sherborne, King Taunton, Taunton School, Exeter school, Maynard, Torquay Boys Grammar and Blundells, among others.

Former pupils include 14th century theologian Boniface; more recently, bass player Orlando le Fleming; Chris Martin – lead singer of Coldplay (who apparently once said, 'ECS is where it all began'); Hampshire CCC manager, Giles White and Dave Webb, ENO.

Remarks: Founded in the 12th century as a choir school, ECS is one of 35 choral schools in the UK, and the only independent boarding school in Exeter. As one parent put it, 'ECS is a rare kind of school,' and we agree. The Chantry, the prep school, and Hall House, the pre-prep, are on either side of the magnificent Exeter cathedral; an impressive backdrop to learning by anyone's standards. Although the multiple sites mean there is a lot of to-ing and fro-ing, it also means that the school feels very much part of the city. In fact one of the opening clips on the local news shows a line of happy children in royal blue tartans and sunny sweatshirts snaking across Cathedral Green.

Hall House is a former canonry and houses reception up to year 2. Securely enclosed by ancient Roman walls (and keypads), it is welcoming, bright and playful. A new 'spongey' all-weather playground separates the main building from the nursery, which was purpose-built in 2015. This is a fantastic area, free-flowing from inside to out. From the cosy keyworker areas and rooms, little ones (all in uniform) can play under awning in an area that leads to the shared playground one end, and the Woodland Garden at the other. This is a child's dream. Centred around a huge hawthorn oak tree, there's a mud kitchen, a bug hotel and The Hide, their very own shed to bird watch, play games or make dens with pipes, tarps and crates. Beyond this there is a terraced garden with allotments for each class and the gardening club. Worried about noise from the city's neighbours? Next door is the bishop's garden.

Classes are small, between 11-18 pupils. And the classrooms are imaginatively set up; we saw one with a zoo area, another with a bakery café. The creativity continues into The Bookwormy, the library, that has a car for a bookshelf and bug beanbags. On our visit, pupils were just back from swimming and were settling down in comfy tracksuits, devouring healthy snacks, ready for storytime. The balance feels just right here; 'there is an expectation for children to do their best and give their all at any task, and there is an academic push, but it is a gentle, perfectly pitched push,' parents said. 'My son has only been at ECS for a year but the school has made him more inquisitive and he has learned so much already,' said one. 'Even this morning, at the age of just 4, he was explaining to me why he could hear building work echoing as he walked across Cathedral Green.'

Pupils walk to the Chantry for lunch or to the cathedral for worship. For sport they are minibussed around the city; there never seems to be a dull moment here and it adds to the charm of this inner-city school. School begins with daily morning worship in the vast cathedral chapter house. This includes spiritual readings, hymn practice and a chance to 'just be'. The Chantry houses the offices, plus years 3 and 4. Other buildings including Evans for years 6, 7, and 8 are dotted around nearby in spaces requiring passcodes. It feels like a maze but it's not; it's full of character. Walks between buildings are across pedestrianized walkways, and glimpses of the cathedral, pretty cobbled courtyards, small peaceful gardens and cleverly planned playgrounds areas make it all feel really rather special.

The boarding accommodation is made up of three Georgian houses with 22 boys' beds and 18 girls' beds for 7-13 year olds. Currently there are six full-time boarders, 12 weeklies and a large number of flexi-boarders. All are from the UK, most live within an hours drive, and around half are choristers. Girl and boy choristers sing on alternate evenings so pupils do get downtime, but this adds to the irregularity of the boarding numbers throughout the week. One parent said, 'The girls are at home there and I know they are happy.' The large dorms have three bunkbeds each and a piano, or in some cases, a harp. Older pupils can have the privilege of a double room with two single beds. Decent showers and toilets. Efficient laundry system; even flexi-boarders get their own clean laundry basket. There's a comfortable common room, a TV room, a classroom to do prep, and the Cosy Club in the basement with sofas, DVDs, a games table and a crafts area. The boarders also have three gap students from Australia to keep them company. One parent said, 'To my eyes, parts of the boarding house could do with a lick of paint!' and this is true, but the new housemistress is on a mission and is gradually upgrading the whole place. After supper, prep, choir practice and Mrs Jolly's Hot Choccie Trolley, there's not much time for activities during the week. At weekends there can be anything from a handful of pupils to 25, and activities include trips to Haven Banks, Dartmoor or beaches. Recently boarders learnt to make sushi and hosted a Spanish tapas evening and an Irish evening.

As you would expect music plays a big part at ECS. One parent told us, 'Her music has gone from strength to strength and she has gone from a child who never stopped singing to a violinist, pianist and a member of Devon County Junior Choir with a place as a cathedral chorister. Yet the music hasn't taken over and she is developing a real love of hockey and netball.' Plans are afoot to create a music centre 'that is befitting of the standard of music that we're known for,' says the head. There is planning permission to pull down or extend the current music and drama building to make this happen. The design technology room has also recently been refurbished and the food technology room is equipped with a large and sunny kitchen. Most classrooms now have smart whiteboards or projectors. And there is talk of moving the ICT suite to a more central part of school and converting the current room into a hub, fully equipped with iPads and beanbags.

Mornings are for core lessons with form teacher and afternoons are for specialist lessons and sports. We were told, 'The English department in particular has exceeded our expectations – my eldest son has studied TS Eliot, Roald Dahl, Ted Hughes, Seamus Heaney, Shakespeare, Michael Morpurgo and Michelle Paver in the past three years with compelling lessons and homework that have both stimulated and stretched him.' Specialists teach science as separate subjects. French, from reception, is very popular. As is the teacher's dog. This is not unusual at ECS; there are several dogs. We met Ted, a rather floppy puppy who was thrilled to have tickles as pupils made their way between lessons. Latin is taught from year 6. The arts are just as impressive; we saw some fantastic (and huge) decorative masks on display in the art studio. Pupils are encouraged to think big and express themselves. For drama, year 4 recently performed Splash, a musical based on Noah's Ark. And every year 8 performs their leaving review. During a week of camping on Dartmoor, pupils work on sketches, singing and dancing (in-between other activities).

Learning support can cater for mild needs including dyslexia and dyscalculia, at extra cost. Small classes are also very beneficial and a real selling point to many families. Parents told us that ECS 'has offered an exceptional level of carefully selected and special, additional help specifically for my children. We are encouraged on a nearly daily basis with progress.' Another parent of boys with very different abilities and needs said, 'We were amazed at how quickly and accurately the teachers understood what made each of our boys tick and used the knowledge to help them both move forward.' In fact we were told several times over how pupils really do receive 'an all-round education.' One parent told us, 'her love of reading, spelling, maths and sport have all been developed at the school but I have also seen her become a kinder and more considerate child.' Another parent suggested that a school counsellor would be a welcome addition, but pupils can contact the independent listener who visits the school, if they wish.

The school doesn't have its own sports facilities but makes good use of some of the best facilities in a traditionally sporty city. All-weather surfaces at the main university campus, other facilities at St Luke's and outside the city at Pinhoe complete the mix. Cricket is played at the county ground whilst judo, squash, swimming, cross-country and athletics are all catered for. Climbing, kayaking, cross-Dartmoor walk and annual expedition add to the excitement. As do the additional inter-house competitions. A new innovation this year was the introduction of U7 festivals for netball, soccer and athletics. As well as some pupils playing county-level hockey and taking part in the National Prep Schools Athletics Championships, one girl was selected as part of the GB sailing team in the Cadet world championships. And another was accepted into the England Pathway Netball Satellite programme. To manage these budding sportsmen and women, and the 60+ fixtures per term, the head is on the hunt for a new director of sport to, quite literally, up their game.

All sports clubs are after school, and all musical activities take place throughout the school day. The library is open to all at breaks and lunchtimes. The librarian reads with all year 3's to get to know them and their abilities and tastes. She recently ran a library Olympics reading competition that pupils have already asked to happen again. Judo after-school club is currently very popular and other clubs include fencing, ukulele, indoor cricket nets, maths, drama and poetry, bell ringing, tennis and cooking. Equestrian club takes place at weekends. Parents are very happy with the activities on offer, one saiying, 'After-school clubs cover an incredible variety (and are inexpensive) – but if you're running late for pick-up even after this time, ECS happily keeps them for prep and supper if needed. As working parents this has been perfect and takes the stress out of being stuck in a meeting and unable to contact the school.' Local trips make the most of the local area with Roman walks and trips to local museums and interests. Years 5, 6 and 7 go to France for a week every two years, year 8 goes camping on Dartmoor, plus there's a Buckfast Abbey choir camp, and hopefully some sports tours soon.

The only real grumble we heard from a number of parents was that 'The food is not great,' and 'the school dinners are very unappetising.' We have no doubt that the head and his team will be onto this with a fix straight away. This city prep school isn't perfect but it's definitely doing it's best to head that way. It's full of charm, balances academia and childhood brilliantly, and most importantly, it gives pupils and their parents exactly what they want and need.

Exeter School

Victoria Park Road, Exeter EX2 4NS

Pupils: 1,103 • Ages: 7–18 • Sixth form: 198

Fees: £11,100 – £12,315pa

Tel: 01392 273679
Email: admissions@exeterschool.org.uk
Website: www.exeterschool.org.uk

Headmaster: Since 2003, Mr Bob Griffin MA (50s). Educated at Wallington High School for Boys, then Christ Church, Oxford, where gained first in modern languages (French and Spanish). Taught at Markham College in Lima before becoming head of modern languages at Haileybury. Came to Exeter from RGS Guildford, where he was second master for five years.

Pupils like him, staff respect him and parents rate him. 'One of the school's real strengths,' we were told by one mother. Another said he 'combines warmth with gravitas' and 'empathises with wider parental concerns'. Still teaches a little and often covers for staff absences. Solid, no-nonsense kind of skipper who keeps his ship on an even keel. Cares deeply about his school and doesn't look ready to move elsewhere. Takes time to get to know everyone and 'just joins in'. Head's wife works at nearby university. Son and daughter both went through the school. Popular with pupils we met, who described him as 'fair' and 'not beyond a practical joke or two'. Enjoys all things Hispanic, walking on Dartmoor and choral singing. Believes in steady development of facilities rather than headline grabbing expansion. Proud of pupils' achievements and of how school has raised its game.

Head of junior school: Since September 2015, Mrs Sue Marks. Began as a medical scientist working in pathology and clinical biochemistry. Qualified as a teacher in Essex and has been involved in primary teaching now for over 20 years, most recently as head of early years and then head of junior school at St Joseph's School, a co-ed independent day school in Launceston, Cornwall.

In 2012, she received The Astra Zeneca Primary Science Teacher Award and was invited to become a fellow of the PSTT College (Primary Science Teaching Trust), which promotes the provision of excellent primary science throughout the country.

Lives on the edge of Dartmoor with her husband and two children, both of whom enjoyed a most successful sixth form experience at Exeter School and are now busy with their further studies. She is also a keen runner and has recently completed her second London Marathon, running for Cancer Research UK.

Academic matters: Fair degree of academic rigour in the junior school (spellings, 3Rs and fairly trad subject mix), but emphasis placed increasingly on individualised learning, with IT playing an important rôle. Following a recent parental survey, less onerous homework, to allow children time to pursue outside activities in their own neighbourhoods – 'A better balance,' one parent told us. Specialist rooms (art/DT and IT suite) also on first floor and final year makes more use of whole school facilities. Clear emphasis on making learning enjoyable – fancy dress competitions and treasure hunts go hand in hand with events like World Book Day, when children's authors come to talk to pupils. Previous head was even dressed as Cruella de Vil during a recent inspection (apparently no inspectors went missing

E

afterwards). House competition includes fun challenges, like 'best flipper' on pancake day. Staff expect high standards, which are achieved by all, including those who start shakily. Junior school SENCo provides screening and support for dyslexia and numeracy issues as required.

Top notch results are 'just a part of what the school does well,' say parents. In 2016, 55 per cent A*/A at A level and 82 per cent at GCSE.

Not a hothouse, but slackers will be pulled up sharply. Regular reporting to parents (includes early warning on promotions and demotions) is a cornerstone of the school. More of an old grammar school work ethic, which most parents relate to easily. Larger top sets (up to 24) in languages and maths allow the less able to get more individual attention in lower sets (10 to 14). Inequalities of choice in modern languages now resolved by a carousel of two terms each in French, German and Spanish in years 7 and 8. Broad choice of options at GCSE, plus RE for all. Twenty-five subjects on offer at A level. Maths and science lead school's results tables but performance is impressive across the board.

Laboratories (all 12 of them) date back to 60s but have been upgraded in terms of kit. Classrooms we saw were all equipped with interactive boards and digital projectors. Staff appointments from state and independent sectors are handled with considerable care, so mix of youth versus experience is about right.

Experienced learning support co-ordinator provides help where needed; staff and parents now realise that special needs cross the whole ability spectrum. Dyscalculia is handled within maths department. 'Pupils are delightful,' says special educational needs coordinator, 'and average ones leave with a cracking set of results.' Strategy sheets for pupils receiving support are updated twice termly and are available through school intranet to all staff. Recent needs addressed include a registered blind pupil, hearing impaired, cystic fibrosis and mild autism.

Amazing programme of enrichment activities – mock trial on day we visited – centred around Crossing club for seniors (includes Oxbridge entrance preparation) and Catalyst club for middle school.

Games, options, the arts: Busy is an understatement here, with large numbers of pupils and staff occupied after school and at weekends. All main games are played well, teams at all levels and pupils reach county, regional and occasional national representation. Older pupils branch out into wider range of sports. Strong PE staff (five full-time in senior school), some extra performance coaches where required and loads of support from rest of staff. Large and modern sports hall with well-equipped fitness area upstairs, dance studio, squash courts and a climbing wall. Kayaking hugely successful. Other leisure activities include croquet and ultimate frisbee. Main sports are netball, hockey, rounders (for girls) and football, hockey, rugby, cricket (for boys). Cross-country, squash and swimming for all. Surprisingly full fixture lists for older juniors, and inclusive approach to participation means results are mixed. Initially unsporty children tend to catch on – 'My daughter even plays in a local hockey team now,' reported one parent. Lots of visits (a residential trip at end of year 5) and wealth of activities.

Extensive sports fields with Astroturf and a variety of hard surfaces for tennis and netball. Outdoor heated swimming pool in centre of school; competition standard pool under construction. Some parental concern that a successful sporting year group could be hard to 'break into' if children joined it later. Sports tours overseas are well subscribed. Annual Ten Tors challenge is taken very seriously (more candidates than places available ensures competitive edge) and involves teaching and ancillary staff as well as parents (former Rifles lieutenant colonel leads the school's campaign) over a number of weekends.

Large numbers of juniors take instrumental lessons and sing in choir. Regular concerts (some for charity) and drama (recent nativity play was in French). Annual highlight involves all year 6 leavers at the end of summer term. Pupils also participate in outside music festivals and competitions. Parents like to meet informally for coffee in local cafés and support the school with practical help as well as fundraising. Senior choirs, jazz bands, orchestras provide glittering programme of concerts throughout the year. One parent said her children had found the approach to music 'too serious', whilst another said that hers had 'flown musically' since joining. Choral society pulls in staff, parents past and present and pupils for high profile performances in Exeter Cathedral. Other concerts are charity fundraisers. Some reach top grade/diploma level and regular participants in national choirs or orchestras. Outreach work at local state primary school involving input from sixth form musicians. We witnessed a lunch-time rehearsal for the junior orchestra – 'work in progress,' we concluded, but range of levels and instruments showed strength in depth.

Good art studios (doors open from 8am to 6pm), with plenty of talent in evidence. Potential quickly harnessed by experienced staff and displays in exhibition gallery bear witness to this. Drama has been headed by a couple who arrived from Paris over 20 years ago – inventive, diverse and of a high standard. Wide range of productions for seniors (most recently Pirates of Penzance) and juniors, with performances in main hall. More intimate pieces in drama studio, which has raked seating.

Strong CCF contingent attracts about two-thirds of pupils, though some opt for D of E or community service. Visits and trips abound. Recent ones include year 9 battlefields visit to France and Belgium which involved over 100 pupils, annual art visit to St Ives, geographers in Alps spending a day on the Argentière glacier, joint classics and geography visit to Bay of Naples (taking in Solfatara volcano and Pompeii).

Background and atmosphere: Founded in 1633, originally for sons of freemen of Exeter. Collegiate feel attributable to famous Victorian architect William Butterfield (who also designed Keble College, Oxford). Links to city's St John's Hospital account for presence of one of three surviving Blue Boy statues over doorway of Exonian Centre (houses archives and provides meeting space for governors' meetings etc). Twenty-five acre site is only a mile from city centre and provides views to open countryside and Haldon Hills beyond. Recent fill-ins and additions have been skilfully matched with original brickwork. Central tower (in brick not ivory) houses office accommodation and staff rooms and is especially well integrated.

Juniors in lovely Georgian house adjacent to senior school. Recent remodelling has provided improved facilities, including four additional classrooms on first floor. School has doubled its numbers in recent years. Period architectural features lend an air of graciousness and classrooms have made good use of the generous amount of space. Pupils benefit from shared facilities with senior school (eg Astroturf, swimming pool, music school, auditorium with large stage for productions). Own multi-purpose hall. School chapel is also used regularly.

Post-war school became boys' direct grant reverting to independent status in 70s. Girls appeared at sixth form level in 1980; fully co-ed since 1997. Present ratio in favour of boys looks set to stay, given proximity of two well-established girls' schools. Girls we spoke to thought co-ed worked well and was 'a better preparation for later life.'

No hint of toffishness, though range of extracurricular activities is more akin to an expensive boarding school. Pupils at all levels look smart; some flamboyance evident amongst sixth form boys in particular. Generally busy but occasionally relaxed sixth formers can choose how to use their free time. Many go to the well-equipped and refurbished library, while others choose to work in the sixth form centre study room and/or hang out in the comfy seating in the large common room next door (breaktime bacon butties a particular favourite). More than adequate school lunches served to majority of pupils (only 20 per cent opt for packed lunches) in multi-purpose hall.

Pastoral care, well-being and discipline: New junior entrants are assigned a buddy from year 6 who helps them through the initial stages. Senior staff visible around site outside lesson times. Sixth formers allowed off-site at lunchtimes, but most don't have time. Mainly self-managing discipline, given school's positive approach, but potential troublemakers risk being weeded out at end of year 11. School marshal, alias CCF instructor, pops up unexpectedly and helps to ensure order. Well-established house system monitors progress and well-being. First line of contact for parents through heads of house now made much accessible through email. Parents praise this system and say that 'a response is always forthcoming quickly and any query investigated'.

Combination of a weekly assembly in the main hall (PowerPoint presentation with a moral twist followed by extensive laudations for conquering sports teams when we visited) for the whole school. Smaller chapel and other gatherings for houses are well established. Sixth form has own programme, with outside speakers plus lots of HE and careers input.

Pupils and parents: Increasing numbers of girls, who now make up about 40 per cent of pupils. Predominantly from professional families. Bright and 'expected to deliver' academically. Popular as a 'family choice' for sons and daughters. New year 7s all go on early residential weekend to an outdoor education centre at Dartmeet. Senior pupils (many have come right through from the junior school) provide leadership in hands-on rather than authoritarian way. Sixth formers we encountered were refreshingly articulate and enthusiastic. Extensive playing fields good for letting off steam. Mobile phones (which are allowed if used sensibly outside lessons) were hardly in evidence. A few pupils cycle to school.

Former pupils include Olympic yachtsmen Stevie Morrison and Ben Rhodes, former MP David Bellotti and actor Matthew Goode. Other alumni range from explorers, business, military and media people. ESPA (parents' support group) is very active, with social events and fundraising through year.

Entrance: To junior school mainly at 7+ and 8+. Increasingly from state sector, but also from pre-prep in Exminster (many other local pre-preps have closed in recent years). Applicants may also enter at other ages where places are available. Selection is by informal assessment and report from current school.

School report and January examination for senior school (no longer required for most junior school pupils). School considers potential as well as achievement. Entry from prep schools and others at 13+. Sixth formers selected by GCSE results (minimum three As and three Bs at GCSE), school reference and interviews. Catchment area spread far and wide and includes over 60 feeder schools, but mainly within a 20 mile radius.

Exit: Almost all juniors (95 per cent in 2016) to senior school at 11+ with progression normally seamless unless applicant has joined in year 6. A trickle go to state selectives – usually Colyton or Torquay Grammars. Some 10-20 per cent leave after GCSEs. Three Oxbridge places in 2016; rest to a range of destinations and courses eg St Andrews, Manchester, London, Southampton, Plymouth. Twelve medics and two vets.

Money matters: 'Honest to goodness value for money', with flat fee from 11-18. 'Typically, both parents work and grandparents may chip in,' we were told. Range of awards at 11, 13 and 16 including three 100 per cent bursaries at 11+ and five at sixth form entry, including two for scientists, funded by former pupils. Governors' means-tested bursaries also help parents unable to afford full fees, and there are various academic and music scholarships.

Remarks: Unpretentiously successful. Offers a stimulating learning environment with every opportunity for boys and girls to play and work hard.

The Fallibroome Academy

Priory Lane, Upton, Macclesfield, Cheshire SK10 4AF

Pupils: 1,499 • Ages: 11–18 • Sixth form: 320

Tel: 01625 827898
Email: info@fallibroome.org.uk
Website: www.fallibroome.academy/

Executive principal and CEO: Since 2002, Peter Rubery BEd (MMU) MEd (Liverpool) MBA (LINCOLN) FRSA, previously headmaster of Ercall Wood Technology College, Wellington; joined as headmaster, a role which evolved into principal and finally into the grandly titled executive principal and CEO of the multi-academy trust of which Fallibroome is part.

Although understated in his chat, it is clear Peter Rubery is one of life's quiet innovators. Pseudo-corporate lingo about 'continuous improvement' might roll off his tongue (he did an MBA in international educational leadership), but there is nothing empty about his rhetoric; under his visionary leadership, the school has clocked up a number of trailblazing firsts. It was one of the first schools to convert to an academy; one of the first to become a college of performing arts, one of the first to be designated an outstanding teaching school, and latterly, one of the first to create a multi-academy trust. So what is the significance of all this? Well, it's huge; the associated fiscal incentives for early adoption of all these initiatives has created a mighty lot of funds which has resulted in Fallibroome being able to boast the sort of jaw-dropping, high calibre facilities (theatres, recording studios, enormous sport pitches and floodlit tennis courts) which, frankly, the more beleaguered pockets of the independent sector could only dream about.

Just idly chewing the cud – because he is very easy to talk to – it is clear his eyes are always scanning the horizon for new opportunities for pupils. In passing, he refers to having attended a couple of TED conferences (the world-famous event around Technology, Entertainment and Design), after which he 'happened to meet' TED's founder, Chris Anderson, only to discover that TED was looking to replicate its formula to a youth audience via a franchised version, TedX. Blink your eyes and bob's your uncle and Fallibroome has started hosting TedX conferences (since 2009) with around 450 of its own over-16 students attending and 150 students from other schools. The live streaming of all its talks are held in archived recordings on the TedX website and a couple – a fairly huge honour, this – of the Fallibroome youth TEDX speakers have made it onto the main TED website. (An achievement you won't see every day on a university application form, that's for sure).

And this is by no means a one off example of serendipity and force of will happily colliding; having learnt about the world famous Venezuela Youth Orchestra (a community project which cascaded music teaching down to underprivileged

F

children resulting in a world class orchestra), he decided to model it at Fallibroome (as you do), likewise cascading musical knowledge down to the primary schools via peer tuition. So what next for Fallibroome – a world class orchestra perhaps? Watch this space.

What's more, at the time of our visit, the school had just released an extraordinary video, First day at Fallibroome. No empty marketing exercise, it was a carefully choreographed theatrical extravaganza with every pupil and teacher taking part; five days after its release, it had clocked up 37,000 hits globally and shortly after made it onto regional BBC news. What a joyous 11 minutes; a single tracking shot inside the school, pupils singing, dancing, showcasing what the school offers: scientists doing experiments with fire, orchestras playing, actors reciting, linguists dancing flamingo, woodworkers sawing away, sporty types dribbling footballs. A more inclusive, dazzling display, we had rarely seen.

So, with all this innovation bubbling away, was he tempted by the new fare offered by the education secretary and harbouring secret thoughts of converting to a grammar? Squashing the suggestion like a fly he is, he says, 'resistant to the whims of politicians' and only 'responds to opportunities, not fads'. Every initiative he has pursued, he emphasizes, has been to create greater opportunities for pupils. We believed him; offering its non-selective intake as wide a choice as possible seems to be the Fallibroome ethos and is evidenced in every nook and cranny of this creative school.

An obvious team player, he refers frequently to Francis Power – now headmaster, previously deputy head – and to whom Peter Rubery attributes much of the school's success, as well as his dedicated team of teachers.

Not surprisingly, having started out as PE teacher, he is keen on team sport and used to play in the national volleyball squad. And showing a little of that cultural diversity he so wants pupils to foster, he loves music, the blues in particular. But there ain't no Muddy Waters about this visionary man or his splendid school.

Academic matters: At GCSE in 2016, 34 per cent of entries got A or A* (84 per cent A*-C in maths, 80 per cent in English) and 79 per cent of pupils got 5+ GCSEs A*-C grades. At A level 29 per cent A*/As.The school does particularly well in maths at A level with 23 per cent of entries getting A* and 57 per cent getting A* in further maths in 2016. Generally, across A levels over the last few years in core subjects (sciences, maths, languages, English) between 45-50 per cent of the entries entering per subject get A or A* (with the exception of biology at 36 per cent and English literature at 41 per cent). Both genders fare about the same and subjects tend to have an even split, possibly with more boys opting for science but only marginally.

From year 8, students are taught in ability groups in English, maths and languages but no pupil should ever rest on their laurels or feel trapped; there are termly reviews and mobility between groups. As for languages, all pupils start with French plus either Spanish or German. About half take one or more to GCSE and about 14 continue to A level.

To adopt the corporate language which is scattered through Fallibroome's prospectus, its key USP is the breadth of its curriculum. So beyond the more traditional core A level subjects, pupils can opt for psychology, sociology, dance, music technology or media studies.

Average class size is 30. It's a national teaching school so there is a strong focus on improving teaching quality. That's the theory – what about the practice? The parents we spoke to grumbled a little about high staff turnover over the last 12 months and the inconsistency in teaching styles which resulted, as well as the detrimental impact on pupils when teachers left at a crucial time. One parent said her child had had four changes across four GSCE subjects at crucial times.

So it's not all golden; one parent felt her child had clashed with a teacher in a core subject and that pupil, along with a few others, had resorted to private tuition to fill the gaps where he had 'come into his own' in the subject. Conversely, the same parent praised the school's flexibility; when her child wanted to swap a subject at GCSE, a successful transition was made. Likewise another parent said he felt the 'individualized care and attention for students' was staggeringly good; the staff were 'very supportive in helping pupils reach their potential'.

The school facilities certainly help back up the teaching – there are nine science labs and every teaching room has e-learning facilities so the use of new technologies is embedded. One parent commented on her child's 'fantastic' IT knowledge, saying the school was 'always one step ahead'. There was, for example, a significant investment in iPads and wireless, which Peter Rubery felt allowed for more tailored ways for pupils to receive feedback. The IT suites – open to 'booking' for any lesson – had, he said, the highest quality of equipment (the best kit being crucial for high achievement in computing or electronics).

SEN students are catered for extremely well too under the school's Quality First Teaching initiative. Different strategies are adopted for different subjects and inclusivity is a driver. Where the student has a statement/EHC plan – there were 23 in place at the time of our visit – they will receive the specified help which may include one-to-one with a teaching assistant. Those without a statement may receive specialist support outside lessons. According to Peter Rubery – and their vast database of metrics can no doubt back this up – SEN students make faster progress than their non-SEN peers.

The school also offers BTecs and other vocational qualifications.

Games, options, the arts: Fallibroome's status as a college of performing arts has resulted in an embarrassment of riches. The glossy What's On programme for 2016-17 is worthy of a West End theatre: spanning all types of concerts, theatrical offerings from Shakespeare to new writing, it even includes a play which came out of the National Theatre Connections Programme. Pupils don't just perform, either; they refine their craft in workshops with the professionals and go on arts trips all over. The impressive performance photos all around the school reinforce a sense of vibrancy, slick production values and widespread participation. Parents spoke with awe about ambitious musical productions, especially an outstanding performance of Les Misérables. What's more, one parent, who referred to such evenings as a 'parade of brilliance', was quick to add that those who tried hard to, say, learn a musical instrument but who weren't necessarily the most talented, got recognised at the school's awards evenings for effort. The same parent also said the creative culture meant, refreshingly, boys plunged into music and dance without any self-consciousness. The extracurricular music similarly runs the gamut; orchestras, choirs and ensembles. If you want to compose, do folk or rock guitar, play in a string quartet or a samba band, it exists.

With sport, there is a decent spread and the facilities to back this up, such as an all-weather pitch. In 2015, the school's netball team won the National Netball Champions (the first comprehensive school to win the title). Although parents of boys who were keen footballers seemed peeved, saying a greater emphasis was placed on rugby (Peter Rubery didn't necessarily accept this but did make the point that rugby was 'the sport' in independent schools. Enough said). One parent of a talented footballing son said he didn't get the opportunities he would like to play competitively. That said, the school boasts a former Manchester United player (not to mention an ex-Olympic gymnast). The school doesn't have its own pool but the leisure centre is, quite literally, next door.

There are all the usual clubs and societies – not quite as plentiful an array as one might find in pockets of the independent sector, but there are still some unusual ones, such as training in TV (camera work and editing), and when we visited we noted the school had won the British Orienteering Championships in 2015 (unique for a comprehensive school). One parent said, 'whatever they're interested in, it's happening in the school'.

At sixth form stage, there is an enrichment programme; one inspection report said it was 'outstanding and sets a benchmark for sixth form extracurricular'. So pupils might form part of management teams, debating teams, gain work experience in South Africa (the school's commitment to raising funds for charity means it supports two schools in the rural western Cape) ....or if they fancied it, take up Mandarin. No, really. When it comes to writing their personal statement at university application time, these pupils are not going to be scraping that barrel for something arresting to say.

Background and atmosphere: The buildings are mostly modern red brick and, over the school's 36 year history, the many additions have evolved in an organic way. The modernity has a clean, Scandi-feel, sunk as it is into woodland lined grounds, vast playing green fields always in sight.

Every wall carries something inspiring which would surely prise open the most closed of adolescent minds. Dazzling art displays are everywhere you look and large, attractively framed photos of school trips, from Iceland to the Isle of Man, show tired but happy groups of young adults. These are placed alongside all the beautiful photo stills from dance, theatre and music performances. The school's ethos – Trust, Respect, Optimism – hangs in a banner in one of the entrances and even to sceptical corporate-averse minds such as ours, manages to sound full of gusto. This school really does seem to do what it says on the tin.

The facilities – from the relatively new sixth form centre, described by one parent as 'like being at university', to the recording booths – are extraordinary.

Pastoral care, well-being and discipline: Peter Rubery is keen to reinforce that there has been a big investment in this area; a pastoral support centre opened in 2012 with a student counsellor and a behaviour support coordinator for more troubled students. Plus, all the usual courses are run in the RESPECT module on drugs, use of online, social media.

Learning managers (heads of year to you and me) monitor the welfare of their group of pupils and are the first point of contact. The pastoral system is overseen by two assistant principals, responsible for years 7-11 and 12 and 13 respectively. One parent, whose child had had a few integration difficulties when he started school, referred to the high levels of teacher support, spurring him on to become involved in music; he was quickly assimilated into broader friendship groups. Another parent stressed the pastoral system was not 'cut and paste' but reflected the caring culture; when his child encountered difficulties in sixth form, massive efforts were made to make him feel valued.

None of the parents we spoke to had encountered bullying, but of course with a school of this magnitude, it exists. Peter's Rubery's response, when asked, was to imply to zero tolerance. And we were inclined to believe that.

It's a big school but Peter Rubery is hot on uniform; the pupils wander in herds of bottle green blazers, while sixth formers wear business clothes. A recent inspection report found behaviour to be 'exemplary'. Pupils are motivated into good behaviour with carrots not sticks (house points, letters of commendation – but also attempts to channel a pupil in a more positive way via interests). If this doesn't work, the metaphorical stick kicks in; the usual panoply of detention-type punishments. One parent referred to the 'spectrum of behaviour issues' which existed but felt there was a 'very well designed system of escalating sanctions'; all pupils knew where they stood, it was very effective. Another parent felt it was a respect, not fear-based system; children were encouraged to self-manage.

Pupils and parents: Fallibroome pupils are drawn from a number of areas, from Cheshire 'wealth spots' like Prestbury to less affluent areas like Upton Priory, so it's a diverse bag. The parents we spoke to found the web portal, The Parental Gateway, helpful in updating them. One parent, a working mother, found being able to book appointments online helpful. All were complimentary about the school – emailing a teacher was, one said, 'an efficient business'. The only grumble from one was that registering a child's absence was troublesome (having notified the school her child was ill, she would invariably get a follow up later asking why her child was not at school). An irritant rather than a complaint.

Another parent felt that while the children were given heaps of information on universities, parents needed more to help guide them (adolescent monosyllables not always being the best conduit). Conversely, another parent waxed lyrical about the very detailed reporting on each child – postcards, texts, emails – to flag up progress or even if a pupil seemed a bit off colour.

The parents at this school are busy working people; they admire the school, shout from the touchlines at matches and give rousing applause at concerts, but they don't have the time to be caught in a quagmire of pushy parental competitiveness.

Entrance: Applications from pupils from the seven feeder primary schools (Bollinbrook, Broken Cross, Mottram St Andrew, Nether Alderley, Prestbury, Upton Priory, Whirley) are prioritised, along with other criteria, such as siblings at the school. It usually has a waiting list of well over 30 pupils. All students are invited to spend a day during the summer term to acclimatise.

Exit: Some 60 per cent stay on into sixth form. Every pupil must have 5+ A*-C grades at GCSE and Bs in any subject they wish to pursue at A level. In 2016, three to Oxbridge, with about 40 per cent to Russell Group unis: eg Southampton, Bristol, Durham, Warwick, Edinburgh, Newcastle, Leeds, alongside the very popular Manchester and Liverpool. Spread of courses from sciences and social sciences to business and engineering. The spotlight on performing arts means that many go off to drama or music school – 14 pupils in 2016. Recent destinations have included the Central School of Speech and Drama, the Guildhall School of Music, Leeds College of Music and BIMM Manchester.

Remarks: This large, wonderful school offers an educational smorgasbord which is as rich and as plentiful as you will find anywhere. It is a place where your child will firm up their identity as a young adult, discover intellectual passions and open their mind to reach academic heights. If you want this for your child, then keep your fingers crossed for a place. If you are wavering between state and independent education for your child, visit this school as a priority.

Farmor's School

The Park, Fairford, Gloucestershire GL7 4JQ

Pupils: 912 • Ages: 11–18 • Sixth form: 225

Tel: 01285 712302
Email: dtaylor@farmors.gloucs.sch.uk
Website: www.farmors.gloucs.sch.uk

F

Headteacher: Since 2013, Matthew Evans, previously deputy head of the Henry Box School in Witney. Has won a national teaching award for achievements in enterprise education; his first leadership post was coordinating a school's business and enterprise specialism.

Academic matters: A comprehensive school taking the full ability range and achieving very good results: 71 per cent got five or more GCSEs at A*-C including maths and English in 2016; 33 per cent A*/A grades. At A level, 53 per cent A*-B grades. Sciences very strong throughout, as are languages (French and Spanish plus Latin at GCSE). Art and design students do extremely well at A level, as do English, business, sociology and media studies. A great strength is range of subjects – 24 at A level plus a handful of vocational subjects, including engineering. Specialist teachers for every subject.

Lots of enrichment activities at all stages outside the standard curriculum. Well-organised library with full time staff, plenty of PCs – 350 networked throughout the school; pupils can access their own work and also have protected internet access for appropriate study. Dedicated spaces for sixth formers to study and or socialise.

Good support for those needing additional help, especially with literacy – mostly delivered in class, but on a withdrawal basis if need be. Classes are not small – 25 to 30 is not unusual in the lower years, but smaller for GCSE years (around 20) and sixth form groups. Good careers advice – the school has Investor in Careers status, with a week in year 12 dedicated to post-18 options.

Games, options, the arts: Good sports facilities – though no swimming and no all-weather surfaces – but rugby, football, hockey, netball, basketball, tennis, cricket and athletics, with many representatives in county teams and regular wins in district and county sports. Plenty of space to run about in. The local on-site sports centre is shared by the school and local community.

Wealth of foreign trips, mostly sports and language related – including destinations such as Ecuador, Paris, Berlin, Iceland and Russia as well as World Challenge trips to Bolivia and the Galapagos Islands – organised by enthused staff and, says the head, very well supported by parents. A great drama studio with plenty of lighting and sound equipment – a proper green room etc. Performing arts GCSE growing in popularity, a recording room and practice rooms for musicians – in fact quite a buzzing music block; about 150 take individual music lessons and plenty of opportunities to join in choirs and orchestras. Regular concerts and dramatic productions. Young Enterprise and D of E are also popular

Background and atmosphere: Founded in 1738 with money left by Elizabeth Farmor and Mary Barker to educate 50 boys in Fairford – a picturesque Cotswoldy town in a predominantly rural area. Girls were admitted in 1815, became fully co-educational in 1922. Originally in the centre of town, in a building now the community centre, but in 1961 it moved to its present site in 18 acres of parkland a short walk away, becoming an 11-18 comprehensive in 1966 and an academy in 2011. The 1960s buildings are showing their age rather – not least because 1200 pupils are now being accommodated in a building originally designed for 400. The head says keeping it all in order is 'a constant battle', but some very good new buildings too. An impressive business teaching facility and very good, new science labs. Recent funding has paid for renovations to the fabric of the school, with all the toilet blocks in the process of refurbishment, and a new sixth form learning resource centre (library in old money).

All parts of the school are well ordered – no tatty displays – though possibly more could be done to show off some of the excellent art and textiles work (which has netted amazing A level results but is not prominent round the school). Staff say, 'We can do challenging work with the pupils because the standards of behaviour are so high and pupils want to learn and do well.' Pupils say the teachers are 'fantastically supportive' and that even in this sizeable school, 'you're never anonymous'. Lots of emphasis – from staff, pupils, parents and head – on the quality of relationships all round.

Pastoral care, well-being and discipline: Clear rules, well known and observed. Head says most pastoral issues arise from families under pressure rather than disobedience or disruption in the classroom. Tutor groups of about 30. The atmosphere is unflustered and orderly. Lots of links with external agencies where needed, school counsellors available, peer counselling and buddy reading schemes to promote good relationships and support between pupils at different stages. Drugs/ alcohol etc 'less of an issue than ever' – school takes 'a very strong line' if any misuse is discovered.

Pupils and parents: Intake from Fairford, surrounding villages and as far away as Swindon. A wide social mix, from those who are struggling to the comfortable county set. Parents are very supportive, with an active and positive PTA. They praise the school's good and frequent communication, say staff are very responsive to individual pupil's needs and that pupils, though well supported, are expected to 'get on with it' – high expectations in a friendly environment. Pupils are polite, motivated, personable, fairly well turned out and very pleased to be at Farmor's. They speak with great enthusiasm about the approachability and commitment of the staff, and their willingness to offer support and help.

Entrance: Has doubled in size over the last 10 years and now 'as big as we can get' – impressive, considering that the local demographic dip would have predicted a fall rather than a rise in school numbers. A fairly large catchment – some children travel in from the Wiltshire borders. Truly comprehensive – 'no selection of any description' – though all come with their Sats scores and are put in sets for maths, science and languages (not for English).

Five A*-Cs at GCSE needed for sixth form, with Bs preferred for A level choices, although some leeway allowed. About half the sixth form (which numbers 150 per year) come from other local schools (mostly those that don't offer sixth form provision).

Exit: Around 50-60 per cent stay on for sixth form, with most others going on to vocational courses, some to sixth form college in Cirencester. Most A level students – around 70 per cent – continue their studies at university, although that profile is changing in the current climate to include apprenticeships and management training. Over half go to Russell Group universities with business, sciences and art very popular subjects. Favourite destinations include Cardiff, Nottingham, Bristol, Exeter, Swansea and Manchester. One to Oxbridge in 2016 and two to study medicine.

Remarks: A comprehensive school in the best sense: opportunity and encouragement for every child at the right level and a genuine partnership between pupils, parents and staff.

Godolphin, Salisbury

Milford Hill, Salisbury, Wiltshire SP1 2RA

Pupils: 355; 68 full, 152 weekly/flexi boarders • Ages: 2–18 (boarding from 7) • Sixth form: 102

Fees: Day £6,537 – £19,515; Boarding £17,001 – £32,304 pa

Tel: 01722 430509
Email: admissions@godolphin.wilts.sch.uk
Website: www.godolphin.org

Headmistress: Since 2014, Mrs Emma Hattersley, previously deputy head, pastoral, at Sherborne Girls, before which she was a housemistress at Canford School. Mrs Hattersley trained as an opera singer at the Royal Academy of Music and has a music degree from Durham. Married with three children, she says she took her career break early so that now, in her early 50s, with her children pursuing their own careers, she is able to devote her time entirely to Godolphin. Her actor husband is immensely supportive, to the extent of running 'speakeasy' communications and other workshops in school.

Her calm, unthreatening exterior deceptively understates the determination beneath. Since arriving at Godolphin she says she has identified needs for brightening up areas of the fabric, developing staff and increasing opportunities for charitable activities. In fact she has already started on a programme of new showers, 'nice enough to make the girls feel good', surveyed parents of all leavers, consulted girls and produced her vision document for the future. She has also initiated the Elizabeth Godolphin Award for sixth formers, which gives focus to a programme of self-development and preparedness for work/life demands.

She says she believes in the Godolphin ethos: happiness, warmth, development which is aspirational but 'absolutely not at the expense of well-being'. 'We are not a hothouse' she says, but aim at 'the best we can possibly be in each girl's own style, celebrating diverse talent' and encouraging everyone to 'succeed at the level right for them'. Having taken on a school a little stunned by losing its new head to 'higher things' after three years, she has restored confidence and won parents' and girls' respect with her ability to perceive and develop what is best at Godolphin. A parent commented that 'under Mrs Hattersley staff can really develop their own teaching and pastoral skills.'

Head of prep: Since September 2014, Julia Miller BA MEd (50s). Having studied history at Queen's University Belfast, followed by a PGCE, she taught at Banbridge Academy, Victoria College and Cheltenham Ladies' College (where she ran D of E and was a deputy housemistress). Head of history and head of house at Godolphin, she was appointed head of the prep after 22 years at the school. She clearly loves it and puts huge enthusiasm and kindness into her dealings with children. Her interests include 16th-20th century history, (she still keeps her hand in in the senior school A level course), 20th century historical novels, travel and gardening. Godolphin Prep girls are encouraged to support the local Chalke Valley History Festival.

Academic matters: The junior school prides itself on good, solid traditional teaching all round, 'the national curriculum plus a bit more'. Maths is solid, reinforced by clubs in lunch breaks and 'mathletics' programmes on school computers in ICT room. 'Girls have to write every day and put their skills into practice'. French begins in the nursery at 3 and continues throughout; Spanish and German introduced in year 6. Latin, Greek and science after-school clubs; reasoning group provides extra practice for those aiming for 11+. Nice light library perches on a mezzanine floor above main hall in which on the day we visited the evening's exciting art exhibition was going up competing with some extremely sophisticated rhythmic clapping from a music class. Small class sizes (12 on average), with some really enterprising teaching and a few new teachers including some men. Our allocated guides were, not surprisingly, slightly reluctant to leave a science class in which they were planning sports events taking account of the conditions of planets other than the earth. However they waxed lyrical over the pet's corner, were warmly welcomed by Sister Gill and clearly loved every bit of the school.

One pretty expert parent commented that school's learning support teacher is 'wonderful', championing girls' needs, liaising with staff (even the slightly wary ones) and exceptionally well qualified with an impressive array of degrees in psychology and special needs education. This is a school that fits the style of teaching to the child.

Definitely academic, with Latin up to A level and Greek on offer, though not taken up much for exams. Spanish, German and French also on offer though with a few following through to A level. Spectacular results in maths and art at both A level and GCSE. Other results certainly respectable, with 47 per cent A*/A at A level in 2016 and 68 per cent A*/A at GCSE. Results have been slightly less stellar since 2013, when the boards tightened up on top grades, but the latest results show that the top tranche of really able girls can achieve a sheaf of four A and A* grades at Godolphin.

French, German, Spanish and Latin taught from first year with Mandarin via a club. All available up to A level except currently Latin, and classical Greek done at GCSE via an 'Academic Society', Girls do either double award science or three individual subjects. The usual subjects are offered plus PE, design and food technology, economics, business studies and drama. Godolphin will put on an A level course for one or two students if necessary, so there's not much you can't do, and options are designed round each girl's requests every year. There is a real buzz of enthusiasm from girls and teachers with excitement about geology coming on-stream as an A level next year. Parents are enthusiastic about the level of encouragement and individual attention given by teachers. One commented that teachers support girls' particular interests by finding articles and information for them even if it is outside the curriculum. Able girls enjoy events put on by the scholars and 'Alpinists' (Accelerated Learning Programme) activities, though sometimes the compulsory ones are 'a bit groan-worthy'. Girls say most are really interesting and attract lots of non-scholars too. The REBEL (Recreational Enhancement for Bright Energetic Learners) scheme provides appreciated stimulus for year 9.

The few SEN students have plenty of help organised by SENCo/ed psych much praised by parents. Help is one-to-one, in groups, or takes the form of advice to teachers about learning styles of individuals. EAL is managed by SEN department – up to three lessons a week if necessary. Not many pupils need support, but advice to teachers is available from occupational therapist and maths specialist. Godolphin can cope with mild

G

Asperger's. Healthy, friendly respect and affection between teachers and girls abundantly evident.

Games, options, the arts: Art has a huge and impressive building bursting with stunning work in every medium and hugely talented and enthusiastic staff. Very professional looking fabric design work on display as well as fascinating mixed media landscape work and spectacular studies based on work done in the cathedral. Two spacious studios for drawing/painting, with separate rooms dedicated to textiles, ceramics, photography and 3D; another smaller room full of iMacs for graphic design. This a truly brilliant department, making creative use of visits to and by local artists, who regularly initiate GCSE projects, and welcoming parents and visitors to view two floors of really breathtakingly exciting work – smashing results too. DT is no less impressive, with lots of colourful and innovative constructions in wood and plastic on display. It's not surprising academically gifted girls take up art or history of art here and a record number go on to art related courses at uni. Lucky prep girls also have lessons in the amazing senior art block, where the staff are passionate about encouraging art from the beginning, teaching painting, drawing, ceramics and textiles.

An attractive rotunda houses the performing arts centre with lovely in-the-round theatre, plenty of entertaining space and good practice rooms. Music is very well served, with the head running a popular junior orchestra of girls from prep and senior schools, a head of music who is as encouraging as he is talented, and the meticulous Mrs Sparkhall, who inspires the girls in a choral tradition that wins them the Bernardo's School Choir of the Year and other accolades. Individual lessons still in the unprepossessing and unreconstructed Rose Villa, but pupils and parents don't seem to mind and there's plenty of chamber music, though not much evidence of pop..Instrumental music flourishe in the prep too, especially now there is a joint senior/junior orchestra. One parent was delighted that her daughter suddenly stopped complaining about orchestra practice. Music is even scheduled for tinies in the nursery. All instrumentalists perform in their own annual concert. Occasional workshops take place with visiting musicians. Lots of obviously enjoyable music – enthusiastic rhythmic clapping happening during our visit. Choir has performed at the Bath Festival and Barbican Centre and regularly joins the senior choir to sing in Salisbury Cathedral. Unusual music theory club open to years 1 to 6; girls regularly pass ABRSM theory of music exams up to grade 2.

All the creative forces come together in drama, typified by recent Oklahoma – spectacular and full of home-grown music and dance. Girls also perform with Portal Theatre, a small, professionally run theatre group. Masses of LAMDA exams and smaller performances.

Lacrosse dominates amongst a total of 90 different teams covering all the usual girls' winter and summer sports. Netball actually fields 23 teams, and tennis 14 teams as well as teams in all the major girls' school sports – quite a feat for a smallish school. All sports reach a pretty high level considering the school's size, swimming aided by a sleek 25 metre indoor pool. Highly competitive equestrian stars, and lacrosse and netball high fliers get to county and regional teams. Achievements include equestrians getting into top three at Windsor Horse Show, U13 netball team winning county championships and one girl selected for England U18 lacrosse squad. One hockey lover's parent commented that perhaps it came second best to lacrosse, but acknowledged that there is plenty of opportunity, even so. No lack of outdoor and other related activities. One girl reported enthusiastically on taking part in the Dartmoor Ten Tors expedition after thorough training through CCF (quite unusual in a girls' school).

Three double games lessons each week for juniors, using the senior school's grass pitches and hard courts. Gymnastics for all, lacrosse is introduced in year 5. Until then the main team sports are hockey and netball. Swimming excels with a terrific programme in which all girls swim amazing distances winning handfuls of ASA awards. Everyone swims each week (including for nursery-age children) in fabulous 25-metre swimming pool; the best swimmers are invited to join a competitive swimming squad after school. Extracurricular clubs include kick boxing and yoga; in summer, girls can choose tennis and rounders at break and after school and riders can join senior school equestrian teams.

Boarding: Girls can start boarding from 7 or 8 in the prep, when they join the junior house. Boarding is about as flexi as it goes, with everything from full time to weekly to flexi (one or more nights per week). One parent commented that though full boarding had been ideal for her daughter because they were not too far away, it tends to focus a bit much on activities for foreign students. Current flexibility is dependent on there being some beds available.

Boarders in years 3, 4, 5 and 6 are housed on separate floor in Walters House, which takes the first years of the senior school. This looks like a bit of a compromise because of small prep boarding numbers. Parents report that staff have adapted quickly to the needs of younger girls, but more boarders are needed to reduce the age range in dorms. As there are fairly few of this age group, weekend activities are tailor-made, though small numbers must limit variety. Mobile phone use is rationed and 'prep plus' activities for junior girls are on the up.

Accommodation is simple, modern and not unnaturally tidy, with two senior (13-16) houses and a very friendly well organised sixth form centre over the road via a pedestrian bridge. Complete refurbishment of boarding is still in progress; study bedrooms are comfortably spacious with plenty of storage and common areas. Parents commented on a lot of changes, probably referring to the recent restructuring of the separate prep boarding to be part of junior house.

Shared dining hall adjoins junior and senior houses. Sixth form house has its own dining room, kitchen, study areas, often with staff at hand, careers advice and leisure space with a proper Café Aroma serving the obligatory coffee shop range of expresso etc. Health provision is supervised by the indomitable Sister Gill, who creates an aura of calm, unfussy friendliness much appreciated by all.

Background and atmosphere: Unusually for a girls' school Godolphin has a long history, dating from a bequest made in 1726 by Elizabeth Godolphin, eventually resulting in the establishment in the cathedral close of a school for 'eight orphaned gentlewomen' who followed a remarkably enlightened curriculum for their day. It moved to its present 16 acre site in Milford Hill in 1891, retaining its links with the cathedral, with the bishop and chapter still represented on the governing body. Skilful use of space and the site still has a gracious feel, generated by the mellow red brick of the original building and the lovely open grass pitches with views of the downs enhanced by banks of lavender at the time of our visit. One has to look quite hard to find the few scruffy corners that Mrs Hattersley is determined to clear. The huge gothic school hall has the dusty feel (it certainly isn't, as the school is exceptionally clean and fresh) which old wood, high ceilings and portraits of ex-heads inevitably evoke. Road access is made awkward by several right-angled bends in the road, but efficient planning of parking helps, though parents report it can still be a bit of a maelstrom at pick up time.

Uniform is unremarkable: pale blue shirt, plaid skirt and navy blazer enhanced by stylish boater with crested red ribbons, known as a 'board'. All, however, is concealed by coverall old fashioned pinafores in royal blue for seniors (except sixth who wear own clothes, plus suits for going to the cathedral), red for preps and gingham for nursery. Oddly, girls seem to like this antiquated touch, while one parent attributed the school's exceptionally friendly and unthreatening atmosphere to the fact that no ultra-trendy girl would be seen dead wearing one. This is certainly a school where those who have been bullied elsewhere find general acceptance and support. An exceptionally happy place with few exclusive 'in groups', where the occasional 'falling out' is sympathetically dealt with by friendly staff, evidently liked and trusted by pupils. With its historic cathedral links, this is an overtly Christian school with a chaplain, using the cathedral for services and confirmation, though one parent regretted that it had to be on a Thursday to ensure parent availability.

Prep school feels quite separate from the main site; older pupils, however, appear very much at home in the senior school buildings, especially as the boarding now overlaps in Walters House, which takes 7-13 year olds. Girls play happily in the small outside playground to the front of the school which features the 'friendship bench'. Anyone sitting there is immediately given care and encouragement by other pupils under the wary eye of Miss Miller, whose room overlooks the playground. The nursery has the lion's share of the grounds at the rear with plenty of safely enclosed spaces. The prep has a lovely light atmosphere enhanced by good use of colour and a spacious feel. Not a revolutionary design, but everything done with children in mind, like the whiteboards that pull down to eye level for the youngest children.

Eagle-eyed staff ensure that everyone chooses sensibly at lunchtimes, when girls walk up to senior dining room. Girls may arrive for breakfast at 7:30am and stay on for prep until 5:40pm. School uniform mirrors senior school kit, with red pinnies (worn over full school uniform), straw boaters (known as boards) and blazers. The nursery children look enchanting in their gingham version of the 'pinny'. Student food council meets once every half term to provide direct feedback to school chef, whilst year 6 leads school council and year 5 selects school charities. Friday assemblies (musicians and public speakers have informal opportunities to perform here) close the school week and parents are welcome. Miss Miller has recently introduced a prep version of the Elizabeth Godolphin Award, which means that prep girls take a pride in their self-development in readiness for transfer to the senior school, and the school has a record of the success in their personal education.

Pastoral care, well-being and discipline: Pastoral care is delivered to day girls – known as 'Sarums' – and boarders together through the residential houses, which all have provision for day girls and welcome them to work and relax with the boarders. Lessons end at 4pm, but the myriad of school activities and prep run in three sessions after tea. School houses involve all ages from nursery to sixth form for competitions, fundraising and social events. Personal development is delivered in the PERSIL programme (another quirky Godolphin acronym representing Personal, Ethical, Religious and Social Issues in Life). In the sixth form the Elizabeth Godolphin Award encourages activities aimed at preparation for life after school. Truly all-embracing, it includes Prue Leith cookery (expensive), banking and finance, with car maintenance, emotional literacy, women's boot camp and dawn visits to Stonehenge all part of the bigger picture.

The older girls gave the impression that life is fun in the prep school, and the interaction between staff and pupils indicated a real kindness and affection. Gentle and girly though its pupils may look, the priority undoubtedly is education, and parents report that children gain in confidence. Its close proximity to the senior school gives it some outstanding facilities, but none the less this feels and behaves like an autonomous friendly community.

Firm, friendly, no-nonsense discipline leads to an atmosphere in which girls and teachers are at home with each other. The best is expected of everyone. Rules are few but clearly stated, and parents say problems such as drugs, smoking or alcohol are 'simply not part of the culture'. Girls rarely abuse the freedom they have to go into Salisbury attend socials with other schools, or entertain guests in the sixth form. 'Staff seem to care as much as I do', one parent commented

Pupils and parents: Mostly middle class with a total of about 14 per cent international students, mainly from the Far East. Not a 'toff' school, though pupils are not averse to joining up with Eton and Winchester for social events. Huge day catchment area has bus routes (some shared with Leaden Hall School) from every direction. In an area with ambitious state schools, art and music still attract pupils, as does the excellent pastoral care. Parents are pleased at how open pupils seem, speaking easily to adults and confident in public, but also that younger ones still behave like children.

Past pupils (with houses named after them) include the full spectrum of women writers, Jilly Cooper, Minette Walters and Dorothy Sayers as well as prolific novelist Amanda Brookfield. TV personalities include Dragon's Den businesswoman Deborah Meaden, Katie Knapman of Countryfile, presenters Helen Bishop and Louise Beale, sportswoman Ruby Smith, yachtswomen Hannah White and Nicola Rodriguez as well actress Charlotte Longfield.

Entrance: Entry to prep at all stages following an assessment day in the school and satisfactory report from current school head. At 11+, 12+, 13+ and sixth form. Registered 11+ pupils invited for a preview day and night in the autumn term, before taking entrance exams in the spring term. Uses its own 11+ entrance test – maths, English and verbal reasoning, plus interview and team building exercises. Now organises 13+ assessments 18 months prior to entry.

Exit: Vast majority choose to remain at Godolphin for senior school but can also be prepared for CE. Good record of academic scholarships – some gain music and sporting awards too. Some to popular state secondary South Wilts Grammar School (prep runs 11+ practice sessions for girls' grammar entry) and St Edmund's.

Around 30 per cent leave after GCSE, to local state schools and sixth form colleges. Most sixth formers go on to higher education, plenty art related, and a good proportion of Russell Group universities. Two to Oxbridge in 2016; lots of bright hopes for the future.

Money matters: Scholarships at 11+ and 13+ for outstanding merit or promise in academic work, music, sport or art. Awards are worth 15 per cent of boarding or day fees. In sixth form, scholarships awarded for all of the above plus drama. Additional bursaries may be awarded to scholars in case of financial hardship. Six Foundation Bursaries (worth 70 per cent) are offered to orphans in need of financial support, when one parent has died or whose parents are separated or divorced. An Old Godolphin Association Bursary (25 per cent) is occasionally available to the daughter or granddaughter of a former pupil at the school. Entrance bursaries are available to all eligible candidates (including at 14+) in order of registration – so it may pay to get in early.

Remarks: It seems an idyllic school, almost too good to be true, and there is no doubt that it offers the very best of single sex education. For all its gentleness and Railway Children look, teaching is tip-top, especially now a real effort has gone into IT. Art and music are about as good as you can get and drama and games exceptional for a small school. Girls can really be themselves and the eccentric and the sociable are equally accepted. A very special place to grow up in.

The Grange, Monmouth Preparatory School

Linked with Haberdashers' Agincourt, Haberdashers' Monmouth School for Girls, Inglefield House, Monmouth School

Hadnock Road, Monmouth NP25 3NG

Pupils: 132 • Ages: 7–11 • C of E

Fees: Day £10,452; Boarding £18,999 pa

Tel: 01600 715930
Email: thegrange@monmouthschool.org
Website: www.habs-monmouth.org

Head: Since September 2016, Mr Neil Shaw, previously head of Westonbirt Prep. Read geography at Exeter, PGCE at Nottingham, MA Loughborough. Began career at St George's Edgbaston and became deputy head. His first headship was at Kingswood School, Solihull. Married with two young children, he enjoys cricket, walking and geocaching, a high-tech cross between orienteering and a treasure hunt.

Entrance: Entry at 7+ though other stages considered if places available. Report from previous school and informal written assessment and interview during a morning in school. Boarding from 9 at Chapel House, which is the junior boarding house for Monmouth School, serving the Grange as well, and takes boys up to 13. Full or weekly boarding is encouraged with flexi arrangements for others only if there is a spare bed. Many come from linked co-ed pre-prep Haberdashers' Agincourt.

Exit: Vast majority to Monmouth School – but they have to take the entry exam on the same terms as outsiders. A few try for – and get – scholarships to other schools.

Remarks: Part of the family of Haberdashers' Monmouth schools. The co-ed pre-prep is Haberdashers' Agincourt School. The preps are separated into boys at the Grange and girls at Inglefield.

Since 2009 the Grange has joyfully occupied fantastic new buildings, which are exceptionally well fitted to prep school needs. Not at all 'like Terminal 4', as one determinedly traditionalist pupil commented, it is certainly spacious and exudes purposeful friendliness. Parents and boys absolutely love it. Though the approach to the Grange and to the swimming pool and sports centre next door (shared with Monmouth Boys) might be mistaken for an industrial estate, do not be put off. Once there it is smart, inviting and buzzes with happy activity. The lofty entrance hall cum library and recreation area forms a hub for meetings, activities or quiet reading.

Classrooms, each with their own cunningly designed loos, lockers and cloakrooms, all open out onto huge enclosed all-purpose play space. The supportive parent group known as FROGs (Friends of the Grange) has made an attractive grassed area with play castle and houses. State of the art music, ICT and art departments are more than justified by the myriad choirs, music groups (a Welsh song in progress when we visited), art projects and the impressive IT and cross-curricular enterprises of the Grange Advanced Studies Group. Recent high-profile science activities have included an eel release activity with BBC Countryfile. The Grange is super-eco-aware and there are areas for veg gardening whose produce is ceremoniously served at lunchtime. In the wildlife pond, underwater life is taken lightly enough for everyone to enjoy invasion by a small plastic crocodile, surreptitiously replaced with a larger size every now and again by a friendly catering department – typical of the happy community atmosphere which pervades.

Food is delicious and appreciated by the boys. School is open from 8am to 6pm with a teaching day from 8.35am-3.45pm. Boarders in Chapel House (which takes the top two years from the Grange and the first two years from Monmouth School) are bussed 'home' each evening. Boarding can be flexi but there are activities planned every weekend – normally on a minimal cost basis. Virtually everything a small boy could want is on offer.

'Settling happily is first priority,' one parent commented. 'Then academics can and do follow'. The Grange has a good record of success for children who have not been appropriately challenged elsewhere. Teaching is by specialists all through the school with lots of academic accolades in national and local competitions. Class sizes under 20 and academic programme in line with national curriculum including French (taught from year 3 on) but not Latin, though there is a classics club run by upper sixth from Monmouth School. Most work a year or more above their chronological age in English and maths. An SEN specialist and a learning support teacher occasionally give individual help, but most support is given in class, by the teaching assistant or teacher, providing both for those with specific difficulties and for the other needs associated with high intellect.

With all the sporting facilities of Monmouth Boys available, prep boys have enviable opportunities. The close relationship between the schools allows older boys to help with the many activities, sporting, aesthetic and intellectual – from Mandarin Chinese or philosophy to muddier things: gardening or the blackberry picking organised for the boarders at Chapel House. Senior boys particularly help in the MAT (More Able and Talented) group, offering all sorts of projects which include a variety of languages to a high standard.

A busy, exciting school, absolutely up to date and efficient in everything it does but happy, friendly and remarkably unpressured.

The Grange School

Bradburns Lane, Hartford, Northwich, Cheshire CW8 1LU

Pupils: 1,176 • Ages: 4–18 • Sixth form: 202

Fees: £8,100 – £10,830 pa

Tel: 01606 74007
Email: office@grange.org.uk
Website: www.grange.org.uk

Head: Since September 2016, Debbie Leonard MEd BEd (40s), previously head of Croydon High. Deputy head of Nottingham GHS, arrived at Croydon towards the end of the academic year as acting head for the following year after only brief tenure of predecessor. Has also been deputy head of Thetford Grammar and head of PE and school development at King Edward's Birmingham. Her masters is in management and learning. A very keen sportswoman, she has been a national league hockey coach and plays golf. She grew up in the Lake District and enjoys climbing and walking.

Head of the junior school: Since September 2014, Mr Guy Rands, previously academic deputy head of the senior school. Educated at Abingdon School and Manchester University. Often to be found out swimming (open water 10ks), cycling (coast to coast in a day), running (up Snowdon) or all three (sprint triathlons). Married to Emma with two young sons, one at the school.

Academic matters: French is taught throughout the school, Spanish from years 5 and 6. Very good results. At GCSE, 76 per cent A*/A in 2016. At A level 8 per cent of papers were graded A*-B; 60 per cent A*/A. The school puts this down partly to real academic choices. The school doesn't turn its nose up at offering subjects such as graphic design and IT at A level. 'We need to prepare children for where the world is going.' Logic lessons from year 7.

Many pupils we spoke to said the homework load was very heavy and that homework timetables often weren't followed. However, some parents reckoned this prepared their children for the real world. The school denies any hothousing.

All sixth formers participate in an enrichment programme one afternoon every week, designed to broaden and balance the academic experience. Options include cookery, photography, community work, RocketBall and bridge. Extra support is available for pupils applying to Oxbridge or to universities abroad, and special workshops for those wishing to study medicine and engineering. There's a gap year co-ordinator and a small bursary fund for youngsters embarking on purposeful projects that make a difference to others during their gaps years. 'Service is extremely important. Pupils are privileged to be here, but with that comes responsibility.'

SEN assistance is provided by a full time SENCo, as long as pupils can access the curriculum with no in-class support. All year 3s, 5s, 7s and sixth formers are screened for SEN.

Games, options, the arts: Amazing £3.6m purpose built theatre, of which children are rightly proud, used all year round for drama and stages yearly productions. House drama and art competitions.

Good range of sports including rugby, cricket, cross-country, golf and martial arts, although one junior school mum pointed out there weren't enough teams for most children to represent the school. School has its own sports hall and there's swimming from year 2 at local leisure centre. Pupils playing for county in polo, baseball, football and rowing. Has own boathouse and 33 boats on the River Weaver.

Music department brimming with life and has received much investment. Housed in its own block with specialist classrooms, music technology suite and peripatetic teaching rooms. Orchestras, choirs, ensembles and lunchtime concerts give pupils plenty of opportunity to perform. House system mingles age groups for drama, music and sport.

Lots of extracurricular clubs, including sewing, cooking, chess, storytelling and Lego.

Background and atmosphere: Originally opened as a prep in 1933; senior school was founded in 1978 due to prep school parental demand. The prep school moved to its current purpose built site in 1996. Previous heads have concentrated on exam results but 'now we're firmly established we can offer more and move in different directions.'

Large, bright classrooms in the junior school with lots of high quality work on display. Lots of computers, science room and DT room complete with laser cutter. Lovely, vibrant art studio where we saw some amazing life-sized Olympic figures painted by years 5 and 6. Vast and green outdoor space, with sandpits, wigwams, climbing frames, swings, sensory garden and woodland area. One father asked: 'Show me where you'd find better facilities round here,' and we reckon we'd struggle. Newish sixth form block with café and common room plus work and careers areas 'provides a strong sense of sixth form identity whilst remaining an integral part of the wider school'.

Some complain that the canteen is too small. Pupils say there's 'not enough choice' and the need to pay cash causes long queues.

Pastoral care, well-being and discipline: Parents and pupils praise pastoral support offered by staff. 'All the teachers are so helpful and friendly,' one boy told us. 'But if you go off track they'll push you back on.' One mother we spoke had a child with a long-term illness and lauded the support she received. Peer support in designated room by ChildLine trained prefects.

Pupils felt that bullying was rare but when it happened was handled well. 'Of course bullying happens, but we deal with it swiftly and undramatically. Eccentrics tend to fit in well here – there's a place for everybody.'

Smart grey and green uniform, although many of the girls we spoke to bemoaned the flesh coloured tights.

Pupils and parents: Pupils come from a 25 mile radius in mid-Cheshire and as a result are mostly white, middle class and wealthy. The school offers an extraordinary number of foreign trips and although the head points out that some families are 'making sacrifices to find the fees,' pupils we spoke to didn't feel that funding these trips was an issue. The school has found it difficult to persuade families living nearer to Manchester to consider sending children here instead of travelling into the city. They are trying to tackle this with more advertising and have seen a 20 per cent increase in external applicants for year 7.

Parents are very involved in school life – raising funds, helping with sport and providing work experience. A parents' Christian group prays regularly for the school.

Entrance: Three-form entry to the junior school, with class sizes of 20. Assessment for reception is January of the year of entry and consists of one-to-one assessment and small group work. 'We try to make it a fun morning,' says the head. 'We're watching to see how the children interact with adults and each other. We need to judge whether they will thrive here. However, they are 3 when they come for assessment and we don't have a crystal ball.' Pupils applying for other years spend a day in class and take a standardised assessment the following day. When we asked if priority is given to siblings the head told us: 'We don't like to split families up.'

Four-form entry to the senior school, with 65 per cent coming from the juniors. The rest come from local state primaries and other independent preps. Entrance exam consists of computerised papers in maths, vocabulary, critical thinking and reasoning and written papers in English and verbal reasoning. This is followed by a personal questionnaire.

Exit: Almost all juniors progress to the senior school (exam entry at 11). The few who don't leave due to relocation and those who might not make it through to the senior school are warned by the end of year 5. Some 15 per cent leave after GCSEs. Almost all sixth formers to university, some after a gap year. Lots to Leeds, Durham, Sheffield and Nottingham; generally several to Oxbridge. A few to universities abroad.

Money matters: Fees are in line with other north west independent schools, but beware, exam fees aren't included. Very small bursary fund, plus a limited amount set aside for academic scholars. Music scholarships available in year 7.

Remarks: Although often overlooked, The Grange is really starting to make its mark. An excellent, friendly school, providing a sterling education. A must to consider if you are looking for a co-ed in mid-Cheshire or south of Manchester.

Greenbank Preparatory School

Heathbank Road, Cheadle Hulme, Cheadle, Cheshire SK8 6HU

Pupils: 200 • Ages: 3–11

Fees: £7,815 pa

Tel: 0161 485 3724
Email: info@greenbankschool.co.uk
Website: www.greenbankschool.co.uk

G

Headmistress: Since 2007, Mrs Janet Lowe, Cert Ed (50s). Previously head of infants at Stockport Grammar School. Married to a chartered surveyor, with two grown up children. Enjoys book club and attending performances by the Hallé Orchestra, also an honorary member of the Cheadle and District Rotary. Has a hands-on approach to her headship, taking a weekly story time in reception class, running year 2 and 3 recorder club and teaching RE to years 1 to 6. 'I want to be involved with the children', she tells us. 'I really get to know them and their families'. Parents describe her as 'strong, approachable and forward thinking'.

Entrance: At age 3 into pre-school with some places held back for those that want reception entry. Entry is non-selective, on a first come, first served basis, with the only preference given to siblings. Places can and do become available later so always worth trying. There is also a day nursery on site and many children come from here.

Exit: Recently to Cheadle Hulme School, Hulme Hall Grammar, Stockport Grammar, The King's School, Macclesfield, Manchester Grammar School, Manchester High School for Girls, North Cestrian, St Bede's, Alderley Edge School for Girls and Withington Girls' School.

Remarks: Founded in 1951 in the house that is now the day nursery, now in modern, light and airy buildings on a spacious, green plot. Not much parking on site, but enough space on Heathbank Road for dropping off and picking up.

Mixed ability classes, but school believes strongly in differentiating work so that each child is treated according to their ability. Small groups receive extra support in all the different areas of the curriculum so that no child slips through the net. One mum told us, 'Never once have I felt that my children have been left to struggle. Support is always there'. 'Every pupil is set individual targets and it is up to us to make sure they achieve them', the head tells us.

French is taught throughout the school, with German and Spanish introduced in the juniors. Additionally, year 6s have a French conversation club and are also taught Latin and Mandarin. A part-time SENCo dyslexia specialist and teaching assistants work with small groups and one-to-one. Gifted and talented programme stretches bright pupils and offers a range of educational experiences. Recently children have attended workshops on space, art geometry and poetry.

Good sport including football, rounders, water polo, netball and swimming. Thriving and impressive range of extracurricular activities for a small school, including drama, gymnastics, cheerleading, art, football, cross country and cookery. There's even a mums' keep fit club.

Excellent music department. Nearly half the pupils have individual instrumental tuition, school holds regular music and drama productions and there are infant and junior choirs. We saw a rehearsal for an assembly on Bollywood dancing and both the staff and children looked as if they were having great fun.

Specialist art teacher with her own large, bright room. Art is taken seriously here with pupils regularly winning inter-school competitions, and there is some amazing work hung throughout the school. We were very taken by the Gaudi lizards created by year 6.

Library and computer room staffed by a librarian who also runs popular lunch-time touch typing club. Truly wonderful eco garden, complete with herb and vegetable patch, bird hide and pond. Regularly used for lessons, but also by the science and gardening clubs.

Lots of trips and residentials, including Lake District, London and France. Smart grey and yellow uniform. Before and after-school care offered at extra cost. Children told us that school dinners were 'yummy' and the dinner ladies were 'very kind'.

Small, friendly school that does fantastically well for its pupils. Head tells us, 'it's a combination of fabulous teaching and our commitment that all our children should have very high self-esteem. Then they'll learn and achieve'.

The Gryphon School

Bristol Road, Sherborne, Dorset DT9 4EQ

Pupils: 1,594 • Ages: 11–18 • Sixth form: 411 • C of E

Tel: 01935 813122
Email: office@gryphon.dorset.sch.uk
Website: www.gryphon.dorset.sch.uk

Headteacher: Since 2007, Steve Hillier MA PGCE (40s). Educated in Wiltshire and read geography at Cambridge before embarking on a teaching career in various community schools up and down the land. Of his appointment to the Gryphon, his first headship, he says, 'All the moons aligned: it was a community school with a sixth form in the west country'. Under his rule, the school has gone from strength to strength (currently graded 'good' by Ofsted), providing a valuable counterweight to the considerable avoirdupois of the local independents (Sherborne School, Sherborne School for Girls, Leweston). 'The only difference between us and them is class size', he states, bravely, though no-one could deny the amount of cross-fertilisation between all the Sherborne schools. Mr Hillier also does all manner of worthy things with North Dorset Schools and Somerset Academies in terms of leadership and funding expertise; the Gryphon became an academy in 2012 'to enable us to keep doing what we are doing now', as he put it.

Parents rate him for the job he does though they do not feel that they could get to know him easily – heads of year have far more of a bearing on school life – but they appreciate his presence at most school functions. 'He's everywhere and nowhere at the same time – quite scary, really,' opined one sixth former. We found him expansive and relaxed on his home ground, and justifiably proud of what goes on there. Mr Hillier is married with three sporty children, two at neighbouring Gillingham and one at university; he and his family enjoy active holidays walking and exploring sites 'where history meets geography', and he is a sometime Bath Rugby season ticket holder.

Academic matters: Commendable results by any standards and particularly for a non-selective school. Vibrant, ambitious sixth form with significant influx from other schools has offered vocational options alongside A levels, such as level 3 BTec courses. At A level, 30 per cent A*/A and 54 per cent A*/B in 2016 means five Gryphon students going on to Oxford (head not unhappy about the fact that the Gryphon sends more to Oxbridge than Sherborne and Sherborne Girls combined), several other Russell Group universities and to read competitive and rigorous subjects such as medicine and dentistry. At GCSE, results are impressive, particularly languages ancient and modern (Latin is taught by a visiting member of staff from Sherborne School) and music. In 2016, 23 per cent A*/A grades at GCSE and 70 per cent of pupils got 5+ GCSE A*-C grades (including English and maths). Good showing in vocational choices too. Academic commitment is expected from the off; some parents feel that too much homework is given in year 7.

Pupils speak very highly of their teachers: 'approachable, passionate about their subject, willing to give up their time'. Maths, economics and art were singled out for particular praise – we were less sure about the guillotine in one history class room. Library and computer provision modern and well-resourced, some excitement about the imminent trial of iPads as a portable learning resource reinforces the importance the school places on e-learning.

The proportion of students with SEN is higher than average; we suspect because of the school's excellent provision, which includes a 35-strong SEN team all of whom have their own particular expertise, plus a dedicated space 'the blue room' where the troubled and overwhelmed can withdraw when it all gets a bit much. Here, sessions on self-esteem and anger management are run alongside more conventional catch-up sessions in literacy and numeracy. All new arrivals are screened on entry and school maintains close links with local services such as CAMHS; efforts are made to intervene early and to investigate causes behind disruptive behaviour, rather than merely dealing with it.

Games, options, the arts: The breadth and enthusiasm for sport and the arts make The Gryphon an all-encompassing school and the recipient of the Artsmark gold award. Its site on the edge of Sherborne means ample space for pitches, courts, Astroturf and a leisure centre with fitness suite, dance studio and sports hall (which could do with updating, say parents), also available to the community at certain times. An outdoor pool has been filled in, but swimmers use the indoor facilities of the two independents in the town. Usual offering of rugby, hockey and netball (where some teams are coached by local club coaches) branches out into golf, basketball, karate, shooting and solo star-dance up to national standard. School also has a show-jumping team in this horsey part of the world, though set up and run by parents. Participation rates are high – two hours PE per week are timetabled up to year 11 with options changing every six weeks, 'and there's a team for everyone', according to our small guide, a keen netball player. At the weekly enrichment afternoon for sixth form, sport is the most popular choice at whatever level; members of staff and some sixth formers took part in a 10K Christmas Pudding run for charity. School an undoubted presence in the local sporting scene – 'nakedly competitive,' said one sixth former, grimly – which takes on all comers with relish, particularly the local independents, and with considerable success. The Sports Award evening is a highlight in the school calendar.

Music a real strength here too, in this most musical of towns; school benefits from close relationships with the abbey and the other Sherborne schools, all of whom contribute to the Sherborne Symphonia, a joint orchestra, and lots of other collaborations. Success on the national stage too, with high rankings in the BBC Songs of Praise Choir of the Year and students gaining places in the National Youth Choir and Orchestra. But the school celebrates its own music too, with two full concerts, a carol service in the abbey and a European music tour every year, for both singers and players, and numerous opportunities inside and outside its gates.

Drama and film-making also prominent: musical theatre the runaway favourite with recent productions of Les Misérables, Oliver! and West Side Story, but more adventurously, a version of Dr Faustus updated to 80s London and a feature film of Far from the Madding Crowd in recent years.

Art and design of similarly high standard; some stunning furniture made by recent A level students would grace any avant-garde shop window. 'We're not spoon-fed – we're encouraged to develop our own ideas', said one A level artist. Younger ones work with textiles, food and resistant materials in rotation; school boasts a professional catering kitchen alongside its art and design studios. Photography also popular, and much work is exhibited locally.

Background and atmosphere: Founded in 1992 out of an amalgam of local schools, the Gryphon's undistinguished buildings were purpose built for 800 or so, and now house double that number. The gripe we heard from everyone was lack of space: considerable congestion in corridors at peak times and no room for lockers, but recent addition of two new classrooms specifically for use by the nurture group, new meeting room and refurbishment of foyer and reception areas will help. Outdoor sitting space with nice wooden tables and benches a precious overflow, but surely bleak in midwinter.

Even though it is not much over 20 years old, the school feels agreeably traditional in terms of its expectations, aspirations and values, reflected in its naming after an ancient and noble mythical beast, denoting intelligence and strength. The gryphon appears on the uniform navy blue sweatshirt and all published material – strong branding indeed. School rightly makes the most of its position as Sherborne's secondary school by holding prize-givings and carol services in the abbey.

Relationships between students and staff, which are collaborative and supportive without crossing the boundary into familiarity, are universally praised: 'I want this to be an island of civility, not a shouty school,' states the head. Even the newest/youngest/shyest students feel as though they are recognised as individuals. School appears to cater for all comers: 'I've got one very bright one, one really naughty and one not very bright and it's suited them all,' said one frank mother.

Parents report mostly good communication from teachers via email (it could be sharpened up when a child is absent, for example), but that parents' evenings are a scrum. A local church which has outgrown its premises meets every Sunday in the conference room, and one of its clergy has been appointed chaplain three days a week, but the school does not feel overtly Christian. That said, we did not spot much religious or ethnic diversity, but significantly a few years ago one student felt moved to start a campaign called 'I am Me', celebrating difference and amounting to a powerful statement against bullying – an initiative which gained her a national award.

Pastoral care, well-being and discipline: Exceptional. School has UN 'Rights Respecting School' status and expectations of behaviour are laid down with positive reinforcement under the guidelines which grace every classroom – 'catch them being good' is a policy statement, and the prevailing culture is one of reward and recognition. 'Teachers are good at making us feel our age and giving us the right amount of responsibility, but they don't nag', said one older boy. Everyone we talked to commented on the close eye the school keeps on healthy relationships between students, and a sixth former remarked on the sense of community between the staff. Sanctions, which are not applied in haste, take the form of detentions of increasing length and seriousness.

Pupils and parents: Mostly white and relatively to very prosperous – school has a lower than average percentage of free school meals – and with a genuine commitment to education and a sense that they are fortunate indeed to be at The Gryphon. Masses bussed in from anything up to 20 miles away; 'I was determined to go to The Gryphon, even though we live out of catchment,' said one new girl. Several teachers from local independent schools send their children; yet more blurring of the lines between the Sherborne schools. The students we met were jolly, chatty yet thoughtful – and pleased with their lot.

Past students of note from this young school include two actors (Sam Dorsey and Ben Hardy), one rising star in film production and another at Bath Rugby.

Entrance: Officially 240 places for year 7, which are almost always oversubscribed by 30 or so – no wonder the place is such a squash. Most come from nine partner primary schools but a quarter of the intake from outside the (largely rural) catchment area; this is a highly regarded school locally. Though transition arrangements appear to be good once the kids arrive at school, at least one parent felt more effort could be made to reach children coming from outlying schools.

At sixth form, nearly 40 per cent arrive from local state and independent schools; entry requirements are five GCSEs at grade C or above to include maths and English, preceded by an interview in the spring. A level choices in maths, the sciences and languages require a B at GCSE. Some 95 per cent of sixth form students stay on to complete year 13. 'They're knocking at the door to get in at sixth form', remarked one mother.

Exit: Some leave after GCSE (46 per cent in 2016) to pursue less academic courses at Yeovil College. UCAS guidance gets top marks from students; five to Oxbridge in 2016, and several to the top London unis. A few take gap years.

Remarks: Super much sought-after school at the very centre of its community and taking on the Sherborne independents. Truly a model of comprehensive education at its best – a place for all comers, which children and parents set their heart on, so it bulges at the seams.

Haberdashers' Agincourt School

Linked with The Grange, Monmouth Prep, Haberdashers' Monmouth School for Girls, Inglefield House, Monmouth School

Dixton Lane, Monmouth NP25 3SY

Pupils: 109 • Ages: 3-7

Fees: £4,257 – £7,137pa

Tel: 01600 713970
Email: enquiries@agincourtschool.org
Website: www.habs-monmouth.org

Head: Since 2014, Mrs Jennie Phillips (40s) who burst upon Agincourt from Badminton School and no one's feet have touched the ground since. Passionate and enthusiastic about the key role of these early years, Mrs Phillips has been building on a highly successful enterprise to make the school something very wonderful indeed. Like lots of her staff, she looks and sounds more like an escapee from Hampstead than you might reasonably expect to find in rural Wales. Polished and poised, she is a whirlwind of imaginative energy and clearly adores the children and the whole environment of the school. On the one hand, she has upgraded the IT so it has the all singing, all dancing facilities of a much bigger school, on the other hand she has encouraged the children to build their own chicken house and run. She doesn't believe in wet break times – the children go outside in their heavy duty waterproofs and wellies and make mud slides. Not surprisingly, she has also got rid of carpets in the vicinity of any outside doors. Parents credit her with introducing a modern approach to special educational needs. 'Mrs Phillips recognises that everyone has special needs and the children are given individual input that they wouldn't get elsewhere,' said one delighted mother of twins who attend the nursery.

A maths specialist, Jennie Phillips has firm views on how to encourage children to love maths and insists on at least three differentiated activities going on at one time in a class. 'The children all come to it from different places and I want them all to find activities that they can do and that stretch their understanding at the same time'. She is introducing a new creative curriculum that is school-wide and themed based – it is Turrets and Tiaras next term.

'I want the children to learn how to work together and be inquisitive learners', Mrs Phillips tells us. She has introduced a range of development opportunities for staff and everyone is buying into her vision of 'succeeding together'.

Entrance: Non-selective entry and children come for an induction day. Parents select the school for its size, its surroundings and the sense of a can-do, loving community. The school offers before and after-care as many parents both work.

Exit: More-or-less everyone moves on to the single sex 7-11 girls' and boys' schools within the Haberdashers' Monmouth Foundation, Inglefield and The Grange. However, they are not guaranteed to move right through the school and a few are offered a place on the understanding that they will need support. There are lots of links with the prep schools for the year 2s as the children get ready to move on, and Mrs Phillips regularly takes assemblies in the next schools so the children continue to see her even when they have moved 'up'. Similarly, the heads of the prep schools are frequent visitors to Agincourt.

Remarks: A short distance from the senior school, Agincourt was taken on by the Haberdashers 16 years ago. The listed rectory nestles in a tiny valley with the church on its doorstep. ('The vicar wants us to use it as another classroom', says the head.) As the setting for a nursery and infant school, it is many parents', and our, idea of idyllic. As we arrived, one class was working outside on a gently sloping grassy bank, intently measuring and timing objects, while blossom from the cherry trees floated down in the breeze around them.

With non-selective entry, early intervention to support any learning difficulties is seen as automatic and is free at this stage, either on a one-to-one basis or in small groups. There are regular workshops for the most able and talented. Up to 18 children in each class, and each teacher has a teaching assistant. Children work towards the national early learning goals and there is testing in years 1 and 2, all of which is tightly tracked to ensure appropriate and speedy intervention and keep a check on value-added scores. A new whole school assessment and achievement programme is being introduced.

The school abounds with evidence of the range of activities. There are decorated tiles fired in their own kiln, scary masks, paper mâché lighthouses, some more convincing than others.

All the children can read simple music by the end of year 2. In PSHE lessons with Mrs Phillips, they were writing survival plans for a desert island stint and learning how to apply for jobs and be interviewed. 'We have to always remember to knock on the door and not just walk in', a serious year 2 told us. Reading is a high priority and the school gets both parents and children committed to rapid progress here. There have been curriculum changes this year with a new approach to phonics and a stress on a skills-based curriculum with lots of outdoor learning going on, including a forest school, where the children make ladders and houses with proper saws and axes. We saw the chicken house and run that the children had planned and helped the deputy head to build. They had themselves petitioned to keep chickens and given a presentation to governors, with a full risk assessment including flood risks and what to do with the hens during the school holidays. Not bad at age 6. The extracurricular side of the school is evidenced wherever you look, and the children talk enthusiastically about the sport, chess, music, sewing and the construction/deconstruction club where they engage in activities such as taking apart a Dyson and putting it back together again.

Parents talk about the school being a home from home, with lots of hugs and kisses. The children are gently persuaded into the structure of school and this approach to progression works. Particularly commended was the very individual pace at which each child is taken forward. 'When I read the Agincourt reports, it is as though a member of the family has written them,' we were told.

It is possible that a child that liked to be indoors and was very fastidious about getting dirty might be unsuited to Agincourt. Otherwise the only downside we could find was that the chicken run has had to be given a mesh roof as the buzzards circle overhead in chick season.

Haberdashers' Monmouth School For Girls

Linked with The Grange, Monmouth Prep, Haberdashers' Agincourt, Inglefield House, Monmouth School

Hereford Road, Monmouth NP25 5XT

Pupils: 483; 137 boarders • Ages: 11–18 • Sixth form: 152

Fees: Day £13,929; Boarding £27,009 – £28,635 pa

Tel: 01600 711100
Email: admissions@hmsg.co.uk
Website: www.habs-monmouth.org

Headmistress: Since 2014, Mrs Caroline Pascoe (40s), previously head of Truro High School for Girls. Microbiology degree from Bristol, member of GB rowing squad at 1992 Barcelona Olympics, still adores sport. An officer in the RAF Volunteer Reserve. Worked in Himalayas and continues to lead high altitude trekking expeditions. Married to a very supportive husband, with a son at Monmouth School, and very involved as a family, in town and county life. Much admired and respected by the girls. She knows everyone's names and it is widely held that she 'walks the talk'. As far as encouraging girls to take risks is concerned, in addition to joining them on outdoor pursuits adventures, she learnt a One Direction tune on the recorder and played it in assembly. We were impressed, and so were her pupils. She has developed a Confidence for Life programme which is all about moving outside your comfort zone. She has also encouraged a higher profile for the creative arts on a regular basis – assemblies have been transformed and are much anticipated, being regularly used to showcase dance and music.

Her appointment of an assistant head to lead co-curricular activities is part of her drive to give breadth, as is her development of the expeditions programme. She is creating a generation of proactive girls with high levels of resilience – no worrying about a glass ceiling here. Breadth isn't just about trips to India; Caroline also wants to keep raising academic horizons – 'Girls don't read enough after year 10, ' she tells us. 'We want to see a continuing love of learning here'. She is also committed to building the boarding, which has grown since her arrival.

A can-do, action head, Caroline leads from the front and her constant presence round school, from eating with the girls to supporting everything they are involved in, creates a buzz around the place. The energy and pace you feel everywhere here is coming from the top. Parents find her very approachable and feel she has ambition for the school to drive it forward to greater things.

Academic matters: The results at GCSE and A level are very good and the school says it achieves this without putting the girls under too much pressure. In 2016, 68 per cent A*/A grades at GCSE and 56 per cent at A level. Art, modern languages, maths and science are popular choices. At sixth form level, Monmouth School for boys and the girls' school come together, allowing 30 subjects to be on offer across both schools, which ensures virtually everyone gets the combination of subjects they want. It means some girls will be taught in some subjects at the boys' school and boys at the girls'. This works well. The girls say they like the different perspective the boys bring to subjects and comment on an often-repeated observation that it is noticeably that the girls think before they speak, unlike the boys.

Parents say that the school doesn't heap unreasonable amounts of pressure on the girls, but that doesn't mean that HMSG has any lower expectations that the big London day schools, with which parents were often comparing it. Learning support is available on an individual/shared basis from suitably qualified staff. The girls say teachers will always make time for them if they need a bit of extra help on a less formal basis. Most departments run surgeries for individual help, too.

Links with outside organisations enhance the academic work. Renishaw plc sponsored a STEM competition recently that led to further work supported by the school staff, which led in turn to two girls exhibiting their invention at the NEC, pitching it on Dragons' Den and selling to national retailers.

Games, options, the arts: The school has a deserved reputation for being very sporty, and clearly even the girls who aren't games mad are very proud of the reputation. Those girls told us that respect and resources are given to the arts as well and there is a policy of introducing girls to different sports to help them all find some physical activity that appeals. Girls regularly represent the region and Wales in a variety of sports. One parent told us that her daughters had asked the PE staff if they could start a gym club. Within a few months they had it – well resourced and competing nationally.

Drama and dance are popular, with excellent facilities shared with the local community. Music is strong with 50 per cent taking some additional music lessons. The annual inter-house Eisteddfod gives an extra frisson to these activities. The glass atrium is hung with house flags on such occasions. Art is popular and high quality – lots is displayed around the school. Parents praise the standard of the drama productions.

At senior level, most of the extracurricular performing arts are done with the boys' school along with CCF, shared visiting speakers and a number of societies. It would be nice to have even more, the girls tell us. D of E and other local community service opportunities as well as fundraising for overseas projects. Girls are committed to these ventures both for their own personal development but also, we felt, out of a genuine desire to serve others.

Boarding: The boarding houses are on the school site and are purpose built. They are strikingly attractive and friendly in feel. From year 11 up, girls have rooms of their own. Below that they share in twos or threes. There is a lot organised for the boarders outside lesson time, some trips including the boys' school. Much sport goes on at weekends and in the evenings. There is shopping, cinema trips, salsa evenings, BBQs and generally a purposeful but relaxed atmosphere, which is very appealing and might account for the very low incidence of illness, despite the attractions of the medical facilities – there are soft toys on every bed. It might also account for the equally low level of law breaking. The girls really struggled to think of naughty things that anyone did. The worst seems to be not doing your kitchen duty or being late to breakfast (punishment – go in early the next day).

Boarding is flexible but that hasn't meant the school opts out of providing after-school and weekend activities. This is an active school with high energy pursuits on offer throughout the days and weekends. The meal menu is wide and quality good with meals served in an attractive extended dining room.

Background and atmosphere: Founded in 1892, to offer girls the opportunities that Monmouth School had provided since 1614, the Girls' School was funded by the original bequest of a local man, William Jones, a member of the Haberdashers' Company who made his fortune in Russian. The livery company is responsible for the school and provides financial support and stability, which reassures staff and has allowed for continual development of facilities. Although the boys' school is not far away, the girls' school has its own extracurricular facilities such as an Astroturf and swimming pool. The original Victorian buildings have been enhanced by imaginative, modern expansions such as a glass atrium and sixth form centre.

The school works hard at being a part of the Monmouth community and from those we spoke to, it is liked and respected. We arrived in the middle of the Monmouth Literary Festival – Carol Ann Duffy had been speaking the night before – which is organised entirely by the sixth forms of the three Monmouth secondary schools, the two Habs schools and Monmouth comprehensive. A remarkable achievement involving contacting agents, organising programmes, ticket sales and so on. There is another serious collaboration through the Monmouth Science Initiative, where state and independent schools work together with Cardiff University to bridge the gap between A level science and university science.

There is a lovely sixth form centre with study areas and a cool common room café – 'The boys love it', the girls tell us. 'We have to remind them that they are here for lessons not to drink hot chocolate all day'. Sixth formers still wear a uniform, suits, and tell us that they like it as they don't want to feel separate from the rest of the school. The dropout rate between year 11 and the sixth form is quite small – girls can't wait to wear suits and go to the café, we are told.

Pastoral care, well-being and discipline: The atmosphere is one of calm and sunny good manners. The relationships between the girls and staff are universally praised and we saw lots of warm and relaxed exchanges. 'They are interested in you and what you want to make of your life', sixth formers say. We heard about the much-anticipated annual satirical review put on by staff as part of the sixth form Christmas entertainments, a good indication of strong relationships. There are anti-bullying ambassadors and a buddy scheme working between year 7 and year 13. The girls tell us they would like even more integration between year groups. Prefects apply for their role and are eager for an opportunity to give back to the school. 'It is the school empowering us to experience responsibility', we were told by a successful applicant. The head has opened up the subject of social media and bullying and the girls are aware of the effects this can have and are being helped to combat it. The school is less focused on punishment and more concerned that the girls understand the dangers and causes.

A coloured card system operates for minor disciplinary infringements throughout the school – three yellow cards for something like late homeworks leads to a detention. 'It is really to help us get caught up,' the girls say. There are orange cards for uniform matters – zero tolerance for nail varnish: it gets that naughty. Parents say problems are nipped in the bud early and the staff are open and honest in their communications on pastoral issues. Pastoral care is outstanding, we were told.

Pupils and parents: Pupils come from a wide local area. There are buses coming from Cardiff, the north Bristol area, the Monmouthshire border, Hereford, Newport and the Ledbury area. The calendars for both day and boarding pupils are coordinated across the five Haberdashers' Monmouth schools, which is clearly a huge advantage for parents.

The bursary scheme ensures a good social mix. There are émigrés from the home counties, old Monmouth families, families with very little in the way of income and lots with both parents working hard to afford the fees. Staff commented to us that you find none of the sense of entitlement that some schools engender – pupils seem grateful to be at the school.

The head takes parents' surveys very seriously and we were impressed by how positive she was about parental criticisms. She wants the school to be on a constant improvement journey and uses parental feedback to keep raising the game. School council is valued by her as well as by the girls. This is an example of a school that pays more than lip service to parent and pupil voices. Parents complimented the school on its proactive approach to keeping them aware of current problem issues such as e-safety. 'They are taking care of my education as a parent,' one mother told us. Parents' view of the HMSG 'product' is one of engaging, confident, interesting girls who are keen to try new things, unaffected and enthusiastic. We would agree.

Former pupils include Lisa Rogers, Sandra Huggett and Jackie Ballard MP.

Entrance: About a third from their own prep school, Inglefield House, a third from other independent schools and a third from state schools. Entry is by entrance exam, interview and junior school report. At 13+ by own exam or common entrance. Some join at sixth form following an interview and good GCSE results.

Exit: There is less of the problem than some girls' schools face with large numbers of year 11 leaving for mixed schools. A few will go for financial reasons or because A levels really aren't for them, but most (some 75 per cent) stay on for the final two years. Sixth formers and parents say the school prepares girls very well for university and beyond. There are lots of links with old girls – staff meet up semi-formally with those who are London-based very regularly. There are plenty of opportunities to visit universities and the girls are starting to think about the possibility of apprenticeships. At the moment virtually everyone goes to university – six to Oxbridge in 2016, the majority to Russell Group universities and others to do niche high quality courses such as stage management and technical theatre, agri-food marketing, anthropology and media. A number study science, including medicine (three in 2016) and engineering. A few go overseas – Hong Kong, Holland and Switzerland in 2016.

Money matters: One in five receive financial assistance through a means-tested scheme that reassesses every year from endowment income.

Remarks: Habs has been in Monmouth for 400 years and reinvented itself over that time. The current structure is a selling point, so parents tell us. They like the all through concept with co-ed for the little ones in Agincourt and at sixth form level. Parents frequently used the word 'honest' when describing the school. You feel the fresh, clear air from the Welsh hills permeates the whole ethos. The location is very inspiring. From the sports fields you look out along the Wye Valley and from anywhere in the school you have views down to the rest of Monmouth and beyond. It is a lovely place to live – for the boarders, but also for staff and for families moving into the area.

We wondered if it was all a rather awful shock when girls had to move outside the Monmouth bubble, but we were assured that the school was anything but parochial. There are lots of visits to far-flung parts of the globe and the head's background in overseas work has re-emphasised the idea of a global village. Having said that, there is no doubt that Monmouth feels a very long way from Cardiff or Bristol, where a number of day girls live – no doubt part of its appeal for many families. It has the ambitious feel of a big city school without any of the traffic jams and tower blocks.

One parent summed up the feel of the school well: 'HMGS may lack a little of the pomp, ceremony and glitz of some public schools, but what you get is genuine care and a commitment to help your child reach her potential, whatever that may be.'

Hale Preparatory School

62

Broomfield Lane, Hale, Altrincham, Cheshire WA15 9AS

Pupils: 203 • Ages: 4–11

Fees: £7,410 pa

Tel: 01619 282386
Email: mail@haleprepschool.com
Website: www.haleprepschool.com

Headmaster: Since 1980, Mr John Connor (70s). Says he has 'no plans to retire – and is still there after 35 years'. Previously head of Hillcrest Grammar, Stockport. Married for 50 years, with four children, two of whom teach at the school. Loves to travel and ski. Founded the school in 1980 to put own educational ideas into practice without constraints from governors. A warm, cheerful man, and parents appreciate his hands-on attitude. One mum told us, 'his door is always open. He's in the playground every morning and afternoon, so you can always grab him for a chat.' Head says that if parents have a problem he will normally see them within half an hour, unless he's teaching. 'I want happy children so I pick up niggles fast.'

Entrance: It is really a case of the early bird here. Entry to reception is strictly on a first come basis and usually you will need to register in utero. One form entry in infant school, with 22 in a class. This increases to two forms in the junior school, so there is an additional intake in year 3, but again, it's essential to register in good time as entry is strictly by waiting list. Occasional places may come up as families move, so it's always worth putting your name down. Late entries take the head's 'happiness test' to check they'll integrate successfully.

Exit: Exceptional results considering the non-selective intake. The Altrincham grammars are much the most popular destinations, followed by Manchester Grammar School, Withington Girls' School, Loretto, Sale Grammar and King David School. Classes are run over the summer holidays in year 5 to practise verbal and non-verbal reasoning skills. Head meets all year 5 parents individually to discuss school choices and offers guidance to school best suited.

Remarks: Housed on four floors of a grand Victorian house in leafy Hale. A lack of space in the main building has meant cabins have been erected to provide extra teaching space.

School offers a wide curriculum (13 subjects by year 6) and stretches and challenges pupils. The pace is fast, so extra teachers are used to support children who need help, either one-to-one or in small groups. Head believes in traditional teaching, backed up with modern aids, and insists all pupils' work is marked thoroughly and within 24 hours. He personally looks at every child's books once a month so that he knows how everyone is progressing. French starts in year 1 and is taught all the way through and Spanish in years 5 and 6. Specialist teachers for music, art, drama, dance, IT, science and geography. Orchestra and choirs, with many children learning instruments. Sports are limited by a lack of space, but pupils are bussed to nearby facilities.

The school has never advertised and relies on word of mouth, so most children are local. They come from middle class and ethnically diverse families.

This is one of the area's best prep schools and achieves stunning results. Although it lacks the physical space that other schools offer, it turns out confident, articulate children who blossom in a smaller, intimate environment. One dad told us that when his daughter was asked what she thought paradise was like she said, 'school.'

Hanford School

Child Okeford, Blandford Forum, Dorset DT11 8HN

Pupils: 102; 96 boarders • Ages: 7–13 • C of E

Fees: Day £17,400; Boarding £21,150 pa

Tel: 01258 860219
Email: office@hanford.dorset.sch.uk
Website: www.hanfordschool.co.uk

Headmaster: Since 2014, Mr Rory Johnston BA (Cantab), Mr J to the girls. He's a classicist, a good fit for a school which has always excelled at classics. He's also a chartered accountant, a good fit for a school whose finances needed some grip – he's already upped the numbers and restored balance. Parted company with the City after 20 years and followed the hunch of a friend who reckoned he'd make a good teacher. Previously head of classics and boarding housemaster at Horris Hill. Wife Georgina, Mrs J to the girls, George to parents, works alongside him and heads up pastoral care. Very highly rated. Rory and George have two children.

Sarah Canning, daughter of the founders, head and owner since 1959, handed over to a charitable trust in 2003. Her presence and influence lived on in the background, as also does her legacy: this remains very much the school she made. Now in her 80s, understandably less in evidence these days.

Entrance: Informal, non-selective, girls can come at any time if there's room (lately a big if). Some at 7, most as 8 or 9 year olds, a few at 10 or 11. Locals, Wessex girls, Londoners (regular coach to Battersea) and numerous families posted or working abroad (especially popular with Forces and FCO families). A smattering of Europeans from Spain, France, Poland, Belgium and Germany. Parents as ever unshowy and unsnobby, new money prefers anywhere blingier. Some bursaries and a good deal for Forces families.

Exit: All over, most to boarding seniors – Bryanston, Sherborne Girls, Marlborough, St Mary's Calne and Ascot, Downe House, Benenden, St Swithun's, St Mary's Shaftesbury, Clayesmore.

Remarks: Ask any former parent or pupil about Hanford and you'll be bombarded by passionate paeans in celebration of its glories: its quirkiness, its changelessness, its quintessential Englishness. Evocations of Malory Towers and Hogwarts will ensue, together with a reverent inventory of the school's more bonkers traditions – the manners system which grades girls from Piglet to Royal Guest and the nutty names of the branches on a cedar tree that girls are encouraged to climb. You'll get the sense of a school that has somehow lain undisturbed for aeons, a time capsule, a girly Neverland; a place of butter-coloured sunlight, blissful children, long shadows, honey for tea, the whole timeless-idyll schtick. And to be sure, all of this grabs you when you go and see for yourself. The school's location is paradisal, the manor house beyond beguiling. Stand and be captivated by the genius loci. Blandings Castle must surely be on the other side of the hill.

The cold reality, back in the days before overarching regulatory frameworks, didn't fall far short of this arcadia. This was the school where Tara Palmer-Tompkinson remembers, 'After swimming we used to run naked round the gardens because it saved the bother of tumble-drying the towels.' But Hanford needs to keep moving somewhat with the times; you can't do that sort of drying-off thing any more. Your typical Hanford parent is change averse, though. They expect a head to be a worthy guardian of the Sacred Flame, bringing as much of the past with them as possible while at the same time enabling the school to earn its keep, propitiate inspectors and prepare girls for the world of things as they are. It's a darn difficult trick to pull off.

The problem is not aims, it's means. It always is. Mr J's mission statement contains nothing that Sarah Canning didn't also sign up for, which, actually, every school in the country signs up for – fulfilling potential, nurturing talent, all that caboodle. But here's the rub: in a changing demographic where parents' needs, expectations and above all values are moving on, how can Hanford go on being Hanford?

Hanford has always had a free-radical feel to it. When the Rev Clifford Canning, newly retired headmaster of Canford, founded it with his wife in 1947, they decreed no uniforms and no prefects – which raised eyebrows back then. But the thing that's especially made the school brilliantly different is the spirit in which it's done things, with idealism, creativity and joy, wholly unselfconsciousnessly. The name for this spirit is eccentricity, and eccentricity is hard to perpetuate in process-driven times. Well, Hanford's heritage behaviours are underscored by strong seriousness, they're integral. They're loveable but they're not cutesy. Any head who fails to understand this must answer to those who feel exceedingly strongly about this school, ie, every single person who's ever known it. In the short time he's been at the school Mr J is winning high approval ratings.

His fans like the way he has committed to ensuring that girls enjoy rich, low-tech childhood in the core heritage Hanford way, out in the fresh air, playing, riding their ponies, making up games, tending the chickens, climbing trees, looking after their gardens (they get around a square yard each). They like the way this builds self-reliance and develops friendships; the way it instils, as one parent put it, 'gumption' – these are decidedly not snowflake children. Hanford parents like the adventurousness and muddy knees. They want their daughters to enjoy what they call 'a traditional upbringing' and that's exactly what they get, watched over at an unobtrusive distance, never fussily superintended. A notably horsey school from way back, pretty much everybody rides, but no worries if you don't. In the summer you can enjoy a gallop before breakfast. Ancient, lovely stables, grade II listed – 'more listed than the manor', a groom told us.

Hard to say the same about the sports hall complex, performing arts centre, design tech centre or indoor swimming pool, all of which the school has not got. But it gets by very well with what it does have – a perfectly serviceable outdoor pool, for instance, a halfway decent gym and some terrifically nice grounds. Okay, so a couple of the classrooms have been temporary for the last 30 years; what matters most is who's standing in front of the girls. Hanford's triumphant lack of state-of-the-art facilities does not, mostly, denote a lack of anything indispensable to the raising of 21st century children; indeed, it very much reflects the unmaterialistic mood music here and effectively – to be brutal – deselects the wrong sort of parent. Mr J does entertain architectural daydreams, mind, but wants to build beautifully.

In the meantime, it's amazing what the girls achieve without benefit of stuff. By dint of excellent coaching and that indefinable Hanford spirit the girls are at the very least a match for the schools they play against with their fancy floodlights and their electronic scoreboards. All the usual sports here plus pistol shooting. Yes, pistol shooting. The time, though, has finally come to lay some Astroturf because other schools are reluctant to come and play any longer on Hanford's grass. So that's very much towards the top of Mr J's shopping list.

Masses of music, instrumental and choral – especially choral. Almost everyone plays an instrument. Dedicated music block. Drama very strong as you'd expect of a school which sets such store by play and imagination. Annual homemade production every summer performed outdoors, everyone has a part, natch. Art another heritage strength, seriously good, very well taught. The teacher told us 'The girls are amazing, they just get stuck in to whatever I give them'. Well, uninhibited spontaneity is very much a Hanford hallmark.

Academically tip-top – 'excellent,' as the inspectors express it. Recent influx of new teachers reckoned to be a shot in the arm. ICT now on course and high time too; next stop, please, DT and some engines to play with. The school bangs on an awful lot about scholarships won, around half a dozen a year, and hats off to that, fair dos, but what if your wee lassie isn't a likely Nobel shortlister? Our judgement: what the school is doing for the brightest it's doing for the rest. Just as the brightest are beneficiaries of extra attention (not special sets), so are the strugglers, because this is a very personal school. One parent who had switched her daughter here from somewhere glitzier described her learning as 'transformed'. Good library, newly beefed up. Around 10 per cent of the girls have a SEN and are attended to by specialists. Interventionist support given to anyone needing it as and when. Physical disability not easily accommodated here owing to the insurmountable architecture, wheelchair sadly a no-no. Not the right school for 'substantial' SENs.

If you want the full seclusive, immersive experience of Hanford – because shared experience and the joyous intensity of living together with your friends are what the school is all about – then you board, and that's what four-fifths do. But boarding doesn't suit everyone, nor the fees, so some don't. They have a bed all the same and can stay overnight more or less at the drop of a hat for free up to 20 days a year. Day girls go home after prep at 6.35pm. Dormitories are upstairs in the manor house, hugger-mugger, in rooms that adapt remarkably congenially to the purpose. They were once famous for their super-spartan furnishings and absence of lavatory doors, so we braced ourselves for a spot of memory lane and were almost disappointed to discover that they are cheery, snug and utterly unobjectionable even if, here and there, yes all right, a dab of paint wouldn't go absolutely amiss. Okay, so one prospective parent said she wouldn't expect her pig to live up here, but that only goes to show how much she just didn't get it. Perhaps she had a very fastidious pig. Whatever, we pictured only happy faces having heaps of fun – and reflected on how self-selecting Hanford parents are. What did concern us were the perils of pressure-cooker factors – girls getting on each others' nerves and being beastly to each other. But the quality of supervision by Mrs J, the matrons, including gap year students, is, we find, up to the mark and quickly onto this. One girl (her dad's in the Forces) protested under strong questioning, 'I've been to several schools and this one's easily the kindest.' So there. Mr J is keen to integrate the boarding and teaching staff more closely. Yes, all for that. In year 8 you graduate to a separate house, Fan's, where you get TV and feel more grown-up. A recent visitor reckoned the showers there resembled 'a 1970s campsite block, complete with soggy towels left on the floor. The tack room in the stable is tidier.' It happens.

A lot of people think that Hanford is an alternative sort of school. Couldn't be wider of the mark. Kindness matters most here. Close on its heels comes old-fashioned courtesy, hence the quaint manners league where you begin as a Boa Constrictor and earn your way up through Squirrel, Primrose etc, but risk plummeting to Piglet. It's aspirational, so there's very little Piglet-shaming. By all accounts it works. The same goes for the committee system, which takes the place of prefects. It's designed to bring out the helpfulness in girls, not the bossiness. Mr J, having watched its workings in his first year, finds it works extremely effectively. Both systems contribute to what one parent described as the school's climate of 'support, positivity and warmth' – a place where 'no one thinks they're better than anybody else'. All agree on this but no one can give you the full formula. One teacher said 'We just don't know how it works'. Being single sex has got to be a factor. That and the ban on mobile phones (but not email). Testimony to the extraordinary happiness of the place comes from the same parent: 'I'm sometimes mortified by how keen they are to get back to school'. None of the potential competition issues you might expect from a school without uniform. Why not? A girl explained 'If you wear something nice, it's probably just going to get dirty.'

If Hanford merely recreated a (mythical) 1930s childhood it would be no more authentic than one of those living history TV programmes in the mould of Wakey-Wakey Campers. It's nothing like that. It has judiciously preserved all those abiding elements which nurture the wonder of childhood at the same time as giving girls a good academic grounding and teaching them how to behave. Sounds simple, but who else does it this well? In a market where schools are increasingly differentiated by nothing more than geography, Hanford retains its measurable quality and its elusive magic. The Sacred Flame is alight and well.

Hayesfield

Upper Oldfield Park, Bath BA2 3LA

Pupils: 1,175 • Ages: 11–18 • Sixth form: 250 (including up to 54 boys)

Tel: 01225 426151
Email: information@hayesfield.com
Website: www.hayesfield.com

Headteacher: Since 2014, Miss Emma Yates (early 40s) B Eng (Sheffield). She came to Hayesfield by means of unswerving resolve – 'I knew from the age of 7 that I wanted to be a teacher' – and a swift ascent up the rungs of science teaching and preparatory stages of headship, her last post being at highly regarded Backwell School. Now a staunch advocate of single sex education, her views are reinforced by previous spells at mixed schools, where she experimented with single sex science sets – and watched results rocket. 'I wanted science to become a more equitable experience, where the girls can't just sit back and let the boys get on with it'. This empowering of girls spills over into the rest of life at Hayesfield, where the calm, collaborative, academically serious atmosphere is appreciated by students. 'My science-minded daughter thought she would do better at Hayesfield than anywhere else,' one father volunteered. Small, neat, blonde in her neutral bouclé suit (with its nod to Chanel) and nude suede heels, Miss Yates sets the tone for the professionalism she expects of her school; her students describe her as 'fair, firm, inclusive, driven'. This last attribute perhaps makes her the keen and competent skier she has become in the last few years; she tries to spend 5-6 weeks a year on snow – 'There's always some somewhere!' she says. Presumably her Yorkshire terrier, Sugar, stays home on those trips, but she accompanies her on some school occasions, such as the induction camp-out at the start of year 7.

Academic matters: All comers are catered for, yet results sit comfortably above national averages for all sorts of measures including the English Baccalaureate at GCSE (one of top state schools in the Bath area), where 25 per cent of all entries were graded A*/A in 2016 and 76 per cent gained five+ GCSEs including English and maths. At A level, 30 per cent A*/A and 57 per cent A*/B. To what can this success be attributed? Well, it could have something to do with the Hayesfield Teacher Mind Set, which enshrines in print the non-negotiables of teaching and learning to 'ensure an outstanding learning experience for every student'. Add some committed well-behaved girls (who can do without boys in the classroom till sixth form), the importance they and their parents place on education, the prevailing, though not ubiquitous, affluence of Bath, some super new teaching space – et voilà. All the parents we spoke to praised the commitment of teaching staff, which extends to running pre-exam sessions on Saturdays and in the holidays, as well as more mundane matters, such as being readily contactable and not letting GCSEs 'come rumbling at them like a snowball'.

The lessons we saw tended more towards traditional pedagogy, with students sitting in sometimes somewhat crowded rows facing the front – and not reliant on IT. Rules on the use of personal devices in class are strict; everyone seems perfectly happy with laptops which travel around school on trolleys as required, and reckon there is enough computer provision in school. We enjoyed the rigour of a year 7 English

H

class where girls were conducting a textual analysis of a passage from HG Wells, but felt it was a pity that so little of the French class we went to was done in the desired language, unlike the Spanish class, which was. Hayesfield acknowledges that not all its students will be high achievers, and strives to support them equally to achieve their goals: all subjects are setted except for the creative ones, which is thought to foster a culture of aspiration rather than demotivation. In the mixed sixth form, the pastoral manager oversees those who won't necessarily get to university by encouraging them to apply for and be accepted onto foundation degree courses with less demanding grades – a welcome change from previous years where weaker brethren (and they were brethren) were encouraged to take their poor AS results elsewhere for their final year. School defends current record on keeping students till the bitter end.

Games, options, the arts: For an urban school on two sites, a remarkable number of facilities and outdoor space is shoehorned onto its premises: an Astro, outdoor netball courts and plenty of grass with tables and chairs for relaxation inclement weather. Main games are hockey and netball, but a wider range of physical activities are on offer as part of the comprehensive array of extracurricular pursuits known as Period 6; these take place after school every day and girls are expected to sign up for at least two sessions per week. Lacrosse, cricket, rowing and fencing all feature, and like all the Bath schools, Hayesfield makes use of the top-notch sports facilities at Bath University, a short drive up the hill. Several fixtures a week against local schools of all persuasions and competitions at county level, but one parent voiced her regret that there aren't often enough staff to coach B, C and D teams so that everyone gets a game and a chance to represent the school. D of E is run with Beechen Cliff, the corresponding boys' school about half a mile away, and CCF with best-in-Bath King Edwards.

Art of all kinds prominent: super studios and exhibition space, plus outstanding pieces on display in the atrium of the fabulous new building. The black dress with feather trim incited our envy, and A Gormley would, we are sure, be delighted with the installation of tiny clay figurines inspired by his work. Performing arts given a tremendous boost by the recent opening of the splendid Roper Theatre, named for a local philanthropic family trust which subsidised it in return for its supporting community events. Beauty and the Beast in rehearsal at the time of writing. Music vibrant, too: the timetabling of music lessons and practice time within the school day shows it isn't just an add-on. Two auditioned choirs, Hush and Host, both win awards in the city, but other ensembles provide opportunity to play and sing at any or all of the three main events in the musical calendar, the carol service in Bath Abbey and winter and summer concerts. If the intellectual life appeals, Period 6 offers basic Russian, a polyglots' club, computing, the Hayesfield newspaper – or manifold opportunities to catch up on weaker subjects.

Background and atmosphere: The current school on its split site (divided by function, rather than by student age, in an effort to integrate year groups) provides an insight into education policy changes enacted in Bath, what with previous manifestations as City of Bath Girls' School, Somerset Industrial School for Boys, West Twerton Secondary Modern – we could go on. In 1973 Hayesfield was born, the child of the local girls' grammar and secondary modern, and still makes use of both sites: Brougham (pronounced Broom, for the uninitiated) Hayes and Upper Oldfield Park, some seven minutes' walk apart (hour long lessons allow for the trot between sites). The latter is all Bath stone, high ceilings, lots of glass, stunning modern additions and stonking views, including a new refectory where delicious chicken and leek pie was on the menu, along with equally tasty home-cooked choices. Brougham Hayes is, well, tired and in widely acknowledged need of a facelift, but it boasts a new design studio, equipped with help from Dyson, which provided industry-quality machinery usually beyond a school's budget. But it is the simply fabulous Nucleus, a new science centre, which must be the envy of schools up and down the land. Eye-catching design which included student contributions, serious green credentials and extreme functionality (we loved the write-on walls, also in the refurbished maths rooms, with their formulae-in-progress as well as more permanent aperçus, and the witty and efficacious use of hay as an insulating material in the walls) mean it is far more than a pretty face.

This sense of modish practicality extends to the uniform, which is amongst the most smartly worn (read rigorously enforced) we have seen anywhere: themed colours of black and purple, with a braided blazer, open collared white blouse and choice of a skirt or trousers. That said, Hayesfield sixth formers are attired with marked degrees of quirkiness, liberated from the deadening (and generally wildly off the mark) expectation of 'office wear' laid down by so many schools. The prevailing atmosphere is one of opportunity – it's all there for the taking. 'Special talents will be developed and supported in this school,' says the head, adding that 'Opportunities should not have to be bought. Parents choose Hayesfield as a social decision – girls come from all kinds of backgrounds, reflecting Britain as a whole'. Subject-specific homework clubs abound, and there's an outreach initiative to support girls from a less advantaged part of the city. We also picked up a spirit of enterprise: the vision and amount of private funding bid for and secured for the sensational new buildings on the upper site, the strong links with China through the Bath-Suzhou Education Partnership, and the ski trip to Canada being just three examples. Market forces too: 'You're going to have to develop yourselves as a desirable commodity,' the head instructs her sixth formers

Pastoral care, well-being and discipline: Very highly rated: 'in our experience, second to none,' some enthusiastic parents told us; 'a safe, nurturing and happy environment,' said one; 'staff and pupils are attuned to each other,' remarked another. As for the girls: 'We can go to anyone when things go wrong – the school nurse, the counsellor – anyone!' It was heartening to see the deputy head greeting everyone (and many by name) at the start of the day when we visited. Effective buddy system in place for year 7 intake from the year above. But a clear system of sanctions is also applied rarely and fairly, according to students, starting with detentions for sins of academic omission and commission. As to behaviour: 'No-one has the right to disrupt the learning of other people,' states the head, who does not shrink from sending the persistently disruptive to Beechen Cliff for their lessons, as a step short of excluding them completely.

Pupils and parents: The girls we met were pleased and proud to be at Hayesfield – 'The school encourages them to be confident from the start,' say parents, while the head's view is that everyone should be encouraged to take risks and to 'colour outside the lines. Coping with failure builds resilience', she says. We certainly found students forthcoming, articulate and go-getting: school lists founder member of the Women's Equality Party among its students. Families come from grade 1 listed Georgian piles and from rather humbler dwellings across the socio-economic spectrum. Brothers tend to go to Beechen Cliff; the two schools share an admissions policy, term dates and inset days. Mary Berry is indisputably its most famous alumna, but sports fans will know of Amy Williams, GB's skeleton bob gold medallist and Anya Shrubsole, cricketer.

Entrance: About 180 girls join in year 7 from a variety of local primary and prep schools, mostly in Bath but 20 per cent coming from outside the Greater Bath Consortium; all applications done via the local authority, whose edicts merit careful study. Open days in September and October. School is currently full but not oversubscribed – some parents hedge their bets with abundant Bath independents. At sixth form, 65 new students can join; no more than a quarter of the total sixth form may be boys, although teaching is joint with Beechen. Some parents think that 60/40 would make for a more viable offer, particularly in terms of boys' sports teams and activities. Entry requirements are six GCSEs at grade C or above including English and maths (the unsuccessful are expected to retake) to enrol on A level courses; some subjects require a B for further study. Lower or fewer GCSEs might mean entry to BTec courses.

Exit: After GCSE, around a third leave for other state and independent schools 'in search of boys, in some cases,' admitted one mother. Tiny number (three per cent in 2016) leave in year 12. After A levels or BTec, 93 per cent go on to higher or further education, a sprinkling of gap years, very few straight to work; school is proud to have Employability Chartermark – not many have. A goodly percentage goes to top universities, helped by school's own Oxbridge and élite course programme (including one to Oxbridge, almost half to Russell Group unis and two to study medicine in 2016). More information on destinations for the less exalted would be helpful.

Money matters: Striving to be a cashless school, but parents report frustrations with Tucasi, the system chosen, which fails to flag up low or empty balances. Otherwise, a sensible and egalitarian attitude to money and costs in particular, in common with most maintained schools. We applaud the accounts of wise and compassionate use of pupil premium and bursary funds in cases of financial nightmare that came to our ears.

Remarks: Defiantly, proudly, pre-eminently a girls' school, freshened up by a mixed sixth form. A particular hooray for the school's emphasis on STEM subjects for girls – this is a place where they can literally reach for the stars.

Hazlegrove School

Linked with King's Bruton

Hazlegrove, Sparkford, Yeovil, Somerset BA22 7JA

Pupils: 375; 98 full and flexi boarders • Ages: 2–13 (boarding from 7)

Fees: Day £8,280 – £16,788; Boarding £19,287 – £24,609 pa

Tel: 01963 442606
Email: admissions@hazlegrove.co.uk
Website: www.hazlegrove.co.uk

Headmaster: Since 2002, Mr Richard Fenwick BEd Adv Dip Ed MA (50s). Educated at Bishops Stortford College, bosh shot at London University and now, after gaining a first and subsequent MA at the Open University in education management and shaping a notable career and reputation in prep schools, living proof that education doesn't always work at the same time for everyone. Stints at Bilton Grange (qv) as director of studies and teacher of DT – still a fabulous carpenter, according to his wife – and head of St Andrew's Turi (Kenya) preceded his appointment to Hazlegrove; also Vice Chairman of ISEB since 2011. 'I want Hazlegrove to be a place where children feel safe and loved' he says, 'so that, instead of just surviving at school, they can direct their energies into academic, creative or sporting endeavour'. Tall and lean, Mr Fenwick bounds about the school, taking stairs two at a time; we trotted to keep up. Hobbies include running, surfing, sea-kayaking, golf, fishing and trekking in remote locations (Nepal a particular favourite) during the hols, we were not surprised to learn. Married to Katie, who is more deeply involved in school life than many heads' wives, (she teaches PHSE and wrote an excellent leaflet for parents of new boarders, for example), they have three grown up children. In some ways rather an unconventional and uncompromising head, attributes which perhaps enabled him to turn Hazlegrove from the rudderless place it was when he arrived to the thriving enterprise it clearly is today.

Retiring summer 2017. His successor will be Mr Mark White, currently deputy head (academic) at the Dragon School in Oxford.

Entrance: Broadly non-selective. All hopefuls are invited for a trial day at which reading/spelling ages and mathematical ability are assessed, plus any need for additional learning support identified.

Exit: To a panoply of greater and lesser public schools at 13+, majority in south west England. Between 40 and 50 per cent to the Sherborne schools, Marlborough, Bryanston, Millfield, Winchester, Eton and Wells. Around half to its own senior school, Kings Bruton. The array of awards year after year impresses – 32 gained by 27 pupils in 2016. A recent parent was delighted by the head's efforts in researching a school where Hazlegrove pupils do not usually go. Former pupils include Peter Wilson (Olympic gold medallist in shooting), Maddie Hinch (GB hockey goalie), sculptor Will Newton and author Tobias Jones.

Remarks: A long drive through glorious parkland – we narrowly avoided cows and 4x4s en route – leads to a fine example of 18th century domestic architecture, enhanced by formal gardens. Less sightly parts of what is undoubtedly a well-resourced and purposeful school are mostly hidden away, but facilities and space abound: super indoor pool, two Astros, tennis courts and acres of pitches satisfy the most sporty. Recent additions include new girls' changing rooms and upgrades to swimming pool including new viewing area and additional entrance. Pigs and chickens enthusiastically looked after by pupils, and there's no ducking their eventual fate either. Full use appears to be made of this bucolic setting (faintly marred by the services visible on the A303), recently enhanced by the planting of a five acre Jubilee Wood.

We were enthralled and impressed by a scholarship English class of 13-year-olds who were getting to grips with the complex themes in William Blake's poetry. Parents recognise and greatly appreciate the fine teaching that goes on at Hazlegrove, and acknowledge the head's insistence in recruiting staff only of the highest calibre: 'The quality of the discussions at parents' evenings is phenomenal,' said one mother. But Hazlegrove is no hothouse, though the children are 'pushed enough' say parents, and does very well by the breadth of ability it admits. About 15 per cent of pupils receive learning support. All these lucky children benefit from exciting and innovative ways to learn, such as a Skype call with astronaut Nicholas Patrick in which the whole prep school participated, and the millionaires club which encourages children to read 1,000,000 words in the course of a term. The latter is part of the Accelerated Reader programme, where books are carefully graded to eliminate unsuitable choices. The librarian gets rave reviews.

Sport, music and drama ditto. There's an extensive fixture list with other schools and plenty of silverware in the trophy cabinet. One parent articulated the common tension between winning at all costs/sport for all, and wondered if there could

H

be more chances for less skilled players to represent the school at matches. (School defends its record on this.) As for the music, well, our socks were knocked off by the impromptu marimba recital (we had not met one before either) the head asked a boy to perform when we happened upon him jamming with a couple of other pupils in the music department. Masses going on of all standards, from absolute beginners to one already at grade 8, and a clutch taking grade 5 theory – plus giant outdoor chimes in pre prep playground. Conventional choices for drama, such as Wind in the Willows and The Wizard of Oz put on in purpose-built theatre and much enjoyed by performers and audience alike; pupils also take LAMDA exams. Mandarin club has proved hugely successful and Mandarin introduced for year 5 pupils.

About a third of pupils board routinely (around 10 per cent of these are international pupils), and there is scope for occasional boarders too. Accommodation is fine (quite big dorms with a strong smell of disinfectant in the boys' quarters) with a bit of recent pepping up (includes a new common room) though rules are quaintly old-fashioned: no mobiles, letter-writing on Sundays and proper shoe-cleaning once a week. That said, activities are myriad and sometimes rather trendy: we were shown the film the boarders had devised, scripted and made the previous weekend. The feel of an extended family is palpable, enhanced by the fact that half the staff live on site. In the evenings, seating for meals is rearranged into family-style groups so boarders get to know everyone; a black tie dinner with five sets of cutlery enlivens proceedings from time to time.

Hazlegrove is quite smart and not a typical country prep school. A broad cross-section (says school) of local and not-so-local families drive or bus their kids in from all over the place up and down the A303, and it's the school of choice for many families making the big move out of London. The head defined parents, when asked, as the 'sort of people who don't look in the mirror before they come to pick up'; their occupations include farmer, lawyer, doctor, plumber, cheese-maker, helicopter pilot, entrepreneur, designer, author and chef. There is an active and welcoming social scene and parents, mums in particular, take up the exercise classes and tennis coaching with enthusiasm. Try as we might, we could not find anything to fault about this super one-off school with its quirky head.

H

Hereford Cathedral School

Old Deanery, The Cathedral Close, Hereford HR1 2NG

Pupils: 736 • Ages: 3–18 • Sixth form: 163

Fees: £4,365 – £13,341 pa

Tel: 01432 363522
Email: admissions@herefordcs.com
Website: www.herefordcs.com

Headmaster: Since 2005, Mr Paul Smith BSc. Originally a zoologist (undergraduate at Manchester, postgraduate at KCL), his first teaching post was at Rugby, followed by stints at King Edward's School Birmingham and as head of science at Haileybury, then second master and acting head at Portsmouth Grammar School. A softly spoken, friendly, but determined character. Married with two daughters.

Works hard at getting to know every child and speaks of teaching as a 'humbling experience'. Insists on the importance of staff respecting pupils and not becoming 'myopic' about children who don't fit a particular mould. Emphatic about the importance of strengthening relationships through extracurricular activities. Pupils say he is 'nice, funny, witty and approachable'. Staff say he is 'calm and considered – you can ask him anything'.

Very keen that the school should be 'all round' – not, for example a music academy or languages specialist. Looking to broaden the horizons of the school and has introduced a small number of international homestay boarding students in the sixth form.

Head of junior school: Since 2014, Christopher Wright, previously assistant head at Exeter Cathedral School. Degree from Warwick in industrial economics, and masters in economics. Has taught at Winchester House School, St Edward's Oxford, The Banda School in Nairobi and Moor Park. Married to Jo; their youngest child has joined the school. Likes squash, tennis, scuba diving and surfing.

Academic matters: The nursery (in a new building) has high staff ratios (we saw a group of 15 being looked after by four staff). In the pre-prep and junior classes, groups tend to be no larger than 13 or 14. Setting for maths and English in year 6. The school 'doesn't do' a gifted and talented programme as feels it is counterproductive to label children as either in or out of such a category, says 'it's all about hard work' and emphasizes the importance of respecting the different learning pathways and intellectual growth spurts of different children. There is instead a detailed programme for what the school refers to as high achievers.

No children with EAL when we visited. Learning support is available and carefully tailored. There are two learning development specialists working across the year groups so that any learning support issues can be identified early. A specialist SEN teacher assists those in years 5/6 who require support. French and music from reception upwards, and all pupils are also involved in drama and performance – starting with poetry recital and working up to debating, improvisation and puppetry by years 4/5.

Strong academically, with 45 per cent A*/A and 73 per cent A*-B at A level in 2016 and 56 per cent A*/A at GCSE. At A level, English, modern languages, history, art, music and RS all do very well. Good results in sciences too – no really weak areas. Nice range of A levels – the usual suspects plus Latin, history of art, philosophy and ethics.

As well as receiving half termly grade reports for effort and achievement, with target grades included from year 10, pupils have to fill in a self assessment form every term that is completed alongside their reports – something parents value highly. Staff say this is not a crammer and that the range of abilities is reasonably wide. Nonetheless, expectations are high.

All students take maths (top sets take two AS modules in year 11), two English, and short course RS as compulsory GCSEs. Some 60 per cent take triple award science and the remainder dual award. The vast majority take French or Spanish, although a handful use the curriculum time for learning support. An additional three subjects are chosen from a range of options, GCSE Japanese is offered as an extracurricular addition, and the school is about to introduce Mandarin.

Interactive white boards in most classrooms, school email used to set and receive work – although traditional means are also used, and there is good access to PCs within school for those who wish to use them, including a dedicated area in the sixth form centre. A well-stocked library with its own small IT suite and a galleried, silent study area. Welcoming and evidently well used, also the venue for the school's book clubs, debating club and film club.

Learning support is well organized with all children MIDYIS tested on entry and supported as necessary, either within class or small group withdrawal. A sense of 'open door' for any wanting assistance. Pupils say they can go into the learning support unit for 'anything and everything'. A handful of international students in the sixth form, all of whom are tested on entry, have EAL timetabled into their week.

Games, options, the arts: The junior art room, complete with kiln, is well kitted out and full of exuberant work – willow structures and ceramics as well as the usual paintings and drawings. There is also a small but well put together DT room where the slightly older children begin learning about resistant materials. The creative arts are plainly very important here – a lovely feature is the Olympic Wall in the main garden – a tiled mural which incorporates designs by every child in the school, reflecting on the themes of 2012, co-ordinated by local artist Clare Woods (whose works were commissioned for display in the Olympic Park).

Art, music and design are simply outstanding here. The A level results speak for themselves, and the quality of work on display is excellent, varied and innovative. Complemented by a small but very well-resourced history of art department. Beautiful, naturally lit studio for the use of sixth formers and large light rooms for the lower years. Textile work is also beautiful.

At the other end of the design spectrum, the DT workshops (for both resistant materials and electronics) are well kitted out with and well organized. Some interesting project work, and DT seems to have been fairly successfully sold to the girls, who make up around 25 per cent of the GCSE cohort.

Music is a central part of school life. The school remains the choristers' school for the cathedral but aside from that there are masses of choirs, chamber ensembles, jazz bands and piano trios as well as a music technology club. About half of all pupils take instrumental lessons, and the school is a choral power to be reckoned with. The senior girls' choir (Cantabile) has won the senior children's choir section of the Llangollen International Musical Eisteddfod.

Sporting success is seen as important but participation is also perceived as a means of increasing pupils' confidence and strengthening relationships. Successful teams fielded in rugby (two Welsh U18 players in recent years), cricket (a number of county players – the girls' cricket team have played at Lords several times in the last few years, reaching the finals of Lady Taverners indoor cricket competition), hockey (boys and girls – county and regional players), netball, rounders (two England players) and tennis. Football has also now been introduced for boys and rowing is popular too. Large and well-equipped sports hall. Fencing and swimming also available as options. Spacious, well-maintained sports fields are a 15 minute walk from the cathedral green (slight moan from pupils who have to walk there and back); netball courts are close, though not actually on site.

Sport, teamwork and having a go are considered very important parts of the junior school experience too, with regular matches against schools from Shropshire, Worcestershire, Gloucestershire and Wales. Hockey, netball and rounders for girls; rugby, football and cricket for boys. The children have use of the senior school playing fields and sports hall – and, unusually, says the school, get a completely fair share.

Unusually, CCF is compulsory in year 10, and many stay with it into the sixth form. It runs a huge range of courses including leadership, sailing, gliding and diving. There is a regimental dinner, summer camps, annual field days. The school also runs an annual trek for year 12 students to the Annapurna range in Nepal where it supports a local school. D of E also well supported.

Extracurricular clubs in just about everything – including mycology, Japanese, New Testament Greek and (reassuringly) board games. Definitely a school where all interests are catered for.

Background and atmosphere: Herefordshire is a deeply rural county, and Hereford itself has something of the quiet county town about it. It is impossible not to feel slightly removed from the cut and thrust of the 21st century here. The school, originally for choristers of the 12th century, is set around the stunning cathedral green, and the splendours of the cathedral lend a special flavour to the place. That connection (the chaplain is a minor canon of the cathedral, as well as teaching full time) gives the school an implicitly Christian flavour and pupils clearly appreciate the depth and beauty of the place.

Quite traditional in feel. Monitors (prefects) wear gowns to chapel, as do academic staff. Services are held four times a week in the nave, and much of the musical and artistic excellence of the school seems to feed off the cathedral tradition of creative and artistic expression. Good spaces between the buildings, which are a combination of listed glories and more modern blocks (such as the sports and dining halls). But for all the leafy tranquility, the school is a very busy place, with lots to do, lots going on, and great enthusiasm from top to bottom about the possibilities 'out there'. One of very few schools whose pupils can claim to have founded a charity with a national ambit (The Little Princess Trust). And there is another under construction. Pupils evidently feel that not only do they have a responsibility to do the right thing, but also that they have the capacity to make a difference.

Like the senior school, the juniors is a mixture of old and new. Three schools in one – a nursery, pre-prep and junior school. Also like the senior school, the junior school is almost in the shadow of Hereford Cathedral, and shares very similar links. It is a charming place, with a very embedded sense of nurture and encouragement.

The principal junior school building – a mixture of medieval and Georgian splendours – has more than its fair share of panelled walls and ornately plastered ceilings, although it also has the feel of a slightly overgrown country house in which a school happens to have landed. Brightened by lots and lots of children's work on the walls and attractive displays.

In complete contrast, the purpose-built Moat, tucked into what would have been a terrace in the old school garden, houses the pre-prep. This really is a great environment for children to learn in. It is airy and child friendly, with small classrooms for an intimate learning space and good areas for play, lots of natural light too. The reception class has its own little garden to play in – well-resourced but not overcrowded.

There are separate gardens for different age groups to play in – one for the reception class, one for years 1 and 2 (with new adventure play area), and one for the older children, as well as a lovely wild garden with a pond, lots of homes for masonry bees and ladybirds, wild flowers and so on. The children in year 5 are responsible for the gardening and there is a pond club too.

The junior and senior school combined offer what they hope will be a one stop solution for Herefordshire parents, for children from 3 to 18. As the school also offers a breakfast club from 8am and after-school care until 5.30pm (and has a policy of never shutting, whatever the weather) there is much to attract parents who need a few additional hours around the edges of the day. The catchment area runs all around the county and into Wales, with school buses from Bromyard, Ludlow, Ross-on-Wye and Presteigne (all supervised, and shared with the senior school). A very pervasive family atmosphere – lots of siblings, many parents are Old Herefordians, and many staff educate their children here, so the community is remarkably tight.

Pastoral care, well-being and discipline: Pastoral care is evidently a very integrated part of school life – four school houses, each with eight tutors, so tutor groups are small. Academic staff are positively encouraged to run extracurricular activities and to strengthen relationships and pastoral links through them. Parents are encouraged to email academic and house staff with any queries, and say that any concerns are dealt with 'instantly', and 'children are kept too busy to have time for cyber bullying'.

Pupils say there is no problem with reporting bullying and getting it sorted out if it arises, but that it is rare. They also say that the school system of detentions is applied consistently, but that need of it is infrequent. Staff say they have very little to deal with on the disciplinary front.

Pupils and parents: Senior school pupils are an absolute delight – very supportive of one another, articulate and appreciative. Comfortable in their own skin, but not full of themselves. Extremely positive about the school and proud of their achievements, but no trace of entitlement or arrogance – if they are a little on the quiet side one gets the impression that this is a result of not having to shout in order to be heard. Parents are a combination of local farmers, businesspeople and professionals. Many attended the school themselves. Busy, supportive PTA. Parents say, 'All children have something special – and here the teachers help them find it', 'The school builds self confidence' and 'identifies needs quickly', both academically and pastorally.

The junior children, from the nursery class eagerly talking about their book choices in the school library, to the reception children, busy with puzzles and problem solving, to year 4s enthusiastically reciting poetry, are the best possible advertisement for the school. Each child we spent time with was friendly, relaxed, happy and engaged. Bouncing about full of things to talk about. You can pretty much hear their little brains fizzing. A delightful place to start exploring life's possibilities.

Entrance: Not selective in its lower years and accepts children into the nursery from age 3. There is also an intake in reception and at age 7, although entrance is possible at other ages, subject to space and suitability. As children get older there are interviews and entrance tests and a requirement for reports from their current school. Substantial scholarships are available for boys who join the school as cathedral choristers (from age 7).

Senior school is selective, but with Herefordshire school numbers in a demographic dip, cannot afford to be hugely so. Most of the junior school pupils end up here, and unless there is a particular cause for uncertainty, are offered a place without taking the entrance tests. All external candidates at 11 examined in English, maths and VR. There is also an interview for every candidate. Successful candidates at 11 can defer their place to 13+ if happy in a prep school elsewhere, and there is also a separate entry procedure at 13 (not CE). For the sixth form at least six Bs at GCSE and at least Cs in English and maths GCSE are required plus references, interviews etc.

Exit: The vast majority of junior pupils go on to the senior school on the head's recommendation and without taking the entrance exam. Those whom it is felt would not thrive there are generally counselled in year 2 or 3 to consider alternatives, so there should be no nasty surprises in year 6, and it is rare for the school not to be able to get a child up to the right level by then.

The majority stay past GCSE and into the sixth form though around 30 per cent go to the local, and very well thought of, sixth form college. Two to Oxbridge in 2016 plus lots to other Russell Group – especially Bristol, Cardiff, Swansea, Birmingham, Leeds, KCL etc. A good mix of subjects – including medicine, dentistry, physics, veterinary science, law, history, business and economics. A number too taking fine art and music. Not many into electronics or ICT.

Money matters: Academic scholarships worth 15 per cent of fees available at 11+, 13+ and 16+. Other scholarships worth 10 per cent of fees for music, sports and all rounders (also for art at 13+). A number of bursary awards and some Ogden Trust bursaries for science students joining the sixth form. Previously a direct grant school and actively fundraising to broaden access.

Remarks: Justifiably growing more self-assured, a school with a great deal to offer and an ethos of careful, thoughtful, nurture. Much to impress, with truly outstanding arts and music, a wide curriculum, a great sense of community service and genuine commitment to developing courage, confidence and a sense of adventure in even the quietest child.

Hereford Sixth Form College

Folly Lane, Hereford, Herefordshire HR1 1LU

Pupils: 2,000 • Ages: 16–18

Tel: 01432 355166
Email: sixth-form@hereford.ac.uk
Website: www.hereford.ac.uk

Principal: Awarded an OBE for services to education in 2013, Jonathan Godfrey wears his considerable success lightly. An Oxford chemist, he has made his career in the sixth form college world, having been a deputy principal at the nearby Worcester Sixth Form College before taking up this post in 1997. He is deeply committed to the college and to the sector, chairing the national Sixth Form College Association since 2011. Sharp, generous about colleagues, enthusiastic in his advocacy of the sector, he runs a well-oiled large institution without any need or desire to empire build. No money wasted here on layers of management to increase his own importance. It is a lean machine and a personal one. Jonathan sings in the college choir and plays in the orchestra. Three of his daughters have been through the college and the fourth is still there hoping to read modern languages at university. His wife is an environmental science teacher at the college. He has the huge advantage of long experience of the college and has lost none of his enthusiasm for exciting developments.

Academic matters: This is no sleepy rural backwater. The college consistently comes out as one of the top institutions nationally for value-added exam results and it was awarded outstanding in every area at its last Ofsted inspection. In 2016, 54 per cent A*/B and 22 per cent A*/A grades. There is an impressive range of A levels on offer including subjects difficult to find in smaller institutions such as archaeology and geology. Offers French, Spanish and German. Science is strong with at least two-thirds doing one science, and numbers for maths are huge too. There are also BTecs in IT and performing arts, and the BTec extended diploma in sport and exercise science as well as a one-year GCSE programme. Running parallel to these, everyone follows a general education programme where general studies A level sits along side a progression studies course that includes careers education, personal finance, healthy living and environmental sustainability. It's coherent and delivers on depth and breadth.

About 10 per cent of students have identified learning difficulties and support is tailored to individual need. The students to whom we spoke rated the learning support very highly and said the college was particularly strong on sorting out dyslexic issues. They were very conscious that teaching was aimed at the top end, but described very effective lunchtime surgeries in all subjects to sort out individual difficulties. Set size is around 20.

Wednesday afternoons are when students engage in enrichment activities in a strikingly wide range of high quality areas. There are some lectures preparing those who are thinking Oxbridge – Cambridge regularly brings a coachful of academics to run talks and masterclasses. The highly structured approach to this extension work is unusual even in high performing selective independent schools.

The college attributes its high performance to an insistence on the highest standards and rigorous, effective use of data. Each student regularly receives three grades – a minimum A level grade expectation based on prior achievement at GCSE, a grade which reflects the current level of performance, and then a grade that tutors feel a student is capable of achieving. These are closely analysed by the college and tutors, who talk through concerns and patterns with each student throughout their programme. Not much can slip through the net here, and parents commented on how successful the college is in keeping students on track. 'It has turned my son's attitude to education round', said one parent whose son had had something of an 'attitude' in his secondary school.

The close-knit Association of Sixth Form Colleges allows regular benchmarking of academic progress against other similar institutions and the college makes effective use of this, which is another way of quickly highlighting any areas of weakness that need addressing.

Games, options, the arts: Well aware that at this level, the best schools are offering a lot more that just examination results, the college runs an enrichment programme with the motto 'something for everyone' – and there is. Around two-thirds of students do at least one activity inside the college. These are open to all and there is a comprehensive explanatory leaflet so students can make the most of their two years right from the word go. Most activities take place outside lesson time, but some are directly linked to the subjects a student has chosen and are actually part of their timetable. The most innovative and structured areas are sport and performing arts, particularly music. The large pool of students obviously helps to provide top performers, whether in sport or the arts, but there is vision and rigour here that drives the programmes.

Students can join one of the five Sports Academies in basketball, football, hockey, netball, rugby. These academies allow enthusiastic sports players the chance to develop their talent alongside their academic qualifications through links with local sports clubs and top quality sports coaches – with consistently impressive successes. Each sports player has an individual fitness programme based round the fitness centre, a multi-gym that is also let out to the public when students aren't using it.

The college is the biggest centre for music in the Three Counties. There are masses of ensembles and groups and an elite programme for top musicians which, rather like the sport, gives students opportunities to perform alongside and learn from professionals. A music scholarship programme offers the best performers training on a par with a music college and is not confined to those taking A level music. Not surprisingly, these music scholars are well prepared to take up choral and instrumental university scholarships. The Academia Musica choir, comprising music scholars and musicians in residence, has a performing contract with a record company, performs weekly in British cathedrals and has a substantial calendar of engagements around the UK and abroad as well as in college. We are talking serious professional quality here. The music scholar to whom we spoke was destined for a music degree at university, but had experience and expectations that far exceeded that of the usual A level student. Instrumental scholars form the basis of the Academia Musica Orchestra that manages its own weekly recital series and has played with the English Symphony Orchestra. The repertoire of both the choir and orchestra is as extensive as you will find in any national youth equivalent.

The college theatre company, Upstage Productions, recently performed Romeo and Juliet in Hereford Cathedral, with voice coaching from professionals.

Background and atmosphere: The college started 40 years ago at a time when Herefordshire was moving away from 11 to 18 schools. The majority of the county schools are now 11 to 16, though some have small sixth forms. The strength and challenge of HSFC is its size. You get the brilliant academic and extracurricular option choices and the college works hard to overcome the impersonality that such a large institution could mean. Students say that some do find the size off-putting, particularly at first if they have moved from a small school. However the ones we talked to made it clear they had chosen the college partly because they wanted the stimulus and interaction of large classes.

The site is undoubtedly small for such a huge number of students and the principal is very aware of that. Student social spaces and the library can be crowded during the common break and lunch hour, although these and the dining area have been extended recently. There are new classroom blocks and everything has been refurbished in the last few years. It looks modern, fresh and cared for, and there is a real studenty buzz about the place. It is very different in feel to a traditional school, particularly an all-through school, and some young people are more than ready for this at 16.

Pastoral care, well-being and discipline: This is a genuine half way house between school and university. All students have a tutor who stays with them for the two years and teaches them for one of their subjects. The tutor meets with each tutee for a 'settling-in' interview in the first term and uses this information to build a nuanced picture of each individual, understanding their lives outside of the college as well as their academic needs. Students are also allocated a director of studies, who is another port of call for any difficulties; students told us they rated their director highly.

Parents are still very much kept in the loop. They are invited in for an information session as soon as the student starts at the college, and there are parents' evenings with the student and tutors during the year. A comprehensive booklet for parents sets out all the organisational and administrative details they might need. Any vital information is posted, but parents are also encouraged to email tutors. On the other hand, the college expects to provide support directly to students. There is a well-being centre offering a range of confidential services. The college chaplain, college counsellor and independent well-being adviser are all based there, offering advice and help when needed on issues ranging from emotional and family problems to housing and legal rights. One parent, whose son had had health problems, couldn't praise the college highly enough for its flexibility and understanding, which ensured the boy could get back to college at the earliest possible opportunity.

Students say that one of the advantages of the college over a school is that everything is geared to a very small age group with very specific needs. That is true of the pastoral care and extends to the comprehensive careers department, which is held in very high esteem by students and parents. One parent commented on the patience of the careers' adviser whilst their daughter was agonising over which pathway to choose – a common dilemma for many at this age.

We asked about discipline issues, but no one felt there were any. 'Everyone wants to be here,' said a student, and the deputy principal felt that any disruptive influences were diluted compared with a school by the sheer scale of the place.

Pupils and parents: Herefordshire is a sparsely populated county and some 75 to 80 per cent of sixth formers in the county attend the college. They also come from surrounding counties and Wales. Those in small independent schools looking for a larger environment are attracted here. Herefordshire as a whole has a low average household income, and a high proportion of students used to be eligible for the now-abolished education maintenance allowance. But there are also parents well able to support the strong careers department by offering top quality work experience and interview practice. Two places for parents on high calibre governing body.

Entrance: Open access, though the college considers five Cs at GCSE sensible for those wanting to start on A levels.

Exit: Despite the fact that entry is open, there are significant numbers going on to top universities, including Oxbridge (10 places in 2016) – and reading a wide range of subjects. Cardiff, Birmingham, Swansea and London universities very popular, plus Bristol and UWE. Others to eg sound engineering apprenticeship at the BBC, intelligence analyst in the RAF, quantity surveying and mechanical engineering apprenticeships. A number of parents were lavish in their praise of the way the college prepared students both intellectually and socially for higher education.

Money matters: It is free! There are a few costs associated with certain areas such as foreign travel, but the college has set up a bursary fund for financial hardship. Parents are invited to pay £50 a year into this, which most are able to do. The county council subsidises daily travel for those living over three miles away.

Remarks: HSFC is as good as it gets in the state sector for sixth form education, and it gives independent schools a terrific run for their money. Families who live near enough are very lucky to have this seriously good option on their doorstep.

H

Howell's School, Llandaff

Cardiff Road, Llandaff, Cardiff CF5 2YD

Pupils: 1,075 • Ages: 3–18 • Sixth form: 185 (45 boys)

Fees: £7,829 – £13,317 pa

Tel: 029 2056 2019
Email: admissions@how.gdst.net
Website: www.howells-cardiff.gdst.net

Principal: Since 2007, Mrs Sally Davis BSc PGCE NPQH (50s). Born and schooled in Wales, she left to read geology at Bedford College and spent several years teaching in London; her last post was director of studies at Harris City Technology College, before a wish to return to Wales and the post of deputy head at Howells coincided in 1992, a point at which she was the second youngest member of staff. Totally steeped in state education as both pupil and teacher, she had never considered working in an independent school, 'but this place changes lives, and I wanted to be a part of that'. Nearly a quarter of a century later, she is still there and held in great affection and respect by everyone we spoke to. She cites cementing the community between the teaching/support staff and senior and junior schools as her greatest achievement in her tenure, but we would also highlight excellent results and the highest retention rates post GCSE of all GDST schools, possibly as a consequence of the exceedingly successful co-ed sixth form college.

Not all heads would have the nerve to dress as flamboyantly as 'Mrs D' – a diaphanous black fur-trimmed wrap and sparkly shoes added a touch of exuberance to a sleeveless black dress the day we met her, and she is known for her statement jewellery, some of which she makes herself. A neon sign in the sixth form café designates it 'Sally D's', but not at the expense of her authority in school, which is unquestioned: 'She's strict when she needs to be' said one young lady. Mrs Davis is married with two grown children; she is a keen traveller with a penchant for house-swapping, so she can be part of a community whether in Europe, Canada or the US.

Head of junior school: Since 2006, Mrs Judith Ashill BEd. Born in Cyprus, but definitely Welsh. She trained originally as a nurse, yet wanted very much to go to university, hence her degree from Swansea. In those days, Welsh was compulsory in Welsh state schools and Mrs Ashill did not speak it, so she spent 14 years at Redland High, before 'this job came up, and I could be this side of the bridge'. Her priority for the junior school, other than getting the academic best out of the girls, is its pastoral care, wrap-around in both senses of encompassing the whole child, and topping and tailing the school day. Hard-working teachers, a palette of opportunities and great expectations are the watchwords of Howell's Junior. Her young charges and their parents find Mrs Ashill 'kind, helpful, calm and open-minded'. She is married with two talented hockey-playing daughters, and likes to take one good holiday a year to distant climes.

Academic matters: Junior school teaching is based on the national curriculum and is topic-based and multi-sensory; all subjects are covered in this way. Science teaching obviously effective: Tesco had written to a year 6 science class asking for tips on growing cress. Welsh is compulsory from the start, French, German, Spanish and Mandarin also on offer as chargeable clubs. Girls evidently enjoy their learning: maths, art and swimming come top of the charts, but 'even spelling tests are fun,' and 'teachers explain in more and more detail to us if we find it tricky', said our interlocutors. Any girls with 'additional learning needs', as SEN is known here, receive Read Write Inc teaching where applicable; no stigma attached. The grounds are used as an outdoor classroom, as far as a city site permits; elements of the forest school programme are incorporated.

Latest A level results down slightly from previous years at 51 A*/A; at GCSE, 74 per cent A*/A grades, and definitely (and correctly) seen as the academic option in Cardiff. 'It is very academic, but then I'm really geeky,' remarked one student, disarmingly. Take-up is greatest for maths, biology and chemistry; stand-out subjects in terms of enjoyment and effective teaching are thought to be maths and physics, all giving ammunition to the apologists for girls-only education. Surprisingly small numbers choose English or modern languages at A level, including Welsh, despite having to do two languages in year 7; modern about equal to ancient, where it is heartening to see a smattering of Greek. All four of the sixth form interviewees we met were doing A level maths, and reported a 'healthy perspective' on Oxbridge and support for those applying for medicine. The teaching we saw struck us as taking the best of old and new: during a physics class, teaching was divided between interactive whiteboard and the good old-fashioned kind with pens – no dazzling with technical wizardry. An eye is kept on the world beyond school by academic competitions and challenges within GDST and beyond – Salters for science, maths Olympiads and so on; EPQ and MOOCs are encouraged at sixth form.

SEN is known here as ALN – additional learning needs – and includes the gifted and talented and those with emotional issues alongside generally accepted definitions of special needs. All are screened on entry in year 7, but liaison with the junior school SENCo is close, 'so we know what we're getting'. School provides much SEN expertise in-house, such as its dyslexia unit, run by Dyslexia Action Cymru; other measures include a modified timetable with fewer languages. 'The learning support room is seen as a place of safety – it's sometimes rather hard to get rid of people!' said one member of staff. Support is not restricted to those with identified needs, but, for ordinary mortals, is provided by the pastoral team.

Games, options, the arts: Hockey, netball and athletics are the main compulsory sports on offer in the two winter terms, tennis and rounders in the summer. Sixth form boys play rugby, football and hockey. Facilities include a swimming pool, tennis courts and a rather tired gym; at last has planning permission for an Astro and new pavilion, due for completion in 2017. School competes locally in the Cardiff and Vale Schools fixtures, within GDST and individuals on occasion for Wales; somewhat improbably, it enjoys considerable success at ski slalom. D of E numbers are highest in Wales; riding much more recent with a small but keen following.

Art is taught thematically exploring various media for the first three senior years; at GCSE and A level, it is coupled with design as a joint course. Art and photography can also be done as clubs. We cast covetous eyes on a marvellous swimsuit made of shells... Performing arts, whether song, dance, theatre or poetry, come together in the fine tradition of the school's annual Eisteddfod, hotly contested and enthusiastically embraced by all, but there is plenty else going on all year. Foundations for music laid early here, with the help of a specialist music room – quite right for daughters of the land of song, who have lifted their voices in St David's Hall Cardiff, Wales' premier concert hall. Musicians of all standards and talents will probably find an ensemble, and if not, are encouraged to start one. The senior four-part female auditioned choir has been as far as Beijing on tour. Theatre tends towards lighter tastes – Beauty and the Beast, The Sound of Music; willing staff with (or without) dramatic leanings are co-opted into the house pantomime competition; serious plays also staged, school assures us. Debating and public speaking also strong here, inside and outside school. Masses of clubs on offer, from the cerebral (philosophy) to the physical (tag rugby), by way of the environmental.

Background and atmosphere: Howell's particularly interesting back story is amply explored and illustrated in the best school history we had ever seen, the salient points being that its founding in 1860 was the eventual result of the legacy of a wealthy Tudor merchant, Thomas Howell (a member of the Drapers Livery Company, which still funds the school to some extent), one of whose clauses provided for the dowries of four orphan maidens, of his kin if they could be found; if not to 'four other maidens of good name'. After protracted difficulties in tracing descendant maidens and staving off claims from girls who were neither maidens nor orphans, an Act of 1852 was passed to set up two boarding schools in Wales for the 'education and advancement of deserving maiden orphans'. Job done: splendid new buildings (a mix of medieval, ecclesiastical, Tudor, gothic, Rhineland schloss and French château – truly) were erected in the (then 'primitive and unsanitary') village of Llandaff, now subsumed into Cardiff.

Housed in a couple of sunny brick houses (one once lived in by Roald Dahl) with an eye-catching curved extension on a corner of the main campus, the junior school has the advantage of its own site and super well-equipped playground, yet shares the senior school facilities just a walk away.

In 1980, Howell's joined the GDST, benefitting from its voice for girls' education, and opportunities for all manner of competitions while at school, and networking beyond – but it manages to keep its Welshness, a vital part of its identity. 2005 saw the admission of boys into the newly constituted college, the renamed sixth form; unlike a similar initiative at its sister school in Bath, this has been a huge success, and numbers of boys remain steady at about one third, and enough (crucially) to muster a rugby team. The girls appreciate doing male-dominated subjects like engineering, little pressure to wear make-up and 'the chance to get my weird phase out of the way' before chaps arrive in year 12. ('We do "odd" well', says Mrs Davis). The atmosphere is one of fun and great affection for the school from its pupils past and present, but certainly not at the expense of hard work and scholarly ambition. Much of this appears to be fuelled by cake: nowhere have we been offered so much so regularly, on top of a tasty lunch where choices were two kinds of pasta, baked potatoes, a salad bar and sandwiches in extremis.

H

Pastoral care, well-being and discipline: Parents greatly appreciate that 'the [junior] school works with all their pupils to ensure they find their own individual niche or specialism where they can succeed and be recognised for their achievements'; that it isn't just a proving ground for the rigours of the senior school. The academic standards are beyond reproach but 'it's also good at manners, music and making sure no-one is mean'.

Senior school pastoral side also highly praised by students and parents alike. One mother summed it up: 'The teachers really are interested and care for their pupils. The school responds swiftly to problems that may turn into something bigger – like bullying – and has a network in place to help any student who is overwhelmed or feeling nervous'. Another spoke movingly of the care the school had taken of her and her children during a particularly difficult time. 'I believe in the concept of mental wealth, which I extend to my staff,' says the principal. Students reckon the balance between reward and sanction is about right: they appreciate the freedom and latitude given them at sixth form and celebrations of all manner of school life, as well as the good cop/bad cop apparently played out between the principal and her deputy. The evils of city life do not appear to impinge greatly on Howell's: we heard no tales of drink, drugs or inappropriate goings-on

Pupils and parents: 'Courageous, creative, caring and willing to have a go,' according to the principal, from families with widely differing economic backgrounds, and whose belief in the importance of education means, in some cases, sending their children considerable distances to be there. Extensive bus routes from a 40 mile radius include Newport and Merthyr Tydfil.

Entrance: Main points of entry to junior school are at year 3 and year 5, but encouraged at other times by arrangement. Girls are assessed over the course of a day, using NFER and non-verbal reasoning; if the latter shows potential, they are likely to be accepted. Nursery and reception hopefuls are informally assessed.

Senior school entrants arrive from the junior school in year 7, but also from over 20 local primary schools, by means of exams held each January in maths (no calculators permitted) and English; rubrics can be in Welsh for native speakers, but written answers must be in English. Questions are on topics covered at school; girls should be working at Sats level 4, but school 'looks for evidence of level 5 work'. All hopefuls are interviewed and spend a day at school. For the college (sixth form), a minimum of six GCSEs are required, with at least a B in subjects taken for A level. Scholarships give typically a five per cent reduction in fees and are awarded for academic excellence (separate exam for sixth form but not at year 7), sport, music, art/DT, drama.

Exit: Juniors mostly to the senior school by means of its entrance tests; parents are told in year 5 if there is likely to be a problem. Limited tutoring goes on outside school; we heard of one small person being 'tutored for stress' but we suspect this is unusual and probably unrelated to school. 'We take well-being very seriously,' we were told – and we don't doubt it.

A handful leaves after GCSE, but vast majority to a range of university courses up and down the land; a bias towards Welsh universities (particularly Cardiff) and some across the bridge in south west England. Lots of medics (six in 2016), a smattering to Oxbridge (four in 2016), several to Birmingham and a few gap years. Careers and UCAS guidance comes in for particular praise. Close and fond links with previous pupils mean a strong Hywelian Guild. Alumni are represented across the professions, academia, arts and sports; the most famous are Ann Cotton, founder of Camfed, Hannah Mills, an Olympic sailor who won gold in 2016, and Charlotte Church, of whom no more need be said.

Money matters: Very good value for money, like all GDST schools. Option to pay fees monthly. Deserving cases for financial help in the form of bursaries are considered centrally by GDST; a couple supported by HSBC each year. Additional support for sixth form studies provided by Welsh government in the form of an allowance paid to lower income households, an initiative phased out some years ago in England....

Remarks: Howell's looks and feels like a good old-fashioned girls' grammar, but is so much more than that. Masses of fun, laughter and cake make the task of scholarly slog so much more palatable; everyone appears to come up with the goods without buckling under the pressure. 'Every inch of Howell's seems to exude care,' observed a parent. Expect Welshcakes and pink branded lip salve in your goody bag – and hulking lads in the sixth form. 'I'm disappointed we have had to wait this long to be able to get my son there,' said a happy parent of three Hywelians. Any sooner, though, and it would alter the unique character of this Cardiff institution.

Huish Episcopi Academy

Wincanton Road, Huish Episcopi, Langport, Somerset TA10 9SS

Pupils: 1,518 • Ages: 11–18 • Sixth form: 140

Tel: 01458 250501
Email: office@huishepiscopi.somerset.sch.uk
Website: www.huishepiscopi.net

Principal: Since 2013, Andrew Davis BSc PGCPSE NPQH (40s). His degree is in applied science and he is particularly interested in astrophysics, climatology and sedimentology. Was principal of Dawlish Community College for seven years (school became one of the highest performing schools in Devon during his tenure). Previous posts as deputy principal at Exmouth Community College, one of England's largest schools, assistant principal at Plymouth High School for Girls and head of science at Holyrood School in Somerset.

Main interests are in developing teaching and learning and curriculum design to raise standards of achievement and ensure that schools 'are designed around the students as an individual rather than the student fitting the system.' Married to a teacher and has three children. His outside interests are family, cycling and reading.

Academic matters: Clearly benefiting from its new academy status, with its newish sixth form the icing on the cake. Operates two distinct bands in years 7 to 11. Two top ability groups identified within each band for English and a number of other subjects. 'Tight' setting in maths and science. Impressive approach to foreign languages, with lots of effort made to broaden horizons. Global Gazette magazine is published annually and highlights new initiatives like Mandarin classes. Most pupils try a second language from year 8 and continue with one or two languages from year 9. Some take Latin as an extra.

Three vocational BTec National Diploma courses available. Sixth form students are encouraged to take up the Extended Project Qualification. GCSE results have improved consistently; in 2016, 71 per cent achieved five or more at grades A*-C including English and maths. A level results in 2016 saw around 40 per cent A*-B grades. Good results also at key stage 3 and school is in top 25 per cent nationally in value added tables. Lessons we saw in years 8 (German) and 11 (history) certainly held pupils' interest and used lively resources to full effect. Parents say teachers 'work incredibly hard' and pupils latch on to those who show 'passion for their subject.' Much effort has been put into training and recruiting staff to teach to A2 level. Head of sixth form came from similar role in Bristol and has made huge impact. We saw an English language class that involved students in careful analysis of material and perceptive discussion with their lively teacher.

Timetable works on basis of a 50-lesson fortnight with maths, English and science getting seven, six and five lessons respectively at key stage 3. Strong emphasis on ICT – laptops on trolleys available on demand and new sixth form IT hub bristles with iMacs. Science is well funded and generous laboratory provision allows pupils 10 lessons of science per fortnight at key stage 4. Strongest candidates take triple science. Study centre is a continuing multi-media success and at the heart of the school's learning. Pupils actively involved in book selection, reading for pleasure lesson in years 7 to 9 and a scheme for accelerated reading. Recent Readathon raised £1,500 for Roald Dahl Foundation (£300 given back in form of new books for library).

At GCSE, along with compulsory subjects, pupils choose four from 16 optional subjects. Class sizes vary according to subject and ability. Large labs accommodate up to 32 pupils in top sets, allowing lower ability groups of 16 to 19. Less flexibility in other core subjects. Links with Yeovil College enable some pupils at key stage 4 to follow vocational courses such as engineering and animal care. PSHE course where topics include dealing with stress and depression.

All year 7 children are screened for specific learning disabilities on entry. Close liaison provides plenty of information beforehand from feeder primary schools. Special educational needs co-ordinator works with whole staff to support pupils within normal timetable. Eighteen learning support assistants work alongside mainstream teachers (some work in specific subject areas). Special needs include Down's syndrome and cerebral palsy. Pupils with Asperger's syndrome get help with socialisation and use of free time in school.

Games, options, the arts: Longstanding reputation as a sporting school, especially in boys' football, rugby, girls' hockey and cross-country. Huge numbers involved on extracurricular basis. Pupils achieve individual representation at area level and school has produced national champions in athletics and high national placings in cross-country. Participation stretches to biathlon and inter-school swimming. Young leaders award for years 8 and 9 gets pupils to direct younger ones in sports activities. PE/sports studies is a popular GCSE/BTec option. School shares its purpose-built leisure centre with locals (a real bonus for this rural community). It includes fitness centre, dance studio and superb squash courts. There are also floodlit multi-use outside courts, a heated 25-metre open air pool, extensive playing fields, plus full size all-weather pitch for hockey or football. Sixth formers get free use (even out of school hours) of the leisure facilities (now managed by school).

Music has come on leaps and bounds in recent years – choirs, jazz band, orchestra and lots of instrumental tuition. New drama studio with raked seating – recent productions include I Hate Shakespeare and Moulin Rouge. Lower school hall doubles up as a drama studio for younger pupils.

Artwork is well displayed throughout school (fashion a particular interest). Innovative and enthusiastic department succeeds in getting students into specialist art and design courses. Wide range of extracurricular clubs and activities (some payable), including badminton, parcours and Taiko drumming. Loads going on at lunchtimes and after school. Busy schedule of fieldwork and trips overseas – recent expeditions include AS art, history and French students to Paris and year 10 to 13 linguists to Brussels (funded partly by the EU) to attend a session of the European Parliament.

Background and atmosphere: School motto is 'Conemur' – Let us strive – which head feels is as appropriate now as ever. Was in first group of 30 'high performing' schools to be offered academy status. This has resulted in extra funding and coincided nicely with the addition of a sixth form. 'Independent school education without the fees,' suggested one member of staff. Single-storey red-brick front to school dates from 1939, with seven subsequent additions behind. Eye-catching sixth form wing ('illuminated walkway looks particularly impressive from the main railway line at night,' said students) has transformed look and feel of the school since we last visited. East wing contains art suite, photographic studio and media hub. Conference suite provides flexibility for talks or use as a teaching area. Still feels like a small school from the front entrance, but on entering the sixth form there is a definite 21st century ambience. Twenty-one new classrooms and three new science labs have been added recently. For many years was a 'lovely secondary modern,' able to go comprehensive slowly and steadily. Certainly not nine-day wonder, it has built up a reputation locally as a school which 'gets the best out of children.' 'You very rarely hear shouting,' said one teacher whose experience elsewhere had obviously been very different.

Smooth transition arrangements for children moving up from primary schools – a concert by primary schools was in rehearsal on the day we visited. School opens up inside like a Tardis, but the original appeal of the place hasn't been lost. Main assembly hall (which doubles up as a canteen for years 9-11) has been refurbished but can only accommodate one year group at a time. Corridors are congested during lesson changeovers given recent increases in numbers but hour-long lessons limit pupil traffic and enhance work ethos.

Pastoral care, well-being and discipline: School believes in dealing with any issues quickly and emphasising positive behaviour. 'It's about removing barriers to learning and supporting pupils in their achievement,' explains assistant principal. Golden rules are set out for all. School council is active and helps allocate rewards. Year 7 head oversees transition from primaries and visits all feeder schools. One mother of a shy daughter praised the way 'staff even visited our home during the holiday before she joined to reassure her.' Ten tutor groups for about 260 year 7 entrants. Year 10 and 11 pupils act as form friends to years 7 and 8. Prefects are chosen from years 10 and 11 (sixth formers play no formal disciplinary function in the secondary school). Tutors follow pupils from year 7 to 11. No house system but inter-form events by year group range from year 7 benchball to whole school cross-country. Recovery room operated for any pupils withdrawn from lessons. Attendance is carefully monitored and there is a close watch on cyberbullying. Mobile phones aren't allowed for secondary pupils – 'but we don't go looking for them,' say staff. School has taken over former parish rooms to provide a discrete student guidance and learning centre (caters for up to 40 pupils) – under dynamic staff leadership and tackles head-on the educational, emotional and social needs of the disaffected few. Additional support for all pupils includes health clinic run by NHS nurse, careers adviser, part-time counsellor and family support worker.

Pupils and parents: A genuinely friendly place. Secondary pupils and sixth formers come from a 200 square mile catchment area. Increasingly oversubscribed. Copes well with all types. 'Local professionals don't need to fork out on costly alternatives,' one mother told us, while another said: 'We moved here from London having been tipped off about the school.' Sixth formers have worked hard to create a good social and student life. We were told that some who started at colleges soon had second thoughts and came running back to join the new sixth form. From 60 in its first year, more than 100 entrants a year now and look set to rise. Parental views are sought and involvement is maintained through regular newsletters. Turnout at parents' evenings is usually about 90 per cent. No formal parents' association but lots of support for events throughout year. Huish-i is being developed as a virtual learning environment and forum for communication with parents.

Standard school uniform, including a blazer. Most girls opt for trousers in the winter. Generally well presented, with some scruffiness at the edges. Sixth formers we saw were dressed sensibly and not on a fashion parade. School day finishes at 3.20pm, with armada of coaches to ferry pupils home. Pupils' contributions valued at all levels. 'Lead learners' are identified and 'learning without limits' programme has set up links with Sekondi-Takoradi School in Ghana. One year 8 boy is currently leading a successful Amnesty group, while others run an environmental action team. Prize-winning school garden, healthy eating programme and lots of eco initiatives. Chair of school council is member of UK youth parliament. Democratic to a T elections held under single transferable vote system. Pupils are even involved in interviewing new staff.

Interesting array of former pupils include fashion designer Alice Temperley and Bob the Builder creator Sarah Ball.

Entrance: Parents move to be within the catchment area (includes about 30 villages across mid-Somerset). Twenty per cent of pupils come from outside the catchment area – by straight line distance from the school.

Exit: Sixth form opened in 2010. So far some 50 per cent of pupils progress into sixth form and then to university. Others leave for colleges, apprenticeships or employment. One to Oxford in 2016; others to study eg maths at Warwick, international relations at Exeter and theatre and performance and Bristol.

Remarks: This trail blazing 11-18 academy in rural Somerset just goes on improving. Newish sixth form is the icing on the cake.

H

Inglefield House

Linked with The Grange, Monmouth Prep, Haberdashers' Monmouth School for Girls, Haberdashers' Agincourt, Monmouth School

70

Hereford Road, Monmouth NP25 5XT

Pupils: 144; 4 boarders • Ages: 7–11

Fees: Day £10,452; Boarding £18,999 pa

Tel: 01600 711100
Email: admissions@hmsg.co.uk
Website: www.habs-monmouth.org

Head: Since 2013, Mrs Hilary Phillips, mid 40s, who came from a London prep school where she had been director of pastoral care, head of French and PSHE and classics teacher. She has the professional appearance of a stylish London head who is used to the competitive south east prep school bear pit. She arrived to a caring and nurturing school, and she wanted to maintain these qualities but bring to it a bit more of the south east edginess. She has widened the scope, opened the school out more to the wider community and brought in what she describes as a 'healthy competitiveness'. She has sharpened up the academic side of the school, introducing rigorous monitoring, and is hot on differentiated activities in every class. She has also introduced the St Cuthbert Diploma, which is a sort of Inglefield baccalaureate. This is awarded by careful tracking of each girl's progress – not just academic, but extracurricular contributions and the development of social skills too. It is personal to each girl and reflects Mrs Phillips' genuine commitment to valuing the whole person.

Parents have welcomed her openness. She has got them contributing to the school by helping with and running clubs. 'Mrs Phillips has encouraged us to come to her with ideas and any concerns. She doesn't want us standing round the car park gossiping and moaning', a parent told us approvingly.

Entrance: Applicants come in for a Saturday morning. It is supposed to a fun time, and the school puts on sports activities, but they also do a maths assessment, a piece of writing and a non-verbal reasoning test. Almost all the girls from Agincourt (the mixed 3 to 7 Habs Monmouth school) come into Inglefield and the head tells us that there should be no surprises for those parents, who have been given a very good idea by this stage if they will make the grade for Inglefield.

Exit: Virtually all the girls go on to the senior school. The head says it is not an 'old fashioned' selection process to get there. Neither school is interested in girls who fit neatly into a traditional academic mould, although the senior school is obviously offering an academic curriculum. 'We want every girl who leaves us being able to say "I can do this well",' the head tells us.

Remarks: Inglefield was opened as a distinct school in 1990 – before that it was just a department of the senior school. Now there are two classes in each year with a maximum of 20 girls. There is a real variety of parental backgrounds – local farmers, those who have moved out of London for a more outdoor life with their family, those where one or both parents commute into London on a weekly basis.

The school uses standardised tests to benchmark the girls on arrival and identify each one's needs. Interim grades ensure early intervention throughout the year, and parents receive these along with two parents' evenings a year for each year group. We liked the head's obvious preference for face-to-face conversations rather than impersonal reports and emails. There is one-to-one learning support from a dedicated teacher if necessary, for which parents pay extra, but the head tells us that there is not a great deal of need. There is no setting, but girls sit with others at the same level as for maths and lesson plans include at least three levels of activity. The girls we spoke to loved maths and said the teachers wanted them to 'find our own ways of getting the answer'. Strong science is seen all around the school. It was good to find the girls well informed about geology, a science much needed but slightly undervalued in schools these days. PSHE, called 'confidence for life', is wide ranging and includes Apprentic-style activities where the girls give a presentation with a business plan for a new product.

The importance of the extracurricular life reflects the school's active aim of ensuring everyone discovers what they are good at and love. The head is keen that girls of this age find something physical that they enjoy to take with them through life. Sport is pleasingly inclusive. There are a lot of matches and the girls say that everyone gets a change to play. The head herself is a keen sportswoman. They use senior school sports facilities and theatre. The Eisteddfod is major annual fixture, watched by everyone, which includes academic as well as artistic competitions. There is poetry, music, dance and song-writing. The title of the competition poem this year was 'If the moon could talk'. The winner sits on grand chair and is crowned. Then everyone sings the Welsh national anthem – our guides sang it unselfconsciously and confidently to us – peace is declared and competitive rivalries forgotten.

We were interested in what the girls, who had mainly been taught with boys before coming to Inglefield, thought about their single sex experience. Apparently they still go on trips with the boy,s but were pleased they could play all the parts in the school plays and throw themselves into a recent re-enactment of the Battle of Bosworth – no boring learning about domestic life in the Middle Ages here.

The girls are very proud of their school council – there is none of the cynicism that you can get in senior school with criticisms of pseudo democracy. 'We bring our ideas to make Inglefield even better,' the girls assured us, and said that the gardening and sewing clubs came about because the need was raised through the council.

We got a real sense of community from talking to the girls. They look out for each other and know that the staff are doing just the same. When it comes to Charity Day and making their own stalls, the girls assure us that teachers are checking no one is left out. The dinner ladies keep an eye on what everyone is eating – not too many carbohydrates, one girl told us seriously. They are very proud of their school, not so much because of great success stories but more because of what adults would see as the balance and creativity of what is on offer. The art is all around, with some wonderful collages. There is evidence of lots of focused day and residential trips. There is a practical emphasis with projects like the geography scheme to make the playground more eco-friendly.

Parents confirmed the excellent liaison between Agincourt on one hand and the senior school on the other. The heads from each school regularly visit Inglefield, taking assemblies and talking to the girls. Senior girls help with junior clubs, coach music and academic subjects as well as taking the lead in the technical side of school productions, and run some linked assemblies. They also run the hugely important and popular annual Eisteddfod. Parents tell us that while each school has a very distinctive feel about it, progression really works, and you can see the girls flourish and develop at each stage.

King Edward's Junior & Pre-Prep (Bath)

Linked with King Edward's School (Bath)

North Road, Bath, Somerset BA2 6JA

Pupils: 182 (roughly two-thirds boys) • Ages: 3-11

Fees: £7,845 - £10,560 pa

Tel: 01225 463218
Email: admissions@kesbath.com
Website: www.kesbath.com

Head Teacher: Since 2008, Mr Greg Taylor, BA (education, Exeter), who joined King Edward's from the George Ward Secondary School in Allington with experience of 'special' education. He progressed from head of PE, then maths to deputy and eventually to head of junior school. He is also a serious sportsman, especially about football, which he played professionally from 14, and has four children.

Head of the pre-prep since 2008 is Ms Jayne Gilbert, whose teaching career before King Edward's was initially in the state sector before moving to a British International School in Penang, then returning to be deputy at Bedales pre-prep from which she was appointed to King Edward's.

Mr Taylor and Ms Gilbert share a refreshing accessibility. On our arrival, Mr Taylor was busy arranging tables in the sun so that the parents coming in later could enjoy an informal meeting with tea and cakes, while Ms Gilbert was about to join a group of parents for coffee and feedback in the pre-prep dining room.

Entrance: Though it is possible to start in the nursery and go all the way through to sixth form, there is also entry at pre-prep level and into the junior school at 7. Both take about half from other local schools. Good to get in early, as entry to senior school is competitive, but the vast majority pass the entrance exam, having flourished in the junior system

Exit: Most progress to the senior school, whether they join at 3, 4 or 7. There is an entry exam to pass, but anyone who is really unlikely to cope will have been forewarned and advised about alternatives. There is lots of competition in Bath, so a few move elsewhere locally or away to boarding school.

Remarks: The junior school nestles at the far end of the KES site surrounded by garden and wildflower meadows, giving masses of opportunity for ecological study. It is cunningly designed so that the class units, each with its storage, display and cloakroom area, feel rather like a little houses in their own right, built in a staggered line to get the best of the sun and view. The school remained in the original King Edward's building in Broad Street until 1991, when a benefactor sponsored the construction of the new buildings. Behind the little street of classrooms is a unifying hall and library space on two levels, essentially a gallery running round an attractive school library. A few extra wings house the school hall, music department, labs and dining area.

The feel is definitely more like a very good state primary school rather than a traditional prep school. Masses of artwork and displays everywhere – the school is constructed to encourage this, and the whole environment is both absolutely child friendly and encourages ecological awareness. Divided from the main school by a band of trees, the site, overlooking Bath's panorama, has a wildlife meadow, delightful wild pond and lots of wonderful stone blocks and trees for climbing. Adventure is encouraged, though carefully supervised. The latest project is the greenhouse, where children are growing their own veg – tomatoes from last year were still going when we visited – and doing wonderful experiments involving breeding and releasing butterflies into the wild. Specialist subject teachers, for languages (French from year 3, with German and Spanish from year 5), science (with a smashing, well-equipped lab), maths etc.

Parents comment that the key to education here is inclusion and encouragement rather than educational pushiness. 'Effort is rewarded as much as achievement and the school does not feel the need to get children to peak at junior level'. As in the senior school, the integration of pastoral care and academia is taken very seriously. New children are encouraged to support each other in a scheme which allocates different 'talk partners' each week. 'Working with everyone in turn, not just friends, creates cohesion,' one parent commented. 'They really value citizenship and social awareness. Friendships extend across year groups and classes and pupils won't stand for bullying or turn a blind eye to it'. SEN is integrated with the senior school department. Tests at appropriate levels and plenty of help available.

Sport is competitive but, according to parents, very inclusive – everyone encouraged to participate. Boys do a short rugby tour and girls a hockey tour, playing matches all over the country. The same applies to music, with lots of singing, a yearly young musicians' challenge and an inclusive scheme in which a different instrument is taught to all pupils in each year group. We enjoyed the first session of the ukelele band, but other years do gamelan etc and in year 6 steel drums, which are said to be 'just incredible!' The art programme is enhanced by taking part in a National Gallery competition, which has culminated in pupils' sculpture and painting being on show there several years running. Drama, dance etc all included, with an impressive filmmaking project on the year 6 French trip.

Pre-school breakfast club from 8am in the new Wessex Building is open to juniors as well as seniors and there are after-school activities and supervision until 6pm in the junior school.

The pre-prep is separate from the senior and junior schools in a 'leafy suburb' on the other side of Bath, but there is a staffed minibus between them which means parents with children in both can make one drop-off and know children will be supervised from there on. It provides an ideal environment for little children, with cleverly planned outside areas equipped with every kind of equipment and divided into age-related areas. On our visit there was a lovely activity, involving walking around the shapes of letters, going on in one place, while the real tinies were enjoying their miniature tricycles – good for directional skills.

All year groups have weekly forest school visits. More conventional classes are in large double areas with two classes in each year group, semi-divided so they can work separately or together. SEN experts are brought in at an early stage to do specific tests where necessary, so emerging problems can picked up and special help given if expected progress is not being made. Lots of music and PE both indoor and out. Art specialist works in all three schools.

Sensible simple navy blue uniform with white shirts, but masses of tough-looking coveralls for outdoor stuff and also for art and craft. Spacious dining room where staff like to eat with children and healthy eating is promoted. Parent contact seems to be high priority and a parent group was enjoying coffee and discussion with Ms Gilbert on the day of our visit.

Before and after-school care provided in Teddy's Lodge, a small house on the edge of what once must have been the front lawn to the main Edwardian House, but is now convenient car park. This is a cosy space that has become something of a community centre for the area, offering parentcraft and similar workshops, such as craft, music and dance for babies and toddlers during the daytime. A calm and gentle environment with children everywhere just happily getting on with things.

KES feels like a happy school. Pupils are friendly but not over-sophisticated. Parents feel included, have well-organised channels for feedback and suggestions, and say there are 'no serious gripes'. The synchronisation of information through careful co-operation between teaching and pastoral staff and the heads in the senior, junior and pre-prep sectors is truly impressive, and everything is directed towards the well-being of pupils. No wonder they enjoy their education and do so well in it.

King Edward's School (Bath)

Linked with King Edward's Junior & Pre-Prep (Bath)

72

North Road, Bath, Somerset BA2 6HU

Pupils: 769 • Ages: 11–18 • Sixth form: 229

Fees: £13,365 – £13,575 pa

Tel: 01225 464313
Email: admissions@kesbath.com
Website: www.kesbath.com

Headmaster: Since 2008, Mr Martin Boden MA (mid 40s), a French and German graduate of Jesus College Cambridge. After his PGCE he was invited back to teach at his old school, Bolton School, progressing from there to head of German at Cheadle Hulme School, then head of modern languages at Bradford Grammar, from which he came to King Edward's as director of studies. Appointed as an exceptionally young head, he has brought the school a stability and capacity for development with his clear vision and strong sense of ethos, which have have been the key to both pastoral care and hence academic success. In his time the academic standard has become even stronger, due, according to Mr Boden and to the ISI inspectorate, to unrivalled outstanding pastoral care underpinning really good teaching. Parents definitely agree. Meanwhile, the sporting reputation of the school remains undiminished, whilst art drama and music have flourished under his regime.

Dedicated to the grammar school tradition of accessibility, he has both kept the fees unusually low 'by lots of good housekeeping' and encouraged entry from bright pupils from less advantaged families through bursary provision. He is insistent that though the school is selective, it is not super-selective, despite the fact that its results put it in the super-selective league. As director of studies, he masterminded the now well-established two-week timetable with hour long lessons, giving an 80 minute lunch break for an overwhelming number of activities and staggered access to the fantastic new dining facilities. Next on his wish list is a proper performing arts centre. He cites concert and cinema going as the only recreational activity he still manages to fit into a life as headmaster and father of two small children currently entrusted to the nursery and pre-prep at King Edward's. Married to head of geography, Jane.

Academic matters: This is a seriously academic school. In 2016, 63 per cent A*/A and 88 per cent A*/B grades at A level, with astronomical results in maths, further maths and English literature. All three sciences, Latin and photography are pretty distinguished as well – so they certainly excel in humanities as well as science.

At GCSE in 2016, the A*/A per cent was down to 72 per cent (from 2014's 82 per cent). Normally some stunning results in individual subjects including maths, sciences, both Englishes and languages with Greek and Latin surpassing the excellent French, German and Spanish. One parent commented that Mandarin had been considered but had not materialised.

As well as the strong, sympathetic pastoral back-up to stimulating teaching, there is an all-embracing and friendly SEN department picking up quickly on children needing support or help. A three-strong team covers the senior and junior schools with a part-timer in the pre-prep. Lots of monitoring done via standardized tests, at crucial stages and when problems crop up so potential issues are picked up early. Appropriate supportive help, either one-to-one or in small groups. They are expert in most common areas of difficulty and have good liaison with staff and exam officers as well as providing encouragement and sympathetic back-up.

Parents comment that lessons seem to be really enjoyable and pupils are not overburdened with homework. Plenty of tests in class, but they take them in their stride. The prevailing atmosphere is that while academic study is interesting, serious and needs effort, it is also exciting and even fun.

Games, options, the arts: Sport as strong as ever. Oodles of teams, particularly in rugby, netball and girls' and boys' hockey, in fact, in just about everything except lacrosse. Sport is taken seriously with teams doing a pre-season sports training sessions before the autumn term to get off to a good start and a sports physio set up in the school medical centre, but the team practices in progress on our visit still looked a lot of fun. It seems to work, as teams in just about all sports reach national school final level, and there are individuals at national and international competition level.

Rugby and netball, which are outstanding, do a regular overseas tour, most recently to South Africa. Smashing sports hall with teaching area, cricket nets, all weather ECB-accredited cricket lanes and the usual indecipherable tube map of sports markings on the floor. Extensive playing fields at Bathampton, a very short minibus-ride away, and cricket practices get the benefit of Bath Cricket Club. (Everyone has a two-hour weekly games slot, so plenty of time for travel etc.) Huge new all-purpose Astroturf with viewing area and lots of tennis and netball courts on site. Using the University of Bath Olympic training swimming pool and athletics track seem a better option than building their own.

Arts and music excellent and getting stronger. Drama has smashing GCSE results and thriving theatre groups, one of which took Jackie Kay's 'Takeaway' to Edinburgh, and were thrilled that the writer came to see it. Orchestra has a new link up with the Bath Philharmonia, doing joint concerts and workshops, and choirs have similar musical links with the abbey, since the original school was just up the road from it. The music we heard was of a high standard with bags of enthusiasm from pupils and from staff in other disciplines. The calendar shows a swathe of workshops, masterclasses and concerts. Contemporary music is encouraged by the school's resident composer and there's plenty of scope for enjoying film scores and more popular stuff. Sadly, take up of academic music at exam levels is very small, but drama and art are much bigger and super-successful. Drama currently has use of a large well-

K

equipped theatre in mid school and a smaller studio in the sixth form area. Music has lots of soundproof teaching and practice rooms, some curiously lined with what looks like sea blue formica, but which is actually proper efficient soundproofing. There is plenty of space, but the proper performing arts centre on the school's wish list would clearly be a bonus.

Art and masses of heavy duty DT equipment occupy a separate building. Art is up above with a Swiss-looking balcony giving panoramic views of Bath's sweeping terraces. A Level classes we visited were just getting down to some really thorough but fascinating drawing technique. DT looks very suitably industrial and up to date.

On the day of our visit the Socrates Club was absolutely packed with 50 or more pupils and staff eagerly debating the problems of migrants in Europe with real concern and some discernment. The knitting club, however, had no takers, though it had done well the previous year. The range of options is impressive, including the academic, such as the Battle of the Books club, as well as music, drama and masses of sports. CCF, D of E. Outdoor pursuits such as Ten Tors can be taken for granted, and there are both curricular and extracurricular opportunities for trips local and further afield, including prestigious ones like the South Africa tour.

Background and atmosphere: This was one of boy King Edward VI's many original grammar schools, as the lovely little roundel coloured glass window in the junior school proclaims. It was originally in a small neo-classical building in Broad Street just up from the abbey, and moved up to this rural-feeling site in the 1960s. The elegant Nethersole House on which the school is centred still gives rather old-fashioned room to RE, philosophy, history and classics, plus SEN and the headmaster's office with accompanying meeting and admin space. Flowing along the hillside, the hotch-potch of undistinguished purpose-built facilities benefit from the sweeping grassy slopes and mature trees. B Block, a new stylish and high tech building, has labs (separate ones for practicals and ordinary teaching) and other subject areas.

The site has been transformed into an organic whole by the brilliant addition of the new Wessex building, opened by the Earl of Wessex in summer 2015. The attractive dining suite with café-style verandas overlooking the central all weather pitch links the sporting and academic areas. Pupils seemed to be enjoying the food, with a choice of hot meals, salads or sandwiches. The dining room overlooks a sunny (on our visit) terrace with fountains, and milling-about and sitting areas including a miniature Greek theatre. The top floor has flexible lecture cum co-curricular and entertainment facilities, while the basement, cunningly dug out of the hillside, houses one of the very best school libraries.

Manned as long as the school is open, it offers cleverly placed reading, discussion and research areas, even a corner with whiteboard walls for teaching/conferencing. It was hearteningly full of older pupils busy working, reading or having serious-looking discussions – though this may have been partly due to the sixth form being temporarily out of its quarters while last minute refurbishments there were being completed, due for occupation the next day. Even so, it seemed a good demonstration of genuinely independent work, with help at hand when necessary. The stray new boy, clearly confused about where he should be, was sympathetically directed to the right class.

The refurbished sixth form centre was near enough completion to be inspected and has spacious study and IT areas as well as a modern spruced up social area complete with coffee shop. The school day runs from 8.40am registration until 4.00pm, but there is a breakfast club from 8.00am and the library is open for study etc until 6.00pm. Definitely a day school feel, with main activities at lunchtime, though there are masses of clubs and team practices after school and matches on Saturday, with major performances and rehearsals in the evening.

Neat uniform with navy blazers, grey trousers/skirts (or Lindsey Tartan for younger girls) and a particularly smart V-necked jumper with the KES Tudor Rose on it. Girls, in particular, like to wear the stylish games uniform (navy with dark red and white) in the afternoons if they can get away with it (only worn for sport not for classes, say the staff). Sixth form boys in smart suits (like young estate agents), though the girls' interpretation of suit-equivalent clothes seems rather more casual, and parents would support tightening up here. The complete uniform list is formidable, but there is a good secondhand shop, now with a plentiful supply of games items (rather expensive new) after a short hiatus when suppliers changed.

Pastoral care, well-being and discipline: The school rightly prides itself on its pastoral care. Bonding trips and activities for new groups in year 7 start a process of building a cohesive and supportive community in which pupils feel confident enough to take any concerns for themselves or others to staff. Exceptionally good collaboration between academic and pastoral staff ensures that needs are identified and supported. In lower school this is delivered via heads of years who coordinate with the form teachers, who 'lay eyes on' pupils twice daily at morning and afternoon registration. Both get to know them really well as they stay with them as they move up through the years. In sixth form tutors supervise groups of about 15 pupils. Pupils were enthusiastic about the trust, sympathy and expertise of their teachers.

Part-time school chaplain doesn't push religion but is exceptionally supportive to church-going families and runs a prayer group. The school recognises the mix of faiths among pupils, describing itself as non-denominational. Parents comment that though some may have a healthy disrespect for formal religion, they still sing very enthusiastically in the abbey. Throughout the lunch hour we came across teachers chatting or in serious conference with pupils. Special care taken with university preparation, including a special Oxbridge and medicine applications help forum.

Though the head had to take a tough line when he started, the atmosphere now seems to be a happy combination of academic and personal rigour underpinned by care and respect. Pastoral care was particularly commended by the ISI and the head's belief that care for pupils is absolutely key to academic achievement is central to the exceptionally close working relationship between head pastoral and academic staff – no slipping through the net here.

Sixth formers are expected to be rôle models and mentors to the lower school: in the lower sixth they can try out being deputy prefect for three weeks before standing for election. Forty per cent of upper sixth then become prefects, with 10 or so senior prefects, from whom a head girl and boy are appointed. There is also a mentoring system targeting less confident pupils, including those in the junior and pre-prep, which both mentored and mentors value highly.

Pupils and parents: Pupils seemed relaxed and pretty well organised. Some more open than others, but all appeared to have a sense of purpose and were polite and natural. The head likes to remind them that having all those opportunities does not make them better people. Parents, from all walks of life, include the very well-heeled but also lots who have to work hard to afford what one described as 'unbelievably good value'. Academically ambitious for their children 'but not at the expense of all the extras,' they support the school in all it does, by active fundraising for extras. In common with most co-ed schools, about 60 per cent boys.

Famous Old Edwardians range from Thomas de Quincy, The English Opium Eater to comedian and TV presenter Bill Bailey, with more recent additions of actor Tom Payne, author Lawrence Norfolk and quite a panoply of distinguished academics and military men.

Entrance: At 11, by passing an entrance exam in maths, English and verbal reasoning. Some 100 or so places up for grabs. Half come from junior school and take the same exam, though parents can be confident that the school would have been in discussion with them if a child were unlikely to pass it. Head says that the few children who 'would not cope' are gently steered elsewhere, and though thorough, the entry test is not unreasonably stringent. Since the whole ethos of the school is that pupils – whether super-confident or more fragile – 'absolutely flourish', it is clearly sensible that children unsuited to flourish in this supportive atmosphere are directed to an appropriate environment. Most of the other half come from local-ish primaries.

Some 25-30 external sixth form places offered, on strength of good GCSE passes (A*/A desirable for A level subjects), interview and references from previous school. Sixth form entry tends to attract girls from local single sex schools.

Exit: Lose a fifth after GCSEs, odd one at end of year 12. Of those who stay, 90 per cent in 2016 to first choice uni (Russell Group for eight out of 10) with about 10 annually to Oxbridge (14 in 2016) and lots to well-established mainstream courses, including one medic in 2016, as well as a sprinkling of drama and art. School is exceptionally helpful to those few with unexpected results, helping to ensure they have a suitable offer by the end of results day.

K

Money matters: Exceptionally good value, according to parents. Lots of trips, most pretty inexpensive, but no pressure to take part in the more expensive ones and lots of pupils fundraise for these themselves. Approximately 15 per cent of pupils receive means-tested bursaries, total fees in exceptional cases; the head very keen to encourage able but less affluent candidates to apply.

Remarks: This is a school which achieves its exceptionally high standards by support and inspiration. 'Teachers are exceptional', one parent said, 'a real inspiration to our children'. The atmosphere is relaxed and constructive, which is probably why the results are so impressive. Parents say teachers have the knack of identifying an area where a pupil can shine and the confidence gained infuses everything else. Pupils accept that, in the few subjects they may not enjoy, effort is worthwhile. High standards are expected and achieved, but the achievement is grounded in confidence, trust and support rather than academic pressure. Though highly academic, certainly not an 'academic hothouse', but a school where even the process of getting into Oxford can be happy and relaxed. The synchronisation of information through careful co-operation between teaching and pastoral staff with the heads in the senior, junior and pre-prep sectors is truly impressive. Everything is directed towards the well-being of pupils. No wonder they enjoy their education and do so well in it.

King's Bruton

Linked with Hazlegrove School

Plox, Bruton, Somerset BA10 0ED

Pupils: 349; 229 full boarders • Ages: 13–18 • Sixth form: 123

Fees: Boarding £30,687; Day £21,330 pa

Tel: 01749 814200
Email: office@kingsbruton.com
Website: www.kingsbruton.com

Headmaster: Since 2009, Mr Ian Wilmshurst MA PGCE (early 50s). A Scotsman by birth and, in his own words, born into and schooled in the Edinburgh educational mafia (his father taught at the Edinburgh Academy, even now his sister is deputy head at Fettes), the last thing he was going to do was teach. But wind the clock forward a few years, after reading geography at Cambridge and the briefest of flirtations with the army, he returned to his old college for his PGCE, after two terms' trying teaching out at the Dragon School. The roll call of schools where Mr Wilmshurst has taught since then is impressive: Highgate, Merchiston Castle and Royal Hospital where, as the sole deputy head, he had terrific exposure to the top job.

On arrival at King's Bruton, he had cause to call on that invaluable experience: at several years' safe distance, he candidly admits that he had plenty of work to do on appointment. Seven years on, he has increased numbers (it's now full for girls) so setting it on a secure financial footing, without sacrificing the welcoming and cosy feel of the place, revitalised the sport and brought the alumni on board. A very different place indeed – and one whose merits he was determined to show us, after spending some time rubbishing what he considered our previous lukewarm and out of date write-up.

Though initial impressions are of unremitting seriousness and focus (no lazy national stereotyping here), we uncovered a compassionate and reflective side, not afraid to discuss the seamier side of education. Not only easy to chat to on the touchline, according to parents, but also 'approachable and kind,' according to one mother whose family had been through a very rough patch. 'Not pretentious – what you see is what you get,' opined another. By his own admission, Mr Wilmshurst is not at all musical (though he certainly appreciates it): his hobbies revolve round sport – a sometime rugby player and cricketer, he now enjoys golf and cycling in particular. Married to Helen, who is a tutor here, he has two daughters, both in the school.

Academic matters: Not very selective, King's prides itself on accommodating all academic abilities: 'One of my priorities is to keep the balance between SEN and Oxbridge,' says the head. No room for slackers, though: everyone is expected to achieve all they are capable of and the whole sixth form does the EPQ. 'We reckon our top 30 per cent is comparable to academically selective schools,' he told us. All assessed for SEN on arrival, then setted in maths and, interestingly, French; classes are then compiled on ability.

Twenty-four subjects on offer at (I)GCSE with particularly strong languages, in scope and in grades, though this may well reflect the numbers of overseas students wanting an almost effortless GCSE. Not applicable to Latin, however, with 60 per cent A*/A grades in 2016. Biology and music also well above the average percentage for A*/A grades (100 per cent for music in 2016), which varies overall between 35-44 per cent (39 per cent in 2016).

At A level, the percentage of A*/B grades reached a four year high in 2016 at 66 per cent, with 31 per cent A*/A grades and nothing below a B in rarer subjects (art, music, some languages) and maths, further maths and history consistently good performers. Small numbers can make results fluctuate considerably, and mean that classes are all mixed ability except for maths. Sixth form timetable allows for the odd maths and English GCSE retake, and it is extremely rare that anyone would be thrown out for poor grades either then or at AS – not unknown, sadly, in other schools. BTec – 'after A levels reverted to a linear format, we felt we wanted alternatives for our less academic students,' the head told us – also offered in health and social studies, sport and hospitality. In 2016, distinctions, starred and otherwise, were scooped in all subjects. We were lucky enough to sample the (delicious) edible submissions at tea time the day we visited, complete with immaculate napery and serving staff. Initiative generally reckoned to be a success, providing access to good universities: Exeter, Bath, Portsmouth inter alia.

SEN was described to us (in a wonderfully mixed metaphor) as the engine room where difficulties are unravelled. The staff of three, plus other prominent teaching staff with SEN qualifications, address a range of special needs: mainly dyslexia and dyspraxia, but also processing difficulties. Speech therapist and ed psych visit routinely. Two dedicated EAL staff to support the 40 students for whom English is not their mother tongue.

Games, options, the arts: 'Everything we touch turns to gold,' we were told, with not a little chutzpah – but it is true that the hockey in particular (girls' and boys') scales heights which would be remarkable for a much bigger school, such as reaching national finals eight times in the last four years and the U16 girls third in the national schools final. But, joyously, everyone gets a game and to represent the school, and are coached from the start by the hockey pro and director of sport to identify any burgeoning talent – 'but we manage expectations in the minds of pupils and parents', we were sagely assured. Rugby, netball and athletics also prominent and successful. No pool, but school makes use of the 25m pool at Hazlegrove; two élite swimmers currently train in Yeovil. Spor tphobes accommodated with a range of recreational options, including volleyball and frisbee. Facilities fine (eg floodlit Astro) but not extensive, owing to the limitations of the school site; plans are afoot to develop underused parts of it.

Music, likewise, is of a scope and standard befitting a much bigger school, and the complementary talents of voice and instrumental heads of music mean a fruitful cross-fertilisation of choral, jazz and orchestral music. From the military band, whose stirring strains and precise marching we were witness to on the most impeccably diagonally striped lawn we had ever seen, to the intense practice of a self-directed trio of violin, cello and piano, there truly is something ancient or modern for everyone. Music tech offered at A level: a handful of students have gone on to study the highly specialised Tonmeister degree course at Surrey. Fifty concerts a year give even beginners a chance to conquer performance nerves. Music scholars receive Kodaly and Alexander technique lessons. The new music school to be built to mark King's 500th anniversary will provide a more fitting home for it all.

Drama well provided for in Fitzjames theatre, where everyone – not just those studying GCSE or A level theatre studies – is encouraged to get involved, whether treading the boards or backstage in lighting, sound or set design. Two house plays per year on rotation, alongside whole school, sixth form and junior productions, in close collaboration with the music dept. Recent shows include Twelfth Night and Oliver! (yawn) but we were impressed that current theatre manager also writes new material. Annual trip to London takes in workshops as well as several shows.

'Not everyone is going to be a painter,' says the head of art, whose department – housed in a stunning former mill, complete with new gallery opened in 2016 – offers an exceptional range of media (3D design, sculpture and digital media, for example) to students who might go on to take a GCSE in art, craft and design. New students experience the whole enchilada, and enjoy the annual team video competition. Unusually, history of art is laid on as an A level – with outstanding results. Of course it does no harm at all to have the internationally renowned Hauser and Wirth gallery just down the road, with its education director keen to be involved. Former students have made waves in innovative artistic careers all over the world, to include a commission to beam multicoloured images onto the Sydney Opera House.

Trips (historians to Poland, linguists and musicians all over Europe, adventurers to Costa Rica) and all manner of physical and artistic exploration abound, with strong showings at CCF, DofE (where expeditions can now be done on bicycles!) and that perennial west country ordeal, Ten Tors.

Boarding: Two-thirds of students (13 per cent from overseas) board in seven single sex houses where day students are fully integrated. The school's long history – all 500 years of it – means no homogeneity in houses: Old House is where it all began, whereas the girls of Wellesley House occupy an elegant Georgian mansion of cream stucco several minutes' walk from the main school. Dorms of up to four to start with; most have single rooms at sixth form. Parents rate the care given to their children, both pastorally and health-wise, and appreciate the option of flexi-boarding. 'There's a good critical mass staying in at weekends and my children like Saturday nights and the chance to chill on a Sunday at school,' one mother reported, in tones of faint regret. More space in the girls' houses would be welcome, but school tells us that places for girls have all been filled. One local pub will deliver late night cheesy chips to boarding houses on request.

Background and atmosphere: Very ancient (sits on the site of a Benedictine monastery dissolved in 1537; one wall survives), but doesn't shout about it; much will be made of the 500th anniversary in 2019, however. One of several distinguished schools in Bruton, where three generous benefactors born in this small Somerset town built of golden stone decided to found the first of them. Varying fortunes meant it was down to just one boy in 1812, but the first half of the 20th century saw it increase in numbers approximating the ones it has today, and take over buildings the other side of the busy road to Castle Cary and elsewhere in Bruton. Charming and quaint but not posh, the school works with its venerable buildings, not against them, using the parish church for whole school services, but its own simple beautiful memorial hall for assemblies.

Parents and students love its size, praising the friendliness and the fact that no-one appears to slip, drift or hide. 'Everyone is valued,' one mother told us; 'even if they aren't especially good at anything, they can just jog along'; another liked the fact that fewer students meant that her children would have to get involved in everything. The school cites its strong Christian ethos and celebrates major festivals and rites such as confirmation, but we did not get the sense that religious belief is imposed upon the unconvinced or the agnostic (respect is non-negotiable, that said): the exuberant chaplain is so down with the kids that his weekly and legendary TGI (Friday) sessions attract many comers and make the deeper exploration of faith voluntary and fun. 'It's not your belief in science that holds you together when tragedy strikes', as he puts it. A handful of Catholics and Muslims fit in comfortably and lend diversity.

Pastoral care, well-being and discipline: No adverse remarks about pastoral care whatsoever, and the tutor system, with its overview of the whole child, came in for high praise from parents; likewise health care and communications with houseparents, meaning that many problems are nipped in the bud. Though King's students might seem a biddable lot, transgressions are treated seriously – and publicly: drinkers can expect to wear uniform at the weekend, for example. We liked the sound of the relationship policy, which cleverly omits any assumption of gender in these more enlightened times.

Pupils and parents: 'Not arrogant, good company and unassuming,' says the head – and we could not disagree. Most day pupils arrive from immediate vicinity; boarders from southern England, Europe, SE Asia and Kenya. All integrate so well that day pupils often come or stay in at weekends to join in with whatever is going on; we picked up some discontent from day parents at the long days and six day week which is more suited to boarders than their daily counterparts. More likely that one would find a child of a (successful) cheese farmer here than of a merchant banker, though the head claims to attract the same day pupil market as Millfield.

Entrance: At 13+ by means of common entrance from suitable prep schools (an average of 50 per cent is expected), though common entrance is neither common nor an entrance exam, in the head's view. Scholarships are awarded on the basis of papers in six subjects, plus a cognitive ability test. Children not prepped for CE can enter the school by means of reports from previous school and interviews, which seems much more like Easy St. About 40 per cent come from Hazlegrove, the rather smarter prep school linked to King's; others from anything up to 15 other prep schools and secondaries. At sixth form, the bar is lowish at five GCSEs with a B at subjects to be taken at A level, plus interview and references. Places in other year groups occasionally come up. The welcome extended to all new pupils was praised.

K

Exit: A handful go elsewhere after GCSE on economic grounds. Of those who stay for sixth form, only about three-quarters get to their first choice university. One to Cambridge in 2016 (with a choral scholarship), one medic and each year one or two to American universities. Some criticism was voiced about support for UCAS preparation, specifically that the school cut up rough on occasion about Saturday commitments clashing with university open days. Famous alumni include some heroes (Hugh Sexey, auditor to Elizabeth I, RS Blackmore, author of Lorna Doone), one villain (William Dampier, 17th century buccaneer) and one comedian (Marcus Brigstocke). The affection between the school and its former pupils is mutual: a higher than normal proportion of OBs come back to work at there – in proper jobs, after the school got rid of gappies. Since 2006, 150 leavers have been to work in their gap years at the Indian orphanage where the school has established strong links.

Money matters: Not a wealthy school in terms of its own assets or the families who come there, but restored to sound financial foundations under current head. Scholarships available to a maximum value of 20 per cent of fees; bursarial help available on application.

Remarks: A down to earth, unpretentious, happy school for virtually all comers in increasingly trendy Bruton (one might run into Mariella Frostrup or other celebs down from London) 'where no-one is ever made to feel second class,' according to one mother, but achieving remarkable success in the sporting arena. 'You get all the big names – then there's li'l ole us!' marvelled a proud hockey player.

King's Hall School

Linked with King's College (Taunton)

Kingston Road, Taunton, Somerset TA2 8AA

Pupils: 314; 40 full, weekly/flexi boarders • Ages: 2-13 • C of E

Fees: Day £7,335 – £15,675; Boarding £17,430- £22,665pa

Tel: 01823 285920
Email: admissions@kingshalltaunton.co.uk
Website: www.kingshalltaunton.co.uk

Headmaster: Since 2009, Mr Justin Chippendale BSc (late 40s). His education and subsequent career have caused him to shuttle between Oxford and Taunton, starting at the Dragon, thence to King's Taunton, back to Oxford Brookes for a degree in biology, exercise and health, a stint as housemaster at the Dragon, a detour to Chafyn Grove as deputy head, then back to Taunton. Affectionately and inevitably known as Mr Chips, he works hard to put the child's experience (of personal development, academic stimulus, physical challenge, artistic exploration and so on) as top priority at King's Hall, closely followed by the quality of relationships: between staff and pupils/parents/each other. 'I work on the invisibles and immeasurables', says he. But that's not to endanger academic expectations: 'It has to be cool to work, and ok to talk about work here,' he adds, and makes it his business to ensure that his charges (and their parents) make well-informed suitable choices for their next schools, even when the majority go on to King's Taunton.

Mr Chips is a keen sportsman and retains the physique of a rugby player, still occasionally coaching. Married with three children at the school, he enjoys entertaining parents 'in order to understand each family's own context' (though a few grumble about not being on the head's dinner list), and he is generally well-liked by both pupils and parents. 'He knows everyone, takes a real interest in us, and we love the Chips Challenge,' opined pupils, who might be asked to research an arcane matter, solve a puzzle or achieve a physical feat.

Entrance: Many join the pre-prep (school also comprises a nursery from 2), but some come from local primary schools and London at 7+. From years 1-4, new children are informally assessed during a welcome day; from years 5-8 they are tested in maths, English and verbal reasoning for which special preparation is not required, says school. Quite an intake also welcomed into year 7 for the final two years before moving on at 13+.

Exit: The majority to King's College at 13+, but a good sprinkling to the Sherborne schools; also the likes of Eton, Harrow, Winchester, Downe House, Cheltenham Ladies' College and Marlborough, some with scholarships. Every child gets into the school of his/her first choice, apparently; 'We didn't get the hard sell for King's', said one mother with a sigh of relief. Famous ex-pupils include actress Juno Temple, founder of Everyday Sexism project Laura Bates, and mad adventurers Ross and Hugo Turner.

Remarks: Sited in the mellow golden former home of the Yea baronetcy Pyrland Hall, dating from 1760, and surrounded by 50 acres of parkland and woods, this is an idyllic setting just minutes from Taunton. But it's not precious – pupils here make the most of the space, freedom and mud to pursue a terrific range of activities and outdoor pursuits beyond the school day which finishes at 4.30pm, mountain biking and archery being just two. Some 15 acres of pitches, an Astro and a sports hall mean all major sports are well catered for and fulfil all expectations, but an indoor pool is undoubtedly on the parental wish list; as it is, swimming is an extracurricular activity until the school's outdoor pool is opened in the summer term. But it all amounts to a slice of gracious enough living for the young.

King's Hall is reckoned to be Taunton's smartest and most academic prep school, partly because it's the only place which prepares children for common entrance (and scholarships) at 13+, still the measure and starting point for the most prestigious public schools. From year 3, children are taught in classes of about 15 by specialist teachers. All begin French in year 1 but there's the opportunity to pick up Spanish from year 5 or Latin from year 6. Science and geography get thumbs up from pupils, but 'We don't go to any lessons and think 'Oh no!', said one. Prep amounts to two half hour subjects per night for the oldest: 'It's ok to make mistakes and they will be explained to you again,' said another. One mother observed that some children are held back until they have learnt some basics by rote, and wondered if there should be more 'aspiration and challenge before they have everything right'. Both prep and pre-prep have own library. Some 49 children are currently on the learning support register; school has policy of not withdrawing children from vital lessons to have their two half hour individual sessions per week.

Pastoral care for the children highly rated; class teachers assume pastoral responsibilities in year 3, tutors with mixed horizontal tutor groups thereafter. The newly formed Friends of King's Hall provides purely social events for parents, and is working on extending its reach to everyone. We liked the enshrining of the school rules into six positive exhortations, such as 'do work hard, and do be honest'.

About 50 children board in a variety of arrangements; school entices children with regular year group boarding nights and film nights for the whole prep school. One busy mum told us her youngest had boarded just for a night at the age of 5 – and loved it. The sole boarding house has separate areas for senior boys, junior boys and girls, each with its own common room and quiet areas. 'It's fun and as homely as possible – I board to relax!' one boy told us, and all reckoned that boarders of all persuasions are well integrated. Parents tell us that facilities have improved, but the school 'doesn't have that horrible bling-tastic feel that the other Taunton schools have'. Well, thank goodness! Day pupils are welcome to join in the weekend activities with boarders, which might include dry ski-ing or making the most of the beautiful Quantock Hills nearby for a 16 mile orienteering exercise; facilities at King's College are also on offer at weekends.

The arts are well catered for too. Pupils' art was displayed everywhere we went and the design side has facilities for 2D and 3D design. Three major productions a year for years 4, 6 and 8 put on in the school's theatre or outside in the rose garden are complemented by prizes for acting and poetry recital at local festivals. About half the children learn a musical instrument, achieving grade 6 or 7 in rare cases, and the new director of music has gone down well.

So what's it really like? A question probably best answered by the pupils: 'I look forward to going back'. 'The weeks pass really quickly'. And to sum up? 'I don't instantly feel like the walking dead when I arrive'.

Job done, Mr Chips.

King's College (Taunton)

Linked with King's Hall School

South Road, Taunton, Somerset TA1 3LA

Pupils: 460; 285 full boarders • Ages: 13–18 • Sixth form: 190 • C of E

Fees: Day £20,985; Boarding £30,900 pa

Tel: 01823 328204
Email: admissions@kings-taunton.co.uk
Website: www.kings-taunton.co.uk

Headmaster: Since 2007 Mr Richard Biggs (early 50s) BSc MA, a product both of the UK's and South Africa's finest: his first degree (physics) from University of Cape Town, his masters (maths and philosophy) from Oxford as a Rhodes scholar. Some barely discernible vowels hint at his upbringing in South Africa; his subsequent career has been entirely in the UK, at Magdalen College School as teacher of maths and physics then director of studies, from where he was promoted to deputy head at Lancing, thence to King's. Now into his eighth year of headship, he can look back with justifiable satisfaction at his achievements since he started, mainly an increase in numbers and improvements to facilities. 'We can really concentrate on academics now, without being over-selective – the market in this part of the world wouldn't stand for it', he says.

Much liked by parents and students alike, who find him 'very bright, approachable and friendly', but we imagine he fixes miscreants with the eye of a basilisk when required. 'Runs a good ship,' remarked one mother succinctly, and writes a jolly good blog. A musical challenge to pass grade 1 on an unfamiliar musical instrument spurred him on to grade 8 proficiency on that most recalcitrant of instruments, the French horn ('a bit of a devil to play') and a seat in the school's wind band. He is married to Sarah, who edits the school magazine and oversees boarding house design, and has two sons in the school. When term ends, he escapes to his cottage on the north Cornish coast with his family for some rugged maritime r'n'r.

Academic matters: Academically inclusive, as attested by recent A level results, 31 per cent A*/A in 2016 (62 per cent A*/B) and yet do not quite achieve 100 per cent pass rates in all subjects. A sprinkling of U grades perhaps indicates that students are permitted to pursue their dream subjects, even if they are unlikely to get top marks; several popular and rigorous subjects (eg chemistry, biology, maths) receive grades from superb to dire, via mediocre. At GCSE, it is a similar story. In 2016, 39 per cent of grades at A*/A. A modern language is expected at GCSE; many study two, and minority languages (German, Japanese, Latin, Russian, inevitably Chinese) laid on for just one taker on occasion. Sciences can either be taken separately or as a dual award. Good range of SEN catered for, and 70 pupils currently receiving extra support; highly praised by a mother of four very different children whom we spoke to: 'My dyslexic child did as well here as anywhere; he received massive support, which meant he exceeded his predictions'. A BTec in sport in collaboration with Exeter City FC and Exeter Chiefs Rugby Club recently introduced.

Games, options, the arts: Make no mistake, this is a sporty school. Masses going on, and no exeat weekends mean a full programme of fixtures against other titans of the west country:

Millfield is the one to beat. Football and rugby top sports in the winter terms, cricket the undoubted Queen of the May in the summer; school is a centre for cricketing excellence as befits its location in Taunton, home of Somerset county cricket with which the school has close links. Year round facilities (as well as beautiful pitches in the heart of the school) mean this is truly a top school for cricket. Hockey and netball also popular with plenty of opportunities for matches. We thoroughly applaud girls' football, cricket and hockey being promoted and resourced as well as the boys' games.

Minority sports include tennis, swimming, golf and athletics, whilst riders' lives are made easier by the offer of stabling near school for boarders' mounts, and the possibility of integrating riding into the school day for day students. Again, chances to compete and bring home the silverware are legion. Usual range of outdoor roughy-toughy stuff like D of E, Ten Tors, CCF and its precursor, the Chindit programme for year 9.

About half the school learns a musical instrument, brass especially popular and school has notable jazz band. Some grade 8 and diploma level players among senior students. Singers abound, their repertoire from the popular to the highbrow, from rock bands to the chapel and chamber choirs, via the new barbershop quartet, Quartones. Performance of whatever standard is encouraged.

Musical talents useful for annual school musical too: recently Guys and Dolls, Les Mis, and The Wizard of Oz. One significant play per year, sometimes Shakespeare, many other less elaborate productions in school's own theatre, black box drama studio, recently built amphitheatre – or, memorably, in a pod of the London Eye.

Four floors of art school, including new art studio, mean there is room enough for a gallery as well as studio space, where visiting artists can exhibit; one created a willow sculpture of the school's emblem, a pelican. Fine art is the basis of work here but digital media such as film and photography also laid on, and textiles GCSE is a new addition. We were especially taken by the newspaper tutu. King's has stand-out DT, which has won Arkwright scholarships and GSG awards on several occasions. A car in varying states of (dis)repair lurks in the DT studio for budding mechanics and designers to get their hands on, but the range of objects emerging from this studio combine beauty and functionality in equal measure: the tree-hung beehive is definitely on our wish list.

Despite the wealth of extracurricular activities on offer, 'the school does not push the kids into doing things, but once they sign up, they are expected to commit', according to one parent. 'Some parents don't like this, but the kids can then take credit for the activities they do, which makes them into secure self-starters'.

Boarding: Nearly two-thirds of students board, and it's the real deal: no flexi or weekly, they either board, or they don't. Busy and obligatory Saturdays mean a short weekend, during which a good range of activities is devised and offered by a designated co-ordinator; some of the students seize the advantage of being near-ish to the coast to surf and sail, some might choose to relax, swot or pop home instead. However, pupils may sign out on certain weekends as long as they don't have prior commitments. Around 12 per cent of boarders come from abroad: Chinese and Germans predominate, but the head actively explores different markets and will cap the overseas quota at 15 per cent. Military families now have their own liaison officer. Boarders stay in touch with home by email, Skype or Facetime. Devices belonging to younger students get handed in at night but enforcement varies from house to house, we were told. Boarding houses were, in our view, so-so: the girls' house we saw had a bitty lay-out separating year groups, but at least some baths still remain for muddy hockey players to soak it all off. Boys' boarding appears to be more integrated between year groups and definitely fewer frills – communal space boasted but some grubby leather sofas ('Eek!' said school 'Not typical') and a huge TV. Day students get one night a week boarding included in the day fee.

Background and atmosphere: A Woodard School, one of about 30 founded by a visionary Victorian cleric, where, these days, Christian values of understanding, diversity and tolerance – 'religious literacy' in the words of the resident chaplain – are inculcated without a whiff of evangelism. The chapel (white, light, beautiful with a decent organ and great acoustic) and collective worship are big parts of school life; all faiths and none are made welcome. But the roots of the school go back to an ancient boys' grammar, founded in the 16th century, but relocated to its current Victorian gothic pile in the 1860s.

It's fair to say that it still feels and looks quite traditional, with conventional uniform with designer tweed jackets and blue shirts, and neatness being identified as a virtue. The dining hall boasts not ancestral coats of arms, but sporting achievements painted on shields all over the walls. We did not have the chance to sample its wares, as we were instead treated to quite the grandest lunch we had ever been offered in the headmaster's dining room: curried monkfish followed by fig beignets washed down with pink bubbly – reader, we succumbed. Not surprising to read that 'the art of tying a bow tie has been revived' at King's: its reputation as being Taunton's smartest school seems entirely deserved, and its parents are disparaging about the others, their attitude on the sports fields in particular. Whilst the façade is impressive, some of the other buildings hit low points of British school architecture – with the exception of the new library whose modern touches integrate wonderfully with the warm reddish Somerset stone.

Pastoral care, well-being and discipline: Highly rated, particularly in the person of the deputy head pastoral, and a sine qua non of Woodard schools. 'Pastoral scaffolding,' as the school explained it, includes tutors, house staff and the school chaplain, who doubles as an additional school counsellor (as well as coaching several sports); parents can raise any concerns they have through the parent portal. Considerate touches include a Facebook page for Chinese non-English speaking parents. 'Any breach of good manners and good sense' will attract censure; punishments range from detention to more community-minded activities like litter-picking, but not in orange jumpsuits. The ultimate sanctions of suspension or exclusion are rarely, if ever, necessary. Commendations are given for all manner of good works and we liked the sound of the Ferrett Prize for 'all round unobtrusive contribution by a member of the 4th Form' – if you can spot it.

Pupils and parents: Unpretentious, happy to be there and grateful for all the opportunities the school offers. A boy from Hong Kong told us that he and his family had 'looked at every school in the country and chosen this one'. Families come from a wider geographical area both in the UK and abroad than the other Taunton schools, and inevitably some parents use the fast railway line to London to commute; the professions, the military, agriculture and the county set are all represented. The school welcomes parents new and existing (but perhaps not vegetarian) with a hog roast at the start of every year.

Entrance: Ninety arrive in year 9 by means of common entrance (passes expected in all subjects but school a bit coy about revealing pass mark), or by school's own papers in maths, English and verbal reasoning. Many, but not all, come from King's Hall, the school's associated prep school; others from prep schools in the south west or from overseas. A handful come into year 10 to start GCSE courses, where space permits. Twenty-five new into the sixth form after 'satisfactory performance at GCSE' or school's own papers for those without GCSEs.

Exit: About a dozen peel off after GCSE, some to the very good and free sixth form college across the road, Richard Huish. Leavers' destinations in recent years include a sprinkling to Oxbridge and a bunch of conventional destinations up and down the land, 46 per cent to Russell Group, including Bristol and Durham. Some less orthodox choices like the Philip Green Academy for retail and the Academy of Contemporary Music. Several students apply post A level. All become Old Aluredians in any event – surely in the running for the most arcane alumni title. OAs of note include sportsmen/women (cricketers Jos Buttler and Roger Twose, hockey player Maddie Hinch, rugby player Tom Voyce), broadcasters Jonathan Meades and Dominic Wood and actress Juno Temple.

Money matters: The difference between day and boarding fees is closer than at the other Taunton schools but broadly in line. Scholarships for academic, sporting and artistic prowess plus DT, to a maximum value of 20 per cent of the day fee, are awarded at 13+ and sixth form. Academic scholars are expected to contribute to the intellectual life of the school, not just pulling in stonking exam results, but also attending weekly meetings at which papers are presented.

Remarks: Look no further for a traditional public school with distinctly sporty leanings sited in a county town. A Somerset institution housed in a suitably imposing stone monolith and serving its environs.

King's Hawford School

Linked with King's St Alban's, The King's School (Worcester)

Hawford Lock Lane, Worcester WR3 7SD

Pupils: 326: 206 boys, 120 girls • Ages: 2–11 • C of E

Fees: £6,864 – £12,360 pa

Tel: 01905 451292
Email: hawford@ksw.org.uk
Website: www.ksw.org.uk

Principal: Since 2006, Jim Turner (early 50s), who is not in the flashy CEO-style head mould. He is comfortable feeding the chickens that are on site and breeding the birds that the children delight in watching. But alongside the gentleman farmer image, there is a man who cares passionately about the sort of education that is right for young children. The children are learning from doing – and a lot of the doing goes on outside. Jim Turner's first headship was in Sunderland and the children tell us that the trials and tribulations of the football team there are a running theme at assembly time. He has been at King's Hawford for 10 years and to say it is just a place of work for him would be travesty – he lives and breathes the whole school. Parents say that he is more comfortable around the children than around them but that is the way everyone likes it. The children want to tell him about all their successes and they want his approval and praise. People often say a good head knows all the children – at King's Hawford that means a lot more than just knowing everyone's name.

Entrance: The school pretty well fills up at kindergarten and only occasional places become available later on, if someone moves out of the area. Certainly at kindergarten level it is fairly non-selective. Children visit the school and are informally observed.

Exit: Most go on to the senior school King's in the centre of Worcester. A number win scholarships there each year. Parents are given plenty of warning if their child might not pass the exam.

Remarks: When we arrived the whole school was outside engaged in a cross-country run around the 23 acre site. The school is just to the north of Worcester and has all the open-air feel of a rural paradise. As well as the extensive grounds, the children are encouraged to make full use of the adjacent river, canal and farm. They embrace the full forest school curriculum, working on real tasks with real tools. They start using the school's own swimming pool from the age of 3 and from 7 they paddle canoes on the canal. They learn to be confident around water and this relevant life skills approach characterises everything about the school.

The head and parents described the site as 'a children's village'. Apart from the deliciously quirky, original Georgian house where there are now some classrooms and a dining hall, the buildings are all low level and spread out, giving plenty of space for chickens and children to run around. It is a school where children climb trees (' I often wonder what a health and safety official would say,' said one parent wryly) and get muddy ('You have to expect to have the washing machine on every evening,' another told us.) You feel the children are not confined in a way that many schools have to restrict movement. 'The children never stop moving,' one parent told us, and we saw no child who looked even a tiny bit overweight. There is a brand new sports hall/performance space where the architects have taken the concept of a barn to enhance the village feel of the site.

Drama, music and dance are all prominent for everyone. The children can read music by the time they leave, they all learn an instrument and over 80 sing in the choir that takes part in local festivals as well as school events. There are about 60 in the school orchestra with masses of formal and informal opportunities to perform. Sport is also hugely popular with two sports afternoons a week and the children have had national successes – the U11 netball team had just competed in the national finals when we visited. The head believes in giving children lots of opportunities – he wants them to be open, eager and wanting to try out the new, so the extracurricular programme is extensive – construction and sewing, story tellers and IT, cartoon/comic drawing and bridge to name just some of the startling range.

Somewhere in the midst of all this, the children have the normal school lessons – though even here it is in fact quite unusual. The 3 year olds learn German. Years 5 and 6 take three modern languages. They are taught old-fashioned loop handwriting and the forgotten arts of carpentry and cookery. There is no IT room but the school is dripping with technology that the children can take outside the classroom and use. There is a school radio that you can access from the website which the children run. After the cross-country that we watched, the current radio team did interviews with the runners for next week's radio show. The head says there is a bit less time for traditional English and maths than some other schools give, but he points out that the children nevertheless achieve highly, the vast majority getting places at the King's senior school. Class sizes are small – 16-20 – and in year 3 and above, the two classes are split three ways for English and maths. There are tracking systems in place to pick up any progress problems and support teachers are used from year 1 onwards if a need is identified. Additional support is not charged to parents. Nor is the wrap-around care offered from 7.45am to 6.00pm, except at kindergarten level. The after-school provision has recently been restructured so there is a supervised prep time before activities, allowing the children to go home with no school work to complete – totally in keeping with the school ethos of letting children be children and not tiny undergraduates.

The children are happy, healthy, open and engaged – far more interested in getting on with their next activities that making polite conversation to visitors. This is not a school for children who want to sit in front of a PlayStation all day. Parents say King's Hawford has a warm, close community, village school atmosphere with all the opportunities of a much bigger school. 'It is no hothouse but it gets the results,' we were told. The discipline seems to work on the basis that highly motivated and challenged children behave well, and parents love the fact the school doesn't have to be disciplinarian in any way. The parent body is pretty mixed – lots of doctors from the local hospitals, established farming families and business people.

'No one gives up at King's Hawford', said parents, watching the cross-country races. 'Everyone is encouraged and they all believe they can do anything.'

This is a 21st century Swallows and Amazons school. We want to ship Department of Education officials out here to see what can be done away from the deadening performance table approach to education.

King's St Alban's School

Linked with King's Hawford School, The King's School (Worcester)

Mill Street, Worcester WR1 2NJ

Pupils: 200 • Ages: 4–11 • C of E

Fees: £6,552 – £11,853 pa

Tel: 01905 354906
Email: ksa@ksw.org.uk
Website: www.ksw.org.uk

Headmaster: Since January 2016, Richard Chapman (early 40s). He was educated in the Midlands (Solihull School, where he was head boy) and read economics at Bristol. He worked briefly as a trainee manager at Marks and Spencer, then balanced his early teaching posts with a stint as a semi-professional rugby player. He was head of sixth form and coach of the 1st XV at Warwick School before joining the King's Foundation in Worcester as second deputy in 2007. He went on to become senior deputy at King's before being appointed head of King's St Alban's. He knows the school and the area very well and is bringing considerable experience to his new role.

He still enjoys sport and continues to play cricket. He is determined to grow sport at King's St Alban's having just appointed a new head of boys' games. His favourite time of the week is celebratory assembly on Fridays when a huge range of the children's achievements at all sorts of different levels are applauded. He revels in the youthful exuberance all around him. 'What I love to see is the children outside having fun playing tag one minute, then the next coming into the classroom and settling down calmly and purposefully to a challenging academic lesson'. Father of two children both in the Kings' Foundation, Richard is clearly relishing the opportunities to grow the reputation of the foundation at the bottom end. He has plans to move IT forward, away from being a discrete subject to an integrated teaching and learning resource, while boosting the status of the library to encourage a love of reading. He is having considerable success with the growth mindset work that he has introduced to build confidence and resilience. Parents who already knew Richard from his senior school days were delighted when he took on King's St Alban's. They see him as being outward facing, very determined and with a competitive edge to him that can only be good for the school. They like the fact that he drops in on clubs and activities as well as lessons.

Entrance: Reception up to year 3 involves spending some time in the school with the appropriate class, being observed. From year 3, there are entrance tests in verbal reasoning, English and maths, which normally take place in the spring term for September entry, but the school will arrange for individual testing at other times of the year. Typically, there are three forms in years 5 and 6 and two in the younger years. Class sizes are usually between 15 and 20.

Exit: The vast majority of children go on to King's senior school. This year 12 won scholarships. A few go into the state sector or to boarding schools. Parents felt the children were very well prepared to move on to King's. For example from year 4 the school starts to build homework steadily so the children are ready for the amount of work they will be expected to do in year 7.

Remarks: King's St Albans was originally a traditional prep school starting at 7 years old. Seven years ago, it expanded to take children from age 4 by buying an adjacent house and converting it into bright, light, children-friendly spaces. Partly because of this, the buildings have an attractive non-institutional feel about them and the resources in the pre-prep reflect the best modern educational practice; it is a purpose built pre-prep department. Every bit of space is imaginatively used to provide outdoor play and activity spaces.

Teaching in the pre-prep is topic based and becomes more subject focused as the children get older. The teachers describe it as traditional but creative and rigorous. Parents tell us that teaching is both nurturing and challenging. 'Teachers show them that they can do more than just well enough'. The small class sizes, enhanced with the use of teaching assistants, ensure that informal assessment is a daily feature and any learning concerns are picked up very quickly. Generally these will be supported in the class room but the senior school SEN specialist can assess and support if necessary. A few children have additional lessons outside normal class time, at no extra charge. Also in the main fee package is wrap-around 8am-6pm care if parents need it, and quite a number do. Lots of families have both parents working. The after-school structured prep and activities are run by teachers.

The children are enthusiastic and serious. Everyone loves sport and the aim to have everyone involved clearly works. The older children we saw were very much enjoying their PSE discussions on a range of social issues. The head has introduced debating to stimulate new intellectual channels for the children. The choristers, who are from year 3 upwards in particular, have a highly structured timetable with long days. Music features prominently for everyone whether a chorister or not. All year 1s have a 'violin experience', lots play instruments and there are a number of different music groups. The head is keen to present aspirational experiences to the children, and choirs from the cathedral and senior school regularly come to perform. The creative arts are a very strong feature generally. Children spoke enthusiastically about Creative ConneXions, an annual occasion that is the culmination of various arts events that go on through the year. There is dance, poetry and singing. The nearness of the senior Sschool is a resource the head is keen to exploit even more. He is encouraging sixth formers to support clubs in order to get a real buzz to the already extensive extracurricular side of the school.

The facilities, as you would expect, are excellent. There is a fully equipped science lab, brilliant for the year 6 annual science week, art room, a swimming pool and sports hall. The school has its own chapel and a lovely light library. King's has an outdoor education space in Wales which the pupils utilise at various stages – a much-anticipated adventure. There are plenty of trips out of school, a particular favourite being Year 6's visit to Normandy.

The school is very positive about relations with parents. In the lower years, reading records go home daily. There are assemblies to which parents are invited two or three times a year, and at the start of every academic year there is a curriculum evening for each year group where teachers share the school's methods of teaching as well as the actual material. Parents appreciate the school's conscious work on developing character. The key words that provided the focus for everyone on the week we visited were concentration, enthusiasm and curiosity. These themes are shared with parents, who like the way the school uses moral scenarios to help the children with their own daily decision making. Discipline is described by parents as very understated. 'When a bell rings in the playground, everyone stops and goes in – no teacher has to raise their voice'. Parents told us any concerns are picked up quickly and dealt with discreetly as far as the children are concerned.

A number of teachers told us that children at the school do not have to fit a particular mould and that all can thrive. Parents say it is a 'really happy school' and the children we met bore this out. 'They care about celebrating children's individuality', one parent told us. The new head is very ambitious for the school and has already made some timely innovations to this already very nurturing and successful school.

The King's School (Chester)

Wrexham Road, Chester, Cheshire CH4 7QL

Pupils: 1,073 (including 353 in infants and juniors) • Ages: 4-19 • Sixth form: 209: 123 boys/86 girls • C of E

Fees: £8,490- £12,888 pa

Tel: 01244 689500
Email: admissions@kingschester.co.uk
Website: www.kingschester.co.uk

Headmaster: Since 2007, Mr Chris Ramsey MA (late 40s). Previously head of King's College, Taunton, deputy head at Cranleigh, head of languages at Wellington College. Educated Brighton College and Corpus Christi, Cambridge. Quick thinking, fast talking, intensely communicative in person and via his weekly blog. Rocked the boat initially with his energetic challenge to the status quo, but all seems plain sailing now. Not expecting further squalls from recent big changes to curriculum; 'we've been two and a half years planning for them and by and large the whole community's on side'. Three children in school from the juniors to the sixth form. He's 'thought provoking, very interesting, a very good teacher,' pupils say, 'and he's at every performance, engaged with everything'. Pastoral and academic deputies also very much involved in senior team leadership of this big school.

Moving on in July 2017 to head Whitgift School. His successor will be George Hartley (40s), currently principal of Elizabeth College, Guernsey. Geography degree from Cambridge and MSc in environmental science from Imperial. He has also been head of sixth form at Berkhamstead School, and taught at Highgate School, Queen's College, Taunton and Eton College. He is married to Merewyn and they have two children.

Head of junior school: Since September 2016 is Margaret Ainsworth LLB PGCE, previously head of Willow Lodge, the infants' school, and before that deputy head at The Queen's Lower School, Chester.

Academic matters: Extremely ambitious; no complacency here with big changes to stay ahead of the game. Peer-reviewed books in junior school classroom libraries help others choose good reads. Curriculum includes Spanish for four years and German and French in the final year. Progress assessed with internal testing and Durham University's INCAS scheme. The latest ISI inspection described the quality of educational experience as 'outstanding' and said, 'The junior school provides pupils with an excellent all-round education'. 'They put you under pressure to do well, but when you do, it's really rewarding,' say pupils. 'There are big exams, but then they really let you off the hook.' Year 4s (top juniors) talk of a daily hour of homework, an hour and a half at weekends, and everyone's keen to earn house points for work, effort and behaviour.

Strong at GCSE with 74 per cent A*/A in 2016. IGCSEs now in most subjects. Pupils sit 10 subjects, from a choice of 22, 'aiming for quality not quantity', with a stronger enrichment programme from Mandarin or astronomy to community service. In sixth form a big emphasis on LVI extended projects. The whole school has moved to a two week, five daily period timetable. A levels in 2016 achieved 87 per cent A*/B grades, 62 per cent A*/A.

Pupils are quick to give 'fulfilling my potential' as a top reason for coming here and praise the teachers for being 'interested in what benefits us as a person across the board, especially the heads of department; being passionate about their subject is instilled in the life of King's'. Teachers must expect head to pop in to lessons, 'to take an interest, be visible, be encouraging', in a spirit of respectful, constructive criticism. Aside from traditional academic prowess, provision for music, art, DT, ICT etc is temptingly good including a state-of-the-art 3D photocopier for realising CAD (computer aided designs). Yearly Arkwright scholars reflecting splendid DT; plenty of prizes in other national Olympiad challenges.

The bright modern library, open from 8am–5.30pm, attracts 800 visits a day to its 16,000 resources, which include 85 journal subscriptions. During our visit in exam season there was a convivial but studious burble of joint revising here, and in fact elsewhere, too, in corridors and round the entrance foyer art exhibition. Plenty of computers everywhere, whiteboards and netbooks in some classes.

Games, options, the arts: 'What I love about King's,' a senior pupil told us, 'is the plethora of opportunities here'. He was directing his own production of Waiting for Godot in the new theatre, using two weeks of the summer holidays to rehearse his cast. Would this be his extended project? 'Well it could be, but I also want to look into whether Dostoevsky deserves his reputation as a dark author; personally I don't think he does so I want to argue his case'. Yes, he hoped to read English at Oxford but, outwardly at least, he was modestly not expecting an offer. The whole school was buzzing about the newish Vanbrugh Theatre, which has 250 foldaway raked seats, 200 seats in the stalls and a gallery, plus, up a spiral staircase, thespian dressing rooms complete with light-flanked mirrors.

Every weekend some 150 pupils make the most of the boathouse and coaching on the Dee, continuing a 134 year old rowing tradition. King's grows a steady supply of national rowers (most recently Tom James, Olympic gold medallist, Chris Bartley, Olympic silver medallist and Olivia Whitlam, world U23 champion and Olympic finalist), and makes its mark at the National Schools' Regatta. Fiercely competitive in all sport from excellent facilities, 'the only thing missing is lacrosse,' say pupils. Acres of pitches, courts, floodlit Astro and tradition of inter-house sport so all can take part. The 18m pool is the only facility seniors seem lukewarm about: 'It's a bit jaded, only big enough for the juniors really'. Junior school pupils fiercely proud of sporting successes, especially in cricket and swimming.

Fabulous music school boasts bright recital hall with floor to ceiling apex windows, recording studio, classroom full of computers and six individual practice rooms. About half take individual instrument lessons in school and pupils enthuse: 'if there's an instrument you want to play they'll find a teacher for it'. Twenty-five orchestras, ensembles and choirs, including Schola Cantorum, which leads services in the cathedral. The music head, described as 'fantastic' by parents, has direct phone and email on school website. CCF here 155 years old in 2015 and there's a minority but well-worn path into the armed forces from King's. Over 120 other activities from D of E (80 per cent take bronze, about half silver), Model United Nations, charities, and clubs from Scrabble to meteorology.

K

Background and atmosphere: Founded by King Henry VIII in 1541, the school left its city centre cathedral site in 1960, and in 2011 celebrated 50 years on the Wrexham Road site just inside the city's by-pass. Today school rents 32 verdant acres from the Duke of Westminster. A generous school flag flies from the copper-capped tower, fluttering over rangey modern buildings in spic and span grounds. Beyond the secure reception area that's open all year the atmosphere is purposeful and businesslike, and the classrooms spacious. The dining room and one or two corridors form bottlenecks at busy times but polite pupils naturally wait their turn, holding doors open for adults. And despite the throng of life and busy corridors, in the middle of it all a happy duck and drake rear their annual brood in one of two attractive quads. Junior school pupils appreciate the outdoor 'buddy bench' and centenary adventure trail with solar powered timers. Confident children work and play hard here. 'We are an academic school,' says head, 'but we also emphasise music, games, drama, fun – it's very important the pupils have fun.' (The 15 foot giant Henry VIII, a masterpiece pupil and staff creation for town parade and junior's centenary celebration was a case in point.)

Pastoral care, well-being and discipline: Pupils describe this as 'a very friendly school' and parents praise the effort made to help children settle in here at all levels. Junior school children feel they have an effective voice through school council and a suggestion box for all. Delighted parents fall over themselves to praise 'the way children's confidence grows here' and the compassionate way school works to accommodate any problems. New learning centre recently added. Prefect and sixth form mentoring and form tutors form backbone of senior school pastoral care. Last ISC inspection mentions 'the excellent relationships between pupils and staff..engendering an atmosphere of trust and security'. Emphasis on integrity and honesty so, for example, under 13s who give false dates of birth to start a Facebook page are asked by school, 'what does that say about you as a human being and is that the sort of human being you want to be?' 'Their Facebook pages usually disappear after that'. Regarding network communication generally, head urges pupils to 'be kind, be kind, be kind'. Strong cathedral links endure, although the feel is of a Christian school with a small c. One of two weekly assemblies includes a two minute 'Quite Interesting' public speaking slot for pupils to share their interests, 'to develop a zest for learning'.

Achievement is recognised in many areas, 'not just for the goal scorers and A*s'. Choosing not to fulfil responsibilities, such as not storing bags correctly, brings the consequence of sanctions such as detentions, simple as that, but discipline doesn't seem to need to be heavy-handed; it's a pretty civilised community. A full-time nursing sister and assistant staff the sick bay.

Pupils and parents: Proportion of girls has grown to 35 per cent (over 40 per cent in sixth form) since their arrival in 2003 and the school now feels properly co-ed with girls of all sorts, not just robust pioneers. Despite school becoming more image-conscious under Mr Ramsey, pupils remain disarmingly normal and charming, a very nice bunch. Head describes intake as 'very varied, we don't just have one type of boy or one type of girl' and says 'we don't have many girlfriend and boyfriend issues, the atmosphere is just cordial and friendly'.

Largely middle class and white, professional or farming backgrounds. From Chester and Cheshire, the Wirral and North Wales, in their distinctive navy, green and white striped blazers and ties. Sixth formers move on to crested navy blazers with ties denoting activities and status and senior prefects get to wear academic gowns for special occasions. Conveniently for parents there's a uniform shop on site. Less convenient they tell us (to a man) is the car park jam up at collection time; 'there are 1,000 pupils here, we try to keep it moving but it's a big school and parents just need to accept they have to be patient,' is head's response. Many use fleets of buses, some shared with Queen's. The glossy Herald news and annual King's Eye celebrate the many varied happenings here.

Entrance: For reception, assessments through play-based activities. If 'progress and behaviour is in line with expectations,' says school, will move into junior school from year 3 (year 1 here) when children from other schools also join – examination relates to key stage 1 requirements, designed to assess potential as well as achievement. Tests in maths, written English, reading and reasoning, as well as play activity and a talk with staff. 'We're looking for an above average level of competency and the potential to do well – it's not an interview, but you can learn a lot from how, for example, a 6 year old draws'. Entry at ages 8, 9 and 10 is sometimes possible, although head says numbers have increased slightly despite recession. Movement from junior to senior by internal assessment; from elsewhere by 11+ exam in January, with English, maths, verbal and non-verbal reasoning and an interview. Quiet warning bells sounded a year or two early in junior school if seniors might not suit, although all may compete on level playing ground with outside applicants by taking the external exam. Seniors are selecting from the top 25 per cent and looking for the brightest 100 regardless of gender. Sixth form requires A* or A in intended subjects and seven GCSE Bs or above.

Exit: Some 90 per cent of juniors move up to senior school. The opening line on school website states, 'From your child's first day at The King's School at 7 years of age, we are preparing them for graduation and beyond'. University is unapologetically assumed from the off and school prides itself that over half go on to a university from The Times Top 30 list. Annual handful to Oxbridge, 10 places in 2016; eight medics and one vet. Durham, Leeds, Newcastle and UCL also popular; one lawyer off to Maastricht. Sixth form support for course and university choice very strong, with all UCAS applications submitted by end of October.

Notable old boys include TV's Martin Lewis, Ronald Pickup (actor), Nickolas Grace (actor), Sir John Vanbrugh (architect),

Steve Leonard (TV vet), Freddie Owen (cricketer) and Admiral Sir Peter Dennis who, after leaving in 1730, reportedly invented mayonnaise, and eight Olympians – four in 2012, including gold medal rower Tom James MBE.

Money matters: About 80 senior pupils receive some kind of means-tested bursary; 10 have free places, with plans to increase bursary provision to help more pupils over next decade, returning somewhat towards school's founding principles of helping 'poor, friendless boys'. King's Scholarships awarded during first three years; others in sixth form. Lunches compulsory adding £720 a year.

Remarks: Purposeful, confident co-ed school with top-notch facilities and acres of space, producing uber-capable young adults who are nevertheless, friendly and unassuming.

The King's School

Cadhay Lane, Ottery St Mary, Devon EX11 1RA

Pupils: 1,070 • Ages: 11 –18 • Sixth form: 180

Tel: 01404 812982
Email: office@thekings.devon.sch.uk
Website: www.thekings.devon.sch.uk

Headteacher: Since September 2016, Rob Gammon, previously head of Robert Blake Science College in Somerset. He has a PE, sports science and physics degree and was deputy head at King's School before taking up his headship at Robert Blake in 2013.

Academic matters: In 2016, 21 per cent A*/A, 48 per cent A*-B grades at A level and 31 per cent A*-A at GCSE (72 per cent achieved 5+ A*-C grades including English and maths). Fifty-six per cent A*/A for EPQ. Strongest subjects are also the most popular – geography, biology and maths, all with 50/60 students at A level. GCSE results are above average and students of all abilities are doing well. All classes are mixed ability except for maths.

Twenty-eight A level options including dance, media studies, politics, photography, psychology, sociology and law. At GCSE the school offers a range of technology subjects including food (catering), electronic products, resistant materials and textiles alongside the usual curriculum subjects. Vocational BTecs and NVQs in animal care, children's care, engineering, beauty therapy, vehicle maintenance and hairdressing are also available. French and Spanish are offered at GCSE and A level, but not compulsory. Around half take a language at GCSE, and but tiny numbers at A level. East Devon Sixth Form, as it's called, is looking at using links between neighbouring schools to teach languages remotely and pool resources.

ICT available as a vocational GCSE-level qualification and at A level. The school is not overrun with computers, with around 250 in total. Apparently it's not unheard of for sixth formers to grab empty PCs from the back of other classes. Technology is not top of the priority list here.

Large skills for learning department run by the deputy head, who is the school's SENCo. Fourteen pupils are statemented, including for Asperger's, Down's syndrome and ADHD. Other pupils are given extra support in literacy and numeracy. There's a life skills room for those needing specialist help for everyday skills including cooking. One parent said, 'Pupils are always looking out for those needing support', and we saw this for ourselves on our tour of the school. The skills for learning department is also responsible for gifted and talented pupils. 'In our view being gifted/talented is as much of a special educational need as a specific learning difficulty.'

Games, options, the arts: King's is a sports college, so there's plenty on offer here. Girls' and boys' teams for football, hockey, cricket (girls are East Devon champions), plus rugby, volleyball, table tennis, badminton. Two hours of PE a week with fixtures after school and at weekends. School believes sport and exercise are integral to learning and motivation. Ten Tors and D of E are very popular. After the success of the netball and rugby tours in South Africa, 2016 saw a hockey tour. There's a sports hall on site, a sports field a short jog away, Astroturf, a multi-use hall for dance and tennis plus use of the leisure centre opposite.

'The music department isn't great', say parents. A few take it to A level. Limited facilities, no mention of a choir or orchestra. Dance is more popular and is taught in collaboration with other local schools. Drama is a strong subject, taught at GCSE and A level, and a popular university choice. We saw a GCSE class working on their group assessment pieces. Pupils were working well together, and the groups were tailoring their pieces to take into account the mix of ability (including pupils with Asperger's and Down's syndrome). This meant that some were using scripts and others were sticking to improvisation. Recent major productions include Bugsy Malone, We will Rock You and Annie. A fashion show is planned for next year

Art and textiles are popular subjects and we saw some creative and imaginative pieces, from life-sized portraits to sculptures and screen-printing. Bunted stretched across the classrooms, equipment was piled high and displays were haphazardly dotted around. It felt chaotic, but the results were creative and the students seemed interested and enthusiastic. There are separate classrooms for sixth form art and photography (the latter has exclusive use of the school's Apple Macs). We particularly liked the street photography on display.

The catering department recently won a national catering department school award, and when we were there the kitchen was buzzing with activity. Pupils (mainly girls) were perfecting their Viennese biscuits, while another class's flapjacks were cooling. The annual year 10 restaurant evenings see students take over a local restaurant for the night. From ordering to managing front-of-house, they create and serve seven courses for 54 covers. The standards are impressively high and all money raised goes to charity.

Clubs are mainly at lunchtime and include sports clubs aplenty, a Lego club, astronomy, a green team, and a walk and talk club (encourages girls to exercise). One parent said, 'My daughter has grown in confidence, joining quite a few clubs at school and is in the drama production, likes singing, has done gardening club, table tennis club, drama, and now joined the teen health club'.

Not many trips or travel – no language exchanges – though there's an annual trip to Paris, Barcelona or the Ardèche. The school has a link with a school in Ethiopia, but due to safety concerns the annual sixth form trip has been replaced with a trip to India. Regular RPE (religion, philosophy and ethics) trips, most recently to Ground Zero, Istanbul and Morocco.

Sixth formers are lucky to have a new block, built in 2009 and extended in 2012. Parents say 'the sixth form is outstanding.' Particular praise was heard for the number of opportunities for them to develop their leadership skills. The sixth formers lead on house competitions, clubs and charity events and put on a sell-out variety show every year. A parent of an ex-pupil told us, 'They had the space to grow into adults without having to let go of anything before they were ready.'

Background and atmosphere: The school's history can be traced back to a 14th century choir school. This was replaced in 1545 by Henry VIII with a free co-ed grammar, The King's School. It moved to its current site in 1912 and turned comprehensive in the 80s. It lies about 10 miles east of Exeter and is an impressive sight on the approach to Ottery St Mary. One parent told us, 'We drove around Devon looking at schools and where they were. We chose King's because it rated highly in the league tables, it's a beautiful building that looked cared for, it's in a lovely part of the county, and it was oversubscribed – everyone wanted to go there.' Considering its heritage, there's not a great deal of history or tradition here. There are cups that date back 50 years or so and the main hall has a small gallery of old school photos, but the wooden award plaques only date back to 2004 – the year the previous headteacher joined.

The site is small. Old, tired buildings alongside crisp, white, new ones. The school has a long wish-list of facelifts and replacements but, as always, funds are hard to come by. Since it become an academy in 2011, an on-site business manager has been appointed to help plan these developments. A fantastic new block was built a year ago to house the English and PSHE departments. And the science department was upgraded just two years ago. More, please!

DT block, again, needs an upgrade. Canoes hanging from the rafters, machinery everywhere, somewhat chaotic feel. Same applies to the art and photography classrooms. The older buildings feel tired and a bit unloved, even tatty in places. A lick of paint wouldn't go amiss. Nor would a de-cluttering session. The school has outgrown itself, the maths department is crying out for three more classrooms and parents mentioned that 'There could be minor improvements such as locker facilities, especially useful on wet days or when they have a lot to carry.'

K

The library (a bit of a sauna at times) is very well used, always booked out for classes. Pupils are actively encouraged to read and use books rather than relying on the internet. When we were there the library was about to be used for a session with guest speaker, Francis Cornish.

Tasty choice of food on offer at lunchtimes. It's all made on site and the catering team has recently won a healthy food award. Chips once a fortnight.

'The house system is the pastoral bedrock of the school.' The houses have been named after local families: Coleridge, Kennaway, Patterson and Raleigh. The students are very loyal to their houses and thrive on the competitions. There's lots of opportunities to lead, mentor and work with other age-groups and abilities. The annual competitions include drama, music and dance productions, sports competitions plus debates and public speaking. Parents praise is high for the house system here. 'My children have certainly thrived and become confident young adults who talk to us about anything'.

The school encourages students to run charitable events from coffee mornings and sleepovers, to mini-enterprises and fun days. Local charities and the school in Ethiopia have all benefited. Latest mini-enterprise entrants included coasters made from CDs and a top trumps card game using staff photos. The MAD (Make a Difference) group helps to raise racial awareness in the school as well as visiting local elderly people.

Pastoral care, well-being and discipline: There are strong relationships between staff and students and the school takes great care of its students – as a result they feel extremely safe. Bullying problems at the school are mainly social media issues, and the school deals with each case accordingly. There's a strong student support team and a teen health website. It's a community school and on the whole, pupils seem happy to be there. One parent said, 'We felt The King's School had an excellent reputation, with no pupils hanging around Ottery at break times as we had seen with other local towns,' There's only been three exclusions over the last decade for behavioural problems. The school is keen 'to look for another way' and give students another chance, particularly those from more disadvantaged backgrounds.

Pupils and parents: Parents are local farmers, civil servants, doctors. Many moved to be in the school's catchment area, and haven't regretted it. 'This [school] really made us all feel that we belonged,' said one. Another said, 'I have a lot of praise for the school as staff are easy to approach.' Parents of a recent leaver anonymously donated a new language lab to the school – they said the money could have been spent on a private education and they wanted to give something back to the school. Very happy parents indeed.

Entrance: The admission process is based on the catchment area and has a set 180 places. It's oversubscribed, a problem that is going to be even more complicated when the housing estate is completed opposite the school.

Sixth former entrants need at least five C grades or above at GCSE and are invited for an interview.

Exit: About two-thirds stay on after GCSEs, and some 60 per cent of sixth formers go onto university. Bristol is the most popular choice, then Plymouth, Birmingham and Cardiff. Occasional Oxbridge places. Popular courses include maths, geography, science, media and law.

Famous leavers are unsurprisingly sporty: British Olympic runner Jo Pavey and Mary King MBE, British Olympian equestrian.

Money matters: Pupil premium fund is available to help families on lower incomes. A bursary fund is available for sixth formers. Plus there's the Foundation & Jubilee Trust which has helped raise money for the school (all-weather sports pitch, stage lighting, new computer network), as well as helping individual students with travel and equipment costs.

Remarks: Good rural comprehensive. Definitely in need of funding to improve facilities, but against the odds, achieving above average results and producing well-rounded students of all abilities. With an obviously supportive team of staff, The King's School is a community school where children can thrive at their own pace in a mixed and safe environment.

The King's School (Worcester)

Linked with King's Hawford School, King's St Alban's School

5 College Green, Worcester WR1 2LL

Pupils: 911 • Ages: 11–18 • Sixth form: 269 • C of E

Fees: £13,080 pa

Tel: 01905 721700
Email: info@ksw.org.uk
Website: www.ksw.org.uk

Headmaster: Since 2014, Mathew Armstrong MA PGCE. He has degrees from Oxford in modern and medieval languages and from Birkbeck College, London in Renaissance studies and English literature. He taught at Winchester and spent 11 years at Charterhouse, where he was assistant head. He had previously been a business analyst for McKinsey and Co, where his wife still works.

Following on from a long-serving and distinguished head, as Matthew has done, is a challenge anywhere, but particularly so at an ancient school such as King's, so steeped as it is in tradition. Nevertheless, his gravitas, combined with personal charm and approachability, is winning everyone round. Parents were initially nervous ('We had the jitters', one parent told us) that his vision for raising academic aspirations would be too narrow a focus, but they are now seeing that this can be done while retaining the other qualities of the school. The pupils find him friendly and accessible as well as impressively intellectual.

He is concerned to widen the diversity of the intake and wants King's to be at the very centre of the Worcester community and has already managed to build a terrific leadership team around him who share his vision. Together, they want to put King's firmly on the national map, so that it moves beyond being the local go-to school and leads the way in innovative teaching and learning approaches across the country.

Academic matters: The school produces consistently strong exam results year on year. In 2016, 47 per cent A*/A grades at A level (70 per cent A*/B) and 69 per cent at GCSE. Nine Oxbridge offers for 2016. Maths is very popular, as is biology, and also art and DT. Computing now introduced. Latin and classical civilisation are offered at A level and GCSE as part of a rich choice that also includes three modern languages, politics and drama/theatre studies. Pupils take a national standardised assessment on entry and the data is used to examine value-added at GCSE. The overall value-added scores have been consistently above national averages, with 2015 data suggesting that pupils achieve approximately half a GCSE grade better in each subject than would normally be expected from their baseline scores.

There is currently a huge drive in teaching and learning – 'persistent innovation shared across subjects,' is how one senior leader described the growing aspirational culture. The leadership team is determined to share the expertise that is already in the school more widely and is encouraging teachers to engage with other outstanding schools. Teachers model the excitement of the intellectual life for the young people. This is a dynamic place to be working and it is out to attract the top teachers nationally. Hard work and commitment are seen as the norm for both staff and students.

Reporting has recently changed to reflect effort as much as actual achievement. Parents are taking a bit of time to adjust to the new timetable and format. Everyone is monitored carefully through regular, formal and informal assessments and there is a particular drive to ensure that the scholars are strong academic role models for the rest of the school. House tutors, year group tutors and the pastoral team actively discuss the effort grades with students after each reporting event and swift action plans are implemented if a student is not exceeding expectations. Reports no longer have target grades – everyone can aspire to top grades. There is an innovative academic enrichment programme before lessons start, aimed at introducing students to new ideas. The scholars attend but it is also open to all senior pupils.

There is an experienced learning skills department offering support in a range of ways. Emphasis is placed on encouraging students to become independent learners. Some pupils find that a short course of half a dozen lessons is all they need to give them a boost and set them on their way. Typically, these sessions cover study and revision skills and exam technique. Others may require lessons over a longer period that cover language skills and problem-solving. Students are taught mainly in small groups or in one-to-one half-hour weekly sessions. In specific cases there may also be some additional support from external agencies. Students are not withdrawn from core subjects. Many of the lessons take place before or after school, or during the lunch break, or for older pupils during study periods. There is no charge for support. One parent with a bright but underachieving boy who had hated his previous school described the learning skills department as 'amazing'. It had turned her son around completely – he now loves school and is doing very well. Perhaps more importantly, he no longer needs the additional support.

Departments have impressive departmental libraries, some more extensive than others. Sixth formers value working in these spaces as well as in the school library, which focuses more on fiction as a result.

Games, options, the arts: Everyone we spoke to said there is something for everyone. The games facilities are wonderful. A new building (the Keyes Building) incorporates a state of the art, national standard sports hall, indoor climbing wall and a gym to die for. The architecturally exciting Michael Baker boathouse juts out over the river which edges the school and, across the river next to the Worcestershire County Cricket Ground, there are extensive playing fields. The boathouse is so stunning that it is also in demand for small concerts and other events. There is every opportunity both to participate and to excel in a range of sports. Keen sportspeople represent the county and there have also been national successes. Dance is taken seriously by both boys and girls and is benefitting from a new dance studio with sprung floor.

Music, as you would expect in a school with close links to a cathedral, is strong. A large number of students learn instruments and there are lots of ensembles, choirs and orchestras. The school has a variety of venues for concerts including the wonderful College Hall, the old monastic refectory dating in part from the 12th century.

There is lots of drama – a big annual production and smaller ones, in the 300 seater theatre or the brand new drama studio, which boasts top quality up-to-the-minute technology. Art is very popular and there are excellent examples around the school. A level artists have their own studio space.

A few of the other highlights, according to some pupils, are the CCF, D of E, Model United Nations, dance club and an annual Jaguar Landrover activity to build a 4x4. We suspect if we had spoken to other groups we would have had another list because there is such a rich range.

The school runs a lot of trips, both domestically – the school has its own outdoor education centre in Wales – and overseas.

Background and atmosphere: A 16th century foundation, originally the choir school for the cathedral, today's school nestles behind Worcester Cathedral and the heart of the community is College Green. For such a city centre site, it is extraordinarily well hidden from view, and that may partly explain why it feels like a world of its own that cocoons students and adults alike. Buildings range from 12th century to 2016, but it is by no means the hotch-potch that it sounds. Each century has produced its own architectural gems and the overall effect is one of great charm; tradition shoulder to shoulder with the contemporary. The classics and Latin departments are housed in the medieval Edgar Tower, accessed via a romantically precipitous spiral staircase. The ascent is worth it just for the views over Worcester. It is possibly not a site for a permanently physically disabled child.

There is a palpable excitement about the school. The sense of a British cathedral tradition is in the air the children breathe, but there is also the feeling of a school gathering itself for a leap forward from this wonderfully secure and comforting position into a more high-octane stratosphere. Parents repeatedly told us it was the feel of the school that attracted them, and that the close links with the cathedral create more than just a religious heritage but also a deep sense of respect that comes from tradition. There are a small but increasing number of Muslim families choosing the school because they believe it enhances the values they foster at home.

The historic boarding aspect of the school has left its mark both in the strong house system and in the rich extracurricular life. King's feels more like a seven day a week school than most city day schools. It is increasingly outward looking. Pupils have always been encouraged to develop a sense of service to the wider community. This is now both global and local; there are links to the Himalayas, providing educational and medical resources, and close connections are fostered with the local business community.

Parents, teachers and students speak of the exceptionally warm relationships that the school generates. 'There is a place for everyone,' one parent told us. 'My children couldn't be more different but they both feel a close part of the school community and so do I'. 'This is a school with a heart and soul', one relatively newly arrived teacher observed. There is a strong sense of community and inclusivity.

Pastoral care, well-being and discipline: The school has used its past boarding structure to excellent effect. Years 7 and 8 operate as a slightly separate group with a form structure; then, when pupils enter year 9, the full house system kicks in. This means that the school can use the early years to build a sense of belonging and identity amongst all the children, who enter not only from the two junior schools but also from a lot of other feeder primaries. Parents confirm that younger pupils are very happy to share concerns with sixth formers as well as staff and we witnessed the huge excitement and affection generated when our senior guide bumped into a group of year 8s that he mentored. Pupils all spoke about how much they appreciated really getting to know well students in other year groups. While many schools use the house system to stimulate competition, the heart of the system at King's seems to beat around the importance of relationships – though of course the competitions are there too.

Parents feel that house staff handle any pastoral concerns very discretely and also promptly. There is also a school counsellor. Discipline is along fairly conventional lines – 'we are tough when we have to be,' one member of the senior leadership team told us. Parents feel there are few discipline problems and when there are, parents are fully involved and generally supportive of the school's line.

Pupils and parents: The school has been co-ed for a number of years and it feels like that. Pupils are unpretentious and charming, very aware of how fortunate they are to be at such a distinctive school. A number of parents told us that it was the demeanour of the senior pupils that had clinched their decision to send their offspring to King's. There is a very attractive air of relaxed confidence about them – you feel they are comfortable with themselves and the world. Former pupils flock back to the school, sharing all sorts of experiences and expertise with the present young people. Pupils travel considerable distances to attend and there are signs, which the head intends to fuel, of families moving out of the home counties for the school. We could well understand why a family who had the option would make that move. Family backgrounds are mixed – some old Worcestershire moneyed families, professionals, business people and those who need the bursary support to keep children there. It is not particularly mixed ethnically, reflecting the Worcester population rather than that of the wider West Midlands, but the Muslim families that are there say there is no hint of racial prejudices.

Entrance: About two-thirds join from the two junior schools, King's St Alban's and King's Hawford. Parents say the transition is very easy for them. The school goes out of its way through the pastoral structure to ensure everyone quickly feels part of the community.

Entry is primarily at 11+ but there are places at 13+ and 16+. At 11, entry is by examination in maths, English and verbal reasoning. In the sixth form, it is dependent on GCSE results, a cognitive abilities test and an interview.

Exit: Just over a quarter left after GCSEs in 2016, a very few more at end of year 12. About 95 per cent go on to university and many get into the top ones. Currently the most popular destinations are Exeter, Birmingham, Bristol and Loughborough, and a growing number are getting Oxbridge places – eight in 2016. The range of subjects is genuinely wide, including all the main academic subjects, medicine, engineering and also applied academics such as real estate and rural management.

Money matters: Fees about average for a large day independent school outside London. In 2016, 20 11+ academic scholarships, three music scholarships; four academic exhibitions and four music exhibitions were awarded. For 13+ entry, five academic scholarships, one music and five exhibitions were awarded and at 16+ there were seven academic scholarships and two leadership awards. Both new entrant and hardship bursaries are available up to 100 per cent of fees, with up to 90 pupils generally getting bursary funding. The head's aim to wider access includes a drive to increase bursaries.

Remarks: This is definitely a school on a journey. It has taken the new head a bit of time to get everyone on board, but now they are. He wants to make it the school that people move out of the south east for and we think he will do it. The environment and pupils can't help but charm, and there is a sense of revving up to take on the national big names in independent education. It is becoming the go-to school for ambitious teachers, which can only make it that much more attractive to parents and their children.

The King's School in Macclesfield

Cumberland Street, Macclesfield, Cheshire SK10 1DA

Pupils: 1,206 • Ages: 3–18 • Sixth form: 240 • C of E

Fees: £12,225 pa

Tel: 01625 260000
Email: admissions@kingsmac.co.uk
Website: www.kingsmac.co.uk

Headmaster: Since 2011, Dr Simon Hyde MA DPhil (late 40s). Born in Macclesfield and an old boy, degree in modern history at Oxford, doctorate there and at the University of Bonn plus a bit of teaching, history master at Loughborough Grammar for three years, swift ascent to senior teacher and head of humanities at Oakham, deputy head at Haberdashers' Aske's Boys, Herts, for seven years, where he was responsible for school development and strategic planning.

Approachable, balanced, financially shrewd, good sense of humour, ambitious in a realistic way for the school, appreciative of staff. High approval rating from all the parents we spoke to, who praised his communication skills – 'a breath of fresh air', 'very impressive and dedicated', 'terrific..not a strutter..makes the parents chuckle in the first five minutes'. Has seized the opportunity to make a number of new senior appointments (enjoys full backing of governors) – young energetic types: previous deputy head (who, sadly, died in Dr Hyde's first year) replaced by two, one for academics, the other i/c development – 'to take a long view'; overall director of sport; head of IT (much to do here). In his first year taught a year 10 history and lower sixth politics group to establish his teaching credentials to staff and pupils – clearly loves teaching.

Very keen for school to be centred in the local community – working with council to support its regeneration plans, encourages sixth form outreach work with feeder primaries and community use of facilities. Wants to acquire funds to invest in infrastructure improvements (new Astro and sports centre, better IT) and extend bursaries, and to raise academic expectations (without losing any of the fantastic extracurricular opportunities). Would like the pupils to 'look smart and have fun'.

Judges national and international debating competitions (ran the regional ESU Mace and judges at world schools comps). Interested in German culture and likes reading historical and detective fiction (the classy Swedish kind, Henning Mankell's Wallender series, so definitely on the side of the angels).

Junior school head since 2009, Mrs Caroline Hulme-Mckibbin BEd (early 40s), educated at Altrincham Girls' Grammar and Homerton College, Cambridge. Taught in state primaries in Trafford then at King's Junior when co education introduced; became academic head. After a career break to have family returned in 2003 as vice principal; 2005 head of Alderley Edge School for Girls' junior section. Friendly and easy to talk to, teaches RS, art, PSHE and ICT to various years and runs philosophy club, about which she is 'passionate'. Husband a business consultant, two girls of 13 and 15 at Altrincham Girls' Grammar. Interests include netball umpiring, theatre, reading. Wants children to believe they can do 'anything they set their minds to', and to think flexibly.

Academic matters: Diamond structure – co-ed infant and junior school, single sex years 7-11, co-ed sixth. Achieves well above national average in reading, writing and maths at key stages 1 and 2 (covers national curriculum with extras); sets for maths all years; more specialist teaching in juniors – French, music and and sport; homework from year 3. Infants do EYFS curriculum plus French and music – all achieve expected level for age and many achieve higher. Emphasis on developing learning and independent thinking skills. No noticeable gender gap, though girls tend to do better at writing, boys at maths – lots of extra reading and writing activities for boys to develop skills, more boys at level 6 in literacy recently. Max class size 20-24 – may split into smaller groups for focus work. Happy, lively children wearing version of senior school uniform.

Very consistent at A level – 2016: 78 per cent A*-B, 51 per cent A*/A. Wide range of academic subjects (no IB nor vocational options) including economics, business studies, government and politics, geology, psychology, philosophy, sport and PE, computing as well as IT, Latin and classical civilisation (small but steady numbers). History and psychology very popular, then biology, economics, maths, chemistry; no drama, but can do theatre studies in year 13 extended studies programme, which allows a fifth AS in, eg, critical thinking, or LAMDA, public speaking, Japanese, sports leadership qual; all complete ECDL then too. Max class size 15, but year 13 sets can be as small as five. Much proficient use of electronic whiteboards throughout, but we enjoyed the English language class demonstrating that low tech skilful questioning can also engage students successfully.

GCSE very consistent too – 2016: 59 per cent A*/A; all do at least nine, with a modern lang (Spanish most popular); can do separate sciences; options include drama, religion & philosophy (excellent results); all work on ECDL. Gender divide closing here (but not at A level).

Very broad curriculum in year 7 – 17 subjects, including three modern langs (French, German, Spanish – several native speakers on staff), choose two in year 8, two or three in year 9; setting in maths from year 7; max class size 25; children encouraged to go beyond homework. Separate sciences in year 9 and have to choose two from art, music, technology and drama. Praise for teachers from a disconcertingly poised and articulate, very new year 7 boy – 'They're fun and good at what they do'; 'They're firm but help you understand,' added a voice from year 9; 'You're encouraged to learn independently, not just rely on the teacher,' from a year 13. According to parents, the teachers know their pupils well as individuals, expect them to work hard, do the best they can, but recognise not all will excel. Various kinds of commendations for especially good work or effort – certificates, letters and postcards to parents, assembly presentations. Several computer suites, huge language lab in girls' division with masses of PCs.

All departments impressively active outside the classroom – workshops, trips, lecture visits, science shows, exchanges; success in a wide range of external competitions; psychology department has 'adopted' a female Bonobo at Twycross Zoo. Lively English – strong creative writing, eg slam poetry workshop, literature quizzes, play trips, videoed performances of book reviews for World Book Day by year 7-9 classes, participation in BBC News School Report Day; trip to BBC at Salford for boys to work with film-making equipment.

Scholars have extensive enrichment programme – eg extra modern language in year 9 or Latin; some activities run by sixth formers, who create and deliver workshops at feeder junior schools; residentials on very stimulating topics going well beyond the curriculum for years 8-11.

SENCo confident school can accommodate mild versions of dys-strata, Asperger's, ADD/ADHD, visual and hearing impaired plus physical disability (but boys would find the last more problematic, owing to the geography of their part of the site). She is a qualified dyslexia and literacy specialist, with two p/t dyslexia specialists and TAs for class support, in and outside class. Extra charge for individual dyslexia session (pairs possible); all departments have a member of staff who links with learning support department. Infant and junior division learning support co-ordinators overseen by foundation head of learning support. All year 7s and later entries screened for dyslexia. Well resourced generally – school 'happy to provide what's needed'. Homework club at lunchtime provides refuge for less secure pupils.

Games, options, the arts: Very strong sports – 25 acres of playing fields (main ones for matches, Derby Fields, one mile away); Astros with floodlighting; four new netball courts for girls; boys' and girls' divisions have large gyms but no modern sports; hall (yet). Wide range – the usuals plus golf, sailing, orienteering, fencing, skiing: caters for the keen and those who just want enjoyment. Very successful rugby (boys and girls), hockey, trampolining, netball and cheerleading: witness a cabinet crammed with elaborate, glittering red, blue and silver trophies (no English modesty here) – a shelf literally collapsed beneath their weight; riding, swimming (despite having to use the town's leisure centre). A 2012 women's Team GB gymnast, two girl British biathlon champions; several pupils represent their county or region. Girls' and boys' sports facilities recently upgraded – include county-size Astro, half-size Astro, cricket nets and four tennis courts.

Music huge and very impressive – full and string orchestras, various bands, including jazz – Big Band highly regarded locally; various choirs; lots of concerts at school and in the community; participation in youth orchestras (Halle,Wigan jazz, Stockport symphony, guitar ensemble). Some in Cheshire and national youth choir; recent tour to Budapest. Wide range of music including film, blues and barbershop.

Unusually ambitious plays produced – Cyrano de Bergerac, Candide, The Rivals, Arturo Ui (a girl took lead role, another plays in first cricket team); biannual musical; art department creates excellent sets and props. Whole school productions plus separate boys' and girls' ones; years 8-10 panto. Years 5-6 production of Guys and Dolls (ambitious).

Tremendous multi media art (we saw more 3D than 2D), displayed throughout the school – we were struck by some interesting glass work (own kiln, gets remnants from local window company), very realistic cakes made of coloured felt on a stand and expressive year 8 ceramic masks. A level students have produced video and sound installation exam pieces. Annual residential in North Wales; 12 students selected for Cheshire GCSE gifted and talented residential. Busy DT – talks, trips, competitions, eg Lego League. Junior art and DT in darkish Portakabin (school says light on a sunny day).

Heaps of (mixed) societies and activities – D of E, sixth form community action, sound technology, arts and philosophy soc, European youth parliament, Amnesty International, debating, fair trade, Arabic. Junior clubs in school day run by teachers – eg puzzle,drama, construction. After-school sports practices run by staff plus some after-school clubs run by external agencies (with charge), eg golf, Spanish, drama. Vigorous financial arm – Young Enterprise, investors club – 30 teams across the three divisions competed in student challenge, sixth form economics department honoured by Bank of England for 10 years' outstanding contribution to their National Target 2.0 competition. Sixth form council; charities and social committee raises thousands of pounds; sixth formers help run clubs for younger pupils in senior and junior schools. Good careers programme – work experience week for all in year 10, more possible in sixth form, one full-time careers officer.

Fab trips – Cerne, skiing in Colorado (pricy), château study week in Normandy for sixth form linguists (tasty), also (mixed) chateau trip at end of year 7 (memorable); year 13s can do work experience in France with a company, returning just before their oral exam. Rugby tour to Canada, hockey to South Africa, history trip to China, diving in Egypt, World Challenge to India. Very testing outdoor activities trips – coasteering (involves jumping off cliffs into the sea – must be heart-stopping for parents), canoeing, surfing; mixed ages for these leading to friendships across years. The pupils we met all very appreciative of this wealth of opportunities – the only downside was finding enough time to fit in all they wanted to do.

Background and atmosphere: Founded by Sir John Percyvale, Lord Mayor of London, in 1502, as a grammar school. Moved to present site in 1854; in 1946 became independent fee-paying school. Girls were introduced into the sixth form in 1986 and in 1992 new girls' and (by now) co-ed junior divisions established in refurbished ex-Macclesfield High School in Fence Avenue, about a mile away, followed by infant department in 2007. Lovely views of the Peak District (but some drab corridors in the girls' section). C of E with ecumenical ethos.

The boys' and sixth form campus is very large, mostly pleasant red-brick or sandstone and harmonious modern additions around a central green fringed with trees. A bridge over a street leads to recent, £2.5 million sixth form block and practice pitches. Colourful, attractively cluttered Alan Cooper library with masses of magazines and DVDs as well as books, wooden beamed sixth form study area on upper floor, honours board for First World War war dead on wall, with an OB's medals beneath it. Separate junior library with lots of fiction. 'The school will get you any magazines, newspapers and books you need,' according to a sixth former. Sixth have common room, study area and café in own centre.

Separate girls' division (370 girls, three forms of 25 per year) and boys' (500 boys, four forms of 25) reduces gender stereotyping re subject choices – several boys choose art and girls maths and science at A level – and allows flexibility of teaching approaches; year 11 house captains and prefects allow more and earlier opportunities to develop leadership skills, eg mentoring younger pupils, supplemented by plenty of co-ed activities and trips.

Junior school has spacious, well-resourced classrooms with colourful displays throughout. Extensive grounds overlooking hills; uses main site facilities – assembly hall, IT suite, library. Outdoor classroom – a wildlife study area, the Gingko meadow. Charming play area for EYFS with little willow beehives (for children, not bees).

Academics well balanced by the extracurricular – head of boys' division observed that the introduction of music at start and end of assemblies encouraged respect for more than just sporting prowess: all achievements celebrated. School council meets every three weeks, issues frequent questionnaires to canvass views, proposals heeded. Parents and pupils feel it has a friendly atmosphere. Food praised for quality and choice (smart cards used); sixth allowed into town in lunch hour.

Almost all the pupils do look very smart – indeed we wondered whether one very elegantly turned out sixth former in suit with waistcoat was a member of staff (but were relieved to see at least one boy with a tie veering towards half mast).

Pastoral care, well-being and discipline: Older pupils do reading work with juniors, helps transition to senior school. Infants have playtime buddy system – year 2 helpers in red caps, plus 'buddy bench'. Year 6 taster day (our year 11 tour guides still remembered their fish, chips and chocolate cake lunch); year 7s said older pupils very helpful if you get lost; bonding form residential trip early in first term. Sixth formers train as peer supporters for years 7-9. We were assured bullying not a problem – the school would stop it immediately: 'It's something King's wouldn't tolerate because it just shouldn't happen'. Mixed age activities encourage general friendliness and there's 'always a teacher you can talk to about problems', as well as the nurse or heads of year. Sixth in tutor groups of 12; induction morning and welcome evening organised by year 13s for new year 12s.

We were pleased to see the 'every child matters' values displayed in the cheerful entrance hall – be healthy, make a positive contribution, enjoy and achieve, economic well-being, staying safe – especially now they have receded into the background at the Department for Education. Weekly award for children who have shown especially positive qualities in memory of former deputy head boy who died at 12 years.

Pupils and parents: Extensive catchment area, about 20 mile radius – lots of bus routes, 10 minute walk from train station to both sites. Three-quarters white British. Lively, confident, happy and energetic pupils. According to head of girls' division, 'Quirkiness and slight eccentricities are liked', girls of different types 'rub along well' – but they need to want to learn, to be happy.

From various backgrounds (majority professional, some farming families and a sizeable minority of blue-collar workers) – 'very rounded parents,' one told us; AstraZeneca based locally, also commuter belt for airline companies at Manchester Airport. Praise for speed of response to queries – 'totally fabulous lady in the office, who will put you in touch with everyone you need to communicate with'; 'Teachers get back to you soon if you phone'; email alerts, regular letters with email addresses of people to contact.

Entrance: Infants' (3-7 years) places offered by date of application (registration from birth). Juniors: full day at school in January – assessment in literacy, numeracy and VR in morning (looking for above average ability), afternoon activities with a regular class. Before this report on academic progress, interests and potential requested from current head. Numbers rise in years

K

3-6 – some influx from state schools, often in year 5. External candidates who join King's Juniors before or at the start of year 5 no longer need to sit the 11+ entrance exam for transfer to senior school; later joiners and outsiders take 11+ exam mid January – English, maths and VR; plus science and languages for year 9; the last minus VR for year 10 plus interview with child and parents. Belongs to Greater Manchester Consortium of schools, so follows its timetable for year 7 applicants (check deadline dates on website). Roughly 10-15 per cent entry to sixth from outside – need at least four As and two Bs at GCSE, plus interview (parents as well) and reference from current school.

Exit: Virtually all juniors to senior school – need to sit entrance exam; regularly win scholarships (strong music). Some preparation in year 6, but not 'slaves to the entrance exam' (hooray!)

Some 10-20 per cent leave post GCSE – mainly to take vocational courses at FE colleges; some may want a more relaxed, less structured atmosphere.

After A level students depart to a wide range of universities – Nottingham most popular, then Nottingham Trent, Manchester, Newcastle and Birmingham; six Oxbridge 2016 and five medics (current hopefuls praised help with preparation). Broad mix of subjects including biomedical sciences, veterinary sciences, geography and law.

Money matters: Means-tested bursaries – strong performance in entrance exam needed; scholarships for outstanding performance – worth £1200pa; two music scholarships awarded at time of entrance exam worth £600pa towards cost of musical tuition – need at least grade 3. Quincentenary bursaries for new sixth formers. Sibling discount.

Remarks: Interesting marriage of traditional values – suggested by cabinets of silver cups, old whole school photos and honours boards in reception – with progressive educational approaches. Dedicated, astute heads augur well.

Kingsbridge Community College

Balkwill Road, Kingsbridge, Devon TQ7 1PL

Pupils: 1,383 • Ages: 11–18 • Sixth form: 329

Tel: 01548 852641
Email: admin@kingsbridgecollege.org.uk
Website: www.kingsbridgecollege.org.uk

Principal: Since 1998, Roger Pope, originally from Bristol, studied English at Cambridge. After teaching in Oxfordshire, he spent four years in Hong Kong, then headed home to be head of English at a school in Somerset. Last stop before Kingsbridge Community College (KCC) was a deputy head role at John Bentley School, Wiltshire.

Married with three children, all former KCC pupils, two are now at Oxford and the other is at King's College. Roger is a very happy customer of the school, he says proudly. One of the key words at KCC is 'calm' and Roger himself seems exactly that, calm. 'He is empathetic and approachable for students and parents and at the same time maintains discipline and standards,' one parent told us. Another added, 'The head teacher is superb, very highly regarded in the community.' After 17 years here, KCC is undoubtedly his home from home, and he's obviously happy here. Hobbies? Dingy-sailing in local Salcombe on Saturdays.

KCC is now part of a multi-academy trust that includes Dartmouth College and four primary schools. Roger is executive principal of the trust, plus he is on the board of regional head teachers. KCC was one of the first schools to be designated as a teaching school, and over the last two and half years over 600 people have been trained here. Roger says this keeps them at the forefront of teaching and ensures they are all continually developing.

Since Roger became head, the college has benefited from an impressive amount of funding and a complete makeover. Most recently there has been the addition of a new science centre, plus an all-weather pitch with floodlighting. The school has some of best facilities we've seen in the area. Ofsted rated KCC outstanding, and parents believe the staff are the key to its success; 'Roger is amazing. And so are the teachers. They all work unbelievably hard, in and out of school hours, and show an unwavering commitment to the development of the students.'

He is spending increasing amounts of time on his role as executive principal of the multi-academy trust.

Academic matters: In 2016. 64 per cent A*-B grades at A level. At GCSE, 79 per cent achieved 5+ A*–C grades including maths and English (39 per cent A*/A grades). Most subjects are taught in ability sets. A language, either French or Spanish, is compulsory, as is RE and a GCSE in IT business and communication systems. Twenty-five options at A level plus BTecs in science, sports, music, media and design. The college also offers work-based learning programmes, with local placements in childcare, customer service, business administration and retail.

Maths and science are very popular at A level – there are two or three sets for each subject. There are currently 90 students taking chemistry – that's one in four sixth formers. This may have something to do with the new science block, opened in March 2015. There are 12 practical labs that are designed to encourage working together in groups, pairs or as a class. To celebrate the opening of the building, there was a Science Week. Students made rockets, got involved in dissections and ate insects from Paignton Zoo. The week ended with the annual Saturday Science event when families came along too. Two of the younger KCC students (aged just 12 and 13) recently won the Faraday Challenge for building the best rocket – their launch vehicle, equipped with LED warning lights and brakes, sent their rocket more than 4m into the air.

A new project, the Learning Café for year 11 students, has been a huge success at KCC. The staff here obviously know that the way to a teenager's heart is through their stomach. So in exchange for some decent grub, pupils turned up regularly, and in their droves, for their revision classes. One parent explained to us, 'I have been extraordinarily impressed by the support his year group has received throughout the GCSE period. This has included (a) an evening explaining revision techniques and approaches to parents (invaluable); (b) after-school Learning Café for all subjects; (c) continual revision sessions throughout the exam period itself; (d) additional exam/revision sessions including on a Sunday which I thought was well beyond the call of duty; (e) Facebook updates and reminders for students.' Another said, 'I know that the school has excellent GCSE results and is constantly striving to improve them, but this year, as a parent of a GCSE child, I really saw the commitment, time and investment that all the teachers put in – not just for the students but for the parents as well.'

The learning support department is in the student support centre. There are 18 TAs and specialist teachers providing one-to-one, group or in-class support. There is a lower than average number of pupils with SENs at KCC. However, that doesn't mean that the facilities and teaching are not of a high standard.

In the English centre, built in 2010, there are small rooms used solely for one-to-one literacy sessions. Ofsted said, 'Very effective and targeted support for students with learning difficulties and/or disabilities, particularly in literacy and numeracy skills, allows them to make outstanding progress.' One parent, whose child has recently been diagnosed with dyspraxia, said, 'KCC staff have faith in his abilities and understand how to manage and motivate him to do his best.... In fact many of the subject teachers have gone above and beyond to provide [him] with extra support and mentoring.'

Games, options, the arts: Great sports facilities and lots of success all round. On site there's a gym, a floodlit all-weather pitch, playing fields, a sports hall, tennis, netball and basketball courts and a dance studio. They use the swimming pool in town. One parent told us, 'Football has always been the poor relation in terms of sports at the school – rugby is king here.' The year 9 rugby team represented Devon in a non-selective state school competition, and one boy not only plays for Exeter Chief U15s, he's also been selected by England Rugby to take part in a development camp. The girls are also doing well; the year 10 netball team won a recent tournament and both the boys' and girls' badminton teams reached the county finals. However, one parent said, 'Most team sport clubs tend to end up just being populated by the kids who are best at that sport. Another team for the less able would be good and may encourage others to take up things they thought they weren't good at.' Surfing is unsurprisingly big and KCC was crowned champions again at the South Devon Inter Schools Surf Competition. It also includes the taekwondo world champion and the judo national champion, plus two brothers who have just taken part in a GB ski camp. Outdoor pursuits like Ten Tors and Duke of Edinburgh are very popular, as are gymnastics and dance. Last year's house gym and dance show saw 164 students taking part in, choreographing and organising their own entries into the competition, bringing sport, music and dance together.

Incredibly high standard of artwork displayed around the school. On our visit we saw scary clay pieces entitled Man and Machine, contemporary dresses by the textiles students, kitchen designs by the graphic designers and superimposed photos of trees by the budding photographers. A recent exhibition in town called Sixth Sense saw the highest numbers of external visitors ever. Sixteen students from year 10 were selected to exhibit their work at the Centre for Creative Industries at Exeter College. Another interesting project we heard about is called My Place. It's the collaboration of KCC students with the Exeter Royal Deaf Academy to learn more about art and British Sign Language as well as discovering their different learning environments.

The art classrooms and photography department are all very well equipped. As is the technology department – there are lathes, welding machines, a forge, a 3D printer and a laser cutter. When we were there, students were designing clocks on laptops, to be produced using the laser cutter and 3D printer. The results were impressive. We saw an amazing display of sixth form product design pieces. There was an up-cycled chair made from car doors, art deco iPod docking stations, lamps, boat storage and a POS display made for local company South Devon Chilli Farm. The facilities and equipment available to the students gives them the opportunity to be really creative. They're also encouraged to go on design residentials, most recently to London, where they not only had workshops with successful designers, they undertook a series of design and research tasks in the Science, Design and Brunel Museums. KCC regularly invites local companies to run design and manufacturing workshops to give pupils of all ages real life examples from a business point of view.

Excellent facilities for drama. Productions take place in the main hall where, at the push of a button, tiered seating for 200 people appears from the walls. Plus there's a professional lighting rig and sound booth providing opportunities for everyone, not just actors, to get in involved. Past productions include Jesus Christ Superstar and Miss Saigon; this year it's The Sound of Music. The drama studio is a similar set up to the main hall, just on a smaller scale. The drama department recently collaborated with the GCSE business students and promoted their 'fantastic' production of Richard III for the Shakespeare Schools Festival. They entered a national student marketing project competition and won second place for 'a brilliant and cohesive marketing campaign.'

The music building is yet another well-designed space: light and airy, with a huge main room and eight individual practice rooms. When we were there, a group of girls practising outside performed their latest xylophone composition for us. Apparently around 200 pupils learn instruments, plus there are choirs, a big band, a jazz band, and samba and singing clubs. There are concerts and performances all year round. Recently the year 13 BTec music students performed in their final concert, plus there was an evening of vocal musical theatre and jazz pieces from the 1930s/40s, called Puttin' on The Ritz!

Most stay on for A levels at KCC. The new sixth form centre provides them with their own study room, seminar rooms and a café with outside seating area. Upstairs is the media department equipped with Apple Macs and the latest editing software. The building has been designed to give them an insight into university life. It also celebrates their work, with displays everywhere. All sixth formers take part in leadership and enrichment activities. The choices include mentoring, supporting teachers, working for a charity, doing work experience, taking a sports leader award, and practising mock interviews. The college constantly strives to raise aspirations and parents told us, 'Study, support and advice on careers has been very good, and guidance through the UCAS medicine application was superb.' There are also regular guest speakers and visits, most recently the army medical services, the RAF cadets and the royal marines. One parent told us, 'Our studious daughter is thriving. She wants to be a midwife and is being given every encouragement.'

There's a huge range of extracurricular activities. As well as the usual sports, drama and music clubs, there's trampolining, busking, animation club, a radio station and science clinics. Students gain house points by taking part, which gives them an extra incentive. Annually there's Challenge Week for years 7 to 10, that could be anything from a week surfing to a cultural trip to Iceland. During this week, year 12 goes on work experience. All Year 9s do half a term of citizenship, where they work once a week in a setting such as a charity shop or an old people's home.

Other trips include regular visits to theatres and galleries. Annual language exchanges and ski trips plus expeditions biannually to places like Ecuador, Kenya, Argentina and Peru.

Background and atmosphere: Founded in the 16th century as Kingsbridge Grammar School, it moved to the current site in the 1930s with just 200 boys. There are now some 1,440 students, 360 in the sixth form. Kingsbridge is a traditional market town situated in the South Devon area of outstanding natural beauty. It sits at the head of its own estuary and is surrounded by lush, green rolling countryside, making it hugely popular for sailing and watersports as well as walking and hiking. In 1976, KCC became a comprehensive and was stretched across two sites, until the current head moved in and sorted it out. It's been on one site since 2002, and has had more than £14 million invested in new buildings and facilities. The head and his team have led all the funding, development and design. The library was built off of the entrance foyer to make it a focal point of the school, at its heart, so to speak. Each department has been well designed and equipped with screens and use of laptops.

Major recent developments include the new English centre, the sixth form centre and a science block. It is a fantastic learning environment, thoughtfully designed inside and out.

There are multiple cafés, so no queues at lunchtime. One specialises in pasta and curry, another in paninis and wraps. Plus there's a salad bar and a free piece of fruit with every meal. The whole site is very well maintained and has unexpected additions like a climbing wall on one side of a building, and a totem pole, made on site by local stonemasons with KCC pupils.

The school is part of a multi-academy trust (Academies South West), which is consulting on merging with another (Templer Academy Schools Trust) in 2017 to form a single trust of six primary and three secondary schools.

Students are well presented and polite; they seem happy, relaxed and calm. And they all look noticeably healthy – all that surfing and country air is obviously working wonders on these teenagers.

Pastoral care, well-being and discipline: There is a large student support centre that houses the learning support department, careers advice, pastoral support and the school nurse. We spoke to one parent who told us, 'While working briefly as a governor at the school, I had the chance to work with the pastoral care team, which left me in awe at the amount of effort they put in to help the development of children less fortunate than my own.' Another said, 'KCC is in a relatively well off area, but of course there are pockets of deprivation – not uncommon in rural areas – and I think it's very important to note that KCC doesn't just work with "nice middle class kids" – they constantly strive to get every child to achieve to the very best of their ability.'

Lower than average number of pupils have been excluded; the last was four years ago. The head says, 'We can't guarantee bullying won't happen, but we can guarantee we will deal with it.' They will invest as much time as necessary to try to change attitudes and behaviour at a deeper level. Recently, the head decided to mentor one troublesome lad rather than exclude him – when he left (with qualifications under his belt) he sent a card that said, 'Thank you, you changed my life.'

Pupils and parents: Due to its locality, KCC is at the centre of the community here. The majority of the teachers and staff have or have had children at the school. The catchment area doesn't sprawl across large rural areas; everyone lives within a small area, and so people tend to know each other. A fair number of families have relocated here; one mother told us, 'Before moving to the area we chose to come to Kingsbridge because of the quality of the school. We considered private schools after GCSEs but decided to stay with KCC, and in comparison to children who moved to private schools at that stage, for our children it has proved to be beneficial. It has totally lived up to our expectations.' What could be improved? 'Sixth form transport for rural areas. A big cost for parents living outside Kingsbridge.'

Entrance: Based on the designated catchment area. Good induction and settling in period, one parent told us; 'This was seamless and well managed with transition days and sporting events. [My children] were very proud to have started and to "belong" to KCC.' Another added, 'Fantastic. Made our shy daughter feel very secure.'

Entry to the sixth form requires five A*-C grades at GCSE. Entry onto NVQ Level 2 courses are by interview with no prior qualifications required. Attendance and attitude are the main criteria.

Exit: On average 75-80 per cent of pupils stay on for sixth form. Around 70 per cent of sixth formers go onto university. Four to Oxbridge in 2016. A higher than average number of students study medicine. Other popular university choices include Falmouth and Plymouth.

Money matters: Pupil Premium funding is available. There is also a trust fund to help with trips.

Remarks: A large, but friendly community school. Fantastic facilities and so many opportunities for all types. KCC works on traditional values like respect and good behaviour, but provides cutting edge opportunities – not just equipment, but also their approach to learning. If you live in Kingsbridge, you are very lucky indeed.

Kingsley School

Northdown Road, Bideford, Devon EX39 3LY

Pupils: 400 • Ages: 2–18 • Sixth form: 68

Fees: Day £5,685 – £12,900; Boarding £16,485 – £25,020 pa

Tel: 01237 426200
Email: admissions@kingsleyschoolbideford.co.uk
Website: www.kingsleyschoolbideford.co.uk

K

Headmaster: Since January 2017, Mr Pete Last, previously deputy head pastoral, senior housemaster, head of boarding and housemaster of a boys' house at Stowe School. Educated at Alleyn's School, London and Cambridge, where he read geography, Mr Last has also completed a masters in educational leadership at Buckingham University. Married to Debs, an art specialist. Both from Kent but met in India while working at Hebron International School in Ooty. Returned after six years to teaching posts at Lord Wandsworth College in Hampshire, also running a boarding house, before moving to Stowe after nine years there. Mr Last is passionate about education (and Arsenal) and 'is looking forward to helping to lead Kingsley forward into a new and exciting chapter of its history.'

Head of junior school: Since 2014, Jane Bruce. Previously head of prep at Millfield, Somerset. Specialist SEN teacher with a diploma in dyslexia. Teaches English to year 6, classes in the Grenville Dyslexia Centre, plus in-house teacher training across the whole school. She believes the staff work well together, taking classes for either the junior or senior schools when needed and sharing knowledge. Parents agree, 'It is a friendly school and the staff seem to work well together for the good of the pupils and the school as a whole.' Some classes are small and are currently boys predominate. Jane recognises that this can worry some parents, but believes it could actually give them an advantage. Year groups are united to make up the sports teams for example, and ultimately make friends across the school. Other parents are not so worried; one said, 'I felt that the staff took time to get to know [my children] – the real benefit from having small classes.'

Academic matters: Throughout the school, teaching is based around the national curriculum, 'but not as a be-all and end-all in itself.' For example, 4-6 year-olds enjoy swimming, forest schools, arts and crafts and French. Afternoon performances of French songs are sell-outs, apparently. The 7-11 year-olds have classes in food technology, personal, social, health and moral education, Spanish and design technology.

Unwilling to give out current exam results, though A levels tend to average 20-30 per cent As and 40-50 per cent A*-Bs, with under 30 per cent A*/A at GCSE.

Fourteen A levels on offer, plus BTecs in outdoor education and performing arts, a Cambridge Technical in sport, a diploma in food, and the Extended Project Qualification (EPQ). French, Spanish and theatre studies offered if sufficient demand. Maths is strong and around 60 per cent opt for it at A level. Other top performing subjects include English and geography. A language is compulsory up to Year 9. BTec in engineering is available at GCSE level, replacing DT.

Kingsley School admits 25 per cent dyslexic pupils. Other SENs are catered for, mainly those associated with dyslexia, like behavourial issues, but nothing too complex. The Grenville Dyslexia Centre is on the school campus. The centre has just been refurbished and apart from classrooms, there's an ICT suite and a colourful common room. Pupils are taught English and maths in dyslexia-only classes, by qualified SEN teachers. Classes are small, 5-10 pupils. One-to-one tuition, and support in after-school prep sessions is also available. One parent commented, 'My younger child who is dyslexic has been given strong support from the dyslexic centre staff and enjoys attending it. It is a friendly and inviting place to be and recently had extras added to entice the pupils, such as tea and toast! We (both parent and pupil) have been asked (questionnaire form) how the centre could improve on the support and teaching and so I can see that they are striving to keep up and ahead with pupils' and parents' expectations.'

K

Following comments from recent inspections, the school has addressed the way the school staff and Grenville staff share information. There are now regular and formal meetings where teachers exchange information on individual pupils, and discuss how best to teach them. Teachers use visual aids for all lessons, for example, and reminders of current topic or homework tasks are clearly displayed on the wall. IEPs are followed and individual attention or needs are highlighted. One teacher told us this is all done in a subtle unobtrusive way 'without anyone blinking an eye.' One parent said, 'It is a friendly school and the staff seem to work well together for the good of the pupils and the school as a whole.'

The results are good, the value added is impressive; SEN pupils do well, they are given good support in classrooms and also exams. One pupil who left recently with A level grades A*, A and B, was told by his previous school he would never amount to anything. With hard work and the specialist support of the dyslexia centre he has more than proved them wrong. Pupils are given the chance to opt for fewer subjects, sometimes dropping a language, if it helps them to focus. There is 'no stigma' at Kingsley and children are given the confidence to learn. One parent said, 'Kingsley School has positively changed our son from a child who found school life very difficult. He was a boy who was very passive and feared failure, he felt that he was not an achiever and his contribution was of little value. The reason for this is that our son is profoundly dyslexic, but in the six years that he has attended Kingsley School, we have seen him grow into a very confident and happy young man.' We heard similar stories from several parents. One parent of an overseas boarder said, 'He identifies completely with the school and we are very happy to see his progress in developing self-confidence and regaining fun in learning.'

The centre's mantra is 'Don't make dyslexia an excuse.' This approach relies upon a nurturing, safe-to-learn classroom environment, and interactive, hands-on, multisensory and memorable teaching methods. In year 7 they focus on spelling and touch-typing. In years 8 and 9, the focus is reading, using a scribe and learning to use software like Dragon Dictate and Read and Write gold. And in years 10 and 11, it's speed-reading, exam strategies and dealing with exam stress. One parent confided, 'Before he started at Kingsley School at the age of 9 years, we had very little expectations for [him], but now we have a son who is a year away from taking his GCSEs and we are approaching them with a confidence for his future and that is solely down to Kingsley School.'

Games, options, the arts: In line with the school's 'quirkiness', the main sports are judo, handball and surfing. Judo is up to Olympic standard, one pupil plays handball in the U19 England team, and another is a member of the GB surfing squad. Surfers and windsurfers do well in local, regional and national competitions and pupils regularly win national titles in gymnastics, netball, judo and biathlon. The U15 girls' football team reached the finals in the North Devon schools championships, and there are regular weekend fixtures for rugby, cricket, hockey, athletics, table tennis, swimming and cross-country. Golf has just recently been introduced, too. There are three sports fields, an all-weather pitch, tennis and netball courts, a sports hall and a gym. Local sports clubs use the school's facilities out of hours, including a fencing club and Bideford Football Club.

Music, singing, dancing and drama are a big part of junior life here. The junior choir practices during the lunch break for concerts and regular performances at local nursing homes or festivals. Most pupils learn an instrument, and as well as extra singing and drama lessons, ballet, tap and modern dance are also available. Plenty of opportunities to perform with productions like Peace Child, Charlie and the Chocolate Factory and Joseph. Productions are led by years 5 and 6, but everybody gets involved making props in forest school or painting sets in art classes.

The music centre is sufficiently equipped with Apple Mac technology plus a rehearsal room and recording studio. There's a choir and a small orchestra – numbers are limited so quartets and ensembles are more common. Regular performances like 'An evening of ...The Bare Necessities...Pie Jesus...My Favourite Things to Guns and Roses...' End of term concerts and annual collaborations with the drama department include A Midsummer Night's Dream, and more recently Alice in Wonderland. Kingsley has a drama studio plus a fantastic theatre with seating for around 400 (also used by the local film club). It links to the library that is occasionally used for functions – like the Mad Hatter's Tea Party before this year's production of Alice In Wonderland. Kingsley also participates annually in the National Theatre's Connections programme and has been lucky enough to perform at the Theatre Royal, Plymouth and the Bristol Old Vic.

Art is important at Kingsley juniors and we were pleased to hear how much they make the most of their beautiful surroundings. For year 1 a typical class on natural art may involve a walk around the grounds followed by a session creating their art pieces, inspired by recent lessons on certain artists. Another class, who were inspired by a trip to a local art gallery, have been making ice sculptures. Art department commands the whole of the top floor of the main building, School House. Two huge studios, plus photography facilities. As a department, they specialise in portfolio building. Some great, and very large pieces on display, with plenty more space to fill. Sixth formers were taking advantage of the lunchtime peace on our visit. Annual exhibition at the local Burton Art Gallery.

After-school clubs and activities run Monday to Thursday from 4pm – 5pm. Activities offered includes choirs, Mandarin Chinese, judo, trampolining, sports, debating, drama, science, orchestra, surfing, yoga, gardening and the Duke of Edinburgh Award scheme. The local scouts and cubs are based on the school campus and are very popular. Plenty of local trips to places like the Eden Project, Cheddar Gorge and Exmoor. In year 6 there is a residential trip; last one was to Somerset for abseiling, grass sledging and circus skills. Senior school pupils have cultural trips to London, Paris and Iceland.

Boarding: Currently around 110 boarders from year 5, 70:30 boy:girl split, 65 per cent from overseas (two-thirds Asian and a third European). Majority are full-time boarders. Some short-term boarders from Spain and Germany, usually to brush up on their language skills for a term or two.

Three large, well looked after boarding houses on the school campus. Belvoir House, just a short walk from the main school building, is the girls' boarding house and is surrounded by sports fields, with views over the woods. Carisbrooke (junior boys) and Longfield (senior boys) are beside each other.

The houses are run by houseparents plus assistants. Most have children attending the school. There are also gap students and two house prefects, which adds big brother or sister role models to the mix. Brilliant pastoral care. One parent said, 'He felt immediately at home and still appreciates the warm-hearted atmosphere of the school and the boarding complex.' The houseparent we met in the younger boys' house really does run the house like a mum: she was friendly, welcoming and has created one of the best family homes we've seen. The fairy lights are always on when the kids come home, there's bowls of fruit and plants in the lounge, two dogs and even a boyfriend/girlfriend sofa. Next to the huge lounge there's a pool table and table tennis table. Nestled amongst the fun is an open-plan office, cleverly tucked away but also allowing an adult to be around at all times. Decent kitchen; they would like to upgrade it but the boys don't want this: they love it the way it is, apparently. Rooms are doubles or triples, the odd single for older pupils. Smallish rooms but the communal areas more than make up for them. Only one dorm, sleeps six, used for flexi-boarders or short-termers. Decent wet rooms.

Plenty of activities and opportunities to get out and about, at weekends and in the evenings. But pupils are also given the time and space 'to be kids,' including downtime and fun, just like home. No Saturday lessons but there are sports fixtures or shopping trips in the afternoons, and activities like quad biking, combat zone, cinema, bowling, climbing, theatre, zoo, theme parks and local city trips on Sundays. Chapel is held on the first and last Sunday of each half of term. As soon as the weather brightens up, surf's up, and as much time as possible is spent making the most of north Devon's beach life. Awesome. One parent told us, 'He enjoys it very much. He likes living in this big family.'

No set exeat weekend, a real plus for Forces families. Kingsley also runs its own guardianship scheme so overseas boarders can now stay at school, in their own rooms, during half-terms. Around 50 boarders are currently taking advantage of this scheme and enjoying the extra activities on offer for them.

Background and atmosphere: In January 2009, Edgehill College and Grenville College came together under the aegis of the Methodist Schools, to create a new independent school. Previously there were three independent schools in Bideford; Edgehill College was founded in 1884, Stella Maris Convent in 1929 and Grenville College in 1954. Edgehill and Stella Maris were girls' schools, while Grenville was for boys until its merger with Stella Maris in 1994.

Now there are around 250 in the senior school and 150 in the junior. School House is the main building, an inviting white building with a 'Kiss and Drop ends here' sign cheekily sending parents on their way. Inside a stairwell and lift run up the centre leading to recently refurbished science labs, classrooms and the art department. Northdown block is a separate building with classrooms and junior common rooms predominantly for younger boys. The school is 'device free' for years 7, 8 and 9. The sixth form centre is separate, in another spacious building. Well-equipped with a modern café area, social area with pool table, table football, piano and large dining table. Several study rooms for small groups, all being well-used on our visit. No uniform but there is a dress code, loosely described as 'business dress'. Sixth form social events take place throughout the year culminating in the summer ball. Leadership opportunities and positions of responsibility are available as prefects, sports captains, competitive house captains and within the boarding houses. Students are also encouraged to act as mentors to younger students. Work experience opportunities are available in the junior school.

Situated on the same campus as the senior school, the junior school has use of all facilities including a purpose-built theatre, a multi-sport gym, 25 acres of playing fields, woodland, an adventure playground and a forest school. They have their own very decent-sized hall that opens out onto their own playing field.

This small, friendly school offers a bit more than just a standard education, whether it's planting trees, or singing French songs, or introducing a new sport. They extend this invitation to other schools regularly through sports, and also the annual children's festival, packed with bands, street dances, cakes, bouncy castles, welly throwing, face painting and candy floss. And last year, they even managed to sneak a chocolate-themed week onto the curriculum. This approach to learning particularly helps children that may need some encouragement, or are struggling to learn. As one parent put it, 'Kingsley School takes the child, and has in place lots of systems and strategies to help with the development of confidence and self-esteem.'

Pastoral care, well-being and discipline: Not formally rigid, 'but clear red lines.' There is an open, and perhaps laid back approach to life at Kingsley, but that does not mean that things get overlooked. Parents said, 'We welcome very much the straight rules concerning for example, smoking, leaving the school ground and so on.' This is a small school community and along with good pastoral care including form tutors, heads of years, house parents, school sister and the chaplain, pupils are given the 'confidence that they will be heard' and 'can have their say,' even if the school doesn't always necessarily agree. As a Methodist school, Christian ethos and values are embedded into life here in a subtle rather than preached way. One parent believed, 'Pastoral care and academic encouragement are key points to the school and are their strengths I feel.'

Pupils and parents: Day pupils come from a wide local area and school buses go as far as Croyde to the north, Blackmoor Gate to the north east, North Molton to the east, Winkleigh and Torrington to the south, and Kilkhampton and Holsworthy to the south west. Termly airport buses for overseas boarders.

The school communicates well with parents with the usual channels of emails, letters and reports. Queries or concerns are responded to quickly, 'usually within a matter of a couple of hours. This has always impressed me,' one parent told us. They went on to say, 'We also have phone calls (at the start of the school year and sometimes throughout the school year) from the form tutors to make sure that there are no concerns.' Another said, 'Show my homework is brilliant for keeping up to date on homework that is due. We have regular contact with the dyslexic centre and in fact any teacher is readily available to speak either personally or via email.' Another parent went on to say, 'The teachers all seem professional and friendly and I feel that they care for the well-being of my children. I feel that they act as a team and alongside of myself, as a parent, want to encourage my children/all pupils to achieve their best.'

Entrance: Non-selective entry to junior school. There is also a nursery that offers dedicated year-round 8am-6pm care for children from three months. One family who relocated looked at several schools in the area, and said 'in the end it was decided upon Kingsley as the final say was what the children themselves wanted.' Another told us, 'When school started, the children seemed to settle in quite quickly and find their way around the school easily.'

Open days, plus taster days and nights available. Entry to senior school by entrance test and interview. Entry at sixth form is a decent set of GCSE results (some subjects have their own minimum requirement), school reports, and the right attitude.

No problems with settling in: 'From day one he absolutely loved it! For a child who finds learning so difficult we have never heard him say he doesn't want to attend,' said one parent. Another told us, 'The invite to attend school the day before school started in the autumn term was a good idea as it gave the children a chance to meet some teachers/form tutors and others from their class. When school started, the children seemed to settle in quite quickly and find their way around the school easily. I felt that the teachers took time to get to know them.' There is also a boarding induction programme which includes a local activity like climbing followed by afternoon tea and sightseeing.

Exit: Some 80 – 90 per cent of juniors go on to the senior school. Assessment is for awards and scholarships. Parents told us, 'It was a very smooth transition from Kingsley Junior School to the secondary school.' In their final year at the junior school, pupils and parents are invited to the senior school to meet teachers and have a tour, including the year 7-9 centre; a dedicated area for younger senior pupils which includes their own common room.

Some 50 per cent of day pupils leave after GSCEs to go the local free colleges. Most boarders stay on to the sixth form. Nearly all go to university eg Falmouth, UWE; others may take a gap year, go into employment, or return to their home country to continue their studies.

K

Money matters: Academic, performing arts or sports scholarships available at 11 and 13. Sixth form scholarships are based on GCSE performance, or excellence in music, drama, art and sport. Means-tested bursaries offered, plus bursaries to Forces families, and sibling discounts. In the senior school, the fees for the dyslexia department and EAL are additional.

Remarks: What teenager wouldn't want to combine school life with that of beaches, surfing and friends from around the world? That may all sound too much like fun rather than education, but Kingsley has got the balance right; a great campus, an open, caring approach, and specialist teachers. The dyslexic children at Kingsley progress further than anyone's expectations and so it's not surprising that one parent told us, 'We can honestly say it was and will remain the best decision we have made for his education.'

Kingswood School

Lansdown Road, Bath, Somerset BA1 5RG

Pupils: 768; 180 boarders • Ages: 11–18 • Sixth form: 236

Fees: Day £14,382; Boarding £22,608 – £30,999 pa

Tel: 01225 734200
Email: admissions@kingswood.bath.sch.uk
Website: www.kingswood.bath.sch.uk

Headmaster: Since 2008, Simon Morris MA PGCE NPQH (early 50s). Educated at Ipswich School (he is one of three current HMC heads – the others are Mark Bailey, high master of St Paul's, and Nick Gregory, head of Wycliffe College – to have attended the school). Read modern and medieval languages at Cambridge, then went into the City, where he qualified as a chartered accountant with Arthur Andersen. He grew up in a boarding school (his father was deputy headmaster of The Royal Hospital School) and admits that 'the call of teaching was pretty strong'. PGCE at Canterbury Christ Church University, followed by first job at Warwick School (he became head of German after a year). Head of modern foreign languages, then housemaster at The Leys. Deputy head at St John's, Leatherhead for seven years prior to Kingswood headship. 'I'm not saying that every day is easy but I have never regretted my change of career,' he says.

First-ever non-Methodist head of Kingswood. Intensely proud of the school – particularly its sense of community and breadth of opportunity. Passionate about instilling high but attainable standards in every individual and results have risen under his leadership. School isn't highly selective but head says pupils have to be 'academically able' – or as he puts it, 'doers who want to get stuck in and have a go at things'. Supported by two deputies (one academic, one pastoral). Taught languages when he first arrived but now teaches PSHCE to year 7 pupils. 'It's a brilliant way to get to know them,' he says. Visible around the school, approachable and easy to talk to – 'a round peg in a round hole,' as we said last time.

Wife Caroline teaches modern languages at Kingswood (she has lots of state school experience too) and they have three children. Elder two were pupils at Kingswood and are now at university (one doing medicine at King's College London, the other reading geography at Sheffield) and the youngest is still at the school. A keen sportsman (cricket and golf), he also enjoys travel and reading. Lives in a house on-site but family (plus labrador) decamps to their house near Axmouth in the holidays.

Academic matters: Results are easily as good as other co-ed schools with illustrious names. In 2016, 61 per cent A*/A at A level. At GCSE, 64 per cent A*/A. School says it does brilliantly on value-added – apparently in the top 20 nationally. Masses of subject choice, with 24 subjects on offer at A level and more than 20 at GCSE. Most students take three A levels (some add the EPQ) and a few, particularly mathematicians, do four. Impressive deputy head (academic) has focused on academic development and says the school does everything it can to give students 'total free choice' of A level subjects. 'We don't pigeonhole anyone here,' she says – a claim borne out by a talented artist who at the time of our visit had just won a place to study medicine yet had managed to do A level art too.

At GCSE the majority take 11 subjects, with all doing English, English literature, maths, three separate sciences (a few do double award) and religious studies. Most take at least one language (French, Spanish or German) although some requiring study support may not. Study support department has three full-time staff and runs an informal drop-in centre for students needing help with anything from managing their time to learning how to revise. Independent support programmes in place for those with specific learning difficulties such as dyslexia and dyscalculia. One mother told us: 'The school isn't just interested in the kids who are going to get three A*s at A level. They mean it when they say they are interested in children with all kinds of talents and skills.'

Games, options, the arts: Sport is a big deal here and there are lots of unbeaten teams. Main sports for boys are rugby, hockey, cricket, tennis, athletics and swimming while girls do hockey, netball, tennis, athletics, rounders, cricket and swimming. School fields at least two teams per year group, with 30 fixtures against other schools each week. Up until year 10 all pupils do a double period of PE every week, plus games. From year 11 some opt for social sports, including aerobics (80 pupils doing this when we visited), cycling, cross-country, multi-gym, orienteering, equestrian sports and more. 'We try and give them more options as they go up the school,' explains the director of sports and PE.

Great facilities, including eight rugby pitches, three cricket squares, two Astroturfs, sports hall and new pavilion. Some pitches are a half-mile walk up the hill but it keeps everyone healthy. School a tad defensive about its 100-year-old swimming pool but says it is 'a great pool to teach in'. Strong links with Bath Rugby Club and the University of Bath.

The arts are outstanding and there is an annual award ceremony for artistically talented pupils in art, drama, DT and music. A third of pupils learn a musical instrument and there's something for performers of all styles and standards. Recent highlights include a performance of Fauré's Requiem, the jazz orchestra playing at the opening event of the Bath International Music Festival and the annual Kingswood Voices Festival, which celebrates the contribution that singers make to the school life.

Drama department has two spaces – a 366-seat theatre and a drama studio. Up to 30 students take drama GCSE each year and between six and 12 do drama and theatre at A level. Three major productions a year and pupils are encouraged to get involved in lighting, sound, stage management and scriptwriting. Unusually, there's a comedy improvisation event for budding comics called Exit Stage Right, loosely based on Whose Line is it Anyway? Art is glorious. Housed in a three-storey arts and crafts style building, it boasts top-notch facilities for drawing, painting, printmaking, sculpture, ceramics and photography. Annual summer art and DT exhibition is a highlight and we saw some breathtaking work, including a vast wire sculpture of a birds' nest by year 8s, a portrait made from tights and pins and a 12-ft long drawing of hands. Sadly, the pupils' monogrammed smocks of old have given away to smart grey aprons embroidered with the Kingswood logo – 'the smocks were too hot,' says the head of art.

Boarding: Even though day pupils outnumber boarders, Kingswood feels like a co-ed boarding school with day pupils. Seven day/boarding houses, some of which are in the process of being updated. The first to be completed, Hall House (for 42 year 9 to 13 boys), is one of the most stylish boarding houses we've seen in a long time, complete with outdoor decking area, wholesome bedrooms (12 en-suite), the housemaster's prized vinyl collection in the common room and views across Bath to the Mendips. We particularly liked the kitchen rules painted on the boys' kitchen wall: 'If it smells, throw it away. If it's dirty, wash it. If you get it out, put it away. If it's on, turn it off.'

Westwood, for year 7 and 8 pupils (170 day pupils and 30 boarders), provides a gentle introduction to the big school. Homely and sprawling, the four-storey building is a hive of activity, with the housemaster's friendly border collie running around with the children after school. Girl boarders live on the second floor, boy boarders on the third, all in dormitories of six to eight and out of bounds to day pupils. The Westwood pupils are allowed to grow up in their own time and, rather sweetly we thought, are read a weekly bedtime story – Ted Hughes's The Iron Man has been a particular favourite. Boarders love the place. 'I'm an only child,' one boy told us, 'so being here is like having lots of brothers'. No Saturday school for anyone these days but a vast array of weekend activities. Sports matches on Saturdays and trips to places like Drayton Manor and Legoland on Sundays.

Background and atmosphere: The only school founded by John Wesley, who believed that education should engage the heart as well as the head, and the first Methodist one. School opened in 1748 for the sons and daughters of Wesley's friends but was soon restricted to the sons of Methodist preachers and leaders. Went co-ed again in 1974.

School moved from Bristol to its current site (just across the road from the Royal High School) in 1852 and has occupied an imposing collection of purpose-built Victorian gothic buildings on the steep northern slopes above Bath ('Satan's throne', according to Wesley) ever since. Even on a grey day, the views from the school are magnificent. Pupils from all denominations and faiths.

School is ideally placed – a 20-minute walk down the hill into the city, but with a country feel about it. Other buildings of varying age and beauty are dotted around the school's 214 acres of manicured grounds, including the chapel (too small these days to house the whole school, which gathers for religious and secular assemblies in the theatre).

Central dining in splendid gothic hall, with pupils allowed to sit where they like. Food is good, with plenty of choice. We much enjoyed the Moroccan potato salad and lemon couscous with pumpkin seeds on offer when we visited. Uniform is tidy and businesslike, with girls in black blazers, white blouses and tartan skirts and boys in black blazers, charcoal trousers and school ties. Sixth formers wear dark suits – girls in years 12 and 13 are allowed to wear natural make-up, nail varnish and modest jewellery. Sixth form housed in The Dixon, slightly scruffy but much loved sixth form block, completely with cabin-like studies, kitchen and chill-out space.

Pastoral care, well-being and discipline: Head says school is 'non-confrontational' and that discipline structures are clear. 'We are quite prescriptive in terms of what is acceptable and what isn't,' he adds. 'I refuse to be complacent but we don't have a huge discipline issue. We educate pupils to make sensible choices.' Pupils and parents agree. Parents describe pastoral care as 'outstanding' and say communication between school and home is excellent – high praise for the head's regular drop-in sessions and the school's weekly newsletter.

Impressive support structure from year 7 up. Pupils are in house-based tutor groups of around 10 (tutors change in years 8,10 and sixth form). Tutors have day-to-day responsibility for pupils but there's a raft of people to help if issues arise. These include housemasters and housemistresses, head of boarding, medical centre (open 24/7) and chaplain. PSHCE for all, often linked to assemblies. Clear system of sanctions, with emphasis on support and redirection rather than chastisement.

Prefect body is known as PR, with head boy and head girl, deputies (one deputy head boy and two deputy head girls recently) and senior prefects. School council meets once a week – recent topics of discussion range from school menu suggestions to exam timetabling issues. 'We want them to air their views,' says the deputy head (pastoral). Very comprehensive pupil and parent handbook details everything from the school's philosophy and aims to behaviour, health and dress.

Pupils and parents: Moderately to exceedingly affluent families, but not particularly posh. Lots of medics, lawyers, business people and an increasing number who have relocated to Bath from London. Around 10 per cent of pupils from overseas (more than 20 different nationalities represented).

Pupils are polite, friendly, unpretentious and confident. A mother whose two children are weekly boarders told us: 'What I love about Kingswood is that the pupils are an eclectic lot – you've got the city children, the country children and the overseas boarders. I wanted my children to grow up kindly and nicely and they really have here, while at the same time being stretched academically.' Most day pupils come from the north side of Bath (crossing the city during rush hour is horrendous and there are plenty of schools south of the river). Pupils come from as far afield as Calne, Chew Valley, Wiltshire, south Gloucestershire and north-east Bristol. Famous alumni include actor Tim Curry, director and writer Jonathan Lynn, the historian and writer EP Thompson and Reggie Tsiboe, one of the lead singers of pop band Boney M.

Entrance: Increasingly competitive, although year 7 recently expanded from four form entry to five form entry. 'More are applying but we are taking more,' says the head. Main intake is in year 7. Around 50 per cent join from own prep school (they share the same site). Others from 20 preps and primary schools (St Stephen's down the road is a major feeder). Maths, English and non-verbal reasoning tested, plus report from current school and interview. Coaching discouraged. Up to 20 pupils start in year 9, with applicants taking exams in English, maths, non-verbal reasoning, science and a foreign language, plus report from current school and interview. At sixth form stage (20 to 30 newcomers arrive in year 12) students need a minimum of four Bs and 2Cs at GCSE or equivalent.

Exit: Virtually all stay for sixth form. A handful leave, usually due to financial reasons. Almost all to university (four to Oxbridge and seven medics in 2016) – Leeds, Exeter, Birmingham, Warwick, Durham, Cardiff and Oxford Brookes popular. A few to US universities. A high achieving pupil recently opted to do an apprenticeship with Barclaycard.

Money matters: Academic and special talent (art, DT, drama, music and sport) scholarships offered at years 7, 9 and lower sixth. John Wesley awards available to boarders in year 9 and sixth form – for 'candidates who show the potential to offer a significant all-round contribution to the life of the school'. Head is keen to increase bursary provision throughout.

Remarks: A terrific school, with a culture of creativity, kindness and academic hard work. Kingswood has a strong sense of community, achieves fine results and is definitely on the up.

Knighton House School

    85

Durweston, Blandford Forum, Dorset DT11 0PY

Pupils: 123; 48 full, weekly, flexi boarders • Ages: 3–13 (boarding from 7)

Fees: Day £6,975 – £16,380; Boarding £21,600 pa

Tel: 01258 452065
Email: admissions@knightonhouse.co.uk
Website: www.knightonhouse.co.uk

Headmistress: Since 2014, Mrs Sarah Wicks, previously deputy head. BEd from the University of Hertfordshire; taught at a state primary in Mill Hill and the Royal Masonic School before joining Knighton in 1995 as head of drama and junior class teacher. She's been there ever since, rising through senior mistress to deputy and then head.

Retiring in July 2017.

Entrance: Any child welcome, more or less at any time so long as space is available. Summer term is a popular time to start and it isn't unusual for girls to come mid-year, sometimes from less happy environments. No entrance exam but the school holds non-compulsory taster days – 'more for the girls to have a look but of course it helps us understand their needs.' There is a scholarship exam, though. Families are mainly local (most from under an hour away), but some from London, plus a handful from Spain or France each term.

Exit: Most stay until 13 when they go to Bryanston (obviously convenient as they're so close), St Mary's, Shaftesbury (parents say that 'it's the same sort of friendly school') and beyond that to anywhere and everywhere, including Marlborough, Canford, St Mary's Calne, Godolphin, Leweston, Oundle, Sherborne Girls, Downe House. Good handful of scholarships (seven out of a class of 15 in 2016) – for music, art or sport as often as academics. Pre-prep boys mostly go on to Sandroyd, Clayesmore or Port Regis.

Remarks: Perched on a windy hillside just by Bryanston's back gate, this happy and quirky little school was founded in 1950 by the parents of Private Eye co-founder Christopher Booker. A rambling rectory-type house with a rather grand staircase (out of bounds), it's thought to have been the dowager home of the Portman family (Dorset worthies) and is surrounded by orchards, stables and paddocks. Mish-mash of old coach-houses, now used for labs and boarding, and stables full of ponies. Classrooms are serviceable rather than plush and there's a purpose-built multi-use hall and lavish music block. Everything looks a bit haphazard but place is bursting with displays of pupils' work and exceptionally well equipped.

Flexi-boarding is popular, and all weekend boarding is free (a major fun event, sometimes in school, sometimes a trip, is offered every weekend). Almost half the girls in the prep board and everyone gets her own bed, even the two-night-a-weekers.

Refurbished dorms for two to eight (with bunk beds) in the main house for the younger girls, who 'like the bigger dorms'. Plentiful loos, showers and even two end-to-end ancient claw-foot baths. Matron, loved by girls and parents alike, has a four-bedded sick room which girls are busy brightening up. No medical nurse, but extremely kind treatment of minor ailments. All boarding staff have first aid training and there is masses of induction and proper training for gappies (Antipodean and local). Smashing food, all locally sourced and cooked by popular chef and team. One parent told us: 'Even my super-faddy daughter actually eats it, especially with the new salad bar'. Teachers sit at the tables to supervise and teach manners and there is a regular 'French' table. Practical, if eye-catching, scarlet dungarees are worn with apparent relish by all except the top form, on trips or to the village church on Sundays. Then it's the girls' 'best' or, as they put it, 'worst' uniform of box pleated grey skirts, red jerseys, checked blouses and dark grey kilts; grey cloaks for cold weather. Oldest boarders have a flat above the labs and get quite bit more freedom: tuck cupboard, some cooking equipment and a more grown up atmosphere to suit their responsibilities and imminent transition to senior school.

Academically adventurous, with no national testing, though pretty thorough assessment, according to the latest inspection. Curriculum includes Latin (a scholars' parent regretted the recent demise of Greek) French from the second year, three sciences in very well-equipped though old-fashioned-looking labs, enjoyable English and maths. Small classes, maximum 18, with some setting in maths, science, French and English. Parents feel that bright girls are stretched and strugglers supported.

State-of-the-art IT with ambitious animations projects for everyone and masses of computer use within all areas of the curriculum. Very good SEN department with two staff, for girls with mild learning difficulties. DT is mainly cooking and sewing but with a bit of woodwork, ceramics etc thrown in for everyone. Two libraries – reference and fiction. Art is enterprising, with emphasis on cross-curricular uses and fun – lots of innovative 3D work. Junior and senior plays produced every year. Lots of clubs, including German and Spanish. There is a contingent of Spanish pupils and Knighton teachers are busy forging links via the Comenius project with Turkey and Estonia to broaden the school's outlook.

Lots of sport for those who want it, with some outstanding successes in tennis, swimming and running. However an unsporty parent told us: 'There doesn't seem to be too much emphasis on sport, which is a plus for me... but manners are very important, which is great, and all the teachers are very well spoken.' Astroturf, playing fields and a swimming pool in a converted sheep dip/storage tank on the hillside – mainly for recreation as real swimming takes place in nearby Blandford or at Bryanston.

But it's the ponies, the music and the friendliness that girls and parents find irresistible. More than half ride and one parent reported that experienced riders are very patient and encouraging with those who start riding at school. Many bring their own ponies and other girls use them too. The stables are close enough for early morning pony visits, (as are the other pet areas and the guinea pig village) and there's an all-weather arena and cross-country course. Friendliness is a defining characteristic. A new parent reported that her daughter, previously anti-school, actually jumped for joy at the end of her first school holidays, while another was delighted to find her two-mornings-a-week toddler was recognised and made a fuss of by older girls. Girls say bullying just doesn't happen 'because we like each other, not because we are told not to,' and a mother told us that a potential incident had been dealt with effectively and kindly for all concerned. The girls we met during our visit were chatty and interested, but not precociously over-confident.

Music has an attractive, dedicated building with a recital room and masses of individual practice rooms. Almost all girls have music lessons, sing and take part in different bands and groups. There's a serious orchestra and small concerts held every Friday to which parents can come. Head of music teaches individual singing and the superb chapel choir sings at the weekly Saturday service, local churches and weddings and has performed grand local venues like Milton Abbey, Lulworth Castle etc. Girls actually get up early for music practice as well as for ponies.

Bright and cosy co-ed pre-prep (The Orchard) and nursery bring in local families, and a weekly toddler group is growing by the hour. ISI inspectors judged it to be outstanding. Children learn at their own pace with masses of careful planned but attractive stimuli. A series of enclosed garden spaces dividing the pre-prep from the main school is evidently much used.

In lots of ways Knighton House seems almost too good to be true. Assessment, checks on new staff, training and above all IT and maths have all been given new rigour recently, without detracting from the essential homeliness of the school. Education and boarding standards are well up to date but the school still has the feeling of one busy, happy and highly motivated family. Parents, who are fed delicious cakes when they come to collect their daughters, wax lyrical, seeing it as a chance for girls to enjoy their childhood in this protected nook. Mooted merger with Hanford in 2014 died amidst parental disquiet and failure of respective boards to agree terms.

As a free-standing girls' boarding prep school, it is one of the last of a dying breed – barely a dozen left in the country. Not smart, glossy or fashionable but a perfect rural idyll in which girls can become confident and well prepared for life.

Lady Barn House School

Schools Hill, Cheadle, Cheshire SK8 1JE

Pupils: 483: • Ages: 3–11

Fees: £6,813 – £7,782 pa

Tel: 01614 282912
Email: info@ladybarnhouse.stockport.sch.uk
Website: www.ladybarnhouse.org

Head: Since September 2016, Mr Mark Turner BA PGCE NPQH (late 40s), previously head of prep at Warwick Prep School. Educated at Berkhamsted, 'where a marvellous teacher inspired me to love Latin and made me want to become a teacher myself,' and at Exeter, where that inspiration came to fruition with a first class honours degree in classics, followed by postgrad teaching qualification at Cambridge. Broadly experienced in both state and independent education. Taught history and classics at a comprehensive before moving to Dean Close Prep where he became, at 26, the youngest housemaster in the history of the school; then nine years in state education in Gloucestershire in various senior roles, then RGS Worcester Prep, where he was deputy head, before the move to Warwick. 'I like independent schools because they are independent and free. Less interference from governmental edicts. We can get on with teaching and inspiring.'

A bright cookie but not a desiccated academic smelling of water biscuits, nor a pinstriped, ruthlessly ambitious, jargon-spewing head. He is, as a former colleague put it, 'a thoughtful man who cares about learning and opportunities.' 'Very approachable and wise,' one parent told us, 'and with a lovely sense of humour.' Certainly a modest man. At Warwick he sought to enlarge the activities on offer and to inculcate a sense of enquiry and experiment in the classroom. 'We want spirited, inquisitive children and staff who can encourage those qualities. Education is a serious business but children don't need to know that.' On the subject of exams, which are taken seriously, he observes, 'you don't fatten a pig by weighing it.' Not an overtly sociable head, he's not interested in being invited to dinner parties or race meetings, but 'knowing parents ensures we operate with consistency. Besides, we're all in this together.' Parents speak highly of his warmth and professionalism.

In an age when 'failure' is seen by some educationalists as a taboo word, he has interesting comments about the importance of supporting and helping children cope with failure and disappointment. 'Everyone will fail at something. It's what you learn from it which is important'.

Married to Jane; one 'very musical' daughter.

Entrance: An open intake of two early years classes of 22 at age 3 with a waiting list which fills up well in advance. 'We do encourage parents to wait until their child is actually born,' says school. A third class added in reception with an activity-packed, half day assessment 'looking for potential, evaluating maturity and the facility to absorb and apply information. It's always a positive experience and everyone has fun'. Children in nursery are not assessed for entry to the prep as any concerns will already have been flagged up. Largely families from Cheadle, Stockport and South Manchester, but the reach is broadening and more and more children make the journey from Altrincham, Alderley and beyond.

Places do come up higher up the school and it's always worth a try. Infants and juniors are invited to a friendly trial day with fun activities and the usual written tests. A parent of a late entry to the junior school said, 'The head understood my daughter better in one day than anyone during the three years at her previous school.'

The informative website answers most questions but school says, 'Word of mouth is our best marketing tool.' Competitive fees include the cost of all trips relating to the curriculum, long and short including, in both years 5 and 6, an activity-packed week in a hotel on the south coast. A few comprehensive but strictly means-tested bursaries available.

Exit: Impressive number to MGS, Manchester High and Withington at 11, and some opting to stay co-ed at Cheadle Hulme. Stockport Grammar and King's Macclesfield are also popular destinations and also, increasingly, the Altrincham grammars. Links with the secondaries are strong and feedback is always good: 'Lady Barn pupils settle quickly.'

Fewer are opting for early moves. Year 6 is viewed by both school and parents as a precious time, 'a reward after the exam process,' where the children flourish with extra responsibilities and a timetable rich in projects and trips. All are prefects and reading buddies to the infants, and are role models for the younger years.

Remarks: A thriving and happy school set within a large Victorian house extended by three further buildings, which children move confidently between. Bordered by leafy Bruntwood Park, conveniently placed for the juniors' cross-country running. Classrooms are vibrant and busy, and colourful work by the children spills into the corridors where it meets numerous photographs of school events, achievements, trips, visits and visitors. Smart, focused children in their signature royal blue blazers sit in rows of front-facing, flip-up desks ('they teach a child to be organised,' school insists).

Teaching is traditional but enthusiastic, 'tremendously energetic and so thorough,' according to parents. The school has a reputation for being a hothouse but parents (and the school) strongly refute this. The impressive results would make it easy to believe, but 'it's an outside opinion,' one parent assured us. 'The spadework is done throughout the years – there is no endless trawling through past papers in year 6.' There are no sets or streams and school firmly rejects Sats: 'they close down the curriculum.' Their methods are tried and tested: 'a winning formula honed over years, cherrypicking new ideas and integrating them as we see fit.' 'They can be a bit slow to modernise,' said one parent, but significant investment in smartboards – now in every class – new laptops for independent research and the adoption of email to communicate with parents are recent and welcome attempts to address this.

Help is there for the struggling, and a SENCo supports children with mild dyslexia – but parents all agree that children with significant learning difficulties would struggle to keep pace at Lady Barn. General consensus among parents is that homework is not onerous, although 'occasionally I do wish we could have a break,' sighed one mum.

Specialist teachers each have their own designated space – a wonderful art room with a kiln, and a science lab uniquely designed for prep-sized children, complete with a pets' corner – home to the not-so-fluffy Galileo the gekko and Aristotle the axolotl. French is taught from kindergarten with an emphasis on the whole cultural experience, to prepare for a trip to Normandy in year 6. They also start Spanish and Latin in year 6 and, from year 1, there are clubs for Mandarin and German. The stunning, cosy library in the eaves is always open and used from time to time by visiting authors for workshops. The dance and drama studios, separated by a movable screen, can be merged to create a single, airy hall, but the spacious gym with a large stage, fully equipped with lighting rigs, is the home to both assemblies and ambitious school productions. Lunches are compulsory but the overhauled menu has proved to be very popular. Outside, early years have their own contained soft play area and there is a multi-purpose, all-weather pitch also used as a playground space. Otherwise, the playground spaces are relatively small, one area within the car park, sectioned off by moveable fencing.

A huge range of extracurricular clubs fills any gaps left in the day, before, after, at lunchtime and on Saturdays, with everything open to both boys and girls. Lots of sport, with successful teams and clubs for all. Girls play football, boys do ballet (not many), there's street dancing, Scrabble and all sorts of diverse activities. Drama is taught as a stand alone subject but most impressive is the music. Four choirs, an orchestra, several ensembles, over 120 individual music lessons and a samba band. Even the parents and staff have their own choir and orchestra, with soirée concerts and performances on open days, and apparently a samba band is on the cards for them too.

Trips, and there are many, both local and further afield, develop independence and confidence, and encourage considerate behaviour. They start in nursery, but overnight trips begin in year 2 with a weekend away with teddies and sing songs. 'The staff enjoy them as much as the children and they are an excellent way to build an invaluable bond with every child.' Good behaviour and effort are monitored and celebrated. A house system starts at age 7 and there is a weekly update in assembly of credits earned, encouraging the competition. The early years have kindness assemblies to reward their good behaviour and the juniors have half termly merit assemblies to which parents are invited. Every child is given an award for some personal achievement or caring attitude. 'These really mean something to the children,' said one parent; and they perhaps contribute to the exemplary behaviour.

Parents are friendly and there is a mix of background and ethnicity, although predominantly middle-class. They seem to love the school and the complaints are few, but they all grumble about the congested pick-up. The extended wrap-around care, which begins at 7.45am and finishes at 6pm, has gone some way to ease this, and school continues to address it. Family involvement is encouraged: 'We are all part of a child's educational journey,' and parents participate in many activities including twice-yearly weekend camps, music, dads' cricket and mums' rounders matches, and even a parents' race in the annual swimming gala – not to mention all the usual quiz/bingo nights etc. The termly Lady Barn Chronicle and weekly newsletters keep parents up to date. 'The communication is fantastic, everything is pre-empted,' said one parent. 'There is a system for everything, nothing is left to chance. The school runs like a well-oiled machine.'

Leighton Academy

Minshull New Road, Crewe, Cheshire CW1 3PP

Pupils: 486 • Ages: 3–11

Tel: 01270 685185
Email: head@leighton.cheshire.sch.uk
Website: www.leightonacademy.com/

Principal: Since 2014 Joanna Young (40s), previously vice principal. She has worked at Leighton for 13 years, as a teacher and foundation stage coordinator.

Entrance: Places are allocated in line with Cheshire's schools' admission policy; first to those resident within the catchment zone, together with looked after children, then siblings, followed by those not resident but attending a catchment feeder school, those with exceptional domestic reasons and, finally, those living nearest the school.

Exit: To a variety including King's Grove, Ruskin Sports College, Sir William Stanier, Sandbach High, Malbank, Brine Lees and St Thomas More Catholic School. Increasingly parents are opting to go further afield to schools in Sandbach.

Remarks: Truly comprehensive; pupils come from leafy suburbs and areas of high deprivation, yet school's a great leveller, offers equal ops and a bit more for those who don't get the support from elsewhere. Changing demographics and the school's reputation mean it's now oversubscribed; at one time middle class families wouldn't consider Leighton, now it's a first choice school.

Parents certainly approve; they were to be found in their droves at the start of the school day. They're welcomed into school, encouraged to work, play or socialise with their child. Praise for the school was unanimous; we tried to find a disgruntled one but they must have been taking a day off.

The school's achievements and awards rival those of many prep schools, and when you walk down the picture-filled corridors it's hard to imagine you are in a deprived area, though the facilities aren't all state-of-the-art. The real strengths lie in the attitude and accomplishments of the staff – there's an artist in residence, a German teacher with links to the Goethe-Institut, a speech therapist (2.5 days a week) and four reading recovery teachers. International outlook extended by links with a school in Kenya.

Leighton caters well for all children, whether they are high or low achievers, and much is expected of all. Mainstream SEN provision is excellent and all pupils are closely monitored with timely intervention as necessary. Trips and tours mainly day and curriculum orientated. School teams play in football and netball leagues, plenty of clubs and activities.

Excellent value added. All children are closely monitored and finely targeted with a range of expertly delivered interventions, reading recovery etc for those in need. Children are attentive, well behaved and interested, then again lessons are fun and we suspect the children aren't always aware of just how much they're learning or how far their teachers are pushing them. There are currently six masters degrees and an ongoing PhD in the staff room.

Leweston School

Sherborne, Dorset DT9 6EN

Pupils: 366; 100 full, 82 weekly/flexi boarders • Ages: 2–18 (girls), 2–11 (boys); (boarding from 7) • Sixth form: 65 • RC

Fees: Day £5,700 – £18,495; Boarding £16,662 – £31,221 pa

Tel: 01963 211010
Email: admissions@leweston.dorset.sch.uk
Website: www.leweston.co.uk

Headmaster: Since 2015, Mrs Kate Reynolds MEd LLB PGCE, previously head of EAL at the school. Law degree from Bristol, and practised until 1994, when she obtained an English PGCE from Bath Spa University. MEd in education leadership from Buckingham. Worked at Gillingham and Sherborne Schools before joining Leweston. Married to Giles, also a teacher; they have four children.

Academic matters: Very much on the up. Happy children in small classes in junior school follow a range of subjects including French and Latin, and sciences in dedicated lab. We were impressed by a lesson which used the patterns in Roman mosaics to demonstrate symmetry. Outdoor learning in Enchanted Wood important.

A level results in 2016 76 per cent A*/B grades and 51 per cent A*/A. Pre-U is offered alongside A levels in music, history, English and history of art, and results are sound, with very few girls getting below a C or equivalent. Twenty-three subjects on offer at A level, with compulsory courses in various things which round out the syllabus, including the global perspectives part of the Pre-U and the extended project. School justifiably proud of the fact that 90 per cent of applications to medical school have met with success in the past five years.

At GCSE, 34 per cent A*/A grades in 2016. Ten subjects out of 20 on offer is the norm; a language and RS are compulsory. Some subjects can be taken early. The fact that the timetable can be tweaked to accommodate any combination of subjects is a huge plus – and very much to the director of studies' credit. Value-added scores are particularly high for Leweston. Greater numbers being interviewed for Oxbridge and recent success in the British Maths Olympiad all add to the sense of a school whose academic star is in the ascendancy. Parents enthuse about maths, English, Spanish, geography and music in particular.

SEN provision deals with mild end of normal issues, including ADD and ADHD, but can accommodate moderate learning difficulties. All girls tested for SEN on entry and school has CReSTeD status. The gifted-and-talented are not neglected either. EAL also catered for; in fact huge enthusiasm voiced for the school by overseas girls.

Games, options, the arts: Conventional offering of hockey, netball and tennis enlivened by squash and badminton courts and, recently, by the transformation of the gloriously sited outdoor swimming pool into a year-round facility by the construction of a perspex roof with retractable side panels. Over 40 green acres go some way to explaining the school's success in track and field events, particularly cross-country and, interestingly, football. Three sportswomen of international standing indicate a school which punches above its weight. Horse-minded boarders can have their mounts at livery: riding lessons can be arranged in either of the two arenas at the school, and teams take on other schools at dressage, show-jumping and eventing. Some kind of sport is compulsory for everyone, including sixth form – all activities are registered. Quite apart from the benefits of exercise (to work off the excellent food), compulsory sport 'gives girls the opportunity to try out different things, and instils a sense of commitment', says the head. All levels of D of E also available. Now a GB Modern Pentathlon Training Academy, running dedicated training programmes and a number of popular training camps and competitions throughout the year; a coach has recently joined staff ranks to develop swimming, riding, shooting and fencing – the building blocks of modern pentathlon. Head keen to develop boys' sport at junior level (junior school now co-ed throughout) and has appointed a director of sport to address this.

Music is a key part of school life and the lure of nearby Sherborne, with the abbey (home to the carol service) and its joint Schools Sinfonia Orchestra, is enough to make any school raise its game. Three recent top performers achieved diploma-level music. A variety of ensembles provide somewhere for any aspiring or shy musician to play or sing, and the joint forces of

L

music and drama come together to produce a musical, most recently Sweet Charity; also collaborations with Sherborne School, plus other male bastions requiring girls. Good showing in Dorset and beyond, notably at the Mid Somerset Festival in Bath for music, drama and recitation. Art and design strong too; we particularly liked the textiles, whose remarkable creations would (and do) grace any catwalk. In fact there is an increasingly well-trodden path to colleges of fashion from Leweston. Many sixth formers take up the option of Leith's basic certificate in food and wine with gusto – a professional qualification and simply essential for those stints as a chalet girl in one's gap year – while all girls have to do survival nutrition and cookery (new home economics room).

Boarding: Boarders up to year 8 share the Junior House; older girls have increasingly more privacy and greater independence. Saturday morning prep and lectures, with sports matches in the afternoons; the evenings may see joint socials with other local schools, whilst Sundays are spent relaxing, riding, cycling, visiting the beach or local attractions.

Boarding has had a shot in the arm and numbers are rising, particularly at sixth form level, now standing at about 50 per cent. 'There was some lack of clarity about it', says school, 'but putting all the junior boarders in one house has improved matters.' School could still do with more local boarders – 'there needs to be a critical mass', according to one mother, who also remarked that her daughter did not enjoy staying in at weekends – weekly boarding is an undoubted trend. Interestingly, Leweston was one of only 10 schools recently chosen to trial the new BSA Boarding Skills Award, a kind of D of E of boarding (but without the yomping): 'to be used as a currency for employability alongside academic results', according to those who devised it. (Everyone passed.)

L

Background and atmosphere: Founded originally in Sherborne in 1891 by the fearsomely named Religious of Christian Instruction (a group of nuns hailing from Ghent), the school moved to its current home three miles away in the Palladian manor of Leweston in 1948, which was purchased from the Rose family (of lime juice fame). A palpable sense of Catholicism still prevails, but not the nasty exclusive you-can't-take-communion-here kind; we felt that girls of any faith, and possibly none, would be welcomed. No nuns these days, but the chapel is central to school life, and the tiny exquisite 17th century Trinity chapel in the grounds hosts smaller weekday masses.

Juniors a rather idyllic small school which has benefited from the beautiful grounds, space and sporting facilities of the senior school since moving from Sherborne in 1993; it now occupies the former coach house of the manor.

Senior school in a pleasing mansion of golden ham stone which sits at the end of a long drive through the park, somewhat marred by later necessary additions, some of which (eg classrooms round the back) are barely fit for purpose, say parents. They are also well aware that the facilities 'don't compare with Sherborne Girls', although a welcome new sixth form den with a café and Wifi has recently been opened. Somehow, though, the relative modesty and make-do-and-mend feel rubs off on the girls, who are appreciative, charming, bright and definitely going places. 'I chose it for my daughter because of the kind of girl who goes there', said one mother, herself an Old Antonian, as former pupils are called. A very accepting culture was also widely praised – of girls from abroad, and of personal quirks, for example – making it a place where girls can truly be themselves, whether that means not growing up too fast, or fleeing bullying at other schools. 'I am thrilled that my daughter has been able to do loads of sport, which she loves, instead of being made to stick just to academics and music, which she's good at', said one happy mother, 'and she's been able to stay younger for longer'.

The social pressures of being right in Sherborne with 600 boys are of course less marked at Leweston, but some parents feel that more use should be made of opportunities for joint productions and sports training, and voiced faint irritation at the fact that there is a 10 per cent sibling discount between Sherborne and Sherborne Girls – but not with Leweston. However, joint trips to Cordoba and New York, as well as musical, dramatic and social endeavours.

Pastoral care, well-being and discipline: Discipline was not mentioned – these girls seem a biddable flock – but pastoral care gets a big thumbs-up. High staff:pupil ratio at 1:7 means no-one feels out of her depth without a life-belt.

Pupils and parents: The majority, nearly 80 per cent, British; a sizeable minority of girls from SE Asia and a good mix of Europeans make for a reasonably cosmopolitan feel to the place (around 30 per cent of boarders are from overseas). Most UK residents are very local; one mother said she felt at a disadvantage coming from Hampshire, as it was hard to get to events during the week. A sprinkling from London. All we met seemed down-to-earth and unpretentious, with realistic expectations of school and life generally

Entrance: Essentially non-selective into junior school. Children are encouraged to come for a taster day during which teachers will informally assess them in the classroom. Little ones come for half a day. All newbies are tested for SEN on arrival; support is given from the learning success co-ordinator (sic) and her team.

Senior school at 11, 13 or into sixth form, but at other points by arrangement. School sets own entrance tests at 11 (academic, numerical and perceptual reasoning), relies on common entrance at 13 and on six 'good GSCE passes' at sixth form. Everyone has an interview with the head.

Exit: Majority of junior girls move up to senior school via its 11+ exam. Up to a third pull stumps after GCSE, possibly in search of boys. Those who stay are glad they did; in fact we were told of one girl who tried a neighbouring school but headed hot-foot back to Leweston after a couple of weeks. University choices span the length and breadth of the land, with a variety of degree courses, from English and history of art to maths and medicine. Spanish most popular as language degree course. In 2016, one to Oxbridge and one medic; and others to eg UCL, Exeter, Essex, Nottingham and Cardiff. Eminent old girls include Kristin Scott-Thomas, Erin Pizzey and Serena de la Hay (whose Wicker Man can be seen from the M5).

Money matters: Cheaper than many competitors by over £1000 per term for boarding in some cases. Scholarships in art/DT, drama, music and sport to the value of 10-30 per cent, 50 per cent for three scholars of exceptional ability across all disciplines at 11+. New 100 per cent academic sixth form scholarship for outstanding local applicant coming from a state school in Dorset or Somerset.

Remarks: Gaudere and bene facere, rejoice and do well, so says the school motto: Leweston girls certainly do both. Hidden gem in a sleepy hollow, definitely meriting a look from those seeking to escape the glitzy rat-race that some girls-only education has become.

Loreto Grammar School

Dunham Road, Altrincham, Cheshire WA14 4AH

Pupils: 1,062 • Ages: 11-18 • Sixth form: 283 • RC

Tel: 01619 283703
Email: admissions@loretogrammar.co.uk
Website: www.loretogrammar.co.uk

Head Teacher: Since 2006, Mrs Jane Beever MA PGCE NPQH (early 40s), first lay head. Educated at a Catholic grammar in Liverpool, read French and Italian at Liverpool and Leeds universities; previously deputy head at Loreto. Head is also a national leader in education.

Easy to talk to and approachable (weekly drop in time for parents), humorous and realistic. Girls value her knowing them all by name and the interest she takes in them at chance meetings. Believes in providing a structured environment with clear rules but is very mindful of individuals – 'We are a very human establishment'. Enjoys walking – 'but my outside interests are mainly Loreto, in England and abroad!'

Academic matters: Specialisms in science and maths. Glowing Ofsted re curriculum, achievements, teaching and learning, sixth form and relationships – girls develop an affection for their teachers; a number we met expressed appreciation of their teachers' friendliness, helpfulness, generosity with their time and skill ('amazing teaching').

In 2016, 76 per cent A*/B grades and 48 per cent A*/A at A level (continued improvement). Offers 30 subjects (will run them for just one to three students) including ologies, economics, Latin, sports science, textiles and resistance materials (but not food tech, which some girls would like). All do a general RE course with broad-ranging outside speakers, eg Loreto Sisters working with trafficked women (led to girls' active involvement in a local campaign) and street children in India.

High GCSE achievement – in 2016, 66 per cent A*/A grades; 98 per cent achieved five + GCSEs including English and maths. Outstanding RS and expressive arts, very good separate sciences (increasing uptake), English, Latin, geography, music, art, food tech, textiles. All do RS and a modern foreign language (Spanish and German too).

Successful in the usual national academic comps, plus engineering, Mandarin Chinese speaking, Model United Nations and film script writing, at regional or national level.

Five forms of 30 at key stage 3 (setting in maths, science and mod langs from year 8), reduced to six forms of around 25 at key stage 4; sets of 12-20 for A level. Well-endowed with modern ICT and science facilities and a developed VLE (eg revision chat rooms). Very focused on constant improvement – uses independent advisors and involves girls.

Well-qualified, sensitive and innovative SENCo – would try to accommodate all needs, including physical disabilities (a blind student did very well), but mostly focused on dyslexia (no extra costs).

Games, options, the arts: Limited space on site for sports and PE – just trad gym plus school hall and a few all-weather courts; sports grounds with Astroturf close and uses nearby leisure centre eg for swimming. Not that this holds the girls back – success at regional to national levels in standard sports plus several individuals at national level in eg gymnastics, karate and boxing, with a world champion kickboxer to boot.

Impressive music – high level choral singing (Canatamus groups regularly in TV recordings), major annual concert at Manchester's Bridgewater Hall. Large drama studio with upper level and much stunningly good art – check out the gallery on the school's website and prepare to be bowled over; a well-established, full-time artist in residence. We were particularly taken with the sparky school magazine, Loreto Life – more impressive creative pieces than we often see and plenty of humour.

Wide-ranging choices in the additional life skills courses – at key stage 4 including self defence, voluntary work via the St Vincent de Paul Society, teaching science or helping with enrichment groups in primary schools, web design; for sixth formers EPQ, general studies, AS science and society or critical thinking, career-linked programmes such as Medlink and vet Medlink, Headstart courses in STEM subjects.

Various clubs and competitions and substantial sums raised for charities, notably their sister school in Kolkata, India, where sixth formers visit bi-annually; exchanges to Spain, Italy, France and Germany; two enterprising Chinese girls present their own regular local radio show. Leadership encouraged at all ages; the school council, says head, 'has teeth – and they show it!'.

Background and atmosphere: Under the trusteeship of the Sisters of Loreto, the school's origins derive from foundress Mary Ward, a splendid sounding 16th/17th century Yorkshire nun who pioneered early experiments in the Christian education of girls, convinced they should have the same opportunities as boys, since women 'could do great things if men would stop making them believe they could do nothing'! She set very high standards of teaching in her schools and her ideas were developed by two remarkably enlightened and innovative 19th century sisters.

Began as a small private school in the YWCA quarters in Altrincham, 1909, with four nuns as teachers; 1946 registered as an independent grammar school for girls. In 1972 the prep and grammar schools became separate; 1997 awarded grant maintained status, then became a voluntary aided school in the Trafford LA, 1999. Now an academy.

Its fundamental values of truth, justice, freedom, sincerity, joy, excellence and internationality derive from Mary Ward's vision of a life of service – 'No half measures – no half women' – and are physically visible around school, as well as in the strong sense of a supportive community based on mutual respect, plus the national and international extent of its concerns – all take part in a weekly current events quiz and it belongs to a network of over 120 Loreto schools in different countries (has an international school award). Seeks to turn out 'women of courage who are alive to the needs of humanity and committed to making a better world' and, according to a parent, 'instils confidence in all the girls'. Their Catholic faith is central – daily worship in the form of class, year and whole school assemblies, services and masses, plus retreats.

The architecture is a blend of traditional and modern – the quirky 90 year old part is the original convent, with pleasant red-brick façade, much wood within, a central 'Crush Hall', where the student services desk is sited, and very special chapel decorated in white, blue and yellow, graced by stained glass windows above half height alabaster arches, a floor-to-ceiling modern tapestry and very comfortable chairs (no austerity here) – clearly a much cherished space. Some classrooms lack space and the narrow corridors can get congested, but the girls we saw in transit behaved very sensibly.

The most recent building, containing refurbished science labs and ICT suites, is only some 10 years old, with a new third storey. The sixth formers have an attractive, fresh common room and the library has also been upgraded – lots of fiction and other well-used-looking books; a small 'chill out zone' furnished with bean bags and comfy chairs; access to PCs and laptops – very focused girls at work.

The uniform consists of dark blue skirts with cream blouse/shirt, tie and very, um, striking blazers with navy blue, gold, white and maroon stripes: a full classroom made this editor think of a convocation of outsize maroon wasps. Girls say they make them look like deckchairs, but we were assured, 'You get used to them,' and one admitted she had become fond of hers. Business wear for the sixth. Drop-off time parking to be avoided, as a few schools bunched along the road.

Pastoral care, well-being and discipline: High praise for pastoral care in inspection reports and from parents we spoke to – the usual structures plus a lay chaplain and access to an external counsellor. Year 12s mentor year 7s, who also have a year 8 'buddy' when they start. Taster visits and a 'marvellous' open day for year 6s, plus transition programme for post-18 planning.

Focus more on relationships than rules – girls treated as individuals; exclusion very much a last resort. Discipline not 'a major problem', according to head and deputy head – 'It's very rare for a girl to kick against the traces'; 'friendly but firm – they have a healthy respect for the staff' (parent). Various rewards, eg celebration lunches ('We see good food as very important' – head), Fantastic Fridays (weekly meeting with head for academic achievers), Bright Stars (recognition for the less outstanding but steadily virtuous girls who might otherwise go unnoticed).

Pupils and parents: Four or five main Catholic feeder primaries, plus 30-40 smaller ones – Altrincham, Manchester, Stockport, Warrington and beyond. A broad range of socio-economic and ethnic backgrounds but majority from high social class areas; almost all baptised Catholics with a few of other faiths – has had a Muslim head girl. Happy, secure, polite, considerate, supportive, serious-minded girls.

Parents in general very pleased – 'Can't fault it'; 'absolutely delighted' (mother of four) – and Mumsnet concurs, though one had wanted more detailed support with medical school application. Plenty of contact, eg newsletters, online access to girls' progress, open weekly mass, invitations to science activities, and their views sought regularly.

Entrance: Governing body controls decisions re admissions, Trafford LA co-ordinates. Takes top 40 per cent of ability range. Very over-subscribed – main requirement is to be a baptised Catholic child; also uses baptised other faiths, placing in exams and distance from school.

Year 7: closed NFER tests in VR and English plus closed school tests in creative writing and maths (no practice papers available).

Sixth form: just dealt with by school, not LA; 15 places for external students, who 'will be expected to support the ethos and values of the school' – need at least six GCSEs A*-B including English and maths; above criteria for over-subscription.

Exit: Some 15 per cent leaves after GCSEs. Has a partnership with Loreto College in Manchester, so girls can do a subject there and the rest in school. Almost all (90 per cent in 2016) to university for a broad range of subjects – English, history and business common. Six medics in 2016. Others have gap year, start art foundation course or move into employment. Around two-thirds to Russell Group – Sheffield, Newcastle and Manchester popular, usually several to Oxbridge (though none in 2016).

Remarks: Exceptionally high standards reached in all endeavours, in an orderly, nurturing atmosphere that does not exclude humour and originality. Kindness rather than competition prevails, with a deep awareness of the spiritual dimension.

M

Malvern College

Linked with The Downs Malvern

College Road, Malvern, Worcestershire WR14 3DF

Pupils: 670; 80 per cent full boarding • Ages: 13–18 • Sixth form: 330

Fees: Day £23,043 – £23,763; Boarding £34,779 – £37,104 pa

Tel: 01684 581500
Email: enquiries@malcol.org
Website: www.malverncollege.org.uk

Headmaster: Since 2008, Antony Clark MA HDE (50s). Widely regarded as a safe anchor for the school, he has been at Malvern long enough to make his own significant mark. He brought all his experience of being head at two schools in South Africa, and Gresham's for six years, to Malvern. He has focused on growing the school (it is now up to capacity, he tells us) and on developing the academic culture within the school, and is overseeing the three international school offshoots in China and Egypt. His wife is a lecturer in law and enjoys being involved in the school as much as she can. Antony is seen by the pupils and parents as a measured and balanced head, a bit distant, but the pupils feel he does know them and they respect the aura of authority that exudes from him. He sets clear boundaries and parents as well as pupils know just where they stand with him.

Academic matters: The school offers an interesting academic dynamic. On the one hand, there are super bright European students who are there for the IB and do very well indeed. Then there are the home grown pupils who are much more mixed ability. The common entrance pass mark is a relatively modest 50, and about 20 per cent of those coming in at year 9 receive some level of learning support. A levels at 70 per cent A*-B grades in 2016, but school is coy about other results apart from high flyers. The school says that it wants to be open to as wide an ability range as it can, partly because it is interested in a broad range of talents and partly because the it wants all the family to come, not just the bright one of the clan.

Parents rave about the level of academic support. There are carefully tailored individual programmes, and whatever their level, pupils say their teachers really know their strengths and weaknesses. Pupils are highly encouraged to focus hard on their academic work. Some parents feel there is rather too much pressure and the school is expecting pupils to spin an awful lot of plates, but others recognise that this is what gets the results that would not have been forthcoming in a school with less resources to put into teaching and learning. Parents are full of praise for the availability of teachers and the tight level of communication between staff that ensures each pupil is getting the academic support and challenge they need.

The head has upped the academic profile in the school by very visibly encouraging intellectual societies to flourish, with a range of top quality outside speakers as well as opportunities for sixth formers to present papers reflecting their own intellectual interests. Here is the stretch and challenge that the bright sixth formers need. The head has also been keen to develop ideas about teaching and learning among his staff, has established a staff group to move ideas forward and initiated peer to peer observations to help share the very best practice.

In terms of subjects, the range is much what you would expect in a well-resourced school catering for a mixed ability range where the sixth form is split more or less exactly in half between IB and A level. Parents talk about how strong history, economics, English, maths, classics and modern languages are. Sixth formers also enthuse about politics and business studies. Science is about to have a real boost with the opening of a modern science centre named after a past pupil, the current prime minister of Malaysia, Najib Razak. Teachers and parents told us that there is a lot of effort put into constructing sixth form timetables that will really play to the strengths of the pupils, resulting in some strong results and a thoroughly valuable sixth form experience for those of fairly modest academic ability as well as the high flyers.

Academic facilities are strikingly good across the board. The internet access has just been speeded up, much to everyone's satisfaction. Not every department has the spanking new facilities of the sciences, but music, which is housed in one of the older buildings, shows that energy, enthusiasm and high achievement are certainly not dependent on buildings alone. The library has all the aura of an ancient seat of learning with the buzz of a 21st century learning resource centre. Pupils commented on the helpful library opening hours.

Games, options, the arts: Sport is outstanding – and there is a lot of it. The sports facilities are excellent, with a splendid new sports centre that incorporates a generous function room for lectures and dinners, all of which are available for community use on occasion. We were pleased to hear of the girls' football teams' successes. There are special programmes for the elite sports players with high quality coaches and professional contacts, but everyone is expected to participate in games at some level. We spoke to parents who had specifically chosen the college for its sporting excellence and were delighted with how it had delivered, but also to one or two with unsporty children who resented the amount of time they had to spend on games, especially if they had really strong other passions – such as music – that required a big time commitment. We would recommend a parent whose 13 year old is clearly not sporty to think hard about whether the other, considerable, attractions, outweigh all that compulsory games.

The other attractions certainly are there. The art is phenomenal and spreads way beyond the art building itself. The whole school is enhanced with a great deal of the pupils' artwork in a brilliant variety of media. It was wonderful to see pupils encouraged to work on a large scale, with great big canvases giving the senior art areas the feel of an art school. Pupils told us that they are invited to use the art building outside of lesson time and it is clear that there is much enthusiasm for doing this. DT is another strength, and both boys and girls spoke passionately about projects they were undertaking there. Drama is housed in a well-adapted old gymnasium, and again there is masses going on, both within the houses and at school level. Thespians benefit from the very close proximity of Malvern Theatre, which has a number of pre-West End runs, and there are house trips to see various productions. Music is very strong too, particularly choral and chapel singing, but there is a huge range of ensembles and orchestras. Every year 9 learns a musical instrument. Those looking for choral scholarships at Oxbridge are well prepared, and the school has had success here. The music offers welcome links with the local community – the brass band played at the switching on of the Malvern town Christmas lights, and the choir were doing three carol services in the town during the week we visited.

Most of the school is involved in CCF at some stage and D of E is also offered. The school makes the most of the wonderful Malvern Hills, with various hill runs being an important part of the annual school calendar. Both IB and D of E candidates involved community service, and the school has links with a local school for blind children.

'It offers all a great school should – and more', one parent told us.

Boarding: Eighty per cent of the school are full boarders. There is no flexi-boarding (though day pupils can stay the occasional night for official school events) but there are two compulsory weekends out of school each half term. Day pupils are incorporated into the boarding houses and have the same study space as the boarders. Pupils eat in the houses and house staff make the most of this opportunity to understand exactly what is going on in the daily life of their charges. Non-house staff and other visitors eat with the pupils at lunchtimes too, and the atmosphere is warm, stimulating and highly conducive to developing the best social manners. Pupils and parents say they know the house staff are there for them and will give unstintingly of their time to offer support.

The school suits high energy all rounders and there is a tremendous amount on offer round the clock. One or two parents felt the demands on the pupils were almost too great, with very little down time, but the pupils we met absolutely thrived on the high octane atmosphere and recognised the diversity of gifts that make up a flourishing and healthy community.

Background and atmosphere: The school is very cosmopolitan in feel and outlook – about 35 per cent are from overseas, and there are about 40 different nationalities represented at the moment. This global feel is grounded in the quintessentially British landscape of the Malvern Hills. The site is stunning, set on the side of the Malverns with spectacular views. There are 11 houses (six boys' and five girls') around the 250 acre site – many in huge 19th century villas that could well have been the houses of the successful financiers of the Empire who made their home in this health resort for the Victorian rich. Malvern is a delightful and slightly quirky town to wander around – staff and parents can feel as relaxed as they could anywhere in permitting pupils to go out to do a bit of shopping or have a coffee.

The Victorian foundation of the school, 1865, with that glorious mid 19th century architecture that exudes confidence in Church and Country, is an essential part of the school's feel today. Everyone goes to the chapel four times a week for a broadly Church of England service, where hymns are still sung and prayers said although the emphasis is on wise words that will speak to those of all persuasions. There are non-Christians in the school – dietary and other religious observations are happily accommodated – but this is a Church of England foundation and you do feel that is a living reality. The head tells us that past pupils really value the regular worship as they move out into the wider world.

Pastoral care, well-being and discipline: Everyone to whom we spoke valued the pastoral care highly, even parents who had other grumbles. The emphasis is on the individual needs – there is no one-size-fits-all here. One parent told us how accommodating everyone was when her daughter suffered a bad sports injury, and pupils spoke about the staff with genuine warmth. Staff, too, showed a strong sense of loyalty to pupils who had come up through the school, wanting to ensure they had the smoothest possibly transition to the next stage and making it clear each pupil was valued for themselves not just for their A* exam results. The atmosphere felt well-disciplined without being too formal. The rules are clear and everyone recognises a no-nonsense approach to any transgressions, but it is rewards rather than punishments that reinforce the school's strong moral values.

Pupils and parents: Among the alumni of the college are at least two Commonwealth prime ministers, two Nobel prize winners, an Olympic gold medallist and many other notables from the worlds of science, law, the military, business, politics, sports and literature – including CS Lewis. The school produces an eclectic range that bears out its claims to suit the all rounders.

There are a lot of wealthy families forming the backbone of the school. Bursary help is available and we heard of families who were pooling generational resources to send children to the college, but one or two parents speculated that this might not be a comfortable school for a child whose parents were really having to push the boat out financially to pay the fees. The international clientèle rubs shoulders with the children of successful Hereford farming families, of London commuters, and of the technological elite who can choose to live in such a delightful part of the country.

The school has been co-educational for about 20 years and there are now more-or-less half boys and girls. Some said that the families put children under some pressure to look good as well as do well, and we certainly saw none of the much publicised childhood obesity here. Housemistresses are aware of teenage girls' desire to look slim and beautiful and on the alert for any obsession, but the girls we met relished the outdoorsy, sporty opportunities of the school and didn't appear to be under pressure to present as cover girls. Both boys and girls appeared pleasingly extrovert and outward-looking. Perhaps not a school for the very quiet and reflective who need a lot of time to themselves.

Entrance: Most families start looking two or three years before entry and some houses fill up faster than others. There are open days, but most families have personalised tours. In some cases there is pre-testing, but the main admission is through common entrance at 13+, or for those coming from non-common entrance schools, the school's own tests in maths, English and science. About 50 join the sixth form each year and they normally do tests in the subjects they want to study at A level or IB, including an English and maths paper as appropriate. The interviews are important too, as are school reports.

M

Exit: Almost all the sixth form go on to higher education. Those staying in the UK are attracted to campus and collegiate universities like Durham and Exeter or the big Russell Group names; five to Oxbridge in 2016. About a third go on to US, Canada and mainland Europe top institutions, and may put in UK applications as well to see what comes up. This group is aiming high – one boy had an interview at Trinity, Cambridge the week after we met him, but it was sixth on his list behind US and Canadian top universities.

Money matters: This sort of education, staffing level, facilities, opportunities and general ambiance does not come cheap. There are means-tested bursaries and scholarships for a wide range of talents. Pupils can accumulate these but learning support and EAL tuition come as extras.

Remarks: This is a school for the international set, and those who come from the local area, or even 'over the hill' – as the other side of the Malverns is described – undoubtedly benefit by having their horizons expanded beyond the comfortable values of the English shires. There are huge opportunities for pupils to learn from different cultures here and the college does well to work on its links with the local community, so it is not just the moneyed international culture that pupils assimilate, delightfully appealing though that is. There is a wholesomeness about Malvern for those who lift their eyes to the hills that can balance the daily busyness. The offshoots in China and Egypt will add to the global dimension and set everyone looking to the far horizons – not just at the opportunities but also, we hope, at the challenges. This is a school deeply bedded in the British public school tradition but with its sights now set across the globe to prepare the pupils for world citizenship.

Malvern St James Girls' School

15 Avenue Road, Great Malvern, Worcestershire WR14 3BA

Pupils: 356; 150 full, 16 weekly, 31 flexi boarders • Ages: 11–18 (boarding from 7) • Sixth form: 125 • C of E

Fees: Day £15,180 – £19,005; Boarding £25,275 – £34,110 pa

Tel: 01684 584624
Email: admissions@malvernstjames.co.uk
Website: www.malvernstjames.co.uk

Headmistress: Since September 2016, Mrs Olivera Raraty BA PGCE, previously deputy head academic at Notting Hill and Ealing High. History degree from Leeds and PGCE from London University; began her teaching career at Francis Holland NW1. Has taught history and politics at both day and boarding schools, including a long stint at Wycombe Abbey, where her posts included head of department, head of year and assistant director of studies. Married with two daughters; enjoys baking and hill walking.

Academic matters: Respectable results both at GCSE and A level. At A level in 2016, 65 per cent A*-B and 35 per cent A*/A. At GCSE, 62 per cent A*/A. Most girls take 10 or 11 GCSEs. Many sixth formers also take SATs for the US universities. An increasing use of IGCSEs to stretch the girls and increase flexibility. The school is 'not tempted' by the IB but promotes the education enrichment programme, running alongside the A level curriculum, which has been designed to give the girls the opportunities, especially in terms of creative thinking and learning resilience, to glean many benefits traditionally seen as an 'IB preserve'. The school also offers critical thinking for years 10 to 13.

Lovely facilities – an excellent purpose-built science block, beautiful and spacious art block, good drama studio and plenty of computers for girls to use in class and for prep. Virtual learning environment allows submission of work online to teachers. Small class sizes – never more than 18. Well organised and supported prep time at the end of each school day.

Teaching is highly responsive to the needs of individual girls – the school has an excellent reputation locally for untangling able girls whose dyslexia/dyspraxia has been a stumbling block to them elsewhere, and learning support is woven into the school structure. 'We welcome the full spectrum of learning profiles.' One-to-one support is available for dyslexia, dyspraxia and EAL at extra cost.

A good choice of modern foreign languages at GCSE and A level, and a modern language at GCSE is 'as close to compulsory as it can be'. French, Spanish, German, Chinese, Russian and Latin taught. A well-stocked and well-set-out library with specific areas set aside for sixth formers. Academic reports are termly, with progress checks every half term.

Games, options, the arts: Fantastic sports facilities – newish and splendid sports hall – and plenty of opportunities to make use of them. Where girls show exceptional promise and talent in sports (currently national representatives in lacrosse and golf)

their curriculum commitments will be adjusted to allow them to flourish on the sports field. Growing an equestrian team which makes use of the facilities at Hartpury Equine College. Many outdoor pursuits also supported – not least by virtue of being at the foot of the Malvern Hills. Lots of girls involved in Duke of Edinburgh too.

There are plenty of opportunities to get involved with music groups or to take individual lessons. Very good drama facilities, and for those interested in life a step beyond there are debating societies, involvement in Model UN, volunteering opportunities at local schools, fundraising for local charities and so on.

The lovely artwork on display around the school deserves a mention, and the textiles department produces some breathtaking pieces. Girls who want a go at pottery, painting, stitching or drawing will have a ball here.

Boarding: Boarding is done by age group with a prep house, two houses for years 9-11 and two sixth form houses. Boarding houses are well set up and comfortable, with plenty of space and privacy for older girls, and nice common rooms. Sixth form boarding life aims to ease transition between school and university – girls are supervised but encouraged to take responsibility for establishing good habits of independent study, dealing with their own finances, travel arrangements – and laundry. Sixth formers may also go into Worcester or Birmingham at the weekend as long as they are in a group.

Day girls are well integrated with boarders – each day girl assigned to a boarding house and many using flexi-boarding either regularly or occasionally. There is no Saturday school but plenty to keep girls busy at the weekends including croquet, reeling, discos and barbecues plus trips into nearby Worcester and Birmingham. Reciprocal social arrangements with nearby boys' school.

Background and atmosphere: The school is well situated in the centre of Malvern, directly opposite the train station, in the building which was once the Imperial Hotel. Founded in 1893 as Malvern Girls' College, it was renamed Malvern St James following a merger in 2006 with St James' School in West Malvern. The surroundings are lovely, with the hills stretching up behind the town, and the buildings feature lots of high ceilings, generous rooms and well-lit spaces. Younger girls seen skipping about chatting and hopping, older girls seem calm and happy. 'We'd notice someone walking round with her head down (or her nose up) straight away.'

The atmosphere is calm and relaxed but with an underlying energy and a sense of fingers on the pulse. Small enough for the headmistress to know every girl by name. The school has a full-time chaplain and there is a sense of respect for and interest in a diverse collection of girls from varied backgrounds. A mixture of UK and overseas students, although the head has now capped the number of international students. Pupils come from the very local to the far-flung – Thailand, Brunei, Russia and Nigeria amongst others.

Food is good – recently brought back in house to improve standards and, according to our sources, successfully so. There are always halal and vegetarian options available and the staff eat with the girls.

A strong commitment to sharing facilities with the local community. The school is well liked by the locals, who say the pupils are polite and never give any trouble. Few rules, relatively late curfews by comparison with other local boarding schools – the girls are given a lot of responsibility, self-discipline is encouraged and the girls respond positively. A family atmosphere – 'the school is all about good relationships'.

Pastoral care, well-being and discipline: Pastoral care permeates the structure of the school, with school staff and older pupils committed to maintaining the highest standards. Prefects are trained as 'sixth form listeners' by Childline and know exactly what to do and when to pass concerns on to staff. Prefects are elected by a combination of sixth form and staff votes. Zero tolerance of drugs – but these are very rare. Sixth formers are encouraged to attend and host dinner parties with members of other nearby schools. Alcohol consumption is restricted to two glasses of wine on such occasions, but not allowed on school premises otherwise, though 18 years olds are allowed to go to local pubs.

Prefects, staff and parents all say that bullying 'does not happen'. Girls are allocated to small tutor groups of about 12 and each form also has a prefect. The school says, 'There is nowhere to hide', and the combination of house staff, peer support, small classes and an open door policy mean the girls always have someone to talk to. 'We train the girls to manage themselves and the girls are comfortable being themselves.'

Girls of all ages mix well.

Pupils and parents: Pupils and parents come from all over the place. Day girls live up to an hour away (minibuses from very nearby and also from Hereford and Ross-on-Wye). Some boarders are local too; about a quarter of pupils are from overseas. The girls we met were cheerful, polite, welcoming and thoroughly enjoy being at the school. Parents say, 'It's lovely, friendly and happy – and every teacher is up to speed'.

Clara Furse, the first woman chief executive of the London Stock Exchange, the late HRH Princess Alice, Duchess of Gloucester and the childcare expert Penelope Leach are former pupils of St James's School, while Malvern Girls' alumnae include the writer Aminatta Forna. More recent former pupils include BBC correspondent Hannah Hennessy, journalist Elizabeth Day, surgeon Abbie Franklin and city high flyers Helen Freer and Elizabeth Sharpe.

Entrance: Prospective pupils are interviewed by the head – via Skype if need be – and all face formal assessment tests. Formal interviews and often quite a long 'courtship' including taster days etc. Prep department provides a growing number into year 7, with others coming from local primaries and prep schools (boarding and day) like Hatherop Castle, The Elms, Abberley Hall, Godstowe and The Croft. At 11, girls sit cognitive ability and comprehension tests, while others do common entrance at 13. Main entry points are years 7, 9 and sixth form. Girls looking to enter sixth form must take a written paper in one of the subjects they wish to study at A level and a general essay paper. All international students must take an EAL test. Not highly selective, but girls 'must be intellectually curious, with a good IQ' and 'able to benefit from what we offer'.

Exit: Around two-thirds stay on after GCSEs. Virtually all sixth form leavers to university. A handful to Oxbridge most years and a good number to Russell Group destinations. Recent destinations include many to London: LSE, UCL, King's, Queen Mary, Royal Holloway and Imperial; medicine, music and mathematics amongst the courses chosen.

Money matters: The school offers a number of academic, music, sport, art and drama scholarships, which are worth between 10 and 20 per cent of fees. Bursaries are also available and may be combined with scholarships. The maximum bursary/scholarship combination available is 40 per cent of fees.

Remarks: A school that is different, 'not tethered to league tables', with a lovely relaxed atmosphere, yielding impressive results in the classroom and on the sports field. Happy, confident girls and staff.

Marlborough College

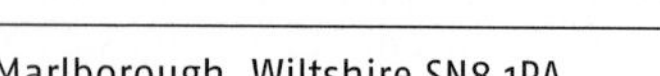

Marlborough, Wiltshire SN8 1PA

Pupils: 937; nearly all full boarders • Ages: 13–18 • Sixth form: 399 • C of E

Fees: Day £29,985; Boarding £35,280 pa

Tel: 01672 892300
Email: admissions@marlboroughcollege.org
Website: www.marlboroughcollege.org

Master: Since 2012, Jonathan Leigh (60s), previously head of Ridley College, Canada and before that head of Blundell's School and second master of Cranleigh School. Married to Emma, also a Cambridge history graduate, they have two grown up children and the obligatory black lab. Educated at St George's Windsor where he was a chorister, thence to Eton. Degree in history from Corpus Christi College, Cambridge, where he was a choral exhibitioner. He still sings (tenor) and on leaving Cambridge thought seriously about going professional, but instead 'drifted' into teaching and consolidated this drift with a PGCE.

Mr Leigh seems to be the go-to chap if you want to do something structural and potentially controversial at a school. He took Blundells co-ed and taught Canada to love the IB at Ridley College. He is a great advocate of the IB but for some reason the qualification (brought in by previous master) failed to 'take root' at Marlborough and, pragmatically, he de-introduced it here. 'It's very hard to run a dual system', he told us, 'especially since A levels have been toughened up. You need a critical mass to make the IB work and it didn't attract the take up at Marlborough that it has elsewhere.' Under 20 candidates is indeed very far from a critical mass – it's a shame though, the results were pretty good (average 36).

M

Since accepting the post of master, at a time when he might have been contemplating retirement, Mr Leigh and his wife have thrown themselves into Marlborough life and society, much to the admiration of parents (Marlborough parents, we have discovered, don't hold back) who describe him as 'charming and user-friendly.' He's perhaps a little shy at first,' we were told, 'but he's a modest and gentle man who's terrific with the children.' Mrs Leigh is equally popular: 'she's brilliant at fundraising events' and 'great company'.

Marlborough is a big school but the master is diligently applying himself to meeting all its pupils, having breakfast or lunch with groups of four to six at a time. He also 'teaches a bit' – an upper sixth elective course on his specialist subject, Middle Europe 1400-1715.

Unsurprisingly, Mr Leigh is an opera lover; his favourites are Samson and Delilah and The Magic Flute. Somewhat more surprisingly he's part of a 50 strong flat racing syndicate and has shares in two horses (both winners, apparently). Syndicate is called The Fifty, horses are called, wait for it, Fifty Shades of Grey.

We found Mr Leigh thoughtful, diplomatic, quietly humorous and without the hubris that is sometimes par for the head course. He has provided Marlborough with much more than a 'safe pair of hands' and parents agree that the College is extremely lucky to have him. 'I only wish I could have started here 10 years earlier,' he says.

Academic matters: In our last review we remarked that what with A levels, the pre-U and IB, Marlborough offered something for everyone. But clearly everyone didn't want quite that much choice. IB has quietly expired and 2015 leavers were its last takers. Academic head hadn't turned his IB poster to the wall (maybe he never will) and delivered a touching eulogy about the bountiful legacy of the qualification's brief life. Its general goodness will float around like educational ectoplasm, enriching the remaining qualifications. He didn't actually say that. He did say, 'Marlborough already offers much of what the IB contains, more so now that A levels are returning to the linear format.'

College motto is Deus dat Incrementum ('God gives the increase') but steady advance of exam results may have less divine origin. Admissions criteria are now somewhat more academically demanding (although prep school head's reference is still crucial). CE result mainly used to 'keep them on the boil and help us with setting'. In 2016, 57 per cent A*/A grades at A level and Pre-U equivalent; at GCSE, 75 per cent A*/A grades. Stand out results in A level art, drama, sciences, geography and maths but good tail of non-vowel grades as well. Astronomers fare well, but then they do have the famous Blackett Observatory to aid their stargazing – local schools also get their turn to view the cosmos from a field in Wiltshire. Parents singled out teaching in philosophy as 'inspirational', and its popularity at Pre-U, not to mention the results, endorse this. We know, we know, it's not all about exams and comparisons are invidious, but just out of interest that puts Marlborough some way ahead of many co-ed rivals.

Exam syllabi excepted there seems to be an (admirable) ideological aversion to the churning out of standard curriculum fare at Marlborough. Shell (first year)'s first taste of their new school's academic approach is 'Form', a multi-disciplinary enquiry into the 'origins of human civilisation', no less. These lessons take the place of separate English, history and RS lessons. Run in parallel with this is the 'Artemis' PHSE course: new pupils take part in guided discussions within their boarding houses. All do two modern languages and Latin, some may also take ancient Greek. Sixth formers can choose from around 35 'electives', mini courses that teachers – including the master – devise to impart specialist knowledge on subjects from cryptic crosswords (now that's a life skill) to special relativity or conducting – the baton, not electrical, kind. These must be as much fun for the staff who run them as they are for pupils.

Average class size is 15, eight in the sixth form. Approximately 100 students have learning difficulties such as moderate dyslexia, dypraxia and ADHD. School says a great deal of thought goes into assessing pupils with SEN to ensure Marlborough is the 'right learning environment' before places are offered. Learning support department works one-to-one and provides a programme of support appropriate to the individual's needs. School also helps a number of students with planning and organisation.

Games, options, the arts: It's no surprise that we filled an entire notebook and ran out of ink during our visit to Marlborough; there's so much on offer beyond the academic timetable. Lest we also deplete our stock of superlatives, suffice it to say that art, drama, sport music are all very, very good. Generous facilities and 'inspirational' specialist teaching help every pupil, from the most talented to the least coordinated, play, sing, throw or create something to be proud of.

The college may have been co-ed for nearly 50 years, but on the sports field rugby is still king. Four England captains and 38 internationals is indeed a noble heritage. 'The first X1 get clapped onto the pitch at the start of the season,' one parent told us. 'They are the undisputed heroes,' said another. These were observations rather than criticisms and everyone agreed that there are so many fixtures everyone gets the chance of a good match. Besides, the girls are doing just as well: the U14 hockey team recently retained the Wiltshire County Championship and several girls have been picked to represent their county and country in sports such as netball, sailing, lacrosse and athletics. Long tradition of excellence in shooting. Most sports including fly fishing and clay pigeon shooting take place within the college grounds, but there's also a off-site programme that offers beagling, canoeing, caving, coasteering, mountain biking, mountaineering and sub-aqua.

Seemingly universal admiration for 'amazing' drama and music, although the former gets more takers at A level than the latter. Performances and teaching take place in the Bradleian studio theatre and on the flexible stage of the Ellis Theatre that seats up to 400. There are three ambitious audition-only main school productions a year, a musical every two years and a house play festival each summer. Nearly half of pupils take individual music lessons and house music competitions get everyone doing something tuneful. There's a symphony orchestra, choirs, loads of ensembles and plenty of opportunities to perform in the college as well as nationally and internationally. Chapel choir has made several recordings and recently returned from a tour of France. Organ scholars get to learn on the beautiful and recently restored Van Beckwith teaching organ. The department also has an impressive concert programme of visiting professionals and partnerships with the Southbank Sinfonia and individual musicians including Julian Lloyd Webber and Ioan Davies, head of chamber music at the Yehudi Menuhin School.

The college is a founder member of the CCF and has 300 cadets and a 25m indoor range. Those who choose not to join the CCF take part in a variety of service activities, working at primary schools, with younger children in the homes of local families or at a school for children with learning difficulties in Swindon; another group helps at a local riding for the disabled group. There are also opportunities to work with the elderly or on conservation projects.

There's a real energy and buzz at Marlborough; you can feel it. Pupils are busy, busy, busy. Maybe too busy, sometimes. Sensible advice comes from several parents: don't try and do it all, especially in the sixth form. You can't star in the play, play in the firsts and come first in the tests. 'You can do your academic work and one other thing well,' we were told. School says most do more than one thing well but they are vigilant about possible overload. Girls especially can feel the strain: 'The boys are more laid back but girls put themselves under tremendous pressure,' said one mother.

Boarding: Sixteen boarding houses (six boys, six girls, four mixed) are run by housemasters or housemistresses who live there with their families; they are supported by resident tutors, dames and other members of the pastoral and support staff. Vertical (mixed age) boarding promotes cohesion between year groups and house loyalty is fierce. 'It's really competitive,' several parents told us. Plenty of opportunities to do battle – house shouts (singing), plays, matches and so on.

Every house has its own character, dictated as much by its position and architecture as the team running it. In Hermitage, one of the older houses, we admired a wonderful ground floor bedroom with huge marble fireplace. This prize billet is given to the chap (it's a boys' house) the housemaster thinks is the hardest working, and its occupant looked very proud to have been chosen.

While we did spy some distinctly less than fancy corners as we ran behind a very long-legged housemaster, most boarders at Marlborough seem to get a pretty good deal. Some of the recently refurbished accommodation we visited looked fit for an interiors magazine – walls painted in the sort of modish shade that might be called Vole's Whisper – and, in one, a spectacular glass wall in the kitchen/dining area that overlooked playing fields.

Shells (first years) sleep in four or five bed dorms, graduating to twin and then single rooms from Hundreds (fifth year) up. Occupants are moved around every half term or so. Shell have supervised prep (no gappies, house prefects do this job), Removes (second year) have separate shared studies, after that pupils work in their own rooms. Pupils may Skype their parents (or vice versa) any time apart from during prep; 'we are flexible because of time zones'. Sensible rules re mobiles etc. Meals are taken centrally but continental breakfast, snacks and drinks available in houses.

Although we didn't inspect all 15 houses, we very much liked those we saw. Considerable thought and expense is going into boarders' surroundings and we're sure the refurbishment programme will eventually transform even the ugliest corners. We often say that boarding school accommodation is of a higher standard than university rooms, but at Marlborough some would surely outclass many homes.

So we asked, how can parents ensure their son or daughter is in the 'right' house? Short answer is, you can't. 'There is no 'best' or 'right' house', we were told firmly. What, no sporty house? No musical house? No. 'Parents must come to house open days and visit as many as they can – at least four; some end up seeing six or seven.' Applications are then made to three but school is in charge of mix and has final say. And parents, while you are inspecting the houses you can be sure members of staff are giving you a surreptitious once over.

Background and atmosphere: Marlborough has both in spades. Surely there is no other school on earth where one can walk out of a glorious Victorian gothic revival chapel (stained glass by Burne Jones and former pupil William Morris, sculpture by Eric Gill) and come face to face with a neolithic mound. 'Merlin's Mound', as it was dubbed by the 12th century tourist board (complete with 17th poetic grotto at its foot), is the second largest man-made mound in Europe. 'Mound' though alliteratively effective, doesn't really describe its stepped shape: it looks more like a fancy Victorian pudding mould. In the 10th century the mound was recycled into the motte of a motte-and-bailey castle – its moat flows beneath the performing arts centre.

M

Take a few paces more and you will see the Memorial Hall, a neoclassical theatre and assembly hall built in 1925 to honour the 749 men who fell in 1914-1918. Constructed upon a floating 'raft' over the water meadows, the 'Mem' no longer holds the whole school (actually it could, but not if school wants to stay on the right side of health and safety legislation). Apparently the acoustics are excellent and the beautifully preserved interior remains very evocative. The hall is to be restored in time for the centenary of the end of the Great War in 2018. Peeping out from behind the Mem is the 'most architecturally important building in the school', a white painted 1930s concrete science block with ocean liner style aluminium windows and topped with a gourd (head of science at the time was Mr Gourd). It is hoped that this building can be converted into a new design centre.

Forgive all this talk of bricks and mortar – we know schools are about people – but somehow the eclectic mix of ancient and modern across the school estate embodies the breadth and quality of a Marlborough education. We were fortunate enough to be shown around by the head of admissions, an architectural historian. He describes the college site as both 'its greatest asset and a glorious problem' and knows the provenance of every wall and window. If ever a chap was in his happy place...

Marlborough College was established in 1851, the Church of England's response to a shortage of vicars. It wanted to provide a good, affordable education for clergymen's sons from the south west of England on the assumption that these young men would go on to take the cloth. List of clerical OMs testament to success of this operation. School was established in an 18th century mansion and former coaching inn which was gradually joined by Georgian, Victorian and Jacobethan buildings including the former town gaol (now converted into a gym). The master's garden looks down to the River Kennet but alas, the Tennyson tree, a glorious copper beech planted by the poet laureate (his son, Hallam, was a pupil), is no more. Its huge canopy of leaves proved too heavy to bear and crashed down during a summer storm.

Marlborough claims to be the first public school to go co-ed (sixth form only, 1968). Surely Bedales, founded in 1893 and fully co-ed in 1898, should get that prize. But let's not quibble, it'll be 50 years in 2018 and even if boys still outnumber girls in the lower years it definitely doesn't feel like a boys' school. Marlborough College Malaysia was established in 2012 and has already doubled in size. This is not a franchise but a 'genuine expansion of the home school', with linked management and governance.

It's impossible to cover everything that goes on at Marlborough in this review. The school is a 24 hour educational, creative and cultural challenge to teenage apathy and we can only stand back in admiration. 'We ask a great deal of our staff,' the master told us; 'during term time there's no such thing as working hours.'

Pastoral care, well-being and discipline: All food is prepared in house and eaten in the large communal dining hall. Lunch is staggered between 12 and 1pm, an arrangement that we hope has improved the lot of Shells who we hear sometimes used to go hungry, elbowed out of the way by older children. Pupils eat with their friends at long wooden tables, there's plenty of choice and what we tried was delicious. Breakfasts and lunches get full marks but (and we heard this from several quarters) supper could do better – not an uncommon complaint at boarding schools, must be something to do with leftovers. Former pupil John Betjeman wasn't a fan of this meal either, although we're sure it's much nicer than what he got in the 1920s.

So what about discipline? It hasn't always had a robust reputation at Marlborough, although our impression is that it is now an extremely well run school. A rummage through the college's many 'policies' leads somewhat circuitously to chapter and verse. Suffice it to say that 'explicit or intimate sexual relations' will get you suspended or excluded. Likewise drugs, alcohol, bullying, theft, use of weapons and a whole load of other nasties. Prefects can go to some of the town pubs but on the whole partying is an in-school affair (there's a policy about it on the website) or – and this sounds like more fun – takes place at friends' houses during the holidays or on exeats.

M

Relations between boys and girls seemed friendly and relaxed, more best mates than Romeo and Juliet. 'There's great banter between the girls and boys,' a father told us. 'There's the odd bit of snogging in the bushes but nothing serious,' said another parent. While we can't comment on the activity we can confirm that the school grounds are well supplied with shrubs of all kinds.

Great praise for housemasters/mistresses, tutors, dames and all others directly involved in pastoral care. Parents like the 'clear' chain of command and felt that anxieties or problems were dealt with swiftly. Good medical care, plenty of joined up thinking and sharing of information (where appropriate) in cases of illness, stress etc. Medical centre or 'Sanny' looked rather forbidding and was described by one parent as 'grim' (building, not people).

House identity is great for bonding but there are still a few grumbles about pupil hierarchy and the lot of the youngest. Efforts are being made, there's a mentoring system and older children write to new pupils before they start, but maybe there's still room for improvement here.

Pupils and parents: Traditional full boarding families broadly sums up the type you will meet here but school doesn't (and doesn't want to) feel like the 'default outcome of a dinner party conversation.' Yawn. It's sparkier and quirkier than that – fish pie and a decent Muscadet at the kitchen table with slightly naughty friends perhaps, rather than 'faine daining', competitive parenting and house prices. Less country than schools further south but 'not too London' either. Some very local day pupils, six per cent international students.

Pupils are a great advert for co-education – self-assured, good company, the sort you could see fitting in anywhere. Many parents get to know their children's friends socially at weekends (exeats, privis) or during holidays. 'They're a great bunch', we heard, 'the sort who always help clear up after a party.'

In addition to ranks of clerical and military worthies, notable former pupils include artists: William Morris, Graham Shepard, Lauren Child; writers: John Betjeman, Louis MacNeice, Siegfried Sassoon, Bruce Chatwin, Frances Osborne; actors: Wilfrid Hyde White, James Robertson Justice, Michael Pennington, Jack Whitehall; politicians (and their spouses): Hallam Tennyson, Rab Butler, Christopher Chope, Mark Reckless, Sally Bercow, Samantha Cameron; plus Sir Francis Chichester, Mark Phillips, Simon Fanshawe, Mark Tully, Frank Gardner, HRH Princess Eugenie of York and HRH Duchess of Cambridge (she was a prefect). Quite some school reunion that would be.

Entrance: Parents are advised to start the process (visiting boarding houses etc) at least three years in advance. According to the director of admissions, 50 per cent of the decision to admit a child rests with the prep school head's reference, 10 per cent on the ISEB test (to check the academic part of the head's reference) and two interviews in a boarding house by HM and a tutor to verify other aspects of the reference. CE's biggest use, he maintains, is to help with setting once a child joins. Important part of the interview is to discover whether a child will be boarding by consent or 'compulsion'. No one wants the latter. Nor do they want children who have been tutored, 'we're looking for potential for happiness.' Someone will be offering to coach children in that soon.

Consensus from many parents that Marlborough is a great family school. School says it does its best to accommodate siblings, but warns, it's not automatic. 'We can't be a closed shop and sometimes this isn't the right place.' Pupils come from over 100 preps but main suppliers are Beaudesert, Cheam, Cothill, The Dragon, Farleigh, Highfield, Lambrook, Ludgrove, Pinewood, Twyford and Windlesham.

We have in the past heard from parents somewhat bruised by Marlborough's 'brusque' response to admissions enquiries. School horrified to learn this: 'we go out of our way to be welcoming and give people time'. Certainly all the front of house staff we met could not have been more charming and less intimidating.

Exit: Very few leave post-GCSE, certainly no kicking out for under par results. Influx of girls in sixth form swells numbers. Big improvements in careers advice; we loved the huge signposts showing all the directions OMs can take. As previously, Edinburgh, Manchester, Bristol, Exeter, Durham and Leeds popular destinations; much the most popular courses are in history, art history, modern languages. Eighteen Oxbridge places in 2016, nine medics and 24 to the US.

Money matters: Fees on a par with other similar schools. Still lots of scholarships (more honour than hard cash) but before you bask in the warm glow do check small print and talk to your child about the expectations that go with these.

Means-tested bursaries of up to 100 per cent available and school may assist in individual cases of hardship. Marlborough is one of 'very few schools' who have followed the Charity Commission's advice and transferred all scholarship funds into bursaries. College is currently raising an appeal for substantial additional bursary provision.

Remarks: The college defines its 'triple foundation' as 'rigour, respect and responsibility', an ethos that is at once modern and yet in keeping with its Anglican traditions. Pupils at

Marlborough are part of a diverse, creative and academic community – 21st century co-ed boarding at its very best. To paraphrase lines John Betjeman wrote after revisiting his old school in the 1960s, Marlburians 'Live in a world as rich as is a king's. How sweet are tastes to them, how deep their dreams. How hopeful and how possible their schemes.'

Marling School

Cainscross Road, Stroud, Gloucestershire GL5 4HE

Pupils: 857 • Ages: 11–18 • Sixth form: 274

Tel: 01453 762251
Email: admissions@marling.gloucs.sch.uk
Website: www.marling.gloucs.sch.uk

Headteacher: Since 2010, Dr Stuart Wilson PhD (50s). Brought up on the south coast, he took a first in geology from Bristol, staying on to do a PhD, then worked as an engineering geologist for a few years before coming to the realisation that 'nothing I had worked on had ever been built' and being inspired by spending a day shadowing teacher friends. He loved GCSE science teaching but his move to Cleeve School in Cheltenham provided A level experience and the requisite senior management roles before his appointment to Marling. That time fell in a low point in the school's fortunes, and part of the appeal of the job was to drag it out of the stagnant waters where it lay. What a transformation has been wrought in five years: Dr Wilson is determined not to rest on the 'outstanding' laurels awarded by Ofsted in 2014, and to press for further improvements, not least a new creative arts centre to complement the recent additions for science, mathematics, humanities and dining. 'He has reinvigorated and reshaped the school,' said one father.

Outwardly relaxed (though setting a high sartorial standard in suit and tie), Dr Wilson's undoubted ambitions for the school extend beyond its boys and buildings to its staff. Marling is now a national teaching school and the lead in a teaching alliance of some 10 local schools; it provides opportunities for career advancement for teachers and leaders, and trains those wishing to learn on the job via Schools Direct. Growing its own talent is part of the culture of aspiration and advancement alive and well at Marling.

Dr Wilson is married to the bursar at a local school, and his son attends yet another. Out-of-hours pursuits include walking, skiing, the allotment, travel to further flung parts of the world and, recently, fly-fishing. When asked to describe him in three words, the group of boys we talked to decided that 'inspiring, positive, helpful' summed him up; one bravely elaborated, telling us he was 'superficially stern, but warm personally'. Parents find him visible and approachable; his presence at parents' evenings is especially valued.

Academic matters: Proud to be a boys' grammar in a world where both are increasingly rare. Selective entry, followed by screening for all, thrice yearly tracking, setting of potential grades and 'constructive specific comments' in marking (HTIs – how to improve) keep most noses to the grindstone most of the time. Results are generally good, but then they jolly well should be: GCSE A*/A grades at 47 per cent in 2016; A level A*/B grades dipped to 66 per cent, with 32 per cent A*/A. Top subjects in the boys' view are the sciences, Latin, psychology, philosophy'n'ethics, RE – so we were not surprised to learn that debating is also popular. At A level, maths, the sciences and history are far and away the most popular subjects; modern languages barely get a look in, though three are offered. STEM was happening here almost before the term was coined: this is the school that once built a plane – which flew and landed safely with students on board. And there's a cosmic ray detector on the roof as part of a research project with Birmingham University. Parents appreciate that it is not a hothouse and that 'there is not a stupid amount of homework', but we found some who thought the boys could be pushed harder. The sixth form is run jointly with Stroud High School.

SEND boys are overseen by a SENCo with a place in the senior leadership team, and three specialist members of staff. The focus is on literacy rather than numeracy, which is catered for within the maths department. Liaison between teaching staff is close, and those needing extra help – but not deemed to have SEN – get it. Awareness of boys on the autism spectrum is good; the school has also just trained its first mental health first aider.

Games, options, the arts: Yes, lots of games here, principally rugby, football, cricket and athletics, but other sports catered for in the sports hall (and fitness suite) across the road, such as basketball, indoor tennis and fencing. All taken quite seriously and Marling first teams set out to crush local and not-so-local opposition. Recent success at county level in running, table tennis, handball and badminton. We heard widespread criticism from parents that only the first teams mattered, that no-one else got an external game or a match, and from one boy that he 'wouldn't put himself forward – the school is only interested in Team GB'. 'However,' the head counters, 'the school is working hard provide opportunities for a wide spread of boys, with A, B and sometimes C teams made available to play other schools in the younger years.' This more inclusive note also sounded by the school's participation in Get Set Ready for Community Action, which looks at projects which could be carried out locally in the run-up to the Olympic and Paralympic Games in 2016. D of E strong here and trips (skiing, New York, Pompeii inter alia) sometimes run with Stroud High get thumbs up.

A similar taint of élitism lingers about the drama and music too, according to parents – commendably high standards and plenty of it for those who arrive accomplished or who quickly become so, but not many crumbs for the less gifted. House competitions go some way to address concerns and at the time of writing, recruitment was underway from years 7-11 for a Christmas production of Elf. But there's a limit to what one drama teacher and 1.2 music teachers can achieve in a school this size. Some joint ventures (eg orchestra) with Stroud High (and its girls!), just next door.

A brighter picture emerges with clubs, some which cross age boundaries: we loved the sound of the 'greedy reader' and the green power car team; enthusiasts are also rebuilding a Jaguar with help from company engineers.

Background and atmosphere: Founded in 1887and named after local benefactor Sir Samuel Marling, it was fortunate enough to inherit endowments and roots from far older defunct schools and educational charities, and has stuck resolutely to its grammar school foundations, mounting a campaign in the late 1980s to keep that status. These days, it's a somewhat divisive topic locally, some parents reckoning that it and Stroud High (the girls' equivalent across the playground) cream off the academic crème de la crème, leaving the town's comprehensive schools the poorer in several respects. If true, this is set to get worse, as both grammars increased intake by 30 in 2016, leaving them open to charges of aggressive and predatory actions. That said, the boys are happy and feel lucky to be there: 'It's an aspirational environment', said one and 'We're intellectual rather than privileged,' added another with a wink. Rest assured

M

that the work gets done: Marling boys have a serious attitude and the prevailing winds are ones of solid academic graft.

It certainly looks and feels like a good old-fashioned grammar school with its beautiful darkly panelled vaulted school hall, portraits and parquet as standard. The cloister – the quaintest and most charming example of redundant school architecture we had ever seen (useful when it rains) – links the two original buildings, good solid Victorian monoliths as they are. Elsewhere some stunning modern building, with new West Block recently unveiled and creative arts block under construction, adds contemporary counterpoint – and luckily the functional green tin sports complex is safely out of shot across the road. IT is not overwhelming; despite wireless access all over the site, this is not a place where everyone has a laptop or iPad tucked under one arm. 'The return of linear A levels mean manifold three hour papers – which need handwriting!' as the head expressed it. The boys appear to toe the line as far as uniform and hairstyle go, and to keep banter within limits, in class at any rate. 'It's not a laddish culture,' opined one mother, but others demurred: 'You can be bright, but it's harder to be a nerd'. 'Non-conformists can be bullied', said another.

Pastoral care, well-being and discipline: Reservations about isolated bullying apart, pastoral care is highly rated by all we talked to. Response to parental concerns is quick and effective, and the school will contact parents over any unease it may have. Heads of year come in for particular praise. The boys reckon the balance struck between sanction and reward is about right, and that the reasons behind any punishments are fully explained. 'Clarity and consistency,' says the head confidently. Sixth formers appreciate being treated like the adults they will soon become. Plenty of accessible and sympathetic members of staff to talk to when things go wrong in whatever sphere of school life.

Pupils and parents: No catchment area, but most students arrive from a 10 mile radius of Stroud by a web of buses, public and private. The furthest flung might come from Swindon, an educational desert, or Cheltenham, which isn't. It need hardly be said that families whose sons are at Marling set much store by schooling and might be glad to have many of the advantages of independent education without the price tag. 'We're proud that parents see us as an alternative', concludes the head, with a refreshing lack of chippiness. His boys are lively, funny, thoughtful – delightful in fact, but not too burdened by the weight of academic expectation the school or their parents place on them. Parents enjoy an active association with staff involvement which raises considerable funds for the school and a good sideline in second hand uniform.

Entrance: Quite selective, aiming at the top 25 per cent of the ability range for its 150 year 7 intake. The seven Gloucestershire grammar schools share the same CEM 11+ entrance test (verbal ability, numerical reasoning and non-verbal reasoning) devised by Durham University, for which tutoring is very common; some parents disapprove massively, however, on the grounds that such selectivity is local government policy and that the playing field should therefore be level. Those who don't make it can have another crack in subsequent years for entry in year 8, 9 or 10. Fortunately, Stroud's other comprehensive schools are well regarded, as is Deer Park in Cirencester. At sixth form, another 25 per cent arrive with the requisite number of GCSE grades (at least five, with a C or above in English and maths and no lower than a B in subjects to be studied at A level).

Exit: Very few after GCSE (around 20 per cent) – why would they, with the scope and lure provided the combined sixth form offer with Stroud High? School will pick out likely lads for Oxbridge and Russell group (two to Oxbridge in 2016) – though they can also 'self-identify'. Requirements exacted by medicine, veterinary or overseas universities also catered for. 'Local options, perhaps less prominent but given no less support,' the head confirms, as are apprenticeships and other non-university destinations. Strong leaning towards maths, engineering and science courses, but English, humanities and politics also prominent. The sixth formers we met were extravagant in their praise for UCAS support and for Futures Day, where speakers from universities, employers, gap year volunteering providers set out all conceivable (acceptable) options. The Old Marlingtonians' Association another useful resource for careers advice.

Remarks: Stroud can be proud of this school, which maintains a high academic profile and traditions for boys without any risk of their becoming arrogant, stuffy or sexist. Bringing home the silverware, literal and metaphorical, matters – but please could everyone have a game? Or a part?

The Maynard School

Denmark Road, Exeter EX1 1SJ

Pupils: 356 • Ages: 4–18 • Sixth form: 80

Fees: £5,400 – £12,585 pa

Tel: 01392 273417
Email: admissions@maynard.co.uk
Website: www.maynard.co.uk

Headmistress: Since September 2016, Sarah Dunn, previously deputy head of Plymouth College. Studied at Exeter and Oxford (PGCE); started as a biology teacher at Torquay Boys' Grammar, working her way up to become deputy head of sixth form and head of careers. Joined Plymouth College in 1995 as deputy head and introduced girls throughout the school.

Head of junior school: Since 2006, Mr Steven Smerdon, originally from Bath, educated at Exeter University. His career has taken him to Edinburgh, Australia and back to Exeter again. Friendly, welcoming and enthusiastic. Teaches RE and drama and is child protection officer for the whole school. In his 40s, he enjoys the great outdoors and is a keen cyclist. Maynard Junior is above average academically, but he says, 'the most important thing we teach is how to get on with people.' Parents say, 'Mr Smerdon clearly loves his job and the girls love him'.

Head of the pre-prep Mrs Emma Cook, previously at Beaudesert Park School, where she was a year 2 teacher, head of years 1 and 2 and acting head of the pre-prep.

Academic matters: Classes are small in the junior school – between 10 and 20. The music class we saw was relaxed and the teacher was encouraging each girl to 'have a twirl'. Instilling confidence is high on the list of priorities here. One classroom door boldly declares: 'We are warriors not worriers'. There is a very high standard of work on display and we saw some impressive written work. There is a teaching assistant for one-to-one reading sessions and the end results have been remarkable. A breadth of reading is encouraged and the library provides a cosy reading area. As part of the school's Buddy program, girls of differing ages read together once a week.

All new girls are screened for dyslexia. There are currently three pupils at SEN level plus one visually impaired. These children have one-to-one specialist teaching outside the classroom for dyslexic type difficulties, including use of a structured spelling and reading scheme, study skills, support for sequencing and memory difficulties. The teaching assistant also covers one-to-one sessions for numeracy. This is all overseen by SENCo. The head is keen to emphasise that 'self-esteem is the most important aid to learning and the whole school works to improve this in all our girls.'

Computing is a rapidly growing area of the junior school. There's a large ICT room and coding lessons have been introduced. Staff have been given extensive training and currently year 6 are all busy making their own apps, years 3 and 5 are using Photoshop and year 4 are working on their own animation project. The head is very focused on safety, and not only runs Cyber Safety programmes for the girls, but there are sessions for parents too. The girls are given limited homework, just enough to prepare for the senior school. The general consensus is that 'home life is deemed as more important at this age', particularly as a fair few travel long distances every day.

Academically selective, Maynard is one of the highest performing schools in the South West. The main reason for most parents choosing the school is 'the academic focus'. Results are good year on year, though with a disappointing dip at A level in 2016, when 55 per cent of grades were A*/A (84 per cent A*-B). At GCSE 66 per cent were A*/A.

Girls take 10 GCSEs. Maths and sciences score particularly well, with many girls continuing these subjects at university. Three modern languages, French, Spanish and German, are offered. ICT is delivered through the higher level EPQ. Girls with LDD are supported well, enabling them to make as much progress as their peers. One parent of a girl who had only just started a few weeks previously said, 'They handle her dyslexia with care and attention to detail. During the first full week she had reading aids, and all her printed work was done on blue paper to help with her reading.'

iPads are being rolled out, starting with year 9. All staff have iPads and have had extensive training, including cyber safety. Sessions for parents on safety are available too. Staff keen to 'respect all traditions of this old school whilst meeting the challenges of the 21st century.'

Classrooms displayed impressive and interesting work, particularly the classics room; the annual Roman Banquet looked like lots of fun. In the food and nutrition room, there was a particularly happy class whipping up a chickpea curry, and over in a science laboratory we saw a GCSE class working out how to test the hardness of water. The teacher had a 'get on with it' attitude, encouraging the girls to think independently and learn by their mistakes. Good, practical teaching.

At sixth form, there are 23 AS and A2 options plus an Extended Project Qualification on offer. Parents say that with such good standards across the board, girls find it hard to choose which subjects to specialise in. Not a bad dilemma to have. We saw classes of sixth formers having maths and science lessons, more than expected at a girls' school. Many go on to study engineering, economics or sciences at university. One teacher believed this was one of the benefits of being a single sex school. A parent agreed, saying she felt 'the school will give [her daughter] confidence to pursue any career she wants and will not pigeonhole her, or any pupil, into "female" pursuits.'

Games, options, the arts: Parents say, 'It would be nice if the school had its own grounds and more facilities for sports activities' – but this is a city school and space is limited. Some say, 'the lack of facilities means that the sports department staff work even harder to ensure that the school puts out as many teams as possible.' This seems to be the case and there's enough choice here for everyone to find a sport they enjoy. For a small school, there's a good number of girls excelling at swimming, netball, hockey and athletics at county level. Other sports on offer include badminton, tennis, rounders, gymnastics, dance and fencing. On site, there are three netball/tennis courts, a huge and impressive sports hall, plus a gym. To compensate for its lack of grounds, the school acquired a sports field last year, just 10 minutes' walk away. They also make good use of the Astroturf at the university, and the local swimming pool.

Art and music are in one creative building. There are two art studios plus dark rooms. There were some very impressive life drawings and textiles on display as well as some abstract work. The sixth form art studio is light and airy and is in constant use throughout lunchtimes and free periods. On our visit, there was an Art in Residence Day for sixth formers. The girls have a whole day with a local artist to explore ideas and ultimately give them a break from the curriculum. We were really impressed by this approach: the girls are provided with a good work/life balance that can only help them in the future when they're juggling it for real.

Upstairs in the music room, a class was split into small groups dotted around the various practice rooms. The theme was Elements of Rock 'n Roll and the teacher looked as if he was having just as much fun as the pupils. There's a good mix of music on offer, ranging from jazz bands and choirs to orchestras, and most girls learn an instrument. The head of music was very excited about an upcoming trip to Italy where the choir will be performing in Venice and then Verona.

Drama can be studied at both GCSE and A level, and LAMDA classes are available. There are usually 8-10 productions a year plus an annual performance that involves girls from all years. Past productions have included Sweeney Todd, The Fantastic Mr Fox and The Just So Stories, all performed in the large oak-beamed school hall, and practised in the adjoining drama studio. There are theatre trips on offer for all years including an annual trip to Stratford for sixth formers. The school regularly invites local theatre companies to come and perform at the school, giving the girls an opportunity to meet the production teams directly.

However, 'It is beyond the curriculum where the real difference is made,' said one teacher. This particularly applies to the sixth form, where the girls are encouraged to be independent and develop in all areas of life to prepare for university and work. The Aspire Plus programme focuses on university and helps with applications by asking 'Who do you think you are?', encouraging girls to look at their core skills and interests. The weekly extension studies programme includes car maintenance, critical thinking, philosophy, politics and cookery. There is a Voluntary Work Scheme plus the Young Enterprise Club where girls liaise with local businesses to develop products, sell them and make a profit. Outdoor challenges like Duke of Edinburgh and the Ten Tors challenge are extremely popular, as are foreign exchanges. There is a biennial ski trip and trips to Greece and Italy with the classics department, plus an upcoming trip to Iceland. Older girls have raised their own funds to go on World Challenge trips to India, Borneo, Morocco and Venezuela in recent years. Recently, the sixth formers went on an expedition to Peru to help with an irrigation scheme in the Sacred Valley. Adventures and challenges are really big here.

The junior school shares the senior school sports facilities. For a small school they have done well to win the Sainbury's Silver Award for Competitive Sport and they regularly participate in sports festivals with other local primary schools.

Extracurricular activities are aplenty. There are events that involve the whole school like the Forensics Day and Multicultural Week, plus an abundance of charity activities and fundraising – Save The Arctic Fox is currently top of the list. Lunchtimes are extended to accommodate the numerous clubs – sports, cooking, drama, music. Many are run voluntarily by the sixth formers who also act as mentors. Parents say, 'We like the very calm, friendly and supportive attitudes shown not just by the teachers, but also by the girls in the senior school.' Home time is later than normal due to long lunchtimes and the school also helpfully provides free wrap-around care from 8am to 5.30pm.

Background and atmosphere: Founded in 1658 by Sir John Maynard, it's the third oldest girls' school in the country and is a registered charity. The school moved to its current city centre site in 1882. Old and new buildings work well together, the latest addition being The Murdin Link built in 2008. It brings the senior and junior school together and houses year 6, textiles, food and nutrition and ICT. There's a beautiful oak-beamed school hall, decorated with stained glass windows and wooden plaques of past awards, that remind you this is a traditional school at heart. Colourful, bright murals are dotted around the outside of the school and there are pockets of gardens, an allotment, an outdoor classroom and play areas. The school grounds feel bright and calm, and there's a feeling of space, even though it really is very small and in the city centre.

Lunch is self-service and 'lovingly' created on-site by the very popular chef. All produce is locally sourced and all dietary needs catered for. Sixth form girls say they rarely bother to bring packed lunch. In fact, they say, they rarely bother to go out of the school even though they can. They prefer to run lunch clubs, or use the art studio or library. Seriously well-behaved girls.

There is a well-balanced mix of male and female teachers. Until recently there has been a very low turnover of teachers, but retirement has seen some newish appointments. One is Tom Hibberd, head of sixth form, relocated from a large boys' school in south London. He says the girls have been very welcoming and the staff couldn't be more supportive. Having just finished his first month, he said he was impressed how the 'girls thrive on autonomy and motivate each other', worlds apart from the boys' school, no doubt.

Junior school in a modern, bright building in the middle of the campus, which opens out onto the tennis courts and feels very much part of the senior school. Photos of recent trips and events are displayed at the entrance. The girls obviously thoroughly enjoy the adventure trips on Dartmoor and Haven Banks. There is a lot of emphasis on teamwork and they've even got their own Green Team. The school is very involved with the Devon Wildlife Trust and there's been training days on glow worms, making bird boxes, and building bug and butterfly hotels. There's an allotment in the play area and the girls grow their own vegetables to cook in the food and nutrition classes. This really is a country school at heart. The outdoor play area is small and quirky. It has a shop area that gets very busy at peak times, dealing in leaves. A favourite tree was once threatened with being chopped down – the girls literally tied themselves to it in protest, apparently. There's even an outdoor classroom made from recycled materials and old tyres, a past head girl legacy and parents' project.

'There is a palpable sense of community support and mutual respect,' said one parent, and it seems the girls really are happy to help each other and others. There is also a new voluntary scheme – Kissing It Better – where sixth formers visit old people's homes, sing, chat, play Scrabble and get to know the older generation.

Pastoral care, well-being and discipline: The Maynard claims to be 'expert in girls', and to treat them all as individuals. During our visit, we really got the sense that this is true, they really do care. One parent said, 'I applaud the school's approach to a democratic education...they accept that everyone learns in different ways. I have direct experience of this with one of my daughters, who had serious health issues and was unable to follow the standard route.' The girls feel valued and there is mutual respect between pupils and staff. Girls say bullying rarely occurs and there's a system for reporting and dealing with it.

There's great autonomy, particularly for older girls. Independence is possible because of the small numbers, enabling staff to keep tabs on the girls fairly easily. No rebellious actions to report. No set school rules. Girls are encouraged to behave responsibly and they are rewarded with a fair share of independence and respect. This seems to work very well.

All junior school staff are available at the school gates at the beginning and end of each day.

Pupils and parents: Parents are medics, farmers, solicitors, from all walks of life and all 'very hard working', according to school. Some girls are funded by grandparents. Some live locally, others travel up to an hour to get to school. Parents say they can be as involved in the school as much as they like, there's no pressure. The parents' association does lots of fundraising and socialising and is run predominantly by mothers. One parent questioned this, suggesting that 'the school is maybe missing out on a broader perspective or set of views?' Sounds like the dads want to get involved. Families are regularly invited to music and dance recitals or mini-productions. Most recently they were invited to a Dine With My Daughter day to taste the culinary delights of the school's kitchen, all cooked on site with local produce.

Old girls and parents regularly come back to share their experiences at university or work or to discuss job opportunities. While we were there, a recent leaver was back from Cambridge to chat about her biochemistry degree and another leaver was due to visit to chat about her internship at Accenture. Old girls include Professor Dame Margaret Turner-Warwick – first woman president of British Medical Council; Claire Morall, author, short-listed for Man Booker Prize; Diana Brightmore-Armour, MD Lloyds TSB corporate banking division.

Entrance: Assessment for reception to year 2 in new pre-prep by 'a series of informal and play-based activities'. Assessments for junior school (7+) are taken seriously as girls are not expected to resit for entry to the senior school (although places are not guaranteed). Having said that, parents say it's 'very straightforward' and 'there was no untoward stress placed on the children.' Girls sit tests in English, maths, reasoning and reading plus an interview for all girls from 7-15. We were pleased to hear that they look for potential, not just current ability. Taster days are encouraged.

Sixth form entrance is based on an interview, GCSE grades and a reference from the previous school.

Exit: Junior school girls have no exam for entry to the senior school, and 90 per cent move on there. In fact, the girls already feel part of the senior school by the end of year 6. They wear senior uniform, can use their own bags and have some lessons in the senior school including a term each of French, Spanish and German. Homework is slowly introduced, too. It's an effective, smooth transition. It does come with a senior school price tag, though: fees go up for year 6.

Some 30 per cent leave after GCSEs. Nearly all sixth formers go to university, a few after gap years. Bristol, Cardiff and London universities are the most popular destinations. One to Oxbridge in 2016 and six medics. Other popular courses include veterinary science, engineering, economics, maths and the arts including fashion.

Money matters: There are a variety of bursaries and scholarships available and the school is keen to make this an affordable education for all. One parent said, 'This is also what I love about the school, the diversity of families. There are families who can easily afford the fees, and those that work two jobs to do it. This makes my children aware of the different backgrounds of their peers.' All parents questioned agreed it was 'a good deal financially'. Means-tested bursaries can cover up to 45 per cent of fees. There are also five scholarships offered at senior level, plus sports, arts and music scholarships at sixth form level. Recently introduced eight new 13+ scholarships, four in sport and four in performing arts. Two of each category to existing students, others to new entrants. Nineteen new Maynard awards, a combination of scholarships and means-tested bursaries. Five of these, for sixth form entrants, offer 100 per cent fee remission. The school offers sibling discounts, provides free wrap-around care from 8am-5.30pm, provides all textbooks and subsidises educational trips whenever possible with the help of the parents' association fundraising

Remarks: Friendly and unpretentious. Not the best facilities but good for a small city school. They provide a caring environment that promotes hard work – 'There is a very clear focus on ensuring that everybody achieves to their maximum, but not in a po-faced way,' say parents. Girls are happy and parents truly believe in the school. One parent of a nervous, studious girl said, 'The Maynard has allowed her confidence to grow...I am certain that the time she spends at school is a big part of what makes her happy'. Another agreed, saying 'I know my three (very different) girls will thrive and leave with good results, as well rounded women, knowing that if they work hard they can achieve anything they put their minds to.'

Millfield Prep School

Linked with Millfield School

Edgarley Hall, Glastonbury, Somerset BA6 8LD

Pupils: 463; 120 full, 46 weekly/flexi boarders • Ages: 2-13 (boarders from age 7)

Fees: Day £8,250 – £17,550; Boarding £26,640 pa

Tel: 01458 832446
Email: office@millfieldprep.com
Website: www.millfieldschool.com

Headmistress: Since 2010, Mrs Shirley Shayler MEd BSc PGCE. Educated at Carrickfergus Grammar School, Northern Ireland, degree in biology from the University of Stirling, PGCE from Queen's University, Belfast, masters in educational management. No stranger to Millfield, having taught biology at the senior school 1989-2002 and undertaken an impressive spread of pastoral and extracurricular rôles including coaching first XI girls' hockey and being a houseparent. Deputy head of Taunton School for four years then head of Stonar for another four plus years doing much to expand and improve the sixth form. Lives on site with husband Gary, biology teacher and head of careers at senior school, and daughter, Caragh, who attends Millfield Prep and rides a school pony.

'Delightful' and 'caring' but steely when need arises. Parents we spoke to all thought she was 'a good head who works hard' and commented on how 'she has won respect through not being afraid to stick to her guns.' Loves being back at Millfield: 'a way of life rather than a job,' she commented to us. Really believes in educating 'whole child' and in releasing children's potential. Often seen walking family labrador (she recently delivered seven puppies). Still involved in hockey and also enjoys swimming, cycling, skiing (annual family ski trip is a highlight for Shaylers), reading and the theatre. Vision for future includes providing more enrichment à la Dragon's Den-style enterprise activity, more involvement in the local community and further developing pastoral care.

Entrance: Many admitted via interview and report from previous head (eg from prep schools finishing at 11). Some arrive from pre-preps or local primaries and others from as far away as Venezuela or Hong Kong (we have seldom seen such a varied list of feeder schools). LDC tutor involved at interview where there are special learning needs. Can be flexible – will always make the effort to take pupils and has been a sanctuary for pupils unhappy or failing to thrive elsewhere: 'IQ not the only arbiter; we need to see the child, not just a collection of data.' Can and will take when space available; means-tested bursaries available in cases of genuine need and a number of scholarships (all the usuals plus chess) for entry into years 6, 7 and 8. The former depend on success in the scholarship exams which can be sat each January.

Exit: Most proceed to senior school. Dozen or more scholarships won annually to senior school: academic, art, music and sport. Transfer automatic subject to good behaviour and satisfactory academic standard. A small number move elsewhere, mostly to other independent schools.

Remarks: Millfield provides a top notch experience in almost every sphere. Lively boarding community which doesn't high tail it home at weekends (apart from exeats) – around 40 per cent of boarders are from overseas – and still includes Sunday chapel. Boy and girl numbers pretty equal throughout. Many sign up for complete (2-18) Millfield experience. Parents underline how school 'instills confidence and maturity' and how it 'has brought a global dimension to rural Somerset.' Prep campus benefits from more acreage than its senior partner. Centrepiece is an elegant Victorian home of former local landowners. Oak-panelled hall leads to head's capacious study (now made-over to suit her taste) overlooking grounds. Internal standard of classrooms, sports and other facilities more than compensates for lack of architectural cohesion on a site that has grown like Topsy. Unusual external touches include a huge outdoor chess set and the multi-coloured climbing wall. Children seem quite content, scurrying around like worker bees under the queen's command. Main entrance sits on a bend of A361 on the Pilton side of Glastonbury opposite (and safely accessible via footbridge over main road) school's small chapel, nine-hole golf course and Edgarley Manor (a boys' boarding house) at the foot of the famous Tor.

Show starts with Millfield Minis, a three-day-a-week event for local parents and toddlers using pre-prep hall from 10.00-11.30am. There are even Minis' swimming, tennis and trampolining. Pre-prep department caters for pupils aged 2-7. Safe, ideal location within former walled garden. Reception area shouts creativity and fun; classrooms are flexible learning spaces with eye-catching displays, live animals and loads of interest. Outdoor raised beds for veggie growing, safe play and exploration including Forest School (two teachers trained leaders) nearby. Pond includes underwater camera for pupils to watch submarine activity on linked computer screen. We liked the three little pigs guarding the gazebo and outside quiet area. Cosy library to make reading fun and indoor tumble room for scrapes without scratches. Read Write Inc a favourite phonic approach, number games abound and we saw some beautiful progressions of pupils' cursive handwriting on display. Humanities and science themes run alongside core learning. Music, art and drama all play a big part.

Children coming into pre-prep are automatically assessed for learning support: one-to-one groups and lessons for those who need extra help from two specialist teachers who work closely with school's learning development centre. Parents appreciate the experience of many long-serving teachers and the extent to which it is 'an inclusive environment' rather than pushy.

Most of the prep school buildings are modern (if not of any particular architectural merit) and provide well for a community of around 400 children. The large, refurbished assembly hall serves for school's frequent drama productions and activities such as fencing and gymnastics. The well-stocked library is above the dining complex (probably the best we've seen in a prep school: all shiny service counters and friendly staff). Food is plentiful and varied.

We observed versatile teaching across a broad curriculum in small classes (maximum is normally 16) from an experienced and friendly staff. Years 3-5 are taught by group tutors for most lessons. Setting from year 3 in English, maths and languages with mixed-ability tutor groups. From year 6 all lessons are taught by subject specialists, with tutors continuing to have pastoral oversight. Academic standards are reassuringly high. Despite many children needing extra English, the school's 'language for all' policy ensures that every child can take Spanish as part of their programme. French and Latin are on the main menu with some linguistic side orders also available (eg Mandarin, Russian and Japanese).

The five science labs are still housed in very adequate temporary accommodation close to the main teaching areas, and teachers we spoke to were in no rush to move into a new building. Young number crunchers perform well in competitions such as UK Maths Challenge and we were told that children particularly enjoy using MangaHigh software. Splendid IT suite where we saw some pupils operating robots they had programmed; good use made of smart boards and digital projectors in all subjects. Scholarship group starts in year 7 and we saw some year 8 scholars preparing for Salters chemistry festival at Bath University. Strong eco bias (Green Flag holders) with regular focus on environmental issues (eg switch off fortnight) and annual eco day. Pastoral team overseen by experienced deputy head: each child is watched over by group tutor, responsible for welfare and progress, and first port of call for anxious parents. Reports are termly, with grades for effort as well as attainment. Parents contacted every half-term regarding progress.

Millfield is not a special school, but it attracts pupils with a range of problems from mild literacy difficulties to those with a diagnosis of dyslexia and/or speech and language difficulties. The language development centre (LDC) is a centre of excellence with five full-time and four part-time specialists plus a classroom assistant. Strong liaison throughout between LDC, pastoral and academic staff as well as with senior school. If reading or spelling is more than a year behind chronological age, this is flagged up, 'But data is not the only aspect taken into account when determining a pupil's current needs.' Speech and language therapist works closely with both the prep and pre-prep. Parents praised how their daughter, previously in a specialist school, was now 'blossoming' at Millfield through the combination of specialist help and 'an emphasis on the positive side of everything.' Group help at both ends of the spectrum included in fees but one-to-one support and recall to therapists are chargeable. Special programme (Potential Academic Curriculum Excellence or PACE) undertaken by super-bright. EAL teacher uses academic lesson time with over 30 international students to immerse them in English before they are progressively fitted into mainstream curriculum.

Sport is a big deal here and a pull for many parents: five PE specialists and a number of ex-international coaches. Sixty pupils in swimming squad alone, partnership with LTA to provide top class tennis coaching, and bubble over one of nine courts on site (pupils go to senior complex if necessary) ensures practice continues through winter. Stonking sports hall (includes large spectator area and four squash courts – two of which are glass backed), equestrian centre with extensive stabling and arenas for dressage and show jumping, a nine-hole golf course just for Millfield prep, a fine 25-metre pool (ditto), new sports pavilion and all sorts of courts, pitches and fields to cater for every conceivable sport and activity (seven county champions in athletics alone).

Rising stars can miss a regular PE lesson to receive individual coaching (eg from ex-first class cricketers). U13 girls had just won national (not just preps) cricket title at Lord's when we visited. A powerful presence across all major sports at county and national levels. School is not invincible and meets some stiff competition on the prep schools circuit. Individuals star in many disciplines: fencing, tennis and golf being recent examples. Even the chaplain has a sporting seam running through him (he was going off with a golfing group when we met him). Millfield brain does as well as its brawn with chess teams defending an enviable reputation in tournaments at all levels.

Cracking music department under long-serving director: attractive modern recital hall (seats 200), classrooms and practice rooms; wide range of instruments, 350 individual lessons, 29 music ensembles and 18 annual concerts. Junior baroque chamber orchestra plus four choirs and a chapel choir. Pupils selected for national children's choir and orchestra. Annual highlights include home-grown Young Musician of the Year competition and a rock and pop concert. Drama lessons lead to many pupils becoming involved (on stage or behind the scenes) in one of four major productions held annually. Staff sometimes have to write plays to suit Millfield's large casts. Parents have been amazed at positive effect of school drama on their children. Art (including popular after lessons clubs) is strong as evidenced by displays around school, from print-making to ceramics via ICT, with critical discussion an integral part of its teaching. Good environment in both drawing and painting studios; innovations downstairs included an ex-government printing press bought for a song and stone carving taught in warmer months by talented working artist and done under a lean-to adjacent to art department. Picture of the week chosen from pupils' artwork for insertion in school's newsletter. Design facilities are more akin to a senior school and include CAD design and a laser cutter. Products range from torches to clocks. Textiles aplenty downstairs and food science upstairs encourages innovative cooking which even includes an inter-house competition.

House system is used for internal competitions of all kinds (not just sport). Apart from Edgarley Manor (boys' boarding house) across A361, remaining four boarding houses are on main site: all modern with capacity for 38 boarders each. No large dorms: boarders either in two, four or six bed units (early swimmers kept in rooms together to avoid disturbing others when they get up to train). More of a home from home than an institutional feel and bright colours help keep spirits high. Year 8 allowed to do prep in rooms; otherwise, boarders are supervised in school between 5pm and 6pm. Well-equipped common rooms and cosy kitchens for snacking and chatting. Extra tuck part of house reward system. Boarding houses have outside play areas including tennis court and enclosed field. Medical staff available 24/7.

Minibuses ferry day pupils (early rises for some) from outlying villages in time for 8.25am start. Younger ones can leave at 3.45pm but majority of stay for activities until 5pm. Great choice includes sailing at Durleigh, sub-aqua group aiming at PADI junior qualification and caving on Mendips. Weekday activities include Airfix modelling and touch typing, as well as sports from pop lacrosse and indoor go-karting. Diverse theme days and stimulating educational visits to destinations as distant as Rome or as close as Glastonbury Abbey all add to broad mix. Charity fundraising and activities within the local community are also given importance.

We liked the way that so many year 8 pupils get leadership roles on a rotating basis and how 20 of them trained with Kidscape to become peer mentors. Former pupils include 10 current first class cricketers (including half of Somerset CC first XI), rugby stars: Matt Perry and Chris Robshaw, Olympic hockey brothers: Simon and Richard Mantell, Euan Dale (Scottish

M

swimming medallist), Joey Barrington (squash international), Ruth Kelly MP and Max Milligan (photographer, author and explorer).

Happy school with genuine excitement at every level. Pupils find their niche here (be it academic, sporting or creative) and 'want to do well.' Facilities to take your breath away but school produces well-rounded individuals rather than arrogant know-it-alls. 'My daughter was dancing with the daisies before she joined Millfield,' said one mum, 'and now the change is unbelievable.' Parents testify to extent that 'academic and less academic pupils can flourish alongside each other.' Hard to do better than this if the package suits.

Millfield School

Linked with Millfield Prep School

Butleigh Road, Street, Somerset BA16 0YD

Pupils: 1,255; 924 full boarders • Ages: 13–18 • Sixth form: 587

Fees: Boarding £35,775; Day £24,030 pa

Tel: 01458 442296
Email: admissions@millfieldschool.com
Website: www.millfieldschool.com

Head Master: Since 2008, Mr Craig Considine MEd (mid 50s). Firmly rooted in the southern hemisphere until his appointment to Millfield – a degree in applied science in human movement (that'll be sports science then), a masters in educational leadership from Melbourne's top universities, director of co-curricular at Geelong then head of Wanganui Collegiate School in New Zealand – he brings some welcome Antipodean directness to one of 'the big names – not one of the old names', as he puts it. A previous (British) head of Geelong had suggested Mr Considine could do worse than look at Millfield for ideas for sports facilities; along with those, he was also aware of and intrigued by Jack Meyer's (Millfield's founder, of whom more anon) work on word blindness, as dyslexia was then called, and its links with top flight cricketers. In the ensuing years, Mr Considine has concentrated on improving academics and dispelling perceptions of Millfield as a place for the well-heeled, dim and sporty, but keeping, nay enhancing, the remarkable scope of activities outside the classroom. 'It's all about balance,' he says, 'We can be all things to all people, but it's still about results – and the school needs to be on more prep school radars'. He is proud of the successful attempts to work ever more closely with each student through increased staffing levels: 'We've increased the number of resident staff to take some of the responsibility from houseparents – I could possibly be lampooned for the burgeoning management team', he admits.

A considerable athlete himself – he represented Australia in the decathlon and played professional Australian rules football – his study overlooks the hockey pitches, and his love of sport is still evident in his physique and Twitter feed. Family consists of five grown up children, including two daughters sometimes based in Australia. 'This is a not a job you can get away from,' he asserts, but he loves the proximity and cultural richness of Europe. We found the mix of Antipodean directness with insight and deep appreciation of matters ancient and modern (Avalon meets the iPad) very refreshing in this unexpectedly thoughtful head, who generally meets with parental approval, and was variously described as approachable, willing to listen, humble and not very polished; 'he doesn't work the room,' one parent remarked. Might he be content with being summed up as 'a good bloke'? Very probably.

Academic matters: Our previous review said that 'academics will never be the point of Millfield' and that remains true, but the head has devoted considerable efforts to beefing up the intellectual offer with, amongst other initiatives, an enviable programme of academic enrichment, including a lecture series and subject conferences which any young person would be foolish to miss, given the calibre and repute of speakers (scientific colossi Robert Winston, Maggie Aderin-Pocock and Jim Al-Khalili on the same platform!). Brainboxes are invited to join Eureka! or Think Tank, mixed aged groups which meet fortnightly 'to develop the skill of argument analysis'. GCSEs currently graded 25 per cent A*/A, down from previous years; depending on ability and aptitude, students might do any number between six and 12, including core subjects but not necessarily a foreign language. A level results 56 per cent A*/B, 28 per cent A*/A, with a staggering 33 subjects to choose from, including world development and classical Greek.

Onward destinations are manifold, both in the UK and North America in particular; just one to Oxford in 2016 'but then we don't have a lot of kids saying Oxbridge is where they want to go,' the head remarked. One parent was critical of Oxbridge preparation – or lack of it, feeling that the school was much more interested in and geared up for applications to American universities; the school is a SAT centre, but that same father reckoned that the top results at Millfield are as good as anywhere. But it is heartening to see the range of qualifications on offer at Millfield: for the less academically inclined, BTecs attract growing numbers, along with the British Horse Society's Preliminary Instructor's certificate and the ever popular Leith food and wine course – just the thing for running that chalet in Verbier in one's gap year. Judging by the longevity of some teachers' careers there, teaching at Millfield can be a job for life, leading to some dissatisfaction with the calibre in some quarters, and a sense that some old timers could usefully be moved on. The head is addressing effective recruitment at least by providing the kind of accommodation designed to attract top notch staff. Class sizes noticeably small here, max 14; the staff pupil ratio is the lowest this editor had ever seen, at just 1:6.5. Students are generally grouped into ability bands via literacy tests, then into sets within those bands, but some A level language and science classes are taught across the ability range.

School's website cites 'sophisticated use of digital technology for learning' but this greatly understates the almost total integration of iPads throughout the school (closer at the younger end). Every student must have one, and through it, almost everything flows, in and out of the classroom. That said, it does not replace live teaching, but aids it: we were privileged, if not faintly repelled, to witness the dissection of a horse's lung, where the lesson went on to explore human lung capacity at rest and after exertion via an iPad app, one boy gamely leaping up and down outside as a live experiment. Unhelpful chatter from Facebook, Instagram and Twitter is blocked in lesson time, and there's a tracking system which monitors any reprehensible activity. 'But what about old-fashioned skills like note-taking?' we asked – and received a somewhat prickly assurance that these were also taught. 'We're about adapting, not adopting' the head said pithily.

SEN provision underpins much of Millfield's successes and its appeal. When we asked the head about Millfield's being viewed as a haven or magnet for SEN, his response was unequivocal: 'Well it is! We make strong assessments of SEN which we normalise here, and occasionally have to say no to those whose learning we cannot support'. Just over a third of students have an identified need, addressed and supported by a team of SpLD experts in the exceptionally well-resourced learning support centre (no fewer than four educational psychologists on the staff), sited right at this rambling school's heart. Support is based on literacy, the key to the entire curriculum, but help is available for all manners of barriers to learning including dyscalculia (sometimes delivered to milder cases among younger students by sixth formers alongside the maths tutor), dyspraxia and organisation skills. Just about everyone gets GCSE English and maths at grade C – hurrah – but retake classes are run in year 12 for anyone just missing that important hurdle. The sheer numbers receiving support means a total lack of stigma: our delightful young guide came straight to the point during our tour: 'I am very dyslexic and here I get all the help I need'. Close liaison between teachers, house staff, tutors and SEN staff provides continuity and reassurance.

Games, options, the arts: Genuinely exceedingly difficult to know where to start! This is unquestionably the place for your budding Olympian, and the fact that it has produced so many top flight athletes and sportspeople is no accident. Both provision and facilities abound, from the famous 50m Olympic swimming pool with all the wizardry and coaches associated with training future national champions to the recent acquisition of a stretch of the Huntspill river (a world class water facility, apparently) and Swingulator which trains oarsmen/women on dry land. It is typical of the Millfield seriousness of purpose that, having only introduced rowing a few years ago, investment in a year-round programme including nutrition, video analysis and diverse training has resulted in this Jonny-come-lately beating many established rowing schools and even universities. But whatever Millfield does – and it does almost everything – it does exceptionally well, devoting considerable sums, land and care in recruiting top coaches to its unequalled sporting offer. We could wax rapturous about the provision for riders, comprising a polo ground, cross-country course and gallops, or about the fencing salle, but the more usual school sports are outstandingly provided for also. The school's level of commitment has to be matched by that of the students': a daily 5.40am reveille is quite common for élite swimmers, for example. Parental opinion about the school's attitude to sporting élitism varies: clearly some send their offspring here exactly for that, others feel that the push for excellence has rather meant other kids being 'left to get on with it', in the words of one father. At junior levels, by contrast, we found some frustration that previous top prep school players (rugby, but maybe other games too) were regularly substituted, meaning that they played less often/for less long than they were used to, demotivating them at times.

M

Art and DT all happen in the same gorgeous spacious block; needless to say, all equipment is bang up to the mark and, claims school, equals some university facilities. The nationally known Atkinson Gallery hosts four major exhibitions a year; when we visited, the most innovative work coming out of the UK's top art schools was on show. We wished we had taken more note of the Millfield sculpture trail as we trotted about the extensive site: new work is regularly commissioned or purchased. Music facilities marvellous – lots of it, very high spec too – and the exposure to the musical life a part of every Millfieldian's first year, when learning an orchestral instrument is compulsory. Major concerts often take place in the sublime contrast of Wells Cathedral, where the choir sings also regular services. It was an unexpected delight to happen across a member of the music staff practising Poulenc for his own pleasure. Drama is popular and very well-resourced, with several studios as well as the Meyer Theatre. Just one whole school production a year but a ton of other things, such as a sketch show and a Spanish play, and opportunities to get involved in all goings-on back stage. Applications to drama school are exceptionally well supported here, and success rates high in this competitive area.

The Millfield Activities Programme (MAP to its friends) offers 100 different pursuits for all students up until year 12, and is intended to offer breadth – alongside élite sport, for example. French cinema, German card games, skiing race training, silversmithing – it's all there for the taking. Local volunteering opportunities with a range of charities provide an outlet for altruism and perhaps a chance to reflect on all that privilege.

Boarding: Three-quarters of students board in 19 boarding houses scattered across the 240 acre campus. We were whisked around a selection of them in a golf buggy, on account of the sheer scale of the place (not because we had visited unsuitably shod in stilettos). Year 9s have their own houses for that vital first year, to ensure solid friendships across the year group and to integrate the large numbers who arrive from Millfield Prep. After year 9, students have a say in their final house, but staff are careful to try to avoid the forming of cliques. Most rooms are twins, singles further up the school, some with ensuite shower rooms; all was clean and functional rather than luxurious, and we noted the congenial common room space with pool tables and ping pong, rather than more screens; all i-anything is handed in at night to a named charging compartment. Pleasant outside space specially designed for barbecues and summer socialising. House staff come in for praise: one housemaster was described as a 'cracking bloke', and parents like the high staff:student ratio and the 15 bed medical centre, with physio clinic. We did, though, pick up a sense of social divide between the day students and boarders, and one father said bluntly that the former are 'disproportionately bright'. Boarders and day students alike eat in the magnificent cafeteria, where the range of choice is enormous, not say bewildering; menus embrace all sporting diets. The tortilla and salads we chose from the Spanish counter as part of the world food bar was delicious, and it was made even more authentic by the Spanish staff jabbering away on the next table. Further flung boarding houses have the occasional dinner in their own dining rooms on special occasions.

Background and atmosphere: For one of the UK's most successful boarding schools, Millfield is really quite a new kid on the block. Just over 80 years ago Jack Meyer, a bright young civil servant and accomplished cricketer, went out to work with the Indian Civil Service. Attracting the notice of a passing maharajah as a jolly good chap, 'Boss' Meyer, as he became known, returned to the UK in the mid 1930s at his request with seven Indian boys, six of them princes, to found a school – Millfield, initially set up in a private house of that name rented from the nearby Clark family (of shoe fame). Innovation was the name of the game from then on: co-ed from 1939, as much emphasis on excellence and opportunity in sport and the arts as on academic success, and from 1942, an interest in and commitment to overcoming dyslexia and other barriers to learning, following the arrival of the 'word blind' son of the then deputy PM, Martin Attlee, who (most unusually for dyslexics of the time) went on to higher education.

These three markers have defined the school ever since, sometimes unfairly, but the feel and look of the place is fresh and contemporary – no hallowed portals here. Instead, buildings of all materials, types and function ('No great architectural merit,' said one father, drily) are scattered across the huge site, more akin to a small university campus, whose grassed areas were strewn with crocuses at the time of year we visited. A culture of entrepreneurship still prevails: on the school's part, ambitious plans for a new enterprise centre, on the part of one new sixth former, encouragement and plaudits for setting up his own charity club to raise funds for less fortunate youngsters. No overwhelming sense of entitlement, privilege or history among the students either; all the ones we spoke to expressing in forthright terms their good fortune at being there. Uniform unexceptional – standard issue navy suits with the finest of pinstripes and v-necked jumpers for the girls below sixth form, but boys get to buy their own suits: we saw one dandy clad in immaculate Prince of Wales check. 'Not fair,' opined one mother – but the fact that it's cheaper than designer options doubtless chosen by some boys must compensate.

Pastoral care, well-being and discipline: The head is concerned that no-one gets lost, overlooked or presumably away with too much in this big school, and has increased house staffing levels considerably to ensure none slip through the net. The general levels of affluence and huge geographical catchment might cause some to make simplistic links with illicit contraband like drink and drugs, but this passed unmentioned by all those we spoke to. Parents are mostly happy with the way in which their concerns are dealt with, and students feel that punishments are fair and appropriate; sixth form gating is a particular deterrent to wrong-doing. The fact that academic work is commended both for achievement and effort goes down well also. What most schools call PHSE has been redesigned as Positive Education – a through-going programme covering, inter alia, resilience and emotional intelligence; this is reinforced in day/boarding houses as well as in class. A dedicated email address exists to report any incidents of bullying.

Pupils and parents: Everyone, nay everyone, talked of the diversity of families – the much-vaunted Millfield Mix – and given the range of bursaries on offer, this is not as fanciful as it might appear (OK, OK, a few children arrive by helicopter, but others in much humbler hatchbacks). 'We work on the Robin Hood principle,' says the head. Maybe its sporting prowess, international clientéle (20 per cent come from overseas but no one nationality predominates) and openness to a wide intellectual spectrum create the 'egalitarian feel of a southern hemisphere school' that the head is keen on, but there's certainly 'a lot less tweed on the touchline than there is at Radley,' as one dad put it. The students we met looked us in the eye and shook us firmly by the hand – 'confident in the qualities that make them wonderful,' in the words of the head. Worth noting that there are roughly 60 per cent boys.

Entrance: Mainly into year 9, many from its own large prep school, but from 120 other prep schools all over the world. Thirty-five places are available in year 10. Places are offered on the basis of an interview with a senior member of staff and a computerised verbal and non-verbal reasoning assessment for which it is not possible to prepare. Overseas applicants sit the UKiset test. Sixth form entry for the 130 who join at this point depends on a minimum of six passes at GCSE including English and maths for those doing A levels; just four for those doing BTecs

Exit: A handful seem to leave in the first couple of years, about 20 per cent after GCSE and unusually, a scattering at the end of year 12. Those who stay for the duration praise the quality and administration of the support given university admissions, whether in the UK or abroad. One to Oxford and one medic in 2016; Cardiff and Oxford Brookes currently top of the pops in the UK, and American universities leading the field by miles for study abroad (21 in 2016), some awarding sports scholarships, particularly in hockey and tennis. Surprisingly few gap years. Famous alumni, especially sporting ones, too numerous to list, but stand-outs are Gareth Edwards and Chris Robshaw (rugby), Duncan Goodhew, Joanne Atkinson and James Guy (swimming). Eight Old Millfieldians competed at Rio 2016 and won four medals between them (swimming, rowing and rugby). But Old Millfieldians are also to be found at the top of their game in journalism, finance and even one mediaeval history don among the dreaming spires.

Money matters: In the past it enjoyed the reputation of being the most expensive school in the UK, but at the moment it comes in at less than Eton. It would, however, be easy to go large on the extras (endless racks of monogrammed house team kit etc) in the school shop, where items can be bought and bunged on the bill with the houseparent's permission. Some activities are chargeable where outside staff are brought in (eg polo); specialist therapy such as speech and language and vision, EAL, individual learning support also. Scholarships (including for design & innovation and chess) awarded to a maximum of 15 per cent of fees, but a generous 50 per cent for exceptional all-rounders into year 9. Extensive bursary provision which goes to 100 per cent in cases of phenomenal hardship

Remarks: A big open-hearted school welcoming all talents but not, we think, none. Only the best will do, in terms of facilities and IT and its ambition seems boundless, as the head turns his attention to the academics and the new centre for enterprise. Besides, where else would you meet princes and paupers?

Milton Abbey School

Blandford Forum, Dorset DT11 0BZ

Pupils: 240: 170 boys, 70 girls; 215 full boarders • Ages: 13–18 • Sixth form: 126: 93 boys, 33 girls • C of E

Fees: Day £17,895; Boarding £35,340 pa

Tel: 01258 880484
Email: admissions@miltonabbey.co.uk
Website: www.miltonabbey.co.uk

Headmaster: Since 2014, Magnus Bashaarat MA PGCE (40s), previously deputy head of Stowe. Educated at The King's School, Canterbury (he and Stowe head Anthony Wallersteiner were contemporaries there), followed by University of Edinburgh, where he read English. After work experience at the York Evening Press he decided to become a journalist and worked for the Observer and Evening Standard for a while. He changed direction after taking a course in teaching English as a foreign language – found he loved 'standing up in front of a class and helping people to learn.' PGCE at King's College London, followed by two years at Sherborne and a 15-year stint at Eton, where he taught English and drama and was a housemaster for seven years. He also did a year at Sydney Grammar as part of a teaching exchange with Eton. Moved to Stowe in 2009 and spent five years as deputy head. He says Milton Abbey is similar to Stowe – 'just on a different scale' – and that its size means 'everyone is seen as an individual, everyone is valued and pupils have a very good relationship with staff.'

Mr Bashaarat is dynamic, forward-thinking and hit the ground running when he arrived. He didn't teach during his first year at Milton Abbey but now teaches an English GCSE retake set. 'It's lovely to have contact time again,' he told us. He's adamant that a head shouldn't be a remote figure and makes a point of seeing the pupils as much as possible, chatting at lunch, running a school cycling group and popping into the boarding houses in the evenings. 'This place has a very honest, nurturing ethos and pupils are very well looked after,' he says.

M

His wife Camilla used to work in communications for the NHS and now runs Milton Abbey's parents' association, or MASPA as it's known (everything from a yoga retreat in Norfolk to a trip to Champagne in France). They have three children – sons at Stowe and Eton and a daughter at Sherborne Girls. In his spare time, he cycles (his road bike is propped against the wall of his study), rows at nearby Canford and goes to the theatre as much as he can. He likes 'serious drama' and if he can't get to London drives to Poole, Salisbury and, a new find, The Tobacco Factory in Bristol.

Academic matters: Milton Abbey's strengths lie in its value-added. School doesn't publish its GCSE and A level results (though 10 per cent A*/A at GCSE in 2016), taking the view that students have such a broad range of ability that their achievements wouldn't be accurately represented by what the head calls the 'crude mechanism' of league tables. 'The value added we get for our pupils wouldn't be represented by the league tables,' he says. Students range from a boy who got three A*s at A level in 2015 and headed to Oxford to read archaeology and anthropology to those who find formal academic learning 'really difficult' and opt for a more vocational route. The school talks a lot about 'parallel learning pathways' and prides itself on tailoring an academic programme to suit individual students. At sixth form, a third of pupils take A levels, a third take a combination of A levels and BTecs and a third take BTecs. In year 11 youngsters attend an options evening, when they discuss individual sixth form choices with tutors and heads of department. Pupils' GCSE profiles are taken into account and subject combinations are based on advice from tutors and teachers (no chance of doing physics A level and a BTec in hospitality). Pupils are encouraged to pursue their passions and interests and all the usual A levels are on offer, plus economics, politics, history of art and music technology.

M

The school is ahead of the curve when it comes to vocational learning. Milton Abbey says it offers the broadest range of BTecs in the independent sector and is one of the few schools to offer BTecs at extended diploma level – equivalent to three A levels. BTecs (available in countryside management, performing arts, enterprise and entrepreneurship, equine management, hospitality, creative media production and sport) aren't an easy option though. They are made up of continued assessment, with a small percentage of the course assessed by exam at the end of two years. The school's 2015 ISI report commended its approach, saying that 'pupils, who come with widely different educational backgrounds and needs, often suffering a negative experience of education elsewhere, are enabled to rebuild the foundation of their knowledge and skills, as well as the self-confidence needed to progress.' The assistant head (academic) concurs with this. 'We're all about getting the best out of our pupils,' she says.

Pupils take between seven and nine GCSEs, with everyone doing English, maths and a science. Class sizes are small – average of 12 up to GCSE and six at A level. 'The small class sizes mean that we have much better outcomes for learners,' says the head. Pupils are streamed by ability for the core subjects. Lessons are now one hour long – school says this helps pupils to concentrate better.

Milton Abbey is resolutely mainstream but learning support, with four teachers and six teaching assistants, is the biggest department. Some pupils are screened before they start and around two-thirds access learning support in some way – for a wide range of difficulties, including dyslexia, dyspraxia, dyscalculia, mild Asperger's). Learning support assistants provide additional help in lessons and there's one-to-one or group support outside lessons too (charged on top of the fees). EAL support and study skills support on offer. Some pupils have learning support lessons instead of doing French or Spanish. The department is very welcoming, with its door permanently open to help anyone who wants to drop in for revision tips, essay planning and time management. 'Quite often their self-esteem and confidence is low and it's our job to raise that,' says the head of learning support.

School library has 9,000 resources and pupils are encouraged to read books for pleasure as well as for study. Robert Muchamore and Meg Rosoff are two current favourites – 'we like to get the pupils in the habit of reading,' the school librarian told us.

Games, options, the arts: Sport is taken seriously here but the emphasis is on enjoyment and there's loads on offer. Rugby, hockey, cricket and football predominate but golf (there's a course in the grounds), sailing and polo have a strong take-up too. The fixtures list and results show the school punches above its weight on the sports field. Relatively small number of girls means everyone gets the chance to represent the school at hockey, netball and lacrosse during the winter and tennis and rounders during the winter. Facilities include a 25-metre swimming pool, two gyms, squash court, all-weather pitch, sports hall and outdoor pitches galore. Everyone does games on Tuesdays, Thursdays and Saturdays but the sportiest do far more. Wednesdays are given over to CCF or community service (including visiting the elderly, taking dogs for walks and cleaning the local church). There's all manner of country pursuits, like fishing, ferreting (you can bring your own ferret, although none were in residence when we visited), clay pigeon shooting, beagling and mountain biking.

It's possible to combine a burgeoning equestrian career with school life. Pupils can bring their own steeds – many of the keenest riders take a BTEC in equine management and keep their horses at the school stables (each individual stable is labelled with the inhabitant's name – Sparky, Dolly and the like). They manage the day-to-day care of their horses and can choose to ride instead of playing other sports.

Art is a popular subject and we saw artwork that was easily on a par with larger schools. A year 12 boy showed us an astonishing oil painting inspired by renaissance art that he'd worked on over the summer. School puts on a big drama production in its theatre every year and there's a vast array of music. Hymn practice is held in the Abbey every Friday, when the whole school gathers to sing at the tops of their voices. 'The volume creeps up bit by bit and it sounds wonderful,' a sixth form boy told us.

Milton Abbey runs the innovative Entrepreneurship in Residence competition, aiming to inspire pupils with ambitions to launch their own business. Top-notch designers like Anya Hindmarch, Johnnie Boden and Cath Kidston have fronted the scheme in the past and now David Ross is leading the next generation of young entrepreneurs. Unlike some boarding schools, students do work experience – usually with school alumni (an Inner Temple barrister and a Coutts banker were among those who volunteered this year). Other activities include D of E, farm club and the Ten Tors expedition across Dartmoor. School is a member of Round Square, a worldwide organisation that encourages young people to broaden their horizons and gain greater understanding of the wider world through exchange trips, community work and themed activities within school.

Boarding: Milton Abbey offers full boarding or day places – 'we don't have anything in between,' says the head. Two three-day exeats a term to allow for longer journeys home. Five boarding houses – four for boys and one for girls. We visited the two newest houses, both wholesome and welcoming, with disabled access and underfloor heating. Each has a housemaster or housemistress, resident tutors and two matrons, who take charge of laundry and cleaning, offer support to pupils and help them to prepare for life beyond school. One matron told us she'd just taught a boy how to iron his shirt – 'it was important he learned how to do it himself.'

Common rooms in the boarding houses are equipped with TVs but these aren't allowed on during the day. There's no mobile phone signal on much of the site so phones are less of a problem here than at other schools. Most use the old-fashioned landlines in the boarding houses to phone home.

Background and atmosphere: Milton Abbey, with 76 acres of rolling countryside, is one of the prettiest schools in the country. You can't fail to be enchanted by the ancient abbey nestling in a wooded Dorset valley, one of the finest Capability Brown landscapes in the country, 15 minutes' drive from Blandford. 'It's deeply rural, but not remote,' is the head's description. We visited on a sunny day but were assured that it looks lovely in the rain and mist too. The school was founded in 1954 and occupies the converted monastery buildings. The vast abbey belongs to the Diocese of Salisbury but the school has full use of it, with services four times a week. Milton Abbey also has its own farm (complete with pigs, sheep, goats, turkeys and chickens), makes its own honey and grows flowers, fruit and vegetables.

Pupils eat all their meals in the Abbot's Hall, a grand dining room complete with stags' heads and a huge mural of the school painted by a parent to commemorate the school's 50th anniversary in 2004. Pasta, salads, wraps and paninis on offer at lunch-time, as well as hot meals, plus snacks at break, fresh fruit and cake in the afternoons. 'No one goes hungry,' grinned one boy. Uniform is smart. Younger girls wear tartan skirts and blazers while sixth form girls are clad in grey skirts and tweed jackets of their choice. Boys wear tweed jackets, grey trousers and ties.

Pastoral care, well-being and discipline: Pupils keep the same tutor from year 9 to year 11, and see them two or three times a week. In the sixth form students get a say in their choice of tutor – often someone who teaches them or whom they have a good relationship with. School operates a system of rewards and sanctions when it comes to behaviour – awards given for good work, sporting achievements and acts of kindness.

Good communication with parents – school has introduced a new parent portal where parents have access to weekly notes on everything from a missed prep to an academic triumph. Pupils told us that 'there aren't hundreds of rules. They give you a degree of trust.' Student voice is considered important. Head boy and head girl (who meet the headmaster every morning), heads of houses and a raft of prefects – called 'pilots' here.

Pupils and parents: Pupils come from 120 or so prep schools and from all over the country – quite a few from London and from as far afield as Northumberland. International students from France, Italy, Germany, Italy, Kenya and the US. Day pupils ('our day fees are really competitive,' says the head) tend to live within a 30-minute drive. School minibus service covers Blandford, Wimborne, Poole, Dorchester, Shaftesbury and Salisbury. Day pupils leave at 6pm but there's the option to stay on for activities and prep if they wish.

Despite such privileged surroundings, the pupils we met were outgoing, enthusiastic and delightfully unsnobby. Sixth formers summed the school's appeal up in a nutshell. 'For the people it's right for, this is the best school in the country,' one boy declared. 'I love it. My sister's at Millfield and her year group is as big as this whole school. Here, everybody knows everybody and the support you get is second to none.' A girl said she liked being 'a big fish in a small pond' while parents told us they love the family atmosphere, plus the fact that their children get loads of country air and aren't glued to their phones, tablets and laptops.

Former pupils include Professor Jonathan Freeman-Attwood, the principal of the Royal Academy of Music, photographer, screenwriter and TV director Harry Hook, restaurateur Oliver Gladwin, sculptor Robert Rattray, documentary maker Anthony Geffen and Professor Alastair Bruce, royal, religious and constitutional affairs commentator for Sky News.

Entrance: School is 'inclusive and non-selective.' Around 70 per cent of pupils do CE – pass mark is around 50 per cent but school is flexible on this and says 'there's no hard and fast rule.'

Applicants attend a taster day to see if the school suits them. Usual entry points are 13 and 16 but a handful of pupils start in year 10, often because they didn't settle at their original choice of school. Milton Abbey doesn't chuck pupils out if they don't make their GCSE grades either. Head believes that when a school accepts a youngster at 13 it should stick with them for the duration.

Exit: School loses around 10 per cent of pupils after GCSEs – largely due to relocation or for financial reasons – but larger numbers choose to join from other schools with 35 new lower sixth pupils in 2016. At 18 or 19 pupils choose a plethora of routes. In 2016, destinations included universities of Sussex and East Anglia plus the Royal Agricultural College. School has strong links with international catering colleges, such as Glion and Les Roches in Switzerland, and several pupils have headed to these in the past.

Head points out that 'a degree isn't a guarantee of a job' these days and is keen on courses that 'will facilitate future employment.' He admits that if he was choosing a degree now he would probably go for vocational journalism and media rather than English. School has forged a close relationship with The Arts University Bournemouth, which specialises in art, design, media and performance across the creative industries.

Money matters: A range of scholarships at 13+ and 16+ – academic, all-rounder, art, DT, drama, music and sport. All worth 10 per cent of the fees, although these may be increased 'where financial need is demonstrated.' School also offers means-tested bursaries, plus scholarships for day pupils living in Dorset.

M

Remarks: Milton Abbey's setting, countryside expertise and innovative mix of qualifications give pupils, some of whom may not have thrived elsewhere, a host of opportunities to shine – both inside and outside the classroom.

Monkton School

Church Lane, Monkton Combe, Bath, Somerset BA2 7HG

Pupils: 704; 253 boarders • Ages: 2–18 (boarding from 7) • Sixth form: 163

Fees: Day £9,312 – £19,995; Boarding £19,965 – £31,890 pa

Tel: 01225 721102
Email: admissions@monkton.org.uk
Website: www.monktoncombeschool.com

Principal: Since January 2016, Christopher Wheeler, previously principal and CEO of Hillcrest International School, Nairobi, Kenya. He has an English and philosophy degree from Durham and a PGCE from Bristol. Taught English at St John's, Leatherhead; then he moved to Peponi School, Kenya, as deputy head, boarding housemaster and head of English and drama. Back in the UK he became a housemaster at Brighton College and then head of St Christopher's, Hove, part of the Brighton College family of schools. He is married to Georgie, who teaches English and sport and is a keen rider. They have three young children, who have joined the school.

Head of prep: Since January 2017, Martin David, previously deputy head at Hazlegrove Prep. He has also been deputy head at St Andrew's Turi in Kenya. An old Montonian (he went through both junior and senior schools), he teaches maths and coaches a wide variety of sports teams. A committed Christian, he is married to Nicola and they have three young children.

Academic matters: Prep school academically sound and according to our pupil guides offers a stimulating and enjoyable education. Despite its non-selective ethos, a parent told us that there are plenty of 'incredibly able' children about. Two-form entry in years 3, 4 and 5; streaming from year 5 and an extra scholarship stream added in year 6. Saturday morning school for year 4 and above. Smallish classes (16 to 17). Lots of emphasis on finding out what a child has to offer. Masses of reading lays a foundation for this, with a programme of author visits and a library offering books, board games and beanbags. Long established learning support staff – 'a cracking team' – offer in-class support, handwriting and spelling groups.

In 2016, 71 per cent of GCSE grades A*/A, and 36 per cent of A levels (71 per cent A*/B). For a 'not particularly selective' school which has 'a default position of supporting a pupil's ambitions, even if they are a long shot' this is fairly respectable. Pupils say they enjoy lessons, work hard and get lots of encouragement. Exams still feel on the tough side to them, so those we met were proud of their results and parents gave across-the-board thumbs up – 'the brightest are definitely stretched.' School is currently upping its academic image. Though intake at year 9 'gets a gentle ride' (gives them a chance to settle between CE and the start of GCSE syllabus) bright children are taught 'up to their level.' Class sizes 18 to 20 up to GCSE, smaller thereafter.

Safe curriculum for GCSE, with few soft options. Mandarin now available at KS3. Increasing number of subjects going to IGCSE. One or two languages for all except extra English candidates at GCSE. Latin but no Greek. In science top set do three separate sciences and the rest dual award. A level courses include photography, theatre studies, sports studies, DT, critical thinking, psychology, politics and textiles – music technology BTec recently added. Some smashing maths results – shiny new £4 million maths and science centre may have helped, plus programme of university links enabling sixth formers to get placements in science research departments. Smartly refurbished arts and crafts library, now renamed learning resource centre.

The learning support unit is sound but the school is no longer registered CreSTed as Monkton provides only for minor difficulties. Nonetheless it is inclusive and copes well with unusual children and physical problems. Students get up to 45 minutes a week one-to-one and teachers are tuned into special needs and work with the learning support unit. Study skills on offer too.

Games, options, the arts: Strong for a smallish school, with the expected trio of rugby, hockey and cricket for boys and hockey, netball and tennis for girls. Male and female tennis players sponsored by LTA via the University of Bath. Rowing's the in thing – perhaps not surprising with a new Olympian rowing coach Matt Wells (won bronze at Beijing). Several former pupils have achieved national and international rowing success, including Steve Williams (who won Olympic golds in 2004 and 2008) and Alex Partridge (who won silver in 2008). Pupils don't have to be sporty – but the surroundings encourage them, as do the facilities – new Astro surfaces, good sports hall, picturesque cricket. Great opportunity for competition in top years of the prep as the corresponding years in senior school play friendlies against them.

Music of every genre in the prep – a culture of singing and oodles learn instruments. Some top notch music scholarships to senior schools for the best.

Senior school music has had a huge boost with new £3.2 million music school (opened by Felicity Lott and Richard Stilgoe) complete with magnificent wood-lined auditorium, multitudinous teaching and practice rooms and larger rehearsal rooms, all the electronic mod cons of recording and manipulating music. Some pretty impressive piano playing doing justice to the brand new Steinway during our visit. List of successful ex-Monkton musicians is growing. Every sort of music, including lively jazz, professional sounding big band and rock bands (always the sign of a truly musical environment).

Art and drama has a plethora of expert staff and a chance for everyone to join in. Art and DT rooms extended and refurbished – exhibition space plus print-making, textiles, photography and CAD areas; A level artists rival mathematicians in the success rates. Lots of exciting stuff – sculpture, photography and first-rate painting. Lashings of drama, with ambitious productions (Shakespeare and Dickens as well as more contemporary shows) and good enough facilities, though they are in the list for development. Visiting artists and workshops, links with local galleries and University of Bath. Art trips abroad every other year, plus exchanges, music trips et al.

CCF is an attractive option. School building up community service. D of E on the up. Other activities include poetry, creative writing and Dearlove Society (focuses on European intellectual life – Camus, St Augustine, the influences of classical Greece – and ends the year with a frisbee competition in Greek robes).

Boarding: Prep school boarders live in Hatton House which overlooks the golf course and has views across the valley. Boarding numbers have increased in recent years as has the number of pupils from abroad. Up to 70 pupils stay during the week in the prep with around 30 or so in at the weekends. Plenty going on at weekends including trips to Wales, Dorset Coast, rock climbing, cinema and shopping in Bath. After church on Sunday there's roast dinner and time to relax. Computers rationed for boarders, but with dedicated daily Skype time for keeping in touch with home.

Flexible boarding available up to year 9, which can include three, four or five nights a week. From year 9 it's full boarding or day; however, boarding pupils may go home after Saturday morning lessons unless they are in a sports team, returning on Sunday night or Monday morning. Day pupils can sleep over if necessary, however (they get 10 boarding nights a year free of charge), and most go home so late it hardly seems worth it. One boarder said it didn't matter if his friends were day boys because he had so little time when they weren't there and anyway he got on with everyone. Houses are run like families, with pupils learning to take responsibility. The number of day pupils who come in at weekends is good measure of how much there is to do. Full Saturday programme of morning lessons followed by afternoon sport mean other weekend activities are necessarily fairly low-key – film nights, barbecues, informal concerts. Seven boarding houses – four for boys, two for girls (school has plans to expand) and the one junior house.

Background and atmosphere: Campus still has a whiff of the school's clerical foundation. Founded in 1868 by the evangelical Revd Francis Pocock, school started with five pupils. School is still popular with clergymen and missionaries. Since merging in 1992 with girls' school next door it's been fully co-ed, with a prep and a pre-prep. The setting at the bottom of a deep-cleft valley is ravishing – sufficiently isolated to feel safe to parents but handily near Bath for weekend shopping and other forays, say pupils.

The school is centred on its strong Christian tradition. This is embodied in the attitude of staff to children and symbolised by such groups as the International School Society and array of social projects it initiates at home and in far-flung places. Pupils definitely buy into respect for each other's needs and personalities. A parent reports a commendable understanding of the occasional oddball. The vibrant Christian Union is run entirely by the students and around a third attend every week. No Sunday service but a large number go into Bath or to local services (often those aimed at university students) of their choice.

Fiendishly hard to find down a genteel residential cul de sac, prep school has a dramatic hilltop setting with great downland views. The stunning sweep of the cricket pitch and leafy lawns isn't spoilt by the mish-mash of school buildings tacked onto the back of the manor house. New pre-prep and nursery building which links to the prep school and includes new play spaces. The school's evangelical Christian ethos underlies all aspects of education here. A happy place, where much is expected and much achieved. Staff, and therefore pupils, work to the highest Christian principles of honest work, self-discipline and concern for the needs of others. 'It teaches how to be a good person,' said one firmly non-Christian parent, 'and allows children to be accepted and to make their own minds up.' Pupils come first, education next but never as second best. Though open-minded, and progressive in the ways which matter, this is an unashamedly and all pervasively Christian foundation.

Pastoral care, well-being and discipline: 'Pastorally brilliant,' say parents, many of whom add that this was their reason for choosing Monkton. The house system (mixed ages but single sex) involves boarders and day pupils alike and husband and wife houseparent teams include both in their care. Houseparents are profiled on boarding pages of school website with family photos, lots of background information and homely details about dogs, baking etc. Reassuringly un-corporate.

Academic tutors attached to houses, though in the sixth form pupils choose their own tutors, The system aims to support, inspire and encourage good working habits and is part of the network of personal support which characterises Monkton. Induction for prefects teaches them to be kind, not martinets. Definitely no sense of parading prefect privilege, though they are proud of their level of responsibility

The trust between pupils of all ages and pupils and staff is very evident, for instance in the dining hall where the interchange is informal and considerate. Statistics show no bullying. 'We pick it up before it's a problem,' said one tutor. 'If you know a child you can see when something is wrong.' One might wonder if this is a little too trusting? One parent definitely felt that cooping up large number of teenagers in a small valley brings its own problems and that pastoral staff have sometimes been a bit naïve, though principal is tougher than his charm suggests. Problems are tackled and for teenagers this is a safe place where they can be themselves and there is unfailing support for the troubled.

Prep school children carry journals and too many negative entries result in Saturday detention – but slates are wiped clean every quarter term. The worst sanction, exclusion for disruptive behaviour, is hardly ever needed. Tutors know children well enough to sense when something's wrong so potentially bullying is picked up quickly but 'children do fall out' and need a 'chat.' Enthusiasm for school meals and even more for the three nurses who care for boarders (and day children when needed).

Pupils and parents: Popular, of course, with evangelical Christians and those who want the values, but plenty of non-subscribers too. Seven-day boarding week is good for the many Forces' families. Wide geographical range, including 10 to 15 per cent international students (20-plus nationalities). International tradition strong and long established. Some need ESL support, but all are tested in English before arrival and many go straight into mainstream English classes. Cultural acclimatisation is thoughtfully addressed too.

School is handy for both ends of the M4, so London and Wales mix harmoniously. Children seem friendly, unpretentious and modestly confident.

School's church connections only account for part of the exalted list of past pupils promoted to glory on earth – former spymaster Sir Richard Dearlove, songwriter and humourist Richard Stilgoe, blockbuster novelist Bernard Cornwell, Piers Forster (who shared a Nobel prize for climate change). The development department is doing a professional and very enterprising job keeping the school in touch with old Monktonians in the worlds of business and arts.

Entrance: Essentially non-selective into prep. Parents pleased that the entry policy allows a wide range of abilities and types, though they're even more pleased that the standards achieved at Monkton Prep rival schools that select. 'The best prep school in England,' one told us. Boarding numbers have doubled over the past few years, so the feel is definitely of a boarding school with day pupils, especially as there is a significant tranche of pupils from abroad (some 35 per cent of boarders). Informal interview for pre-prep. For the prep at age 7, interview plus tests (English, maths and verbal reasoning).

Monkton senior looks for 50 per cent plus at CE. Standard rising. Special needs evaluated to make sure a pupil will cope comfortably with what has become a slightly more academic curriculum. 'Definitely pulling out of their less able image,' a parent commented, but parents of 'strugglers' are delighted with unexpected A*s and As. Pupils come from Monkton Prep, St Andrew's School (Turi, Kenya), Castle Court, Mount House, Rose Hill, All Hallows and Summer Fields.

Exit: Some 80 per cent from the prep to the senior school at 13, but others to eg Marlborough, Sherborne, Prior Park, Canford and King's Bruton. About 75 per cent go through to sixth form (further five per cent leave after year 12). Up to 10 Oxbridge applications per year – though only a smidgeon get in (five in 2016). A tranche to good solid courses and good solid unis including UCL, Imperial, Durham and Nottingham, and plenty to useful-looking vocational courses including art college, not on the whole the whacky sort. Plus some to US and other countries.

Money matters: Bursaries on offer to children of missionaries and clergy – means-tested. A clutch of academic, art, drama, music and sport scholarships on entry to years 7, 9 and 12. Has secured a £2 million donation for the school and is embarking on a £35 million development programme – seriously confident in straitened times.

Remarks: A school that sees itself as on the up, its image polished by a super-efficient development department busy developing everything in sight. Governors clearly have no fears for the future. Despite the ongoing makeover, its Christian ethos shines out in the unforced friendliness and directness of its pupils and through the disciplined but loving care of its staff. Service to others comes first, but confidence and academic achievement are treasured as the means of achieving it. One parent said, 'I thank my lucky stars every day that I found Monkton.' These boys and girls go on to do well and to do good.

Monmouth School

Linked with The Grange, Monmouth Preparatory School, Haberdashers' Monmouth School for Girls, Haberdashers' Agincourt, Inglefield House

Almshouse Street, Monmouth NP25 3XP

Pupils: 511; 150 full boarders • Ages: 11-18 (boarding from 9) • Sixth form: 164

Fees: Day £14,907; Boarding £27,009 – £28,635 pa

Tel: 01600 713143
Email: admissions@monmouthschool.org
Website: www.habs-monmouth.org

Headmaster: Since 2015, Dr Andrew Daniel, previously senior deputy head at Wellington School, Somerset. A former pupil of UWC Atlantic College, Dr Daniel graduated with a starred first in geophysical sciences from the University of East Anglia and University of Washington, Seattle. He was awarded his doctorate from Liverpool University on the mathematical modelling of plate tectonics in Patagonia. He was head of mathematics at Taunton School and responsible for the academic life of Aiglon College in Switzerland before joining Wellington.

Married to Alison, an oceanographer; they have a young daughter and son. His interests include mountaineering, hill walking, cycling, coaching squash and the French horn.

M

Academic matters: Good performance at both GCSE and A level over the last five years, with consistently impressive grades for high fliers – though whole year averages fluctuate a bit. In 2016, 50 per cent A*/A at A level. More telling is that between 20 and 35 out of around 85 candidates regularly get three or more A*/As. There is a small tail of C, D, E grades which probably reflects the school policy of allowing enthusiastic hard workers to 'have a go' (they only need five B grades at GCSE to join sixth form).

At GCSE results are consistent, with 68 per cent A*/A grades in 2016. English, maths and science (now IGCSE 'because it's more rigorous') have a pretty impressive clutch of top grades and minimal below C. All take core subjects of English, maths, three separate sciences (a few do double award) plus a modern language (French, Spanish, German, Russian or Mandarin – Welsh can be arranged as an extra). Latin (good take-up) and Greek (a few) right up to A level. Lots of A level choice – around 30 options in conjunction with Haberdashers' Monmouth School for Girls. Arrangement gives flexibility amounting to virtual freedom of choice as well as spin-off benefits of mixing with girls for curricular and extracurricular stuff.

The Monmouth Science Initiative gives boys the chance to work alongside scientific development at Cardiff University and is extended not only to the girls' school but also to local state schools, with clear feedback that it is making a significant difference to potential science high fliers. Learning support on an individual/shared basis from qualified staff, although additional charges apply for numeracy and literacy support.

Parents say individual teaching staff are exceptionally encouraging to enthusiastic pupils, though one commented that you have to push quite hard to do more than the statutory 10 GCSEs. 'The school could vaunt its academic image more but likes to be seen as inclusive,' said another. Lessons in study skills for all and sixth formers are encouraged to tailor choice towards career. Lots of additional help from local experts in minority subjects.

Games, options, the arts: Sport is tip-top here and Monmouth (comparatively small) has consistently challenged the giants of school sport in rugby, rowing, soccer and cricket. Rugby is top dog, though parents say other sports have had more of a look in recently. Not content with schoolboy competition, pupils have played for the Newport Gwent Dragons, Junior Welsh and other professional and semi-professional teams. Recent head boy is combining medicine at Cardiff with his professional Welsh Rugby commitments. This, and the fact that former Wales and Lions player John Bevan is a teacher first and rugby coach second, typifies the school's approach to sport as something to be done alongside life rather than an end in itself, though it doesn't stop them taking some significant trophies. As well as coaching the 1st XV he takes the younger boys on tours to Blackpool, Ireland and Italy.

Rowing, not surprisingly as the Wye surges right past the games pitches, has a strong though small take-up. It's in the tent-and-sandwiches league rather than turreted-pavilion-and-champagne at the posh school competitions, but still manages to sweep the board. Tennis, cross-country, squash, golf and sailing all flourish. Several teams in each year group – gives more boys a chance to represent the school and helps identify potential.

A bewildering range of activities available – artistic, intellectual, sporting, and practical. Juniors (11 to 13-year-olds) must do two a week and everyone does either CCF or some form of community service. In A-Z terms astronomy to water polo (no zoology) gives a flavour of what's on and it's good to see literature and poetry enjoyed by boys (something the head sees as too easily excluded by gender stereotyping in co-ed schools).

Perhaps the music school looks a little elderly in comparison with the jazzier modern developments, but it is comprehensive and bursting with energetic activity. Around 40 per cent play instruments and enjoy a plethora of groups, choirs, bands and orchestras. A recent deputation from the Haberdashers' Company was staggered to find themselves entertained by a full scale performance of Carmina Burana, involving the second year en masse. A good record of music college entry (recent leaver offered four scholarships to different academies) and parents feel the school gives boys a musical resource for life. The usual gamut of school visits, choir trips and exchanges.

Drama studio and new 500-seat theatre (as well as being used by the school it hosts a programme of public performance art, including ballet and world cinema). Quality art – the venerable but well-equipped art block full of boys working in a wide range of media.

Boarding: Over a quarter of the senior school boards (full or flexi). Around a third overseas. By sixth form, ratio of day to boarding is 60:40. Still has Saturday morning school for all but the sixth form – not universally popular with parents, but how else would the school have time to run outside all those activities? Plans afoot to increase boarding capacity. Five boarding houses have sensible rather than luxurious accommodation for boarders though the old Grange (prep school) buildings make a shamelessly luxurious sixth form house.

Background and atmosphere: Founded in 1614 as a local 'fre schole' by William Jones, a member of the Haberdashers' Company (one of the oldest Livery Companies in London), it became a 'public' school in the 19th century to expand its boarding beyond the locality and was a direct grant school until 1975. Part of the Haberdashers' family of Monmouth schools, which includes Agincourt (pre-prep), the Grange (boys' prep), Inglefield (girls' prep) and Haberdashers' Monmouth Girls'.

Rebuilt in the 1880s, with a magnificent Jacobean-style main building, it occupies and gives character to a significant part of Monmouth. Sensitive restorations, acquisitions such as the lovely mansion and gardens of Chapel House, bursting with happy junior boarders, the ex-pub housing the maths department and rows of almshouses (now staff offices) complement the new buildings that house the prep school and swimming pool. The William Jones building provides new classrooms, meeting space and admin centre. Pleasant grassy areas break up the hotch-potch of main buildings but it's something of a maze. Gorgeous playing fields bordering the Wye are reached by a pedestrian tunnel under the busy A40.

Uniform is plain navy blazer and grey trousers, replaced in the sixth form by a 'smart' business dress code. Food, boys say, is pretty good at lunchtime and OK-ish in the evening.

Pastoral care, well-being and discipline: Tutors are the focal point for monitoring academic performance, while housemasters look after pastoral well-being. One parent commented that no trouble is spared to find specialist help where needed and to support boys in difficulties. School rules are sensible and concentrate on the standard of behaviour expected, rather than a prescriptive list of dos and don'ts. Relations between staff and boys appear relaxed, but are formal enough to engender respect. Clear policies on drinking, smoking and drugs – not considered a problem, but boys are made aware of the damage they could do to themselves.

Pupils and parents: School attracts boys from south west England and south Wales, plus a few from Hong Kong etc, but is spreading the net wider and is popular with Forces families and expats. Definitely unstuffy and produces confident but considerate young men who are open and independent. Notable old boys include Christopher Herbert, the Bishop of St Albans, David Broome, Eddie Butler, Major Dick Hern, Lord Moynihan, Lord Ezra, Steve James, Keith Jarrett, Tony Jordan, Victor Spinetti and recent silver medallist Olympic rower Tom Lucy.

Entrance: Three-form entry at 11, from its own prep department and local primary schools. Both groups sit the school's own entrance exam, with scholarships awarded on that performance alone – no supplementary papers. School at pains to stress that there is no pass mark, but looking for potential – great store put on interviews. A further one-form entry at 13 from a growing list of prep schools – based on CE. Foundation scholarship exam or an entrance exam for those at state schools.

Exit: A dribble (some 10 per cent) leave post-GCSE. Majority to sound universities – Swansea, Bristol, Cardiff, Exeter etc – with engineering, business and economics very popular. Quite a few gap years. Eight to Oxbridge in 2016.

Money matters: About a third of the government assisted places now replaced by the school's own scheme and this offers a number of scholarships and bursaries. One in three get means-tested help with fees in the senior school. Day fees about what you'd expect from similar schools but boarding is exceptionally good value.

Remarks: A school that sets out to serve its community and has now been discovered by the wider world, with high quality education and a real flair for sport and the more aesthetic life skills.

Moor Park School

Moor Park, Richards Castle, Ludlow, Shropshire SY8 4DZ

Pupils: 224; 15 full, 120 flexi boarders • Ages: 3m – 13 years (boarders from year 3) • RC

Fees: Day £7,140- £15,930; Boarding £19,560 – £23,475 pa

Tel: 01584 876061
Email: head@moorpark.org.uk
Website: www.moorpark.org.uk

Headmaster: Since 2015, Charlie Minogue. It is never easy taking over from a popular longstanding head, but the word among parents is that Charlie is different and brilliant. He has won their hearts by singing Can't Stop Me Now with the parents' band at a school ball, wearing his kilt. Before Moor Park, Charlie worked at Aldwickbury School (deputy head), Harpenden and St Paul's Cathedral School, having started his career in a secondary state school, an experience that has shaped his educational values. 'That first school taught me to never give up on a child and always be aware of what else is going on in their life. No-one is only a school pupil.' He is not a practising Catholic but very drawn to the moral framework that the Catholic foundation provides and subtly underpins everything about Moor Park.

There is a gravitas about Charlie that is balanced by boyish good looks and a twinkle in his eye. He knows all the children by name and what they are up to. The children are clearly keen to win his approval and attention. While we visited, one boy came up to him to arrange to be his partner in a golf match on the school's nine hole golf course that evening and it was clearly the highlight of the boy's week.

Charlie, his wife and two children are loving the open air life that the Shropshire 85 acre estate allows after the restrictions of the south east. Both children are at the school and Charlie says that when they went back to Harpenden to meet up with friends, his son commented, 'It was nice seeing them, Dad, but we can be outside so much more now and never seem to use our mobiles much'. Smartphones are not a feature for the family at Moor Park – there is far too much climbing trees for that. Charlie's wife is totally involved in the school, entertaining visitors, teaching the double bass, running the marketing. 'She's fantastic,' one parent told us. She exudes charm and common sense and is a very reassuring presence for parents of boarders. The couple have exciting plans for the school, including a performing arts development. Parents like the fact Charlie has an open door policy for them. 'Don't moan in the car park', he says, 'Come and tell me'.

Entrance: The school is non-selective. Assessments take place either prior to or at joining to establish educational needs. Some children come from the nursery all the way through the school, but more join throughout the years. Some parents send them for the last few years as a preparation for senior full boarding.

Exit: The UK's best known senior schools figure as destinations including Eton, Winchester, Radley, Cheltenham, Shrewsbury, Moreton Hall, Christ College Brecon, Malvern College, Hereford Cathedral School and Ellesmere College. Of the 18 leaving in 2016, 14 had awards at their chosen school including an academic scholarship to Harrow. School prides itself on the advice it gives parents regarding the most appropriate senior schools for their children.

Remarks: In physical terms, this is the site to die for. Parents talk of the delight of seeing distant deer appear through the early morning mist as they drop their children off. The original house is Queen Anne, much developed in the late 19th century and includes Arts and Crafts features such as Morris stained glass. The entrance hall is inviting, with a big fireplace and imposing staircase that boasts remarkable tooled leather wallpaper and leads up to the boarding area for older children. Just off the entrance hall is the chapel, the old ballroom with a wonderful ceiling. The 85 acres includes a deer park, lake, terrace, lots of woodland and lawns.

But this is no sterile stately home. The delight of the grounds and buildings is that all are used both formally and informally for the children to have a full outdoor life and rich childhood. The dormitories in the old house are in the quirky top rooms with slanting ceilings and irregular lines. The old coach house has made a spacious pottery and art space. Outside, full use is made of the stream as part of an assault course – mud runs are the fun activity of the moment. There is an outdoor classroom in the woodland where the children have poetry lessons and there is an Astroturf. The night before we visited, there had been a bonfire in the woods where the children had baked their own bread. 'Awesome', said the year 8s. Around the main house are lots of small outdoor areas and as you turn a corner, you find a swing with a group of girls playing, then round the next a small grass area with half a dozen boys playing cricket, then you see individual raised beds for vegetable growing for the incipient gardeners. You couldn't get further from the typical urban fenced-in school playground. There is a big sports hall, a swimming pool, excellent outdoor sports facilities as well as a large multi-purpose space with banked seating for performances and whole school assemblies.

M

The school is non-selective and caters for the full ability range. There are two children on formal SEN statements and also a lot of academic scholarships to highly regarded senior schools. When children join, there is an assessment of their academic needs and if necessary a plan is put in place with the SENCo ('She's a brilliant asset,' says the head). The school works successfully with children who have dyslexia or dyspraxia or are on the autism spectrum. One parent told us how quickly the teachers picked up on her son's dyslexia, despite it having been undiagnosed for years at another school. There are two forms most years with up to 16 children in each form, so class sizes are small enough for a lot of one to one support as a matter of routine, which the children are quick to point out and appreciate.

The children do well in terms of acdemic outcomes and the head is delighted that, having created a new academic committee, teachers are starting to talk to each other more about teaching initiatives. A new post common entrance programme brings real enrichment to the educational experience of the year 8s, preparing them for the challenges ahead. The maths department runs a shares competition, and there is a developing emphasis on emerging technologies, thinking and creative skills.

Art is undoubtedly one of the outstanding strengths of the school – the standard of work is way above what you would expect for children of that age. The DT workshop is home to an enormous crocodile made by the children that hangs from the ceiling and the emphasis is on teaching crafts using the professional-looking array of tools and equipment. The children have made a compostable loo for the woods and a hovercraft as well as tables and chairs that can actually be used. Everyone up to year 2 has woodland time each week.

The children say there is always lots to do and that the best thing about the school is the freedom. Sport is huge and very successful – the girls' U12 hockey team had just been in the national finals when we visited. Children take part in equestrian eventing and triathlons feature. Many are involved in out-of-class musical activities. We were impressed by a flautists' group that arrived in the school chapel for their lunchtime rehearsal and just got on with it before any teacher appeared. Those involved in speech and drama regularly take part in local festivals and competitions and again do very well. There are school plays and concerts. Weekend activities are wildly anticipated. These are often themed – a Bake-Off weekend, a Camo weekend with the highlight being Capture the Flag at night. They also climb trees.

The emphasis is on flexi-boarding. There are full boarders, some of whom are foreign nationals coming over for perhaps a year or even a term, mainly from Europe. A lot of children dip in and out of boarding on a weekly basis and that works well both for the children and families. Everyone is welcomed for special boarding weekends. It all feels very relaxed. There is a separate purpose-built boarding house for younger children, The Tree House, a wooden building that has impeccable eco-credentials. This allows for 10 girls and 10 boys to board at any one time and children typically stay for two or three nights a week. Parents see this as an excellent introduction to boarding.

Pastoral care is regarded as outstanding. The children say that staff sort out any problems very quickly and the head tells us that he was very struck, coming new into the school, how very positive the weekly staff pastoral meetings are, with is a sense that everyone is supportive of the holistic approach to pastoral care. The children and staff comment on how the children all look after each other, particularly in the boarding context, where the older and younger children play together all the time. Parents describe how if there is a relationship upset between the children, the staff are very good at dealing with it sensitively, getting everyone to sit round and have a general discussion about being kind and thoughtful.

There are daily assemblies in the middle of the morning to give the children a sense of calm and something outside their busy daily lives. Mass is held each week and although now most children and staff are not Catholic, that tradition is very visible and very much a part of the school's fabric. The children said that one of their most memorable events in the school calendar was the Benedictus at the end of the Michaelmas term. 'They trust us to hold the candles and the sheet of paper with the mass on', we were told by awed children. The school is concerned to ensure that those who board have some time just to be quiet by themselves, and the small bedrooms help this. Having said that, children who were very introspective or fixated on their play technology might not settle here. The head said that staff have to like the outdoor life, and we would say the same for children. If your child really doesn't enjoy getting muddy, Moor Park would be a bit wasted on them.

About half the children are fairly local – school minibuses bring children in from the rural areas. Traditionally it has been a school for established farming/land-owning families and those wanting a preparation for the big Catholic boarding schools. Nowadays there are increasing numbers of escapees from the home countries. Families tend to share a belief in a holistic education and want their children to enjoy every minute of their childhood. 'Moor Park is unflashy', one parent said. 'Everyone's car is dirty'.

Moor Park is the most magical bubble. Children have a childhood experience that will never be forgotten and will shape them whatever life brings. The school develops skills that prepare them for life outside. They leave with the ability to interact positively with others of all ages, with a striking degree of self-reliance, and a sense of knowing themselves and knowing the delights of our natural world – things which can never be taken away. Parents can't bear to think their children will ever have to leave. 'It is a blessed place,' one said to us.

Moreton Hall School

Weston Rhyn, Oswestry, Shropshire SY11 3EW

Pupils: 303; 201 full boarders • Ages: 11-18 (junior boarders from 7) • Sixth form: 125

Fees: Day: £24,900 – £26,940 pa; Boarding: £30,900 – £32,700

Tel: 01691 773671
Email: registrar@moretonhall.com
Website: www.moretonhall.org

Principal: Since 1992, Jonathan Forster BA PGCE (50s) who still 'just loves every day at Moreton Hall'. His daughters have been through the school and he and his wife, who's heavily involved in school life, can testify as parents to what a wonderful place it is bring up children. Jonathan – who has a degree from Leeds and was previously housemaster and English teacher at Strathallan – rescued the school from imminent closure, and he has continued to drive it at a pace that speaks of a life-long mission and endless creative energy. He is always ahead of the game, ensuring the school leads not follows market demands. He has kept true to the liberal educational vision of its founders and provided that liberalism with a modern twist, to give Moreton Hall girls the edge when they enter the adult world of work. Jonathan says he has been empowered by the environment, and it must be mutual, because his entrepreneurial spirit, his thinking outside the box, shows in the girls and in the whole ethos of the place. He has done remarkable things and when he eventually does leave, it will take someone very special to take his place.

Academic matters: Academic results are strong, with an improvement at A level to 40 per cent A*/A grades; GCSE 70 per cent A*/A, and the value-added scores at both GCSE and A level are usually huge. Its increasing success draws in star teachers and bright girls, so it's all on an upward trajectory. With lots of living accommodation on site, the job becomes a lifestyle choice for teachers as well as families. There is no deadening insistence on the latest Department for Education pedagogy here. The principal is far more interested in bringing in people who have done things – the English department boasts a writer, the art department has practising artists and the girls told us that their chemistry teacher had been testing perfumes before joining Moreton Hall. There is a strong science drive in the school (innovative science centre includes medical science facility – the first for any UK school) and well over half are taking at least one science A level. Close links to Keele University and the orthopaedic hospital at nearby Gobowen,

Though edging up all the time, the ability is quite wide on entry, which makes the results particularly encouraging. It's down to excellent teachers as well as small class sizes. The girls describe their teachers as 'passionate and enthusiastic' and are very aware that they are there literally all the time. 'They give you as much extra as you need,' said one sixth former who told us that when she was working late on a piece of work, she had emailed her teacher with a query at 11pm and had a reply.

There is no extra charge for learning support, whether it is Oxbridge preparation or getting through GCSE maths. Teachers are there for the girls whatever their needs – no sense of children having to fit into rigid school systems here. One parent commented on the flexibility the school offered in terms of curriculum – girls can study more or less any combination of subjects they want at GCSE and A level.

Games, options, the arts: It's in this side of school life where its radical and constantly progressing nature really shines. In sport it embraces that most traditional of girls' sports, lacrosse, where the Moreton Hall teams win everything this side of London and a fair bit nationally as well, but there are masses of other successes and opportunities with the fabulous sports facilities on site – a nine hole golf course and grounds that mean cross-country really is cross country.

Lots of music goes on, classical and popular, with girls performing regularly to both large and small audiences. Drama is hugely popular and professional. 'Musical theatre can consume everything', said one non-thespian parent, worrying about exam results, but the girls are queuing up to take part.

All this is nothing like enough for Moreton Hall. The school is strong on connections and is extraordinarily well linked with a network of influential men and women whom Jonathan brings into the school for inspirational talks. Outside London this is not easy, and you would never guess this school was in the depth of gorgeous Shropshire. Dame Jocelyn Bell Burnett, world famous astrophysicist, had just been when we visited, and strong links with Keele University produce a steady flow of high-powered visitors. These not only enhance academic lessons but often come to speak at one of the many societies to which parents also drop in. There is wine-tasting, a feminist society, a medical science group, share dealing and so it goes on, reflecting the scope of opportunities for young women in the 21st century world.

All the girls get involved in the English Speaking Board to enhance confidence, presentation skills and the ability to think on their feet. One parent said, 'Everyone gets a 2.1 from Bristol or wherever these days, but Jonathan Forster really understands that the girls will need a lot more than that – he is giving them the life skills to succeed.'

Moreton Enterprises is part of this – a unique business venture consisting of a shopping mall run entirely by the girls. There is a branch of Ryman's stationery, Barclays Bank and home grown shops. The girls have business mentors, but basically the lower sixth operates as a small business turning over £50,000 a year. It is seriously impressive.

Boarding: About 90 per cent are boarders, and there is Saturday morning school, but apart from that, it is pretty flexible. One parent felt that girls new to boarding could be unsettled by friends coming and going, but we didn't find any girls who worried about this. The school wants girls to love boarding there and they do, partly because of the very special staff and partly because there is so much going on. 'It's like a long sleep-over but with loads to do as well,' said an enamoured 13 year old who had started as a day girl and then converted to boarding after a few taster nights.

We asked the sixth formers whether they felt a long way from all the city lights and boys, but were assured they saw quite as much as they wanted to of Shrewsbury School boys and often stayed Saturday night with friends in Manchester or Birmingham if they could fit it in between rehearsals, choir, talks. 'But it is just so lovely to come back,' they said with heartfelt sincerity.

Senior boarding accommodation is single or double (very popular in holidays with overseas adults as well as children), adding to the home from home feel. Junior girls and boys, often boarding one or two nights a week, have their own cheerful dormitories.

Background and atmosphere: As you would expect from girls who run a business at the age of 16, they are confident and at ease with themselves. They work and play hard, but there is something in the rural Shropshire surroundings (the school is set in 100 acres of parkland) that takes any unattractive edge off the ambition and drive. We felt that every girl in England should have at least a term in this environment.

The school was started by women educationalists 100 years ago, and Jonathan holds firm to their liberal view of education. He has used the school's centenary year to ensure the girls know about the strong female role models in the school's past. 'It was never meant to be like other schools,' he tells us. 'The Lloyd Williams family wanted a school where girls could enjoy the country and experience a rounded education that would set them up for life and all the different people they would meet'.

The very English country landscape and original school building, a moated Tudor house with the current façade dating from William and Mary, are balanced by new state-of-the-art purpose built areas. There is a stunning new science block planned in a collaboration with Keele University and local state schools. The facilities are used by the university to run science taster session for local students with a particular emphasis on medical careers. The library is both welcoming and very modern. One girl talked about working in the library before her GCSEs and being able to take her kettle, mug and biscuits in there for a real go at her revision – good for the librarian.

Pastoral care, well-being and discipline: The principal wants the girls to love Moreton Hall as they would love their home, and to care for the school and each other in the same way. From what we saw, they do. There was a genuine warmth between the older and younger girls and a sincere appreciation for their surroundings and the attention they receive from teachers and boarding staff. Given the entrepreneurial energy about the place, the girls are amazingly relaxed. One member of staff said, 'They have time and space here so you don't get a frenetic atmosphere building up where no one has room for anyone except themselves'. These are not privileged princesses who think the world owes them. They are self-disciplined young women who have learnt in school that you can make a difference and live happily together. The centenary pageant included everyone who is a part of the school – not just teachers and girls. It's an inclusive place. Discipline was not a word we heard mentioned, and for a school that can happily host tribute bands in the outdoor amphitheatre on the last night of the summer term without a qualm – who needs lots of rules and punishment?

Pupils and parents: Some 80 per cent of the boarders are from the UK, a deliberate policy, and about 90 per cent of those girls are from within one to two hours travel. The school caters for business, diplomatic and professional families where often both parents are working and see the boarding option as a lifestyle choice, with the girls having endless activities and friends on tap. Communication, both formal and informal, works very effectively. Overseas parents tell us the school makes brilliant use of modern technology and emails are responded to very quickly by both the head and staff. Parents are supportive both in terms of social events and also by acting as mentors for the business enterprises. They can drop in to more or less any event going on, and the division between home and school seems very fluid compared with many schools. One parent said, 'There are very traditional families who find it all rather liberal, but the principal soon shows them it works'. The principal and staff are well known for their assiduous attendance at school events and their detailed knowledge of the girls and their families.

Alumni include Zanny Minton Beddoes, editor of The Economist, Thea Musgrave, composer and musician, and Dame Linda Dobbs, high court judge.

There is a separate study centre for overseas students and multi-activity holidays for children and their parents.

Entrance: Many of 11+ entrants from co-ed junior school, Moreton First. Then further entry points at 13 and 16 into the sixth form. Number from overseas capped at 10 per cent. Test, interview and school report to determine entry. Oversubscribed at various points, particularly in sixth form. Once girls are there, the school sticks with them and very few leave – including hardly any year 11 leavers (some 10 per cent).

Exit: Almost all to university including impressive 10 to Oxbridge in 2016, plus three medics and one vet. Leeds very popular (including for physics and biology), then Bath, Exeter, Liverpool and Oxford Brookes. Not surprisingly, given their experience in school, a remarkable number of Old Moretonians are running successful businesses.

Money matters: The school has worked hard to increase means-tested bursaries, particularly to allow local girls from state schools to join the sixth form. Everyone pays something, but the aim is to give girls who would otherwise not have the opportunity a chance to experience the high-powered, aspirational world of Moreton Hall.

Remarks: It is outside the radar of parents who don't look beyond the home counties but more fool them – they are the ones missing out here. When asked why he had chosen Moreton Hall for his daughters, one parent looked vaguely bemused and said, 'Well, why wouldn't you?' We agree. This is a school with a difference, rigour in everything but going about it in a way that shows girls they can lead the world in a new way. And they will.

Mount Kelly Prep

Linked with Mount Kelly

Mount Tavy Road, Tavistock, Devon PL19 9JL

Pupils: 299; 37 boarders • Ages: 3–13 (boarders from year 3) • C of E

Fees: Day £6,900 – £13,200 pa; Boarding £17,250 – £22,500 pa

Tel: 01822 813193
Email: admissions@mountkelly.com
Website: www.mountkelly.com

Head of Prep: Since September 2016, Dominic Floyd, previously assistant head at Hazlegrove. Geography degree and PGCE from London University; taught geography at Cothill House and Westminster Under School; director of studies and deputy head at Polwhele House; head of Ashdown House. He and his wife Maria have three young children and his interests include micro-adventure, hiking, tennis and golf.

Entrance: Wide ability range – tests in English and maths 'more for benchmarking than selection,' says head. Most entrants attend a taster day in February prior to admission. Majority join the pre-prep at start of year 3, but growing numbers delay start until year 7, transferring automatically to the college at 13.

A few means-tested bursaries available.

Exit: Pupils prepared for 13+ transfer to the College at Mount Kelly or elsewhere. Presumably any pupil wanting to 11+ transfer elsewhere is prepared for this. The hope is for the majority of prep children to move into the main college at 13 and about 80 per cent do so.

Remarks: In the merger which established the Mount Kelly Foundation in June 2014, Kelly Prep children moved into the sumptuous Mount House facilities, which are conveniently adjacent to the main Mount Kelly College buildings. A bridge over the road (still at planning stage when we visited) will mean that the prep will benefit from the college's impending Olympic size pool and college pupils gain access to the prep's sports hall, extensive grounds and other impressive facilities.

Stunning grounds include a trout stream (ideal for fly fishing) and a beautiful lake (great for science) bordering on Dartmoor National Park. A recent team of inspectors dubbed it 'an inspirational learning environment'. The prep is based in and around an elegantly proportioned, stone-built Georgian manor house with an assortment of additions, some historic and some ultra-modern purpose built. The attractive hall, accessed rather curiously through an office rather than its lovely glass doors, fulfils a variety of functions including regular assemblies and church services. The head's oak-panelled study leads off on one side and the school dining hall on the other. Upstairs are all the boys' and girls' dormitories in separate areas plus the sick bay. Dormitories of between four and eight are extremely well designed, with bathrooms etc between each pair of dorms. Boys' rooms are clean, fresh and pretty tidy, while the girls obviously like to express themselves more freely via plenty of pictures, and personal touches.

A plethora of buildings clusters behind the main house, some old and definitely unusual – the original stables have been converted in a variety of ways, including the 'giraffe house', which features a climbing wall, plus some really impressive purpose built facilities: the modern sports hall (with two squash courts), two large science laboratories and impressive music school. Music had a bit of a hiatus after the merger but seems to have recovered to 'even better than before', partly thanks to the 'best singing teacher in the universe'. 'Proper' church choir contributes to festivals etc and music is definitely 'in'. Full orchestra, jazz band, woodwind, choir, rock band all perform regularly. The school has a record of music and art scholarships, and the inviting art department had work on display which more than explained this.

Prep schools with such an array of enterprising ventures are few and far between, especially in deepest Devon. Recycling motivates the highly organised CDT department, where self-sufficiency and sustainable technology become second nature, and everything from day-old chicks to bicycle wheels finds a use. It is masterminded by an enthusiast who also runs a small farm in the school grounds. All ages contribute and 'truly love it'. Amongst animal and other agricultural activities, pupils are building a sustainable hut which even provides it own electricity (solar micro generators) while the tractor runs on the kitchen's recycled vegetable and the water supply comes from a borehole.

Most of the classrooms are an extension of the main building: attractive internally – some with stunning displays – and all with high level of equipment (smartboard in every classroom). Eighteen PCs in IT suite and staff are mostly IT savvy. 'Some fantastic teachers with a wide variety of styles from formal and well organised to lots of fun' – but all of them kind and good at building confidence. The recurring theme from parents, however, is that teachers are kind while children enjoy lessons and are happy. 'Mix of old timers and new blood on staff works well,' commented one father. Average class size is about 16. Curriculum is designed to allow pupils to go off piste and generate individual enthusiasms. High quality of written work wherever you look; motivational French lessons was another strong point noted.

Director of studies acts as SENCo with some 35 pupils on special needs register. Pupils are screened for dyslexia and a dedicated education psychologist will develop an IEP if required. Two part-time SpLD staff give one-to-one help where required.

Pre-prep in purpose-built, low level accommodation for 60 children up to end of year 2 with discrete outside area. High level of care and individual attention – most pre-preps transfer seamlessly aged 7. Lots of fun and outdoor experience for this end of the school, as well as developing strong foundations in the classroom basics.

Boarding ethos is all-important, especially to day pupils. One who begged to do a term's boarding loved it and found it problem free. No cliques or bullying and the occasional loner supported and encouraged. The new régime has relaxed some of the compulsory weekend elements but includes Saturday evening pick-up after activities, then low-key, on-site Sunday programme. Ten couples/families live on site and rotate weekend duties. Early signs are encouraging, with boarding numbers apparently on the increase. All staff stay here until 6pm every day; prep finishes at 7pm for older pupils (younger ones have clubs) and duty team of staff remains until dorm staff take over at 8.30pm. Most pupils spill out into grounds after prep but there are also lovely hidey-holes in the subterranean library for dedicated bookworms, and a lovely decked space for quiet relaxation complete with multi-lingual telephone box.

Five days a week sport here – facilities include fine pitches, heated outdoor pool (very popular) and full size Astroturf; national/regional successes principally in rugby, cricket and girls' hockey. Boarders love to play in the nets or swim after prep in the summer. Pony-mad pupils get a look in with the local hunt and inter-school equestrian events. The Shackleton Award scheme (junior D of E award type project aimed at building confidence) was in full swing doing splashy things down by the enchantingly beautiful lake during our visit. The exceptionally beautiful grounds with waterfall and sloping lawns are meticulously managed by a groundsman who is endlessly kind to pupils, and even to parents with engine trouble or no petrol.

Pupils are well turned out – variety of dress according to age and season; they come mainly from Devon and Cornwall, professional, farming and Forces families plus a few from London or elsewhere (very few overseas). Twice-termly lectures, alternating between the prep and the college, for parents and pupils across the Foundation, tap parental know-how: recent outside speakers have included explorer Pen Hadow and yachtswoman Tracy Edwards. Lots of local visits for all ages, annual trips to Northern France for the older pupils and regular ski trip to Alps. Former pupils include Phil de Glanville (England rugby captain), Adrian Lukis (actor in Pride and Prejudice), former foreign secretary and SDP co-founder, Lord David Owen, and explorer, long-distance swimmer and environmentalist, Lewis Pugh, to name but a few.

This combination of traditional prep and local junior schooling has given the far west a potentially remarkable school. One parent commented that the last few days of summer term are a triumph and say it all. Pupils leave, some to take up academic, sporting or artistic scholarships at the college itself, or other schools, able to 'catch a fish, thread a sewing machine and bake a cake', full of the confidence to face the next step eagerly.

Mount Kelly

Linked with Mount Kelly Prep

Parkwood Road, Tavistock, Devon PL19 0HZ

Pupils: 570; 148 full, 20 weekly/flexi boarders • Ages: 13-18 • Sixth form: 130 • C of E

Fees: Day £16,710; Boarding £27,150 – £29,100 pa

Tel: 01822 813193
Email: admissions@mountkelly.com
Website: www.mountkelly.com

Head Master and Principal of Mount Kelly Foundation: Since 2014, Mark Semmence, previously assistant head at Rugby School. An economist with degrees from Durham (BA and MBA), London (PGCE) and Warwick (MA), he taught at Ludgrove Prep, then worked in international sports marketing before returning to teaching. Played cricket for England Schools U19 and Durham University; a member of MCC Youth Cricket Committee. Married to Alison; they have two young daughters. Mr Semmence cites architectural history as one of his interests, which is probably just as well as he has inherited a building whose Victorian architect clearly thought that the naval officers it aimed to produce required a medieval monastic training.

He is certainly equal to the challenge, having managed to pull off a universally excellent Independent Schools Inspectorate review within six months of taking the merger of Kelly College and Mount House into the Mount Kelly Foundation. This has involved a restructuring of both staffing and of the way the prep and the college relate. Parents comment that he has been 'ruthless about upping academic teaching standards'. Masses of 'rebranding' has been done to tempt both local day pupils and traditional 'public school' boarding. He must have done a remarkably thorough and well-planned job, as ISI normally requires 'embedded values': hard to achieve in six months. He has also acquired a swimming pool left over from the London Olympics. Wow!

Academic matters: Mount Kelly is one of those schools brave and sensible enough to eschew the 'league tables'. A level results commendable, especially for a school which is not academically selective, with maths definitely impressive at all levels. In 2016, nearly a third of grades were A*/A, with 15 per cent at A*. AT GCSE, 49 per cent A*/A grades.

Class sizes are small – sometimes very small at A level. Currently the school will put on a course for one pupil – sadly necessary since the take up in modern foreign languages, art and music is select but able. Pupils we spoke to were full of praise for the extra help offered by their teachers when necessary. A good range of solid academic subjects on offer, with excellent language and IT areas. Parents spoke of the expert and sensitive advice they had had from staff when trying to help their children choose the most suitable subjects for them. Perhaps fewer now feel the urge to go further afield for a 'real academic education'. Parents and pupils speak very highly of the help given to those with special needs.

Games, options, the arts: Mount Kelly is rapidly becoming synonymous with swimming. Its reputation, built up over 30 years, is currently growing under the tutelage of Robin Brew, ex-pupil and international and Olympic swimmer, who heads a team of coaches of similar calibre running a comprehensive coaching programme for swimmers with competitive ambitions. The programme is built round the academic day and so is considerably less stressful and probably less expensive than the constant travel, early mornings and compromises with school that many young swimmers have to make. A parent commented that only one or two British schools have anything like comparable swimming and coaching facilities, and that Mount Kelly's pastoral care for such pupils is leagues ahead. To crown it all, a third pool to latest Olympic standards purchased from the London Olympic site is being installed. No wonder the school boasts that, on average, a Mount Kelly swimmer a year has represented the UK either nationally or internationally.

Non-swimmers, however, are far from sidelined. Pupils spoke with enthusiasm of music, debates and outdoor activities, and there are myriads of curriculum supporting events. It's a lively place but also cheerful, friendly and definitely not frenetic, even at exam time. It is old fashioned enough to insist on school blazers with ribbons and badges festooned all over athletic gods and goddesses, but musicians, artists, thespians and prefects can be equally decorated – the school is just good at celebrating and acknowledging. The pitches and grounds in both prep and college areas are superbly managed and the acquisition of the Mount House School site has brought the one missing element, a fantastic sports hall. It will be a real boon for the seniors once there is a bridge across the A386 into Tavistock. Sport plentiful but traditional – rugby and cricket for boys and hockey and netball for girls. Both girls and boys play hockey and compete in a mixed summer league.

A splendid and most interestingly designed performing arts centre with superb facilities for music, drama and debate – to say nothing of interval entertainment – is close by, as is the art building with evidence of creative painting and pottery. Since the college snuggles into a valley on the edge of Dartmoor, it's hardly surprising that outdoor education, D of E, CCF and all those sort of things are available and popular. Huge numbers of girls as well as boys complete the 125 mile canoe marathon from Devizes to Westminster and the Ten Tors expedition, as well as training as divers, rifle shots and mountaineers.

Boarding: Despite its monastic appearance, the renovated sections of boarding are exceptionally well done. Clever planning means that day pupils and boarders can socialise on the lower floors with plenty of well-equipped work and milling about space, while the bedroom floors above remain private. We were not taken to the 'unreconstructed' areas but, since two out of four houses are already redesigned and the others proceeding apace, most pupils entering now will not see them either. The four houses are divided into girls' sixth form, boys' sixth form and two co-ed houses for years 9-11, each managed by housemasters with a team of tutors drawn from academic staff as well as non-teaching matrons. Full medical service on hand. Boarders spoke enthusiastically of the sixth form centre and the activities arranged at weekends. Flexi boarding is very flexi.

Background and atmosphere: The buildings, tucked under the edge of Dartmoor just outside the pretty little town of Tavistock, have historical connections with the Duke of Bedford, who donated the land for the college, founded in 1877 by an Admiral Kelly. Despite its gentle lawns and lush green pitches, it's a craggy looking place, all gothic arches, dark wood and stone staircases, echoing corridors and lots of pointy bits. Academic mustiness, however, is banished by skilfully placed features of interest, pictures, honours and information about the school's past and the pupils' futures. Handsome library presided over by enthusiastic librarian and dusty looking (actually it isn't) chapel still exuding an odour of past sanctity, used four times a week.

Attractive new buildings higher up the hill behind the Victoriana, one of them the delightful Conway House, where the younger boys and girls live in comfortable harmony before joining the senior houses. Co-ed has been going here for nearly 40 years, so it all feels very relaxed and natural.

Pastoral care, well-being and discipline: Lunch in the dining room (masses of choice – cooked meals, salads and faster-looking stuff – particularly delicious lemon posset) was a good insight into the relationships between staff and pupils. Enough mutual respect and genuine affection to allow friendly banter on occasions. The pupils were forthcoming, friendly and honest in their conversation with us, though we were not shielded from meeting the odd awkward customer – treated with helpful sympathy and understanding. While accepting that bullying was always a possibility, they felt that the tutorial system in place was a good safety net and protection – always someone to talk to; above all they said they genuinely like the staff. Pretty common sense school rules result in very little indiscipline. Pupils all looked smartish, though lots dressed in mufti or sportswear towards the end of the day.

Pupils and parents: Parents come from a broad spectrum. Mount Kelly is trying to bridge the gap between being a good local option for the West Country and an upmarket public school. Boarding is boosted by swimmers from England and abroad (around 25 per cent of boarders are from overseas). One parent commented: 'My son can swim but hates it. But he gets stuck into lots of other things and that's the point. I take the view that excellence breeds excellence.' Others praise the community feel among parents, stressing how welcoming they are to families who move to Tavistock for schooling. The pupils we met and observed were open, friendly and trusting, and we noticed how much family-like interaction existed between the different age groups. Though there is definitely a sense that Mount Kelly is on its way to joining the league of 'top schools', it still feels a friendly, relaxed place where children can be children as much as is possible in this day and age.

Entrance: At 13+, about 75 per cent of entries come from the prep. Academically, the emphasis is on literacy and numeracy, with as much attention paid to potential as to knowledge. Entrance at sixth form is based on GCSE results (or equivalent) – normally about 20 new sixth formers joining each year. The important thing is to be alert, bright-eyed and willing to be taught. That applies as much to rugby players as potential Nobel Prize winners.

Exit: Three-quarters go on to the sixth form. Nearly all of these to university. A sensible number to well established ones all over the UK (and occasionally USA) to do old fashioned academic subjects and one or so a year to Oxbridge (one in 2016) proves they can do it.

Money matters: Scholarships and bursaries are available. Forces families may receive 10 per cent discount – don't be afraid to ask.

Remarks: Definitely worth watching. The signs are that it may succeed in providing an excellent environment for girls and boys set on local schooling as well as building up a boarding clientèle based on academic success enhanced by the lure of swimming. A sound, progressive place, where effort is rewarded and friendships flourish, unhampered by snobbery or over-sophistication, and on its way to giving the West Country a really fantastic school. Numbers up in the college with more boarders this year, so the signs are positive.

Okehampton College

Mill Road, Okehampton, Devon EX20 1PW

Pupils: 1,390 • Ages: 11–18 • Sixth form: 180

Tel: 01837 650910
Email: admin@okehamptoncollege.devon.sch.uk
Website: www.okehamptoncollege.devon.sch.uk

Executive Principal: Since 2005, Daryll Chapman, originally from Kenilworth in Warwickshire, grew up in Derbyshire. Started his career playing professional football for Derby before training to become a PE teacher at a specialist college for physical education in Bedfordshire. After four years teaching at Cavendish School in Hemel Hempstead, he became head of PE at Misbourne School, Bucks, later becoming deputy head at a school in Aylesbury. Daryll joined Okehampton College in 2001 as vice principal, taking on the role of principal four years later.

Married with three children; his youngest has just joined OC. He's looking forward to seeing the school through her eyes. His eldest daughter also went here so he knows how valuable this insight can be. No longer teaches PE, but he does teach maths to some of the more challenging students. Still playing football? No, he smiles, more of a spectator these days, and too busy ferrying his children around various athletics events across the county.

Daryll's adamant that the school isn't run like a business; it's a community. 'It's important to give the local children the opportunity to work and grow together,' he says. It's a big school, currently over 1,300 students, but he is more than happy to continue to grow, fully confident of their ability to cope with this. He also strongly feels that they haven't lost their personal touch at all. We agree – the school didn't feel as big as it actually is. He believes in traditional values, meaning 'old school' values like being 'firm but fair', but not traditional in the sense of heritage and customs. Positive comments all round from parents, one saying, 'very impressed with Mr Chapman, he is part of the reason we didn't look around elsewhere.'

Academic matters: In 2016, 63 per cent A*-B grades and 33 per cent A*/A grades at A level. At GCSE, 67 per cent got C+ in both English and maths. Ofsted said, 'All students make excellent progress from their generally below-average starting points.' Maths is a strong subject, and results have been in the top five per cent value added over the last four years. In science, another popular subject, students have recently won bronze awards and commendations in the National Physics Challenge.

Twenty-five A levels offered, plus BTecs in business, sport and dance. Vocational options cover catering, childcare and customer service. French is compulsory at key stage 3; German and Spanish are also offered. The school supports EAL students who wish to take a GCSE in their mother tongue. Recent examples include: Polish, Dutch, Russian, Portuguese, Japanese and Spanish, but only in small numbers. Parents all agreed they were 'very pleased with the quality of teaching'. One teacher even called the college a 'career stopper,' happily refusing promotions elsewhere to stay there.

Large learning support department that recently won a Devon Dyslexia-Friendly Award. Twenty-five TAs, three special needs teachers, two literacy tutors, two numeracy TAs, all headed up by their SENCo. More than a quarter of students at OC have a recognised need. This includes the gifted and talented high achievers, as well as those needing support with reading or writing. One parent told us their child is 'studious and anxious and [we are] very pleased with the level of emotional support offered.' The site has been specially adapted for those with physical disabilities. There are wheelchair ramps, automatic access doors and yellow lines for partially sighted students. SEND is considered a priority and there's an ongoing teacher-training programme. Support is tailored to meet individual needs. Small groups for literacy and numeracy, a social skills group, a buddy system for reading and socialising, plus in-class support. There's also a number of clubs – breakfast club, break-time club and after-school homework club when learning support staff are on hand to help.

Games, options, the arts: Excellent sports facilities. Astroturf, four floodlit tennis courts, extensive playing fields and a sports hall. The town's leisure centre is attached to the campus so although they don't have sole use, they have access to the dance studio, sports hall, fitness suite and swimming pool. The school offers all the major games, plus gymnastics, trampolining, dance aerobics, athletics, cross-country and fitness courses. Outdoor pursuits are very popular: orienteering, canoeing, sailing, windsurfing, and moor walking. Notable success in table tennis – they are currently the national U13 table tennis champions, having county champions in their midst. One girl plays cricket for Devon county, one boy was recently crowned national judo champion and three students have represented England schools in athletics.

Good drama faculty (faculties, not departments here), popular and a good exam pass rate. There are regular trips to the theatre, plus opportunities to take part in dance and drama workshops with visiting theatre companies. Latest productions include Les Misérables with over 100 actors, and Kitty Jay, a Dartmoor legend, performed both at Castle Drogo and at the college. The school has its own 200 seat theatre with a professional lighting rig and a sound booth. The next big production is going to be West Side Story. Sixth formers regularly visit London for plays or to take part in National Theatre acting workshops with professional West End actors and directors.

Art and textiles are offered at GCSE and at A level. Plenty of opportunities to visit galleries locally, plus in London and Paris. There are three art rooms, and a sixth form area. Textiles is popular and the classroom has spectacular views of the sports fields and the moors beyond. Very good art on display, landscapes no doubt inspired by the surrounding area, and a huge number of papier-mâché shoes, no doubt inspired by, well, the love of shoes.

Music is in a purpose built area, including an upper floor with four practice rooms and sound booths. Well resourced, each classroom has a piano/keyboard, drum kit, amps and guitars. When we were there, students were recording their individual exam pieces on the drums in one room, and practising as a band (teacher on drums), in another room. The whole building was alive with activity and ad hoc practice sessions. The school encourages individual lessons and although parents contribute, there is a charity set up to help keep costs down. Wide range of ensemble activities, including orchestra, big band, little band, junior and senior choirs. Big Band has travelled to New York, Hong Kong, Paris and recently Barcelona. Two major concerts each year at Christmas and Easter.

There's a well-resourced and modern building for technology and ICT. Six large suites dedicated to ICT, plus a sixth form suite, and Wi-fi covering the whole school. For technology, there's professional standard catering equipment, two labs for resistant materials, two labs for electronics, a CADCAM suite and workbenches. All hand and computer skills are covered here.

The school offers a good range of extracurricular activities and even provides late buses to ensure that everyone can take part. However, the head did say, 'my only disappointment is that more of them do not take advantage of these opportunities.' Annually there's a curriculum extension week and recently students have gone sea fishing, cycled along the Devon coastline, travelled to France and Germany, and taken part in cooking, drama and even magic courses. Other trips include regular French exchanges with a school in Brittany and recently, cultural trips to Germany and Poland.

Background and atmosphere: Founded in 1910 as a grammar school, the college is set in a large park, surrounded by woodland and Dartmoor, and bordered by the Okement River on one side, and rolling farmland on the other. It really is a beautiful country setting. There's a good mix of old and new – there's the original Victorian building with its large arched windows, a modern three-storey block, plus 70s buildings, all linked by covered walkways. It's easy to find your way round. The site feels open, friendly and has interesting touches of courtyards, picnic tables and even its own trickling leat.

There have been a few developments in recent years including the refurbishment of three science labs and a library. The most recent development is the addition of a second floor in the lunch hall creating an upstairs dining area. It feels more like an airport café than a school dining hall and we could see why the pupils love it. Sixth formers have their own café (year 11 can get passes as rewards). Lunch is cashless for everyone and nobody is allowed off site.

The student council is busy at OC. To date they've created a 'peace garden', improved the toilets, sorted the bus shelters and are even allowed to get involved in the interview process for senior staff members. They take the lead in raising money for charity and run events like the annual school sponsored walk across the moors. The school also has its own weekly 'memory café' for local people and their loved ones who are affected by dementia. Students work at the café as 'dementia ambassadors.'

Okehampton College is seriously green. It is featured in Sustainia 100 as one of the world's 100 best energy projects. In 2013 it won the Zayed Future Energy Prize (Global High School category), and also received the Ashden Award for sustainable energy from Sir David Attenborough. There are solar panels aplenty, a biomass boiler, on-site waste composting, allotments, polytunnels and a heap of activities and clubs that students can get involved in. As well as the environmental benefits, the pioneering energy work produces savings for the school and gives pupils real working examples of energy efficiency, recycling, renewable energy and sustainability. One parent told us her son had gained a lot from one of the clubs, STEM; 'He was in it from year 7 and he gained a lot of confidence in presenting through it as well as learning about energy efficiency.'

Pastoral care, well-being and discipline: No 'rules' boards. 'Respect' is the big word here. The head believes that pupils should be treated with empathy and sensitivity within a culture of high expectations. He calls it 'the sensible approach – work with them, but be firm but fair'. OC is a big school and there are children from all walks of life here. There's a low rate of exclusions; the school is prepared to support them rather than isolate them – due to the school's location, some children live in very rural areas. There is a good student support department here, plus vertical tutor groups and clubs or drop-ins where pupils can ask for help. Ofsted was very impressed and said OC is 'an outstandingly caring and supportive community where students flourish and develop as individuals.'

Pupils and parents: The catchment area is huge – over 400 square miles – so there are school buses to ferry them around. This part of Devon is very rural and so the college is central to the social lives of everyone as a community. Pupils are 'enthusiastic and happy to go to school', but a number of parents 'would like to see a smarter uniform, shirt, tie and blazer.'

Entrance: Based on catchment area. Eleven feeder primary schools and lots of opportunities for prospective pupils and parents to get to know the school. One parent confirmed they were 'very pleased with how the transition is handled.' When we were there, we bumped into two primary school pupils on a tour; they were really excited about the upcoming science and sports tournament day as part of their induction.

Entry to the sixth form requires five GCSEs, usually including a grade B in the chosen subject.

Exit: On average, 50 per cent stay on for sixth form. The majority who leave go to Exeter College or specialist colleges for land-based studies or art. The sixth form here, graded as 'outstanding' by Ofsted, isn't separate from the rest of the school and can't provide the lifestyle offered by Exeter College. There are potential plans to convert the now unused 'skills centre' as a sixth form area, but this is still only a maybe. The building was originally built to offer on-site vocational training in construction, hairdressing etc but has since been left empty. As a sixth form centre it would work well, but we're still not sure it would win over those set on city life.

The college offers plenty of careers advice and support, with trips to universities and careers lessons to raise aspirations. Most students go on to university with many getting their first choice eg University of the West of England, Bournemouth, Bath Spa, Plymouth, Exeter, Portsmouth. One off to study medicine in 2016. Famous leavers include Steve Holliday, CEO of the National Grid, and Matt Woodley, Radio Devon's breakfast DJ (now a parent here).

Remarks: Good rural comprehensive. Good results, friendly atmosphere and, as one local business put it, 'confident kids.'

Packwood Haugh School

Ruyton XI Towns, Shrewsbury, Shropshire SY4 1HX

Pupils: 213: 150 boys, 63 girls; 93 boarders • Ages: 4-13 (boarders from 7) • C of E

Fees: Day £8,100 – £17,250; Boarding £21,750 pa

Tel: 01939 260217
Email: headmaster@packwood-haugh.co.uk
Website: www.packwood-haugh.co.uk

Headmaster: Since 2012, Clive Smith-Langridge. Limbered up for the role by spending 16 years in marketing before switching to boarding schools (was previously deputy head at Walhampton). Brings essential savvy plus the experience of having captained a Chile cricket XI vs Brazil. In an evolving boarding market, Packwood is lucky to have his sort of business nous and strategic expertise: finances are sound, numbers healthy, pupils and teachers audited and fine-tuned. Appointed in tandem with his wife, Sally, who glories in the possibly puzzling title of Headmaster's Wife, a post you'll find in many prep schools. Hers is a salaried role with responsibilities on the pastoral side. Parents very much like this proxy-parent, family-feel arrangement. Clive and Sally have two daughters.

Entrance: Co-ed (some two-thirds boys), non-selective. Informal assessment for prep – Eng and maths. No assessment for pre-prep, Packwood Acorns. Range of scholarships. Bursaries for Forces families and local children, one of whom is off to Eton. Children come from all adjoining counties and north Wales. Some, sons and daughters of devoted former pupils, journey from afar. Less than 10 per cent from overseas – Spain, Japan, China.

Exit: Packwood has long furnished the top public schools. Lots to Shrewsbury, others to usual suspects – eg Rugby, Malvern College, Eton, Harrow, Wycombe Abbey, Moreton Hall, Stowe, St Edward's. They know it's important to get it right, so a smattering to Sedbergh, Ellesmere, Wrekin College. Eminent one-time pupils include Mark Rylands, Bishop of Shrewsbury; Tom Salt, head chef at Manicomio; Tom James MBE, double gold medal winning Olympic rower; and Rhys Bevan, Toby Fairbrother in the Archers.

Remarks: A time-honoured top-tier prep school which celebrates its headmasters by inscribing their names in gold on the panelled ceiling of the entrance hall. Co-ed since 1968; we await the first headmistress. Former pupils celebrate glorious character-building idiosyncrasies, all now superannuated (Molesworth, where art thou?). Packwood is fully C21-compatible with heritage values – country prep school, 'proper boarding', traditional values, old-fashioned manners, fresh air, friendship, give it a go, play out of your skin. The food's great – official. So nothing here evokes St Custard's. But there is a skool dog, the head's border terrier Belle, never cheerfuller than when egging on the troops from the touchline on match days.

There's none of your oligarch-magnet hotel-quality accommodation and associated blingy 'facilities' here. We're not talking spartan, we're talking quite comfy enough – in the case of the girls' dorms, very nice indeed, because of course girls are domesticable in a way that boys generally aren't (boys here tend to call each other by surnames, girls by first names). What else do you want? Purpose-built theatre? Tick. Sports hall? Tick. Swimming pool? Tick. All-weather surface? Tick. Er, golf course? Yep. Lamasery? Oh yes, got one of those (it's a quiet room set aside for contemplation.) Spinney? Yes, that's where we go to make dens and Packwood Acorns have their outdoor school. Everywhere you go you don't see children staring moodily into the middle distance of their smartphone screens. None, we asked? None, said the head (a non-negotiable no). Don't need them. They can Skype home from their dorm in the evening. All good.

Packwood is a classic country house prep school set in a mere 66 acres of lark-filled Shropshire. It is not set haughtily apart, though; you happen on it off a side road, you don't motor up an avenue to get to it. It adjoins the splendidly named Ruyton-XI-Towns (always XI) with which the Smith-Langridges have forged friendly relations on several fronts. There are collaborative links with local schools; many who work in the school live in the village; and Packwood boys and girls sing in the church choir. There are activity days to which all and sundry are invited. Some prep schools orbit real life. Not Packwood.

Honours boards, honours boards everywhere. There's no mistaking what's expected of you. Oppressively so? Not so far as our inquisitorial investigations revealed. Aspirational, more like. In any case, pupils know perfectly well who their brainy peers are and where they stand in relation to them. More to the point, how does it feel to be in the wake of them? For one dyslexic pupil, no problem, the learning support is great, some of the brightest have it too and anyway your friends don't measure you by how many marks you get. Hats off to the teachers, though: for an open access school all these scholarships represent an extraordinary achievement. Hurrah for the SENCo, too. Parents praise the way their children are 'pushed and stretched'. Mr Smith-Langridge has upped the game in terms of monitoring individual progress and thereby also the effectiveness of the teaching. He likes his data and he wants more of it. But he doesn't want to run a hothouse or a sweat shop. For him it's all about making the best of all the opportunities of the long, boarding day – and not just academic opportunities, either. He and his colleagues delight in the richness of achievement of all their charges according to their lights, not just their honours-board-worthiness. Art is good, drama on the up, music ubiquitous and top-notch.

If boarding isn't done well, 'twere well it were not done at all. Packwood has intelligently reinvented it and, just as important, made it a specialism, because no one wants to board at a school where most children go home at night. Boarding is phased in, there's a range of flexi-options and the majority graduate to full-time in preparation for their senior school. Weekends are busy with numbers boosted by those returning late on Saturdays from sports fixtures in faraway schools. Boys are in the big house, hugger-mugger, as they like it. Girls have their own residence. A number of teachers live in school, there are houseparents and there are lovely matrons. There's masses of care and oversight from warm, watchful adults who know these children and mind about them. There are bright posters bearing improving/banal quotes on the walls (we'd have preferred quotes by the children). Beds are cosy and teddy comes too. But take a look at the boys' washbasins, tidy as can be, and you'll see there's rigour here: this is no sleepover city, it is home from work; talking after lights out is a big no-no. A happy school is a deceptively rigorous place and all the happier for it. All parents praise Packwood's code of conduct and the way the children buy into it. Said one parent: 'They know when they've done wrong and genuinely feel contrition'. Another indicator of emotional health: Packwood children are no respecters of age and happily chat to those below and those above. There are boarding captains, older children to whom the younger ones can turn for counsel. And here's the point. We were accompanied by a viscerally antipathetic visitor to whose mind boarding is a bad, weird thing to do to a child. She visibly melted, the more she saw and heard, and ended up easily envisaging her grandson here, happy as a sandboy. One recent parent wistfully said she wished she'd known about Packwood for her other two girls.

Yes, the children really are terrifically nice and lit up, their manners are excellent, they're very at ease among adults, they're great company. It's easy enough to see how an outdoorsy, team-sporty child will thrive here, and the school aims to enable every single child to represent the school at something. There's a big games playing tradition at Packwood, another heritage touch, and not just in main sports. To survey the offering all round is to find yourself muttering clichés about punching above their weight. Like all knackered clichés, it exactly pinpoints the truth.

So what of the ones who are indoorsy, solitary, geeky? They're the ones you worry about, so we pried. Unlikely as it may seem, more than you'd think take to fencing; indeed, Packwood is nationally famed for its swordsmanship. And for its horsemanship. Some take to cross-country running (very strong here). We learned of one child who managed deftly to schedule guitar lessons in games time. All the parents we spoke to assured us that eccentricity in all its guises is simply not an issue. And then Mr Smith-Langridge recalled the boy who loved knitting.. and no one gave him a second glance. It helps to be gregarious, though, obviously, it's in the nature of the place. And at least a bit fresh-airy. Outside, after all, is where it happens every afternoon.

Packwood has a devoted fanbase of parents. Former pupils keep in close touch and their feats serve as an inspiration to the present generation. The school has shrewdly and effectively remodelled itself to align with the needs of today's working parents and carried with it the best of the old values. Our view: you get the best of both.

P

The Paragon School

Linked with Prior Park College

106

Lyncombe House, Lyncombe Vale, Bath, Somerset BA2 4LT

Pupils: 267 • Ages: 3–11

Fees: £8,745 – £9,735 pa

Tel: 01225 310837
Email: admissions.paragon@priorparkschools.com
Website: www.paragonschool.co.uk

Headmaster: Since 2012, Andrew Harvey BA PGCE (late 30s). Brought up and educated in Dorset (Milton Abbey) with a degree in history and theology from the University of Derby, he taught briefly before joining the Royal Dragoon Guards for three years 'mainly for the rugby – but also the leadership values', though he always intended to return to teaching; 'I'd conk out if I did it for 40 years, though'. Mr Harvey's career has been forged in prep schools (most recently Lambrook), except for a stint as head of pastoral care at Sherfield School, and it is here that he appears to feel most at home. The unstuffy atmosphere and Bath location of The Paragon appealed to him, but it was the fact that he and his wife Anna thought it would be the ideal school for their two small daughters that swung it. Mr Harvey follows a charismatic predecessor, but he has gone down well with parents, who find him visible, very approachable and hands-on – he pops into every class every day. The children find him 'funny', 'jolly' and 'religious' by turns and 'he doesn't like spending time in the office', said one perceptive little chap. The deputy head, who has been at the school for aeons, is a whizz at systems, so provides a good foil for the 'incredibly personable' (so says one mother) and omnipresent Mr Harvey. Hobbies include rugby, cricket and squash, and reading up on matters educational.

Entrance: Main entry points are at nursery, reception and year 3, though children are welcomed at any stage; most come from Bath and the villages south of the city. Three open mornings a year, after which an individual visit and interview with the head will generally secure a place; he is, however, not afraid to turn away children whose behaviour or academic delay would stretch the teachers' resources and disadvantage the class. Trial day provides opportunity for informal assessment

Exit: The majority at year 6 to Prior Park College, up the hill from the Paragon and part of the same foundation (along with Prior Park Prep in Cricklade, but Anglican rather than Catholic, unlike the other two), but some to other Bath schools, state and independent. Anyone wanting traditional common entrance at 13+ would need to go elsewhere for years 7 and 8, and a few do. In some years, nearly half the children gain an award of some kind into their next school – more given for sport than anything else. Any doubtful runners for Prior Park are given the nod in year 5; that said, the schools' learning support departments work closely together.

Remarks: Tucked away in a wooded dell surprisingly close to the centre of Bath, The Paragon now occupies what was a private Georgian house with a mineral spring still in its grounds, but it owes its name to its century-old origins as an educational gymnasium in the street of the same name in the city. Its seven and a half secluded acres comprise pitches, both Astro and grass, a conventional playground for younger children but – gloriously – masses of wooded slopes too, complete with a yurt and a tepee. Head, parents and children all very keen on outdoor learning; the school really lives it (eg acting out scenes from the Bayeux Tapestry) with help from Swainswick Explorers, instead of merely taking children outside to read on sunny days, as some do.

Classrooms are split between the main building and the charming stable block a minute's walk away. Not a school which bowled us over with technological wizardry; rather we liked what we saw and heard going on in classrooms, where one lucky English class was rewriting Cinderella in the style of Roald Dahl. Year 6 reading books lying about on desks impressive for children of that age. Head determined to extract more academic juice than has sometimes been the case before – to that end, he has lured his new director of studies from his previous school and introduced philosophy to the curriculum – yet remains a school where children can continue to be children until they leave. One parent felt that it's not a moment too soon to raise academic standards, and that attainments in maths in particular could be higher, given the small class sizes and biddable children. The head is certainly conscious of local competition in the form of KES Junior and excellent Widcombe Primary.

Sport is a serious matter, and even the tiniest children are taught the basic skills of the major sports. 'Rounders is a silly game,' says he, so is keen to introduce cricket to the girls, and has just appointed a head of girls' games to beef them up; high quality coaches also take regular sessions. School performs amazingly well in competition, especially considering its size; rugby, hockey and swimming stand out. Though its own facilities are limited, the pitches and swimming pool at Prior Park are but a short ride in a liveried minibus up the hill.

Music gets thumbs up from parents too, and the majority of prep school children learn an instrument, many achieving grade 3 or 4 by the time they leave. Local successes and two accepted into Young National Schools Symphony Orchestra. New music centre The Lodge apparently looks like a Swiss chalet.

We loved the expansive displays of art on the walls: a mixture of work based on established artists and the purely creative, but most of all we loved the craft room, up a mysterious staircase, and pervaded by the scent of lavender, where dear little bags were being made for charity. Paragon children emerge being able to sew on a lot more than a button. Drama is performed in the hall which doubles as a gym and the dining hall – a theatre is on the head's wish list. Noye's Fludde is currently in rehearsal with Prior Park, and we are sorry not to have seen La Neige Blanche et les Vingt Nains.

Everyone raves about the family feel of The Paragon, further enhanced by teachers now lunching with the children at the same tables. 'It's done wonders for their manners,' said one mother approvingly. Indeed: one boy we lunched with (pasta, pasta or pasta the day we visited) nearly choked rather than speak with his mouth full. Definitely time to get rid of the garish 'prison trays' the children eat off, though – staff get plastic plates. Active PTA raises funds but also has a strong social agenda and an impressive newsletter, The Paragraph.

The Paragon is unquestionably taking on a higher profile in Bath's competitive educational market place, but there remains an interesting contrast between its flamboyant rebranding (surely the most pukka uniforms locally, with red stripes in abundance for all) and its quirky relaxed feel, for which many parents choose it.

Parkstone Grammar School

Sopers Lane, Poole, Dorset BH17 7EP

Pupils: 1,291 • Ages: 11–18 • Sixth form: 391 (including 53 boys)

Tel: 01202 605605
Email: enquiries@parkstone.poole.sch.uk
Website: www.parkstone.poole.sch.uk

Headteacher: Since 2013, Mrs Tracy Harris. Was previously deputy headteacher at South Wilts Grammar School for Girls and has a strong track record in selective single sex education. Educated in the south west and studied history at Exeter University. Her husband Ian is also a teacher and she plays in a brass band in her spare time.

Academic matters: Results at GCSE and A level generally live up to its local reputation for excellence. Almost all do three sciences at GCSE, with pretty spectacular results; in 2016, 62 per cent A*/A grades across all subjects. At A level, maths, English, biology and chemistry have a high take up rate and pretty impressive results. In 2016, 73 per cent A*/B grades and 39 per cent A*/A overall.

This is a maths, science and modern languages academy with a wide choice of other subjects: drama, electronics, textiles in addition to usual GCSEs; plus computing, food, media studies, graphics, geology and politics at AS and most of these at A level.

Girls learn French, German and Spanish in year 8 and choose between German and Spanish on year 9. Most (85-90 per cent) continue with at least one language to GCSE, and girls can do up to three. No Latin, Greek or eastern languages at present, though Italian is now on stream. Girls are absolutely confident that the school would support anything they really wanted to do. Astrology currently on offer.

Sixth forms are sufficiently coordinated for girls to be able to slot into all-boys Poole Grammar School courses if Parkstone can't offer the combination they want and vice versa. Further maths, computing, geology and graphics A level courses available at Poole Grammar; the boys come to Parkstone for sociology, theatre studies and politics.

Large classes of up to 30 plus in lower school but very good monitoring. Subject prefects are good at providing help schemes and revision clubs with lots of encouragement from staff. Exceptionally good staff-pupil relationships with girls declaring, 'at risk of sounding cheesy, our staff are amazing, inspiring, working really hard to give us good lessons and ready to do anything to help.' SEN help available and an atmosphere of trust makes emotional, organisational etc support easily available. A small percentage with SENs including physical/medical and emotional difficulties and school can support those with mobility problems. Almost no EFL needed.

Homely library, evidently much used for borrowing, as well as study in the sixth form computer section. Help on hand and girls encouraged to read anything they fancy.

Games, options, the arts: Well-known in Poole for their lavish joint musical productions with Poole Grammar, but these are led by Parkstone. Lots of smaller drama things going on, often with Poole via theatre studies; art gets a smaller take up. Music is important and has the most attractive building on site, purpose-built and homely in brick complex shared by sixth formers who use it as a class base. Orchestras and groups (string, saxophone, choir etc) abound.

All girls do PE to the end of year 13, and rugby, cricket and football are popular. Netball and cricket strong – national finalists in recently; but sport cannot be underestimated in a school boasting three Olympic athletes (sailing, volleyball and beach volleyball) amongst its recent past pupils. There's a fantastic sports hall with stunning beechwood sprung floor, masses of tennis courts and room for everything else, but sixth formers can do their own thing off-site in local clubs etc.

Extracurricular options extensive and adventurous; some shared with Poole Grammar. Twenty or so clubs include, of course, debating, books, films and drama etc but also some further educational opportunities: Japanese at several levels, Mandarin Chinese, Russian plus engineering and robotics. Parkstone girls have built three racing cars from scratch – as opposed to one from a kit at Poole – and raced them nationally, winning commendations for their exceptional teamwork. As a team, the school has been totally behind a member of staff walking 630 miles of the south coast path to raise funds for several charities, plus a bit for the school's technology department. Parkstone has a British Council award for its links and work with other countries – Zambia and Kenya particularly. Trips on offer for languages, skiing etc, with Poole Grammar providing geology and other exciting options. Concert band and choirs recently did open air concerts in Rome and performed in Barcelona. Girls say that financial help is available and they can spread the cost – and regard trips as unprecedented opportunities.

Background and atmosphere: The school started as co-educational in Parkstone and has been at its current site since 1961. Its 20 acres abut residential lanes of bungalows and industrial areas – the derelict Poole pottery is just up the road. The nearby sewage works, which occasionally make their presence felt, were not detectable on the GSG visit. The buildings reflect their surroundings and even the bandbox-new £6 million technology, maths and art block could be mistaken for a factory, though the long wide interior corridor with its distant glass wall opening on to silver birches is a felicitous piece of design. This was funded to provide the extra facilities needed when the Poole schools, hitherto starting in year 8, begin to admit year 7 pupils in 2013.

New £1.8m sixth form hub, and sixth formers have also had access to the spacious and welcoming dining area at all times, and foung it a good place to work. Early risers can use its café at 8am. Food, say the girls is really good, with plenty of choice and cheap too. 'You can order an omelette and have it made in front of your eyes!'

The language block, dating from 1995 but looking curiously like a 70's product, is well-equipped, and a deceptively large new lecture theatre, full of girls being given some gruesomely graphic anti-drugs education on our visit, has been squeezed in between buildings.

Pastoral care, well-being and discipline: Big tutor groups, with the same tutor for the first four years, get an hour's tutor time/PSHE each fortnight. Mentoring schemes help new girls fit in and are continued for those who need it. All staff take a positive role in pastoral care – the school stresses, and the girls confirm, that any member of staff can help any girl, not just their allocated charges. Uniform quite stylish and, surprisingly, girls like pale yellow shirts, grey v necks with striped edges and crested and multi-pocketed black blazers. Expensive-ish, 'but cheaper than us having to provide constant fashion updates.' Sixth formers value an own-clothes-but-suitable-for-work dress code.

School has a few rules about jewellery etc and girls do not take advantage of this. Few problems, but girls say they make their own pressures and find the staff are good at recognising the signs and helping them to cope with stress. Girls' trust in staff and respect for the amount of trouble they take to support them is impressive.

Pupils and parents: Poole has a largely white Anglo-Saxon population with both some very affluent and some very underprivileged areas, and families come from all over. Parkstone's reputation is good enough to attract those who could afford independent education and the school is keen to make sure those who most need Parkstone find it accessible. Sixty-five per cent come from Poole, the rest from up to an hour away. Around 40 per cent of girls come to school by bus – local bus company, city bus or via private arrangements made by parents. One of the nicest things about the girls is their awareness that not all their primary school friends get the opportunities that they do – which both motivates them to make best use of their chances and to want to make things better. Parent-staff association raises lots of funds for extras like minibuses and special equipment.

Entrance: Poole changed from a three-tier (junior, middle and senior) to a two-tier system in 2013 and girls now enter the school in year 7 at the age of 11.

There are between two and three applicants for each of the 180 places in a year group. All girls now have the right to take the Parkstone test (late September – register by mid-September – exact dates etc available from the school) before they commit themselves to choosing which schools to apply for. School has recently changed test to separate multiple choice English, maths and verbal reasoning tests. Previously, successful Poole applicants automatically got places, and those outside the town were allocated the remaining spaces in rank order of score. The new admissions code now allows pupils to take the test before applying. They will be told their test score and whether or not this meets the required standard (but not whether they have got a place) before the deadline for applications. Once they have applied, they will be ranked according to results, but further candidates not yet tested will also go into the pecking order, so things are not clear cut. Best advice is probably to take the test at first opportunity, though it may mean a bit of a wait to know if you have gained a place. An independent admissions appeals panel can and does allocate further places – occasionally up to about 40 as parents are very well aware of the excellent education on offer here.

Girls come from all over Poole, but some schools are better than others at raising awareness: Broadstone Middle School, Baden Powell and St Peter's School, Canford Heath Middle School, Oakdale Middle School and independent preps like Buckholme Towers, The Yarrells and Castle Court in Corfe Mullen.

Can take up to 50 girls at sixth form – currently, the school requires a bare minimum of six GCSEs at A*-C, with at least a B in subjects to be studied at A level; specific entry requirements for each subject can be found in the sixth form prospectus/ website.

Exit: A few – some 15 per cent – go after GCSE – either to good local sixth forms or occasionally to independents; others join from elsewhere. At 18, nearly all to uni. South west ones to the fore, eg Southampton, Bournemouth and Portsmouth, though a sprinkling everywhere, with a high proportion to the older, well-established universities, including Oxbridge (four places in 2016, plus six medics). Law popular, masses of scientific courses and a very wide spread of other subjects. Two off to study degrees sponsored by Capgemini and KPMG.

Remarks: A hive of clever, purposeful girls, who nevertheless have wide interests. Unpretentious but high powered, Parkstone gives girls an exceptional level of support and a rich experience. The enthusiasm of the girls speaks for itself.

P

Pate's Grammar School

Princess Elizabeth Way, Cheltenham, Gloucestershire GL51 0HG

Pupils: 1,097 • Ages: 11–18 • Sixth form: 456

Tel: 01242 523169
Email: office@pates.gloucs.sch.uk
Website: www.pates.gloucs.sch.uk

Headmaster: Since 2012, Mr Russel Ellicott BA. Read history at Royal Holloway and then completed his PGCE, became a teacher of history and PE first at The Crypt School in Gloucester, then at Marling School in Stroud before moving to Pate's in 2007 as deputy head. Married with two children. Teaches GCSE history. Passionate about cricket – and had carefully selected his headmaster's XI for the Cricket Festival in the week that we were visiting.

Friendly, direct and effective. Doesn't appear to be a man to thrust himself into the limelight – a careful, analytical listener who interrogates assumptions. Enthusiastic, organised and strategic. Keen to turn the school more 'outward', to be a 'magpie' of best practice in other schools and to go 'beyond outstanding'.

Says pastoral care and creating a happy school are 'what we are here for', not just for pupils but for staff – 'there must be a work life balance'. Passionate about developing and distributing leadership within the pupil and staff bodies (large numbers of staff involved in leadership projects and research into learning strategies). Staff say he is 'warm, open, supportive', 'won't make false promises' and 'will give anyone an opportunity to do anything'. Parents say he is 'wonderful with the children, quiet and calm, completely engages them'.

Academic matters: Extremely impressive results: strong across the board. In 2016, 87 per cent A*/A at GCSE. All take triple award science, maths, English language and literature. The vast majority also take a modern language (French, German, Spanish, Mandarin). Lots of other options including Latin, DT, PE, RS and drama. There are five one hour periods a day and the GCSE syllabus, as with some other academies, is taught from year 9 so options have to be chosen in year 8 – parents say there is lots of help and information with this. However, the longer lesson times and three year curriculum leave masses of time for enrichment and mean that Tuesday afternoons are generally free for extracurricular activities, most of which are sixth form led.

Intranet and VLE are fully integrated into teaching and learning. Well organised use of a good library, a good supply of laptops and networked computers, and very good technical support.

Results at A level are excellent: 70 per cent A*/A in 2016, with sciences particularly strong – maths, physics, chemistry and biology are the most popular subjects here. However, you would have to search long and hard for a weak area. A good range of subjects too – including Arabic, Latin, politics, psychology, theatre studies.

Pupils remark on the helpfulness and availability of staff, and staff speak very well of the students – but no-one comes to Pate's without an enthusiasm for learning. For those on the SEN spectrum (about 15-20 in the school at any one time – mostly high functioning Aspergers/ADHD) there is careful, tailored support.

Games, options, the arts: All the usual sports; athletics and cricket are particularly strong. A large and well-maintained sports hall, fitness suite and climbing wall. Less gifted sportspeople get a chance to compete in inter-house competitions, and a large number of students take PE at GCSE, some at A level too.

Large CCF, an active Duke of Edinburgh programme, outdoor pursuits most weekends. Very good art facilities with lovely light studios and art rooms, and a rather charming gallery which has risen out of the shell of the old school kitchen. Lots of student work on display around the school and very good GCSE and A level art results.

Music at the school is very strong – good exam results, as well as plenty of opportunities to perform: lots of ensembles, choirs, charity concerts and recitals. There are orchestras as well as composition classes, a good range of school instruments available to those wishing to learn and good practice rooms. Music is strongly linked with drama and dance, also popular. There is a small performing arts space for those productions not suited to the full 'school hall' experience.

Debating, film, Latin, 'wearable art', kayaking clubs – lots to do. Sixth former organise many of the activities, part of a school-wide policy of sharing and encouraging leadership. Parents say 'there is something for everyone'. In addition, many students are involved in charitable fundraising, and the school has a very popular charities committee with a 'keenly contested' application process. As many pupils have a long commute, the majority of extracurricular activities are scheduled for lunchtimes and Tuesday afternoons.

Background and atmosphere: The school was founded over 400 years ago by a local – the eponymous Richard Pate. It was a free grammar school for boys until 1904, when a girl's school was added, the two merging about 20 years ago. It has recently been substantially rebuilt, and has added a lovely new refectory and IT suite. Pate's is not exactly set in rolling parkland – it's at the less glamorous end of Cheltenham, and perimeter fences make the initial impression somewhat forbidding. However, the school buildings are uniformly well designed, and based round a large quad which gives a sense of openness. There are good sized playing fields to the back alongside a very well set up sports hall, and generally the school is well maintained and well equipped. Food, according to the pupils, is good, varied and healthy. The atmosphere is one of confidence, aspiration and determination – the pupils and staff seem comfortable, confident and happy.

Pastoral care, well-being and discipline: Pastoral care, which has long been a high priority for the school, has been reorganised: alongside the tutor groups and house system (four houses from Y7 up) there are now individual year heads for every age group plus a personal development lead tutor (focussing on co-ordinating the usual PSHE stuff plus financial and economic know how, personal resilience etc). A school counsellor comes in twice a week and a SENCo acts as lead for pastoral interventions in the case of illness, eating disorders or similar. We sense that pastoral care is highly tuned here and co-ordinated well with outside agencies where appropriate.

The school takes the opinions of its students seriously – members of the student council sit as associate governors of the school and their input is described by the chair as 'exceptional'. We have a strong impression that students are treated with great respect and care by governors and staff, a respect which is appreciated and reciprocated. Parents say discipline is 'quiet, never heavy handed'; and that the the interest in looking after every child is 'heartfelt'.

All Y7 children get birthday cards from the head, and small groups of Y8s get birthday cake in the head's office. Little in the way of a formal disciplinary system in evidence – although there are occasional withdrawals from lessons for an afternoon for those who overstep the mark.

Pupils and parents: Pupils are largely from around Cheltenham but they also come from further corners of Gloucestershire, and even Worcestershire, West Oxfordshire and Herefordshire. Most parents are middle class and aspirational, with many coaching their children very determinedly to get a place, but the school is also very keen to encourage entrance for those from less advantaged backgrounds and to make it 'a school for everyone'. There is an active PTA and communications between parents and school are generally very good, with good turnouts to parents' evenings and positive responses to reports. The pupils themselves are friendly, confident and happy. They say they chose the school because they 'want to learn', that 'teachers don't talk down to you' and that the best thing about the school is the 'incredibly kind' people in it. Parents with children who have been through Pate's and gone on to university say they feel 'they have been better prepared for further study than their peers'.

Entrance: Highly over subscribed- about 10 candidates per place for year 7. Two opportunities for entrance: at year 7 and again in the sixth form where there are an extra 50-60 places available. At year 7, selection is via the LA but using Durham University CEMS test (register in June for test in September) and places are offered strictly to the 150 top scorers at the beginning of March. Applicants will already have self-selected to some extent as the school is known for its very high academic standards. The competition is quite tough – not for the faint-hearted. Work is ongoing to make the tests less coachable, so that the school is accessible to 'anyone who is bright enough to be here'.

External candidates for the sixth form are expected to have As, preferably A*s, predicted in the subjects chosen for A level study, and strong results are expected across the board. Internal candidates have to meet the same criteria as external candidates. Places for the sixth form are offered by the end of April (apply by February).

Exit: Very few leavers after GCSE. All sixth formers to university – impressive 36 Oxbridge places in 2016, and 18 medics. Exeter, Cardiff, Bristol, Nottingham all popular; a trickle abroad (Princeton, Milan). All sorts of subjects – lots into sciences, but also business, languages, law etc. Lots of support and help in choosing courses and putting UCAS forms together, say parents. Developing contacts with alumni.

Money matters: Financial assistance to help ensure that no-one is excluded from wealth of extracurricular bits and pieces, trips abroad, skiing expeditions etc. Gets funds from the Pate's Foundation.

Remarks: Continues to be really outstanding academically and pastorally, with no sense of slowing its pace. Pate's offers a great combination of academic excellence and extracurricular enrichment. A very strong sense of kindness and community, but still committed to the individual. For those who seriously aspire to excel intellectually and personally, this is a fantastic place to be.

P

Perrott Hill School

North Perrott, Crewkerne, Somerset TA18 7SL

Pupils: 218; 8 full, 64 weekly/flexi boarders • Ages: 3-13 (boarders from age 7) • C of E

Fees: Day £9,225- £14,400; Boarding £18,300- £22,080 pa

Tel: 01460 72051
Email: admissions@perrotthill.com
Website: www.perrotthill.com

Headmaster: Since 2015, Tim Butcher. Originally from Winchester, Tim was educated at The Pilgrims' School, where he was a Quirister, and later at Lancing College. The 'voice of an angel,' parents told us, he is passionate about singing and after a stint of directing children's theatre and working in holiday camps, he toyed with the idea of becoming a voice coach. However, marriage and a family steered him towards a teaching career and by the age of 24 he was head of history at his old school, The Pilgrims. He then went on to become housemaster of choristers at The Chorister School, Durham Cathedral, and lastly, deputy head at Winchester House for five years before joining Perrott Hill. Tim lives on campus with his wife and three children and one parent told us he 'is reassuringly the right person to bring the school into its next phase of growth.' Another said, 'He is very visible, equally accessible to children and staff and evidently delights in the wondrous process of acorn to oak.'

Entrance: Non-selective, entry is at the discretion of the head following an interview with the parents and consideration of previous school reports. Scholarships awarded for academic, sport, music, drama and art/DT excellence. Means-tested bursaries also available. Overseas pupils should be at Basic Level A1 in English and are expected to complete a minimum of one term and preferably three terms; no short study programme. The EAL specialist teacher can offer two weeks intensive tuition to bring pupils up to speed. The school will consider all children, but may not offer a place if any special educational needs cannot be supported.

Open mornings every term. 'As soon as we saw Perrott we were bowled over by the warmth of the teaching staff and parents, the happy positive and politeness of the children as we looked around and the stunning setting of the school and grounds.' There's a taster day plus a test day. Test day is a short academic assessment to ensure the school can meet all educational requirements. According to parents, these days are far from daunting. 'They are seamlessly arranged for the new little person to snuggle into the class: the experience is homely, smiley, personal and fun.' There is also a 'new pupils' day' at the end of the summer term and lots of help to settle in once started; 'The settling process was great, they had two buddies, they were there to meet them in the car park on any settling days and the first week of starting. They also wrote them welcome cards.'

Exit: Nearly all stay until 13. (This year only three pupils left at the end of year 6 to go to Colyton Grammar.) In 2016, over half of all leavers won awards or scholarships to their schools of choice. These included Blundell's, Canford, King's College Taunton, Leweston, Millfield, Queen's College Taunton, Sherborne Girls, Sherborne, Taunton School and Wellington

School. Other destinations include Harrow, Winchester, Eton, Bryanston and King's Bruton.

Remarks: Founded in 1946, Perrott Hill is situated in 28 acres of beautiful grounds and woodland close to the Somerset-Dorset border. It is a traditional prep that embraces its surroundings and promotes good country living, a big selling point for many parents. One told us, 'They love the outdoor opportunities; double woods sessions, golf before lunch, farming in the afternoon – they didn't get to do that in London!'

The school day is long, from 8.20am-5.45pm, but all the (many) activities on offer are fitted into these hours. One parent told us, 'There were many opportunities for the children, the hours of care suited us and the nurturing environment suited our children.' Activities include ballet, karate, fencing, riding, gymnastics (at extra cost) and unpaid activities such as art, sports, eco-club or playing in the woods. From year 5, there is school on Saturdays until 4pm (for day pupils and boarders). There are lessons, sports fixtures and the highlight of the day is the French lunch. Not all pupils and parents are enthusiastic about the extra day but they all agreed 'you soon get used to it.' During the school weekday there are two long breaks of 40 minutes, one in the morning and one after lunch. Pupils are not only encouraged to rest or play in these periods; they are given the chance to read or to work on an art project. We saw plenty of these projects in the small but very productive art studio. One pupil, inspired by his recent travels, had created a collage of a world map showing flight paths. A class trip to Lulworth Cove was another inspiration. Art is obviously very popular and the teacher sets up still life projects and even life drawing sessions – the last one was a geisha. Parents are invited to take workshops too. One parent who used to work for John Galliano ran a 'punk' workshop recently, another ran a photography session. One parent said, 'The art department is fantastic at school and with the resources it has bats way above other schools, but we would love there to be a bigger art room and facilities as it is such an amazing department.' We will definitely second that.

The head is planning on creating a similarly creative environment for science. Now the new sports hall is complete, the old changing room will be refurbished as a 'science suite'. The labs will be set up with movable benches and storage to allow room for experiments of all kinds and flexible teaching. There will also be a 'tinker room' full of Lego, Meccano, BBC micro-bits and anything else that can be used for 'free-flow projects' at break times. Although many parents love that screens are few and far between at Perrott (fibre-optic broadband only reached them last summer), the head feels it's important to find a balance and prepare children for the real world. This is a creative and fun way to do it.

The location and outside environment are stunning; in fact it's hard to believe that anybody could have a bad day here. At the back of the main school building the library opens out on to a terrace, a rose garden, the monkey woods (a maze) and fields for as far as the eye can see. There are playing fields with an athletics track, cricket pitches and nets, rugby and football pitches and a pavilion. Plus two hard courts, a climbing wall, an Astroturf, a sports hall, a heated swimming pool, and not one but two golf holes and a practice putting green. Nestled under the trees is forest school with a newly built roundhouse and large fire-pit. When we visited, it was alive with activity; one group was rubbing flints to make fire, another was learning to saw and a thride group was making donuts – normal and gluten-free, of course. Other culinary delights have included wild garlic bread and nettle soup, all foraged and picked themselves.

Not far from the forest school is the new music centre. Fundraising for this has included staff taking grade 1 music exams, and an auction to become head for the day (head becomes a pupil, of course). Environmentally sensitive, it sits in the natural slope of the hill, clad in cedar. Concertina doors open out onto the decking looking across the Somerset hills. Fantastically inspirational. The department is run by 'an excellent music teacher' who has set up a good-sized string orchestra for such a small school (all year 2s learn violin for a year), and a choir that has been to Venice, Prague, Rome and London. As well as musical performances, there are plenty of drama productions too, all taking place in the well-equipped theatre. Most recently year 6 performed Why the Whales Came, and the leavers' production will be Beowolf.

Class sizes are small, average of 12 to a class, with two classes in most years. Years 6 and 7 are streamed in preparation for common entrance. Excellent learning support department, highly praised by parents. One told us, 'My child, having received learning support for a few years is now leaving with scholarships, has been made a prefect, his confidence has increased and his academic ability has improved enormously.' Another told us, 'He had lost his confidence and with the individualised teaching and fantastic learning support it is like Pandora's box has been opened, it is so wonderful to see.' The head of SEN is a literary specialist and there is an in-house team of five assistants plus an external team, Sound Thinking, who provide speech and language therapy and educational psychology. The school provides good support for dyslexia and dyscalculia and extra tuition can take place instead of Latin or French, at an extra cost.

The school offers full, weekly and flexi-boarding. Boarding has become increasingly popular, especially for those planning to go on to board at senior school. Currently there are 8 full boarders and 24 weekly. There are six pupils from Spain, one from France and the rest are from the UK. In fact a large number are fairly local. One parent said, 'They love it! We live only 15 minutes away and the older boys choose to weekly board and flexi board. Sometimes they don't want to come home – they have a lot of fun!' Flexi boarders must book regular days; the school is keen not to be used as a hotel. There are currently 40 boarders (girls and boys) in for one to three nights, mainly from the older years. Flexi or weekly boarding is available from year 3, and although numbers are currently low, interest is growing in the lower year groups. Full boarding available from year 5. Due to the high demand (there is a waiting list) the school is converting the old music suite into two senior boys' dorms and a shared common room over the summer. Dorms are a good size and there are decent separate common rooms. Parents said, 'The boarding house is very family orientated and they have a lovely time in the evenings when the houseparents are very involved with activities with the boarders.' Evening activities include reading, music practice, watching TV, art, ICT, games in the sports hall, tennis, football, skateboarding, rollerblading. There are 'family weekends' spent with the houseparents and then there are 'activity weekends' when day pupils can join in too (up to 40 pupils). Past weekend themes have been Inspector Gadget, Indiana Jones (with an assault course), Harry Potter and Making a Musical. 'The boarding staff are fantastic; my children have always been very happy to board, although we tend to build it up over a few years as they get older, and have more stamina,' parents told us.

The best thing about this school is that the pupils love it, something we couldn't help but notice on our visit. One parent said, 'She will not hear a bad word against it or anything to do with it and cannot under any circumstances be persuaded to stay at home if she is under the weather.' And the academic results are undeniably impressive. But the most important thing for many parents is self-belief and confidence and the school does a great job here. One parent told us, 'My eldest was very shy and within a year was in the final of the school poetry recital performing in front of the whole school and parents – in less than one year!' With confidence and self-belief you can go far.

Pinewood School

Bourton, Shrivenham, Wiltshire SN6 8HZ

Pupils: 421; 124 weekly/flexi boarders • Ages: 3–13 (boarding from year 5) • C of E

Fees: Day £8,745 – £16,830; plus weekly boarding supplement £4,110 pa

Tel: 01793 782205
Email: office@pinewoodschool.co.uk
Website: www.pinewoodschool.co.uk

Head: Since 2002, Mr Philip Hoyland BEd (50s), educated at The Downs, Malvern, followed by Cheltenham College. Read English and education at Exeter; previously housemaster, then deputy head, at The Dragon. Married to the warm, compassionate Henrietta; they met at Ludgrove when she was under-matron and he a rookie teacher (they have three grown-up children). Very much a partnership, her gentle humour a foil for his sense of adventure; both fully involved with the school (she is head of girls' boarding and central to much of school life).

Articulate, charming, a gentleman, Mr Hoyland wants education to be explored, and enjoyed. Seeks to offer 'non-conformist, old-fashioned values, coupled with innovative learning.' More than a sense that his Quaker heritage (his great-grandfather was businessman and philanthropist George Cadbury) shapes his views. Says, 'we work hard to ensure we have happy children here, it is difficult to do anything if they are not; children need to take risks, to be excited'. We watched as gaggles of animated youngsters flocked to his side, eager to tell of their day, show off work, badges, awards. Parents say he is kind, an intellectual and fantastic with the children, 'they adore him', but seemingly he's not always quite so good with parents: 'He's not a gushing head and if you expect your child to always be the star of the show you're probably not going to get on too well here.' Other mutterings that he backs staff over parents, but all unanimous that he really has propelled the school forward.

P

Entrance: Mainly via nursery and pre-prep; register early. Unselecitve, but prospective pupils come in for a taster day. Deliberately takes broad-ish ability range, 'deal with what we get', but always considers what is in child's best interests (occasional one helped to move elsewhere). Assessment for entry into prep. Handful with parents at nearby Defence Academy (nominally for a year or two, but many convert to boarding and stay). Most years full with waiting lists, though movement, especially of day children, and flexibility for additional groups, means places materialise.

Exit: Primarily Winchester, Marlborough, Radley, Cheltenham College, Wellington, Sherborne, Sherborne Girls, Dauntsey's, Cheltenham Ladies' College, St. Edward's Oxford, Our Lady's Abingdon, Bryanston, St Mary's Calne, Tudor Hall and Abingdon. Occasional early departure from parents who believe school isn't pushy enough, yet they annually win a clutch of scholarships (art, music, academic and all-rounder) to a selection of schools.

Remarks: Founded in 1875, moved to this pretty Victorian Cotswold stone house in 1946. Nursery and pre-prep in former stable block with fantastic play area in old walled garden.

Noughties, and the arrival of the Hoylands, saw shift from a school languishing in the doldrums – 'it really was falling down,' said one parent – to one riding a wave, albeit with choppy interludes. 'There was too much complacency; we had made strides but not leaps', admitted the head. 'Our parents were shocked but it allowed the final clearing of driftwood'. Now vast majority of teachers are head's own appointments; admits he has taken a few risks, going for the fizzy or alternative to encourage excitement and develop a joy of learning. This strategy hasn't been lost on the youngsters; pupils were eager to tell what they had learned, and how: 'Exciting teaching, kind teachers, some a bit mad but the good thing is you remember what they say, it stays with you and they will always help'. We saw super maths model villages (lots of nets and shapes, fashioned into 3D high streets); we even gently teased our charming guides about the designer outlets and Jack Wills stores; they responded with good humour, enthusiasm and grins. We were dragged to the plush changing rooms (complete with under-floor heating) but the boys didn't swallow our tease that we especially loved the girls' sauna and steam room (alas not yet!). They got their own back with tales of 'breaking the ice' in the outdoor pool – not literally, but an annual event that usually sees the head dive in first, followed by a posse of pupils.

Only the caffeine kept us from drifting off as the head recounted the extensive building work but, as we toured, we began to appreciate how fundamental the redevelopment has been to the Pinewood metamorphosis, with library rehoused in renovated Orangery, super performing arts centre, new sports hall etc. Pupils certainly appreciate the changes, possibly nowhere more so than in science where the newish labs have opened a whole world of discovery and experimentation. Indeed, we were hijacked by an endearing chap who insisted on explaining his classification diagram (task carefully differentiated) and cheerfully showed us the errors his partner had made, and how they were putting them right. Refreshingly, this is a school where children are encouraged to make mistakes, take risks, explore their learning and get it right.

French from 4, Latin from 10, Greek and philosophy for scholars, enrichment for anyone who will benefit. Classics, French, science and maths top the popularity bill but, unusually (for a prep school), history and geography under kids' radar: 'They lack the zing of other subjects,' was parental response. (Indeed, school has announced that it will free the children somewhat from the 'treadmill of examinations' by no longer offering history, geography or RS at common entrance.) ICT important for all, even wee ones are encouraged to Google. Usual plaudits for art, groans that DT had been chopped for older years and applause for drama and music (including ensembles, jazz band, a chorus of choirs and inclusive performing opportunities). Daily sport for all ('cept Thursday which is given over to activities); every child has ample opportunity to represent the school. Lots of motivational messages on notice boards and gentle reminders: 'win with honour, lose with dignity.' Thanks to new sports director, PE back with a bounce, carefully thought out, planned and linked to games programme, health etc. A hardy bunch, practise in all weathers; used to lose at everything but no longer the case, indeed they are recent National Junior Cross-Country Riding Champions and recently became mini schools show jumping, cross-country and eventing champions.

Solid learning support and a genuinely multi-sensory approach mean those with mild dyslexia, dyspraxia, ADD (Bluetac et al for fiddlers), high functioning ASD are well served. Access arrangements and laptops if needed. OT, speech and language therapy, play therapy, in-class learning support plus one-to-one or small groups as required (most incur additional fee) but not the place for those with moderate or severe needs who need frequent, or intensive, support.

Quietly Christian (aside from the rousing hymns), emphasises tradition, kindness, fun and adventure. Think greenhouse not hothouse; tender plants (and tough weeds) will be nurtured, watered but not pruned, though delicate darlings might flounder: 'We are about climbing trees and falling out.' Very much preparing children to make choices.

Boarding genuinely popular and on the wish list of many; handful of full boarders (fortnightly exeats mean grannies and guardians essential for boarders from far-flung corners). Comfortable, squidgy, homely accommodation and great food, including imaginative vegetarian choices, continental cuisine and school-dinner stalwarts. Squabbles usually sorted over a mug of hot chocolate in Mrs Hoyland's kitchen. Unpleasantness dealt with promptly, no complaints from anywhere on that score; only slight grumble from parents is that communication dwindles as pupils move through the school. Reading room (much loved by youngsters) and old chapel provide quiet spaces, with games room (table tennis, air hockey, snooker) for the active. German spotlight (risk assessed) a unanimously favourite pastime. 'It's so dangerous,' said one wide-eyed youngster, then quickly added, 'well, only kind of', doubtless concerned that we might be among the spoilsports keen to curtail anything remotely daring.

Parents proud that it remains steadfastly a local school; majority live within an hour's drive. True country prep, car park more mud-splattered four-by-fours than flashy Ferraris. Concentrates on extending childhood – the pre-pubescent 'up-do, make-up and manicure' brigade would either roll up their sleeves and regain their innocence – or, likely as not, hate it. Very much for those happy to don a boilersuit, roll down a hill, climb a tree, play hide and seek or chase through a meadow.

Wellies essential, rain or shine, outdoors as important as in. Annual activities week for each year group the icing on a well-filled cake. Pinewood is one of the country's leading outdoor schools (they even have an award to prove it). It's not just the Astro and sports pitches but the treetops adventure, outdoor classroom, fairy garden, child-friendly woods, super sensory gardens; colours for the youngest, then scented, smelly, touchy feely and finally a polytunnel of polygons, plants, maths and more.

Pre-prep headed by the energetic, triple-hatted director of learning. Suits the worms, germs and stones brigade; aims for children to fall in love with learning (we suspect most tumble head-over-heels). Children encouraged to explore their learning through carefully planned in and outdoor activities. Parents genuinely welcome to spend time with their child at beginning and end of the day; no classroom barriers here. Learning is multi-purpose and multi-sensory, extending well beyond the regular primary diet. Learning of 'oo' in moon includes the baking of tasty m'oo'n rock cakes and tracing sounds in sand. Parents appreciative – 'they are really good at getting the basics firmly in place' – though another added, 'Lots end up having learning support which costs extra,' adding cynically, 'You wonder if so many really need it or if it is just prevention better than cure mentality.' School disputes this, saying only 18 per cent of pupils have learning support with fewer than two per cent in pre-prep (equating to handful of pupils max) – so seems perception is misplaced. Curriculum 'wow' days have seen youngsters take off on a variety of adventures including transatlantic travel: office converted to aircraft, check-in desk, tickets, airline food, sick bags – an experience so real, one boy cried at the thought of flying without mum.

Good at building confidence; suits the London day school refugee, but not a place for the smart London set, nor for those into clicking heels and clucking 'Yes sir, no sir.' If you could recreate the secret garden you'd probably do it here; active children fizz with enthusiasm, happily maintaining the innocence of a bygone era but with the benefits of modern technology and teaching. A genuinely wholesome school that emphasises cooperation rather than competitiveness, confidence not arrogance and and team before me. Especially good for the creative boy or girl with boundless energy, sporty or not, and limitless curiosity.

Plymouth College

Ford Park, Plymouth PL4 6RN

Pupils: 700; 155 full/weekly boarders • Ages: 3–18 • Sixth form: 140 • C of E

Fees: Day £7,620 – £15,420; Boarding £25,995 – £29,790 pa

Tel: 01752 505100
Email: mail@plymouthcollege.com
Website: www.plymouthcollege.com

Headmaster: Since 2015, Jonathan Standen, originally from Tunbridge Wells, studied ancient history at Nottingham University. Previously, head of The Crypt School, Gloucester. He has also been deputy head at St Augustine's Catholic College and Bishop Wordsworth's School and assistant head at Hardenhuish School, all in Wiltshire. Lives on site with partner Suzie and their son. In days gone by he has been a ski instructor, a rugby coach and a cricket coach, but these days he enjoys a round of golf.

Some positive parent reviews: 'I'm impressed with the new headmaster and I feel he's keen to improve the standards at the school,' said one. 'There has been a shake up of staff and he's good at communicating with parents – via a newsletter – and keeping us informed of changes.'

Prep school head: Since 2007, Christopher Gatherer BA Cert Ed. Originally from the northwest, studied English at Keele. Taught at Sherborne, then joined Plymouth College in 1982 as head of year 7 in the senior school. Teaches drama and PSHE to years 5 and 6 and takes storytelling sessions in reception once a week. 'The head teacher has a wonderful rapport with the children which he establishes early on by telling the children stories about his "Wolfie" character.' Popular with parents too: 'He takes pride in the successes (big and small) of each individual and is quick to praise good behaviour or discipline unacceptable behaviour. A remarkably energetic and motivated man who the children look up to.' Another parent summed him up by saying, 'He clearly loves his job and is very good at it!'

Academic matters: Prep school children are taught 'not to fear failure.' Pupils we saw and spoke to were confident, articulate and very keen to answer questions. Parents said, 'The school are adept at identifying strengths and encouraging individuality, whilst gently exposing them to new ideas and challenges within their capability.' One of the school's strengths is specialist teachers. All subjects are taught by specialists in years 5 and 6, plus music, sport, French and ICT in years 3 and 4. Music and sport are taught by specialists all the way through from kindergarten. French is taught from year 3 and Spanish from year 5. Methods of differentiation are used to teach maths and English all the way through the school with setting from year 5.

The learning support department in the prep can help children with mild needs including dyslexia or dyscalculia. According to parents, the support is good but 'the extra resources are very limited.' One parent told us they are paying for home tuition to fill the gaps. However, others told us how the learning support has helped improve their child's confidence dramatically. 'The school has instigated appropriate support and tailored lessons and homework to meet her ability and needs and, importantly, helped her understand why she finds learning so difficult, and provided her with strategies to cope whilst integrating her with the rest of her year so she doesn't feel different.'

In 2016, at A level, 65 per cent A*-B and 34 per cent A*/A grades. At GCSE, 40 per cent A*/A grades. Plymouth College achieved the highest average point score at A level in Plymouth, beating all three neighbouring grammar schools. Twenty-two options at A level offered. Top performing subjects are maths, science, economics and business studies. Most do three A levels plus one elective subject eg EPQ or a BTec in sports leadership, ICT, performing arts. A one year IGCSE course is available in year 11, popular with international students. Also offers the sport baccalaureate, which is based round the BTec level 3 extended diploma in sport (outdoor adventure), and includes topics such as fitness, nutrition, coaching and leadership. Plymouth College is well known for producing top athletes including swimmers, modern pentathletes, fencers and divers. For the last seven years, the college has been the top swimming school in the country. All athletes are supported through their rigorous training programmes as well as their academic studies. One parent told us, 'We chose Plymouth College because it gave the opportunity for her to develop her swimming (she had swum competitively from a young age) whilst also stretching her academically.'

Class sizes are small, around 13 per class. Setting or streaming in maths, science, and English from year 8. As well as the standard GCSE options, the school offers some that can be studied as an after-school activity, including philosophy, Greek, computing and film studies. Most pupils study two languages of French, Spanish or German. Extra support in maths and English can be provided for those that only take one language.

The head of the learning support department is a qualified educational psychologist. In-class support and individual tuition is provided for mild needs including dyslexia, dysgraphia, dyscalculia, and dyspraxia, though some parents felt that 'earlier identification and intervention' would be helpful. One parent, who had eventually organised her own child's assessment, commented: 'The SEN department has improved hugely since then, but integration in teaching and lessons as well as regular SEN feedback still needs improving.' All comments on teachers, including SEN, were positive; 'supportive and communicate well' and 'very committed and enthusiastic.'

P

Games, options, the arts: As expected, top sports facilities here. There's a large sports centre, a cardiovascular gym, two squash courts, a weights room, a climbing wall, Astroturf, playing fields and cricket nets. Plus a fantastic 25 metre indoor pool (the elite swimmers use the Life Centre facilities in Plymouth). As well as swimming lessons the pool is used for inter-house galas, water polo and lifesaving competitions. Around 50 pupils swim at national level. Past pupils include Tom Daley, Olympic diver and Cassie Patten, Olympic swimmer. However, it's not just in the water that the college succeeds. Other former pupils include Henry Slade and Paul Ackford, both England rugby international players. Two current pupils play football for Plymouth Argyll, another plays cricket for the Surrey county professional team, and one girl has just been selected for the U15 south west England rugby team. No problem if you're not a top sportsperson: 'He has not felt out of place among elite sports people even though he is an amateur,' a parent told us. Other sports offered include basketball, badminton, hockey, netball, gymnastics, cross-country running, golf and equestrian.

There are plenty of opportunities for prep pupils too. Apart from swimming, there's athletics, rugby (the U9s have been unbeaten for the last two years), cricket (some pupils have reached county level), hockey, netball, football (one girl plays for Devon), gymnastics and cross-country. Some take part in biathlon events through the pentathlon programme at the senior school, and recently one pupil became a national finalist and has now gone on to represent GB. There are also plenty of inter-house competitions that carry on into the senior school. Parents told us, 'The teachers are all very nice, some more enthusiastic than others, but I guess that's like anywhere. We really like the new sports teacher as he is really shaking things up in that department and getting the training and clubs all sorted.' Don't be put off if your child isn't sporty, though; one parent said, 'Our child struggles in sports but the sports teacher has been really encouraging. Children also encourage one another in sports and other activities.'

Each prep class performs a drama production every year. Most recently there was Snow White by year 4, Midsummer Night's Dream by year 6, Ballooning Round The World by year 2, and Rapunzel, starring reception and kindergarten. Peripatetic training is available for LAMDA exams and some pupils go on to perform at Plymouth's Theatre Royal. Pupils all learn musical instruments: recorder in year 2 the recorder, violin in years 3 and 4, and playing and composing on keyborads in years 5 and 6. Some set up their own bands. There are regular concerts and recitals plus 'first steps concerts,' just for beginners.

For the more arty senior school types, there's a new drama studio (recently opened by ex-pupil Michael Ball), and plenty of productions to get involved with. The latest whole school production was Beauty and the Beast. And the latest house drama was Scrooge – each house had to adapt the original story giving it a modern twist or unexpected makeover. Most pupils learn a musical instrument; even the harp is offered. As a traditional school, there are plenty of formal music concerts but informal guitar and piano evenings are popular and recently there was a woodwind, vocal and brass evening. Clubs and groups include choir, chamber choir, rock school, flute group, orchestra and string orchestra. One talented pupil recently won a place at the prestigious Royal College of Music for vocal studies.

The art department is split across the site. There is a small sixth form classroom adjoined by a computer suite for photography and graphics. Plus there is the Art Haus, a small two-storey cottage, hidden by trees, appropriately decorated with a graffiti-type mural. One classroom downstairs, and another upstairs with a handful of PCs and a dark room. Department produces good results.

Extensive list of extracurricular activities. Many take advantage of the school's location; sailing in Plymouth Sound, and adventures on the moors including the Ten Tors and Duke of Edinburgh schemes. Plus there's caving, climbing, mountain biking, sea kayaking, SCUBA diving, canoeing, white water kayaking, mountain and hill walking, camping, bushcraft and gorge walking. Then there's the Combined Cadet Force; from year 10 onwards students can opt for navy, army or RAF. Other clubs include sports like archery or snooker, music clubs like school of rock or samba club plus there's a model railway club and a Young Entreprise group. With around 40 activities on offer each term, there's something for everyone. An activities fair is held at the beginning of the autumn term to find out what's on.

Sixth formers have their own enrichment programme. They can choose from Duke of Edinburgh Award, Combined Cadets (CCF), Ten Tors challenge, financial studies, politics, cookery, journalism, photography or volunteering placements. The latest addition has been a pre-med course. Medicine has been a popular university course choice in recent years and the new enrichment course prepares students for their medical school applications alongside studying for their A levels. It is heavily supported by parents and ex-pupils, many of whom are GPs and consultants.

All pupils benefit from regular local trips to the theatre, art galleries, ancient castles, plus field trips to South Devon beaches and Dartmoor. Further afield there are day trips to France and London, overseas residential trips to Ireland and Greece, German trips to Berlin, physics trips to Switzerland, ski trips and language exchanges. Recent sports tours include South Africa with Rugby and a cricket tour to Sri Lanka. Annual charity expedition to Malawi. The prep school has local day trips throughout the year plus year 6 goes to France for a week and year 5 goes to an eco-camp in Cornwall for a night.

Boarding: Currently, 150+ boarders in six boarding houses; a row of large villas dating from the mid-19th century. On the main school site is a boys' house, a girls' house and three smaller houses/annexes for sixth formers. The Captain's House, specialist accommodation for the elite swimmers, is on the prep school site, 10 minutes away, housing around one third of boarders. One parent told us, 'The boarding facilities were initially disappointing but have improved dramatically....A tremendous amount of work has been done to improve the accommodation.'

Around 50 per cent of all boarders are from the UK. Other boarders are from over 40 countries around the world including Germany, China, Hong Kong, Australia, the Caribbean, Estonia, Bangladesh, Bolivia, Italy, Russia, South Africa, to name but a few. Some pupils come from military backgrounds, but not as many as expected: just three in the girls' house. Weekly boarding is available, but we were told the majority of boarders are resident at weekends these days. Flexi boarding is offered for up to 14 nights per term. If your child is going to be a full boarder, do check how many of their age group will be around at weekends, particularly in the lower years, to ensure they have plenty of company.

Currently, some 40+ boarders in the girls' house. Fifty per cent are athletes – swimmers, divers, pentathlons etc. The house is run by a friendly, approachable housemistress who lives in the basement with her husband and three young children. Parents told us, 'The current boarding staff are exceptional in creating an environment in which both our girls are currently thriving.' Rooms are mostly doubles and a few triples, with older girls together at one end of the house. One room has been specially adapted for a disability but there is no wheelchair access available. All the newly refurbished bedrooms and bathrooms are lovely. The housemistress is now looking forward to updating the common areas – one room will be a games room and the other a large lounge. There is also an arts and crafts room and a homely office area with sofas for girls to pop in for chats any time. There are regular (and impromptu) informal discussion groups to chat about current issues or 'things on their minds'. This is a busy house; some athletes start training from 4am and others are training until 9pm. There are a lot of comings and goings and the housemistress does a great job staggering food times and everything else in this house. She says it keeps the house alive and interesting, buzzing. Boys and girls are free to socialise between the houses, cooking food in the kitchen, playing games, chatting or watching TV.

'Mr Tippetts is the head of boarding and an impressive man,' parents told us. 'He's a calm but effective leader.' He has been been at Plymouth College for the last 19 years and lives there with his wife and dog. Popular with the boarders; one told us that many boys, him included, have found that Mr Tippet has fitted into the father figure role perfectly for them. He runs the boys' house with a good balance of discipline and fun. If he finds a bed unmade, he will hide the duvet as punishment, so beware. Plenty of common areas including a TV room with projector, table tennis room, pool table room, music room with table football and a prep/study room with PCs. The junior kitchen is new, but the best makeover of all is the sixth form area. There is a fantastic new kitchen with a stunning open-plan lounge, wooden floors, sofa and large dining table. The annexe, or the Boat House, is also new and provides sixth formers with very small but private single rooms. Great for the transition to university life.

In the Captain's House, boys are on the ground floor and the girls on the first floor. The staff are experienced in the training and needs of elite athletes; it is a unique environment supporting over 40 performance swimmers with high levels of pastoral care, specialist nutritional needs and complicated logistics. There is a regular minibus service between the boarding house, the pool and school. One parent whose child swims for GB said, 'The boarding house dedicated to swimmers is ideal....The only problem [my child] sometimes has is the transport arrangements from school to the boarding house.'

In the evenings and at weekends, the boarders can use the school facilities. Most evenings there is a game of football or dodgeball in the sports hall, or games on the Astroturf. The swimming pool is open at weekends. Other weekend activities include trips to the beach for surfing or paddle boarding, or days out to Adrenaline Quarry or the Eden Project. Regular trips to the cinema, 10-pin bowling, ice-skating, paintballing, boat trips, pitch and putt golf, moorland walking, and dry-slope skiing. No exeat weekends but the school closes at half term.

Background and atmosphere: Founded in 1877 as Plymouth High School for Boys, the school moved to its current site at Ford Park in 1880, changing its name to Plymouth College three years later. The prep school moved to a different site in Hartley Road in 1947. There have been a number of mergers with girls' schools (the school became fully co-ed in 1995), and most recently with St Dunstan's Abbey School for Girls in 2005. It was then that the prep school moved to its current site in The Millfields, the old naval hospital, three miles away.

The prep school is in the old naval hospital building and there are no concerns about security here; it's on a gated development, all visitors are stopped and questioned at the entrance. Inside the school building, some original naval hospital facilities and memorabilia are still in place; even the disco ball is still hanging in the old dance hall, now the school theatre. At back of school is a large walled field. 'Our very own Lost Gardens of Heligan,' says the head. It is a real pocket of calm. The field is used as an athletics track, or a cricket, rugby or football pitch. There is also a long jump pit and a netball/tennis court. The sports hall was built in 2005 and is used for a multitude of activities especially on rainy days, the norm in the south west. The chapel is surprisingly light; a white ceiling set against black beams makes it feel bright and open. It's a lovely little chapel used for daily assemblies, all including some religious content.

The latest development is the early years outdoor classroom. Built a few years ago, it is still a work-in-progress, but to date there is a wooden castle, trees (regularly and enthusiastically watered from the central water pump), and a sunken-decked mini-ampitheatre for teaching and outside performance. This is a great space to play, and as the garden grows, the children will be able to learn and grow with it. Early years is about learning just as much as play, and the two are very much inter-linked. The annual 'messy Monday' for reception involves a great deal of puddle jumping, as well as collecting leaves and sticks to analyse (and paint) later. The classrooms are colourful, with lots of creative displays from pirates to farm shops to ladybirds. The building is wheelchair accessible with a lift. There are two libraries, an infant one and a junior one, plus an art classroom for painting and pottery, and a better than average science lab. Outside in an outbuilding is a well-equipped food technology classroom.

The senior school site is tucked behind the hustle and bustle of Mutley Plain in Plymouth. It is surprisingly big considering its urban position. The main buildings are grand Victorian villas, very impressive from the outside, in need of a little attention inside. However, work is underway and it's looking as if these original family homes will be restored to their former glory. The main building is huge. With its high ceilings, stone steps and beautiful ornate windows it's stunning, but in places it feels cold. The library is grandiose and the classrooms are traditional; original wooden benches in the science laboratories, everything you'd expect in a school as old as this.

Decent sixth form centre with bistro and lounge area to socialise or work. Very small and uninspiring quiet study area upstairs. Sixth form social life is thankfully much more vibrant and fun with a freshers' ball to kick it all off, followed by a Halloween ball, quiz nights, DVD and pizza nights, and an end of year ball.

The active school council 'gets things done.' Members planned and created the outdoor classroom, set up and now keep a flock of rare chickens at the school, have installed a wildlife pond, and successfully campaigned for a salad bar and pasta bar. Their latest project is the Gutter Grow system for cultivating fresh herbs, vegetables and fruit on the roof of the school canteen.

Pastoral care, well-being and discipline: Very good pastoral care. Parents told us, 'Staff work hard to integrate the different nationalities and the welfare and medical support is outstanding. Both our [children] have had medical issues that have been dealt with comprehensively and with compassion.' There is a school nurse plus a day matron in each boarding house, also in charge of physio for the athletes. Out of hours, responsibility lies with the boarding staff, all first aid trained. For athletes there's a 'playground to podium' ethic, which involves regular communication between boarding and pastoral staff, parents, coaches and the athletes themselves. Sixth form course include coping with stress and mindfulness as well as eg money management.

The weekly prep school awards assembly welcomes parents. Awards can be for earning house points, reading books, helping others, being polite, thoughtful, kind, cheerful or just generally positive. One parent told us, 'They are very clever at ensuring every child feels valued.'

P

At a small school with a strong and very competitive house system, pupils have opportunities to make friends across the years. Boarders, athletes and day pupils live, study and train together well; pupils seem to make good lasting friendships that continue beyond their school years. Plymouth College has a Christian ethos but it is 'understated,' the head told us.

Pupils and parents: As well as Plymouth itself, day pupils come from south east Cornwall, west and mid Devon and the South Hams. The school provides a daily bus service. Parents are doctors, surgeons, teachers, business owners, engineers, members of the Royal Navy, RAF and the army. Parents of all pupils we spoke to said they were happy with communication between school and home. One said, 'Communication has always been superb with easy access to teaching, boarding and support staff with prompt responses to issues. This has been tremendously important in living at some distance from the school.'

Entrance: Open days and taster days including an informal assessment. Kindergarten is part of the school so children are assessed (informally) to ensure they are ready for a school environment. One parent whose child started half way through a term said, 'On her trial day, she was chaperoned by two lovely girls who took the responsibility of showing her around very maturely.' Settling in was good too: 'Once there, the other boys and girls in her year were kind and considerate and we were amazed at how quickly she found a genuine sense of belonging.'

Senior school also non-selective, but entrance exams in maths and English 'to maintain minimum standards,' and for scholarships. Around 50 per cent of intake is from the prep school. One parent told us, '[Our child] settled in well into year 7 with a great head of year leading the team and a weekend away in Whiteworks, Dartmoor. It's a good thing to do in the first few weeks of term.'

For sixth form entry, pupils are expected to achieve at least six GCSE passes at grade C, including English and maths, and three passes at grade B or higher. International students are assessed for English speaking and writing skills.

Exit: Some 60 per cent go on to the senior school, the rest go to local grammar schools. One parent said, 'One of the biggest advantages has been the promise of a place at the senior school. The knowledge she can enjoy an excellent next step education without the risk of rejection has been very reassuring.' The transition starts in year 5 with activity days, plus the prep school DT teacher is also the head of year 7.

On average, 25 per cent leave after GCSEs to go to local colleges or grammar schools. The same number (around 20 pupils) will join the sixth form. Some sixth form boarders are particularly attracted by the sports programmes on offer, others by the fact that nearly all sixth form pupils go on to university. Several have gained sports scholarships at American universities in recent years. Other popular university destinations include Bristol, Cardiff, Exeter and London. Most popular courses include architecture, business, economics/accounting, engineering, law, medicine and sports science.

Money matters: Scholarships offered include all-round, academic, art, drama, music, performing arts and sport awards. Means-tested bursaries also available, as well as discounts for siblings and military families.

Remarks: To date, the academic, and particularly the sporting successes, have been impressive. The refurbishments have enhanced the boarding areas positively. Elite athletes plus day pupils and boarders of all abilities and nationalities study, train and live together harmoniously. Pupils are able to develop at their own pace, and most importantly gain confidence. One parent confirmed, saying, '[My child] is now oozing self-esteem, loves going to school.'

Plymstock School

Church Road, Plymstock, Plymouth PL9 9AZ

Pupils: 1,511 • Ages: 11–18 • Sixth form: 243

Tel: 01752 402679
Email: info@plymstockschool.org.uk
Website: www.plymstockschool.org.uk

Headteacher: Since September 2016, Robert Diment BSc PGCE NPQH, previously deputy head.

Academic matters: Generally around half get 5+ A*-C grades including English and maths at GCSE. At A level, over 40 per cent A*/B in 2016. Offers 25+ A level courses, besides good GNVQ, NVQ, RSA opportunities via a training consortium.

Lots of awards. Enhanced specialist provision – centre for communication difficulties and intensive numeracy and literacy programme for SEN in years 7 and 8. Good extension studies for gifted/talented students through faster moving classes, earlier entry into subjects; supportive services include reading and homework club.

Games, options, the arts: Excellent reputation for county, national and international sporting achievements – hence has specialist sports college status. Enviably large, outdoor floodlit sporting area with flat grass track and netball/tennis courts. Newly completed third generation artificial football pitch and very large sports hall. Parents believe separating boys' and girls' groups for PE works. The less academic will not fade here and budding actors still have a chance with drama and performing arts A level. Growing percentage of students do PE, dance and sport studies. The art adorning the corridors shouts high quality. Parents impressed with varied range of musical and dramatic performances from Shakespeare to rock and roll. Work experience in Germany popular for A level German students – a big confidence booster.

Background and atmosphere: Very attractive school with garden courtyards. Teachers, students and parents work well together. Quiet and hard-working atmosphere of which it is proud. Recent investment of £5m has replaced temporary classrooms with well-resourced dance and drama, modern languages, mathematics, pottery and sport areas. Science, technology and humanities refurbished. Keeps up with leading edge ICT development – electronic whiteboards in every department, digital music recording. Wheelchair friendly.

Pastoral care, well-being and discipline: Bullying or behavioural problems are dealt with quickly. It's 'cool to be clever at Plymstock' so ridiculing high achievers – 'boffs' – is out. 'Unreserved support' for any necessary punishment is expected from parents.

Pupils and parents: Mixed social backgrounds, although Plymstock is more affluent than many parts of Plymouth. Parents are 'proud' to send their children here – 'It really encourages individuals to celebrate their talents'. Students believe they achieve because the teaching is good. Olympic swimmer and gold medalist Sharron Davies came here before winning a scholarship to Kelly College (now Mount Kelly).

Entrance: Pupils from eight feeder schools: Oreston, Elburton, Hooe, Dunstone, Pomphlett, Goosewell, Downham, Wembury – belonging to the Plymstock (Plymouth) area Academic Council. This family of schools communicates well. One per cent choose Plymouth grammar schools instead.

Exit: Approximately 75 per cent of year 11 students progress to sixth form, others head for the local college of further education, the College of Art and Design, employment based training and other schools. Most to university, including occasional Oxbridge, to read eg maths, law, French, biology. One law firm apprentice in 2016.

Remarks: Highly successful and good all-round comprehensive in a pleasant suburb of Plymouth.

Poole Grammar School

Gravel Hill, Poole, Dorset BH17 9JU

Pupils: 1,197 • Ages: 11–18 • Sixth form: 310

Tel: 01202 692132
Email: office@poolegrammar.com
Website: www.poolegrammar.com

Headteacher: Since 2014, Andy Baker, previously deputy head. BA from Lancaster (politics and economic history), PGCE from Keele and MA from Middlesex (social and industrial history). Taught at schools in Essex before joining Poole as deputy head in 1993. Likes pottery, skiing, period property restoration, music (listener and performer). Married with two grown up children.

Academic matters: Specialises in maths, computing and cognition, so it's no surprise that maths is top of the pops at A level, closely followed by the three separate sciences, which everyone does at IGCSE. All students take French, Spanish or German to GCSE, though no classics or eastern languages. Fantastic results in maths and chemistry but also, impressively, in English, RE, geography and history. Exciting ICT with everyone doing the short course ICT GCSE at the end of year 9. In 2016, 57 per cent of GCSE grades A*/A.

Boys take four or five subjects at AS and narrow down to three for A level. About 30 subjects to choose from. Joint sixth form teaching in many subjects with Parkstone Grammar School (girls) means almost any combination of subjects can be timetabled. Lots of enrichment choices in AS levels and a few unexpected AS subjects, including archaeology, critical thinking, theatre studies and media studies. English language is a popular A level, plus computing, the inevitable sciences and above all maths, while most boys take general studies. Nearly thirty per cent A*/A grades in 2016. Masses of add-ons: boys can take the AQA Baccalaureate virtually in their stride if they do the right mixture of subjects. Accelerated courses in maths etc supplemented by school extension courses, mainly in form of IGCSE in preparation for A level. Poole has Cisco and Microsoft Academy status and students can earn the CCNA networking qualification in the sixth form.

Setting only in maths, from year 9. All pupils do two weeks' work experience in year 11. Class sizes not more than 30 and some much smaller groups in sixth form.

Less of an academic sausage machine than you might expect. Surprisingly for a grammar, SEN is one of school's specialisms – head sees it as truly cross-curricular and serving the needs of the most able, gifted and talented, as well as those with identified academic difficulties. Excellent results for disabled pupils and those coping with profound deafness and other personal challenges. One former pupil with severe cerebral palsy has just finished a computer science degree at university, with outstanding results. A five-strong department recognises that almost everyone has some sort of need, hand-in-hand with the belief that supporting pupils through any kind difficulty will be beneficial to their academic performance.

Games, options, the arts: Boys are adamant that music, art and the humanities are important to the school. Exam take-up in art and music belies this, but the life-like and often enormous paintings and drawings in the art department and the impressive new music department, with its record of concerts, musical and drama productions (often with Parkstone

Grammar), all justify their pride. A completely pupil-led play – written, performed, produced, managed by pupils – is on the bill. Popular orchestra and huge year 8 choir etc.

This is a pretty sporty school. Head believes the largely Poole-based population makes for a sense of identity and commitment to teams. Sport is compulsory for all and a good tranche of boys are in teams. Football is the most popular sport, but rugby, cricket (on 'the best cricket square in Poole') and athletics are probably more successful. Sports hall rather outmoded now, ditto the fitness room, but good new outdoor facilities. No pool but pupils use nearby Dolphin pool, which currently occupies the school's original site. Distinguished past and current athletes have trained through local clubs as well as in school. Inevitably there is sailing (at Hamworthy), plus squash, outdoor education etc off the premises. Parents say sport is good but that school also encourages pupils to use excellent local facilities and clubs, where specialists can (and do) excel in minority pursuits like trampolining.

Bags of clubs at lunchtime and after school. These include philosophy, debating, classics... and lots of subject-specific extras. Enterprise and languages well catered for as well as Formula 24 Greenpower car club, aero modelling et al. Big theatrical productions on alternate years, with smaller studio plays in between and some boys opt into Parkstone Grammar's big musicals. Terrific range of DT rooms, including a brand new food lab complete with rhubarb growing by the front door. Masses of trips – language visits, expeditions to Second World War sites and popular geography beano to Iceland post-GCSE.

Background and atmosphere: Poole bucked the usual trend and the school started as a co-ed in downtown Poole in 1904, before splitting into boys' and girls' grammars in the 30s. Present site in Gravel Hill, a nondescript wooded artery into Poole famed for its speed traps, has acres of well-groomed space, including good pitches and athletics space. The original red-brick 60s blocks marry well with the square glass and brick modern extensions, giving a pleasant though unremarkable whole. Inside the new bit, with libraries (always manned), state-of-the-art music and drama and some pretty smart classrooms, is bright, light and user friendly. Boys keen on the little work carrels tucked in at the top of the stairs. Reception area bristles with achievement certificates (over 40 of them) and trophies, plus huge historical photos of the school. Main dining hall serves locally sourced largely organic food ('delicious,' according to one pupil we spoke to) and certainly a majority of pupils and staff vote with their stomachs. A Gold Food for Life award earned partly for the supply of fresh fruit and vegetables planted in the school grounds and partly for the school spreading its culinary largess to a swathe of Poole primary schools using their catering – a nice income for the school. Chef recently presented with catering worker of the year award at 10 Downing Street.

School has academy status so has more freedom in what and how it offers. Part of the South West Academic Trust (consisting of several grammar schools and Exeter University), it takes a lead in local academic matters and is formally linked with several primary and special schools. Proud of its lead in staff training – all in-house by own staff – and of the links forged with schools in Europe and further afield. There are nearly as many female as male staff – possibly why the atmosphere is so normal – though heads of department are mostly men.

School has now expanded to include year 7 and has a remarkably calm feel for what is essentially a hothouse for more than 1,200 teenage boys. Humanities and enterprise flourish, lessons evidently absorb attention and boys are enthusiastic about all aspects of school. Adding 'cognition' to the potentially 'nerdy' specialisms of maths and computing allows the staff to boost their care of individual boys, whatever their needs.

Pastoral care, well-being and discipline: Heads of year take responsibility for all boys in the year. Head of year 7 makes sure the little lambs settle and takes them into year 8. There's a remixing of forms in year 9 which then remain static through to year 11. Uniform requirement relaxes over the years – from blazer and tie for years 7 and 8 to jumper and tie for years 9,10 and 11, to ties only (not literally) in sixth form. Out (either temporarily or permanently) for bringing drugs on site. Bullying could result in exclusion – either entirely for a time or in school's exclusion room, though there are few reported incidents. Strong mentoring of year 7 and 8s by senior boys is valued by both. Prefects are a very select few elected by senior boys and staff. Parents praise the discipline here and the rapt and concentrating faces in lessons certainly bore this out. Social events arranged with Parkstone Grammar for all year groups and older boys mix take lessons in both schools.

Pupils and parents: Head says has a particularly wide social mix because it positively seeks to provide first and foremost for the bright boys of Poole – so is less open to 'advantaged' children from further afield. Small but varied ethnic minorities – 19 languages spoken other than English and bilingual boys increasingly encouraged to do GCSE in their mother tongue. Ability range broader than you might expect, perhaps because of Bournemouth School just down the road, some very good local comprehensives and also because entrance policy favours local pupils above potentially brighter but more distant applicants.

Entrance: Complex and intensely controversial. School admits pupils who have passed the test and who live in Poole, irrespective of where they go to primary school. Takes some pupils from outside the borough. Applications by early September; tests in maths, English and verbal and non-verbal reasoning – common to Poole schools consortium – in late September. Results (whether or not the boy has met the required standard – not a guarantee of a place) sent out in mid-October, in time for local authority school applications. Main feeder schools include Broadstone, Oakdale and Canford Heath Middle Schools and Dumpton Prep.

Sixth form entry is much less competitive – surprising that more people haven't caught on. Applications depend on 'satisfactory achievement' at GCSE.

Exit: Occasionally boys defect after year 8, in search of small classes at local independent schools. Some 10-15 per cent leave after GCSEs for vocational courses, apprenticeships or sixth form college. Three sixth form leavers to Oxbridge in 2016, and one medic; others to universities like Durham, Exeter, Southampton, Bath, Bristol, Imperial, UCL, Kings, Warwick and Nottingham. Bournemouth popular for media programmes.

Remarks: A high achieving school for the bright boys of Poole.

Port Regis

114

Motcombe Park, Shaftesbury, Dorset SP7 9QA

Pupils: 300; 60 per cent boys; 180 boarders (full, weekly and flexi) • Ages: 3-13 • C of E

Fees: Day £8,670 – £17,997 pa; Boarding £20,250 – £24,300 pa

Tel: 01747 857914
Email: admissions@portregis.com
Website: www.portregis.com

Headmaster: Since 2016, Mr Stephen Ilett (50s). Educated at Rossall School in Lancashire, where his father was a housemaster, and Lincoln College, Oxford, where he read history and played rugby for the university's first XV. Spent 18 years working in the City (for Lloyd's of London) before moving into education. Reckons his early career equipped him well for headship. 'I held positions of responsibility in the City and ran teams of people so I'm used to keeping all the balls in the air,' he says.

First post was teaching French and coaching rugby at Caldicott. He was promoted to director of studies within two years. After eight years at Caldicott he became head of Milbourne Lodge, the Surrey co-ed prep. Five years later he took the reins at Port Regis. 'Port Regis has the reputation of being one of the best schools in the country,' he says, 'and when the headship came up it was too tempting to turn down.'

A keen linguist, he taught modern foreign languages at Milbourne Lodge – 'I love teaching French,' he says. When he arrived at Port Regis the timetable was already in place but he's planning to teach life skills to pupils during the next academic year. He believes Port Regis's stand-out qualities are its facilities ('which are genuinely acknowledged to be second to none') and the high calibre staff.

Married to Amanda, who is Port Regis's marketing manager, and they have five grown-up children between them. They are passionate believers in the benefits of boarding and are keen to show that Port Regis is 'very friendly, very caring and very nurturing'. In his spare time the head likes cricket, golf, travel, reading and walking his two dogs. They live in a house on site.

Entrance: Main entry points are nursery and year 3 but children join all the way through the school. Pre-prep is first come, first served while entry to the prep is via an interview with the head, assessment (verbal and non-verbal reasoning) and report from previous school. Children join from a raft of preps and from local state primaries (including Motcombe, Semley, Wardour and Ludwell). Virtually all pre-prep children move up to the main school (no assessment required).

Exit: Leavers head to an impressive array of schools – a total of 26 in 2016. Destinations include Bryanston (29 per cent in 2016), Eton, Marlborough, Benenden, Canford, Downe House, Godolphin, Harrow, King's Canterbury, Millfield and Sherborne. Fifty-five per cent to co-ed schools, 45 per cent to single sex, with a good smattering of scholarships and exhibitions (33 in 2016). Senior schools tell Port Regis that Port Regians are children who are 'resilient, self-reliant and know how to get on with things'. Most pupils stay until 13 (one or two girls leave at 11 for schools like Wycombe Abbey but school doesn't encourage this).

Remarks: Located in 150 acres of sweeping Dorset parkland, yet only a couple of miles from the hilltop town of Shaftesbury. Visitors gasp at the setting – it could easily be mistaken for a senior school, with its long drive, stunning architecture, modern classrooms, central lake, huge treehouse and extensive playing fields and grounds. Main school building is a Victorian mansion built in 1894 by Baron Stalbridge but it is surrounded by a collection of stylish, purpose-built additions. School was founded in London in 1881 by Dr Alfred Praetorius. It was later bought by a couple called Mr and Mrs Roderick, who moved it to Folkestone. When they retired it was incorporated into a school at Kingsgate, Broadstairs and named Port Regis (Latin for 'Gate of the King'). It moved to Motcombe House in 1947 (via stints at Bryanston and St Albans). First admitted girls in 1972.

Mildly selective – head says the school is 'a broad church' – but academic results are very good. Setting from year 5, with scholarship sets introduced in the last two years (year 8 scholarship group is called Alpha, year 7 scholarship group is Beta). Maximum class size of 15 throughout. French taught from the start and Latin from year 6. Spanish on offer from year 6 and there are opportunities to study Italian, Russian and Mandarin outside the main curriculum. Ancient Greek is taught as an after-lunch club for children in years 6, 7 and 8. Staff give it a try too. When we visited the director of studies had just signed up.

Pupils have a form teacher till the end of year 6, then get the chance to choose their own tutor for years 7 and 8. Excellent learning support department led by dynamic head (who used to be head of science and also teaches mindfulness). A fifth of pupils access learning support, mainly for dyslexia, dyspraxia, ASD, mild ADD and speech and language therapy. School has produced a senior school guide to help parents choose the next schools for their children and head meets parents to discuss choices when children are in year 5.

Well-known far and wide for its sporting prowess, school offers a plethora of sport. Boys play rugby, football, hockey and cricket while girls do hockey, netball, rounders and tennis. As well as acres of playing fields there's an Astroturf, nine-hole golf course, rifle range, heated swimming pool and impressive indoor sports complex that serves as a national centre for junior gymnastics. School does particularly well at hockey, rugby and athletics (11 pupils qualified for 15 different events at the 2016 IAPS national athletics championships).

Art, DT and pottery (there can't be many prep schools with a whole room devoted to ceramics) are amazing. We were particularly taken with a vast sculpture of a pear core created by a 13-year-old pupil. The year 8 guide who showed us round the DT department told us: 'This is a place where ideas can be formed.' Many senior schools would give their eyeteeth for facilities like these – everything from a 3D printer to a laser-cutting machine (great for making stickers). The children really let their imaginations run riot here. We saw an iPod speaker inspired by an old-fashioned toaster, a hanging chair and a lamp that projected a bat-shaped shadow on the wall. 'They surprise me all the time with their designs,' beams the head of DT. Annual summer exhibition gives pupils a chance to show off their creative flair.

Music is top notch too. Every 7-year-old learns the recorder and how to read music and every 8-year-old learns the violin. Music is taught in the striking Farrington Music School, an octagonal-shaped building overlooking a small lake known as 'Bob's Pond'. It boasts a 132-seat recital hall, music technology room and 17 teaching rooms. Wind, brass and string ensembles, chool orchestra, senior and junior choirs, samba band, swing band and lots of other groups, all of which put on regular concerts. Plenty of drama. Each year group puts on a play and there's a leavers' show at the end of the summer term. More than 70 activities and hobbies (we'd love to do them all), including aerobics, backgammon, beekeeping, film animation, computer coding, friendship bracelets and trampolining. Debating, or 'persuasive talks', are very popular, with children encouraged to discuss the issues of the day.

School is firmly committed to boarding. 'It feels like a second home really,' one boy told us. Around 60 per cent of children board in some way, whether it's full boarding, flexi-boarding or the odd night here and there (via an efficient online booking system). 'We have tried to listen to what our parents want,' says the head, who introduced flexi-boarding on his arrival. Apart from half term and holidays, the school never shuts. While some boarders go home at weekends, 70 to 80 children (a third of the main school) stay at school. Around 20 per cent of pupils live abroad – their parents include non-EU internationals, expats and servicemen and women. Lots on offer for the boarders – staff and 12 gap students put on activities like face painting, cooking, weekend walks and trips galore. Most staff live on site.

Boarding facilities are top notch – way better than some senior schools we've seen. Junior boarders (years 3 to 6) are housed in the main school building – girls on one side, boys on another. Dorms of four or six, each with a dorm captain. Older boys and girls have separate boarding houses in the grounds. The girls' boarding house is stunning, complete with disco lights on the hall ceiling, a double tier sofa to snuggle up and watch movies at weekends and breakfast bar stools made from riding saddles. Each girl has her own 'cubie', with a bed, desk and wash basin – separated with a stylish bead curtain at the door. There's even a retro caravan in the garden (the enterprising bursar snapped it up on eBay). The senior boys' house is pretty nifty too – the games room ceiling is decorated with real surfboards. A lot of thought has been given to helping new children settle in. New pupils get a shadow to guide them through the early weeks.

Year 8s given responsibility – there's a head boy and head girl, plus dorm captains for boarders. No prefects. 'We don't think it's good to single out children at this age,' says the head. Children encouraged to be children for as long as possible. No electronic devices or mobile phones (apart from pupils whose parents live abroad). Boarders can Skype their parents on the boarding house computers. Pastoral care is very much at the forefront, with form tutors and houseparents the first port of call when problems arise. Very few behaviour issues here. Indeed, Port Regis is hot on manners, pleases and thank yous and holding doors open for visitors. Boarders write letters home every Tuesday. School is also planning a kindness day – 'we want children to understand that it's cool to be kind,' says the head. 'It's not to be derided. It's a real strength.' Slightly more boys than girls but school has appointed a head of girls' games and a senior tutor, who is effectively head of girls (she is also head of classics, has a PhD from Cambridge and has written two critically acclaimed books).

P

School food is among the very best we've tasted. Head chef (whose family runs a local restaurant) and his five-strong team cook up to 1,000 meals a day – breakfast, lunch and supper, using fresh locally sourced ingredients as much as possible. We happily tucked into a lunch of fillet of sea bass (freshly caught off the coast of Brixham) topped with caper and lemon sauce, spinach and roasted new potatoes. Salads and vegetarian options always on offer – avocado and chargrilled peppers, quorn wraps and lentil soup when we visited.

Pre-prep (with 52 pupils) is housed in a stable block, just a few minutes walk from the main school. Idyllic setting, complete with forest school, enclosed playground, rose garden for imaginary play, loads of outdoor space and plenty of scooters and helmets. When we visited children had been picking apples and were about to cook their own apple crumble. Head of pre-prep is a former GB underwater hockey player and is passionate about outdoor learning.

Pupils are chirpy, enthusiastic and refreshingly down-to-earth. We saw a group of year 4s, all dressed up as chimney sweeps, street children and lords and ladies of the manor, throw themselves with relish into a Victorian Day workshop led by a guest speaker. Parents say there's 'a buzz about the school' and like the way it treats every child as an individual. A mix of local families and those who have moved to the country in search of a healthier, less pressurised lifestyle. Some from London – school is only two hours from the capital and Heathrow by train. Day pupils come from as far afield as Sherborne, Salisbury, Bruton and Warminster, mostly places within a 40-minute drive. School is building up a network of minibuses for day pupils. Parents are very involved in the school, attending quiz nights, balls, the Christmas fair, debates and lectures.

Illustrious alumni include the abstract painter Adrian Heath, former Press Council chairman Sir Louis Blom-Cooper, fashion designer Jasper Conran, singer/songwriter Bo Brudenell-Bruce, Olympic medallist horsewoman Zara Phillips and historian Jonathan Gathorne-Hardy.

As we've said before, it's difficult to find fault with Port Regis. It has sometimes been seen as the preserve of the very rich but in reality children come from a wide variety of backgrounds. Scholarships and means-tested bursaries on offer too. The pupils we met clearly love the place and as a parent told us: 'If anyone is going to bring out what your child is good at, Port Regis will.'

Prior Park College

Linked with The Paragon School

Ralph Allen Drive, Bath, Somerset BA2 5AH

Pupils: 602; 95 full, 64 weekly boarders • Ages: 11–18 • Sixth form: 200 • RC

Fees: Day £14,415 – £15,915; Boarding £24,285 – £30,510 pa

Tel: 01225 831000
Email: admissions@priorparkschools.com
Website: www.priorparkcollege.com/

Head Master: Since 2009, Mr James Murphy-O'Connor MA (Oxon) PGCE (40s). Historian. Educated at St Benedict's, Ealing. Degree at Greyfriars Hall, Oxford, PGCE at Peterhouse, Cambridge. Thence to Stamford followed by Sherborne, where he was a housemaster. First headship was the brand new Sherfield. Says 'Prior Park is in my DNA' and justly, for his father, Jim, was educated here along with his four brothers. Jim played rugby for Ireland, his younger brother Cardinal Cormac is the retired Archbishop of Westminster and still engages with the religious life of the school. James is married to Ali, four children, all former or current students. Keen on the arts, fan of F Scott Fitzgerald and Thomas Hardy, plus Picasso's 1920s art. Passionate Tottenham Hotspur and Ireland rugby fan. Enjoys retreating to family cottage amongst the mountains and wild Atlantic beaches of his beloved Mayo in Ireland where dalmador (dalmatian x labrador) Holly runs free.

By present day standards Mr Murphy-O'Connor's has already been a longish innings, but he's not ready to move on yet and talks like a man with an as-yet unfulfilled vision for the school. His focus is the human level, improving the school experience of all students, making sure they are nurtured, safe and throwing themselves into everything on offer. Often to be sighted out and about at the start of the day, 'chatting and welcoming', students note admiringly that 'he knows your name and things about you from day one'. Well-being issues come first in his book – not that the snazzy new sports centre is anything to sneeze at. Scorelines from academic through to sporting have risen measurably on his watch but his legacy will be the emotional health of the school community – which is inaccessible to units of measurement. This isn't a bandwagon response to recent alarm bells about teenage mental health issues, it's where his and his school's heart have always lain. At the time of our visit the big news was a fledgling peer mentoring scheme, a give-something-back enterprise originated by sixth formers intended to enable them to offer discreet advice and emotional support to their younger fellows. Rather than take ownership of the initiative, Mr Murphy-O'Connor was characteristically taking the route of empowerment. This is what his school is all about and all parents we spoke to said it was the pastoral care and evident happiness of the community that got them reaching for their registration form.

In a Catholic school whose roll numbers 65 per cent non-Catholics, Mr Murphy O'Connor unabashedly decrees Catholic values of kindness, service and 'being the person God wants you to be' – he says 'every child is precious'. No lip-service here. None of these values is objectionable to parents of a broadly secular disposition, to whom they are also humanist values which they want their child to imbibe. Discussion of topics like abortion and homosexuality hears out and respects all points of view. Non-Catholic students express no uneasiness.

Prior Park delivers, says the head, a rounded education. Lots of heads say this. When they do, cock an eyebrow – we did – for this is an inexact term. It can mean an educational philosophy, it can mean that the students here aren't terribly good at exams or, when employed by a school that is terribly good at exams, can mean all too little. Which is the case here? The way to find out is to investigate whether, down on the shop floor, teachers and students are walking the talk. What we found by dint of interrogation is that they most emphatically do. Yes, they echo and act out what their head says, and never in a dutiful, parroty way. It is highly unusual to visit a school and hear the words of a head made flesh like this, the more so given the disposition of young persons to subject the exhortations of authority figures to ruthless due diligence. But they like what their head wants, they really do. They want it too. Work matters most, but everything else matters too. One parent told us that your typical Prior Park student is 'accomplished, compassionate and humble'. No divergence here from Mr Murphy-O'Connor's primary purpose. Another said, 'Each student, honestly, matters to him.' Another: 'He's passionate about encouraging pupils to become rounded.'

Academic matters: No point in looking at Dept for Education performance tables for raw data and comparison tables because the school, along with others, is boycotting them. Why? Because in the head's book there's more to education than exam results, performance tables take no account of 'creativity and inspiration', and the only true measure is how far a school raises its students. So he'd happily sign up for value-added league tables.

Headline figures vary little from year to year. In 2016 at GCSE 86 per cent A*/B grades, 60 per cent A*/A; at A level 42 per cent A*/A. So: the school does consistently well by its broad-ish intake. This is not an exam factory because there is no relenting in the commitment to all-round personal development, neither is roundedness achieved at the expense of best-possible exam results – a neat trick which the school pulls off adroitly. There's pressure all right, but it's judiciously applied and it works because – this is the culture of the place – teachers know their students very well as people, they pick up on stress, lethargy and waywardness just like that and make time to support. One student said, 'They always help when you're finding it difficult and get you back for a bit of tuition to help you through.' Another said, 'No teacher here would ever turn down a request for help'. Call this rigour through kindness if you like, there's a lot of mutual respect going on here. The PHSCE programme is substantial and delivered with purpose.

Prep (homework) is supervised up to sixth form. The relatively long day here (no Saturday school) means that you can break the back of it before you get home. Parents like this: 'There's usually not all that much to do at home so we can relax together as a family'. As you age it increasingly spills over, of course.

There's currently a curriculum review in progress which aims to fine tune already estimable value-added scores. Having rejected the International Baccalaureate, they aim now to offer a bespoke version. The outcome the head seeks is 'an educational framework that enshrines our values.'

No statemented students accepted, but SEND provision supports milder SENs and intervenes when disparity emerges between a student's potential and ongoing achievement, or a student needs, say, organisational strategies or exam-stress support. Extends to students who develop mental health issues. Parents speak well of the expert sensitivity of the support given to their children. Mobility impaired students accepted where possible, but the school's architecture is a constraint.

Games, options, the arts: Sport, says the head, is 'one of the things we do'. Puts it in its place nicely, neither bigging it up nor doing it down and underlining his commitment to celebrating achievement in all areas equally, each student according to their lights. Parents like the way the school 'encourages everyone to give it all a go regardless of ability.' Hockey's what they do best in shop-window terms (national champions 2016). Netball is strong, rugby has an ex-England international coach, the rest competitively respectable given the size of each year's intake. Spacious playing fields, plentiful Astroturf. Sport for all, they say, greatest involvement by the greatest number, borne out by number of teams per sport sent forth to battle for their school every Saturday – around 10 on good day. Individuals regularly play at regional and international level. One of the lessons we learn from sport, they say, is humility. That's so Prior Park. No, it's emphatically not a philosophy of loser takes all, they love to win. Spanking new sports centre, source of great pride, opened in 2015, includes multi-sport gym, fitness suite, you name it. It's been a boon for the less gamesy types.

Art and design happen in and around a refurbed dorm. Fine art good, photography especially strong just now as is textiles. Healthy numbers, decent results. Design technology in a good place, partnerships with local industries, lots of energy input from staff. A bit boy heavy but efforts being made to bring in the girls.

Music universally praised. Inspirational head of music also performs with singing group Opus Anglicanum. No elitism here when it comes to genre: anything goes from Gabrieli to grime. In cases of indie genres his smart ploy is to offer 'hands-off facilitation' thus enabling students to retain ownership of their sounds. High-end choral tradition longstanding and outstanding, biennial opera, multiplicity of ensembles, concerts formal and informal, for they love to go live and give others 'an experience of the sublime'. Two, yes two, musicals every year, all singing, all dancing – one parent said, 'Never a duty date, I simply can't believe the standard they reach'. 'Blows my mind,' said another. Music here reaches all parts and catches up those who never knew they could. There's an inter-house music competition including student-rehearsed house song in which everyone sings and thereafter dwells on, marvelling fondly, for the rest of the year. A level numbers small, but of these a good number go on to top music colleges. Chapel choir is 90 per cent day students who come in every Sunday to sing at mass. What does that tell you?

Drama's right up there with music (let's call it a dead heat). Up to 14 productions of all sorts a year, much of it high-end stuff. Staff (superb) all come from professional theatre, that's what makes the difference. Fabulous Julian Slade theatre (1993) largely funded by Cameron Mackintosh's Foundation – he's a former student – palpably redolent of the magic created in it down the years by dint of passion, sweat, discipline, creativity and self-discovery. It's the real thing all right. Mackintosh also funded the excellent dance studio.

You get to do your after-school activities in school here. Recreational options, both lunchtime and after lessons, are multifarious and eclectic, embracing a diversity of endeavours from tricky physics to knit-and-natter. More than 60 to choose among. There's a Saturday (morning) Active programme whose breadth spans street dance and cookery. There's a CCF – voluntary sign-up from year 8 upwards – and there's D of E. There's even an equestrian team.

Sixth formers have their own after-school (ad)ventures. They concoct a social programme – film nights, music nights, BBQs etc. The charities committee coordinates competitive fundraising for good causes and the best house wins a cup. Then there's Prior Concern, which sends forth students to do their bit for the homeless, nursery-age children and the elderly. Catholic values in action.

Boarding: Some 160 students board from age 13, around a third of them girls. Of these, around 50 are weekly and flexi boarders. Roughly 60 full time boarders are international students. Stopover beds for day pupils. We had reservations about the boys' accommodation in St Paul's. Gorgeous as the building may be on the outside, its bigness seemed inimical to snugness on the inside. This is an adult perception; the students reckon it does very nicely. Boys live alongside residential staff and their families. Girls occupy the unarguably cosier Priory nearby. Prep is supervised by a teacher. Weekend activities, the bugbear of any boarding regime, continually addressed. Mass on Sundays compulsory. To be honest we wondered about the head of boys' boarding being an ex-Marine – until we met him. Bit of a martinet? No way. He's a man who understands the vital importance of addressing individuality in all its manifestations.

Background and atmosphere: Run by the Christian Brothers 1830-1981. Palladian mansion built by quarry owner Ralph Allen to advertise the golden glories of Bath stone. This a grade 1 listed building standing two miles from the centre of a UNESCO World Heritage city. Stunning view down from the portico stops all the clocks. Inside, architectural grandeur doesn't always adapt readily to the needs of a 21st century school and can play the part of an awkward host. 'Don't agree,' say the students as you fight for breath up an endless spiral staircase; 'it's quirky, it's part of the charm'. A parent concurred: 'Yes, all right, it's a bit shabby in places but in the nicest way – a bit basic but kids love it.' Lovely chapel, lovely name, Our Lady of the Snows, used also for weekly assemblies – all get in, just. Science block purpose built. Years 7 and 8 in their own standalone house, Baines, overseen by greatly-liked housemistress and team. Compulsory residential course early in year 7 and team building day for year 8 students underpin community values.

Amazingly posh architecture notwithstanding, the social climate here isn't the least snooty; this is a down to earth place where ordinary people go to school, a place whose unpretentious personality answers the values of the sort of parent who celebrates 'a school that doesn't set itself apart from the city but participates in local events.'

Pastoral care, well-being and discipline: There's a culture here of looking out for each other, teachers for students, older students for younger ones – one parent said, 'they got to know my daughter very quickly and genuinely appreciated her as a person.' It's a palpable culture, one you pick up on as you tour and chat. Intervention is prompt. One parent said, 'It is a fantastic strength of the school that they are so diligent with the students' well-being.' This doesn't all come about by wishing it so or generating policy docs, it derives from expectations, watchfulness, example-setting and buy-in. It works because it's hard work and it conditions behaviour because it is underpinned by tenacity. Above all, it's what the students want. So, said one parent, 'There is no room for anyone to bend the rules. Boundaries are set and are the same for everyone. This has created a school of pupils who take pride in how they are being perceived by everyone.' Another said: "We are constantly amazed by the school's ability to encourage and maintain an exquisite level of behaviour and compliance without the need to instil enormous amounts of discipline.' Concern for well-being shirks no issue raised by social media, a major concern; sexting, by way of example, is a regular assembly topic and parents join in the discussion. We asked one parent if social media was a regular discussion topic. 'No, it's a constant conversation.'

Pupils and parents: Co-ed since 1982, almost 50:50, boys slightly more numerous. Common rooms are same-sex, lessons and dining mixed. Some 35 per cent of students are Catholic. Year 7 entrants from, equally, local state schools and Paragon Junior. At year 9 a wodge from the prep school in Cricklade plus a smattering from other preps and international schools. Sizeable contingent of parents are dahn-from-Londoners, who have colonised Bath in recent years – yes, even raggle-taggle Walcot Street has capitulated to the hipsters. This monocultural tendency is mitigated by the school's international students, never more than 10 per cent of the roll. To cope with demand from overseas the school has just launched Prior Park Gibraltar. With two outstanding (Ofsted) state schools and four rival independents in Bath alone, the education market locally is working well, with competitive pressures driving up standards and heightening distinctiveness.

For day students, buses from all corners up to 30 miles away. Parental involvement welcomed: twice-monthly coffee mornings hosted by PoP (Parents Of Prior), which even has its own private Facebook page. Regular parent forums with the head so he can hear what you think. Weekly newsletter from the head. Listings of parent phone numbers by year group (voluntary) a nice touch. Businesslike, highly functional website. Parents really like the 'wonderful feeling of community'.

Entrance: Selective. Don't miss the application deadline – details on the website. Tests for 11+ entrants; CE and scholarship at 13. At any other time, report and interview. Around 20 join post-GCSE from other schools, telling you something about the strength of the sixth form, whose entrants need a minimum six GCSEs with As in A level subjects preferred.

Exit: Very small exodus post-GCSE, most to vocational courses. Sixth form leavers are Russell groupies, most of them, Exeter, Manchester and Cardiff especially popular. Good and varied balance of arts and sciences. Four to Oxbridge, 2016, about average, plus three medics.

Money matters: Customary range of scholarships up to a value of around 25 per cent, more in deserving cases. Bursaries can be standalone or added to a scholarship. The head says he likes to help where he can, and in another clear-cut case of walking the talk an examination of the accounts reveals that the school awards roughly half as much again in bursaries (as a percentage of income) as other Bath independents. Some carry-over scholarships from prep school. Discounts for siblings. Lunch bundled with fees but not transport. Taking account of the long school day and the 4-6pm activities programme, good value for money. The head says, 'We recognise that we have a lot of working parents who stretch themselves to afford the fees. We don't want to let them down.'

Remarks: Confident in its Catholic values, happy in its own skin and distinctive in its commitment to a genuinely all-round education, this is a school which inspires esteem and affection in equal measure.

Queen Elizabeth's Hospital

Berkeley Place, Clifton, Bristol BS8 1JX

Pupils: 685 • Ages: 7-18 • Sixth form: 157 (co-ed from 2017)

Fees: £8,925 – £13,659 pa

Tel: 01179 303040
Email: headmaster@qehbristol.co.uk
Website: www.qehbristol.co.uk

Headmaster: Since 2000, Stephen Holliday MA (early 50s). Educated at Batley Grammar School and Jesus College, Cambridge, where he read history. Worked for British Rail as an operations manager in Dundee and Glasgow before hearing call to return to school life. After six years at Dean Close in Cheltenham, where he became a boarding housemaster, Mr Holliday joined Giggleswick School in his native Yorkshire as head of history. Ventured across the Lancashire border to become deputy head (pastoral) at Queen Elizabeth's Grammar School in Blackburn before moving to current role. Since 2013, he has been treasurer of HMC, which represents the heads of many independent schools.

At QEH, he has overseen closing of boarding and opening of junior school in the same premises, developed a new sixth form centre, and a new science/arts block in under construction. He is a Methodist local preacher, and parents describe him as 'honest' and 'forthright'. He is married to Gail, a teacher at Redland High School, and they have two sons, one at Durham University and the other a pupil at QEH.

Mr Holliday loves watching all sport, especially cricket, and is a keen fan of Leeds Utd. He has presided over a change from the previous rugby-dominated culture at the school to one that gives equal weight to rugby and football. 'Market forces,' he says. 'Boys just want to play football.' QEH shares its sports facilities three miles away at Failand with Bristol City FC. He admits he does not remember all boys' names, although he still teaches year 7 at the start and end of their first year to help get to know them. He has recently started teaching A level history, 'a complete indulgence', he admits.

Head of junior school: Since 2008, Martin Morris BEd BA (50s). Educated at Downsend Prep, Dauntsey's, Exeter University and OU. Taught biology and physics at Sedbergh, then moved to Leighton Park School in Berkshire. Appointed head of Catteral Hall in Giggleswick in 1995, then became head of Kingham Hill, Oxfordshire in 2000. After decades as a boarding houseparent, he arrived at QEH Junior a year after it opened in the former boarding houses of the senior school.

Married to Gill, a boarding housemistress at Haberdasher's Monmouth School for Girls, and they have seven grown-up children. Pop art portraits of them all, painted by one of his daughters, line his study walls. Four grandchildren.

A keen sportsman (and West Ham fan), head plays league cricket, coaches and plays hockey and has run three London marathons, numerous half-marathons and fell races. He is on IAPs sports committee and HMC junior school committee. Interests include music, bird-watching, gardening, cooking and amateur dramatics. Mr Morris is leaving in July 2017.

Academic matters: Junior school head teaches year 6 science and year 5 RE and builds his syllabus around topics suggested by the boys – 'unashamedly, things that will excite them,' like the Bloodhound project to build a 1000mph supersonic car in Bristol. Year 3 pupils mainly learn with class teacher. From year 4 upwards, subject specialist teachers for maths, English and science. French taught by senior school staff and some senior staff help out with coaching games. Years 3 and 4 have cross-curricular topics, incorporating history, geography, RE and ICT and integrating it with literacy, numeracy, and creative subjects. Years 5 and 6 have some of these subjects taught discretely, but also follow topic themes, including Azerbaijan and China as well as the Romans and Second World War.

ICT is up-to-date but unobtrusive. Year 6 boys use laptops in their classroom. Maths lessons largely follow national curriculum. English too, though teachers say 'we are not confined by it'. Shakespeare and poetry feature strongly. Lots of creative writing, again based on active experiences, using Pie Corbett's Talk for Writing. Reading is regarded as key. Regular reading weeks, when homework is dropped in favour of half an hour's reading every night. Pupils participate enthusiastically in Read 4 My School, a national online scheme involving reading and reviewing books. Boys praise the library for being well stocked with titles of interest, including 'speedy reads' and 'riveting reads'. Years 3 and 4 generally get 20 minutes' homework a night, while years 5 and 6 get 30 minutes. SENCo shared with senior school.

Results buck national trends, with boys consistently performing well at GCSE and A level. Proportion of A*/A passes at GCSE 65 per cent in 2015; at A level, 80 per cent A*-B and 54 per cent A*/A. Boys sit 10 GCSEs; school has moved to IGCSEs in sciences and languages as well as English and maths, for rigour, better preparation for A level, and more consistent marking scheme. 'Boys enjoy them more and they are more fun to teach,' says head. Maths and French setted from year 7, English from year 10. Class sizes 22-25 until year 9 then much smaller.

Maths is strong throughout school, and is most popular A level subject, with kudos among boys who are 'proud of being maths geeks'. Those who take maths and further maths dub them 'hard maths and double hard maths'. Separate sciences from year 7. More than half of sixth form studying one or more science subjects. Plans for new block would increase number of science labs to 10, extend art department and give more space to music and to design tech. Spanish most popular language choice, followed by French, with German third. Latin on offer at GCSE and A level and some study ancient Greek A level in their lunch hours. Small numbers enable QEH to tailor curriculum to individuals in response to occasional demand for a subject such as photography or music tech.

School says recession has affected A level choices, with many having a sharper focus on career prospects and aiming for medicine, science, engineering. Rise in business studies and economics and fall in arts, music, drama, languages. Head 'hopes they bounce back' and notes that some students 'still delightfully go with the flow'. Some concern too about changing university landscape, with worries that unconditional offers are unhelpful to boys. Detailed Oxbridge preparation valued highly.

Importance of reading emphasised. Good library, with boy-friendly titles and a strong range of periodicals. Regular reading weeks, where homework is replaced by sharing of books. Otherwise, homework goes from an hour a night in year 7 to two hours in year 11. Parents rate 'high standard of teachers across the board'. 'Staff are inspirational, and aspirational for the boys,' said one.

Games, options, the arts: Great atmosphere of creativity throughout the junior school, with excellent use made of the split-level classrooms. Music and drama are strong – lively rehearsals for the house singing competition were taking place during our visit. Boys learn a host of instruments including piano, flute, clarinet, saxophone, trombone, cello and drums and have the chance to play in groups and an orchestra. There's a mind-boggling range of clubs, which take place before school, at lunchtimes and after school and include problem-solving, brain-boosting, Lego, debating, general knowledge, chess, Italian and robotics as well as arts, music and sports.

Boys use the sports ground at Failand – a 10-minute coach ride away – twice a week for rugby, football and cricket. Facilities hared with Bristol City Football Academy.

The school opens on to Brandon Hill, a Civil War battle site, and is within walking distance of the SS Great Britain, Bristol Museum and Art Gallery, the Royal West of England Academy, @Bristol science centre and the M Shed museum. Trips further afield include an Easter ski visit. Outdoor pursuits popular, with year 5 and 6 boys taking part in the QE Award, similar to D of E, but tailored to their age group.

Aim is for students to be not only well qualified, but well educated, hence phenomenal range of activities in senior school. Sport has always been a strength, but these days is now just one element in a wide-ranging offer. One term rugby, one term football in winter; athletics, cricket and tennis in summer. Weights room and fitness room popular. Outdoor pursuits growing; almost half of boys opt for bronze D of E and up to 30 a year achieve gold. School teams highly successful in Ten Tors. Boys encouraged to take risks. 'They do allow them to do quite crazy things sometimes,' a parent says. Extreme example is Lewis Clarke, who was permitted to abandon his GCSE studies for two months to become, at 16, the youngest person to walk to the South Pole.

Thinking skills important too. Some year 9 pupils undertaking the Extended Project Qualification, a 'mini-dissertation' usually confined to sixth-formers. QEH is pioneer of Future Problem-Solving, a six-step scenario project to solve a global issue. Debating is a strength.

Many opportunities arise thanks to QEH's 220-seat, purpose-built theatre. Music highly valued. Various orchestras and ensembles. At least half a dozen boys in National Youth Orchestra. One student has won a place at the Yehudi Menuhin School. Lessons offered in almost every instrument – even bagpipes. Annual Battle of Bands and Unplugged events. Choirs are of high standard and boys are proud to be involved, even up to sixth form. Choir is only occasion when traditional bluecoat uniform is worn. Old boys recall this with pride but some sons less keen on 'all that old stuff'.

Q

New £3.5m development now open gives increased space for art and music, as well as science, including new ensemble rehearsal space and practice room and a ceramic studio.

Many trips, both those related to curriculum and extracurricular activities – WW1 battlefields, Iceland, Pyrenees, Slovenia, Morocco, China, Himalayas etc.

Many links with Bristol girls' schools for social and learning activities including cookery, quizzes, salsa dancing and philosophy.

Background and atmosphere: Imposing grade 2 listed Victorian building on Brandon Hill. 'Looks intimidating from the outside,' one pupil observed. Hogwarts-style features inside too, with stone staircase leading to 'headmaster's landing'. But atmosphere is overwhelmingly friendly and respectful. Total of 60-70 staff, including several who've been there more than two decades and some recent former pupils who have returned as teachers. Parents value the stability, but head likes to see young teachers move on and further their careers. Long-serving staff note there are many more female staff now, and boys are no longer addressed by their surnames.

Technology is up to date. Wifi everywhere (not an easy task in such a building), laptops, whiteboards, projectors where needed. Head is considering more use of iPads and students' own devices, but says he will 'only move in that direction when I am sure it will improve teaching and learning'. As he points out, exam system is still paper-based. One good example of using technology is where dyslexic boys photograph the board with their iPhones so they can have more time to study it.

Meals are prepared in £400,000 new kitchen and eaten in the hall, where a hand-sanitiser adds a somewhat incongruous though probably necessary note. The food is good. School believes strongly in a healthy diet and 'boy-sized portions' to fuel learning in and out of lessons. The Yard, one of the biggest tiled areas in Europe, provides an excellent space for running around.

Pupils belong to one of four houses – Bird's, Carr's, Hartnell's and Ramsey's – named after benefactors, and are intensely loyal. Those who excel are awarded house colours.

School's motto is 'While we have time, let us do good' (dum tempus habemus, operemur bonum), and charity fundraising and help for others are major focuses. Pupils listen to reading at a state primary as well as helping out at QEH Juniors.

Boys will be boys – that's the starting point for the junior school's entire approach. Curriculum geared to capturing interests. 'We have tried to develop a prep school feel, with an emphasis on preparing them for senior school,' says the head, adding that the style and teaching are 'very practical.' Competition is encouraged 'but is not the be-all and end-all.' Outdoor space at the junior school includes a climbing wall. Boys have access to the huge senior school yard at break-times to run around and let off steam, but any who prefer to stay indoors and read can do so. One parent said the confined site and lack of green space was 'not great – though none of my boys has ever complained.' There is a garden where year 3 boys grow vegetables, and a grassed area,

Pastoral care, well-being and discipline: The school prides itself on 'strong but unobtrusive pastoral care' and parents and boys confirm that this is very much the case. For a school that unashamedly promotes 'boys being boys', there is a surprising emphasis on emotional intelligence. 'They embrace each child and what he has got to offer. The school has met both my boys' very different needs in a superb way. I only wish my daughter could go there – though that would mean the school changing, and I don't want that,' says a parent (school sixth form is becoming co-ed in 2017, however). Boys are trained well to participate in peer mentoring, peer support and 'ebuddies' schemes, which are highly valued by all. 'It is not a monoculture. There is not an unpleasantly masculine atmosphere,' said a mum, who admitted she had previously been against single sex schooling.

The philosophy that boys should be 'stretched not stressed' also appears to work well. 'They have got tabs on them but in a very subtle way. They seem to know when to push the buttons to get them to perform well – in time but not too soon,' a parent observed.

School rules are short, simple and sensible – from time-honoured 'all roofs out of bounds' to the 21st century 'no social networking posting that affects well-being of another boy or brings school into disrepute'. Not to mention the classic 'facial hair must not be grown unless specific permission has been obtained from the headmaster'.

One parent praised help for son's dyslexia; another said support used to be patchy – but unanimous plaudits for the way the school prepares boys for the outside world. Sixth form offers sessions on cooking, sewing, budgeting, car and bike maintenance and healthy eating.

Staff, parents and pupils value the family atmosphere and careful pastoral approach at the junior school, which helps develop confident, well-rounded boys. 'The staff are sensitive and they really know the boys,' a parent told us. 'They help them, but in a subtle way.' School has links with girls' schools like but it is the single-sex education that is the big draw for parents. 'It means they can have a go at anything without any constraints or worries – they don't have to feel embarrassed,' we were told. One mother added: 'I had never intended my sons to go to a boys' school. They don't have a sister. But QEH has worked for them so well and I have no regrets. Most of all, it's really good fun.'

Pupils and parents: Changing demographic since demise of assisted places – 85 per cent now pay full fees. Stronger academic record means QEH now attracts the sons of university professors and doctors. Ending of Saturday lessons in the final years of the 20th century has also attracted a wider range of families. School aims for a wide social mix, and there are more pupils from modest backgrounds than might be imagined. Some boys with mild Asperger's, ADHD, dyslexia. Two boys with specific health needs are being funded by the local authority. School says it deliberately and as a matter of principle does not record black and minority ethnic numbers, because it believes all boys are equal. High proportion of gifted and talented pupils; enrichment programmes for all abilities. Some international sixth form students stay with local families.

Notable old boys include screenwriter Ashley Pharoah, football commentator Jonathan Pearce and racing driver Dino Zamparelli.

Entrance: Main junior intakes are years 3 and 5, but increasing demand to join in year 6. Some children come from independent schools but most from local state primaries. During assessment days, boys work with head on maths, reading, writing and verbal reasoning. 'I hate the idea of a formal exam for children of that age,' he says. 'I'm looking for potential – a spark of inquisitiveness and imagination.' No SEN statemented children on roll; a few with mild dyslexia. A joint venture co-ed pre-prep school at Redmaids' High Junior School takes 3-7 year olds.

About 150 applications a year for senior school. Places for 75-100 at 11. Entrance exams in verbal and non-verbal reasoning, maths and English. There's also an interview. A handful of pupils also admitted at 13+ after taking similar entrance exams and submitting a report from their school. Entrants to the sixth form (including girls from 2017) must have a minimum of six Bs at GCSE; higher for external applicants.

Exit: Almost all juniors progress to senior school via entrance exam. Parents warned well in advance if this does not look like the best route for their son. Almost all stay for sixth form. School will discuss with parents and pupil well in advance if this is unlikely to be the best option. At 18, most progress to leading universities, sometimes after a gap year. Eight Oxbridge offers in 2016 and five medics.

Money matters: When it first opened in 1590 with a Charter from Queen Elizabeth 1, the school was specifically charged with the education of poor children and orphans. Nowadays, only 15 per cent of pupils receive some financial help. No bursaries in junior school but two academic scholarships offered in year 3. Scholarships for music, sport and academic ability are worth 10-50 per cent of senior school fees. Some bursaries are awarded, with old boys increasingly supporting the school, in some cases funding 100 per cent of a needy pupil's education. Head would like to offer all bursaries, rather than scholarships, but says he is prevented from doing so by the 'Bristol market'.

Remarks: It is rare to find a school that so accurately reflects all the claims in its impressive literature. QEH has adapted to meet the needs of each age but remains true to its history.

Queen's College (Taunton)

Trull Road, Taunton, Somerset TA1 4QS

Pupils: 713; 192 boarders • Ages: 3–18 (boarding from 8) • Sixth form: 188

Fees: Day £6,000 – £17,400; Boarding £13,290 – £32,580 pa

Tel: 01823 340830
Email: admissions@queenscollege.org.uk
Website: www.queenscollege.org.uk

Head: Since September 2016, Dr Lorraine Earps, previously deputy and then acting head here (following the resignation of previous head Chris Alcock in May 2016, following allegations that he had breached the school's code of conduct). Degree in chemistry and biochemistry from Southampton, plus a doctorate in protein chemistry; taught in the state sector for six years; has also been head of chemistry at Stockport Grammar and director of studies at Withington Girls. Married with a son.

Junior school head: Since 2010, Mrs Tracey Khodabandehloo BEd MEd PGDip (50s). The name must be the most exotic in all the GSG canon, but it soon comes rolling off the tongues of all but perhaps the tiniest children. Brought up and educated locally, Mrs Khodabandehloo was a parent at the school when the headship came up; she was pursuing a successful career as a state school head of 15 years' standing, looking not to join the independent sector, but 'when a job came up in the school I passionately believed in, I had to take it'. She has enjoyed breaking free from narrowness in the maintained sector: of the curriculum and measures of success, most of which seem to be data-driven, and has revelled in resetting the curricular bounds. That said, there are, in her view, benefits which could usefully be employed by independent schools, such as pitting their academic data against national norms and developing formal professional links with teacher training institutions. Warm, motherly and compassionate, Mrs Khodabandehloo believes in, embodies and inculcates the family atmosphere and strong relationships for which all different parts of Queen's is famous, whilst prioritising an environment where learners are motivated and learning flourishes. Her three children are now grown and in fruitful careers of their own – one setting up a business using the skills learnt at Queen's business department. Spare time might see her riding in the Quantocks or perfecting her craft as a barista in a local church coffee shop; holidays are spent travelling, especially to Barbados.

Academic matters: The fact that most of the junior school pupils go on to the senior school at 11 means that air of fevered preparation for entrance exams to premier league independent schools is absent here, and consequently that they can enjoy a more relaxed pace. But that doesn't mean lack of rigour (eg knowing up to 12x12 by the end of year 4) or breadth – they learn French from the off and the school prides itself on its specialist teachers. Younger pupils are taught largely by form teachers, but from year 5, subject teachers take over. While Christian foundations underpin much of the religious and PHSE syllabi, we were impressed by the airtime given to other significant religions and their deities, prophets and manifestations. Independent and interlinked learning definitely encouraged, with topics spread across traditional subject boundaries.

Classrooms are bright and busy with plenty to draw the eye – children's work included; good to see a science lab and art studio too. All pupils are screened for SEN on arrival and provision for the milder end of the spectrum is woven into the life of the school; we were told that even when the need for intervention had passed, pupils still revisited the learning development department. Key SEN personnel at each stage of a Queen's education liaise closely.

One of the top of the Taunton schools pops for A level results in 2016, at 65 per cent A*/B, and 37 per cent A*/A, plus a respectable 47 per cent A*/A at GCCE, suggesting sound value-added at sixth form. But they appear to achieve this without excessive pressure: 'I spend more time taking the pressure off, than laying it on', said the previous head. That said, he had, during his time, concentrated on the middle band, moving Cs to Bs, and Bs to As, as well as catering to different learning styles – testament to his success is a severely dyslexic boy now reading law at Exeter. He also binned Saturday school – 'The kids at the other Taunton schools are tired!' he asserted. Class sizes average 17, and there's a choice of 24 subjects for GCSE and A level. A modern foreign language is compulsory at GCSE; business studies and ethics & philosophy more unusual options. Students are grouped by ability for core subjects but mixed for options. At A level, option blocks are changed yearly in an effort to accommodate individual subject choices and the school's flexibility at the start of sixth form while A level choices bed down is appreciated. Critical thinking, EPQ and TUG (top universities group) offered alongside these. One parent we spoke to chose Queen's specifically for its academics, another because her child 'did not shine academically, but has not been made to feel inferior by staff or pupils'. Stand-out subjects for the students are geography, chemistry and maths – 'but the sport and music are also amazing', our guides reported.

SEN support is provided through an integrated approach with the learning development unit (sic), where an electronic register shared with teaching staff records and tracks the needs of the high-ish proportion of SEN students. 'We haven't and don't wish to acquire dyslexia-friendly status,' says school, but it appears to serve its SEN population well, maths support in particular provided by the same teacher throughout the school, using traditional methods. Active EAL programme for the 100 or so overseas students.

Games, options, the arts: Sport is important – more a question of a game for all than winning at all costs. The junior school shares the Astro and pitches with the senior school, timetabled so that younger players are not trampled by the first XV, along with the gorgeous swimming pool adorned with its mosaic dragon. Just the place for sportsmen and women, but 'equally OK for incredibly anti-sports daughter,' according to one mother, who added that it is 'much more geared towards music, drama and the arts than the other Taunton schools'. Nonetheless, Queen's excels at sports and has just opened academies for both hockey and cricket (for which Taunton is famed), not just for its own promising players, but also for high flyers locally. Thirty acres of pitches, two Astros, an indoor pool – swimming is a strength here – and well-equipped sports hall make for a comprehensive offering. 'Rugby and hockey have been fundamental to my son's time her,' stated one mother. Off site, riding, sailing, canoeing, climbing and caving in nearby Mendip suits those with less of an eye for a ball, but everyone is encouraged to explore the great outdoors: almost all do at least bronze D of E, and a high number complete gold.

Performing arts shine too – school boasts largest performing space(s) of any school in the south west: two theatres and a studio big/smart enough for more intimate productions, and uses expertise of Somerset College's specialist film and TV make-up course. Recent shows include Seussical, Coram Boy, Macbeth and Storm Boy, adapted from the book by the head of drama, a published playwright. Junior school plays and concerts take place in its own hall – performed with similar panache and enthusiasm as those at the senior school. A massively ambitious arts festival, Quartz, takes place at school each October, which brings in actors, musicians, dancers and artists of all persuasions for performances and workshops. Dancers extremely well looked after in terms of facilities and the school's own academy of performing arts, which attracts the likes of Birmingham City Ballet to give classes; strong on contemporary dance too, such as street jazz. Musicians jolly fortunate, too, to have a dedicated concert hall as part of the music school, complete with Steinway and 30 stop organ, plus music tech facilities. Choirs and ensembles abound – we were intrigued by the 'exuberant arrangements' apparently played by Sound School, a sax ensemble. Trips for local and international (recently Germany and Italy) performance and trophies from Taunton Festival round off an extensive, if traditional, musical offering.

Art of all kinds is housed in a gorgeous art school overlooking the cricket pitches; students are exposed to all media, techniques and materials so that they are well prepared for GCSE art and design. Painting, ceramics and textiles are areas of particular expertise, but all benefit from trips here and abroad (Barcelona and New York, inter alia) as well as the influx of visiting practitioners at the annual Quartz Festival. But despite the range of diversions to choose from, some parents still feel it's too narrow, and that a shove could usefully be applied to the idler students to sign up to more of them.

Boarding: More than a third of students board, and some parents, at least, appreciate the finishing time of 4pm, which suits those who come daily. The absence of Saturday school does not mean a fallow day, however: au contraire, there's a full programme of activities or rehearsals in the morning, with sports fixtures and expeditions in the afternoon. Younger boarders are accommodated in charming Cotlake House, a home for 8-13 year olds with a delightful family feel which crosses the transition between junior and senior parts of Queen's. We liked the handbook greatly, with its dedicated section on cultural differences for overseas boarders, stating an insistence on eating with a knife, fork and spoon, rather than (in some cases) more habitual chopsticks. Importance placed on emotional welfare comes cross very strongly, with regular liaison between staff and parents, particularly crucial when boarders below year 7 are not permitted a mobile or iPad; other methods of communication, such as good old-fashioned email, are made clear and there are communal in-house computers.

We felt some of the senior boarding accommodation was on the cheerless side of acceptable; doubtless legally compliant, but the bare walls and lack of personal touches in some of the dorms was a bit bleak – and a bath list a relic from an earlier age. The continuing refurbishment cannot progress fast enough. That said, the evident warmth of the staff and close friendships between year groups compensate for any dreary living quarters awaiting tarting up. Food generally reckoned to be good: a tasty choice of stew with Yorkshire pudding, cheese and onion pie, breaded chicken or salad bar the day we visited is not, though, perhaps enough to satisfy every palate, witness the group of Asian girls we saw tucking into noodles in one of the house kitchens... The boarding community enjoys eating together in the evenings and the tweaking of boarders' teas with extra carbs and meat to suit sportsmen/women is appreciated.

Background and atmosphere: Originally and fabulously named the West of England Wesleyan Proprietary Grammar School and founded in 1843 by local Methodists dissatisfied by the kind of schooling accessible to nonconformists, Queen's was renamed for Queen Victoria's golden jubilee in 1887. A run of imposing Victorian gothic buildings redolent of the timeline along a stretch of road leading out of Taunton to the village of Trull; modern additions are concentrated behind the original buildings, leaving a view across the extensive sports facilities to the distant Quantocks. A super sixth form centre has been created from a former rather ugly civil service club, now greatly appreciated by its new occupants who enjoy areas for silent study, as well as space to chill, chat and rustle up those staples of British education – toast and coffee. In the view of one parent, it gives students 'independence, self-respect and responsibility'. Sharing the same stretch of road and major facilities as Queen's College, if not its architectural merits, is the junior school.

Founding Methodist values still prop the place up today: tolerance, friendliness and a lack of pretension underpinned by Christian principles and practice define it; a full time chaplain is on the staff. Individuals are valued, quirks and diversity welcomed: 'We looked at several schools,' one mother told us 'but this one had a good feel and was right for both my very different children. My son was initially shy but has really grown into himself'. Other parents praise the school's 'gentle approach' which builds confidence in the diffident, as well as 'the lack of social/wealth/class issues'. Hurrah for that.

Pastoral care, well-being and discipline: Queen's Junior is not, thankfully, an academic proving ground for the next pressured stage, but a place where 'We're really good at the individual – any parent wanting their child's passions, skills and talents unlocked should look no further,' as the head says – and we'd be inclined to agree.

Pastoral care highly rated by students and parents alike, from the tutors to the house staff. Close attention is paid to every child – 'We notice if anyone is off-colour'. No in-school counsellor, as staff feel that students would be 'naturally suspicious of anyone from inside school'; the view from one girl we spoke to was that she wouldn't know who to talk to if she had a problem – 'there are just so many options'. An extensive reward system recognises not only achievement but also students who have triumphed over adversity in some form. Discipline was not a word we heard much – we suspect that it doesn't rear its head that often – but 'to incur the disappointment of the head is a crushing blow,' one mother told us. Prefects have the power to administer 'fatigues' for minor infringements of rules or poor behaviour.

Pupils and parents: Mostly pretty local (Somerset, Devon and Dorset), augmented by a contingent of overseas boarders such as Forces' children and an array of nationalities, with Russian and SE Asian predominating. 'Queen's wouldn't suit very competitive sporty, hearty, Sloaney families,' we were reliably informed. Parents tend to be loyal and to involve themselves in the life of the school, but some think school communications need a kick in the posterior: poor grammar, six copies of the same email just two examples

Entrance: Junior school essentially non-selective at all points of entry, but low-key assessments are carried out in the classroom setting during taster and assessment days. About 60 per cent of senior school entrants come from the junior school without let or hindrance, unless they are trying for a scholarship or have specific learning difficulties. Others arrive from local primaries at 11, yet more from the odd prep school at 13+ and all sit tests in English, maths and verbal reasoning. At sixth form, the bar looks quite low at five GCSEs above a C with 'preferably A*/B' for subjects chosen for A level, but hopefuls are also required to take two papers in their likely A level subject choices. Children from overseas take a paper in English as an additional language.

Exit: Mostly and automatically from the junior to the senior school at the end of year 6; standardised scores in English and maths are passed on for setting purposes. In very rare cases, doubtful candidates are identified in year 5 and gently encouraged (and indeed supported) to look elsewhere.

About 30 leave after GCSE, many to local excellent (and free) sixth form college in Taunton, Richard Huish. Almost all sixth form leavers go on to their chosen degree courses up and down the land – Warwick, Cardiff, Swansea, Bristol and Southampton popular. Some gap years. Notable alumni include Sir Nick Harvey (long-standing MP for N Devon), Lord Widgery (former Lord Chief Justice of England and Wales), and clutch of other luminaries across the professions, armed forces and arts, including a Prime Minister of Newfoundland and Elephant Bill, an army officer known for his work in Burma in World War Two.

Money matters: Fees about 10 per cent lower than comparable schools for UK students, but work out about the same for those from overseas. Lunch is charged separately for day students; learning support, EAL and any kind of extra tuition cost extra. 'Singing lessons are a bit steep,' remarked one parent. Usual range of scholarships on offer, more bountiful than many at a maximum of 25 per cent for a major academic award. Sibling discounts more generous than some we have seen, too.

Remarks: A Taunton institution which distinguishes itself from the local competition by its family feel, yet continues to cut the academic, sporting and artistic mustard year after year, Queen's is a welcoming, inclusive, unpretentious place which could sell itself better. A lick of paint here and there wouldn't go amiss either.

The Queen's School

City Walls Road, Chester CH1 2NN

Pupils: 666 • Ages: 4–19 • Sixth form: 104

Fees: £8,988 – £12,825 pa

Tel: 01244 312078
Email: admissions@thequeensschool.co.uk
Website: www.thequeensschool.co.uk

Head: Since 2010, Mrs Sarah Clark MA (early 40s). Read history and classics at Newnham College, Cambridge. Previously deputy head at Wellingborough School in Northamptonshire. Married to a history lecturer, with two teenage children. Avid supporter of Chelsea FC and loves to cycle, paint and write fiction. Active and breezy, she spoke to us exuberantly about working in single sex education. 'Girls can really be who they want to be here. They don't hold back because they don't feel they need to be cool in the same way they would if there were boys around.' Girls describe her as 'chatty and down to earth,' and say 'she's really in touch with people our age. She even takes part in the sixth form panto.' She is also a bell ringer for the local church.

Head of lower school: Since September 2014, Mrs Rachel Cookson BA (London), PGCE (Bristol), 40s. Taught at state primary schools in Bristol and Macclesfield, then joined the original infant team at The King's School, Macclesfield, helped to set up the new division and stayed for 13 years. Moved to Terra Nova Prep as head of EYFS then head of pre-prep and nursery before joining Queen's. Husband is a company director; two sons.

Academic matters: Two form entry throughout lower school, with 22 per class in infants, rising to 24 in juniors. Gentle, fluid setting from year 3 in maths and English, then more formal setting from year 5. Spanish is taught throughout the school, with French in year 6. Curriculum is thematic in infants, with outdoor space used as much as possible. Specialist teachers for languages, music, PE, art, drama, ICT and ceramics. SEN children given help by three members of staff but head says they need to be 'bright children who can keep the pace.'

An academic school; 52 per cent A*/A grades at A level (82 per cent A*/B) and 66 per cent at GCSE in 2016. Language provision is worth noting. All year 7 girls study Mandarin, with the option of continuing it in year 8 right up to A level if they wish. A trip to China is run every other year, subsidised by the Chinese Government's department of education. Main European language is Spanish, with Latin also taught. School has introduced the Pre-U in art after teachers became frustrated with the subjectivity of examiners at A level. We saw some breathtaking artwork in the bright, airy studios in the school eaves.

Critical thinking in year 12 for everyone. One girl we spoke to felt exam results could feel 'like the be all and end all at times here,' but others felt that the pressure was manageable. Part time SENCo can offer one-to-one support if needed to a broad spectrum of SEN, although girls must be able to keep up with the fast pace of work. Introducing own sixth form baccalaureate – A-levels, additional units of academic study, enrichment activities and the EPQ. Widely stocked library, spanning many rooms, with plenty of workspace, but some girls say its relatively early closing time of 4.15pm can be inconvenient.

Games, options, the arts: New sports pavilion with changing rooms, spectator space and kitchen opened by Olympic bronze medallist gymnast and old girl Beth Tweddle. Girls complain about the lack of sporting space but the school achieves success in both team and individual events. New fitness suite, tennis courts and Astroturf have been resurfaced and the school has recently introduced rowing and sailing.

Music and drama both popular. All year 7 girls encouraged to try different instruments and around two-thirds take individual tuition. Wide range of extracurricular clubs and activities, including podcasting and riding, with young journalists' club, St John Ambulance Badgers (programme for 5 to 10-year-olds), skipping and fencing for lower school.

Background and atmosphere: Founded in 1878 by the Dean of Chester to educate 'the daughters of the middle class.' Moved to its present location (once the site of the city gaol and house of correction) in 1882, a short distance from Chester racecourse. The school has expanded over the years as neighbouring houses and a hotel were bought. However, space is limited and any changes are encumbered by the need for archaeologists to hunt down Roman remains. Sixth form areas could do with a make over.

Lower school is housed in two Victorian buildings with modern extensions. New reception building, Honeybee House, has increased facilities for play and learning. Large grounds enable the school to boast fantastic facilities, including a swimming pool (shared with senior girls), sports fields, netball court, science, art and cookery rooms. Our guides were extremely excited to show us the pet chickens they had incubated themselves. One mum told us: 'My daughter's experience is so broad here, but in a real practical sense. They do everything.'

Pastoral care, well-being and discipline: All new girls teamed with a peer buddy. Older pupils mentor younger ones. Sixth formers have the liberty of being able to pop into town for lunch. Pupils told us they feel comfortable talking to their tutor or head of year about any problems. A number of pupils we spoke to reported incidents of bullying via Facebook, mobiles and emails and some felt that the school didn't do enough to combat this. The school, however, feels it deals with such episodes firmly and this is backed up by the ISI inspection.

Pupils and parents: Mostly white and middle class, with a small percentage of British born minorities. Some foreign families brought to the UK by work. Most pupils live in Chester, but a good bus network brings pupils in from other parts of Cheshire, the Wirral and 20 per cent from North Wales. Notable old girls include Vivienne Faull, the first woman to become Dean of an English cathedral, and Olympic gymnast Beth Tweddle.

Entrance: By informal assessment for entry into reception and formal assessment in English, maths and verbal reasoning for later entry. Head or her deputy visit all prospective reception class parents at home and the school has links with nurseries within a 40 mile radius to raise awareness of the school.

Around 40 per cent of senior school entrants from lower school, the rest from other preps and state primaries. Girls take 11+ exam in English, maths and verbal reasoning. Written reports from current schools are important and all candidates are interviewed.

Exit: No stressful exams for these lower school girls at 11 as they are virtually guaranteed a place at the senior school (any problems flagged up in year 5). A few leave to enter the state grammar school system. Transition is made as seamless as possible by getting the girls used to moving around for lessons, subject specialist teachers and mirroring senior school routines.

In 2016, 18 per cent left after GCSEs. Queen's girls are very successful academically, with most making it to redbrick universities – almost all to first choice. Handful to Oxbridge most years and around 10 per cent to medicine. Durham, Leeds, Newcastle, Manchester and Birmingham very popular. Steady trickle at 16 to sixth form colleges or boarding.

Money matters: Small number of honorary scholarships are awarded to girls who perform exceptionally well in school's entrance exam. One Hastings bursary awarded every year and one Owen Jones bursary, with preference given to freemen of the City of Chester. Aside from this, the school has a small bursary fund, although when asked the head refused to reveal how much this was worth.

Remarks: Elegant campus within the city walls for girls who aspire both academically and personally. Those who might struggle with the high expectations may be happier elsewhere. One girl told us: 'It's not good here to be able to spell anything with your exam results.'

Redmaids' High Junior School

Linked with Redmaids' High School

Grange Court Road, Westbury-on-Trym, Bristol BS9 4DP

Pupils: 148 • Ages: 7–11

Fees: £9,060 pa

Tel: 0117 962 9451
Email: juniors@redmaids.bristol.sch.uk
Website: www.redmaidshigh.co.uk

Headteacher: Since 2015, Mrs Lisa Brown. She has a BSc in psychology from Leicester and a PGCE from Oxford Brookes. She joined the school in 1995 and was previously year 3 class teacher, also overseeing science, DT, pastoral care for new girls, and links with QEH.

R

Entrance: The head selects year 3 pupils by one-to-one assessment and year 5s do a small group assessment. Up to two classes in each year group. Girls come from a wide range of local state and independent schools. Recruitment is influenced by positive word of mouth and assessment begins in the autumn term. Some parents wish they could start girls at year 1 but school suggests that might mean so long in one place that the senior sixth form might suffer – and it's too good to risk.

Exit: Most to senior school. Normally automatic entry (including scholarships via entrance examination) except where head indicates child will not cope. This would be flagged by the start of year 6 and parents given advice about alternatives. Parents of averagely bright girls can be pretty certain they will get in but shouldn't take it for granted. A tiny trickle go to state education or scholarships to other Bristol independent schools, not seriously increased by hard times financially or the current advent of academies and free schools in Bristol.

Remarks: Wonderfully welcoming, homely feel despite impressive facilities. A wet indoor break time buzzed with happy children using every inch of the school for play. Girls are lively and friendly, neatly dressed in red kilts and jerseys with white blouses in winter. Summer uniform is red and white striped dresses with sailor collars and red cardigans.

The curriculum allows for some 'proper' subjects. 'Girls get on with learning rather than spending all their time getting ready to learn as in some state schools' (a parent). 'Homework is about consolidating what's been done not just endless projects' (another parent). Good academic standards with written work on display but plenty of IT, art (smashing little art room staffed from senior school and an after-school club), PE, weekly swimming, with every facility except a pool on hand. All girls now learn French (replacing Mandarin). Entrants are screened for dyslexia and given specialist support on site where necessary.

On same campus as senior school, and using its dining room and sports areas, but still having their own grassy play areas. A Wendy house and play castle, 'both with proper upstairs floors', were donated by parents, as were the raised beds in the 'allotment' with lovely pumpkins ready for Halloween, and professional looking lighting in the new hall. Everything is pristinely well-maintained but there's no restriction on putting a nail in the wall to hold up a circus tent or covering classroom with brightly coloured work. Some classrooms have their own cloakrooms and loos, with décor of swimming fishes imaginatively designed by the class, and some share between two. The drama room is full of Shakespeare – literally a life-size collage figure – and girls get to know his plots early as well as winning drama awards themselves. The music room bursts with keyboards and other instruments including the various parts of a gamelan. Lots of singing and masses of music generally, with orchestra, brass band and choir. Computer technology etc taken for granted.

Wide choice of clubs and activities. Robotics with Lego is popular, as are fencing and caving. You only pay extra for things done by outside organisations, and even the residential week at Skern Lodge outdoor education centre is included in the fees, as is after-school supervision – though breakfast club has to be paid for. Loads of visits including a ski trip with QEH boys.

Parents feel this a friendly, nurturing place able to draw out the best from the most reticent child and harness the most ebullient. Difficulties such as unkindness happen but they are not allowed to grow into problems. Their greatest fear is that success in games may mean that the A team get all the attention, but there's no sign that anyone is left out at present. Not a snooty school where the car you drive matters, but one where parents are prepared to make financial sacrifices to access it for their daughters.

Has recently built two new classrooms. The school has now legally merged with Redland High School, although most Redland High girls will be taught on their current site during 2016/17. The school will not be on one site until September 2017.

Redmaids' High School

Linked with Redmaids' High Junior School

Westbury Road, Westbury-on-Trym, Bristol BS9 3AW

Pupils: 470 girls, all day • Ages: 11–18 • Sixth form: 125

Fees: £13,320 pa

Tel: 01179 622641
Email: admissions@redmaids.bristol.sch.uk
Website: www.redmaidshigh.co.uk

Headmistress: Since 2001, Mrs Isabel Tobias BA PGCE (50s). Read English at New Hall, Cambridge and started work in publishing. Began teaching at Henrietta Barnett, London from where she moved to Royal High School, Bath as head of English then deputy head before taking up headship at Red Maids'. Keen to be forward-looking and modernise, she nevertheless really listens to her girls and respects their sense of tradition. Kept the school's original red capes and bonnets for a coveted few to wear in the annual founder's day procession through Bristol.

Originally head of the Red Maids' School, she maintained the headship when it merged with Redland High in 2016 to form Redmaids' High.

Her own children being largely off her hands, she has a bit more time to enjoy Bristol's theatre and do more walking and reading. Deeply involved in all that goes on in school, she is obviously proud of the girls' achievements in all fields.

Terrific new sixth form house has materialised under her management as well as numerous exciting projects, such as a joint observation of cosmic rays with Bristol Uni using equipment on the school roof, funded jointly by school and parents, with year 12 physicists processing and interpreting data. She was also responsible for introducing the IB, which now has a take up of about a quarter of sixth formers. South west chair of the Girls' Schools Association and an ISI inspector.

Academic matters: The only Bristol school offering A levels and IB; some A level girls also enter for the Extended Project Qualification with distinguished results. Choice of languages includes French, German, Spanish and Russian with everyone doing at least one to GCSE. Psychology, English and history consistently popular A level subjects alongside maths, biology and chemistry, with a proportion of girls moving on to medical school every year. Latin but no Greek. All girls take either three separate sciences or do the dual award science plus additional science.

Some pretty impressive GCSE results recently with 70 per cent A*/A in 2016. English, maths and science all done as IGSCEs 'because they are more academically demanding', with English thus avoiding the recent mess up on grades and doing exceptionally well into the bargain. Splitting the sixth form between IB and A level means groups are really too small to identify trends, but results have gone steadily upwards over the last few years. Average 37 points in IB in 2016; 37 per cent A*/A grades at A level.

Choices at both are wide enough for most needs with lots of creative stuff. Shiny new food technology kitchen. Resistant materials (the tough stereotypically male bit of technology, harder for schools to do as it's expensive) is incorporated into textiles, which may look more girly but is certainly not sidelined. Surprisingly for a 'not religious' school, a goodish take up of philosophy and ethics. Spirituality and 'thoughtfulness' definitely encouraged. Even its small group of IB students earn it a 'top IB school' status.

A small proportion of SEN but the school is 'accessible' and has one partially sighted pupil, supplying every required facility, and the few dyslexics are well and considerately catered for. Almost no need for EAL but there is a Talented and Gifted programme targeted to stretch the brightest. The weekly sixth form Academic Symposium is part of this, presented alternately by girls and academic outsiders on topics such as stem cell issues. Similar initiatives in place for younger groups too.

Games, options, the arts: Enormous sports hall with dance studio and fitness centre upstairs for 'unsporty' sixth formers as well as acres of Astroturf. Endless teams for hockey, netball, etc plus football and some high flying tennis stars. Options include fencing, basketball, and gymnastics. Staff are very hot on encouraging girls to join local sports clubs as well. Strong music department includes iMacs (Sibelius and recently Logik, ie music writing and multitrack recording programmes) for composition. Over half the girls learn a musical instrument (including singing at a very high standard with choir, chamber choir and barber shop group). Three orchestras, ensembles etc and frequent musical productions on stage, though girls looked a little surprised when asked about pop groups. Absolutely fabulous art department, and that's saying something in Bristol, where the competition at school level is strong. Some delectable fashion design too; dresses made from sweet wrappers are popular, say sweet-toothed girls.

It was interesting to see several girls sporting neat black moustaches in preparation for the evening performance of Twelfth Night at the new Bristol Tobacco Factory Theatre. Big adaptable performance space in the 300 building (named for school's 300th birthday) with an energetic American head of drama who is galvanizing the school's already enthusiastic performances. Whizzy new performing arts centre under construction. Quite a high proportion of male staff, giving plenty of good role models. A well-tried programme of annual concerts, joint productions with QEH and an annual whole school festival alternating between drama and dance allows girls at all stages to perform at progressive levels without missing out on games.

Working library stocked with books, rather than computers and gadgets (plentiful DVDs too) with some working space for after-school homework, supervised at all times. Masses of clubs – a whole wall full of club posters in the dining room and trips of every sort both educational (exchanges or China with QEH boys) and philanthropic, and some impressive international links: Emma Willard School in USA and Pymble Ladies' College in Melbourne, Australia. They really did build a small school in Cambodia and start a charity for Moldovan children. They do pretty well in all the school speaking, debating and the like competitions and have all sorts of whizzy projects such as a link with local GKN Aerospace where there's an ex-Red Maid 'young engineering ambassador'. Career advice includes the gamut of conferences and top local speakers from all disciplines. Special conference on medical and engineering careers open to all SW schools now and annual event.

Background and atmosphere: The original 'Red Maids' benefited in1634 from the generosity of Bristol mayor and MP, John Whitson, who having been widowed thee times and lost a daughter from each marriage, died, leaving no heirs but bequeathed £90 per year to provide a dwelling house for 'one grave, painful woman and modest woman' and 'forty poor women children' who would be taught to support themselves. As, amongst other things, he imported red dye, they were to 'go apparelled in red cloth.' It is the oldest surviving girls' school in the country and moved from inner Bristol at beginning of the 20th century to its present 12 acre site. Wide lawns and green Astroturf shaded by a winding avenue of lime trees are edged by an array of purpose-built school buildings centring on the pillared mansion bought with the site. An impressive array including the huge 1930s '300' building housing much of the teaching areas, the 1950s Denmark Hall and airy 2011 sixth form centre complete with teaching and recreation areas, cafeteria, 'film theatre', as the girls call a resources room, and careers library. Sixth formers have special electronic passes so it really is their exclusive domain. School recently completed £2 million development, including new library and expanded dining room, with more in the pipeline. WW2 air raid shelter is hidden under a bank in the grounds, complete with anti-Nazi graffiti – a popular attraction for local primary schools.

While valuing its purely altruistic beginnings, the school is forward thinking in all respects and firmly 'not' rather than 'non'-denominational with assemblies covering all kinds of issues, though the head is supportive of individual religious observance.

Girls were quite enthusiastic about the food: much healthier than it used to be and things like Caesar salad made specially for you as well as masses of pasta etc. Breakfast club runs from 7.45am.

The merger between the Red Maids' School and Redland High, to form Redmaids' High School, has been completed, though the schools remain on their own sites during 2016/17. Redmaids' High will operate from the current Redmaids' site from September 2017.

Pastoral care, well-being and discipline: Houses are named after John Whitson's merchant ships but main pastoral care is through form teachers who meet girls twice daily. Excellent 'big girl/little girl' buddying system – Mrs Tobias was persuaded to let them keep the name – for new arrivals. 'Big girls' meet their new girls on induction day and write to them in the summer holidays as well as shepherding them through their first term. It's all part of the culture of respect for each other's feelings that she sees as instrumental with dealing with bullying. 'Of course girls are sometimes unkind and sometimes upset', but staff talk to all concerned as long as they know about it and it's tackled along with other life skills in PHSE. The girls we met say bullying doesn't happen. Head of year 7 oversees transition from wide range of state and independent feeder schools; pastoral evenings in autumn term for years 7, 8, 9 and 10. The senior tutor is in charge of pastoral for whole senior school including sixth form. Plenty of chances to 'develop leadership potential' as girls can be appointed to positions in houses, school clubs and tutor groups as well as head girls, head almoners, games captains and house captains. Sanctions include detentions or at worst suspension or expulsion, but the school favours a positive behaviour code and encouragement. A clear list of policies and appeals procedure on the website means it's easy to know where you are with things.

Pupils and parents: Friendly, open girls from a wide social and ethnic background, though the majority look distinctly English. Though sounding quite sophisticated, and some very academic, girls on the whole look natural and not artificially grown up.

Girls look neat, wear simple red jumpers over a white blouse with red skirts for ages 11-16, not expensive though there were some crumpled pleats and current jumper goes out of shape easily, according to one parent. Sensibly interpreted dress code for sixth formers. Parental discussion group meets regularly with head. Former pupils include novelists Susan Lewis and Kate Sedley, TV anthropologist and presenter of Coast Dr Alice Roberts, Helen Marsden, winner of a WISE (Women into Science and Engineering) excellence award, and Daily Express journalist Tina Moran.

Entrance: Year 7 intake has increased recently to around 75 per annum. Candidates (including those at junior school) sit entrance exams in January in English, maths, verbal and non-verbal reasoning. Brief interview with headmistress for all including short presentation on subject of girls' choosing. For sixth form entry, minimum six grade B GCSEs with A*/Bs in chosen IB or A level subjects plus interview with director of sixth form.

Exit: Some 20 per cent leaves after year 11 for colleges or co-ed or maintained sixth forms, but majority stay despite the advent of academies and free schools in Bristol. All sixth formers go to uni (Nottingham, Exeter, Leeds and Southampton popular); two Oxbridge places in 2016, five medics.

Money matters: One of the very few girls' school with a good scholarship and bursary programme, thanks to the founder; all development is paid for, not funded by loans, so it's really financially stable. Two major awards of up to 100 per cent, plus two music and one sports scholarship awarded at 11+. Entrance scholarships at year 9 (13+) and sixth form (year 12) for external candidates. A number of bursaries available.

Remarks: Far from a stuffy school, despite its historical cachet and strong academic record. 'Staff care hugely' and 'girls are genuinely proud of their school,' say parents. It feels like a school on the up. Head definitely has her eye on the future of her girls. We will watch with interest how the newly merged school develops.

Rendcomb College

Rendcomb, Cirencester, Gloucestershire GL7 7HA

Pupils: 503; 107 boarders • Ages: 2–18 • Sixth form: 78

Fees: Day £7,005 – £21,990; Boarding £20,850 – £30,540 pa

Tel: 01285 831213
Email: admissions@rendcombcollege.org.uk
Website: www.rendcombcollege.org.uk

Headmaster: Since 2015, Robert Jones, previously deputy head at Shiplake College. Educated at Swansea (economics), Worcester (PGCE) and Buckingham (MBA); has also taught economics and business at Canford, Clifton College, King's Worcester and Dauntsey's, coached rugby and rowing and run day and boarding houses. While at Shiplake, he undertook successful major reorganisations of the timetable, pastoral care and teaching systems – so unlikely to rest on his laurels here. Two children.

Head of juniors: Since 2015, Victoria Beevers, previously deputy head at Dean Close Prep. She has also taught at Cheltenham College Prep and Thomas's. Married to Al, she has one daughter and is a keen runner and cyclist.

Academic matters: Specialist teaching for music, PE and languages from reception with more subject teachers from year 3 onwards. Small classes (between 10-15) mean children receive individual attention and can learn at their own pace. 'Teachers can set challenges for the most able while ensuring nobody gets left behind,' a parent told us. All screened for dyslexia; SEN support described as 'on the ball'.

Pretty sound academics and the trend is upwards: in 2016, nearly half of both GCSE and A level grades A*/A. English, science (double and single), maths and further maths strongest contenders at both levels with history (surprisingly), French and music least popular A level options.

Classes of maximum 18 and smaller in the run up to GCSEs mean lots of individual attention. Good range of A level options including psychology, economics and business studies inevitably means that there could be just one or two in some of these classes. Compulsory study skills sessions recently introduced. Whether tutorial sized classes are a bijou bonus or a bit of a one man band depends greatly on student teacher relationships. Sixth formers generally seem to enjoy the small groups and getting to know teachers well in a more reciprocal environment. School's emphasis on personal development and independent learning goes up another gear after GCSEs, when in addition to more freedoms and responsibilities, pupils are encouraged to take the Extended Project Qualification and participate in a varied enrichment programme.

Perhaps those language and literature results are helped along by the inspiring view over the Churn Valley enjoyed by the English department classrooms. Teaching we observed was an energetic mixture of old school dry wit, lively discussion and subtle encouragement – an admirable combination only found in places where teachers know their pupils really well. Science, maths and ICT departments are housed in the former stables across the (very quiet) lane from the main school site, so commuting between lessons can take time and pupils sometimes 'get a bit soggy' when it rains. Economics gets 'half a stable' – sixth formers think it should 'join up with business studies and become a full size department.'

School takes children with dyslexia, dyspraxia, mild Asperger's and SpLDs. Learning support and EAL sessions arranged around pupils' individual lesson plans, and parents describe the former as 'astonishing' and 'inspirational' (not to mention 'very well organised, switched on and professional'). Another parent praised the way the school accommodates the 'eccentric' child saying that the same amount of effort goes into supporting the highly academic as it does those with SEN.

Rendcomb is highly regarded for its inclusive approach, but such a reputation can sometimes work against a school. It was clear to us (our opinion confirmed by parents and university destinations) that the very bright are equally well served – particularly if the competitive cut and thrust of a large, highly academic school would be likely to stifle, rather than bring out, their best. School seems to have a real knack for building pupils' confidence; one parent told us that she had been 'astonished' by her child's academic progress, 'She used to struggle, now she's flying'.

Games, options, the arts: With just under a third of pupils achieving A*/A for art at GCSE, it's surprising that no more than one or two continue with the subject at A level. Facilities in the purpose built 1960s block are ample with large, light studios and there's a real creative buzz, enhanced by the sound of music drifting down from upstairs practice rooms. Pupil and professional art is on display including, when we visited, a large ceramic hare at the main entrance to the school; pupils have also exhibited at Calcot Manor and The Paragon Gallery in Cheltenham. The beauty of the Gloucestershire countryside, not to mention the school's architectural features such as arts and crafts style stained glass panels and ornate plasterwork, would inspire anyone. Well, nearly anyone. As we cooed over this view or that cornice our sixth form guide admitted that he'd been there since he was 4 and had 'stopped noticing', but knew he'd look back and realise how lucky he'd been.

All junior school children encouraged to try out instruments in taster lessons, there's a junior orchestra and choir and pupils can take ballet and LAMDA classes. Otters (infants) and juniors perform in their own, separate, concerts and plays – that way there's room for everyone to have a moment in the spotlight. Masses of music in the senior school with orchestral and singing groups to suit all inclinations and abilities and excellent GCSE results although, as is often the case, there's minimal take up at A level. The same goes for drama and theatre studies, but even if drama's not first choice as an A level, Rendcomb fosters some dynamic talent, with a student group recently taking a play written and directed by themselves to Edinburgh, and a new performing arts centre. Newly introduced music technology A level (with all the kit) may change this; the proposed performing arts centre certainly will. Current venue, the Dulverton Hall, was originally the house's orangery – hence the cast iron pillars. It's had a rough life, having previously served as a gym – presumably after the glass had been removed – and is crying out for restoration. Beautiful reading room also used for concerts etc.

Sport is inclusive with junior school pupils benefiting not only from the heated outdoor pool and senior school pitches but also Rendcomb's possibly unique claim is that every pupil will at some stage represent the school at sport. The prevailing attitude to team sport here is very different: the fact that a place in the first team may be open to what in other places would be a third team talent delights pupils and parents alike. 'My daughter would never have got a look in elsewhere', one mother told us, adding that the more able at sport develop leadership skills early on because they 'get to motivate and bring on others in their team'. Facilities include plenty of pitches, tennis and squash courts, a climbing wall, golf course and an open-air pool. There's a packed fixture list and they 'play good schools and learn, whether they win or lose.' Quite a few pupils are county and national level players and school teams have recently competed and won in lacrosse and shooting competitions. All this notwithstanding, Rendcomb is probably not going to be first choice for the highly competitive, sports-mad child. Other sporting options include riding (and polo), mountain biking and even fly-fishing on the River Churn that runs through the grounds. The delightful director of sport (who would certainly have inspired this PE-dodging writer) is keen to make even more use of the college's 230 acres and get students to see fitness as a habit for life. To this end he tries to ensure that all the sixth formers keep doing 'something' in the sporting line – a noble aim and one in which we're sure he'll succeed.

Generous range of co-curricular options including D of E. If you go down to the woods today you shouldn't be surprised to find science, art, creative writing and even drama going on. The forest school is the real thing, a bosky paradise complete with 'eco bog' and log cabin. At least once a week, come snow, rain or whatever else the west country weather delivers, all the juniors don wellies and head for the woods. Pupils make shelters, search for slugs, construct bird feeders, survey plants and animals and generally get messy. They experience the changing seasons, pond dipping for tadpoles in the spring, blackberrying in autumn. Not surprisingly this and other endeavours have led to the school achieving a coveted international eco-school green flag award. Outdoor education extends, via bushcraft, all the way to sixth form leadership challenges. School 'sends a powerful message encouraging kids to grab every opportunity,' a parent told us.

Plenty of trips, big and small, to Bristol Zoo, Roman Bath and Chedworth, the Cheltenham Festival, London and, closer to home, the village post office and church. Coastal expeditions end with rounders on the beach at Weston-super-Mare and ice-creams for everyone. Can we come?

Boarding: Boarding was described to us as 'laid back' and we rather agree. Rules is rules, of course – we're not talking about lax discipline – but sometimes school boarding accommodation can be a little sterile. Here it was good to see such characterful and welcoming surroundings in the junior boys' house, The Old Rectory. With its worn and polished flagstone floors, Delft tiled fireplace and jumble of colourful beanbags in the cinema room, it was more home than house. Boys get to name their own dorms – currently Harry Potter characters – and bedside tables were littered with books, mugs and evidence of snack attacks. House parents have decorated the walls with huge photo collages. Day pupils are assigned to a boarding house and have book lockers there.

Sixth formers live in Park House – girls' and boys' wings separated by a common room and kitchen. Park House was built in the 1970s and, predictably, is not a thing of beauty, but study bedrooms are serviceable and the atmosphere convivial and relaxed. All sixth form students get a taste of independent living with their stay in 'the flat', in the village. Groups of four (students don't get to choose) are given housekeeping money and live there from Monday to Friday. They have lunch at school but must manage the rest – buying provisions from the village shop and arranging domestic chores. The results are variable – sometimes it runs like clockwork, sometimes mummies deliver food parcels and help clean up at the end.

Sensible rules about phones and technology in general and the school internet is turned off at 11pm – not popular with older students burning the candle to finish essays. Mobile phone reception was described by one parent as 'dire' (we agree). Discipline, when necessary, is firm but fair; small numbers and strong sense of community mean that unkindness, unhappiness, bullying etc quickly spotted and dealt with.

Background and atmosphere: Rendcomb was founded in 1920 by Noel Wills (of the philanthropist tobacco family) as an idealistic experiment in the 'power of opportunity and environment'. Wills believed that 'the true aristocracy among men is in reality simply an aristocracy of brains and character.' Initially the school provided 40 local boys with a free boarding education and preparation for entry to public schools. Wills was inspired by the ideas of educationalist J H Simpson, persuading him to leave his post at Rugby and become founding head of Rendcomb College. Under Simpson, Rendcomb started taking boys from age 11 and preparing them for university. Contrary to the Spartan regime that then prevailed in most public schools, Simpson and Wills shared the Platonic view that students flourish in beautiful surroundings and should be educated together regardless of class differences. Revolutionary stuff.

While the school has inevitably evolved over time, its founder's influence remains. For instance, there are no house competitions, thus enabling the whole school community to work together rather than dividing tribally. The emphasis on learning to lead, rather than win at all costs, was also well understood by the pupils to whom we spoke. As Noel Wills wrote of his school in The English Review in 1924, 'Work and games are abundantly worthwhile. Neither is the former rewarded by prizes, nor the latter by colours.'

Pretty much equidistant between Cheltenham and Cirencester, Rendcomb is in Cotswolds profond. This is Laurie Lee country – steep wooded valleys, ancient hedgerows, lush pasture and winding streams. School and village are as one – the post office (school played a key role in saving it from closure) is also the tuck shop, there's a surgery and even though the pretty church can't quite accommodate the whole school (carol service is held in Cirencester), it's still used for eg junior school assemblies and monthly boarders' services.

It may look more like a country house hotel than a school from the outside but on the inside, though clean, Rendcomb is well worn. Heating and maintaining a building like this with its huge windows and stone corridors must be a bursar's worst nightmare. The Wills family remain as trustees and, with the board of governors, are still very much involved in the school's educational and charitable ventures. Parents generally like the fact that it's 'not flash', and one commented, 'It's not about the latest facilities, it's about giving children an appetite for learning.'

The junior school, while attached to main school building, occupies somewhat more utilitarian surroundings of former senior day house. Large ground floor nursery classrooms, well resourced and full of colourful displays, lead into secure outdoor space. 'It's all about free flow and adventure play,' we were told as girls in stripy red and white summer dresses and boys in red polo shirts and sensible navy tracksuit bottoms buzzed about happily. 'Otters' (or pupils in reception and years 1 and 2) are equally busy and creative – their work, along with that of the older juniors, is beautifully displayed everywhere.

Rendcomb's visitors are (or perhaps, were) met, somewhat broodingly, by a huge marble statue of King Saul that 'came with the house'. We got the impression that the poor old chap wasn't entirely popular, and he certainly seemed out of kilter with the school's welcoming atmosphere. We're not sure whether King Saul was beloved of old Rendcombians, but it seems that his days as gatekeeper are numbered. School was rather coy about his fate, but we gathered that he was off to a new home in the USA, having boosted the performing arts centre funds. Let's hope he cheers up.

Pastoral care, well-being and discipline: School says there's 'no hierarchy' at Rendcomb, and along with the school council is keen to see even more collaboration between year groups. A sixth former told us, 'It's a small community but there are lots of characters here and we all grow up together. It's good for team spirit.' Parents hugely appreciative of the individual care their children have received; one mother with two very different children said that 'each got exactly what they needed'. The UK guardian of an international student who had previously disliked school told us that he had 'blossomed' and now 'loved boarding'. She also praised the excellent communication from teachers and house parents.

Pupils and parents: Most families are from within 20 minutes' drive – school is equidistant from Cirencester and Cheltenham although majority of families are from villages in between. Some also from Swindon plus a handful of US families from nearby airbase. County set still feature but parents say it's a broad social mix – gingered up by increasing number of ex-London families. Active and engaged parents' association runs socials and fundraisers, 'really friendly and welcoming' said one new member. Quite a few had chosen Rendcomb despite their children having gained places at local grammars, 'We wanted a school where the focus wasn't so narrow,' said one. About 65 per cent of boarders from abroad, a considered mix of European and those from further afield. 'It gives the students a great network after they leave.'

Entrance: Into nursery at rising 3 from local pre-schools. Shadow/taster day for youngest. Assessments in English, maths and VRQ plus report from current school for 7+, with a new scholarship available. At age 11 majority come up from junior school plus others from local primaries; influx from preps such as Airthrie, Beaudesert, Hatherop, Pinewood and Prior Park at age 13. Candidates for sixth form need minimum of GCSE grade B in subjects to be studied, plus reference and interview. School takes pupils with SEN who can cope with the curriculum; all are assessed individually. Nature of site means it's unlikely to be suitable for pupils with more than minor physical disabilities.

Exit: Majority (80+ per cent) of juniors progress on to the senior school at 11 via the entrance examination; others to eg Pate's Grammar, Marling School, Cotswold School and Stroud High.

Degree subjects as diverse as one would expect, from politics and international relations to sports and exercise science to speech and language therapy. London colleges, Bristol, Edinburgh, Exeter and Birmingham currently popular. One to Oxbridge and one medic in 2016; also one off to Keiser University in Florida with a joint academic (political science) and lacrosse scholarship.

Money matters: Very good value, especially boarding, compared to nearby competition. Music lessons, SEN and EAL support are extra. Academic, choral, sport, music and art scholarships on offer. Noel Wills full bursary awarded annually to one local state primary pupil.

Remarks: Rendcomb remains true to its founder's gently progressive vision. This is a genuinely civilised and humane school where chalk and cheese flourish alike in one of Gloucestershire's happiest valleys.

RGS Worcester

Upper Tything, Worcester WR1 1HP

Pupils: 765 • Ages: 11–18 • Sixth form: 210

Fees: £11,952 pa

Tel: 01905 613391
Email: office@rgsw.org.uk
Website: www.rgsw.org.uk

Headmaster: Since 2014, John Pitt, previously second master at Whitgift. History degree and PGCE from Cambridge. Began teaching at Whitgift, rising to head of sixth form; moved to Portsmouth Grammar as academic deputy head; returned to Whitgift in 2007. Married to Anna, also a teacher; they have three young children. Particular interest in sport, especially sailing, rugby, hockey and cricket.

Academic matters: Doing well alongside other local schools – King's Worcester, Malvern College, Bromsgrove School etc. Fully co-ed following its merger with Alice Ottley in 2007 – numbers of boys and girls evening up. Academically very sound across the board, with 57 per cent A*/A grades at GCSE in 2016, and at A level, 42 per cent A*/A grades (73 per cent A*/B). About 70 per cent of pupils take triple award science at GCSE. Has a particular reputation for its science, engineering/design and maths teaching, and though quite boy heavy in these subjects, the girls also make a good showing.

Lots of Arkwright scholarships, three different DT subjects taught at GCSE, and strong in art and textiles as well, giving a creative edge to technical subjects. Impressive labs and well-lit, well-equipped classrooms. School has embraced digital technology – good use of electronic whiteboards and iPads play an important role, enabling easier access to learning resources; now offers computing GCSE (A level option to follow in 2016).

R

Economics, politics and business studies are popular choices at A level too. All study a modern language in year 7 and take on a second, plus Latin or classics, in year 8. All take a modern language at GCSE (French, German or Spanish), though not especially popular at A level – a fair number take French but few go on to study German or Spanish.

Attainment and attitude are graded every half term, with pupils given specific objectives. Most GCSE classes are small – under 20. Private reading is timetabled for lower school pupils and takes place in a well-resourced and attractive library, with lots of guidance and monitoring of who is reading what. Well-equipped language lab with stacks of Macs, which doubles as an ICT suite.

Staff are very enthusiastic about the school, positive about the pupils and parents, and say that the school management is also very supportive in promoting the personal and professional development of its teaching body.

Games, options, the arts: Very busy! Lots of sport (rugby, soccer and cricket for boys, netball for girls, rowing, hockey, athletics for both). Rugby and cricket are regarded as particularly strong and netball has been very successful recently. Rowing is increasingly successful with a number of RGS rowers attending GB trials. Regular Saturday fixtures, though no formal Saturday school. Fitness suite, two sports halls, all weather pitch and lots of space on playing fields at RGS The Grange just north of the City Centre. CCF and Duke of Edinburgh awards are popular with a number of gold awards each year.

Masses of clubs (literature, debating, model making, dance, chess, choirs etc) and lots of school trips – staff say they have trouble fitting them all in. Lots of music – 14 ensembles including three jazz bands, a gospel choir, junior and senior choirs, chamber choir etc. About 15 peripatetic instrumental teachers, 10 practice rooms. About a third of pupils are taught an instrument through school. The principal teaching areas for music are being improved, with soundproof recording areas and new lighting and seating in the pipeline. Nice theatre with full lighting box – and drama is quite popular at GCSE. Lots of pupils also take Lamda exams and school plays attract large numbers of eager participants.

Parents and staff love the range of activities but also say this can be very demanding – the phrase 'trying to fit a boarding school offering into a day school timetable' has been used. Newish head of co-curricular activities aims to co-ordinate and manage this aspect of school life.

Background and atmosphere: A very ancient school, dating back to the seventh century. At the northern end of central Worcester, and benefitting from very large playing fields at its junior school (RGS The Grange, which is just outside the city). Mostly Georgian and Victorian buildings, well maintained and with a nice balance between preserving the character of the architecture and functioning fully in a 21st century market. The library is a good example of this. Generally well-maintained and pleasant – there are enough open spaces and gardens to give a sense of light and movement and there are pleasing displays of the pupils' work throughout the school.

Facilities are very good – from the DT workshops to the sports fields – and there is no sense at all of resting on laurels. The management of the school is being reorganised to put all teaching on a faculty-based foundation, a move designed to improve coherence and depth across the board, and there is a sense both of excitement and determination amongst staff to keep pushing at the edges of what can be achieved.

Parents describe it as 'a school that wants to win' and say their children 'can't wait to get here'. All seem to feel that the merger with Alice Ottley has been a happy marriage which has produced a school offering more than the sum of its parts. There is an atmosphere of steady attention and diligence about the place, and staff are fully engaged with what seem to be quite radical curricular and management changes. One of a number of strong schools in Worcester- a very positive place with a great deal to recommend it.

R

Pastoral care, well-being and discipline: A strong ethos of 'right, wrong and good manners'. Pastoral support is provided both by prefects and by form tutors and year heads. There is a strong 'family feel' and pupils emphasise that pastoral support is everyone's responsibility. Staff are 'always there if you need help'. The school's anti-bullying policy has been reviewed recently and is strong. Parents say, 'the school was already getting it right'. A CEOPS programme on internet use is offered annually to parents and pupils. Very few disciplinary glitches in terms of drugs or alcohol. Students, parents and staff speak highly of levels of care and speed of response in the event of any issues arising.

Pupils and parents: Retains something of its original grammar school flavour. Parents like the friendliness, open door feel and academic breadth of the school. Many pupils from the north of Worcestershire – Kidderminster, Droitwich, Birmingham. Parents engaged in commerce, medicine, law etc. A lot of 'ordinary people who work hard to pay the fees'. Wide catchment and just a few minutes walk from the station at Worcester Foregate – transport links to Malvern, Evesham, Tenbury Wells, Bromsgrove etc. Pupils seem calm, purposeful, polite and friendly.

Entrance: In year 7 about 50-60 per cent come from the school's junior feeders – RGS The Grange and RGS Springfield. Others from Abberley Hall, Winterfold House, Dodderhill and other local prep schools. Some others join at 13 via CE, and others again post-GCSE (entrance requirement of six Bs at GCSE for sixth form). A handful from feeder schools are 'counselled out' in years 5 and 6. Of external candidates at 11, around 75 per cent offered a place.

Exit: Some 30 per cent leave after GCSEs. Of those, most will go to local sixth form colleges. Post sixth form the great majority go on to university. Two to Oxbridge in 2016; three medics and one vet. Lots to Russell Group; Nottingham, Cardiff, Imperial, Oxford Brookes and Southampton are popular. Lots of engineers off to Bath, and Loughborough. The popularity of engineering, product design and technology-based degree subjects reflects the school's strength in DT and sciences, but others go on to study music, art etc. Many alumni also go into business, one currently managing the Poole Lifeboat service – quite a few out of the normal boxes.

Money matters: Some scholarships at 11+,13+ and 16+ worth up to 33 per cent of fees – awarded for academics, sport, music and art. Bursaries of up to 100 per cent. Some packages of support are also put together with organisations such as The Ogden Trust and The Rank Foundation. Keen to improve access for children from poorer backgrounds and not to leave them feeling marginalised or 'sweaty palmed'.

Remarks: A friendly, grounded school with its sights set high. Suitable both for the very bright and those whose potential is yet to be unleashed. Strong academics across the board and managed with a real vision for excellence. Good value for money.

Richard Huish College

South Road, Taunton, Somerset TA1 3DZ

Pupils: 1,786 • Ages: 16–99 • Sixth form: 1786

Tel: 01823 320 800
Email: enquiries@richuish.ac.uk
Website: www.richuish.ac.uk

Principal: Since 2013, John Abbott, originally from Blackburn, studied sport and exercise science at Manchester Metropolitan University, then completed a masters in sports psychology and exercise physiology. Previously assistant principal, John joined RHC in 2003 as faculty director for maths and sciences, before being promoted in 2009. Prior to that, he was section leader at Bridgwater College. The father of two young girls, John is a keen sportsman, particularly passionate about squash and basketball. He ensures all 1,500+ students know him, through tutoring and recording video messages for college induction tutorials and other messages. Plus his office is in a prominent position at the front of the college, and he does his fair share of bus duty. One parent told us, 'He is a calm, inspirational leader who wants the best for every student in his care. John, and all the teachers we met, are committed teachers with the best interests of their students at heart'.

The college strategic vision is 'to provide exceptional education and training through the delivery of a holistic academic and vocational curriculum'. It can deliver this because its offering differs from an average school sixth form. John told us there are three reasons for this. Firstly, the college has an 'adult approach.' Secondly, students that were 'top dog' at school find themselves amongst other 'top dogs'. This in turn creates a collective energy and competitiveness, and raises the aspirations of all students – they thrive on it and achieve so much more. Thirdly, there is greater freedom of choice at the college. Due to the high numbers, they can offer a wider range of courses and provide greater flexibility around subject and enrichment choices.

Academic matters: In 2016, 54 per cent A*-B grades at A level (24 per cent A*/A). One of the best sixth form colleges in England, in the top 10 for A level results for the last eight years. Consistently good results at BTec level too, 67 per cent achieving three distinction* grades in 2016. RHC is a Beacon college designated 'outstanding' by Ofsted.

Over 35 subjects offered at A level. As well as traditional school subjects, the college offers archaeology, critical thinking, environmental studies, law and philosophy. There are BTecs in applied science, business, media, health and social care, popular music, music production, IT and sport. Most popular courses are psychology, biology and maths. Best value-added results are in science and maths. Statistics recently revealed by the A Level Performance System (ALPS) show that Huish ranks in the top 100 out of 1,164 for the value it adds to students. Value added is measured by comparing students' predicted achievement based on their GCSE results with their actual achievement at A level.

Students enrol on a study programme which consists of a core of three A Levels, an extended diploma or a combination of A Levels and subsidiary diploma. Any combination is possible; the college has the resources to be able to offer this without exception. As long as the students achieve the grades for entry, all are accepted. The college is fully inclusive and adapts facilities if necessary. The campus is accessible for wheelchair users, and there are lifts and ramps in all buildings. If needed, the college can provide specialist one-to-one study support, specialist equipment and software, support during exams and links to external specialists. Praise from students themselves includes, from a wheelchair user with chronic pain: 'I am very grateful for the compromise [a reduction in timetabled lessons due to hospitalisation]...it is going to mean a significant increase in my attendance.' From a student with sensory integration dysfunction: 'all my exam scribes have been excellent.' From a student with visual impairment: 'I am thoroughly enjoying it, all the subjects have been able to adapt resources and I feel that I am keeping pace with the class.'

Games, options, the arts: Sport is huge here. Student participation is nearly double the national average compared to other colleges, and many students compete at a national level in basketball, volleyball, hockey, squash, cross-country, trampolining, swimming, table tennis and badminton. Hockey men's and women's 1st teams are reigning South West League Champions. Again, thanks to the high volumes of students and great facilities, the college regularly has fixtures for 1st, 2nd and 3rd teams for most sports, meaning that all abilities can get involved. There is also the Active Huish scheme, part of the enrichment activities, which encourages students to take part in a more relaxed atmosphere, and can be anything from football to ultimate frisbee or dodgeball. Academies for cricket, tennis, football, golf and recently rugby union are offered. One student recently chose to come to the college solely because of the excellent reputation of the cricket academy, even though it meant a daily three-hour commute.

New two-storey state-of-the-art sports hall, including a full sized multi sports arena, a viewing gallery, changing rooms, a gym and a classroom, next to the sports fields. Most sports activities take place on campus, but some facilities are used at Taunton Vale Sports Club, The Wyvern Sports Club and Kings College.

Along with sport, music is hugely popular. There are concerts and gigs including performances from the choirs, orchestra, jazz bands, big bands, and ensembles. To date there are 35 pop bands, and they all do gigs. The teachers at the college set up tours for them in local pubs and venues; this is a big hit with the budding musicians, their friends, and of course the parents and teachers. They have a big following and annually the college hires a venue for two nights to showcase their greatest hits. The college even has links with the organisers of the John Peel stage at Glastonbury, giving bands the chance to perform, and media students the chance to work on the filming with the BBC crew. On campus there's a recording studio, four rehearsal rooms, and Apple Macs galore in the music technology room. The standards here are very high, and just this year two guitarists have been accepted at the Royal Northern College of Music – a highly competitive university where only musicians who have passed grade 8 music exams are considered for interview. Another success story is the student who wrote and conducted his own rock opera featuring a full orchestra, choir and soloists.

The drama department puts on three big productions a year. When we were there, we saw Sweeney Todd in rehearsal in both the dance and drama studios. There must have been at least 50 students involved in just that one part.

The art department is split into three large studios. Wide range of creative media including painting, drawing, mixed media, installation, print making, 3D, textile arts and contextual studies. There are also facilities for dyeing and constructed textiles, a dedicated print room and a large scale printing press. There is a weekly life drawing class too. Good photography facilities including a studio and a dark room. For Apple Mac enthusiasts, the top software is available in the media and film studies departments. Recently students have produced a film called Hitting the Road, aimed at giving bikers practical advice to stay safe. It is so good that Somerset Road Safety has commissioned it.

All enrichment activities take place during the school day as most students are restricted by bus timetables. For this reason, the college day finishes at 4.35pm. There are subject enrichment activities such as politics, debating and public speaking. There's Active Huish for sports, a wide range of musical activities, the Duke of Edinburgh Award Scheme, BELA, and drama and dance productions. Plus trips – volunteering in Sri Lanka, trips to Iceland, ski and snowboarding in France and archaeology trips to Rome.

Background and atmosphere: Originally founded as a grammar school for boys in the 18th century by Richard Huish, college has just celebrated its 400th birthday. It became a sixth form college in 1993 and since then has grown from 660 full-time students to nearly 2,000. It has expanded again to include Huish Business School for adults (adult students make up less than five per cent of the college's full-time equivalent students), International Huish, and even a driving school.

The 20-acre campus, in the south of Taunton, is predominantly sports fields. The college itself is alleged to be on the site of an old Arboretum and each building has been named after trees – Redwood, Willow, Juniper, Hawthorn, Cedar, Maple and Beech. Most buildings are new and they have all been designed with the same footprint. Each department has its own study centre, which is more informal than the learning centre (library); students can work in groups or chat while working. Learning resource centre at the heart of the campus. There are two silent zones, PCs, and a careers area with two staff on hand. Over the last three years, there has been an impressive programme of improvement and new building. The Juniper building is a purpose-built centre for a range of media studies, including state-of-the-art editing suites. The newish Cedar Building accommodates a range of teaching in 10 classrooms, and all laboratory facilities have been upgraded to meet the growing number of students wishing to study science. Finally, there is the new two-storey café, complete with Costa restaurant, at the entrance to the college. The next project will be a new space for art and music.

The college has long-been Wifi enabled. There is a remote desktop service available for all students and staff, plus a laptop loan system. Students can borrow laptops for free all day. Simply scan the lockers with an ID card, take a laptop, return when finished. No printers on campus; all have been replaced by multi-function devices; more convenient, greener and cheaper. Students can log on to any device and print their work. No regular bins on campus either: after rigorous campaigning by the environmental group, they have all been replaced by more eco-friendly recycling bins.

Pastoral care, well-being and discipline: There are three clear and simple expectations of students at Huish: be on time, do the work given (if you can't, ask for help), and be nice. No strict policies or statutory rules – one of the differences between a sixth form college and a school. One family told us, 'We did consider other colleges, but chose Richard Huish mainly due to the respect the teachers gave the young people and how they treated them as adults.' They went onto to say, 'At this stage parents obviously need to be involved/kept in touch but I found that trusting [my son] and his teachers to work together as a team resolved most issues.'

All students have their own tutor and all tutorials are one-to-one. There are group tutorials initially when the term starts, but these are the exception. Each tutor then assesses each student individually and sets out a plan based on individual needs. For example, a tutor may decide to see one pupil weekly and another less frequently. Students are encouraged to speak to their tutors and ask questions whenever needed. They are also made aware, through tutorials and signposting throughout the college, of the help and counselling on offer at the school, should they need it.

We heard from parents that could not speak highly enough of 'the support and caring nature of the staff at the college.' One parent whose child had had some difficulties said the 'tutor is amazing and has been a real rock for our [child] through a very difficult time, going over and above to [help].' Another family told us that when their child had to extend their studies due to unforeseen medical issues, the college was more than accommodating and supportive. The college provides 'fantastic out of lesson support,' they said.

Pupils and parents: This is a college for the students. This is very apparent on the website: student case studies and videos, student quotes and stories; it is aimed at students, not parents. Of course parents are involved, but it is obvious they are not the main customer. Parents we spoke to were happy with this approach. 'Communication has been fantastic and staff are very approachable,' said one. Another confirmed this, saying, 'Richard Huish newsletters kept coming, informing us of the college's activities, and termly reports were very informative, covering the areas which parents like to know: attendance and level of work quality. Contact details were available if we needed to contact the college and when we used them we had prompt, honest responses.'

The students we saw looked presentable and happy. Green hair after Halloween is standard. There's bound to be a real mix of people here due to high volumes, and individuality is encouraged. The college isn't producing clones as some schools tend to do; they are encouraging the students to develop with confidence, and providing them with the best tools and environment to do so. A parent said 'He had loads of potential, but was headstrong. We hoped Richard Huish would channel all that enthusiasm in a positive way and help him to mature and fulfil his potential; they did exactly that. I feel this was achieved by working with him almost as mentors, not teachers, and by treating him as an adult. I think if he had stayed at a school sixth form he would still have felt like a school boy, not a young adult.' Another parent gave a similar view, '[...] has benefited more than he would at a school sixth form. We can see he has become more independent and self-driven and studies hard to a high standard, which has all been encouraged by the college.'

Entrance: Requires five GCSEs at C grade or above including maths and English language. Offers a 12-month GCSE resit programme for those that may have just missed a grade – around 60-65 students are currently on this. Students apply from all over Somerset, and some from as far as Devon and Dorset. The college produces handy information leaflets for each course so students can easily find out the essentials. There is a flexible approach to study; students are able to take combinations of A levels and BTecs, and the college invests time into making sure they choose the right courses. There are taster sessions for prospective students, then a taster day in the summer term. There is also a two-week period at the beginning of term when changes can be made. Good parent feedback all round on this. 'Starting at college is always daunting, however Richard Huish made it a controllable process, offering flexibility, points of contact for concerns with a sensible amount of time allowed for it. Plus I feel it was the start of a process where students took responsibility for their future and started to stand on their own feet by seeking answers to any concerns.'

Exit: Around 75 per cent go onto university, with a third gaining Russell Group places. The most consistently popular subjects are psychology and law, with nursing, sport, history and English always in the top 10. In 2016, nine Oxbridge offers, one student off to the US on a scholarship and another heading for the Royal Welsh College of Music.

Former pupils include science fiction writer and inventor Arthur C Clarke, a former pupil of Huish's Grammar School, Andrew Castle, former British number one tennis player and television presenter, William Gibson, professor of history, Rebecca Huxtable, former co-presenter on Radio 1, Keith Parsons, cricketer and Andy Robinson, former head coach of the England national rugby union team.

Money matters: The college can help with travel costs, and college discretionary bursaries are available. Eligibility depends on household income or benefits received. There is also a Care to Learn scheme to help young parents, and a 19+ means-tested bursary offered. The Heathcoat Trust Bursary is for students from the partner schools of Uffculme, Cullompton and Tiverton High Schools who apply to university; it is worth £3,000 over three years.

Remarks: The results from this college are impressive year on year. The facilities are enough to make any teenager (or young adult) want to learn. The opportunities are endless due to economies of scale. College life here is far more exciting than at many a school sixth form, and the adult approach to learning is a positive step towards university and work for many. Some parents may find it hard to take that leap of faith, but from everything we saw and heard, we think it's worth it.

Rougemont School

Llantarnam Hall, Malpas Road, Newport NP20 6QB

Pupils: 579 • Ages: 3–18 • Sixth form: 108

Fees: £6,999 – £12,696 pa

Tel: 01633 820800
Email: registrar@rsch.co.uk
Website: www.rougemontschool.co.uk

Head: Since 2014, Mr Robert Carnevale. Read applied physics at Bath, specialising in nuclear energy. PGCE from Cardiff and MA in education management. Joined Rougemont as head of physics in 1998; soon asked to take over sixth form pastoral role; progressed to director of studies then deputy head (academic). Ten years' experience as a school inspector for ISI and Estyn (in Wales); an examiner and principal moderator in A level physics.

Academic matters: Not an academic hothouse by any means, but the school produces good results for its intake. Value-added scores are high, and exam results very respectable: 58 per cent of GCSEs at A*/A in 2016 and 43 per cent at A level (71 per cent A*/B). Refreshing (relative) lack of concern for league tables means that pupils are encouraged to have a go at subjects they are interested in, even if they are unlikely to get the top grades.

Science is a strong point, and sciences are taught separately from year 7. French is the main foreign language, while German is being phased out and replaced by Spanish as an optional second language from year 9. All but a handful take a language GCSE. French and maths are setted from part-way through year 7, English from year 9. Most take nine or 10 GCSEs. Latin reintroduced for all in year 7 (optional from year 9).

Maths and science are the biggest focus at A level – around half to two-thirds take maths, and a third take physics. Mainly traditional subjects on offer – economics rather than business studies, for example, though the latter is available at GCSE – but a few takers for media, sports and theatre studies. Art is a growing strength – the displays of coursework during our visit were outstanding.

Wide range of gifted provision, from fiction writing and code breaking in the juniors to maths challenges, reading groups and extended projects in engineering, media and music for seniors. Open university courses are a possibility for sixth formers. The main SEN provision is for dyslexia – a team of four specialist staff teaches juniors and seniors individually or in pairs. No current demand for EAL support, since a nearby Korean-owned plant shut down, but can be called on if necessary.

Games, options, the arts: Junior-level sports are very successful, particularly hockey and rugby, with lots of local and regional trophies in the cabinet. At upper school levels, the school's teams are developing well. Some strong individual players, including county, national and international level team members, but finding enough good players to make up a winning rugby or netball team in a smallish co-ed school can be hard. At least the on-site sports facilities make it easy to get plenty of practice. Regular international sports tours and other overseas trips (skiing and so on).

Drama popular as an activity, less so as an exam subject. Lots of in-house performances, but also some for wider public, such as an annual link with Gwent police to put on an anti-drugs play, Wings to Fly, with audiences drawn from other local schools. Still lacks a really good large performance space – next on the development list. Full range of music going on, with two orchestras (training and main), brass, wind and jazz bands, and school choirs. Full school concerts twice a year, as well as house music and smaller shows.

Young Engineers scheme, for sixth formers studying physics, gives an opportunity to work with local companies on real-life problems, and compete with other schools across Wales – has won prizes most years. An Exxon Mobil subsidiary in Newport offers work experience to one budding chemical engineer every year. Also young enterprise scheme, Duke of Edinburgh's award, public speaking, chess and so on – 'We try to find something for everyone'.

Background and atmosphere: Has evolved from a small junior school focused on prepping for local grammar schools to an all-through independent. The original owners sold up in the 1970s, the first A levels were taken in the 1980s and it moved to its present site in 1995. Currently running at well below maximum capacity of around 750 in the whole school.

The site is huge and green, with playgrounds, gardens, sports fields, and even woodland areas to learn and play in. Juniors look sweet in their red-trimmed grey blazers, seniors more businesslike in their black uniforms. The low-slung, purpose-built blocks (apart from the Victorian mansion which now houses the juniors) could be mistaken for a state school, but the academic gown hanging in the head's study is a reminder that this has been an HMC school since 2000 – gowns are worn for formal assemblies and major school events. New science and technology building; sixth formers have refurbished block with new café.

Almost the only clue that the school is in Wales is the names of the houses: Caradog, Dyfrig and Gwynog, named after Welsh saints. The Welsh language is not formally taught, but some staff are fluent, a Welsh club and the chance to participate in regional Eisteddfods.

Pastoral care, well-being and discipline: Pupils seem relaxed with teachers, confident with visitors, and at home in their environment. They like the heavy teacher involvement in the PTA and in extracurricular activities and trips, which give them a chance to get to know teachers on a more personal level. Also good for inter-year friendships and support.

The school's policy on welcoming children who have been bullied elsewhere means that any hint of bullying is not tolerated. In the younger years, problems are dealt with in circle time; later on, always someone, whether a staff member or another pupil, to talk to informally if you have a problem, the children report. Rarely a need to escalate to formal measures.

Expulsions are extremely rare, and discipline issues tend to be minor. Two pupils suspended (briefly) recently: one for a driving offence outside school and the other for bringing a penknife to school – with no ill-intent, but rules are rules.

Pupils and parents: No one would call this a posh school – 'We are not – and do not want to be – socially exclusive'. The typical parent would be a doctor or local small-business owner, but you find all sorts here.

Broad intake geographically as well as socially. The only independent secondary in Newport, but also serves the surrounding area: school minibuses bring pupils in from a 25-mile radius, with an extra coach from Chepstow. Fewer come from the direction of Cardiff, as more independent competition over there.

The main aim of the PTA (recently renamed from the 'parents' association' to make a point of teacher involvement) is to have fun and socialise, rather than raise funds. The school does have ambitious plans for a new dining/performance block as the final element in the development of the new site, but the £2m projected budget means it is still a few years off and may require outside financing.

Entrance: Junior school entry virtually non-selective, and most continue on to the senior school. Around a third are new in year 7, mostly from local state primaries, and small numbers join in years 8 and 9. Senior school selective, but not excessively so – 'We can offer something to a wide range of abilities'. About five to 10 newcomers in the sixth form each year. Potential newbies are encouraged to come and spend a day – or even two or three – in the school to get a feel for it before making up their minds.

Progress from juniors to seniors is almost automatic – no need to sit a test unless trying for a scholarship – but the school reserves the right (very rarely exercised, though) to advise parents their children are not suited to the upper school. Outside candidates take a test for entry to year 7 and up.

An average of five Bs at GCSE required to join the sixth form for both internal and external entrants, though most have much better results under their belts.

Exit: About 65 per cent move through to sixth form. Lots stay in Wales for university – the financial incentives to do so are strong – but of those who venture further afield, popular destinations include Bristol UWE, Bath, Portsmouth and Exeter. Largest numbers go into engineering and medicine/biomedicine (two medics in 2016). 'One or two a year' who don't go on to university.

Money matters: A newish school so no endowment fund to fall back on, but roughly five per cent of fees are allocated to bursaries and further funds to scholarships. Bursaries for deserving newcomers, including some who have struggled with bullying or other issues at previous schools, or existing pupils who might otherwise have to leave the school in exam years due to financial difficulties. Sixth form bursaries depend on academic ability as well as financial need.

Remarks: Relaxed and friendly school with an inclusive approach, aiming to give everyone a chance – or even a second chance – to do well at something. Academic standards are high, but not the be-all and end-all.

R

Royal High School, Bath

Lansdown Road, Bath, Somerset BA1 5SZ

Pupils: 761; 140 boarders • Ages: 3–18 (boarding from year 5) • Sixth form: 155

Fees: Day £9,249 – £13,116; Boarding £24,135 – £28,374 pa

Tel: 01225 313877
Email: royalhigh@rhsb.gdst.net
Website: www.royalhighbath.gdst.net

Head: Since 2015, Mrs Jo Duncan MA, previously head of Princess Helena College. Educated in N Ireland; studied English/theology at St Andrews and then PGCE at Homerton College, Cambridge. Taught RS at The Latymer, then moved to Benenden, where alongside teaching RS was also deputy housemistress, part of weekend activities team and award officer for D of E. After seven years, appointed head of Princess Helena. Is an ISI boarding inspector. Loves travel and has organised and led trips to eg India, China, Belarus and Israel. Married to Murray, a lawyer, and they have two children.

Head of junior school: Since 2013, Miss Heidi Hughes BSc PGCE MA. Previously deputy head of Royal Russell Junior School, Surrey. Prior to this she was a member of management teams at British schools in Singapore and the Philippines. A strong advocate of linking learning in and beyond the classroom, she welcomes parental involvement. Outside school, her interests are sport, travel and family. She often volunteers at local sporting events (including the London 2012 Olympics).

Academic matters: Praise abounds for the teachers: 'enthusiastic, committed, gentle, nurturing, yet they challenge the girls', and keep them tested and stretched. Small classes must help. Any suggestion of hothousing strenuously rejected, however. Collaboration is the name of the game here: maths surgeries (for parents) very well attended, and any hint of SEN identified and discussed with parents early on. Languages particularly vibrant, with French from nursery to year 6, Spanish in years 3 and 4, Mandarin for year 5 and Latin in year 6, with emphasis on oral communication led by native speakers where possible – we were reluctant to leave the Mandarin class we visited. The curriculum is broad and not exam-led – the GDST has abandoned year 6 Sats, although other initiatives from the state sector such as Sing-Up, Healthy Schools and Artsmark (gold, in RHS Junior's case) sought and achieved.

In 2016, 76 per cent A*/A grades at GCSE and 52 per cent A*/A at A level. Pupils taking IB achieved average of 37 points. Wide choice of subjects plus IB must make the 35 per cent exodus of girls after GCSE particularly galling, but we imagine that's not really about options. Relatively small classes where active participation is encouraged makes for a happy flock. A level classes run for sole takers, on occasion.

Achievements recognised both inside and outside GDST, with successes in Maths Challenges/Olympiad, Nuffield Bursaries, Nomura Scholarship and Young Science Writer prize recently awarded; one parent, however, had reservations about the quality of advice offered for Oxbridge during UCAS. The school's recent ISI report judged its academic offering to be 'excellent' and its value-added scores are high. That same report also sounded a cautionary note that GCSE pupils should be allowed to lift their nose from the grindstone from time to time..

SEN gets a thumbs-up from parents. Early identification of problems in the junior school means the senior school is well-equipped to deal with their own new intake. Parents cite a supportive culture with no stigma and teachers who employ a variety of techniques to help, not just with the three Rs but also with organisation, presentation and strategies for revision. 'Concentration on their performance skills builds their confidence enormously,' remarked one father, a leadership expert. Extra help is paid for.

Games, options, the arts: Art, music, dance and drama all impress in the junior school, particularly a recent production of Alice in Wonderland.

Enough going on in school time to satisfy further-flung girls bound by school bus departure times. Lots on offer from Dance Storm to D of E. All the games and sports you would expect are played on the school's own facilities: Astro, tennis courts and sports hall on campus, larger grass pitches and athletics a short drive to more level but windswept terrain on top of Lansdown. Swimming in the outdoor pool in summer or at the university across the city – the facilities and coaching are worth the drive. Hockey and netball particularly strong and the school puts on a good showing locally and nationally. One girl, whose sister left in search of springier pastures after GCSE, said she couldn't possibly think of leaving because of the sport. Sporting interests which fall outside the curriculum well catered for too, eg judo, fencing and aerobics, and individual talents encouraged, not just amongst the pupils: a teacher is a serious Olympic prospect in archery. A full voluntary activity programme is offered on Saturday mornings, but members of school teams are expected to commit at least some of their weekend to their sport – maybe going on tour to Barbados compensates. It is, however, quite possible to blag your way out of sport completely in the sixth form, it seems.

Wonderful art emanates from the fantastic new art school, where light airy studios with panoramic views give students every opportunity not only to create masterpieces but to exhibit them as well. All you could wish for, including ceramics, textiles, sculpture and photography. RHS has long been known for its music and drama; these remain strengths, though one parent reckons that music has perhaps lost a little of its sheen in an attempt to 'become more democratic', as she put it; 10 ensembles seem to us to be a sign of a healthy musical life and a recent choral scholarship to Cambridge, soloists in Bath Abbey and the current leader of the county orchestra suggest that music produces the goods. Associated Board results confirm this, with most entrants getting merits or distinctions.

The jewel in the crown is drama: loads of plaudits from the Mid Somerset Festival and LAMDA. Single sex schools do of course demand versatility on the stage from their pupils, though boys are imported from local boys' comp, Beechen Cliff, to form Bathos (!) theatre troupe, and no poverty of dramatic ambition: recent productions include The Crucible and musicals and Gilbert and Sullivan are staged to general acclaim. Strong support given to girls keen on the tech side too with the opening of an new media centre offering activities from sound recording to green screen CGI filming. The centre, which is now known as The Sophie Cameron Performing Arts Centre, named in honour of a former head girl, hosts key cultural events throughout the year.

Boarding: Two or three bedded rooms for 9-16 year olds are on the upper floors of the main school building (just a few year 5 and 6 boarders); some sixth formers have study bedrooms in Level 6 in the main house, others in Gloucester House, a purpose-built sixth form building nearby. Recent refurbishment of common rooms and parts of boarding houses. Usual weekend offerings include eg ice skating, shopping, theatre trips, bowling.

Background and atmosphere: Victorian stone monolith stands back from the road up a drive through an off-puttingly narrow archway. First impressions of austerity are dispelled by the warmth and courtesy of staff and pupils and by more natural light at the back of the main building – the library is lovely, though other parts could use a lick of paint here and there. It all feels rather traditional, despite mod cons, and the girls fit in. Edgy it isn't, despite valiant new initiatives such as the sixth form college (with its brief introduction of boys) and IB. The Royal High has blazed something of a trail within GDST as its only school to offer boarding (a legacy from the amalgamation between Bath High and the Royal School in 1998). The school draws a distinction between the experience of the first five senior years and the last two, by housing the sixth form college in a separate block with teaching space for small groups, space to chill for larger ones and a café, in a genuine attempt to address the gap between school and university. Each sixth former is issued with a bright red laptop, all wired up to the school intranet and ready to go, a move universally welcomed, coming as it does with full technical support. Further down the school, it feels reassuring – a place where girls can be girls and pursue trad 'male' subjects without distraction or fear of censure: the shortish school day (finishing at 4pm but with an option to stay till 6pm) and proximity to town mean plenty of opportunity to socialise after school.

Junior school has moved into a stunning listed building, Cranwell House, on a much larger site with better access than its previous home, and ecologically diverse landscaped grounds.

Parents report a happy school with an inclusive culture, where results aren't everything, and achievement of all kinds is celebrated. Social awareness is also inculcated and a sense of the world beyond school, with a good current affairs programme, Model UN and a partnership with a Kenyan school, as well as the 20 or so foreign pupils. Most look nowhere else.

Pastoral care, well-being and discipline: Sense of community in junior school built on close links with parents and the fact that the whole school lunches together, eating proper food with knives and forks; manners, poise and common sense mark out Royal High girls, according to one happy parent, tired of being mown down by boisterous counterparts in other schools. Quaint formalities too, eg where girls are dismissed with a handshake from teacher at the end of the day. Everyone has a 'book friend', where the littlies and year 6s share books and read to each other – our guide's book friend came and hugged her in the playground – says it all, really.

Girls are well looked after and look after each other. The detailed PHSE programme ensures they are as savvy as the school can make them about the pitfalls and downsides of teenage life – and sanctions for those who transgress. Anyone caught smoking, drinking or with drugs can expect the heave-ho or suspension for shop-lifting. Sixth formers lead discussions about aspects of contemporary life with the younger ones; sessions have included celebrity culture and Fairtrade. Conduct within school, and occasionally beyond, is governed by a system of merits, commendations and debits – the emphasis, according to the school, very much on praise rather than blame, although we picked up the odd gripe from parents about heavy-handedness over petty things. Support structures and expertise in the problems besetting teenage girls, eg eating disorders, definitely in place, though.

Pupils and parents: 'Hard to generalise,' but school says RHS girls share the values of open-mindedness, respect, courtesy and a sense of their own individuality. We found them polite, articulate – and perhaps a touch inhibited by the presence of a senior teacher over lunch, for reasons of safeguarding, note. A good cross-section of parents – most professions and some media types represented, plus humbler occupations, and of course the 20 or so overseas boarders. Not a snobby school – girls come from anything up to 20 miles away by bus or train; the school runs a minibus from the station and, as well as its own, two buses run in collaboration with King Edward's across the city.

Famous old girls include Mary Berry, Baroness Elspeth Howe and the last head of Queen Anne's Caversham.

Entrance: Into junior school by assessment and interview with the head. Nursery school pupils are expected to transfer to the junior school and have first choice of available places. Seventy-five girls arrive in year 7, having passed examinations in English, maths and verbal reasoning the previous January, plus interviews with the head and year 7 co-ordinator. Academic taster days for year 6 prospective applicants. The main route in is from the junior school, but girls come from local independents and primaries too across Wiltshire, South Gloucestershire, Somerset and Dorset as well as from overseas. More will arrive in year 9 after entrance exams in English, maths and science and the offer of scholarships at this entry level, then another intake in lower sixth, where six GCSEs, with A grades for A level subjects, are required. Transition arrangements come in for particular praise at year 7.

Exit: Virtually all (95 per cent) ofjuniors go on to the senior school by way of the transfer exam in year 6 – 'a rite of passage,' says the head, who will have suggested, very nicely and well in advance, that doubtful runners look elsewhere. For everyone else, the exam is used for setting and awarding scholarships. A few to King Edward School (co-ed independent) or Hayesfield (state).

Some 35 per cent leave after GCSEs to go to local co-eds, state and independent; others join. After A levels or IB, pretty well everyone makes their first choice destinations, embracing a range of courses from the vocational to the theoretical. Bristol, Durham, Exeter, Edinburgh and London universities currently the most popular destinations. Several to Oxbridge most years (three in 2016), despite some caution on the school's part about putting pupils forward. Gap years the exception rather than the norm. GDST girls become members of GDST Alumnae, the Trust-wide network for communication and support amongst former pupils, which offers the inside track on various universities and professions.

Money matters: Remarkably good value for money – unusually, exam fees, books and insurance are included, though most extras and lunch are paid separately. Forces' offspring get a 10 per cent discount. Boarding fees are significantly cheaper than any boarding establishment we know of – how do they do it? Thrift extends to sensible and well priced uniform. Scholarships and bursaries offered for academics, art, music, drama and sport; bursaries for bright girls whose parents could not otherwise afford it also available, as is short term assistance for temporary hardship cases.

Remarks: Consistently good girls' day school, as befits the GDST, with some interesting departures – boarding, a collegiate sixth form offering A levels and the IB. A safe bet which should fulfil almost any girl, but not perhaps for the rebel.

R

The Ryleys School

Ryleys Lane, Alderley Edge, Cheshire SK9 7UY

Pupils: 220: 140 boys, 80 girls • Ages: 21m–11

Fees: £9,741 – £10,959 pa

Tel: 01625 583241
Email: info@theryleys.com
Website: www.theryleys.com

Headteacher: Since 2014, Mrs Claire Hamilton BSc PGCE (early 40s). Attended Stockport Grammar School, degree in applied biology at Hull University, taught at Kimbolton Prep. Seventeen years' service here – deputy, then acting head. Teaches science to year 3. Seen as very approachable, relaxed, natural, friendly manner with the children, realistic, good sense of humour, very experienced in advising parents on secondary schools. Committed to an inclusive approach; introducing greater use of technology and tracking data. 'Mrs Hamilton has ignited something in the staff...teamwork is phenomenal now' – member of staff. 'Lovely, brilliant, very organised and hands on with the children.' 'She's given the school stability..she cares about all the pupils' – parents. Enjoys fitness and cookery.

Entrance: Pre-school children observed interacting with others at a taster day – looking for social development and readiness to learn. Non-selective – maths and English assessments for older children used as baseline tests.

Internal scholarships awarded in years 4 and 5 for academics, arts and sport, on the basis of written tests or teacher assessment plus interview with head (10 per cent reduction of school fees).

Exit: Children get into schools of their choice, including high powered selectives such as Manchester Grammar, Manchester High, Withington Girls, Cheadle Hulme, King's School, Altrincham Grammar, Stockport Grammar, St Ambrose College.

Remarks: Situated in Cheshire on southern outskirts of Greater Manchester. Established in 1877 as a day school for sons of local families; co-ed since 2009. Ratio of boys to girls evening up as increasing numbers of girls feed through. Early 1990s main red-brick building has several staircases and narrow corridors (some tired-looking walls in need of painting), various extensions. Attractive, very blue, open air swimming pool, climbing wall, pleasant grounds (but only tarmaced play areas – no big field), smallish library.

Average class size 15 (20 max); flexible setting for maths. No Sats (hurrah!) – goes beyond national curriculum. Specialist teaching from pre-school in French, music, dance, PE, plus art from reception; for all subjects from year 3, including design and technology, ICT. Spanish in years 5 and 6, Latin as after-school club. No particular gender gap – some very impressive writing on display by girls and boys. Rigorous monitoring of progress in English and maths. Success in national maths challenges; participation in international interactive quiz. Two IT suites of 20 computers, class sets of iPads. Inclusive approach to displayed work. 'The teachers have a great relationship with the children – there's a genuine desire for them to be happy and do well' (parent).

Scholars enjoy free Saturday enrichment trips and activities, eg a tour of the BBC at Media City, workshops at the Royal Exchange and Barclays Bank, performing on the set of The Little

Shop of Horrors, a trip to Jodrell Bank; in class and after-school extension opportunities for the very able.

Very strong on EAL and special needs support (free unless one-to-one teaching assistant required) for a broad range of physical, learning, communication and behavioural needs; would take any child that could access the curriculum, apart from those with severe emotional/behavioural/social needs, but nature of site problematic for a very physically disabled child. New SENCo brimming with energy and commitment. Close collaboration with parents – 'She doesn't see SEN children as a problem but as a challenge – she gets it,' said the parent of a child whose needs were identified very quickly in the nursery and who was helped with the assessment process. Has has seen her child flourish and catch up with peers.

Two Astros, one not on site; all the trad sports plus triathlon, success at regional level – inclusive approach to teams. Several sports scholarships to senior independent schools; ski trips and sports tours.

Music flourishes – various ensembles, lots of public performances (national concerts with French choirs), broad range of styles. Much drama – specialist teacher from year 3; visits from writers and theatre companies; high quality productions – Jonah and the Whale, The Wizard of Oz, Bugsy Malone, The Sound of Music. LAMDA and ESB public speaking/interview skills awards; participation in local festivals. Interesting art (teacher is an artist) using different materials – scholarships to various boarding schools, prizes in local and regional competitions. Well equipped DT room (dedicated, long-standing teacher) – high quality work and materials. Year 6's kit car, the Ryleys Rocket, built from recycled plastic, came third when raced – girls as involved as boys. Lavish menu of academic, sporting and creative clubs, including street dance, Spanish, sailing and coding. Outdoor pursuits and modern language residentials.

Very strong on pastoral care ('fantastic..the form tutors are very supportive..you get a very quick response to emails and feel well looked after' – parent) and rewards – house cup comes with huge, child-friendly cake decorated with icing in house colour. Three grades of badge for good manners. Children we spoke to definite that bullying not a problem, but they all knew who they could turn for help. Year 6 buddy year 3s, assisting them with the extra expectations of the prep section.

Three religious assemblies a week, head boy and girl, prefects, library monitors, plus school council. Very trad uniform – girls in grey pinnies/skirts; boys in grey shorts/trousers; black blazers with yellow stripes – resembling inflated wasps – that have to be worn almost all the time ('unless there's a heatwave') which reduces their life, commented a parent.

Mainly local professional and business families, wide range of nationalities and faiths. Very good communication with appreciative parents – weekly newsletters, helpful handbooks, coffee mornings, focus groups. 'The teacher's door is always open.. they work on problems before they grow..everyone works as a team'. Friendly PTA has very active social committee.

Open, confident, happy children – 'There aren't lots of tests.. you do fun things too.. teachers are helpful – they don't get angry', tolerant and considerate. No food grumbles (reasonable amount of choice).

Pre-school (nursery) from 21 months highly praised in ISI report – cheerful, busy atmosphere, bright, spacious classrooms with attractive displays; parents very happy – 'The staff are amazing..very enthusiastic about developing the school and helping parents'. Well-equipped playground. Good choice of clubs including sewing, Spanish, newspaper and computer programming. Rainbow awards for a delightful range of attributes such as 'enthusiastic writing', 'being a super role model to her peers', 'sharing his magnets with his friends'.

'Getting back to where it was after a dip,' under the leadership of a very capable, well-liked head. Blends the traditional – old fashioned jars for marbles representing house points, school caps reminiscent of Just William, pudding basin hats for the girls, honours boards bearing the names of fallen World War 1 old boys – with the 21st century – a new board for head girls, coding and an alphabet soup of tracking systems. Offers a secure, small scale, nurturing experience combined with high academic achievement.

St Ambrose College

Hale Road, Halebarns, Altrincham, Cheshire WA15 0HE

Pupils: 998 • Ages: 11–18 • Sixth form: 218 • RC

Tel: 01619 802711
Email: office@st-ambrosecollege.org.uk
Website: www.st-ambrosecollege.org.uk

Principal: Since 2015, James Keulemans BSc NPQH, previously head of Our Lady's RC High. Geography/biology degree from Coventry and PGCE, geography from Sheffield.

Academic matters: Selective on intake, boys are able, highly motivated and supported by parents with high aspirations for their sons. Consistently high-achieving school, value-added especially good. In 2016, 56 per cent A*/A grades at GCSE and 69 per cent A*-B grades at A level, with 34 per cent of grades A*/A.

Decidedly and unashamedly traditional and academic; no vocational subjects here and no media studies. All boys take a minimum of nine GCSEs at the end of the fifth year. Boy-friendly infrastructure and teaching styles. High in value-added across the board, academically and socially. Way ahead of most schools in use of technology; scrapped whiteboards in favour of graphics tablets and podcasting. Teachers offer online support as needed after hours.

Multi-media language labs for French, Spanish and Latin, Italian Society also available. Enriching language trips overseas – Le Mans 24 hour race track especially popular. Overseas work experience also on offer for sixth formers. New building widening curriculum opportunities for expanding technology, drama and cooking.

Distance learning with universities an option to challenge the most able, online tutorials changing, revitalising and transferring knowledge through a wide range of opportunities. Very small number of statemented boys, one member of staff assigned to support SEN.

2016 GCSE Results;

Games, options, the arts: 'Competitive, testosterone-fuelled house events,' say the boys, whilst adding the party line that 'it's not the winning but the taking part that counts'. Lots of sport and big rivalry in rugby, cricket and athletics. Athletics under-15 side are Trafford champions; under-15 rugby side reached quarter finals of Daily Mail Vase; under-16s county rugby union winners; two pupils playing rugby for national under-16 and under-18 sides. Wow-factor facilities in the new building include superb sports hall and pool and there is no shortage of outdoor space. Soccer, cross-country, basketball, table tennis, badminton also available. Sports teams tour widely – Barbados, Vancouver, South Africa, Italy, Holland, Australia, South America, New Zealand, Fiji, Hong Kong and USA.

Music suite and well-stocked library; the school is generously resourced, hard to think of something they don't have. Plenty of extracurricular activities on offer; D of E strong. Boys are actively involved in the liturgical life of the school: assemblies, prayer groups and holy mass regularly celebrated.

Background and atmosphere: Christian Brothers' Roman Catholic boys' grammar school with selective intake. Founded by the De La Salle Brothers in 1940; after evacuating Guernsey, taken over by the Irish Christian Brothers in 1946; Blessed Edmund Ignatius Rice still at its core. Awarded maths and computing specialist college status; rated outstanding by both Ofsted and the Catholic Diocese of Shrewsbury in recent inspections. Long-standing traditions and high aspirations, both academically and spiritually, all housed in newly state-of-the-art facilities.

No official catchment area; boys come from a 30 mile radius and full range of social spread of intake, right across the board, and proudly so. Boys from Moss Side rub shoulders with sons of multi-millionaires, but nobody really cares too much. Much opportunity for reflection away from the college: annual trip to sister college in Sierre Leone, much hard work and fundraising involved, including work in slums and on rubbish tips – this is no holiday; first year boys enjoy a retreat at St Cassians during their first few weeks; older students head to Myddleton Grange and provide regular assistance at Cornerstone, the Christian Brothers' project to help disadvantaged and vulnerable homeless people. Sixth formers join Old Boys on visits to Lourdes, a profoundly deep and lasting experience for all involved. Looking after the margins of society deemed important: strong links with Revive, a refuge for asylum seekers in Salford – 'in some cases silence is dangerous', Saint Ambrose. Very clear on the reason why: 'it's not about you feeling better, it's about someone else feeling better because of what you have done,' says the head. And they live out that message here.

Four college houses led by student house captains.

Pastoral care, well-being and discipline: Consciences worked on rather than harsh restrictions imposed, underpinned by Christian values. Emphasis on self-discipline and taking responsibility for your own actions. Rewards are age-appropriate and poor behaviour is quickly checked and fairly and duly punished. House points can be won for academic excellence and any activity which can be defined as service.

School community takes its model from the family, and rewards and disciplines accordingly, 'fairly' say the boys – 'behave yourself, work hard and wear your uniform, everything else is negotiable'. An all-boys' school that speaks comfortably about the importance of valuing people and relationships is a breath of fresh air – here are articulate young men who genuinely value being 'a part of something' – they live it, they breathe it, they feel it, happy to quote rugby statistics one minute and the words of St Ambrose the next. They smile when referring to 'their Holy Trinity' – food/rugby/chapel (though not necessarily in that order).

S

Pupils and parents: Parents and boys are from a wide range of backgrounds, professional/local business/self-starters/trades. Current parents appreciate 'the high morale and Catholic standards which it upholds and works into daily activities' and the fact that the 'sporting facilities are second to none and allow boys to excel in their chosen sporting activity'. The 'caring and compassionate approach' is also of high value to boys and their parents as delivered by 'highly qualified, committed, caring teachers and staff, as well as high standards of discipline'.

The new building took longer than expected to complete, and whilst some parents bemoaned that fact as their sons were at the tail end of their academic career now, they were immensely proud of the school's advancement from tired old premises, and know that their boys have 'had a great time and done extremely well' regardless. 'Classrooms do not maketh the man' apparently – though the stunning new buildings have quite an impact, not only award-winning architecturally but also in bringing the school's hopes, dreams and aspirations together.

Former pupils include king of skiffle Lonnie Donegan MBE, graphic designers Peter Saville and Malcolm Garrett, Damien Hinds MP, Paul Maynard MP, Greg Mulholland MP, Keith Breeden Royal Society of Portrait Painters, Martin Baker organist and master of music at Westminster Cathedral, Dr Kieran Moriarty CBE consultant gastroenterologist. Long established Old Ambrosians and Parents' Association.

Entrance: Most enter at 11 via competitive entrance exam comprising verbal reasoning, English and maths tests, taking top 30 per cent of ability range. Admissions policy includes lengthy and detailed over-subscription criteria as demand for places is high and school is invariably over-subscribed. Boys come from a plethora of schools to include the local St Ambrose Preparatory School.

Exit: The majority of boys stay on into sixth form (12 per cent left after GCSEs in 2016 and similar numbers at end of year 12); new boys join and add to the numbers. Pupils are well-taught and well-advised and most proceed to good universities – Sheffield, Sheffield Hallam, Newcastle, Durham, Edinburgh, Nottingham and Leeds popular. A number to Oxbridge each year: one in 2016, and three medics.

Money matters: Some funds available for uniforms, lunches, transport as necessary.

Remarks: First and foremost a Catholic school with a Catholic ethos, strong and clear convictions that sing through the hearts and minds of both staff and boys.

St Brendan's Sixth Form College

Broomhill Road, Brislington, Bristol BS4 5RQ

Pupils: 1,725 • Ages: 16–19+ • RC

Tel: 01179 777766
Email: info@stbrn.ac.uk
Website: www.stbrn.ac.uk

Principal: Since 2012, Mr Michael Jaffrain. Originally from France and briefly worked as a bank cashier at the Bank National of Paris, before moving to England to become a language assistant at South Cheshire College. Thence to Shrewsbury Sixth Form College, from where he was appointed assistant principal at St Brendan's in 2010. Approachable, bouncily enthusiastic and easy to talk to, Mr Jaffrain likes to have contact with and personal knowledge of his students, despite the size of the college, and to be at the centre of activity. Since arriving he has relentlessly pursued his aims of 'developing concrete, working partnerships with other educational establishments, leading innovation and change, developing close ties with business and becoming an outstanding college focused on excellent quality in teaching and learning.' He has repositioned the college's academic status by terminating level 1 (sub GCSE) entry, which was very small and 'which other more specialist institutions can do better', and 'concentrated on raising the aspirations of students at level 2 (GCSE etc) and level 3 (A level etc)'. Amongst all this he still finds time to be an enthusiastic rugby fan.

Academic matters: College offers two main levels of post-16 study: level 3 (over 70 different A levels and BTecs), and level 2 (GCSE retakes for those who have not passed English and maths at school plus a number of BTec courses providing the equivalent of four GCSEs at grades A*-C). The college is just beginning to extend into first year degree level with a new psychology course, aimed at encouraging more students to raise their sights to university. The City and Guilds CAD course provides a back-up for A level design students, whilst other level 2 and 3 courses include BTecs in applied biology, business, IT, law, media, music technology, performing arts, public services and sport.

A cohort of over 1700 students means that there is an exceptionally wide choice of courses and more popular courses consist of several groups. This means that students can pick freely without the timetabling restrictions inevitable in even the largest school sixth form. A level results are above national average, with growing number achieving four or more A grades. Sixty-nine per cent A*-C grades in 2016. Results for those who enter the Advanced Graduate Programme, for the most academic students, compare favourably with the best in the school league tables, though the entry requirements are less stringent (an average of at least B at GCSE). Advanced Graduates also get specialist options including extra help for Oxbridge and other high demand applications, and are encouraged to take the Extended Project Qualification (EPQ), which develops research skills, time management and a whole host of other skills.

A suite of learning development provision allows students to drop in if needing study skills or just a bit of help on a one-off basis. About half do at some stage. Some 200 of these students have regular support or exam entitlements and are helped, either one-to-one, or in small groups, with special arrangements for them such as a relaxation of age limits. Though the college no longer admits level 1, students the last cohort who recently left are doing very well, thanks to the specialist help given. A high percentage of pupils receiving learning development support achieve better grades than predicted, and do at least as well both in terms of results and value added as other students. ESOL candidates from abroad have to complete GCSE or an equivalent in English before embarking on A level. All areas of the college are accessible to wheelchair users.

Students seem happy to take the RPE (religion, philosophy and ethics) course, one of the few compulsory aspects of the college, commenting that 'the philosophy bits are really interesting,' though the ones we met were non-committal about the religious content.

Games, options, the arts: While absence of compulsion is highly valued by students keen to get away from schooliness, most acknowledged that there are great opportunities and even the least sporty could enjoy yoga, using the comprehensive fitness gym or popular sprung floor dance studios. Enthusiastic dancers, including some boys, were energetically rehearsing for a production during our visit. Lots of spectators for the netball match in progress, and more queuing up to watch impending basketball. Exceptional facilities for most sports, though no pool (but there is an Olympic one just up the road) and programmes such as Total Pro Soccer (TPS) for boys and girls allow students to include sport in their portfolio of qualifications. Since its introduction in 2014, several students have gained US sports scholarships, and the success for students applying to sports-related HE courses and apprenticeships has tripled. Lots of dynamic overlap with arts, especially for theatre productions.

The arts equally well served. BTec performing arts courses incorporating musical theatre, dance and acting are especially popular. Film students very innovative and even have their own Oscars evening. Trad music A level is limited, as is the chance of orchestral experience in college – no hoards of up-and-coming younger pupils to swell the second violins and half the cohort leaving every year makes this difficult – but lots of singing, with a popular choir doing public things like welcoming the Georgian rugby team ahead of the Rugby World Cup, and singing at Bristol matches. Production and studio engineering also on offer. Parents speak warmly of the support given to students in entertainment studies, facilitated by fantastic links with Bristol Old Vic, BBC and ITV for internships and career opportunities.

Exceptional art, with some magical work going on in both graphic communications and straight art A levels. Students benefit from highly sophisticated printing and IT facilities, encouraged by an ex-professional design teacher who inspires such stunning work as the variations on an underwater theme displayed on the day of our visit. Art is as impressive. One fine art A level student, working on expressing emotion through physical disease and malformation, eschewed the 'pretty', while others were using entrancing flower and seaweed images with a really professional-looking finish. Some spectacular results in graphic communications and sound all round.

Background and atmosphere: Originating from a boys' independent school founded by the Christian Brothers in 1890, St Brendan's finally evolved into a co-educational, Catholic sixth form college in 1979. Masses of recent building work has produced a harmonious, if brightly coloured, modern-looking campus, into which the few surviving but updated original buildings fit comfortably. While the access is unprepossessing and the security impressive (but friendly), the grounds themselves feel spacious, informal and park-like. Plenty of inviting-looking areas for outdoor relaxation in summer. Students look informal but not, on the whole, scruffy, while there was only one bit of litter in evidence – and that was towards the end of the day. Most students enjoy using first names throughout all levels at the college, finding it subtly alters relationship between students and teachers, giving them confidence to respond and question, though one student admitted that a few students hang on to the familiarity of 'Mr/s' or 'Sir'.

Lots of work-friendly places in the spacious library where a quiet and studious atmosphere seems taken for granted. It remains open until 5.30pm and has extensive computer facilities. Computer 'break out' areas (20-30 computers for general use) nestling in handy corners all over the college including one internet café/IT work area adjacent to student canteen where a staff member is on hand to help.

Flexible auditorium with raked seating for about 250 provides performance and lecture space. Assemblies held here to celebrate Christian festivals. The tiny rotunda chapel, the central feature of the original school, is still central. The chaplain offers an informal welcome to all with masses etc for Catholic students, who are very much in the minority of only about 12 per cent, but college is the favoured choice of a number of other Christian churches in Bristol. A parent commented that the Catholic ethos gives the college a calm and caring feeling, nurturing 'bright young people keen to make difference but not afraid to be different'.

Activities, visits and sports rely heavily on input from a strong students' union, committed to providing social life and doing charity fundraising, which also has a student rep on the college governing board. It definitely feels more like a college than a school.

Pastoral care, well-being and discipline: Unlike uni, however, the pastoral care is exceptional, and valued by parents and students. Problems are identified and action taken effectively. One parent reported that her daughter's exam nerves – a product of no previous experience of formal exams – was effectively tackled by teachers and tutors. Qualified counsellors/psychologist on hand to meet both referred and self-referred students. Staff says the newly inaugurated faculty system has allowed more time for proper evaluation of lesson and support of teachers, in order to make teaching even more effective.

Masses of feedback to parents and lots of encouragement to students to undertake activities to support their courses – revision programmes, catch up sessions and such. Since there are several groups studying each subject it is usually possible to find a repeat lesson for something scantily understood. A tight rein is kept on attendance and progress. Role of student support managers is pivotal: each has 10 tutorial groups for 45 minute periods a week in groups of 25 or individually. In cases of poor work or behaviour students can be placed 'on contract'. Retention over year is 94 per cent, which is high compared with FE institutions and school sixth forms. Rolling programme of fairs, visits, speakers tutorials and careers advisors ensure that course choices lead to ongoing opportunities.

Very strict guidelines on alcohol and drugs, with surprisingly few incidents. For the few problems that do occur rehabilitation is aimed for and often achieved, but no quarter given to those who do not respond to help.

Attractive canteen with plenty of choice, though what sells seems to be mostly breakfast type fast food.

Pupils and parents: Huge catchment area from Gloucestershire, the boarders of Somerset, Dorset and Wiltshire with First Bus routes offering a student ticket which can be used for any journey in the city. Cars permitted but only with a parking permit given on first come basis – so apply early. Fifteen per cent ethnic minorities. Being part of Bristol's south east area partnership alongside City of Bristol (FE) College has opened the doors to many more non-Catholics. Usual choice for Catholics from Bristol and Bath Catholic Collegiate for whom it is the only denominational post-16 option. Increasing uptake from ex-independent school pupils.

Entrance: All students are admitted to the college rather than to a specific course or level. Choices are confirmed or made post-GCSE or equivalent results via extensive interview and discussion. Disappointing GCSE results can be rescued with a year consolidating GCSE before starting A level or its equivalent. As the college manages to offer the third year post-16 without any fees, this is an excellent option for someone needing to sort out disastrous GCSEs.

Impressive, university-style prospectus makes task of selecting courses much easier. About 12 per cent of entrants come from Catholic Collegiate schools, where they are interviewed prior to admission and meet student ambassadors from St Brendan's. Parents generally like to attend these meetings and are welcomed. Remainder are interviewed at college. Over 70 feeder independent and state schools covering area between West Wiltshire and North Somerset.

Exit: Academic ambition definitely on the up. Majority proceed to wide range of degree courses including three to Oxbridge in 2016. Many to vocational and arts-related courses eg one off to Falmouth to study textile design. Some into employment or to 'elite apprenticeships' – eg a finance apprenticeship with the MoD – encouraged by the college's strong links with industry around Bristol. Under two per cent leave 'not in education, employment or training' (NEET).

Remarks: Fantastic environment post GCSE for both high fliers and those needing to salvage something from weak GCSEs. Ideal transition from school to uni or work. All the support and expert guidance of a good sixth form developed by staff with sustained concentrated experience in sixth form teaching and pastoral care. St Brendan's offers opportunities that many schools cannot provide. Atmosphere deceptively like uni but underpinned by stringent but informal academic supervision and genuine generous care for students. A very special place.

S

St David's College

Llandudno, Conwy LL30 1RD

Pupils: 240: 154 boys, 86 girls; 100 boarders • Ages: 9–19 • Sixth form: 74

Fees: Day £6,900 – £16,950; Boarding £16,620 – £31,440 SEN: Day £10,035 – £20,505; Boarding £19,755 – £34,575 pa

Tel: 01492 875974
Email: hmsec@stdavidscollege.co.uk
Website: www.stdavidscollege.co.uk

Head: Since 2008, Mr Stuart Hay BEng PGCE (early 40s). Joined as deputy head from Warminster School, where he was head of electronics and product design. After gaining his electronic engineering degree and PGCE at Bath University, he taught in both independent and maintained sectors.

He is married to Lucy and they have three children, Ben, Milly and Thomas. Ben, the eldest, attends the school and appeared to be loving it when we came across him in a lively reading class. Mr Hay's main interests are mountaineering, road cycling, mountain biking, racquet sports and St David's. Parents speak very highly of Mr and Mrs Hay. 'It may sound corny,' said one parent we spoke to, 'but their happy family really seems to include all the pupils, whether it's Mrs Hay's cooking activity or Mr Hay sea kayaking round Anglesey.' All the parents we spoke to, and they were queuing up to do so, spoke of the open and natural friendliness of Mr and Mrs Hay and their involvement around the school. 'Mrs Hay is really super,' said a number of children, who assured us she was not their mum. Mr Hay is much admired for the sensitive, generous minded and understanding way he encounters pupils, staff and parents. 'He's astonishingly energetic,' an admiring mum told us.

Mr Hay took a lot of persuading to become headmaster. He was reluctant to lose the close contact with the pupils and the opportunities to teach them and to share in their activities, especially the outdoor pursuits he likes so much and which he believes are so important for the development of the pupils. He most emphatically does not belong to the pompous bullfrog style of head: he is a listener who really does seem to put the welfare of his pupils first. 'He's no softy,' said a father to us. 'He's good at judging pupils' abilities and how far he can encourage them without expecting too much. He'll push if he feels that is necessary, but essentially he does that through encouragement, because he knows them.' We found him extremely thoughtful and pleasantly modest, warm in manner, wholly committed and with what seemed an inner calm. He is completely genuine and, incidentally, very good company.

Academic matters: What a joy it was not to have examination results and league tables thrust under our noses. There is a belief in some quarters that education is dead and has been replaced by a slavish seeking after grade levels and that dreaded, often misused, word 'targets'. At St David's there are individual goals for each pupil but they are personal rather than political. Education at its best is very much alive and shining at St David's. The reticence they have in not trumpeting their grade results is for no reason other than the firmly held conviction that grades are not the most important aspect of life at this school.

Average class sizes are 10 and every teacher is a qualified dyslexia teacher. An infinitely better system than that where a pupil is given one session of help a week and then goes back to a class where the teacher is making no allowances at all. That happens in a number of schools. This school was one of the first to adopt a multi-sensory teaching policy and we witnessed some marvellously lively, creative and stimulating teaching from a staff who seem universally dedicated and fun. None more so than those we met in the Cadogen Centre, a specialised building where each pupil enjoys one-on-one teaching with a programme individually planned for them after careful discussion with their class teachers.

The facilities for IT are excellent and we had a wonderful time with some very bright sixth form pupils who were about to go off for an exhibition. Not only was the work they were doing as part of NVQs in CAD outstandingly good, but so were the fluent and perceptive comments which accompanied the work. 'Dyslexics often think out of the box,' a teacher told us. Recently a young man from St David's, who while there had attended one-on-one lessons, graduated in architecture at Manchester University. Another is reading nuclear physics. There are so many success stories.

Games, options, the arts: To gaze down from the beautiful terrace in front of the house is to marvel at the immaculate state of the games pitches, the superb Astroturf and the lure of mountains beyond. Virtually every game you can think of is on offer, and other schools talk of the verve and energy with which St David's teams perform. In addition there is a shooting range, an indoor climbing hall and vast amounts of equipment for outdoor activities, one of the distinctive features of the school. The excellent prospectus and online introduction to the school reveal the depth and breadth of the activities on offer. There is an activity, an expedition, a challenging outing once a week, but lest anyone think this is an attractive offer replacing academic pursuits, think again. The school academic day continues until 5pm Monday to Friday and there are additional lessons, activities and games sessions timetabled on Saturday mornings. When questioned about Saturday morning lessons, 'Fair enough,' said the boy we asked. Sixth formers can take a BTec in sports (traditional or outdoor ed).

A particularly popular activity is 4x4 off road driving in a spectacularly battered and mud caked old Land Rover. The school really is a paradise of activity, challenge, determination, broadening horizons and going beyond the syllabus.

Very lively art in an old building where budding artists can express themselves without worrying about spilling paint. Those are often the best buildings for producing the exciting art work. There was plenty here and in the photographic section adjoining. Such creativity and such joy, delight and encouragement.

Boarding: The boarding houses (three for boys and one for girls) are bright, airy and friendly; the house teams dedicated and involved. Boarding seems to work well, which is probably one reason why pupils come from so far afield from throughout the UK. Huge variety of indoor and especially outdoor activities available at weekends.

Background and atmosphere: In 1965 a deputy head from Cheshire, John Mayor, upset by the way boys and girls with learning difficulties were smothered, if not dismissed, because they were seen as lazy or stupid, decided to found a school where their needs were addressed. It was founded on three main principals: a determination to respect, understand and help the pupils; adventurous outdoor activities where the young could experience freedom and excitement; and all this within a gentle Christian ethos. Fifty years later the school largely continues to follow those guidelines. And it shows. We met happy pupils who spoke confidently and unselfconsciously about how miserable they had been on arrival, with a bleak and cheerless outlook on life and no self-esteem at all. For some, St David's was last chance saloon, and some of them were far from home. They spoke of the warmth of the welcome they received from the whole community.

'Community' is a word which sits easily on the lips of pupils eager to talk about their school. And that's not a cliché either: they really do feel as if the school belongs to them and they to the school. There's a very real closeness. They talk of the increasing delight they derived from their lessons; the love and interest shown by the teachers; the friendliness of their contemporaries. 'It's just everything,' said a young boy, struggling to articulate the indefinable. 'Surely there must be some things you don't like?' we pressed. 'Of course,' came the reply, 'but there's far less to worry about than there was at my previous school. It could be very depressing there and a bit scary on occasions.' What they all agreed on was the 'overall atmosphere'. They looked surprised when we suggested that that came from them. These young have not been stuffed with cheesy old clichés raked off that useful pile plundered by professional prospectus writers or that irritating band of media trained heads. These are real people making real discoveries about themselves. Perhaps it is not a coincidence to have a parent describing the head as a real person.

Pastoral care, well-being and discipline: Within the academic, as well as the sporting and sporty side of life at the school, there are practical and generous ways in which pupils help each other. This is manifest by the way in which older pupils help younger pupils with academic subjects as well as more personal, private anxieties. The people we spoke with were unanimous in the feeling that there was always someone there to help. A word they were fond of evoking is 'banter.' Affectionate teasing. One of the most moving moments of our tour was when our guides pointed out the Prayer Garden, 'or whatever you like to call it. You can approach it in any way you like, but it's essentially a place for reflection. You can take it or leave it.' It's a lovely touch, and the statue in front, created by Nick Elphick, an old boy of the school, is a thought-provoking addition. This is not a threatening environment. Discipline is sensible, thoughtful, considerate. It seemed as natural as breathing.

Pupils and parents: From a wide range of primary and prep schools. Day pupils from across the whole of North Wales. Boarders from all over the UK, a small number from overseas. Inclusive entry helped by quite a number of pupils being funded by their local education authorities. Apart from those with special educational needs, many parents choose the school because of its broad all-round education and its small class sizes. Recent extension to boarding provision due to increase in pupil numbers.

Entrance: The majority enter aged at about 10 after an interview and a report from their school (although some join age 9 into year 5). A large number come from local primary schools, but others come from far afield. We heard how sensitively the business of arrivals is handled. Always a sign of a happy school. A few leave and a number come into the sixth form, attracted by the reputation of the teaching and the breadth of subjects on offer. The sixth form handbook says that the most important qualities for entry into the school are commitment and enthusiasm. That handbook is, incidentally, one of the best of its kind we have ever seen.

Exit: Around 15-25 per cent leave at 16. The school goes to tremendous lengths to help the boys and girls choose the courses that match interests and abilities. The vast majority do go on to further or higher education. Technical subjects seem the most popular, but not exclusively so.

Money matters: The school works hard to keep the costs down. The wonderful expeditions are very carefully budgeted. No swanky hotels. Parents we spoke to said that they felt the school was very thoughtful about money matters and we got the impression that those who ran into severe financial difficulties would be carefully listened to.

Remarks: This is a very special school, almost a magical place. Pupils develop in an unsentimental atmosphere of love and generosity. The staff are almost as amazing as the pupils and, yes, there is plenty of banter along with the seriousness. Over the years a strong bond has matured with Kampala. Pupils and gap year students are deeply and genuinely involved. 'The projects we are involved in come from the dreams of our own pupils,' says that handbook. The same could be said about the school as a whole.

Saint Gregory's, Bath

Combe Hay Lane, Odd Down, Bath, Somerset BA2 8PA

Pupils: 958 • Ages: 11–18 • Sixth form: 151 • RC

Tel: 01225 832873
Email: stgregorys_sec@bathnes.gov.uk
Website: www.st-gregorys.bathnes.sch.uk

Headmistress: Since September 2016, Ann Cusack, previously deputy head at St Augustine's Catholic College in Trowbridge. She has worked at a number of secondary schools in London and Norfolk as well as the west country.

Academic matters: Excellent results, particularly for a non-selective school. Performance at GCSE has shown steady and sustained improvement; in 2016, 30 per cent of grades were A*/A. Interestingly, the school has kept figures on the English Baccalaureate (five traditional academic GCSEs in maths, English, a science, a language and history or geography) long before Mr Gove deemed it desirable. Nevertheless, some parents grumble about the amount of homework – too much of it, material not previously covered in class, too many negative comments – this last remarked upon in a recent interim inspection. A level results 42 per cent A*/B grades

S

School has specialist language status; Spanish is particularly strong, but we were also impressed by the lively German class we popped into, where pupils were speaking unselfconsciously in a supportive environment. Polish and Italian were also put on last year; Japanese on demand.

All new pupils in year 7 are streamed according to ability, with some adjustments made for English and maths; at the start of GCSE courses, they are assigned different pathways (fittingly and tactfully named Canterbury, Glastonbury and Walsingham) designed for a range of abilities, and incorporating some vocational courses at Bath College to be taken alongside fewer GCSEs. Parents reckon their offspring have a clear idea of their individual targets and next steps; they like the culture of endeavour. 'My daughter wants to be a medic, and the school's right behind her,' said one mother.

But we did pick up some dissatisfaction with the maths teaching – when tackled about it, the school said that 'the results and final outcomes were very good and well above national averages' – when in fact maths has the lowest pass rate of any subject at GCSE – and 'that some variation in 50 teachers was inevitable'. Granted.. but at least one mother reckons that private tuition 'which nice middle class parents resort to' masks true results. That said, there are plenty of maths clinics, one entitled 'Revision to ensure that grade C'.

Around seven per cent of St Gregs' pupils have some special educational need – all are screened using NFER on entry, which tests numeracy, verbal and non-verbal reasoning. Dyslexia expert on staff, and TA dedicated to children whose first language is not English. Ofsted praised support given to pupils with learning difficulties, disabilities or any other kind of vulnerability.

Games, options, the arts: Designated specialist college of performing arts, and strong local reputation. Recent production of The King and I was 'fabulous', according to one mother, who chose the school on the strength of its drama; 'very good and lots of it,' said another. Gilchrist Studio is a dedicated performance space and the school has actively sought grants to refurbish its art and music facilities to good effect. The (small) choir sang beautifully at the assembly we went to; music is well-resourced and prominent, and dance enjoys a good following.

Opinions divide on the question of sport, however. Ask the school, and you will be told about the Olympic swimmer (currently seventh best in the world), three England athletes, two cross-country runners and a rugby player, a Royal Ballet pupil (who spends half her week in London) and an impressive list of county players – plus the 1st XV who had just thrashed arch rivals Beechen Cliff. All this is quite remarkable – but pupils and parents find attitudes to sport inconsistent and facilities just about adequate.

The jocks complain that the top brass prioritise academic performance over everything else, and that tutors don't cut them enough slack, or give them enough credit for the glory they bring the school. A home pitch, team shirts and fixtures with local independents in this rugby-mad city are on their wish list. One parent reckoned that there were not enough matches for girls, and that team practices were stymied by bus departure times – the school's response was that parents are in fact quick to co-ordinate lifts.

Good range of trips offered to complement most subjects and interests, eg China, New York, ski-ing. D of E recently introduced (what took them so long?) and recently an adventure trek to Namibia, for which pupils were expected to raise sizeable fun ds.

Background and atmosphere: Founded and built in the late 70s (in buildings less grim and better preserved than you might think) by Clifton Diocese, to make a logical progression from the eight local-ish Catholic primary schools which feed it. All nine schools have become the South Clifton Catholic Federation 'to provide an even better Catholic education for young people in the area' and to show solidarity in the face of the 'significant lobbies (..) who argue for an end to faith schools'.

That describes St Greg's: from the huge banner which dominates reception 'In Christ we flourish' to the creed written by the pupils, this school proudly wears its Catholic heart on its sleeve – but it's a big and inclusive heart. Everyone, nay everyone we spoke to mentioned the strong family atmosphere and the forces for good which prevail in the school, which embraces the handful of non-Catholics who attend and where 'bullying is jumped on'. A sense of religious observance was palpable, and pupils accept large doses of spiritual input (and revival of old edict of no meat on Fridays) along with the three R's. 'Our kids are taught not to be embarrassed about their faith', says the school. At a time when Catholic education is in paroxysms of guilt about the dodgier aspects of its past, such pride in its best manifestations is cheering. 'My children don't know who is Catholic and who isn't – all are blessed,' one mum commented: says it all, really.

School sits just inside the city boundary on top of one of Bath's seven hills (like Rome, but greyer) and overlooks sweeping countryside to the south. Piazza with picnic tables and chairs, recently created at centre of school at pupils' request, enhances break times, and year 7s have a designated area to call their own.

All are assigned to a house on entry (named suitably after popes) and within that, tutor groups. Transition arrangements from primary schools are good, though some parents would rather newbies from the same school weren't always put together.

Pastoral care, well-being and discipline: Pupils feel exceptionally well looked after by their tutors and appreciate the high standards of behaviour, which make life bearable for all. Bus monitors, selected from senior pupils, oversee any over-exuberance on the way to and from school, even on public buses. Bad behaviour inside or outside school is counselled in the first instance, rather than censured.

But once sanctions apply, they appear pointless to some, eg writing out 'Your parents are very disappointed in you' X times, or an excuse to escape going outside in winter. A compulsory session or two at the after-school homework club might meet the case better, say pupils, who also mentioned some inconsistency from teachers. Understandable disquiet at the introduction of CCTV in the loos (not in cubicles, we were assured) as a deterrent to vandals. No complaints from parents, however, in this climate of guidance and gentle correction, rather than brute force.

Pupils and parents: Some 75 per cent Catholic, socially mixed but sharing the same values in education. 'Most of our children come with the right expectations – we encourage debate but ask for respect for what the school stands for,' but a young person who had 'turned his or her face against religious expression' might not thrive here. We found the flock thoughtful and grounded, with a refreshing lack of cynicism. Notable alumni? School is on the young side to have produced anyone with a long and distinguished career, but observers of the current music scene should search out Hannah Collins' début solo album.

Entrance: Intake of 160 into year 7. Governing body responsible for admissions, although applications are made through normal LA channels. Vast majority of pupils come from Catholic primary schools as far away as Wells and Chippenham. A sprinkling from others – some parents are reckoned to have dredged up any vestige of Catholicism to get them in. Some tactics – such strategic late baptisms – frowned upon by other parents. 'Catholic children are admitted by baptismal certificate, not by how their parents practise,' states the school. Oversubscribed – and the criteria are applied in strict sequence, so that even sibling cases have gone to appeal.

Exit: Now has a joint sixth form with St Mark's – the New Sixth Bath – with all classes at St Gregory's and teachers from both schools and around 40 per cent go on to this. Leavers to eg Exeter, Plymouth, Manchester, Warwick and Birmingham; one to Cambridge in 2016 (economics), two medics and a vet.

Money matters: Catholic education is not fully funded by government, so schools have to find 10 per cent of capital expenditure; for St Greg's some £10,000. Parents are asked to contribute and gift aid any donation they care to give; requests go out every autumn. Active parents' association funds extras and all Name and Praise book tokens (given out in assembly for commendable work or behaviour) – it does well, raising around £7,000 per year.

Remarks: Top choice non-fee paying Catholic secondary in the area, in our view. Long journey times from huge catchment area and hotly contested places are testament to the thirst for this kind of spiritually-led education, which turns out great results and thoroughly nice kids. We will watch the development of the new joint sixth form with interest.

St John's-on-the-Hill School

Castleford Hill, Tutshill, Chepstow, Monmouthshire NP16 7LE

Pupils: 188; 10 full, 20 flexi boarders • Ages: 4–13

Fees: Day £7,899 – £13,002; Boarding £18,297 pa

Tel: 01291 622045
Email: Office@stjohnsonthehill.co.uk
Website: www.stjohnsonthehill.co.uk

Head: Since September 2016, Ruth Frett, previously housemistress at Cranleigh School. She has an English degree from St Andrews and moved on to Trinity College of Music, performing all over Europe as professional singer for 10 years. Four children later, she moved into teaching, via London primary and prep schools, becoming head of middle school, head of RS and chaplain at Cranleigh Prep. She currently teaches RS, classical civilisation and drama, and coaches netball and rounders.

Ruth is married to Dan, an American who works for a software company in the City as well as serving as a priest at their local parish church. Their four children range from late teens to mid 20s.

Entrance: Mixed ability entry. Assessment is based on a 'taster day' in English and maths plus report from previous school. Procedure is 'painless,' say parents, who compared it favourably with other schools. Pupils may enter at any point provided spaces are available. Main catchment area is Newport/Cardiff through Monmouthshire to Forest of Dean and west Gloucestershire. Boarders come from all over.

Exit: Has reputation for gaining scholarships near and far. Most popular: Dean Close (around a quarter), Monmouth (boys and girls), Kings Gloucester, Christ College Brecon, Marlborough, Rougemont, Clifton College, Cheltenham College, Malvern College.

Remarks: Perched above river Wye, a short stone's throw into England, school overlooks Chepstow in Wales. Founded in 1923 in a rambling Georgian manor (rebuilt in 1805 after a fire). Succession of proprietorial heads until '60s but co-ed and charitable trust (incorporating former Brightlands School) since then. New buildings (and new conservatory entrance area) fit well into overall scheme of things on a pleasant eight-acre site (plus 12 more acres of playing fields across the road).

Spectacular growth of nursery education (now provided on three sites, including one in Newport) – 70 per cent of pre-prep intake comes from the school's own nurseries. Our visit on a 'Foodie Friday' coincided with 'wormy pasta salad' on classroom menus. Highly professional early years teachers and assistants ensure tinies are happy and cared for. Impressive range of activities for these tots – stimulation in the nursery section includes sensory and soft play rooms plus safe outdoor play areas for all.

'Seamless' progression to reception level on Tutshill site where children 'learn to read without noticing,' say committed staff. Phonic introduction alongside activities such as puppets and story telling. Loads of measuring and counting too. Each day begins with assembly in spacious hall; weekly link-up with nursery from below and to prep (in their hall) once a week. Communication between teachers and pre-prep parents includes 'wow cards' and home-school link books. Wide corridors in this modern, purpose-built building boast frequently changed displays including output of creative arts club and strong evidence of cross-curricular work: eg 'forces of movement' incorporating art, science and ICT work. Smart boards in each year group and laptops already in use at this level, not to mention school intranet on plasma screen. Huge choice of readers ('Fireflies' non-fiction popular with boys). Tea after school for those involved in clubs, activities or post-lessons care.

Pupils leave the swish pre-prep for the cleverly converted coach house which accommodates years 3 to 5 in what a previous head described as 'a bit of a Tardis.' Smallish but cheery classrooms (maximum class size is 16) for these years.

Much better than average prep school facilities for science: junior (in a quaint outpost) and senior (modern) laboratories with well-qualified teachers to match. Lovely dining area combines best of cafeteria and sit down traditions whilst civilised entrance (with memorabilia on show) and meeting room (referred to as the Embassy) add gravitas. Prep is awash with subject specialists (some escapees from state sector, others ex-other independents) who can take pupils as far as they want to go. Art teachers (ex-Monmouth senior) explained how they are adapting OCR syllabus for St John's and thereby widening pupils' artistic horizons. We appreciated the ongoing Picasso exhibition whilst annual Arts Week gives pupils a chance to let their creativity run wild. Athletic head of DT (he manages British universities' cross-country team) oversees a well-resourced area which includes 3D model making.

Somewhat dated school hall serves for assemblies as well as concerts and school productions (recent one was a full blown Grease.) Music has a large classroom base plus three individual practice rooms. Everyone in year 3 gets a violin and learns to scrape – like it or not. Orchestra and wind band plus choirs (school subs for Newport cathedral choir and also sang at recent IAPS conference) are all well supported and three ex-pupils have graduated to National Youth Orchestra. Specialist ICT rooms are well used but school maintains a healthy balance between new technologies and more traditional approaches.

Sports facilities include half-size Astroturf and hard tennis/netball courts, attractive 15-metre swimming pool and oodles of playing fields. School more than holds its own against larger preps with an impressive fixture list (includes Millfield and Cheltenham College). Wide choice of sports features rugby, soccer, cricket (boys and girls) as well as netball, rounders, swimming, tennis and golf. All pupils encouraged to participate as best they can.

Refreshingly open, happy pupils – well turned out and polite nonetheless. We observed a school council meeting chaired effectively by a year 8 boy. Plenty of evidence of pupils' ideas bearing fruit eg new homework diary and rewards system not to mention refurb of pupils' loos. Pupils also discussed making a new outdoor classroom interactive – cutting edge stuff for 12-13 year olds. Large number (33 last time) go for a whole month's exchange with host schools in Stirling and Cape Town, South Africa. Led (10 visits so far) by a staff member who hails from those parts. Does wonders for pupil personal development and bonding. Pupils wax eloquent about how they are all 'given a chance' by 'kind teachers' and how 'friendship' is the magical ingredient at St John's. We were shown a wide variety of pupils' work – impressive in its quality and diversity. Alumni include Olympic show jumper, Richard Mead, Welsh rugby player Marc Batten and Rebecca Watts (in first group of ordained women priests).

Fleet of minibuses ('drivers are really kind,' say parents) to ferry day pupils twixt home and school. Boarders get a good deal here with lovely, mixed (not the dorms) accommodation, dedicated and well qualified houseparents who 'go the extra mile' to develop a family, 'home from home' atmosphere. Bathrooms recently upgraded. Houseparents even cook for boarders on Saturdays (take-aways are not unknown) but school roast on Sundays is 'to die for,' they confess. Junior boarders write home (plus ICT and reading) on Saturday mornings whilst their seniors are in lessons. Dorm points add up so that winners get a reward outing. Regular Boarders' Bugle adds to monthly school newsletters to keep boarding parents well informed. Flexi-boarding clearly popular with parents. Active Parents' Association have raised loads of dosh for worthwhile projects plus social and sporting events such as the summer ball and PA Golf Day. Parents help children's fundraising through their four houses to benefit of a wide range of local, national and international good causes.

Great 'family' school for youngsters with 'gunpowder in the barrel' – 'we'll take them as far as they want to go,' insists school. Parents were at a loss to pick out a single outstanding feature – 'excellent teachers'; 'all pupils get involved'; 'a super school in all respects' was the consensus. Recently acquired by Dean Close School (Cheltenham), with same board of trustees.

St Laurence School

Ashley Road, Bradford-on-Avon, Wiltshire BA15 1DZ

Pupils: 1,351 • Ages: 11-18 • Sixth form: 243

Tel: 01225 309500
Email: admin@st-laurence.com
Website: www.st-laurence.com

Headteacher: Since 2013, Fergus Stewart (early 50s), a chemist by academic discipline, with an MA from Oxford and a PGCE from Nottingham. Despite the Scots name, upbringing and colouring, Mr Stewart has spent most of his career in Wiltshire, latterly as deputy head of Nova Hreod (no, it's not a misprint) school in Swindon, before moving to 'that good school that I'd always been aware of in the corner of the county'.

An unequivocal believer in comprehensive education, Mr Stewart expresses his two key aims for his school to be academic excellence for all and the development of well-rounded young people – and holding those in tension. So does he achieve it? Ask parents, and you will find a pretty satisfied lot: 'Thrilled, blown away by it', said one mother with sons with very different needs. 'It shames the private schools'. Everyone we spoke to had chosen the school over local independents and state options. Mr Stewart has gone down well with these same parents, who find him approachable, receptive to suggestions and, crucially, quick to respond to concerns raised with him. We found him very much on-message (as befits a newish head), but we did uncover a fisherman, a runner and a walker not averse to

S

enlivening his peregrinations with a pub lunch. Mr Stewart is married with cats, two children at university and one at school.

Academic matters: Curriculum is predominantly broad and academic, offering GCSEs and more than 20 subjects at A level, but there are vocational options such as BTecs in a few subjects and ESPE (employability skills and personal effectiveness) which helps the less academic with pre-16 education and training. 'We teach the classes in front of us,' says Mr Stewart, though the raw material at entry is more promising than at many comprehensives. Results at A level variable with 48 per cent A*-Bs and 19 per cent A*/As in 2016. 'My boy was very happy at the school and came out with his three As', said one delighted mum of an undergraduate. At GCSE, 79 per cent of students got 5+ A*-C grades including English and maths; 26 er cent of grades were A*/A.

Teaching staff come in for high praise: 'encouraging, supportive, they clearly enjoy what they do, committed – volunteering to help strugglers in their own time, very good at understanding individual children, particularly the problematic ones' were some of the comments made to us by parents; 'they are incredibly proud of the school,' adds the head. Their commitment is evident by the long list of revision and catch-up sessions laid on in the 3-2-5 sessions after school. Clear expectations are set, and individual targets recorded in possibly the best student diary we have ever seen, equipped with the periodic table, a world map and a trigonometry crib sheet. Only irregular verbs and musical notation were missing.

Sixth formers have their own new centre with common room, IT facilities and study areas.

For the first year, teaching is done in mixed ability sets, but maths and languages are set from year 8. SEN provision and care is highly rated, where the balance between those needs and other students' progress is finely struck.

Games, options, the arts: St Laurence is known locally for its music, as the Wiltshire Music Centre is built in its grounds and the school has day time use of its excellent facilities: 'the finest acoustics outside London', apparently. Some musicians achieve diplomas before they leave; music is timetabled. When we visited, two St Laurence girls had just won the Amnesty Young Songwriter competition – sadly, technical difficulties and time constraints meant we did not see it performed, but we were treated to the wonderful GCSE dance display which was that day's house assembly. Productions range from Hamlet to Joseph, via Les Mis, and include less formal and highbrow events, such as the 70s gig night.

Sport also prominent: rugby, netball, hockey, football and athletics the main ones, but also HRE (health-related exercise), for the ball-phobes, presumably. National swimmer and skier among current students. Advantage also taken of nearby river Avon for rowing, and as training ground (water?) for Olympic and European kayaking champions. Staff also don their whites on occasion, taking on Prior Park at cricket – and winning.

Art comes as part of a rolling programme with design and technology; parents like the range of opportunities younger pupils experience, such as cookery and textiles, 'where boys are free to explore things which might be considered a female preserve', as one mother put it. There was certainly a selection of smelly boys' shoes outside the dance studio. The new Mac suite is also 'as good as anything you would find at a private school,' opined the same lady. Extracurricular activities are many and varied, much taking place off site and at weekends, such as D of E, Ten Tors, a ski trip (where staff have gone to considerable lengths to include at least one pupil with SEN), French and German exchanges every year, plus a practical building trip to Romania with a local charity, a spiritual trip to India and World Challenge to Nepal.

Background and atmosphere: Very much the town school of the charming, historic and prosperous town of Bradford-on-Avon, with its honey-coloured buildings tumbling down to the river (we could get quite carried away), and determined to remain at the centre of the community; each September the school holds a street party for all residents. Built in the 70s from an amalgam of previous schools on a site at the top of the town, where there is still a fine Roman mosaic floor buried under the sports pitches – seems a pity. As the town's only secondary school, there is a very inclusive feel about the place, appreciated by parents and students alike. A heartening initiative is the pairing of children with special needs with abler companions on an away-day, all of whom can miss a day in the classroom without detriment, or (better) to their mutual benefit. 'The staff have really stuck with my daughter who has ADHD,' said one mum. The Christian ethos of the school is apparent – it is a Church of England school – and the head's personal faith is clearly important to him, but regular church-going plays no part in the admissions process. Neither is it touchy-feely to the exclusion of real endeavour and winning, whether places at Oxbridge/Russell group, on the rugby pitch or eventing at nearby Stonar – but all achievement is celebrated. Despite its ancient setting, the buildings are largely unremarkable, with the exception of the new Moulton maths block, named for its benefactor, local cycle manufacturer Moulton Bicycle Company, which boasts the latest eco-wizardry, including a turf roof.

Pastoral care, well-being and discipline: Very much a place where achievement is talked up, and positive reinforcement rules. Vivos (sic) – an electronic points system – are awarded for good work, mannerly behaviour and everything one would wish to encourage, then totted up and go towards house totals for ceremonies at the end of term. We heard very little about discipline from anyone. The vertical tutor groups were universally praised – as well as offering support to younger students, one parent suggested that they also reduce bullying, as bullies would not want to be known as such by their tutor group and risk consequent disapproval. Tutors appear to play a more meaningful role here than many who bear that overused title, and teachers praised for knowing children as individuals.

Pupils and parents: Representative of the town and surrounding (affluent) villages. A lower than average percentage of children on free school meals and predominantly white, but, as the head points out, the absence of notorious estates in Bradford-on-Avon does not mean an absence of pupils with difficult home circumstances. 'We try to reach less confident parents who find negotiating herds of middle class parents very daunting', says he. When asked to describe a typical St Laurence student, he replied, 'Terrific, in terms of sociability, openness and enthusiasm.' We will have to take his word for it, as we met but two of them when we visited.

Entrance: At 11, 220 places applicants mostly from five local primary schools, but a significant number from outside the catchment area, including some from local prep schools; oversubscribed. As an academy, the admissions policy is set by the governors but applications are made through Wiltshire LA. Transition arrangements highly praised. At sixth form, applications are made direct to the school: five GCSEs at grade C or above including English and maths are required, with Bs in A level subject, four for BTec courses. All hopefuls are interviewed at the school.

Exit: About a third leave after GCSEs, the majority of those to further education. Negligible, if any, fall-out at year 8 when children could go to local independents at 13+. 'We didn't even consider it,' said one mother who might perhaps have wavered at year 7. In 2016, one Cambridge place (maths) and two medics;

vast majority of sixth formers got to university. Famous former students are mostly sportsmen and women, in rugby and water sports.

Money matters: Lots of extras on offer, such as trips, for which parents pay, but amounts seem very reasonable, payment terms are long and gradual and anyone likely to experience difficulty is encouraged to say so at the earliest opportunity. Very active parents' association, which, as a registered charity, maximises its revenues by tapping the CSR resources of parents' employers, as well as dealing with second-hand uniform and holding fundraising events to provide extras, such as special effects for drama and data-logging equipment for the science labs.

Remarks: Comprehensive education does not get much better than this. Parents in a position to choose from the entire range of education on offer in the UK choose St Laurence. If you live locally, why look anywhere else?

St Mary Redcliffe and Temple School

Somerset Square, Redcliffe, Bristol BS1 6RT

Pupils: 1,702 • Ages: 11–18 • Sixth form: 621 • C of E

Tel: 01173 772100
Email: enquiries@smrt.bristol.sch.uk
Website: www.smrt.bristol.sch.uk

Headteacher: Since 2005, Elisabeth Gilpin MA, formerly head of St Augustine of Canterbury Joint Roman Catholic and Church of England school in Oxford. A science teacher by background, she has also taught in schools in Bath and West Sussex. As a state-educated Oxford graduate, she is keen to encourage the most able students at her comprehensive to aim for Oxbridge. She is a National Leader of Education and vice chair of Anglican Academy and Secondary School Heads Association.

Small in stature, she is big on enthusiasm for young people and hopes for their future. Her joy at her students' successes means that on results day she is as likely as they are to be leaping into the air for the photographers. She embodies the school's belief that 'the glory of God is a human being fully alive'.

She is married with a teenage son and loves salsa dancing.

Academic matters: SMRT is consistently one of the highest achieving state schools in the west of England, with 76 per cent of students gaining at least five A*-C GCSE grades including English and maths in 2016 and 32 per cent of grades A*/A. In the large sixth form, 80 per cent of grades were C or above. The school was one of the first to be rated outstanding by Ofsted under the new, tougher framework, and it was also judged outstanding in its latest diocesan inspection.

The curriculum is mainly an academic one, although some BTec level 2 courses are offered. Humanities have always been a strength; SMRT became one of the first humanities specialist schools in the country in 2004 and has worked with other secondaries to support them in these subjects, leading to the development of a successful revision website called Take Five. Unsurprisingly, there is a strong emphasis on RE and 'values-based' learning.

The school says it will be flexible with how and what it teaches 'where that is useful', but resists changing to meet every new idea. Mrs Gilpin says: 'We keep the best of the traditional approach and combine it with up to date teaching methods.'

The KS4 and KS5 timetable is built each year to take account of student choices and, because of the size of the cohort, can accommodate some unusual combinations. The sixth form offers about 40 A level courses. 'We want students to go where their strengths are. What makes us distinctive is the balance we can provide,' says the head.

Parents seem generally happy with what is on offer, although one expressed a disappointment with modern foreign languages in KS3. 'I don't like the system of alternate years being taught French and German – in my opinion it would be much better to either do both or give pupils a choice from year 7.' The amount of homework is quite high, which is welcomed by some parents and is a slight concern to others.

SMRT, which has more than 1,500 students and 180 staff, has been designated a school of excellence for gifted and talented as a result of its position as a high performing specialist school. It is now, in alliance with partners including the University of Bristol, Bristol Diocese and the AASSH, seeking teaching school status.

It has an unusually large leadership team of nine, including the head, which Mrs Gilpin says helps enable it to be outward-facing, sharing its successes and learning from others.

Games, options, the arts: A recent £23 million modernisation enhanced the sporting offer. The swimming pool was retained so swimming lessons continue – not to the delight of all students! – and the gym was also kept, to be used for dance lessons. A huge new sports hall, the width of four badminton courts, provides a full-sized basketball court that is used by a professional side, Bristol Storm, as well as students. Volleyball is also a popular option. Outside, there are more facilities than might be expected on a cramped inner-city site, including tennis and netball courts and a long-jump pit. Moves to floodlight the new all-weather pitch are progressing. For field sports, students have to travel to grounds at Brislington and, from this year, some slightly nearer in Knowle.

Music is a strength, both within lessons and in extracurricular activities. The staff have a range of talents and are supported by visiting teachers, and the facilities for practice and performance are first rate. The gospel choir is a particular highlight, as are the annual musical theatre productions. In recent years, shows have included Little Shop of Horrors, West Side Story, Hairspray and Les Misérables.

The public art aspect of the redevelopment of SMRT involved the Bristol-based photographer, Martin Parr, making a pictorial record of a year at the school. It began with students wearing the former grey uniform and ended with them in their new raspberry sweaters. Eight of his shots are displayed in huge format around the building.

Students take part in the Duke of Edinburgh Award scheme and there are regular World Challenge expeditions to eg Ecuador. The school has a long-established partnership with Ikoba School in Uganda as part of links between the Bristol diocese and the church in Uganda and the Bristol-Masindi Schools Partnership. Staff and students take part in exchange visits.

There's also an emphasis on green issues and on what Elizabeth Gilpin describes as 'creative, confidence-building opportunities'. A student won the television The Speaker competition a few years ago and every year students enter the citywide Gabblers public speaking contest. Young Enterprise, Envision, Christian Union and voluntary community service are among other activities.

Background and atmosphere: It is hard to believe this is such a big school – it is so quiet! The atmosphere is calm and the building is modern, functional and well-ordered. Facilities for students such as breakfast provision and the learning resource centre are available off the covered 'street', which works well for those who arrive early from outlying areas of Bristol. The school says the standard of behaviour was always good but has improved thanks to the well-designed wide corridors and social spaces. Students are proud of the new building and look after it well. Memorabilia from the school's 430-year history is on display.

SMRT is clear about its high expectations for creating a school community of hope based on Christian principles and featuring good relationships, safe boundaries and empowered learning. What this boils down to, it says, is that it wants every student to be able to say: 'I feel safe; I belong here; I enjoy learning and achieve well; this school helps me to make my hopes for the future come true.'

A parent commented: 'There is a compassionate ethos which seems to be shared by staff and pupils. Teaching in most subjects is excellent and expectations are high, which leads to great results. Communication between the school and parents is open and supportive.'

Worship is an important part of school life and one of SMRT's most distinctive features. Services take place in the historic and beautiful St Mary Redcliffe Church at the start and end of each term and for the annual Colston Day. These are supplemented by regular clergy visits and house assemblies.

Pastoral care, well-being and discipline: SMRT has clear systems in place for behaviour. Students are given levels from A* to E. The highest grades are not merely for complying with rules but must include behaviour that supports and enhances learning for others. Anyone who needs help gets it in the appropriate way and liaison with parents is strong. Learning support is an integral part of the school. 'We generally intervene early to sort things out before they become a problem,' says Mrs Gilpin. There has been only one permanent exclusion in the past three years. Attendance levels are good too – close to 96 per cent.

The school is proud of its pastoral care. Children come into year 7 from schools in every Bristol postcode and some will not know anyone else when they arrive. Year 7s register in a separate place, the Temple Colston building, and have their own house.

A parent whose child started recently said: 'The school was excellent during the induction day in showing the children where the bus stops were, so that this was never a difficulty for her. Since starting, the school has carried out several assessments across all subjects and found work at exactly the right level for our child. She has made friends very easily and the children were given time to adjust to the new school before homework was set. Everything has been paced very well. We are delighted and are full of confidence that she is being very well taught and cared for.'

Vertical tutoring has become trendy in recent years but at SMRT years 8 to 11 have been organised in mixed age tutor groups since 1966 as part of the school's Christian family ethos. Students are allocated to one of four houses – Canynges, Cartwright, Colston and Francombe (moves to modernise the traditional names were resisted). 'It is a way of creating smaller units of belonging within a large organisation,' says Mrs Gilpin.

The sixth form is in a separate building, the Redcliffe Sixth Form Centre, about five minutes away from the main site. Students come to the school to run clubs and mentor younger children. Some feel they would like to integrate more with the rest of the school while others value the independence and the more college-like atmosphere. Parents value the supportive atmosphere of the sixth form, which takes in external students as well as those from SMRT.

'The sixth form is excellent – support for learning and for the university application process is very strong and there is a very good rapport between students and teachers,' said one.

Pupils and parents: Pupils come from a range of communities across greater Bristol. Elizabeth Gilpin describes the school population as 'uniquely socially diverse' and says, 'We are passionately committed to social inclusion and want everybody from every background to achieve their best'. The school has a comparatively high number of children in care among its pupils. Mrs Gilpin says the admissions policy is deliberately structured to create a rich ethnic mix. The school has a higher than average number of students from black and minority ethnic backgrounds – over a third. Some parents from predominantly white areas have made positive choice to send their children to SMRT because of this diversity.

The school takes pride in students of all backgrounds who overcome challenges. One lad with Asperger's and sensory neuropathy gained four A*s at A level and won a place at Cambridge recently. The experienced sixth form team helps support a number of students into Oxbridge and medical school every year.

Communication with parents via monthly newsletters and a comprehensive website is good. One parent of a sixth-former who joined SMRT from another school said: 'She has had a great start in all her classes where the staff have made high expectations very clear from the outset and been supportive where needed. Our daughter was able to take all the A level subjects she wanted to study and has already been on art and physics trips. There are so many extracurricular activities in the large sixth form that there is bound to be something to suit the vast majority of children. Thanks to the excellent online school calendar and sixth form newsletter, we already know the key dates that our daughter and we need to be aware of this year in terms of mock exams, university applications, parents' evenings and more. There are plenty of opportunities to develop leadership and communication skills too.'

The school runs regular training and briefing sessions for parents, which are much appreciated.

Entrance: SMRT is an Anglican voluntary-aided school and admits children from all Christian communities in the Bristol area. More than 80 places of worship are represented, including mosques. The school offers 216 places each year. Sixteen are reserved for children of any faith living in immediate vicinity of the school and four are allocated to children of other faiths. Priority is given to those who attend church most regularly.

SMRT has come under fire from the Fair Admissions campaigners, who accuse it of selecting wealthy pupils by the back door because it has a low proportion of students on free school meals compared with the numbers living in its immediate locality. But the school says this is a misrepresentation, as few teenagers live in the tower blocks close by and the number of places it has available is sufficient to meet demand.

Exit: The majority of year 11 leavers (about two-thirds) go into Redcliffe sixth form. A high proportion of year 13 leavers (around 70 per cent) go to university. Degree subject choices include maths, physics, geography, history, English, film, journalism and psychology. In 2016, five to Oxbridge, including one to read medicine, plus three more medics elsewhere, supported by strong links to local university departments.

Money matters: Children in care, care leavers and students in receipt of income support are guaranteed a non-discretionary bursary. Beyond this all awards are discretionary and depend on the availability of adequate funds and the volume of eligible applications.

Remarks: A school so firmly based on a second century line from St Irenaeus might seem incongruous in the 21st century. The words 'The Glory of God is a human being fully alive' could even be a tad embarrassing to some believers (and to some teenagers) – yet at SMRT they are embraced without apology and feel totally natural and right. They provide the roots on which a happy and thriving school has been built.

St Mary's Calne

    134

Curzon Street, Calne, Wiltshire SN11 0DF

Pupils: 346; 282 boarders • Ages: 11–18 • Sixth form: 110 • C of E

Fees: Day £27,150; Boarding £36,450 pa

Tel: 01249 857200
Email: admissions@stmaryscalne.org
Website: www.stmaryscalne.org

Headmistress: Since 2013, Dr Felicia Kirk MA PhD (early 40s). Born and raised in Maryland, USA, Dr Kirk's distinguished academic career in languages, both ancient and modern, took her to the École Normale Supérieure in Paris, where she met the Brit she would later follow to England and marry, leaving the groves of academe for the real world of teaching children. Her first job was at the Royal Hospital School in Suffolk, followed by a move into girls' education as director of higher education at Wycombe Abbey, then latterly as head of sixth form at Ipswich High School. Of her move to Calne, she says, 'I missed the boarding, and I liked the fact that the school is small, yet ambitious'.

Totally committed to girls' education, she intends to build on breadth of opportunity at Calne 'unencumbered by gender stereotyping'; building both literally and figuratively, that is, with an ambitious 10 year development plan to squeeze every last square inch (OK, centimetre, then) out of this school's compact site, with increased provision for arts, sports, a new library and more science labs. Any faint question marks about an American leading this very British institution are utterly dispelled on meeting her – she's hardly even mid-Atlantic in accent, and elegantly clad in a tweed jacket with velvet collar the day we visited – and parents appreciate the richness brought by experience from elsewhere, as well as her plans for the place: 'The school needs more than academia to keep it at the top table,' said one mother. Try as we might, it was impossible to break through her professional, though charming, veneer. Her girls describe her as enthusiastic and easy to talk to, are pleased to see her walking her dog in trackies and to receive a birthday card in their first year. 'Plus she's innovative,' said one. What does that mean again? 'It's new stuff like introducing company jumpers,' said a helpful friend.

Dr Kirk is married to an accountant. Her home is in Suffolk, where she also keeps her retired eventer.

Academic matters: Undoubtedly what the school is about, but not all it's about. At A level, 54 per cent A*/A grades in 2016. Stand-out subjects are maths, history, Spanish and Latin.

At GCSE, results have crept up over recent years to the point where 78 per cent were A*/A in 2016. Geography, Latin, art, and music excel here. Results are more exciting than the classrooms which produce them, and teaching does not appear to be as reliant on IT as is the case in many schools we see; that said, refurbishing the labs cannot come a moment too soon. Library provision too is good but scattered, and will be consolidated under the development plan. Enrichment week – inter alia, gung ho girls in camouflage crawling enthusiastically under netting taking orders from an army officer – was in full swing when we visited, but we were pleased to note an A level history class of about six discussing Mary Tudor's relationship with the clergy, rather than the apparently ceaseless rehashing of the two world wars. Ditto Northanger Abbey read in its entirety in year 9 – none of these bite-sized chunks beloved of modern exam setters. Recent success enjoyed in prestigious maths and German Olympiad competitions too. SEN provision is as expected at a school of this calibre – definitely the mild end of dys- spectra – though everyone is tested on entry. About eight per cent of girls have an identifiable educational need catered for; provision equally is made for EAL and the very brightest sparks too.

Games, options, the arts: An astonishing amount of sporting facilities is crammed into this compact site, with more planned. A full-sized Astro and new netball/tennis courts (all floodlit) opened in the few days before our visit form part of an ambitious upgrade of the sports offer, which has already seen the leasing of pitches plus track and field facilities a short distance away, making the hosting of fixtures with other schools easier. Lacrosse is the winter sport on offer, alongside netball, which is played against schools not offering lax; hockey is played in the spring term. The youngest girls all represent the school early on; later, team practice becomes optional and from year 10, girls can drop ball sports altogether, as long as they do something to get them off the couch and away from the toaster. Tennis, swimming, fencing happen all year round, rowing and sailing in summer. Though no horses reside at school, show-jumping and eventing are a successful part of the sporting calendar. Skiing is prominent too: as well as the usual ski-trip, school also takes part in the quaintly named but deadly serious British Schoolgirls Races in Flaine each year, to some acclaim.

The arts take centre stage. Huge portraits adorn the entrance (colloquially known as the goldfish bowl), and paintings most of the walls. Sculpture is big here too – long before art becomes a GCSE option, junior girls experiment with life-sized figures. A full size war horse and cavalry officer in the early stages of construction out of wood and chicken wire has to be built in a gazebo outside the art school: 'I can't wait for the new studios,' remarked one member of staff with feeling. Drama a high point too: an inspirational head of drama who retired a few years ago left a legacy of adventurous excellence, which is not limited to an annual musical, Shakespeare (recently an all-female Hamlet), performances at the egg theatre in Bath and at the Edinburgh Fringe. Tess of the d'Urbervilles was on the week we visited – we were charmed by the hay and ancient agricultural machinery strewn throughout the foyer of a somewhat tired theatre. Quite the glossiest programmes we had ever seen. Much of the singing harks back to its roots in the English choral tradition, to be expected in a school where chapel is still central to its life, but its reach extends to the charitable, profitable and glittery: a concert at Chelsea Old Church with a sideshow of celebrities raised £19,000. A symphony orchestra, jazz band, opera, string and flute groups complete the offering, which both brings top performers into school, takes musicians out of school (not only in the UK but abroad to Paris and so on) and music to local venues and primary schools as part of its community outreach. Generously resourced and imaginative in scope, the music department recently commissioned an opera to commemorate the start of WW1.

Boarding: The majority board, housed in year groups and moved into accommodation of increasing luxury each year as they progress up the school; day girls belong to houses along with their boarding counterparts and integration seems seamless. The new lower sixth house with its en-suite bathrooms and groovy décor (not sure about the bilious green chairs, however) will surpass anything likely to be encountered in most freshers' lodging, or even at home. House unity, as generally understood, is generated through companies, five groups of girls of all ages named after former bishops of Salisbury; a coloured band on the regulation navy jumper denotes it, and the company shout (known elsewhere as house music) loudly affirms it.

Background and atmosphere: Founded in 1873 by the then vicar of Calne, as a place where girls would receive an excellent academic grounding and would be able to develop their individuality within an Anglican foundation, the school still delivers on all three fronts. Its compact site right in the small somewhat undistinguished (yes, the last entry said that, but we agree) Wiltshire town means a lack of rolling acres and constant improvement, redevelopment, refurbishment rather than expansion of existing facilities, resulting in a startling mix of architectural styles redolent of the time they were built. No pretty gardens or places to escape to for a quiet cig, that we could detect – maybe that is why vice seems so notably absent. Parents like the fact that the school is not London-y, though there is a posse from London and buses run at the start and end of every term and half-term.

It all feels quite cosy and its size is frequently mentioned as a positive by both girls and parents. Uniform is ubiquitous kilted skirt and light blue blouse. Sixth formers' dress code is quite relaxed, and perhaps because there are no boys, make-up is minimal. Unquestionably a female preserve or possibly a refuge, but not a nunnery: 'It's easier and less distracting not having boys around,' said one little scrap, though the junior dorms were full of pictures of boys (and ponies), known or dreamed about. Older girls regret the lack of socials with boys' schools, though the mixed lacrosse match is possibly a less stilted encounter.

It all feels rather traditional, despite the 14 per cent from overseas, partly on account of daily chapel, not always religious, but serious and, when the occasion demands it, reverent.

Pastoral care, well-being and discipline: Highly rated by both girls and parents. Each girl is allocated a tutor (who can be changed in the unusual event of it not working out) and has a weekly individual meeting. Between the housemistress and tutor, 'it's like having a mum and dad at school,' said one. Plenty of avenues to seek help if ever things go wrong, and generous provision for anyone needing medical attention, with a fully equipped, permanently manned medical centre. Not only is good work (both absolute and relative) rewarded by 'blues', but so are other virtues such as kindness, punctuality and tidiness. A 'good egg' prize is awarded each year for the sort of qualities which make a community run joyously. Miscreants who talk after lights might be made to do the house washing up the following day; major sins attract an escalating scale of punishment. Smokers' fines are donated to cancer charities.

Pupils and parents: Well-mannered and forthright with plenty of get-up-and-go. 'If you want something started, ask a Calne girl,' said the head. The ones we met were certainly privileged but not in the slightest bit tiresome. One mother said she chose the school because she wanted confidence not arrogance instilled in her daughters; something the girls in Grosstete company might be particularly mindful of. The school appears to run on old money, rather than new – 'The car park is full of Audis, Volvos and battered old Fords,' one parent observed – with a tangible affection from its former pupils, some of whom send their daughters. Considerable camaraderie on the lacrosse touchline too.

Entrance: Registration is advised three or four years ahead of proposed entry at year 7 (LIV in school parlance). Places conditional on entrance exams (either CE or school's own 11+ exam) are offered after an assessment day held in the September one year before entry. Process for 13+ (year 9, UIV) starts a year earlier; assessment day held almost two years before entry. Bright sparks are invited to apply for scholarships. Girls come from the smarter prep schools in the south and south west, some from London, some from school's own prep, St Margaret's, and a few from local primaries.

Around 15 new into sixth form with good GCSEs, sparkling in subjects to be taken to A level

Exit: A handful – some 15 per cent – leave after GCSE in search of (in no particular order) boys, brighter lights, wider subject choices, more freedom; the rest to top notch universities up and down the land or art foundation. A handful to Oxbridge every year (five in 2016), the majority of the rest to Russell group. In 2014, nearly half the cohort – an unusually high number – did not go straight to university; online speculation bubbled, yet the school assured us that more girls were taking gap years and that those wishing to apply to university post A level were equally well supported through UCAS even though they were no longer at school. School takes great care over the next stage: hosting a higher education conference for GSA, Oxbridge aptitude testing in school and Futures, a new half termly publication covering exclusively university applications, developments and more adventurous overseas options, plus alumnae experience. Increasing number of gap years. Famous OGs include Laura Bechtolsheimer, Olympic dressage medallist, and writer Lucy Hughes-Hallett (plus David Cameron's sister).

Money matters: Not a rich school, but one husbanding and developing its resources to ensure its place amongst the UK's top girls' schools. Usual range of scholarships offered, including a choral scholarship at 13+. A nominal five per cent fee reduction is given, but up to 40 per cent depending on means-testing. Two sixth form scholarships to internal candidates and one to external on offer too. A foundation scholarship of up to 100 per cent of day fees at both year 7 and sixth form is aimed exclusively at state school pupils for whom 'reasons of financial restriction' would otherwise preclude going there.

Remarks: A school for clever girls? Certainly, though 'it doesn't matter if they're not – they're usually good at something else.' Quintessential English girls' boarding? Absolutely. Social cachet? Unquestionably.

St Mary's School (Shaftesbury)

Donhead St. Mary, Shaftesbury, Dorset SP7 9LP

Pupils: 200; 130 boarders • Ages: 9–18 • Sixth form: 70 • RC

Fees: Day £15,750 – £19,950; Boarding £19,500 – £30,990 pa

Tel: 01747 852416
Email: registrar@stmarys.eu
Website: www.stmarys.eu

Headteacher: Since January 2016, Mrs Mary Arnal MSc, PGCE, FRSA, previously head of Sherborne International School, and before that head of the prep school at St Teresa's, Effingham.

S

She is an applied linguist with a masters from Edinburgh, and has a background in university lecturing and teaching in the UK and overseas, including being senior housemistress at St John's School Leatherhead. Her specialist subjects are English language and philosophy and she has experience teaching the IB in Spain, where she was director of studies at a school in Madrid. She has also taught and lived in Peru. She describes herself as English by birth, Irish by blood and Spanish in spirit.

Mary is married to mathematical analyst, Don Antonio Arnal; they have two children.

Academic matters: Popular A level subjects include English literature, history and history of art, geography, fine art and photography. Steady uptake of science, economics, business studies, maths and modern languages. For a small school with pupils of mixed ability, results are consistently good. In 2016, 72 per cent of A levels graded A*-B and 48 per cent A*/A. Drama AS level continues to broaden the range of subjects available.

GCSE results also good with 56 per cent A*/A in 2016. Girls do well in English literature, modern languages, science, the humanities and art. Languages department has introduced iGCSE exams throughout and runs a language 'circus' where girls can try Spanish or German for a term; six-week taster sessions in Italian and Portuguese also on offer. French exchanges for those interested.

Parents praise 'very experienced teaching staff' for their dedication, openness and lack of pretension. Some have been there for years, but head says the average age is beginning to come down. General consensus is that self-motivated girls are very well supported. 'If you do want to be bothered [with work], the teachers will bend over backwards.' One commented that the school 'hides its academic light under a bushel', although all agreed that 'the teaching shines'.

Three dedicated SEN rooms at the top of humanities block helps those with mild learning difficulties (dyslexia, dyspraxia) as well as running revision sessions and helping girls to improve their grades in maths and English. At the time of our visit, 46 pupils (up to three at a time) were receiving EAL coaching.

Games, options, the arts: 'Sport for all' is school's aim and girls play all the usual sports up to GCSE plus a few less common, eg water polo, yoga, pilates and zumba. School will lay on an activity if there is sufficient interest, eg scuba diving. In years 10 and 11 girls have access to the school's fitness suite and can begin the sports leaders programme which continues in sixth form for those taking A level PE. Circuit training and conditioning machines used for school's elite athlete training programme. Large sports hall and 25m pool sit side by side, surrounded by Astroturf pitch, netball and tennis courts. Swimming and tennis available year round. A few girls play hockey at county level and train at the county netball academy, with some year 10 girls put forward for LTA tennis league each year. Regular match fixtures and swimming galas throughout the year; teams hold their own and win against much larger schools.

S

Stunning, spacious art block opened in 2014; the creative arts are a real strength here and evidence of this hangs in corridors throughout the main school building. 'Art is outstanding and all visual arts are very good.' Busy textiles room with lots of sewing machines humming; textiles and design taught in six-month blocks, fine art all year. Photography offered at GCSE and A level and textiles at GCSE. Trips abroad to exhibitions in Paris, Florence and Barcelona for sixth formers.

Excellent music block, with 25 individual practice rooms, small concert space, music technology room and dedicated classroom, plus a well-stocked music library with archive material and CD recordings. Some 60 per cent learn a musical instrument, 15 per cent study two and some learn two instruments and singing. Each term, around 40 girls take ABRSM and Trinity Guildhall practical exams. Instrumental lessons rotate through the school day up to year 9, after which they are fixed; practice is timetabled. Ensembles include school orchestra, percussion and wind bands plus a rock band; others are formed depending on instruments and girls are encouraged to take the initiative. Everyone sings each week, either in class or as a form. Young maths teacher runs a GLEE club. 'The school needs a bit more singing outside the chapel choir.' Two school choirs, one of which is the 'awesome' chapel choir which rehearses three mornings a week for chapel assemblies, Sunday mass and tours abroad. St Cecilia's pupils' concert takes place each year. Regular outreach to primary schools and local choirs, including annual Choral Day.

Extensive range of extracurricular activities, clubs and societies on offer; these include equestrian polo, rock climbing and a young enterprise scheme. French society is very popular and includes a literary circle. Sixth formers can qualify for Leith's Basic Certificate in Food and Wine in well-appointed cookery school. Several drama productions across the age range each year and LAMDA exams are popular. D of E awards are a big part of school life, with two-thirds completing these every year. In keeping with school's Catholic ethos, girls fundraise and lead charitable expeditions to countries such as Rwanda, Chile and Zambia to work with schools and orphanages. The Mary Ward Lecture Series encourages girls to think through listening to speakers on topics such as war theory, bioethics and religious pluralism.

Boarding: Boarding arrangements work well; years 7 and 8 board separately in individual 'cubies'; day girls are welcome to visit the boarding house. After this, girls move into one of four houses where they sleep in single, double or four-person bedrooms. Some bedrooms are small, but each house has a spacious common room and a kitchen. Rooms rotate regularly and day-to-day housekeeping is efficient. 'A brilliant woman runs the laundry and the shift system for washing clothes works.' Parents full of praise for sixth form housemistress. 'She's seen everything and can deal with anything.' Girls in sixth form are given independence, eg preparing their own breakfast and entertaining outside friends to dinner parties.

Two-thirds are full boarders, so school doesn't empty out on weekends, though flexi-boarding is available. Day girls can go home after lessons, but many choose to stay on for clubs, homework and supper. Supervised prep sessions on Saturday mornings and plenty to do on weekends. Long, wrap-around green kilts up to year 11 are very popular with the girls; sixth form uniform phased out in favour of smart home clothes.

Boarders are escorted to and from various airport terminals by school minibus on exeat weekends, at half-term and at the beginning and end of term; those going to London on exeats can travel by escorted coach to Richmond. Parents confirm that school is very aware of where girls are.

Background and atmosphere: St Mary's was founded in 1945 and can trace its origins back to Mary Ward, an English Catholic nun who championed the rights of girls to receive an education, despite living in hostile Tudor times. Imprisoned for her beliefs, she succeeded in establishing a school for girls in York before her death in 1645.

With the school set in 55 acres of parkland and approached down a winding, tree-lined drive, there is a sense of leaving the outside world behind as one arrives at an imposing early Victorian mansion. Sensitive efforts have been made to modernise the interior, with glass screens to let in light. Spread around the main house is a collection of buildings ranging from ultra-modern to slightly frayed labs and other older classrooms. New and old nestle side by side and somehow manage not to look incongruous, but the impression is of much brown and green.

In contrast to the school's cooler colours is its warm, family atmosphere. Teachers, parents and girls alike champion it as safe and nurturing. 'It's a very caring school which fosters life-long friendships.' Walking round, we were struck by the genuinely supportive relationships between girls of all ages. 'If you could bottle the atmosphere at St Mary's, it would be invaluable.'

Head has reinstated years 5 and 6.

Pastoral care, well-being and discipline: Strongly underpinned by school's Catholic faith, pastoral care is 'brilliant' and 'house assistants are excellent'. 'Somehow the school makes the girls very caring and respectful.' Full-time chaplain lives on campus, with school's own priest in residence from Thursday to Sunday. Anglican minister visits once a week to lead the Eucharist. 'The school operates more on praise than sanction,' said one parent. Any misdemeanour earns the culprit a lavender ticket, 'lavvies' to the girls. Punishments range from parental meeting to suspension. 'The girls want their community to work – we have to deal with so few sanctions.' Strict on smoking and alcohol, the odd suspension has happened for having one too many at socials with boys' schools.

Despite being 'in the sticks', parents insist their daughters don't feel cut off as school allows enough freedom. Thirteen-year-olds don wellies and stride off in small groups over the fields for Saturday afternoon shopping in Shaftesbury; older girls catch the train to Salisbury. School puts on a bus to Bath if enough girls wish to go.

School meals served in cafeteria with staff on hand to supervise; good food with several choices including a vegetarian option, plenty of fresh fruit, cheese and puddings.

Girls are allowed mobile phones, but no Skype or Facebook until year 11. School Wifi switched off at night. School says that trust between staff and pupils forms the basis of school community; 'older staff are very good at dealing with any minor teasing or bullying'.

Pupils and parents: Girls joining in years 5 and 7 come from local primaries, London day schools and boarding preps, eg Leaden Hall. Intake doubles at 13+ from prep schools such as Farleigh, Sandroyd and Port Regis. Some foreign nationals join the school later. Average year group numbers 55, with 70 per cent of families within an hour's drive. Some 15 per cent from abroad, mostly Mexico, Spain and Hong Kong, with a few from Nigeria, Japan and the rest of Europe. There are 25 military families, though no extra bursaries for Forces. Parents are a mixed bunch, some wealthy, some not, whilst girls are natural, unspoilt, polite and articulate. 'The girls like themselves, know themselves and are very confident in their own skins.'

Entrance: Main entry points are at nine,11 and 13, although girls can join in any year. Entrance examination day takes place in January and includes tests in maths, English and verbal reasoning plus an interview. At 16, girls need a minimum of eight GCSE C grades. Families must be 'sympathetic to the Catholic ethos' of the school.

Exit: Up to half leave after GCSEs. Most sixth formers to Russell Group universities throughout the country, eg Bristol, Exeter, UCL, Manchester, Newcastle and Edinburgh. Oxford Brookes also popular. One to Oxford in 2016 (English), plus one medic and one vet. A good handful to art college each year, eg Bournemouth, Falmouth and Plymouth. Most choose arts degrees; good to see that a sprinkling of girls opts for the sciences, eg anatomy, biomedical sciences, physics and nuclear astrophysics. A small number pursues practical courses such as agriculture, publishing and events management.

Money matters: Usual range of 9+, 11+, 13+ and 16+ music, academic, sports and art scholarships on offer together with one 11+ Catholic Local Primary Scholarship. Head's Scholarships 'for excellence' plus means-tested bursaries worth up to 50 per cent of school fees are available at school's discretion.

Remarks: In the past we have described St Mary's as 'a jolly nice girls' Catholic boarding school' but this belies its true character. A reasonably pacey school, St Mary's is performing pretty well on all fronts, albeit with great modesty. 'They don't blow their own trumpet enough,' remarked a parent. With lower fees than many independent schools, this school is quietly delivering excellent value. Girls wanting to be educated with boys and/or dolled up to the nines should look elsewhere, but those looking for a warm and caring environment where they can achieve and be themselves will be right at home.

St Peter's School

Harefield, Lympstone, Exmouth, Devon EX8 5AU

Pupils: 281; 10 flexi boarders • Ages: 3-13 (flexi boarding from 7)

Fees: Day £7,140 – £12,255; Boarding £18,435 pa

Tel: 01395 272148
Email: hmoffice@stpetersprepschool.co.uk
Website: www.stpetersprep.co.uk

Head: Since September 2016, Charlotte Johnston, previously deputy head (academic) at Edge Grove School in Herts. Studied English and history of art at Birmingham; PGCE primary from University of Herts; MEd from Buckingham. Worked as a change management consultant for PwC; after starting a family she retrained as a teacher and joined Edge Grove in 2002. She and Oliver (a police officer) have two children.

Entrance: Non-selective: 'not saturated with tests on taster days,' we were told. Takes rising 3s upwards; staff will decide on admission either into KG or nursery class (voucher system operates but those not aiming at pre-prep go to back of the queue).

Exit: Most remain to 13 and proceed to south-west independent day and boarding schools (eg Exeter, Blundells, Wellington, Taunton). Up to two-thirds obtain scholarships; net is being cast wider to include Badminton, Canford and Sherborne. Small number leaves at end of year 6, mainly to Colyton and Torquay grammars.

Remarks: Founded in 1882, St Peter's enjoys a stunning position (a sign near the main entrance invites visitors to 'please enjoy the view') overlooking the Exe estuary. Built for a local notable in late 1820s, Harefield House was in the hands of the Peters family (a portrait of late Admiral Sir Arthur Peters can be seen on the main staircase) for a century until 1949 when the then head, Mr Theophilus Rhys Jones (grandfather of HRH Sophie), moved the school here from Exmouth. Current bursar and a former head are co-proprietors; school is run by an executive management team, assisted by a broad-based committee of reference; estate trustees have considerable say on development issues.

Produces 'aspirational pupils' of all abilities; hugely committed staff are encouraged to 'go with their own ideas.' Home-grown baccalaureate encompasses three key learning skills: curiosity, finding and presenting. Core academic areas are balanced by creative and performing arts, plus sport and personal qualities. All children are marked throughout school for effort. Emphasis on personalised learning: children present their understanding using any medium which suits them (which may well not be essay writing). Senior schools have shown considerable interest in this approach. Experienced academic team track children's achievement with emphasis on early intervention.

Co-educational since 1974, balance between sexes fluctuates from year to year; overall numbers close to capacity. Small (14 bed) flexi boarding facility with houseparents in charge; separate dormitories and combined games and common room areas. 'School makes a fuss of the boarders,' said one boarding mum whose son 'simply loves it.' Friday night provision entails sprog collection by 10am on Saturday.

Site includes three main outside areas. Lovely cricket pitch with own pavilion (highlight is annual game against Lympstone village team); adventure playground, separate 10-acre field nearby (used for athletics and rugby) is reached via safe path which snakes its way through much-used forest school woodland area; adjacent smaller field used for pre-prep sports as well as daily activities. New Astroturf for mini hockey and tennis; outside heated swimming pool in use between May and September. Refloored sports hall (squash court also in complex) provides a full size basketball court; doubles up as a venue for assemblies and smaller scale productions.

Discrete early years' section located in somewhat dated timber-clad classrooms: 'we're more interested in what goes on inside,' a mother told us. Carefully zoned outside play areas; new outside performance facility has sound system provided through parental fundraising. Cosy KG classroom boasts highest staff:pupil ratio. Easy transfer to nursery (shell 3) and 90 per cent proceed to reception (shell 4) classes. Forest school and outside learning an important element: we saw tinies enjoying hot chocolate by a camp fire.

We liked the way that planning, monitoring progress and regular information sharing with parents all figure prominently as part of a whole school approach. Goals for youngest broken down into 'stepping stones'. Wide range of reading resources; some nursery children are 'reading ready', we were told. Obvious focus on language development: separate 'time to talk' area promotes confidence; home/school diaries used daily; plenty of imaginative numeracy work: we saw youngest children measuring paper worms and making numbers with them. Lively classroom displays are linked to changing themes. Rôle play areas mutate from fairy castles to butterfly gardens. Regular pre-prep assemblies: classes take turns to present items. Music and French from the start.

Junior years in separate red-brick building. Streaming in English and maths from year 1, and from year 5 upwards teaching is subject-based. Top set all sit CE 11+ exams. Separate scholarship and CE sets in years 7 and 8. German and Spanish introduced in addition to French from year 7 plus Latin for scholars. High proportion of all-round scholarships obtained attributed to breadth of school's curriculum.

Seniors shuttle for lessons between outside classrooms, the main house and modernised science laboratory in wing of the sports hall. Refurbished library on ground floor of main house is focus for research including computers, book related activities throughout year eg for World Book Day. Large music room is used for classroom teaching and rehearsals. New ICT suite on first floor provides for class-based work and is carefully monitored. Large art and DT area in separate hut buzzes with creativity: scholars have own carrels and produce work which impressed us by its range and quality. Every pupil had picture in last art exhibition.

Two formal parents' evenings during year; staff often meet parents after school in flagpole area to sort out small concerns. Email access to all staff and regular newsletters.

Sixty-nine children currently on learning support register; two children are statemented. Strong, switched on remedial help with 'open doors' policy: 'nothing should ever be a shock to parents,' said SENCo, who came to St Peter's with 11 years' experience at Belmont Primary, Chiswick. Range of difficulties includes SpLD and mild Asperger's; to date no child has failed to get a place at a mainstream senior school.

Exceptionally strong sports record maintained over long period with more than a handful making at least county level representative teams. Usual major games for boys and girls; school has really shone at rugby (undefeated 1st XV), netball and squash recently; two boys recently represented English prep school U13 rugby team on tour to France and school also has current England prep schools' U13 squash champions. All children participate at some level; good fixture lists with south west schools, matches on Wednesday afternoons.

Sixty per cent of pupils have individual music tuition; director is supported by 14 peripatetic staff. School hosts Devon Youth Choir/Orchestra and Brass Band. Regular music assemblies, concerts and performances for soloists and groups throughout year. Activities include chamber choir, woodwind groups, brass ensemble and pop cantata. External festivals, competitions and evensong at Wellington School. Most recent tour to Edinburgh. Large scale dramatic productions staged in Exeter's Barnfield theatre.

Jolly lot of pupils with lots to do. No mobile phones allowed during school day. Staff will 'all go the extra mile,' we were told. 'The way everyone joins in to help with school productions speaks volumes,' said deputy head who runs Cross Keys (outdoor adventure) programme. Pupils get the Swallows and Amazons treatment and leave knowing they are achievers. Plenty of after-school activity with full range on Friday afternoons. Options start in year 1 and include drama, yoga and horse riding, not to mention cooking and sailing. Visits start early on and full blown tours feature at upper end and include year 7 stay at Château de la Baudonnière, artists staying in St Ives and ski trip to Andorra.

Pupils come from wide catchment area; many use fleet of liveried minibuses. School day for seniors ends at 5pm. Year 8 pupils take on responsibilities and have own social area. Children meet in tutor groups at start and end of each day. Holiday programme (site closes for only one week in summer) is heavily oversubscribed. Supportive Friends of St Peters run fundraisers and social events such as annual ball and more recently (de rigueur given head's origins) Burns Night celebration. Notable alumni include Olympic yachtsman Ben Rhodes, journalist Anna Tyzack and children's TV entertainer, Dominic Wood.

Bursaries granted on individual basis; substantial number of internal scholarships awarded for years 7 and 8 at head's discretion.

A school with a 'real heart' that may be short on some mod cons but compensates by giving value for money. Unique blend of progressive philosophy and traditional standards in a beautiful setting. Obviously happy children who achieve beyond expectations. A breath of fresh air in every sense.

Sale Grammar School

Marsland Road, Sale, Cheshire M33 3NH

Pupils: 1,250 • Ages: 11–18 • Sixth form: 350

Tel: 01619 733217
Email: office@salegrammar.co.uk
Website: www.salegrammar.co.uk

Headteacher: Since 2010, Mr Mark Smallwood BEd MA PGDip NPQH (early 50s). Studied at Manchester and Lancaster Universities (physics), taught in a number of state schools in the North West and for three years in the Bahamas; previously head of Fearns Community Sports College in Lancs. Teaches one lesson a week (IT, general studies). Married to a primary school teacher; three children – two at university, one in year 6. A Manchester United supporter and plays the tuba in a community wind band. Approachable, balanced, good sense of humour, well liked by children and parents, 'He's pragmatic, listens well, is fair and firm when necessary', relates in a natural, easy way with pupils, very visible around school.

Academic matters: High performing specialist school in visual art, science and maths. In 2016, 47 per cent A*/A grades at A level (76 per cent A*/B). No marked gender divide. Twenty-four subjects including philosophy, psychology, sociology, business studies, economics, politics, PE, performing arts, AQA Bacc, EPQ (perspectives on science), but no ICT; will run courses for very small numbers. Particularly successful geography, maths, physics, art, business studies, sociology; big numbers for separate sciences, English, maths, history, psychology.

In 2016, 60 per cent of GCSEs were at A*/A. Generally strong, especially separate sciences, French, geography, art, expressive arts. Spanish and French IGCSE, plus possibility of psychology; most achieve eight/nine at C or above; girls do better at very top grades. All do ECDL computer qualification in year 9; ASDAN (personal and social skills for life) taken via PSHE – good idea to give an extra qualification for what is usually an unexamined course.

Classes 20-30 at key stage 4, 5-16 at A level. Lots of extension activities by all departments and pupils encouraged to go beyond syllabus in homework (called 'extension studies' to promote this). Active learning week at end of summer term for year 7s (arts), 8s (humanities), 9s (camping), 10s (work experience), 12s (eg more work experience). Many opportunities for the most able students, eg university language enrichment course, poetry slam competition. Teachers praised by pupils we met as always ready to help – individual or revision sessions outside the classroom. Tiptop ICT facilities – home access to school network, masses of PCs and laptops, much use of electronic white boards, by staff and students.

Can accommodate all SENs provided entrance exam passed – in-class support if needed, outside for, eg spelling; SENco qualified to test for special exam considerations.

Games, options, the arts: Trad gym, good size sports hall with climbing wall, own Astro, uses off-site facilities for swimming and hockey. Usual sports including rugby, plus (successful) girls' football, lacrosse, indoor rowing, table tennis, trampolining, taekwondo; national and county players. Sports leadership qualification; sports tours to Cape Town, Malta.

Various ensembles, choirs and bands – wide range of instruments taught and music played; all year 7s take part in Christmas concert, spread over two nights. Annual school play is a big musical, eg Oliver! (girl Mr Bumble), West Side Story. Limited facilities, new performing arts centre on wish list. Plays performed in school hall; the drama studio lacks stage lighting and rehearsal space doubles as sixth form relaxation area (furnished, oddly, with a complete set of Hansards 1970-2000 donated by local MP). Also dance (boys too) and LAMDA. New music and PE facilities.

Outstanding visual art – excellent work in various media on display around school (year 12 artists successful in national competition). Input from professional artists and latest technology (iPads); ceramics area – own kiln. Interesting community projects, eg providing installations for Manchester hospitals. All take GCSE technology – choice of resistant materials, electronics, textiles (particularly strong results), food tech and graphics: not too influenced by gender (though we did see only one girl in an otherwise all male electronics class).

Good range of extracurricular clubs – debating, media team (produces high quality newsletter and monthly bulletins), science: medical/engineering/astronomy, chess, Spanish film, YE, expressive arts; community involvement as part of enrichment programme for sixth. International school status – works with twinned schools in South Africa; World Challenge to South America and Namibia; cultural exchanges with South Africa; annual trips to Spain and France. Plenty of careers advice.

Background and atmosphere: Pleasant red-brick original building with interestingly designed, spacious, modern additions. Light, wide corridors, spiral staircases and brightly coloured, fresh decoration – all well maintained. Much purple (school colour) throughout – fetching silver and purple ties, screensavers, sofas, pale purple brickwork... Attractive LRC primarily for sixth but shared with other years – lots of PCs but not many reference books: sign of these digital days. Sixth form also housed in Claremont Centre in town, 15-20 minute walk away (shuttlebus service), where some subjects are taught and assemblies held – new sixth form centre under construction. Cheerful, light, modern canteen – pupils speak well of food. We liked the key stage 3 quad with four wooden shelters and metal benches for packed lunch eaters. Lack of room for expansion is the main problem – existing space, eg a car park, has to be used cannily for any new build.

Formed from amalgamation of Sale Girls' and Boys' Grammar Schools 25 years ago. Outstanding last full Ofsted, 2006, endorsed by 2010 interim assessment. An academy trust grammar – partnerships with University Hospital South Manchester, LIME (arts in health charity), Findel plc, Manchester Metropolitan University, the Manchester Museum of Science and Industry. These provide expertise and resources used in educational and community projects (community engagement award for primary school and family learning work) and activities, as well as work experience opportunities for pupils and professional development for teachers.

Atmosphere is orderly and purposeful – a quiet hum and sensible movement between lessons. Head boy and girl elected by pupils – no prefects. Four houses (called Halls) with officers; activities led by sixth formers. Each house has own council, occasionally assembling for whole school council – seen as effective. House points for achievements, including community contributions and charity activities – end of year 'thank you days' for pupils who've accumulated the most points feature fun activities such as BMX riding, laser tag, cupcake decorating. 'Strong community spirit', praised a parent, which is developed in children 'as soon as they arrive'.

Pastoral care, well-being and discipline: Pastoral care a strength – traditional structure with form tutors, heads of progress and learning (ie heads of year) and key stage managers. Separate student services reception desk; counselling provided by professionals plus mentoring of younger pupils by years 11-13. Year 7s settle in easily, thanks to general friendliness and three day outdoor pursuits residential in their first term. Bullying very rare and would be dealt with effectively. 'Sensible, responsible and respectful' behaviour code; strict on not using mobiles in school; exclusions very unusual.

Pupils and parents: Pupils from over 50 feeder schools, mostly Trafford. Middle class, but not all well off; 70 per cent white British; lively, involved in lessons, happy with school, especially sporting and extra curricular activities. Regular communication with parents via newsletters, emails, questionnaires; lots of parental support. School and public buses plus Brooklands Metro station a short walk away.

Entrance: Takes around 180 for year 7 – top 40 per cent of ability range; over subscribed – 1600 for 180 places. Tests early October of year 6 in VR, NVR and maths; apply to school from mid April of year 5 to take exam; also have to complete Trafford LA common application form. Oversubscription criteria: looked after children; priority postcodes (may use proximity to school measured by straight line); then for those from outside this area rank order in tests, again possibly using proximity.

Sixth form: five GCSEs including two As, three Bs, at least C in English and maths; takes 40 external candidates (always oversubscribed).

Exit: Post-GCSE in 2016,18 per cent left most to FE colleges for non-traditional subjects, plus three per cent at end of year 12. Usually around 80 per cent of year 13s to university, mainly in the north west, high proportion of Russell Group – Manchester, Sheffield, Leeds, Durham popular, six to Oxbridge in 2016; others to jobs, eg Royal Bank of Scotland apprentices.

Remarks: High achieving without being highly pressurised, with learning opportunities going beyond exam syllabuses. Aims to provide a blend of tradition – academic rigour and high expectations, with innovation – up to date technology and opportunities for the development of the whole child – and makes a very good job of it.

Salisbury Cathedral School

The Old Bishop's Palace, 1 The Close, Salisbury, Wiltshire SP1 2EQ

Pupils: 208; 18 full, 37 weekly/flexi boarders • Ages: 3-13 (boarders from age 7) • C of E

Fees: Day £8,175 – £14,715; Boarding + £6,915 pa

Tel: 01722 555300
Email: headsec@salisburycathedralschool.com
Website: www.salisburycathedralschool.com

Head Master: Since 2013, Mr Clive Marriott MA BEd (40s). Educated at Queen Elizabeth's School, Crediton and read geography at Winchester. Spent eight years in a large maintained primary school in mid Devon before spending 14 years as deputy head of St Paul's Cathedral School. A very warm, welcoming and genuine man, he is clearly well liked by staff and pupils alike. Began as he means to go on by slimming down the management team, streamlining school process and appointing key stage coordinators to develop the curriculum.

Acknowledges the difficulty of driving some cultural changes, but says, 'What keeps me going is the fact that I'm doing it for the children.' Wants to 'keep raising the bar' of academic standards without losing sight of school's breadth and happy ethos. It's clear that the children are his firm focus as the walls of his study are full of pupils' artwork.

Wears his choir school head's hat with ease in understanding the importance of maintaining good relations with the cathedral and attends nearly every service. Recognises too that the school isn't just about the choristers and is strong on pastoral care for everyone. Would like to banish the term 'non-chorister' for school's other pupils and always appoints head boy and head girl from among year 8 students who are not in the choir.

Has needed his considerable people skills to calm anxious parents, concerned about cathedral's proposals to move the school from the Bishop's Palace into modern, purpose-built classrooms. At the time of writing, the dean of the cathedral has written to parents to tell them that this is now 'off the agenda'. A keen amateur musician, with interests in church music and musical theatre, loves the outdoors and lives by the sea in north Devon. Enjoys cross-Channel sailing and the delights of French culture and cuisine. Fascinated by urban design and especially the architectural landscape of the City of London. "When asked if I have a family, I simply say, 'Just look around you'."

Entrance: At all stages. Hugely oversubscribed chorister places – uniquely, it has parallel boys' and girls' choirs with entirely equal treatment – are offered as a result of a voice trial, academic assessment and interview; there is an informal test for others. Scholarships are available for music, sport and academic ability at 7 and 11. Day children come predominantly from local primaries and boarders from a wide area: 'choristership knows few boundaries'. A few Forces children and occasional Spanish and South African boarders (none needing extra English). Following the recent merger with all-girls Leaden Hall, there is a good gender balance in the school. School's governing body is genuinely endeavouring to keep a lid on fee increases.

Exit: Mainly at 13 to a range of schools eg Bryanston, Canford, Sherborne, Warminster, Dauntseys, Eton, Bedales, St Swithun's, Monkton Combe, Marlborough College, King's Taunton, many with music awards, but also with sport and all-rounder scholarships or exhibitions. One or two gain specialist music school places. A handful leaves after year 6 to Salisbury's grammar schools or independent schools such as Godolphin and Leehurst Swan (school runs 11+ practice sessions) but only the odd intrepid explorer manages to navigate the choppy waters of the 13+ exam for late entry to the grammar schools (boys' grammar often full). Academic scholarships pop up occasionally – the school says, 'Scholars are being given greater focus and we are proud of the results.'

Remarks: One of the oldest schools in the country; founded in 1091 by St Osmund to educate the choristers of his cathedral at Old Sarum. Moved to its present home, the former 13th century Bishop's Palace centred in 27-acre grounds within the Cathedral Close, in 1947. In the shadow of Salisbury's magnificent spire, its setting is idyllic and appreciated by parents and pupils alike.

School was an early adopter of the Independent Curriculum. Small class sizes (12 on average) are a big draw for some parents. Strong on science teaching; year 8 pupils regularly do well in chemistry competitions at Southampton University. Geography also good; field trips conducted thoroughly and children encouraged to think independently. French and English teaching much improved. Maths, a long-standing thorn in the school's side, also looks to be on the up. Latin for all from year

6; classical history trips to Italy round out non-linguistic studies (budding classicists don't leave translating Virgil, however). No scholarship set, so able children rely on individual teachers to stretch learning (some do). Regular study-skills workshops introduced for years 7 and 8, plus year 8 maths-skills sessions and English grammar and etiquette lessons for year 5.

Library is very well stocked and organised. All classrooms have whiteboards. Good ICT facilities. Imposing Big School Room, its walls lined with portraits of past Bishops of Salisbury, is an unusual venue for school assemblies and plays. Lovely ancient chapel in main school is used for morning worship twice a week. Welcoming SEN room provides help for 'mainly dyslexic' children.

Music is clearly the school's greatest strength. Some 85 per cent of pupils play at least one instrument; some learn three. Music Circus in years 3 and 4 allows young musicians the chance to try out a wide range of instruments free of charge and determine which they would most like to play. Further up the school, young organists revel in the opportunity to play the cathedral's Father Willis organ. There is a school orchestra, concert band, myriad lunchtime and after-school music ensembles and an annual friendly, non-competitive music festival. 'Everyone' sings and there are three school choirs as well as the two cathedral choirs. Jazbytes, the school jazz band, occasionally performs in public and invariably brings the house down. Weekly, informal Monday lunchtime concerts allow players the chance to perform in front of a kind audience (staff, pupils and parents). Practice sessions are scheduled for boarders and a few day pupils. Music department enters dozens of candidates every term for ABRSM exams and most pass with merit or distinction. A good number pass grade V theory every year. A child doesn't have to be musical to come here, but it would be difficult to leave without a song on the lips and some appreciation of classical and choral music.

Sport continues to improve thanks to new sports teachers. Good Astroturf, three rugby pitches and generous scholarships attract sporty children. All-inclusive approach means nearly everyone gets a chance to represent the school (usual list of prep school sports on offer) and fixture card is healthy. First rounders' team had an unbeaten season recently and all senior teams put in a respectable performance. Wednesday afternoons devoted to sport. Match teas for parent supporters are 'the best on the local circuit'; the school does these beautifully in summer, complete with home-made cakes and a marquee on the lawn in full view of the cathedral spire. Parking for matches on Wednesdays can be a challenge if lots of parents turn up, as can escaping from school afterwards.

School chaplain promotes a strong Christian ethos in and out of RS lessons; her Friday morning services in the cathedral for the whole school are legendary (balloons have been known to lodge themselves cheerfully in the organ pipes). A good number of parents attend every week and exemplary values are enthusiastically encouraged – Esther Rantzen spoke eloquently about bullying at one year's speech day. As most pupils meet the school's high moral expectations, serious issues are notable by their absence. Upbeat, happy, 'busy bee' school atmosphere possibly explains why the rare case of low-level unkind behaviour lurks below the radar (any concerned parent is always given a prompt hearing) and school staff may need to fine tune their pastoral antennae and ensure that disciplinary procedures remain consistent.

Switched on to the needs of busy parents; day pupils may arrive from 8.00am (to the strains of choristers at morning rehearsal) and stay until 5.30pm at no extra charge. Day prep sessions are easy going; boarder prep is more effectively supervised. No Saturday school, although there is morning music practice for choristers. Other boarders staying in school take part in separate activities. Excellent range of clubs on offer at lunchtimes and before and after school: chess, ukulele, rock band, general knowledge, archery, football, golf, swimming, drama, photography, street dance and sewing are just a few. 'Eco' club tends the lake in Palace grounds (useful for practical science). School musical every year (Guys and Dolls, Oklahoma!, Fiddler on the Roof). Everyone in the prep school can be involved; choristers do not automatically win main singing roles. 'It's the highlight of the school year, and such fun.' Unusual exchange programme with a South African boarding school – two year 7 pupils can spend a term in Graaff-Reinet. Yearly ski trips in Easter holidays. Annual history excursions to France, alternately visiting World War battlefields and Normandy beaches.

Boarding house tucked behind a cream tea shop five minutes' walk away, so boarders (nearly all English) stride off to school for breakfast and do not return until 7 or 8pm. Boarders' bedrooms are wholesome, if rather cosy, with largish dorms for youngsters shrinking to doubles for older children; lots of common areas downstairs. Excursions planned most weekends for those staying in. In term time there are always two choirs in residence and day choristers are required to board twice each term – most regard this as a treat and look forward to 'chori hols' at Christmas, Easter and in July. Boarding house staff works hard to punctuate the choristers' duties with rest and fun (choir parents quip that a closed school kitchen on the final day three times a year isn't so much fun for them).

Chorister life runs like clockwork thanks to cathedral's supremely organised director of music and a chorister tutor who puts in hours beyond the call of duty. Musical standards are consistently good and choirs undertake regular concerts, recordings and live broadcasts in addition to their regular weekly services (duties shared equally between girls' and boys' choirs). Choristers play a full part in school life and are treated much the same as other pupils, although they clearly have an extra workload before and after school. Foreign choir tours no longer an annual event, more's the pity.

Pre-prep housed in classrooms tucked away in a corner of the Palace grounds, overlooking a pleasant area of lawn. Takes pupils from age 3; these youngest children are charmingly known as Ladybirds, moving up to Dragonflies (year 1) and Busy Bees (year 2). The head – 'a wonderful teacher' – is well supported by committed staff. Approach to early education isn't pushy; nevertheless children thrive and emerge happy, balanced and confident. Red Badges are awarded each Friday for effort, achievement or any other positive contribution and winners are applauded at Monday assemblies. The best class wins the privilege of having Mr Gnome to stay for the week. Has its own sports day and prize giving, an informal lunchtime concert each term, and takes part in the annual music festival. Staff stage a play every summer in addition to the customary nativity. Weekly timetable includes RS, French, games and ballet; pupils use the main school's library, gym and ICT facilities. Year 2 pupils have the chance to experience Music Circus. Own play area and sandpit; teachers are very good at ensuring children play outside every day. Golf coaching sessions, football and gardening clubs, trips to Salisbury Museum and grandparents' tea parties all keep young ones cheerful and interested. No surprise that numbers here are on the up.

Informal atmosphere – cheerful, super-efficient school secretary does much to keep it that way. Head's PA is also a gem, unfailingly helpful and courteous. A tight-knit school where each child is known well, most pupils are very happy and care about one another. 'It's the kind of place where you can go up to some of the teachers and give them a hug.' Former pupils include MPs Robert Key and Michael Mates, actress and singer Amy Carson (Kenneth Branagh, The Magic Flute), organist Bernard Rose, composer Peter Gritton and Sir Anthony Lewis, former president of the Royal College of Music. Judging by the strength of the alumni association and the lasting friendships between former pupils, SCS is a happy and very special place to spend your early school years.

Following merger with Leaden Hall (March 2016), younger children are on the Leaden Hall campus and the older ones on the Salisbury Cathedral School site for the next few years at least. Clive Marriott heads the merged school.

Sandroyd School

Rushmore, Tollard Royal, Salisbury, Wiltshire SP5 5QD

Pupils: 200: 134 boys, 66 girls; 95 full, 57 flexi boarders • Ages: 2–13 (boarders from 7) • C of E

Fees: Day £8,280 – £19,800; Boarding £18,990 – £24,000 pa

Tel: 01725 516264
Email: office@sandroyd.com
Website: www.sandroyd.org

Headmaster: Since September 2016, Alastair Speers (late 30s), previously senior housemaster at Oakham. Alastair and his wife Alice (an English teacher) grew up in Dorset and have strong links locally. Alastair attended Sherborne School, whilst Alice went to Bryanston. He has a degree in building engineering and management from the University of the West of England; worked for six years in architecture as a consultant engineer, before completing his PGCE at Cambridge. Has recently completed a masters in education leadership at Buckingham. Keen on rugby, cricket, skiing, sailing, squash and performing arts. They have two young daughters.

Entrance: Pupils join at all stages, although school policy is to keep numbers below 200, hence there is a waiting list in some year groups. The Walled Garden (pre-prep) takes children from the age of 2. Many join the main school in year 3 from local primary or pre-preps (mostly in Wiltshire and Dorset) and the first full boarders start in year 3, when the school doubles in size. Some come at 10 or 11 from further afield, specifically for senior boarding. Not selective, but all those joining aged 7 and above have an informal interview with the head and are assessed in reading and reasoning. School stresses that tests are not pass/fail exercises.

Means-tested bursaries are available on an annual, case by case basis. Single 100 per cent bursary from year 7 (joint award with Bryanston) is awarded to one child. A further 100 per cent bursary (in conjunction with Radley, St Mary's Calne and Downe House) is available for children of servicemen or women killed or wounded on operational tours.

Exit: Most leave at 13 for eg Eton, Harrow, Radley, Downe House, Marlborough, Winchester, Bryanston, Canford, St Mary's, Sherborne, Dauntsey's, Blundells, Downside, Clayesmore; otherwise to schools far and wide. A good handful leave with sport or all-rounder scholarships or exhibitions and some win academic, music and art awards.

Remarks: Founded in 1888 by the Rev Wellesley Wesley as a 'small coaching establishment' for aspiring Etonians at his own home, the school quickly flourished. It moved first to Surrey and in 1939 to Rushmore House (the Pitt-Rivers' family home) on the Wiltshire/Dorset borders. School purchased the house and 57 acres within the 400-acre Rushmore estate in 1966. Like most elegant country houses, it sits at the end of a long, winding drive in solitary splendour, surrounded by playing fields, woods and parkland.

Beautiful entrance hall with open fireplace, cosy sofas and lovely wood panelling; head's study is bigger than some studio apartments and has a stunning view of open countryside. Entire school (except pre-prep) is in the original house, although there have obviously been significant additions and alterations, eg theatre, chapel, classrooms and girls' boarding wing. Everything connected by lots of passages (even our pupil guides managed to miss out half the school first time around) but there is an order to the layout once you get the hang of it. Bright, spacious classrooms on the far side of the house are mostly ranged along two main corridors and also have marvellous views. Still feels very much like a country home in the boarders' quarters (sitting rooms and comfy sofas) where houseparents have apartments. Although it is now less traditional, we were pleased to see that some 'old style' disciplines remain, eg shoe polishing, letter writing and good manners.

Still true to its original purpose, the school fosters a 'cool to work and achieve' ethos and parents confirm this. 'If you are destined for Eton, you will get there.' Children get lots of support along the way, with each child assigned to a personal tutor who monitors academic progress and keeps an eye on extracurricular activities. 'Tutors always have time to talk to parents and seem to know the children very well.' Strong in most areas of the curriculum thanks to good teaching and positive attitudes, together with small classes of no more than 16. Saturday morning lessons start in year 4. Teachers reward effort and achievement with 'alphas' and discourage slacking with 'omegas'. Pupils collecting enough alphas are treated to an outing and those given omegas have to do penance with a chore.

Maths is set in years 7 and 8; able mathematicians in year 6 join advanced classes. French from year 4 and Latin from year 5. Year 3 also gets a taste of French, German and Spanish, whilst year 8 is introduced to Greek. School has scholarship sets in English, maths, French and Latin. Year 7 pupils go on an annual residential trip to a château in Burgundy. Two very well-appointed ICT suites and an excellent, bright, modern science laboratory. SKULL (skills, knowledge and understanding for lifelong learning) educates beyond the classroom, eg study skills, art appreciation and career skills for older pupils, financial literacy and European culture sessions for younger ones. RATS (reasoning and thinking skills) culminates in a GCSE in year 8. General knowledge questions set for whole prep school every week and tested every Friday. At the time of our visit, there were 32 pupils in the learning support unit and nine pupils with EAL requirements – mostly Spanish pupils at the school for one year. SEN classrooms are welcoming, light and bright (with those brilliant views again).

A very sporty school – games every day and Wednesday and Saturday afternoons devoted to matches and sport. Lots of boys' teams, eg four senior boys' rugby teams with an A and B side at every level, means everyone gets the chance to play for the school. As well as the usual prep school sports for boys and girls, there is tennis and squash coaching, plus archery, shooting and clay pigeon shooting, plus a girls' cricket team. School surrounded by acres of green space for games and has wide expanses of grass pitches, plus an all-weather pitch, cricket pitch, new netball and tennis courts. Local primary schools invited to enjoy the facilities from time to time. New sports hall. Many individual sporting accolades, eg finalists in IAPS national swimming and athletics championships; some selected for Wessex rugby and U14 and U13 county hockey teams.

A third of the pupils have riding lessons, either on school's ponies or their own (ponies are welcome to board) – eager beginners up to advanced equestrians. In our enthusiasm to see the whole school, we vaulted a stile and strode off across the paddock to watch a lesson. Naturally, the pony promptly morphed into a Thelwellian devil and refused to jump anything (much to the chagrin of both pupil and instructor, to whom we apologised profusely). Previous head confessed ruefully that he couldn't see the appeal of riding when his charges fell off! Clearly they don't come off too often, as senior boys' show jumping team has competed in the National Schools Equestrian Association finals.

Arts appear to be in rude health; music is on the up with newish head of music. The chapel choir, which now practises several times a week, sings Sunday morning service in the school chapel and has sung evensong in Salisbury Cathedral. There are two further choirs, a school orchestra, string ensembles, brass and saxophone groups, a jazz band and the School of Rock. There are concerts every term and an annual school musical. Eighty per cent play an instrument and music lessons are rotated through the timetable; practice sessions are timetabled and checked. All the usual instruments on offer, plus some less likely, eg tuba, banjo and bagpipes. Music theory and aural training are also available. All pupils in year 4 receive free tuition for one term on an instrument of their choice.

Fantastic theatre, probably the best we've seen outside senior schools, used by all ages from reception upwards. Every year group in the prep school puts on a play and reluctant thespians are encouraged to help out with lighting, scenery and sound. Lovely bright art studio affords plenty of space and light; next door is a small exhibition space for art scholars to display their work. Very well-equipped DT studio, with computers for designing projects (doubles up as a bike repair shop on Wednesday evenings). Lots of activities on offer during designated 'hobby' afternoons, after school and at the weekend, including astronomy, philosophy, scuba diving, pony care, survival skills and den building in woodland belonging to the Rushmore estate. Great climbing wall perches at the back of the main house.

Boarding provision is very well organised, with a junior house for boys and girls, middle house for boys and senior boys' and girls' wings. Senior girls' wing accommodates those in the top two years. There is flexi or weekly boarding lower down the school, but by year 7 children are expected to board full time and a busy programme at the weekend means most do. As 60 per cent of teachers live on site, every house and wing has its own houseparents as well as a team of matrons. Pastoral care is 'fantastic' and parents praise swift communications between home and school. Any unkind behaviour is stamped on quickly; a parent commented that 'school culture provides very little room for bullying.' Girls' dorms are probably the prettiest we've seen, with lots of pink and attractive lampshades and curtains. Boys' dorms are plainer and slightly more spacious in the senior wing, with three or four to a room. Older pupils have desks in their bedrooms and can choose to do prep here if they wish. They also have their own common rooms and kitchens, where they can make toast and cocoa (and learn to wash and tidy up). We were amazed to learn that school washes day pupils' sports kit as well as all the boarders' clothing. The laundry room resembles a commercial operation – rows of machines and banks of shelves for clean towels, shirts etc.

School lunches are generally good and served in a large bright, airy dining room; snacks of fresh fruit are available throughout the day. Some mothers felt school teas could be healthier, but supper seemed wholesome enough (milk, cereal, bread and fruit). Mobile phones are not permitted in school; overseas boarders are allowed to Skype their parents and others can buy phone cards to call home. There are two obligatory 'weekends in' per term, but on most Sundays children are allowed out for lunch with their parents after chapel. Many choose to remain at school with their friends to join in afternoon activities, eg football, cycling, cookery and hacking across the Downs. 'My only concern about boarding is that my children would rather be at school than at home,' said one mother wistfully.

The Walled Garden (pre-prep) is built on to an original wall surrounding the formal gardens to one side of Rushmore House. A sympathetically designed, unusual curved fibreglass ceiling lets in plenty of light without spoiling the existing aspect. Children are taught in small classes, often by a specialist teacher, with a strong focus on numeracy and literacy. The Walled Garden has its own hall for drama and assemblies (which doubles up as an art studio). A new library has recently been opened. Pre-prep pupils use the main school computers and swimming pool, walk up to the dining room for lunch and can stay on to take part in after-school activities. The playground is packed with activities such as sandpit, musical instruments, bikes, trikes, chickens, wormery and a recently opened Bug Café.

School is 'a happy mix of local and less local folk', with students from all over – a few Spanish there to learn English, with others from Germany, Norway, Japan and Mexico, plus a few expats from Hong Kong, Nigeria etc. School escorts pupils on the train to London on exeat weekends and at half-term, it arranges taxis to airports for overseas pupils. Pupils are uniformly polite, display excellent manners (standing up for the head and visitors to the classroom) and perhaps more important, are utterly unpretentious. A luminary roll call of former students includes Sir Terence Rattigan, Sir Ranulph Fiennes, Lords Carrington, Gladwyn and Wilberforce, Archbishop Ramsey of Canterbury, Rt Revd Roger Wilson, Bishop of Chichester, Professors Hawkes, Godley and Dummett, Randolph Churchill, Ian Gow and many other British and foreign dignitaries.

A very happy school, offering a well-balanced education in spectacular surroundings. Not a hothouse, but prepared to 'push when necessary' to prepare for senior school. There is lots of sport, so those allergic to games might not feel totally at home here. Has retained the best of traditional boarding school values and consigned the outmoded to the dust. We'll watch the top scholarship tally in years to come with interest.

Sands School

48 East Street, Ashburton, Newton Abbot, Devon TQ13 7AX

Pupils: 81 • Ages: 11–17

Fees: £9,900 pa

Tel: 01364 653666
Email: enquiry@sands-school.co.uk
Website: www.sands-school.co.uk

Head: No one. Everybody. Sands is a democratic school, a co-op, so there's no hierarchy. All decisions are taken collectively by teachers and students at the weekly, student-chaired school meeting, one person, one vote. This applies both to day-to-day decision making and strategic planning, which you'd expect to be the job of governors but at Sands the governors don't govern in the usual sense, they don't even get to vote. Nor do parents, by the way.

So Sands has a rationale. But it is not in thrall to a Big Idea. There's no guru calling the shots here – no Neill, no Steiner, no Hahn, though they do own up to a dash of Tagore. The point is, Sands is not the keeper of anyone's flame and this frees it up to respond to the here and now and reinvent itself as it sees fit. It

S

makes it up as it goes along? Yes, that's exactly what it does, it's in a state of continuous evolution under the influence of the democratic process. And if that makes Sands sound like some sort of counter-cultural cloud cuckoo land blithely defying societal norms, inspired by a school motto of 'If it feels good, do it', sorry, it's all much more down to earth than that. When you visit, Sands feels at first little like a school what with students sprawled on the grass chatting when surely they should be in class, dammit. Go deeper and you discover both the strong seriousness that drives the school and a reassuring mundanity in, for example, the way it pairs rights with responsibilities: 'Everyone in the school has the right to eat school lunches, but if you choose to do so, you then have the responsibility to do your fair share of washing up.' This essential pragmatism is testament to the school's trust in the common sense and goodwill of its teachers and students and expresses itself in the down-to-earth simplicity of its core value: 'We believe that everyone should be treated equally, be happy, and have access to a good education.'

Mark Twain said: 'If voting made any difference they wouldn't let us do it', a sentiment with which students in some democratic schools would agree. The perils of kidology are obvious here. Teachers, by virtue of an accumulation of life experience and the accretion of wisdom, could use the force-field this creates to dominate debate in school meetings – even to spin off into something cultish. They acknowledge the perils of dominant personality syndrome: 'We carry great authority as the owners of the knowledge and skills that children want to access. With the best will in the world, this does create huge inequalities between the possessors of learning, the teachers, and the consumers, the students.' They guard against undue influence, in our observation, by exercising respectful self-restraint. The best decisions, they say, are made when everyone decides together – an empirical appraisal. In the school meeting we attended you could see the adults swap glances at one point as a motion approached a vote. They seemed to be sharing something like 'We'll possibly need to come back to this and debate it some more – that's okay.' Because of this, students engage full-bloodedly and amazingly articulately in debate, justly confident that their voices count equally. They do. And they do get to decide everything – from humdrum practicalities and discipline issues to admissions and staff appointments. One parent told us, laughing, 'all this democracy isn't always welcome at home – they're forever questioning things'.

When, say, Ofsted comes calling, Sands' public-facing spokesperson is Sean Bellamy, one of the school's founders. He rejoices in the title of administrator. He didn't put himself forward when we visited, a student took charge of us; we only got to speak to him by hunting him down at lunch.

In addition to the customary legal duties of charity trustees, the responsibility of the governors is to defend the school against corruption of its foundational values – eg, by dominant personalities or entryism. Both they and parents can lobby the school meeting and have their views debated, but the autonomy of the student-teacher body is everything, hence the school's arm's-length position on parental interference. Budget setting remains with the governors.

Academic matters: Some seriously bright and thinkerly teachers here inspire a reverence for learning, no question. Sands teaches up to GCSE, 'flawed' as it is. Students sit exams when they're ready; the school is more interested in promoting self-discovery and personal development as essential factors in awakening innate talent and promoting self-directed learning. No teaching to the test, no fact-cramming, no coercion, no competition. Osbert Sitwell once said, 'My education takes place during the holidays from Eton'. Chances are he could have fitted it into term times at Sands. There's hardheadedness to this approach. Sands believes that the emphasis in mainstream schools on factual recall and the application of ordered methodologies prepares children for the very jobs that computers will soon do better. The future, they reckon, lies with soft skills: creativity, collaboration, communication and lateral thinking.

Classes – ave 12 – comprise a mix of ages. The school acknowledges that 'kids increasingly feel like they have to do exams more than they ever did'. Some students go for it big time, bag all the GCSEs they can and go on to soar; others go for no more than they need for whatever's next, regarding GCSEs as negotiable currency – necessary 'bits of paper' – 'You do what you need do'. One arty student had settled for just four, three for art school and one for fun and felt 'in no need whatever of any more' – her time was better spent painting. She's not typical. No one's typical. Unsurprisingly, the school isn't remotely interested in looking good in league tables and the record shows that it doesn't. Don't read that as blasé; they take aspiration seriously (but in 2016, 33 per cent of GCSE grades were A*/A). Ofsted, never knowingly effusive, said in 2013: 'Pupils' achievements are good, as a result of good teaching, an effective curriculum and the excellent learning environment.' Market forces determine what makes a good teacher: students empty-classroom those they reckon aren't up to it. All staff – 50:50 male and female – are appraised by students, who are also integral to the selection process. All are qualified, most have worked at mainstream schools. No shortage of recruits: the recently advertised post of art teacher lured more than 100 applicants.

Going off-topic in classes in pursuit of fruitful and fascinating digressions is normal. One student said 'I still remember the arguments I had with Nathan, my maths teacher, about philosophy and climbing'. If you want to pursue an interest in astrophysics or circus skills, they'll fix it for you. If it snows, they drop everything and go up to the moors. If you're in the middle of a great painting, you can go at it three days straight. The last week of the summer term is devoted to camping beside the sea.

If a mainstream school is a place of decrees and proclamations, Sands is a school of delicate balances, sensitive negotiations and unrelenting tensions. Sure, you don't have to go to lessons if you don't want to... 'but we only offer places to students who want to learn'. If you opt to attend, make sure you get to class on time or you'll face a sanction. You don't have to do subjects you dislike... 'but we'd like you to give them a second chance'. There's a criticism made of schools like Sands that freedom to bunk off when you feel like it can be lethargy inducing, and they work hard to demonstrate the link between hard work and joy in achievement. Most students do go through a phase (or two) of skyving and larking in a spirit of, say, Hey, party! or adolescent angst. One mother described her initial feelings of 'Oh my God, what have I done?' but had learnt that all's well that ends well. You won't be surprised to learn that this is no place to stand and watch students, like heroes of Soviet labour, march in shining-eyed cohorts past developmental milestones bang on time. They breeze on by when they're good and ready.

Special needs are addressed by all teachers and three specialists. Everyone chooses their academic tutor, with whom they devise their timetable. Tutors liaise with parents and also have a pastoral role, acting as advocate of last resort for any tutee in especially hot water. There is no staff room at Sands, no uniform, no us, no them and no bells, obviously. Imagine.

Games, options, the arts: You've sussed there's not a lot of snarling, tribal rugby going on here, what with the lack of numbers and the absence of playing fields, not to mention a general disinclination. Not that they're against competitive team sports. Students who want to play at a decent level join local clubs. The school promotes, on a broad front, in line with demand, anything that's hilarious and physically active, including tree climbing, swimming in the river, hockey, football, weight training, kung fu, skateboarding, surfing and cycling. Music making tends to be similarly ad hoc but of a higher order of accomplishment – instrumental specialists brought in according to need. Concerts happen as and when. The Performing Arts BTec serves as a focus for musicians as also for dance, drama and art students. The tenor of Sands is markedly arty – 'we're known for our art'. And crafty. Woodwork thrives under the auspices of the well-loved Peach. The art room is heaven on earth.

Background and atmosphere: Arose from the ashes of Dartington Hall in 1987, but not as a reinvention. The radical difference is that Sands was co-designed by students and teachers, it's not the offspring of a single seer, and it's fuelled by dreams and intuitions, not certainties, in a spirit of 'We'll know what we think when we see what we do'. Call it creatively muddling through if you like – creativity implies ferment. The school's name derives from the salutation used by David Gribble, a founder, in letters to the other two founders, Sean Bellamy and Sybilla Higgs – 'Dear S and S'. Geddit? The school has evolved under continuous and, it has to be said, unsparing self-examination – what you see is where we are. It reckons it's in better shape now than ever, but it's still light years away from complacency – 'Oh no, we're not perfect'. Admin is, though. Bursar Peta runs a tight ship.

The school occupies an early Victorian townhouse with a nice garden in the middle of Ashburton. Expect no hush (so fashionable just now) for hush there is none, not ever, there being masses going on in all directions. This an infectiously friendly, happy place where everyone meets your eye – they are the only young persons we have ever met who don't talk up to you or down to you but treat you exactly as if you were one of them. Scuffed but comfy – the building, that is. Lived in. Fit for purpose. Zero prestige facilities but everything perfectly serviceable. Classrooms roomy. New science block coming soon. Toilets are marked male and female but actually they're inter-gender. Skateboarding is mostly outside. They all know each other, of course, and mostly rub along together just fine (lots of high fives and hugs) – 'We're one big happy dysfunctional family!'. Most impressive, we thought, was the spirit in which they equably received probing, challenging questions – they never bridled. Parents do their bit with, say, an occasional paintbrush. The school likes having them around as long as they don't start backseat driving. Food is excellent, plentiful and vegetarian – to get around H & S concerns. Despite the high student-teacher ratio and small numbers, finances are sound and there's a good reserve.

Pastoral care, well-being and discipline: There are complex and ever-present tensions to be addressed here, strenuously and unendingly – free expression vs foul language, exam results vs self-directed learning, the individual vs the community, spending time vs wasting time, parental input vs student autonomy... It all calls for courage, care and steadfastness and must be nerve-racking. A do-as-I-say regime would be – you see it so clearly here – oh, so much easier.

In the words of one student, 'everyone here has their own backstory'. Actually, not everyone here has a backstory, though there's an easygoing perception locally that they're all a bit bonkers. We spoke to parents whose children had no prior hangups, one whose son is quite interested in becoming a policeman. Backstories involve unhappy experiences of mainstream schools because of bullying or a cast of mind that will not surrender to demands for conformity and obedience. Sands is a happy landing for characters, daydreamers, dyslexics, eccentrics, refusers and mavericks, some statemented, others not, some angry, some muddled, some howling. 'People come here to be saved,' a student told us, and when they arrive – some of them funded by the local authority – it can take time for their sails to fill, and during this phase they may bunk off big time until they feel calm and validated, ready to come in and do some work. For such, Sands is a therapeutic environment. Teachers reconnect them with their best interests by talking, listening and above all respecting. Parents whose daughter who had become impossibly wild and furious told us how amazing the school had been. At a crisis, one of the teachers sat with her on the floor of toilet for three hours. It was a turning point and now she's 'as lovely as we always knew she was – lovelier.'

Liberal regimes that work require everyone to go the extra hour. We watched the school meeting debate sanctions for two students who had been making others unhappy. They were present, there were adversarial episodes – it's quite something when your peers hold up a mirror to your conduct. As a student told us, 'You get big life experience here, but it doesn't work for everyone.' Another said, 'Actually, there's not much here to rebel against.' And although the school clings to the conviction that 'there are no bad kids – difficult kids but no bad ones', some, rarely, don't go the distance and are excluded.

There are rules. Not many, most of ancient heritage, a bit like common law, not written down. You have to take your shoes off before you go upstairs so as not to ruin the carpets. Everyone has to play their part in washing up and cleaning the school at the end of the day. It's quite something to see a teacher doing the pot wash. If you want to smoke, a student told us, 'Go and do it alone, not somewhere idiotic and public like a bus stop'. These are longstanding conventions rooted in common sense. And the greatest of these is: 'you have to want to be here'.

First stop for infringements, disputes, etc is the school council – sic students and a teacher – who arbitrate and make recommendations to the weekly school meeting, which is the ultimate arbiter and ratifier of everything.

Pupils and parents: Just 15 mins by road from Totnes, epicenter of a region famously populated by counter-cultural, freethinking folk of all hues. A good demographic for Sands, you might think. Yes, some parents are principled objectors to 'factory schooling' but others are just like parents everywhere, swayed not by ideology but what works for their children. It's all about size, teaching to students' needs and personal and intellectual development – 'Our friends just can't believe the difference in them'. Many parents scrattle about somewhat to find the fees – one mum cooks lunch to help pay hers. It's not for the social cachet they go short in a good cause, but because they reckon the school brings out the most in their kids. Others, whose children the school has restored to emotional health, echo the words of one such: 'Sands is a lifesaver.' There's an early-stage PTA.

Students span the spectrum from exotic to withdrawn; all are incredibly easy around adults, they're supportive of each other and most radiate purpose. Not all, some are getting there. They're not chauvinistic, they're not inward-looking, they don't think Sands is the only school in the world. Any number told us 'This school isn't for everybody'.

Entrance: Come and do a taster week, get to know everyone, decide if you like it. Interview at the end of the week, after which your application goes to the school meeting. They won't have you if they feel they can't meet your needs or you have been a serious pain. Roughly 20 per cent from home education, 10 per cent each from Park, Totnes, S Devon Steiner and local primaries; 20 per cent from local secondaries in yrs 7 & 8 – 'some last less than a week before they are on the phone to us'. School website very informative.

Exit: A range of further ed choices, sixth form or FE vocational mostly – Exeter College, Kennicott sixth form and Plymouth Art College – thence to uni, some even unto Oxbridge. Is the school is a good springboard? Transition may be difficult but, having taken ownership of their education, these students know themselves and what they want, making them, arguably, high-value applicants.

Money matters: Fees on the low-ish side for an independent day school. Expect to shell out a bit extra for the odd school trip and over-the-odds special needs. A few bursaries, income based, offering up to a third off.

Remarks: The decline of difference in all mainstream schools has left Sands looking decidedly far out, incapable of appraisal by prevailing quantifiable outcomes. If you reckon it might well be the right school for your child the only way you'll know is by going to see, whereupon your guts will tell you just like that whether these kids are on an incredible journey or the high road to havoc. If you are persuaded of the former, you may need to move house.

Sexey's School

Cole Road, Bruton, Somerset BA10 0DF

Pupils: 556; 224 boarders. • Ages: 11–18 • Sixth form: 163 • C of E

Fees: Boarding £9,975 pa. Day free.

Tel: 01749 813393
Email: admissions@sexeys.somerset.sch.uk
Website: www.sexeys.somerset.sch.uk

Head Master: Since 2013, Irfan Latif BSc (40s). Educated at Emanuel School – as a sixth former he helped to rescue injured people from the 1988 Clapham rail disaster. Read chemistry at King's College London, followed by a PGCE. First teaching post was at Kidbrooke School in Greenwich (where Jamie's School Dinners began). Taught at several independent schools, including Haberdashers' Aske's Boys', Whitgift and St Benedict's in Ealing, where he was head of chemistry and director of science. He was previously deputy head (academic) at Bedford School and says Bedford's then head John Moule (now warden of Radley) was a huge inspiration to him.

Describes his appointment to run Sexey's as 'serendipity.' With boarding fees at independent schools on an upward trajectory, he feels that state boarding is the future. 'We are like Essential Waitrose,' he jokes. He has kept the traditional aspects of Sexey's (which celebrates its 125th anniversary in 2016) while ensuring that it is cutting edge when it comes to teaching and technology. He has used his knowledge of the independent sector to good effect, changing the school's house system, academic structure and governance, taking a close look at feedback, assessment and pupils' progression and introducing far more sports fixtures. Firmly believes in giving a wealth of opportunities to all and encourages students to work hard and flourish. 'We're in the business of transforming lives here,' he says. 'But it's not a holiday camp. They are here to work.'

Head knows every pupil by name. He has an open door policy for students, writes a comment on every child's report and is much in evidence around the school. Still teaches six periods of chemistry per 10-day teaching cycle – to GCSE pupils last year and A level students this year. 'I arrange my meetings around my teaching, not the other way round,' he says. Lectures at the Royal Institution of Great Britain, is a fellow of the Royal Society of Chemistry and is also a magistrate. 'He never sleeps,' jokes a colleague. Head puts it differently. 'There's no point sitting around,' he says. 'If a parent has entrusted me with their most precious commodity then I have to deliver on all fronts.' His teacher wife Jocelyn is very involved in the school, including organising fundraising events for Macmillan Cancer Support (founder Douglas Macmillan was a pupil at Sexey's). They and their two young daughters live in a house on the school site.

Academic matters: Results are consistently good. At GCSE, 83 per cent bot 5+ A*-Cs including English and maths in 2016, with 28 per cent of grades A*/A, and at A level, 33 per cent A*/A grades, 63 per cent A*-B. The Department for Education recently named Sexey's as the best performing state school in Somerset and Dorset for GCSE. Most pupils take 10 subjects at GCSE, with around 38 per cent doing triple science.

New deputy head (academic) has launched major focus on teaching and 'supporting students to be successful' and school continually looks at how pupils can improve. Strategy has paid dividends – school recently won two national awards for being in the top 10 per cent of schools for progress made by pupils between key stage 2 results and GCSE and in the top 10 per cent nationally for high attainment. Year 7 to 9 pupils are set for maths, science and languages (French and German). Average class sizes are 22 at key stage 3, fewer at key stage 4 and 10 to 12 in the sixth form. Good SEN provision – SENCo and her five-strong team offer literacy and numeracy support in small groups to pupils who meet county criteria. One boy increased his spelling age by 22 months after 10 weeks of specialist literacy classes.

At A level, all the usual subjects, plus business, government and politics, media studies, photography, psychology and sociology. Sport and exercise science is the only BTec available. School is continuing with AS levels and pupils must achieve three Ds in year 12 to continue into year 13. One or two opt to retake their AS exams each year. Impressive head of sixth form keeps a weather eye on all and advises on higher education and career choices. A third of sixth formers do the EPQ and all year 12s do work experience.

School is forward thinking when it comes to technology. Prep diaries have been dispensed with and students use the Show My Homework app – so pupils and parents alike can see the prep that has been set and when it's due in. School has introduced philosophy as a discrete lesson for year 7 to 9 pupils and Mandarin as an after-school enrichment subject. Younger pupils do food technology for three years (everything from nutrition and healthy eating to cooking and food safety) and the subject is offered at GCSE and A level too.

Games, options, the arts: Sport has progressed in leaps and bounds in recent years. School now plays loads of matches against independent and state schools (including two Saturday fixtures a term, one for boys, one for girls) and holds its own against the likes of Millfield and Dauntsey's. Parents contribute to a voluntary sports subs fund to help cover transport costs to matches – but there's no compulsion. When we visited, the under-15 girls' cricket team had just beaten their rivals at Millfield and King Edward's, Bath respectively. All age groups do at least two hours of sport each week. Rugby, hockey, netball, cricket, football, equestrian pursuits, sailing – you name it, they do it. Sports hall with weights room and gym, 18m heated indoor pool, good pitches and five hard tennis courts that double up for netball and five-a-side football. Emphasis is on healthy, active lifestyles and sixth formers can also choose activities like yoga, keep fit and Pilates. Dynamic new director of sport says her aim is to broaden the PE curriculum for all – 'the girls want to do football and rugby and the boys want to do basketball and hockey,' she says.

Loads of music, drama and dance on offer. Around 130 pupils play instruments (lessons are rotated so pupils don't miss the same lessons each week). Music department is housed

S

in former head's house and includes large classroom, recording studio and practice rooms. Reasonable numbers take music at GCSE but the subject isn't offered at A level. Performance groups include choir, wind band and folk group. Yearly drama production (Little Shop of Horrors in 2015) – studio space for smaller productions and traditional hall for major performances. Drama and theatre studies available at GCSE and A level. Art is breathtaking. We were particularly impressed by a montage of year 10 kaleidoscope paintings inspired by artist Brian Moss. The school has wisely formed close links with Hauser & Wirth Somerset, the stunning contemporary art gallery just a mile up the road.

A plethora of extracurricular activities – including circuit training, creative writing, radio club and Warhammer. Two boys who are gardening enthusiasts are developing the school's centenary garden. D of E, plus Army Cadet Force and Air Training Corps (at nearby Castle Cary). Pupils produce their own termly school magazine – recent issue included an insightful advice column on coping with exams.

Boarding: Boarders (weekly and full boarding available) account for nearly half of the school roll. They occupy three vertical, mixed boarding houses – Coombe, Lisbury and the newest, Macmillan, which opened in 2011. Boarders' dorms are mainly for two or three pupils. All well-kept and wholesome. Each house has its own houseparents, most of whom have teaching or support roles too. After-school activities between 3.40pm and 5pm every day, then boarding team takes over. Two hours of prep a night for most – year 7 to 9 boarders are supervised, older pupils can work in their rooms.

Loads of weekend activities – everything from foraging to theatre trips. Younger pupils are allowed (with permission) to visit Bruton once a week, older pupils twice a week. The mother of a year 7 boarder told us that she likes being able to drop her son off on Monday morning and pick him up on Friday afternoon. 'I feel we get the best of both worlds,' she said. 'There is no Saturday school so we get a proper family weekend.'

Background and atmosphere: School is named after Hugh Sexey, the son of poor parents who rose to become royal auditor to Elizabeth I and James I. After his death in 1619 the trustees of his will established Sexey's Hospital, which still provides care for the elderly today. The trustees later established a school for apprentices within the school grounds but it closed 200 years later. The current school was founded in 1891 and was the inspiration of East Somerset MP Hugh Hobhouse, who drafted the 1902 Education Act (his great, great grandson is a boarder at Sexey's). School later became a grammar school and then metamorphosed through voluntary controlled, grant maintained to voluntary aided. Went co-ed in 1977 and expanded its boarding provision in the 1980s to become one of the largest state boarding schools in the country. State boarding schools provide free education but charge fees for boarding.

The school's expansion over the years has resulted in a hotchpotch of architectural styles (some new, some old) squeezed into a narrow, 30-acre site, with a main road on one side and a picturesque valley on the other. Some areas of the school are slightly tired looking but the glorious countryside that bounds it on three sides more than makes up for it. In recent years Bruton, with its ancient streets of stone and stucco houses, has become one of the most sought-after places to live in the country. So many showbiz and fashion names have houses in the area – Cameron Mackintosh, Dominic West, Rhys Ifans, Sam Taylor-Wood and Mariella Frostrup to name but a few – that it's been dubbed 'the new Notting Hill' and the opening of Hauser & Wirth has added to the cachet. Mariella Frostrup was the guest of honour at the school's 2015 speech day, cautioning students about the power of social media.

Year 7 to 11 pupils wear blazer and tie uniform (burgundy polo shirts in summer). Head recently changed dress code for sixth formers – they now wear business suits. Most like this, a few don't. 'I'd been waiting for five years to wear my own clothes,' a year 12 girl told us. Sixth form has its own common room with views over the Somerset landscape and a pervading air of studiousness when we visited at exam time. Sixth formers who have passed their driving tests are allowed to drive to school. We asked a year 12 group what they'd miss about the school when they left and they unanimously said 'Squares' – a playground game invented by Sexey's pupils. Parents praise the school's sense of community and family atmosphere and say that its size means that teachers know every child. 'Children feel proud to say they are at Sexey's,' the mother of a year 11 told us.

Food is excellent. Most have school dinners, with only a tiny handful bringing packed lunches. Everything is cooked in-house by talented chef (a former chef de partie at Heathrow) and his 20-strong team. Six hundred lunches served every day. Food is locally sourced where possible and halal, vegetarian and gluten-free options are available. Bustling canteen, with pupils allowed to sit where they want.

Pastoral care, well-being and discipline: Every pupil (day and boarding) belongs to one of four houses, each of which has a head of house and team of tutors. Lots of healthy inter-house rivalry – houses compete in sport, music, drama, enterprise, poetry and more to win the annual Bint Shield. Vertical tutor groups, with 15 minutes of tutor time every morning. School takes a huge amount of care in helping pupils' transition from primary school. Pupils due to board in year 7 come and stay for a boarding weekend in the July before they start. 'It means they're not sitting at home worrying over the summer holidays,' explains the head.

School is very keen on creating a culture of well-being and happiness. The key words at Sexey's are tolerance, respect and kindness and with that in mind the school has created The Sanctuary, a quiet place for children to go and reflect or chat about anything that's bothering them. 'The pastoral care is second to none,' a mother told us. 'The communication between teachers and parents is good too. They seem to take pride in going that extra mile.' As a C of E school, it prides itself on its close links with Diocese of Bath and Wells and St Mary's Church in Bruton (boarders regularly attend Sunday services there). School san, staffed by rotating team of three nurses, is open 24/7 for boarders. Active school council, plus head boy, head girl and raft of prefects.

Pupils and parents: A real mix. School prides itself on its diversity and pupils come from a wide variety of backgrounds – from horsey types who compete in the school equestrian team to youngsters with 'chaotic' home lives. Boarders come from all over (from Spain to Hong Kong) but must be UK nationals, hold an EU passport or be domiciled in the UK. Quite a few boarders are from army families, others from RNAS base at Yeovilton. The students we met were friendly, enthusiastic, down to earth and unpretentious. A sixth former reckoned she might have been a 'bit of a brat' if she'd gone to an independent school but said no one was like that at Sexey's.

Parents are very involved – thriving parent and staff association, with spring ball hosted in the school hall every year. Former pupils include the late Ned Sherrin, Million Dollar website creator Alex Tew and BBC wildlife film-maker James Brickell.

Entrance: Demand for day places is intense. Day admissions are handled by Somerset County Council but there's virtually no chance of a day place in years 7 to 10 unless you live within two kilometres of the school. Boarding numbers are increasing so boarding places are easier to come by. Main intakes are year 7, year 9 and sixth form. Head and head of boarding interview prospective boarders and reference from previous school required.

No new pupils admitted in year 11 and no catchment area rules for day pupils in the sixth form. Around 60 new pupils join the sixth form each year. Minimum of five GCSEs at A*-C needed, plus some subject-specific requirements.

Exit: Up to 60 per cent leave after GCSE, mainly to take vocational courses at FE colleges in Street and Yeovil. Some to do apprenticeships.

After A level 96 per cent go to university. A wide variety of courses – from physics and biomedical science to law and history. Universities in the south west are perennially popular – Exeter, Bath, Falmouth and Plymouth – but an increasing number are going further afield, to places like Durham, Leeds, Manchester and Southampton. A few do art foundation courses and one or two go to Oxbridge most years – one vet to Cambridge in 2016 and one medic to Edinburgh.

Remarks: If you want your child to be a day pupil and you're lucky enough to live in the (tiny) catchment area then applying here is a no-brainer. If you want your child to board then Sexey's offers all the advantages of boarding in a small school – but without the enormous price tag or social pretentiousness.

Shebbear College

Shebbear, Beaworthy, Devon EX21 5HJ

Pupils: 339; 67 boarders • Ages: 3-19 • Sixth form: 60

Fees: Day £12,525; Boarding £18,390 – £24,750 pa

Tel: 01409 282000
Email: info@shebbearcollege.co.uk
Website: www.shebbearcollege.co.uk

Headmaster: Since 2013, Simon Weale MA (Oxon). Previously deputy head at Brentwood School and before that, head of sixth form at Reigate Grammar School, head of year at Latymer Upper School, London, and history teacher at Judd School, Tonbridge. He has relocated from the south east to one of the most rural areas in Devon. Married with three children ranging in age from tot to teens. A keen sportsman, he has played cricket for Oxford University and was captain of Teddington Cricket Club. He played rugby for London Cornish RFC and hockey for the London Schools Hockey Association. Still plays cricket. In fact he can literally step from the headmaster's house in his whites straight onto the cricket field to play, something he can't wait to do again this summer.

The Old Shebbearians and governors seem to have a tight rein over the school's developments; it is 'their baby.' The aim is to 'preserve but improve through careful change.' One parent said of the headmaster, 'I feel he has a good long term strategy for the school but at times does not sell himself or the school as well as he might.' Another said, 'I like the headmaster enormously. He has a great sense of humour and is happy to listen to issues and pass them on appropriately. However, he appears somewhat shy and I believe is seen as being unapproachable by some parents due to this.' What do the pupils think we asked? 'I know my daughters have the utmost respect for him while having no qualms if they needed to speak to him. That is just as it should be,' we were told.

S

Head of prep school: Since 2012, Mike Furber BEd. Originally from York, Mike qualified as a teacher in London before heading off to Nigeria and then Thailand to teach. Once back in the UK, he settled with his wife in the local village, Shebbear, where they've been for 17 years with their now teenage sons. Previously deputy head of Bradworthy Primary School, also north Devon.

Academic matters: Years 1 and 2 are taught together, a challenging task carried out by their class teacher with the support of a full-time teaching assistant. The class of around 15 is split for group work to accommodate and cater for the varying abilities and needs. Pupils benefit from senior school specialist teachers in French, ICT, music, PE and gymnastics. French is taught from year 1, Spanish from year 6.

In 2016, at A level, 29 per cent of grades were A*/A and 53 per cent A*-B. At GCSE, 37 per cent A*/A grades. Parents are happy with the teaching, progress and results, saying, 'Academically I feel the teachers understand both children's strengths and weaknesses and work with them so they achieve their best.' Another agreed, adding, '[My children] may not be grade A students, but they are encouraged to give it their all.'

Seventeen subjects offered at A level. Maths and science are strong at this level; at least half of sixth formers opt for maths or a science. One pupil was recently ranked number one in the country at the Maths Challenge UK, and another is now studying at Cambridge. Art and music have produced top marks at both levels, with 12 out of 13 pupils achieving an A* or A at GCSE art in 2016. No plans to add BTecs or other vocational qualifications. Religious studies and a language are compulsory at GCSE. Spanish is taught from year 7 and French from year 8. As an international school, some pupils take qualifications in Italian, German, Russian and Cantonese. EAL also offered.

All pupils are annually assessed for reading comprehension, spelling and writing skills. Learning support is then provided as needed, at an extra cost. A foreign language can be dropped if extra tuition is needed. One parent told us, 'She needed some additional help, but wasn't bad enough to get any at the state primary school. Shebbear offered, gave, and are still giving her the additional support she needs.' The learning support department produce Individual Teaching Plans (ITPs) twice a year and Individual Education Plans (IEPs) for all pupils with a statement/EHC plan. The department uses a number of tried and tested methods to help pupils, including a handwriting scheme using music, coloured reading rulers and overlays to help dyslexics. For pupils that find it difficult to retain information and to concentrate, they motivate them using multi-sensory techniques, educational puzzles and computer programmes. This provides structured learning, in a playful, fun way. Assistance during exams is also available, including reading, scribing, word processing, prompters, transcriptions and extra time. Nurses assess pupils too, and any seen to be showing signs of fine motor skill difficulties can take part in exercise classes designed for neuro-developmental delay. The school can also provide a number of resources including special pens and grips to help.

Games, options, the arts: All the traditional sports are played here. For boys, the major games are rugby, hockey and cricket, and for the girls there's hockey, netball and rounders. Other sports on offer include basketball, football, surfing, horse riding, hiking, table tennis, badminton and trampolining. There are several playing fields, an all-weather floodlit pitch, cricket nets, a dance studio, a gym overlooking the sports hall, and a weights room. For a small school the teams do pretty well; the U15 and U14 rugby teams are strong (an ex-head-girl now plays in the England women's rugby team), and the U14 cricket team recently won the Devon Cup. Latest sports tour travelled to Barbados and St Lucia where the boys and girls played football, netball and cricket. Next tour is a trip up to London for matches and tournaments. Swimming lessons start in year 3 and some prep pupils play in senior school teams.

When we were there, preparations were underway for the upcoming performance of Oliver! Two casts performing over four nights. The art teacher was busily working on a very impressive set in the main hall; he definitely has a great eye for design, and a passion to match. Past performances include Sweeney Todd and The Rocky Monster Show and, more recently, An Evening of Music Drama and Readings from the First World War. Prep school productions have included Joseph and His Amazing Techicoloured Dream Coat, Panto Pandemonium and Pirates of the Currybean. The senior pupils here have even been lucky enough to take part in a drama workshop with actor Joseph Fiennes.

Shebbear has a strong musical reputation and the music department is run by a husband and wife team. Brand new music centre with recording studio and Steinway concert hall. Several budding musicians have gone on to top music colleges, some with scholarships. In year 1 everybody learns the Irish whistle, year 2 the violin, years 3 and 4 the recorder and years 5 and 6 the keyboard. There are plenty of musical activities and groups – choirs, orchestra, flute group, saxophone group, brass ensemble and a string group. Plus regular performances such as informal chamber concerts for the younger ones, gig nights for the teenage rockers, and formal concerts for ensembles, choirs and orchestras. Recent visits by professional musicians have included Voces8 and Festive Flutes.

The art department is on two levels in the main building, with separate pottery, woodworking and food and technology areas on the ground floor. The top level has a large studio for sixth form use, as well as an ICT suite (for all pupils). The downstairs level has another large studio. There is screen-printing equipment as well as a cylinder and roller press, plus a kiln room. Artwork is displayed everywhere, no wall is left uncovered, and good use is made of the ceiling, too, with plenty of pieces dangling overhead. The art teacher is keen on pupils being able to compare and contrast their work, learn from each other, and be able to go back to pieces and give them more attention. We felt this approach gave the space a real creative edge, a great way to motivate and improve. Standards of work were in some cases very high. Regular visits to art galleries, local cathedrals and museums for all, plus A level students can visit London, Barcelona and Paris. Weekend workshops and some evening classes are on also offer, including life drawing.

Extracurricular activities include the usual array of sports, science, drama and arts clubs, plus a few more unusual offerings such as archery, shooting (rifle range is just behind main school building), Minecraft, wildlife studies and gardening. Given the location, outdoor pursuits like Ten Tors, Duke of Edinburgh and army cadets are also readily available and very popular. There are other projects like World Aims and Eco-Schools, which pupils can get involved in events like the Global Student Forum and Model United Nations, campaigning for War Child, Amnesty International and Christian Aid. There are also Fairtrade events such as the recent fashion show, plus a daily Fairtrade tuck shop. Recent trips abroad include a trip to Poland visiting Auschwitz, and a sixth form charity expedition to Uganda.

The prep makes good use of its rural location. There is a forest school and pupils are often out on walks on campus, learning about birds, pond dipping or naming plants and trees. Pupils plant potatoes to grow, harvest and then make their very own potato wedges. They also get out and about to local farms, collecting eggs to bake in cakes the next day. Regular trips to the seaside to learn about sea creatures and rock pools. Other recent trips include Tiverton Museum, Dingles Heritage Centre where they learnt about the life of a travelling fairground family, and a whole school trip to Paignton Zoo. Year 6 went further afield to Dorset for their annual PGL residential. Lots of fundraising events too, the last being for South West Children's Hospice when pupils did sponsored cycling, skipping marathons, gym challenges, and of course sold lots of cakes.

Boarding: Just over a third of boarders are from Hong Kong and China, a third are from the UK and the rest are from Europe. A large number of the UK boarders – including four 7-year-olds – are from Forces families. One parent told us, 'We chose Shebbear because it had such a homely feel and the head of boarding made a lasting impression on both of us. The location was and still is stunning, and the facilities for the boarders are very good. I also felt that the school really understood the needs of military children and in this I haven't been mistaken.' They went on to to say, 'When asking for time off in special circumstances eg bereavement and holiday when dad was back from Afghanistan, the school have been understanding and always honoured my request.' One girl, who recently left the sixth form, boarded here for 12 years.

The older boys' boarding accommodation, Pollard, is in the main school building and currently houses the majority of boarders. Pyke House, which has just been reopened, is for the 11 to 13 year old boys, and is above the prep school kindergarten and lower years classroom. There are currently 12 boys there. The girls' house, Ruddle, is across the campus and has around 25 boarders at the moment. Most rooms are doubles or triples; sixth formers are offered singles if they would prefer. All rooms have internet connection and are good sized, well maintained and homely. Common rooms or lounges are also decent sizes with power hockey and snooker tables in the boys' houses and a decent kitchen in the girls'. The girls often invite the boys over for meals and cooking evenings. Parents said, 'I have always been completely happy with the rooms, the pastoral care and the general facilities. My girls have been properly cared for and helped if feeling homesick or angry or just plain miserable. I have been able to ring the houseparents if I've been worried and within minutes they have been with my child and then calling me back with an update.' The majority are full-time boarders but families do make use of the flexi arrangements occasionally. Weekly boarding is becoming more popular and some are opting to do so during the summer term so they can revise at school during the week.

School facilities including the sports hall and library are open to boarders in the evenings and at weekends. Swimming is on Mondays, there are shopping trips at weekends, plus visits to National Trust places, theme parks, cinemas, theatres, paintballing, surfing, cycling, and horse riding by arrangement. Summer is when the school really comes into its own, lovely light evenings and sprawling countryside, perfect for barbeques, picnics or evening sports. There is no school on Saturdays at Shebbear, just sports fixtures. Plenty of social events throughout the year including the summer ball, discos, themed parties and talent contests. In the summer holidays the school is used as a language school.

Background and atmosphere: Founded in 1841, Shebbear College is one of the oldest schools in Devon, currently celebrating its 175th year. Originally set up as Prospect College by Bible Christians in 1829 (the emblem 'PC' still remains on the main gates today), it was re-founded by the Bible Christian Church as Shebbear College over a decade later, and eventually became part of the Methodist Church. It became co-ed in 1992. Set in 85 acres of the North Devon countryside, this is as rural as it gets. In fact it's surprisingly rural, so be prepared. Nearest cities are Exeter and Plymouth, both about an hour away, nearest big town is Barnstaple, half an hour or so away. The school rents out 65 acres of the land to local farmers but has plenty of room left for the main campus, several playing fields and a good cross-country course. Prep has its very own adventure playground fully equipped with wooden pirate ship and climbing ropes and frames. The campus itself is very flat, open to the elements, ensuring any cobwebs are blown away as pupils make their way between buildings. The main building used to be an old printworks and some of the original 100-year-old tables are used in the dining area.

Great science block; all the laboratories have been updated in the last 18 months. Lovely, modern, bright classrooms; we particularly liked the biology lab, equipped with a hamster colony and tubes for them to run across the ceiling. There's also a resident python. The junior lab is used by year 6 pupils from the prep school. They were recently treated to a lung dissection; just one little one fainted. All part of the preparation for senior school, apparently.

New sixth form block is open to all pupils on the ground floor, but sixth formers have exclusive use upstairs. Downstairs toilets have underfloor heating, much to the delight of girls here who regularly take their shoes off on a visit. There are also changing rooms and a kitchen. The building opens out onto the cricket pitch so the ground floor is used for cricket match teas in the summer. Upstairs, the sixth formers can look out across the Devon countryside on all sides. There's a modern kitchen, sofas, a study room and a quiet area. It's all open-plan, divided by glass windows rather than walls. There are separate tutor rooms and a small classroom too. The large viewing balcony runs all along one side of the building, looking over the cricket field. This is no doubt well used in the summer.

Sustainability is high on the priority list at Shebbear. As an Eco School they have been awarded a Green Flag award. They have two biomass plants that provide heat and hot water to the main buildings, and solar panels that provide around five per cent of the electricity. A wind turbine was opposed by locals, but Shebbear is undeterred; they are now planning electric car charging points. Even the minibuses are eco-friendly: all run on biodiesel made from oil from a local pasty company.

Pastoral care, well-being and discipline: Polite, well-behaved children, standing when an adult enters the room and opening doors is standard here. One parent said, 'It is very important that our children should be kind and have good manners and these values are constantly reinforced through example.' Good pastoral care, as well as tutors (each pupil has a designated tutor who is responsible for overseeing both academic and social progress), houseparents and nurses, there is also a full-time resident chaplain. Chapel is every day except Wednesday, and although the school's Methodist roots are central to the school's ethos, students of all faiths and none make up the community – less than 10 per cent of pupils are Methodists. One parent commented, 'Both of my daughters have and are excelling themselves academically and I have to put this down to the quality of the teaching staff and the environment they live in. They are happy, cared for and have a fantastic group of friends around them.'

S

Pupils and parents: There is no school gate life at Shebbear; pupils come from a very wide area, so free buses are provided. Destinations include Tavistock, Bude, Holsworthy, Launceston, Okehampton, Bideford, Dolton, Bridestowe, Hartland, Merton, Petrockstowe and Torrington. Buses leave at 5pm daily Monday to Thursday so everybody gets the chance to participate in after-school clubs. One parent told us, 'Our daughter was not getting on very well at the local school, always came home very tired, grumpy... Despite a longer day at Shebbear she still comes home tired, but is happy and achieving lots.'

The school keeps parents updated with regular newsletters. 'The school is good at communicating to parents. We have email addresses for all the teachers, who are very approachable and are good at coming back with answers to any queries,' parents told us. The only grumble from parents was around sports fixtures – 'Organisation at times could be better – particularly with regard to matches where the children don't know until the day before whether or not they are playing.' One parent added, 'Often it is left to the children to communicate changes, which they do not always do.' And the only grumble from pupils, 'The food is the only thing which our children occasionally complain about!'

Entrance: Entry to Shebbear is not selective but there is an entrance exam to the senior school for assessment purposes and scholarships. Open days and taster days, including boarding, are available, plus induction days once accepted. Smooth transition from the junior school, which makes up nearly 50 per cent of the senior intake. Others come from local primary schools including Bradworthy, and also from St Petroc's in Bude.

On settling in, one family told us, 'The entrance process was slightly daunting for our elder son who is not particularly confident. It took him a whole year to settle but we had a lot of help from the pastoral team who went to great lengths to try and make him feel comfortable; they even established a new club based on his main interest.' A parent of a boarder told us their story: 'The entrance process was simple and straightforward. The settling in time was awful for me as I felt like I had lost a child. The boarding mistress and staff were incredible and made my daughter feel immediately at home. They also gave me regular updates as to how she was doing which made me feel a million times better.'

Exit: Nearly all prep school pupils move up to the senior school. Some 66 per cent stay on there for sixth form. Many pupils come from farming families so some pupils leave to go on to vocational colleges to study land-based courses. Most sixth formers go on to university. Popular destinations include Exeter, Plymouth, Bath, Falmouth, Durham and York. One to Oxbridge in 2016 and one won a scholarship to study cello at the Royal Welsh School of Music. Some boarders return to their home country to study.

Money matters: Shebbear offers academic, all-rounder, music, art, drama and sport scholarships at year 7, year 9, and sixth form entry. The Boarding School Allowance (BSA) is provided to help children of service families, plus there are means-tested bursaries, a college bursary scheme, a Methodist church bursary scheme, siblings discounts and allowances for old Shebearians, families in the parish of Shebbear and Methodist ministers.

Remarks: Shebbear is a traditional, historic school set in rural countryside. Pupils come from far and wide, and particularly for military families, Shebbear is a good choice. It is small and many parents praised its family atmosphere. The school makes the most of its rural setting with its sustainable approach, good sports facilities and outdoor pursuits. The new buildings are great assets; hopefully this is just the beginning and Shebbear will continue to develop and move forward. Parents commented, 'We did look at other schools but chose Shebbear because of its excellent reputation for pastoral care, the very good relationship between the teachers and children based on mutual respect, and the lovely family atmosphere.'

Sherborne Girls School

Bradford Road, Sherborne, Dorset DT9 3QN

Pupils: 473; 410 full boarders • Ages: 11–18 • Sixth form: 174 • C of E

Fees: Day £19,740 – £24,300; Boarding £26,850 – £33,300 pa

Tel: 01935 812245
Email: registrar@sherborne.com
Website: www.sherborne.com

Headmistress: Since 2006, Mrs Jenny Dwyer BEd (late 40s), formerly head of Prior's Field. Educated at Bradford Girls' Grammar and then read maths at Homerton College, Cambridge. First job at Benenden (teaching/housemistress), then went on to Queen Anne's School, Caversham, where she was deputy head responsible for pastoral care. 'Glad to be back in full boarding', she asserts that 'all girls, not only the very brightest, should have a chance of a seriously good education'. Boarding numbers are up by more that 20 per cent since her arrival and the school is nearing completion of a huge development programme of new buildings and thorough refurbishment of old.

Married to a 'very supportive man', they have two sons (educated at Charterhouse and Milton Abbey). Keen on maths, hockey and dinghy sailing at her home on the Norfolk coast. Pastoral care is her particular passion. Vivacious and easy to talk to, she appears full of creative energy and very stylish. Her most obvious attribute, apart from the ability to negotiate stairs and rough ground at speed on needle thin three-inch heels, is the ability to get people talking freely and confidently. She also listens to what they say.

Academic matters: The number of girls taking IB has grown. Sherborne Girls now offers it as the boys' school dropped it from their curriculum (boys can still do IB with the girls). Mrs Dwyer says girls thrive on its rigour and staff return from IB training courses full of enthusiasm which filters down to everyone. Evidently it's horses for courses, as one girl said she had started it but found she preferred A levels. Results generally pretty impressive, though average point score dropped to 33 in 2016.

At A level greatest uptake is art history and maths. Wide range, including Russian, Japanese, theatre studies and DT reflects broad curriculum. In 2016, a disappointing 35 per cent of A level entries were graded A*/A. IGCSE now used for sciences, maths, and English. Mandarin recently introduced. Sciences amongst strongest results. In 2016, 61 per cent of GCSE papers were graded A*/A. One parent commended the school for being hot on picking up and remedying any weakness in the curriculum.

New labs, each with practical and teaching areas, don't even smell of chemicals and announce their purpose to the world via curious sundial on the squat turret. Adjoining is the bright refurbished language department with lots of lovely language IT. When Sherborne refurbishes it's root and branch, not just a lick of paint. French, German, Spanish (plus Latin) on offer and native speakers of other languages can study them to GCSE. New languages, including Russian, introduced in second year – they also get a Prue Leith Cookery School course (the sixth form can brush up on Prue Leith too).

There is flexibility to take subjects jointly with Sherborne Boys' at A level and IB. Theatre studies is genuinely a joint enterprise but has quite a small take-up.

Much setting and streaming from age 13. No form tutors; girls meet individually with personal tutors moving to a new one approximately every two years. The Junior Diploma is an initiative to keep girls consciously reflecting on their own competencies in the foundation areas of knowledge, learning skills, personal attributes and contribution to the curriculum. About 20 per cent of pupils have mild special needs; they may get extra lessons outside hours.

Games, options, the arts: Sport has a high-ish profile now at Sherborne and girls' teams are definitely up with the best in Dorset. They are old hands at the increasingly popular lacrosse and have hosted ELA lacrosse finals for 1st and U15 teams throughout UK. The girls are proud of their record and Sherborne holds pop lacrosse tournaments for prep and primary schools. Even the less sporty get encouragement.

Hockey (county champions and have provided England team members) and netball seriously competitive. All levels of players have access to good coaching. L4 and U4 have sport every day, L5 to U5 have at least three sessions per week, plus activities. The Oxley Sports Centre, with indoor pool, fitness suite, gym, dance studio plus floodlit Astro is getting a facelift, and offers first class facilities to girls and to the town in a smooth-running shared arrangement. Plenty of grass pitches and 27 tennis courts (eight floodlit), mostly artificial.

Bags of other sporty things. Riding team does well in National Schools' Show Jumping at Hickstead, polo, ski trips, various martial arts, dance etc and opportunities via Sherborne Boys' for things like rifle shooting as well as everything (almost) put on for the town in the Oxley Centre.

Art block with libraries, photography and printmaking, has cunning wooden bars across the wide stairwell and entry, allowing for effective display of textiles etc. There are ambitious plans to link this with a new performance centre in the next development phase. Masses of accomplished architectural studies all over the school as well as a few landscapes that might be mistaken for one of the modern masters. Head of art is an inspirational teacher. Good studio space for A level candidates who appear virtually to live here. Weekend workshops offered on juicy topics eg book-binding, stained glass, paper or jewellery making. Overseas trips made jointly with history of art dept. Computer-aided design and manufacture suite.

The lovely singing from above when we arrived was Friday choir practice. Several choirs sing in the abbey and even Salisbury Cathedral and benefit from having accessible boys' choirs. Sherborne Choral Society runs jointly with boys' school, one area in which their proximity really enables girls to keep up in an area notoriously hard for girls' schools to build a good tradition. Sherborne Schools' Symphony Orchestra skims off the cream of musicians from Sherborne Girls, Sherborne Boys and nearby Leweston to produce two joint orchestras. Singing, chamber orchestra, jazz band, senior choir, elite madrigal choir etc etc. Girls enjoy music and even take up instruments when previous experience has been off-putting. Current music building bursting out of its breezeblocks into huts alongside, so the new performing arts centre is eagerly awaited. Joint musical theatrical productions with Sherborne School and some separate drama.

'A plethora' of societies and clubs for intellectuals (from astronomy to current affairs), the arty crafty (life class – gardening), domestic goddesses (cookery – all sorts) or sporty types (ballet – yoga). D of E gets about 150 and 40+ go on to gold.

Lots of charitable activities including a lovely project for the juniors in the New Aldhelmsted West (just say West) with past pupil Camila Batmanghelidjh CBE, who opened the house. Trip to Nepal exploring and helping in an orphanage – plus all the usual exchanges and field trips such as sea kayaking and trekking in the Spanish Picos. School exchange links with Toronto and Tasmania.

Boarding: Sherborne is one of the few true boarding schools remaining with only about 40 day girls (seven per cent). Day girls are allocated to boarding houses and given their own space (some even their own bed) there. They can stay for the occasional night. No flexi-boarding and there is Saturday school. The majority want to be in on the weekend activities. Ideal for expat parents. Day girls allowed home at 6pm but some stay to do prep until 8pm.

Massive refurbishment of boarding houses means all have pleasant meeting, working, library and dining areas plus 'drawing rooms', for entertaining or watching Downton Abbey. Some girls sleep in cubicles (partitioned compartments in a dormitory – they claim not to make a habit of vaulting the partitions) but most in double or single rooms. Upper sixth girls move into Mulliner with individual study bedrooms and bit of independence. After February of their final year they are allowed into Sherborne pubs.

Background and atmosphere: Founded in 1899 by the Wingfield Digby family – local bigwigs owning Sherborne Castle – the main building is a rambling Victorian warren in the pretty local hamstone. Meticulous planting makes an attractive site with the main boarding houses and teaching facilities forming a crescent round a green expanse of playing fields and lawn on the edge of the town. Still a few 'huts' for drama and music but the five year development plan is already nearing completion after only four years, making way for the next performing arts phase.

Recently completed Aldhelmsted West is a fabulous environment for the first two years with sunny dining room, laid out for birthday tea on our visit, work rooms for homework, lots of comfortable play space and room for music practice. Parents get involved in sports as West positively encourages them to get to know one another. Several live-in staff and a housemistress' house attached with openings onto all three floors. Good big bedrooms, mostly for four, with loo and shower en suite.

The undoubted advantage of an all boys' school in the same small market town means the girls can share entertainment and have sensible and reasonably safe access to town life, a situation envied by similar girls-only schools in the area. Younger girls can go into town at weekends. Lower sixth can go as far as Yeovil, Exeter, Salisbury. Upper sixth girls allowed into the sixth form bar at Sherborne Boys. Common features include coordinated term dates, some A level courses, IB, social events, two joint plays, the Academic society and Epicurean society as well as music.

Pastoral care, well-being and discipline: School rules are straightforward, based on 'keep safe and consider others'. Exclusion for dealing drugs; experimenters can 'expect' to go but 'touch wood no issues' and smoking not really a problem. 'Robust' attitude to alcohol, shared by boys' school, includes possibility of breathalysing. Daily living still done the old school way with all meals in houses with their own separate kitchens and dining rooms. Formal lunches (sixth form do table plans, staff at each table), but cafeteria-style suppers. Hot drinks machines for girls to entertain friends, male and female, in the downstairs areas. Afternoon tea at 5pm and supper at 7.30pm means sensible pre- and post-supper time for supervised prep and activities. Girls say food's pretty ok.

Resident housemistresses, some with families and pets (one house is pet free for allergy sufferers), run the houses like homes with minor medical help and a friendly ear available during the day. Proper school san. The popular school chaplain teaches, offers confirmation etc and keeps an eye that all denominations get spiritual support. Has the right balance of welcome and warmth with respect for girls' views, say parents. Teams of house tutors give personal and academic support on an individual basis. Issues (homesickness, cliques, etc) do crop up but they are very well resolved, said one parent.

Pupils and parents: Still lots of old west country families but also Forces families, diplomats, Londoners with south west connections (Sherborne is on the main line to Waterloo). About 10 per cent come from Hong Kong and elsewhere: Dubai, Nigeria etc plus Europe since IB was introduced. Around 25 need EAL support of one lesson per week. Recently awarded the DfE International School Award in recognition of the international dimension being a key part of school ethos. Sixth form are let out of uniform but have regulation black tailored suit (with a quite skimpy skirt) worn with their own accessories.

Old girls – Camila Batmanghelidjh, soprano Dame Emma Kirkby, violinist Ruth Rogers, writers Sophie Kinsella, Santa Sebag Montefiore, Dames Deirdre Hutton of the Trading Standards Institute and Juliet Wheldon, who was legal advisor to the Bank of England. Sherborne old girls are exceptionally efficient: organised into regional circles, they support all sorts of school initiatives, their own charitable causes and a careers information network. Such benevolent networking may lie behind the remarkable collections of speakers who visit Sherborne – AC Grayling on the day of our visit, Germaine Greer, recently, Becky Anderson of CNN, Matthew Pinsent, Simon Weston, Ann Widdecombe, Griff Rhys Jones.

Entrance: Visit, registration, 'at work days', taster weekends, deposit paid, then scholarship exams, common entrance papers or own entrance exams in maths, English and reasoning plus an interview. One form enters at 11, a few girls join at 12 but the majority (three forms) enter at 13. Mainly from Hanford, Port Regis, Hazlegrove, Knighton House, Sherborne Prep, Leaden Hall, Perrott Hill, Cheam, Bute House, Newland, Thomas's, Mount House Farleigh, Forres Sandle Manor, Twyford and Sunninghill. About 20 join for sixth form – at least five grade B or above GCSEs required for A level or IB.

Exit: A few leave after GCSEs, mainly to sixth form colleges. After A levels, practically all go on to university to read a wide variety of courses (modern languages, theology, lots of sciency things including medicine). Edinburgh, Exeter, Durham, Newcastle, Bath, Warwick, King's College London, Sheffield, Cardiff (medicine) and Bristol (veterinary medicine) currently leading the pack. A few to Oxbridge most years (none in 2016) and several to art schools or to study academic art history.

Money matters: Boarding fees about what you would expect, on a par with co-ed fees for boarders though less than the boys. New fee structure for day students with two options: day boarder (with the option for overnight stays) or day girl (no overnight stays, but her own space for storage and study in a boarding house). The school hopes the new cost structure will offer a competitive day fee to local families whilst still ensuring that day girls feel fully involved in the busy life of a boarding school.

Scholarships generous for a girls' school. Academic, art and music awards pay up to quarter of fees, plus bursaries based on need. Music scholars get up to three lessons per week – more than at most schools. Nearly 100 girls are receiving some sort of award or bursary. Currently appealing for bursary fund. School has also introduced elite swimming programme for which scholarships are offered.

Remarks: No longer the stuffy warhorse of girls' education, though its academic standards are undiminished. Parents appreciate that its good teaching avoids hot housing and encourages a balance of activities. A real gem amongst the girls' only full-boarding schools with all the advantages of its symbiotic proximity to Sherborne School.

Sherborne Preparatory School

Acreman Street, Sherborne, Dorset DT9 3NY

Pupils: 265; 35 full, 15 flexi boarders • Ages: 3-13 • C of E

Fees: Day £8,790 – £16,380 pa; Boarding £22,425 – £23,460 pa

Tel: 01935 812097
Email: registrar@sherborneprep.org
Website: www.sherborneprep.org

Headmaster: Since 2015, Nick Folland (50s). Educated at Exmouth Community College, one of the largest comprehensives in the country, and Loughborough University, where he read PE, sports science and geography. Worked with deaf children for three years, did a PGCE at Loughborough and then moved to Blundell's. Played professional cricket for Somerset for three years before taking a housemaster's post at Blundell's. Appointed as inaugural head of Blundell's Prep and after a decade there took on the headship of St John's On-The-Hill prep in Chepstow, where he spent four years.

Married to Di, a charming Australian speech and language specialist who is immersed in school life. They live in a house owned by the school, a five-minute walk away. He has two children – a daughter in the sixth form at Blundell's and a son just starting his law career. Head is go-ahead, energetic (his wife describes him as a 'can-do person'), refreshingly down-to-earth and popular with parents. 'I'm a pretty open book,' he says, 'and if there are things to improve then I get on and improve them.' Very proud of the fact that the school is not selective yet gets excellent results. 'I'm really enjoying the job,' he says. 'The children are what it's all about and they are wonderfully positive and really want to achieve.' His hectic schedule means he doesn't teach these days but he's very visible around the school, lunching in the dining hall, chatting to children in the corridors and coaching the under 9s rugby team. Plans are afoot for him to coach netball in the coming year. He isn't in the least fazed by taking on a new sport – 'I'm a gamesy person,' he says. Enjoys sport, film and travel in his spare time.

Entrance: School is non-selective and unpretentious. Entrance is by interview with the head and previous school report, plus informal assessment when pupils come in for a taster day before joining. Most pupils start in the pre-prep or year 3 but there is a steady trickle joining from years 3 to 7 and at least ten new starters arrive in year 7. School is happy to consider new pupils all year round, not just those starting in the autumn term. Academic, music, sport, art, DT and all-rounder scholarships available – school says 'talent and enthusiasm are especially sought'.

Exit: Sherborne Prep is independent of Sherborne School and Sherborne Girls but has strong links with both. Around half of the pupils head to the Sherborne senior schools. Others go to Eton, Harrow, Winchester, Cheltenham Ladies', Marlborough, Bryanston, Canford, King's Bruton and Charterhouse, more than a third with scholarships.

Remarks: Founded in 1858, the school moved to its present location, just off a quiet Sherborne side street, in 1885. Went co-ed in the 1970s. The school site combines the best of both worlds – it's five minutes' walk from the centre of town but has 12 acres of grounds (including five acres of sports fields) for children to play in.

Despite its traditional exterior, Sherborne Prep is impressively forward thinking. The dynamic head of teaching and learning (she's also the head of languages) helps children to work out what type of learners they are (visual, auditory, kinaesthetic) and has brought in a self assessment programme that encourages pupils to give themselves scores for collaboration, participation, conduct and independence. The head of the pre-prep has introduced a Singapore maths programme called Inspire Maths to develop pupils' number confidence and mental arithmetic skills.

Teaching is excellent throughout. Teachers are a dedicated bunch, full of ideas and enthusiasm. A parent described them as 'outstanding, with a diversity of styles and approaches'. We met the deputy head (academic), who attended the school herself and had such happy memories that she decided to return, and a humanities teacher who has been at the school for 41 years. Exam results are first rate but a member of staff emphasised that the school isn't an exam factory. 'Exams aren't the be all and end all,' she said. 'They are part of the journey. People get so focused on exams and it's important to realise that they are just a stepping stone.' As well as their form tutors, who they see every day, the children get to choose their own independent tutors – anyone from the teachers to the head of maintenance.

Classes are mixed ability, apart from scholarship sets at the top of the school. Maximum class sizes of 18, but rarely more than 16. Three classes per year group in years 6, 7 and 8 and two per year group for younger pupils in the prep. Learning support (accessed by 13 per cent) is provided by the 'Learning Hub'. Children receive one-to-one help or work in small groups.

Languages are a particular strength of the school and are taught from the pre-prep upwards. Reception children do a bit of Italian (learning through music, drama and cultural aspects) while year 1 and 2 pupils learn Mandarin. 'The idea is to give them a foundation in the idea of appreciating languages,' says the head of languages, who has developed a website called Language Prep to make languages fun and accessible (it's used by other schools too). Years 3s do German, year 4s Italian (with a focus on ICT and cooking) and year 5s and up French and Spanish (ready for their senior schools). Latin is taught from year 6. Debating and public speaking are notable. When we visited a year 8 boy had just won the local round of the Youth Speaks competition, speaking without notes about finding strength through adversity. No lessons on Saturdays. School runs an optional programme of activities – children come into school in their home clothes and take part in three-hour clubs (everything from forest school and pond club to circus skills, cartoon character drawing, LAMDA and sport). Saturday lectures for year 7 and 8 children and parents tackle a raft of unusual subjects – the history of salt to 'is levitation possible?'

New head of sport (previously at Glenalmond) is keen for every pupil to get the chance to wear a team shirt during their time at the school. Main sports for boys are rugby, hockey and cricket and hockey, netball and cricket for girls (rounders less popular these days). Hockey is particularly strong, with under-8 and under-11 girls winning a string of tournaments in recent months. Sportiest pupils get pro-cricket and hockey training but school also has a 'team of the week' award, where individual children are commended for their efforts in promoting school values on the games pitch. School mainly uses its own playing fields but also has access to the facilities at Sherborne School, just over the road, and the swimming pools at Sherborne School and nearby Sherborne Girls. The children get loads of fresh air, running off steam in the grounds at break and lunchtimes. Pupils enjoy playing conkers (a previous head thoughtfully planted a row of chestnut trees for precisely that purpose).

Parents are full of praise for the school's music, drama, art and DT. A father with two older children and two at Sherborne

Prep said a year 7 play he'd recently seen was 'creatively delivered and outstanding', far better than productions he'd seen at senior schools. Music is integral to the prep and the school provides 14 choristers for the choir at Sherborne Abbey. More than half of the children play a musical instrument and the new director of music reckons numbers will rise to 75 per cent before long. A host of opportunities for budding young musicians, including full orchestra, senior choir, junior choir, chamber choir, brass ensemble, jazz ensemble and piano trio. The art room is a vision to behold – light and airy, with views of Sherborne Abbey and the children's work proudly displayed everywhere. Head of art is a successful artist from Spain who encourages the children to explore different art forms, including drawing, painting, sculpture, film and experimental media. 'They never have the same lesson,' he says. He allows children to use the art room at break times, on the proviso that they clear up afterwards, and also teaches art to parents during the spring term.

The pupils are spirited, chatty and well mannered. They stand up when visitors enter the room and are keen to talk about their school. Asked what they like best one said: 'The teachers. They understand you as a person.' Another told us that the teachers have 'a fun way of teaching' while a third described the school as 'small and cosy'. A boarder waxed lyrical too. 'It's easy to make friends here,' he said. 'It's more like a family.' They all gave the Sherborne Prep uniform the thumbs up (especially the navy blazers with jaunty green trim and assorted badges), but the school's sweet and sour chicken wasn't quite so popular. Senior schools say Sherborne Preppers are mature, independent and like 'having a go'.

School has 35 full boarders but offers flexi and occasional boarding too. Boarding from year 3 upwards but few board before year 5. Seventeen international pupils when we visited, from France, Japan, Thailand, Korea, China, Russia and Spain. Two boarding houses – one for boys, the other for girls. Both very homely and friendly, with a plethora of weekend activities to sign up for. Day pupils come from Sherborne itself and from as far afield as Dorchester, Shaftesbury, Shillingstone, Langport and East Coker. Five minibus routes at present. Parents range from architects and business people to writers and directors, many of whom have swapped London for the wilds of the West Country. A mother told us she couldn't 'sing the school's praises highly enough.' She added: 'It's a very warm, unsnobbish, lovely place.'

Pre-prep and nursery housed in a separate building on the main site. Head of the pre-prep says there's an outdoor ethos, with children spending lots of time outside (clad in wet weather gear on rainy days). 'You don't know until you try' is her motto and there's a plethora of after-school activities, including recorder club, ballet, golf and cross-stitch.

Sherborne Prep is an exciting school. Full of character and great ideas, it's friendly, unsnooty and fun – and achieves top-notch results.

Sherborne School

Abbey Road, Sherborne, Dorset DT9 3AP

Pupils: 552; 549 boarders • Ages: 13–19 • Sixth form: 242 • C of E

Fees: Day £28,350; Boarding £35,025 pa

Tel: 01935 812249
Email: admissions@sherborne.org
Website: www.sherborne.org

Headmaster: Since January 2016 Dr Dominic Luckett, previously head of Mill Hill School. Educated at the University of Leicester, where he obtained a first class honours degree in history, and at Magdalen College, Oxford, where he completed his doctorate on Henry VII. Taught for 11 years at Harrow School, where he was head of history and an assistant housemaster, before moving to Worth School as deputy head. In 2007 he was appointed headmaster of Mill Hill School and chief executive of the Mill Hill School Foundation. Married with two children and has published various articles on early Tudor history, is an inspector with the Independent Schools' Inspectorate and a member of the council of the University of Leicester. A tall, softly spoken and sincere man, his interests include paragliding, skiing and hill-walking.

Academic matters: Newish academic deputy, Tim Filtness, has gone down well both with boys and parents and is busy ensuring that academic life is 'at the centre of the wheel, with everything else forming the spokes', as he put it. Boys encouraged 'to become much more independent about their learning', and at the same time they are incentivised to do well by the payment of £10 per 10 commendations! Nine or 10 GCSEs is the norm out of the 20 subjects on offer; virtually all do separate sciences (all science is at IGCSE), and at least one language and one humanity, from a list including Latin/Greek, is compulsory. Results are good rather than stellar, though best ever this year, with A*/A grades awarded to 67 per cent of GCSE entries in 2016. Individual subject stars tend to be art, all three sciences, history, RS and German. A*-B grades awarded for 78 per cent of A levels taken in 2016; 52 per cent of grades A*/A.

No plans to raise the bar at entry, but those who did not achieve their target GCSE grade in the exams held in the last week of the Michaelmas term were required to come back a day early in January to resit them. Teaching is praised by boys and parents alike: stimulating, with levels of banter which do not overstep the mark (mostly). 'They teach the subject, not just to pass exams,' said one mother, approvingly. Learning support, housed in the top corner of the beautiful science block, was pointed out with the wave of the hand by our guide, whose own needs, hitherto unrealised by him, had been identified and acted upon by its staff. 'Sensationally good, and I still pop in there for extra help', he said, unprompted. All boys are screened on arrival, and sessions on learning styles and study skills are timetabled, as are revision classes as GCSEs loom. Subject teachers work closely with learning support staff in individual cases – all quite unobtrusive, but clearly effective.

Games, options, the arts: Gosh, where to start! Sherborne does everything rather well in the sporting line (except rowing), and it's an important part of life here. Acres of verdant pitches (including the hallowed turf of the Upper, a piece of which went to Rwanda as part of a cricket pitch the boys constructed in 2008), tennis courts, Astro the school has in abundance. Twenty-six sports on offer – including fives, polo and real tennis outside the mainstream; clubs and/or trips cater for minority tastes like surfing, canoeing and skiing. Simply masses of fixtures for all standards and tours (recently Australia and Dubai) for top teams. Main sporting rival is Marlborough. Boys get to try most things out in their first year. Pool and fitness suite on site used by local community, and school has sports physio on the staff. Prominence in the regional or national arena actively promoted by director of sport, who says 'I don't want us to produce good players on an ad hoc basis'. Strong tradition of CCF, Ten Tors and D of E too, actively supported by boys and staff alike.

Arts too are tops here. Strong drama emanates from Powell theatre and Victorian Big School Room, neither one ideal performance spaces on grounds of size or original purpose. Lots of productions on school and house level, plus lavish musicals with other schools, Sherborne Girls particularly, but also Leweston and local comprehensive, The Gryphon (all GSG schools). Foreign language plays too, and productions to Edinburgh Fringe. School has produced several notable thespians: John le Mesurier, Jeremy Irons, Hugh Bonneville and rising star Charlie Cox, the two latter (type) cast as posh chaps in Downton Abbey, and Charles Collingwood, landowner and former Lothario, Brian Aldridge in The Archers.

Music has been rehoused in a splendid newish facility, a contemporary yet sympathetic addition to Sherborne's fine buildings. All is state-of-the-art here, so that rock bands (v big here, at least 10 in school) and string quartets can rehearse in neighbouring rooms without conflict. Gorgeous 120 seat recital hall graced with one of several concert grand pianos, all bought new. Technically top notch recording and music tech facilities too; provision, teaching and charismatic head of music, who has returned to teach at his alma mater, all combine to produce some outstanding musicians of all timbres. Practice time protected in an hour after lunch (Q time). Music is a much-loved part of Sherborne for many boys, past and present: 'My son isn't particularly musical, but still plays the piano,' said a parent. Singing, whether in the sublime setting of the abbey twice a week, chanting on the Upper or in the revived house song (banned for a few years for being too rude), matters a lot. Hymns for Sunday services are practised with gusto at Congo and everyone knows the school song, with its rousing chorus of 'Vivat! Vivat! Vivat!' How sad that limited space in the abbey constrains some lower school parents from attending the carol service, an exposition of the finest English choral tradition.

Visual arts have super, dedicated block and permanent exhibition space, where teachers' art is displayed alongside pupils'. Scope for fine art, digital media and DT enormous and very well resourced. Boys love weekend availability, when dabblers seeking light relief are as welcome as fevered public exam candidates hard up against a project deadline. Artworks shown all around the school, which also collaborates with local galleries to put on exhibitions and shows in the town. Impressive results at all levels.

Boarding: Boarding houses all over the town – some in existing buildings (Wallace and the Digby used to be hotels), some purpose-built (Lyon). Accommodation comfortable but certainly not luxurious. Boys in their first year have tended to be housed in one enormous dorm, with individual sleeping compartments for a modicum of privacy, though school tells us they are now mostly in smaller units; thereafter twin rooms and, finally, single rooms at sixth form, sometimes before.

Previous head's mission was to change the culture in boarding houses, where, to an extent, house custom and practice was down to the senior boys; in some, 'chores' (younger boys might nip down to the chippy on behalf of sixth formers, for example) still persisted. No longer. Senior boys are now heavily involved in the pastoral education (not 'care', note) of the younger boys – and assertive, not aggressive or submissive, is what they should all strive to be.

Background and atmosphere: Beautiful school forming a substantial part of a charming and well-heeled Dorset market town, fashioned from gloriously golden ham stone. Founded as a grammar school by Edward VI in 1550 (and still using some of those ancient buildings), yet tracing its origins back to the eighth century, it travelled a somewhat rocky road until a period of mass expansion and financial bolstering up in the mid years of the 19th century. School's heart is in the Courts, surrounded by the most historic of its mostly exquisite architecture, boasting two cloistered walls and sharing one with the abbey, and main school facilities, including the dining hall are centrally located. Additions sensitively designed so that they blend well – Pilkington science block an outstanding example. Boys walk through the town on their way to and from lessons. 'I can't believe the freedom, Mum', marvelled one new boy on arrival.

Atmosphere is one of entitlement – to fabulous surroundings, facilities and opportunities – yet it does not feel horribly posh: no anachronistic uniform here, but supremely practical navy blue shirts and jumpers, which don't show the dirt. Suits and ties at sixth form. Definite masculine and work-a-day feel to the place and female staff in an obvious minority. 'Sherborne remains a place where boys will be boys – and girls are welcome,' says the school. Tremendous house loyalty and fierce though good-natured competition between them. Much made of the ideal combination of single sex education provision within the same town, with plenty of opportunities for socialising.

Pastoral care, well-being and discipline: Our previous write-up alluded to the 'occasional Sherborne refugee [from bullying] at other schools', something the previous head was determined to strike out. To that end, he completely overhauled the pastoral guidelines (which have long included an entire section on culture shock for international boys). He was also keen on the idea of value-based leadership promoted by the Bloxham project; school chaplain Lindsay Collins (a senior female appointment which raised a few eyebrows) is a trustee.

A close eye is kept on all boys by their tutors, who meet them at least once a fortnight and who oversee their well-being in and out of the classroom, and by the house staff, particularly matrons, whose status has definitely been raised. It would be difficult for anyone to go on being unhappy for long without someone noticing, according to the pastoral deputy. Bullying swiftly jumped on, school claims, and 'I'd be disappointed if a delicate flower or a quirky chap couldn't survive', the previous head told us. We will see – Sherborne's reputation for a robust environment (robust, mind, not tyrannical) will take some dismantling, even if it no longer reflects the place.

Sanctions have been simplified and far more rigorously enforced too, to some dismay among boys. 'Heavy-handed,' said one, with numerous house gatings on a Saturday evening being handed out for academic shortcomings, as well as the ever-present smoking and drinking offences. 'OTT!' said another, outraged at being gated for being 'one minute late'. 'Clarity of expectations', says school, which, in the previous head's first term, suspended 30 boys for different things; suspensions rarer now boundaries are better defined.

Pupils and parents: Varies from long-established families to first time buyers, but we nearly laughed when the previous head talked about 'a wide economic mix' – with fees over £30k per annum. Catchment tends to be London extending westwards and eastwards from Devon and Cornwall but not much further afield. Members of all professions, the Forces and local gentry send their sons. Turns out confident (perhaps not confident enough, said previous head – but he was an Etonian) and likeable boys, who form many enduring friendships at school. So many people we spoke to remarked that they 'had never met a Shirburnian they didn't like'. Sprinkling of boys from other countries who enhance the place. Limited opportunities to meet parents from other houses socially is a pity, say some; school does put on fantastic events such as Commem (Speech Day), but jollifications are organised within houses, as are refreshments at parents' evenings and the carol service – if you can squeeze in. Parents report improved communications from school, especially by means of the parent portal, where every aspect of their son's school life can be viewed.

Notable old boys include Sir Alastair Pilkington, John le Carré, Chris Martin (Coldplay), Gulf War commander Major General Sir Patrick Cordingley DSO, political commentators Peter Oborne, Tom Bradby, newsreaders Chris Vacher, Simon McCoy, in addition to many others who have reached the top of the tree in the diplomatic service, academia, the church or the sporting arena.

Entrance: At 13, by entrance exam – either CE, scholarship papers or school's own papers. Average of 55 per cent expected at CE. Process starts a minimum of three years in advance by registering and paying a non-refundable fee, currently £100; pre-test in year 7 with guaranteed places for successful applicants, who sit CE as normal. Parents wanting a particular house advised to say so and register early. They may not then know who will be housemaster when little Johnny goes – housemasters remain in post for 10 years, with a further two by mutual agreement. Boys spend a day at school two years before they start. Final confirmation (subject to meeting entrance requirements) plus hefty but refundable deposit 18 months before entry. At sixth form, entry requirements are five GCSEs at grade C or above, with A level subjects at grade B or higher. School not shy to suggest to weaker candidates that they look elsewhere for sixth form. Handful of newcomers (some from abroad) join at this point.

Exit: Around 90 per cent stay on after GCSEs. Almost all to higher education and university of first choice. Inordinate care taken over UCAS advice and applications. Exceptionally well researched and well resourced programme, which extends to boys who defer or redo UCAS after they have left. Surprisingly small numbers to Oxbridge (five in 2016). Top choices are Newcastle, Durham and other northern universities, old and new. A dozen or so to London; Bristol, Cardiff and Oxford Brookes also popular; increasing interest in US universities. Some to medical school or music college, others to land-based careers. Wide range of degree courses taken.

S

Money matters: Six scholarships of up to 20 per cent and six exhibitions of up to 10 per cent of fees offered at 13+, on basis of 'academic potential and proficiency'. One closed exhibition to 10 per cent of fees offered to sons of the military. Academic scholarships also offered at sixth form, plus awards for artistic, sporting, musical and practical abilities at both entry points. A third of boys receive some financial assistance. Sherborne Foundation supports occasional exceptionally deserving cases, as well as helping the school's wish list to become reality. Expect extras on the bill for trips, all learning support, plus of course the siren call of the school shop.

Remarks: First class boys' boarding in spectacular golden setting, which succeeds in combining the best of ancient and modern without diminishing either. Sharpening up of the academics will secure its place in the galaxy of the greatest English public schools. Stat of flux caused by sudden dismissal of previous head should stabilise as new head makes his mark.

Shrewsbury High School

32 Town Walls, Shrewsbury, Shropshire SY1 1TN

Pupils: 640 • Ages: 3–18 (boys 3–13) • Sixth form: 110

Fees: £7,179 – £13,521 pa

Tel: 01743 494000
Email: admissions@shr.gdst.net
Website: www.shrewsburyhigh.gdst.net

Head: Since 2012, Mr Michael Getty, previously deputy head of Hill House in Doncaster which, shortly after he left, won the independent school of the year award. Schooled in Liverpool, he went north in search of university, heading to Newcastle to read economics. Began his teaching career at Durham High School for Girls as head of economics, and remained there for nine years, during which time he became head of sixth form. He also spent time teaching overseas at the New English School in Amman, Jordan, and for three years was assistant head at Sheffield High School, another GDST school, before going to Hill House. He is Shrewsbury High School's first headmaster. Married to an Ofsted inspector; they have two young children, both of whom are in the prep school.

Mr Getty showed no signs of fatigue when we met him towards the end of his first year at the helm. He appeared irrepressible, and as we listened to ideas tumbling out, he looked just like a boy who has found himself in a sweet shop with the freedom to buy whatever takes his fancy. He simply could not stop smiling. He has reason to smile: he has great financial support from the GDST and has already added to the buildings and facilities he inherited. Many of the girls talk of innovative ideas, the head's willingness to listen and see how their ideas can be initiated. 'I really think he puts the girls first,' said one girl. 'Phew!' was the response of the head, 'job done.' Not quite yet. Many of the parents appreciate Mr Getty's innovations and changes; others remain to be convinced though, as he pointed out, interest in the school has increased dramatically.

Head of prep school: Since September 2015 is Kate Millichamp, previously assistant head of Wolverhampton Grammar Junior School which she helped set up with the head after joining school in 2007. Before that was at Brewood Middle School for seven years, teaching maths and art to years 5-8.

Academic matters: Shrewsbury High School has always prided itself on its success in A levels and GCSEs though recent results have bucked the trend, dipping disappointingly. Forty-one per cent A*/A grades at GCSE in 2016, with 31 per cent A*/A grades at A level. The head has trenchant views on girls' education and the direction in which it is moving. As a result, two houses have recently been bought backing on to the secret garden of the school and complementing the delightful collection of buildings clustered around. One is destined to be the Business School, the place for business studies, economics, for manufacturing and selling, for enterprise. The other is already an amazingly swish sixth form centre with an eye on university-style living.

The head was characteristically enthusiastic about it when he showed us round the day before the keys were due to be handed over. 'Here, through technology linking up with the outside world and the main school network, girls will be able to research, explore, experiment. Independent learning, as they prepare for university study. As well as banks of iPads and laptops, the girls are also able to connect their own mobile devices, such as tablets and phones, to our own network. This is a great symbol of how we are trying to combine an awareness of the girls' lifestyles with a forward-looking take on independent study in preparation for college.'

Well, not many universities have computer rooms hung with chandeliers (sic), cooking facilities with granite work surfaces, common rooms with chandeliers (encore), leather sofas, arm chairs and side tables, a patio for elegant luncheons overlooking the gardens and a gym next door. For some schools, doing your own washing and being allowed a glass of cider in the school bar is the only preparation for university. Mr Getty says schools should be preparing girls for the sort of careers they will be following after university, such as management, architecture, engineering, running businesses, leadership and much else. But the school needs to be more than academic. That's why in addition to academic awards the school has introduced scholarships for sport, art, drama, music and all-round promise. There is more than one of each available if the standard merits.

Despite this new sixth form centre representing a preparation for university and life beyond, some may gasp at a charitable institution spending £1m so luxuriously. Chandeliers, forsooth! Instead, the 'SHS was shortlisted in the UK Independent School of the Year Awards, 2013. In this case The High School has been listed for the Outstanding Strategic Initiative Award in recognition of the school's highly ambitious recent development.' Some might say it can afford to be ambitious.

The school is alert to the fact that the sciences are becoming increasingly popular in girls' only schools and, in the case of Shrewsbury High, even physics. So how can the school increase the momentum and raise the interest in physics? Enter them for the competition to design an electric car in the national Greenpower electric racing car competition involving 400 schools. Rumour has it that the girls have been drawn to race Shrewsbury boys at Brands Hatch next year. Watch this space. Buy a crash helmet.

All this is trendy, ground-churning stuff, but what of the old fashioned virtues? Well, there's a delightful library with decent books – oddly enough, that's not always the case with schools these days. We saw some inspirational teaching in the arts and in the superbly equipped IT facilities and science labs, and in the magical cottage which houses the very lively and successful music department. We saw an excellent art exhibition and met talented, enthusiastic and happy artists. Drama is extremely active and popular with a recent performance of Noye's Fludde taking Shrewsbury by storm and involving a number of schools around the town. There's no doubt there's a lot of lively creativity about.

Games, options, the arts: A fabulous sports centre in part of the main complex offers a tremendous variety of sports; the river nearby beckons oarsgirls; tennis courts, lacrosse, hockey: they're all available – no doubt helped by new floodlit Astroturf; and recently the school enjoyed county championship successes in athletics, netball, rounders, hockey and cross-country. All this without seeming at all hearty. Optional activities abound and the range of possibilities listed in the enrichment programme is endless, from jazz ensemble to Duke of Edinburgh, from helping in primary schools to yoga.

Background and atmosphere: A GDST school which, since its foundation in 1885, has been a distinguished feature of Shropshire education. The bridge which separated it from Shrewsbury school for boys – the Santa Trinità Bridge of the West Midlands – witnessed much to-ing and fro-ing, both in terms of shared activities and social encounters. When Shrewsbury School decided to take girls, following a brief period of girls only in the sixth form, shock waves permeated throughout the county, rendering life difficult, challenging and unsettling for, in particular, the High School. Initially, girls flocked to Shrewsbury School sixth form, and Mr Getty's predecessor was understandably upset. Mr Getty says he is very calm about it all. 'To be honest, we don't notice,' he says. 'We are full for year 7 and numbers in the sixth form have increased by 25 per cent. We're busier than ever.' Girls only versus coeducation. Game on. You pays your money......

For over 100 years the impressive black and white house, which is the first house you see after you've been let in through the electric gates to the prep school, was the main building of a boys' only prep school called Kingsland Grange. From 1964 for about 30 years the wonderful Groves brothers, Alan and Dick, both Old Salopians, ran the school with marked success, particularly on the sports field. But there were always scholarships and some music. Boarding, in common with many schools, became less popular and eventually the school, while remaining strong, became a day school. In 2007 the school merged with Shrewsbury High and the wealth and vision of the GDST began to kick in. It wasn't just the railings outside the school being painted blue which signalled to the world a new ownership; the 13 acres of land were skilfully, sensibly and attractively landscaped so that the view from the outside of the house is even more delightful. We met children who actually pointed out their favourite views. In amongst the trees and valleys a cross-country course has been laid out as well as new cricket pitches and other games fields. William Kent, it is famously said, 'jumped the fence and found all nature was a garden.' He'd have been pleased with what has been done in this campus, and amazed that apparently some of nature has jumped onto the roof. There has been some marvellous new building: a wonderful new dining room with, it is said, delicious food; new bright classrooms kitted out with modern gizmos; a superb sports hall; a science lab; and a design and technology workshop. This building boasts its own solar power generation unit, sun-pipes for illumination, and, wait for it, Mr Kent, a green roof planted with sedum to keep the building cool in summer and warm in winter.

Meanwhile, back in the old house with the wonderful main staircase, the higgledy-piggledy back stairs and the late Victorian stained glass windows, with dance music filling the hall (not the head practising), that venerable old house has been fully refurbished and modernised with state-of-the art technology and the music department. Music is particularly strong in the prep, and a number of excellent music scholarships have been won to top schools. The adventure all begins in a wonderfully imaginative nursery with magic grass, a Once Upon a Time chair in the trees, and bright, glorious teachers.

Wandering around the senior school, lost in the warren of buildings – some old and institutional; others plate glassed and modern – the visitor must be struck by the open friendliness of the girls, the smiling faces, the courteous offers of help. This feels like happiness and those to whom we spoke did not deny it. 'It's good fun here. The days are packed.'

Pastoral care, well-being and discipline: There seems to be a happy relationship between staff and pupils, and the provision for pastoral care, support and help over academic matters and guidance over more personal issues is well in place, and much appreciated by those to whom we spoke. Rules are clearly delineated, and on the whole the existence of those recognisably blue uniformed children in town is a welcome addition to the social mix. All senior school girls have personal tutors and form teachers, and parents are invited to discuss worries and concerns. This is, after all, a day school. One of the most appreciated aspects of care is the help and advice given not only with choice of GSCEs/A levels but with university and what to read there. We spoke to a mother whose daughter had benefited enormously from the various layers of academic support. She was delighted with the outcome. It feels like a very cheery school. One parent told us, 'it's almost too good to be true.'

Pupils and parents: Yes, SHS students appear confident, outgoing, friendly and stylish. Not really a school exclusively for toffs. Nor plebs. Most parents come from the professional classes, with some farmers and a hint of county. A good Shropshire mix. The catchment area is large and the newish head has introduced an extraordinary bus service from Church Stretton, Ludlow, Oswestry, Bridgnorth, Ellesmere, Welshpool. All about an hour away and most passing by or close to other girls' schools. SHS is no shrinking violet, any more than the students themselves, let alone the marketing department.

Entrance: Entry into the nursery for girls and boys from age 3 'with no formal testing.' Places in reception by means of formal assessments during a day spent at the school with the class that the pupil might eventually join. Parents are advised of any areas which might need special attention from a tutor. So it isn't just in London that the young are being specially prepared, though parents assured us it wasn't as gruelling as that extract from the prospectus might suggest. In truth, children would probably be accepted at any stage if they were up to it and space was available. Music, academic, sports and all-rounded scholarships for boys entering year 7.

Entrance at 11+ into the senior school is by examination in verbal reasoning, non-verbal reasoning and quantitative skills. Intake is not overly selective and staff are good at helping those with learning difficulties, including dyslexia. As for girls who wish to enrol in the sixth form, they are expected to achieve a minimum of six A*-B grades at GCSE with at least Bs in those subjects they wish to take on to A level. Mr Getty said that no girl would be asked to leave purely on the strength of her grades in AS, 'though clearly new strategies might have to be drawn up in the best interests of the pupil.' It is always worth asking that question when visiting schools. You won't always get a straight answer: more and more schools are weeding in the interest of league tables.

Exit: Most girls move up to the senior school at 11, after verbal reasoning, non-verbal reasoning and quantitative skills tests. Boys mostly remain at the prep until 13, though a few also leave at 11 to local grammars. Boys are prepared for CE or scholarship and most progress to Concord College, Shrewsbury School, Wrekin College or Ellesmere School. Shrewsbury School is no longer the automatic first choice for parents of talented boys, 'perhaps because of the fees in this difficult (financial) climate,' the head told us. One parent suggested another reason. Lots of really good scholarships have been won recently.

S

Around a third leave for sixth form elsewhere – for co-education, boarding, a change – but on the whole the majority stay. Popular destinations include Cardiff, Newcastle, Sheffield, Bristol and Durham. Wide range of subjects – classics, dentistry, anthropology, management, psychology, medicine and engineering.

Remarks: The school is not in the middle of town as has been suggested: it is actually on the site of the old medieval town walls overlooking the river and Kingsland. The school has recently taken out an 80-year lease on the only remaining wall tower. Close to the sixth form centre, it will be used as a museum, curated by interested girls. It's another example of the zany, the original, the questing way in which the school is seeking to extend horizons, to encourage research and inquisitiveness: to enliven. Newish buildings, equipment, facilities, money pumped in. There's a fresh approach and much excitement and buzz. But, of course, none of this is of any use unless there is a reason, a plan. The thought behind the action is as important as the action itself. What lies behind all this is new stuff is how the years ahead are perceived. Will it be chandeliers? The main theme seems to be preparation. That, after all, is what schools are for. This is a school well worth visiting if you live within an hour's drive. Do check it out.

Shrewsbury School

The Schools, Shrewsbury, Shropshire SY3 7BA

Pupils: 788: 612 full boarders • Ages: 13–18 • Sixth form: 364 (104 girls) • C of E

Fees: Day £23,625; Boarding £33,750 pa

Tel: 01743 280552
Email: admissions@shrewsbury.org.uk
Website: www.shrewsbury.org.uk

Headmaster: Since 2010, Mr Mark Turner MA PGCE (50s). Educated at Rossall School where he was head boy, followed by Mansfield College, Oxford where he was an army scholar and read geography. Served with the Royal Artillery for four years before completing a PGCE at Cambridge. Housemaster at Oundle and then headmaster at Kelly College (now Mount Kelly) in his early 30s, followed by Abingdon for eight years. Married to Elizabeth, also an Oxford graduate, who teaches religious studies; they have two sons. Spends spare time in Devon where he can indulge his twin passions of bass fishing and lobster potting.

A 'crisp and keen administrator' who wants to 'retain the best of the past with the cutting edge technology of the future' and to up the academic ante. Having a close look at teaching styles and practice and work ethic, but does not want the school to become overly selective – believing in rigour rather than elitism. Cuts a slightly remote figure; parents and boys still feel that they hardly know him. Abingdon parents felt that Mr Turner's military demeanour and focused approach was just what that school needed – and we agree – but while many Shrewsbury parents feel that discipline did need tightening up, some are concerned that he is bearing down on eccentricities and traditions, and is too pernickety and keen on process. Capable and ambitious.

Academic matters: In 2016, 91 per cent A*/B at A level/Pre-U and 70 per cent A*/A – a comforting indication that this is a school that does not chuck out kids at 16. Particularly good showing at maths and further maths. Forty-eight per cent A*/A in IGCSE (most subjects) and GCSE in 2016. Wide choice at A level/Pre-U – usual academic subjects plus ceramics, photography, computing, design, theatre studies, PE and most combinations can be accommodated. 'Clinics' offer support for anyone who is struggling. Vibrant academic life outside main curriculum – voluntary complementary study programme in sixth form, some examined and some not eg global perspectives Pre-U, BTec in public services, extended project, sports leadership programme, Russian, Arabic, law and book-keeping for beginners as well as debating societies and Model United Nations. Range of academic societies with presentations by pupils and visitors. School hosted the International Young

Physicists tournament and received a gold medal in the British Biology Olympiad.

About 130 pupils with SEN – mainly mild dyslexia. One full- and five part-time members of staff provide support. EAL offered but pupils must be able to follow the curriculum. Plenty of careers and university advice includes help finding work experience and talks on what employers are looking for. The school offers tuition for SATs (American university entrance exams) and is a registered SAT centre. Lectures from universities, agricultural and art colleges and the world of work plus lower sixth talks on interview technique and an interview coaching course (charged for).

Low turnover of staff – loyal band, some were at Shrewsbury themselves. Increasing number of NQTs but most changes come from retirements. Hugely supportive staff who 'bring out the best in everyone and take children as far as they want to go academically'. One parent told us, 'The school has brought out things in my son that none of us knew he had'.

Games, options, the arts: Sport taken seriously here both at house and school level but still with an emphasis on 'fun, friendship and fitness', as the school puts it. Wide range of sports; big on rowing, girls are now also afloat in numbers – lots of national competitions, significant presence at Henley and many Shrewsbury boys have represented their country on the water. Newish Yale boathouse with training room and indoor rowing tank. New head of rowing is from Abingdon – so interesting times ahead on the river. The elite can take it as a major sport for all three terms, the rest compete at house level. A leading fives school (Eton variety) with 14 courts – a recent pupil was one of the first girls to be awarded a half blue at Oxford.

Venerable cross-country running club known as The Hunt is prominent on national circuit. Stunning cricket pitches described by Sir Neville Cardus as 'the most beautiful playing fields in the world'. Top class indoor cricket centre also used by local and regional clubs, funded by the Foundation. Recent winners of the national boys' cricket 20:20 championships.

Masses of non-team sports including canoeing, kayaking, climbing, mountain biking, and sub-aqua club. Outdoor pursuits and hill walking weekends to Tally, the school's own cottage in Snowdonia, with the aim of having 'serious fun'. Thriving CCF and Duke of Edinburgh up to gold.

Rich and impressive musical tradition with numerous ensembles and choirs (places in the chapel choir particularly sought after), annual house singing competition. Pupils often take productions to the Edinburgh Fringe and perform concerts in London and Birmingham. All new pupils offered a free lesson on an instrument of their choice and there are several Steinways and an organ to practice on. Two major drama productions a year a well as house plays.

Buzzing art department with mezzanine art gallery where upper sixth students can hold solo art exhibitions – particularly strong ceramics. A number go on to art school each year.

Dozens of societies, both academic and not so academic, from millinery and wine tasting to bee-keeping and the green power electric car racing team. Witty and irreverent school magazine follows in the satirical tradition of the Old Salopian founders of Private Eye.

Community service popular, but not compulsory; involves work in old people's homes, schools, charity shops etc – oh, and a trip to Malawi. School has close links with Shrewsbury House community centre in Liverpool, known as The Shewsy; sixth formers can spend a week there and see another side of life and children come back for a return match to Shrewsbury.

Boarding: Eight boys' boarding houses, of about 60 beds, two day boys' houses and three girls' houses – mixed day and boarding. Housemaster or mistress, matron and team of four or five tutors in each house. Boys' houses scruffy and comfortable – girls' houses newly built or refurbished with en suite bathrooms – some harrumphing from the boys about this but their houses next on the list for refurbishment. Boys start off in dorms and then graduate to study bedrooms as they move up the school.

Background and atmosphere: Founded in 1552 by Edward VI, the school throve, faltered and then revived in 1882 when it moved across the river into the old workhouse-cum-lunatic-asylum. It was named as one of the 'great' public schools by the Clarendon Commission in 1886 along with Eton, Harrow et al. Set in 100 acres high above the river Severn with distant views to the Malvern hills. Sir Arthur Blomfield's chapel was one of the first buildings to be built and is very much the centre of the community, with its vibrant red and blue interior, striking modern ceramics and pew runners representing the River Severn. Not everyone can fit in the chapel so houses take it in turns to have a Sunday lie-in.

Elegant Edwardian houses cluster round the cricket pitch connected by immaculate lawns and fine avenues of trees. Programme of refurbishment under way and new buildings (more to come) blend into the landscape overseen by imposing statues of famous old boys Charles Darwin and the warrior poet Sir Philip Sydney.

The ancient Chained Library, open on Sunday mornings, contains some remarkable books including John Gower's Confessio Amantis, printed by Caxton in 1483, and Newton's Principia, which the school bought on publication in 1687, as well as books, manuscripts and letters of Charles Darwin.

The first girls joined sixth form in 2008 and school started taking in girls at 13+ and 14+ in 2014, aiming for 65:35 ratio with scope for numbers to increase to 780. Parents divided on this change between the huffers and puffers and those who felt it was a bit of a pity but probably inevitable. The blow softened by the evident high quality of the current sixth form girls, and the long lead time that means that all who joined for a boys' school with girls in the sixth will get just that. In our view Shrewsbury boys will adapt well to co-ed – a civilised and courteous lot.

Pastoral care, well-being and discipline: Strong sense of community and a family atmosphere with many staff living on site. 'Staff totally committed and often find it difficult to leave' but still a healthy number of young teachers. Comfortable relationships between staff and pupils who are still expected to call teachers 'Sir'.

The house system 'preserves the innocence of school days but makes sure children are ready for the next stage,' said one happy mother. Children not allowed out on Saturday night without good reason (granny's birthday dinner likely to be as exciting as it gets) and they mostly keep to their side of the river anyway. It is too far away to 'bunk off to the King's Road on a Saturday night', said another. Strong house loyalty with lots of inter-house competitions in music, drama and sport. Enormous dining room where everyone can eat together – pupils sit in house groups with tutors. Food much improved in recent years – lots of choice, praised by children.

Sixth form common room, known as Quod (no one knows why) with separate social and study areas and a shop, is run by a committee of sixth formers who organise talks, lectures, film nights and socials. Sixth formers choose their own tutor and anyone who wants to be a prefect, known as a praeposter, has to write a letter of application to the headmaster.

The chapel is central to school life but Catholics can attend services at the cathedral across the river and other faiths are accommodated. Whole school policy on bullying is underpinned by extreme vigilance from housemasters (a comfortable and friendly crew): none of the parents we talked to mentioned bullying as a concern, and we heard no grisly stories from the boys either. If there is clear evidence of drug taking a pupil will be asked to leave, if it is unclear they have to comply with a testing regime. When asked about drinking, children said there was 'no point as you would only get caught', and there is no doubt in their minds as to how Mr T would react.

Pupils and parents: An eclectic mix of landed gentry, City money, local farmers and intellectuals, all happy to keep their children away from the rat race of the south east. From all over the country including London but most live within a couple of hours of the school. About 10 per cent from overseas. Fleet of coaches ferries children home for exeats – as one father said, 'the school has something special and it is worth the long journey'. Lots of children of Old Salopians, sometimes fourth or fifth generation.

A school with a genuine sense of individuality, 'where you can really be yourself and where everyone's personality has a place,' according to one sixth form girl. Described by a parent as 'interesting, interested and able to get on with people from all backgrounds'. Lovely quirky Salopian sense of humour can be seen in the Blue Chair Charity set up some years ago to raise money for leukaemia research. Old Salopians take two blue chairs with them on their gap year and photograph them in unusual places – they have been spotted outside the Blue Mosque in Istanbul, and at the Taj Mahal; one fell down a ravine and had to be rescued and another is being held hostage on the Somali border and an £8,000 ransom has been demanded. The 8,000 members of the old Salopian Club have a great bond and sense of community. Most famous old Salopian of all is Charles Darwin, who was at the school from 1818-1825. Others include Sir Martin Rees, cosmologist and astrophysicist, Richard Ingrams, Willie Rushton and Christopher Booker, who cut their satirical teeth on the school magazine The Public Nose and went on to found Private Eye, and Paul Foot, who was a major contributor; also Michaels Palin and Heseltine.

Entrance: Fairly broad church and also looking for potential. Most come from about 12 preps within about two hours of the school. Entry mainly via CE (55 per cent required) or academic scholarship (held in the May before entry). School's own tests in English and maths for those at non-CE schools. A few join in the fourth form (year 10) if things have not worked out elsewhere but must be able to 'hit the ground running' some 25 boys and 50 girls join for sixth form – a number of boys come from local state schools.

At sixth form entry they are looking for candidates who will make a contribution to school life – sport, music academic, drama. Assessment weekend in Nov prior to entry – candidates can choose three or four subjects in which to be assessed, plus a reference from current school, interview and personal statement.

S

Exit: About 50 per cent take a gap year – Shrewsbury International School in Bangkok useful source of employment for gappies; travel scholarships available for interesting and challenging gap years. About 98 per cent to university, 12 in 2016 to Oxbridge; otherwise mainly Russell Group – Bristol, Newcastle, Leeds, Edinburgh. Anyone who does not achieve at least five Bs at GCSE will be asked to leave – parents get plenty of warning if this is likely to happen.

Money matters: Scholarships and bursaries a tradition since the school was founded. Not a rich school but very supportive Old Salopians and parents put their hands in their pockets for the annual Foundation appeal, a telephone campaign staffed by sixth formers and recent leavers. Range of Foundation awards and scholarships worth up to 50 per cent can be topped up with a bursary – testing, interviews and consultation with prep schools (and some primary schools) for talented children who can't afford fees. Academic, sports, all-rounder, drama, music, DT and arts awards offered. Sixth form Margaret Cassidy Sports Scholarship worth up to full fees for talented footballer, cricketer or oarsman, and Alex Wilson day boy scholarship also worth up to full fees, for academic and sporting excellence (we assume girls not eligible for these).

Remarks: A school where individuals and individual talent are truly celebrated and where there is a 'breadth of opportunity without pressure cooker atmosphere'. Produces people with a wonderful and quirky sense of humour who are not afraid to be different.

Sidcot School

Oakridge Lane, Winscombe, North Somerset BS25 1PD

Pupils: 656; 170 boarders • Ages: 3–18 (boarding from year 7) • Sixth form: 161

Fees: Day £7,410 – £16,590; Boarding £24,900 – £31,410 pa

Tel: 01934 843102
Email: admissions@sidcot.org.uk
Website: www.sidcot.org.uk

Head: Since 2012, Mr Iain Kilpatrick BA Med FRSA PGCE, a former RBS banker who saw the light and turned to schoolmastering in the mid-90s, by way of a degree in English from Stirling and a PGCE from Edinburgh. Though English-born, Mr Kilpatrick's upbringing, education and career until Sidcot has been north of the border, but 'Much as I love Scotland, there's not a huge diversity of schools. IB was quite a draw, plus the mix of day and boarding, the area and the size and atmosphere at Sidcot'. Having thrown himself wholeheartedly into the holistic life of Strathallan and during his first headship of Beaconhurst, an all-through day school, he has shown himself ready to do the same at Sidcot, and is often to be seen around school, at its performances and indeed away matches.

Parents reckon he has smartened up the place and the people in it, made it 'more corporate' (for good or ill), and on occasion let technology obfuscate the message – some parents would be perfectly happy with good old-fashioned letters or emails, rather than having to download an app to check what's going on. Some also suspect that he is eyeing the academic performance of the Bristol independents with which Sidcot competes for Bristol families – with a view to upping Sidcot's game. Personally, he is dapper and articulate – 'Not to be messed with,' said one mother – and possessed of a good firm handshake. His students find him 'Scottish, smiley, interested in everything you do, with the power to make things happen'. Married to Katrina (a pharmacist), he has a son and a daughter in the school, and is very family-minded: 'children are an endless source of optimism, humour and entertainment'. Though he admits to being that kind of annoying person who always enjoys their job, he takes much pleasure in the countryside (walking and golf), as well as theatre.

Head of junior school: Since 2012, Ms Claire Lilley (early 40s). Educated at Tunbridge Wells Grammar and Homerton College, Cambridge, where she did a BEd in music. She worked at Sidcot as a year 5 teacher and after a foray down a different career path realised that teaching was what she truly wanted to do: 'I felt as though I had come home when I came back to Sidcot in 2009,' she says. A rapid ascent through the hierarchy culminated, after a proper selection process, in her appointment to the headship.

Tall and blonde, with an infectious laugh – 'you can always hear Ms Lilley,' said one boy – she is described by pupils as friendly, cheery and 'really in control but does not have to shout to get her point across.' Has a young daughter.

Academic matters: No entrance exams for the senior school and no Sats – 'we think labelling children according to their intellectual ability is counterproductive,' says the junior school head. But that is not to say that the teaching lacks rigour or focus. 'We follow the national curriculum, but are not slaves to it, and we certainly don't expect children to come in and conform to the way we teach. We look for a learning style that suits each child.'

Closer tracking to monitor progress continues to be introduced (not that the children are necessarily aware of it). Languages are strong: there is even a competition to recite a poem in a foreign tongue. Now a forest school from the nursery onwards, whose benefits include managing risk, getting up close and personal with nature, teamwork, cross-curricular learning and making an Iron Age round house. Phew! Alongside the three Rs, children here also learn emotional intelligence, to have a voice and to learn independently: each pupil has to research a topic to present on a double page spread in any way which appeals – writing, pictures, photographs, diagrams. Anything goes and is peer-reviewed. Work is often marked by two stars and a wish – the stars for things done well, a wish for something to be done better next time. The friendliness of the school is noted and appreciated by the children and SEN support is extensive and totally without stigma.

Results are solid if not stellar, with 33 per cent of GCSEs graded A*/A and 34 per cent at A level (58 per cent A*-B) in 2016. That said, maths is acknowledged as being exceptionally well taught. Year 11 Pathway (up to seven GCSEs taken in a year) scoops up students who need GCSEs, and fast – perhaps because they have bombed elsewhere, perhaps because they plan to do A levels or IB and need the ground work, or because their English requires a shot in the arm. IB (taken up by about one in five) average score was 30 in 2016. Resolutely not an academic hothouse, which is a large part of its appeal – 'Being force-fed academically just because she is bright would not suit my daughter,' remarked one mother – yet parents are confident that bright children will be sufficiently inspired and well enough taught to achieve all of which they are capable.

Mr Kilpatrick is keen on breadth, and has introduced the Sixth Form Passport, comprising the CAS elements (creativity, action and service) of the IB syllabus for all sixth formers, plus 'post-school survival skills'; EPQ is also encouraged. SEN students with mild to moderate learning difficulties, as well as social and emotional issues like anxiety and (a lack of) social skills, are well provided for by well regarded and qualified staff in a light and colourful room; school has CReSTeD status, and staff work closely with English and maths depts. Integration and acceptance are total here – everyone is screened on entry, and periodic assemblies on dyslexia to raise awareness mean it's just part of school life. The undiagnosed are also welcome to ask for support, for example at exam time, and 'Everyone who needs support, gets it,' according to one parent. 'The teachers will help you hundreds of times till you get it right,' affirmed one child.

Games, options, the arts: Twenty acres of pitches, including new all-weather pitch, and a multi-purpose sports hall with the nicest school pool we have ever seen – lifeguarding and kayak tuition also happen in it – mean there is plenty on offer at Sidcot. The size of the school causes some parents to bemoan the strength and depth of rugby talent – but naked aggression is possibly not the Quaker way. Sidcot is not, perhaps, the place for an élite sportsperson – more serious players often belong to local clubs – although a pair of sisters have achieved considerable regional and national success at swimming, both in the pool and open water. The equestrian centre has opened to the public for livery, Pony Club and equestrian studies. Its purpose for the school seems to be more to provide qualifications (BTec, BHS) and opportunities for students to ride (some boarders bring their own steeds) than to identify and kick on young, promising riders. All benefit from an indoor and outdoor school (floodlit) and 160 acres of glorious country to hack in. Plenty else for those unmoved by ball games or horses, such as trampolining, archery, TV production, debating and so on. New sports development director giving increased focus on life skills acquired through sport.

Arts are housed in a new light, airy centre which accommodates visual arts, drama and music. Visual arts astound in particular. We witnessed the most controversial A level art exhibit we had ever seen, depicting the conflicting duality of Muslim women, the siren beneath the burqa. Ceramics and textiles also noteworthy. All manner of artistic media are on offer, and those not studying art are welcome to scratch any creative itches at a club or society. DT and product design stand out too: from a man-powered bushfire extinguisher to an iPhone-powered record player – a range of practical, aesthetic and downright eccentric projects are realised. Seven drama productions a year; recent ones include Into the Woods and A Midsummer Night's Dream (directed by students) performed in the grounds; facilities exist to make film and radio also. International students are encouraged to take part, partly to improve their English – but Struwwelpeter in Chinese was surely not to be missed. School takes a show to Edinburgh every other year. Sidcot's music, the school readily admits, would appeal more to fans of One Direction than the Endellion Quartet, resulting in some of the school's most talented classical musicians choosing to take their lessons in Bristol, rather than at school – but they don't half sound impressive at concerts. The auditioned choir (all girls, necessarily limiting the repertoire) tends towards 'the Gareth Malone end of the spectrum', quite possibly because there has never been a tradition of church music. Facilities and tuition designed rather for music tech, creativity and composition.

Outdoor stuff on offer such as D of E, and good use is made of the extensive grounds for gardening, beekeeping and the construction of a nature trail, inter alia. Trips include a French exchange, Tanzania, Vienna for culture/art/language. PASS – Programme of Activities for Sidcot School – 'a co-curricular initiative based on our key values of integrity, stewardship, self-reflection, adventure and community'.

Sports and music are junior school favourites: everyone adored composing music for Tom and Jerry on the computer and the pop choir is – well, popular. Separate PE for girls and boys from year 3. Trips, laid on every year for each year group, also get thumbs up: a camp-out in the grounds for the littlest, progressing all the way to outdoor pursuits camp in Okehampton for year 6.

Boarding: Majority full but a few flexi boarders; around half from overseas. The five boarding houses are sprinkled through the grounds, facilities are clean, tidy yet homely; we were struck by the warmth and knowledge of each boarder displayed by the house staff. Three or four share a room in the younger years; sixth formers in ones or twos. Usual range of sporting and artistic activities after school and at weekends, plus trips to eg cinema, ice skating rink, local festivals.

Background and atmosphere: Sidcot's USP: everyone, nay everyone, we spoke to singled out the atmosphere at the school as being the reason for being there. The school's proud Quaker origins (dating from its founding in 1699), history and traditions are lived out every day, giving it a curiously contemporary feel which is so much more than lip service. The school's first ever founding director of peace and global studies has recently been appointed, with a brief to 'bring 21st century Quakerism to life' right through the curriculum, weaving in themes such as social justice, conflict resolution and global responsibility. Sidcot is now a 'change-maker school', as a member of the Ashoka movement, which aims to 'empower the next generation to lead social, environmental and economic development'. Specifically, the atmosphere is one of respect and tolerance – for those of all faiths and none, for different nationalities, for different gifts, skills or shortcomings, for each individual. Quaker half hour is held every week and presided over by sixth form elders, at which teachers and students have equal rights to speak and to be listened to.

We had never met a more thoughtful bunch of young people. 'The children look out for each other, and the school does its best to bring out well-rounded young adults'; 'a home from home for your child, with similar principles as the ones we have brought them up with at home'; 'the teachers are accountable to the children' were just some of the views we heard. One mother described her daughter as a 'bruised and tender plant when she arrived at Sidcot', but who 'had turned into a strong, forthright and confident young woman, which is moving to see'. We heard about several instances of parents choosing Sidcot for its ethos (dread word) over other schools whose academic, sporting or musical prowess was more notable. Learning is conducted in a calm and conducive environment, where 'punishment is not a word we use,' said one member of staff; some parents though feel on occasion that the benign Quaker view of children needs to be tempered with a dose of realism when it comes to high jinks in class.

The Quaker foundations and conventions are not lost on the juniors, either. 'The elders are year 6 and we sit silently in a circle with our teachers at our Wednesday assemblies. We think about stuff like keeping secrets.' Perhaps because the children and their achievements in every field are fêted, there is no need for anyone to feel undervalued, 'We absolutely do not brag at this school,' said one perceptive year 6

Conveniently situated just beside the A38 running south from Bristol (thankfully with a bridge over it to get to the sports fields), the school's main façade is a pleasing white stucco building, with the inevitable less sightly additions behind it. The main complex of buildings is compact and extremely well signed, but there are some charming gardens in among them, covered in brightly coloured gazebos on the scorching summer day we visited, to represent each of four virtual houses. Sidcot has no physical house system, though there are (of course) five separate boarding houses sprinkled through the grounds, plus the meeting house: a little oasis of calm and quiet just metres from the main building. We were enchanted by the ponies grazing beyond the fence bordering the garden to one of the girls' boarding houses, with a tantalising glimpse of the Mendips behind.

S

Pastoral care, well-being and discipline: Respectively, exceptionally good and deploying the lightest of touches. We did not uncover any rebels, tearaways, lads or ladettes, and when quizzed, students listed acts likely to attract reproof as 'not listening, disobedience, laziness, doing what you want'. Hardly hanging offences. Censure from one's peers would be a greater deterrent, we sense. According to parents, the head is adamant about drink and drugs in school – one strike and you're out. Sidcot has no bar, unlike most boarding schools with a vibrant sixth form.

Pupils and parents: An intriguing mix of individuals conforming to shared expectations and outlook, but card-carrying Quakers a small minority. Though the students look conventional enough, with uniform on the posh side (striped shirts, blazers), we suspect that Sidcot families conform to fewer than usual independent school stereotypes. When asked what sort of parent would send a child to Sidcot, the head replied, 'Guardian readers indifferent to sipping sherry on the lawn on speech day, whose children see diversity as a strength, who are prepared to stand up for what they believe in'. According to the junior school head: 'The kind of parents who send their children to us are normal, down to earth and just want the best for them – some make considerable sacrifices for them to come here.' A few locals, refugees from Bristol schools and nearly 20 per cent from overseas thrown into the mix. Notable alumni include Sir George Trevelyan (dubbed the hippies' champion), geologist Robert Shackleton, founder of Macmillan Cancer Support, Douglas Macmillan, Zoe Wanamaker, Justin Webb, and Deborah Warner.

Entrance: All junior school hopefuls attend a two-day taster session, including assessments in maths, reading and spelling, non-verbal reasoning plus an informal interview with the head – but the policy is non-selective. Children are welcomed in at all stages; quite a few arrive in year 5 instead of starting middle school as they would under Somerset LA. Scholarships on offer from year 1, 'both talent and academic.'

Sidcot is academically non-selective so transfer is automatic (and highly praised) from the junior to the senior school; otherwise applications are taken at any stage except into years 11 and 13, and places offered on the basis of previous school reports and interviews at the school to 'children who will benefit from an academic education and activities at Sidcot and who will contribute to and benefit from the ethos of our school community', to quote the admissions policy.

Exit: The majority of juniors to the senior school (around 80 per cent), whence entry is automatic. Baseline assessments are done for setting and monitoring purposes. A few after GCSE for a change if they have been there since nursery, some to a greater range of courses and subjects post 16, and quite possibly the brighter lights of Bristol. Destinations comprise old and new universities up and down the land to do an array of courses, with a leaning towards art and design; some gap years. One to Oxbridge and one to Newhouse School of Public Communications – Syracuse in 2016, plus five biomedics.

Money matters: Fees are stepped according to year group, and a loyalty discount (about 12 per cent for boarders, seven per cent for day) applies to anyone staying on to sixth form. In general, fees are noticeably lower than local boarding competition in Bristol, but more expensive than the Bristol day schools which have no boarding infrastructure to fund. Ten per cent sibling discount. Quaker families on occasion receive 100 per cent remission of fees. Scholarships awarded for academics or talent; level of funding is discretionary.

Remarks: A school more likely to produce the head of an NGO than a merchant bank. For those untroubled by notions of social pretension or academic snobbery, yet for whom a considerate altruistic atmosphere really matters, this is just the place

South Dartmoor Community College

Balland Lane, Ashburton, Newton Abbot, Devon TQ13 7EW

Pupils: 1,600 • Ages: 11–18 • Sixth form: 300

Tel: 01364 652230
Email: enquiries@southdartmoor.devon.sch.uk
Website: www.southdartmoor.devon.sch.uk

Head teacher: Since 2010, Hugh Bellamy; originally from Taunton, studied history and education at Homerton College, Cambridge. He spent the early part of his career as deputy head at a specialist dyslexic school before becoming special needs co-ordinator at schools in Somerset and Wiltshire. During this time he was also a course tutor for the RSA teacher training diploma. He went on to become deputy head at West Somerset Community College for six years, before taking on 'missionary work' at George Pindar Community College in Scarborough. In seven years the school went from 'failing' to being crowned 'the most improved school in the country.' Hugh is a firm believer in 'building learning power', a principle based around six key approaches to learning, and it is this tried and tested strategy that he has introduced at SDCC.

Married to a primary school head teacher, and father to two daughters, one a teacher and one an ecologist, Hugh says they are all very pleased to be back in the south west. As busy as he is, running has become a major part of life and he's even got his colleagues hooked. Recently, 36 teachers ran the London marathon with him – the school raised a whopping £60k. Last year he did it again, and is now in training for the Florence marathon and the London-Brighton race.

Hugh still teaches English and is also the executive principal of the new project, The Atrium Studio, which opened in September 2015. This new school is for 13 to 18 year-olds, specialising in the built environment. It sits under the umbrella of the South Dartmoor Academy, which includes SDCC, four local primary schools, a sports centre, an activity centre and a learning centre. The main objective of the Academy is to run a 4 to 19 curriculum, pulling in resources and working closely together. The Atrium will eventually take 375 students and reduce the numbers at SDCC – Hugh knows the school has become too big; it's much larger than the average secondary school.

Academic matters: In 2015, 53 per cent A*-B grades at A level and 25 per cent A*/A. At GCSE, 61 per cent achieved 5+ A*-C including English and maths. GCSE grades are good, above the national average and increasing. Post 16, SDCC offers 40 different courses ranging from vocational NVQs through to A levels and AQA Baccalaureate. The A level results have been rated in the top 10 per cent of colleges for value added progress. Vocational options with on-site facilities include catering, land-based studies, vehicle maintenance and hair and beauty.

Strong subjects across the board include art, photography, history, music and dance. Maths has improved so much that one of the teaching staff is now supporting schools across the country and advising the DfE. One language, either French or Spanish, is compulsory at GCSE. Science is popular, there are regular science café events, and students recently reached the finals of the National Science & Engineering Competition, representing the south west in Parliament. Parents say they'd like to see more such events; 'Our son took part in the Big Bang competition ...This was a fantastic experience for him and he loved every minute of it..I think it would be great if there were more opportunities like this. When young people are excited and enthusiastic about things they learn so much more.'

All special needs are looked after by a large teams of TAs. There are 53 statemented pupils and a specialist resource base for eight students who display autistic spectrum disorders. Ofsted said, 'Disabled students and those with special educational needs make good progress.' Student support operates at a number of levels, helping with exam stress, anxiety and problems at home. For younger pupils not really ready for secondary school there's a Learning Enrichment Centre. The focus is on support with literacy, numeracy and thinking. The classroom is bright, colourful and uses fun primary school-type learning displays. When we were there students were getting ready for a pizza night, all to be cooked in the oven they had worked hard to make and decorate with individually painted stones. They cheekily told the head he would get a free pizza – it looked as if it was going to be a fun night!

Games, options, the arts: SDCC specialises in sport and it shows. The hockey team was the first team from a state school ever to be the national indoor hockey champions in 2012, and the girls' cricket team has been a national finalist for the last two years. A recent sports academy dinner raised almost £3k and was hosted by veteran footballers Joey Jones and Mickey Thomas. Plus there's an annual football tour to Sweden for the Gothia World Youth Cup, and links with Chelsea Football Club. There's a golf academy on site too, and plenty of other opportunities for sporty types. One parent told us, 'Since joining SDCC my oldest daughter has become more confident and is willing to take part in anything; she has also excelled in sport, taking part in hockey at county level and cross-country at national level.' Another student was recently crowned National Juvenile Mountain-biking Champion, and there's been success in life-saving, horse-riding and even go-karting. D of E is popular, a part of life, and SDCC is the only school to have taken part in the Ten Tors every year since it began.

Brilliant sports facilities. Astroturf, all-weather cricket nets, football pitch, hockey field, netball, basketball and tennis courts, golf facility including a driving range, sports hall, dance studio, and a sports centre equipped with spinning bikes and a full gym.

Music is popular, with lots of bands, some even playing at gigs outside school. Facilities are good, huge classrooms with practice rooms set to one side, and lots of opportunities to get involved, whether it's in the choir, orchestra (one pupil is a harpist in the National Youth Orchestra) the annual Live Sessions performances, or even the recent production of Carmen. Dance is also a big hit, and Body Language 2015 was apparently a sell-out. Drama productions of late include Bugsy Malone, Oliver! and Aladdin.

Not a great deal of art displayed around the school, except in the sixth form house, but the exam pieces we saw on our tour were of a high standard. One particular piece, a stone and shell formation, was impressive but unfortunately students were at a loss as to how they were ever going to move it. Decent photography department including an Apple Mac suite, a studio and a dark room.

There's a good selection of lunchtime clubs and activities plus skateboarding and a boys' dance project (street dancing or break dancing). There's an annual enrichment week for years 7, 8 and 9, with the opportunity to do something different for a week: gardening, surfing, water-sports, sea-fishing, climbing – the list is endless. Trips abroad include annual football tours, ski trips, language exchanges, classics trips to Pompeii, and for sixth formers there's World Challenge trips and cultural excursions to France, New York and Italy. There are annual visits to Thailand, as the school has links there through a project run by the British Council and Youth Sport Trust. Teachers also get the chance to do exchanges – we saw an Australian history teacher taking a class while his English counterpart was no doubt enjoying life Down Under. Other exchanges have taken place in Spain, France, Thailand and India. SDCC is a training school, so there's a regular turnover of younger staff.

Background and atmosphere: South Dartmoor Community College has existed in a range of guises and under a number of names since 1314, making it one of the oldest schools in the country. Initially founded by the church, it became a grammar school in the 16th century and managed to survive the interventions of Henry VIII and Edward VI. In 1845 the school started taking boarders, and it became co-ed in 1912. It then fell on hard times and closed in 1938. It re-opened 20 years later as Ashburton School, and has grown and grown ever since, as well as changing its name.

It's a large site, more like a higher education campus than a school. A mix of one and two-storey concrete blocks, temporary prefabs, and tented areas. The entrance is uninviting and confusing, and there's a lack of signage to car parks or reception (although plenty of advertising boards for local companies). However, entrance and car parks developed as part of Atrium Studio projecy. Currently the mass coach exodus at 4pm is a hideous diesel cloud overrun with coach drivers. Due to its location, the school covers a large catchment area, and apparently there's an eye-watering £1.3m spent every year on coaches. They are therefore very pleased to have just been granted funding for five new minibuses.

More funding has also just confirmed for a new dining hall. This will replace the strange tented pagoda at the front of the site and will mean that the school hall can be used solely for assemblies, productions and performances. When we were there the spring concert was being set up (after lunch had been put away). The line-up included pieces from the choir, orchestra, and jazz and folk bands – plus the house band that's been around for 20 years, of course with new members.

The on-site vocational facilities include a full working restaurant where students cater for staff once a week. Outside the DT rooms there is a vehicle maintenance garage with an old banger and motorbike to tinker with. The hair and beauty salon is run by a local professional company and Bright Beginnings is the social care department. We saw a class of girls who were blowing eggs with the challenge of 'caring' for them for the next 24 hours. Some had exploded, much to their amusement, and ours.

Maths and English are in the in same block as the huge and impressive library. High ceilings and lots of light create a modern learning environment equipped with pods of PCs and an additional media suite. English classrooms have been given names like Duffy's Den, Tolkien Tower. There's one large ICT suite with 60 PCs plus six smaller suites. The science block is the newest addition to site, built way back in 2002, so the latest construction and developments are more than welcome and needed.

Food is catered for by the on-site café, Scoffers. It's well-liked and nutritional. Outside, the covered eating area is decorated with large colourful graffiti letters, much more appealing than the huge one-way and no-entry signs on the school corridors inside. Admittedly it's a bit of a maze, and there are a lot of pupils to herd, but they're not the most friendly or welcoming of signs. Unfortunately, they're not big on creative displays here either. Maybe this is one of the negatives of being so big: they have to stick to practicalities rather than making it look good. Also, we were told, younger students can sometimes feel a bit lost in the crowd. One parent said, 'I think the way they organise the timetables seems very complicated and could be improved. When he attends lessons there are one or two friends that stay the same, but generally the pupils get mixed up for every single lesson. I am not sure this is completely necessary and it did make it more difficult for him to make friends in the first few months at school.'

The sixth form is in Place House, a large Georgian building (gifted by Glendinnings) set in its own grounds, and in our view the most impressive part of the school. On the way (it's all uphill, you need to be fit), we passed the outdoor classroom, tennis courts, and a bunch of students taking a break from building a dry stone wall, and toasting marsh-mellows by a fire. This is Devon, after all. Dilapidated barns at the back of the sixth form building have been tagged for a future renovation project. This grand building sits pretty at the top of the hill overlooking the Glendinnings quarry below. The surrounding land has just been donated by the said Glendinnings and is going to be used for farm studies. Inside, the building continues to impress with original cornices and huge marble fireplaces. The modern extension has been designed thoughtfully and the two buildings blend well to create a fantastic place to study – the sixth formers seemed suitably happy as a result.

Sixth formers are given the chance to show off their leadership skills by acting as learning mentors for younger pupils. They also organise social events such as ice-skating, meals out and an annual leavers' party. There's a sixth form magazine and a very active Young Enterprise club, and they can even gain an Employability Award (supported and accredited by the Devon and Cornwall Business Council) that officially recognises extracurricular activities and achievements.

The school council has managed to improve the canteen, set up regular mufti days for charity, plus improve the recycling. As a school, they have raised a great deal of money for the charity Whizz-kidz through marathons and other events. The house system, named after local tors, also raises money for good causes. One group recently designed t-shirts for the YMCA. This is a community school and its carnival float sits proudly in the car park waiting for its next outing – apparently Star Wars is the theme this summer.

Pastoral care, well-being and discipline: It's all about taking personal responsibility at SDCC. And it seems to work a treat. Ofsted noted, 'Students' behaviour is outstanding, in lessons and around the school. Students are polite and considerate, and have excellent, respectful relationships with staff.' The general consensus from parents and pupils alike is that they 'feel safe.' Apparently any bullying, including cyber bullying, is rare and is dealt with swiftly by staff. There's a students' support group that has been specially trained to help any of their peers. Plus there are tutor groups and heads of houses. The large support department is on hand to help at all times. The number of exclusions is below average. The head says they take a hard line on issues like bullying, drugs or behaviour, but they use a restorative approach, and he believes that the pupils look out for each other. Parents confirmed to us that their children are happy at school.

Pupils and parents: Families come from far and wide due to the large catchment area. Some even live beyond it. Parents are nurses, builders, teachers, fitness instructors, computer programmers, a whole range of occupations. The school has a Parents' Forum which is used as a sounding board for ideas and feedback. One parent said, 'We have always been happy with the way they have dealt with any concerns or issues that arise.' Generally they feel the school is open and good at communicating. 'At parents evenings, the staff have been very easy to talk to and helpful, and clear about the next steps in order to progress. One teacher who was not able to attend one parents evening even phoned all the parents later that week with an update on progress. Regular progress reports are also very helpful.' Parent support advisors are available too, and regularly set up parenting courses and support families in need.

Entrance: Large catchment area, due to its location on the edge of the moors. Children from outside the catchment area will also be considered. There's an induction week in June for all newcomers. 'There are lots of opportunities for children in year 5 and 6 to go to workshops at SDCC and they spend a week there in the year 6 summer term as well. By the time they get there at the start of year 7 it is quite familiar and not too overwhelming.' As an academy, teachers from the four local primary schools work with SDCC to ensure a smooth transition for the pupils from primary to secondary. Based on parents' comments, this is working well. Sixth form entry is dependent on grades.

Exit: Around half of sixth formers to university, with around 30 per cent of them at Russell Group universities. Popular choices are Falmouth, Plymouth, Bristol, Cardiff and Exeter. One former student recently gained a first from Oxford in biochemistry, and another gained a first in economics and politics from Leeds. Around 15 per cent of leavers take a gap year, 25 per cent into employment, apprenticeship or training, and 15 per cent to local FE colleges.

Famous leavers include the comedian Josh Widdicombe, Julian and Chris – the plasterers from DIY SOS, CBeebies presenter Ben Cajee, and singer Jo Harman, hailed by the press as 'the finest female soul and blues vocalist in the UK'.

Money matters: Pupil premium funds are available to help with trips, uniform, equipment, school meals etc. There's a year 7 catch up premium, which is funding that can be used to provide literacy and numeracy catch-up support. Plus a learner support bursary for sixth formers.

Remarks: Great if you're sporty or musical, plus there's a good range of extracurricular activities and an impressive sixth form centre. But we felt the site lacked colour and stimulation, and it's just too big. It has, however, been undergoing major changes – the building improvements are making a positive difference, and the new Atrium school will help to reduce numbers. The results are improving year on year, and more and more students are going on to good universities and careers. One parent we spoke to said, 'I think that they could have been pushed harder academically as in many cases teachers were happy with mediocre progress when we felt they were capable of more...but I could not have hoped for a more rounded education for our children, who were all very happy at school. They did have to work hard to achieve their grades, but they have learnt to take responsibility for themselves and knuckle down.' Improving all the time.

South Devon Steiner School

Hood Manor, Dartington, Totnes, Devon TQ9 6AB

Pupils: 300 • Ages: 3–16

Fees: £3,465 – £6,585 pa

Tel: 01803 897377
Email: admissions@steiner-south-devon.org
Website: www.southdevonsteinerschool.org

Head: The first rule of Steiner. No headmaster. No headmistress. No hierarchy.

So who runs the school? 'It's a flat, republican management model.' The school council covers the governance and delegates management to the steering group. The management is split into three 'realms', the Cultural, the Rights and the Economic. The Cultural is the realm of ideas, the teachers and the teaching. The Rights is open to all employees, and creates all school policy, vision and planning. The Economic realm speaks for itself. This relatively new structure is 'constantly evolving to try and simplify the decision-making process, and keep the "big" personalities at bay.'

Then, there's the parents. They are heavily involved, not only in a practical hands-on way but also financially.

Part of the Steiner Waldorf Schools Fellowship, the school follows the teaching practices and educational philosophy of Rudolf Steiner (check these out if you are considering the school). It's a co-ed school for 3-16 year olds, educating 'the whole child through hand, heart and mind'. It's not just about academic development, it's about the spiritual and physical well-being too. It's a philosophy based on an appreciation of nature and life.

The second rule of Steiner. Brush all cynical thoughts aside.

Academic matters: Due to a full Steiner curriculum, mainstream qualifications are pretty thin on the ground – the school only offers four GCSEs in maths, English lang and lit and German or French. Teaches the Steiner School Certificate, that 'allows students to explore subjects independently, and in-depth, with increasing specialisation and extension into preferred subjects'. Currently teaches to level 1 in classes 9 and 10, but in 2017 hopes to add classes 11 and 12, studying to levels 2 and 3 and hence to university.

So what about the national curriculum? Steiner teaching and education is a completely different ball game. As one parent put it, it's 'a lovely environment where emphasis is not on cramming knowledge'. Or as the school describes itself, it's providing an 'unhurried and creative environment for learning'. Definitely no exam pressure here. No Sats. No reading or writing before 7.

However, it can't all be about being at one with nature and outdoor classes, can it? Well, it is until age 7. This is how they do it in Scandinavia and the results there prove it works well. In the early years there is an emphasis on play and imagination. No formal learning: think songs, poems, games and plays, handicraft, baking, painting, woodwork and gardening. It's all based on 'rhythm and repetition'. One Ofsted report says positively 'children are immersed in the rhythm and rhyme of language, including verse, song and stories'. Numeracy and literacy are taught through music (pentatonic music, a five-note scale theory), storytelling and eurythmy (physical expression). These themes are continued throughout the children's school life. In the middle years, in Steiner philosophy, this grows into curiosity and investigation, and in the upper school into creativity and a deepening of knowledge. Throughout the school years the curriculum is broad and subjects are treated as inter-dependent, with practical skills like metal-work, gardening and craft being taught alongside core subjects such as sciences, history, geography, English, modern languages and maths.

Unusually, one teacher takes on the hefty responsibility of taking pupils through all eight years of their school life or journey. Teachers cover not only literacy and numeracy but also bring history, geography, art and the sciences into the classroom. Languages, music, sport and crafts are covered by specialist teachers. Teaching is based around the daily two-hour main lessons. These are based on themes and last for three weeks. Subject themes could be anything from the Industrial Revolution to Ancient Greece. Steiner teachers have the freedom to choose when, what and how to teach, based on their pupils' needs and abilities. Lessons are all taught using movement, games, poetry and music.

One subject not on the agenda at all until the upper school is computing. This will no doubt raise a few eyebrows. The Steiner way discourages computers and TV at home until at least 7 years old. As lovely as it is to keep children as wholesome as possible and away from the influences of electronic media, the reality is that it's everywhere. Used in the right way it can encourage creativity and imagination. Surely there's a happy medium here? Not at Steiner.

Financial constraints mean that the school cannot provide a full range of learning support. They do accept some children with specific learning needs and they do have a learning support team to facilitate this. However, only one child is statemented and apparently there are others that should be, but it is now hard to get local authority funding. This is a shame as it seems that this sort of education is particularly favoured by parents of children that struggle with mainstream education, and would benefit from a Steiner education, if the special needs support was available.

Games, options, the arts: Not much in the way of sports facilities, none indoors. There's a basketball pitch and a small sports field on site plus a hockey pitch a short cycle away. Competitive sports don't play a huge part in the day and football is particularly restricted. Especially in the playground. There is, however, lots of enthusiasm about the annual Inter-Steiner 'Greek Olympics' that goes on for several days and is hosted by a Sussex Steiner School. Cycling is massive here. There are good cycle paths around the school and whole classes cycle to sports facilities on a regular basis. One ex-pupil even went on to become a professional cyclist and raced internationally for Team GB.

There's a strong emphasis on the practical side of education – other main lesson themes include farming, house-building, botany and natural sciences. One class recently built 50 bird-boxes. The children are now out there every day, with their binoculars, keeping diaries and sending their data to RSPB to be collated for a local bird survey. We saw a surprisingly good climbing frame recently designed and built by class 3 as their building project. While younger pupils are mastering the art of whittling, the 9-year-olds and above are getting handy with saws and axes. Pupils also have their own group allotments and are 'recycling experts'. The outdoor classroom packs in fruit trees, larger allotments, a polytunnel, chickens, sheep, a cob building and a kiln. Pupils are involved in every process you can think of here, even sheep shearing. The outdoor classroom teacher keeps his projects in line with the main lesson themes. So, when his class of 12-year-olds were designing a market garden, they were also having business maths lessons to support it. The project took them from design through to implementation and on to selling for profit. In a similar way, the Roman roads, or paths, in the Little Garden were laid when the class was learning about the history of Rome.

Eurythmy is central to Steiner education. It's an expressive movement art originated by Rudolf himself. It's used as a teaching tool but is also taught as a lesson in the main hall, where they also hold weekly assemblies, drama productions and music performances. Music is in the manor house; younger classes are taught flute and recorder and there's an orchestra from class 5 upwards. One major production every year is Shakespeare, in costumes made by the 14 year-old actors themselves. The latest one is Romeo and Juliet. The GCSE students return to school after they've sat their exams to work on a last drama production – a chance to end school on a high note.

Pupils are taught the history of art as well as techniques. Paintings are done 'in the style of' rather than using traditional teaching methods. Crafts are huge: there's a handwork room for sewing, knitting and crochet, a woodwork hut and a forge for metal work. Pupils also trying spinning and weaving.

There's not much in the way of lunchtime or after-school clubs, but the school does provide afternoon care for parents who struggle with the half-days for younger pupils. There are many trips and exchanges for all ages, including cycling trips around France, canoeing, camping and canoeing on the River Wye, working on farms, geology trips to Cornwall and a summer language school. One parent said her 15 year old daughter had spent seven weeks in Germany on an exchange and three months in France on another. The trips are 'life-changing,' said another parent, and apparently the students come back with a 'I can do anything now' attitude. In true Steiner style, pupils are even encouraged to go on a trip before their GCSE exams to de-stress.

Background and atmosphere: Founded over 30 years ago, South Devon Steiner lies just a stone's throw from the beating drums and burning incense of Totnes. Surrounded by organic farms and rolling Devon hills, it's without doubt the perfect setting for a school with such an unorthodox approach to education. Driving up to the school and wandering around the grounds, you can see why parents fall head over heels for this place. The school inspection report says that 'the outdoor environment is outstanding and promotes the pupils' personal and physical development extremely well.'

From Hood Manor, the main building, steps take you up to the rest of school sprawled across the Devon countryside. We passed a handful of boys casually playing basketball, while a few others were climbing trees. The large hall towers over the more makeshift-looking structures. Planning permissions for an extension for the music department and a new sports hall have been granted for some time now, but unfortunately it's just the funds holding them back. The Bunk House, built in partnership with South Devon College Apprenticeship Scheme to house conferences and teacher training, should be a much needed source of income for the school.

Classrooms feel homely. Rows of muddy wellies and cycling helmets in every one. Old-fashioned wooden desks and chairs – each child has their own designated desk, used for lunch as well as teaching as there's no canteen. Most surprisingly there are blackboards, almost vintage, but used very creatively by all the teachers. We saw impressive chalk artwork on the boards of every classroom. Masterpieces ranged from Mesopotamia to Charlotte's Web. As well as the teachers' artwork, pupils' work is displayed everywhere too. One class had recently been learning about the Renaissance, so they had painted artwork on the ceiling. Another class, studying geography, had made world maps from play-dough.

The kindergarten world is in a very festival-like setting and cut off from the rest of the school. Each of the four buildings have an outside area shaded by a rustic awning. When we were there a little girl was in the tree house, happily whistling at the birds and listening for answers. Beautiful. Keeping in rhythm with the seasons is important here, but come rain or shine, the day always starts outside, usually by a fire.

Fundraising is essential to keep the costs down for parents and improve the facilities here. A recent success has been a new bike shed for all those budding cyclists. There's also a group set up by parents and the local community to improve the cycle paths and roads around the school. There are two large fundraising events a year, summer and advent. Parents enthused about these and said they were a lot of fun. And also very profitable: the last advent fair made a whopping £12K. Parents, children and local community seem to work well together here. As part of National Tree Planting Week they planted 600 trees, including hazel, rowan, elder, hawthorn, crab apple, dog rose and blackthorn. Ultimately, the planting, growing and caring for these trees will become part of the children's education.

S

Pastoral care, well-being and discipline: One of the golden rules at Steiner is to 'educate with love'. The teaching also encourages 'awareness of others' needs' and respect for each other. As a very small, close-knit school with both teachers and parents around in force at all times, not much seems to go amiss. However, if bullying does get spotted, all parties will work through the problems together. Pupils included.

As for behavioural problems, the school asks that parents follow the school guidelines at home to provide continuity. Parents admitted that this can be quite a challenge if they have come from a state school environment, but the school is willing to support parents and work through any problems they may have.

If a child needs to be disciplined in the classroom, they are sent to the Quiet Room to 're-centre', and if necessary, fill out a Reflection Form. If there are repeated instances then the parents will be called to the school to discuss. The school does not tolerate smoking or drugs.

Pupils and parents: Local; many have relocated just for the school. Pretty much everybody that works here has, or has had, children at the school. One parent described the school as 'extra support, a family', and it does have a definite sense of community.

As part of the deal financially, parents have to commit to workdays – two Saturdays a month, lunch provided. They take on maintenance jobs, painting, changing bulbs, gardening, anything that needs doing. There's also a cleaning rota for each child's classroom. This involvement gives parents 'ownership' and means that children see their parents as part of the school. It also means they get to keep a pretty close eye on things.

Parents are expected to take part in the summer and advent fairs by cooking, making crafts or organising. This could seem daunting to some, but apparently 'there is no pressure to take part if it isn't for you. In terms of crafts, personally I can't roll a ball of wool let alone knit anything; it's not an issue.' Phew.

Entrance: The admission process is three-pronged – an application form, an interview and a three-day trial. All three stages assess the child's and the parents' suitability, and of course the school's suitability for the applicants.

Oversubscribed. There's a waiting list for most classes. Apparently some children are being home-educated while they wait for spaces to crop up, but this really is a 'one out, one in' system so it could be a long wait. The prospective parents we met said their children were 'struggling in the state system, too much pressure'. Parents are desperate for some kind of alternative to the 'test' culture of mainstream schools. So for some families, it really is worth the wait.

Once in the school, pupils are reassessed for the lower and upper school to ensure that the school can continue to provide their educational needs.

Exit: At 16, most pupils go onto local colleges, Exeter College, Kennicot, and South Devon College. Teachers we spoke to were adamant that the local colleges are happy to take references for the Steiner pupils rather than basing admissions on GCSEs. This seems to work well and a decent number of students have gone on to do A levels or the International Baccalaureate, and then university courses. Others may do more GCSEs and then apprenticeships. The school is planning to open a sixth form in the future, with classes 11 and 12 from 2017. However, there are practical and financial issues.

Former Steiner pupils have had great success in some very diverse and interesting areas. Their stories are full of foreign travel and many have either studied abroad or ended up settling in pastures new. A few random examples: a high rise window cleaner, someone with a doctorate in nanoscience, a midwife, a champion surfer, an opera director, a weather forecaster, aid workers risking their lives in war torn areas, a designer for Tom Ford, a top level computer programmer for Microsoft and even a dog whisperer.

Money matters: Parents must contribute financially at SDSS – although a few new Steiner schools are now state-funded or 'free' schools, this one was turned down in 2011. The school is very keen to emphasise that parents are not paying for their child's individual education – this is not a 'private' school – but are contributing towards the upkeep and on-going costs of the school. 'Financially tough' was one parent's comment, but the school does its best to keep costs down. Parents have to contribute their own time, skills and abilities in lieu of cash. Committed parents only need apply.

Remarks: The Steiner way, it's a way of life for the whole family. Parents agree that 'It produces confident, creative and genuinely independent thinkers.' But, as one parent put it, 'If you are freaked out by the "religious, cultish" (or indeed "health and safety") connotations of someone lighting a fire, or you don't believe in telling children fairy stories, you won't like it. Equally if you want your child to be immersed in technology from a young age and you are looking for academic "hothousing" it isn't for you.' For those parents that are prepared to take the leap of faith, the advice from current parents is 'Make sure you do your homework' beforehand, and then, 'Trust in the process'.

Our view is, if you're not sure about Steiner, if you don't love it, then don't even consider it. The teachers and parents at SDSS are fully committed and passionate about the school and its philosophy. You need to be too. Totally, wholeheartedly committed. Not necessarily an eco-warrior but maybe just a bit more than a hippy at heart.

South Wilts Grammar School for Girls

Stratford Road, Salisbury, Wiltshire SP1 3JJ

Pupils: 997 • Ages: 11–18 • Sixth form: 325

Tel: 01722 323326
Email: head@swgs.wilts.sch.uk
Website: www.swgs.wilts.sch.uk

Headteacher: Since 2011, Michele Chilcott BSc PGCE NPQH (mid 40s). An environmental geographer with a degree from Wye College (now Imperial) and a PGCE from Oxford, Mrs Chilcott taught in a range of secondary schools in southern England before coming to South Wilts as assistant head in 2004. Clearly still enthusiastic about her subject, she teaches all of year 7, partly as a means to get to know them all, lives on the coast (well away from school) and is a keen and adventurous traveller: 'I don't want to visit the same place twice', she says. She's also very pro single sex education: 'Coming here means girls can still be girls at 11', she says, 'before going on to excel in traditionally male subjects like maths and sciences'. Highly regarded by her girls and their parents, if not terribly visible ('Superb', said one father simply, and 'She knows where she's going and is really hot on recognition – and not just for academics', according to one girl), we found her understandably keen to talk about the school, but somewhat guarded as a person.

Academic matters: An outstandingly academic school and makes no bones about it. Highly selective at entry, with three bright girls trying for every place at 11+, its results jolly well ought to be good – and they are. In 2016, 76 per cent A*/A grades at GCSE and 47 per cent at A level, results which place South Wilts among the top 100 schools in the country. Preparation for such stellar performance starts early: these girls work hard from day 1, with an amount of homework which is sometimes baulked at, even by parents, but 'when my daughter said she was jealous of the little homework her friends at the local comprehensive got, I just said that's the deal at South Wilts', said one. Teaching appears traditional; everyone was sitting at desks facing the front in the lessons we saw. Subject choices are wide – most girls take 11 or 12 at GCSE (some at IGCSE) and 33 subjects are offered at A level in conjunction with neighbouring and similarly excellent boys' grammar Bishop Wordsworth. AS Latin now on offer, but there is neither photography nor media studies – though communication studies is included. The top five per cent of this exceedingly bright bunch are tracked and encouraged to enter national competitions, such as maths Olympiads etc, though this is open to all, and specific support is laid on for any girl considering Oxbridge, medical or veterinary school. Progress is closely monitored: parents appreciate the frequency (three per year) and quality of reports, but one mother described parents' evenings as 'a time-wasting scrum', which would be better replaced with exception reporting if things go awry.

All girls are CAT tested on entry, and school employs a dyslexia expert. Extra time can be given for 11+ exams, where girls come with a recommendation from primary school; South Wilts is keen to open access to very able girls with SEN. Once in situ, there is help available for spelling, handwriting and organisation, such as scheduling work and completing exams. An assembly at the start of sixth form deals expressly with barriers to learning and where to seek help for them.

Games, options, the arts: Plenty of all these on offer – this school is not just about what goes on in the classroom. Extensive grounds (for a city school) include tennis and netball courts, hockey pitches and – jewel in the crown – an all-weather athletics track. Sport of some kind is compulsory up to the end of year 11; school has Healthy School award. For a school which has neither a pool nor horses, its success at swimming and riding is commendable, and it brings back quite a bit of silverware from local-ish state and independent schools and from regional contests; national badminton player a current pupil too. Minority choices include trampolining and tap-dancing – plus some alternative sports (ultimate frisbee and American football inter alia) laid on by a sixth former as part of the Sky Sports Living Programme.

Arts scene also strong, as befits a school which holds the gold Artsmark award. Masses of music (a third of girls take music lessons) for all standards: three orchestras, wind band and guitar group, plus three choirs, one of which is good enough to sing at weddings and at evensong at Queen's College Oxford, where several of the choral scholars are ex-South Wilts. School takes full part in the musical life of this cathedral city. Recent drama productions include Grease, A Midsummer Night's Dream and Animal Farm, the latter in collaboration with Bishop Wordsworth; there's also an annual Oscars ceremony. Visual arts are clearly a strength too and on display all over school. In 2013 the Arts Award was run for the first time; two lower sixth girls gained their gold straight off.

Packed schedule of clubs at lunchtime, some for just for fun, some with more serious intent, such as the pond club, which helped the school gain its green Eco Flag; good take-up for D of E too. A wide range of trips and jaunts – most are educational, for linguists, historians and geographers – but also ski-ing just for fun. School proud of its international links with schools in France, Germany, India and China and has sent staff and pupils on exchanges to all those countries.

S

Background and atmosphere: Four-square brick buildings in a leafy suburban street, dating from 1927 when the school was founded, convey the impression of no-nonsense academic seriousness we imagine the school would wish for. The usual collection of 'temporary' buildings providing extra space do not encroach too much on to the grassy grounds, where girls were relaxing at lunchtime in sizzling sunshine the day we visited. Bits of the school could do with a coat of paint, but we loved the new learning resources centre (aka library) with its sofas and beanbags, and super new sixth form block, complete with lounging Bishops' boys, sofas, toasters and kettles. Canteen kitted out with garish chairs seems small for the number of girls passing through it at lunchtime; much of the sixth form prefer nearby Waitrose. Practical and good value uniform (kilts, polo shirts, sweaters in navy and bottle green) in keeping, and sixth formers tidier than many we have seen. Fearsome reputation for academic rigour borne out by a sense of intellectual endeavour we could almost smell: 'I was bullied for being clever at my last school,' one girl admitted, 'so I wanted to come to South Wilts because everyone would be a boffin'. All this is not at the expense of fun, however: 'The girls have rather a jolly time while learning really quite a lot,' as one mother put it. Local opinion that the school might be 'boring' is stoutly denied by the girls, who appear to enjoy the fact that they can pursue whatever subject takes their fancy without fear of ridicule, 'though having boys here would mean fewer arguments', said one. It seems a happy place for staff too: one father commented on the positive relationships between staff, their commitment to the place and the rapport between them and the girls.

Pastoral care, well-being and discipline: Gets the thumbs up from parents, as does the school counsellor from the girls, though this is not a touchy-feely school. Parental concerns are dealt with swiftly and effectively; the only real gripe we heard, and which is common to most state schools, was the lack of medical facilities (eg sick room) and trained staff. Sanctions mostly handed out for poor behaviour, and certainly for late work, and take the form of detentions at break, lunchtime or in the most serious cases, Friday afternoon. 'We're generally pretty well-behaved,' said our sixth form guide, 'but the school would certainly act if something outside school like drink or drugs was affecting academic performance' – we did not feel anyone was much troubled by this

Pupils and parents: Girls unpretentious, bright and not afraid to admit it. Refreshing lack of preoccupation with personal appearance: hardly any make-up, micro-minis, body art or piercing – no boys to impress, see. Parents clearly relieved their daughters got in and grateful for all the school offers; there's an active PTA, raising about £10k per year, which has a 'symbiotic relationship' with the school, said one dad. All seem remarkably content with their lot; the only things on the wish list might be a proper sports hall and better lights at the entrance. 'Not a hotbed of ethnic diversity' our last write-up noted, and little has changed.

Entrance: By way of the 11+ exam in VR, maths and English in the previous September; passing the exam does not guarantee a place at the school, to which applications are made through the LA once results are known. Coaching for the exam is endemic – 'You play the game, because everyone does it,' according to one parent, 'but it's not the place for someone who has been coached to the max just to get in'. Girls come from 58(!) local primary schools and several prep schools; those who don't make it often to go to independent schools. Now has 150 year 7 places.

At sixth form, about 80 girls arrive with a minimum of six GCSEs above a C, with at least a B in any subject to be taken at A level and Bs in maths, English and the sciences. In our view, this is quite a low hurdle for a school of this calibre, and a few newcomers find the academic pace daunting initially, though the school does its best to integrate them on arrival.

Exit: About 10 per cent leave after GCSE, mostly to local sixth form college – more choice and greater freedom. Those who stay get into top universities – a good handful to Oxbridge (12 in 2016), the rest to worthy runners-up, such as Bristol, Cardiff and Birmingham universities. Broad range of subjects; geography, politics, biomedicine and philosophy most popular recently. Careers revealed at a recent reunion included an architect, doctor, opera singer and controlled risk consultant.

Remarks: Unapologetically academic no-nonsense girls' education. Certainly not no-frills, though: this school has a range of activities to nurture all talents – and none. When we put it to the head that her school was so good it could be independent, her face gave her away: 'We're a state school and the only form of élitism we go in for is academic. We're here to serve the community'. Sums it up, really.

Stockport Grammar Junior School

Linked with Stockport Grammar School

Buxton Road, Stockport, Cheshire SK2 7AF

Pupils: 424 • Ages: 3–11

Fees: £8,262 – £8,505 pa

Tel: 0161 419 2405
Email: sgjs@stockportgrammar.co.uk
Website: www.stockportgrammar.co.uk

Head: Since 2014, Tim Wheeler (BA MA PGCE FRSA, Sheffield, Cambridge and Bath). 'Respect without awe' is his preferred style and it shows; during our visit, smiley children wander up to him to enthuse about various charitable projects they want to initiate and he, with perfect recall of their last conversation on the topic, is able to give them next steps and arrange a further chat. Previously headmaster of Hereford Cathedral Junior School, before that director of studies at Bilton Grange, he worked for several years as an educational consultant specialising in strategic school improvement. It seemed to us this latter consultancy experience is key, because two years into the post, he has introduced widespread changes: a new discipline regime, an expanded learning support department, a new maths course. It goes on.

No thumping management consultancy style here, though. Subtle change by stealth seems to be his method, tweaks here and there which people can embrace at their own pace but which, after a while, result in innovation. Staff are a blend of longstanding and new, so experience and a sense of renewal co-exist. All the parents to whom we spoke loved the school and effervesced about their children's happiness and progress. They felt he had implemented lots of positives; that he was quietly but actively 'shaping the future of the school'.

His philosophy is simple: '"They are just children",' he says, "should be plastered across the wall". He translates this longhand by saying that we must never forget they are children but at the same time we must never limit them on the basis they are 'just children'. It is a very balanced, very human approach. Very him. School, he maintains, is a place to make 'mistakes', to learn, to deal with friends, to navigate social groupings, as this is what will enable them to go forwards in the world after leaving the junior school. One parent underlined this, saying she felt children were really encouraged to be 'independent, empowered; fully prepared for the senior stage'.

A keen long distance runner, marathons in particular, usually in daft costumes because of his passion for charity work, it is clear the important thing to him is always to try – to dig deep, have grit, with the belief that inspiration can follow. He exudes warmth and enthusiasm for life; music is a great love, and although he tells us he doesn't consider himself to be the best bass player in the world, he says he can raise his game when playing with gifted musicians. This seems to be intrinsic to his attitude to learning, which is all about perseverance, hard work and inspiration. A sports lover, he cites Andrew Murray and Mo Farrah as inspirations for children, describing what they have as the X factor – not just raw talent but the capacity to work very hard at honing that talent to make it into something great.

Entrance: Most come up from the nursery. At reception stage – there are two classes of around 20 children – entry is mainly a matter of simple observation; looking at what a child does, how they interact and respond to simple instructions. A great many children, though, apply in year 1 or 2; here they are invited in for a sample day and, again, subtly observed to see how they respond to basic tasks. The taster day includes tests – English, maths, reading and some non-verbal reasoning – but it is all done with a light touch so children don't feel intimidated. It's not about judging them, Tim Wheeler stresses, but about working out whether this is the right school for the individual child to be happy.

Exit: Almost all children take the entrance exam for the senior school and move across. Prior to that, there are taster days to provide a slow integration. Bravely (we thought), Tim Wheeler says he has 'downgraded' the status of the entrance exam so that it is part of what the school does, rather than 'everything'. All the classroom work – albeit without pupils being aware – is preparation for the exam in itself. By year 5, they are doing a few past papers but care is now taken to ensure this does not disrupt the curriculum.

He says children who would not thrive at the senior school are nicely eased out. By year 2, the school has a sense which children need an alternative environment, and an extended conversation begins with the parents, often lasting a couple of years, where the child's welfare is discussed and parents and children supported towards a decision around year 4 or 5. When children leave the junior it is usually related to a special needs issue; we were told that that there were three dyslexic children in the school and only two of those would be able to go forward to the senior school. Only occasionally do children leave for other reasons, perhaps due to a sibling being at another school.

Remarks: From the moment you step through the door into the entrance hall flooded with light – a collaborative space where a community of animated children gather in throngs of chat – there is an overwhelming sense of vibrancy, warmth and happiness. This is reinforced by corridors and classrooms, which are an explosion of colour with innovative art displays everywhere you look.

At infant stage, in addition to English and maths, subjects include modern languages, computing and music. The junior school has a broader curriculum with science and the arts integrated. Work is differentiated with a bespoke plan for each child – bespoke is the watchword at this school. The reporting system on the merit card, for personal improvement and development, has recently been tweaked; the grades are less prominent and it is now more about the pupil's individual progress. English and maths, Tim Wheeler says, can be assessed 'as an absolute', but each child's individual 'upward trajectory' is the important aspect. Bespoke, you see. Parents tell us that their children have fantastic form teachers who 'won't allow mediocrity' but drive them as individuals to achieve in a positive way.

Children move between iPads, Chromebooks and exercise books with fluidity so the value of all is appreciated, although one parent wondered if technology needed to be used to a greater extent and felt it was quite a traditional way of learning. Lesson plans are done with rigour but they are not a 'straitjacket', Tim Wheeler says. So are the more able children pushed? While the head thinks it should be every teacher's mission to be proactive about this, one parent did tell us that she had to really pursue extra work for her child, adding: 'If there is a push, it works well'. However, another parent said one of her children, who was a little slower than his siblings at learning, had been given excellent support. Teachers, she said, were always responsive to concerns. As a result, her child had made huge strides forward and this was recognised and celebrated: 'It's not about A grades, effort is rewarded and recognised'.

Learning support therefore extends to all children who are below the high academic thresholds the school sets. Around one quarter of pupils in the school have received some kind of 'intervention'– a bespoke programme to help them improve – in the past year. The learning support teaching team has been expanded and the goal is to identify any needs or issues early on and then set up any appropriate additional help. Based on their assessment score, a number of children receive first stage intervention (some extra classroom work and and usually some time in a booster group). If further support is needed, they may provide some small group work. The third stage involves a small number of children receiving a small amount of one-to-one support. The overall aim is to get children to the point where they can manage effectively in the classroom. In the last academic year, two dyslexic children both received some one-to-one support, in addition to their local authority funded support (there is no charge for the extra teaching in the school).

A sports fan, Tim Wheeler has introduced a card system akin to football rules to maintain good behaviour. One or two breaches of school rules – such as eating in the classroom – might result in a yellow card. Three yellow cards and you have a red card – no dramatic football send-off ensues, but the parents are called. Although an effective tool, it is not, he says, enforced with excessive rigidity. One parent we spoke to felt it reinforced the importance of respecting each other and embedded basic manners within the children. All seemed to appreciate it and feel its positive impact. Certainly all the children we saw were happy, bubbly and seemed to deport themselves admirably.

S

As for empowering the children, they are gradually given responsibilities: first in their form, then later via more expansive opportunities, such as the school council. All year 6 children are now prefects with discrete areas of responsibility which, says the head, 'won't eat into their time'. He is very respectful of the latter, always bearing in mind that children need their downtime as well.

All parents commented on the 'amazing' range of activities on offer; alongside the usual sports, more unusual options include archery, puppet making and fencing. Specialist teachers are hired when necessary and new activities are evolving all the time. Lacrosse, fondly remembered by old Stopfordians, has recently been resuscitated due to a member of staff's enthusiasm and had a huge take up. The inclusive nature of these activities is also key (it is very much part of Tim Wheeler's leadership to encourage a 'have a go' culture). One parent said because her child could play at both formal and informal concerts, it had encouraged her desire to perform. Many sport clubs do not select exclusively by talent; there are some which have been broadened for children who just want to see what they might be able to achieve if given the chance. Everything is gender-inclusive; one parent appreciated that her boys had been encouraged to sing in choirs. The drama productions – a recent one being Beauty and the Beast with a cast of 80 – are wide ranging. Children can use the sports centre in the senior school grounds (alongside its cheery all-weather turf) which one parent identified as being very helpful in breaking down barriers between the two schools.

Pastoral care seems very strong also. A parent whose child had specific health needs, on which her daily well-being depended, was glowing about the emotional and practical support she had received, the delicacy and tact with which it had been handled, and how this had enabled her child to breeze through school with no disadvantages or attention being drawn to her predicament.

Like its parent school, it proudly bears its locational name – Stockport – a tag which usually precludes the starry footballer parents which are often seen prospecting for schools in the north west. Stockport parents may not necessarily have reams of spare cash, but what they do have, they want to channel into education. It tends to pull in parents from surrounding areas and is very much a local school. Where parents in other high profile schools in the area might be termed 'driven', Tim Wheeler says Stockport Junior parents are very 'grounded, solid and loyal. Certainly this grounded and very local school provides a wonderful platform for local children to discover, grow and aim high.

Stockport Grammar School

Linked with Stockport Grammar Junior School

Buxton Road, Stockport, Cheshire SK2 7AF

Pupils: 1,020 • Ages: 11–18 • Sixth form: 240

Fees: £11,034 pa

Tel: 01614 569000
Email: sgs@stockportgrammar.co.uk
Website: www.stockportgrammar.co.uk

Headmaster: Since 2005, Andrew Chicken BA (London) MEd FRSA. 'We are not in the business of gentrification,' he says, casting a firm eye in our direction. He was previously head of Colfe's, temporary head of Cheadle Hulme and, before that, taught at Manchester Grammar. This school upholds the ethos of the old grammar school system (although perhaps not so 'old', if the prime minister is to be believed about plans for a new wave of trad grammar schools). A school, he says, warming to the theme, is about the 'promise of pupils in every community. Community, affordability and accessibility.'

'Grammar common denominators' are therefore ubiquitous: references to the 11+ abound and there is a clear emphasis on good old-fashioned 'qualitative teaching across traditional subjects'. No matter how senior or managerial a teacher's role, stresses Andrew Chicken, they still have to teach lessons in his school. Standards matter. We spoke to a parent who told us the head is outside the school each week, a 'visible presence', keeping a wary eye on haircuts and smartness.

Yet it's clear to us that the strong backbeat underpinning the 'grammar-ness' of it all is social fairness: the school is and should always be, Andrew Chicken says, a 'true representative of the broad constituency of Stockport'. Strongly committed to ensure a 'full range' of pupils attend, it seems the school backs this quiet drive for diversity with some filthy lucre; the generosity of its bursaries (120 pupils are benefitting currently) allows for a far more diverse community than is perhaps the case in other independent schools in the Manchester area. Unlike a lot of rather cloistered (in all senses) headmasters, he spent part of his life teaching in rufty tufty-ish south east London. Stockport, he points out, is the most socially polarized area outside of London, and its bursaries are a measure of how committed the school is 'to making sure doors are open'. With or without bursary assistance, he is clearly very proud that over half (53 per cent in 2016) of the children joining the senior school at age 11 are from state primary schools (in addition to those joining from Stockport Junior and other independent preparatory schools).

We found him a very easy man to talk to – approachable and amenable – and he was described by one member of staff as a great listener. Married to a former teacher at Withington Girls, he is steeped in the educational offering of the north west. The art-covered walls of his office are crammed with pictures of local Stockport scenes – he is a keen hill walker in the local area – but more importantly, like all self-respecting, card-carrying northerners, he is a lover of football and a longstanding season ticket holder to Manchester United.

Academic matters: Roll call per year is around 150-155 (sixth form 120-125) and classes tend to be around 25 pupils. The curriculum is solid and traditional with the usual spread of subjects covered at GCSE, pupils being enrolled for nine or 10 subjects. Some extracurricular subjects like further maths, Greek and astronomy are also on offer. The headmaster flagged up maths and single science subjects as being particularly strong in the school (and with frive female physics teachers, he felt gender across these subjects was 'not an issue'). A quick glance at the school's A level results and chosen areas of study at university confirms this to be true.

Languages also figure highly, with everyone in the first year onwards studying both French and German, then picking up Latin in the second year and in the third year choosing three languages out of French, German, Spanish and Latin. Yet the take-up at A level is modest; there were 26 language entries in 2016 with three A*s and nine A grades; interestingly, German was much the most popular language.

Overall, in 2016, 52 per cent of all the A' level examination entries were awarded A or A*, and 62 per cent at GCSE. So the results are strong and solid; and the teaching likewise?

The last school inspection was carried out in 2011 – another one is due soon – and the faint grumble in that was that teaching was too directed and gave insufficient scope for pupils to explore. Digging around this we did, in fact, encounter one or two grumbles ourselves; one parent suggested that her children took the rather jaded view that the quality of the teacher you got was the 'luck of the draw'. 'If your child is motivated and driven,' she said, 'they will do well, they will go seek', implying it was not necessarily great news if they did not 'go seek'. Conversely, another parent said that when she had encountered a teacher whose standards seemed a tad dubious, the school had immediately listened, swung into action and did all they could to rectify the matter. This latter parent found that the academic environment was very nurturing, with her less academic child being supported as much as her academically high flying older sibling. 'She's encouraged to do as well as she possibly can.'

The school can also accommodate a range of SEND requirements for pupils who have passed the examination (these may include physical disabilities, sensory problems, English as an additional language and specific learning difficulties). A learning support department works with pupils, parents and teaching staff to ensure pupils make progress in line with their ability. Specialist timetabled teaching – and there is no additional charge for this – is made available to pupils in small groups to address their individual needs and help support curriculum studies.

Games, options, the arts: Like most other independent schools in the area, Stockport Grammar, with its vast grounds and great sports centre, offers a breathtaking choice of activities. Every parent we spoke to waxed lyrical about this. The core sports fare well; at the time of our visit, the girls' hockey team had excelled, so too the boys' rugby. For the more specialist pursuits, such as for climbing and golf, there are specific tutors.

There is a wide range of general clubs also, including some unusual ones like Big Band, Japanese, philosophy and some fun challenges; a MasterChef competition, judged by a Bake-Off celeb, had clearly gripped the school's imagination. Amongst all this activity, participation, specifically inclusivity, is an important driver; one parent summed it up: 'If you turn up to practice, you will get a go'. So, by way of example, there is swimming training for the gala and swimming for fun. Andrew Chicken also tells us the turn out for voluntary extracurricular trips is good, a recent battlefields' trip attracting 80 out of 150 pupils. There didn't seem to be a gender divide about activities either; a noticeboard showed photos of boys and girls involved in a dance show (a parent told us that a male dance teacher had being hired to run a dance day specifically for boys to encourage participation).

Music is strong with an extensive concert programme (more than 400 pupils learn instruments). Two sixth formers in 2015 were selected for the National Youth Orchestra, one for the National Music Theatre. Diverse plays and shows run the thespie gamut, from modern drama to the classics; one play had a cast of 86, with 50 people involved in the production side, so inclusivity is a big driver here too. For aspiring politicos, there is also lots of opportunity for debating and public speaking. The school team at the Model United Nations conference fared well, with lots of commendations and 'outstandings' awarded.

If your child's tastes run more to the more quietly cerebral, however, there are other interesting projects; lower sixth historians had produced the first edition of SGS Historian, a super little magazine looking at figures who shaped history, which gave them a flavour of editing and publishing.

Background and atmosphere: Stockport Grammar is one of the oldest schools in the country, having been established in 1487 by Sir Edmond Shaa, who became the 200th Mayor of London. (Being a historian, Andrew Chicken is passionate and very knowledgeable about the school's history.) The move to its current site took place in 1915 and this, the old part of the school, is utterly charming and all cloistered-up. The school's expansion, with the addition of several attractive, modern, airy buildings (the library being a recent addition in 2005, purposely placed at the heart of the school to feed those intellectual watercooler moments) means it is spread out over a large, if attractive, site with flashes of green everywhere. We imagine this involves a lot of dawdling between lessons, but while it makes for a slightly fragmented feel akin to a campus-based university, it is nonetheless impressive in its sweep and facilities.

Pastoral care, well-being and discipline: Form tutors are the first port of call for pupils in the event of any problems, and they in turn liaise with heads of year, as well as heads of lower school, middle school or sixth form, who all work closely with the deputy head pastoral. Aware of the pressures pupils are under, Andrew Chicken has expanded the pastoral staff and school counselling facility in order to provide the all-round care which the he perceives to be 'essential if children are to navigate the den of adolescence and flourish in and out of the classroom'. The school seems pretty clued up in this respect and there are heaps of talks for pupils on the dangers of misusing social media and the internet.

There may, however, be an uncomfortable chink in this pastoral care. One parent we spoke to, while acknowledging all the good work done by the school, had experienced the trauma of her child being bullied. She felt let down, that the whole matter had been brushed under the carpet, with the bullying policy being enforced weakly with no clear outcome. She also felt the remedies offered in such circumstances – counselling – were so conspicuous (pupils having to leave lessons to attend) as to intensify the problem for victims rather than aid the recovery. The after care, she said, was 'non-existent'. She summed up the school community in this respect as having 'lots of grit. It is a tough environment'.

One person's grit is, of course, another's pearl; other parents spoke glowingly of their children's happiness, saying the teachers seemed genuinely interested in what made each child tick. One recalled that at the parents' interview on entrance, a teacher had gushed they wanted every child to have their 'ray of sunshine'. She felt her own three, very different, children had found just that, each progressing very successfully through the school. 'Every achievement is really valued; you are no better just because you are A* pupil.' Lots of the parents we spoke to really reinforced how happy their child was at the school and how well rounded they had become with all the diverse activities on offer.

Another parent paid tribute to the pastoral care, saying she had been 'bowled over' by staff who had 'bent over backwards' when her high-achieving academic child hit tricky times in sixth form for personal reasons. Teachers had rearranged their diaries to help her; sought her out at lunchtimes to chat and altogether provided her with outstanding care, encouragement and support which was enabling her daughter to rally again at a critical time.

Pupils and parents: Stockport Grammar parents do not seem to be of the extremely affluent, sharp-elbowed variety. Or, as the headmaster put it, parents are 'proactive and representative of its broad social intake'. Most told us they didn't need to go into school to check on progress; the usual channels – newsletters, the parent portal, parents' evenings – were sufficient. When they did need to raise an issue, most said you could speak to a teacher direct on that same day. One parent she said that she felt that it was a 50:50 partnership with the school: 'if you work in conjunction with the school, you get the best out of them'. So all very fluid, relaxed and not too competitive.

Entrance: Children joining from local state and independent schools and from the junior school are encouraged to visit for taster days, including tests, in year 5, and open events. Stockport Grammar Junior children integrate gradually with activities in the senior school. Around 370-400 children from other local schools take the comprehension, essay, maths and verbal reasoning papers, competing for 90 or so places (60 of the 150 total are generally taken by Stockport Junior pupils). There also informal interviews for parents and the pupil and a school report. Those who apply for entry later on, up to year 10, sit maths and English papers.

Sixth form admissions by interview with generally 6+ A*/A grades required at GCSE.

Exit: Around 20 leave after GCSE, usually for a fee-related issue or occasionally because sixth form is not for them. Five to Oxbridge in 2016 and three medics. Others off to study eg anthropology at Durham, maths and philosophy at Edinburgh, engineering at Nottingham, fashion marketing at Nottingham Trent and French and international management at Bath.

Money matters: The school is committed to keeping fees as low as possible and Andrew Chicken flagged up how reasonable they are compared to other schools in the area. The school bursary scheme, a significant part of the fabric and ethos of the school, provides assistance with school fees, meals and sometimes travel costs. Bursaries are based on family income and a child's performance in the entrance exam. Music scholarships are also available and Ogden Trust Bursaries in the sixth form. In addition, Shaa Scholarships are offered to children based on 'outstanding performance' in the entrance exam.

Remarks: If you think that the old grammar school system was one of the best things about Britain as it was, and as it could be, then this is the school for your child. They will receive an excellent 360 degree education in a relatively diverse environment, where achievement at every level is celebrated, allowing all pupils to thrive.

Stonar

Cottles Park, Atworth, Wiltshire SN12 8NT

Pupils: 327; 75 full/weekly boarders • Ages: 2–18 (boarding from 8) • Sixth form: 42

Fees: Day £8,130 – £15,795; Boarding £19,455 – £30,210 pa

Tel: 01225 701741
Email: admissions@stonarschool.com
Website: www.stonarschool.com

Head: Since 2015, Dr Sally Divall MA PhD PGCE, previously deputy head academic. Following a BSc and PhD in natural sciences at Cambridge, Dr Divall has worked variously at BP, the Bristol Exploratory, as a visiting lecturer at UWE and as a research fellow at Bath University before joining Stonar in 1999. Providing a welcome stability after several predecessors failed to stay long in the saddle, she has two grown up daughters and is a qualified mountain leader. Away from work she enjoys off-road running and mountain trekking.

Head of prep: Since 2009, Mr Mark Brain BA (Ed), formerly deputy head of Kelly College Prep (now Mount Kelly Prep). Engaging sporty, outdoor type, married with a young family, so very at home in this setting. Has experience of state and maintained sectors, as well as secondary. Busy building numbers of boys at the prep, following the decision to make the prep school fully co-ed since 2011, and now the senior school is co-ed too.

Academic matters: Completely non-selective, and does well by its pupils. Sound teaching, a staff to pupil ratio of 1:6 and rigorous tracking using all the gismos at the school's disposal (CAT, Alis, Yellis) have been put in place to squeeze every drop of potential

S

out of them. 'We want the best academic development for every child – but not at the expense of everything else'; we should think so too.

School's results shine more brightly when looked at in relative rather than absolute terms: value-added scores compare well with competitors (nearly 36 per cent A*/A grades at GCSE in 2016 and 23 per cent at A level). That said, clever children also get results which stand up anywhere, but 'Not the school to choose if you want your son or daughter to go to Oxbridge,' opined one mother. Good single science results at GCSE, but more effort perhaps needed for weaker scientists, where not everyone manages a C even in core and additional syllabuses. French from the pre-prep and Spanish from year 5. Spanish far and away the most popular modern language at GCSE; a two year certificated classics course including basic Latin in years 8 and 9. Twenty-six subjects on offer at GCSE but a mere 15 at A level (18 on demand, says school); mention must be made, though, of the vocational options up for grabs in sixth form such as the British Horse Society Assistant Instructor qualification, sixth form cookery course including the Leith's Toolkit and ECDL. Parents appreciate these alternatives and the clear indication given by the school when their children are not A level material. Pupils are now benefitting from a lively programme of cultural, academic and inter-school exchanges and events between schools in the NACE group.

SEN well catered for: about a third of pupils have some kind of identified need, mainly dyslexia, but visual and hearing impairments as well as ASD also accommodated.

Games, options, the arts: None can hold a candle to Stonar's equestrian education. The celebrated cross-country courses and show-jumping arena border the drive and lift any rider's heart (this editor's included) and provide a permanent home for the Inter-Schools One Day Event, ISODE. The equestrian facilities (an indoor and outdoor floodlit school, stabling and grazing for 70 horses) and resources thrown at it deserve their reputation. This is further burnished by the director of riding, Darrell Scaife, an international event rider of some repute in his first role of this sort. His aim is to produce horsemen and women, rather than solely competition riders, and he starts with the building blocks to successful riding: position, anatomy and movement. He's also much interested in learning styles and in equipping his riders to bring on young horses; in fact he has persuaded the school to purchase, with help from sixth form fundraisers, a youngster for his riders to develop. It may all sound rather high-flown, but Mr Scaife has come from Brixton where he is still involved with Ebony Horse Club, which gives inner-city troubled youngsters the chance to ride, and has arranged a highly successful exchange – an eye-opener for all concerned. 'No glamour and plenty of muck', he says and the busy pupils, who do everything for their steeds, whether owned or loaned, bear this out. Clinics from visiting luminaries like Tina Cooke, competitions and trips to national shows and events, plus an exchange with an equestrian overseas boarding school, give riders lots to aim for. New rider development programmes give individual equestrian and academic timetables.

But the riding is prominent, not dominant. About a third of the pupils ride, but those who don't are in no sense second class citizens – and they don't have to get up early to muck out. All usual sports on offer for them (hockey, netball etc but also full contact rugby coached by a Welsh rugby international, no less) and parents like the fact that small numbers mean players of modest ability get to represent the school. Tennis courts grace the front of the main house, and usual independent school provision of floodlit Astro, sports hall, fitness suite and squash courts, 'but the swimming pool is tired', said one parent. Recently upgraded, says school. D of E and lots of trips – to Cornwall for the artists, to Le Touquet as a combined offering for the modern languages and food tech departments, plus skiing and Challenge Romania, where girls build a home for a destitute family in the course of one formative week, preceded by raising the funds for the opportunity to go. Back at school, there are allotments and chickens to be tended – and their produce to be enjoyed. Goats and pigs to follow.

Better known for its drama than its music, perhaps. Vibrant drama dept puts on (amongst other things) a Shakespeare play every year to great acclaim – and not just the easy ones either: Henry IV was a recent choice, whilst the prep put on A Midsummer Night's Dream. Tons of silverware comes home from the Mid-Somerset Festival and is displayed in the front hall. Small class sizes mean all hopefuls get to star – in a performance space which is functional rather than flashy. About a third of pupils take music lessons up to grade 8, but lots of scope too for the more technically inclined, with a well-equipped recording and music tech studio. Concerts at notable Wiltshire Music Centre in nearby Bradford-on-Avon as well as local venues and in school. No singing in assembly, though, when we visited, but a certain amount of bopping and lip-synch-ing in seats, as Aretha Franklin's Respect launched the (entirely secular) topic for the day.

Visual arts housed up stairs in a series of studios; we were lucky enough to see the end of year exhibition hung the height of an airy staircase. The huge dark-room, kilns and Macs ensure all types of artists are well provided for.

Boarding: Sixth form, senior and junior boarding houses have recently received major refurbishment (including a new wing for boys). Upper sixth boarding offers individual study bedrooms and lots of communal space in purpose-built York House. Popular choice for short term stays for overseas children: it was day one for a couple of Hungarian girls when we visited, who appeared to be managing valiantly, helped by smiley staff and children.

Super homely feel, particularly from house staff and nursing sister; tasty food also an important morale-booster with such limited opportunities for shopping. Parents and pupils love the sense of family, and house staff seem nothing short of cuddly. Communication between home and school on the boarding side is reported as good; issues raised are dealt with. 'We've found the school open and accommodating,' one mother confirmed, and pupils have opportunities to ask for help with any aspect of their school lives.

Background and atmosphere: Looks and feels like a slightly run-down country house. The school moved to its present home in 1939: it was evacuated from Sandwich and never returned from the Grade 2 listed Cottles Park, a very pretty Strawberry Hill gothic mansion sitting elegantly in acres of rural Wiltshire about eight miles from Bath. 'No muddy boots!' on every outside door – we'd never seen so any pairs of Hunters and Du Barrys gathered in one place. Gracious panelled hall and head's office soon give way to unfortunate corridors along which purposeful pupils scurry, sometimes in regulation navy jodhpurs and fleeces. Again, functional but not flashy.

Less pretty additions hidden behind the main house, as are all the stabling and manèges, and all that green space and lack of traffic – barring a few Land Rovers and horseboxes – is beguiling. But it is very rural, with intermittent mobile signal – 'definitely not for metropolitan types,' say parents, which is perhaps why they chose it, and for the fact that girls can be girls without having to keep up appearances (now has boys in the younger years, but we saw no make-up, jewellery, tattoos or short skirts) or grow up too fast. The girls like that too.

'At least they're not hanging about on street corners,' said one mother. Super homely feel, particularly from house staff and nursing sister; tasty food also an important morale-booster with such limited opportunities for shopping. Offers 'a healthy antidote to a results-driven culture – a niche which should be carved out,' raved one mum, with an ear for a sound-bite. Very inclusive, the sort of place where three squeaky notes on a violin from a nervous first time performer would raise the roof.

Bought in 2013 by NACE, a European education group with 21 schools in Europe, India and the US, with development prospects both in academic and bricks-and-mortar terms. Investment in boarding and sports facilities has been swift and evident.

Pastoral care, well-being and discipline: Highly praised. Discipline was hardly mentioned, but sins listed include lateness, untidiness and lack of co-operation. Drink and drugs in school will usually result in suspension, or the boot, depending on the severity of the incident, as will persistent smoking. School anxious to stress that such issues are extremely rare: 'but we've got the policies'. Sanctions start with a green slip progressing to detentions, 'internal exclusion' before sending hard-core miscreants off site on a temporary or permanent basis (not many of those). What did impress, though, was the self-discipline of riders, who need to be up at 7am and to fit all the care and exercise of their mounts in and around the school day.

Pupils and parents: Day pupils come from about a 35 mile radius, but boarders from much further eg London and home counties; around 70 per cent from overseas, predominantly SE Asia. 'I was so shy when I came here', said one charming, bright, Hong Kong Chinese girl, misty-eyed at the thought of leaving but destined for Imperial. Parents refreshingly down-to-earth, and free from the hoof-mark of arrogance and pretension which sometimes brands the horse world. Pupils seemingly more than content with their rural lot, and unencumbered by pressures from mobiles/social media, none of which function reliably at Stonar. 'Sparky, energetic, quirky but not cliquey,' according to the head. Parents speak well of school events, such as firework night and the end-of-year ball, a splendid affair, judging by the billowing expanse of marquee we saw when we visited.

Friendly integration between nationalities and year groups appears to be standard, but more between day pupils and boarders would be welcome; particularly marked at sixth form, where day pupils are allowed into the upper sixth boarding house only by invitation. 'But they can all use the sixth form centre', says school, with justification.

Entrance: Non-selective entry, mostly into nursery at 2 or reception at 4. Assessment and interview for all higher up, 'to ensure that children will thrive at the school'. Senior school applicants do sit an entrance exam in January, preceded by a taster day in November, for setting purposes once they arrive in year 7. Scholarships are offered for academic ability, drama, music, sport and riding. Boys now admitted into years 7 and 8 with intakes in years 9 and 12 too in 2017, and the school will be co-ed throughout by 2019.

S

For sixth form, admission depends on an interview and report from current school; same range of scholarships on offer, plus all-rounder. Figures from the school suggest quite a few comings-and-goings in most years.

Exit: Well over half of the juniors go to the senior school, by means of entrance exams for setting purposes only; the senior school too is non-selective. School says pupils sitting exams to move elsewhere (recent destinations include Dauntsey's, Warminster, King Edward's Bath, Royal High School Bath and St Laurence) are fully prepared and supported with this.

Quite a few – some 50 per cent – peel off after GCSEs, in search of brighter lights, boys and wider A level choices in Bath or Chippenham; some parents reckon it's all a bit sheltered and quiet for sixth form, and not a realistic preparation for life beyond Stonar's Cotswold stone walls. Of those who stay, the majority head straight off to further education, in many – but not all (eg Sandhurst) – cases to university. Degree courses range from pharmacy to environmental science to agriculture at universities including Exeter, Durham, Cardiff and Hong Kong. Distinguished old girls include big names in riding such as Junior and Young Rider gold medallist, Georgie Spence and twice Olympic short-lister Lucy Weigersma; actor Romola Garai and controversial author Gitta Sereny.

Money matters: Fees cheaper than many competitors, which is commendable, given the high staff:pupil ratio. Extras on the bill, as expected, but riding good value at about £300 a term. Scholarships to a maximum of 15 per cent of fees, even if more than one awarded; Forces and sibling discounts. Bursaries means-tested, generally to a maximum of 50 per cent off day fees.

Remarks: Stonar's reputation as being a place for the dim and horsy is undeserved and out of date. Not a hothouse, but the distinction made between exhorting pupils to do their best and exerting too much pressure is well made. Hunter wellies essential, ability to drive or at least negotiate an oncoming horse-box highly desirable.

Stover School

Stover, Newton Abbot, Devon TQ12 6QG

Pupils: 370; 57 boarders • Ages: 3–18 (boarding from year 5) • Sixth form: 60

Fees: Day £7,680 – £12,420; Boarding £16,290 – £25,440 pa

Tel: 01626 354505
Email: registrar@stover.co.uk
Website: www.stover.co.uk

Head: Since 2014, Richard Notman BSc. Studied finance and stats at Birmingham University but soon discovered he was not made to be an auditor. After taking his PGCE in Manchester, he spent the next eight years in inner-city comps before teaching maths at Withington Girls School and then becoming head of maths at Alderley Edge School for Girls. From there he went to Longridge Towers, Northumberland as deputy head, and finally Cundall Manor School, Yorkshire as head teacher before he swapped the moors for the Devon hills.

'A breath of fresh air', said one parent. He is more than up for the challenge and is excited to be at Stover. He says he 'can cherry pick the best of state and independent practice' and feels he now has the experience, knowledge and confidence to take the school forward. Plus it's rural, small, non-selective, 3 to 18, and co-ed; everything he wants in a school. It's not just a new life for him though; his wife and young family have moved to live in the school grounds, and his two children are settled in the prep school. He's keen to make this a family venture, and one parent told us, 'Both Mr Notman and his wife Helen have done everything they can to integrate their family into the school and make themselves known and accessible to all. They are a tremendously friendly family, and have placed emphasis on getting to the root of what the parents and children of Stover want changed and improved.'

Some major changes (or 'tweaking' as he calls it) are already under way and parents have been impressed so far.

'Communication from the school has been excellent in this matter,' they say. Research-based learning has been introduced and teachers have all taken it on board enthusiastically. Parents said, 'He has focused the staff on the bigger picture and has given a renewed energy across the school.' Pupils are 'very inspired by his assemblies and messages he is getting across.' His to-do list includes major makeovers for the sixth form and boarding; getting parents more involved; and making as much use as possible of the extensive grounds. One parent told us, 'The new head has been fantastic at attracting new children, as Stover was good but too small.'

Head of prep school: Since September 2016, Mr David Burt, previously head of primary at Compass International School, Madinat Khalif, Qatar. He has a degree in geography and sociology and a PGCE in primary education. Originally from the Isle of Wight, his hobbies are based around the outdoors and the sea: he is a keen fisherman who likes nothing more than spending a few hours on a beach or in a boat attempting to catch fish. He also enjoys watching and playing a wide range of sports and is an avid gym-goer. He is married and has two small children.

Academic matters: At GCSE in 2016, over 60 per cent A*-B grades. At A level, 38 per cent A*-B. Newly introduced vocational qualifications: BTecs in home economics, sport, ICT and performing arts. Maths is a strong subject with top grades at both levels. Stover has performed well in recent Regional Maths Challenges. Chemistry another strong subject with three students recently winning places at the prestigious Salters Chemistry camps. Photography very popular at A level. Spanish is taught from reception and French from year 3.

Stover welcomes pupils of all abilities. One parent said, 'It's a non-selective school and does very well in terms of exam results given its mixed ability (and after the grammar schools cream the top academics off).' A boarding school with 15 per cent of overseas students, English is not everyone's first language and this is sometimes reflected in the grades. Parents speak highly of the learning support department, and a whole range of learning difficulties are well looked after here, with one-to-one specialist support for autism or Asperger's. One said, 'When extra help is required they have the staff to support your child and our daughter was given her own "adult" in maths to sit with her and help her on a one-to-one basis, which helped hugely.'

Along with the introduction of research-based learning, Stover is setting up 'bring-your-own-device'. It is planning to invest heavily in a new (and safe) server instead of upgrading equipment. This will give teachers a new teaching aid, encouraging pupils to research online and become more tech savvy on their own computers. The ISI inspectors reported that 'teaching was excellent,' but we heard some concerns from parents about its quality. One said, 'I think there should be a review of the current teaching staff to ensure any weaker members of the team receive up-to-date training to help them improve their methods.'

Games, options, the arts: Extensive grounds and good sports facilities. Pupils 'relish the 60+ acres at Stover.' There are six all-weather floodlit tennis courts (some recently resurfaced), netball courts, a gym, plus football, rugby, hockey and cricket pitches. The only drawback is that Stover is a small school and there aren't always enough players of the same standard to make winning teams. One parent said, 'They seem to punch above their weight and have won hockey and netball leagues recently against much bigger schools.' However, other parents agreed that there's room for improvement: they would like to see 'a bit more sport and a few more fixtures in the senior school,' as well as 'investment in a school swimming pool.' Extracurricular activities include table tennis (big here), judo, fencing, clay shooting and more recently a Stover riding team. With the school on the edge of the moors, D of E and Ten Tors are very popular and are a part of life here. The head has linked up with Devon Schools Sports Partnership so that other local schools can make use of the grounds too. They hosted the Devon Schools' Area Athletics Cross-Country Championships 2015 with over 350 competing athletes.

Good music department. One parent said her daughter 'has been inspired by the head of music....they have nurtured her talent; she was very disengaged with it when she first joined.' Most pupils learn an instrument – the ukulele is popular in the prep school – and there's plenty of concerts and groups to join: the orchestra, brass and jazz bands and choirs. Another parent said, 'Stover has several choirs and is very good at singing and music. They win almost everything in local and regional competitions. My son's year even went to Bruges Cathedral after winning one competition.' Productions, assemblies and concerts all take place in the dome-shaped Jubilee Hall which also houses a recording studio and practice rooms (more rooms recently added).

As well as music, performing arts and public speaking are strong themes throughout the prep and senior school. Regular productions and plays, including one each year for the prep and the pre-prep. 'The ones I have seen are very well produced. I went to Bugsy Malone the other year and the Match Girls last year. So, very different ones,' said one parent. Stover also offers LAMDA speech and drama lessons with Stagecentre plus performance exams.

The art department has a building to itself. It's well set out with art downstairs, a separate sixth form area at the back, and photography upstairs. Art studio the latest add on. Pupils 'love being able to go outdoors to learn – in science and art they will often make use of the natural world around them.' Great displays and some impressive work including a John Lennon mural, and large fish sculptures inspired by a recent trip to the aquarium. We were particularly impressed by the photography upstairs, including some portraits taken on a trip to Brick Lane. More than 10 students taking A level, a high number for such a small school.

Clubs or daily activity sessions take place at lunchtime, with a late-ish school finishing time of 4.30pm. Mixed messages from parents on this. It suits some, but not all. When we were there we saw the Ukulele Club doing karaoke, and the Ready Steady Fry club had just finished making dough in the well-designed home economics room. Other activities, apart from the usual offerings, include bush-craft, astronomy, Dragons Den, the Raving Reporters, Knitting Club and Man Choir. There's also plans to make more use of the grounds and set up horticultural and farming activity clubs.

Day trips from reception, residential trips from year 4, with a night away, then a three-day trip to Cornwall in year 5, three days in Mount Batten for year 6. As well as language trips abroad, there are regular theatre trips, art trips to galleries locally and in London, field trips to Dartmoor, history trips to Flanders, and a recent sixth form expedition to Tanzania.

S

Boarding: Good balance of boarders and day pupils. The head sees Stover as different, not as 'regimented' as other boarding schools; he says it's ultimately 'a school, that has boarding provision.' Admissions criteria have been changed and there is now much more focus on language (interviews by Skype). There is also a more varied mix of nationalities (currently 17), with pupils coming from Bulgaria, Serbia, Russia as well as China, Vietnam, Spain, Germany and Cuba though Brits now in the majority in both houses. The plan is to recruit mainly full boarders and offer the flexi option in a very limited and controlled fashion – they don't want it to 'feel like a motel.' Short stays will still be offered during the summer as these serve as good tasters, and day pupils will still be able to take advantage of the wrap-around care.

Girls board on the opposite side of the main school building to the boys. Both areas have been recently refurbished. The boys are lucky to be in the original part of the building with high ceilings, ornate cornices, huge bay windows with shutters, original fireplaces, domed ceilings, arched hallways and great views. It's very tidy; the military background of their houseparent keeps them in check, apparently. He's also well known for getting the boys together for regular evening chats round the dining table. Cheerful rules boards dotted around – live, laugh, love etc – make it feel homely. The large dorms feel light and spacious.

The girls' side, without the original features, is less impressive. The common room felt stuffy, and although it was equipped with PCs, a Wii, a drinks area and dining table, it didn't have the same inviting feel as the boys' room. On the plus side, the girls do have single, double and treble rooms as well as dorms. When we were there the girls were obviously getting ready for the prom, dresses proudly displayed on most wardrobes. Good-sized showers and bath facilities. In fact all the facilities are good – kitchen areas, drinks area and laundry facilities all promote independent living as much as possible.

Usual rules for mobile phones and such, but all seemed pretty relaxed. The boarders here really get to know each other, and the staff, well. Parents say it has a 'friendly, family atmosphere.' Some students even come back for more. Gap year students help out with admin duties, evening activities like football or tennis, and weekend trips to the cinema, the beach, shopping and just recently Stonehenge and Thorpe Park.

Background and atmosphere: Stover School is set in beautiful grounds, 64 acres of parkland located between Dartmoor and the sea. Founded in 1932 by two sisters on the Stover Estate, the object was to help pupils lead independent lives. Boys and girls have been in the prep school since it started in 1996, and boys in the senior school since 2005. he Clock House, built in 1843 and housing the prep, was originally stables and is set around a charming cobbled courtyard. Several of the classrooms have interconnecting doors and are linked by very narrow hallways and stairs. It's small, some would say it feels cramped; others would say it's full of character.

The main house, built of granite ashlar, is an impressive sight as you drive in. With its double flight of portico steps it wouldn't look out of place on a film set. Inside, the grand entrance hall continues to impress with high ceilings, beautiful plasterwork and ornate fireplaces. The school is proud of its heritage and cups, plaques and photos adorn the corridors. The rest of the school is housed in various well-designed buildings and wooden outbuildings in the perfectly manicured grounds.

S

The Millennium building is modern and bright with science labs downstairs, and maths upstairs. Floor to ceiling windows, new equipment and colourful murals by a teacher make the labs cheerful and inviting. Small class sizes also mean that there is always enough equipment. Fish, gerbils and even an adopted stray ginger cat add to the happy vibe here. Recent trips include The Big Bang and the Eden Project. Upstairs are two bright and sunny (when we were there) maths rooms, linked by a large balcony, also used as form rooms.

Separate wooden buildings or cabins are used for English, humanities and modern languages. All freshly painted – we could still smell the paint – something else the newish head has done to freshen up the school.

Amongst the acres and acres of land, there's a large playground with a sandpit, a wooden pirate ship, a football pitch and even an outdoor chess board. The new outdoor classroom has replaced the forest school that was destroyed by bad weather. There's a pond, a fire pit and parents have recently planted fruit trees. They are keen to make as much use of the grounds as possible with activities like bushcraft and gardening club. The nursery is next to the playground and is a homely space for toddlers from 8am to 4pm. The school provides wrap-around care from 7.30am until 6.30pm for prep school pupils from 6 years old.

All pupils agree full-heartedly on two things at Stover. Firstly, it's friendly. And secondly, the food is excellent. We saw long queues of hungry pupils looking forward to the curry of the day. One said, 'I love Roastie Wednesday and Fishy Friday!' and apparently lots of pupils happily get dropped off early in time for the boarders' breakfast.

Parents like 'the friendly, family atmosphere.' One told us, 'We chose Stover for a number of reasons – yes, the grounds are lovely and the buildings beautiful but a school needs to give more than that. We were inspired by the ethos of the school as a whole. You don't have to get the highest scores in maths and they aren't going to force your child into a shape they don't naturally fit. [Stover] helps them to excel in the areas they have a passion for.'

Pastoral care, well-being and discipline: Well-behaved, well spoken and polite. Good behaviour is part of life here and is instilled at a young age – walk into any prep class and they will all stand. The pupils we spoke to seemed happy and proud of their school. Due to its small size, problems are spotted quickly and dealt with swiftly. Everybody knows everybody, but there is a solid support network of house parents, tutors, the school nurse, the school counsellor and the school chaplain if needed. The chaplain takes an active role in school life as well as regular collective worship and running the Christian Union Group.

The house system runs all the way through the prep and senior school and helps to give the pupils a sense of belonging. It's also great to bring out the competitive streaks. There are three houses, but strangely they are then split into boys and girls, making it six houses in all. The pupils we spoke to had no idea why it was like this as the only aspect they are separated for is sport. Presumably this is just a hangover from days gone by when boys and girls didn't mix. Strange that it hasn't changed with the times.

Pupils and parents: Day pupils from Newton Abbot, Exeter, South Hams, Torbay, Bovey Tracey, Plymouth. Boarders mainly from overseas. Parents mostly in professional occupations. Good bus service, or parents can take advantage of the wrap-around service from 7.30am to 6.30pm.

Communication is good, there's even a parents' app for news, events and photos. Plus Soundcloud to access all the latest music. Friends of Stover are always busy fundraising, and the upcoming Summer Ball was causing a bit of a buzz. 'There is also a monthly Friend's of Stover coffee morning where parents meet with the headmaster and his wife, and can exchange information, chat and generally catch up, which is lovely,' said one mother.

Entrance: Main entry points at 4, 7 and 11. By interview, school reports, and a taster day where academic ability and attitude to learning are assessed in an informal manner. One parent told us, 'They focus a lot on getting big friendship groups and not allowing cliques in prep school; new pupils are embraced.' Another said, 'We all found the entrance process very good. The older two started half way through the year but, they didn't seem to have any problems fitting in and finding their feet. The staff were welcoming, helpful and informative and communication with us was good. Since starting we have not had one single morning that they haven't wanted to go to school.' The school also has a system of parent class reps to help the new parents settle in – 'one parent per class keeps a database of details so that round-emails can be distributed with details of coffee mornings, birthday parties and play-dates – you soon feel like part of the furniture even when you've only been at the school for a matter of months!'

Exit: Most prep school pupils move up to the senior school, with a few peeling off to local grammars. Around 20 per cent leave after GCSEs, mostly to non-fee-paying alternatives. Popular university choices are Plymouth, Exeter, Bristol, Cardiff and Falmouth; courses in 2016 included forensic science, silversmithing, goldsmithing and jewellery, practical film-making and civil and coastal engineering. One leaver worth a mention is Debra Newbury, awarded the MBE for her services to transatlantic rowing.

Money matters: Academic, music, art and sport scholarships available at most ages up to 20 per cent of day fees. Two means-tested scholarships at year 10 and sixth form, the Maurice Key and Laurus scholarships offering up to 100 per cent of day fees. There's a maths scholarship available to international sixth form students covering 25 per cent of fees at Stover and 10 per cent of fees at Plymouth University. Armed forces and the police force are offered a 10 per cent discount.

Remarks: Stover is a small, friendly school. It's for mixed abilities, and for those that wouldn't suit a larger mainstream setting. It's undergoing some major changes. For the better. Everyone agrees there are 'exciting times ahead'. As one parent put it, 'It was a good school in many ways, but now I think it has the chance to be really outstanding.' And having met the heads, we think this is just the beginning. One to watch.

Stroud High School

156

Beards Lane, Cainscross Road, Stroud, Gloucestershire GL5 4HF

Pupils: 891 • Ages: 11–18 • Sixth form: 279 (co-ed joint sixth form)

Tel: 01453 764441
Email: admin@stroudhigh.gloucs.sch.uk
Website: www.stroudhigh.gloucs.sch.uk

Headteacher: Since 2014, Mark McShane, previously deputy head of Gloucester High School for Girls. He has spent all his teaching career at grammar schools in Gloucestershire, and has also been assistant head at Pate's Grammar School. He is married to Alison, and they have a young son and twin daughters.

Academic matters: Selects bright girls at entry and does well by them. Results are excellent, despite staff's constant refrain, 'We're not an exam factory.' Pupils take 10 compulsory GCSEs from a range of some 30 subjects. Less mainstream subjects include astronomy and photography. The school has a long history of outstanding academic achievement; in 2016, 68 per cent of GCSE grades at A*/A. At A level, 42 per cent A*/A and 71 per cent A*-B grades. Everyone takes a science subject and some 20 per cent of leavers go on to study a variety of science subjects. Modern foreign languages specialist status: good recent A level results for French, Spanish, Russian, more mixed at GCSE for German and Spanish. Staff go to great lengths to offer flexibility. 'The more unusual the subject combinations, the better I like it,' says one pupil. 'We don't do columns of subjects here.'

The school forms part of the Stroud District Partnership, a collection of nine local secondary schools and Stroud College that between them offer a wide range of subjects and diploma courses, though in practice just a handful of students seem to cross over. Specialist science and maths status, which has helped provide funding for an army of interactive whiteboards, and opened up new initiatives: a recent project involved building a plane from scratch. English, maths and psychology are currently the most popular subjects in sixth form, with very good results. Joint sixth form teaching with the boys has not affected girls' results, and the verdict seems largely positive. 'It has made things more chilled and sociable, in and outside school,' says one sixth former. 'The boys bring a lot of fun to everything.' Another confides: 'At first, we all mill round the new sixth form block being social, then gradually – usually after the boys have a bit of a shock with their ASs – everyone gravitates upstairs to study.'

Very dedicated staff: about half are early 40s and under. 'Staff don't just go that extra mile, but two or three,' remarked a parent. Year 7 is taught in four tutor groups of around 32. Year 8 onwards divides into smaller groups of about 25, up to sixth form. You can hear a pin drop, walking round during lessons. 'My brothers teased me I was off to school with the nerds,' said one girl, 'but everyone just wants you to do your best – it doesn't matter what sets you're in.' 'No stigma' for the school's 20 or so pupils on the SEN register. SENCo works alongside all members of staff. Pupils can have one-to-one mentoring. Some who find coping with a whole school day difficult due to their medical conditions are on reduced timetables. Other SEN students say they feel so supported by their peers and teachers they cope without teaching assistants. A few use laptops in lessons and examinations.

Games, options, the arts: Lots of sports on offer, from netball, athletics, hockey, rounders, tennis to football and basketball. Large, well-equipped sports hall and newly renovated gym. Girls compete at national level in athletics (including one tipped for potential Olympic stardom), cross-country, rounders and swimming. Recent overhaul of the tennis courts seems to have paid off, with the school reaching national finals of the prestigious Aberdare Cup for past two years running. School represented at regional level in netball and hockey, plus county level. 'There are lots of fun sports as well as team sports,' said one girl. Recent attempts to boost numbers for fun sport clubs.

Around one-third of girls take a musical instrument, with singing lessons very popular. Regular school concerts open to all ability and a range of choirs, orchestras, ensembles and groups. Gospel choir performed recently with Mica Paris, the senior choir sings at Cheltenham Festival. Wide range of clubs available within school day: popular ones include badminton, street and contemporary dance. Notices are posted on in-house plasma screens dotted around school, in assemblies and the fortnightly newsletter. Art and drama good and very popular. Terrific – and well-used – photography room.

Success in national competitions – Investment Challenge, Young Consumer of the Year – and local ones: the High School Food Team won at an enterprise day at Calcot Manor. Lots of trips, plus visits, exchanges and work experience in France, Germany and Spain. Foreign trips seem to be expanding: recent destinations include New York, St Petersburg and China. (One girl quick to point out: 'Not everyone has the money to do things but there's enough going on that you don't feel you miss out'). Very strong ICT department, which permeates all levels: as a tool for staff to track pupils' progress, and giving girls excellent access to computers, plus a range of music technology and software and state-of-the-art multi media equipment. 'Nothing's ever locked up and we have no vandalism,' said a teacher.

Background and atmosphere: The school was started in 1904 by far-sighted local dignitaries to give girls an education similar to that enjoyed by boys at Marling School. In 1911 the school moved to its present site beside Marling, set just off the main road into town (mayhem at drop-off/pick-up). The school's first fourth generation pupil started recently, and the School Birthday and prize giving remains the celebratory highpoint of the school year, with cake for all. The original red-brick, creeper-clad main building can feel cramped inside, but is sunny, both in aspect and atmosphere. Some old pre-fabs remain, and the school remains divided from its former junior school site by a car-crammed residential street, but there has been a feverish programme of building and refurbishment over the past few years, and the school is justly proud of the smart new sixth form block.

'The school's come rocketing into the 21st century,' said one parent, and there is a real sense of a good school sharpening up still further. This shows in various ways, from a smart new uniform, introducing burgundy jackets – 'not "blazers",' the girls explain – although pupils voted to keep their distinctive candy-striped shirts, to an overhaul of the way the school tracks and monitors pupils' and teachers' progress throughout school, to the building programme, and removal – both physical and psychological – of walls between the girls' and boys' schools.

Pastoral care, well-being and discipline: Lots of support systems in place. Girls struggling, for whatever reason, are mentored by designated staff, whom they can choose. Girls think buddying system and peer mentoring work well. Active whole school council, with all senior pupils eligible to be termly prefects. Separate sixth form council. 'We're encouraged to be independent in improving the school,' said one girl, eg some year 11s set up their own informal homework club, The Space (known as 'the Biscuit Club'), which has become a focal point for other year groups too.

'I like to think we're nurturing the next generation of eccentrics,' said one teacher. 'The girls are very eco-minded, always checking my recycling bins,' said another. Stroud High girls are continually described as 'quirky', 'original', 'vocal' and 'feisty' by parents and staff alike, and so they are, although not dauntingly or overwhelmingly so. This is Stroud, after all, and the school reflects the town's liberal-minded, arty/artisan ethos – what one teacher calls 'the Stroud effect'.

Which is not to say discipline is airy-fairy. 'It's about recognising things can go wrong and positive behaviour management'. School adopts a graded approach to discipline, starting with a warning, then room detention. The ratio of praise to sanctions is about 6.1. 'It's not about hanging people out to dry.'

Pupils and parents: Interesting, fun and fair-minded girls have a touching sense of their good fortune, and a strong sense of the world around them. They raise huge amounts for charity, and are 'always coming in with fundraising ideas.' Some pupils travel from as far afield as Ross-on Wye, Malmesbury, and the fringes of Bristol, but majority are from Stroud and surrounding area. Energetic parent-staff association and strong governing team.

T

Entrance: Approximately three applicants for every place. Now sets Durham University CEM verbal, non-verbal and numerical reasoning tests (supposedly tutor-proof) in September. Pupils come in from over 50 partner schools which vary from year to year. Additional places at sixth form, with minimum requirement of five A*-B at GCSE.

Exit: The majority of students achieve their first choice university destination. Three to Oxbridge in 2016 plus five to medicine and veterinary medicine. Students are given careful careers advice, including opportunities for higher apprenticeships and management training schemes.

Remarks: Really warm, vibrant school that offers bright, sparky girls a combination of single-sex education and co-ed. Girls go it alone up to sixth form, then join forces with the neighbouring boys' grammar to form the Marling School and Stroud High School sixth form. The two sixth forms share faciltiies but are not a joint sixth form. The sixth form is nicknamed Downfield.

Talbot Heath School

Rothesay Road, Bournemouth BH4 9NJ

Pupils: 565; 40 boarders. • Ages: 3–18 • Sixth form: 65 • C of E

Fees: Day £6,111 – £12,825; Boarding £21,654 – £22,719 pa

Tel: 01202 761881
Email: office@talbotheath.org
Website: www.talbotheath.org

Head: Since 2010, Mrs Angharad Holloway, previously head of MFL and IB at Royal High School, Bath. Married, with two girls at the junior school. Mrs Holloway has made some 'fantastic changes,' said a parent, who described the the previous head as somewhat old fashioned. Not so Mrs Holloway, who is gently updating school, curriculum and thinking with a largely conservative constituency of parents. Lively energy – 'enthusiastic all the time,' said one mum. Not goaded by Jeremy Paxman on his visit, so unlikely to be shaken by much.

Keen her girls should have coping strategies for life, and teaches women and leadership to her 12 year olds, who end the course understanding not just about leadership, but also work/life balance and the right to flexible working. Teaches international politics to 11 year olds to broaden their horizons. Most desired quality for her girls on leaving school – resilience. Quite.

Head of junior school: Since September 2016, Mrs Sally Weber-Spokes, previously deputy head academic at Clayesmore School. English and music degree from Leeds and PGCE from Bath. Has been head of English at The Beacon School in Surrey, spent five years as director of studies in Nairobi and joined Clayesmore in 2008. Sings with the Bournemouth Symphony Chorus. Other interests include the piano, snowboarding, travelling. Married with two sons.

Academic matters: Academically rigorous – girls in year 2 are doing mixed tables tests each week, though it was emphasised that they are trying to beat their own score and time, and the ability level will vary immensely between the girls. English and science particularly strong, said one parent. French from year 1. Craft, food technology, woodwork and reasoning taught in cycles. Lots of physical exercise, four PE sessions a week by the time pupils are in year 4. Class sizes no more than 20. Despite the focus on academic work here, a lot of girls get tutored for entrance to the (ferociously competitive) grammar schools.

Learning support available for those with mild learning disorders. One-to-one support available for no extra charge, and support can be given to those who need a bit of extra help in the run up to the senior school entrance exam.There are also maths and literacy clinics available for those who need a bit of an extra shove – always in assembly time. 'It's important that they don't miss out on social time.'

'A first class education for girls,' say parents, who expect results – '[the] priority's always academic,' said one. And they achieve good results. In 2016, 67 per cent of A levels were A*-B

(41 per cent of these A*/A). GCSEs – nearly 54 per cent A*-A. 'We do it well,' says the head. 'We are not a hothouse, but [we] do wish each girl to give of her best.' This is strongly felt in the atmosphere of this school. It's not a school where it is cool to muck around. Girls are very aware of why they are there and the importance of exams – 'all the girls want to achieve,' said a parent – but there are light touches. One mum described how her daughter had the school webcam – situated in a nesting box in the woods – on while she revised, so she could keep an eye on the babies.

A great school for value added. Entry requirements not stringent, so the high standards achieved in exams are all the more remarkable. At least in part due (says the head) to being an all-girl environment where girls can flourish – there is not that 'second's hesitation' before a hand goes up. Attracts a number who didn't make the grammars, who do very well – 'I think it's because...the staff genuinely care that the girls do well. Parents' evenings are very businesslike – this is what we need to do for your daughter, and this is how we will do it.'

'Subjects are traditional,' said a parent, 'nothing weird.' It is a conventional and fairly short list (classical civilisation finds a natural home here), but with Mrs Holloway at the helm, with her aim of holistic education, parents can be confident the girls are not being limited. Good take up (around 40 per cent) for A level chemistry and biology – the girls say the teaching of biology is outstanding. Physics is not so popular (just 10 per cent), and the results are less stellar. The head has set up a number of projects with local universities: music, drama – even forensic science; and of course there are her own pet subjects – international politics and women and leadership. Extended Project is also available. Languages are limited to French, Spanish and Latin, and some would like to see German back on the curriculum (it was dropped due to low uptake). But extracurricular Italian was implemented to assist a girl who wanted to study modern languages at university, and attracted a number of other takers, all enthusiastic about achieving GCSE Italian in a year. 'They provide extra if they can,' said a parent.

Sixth formers spoke with great enthusiasm of coming into school with extracurricular questions about favourite subjects and discussing them with teachers during lunchtime – 'It's like we're exploring and learning about it together.' Lunchtime lectures are very popular with sixth formers – one spoke eagerly about listening to Professor Frances Ashcroft talking about ion channels – 'they suddenly fitted in to life.'

Good computer provision: science block has dedicated space for computers, CAT block has a computer room for younger seniors, and lower and upper sixth each have a computer room.

Learning support gets a thumbs up from the girls – apparently no stigma here. 'They help a friend with her spelling every week,' said one matter of factly. Unusually, extra sessions from learning support are free here. Around 10 per cent have support for a range of mild learning disabilities, and they can drop a subject to make life easier. Girls have the highest opinion of teachers, who apparently go out of their way to help those who are struggling. One pupil, who had what she described as a 'maths crisis', spoke with enormous praise and affection about the maths teacher who devoted so much time to helping her regain skills and confidence. Lunchtime maths and science clinics available for those who are struggling.

Girls who speak English as a second language are welcome, providing they pass the entrance exam. Specialist in-house EAL lessons, and will be supported by staff in class. Children from many countries, including Russia, Spain, Germany and Jordan.

Lots of change in the staff in the senior school – around 50 per cent in the last four years (but largely due to retirement). Three classes in each year. Small class sizes (maximum of 20) please parents, who believe they promote good relationships between staff and pupils – and of course get those results.

Games, options, the arts: Dedication to sporting excellence described by parents as 'second to none'. Special tennis programme designed with the nearby West Hants tennis club. About 10 girls are enrolled on the programme, and it is pricey, although the school awards a scholarship to tennis players, so that they are not paying overall more than a regular full fee payer. There is no wish to expand numbers of elite tennis players, so competition to get a place is fierce.

Specialist programmes are not limited to tennis: Talbot Heath has 20 girls at national level in 14 sports, including tennis, netball, rowing and badminton, and there are Youth Olympians among the pupils. This school is small enough to tailor-make education for individual girls, and flexible teaching accommodates the need for elite athletes to train and travel around the country to tournaments, whilst still providing a rigorous education.

But although there are the elite – and yes, they are cool – genuine efforts are made to encourage all: there are some 56 rowers and 70 netball players of all abilities who turn up to training sessions. One parent said they are always coming up with weird and wonderful sports to keep the girls engaged.

'[Sporting] facilities are not as good as at more expensive schools,' said a parent, 'things need to be bigger and better.' In particular, a new pool to replace the 'tired' existing outdoor pool, or at least a cover so year round swimming would be possible, said another. The pavilion on the sports field is a bit ropey (and match teas 'could be a bit nicer' too), but although facilities are not as 'fantastic as they could be...it doesn't really matter,' said one. 'The staff are the thing, and they're amazing, and they work really long hours.' The level of sporting excellence at this school suggest their facilities are indeed secondary to success.

Excellence here is not limited to sports: there are members of the National Youth Ballet, the National Youth Choir, the National Children's Orchestra, the National Youth Orchestra and Wessex Youth Orchestra. Those outstanding in certain areas can drop a subject and have a reduced timetable to accommodate their specialist subject. Many win classes at the Bournemouth Music Festival, and there are monthly informal concerts for parents and friends, as well as more formal affairs.

Drama is popular: and although the drama block is a bit scruffy, it is clearly well loved, with an effective (if claustrophobic) curtained black box space. There are five productions a year, using the black box or the decent sized stage in the school hall. Girls often write their own adaptions – The Lion, The Witch and The Wardrobe was in dress rehearsal when we visited, written by 14 GCSE drama pupils. At another recent production, a parent described things as being '... stuck together...Heath Robinson style,' but the parents we spoke to appreciated the team spirit and the 'all hands on deck' feel, and pupils certainly have a wonderful time.

There's a well-attended debating society, very popular with girls after their stint with the head in international politics. Art is a strong department, say parents, although conditions are rather cramped. The CAT block includes a room with a battalion of sewing machines – certainly the warmest in the school (everywhere else kept at a fairly brisk temperature; no falling asleep in muggy classrooms here); there are old but well-preserved cookers in the food technology room, where lower sixth is taught a range of low cost dishes in preparation for university.

Boarding: Glossy new facilities in St Mary's boarding house (after a mediocre report from Ofsted). Spacious shared dormitories for those in years 6, 7, 8 and 9, with a cubicle effect (giving semi privacy) created by desks and cupboards, all in crisp new pale wood. No bunk beds. Own rooms from year 10, which increase in size considerably for those in upper and lower sixth. The boarding house has a rather clinical feel at the moment (it has only recently been finished), but the art department is going to provide some pieces to make it feel a bit more homely.

Bathroom facilities clean and new – 'the shower's better than home,' said one girl feelingly. Food varies from average to good, depending on the chef that day, say boarders. Practice room with a piano, and comfy lounges with TV and Wifi. Boarders can have laptops, Kindles and phones – although latter removed at night.

The 40 or so boarders mix across age groups – which creates a family feel, says the housemistress. Boarders seem very happy and well cared for. Most stay at school for the weekend, and are kept busy with a variety of activities, from ice cream making and adventure days to archery and shooting, evena pamper afternoon with homemade facial scrubs (inspired by a trip to Lush).

Background and atmosphere: School formed in 1886 by Mary Broad to provide a first class liberal education for girls. She shocked the locals by exercising her girls on the local common and taking them on trips around Europe.

A lovely environment, surrounded by woods (although the pines do gloom a little). Woodland area with tents and wigwams for the early years, all carefully made from wood and camouflage – used under supervision, of course. Flocks are watched closely here – few trips to A&E from this school. Hard surface play areas to use when the woods are muddy. The juniors have a special area of woodland, carefully fenced off, complete with log cabin. And no, they sadly aren't allowed to climb the trees.

Rather forbidding architecture, daunting on approach, though windows attractive 30s fare. Lovely modern hall with glorious wooden roof, and craft area upstairs. Juniors use the senior school facilities and specialist teachers where appropriate. Juniors and pre-prep occupy separate wings, with a courtyard eco-garden separating them – it looked a bit sparse, but it was carefully explained that this is a working garden of useful plants – a description that could aptly apply to this school.

Inside the junior school a feeling of order and purpose dominates – displays are as likely to be of written pieces of work, as of art – and goodness, the handwriting is good. Clearly something emphasised here. Girls were keen to show off their work, and very proud of their efforts. There was much enthusiasm in the classrooms, hands reaching to the ceiling and girls practically leaving their seats in an effort to answer questions.

'Traditional' is a word which comes up a lot when speaking to parents (although the current senior school head is certainly blowing away any remaining dusty elements). Curriculum, staff, behavioural expectations – all traditional, and parents like it. Attractive to one parent for being 'well structured, organised and friendly, [with a] structured discipline.' It is a disciplined environment – although it didn't feel stifling. But rebellious and disruptive girls would certainly stand out; and if their behaviour continued, would need to find a home elsewhere. C of E school, but focus primarily on fundamental values, so those of all faiths fit comfortably. Don't have to attend faith assemblies, but most choose to.

Rather foreboding buildings in the pine woods (but what a lovely smell). Some 30s charm, particularly a gorgeous gym which looks as though it has been perfectly preserved since the building's inception (there's a modern sports hall too). Even has original WW2 bunker classroom, complete with toilet buckets bearing TH emblems. Flags festoon the ceiling of the language corridor. There is art, and it's very good, but it's not spread lavishly around the place (apart from a few entrance displays: a sleepy china pig in bed with many covers, pop art shoes, and the school birthday quilt which all pupils embroidered). School is extremely well ordered, with tidy notice boards.

Chosen by one parent who moved to the area for the selective grammars, but fell for Talbot Heath. She 'loved the calmness... the silence during lessons, and the sense of purpose [in the school]'. One pupil, who chose the school after looking at three in the area, did so on the basis that it was the most welcoming, and said they 'focused on me as an individual.' The individual point is one frequently mentioned by parents, particularly in the context of the local school options: the grammars are big and impersonal, you're just one of the crowd; here teachers treat girls as individuals and want them to succeed. The grammars expect 14 GCSEs. Only nine or 10 taken at Talbot Heath, to make time for the rest of life – for sport, music and drama. One sixth former said she felt she had learnt that you need to spend time doing things just because you enjoy them.

Navy uniform, with a super blue cloak for the juniors (or coat alternative for the self-conscious). No uniform for sixth formers, and although there is the standard no-denim rule, girls succeed in looking very relaxed in skirts and leggings. More comfortable than smart, but these girls have a tremendous sense of purpose. Sixth form common rooms with kitchen facilities, with which they are tremendously pleased. The girls appreciate being treated more like adults in the sixth form, and like the tutorial feel of some of the lessons – cosy further maths lessons for two at the moment. The sixth formers we met were friendly and articulate, but didn't have that public school confidence bordering on arrogance.

Communication good – they do take notice of feedback, said a parent who had protested about the large amount of homework expected of year 9 compared to other independent schools. Another said 'food...is the biggest moan,' but she thought the school was trying to address the issue (on the day of our visit it varied from average pasta to excellent sticky toffee pudding). Parent Staff Society (PSS) meets every three months and responds to every point raised: apparently the PSS works hard to try and keep parents involved after the increase in independence expected of the girls after the move to senior school. Parent portal has got better recently, and the school is proud of its new website.

Pastoral care, well-being and discipline: Junior girls were friendly and articulate, with ready smiles. Leapt to their feet as we toured the school and were very prompt with their 'good morning' chant. School is strong on discipline; or 'strict in a nice way,' as one parent put it. 'Old fashioned values [and] a lot of respect,' said another. Traditional system of demerits plus stars and badges for rewards. Praise for exceptional performance, but also exceptional behaviour of any sort. Harold the toy hare goes home each week with someone who has been especially kind.

Community and the high level of pastoral support greatly praised by parents: 'they always find time for the girls'. Very strong on anti-bullying – anything dealt with very efficiently, agree parents. All girls 'feel slights' and the school says it manages them carefully. They will sit down with someone who is upset; but it often just comes down to thoughtless comments.

Transition (at 11) between junior and senior schools is easy, say parents. Year 6s go to the senior school daily for lunch to help them find their feet. Own school exam to gain entry to senior school. Girls are well prepared and most, but not all, pass. For those who don't make it, every assistance will be given to help find a new school.

This is a strong community, and there is a great feeling of vigilance here. Teachers will go out of their way to support pupils, and parents had high praise for their efforts. It's a very supportive environment, and several parents commented on the girls' tendency to encourage and care for each other – 'they positively want each other to succeed'.

Senior school head says there is a strong ethos of respect and care, so those who don't follow this stand out a mile, fitting with school motto – 'honour before honours' (one does feel a hint of Malory Towers here). The school aims to resolve any issues rapidly, and through discussion: 'this is a talking school,' says the head. Differences of opinion are usually sorted by consultation. One parent described how a personality clash between her daughter and another child was sorted out amicably and quickly by coming in to discuss it. Staff are very approachable, say parents, and it's easy to come in and talk.

Usual system of sanctions for unsatisfactory work or behaviour. No one we spoke to had come across drug taking of any sort – of course they experiment at some point, said one parent, but the strong school culture militates against it, at least on school premises.

Pupils and parents: Pupils both from the immediate area and further afield, by bike, train and school buses. About three-quarters of boarders from overseas, and Forces parents – also the tennis whizz kids, who work long days and find it helpful to be on site.

Some comfortably affluent parents, but most feel it's a big decision to pay for education, and those who fork out have academic results as their main priority. Typically both parents work, and they don't have elaborate holidays. Wouldn't suit one-dimensional girls, suggested one parent; nor, with its academic emphasis, those looking for a more vocational education. Not a posh school.

Former pupils include Judge Cosgrave, Lady Faithful (social worker and reformer), Charlie Lee-Potter (journalist), Pat Smythe (show jumper), Natalie Clein (cellist), Dame Shirley Williams (politician), Kate Royal (opera singer), Nicole Faraday (actress), Caroline Gledhill (engineer) and Frances Ashcroft (geneticist).

Entrance: Not selective until year 2, and pretty much takes all comers. From year 2 onwards girls are tested in English, maths and verbal reasoning, with a head teacher's report.

Own exam at 11+ – maths, English and verbal reasoning. Waiting lists for some years, currently 10-12. Most juniors pass the exam to progress to the senior school.

Exit: Nearly all juniors to the senior school. Most of the rest to local grammars, a few to other state schools. Lose some to the grammar, mostly for financial reasons, although around 30 per cent depart before sixth form to study something more unusual. They depart after sixth form to universities all over eg London, Exeter and Southampton; two to Oxbridge in 2016. Subjects range from veterinary medicine and law to animal behaviour.

Money matters: Parents say the school is cheaper than many independent schools in the area, and very good value for money. 'Prices could go up, and we would still go,' said one parent with enthusiasm. 'Bargain,' said another. Around a quarter of pupils are on scholarships or bursaries of around 10-20 per cent.

Remarks: Does what it says on the packet: a first class education for girls, provided with a great sense of purpose and vigour. Though academic, sport also strong, and excels in accommodating sporting and other extracurricular specialists. Feels like a very safe and caring environment. Better introduce boys yourself along the way though, suggested one parent, or some girls could go a bit crazy at university.

Taunton School

Staplegrove Road, Taunton, Somerset TA2 6AD

Pupils: 1,496; 348 full/flexi boarders • Ages: 1-18 (boarding from 7) • Sixth form: 280

Fees: Day £6,785 – £18,375; Boarding £10,900 – £34,050 pa

Tel: 01823 703700
Email: registrar@tauntonschool.co.uk
Website: www.tauntonschool.co.uk

Headmaster: Since 2015, Lee Glaser, previously deputy head for five years. Read maths at Liverpool University before qualifying as a chartered accountant with Coopers and Lybrand, and then teaching at Millfield School as senior master and director of sport.

Head of prep: Since 2013, Mr Duncan Sinclair MA HDE. Born in Zimbabwe, he moved to South Africa at the age of 7. Read English and environmental science at the University of Cape Town before completing a higher diploma in education. Began his teaching career in Cape Town, also coaching cricket, rugby and athletics. At the same time, he enjoyed a secondary career as a semi-professional rugby player representing Western Province as a second row forward. Moved to St Michael's Preparatory School, Kent, in 2002 where he was year 4 teacher, head of geography and PSHE and deputy head and completed his MA in educational leadership and management. In addition to taking part in competitive cricket and hockey, Mr Sinclair plays the clarinet, trombone and tuba and is a keen chorister. Married to Georgina, a primary teacher with a PE specialisation; they have a young son.

Moving on in July 2017 to head Yardley Court, part of the Schools at Somerhill. His successor will be Andrew Edwards, currently head of Park School in Bournemouth. French with German degree from Manchester; became a lawyer and worked in the City before turning to education. Has also taught at Port Regis School and Castle Court Prep. He is married to Robyn, a sport, French and primary school class teacher, and they have two sons.

Academic matters: Results are sound considering the non-selective intake: 34 per cent A*/A at A level in 2016, 51 per cent at GCSE. IB diploma average score was 32.

Alongside the IB, Taunton maintains a broad curriculum culminating in 23 subjects at A level, including photography, music technology and critical thinking (a school passion and something of a hallmark). Mandarin and Chinese literature are offered as part of the IB syllabus.

Taunton's goal seems to be to produce young people that are highly motivated, fully developed and ready to meet the challenges of the 21st century. It may not be a strongly religious school, but there is whiff of Victorian 'muscular Christianity' in its ether: 'We believe we should prepare pupils for the next 50 years of their lives, not just for the next five. Our job is to equip them with values and experiences for a future anywhere in the world. We are not interested in producing children who are clones of their parents; we want them to be themselves.'

In keeping with its commitment to being prepared for change, Taunton is planning a radical overhaul of teaching in science and technology. New facilities for departments of engineering and life sciences will be created to make the academic structure more relevant to new technology and contemporary employment prospects. New courses will include robotics, electronics and computer programming plus co-curricular projects like biochemistry and green power.

Strong special needs ('learning success') department. All pupils are assessed on entry and provision is put in place, if appropriate. The department consists of a full-time head of department and five part-time teachers and is housed in its own area, which is bright and homely. There is also a 'gifted and talented' extension programme.

Games, options, the arts: The heads of art, music and drama are role models for their pupils. They spoke with passion about the importance of their departments and the value of their subjects to the youngsters. We were treated to Bach on the chapel organ (a spontaneous moment, not a pre-arranged performance) and a drama rehearsal by a group of boys who all seemed to be in touch with their inner Kenneth Branagh, and witnessed myriad examples of paintings, sculptures, installations and photography.

Lessons are offered on an astonishing variety of instruments. There is an orchestra, a jazz band, a clarinet ensemble and a percussion group amongst other formal and informal groups. Some 60 per cent of pupils learn at least one instrument and there are over 100 in the (voluntary) choir. A smaller and selected singing group, coached and conducted by a flaming-haired Celt who could charm sweet music out of a buffalo, has recently sung in Venice. Previous destinations have included Rome, Barcelona and Prague.

The design technology department is a delight, with tools and machines from modern digital gizmos to old fashioned benches, vices and even a huge anvil a traditional blacksmith would be proud of. It is also the proud manufacturer of a 'Greenpower' car. When we asked about the teaching of craft skills, the answer was short and sweet, 'The pupils confront the task, work out what skills they need to meet it and then acquire them; they could involve a laser or a carpenter's mallet and chisel.'

Sport and exercise are high priority for staff as well as pupils: the registrar is an ultra-runner and the head of classics, in addition to a PhD in classical literature, has the muscles of a body-builder. When he's not describing the deeds of the heroes of the Trojan War, he can be found pumping iron in the school's new fitness centre, an amazing facility that looks like a private members' gym and which earns outside revenue for the school.

There is an abundance of more traditional fields of play, including 20 tennis courts, three gymnasiums, two swimming pools and a pair of Astroturf pitches. Competitive sport thrives at all levels and county-level participation is given precedence over school fixtures. As a consequence, results are excellent and individual achievements impressive.

The range of extracurricular options at Taunton is fascinating. Radio astronomy, green power, rifle shooting, Warhammer and vocal funk are just a few of the more unusual on offer. There's also healthy uptake for D of E and CCF, and we were assured that the senior wind band was an ensemble of musicians, not a nickname for the staff common room.

T

Boarding: Around 60 per cent of boarders are from overseas. Five senior boarding houses – three for boys and two for girls – plus one co-ed prep boarding house. The prep school dormitory arrangements (girls' named after hills and boys' after rivers) were very popular with our guides, as were the (segregated) common rooms with televisions, presided over by a splendid matron who said she enjoyed being at 'the hub of things'. Tasters are available. Most stay at weekends, when there is a rota of activities which includes conservation projects, clay pigeon shooting, cycle trips along the local canal, house cookery, fishing, house outings to theme parks and castle visits and picnics. All very jolly.

Background and atmosphere: Taunton's grand neo-gothic Victorian exterior conforms to the popular image of a traditional independent school. The tall clock tower and spire overlooking immaculate lawns and flowerbeds is archetypal, likewise the long corridor of gothic arches and wood panelling. But don't be fooled, this school is far from being educationally conservative, declaring, '...we have little time for social pretence,' and is proud that it has 'no snobs and no yobs'. Typically, a recent trip to China was subsidised at a fixed price of £200 per head to ensure that as many children as possible had the chance to go.

Established in 1847 as an inter-denominational foundation for the sons of nonconformists, and co-ed since 1973, Taunton still has a radical feel. Overtly non-selective, the banner headline for its very glossy, highly professional marketing literature (also emblazoned on its huge fleet of buses) is 'Offering More'. For that, read 'more' than a narrow commitment to academic success; 'more' than sport; 'more' than a single focus on a particular kind of education. Taunton's goal seems to be to produce young people from John Newton's mould: highly motivated, fully developed people ready to meet the challenges of the 21st century.

Staff, parents and pupils alike claimed that, despite its strong work ethic and drive to succeed, Taunton is a very friendly and relaxed place to live and work. Our experience, from two nourishing visits to the dining hall and a parents' evening, where we were left to roam and natter to our hearts' content, suggests that Taunton has got the balance exactly right. The staff mingled jovially, the parents smiled appreciatively and the youngsters behaved like responsible young adults.

Our charming 'minder' was a model English gentleman, except that he was Bulgarian, a product of the school's strong international perspective. Taunton International School, a 9 to 17 adjunct to the main school, serves as a proving ground for foreign students preparing to join the English system, and runs a programme for Taunton youngsters hoping to go to university in America.

Pastoral care, well-being and discipline: The matter of bullying is tackled thoroughly in the prep. 'Buddy Groups' – vertical rather than horizontal – meet regularly, as do form captains. In groups and assemblies all are constantly reminded that 'different people have different sensibilities.' Leavers' questionnaires deal with the topic and regular self-assessment reports provide opportunities for airing anxieties. There is even, rather touchingly, a Friendship Bench overlooking the playground. The story is told of an exhausted member of staff plonking himself on the bench only to be approached by a young child asking if he had no friends.

The core of the pastoral system at Taunton is the five boarding houses and six day houses. Each housemaster/mistress is responsible for each pupil's well-being and progress and is the first point of contact for parents. They are supported by a house assistant and a team of house tutors. There is a chaplain, a health centre and school prefects. Peer monitoring is encouraged and an 'independent listener' is available by phone.

School is savvy enough to realise that society's ills lurk everywhere and that to keep them at the gates takes constant vigilance. School believes that experienced house staff are vital. They must be able to 'read the tea leaves' and sniff and smell for problems when they are brewing, not when it is too late. Reassuringly, school does not pretend that Taunton is free of the problems that afflict us all, but is confident that most are nipped in the bud, or, on the occasions when they become more serious, are dealt with quickly and appropriately. Parents concurred with this: 'The school is relaxed, but the children know where the boundaries are'. The young people we spoke to agreed. 'The senior staff set a good example, they're easy to talk to, but you respect them because we all know how much they do for us'.

'Most problems are dealt with in our houses, even if they've come in from outside. It's very unusual for anyone to be unhappy here'.

Pupils and parents: Taunton is a modern school for modern times. We met confident, articulate young people and grateful and contented parents. The staff were evangelists for their subjects and it was easy to imagine the positive impact they have on their students.

Parents are a cross-section of society from a huge catchment area; bus routes run from as far away as Bristol, Exeter, Yeovil and Minehead. We met farmers, teachers, nurses, small business owners, civil servants and military personnel; all were gushing in their praise: 'lovely school', 'good kids', 'the staff are great'. Several parents praised the school's inclusivity. 'Even though we live on Exmoor, we thought it was worth the effort. Both our boys have flourished, especially one of them who had dyslexia, he's flying now.'

Entrance: There are three rungs to the school's ladder. Entry into the nursery classes; then the pre-prep; and finally at 7+ the prep school itself. The first two rungs involve no formal assessment, but rather familiarisation sessions to ensure all parties are happy. Entry into the prep school in year 3 is when those moving up from the pre-prep are joined by some half dozen or so new pupils. Since the prep school year groups grow in size from 36 in year 3 to 72 in year 7, entry is usually possible at all ages. Potential prep school pupils spend a day in the school individually or in pairs, joining their peers for lessons, before sitting papers in maths, English and non-verbal reasoning.

Seventy per cent of the senior school intake comes from the prep. External entrants take common entrance, but school insists that the interview is more critical, as is the report from the child's previous head.

Entry at 16+ normally conditional on a minimum of five GCSEs at grade A* to C, but, again, the interview is also important.

Exit: Most prep school pupils move up to the senior school. No CE but children are setted according to the prep school exams and detailed reports. The headmasters of the prep and senior schools have regular meetings, anyway. Entry to the senior school is almost, but not quite, automatic. Occasionally pupils are recognised as not being up to it and are 'diverted to somewhere else where they can succeed.' The school aims to help the parents select a suitable alternative and to avoid sudden hatchet jobs. Occasionally parents do choose to send their children elsewhere; in the last few years pupils have won scholarships to Winchester, Millfield and Sherborne School for Girls. 'Staff love the challenge and it's healthy to have some variety.'

Up to a quarter of students leave after GCSE. Taunton does not offer vocational courses so it believes most leavers at this stage have reached their academic ceiling and need to go elsewhere to continue their education or vocation. Post A level, 96 per cent of leavers go to universities or colleges (UK and abroad). Four medics, a vet and a dentist in 2016.

Money matters: There are scholarships at 11, 13 and 16 for academic, music, art, sport and all-rounders.

Remarks: Prospective parents can be confident that whatever the future holds, the Taunton School team will give your children the best possible chance of meeting its challenges.

The Thomas Hardye School

Queen's Avenue, Dorchester, Dorset DT1 2ET

Pupils: 2,150 • Ages: 13–18 • Sixth form: 780

Tel: 01305 266064
Email: admin@thomas-hardye.net
Website: www.thomas-hardye.net

Headteacher: Since 2011, Mike Foley BA MEd (50s). Educated at The John Fisher School in Purley, Surrey, then St Mary's University, Twickenham, where he read history. He originally planned a career in law but decided to do a PGCE first – 'someone said it would stand me in good stead' – and found that he loved teaching. More than 30 years on, he still loves it. When we met him he was looking forward to teaching an A level history class on his favourite subject, the English Civil War. First job was at Kesgrove High School in Ipswich, where he had 'an inspirational' head of department. 'He still inspires me to this day,' he says. 'One simple thing I took on board was that when students walk into the classroom you should have the room set out for the lesson. They immediately know you mean business.' Worked at a range of schools before becoming head of Great Cornard Upper School in Sudbury, Suffolk (now Thomas Gainsborough School) for nine years. Along the way he did an MEd at Cambridge.

The Thomas Hardye School was already an outstanding school when he arrived and friends joked that becoming head would be like taking over at Manchester United. 'But I always have this philosophy that no matter how good something is it can always be better,' he says. Sure enough, the school has gone from strength to strength under his leadership. One of his key aims from the start was to ensure that even though the school is huge 'we make sure that every youngster is monitored, looked after and cared for.' He brought in a new college system, dividing the school into four mixed-age colleges. Each college is led by a teacher but also has a guidance leader – a non-teaching member of staff who is responsible for pastoral care and day-to-day issues. Rather than staying at their desks, the school's leadership team is out and about throughout the day, including breaks and lunchtimes, ensuring that problems are picked up quickly and dealt with.

Head firmly believes that it's crucial for pupils to get off to a good start the moment they arrive in year 9. 'People establish patterns of behaviour from day one,' he says. 'When the year 9s come in all the staff are available and we make sure that no one leaves school that day with a worry – or if they have a worry we make sure we know about it.' At the start of the autumn term he emphasises to year 11, 12 and 13 students that they have 32 weeks at school before study leave and by half term almost a quarter of the year's teaching time will have gone. 'We tell them that every lesson and every day has to count,' he says. Wise words indeed.

Wife Teresa is a secondary teacher and they have four children – the elder two are at university and the younger two are pupils at Thomas Hardye. He's a season ticket holder at Crystal Palace and enjoys sport, skiing, reading and travel.

Academic matters: In 2015, 67 per cent A*-C including English and maths; 36 per cent A*/A at A level and 83 per cent A*-C. All the usual subjects on offer at A level (maths the strongest subject), plus accounts, business studies, economics, electronics, food tech, media studies, performance studies, sociology and travel and tourism. Also offers the EPQ (extended project qualification) and CACHE diploma in childcare and education.

School achieves impressive value added scores. Most recent was 1030 – the equivalent of every pupil achieving half a GCSE grade higher in all their subjects than students of similar ability nationally. Assistant head attributes this to 'high expectations, purposeful atmosphere, focus on learning and the dedication of the staff.' Although year groups are big (between 400 and 450 pupils), class sizes are relatively small. GCSE classes, for example, tend to be between 10 and 22. Pupils are set for maths while English is taught in mixed ability classes. Most do a language (French or German) at GCSE. Science is strong here – 18 labs, enrichment activities and community lectures ranging from 'what are black holes and how can we study them?' to 'the story of the aurora.' School has appointed an industry partnership development manager who forges links with local companies. School is above average when it comes to numbers of girls taking STEM (science, technology, engineering and maths) subjects but is determined to improve further. Also working hard to close gap in attainment of pupil premium students (a total of 120 in the school).

School has a physical disability base and a speech and language base, each with 15 pupils. Six per cent of pupils on SEN register – support given one-to-one, in small groups and before start of school. Head takes the view that 'everyone is a learner, no one is the finished article' and teachers are encouraged to do their own research projects too. School operates on a two-week timetable but pupils say they soon get used to it. Impressive library, opened by novelist Tracy Chevalier in 2010, with 22,000 resources, 32 laptops and 14 computers. Librarians encourage reading for pleasure and popular choices include John Green, Robert Muchamore and Manga.

Games, options, the arts: Sports facilities are excellent – floodlit Astroturf, sports hall with climbing wall, fitness suite and dance studios and acres of playing fields, plus use of neighbouring leisure centre (with two swimming pools, no less). School concentrates on traditional sports – rugby, football (boys and girls), netball, cross-country, athletics, cricket and swimming. 'We're a very sporty school,' the dynamic deputy of PE told us. Outdoor education is part of the curriculum, with activities like sailing (the Jurassic coast isn't far), kayaking, water polo and the Basic Expedition Leaders Award.

Art, music, drama and dance departments buzz with activity. Art department has six staff, all with different specialisms – from painting and sculpture to printmaking and animation. More than 180 individual instrument lessons every week and loads of ensembles to join – orchestras, concert band, wind band, jazz orchestra, rock groups, chapel choir, the list goes on and on. Music popular at GCSE and A level. Music and dance tour abroad every two years – they're off to Rhineland in 2016. Drama in school's own theatre and two performing arts studios. Regular student productions, with frequent visits by professional performers and companies too.

Loads of extracurricular clubs at lunchtime and after school – electronics, Raspberry Pi, murder mystery, fossils to name but a few. CCF, D of E, Model United, plus a host of charity events and trips. Sixth form pupils visit the US and Russia in alternate years.

Background and atmosphere: Thomas Hardye founded the first free school in Dorchester in 1569, with five pupils on the school roll. The school has nothing to do with renowned Dorset novelist Thomas Hardy, who somewhat confusingly attended Mr. Last's Academy for Young Gentlemen in Dorchester in the 1850s. School doubled in size in 1993 when it amalgamated with a girls' school. Today it's even bigger, with more than 2,000 pupils and 780 in the sixth form alone. 'I think we're the biggest school-based sixth form in the country,' says the assistant head. Belongs to Dorchester Area Schools Partnership (comprising 15 first schools, three middle schools and Thomas Hardye itself), which means there's masses of collaboration, especially when it comes to staff training and development. School is situated at the end of a long, tree-lined avenue on the edge of Dorchester. Swish office and reception area in central redbrick building, plus lots of modern additions, including £2.7 million English and modern languages block with glass atrium.

School has a real 'can-do' approach. Younger pupils look up to sixth formers and sixth formers mentor the younger ones. 'There is nowhere else like this place on terms of the atmosphere and ethos,' the assistant head told us and as we walked round the school with two keen as mustard year 10s we had to agree. Despite its size the atmosphere is calm and purposeful, no rushing about or chaotic corridors. 'It's quite a grown-up sort of place,' agreed one of our young guides. 'We don't have a lot of rules,' the head told us. 'We give pupils a degree of responsibility and they respond to that. Behaviour here is outstanding. That's not to say we don't have some difficult youngsters but the vast majority are a delight.' No permanent exclusions in recent years and fixed term exclusions 'very low.'

Smart uniform – blazers, white shirts and college ties, plus grey skirts or trousers for girls and grey trousers for boys. Sixth formers can wear what they like, within reason. School says (very sensibly): 'We do not think that denim shorts, very short skirts, skintight leggings or clothing with inappropriate slogans are suitable for school.' Sixth formers have their own centre, with a huge common room, study area and mini-canteen. Main school canteen opens for breakfast at 8.15am.

Pastoral care, well-being and discipline: Prospective parents often worry about the sheer size of the place but it doesn't seem to be an issue once pupils start. Children are divided into manageable-sized year groups and colleges and say it works well. Good induction – thanks to Thomas Hardye's partnership with local primary and middle schools most pupils know the school reasonably well by the time they arrive in year 9. 'And we get maps to help us find our way round,' said a year 10 girl appreciatively.

Pupils join one of four colleges, all named after the original signatories of the school's 16th century foundation deed – Henning, Napier, Stratford and Trenchard. Each college has a college leader, deputy college leader and guidance leader (one of whom is an ex-police officer). All four colleges are further divided into five year 9 tutor groups, five year 10 tutor groups and five year 11 tutor groups and pupils see their tutor before lessons and after lunch every day. School's 2015 Ofsted report described its pastoral leadership as 'remarkable' and noted that the college system meant that all pupils 'are known as individuals.'

Pupils and parents: Pupils come from a vast range of backgrounds, from very disadvantaged families to the incredibly privileged. Head says that one of the things he's most proud of is the school's 'inclusivity.' Before he arrived a parental quibble was that they'd like to be more involved. School has addressed this by running a parents' focus group to share ideas and trial new initiatives.

Entrance: At 13, most pupils come from three middle schools, two in Dorchester and one in nearby Puddletown, plus a few from Weymouth and a handful from Sunninghill, a Dorchester prep. At 16 the catchment area widens considerably, with pupils travelling from as far afield as Bridport, Lyme Regis, Axminster, Sherborne, Poole and Bournemouth. Most arrive by bus (there's a 16-19 bursary fund for students who struggle with the cost of transport, trips and equipment) but a few drive (there's plenty of parking). School asks for at least five Bs at GCSE but says 'everything is case specific.'

Exit: Around 10 per cent leave after GCSEs, for apprenticeships, employment or to do vocational courses at Weymouth College and Kingston Maurward College. At 18, 90 per cent to higher education, including half to Russell Group and an average of 10 to Oxbridge each year (eight in 2015). Popular destinations include Exeter, Cardiff, Bath, Southampton, Bournemouth and London.

Remarks: A well-run, purposeful comprehensive. Its impressive results, value added scores, high expectations and excellent leadership show a school at the top of its game. Rather than resting on its laurels though, Thomas Hardye is determined to get even better.

Thomas Telford School

Old Park, Telford, Shropshire TF3 4NW

Pupils: 1,339 • Ages: 11–18 • Sixth form: 447

Tel: 01952 200000
Email: jhart@ttsonline.net
Website: www.ttsonline.net

Headmaster: Since the creation of the school in 1991, Sir Kevin Satchwell BA, OU education degree plus a diploma in educational management. Taught PE, ran his department in two schools, then deputy head in Kirkby and head of Moseley Park in Wolverhampton, before being appointed as TTS's founding head, with the brief 'to raise educational standards in Telford and Wolverhampton'. Softly spoken, direct, utterly committed to engaging the children, 'the child comes first, always'. Says there is nothing better than being in the company of his pupils, 'it's uplifting'. Uncompromising about the delivery of exceptional outcomes; thinks nothing of overturning conventions (eg the school has two three-hour learning sessions a day) and sees teachers not as imparting knowledge but as catalysts in the process of enabling children to become autonomous learners, 'it's not about being the fount of all knowledge'. Gives the children real responsibilities: 'We gave them the choice between outdoor learning areas and a swimming pool. They chose the pool'. 'Sir Kev' remains part of the personal tutor team, holds regular working lunches with students of all ages, and runs one of the school football teams. An exceptional man adored by his pupils; 'When he talks you feel he talks directly to you'.

Academic matters: The academic standards are at the heart of the school, and 98 per cent got five GCSEs at A*-C including maths and English in 2016 (following its full house in 2014), with 42 per cent of grades A*/A. For a school that takes children from the full spectrum of ability, this is an extraordinary result. With its unusual timetabling (two three-hour sessions a day) and longer working week (each child has about 30 hours of lessons a week compared to a state school average of 24), each pupil has simply more time to get to grips with the curriculum. What's more, GCSEs are taught over three years so students have an extra year of 30 hour weeks to get up to speed. It works. The whole year's curriculum is prepared the previous summer and is available to the students online at any time. Teachers are there to 'facilitate, share and excite,' but all teach the same lessons, planned centrally in advance. At A level, 21 courses are offered, plus BTecs in hospitality, performing arts and sports. Results are strong – in 2016, 66 per cent A*-B, 43 per cent A*/A.

Reports are sent to parents every four weeks, to be signed, commented upon and returned, very tight oversight of academic work. In addition to the normal compulsory curriculum, everyone takes business GCSE and a modern language. Geography and history provide the springboard for lots of trips abroad – Belgium, Spain, Italy. Help is available to those who might not be able to afford such trips without assistance. As a technology college, sciences, maths and business make a particularly strong showing, but vocational courses are also very popular – a lot of performing arts courses available in the sixth form as well as sports studies, hospitality and health & social care. Modern language dept is described as a 'small but strong' department and offers a choice of Spanish, French and German.

Learning facilities are impressive throughout – stacks of networked computers, well-equipped labs, DT rooms and workshops. Learning spaces are large, well lit and well maintained. Strong careers advice too, with a walk-in service for sixth form students, lots of support and ideas posted through the school website. Good support for those with special educational needs and the buildings are readily accessible to those with physical disabilities.

Games, options, the arts: Excellent sports facilities including a fabulous gym, floodlit pitches, Astroturfs and a massive swimming pool. Lots of cricket, hockey, athletics, football, recently rugby as well. Sportsmark. Strong student representation at district and county level. Many students also involved in D of E, and over 100 taking individual music lessons. Performing arts are very strong with many opportunities to play in the school bands, sing in the choir, etc. A great theatre which is used to stage some stunning productions – good dance too. In addition public speaking, Young Enterprise and a host of placements available to gain work experience with local industry and business. This interaction is a feature of the school which is clearly valued both by pupils and parents.

Background and atmosphere: The school buildings themselves are kept to an extremely high standard – no loose plaster on the walls, no dirty floors or damp smelling corridors. No bells ringing, no mess anywhere. The work of the students is displayed proudly, and the school media team produces weekly videos of the pupil of the week, and the school news, uploaded onto the school website. Students say, 'it's hard work,' but 'you get out what you put in', and, 'we work as a team'. Staff remark on the respectful, collaborative relationships with children and the unequivocal support from parents. Pupils, parents and staff all remark on high levels of expectation, courtesy and co-operation.

The school is housed in an attractive purpose-built campus; plenty of open spaces, including open areas where two or three classes are taught simultaneously. The 'work hard, play hard' ethos seems to permeate. Everything, from the toilets upwards, is built, maintained and presented beautifully. Uniform is worn neatly, top buttons done up – older pupils say, 'it matters because the little things lead to big things'. It's a pretty secular place – with a multicultural catchment area, it has all the standard RE and PSHE, and plenty of information about the diversity of life – but not much in the way of formal religious content of any sort, if that's your bag.

An 'incredibly supportive governing body' (the principal sponsors of the school are Tarmac and the Mercer's company) has enabled ongoing enhancement of the school's resources in IT, sports facilities etc.

Pastoral care, well-being and discipline: The school takes great care of its pupils – not least in facilitating access to what's on offer: it runs coaches to and from Wolverhampton – all of which are stewarded, and later coaches also run to enable all to participate in extracurricular activities. There is daily time in tutor groups, which run vertically through the school – this seems to work very well, giving older pupils responsibility and younger pupils role models. Zero tolerance of bullying and a strong sense of mutual respect between pupils. In a large school, which appears to run on rails and might tend towards the overwhelming, pupils say that tutors work hard at nurturing diffident pupils and unearthing their talents.

Pupils and parents: The students are remarkable – speaking passionately about the self-discipline and sense of aspiration the school has fired in them, confident, articulate, polite, focused, and open. Parents, like their children, come from the full spectrum of Wolverhampton and Telford – single parents struggling to make ends meet alongside the businessmen and women of the area. They wax lyrical about the school, feel 'part of the team', and are very positive about the monthly reports home. They speak highly of the pastoral care and the 'family feel' created by the tutor groups, saying any disciplinary issues are dealt with quickly and fairly, 'every child in the school is a credit to the school'. They also love the values the children absorb, 'respect, discipline, courtesy'.

Entrance: Massively oversubscribed (1300 applicants for 182 places in year 7). No sibling or medical preference. Applicants divided into nine ability bands, with smaller percentages taken from highest and lowest bands – but they also have to provide their year 5 school report, and those in each band who score highest on aptitude for science, technology and maths get preference. Head also takes into account 'those applicants most likely to benefit from the education on offer at the School and who have the strongest motivation to succeed'.

The catchment area is basically Wolverhampton (around 30-40 per cent of places) and Telford Town (60 per cent) in accordance with 'the criteria embodied in the funding agreement between the school and the Education Secretary' when the school was founded. Granted the competition for places, it is well worth checking the details of the process early with the school's admissions office – generally, applications close in mid-September of the year prior to admission.

Parents get an opportunity to look round the school whilst the assessment of candidates is taking place, but there is no opportunity for individual visits. Some places available after GCSE – especially popular for those wanting to pursue the BTecs in performing arts and sports. Applications close in the October prior to admission.

Exit: Up to 80 per cent stay on for the sixth form and of those a large number go on to university – some 50 per cent to top universities or stage school. Eight to study medicine plus three to Oxbridge in 2016. Sheffield, Nottingham, Manchester, Liverpool and Birmingham are popular destinations. As might be expected, sciences and business are particularly strong, but there is also good representation of humanities, languages and performing arts.

Remarks: This school is exceptional whichever way you look at it, with some approaches radically different from those of conventional comprehensives. Led by an innovative and uncompromising head, who is unapologetic about a relentless drive for academic excellence, it caters for the whole spectrum of ability and background. A culture of very high expectation produces appreciative, confident and capable pupils who are delighted to be at school. No wonder that it's so heavily oversubscribed.

Torquay Boys' Grammar School

Shiphay Manor Drive, Torquay, Devon TQ2 7EL

Pupils: 1,117 • Ages: 11–18 • Sixth form: 320 (including 44 girls)

Tel: 01803 615501
Email: enquiries@tbgs.torbay.sch.uk
Website: www.tbgs.co.uk

Head: Since 2014, Peter Lawrence BSc. In his 40s, originally from the Midlands, he studied maths at Exeter University and taught at TBGS for five years in early part of his career. Left to become a head of department and taught in three comprehensives in Devon before moving to teach in Jersey. Returned to TBGS in 2001, taking roles as head of house, assistant head and then pastoral deputy head.

Now firmly settled in south west (Exeter Chiefs Season ticket holder), with his wife (she teaches maths at TBGS), he is the sixth head, and modestly proud. He says, 'it's a privilege', something he's reminded of every morning as he drives into school. His predecessors had long careers. Pete is definitely in for the long haul, but laughed at the thought of being head in 30 years. Well, you never know.

He's friendly and open, and made us feel relaxed on our wander round the school, a school he is more than happy to show off. A keen sportsman, he plays five-a-side football every Sunday (regrets it every Monday morning). He says, 'Our school mantra has long been to maintain the best of the old and combine it with the best of the new'. Parents rate him as excellent.

Academic matters: In 2016, a disappointing 32 per cent A*/A at A level (63 per cent A*-B), and 67 per cent A*/A at GCSE. Top scores in maths (regular national Maths Challenge successes), English and science. Twenty-two subjects on offer at A level. The school works with neighbouring Torquay Girls Grammar School to ensure that all options are available. One parent said, 'The school went out of its way to try and find a solution rather than asking [my son] to change his fourth option.' Choice of A level or IB in the sixth form (average score of 37 in 2016); girls can join the sixth form, but must study IB. The school also offers a range of BTecs such a health and social care and travel and tourism, in conjunction with Torquay Academy, though in reality all TBGS boys opt for A levels or IB.

TBGS has sponsored Torquay Academy (formerly Torquay Community College) and set up the Torquay Boys' Grammar School Multi-Academy Trust. The aim is to help raise standards and provide all students in Torbay, regardless of ability, the same opportunities and access to a top rate education.

Good range of MFLs on offer: Spanish, French, German, Japanese and Chinese. Now a Confucius school promoting Chinese; around 75 year 9 pupils are currently studying it, and the annual trip to China is in great demand though A level not currently offered. Every subject department has access to a dedicated IT suite; no shortage of computers, with around 800 in total. There's also a boardroom with 25 computers, dual flat screens and Reuters links, all thanks to a previous business and enterprise sponsorship. A good insight into the real thing, and high numbers of students are choosing economics at university.

SEND panel for pupils who are dyslexic or have problems with numeracy; two are currently statemented. SEND panel also deals with all emotional support and counselling for the pupils. Ofsted report says, 'This drive for academic achievement is balanced by a deep commitment to students' wider personal and social development.' Achievements, academic or otherwise, are all commended regularly. Pupils are given 'effort grades' for each subject on a termly basis, and screens around the school announce the latest Student of the Week award. One parent said, 'It really does encourage the students to do well.'

Games, options, the arts: National football champions three times in recent years; one recent ex-student has been selected for the U20 England rugby team this year; cross-country, hockey, athletics, cricket and tennis also on offer. Strong tradition in swimming and water-polo. Ex-pupil, teacher and swimming champion from the 1940s now coaches the very successful teams.

As expected, facilities are impressive. Sports hall large enough for four badminton courts, with viewing gallery (also kitted out for seminar-type lessons for A level PE students). Astroturf shared with TGGS next door, plus a half-size one. Five hours of PE a fortnight. Matches on Wednesday afternoons or after school. Outdoor education classes for years 7, 8, 9 include lifesaving (beach and pool), potholing, canoeing, rock-climbing, orienteering and sailing. Large numbers of students take on Ten Tors (school holds 45 mile record time), D of E and occasionally Three Peaks Challenge.

Parents say, 'The school has a very strong music department, which encourages musicians and puts on numerous concerts, including a musical, every year.' New block with light and spacious rooms. All year 7 students are given the opportunity to learn a brass or woodwind instrument for a year and take part in the annual concert. Many continue with private lessons. Jazz band recently played at Montreux Jazz Festival. Upcoming trip to Grenoble for the orchestra and choir. Full scale musical each year at end of spring term; tickets on sale for The Sound Of Music when we visited.

Recent improvements to the drama facilities include a new theatre and a well-equipped studio. Media studies also popular, students heavily involved with film-making, local radio and podcasts.

Brilliant art department in the newly refurbished Manor House. The art on display was of extremely high standard, with a huge variety of styles and techniques: aboriginal paintings, cartoons, pop-art, portraits, masks, sculpture and digital design. Average of 30 students in each sixth form year study art.

DT also has well-designed space, with workshops set around a central foyer and spiral staircase. This is a good example of the old working well with the new. As well as the traditional workshops, there are CADCAM suites, laser-cutters and the latest production software. Good displays showing the history of product design – The Mini Story and The Story of the Portable Music Player. Cabinets full of clocks by year 7 plus impressive A level assessment pieces on display.

Huge choice of clubs and activities at lunchtimes and after school; they even offer mountain-biking, fencing and golf. The orienteering club recently won the national championship, so they're now off to Turkey to compete in the World Schools competition. Chess is also prominent, and top players have gone on to win at national and international level. Local Air Training Corps has HQ on site, and the school has its own scout troop. Astronomy club is lucky enough to have a refurbished observatory with a brand new Celestron C1400 telescope on site. The school's patron was famous astronomer, Sir Patrick Moore, and is now Chris Lintott, Sky at Night presenter, a past pupil.

Trips aplenty. All the usual foreign exchanges plus departmental trips – art to Barcelona, philosophy and applied ethics to India, biology to Costa Rica, geography to Snowdonia and Iceland.

Background and atmosphere: Founded in 1904 as the Pupil Teacher Centre, it relocated in 1915 and became Torquay Secondary School with just 170 boys. In 1983 the school moved to its current site, a stone's throw from Torquay town and the English Riviera. From 750 boys in four houses, they now have nearly 1,120 boys and girls in six houses. Extensive building programmes have taken place on the 40 acres through grants and investments, and the result is a well-presented and well-planned campus. A good example of this is the Cavanna Centenary Hall, which houses assemblies and theatrical productions.

Past glories and present day achievements are on display in the entrance foyer, along with uniforms of days gone by and rows and rows of school photos. Past pupils (many are parents of current pupils) love roaming the corridors studying these at school events.

Each subject area has its own IT room and each area corridor is filled with subject-led designs and artwork by pupils, or latest achievements and competitions. This immerses you in each subject, sparking interest in a fun and colourful way. The Ofsted inspectors wrote: 'The school is enthused with a lively and open atmosphere which encourages innovation and underpins a relentless drive to provide the very best education for the student'.

The Manor House is by far the oldest building on site. It has been a home, a hotel, a nightclub and a sixth form for the neighbouring girls' school. It now belongs to TBGS and was refurbished in 2013 into an impressive space for art. The old character remains with a grand, winding staircase and tall windows overlooking the grounds. Perfect gallery spaces. The stable block opposite houses a few offices and a quaint quiet study area for sixth formers. Incredibly low oak beams and a tea and coffee area make this a decent get-away-from-it-all room. One parent said, 'The environment is excellent – one that encourages the students to study – which is great, particularly if they're not very studious!'

Refurbishment of the Manor as an art centre meant the school could upgrade and expand the science laboratories. The school's annual science fair is a real crowd-pleaser and gives pupils and parents alike the opportunity to experiment and to learn – think rocket launchers and explosions.

There is a strong house system at TBGS. One parent said, 'Belonging to one of the six houses gives the students a sense of identity, and works very well for inter-house competitions. Each house [Blake, Davys, Frobisher, Gilbert, Hawkins, Ralegh – named after British seafarers] also organises events to raise money for a nominated charity each year, which builds friendships and team-building skills.' Pancakes for Malawi was one of the latest events.

Pastoral care, well-being and discipline: Parents agree that 'the school is very good with its pastoral care, which ensures that any problems are sorted out smoothly and efficiently.' Key words are 'respect' and 'responsibility' and the school hopes to develop 'well-rounded students who have a strong moral compass and compassion for others'. One parent said, 'Teachers are excellent at resolving any difficulties', and bullying is dealt with immediately and sensitively. Bullying tends to be 'boys' banter that goes too far' and is dealt with accordingly. No recent exclusions to speak of and only a few suspensions for behavioural problems. Zero tolerance on drugs.

The school employs a full-time counsellor and there is a pastoral support team. The house system also helps, by breaking the school down into smaller groups and giving the students more individual attention from heads of houses. Seniors are encouraged to take leadership roles. Year 13 students mentor years 7 to 9. Active school council – recently acquired a new recreational Astroturf as pupils complained they had nowhere to go when it was muddy. The power of a council.

Pupils and parents: Mainly local, but some live as far as Plymouth or Exeter, and many have relocated to be near the school. Parents' association changed some time ago from being a fundraising machine to running social events (no pressure to contribute). Wine & Wisdom night particularly praised. The charitable trust takes care of fundraising now.

The list of famous leavers is long. One recent addition is Olympic rower, Bill Lucas. CEO of Rated People, Chris Havemann, is the next ex-pupil booked in for speech day. Others include Chris Read (Nottinghamshire captain and former England wicket keeper); former Wimbledon tennis player Mike Sangster; newspaper mogul Sir Ray Tindle; Marcus Bateman (world champion rower); six times British swimming champion Malcolm Windeatt; Professors Simon Whittaker (St John's, Oxford), Ian Diamond (vice chancellor, Aberdeen University) and David Southwood, president of the Royal Astronomical Society. One former languages graduate, Marcus Richardson, now fluent in Serbo-Croat, became interpreter at the War Crimes Tribunal at The Hague, and Tom Ewing is one of the UK's top fund managers.

Entrance: Takes top 25 per cent. Same entrance test as two other local grammar schools. Recently changed to two CEM 11+ tests, plus maths and English. Some 270 try for 156 places. Around 70 primary schools feed in. 'The entrance process was very well organised and the school made them feel at ease,' one parent told us. 'Current sixth formers were there on the test days to assist the teachers and to look after the boys. The sixth formers were mature, courteous and excellent role models for the school. Between tests there were impromptu games of football, which helped to make the day more relaxed.' Another said, 'On the first day at TBGS there are only year 7 and year 12 pupils at school, which gives new pupils a chance to settle in and get their bearings.'

The equivalent of three As and three Bs or above for entry to sixth form. Of around 360 pupils in sixth form, around 80 are newcomers – many of them girls, who must take the IB.

Exit: In 2016, 15 per cent left after GCSEs. More than 95 per cent to university, vast majority to Russell Group universities including Oxbridge (eight places in 2016, plus one to Harvard and six medics). Other favourites are Cardiff, Bristol, Bath, Southampton, Exeter, Warwick, London. Most popular courses, engineering, science and maths.

Money matters: Families can apply for help with costs through pupil premium. All trips can be paid for in instalments. Bursaries available for sixth formers

Remarks: One of the top 20 boys' schools in the country. Deservedly so. Fantastic facilities and teaching that produces top results and very successful young men and women. Every area is given the same attention and passion, whether it's sport, maths, languages or arts. All types will find their niche here. As one parent put it, 'TBGS has been extremely supportive to all of my sons and has nurtured their individual talents. We couldn't have asked for any more. TBGS gives every child the opportunity to achieve their full potential.' Brilliant.

T

Torquay Girls' Grammar School

30 Shiphay Lane, Torquay, Devon TQ2 7DY

Pupils: 944 • Ages: 11–18 • Sixth form: 253

Tel: 01803 613215
Email: admin@tggsacademy.org
Website: www.tggs.torbay.sch.uk

Headteacher: Dr Nick Smith MB BS PGCE NPQH, a pragmatic, determined man in his late 40s, has been in the hot seat at TGGS since 2007. A qualified scientist who practised medicine for a couple of years – and yes, he did work at London Zoo looking after the penguins – he has brought the clear thinking of a trained empiricist to his task at TGGS.

Dapper, self-effacing and charming, he has brought vision and vigour to an old-fashioned grammar school. 'He knows what he wants and is relentless in achieving it' was typical of the comments we heard from parents. But we got the distinct impression within the school that the culture was not just geared towards better and better results. 'Caring for others' and 'working in a happy and caring environment' were the kind of phrases mentioned often and there was much evidence that these were not just platitudes.

Universally admired by pupils, parents and teachers alike, Dr Smith could deservedly rest on his laurels at his home on Bodmin Moor, where he lives with his wife (and fellow teacher) and two children, and from where he yomps across the Cornish wilderness (he's a former marathon runner), but he is not finished yet.

Although his justifiable claim that TGGS is very successful in 'adding value' to his incoming cohort, he wants to do much more, especially in terms of enhancing the aspirations and ambitions of his female pupils. Of course, phrases like these are often spoken by headteachers, but this man has a gleam in his eye when he uses them that is very convincing.

Ideally suited to lead an academy school, he relishes the independence it gives him and is not daunted by the chief executive challenges that come with the autonomy; in fact, he relishes them.

Academic matters: TGGS is, first and foremost, a school that sees the achievement of outstanding academic results as its primary responsibility. The girls are encouraged to work hard and aim high. There is an aura of quiet industry about the place. There was an absence of the more typical mayhem of narrow corridors channelling too many youngsters to the next lesson and of doors being slammed with teachers bellowing orders over the din.

But the girls do not learn by rote, nor do they learn just to pass examinations. Here are the school's 'Four Common Teaching Elements', a praiseworthy benchmark for the staff: Are the girls told why they are doing this work? Are the girls made to think? Does the lesson maintain the girls' focus? Are the girls shown how to improve?

Results generally continue to progress in a steady climb and the school has the graphs to prove it. In 2016, A level figures show 83 per cent A*-B grades across 24 subjects (including a few subjects shared with Torquay Boys' Grammar School) and 51 per cent A*/A grades, with GCSE at 73 per cent A*/A – a distinct improvement on the year before.

The curriculum is described in great detail in a lengthy booklet, part of an elaborate set of marketing brochures (although they would all benefit from some diligent proof-reading) which are not unlike the glossy sales material of a private school. There is plenty of detail for each department, a 'Careers' box, which lists the likely employment destinations in that subject area, and useful lists of 'Students will need to', which itemise 'compulsory' and 'optional' study requirements. At 40 pages of A4 in a small font size, it is a heavy read, but a good one.

The school is proud of its membership of the South West Academic Trust, an elite 'Russell Group' of nine Wessex schools in association with the University of Exeter, which brings shared values and commitment to excellence.

Although TGGS is a humanities specialist school, with geography being particularly strong, it has strengths across the curriculum, including good biology, maths and art departments. It also offers the AQA Baccalaureate in the sixth form and has introduced innovations like academic mentoring, where older girls support younger ones in a Big Red Bus bought specifically to provide a novel environment for the initiative. Although it is something of an endearing gimmick, it works; the girls cherish it – 'It's our space, we love it' – and Dr Smith readily embraces gimmicks that produce results.

The school has kept pace with technological change and many teaching spaces bristle with digital gizmos of all kinds. Those of us in the older echelons of the population might be daunted by it all, but we were impressed that both teachers and staff talked about learning together through the internet and that whiteboards, YouTube and social media outlets are as much part of the teaching fabric as blackboard and chalk were in the past.

Another important didactic tool is the list of learning skills, which gives 16 semantic anchor points for the school's aspirations. Key words like Concentration, Resilience, Collaboration and Creativity are recited like a catechism throughout the school by both staff and pupils. It is a somewhat clichéd mechanism, but again, it works and focuses everyone on the school's aspirations.

There is an admirable procedure to support those girls who find the rarefied intellectual atmosphere difficult. The incoming intake is assessed by the MidYIS cognitive test and all the girls are then colour-coded on a huge display board in the staffroom. This then becomes the touchstone for the girls' progress throughout their school careers. Significantly, there are clear strategies for girls who are at the bottom of the league and those who start to slip downwards. In some years it can be as many as 15 (slightly more than 10 per cent of the intake), in other years it can be as few as five.

Driven by its own imperative of ensuring that all girls achieve a minimum of five A*/As at GCSE, underperforming girls are supported by a study programme hallowed silence in the school's study centre, run by two full-time members of staff. Girls can be taken off timetable, or subjects dropped, to create more time to concentrate on other priorities.

Each of the senior staff, including the head, 'adopts' up to five girls in this category and becomes their mentor through this remedial programme. All the while, the objective, in a telling phrase, is the desire 'to get them through', a worthy sentiment that is mirrored in the school's approach to any girls who may be having emotional or behavioural problems, or issues at home. At examination time they can engage in a study programme which provides breakfast, keynote sessions and revision in the library.

Games, options, the arts: There is a wide range of sports on offer, both within the curriculum and as out-of-school activities, some more esoteric than others. They include aerobics, cricket, fitball, boxercise, hockey, netball, tennis, badminton, rounders, swimming, outdoor pursuits, athletics and football. There are also options offered externally in scuba diving, mountain biking, dry-slope skiing, squash, horse riding, sailing and windsurfing. Fixtures are frequent and at all levels and there is success at local, county and national level.

It is a huge list; but is sport a major priority at the school? It appeared to us to be more about 'rounding' the girls, and an opportunity for them to let off steam, than central to school life.

Facilities are good and improving, including an Astroturf, plus a second one shared with their neighbours (Torquay Boys'), and a brand new sports hall, replacing the antiquated, yet evocative, previous hall, which had the wooden wall bars and climbing ropes many of us remember from our own school days – ah, happy memories!

There is a very strong art department with commendable results and its impressive work is on display around the school. The music, media and drama suites are modern and there is a range of drama productions and performances from the orchestra, choir, flute group and jazz band. New amphitheatre for performing arts built to celebrate the school's centenary in 2015.

There is a somewhat whimsical House Culture Calendar, which includes several Dr Smith 'traditions' designed to bring the school its own idiosyncratic identity. They include the House Shout, where the girls and the staff in each house sing a song of their choice at the end of term assembly, and the formal handover ceremony of the head girl's jacket – as at the Augusta Masters' golf tournament.

These 'Smith traditions' are a consequence of something he was told when he arrived at the school in 2007: that the school was proud of its long-standing traditions. But when he asked what they were, he found that nothing of substance was forthcoming, other than that the school had been around for a while. Thus, his innovations: the Culture Calendar, Big Red Bus, 'Shouts' and other clever mechanisms designed to bring an old-fashioned school into the 21st century.

The list of clubs, trips and activities is exceptional. Not surprisingly, given the school's proximity to the marvels of Dartmoor, the Duke of Edinburgh Award is prominent, as is the Ten Tors Challenge. The school owns a residence in Brittany, to which all pupils go twice in their school career, while the current rota of trips includes: China, Cuba, Iceland, Mongolia, Nicaragua, Croatia (to study Adriatic dolphins) and Kenya, where TGGS supports a local school. Interestingly, when we questioned the unusual choice of Mongolia, the answer came back quickly, 'Because that's where the girls wanted to go.'

Background and atmosphere: 'Never judge a book by its cover'; this aphorism sits well with TGGS. Its central building is a 1939 structure with an unconvincing claim to be art deco; it is better described as pre-war drab. It is the school's least endearing feature, although new buildings, including a new dining hall and sixth form centre, help alleviate the dour central block.

Not surprisingly in this jaunty institution, nobody within the school seems to bemoan their dreary abode. In fact, they tend to nurture it like an aging relative: 'Yes, it's a bit cold in the corridors and some of the rooms are cramped, but we love it; it's our home.'

The central reception area is a motif of the school in miniature. Compact and brightly decorated, four black and white portraits of former headmistresses hark back to the old days. But everything else reflects the new TGGS. No photographs of the staff in their austere academic robes here, rather a collection of pen pictures of smiling faces, including all the non-academic staff. A new archive corridor includes a 100 year time line to help mark the 2015 centenary.

Pastoral care, well-being and discipline: The school boasts, legitimately, much pastoral care and little need for discipline. Of course, bright girls are not without problems, both behavioural and social, and TGGS has a strong pastoral care regime led by the heads of year. Inevitably, the school has 'problem' pupils like any other, but places a strong emphasis on human relationships and core values.

There is strict code on bullying; a phenomenon that pupils and parents are unanimous in reporting is almost non-existent. They are equally adamant that ill-discipline is a rarity. In an affirmation of this, the girls we spoke to were at pains to explain that they felt it is their responsibility to deal with most issues and that they hope members of staff would only need to become involved on rare occasions.

Problems are dealt with according to very clearly defined procedures. The school is proud of the commendable belief that the first line of defence in dealing with issues is the girls themselves and that it promotes an ethos of support and mutual care between them, an article of faith that was confirmed by the girls we spoke to.

Further bulwarks are the class tutors, year heads (who follow their year group up through the school), the school's own dedicated personal counsellor, a part-share of careers adviser and a visiting nurse. Finally, Dr Smith's three deputies oversee the heads of year.

When we pressed Dr Smith about where his threshold on behaviour was fixed, it was clear that he would have no hesitation in excluding a girl whose behaviour was unacceptable. Reassuringly, we were left in no doubt that he meant what he said.

Wholesome food is a top priority and a recent innovation is a cashless service (operated biometrically by thumb print) which allows parents to monitor exactly what their daughters are eating. Indeed, the entire school is cashless and every parent has an online account. The new kitchen and servery gleam and are staffed by a very cheerful group of dinner ladies.

Pupils and parents: There is a strong consensus in this focused and happy school between parents and pupils about its ambitions and ethos. 'The school punches well above its weight', 'There is a strong emphasis on decency and human values', 'The rapport between the girls and their teachers is remarkable', were a few of the positive comments from parents.

Pupils were equally voluble with their positive comments: 'It's like nowhere else', 'The staff are always there to help', 'We want to do well for them'. When asked about the school, the word 'pride' came up repeatedly from the girls. They also stressed that the pejorative terms, 'nerd' or 'boffin', sadly so common in the adolescent vocabulary, are not in the lexicon at TGGS. 'We are admired for being clever here', 'it is easier to succeed here than at schools our friends go to'.

School uniform is an uncomplicated navy blue for the main school and a black and white ensemble for sixth formers. However, the current vogue of pulling skirts up as high as they will go is a blight at TGGS, just as it is in so many schools.

Famous alumni are impressive, as they should be of course, and include leading academics, people in the media, lawyers and doctors. But Dr Smith is very committed to new employment opportunities for his girls. Because women remain underrepresented at the highest levels in many areas of employment, he feels his continuing mission is to expand the personal development of his charges, while maintaining the school's lofty academic standards. 'Encouraging future leaders in industry, finance and commerce' is his avowed cause.

Entrance: TGGS is over-subscribed and admission is based solely on ability. There are 150 places available at 11+. Selection is determined by verbal reasoning, maths and English examinations in two sessions and the intake represents the top 25 per cent on the academic scale.

About 60 girls join the sixth form from other state schools. The entry requirements are seven GCSE A*-B, plus some subject-specific requirements set out in the school's sixth form prospectus.

Exit: Some 80 per cent of girls stay on for the sixth form. Some 90 per cent to their first-choice university, around three-quarters to Russell Group institutions; three to Oxbridge in 2016 and four medics. There is a broad range of future careers for TGGS girls. A recent cohort included a typical spread of lawyers, teachers and jobs in other public sectors.

Remarks: 'Definitely one to watch' was a key phrase in our previous report. We also proffered the thought that it was time for the school to claim a 'bigger share of the limelight'. Sharp eyes would now readily attest that TGGS has indeed moved directly into the bright glare of the academic elite of the South West.

Not for nothing has the school been awarded an 'outstanding' accolade by Ofsted. If you are looking for a single-sex haven for your daughter, which places great emphasis on intellectual gifts and the future employment prospects of its girls, this is the school for you.

It does not disregard those towards the lower end of its academic intake, indeed it offers them great support and encouragement, however, it is unashamedly about nurturing excellence for as many girls as possible.

It firmly believes in creating a cheerful and caring environment and in producing rounded individuals, but is candid in stating that its primary concern is academic success.

Trinity School

Buckeridge Road, Teignmouth, Devon TQ14 8LY

Pupils: 500 • Ages: 2–18 • Sixth form: 80

Fees: Day £7,365 – £ £11,715; Boarding £18,060 – £26,115 pa

Tel: 01626 774138
Email: registrar@trinityschool.co.uk
Website: www.trinityschool.co.uk

Headmaster: Since September 2016, Mr Lawrence Coen BSc Hons (Aberystwyth), PGCE (St Lukes, Exeter), NPQH. A science teacher, specialising in biology, Mr Coen was previously senior deputy head and spent time as a residential boarding master, as well as being involved in sport and co-curricular activities at the school.

Prep school head: Since 2012 Rachel Eaton-Jones. Previously deputy at Wellington School, Somerset, she studied psychology at Bristol. Educated at boarding school herself, so Trinity is familiar territory. Although it is a traditional school, Rachel feels they are more 'contemporary' here, encouraging pupils to ask questions rather than just being told, and ultimately taking responsibility. The school is without doubt friendly. Rachel's office is a treasure trove of bits and bobs to amuse and comfort any child. Her door is always open. Parents have nothing but praise: 'The current headmistress is a real reason why I chose to have [my child] attend the prep school.' 'The head teacher manages that wonderful combination of care and love with growth, encouragement to reach their potential. Her energy is infectious and an asset to the school.' Numbers have shot up since Rachel was appointed, and the increase in pupils going to secondary grammar schools is another sign of the prep school growing stronger and stronger.

T

Academic matters: In 2016, 14 per cent A*/A grades and 31 per cent A*-B at A level. At GCSE, 11 per cent A*/A grades and 52 per cent achieved 5+ A*-C including English and maths. Results have been down over the past two years (since 2014), and can vary from year to year. Trinity is a non-selective school, catering for a wide range of academic ability. Numbers have doubled in the last 20 years to 500. Classes are still very small – rarely reach double figures. At all levels in recent years, girls have achieved far better results than the boys, although this may be a secondary effect of SEN/EAL currently being more heavily represented amongst the boys.

Nineteen options at GCSE, 18 A level subjects offered, plus BTecs in performing arts, music, sport, IT and travel and tourism. BTecs were introduced in 2014 and are becoming popular; seven pupils opted for a BTec in sport in 2016. Strong subjects across the board include maths, business studies, economics, art and psychology. A language is not compulsory at GCSE; psychology can be taken instead. RS is compulsory; everyone takes ICT at KS3 but can drop it at KS4 if taking single sciences.

Some 22 per cent of pupils have special educational needs, double the national average. Experience with dyslexia, ADHD, pragmatic and semantic disorders, autism spectrum disorder, non-verbal language difficulties, dyspraxia and general learning difficulties. Complex needs and some behavioural issues may not be catered for. The school is aware that they cannot cater for too many pupils with special needs, therefore some may be turned away after assessments. One-to-one specialist tuition with qualified SEN teachers is charged by the hour. All staff are given on-going training in-house and updated on individual pupils' IEPs. When we were there a deaf scriber and BSL signer were supporting a profoundly deaf student in a biology class. One parent told us, '[My child] has language delay and needed educational support... They have adjusted the teaching materials according to his abilities.' Other parents explained how Trinity has helped their children to become more confident. We hoped [my child] would work hard, have fun and meet new people and develop confidence. [S/he] is developing in all ways already and we have seen a huge increase in self confidence.' Providing a supportive learning environment for children that lack confidence, or have had a bad experience of learning, seems to be what Trinity does best. A parent of an oversea boarder told us, 'He had shut himself off from learning; he just lost interest in school totally. Confidence completely drained away from him.' Now, he is 'happy' and 'interested' in school again; 'teachers have been excellent at supporting him.'

Every member of staff we spoke to said they had been at Trinity for a long time, several more than a decade. Parents say, 'The teachers are extremely dynamic, passionate and enthusiastic about their topics and are always available to communicate with parents.' For some, Trinity's size is a great benefit, particularly the small classes, but sometimes this can be limiting. One parent mentioned this to us: 'For its size I think it does an excellent job but I think a larger year group, particularly in [my child's] year would be beneficial. This is not the fault of the school.'

Games, options, the arts: Great opportunities for sporty types. For such a small school they celebrate a good deal of success. Medals aplenty for the last two years in national ISA swimming and athletics championships. Tennis is a major sport and several play at county and national level, one even at international. The U13s are Devon county champions. Trinity came second in the SW schools climbing championship, and U16 runners up in the netball ISA SW finals. U11 ISA SW football champions, U9 rugby winners of local tag rugby festival, U9 South Devon badminton champions, mixed hockey Devon U11 champions, third year in a row, two pupils have been selected for the Devon U10 cricket squad, and another is the Devon U8 county tennis champion. One family with two children at the school commented, '[Our children] are both extremely sporty and have represented both Trinity and the south west in the ISA championships (daughter – netball, cross country, athletics and swimming; son – cross country, athletics and aquathon). My daughter also embraced all extracurricular activities available and was a member of the CCF and took the D of E Award.'

Facilities include an outdoor 25m heated swimming pool, a small gym, a multi gym, three tennis courts (one indoor and two floodlit), one pitch and one hard-court. Use of local facilities include Broadmeadow and Dawlish Sports Hall, Dawlish Swimming Pool and Dawlish Astroturf. There is a tennis academy on site, run by former junior international player Mark Syms, plus an indoor cricket academy. Pupils can sign up for individual, group or squad training in both. Trinity takes full advantage of its coastal location and pupils can take part in surf lifesaving, rowing, sailing and other watersports. At the national surf lifesaving championships, Trinity won two golds, one silver, and one bronze. One pupil has been selected for a GB sailing squad. However, table tennis is not on offer competitively and one parent from the Far East said, 'it is a real pity that this sport is left out at Trinity.'

Combined Cadet Force is compulsory in year 9. Very popular. Activities on the cards the week we visited were sailing, a powerboat course, and helicopter rides over Teignmouth. CCF meets once a week, and there are also weekend activities and holiday camps. Cadets take part in Ten Tors and the Duke of Edinburgh's Award scheme. Plus they can play in the National CCF Band, and last year the CCF team raced in the Tall Ships' Race from Falmouth to Greenwich, coming in second out of 50 ships. Cadets can also take a level 2 vocational award called BTec Public Services First Diploma. This equates to four GCSEs.

Good art facilities including a kiln and a printing press. Fantastic studio which was the star of the show for us. Unlike much of the school, it is large and spacious. A huge diamond shaped window almost fills one end of the room. The art teacher says the mix of nationalities creates an 'international flavour.' Some of the sixth form pieces on display were particularly abstract and demonstrated thinking beyond their years. No surprise that Trinity won two golds, two silvers and two bronzes at the recent ISA national art competition. One recent leaver (head girl 2013/14) has just had her first exhibition of art work open at Living Coasts in Torquay.

Music department is well-equipped with the latest Apple computers, a grand piano, drum set, keyboards and electric guitars. The senior school choir has been named South West choir of the year – again, they've won three out of the last four years at Torbay Festival. They have performed at Teignmouth and Exeter Festivals and the Devon County Show. Individual music lessons available, plus clubs including Big Band and a recorder club. The junior school choir involves all children from years 3 to 6, plus there is a chamber choir, entry by audition. They have performed at the Devon County Show and Powderham Castle. Most junior pupils learn an instrument, plus there's a string ensemble, a recorder club and a ukulele orchestra after school. An inter-house music festival is held annually as well as a summer concert, and regular 'tea-time concerts' to give everyone a chance to perform. Trinity Prep has been awarded Best Primary School at the Torbay and South West of England Performing Arts Festival for five out of the last six years. Recent joint junior productions between the drama club and music department include the musicals Doo-Wop Wed Riding Hood and The Rocky Monster Show.

Last major senior drama production was Les Misérables. Rehearsals were underway for Joseph And The Technicolour Dreamcoat in the drama studio. The band accompanying were BTec music students. Plenty of after-school clubs for aspiring thespians, including theatre workshops and public speaking. Last year four pupils won at the poetry recitals at Paignton Festival. Other options for extracurricular activities include anything from chess to salsa dancing to public speaking or judo, fencing or even cross-stitch.

Every half term, there is a 'life skills day' when everybody in the junior school takes part in a round robin of three activities in house teams, so year groups are mixed. Activities include building shelters, survival skills, internet safety exercises, storytelling in the tipi, and more recently creating pizza toppings and meeting a police officer.

Residential trips start in Prep 2 with an overnight stay at the school. Older pupils go to Heatree activities centre or Manaton on Dartmoor. Year 6 go up to London for museums and West End shows. Regular trips to Normandy for French and history classes. Geography students to Iceland. Plus cultural trips to Berlin, and skiing in the Alps. In the UK, there's an adventure and challenge week in Wales. For sixth formers there are volunteer opportunities on the Grass Roots Project in South Africa. The students work in township schools teaching, developing sports fields and building vegetable gardens. 2015 saw the introduction of a second project choice, an orphanage in Johannesburg.

Boarding: 'The boarding staff provide excellent pastoral care in a safe, loving and caring environment. They also encourage each individual with both their school studies and extracurricular activities,' said one parent. Boarders currently range from 10 to 19 years, and there are around 25 pupils in each of the three houses. The majority are full-time, there are occasional flexi-boarders and some European short-termers to brush up on language skills. Some 75 per cent are from overseas, a third from the Far East, a third from Europe and a third the rest of the world. Around 50 per cent of the sixth form are boarders. Two year 5 pupils are currently full-time boarders. A parent of one told us, 'He was homesick the first night, but the houseparents kept him busy so that he didn't have time to think too much. He settled down very quickly, much quicker than I expected. The houseparents are simply the best. They looked after him so well. He loved them. They would send me emails to tell me how he is doing without me asking.'

The houses are split into girls, younger boys and sixth form boys. The girls' and younger boys' accommodation are on separate floors. Each are set out the same, one long corridor with bedrooms on one side and toilets/bathrooms opposite. At one end of the corridor is the common room, and the other is the houseparents' accommodation, in the middle an office. Although it is not set up to replicate a family home like many boarding houses, the atmosphere was warm and friendly. One parent said, 'We looked at a few schools and liked the homely atmosphere at Trinity.' The boarding accommodation is part of the school building and as such pupils don't leave school 'to go home'. For some this may make a difference. Rooms are nearly all doubles. Some sixth formers have singles with either shared bathrooms or interconnecting shower rooms. Communal areas are small but there were no complaints from any of the boarders we met. The older boys' house is bigger, arranged into two wings – one for the upper sixth and one for the lower sixth. A shared kitchen and a common room, with a darts board and pool table, join the two wings. The houseparent lives there with his wife and two small children who apparently love helping with wake-up calls in the morning. Only sixth formers are allowed to study in their room, but all boarders are allowed back to their rooms at lunchtime. We saw quite a few taking advantage of this rather than socialising with fellow pupils over lunch.

Activities in the evenings and weekends can be 5-a-side football, cinema, climbing, go-karting, paintball, or anything the pupils' request. Each house votes for their house captains who then assist the boarding staff in the running of the house. At the weekend there's always one evening where the boys and girls mix, 'classic movie night' is one. All activities are compulsory for the younger ones. From year 9, pupils can go into Teignmouth, and from year 11 they can go to Exeter, back in time for supper. Occasional evenings out are allowed if arranged in advance with set home times. Church on most Sundays in Teignmouth for everyone.

Regular Skype calls to parents, plus updates from houseparents. One parent said, 'Houseparents are simply the best. They looked after [him] so well. [He] loved them. They would send me emails to tell me how [he] is doing without me asking. They are really excellent.' Other parents told us, 'Very safe environment with a lot of activities.' And 'he made a lot of friends.' Plus, 'Clear rules help the boarders to orientate.' All parents agreed their children settled well; one told us, 'He settled down very quickly, much quicker than I expected, in fact since day two at Trinity he didn't need help from his guardian at all except during exeats and term breaks.' Exeats in the middle of each half term, one being compulsory in the autumn and spring terms.

Background and atmosphere: Founded in 1979, the school used to be a girls' convent school. Set in a stunning location in Teignmouth, the school has views over Lyme Bay and the English Channel. Not far from the rugged moors of Dartmoor and the surf beaches of South Devon, Teignmouth is a traditional English seaside town. It is a quiet town, not known for nightly rowdiness like other nearby hotspots. This is part of the attraction for parents; it's safe. 'The smaller size of the boarding school in a safe area was attractive given [he] was travelling on his own,' said a parent of a boarder.

The main building is old; narrow corridors, even narrower wooden winding stairs, and panelled wood. The red library on the red corridor is in the oldest part of the building. Induction sessions for all newbies. It's set on two levels, with a reading room to one side and a large teddy in residence in the middle. The reading room is also used for lunchtime films plus the girls' and the boys' (separate) 'brew clubs'.

Up the stairs is the chapel and the boarding accommodation. At the very top of the building, aptly named The Attic, is the sixth form area. Here there is a (very warm) study room, a quiet zone and a common room. The head of sixth form also has his office here. Basic and functional, but ideally located at the top of the school away from everybody else. Currently 80 students. The new building links into the original building with a courtyard in middle. In the new part is a DT lab with laser cutter and CNC cutter, four science labs and three ICT suites.

The prep school is set apart from the senior school but shares its facilities; outdoor heated swimming pool, playing fields and tennis and cricket academies. In addition, they have their own tipi, a forest school (busily sawing up Christmas trees when we visited), and a film studio in their ICT suite that uses green screen technology. Classrooms are bright and cheerful.

The school's motto is 'Optimism, Confidence, Charity.' In the last year they have raised over £4500 for local, national (mainly British Heart Foundation) and international charities like the one in South Africa. Annually there is a Giving Nations' Day when pupils set up stalls and sell their wares for charities around the world. Students are also encouraged to volunteer to help in the prep school or work in a local elderly home. Trinity has won the school float contest in the Teignmouth Carnival for the last two years.

For sixth formers, there's quite a social calendar to keep up with. They kick off the year with a disco or gig night, followed by quiz nights, a fancy dress party and a film festival. That only takes them up to the Christmas festivities. Then it's the Valentine's ball, a prefect dinner, a summer barbeque, a beach barbeque, and finally the sixth form summer ball.

Pastoral care, well-being and discipline: One prep school parent told us, 'There is no one size fits all approach, each child is given the right opportunity for them to develop their own strengths.' Another summed it up for the majority: 'It has been the perfect start in school life for my children.'

'The head teacher and all of the staff involved in pastoral care have been excellent,' said a senior school parent. Another told us that they chose Trinity because 'I wanted a caring supportive environment which I felt was important as I am a single parent.' Form tutors, key stage heads, boarding staff, two qualified nurses, the school chaplain, and a school counsellor are all available to support the pupils. The school also runs pastoral review meetings every half term to share information amongst staff, and discuss any potential issues or support needed.

The prefect system, including the pastoral prefects and the mentors, provides peer support and ultimately friendships across the years. The house system also gives pupils the chance to make more friends throughout the school – and it is taken very seriously; pupils love the competitiveness. There are regular sports competitions, talent shows, science and maths challenges.

Trinity is a Christian school built on a joint Anglican and Roman Catholic foundation. The school chapel is central to the spiritual life of the whole school community. Mixed year chapel services throughout the week plus hymn practice every other week. Since 2014, the school has employed a full-time chaplain, a C of E priest. As well as formal celebrations, chapel and assemblies, his role includes the pastoral care of pupils and staff. He also teaches PE and looks after the boarders a few nights a week; he is keen to get to know everyone. He is also keen that the school becomes a part of the local community and that pupils 'don't live in a bubble.' He encourages them to 'look outward' and participate in local charitable events. Pupils we spoke to were happy with the school's approach to religion and said 'it's not pushed, it's a way of life' at Trinity.

Zero tolerance on drinking, smoking and drugs. Persistent smaller offences lead to detentions. Further persistence leads to suspension and expulsion. Trinity works with pupils and parents as much as possible to prevent this.

Pupils and parents: Parents of day pupils are mainly local professionals. Recently many more people are relocating to Devon and commuting into London. Some pupils come from as far as Totnes, Paignton, Ivybridge and Honiton. This is the advantage of having a train station on the doorstep; pupils can catch the train to school and jump on the school shuttle. The recently completed Dartmouth bypass should also help bring more pupils from that part of Devon. Escorted airport bus service for boarders. Parents all agreed, 'Communication is good, proactive and responsive. No complaints.'

Entrance: Entry is by registration fee, recent reports, and a taster day including a verbal assessment for KS1 entrance, and a written for KS2 entrance. Assessments are to ensure the school has the appropriate provision is in place, not as a selection process. They rarely turn anyone away, unless special needs are too complex. For entry to reception, several trial mornings in the summer term to ease transition. One parent told us, 'Taster days worked well and he clearly enjoyed them. When being shown around the school, the sixth former showing us around was open and honest, which provided a credible experience.' Three open days for prospective parents every term. 'We were shown around by the pupils who were confident, enthusiastic and excellent ambassadors for the school. We looked at them as excellent role models and thought if our children could turn out like them we would be extremely proud, which they have and we are!'

For senior school entry, registration fee, entrance test and interview. Copies of school reports if applicable. For sixth form entry five GCSE passes at grade C or above. Overseas students must complete a personal statement and English skills assessment. Only those with good use of the English language are accepted onto the standard curriculum from year 10 upwards, but there is a pre-A level course enabling those with weaker English to enter the sixth form. At this level there are usually 10 new European boarders, 10 new international boarders and six UK pupils, usually two of which will be boarders. Parents commented, 'The school was very helpful in helping the children settle in. I could not have asked for more.' Another confirmed, 'The children now feel at home at the school.'

Exit: Around 60 per cent of prep school pupils go onto the senior school, 20/30 per cent go to local grammar schools and 10 per cent to other local schools. Around 40-45 per cent leave after GCSEs to go to the local grammar schools or vocational colleges. Around the same number of new pupils join the sixth form. Around 65 per cent to university. A good number of pupils go to Russell Group universities; some overseas students return to their home countries.

Money matters: Sport, music and performing arts scholarships available, mostly at 11+, offering up to 50 per cent off fees. The Notre Dame Award is an all-rounder scholarship. Limited number of means-tested bursaries. Armed forces discounts available plus sibling allowances.

Remarks: Trinity School is a small school that provides a safe and supportive environment for pupils of all abilities – particularly those who may have struggled to learn in the past, or lacked the confidence or support to reach their potential. Trinity ticks all the boxes, but it doesn't push any boundaries, it just does what it does well. Sport is a good example of this. One parent told us that they chose Trinity as 'We were amazed by the fact that every pupil is treated as an individual and they recognise their strengths and weaknesses, and Trinity view these (as we do) as just as important as academic prowess.'

Truro and Penwith College

College Road, Truro, Cornwall TR1 3XX

Pupils: 6,500 • Ages: 16+

Tel: 01872 267000
Email: enquiry@truro-penwith.ac.uk
Website: www.truro-penwith.ac.uk

T

Principal: Since 2010, David Walrond MA MBA PGCE (50s). Read English at Exeter University (followed by MA in 20th century religious verse), PGCE at Jesus College, Oxford and an MBA in education management at Leicester University. Previously director of curriculum, quality and planning at Truro and Penwith College for seven years. Has worked in post-16 colleges in London, Hampshire and Cheshire and was an associate Ofsted inspector for five years. Early in his career he lived in Italy for four years, doing everything from driving a forklift truck to lecturing in English at Padua University – 'a real life education,' he says.

Although his PGCE was in secondary education he has always worked with post-16 students. He believes that '11 to 18 is too big a phase to teach under one roof,' whereas a post-16 college can specialise and teach a vast number of subjects (50 here) in any combination. 'We understand this age group and its challenges very well,' he says. Still teaches the occasional English literature lecture at the college – he regarded this as an honour but jokes that he now realises that no one else wanted to teach Victorian poetry. Hugely proud of the college's myriad achievements, including the fact that it has held Investors in People status for 15 years and has twice been listed as one of The Sunday Times 100 Best Places to Work. On the academic front, it was the first FE college to be awarded outstanding status by Ofsted, is the best performing state A level provider in Cornwall and is in the top two per cent nationally for progress made from GCSE exam results. As the principal says: 'We add value.' He takes his responsibilities in post-16 education very seriously and gave evidence on career guidance for young people at the House of Commons education select committee. Unlike some heads he doesn't denigrate subjects like media. 'Media can be a fantastic career,' he says. 'We have a hugely successful media and creative industry in this country and it can be a very profitable thing to get into.'

Principal is based at Truro campus but drives down to the Penwith campus in Penzance once or twice a week (his Penwith office has the best office outlook we've seen in a long time – a stunning view of St Michael's Mount). Married to Carol and has three children – the elder two attended Truro and Penwith and are now at university and the youngest is doing the IB at the college. In his spare time he enjoys music (Bach in particular), cricket, literature and languages.

Academic matters: Results are truly impressive – even more so given the number of students (2,200 currently doing A levels or IB) and the range of ability. In 2016, nearly 31 per cent of A levels were A*/A and 61 per cent A*-B. College also offers IB – average scores (36 points in 2016) make it consistent high performer compared with other non-selective state providers. Teachers are post-16 specialists 'who love their subject.' A girl hoping to study forensic science at university said her tutor 'had made maths enjoyable' for the first time in her life. Recently designated as a maths hub and 300 students take maths A level every year.

The college is big but classes are small – 15 on average, although the sciences are sometimes larger. College monitors students' attendance (students register electronically at the start of classes so staff have up to the minute data on attendance) and tracks their progress throughout their time here. A budding medic described the college as 'a stepping stone to adulthood, from calling your teacher "Sir" to being friends with your tutor,' but added: 'We all know that if we want our grades we have to work.' The college offers French, German, Spanish and Italian at A level but college 'will adapt to what people want to do' and if there is a call for other languages staff will do their best to offer them. Parents' evenings once a term – students attend with their parents.

College day runs from 9.15am till 4.15pm, with time for private study in between classes. There's plenty going on in the evenings and at weekends too. Revision sessions and extra classes on offer in the run-up to exams and students can email their tutors for help. 'This place helps students to be the best we can be,' said a teenage boy, while a girl told us: 'Coming here has made me grow as a person.' College runs a range of academies to support gifted and talented students and promote excellence – these include an academic academy, medics academy, STEM academy, music academy and 11 sporting academies (from cricket and rugby to sports leadership and, not surprisingly given the location, surfing).

A host of vocational options exist and are given the same parity of esteem as more traditional academic routes. Total of 1,400 students on two-year level 3 vocational programmes – anything from bricklaying and carpentry to hospitality and catering. Hair and beauty students are based in a very professional looking salon called FACE (staff and students get discounts) and a nail technician student recently scooped silver in advanced nail art at the World Skills UK competition. Another won gold in the computer games development section of the same event. Apprenticeships are growing in popularity – everything from art and design to computing and IT. College has close links with Rick Stein and is the training provider for the chef's apprenticeship programme.

College offers diagnostic testing when students start. Learning support tutors work with students on literacy, numeracy, revision skills, exam technique, essay writing and more – one to one, in small groups or in workshops. Broad range of students includes those with profound and multiple learning difficulties and university undergraduates (college launched higher education provision in 1998).

Games, options, the arts: College offers Study Plus – an enrichment programme of activities like drama, driving theory, IT, languages, music, photography, skateboarding and work experience. D of E is popular, plus fundraising for charity and trips abroad (either as part of students' studies or for enrichment). 'There are far more opportunities here than there were at school,' a student said approvingly. College has its fair share of sporting successes – 'you'll find the most able sports people in Cornwall here,' we were told. England rugby player Jack Nowell is a former student and college wins scores of sporting honours every year.

Art, music and drama, as we said last time, are seriously top notch. Even if the arts aren't for you there are plenty of other pursuits. A teenager heading for university told us that while she'd been at the college she'd trained as a barista, learned Makaton and volunteered with a local food bank.

Background and atmosphere: When the college opened in 1993 it expected to take 500 students from Truro and the surrounding area, but more than 700 turned up on the first day. The reputation of the college is so impressive that students make longer and longer journeys to attend (up to 90 minutes travelling time in some cases). Indeed, some students from further afield lodge with host families during the week. The college merged with Penwith College in Penzance in 2008.

The Truro campus, three miles west of the city centre, is purpose built, architecturally striking and wonderfully resourced. It is the sort of place that tempts fee-paying parents to chuck their chequebooks aside – and the list of students' previous schools shows that many do just that. Breathtaking facilities, ranging from the White building, an art and design department filled with gleaming Macs and light, airy studios, to the Mylor building, which houses science, music, dance and the performing arts. The buildings all have their own libraries and IT suites and are bright, well equipped and immaculately kept – no litter or graffiti here.

The college has a university campus feel – bells don't ring, there's no uniform and students address lecturers by their first names. The principal reckons that in today's society, where teenagers are 'protected and often infantalised' by their parents, the college prepares youngsters well for university. He says that students learn to be self sufficient and independent here, while being supported through their studies. The size and bustling atmosphere can be bewildering at first but it's not a place where students feel lost in any sense of the word. Plasma screens in each building give news about what's going on and, as we discovered ourselves, students are happy to stop and point newcomers in the right direction.

Pastoral care, well-being and discipline: Students spend their working lives in 15-strong tutor groups. Every student has a tutor (usually a lecturer who teaches them) who is the first port of call for advice and guidance. Very effective student services department offers help on everything from careers to a lost bus pass and from money worries to problems at home. Student counsellor for graver problems. College runs a series of induction days for new students before term starts in September.

Staff told us that students know what is expected of them and discipline isn't an issue. No drink or drugs – college tries to educate youngsters about drugs and alcohol issues and provides help for those who ask for it. Designated smoking areas. A plethora of canteens and snack bars throughout the college, even a mobile burger bar – all cashless and paid for by card.

Pupils and parents: Cornwall is the poorest county in the country – 51 per cent of students at the college received the Education Maintenance Allowance (EMA) before it was abolished in 2010 – and students come from a cross-section of backgrounds and from state and independent schools.

None of the students we met were intimidated by the size of the place. One boy told us: 'If school had been more like this college I would have liked it more' while a 17-year-old girl in her second year said the college had exceeded her expectations. 'I wanted to be more independent and this seemed like an amazing place to study,' she said. 'Before I came here I was at a school with only 300 pupils but everyone is so friendly here that I knew straight away that I was in the right place. It's more grown-up and more informal than school, but you are expected to work hard.'

Entrance: Students applying to do A levels need at least five Cs at GCSE, preferably Bs in the subjects they want to study at A level. However the principal stresses that the entry requirements aren't set in stone. 'If we had a very rigid entry it would be selection by school,' he says. 'Not all schools perform equally well.'

Entrants complete an application form (either online or by post) and then attend an interview (parents can come too). 'Interviews are very friendly,' said a member of staff. 'We ask students why they want to come here and what their goals are.' Those who don't get their grades are invited in to discuss their options and some retake English and maths GCSE at the college. 'The college doesn't give up on people,' we were told.

Exit: 'We understand higher education very well here,' says the principal, adding that the college processes a staggering 1,500 UCAS forms a year. Between a dozen and 20 to Oxbridge every year (15 in 2016) and around a quarter to Russell Group.

Money matters: Subsidised travel available to full-time students under 19 who live further than three miles from the college. Bursary fund assists students with travel, essential equipment and trips – all means tested.

Remarks: Exciting and forward thinking. Truro and Penwith College is at the top of its game and thoroughly deserves the accolades heaped upon it. Offers a broad range of qualifications for all and provides the perfect bridge between school and higher education. Despite its size, it is nurturing, inclusive and achieves glittering results.

Truro High School

Falmouth Road, Truro, Cornwall TR1 2HU

Pupils: 398; 42 full boarders • Ages: 4-19 • Sixth form: 50

Fees: Day £5,340 – £12,603; Boarding £21,999 – £24,615 pa

Tel: 01872 272830
Email: registrar@trurohigh.co.uk
Website: www.trurohigh.co.uk

Headmaster: Since 2014, Dr Glenn Moodie, early 40s. Originally from New Zealand, he studied classics and ancient Greek at university before coming to the UK to study a PhD in classics at Bristol, and a PGCE at Leicester. This is his first headship; he was previously at Wycombe Abbey as director of studies, and prior to that, had teaching roles at Uppingham School and Clifton College. Currently teaches Latin and history of art to sixth formers. Married to Vanessa, a primary school teacher; their daughter attends the prep. They are still adjusting to life in Cornwall, but he says the drive to school often evokes nostalgic memories of New Zealand, which makes him smile. What he loves about Cornwall is that many people are there because they have made a choice; they want a better work/life balance and their perspective on life is different – health and well-being are paramount.

Truro High School is the only single-sex school in Cornwall. The school says, 'An all-girls education is liberating with students able to be themselves and take on challenges without fear of censure.' However, the co-ed idea was thrown into the ring just as Glenn started and it definitely stirred up the parents, many of whom are 'more wedded to the idea of single-sex education.' One parent sympathised, saying, 'Dr Moodie had a tricky start with the whole co-ed question – which we believe was essentially down to the governors. Everything has settled now.' In the end, the governors decided to stay all-girls, as they have been for 135 years. Another parent told us, 'The co-ed idea was very badly handled, but communication has been much better since. I would like the head to be much more visible, especially at events where parents are in school. It is his school, he should be there "pressing the flesh".'

In years gone by, there was a co-ed sixth form at Truro High, and although this could be suggested in the distant future, the whole co-ed matter has now been parked indefinitely. Things have without doubt settled down now, and confidence is improving. 'We feel the head teacher is extremely diligent, approachable and non-judgmental and that he puts the interests of the school first and foremost.'

Head of prep school: Since September 2016 is Annabel Ramsey, previously a class teacher here for two years. Brought up in Falmouth, she has a BEd from University College Chester, and began teaching at a junior school in Wootton Bassett, moving to Porthleven School and then Archbishop Benson CofE primary as deputy head. She joined Truro Prep after a year's sabbatical touring south east Asia and Australia. Loves to explore the world – whether it be close to home on the Cornish coastline and surrounding villages or far flung places in other continents. She is a great fan of the theatre, visiting at every opportunity, with a particular passion for Les Misérables.

Academic matters: Prep school classes are very small and often the younger ones have lessons like RE together. On our visit we were treated to an impromptu demonstration on how to use an abacus (made by the girls), plus a poetry reading. The poem had been written in the last 20 minutes and the subject was anything to do with National Maths Day. The young poet had chosen shapes as a theme and the result was most impressive. Another treat was hearing about the Egyptian Extravaganza, 'Tomb Time.' Girls showed us their mummified Barbies in shoe box tombs and explained how they had mummified tomatoes. The girls were polite and confident, but not overly precocious. They were enthusiastic and excited to show us their work, but it's clear they know their boundaries.

In 2016, 45 per cent A*/A grades and 72 per cent A*-B at A level, a big increase on last year; 56 per cent A*/A at GCSE. The school is regularly top of the county league for A level and GCSE. Twenty-one subjects on offer at A level. Maths and physics are strong, and all girls take separate sciences at GCSE. English is consistently good at both A level and GCSE. Latin holds up very well at GCSE and is still there at A level. MFLs include Spanish, French and German, as well as EAL and a Japanese club. Religious philosophy is compulsory.

With so few pupils, all classes are small, and at A level some are even one-to-one. Very low turnover of staff but a few recent retirements have made way for some welcome new blood. Parents told us, 'We are impressed by and have every confidence in the head teacher and all the other teachers who have been involved in our child's education.' Another was a bit more critical: 'I think the teachers are pretty good, but listening to the girls talk about them, I think covering illness etc could be better handled. I still feel there is a lot of stuff which goes unchecked, spelling errors in work displayed on the wall etc, errors in reports.'

According to the ISI inspection report, the school 'provides a good education....the curriculum is good, successfully providing for the needs of all pupils including those with EAL and SEND.' All staff are trained in assessment techniques and the school provides extra study support for those pupils in the prep and the senior school with dyslexia or dyspraxia. The small class sizes enable regular monitoring and support.

Games, options, the arts: Facilities are pretty good. There's a 25 metre heated indoor swimming pool, full sized Astroturf, a playing field, two netball/tennis courts, and an athletics area for long/high jump, javelin, discus etc. There's also a separate dance studio building, historically only used for ballet, now packed with yoga classes, and street and lyrical dance ensembles.

Netball and hockey fixtures are weekly and the school has won 37 county team sport titles over the past five years. Twenty-five girls represent the county and nine play either hockey or netball for West of England. Girls' football and tag rugby are now included in the curriculum and the new rugby club on Mondays was hot news of the day. Proper rugby, not tag, we were informed. They even had the Cornish Pirates in for a session. Swimming is popular, as is horse riding; they have their own team. Outdoor pursuits like D of E and Ten Tors are a part of life here. Third fastest all-girl team in Ten Tors challenge on Dartmoor recently.

Most girls learn an instrument and there's a 120-strong choir and a 60-strong orchestra. The new music building has six individual practice rooms and a large main room set up with instruments aplenty and 10 iMacs. Groups include a jazz band, samba band, flute choir, chamber choir and a ukulele club. Recent choir trips and tours include Belgium and Hong Kong.

At the end of our prep school tour, the head teacher was off to help with the singing auditions for the upcoming production, Cinderella Rockefeller. On our way out we were lucky enough to sneak a peek at the reception class rehearsing Noah's Ark. The prep school is passionate about putting on plays and musicals, and of course the annual nativity. They even put on an open-air production of The Princess and the Frog by the school pond last summer. Music is a big part of life here too, with many taking part in the junior choir, and the majority learning instruments.

The performing arts centre has a small theatre used for presentations, as well as larger productions. Rehearsals were under way for Into The Woods, the year before it was The Importance of Being Earnest. Girls are keen on debating and participate in competitions organised by the ESU and the Cambridge Union. Large numbers doing LAMDA qualifications and Rotary public speaking competitions. One parent told us, 'I think Truro Hugh ultimately gave my daughters self belief. My youngest became the member of the youth parliament for mid Cornwall; she had been taking extracurricular lessons in speech & drama, and debating society. These little extras can make a huge difference to one's future.'

Art is set in yet another outbuilding; rooms are a good size and sixth formers have their own area. Plenty of girls go on to do the prestigious Falmouth foundation course. Textiles also popular and former pupils have gone on to get firsts in design courses, and land jobs at Mulberry or Karen Millen. Head of department once worked for Laura Ashley and knows not just the creative side, but also the logistics of production and manufacture. On our visit there was a lot of excitement about the fashion show that night. Proceeds going towards The Mermaid Centre at Royal Cornwall hospital and purchase of a laser cutter for the department.

Up until GCSEs, girls alternate terms of textiles and food & nutrition. The latter includes food science and is popular, with some even taking it at degree level. One sixth former told us she's signed up for a Cooking for Uni course as one of her enrichment options on Wednesday afternoons. Other options include ceramics, life drawing and photography.

Football, rugby and engineering are also available and enthusiastically taken on board. The school is adamant that there is no pressure, and girls are given the space and confidence to choose. There has been a big drive towards engineering, with guest speakers and events on Women In Engineering. The school also has its own racing car team with five cars. With help from the local community, the girls are raring to go and compete in national racing events.

As you would expect in this part of the country, plenty of outdoor learning in the prep school. This could be anything from bird watching to taking care of the bug hotel and studying worms. Gardening club is popular; recently they have been very busy planting trees in a local park for a community project. There are regular trips to local art galleries and museums, and the older prep girls have been enjoying enrichment activities based on the theme 'When I grow up I want to be....' This has led to trips to a local wedding dress designer and an artist, so far. Who knows what will come up next, a fireman, a pilot, an astronaut? Let's hope so. There's annual residential trips for years 3 to 6, most to Barton Hall, and plenty of other fun days out for the whole school. There's the Royal Cornwall Show trip where the choir sings and girls enter pieces for Best In Show. There's Ladies' Day when girls design and create their own hats and race on hobbyhorses. There's even an Annual Pet Show. Don't panic if you don't have a pet, get creative and make one – pineapples make great turtles, apparently.

Boarding: 'The fact that both girls loved weekly boarding had a huge bearing on their success at school.' Majority of full boarders are from abroad but the school promotes its flexi facilities so families can use them whenever necessary. No plans to change the boarding; the head says it provides the school with some essential cultural diversity, something Cornwall rather lacks. The German students tend to come just for a term to improve their English, but other boarders from Russia, China and Australia and the local islanders from the Scillies are more permanent.

Two boarding houses – Dalvenie (years 8-10) and Rashleigh (years 11-13). Trips for all boarders on Saturdays and Sundays. Treasure hunts in town for the new girls, beach trips, horse-riding, shopping in Exeter and visits to the Tate in St Ives and the Eden Project. For nights in, there's swimming, plus pool parties with inflatables, barbeques, baking and movie nights. Boarders all participate in after-school clubs, and the older girls are allowed into town in pairs – back for supper at 6pm.

The younger girls are four to a room with communal showers and toilets. The older girls can opt for either two in room, or individual rooms, all with ensuites – very much like university rooms (actually a little better). In Dalvenie the common room has a TV, Wii, a pool table, piano, PCs, a dining table and a comfy sofa area. Rashleigh was refurbished a few years ago and the lounge is really rather grown up, set out like a large apartment with sofa/TV area and a fully fitted kitchen. Next door is a quiet room with pianos, a room for the girls to be able 'to get away from it all'. Girls do their own laundry and have a council and regular meetings. Houseparents live on site with their families (and cat). Their daughters also attend the school, so it really is a family affair here.

Background and atmosphere: Founded in 1880 by Bishop (later Archbishop) Benson (first Master of Wellington College) who built Truro cathedral and gave Henry James the idea for The Turn of the Screw. Situated close to the centre of Truro, the school has been on the same site since 1896. The aim was to provide an academic education for girls within a Christian community. The school retains its founding links with Truro Cathedral and commitment to a Christian ethos but welcomes girls of all faiths or none. Hymns are sung in assembly once a week, girls attend services at the cathedral threes times a year, plus twice-termly church services at the local parish church have recently been introduced.

The main building is partly castellated and made of Cornish granite, not a grand entrance but a welcoming one. Inside, narrow corridors, wooden staircases, plaques dating back to 1800s, fairly antique toilet facilities, in need of a lick of paint here and there. Outside, the site is very well-maintained, the gardens are lovely, but overall it feels a little disconnected as outbuilding after outbuilding appears, as do seemingly ad-hoc extensions. Shining stars are obviously the most recently built language centre, music block and performing arts building.

The library seems well-used and well-resourced, with a separate sixth form area. School is definitely not overrun with computers, but given its size maybe this is reasonable. Best IT resources appeared to be suite of iMacs in the music room. Wireless internet is available in certain areas of the school and to sixth formers. All social media is blocked until 4pm, when the boarders can log on.

'The sixth form building is fantastic,' say parents. Both floors have workstation rooms with individual carrels – the girls call these 'caroles' and personalise them as much as possible. Most amusing was the fact that the girls were using wine glasses for water (it was definitely water); young ladies at work. Shared common room opens out onto garden. Kitchen with dishwasher, toaster and coffee machine. Girls seemed happy and relaxed, chatting away over a mountain of toast. Lunchtimes in town are allowed but they rarely go, occasionally on birthdays.

The prep school is in a small, unmodernised building next to the boarding houses. The playground is pretty standard, quite bland, but the inside of the school is a different story. Photo collages fill the stairway, and classrooms and corridors are brimming with artwork and displays. We particularly liked the paper mâché tree in the library, adorned with butterflies, and even a fluffy squirrel.

Pastoral care, well-being and discipline: Discipline problems are rare and pastoral care is led by the form tutors and houseparents. There is also a nurse on site. Good mentoring and prefect system means that girls of all ages get to know each other – lots of impromptu hugging on our tour as our guide saw her younger friends. This is a small, friendly and unintimidating school. One girl told us how she was bullied in her last school and that she couldn't have felt more welcome when she started Truro High. She made friends easily and says she has never looked back: 'Coming to Truro High was the best thing I've ever done.'

One parent of a boarder told us, 'Only last week my youngest, now in upper sixth, was not feeling very well, but a quick call to the boarding house reassured me. One of the senior members of staff has been there many years and I have formed a good relationship with her. Boarding in Truro High really worked for my girls, it's fun, friendly, relaxed.'

One prep school parent enthused, 'We were delighted by the atmosphere of the place. The wit and dynamism between children and teachers, the warmth between the girls – the spark was exactly what we were looking for (and what was lacking at the other schools).'

Pupils and parents: Parents are professionals, company directors and the like; many have relocated and now commute by plane or train to London. One told us, 'We are not particularly enamoured of the attitude which is common amongst some of the children and parents of the top tier private schools so were looking for a "third way" of excellent schooling without some of the arrogance, stress levels etc found elsewhere.' They went onto to say, 'We wouldn't have moved to Cornwall if it wasn't for Truro High.'

Others said, 'We were delighted by the atmosphere of the place. The wit and dynamism between children and teachers, the warmth between the girls – the spark was exactly what we were looking for (and what was lacking at the other schools).' Communication from the school to parents is good. 'There is a huge amount of information to share and parentmail does the job well. Teachers are approachable and helpful when required. Communication regarding the general management of the school has improved.'

Uniform up to year 11 is a Balmoral tartan skirt and green pullover. Sixth formers could easily be mistaken for staff – very mature, not a rebel in sight. Parents enthused, 'Can't speak highly enough of the culture of Truro High. Our girls come home at the end of the day with a smile on their faces. They look forward during the holidays to going back to school.'

The school has recently had a publicity makeover thanks to the new director of marketing, a former ITV Cornwall news presenter. Smart promo packs, new-look magazines, local news articles, radio plugs and a Facebook page that is updated several times a day. An old girl herself, she has two daughters at the school and continues to fly its flag by setting up events like the fashion show in conjunction with local businesses, and letting parents use the grounds – one recently put on a refugee in crisis event.

The school is also strengthening its relationship with local community and parents with events such as 'family swim days' at weekends. Anyone is welcome for a small token that is then used to pay the (qualified) sixth formers to lifeguard.

Old girls include Dame Lynne Brindley (master of Pembroke College, Oxford), TV presenter Hannah Sandling, comedien and writer Morwenna Banks and mezzo soprano Anna Burford.

Entrance: Prep school entry by a taster day and informal assessment. Once accepted, there is a 'buddy system' to help all the girls settle in and feel at home. Boarding is available from year 3 upwards, but no boarders at present.

Senior school entrants mainly from own prep plus Polwhele House, Roselyon, St Piran's, Bolitho and Truro prep. A decent number are from local state primaries. Biggest overseas market currently is Hong Kong; others from Russia, Germany, Spain and Australia.

Applicants for the senior school are invited to a taster day (boarders have a trial night), then sit an exam and interview before admission. For sixth form entry, GCSE grade A*/A in proposed A level choices, plus interviews for UK candidates and test papers/school assessments for overseas students.

Exit: Almost all juniors go on to senior school. No further assessments to transfer, but girls do sit the entrance exam to determine setting. For academic reasons some may be asked to look elsewhere, but these situations are reasonably rare and are handled early on with parents.

On average half leave at 16 to go to (free) Truro College up the road, Truro School or co-ed boarding elsewhere. One girl off to study medicine at Cambridge in 2016 and one to study veterinary science at Nottingham; other popular choices this year include law at Southampton, English literature at Edinburgh, astrophysics at UCL and chemical engineering at Manchester.

Money matters: Academic, music, drama, sports and art scholarships available, plus means-tested bursaries at year 7 entry, and into sixth form.

Remarks: Truro High School is unique in Cornwall. It's a small, all-girls school that delivers on qualifications, but nurtures and cares. One parent said, 'We wanted all girls, so it was a no-brainer.' But most have been overwhelmed by the 'spark' and 'atmosphere' of the school. A few minor grumbles about teachers' spelling and communication, but all we saw were happy, well-behaved girls. One parent said, 'I thoroughly recommend Truro High, for sciences and humanities, for quieter children and more vocal – I have one of each!' It's the type of school that needs to be visited; parents will know immediately if it's right for them or not.

Truro Prep School

Linked with Truro School

Highertown, Truro, Cornwall TR1 3QN

Pupils: 260 • Ages: 3–11

Fees: £8,550 – £12,225 pa

Tel: 01872 272616
Email: Prepenquiries@truroschool.com
Website: www.truroschool.com/prep

Head: Since September 2016 Ms Sarah Patterson BEd, previously deputy head at The King's School, Canterbury since 2012. Degree from Birmingham; has taught in a variety of schools including prep schools in Kenya and Chile. She has been head of English and director of studies as well as class teacher and deputy head.

Entrance: Pupils join nursery in the autumn term after their third birthday. Entry to nursery is first come, first served but school emphasises from the start that it is 'education, not childcare,' with children encouraged to do two full days and gradually build up to four or five. School likes parents and children to visit first. 'We don't like to offer places to people who have not been to see us.'

For entry into reception, year 1 and year 2, admission is based on a taster day and informal assessment. For prep (years 3 to 6), entry is selective, with English, maths and non-verbal reasoning tests, informal chat with the head and taster day with their year group. Children joining in year 6 and aiming for the senior school have to take the Truro School entrance exam along with external applicants.

Exit: Vast majority head to senior school at 11. Progression to senior school is by head's recommendation – parents get a letter when their children are in year 5 to say whether they've got a place or not, although they still take the entrance exam 'as an assessment exercise.' A handful of pupils go elsewhere, including Truro High (girls), Mount Kelly and the occasional scholarship to Millfield.

Remarks: An idyllic, 10-acre setting at the end of a winding, rhododendron-bordered drive, surrounded on all sides by the local golf course, extensive woods and sports grounds. Originally known as Treliske School, it was founded as Truro School's prep in 1936. Victorian main school building is grade II listed manor house and boasts a wealth of period detail and stunning art collection (we particularly admired the Terry Frost painting in the hall).

Academic standards are good, with teachers praised for their ability to bring out the best in everyone. All pupils have a form tutor whom they see for registration, reading period and 10 minutes at the end of the school day. Specialist teaching from years 3 to 6. Pupils set for English and maths from year 3. On the languages front, pupils have taster year of German in year 3, taster year of Spanish in year 4 and start French in year 5. 'We think year 5 is the right time to start French. By then we have identified able linguists and they are put into an accelerated group.' No Latin on offer – 'there's no time.' SEN department offers individual and in-class support. School has pupils with mild dyslexia, cerebral palsy, hypermobility needs and some with autistic spectrum behaviours. Maximum class size is 20 from year 3 to 6, 16 from reception to year 2 and 30 in the nursery. Half the year 3 to 6 teachers are men and school has appointed its first male year 2 teacher.

Year 6 'is a fantastic year,' with all year 6s taking the Truro Prep diploma, a mix of core academic subjects (English, maths and science), humanities, performing arts, creative arts, sports and outdoor activity and life skills (including IT, languages, first aid and cooking). It's 'good, solid preparation' for life in the senior school. We reckon that with its research project and cookery lessons (everyone has to cook a two-course meal) it'll set them up well for the university years too.

School is hot on reading and staff urge parents to read with their children – not just idly listen while they concentrate on doing something else. 'We want them to sit down together and share a book.' More than a third of pupils play musical instruments – all year 2s play the recorder, year 3s try their hand at the violin and year 4s learn violin, cello double bass or brass instrument for a year in small groups.

Nursery and pre-prep housed in spacious, modern building, separate from main school and with own gated grounds. Built in 1991, it was extended in 2009 and has a forest school, Enchanted Garden and Magic Tree – all wonderfully Enid Blyton. Nursery staff give parents a video record of their children's early years – saved on a memory stick at the end of each term.

As you'd expect, children spend lots of time outdoors here – playing in the woods, working in an outdoor classroom designed and built by the DT teacher and growing fruit and vegetables at the gardening club. School brims with imaginative and creative ideas – a groups of pupils recently made a racing car and raced it at Newquay Airport while others started a company called Cornish Jammers, making and selling strawberry jam. In typical forward-thinking fashion, prep has also applied to set up a partnership with local state and independent schools to make their own apps. All pupils do ICT, including coding and animation. Sport is hugely important too – particularly rugby, football, cricket, netball, athletics, tennis, swimming, sailing and kayaking. Everyone learns to swim by the age of 7. Like the senior school, which runs a fencing elite academy programme, the prep is excellent at fencing. A pupil who started fencing sabre at the prep has been ranked second in Europe at under-17 level and current pupils won gold and silver medals at recent IAPS fencing championships.

Around half the pupils are Truro-based while a fifth live near the A39 corridor to Falmouth. Others travel long distances to the school, from the likes of Wadebridge, Fowey, Padstow, St Ives and Helston. School runs a very popular early birds breakfast club for pupils, parents and siblings from 7.45 to 8.15am, offering bacon butties, croissants, cooked breakfasts etc. For pre-prep children there's a tea club from 3.45 to 5.30pm (£1 per 15 minutes), while prep pupils can stay till 5.45pm for homework club (free), clubs and activities (everything from sailing and kayaking to chess and dance). Mindful of some children's long journeys, school offers a packed tea for them to munch on the way home – parents order in advance and it goes on the bill. Lunch said to be excellent – everything cooked in-house, organic and local food where possible and served up café style. Navy uniform is smart and practical and everyone keeps a pair of wellies in school for rainy days (there are quite a lot of them in this part of the world).

A happy school, where children get the chance to learn, have fun and grow up in their own time – as well as make the most of the glorious countryside and coastline. Parents (half of them recent arrivals to Cornwall) are hugely supportive and appreciate the prep's distinctive Cornish vibe. 'It has a very friendly, laid-back atmosphere,' one mother told us, 'but it gets very good results too.' Another said: 'It reflects the area. It's not a hothouse and it offers exactly the right balance of work and play.'

Truro School

Linked with Truro Prep School

167

Trennick Lane, Truro, Cornwall TR1 1TH

Pupils: 790; 80 boarders • Ages: 11–18 • Sixth form: 205

Fees: Day £13,215; Boarding £22,230 – £25,875 pa

Tel: 01872 272763
Email: jeg@truroschool.com
Website: www.truroschool.com

Headmaster: Since 2013, Andrew Gordon-Brown BCom MSc QTS (40s). Educated at Hyde Park High School in Johannesburg, read commerce at University of Cape Town and then qualified as a chartered accountant. He rowed for South Africa in the 1992 Olympic Games (team came a creditable eighth) and set his heart on rowing for Oxford or Cambridge. He achieved his dream when he completed an MSc in agricultural economics at Keble College, Oxford and picked up a rowing blue along the way (he rowed for Oxford in the 1994 Boat Race). After 12 years in banking and financial services, working for blue chip companies such as Deloitte, UBS and JPMorgan Chase, he had a 'Damascene conversion' and decided to become a teacher. 'I turned my back on the big bucks,' he told us with a smile. Achieved his QTS via the University of Gloucestershire, taught economics and rowing at Radley for four years and then spent five years as deputy head at Stonyhurst College in Lancashire.

Dedicated, energetic and charming, he has always loved Cornwall (his family owns an old farmhouse on The Lizard) so jumped at the chance to take the reins at Truro School. Keen to use his business background to help pupils, he teaches careers guidance to year 11s and runs financial literacy classes as part of the sixth form's enrichment programme. Has a very global outlook and tells students they should see the world 'as their labour market.' He holds regular lunches for year groups and describes pupils as 'wonderfully unpretentious.' 'Unlike in bigger conurbations, they don't have an edge to them,' he says. Discipline isn't a problem either. As he puts it: 'The teachers teach, the pupils learn and the parents are very supportive.'

His wife Harriet (who was on the same MSc course as him at Oxford) is very involved in school life and they have three children, the eldest at the senior school, the younger two at the prep. They live in a house on the school site.

Still a keen sportsman, he enjoys running, cycling and going to the gym. His family has just bought a boat – 'but I'm a novice sailor' – and he sings whenever he can (most recently in the Truro School Choral Society performance of Faure's Requiem at Truro Cathedral).

Academic matters: It's cool to work hard here – and the pupils do. Fifty-five per cent of GCSEs were A*/A in 2016, with English lit, maths and physics all strong performers. At A level, 33 per cent A*/A, with maths leading the field. The sciences and maths are particularly strong and many go on to be medics, dentists, engineers and, perhaps not surprisingly given the location, geologists. The school is one of only 230 in the country to offer geology – 'we've got a department that isn't far off a small university department.' School runs more than 20 subjects at A level, including business studies, economics, PE and psychology. Thanks to a bit of timetabling wizardry, students can take any combination (for options submitted in the preceding spring term). EPQ on offer too.

Everyone does at least one language at GCSE and some take up to three (students can study a third language from year 9 in extra twilight sessions first thing, at lunchtime and after school). Mainly French, German and Spanish but the school will do its best to accommodate requests for others (students have taken Chinese, Dutch and Russian in recent years). Exchange trips for younger pupils and work experience in France and Germany for older ones, with CVs written in French and German of course. Music is offered to talented musicians off-timetable as an extra GCSE.

Learning support department with full-time head and two part-time staff. School caters for students with moderate learning difficulties – dyslexia, dyspraxia, dyscalculia, dysgraphia and Asperger's. All students are tested during their first year at the school – extra support given individually or in small groups (no extra cost).

All pupils are encouraged to be the best they can (school motto is 'To be rather than to seem to be') and they get regular progress reviews, on attitude in lessons, ability to study independently and organisation skills, as well as academic achievement.

Games, options, the arts: A very sporty school, with county champions in rugby, hockey and netball. First XV regularly gets into the last 16 of the NatWest Schools Cup and a sixth former was recently selected for the England U18 XV. Teams often have to travel long distances to compete but pupils don't seem to mind. The school has 40 acres of playing fields, Astroturf, eight tennis courts, cricket pavilion and grounds, climbing wall and a 25m pool, but the jewel in the crown is the new Sir Ben Ainslie Sports Centre, opened by the man himself, which boasts an eight-court sports hall, two squash courts, fitness suite and dance studio. It's used by the local community too – 400 members signed up in a flash when it opened. The days of the school being regarded as 'the rich kids on the hill' have long gone. The school also excels at fencing and runs an elite academy programme. Several youngsters fence at national and international level and are aiming for the 2020 Olympics. A girl in the upper sixth is currently ranked fifth at senior level in the GB. As the head reminded us, 80 per cent of Cornwall's county border is sea, so the school makes the most of the plethora of water pursuits on the doorstep – like sailing, surfing and snorkelling.

The music department buzzes with activity from dawn till dusk. A third of pupils takes instrumental lessons and there are orchestras, choirs, bands and jazz bands to join. Pupils frequently selected for National Youth Orchestra and National Youth Choirs. Around three or four a year take music at A level. School has a strong relationship with Truro Cathedral – it recently announced a new partnership whereby girl choristers aged 13 to 18 will join the cathedral choir and get a 25 per cent scholarship from the school.

Drama is top notch. When we visited, the school was gearing up for a production of Sweeney Todd, complete with an ambitious two-storey revolving stage. Theatre was opened by Sir Tim Rice, and as well as school productions and Friday lectures for the sixth form, it opens its doors to touring companies. Art is superb – everything from oil paintings and life drawing to sculpture and ceramics. The head's study, corridors, boarding houses and art department are lined with stunning artwork. School has strong links with nearby Falmouth University and with local artists (some of their work is exhibited at school's new Heseltine Gallery). We loved the graffiti-style mural painted up the side of the gallery steps – pupils came up with ideas and street artist Cosmic spent five days on a cherry picker creating it. Theatre studies and art are popular at A level. So is DT, which is taught in a proper workshop. Many of the pupils' creations are inspired by the sea. We spotted model yachts, a gadget for cleaning boat chains and a rocking hammock.

Wednesday afternoons are given over to extracurricular activities – everything from sport and music to surfing and war games. Truro pupils certainly don't lack fresh air, that's for sure. D of E is huge here (over 100 take part each year) and there are always school teams in the gruelling Ten Tors Challenge across the wilds of Dartmoor. World Challenge on offer, plus a raft of expeditions at home and abroad.

Boarding: Small number of boarders but head says that he has 'given boarding a bit of a push', and recently opened an additional boarding house for girls. There are now four boarding houses (two for girls, two for boys), all small and homely and each with a resident housemistress or housemaster. Boarders do 90 minutes prep a night in the library, overseen by staff and sixth formers. Lots of activities organised for them at weekends, particularly for the youngest – kayaking, coasteering, surfing, barbecues etc. Older pupils get time to socialise with their friends – 'it's important not to timetable every part of their day,' said a housemistress. Some flexi-boarding available.

Background and atmosphere: Gloriously situated on a hill overlooking the River Truro and the cathedral (you get tantalising glimpses of it as you walk between the buildings). A Methodist school founded in 1880, it opened with 35 boys and two teachers in a schoolroom in the centre of the city and moved to its current site in 1882. Original gothic building in local stone has been much added to – it's 'a bit of a warren,' said a parent – but it adds to the charm. School went co-ed in 1990 and these days 40 per cent of the pupils are girls. Buildings include a lovely 1920s chapel (year 7 and 8 pupils attend twice a week and year 9s and above once a week) and library with 18,000 resources. Whole school assembly every Tuesday. Library staff are dynamic – they produce own reading for pleasure guide, say John Green (The Fault in Our Stars) is the most requested author right now and invite the likes of Meg Rosoff and Patrick Gale to do author events.

Food gets the thumbs-up – 800 lunches served up every day, payment by lunch cards and lots of choice. Boarders eat in the main school, although they can make toast, pasta, hot drinks etc in boarding house kitchens. Sixth formers have to be in school every morning but if they haven't got lessons, they are allowed out after 12 noon. They also have their own café and sixth form centre, complete with common room, study area and thumping music at break time.

Pastoral care, well-being and discipline: School has clear expectations of pupils but everyone we spoke to reckoned it's a fair, equitable place. Prefects are trained to play a big brother/sister role to younger counterparts – all adding to the friendly atmosphere. Most lower sixth pupils do a 16-week peer counselling programme led by the chaplain (who's known as The Rev). When we asked if the school is strict, a year 7 pupil told us: 'There are lots of rules but they are reasonable ones.' Homework is pretty sensible too – starting at 20 minutes a night per subject (up to three subjects a night) and rising as youngsters get older. Good support for new pupils – sixth form prefects look after younger pupils and maps doled out to help them navigate their way round the site. The only improvements year 7s and 8s could think of would be a mini-buggy or ski lift to transport them around the campus. We can't see it happening any time soon.

Deputy head is responsible for pupil progress and welfare. Tutor groups organised by year and tutors are pupils' first port of call if there are any problems (they can also go to their head of year, chaplain, medical centre, school counsellor and sixth form peer counsellors). Head boy and head girl, plus deputies and a raft of senior prefects, and a house system in place. New head is said to be stricter on uniform than his predecessor and pupils are well turned out. Sixth formers wear business dress – 'we have our own fashion sense but we have to look smart,' said one. No jeans and trousers must have a crease.

Pupils and parents: The youngsters we met were down-to-earth, motivated and refreshingly modest about their individual achievements. Our guides included a talented 800m England schools champion and a jazz singer who's in the National Youth Choir, but we had to drag the information out of them. 'Anyone can fit in here – even if they are quite shy,' we were told. Pupils come from all over Cornwall – around half from Truro itself, but others from up to an hour away and as far afield as St Austell, Bodmin, St Ives and Penzance. Many travel long distances by train (a fleet of double-decker buses ferry them from the station) and parents have organised minibuses from places like Helston.

The boarders include weekly boarders who live in the Scilly Isles, children of expats and a small number of international students from countries like Germany, Spain, Italy, Hong Kong, China, Nigeria, Georgia and Ukraine (around 40 with EAL requirements). Everyone mixes in together – 'it's a really friendly place,' a sixth former told us.

Parents are an eclectic group – lots of doctors, accountants and lawyers plus farmers, holiday park owners and entrepreneurs. Just like their children, they are genial, unpushy and appreciative of the school. As we said last time, there's 'nothing flash or lah-di-dah here.' A mother who'd moved from Surrey told us: 'The teachers are incredibly supportive and down-to-earth – questions and queries always get dealt with, and unlike my son's old school, I never come home grumbling.' Parents also said they approve of the way the school treats youngsters as individuals and seeks to discover everyone's talents.

Distinguished former pupils include former M&S chairman Lord Myners, actors Robert Shaw, John Rhys Davies and Nigel Terry, baritones Benjamin Luxon and Alan Opie, sopranos Lynette Carveth and Saffron Jones, quadruple Olympic gold medallist sailor Ben Ainslie, chess grandmaster Michael Adams and Queen drummer Roger Taylor.

Entrance: Around 40 per cent of the pupils come from the school's own prep, the rest from a host of state and prep schools. School is moderately selective (around 110 applications for 85 year 7 places) and main entry points are at 11, 13 and 16. Admission before sixth form is by entrance exam, school report and interview. For pupils joining sixth form, predicted GCSE grades, school report and interview.

Exit: Around a third leave after GCSEs, either because they want a change or to do subjects not offered by Truro School (many head off to the mighty Truro and Penwith College four miles away, although new head says he is determined to increase retention). After the sixth form most go to university (80 per cent straight from school), including a handful to Oxbridge. One to Oxford in 2016 but another pupil turned down a Cambridge place to study physics at MIT. Maths, sciences and geology are the most popular subjects and Cardiff, Exeter and Bristol the most popular destinations over the last five years, with a few off to Europe or the US. The school offers a specialised careers programme for budding medics, dentists and vets.

Money matters: Academic, art, music, drama, fencing and sport scholarships worth five to 10 per cent of the fees offered. Not a rich school – no endowments – so relies on prudent husbandry and strives to be as inclusive as it can afford to be. Some means-tested bursaries and headmaster's boarding awards (fee discount of 25 per cent) for boarders.

Remarks: A friendly, high achieving school with a real sense of purpose. It combines the best of old and new, makes the most of the bracing Cornish sea air and encourages pupils to find their own niche, whatever it may be.

Uffculme School

Chapel Hill, Uffculme, Cullompton, Devon EX15 3AG

Pupils: 1,020 • Ages: 11–16

Tel: 01884 840458
Email: secretary@uffculmeschool.net
Website: www.uffculmeschool.net

Head teacher: Since 2007, Lorraine Heath, living in Taunton, grew up in Yeovil and studied at Exeter University. Never straying far, she taught English at several schools in Somerset before working as an English advisor for the local authority for a year. After five years as deputy head at Ladymead (now Taunton Academy), she joined Uffculme. Already a very good school, she was determined to make it better.

Lorraine met her husband, also originally a teacher, at Exeter University. He now runs his own business. Her eldest is at university studying philosophy and her youngest is still at school. Any hobbies, we asked? Her friends would say 'shopping and champagne,' she laughed, but in reality it's the gym and time with her family. Definitely 'doesn't do camping'. When invited on a trip by her staff (very outdoorsy, here), she politely declined – 'nowhere to plug in her hair straighteners'. Fair point, we agreed.

Lorraine still teaches – currently GCSE media studies. She likes to be part of the team and wants to get to know the students. One parent said, 'She has the right blend of professionalism and friendly approach. Students respect her, trust her and like her...The teachers all follow her example too. They are friendly and approachable and all teach with amazing diligence.' She says of the school's success, 'The trick is not to overcomplicate – keep it simple – do the right things well.'

Academic matters: In 2016, at GCSE, 86 per cent achieved 5+ A*-C grades including maths and English, with 40 per cent A*/A grades. Results are consistently far above national averages and make Uffculme one of the top performing comprehensive schools in the country; rated outstanding by Ofsted at last inspection. One parent told us, 'We chose Uffculme because of its great reputation. The reputation continues to be good in the area as the academic results have been so impressive.'

Alongside core subjects, all students must take PE, ICT and RE. The majority here take all three sciences separately – when we were there almost an entire class put up their hands when asked if they had chosen separate sciences. Parents would, however, like to see them 'push languages more and offer Spanish and Latin.' For most subjects pupils are taught in ability sets; one parent told us, 'Teachers deal with the mixed abilities well, pushing and challenging in good measure.' Another said, 'The teachers are inspirational, lessons are fun, motivating and engaging.' Some students – around 15 a year – combine fewer GCSEs with vocational qualifications at local colleges. This involves a day a week at either Exeter, Petroc or Bicton Colleges studying mechanics, land based studies or hairdressing, for example.

'Students who receive the pupil premium, disabled students and those with special educational needs all make very good progress', says Ofsted. Good learning support department, with specialist teachers. Students are supported in lessons, in small groups or one-to-one. All pupils take screening tests on entry to the school and there is plenty of literacy and numeracy support for year 7s. One parent we spoke to whose child has significant learning difficulties said, 'We firmly believe that a good quality education should be available locally, within our community. This is sadly more difficult to achieve when your child has significant learning difficulties; however, Uffculme school gets it right, expecting the best from all its students whilst supporting, coaching and nurturing their whole development.' Another parent told us, 'We chose Uffculme because it seemed the only place that seemed able or willing to cater for a child with extreme academic intelligence but also intense special needs. Our decision was based on the learning support team with its clear expertise, understanding and experience of similar children. In particular the HLTA with a specialism in autism gave us confidence.' They added, 'Certain special teachers have genuinely touched and transformed my child's experience of school with a shared enthusiasm for learning.'

The Aspire programme was started in 2013 as a way of supporting student aspirations to gain entry to highly competitive universities. Any year 10 students predicted top grades can attend a regular mentoring session to keep up to date with their academic and emotional progress. There are college and university visits, plus guest speakers and lessons on how the process works. However, it's not just about university and careers; the programme challenges the brighter kids with tasks that they might fail, and teaches them to cope with that failure.

Games, options, the arts: Lots of sports success with some pupils competing at a national level in women's rugby, golf, sprinting and cross-country. The U13 and U15 girls' rugby teams are county champions, as are the U12 boys' team. In basketball, it's the girls winning again – both the U14 and U16 teams are regional winners, and are through to the last eight in the country. Past pupils include an Exeter Chiefs player, a national BMX champion and those playing hockey, rugby, wheelchair badminton and golf for England, plus sailing and horse riding for GB.

Good facilities. Playing fields, plus tennis, netball, basketball courts and a large sports hall. Health & fitness is in a separate building, run as a separate business by the school, with pupils given full and exclusive use during school hours from 7am. There's an impressive fully equipped gym, spinning bikes, weights and a huge dance studio with double-height ceiling (for trampolining). The only thing missing here is an all-weather pitch, but there's one in nearby Cullompton. Uffculme is also very big on outdoor pursuits: canoeing, kayaking, surfing, sailing, climbing, caving, mountain walking, skiing, and of course the Duke of Edinburgh and Ten Tors.

Drama is very popular. As well as drama clubs at lunchtimes there's a major production every other year. Last time it was Les Misérables, and now they're working on The Lion King. With over 100 in the cast and many more involved in costumes, props and music, the drama teacher was suitably excited. He was particularly keen to make use of the music department's African drums and drummers. A new drama theatre is under construction.

Good music department, another popular subject. Concerts are held every term and there are various groups such as the jazz band, choir, singing groups, samba band and other band ensembles. There's a large recording studio, plus the main classroom, and a separate tech room. Individual music lessons are available and if music is chosen at GCSE, the school pays for the lessons to support pupils who are in need of financial assistance.

The school has a good reputation in art and some impressive work is displayed around the school. The art department is in a recently refurbished building, and it's brilliant. In the entrance there's a large papier-mâché tree, huge canvas pieces, murals and 3D pieces. Upstairs are two fantastic studios overlooking the playing fields. Very high standards of artwork; some could easily be mistaken for sixth form work. Students annually exhibit their exam pieces at the local Coldharbour Mill exhibition, and some even sell them there. There are regular visits to art galleries, as well as theatres and concerts.

Extracurricular clubs take place mainly at lunchtime, with sports and revision classes taking place after school. Clubs include chess, computers, scrabble, film, religious groups, book clubs, plus the usual array of music, drama and sporting activities – however, surf club in Croyde on Friday afternoons sounds particularly appealing. There's an annual summer activities week for years 7, 8 and 9 (most popular is the cycling and camping trip to France) and a work experience week for year 10. On average there's six opportunities a year to go camping or on residentials on Dartmoor, Exmoor, Wales or on the coast. There are regular exchanges with France and Germany, as well as skiing trips and an opportunity to travel to China.

Background and atmosphere: Uffculme School was founded in 1954 as a secondary modern with around 200 pupils, turning comprehensive in the 70s. Situated in mid-Devon, Exeter and Taunton are equidistant, Exmoor and Dartmoor are within easy reach, and the north and south coasts are just a short drive away (surf boards and kayaks optional).

It feels a lot smaller than it actually is. It's a small site but it's not cramped. New blocks have been added as and when funding has allowed. The latest addition is the history block with light, airy classrooms all fitted with large screens. Most impressive is the science block. Seven brand new labs, walls of windows and large open hallways decorated with creative scientific abstracts. The art building (built way back in 2013!) used to be the science block but the head won funding to refurbish. She seems particularly good at this; the key, she says, is to 'never give up.' Below the art studios, there's the Art Café. This is year 11's own dedicated space, designed by and run by them. It is far better than most sixth form areas we've seen. There are PCs, an outside picnic table area and barbecue, a radio blaring, café style drinks and snacks, comfy seating. It's the perfect introduction to sixth form life. Parents say, 'The Art Café has helped them to feel more independent and to grow into being year 11 students so that they are ready to move on.'

Uffculme is wireless enabled, and along with the use of laptops and tablets, there are three dedicated ICT suites, each with 30 PCs. In the library, as well as books, there are laptops, digital cameras, video cameras and microphones. There are regular authors' workshops, most recently children's writer David Almond (Kit's Wilderness).

The school feels calm, well managed, and most definitely well maintained. Traditional values like good behavior are a priority, but this doesn't go as far as standing to attention in class. And there are no bells between lessons; it's fairly informal and relaxed here. The head has done a great job in ensuring that the interiors are 'vibrant and attractive', and even 'pretty'. The school feels welcoming; there are photos to make you smile, artwork to inspire, and the stunning views are an added bonus.

Pastoral care, well-being and discipline: 'Pupils are treated with respect at Uffculme and as a result they are very mature,' said one parent. Ofsted agreed, saying, 'Behaviour is exemplary.' The pupils here are provided with fantastic facilities and in return they look after the school and are proud to be part of it. However, it's not just about the material environment; one parent told us, 'I don't know whether [they] would have faired so well in a different school. I put this down to the pastoral component of the school and the supportive style the teaching staff have for each other and the children.'

There's a student nurse, welfare officers, parental support advisors and weekly lunchtime drop-ins with a youth worker. There are tutor groups and a flexible learning centre for those that need to study away from others for one reason or another. Low rate of exclusions. One parent told us, 'They deal with issues without the involvement of parents as much as they can; however, they do call in the parents if things go up to a more serious level.' Another said, 'Issues are dealt with very professionally and personally. The teachers really care about the pupils.'

Pupils and parents: Real mix of families. 'Economically diverse,' we're told. Some are local, some have relocated. 'We were looking around the Exeter area but we heard about Uffculme's great reputation through estate agents and we refocused our house search on villages in the catchment area for the school.' Parents are directors of companies, nurses, estate agents, farmers, doctors; the list is endless. There's a large and active PTA; the last annual craft fair raised almost £6k.

Most parents say they based their decision on local reputation. 'We didn't look at other schools as Uffculme had such a good reputation.' Parents feel involved in the school; one told us, 'The school is great at communicating with parents. The thing they do incredibly well is celebrate the successes of the students. Not just academic but sports activities too.' The school promotes participation and the head and her teachers are frequently seen at local, regional and national events supporting their students. The badge system encourages participation and celebrates success and achievements too. One parent said, 'Uffculme has helped her to think, to aspire to succeed and to see the bigger picture.'

Entrance: Based on catchment area. Seven feeder primary schools, and Uffculme Primary School recently became part of the Uffculme Academy Trust. One parent said, 'it was either Uffculme or Blundell's.'

Good transition. Uffculme's teachers visit the primary schools and set up plenty of opportunities for children and parents to visit the school. 'The process was great; they used to come to Uffculme for sports from primary school which really helped them to settle in. The sports teachers were familiar and friendly, having worked with them before. They also had a wonderful teacher who came to their year 6 lessons and talked about life at Uffculme.' Once started, pupils are split into tutor groups, and in the first few weeks they take part in a variety of team-building activities to give them all a chance to make friends and settle in. Children with special needs are given an 18-month transition phase, and one parent told us, 'This meant that when September came she was absolutely ready to start and coped exceptionally well with the change.'

Exit: Most choose to take advanced academic or vocational courses at Petroc in Tiverton, Richard Huish College or Somerset College of Arts and Technology in Taunton, Exeter College, Bicton College or the sixth forms of independent schools and other colleges. Any famous leavers? Joss Stone, of course!

There are mixed feelings on the lack of a sixth form. Historically there's never been a sixth form and there probably never will be. On funding issues alone, the local colleges are very good so it would be hard to compete. 'My son is definitely ready to leave as he is in a hurry to grow up. I think the year 11 Art Café helps the children adjust towards becoming more independent.' 'The addition of a sixth form would be an excellent improvement to the school. [My child] will be very sad to leave the school and wishes there was a sixth form there.' The jury is out on this one.

Money matters: South West Regional Winner at the Pupil Premium Awards 2015, receiving £100k. This funding is mainly being used for the year 7 Catch Up programme to help improve literacy and numeracy. It will also be used to provide free meals and breakfasts, uniforms, books and emotional support. The school has its own charity trust to help with additional costs like music lessons, extracurricular activities and trips.

Remarks: Great. Stimulating and creative learning environment; fantastic place to go to school. Strong head teacher with a good team – the results speak for themselves. The general consensus is that 'Uffculme offers pretty much what the local private schools offer.' Children of all abilities fare well here. We might just have to look up a few estate agents ourselves.

UWC Atlantic College

St Donat's Castle, St Donat's, Llantwit Major, Vale of Glamorgan CF61 1WF

Pupils: 367; all full boarders • Ages: 15-19

Fees: Boarding £28,105 pa

Tel: 01446 799000
Email: jan.bishop@atlanticcollege.org
Website: www.atlanticcollege.org

Principal: Since March 2017, Peter Howe, currently head of college at UWC Maastricht in the Netherlands. Degree in accounting, finance and economics from Queen's University in Ontario and PhD in art and architectural history from University of Toronto. Had a brief stint in sales and marketing at Procter and Gamble before switching to teaching, and spent 13 years at Canadian universities. His UWC career began in 2005, as the IB coordinator and head of economics at the Italy-based UWC Adriatic. Later, he became the school's deputy head and director of studies and ultimately, its rettore (head of school), before moving to Maastricht in 2012.

Academic matters: Education starts with the IB but, like the battery-powered toy bunnies in those long ago TV ads, keeps on going long after other schools have ground to a halt, courtesy of the Atlantic College Diploma, the compulsory, wrap-around co-curricular programme introduced in 2012.

Diploma extras take up a good 30 per cent of pupils' time, 'and probably more,' requiring the academic component of the IB (no picnic at the best of times) to be breezed through in just five mornings plus an afternoon in the classroom each week. Pupils choose one of four 'experiential' faculties, each big on the redemptive powers of active, selfless participation (very Kurt Hahn), that add to the IB's magnificent seven and tick off its creativity, action and service component en route.

There's outdoor (focus on those in peril on the seas – past pupil and teacher developed now best-selling RIB boat, then, combining brilliance and philanthropy in equal measure, selflessly donated patent to the RNLI); social justice (first hand encounters of a robust kind, including work with refugees and prisoners' families); global (everything from organising peace events to sharing a dorm with traditional enemies); and environmental, where commitment to sustainability is no light matter (students, who recycle everything, deeply miffed by college's failure to consult over green disposal of fittings following boarding house refurb).

It's education the immersive way, students picking a theme that interests them and following its thread through their studies – real world, practical applications dovetailing with academic side. Someone with an interest in Middle East might study Arabic, prepare an extended essay in world studies, help set up a project week in Jordan and, through this, 'understand the UWC mission in the way they choose to develop their strengths,' says head of curriculum.

At its best (which is much of the time) diploma activities feed back into lessons, making for a buzzy classroom atmosphere where passionate debate is a way of life. There's nothing like hearing about refugees' experiences then discussing them back at base to add bite to economics or geography lessons. 'Makes it much more interesting and stimulating. I think it affects their exam grades, too'. Worked wonders on inspectors too, who assumed students leading lessons (spreading the word to peers in other diploma facilities is part of the syllabus) were teachers and had graded them outstanding before misunderstanding pointed out.

Structure won't be for everyone, particularly those with league-leaping performance as sole aspiration. College holds trenchant views on results, which are 'meaningless after a few years. It's the outcome that is important. We measure the success in the effect our students have on the world'.

Despite this, has earned itself plenty of bragging rights, with average IB score of 35 in 2016, including a good proportion of bilingual diplomas. If not at the very top of the tree, it's well ahead of the world average (around 30) and not to be sniffed at, particularly as for some students, who are selected on potential rather than educational back story, this may be their first ever brush with formal schooling.

Hot spots include spectacular languages (nine mother tongue or foreign options and a further 21, including Khmer, Mongolian and Welsh, as self-taught subjects). Maths and science are also very strong, say students – big clue to expectations the vast university physics textbook toted with pride by first year student.

With run of the mill IB students elsewhere already reckoned to be worked more intensively than A level counterparts, it's useful to arrive with work ethic fully formed and be good with stress, say students, who rapidly acquire super-efficient learning techniques.

Pre-diploma programme sees some 20 15-16 year olds who aren't yet ready for full-on IB experience doing one year IGCSE course (26 per cent A*/As in 2016) alongside co-curricular activities.

In the main, it's attitude of mind that determines student suitability. 'Not for the weak-hearted,' thought one. Just as true for teachers, many with similar international background. Total conversion to college philosophy the norm and few move back to conventional posts afterwards. Once recruited, becomes a forever post, others paling into comparison. 'You're spoiled for life', thought one, while college newsletter praised students' freedom to 'chase academic hares into the undergrowth of learning [...] keeping an eye on the syllabus and sometimes even a blind eye'.

Generous with their time (lots of impromptu one-to-one sessions were under way in final run up to IB exams), teachers praised for effective problem-spotting system that kicks in early, tutors the first point of call, subject specialists alerted and involved as necessary.

Other areas (notably EAL, learning needs, gifted and talented), formerly a bit piecemeal but are having policies written and in some cases coordinators, including SENCo, appointed. Essential, given some pupils' patchy educational history and/or imperfect grasp of English (no minimum language requirement for EU students). Lack of screening during committee-based recruitment system also means learning needs (mostly mild Asperger's, SpLD and ADHD) will only be picked up on arrival, though good to see real commitment to disabled access. Wheelchair access determinedly provided wherever possible, whole classes relocated if necessary when it isn't.

Overall, exceptionally demanding curriculum covers emotional, intellectual and practical terrain that many adults would find hard going. Though something you'd hesitate to impose elsewhere, impressively mature bunch here take it in their stride. Only student doubt was perception that college is putting greater focus on IB scores. College is adamant this isn't the case.

Games, options, the arts: Whichever diploma faculty they choose, students are unlikely to spend much time sitting on their hands, all areas being long on activity. Derring-do comes with the territory no matter what the gradient, acquisition of skills in graceful failure as important as trappings of success (fallibility reckoned by Kurt Hahn to be essential part of the learning process). As a result, there isn't much pupils here would say no to, from consorting with top scientists and politicians at climate change summit in Fiji to qualifying as a music therapist.

Outdoor faculty is the most obviously action-packed of the bunch. Students join either aquatic water activities team (kayaking and surfing on offer but highlight lifeboat training at college's own RNLI station) or sign up to Terra Firma, which features mountain walking, navigation, emergency first aid and climbing (Brecon Beacons, a few miles inland, the venue for unlimited yomping).

While physical activity is compulsory, organised sport isn't. Stems from character building the Kurt Hahn way, which almost heretically relegates organised games to an 'important but not predominant' position in the hierarchy.

What happens and whether it happens at all is largely down to pupils. Though specialist coaches visit (pupils seemed slightly hazy about the details), there's no head of sport and activities vary from year to year depending on each cohort's enthusiasms. As a result, vast games field is intermittently used. Only sound on a fine spring afternoon was the bleating of newborn lambs from on-site farm. Anyone expecting pitches groaning with glory-seeking team endeavours may well be in for a bit of a shock.

Similarly, though IB studies are efficiently catered for with public showcases including drama reviews and weekly music recitals, there's not much in the way of large scale musical or dramatic endeavours.

Boarding: Seven boarding houses. Their distinctive characters, reflected in not always flattering secret student nicknames (we know what they are, too, but had to promise not to tell), are home to just under 50 pupils each. Pastoral care efficiently provided by brace of well-liked houseparents. Facilities are 'simple', says college, and they're not wrong. Perfectly acceptable though, with extensive communal drying rooms and welly racks (essential given climate) and enough single showers to ensure sufficient privacy for those who find communal versions problematic. Pre-diploma pupils have their own house.

There's the odd idiosyncrasy when it comes to equipment – irons are allowed in dorms, kettles are not (one boarding house has just been rebuilt following a fire). But this is outweighed by impressive, all-round sensitivity, subtle pooling of kitchen equipment in mixed common rooms avoiding distinctions between haves and have-nots, daily deliveries of communal food essentials.

Background and atmosphere: For mood and idealism, think educational version of Star Trek, the crew's goal less about finding 'strange new worlds' than improving the one they're in, one dilithium crystal at a time. While hippies might give peace a chance by putting flowers in gun barrels, Hahn's solution to unify Cold War ridden world of the 1960s and ward off what he saw as the physical and moral decline of the young was to found a school (two, if you count Gordonstoun, many more if you allow Round Square schools).

Here, the aim was to create a harmonious blend of nations and cultures, pairing opposites of every sort, oppressors and oppressed, poor and rich, who by living and studying together would develop shared outlook and common purpose (though took until 1967 before they got round to adding girls).

College remains a one-off in the UK and was the first of what is now 12-strong United World Colleges international movement. Its niche status and relatively low profile (even amongst heads, let alone the average parent) is, however, in inverse proportion to behind the scenes clout. Former students are embedded in some of the most powerful organisations and political administrations in the world, from the Chinese and US governments to top banks, providing under the radar alternative to conventional old boys' (and girls') network and one with huge clout.

Setting – in 800-year-old castle by the sea – is out of this world and much appreciated by production companies (has featured in Dr Who). In addition to as many corkscrewing staircases as you can shake a medieval flail at, castle interior features terrific library, galleried and home to municipal quantities of books including Harry Potter (a college favourite) in assorted translations.

Appearances are slightly deceptive. Assorted chunks of apparently authentic gorgeousness such as stone entrance to dining hall pillaged wholesale from Boston Church in Lincolnshire by former owner, the newspaper magnate William Randolph Hearst. His wholesale salvage sweep also included the carved heads adorning the breakfast room ceiling – Lewis Carroll's inspiration, apparently, for Tweedledum and Tweedledee.

Lessons in many cases a perfect match for surroundings. History lessons compete with hard to improve vistas through arrow slits to wooded hill beyond, art and music located in nicely converted stable block. Other subjects are taught in three 1970s teaching blocks (science and maths, perhaps appropriately, in crumbliest and flakiest), all apparently constructed, together with admin centre, by embittered town planner having a bad day and featuring urban-style mini-underpass.

With just one communal TV to its name, a climate that's far from tropical and the nearest cinema nine miles away by land (or 13 if teamed with a bracing swim across the Bristol Channel), this is a place that needs decent social events more than most. Until recently, though, it wasn't getting them, felt pupil. Far better now, with weekly disco (noise levels bravely borne by principal, who lives opposite), boarding houses charged with weekend event organisation, and much more to do.

The sense of being a body apart is reinforced by two-term structure that follows the beat of the IB drum – with the result that pupils only have four days off between January and May and are then off on holiday until early August when second year pupils arrive back for a week's bonding before new intake turns up.

Physical apartness makes it something of unknown quantity within the local community. 'Out of my league,' thought one local. 'Feels exclusive – if you can afford for your kids to go there, you're doing well'. No wonder the college is contemplating a hearts, minds and meters job to get locals, starting with taxi drivers, who are probably the college's most frequent visitors, on side.

Pastoral care, well-being and discipline: New arrivals are paired with 'excellent' buddies, big on tea and sympathy (favour returned when it comes to exam time). Their first task is probably to settle nerves after meeting and greeting ceremony, where they're drummed in with chorus of pots and pans pillaged from common rooms by second years ('it leaves terrible dents', said one pupil, who as kitchen monitor was charged with subsequent search and rescue mission).

With full boarding the only option (though parents can come and stay nearby at beginning and ends of term), inner core of steel probably helps, given policy of picking room-mates for differences, the more apparently irreconcilable the better. 'We would always put Israelis and Palestinians together', says principal, who is spearheading drive to recruit Syrians from both sides of current conflict.

Pupils aren't just in favour of approach but drawn to college because of it. Beliefs that elsewhere would be on collision course (there's a strong LGBT movement, for example) spark enduring friendships and sometimes more, with potential for heartache when relationships breach cultural barriers.

Whether deliberately or by chance, student bonds are well and truly cemented by decision to involve them in the nuts and bolts of college operations. Open book policy on everything from finances to rebuilding ensures that student voice isn't merely heard but is a force to be reckoned with, from spontaneous orations in assembly on whatever issues take their fancy, college-related or otherwise (polemic following death of Mrs Thatcher made for edgy listening) to indignation over any perceived high-handedness. 'If they give us a voice, that's what they have to expect', said one.

So while there's considerable disquiet over new pre-IB year, it's as nothing compared with fury, manifested in banners and even anonymous notes, following introduction of boarding house locks (sadly an inspection non-negotiable). It's just as well college pre-empted decades of conflict by ditching uniform in the 1970s. 'Pupils fear change' – might be right at that, what with tolerance for far more obtrusive but longer-standing security measures such as airport-style library security gate and 11 separate entry codes (a school record, we reckon) covering everything from Mac lab to harp storage. No wonder one pupil adopts low-tech approach of banging on the window to attract attention instead.

Impressive maturity means that nobody sweats the small stuff. Courtesy on both sides is a given, teachers generally liked (only one got thumbs down) and while big issues go to the wire, there are minimal rules elsewhere, nous and good sense taken as read. 'We don't need a rule about using phones in lessons when it would clearly be rude', a pupil told us.

Pupils and parents: Easy to gush over pupils' self-assurance and intelligence which carries all before it (just one non-show in recent memory, pupil so overcome with nerves that unable to board the plane). A sassy bunch, it's no surprise that many have persuaded their parents that this is the place to be and in one case at least secured the sponsorship to pay the fees.

Though fees are 'low compared to other top boarding schools', says college, they are still high enough to skew social mix towards luxury ingredients rather than salt of the earth. Or in UWC words, 'similar people simply born in different places'. A pupil says that this 'isn't the place for the materialistic or those who believe the world can get better with money alone'. Parent philanthropy is a way of life, one family funding not only their own child but three others, too. Similar acts of generosity both widespread and long term.

Five-strong development department works with alumni who include King of the Netherlands, chairman of Shell and vice-president of European Bank to get that giving feeling early. And give they do. Vocal and passionate espousal of college and ideals often continues for life, endorsements from everyone from Nelson Mandela to Queen Noor of Jordan setting the tone. It's resulting in growing numbers from the poorest and most war-torn regions of earth.

Some local recruitment, extending to deprived Liverpool, Birmingham and Valleys schools, requires a bit of careful eggshell treading to avoid Orphan Annie connotations, college raising grateful poor to a life of privilege. So far so good.

Entrance: 'The world is our catchment area', says college (90 nationalities currently). Makes a refreshing change from same old distance from home criteria, but downside is labyrinthine admissions process requiring minotaur-seeking levels of persistence (though no string). Think Oxbridge inter-college pupil swapsies at admissions time, add international dimension requiring agreement between parents, students and UWC staff who may all be on different continents, and it's not surprising that entrance process is officially badged as 'extremely complicated'. On the surface it's highly competitive, too, with nearly 100 nations jostling for places, just 20 available for UK nationals and a further 17 places in other UWC colleges.

Would-be pupils submit applications either to one of 140 UWC national committees, often staffed by alumni, or direct to colleges – specific requirements as individual as they are. Though they can express college preferences, they're assumed to be signing up to UWC aims rather than a location, and so could end up being offered a place somewhere completely different. Loving care is advised to ensure that focus on community work and support for UWC ideals shine through. Also useful to ensure academic endorsement (no GCSE minimum grades specified, every application considered on merit) is from teacher '... who supports the idea of you going to a UWC'. (Our tip: use the word 'mission' at least once).

Shortlisted UK candidates have an overnight stay at the castle, followed by informal 20-minute interview with committee members, alumni and, unusually, former rather than current teachers. Final decision communicated around three weeks later (though can take longer). Whole process is an excellent Kurt Hahn-style challenge and, if you meet the age criteria (students normally start aged 16 or 17, though there's some flexibility), there's the chance to do it all over again the following year.

Exit: It's off to better things not just for pupils, but with 70 per cent ultimately ending up in humanitarian-linked careers, for the world as a whole. While US admissions tutors zoom in early, like dealers at a jumble sale before the doors open to the general punters, other top unis aren't far behind.

US is the most popular university destination overall with close to 40 per cent of places (college doesn't train students to take SATs, but is a test centre), followed by UK (28 per cent – vast majority to Russell group members, including two to Oxbridge and four to study medicine in 2016) then Canada and Europe, with a few to Asia. Recent destinations include Harvard, Cambridge, Brown, MIT, Yale, Princeton, UCL, Sherbrooke and Cornell.

Around 18 per cent take a gap year or go off to complete national service. Courses many and various. A pupil we spoke to hoped to major in physics with laudable aim of investigating travel across vacuums in outer space.

Money matters: Admissions process supported by large fundraising and development department working overtime to bring in the dosh. Latest initiative themed to college's 50th anniversary (think of a number, any number, with a 50 in it and hand it over) is generating over £2 million a year, almost all used to fund scholarships. Other countries chip in, too (Norwegian government funds 10 of its own students, for example). In all, over 55 per cent of students have some sort of financial support.

Remarks: Once a glorious experiment, still out on a limb (and, we suspect, in no hurry to shed iconoclastic status), Atlantic College provides an education as remarkable as the feisty, impassioned students it attracts. The ticking of admin boxes may annoy, but it's a necessary evil that parents will welcome. Its location may be isolated but its perspective, genuinely global, is anything but. Just don't expect a picnic by the sea.

Wellington School

South Street, Wellington, Somerset TA21 8NT

Pupils: 965; 105 full, 17 weekly boarders • Ages: 2-18 (boys board from 11, girls from 13) • Sixth form: 180 • C of E

Fees: Day £5,970 – £14,355; Boarding £21,600 – £29,610 pa

Tel: 01823 668800
Email: enquiries@wellingtonschool.org.uk
Website: www.wellington-school.org.uk

Headmaster: Since 2014, Henry Price MA (40s), previously senior housemaster at Rugby. After reading classics at Oxford, started teaching career at Sydney Grammar School (Oxford Classics Fellow), before moving to Sherborne. At Rugby for 13 years; was head of classics, housemaster, coached rugby, cricket and netball, and was involved in 'trips, debating and much more'. He is a governor of Skinner's Academy in Hackney. Married to Mary, whom he met at Oxford, and who is training for her first triathlon; they have four young children. Holidays are spent on the beaches of Anglesey and walking in Snowdonia.

Head of prep school: Since September 2010, Adam Gibson (mid 40s). A Wellington pupil himself, he was previously head of Manor House Honiton, which closed in 2010. He is a triathlete and takes a running club at the school as well teaching some ICT and maths. Adept at analysis, having had an earlier career in information systems, he is dab hand at tracking and assessing pupils' progress. Achievement is monitored in conjunction with their cognitive ability and quick action taken if potential is not being realised. Despite these skills, he is essentially a people person. He and his deputy meet children and parents in the playground each morning so that he can assess each child's mood, pick up parental concerns. 'A child should be happy, confident, prepared to experiment and think differently. Every child should be inspired every day.' Looking round this delightful school it is easy to believe in inspired pupils. Mr Gibson has a son in the senior school and is pleased to find that the spirit of the school is similar to his day.

Academic matters: One prep school classroom boasts a real ex BBC Dalek, while a wall we passed was covered with writing exercises in which some observant children had enjoyed 'comparing father with a gorilla' – the children's writing was workmanlike and the gorilla had the advantage. Lessons, even the serious ones, looked fun, from the enchanting animal songs in the nursery to the studious reading in an older year. Children are screened both for learning difficulties and for physical mobility – 'the motor skills are so vital to development'. Learning support team works in class and withdraws pupils where necessary, giving particular attention to the exam year.

Wellington sits comfortably between its local Taunton independent rivals in academic achievement and considerably higher than the nearest sixth form college. Over the past 10 or so years it has had pretty consistent sound results at GCSE and A level. It is proud of 66 per cent A*-B and 40 per cent A*/A grades at A level in 2016. While it's not right at the top of the national league tables, recent scores in maths and science, both IGCSEs, are impressive. (In 2016, 53 per cent A*/A grades overall.) Classes average 22, but not larger than 25. All study French in the first three years and pick up either German or Spanish and Latin. All do RS, Eng lang and lit, maths (IGCSE), either three separate sciences (IGCSE) or dual award, and at least one language (if two taken one has to be French ie can't do Spanish and German). State of art language IT, in use on our visit. Outstanding classics department gives Latin an exceptionally high take up. Music and drama on offer in a basically standard selection, except for Greek, which has grown from a club started 10 years ago, and is taught in spare time. A level offers a free choice and generally manages to timetable it. Economics and classical subjects get a small take up as do all mod langs, with maths (plus further maths) and physics topping the bill, both with very good record of A*/As. Plenty of options for less academic students, whose results are more than adequate. High fliers – quite a few of them – with some fast track arrangements when parents request it.

Extensive new labs are well designed (by teachers) with separate areas for study and practical work. Aristotle the axolotl (Mexican amphibian with external gills) is lovingly looked after by the physics technician, typifying the enterprising flexibility of the school. Though large and exceptionally well-equipped, the labs are functional rather than spectacular, with lots of bare breezeblock – reflecting the common sense economy which has allowed the school to undertake massive developments over the years. Spacious but understated new English teaching block also houses a comprehensive SEN department (SEN help offered at need on individual or group basis by qualified staff of three, though charges for extra English for foreign students) and an enormous exam hall. It means other spaces don't get blocked at exam time and gives assembly and function space. One year GCSE programme for students from abroad allows them to get up to five basic subject passes in order to do A levels in sixth form or IB elsewhere.

Games, options, the arts: Even those reluctant to exercise seem to get a look in. A parent commented that boys and girls alike are encouraged but not forced, and the truly non-sporty get support, a few concessions but enough exercise. Lots of teams for everything with girls' hockey and boys' cricket getting players to county level, while girls' netball is making a splash locally. There's definitely a rugby set, parents say, with 10 teams posting enthusiastic reports of results in the school mag. Most of the usual summer and winter sports (no soccer?) with athletics outstanding. Elite cricket and athletics programme. Fantastic pale blue Princess Royal Sports Centre (she opened it) with its own department of sports medicine, huge adaptable sports hall with viewing and teaching spaces and fitness suite. Lovely dance studio is also home to fencing with a small but very distinguished take up reaching national level.

Masses of sport at the prep too, with rugby number one for boys and netball (now at national level) for girls. Though it's pretty competitive, one parent recounted with gratitude that her eager but disappointed son had been completely consoled by spending match time learning to make a cake. Wellington Prep holds the national under 11 title for cross-country.

New music block is rather small, which belies the emphasis on music (an 'all Steinway school'). Regular chapel sung services, lots of orchestras and small groups orchestral, choral, classic and pop, include 'Girlforce9', a self-generated a capella choir. 'Cushion concerts' in lunch hours for lower school as well as the usual full school ones and masses of encouragement for all types of music, such as the summer 'fretted strings' celebrations for guitarists. The prep school music department has an orchestra where even beginners can join in. As well as classrooms, the upper floor, arranged around the wide corridor with windows down to the central atrium, has dedicated art space, music teaching rooms for class (with lots of instruments and keyboards) and individual lessons.

Drama uses the main school hall converted to a blacked-out all-singing-and-dancing venue, opened by past pupil David Suchet. A bit of a desecration of what must have been a gracious, light-filled school hall (not a permanent one, says school – curtains frequently drawn back for events), one of the few original buildings, but allowing frequent huge musical productions which pupils clearly adore. There's serious stuff as well: The Crucible, Odysseus, Tristan and Isolde. Brilliant posters and some outstanding theatre photography attest to the quality achieved. Smashing photography in lots of the school's promotional bumf must emanate from the influence of the art department. Its policy is 'to encourage self expression', but the work on show in the cramped department bursts with exceptional observation and drawing as well as tremendous imaginative use of material, extending to 3D and photography. Some of the best school art around.

Prominent CCF means that school is full of service (all three) uniform every Friday and drilling seemed to occupy most of the afternoon we visited. Year 11 was embarking in huge numbers on a weekend camp. Air force cadets get a flight before they leave sixth form, navy actually get to sea plus plenty of free sail training etc and army cadets were handling some alarmingly real guns.

'Almost too much to do,' a parent commented. Twenty or so activities on offer, from semi-academic to energetic, as well as all the sport/music/drama/CCF programmes. The usual exchanges and visits abound. A sample school mag reported 15, 10 of which were abroad – New York, South Africa, Greece and Alps for skiing etc (not counting CCF and D of E) and Barbados, the Arctic Circle and Tunisia are in the pipeline. Occasional financial support for trips central to curriculum.

Younger prep children get out of the town environment for forest school days spent in their Blackdown hills site, wellies, anoraks and all. In all weathers, snow, rain or shine – except for high winds (dangerous in forests) – they enjoy a muddy natural learning environment, exploring and gaining skills such as making clay oven damper bread and eggs scrambled in a plastic bag. Older children have nature study day projects and a survival course, successful enough for pupils to enjoy teaching their parents a thing or two when they are allowed to join in.

The recently devised 'Aces' scheme encourages pupils to take responsibility for their own development and learning. Pupils have a termly tutor interview to reflect on their underlying skills, based round competence in action, communication, exploration and self-development.

Boarding: Boys can board from 11, girls from 13. Top juniors and first two years of senior have mixed boarding in Overside. Senior boarding boys have two houses, and one for senior girls. The vast majority of day pupils are split into three boys' and three girls' houses. Fairly basic accommodation in comparison with the five star rooms of some schools, but boarders seem contented, and there are all the trimmings of common rooms, kitchens, showers etc and the odd bath for easing the rugby stiffness.

Background and atmosphere: Founded in 1837 as Benjamin Frost's Classical Mathematical and Commercial Academy, occupying the great hall, where all teaching took place, Wellington morphed into the West Somerset County School. In 1945, as Wellington School, it became the first direct grant school and became fully independent in the 1970s. Girls infiltrated it from 1972, and in 1997 it added Wellington Junior School, now called Wellington Prep. The current site straggles across a busy-ish road (no over- or underpass) in the little town of Wellington, birthplace of the Iron Duke. A mixture of Georgian-type houses converted into sixth form centre, head's house and san, and facilities purpose built or acquired over its 175 years rejoice in styles of these various times. A huge tree-lined green expanse edged by new labs, pool etc creates central campus. It softens the red-brick neoclassical great hall and gothic spikes of the chapel, built to commemorate the fallen of WW1, with a stunning blue star-studded ceiling, carved oak pews and angel decked organ. Used for daily assembly and masses of music it is, physically, the central point of Wellington.

Smart, refurbished reception and head master's offices – definitely welcoming; comfortable library with terrific AV, friendly round tables for clean cafeteria style dining, serving a choice of Friday fish, on our visit, including popular but rather small portions of moules marinières. Lunch is extra but very few opt out.

Parents wax lyrical about the prep school. Several, with children recently moved, note their offspring blossoming in attitude and confidence. The building, Mr Gibson considers, needs trees to soften its edges. Meanwhile, the playground is full of timber play equipment, puzzles and trails painted on walls and tarmac, a lovely Wendy house for tinies, and even the fence posts are shaped like coloured pencils. In the library, colourful little mats looking like open books invite children to sit and read, while the big central atrium has a chess board carpet. Assemblies, indoor PE, lunches and anything needing space happen here, but carpets are spotless even at the end of the day.The surrounding corridors are wide enough to have recesses with seats and table for extra teaching or just chatting. Enchanting toddlers group, 'Little Wellies', for pre-school age; brand new nursery for two year olds.

Pastoral care, well-being and discipline: Pastoral care is delivered via the houses, with each pupil allocated a tutor who takes pupils right through the school and is first point of call for parents. Problems are dealt with sensitively, say parents, and children given every support in settling and studying. No recent incidents calling for ultimate sanction of permanent exclusion. Parents agree that neither drugs nor drink are rife, and say pupils know where they stand on this (urine tests for suspects) and other matters of discipline. Plenty of responsibility for house and school captains, and for lower school prefects.

Pupils and parents: Definitely not a toff school, but lots of Somerset families – inevitably farmers and businesses relating to farming. Professionals and families where both parents work to cover the fees. A few expats and a tranche of international boarders (about 65 per cent), some of whom come in via the school's one year GCSE programme. Huge majority of day pupils come in by bus from Exeter and Chard to the south, Minehead and Dulverton to the north west and beyond Bridgewater to the east.

Despite the usual reservations of some parents and pupils that kilted skirts don't suit all shapes, and regulations are not always enforced, Wellington uniform of blue crested blazer (quite expensive), white shirt and grey trousers/skirt is worn with evident pride by pupils. Not a half-mast tie or dipping hemline in sight. Second hand shop.

Past pupils include David Suchet, Jeffrey Archer, the late Keith Floyd, actress Carly Bawden, ex Black Rod Sir Freddie Viggers, mathematician and author Simon Singh and marine biologist, Dr Jon Copley.

Entrance: Not selective into the prep, but those who won't cope are 'turned away gently'. They won't admit anyone who won't make the senior school.

Main senior entry at 11, with 30 per cent from junior school, then at 13 and to lower sixth. Pupils can enter for any year, but if it is half way through an exam course and the syllabus does not match, they may be advised to repeat a year. Broadly selective, tending to discourage potential non-copers. At 11 all, including juniors, take the school's own exam in January. At 13 from prep schools, exams in maths, English, science and a subject of their choice from modern languages, history or geography.

International pupils can enter via one year GCSE programme and pay a higher fee to cover any extra tuition needed.

Exit: Over 90 per cent go on to the senior school; the remainder are either scholarship winners to other schools or go to the state system. Prep school children take the same exam as outsiders. Almost 20 per cent leave after GCSE, often to Taunton's Robert Huish College, which has a good reputation. The head points out that some parents make a strategic decision to fund years 7-11. Vast majority from upper sixth to uni, about half in mainstream subjects to established courses. Five to Oxbridge in 2016, and one medic; lots of mathematicians, linguists and classicists. Tiny trickle straight to Forces or training.

Money matters: Both boarding and day are pretty good value in comparison with similar schools. Scholarships, both academic and talent related (music, drama, sport), between 10 and 50 per cent of fees awarded at years 7, 9 and 12 by examination, audition etc. Scholarship holders can apply for means-tested bursaries of up to 100 per cent. The school spends cautiously, avoiding the flashily expensive, but has nevertheless achieved tremendously improved facilities over the last six or seven years.

Remarks: Can't think why Wellington hasn't featured in Good Schools' Guide until recently. Friendly, purposeful and busy, it is a solid, well-managed school, neat but not glossy, giving its pupils a sound education and masses of high points in developmental experience. Its flexible and approachable style means happy pupils and happy parents.

W

Wells Cathedral School

The Liberty, Wells, Somerset BA5 2ST

Pupils: 796; 245 boarders • Ages: 3-18 (boarding from year 5) • Sixth form: 200 • C of E

Fees: Day £7,272 – £17,895; Boarding £20,970 – £29,948 pa

Tel: 01749 834200
Email: main-office@wells-cathedral-school.com
Website: www.wells-cathedral-school.com

Head: Since September 2016, Andy Kemp, previously deputy head and maths teacher. Several degrees and postgrad qualifications from Warwick in maths and maths education, plus an MBA in educational leadership from the Instutute of Education. Taught maths and ICT at Warwick School and moved to Taunton School as HoD; joined Wells as director of studies before moving upwards.

Head of junior school: Since April 2014, Mrs Julie Barrow. A longstanding member of the junior school staff, and still very much involved in the day to day delivery of the curriculum at all levels of both pre-prep and prep. Her appointment has delighted parents. 'The school is thriving under her care,' wrote one parent, 'she is down to earth, has a great sense of humour and clear leadership skills. She also has a truly professional and committed team around her.' Another grateful mother added, 'Mrs Barrow is the most wonderful, kind and caring head teacher. She is always approachable, and in every instance the child comes first.'

Previous senior school head, Elizabeth Cairncross, is now principal of the whole school. Read English at London University (Bedford College, now joined with Royal Holloway College). Formerly deputy head of Christ's Hospital, Horsham, where she had been a teacher since 1986. A passionate believer in co-education, and radiates calm confidence in the school. Not an elite musician herself – a useful asset here, she believes – but came to Wells because 'the Wells way is to look at what's the best way and it was that creativity that attracted me.'

Impresses as a true scholar, who thinks hard about life, the universe and everything; and as a modernizer who is nonetheless at home with tradition. Hugely popular with parents, who queued up to give praise: 'An inspirational leader, who doesn't take any flannel, is very focused, and manages to juggle the many facets of the school with skill and aplomb'; 'Clearly not a head who rests on her laurels, and there is a definite sense of a school wishing to explore new ways of working and not being satisfied with the status quo'; 'An excellent role model with high academic standards'; 'What I love is that the children absolutely and 100 percent come first for her' – etc.

Academic matters: Wells's unique selling point is flexibility. The school goes out of its way to address individual needs and preferences, and the results are highly creditable. In 2016, 64 per cent of GCSEs and 43 per cent of A levels were graded at A*/A. Compared with the other specialist music schools, offers a broad and challenging curriculum, with a good range of languages on offer: French, German, Spanish, Italian, Mandarin and Latin. Really excellent maths provision, owing to the innovative Specialist Maths Scheme, which allows able students an extra three hours of maths per week and aims to turn out creative mathematicians who can think beyond the syllabus.

Why maths in particular? School says, 'It grew out of the music – we already knew how to specialize and be flexible.' Science labs endearingly shabby, but science teaching is 'very good, one of the strengths of the school,' according to a parent, and the pupils we spoke to – one of whom was off to Edinburgh to read medicine – agreed. Humanities also popular: one mother wrote, 'The school is now providing some really exciting and interesting history, philosophy, etc.' No IB – head dislikes the amount of assessment involved, and prefers the depth of A levels (Cambridge Pre-U also offered in history). Everyone praised the teaching staff's willingness to give students the support they needed and to work constructively with all pupils, including those for whom music came first. Small class sizes and kind, knowledgeable staff, many of whom have been here for years and have a huge loyalty to the school.

SEN well catered for, with specialists in both the junior and senior schools ('second to none,' according to the mother of a dyslexic pupil), and school excels at adapting its provision to the individual student, an approach head clearly relishes: 'In 10 years' time, all schools will have to offer bespoke programmes for everybody.' One mother ran out of superlatives when describing the way the staff had worked with her to draw up a care plan for managing her child's epilepsy. At the other end of the scale, parents rated the way their bright children had been stretched and challenged: 'The teaching is really good for an able child, and the maths has been wonderful.'

Given that Wells isn't overly selective in terms of academic ability, we were much struck with the school's achievements in this area and asked how it was done. 'By tailoring, by playing to people's strengths, by being can-do, and by having staff prepared to put the grounding in place,' was the answer. Parents agree: 'The children do incredibly well there, but it comes without the hothousing stress that other nearby schools create,' said one. 'They're really, really good at getting the best out of their pupils, no matter what their level is,' wrote another.

Games, options, the arts: Wells is one of five UK schools accorded specialist music school status by the government's Music and Dance Scheme and, as you'd expect, the music here is very special indeed. We heard a stunning young violinist rehearsing Korngold's violin concerto with the school's equally stunning symphony orchestra, which pretty much set us up for the day. For those who love music, there's a pulse-racingly good range of ensembles and other opportunities offered by the nine performance faculties: brass, composition, choristers, jazz, keyboard, percussion, strings, vocals and woodwind. The new Cedars Hall offers a world class concert venue within the school grounds, adding to the school's already-top-notch music facilities. Quirkier aspects of music also catered for: the percussion suite includes a World Percussion room, complete with its own Indonesian gamelan – other specialist music schools, please take note. All children in year 1 are offered free violin lessons, and the lovely end-of-year performance we heard testified to their impressive progress in this area. Fantastic and inclusive junior choir performs in concerts and all children aged 3 to 11 are involved in the school shows. For the specialists, there are two highly-regarded sets of junior choristers, one for boys and one for girls.

Parents and students alike praised the inclusivity of the music provision at Wells, saying that all pupils had the opportunity to take part and to excel if they wished, and many felt that the music benefited pupils in ways beyond the music itself: 'I think that being in a place where musical excellence is encouraged has inspired excellence in other areas,' wrote one mother, and others said similar. May not suit young musicians seeking the hardcore, all-or-nothing ethos of the other specialist music schools, but the parents we spoke to felt this was a strength: 'That's the real and very special feature of Wells,' wrote a father. 'It makes highly skilled musicians feel normal and grounds them in real life.'

Better sports than at any of the other specialist music schools, and pretty good for any school. Lovely new sports pavilion, all blond wood and glass, fronts the tree-dotted cricket pitch that boasts 'one of the best wickets in Somerset,' according to proud students. Teams are fielded in cricket, rugby, hockey (boys and girls), netball, rounders, tennis, swimming, soccer and basketball, and everyone who wants to participate will get the chance. Again, inclusivity is the watchword. 'I love that the emphasis is not on winning at all costs,' wrote one parent. 'Sometimes the order will be changed to ensure that the lower order players get to play the key positions, even if that means we are likely to lose the match. I think this is brilliant, although not all parents agree!' It's not all losses, either: remembering a recent victory against Millfield clearly raised our tour guides' testosterone levels. Excellent covered swimming pool used all the year round. Dance studio is home to compulsory dance for both boys and girls up to year 9.

Flourishing drama with at least two productions per year, and remarkably good art and photography, reflecting the very creative ethos. A huge programme of clubs and societies, everything from jewellery making to CCF. School embraces the forest schools initiative – children in years 1 and 2 learn to eg build shelters and cook on open fires.

Boarding: The boarding provision was given the thumbs up by everyone we spoke to, with all boarders confirming that they enjoyed their time here ('It's really nice! Lots of activities at the weekends,' said a sixth former who joined in year 12). Very small numbers of boarders in junior school (currently nine), all of them housed with the older pupils – didn't sound ideal to us, but no complaints of any kind reached us. Boarding houses are frankly dilapidated – the ones we saw, at any rate – and numbers to a room rather high for this modern age, with four or five being fairly normal. Living in one of the country's prettiest and oldest towns has its flipside, perhaps. But the students seemed cheerful enough about it, and although we dug hard, we couldn't unearth any complaints. Appraisals of the food were mixed. 'Like the food I had to endure when I boarded 25 years ago!' said one parent, while another countered loyally, 'I'm told it's amazing!' But again the students, all of whom seem to radiate good health, seemed happy with it. We ourselves were served a pleasant and wholesome lunch, so can't comment on this further.

Background and atmosphere: Tracing its roots back to 909, Wells is one of the world's oldest schools, and wears its age beautifully; there surely can't be a lovelier place of learning anywhere. Whether picking our way down the cobbled Vicar's Close, where we heard mellifluous treble recorder playing drifting out of the mullioned windows, or wandering about the many elegant Georgian buildings cocooned in greenery, we thought that growing up here must be a gift. 'I am not sure our children yet realise just how lucky they are,' agreed one parent, 'and when I visit I do have to pinch myself sometimes.'

Co-educational since 1969, and a specialist music school since 1970, and remains the only such within the setting of a normal school, something which parents clearly value. Music department housed in gorgeous – if rather cluttered – medieval building directly opposite the cathedral. We liked the library with its stock of 2,000 vinyl records plus turntable, although it did seem too small for quiet study, and one parent said that this was a problem throughout the school, describing the boarding houses as noisy. Junior school on a cloistered, lovely, leafy, tree-dotted site with a very nice games courtyard and a delightful early years play area. All rooms made attractive and colourful, and when we visited on a blisteringly hot day, they were refreshingly cool.

This is undoubtedly a very happy community; everywhere we looked we saw a kind of upbeat tranquility blended with lively creativity. One mother spoke for everyone when she wrote, 'What I love about Wells is the happy and welcoming atmosphere. Everyone has a smile – and it is really infectious!'

Pastoral care, well-being and discipline: Highly praised by everyone. The school motto is 'Be what you are' ('Esto quod es'), and all parents commented how confident and happy their children had become since starting at the school, and on the good friends they'd made there. Indeed, we spoke to parents whose children had previously been miserable – in one case at a top academic school, in another at a different specialist music school – but were now simply loving life after transferring to Wells. School communications on pastoral issues rated by parents as prompt, efficient and helpful. (Exception to this appeared to be some of the music teaching staff, who, some said, were reluctant to keep parents in the loop and clung to an outdated 'what goes on in my lessons is my business' attitude.) One parent wrote, 'We love this school. It expects high standards of behaviour and achievement but allows children good levels of independence and autonomy in reaching these. The children learn to motivate themselves. They are supported and nurtured and helped with strategies and tools, but they are not micro-managed.'

Focus is on 'mutual consideration, respect and courtesy,' and discipline problems are few. Children are charmingly polite, but very much themselves: 'Hullo, Mrs Cairncross!' exclaimed a 6-year-old lad with grave propriety as we walked by, 'I looked away and when I looked back again you'd popped up!' Older students showed the same style of courteous assurance, duly matured.

One parent, whose child had moved to the junior school after an unhappy time at another school, commented, 'My daughter is now the happiest child you could ever meet. She goes into school smiling and comes out so excited about her day.'

Pupils and parents: Day pupils drawn from large local radius – school operates bus routes to bring children in from Bristol, Bath, Taunton, Yeovil and comparable. Boarders come from all over, but a significant proportion still from the south west, perhaps because Wells remains off the beaten track: the nearest train station is Castle Cary, some 13 miles away. International students bring cultural diversity: they are welcomed into the purpose-built International Centre and offered very good EAL support. Parents mostly hardworking professionals, keen for their children to turn out right on all fronts – many families choose to send all their children to Wells for their entire education. Pupils are well-mannered, well-spoken, well-adjusted, well-turned-out, and very likeable.

Entrance: A broad church academically and, as always with Wells, flexibility is key. Informal assessment for the pre-prep plus meeting with its head, Janet Bennett. At junior level, more formal tests but still 'friendly'. Chorister auditions held in January each year.

Children can join the school at any point in their school career, even year 13 – the school works to make it a success. At the usual senior entry points of age 11 and 13, however, a formal entrance assessment is held in maths and reasoning, and satisfactory report from previous school is required. Entry to sixth form is subject to interview and at least six grade C passes at GCSE, with grade B or above in subjects to be taken for A level. Auditions for music places currently held in November (sixth form) and January (all age groups) after a pre-audition meeting.

Exit: Almost all juniors move up to the senior school, after sitting an entrance test to gauge academic levels. Some 10 per cent after GCSEs. At 18, almost all to higher education, with a high proportion to Russell group universities, or to music conservatoires in the UK or abroad, many with scholarships. Others off to study eg environmental science, history of art, psychology or engineering. Two Oxbridge places in 2016.

Money matters: Historically, not a wealthy school, but Wells has made what it's got go a very long way. An unusually wide variety of scholarships on offer: maths, music, sports, creative arts, academic and all-round. Most of these worth no more than 10 per cent, but a sliding scale of means-tested bursary assistance is also available, and school is working overtime to build up its endowment and reach a 'needs-blind' point of admissions. Funding of up to 100 per cent available for some 'elite' specialist musicians via the government's Music and Dance Scheme. Special provision pupils – children who are musically gifted but want to follow the full academic curriculum and keep their options open – often receive financial support for their music tuition.

Remarks: As one parent summed it up, 'We really love this school, and believe that by sending our children here we are giving them the best possible start in life.' A magical place, where children grow into kind, confident and accomplished young adults.

Wellsway School

Chandag Road, Keynsham, Bristol BS31 1PH

Pupils: 1,330 • Ages: 11–18 • Sixth form: 275

Tel: 01179 864751
Email: enquiries@wellswayschool.com
Website: www.wellswayschool.com

Principal: Since April 2016, Matthew Woodville, previously head of Oldfield School in Bath. Degree in law from London; worked briefly in the corporate world before training as a geography teacher. He was rapidly promoted to senior leadership, including becoming director of post-16 education at St Laurence School in Wiltshire and assistant principal at Oasis Academy Brightstowe in Bristol. He is married with two children.

Academic matters: Specialist sports and science college. Fine results for a non-selective school in a not solely middle class area. In 2016, 84 per cent got five or more A*-C GCSE grades including English and maths (28 per cent A*/A). Some 60-70 per cent stay on for sixth form – nearly a third A*/A grades and 64 per cent A*-B in 2016. Vocational students impressively averaged Distinction*, and 75 per cent of those taking the EPQ got A*/A grades. Sixth form study centre with computer suites and quiet study areas. Very strong departments led by specialist staff. Sound provision for statemented pupils.

Games, options, the arts: Heaps of teams in all sports. Artificial pitch. Annual French trip for year 7, ski trip, water sport trip. World Challenge expeditions have been to Ecuador, South Africa and West Canada. Currently running Wellsway Challenge to destinations in Europe.

Innovative and fabulous art department. Dedicated staff stay long after school hours to keep facilities open. Mad on musicals – staged Return to the Forbidden Planet, Barnum, Grease, Guys & Dolls, Billy, Cabaret, My Fair Lady, Animal Farm and Oliver!

Background and atmosphere: A once thriving market town between Bath and Bristol, Keynsham is a town of churches – five Anglican, one Baptist and one Methodist, denoting its past trade wealth. A spacious campus amongst green fields is cheek by jowl with Chandag Junior and Infant Schools. Highly motivated staff aged 22 to 60; seem far less frantic than most at large comprehensives. Many of them have own children here and the relationship between staff and pupils is that of a close-knit village school. Bulletin boards bursting with news or press cuttings of ex-pupils making local headlines. Now part of a multi-academy trust.

Pastoral care, well-being and discipline: Policies on everything from asthma to child protection. School rules insist that anyone being bullied report it. Comes down ton-of-bricks on anti-social or violent behaviour and nips any incident in the bud by locating pupil's parent instantly. A counsellor is on staff. Sixth formers become 'buddies' to any year 7 who request one and may coach sports/share lunch and chat/solve bigger problems.

Pupils and parents: Local business folk, many old girls'/boys' kids, every class and creed. Very loyal. A weekly newsletter keeps parents well-informed and asks parents to monitor homework and control absence. Excellent, informative website. Uniform of green blazer/black trousers/skirts. Strong on community service and raising funds for charities.

Entrance: Oversubscribed. Wellsway serves Keynsham (to the east of the River Chew), Chelwood Village, Compton Dando, Corston, Marksbury, Newton St Loe, Priston and Saltford. Children from within this area whose older sibling will be attending the school on the admission date come first, followed by other children from the area, then other siblings. Five Cs at GCSE preferred for sixth form entrance.

Exit: Around 60-70 per cent of GCSE pupils continue on to sixth form here, 20-30 per cent to education elsewhere. After A levels most go to university eg Bournemouth University, Cardiff, Birmingham and Bath Spa. One to Oxford in 2016, two medics and two lawyers, and six to apprenticeships including MoD and Dyson. A few to a gap year and a sprinkle to art foundation or drama school.

Remarks: Confident pupils with high expectations well prepared for life. Loveliest bunch of teachers in the county.

Westonbirt School

Westonbirt, Tetbury, Gloucestershire GL8 8QG

Pupils: 290; 117 full boarders • Ages: 3–18 (boarders from year 5) • Sixth form: 49 • C of E

Fees: Day £14,985; Boarding £29,250 pa

Tel: 01666 881301
Email: admissions@westonbirt.org
Website: www.westonbirt.org

Head: Since 2013, Mrs Natasha Dangerfield BA (40s), previously deputy head and head of boarding at Harrogate Ladies' College. Also taught at North Foreland Lodge and Downe House and was director of pastoral care at Gordonstoun School. Mrs Dangerfield studied physical education and English at the University of Brighton and thought she wanted to be a physiotherapist, but while working in sports camps she met teachers who inspired her to change direction. Parents describe her as 'dynamic', and 'approachable' and a great role model for the girls, 'she speaks their language.'

Westonbirt inspires fierce loyalty and we got the impression that any head who messed with the school's fundamental character would do so at their peril. Most agree that her changes so far have been the right ones – modernisation of some material aspects, gentle 're-booting' in other areas. The fact that she is a parent herself (she has three young children, two boys and a girl, who attend the prep) must be a good ice-breaker. Her husband works in the fire service.

The combination of over 200 lively girls and a grade 1 listed building must be a little worrying, we suggested to Mrs Dangerfield. 'This house is built so well that everything is in pretty good order,' she told us. Fortunately, the Westonbirt Trust takes care of historic preservation; 'To put Venetian silk back on the walls is not our responsibility.'

Lacrosse is Mrs Dangerfield's sport (back in the day she played for England) and she continues to coach – even taking pre-season training for her school team. 'I'm not very good at standing on the sidelines,' she confessed.

Prep school head: Since September 2016, Mr Sean Price, previously assistant head (pastoral) and year 5 form tutor. He joined the school in 2013.

Academic matters: Specialist teaching from nursery upwards for music, French, swimming, ICT, art, science and DT. Parents describe teaching as 'really good' and 'thorough', several told us that they particularly liked the attention paid to public speaking. Everyone is encouraged to find their voice, both in lessons and by contributing to class assemblies: 'When she started my daughter was very shy, but she's flourished and has so much more confidence now.'

In a year 2 class we saw boys and girls writing first person descriptions of life as a WW1 soldier. Children had brought in family photos and memorabilia and were using these along with poems and other resources for inspiration. Pupils were fascinated by the topic and their imaginations were up and running; mini whiteboards were covered with words and the room was buzzing as children discussed their ideas. The class teacher and teaching assistant were on hand to guide but this lesson was pretty much running itself.

Numbers are rising and as the school starts to attract more families the range of potential secondary destinations becomes wider. While the majority of girls will go up to the main school some feel that advice about, and links with, other senior independents could be improved. Parents told us that they welcomed what they see as a 'rebalancing' from previous 'over emphasis' on 11+ grammar school preparation and hope this balance can be maintained for the benefit of the boys and girls who are headed elsewhere.

In 2016, a upswing to 27 per cent A*/A (50 per cent A*-B) at A level. At GCSE, 44 per cent A*/A grades. Highs and lows in all subjects reflect the relatively non-selective intake. While there has certainly been a tightening up of standards and a review of the subjects on offer, head has no plans to change entrance requirements. Focus here is on helping girls reach their potential, whether that's 10 A*s at GCSE, or three 'good' A levels.

Parents have told us how well their daughters are doing and the University of Durham has put a number on it: Westonbirt is in the top five per cent of schools in the UK for value added. This objectively assessed measure calculates pupils' academic improvement between the ages of 11 and 16. Analysis by the

University of Durham shows that girls here achieve almost a grade higher in each subject at GCSE than expected.

All learn French in year 7, Spanish, Mandarin and Latin 'tasters' in year 8 and all learn touch typing. In addition to academic subjects, girls in all years follow a 'skills for life' programme that focuses on practical (communication and study skills) as well as personal and social development. With an average class size of 10 (maximum 15), girls here receive what is practically customised teaching; the parents of several girls who had joined from large preps were astonished at their daughters' progress. 'She thought she was bad at maths and science but now she's so confident and doing really well.' Subject teachers set targets and academic progress is closely monitored by tutors. In a year 7 maths class the atmosphere was collaborative rather than competitive, girls attempting questions confidently, undaunted if they were wrong. Even we wouldn't have been scared to hazard an answer.

Choice of 25 A level subjects – all the usuals plus history of art, classical civilisation and business studies. School says that it is able to accommodate most combinations. Enrichment for sixth formers includes a lecture programme and weekly personal finance lessons.

Technology was somewhat prehistoric but is now much improved and used in lessons 'appropriately and with relevance,' although Mrs Dangerfield's announcement of the 'death of the handout' might be a bit previous. iPads now on kit list although school will lend if necessary. Great boon for dyslexic girls who can use the speech facility for essays. Apps etc stored in the 'Westonbirt cloud' and controlled by school. As we were visiting the science, art, design and technology block, we spied a classroom of very overgrown schoolgirls and boys, concentrating hard. 'Oh, that's the teachers,' our guide said. 'They're having an IT lesson.

'Outstanding' learning support department caters for wide range of SpLDs including dyslexia, dyspraxia, dyscalculia and mild speech and language impairments. Gifted and talented programme also in place.

Games, options, the arts: 'There's so much drama at Westonbirt!' we heard. Ditto singing, dancing and playing of instruments. Emphasis is on enabling everyone to perform, whether it's in the intimate setting of the Camellia House – a charming venue, used for recitals, 'little plays' and socials – or in the 450 seat Orangery Theatre. Fresh air fiends can also tread the grass of the amphitheatre in the grounds. Music practice block suffers somewhat by comparison with the smart Marriott Centre, home to brand new recording and music tech kit. Three choirs and weekly whole school hymn practice keep everyone in good voice. Huge art studios looking out onto peaceful pastures, DT workshops with laser cutters and CAD equipment.

Swimming is big here with lessons for all in the 25m pool in nearby school sports centre. Twice weekly for the nursery water babies (the aim is that all should be able to swim by the time they leave reception) and an hour a week for the rest. Schol very appreciative of the parent volunteers who bravely don their costumes to help out. It's paying off: Westonbirt Prep recently won silver in the national IAPS finals – the smallest school ever to make it through.

Mrs Dangerfield is applying her expertise to senior school sport. Local opposition is formidable, and while no one expects Westonbirt to carry home the silverware at every match, there was room for improvement. Sensible trend in this and other girls' schools is a shift from privileging team sports to an equal emphasis on health and fitness – that way you can keep everyone doing something.

No shortage of running around space here and opportunities to play for the school abound, whether it's lacrosse, netball, tennis, golf (there's a nine hole course), riding or polo. In the £3m sports centre, opened by near neighbours the Prince of Wales and Duchess of Cornwall, there's dance studio and fitness suite. Very popular is the new all weather wicket; 'now we can invite other schools to play at home.' All weather facilities for other sports still on school's, and parents' wish lists. Parents tell us that there are plenty of fixtures and the school is more than able to take on and win against other, often larger, opponents. Or you could just take a book and find a secluded spot in the gardens.

Forest school is just a few minutes away in The Spinney – huge old trees make it a magical place, ideal for dowsing, worm charming and cook ups over the fire pit. Wellies and waterproofs, not to mention a canopy slung between trees, mean that outdoor learning can take place whatever the weather. 'It's an open challenge to create, do and be resourceful,' we were told. Muddy fun for the youngest and the older children love it too; their activities are linked to class work – whether it's science, nature, poetry or drama. 'It's great for self-esteem. It can bring out unexpected talents from a child who may not shine in the classroom.'

As befits the alma mater of Baden Powell's daughter, the school has a girl guide troop – 1st Westonbirt Guides, although members tend to be from local villages rather than the school itself. D of E to gold level offered plus clubs and activities from app design, through gardening and poultry, to zumba.

Sixth formers have the opportunity to enrol on the very popular Leith's certificate in food and wine. Westonbirt was one of the first two schools to run this course, and to have Leith's on your CV is great for holiday and gap year jobs such as a spot of chalet girling. For those whose ambitions go beyond holiday jobs, there's the Young Enterprise scheme and a separate business school with office space and classrooms – A level business studies is taught here.

Boarding: Years 5-8, day girls and boarders, live together in Beaufort House. This junior house is a stepping stone between prep and senior school. There are three senior houses for years 9, 10 and 11 – Badminton, Dorchester and Holford – plus the sixth form. Girls in Holford sleep in what were the family state rooms on the first floor, little beds dwarfed by grand proportions (grade 1 listing is not at home to subdivision). Priceless silk wallpaper, preserved under Perspex, rubbing shoulders with One Direction posters. Beautiful painted panels on the wardrobes and tall wooden shutters instead of curtains. All day girls get one free night of boarding per term and sleepovers are very popular. Wonderful views over the park from common room 'perfect for moon watching'. We asked girls what they thought of the food and the general consensus was breakfast fab, lunch pretty good (we can vouch for that) but catering seemed to run out of steam by supper time. We hope this is on Mrs Dangerfield's to do list.

In the sixth form house every girl has her own study bedroom so day girls can decide at the last minute to stay overnight. There's a dining room, kitchen, laundry facilities, yoga room and bar/café. Not surprisingly, over three-quarters of sixth formers board. Many like to remain in school over the weekend, because it 'helps them stay focused on their studies'. An international student (around 20+ girls are from abroad) told us how much she appreciated learning in such 'serene and calm surroundings.' We loved the spacious common room, newly decorated in a modish putty colour ('seagull'), a simple vase of marguerites on the coffee table.

Background and atmosphere: Westonbirt is one of the 'Allied Schools', an umbrella body for eight Martyrs' Memorial Trust schools including Canford, Stowe and Harrogate Ladies' College. It was founded in 1927, acquiring Westonbirt House and 210 acres of park and garden from the Holford family who had lived on the estate since the 17th century. The house itself, built in Jacobethan style (later than, though not dissimilar to, Highclere Castle), was completed in 1871 and used by Lord Holford as a country retreat (his main residence was Dorchester House, Park Lane, now site of The Dorchester Hotel). Just over the road is the world famous Westonbirt Arboretum, another of Lord Holford's enduring projects. When the head told us the house was 'well built' she meant it – constructed around a steel frame, it had all the mod cons of its day (gas lighting, central heating), not to mention fire-proof cavities between each wall and floor. Interior décor was in the distinctly un-modern classical style, with splendid marble halls and corridors on the ground floor, richly gilded wood and plasterwork and intriguing architectural details wherever you look. Friday notices and vespers are held in the galleried great hall, and year 11s dine under a ceiling festooned with plasterwork goat skulls.

As we sighed over the refurbished Gentleman's Library, enjoying the irony, we wondered what the girls thought about studying in such sumptuous surroundings. 'It is a bit like Downton Abbey', one confided, and we would not have been surprised to see Hugh Bonneville and his arthritic labrador taking a constitutional in the Italianate garden. What a place.

Prep shares the beautiful grounds, if not the breathtaking architecture, of senior school, occupying a former boarding house and san. Classrooms are light and spacious with fantastic views over woods and meadows. Almost half the pupils are boys and there are three full-time male members of staff.

Pastoral care, well-being and discipline: Pastoral care has always been one of Westonbirt's strengths. In a small community with a high staff to student ratio, problems become visible sooner. Parents say that friendship troubles and the like are dealt with fairly and swiftly. 'Everybody has to get along,' we were told, and 'the older girls look out for you.' Not really the place for 'tricky' personalities, observed one mother. We agree; Westonbirt girls are more likely to ride the horses than frighten them.

Girls are encouraged to take responsibilities such as organising social events – planning for a charity ball was under way when we visited. There's a 'much improved' programme of socials with boys from Abingdon, Radley and even co-ed Cheltenham College. A less welcome visitor is the school's lone peacock, Westy, who frequently has to be escorted off the premises. We hear that the class of 2014 bought him a friend, christened (you guessed it) Birty.

Pupils and parents: From all over the UK, although majority of families live relatively locally. Easy to reach from Bristol and Bath and handy for M4, Heathrow and London. Parents tell us it's 'not posh.' Hmmm. It is, but in a quiet way. Nearest places to spend pocket money are Cheltenham and Bath, although you could do some damage in Tetbury. Smallish cohort (some 25 per cent) of international students from all corners of the globe – as elsewhere, more attention being paid to the mix.

Former pupils include the Hon Mrs Betty Clay (Lord Baden-Powell's youngest daughter), Mercia MacDermott (historian); Anna Hornby (painter); Salma Sobhan (academic and human rights activist); Patsy Toh (pianist); Georgia Byng (author of the Molly Moon series of children's books); Lady Natasha Rufus-Isaacs (designer, founder of Beulah London); TV presenter Ruth Watson; TV producer Patricia Llewellyn; Lady Jenny Bland; Jenefer Greenwood, OBE.

Entrance: Prep school entry by visit then taster day when child is informally assessed in classroom setting. Senior school entry includes many from the prep, rest from wide range of preps and local primaries. Non-CE candidates sit school's own entrance exams in maths and English plus an online adaptive test. Head likes to interview everyone in person (or via Skype). For entry to the sixth form girls need at least five A*-C grades at GCSE (including maths and English), with A or B in subjects to be taken at A level.

Exit: Eleven plus entry to senior school for most prep school girls (five per cent fee discount for those who continue from prep to senior). Boys and some girls to local grammars or other independents. A few girls leave for pastures new after GCSEs but are replaced by others from elsewhere doing the same thing. After A levels more than half depart for Russell Group universities to study everything from aeronautics to zoology. Business and management popular choices. Occasional one or two to medical school (one in 2016), likewise Oxbridge; one to the Royal Agricultural University and one to Toronto in 2016.

Money matters: Fees restructured from 2017, with flat rate boarding fees and day fees reduced by some 25 per cent. Academic, art, drama, music, sport, performing arts, organ and choral scholarships up to a maximum of 50 per cent of day fees. Means-tested bursaries may be available – applications considered on an individual basis. Fee reductions for siblings, Forces and clergy families. Girls transferring from prep also get a five per cent discount throughout their senior career. Sixth form bursaries offered to girls from local state schools.

Remarks: Westonbirt has always been highly regarded for inclusivity and exemplary pastoral care, but perhaps its other strengths have been overlooked. Until now. Parents told us that 'there's a new energy, a real buzz' about the place; one described it as 'added sparkle', and they're right. Inside this solid Victorian stately home we found a vibrant and forward thinking community of young women, hugely appreciative of their beautiful surroundings but very well prepared to take on the world beyond Gloucestershire.

Wigmore School

Ford Street, Wigmore, Leominster, Herefordshire HR6 9UW

Pupils: 464 • Ages: 3–16

Tel: 01568 770323
Email: admin@wigmore.hereford.sch.uk
Website: www.wigmore.hereford.sch.uk

Headteacher: Since 2015, Mr Dean Curtis, previously senior deputy head and acting head.

Academic matters: Now an academy, in federation with what was the neighbouring primary school. The school is a designated National Support School providing support and guidance to other schools and is recognised by Ofsted for its innovative and successful approaches to learning, leadership and quality assurance.

Very good GCSE results. In 2016, 77 per cent got 5+ A* to C including English and maths and nearly a third of all grades were A*/A. Apart from the normal Sats at the junior end of the school, all children are tested at year 7 and there is setting for all core subjects in KS3 and KS4. Pupils have a good range of GCSE options to choose from – either dual award or (increasingly popular) triple award science, French or Spanish, and a dual award in IT, as well as geography, history, RS, drama, DT, art, music and PE.

All pupils benefit from a newly developed Student Support Centre, which comprises both learning support for those with specific learning needs, and careers guidance. In addition to two SENCos (one for the junior end of the school, one for the senior) the school, by using the income it gains from supporting other schools, funds a careers adviser and a counsellor – regarded as absolutely critical in the current harsh economic climate. The school was the first in the country to receive the IAG quality mark for its careers guidance. Work placements and university visits for all in year 11. Excellent IT facilities, well integrated into all areas of learning – lots of computers, iPods and video conferencing to enhance learning and enable some innovative projects.

Pupils are consistently encouraged to aim high. Reports to parents are sent every term with grades for progress, effort and behaviour. Staff are particularly aware of the potential for cultural isolation: ethnic minorities are practically non-existent in this corner of Herefordshire and great effort is made to ensure that the children are acquainted with the full spectrum of faiths and cultures, with visiting speakers, 'exchange' trips to Muslim schools in Birmingham etc. French trip every year for year 8, three-day trip to London for year 9, a high uptake of French exchanges and Spanish trips.

Games, options, the arts: Over 85 per cent of pupils participate in after-school sports activities – dedicated parents do a great deal of ferrying in this deeply rural area. Aerobics, zumba and badminton, as well as rugby, cricket, netball, athletics. Circus skills for the juniors too. Games provision is impressive, with a huge sports hall, fitness room, cricket nets, 400m track and a large hard play area.

A high level of participation in all sports, and staff ensure that all who show enthusiasm get a chance to represent the school. This inclusive approach is no barrier to excellence. A number of children participate at county and national level (including netball and women's football). A great food technology room, buzzing with activity and enthusiastic chefs. Has Healthy Schools status, an award-winning kitchen manager, a choice of at least five main courses a day and 'no problems with obesity'. The school has also been awarded Artsmark gold, a recognition of the very good work it does with sometimes limited facilities – there are some very interesting pieces on display in the hall and around the school. A lot of very good drama, inside and outside the classroom – Shakespeare to home-grown as well as a strong debating team.

A well-equipped music room, plenty of school bands and orchestras and a popular singing group as well as three choirs. Range of instruments taught by peripatetic staff directly contracted by the school ('we weren't happy with the county music service') – around 100 of the children take instrumental or singing lessons; some nice new practice rooms.

Background and atmosphere: In a pretty village in a rather remote corner of Herefordshire. Lots of fantastic outdoor spaces. The building itself is no architectural gem but is well maintained, and there are some new classrooms as well as the new Student Support centre. A general sense of being well organised and tranquil. Children know what is expected of them.

The school is calm, happy, purposeful. 'Our environment, our atmosphere is of high standards, high expectations'. Despite high class numbers (we saw a couple of groups pushing 30), work is done with great concentration and care. There is no disruption and very little poor behaviour – 'the children won't have it'. Children are polite, focused, well turned out and very happy. Pupils appreciate the opportunities and care that they receive at Wigmore, 'Everyone is included, it's really friendly.' A huge emphasis on being part of the local community – the sports facilities are open to the public at weekends, the school runs wrap-around care for working parents, and now has a nursery unit in response to local demand.

Pastoral care, well-being and discipline: A team of deputies head up the pastoral care system, which is rooted in tutor groups. PSHE is known as life skills here, and carefully vetted outside agencies are used to support the resources and learning about sex, drugs, alcohol etc. Staff are aware that pupils from this corner of the world may find the city lights pretty overwhelming when they move on, and are committed to equipping them with the information and maturity to cope as they do so. No exclusions in the last few years, very few disciplinary issues. Of greater concern pastorally is the increased pressure families face as the economic downturn continues to bite. A strong policy on bullying. School says parents 'want their children to be loved – and we do – we look after them with loving care'.

Pupils and parents: The catchment area is predominantly agricultural land and the pupils and parents are mainly of farming stock, although some from the professional classes and some from the much more deprived end of the social spectrum. Many parents attended the school themselves and are very supportive of the staff – they have to be if the extracurricular sports offered after school are going to work. Staff say relationships are very positive, with close to full attendance at parents' evenings, 'parents recognise the quality of what we provide'. Parents say that communication from the school is excellent and that their children are well looked after, disciplined effectively, and happy.

Entrance: The school is a federation of Wigmore Primary and Wigmore Secondary, providing an all-through education since 2007. Those attending the primary are automatically entitled to a place in the secondary school, which also takes pupils from six other local feeder schools. It is wholly non-selective (about 20 per cent on school action plus of whom roughly a quarter have a statement). Accepts pupils on the traditional LA criteria of catchment area, siblings in school and so on. Oversubscribed, with a waiting list for each year group and a substantial number of disappointed parents on appeal to the LA. It is essential to be within the catchment area, but this is quite large (running north to Ludlow and west towards Presteigne) and, generally speaking, being in catchment gives a fairly good chance of a place.

Exit: Most go on to take A levels at Hereford Sixth Form College (very good academically) or Ludlow Sixth Form College. Others go on to local agricultural colleges such as Hartpury and Holme Lacy, with others heading for apprenticeships. The school estimates about 60 per cent end up at university, though this percentage has fallen a little over the last two years due to difficult economic circumstances. The school positively encourages students to look at overseas opportunities (such as the Netherlands and the US) as alternatives to the UK for higher education.

Remarks: A delightful and extremely successful school. Relaxed, happy, community feel with very high expectations and a heartfelt concern for each individual. Children are encouraged not only to learn but also to take responsibility for themselves and one another. Achieves results in a non-selective state school of which many selective independents would be proud.

Wilmslow Preparatory School

Grove Avenue, Wilmslow, Cheshire SK9 5EG

Pupils: 118 • Ages: 0-11; co-ed up to year 2

Fees: £8,955 – £10,365 pa

Tel: 01625 524246
Email: secretary@wilmslowprep.co.uk
Website: www.wilmslowprep.co.uk

Head: Since 2014, Mrs Helen Rigby BEd NPQH. Was a parent at the school and joined the staff as reception teacher in 2001. Appointed deputy head in 2005.

Entrance: Non-selective, although officially by assessment and interview for older children, which in practice seems to mean school checking it can meet their needs. It usually can, thanks in part to a three-day-a-week SENCo providing extra help, including a gifted and talented programme, who's described by parents as 'pro-active and great at liaising with us'. Space in most years.

Exit: Sound results bagging a spread of excellent, almost all selective, secondary places. Withington and Manchester High School for Girls both popular destinations. 'There's lots of preparation for entrance exams, and extra for Withington because it's so hard,' girls tell us; 'they do stretch you but it's not too pressurised'. Most to King's Macclesfield, Cheadle Hulme, Alderley Edge School for Girls, Stockport Grammar, The Grange and Morton Hall, some with academic, sports or music scholarships.

Remarks: Hugely well-to-do Wilmslow has a reputation for glitz, but despite WPS's location at the very heart of this leafy South-Mancunian suburb, there's little of that here. Instead it's refreshingly unpretentious, a small, happy prep of well-mannered, busy, confident, green-clad girls (and, increasingly, boys). With just over 100 pupils across eight years, numbers are bijou with an average class size of 15, but school claims 'we punch above our weight' in both curricular and extracurricular realms – WPS shines at the Alderley Edge Music Festival and in sport it holds its own against much bigger schools. Bespoke teachers for music, drama, science, French (from kindergarten), IT, sport and art help. As do designated rooms for most of these too, with a separate art block, 'no fun running across the playground in the rain', nevertheless with impressive art and ceramics from its own kiln.

The older play area boasts a living willow igloo and tunnel, and by the fun early years' Astroturf patch, veg growing boxes are verdant. The playground underwent a makeover in 2012 with lots of new equipment. Inside, the former busy vets' office has become a post-royal-wedding fairytale castle complete with sky-rocketing (runner) beanstalks. The buildings are Tardis-like on a road with limited parking, but staggered finish times mean parents feel pick-up 'isn't too bad'. A galleried sports hall sits a few yards down the road, oddly with just one domestic house in the middle of the overall plot, but there's still room for a planned all-weather tennis court. Replacing the music and drama prefab buildings is on the cards too. One parent told us, 'What they get here are the tools of politeness and confidence without being obnoxious', and another that 'this small friendly school has cared for my daughter like a family'. When we raised the idea of a culture shock moving from this protected environment, where little straw boaters hang sweetly on pegs, to the hurly burly of a large secondary school, the parents roundly responded, 'No, they're fine, they've done so much public speaking here, they're so confident'. And they feel the school's size brings a parental bonus of sociability, with form parent reps organising, among other things, termly get-togethers. One mum with four girls here said, 'Yes, it's true; I certainly drink a lot of coffee.'

Winterbourne International Academy

High Street, Winterbourne, Bristol BS36 1JL

Pupils: 1,880 • Ages: 11-19 • Sixth form: 368

Tel: 01454 252000
Email: office@trfwia.org.uk
Website: www.trfwia.org.uk

Principal: Since 2015, Mr Richard Haupt who has worked at a range of independent and maintained schools. He was head of economics at Gillingham School in Dorset, assistant principal at Angley School in Cranbrook, deputy head at Matravers School in Westbury and assistant dean at Yeovil College and has also been head of sixth form at a Hastings-based school. His appointment follows a disappointing Ofsted review earlier in 2015, which rated the school as requiring improvement.

Academic matters: Parents enthuse, 'They're not shy of trying new things'. First in the region to offer the International Baccalaureate, though no longer offers it, and relaunched as an academy (2009), with a federated sixth form with the nearby Yate International Academy, offering some 30+ A level subjects plus a few applied A levels.

Some of the 'extra bits' of the IB curriculum still offered, including the creativity, action, service section, and the school has also introduced critical thinking to A level students.

Academy status has given the school freedom to pursue the IB Middle Years curriculum in lower years. Languages a priority, in keeping with international school status – nearly everyone takes at least one language at GCSE, but only small numbers at A level. Most popular A levels – general studies, psychology, biology and maths. At least one non-European language, most likely Mandarin, on the menu soon.

Classes are setted by ability in some subjects from year 7 onwards. All types of SEN are catered for, but the numbers are fairly low – 20 or so with SEN statements in the whole school, with another hundred or so getting some support from the SEN team and teaching assistants. Only a handful of EAL students.

Specialist technology school status has now been dropped, but the high-spec DT and ICT suites remain, along with links with industry, notably Airbus (nearby at Filton) and CISCO.

Results above average for a non-selective school: in 2016, 73 per cent of pupils got 5+ A*-C grades at GCSE including English and maths. At A level, 61 per cent of results were graded A*/B and 34 per cent were graded A*/A in 2016.

Games, options, the arts: A very sporty place, especially since the opening of the sports 'village' (2010), including sports hall, all-weather pitch and refurbished swimming pool. Some of the gym rooms not yet fully equipped, but the main sports hall is a vast improvement. Full-size pool popular with pupils, their families and locals, who can use it out of school hours.

Rugby is the biggest thing here, and not just due to the Welsh head's influence. The 'rugby academy' offers training to all, and produces strong players for the school teams and beyond: one former pupil has been selected for the England rugby squad. Other sports are not neglected: several footballers are training with professional teams, and school teams for just about everything do well in local leagues.

Drama, music and debating standards are high – the academy gives the local independents a good run for their money in regional competitions, and often comes out on top. Art and drama have plenty of space and enthusiasm – lots of school productions, and some impressive art displays around the school. Library disappointingly small for the size of school, but at least they still have one.

Overseas trips limited, as not everyone can afford to go, but video conferences with an imaginative range of partners (from astronauts to school children in Afghanistan) help make up for it. The international outlook pays off for some students with gap year plans – the school has had five leavers over several years picked for the Prime Minister's Global Fellowship, which awards funds for work in developing countries.

Background and atmosphere: Formerly known as The Ridings High School, the school became Winterbourne International Academy in 2009, part of a Ridings Federation with the smaller Yate International Academy. Not many visible signs of change, apart from the appointment of the head, and smart new blazers and ties on years 7 to 11 (sixth formers must dress as 'young professionals' – open to quite broad interpretation, but most seem to have got the idea that it is not jeans and hoodies).

The modern red-brick office-style building at the entrance to the school campus used to hide a rather dilapidated core of 1950s classroom buildings lurking behind it. But huge nearly £20m capital investment programme has now seen fantastic new buildings facilities for sports and arts.

International status seen as a big positive by some parents, others not bothered about the languages and extra bits but like the good results and the sports.

Pastoral care, well-being and discipline: A big school (intake is 302 a year), and possibly a bit daunting for the younger ones. To ease the newbies in, year 7 tutors start visiting feeder primaries from year 5 onwards to get to know the likely applicants. Year 6s come to school taster days and even the annual panto.

A part-time in-school counsellor is on hand, and other referrals can be arranged. House system introduced, but most pastoral care organised via tutor groups. Vulnerable students have older students assigned as peer supporters, and sixth formers are attached to each year group to provide more general support.

Behaviour expectations clearly laid out in personal planners, and parents and pupils have to sign a home/school agreement. Principal says exclusions are down since the school became an academy, and there is low tolerance for disruptive behaviour. Disciplinary measures include detentions and referral to an in-school behaviour unit. The pupils working at desks outside the principal's office on our visit didn't look pleased to be there, but they were quiet and getting on with their work.

Repeat offenders get referred to the Behaviour for Learning Centre – an alternative to exclusions, with specialist staff, where troubled and troublesome pupils follow the same curriculum as their classmates as far as possible. The aim is to reduce outright exclusions and eventually reintegrate pupils into the rest of the school.

Pupils and parents: Cover the whole range from well-off families in commuter villages to those getting the bus in from some more deprived areas on the fringes of Bristol. Comprehensive intake, but on the bright side. Not many non-native English speakers, and the few there are tend to catch up quickly. An international touch comes from engineering staff at nearby aerospace companies, which have strong French links and some overseas workers.

Entrance: There are good reasons why so many Bristol families move to the other side of the M4 when their children are nearing double figures. Many Bristolians would love to get their children into this place, but if you don't live in a small corner of South Gloucestershire – namely, first area of prime responsibility: Winterbourne, Frampton Cotterell, Coalpit Heath, Frenchay and Hambrook and consortium area of prime responsibility – you are most likely out of luck (unless you have a sibling already there or a special educational need). The academy is heavily oversubscribed, and catchment-area based admission rules haven't changed with the shift to academy status. No entry tests for banding as used by other local academies. Applications through South Gloucestershire council in October before year of entry.

For the sixth form, minimum B grades at GCSE expected in A level subject picks.

Exit: Growing numbers in the sixth form – well over half stay on, but some leave at 16 for work, training or more vocational courses at local colleges. Sixth form leavers go anywhere and everywhere, some 80 per cent to some form of higher education, including Oxbridge and Russell Group universities, but a few straight to employment or training.

Money matters: Academy now manages its own budgets and can shop around for better-value outside services. Parents' association has active fundraising programme – lotteries, quiz nights etc – and partners in industry have helped out with equipment and some funds in the past.

Remarks: Deservedly popular commuter-belt comprehensive turned academy, with big ideas, new buildings and an eye on the wider world. Good results and a strong sporting tradition keep its feet on the ground.

Writhlington School

Knobsbury Lane, Writhlington, Radstock, Somerset BA3 3NQ

Pupils: 1,500 • Ages: 11–18 • Sixth form: 316

Tel: 01761 433581
Email: info@wsbe.org.uk
Website: www.wsbe.org.uk

Head teacher: Since 2011 Mr Mark Everett BSc MA PGCE NPQH (early 40s). By his own admission, an Army brat from 'mostly around Manchester'. He read physics at Nottingham as an officer cadet, but had a crisis of conscience at the end of the first Gulf War, at which point he turned his back on officer training and worked in a cheese factory after graduation. His patience with other cheese-makers indicated that he might make a good teacher, so he enrolled on a PGCE course at Hull, going on to forge a successful teaching career in some pretty rough inner city schools in London and Southampton. 'I've seen it all', he says, and this gives him an unshakeable belief in the value of truly comprehensive education: 'No school should isolate less advantaged kids when the social profile of the school changes; our job is to ensure that everyone, irrespective of background, goes on to achieve more than his/her entry assessment would suggest'. His military background still obvious 20 years on in terms of his physique, energy and confidence – we were amused that he turned out of his office for us to chat to pupils, one of whom dared to swivel around in his big black chair. Generally respected by parents and pupils alike for his local and global ambitions for the school; an 'excellent front man – who should not lose sight of standards closer to home such as behaviour and uniform,' according to one mother. Married to another teacher with a small son, and admits to a love of surfing when time permits.

Academic matters: For a completely non-selective school in a socially mixed, if not ethnically diverse area, 64 per cent A*/B grades at A level in 2016 is impressive (though GCSE results hard to find). Academic superstars need not fear that they will not sparkle here.

This was the first school where we have been handed an academic paper as a going-home prize. A few years ago, a year 11 pupil carried out research in Sikkim, where he compared historical records of altitudes where orchid species grew with present data, as a means of recording climate change. He was awarded Young Biologist of the Year for his pains.

Parents have noticed a greater emphasis on top universities, not merely local ones. 'I didn't know what Russell Group meant till I heard the head go on about it', admitted one dad. We were put in our place by one little brain-box, who, when we asked if he was aiming for Oxbridge, said 'No, MIT actually'. But the school appears to look after everyone by assigning each student to a pathway according to his/her intellectual lights – academic, applied learning, sport or STEM. This assumes particular significance in year 10, at the point where choices made will affect sixth form courses of study; a meticulous and collaborative process, resulting in an agreement signed by parents. One parent felt, however, that his child had been written off academically and that the school could do better at recognising his other achievements and attributes, another was disgruntled that her child had changed GCSE subjects without any word from the school, and yet another that her bright son was frustrated and bored in mixed ability sets.

The design of the building and emphasis (plus funding) given over to technology results in innovations in teaching: every child has an iPad to be used as a learning resource and means of communication – 'makes life a lot easier for my dyspraxic son too', said a father. The school has learning zones, where a whole year group can be accommodated: we were impressed by the purposeful way in which 90 children were getting on with their differentiated work with just one teacher and a couple of TAs overseeing them. Traditional methods still employed where effective too: one class was studying graphs of rainfall, sitting in rows, facing the front and paying attention.

SEN, and in fact any intervention for all abilities, has been brought right into the centre of the school in the atrium, where small groups brought out of class work on literacy and numeracy under the watchful eye of a staff member. We wondered if it would be distracting or stigmatising but were assured not – quite the reverse, in fact. Some parents report a lack of communication between SEN and subject teachers, however.

Games, options, the arts: School is fortunate to have a community sports centre on site; with its sports hall, gym and squash courts, the only thing it lacks is a pool. As well as rugby pitches, there's an Astroturf (used by the FA); indoor nets and an outdoor pitch cater for cricketers. A tennis centre run in conjunction with the Lawn Tennis Association. Several local clubs and members of the public make good use of the facilities. Recently launched outdoor education programme means students will be able to take up D of E and Ten Tors. School has been selected for training by Bath Rugby. A smattering of outstanding sportsmen/women (Commonwealth Games hopeful for target shooting, one year 7 boy chosen to play football for Welsh National side, another for the World Trampoline Championships, a sixth former offered 13 (!) tennis scholarships to American universities) mean Writhlington is always in the news.

Musical life also abounds, with all year 7s offered free instrument tuition for their first term. A Musical Association has been in existence for 20 years, its primary aim to raise funds to support the school's many musicians with instruments, transport and more recently, snazzy waistcoats for band members. Happy collaboration and perhaps rivalry with nearby Downside, particularly at annual Battle of the Bands. Individuals excel too; recently two girls got grade 8 singing, one with distinction. Facilities top notch, with high tech recording studio particularly praised – and let out to local groups seeking low-cost recording facilities. Productions of all kinds staged in 400 seat theatre where recent drama productions include Little Women – the Musical and The Tempest. Students can choose a performing arts option from year 10-13, which covers not just acting, but production, direction and technical support too. Art occupies four specialist rooms on the first floor, and from year 10 students have options in either art or art and design; their work is exhibited on occasion in Bath and Bristol's most prestigious venues.

Extensive enrichment programme with plenty of clubs in school time; enterprising parents and staff enhance offering outside school with such ventures as the equestrian team, run by the head's PA.

Background and atmosphere: Fifteen years ago, 'Writhlington was a dump, and no child of mine will ever go there,' declared one mother, recalling with a shudder its depressing concrete buildings, windswept site and low aspirations. Historically, it had served the mining community in and around Radstock; it is now federated with the town's other schools, so relations are greatly improved between them. Enter a dynamic and visionary head and an exceptional business and finance manager, whose success in pulling the place up by its bootstraps and securing some of the last funding available under the Building Schools for the Future programme resulted in £42m worth of brand new buildings of truly innovative design, a recipient of an award from the British Council for School Environments ('but looks like a prison', say locals).

'However, it is what goes on behind its doors that I believe makes Writhlington simply remarkable', says the current head, an opinion largely shared by the parents we spoke to, including the mother cited above. Very much the comprehensive of choice for the area now, where students are given myriad opportunities to shine, and where success of all kinds is recognised. The new buildings, insistence on higher standards of turn-out than many schools we know and the weekly appearance of the CCF in their uniform make for a smart, clean, rather business-like school. Thriving sixth form retains many of school's own students and attracts others from the area, including from local independents.

Business and enterprise accreditation plays out in practice with the school's strong links with local businesses; it also belongs to Career Academies UK, so that students taking that curricular pathway have access to a mentor, paid internships and contact with leading businesses. Because of the school's non-selective intake and inclusive philosophy, university is (refreshingly) not regarded as the be-all-and-end-all of sixth form achievement. One father, however, commented wryly that the students needed to see more of, and be ready for, the realities of the working world.

Parents and their offspring recognise that the school successfully brings the world to the school, with its offer of Mandarin, the China exchange and the increasingly famous orchid project, which has recently ventured to Rwanda to teach schools there laboratory and conservation techniques, and to promote science education. The trip was funded by orchid sales from the school, which now has a new hybrid named Oncidium School Days in its honour by a previous student.

Has recently opened the Mendip Studio School, offering STEM courses to 14-19 year olds.

Pastoral care, well-being and discipline: Appears to be a school where concerns are acted upon, and where students have places to go when things go wrong. 'The support and guidance staff sort you out and cheer you up,' was the consensus from the group we spoke to. Parents generally approve of the discipline, but one felt that those meting out punishment should be answerable for their actions; the students' view was that it was 'quick, effective and tailor-made'. The fact that achievement of all kinds is celebrated was universally praised, but part of the reward system consists of a trip for the class, for which the parents pay – to the outrage of some, who consider that to be socially divisive. 'And what about recognition for the kids who are good all the time across the board?' said a mother plaintively: 'The system specifically aims to reward those whose work ethic is consistently high,' says the school in response

Pupils and parents: Very mixed, as befits a truly comprehensive school. Catchment is economically varied (though a lower proportion of free schools meals than the national average) with dreary Norton Radstock at its heart, yet prosperous little villages and madly arty Frome close by. Two university academics we met chose it over other local options. Building purpose-built for kids with limited mobility, which gives it a lovely inclusive feel.

Entrance: An open day in September and subsequent open mornings helps decision-making, thence applications are made through the local authority, BANES. Year 7 intake is over 250 from several local primary schools, and other years are already oversubscribed. Sixth form numbers are lower: entry requirements are five GCSEs at A*/C including English and maths; some A level choices will require specific grades. Open day in November each year. Great care taken over information available for new students on the website, such as several student video clips.

Exit: Post-GCSE, some leave for college and a few to apprenticeships or work. Some 70 per cent of sixth formers go to university, and most of those to their first choice, including Royal Veterinary College, LSE, Exeter, Cardiff, Manchester, Sheffield, Nottingham, Bristol, Southampton, Kent and Bath.

Remarks: This school is a phoenix rising from some pretty unpromising ashes. The process of bringing it back from the moribund, if not dead, started long before the dramatic new build of 2010, and now it has the setting to reflect its considerable aspirations. The school aims to make these attainable for everyone. 'The whole place makes me feel as though I wanted to go back to school', said one father, a little wistfully

W

Wycliffe Preparatory School

Linked with Wycliffe College

Ryeford Hall, Stonehouse, Gloucestershire GL10 2LD

Pupils: 323; 61 full, 25 flexi boarders • Ages: 2–13 (boarders from 7)

Fees: Day £6,600 – £13,410; Boarding £18,090 – £25,500 pa

Tel: 01453 820470
Email: prep@wycliffe.co.uk
Website: www.wycliffe.co.uk

Headmaster: Since 2003, Mr Adrian Palmer BA (rapidly approaching 60 but with no intention of retiring). An ex-maths and PE teacher, he had a spell as head at Warminster Preparatory School then moved to Rendcomb, where he started the junior school and built up numbers rapidly before moving to Wycliffe. Though he works closely with Wycliffe College as part of the overall leadership team, he enjoys the freedom and respect accorded him by the new head of college, which gives him complete control of development in the prep school. Married to Julie, a lynchpin in the school, managing SEN and, as author of The Write Path, assisting everyone to develop legible handwriting; they have son and a daughter who both went through the prep and the college.

Exceptionally talented at inspiring children and setting them at their ease; they positively bubble with delight at his arrival, and are reluctant for him to depart. His office boasts masses of impressive artwork with a stunning pencil portrait of him done by a pupil. His 'persona' is emphasized by a lurid collection of over 200 ties, which are the source of endless discussion and delight to pupils. Though he does not teach, he is very much in evidence around the school at all times, personally showing round every prospective parent and aware of the individual needs of every child. He has developed a simple but effective effort grading system which pervades every classroom, based on skills like persistence, cooperation, organisation etc, which accounts for the confidence with which one pupil told me that coming top was less important than fulfilling potential and achieving a personal target grade. End of year exams for the top three years are intentionally tough with 'opportunities provided' for revision, so that children can learn to deal with this situation.

Utterly pupil-centred, Mr Palmer, and hence the school, believes in pupils enjoying their education. Responsibility appointments, prefects, etc are made 'when children are ready for it' throughout the final year, and head boys and girls hold the post for part of the year only so that leadership is shared out. He runs the school with a light and humorous touch, an example being the hanging model of a bee in the dining room, left after a food info project 'because it was fun'. While his approachability is clearly appreciated by pupils, staff and parents, his professionalism is evident everywhere. Everything runs like clockwork.

Entrance: Over 60 per cent from the nursery situated across the road from the main prep school, via a charming bridge built in the 1930s, which is 'the only way pupils ever cross this busy road'. Pupils join from other schools via relaxed interview and a good report. Moderate learning difficulties can be given appropriate help. An increasing number comes in at 11+, when scholarships and awards in music, drama, dance, sport and art are available. Fleets of buses from all over the place. Parents may apply at any time of the year and pupils may join whenever there is room.

Exit: Typically all but one of the year group we talked to were going on the senior school. Exams are for setting purposes as transition is very nearly automatic and the school gives plenty of warning to parents if the senior school would not be appropriate. Pupils who need to go elsewhere are prepared for CE etc.

Remarks: The campus is divided by a main-ish road with the prep, lower prep, teaching, drama, sports hall and pool (used by seniors as well) nestled tightly but comfortably on the smaller southern area. Nursery, boarding and massive playing fields are over the bridge to the north. Teaching facilities include bang up to date Etheridge Hall, an attractive modern and spacious class and subject room centre with latest high-tech facilities, and large common room for year 8 pupils (tea and toast making facilities). In contrast the largely unreconstructed original house, with its high ceilings and steep stairs, houses the library (undergoing recataloguing by the new real librarian) and lower forms. It's not very accessible, though the school will switch what's taught where to accommodate anyone's needs. The main campus is an amazing hotchpotch attractively united by some remarkably well-designed gardening and wonderful views. Early years have disguised portacabins, airy and well equipped inside with colourful enclosed outside soft play areas. Little sheltering pagodas with blue roofs harmonise the haphazard older buildings, which include a hugely impressive art room, full of deconstructed cubist guitar paintings and occupied on our visit by a class learning to make Egyptian cartouches.

Gym and good sized indoor pool are serviceable but undistinguished, and juxtaposed with a massive and essential boys' changing room in Tesco's Toytown style, and a really state of art modern theatre building, much used for really exciting performances – Hairspray, The Lion King etc. Far better equipped than many a semi professional senior school theatre. A cunning portrait of the head done in string on the tennis court fencing typifies the friendly, quirky atmosphere of the school. An inspirational addition evidencing its serious core is the stunning sensory garden with open-air pavilion for either teaching or just sitting and thinking.

Everywhere is well equipped. ICT is taught as 'a discreet subject' and from the age of 7 each pupil has two lessons a week. Pupils talk enthusiastically and cogently about their activities. Good labs, French taught from tinies on and German and Spanish from year 8. The prep school provides carefully appropriate tuition for a very wide range of abilities and has demonstrated this by its affiliation to both CResTed, which confirms its good SEN provision, and NAGC, which accredits work for gifted and talented pupils.

Pupils genuinely believe that there is no bullying and that any potential problems can and will be sorted out by sympathetic but firm pastoral staff. Parents confirm that the merest sniff of trouble is dealt with well. A zero tolerance of bullying and a real sense in older pupils of their responsibility to take care of younger ones make it 'a bit like a family,' one said. A boarder explained that there was no need to be homesick because some members of staff are really like another mother.

Lots of Forces boarders and a few from abroad – occasionally short term visitors like it enough to want to stay on for the rest of their prep years. Weekends great fun and, though boarders are allowed out, there tends to be in inflow of day pupils staying for special activities rather than a general exodus. The boarding houses (one each for boys and boys and girls of all ages, with a connecting lobby) are at the top of the site and have splendid views. The large dormitories have been split into rooms taking two to four pupils with loos very near and showers – some definitely catering for privacy and some less so – and baths downstairs. Boys and girls are allowed to visit each other's common rooms under supervision. Lovely touches abound, like the heart-shaped 'memories' collage of photographs. All prep is done in school so work doesn't come home, but mobiles and computers are allowed during waking hours in the boarding houses – handed in at night and during lesson hours. It's all feels very secure, homely and not too tidy, with the inevitable bunk beds which children seem to like.

Food is 'pretty good now', especially breakfast with croissants and pain au chocolate. Pupils were anxious to assure me that there is masses of choice and all food groups a represented. Dining is informal with a separate round table area for little ones. Early bird day children welcomed into boarding houses and taken down to breakfast by helpful prefects. At weekends boarders go up to the college for Sunday lunch – one parent said this was the only feature of the school she had reservations about, but not a serious one. Noticeably kind and motherly kitchen staff. Teachers sit with pupils. Saturday morning school (for years 6, 7 and 8) is one of the few things pupils could think of that they didn't like – but then they decided that actually it's fun 'on the whole'.

Sport is really important, and as well as the usual rugby/soccer/cricket for boys and netball/hockey/tennis and rounders for girls there are some distinguished athletes – one girl reached national biathlete standard, and other children who are interested in special sports or excel in any area are taken to local clubs in the evenings and get absolute top coaching, with some spectacular results. Masses of other activities after school, and day pupils can go home at 4.45pm or stay later for prep and activities.

The nursery is next to the boarding houses, surrounded by little secure areas for digging, outdoor play and exploration. More log-clad portacabins make a light-filled flexible space with all the nursery equipment imaginable. It is filled with small children absorbed in play activities or books, dressed in cheerful red tops or cardies with bright gingham dresses for girls, quite different to the smart jerseys and girls' kilts of the older pupils. Good library – 'the nursery eats books,' said one teacher. Other meals are taken in the nursery dining room. It all feels happy and purposeful, provides after-school care and has terms which are much longer than school ones to provide a consistent service. There are even beds are even available for occasional rest time.

Parents get a chance for input as Mr Palmer has parent forum groups, and one noted that several suggestions had been taken up and were working well. Those stationed abroad are particularly grateful for a parent community prone to scooping up boarding children with absent parents and ensuring they get to birthday parties etc, and being on hand to offer visiting parents a bed for the night.

The key feature of Wycliffe Prep is its happy atmosphere. Children and parents enjoy their experience of the school as well as getting second to none opportunities in sport, music and drama, combined with some exceptional teaching. Its atmosphere, creativity and endearing quirkiness are typified by an extraordinary portrait of Mr Palmer, done in string on the wire-netting fence to the tennis courts – smiling, as usual.

Wycliffe College

Linked with Wycliffe Preparatory School

Bath Road, Stonehouse, Gloucestershire GL10 2JQ

Pupils: 400; 217 boarders • Ages: 13-19 • Sixth form: 175

Fees: Day £17,430 – £18,990; Boarding £30,540 – £31,785 pa

Tel: 01453 822432
Email: senior@wycliffe.co.uk
Website: www.wycliffe.co.uk

Head: Since 2015, Nick Gregory, (40s) who was pastoral deputy head at Mill Hill School in London. He graduated in French and Spanish at Nottingham, then spent eight years at Barclays, including time in Madrid, before teaching, modern languages first at Barnard Castle School, County Durham, then at Merchant Taylors' School, Northwood. He then became boarding housemaster at Old Swinford Hospital, Stourbridge. He and his wife, Helen, have three sons, two of then at Wycliffe. He believes school needs to be more than a teaching machine, somewhere that gives a lived and valued experience which will lay a foundation for life. Despite the popularity of his predecessor, senior pupils say he has grasped the traditions and special nature of Wycliffe and that he knows them well as individuals.

He took over an already flourishing school and is mainly concerned to develop the good practice and vision he has found. 'No major changes planned' but there have already been a few changes in staffing. He is 'nurturing boys' sport from the bottom up' to ensure that there are promising signs of success (girls are doing pretty well at present). He aims to support 'the gifted and talented pupils the school attracts, while maintaining access to all academic levels, and supporting bringing out the best in those with difficulties'. He expressed his approach very simply as enabling his pupils 'to be good people'. His pastorally orientated philosophy works on the premise that young people learn and are motivated when they are confident secure and feel valued. If the these sound like 'soft' skills, he is also determined that the school will be supported by the best in teaching and technology, and have well structured opportunities from tutors, careers advice, business links and university access. Parents consider that he is bringing a needed touch of academic edge to the school. Exceptionally accessible and easy to talk to, Mr Gregory is also someone who works fast and gets things done quickly. 'A force of nature,' said one parent! He and his family live on the premises, and when he actually gets some time away he likes to spend it giving full time attention to his family life in their house in southern Spain.

Academic matters: Considering that the school has an open access policy with exams only used for purposes of setting or scholarships, GCSE and A level results are very respectable. There is no doubt that gifted pupils do really well, with the relatively few high fliers, including those who have been right through the Wycliffe experience and some more recently arrived from abroad, getting straight A*/A grades and, in 2016, making it into Oxford, Harvard, Imperial College and St Andrews. 2016's 27 per cent A*/A and 56 per cent A*-B represent an improvement on the slight 'glitch' of 2015. Ninety per cent of all leavers achieved their first choice of uni. Mr Gregory says the long-term aim is least a third of A levels A*/As and two-thirds at B or above. Choice is impressive with over 30 A level subjects including BTec equivalents in travel and tourism and sport, both of which have impressive results. Languages (French, Spanish, German, Russian and Japanese) have good take up as does maths, with a consistently sound record, though whilst economics and business studies are also much in demand, As and Bs are thin on the ground.

2016 GCSE results improved on 2015 despite the national downward trend. Some spectacular results here in maths, further maths, German, Russian and Chinese – the latter possibly accounted for by some native speakers.

Value-added is key to the school's approach and all the statistics indicate that this is impressive. (It is worth pointing out that value-added is particularly difficult to assess in very high achievers, and pupils and parent satisfaction is probably a much better guide.) Masses of help available when needed – with teachers exceptionally ready to go the extra mile with one-to-one and special help. Lots of careful supervision and expert help on subject choice. Study leave is only allowed at A level, and even then those who need guidance with revision are advised to stay in school. Teachers always keen to help even after exams have started. Boarding and day pupils have study space in their houses and the library, which is also a fabulous multimedia resource centre. Very popular, spacious and well planned, with plenty of help on hand; it was very full and had an extremely studious feel on the day of our visit. All this is underpinned by a careful tutorial programme and rigorous tracking of pupil progress which stops pupils slipping through the net. PHSEE provides life and study skills and every year group has courses such as teamwork, problem solving etc, aiming to develop skills as useful in life as they are in academic approach.

Newish labs, biology sporting a fish tank that wows prep school visitors. Classrooms jigsawed into every part of the buildings with plenty of the relevant IT etc, and without exception those we passed looked busy and purposeful.

Extensive remedial and special needs programme with lively, sensitive and fully qualified teachers who help and support. Pupils are automatically assessed on entry to the school, as much to identify gifted and talented as those with learning difficulties. Wycliffe has received accreditation and plaudits from both CResTeD (for SEN) and NAGC (for specially talented), which endorses the quality of teachers' work with pupils. Emphasis is on differentiated teaching as well as individual help. EAL support is on hand.

The 'development year' is a pre-A level course designed to give pupils from abroad both basic English and some GCESs or equivalent on which to ground A level study. Some 30 or so pupils each year from all over the world benefit from this, with 15-20 staying on into the sixth form and contributing a range of sporting and other skills. Mr Gregory, parents agree, has certainly 'turned up the gas' a bit on the academic side but not, they also agree, at the expense of Wycliffe's happy and supportive community feel.

Games, options, the arts: Sport is a vital aspect at Wycliffe and a number of parents cite it as their deciding factor in choosing the school. Facilities are excellent, with smashing new Astroturf and smart multipurpose sports hall (full of aspiring small cricketers avoiding the rain on our visit) with professional standard squash courts, fitness gym and viewing areas. The pool is on the prep site. Massive pitches and lawns surround the school. Teams in hockey, netball, rugby and tennis reach county level at least on a regular basis, while individuals perform at national level in a huge range of sports including rowing, biathlon and an abundance of all branches of athletics. Girls' teams have acquitted themselves particularly well recently, with recent district and county successes at netball, hockey, rounder and tennis. Squash is truly exceptional, with boys' and girls' teams winning national events, and the school has an

W

internationally-renowned programme that pupils from across the world come to join as boarders, producing recent British and European champions.

Choral singing – with a 75-strong chapel choir and the upmarket Vox chamber choir for the real elite – is the heart of performance music, but a vast swathe learn instruments with a few getting to grade 8, and National Youth Orchestra or Choir standard. No full orchestra, but lots of thriving ensembles and an emphasis on music technology. Several take A levels in music and music technology each year, with some progressing to uni on the technology side. Fantastic support and inspiration from the two exciting musicians who head the department.

Strong drama boasts established theatre studies and emerging film studies, with pupils carrying both of these on to post-school study and ambitious school productions. The Sibly Theatre, named for the founder, now looks a little dated, so not quite as slick as the junior theatre, but bigger and very well equipped with studio spaces behind the stage.

Art inhabits its own building with a chaotic barn-like upper art room and pottery, classrooms and other media below producing some striking work, which reflects the team of professional artists. Sadly we missed the A level work, which had been packed up for dispatch, but there was some exciting painting and in most years the results are A* studded.

Not surprisingly for a school offering a whole life experience, the range of co-curricular activities is wide and diverse. Up to GCSE pupils have to opt into two activities weekly. Since the alphabet of activities starts with astrology, beekeeping and cryptology, continuing in the same vein, this is no hardship. Opportunities to take up fencing or yoga, the staples of CCF and Duke of Edinburgh, and academic extensions such as robotics, studying newts or serious debate are an integral part of what Wycliffe is about, and a chance for every pupil to excel – and they do.

Beyond this there is serious programme of exchanges, visits and expeditions: cricket to Barbados, squash to Canada, hockey and netball to Sri Lanka. Language visits include Japan and there are careers and education trips to theatres and museums etc, and year 12 is launching a charitable project in Costa Rica.

Boarding: Having pupils from all over the world, plus Brits who live some distance away, means there is a solid core in school at weekends. Some locals choose to stay as there seems to be a thriving social scene, so boarding really is a good bet for Forces families or expats.

Boarding houses with full and flexi boarders plus attached day pupils form the core of the social life. The system is a real mixture with a designated sixth form house but some sixth formers in the main school houses, and a day pupils' house, as well as some day pupils in the main boarding houses. Loosley (named after the third and most illustrious Wycliffe head) houses the sixth form – both boys and girls – with spacious common rooms, small kitchens and laundry areas for washing casual clothes and a campus feel for milling about. Sixth formers in mixed age houses can drop in on Loosley. The mixed day house, with generously broad corridors, brightly painted studies and common rooms with balconies overlooking the green sward, is clearly much appreciated.

Rooms (for two to four and the odd single for prefects or heads of houses) are fairly basic and include work space. All boarding accommodation is utilitarian rather than palatial, though some houses are being upgraded in a multi-million pound project – the new Ward's and Ivy Grove houses look as though this is are worth waiting for. Pupils with study periods can use their rooms – so the houses are certainly not unnaturally tidy. Plenty of loos and private showers, with a bath available in each house. Houses looked after by friendly and very approachable non-teaching staff, who seem to be available throughout the day as well as in the evenings, plus a teaching houseparent in charge of each house.

Sixth form boarders are allowed a pint or glass of wine at weekends and the occasional early evening visit to the pub in the neighbouring Cotswold town of Stonehouse, which despite its quiet atmosphere is conveniently on the main line from Paddington.

Background and atmosphere: The parkland feel of the huge grassy campus is created by wide, well-maintained pitches (cricket/rugby and some Astroturf) sited amid trees and well-kept garden. A succession of buildings, some inspired and some less, has divided the whole into a series of campus 'rooms', each with its lawns and distinctive buildings, ranging from the elegant Georgian Haywardsend House, though the bizarre exterior of the Sibly Theatre (really good facility inside) and the workmanlike labs to the inspired modern wood and glass of the huge curved dining area, serving delicious food with a tantalising variety. Sunday brunches 'are to die for'. The last looks out on a massive expanse of new, green Astro used for hockey etc in the winter and tennis in summer. It is spectacularly edged in dark purple, which echoes the head's penchant for this colour – which, conveniently, is the school colour, emphasized by the pale mauve of the large Wycliffe sign boards and, more attractively, by the wisteria which swarms over several of the buildings.

Founded by the Sibly family in 1882 and named for the pioneering Christian spirit of John Wycliffe, the school now goes out of its way to make this spirit accessible to all denominations and races. Pupils and parents set immense store by the Wycliffe ethos, friendly, nurturing and pupil centred. A sixth former commented favourably on Mr Gregory's evident efforts to know the school history. A busy campus with friendly staff and well-mannered but unaffected pupils strolling purposefully around. Inside and out there is seating dotted around inviting conversation with a sense of reasonable privacy. The school has been fully co-educational for more than 30 years and it feels absolutely right. The happy purposefulness of the place is most evident in the exceptionally user-friendly library, full of pupils working quietly and calmly (it was almost exam time) with help on hand. It is designed to divide into areas for quiet study, computer research, reading and even discussion and is clearly a real centre of academic life.

Pastoral care, well-being and discipline: The house system is the pastoral structure for both boarders and day pupils. The houseparent, matron, house staff and a team of house tutors are supported by prefects and responsible sixth formers, who provide the essential links between staff and pupils. Both pupils and staff give the impression that the relationship between them is free and easy. Students say there is little or no bullying, certainly nothing serious. 'It's just not what we do and absolutely not tolerated'. One parent reported that he was informed of a minor incident which his son had not mentioned because 'it was not a real problem'. It had clearly been nipped in the bud before it became serious. Communications are excellent and parents who want frequent updates are well satisfied. Pupils from abroad seem to mix in well – a table of very all-inclusive chatterers in the dining room proved on our enquiries to consist of a real mix of recent and new pupils, from both the locality and as far away as Latvia and the Ukraine. Awkward moments, like the transition from prep school, are extremely well handled, according to parents.

All faiths catered for and the chaplain is very open and inclusive. Pupils evidently felt real affection for the beautiful chapel, and recounted its history with pride: rebuilt post war by pupils and staff incorporating wood from a pier on the Isle of Wight and stone from a bombed church.

All is underpinned by clear procedures and regulations. Support runs deep in the community, typified by the head, who after just under a year was able to give minute details of every pupil we met.

Houses do lots of social, competitive and charitable events, which give creative opportunities involving everyone in mixed age groups in cultural and aesthetic activities: singing, drama, film quizzes etc. Usual structure of prefects etc clearly relishing their responsibilities.

Pupils and parents: Plenty of army families but also lots of locals as well as a high proportion from abroad (30 per cent, which means about 60 per cent of boarders): Europe, ex-USSR countries and the far east. The chair of the PA says parents who want to take a large part in their offsprings' education are given real support, but those with a less hands on approach seem equally satisfied. Head finds pupils refreshingly unaffected in comparison with the London set. Parents here are exceptionally supportive of each other, and those from further away say they get invitations to stay and offers to entertain their offspring.

Entrance: The majority of pupils joining in year 9 come from the school's own prep school, though recently increasing numbers come from other prep schools as well. Entrants sit exams but only for setting purposes. The school really prides itself on value added, which is one of its key aims, and only turns down those with learning difficulties too severe to be managed well at Wycliffe. Entry into the sixth form usually requires at least five GCSEs at grade C or above, but they do consider, more carefully than many, the question of potential, and the variety of academic pathways post-16 allows pretty much anyone to be accommodated appropriately.

Exit: Just over one-third leave post-GCSEs to vocational courses and sixth form colleges. Over 97 per cent of the sixth form go on to university with a few Oxbridge places. A number apply successfully to USA and other unis all over the world, and when the specialist adviser on US places moved on, the replacement was expert in international university entrance. 2016 saw one pupil going on to Harvard and one to Oxford. Some art foundation courses and drama school, otherwise business-related careers very popular, as are law and digital/creative courses.

Money matters: In terms of endowments, the school is not particularly wealthy, though it stresses that it is 'strong financially.' Scholarships are available at 13 and 16 for academic excellence, art, music, DT, ICT, drama and sport (10-20 per cent). This seems to be a particular draw in sixth form and there are a few pupils with exceptional circumstances who get pretty full financial support from the school, dependent on school reports and financial circumstances.

Remarks: A school which offers a way of life as much as an education. That the Wycliffe experience clearly breeds the confidence and openness is evident in its pupils. Definitely hotting up academically under the new head, but still faithful to its broad academic ability range. If success increases demand, will it be able to maintain an open admission policy? At present it is doing a remarkable job of being 'all thing to all men' – and women. A real gem of a school.

South East England

Berkshire
Buckinghamshire
East Sussex
Essex
Hampshire
Hertfordshire
Isle of Wight
Kent
Oxfordshire
Surrey
West Sussex

Northampton
Cambridge
WARWICKSHIRE
Bedford
BEDFORDSHIRE
Milton Keynes
Stevenage
OXFORDSHIRE
BUCKINGHAMSHIRE
Luton
Harlow
Oxford
Enfield
Ilford
Harrow
GREATER LONDON
Swindon
London
Reading
Croydon
SURREY
Basingstoke
Guildford
HAMPSHIRE
Winchester
WEST SUSSEX
Southampton
Brighton
Worthing
Portsmouth
Bournemouth
Isle of Wight
M1
M11
A1
M40
M4
M25
M3
M27

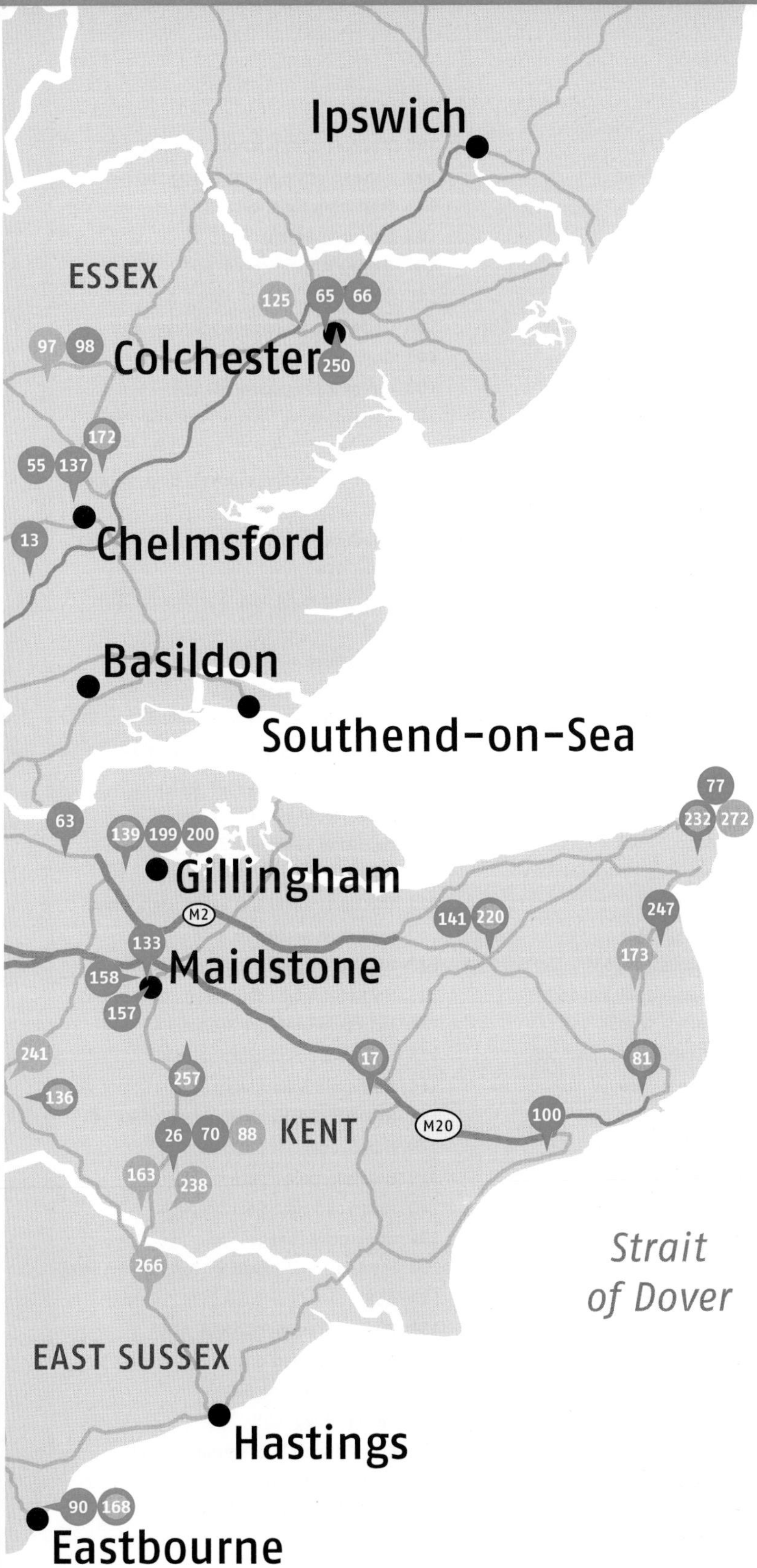

Ipswich
ESSEX
125 65 66
97 98
Colchester
250
172
55 137
Chelmsford
13
Basildon
Southend-on-Sea
77
232 272
63
139 199 200
Gillingham
M2
247
141 220
173
133
Maidstone
158
157
241
136
257
17
81
M20
100
26 70 88
KENT
163 238
Strait of Dover
266
EAST SUSSEX
Hastings
90 168
Eastbourne

255
221
217 56 178
82
209
280 87
171
118
59 156
Oxford
67 51
A

182
161
92 7
8
191
270
109 110
Watford
111 112
271 227 131
B

174
4
116
107
99
Woking
132
127 160
104
108
260
73
Guildford
240
145
189
204
C

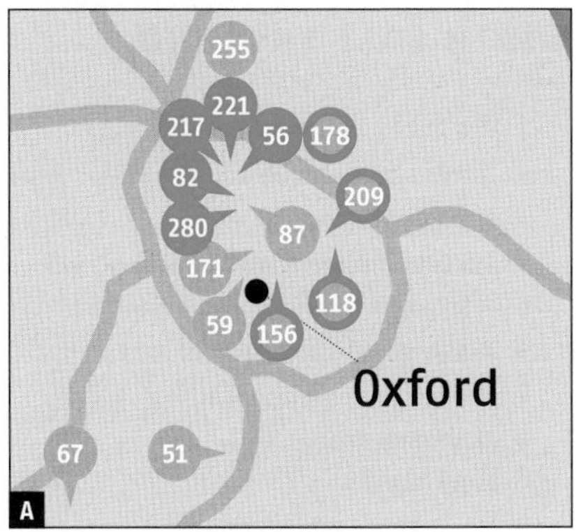

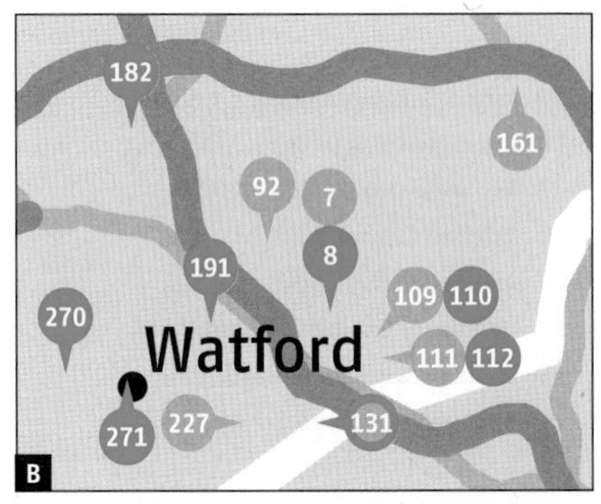

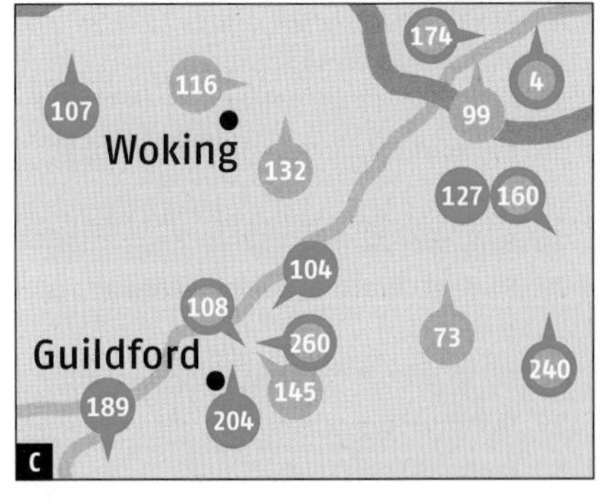

Junior Schools

Senior Schools

Junior & Senior Schools

SOUTH EAST ENGLAND

A

The Abbey Junior School

Linked with The Abbey School Reading

30 Christchurch Road, Reading RG2 7AR

Pupils: 366 • Ages: 3–11

Fees: £11,370 – £13,740 pa

Tel: 01189 872256
Email: schooloffice@theabbey.co.uk
Website: www.theabbey.co.uk

Head: Since February 2015, Mrs Nicola Dick-Cleland MA Oxon QTS (50s), previously deputy and then acting head. She joined the school in 2011 and was rapidly promoted to deputy. Has a degree in experimental psychology from Oxford and a teaching qualification from Reading. Was a senior manager at BT (the second most senior woman in BT at the time) before turning to a career in psychotherapy and, later, taking on a role as music teacher at the Dolphin School in Hurst, where her son was at school and where she loved it so much that she embarked on formal teacher training. 'For me, being a head brings together everything I know – leadership, psychology and education – perfect,' she says.

Refreshing to hear her talk enthusiastically about working with adults (many primary heads complain that they miss working with children), she nevertheless has a wonderful rapport with the kids here, whose faces light up when she bounces informally into classrooms. The tone of her communication with the children seems to us just right – warm and cuddly, but with an underlying authority. Parents like her and children tell us she's 'lovely' and 'kind'. Bizarre, then, that our pupil guides had absolutely no clue at all where her office was, although to be fair, she went onto explain to us that she purposefully keeps her office a largely child-free zone. 'I go out to them – an office isn't really an environment for children,' she believes.

Lives locally with her husband, with whom she has two grown-up children. Her daughter was a pupil at The Abbey. An outdoorsy type, much of her spare time is spent walking in the countryside.

Entrance: Nursery, reception and year 3 are the main points of entry. Spaces do appear in other year groups, although there are waiting lists for some. A short morning of informal play and assessment for youngest; tests plus interview for older girls. 'We're not looking for rocket scientists, but a good average, although when it comes to 3 and 4-year-olds, it's obviously an inexact science,' says the head, who adds that conversations with prospective parents are taken into consideration. 'In the end, it's all about whether the family has a fit with a school that has quite an academic pace and depth.' Whilst some parents make enquiries the moment their child is born, others call up mid-academic year, saying their husband or wife just has been relocated to Reading and they need a place at short notice. Increasingly, girls are moving across from state primaries. Class sizes generally 22 maximum, with many much smaller.

Exit: Around two-thirds move up to the senior school, with others going to nearby grammars (eg Kendrick, Sir William Borlase) or one of the good local comprehensives (eg Maiden Erlegh). A handful choose another independent day school, if the senior school doesn't feel quite right for them. Those who leave before the end of year 6 generally do so for relocation reasons. 'I like the turnover we have here,' says the head. 'We have a solid core, which keeps it from feeling like an international school, but newbies never find themselves joining cliques of girls and the mums that go with that. It's a comfortable school to join.' Pupils and parents agree. While the school is, inevitably, a feeder for nearby Kendrick Grammar, girls who gain places at both often choose to stay on.

Remarks: Open the magnificent door to this charming primary school in the university area of Reading and the tone is immediately set by the welcoming, down-to-earth staff and the seemingly endless displays of photographs, artwork, booklets, written work and more that decorates every single room and corridor. 'That's my work!' come the squeals of delight from the girls, making it immediately obvious how much pride they take in their work, and the boards are colourful, bold and tasteful too – a joy to see.

Nursery is based in Knell House, a converted Alfred Waterhouse villa, which boasts decent-sized learning rooms for these 20 children that are light, airy and welcoming (those displays again). One downstairs classroom we visited had a straw-based area that looked so much like a mini-farm that we half expected a live animal to appear. In fact, teachers had set it up to prepare the children for a school trip to a local farm. There's a good outdoor space, complete with Astroturf play area and adventure climbing equipment, overlooked by the church (which the school is closely linked with, including school carol concerts at Christmas). Facilities include a library/quiet room and singing and drama room. Emphasis at this stage is on learning through play – no writing until reception.

Things get slightly confusing when it comes to reception and year 1 as these classes have been relocated just down the road to Abbey Gardens, which was opened in 2014. Originally a judge's lodgings, the school really bought it for its large garden, which has been converted into an impressive all-weather sports pitch surrounded by a 'Willow walkway,' utilised by the whole junior school. But the house itself, built in the late 1800s, also makes for a delightful learning space. A tasteful, purpose-built ground-floor extension has made way for a gym, in full use with playmats when we visited, whilst the rest of the classrooms are based in the converted, but roomy bedrooms, all of which are well-ordered and well-equipped, but also colourful and homely. Even at this age, girls are taught by specialist teachers for PE, music, drama and languages (then sciences and computing from year 3), whilst the remaining subjects are taught by form teachers. We saw spirited girls having a whale of a time with paper, glue and plenty of glitter, as well as engaging in some more advanced activities.

Back in the main junior school, a mix of Victorian and later additions are home to years 2 to 6. Impressive facilities include a great science lab, where year 6 were busy purifying salt, a large dedicated dining room (no packed lunches here and nobody minds) and a computer suite with touch screen computers.

For drama (which is timetabled across many of the year groups) and dance (which is taught as part of the PE curriculum and via clubs), there's a dedicated studio with mirrored walls and deep carpet, along with a larger wooden-floored one and the main school hall. Both the latter double up as performance space – indeed, every year group does some kind of annual production, giving all children a chance to shine and less of a crush for the audience, and girls enthuse about how they get involved in everything from choreography to set design. 'By year 5, we are allowed a microphone,' one girl told us, practically jumping up and down with excitement, adding that they were waiting 'with bated breath to find out the results of our recent auditions.' 'The school plays are the best thing about the school,' more than one girl told us, although for others it was a toss-up between that and the swimming galas.

Music is outstanding here and very much part of the lifeblood of the school. We met the head of music when we visited – a delightful woman who provides two music classes per week from reception upwards, plus a weekly singing lesson – as well as overseeing the 15 peripatetic teachers that teach a total of 210 lessons a week. She also heads up the four school choirs and orchestra and gets the girls publically performing wherever possible, for which they regularly win awards (finalists in Barnardo's Choir of the Year was the most recent when we visited). Plenty of visiting workshops from the likes of composers specialising in children's songs to those teaching world music.

Art, which is mainly done in classrooms, is also notable. In fact, at the risk of harping on about those displays again, a series of charcoal drawings from year 6s showed such talent that they blew us away.

Girls do sport most days. 'We want it to become part of who they are,' says the head, and although it's more about inclusivity than competition, there are fixtures for those who want them. Netball, hockey, athletics, biathlon, swimming (at the senior school), football, Frisbee, gym and dance are just some of the options on offer. 'My daughter's not naturally sporty, but they get her having a go and she enjoys that,' one parent told us.

Languages are strong. Conversational French in reception and year 1; conversational Spanish in year 2; conversational German in year 3; then back to French, which is taught more formally, in years 4, 5 and 6. No setting – 'We don't need to as all the girls are relatively able and whilst they might need help in fractions one week, they might be a whizzy-whiz at 2D shapes the next week,' explains the head, who points to the research that shows that younger children in particular tend to define themselves by what set they're in, 'which can be counterproductive to learning.' Homework only set if it's seen to be genuinely aiding learning, so whilst there are weekly maximums amounts for each year, the girls don't always get it.

Teaching is lively and engaging, which was palpable in every classroom we visited. Head puts it down to well-paid and well-trained teachers (who all but two are female), who are given lots of autonomy in the classroom. This teaching is complemented by lots of visiting workshops – Roman workshops; maths puzzle; zoo lab are a few such examples – and a lively house science quiz was in full swing in the main hall when we visited, with girls all buzzing about it afterwards.

Specialist small group and individual support for mild SEN available, although most extra help is in the classroom, where there is no shortage of teaching assistants, many highly qualified. 'We don't want children to become dependent or resentful of having set extra help every week. We want a learning support model that anyone can use anytime – for instance if they're struggling with a particular maths concept,' says the head.

We found the girls capable and keen to learn – and it is this engagement that eliminates the need for sanctions, according to the head. No school rules here – only values and a class contract, written by the girls and teacher at the beginning of each academic year. 'Listen to others,' 'Respect each other's property,' 'Work hard' etc. Lots of praise for good behaviour, with special merits given in assembly by the head, particularly for effort (more likely for 'Jemima really persisted in her fractions' than 'Jemima got an excellent maths score').

When we asked the girls about bullying, we got a blank look. 'We know what it is,' one eventually said, 'but we haven't come across it.' Head believes this is down to keeping conversations alive about what bullying is and how you are just as culpable if you stand by and watch it – and this, together with an excellent form-tutor led pastoral system, seems to keep them on the straight and narrow. 'I'm not suggesting the girls are paragons of virtue, but there is a sense of community and decency,' says the head. One also gets the impression that the head's psychotherapy background comes in very useful pastorally. 'Children don't come to school to behave badly – and if they do, you need to look at the root of the issue,' she says, as if reading our minds.

Happy relationships also aided by the classes being muddled every two years or more to promote group bonding. Meanwhile, year 5 girls are trained to be 'playground buddies' and set up games, manage play equipment and mediate in squabbles. There's an active school council too.

Residential trips are a big thing here – building up from one night away in year 3 up to 6 nights in year 5 (then back down to 5 in year 6). 'The social and emotional benefits far outweigh anything else,' say the head. Meanwhile, day trips start from nursery (remember that farm) to the likes of Windsor Castle, Legoland etc.

The school day runs from 8.30am to 3.45pm, with an optional (and separately run) breakfast club running from 7.30am and after-school care until 6pm (these cost extra). Full club programme, mainly at lunchtimes, include everything from Lego club to nature detectives and from archaeology club to chess and judo.

Parents range from the very wealthy to the struggling-but-determined to afford the fees and everything in between. Lots of dual income families. You do get the 'My daughter must be top in everything' ones, but head manages it all well and does encourage parental involvement. In fact, one parent told us that this isn't a school to consider unless you're prepared to get involved. 'If you're the kind of parent that wants to hand over your child to the private school system and let them get on with it, this isn't the place for you, which can be tricky if you work full time – but it's a good ethos,' said one. Catchment area quite wide, generally within a 15-mile radius. School bus and kiss-and-drop service seen as godsend by parents. Healthy ethnic mix, with around half traditional white British and the rest as mixed as you can imagine – so for every yummy family from Henley, there's a Russian, Indian, Chinese etc family. Active PA and lots of socialising among parents ('Parents get on really well here – I've made good friends and not necessarily mums of friends of my child,' one mother told us).

The girls we saw were cheery, jovial and excitable, although parents assured us there's room for quiet ones too. The main characteristic you seem to need is being average or above in intelligence, with every parent we spoke to saying that the academically challenged might struggle.

A confident and well-run school that knows exactly where it's going, with happy girls who are stretched and challenged but not pressurised. Whilst many girls will attend The Abbey from 3 to 18, the junior school provides opportunities to help the girls reinvent themselves at different stages along the way. In fact, a word you'll hear a lot here is 'refresh,' which neatly sums up the school's attitude to constantly keeping things fresh and ahead of the game.

The Abbey School Reading

Linked with The Abbey Junior School

Kendrick Road, Reading RG1 5DZ

Pupils: 693 • Ages: 11–18 • Sixth form: 192

Fees: £15,720 pa

Tel: 01189 872256
Email: schooloffice@theabbey.co.uk
Website: www.theabbey.co.uk

Head: Since 2014, Rachel Dent BA QTS (40s), previously deputy head. Grew up in the Midlands and read English at Southampton

University, then embarked on a career in journalism in 1992, although she quickly realised it wasn't for her, quitting her first job at Time Out magazine after just two weeks. Travelled to Egypt to 'find herself' and when she realised she needed some money, she 'blagged her way into teaching English GCSE' and 'never looked back'. Did her formal teacher training back in the UK via fast track QTS at Reading University, then worked at Wisbech Grammar and then Cokethorpe School. Joined The Abbey in 2007 as director of sixth form. Her office is plush, swanky and large – think Farrow and Ball grey and white tones, stone fireplace and fresh flowers.

Whilst she's done odd bits of teaching since becoming head and leads Wednesday assemblies, the general consensus is that she's more of a CEO-type head than a hands-on teaching type (in fact, she'd recently been on a Henley Business School course with CEOs when we visited). A working mum, she is adamant that overworking isn't good for anyone and keenly leads by example to both staff and pupils when it comes to achieving work/life balance. 'There will always be tomorrow' is her mantra. Described as 'modern', 'dynamic', 'energetic' and 'visionary', we found her all these things, as well as warm and relaxed. Particularly keen to make the school's spaces more user-friendly and fit for modern teaching methods. 'I want to move away from traditional wooden desks,' she explains.

Lives locally with her husband and daughter. Regularly spotted walking her two dogs across Berkshire and Oxfordshire in her spare time.

As head of the senior school since 2015, Jan Cresswell – who has a degree in English lit from Durham and has taught English, drama and RE – is second-in-command and most likely 'go-to' person for parents and pupils. Previously head of sixth form at Portsmouth High School, she also served on the senior leadership team of a large co-educational HMC school. She is famed around the school for her fondness for literary references and her warm and persuasive leadership style. 'Rachel's focus on balance was a great fit with my belief that well-being matters most, so I knew I'd love it here,' she told us. 'And the girls are just what you'd hope them to be: energetic, curious and confident – but never pushy.' Since joining, she has overseen a restructuring of the pastoral support system. 'I don't suffer from tunnel vision,' she insists. 'I want the girls to share that sense that the world is a wonderfully exciting place to be – and that they can make a real difference.'

Academic matters: Impressive results across the board. In 2016, 84 per cent A*/A grades at GCSE. Refreshing to find students encouraged to take average of 10 GCSEs (previously it was 11 or 12), with most popular options being geography, history, food tech, textiles and drama (in that order). Choice of double and triple science. Computer science on the up.

At A level, girls can choose from 24 subjects, with the school priding itself on its ability to support some unusual combinations. In 2016, 60 per cent A* or A grades (89 per cent A*-B). IB results also notable – in 2016 one candidate scored the full 45 points (fourth time in school's seven year IB history) and the average was 39 points, making it one of the top IB schools in the country. In fact, it seems incredible that its introduction to the school in 2009 was seen as a brave and controversial move, with IB now as embedded into sixth form life as A levels. Teachers enthuse about how it has opened up the school's global community, made the school much more outward looking, as well as being energising for all sixth form teaching staff.

French and Latin from year 7, with the addition of Spanish or German in year 8. Some setting in year 7 in maths and French, but there's plenty of movement and no more setting until year 9. Sciences split from year 7, making students with strong preferences very happy. No homework for homework's sake here (back to that work/life balance ethos) and no homework at all during certain weeks, such as Intellectual Curiosity Week, Festival of Performing Arts Week.

Much praise from pupils and parents for teachers, who are described as 'committed' and 'enthusiastic', with high attendance at the non-compulsory monthly teacher-led learning innovation group meeting, which focuses on sharing good practice. Don't be fooled into thinking there's a single style of teaching here, however, with much autonomy given to individual teachers, although it is agreed that all teaching is personalised, with lots of attention given to discovering individual learning styles and adapting teaching to these. Whiteboards, computers etc are all present in lessons, but there's not an overdependence on them, as at some schools. 'I always say that if we lost the buildings, we could carry on,' says the head. Informal teacher-student relationships, backed up with a huge mutual respect that was palpable during our visit. 'Teachers are never patronising here, even when you're in year 7,' girls told us.

Around 30 with mild SEN receive one-to-one sessions either before school or in lunchtime (no lessons to be missed); small number (and often none at all) have EAL support from qualified teacher. 'SEN here is more a case of students using pink paper in exams than anyone being statemented,' says head.

Sixth form provides a happy transition between school and university, meaning that girls who would perhaps in the past have left, ready for a change, now stay on because the change is here. Itchy feet cured by no uniform, even less hierarchical teacher/pupil relations, tutorial style lessons where students can bring coffee along, superlative careers support and magic timetabling to enable endless permutations of A level and IB choices. The common room, with its own kitchenette, is fabulous – spacious, yet cosy and highly sociable, with music played during breaktimes and plenty of computers in the corner for those who don't mind studying with the low-level noise. Surrounding this space are 12 sixth-form teaching classrooms, along with an open study area with communal tables for quieter working. Many pupils told us their classes can have as few as two or three students in.

Outstanding careers advice, but there's an emphasis on keeping your options open, rather than pigeonholing yourself from too early on. 'We are constantly encouraged to explore what kind of a person we are – not just what subjects we're good at,' explained one girl. Lots of showcasing of work around the school. Tests and quizzes all part of daily life, but 'they're surprisingly relaxed,' say pupils, explaining that teachers use them largely as a way to feedback on areas students may be falling behind in; how revision techniques could be improved, etc.

Games, options, the arts: If you tour the school, don't make the mistake (many do) of singing the praises of the large, well-kept playing fields that much of the school overlooks – sadly, they belong to the adjacent Reading Boys'. It's the one thing the pupils and parents we spoke to would change. 'It would be great to have more outdoor space,' is a common statement here, although there's also an acceptance that it's a town school and most agree sports facilities still have a wow factor, including a large Astroturf sports pitch, excellent indoor swimming pool (early morning swim fit a popular class) and large sports hall. Main sports are hockey, netball, swimming and athletics, with rugby, football, volleyball, cricket, rounders and biathlons also popular. Fitness options range from belly dancing to zoomba. Very much a case of 'sport for all here,' with an emphasis on inclusivity over competitiveness, although there are plenty of opportunities for girls who do want to compete, with county and national triumphs for teams and individuals. When we visited, the school had an under-19 England netball player, five under-19 England rowers and several regional winners in netball, swimming and ice hockey. 'Even if you don't like sport, they make it fun,' one girl told us. 'I should know – I'm not keen.

But this morning, for instance, we did long jump and shotput and they helped me with technique in such an engaging way that I actually found I'd quite enjoyed it.'

Over a third of pupils learn a musical instrument at school and girls make a big noise in both grade examinations and numerous bands, choirs, ensembles and orchestras. There is a major musical production every two years and an annual overseas tour. Drama is very popular and girls we spoke to love the fact that the absence of boys (no shipping in for male roles) means that they get a chance to play all the star parts. Art is a dazzling department, with lovely big art studios and plenty of striking examples of everything from textiles to furniture on show throughout the school.

The Abbey Edge is an exhaustive (and quite possibly exhausting) programme of clubs and activities from crossword club to film society. It includes Chinese club, book clubs and news quizzes in the library, drop-in clinics for academic subjects (an excellent alternative to an evening's bad tempered homework trauma), D of E (this is one of the biggest D of E schools in the south east, for which the school has a gold award from Buckingham Palace), public speaking, gymnastics, drama, choirs, orchestras, ensembles, West Wing Club, altruistic society and golf. And that's just the start of it. 'It was the sheer breadth of extracurricular activity that made us choose the school, and the opportunities our girls have had as a result means we've never regretted our decision,' said one parent. Where possible, clubs (many of which are student-led) take place during lunchtime, although some are held before or after school. How on earth girls find time to do all this and get great results is an Abbey mystery, all the more astounding when you take into consideration that many girls are also involved in sports and clubs where they live. 'I did swimming training for 18 hours a week during my GCSEs and never once did the school suggest I should give it up, because they recognised that swimming is part of what makes me who I am – classic stuff for The Abbey,' one girl told us. 'More than that, they supported me to do well in the swimming and get my grades and I did.'

School trips plentiful – about 10 a week across the school, ranging from theatres to museums. Residentials include outdoor pursuits courses (home and abroad), battlefields (history), Iceland, Grand Canyon (both geography), France (water sports), Austria (skiing) and much more besides. Vietnam, Uganda and Equador were also mentioned during our visit. Fundraising and volunteer work is seen as important, with 70 girls involved in the Reading Refugee Programme when we visited. This involves girls helping children with homework on a regular basis. 'It helps them understand the real world and actively inspire children,' says the head.

Background and atmosphere: Based in the 'nice bit' of Reading, about half a mile from the university and a quarter of a mile from the town centre, the school was founded in 1887 as Reading High School. In 1914, it departed from the Church Schools Company and took its present name. Located in a leafy street with Victorian villas, it feels far, but not too far, from the madding crowd and is practically next door to both of Reading's massively oversubscribed state anomalies, Kendrick Girls' and Reading Boys' grammars. But while there is some cooperation (careers talks, university presentations), neighbourly relations remain at the polite nod rather than 'come in without knocking' level.

Old girls apparently horrified when they saw plans to demolish much of the Victorian frontage, but less so when the work was completed. The gothic entrance has been retained and old and new blend together pretty well, although – like many schools that have been added onto over the years – some of the buildings 'lack flow' and some areas are less lovely than others. Notable facilities include great science labs (well-equipped but not soulless); large and airy school hall (including balcony) which was all set up for exams when we visited; and library, which – whilst not the most hi-tech or modern – is roomy, well-stocked and welcoming. Lots of break-out areas, many with sofas ('You never feel you're bound to your classroom here,' said one pupil) and a terrific conference room, which is used for girls' presentations, IB exams and board meetings for the Young Enterprise club, and wouldn't look out of place in the likes of Silicon Valley.

Atmosphere is active, busy and buzzy – never silent. 'I don't like it when the school is too quiet,' laughs the head. It's about learning through doing here, she explains, with girls expected to try new things throughout their time here. 'This is not a school for girls who don't like trying new activities. It's fine if you don't like them, but there is an ethos of having to give things a go,' one girl told us. 'If you're all about head down and being shy and retiring, a grammar is probably better.' Other girls told us that highly competitive girls might also struggle, such is the atmosphere of collaboration and support.

Food, which all girls eat (no packed lunches here), widely praised.

Pastoral care, well-being and discipline: Form teachers (who really take time to get to know each girl) are at the heart of pastoral care, all of whom are supported by heads of year. These staff members meet every week for a detailed pastoral meeting, so any problems are picked up quickly. 'The teachers seem to know exactly know when to step in and when not to – the pastoral care is simply amazing,' said one parent. Disappointing to find no school counsellor, although head assured us there are plenty of links to external provision and girls seem very clued up on where to go for support. Our guides also pointed to sixth form buddies, whom you can email if you're shy.

All the usual leadership opportunities – form captains, school council reps, house captains etc – and you get the feeling they're much more than just labels here, with library prefects, for example, running assembles. 'Our leaders are do-ers and they love it,' says head, and pupils concur.

Discipline? Not needed, says the head. 'I can't remember the last time someone had a detention.' Rules? Nope, she says, unless you count those relating to respect. Girls told us that rules do exist and year 7 girls told us you get a black mark (you're not supposed to call it that, but they do) in your planner for crimes against uniform, homework etc. 'I got one yesterday for forgetting my apron for food tech,' one told us. But they all agreed the ethos is more about setting the standards in the early years, rather than focusing on punishment. Plenty of recognition and merits, including for those who are quietly good, who are often overlooked by other systems.

Bullying not problematic. When girls fall out (which, of course, they do), there are good strong tactics to sorting it out quickly and not letting it develop. Plus, girls say there's no stigma to reporting when you're feeling upset about something. Friendship groups, in the main, very wide-reaching. 'If we're trying to organise a night out, we soon find there are 40 people on the list,' a sixth-former laughed.

Pupils and parents: Hardworking and unsnobby, definitely no princesses here. Many from Reading's business community (Sage, Microsoft and Pepsi nearby), with many also in public sector, including academia (university and hospital also nearby). Others from Henley, Windsor and Basingstoke. Ethnic mix much as you'd expect in Reading – that is, mainly white British, but plenty more besides, with a plethora of languages spoken by students. Good transport links: school and public bus network and new Reading train station. Christian values prevalent, but religion is by no means in-your-face and all faiths (including non-believers) are welcome. Old girls include Baroness Brigstocke, Elizabeth Taylor, Helen Ganley, artist and social reformer, and a trio of BBC reporters, Miranda

Krestovnikoff, Kate Humble and Sally Taylor. Alumni seen as increasingly important, with the school having introduced a 'school version of LinkedIn,' as one girl puts it – that is, a social networking tool specifically for Abbey girls, past and present. 'It can open doors,' says one.

Entrance: Main entry point is 11, with around half coming from The Abbey Junior School. Others from independents (Highfield, Dolphin, Eton End, St Pirans) and local state primaries; small intake at 13. Girls sit exams in maths, English and reasoning. Interview with member of staff on their taster day and reference from their current school also taken into account. Sixth form candidates come in for a taster day of lessons in the subjects they want to study at IB or A level. They are expected to gain A*-B in these subjects at GCSE. Same grades required of existing pupils.

Exit: Around 20 per cent leave after GCSEs, mostly to attend local grammars and a few to local comps and colleges. 'Many parents budget for a certain amount of their girls' education and sixth form is not in the game plan,' says head. Almost exclusively Russell Group universities, with popular destinations including Birmingham, Exeter, UCL and Bristol. Five to Oxbridge in 2016. Heavy duty science subjects popular (six to study dentistry, medicine, veterinary and biomedical science in 2016), but also psychology, languages and English. 'Humanities hold their own,' says head, who adds that combined courses are increasingly popular – no doubt largely thanks to the Abbey ethos of staying open-minded about your future.

Money matters: Fees pretty competitive – they have to be and, unusually, they include exam fees, all text books and lunches. Means-tested bursaries of up to 100 per cent available; academic scholarships (10 per cent) at key entry points. Special awards for music (instrumental tuition paid) and talents in sport, art and drama – all with an accompanying enrichment programme.

Remarks: Yes, of course the girls work hard (and joy of joys, it's not seen as nerdy to do so here), but Abbey girls take things in their stride and manage to do plenty more besides. Indeed, for a high-achieving girls' schools, we found a reassuring lack of pressure, although we suspect some legs are paddling furiously below the surface. We also found it pleasantly down-to-earth and grounded. For bright girls, this is a fun, supportive and motivating place to be, providing excellent preparation for the modern world.

Abingdon School

Park Road, Abingdon, Oxfordshire OX14 1DE

Pupils: 1,262; 104 full, 32 weekly boarders • Ages: 4–18 (boarding from 13) • Sixth form: 300 • C of E

Fees: Day £11,265 – £18,585; Boarding £32,265 – £38,625 pa

Tel: 01235 849041
Email: admissions@abingdon.org.uk
Website: www.abingdon.org.uk

Head: Since September 2016, Michael Windsor, previously head of Reading Blue Coat School. First in French and German from Durham; worked briefly in publishing before heading for Bologna to teach English as a foreign language. On his return, did a PGCE at the Institute of Education and then joined King's College Wimbledon to teach foreign languages and take charge of the IB; also deputy head at RGS Guildford for five years. Coached rugby, hockey and athletics, involved in CCF and World Challenge expeditions. Also has an MA in modern German studies from Birkbeck and is an ISI inspector. Keen musician, playing the double bass in classical and jazz ensembles. Married to Shanti, who works at Reading University; they have two daughters.

Head of prep school: Since 2011, Mr Crispin Hyde-Dunn MA (Oxon) PGCE MA(Ed) NPQH (30s). Read history at Oxford. Previously deputy head of King's College School, Cambridge; was head of history at New College School in Oxford. He lives with his wife, Lucy, a medical research fellow at Oxford, in the school house just down the road.

Charmingly fogeyish in his immaculate pinstripes, he presents a rather formal face to the world but has genuine rapport with the boys, all of whom he knows by name (they call him Crispin – more of that later). He is actively involved in teaching – takes the year 8 boys for PHSE every week and when we visited, just a few weeks before CE, PHSE was, understandably, revision techniques for history. He ringfences slots in his diary for both reading with the pre-prep children and 'slipping in and out of lessons across ages and subjects – vitally important'. Also does a share of break duties, part of being a 'visible head'. Parents remarked how perceptive he is, 'really able to get to the nub of what makes a boy tick'. When asked about future developments, he reveals that the governors have agreed in principle to establishing a nursery and that plans are afoot for outdoor classrooms in the forest school tradition. And after that? Astroturf is top of his list.

Describes himself as a 'gentleman racer', his vehicle of choice being a Maserati. Favourite book? That perennial heads' author, George Eliot again, but this time it's not Middlemarch but Silas Marner, 'a story of humanity'.

Moving on to head The Dragon in July 2017. New head from September 2017 will be Mr Craig Williams, MA (Oxon), PGCE (40s). Educated at Bradfield College and studied geography at Oxford. Currently senior deputy head at Thorngrove School. Mr Williams is an accomplished sportsman (2nd XI cricket and football at Oxford) and still enjoys playing cricket. Other interests include golf, historical novels and Manchester United. His wife, Hannah, is also a teacher.

Academic matters: Subject specialist teachers from pre-prep onwards; languages are French plus Latin (taster Greek for the scholars). Years 7 and 8 learn programming in IT (batch of Raspberry Pies about to arrive at time of our visit) as well as touch-typing. Parents praise learning support – boys with dyslexia/dyspraxia or those who need help with core skills are boosted by small group work (usually instead of Latin) or one-to-one sessions.

Abingdon Prep is a leading light in synthetic phonics and has embraced this system with almost missionary zeal, believing it to be particularly suitable for engaging boys in reading and writing. The school has developed its own scheme that is now being taught in 12 other schools and disseminated via workshops etc. In the pre-prep classes we observed boys (grouped by ability, not age) were learning sounds using hand gestures, mime, raps, memory and active games, all kinds of kinaesthetic activities. Parents attend evening sessions to prepare them for what and how their children will be learning in reception. By year 3 teachers really notice the difference and the method is equally suitable for children with dyslexia, helping them develop coping skills.

We encountered the best French lesson we've ever observed – a whole class of unselfconscious 13 year olds belting out their avoir and être verbs to (with true entente cordiale) God Save our

Gracious Queen and the Marseillaise, followed by a brilliant rap complete with hand gestures. One feels this is French that will never be forgotten. The head says that the aim of his school is to provide a curriculum (academic and wider) 'that really inspires boys'; this certainly seems to be the case and all the teaching we observed was energetic, challenging and fun. Parents report that teachers are 'very approachable' and quick to respond to queries.

A top rank academic school, but one with a tradition of breadth: in 2016, 56 per cent A*/A at A level (84 per cent A*-B); 87 per cent A*/A at GCSE, slim but comforting tail of lower grades (no properly human community is ever perfect).

Sciences/maths the most popular subjects at A level, with geography (unusually popular and notably successful), history and economics not far behind. For a boys' school, art, drama and languages (Mandarin, Spanish) fare pretty well, as does classics (a department which receives great praise from parents). Latin for first two years, thereafter optional. Classical civilisation popular GCSE choice for those enthusiastic about the history but less so the languages. RS no longer compulsory for GCSE but English literature has been added (used to be considered 'too narrow') – certain amount of reshuffling in these departments may or may not be connected.

Traditional academic focus: an emphasis on the more rigorous IGCSEs, few of the lightweight 'studies' on offer; previous head allergic to 'ologies', but psychology has recently crept in for A level. Some sixth form subjects (eg theatre studies, politics) taught jointly with nearby St Helen's, as is the new general studies course. Practical activities (DT, computer programming) relatively underdeveloped as academic subjects – but then 'The Other Half'.

Setting when CE boys come in at 13 based on exam performance in core subjects, but reassessed at the end of the first year – with maths and MFL reset during year 9 as well. School would say only a small difference in ability and final outcome between upper and lower strata – but these competitive boys perceive it more keenly. Some comment that potential Oxbridge candidates not so subtly identified and polished up quite early on, but one is assured that all is not lost for the late bloomers. General rule is 10 GCSEs taken in year 11, though native speakers of foreign languages may take them earlier.

The quality of teaching and learning by best practice is very much a focus. Boys say that teaching is 'generally good, some inspiring', and that they get on well with their teachers, but they did not seem to be as critical as those in some other schools, given that they are well behaved and work very, very hard. Teaching 'well beyond the syllabus, made interesting and relevant'. Room too for the robustly eccentric teacher and here, as elsewhere, those who are not standard issue are usually the most popular.

Classroom learning supplemented by plenty of imaginative day trips, many included in the fees if within UK. Annual classics trip particularly praised – 'way beyond what parents could organise for themselves, well prepared, serious, in the style of the Grand Tour'. Advanced level ancient historians encouraged to write talks about sites and deliver them in situ to the younger boys.

Good learning support – all boys screened, will deal with dyslexia/dyspraxia in children who are fundamentally bright enough to keep up.

The usual methods of regular prep and tests keep boys on their toes and most know how they are faring in relation to others, even if they don't let on at home. Detailed termly reports and regular parents' evenings reveal all. Individual teachers respond quickly to specific enquiries by phone or email.

Games, options, the arts: The Other Half, Abingdon's credo for learning beyond the classroom, is an emphatic commitment to breadth in education. Forty pages of stylish brochure lay out the opportunities available and the philosophy behind them. Breadth within breadth: boys cannot do just one sport, or all sport, or indeed all anything, and must 'undertake a period of service-type activity' – classroom assistant in a primary school, charity shop, chatting to grannies among a wide range that is praised by parents for getting the boys really involved.

Sport for all, not just the gifted, though you can just about get away with not taking it seriously after the first few years. The top teams are top notch and the Bs, Cs and Ds are pretty good too. Rugby, hockey and cricket all strong, but come the summer it's the rowers who rule. Oarsmen running the mile down to the beautifully designed wooden boathouse in their pink and white strip pass through one of the more lively residential areas of Abingdon, an educative experience, improving knowledge of the vernacular and self-control. It's all character building and, who knows, may contribute to the Boat Club's string of records and successes at national level (first VIII won the Princess Elizabeth cup at Henley for the third year running recently). Splendid sports centre with eight lane, 25 metre swimming pool. Four pitches by school, others further away. A good range of other sports, no looking down on those who prefer solo to team play, and Real Tennis (at Radley) a rare delight. Regular foreign tours and training trips for the committed can be effectively compulsory – and often expensive.

An impressive sporting programme in the prep too and everyone gets a match, whether it's inter-house competitions or against other schools. In addition to the usual oval and round ball games (numerous rugby pitches across the road reached via a footbridge) boys can choose from activities such as fly fishing, sailing, water polo, judo, fencing and hockey. Like its big brother, the prep has a huge range of Other Half activities including textiles, sculling, word games, films and chess. No lessons on Saturday (though year 8s get revision sessions in the run up to CE), but before booking that mini break parents should be aware that matches and other half activities fill the void.

Though sport is seriously good, it is by no means everything. Strong music in the prep with several choirs, an orchestra, a jazz band and chamber groups. Music is fine and widespread in the senior school too, with ring-fenced time to avoid encroachment, lots of bands, orchestras and choirs, with a composer-in-residence too, though it is not much studied as an academic subject. Despite the extended lunch time, parents tell us that it can still be a problem for the sporty and musical all rounder (a type Abingdon favours) to fit everything in. Art and design technology well taught to all up to the age of 14, and those who continue with art achieve strong results at A level.

Drama is enjoyed, not least because of joint productions with St Helen's and St Katharine's, but is not part of the life-blood of the school. The film unit, though, is something extraordinary – a semi-autonomous organisation staffed by professional documentary makers and animators, with industry standard kit. Over 100 adventurous, inspirational and award-winning short films have been created there since its foundation.

Boarding: Boarding, full and weekly, mostly located in the rather grand houses that form the crescent adjacent to the school. Small dormitories that are remarkably impersonal – each bed with a large, completely unused pinboard above it. We have observed this in some other boys' boarding schools – a certain reluctance to provide hostages to fortune or signs of finer feelings perhaps. Well-organised weekend activities for the full boarders. Food very good – 'great,' said our guides – but everyone seems to rush lunch to get on to whatever else they are doing. The Asian boarding contingent tends to make or order in their own of an evening, local takeaways no doubt grateful for the regular custom.

A

Background and atmosphere: A serene place, even on a gloomy day. Parks and playing fields surround a harmonious assembly of Victorian red-bricks. An old foundation (1256), long associated with the Mercers Company. Fine chapel: weekly attendance compulsory, at the inter-denominational end of the Church of England.

Prep school occupies a large Victorian double-fronted country house just three miles from Abingdon, and the extensive grounds at the back merge into meadows, contented sheep adding to the pastoral charm. Generous running around space plus The Big Adventure, a huge rope and wood activity structure; quiet grassy quad too for reflective moments.

Practical mix of purpose-built additions provides light and functionality; we loved the colourful DT room with octagonal work benches – equipment here would not disgrace a small industrial unit. The head of DT is particularly proud of the pewter and acrylic moulding equipment. She (yes, she) told us plans too for a dedicated cookery room. The library, comfortably full with books and beanbags, is in a barn and staffed by parent librarians. The new drama studio space in another stone outbuilding was, perhaps, a little oversold – not a theatre (prep uses Abingdon's Amey theatre for their productions) but a series of rooms used for drama (taught from year 5) and after-school activities.

Our delightful guides were, if you will, two of Abingdon Prep's premier products – both had recently gained scholarships to the senior school. First stop on the tour was the wonderful mansard art studio, flooded with light and buzzing with creativity. Year 7 boys were briefing year 4 boys on the school's collaborative jubilee project – a splendid circular mosaic of the Queen. (Now completed and gracing the front of the school, with every child and member of staff having had a hand in its creation, cabochon jewel added by headmaster to provide final touch of bling). Three very popular lunchtime art clubs each week.

With a couple of girls' schools nearby, those pupils who want female company do not have to look far; sixth formers have joint lessons, plenty of musical and dramatic co-productions and a shared bus system. Mothers say their sons do better without a lot of girls at the front of the class with their hands up, and generally cluttering up their lives (but then they would, wouldn't they?).

Undramatic uniform of blue blazer, grey trousers and plain blue or white shirt plus any one of at least 30 ties showing allegiance to house, sport or Other Half activity; suits in sixth form. So far, so economic, but watch out if your boy is a team player – anything with the griffin on it hurts. Parent-run second-hand uniform shop can really help here.

Pastoral care, well-being and discipline: An unusual feature in the prep is the tradition of pupils and teachers calling each other by first names. This practice stems from the establishment of the school in Oxford in 1956 when three of its first five pupils were the sons of the founder. It takes some getting used to at first if your ear is conditioned to the more formal practices of other schools and can, apparently, put some parents off. Mr Hyde-Dunn, though not an obvious candidate for such a bohemian tradition, is a sincere champion – 'It's not a gimmick – it is the ebb and flow of natural respect and epitomises a sense of community'.

Houses and long, weekly tutorials are the backbone of the pastoral system, supplemented by professional counsellor. Pastoral care 'not cuddly, but helpful' – staff are vigilant, and we hear that bullying is stamped on pretty fast; reports too of unusual boys being well supported, the best brought out of them. Not all relish the rough and tumble of the house rooms at lunch time (prefects and CCTV still on the losing side against youthful exuberance), but havens for those who prefer to work quietly. Parents full of praise for lower school (ages 11 and 12); boys are kept at a slight remove from the main school to help them ease into the system.

Good behaviour expected at all times but discipline is kept in perspective, perception amongst boys is that things (especially with regard to hair and uniform) are a little less draconian than of yore. Straightforward sin treated seriously – this is a boarding school in the centre of a town so it needs to be – and it's out for drugs.

Pupils and parents: Most day pupils from within the 20-mile radius of the ('unreasonably' say parents) expensive bus network. Parents usual Oxfordshire mix of academics, medics, IT professionals, many working long hours to afford the fees. About half the school's full boarders from overseas – a wide range of countries, and well integrated; those we talked to reported close foreign friends. All in all, they're collected and courteous boys.

Correspondence nearly all electronic and weekly email system works a lot better than letters at the bottom of sports' bags. Active parents' association organises all sorts of social events.

Old boys include MP Francis Maude, actor Tom Hollander, comedian David Mitchell, all five members of Radiohead, and countless others who have proper jobs.

Entrance: No formal academic testing for pre-prep, but boys should be sufficiently mature to settle into a class. Thereafter testing in English, non-verbal reasoning and maths, but Mr Hyde-Dunn says that Abingdon Prep also looks for 'that spark', boys who 'would thrive', rather than relying wholly on test scores – this may include visiting a boy on his home turf.

A good flow into the senior school at 11 from surrounding primaries (mostly with the help of the local tutorial network, if only to get used to the exams: seek out a good one via the parents of pupils who made the grade) and preps like Chandlings that teach for the Abingdon School exam. A larger number at 13 from prep schools including Abingdon's own, via a mix of exams.

A dozen or two join at sixth form – school has raised the bar somewhat and it's now generally A grade GCSEs for subjects to be studied at A level. Interview and school recommendation important at all ages.

Exit: Prep school candidates for the senior school sit their pre-test in year 7 and then CE in the same way as those from other schools. In most years, around 80 per cent go on to Abingdon; others to Magdalen College, Radley, St Edward's. School will have 'an early dialogue with parents' if they think it's best for a boy to depart at 11 (to Our Lady's, The Oratory, Bloxham, Cokethorpe).

Very few leave after GCSEs (plenty of warning to parents, if needed). Almost all to university – currently popular are Manchester, Imperial College, Newcastle and UCL. Good numbers to Oxbridge, 10 in 2016, with four off to the US. Wide range of courses, with engineering and economics prominent; above average numbers choose languages, history and medicine.

Money matters: A range of decorative scholarships, but the money is (as ever these days) in the means-tested bursaries.

Remarks: A premier league boys' school, with a strong commitment to a broad education and academic success. Best suits those robust boys who will knuckle down and do 'a hell of a lot of hard work', but understands that boys need to be amused and not just fed facts.

ACS Cobham International School

Heywood, Portsmouth Road, Cobham, Surrey KT11 1BL

Pupils: 1,410; 78 full, 31 weekly boarders • Ages: 2-18 (boarding from 12) • Sixth form: 331

Fees: Day £7,410 – £25,680; Boarding £36,810 – £44,360 pa

Tel: 01932 867251
Email: cobhamadmissions@acs-schools.com
Website: www.acs-schools.com

Headmaster: Since 2011, Tony Eysele (50s) BSc Natal University, HDE Edgewood College of Education, organisational behaviour degree Heriot Watt University. After two years in the army, started his teaching career in a South African state school before moving into, and progressing upwards in, the independent sector. Headships in Johannesburg and Harare until, in 2004, moved to the UK with his wife and sons and became foundation director at Lord Wandsworth College, Hampshire. One of his sons is now a teacher, the other is a professional athlete. His wife is admissions director at Marymount International School in Kingston-on-Thames.

Enthusiastic, approachable and popular, he says, 'Children in our school are all incredibly happy', and from what we saw as we walked round, we tend to agree with him. Parents say 'very approachable', 'quick to react to good suggestions for change' and 'really does seem to be listening to us'. Has increased the number of staff where needed. It's hard to take over from a long-standing predecessor (who spent nearly 20 years at the helm) but Tony Eysele seems to have handled the challenge well and parents, staff and pupils are all equally happy.

Academic matters: Non-selective so a real mix of ability throughout. A truly international school – 72 different nationalities represented and a multitude of different languages spoken.

In the early childhood years pre-schoolers are prepared gently for the future. They build their social skills and interact with each other, developing their language and communication abilities through play. With such a large range of backgrounds, we were delighted to see them chattering away together and enjoying participating in group discussion and activity.

The lower school contains grades 1-4 and the majority of core lessons are classroom-based. They largely follow the American curriculum, but elements of the International Primary Years programme are also included. These are the preparatory years, when teachers discover strengths and weaknesses and begin to unearth any particular talents. All classes are mixed-ability. No formal exams or tests at this stage, though parents say general testing is continuous – presumably because MAP (Measure of Academic Progress) begins in grade 2.

At around 10 they move into the middle school for four years. This is when their futures begin to be mapped out. Timetables are based on the individual needs of the children, who are grouped by ability within their own age groups. Each child begins to follow a curriculum based on his known strengths and weaknesses. Classrooms are now subject-based, and it's the pupils not the teachers that move. The school is determined to provide a solid grounding and ensure that pupils can work together in teams, sharing their ideas and listening to each other. Exceptionally able children will sometimes be transferred to work with older pupils for particular subjects, thus assuring that they are being properly stimulated and working at their correct levels. Middle school children can be found studying their native language several grades higher than their ages.

At 14 it's high school, still in the same building as the middle school. They are separated by a large marble hall where these older pupils have Wifi access and the use of computers. The curriculum is wide and mixed, with 17 languages currently available. Timetables are based on each child's needs, exams are coming into the picture – decisions will soon have to be made. Some opt to study IGCSEs for a year, though they don't sit external exams in all subjects. For their final program(me), some decide to follow the International Baccalaureate, others take a variety of AP courses (18 available), and the rest work for the American High School diploma and SATs. Much depends on whether they are heading for university in the UK, the USA or continental Europe. This school prepares them for all, thus really meriting the international label. Generally around 80 per cent get 3+ AP scores – average 3.4 in 2016; IB average 33 points. Not bad for a non-selective school.

Games, options, the arts: At a school sitting in 128 acres of country, with plenty of playing fields and its own a six-hole golf course, you'd expect the sports to be good. And they are. Not only outdoors, but in the all-singing, all-dancing sports centre as well. We were fascinated by the swimming pool with its computerised touch pads, enabling the raising of the pool bottom or adjustment of water temperature, at will, depending on activities of users. And as for the dance studio/gym with a professional sound system and sprung wood flooring; the fitness suite for older exercisers where the equipment is card controlled; the international-sized basket/volleyball show court and the café for spectators and participators alike – these children have no excuse for being unfit. PE is compulsory for all the whole way through the school.

From middle school up, all take part in a good mix of indoor and outdoor sports, competing against other schools and, once in high school, in the ISST (International Schools Sports Tournaments) programme Europe-wide. A varied selection of different sports each season, something for everybody. A parent said, 'Sport is a big deal. Even the less sporty children find something they enjoy doing.'

Theatre, drama and music are also 'a big deal'. The amazing new performing arts centre provides everything budding thespians and musicians need. Several drama studios and music practice rooms; a music technology suite and an amazing high tech theatre which some drama schools would die for – even has an automated fly-tower. Instrumental and choral groups to suit all tastes. For those who want it, it's all there. No wonder the middle school singers have won their category in the Godalming Music Festival at least twice and drama students have been selected to participate in the National Theatre Connections project. Plenty of opportunities for students studying theatre for the IB. And for the musicians, it's all there for them as well – there is even a large lift so that a grand piano can take its place on the stage for a special recital. Good artist in residence programme when, for instance, a visiting band spends time with all instrumentalists, working with them and introducing them to new concepts.

Art on display all round, certainly appears to be plenty of talent. Imaginations run riot. Well-equipped studios enable experimentation, self-expression and developing talents to thrive.

Plenty of expeditions and field trips within UK, Europe or worldwide – exploratory, educational or languages involved. Around 100 working for the Duke of Edinburgh Award, at all levels. Recently two current students got their golds – a significant achievement given that most don't complete this till university.

A

Boarding: More than 100 boarders aged 12-18, most full, with equal numbers of boys and girls. About 80 per cent from overseas. Boys and girls in separate wings, but plenty of chance for social mixing. A banner in the entrance hall reads: 'Because we are all different, we are all the same'. Jolly, caring, head of boarding says, 'We are a home from home and, with children representing so many nationalities, this is a great opportunity to understand and embrace different cultures. All are well integrated, no cliques.' Trips organised every Saturday. Supervised prep every evening between 7.00pm and 9.00pm; the younger ones in a study room, the older ones in their rooms with the door open. Rooms look clean and comfortable. Seniors given personal privacy and do their own washing.

Currently building a new boarding house, which will have 59 single rooms for grade 12 (year 13) students plus 27 twin rooms. The four storey house will have lots of social and study areas, with a triple height atrium and views across woodland.

Background and atmosphere: Originally built in the 13th century, the main house at Cobham went through a variety of owners, from the aristocracy to businessmen, until it was acquired by ACS in 1975 in order to create their first American school in England. They now have two others in Surrey and Middlesex, and one overseas in Doha. Originally aiming to provide an American education for families living and working here, they have now become 'international' and the curriculum has been broadened to include the IB programme and enable pupils to attend universities worldwide. Looking round at the huge mix of nationalities represented, 72 at present, the change is merited. And you certainly notice it as you walk round this ultra-modern, high tech school where classroom and studios are fully equipped with every possible learning aid. This is the 21st century.

No uniform, but a code, for both pupils and staff, and those not sticking to it are in trouble. Some parents told us they would prefer to have one, and felt staff should perhaps be stricter on the boundaries, but they also agreed that their children are perfectly happy with the way it is. We noticed no extremes: most pupils we saw looked neat, tidy and relaxed. The head says having no uniform 'means focusing on the child'.

A closed campus, surrounded by its own land, no entry without a pass; this is a safe place for children of all ages. The early childhood village cossets the very young, giving them a sense of security before they move on to the lower school building. Here floors and classrooms are colour coded, all mixed ability, light, bright and welcoming; they only move for specialist classes. Great library, where language books are plentiful and some are colour coded to lend variety to different reading levels. For the first two years children are each lent an iPad for class use; from grade 3 onwards, they are given their own to take home. Both lower school and early childhood have their own playgrounds, while the middle school has its own playing fields, and the high school pupils have their own designated areas during break times.

The technology is blinding in the middle/high school building. From the interactive learning centre in the basement where they appear to be able to reach out all over the world, to the science labs where they can work together with their iPads, to huge divisional libraries again filled with books in a multitude of different languages, you could say the atmosphere buzzes.

And as for fuelling the inner child – the new dining area is high tech. Canteen style, children collect their food, from a range of options, in coded containers, which are then scanned and a thumb scan identifies the child – no money changes hands, and parents are digitally informed what their children are eating. Or, at least, what they are taking to their tables. Big Brother is definitely watching over these children. Selections are such that no-one can get away with eating unhealthy food, and staff are watching carefully for any secret non-eaters.

Pastoral care, well-being and discipline: With such a large range of nationalities, there is a huge need for EAL support, particularly in the lower and middle schools. So, EAL numbers are capped. Children are initially assessed by EAL teachers and given as much support as they feel necessary. Depending on need, this can be in class or out of class, either in small groups or individually. IPads are used for translation and general help.

About 250 pupils have some form of mild to moderate learning difficulty or EAL need. Each one is looked at individually, 'one-to-one case management', and a programme devised for them. Learning support numbers are capped each year and children are only accepted if the school feels it can support their particular needs.

Parents report some communication problems over learning support, as teachers are not always ready to listen but, on the whole, happy with the situation. The holistic approach adds extra dimension, treating the whole child. Excellent occupational therapy room, and imaginative ways of helping. Enthusiastic, sympathetic teachers with specialists at even the youngest age groups.

Head said substance abuse problems rare and dealt with quickly and efficiently on a case by case basis. Can't realistically control what happens outside the school grounds, but does not believe anything serious. As school in own guarded grounds, cases of bringing forbidden items rare. No toleration of antisocial or unkind behaviour. Rules are there to be obeyed.

Pupils and parents: A multi-national, multi-cultural school. Around a third are American and about a third of the rest are from the UK and other English speaking countries – the remainder cover Europe and the rest of the world. Inevitably, turnover quite large in the early years. Lots of expats from various different walks of life, some in transit, some who have decided to settle here – at least while their children are at school. Truly representative of today's mobile world. Excellent bus service, covering a huge area from Godalming to Hyde Park Corner, before and after school, means that quite a few travel from London. Beware the fleet of buses at arrival and departure times.

Parental involvement huge, as you would expect from a largely American school. Also makes relocation and transition easier. Plenty of charity support, organised social gatherings and career advice given.

Students appeared relaxed and happy. We asked one what he would change about the school: 'Nothing, really but maybe lessons could be shorter?'

Entrance: Inevitably, because of the transitory national side of the school, places can crop up at different stages. So it is always worth trying. Academic records examined and references required, but no testing until 13+, when English is assessed. However, school adds the caveat: 'We will take any child at any stage providing we have space and can meet their needs academically and socially'. In the last two years, they will only take IB pupils if they are already following the programme and their courses can be matched. Any child can join the American Programme, even, occasionally, for their last year. But they do have to stay for at least one semester.

Exit: Typically 40 per cent of students to UK universities, 40 per cent to American universities and the remaining 20 per cent worldwide. Every student assigned a college counsellor at high school level. For the first two years they may just consult them, but at 11th grade it is compulsory for each student to work with them. A huge and varied exit list including London colleges and Durham plus unis in Canada Germany, France, Mexico and Spain.

Money matters: Well, it's certainly not the cheapest. But just a look around will tell you why. That said, fees cover pretty well everything, including curriculum related field trips, all books and those iPads. Private corporate owners of all four ACS schools. No scholarships and limited bursaries but some financial aid occasionally available.

Remarks: If you are looking for a large, lively, international school with a multitude of opportunities and facilities to die for, or if you are in transition round the world, then this could be perfect for your child. Shy, retiring children might just get a bit lost, but then again the holistic approach could also help them. Anyone looking for a traditional, structured, English establishment, however, should probably look elsewhere. That said, this school has a huge amount to offer any child prepared to think outside the box.

ACS Egham International School

Woodlee, London Road, Egham, Surrey TW20 0HS

Pupils: 546 • Ages: 3-19 • Sixth form: 117

Fees: £7,080 – £24,020 pa

Tel: 01784 430611
Email: eghamadmissions@acs-schools.com
Website: www.acs-schools.com

Head of School: Since 2010, Mr Jeremy Lewis BA PGCE. British by birth, raised in Cape Town, degrees from Portsmouth and Nottingham plus a masters in education admin from Bath. Has taught in schools from the Isle of Wight to Kuwait, Japan, Hungary, Vietnam and Turkey. Started as a teacher of humanities, then a progression of senior leadership roles – most recently headmaster of Istanbul International Community School.

Wants to make school a centre of excellence for IB teaching and learning, while broadening and strengthening curriculum. Has extensive IB experience: teaching, coordinating, training; brought the IB to Kuwait in the mid '80s. His Irish wife, Carmel, is a career IB ESL teacher and their two children, both at ACS Egham, are IBPYP and IBMYP products. Believes that more pupils are capable of managing the IB diploma programme than some would say.

His two passions are the idea of developing internationally-minded students and football, both formed during his South African childhood (during apartheid). Sees this as a place where parents, too, are engaged in the children's learning. Held by them as a thoughtful, cheery, reflective and genuine person – a very nice man.

Academic matters: Well-established IB diploma programme with the usual range of courses plus new IB sports, exercise, and health science – introduced thanks to the impressive new sports facility. Also offers the IB Career-related Certificate – IBCC. In 2016 IB results produced an average of 36 points. Most students take the full diploma, although they can opt to take individual certificates without doing the full diploma. IB programmes encourage strong communication skills; teachers give students every opportunity to express themselves and are approachable. One parent said her youngster 'produces impressive PowerPoint presentations and has no fear of speaking in front of a group'. Kids very comfortable with visitors and ready to tell you all about what they are learning or doing, from the youngest pre-schoolers (they're aptly known as 'Scramblers') right up to the second year IB students. A hat design activity going on in an MYP art class was less about millinery fashion and more about design and construction plus fun facts about famous hats in art and history. We learnt a few things we didn't know.

Technology throughout. It's an Apple Mac school and generous provision is rolling out iPad programme in two phases. Class sizes vary significantly across the school and across the subjects. French and Spanish are taught in grades 1-12. The native language enrichment programme gives students the opportunity to maintain their own language. Where viable (minimum of three students of similar ages and levels), mother-tongue languages are supported by additional classes, funded by the school. Eleven currently on offer including most European languages plus Russian, Urdu, Hebrew and Japanese. If fewer than three, the school helps find a tutor with classes paid by parents. EAL programme supports pupils in regular classes with specially trained teachers to help each student acquire basic vocabulary and vocabulary relevant to classroom topics. They make the school fit the child. Limited learning support in the school for mild to moderate needs, but mild special needs support is provided and monitored. Some special needs can be accommodated and each case is assessed by the child study team. If specialists are brought in, parents must assume the costs.

Reports are sent by email, and if any problems, the child study team steps in right away to review all options for help. Each term there are student-led conferences with parents and faculty: the school feels that the student is the main player and should take responsibility for their education. ISA (International Schools' Assessment) tests are given to students from ages 8-15, to assess progress and MAP tests (Measures of Academic Progress), a data-led approach originated in the US designed to improving teaching and learning, is also used to help students set goals.

The faculty of 85 full-time teachers brings lots of previous international and IB experience. Lewis is pleased that the level of turnover is dropping and teachers are staying longer. In lower school; the quality of the teacher really makes a difference and parents say some teachers are stronger than others. Reports are that overall ACS Egham teachers are much appreciated and well-liked by students and parents are happy.

Games, options, the arts: Healthy mix of sports available: rugby, soccer, basketball, volleyball, cross-country, athletics, tennis, golf, softball, baseball, track and field. Impressive new sports facility includes a large climbing wall, a fitness suite, dance studio, two gyms and technology to help students analyse and assess their fitness and technique. The new facilities may see fitness, climbing, dance, pilates and judo introduced. Despite concerns about the small size of the school, parents appreciate that chances of making the competitive teams are better. Competition with local international schools and through ISSA, meaning some matches in exciting places on the Continent. Lower school offers soccer, gymnastics, tennis and track and field during the school day.

After-school clubs popular for all ages from crafts to model United Nations to sports. Choir has performed at Royal Albert Hall. Artist in residence programme brings in everything from local poets to painters. Annual drama production. Impressive design tech studio – students work with plastics, metal and wood. Parents highlight the rock weekend, a sort of 'battle of the bands' involving everyone.

Mr Lewis is keen to broaden and strengthen students' sense of altruism and responsibilities towards the local and wider community. He is building collaborative partnerships with local schools including two academies. Community service activities include volunteering with Orbis Eye Hospitals, travelling with 'flying hospital' to Vietnam and Mongolia, nurturing the school's five-year partnership with a school for street children in Kenya, when kids travel out to help in all sorts of ways. Described as 'amazing' by one parent, who said, 'this activity created very real connections. Kids want to go back there and become completely engaged. Exposure to other ways of living helped them appreciate their own privilege.'

Background and atmosphere: Located on the fringes of beautiful royal Windsor Great Park, and bordering Victorian icon Royal Holloway College. Illustrious former occupants of the original mansion house include a 19th century Member of Parliament, a WW1 veteran who fought at Gallipoli and his society wife, and wounded WWII heroes who went there for rehabilitation and retraining. Today it is filled with bright and sunny classrooms and offices. Set in manicured gardens, the mansion now shares the grounds with several architecturally-sympathetic modern buildings designed for educational use by ACS.

Much attention in recent years to improving the campus. The buzz is all about the new sports centre, which has state of the art everything PE, with the exception of a pool. General classrooms in the sports centre supplement the school's teaching space to meet the growing enrolment. The lunch room is noisy but teachers supervise and keep under control. Valiant efforts have been made to improve cafeteria service, particularly the flow of traffic; parents say it's probably not adequate yet for the number of pupils at the school. Though the kids grumble in the time-honoured tradition of kids everywhere and describe the canteen as 'boring', once they're actually sitting down to eat, 'it's okay'.

The other improvement is the IB diploma centre – exclusively for the eldest students with teaching spaces, offices for both IB coordinator and university counsellors for easy access (plus subtle supervision), lounge with kitchenette with microwave, fridge, etc. for lunch or senior munchies attacks. On the day we visited, PTO was there doing a MacMillan bake sale at school; we loved seeing that they had left a tray of goodies for seniors in the IB centre with 'please help yourself and donate' sign next to a little basket filling up with money. Parents say it's early days but the school is protecting this space for the IB kids and the younger students honour that – 'it's like hallowed ground'.

Plenty of room for everyone to learn and play. Generous art rooms, science labs, early childhood provision is all self-contained and lovely setting for first school experience, beautiful grounds and sports fields. Now that the IB diploma centre is finished, parents would like to see enhancements to science labs, and a 'commons' for middle and younger high schoolers. 'If you ask where the heart of the campus is, there's no obvious answer'; but maybe the new gym will change that.

Two well-stocked libraries and a generous budget of several hundred thousand to meet technology needs. Computers everywhere; high schoolers can bring their own laptops and are given an iPod to use as tools and memory devices. There is 'no uniform, just good judgment'.

Egham is one of four ACS International Schools (three in UK, one new one in Qatar). The schools are governed by a board of independent, non-executive directors (who typically have international and UK experience across a range of areas including education, finance, and law). According to the school's website, the board 'supports the development and the day-to-day operations of the schools'.

Pastoral care, well-being and discipline: Despite growth in enrolment, the head strives to maintain a 'small school' feel where teachers and students know each other. Problems are quickly detected and the child study team steps in to review and resolve. The caring atmosphere means that bullying doesn't work here. Parents say, 'there is no anonymity or privacy here so if you are in trouble there's no hiding it.' Health classes, drug and alcohol prevention seminars keep the students informed. Zero tolerance for drugs and drinking – students' unwillingness to disappoint parents largely seems to keeps everyone out of trouble.

Although the school is non-selective, parents say that the culture of the school stresses the importance of hard work and has a way of motivating students. Parents tell of lower school students who want to get on with homework independently and 'without help' from parents. It's not unusual for kids at IB diploma level to organise themselves into study groups to revise or discuss classwork, but balance is important too and students make room in their lives for pursuing sports, musical interests, etc.

Some parents wonder about the smallish size of the high school and comment that higher numbers of students might mean more resources, more options for musical groups, more scope for sports teams. The all-singing, all-dancing Cobham campus is just down the road and parents sometimes question how much of their fees are subsidising other ACS campuses, including developments in far-off ACS Doha. However, as the school pointed out in response to this comment, Egham has invested a tremendous amount in its own right in recent years. Nevertheless, prevailing view is that Egham's smaller size means that there is a strong sense of community and a family feel.

Pupils and parents: The school attracts 'like-minded' internationally-attuned families who are 'looking for a mind-set, not just a curriculum'. Over 50 nationalities, about 22 per cent US followed by 17 per cent British, nine per cent Dutch, and then the rest of the world. Parents stress there is no predominant nationality or culture and many have chosen Egham for that reason.

The head, also an Egham parent, meets regularly with PTO, does the usual monthly newsletters, and four times each year hosts a forum for parents, taking open questions on any topic – no advance submission required. He's pleased with the strong sense of community at the school – verified through an annual independent parent survey that helps keep him abreast of opinions. 'Welcoming and accepting' are words heard repeatedly about the school community. PTO organises lots of activities to help new parents fit in and a 'family buddy' system gives new arrivals first point of contact in the community and tips like where to get a haircut and buy school supplies. Be sure to ask for a copy of Jaguar Tales.

School bus routes cover areas from Maidenhead and Slough to the north, Weybridge to the east, Frimley and Woking to the south, Wokingham to the west.

Entrance: Non-selective school welcomes students with wide range of abilities. Admission based on previous school records and testing scores, references from previous school, family questionnaires. Academic English required to enter grades 8-12, assessed through a comprehensive English test that can be sent to the current school to administer.

Predominantly expats at the school with about 25 per cent annual turnover, so there is transiency and hope of a place. Rolling admissions; students admitted year-round. Feeder schools include local area schools but mostly international schools worldwide.

No open days per se, visits by appointment are normally available year round. Parents say that some families join ACS without understanding the IB, so ask questions. With the scope and relatively long history of the ACS schools, parents often hear about the school 'on the expat circuit', so that, sustained by ACS International's slick marketing, is what brings parents to the door.

Exit: If children leave before graduation, it is most often due to families being transferred. The school offers the coursework needed to satisfy the requirements for an American high school diploma. University guidance is started in grades 9 and 10, and grades 11 and 12 are given one-to-one advisors to help with the application process. Students go to universities in the UK (about 50 per cent), USA, Canada and beyond. Parents are watching to see how a popular teacher recently appointed as college counsellor copes with the dual US-UK university admissions process.

The PSAT is offered to all students in grades 10 and 11. SAT also offered.

Money matters: ACS Egham is privately owned, fee-supported with no endowment. The school relies on income from fees, with surpluses reinvested in the schools to maintain high standards; it is evident that money has been made available to develop the ever-improving facilities and programmes required to serve the growing enrolment. Some parents say the fees are high but that they continue to choose this education because of what it offers. ACS Foundation offers limited needs-based financial aid plus one full sixth form scholarship for a talented pupil coming from a local state school.

Remarks: The individualised approach to education serves a range of different learning styles and academic abilities. One parent summed it up: 'There are always things you'd like to see done differently at any school, but at ACS Egham my kids are thriving and children are learning, growing and developing. Isn't that what's most important?'

Akeley Wood Junior School

Wicken Park, Wicken, Milton Keynes, Buckinghamshire MK19 6DA

Pupils: 313 • Ages: 1–11

Fees: £9,450 – £11,685 pa

Tel: 01908 571231
Email: registrar@akeleywoodschool.co.uk
Website: www.akeleywoodschool.co.uk

Headmistress: Since 2008, Mrs Clare Page BEd (50s). Educated at Ancaster House in Bexhill and Chelsea College, Eastbourne where she read PE and science. Cut teeth at Haberdashers' Aske's School for Girls in Elstree, joining Akeley Wood in the senior school as head of girls' games before defecting to Beachborough School, a competing local prep. Happily returned to Akeley in 2001 as year 6 teacher and head of year 5 before being promoted into current job. Has made changes aplenty during her tenure – 'we've really been on a journey of getting everything in the right place, and every gap is plugged now'. Proud of school's 'vast curriculum' but mainly of the contented brood of children we watch frolicking on the lawns (again, vast) as we chat. 'Happy children learn', she beams. Motherly and approachable – parents say 'her door is always open'.

Entrance: After nursery, not oversubscribed – 'competition from good village schools is fierce', says head. Prospective reception children spend a morning with their peer group in the pre-school, with a visit to the reception class, and are observed in play. Older applicants come for a taster day (two if either party isn't sure) and are assessed in reading and maths, spending time with the SENCo if necessary. 'The idea is that they have a nice day', says head. 'We always try to offer.' Stresses that she likes parents to be honest about any difficulties their child may have and that only those who it is felt genuinely won't thrive or whose needs can't be met that would not be accepted.

Exit: At 11, vast majority (around 75 per cent) make the seamless move to Akeley Wood Secondary School with places guaranteed subject to head's recommendation. Almost unheard of for a child not to be accepted. At time of writing many changes afoot at senior school so worth asking how new staff, curriculum and integration of pupils with SEN is working out. About one-fifth – generally the more academic cohort – leave for selective grammars such as The Royal Latin, Aylesbury Grammar or Sir Henry Floyd, with one or two each year going to Bedford either for transport reasons or boarding and some parents feeling simply that their children need to grow beyond 'the Akeley bubble'.

Remarks: Who knew that just out of earshot of the M1 lay this gem of a setting, approached by winding drive (complete with lambs grazing by its side), leading to idyllic Georgian mansion and a dozen or so acres of dreamy fields and gardens? Two form entry reception class, growing to three in year 3, with lessons for classes up to year 4 taking place almost exclusively in the well converted mansion ('we've extended into every available space', says head.) Years 5 and 6 housed in a separate (although equally beauteous) house just across the garden, although visit main school building for some lessons – 'they love the feeling of being away from the little ones'. School well equipped across the board, thanks to massive investment by owners, Cognita. From the gleaming IT suite (new computing curriculum taught by 'really vibrant' specialist) to the immaculate cricket pitch, adventure playground equipment and multi-purpose sports hall, it feels like there's nothing that a child couldn't do here. Stunning artwork adorns almost every millimetre of wall space and there's even a food tech room with child-sized units – the only one we've ever seen.

Pupils mainly class taught to year 6 with specialist teaching for science, French, IT, music and games. French from year 1 with Spanish or German added in year 6 and clubs on offer along the way for any budding linguists. Setting for maths and English from year 3, with as few as seven children in the lower maths sets.

School boasts 'the most amazing' SENCo, winner of a global award by Cognita. This just one factor in securing Akeley's reputation as a natural destination for children needing extra help, particularly with dyslexia, although also well equipped to work with dyspraxia, dyscalculia and children on the autistic spectrum. Early intervention is part of school culture with SEN programmes including a mix of support either one to one or in small groups, plus initiatives such as touch typing club. 'Children have one chance and we have to get it right', says head. TAs used flexibly across school to enable them to support both those with SEN and the top five per cent of all year groups identified as gifted and able. Do parents worry that their bright child will be held back by such an inclusive culture? Apparently not. Pupils at the top of the academic tree 'continuously stretched', say parents, with extension activities such as maths trips to try coding at Bletchley Park and workshops with published authors, from which 'they come back buzzing'. Also extension work in school and at home. EAL also all in a day's work here, with occasional new joiners (mainly German speakers with parents relocated to nearby Mercedes or VW) arriving with very little or no English quickly up and running.

'Loads' of drama and music, both on curriculum throughout. Four choirs – one for boys only (launched with the promise of biscuits for attendees and now buzzing with a capella performances of Beach Boys medleys in four parts) – perform and compete in local and national shows and competitions such as Young Voices and the Northampton Festival. Around one-third of pupils take peripatetic music lessons. Head says parents are 'blown away' by performances, often scripted by pupils themselves. Inclusivity is the name of the game in the drama department, with main parts cast multiple times in major productions to ensure everyone gets a chance to shine.

School awarded Artsmark in 2014 and now working towards its gold award.

Sport specialist taught from nursery. It's a traditional menu of rugby, football and cricket for boys with netball (coached by Welsh national player), hockey and rounders for the girls. With A-D teams fielded for Wednesday afternoon fixtures most weeks, everyone gets a go at representing the school. Super results too, most recently U11 Cognita Schools Festival winners. No on-site pool but swimming takes place at nearby Wolverton Pool for all year groups – again with plenty of trophies in the cabinet.

House system runs through whole junior and senior school with house captains elected termly, a weekly house trophy and competitions galore for everything from sports to music and art. Copious reporting keeps parents well up to date with two parents' evenings and three full reports a year plus half termly gradings. 'They're continually assessed', reported one parent, 'but not in a stressy way – and they all know what targets they're working towards.'

With just the occasional grumble about school dinners, Akeley parents gush with enthusiasm about the start their children are getting: 'thriving' was used almost uniformly by all we spoke to. Perhaps not an obvious choice if you're looking for an academic hothouse, but an idyllic school where juniors can flourish whatever their ability.

Aldenham Preparatory School

Linked with Aldenham School

Elstree, Borehamwood, Hertfordshire WD6 3AJ

Pupils: 187 • Ages: 3–11 • C of E

Fees: £9,030 – £13,101 pa

Tel: 01923 851664
Email: prepschool@aldenham.com
Website: www.aldenham.com

Head: Since 2011, Mrs Vicky Gocher BA BEd MA (late 40s). Educated to A level at Gwernyfed High School in Powys, Wales followed by Hull University (English) and a PGCE at Roehampton. A vocational teacher ('I knew when I was 16 exactly what I wanted to do'), and always focused on teaching younger children: 'I want to share everything with them,' she says. Completed masters in educational leadership and innovation at Warwick in 2011. Formerly deputy head at Caterham Prep School, having previously taught at Downsend School, Leatherhead.

Purposeful and businesslike in manner, head inherited a young prep school 'riding the coat-tails of the senior school,' and set to work to cement school's reputation and smarten up discipline and behaviour. Consistent with the Aldenham ethos, enthuses about school's nurturing atmosphere – a refreshing approach (some might say USP) in comparison with local pressure cooker rivals. 'A wide range of abilities mirrors life,' she says. Parents approve – she's front of house every morning and 'never says no to a quick word.'

Lives on site with husband and has two adult daughters, both of whom are in the teaching profession.

Entrance: Broad selection criteria – not just academic; school is oversubscribed with around four applicants for each place. Entry at 3+ and 4+ by gentle 'playgroup style' assessment to ascertain readiness and sociability. Applicants for occasional places thereafter assessed in maths, English and reasoning. Two form entry into nursery and one form thereafter. Reception room, to which nursery children transfer 'without batting an eyelid' according to parents, has teacher and two TAs with all other year groups of maximum 22 children having one full time TA.

Exit: Between 50 and 65 per cent to Aldenham School. Entry not guaranteed but 'we won't allow a child to take the exam if they're not going to thrive there,' says head. And all efforts made to help find suitable pastures new for those who won't. Conversations regarding next steps carefully timetabled 18 months in advance, kicking off with a session with head of senior school. School fully supports and prepares for entry to other destinations, with pupils heading off in small numbers to a range of schools including Haberdashers' Aske's, Merchant Taylors', John Lyon, North London Collegiate, St Albans and the Watford Grammar Schools. Happy to support Herts 11+ hopefuls but limited in ability to offered tailored tuition.

Remarks: Nestled in a picture perfect postcard village, yet just a stone's throw from the M25 in the grounds of Aldenham School, location is clearly a big draw for urban families who describe the setting as 'fantastic'. Pupils housed in two low rise structures, the first catering for the pre-prep's two nursery classes, reception class and years 1 and 2. Lovely bright and airy classrooms, decked with cheery displays, which for the younger years lead directly onto wonderful outdoor play zones and gardens, keeping each age group separate while they settle into school life. These segue into woodland where little ones can play on adventure equipment, looking onto further endless idyllic grounds and playing fields. Nursery and reception classes benefit from their own kitchen with hot lunches prepared on site – and picnics in the grounds once a week when weather allows. Parents rave about atmosphere – 'caring from day one.'

Years 3 to 6 are in a functional, purpose-built dwelling with a large multi-use entrance hall with classrooms leading off. Artwork, accolades and information on school initiatives neatly displayed in corridors and in the atrium, ranging from information on how school is working towards eco school status to pupils' impressive achievements outside school (our guide was UK's youngest ever taekwondo black belt) including regional gymnasts and a national team figure skater.

Prep benefits from sharing some of the senior school's facilities (sports hall, theatre and dining room, where years 1 to 6 take lunch) which is not to say that it lacks a few of its own. Super ICT suite boasts a gleaming fleet of computers new for 2015 and year 6 pupils all have a kindle on which to follow the class reader. A stand-alone drama studio was host to initial rehearsals of upcoming year 5 and 6 show, Bugsy Malone, on our visit. Stunning sports field, Astroturf and well organised library, packed with immaculate sets of books. The small, suspiciously tidy art room was sadly bereft of display work on its walls, although some super 3D work in display cabinets compensated somewhat and head assures that art is 'on the up,' with work recently accepted into the prep schools art competition.

School has a gentle, friendly feel, almost like a village school, with a quietly confident mixed ability cohort who, parents say, 'flourish, whatever their academic ability' in this environment which, despite its bijoux headcount, is abundant in space both inside and out. Pupils, mainly hailing from nearby London suburbs (Edgware, Stanmore) and neighbouring towns (Radlett, St Albans) chat with enthusiasm and pride about their school, struggling to choose one thing they think is best.

Unlike senior school where number of boys dominates, here it's exactly 50/50. Excellent cultural mix reflects the local community with every main religion represented. Plenty of London commuters in the parent community, helped with their long days by before- and after-school care on offer, starting at 8am and ending at 5.30pm, with pupils in years 3 and up able to commute on one of eight school coaches. A nine week holiday over the summer is parents' main grumble.

All year groups are class taught with specialist teachers for music, drama, French, art and sport. Head still keeps hand in with the troops, teaching PSHCE. Setting in maths and English almost from the start enables teaching staff to stretch the brightest and support those who need more help. A 'very talented' SENCo assists a handful of children across the school (mainly mild dyslexia or dyspraxia, occasionally mild ASD) with one-to-one sessions held in the aptly named Launch Pad, and joins classrooms to provide booster maths groups where required. EAL well catered for. Despite an atmosphere which parents describe as 'a bit more laid back' than other schools in the vicinity, they say the standard of work is 'amazing... but without pressure'. Dynamic young music and drama teachers enthuse pupils, with a large proportion taking LAMDA examinations and all learning recorder in year 2 and violin in year 3 (but don't let that put you off).

Sport three times a week, comprising games, PE and swimming, which takes place at a nearby leisure centre. The usual culprits of football, hockey, cricket, netball and athletics take centre stage with a wholly inclusive ethos that ensures all those who want to have a chance to represent their house and school. Head admits that with such small numbers of children, the talented ones can feel stifled, as it's not always easy to put out an A and a B team for fixtures, so those looking for a ride on the school minibus to battle it out at fixtures on a weekly basis may need to look elsewhere – or pursue their chosen sports outside of school.

An impressive list of extracurricular activities to broaden horizons at lunch times and after school ranges from Lego robotics and animation to fencing, gardening and choir. Lots of accolades and rewards for achievements from badges for house point excellence to commitment to sports. Head boy and girl are chosen by staff, with opportunities for others to pitch themselves to the masses as prefects or school counsellors.

For parents looking for balance, roundedness and a school where their child will have the space – physically and mentally – to grow, look no further. Unashamedly kind without compromising on quality teaching, this is a school that allows its charges a childhood whilst keeping plenty of options open for the future if the call of the north London academic hothouses proves too loud to ignore.

Aldenham School

Linked with Aldenham Preparatory School

Elstree, Borehamwood, Hertfordshire WD6 3AJ

Pupils: 565; 26 boys, 17 girls full, 89 boys, 17 girls flexi boarders • Ages: 11–18 • Sixth form: 165: 117 boys, 48 girls • C of E

Fees: Day: £15,291 – £21,414; Boarding: £21,099 – £31,386 pa

Tel: 01923 858122
Email: admissions@aldenham.com
Website: www.aldenham.com

Headmaster: Since 2006, Mr James Fowler MA PGCE (50s). Educated at Merchant Taylors' School, Northwood and New College, Oxford where he was a choral scholar. Previously head of sixth form at Brentwood School and deputy head at Highgate. Permeates every facet of school with his relaxed charisma and understanding of what makes parents and pupils tick. Unusually, interviews every candidate with their parents before admission. Is he interviewing the parents as well as the child, we asked? 'Of course,' he says. 'I spend a lot of time helping people understand what we are and are not.' And it's to this level of mutual soul searching that he attributes the happy, enthusiastic nature of his cohort in evidence all over the school, almost all of whom he knows by name and who claim that their voice is 'genuinely heard' by him. It's not just the children who are happy with their leader, either. Parents describe head as 'always available', and 'very good at resolving issues in the right way,' adding that 'his attitude filters down to all the staff.'

Definitely not a head chasing glory in the league tables – and one totally at ease with this status; a breath of fresh air in the ferociously competitive North London landscape. Keen to provide a totally different experience to his urban competitors as applications from London families increase, and determined that his charges feel 'secure and safe'. Single-mindedly focused on school providing 'the best possible pathways' for each student, regardless of academic prowess. 'We celebrate successful entry to art school in the same way as entry to Oxbridge,' he says.

Lives on site with wife and two sons.

Academic matters: Situated in the heart of UK's spiritual home of secondary academia (Habs, Merchant Taylors', North London Collegiate et al), Aldenham stands apart with its unpressurised vibe and mixed ability cohort. Perhaps not a destination for the single minded scholar, although pupils say they are strongly encouraged to hit their own personal best; 'the natural spread of ability makes for breadth and roundedness,' according to head. Although those bright enough to get to Russell Group universities – and occasionally Oxbridge – will do, it's immediately evident that it's the journey that defines Aldenham rather than the destination.

A respectable 22 per cent of A*/A grades at A level in 2016 with 44 per cent A*-B, and 37 per cent of GCSE examinations at A*/A grades. Many subjects have now moved to IGCSE to stretch brighter students, who are also recruited into small study and discussion groups such as 'Les Philosophes' with visiting speakers including Anthony Grayling enabling them to exchange ideas and broaden horizons. 'Parents trust us with children of all abilities,' says head.

Small class sizes of maximum 22 and often down to 10 in sixth form, with setting from year 7 in maths and science. Eleven GCSEs the norm with a broad range of subjects available, from the traditional ('the brighter students tend to gravitate towards sciences,' says head) to dance, textiles and DT. French, German, Spanish and Latin on offer in the languages department. Non-traditional subjects on offer at A level include psychology, media studies, government and politics and computing. Parents and pupils appreciate extra revision lessons at lunch times, after school and even on Saturdays laid on in the run up to public exams. University conversations start in year 12, with a series of events including visiting professionals brought in to 'give insights' into the world of work. Pupils feel well supported and guided through uni application process, although one or two parents felt that school could secure more top level places for the brightest if things were slightly slicker.

Good provision for SEN run in dedicated area by full time SENCo, with around 10 per cent on the register – mainly catering for mild dyslexia or dyscalculia although can deal with mild Asperger's and recently sent one such child to Cambridge. One-to-one teaching rooms well used by overseas pupils requiring EAL support.

Games, options, the arts: In a setting that needs to be seen to be believed – over 110 acres encompassing woodland, playing fields plus full-sized Astro hockey pitch, tennis courts, dance studio, well-utilised weights room and an enormous sports hall (recently resurfaced) plus manicured cricket pitch that lies literally at the heart of the school ('the pavilion is one of my favourite spots,' says head) – sport is integral to life at Aldenham and thrives at all levels, from the most elite to the 'just for fun'. It's football, hockey and cricket for the boys, no rugby, while girls focus on netball, hockey and rounders. School known for its footie prowess, with a handful of boys training with top academies, and also embryonic links with Southgate Hockey Club, but parents say it suits students less inclined towards team pursuits well too. Options include zumba, archery, sailing, tennis, athletics, Eton fives, judo and climbing on its climbing wall – in the words of one parent: 'all that's missing is a swimming pool.'

Two compulsory activities a week, ranging from bell ringing, horse riding and film club to a very popular CCF, make for a long school day which for most ends at 5.30pm. This gives school a unique boarding atmosphere, even for those who do not take advantage of the marvellously flexible boarding on offer. Aldenham is 'synonymous with trips' according to pupils, who enthuse about the 'amazing experiences' they have had on CCF trips to Holland, language trips including a Spanish trip to Cuba, geography to Iceland, choir to Rome and a three week charity volunteering trip to Malawi.

Outstanding art department, unanimously acclaimed by everyone from head to parents and pupils, and so popular that school recently built a superb new art cabin to accommodate the large numbers electing to pursue art A level. Fabulous work on display: huge canvasses, three dimensional installations and sculpture with as much rigorous preparation and development of concepts on show as final works. Pupils say that head of art won't accept anything less than excellence and parents report offspring joining school 'unable to draw' and emerging with A grades. Dedicated textiles room also displays high quality fashion design and DT labs are hives of industry, complete with 3D printers in motion.

Music thrives, with bands, orchestras and choirs galore, run by 'fantastic' and 'passionate' musicians, according to pupils. As with sport, there are opportunities for musicians of all levels to participate, with pupils enthusing that the fiercely competitive annual house music event (compulsory participation for all) is one of the highlights of the year. All year 7s offered opportunity of one term's free music lessons on the orchestral instrument of their choice, leading to many taking it up more seriously. Futuristic music technology equipment puts department very much in the 21st century.

'Really strong' drama on and off curriculum, headed by 'inspirational' head of department who clearly drives excellence and pushes boundaries. 'We're into serious drama,' she says – school refreshingly veers away from the usual hackneyed shows and rarely produces musicals, mainly delivering productions of the Sophocles and Brechtian variety, oft performed in the purpose built 150 seat theatre, but sometimes out in the grounds or as a promenade, which are 'just fantastic,' according to parents. A handful of students are members of the National Youth Theatre and it's not unusual for one or two each year to head off to destinations including Central School of Speech and Drama or LAMDA, and these applications are taken seriously – head says that in the year school sent three students off to drama school and three to med school, both were supported and celebrated in equal measure.

Boarding: Around 30 per cent of the school community participates in boarding life at some level – enough to lend it a 'proper' boarding ethos without any trace of 'them and us' between boarders and day pupils. Boarding starts in year 7 in a small co-educational junior boarding house with 25 beds. No full boarding at this stage, meaning that cohort tends to be exclusively UK based with vast majority never having boarded before. Pupils enjoy a 'home from home' environment here – but still relish having a 'lot more freedom' when they move into one of the four main single sex boarding houses (three for boys and one for girls), each with its own strong identity, that shape the school.

Head keen that students 'experience boarding as part of their overall education,' hence provides excellent flexibility with boarders able to stay from just one night to, for a minority of mainly older, overseas students (some 25 per cent of boarders), full time. Up to sixth form, majority are reasonably local though, with boarders heading home at weekends to homes in north London, Herts and Bucks. 'Terrific' live-in houseparents supervise their charges in spacious houses – not the most luxurious we've seen, but functional (well-equipped kitchens and study spaces) and welcoming with plenty of nooks and crannies for down time and socialising. Boys dorm in fours until year 11 when they double up, with girls mostly in twos and threes then single rooms in sixth form. An ongoing programme of renovations is brightening things up.

Evenings see boarders participate in the clubs or activities of their choice, or gather in the art block, library, media suite or gym. Most popular nights to board in sixth form are Tuesdays and Thursdays when the bar opens and pizza is served in the wonderful sixth form centre. Sunday brunch is 'the best meal of the week', attended by most staff who live on site, plus their families as well as weekend boarders, and whilst there are weekend outings, trips and activities on offer, quite often students, having had a long week and sports fixtures on Saturdays, just 'want to chill.'

Background and atmosphere: Founded by brewer, Richard Platt, in 1597 after Queen Elizabeth I granted him letters patent to build 'the Free Grammar School and Almshouses' at Aldenham for elementary children. The Brewers' Company then had a controlling interest in the school and links remain strong. Original Tudor buildings demolished in the 19th century to make place for two new schools – one providing an elementary education for the local population, the second a grammar school for fee-paying boarders. School now occupies a prime position in protected green belt, attracting pupils from affluent local villages like Radlett and Sarratt, London suburbs such as Edgware and Stanmore and increasingly north London, with parents attracted by the fabulous country campus, handy coach services and inclusive ethos.

Main school building is Hogwarts-esque Victorian gothic with gables, tower and turrets, with additions – some more appealing than others – from subsequent decades. Most notable new facility is fabulous sixth form centre – all white walls, squidgy sofas and sliding glass doors offering panoramic view of cricket pitch – complete with its own coffee shop and bar where years 12 and 13 can socialise, study and generally commune outside of school hours. A few tatty corners in other areas, but plenty of up to date Mac technology and a luxurious feeling of abundant space that more than compensates for grubby paintwork.

An extraordinary chapel (the largest consecrated building in Hertfordshire after St Albans Abbey) which can host entire school – and frequently does – lies across the road that bisects the school. Surprisingly welcoming, the Stanley Spencer altar pieces of yesteryear are but a part of school history now (sold to raise funds during the desperate 1990s) and an attractive ironwork cross and dove now dominates the altar. Despite the diverse religions of the school community (about 60 per cent Christian, 20 per cent Jewish and all other main religions represented) all attend chapel twice weekly to underscore the 'feeling of one community' that's so integral to the school.

Beautiful panelled library complete with mezzanine level, spiral staircase and view of cricket pitch and miniature replica statue of old boy Alfred Gilbert's Eros. There's an annual run on the last day of term for those brave enough, from Eros in Piccadilly to the school's statue, just one of the many traditions that pupils say are 'a huge part of the school'.

Break times see pupils congregate en masse on the field with cross year group socialising in evidence everywhere ('we're like a family – everyone knows everyone,' said one happy pupil). Although not the most polished cohort we've ever seen, pupils without exception seem totally at ease with the school and are arguably one of the most sociable and understatedly confident bunches we've met. Quite possibly one of the happiest too. Girls now make up around one-third of the school – many join in sixth form – and school is content with this balance – 'we'd ideally like 35 to 40 per cent,' says head.

Pastoral care, well-being and discipline: Parents report excellent pastoral care, thanks mainly to the system that places all children in a boarding house, even if they don't board, so staff have a close eye on everyone's well-being. Good sign that many boarders we spoke to live locally and board 'because we love it.' Food has been a small bone of contention although pupils say it is 'getting better'.

The usual disciplinary issues but in the main very few incidents. Suspensions for major breaches of rules (eg boarders driving off campus) but in the main little need to transgress as students given sufficient freedom to spread their wings.

Pupils and parents: Majority of pupils from a 20 mile radius. Lots of busy, professional commuters and London parents attracted by the flexible boarding uniquely on offer here – as well as the atmosphere that they say gives their children 'space to breathe', both literally and metaphorically. Mixed financial demographic – plenty of first time buyers and parents stretching themselves to afford Aldenham – with these children fitting comfortably in with those who can easily cover the fees.

Overseas boarders tend to be in higher year groups. Of these, around 30 per cent from Germany, then handfuls from China, Hong Kong and ones and twos from elsewhere. All are well respected and well integrated – boarding pupils embrace and relish the diversity of their peers. Around 40 boarders stay in school at weekends.

Entrance: Around 60 places in year 7 with between 15 and 20 of these taken by children coming up from on-site prep school and the rest made up of children joining from the state sector (40 per cent) and local 11+ preps. About 30 per cent of year 7 are girls. Another 25 to 30 join in year 9 from a vast array of preps, notably Lochinver House, Orley Farm, Northwood Prep, St Martin's and St John's and further afield The Beacon, The Hall and Davenies. Applicants at 11+ take papers in maths, English and reasoning with the addition of science and a language at 13+. Scholars are interviewed away from their parents.

Late arrivals come from other, more pressured, local schools – not always because they can't cut the mustard but mainly because they are looking for a school that's about more than exam results. And that, here, is what they find. Around 30 places available in sixth form.

Exit: Approximately 30 per cent leave after GCSE to follow vocational courses or A levels elsewhere (mainly state schools or colleges) or to employment. A broad spectrum of destination universities reflects mixed academic intake, with about 20 per cent to Russell Group, a couple each year to art schools (often St Martins) and regular success with applications to top drama schools. Other degree courses tend to veer towards the vocational, many with a business/management focus. One or two to Oxbridge most years.

Money matters: Scholarships at 11+ and 13+ in music, art, sport, DT as well as academic, with a maximum of 15 per cent off fees awarded. Means-tested bursaries available.

Remarks: Head describes Aldenham as 'an extraordinary school for ordinary children' and we concur. An unpressurised environment such as this makes for some of the most contented pupils we have met, and self-motivated children can fare well academically too. Tread carefully if scholarly accolades are top of your wish list or if your offspring need stick rather than carrot, but if it's a rounded and happy child you're after, then Aldenham's definitely one to consider.

Aldro

9

Lombard Street, Shackleford, Godalming, Surrey GU8 6AS

Pupils: 220; 7 full, 55 weekly/flexi boarders • Ages: 7–13 (boarding from 8) • C of E

Fees: Day £15,915 – £17,670; Boarding £21,330 – £23,085 pa

Tel: 01483 810266
Email: hmsec@aldro.org
Website: www.aldro.org

Headmaster: Since September 2015, Mr James Hanson, previously head of the boys's senior school at the Royal School, Haslemere. Studied maths and zoology at Oxford; MPhil in maths education from Brunel. Ten years at Harrow, where he was senior maths master, head of the G&T programme and of rowing, and deputy housemaster. He is married to Jenny, and they have two daughters.

Entrance: At 7+ a largely local intake. School is full and with a waiting list – boarding numbers are up since introduction of more flexible system but generally more competition for day places than boarding. Two form entry. Exam, assessment and reports in January for the following September. Boys come from many different feeder schools – over 30 at the last count, but always a chunk from St Hilary's. A few substantial bursaries available through the Royal National Children's Foundation.

Exit: Expert and practised at feeding the public school system. Aldro boys hoover up scholarships and head off in their 10s to Charterhouse (five minutes away – Aldro seen as a feeder, but isn't officially) in handfuls to Eton and Wellington and ones and twos elsewhere – typically to around a dozen different destinations, including Tonbridge, Sherborne, Radley, Winchester and recently the more local Royal Grammar School, Guildford and St John's Leatherhead.

Remarks: An old-fashioned, traditional school which sees itself as very much part of the 'establishment' of leading public schools. With academics at its core, be aware that the thrust of the place is to get the boys to major public boarding schools. 'It's an unspoken thing, but I very much got the feeling the school wondered why I would want to go anywhere other than those schools – that's the culture,' a parent told us.

Long school days with the youngest boys finishing at 5pm, older pupils going on past 6pm. Boys here are all of above average ability, but still divided on academic lines in year 7 into 'scholars' and 'others' (or 'brainy and thick,' as one son told his

A

mother). School happy to support boys who may struggle in one area and will take those with mild dyslexia or dyspraxia. Around 10 per cent of pupils have some extra help from specialist SEN teachers. But it's probably not for a boy who may struggle across the board – he simply wouldn't get the best out of the place.

Each school day begins with short service in the beautiful chapel – whole school, two hymns and a reading and a few words from the head or senior staff. Then it's straight into lessons. Prep is done at the end of the day, so no homework needs to go home with the day boys; 'wonderful,' chorus mothers, who don't have to chivvy.

It's a fairly challenging academic environment; Aldro boys are undoubtedly hard working, well monitored and generally encouraged to develop high levels of independence, self-motivation and organisation skills. Quite a few longstanding teachers doing what they've always done, with some young blood to leaven the mix. Higher than average numbers of husband and wife teaching combos. Particular parental mention for 'stand-out' science and 'superb' French. Although long-serving head of department has retired, two native French speaking staff are much praised – we spotted Monsieur teaching pétanque during break and school has its own bouledrome. Pupils keen on history teacher operating out of distinctive classroom with mood-setting, old-fashioned fixtures and fittings, who organises chances to dress up and act out characters and events. Seventy per cent of full time teachers are male – great role models for the boys – 'lots of nice teachers,' they told us. Good manners abound – boys will sometimes say 'thank you' after a lesson and staff sometimes say it too, if boys have been particularly productive and engaged.

A pleasingly broad curriculum: boys say the best thing about this school is the variety of things they get to do – drama (in new studio), plenty of art and DT, including pottery, music (two-thirds of boys have an individual lesson every week and masses of practice rooms) and, of course, sport galore. Past feeling that less sporty boys get overlooked has changed as staff work hard to achieve 'sport for all'. 'I like the fact they go back to basics, including working on fitness levels that can be overlooked,' said one parent. Main sports are rugby, football, hockey, tennis, cricket and athletics. Aldro's 1st XV rugby team have been national under-13 champions. New sports centre completed 2015. Boys can also hunt (for fossils), shoot (pistol and rifle) and fish. This place is also tremendously strong on chess and even a model railway – basically, if your son has an interest, this school will ensure he develops it.

Boys really can be boys here – blessed with seemingly boundless bosky grounds, bordered by woods where they make dens and play in the tree house, on the rope bridge and in the rowing lake. 'They have a lot of freedom outdoors and it can be quite a shock after their usually sheltered pre-prep experiences, where they are marshalled from pillar to post,' said one mother. 'It's simply idyllic,' said another. 'And because the boys are free to roam in the great outdoors they get great self-confidence, which has benefits in all sorts of areas.'

Indoors, the main building is arts and crafts, centred around an imported Jacobean staircase. Most of the classrooms are in a much newer 1990s block including the flashy IT stuff and a tip-top library. But generally the school is selected for its reputation, rather than swanky facilities. A glance around the car park on match days will confirm Aldro parents are generally a very well-heeled bunch; the majority are the married upper-middle classes.

Aldro has a distinct boarding school ethos, even though on bald numbers it has many more day pupils. While the school has the occasional boarder at 7 or 8 (these tend to be Forces families), more typically pupils board by 9 or 10 in readiness for their move to a senior boarding school. 'The whole boarding set up is brilliant and was just what we needed by year 7,' said one mother. 'The boys have supper and some time to relax and have fun, but are then brought back to task with prep and revision sessions – fantastic; I couldn't have done as well at home.'

'The boarding is great and be warned, your son will want to try it before he leaves,' counselled another mother. 'We live too close to make it viable, but my son would leave home for school tomorrow if I said the word.' Just seven boys board full time, 20 are weekly and the rest flexi, with an average of about 50 sleeping at school on any one night. In reality 'flexible' means 'pre-arranged part time', though of course the school will try to facilitate the odd night when required. But it takes its responsibility to the regular boarders seriously. 'A boy needs to feel settled and to know who'll be in the next bed on any given night,' says boarding master. Certainly the current arrangements must work well, because since introducing this more flexible approach (in the past it was all or nothing) boarding has flourished here.

Boarders and hanger-on day boys have supper at 6pm, after which the day boys leave and it's 'Mars time' for boarders – from the old advert 'work, rest and play'. But for 'work' school means 'do some', for a rest 'read your book' and 'play' means 'play your instrument'. At 7.15pm an activity, then 20 minutes or so access to phones/iPods before showers and bed (year 6 at 8.30pm). We spotted a Wii gathering dust in the corner of the common room – apparently it comes out in terrible weather – and a (thankfully more popular) pet hamster. Accommodation is typical of modern boarding facilities, functional and homely rather than luxurious, all supervised by young matrons in the 'big sister/concerned aunt' mould.

Parents find the school nicely sociable, usual set up of 'Friends', class reps and so on. Mothers enjoying a tennis morning when we were there. Not tons of extras to find. It's expensive, but that's it – you won't pay for much else. Lunch and books included in fees and not many outings or fancy trips. Thriving and established market in secondhand blazers, so check that out before you buy a new one.

Overall a successful school with a real Christian ethos – no lip service here – and lots of traditional elements: high standards of work, play and simple manners. Good for active, go-getty characters. Not for the faint-hearted – academically or personality-wise. If your son needs brow-mopping and spoon-feeding, think again.

Aldwickbury School

Wheathampstead Road, Harpenden, Hertfordshire AL5 1AD

Pupils: 380; 50+ flexi boarders • Ages: 4–13 (boarding from 10) • C of E

Fees: Day £12,270 – £15,180 pa; Boarding + £29.90 – £36.40 per night

Tel: 01582 713022
Email: registrar@aldwickbury.org.uk
Website: www.aldwickbury.org.uk

Headmaster: Since 2003 Mr Vernon Hales BEd (50s). Educated at Langley Park Grammar School and Exeter University, where his education degree majored in PE. After a year in the state system, he started his prep school career at Papplewick ('great fun') before heading off to New Zealand, becoming deputy head in its then largest boarding prep school. Returned as deputy head and boarding housemaster at Elstree School, then joined Aldwickbury as the school's fourth head. Partnered through entire professional journey by wife Claire, also a trained teacher and now head of marketing at school and 'traditional head's spouse'. Educated his two sons, now late teens, at Aldwickbury and The Leys, where they are full boarders.

Relaxed, warm and jovial with the boys, and 'very visible around the school', according to parents, he recently 'came out of retirement' to resurrect his passion for club cricket and harbours personal ambitions to become a good golfer (must be the stunning course surrounding the school grounds calling). Lives in the main school building and is proud of its unique local offering as a boys' (mainly) day school, based on a boarding school model. Recognises that although sport is very important to boys, he wants Aldwickbury to be an 'all round' school. He speaks with conviction about understanding the distinctive needs of boys in their formative years, describing Aldwickbury as 'philosophically a boys school.' Would like to increase school numbers very slightly 'without losing our small school feel'.

Entrance: Non-selective at 4, the school works with local feeder nurseries to ensure smooth transition for its youngest pupils as they join reception. Recently became three-form entry at the bottom of the school, with 15 to a class, due to increased demand for places. Maximum class size in pre-prep fixed at 18. Boys joining higher up the school are invited in for an informal session with their relevant year group head, where they are encouraged to talk about themselves and take tests in reading, maths and spelling to ensure they can access the curriculum. Means-tested bursaries available.

Exit: Vast majority stay at Aldwickbury until the end of year 8. School loses just a few each year at the end of year 6, 'for either financial or academic reasons', according to head. Feeds about half its boys into year 9 at St Albans School, 'a handful' each year with scholarships. Remainder to schools including St Columba's, Bedford and Haileybury. One or two recently to Eton, Harrow and Shrewsbury and Berkhamstead. 'The key is getting parents to choose the right school for the boy', says head. Parents confirm that he gives them a strong steer in the right direction.

Remarks: Situated a stone's throw up the hill from Harpenden's second (less chi-chi) high street in Southdown, Aldwickbury Mansion, which dates back to 1871 and is full of Victorian character (albeit with a few tired corners), became home to the school in 1948. It makes excellent use of its leafy 20-acre site and has sympathetically incorporated a number of modern buildings to create an appealing and well-functioning school campus. Main school building sits atop grassy terraces and playing fields, affording the head and his boarders a panoramic view of the school grounds. A separate purpose-built pre-prep department was built in 2001, providing the school's youngest pupils with a bright and cheerful base, where they can ease their way into school life without the rough and tumble of bigger boys.

Reception has its own safe haven outside with a small adventure playground area, plus trikes, bikes and a sand table – 'very therapeutic if they've had a tricky morning in the classroom', says head of pre-prep. School places a large emphasis on outside learning at this stage – 'we're not a forest school but we do take on elements of that ethos'. On our visit, reception boys were enthusiastically doing Victorian-style laundry outside. The pre-prep building is festooned with topic-related art and written work and has its own hall for assemblies, activities and performances.

Junior department houses years 3 and 4, when the school starts to 'encourage independence in a gentle way', including the introduction of a more formal uniform. Even maths classrooms are creatively themed and staff overall exude energy and enthusiasm, reinforcing the school's ethos of 'really getting boys'. One year 1 teacher quietly plays classical music CDs when she wants her class to concentrate, and – try it at home – it seems to work. Boys in years 5 to 8 move around classrooms for specialist teaching to prepare them for senior school life.

Lovely heated indoor swimming pool – well used, with weekly lessons for all from reception, plus early morning and after-school swim clubs. Coach house now home to ever-popular DT workshop ('we really look forward to coming in here', say boys) with feel of a real man space where industrious pupils turn out quality projects from wind chimes to fruit bowls. Art room (also in coach house) is a showcase for the boys' enthusiasm. The gym is in dire need of some TLC, but school now has an 'all singing, all dancing' £3.2m hall and music department, plus several new classrooms including science rooms, 'to provide flexibility and accommodate growth'. Also boasts a gleaming modernised dining hall (food to be recommended) and library.

Parents and pupils alike describe Aldwickbury as 'very friendly and welcoming', and the nurturing feel pervades the fabric of the school. 'Definitely not pushy', say parents uniformly, suggesting that league table watchers may want to look elsewhere. Boys have the knack of knowing when to be quiet (quite a feat in a dining hall of rumbling tummies waiting for someone to say grace) and when to let off steam. Confidence and manners, without arrogance, in evidence in all age groups.

A true 4 to 13 school. 'All year 8 boys have jobs' and are given responsibilities around the school, such as helping teachers get younger boys organised in the mornings and listening to year 5 boys read at lunchtimes. With around half the teachers male, the overall vibe is of a school where boys really can be boys. Year groups encouraged to mix at meal times, with lunch taken as 'sections' (that's houses to the rest of us). Boys compete throughout the year for the section cup, not just in their academic lives and on the sports fields, but also with competitions and challenges, including section Scrabble and top autumn favourite, the 'conker-tition'.

Majority of pupils from the immediate environs, with 50 per cent 'sharing the AL5 postcode,' according to head. Remainder from surrounding towns and villages. Very few from further afield. Overwhelmingly Caucasian majority reflects the local community. Most parents in the professions, many dual income, but a by all accounts a pretty grounded bunch and a number 'stretching themselves' to pay school fees. A parents' association set up recently to bring together parents, staff and boys and foster the school/community relationship. Events so far have included discos with local girls' school, monthly tuck shops with home-baked cakes and a dads vs masters cricket match.

French with a specialist teacher from year 1, with Spanish and German added to the mix in year 5 and Latin from year 6. Specialist teaching from year 3 for ICT, art, music and drama. Mixed ability classes 'by ethos' to end of year 5, although head admits to some 'subtle setting' from year 3 and parents of able children report extra work being given to ensure the brightest are stretched. Classes mixed at end of years 2 and 4 which some parents grumble they find 'stressful', although they admit the school 'normally gets it right'. Streaming introduced from year 6, with two or three classes and a scholarship class in year 8. This, however, is not always uniform in its structure – head is determined to 'start from the point of what's best for the boys'. SEN all in a day's work and good provision in place to deal with minor blips rather than more serious problems.

Music taught by male teachers from pre-prep onwards, which really 'turns boys on to learning an instrument', according to head. Around 160 boys from year 1 upwards take music lessons in a wide range of instruments. Abundance of musical groups to join, from choir to guitar groups, including the popular Aldwickbury Strings group, a collaborative effort between staff (including the bursar, a talented violinist) and boys. Drama is 'really important', says head, with participation in plays compulsory up to year 5 to 'build confidence'. Main school play, most recently A Christmas Carol, performed in the round, is optional in years 7 and 8 but most choose to take part, if not on stage, then in lighting or costume, with the occasional rugby player taking charge of make-up.

Sport is the lifeblood of the school, with specialist teaching twice weekly from year 1 and boys from year 3 up having a daily games lesson. Competitive football, swimming and skiing are 'excellent', says head, and boys regularly compete at national level. Team fixtures for all from A-E teams, so everyone gets a ride on the school minibus and a shot at sporting glory. Colours awards on offer for stars of rugby, football cricket et al, but also for drama, music and citizenship, proving that heroes are not only found on the sports fields here. In the words of one boy, 'all things here are valued the same'.

Boarding almost exclusively flexi, with the occasional weekly boarder, but no provision for boys at weekends. The majority of those who board from year 6 are at their 'second home' (as they call it) two or three nights a week, with provision for 33 boarders at any one time. Once the plethora of after-school clubs has finished, there's more fun, with 'non-stop activities,' say boys, followed by weekly film nights in the cosy boarders' lounge and occasional events such as the popular 'chippy night' (one benefit of being so close to the high street). Functional dormitories sleep up to nine year 6 boys, with numbers dropping to four or five in the upper years. No phones with SIMs are allowed but, with all that's on offer, boys have got better things to do than phone home. With the majority of boys living so locally, most are here purely for the fun of it and speak wisely of their new found 'independence' and how boarding has changed them.

Day boys able to join boarders for breakfast from 7.40am and supper for a small cost – handy for commuting parents. All boys from year 5 up stay for prep until between 5.10pm and 5.45pm and there is an after-school club which can take pupils of any age up to supper time at 5.50pm.

Broad range of extracurricular activities to cater for all tastes, from chess, Lego or general knowledge club for the cerebral crowd to skiing, fencing or martial arts for those wanting to try their hand at something more physical. Loads of opportunities to get out and about, with trips aplenty. School makes full use of being on the capital's doorstep, with trips to art galleries and theatres and also ventures further afield (expeditions to France, Iceland and the much anticipated leavers' trip to Dartmoor). A schedule of evening seminars on topics such as 'the history of the Ashes' ('much more interesting than it sounds', says head) is in place for older boys and their parents, and a number of external learning sources are brought in throughout the year. When we visited, boys were buzzing after a visit from a 'mathemagician,' part of the maths week itinerary.

Alton College

Old Odiham Road, Alton, Hampshire GU34 2LX

Pupils: 1,700 • Ages: 16–19

Tel: 01420 592200
Email: enquiries@altoncollege.ac.uk
Website: www.altoncollege.ac.uk

Principal: Since April 2016, Sara Russell, previously vice principal (curriculum).

Academic matters: Offers a very broad range of qualifications to a diverse group of students – anything from Oxbridge to GCSE retakes. The majority of sixth form students study A levels, with fewer following vocational courses. Also educates disabled students from nearby Treloar College.

Excellent range of academic subjects on offer – several young people we met were studying combinations you might expect in any public school sixth form. Achieves pass rates well above the national average. In 2016, 47 per cent A*-B and 22 per cent A*/A grades at A level. Lots of opportunity to mix and match, as also offers A levels in less mainstream subjects such as dance, health and social care, music technology and photography. Some students choose to combine BTec diplomas with A levels to give their qualifications a more practical slant; others follow the vocational route completely and opt for the extended diploma. BTec courses include applied science, art and design, business, engineering, graphic design, ICT, performing arts and sport. Those who haven't passed any GCSEs can re-sit them at Alton.

Students say 'sciences are strong' and results back this up; science labs in Beacon Centre are spacious, well equipped and modern. Maths in good health – six maths A levels to choose from. French looks first-rate. Austen building has recording studios for film and media studies, as well as classrooms for English, modern languages and the humanities.

Learning resource centre has well stocked library and lots of individual cubicles for private study – ICT provision excellent: huge, silent room full of screens and students beavering away. Class size averages 19, with a maximum of 26. Statistics backed up by praise from Ofsted, which rated the college outstanding in nearly all areas after two consecutive inspections. Students achieve local and national success – a team won the UK Senior Maths Challenge and law students were finalists in the Bar Mock Trial Competition regional heats.

Outstanding SEN provision, not least for the learning support provided for students at Treloar College (pupils with severe physical disabilities) who study at Alton whilst boarding at Treloar. Dedicated rooms with computers and tables at the right height for students in wheelchairs. Also caters for a wide array of special needs, from dyslexia and dyspraxia to mental health issues and extra help with literacy and numeracy. Has won an Association of Colleges beacon award for its provision for students with special needs – eg creating a sports unit so a disabled student could complete his course by playing boccia in a wheelchair.

Games, options, the arts: Although sport not compulsory, more than 200 students are enrolled on sport related courses and another 200 take part in extracurricular physical activities. One hundred per cent pass rate for the BTec diploma in sport – 50 per cent with merit and distinction. Large sports hall is located next to playing fields and has a gym with weights and resistance equipment. No swimming pool on campus, but students use Treloar College pool a short distance away. Matches against other Hampshire colleges throughout the year and regularly tops the county schools leagues in rugby, football and mixed hockey. Other teams compete in netball, basketball and badminton in winter, plus cricket and tennis in the summer term. Alternative sports include aerobics, dance, volleyball and women's football.

Michael Gray building houses art and music on three floors; vocational art takes place in two spacious studios on the ground floor, eg fashion design. Top floor is dedicated to A level art, with separate rooms for textiles, painting and drawing. Some very good quality work on display throughout the college and exam results are strong.

Lower floor of Gray Building devoted to music, with individual studios, practice rooms and music technology suites for recording and mixing sound. Music good with all the usual instruments on offer (practice not formally timetabled) – all music and music technology students receive tuition on one instrument free of charge. Visiting peripatetic staff teach nearly 200 students every week, chamber orchestra, jazz band, four choirs (including rock choir) and several instrumental ensembles. Composers' ensemble is on a winning streak – one student won the BBC Proms Young Composers Competition and had her pieces broadcast on Radio 3, while another won the big band section of a jazz competition with her music. College 'jazzers' perform regularly in local festivals and venues, have undertaken a monthly residency in a local pub, performed at the Birmingham ICC and given a short concert tour of France. Two students won places in the National Youth Jazz Collective and others have gone on to study jazz, composition, piano and orchestral instruments at music conservatoires.

Fabulous, modern Berkoff performing arts centre has a professionally equipped theatre, large dance studio with sprung flooring and a busy schedule of performances throughout the year. Stevens Building houses photography studios and darkrooms – one student had her work selected for Royal Photographic Society's International Print Exhibition. Engineering building is distinctly unglamorous by comparison and affectionately referred to as 'the shed'. It nevertheless looked pretty well fitted out to our untrained eye, with lots of practical, blokey activities going on. Sadly, numbers studying engineering stay capped until the new building is built.

Good opportunities for students to flesh out work in the classroom and beef up university CVs – trips to First World War battlefields (English), St Petersburg (art), South Africa (geography), Iceland (chemistry), Berlin (German) and Cuba (photography and biology) organised. Intrepid college students have also got as far as Peru, Tanzania, Bolivia and the Himalayas. Lots of extracurricular opportunities, from Iron Man training in Lanzarote to skiing in Switzerland, chess club, debating society, recreational badminton, grade 5 music theory, first aid and the college magazine.

Background and atmosphere: The first purpose-built sixth form centre in the UK, opened in 1978 with 240 students. It now educates nearly 2,000 16 to 19 year olds and nearly 900 adults following part-time courses. Over £20 million has been invested in the college since 2002 and new buildings have been added.

Feels more like a university campus than a school. The young people we met valued the adult atmosphere and cited mutual respect between staff and students. 'We call our teachers by their first names and we can email them whenever we like,' one told us. Some felt they had outgrown their former schools and said, 'Alton is the right step between school and uni for us'.

University feel continues with college's large refectory serving subsidised meals; also various smaller cafes dotted around where students can buy Fairtrade coffee, sandwiches and snacks. A crèche on site, mostly used by staff but also by a very small number of sixth form students with young children.

Pastoral care, well-being and discipline: Big on pastoral care – well organised programme to monitor student progress. College recognises that 'myriad things underpin academic successes'. Each pupil has a personal tutor, who reports to a senior tutor, who in turn reports to director of learning. Everyone has weekly personal learning and development lessons in the first year and is issued with an individual learning planner. Pupils touch in and out of lessons via an electronic pass and can monitor their attendance, homework and grades via Moodle (virtual site), which also has plenty of learning and revision resources online; student reps use it to give feedback to staff members. We got the feeling that not much slips through the cracks here.

Gifted and talented programme for around 300 students applying to top universities – focus on interview technique (eg how to cope with being stared down by an Oxbridge don at the far end of a table in very grand rooms) and how best to prepare applications to competitive courses, eg medicine and veterinary studies.

Active student union meets regularly with the principal and organises charity events. Student centre offers counselling and career advice and helps students with higher education choices and contacts for work experience. Few problems with discipline – college says, 'The vast majority of young people rise to the standards we expect of them'. Quiet garden in memory of former students provides a peaceful space to relax and reflect in.

Pupils and parents: Many pupils arrive from nine partner schools, although a significant number come from other schools in Hampshire, Surrey and West Sussex. Approximately 10 per cent from the private sector, either because they want a more adult atmosphere or a wider choice of subjects (college hosts a special evening for those transferring from independent schools).

Most families live within 20 miles of the college, a few further afield. Ten subsidised bus routes deliver students from destinations such as Basingstoke and Haslemere. Parents choose the college in the hope that it will ease the transition to university, confirmed by feedback from admissions tutors.

Most students are British, although growing number of students from other ethnic backgrounds, one of whom we met (an engaging Russian who spoke excellent English and clearly has a future in politics). Students are mature, focused and fairly laidback; they have clearly made the transition from school to university 'halfway house'. Not perhaps as polished as the independent school product, which isn't necessarily to their disadvantage.

Entrance: Not selective, but anyone missing the applications deadline is very likely to go on the waiting list. Applications invited from November of the previous year to the end of March for entry the following September; everyone is interviewed twice. First interview takes place by the end of April and the second following GCSE results.

College's feeder schools are Amery Hill, Bohunt, Eggar's, Mill Chase, Perins, The Petersfield School, Robert May's, Weydon and St Nicholas' School. Open evenings held in October and March; guidance meetings scheduled in partner schools between November and April. Welcome event for prospective new students happens in July.

Exit: Given the inclusive intake of the college, leavers' choices are broader than most. Has commissioned and produced a highly detailed analysis of its students' destinations, so we can report with complete confidence that 70 per cent of A level pupils, 50 per cent of vocational course students and 98 per cent of art foundation leavers go on to higher education. A very small number (three per cent) chooses further education, eg Sparsholt College or Basingstoke College of Technology, whilst around 13 per cent seek employment.

The most popular university courses are art and design, business, linguistics, biological sciences, law and physical sciences. Top university destinations are the University of the West of England, Bournemouth, Southampton, Brighton, Surrey, Bath, Exeter, Kent and Portsmouth. Twenty-five per cent of leavers secure places at Russell Group universities and a few gain places at specialist music conservatoires (six in 2016, plus two to Oxbridge).

Former pupils include MP Yvette Cooper, actress Catherine McCormack, scientist Jonathan Tucker, musicians Alison Goldfrapp and Gwyneth Herbert, cricketer Chris Wood, comedian Russell Howard and Ben Southall, winner of the Best Job in the World competition.

Money matters: College foundation offers scholarships worth up to £1,000 to those who demonstrate excellence in a particular subject (disciplines have included art, engineering, law, medicine, music and sport). Bursary scheme subsidises the cost of education for families on low incomes and can be used for any purpose, eg paying for the cost of travel to and from college. Award worth £250 is available to students on the one-year art foundation course.

Remarks: Open access sixth form college which offers a broad range of qualifications and provides a bridge between school and higher education to those looking for a bit more freedom to manage their own education. Gets good results and also scoops up those who have fallen by the GCSE wayside. Provides plenty of support, but may not suit someone who needs a hand held at every step.

Amesbury

Hazel Grove, Hindhead, Surrey GU26 6BL

Pupils: 355 • Ages: Ages: 2–13 (taster boarding years 5–8) • C of E

Fees: £9,705 – £14,850 pa

Tel: 01428 604322
Email: reception@amesburyschool.co.uk
Website: www.amesburyschool.co.uk

Headmaster: Since 1994, Mr Nigel Taylor BSc PGCE MA (50s). Previously deputy head, St Paul's School, São Paulo. Married to Caroline. Attractively self-deprecating with lashings of charm, used to devastating effect on prospective parents who may see the strings being pulled but succumb anyway. Sensibly takes most round himself. 'He was down on the carpet playing with my son,' says mother, who signed up on the strength of it, despite having previously registered elsewhere.

Charm is coupled with a keen intelligence. 'He's quite a political animal,' says a parent, 'but you can't be in that sort of position without some sort of astuteness.' However, he's anything but bland. Just glimpsed red socks are a subtle clue. For a whopping big one, try the mouse mat featuring him going the full Disney in the London Marathon dressed as a fetching Snow White, accessorised with wig, long dress, manly, hirsute arms and seven teachers as his dwarves.

Undoubtedly sincere, too. Read between the lines of the exceedingly well-written, occasionally poetic current prospectus (being revamped, so get in quick in case his sensitive prose is replaced by 50 shades of corporate beige) and you'll find clues to his own experiences.

Was described in previous GSG review as 'streetwise, not posh'. Spot on, he says. Though fits effortlessly into current surroundings (delightful room and study, complete with blazing wood fire of almost Narnian degree of cosiness; you expect Mr Tumnus to appear at any second bearing a plate of crumpets), upbringing took place against a very different backdrop.

An adopted child, he was raised on a tough Leicester council estate, attending 'appalling' primary school which told the most able they had 'finished reading' in year 4 and were cut free to fag for the head. Fairy godparent moment came via sympathetic teacher's subtle interview coaching which ensured he made it to grammar school and thence to bigger and better things.

Sport and writing were his first serious interests. Law, too (still indulges inner Perry Mason with occasional day off to watch Crown Court trials). Logical career choice, sports journalism, hit the buffers when political machinations saw him effectively ousted from postgrad scholarship course at Columbia University. Nothing daunted, he returned to the UK and was talent spotted while helping to run a holiday coaching course at Stowe School and that, in career choice terms, was that.

Clear sighted but unresentful about deficiencies in his own education (and, with an MA in educational management as well as hands on know-how, something of an expert on how it should be done), his pet hate is a system designed for the convenience of adults at the expense of children, public mortification all too often the unintended consequence. As a result, school teems with humane initiatives, including emailed exam results which are 'the business of the child, teacher and parents, that's all.' He wouldn't post details of staff performance in common room, he says – 'I'd have the unions in straight away' – so why should pupils endure it?

Also of note is emphasis on making everyone feel special. Mr Taylor decided early on that it was signally unfair for the most able to have unlimited extra attention to prepare for scholarships while parents whose children required learning support wilted under the extra charges. Now, unless parental requests would involve disproportionate time or funding, they're all included in headline fees. Similarly, subject teachers work with small groups in turn across the ability range so middle ranking as well as high and low achievers get the VIP treatment, initially in English and maths (both highly praised in most recent inspection). Undoubtedly successful and once the golden glow extends to other subjects, too, even more so.

At his 20th anniversary, Mr Taylor is open about having had a touch of the career fidgets 'a few years ago' (common knowledge to parents as well), but having looked round, has decided this is the place for him. He'd be missed if he went. To misquote: 'No head is a hero to his pupils'. Not that this one would want to be. 'My dad says you need adults to treat children as humans and he does,' says a pupil.

Entrance: Through registration plus visit – not a formal assessment but the opportunity for child and school to get acquainted, pupils accepted until spaces filled. Scholarships (academic, tennis and expressive arts) available years 3 to 7 for those 'head and shoulders above other very talented children'; worth applying for, with awards worth up to 50 per cent of the fees.

Nursery flexibility a given, with full days for those who need them (complete with freshly cooked hot meals, served in nursery classrooms; reception eat in dining hall, served like year 1 and 2 pupils at the table) and though school will suggest at least two consecutive sessions a week, there's no minimum nursery stay, with staff on hand to plug gaps at relatively short notice if there's a sudden bulge in numbers, now recovering after a lean patch. Will not adopt government suggestions to ease staffing ratios but up entry qualifications by way of compensation. 'Stupid,' says nursery head. 'It doesn't matter how well qualified you are, you're still only one person.'

Exit: Fall out after year 6, formerly a bit of an issue for the school (as elsewhere), has been largely contained ('resolved' – more girls staying on than leaving) helped by head's decision to stem school gate chatter by bringing the debate back into school and proselytise the benefits of staying to the end. Pupils, in no doubt as to the benefits, all happily cited kudos-factor of being top in the pecking order. Wide range of destinations, day including Royal Grammar, Portsmouth Grammar, St Catherine's Bramley, Tormead, Guildford High, Prior's Field; boarding including Bedales, Bradfield, Brighton College, Bryanston, Canford, Charterhouse, Harrow, Marlborough, Millfield, Rugby, Winchester and Wellington.

Remarks: One of a cluster of preps in this well-to-do area of Surrey, now more primrose path than rat run following opening of Hindhead tunnel – 'Other schools build a new sports hall, we spend millions on an underpass,' jokes head – school is considered a breath of fresh air by its supporters, who extol approach as trad with a twist.

On the surface, it oozes convention, second occupants of Lutyens' only purpose-built school, having moved here in 1917 from Bickley in Kent (was originally founded in 1870 in Redhill) to swap air raids for fresh air. Designed like a scaled down Hollywood set, main building features windows at two-thirds height, with a baby grand entrance and chapel, added 1938, which potentially reduces a wrath-filled God to a Wendy house-sized deity – a much more comforting notion to the young. Even the reception signs, so tiny that this reviewer walked past them twice, may have been boil-washed one too many times.

Some areas, a bit factory second here and there on date of visit, have already been improved, with sagging maintenance shed in the grounds subsequently demolished and staff treated to what head terms a 'luxurious' common room.

There has also been considerable smartening up: blue-canopied entrances on more modern buildings including super new visual and performing arts centre, an attractive and well-equipped example of the genre, as well as impressive giant, echoing sports hall – a yodeller's dream – a new dance studio, refurbished science department and general pepping up of floor surfaces and corridors.

Also notable for exceptional cleanliness. Wherever we went, a mop or broom was sure to be in attendance close by. Much appreciated cleaning team was particularly busy in recently (and handsomely) refurbished separate nursery/reception building – all whiteness and brightness, with space for big, pristine, set piece indoor toys, recently enhanced with modish free flow into secure outside area (complete with inevitable free flow mud), all presided over by caring, multi-tasking staff (capable of spotting child in need of TLC while extolling multiple uses of home-made Play-doh).

While parents appreciate surroundings, heading praise list (which is extensive) is school's philosophy – 'holistic' says one. 'They balance the academic side with lots of other things so that all the children can find a way of expressing themselves.' Approach can manifest itself in an absence of surface polish: hair that little bit longer than the norm; uniform (traditional skirts for girls, boys in viyella shirts with dress down brown guernseys for all – 'only itchy with short sleeves' says plucky pupil) occasionally lacking in parade gloss finish; productions and matches feature all comers.

We'd written originally that these were in consequence 'a tad rougher round the edges' based on parent feedback. 'Inaccurate' says head. 'We are rougher round the edges on a day to day basis, hair is sometimes longer. However, we are neurotic about getting it absolutely right on match days.' Ditto chapel choir and school plays, which are 'super professional.' The trick, he says, 'is to be more relaxed until the moment when it matters and then we are absolutely spot on.'

There's also convention where it matters – 'very strict on how they speak to the teachers, so not liberal in that respect,' said a parent and no shortage of competition. But while two houses, carefully matched for ability, are expected to slug it out for supremacy during the year, what shines through is wrap-round encouragement for everyone, not just the most able, with the slightest flicker of talent breathed into a living flame.

Upbeat approach embraces learning needs, catering for rather more than advertised. One parent who packed tissues before meeting teachers, expecting to discuss behaviour issues, ended up being overwhelmed by praise.

Dyslexia, official speciality, had own separate centre until around four years ago. A new head of learning support, also qualified to carry out assessments, has now been appointed and most support is now provided in class. Considerable flexibility, however. 'If pupils need somebody physically sitting alongside them in the lesson to support them, that's what we'll do – focus is not on one size fits all: it's the right programme for the right child,' says head of English.

Sets the tone for excellent pastoral care, in and out of lesson time, from twinkly matron, popular with the walking wounded and others – 'we have our regulars' – to staff mingling with pupils for 'usually good and never awful' lunches in delightful blue-painted dining hall, dominated by bison's head (which lends its name to major house trophy, though history and significance remain an apparent mystery to all).

Register ensures that everyone eats (older pupils can choose when) though latecomers have to negotiate bottlenecks either side of diddy double doors as two-way queues of well-nourished, 21st century children jostle for supremacy, accompanied by fairly vigorous shoving by all.

It's the only sign of anything other than cordial pupil relationships, with friendships, seen as a huge strength, crossing between year groups, welcome sense of 'freedom to talk,' says pupil and little in the way of conflict. One pupil who had experienced bullying in previous school felt 'there's just not the space for bullies. If you did it, you'd find yourself on your own.' Bonds strengthened by taster boarding week for everyone in years 5 to 8, groups of 10 boys or girls at a time – Mallory Towers lite, big on the hot chocolate with marshmallows element.

Academically, it's emphatically not a hothouse, though parents feel that standards are rising across the board, helped by emphasis on focus group teaching and calm but engaging class lessons notable for levels of discussion (lots of confident participation through the age ranges, reception children working on 'ay' sounds as a group; year 3 children engaged in quick fire mental maths and a school-wide absence of furrowed brows).

English and maths are excellent, remaining subjects being brought into line, recent staff additions generally reckoned to be plugging previous gaps (Latin and French now much improved, felt one mother). Humanities, headed by hugely popular teacher (has starring role in whole school charity remake of Pixie Lott hit, worth three minutes of anyone's time on Youtube) who is also very dashing, notable for dynamic text book light, tech-heavy approach to geography (we enjoyed contrast with low tech lunchtime message system – communicated in chalk, on a blackboard).

Plenty of extras on offer in the form of clubs, too, and if more pupils hadn't taken up Mandarin, it was only, they said, because there was so much else going on, with many ecstatic about performing arts, much open to all and sweeping plentiful numbers of boys as well as girls into their orbit.

Music embraces everything from formal chapel choir to semi-secret bands formed each year, strutting stuff at annual concert. There's plentiful dance and drama including ambitious takes on Shakespeare (a swinging 60s Comedy of Errors and 1920s gangland style Hamlet amongst them) while inaugural action-packed arts week successful but so energy and resource sapping, hoovering up just about everyone, staff and pupils, into its maw, that likely to become every other year wonder.

While arts feature large in pupils' career horizons, sports almost as popular. Aspirations and confidence stem, think pupils, from school's desire to 'want you to like sport.' Taken seriously ('steely' is head's description of sports teams in prospectus), as so it should be, with four grass pitches, one Astroturf and 'very fancy' sports hall, foyer decorated with motivational images of assorted sports, to do them in. No swimming pool and wouldn't be on pupils' wish list in any case. 'It would get cold and crowded and you'd want to get out,' said one, sensibly. Tennis, a big thing, is now offered from nursery, two ping pong tables installed primarily for year 7s and 8s 'and other years when

A

they're away or not using them' also hitting the spot. But, just as school prizes aren't just awarded to 'the obvious people but the ones with the right attitude,' say pupils, team selection favours the also rans as well as the stars. It's a brave strategy, given level of local opposition, main rival prompting something close to pupil bloodlust when you quiz them.

All in all, adds up to an atmosphere that substantiates the blurb. Many a school may claim to be 'academically rigorous'. Not all would also make such a virtue out of also being 'relaxed' (Mr Taylor's prospectus wording). This one does. Parents in search of an education which will deliver confident children who see their futures in terms of unlimited options rather than curtailed ambitions – 'I'd like to be an international sportsman, I just don't know which sport yet,' said one – would be well advised to pay a visit.

Anglo European School

Willow Green, Ingatestone, Essex CM4 0DJ

Pupils: 1,350 • Ages: 11–18 • Sixth form: 300

Fees: None

Tel: 01277 354018
Email: enquiries@aesessex.co.uk
Website: www.aesessex.co.uk

Co-headteachers: Since 2005, David Barrs MA BEd Cert Ed NPQH (60s); educated at London and Bristol Universities and St Paul's College, Cheltenham. Taught in Basildon and Saffron Walden; previously one of the school's joint deputy heads (1994-2005). Interests include the United Nations, cricket, golf and gardening.

Since September 2015, Mrs Jody Gee, previously deputy head since 2007, who has spent most of her career in Essex. She studied at Shenfield High and has taught at Newport Free Grammar School near Saffron Walden and the Plume School in Maldon, where she was head of English, then assistant head teacher.

Apologies for the cliché 'two heads are better than one', but this is clearly the case at Anglo European. The co-heads run the school; they don't 'divide' responsibilities, but are both on hand to take decisions, normally in consultation with the members of the senior leadership who help to ensure things run like clockwork. This leadership model is a legacy of the unexpected death of the previous head; the two, then joint deputies, stepped up to take charge, essentially pitching to the governors that they wanted to share the role. This dream team appears to work beautifully; if one is travelling, decisions aren't delayed, and it leaves both with time to do a little classroom teaching. Parents we spoke to will happily consult either.

The school seems to maintain comfortably high academic standards with a particular international emphasis. Both co-heads have a strong commitment to languages, so we asked what languages both spoke besides English. Interestingly, they both replied, 'none', which is precisely why they are both such strong advocates of the importance of developing linguistic agility in their young charges.

Academic matters: Well-known to many seasoned IB educators as one of the first IB diploma schools (and the first state IB school) in the UK, first offering it in 1977. A pace-setter since its inception, it was one of the handful of schools worldwide chosen to pilot the new IBCC (IB Careers Certificate) programme introduced in 2010.

The school's international ethos is evident in significant ways, from the impressive range of languages offered, to internationally-minded teachers, to loads of educational visits and exchanges.

They offer a choice of IB and A levels – or a mix of both. Sets by ability for maths from mid year 7, other subjects from year 8. Competent, knowledgeable counselling to help students sort which programme, or combination thereof, might best suit abilities, university goals, career paths. In 2016, 32 per cent of GCSEs were A*/A and 68 per cent of pupils got 5+ A*-C grades including English and maths. Average IB point score 35; 52 per cent A*-B grades for A level candidates.

One non-negotiable is that all students must continue to study a language all the way through, if not as an IB subject (one additional language is compulsory for the IB diploma), or A level, then as an asset-examined language (one generally outside the mainstream curriculum). This language emphasis can't be stressed enough. In year 7, students study three languages in addition to English: German, French and Chinese. For year 8, they can continue with German and French, or replace German with Spanish. At the end of year 9, if they are doing well in both their languages, they can begin a third, choosing from Mandarin, Russian, Japanese or Italian. Students who want to take on additional languages, or maintain a mother tongue, may also take lunchtime language lessons (and teachers get lots of praise for their willingness to do this). The parents and students alike talk about this, and truly appreciate the great advantage not only to speak more than one language, but to be spoilt for choice.

The educational exchange visits programme is one of the star aspects of this school. Year 7 students start with a 10 day class visit to a Belgian château with learning activities in France linked to the curriculum. Year 8 students do homestay exchanges with individual host families, whose schools in turn send kids to Anglo European, with students attending classes at the respective schools. The destinations on offer increase as the students move up the school (year 8 to France, year 9 to Spain and Germany, year 10 to Germany, France, Spain, Italy and China), all focused on whatever languages they're learning. Visits aren't mandatory, but very popular. Close to half of the school's 1,350 students participate and return with great stories: clearly a lot of cultural and linguistic learning through this excellent immersion programme.

Citizenship gets a special mention here by all parents we spoke to. Many schools subsume it into the history or PSHE curriculum. At Anglo European it's a 'stand-alone' course encouraging good global as well as local attitudes, all reinforced through the international visits, work placement trips and activities, and the community service programme. One unusual sixth form course is travel and tourism, which is fitting considering the international character of the school.

The choice between A levels, IB diploma or the newish IB Careers Certificate (an interesting blend of academic and vocational courses drawing on IB and A level coursework) or a combination, opens up the most amazing range of possibilities for sixth form, but by no means results in a class system of elites vs non-elites. A level students have the option of taking some IB courses if they wish, for example the Theory of Knowledge course, gaining from the best of both worlds. The sixth formers we met – who represented all three programmes – were confident in the courses they'd chosen, and felt they'd had good advice about the various options.

Classes can have as many as 34 students, but the average is 20. Parents feel the teachers form a strong team, and are themselves international, either nationals of other countries, or repatriating British teachers with international experience. Average age is 40s, and nearly half have been there for over 10 years.

Games, options, the arts: Wide range of extracurricular programmes. Good sports facilities on site – two gyms, a large outdoor field for rugby, cricket, rounders, etc, and a playground for break and other activities. Lots of the usual sports clubs and activities, including trampoline, and some self-defence, but above all Flags, an AE-invented ball game that's a wildly popular break-time tradition. Students say the small swimming pool is 'okay for the younger ones', but serious swimmers prefer to rely on local sports facilities for real work outs. In fact, while one parent said Anglo European would probably not be the best choice for a very sporty student, another mentioned the school's support of a student selected for the England Women's Football (Under 15s) League.

The school has joined an IB scheme allowing 'elite athletes' to do the IB in three rather than the usual two years; other sporting achievements and team victories in rounders, swimming and volleyball are indications of the school's support of sporting excellence. Some 60 students are pursuing the Duke of Edinburgh bronze award.

Students say there's lots to do, although sometimes a bit tricky with a long commute for many of them. They also say that many of them are more interested in the community service, citizenship, work placement type opportunities than school-based activities. Drama gets a lot of mentions and seems to involve anyone and everyone (mostly below the sixth form) who is interested in taking part, not just the thespian set that can sometimes dominate in schools. Plenty of musical outlets with bands, orchestras. (One recent graduate has moved on to the Royal College of Music.) The Eisteddfod is a popular annual event involving everyone (Eisteddfod is a Welsh festival of literature, music and drama) – a sort of school talent show that further extends the school's international ethos – and there is a popular winter arts festival and a Christmas concert as well.

Many of the kids get involved in the World Challenge programme and Model United Nations: the students say that this latter is very much inspired by Mr Barrs' own passion, which must be infectious, judging from the students' enthusiasm for it. He recently arranged for a whole group to go to Geneva to see the UN in action, and this will now become an annual event.

One of the most notable extracurricular features is the school's unique work experience programme. Both parents and students enthuse that this has provided life-changing experiences. The students made a point of commending the school for its continued commitment to this programme, despite recent government budget cuts. There are work placements in both the local voluntary and commercial sectors (restaurants, supermarkets, doctor's offices, banks, a nano-tech lab) and we spoke to students who have worked in New York, Berlin Frankfurt and the South of France. This is a compulsory programme in year 10 and available to any interested student in the sixth form and can be arranged by the school, or by the individual.

Background and atmosphere: Established as a school with an international ethos in 1973 on the site of a former secondary school as part of the local authority's effort to enter into the spirit of Britain's entry into the European Union. At the time Marconi and the Ford Motor Company had operations nearby, employing international and repatriating British families whose children had become fluent in foreign languages, and who were seen as part of the target community for this new school.

Past its 40th anniversary, the buildings look their age – and don't date back to an era renowned for architectural beauty, but rather the typical purpose-built mid-20th century generic state school blue-plan design. They have been well used during these four decades; some of the rooms and public spaces are a bit worse for wear with stained carpets in need of replacement and one or two leaky skylights revealing themselves on the rainy day we visited. But this does not seem to dampen the community's sense of affection for the place, and there is ample evidence of ongoing efforts to expand in response to demand for growth, and to modernise, refurbish and redecorate the buildings over the years – including a new £2.7m building opened in 2015.

Despite lots of student traffic during break and lunch, the students still seem to try to take care of their space (no excessive litter or books and coats left lying about). New humanities and technology building features a Comm room – a video-conferencing centre where AE kids can link up with other schools worldwide. Sixth form student requests have resulted in Wifi provision being installed in their study area. They also have two spaces – one for quiet work and one for 'silent' independent or supervised work.

There are several computer labs around the school, many of which sixth formers can freely access at any time unless they are booked by classes. Younger students use the library. Projectors linked to teacher computers in most all of the classrooms, some interactive smartboards. During our visit we dropped in on year 7s preparing individual computer presentations to introduce themselves at the class assembly. Thanks to the well-liked head of maths, rooms in the maths block are numbered using prime numbers only, and our student guide pointed out a small library collection named after a former maths-loving student, who left his books of maths puzzles and challenges for today's students to borrow. (And they do.)

An outdoor amphitheatre provides a setting for drama or fair weather outdoor classes of all sorts. Throughout the school there are framed plaques and awards going back many years from a variety of organisations (eg World Challenge, International School Award from the British Council, etc), as well as flags representing all the students' nationalities.

Pastoral care, well-being and discipline: Despite it being large school, parents we spoke to were happy with the pastoral care and personal attention. They said that despite the occasional fight, bullying, or even the rare instance of drug taking, it is very controlled – 'students regard school generally as a no go area for drugs.' The kids know the boundaries and the school staff seem to know what is going on; they're accessible, communications are said to be very good, the school is quick to respond, every concern is taken seriously, and the follow up is consistent and ongoing.

The kids, too, tell us that their teachers are readily available; emails sent to a teacher at midnight about homework have been known to get a response five minutes later. It seems at least one teacher never sleeps.

Even parents with concerns were very happy with the way the school responded. 'There is a pastoral director for each year group and the kids know they are there for them. Whether it's because of a missing shoe, or the awkward confusion brought on by personal problems, they are like the school's own mums and dads.' The school is really good at fostering independence. 'They embrace it.'

The welcome extended to new students – from staff as well as other students – 'was a godsend', one parent told us. For students, especially British kids coming back from abroad, the adjustment is tough but the school makes it much easier. There were plenty of 'Can we help you?'; 'Do you know where you are going?' and 'Are you okay?' comments overheard in the first days of school. The students claim that after a few days, no one can tell the difference between the old and the new students.

The school is rightfully proud of the newly-opened 'sanctuary'. This is a quiet and lovely building set apart from the hustle and bustle of the other buildings for the purpose of contemplation, reflection, discussion and prayer. Funded by parent donations and inspired by the Dag Hammarskjöld meditation room at the UN headquarters in New York, it is a welcome oasis; our Muslim student guide said he'd be returning there in a few hours for his Friday noontime prayer. The school has no religious affiliation, but there is an inclusive attitude that helps foster respect and understanding for all faiths.

Pupils and parents: With around 35 nationalities, this place is truly a little UN community in the heart of Essex, and students come from far and wide to study here. Many people talked about the 'Anglo family' in reference to the kids but also the parent community. The students learn so much about each other, their cultures and beliefs, and parents say they benefit too. One parent remarked that in her daughter's class there are 19 mother tongues spoken. 'We've met families from Brazil, Singapore, Nigeria and France...and when the kids have a birthday party they are quick to remind us about each other's diets, saying one can't eat meat, another must eat halal, another is vegetarian..'

The great kids we met were adamant that their diversity is accepted, and being different is normal; that's what attracts many of them to the school. There is quite a wide socio-economic range of students from homes as diverse as Essex country mansions and inner-city flats. One parent described it as 'real world'. The head reputedly warns families on the first day that if you don't like allowing sleepovers in various parts of Essex and London, this is probably not the school for you, as the kids do arrange to see each other out of school hours. So many kids use the train to come and go that the school has designated 'train ambassadors' from year 11 and up who supervise their peers, helping to manage the crowd in a special waiting room created for the students within the station, which is a 10-15 minute walk from school through the picturesque village of Ingatestone.

The bus service run by a 'wonderful' private company covers a broad area. Parents say it even ran smoothly during extreme winter weather conditions.

A number commute by train from east London. We met one sixth former who'd been travelling up to two hours each way since year 7, and thought it definitely worth the commitment. These stories add up to some pretty compelling endorsements. The group of students we met seemed mature beyond their years, yet fun-loving, curious, and proud of their school. There was a genuine sense that these students really appreciate the education they are getting at Anglo European and value what the school and their teachers offer them. Quite refreshing, really.

The parents' association is active; lots of ways for parents to get involved, but no pressure to do so. An alumni association brings former students back for key events, but also for talks on careers, universities, and experiences abroad.

Past students include Douglas McCallum, MD of Ebay, David Abraham, chief exec of Channel 4, professional footballer James Harper, and some actors and musicians of note.

Entrance: Anglo European is an interesting blend of 'local' and 'international' school. As a state-funded comprehensive school (with academy status), they're obliged to enrol local students (feeder schools include Ingatestone and Fryerning Junior School, Margaretting Primary School and Mountnessing Primary School), but there is a priority scheme, with the first three categories being 'children looked after', locals within the three local parishes, and siblings.

Next is the 'international group', and here a point system comes into play with factors such as length of time abroad (and length of time since the overseas experience), ability to communicate in other languages, and extent of the cultural engagement in that context.

There is a very important point that families should know: Anglo European has a 'special dispensation' within the local authority that is highly unusual, possibly unique, within the UK state education system. In order to apply to Anglo European, families need not have proof of local residence. This is a huge bonus as it means that families moving to the UK from abroad seeking an international school can at least apply for places before they arrive.

The admissions secretary, described by parents as 'a gem', patiently explains the process to prospective families who may not be familiar with the system, and she is happy to respond to pleas of help from parents. She herself has lived abroad with her own children, so she is an empathetic ear to have at the end of the phone. Furthermore, with a mobile international community, and no fees to pay, places become available at very short notice, including mid-year. So, whereas the school is non-selective in terms of academics, it is looking for families who will embrace and support the international outlook.

Exit: Our student guide explained they have regular meetings with UCAS advisors from early in lower sixth to consider university options. There is a Higher Education Superfair with days dedicated to explaining the university admissions process. Students are encouraged to attend local university master classes to get a better understanding of what courses entail.

Enterprise education lessons within the citizenship curriculum provide well-organised learning opportunities working in conjunction with 50 local employers, trainers, and higher education institutions for students from year 7 upwards.

A good number of AES graduates go abroad to university, thanks in no small part to interest, awareness and richer CVs after so many AES study trips abroad. The university and careers counsellors are well-briefed on both UK and overseas universities. As one sixth former said, her decision to apply to a top Canadian university was based on the counsellor informing her that, with good IB results, she could qualify for a significant scholarship. Alumni are invited back to school events to talk about their experiences, so it seems that, undaunted by foreign languages or new cultural surroundings, these kids are confident to go out into the big wide world for the next stage of their education. The school is developing relationships with universities throughout Europe and beyond as shrewd internationally-minded Anglo European students have worked out that it is now cheaper to study abroad.

Ninety per cent of students go to university, the others go on gap years or take on apprenticeships. Three to Oxford in 2016 (Persian, chemistry and human sciences), with other destinations ranging from physics and astronomy at Sussex to international relations at St Andrews to mental health nursing at Surrey.

Those opting to leave Anglo European after GCSEs (around half) tend to go to local vocational colleges such as Writtle College for equine and agricultural courses, Colchester Institute, Chelmsford College, South Essex College.

Money matters: There are some low-key fundraising activities organised by the school, the parents' association and the students themselves as part of their philanthropic activities.

The bus service is available at extra cost (paid to bus contractors). The exchange visits incur additional charges, but parents feel they are well worth it, and there is even some means-tested financial support available so that nobody who wants to participate is prevented from doing so on financial grounds.

Remarks: As one parent puts it, you often hear that parents choose a particular school because it fits a certain kind of student. At Anglo European, there is something for everyone because they really appreciate each student's individuality. When the sixth formers were asked about this, the group endorsed the student who said, 'There is this perception that this school is only good for internationals or linguists, but that couldn't be further from the truth. Everyone benefits here.'

Ardingly College

College Road, Ardingly, Haywards Heath, West Sussex RH17 6SQ

Pupils: 984; 299 weekly/full boarders • Ages: 3–18 • Sixth form: 250 • C of E

Fees: Day £8,400 – £23,610; Boarding £12,780 – £32,130 pa

Tel: 01444 893000
Email: registrar@ardingly.com
Website: www.ardingly.com

Headmaster: Since 2014, Ben Figgis MA (Cantab). Previously deputy head at Oakham, where he also taught sixth form history and theory of knowledge. Has also been history teacher, housemaster and head of boarding at Abingdon. Before taking up teaching had a life in media, which he left after concerns about the ethical compromises involved in newsgathering. Keen to provide pupils with a modern education, and a world view. Enrichment is a word which comes up a lot – an interest and excitement in subjects is as important as achieving a particular grade.

Pupils are very enthusiastic about the head and say he's 'balanced' (in comparison to his predecessor who was apparently more hard line). Described by a parent as 'approachable', though still finding his feet; but she said her children all really like him. Loves theatre, and enjoys fly fishing. Just finished Paradise Postponed by John Mortimer. Married to Joanna.

Head of prep: Since 2007, Chris Calvey BEd (40s), previously deputy head at Bishopsgate. Energetic and approachable. There is a gentleness about him – it is easy to see that children would trust him very quickly: beaming smiles and chorused greetings as we toured the school. A parent described the head as 'quite incredible – he knows and cares about every child.' When they were being shown around the school, the head apparently asked a boy who was staring out the window, not paying attention, a question, which he couldn't answer – 'ah, you're thinking about that winning six on Wednesday...' He's really involved with the children; and pupils know their importance to him: recipients of an HMI (Head Master's Initials) school award can interrupt any meeting to receive their award from the head.

Mr Calvey has a good sense of fun – alas the two Segways he ordered to get around the vast grounds were sent back by a horrified bursar. Enjoys gardening and cricket – plays for the village team. The children vote at assembly for which book the head reads next: he's just finished The Fault is in Our Stars, and is about to start Divergence. Married to Nicola, with two children at the school.

Leaving in July 2017.

Academic matters: Independent learning and thought is the great strength in the prep. Children get as much choice as possible, younger children deciding the term's topic – year 2 chose circuses, and all subjects were taught through the circus medium, children learning their tables through juggling; year 3 chose chocolate and for their stunning starter a parcel from Willy Wonka arrived during assembly.

Older children are more constrained by the CE, but year 8s choose the books to study in English – and read many more books when they've made the choice, says the head. Parents like the removal of history, geography and RS from the CE – fewer exams mean less stress and hoop jumping for kids, who instead choose a topic which encompasses these subjects – one child chose the Mafia, another picked Vietnam, and parents are delighted as their children become absorbed and fascinated by their chosen topics.

They're always thinking and arguing, said one mum, not just downloading information off the net: the weekly thunk, posed by the head, is on the school website, and is often a moral question, such as would you like always to be happy? Pupils are encouraged to write a response, the emphasis on there being no right answer, but forming arguments to support your view. Teaching here can be really exciting, and one parent described her un-history minded child coming home enthusing about Thomas Becket and keen for a trip to Canterbury Cathedral, after dressing up as a monk and acting the 'will no one rid me of this troublesome priest?' part out on the playing fields.

There's a large new computer suite (year 4s are already programming apps),and iPads are in regular use. Two-thirds take their own, though iPads are available at school. A grateful parent commented on the help at parents' evening from sixth formers, who were available to help parents with the foreign lands of privacy settings and Instagram. iPad use is carefully policed – a 'poor comment' made by a boy about a girl in a class email chatroom was down within two hours, and she received a written apology from the boy.

Not much prep lower down in the school: years 3 and 4 just have reading, spelling and tables (much emphasis on reading here – the children write reviews of children's books for the local Waterstones, and have a super new library with colourful lava lamp style bubbly water containers alongside the books – to underline the joy of being in the library.) Year 6 has two prep sessions a week; years 7 and 8 have three, which are completed at school, to parents' delight.

One shell-shocked London prep parent, whose children were skilled at reasoning and maths but could do little else, glowed about the balanced curriculum and pastoral care at Ardingly: 'I could see them blossom before my eyes'. She admitted it was a jolt for her children, who were used to being spoon-fed in London, but commended the dedication shown by the staff in providing extra classes for her daughter to catch up. Children are set from year 5, and class sizes usually around 16. Two form entry from reception to year 4; three forms from years 5-8.

Learning support is available for mild special needs. A child may have two half hour support sessions in English and maths each week; more than that is not really do-able, says the head. A couple of children depart each year to find a school capable of providing more specialist support.

Excellent GCSE results, mostly climbing steadily each year. In 2016, 63 per cent of GCSEs A*/A. Subjects are almost uniformly excellent, with sciences and maths being popular high performers, and humanities also doing very well. Only performance in classical civilisation is comparatively underwhelming, though the few opting for Latin get mostly A*s and As.

IB points a very good 37 per pupil. A levels less startling: 44 per cent A*/A, 77 per cent A*-B. The international nature of the sixth form means a good showing in MFLs such as Chinese, Russian and German; but performance is less strong in other areas. A reasonable list of subjects on offer, although one parent said she would like to see the inclusion of some less purely academic subjects, such as sociology.

High take up of IB in this internationally minded school (40 per cent): they're in the top 10 IB schools in the UK, and very enthusiastic about it. The IB way of learning and thinking is here viewed as so beneficial that it has been adopted for A level pupils, who also study the IB core of extended essay, theory of knowledge, and action and service. A parent described her daughter as 'a bit miffed' at the extra work, but can see the benefits of the community service and mindfulness elements. She was rather more dubious about the extra written work, feeling that A levels on their own are quite enough for some stressed teens to cope with.

There are plans to develop science and technology to enhance pupils' preparation for undergraduate study – computer science is now on the timetable, and the head is particularly keen to make sure science options, usually dominated by boys, are appealing to girls.

Ardingly is keen to promote independent learning and one of the parents we spoke to said this was one of her favourite things about the school: she praised their promotion of independent research, thinking outside the box and examining information with a critical eye. 'It sparks their interest', she said. The skills for independent learning start in year 9 with iMind – not, as you might think, a new app, but how the brain functions, mindfulness and a personal project on any chosen subject (from what makes the perfect curry to what makes people interested in the paranormal). In an eye-catching project which illustrates their innovative thinking, pupils built a solar car which was entered for 3,000 km World Solar Challenge across Australia in 2015. Didn't complete the course but was a first for a school in Europe.

Pupils here are lively and interested in what they're doing. We joined an English lesson on The Importance of Being Earnest, and were impressed by an energetic teacher, and pupils' interested and thoughtful approach. A parent commented that she loved the 'relaxed open relationship with teachers', and this was evidently the case.

Learning support good for those with mild disorders. We spoke to a parent whose daughter has mild dyslexia, and whose LS with maths and English helped her get the grades she needed at GCSE. But pupils need to be able to cope on their own at A level.

Games, options, the arts: Grounds are extensive and gorgeous – it is succulently green all around. One of our guides glanced with familiar affection across the fields: one of them, the scene of a recent victory, had become his favourite place at school.

Strong sports department with county and national winners in hockey, football, fencing and golf, and plenty of individual winners too. Pupils were keen to point out that the glory is not exclusively for high performers: pupils in first XI all the way down to the sixth XI go on school tours, and receive school awards, although a parent said she felt that the greatest focus was on the senior A and B teams. A bit boy-heavy in emphasis, said a mum (the girls are probably delighted, she added dryly), with the girls only really excelling in hockey; but the head points out the same resources are put into girls' and boys' sports. A minimum two games sessions a week for all, and day pupils' kit often ends up being laundered at school.

Monday activities include minor sports such as horse riding, and sailing or rowing on the reservoir; and an ever-changing variety of other activities, from bee keeping and book binding to the interestingly named Ardinglay (it's a chicken club). DofE: lots do silver, and a few gold – in canoes and on horseback in recent years. It's not cliquey – the head relishes the fact that footballers about to play in the Boodles cup opted to spend the morning at the Ardingly national Shakespeare conference. You can choose to be very busy indeed; but pupils assured us that not everyone does, and that's fine too. The prep has use of the superb college facilities for games. Three games lessons a week and a PE lesson, which might be swimming, dance, or gym. Lots of clubs, including Lego, knitting, massage, Ardingly adventurers (own version of scouts for boys and girls) and tag rugby for the girls.

CCF is not popular here, to the chagrin of one of our guides, who clearly has a wonderful time. 'I think the parades put people off,' she said wistfully, 'but it's so much fun. There's a section attack on the headmaster's field this afternoon,' she added enthusiastically, as a cannon was wheeled into the quad. 'It just shoots blanks,' she said cheerfully, 'but it makes lots of noise.' It's difficult to argue with the evident joys of shooting a cannon. Almost worth the parades, one might think...

Large number of instrumental lessons and ensembles; in particular the 70-strong flourishing chapel choir which sings at cathedrals at home and abroad – and is a good outlet for exam stress. A vocal ensemble and the London Philharmonic visit to coach and inspire, and Ardingly hosts a concert series which stars national and international musicians.

Drama is popular, particularly with boys, to the delight of the head, who feels that creative art is too often the preserve of girls. They haven't got the posh modern theatre many independent schools boast, and one of the parents commented that the infrastructure could do with a bit of investment, but a gradual programme of modernisation is under way. Pupils perform at the Edinburgh fringe and home grown ArtsFest each year (a post-exam joy here), fun even for those not into drama, who do half day workshops on anything from making short films to mask mimes. Drama is super in the prep too, said a mum. Annual big production in a professional theatre, Oliver! the last one; anyone and everyone gets involved. Lots of singing at this school, with trips in the UK, and abroad; last year to Paris, next year to Rome.

Superb art department with a gallery packed with amazing work – we could happily have spent hours here appreciating the extraordinary creative work on view, showing that art students at Ardingly see life from all sorts of interesting angles, from butterfly dresses to a view inside a body which almost seemed to pulsate. There's a free range element to the GCSE, A level and IB art curricula, with students choosing which areas they wish to pursue; and you can see how much this freedom is appreciated by the quality of the work. Pupils can even have lessons from the sculptor in residence.

Boarding: Feels a bit like a university campus, with boarding houses reached by a path through a tranquil bluebell-lined woodland glade. Boarding houses are modern purpose-built blocks, decorated in house colours. Corridor walls covered in photos chosen by boarders, organised by year, up to lower sixth on the top floor. Very strong house feeling – all must compete in cross-country run, and apparently even reluctant runners are happy to compete for their house. A map of the world decorated with flags and photos shows where each boarder comes from in this truly cosmopolitan school; and there's a list of names of older students from whom youngsters can seek academic help. There's a teacher on duty every night too, but one boy said that older pupils can often help better – they explain things in a different way.

Children may board from year 3, and there are currently 45 flexi boarders in the prep. All prep boarders go home for weekends, but may return on Sunday night (almost all return on Monday, though). Boarding accommodation is immediately above the prep school, rooms varying in size: there's a huge barn-like bedroom for 10 – very popular, with a few letters remaining of the big notice telling boys not to stand up on the top bunks – to smaller rooms for two or four. Houseparents (who are 'lovely', said a parent) are situated in between the boys and girls. Girls' rooms are rather pinker, and (whimsically) named by the girls: Narnia, Pandora and Fantasia (the boys inherited their rather more feisty dormitory names – Hogsmeade, Camelot and Helmsdeep). Showers and basins are all modern and spotless – the kids take good care of them.

There is a feeling of child ownership about these dormitories – it is very much their domain, and it would be easy to feel at home here. Comfy common rooms with squashy sofas and bean bags, and more upright rooms with tables and chairs for working. The girls and boys run their own small tuckshop with mini versions of sweets, where they are allowed to spend their pocket money. The strong community is evident – parents say older pupils look out for the younger ones, and some volunteer for community service, which involves getting up an hour early to help make breakfast or pick up litter. Children generally keep in touch with home by email. They can phone (from the school phone), but there's no point in taking mobiles because there's no reception anyway, said a mum diplomatically.

Parents of senior school boarders were full of praise: one said all her children wanted to board, and really enjoy it. The boarding master responds promptly to emails, and she likes the easy mix between boarders and day pupils.

Rooms for two to four younger boarders, with singles for older pupils. A housemaster admitted rooms are on the spartan side, being limited to bunks, desks and wardrobes; but said he doesn't want pupils lingering in bedrooms: they are for sleeping and studying, and the rest of time should be spent in the common room: spacious, squashy leather sofas, TV, pool, table football, the Times and Telegraph. Girls' houses recently refurbished. Brew rooms (kitchens) on each corridor, and one equipped with oven for more serious culinary matters (used under supervision). Lower sixth supervise youngsters' studying and bedtime rituals, studying supervision being much preferable, said one of our guides, with small shudder at the thought of bedtime duty (they are given advice about how to manage this).

Activities and sports on Saturday – recently a night of cowboy fun complete with hired rodeo bull; the head of boarding was moving with due care for bruises. Sundays for relaxation (gym and pool are open), with a trip out every three weeks. There's a tremendously popular Sunday shuttle to Sainsbury's, with each year group getting £50 for ingredients: serious cooking follows. No making their own breakfast though: kitchens are locked to ensure pupils go to the dining hall for a proper breakfast – 'no surviving on just toast until lunchtime.' Each floor has a disabled loo and lift access.

Around half of boarders are overseas students, including expats, so there's no dominant country and no general exodus at weekends. Every Wednesday the blog is updated to communicate boarders' latest doings to parents. Pupils use own laptops to keep in touch – letter writing is largely a thing of the past here.

Upper sixth has their own boarding house – like Premier Inn, suggested a member of staff; there is some similarity, though we've never seen a Premier Inn in such a lovely setting; or with such a nice gym. Super en suite study bedrooms, kitchens, huge common room, which is divided at 10pm between boys and girls, and opens at 7am. There's even a bar (two beers or two wines limit) but not many choose to drink. Encouraged to do own laundry– some actually do.

Background and atmosphere: Not as stiff and traditional as the cream paper in the guide for parents would suggest. One parent chose the school because the children who go there seem so 'normal', and for the strong sense of community. There's no held breath tension in the corridors here: pupils are relaxed and happy, with an outward looking politeness (pupils enquired after reviewer's journey etc – it doesn't often happen). It's not a leap to your feet school, but there was a genuine friendliness in the courtesy and smiles we encountered on our tour.

Charming red-brick buildings form the older parts of the school, whose atmosphere lacks the rarefied feel which often goes with the presence of quads. Modern and rather nondescript buildings house the music and boarding houses; but the green surrounds offer ample distracting beauty. One of the favourite places of our guides was the terrace, with its stunning views over the Sussex countryside; just below lies the head's garden, viewed longingly by both pupils and the head of prep – it's clearly Eden here.

This Woodard school was originally for the children of clergy; and it is no surprise that there is a clear religious structure here, with a weekly communion service in the chapel for all (including non-believers and other faiths). High church with bells and smells, and what one parent called 'some obscure hymns'. The parents we spoke to liked the weekly service, one saying she felt it was important for children to develop the ability to sit still, be silent and respectful: 'you can hear a pin drop,' she said approvingly. Another, while liking it herself, admitted her children thought it was boring, and said the newish head is revisiting the ethos of chapel with pupils. The head believes there's a value in exposing pupils to chapel, but there is no expectation of them adopting Christianity –'pupils need to feel comfortable and welcome.' Notably, divinity is joined by philosophy in the curriculum, and in the latest edition of Logos, the school magazine, there are articles on the Bible and feminism, and whether the Christian tradition ever treated women with respect. The Sophos philosophical debating club regularly debates pupil chosen topics such as life after death. This is not a school for unquestioning acceptance, and this critical eye extends to its founding Christian ethos.

Pre-prep, headed by Hilary Nawrocka since 2010, is down the lane in the old Ardingly farmhouse. Low-slung farm buildings with beamed ceilings on three sides of the farmyard, a long broad corridor library running the length of one building, so children are always moving past books. Reception dozed peacefully to music at rest time, a lively year 2 were in a circle on the floor: huge excitement as they took it in turns to pull an item from the bag to identify a story. Nursery class occupies the old pig sty, and takes pre-nursery tinies who have just turned 2. Free flow inside and out for nursery and reception. Lots of outside equipment, and a magical place to sit in the felled tree carved into seats and badgers. Weekly forest school lessons for nursery to year 3; forest club for the rest of prep.

Pastoral care, well-being and discipline: Bullying is taken seriously in the prep, and may result in exclusion. A mum whose son was bullied confirmed that the school resolved the matter thoroughly and quickly, and there was no recurrence. Her son received a written apology from the perpetrators by morning break on the day she complained. Children may also be excluded for continuously naughty and disruptive behaviour, but the school tries to avoid using the label exclusion – 'these children just need more support than we can give them,' says the head.

One parent, who loves the feeling of community at the school, said her favourite memory was of the taking of the school photo, 700 children, squeezing onto a stand. Nursery children were last up, crying and upset by the whole exercise. The older children spontaneously started singing nursery rhythms, and within a few rhymes the little ones were laughing and clapping along.

Pastoral care is 'outstanding,' said one parent; 'paramount,' said another, who said the ability to cater well for each child's individual needs is the best thing about the school. What's more, 'they take on difficult kids from other schools and bring them into line.'

Eudaimonia, not a rare disease, but 'human flourishing' al la Aristotle (PHSE to the rest of us) is part of the curriculum throughout senior school. Encompasses the usual sex, drugs and internet warnings; but also friendship, positive thinking and the wonder of every individual.

Firm line on bullying: pupils are encouraged to whistleblow, and expulsions will follow if the situation's unresolvable, say pupils, who also commented on some expulsions a few years ago for smoking dope, which they completely supported – 'we wouldn't have wanted them here,' they said in shocked voices.

The head is clearly just as principled as his predecessor, and has expelled a pupil for being rude and disrespectful to a member of the catering staff. But he seems more likely to understand that children experiment and less likely to damn

A

them for doing so: those who come clean about offences and promise not to reoffend are likely to have a second chance.

Pupils choose their own tutor, whom they meet fortnightly to ensure individual needs are being met – for example in timetables or teaching methods. However, the head also has a strong belief in the values of service and community, and is wary of growing expectations from customer parents to have school life flexed to suit their children. Some requests are reasonable, but there is some danger that children who always having things adjusted to their needs feel everything will always revolve around them: the values of living in and adapting to a community need to be understood.

There's an on campus chaplain and independent listener for those who need to talk through problems confidentially.

The community here is very strong, say parents, which is reflected in the reward structure: the usual system for effort and attainment, but with extra emphasis on becoming a good citizen: ACES (Ardingly Citizenship Exemplary Student award) is given to pupils whose good behaviour models the justice and compassion desired for all pupils at Ardingly. Good citizenship is the avenue for year 8 pupils to achieve monitor and prefect status.

Pupils and parents: Thirty different nationalities in the school, with 28 per cent of pupils coming from overseas. The head deliberately manages the numbers of overseas students, from around 18 per cent in Shell (year 9), up to a third in upper sixth, increasing diversity and international thought as students get stuck into the IB.

Parents include many London professionals, expats, and foreign office. 'There is wealth in the school, but it has a down to earth quality.' There's someone topping up fees by working in Sainsbury's; and then there's a few more who buy their new four wheel drive every February when it's bonus time. Not a posh school, said a parent, although some are incredibly wealthy. The Russian pupil who required an armed guard was refused a place.

Communication is excellent – if anything they over-communicate, said a prep school parent. Easy access to teacher or head with problems. Parents receive reports five times a year which detail effort and attainment. Reports issued in the middle of terms please parents, who can then talk about the contents with teachers –'it makes such a difference.' The senior school head's introduced a weekly email telling parents what's going on, which is much appreciated. Parents are confident they could approach a form tutor or head of house with a problem.

Old Ardinians include racing driver Mike Hawthorn, Ian Hislop, composer Stephen Oliver, actors Terry-Thomas and Alan Howard.

Entrance: Most join the prep in nursery (pre-nursery from age 2), year 3 and year 7, with a scattering across the other year groups. Taster day with assessment of reading, spelling, vocab and maths. Doesn't accept those performing below their age in all tests, and below the standardised performance in maths. For year 7 and 8, entrance exams in English, maths, verbal reasoning and reading, and an interview with the head.

Need 55 per cent at CE, 110 CAT test for the senior school. Written assessments in English, maths and verbal reasoning, and interview with the head. Overseas students need to have fluent English, and pass the same assessments as English counterparts.

Entrance to the sixth requires six or more grade B passes at GCSE, including at least a C in English and maths.

Exit: Majority from the prep move up to the senior school, handful departing elsewhere – recently Brighton College, Wellington and Hurst. Common entrance in all subjects except humanities. Need to pass core subjects to move up.

Some 30 per cent leave after GCSEs, mostly for local sixth form colleges. Lots of sixth form leavers to Russell group universities eg UCL, Exeter, Manchester; two to Oxford in 2016, plus universities in the US, Hong Kong, China and Germany.

Money matters: Over a third of pupils on some sort of support or bursary. Once a prospective pupil gets a scholarship, the level of support depends on need, and is not restricted by the numbers already in receipt of scholarships.

Remarks: A strong and caring community which finds a balance between excellent pastoral care and academic achievement. This modern school with its focus on independent thought would suit those with a broad outlook and interests.

Ashdown House School

15

Forest Row, East Sussex RH18 5JY

Pupils: 137; 88 boys, 49 girls; 97 full and 16 flexi boarders • Ages: 4–13 • C of E

Fees: Day £8,010 – £19,050; Boarding £26,070 pa

Tel: 01342 822574
Email: secretary@ashdownhouse.com
Website: www.ashdownhouse.co.uk

Headmaster: Since 2012, Haydon Moore, married to Annie, with three children, all of whom attend or attended Ashdown House. Mr Moore has had a long relationship with Ashdown House, teaching here since 2002. The head's aim is for pupils to leave with an appreciation of the real world: they are privileged, but need to have their feet firmly on the ground, and show it in a well mannered respect for all those around them, from the head to the school cleaners.

Much liked by pupils, who evidently take his words to heart: he says a joke is only funny if everyone is laughing, one pupil told us seriously. 'He's nice'; 'he listens'; 'I could talk to him about anything'. Parents say: 'The head is very empowering... encourages children to do something that frightens them – love him'; 'very approachable, great relationship with children'.

Entrance: Steady intake all the way through, many coming from local big preps where they are unhappy and 'not flourishing', and others who are relocating from London. Foreign nationals only if English is up to scratch.

Entrance by interview with head and ed psychologist report if necessary. Not selective.

Exit: Parents want a 'named' school, says the head. Some feeling of an expert matchmaking service in the way in which this head matches up pupils with senior schools: 'the biggest and best thing we do,' said the head, who knows the public schools at an individual house level, so he knows where each pupil would fit best and flourish. A subtle art.

Eton, Rugby, Harrow, Benenden et al.

Remarks: 'Slow – free range children and animals', says a sign on the drive, and this is quickly proved by wellied children noisily playing amongst the rhododendrons, Charles and Camilla (turkeys) strolling amongst them. 'There's a lovely feeling of coming home', said a parent.

The rather splendid main house, with its elegant columns, was designed by the Yorkshireman who went on to design the

White House; but here the oval office is a lobby full of wellies and ceramics. 'If they're a long way from home', said a parent in the Cayman Islands, 'you want small school with nice homey feel about it', and this school certainly has that.

'Not a school who focus on petty things', said a parent, 'like top buttons, ties and shiny shoes. It concentrates on the important things, like kindness and being able to talk to grown ups and hold open doors'. Another parent told us that when they were shown around the school, their pupil guides disappeared. The head came out to look for them, and pointed up a tree, where the guides' legs dangled, finished in scuffed shoes. 'Perfect'.

'It is structured – but doesn't look like it. When you walk in, kids are running around everywhere', a parent commented, and the kids say the best thing about school is the freedom. 'In your free time you can go anywhere', said one, including the woods: they're not allowed near the pond or the pit of death (a muddy sink hole), but can climb trees, 'even if you break your arm'. Pupils hone their skills in the Larva Tree and the Spaghetti Tree, progressing to the Love Tree (pupils scratch name of their beloved into the top of the trunk). Not the Welly (Wellingtonia), 100ft+, out of bounds since a pupil, aptly named Everest, made it to the top a few years ago. 'Not cotton wool and cosset', said a parent approvingly. 'They let children take risks and explore their environment'.

Freedom extends to access: there are keypads everywhere, but all the doors are left open during the working day – 'we trust the children', said the head. 'You can wander in, but I don't think anyone ever does', said a parent.

C of E, but it's more about kindness, willingness and helpfulness, say parents; they welcome pupils of any or no faith, and explore many. A parent described arriving at school the other day to see the head sitting barefoot on the lawn with some pupils humming – 'it was a Buddhist thing I think...'

'Academically strong – all sorts of different types thrive there', said a parent. Pupils are streamed from year 6 upwards. Not a frenzied approach to work, and homework pressure is not excessive – year 8, an hour a day, year 7, 45 minutes. And with this calm measured approach, Ashdown feeds top public schools.

Lessons are generally fun, say pupils: not Latin, but DT is extremely popular, and geography and science also got a mention as really enjoyable subjects. Pupils enjoy a half a term at Château Sauveterre to improve their French, and science, geography and outdoor pursuits trips to the Old Malthouse in Dorset.

There's not the usual emphasis on IT -'not the driving force', said the head firmly; though iPads are available as an enabling tool in lessons. Only year 3 has an interactive board – the rest of the school does very well with white boards and projectors. 'Get lost in a book, not a computer game', exhorts the head. For pupils who like playing computer games, they can – but only if have programmed it themselves first.

Class sizes 10, max 15. If numbers reach 18, a class will be split in two. Saturday school is optional for year 3, and compulsory thereafter: lessons until 11, then clubs and matches. The weekend is just a couple more working days for staff, which parents feel is fantastic – 'staff are the school's biggest asset'; 'they're dedicated, like spending time with the kids'; 'they make lessons exciting and interesting'.

Learning support – learning enhancement here – is accessible to all. Wouldn't suit those with severe special needs, but prides itself on helping those with mild dyslexia extremely well, and has successfully helped a profoundly deaf pupil. Learning support is charged as an extra.

Classrooms vary from modern, light and smart in the Jungle block to old and bit shabby, but perfectly functional. Pre-prep (14 pupils) has recently moved into a refurbished bungalow – light and colourful, with trainers in a scruffy tumble on the floor and laminated poppy handprints in flower bed.

Drama is described by a parent as 'an absolute dream', explaining that they don't take it too seriously: lines are handed out the week before, so if you fluff up, no one minds – but it's very good. Everyone's involved – backstage and lighting, if not performing. Farce is popular, as is the annual Mock Trial.

Clubs for evenings and weekends include gardening, cookery, poker and a gentleman's club for the first XV (they learn how to iron a shirt). Strolling through the dance studio (also used for discos and exams), we saw something that resembled a mangled skateboard – apparently the head was rip sticking with kids the evening before.

Art is everywhere – not just the best stuff – with the artist's name dangling on a luggage label from the picture. One pupil said her favourite place in school is the art room: 'cosy... you're not forced to be hard working...it feels free'.

Several pupils said they were attracted to school for the sports; it's odd when you consider this is a small school which is rarely able to field winning teams against big schools. '[You're] not allowed to be a bad loser', said a parent. They play sport every afternoon here, seriously and with much enthusiasm, polo and golf featuring amongst the usual, with the girls also playing football, and cricket (as a club). 'As long as enough pupils to put together a netball team, it doesn't matter there aren't ABC teams – purpose and dedication are installed...', said a parent.

'It's a traditional school', said the head, 'but very, very supportive'. Parents commented happily on his partnership with wife Annie who they say has a leading role in pastoral care, and knows every child.

A parent described the 'extraordinary care' of their son while his brother had heart surgery, and the school's amazing care of both boys subsequently: 'they were willing to take our son... who was a walking time bomb. Ashdown goes out of its way to keep children safe'.

Both pupils and parents told us how good Ashdown is at helping problem children: 'Children who have had a terrible time at other places and been bullied or expelled are turned around by Ashdown', said a parent; 'They don't give up on anyone', confirmed a pupil.

They're very supportive of mental health here, particularly aware of the anxiety that kids can suffer near CE. Children are divided into groups with a supportive mentor and learning support will provide extra help to anyone who needs it, with extra tutoring available in maths and English – 'fantastic', said a grateful parent. For those who are really worried, there is an art therapist and a baking counsellor – 'because no child wants to just sit and talk to someone about their problems', said the head. A CBT counsellor helps pupils by Skype, giving them practical exercises to help them cope with exam stress.

Parents told us incidences of bullying are dealt with by the school 'quickly and efficiently'. 'They don't put up with any nonsense at all'. Pupils say if you behave really badly, you get sent to Mr Moore – 'he doesn't shout', said one boy appreciably. Punishment is a 'pause for thought' (detention). Parents said children could go to anyone with a problem – teacher, form tutor, matron – would get immediate responses from all. Can and will speak to the head if needed – 'very flexible'.

Communication is good, and parents appreciate the school office being open on Saturday, though views vary on school administration, from 'brilliant' to 'a bit dodgy', and another thought that a greater use of social media could make a more efficient school – 'if matches are cancelled, I would like to know'.

'A true boarding school', said one parent, 'with a seven days a week presence'. Nearly 100 full time boarders, flexi-boarders on regular nights, with designated beds. Boarding is a 'way of life,' says the head, in tones of deep dedication; the boarding community takes priority here, and half the staff live on site. A parent thought that it would have been a shock to go directly to boarding senior school, and Ashdown is a 'cosy [first] experience of boarding...' Two fixed exeats a term, and two floating, 'but the children never want to take them', said a parent; 'there are so many things on at the weekend'.

'No rules for rules sake', says the head, who accommodates parents who want irregular contact with their children; for instance, when Foreign Office parents are on tour, Ashdown will care for their kids full time, but when parents are home they can pop in and take the kids out for pizza.

Rules do have their place in the day-to-day mechanics of boarding, which is very structured – much like having strict but kind parents who know the importance of a good night's sleep. 'Not a sleepover atmosphere...', says head. Homesickness is addressed with a mixture of comforting and keeping you busy.

Boarding accommodation is comfortable, though not plush: dorms for 6-12 in bunks and singles with duvets from home, decent bathrooms and friendly common rooms with TV, water cooler, ample supply of fruit and books. Matron can make toast for those who ask. Photos all over corridors – 'I adore this', enthused one parent.

Pupils write a proper letter home every week – 'quite sweet,' said a parent – and parents can phone in to the landings between 7-8pm. The head keeps all devices in his study, but pupils can ask for their mobiles to call parents or use the phone room. Contact home for overseas pupils is arranged taking into account time differences – one pupil leaves morning lessons to Skype her parents each week.

Everyone agrees that the food is delicious and it is no surprise that the chef also runs a restaurant. He has reduced the salt and sugar in food, and bottles of ketchup, used to happy excess by pupils, have been replaced by a one sachet policy. Pupils would like a tuck shop: it's just one chocolate bar on Sundays at this health conscious school. 'There are no fat children here', said a parent bluntly.

Would suit pretty much anyone, think parents, from the over-assertive (whom the school will mellow) to the quiet and shy ('If you can play one note on the oboe, you'll still be in the concert'). 'A sadistic bully would probably be asked to leave though', said one parent, on further consideration. Pupils thought this school would not suit someone who doesn't try hard. But it's not, they say, a school which expels people – 'they give people a chance'.

Ashdown families are generally traditional, wealthy and established. Not many new Porches here. Some 20 per cent from overseas. No scholarships, but can support families if things go wrong.

Ashfold School

Dorton House, Dorton, Aylesbury, Buckinghamshire HP18 9NG

Pupils: 270; 65 flexi boarders (Monday to Thursday) • Ages: 3-13 (boarding from 9)

Fees: Day £6,915 – £15,885; Weekly boarding £19,035 pa

Tel: 01844 238237
Email: registrar@ashfoldschool.co.uk
Website: www.ashfoldschool.co.uk

Headmaster: Since 1997, Mr Michael Chitty (50s). Educated at Clifton College, Bristol then Exeter University where he read economics before following generations of forefathers to Sandhurst. First bitten by the teaching bug on his gap year in Kenya, where he was a student teacher at The Banda School and later, following an army career that saw him rise to the rank of Captain in the Queen's Royal Irish Hussars via Equerry to HRH Prince Philip, when he returned to Sandhurst as officer instructor.

Landed squarely on his feet in his first teaching position at Stowe School, where he taught economics, politics and European studies, always with an eye to his main ambition of becoming a prep school head. Given role of 'adjutant' to ease communications between the head's office, bursary and staff common room before being appointed housemaster of Grenville House (after which he later named one of his two black labradors). Headhunted after six years to become head of Ashfold, which he transformed with his energy, enthusiasm and clear vision. No longer teaches, although he does share boarding duties, but parents say he is 'very hands on' and he still coaches rugby, hockey and cricket teams, as well as clay pigeon and.22 rifle shooting teams, sits with children at lunch times and is always visible at matches and other school events.

Prospective parents unlikely to meet many heads whose former jobs include 'deployment of the British army worldwide' and Chitty does not disappoint, with his overwhelmingly positive, driven – and some might say military – approach to managing his school. An animated and dynamic communicator, he likes to keep up to date with car park chit chat via parents. Says he is running a 'very together school,' and is now 'in a position to do some very exciting stuff.' Appointment of a female deputy has boosted girls' numbers and brought fresh ideas.

Lives in a house on site – as do around 15 staff – with wife Louise, a barrister. Two grown up children, now working, come back for regular visits and often join their parents at their second home near Cirencester, where they enjoy spending weekends sailing, walking dogs and occasionally indulging a passion for cricket.

Entrance: Non-selective, with the majority joining reception from the nursery. Prospective pupils for all year groups invited to spend a day in school for assessment only. Head likes children from state primaries to join by year 2 and will hold places for them to this point. From year 3, places are harder to come by, with waiting lists for most year groups.

Exit: Leavers to a wide variety of schools, with about 50 per cent heading off to board most years. Popular co-ed choices include St Edward's Oxford, Rugby and Stowe with Headington popular for girls and the most able boys opting for Abingdon or Magdalen College. Impressive scholarship record – on average, more than 40 per cent of leavers have won scholarships or awards to their senior schools over the last nine years. Head takes care to place less academic children in next schools where they can shine. Very few to state maintained grammars (just a couple each year), with head discouraging 11 plus unless for financial reasons.

Remarks: The cross country drive through rolling hills and farmland and rising fear that the satnav is playing tricks on you is well worth it for the first sight of Ashfold's stunning Jacobean mansion set in 33 acres of fields and woodland. Rugby pitches in the foreground give the impression of a traditional boys' prep but behind the magnificent building are three hard tennis courts, a well maintained, heated outdoor pool, full size Astroturf, netball courts and a lovely adventure playground, proving that that the girls who make up roughly 40 per cent of the school population are well catered for and now integral to the culture of the school.

Wood panelling, winding staircases and cobbled stable blocks bring Hogwarts to mind, and rosy cheeked, windswept and slightly dishevelled children litter the grassy play areas, giving an overall impression of an idyllic country school – worlds apart from the urban London schools many of its commuter families have left behind. Lacks some of the dazzling showcase facilities boasted by many preps, but every part of the campus is put to excellent use (and in the words of one parent: 'you're a bit restricted with a grade I listing') and the overall effect is of an inspiring, functional and nurturing environment, which, in the head's words, 'celebrates children.'

Purpose-built pre-prep building houses nursery to year 2 in a light, spacious and colourful setting with its own well-equipped playground and large field, complete with bug hotel. Pre-prep children well integrated into the main school, sharing its assembly space (often the village church, situated on site), sports hall and playing fields. Junior department housed in main wing of house, while most senior lessons take place in recently renovated courtyard classrooms.

Largely rural catchment from surrounding villages, with majority of children from hard-working middle class families ('hardly any old money,' said one parent), who travel up to 30 minutes to school. Very few from non-Caucasian families. School keen to prove its country credentials with a flourishing veg patch tended by pupils and weekend challenges set for families, resulting in the presentation of the school's 'countryside certificate' on completion of all 30. Small number of scholarships, with the Stowe-Ashfold scholarship and the Tudor Hall-Ashfold scholarship covering 100 per cent of fees and other awards up to 30 per cent, available for pupils 'who show outstanding academic, artistic, sporting, musical or all-round ability' for the last two years at the school.

Girls have been part of the furniture at Ashfold since the 1980s and now less than 40 per cent are siblings of boys. Although they make up 40 per cent of the total cohort, numbers vary between year groups and are very small in some (as low as three in a class), which is 'a bit of a downside,' according to parents. In some year groups, however, girls actually outnumber boys and parents add that all children get the same opportunities, regardless of gender. School addressing gender balance with increased girl-focused activities such as dance, equestrian and girls' clubs; head feels that current boy:girl ratio is ideal.

Whether arty, sporty, or musical, there's something for every child here ('they look at the child as an individual,' say parents) and academics are solid all round too. Class sizes are small. French with a specialist teacher from 7 and Latin from 9. Some mutterings from parents that they would like an earlier introduction to languages. No setting until last two years 'to allow for the genders' different rates of development,' according to head. Pupils entirely specialist taught from year 4 and move around the school for different subjects from thereon. All children screened for dyslexia aged 7 or whenever they join the school. Currently around 12 per cent of pupils under the SENCo for mild needs (SpLD, dyslexia or dyspraxia). In class support and small group work with a learning support assistant covered by fees. One-to-one lessons with the school's SEN specialist charged as extra.

Parents find channels of communication excellent and are able to email class teachers – who they describe as 'a really talented bunch' – directly with queries or issues. Recent introduction of e-learning online assessments for all children from year 3 up have 'really freed up teachers to focus on creative lesson planning,' says head.

High standard of art on show in and around a lovely bright art room; 'you can't usually see the ceiling for work,' said the head of department when we visited (it was the first week in September), although it would be nice to see a bit more of the pupils' work festooning the walls around the rest of the school. Brand new £1.3m art and design centre opened in January 2016 with facilities for DT, cookery, art, ceramics and textiles.

Almost 60 per cent of pupils learn a musical instrument peripatetically, inspired by the head of music (described by parents as 'magnificent'), a surprisingly young addition to the Ashfold team who doubles as a rugby coach and has 'changed the kids' perceptions of music,' say parents, by injecting the school with lively doses of musical theatre. He even had head singing Greased Lightning (actions and all) in a staff and parents' choir recital. Waiting lists for all choirs underscore the school's renewed collective passion in this area and all pre-prep children learn the violin and recorder from year 1. Lots going on in the drama department too, with recent productions including Sherlock Holmes and The Secret of Immortality and The Wind in the Willows, and plans in the pipeline for more musical productions.

Once children reach the prep school they have an extended day, ending at either 5 or 6pm, depending on age. This enables the curriculum to include daily sport for all, which although adored by most is 'a struggle' for some of the less sporty ones, according to parents. All the usual suspects played to a good level but head exceptionally proud of his U13 girls' hockey team which won the IAPS championship recently and the clay shooting team, also IAPs U12 and U13 champions and runners up at the British Schools and Young Shots Clay Shooting Championships in 2016. He puts this and other sporting successes down to a 'real focus on coaching' with specialist talent brought in to coach rugby, hockey, netball and football (with an ex-Oxford United coach). Gymnastics and indoor games take place in a good sized sports hall incorporating wonderful changing facilities – 'with hot showers,' the head assures. From year 6, those demonstrating talent in other areas are selected to join scholars' groups (academic, art, drama et al) in place of time allocated to games.

Boarding allowed from year 5, where children can stay for supper after games, then take part in one of a multitude of activities on offer (from rifle shooting or fishing to chess and cookery). Given that this takes them up to 8pm it's a bit of a no brainer for parents of children keen to sample boarding life, and up to 30 children board on any given night. Dorms of up to seven beds have been recently revamped and provide spacious, comfortable accommodation in the mansion, girls at one end of the building, boys at the other. Head says, 'it's proper boarding, not a sleepover,' and boarders sleep in the same bed on their chosen boarding nights. Newly refurbed boarders' common rooms, complete with pool table, two flat screen TVs and comfy sofas, provide a home from home feel and open onto the houseparents' accommodation. No mobile phones, iPods or other gadgets allowed with the exception of Kindles – a very popular move with parents. Lights out at 9.30pm and cooked breakfasts are a hit.

School has a Christian ethos but accepts other denominations. Rightfully proud of its pastoral care with parents reporting 'very clear lines of escalation' should things ever go wrong. Three houses (Gryphons, Lions and Dragons) compete in lots of eagerly contested competitions (parents describe the standard of work in the inter-house art competition as 'unbelievable') with the each term culminating in a house cup. Pre-prep pupils presented with star of the week awards for effort and attainment in weekly assemblies. Head boy and girl chosen at the beginning of year 8 amid great excitement; rest of year 8 are all prefects. Head clear that 'leadership is about serving others,' and says he won't have any arrogance in the school, on occasion passing over obvious macho choices for head boy for 'a lovely gentleman with outstanding manners.'

No school buses as head wants parents to bring children into school to keep lines of communication open: 'If a child has had a sleepless night, for example, we want to know about it,' he says.

A

Ashford School

East Hill, Ashford, Kent TN24 8PB

Pupils: 909; 179 boarders • Ages: 3-18 (boarding from year 6) • Sixth form: 162

Fees: Day £8,925 – £16,800; Boarding £29,250 – £36,999 pa

Tel: 01233 625171
Email: registrar@ashfordschool.co.uk
Website: www.ashfordschool.co.uk

Headmaster: Since 2005, Mr Michael Buchanan (50s) BSc PGCE NPQH. Educated at Downside and King's College London, where he read physics and trained as a teacher. Previously spent 10 years at Highgate School in north London, where he left as principal deputy head. Part of his brief there was to bring in co-education, and he has done a similar job at Ashford with great success. Previously head of sixth form at Royal Grammar School, Guildford. Businesslike and charming, he has a passion for physics, sport and choral music – he is a highly experienced, lead ISI inspector. 'Very approachable and a good communicator and you know who is in charge', according to one parent. Still teaches and referees sport when he can. Married with two daughters who attended the school; his wife works for a bank in London. He says the whole family felt welcomed from the moment they arrived at Ashford.

He is a 'very good motivator', according to one former pupil, and has introduced the Adventurous Learning programme that is all about taking people – staff and children alike – out of their comfort zone and challenging in all areas, personal as well as academic. It might be trying something new like speaking in front of the whole class and then the whole school. He 'wants children to develop as self reliant all-rounders who have a sense of responsibility, compassion and teamwork and the resilience to cope with adversity'. He also wants pupils to take responsibility for their own learning and to feel able to make mistakes. Likes every sort of success to be rewarded and feels that learning should be fun. Head and staff lead by example: Mr Buchanan has taken up the euphonium and 40 teachers have taken up other musical instruments to remind themselves what it feels like to be a pupil.

The school has grown by over 150 since he arrived, helped by the massive building boom in Ashford and the fast rail link to St Pancras. He is gradually replacing the ageing school buildings at the same time as driving the rise in academic standards.

Head of prep school: Since 2001 Mr Richard Yeates (50s). Joined the senior school as deputy head in 2000 and became headmaster of the prep a year later. Educated at Exeter University and The Royal College of Music. Previously director of music at King's Hall, Taunton and housemaster at King's College, Taunton as well as being master in charge of the 1st XI cricket. He is also an ISI inspector. His wife is head of the nursery at Ashford, and they have three children who attended the senior school and are now at university or beyond. Mr Yeates is a good communicator and is popular and highly respected by parents and children alike. He believes that the breadth of education offered by his school 'unlocks ability' and enables children to flourish. The school is his home and visitors are welcomed into his house – all adds to the cosy family atmosphere. Music, golf, travel and fine wine are his extracurricular passions.

Academic matters: Pupils set in maths and English from year 3 but plenty of movement between sets and scholarship children are taught within the class. Lessons seem to be enjoyable and interesting; our guide remarked, 'I have never been a fan of science but they make it such good fun'. Accelerated reading programme known as the Millionaire Club has been a great success for keen and reluctant readers alike. Children have to choose a book and do a quiz, and then their name is put on a board. Anyone who reads a million words gets a hoodie. Soundswrite, a first phonics programme, is used to teach reading and writing in the pre-prep. About 20 children have significant learning difficulties, one or two with mild Asperger's or dyslexia, and some who need help with organisational skills. There is one full-time SEN teacher in the prep plus several teaching assistants and a specialist dyslexia teacher. School very supportive of those who do not find academic work easy, so long as they are ultimately likely to be able to take GCSEs.

Broad intake, results improving year on year. In 2016, 71 per cent A*/B and 46 per cent A*/A at A level; at GCSE, 48 per cent A*/A. Particularly good results in science and maths. Everyone takes separate sciences from Year 7. All students learn two languages chosen from Spanish, German and French; German most popular. Pupils from abroad also encouraged to take GCSE in their first language eg Chinese or Dutch. Good range of subjects at A level including Chinese, business studies, psychology, textiles, sports studies and drama. In sixth form Russian, German and Spanish offered as a business language (basic language skills, mostly conversation). Very accommodating timetable and school willing to offer a subject to only a handful of students. Digital literacy programme for year 7. A very tech savvy school – radio voting handsets have proved popular and effective – children text answers to the screen anonymously, useful for shy children but also means there is no chance of a snooze at the back of the class as everyone has to participate. Pupils set by ability in core subjects but there is plenty of flexibility and children can be moved up or down mid term if appropriate. No plans to introduce the IB.

Loyal team of teachers who love the challenge and freedom to innovate and are encouraged to use their initiative. Headmaster likes to recruit those with outside experience who can offer something different. Good mix of old hands and NQTs – school runs a leading and innovative graduate teacher training programme. Biology teacher won a UK top teacher award and also organises the school's rock festival, AshBash. A new higher education advisor has recently joined the team to help with UCAS forms and beyond – he was previously a university admissions tutor. The Oxbridge Club provides extra coaching in problem solving and analytical and critical thinking. Lots of language exchanges and trips that help bring learning to life and 'take school work into the real world,' according to one happy father. A level physicists visit CERN.

Some 35 pupils with SEN ranging from organisation skills to severe dyslexia, dyspraxia, dyscalculia and school can support children with physical disabilities, 'The teachers really go the extra mile for a child who struggles – nothing is too much trouble'.

New International Centre for 21 11-16 year olds offers a one-year intensive English language course.

Games, options, the arts: Prep school sits in 25 acres of grounds and playing fields – just redeveloped to create new floodlit Astro hockey pitch with other facilities in progress – and offers the usual sports including lacrosse and Kwik cricket for the girls. Good results in biathlon, triathlon, cross-country and swimming and a number of children play hockey and rugby at county level. Strong cricketing tradition – England cricketer Richard Ellison is an old boy – there is a pitch on site plus school has use of Ashford Cricket Club for matches and borrows floodlit Astroturf from the senior school.

Good sports facilities at senior school also include two gyms as well as a fitness centre and dance suite, indoor swimming pool and all weather basketball court. Cricket played at the local club a few minutes' walk away and a new sports centre opened in 2013 with Sport England specification. Boys' sport now fully developed and there are senior first teams in rugby, hockey and cricket, but fixtures still a bit sparse as other schools are a 'bit slow to twig that Ashford boys are actually rather good at games'. Teams maintained into sixth form and everyone has to take part in a physical activity at least once a week. Yoga and exercise classes popular, especially with the senior girls, along with street and jazz dance and personal survival. Strong house loyalty and everyone expected to take part in house events.

Plenty of concerts and musical events at the prep, about 65 per cent learn an instrument (school has recently become proud owner of a harp) and there is specialist music teaching from reception upwards. Year 3 pupils have free music lessons for two terms and the school is always on the look out for hidden talent. Good drama with something for everyone leads to blossoming self-confidence, most children are comfortable standing up in public and a 'have a go' mentality pervades. Two plays a year for years 6 and 2 and every class does annual mini production and entertainment.

Lots going on in the senior school drama department from house plays and speech and drama recitals, lower school productions and the spectacular whole school summer musical. Active junior drama club as well as technical drama club for those who prefer to keep out of the spotlight. Drama a popular option at GCSE and also offered at A level and school prepares pupils for speech and drama and LAMDA exams. Vibrant music and art departments: head of music is a colourful character who has transformed the musical life of the school; numbers participating have shot up, as has the standard. Tuition on most instruments available from the bassoon to the organ and school has two Steinway pianos as part of the Steinway schools programme. Lots going on: concert band, chamber music groups, string quartet, rock bands, string ensembles, community orchestra. Concerts every three to four weeks. Head wants music to be 'about performance and enjoyment' with plenty of opportunities for showmanship from 'teatime tootles' in the atrium to singing in Westminster Abbey.

Fabulous textiles and 'big and bold' approach to art; several go on to art foundation courses each year. A group of pupils recently designed a stained glass window for a church in the Holy Land and were then invited to install their work in situ. Another group made some wall hangings for the local hospice. 'We do random and different things and let it all come out', says one pupil.

Lots of healthy inter-house competition in the prep with weekly house points keenly contested – everything from academic, sporting and fundraising events, plus points also awarded for effort and progress. Over 30 clubs and activities to choose from including, sports, music, chess and even dry slope skiing. Saturday mornings are also for sports and activities but attendance is not compulsory. Cooking offered from nursery upwards and by the time they leave some pupils are quite proficient – we watched the construction of some beautiful gingerbread houses. Vibrant art department celebrating different styles: self-portraits, Venetian masks, pop art, funky landscapes and interpretations of Guernica. DT very popular and children often put in extra work on their projects in the lunch break. Numerous trips and visits all covered by fees, including the residential adventure training camp for leavers.

Huge range of clubs and activities in the senior school too, from Lego robotics to cooking and debating – something for everyone and all have to take part until sixth form. Strong debating team has represented the school at the Oxford and Cambridge Unions' competitions and taken part in the European Youth Parliament at the Foreign Office. Amnesty group won an award for 'Best Fundraising Event in UK Schools' with their 'Dare to be Different Day'. CCF popular and about 12 pupils complete their D of E Gold each year.

Boarding: Boarding from year 6 (bussed over to junior school) but very few in this age group. Boarders well supported and cared for; they are also allocated a house and are not allowed back into their boarding houses during the day, which means plenty of interaction with day children. Lots of boarders' activities and birthdays always celebrated. Houses recently refurbished; sixth formers have en suite bathrooms. Six houses, each led by a head of house, a teacher who oversees academic progress and personal development of each child. Children from abroad spend the first weekend of term with a day pupil – helps integration. Close liaison with parents and tutor and regular progress reviews. Lots of leadership opportunities running house events and activities, from community work to the house play. No lessons on Saturday mornings but time devoted to sport, rehearsals and activities – day children always happy to come in and it means the boarders are kept busy.

Background and atmosphere: Founded in 1898 with the aim that the pupils should play an active role in the life of the town and with an emphasis on 'training and development of character', the school moved to its present site in 1913 and became part of United Learning in 1999 (a group of 31 schools). This brought a welcome injection of cash resulting in new buildings springing up all over the place. Senior school is at the foot of the High Street, approached by a narrow lane and enclosed by high red-brick walls with lawns and greenery stretching down the hill. It's a green oasis in the middle of busy Ashford and quite difficult to find if you don't know where to look. Extensive rugby and cricket pitches are a short walk away. It's an international and friendly community – pupils are expected to engage with school life, and head says he 'does not want passengers on board and expects everyone to take part'. Good food, cafeteria style, lots of choice and healthy salad options. Brightly painted Atrium café a popular meeting place, also open to parents at pick up and drop off time.

There has been so much development at the prep since our last visit that the school is hardly recognisable. The Georgian house with arts and crafts additions remains the heart of the place, but now there is a fabulous glass atrium and classroom block with wide bright corridors, all sensitively blended with the original buildings.

Pastoral care, well-being and discipline: Strong pastoral care via house system; everyone is allocated a house on arrival as well as a specialist tutor; new joiners in year 7 also have a sixth form mentor.

Pupils and parents: About 70 per cent day children from as far afield as Maidstone, Sittingbourne and Cranbrook (minibus service). Very few weekly boarders so room for growth here. Families from a broad social spectrum; parents have high expectations and are encouraged to get involved and be part of the community. Twenty per cent foreign nationals, over 24 nationalities and particularly popular with Chinese, Germans, Eastern Europeans and Nigerians – school takes care that no nationality dominates. 'Ashford is very good at taking kids of any type and getting the best out of them', says a parent, 'and I like the way the school takes trouble to develop the kids' characters as well as the academic side.'

Entrance: Not overly selective. Majority join the prep in the nursery and reception and there is also an entry point in year 3, but children can join at any time if there are spaces. At nursery stage children (and parents) meet headmaster and have a taster session. Older children have a taster day and literacy and numeracy tests. The latter are for setting purposes and the only

A

occasion when a child will not be accepted is if it is felt that they would not be able to cope with the curriculum.

About 60 per cent of senior school entrants come up from the prep school, others from local primaries and prep schools eg Sutton Valence, Dulwich and Spring Grove. Wide ability range – some very bright, others who struggle, but all must have the ability to pass at least six GCSEs. Almost automatic entry from prep school but must be within the academic range. Children joining from other schools sit assessment tests in English, maths, science and non-verbal reasoning and take part in a team building exercise. Preference given to siblings where possible. A further 15 or so join at 13+ via school's own tests. Sixth form entry tested in proposed AS subjects and must have six GCSEs A*-B or equivalent, plus English proficiency test if appropriate. Lots of foreign nationals come for sixth form as well as several each year from local state schools.

Exit: About two-thirds of prep school children go on to the senior school, many with scholarships, others mainly to grammars including Judd and Skinners. Some to Benenden and occasionally to Wellesley House and other preps for last two years before common entrance. Will familiarise children with the Kent Test but no intensive coaching. Children's progress tracked via CAT tests so school aware of any weakness and can advise on appropriate next step. There is close liaison with parents and school is expert at managing expectations.

A few leave at 13+ – no coaching for CE but good relationships with other local schools; around a third depart after GCSEs. Sixth formers to a huge range of different institutions from Russell Group (two-thirds) to modern, including a smattering to Oxbridge over the last few years (two in 2016, plus two medics): broad minded higher education and careers advisor takes huge trouble to guide right student to right course.

Money matters: Academic, music, art, drama and sports scholarships offered – usually 10-30 per cent of day fee. Means-tested bursaries for children of clergy, mostly Anglican but will consider other Christian denominations. Twenty per cent discount for Forces families, discounts for siblings. Church Schools Foundation Assisted Places assessed on a combination of academic ability and financial need, worth up to 85 per cent of fees – offered to those entering in year 7, 9 or sixth form. Short-term emergency bursaries available.

Remarks: A forward-looking school with a strong international contingent which is going from strength to strength, benefitting in part from the huge growth of Ashford town. The school has 'changed beyond belief in the last eight years' and appeals to a wide range of families with its strong pastoral care and adventurous learning programme.

Aylesbury Grammar School

Walton Road, Aylesbury, Buckinghamshire HP21 7RP

Pupils: 1,311 • Ages: 11-18 • Sixth form: 382

Tel: 01296 484545
Email: office@ags.bucks.sch.uk
Website: www.ags.bucks.sch.uk

Headmaster: Since September 2014, Mr Mark Sturgeon (40s), educated at Dr Challoner's Grammar School, University of Liverpool (geography) and the Institute of Education, University of London (PGCE). Qualified as an FA football coach whilst at university, then headed to the USA as a volunteer coach where he recognised his vocation to work with young people. Returned to UK for his teaching qualification before landing his first job at Burnham Upper School. Understatedly ambitious, promotion to head of department at Aylesbury Grammar School aged 26, followed by another to head of year 13. A local boy through and through, returned to DCGS as assistant head, becoming deputy headmaster there after four years.

Describes AGS as 'pastorally driven' – high performing but caring and happy. 'We don't want the students to feel extreme pressure.' The focus now is 'to take a closer look at learning and what makes a good learner,' he says. Clear that talent is not just innate and that it's school's job to offer opportunities: 'exam results will open the door, but the boy has to walk through it and we have to give him the tools to do that.'

Retired from first XV rugby (which he took up aged 30) a couple of years ago but keeps competitive playing squash and golf. Still teaches year 8 geography ('I'm the same teacher I always was') and modestly sees himself as the school's custodian – respectful to those who came before but keen to keep improving and defining the future. Married to Angie, a primary school teacher, with three young sons.

Academic matters: Respectably placed in the league tables and climbing steadily – the big guns in South Bucks' leafier suburbs better watch their backs. Broad, traditional-ish curriculum with options including economics, business studies and Latin as well as all the usual suspects. Head's pick of top departments are maths (all do at least one module of further maths in addition to GCSE), sciences, history and geography, adding that languages are 'unbelievably good'. Refreshing for a boys' school. In the languages department all study French from year 7, pus either German or Spanish (students are allocated one of these, rather than given the choice). Latin too from year 7 and plenty of dual linguists at GCSE. Sciences also a specialism, with all taking three separate sciences at GCSE. Most take 11 GCSEs, with 63 per cent graded A*/A in 2016. Top notch value added – features in top 10 per cent nationally, and boys say that their GCSE options are chosen with help from teachers with their degree choices in mind. Strong support wherever needed with drop-in sessions offered for almost all subjects, whether to iron out creases or stretch the most able. Sixth form lecture series recently introduced.

Setting for maths from year 8, with surprisingly small class sizes across the board from year 10 up: maximum of 25 for most GCSE classes, with some history groups we saw with as few as 12 students. Individual target setting enables boys to take ownership of their progress – one of school's key cornerstones. They set their own academic goals and reportedly mostly exceed them. Teaching we observed was mainly of the traditional genre with formally laid out classrooms – but notably boys were attentive and engaged. In the words of one who joined in year 12: 'we all want to do well here – there's no messing about.' That said, a pressure cooker it's not. Boys were clear to point out that whilst those who wanted to chase Oxbridge and Russell Group places were thoroughly well supported, those choosing more vocational destinations were no less so.

Over 20 A level subjects on curriculum, with strong performance across the board: 45 per cent of A levels were graded A*/A and 75 per cent A*-B in 2016 – boys, proud of their achievements, told us 'the academic high scorers are the leaders in this school.' Teachers praised for their expertise and boys appreciate the knowledge that those who have pursued other careers prior to teaching bring.

Super SEN provision – known as Student Support – described by head as a 'phenomenal department'. Over seven per cent of the cohort have identified needs (mainly dyslexia and dyspraxia but also several on the ASD spectrum) and are watched over by one full time SENCo and two assistants. All screened for learning difficulties on entry and supported in small groups. In addition to their ongoing programme, boys benefit from department's creative approach to managing their needs. Tuesday lunch times, for example, see a social club for students receiving help from the SEN team where they can get together and talk over their challenges and triumphs. We heard that for some it was the best part of their week. Absolutely no sign of stigma attached to department – in fact, many boys go there in their free periods 'for a bit of peace and quiet'. Parents included too, with regular 'autism coffee mornings' to share anecdotal advice with one another.

Games, options, the arts: Rugby rules ('massive', say boys) – with students playing at national and county level and strong links forged with Wasps. Glory also achieved in footie (finalists and sometime winners in county cup for several years), tennis, squash, basketball, cricket and handball. Not bad for a school where students' only wish is for more sports pitches. Games compulsory to sixth form, so there's also fencing, hockey, swimming, table tennis and badminton to cater for all tastes, as well as one of the best equipped gyms we've seen in any state maintained school – well used by boys both as part of PE curriculum and in own time. PE available as option at GCSE and A level. Facilities more than adequate and ranging from gleaming (newly refurbed squash courts) to shabby (the old sports hall), as well as a functional newer sports hall and indoor swimming pool (weekly lessons for newbies cater for all abilities). Is there sport for all? To a degree: 'it's not as cliquey as you might think', boys assured us. Most year groups field A and B teams for major sporting fixtures with wannabes able to attend school training as an extracurricular activity. Minor sports such as badminton or squash also well attended with occasional fixtures. Importantly, less starry sportsmen have a host of other activities from chess to creative writing or debating to flex their intellectual muscles.

Music definitely not just a sideline – or seen as a lesser pursuit than sport – one elite rugby playing year 13 boy wistfully told us he wished he had joined the choir: 'It would have been cool to have played for the first XV and have been a chorister.' Music, DT, art and drama all popular options at GCSE and A level. DT covers food, woodwork and textiles in years 7 to 9, and school boasts four spacious DT labs, complete with laser cutters and all manner of equipment to enable boys to spread their practical wings. Art room not the most inspirational we've seen but quality of work high – and school adorned with examples of boys' work at every turn. Productions often in conjunction with conveniently positioned Aylesbury High, and there are colours awards for music as well as sport, underscoring school's ethos of roundedness. Plenty of opportunities for boys to showcase their talents – from a cabaret evening at the Aylesbury Waterside Theatre (definitely worth checking out on YouTube) to intimate solo evenings with musicians performing to a handful of parents.

'Amazing' array of trips and tours both curriculum linked and just for fun, from the ever popular year 7 residential to rugby tours to Australia, ski trips to USA, language exchanges for French, Spanish and German and history excursions to Auschwitz or Washington DC. D of E well run according to parents and 'encouraged'.

Background and atmosphere: Founded in 1598 by Sir Henry Lee, a champion of Elizabeth I. Situated in centre of Aylesbury until 1907, now just outside of the main town in a rather more residential area, with its sister school, Aylesbury High, conveniently located just a few yards across the Walton Road. Buildings, although all highly effective in their functionality, range in their aesthetic appeal. The main school building has definite shades of Alan Bennett's History Boys with its gleaming parquet floors and half tiled walls, complete with large, airy sash-windowed classrooms. A solid showing from the recently refurbed music labs (2015), complete with Macs, rock equipment and lighting for performances, plus studio theatre, recording suite and large multi-purpose sports hall, with enviable gym and weights room, used by all. Other outbuildings – mainly erected in the decade that architecture forgot, the 1960s – serve their purpose well and the only complaints from boys is that they wish they had more fields. Science labs recently refurbished, ditto library, funded mainly by alumni and dedicated parents' committee. Large sixth form area includes snack bar, common room and new area for private study. Others take lunch (typical school dinner fare – pizza and chips, anyone?) in a canteen style setting.

Thriving house system with fierce (but friendly) competition in every area. Two coveted trophies presented to winning houses each year for sporting triumphs and cultural and artistic excellence. House athletics and house quiz competitions are held on the same day so that jocks and brainboxes can bask in equal glory.

Pastoral care, well-being and discipline: The boys we met glowed with pride when talking about their school and were aware of their privileged situation in a way that many grammar students from more affluent catchments fail to be. They praised 'diversity', teachers that 'always try to bring out our best' and 'the confidence the school gives us'. The result of this is very few major transgressions and scant need for a hefty rule book as self-discipline tends to come naturally to most, although parents describe school as 'quite strict'. Pastoral care in strong evidence from head (who sends handwritten notes home to boys for outstanding learning or behaviour) all the way down to the year 8 buddies who are on tap to help newbies with any problems or questions they had experienced themselves when they joined the school. School motto 'Respect and Aspire' is most befitting – we felt that the sixth form boys having elected to continue wearing school uniform rather than business suit spoke volumes.

Pupils and parents: With less than 10 per cent of cohort joining from the independent sector, school has a genuine grammar feel to it – couldn't be mistaken for a private school, but matches – and in some ways exceeds – its slicker South Bucks counterparts in purposefulness, drive and ambition. With one mother commenting 'there's no money in the school' and around 15 pupils in most year groups eligible for free school meals, this surely (listen up, Nicky Morgan) is what selective state education is all about. Entitlement not part of the AGS vocabulary – parents say boys 'all want to work' and the sample we met were likeable, articulate, diverse and thoroughly grounded. School not filled from catchment so boys come from as far afield as Milton Keynes – around an hour each way by bus. Tiring for the youngest, but one such traveller of almost seven years told us 'it's totally worth it.'

Entrance: Via secondary transfer test administered by Bucks County Council in September of year 6. Admission purely on qualifying score (121). Further opportunities for admission at 12+, 13+ and 14+ by Late Transfer Testing if places available. Around 30 places open up in sixth form with boys needing 368 points from best eight GCSEs and at least a B in potential A level subjects.

Exit: Around 16 per cent leave post GCSE, small number at end of year 12. Excellent guidance takes boys to a broad array of universities. Five to Oxbridge in 2016. Significant numbers to Southampton, Nottingham, Exeter, Warwick, Bath and Birmingham. Loughborough a top choice for those interested

B

in pursuing careers around sport. Nine to study medicine in 2016. History, maths and chemistry also popular.

Money matters: Like most state grammars, rather strapped for cash, but dynamic parents, staff and alumni enable school to fund improvements and new equipment. Bursaries available for trips abroad.

Remarks: A grammar school in its purest form: purposeful, determined and socially diverse. In the words of one mother: 'I'd more than happily pay for this school.'

The Beacon School

Chesham Bois, Amersham, Buckinghamshire HP6 5PF

Pupils: 520 • Ages: 4-13

Fees: £10,800 – £16,200 pa

Tel: 01494 433654
Email: admissions@beaconschool.co.uk
Website: www.beaconschool.co.uk

Headmaster: Since September 2015, William Phelps, previously head of the British International School in New York. Theology degree from King's College London and PGCE from Oxford; taught at Aldenham and Abingdon before heading to the Big Apple in 2010.

Entrance: Now three reception classes. Non-selective in the early years, mildly selective from year 3 upwards: 'We want to make sure that they're going to fit in with what we've got, and that we can deal with their needs'. Also takes some five to 10 boys into year 7, including boys from state primaries who have not got places in the local grammar schools, as well as 'those whose parents think they would benefit from two years at the top of a prep school rather than at the bottom of a secondary school'.

Exit: Between a third and half of the boys move on to the local grammar schools at 11 (some 60 per cent take the 11+ exam and around 70 per cent of those are generally offered places). Clear favourite is Dr Challoner's, with a few to other local grammars. Others to a wide variety of local schools including Berkhamsted, Merchant Taylors', St Edward's, Wellington, Stowe, Radley, Magdalen College School, some with academic, drama, music, art or sports scholarships.

Remarks: This is a classic boys' prep, set on the edge of green Chiltern beech woods yet just down the road from the Metropolitan line. Many families moved out of London when they had children and quite a few fathers still commute to the City whilst mum stays at rural home: 'That supports well-mannered, disciplined children.' The school is based round what was once a Buckinghamshire farmstead, with brick and timber ex-barns and farmhouse; now vaulted dining rooms and classrooms.

Pre-prep have their own separate building and playground, giving a cosy and secure start to school life in bright, colourful classrooms. No longer has a nursery, but three reception classes.

Lively, interactive teaching. When we visited, year 3 were writing an adventure story they had spent several lessons planning, year 4 were learning about advertising and persuasion, and year 8 were doing a French crossword. We also saw boys painting intricate pictures of the insides of various types of fruit. Lots of trips to eg British Museum, Hampton Court, Bracknell Discovery Centre and Apsley Paper Mill for hands-on learning.

Two libraries, one for the pre-prep and one for the prep. The main library is in the heart of the teaching area, complete with iPads, which are particularly popular with the boys, and, during our visit, a net containing chrysalises in the process of turning into butterflies. Two full-time librarians are part of the school team and help teachers enthuse boys about reading.

Building work over last year has provided a new three storey building with a 250 seat theatre, eight classrooms, three laboratories, prep room and science study, a new cooking & nutrition room and a new learning support centre.

International Studies is an eight-term programme during years 2, 3 and 4, which introduces boys to the bare bones of a different major world language each term plus elements of that country's culture and geography. 'The purpose is to broaden their horizons, and to get them fired up and excited about learning languages.' They begin French during the final term in year 4, and start Latin in year 6. Some parents are very enthusiastic; others feel that children should learn a language from nursery upwards, 'but we think that inoculates them against fun and interest.'

Non-selective at pre-prep level, so a fair ability spread, though around half of pupils are in the top 10 per cent of the national ability range. Setting by ability in increasing numbers of subjects from year 3 upwards, with specialist teachers for most subjects. 'Fantastic' learning support department gives excellent help for eg dyslexia and dyspraxia with no stigma; plenty of differentiation in class ensures everyone achieves well. At least one boy in a wheelchair has gone happily through the school (his class organised a reunion at a bowling alley to ensure he could take part) with the help of lifts to upper floors.

The previous head pioneered the Beacon Certificate of Achievement (BCA) as an alternative to the narrowness of the common entrance format. Although it follows the same academic path, it also records achievements in sports and creative arts, and 'reflects the full range of prep school education'. It has cumulative and modular assessments as well as end of year exams. 'This suits most boys better, as they are working for immediate goals rather than just far-off exams, and it breeds better work habits.' Half of the boys who don't move at 11 to grammar schools are aiming at local day schools Berkhamstead or Merchant Taylors', which set their own entrance exams.

However, an exam set by only one school clearly has potential disadvantages with moderating standards, and the Beacon is one of 12 prep schools currently piloting the Prep School Baccalaureate (PSB) in the hope that prep schools nationwide will adopt it as a common entrance alternative. It encompasses the same principles as the BCA, but with an added emphasis on skills such as critical thinking, independent learning and teamwork. 'It's rather exciting: we're involved in cutting edge stuff, leading the way in the curriculum.' Some 20 senior schools are happy to accept the PSB, either alongside their own pre-tests or with some additional exams in year 8.

Sport very important, and not just for the stars: a parent reports that her 'geeky' son has greatly enjoyed playing for C teams. Sports hall, Astro pitch, outdoor pool and sports field round the back, with a cross-country course following footpaths across soft Chiltern hills. A climbing wall provides 'a diversion before going home'. Strong programme of matches, with football, hockey, rugby, cross-country, cricket, tennis and swimming teams competing with great success. Plenty of boys are successful at county and national level.

Drama is increasingly high profile. 'We're known to be strong at sport, but boys in particular can get really engaged in the performing arts, and we want to give them every opportunity.' There is a new studio theatre in the Old Barn, but at present the sports hall doubles up as the venue for large-scale performances. 'It is a very good sports hall but a less good theatre.' But boys perform enthusiastically in eg Joseph and the Amazing Technicolour Dreamcoat, and have great success in drama and public speaking exams.

'Superb' head of music encourages everyone to sing and many to play. The Beacon Young Musician of the Year competition is keenly contested, everyone composes and can record their own music; we heard an enthusiastic drumming class. Huge range of peripatetic teachers, many of them professional musicians. There are four choirs, an orchestra, a swing band and lots of ensembles.

Excellent, well-equipped DT department, and strong art with imaginative work displayed round the school. Food tech also popular – fab new Food Technology Centre – with some 40 boys competing in Beacon Mastercook (the winner cooked 'very tasty' coconut pancakes); other after-school clubs for different age groups range from rounders to warhammer.

'Lovely' teachers and a very caring feel, say parents. Newish director of pastoral care is overseeing a structured programme of PHSE lessons throughout the school. 'You can get exam results and win matches, but unless you help boys understand themselves and learn how to deal with pressure, you're not doing your job.' The new programme includes developing emotional intelligence and well-being, and talking honestly about issues.

Parents tend to be 'highly aspirational', and the previous head felt his job was to square the circle between their ambitions for their own sons and the needs of the whole school, 'to look after all the children's interests.' They also tend to get closely involved in events such as food and wine tasting evenings, cake sales and the summer ball, and most are hugely positive about the school. One parent expressed a general view: 'It's given my son an excellent start in life'.

Beaconsfield High School

Wattleton Road, Beaconsfield, Buckinghamshire HP9 1RR

Pupils: 2,000 • Ages: 11–18 • Sixth form: 325

Tel: 01494 673043
Email: enquiries@beaconsfieldhigh.bucks.sch.uk
Website: www.beaconsfieldhigh.bucks.sch.uk

Headmistress: Since 2015, Mrs Rachel Smith, previously deputy head at Langley Grammar. English degree from Sheffield and masters in educational leadership from Roehampton. Has also been head of English at Robert May's School in Hampshire and vice principal of Kings College for the Arts and Technology in Surrey. Enjoys scuba diving.

Academic matters: School has confidently inched its way up the league tables, currently in top 30 of best performing state schools in the country and now quietly outperforming all local competitors – without the hothouse reputation, or bookish atmosphere, of some. Forty-five per cent of all A levels graded A*/A in 2016 (75 per cent A*-B). Top performing subjects are maths ('extraordinary' and 'an extremely well run department'), English literature and the sciences (pupils' favourite), with 60 students taking biology to A2 level in 2016 and 33 taking chemistry. GCSEs similarly impressive in 2016, with 69 per cent A*/A grades.

Dance and computing now part of core curriculum with Spanish, French and Latin ('increasing in popularity') on the languages menu under the watch of the 'outstanding' head of modern languages. Girls take 10 GCSEs plus further maths for top two sets and four subjects to A1 level, with the majority taking three to A2.

Senior girls speak highly of support given during the university application period, with plenty of help on offer for all-important personal statement preparation, guest speakers to advise on all elements of process and parents saying they feel kept well in the loop. Girls report similarly 'understanding' support from the SENCo in relation to help with minor needs such as dyslexia. Parents say school 'gets homework levels rig ht'.

Games, options, the arts: Compulsory games from years 7 to 11 with something for everyone and plenty of opportunity to compete. When asked where their school's strengths lie, girls almost uniformly say that the 'school loves sport', describing the offering as 'incredible', and parents who weighed up the private option when choosing felt Becky High had as much to offer their sporty daughters. The laziest of couch potatoes are tempted to join in, with PE options ranging from netball and hockey to zumba or trampolining for those less competitively inclined. School fields A-D teams for netball so everyone who wants to compete gets a seat on the bus. A love of dance, which takes place in a dedicated studio, pervades the school – the annual dance show manages to include around 300 girls (and some of the more game teachers) in some capacity across all year groups.

Better playing fields than many local counterparts, plus a good sized Astro, add to the sporty feel of the place. 2014 national U16 netball champions plus several pupils currently in development squads for Rio and national level competitions for events including pentathlon, sailing, rowing, skipping and swimming. Competition not exclusively reserved for sporty types, though, with girls also able to shine in events including Masterchef competitions, cake competitions and an annual fashion evening with dresses designed by older girls, hats by the younger ones and canapés for guests provided by the food tech students.

Super selection of extracurricular activities – parents are 'really impressed' – mostly free and often led by the girls themselves. These range from chess, coding and bridge to lyrical, contemporary and hip hop dance, and the ever-popular university cooking club where girls are taught to budget and fend for themselves in the big wide world. Endless opportunities for budding thespians to showcase their talents, including an annual house panto, scripted by girls, orchestras, bands and groups and all-singing, all-dancing shows, most recently We will Rock You and Grease. Tours and trips galore, both curriculum and enrichment-based, with girls heading off near and far to locations such as New York to workshop their dance moves with Broadway performers, an Australian netball tour, to the battlefields for history or Iceland for Geography.

Background and atmosphere: Like the majority of South Bucks grammars, the fabric of the low rise 1960s buildings has a tatty, labyrinthine feel, although girls here are far less cramped than their Challoner's equivalents, and playing fields, whilst not impressive, are adequate. Subject to the restrictions of local authority funding, the majority of improvements are funded by parents of the steadfastly middle-class cohort. The newish canteen brightens up the feel of the school's fabric, with a buzzy adjoining sixth form common room and bright, new GCSE/A level classroom block.

A purposeful buzz pervades the school, although it admits to 'playing catch-up' where technology is concerned. Notably, we didn't enter a single classroom with students sitting, glazed over, in uniform rows. One biology class comprised animated groups of girls drawing life-sized diagrams of the human digestive system, whilst some geographers were occupying a whole corridor creating a wave motion with a tape measure. Every wall is festooned with artwork from all age groups, and chattering girls move noisily around the school, creating the impression of a very happy ship.

Good facilities all round. Two bright, inspirational art rooms run by 'fantastic' teachers showcase girls' creative talents and offer plentiful opportunities for creative expression, from 3D work to collage and painting. No surprise that art is a popular option at both GCSE and A level.

Pastoral care, well-being and discipline: Head says that 'chewing gum and short skirts is as bad as it gets', and school gives perception of a tightly-run ship (woe betide the girl who chats during a fire drill), with a no-nonsense approach to keeping the girls in check. Pupils themselves describe staff as 'firm but fair,' although some rather scathing views were aired regarding head's apparent obsession for skirts of an 'appropriate length' (maximum of four inches above the knee for the avoidance of any doubt).

Teachers deemed to be approachable and flexible in relation to homework as well as – in the main – being 'prepared to give up their time' at breaks and lunchtimes, according to girls, to offer pointers. A close eye kept on any potential lost sheep, with grade cards issued at four points each year stating whether girls are above, below or meeting expectations. All girls with 'belows' are spoken to directly, parents contacted if there are three belows or more, and appropriate development strategies put in place, often with support of peer group mentors.

Plenty of chances for older girls to notch up CV-worthy responsibilities, with a head girl elected by students, teachers and governors in a process that would give some job applications a run for their money, plus over 30 senior prefectures and numerous subject prefectures up for grabs.

Bullying reportedly rare, but girls with any kind of worry can email the school counsellor, who will arrange a confidential meeting with them, and the head of sixth form is described as 'like a mum' and reportedly 'can sort out any problem.'

Pupils and parents: With grammar schools being the holy grail of the South Bucks education scene and hardly an academic competitor from the private sector in sight, it's no surprise that 91 per cent of pupils live in catchment. One third of the cohort join from independent prep schools, with main feeders including High March, Maltman's Green and St Helen's.

Unlike DCHS, neither social nor ethnic diversity are in huge evidence here, reflective of the immediate – but not the broader – catchment. School probably suits girls who like to take on a challenge and can pick themselves up and carry on after a set-back, as well as those ready to develop collaborative and leadership skills. Parents a sociable bunch, with plenty of chances to get to know each other organised by active form parent system – 'useful for when the girls start to go to parties,' noted one.

Entrance: Selective. The mysterious business of catchment waxes and wanes on an almost annual basis according to how many are successful in the much hyped Bucks 11 plus. Slightly less ferociously exclusive than DCHS, mainly due to the lack of a neighbouring boys' school. Despite recent academy status, apparently no plans to change either the selection criteria or the 11 plus exam. Preference currently given to siblings and, in rare cases in this super-affluent demographic, those qualifying for free school meals. Taking in an extra year 7 class from 2016 to give 180 places.

The competitive nature of entry means that many girls join in ones or twos from their junior schools, with even the largest (mainly private) feeders sending just 15 to 20 girls. Events such as picnics in the summer holidays arranged for such girls to meet each other before the start of term each autumn.

Large intake into year 12, mainly from local private schools such as Piper's Corner, or high achievers from local comprehensives looking for a more academic environment. These girls integrate well into this friendly, supportive school, but are expected to hit the ground running and be able to keep up from day one.

Exit: Everyone on to higher education with around half to Russell Group universities and a handful each year to Oxbridge (six in 2016). Strong numbers to study medicine and veterinary science each year, and one or two to international universities. Girls report good support with university applications and preparation of personal statements.

Money matters: State maintained. Active 'Friends' association and highly supportive parent body extremely successful in fundraising, occasionally securing one-off parental donations of up to £10,000. The Christmas Fayre alone raises £17-£18,000. Bus service (around £10 a week if school is not your closest) from surrounding areas morning and afternoon has recently created grumbles following changes of route, with some pupils reporting the bus passing the school to collect further flung girls before looping back and dropping them half an hour later. Small hardship fund for those who need it for extras like school trips.

Remarks: Now Buckinghamshire's top performing grammar and ranked in top 30 of best state schools nationally, 'Becky High' soars above the competition in the league tables, but somehow keeps hold of its relaxed, friendly vibe. Parents and girls fortunate enough to have the choice will find a totally different culture to nearby Dr Challoner's High School and girls will typically fit one mould or the other, with this school offering a gentler transition into senior school and a somewhat more nurturing – some would argue rounded – approach throughout. Despite repeated changes in leadership, something for everyone, with super teaching, excellent sport and plenty of extracurricular to suit all tastes. All that's missing is a brother school.

Bedales Pre-prep, Dunannie and Bedales Prep, Dunhurst

Linked with Bedales School

Alton Road, Steep, Petersfield, Hampshire GU32 2DR

Pupils: 177; 40 full or half, 30 flexi boarders • Ages: Dunannie 3-8; Dunhurst 8-13

Fees: Day £8,628 – £18,957; Boarding £21,141 – £23,724 pa

Tel: 01730 711733
Email: jjarman@bedales.org.uk
Website: www.bedales.org.uk

Headmistress: At Dunhurst since 2011, Jane Grubb, previously of Hurstpierpoint and Brockenhurst. Always had an eye on Bedales, and has clearly found her nirvana. 'I wanted to be

Jane', said the head, talking about her friendly collaboration with children. Parents say – 'I have an enormous amount of time for her'; 'it's clear how much she cares for children and ethos of school, and making [the children] better people'. Has a super sense of humour – a great attribute in a prep school head.

Leaving in July 2017. Her successor will be Colin Baty, currently head of Great Walstead Prep in Sussex. He has previously taught at the prep, and his wife, Debbie, at the pre-prep, before moving to Moreton Hall, where he was deputy head.

At Dunannie since 2010, Jo Webbern, who worked before at Ibstock Place. 'Very lovely and approachable, great with children', said a parent. 'A look or a word from Jo means a lot to these children – they don't want to let Jo down', says Jane. Has 'commit-tea' every Wednesday with four of year 3, to discuss ideas – 'how about a zip wire in the orchard', suggested one. 'I've got a zip wire at home', said another. 'We'll all go around to yours then', said the head brightly. Jo is very careful to write everything down: she ensures the children here feel that their ideas are properly considered and valued.

Entrance: They are looking for children and families who like and understand the Bedales ethos, and this, and an intention to progress through the school, is all that is necessary for entrance into nursery and reception. For entrance to years 1-3, informal assessment of reading, writing and maths. At Dunhurst, English and maths assessments, non-verbal reasoning and interview. Prospective pupils are considered in the round, so although they are looking for average ability or above in academic terms, a pupil could be below average in some areas, with a spark in others. Overall lower scores might be acceptable in a child who is a good worker who won't give up. Prospective pupils spend time with their peers to see how well they cooperate. No waiting lists, but some classes close to full. Eight plus and 11+ are natural points of entry.

Exit: Most progress on to Bedales, after sitting a maths and English test. A small number to other senior schools, including Winchester, Cheltenham Ladies' College, Cranleigh and Bryanston.

Remarks: Pupils sitting on chairs, tables, leaning against radiators. Excited laughter, banter between teacher and pupils, the energy almost tangible. Were they perhaps discussing a forthcoming party? No: it was a lesson on longshore drift. Rare indeed that longshore drift generates such excitement; but this exchange of energy between teacher and pupils was replicated in other classrooms again and again. Pupils didn't leap to silent feet when we appeared – they were engrossed in learning. The point here is not neat quiet rows, but the work you are doing; and the pupils were fully and busily engaged.

No carrot or stick approach to learning here: it's not an awards assembly sort of place. Time is not wasted on the common entrance – years 7, 8 and 9 do a three year pre-GCSE curriculum. A parent commented that 'children are expected to raise questions which require discussion and debate'; another that 'lessons are rigorous and stretching'. Although one parent commented that a greater insistence on accurate spelling would be nice, most felt that high standards were expected, particularly of those with potential.

Parents agree that English, dance, music and art are outstanding, and that there has been a significant effort to raise the game in sciences and maths, which are now also strong – 'pupils do now routinely learn things by rote, such as tables'. One parent commented happily on the cross fertilisation between subjects, giving the example of a school trip where everyone had to make a snack for everyone else: a happy blend of maths, domestic science and altruism.

Class size is a maximum of 20. Years 4, 5 and 6 have a double in intake, with three or four classes a year in years 7 and 8. Children are only set for maths – they're keen to avoid any labelling here. Saturday morning school starts at age 12, in block 1. Parents aren't terribly keen on it, but the kids don't seem to mind.

Homework is integrated into the day, pupils having a number of free periods called Greens for homework, and any LAMDA or music commitments. Parents say it's great for those who are self-motivated and can organise themselves, and love the fact that prep gets done at school, so kids are free when they get home.

No competitive parenting here: one mum told us if people were heard talking about their child's levels of achievement, other parents would raise eyebrows of horror: they were certainly at the wrong school.

Learning support both in and out of lessons – we spoke to a pupil who chose Dunhurst particularly for its SEN support, and to the happy parents of a dyslexic pupil who had regained lost confidence by joining Dunhurst.

'It's not all jazz hands [just because we're Bedales],' says Jane; although it is certainly possible to see that the confident could dance their way through life here. The whole idea of jaw (a weekly lively discussion forum with a speaker) seems made for the self assured to fly, reflected in a parent's comment that this is a school which would best suit those who know their own minds, are self-motivated, and not easily influenced by their peers.

But this caring environment could also suit those who are more tentative. Development of individual rather than the mass is a focus which pleases parents, and shy children can find their feet and their confidence at Dunhurst.

Those seeking a traditional prep school education might be disconcerted by Dunhurst. 'If a parent has pigeonholed a child as just academic then it won't suit them,' says Jane. As a parent told us, 'It's not so much which child the school wouldn't suit, as which parents...'. They described a pupil, lacking self-confidence and happiness, who came to Dunhurst from a traditional school; a recovery at Dunhurst; then subsequent return to the traditional school, and the surprise of the parents when the child fell apart again.

The pastoral care here is highly praised by parents – the clincher for this school. There's much emphasis on well-being; down time, such as meditation, is incorporated into the school day. Jane explained the importance of the Friday custom of staff shaking hands with pupils: knowing the nature of each pupil's handshake means you can tell if something's wrong; it connects you with every child and gets rid of any bad blood before the weekend. 'It's totally unique', said a parent, describing his son's happiness, and his development of social skills, self-confidence and worldliness at Dunhurst.

Bullying not tolerated here, confirmed a parent, who said that older children have a responsibility to look out for the younger ones, and blow the whistle on any bad behaviour. This is mentioned frequently, as is the peer listening network and the school counsellor – to whom the children can self refer. '[The children are] all very tuned in and look out for each other', said a parent. The head says the approach will depend on the severity: if year 4s are getting a bit tetchy with each other, being a good friend might suddenly become a topic in PHSE.

In disciplinary terms, it's not so much which punishment fits the crime, as what can you give back to the community. Offenders might be put on beauty duty cleaning out the green houses; but bring your friends along, some other teachers might join in, and someone brings a radio.

First names between teachers and pupils, and the lack of uniform, might seem strange to newcomers, but there is plenty of respect here – 'when kids talk to adults, they're not

B

frightened', said a parent. Most kids chose to dress very casually – jeans, leggings and hoodies are the norm.

Head, heart and hand are the guiding principles here, and the head part is not just academic; there needs to be something for the soul too, says Jane: time for stillness and thinking; opportunities to appreciate beauty and contemplate life. So there's lots of art, drama, and music; the divine smell of a room devoted to woodwork – 'Dunhurst pupils wouldn't go to B&Q to buy a shed', says Jane. An art room with views over the countryside; a colourful paper model village, with circuits underneath for night time lighting; a table of cupped pottery hands which look as though they are awaiting communion. All do outdoor work – a hand-painted gypsy caravan (Jane's special project) will become a small classroom. There's an outdoor hut with pizza oven, rows of wellies on pegs, mud and clucking hens; tasks range from building to planting to clearing bracken. There was schoolwide participation in RSPB birdwatch.

Wednesday afternoon is activity time, which includes outreach for years 7 and 8 (visiting the elderly or helping at local primary schools), outside work, shopping in Petersfield, cooking in Scoffs (the pupil run café) or sports. Sport is not something which is overemphasised, and you can opt out of matches (as you might expect). There is plenty of sport available, with excellent tennis provision, and access to all the Bedales facilities, including the lovely swimming pool, but 'if you're not strong at sports, it's not a big deal', said a parent.

Communication is good, with a Friday report reviewing the week's events. Staff will contact parents by phone or by email if something is going wrong, and one parent described thorough and regular reporting of his child's medical condition. For parents who have experienced the fluid atmosphere of Dunannie, it is less easy to walk into Dunhurst to chat to teachers, said one parent, but they do always get back by email.

There are up to 80 boarders, around 40 of whom are full or half time, the remainder being flexi boarders, staying from one night a week. Most boarders are from years 7 and 8. Beds are singles, two to six per room. Comfortable clean facilities, showers and baths – the girls protested at the suggestion of segregating the triple bathrooms – apparently simultaneous bathing is a happy community activity (curtains can be drawn if the girls choose). Kitchen facilities are available at certain times, with cereal, toast and fruit on offer (but boarders must go to the dining hall for proper breakfast and supper). Tech must be put away at 8.30pm. Boarders can contact home by phone or email, and most use their own devices, but can use the phone in matron's room at any time. Very few overseas boarders, but pupils can stay at weekends, and trips are organised for those who do.

Dunhurst connects to Dunannie, the pre-prep, but the nursery is separately situated in an old barn, full of light and sunshine, a safe magical world. All the usual tiny person activities, with the addition of an area devoted to planting vegetables, which they subsequently enjoy making into soup. Outside, a large sandpit, and saucepans and frying pans hanging on strings to batter.

Dunannie children take learning outside for around a quarter of each day – 'it's not just an add on here', says Jo; all-in-one rain gear and wellies hang neatly in a boot room – the children learn how to change very quickly so they can maximise their outside time. Vegetable plots from nursery upwards, a willow pod (made by years 2 and 3) and a thatched Celtic hut (made by Bedales students) to play in.

Relaxed classrooms, children sitting happily on the floor, chatting with teachers. Lessons are practically based: year 3 are studying birds, filling paper bags with shells to make up the different weights of birds, following birds' migratory paths on maps, and making their own memory maps for trips around the grounds. Home-made willow bird feeders are hung outside the large windows so the class can appreciate visitors (how many schools would find these random interruptions to lessons acceptable?).

Individualised learning plans for each pupil, with no expectation that they will all progress at the same rate. A child can do a year again if seems advisable for their happiness and development. Very little homework, mostly spelling or reading. Dunannie can cope with quite a profound level of special needs, but will consider carefully how well a child will fit into a class before accepting them. Those with severe needs are unlikely to be able to progress to Dunhurst.

Class sizes up to 20, split into two at year 3, where class sizes are up to 15.

Pastoral care is very strong. The golden rules at Dunannie are to listen and be respectful, and they talk about these rules a lot. Pupils are very caring of one another: one parent told us that when one child made racially explicit comments about another, a classmate reported the issue. It was dealt with immediately, and the matter fully reported to the relevant parents.

Bedales School

Linked with Bedales Pre-prep, Dunannie and Bedales Prep, Dunhurst

Church Road, Steep, Petersfield, Hampshire GU32 2DG

Pupils: 468; 314 boarders • Ages: 13–18 • Sixth form: 195

Fees: Day £27,138; Boarding £34,533 pa

Tel: 01730 300100
Email: admissions@bedales.org.uk
Website: www.bedales.org.uk

Headmaster: Since 2001, Keith Budge, married with three grown up children. Read English at Oxford, and came to Bedales via Loretto and Marlborough. His previous schools, says the head, did not have the child so much at their centre. Neither, presumably, did the pupils call him Keith. Children here own and shape their education; the teachers, says Keith, are their collaborators. Who, indeed, would collaborate with Sir?

The head is deeply committed to the underlying ethos of Bedales (education of head, heart and hand). These are the ideals, says Keith, but 'idealism here has a strong thread of pragmatism running through it'. He also believes that a school needs to constantly reinvent itself: the head originated Bedales Assessed Courses (BACs) as an alternative to GCSEs, and also now offers enrichment as an option instead of a fourth A level – 'an intelligent, brave approach', said a parent. Others say he's 'intellectual and caring'; 'kind, understanding, firm where necessary'; 'tries to see others' point of view'. 'I'm a huge fan', added another parent, who says he does an incredible job with diverse parents and really varied students.

Academic matters: Education is different here, its value much more in itself than the end qualifications – the qualification hoops to be jumped to get to the university to reach the gold-plated job. It's not that Bedales ignores these reasonable parental desires – most students end up at the same universities – but it tries as far as possible to make education of the individual the thing: 'to develop inquisitive thinkers with a love of learning who cherish independent thought'.

Qualifications look different here too, to fit this more holistic vision of learning: 'the wonderful BACs' (as described by a parent) are a living alternative to GCSEs. They focus on cross-curricular, independent thought, with a range of assessment methods from written assignments to presentations and performances: an organic process of learning over time, with few make or break final day assessments. And universities are happy with them too, though Bedales retains a compulsory core of five IGCSEs in English, maths, modern languages and sciences. Parents and pupils like the mixture of assessment methods in the BACs, and they're done and dusted in time to leave a clear month to revise for IGCSEs.

At BACs/IGCSEs in 2016, 55 per cent A*-As. It's a classical looking curriculum, but a global awareness BAC is imminent. Philosophy, religion and ethics (PRE) is one of the most popular BACs, with nearly half of the students taking this option. 'It really makes pupils think, and they carry those skills and that knowledge with them. It's evident in their thinking at A level...a really impressive linking of ideas', said a parent. 'Star course', said another. Classics was also particularly highlighted by parents, who said the quality of teaching is 'superb'. '[students are] really stimulated and pushed to the limit'.

Uniquely at Bedales, there is no dead time after IGCSEs and BACs. Pupils start their A level courses immediately, so they have a month's A level taster before the summer holidays. If pupils don't like what they have opted for, they can change courses before starting A levels properly in September.

At A level, 46 per cent A*-A, 77 per cent A*-B in 2016. Maximum class size is 14 but often significantly smaller. On average seven per cent to Oxbridge over the last five years (three places in 2016). Bedales has recently started enrichment at A level, compulsory for those not taking four A levels. This safeguards time to learn something just for the joy of it; it could include beginners' Russian, oak framed building, dance or astronomy. 'Education at its best', said a parent, another describing her child's delight at doing art again, having given this up to concentrate on academic subjects. Some parents are concerned that enrichment subjects won't be as rigorous as examined courses, and might be viewed by universities as wasted time. But the school believes that enrichment is valuable in itself (hear hear).

The counter-side of all this educational roaming is a strong and structured guidance system: there's a six weekly review by teachers of each student's effort and attainment, and students have a fortnightly one-to-one tutorial. The tutor's job to get students to self-motivate and organise, and help them realise that what they put in to learning is what they get out. This 'got it' moment should happen earlier at Bedales because of the innate value placed on learning, but in the rare case that it hasn't clicked by the sixth form, they will put a military structure in place to try and help.

In this strong community, students are encouraged to help others academically: year 13s can be Badley seniors (from founder John Badley) and help year 9s with their work; others become dons – English dons, physics dons etc – and champion a subject to help others.

Homework is generally fitted into free periods during the day, one parent commenting on the different homework culture at traditional schools: her non-Bedales child swots all evening. Some teachers give loads of homework (don't worry if that leg injury's keeping you at home – you can be Skyped the French homework), others much less. A parent commented that his daughter feels the pressure a bit, but the Bedalian atmosphere helps: 'If she was surrounded by little Miss Perfects it would be much worse'.

Students at Bedales are generally highly motivated, owing, a Harvard study suggests, to a love of learning, and the level of autonomy and choice enjoyed by students here. But 'some don't bother at all', said a parent, who wonders whether a more pushy environment might galvanise the lazy. Here, the approach is to try to find out why children are not performing, and help them develop their full potential. And generally this works much better than an order from above: parents refer to the unusual mutual respect between teachers and pupils – 'a powerful developmental thing'. '[They're a] really gifted staff', said another.

Learning support (LS) is staffed by one full-timer and six part-timers, two of whom are maths specialists, and is charged as an extra. A speech and language therapist comes in as necessary. No in class support here, so students need to be able to cope with lessons on their own. Up to two sessions of support a week during free periods. LS rooms here are dotted around, so students don't have to leave a subject area to go to a particular stigmatised centre. There's close liaison between LS and subject teachers, with LS feeding into every year group review. LS emails home with progress reports, keeping in regular contact.

Around a third of students use LS at some point: the department is happy to provide spasmodic support for particular difficulties, although often short term problems can be mopped up by teachers and supervised study. LS generally supports mild learning difficulties (but can cope with severe dyslexia). Progress rates of dyslexic students are the same as others, with some doing exceptionally well.

Several parents described dyslexic children who suffered from self-esteem issues while attending high achieving, pressurised schools, and the difference in their children once they started at Bedales: 'Bedales is outstanding in the support it offers pupils'; 'it's inspiring pastoral care'; 'they draw out the best in children'.

One couple with a dyslexic child were initially sceptical about Bedales – 'we're not celebrities, just ordinary middle class parents'. Four open days later, they decided to go for it, and describe an open and supportive atmosphere, and a child who now loves school and has regained her confidence.

Games, options, the arts: This must be the only school in the country which has 'appreciation of the beautiful' as one of its aims. 'There is an intense delight in seeing your work grow under your hand...It is the delight of creation, of shaping something that shall have use and beauty, the delight of an artist'. (John Badley, founder). Outdoor work is a key part of the curriculum: from planting, to building a posh pig sty, to putting a new engine in an ancient Land Rover.

Parents eulogise about the music, arts and drama here – 'art is very, very good – they're really pushed and well prepared for A level'. Music receives similar accolades: the BAC is much more demanding than GCSE, dismissed by the head of music as a 'pub quiz': students go from the BAC to music Pre U. Performances take place in the lovely timber-framed Olivier Theatre. Bedales arts feels a thoroughly professional affair, from a display of Matisse, visiting theatre, music and dance, to in-house productions.

'Sport doesn't dominate the extracurricular', says Keith, although he adds that Bedales competes in the usual rounds of county, regional and national competitions. But sport is just one option in the compulsory activities programme, allowing pupils to choose from a range of cerebral, social and physical activities (heads up for the boys – this is not a big rugby school).

Plenty of charity initiatives, D of E, but no students marching around in combat gear – not a natural home for CCF. No noticeable community service either, which parents feel is an omission, and surprising since one of the school's aims is engaging with the local community.

Boarding: Pastoral care for boarders is excellent, agree parents, one saying that the housemistress 'did a better job than we would have done' with his anxious daughter: she 'knew instinctively' what would work.

Comfortable, well-kept single sex boarding houses, with mixed aged dorms, which are a big plus, parents feel. Year 12 pupils take the responsibility of running dormitories and caring for younger pupils, although one parent said her daughter opted out of boarding to avoid being dorm boss, which is a time-consuming post. No flexi-boarding, so those who aren't interested in boarding full time may revert to day pupil status. Year 13 pupils live in a separate, co-ed boarding house as preparation for university. Dorm size varies from two to six beds. To clamp down on overuse of technology, school Wifi is switched off at midnight and the Block 3s (year 9s) hand in their phones at night.

Dorms have a comfortable homely feel even during the day, students returning during breaks to lounge happily on beds and chat or work. Of the school population, 68 per cent are boarders and eight per cent are overseas students.

Laundry is done for younger children; year 13s learn to do their own. Kitchens in boarding houses are open 8.30- 9.30pm, with pasta, bread and butter, and fruit available. Students do kitchen duty twice a week – 'a bit grim' said a boarder. There are activities on Sundays, which are not compulsory. 'Some just slump', said a student.

Students keep in touch with home by phones, text and email, most returning home on Saturday afternoon until Sunday evening. For those left at school – overseas boarders, or those who live further afield in the UK – things can be quiet at weekends.

'It's the ethos of boarding school with day pupils', said one parent, who feels this is a boon – even day students have to do activities in the evening, so can be at school until around 9.30pm.

Background and atmosphere: Nonconformist. No Sir or Miss, no uniform – unless the prevalence of hoodies could be described as such. Emphasis on development of the individual, and collaboration between individuals.

This school is in many ways quite extraordinarily lovely: you can feel the life and energy in the wood when you enter the oak-framed arts and crafts memorial library. It must be inspirational to study in: an 18th century timber-framed barn housing some outdoor work, donated, dismantled and carefully re-erected in a convenient spot; and a new art and design building is imminent, with arching roofs and skylights. There is an integrity about these buildings, their construction and materials: a clear coherence with the school's ethos. Bedales sits comfortably in the surrounding gentle countryside: a world apart in many ways – a 'Bedales bubble,' said a parent – very gorgeous for the lucky students who attend.

The head wants this to be a protected part of life, but says there 'needs a breeze to come through from beyond'. This evident in the fortnightly Jaw, a more inclusive version of other schools' assemblies, with student or visitor led debate on matters of moral or spiritual engagement. 'It opens their horizons', said a parent; 'makes them feel they can do anything'. The breeze is also evident in careers advice, which aims to develop ambition and show horizons, old Bedalians playing their part by mentoring and networking.

'Not pressurised', said a parent, whose academic children benefit from being big fish in a small pond. 'Work is not carried out in a competitive fashion'. She sometimes asks herself whether more pressure might make them do better (her son just failed to get into Oxford) – '[but] the ethos of the school is very attractive, and of more benefit than attending a school which would have helped achieve Oxford. And socially Bedales is the best', the parent concludes. Another parent commented on this positive atmosphere: her daughter was lazy at her old school, but now never wants to be late, is really trying hard and working her best.

'Bedales doesn't do prizes', said a parent, 'it just doesn't believe in them'. An egalitarian, no marks on the wall sort of establishment. This means if you're not very good at something, no one need know. Achievement is celebrated, via a handwritten card, or email, with those doing really well being invited to a Keith's feast.

Pastoral care, well-being and discipline: Pastoral care is the real strength of the school, said a parent – 'if you're vulnerable, if you've had a terrible time, it's lovely'. Another said that 'people are understanding, friendly, kind, and very open'. 'They will find something good about you'. Understandably, in the light of this, Bedales does sometimes find itself receiving serial offenders from other schools. Sometimes it works; sometimes parents are not happy that these kids convince peers to follow them into 'naughty projects'; worth perhaps bearing in mind the comment from a parent that this school suits best children who know their own minds.

'Before we went to the school, we had the impression it was all about sex and drugs', said a parent, who was very pleased to find it was zero tolerance in many areas.'There are a fair number of pupils who smoke', she added, but the school firmly try and stop this amongst Block 3s (year 9); it is harder to control amongst sixth formers. 'They try to keep an eye out, but the kids need some freedom', she added. Parents are pleased that the head talks to them about his approach to drugs, taking into account their views. There are occasional incidents of bullying, said a parent, but they are dealt with appropriately – 'it's harder to get away with here because of the strong integration between the years'.

Many parents spoke of the strong relationships at this school: between pupils, and pupils and teachers – '[it's] as close to family as possible to get'. 'Pupils good at celebrating each other', said another, describing the time when her child had to wear sunglasses for an eye problem, and was teased by a couple of class mates. The housemistress sent out a carefully crafted light email: some kids sent apologies, and the next day all the kids in class turned up in sunglasses in support. The day mistress called the parents and kept them informed. Several parents commented on the unusual level of involvement: at other schools, the doors are closed, school knows best. Not at Bedales. Parents are very involved here. 'It's almost like being at primary school', said one, who said school is very welcoming to parents and 'very, very patient'.

Food was delicious on the day of our visit, though no meat Thursdays, the brain child of the vegan head boy a couple of years ago, is controversial with committed meat eaters, who don't see why they should be forced to abstain.

Pupils and parents: Parents include media, actors, business, celebrities, professionals, scientists, a few bankers ('with exceptional educational views', said a parent), trust fund kids, and a few from overseas. A broader range than there used to be, says the head, with more traditional parents reassured by good behaviour and academic records. 'Good alumni', said one parent practically – 'you're buying a network'.

Communication with parents is generally good: a weekly newsletter keeps parents up to date with what's going on; there are half termly reviews, and termly parents' evenings (not the usual siren when time's up – 'that would not be Bedalian', said a shocked parent). There are a few blips: one said that when a teacher has an issue, this can be slow to trickle through to the parent; another, that there are a few administrative issues: wrong half term dates and occasional typos on the school website, and they were once sent the wrong school report – it's 'sort of charming,' she said, but could be improved. On the other hand, another parent described the head's involvement of parents on the changes to A levels with shocked delight: she had never experienced such engagement at other schools.

Entrance: Maths, English and general ability test for 13+ entry. Just over half from Dunhurst, and most of the rest from preps in London and the south east, in particular Highfield. For sixth form entry, minimum of five Bs, four Cs at GCSE or equivalent points.

Exit: Around a third leave after GCSEs. Pupils depart for a variety of universities and art colleges, a small number of Oxbridge (three in 2016), and many to Russell group, plus some to US. Only a handful to science-based degrees, including three medics in 2016.

Money matters: Scholarships are largely honorific in nature, but the school funds 70 bursaries at a cost of over £1 million per annum.

Remarks: Most children would thrive at this lovely school. Parents described the very clever, the quirky, the academic and those in the middle, all of whom are happy. Not perhaps for a child who needs lots of boundaries, or a large degree of privacy, thinks the head; and it wouldn't, perhaps, suit all parents, who need to be broad-minded about the purpose of education. But for most children, this would be a wonderful place to grow a rooted sense of self, and joy in life and learning.

Bede's School

The Dicker, Upper Dicker, Hailsham, East Sussex BN27 3QH

Pupils: 1,147; 237 full, 70 weekly boarders • Ages: 4-19 • Sixth form: 338

Fees: Day £9,675 – £20,925; Boarding £23,595 – £33,261 pa

Tel: 01323 843252
Email: admissions@bedes.org
Website: www.bedes.org/

Headmaster: Since September 2016, Peter Goodyer, previously deputy head at Colston's School in Bristol. Educated at Rhodes University in South Africa (BA in psychology, postgrad diploma in international relations and PGCE in secondary education) with an MBA in education from Keele, he started his career as a history teacher and sports coach at St Andrew's College in Grahamstown, South Africa. He moved on to St John's Leatherhead (head of psychology and housemaster) before joining Colston's, where he has been interim as well as deputy head. He is married to Laura, also a teacher, and they have a young son.

Head of prep: Since 2013, Mr Giles Entwisle BA (French, politics and economics at Loughborough) PGCE (late 40s). He came from a deputy headship at Highfield, prior to which he was head of year, housemaster and head of MFL at Holmewood House, near Tunbridge Wells. An enthusiastic, ambitious and engaging, career prep school man, he and senior school head Dr Maloney are a mutually appreciative team, sharing a vision of Bede's and its shining potential. Mr Entwisle, a keen skier – so, clear-sighted, focussed and energetic – has a palpable commitment to getting the best out of everyone – pupils and staff alike. Married to a Spaniard and school fosters many links with Spain. Oh – and he is an expert juggler, always useful for a headmaster.

Parents are delighted: 'He's lovely with the children – he knows everyone by name and is getting an excellent new team around him.' 'His door is always open.'

Academic matters: Prep school parents enthuse: 'The teachers are wonderful – so imaginative and approachable!' – and especially about individual needs and pastoral care: 'superb – any problems or hint of bullying are dealt with at speed' and 'they answer emails practically before you've sent them'. Weekly staff meeting to discuss and act on academic or pastoral concerns with head of learning support on hand if needed. Pupil praise too – 'They push you to your potential and we are only 10 in some groups so they can really help you'. Small group specialist work in eg fine motor skills, writing, reading, phonics for tots who seem to be falling behind. All lower classes have a TA to support individuals but some feel this should continue into upper years, 'where they need it just as much if they are struggling with a subject'. As a pupil told us, 'When I'm stuck, if they take time to explain it to me, I really get it!' Individual support – and around 25 per cent on the SEND register here – described as 'good but pricey'.

Unusually large range of GCSE options includes two popular business courses, Mandarin, dance and PE alongside all the more predictable options. Also popular are art, history and geography. Impressive results in art and the sciences in particular. BTecs on offer in nine subjects – including animal management, music performance and business studies. Similarly impressive list of A level subjects includes accounting and computer science. Pre-U rather than A levels offered now in English and music – wise choices. EPQ added recently. Art, again, the stand-out subject in terms of results, but this is not – thankfully – a results-driven school. The point here is to be 'better' – school unfussed about league tables save those which measure value added – and Bede's scores very highly here. 'We prove you can have great results with inspired, holistic teaching.' Parents agree. One – a parent of three – told us: 'It's ridiculous to say it's not academic. My exceptionally bright son is brilliantly taught and is flying. And my other two, who are very different, are well-supported and are equally happy and successful.' In 2016, 45 per cent A*/A at GCSE, and 78 per cent A*-B, 53 per cent A*/A at A level.

Learning enhancement in its own block and central to the ethos of the school. Lots of screening. Years 9-11 have effective revision technique classes, and 'anyone can have learning support in individual subjects or just help with learning in general' – a useful approach. Year 9s also have 'prep project' to learn study techniques. Some 25 per cent of entrants to the earlier years and 12-15 per cent of sixth form entrants come with some kind of, usually mild, SEN. So, additional help is normal here and, as several grateful parents told us, with 'absolutely no stigma'. One parent typified the rest. 'My son has mild SEN problems – I looked at 25 schools and then made a shortlist. They all promised everything but there were cracks in what they said. Bede's learning support finds what they're good at – the teaching is multi-sensory, the classes are alive, the teachers are passionate. My son has grown in independence. He doesn't need support any more.' Others agree: 'They find ways to ensure you don't fail though, on occasions, some more constructive criticism wouldn't be bad,' we heard. Separate EAL dept.

Library not the most impressive aspect of school's provision, though modern fiction stock is good. But why a whole set of Hugh Walpole and no Thackeray? Or were Barry Lyndon and The Newcomes etc out on loan?

Games, options, the arts: Dance is big. Bede's is home to the Legat School of Dance and dance attracts much young talent to the school. One large and two smaller studios – the large one is light and lined with photos from the school's history. For some, dance increases in importance and they leave to pursue careers in this area. For others, academics or other pursuits take over and dance becomes a passionate hobby. Teaching is dedicated and inspirational. Dancers work. 'It has been hard at times but it's so convenient having everything in the same place,' one young hopeful explained. 'Dance can be stressful but the pastoral care here is amazing.' Very good drama, led by lively staff in excellent theatre and studio, encompasses the conventional to the experimental. And not just musicals. Technicians from Glyndebourne help and guide, and major productions shown in Eastbourne theatres.

Let us know if you find more inspired, better equipped or more varied ceramics anywhere. It's a real feature of the school, led by veteran potter in the Old Kennels, with three kilns, a spray glazer, electric wheels and a kick wheel dating from 1945 which he found on eBay. Graduates of this A level go on to product design, architecture, fashion, photography, interior design and textiles – a fabulous hand and eye education. Good music, super art – as good as anywhere we know. Photography, mixed media – all impress. No strait-jacketing here but evidence everywhere of imaginations encouraged to flow and flourish. Endless other activities from beekeeping to the breeding of small animals in the unique Animal Management Centre, where we met some of the 500 inhabitants including a common plec, a sun beetle and a lesser hedgehog tenrec. Links with several zoos. All go to support pupils' studies in the practicalities of animal care.

And then there's the sport. Cricket on glorious pitches – now embellished by the Martin-Jenkins Pavilion celebrating the family's links with the school. Elite sportsmen and women on the staff; many a young sports star in the making stays on here rather than joining some club programme or other, 'because it's just as good and I can do my academics too'. They do anything from athletics to water polo – huge range and super facilities. They don't necessarily win everything but some sports, eg boys' U18 tennis and football, are hard to beat. Everything done with verve and energy.

Prep school sports are exceptional – and not just because of facilities – at both ends of the spectrum. Says Mr Entwisle: 'We're the best cricketing prep in the country' and, as parents told us, 'even the non-sporty get enthused – and they have elite schemes for the really talented'. 'They do wonderful trips, especially for sports and languages.' Children concur: 'We went to Portugal and got trained by Benfica.' Senior school fields etc also used. Several teams in most sports for all years so that all but the child with thumbs glued to his iPad get a look-in, though some sense that more could be done for the less than athletic. Dance is serious so all do dance up to year 5 and many continue. Teachers seen as 'brill!'. Music has a new director and is set to sparkle; art and drama well on the way.

Boarding: Boarding – small in the prep but growing here, unlike elsewhere, with 12 full and eight weekly boarders – currently starts at year 5 (nearly half of boarders from overseas) and is found in two attractive houses over the road from the main buildings, staffed by warm and cheery houseparents with their own children on site and lively Aussie gappies. Plans afoot to develop this provision and school set to become a significant player in prep boarding on the south coast.

Just under half of the senior school board of whom 18 per cent are from overseas. Majority are full boarders, about 70 weekly. The five boarding houses, are, of course, mostly recent and cleverly designed with large, light and airy atria which act as common rooms and off which rooms radiate. This system 'produces community right away – no long corridors in which people can get lost or hide away.' No mixed houses. Younger years in rooms with four beds, later in twos or singles. Good shared bathrooms, no en-suites. Houses staffed mostly by couples/families, their cats and dogs being house pets adored by all but asthmatics. Everyone 'patriotic' about their houses.

Background and atmosphere: Unusually, Bede's Senior grew out of a prep. The prep, founded in 1895, was thriving and, in the 1970s, its then head was urged by parents to provide continuation and the search for premises was on. Could they have done better? They found a house – The Dicker – around 12 miles inland – which had belonged to the extraordinary Horatio Bottomley (well worth looking up if you don't know) – a splendid, early 20th century, arts and crafts-cum-mock-medieval-Tudor extravaganza with a splendid landscaped park surrounded by stunning countryside. Head's own 'salon' is an exquisite blend of the Victorian at its best and the ultra modern. Gorgeous 'old' dining room.

The school opened in 1979 and has, since then, spawned around 40 lesser buildings – everything from pre-fabs to a building described as a Kenyan Safari Lodge, atop which, in an improbable eyrie, sits the school library. Huge 'MPH' houses gym, pool, vast assembly space etc. Sussex flint, free-standing chapel used for talks by chaplain but no heavy-duty religion practised here. Biomass boilers and solar panels – school runs almost entirely on sustainable energy. Plans to lose several lesser buildings and construct a major, multi-flexible, classroom block – pupils are involved in the planning of the project and school pays tribute to their insights and ideas. All nestles in the park – extensive fields, meadows, gardens, plus a large, lilied lake and all, seemingly, in terrific nick. All this and train connections to London are close and quick.

You can't beat the prep for location. At the upmarket end of the grassy Eastbourne seafront where the land curves and rises to the great cliff of Beachy Head, perches an attractive five storey, mock-Tudorbethan pile, its long windows facing the sea. Surrounded by fields on all but its southern aspect, with a cluster of smaller buildings round about, it sits like a benign hen comfortably supervising its offspring, assured that all can run about safely in a healthy, beautiful, open space.

Space is a key asset and to anyone used to, for example, an urban prep or primary, Bede's is a revelation. There are more fields five minutes up the hill and another five minutes inland – all facilitate the range of sports available to these lucky children, who have the look of relaxed freedom that inhabiting such openness gives. Space also in eg the dining hall, one wall of which is just large windows fully open on warm, sunny days, so that the outside and the inside blend. No shortage of facilities, inside and out – big sports hall, 18m pool, climbing walls, decent library – 'they'll get books you want if you ask' – good theatre and lovely, light rooms with the downside that 'if I'm facing the sea I just go into a daydream,' as one youngster confessed.

Two main buildings. Holywell Mount – a large Edwardian house to the right of the main building if you face the sea – houses the pre-prep and nursery. We visited at the end of a long day and were astonished by the bright-eyed vitality of the teachers. They told us of the new topic with which each term is launched in each classroom: 'It's so exciting – they can't wait to come in and see what we're going to do!' And on offer in just some rooms were: Under the Sea World, Ice World, Out of the Egg (and you should have seen the egg!) and Knock Knock – imaginative stuff, inviting exploration and discovery of all kinds.

Pastoral care, well-being and discipline: 'Health and safety are taken very seriously,' prep school parents tell us, as are efforts to integrate newcomers, especially into year 7 when there is a fairly substantial intake. And there is masses to do. 'My daughter was very shy but there are so many performances and so on – her confidence has grown unbelievably.' Transition from other preps and primaries handled well. Integration of new pupils from different cultures, likewise. Integration of day pupils and boarders to be supported by new system of mixing up the houses. Day pupils able to stay until late and each house will have boarding, day and late-staying pupils.

Pupils consulted at each stage. 'We're a real believer in pupil leadership. They make real decisions and decide on their legacy to the school.' Tartan skirt and blouse for girls, who wear suits in the sixth; boys wear dark suits but can move into chinos in the sixth. Most enthuse about the food and all like the range of choice.

Parents testify to the absence of bullying and say that anything more than light banter between pupils is handled sensitively. 'And they don't force you to do things you're uncomfortable with,' a parent averred. 'They allow you to be who you are without mortifying you as other schools do.' Tutors, houseparents and a thoroughly understood system of rules and sanctions maintain the school's tangible peace. Few serious misdemeanours – those few handled 'both formally and personally', according to pupils. Permanent exclusions a rarity. School well up on 'safe' internet use: 'We have a group of kids advising us on what we need to know.'

A happy school – 'It's good at turning out all-rounders,' said several. 'It's pretty unsophisticated and relaxed – you don't get awful pushy parents there – they trust the school to know what it's doing.' And, in the words of a pupil, 'My parents wish they could have come here.'

Pupils and parents: From an ever-widening arc – Bognor to Hastings. The vast majority are local or local-ish. Boarders from hither and yon and likely to grow in number. Everyone from wealthy Sussex farmers to London refusniks, to looked-after children in care of the LA – seamlessly and sensitively integrated. United in being smiley, fulfilled and grateful.

Entrance: Oversubscribed at all points but not by much. This is set to change and far-sighted parents need to get down and register. For year 9 entry from 2018 onwards, applicants invited to a Bede's Experience Day, which will include a group task and discussion, interview, verbal and non-verbal reasoning assessment and a co-curricular activity. Currently, for sixth form, at least five B grades for A levels, depending on subjects.

Exit: Nearly all from the prep move up to the senior school. Far fewer now leave after GCSE and most who do go locally to sixth form colleges. Post-sixth leavers to a great range of places (50 per cent Russell Group in 2016) and courses. Lots to vocational courses eg sports management, advertising, accounting but also maths, medicine, English at Russell group universities and a few most years to Oxbridge. In 2016, two to Oxbridge and two medics; 20 per cent to creative/media/performing arts courses and a further 16 students to art colleges.

Alumni of either the prep and/or the senior branch include Eddie Izzard, Nicky Henson, Jamie Lloyd, footballers Dan Harding and Solomon March and a growing stream of cricketers including Ollie Rayner, Luke Wells and, newbie, Shai Hope.

Money matters: Scholarships of up to 25 per cent and a good and growing bursary fund. But – being a newish school – without massive endowments etc, of course.

Remarks: School says, 'What we want parents to know is that their children will be bloody well taught and we are doing great things with them.' Parent says, 'Look at it seriously – whoever your child is'. Pupil says, 'I am so lucky to be here.'

Beechwood Park School

24

Markyate, St Albans, Hertfordshire AL3 8AW

Pupils: 523; 40 boys, 20 girls flexi boarders • Ages: 3–13 (boarding from year 5)

Fees: Day £10,155 – £15,225; Flexi boarding plus £3,618 pa

Tel: 01582 840333
Email: admissions@beechwoodpark.com
Website: www.beechwoodpark.com/

Headmaster: Since 2015, Edward Balfour, previously head of Northbourne Park School in Kent. Studied education at Homerton College Cambridge; has taught English and drama at RGS Worcester and English at Whitgift, and been head of drama and housemaster at Bradfield College. Married with three young children.

Entrance: The school has a nursery (Woodlands Nursery) which has recently moved to new purpose-built premises on the main school site. All children above nursery age are assessed before entry. For reception children, expect informal assessment (school stresses this isn't about ability but behaviour). Some year groups have waiting lists, so best to get in early.

Exit: The school is praised by parents for 'knowing the children', and parents and pupils alike are carefully navigated through the decision process. St Albans, St Albans High School and Haberdashers' Aske's (Boys and Girls) are popular choices. Other contenders include local grammars, Berkhamsted, Bedford, Merchant Taylors', Uppingham, Queenswood and Haileybury. Respectable numbers of bursaries.

Remarks: Rural setting in west Hertfordshire, with far-reaching views over farms and woodland. That is, if you can find it. Our GPS took us down a muddy single track lane where we had to do a U-turn at a field entrance. According to school staff, this isn't uncommon, though they told us signage has now been greatly improved. The grade 1 listed building and beautiful parkland have a rich history, playing home to barons, nuns and visits from royalty through the years. One effusive parent remarked it reminded him of Swallows and Amazons. We couldn't see any lakes, but we see what he means.

School caters for children up to year 8, with a new on-site nursery (Woodlands Nursery). Class sizes hover around 20. Setting begins in year 4, with a scholarship set in year 8. Pupils are prepared for 11+ and 13+ entry to senior schools. Parents we spoke to were happy with academics. 'The results speak for themselves', we were told. Boy to girl ratio is 60:40 up to the age of 11, when the majority of girls leave. A brave few stay on – 'I like to be different', said one. It is worth checking expected intakes for individual years as these ratios are not for everyone. Ethnic mix reflects the local demographic. Pupils commute from a 30-mile radius, many catching one of the school buses. There is a strong Christian ethos and assembly is held daily. Senior choirs sing at local churches once a term.

Around 10 per cent of pupils receive SEN support in school (principally for dyslexia, dyspraxia and Asperger's). No extra charge for this (three cheers), unless foreign language assistance is also required. Plenty of help offered in early years; children are weaned off one-to-one support by key stage 2. Staff promise the door is always open for children to return, although one

B

mother found this transition hard. 'It feels like my son gets less support now', she told us.

Classrooms vary from bright and modern in the junior school to more formal learning spaces for older children. Regency library was advertised as a wow factor by our young guides. Perhaps a little over-hyped (though we admired their enthusiasm) but it is well-stocked with antique books as well as a broad selection of children's literature. In the generous music block, we were treated to a recorder recital in one of the 15 practice rooms.

As you would expect with generous grounds, sport is important and the school has many successful teams, particularly in rugby and cross-country, though we noticed that pictures of boys holding trophies dominated the news pages of the website. Pupils who don't make school teams are encouraged to develop as athletes with the aim that 'everyone can find something they are good at'. The 'sports for all' programme claims breadth, with sailing (for a select few), climbing and golf on offer alongside the more obvious, although this only truly kicks in from middle school.

Huge numbers of after-school activities – outdoor adventures to touch-typing to Brazilian soccer – are a boon for working parents. Children are actively encouraged to take up an instrument and there are concerts and workshops. Five choirs, orchestra, drama, language clubs – 'my friend has really got into Greek this term' – and cookery are all on offer. Parents applaud the breadth. 'My 7-year-old does cello, football, cricket, drama and papercraft', said one. 'It is a well-rounded school'.

Pupils we spoke to were generally happy, apart from usual minor grumbles like 'too much homework' and 'food could be better'. We can't vouch for homework, but the lunch we sampled was adequate, if a little stodgy (school says there are at least eight salads on the menu at each meal, sometimes more, food is generally considered excellent and menus are well-balanced). Parents are enthusiastic about the school too. We heard comments like 'the teachers know the kids well and have their eyes on the ball', 'it has met our expectations' and 'I wouldn't change a thing'.

Pastoral care is seen as a priority. Pupils 'are aware of values' and enjoy a credit system awarded for good behaviour (our guide proudly showed us her badges and values booklet). School encourages good behaviour by 'supporting and challenging children so there is no time to be naughty'; the bad behaviour that does exist is managed with a debit system. Pupils we spoke to see it as a fair system. We heard no reports of bullying and while it was acknowledged that disagreements can break out, we were assured that teachers can be relied on to 'help them sort it out'. One parent (a former pupil himself) said that 'pastoral care was the key driver in choosing this school for my son', while another told us, 'I do have a few concerns sometimes, but I suppose it's hard to supervise that many children on the playground'.

Flexi-boarding is offered during the week (no boarding at weekends) in clean and modern dorms run by married houseparents. Roughly a third of all children in years 5 to 8 board, many staying a couple of nights each week: 'I'm not ready to board full time yet, so this is perfect for me,' said one pupil. Boys and girls have separate dormitories, but share common rooms kitted out with air hockey, darts and Xbox. No mobile browsing allowed, but pupils can call home whenever they want.

Belmont Preparatory School (Dorking)

Feldemore, Holmbury St Mary, Dorking, Surrey RH5 6LQ

Pupils: 228; 5 weekly, 35 flexi boarders • Ages: 2–13 • C of E

Fees: Day £8,610 – £14;340 Boarding + £3,000 – £6,450 pa

Tel: 01306 730852
Email: schooloffice@belmont-school.org
Website: www.belmont-school.org

Headmistress: Since 2006, Mrs Helen Skrine BA. Following a music degree at Exeter, she took up posts teaching music, English and Latin at Wrekin College, Greenacre School, and Chinthurst Prep and was deputy head at Highfield School, Liphook.

A sound business head comes across when she describes how she has steered the school through the challenges of the recession, but there's also a strong maternal streak. On our tour we came across a boy with a bloodied knee being helped in by his friends. 'Oh my darling boy,' she exclaimed. 'Let's get that knee up. Matron is coming with her blue light on.'

Described by parents as 'very hands on and responsive' and 'a strong but caring leader.' Much praised for pastoral care. 'She has even offered support to our son whilst he struggles to adjust to secondary school,' said one mother. Another said: 'She is completely honest and open when it comes to issues with bullying. We were approached by her regarding our daughter being upset in school, something we found most refreshing.'

Two sons now at university. Her home is next door to the school building, not even a stone's throw away. She's not remotely tempted to move off site for a more private off-duty life, as some heads are. 'Last evening the children were all outside here playing,' she said. 'Some boys came to borrow the dog. I love it. It's a life, not a job.'

Entrance: 'First and foremost I look at the parents,' says the head. Yikes. No need to brush up on algebra though – she means she wants to be sure that they are buying into the school's ethos, which is not of the all-stations-to-Oxbridge variety. 'We want parents who understand what the ethos of this school is,' she says. 'We do a really good job academically but we are also interested in developing the co-curriculum areas and developing the children as people. I really believe school should be fun, not weighed down in endless testing, stress and strain.'

Who wouldn't it suit? 'Some of the tiger mums I met in my daughter's previous school,' says one mother. Another parent concurs, telling us: 'I haven't met any overly pushy parents at Belmont but I imagine that they would struggle to fit in.'

Next on the head's selection list is: 'Does the child have a spring in his/her step, will they throw themselves into everything and will they fit academically in the range of the year group?' Assessment is through reasoning tests and classroom observation. 'We won't take children outside the average range, but we will take low average pupils – sometimes it's just that they're not thriving in their current school,' the head says. Once in, the children are guaranteed a place until 13, unless any serious learning difficulties arise.

Key points of entry are at 2, reception, year 3 – and some come from other preps at 11. Entrance mid-school is well catered for. A mother told us: 'The parents in my daughter's year have been extremely welcoming. A barbecue and trip to

Legoland were organised by the class rep before the start of the academic year so the new children could meet everyone before their first day. Mothers were quick to give me tips and advice about matters such as games kit.'

There's a two form entry per year, and that's the limit. 'I won't go to more than 32 to a year group,' says the head. 'I don't believe big is beautiful.'

Exit: Most parents are buying into private education for the duration – it's rare for a child to leave at 11 for local state secondaries. The head is a big fan of boarding and the children spread their wings far and wide. St John's, Hurstpierpoint College, Lancing, Box Hill, Dunottar, Seaford College, Lancing, Claremont Fan and Manor House all popular recently.

Remarks: The campus is a glorious 65 acres, with children's playtime roaming through nooks and glades – only constrained by dots on the trees, which indicate when they are out of hearing range of the bell. The main school building is based around the one-time home of Edwin Waterhouse (of the Price Waterhouse Cooper accountancy firm), and although the original 1880 house was rebuilt after a fire, it retains its grandeur, with high corniced ceilings, lots of wood panelling and deep window seats. Classrooms for the older children are based here, while years 2 to 4 are accommodated in a modern building, and early years children – two reception and two year 1 classes – have their own buildings arranged around a courtyard, patrolled by three cats.

Specialist subject teaching kicks in from year 5, and children are split into two sets for all CE or scholarship subjects in years 5 to 8. This is flexible, with lots of movement between the sets, and pupils feel it's no big deal to be in a lower set. 'It's exactly the same work – they just slow it down to your speed,' they explained to us.

Parents are overjoyed by the fact there is no homework until year 7 (even then it's not an arduous load, with two preps of half an hour each). Up until then prep is timetabled in a daytime session. 'This is where Belmont differs from most prep schools,' a parent told us. 'They actively keep the pressure off the children and parents right up until year 7. The work handed in is theirs alone, and not the parents'. In addition, the school never sets time-consuming projects for the children where the parents end up spending endless hours making models of Egyptian vases or the like. 'It's such a relief, as a working parent.'

Feedback to parents comes in the form of half termly grades, full written reports twice a year and parents' evenings. There's lots of informal reporting. 'Every parent has the email address of every teacher,' says the head. 'I encourage email and we have a policy of getting back within 24 hours.' There's also afternoon tea with the head on a Friday afternoon, which parents say is a great way to meet other parents and have an informal chat with the head and teachers.

The head is passionate about ensuring that it's not just academic achievement that carries kudos here. 'We get lots of awards for things such as work of the week, good manners, boarder of the week,' said the children. During our visit the head's table was strewn with rosettes and certificates – all being sorted ready for prize-giving at the weekly assembly. 'Winning a commendation certificate from the headmistress is a most sought after prize,' said one parent.

An array of clubs. These can be mixed and matched, most having no requirement to commit for a term – no battles then to haul a recalcitrant child along to a club which he didn't like by week two. Invitation clubs for the most talented run alongside general access clubs.

Sport is very much an all-inclusive affair. The commitment to involve everyone, combined with small year groups, mean that if a prestigious A team is high on your list, it may not be the place for you. 'Some may feel it does not have enough children to pick teams of excellence,' said one parent. 'We feel our daughter plays her major sports externally, at county level, so for us she is learning to be a team player, to lose sometimes, and to enjoy sport.'

Another told us: 'Small class sizes and year group numbers do limit sports team ability levels at times since the teams often have to mix in different year groups. The benefit of this, however, is that every child, however good or bad at sport, gets to play sport for the school.'

Head points out that the school fields U13, U11 and U9 teams that are selected on ability, and says they 'win many more games than they lose.' Parents praise the school's willingness to embrace individual needs – timetabling cricket and tennis sessions with the boys' teams for a very sporty girl, for example.

On the arts side, the head says 'every child is on stage in front of the parents at least once a year.' Bands, choirs and string groups, with teaching from a professional opera singer and a director of drama. The school has its own biannual festival, Bel Artis, where visiting professionals lead workshops for children, culminating with an evening of performance.

The school shares the site with Moon Hall, a specialist school for dyslexia. The two have separate governing bodies and are separate companies, but there's much crossover outside academic lessons. The Moon Hall children wear Belmont uniform and join Belmont for playtime, assembly, lunches and extracurricular activities. They can be in a school play and board alongside the Belmont pupils. Superb option if you have a dyslexic in the family.

Children can be dropped for breakfast from 7.30am and parents have a broad range of pick up times to choose from – at the end of the school day at 4.30pm, after clubs at 5.45pm, after supper at 6.30pm, after prep at 7.45pm, or children can board for an occasional night or any number up to five nights per week. All of this can be done on an ad hoc basis, so there is great flexibility for the working parent. Nearly 100 pupils board in some form, mostly flexi. 'Our daughter begs to board as often as we will let her,' a mother told us. 'It is a wonderfully warm and friendly environment with the boarders doing lots of interesting activities and going on trips.'

Benenden School

Cranbrook Road, Benenden, Cranbrook, Kent TN17 4AA

Pupils: 550 (all full boarders) • Ages: 11–18 • Sixth form: 188 • C of E

Fees: Boarding £35,700 pa

Tel: 01580 240592
Email: registry@benenden.kent.sch.uk
Website: www.benenden.kent.sch.uk

Headmistress: Since 2014, Mrs Samantha Price, 40s. Attended Malvern Girls' College (now Malvern St James), so knows about life at a girls' boarding school from both sides. Read history of art at Edinburgh University and began her career in the Tate Britain marketing department, but soon felt office-bound and switched to teaching. Worked at Reading Blue Coat School, King's Canterbury and Hereford Cathedral School before taking up her first headship at Godolphin School in Salisbury, from whence she was headhunted for her present post. Leaving was a very difficult decision, she says, but she has no regrets: 'Benenden is my dream school, and full boarding is in my DNA.' Married to Iori, an army chaplain, with a young daughter and son.

A passionate devotee of girls' education, and a powerhouse of ideas and energy underneath a warm and civilised exterior. 'I'm very proud of this school. It's a wonderful place to be.'

Academic matters: Impressive: in 2016, 82 per cent A*/A at GCSE and 74 per cent A*/A at A level (A*/B 92 per cent). Pretty much always in the top 50 independent schools nationally. Everything you'd expect on offer, with breadth prized as much as depth: girls study a good range of languages, both modern and classical, and DT, art, music and drama are compulsory throughout the lower school. Science very popular, and is taught in truly amazing brand new science block, all glass and blond wood, opened in 2012: a floor per science, and at least three laboratories per floor, plus designated experiment rooms just for sixth formers, and a 150-seater lecture theatre which hosts a rolling programme of visiting speakers. 'My daughter's teachers have inspired her to be really passionate about science,' wrote one happy father, 'and she has really enjoyed science club.' Classrooms are large, modern and well-equipped, and superb library offers space and quiet.

No plans to introduce the IB: A levels are taught as part of a refreshingly commonsense yet innovative approach which makes any such change unnecessary. Girls can almost always study the combination of subjects they want, and the EPQ is offered to all girls to provide additional academic challenge. Lots of skills and vocational courses on offer which sound genuinely appealing rather than drearily functional. For instance, 'I don't think we'll do a food technology A level,' says head, 'but we might run Cordon Bleu courses, and I'd like to run the Leith's Diploma. Being realistic and practical will be increasingly what gets you ahead.' No danger of gender bias in this forward-looking school, however: DT is one of the most popular options, taught in an excellently-resourced technology block which even sports its own ICT suite. The school has introduced a Professional Skills Programme for the sixth form, which enables girls to work alongside professionals in a variety of fields and develop real-life experience of eg reading balance sheets, developing ideas into business proposals. For younger pupils there's the Benenden Diploma (years 7 and 8) and real life problem solving linked to different aspects of service for year 9s. Entrepreneur and engineer in residence in 2016.

The tutor system allows for a lot of contact time, and parents and students alike praise the caring and friendly approach. SEN department supports those girls diagnosed with dyslexia and dyspraxia, and students can have weekly individual lessons if needed (as with most independent schools, these are chargeable). That said, the school acknowledges that this probably isn't the school for those with more than mild difficulties. Extension programme for gifted and talented throughout the school.

Wherever we looked we saw girls relishing the curricular opportunities on offer. As one put it, 'At a school like this, you get to try everything!' A parent added, 'Academically, my daughter has come on amazingly since she joined the school.'

Games, options, the arts: 'You've got to involve yourself,' observed our tour guide, and there's so much to do here that it really would be crazy not to. Loads of traditional girls' sports, with lacrosse, netball and tennis topping the list; but more niche activities such as scuba diving and pool also popular. Dance is big here: there's a lovely dance studio where girls can learn tap, ballet and contemporary dance, plus a rather ace fitness suite for those wishing to acquire the body beautiful (or just keep fit). New all-weather sports pitch and pavilion.

Fabulous theatre was opened by Helena Bonham Carter, staffed by two full-time technicians from whom the girls can learn lighting, sound and set construction. Professionals would kill to have facilities this good. Drama is concomitantly lively with at least two major productions a year and lots of student-led performances. LAMDA also flourishing. Music block was built in the 1960s and in another school would be something to boast about, but here looks down-at-heel and in fact is due to be rebuilt soon. Masses of music going on notwithstanding – instrumental lessons, ensembles, orchestra, choir, the works. Art and design is particularly impressive, with wonderful work on display: etching, lino printing and some whacky sculpture rubbed shoulders with really beautiful embroidery. How refreshing to find a school where girls can still learn such things if they wish to.

Lots of trips both home and abroad. Good range of weekend activities appreciated by students and parents alike. 'My daughter has thoroughly enjoyed the weekend programme,' said one grateful mother.

Boarding: All students here are full boarders. School is relaxed about letting girls go home at weekends. Boarding rooms are colourful, light and homely – perhaps a little crowded for some tastes, with up to five girls in a room for the lower school, but all the girls we spoke to insisted they liked it that way. Older girls can choose to have smaller rooms and fewer room-mates, and all sixth formers have their own room in a deluxe modern block built especially for them, designed to be a halfway house between school and university. Fully equipped and spotlessly clean, we couldn't help thinking that most university accommodation would be a bit of a come-down afterwards.

Background and atmosphere: Started in 1923 by Miss Sheldon, Miss Hindle and Miss Bird, three teachers from Wycombe Abbey, the school moved to its present site in 1924 and has flourished ever since. Held in immensely high esteem by its alumna, many of whom had gathered to pay it affectionate respect when we happened to visit. Many girls here whose mothers – even grandmothers – attended the school.

The original house, Hemsted, still serves as the school's main building, and must be everyone's idea of what an English boarding school looks like. The magnificent wood-panelled entrance hall and staircase are hung with portraits of the Earl of Cranbrook's family, and coats of arms are etched upon the stained glass. It was actually built in the 19th century, but was designed to look much older, and the effect is frankly gorgeous. We found ourselves thinking of Daisy Pulls It Off, and apparently most newcomers cry 'Hogwarts!' as soon as they get through the front door. It's still possible to board in Hemsted, and the girls that do told us they absolutely love it.

However, a massive programme of refurbishment over the past 20 years has ensured that Benenden can more than hold its own in the 21st century. All the facilities here are stunningly good, and the whole is set in 240 acres of exquisitely landscaped grounds: beyond the playing fields, where we saw girls desporting themselves at lacrosse, are lawns, roses, woods, water features, flower beds, a walled garden, lime tree avenue, all overlooking miles of hills and greenery beyond. 'I love it!' confirmed a cheerful sixth former, adding in proper Benenden patois, 'and you can walk into vill whenever you like.'

Excellent school shop, where students can buy everything needful from shampoo to study aids, and an air of unfussy practicality throughout. Food universally praised (we can confirm the chocolate brownies were to die for), and girls say that their suggestions for the menu are listened to. Impressive building programme has added eight new staff houses to overcome issue of local property prices deterring many good teachers from applying. New school hall and music school will be built in the next few years. This is a school that takes people's everyday comfort seriously, and puts its money where its mouth is.

Pastoral care, well-being and discipline: No real behaviour issues – this is a happy ship, and the care and support given to the girls were praised everywhere. 'It was a big move to the UK for my daughter,' wrote an overseas mother, 'and the house staff looked after her as if she were their own, giving cuddles and love whenever she needed it. They still do so now.' And everyone we contacted said something similar. In addition to her tutor and housemistress, each girl is allocated an older girl or 'big sister' to look after her, and girls spoke to us with fondness about the friends they'd made across the different year groups.

Rules are enforced with a light touch. One mother commented, 'I like the fact that they teach the girls the right thing to do rather than impose really strict rules, eg they don't ban access to the internet – even for the younger girls; they spend time teaching them about internet safety instead.' Girls said again and again that they felt able to be themselves, and mothers frequently commented that their daughters hadn't felt pressured into growing up too quickly.

Considerable privileges and latitude given to sixth formers, who really value the increased independence and are consequently less likely to switch to co-ed at this stage. The school has opened a new cafe bar where sixth formers can buy a glass of wine on a Saturday night (with parental permission). All the girls wear uniform, even the sixth, but it's an unfussy uniform and the girls honestly didn't seem to mind – it's a community that fosters a sensible and pragmatic attitude to life's challenges. As one parent enthused, 'Everything at Benenden is done so smoothly and efficiently. Our daughter loves it and so do we. We are struggling to find a school as good as this for our son!' Another wrote, 'My daughter speaks of being school-sick during the holidays, the opposite of homesick, because she loves everything about the school so much – she is very, very happy at Benenden.'

Pupils and parents: Fees are high, and Princess Anne may be Benenden's most famous alumna, but this is not a school for snobs. About 12 per cent from abroad, many of them expats. Otherwise, families are solid professional London and home counties people who want the best for their children and 'work their socks off to send their girls here,' according to head. Bursary assistance ensures at least some social diversity: one girl on a 110 per cent bursary spoke movingly to us about her own experience: 'The school has helped in every possible way. I've never felt out of place, and I owe them so much.'

Entrance: Forty girls join at 11 and 50 girls at 13. Both intakes oversubscribed, but not dauntingly so. Plan ahead, though: the lists can close a year or more in advance. From 2018 entry, early offers programme means 13+ entrants can be offered a firm place in year 7. Girls have to achieve at least 55 per cent at common entrance, but in practice many applicants will, so the school also uses pre-tests and interviews and works closely with local prep schools to be sure they're getting it right. 'We're looking for sound academic competence and potential. We're a broad church.' Occasional places for other years – the school operates a waiting list. Entry to sixth form dependent on exam, interview and current head's report, but fantastic sixth form opportunities mean that very few existing students leave, so not many additional places available.

Exit: At 16, hardly anyone (just under seven per cent in 2016): occasionally girls may opt for a co-ed experience at schools such as Charterhouse. At 18, about 10 per cent to Oxbridge (12 in 2016), the rest mostly to Russell group universities (half places are in UK top 10) to read a broad range of subjects – engineering and physics currently enjoying a surge in numbers. London, Durham, Bristol and Exeter all popular destinations. An increasing number to US and Ivy League colleges (nine in total, including one to Yale in 2016). Others to British Columbia, HKU and Grenada.

Money matters: Scholarships of up to 10 per cent for academics, music, art, DT, sports and drama. Those who've been awarded a scholarship can apply to the generous bursary fund: a number of girls here benefit from means-tested assistance of up to 80 per cent. The Benenden School Trust also offers up to three 110 per cent bursaries each year to girls coming from local state schools.

Remarks: Traditional girls' boarding brought radiantly up to date, jettisoning what was bad, retaining everything good and adding a huge amount more. An exciting and appealing place: if we were young again, we'd be clamouring to go there.

Bentley Church of England Primary School

School Lane, Bentley, Farnham, Surrey GU10 5JP

Pupils: 215 • Ages: 4–11 • C of E

Tel: 01420 525010
Email: admin.office@bentley.hants.sch.uk
Website: www.bentleyschool.co.uk

Headmistress: Since 2012, Mrs Katy Pinchess (40s); began her career as a buyer of children's books for Waterstones before settling on teaching (her mother was a head teacher, so it's in the blood). Experience includes setting up CET Primary School Westminster, a free school in central London. Returned to Hampshire and joined Bentley C of E after a stint as head mistress of Bordon Infants. Keen to build on 20-year legacy of previous head Phil Callaway, who transformed Bentley from two-room village school into highly sought-after primary through personal dedication and judicious financial management. Parents seem confident that she will step into his rather large shoes and say, 'Everyone's really pleased, she's a lovely person.' Energetic and hands on, she is married with two young children.

Entrance: Sought-after primary school and always over-subscribed. At the time of our visit almost all places were taken by children from the catchment area of Bentley and Froyle. Any remaining out of catchment places (very few) usually go to siblings of a child already in the school. Routinely has a waiting list for reception and years 1 and 2.

Exit: As in previous years, about two-thirds plump for Eggars School in Alton (local state secondary). One third chooses independent education; local private schools include Alton Convent, Churchers, Guildford Grammar and High Schools and Lord Wandsworth College.

Remarks: Founded in 1842 on land given by the Bishop of Winchester, Bentley C of E has been modernised and expanded several times since the turn of last century. Still sits in a pretty bucolic location more than 150 years later, next to a winding country lane surrounded by cottages, fields and hedgerows. It's very easy to imagine how this typical village school might have looked in Victorian times. Charming it may be, but any similarity to old fashioned education stops as soon as one crosses the threshold. Bentley is a vibrant, modern little primary school which punches well above its weight.

Eleven and 12-year-olds regularly achieve outstanding results in year 6 Sats tests (well above the national average). Some 97

B

per cent of students score level 4 or above in reading, writing, maths and science; the one or two that score below this almost always have statements. Two or three manage a stratospheric level 6; 100 per cent get level 4+ in maths and English. With a full-time staff-to-pupil ratio of 1:20 and average class sizes of 30 children, we conclude that Bentley is fortunate to have some excellent teachers, ably supported by learning support assistants in each year group. 'Teachers are so enthusiastic and their energy reflects on the children.'

Most unusually in a state school, everyone learns French. Rest of curriculum as expected; topic work links the disciplines, especially literacy, science, geography, ICT and history. Although classroom atmosphere is relaxed and very friendly, children appear busy, engaged and enthusiastic – even at the tail end of a science lesson just before the lunch bell. ICT provision is good; school has largely moved away from fixed terminals to laptops and tablets; contributions from very active Parent, Teacher and Friend Association (PTFA) keep these up-to-date. Wireless network throughout and interactive whiteboards are in every classroom (not always the case in village schools). Reporting system is fairly informal, via regular parents' evenings and written reports at year end. Head says, 'Meet and chat sessions for parents happen several times a year [for reading, maths and spelling].' Parents add, 'There is very much an open-door policy.' School looks after the gifted and talented as well as those with special needs. Deputy head works with the most able in small groups in years 5 and 6; special needs assistant in every class works with children requiring extra help (almost always classroom-based).

Naturally, Bentley isn't blessed with acres of playing fields like many of its independent cousins, but manages remarkably well with the resources it does have. Reception and years 1 and 2 have their own playground and equipment, fenced off from the 'big children'. Years 3 up use a separate courtyard playground at the front of the school. The 'back playground', a grass pitch at one side of the school, is marked out for games, eg football, cricket, tag rugby, athletics and rounders. Boys' teams drawn up from year 3 onwards – girls wait till year 5, and sadly main focus is on boys' sport. Adjacent woodland area has a trim trail through the trees. School also enjoys the use of much larger, council-owned recreation ground for running and sports matches. The children showing us round said wistfully that they wished they had more access. Sighed the head, 'Health and safety doesn't allow us.' Swimming (at nearby Treloar School's pool) once a week for year 3; year 1 get a taste of tennis. Bentley has nonetheless notched up a respectable sporting record. Recent successes include: national six-a-side football championship runners-up, under-11 county football champions, Isle of Wight rugby champions, under-10 and under-11 country cricket champions (girls were Kwik Cricket county champions and came 4th in Southern National Championships in 2013) and area winners of national dance and basketball finals. Those with a talent for sport get extra coaching sessions from specialists on Friday afternoons. Clubs include netball, fencing and gym.

Music has a higher profile here than at most state primaries and Bentley has a dedicated, if cosy, music room. A big draw has to be Mr Hoare the piano teacher, who plays in a rock band and seriously looks the part. No surprise, then, that at least 50 children are learning the piano. A good handful each learns violin, clarinet, guitar and various brass instruments. Small school orchestra and choir perform from time to time (lots of keyboards and instruments stashed in a cupboard next to the dining hall). A local secondary offers extra coaching sessions to musicians with potential. Two Christmas plays, plus a fully-fledged drama production in year 6 (Bugsy Malone) make full use of school hall. No dedicated art room, but plenty of evidence of creativity on display, eg Giacometti-inspired figures from coat hangers made by year 6. School puts on as many educational visits as possible and firmly believes in residential trips for juniors from year 3 up, eg to Gordon Brown Centre (environmental studies) and Calshot (activities and watersports). 'They do a lot of off-site stuff and pull in experts regularly, such as sports coaches and authors,' said a parent.

Aims to promote a kind environment; regular anti-bullying days are reinforced by discussions in classroom circle time. School's close 'family' feel means that 'new children are treated like celebrities.' The vicar of Bentley (also a school governor) leads assembly once a week. Teachers take the lead in pointing out unacceptable behaviour (we observed a reception teacher doing just that) but no child is ever made to feel the black sheep. Staff will always listen to parental concerns. Classroom assistants are usually parents themselves and are quick to pick up on any problems. 'There's always someone there to look out [for the children] on a motherly level.' Older children are encouraged to take responsibility for younger pupils, eg year 6 students read stories to reception. Good array of clubs on offer after school, from the musical (orchestra, choir, guitar, recorders) through sporting (judo, fencing, netball, gym, tennis, football, basketball) to ceramics and science clubs. Keen swimmers in upper years can go to Treloar pool before school to train. School canteen provides hot meals to around three-quarters of children every weekday (food is fresh, varied and inexpensive). PTFA raises money for the school (typically £15,000 per annum) which helps to fund new building projects, purchase new books and technology, part-fund the very popular Bonfire Night and run one of the school's two minibuses. 'This means we can take an entire class out for a day trip.' Two class reps in each year group organise regular social events.

Located in rural Hampshire, the majority of families are inevitably white middle class, although we did spot the odd ethnic minority face here and there. Parents are very involved in the life of the school, helping out in the classroom, library, after school, on trips and during sporting events. 'A lot of people are prepared to give up time and money to make sure we continue to do what we do.' They stress, however, that Bentley isn't overflowing with pushy types. 'The children all see the school as an extension of their family ... it's more than just a school.' Anyone with young children living within the catchment area and willing to get stuck in to school life will be fortunate if they gain a place.

Berkhamsted Preparatory School

Linked with Berkhamsted School

Doctors Commons Road, Berkhamsted, Hertfordshire HP4 3DW

Pupils: 523 • Ages: 3–11

Fees: £10,065 – £14,265 pa

Tel: 01442 358201
Email: admissions@berkhamstedschool.org
Website: www.berkhamstedschool.org.uk

Headmaster: Since 2013, Jamie Hornshaw BEd, NPQH (40s). Recently completed MEd in educational leadership at Buckingham. Educated at Borden Grammar in Sittingbourne and Plymouth University, where he took his primary teaching degree. Intent that Berkhamsted prep no longer seen as an easy shoo-in to the increasingly competitive senior school, entry to which he wants to be 'seen as a bonus.' Investing heavily in freshening up both the site and the staff room – 'lots of rolling up sleeves and getting back to basics.'

Formerly head of the British School of Paris Junior School. Cut teeth as year 3 teacher at St Peter's Prep in Devon, followed by Hazelwood School in Surrey, teaching years 3 and 4 as well as running sports teams and directing plays. Joined Grove Place Prep in Hampshire as deputy head and head of English and drama before moving to Brentwood Prep as deputy head. Attracted to Berkhamsted by 'family and community ethos,' inheriting it after a shaky period following merger with Haresfoot Prep. Now in the process of 'taking school by the scruff of its neck and moving it up a division' – as stated in his recent prize-giving speech: 'Status Quo's a great name for a band but not an ethos for a running a school.' Parents in favour of improvements made so far. 'He has a great communication style,' said one, referring to head's introduction of new weekly update to share successes, and his Twitter feed, which regularly reminds parents about calendar events and results. Lives on site with wife and two daughters, both Berkhamsted pupils.

Head of pre-prep since September 2015 is Karen O'Connor, formerly acting head of The Rosary Roman Catholic School in Camden.

Entrance: Non-selective entry into pre-prep at 3+ and 4+ currently oversubscribed. Fifty-four places in nursery class and reception, with around half moving up from the on-site Berkhamsted Day Nursery. Six additional places in year 2 and a further 12 in year 3.

Entry into prep more selective, particularly as places for children hoping to join senior school from other preps are becoming harder fought for, especially since addition of new year 5 class, bringing the year groups for years 5 and 6 up to around 90 children in each, with five classes of maximum 20. Standardised testing in English and maths for applicants from year 3 and up. Fifty children recently tested for year 5 with just 15 places offered – 'we don't want to be seen as a soft option any more,' says head. Most make successful transition from pre-prep to prep, with a tiny minority who it is felt won't be able to keep up supported in finding more suitable schools.

Exit: Almost exclusively to Berkhamsted senior school at 11+ (nine sports, music and drama scholarships/exhibitions in 2016). A handful each year head off to state maintained grammar schools and one or two to schools traditionally seen as more academic, eg St Albans.

Remarks: School split between pre-prep, for children from nursery to year 2, and prep, across two different sites, about a five minute drive apart and with totally different vibes. Visitors to the pre-prep, housed on the former Haresfoot site, can't fail to be charmed – if not stunned – by the picturesque setting and seemingly endless acres of land. Superb facilities and spacious classrooms, many newly built for 2015, sit amongst walled gardens tipping off into woodlands, home to the adventure playground and new high wires course. And what could make spelling tests any sweeter than taking them in a 20 acre meadow? Huge sports hall dwarfed the tiny tots we saw rehearsing their show and a new reception classroom block (2015) is the cherry on top of this idyllic setting.

The prep has a more businesslike atmosphere and instantly gives the impression of a very large school – when pupils arrive here in year 3 they leave behind a dreamy country prep environment for one which feels so urban it could almost be in London. A recent facelift, however, has left buildings very smart with few tatty corners, and pupils continue to enjoy excellent facilities – as well as occasionally those shared with the senior school, including theatre, pool, playing fields and brand new food tech room. Slight wistfulness about lack of prep fields to run on at playtimes – especially from parents of boys.

Majority of pupils from two to three mile radius, with many moving to the area for the 3-18 education found here. Very little ethnic mix but demographically diverse – plenty of first time buyers with a bit of old money thrown in for good measure. Lots of dual income commuting families keen to benefit from outstanding wrap-around care and new, modern approach to communication: 'Things like the introduction of electronic booking for parents' evenings make life so much easier,' said one.

Pre-prep offers a gentle and nurturing start to school life. 'We don't support cursive writing being taught from 5,' says head. 'The only benefit is marketing to parents.' Homework – or 'home learning' as it's known here – is optional and the focus is on 'being mindful of every stage of development,' and allowing children to grow at their own pace. Things step up in the prep school with a well-structured timetable and parents praising the fact that 'it suits all academic abilities – those who aren't super bright don't get lost,' and reporting that children are generally pushed to reach their potential and are 'well prepared' for examinations, especially those for entry to senior school. Head concurs: 'In a mixed ability cohort we provide for the strongest and the weakest.'

Traditional, formal curriculum with French from reception and twice a week from year 3, science 'going great guns,' according to head and history top choice with the children due to 'inspirational' departmental head, whose room is 'like a museum'. DT specialist taught from year 3 in well-equipped lab, complete with dye sublimation machine to provide greater links with the art department. Drama on curriculum from year 3. Tasters of Mandarin and Latin in year 6 give pupils an idea of what's on offer at the senior school. Children mainly class taught to year 3 with lessons almost exclusively specialist taught by year 5 in a format 'closely modelled on what they'll experience when they move up to senior school.' Subtle streaming for reading from year 1 and maths from year 2. Maths groups split into sets from year 3 with movement on a half termly basis so 'it's never a white rabbit moment to parents,' says head.

Team of five SEN experts – all dyslexia specialists – work across all Berkhamsted schools, with about 10 per cent of the cohort on their register. Although they are qualified to work across all levels, there is an acknowledgement that 'the pace is fast' once pupils hit the upper prep years and 'they have to be able to cope – it wouldn't be the right school for children with greater needs.' Able to deal with mild to moderate dyslexia, dyspraxia and children on the autistic spectrum. All children screened in year 3 with a mixed programme of in-class and one-to-one help, and those with the greatest needs removed from French.

Parents uniformly comment on 'huge range of opportunities on offer' and this highly evident in music and drama. All children play a stringed instrument in year 2 with peripatetic lessons available from year 1. There are choirs, bands and ensembles aplenty from year 2 upwards and LAMDA on curriculum to year 6. Huge number of productions and recitals on the calendar, with every year producing its own show annually – recent successes: Peter Pan and Wind in the Willows.

Alongside drama, pupils name sport as top dog – and honours boards around the school demonstrate commitment and excellence, not just in the usual suspects but also minor sports like tennis and swimming, although with two games sessions and one PE lesson a week there's not as much coaching as at some preps. It's football, rugby and cricket for boys and lacrosse, netball and rounders for the girls as major sports. New focus on making sport accessible for more children following appointment of new head of sport in 2013, with initiatives like 'sports pupil of the term' – a prize for endeavour, not necessarily achievement – introduced. Competitive successes are 'on the up', according to head, with teams reaching national finals in swimming relay, national champions in rounders and county tennis players and cricketers amongst the cohort. Fixtures up 25 per cent in the past two years and external coaches brought in to re-energise teams. Brand new Eton fives courts getting good use. Compulsory Saturday sport axed in favour of optional house sports festivals, 'where even a D team player can get a gold medal.'

'Fantastic' extracurricular programme, say parents, with clubs on offer three nights a week in the pre-prep (cookery, judo, nature) – mostly included in fees – and clubs from Eton fives to Spanish in the prep. Lots of trips, with pupils going further afield as they move up the school, culminating in a year 6 outdoor pursuits trip to Skern Lodge. Wrap-around care a major selling point for the hard working middle class parent cohort. Pupils can be looked after from 7.30am to 6.30pm up to 50 weeks a year, including the provision of breakfast and tea – a facility used by around 30 per cent of families who are, apparently, 'moving from north London in droves.'

Things are looking up for Berkhamsted Prep now that the head has his feet firmly under the table, major changes have settled and improvements to the sites are completed. A solid choice for parents looking for an all-through, thoroughly rounded education – not to mention immunity to the local 11+ frenzy – in a leafy suburban setting. Without the universal favourite topic of 'next schools' on the dinner party agenda, we wonder what on earth Berkhamsted parents talk about...

Berkhamsted School

Linked with Berkhamsted Preparatory School

Overton House, 131 High Street, Berkhamsted, Hertfordshire HP4 2DJ

Pupils: 1,188 • Ages: 11–18 (weekly boarding from 13 and full boarding from 16) • Sixth form: 379

Fees: Day: £16,770 – £19,665; Boarding: + £6,665 – £11,660 pa

Tel: 01442 358001
Email: admissions@berkhamstedschool.org
Website: www.berkhamstedschool.org

Principal: Since January 2016, Richard Backhouse, previously head of Monkton Senior School. Economics degree from Cambridge, where he was vice captain of boat and ran the college Christian Union; has also worked at Oundle and Bradfield. Married to Debbie; two children.

Mr Richard Petty is head of the sixth form – he was previous head of history, politics and year 11 at Notting Hill and Ealing. Mrs Liz Richardson is head of the girls' section and Mr Richard Thompson is head of the boys' section.

Academic matters: Adheres to a traditional philosophy of education in seeking to provide opportunities for broad development. The wide choice of subjects at A level – 27, not to mention the enrichment studies undertaken in year 12, are consistent with this approach. Quantity does not compromise quality, however. In 2016, nearly 46 per cent A*/A grades and 76 per cent A*/B grades at A level. A level art and photography students in the top five nationally for the AQA exam board in recent years. Maths, politics, geography and English are other areas of strength. EPQ now offered and Berkhamsted Mini-MBA. Care is taken to steer particularly able pupils towards the more academic subjects while others are nudged towards less demanding curricula. The head of sixth form encourages sharp academic focus and pupils to aim high. Staff praised for being readily accessible and other assistance comes in the form of drop-in maths workshops and lectures from leading experts, organised through the local chapter of the Geographical Association, to which the school is host.

While some enter the school lower down having been denied grammar school entry, parents feel that the non-academic would probably not be happy here. Single sex teaching for key stages 3-4 (co-ed in sixth form). As with A levels, results at GCSE have seen improvement over the past few years – around one in three achieve at least 10 A*/A grades; in 2016, 67 per cent A*/A grades overall. Again, good performance in most subjects – modern languages said by school to be on the up with newish head of department; Mandarin now offered from year 7. All are required to take GCSE in RS (full course or short course) and many go on to A level. IGCSEs in English, maths, sciences and RS (full course) to ensure they remain challenged, but the school is apparently not, and will not become, a 'sweatshop'. The learning support department will conduct assessments if requested and supplementary lessons are organised as necessary. Two ESL teachers.

Games, options, the arts: Receives just recognition for its sporting achievements. It recently won the regional lacrosse championships and former and present pupils regularly represent the country and compete at regional and county level across a range of other sports. Emphasis placed on teaching sport well and ensuring that everyone has fun and is able to benefit. Netball and boys' hockey given new emphasis of late. Rugby, hockey, lacrosse, cricket, football, swimming and tennis compulsory, depending on age and gender. The new sports pavilion has opened up wider possibilities both to pupils and the wider community, including squash, aerobics, yoga, badminton and weight-training, and there's a new high ropes course.

Over 50 per cent opt to study singing or an instrument of some kind. A talent competition to raise money for charity and Young Musician of the Year are relatively recent additions to the calendar and audiences are overwhelmed by the diversity of talent. The Friends provide Pimms, soft drinks and strawberries for Proms in the Quad, and all leave with fond memories of rousing and moving performances from solo vocalists and musicians – the ever-popular swing songs from the mixed pupil and staff big band ring in their ears. Drama is a popular option at GCSE and beyond and inter-house competitions to encourage all to take to the stage. Some grumbles from parents that staff compete fiercely for pupil time when schedules conflict, but generally a much appreciated aspect of the school – 'My son's speech at our wedding anniversary was faultless. They even found time to teach him public speaking'. May well have honed his dance floor skills too, at the Strictly Come Dancing fundraiser, one of many community events at which the girls and boys come together.

A tour of the school may well take in the historic armoury. CCF is well established and attracts large numbers of recruits each year. The choice between this and D of E is often a hard one, but few can keep up with the demands of both. In addition to special visits, cadets are offered at least one training weekend a month and the D of E expeditions take candidates anywhere from the wet and windswept Lake District to the altogether more clement foothills of the Dolomites. High level of commitment found with a large proportion completing the award.

Boarding: Boarding houses are within easy walk of the school and indistinguishable from surrounding privately owned flats. Recently refurbished bedrooms, many en-suite, are comfortable, and tasteful pictures, vases of flowers and modern furnishings give a lovely homely feel to communal areas, with quiet and noisier common rooms to suit your mood.

Concentration of overseas students in the boarding house doesn't seem to create a divide between them and the six weekly or 20 or so flexi-boarders (equal girl/boy split). Boarders participate in wider weekend school activities and also organise activities and outings tailored to their interests. ESL lessons are offered; visits to London's Chinatown and markets to buy African foodstuffs reportedly very successful.

Background and atmosphere: Christian foundation school which dates from 1541 and amalgamated with the 1888 girls' school in 1997 and the mixed prep the following year. Boys and girls still have their own campuses but some facilities shared. 'Little school feel, big school infrastructure', and indeed a general feeling that all parts of the school come together and meld peaceably with the pretty and historic town.

The Castle Campus, which mostly houses the boys, plus the sixth form, has some slightly scruffy houses and common rooms but these are more than compensated for by the neat grass quad, well-preserved exteriors and assembly rooms, including the grade 1 listed Tutor hall and 19th century Venetian-style chapel. Some modern classrooms and labs and an ultra-swish new dining hall – little wonder parents queue up for those tasty charity breakfasts. Games on the Eton fives courts provide a popular spectacle and seats under mature trees a traditional girls' meeting place – perhaps not surprisingly, lots of boys milling about nearby.

No-one now suggests the girls, in King's Campus, are hard done by comparatively, enjoying the traditional ('Our art room is more authentic, a Parisian atelier') and the modern – new sports centre and a 500-seat theatre are right on their doorstep, and a more spacious dining hall, chapel and classroom block to the tune of £8 million has now been completed.

Smart suit dress code and sanctioning of moderate make-up help prepare sixth form pupils for life after school. Work experience after AS with targeted placements. Good decision making support in the form of advice from teachers, careers fairs and lunches with parents and others to open their eyes to the world of work – in fact introduction to career choices starts much lower down the school, with research, profiling and guidance interviews in years 8, 10 and 11.

Pastoral care, well-being and discipline: A community school. Many enter the prep early and stay the course. Up until GCSEs, the separation of boys and girls allows them to be themselves and be less inhibited, while extracurricular activities ensure they are not cut off completely from the other sex. Sixth form very much run along the lines of a college, geared towards preparing pupils for the outside world – many choose the school for all these reasons. A great feeling of pulling together and mutual support pervades throughout. A vertical house system facilitates friendships across and in between year groups – 'This is where we meet to do our prep'; 'We come here to do presentations, sharing our knowledge of specialist subjects'. Spiritual teaching in the chapel, with all faiths welcome.

Pupils wearing smiley badges gather up lost souls and answer questions. On more serious or personal issues, pupils and parents are encouraged to communicate directly with house tutors. Is there bullying? Well, yes, some, but the caring attitude of staff and fellow pupils usually keeps it to a minimum – 'The kids are pretty sensible on the whole'. No real worries about drink or drugs, though recently a discussion forum has been established – 'Schools should provide a moral lead beyond the school boundaries'.

Pupils and parents: Generally families live within 40 minutes or so of the school. Small number of MOD and expat families. Number of first time buyers along with the more comfortably affluent. The boarding community largely made up of upper school overseas nationals, mostly from Far East and Africa. Overall mix and town location prevents any feeling that they are living in a rarefied environment. Suits those that are willing to try everything out and contribute across the board. Pupils friendly, open and fun – 'Well-mannered and a pleasure to have in your house'. The Friends organise regular social events, including coffee mornings. Good chance to meet other parents and put views across to the principal who attends when he can.

Very vibrant OB association with regular sporting fixtures against the school, meetings with fellow professionals, reunion dinners and regular charitable donations to support school activities. Most famous OB Graham Greene, whose father was the school's head. Others include explorer Robin Knox-Johnston, composer Sir Alexander Goehr, Sir Kenneth Cork (former Lord Major of London), Michael Meacher MP, musician Antony Hopkins and actress Emma Fielding.

Entrance: Seventy or so move up from the prep each year. Wide range of feeder schools in Hertfordshire, Buckinghamshire and Bedfordshire, including Abbot's Hill, Beacon School, Gateways, Lockers Park and Maltman's Green School. Home-grown thought to have an advantage but all have to take an entry exam. This comprises verbal reasoning, English and maths testing at 11+ and additional non-verbal reasoning test at 13+. Can enter in years 8 or 10, when testing also takes place. Push to raise the number of girls and even out numbers.

Approximately 40 apply for sixth form from outside. One in two turned away, based largely on GCSE results. Minimum requirement of at least five B and two C grades, which may possibly include a short course (usually RS) with A or B in the subjects chosen for A level. A grade required if choices include English literature, maths, modern languages or science. Prospective students meet the head of sixth form and are required to provide a reference from their current school.

Exit: Some 10 per ent leave after GCSEs. Most go on to further education, many after a gap year. Nine to Oxbridge in 2016, including two medics, with three more headed elsewhere; 61 per cent to Russell Group universities with popular destinations including Birmingham, Durham, Loughborough, Sheffield, Leeds, Bristol, Exeter, Nottingham, UCL.

Money matters: Fees for extras considered reasonable and fair. Limited number of academic, music, drama, art and sports scholarships available, awarded on merit. Also bursaries in case of need.

Remarks: Combines the best of a single sex and co-ed school. Study with strong spiritual basis and community ethos produces confident all-round achievers.

Bethany School

Curtisden Green, Goudhurst, Cranbrook, Kent TN17 1LB

Pupils: 343; 123 boarders • Ages: 11–18 • Sixth form: 109; (76 boys, 33 girls)

Fees: Day £15,795 – £17,490; Boarding £24,420 – £29,745 pa

Tel: 01580 211273
Email: registrar@bethanyschool.org.uk
Website: www.bethanyschool.org.uk

Head: Since 2010, Mr Francie Healy. A graduate of Trinity College, Dublin, he began his teaching career at an inner city school in Dublin, before taking up a post as maths teacher at Bethany in 1989. He's never wanted to leave the place, and grew his role to head up the IT department, then through director of studies, academic deputy and deputy headship. He doesn't, however, plan to stay quite as permanently as two previous heads, who are buried in the grounds.

'Genuinely held in high regard by the students. He is also very funny,' commented one parent. Not many heads would go to the lengths he did in a charity raffle which resulted in him changing places with a pupil for the day. He rang the school's uniform supplier to ensure he could be properly kitted out for the day, and queued up with his tuck money at break.

Known for his friendliness to both parents and pupils, it's hard to imagine any stern reprimands delivered in his County Clare burr. As we wandered through the sixth form common room and the boarding houses where pupils were converging at lunchtime, we noticed how relaxed the children remained in the head's presence – there was no straightening up or jumping to attention.

'Loves those children with a passion,' a parent told us.

Academic matters: Bethany is characterised as a mainstream school with a specialist learning support department, and around one-third of pupils receive support for specific learning difficulties, and 45 foreign nationals have English language support. Its day intake is also skewed by the density of grammar schools in the region, which tend to cream off the top achieving pupils at 11. Given its broad ability range, it produced a very decent 23 per cent A*/A grades (46 per cent A*-B) at A level and 13 per cent A*-A at GCSE in 2016.

As a small secondary it also appeals to those not suited to the rough and tumble of bigger schools. 'The small class sizes and, therefore, closer relationships with the staff have really helped her find her feet,' commented one parent. One boy who has moved here from another secondary told us, 'The difference here is the teachers spend more time with you'.

The broad ability range is catered for through setting and an individualised approach. 'Get to know and understand the child, then you appreciate how that child learns and thinks. Then you set targets, and as soon as those are reached, raise them,' is Healy's approach.

Those on full learning support are not expected to study a language. Others who don't have an aptitude for languages are free to choose an alternative subject for GCSE (dance recently introduced). Only those in the top two sets study English literature in addition to English language. 'Bethany treats its pupils as individuals and is really flexible, it will change the timetable to suit the pupils, not the other way round like most schools,' said a parent.

Setting begins in English, maths and science from year 7. We saw this at work in English classes, where one group was tasked with finding unfamiliar words in the dictionary, and composing a sentence with them. All were working on laptops. Another group were looking at how sound and visual effects were conveyed in a piece of writing. The EAL group meanwhile were working separately on language skills.

Science is moving to the three individual subjects (previously all pupils took the dual award), enabling the strong scientists to do all three, and those who are less keen to opt for one or two science subjects. There are two well-equipped labs each for biology, physics and chemistry. Pupils were working on decomposition – looking at bread under what they told us were the optimum 'wet and warm' lab conditions, as well as a dead bird they had handily found outside.

Pupils will also begin a different IT course in 2016, as the school opts for computing instead of ICT, which focuses more on coding.

Mandarin is introduced from year 7, and the school has an exchange programme with Taiwan. This, says the head, is because 28 per cent of the world's economy will be Chinese by 2050.

Food tech is compulsory for years 7 to 9 (split for half of the year with design technology), and in the sixth form, where they do a 'university gourmet for life course' to prepare them for living away from home.

DT has a good following to A level, and the workshops are well equipped with all the kit to cut, stick and mould. A level students were hard at work on their final exam pieces, the range clearly indicating their own interests – a golf cart, electric guitar, go-kart, a desk with a built in fish tank, and a dog house.

The work on display in the art rooms is a joy to behold – some catwalk-worthy costumes on mannequins produced by the A level textile students, and tremendous portraits by the art students. Others working on installation pieces were allowed to take over whole areas of the art room – one based on the birth of a lamb, complete with sound effects, straw bales strewn with lambswool, and film footage.

There is no requirement at sixth form to stick to the traditional/academic subjects. Those wishing to take three creative subjects are free to do so, and the school also offers two BTECs, in sport and business. 'They truly do find what you are good at and therefore make the things you aren't so good at much less important,' said a parent.

Learning support is given either as full support (10 per cent of timetable) or part-time support (3 per cent). This is all timetabled with no sessions outside of school hours, as Healy says, 'pupils with learning support work harder in lessons therefore they are the last pupils who should be getting extra lessons'. So the support is given instead of French in years 7 to 9, and in place of one GCSE in years 10 and 11.

Support for external exams is reportedly excellent, and we saw a small group in the learning support room being coached in revision techniques. In year 9, the learning support team sift through the whole year group to establish who should apply for exam concessions, and who might need to get an educational psychologist's report.

All of the pupils have a laptop or iPad, so use of these in lessons is no big deal, and the school uses Dragon speech recognition and Read & Write Gold dyslexia software.

All children receiving support will have an IEP (individual education plan) which identifies strengths, weaknesses, strategies, and targets. Subject teachers can look up the strategies for that individual child – which might be asking short questions; looking at the resources they are giving out and ensuring key words are highlighted; using coloured overlays; using cards so the child doesn't blurt out the answer; and advising where they should sit in the classroom.

The school's specialism is dyslexia, so this is the area of need where you will find the best support, but parents suggest it is not as focused and effective for other areas of special need.

Parents commented on the stability of the teaching staff – that the same people were there as the child reached the top of the school as when they joined. 'On the very odd occasion that teachers have not been up to scratch, issues have either been dealt with, or the teacher has been replaced,' said one parent.

Games, options, the arts: There are compulsory activities four afternoons per week. Teaching finishes at 3.40pm, and after a 20 minute break, children go to activities which finish at 5pm. The wide range of options includes the likes of chef's school, bushcraft, horse riding, sailing, model making, symphony orchestra, life saving and pilates.

Bethany is a very creative school, and those who like to tread the boards are well catered for. Ex-pupils include the Brit award winning music producer Charlie Andrew, who pops back to cheer on the pupils. Music productions are reportedly terrific – one father's voice was breaking with emotion as he recalled a performance from the previous evening. Music teacher Grant Tunbridge 'turns them into gold', he said.

Everyone does sport all afternoon on Wednesday – alongside the traditional team sports there's options to suit all including clay pigeon shooting, tennis, basketball, badminton and table tennis.

Sport is an inclusive affair, with fixtures matched to schools of similar standard – one or two parental grumbles that standards in sport are not demanding enough. But Bethany also caters for hotshots, with current pupils including a boy ranked third on the European golf circuit, and a pupil placed 16th in the world for sailing. Arrangements are made for the sporting stars to catch up if they need time out of school to attend key competitions. As they were for a boy who had acting commitments, and was allowed to take his A levels over three years.

Sixth formers have a Young Enterprise Company – they sell shares in it, with the aim to give a dividend back. They choose a different product to sell each year, and outside advisers come in to give timetabled sessions on business strategy. Pupils learned an important lesson when they tried to sell scented candles at a Christmas ice rink at the wrong price point.

Boarding: Around one-third of the 355 pupils board, and around 40 per cent of the boarders are international students. One weekend in each half term is designated as a 'home' weekend, but full boarders and overseas students can remain in school for these weekends.

Most weekends will find about 80 students in residence. There's no Saturday school, but Saturday activities – trips to Brighton, London, Thorpe Park, shopping trips, sporting activities – are compulsory. Sunday activities are optional.

There are three boys' boarding houses, one for girls, and a co-ed one for the sixth form. In the sixth form block all rooms are singles with ensuite bathrooms, modern, and a reasonable size. Some sixth formers stay in the houses for younger pupils if they want a leadership role, or prefer to live in the sixth form house – this has smaller rooms, which are not ensuite. Younger pupils' dorms vary from twin to five bed rooms.

The last ISI inspection report relayed pupils' complaints about the food – this has been addressed by a supper boarding committee, and greater sensitivity to the preferences of international students.

Background and atmosphere: None of the usual eau de cabbage, trainers and pencil shavings smells greet you here – instead you catch wafts of strategically placed aromatherapy diffusers.

The school is a mixture of the glitzy and homely. Classroom blocks are utilitarian – you could be inside a comprehensive school. 'We don't do posh,' says the head. You might beg to differ when it comes to the facilities – a swanky £1.7m swimming pool; a fitness room groaning with running machines ('five grand each'), rowing machines, weights and exercise bikes; the cricket pitch and pavilion, tennis and squash courts. A digital performing arts centre with a performance space, practice space, concert space, and the digital equipment to film, edit and make music is in planning.

The school has a strong Christian ethos, and chapel twice a week is compulsory. But head says the sermons have a moral rather than religious bent.

Pastoral care, well-being and discipline: 'Seem to have them on a long flexi-lead which they will let out quite far, but they know when to pull it in,' said a parent.

There's no pussy-footing around on the serious issues, though – boarders are checked for drug-taking by random mouth swabs and the occasional appearance of sniffer dogs.

Pupils are made aware of their relative privilege, and duty to those less fortunate. The head reeled off a series of recent charitable events, including a tour to South Africa where pupils helped to build a school in a township. 'They can bring an idea and know they will be listened to,' says Healy, relating how the school celebrated the Indian Festival of Colour at the behest of three year 8 pupils, who successfully convinced him that its tradition of dousing each other in coloured dyes would be a great post-exam stress reliever. They raised funds for Unicef in the process.

'Bethany has the knack of bringing out the best in each and every child, not only academically, but by drawing out hidden talents, and recognising the gifts and abilities children have that are not measured by grades or traditional accolades,' summed up one parent.

Parents are given email addresses for all staff, including the head, and there's a policy to respond within 24 hours. Healy's first step as head was to make all his correspondences on first name terms. Parents agree this helps to build relationships, and that any issues are dealt with quickly.

Pupils and parents: The school is set in the middle of nowhere but a fleet of buses bring the day pupils in routes from Tunbridge Wells, Sevenoaks, Tenterden, Kings Hill and Frant.

About 15 per cent of pupils are international students, hailing from Russia, Ukraine, Europe, China, Hong Kong, USA, Nigeria, South Africa, Cambodia, and South Korea. The biggest group – around one-third of the total – comes from Hong Kong and China, but the school keeps numbers in any particular year group small to encourage them to converse in English.

Its dyslexia provision is a lure, but its small and nurturing ethos also attracts those pupils who would find the hurly-burly of a large comprehensive too much to cope with, and the parents who want something more holistic, and to avoid the treadmill of the highly competitive schools. The head's own three children have been through the school – the elder two now at university, and the youngest is in the sixth form. His daughter got 10 A*/As at GCSE, proof indeed that they cater for the high fliers.

There's a preponderance of boys, owing perhaps to its one-time legacy as a boys' school, or the fact that boys tend to be diagnosed with dyslexia more readily than girls. 'I would tell prospective parents of girls to check that there are enough girls in the year group, as some year groups have literally a handful of girls which would have made our experience of the school very different,' advised one parent.

However we also heard repeatedly of the friendships that form between different year groups, perhaps making the girl issue less of a thing than it might be in schools where friendships stick rigidly within year groups.

The parent community is also warm and supportive, we were told – to the extent that 'a number of parents choose to remain involved with Bethany once their children have left,' according to one parent.

Entrance: Pupils wishing to join in years 7 to 9 take the school's own entrance assessments. Sixth form applicants need to be predicted at least four C grades at GCSE level, although for some subjects a grade B is preferable. Overseas students can take assessments at their current school, and have their headmaster's interview via Skype.

Where a student has additional learning needs, the staff will, if necessary, go and see them in their current school, consider school and educational psychologist reports, and sometimes suggest that the prospective pupil spends some time at Bethany. They will usually be looking for standardised scores no lower than 90 (where 100 is average), but this can be flexible where a child has a particular ability in some areas. Autistic students are considered if high functioning, and if they can manage appropriately in the school environment (one former autistic pupil is expected to get a first in her university degree). The school promises that if the pupil is not best suited to

B

Bethany, they would always recommend an alternative school to approach.

Exit: Two-thirds to three-quarters of pupils stay on into sixth form, and at this point leaver numbers are matched with new entrants. Those leaving at the end of year 11 are usually those not best suited to an A level curriculum, and they go into higher level apprenticeships or further education courses. Joiners come from overseas, or for the curriculum choice. One girl came because her school wouldn't let her do three art A levels – at Bethany she achieved A* in each of art, photography and textiles.

At the end of sixth form more than 90 per cent go to university (in 2016, included Essex, Brighton, Nottingham, Surrey, Leicester, Leeds, Birmingham and Bangor), and the school's creative bent sees high numbers achieving places at the top art and design colleges – one recently grabbing one of only 30 places in the country on an automotive design course.

Money matters: Scholarships (10 to 20 per cent of the fees) are offered for entry into year 7, year 9 and the sixth form in art, dance, drama, music, technology and sport. Academic scholarships are also offered to a maximum value of 40 per cent of fees. Two special scholarships called Christopher Jackson Scholarships can pay up to 100 per cent of fees, and bursarial awards are available covering 30-50 per cent.

Remarks: What we loved here was the sense of letting children be free to be who they want to be. There's no shoehorning into option blocks, or diktats about studying certain loathed subjects. If they want to do three art A levels, fine, if that's what they're good at. Dyslexic? Then no need to do a language. The result: happy children, free to do what interests them, and all the more successful for it. 'We let the children excel at what they are good at,' says the head. We wish a few more schools would follow Bethany's lead.

If you have a creative, goes against the mould child; or the deep thinker who can't bear the hustle and hassle of a huge school; or a bright dyslexic; or you just can't stand the competitive treadmill of some schools – then you have found your place.

Bishop Luffa School

Bishop Luffa Close, Chichester, West Sussex PO19 3LT

Pupils: 1,451 • Ages: 11–19 • Sixth form: 317 • C of E

Tel: 01243 787741
Email: HeadsPA@bishopluffa.org.uk
Website: www.bishopluffa.org.uk

Headteacher: Since 2000, Mr Nick Taunt. Read English at Exeter College, Oxford, head of English and the arts at Harwich School, then deputy head of Hedingham School. Married with three children, two of whom went to Bishop Luffa. Eloquent – uses language with lawyer-like precision. 'He's not scary and very calm,' said one pupil. Much approved of by parents – 'he's running a Rolls Royce School on an Austin Maxi budget,' said one in admiration. Most frustrated by lack of time: on a tour of the school, it was like trying to keep up with a sprightly white rabbit in a rather shabby wonderland.

Relishes the power to set the direction for a large school but does not sit in grand isolation: sometimes sits in on lessons and teaches the extended project of the AQA Bacc (which includes critical thinking) in the sixth form. Of his pupils and staff, he says, 'I want each individual to shine' – and this is not limited to the A* sort of shining. His vision for pupils: to develop to be independent, reflective and responsive.

Deeply committed to his school – and education in general – he was appointed National Leader of Education. Shares expertise and resources with other schools and colleges – 'because we are all responsible for all the young people in the area' – there is a lower exclusion rate in area as a result. Would only leave Bishop Luffa if he felt he had nothing more to contribute: his packed agenda would suggest this is some way off at present.

Academic matters: 'Judgement on grades alone is unhelpful,' says the head. But the grades are excellent for a state comprehensive all the same: in 2016, GCSE: 80 per cent of pupils got 5+ A*-C grades (including English and maths), 38 per cent of grades were A*/A; A level: 61 per cent of grades were A*-B, 33 per cent A*/A. Pupils say there is pressure to do well, but this is from themselves, not the school. 'At the start of the course they do say the grades people got at GCSE last time and you think you'd really like to do that too. I want to get an A to show my parents and teachers that I can do it.' The head says it's important to find the right pressure: these are important times, don't waste them. But it is not an exam factory.

Class sizes 25-30, and remain on the large size in the sixth form. A tribute, then, to the teaching staff that the pupils feel there is so much individual focus on their learning; and that the results are good. 'Inspirational teachers,' say parents. Pupils say teachers are friendly and approachable, and there are only two scary teachers (out of 95). Lessons are lively: there was a buzz of energetic industry, occasionally bordering on boisterous, in classrooms; attentive silence from sixth formers where the teacher was in full flow. The aim is to get pupils to think for themselves: critical thinking starts in year 7 with Edward de Bono thinking hats and is carried through to sixth form with critical thinking in the AQA Bacc. Lateral thinking plays a big part in end of term exploration days: year 7 designed an airline, working in textiles to design a uniform, in food preparation to make light food etc; sixth formers had a 'day of evil', exploring evil as a philosophical concept.

Curriculum not just aimed at those who are academic. Key stage 3 students cycle through all varieties of design & technology: graphics, product design, textiles, resistant materials and food technology. There are two food preparation rooms; in one, purring pupils constructed trifles from their hand drawn designs – some spoon it up on the way home. These rooms are clearly used to the full: cake making even plays a part in further maths, with a chocolate cake holding the current record for tallest further maths cake of the year. At key stage 4, those who want to pursue a different vocational path take day release to Chichester College.

The geography teacher is very popular and successfully converts non-believers – 'my son didn't like geography until he was taught by [the teacher]' – 'he's the reason my son's doing a geography degree.' Budding mathematicians – and those bored by the subject – will be happy with the innovative teaching of mathematics: results are outstanding and there is a high up take of maths in the sixth form.

The learning support department supports not only children with statements, but any pupils with particular needs, including gifted and talented. The four dedicated teachers and nine LSAs provide individual support, group sessions and in-class support.

Librarians work hard to enthuse pupils and staff with e-research and internet safety lessons, as well as an imaginative programme of challenge and award schemes; some way to go yet: just 36 pupils and staff competed in the recent 12/12 Challenge (to read 12 books or write 12 stories). Professional writers present the awards: Andy Briggs and Vanessa Curtis this year.

Games, options, the arts: Two large playing fields, in constant efficient use. MUGA (multi-use games area), climbing wall, and newish gym. 'They really take sports seriously, I thought they wouldn't. It's as good as an independent school,' commented a parent. Year 10 pupils can get a Junior Sports Leader qualification by learning to teach sport to primary school children. Extracurricular activities open to all pupils irrespective of ability: despite high achievement on sports field (pupils compete and win at a national level, and the school has the Silver School Games Kitemark Award for PE) it's an inclusive club at Luffa. Several parents commented with appreciation that their children had been encouraged to participate: 'My son's rubbish at sports, but has become enthusiastic about them, because the sports coach is so encouraging.'

Plenty of non-sporty options: chess club three lunchtimes a week – 'I thought it would be – you know, lame, but it was quite fun,' two film-making clubs, economics society with regular outside speakers, small but lively debating society, and IMPACT- the Christian Union, led by sixth formers, meets weekly to discuss ideas about Christianity and God. Plenty of opportunities for those interested in music: individual tuition, choirs, an orchestra and bands, with concerts and recitals throughout the year.

Keen uptake of Duke of Edinburgh, currently 10 gold, and 20-30 silver and bronze; demand exceeds places. Lots of trips, including French and German exchanges, ski trips, and field trips. Further afield for the sixth formers: Tanzania, Washington and Pompeii.

Arts thrive at Bishop Luffa (it has the Artsmark), and it's not just for those with a natural inclination: drama, for instance, is taught to all pupils across key stage 3 'to nurture confidence and sensitivity.' The new creative arts centre houses music rooms, recording studio, drama and dance studios, and hosts the Bishop Luffa Summer Exhibition: 'Fruition'.

Background and atmosphere: Built in the early 60s with some modern additions since, uninspiring buildings disguise the excellent school within. Cramped conditions – in some corridors you can touch both walls – and it felt a bit dark in places. However, £2.5m programme of improvements underway. One parent commented that it is hard to find your way around: year 7s are allowed to be late to class for the first week while they get their bearings. There is a quiet area away from the whirl – 'a good place to go to sort out an argument with friend.' The sixth form area is scuffed and packed; a peaceful interior hub houses a small library with 40 computers (you can bring your laptop and plug it in to the network).

Fun displays of art and textiles: clothes made from anything and everything, a fabric chocolate cake and a pink ring doughnut sitting temptingly at the top of a staircase, while a swan made of white plastic bags flies overhead. As you walk down a corridor a florescent green 3D box appears to float in front of you, the word 'think' written next to it – think outside the box. A grubby green wall looks as though it's waiting for a display: actually it's a wall you can lean on to make shapes – a fidget mechanism for restless adolescents.

Recent work to bring the decoration of classrooms up to scratch – 'a few classrooms are still scruffy,' say the kids. The school is tremendously clean, which is much appreciated by children. Year 7 pupils are particularly impressed by cleanliness after recent exposure to evidently unclean primaries – 'there's no half-eaten pizza lying around here.' 'Lit pick' keeps the school tidy – a detention, but also something done during wet break times – 'it's quite fun really'; the head, too, ducks and dives when he spots a piece of litter on the floor.

No religious brainwashing here: the church background shows in the supportive atmosphere. Everyone is important, which is why the two youngest pupils raised the jubilee flag (50 glorious years of Bishop Luffa). The key element is respect, between staff and pupils and in pupil relationships. If you come to Bishop Luffa, you must respect religion, but it's not their brand of Christianity or damnation: the school does have Muslims and Hindus (they can opt out of communion, but must attend the daily act of worship). However, 'not for you if you are anti-religion,' said one parent thoughtfully.

Food is very healthy; too much so for some: 'it would be nice to have unhealthy stuff sometimes,' said one pupil wistfully; outraged others responded: 'we do have chips on Fridays' – pupils are fiercely loyal to their school. 'The pasta is overcooked,' said a long suffering ex-resident of Italy. But this is lost on most of the kids: Pasta King is so popular it has its own queue. One pupil said, 'sometimes you can be hungry' – apparently what's left by the time the end of the queue is served is not so desirable. Year 7s have their own food queue away from the rough and tumble of the rest. No eating in the wrong place – you get a red slip – but dedicated place for packed lunchers inside, and nice new area outside.

Pupils make their own way to school, on foot, bicycle, or train – 'if I drop him off, it has to be around the corner,' said one parent in lowered voice. Pupils are clearly happy to be there; even if most of them would prefer to be there a bit later in the day. All the pupils we spoke to would like to change the early start time (school day: 8am – 2.30pm). 'It's very hard for teenagers to get up at 6,' said one boy in injured tones.

Pastoral care, well-being and discipline: House system provides a sense of belonging and helps children feel secure: support and congratulation at a low key level suitable to the self-conscious age. Pupils assigned to a tutor group in year 7, and stay in the same group until year 13. The day starts with tutorial time and includes a thought for the day. One pupil, who felt his head of house hadn't really appreciated his efforts to change his behaviour, said, 'but I can talk to my tutor. There is always someone to go to.'

Pastoral care is underpinned with imagination: time out of school to visit Dad who works in Gibraltar not seen as a holiday, but essential family time. One parent said, 'They are very sensitive to teenagers. At an options meeting, the talk was not just about options, but also about the fact that kids are growing up and need to have a social life and interests outside school lessons. They really are interested in the whole child.' New year 7s are paired with sixth formers for individual mentoring, and will be greeted by their sixth former outside school on their first morning, so no one goes in alone. One parent commented on her worry when her quiet son started at Bishop Luffa, but how, after a teary first few days, he is flourishing and gaining confidence in its supportive atmosphere. His tutor was in attentive email contact, she added.

Bullying is dealt with quickly, said a parent whose son was a victim, though the head is quick to point out that sometimes it's not so much bullying as thoughtless words. They have a toothpaste assembly to sort this out: it's quick to squeeze out, much harder to put back in again: it's easy to say words...

Disciplinary system: warnings, red slips, then detentions – 'you can get a room 10 for being late' – it's not quite a room 101: no rats or anything scary used to check behaviour at Bishop Luffa. Indeed, this school champions a restorative approach to wrongdoing (all staff have been trained), which works well – 'I used to bunk off last year, but I've really tried to turn it around this year.' There are the problems you get with any bunch of teenagers: occasional smoking in the quiet area, the nicking of valuables (one pupil told us your phone or wallet can get nicked

B

during PE if you don't put them in the valuables locker), and some pressure to have the right gear. You can get a red slip for a uniform problem, such as hitching up skirts or under-age make up (light make up allowed from year 11). A Juliano approach to law enforcement – 'some of my friends have just stopped wearing make up,' said one pupil rather wearily. A parent said, 'Not for you if you don't like your child to be pulled up on behaviour – children have to step up and behave.'

Exclusion for swearing at staff, persistent disobedience, smoking or drinking. Drugs at school would result in permanent exclusion – 'because it is important that all the children can feel safe at school.' Eight pupils have been excluded over the last year, with five permanent exclusions in the last 13 years (three of these for drugs).

Pupils and parents: A true comprehensive, it takes all types. Pupils come from the deaneries of Chichester, Arundel and Bognor, and Westbourne. Many middle class, but not exclusively so.

Past pupils include: journalists Jonathan Thompson, Amanda Ursell, Rupert Winfield-Hayes and Charlotte Hawkins (Sky News presenter); theatre director Paul Millar; actors Linus Roach, Rupert Holliday-Evans, Cara Horgan and Nimi March; footballer Joel Ward; investment manager and founder of the Thirty Per Cent Club Helen Morrissey; explorer Catherine Hartley; musicians Jonathan Ansell (of G4) and Zoe Rahman; Rob Shaw, co-founder of Jack Wills Clothing Co; and poet and novelist Sam Meekings.

Entrance: From West Sussex primaries, at 11, 220 places a year, oversubscribed. The vast majority (165) C of E: prospective parents and offspring need to be regular church goers for two continuous years – 'go from year 3 to be sure of it,' suggested one parent. Thirty places to churches of other denominations, 20 local community places, (no church required) and five special places offered to those in particular emotional need.

Academic sixth form: pupils need to get at least Bs to enter. Around 140 from Bishop Luffa go on to the sixth form, 20 places for outsiders.

Exit: Careers sessions fortnightly from year 7; it's low key and kids can tune it out, say parents, but when you need it, it's there. Around a third leave after GCSEs. Nearly all sixth form leavers to university to university; five to Oxbridge in 2016; five medics/vets; some take a gap year; others to Durham, Bath, Southampton, Bristol, UCL, Nottingham, St Andrews.

Money matters: PFA (Parents and Friends Association) help the less well off pay for school trips.

Remarks: A church school, but not a God club. Principles no one would disagree with: respect for others and helping each person to shine. Excellent results for a non-selective school, but no feeling of being a hothouse. Pupils are friendly and polite. Only downside – the cramped school buildings. One parent said, 'I really feel grateful that my son can go to a school like it. More schools like Luffa are needed! They have a balance between pastoral care and learning, and that is fantastic.'

Bishop's Stortford College

10 Maze Green Road, Bishop's Stortford, Hertfordshire CM23 2PJ

Pupils: 1,163; 48 full, 20 weekly, 84 flexi boarders (about two-thirds boys) • Ages: 4–18 • Sixth form: 252

Fees: Day £8,412 – £18,360; Boarding £18,975 – £28,707 pa

Tel: 01279 838575
Email: general.enquiry@bishopsstortfordcollege.org
Website: www.bishopsstortfordcollege.org

Headmaster: Since 2011, Mr Jeremy Gladwin BSc MEd. Educated at The King's School, Worcester (chorister) and Whitgift School in south Croydon. Graduated from Durham in geography, taught at Shrewsbury School for 15 years, rising to become head of geography and housemaster, then deputy headmaster at the Royal Hospital School, and headmaster of St Edmund's, Canterbury. Decided to apply for second headship as 'the opportunity to lead Bishop's Stortford College was too good to miss'. Recently took a masters in education at Cambridge, focusing on 'educational leadership and school improvement', the completion of which has prompted his appointment to HMC committee for professional development. 'Heads are lonely,' he says; 'they need more support. That way we might be able to tackle the current high rate of attrition.' Also an inspector for both ISI and Ofsted (boarding). Married with grown-up son and daughter. A keen walker, enjoys watching rugby and plays tennis at club level. Loves music, especially sacred choral (weekly attendance at evensong at St John's College, Cambridge is his de-stresser) and classical. A fine pianist. Mild-mannered, considered, down-to-earth type. 'Runs a tight ship; proactive and forward-thinking,' say parents.

Head of prep school: Since September 2013, Bill Toleman BA MSc FRGS (40s), previously head of Yarm Prep School. Before that, deputy head at King's Worcester. Read geography at Nottingham University and has since added an MSc in educational management and leadership and fellowship of the Royal Geographical Society. Affable and so unassuming that when we ask him to describe his leadership style he calls in his PA, settles her in an armchair and closes the door on his way out. 'Approachable and informal,' she smiles, as soon as the latch clicks; adjectives bandied about by parents include 'child-centred', 'fair' and 'proactive'. Certainly in his short tenure to date he has systematically swept away all signs of stuffiness – entrance exams are now sat in a multiplicity of cosy classrooms rather than in serried rows in one huge daunting sports hall, for example, and parents and pupils alike pop in at all hours, keen for a chat. 'If people want to come and see me I'm very happy to see them,' he says, although when the queue becomes too long or other matters are too pressing his PA honours visitors with an appointment in the head's diary. 'The children love that,' she laughs. To his regret, no longer has time to teach his beloved geography, although helps out with fieldwork (most recently accompanying lower third to Walton-on-the-Naze). Enjoys surfing in North Devon and still plays occasional cricket and Sunday rugby. Married, with three grown-up sons.

Academic matters: 'This is a purposeful, happy place to come to school – it has to be,' says prep school head, 'because we're here for a long time.' Pre-prep for age 4 to 7, prep for 7 to 13s. While pre-prep makes use of national curriculum year group terminology, traditional names still charmingly in use in the prep – so lower and upper shell are followed by forms 1 and 2, then lower and upper third (continuing into the senior). Although less than 20 per cent of prep pupils board, school operates a boarding school week for its pupils aged over 7, with long weekdays until 5pm for the eldest and Saturday morning school for all, afternoons for form 1 and above.

'Children work hard here because they want to, not because we make them,' says head; said a parent, 'My son has been coaxed, encouraged and inspired to push himself and achieve the best he could.' Academic streaming begins in year 4, plus setting for maths. Classical civ for years 5 and 6, Latin to add to Spanish, German and French for years 7 and 8. DT and drama on the curriculum from year 3 up. Lots of visits and trips, as well as speakers in – curricular activities included in fees. Bring Your Own Device recently introduced for top two years – prep pupils say they use iPads and equivalent in 80 per cent of lessons and that they really help with self-organisation. Wifi all over.

Academic results have soared in recent years – unrecognisable in comparison to the college of 10 to 15 years ago. Head attributes this to the arrival of girls when the college went fully co-ed in 1995 – not only did they bring self-motivation but they raised the academic bar. A concerted effort to improve results through academic rigour, targeting and 'working smarter' has paid off – now among top 20 UK co-ed independent schools. The 68 per cent A*/B A level grades of a few years ago have given way to 81 per cent in 2016 (54 per cent A*/A). Maths, history, English literature, psychology and physics are most popular subjects, with strongest showing in theatre studies, art, and geography. Out of the running for GCSE league tables due to IGCSEs, which parents gladly accept, but a commendable 68 per cent of passes A*/A in 2016. Prestigious '10 club' – tie for at least 10 A*/A grades at GCSE. Language provision has broadened – on joining senior school, pupils choose two modern foreign languages (most having been introduced to French, German and Spanish in the prep, not to mention Latin). Pre-empts the changes to GCSEs which head fears will discourage language take-up.

Streams and sets for most subjects meet needs of all, including the gifted. A dedicated learning support team of three sensitively supports 30 students with specific learning needs (charged as an extra), including dyslexia and Asperger's. All international students are offered one or two EAL lessons a week and reach IGCSE level (required for university admission). However, this is not solely an academic day school – head recoils at the suggestion of a hothouse. 'We won't sacrifice the breadth that comes with a boarding school curriculum – we just want to do everything well and keep some balance.' Broad-based academic intake – 'results are due to the quality of teaching and learning,' emphasises head.

Bring Your Own Device recently introduced – Wifi all over. Pioneering use of geographical information system technology. Interactive science action centre. Solid traditional teaching facilities too.

Games, options, the arts: Successful sports: unbeaten seasons in rugby and hockey now the norm – several ex-international players offer top level coaching and inspiring role models. County hockey and district netball and swimming champions – swimming a major sport in fabulous pool; tennis and water-polo also popular. Prep pupils national finalists in pretty much everything – rugby, hockey, cricket, netball, even football, although only an after-school club. Standout individuals too, notably swimming and tennis.

'Have-a-go' culture is alive and well in the prep. One afternoon each week devoted to a 'wheel' of activities which changes with the term (street dance and yoga to survival skills). All pupils allocated to a house (either at random or according to family connection) – fierce competition through all manner of contests and quizzes. Highest achieving house wins supper with the headmaster. Fundraising through teddy bears' picnics, film nights, doughnut sales and auctions in aid of the annual chosen charity – £10,000 plus donated every year. Head meets prefects for 'biscuits and a chat' half-termly, and drops into lessons and activities unannounced.

Music important – around 10 per cent of pupils perform to grade 8 or beyond. Pianos in most boarding houses, plenty of airy practice rooms. Much-appreciated resident college musician supports in readiness for exams and accompanies. Orchestra and all manner of ensembles large and small. Twenty concerts a year, including choral work for pupils, parents and staff, plus a couple of ventures into the world of opera. Well-equipped theatre provides venue for some stunning musical and dramatic performances (set for recent production of Cabaret still in evidence, though slowly transforming into Scottish heathland for next epic – Macbeth). New art centre with stunningly mature GCSE and A level work on display in spacious ateliers.

Trips and tours across the globe including India, New York, Malawi, South Africa, Barbados, and a fair few closer to home too. Wide choice of extracurricular activities including D of E (the college is the leading school in east Hertfordshire) debating (standing room only for some hot topics) and community work.

Boarding: Three senior boarding houses – two for boys and one for girls. Full, weekly and flexi boarding, the latter most popular. Saturday lessons and sport mean everyone is at school till Saturday afternoon. Most go home on Saturday nights, but eg paintballing and visits to theme parks organised for those still in school. Own comfortable boarding house for prep pupils. Few full boarders but 50+ stay a minimum of two nights a week – most popular Wednesdays (sport after school) and Friday (Saturday morning lie-in for mum and dad).

Background and atmosphere: Founded in 1868 as a non-conformist boarding school, with aspirations of securing an effective and Christian education on terms that should not be beyond the reach of the middle class generally, originally sited on the outskirts of Bishop's Stortford. Once boys only, now 45 per cent girls. Full-on Saturday school for all from 8.20am until 3.40pm has its detractors, but most accept it's necessary if children are to make the most of all that's on offer.

Despite recent new developments and proximity to town, the 130 acre campus still has a rural feel. Governors canny through the economic downturn and fees have remained relatively low. Indeed, an ambitious programme of facilities upgrade ongoing and due for completion to coincide with the school's 150th anniversary in 2018. New addition to existing pretty Edwardian building under way when we visited, which provides a new girls' day house (replacing the previous one), and there will be another girls' house added. Brand new boys' day and boarding houses are next on the agenda – much more economical to design from scratch than to bring the existing original School House building up to modern living standards; instead it will be repurposed as offices for the head and administrative teams, plus 11 classrooms. By the end of the project, head predicts the college 'won't just be beautiful, it will be magnificent!'

Despite these physical changes, 'We are a large school, but we retain the small-school feel,' says head, and unabashedly goes on to describe Bishop's Stortford College as 'cuddly'. 'A really positive environment,' suggested a parent. Certainly the all-pervading ethos is one of kindness, caring and humanity – a quality the head has discovered is neatly defined by the Zulu word 'ubuntu' (which we went home and looked up – perfect). 'Pupils here are mutually supportive,' says head. 'They work hard. When asked why, they simply reply "why not?"' Head is keen to resist the spoon-feeding culture in favour of promoting independent learning in preparation for life. EPQ is popular in the sixth form as is the college's own research project

B

programme – no UCAS points but an academic challenge and something to talk about at university interviews and mention on personal statement.

Superb library with two-storey bow windows, well stocked with books, DVDs (multi-lingual) and CDs. Ferguson Lecture Theatre is a cosy additional space, where assemblies can be relayed from Mem(orial) Hall, the original, atmospheric school hall. Sixth form Stars in their Eyes a sell-out. Sports hall with fitness suite in the gallery. Five all weather netball/tennis courts. Two floodlit Astro pitches.

Dining hall large and functional; food plentiful and tasty, on a three-week menu rotation (our sixth form guides tell us the pupils' request for 'chicken zinger' through the school council was provided by the catering manager and it was very tasty).

Prep and senior pupils co-exist harmoniously on the site. Main prep building now all sparkling glass and purple carpet, thanks to £3m extension and refurb. Super reception area, hall with stage and roomy classrooms. Art rooms, including kiln, plus science labs across the attractive brick courtyard (complete with happy preppies chatting on steps, idyllically). Wonderful new library with floor-to-ceiling vistas. Shares with seniors music facilities, super 50-metre indoor pool in own timber-clad edifice, sports hall and hard courts, plus pitches as far as the eye can see. No wonder prep children look relaxed, contented – and well-exercised.

Pastoral care, well-being and discipline: Strong pastoral care network begins in the prep with form tutor as first port of call for parents, then heads of year. Pyramid above of senior teacher (pastoral), director of studies, operations, then deputy head and head. 'Compassionate' teaching and learning support for those with mild SEN much praised by parents of children who have benefited – IEPS, one-to-ones, additional time in exams.

Few discipline problems – head likes 'to give pupils a chance to get it right'. Strong house system offers support. 'The school expects a lot from the children and as a parent that is exactly what I want,' said one parent.

Pupils and parents: Prep school parents in the main professionals or city, some farmers – same as in senior as pupils grow up through the school with few additions. 'There really is not a type of child or parent,' said a parent. 'Plenty of commuters as London is so close, but there are farmers and scientists and just about all professions going.'

Pupils 'normal, not arrogant,' says senior school head. 'I'm not keen on elitism.' Most from within daily travelling distance; about 65 per cent of boarders from overseas, including Europe and the Far East. Parents – 'all professions going' – described by one of their number as 'friendly, sociable, aspirational, encouraging of their children'. Appreciate weekly contact by e-newsletter and the twice yearly news magazine.

Long list of distinguished former pupils includes presenter Andy Peebles, rugby player Ben Clarke, writer Dick Clement and educationalist Professor John Ferguson. The world of espionage features prominently via former heads of MI5, Sir Stephen Lander and Sir Dick White, and Peter Wright, author of Spycatcher.

Entrance: Entrance to the pre-prep is by an informal group assessment session and there is a long lead-in for tinies registered to start reception ('messy play' session in progress when we visited). External candidates for the additional 20 places made available at 7+ must sit the entrance exam to the prep school (English, maths and reading), spend a morning in school and are encouraged to meet the head with parents; no assessment required of existing pupils. A further 20 places offered at 10+ and 20 more at 11+ (academic and music scholarships available) to give a total of 100 pupils per year group by lower third (year 7). No sibling discount or preference given.

Senior school pupils are selected via interviews, entrance tests and school references; takes a range of abilities, not just academic high-fliers. At 13 majority come from the prep school but also takes some 12-15 external entrants annually; small number join at 14, in time for GCSEs. Some 30-40 join in the sixth form – entrance is by interview and written tests; need at least five B grades at GCSE with A*-B in A level subject choices.

Exit: Some 97 per cent plus straight to senior school. Remaining handful to other, further-flung boarding schools (in recent years Harrow, Stowe, Millfield, Uppingham, Shrewsbury, Benenden) and a few to state at 11+. As Bishop's Stortford College is selective, prep parents are given plenty of advance warning if their child's ability to keep up after transfer is in question. Other, suitable schools, recommended. Fairly rare occurrence as school prefers to tackle underachievement to keep pupils under its wing.

A handful – some 15 per cent – leaves after GCSEs to study A levels elsewhere. Nearly all sixth formers head to university. Three to Oxbridge in 2016, including one medic; three more medics and one vet. Subjects range from motorsport engineering at Derby to natural sciences at Durham to theatre and performance at Leeds to social anthropology at LSE.

Money matters: Assistance for those in financial need. Academic, music, art and sport scholarships offered. 'A considerable proportion of our income goes on bursaries and scholarships,' says the head. 'If a child is talented but his or her parents can't afford us, we will do what we can to help.'

Remarks: Without five centuries of history to draw on, Bishop's Stortford College isn't widely known, but is among the generation of schools founded in the Victorian era that are quietly succeeding. Local word-of-mouth is enough to keep it oversubscribed – without needing to worry about recruiting for tomorrow, the head and governors can look further into securing the college's position well into the future.

The Bishop's Stortford High School

London Road, Bishop's Stortford, Hertfordshire CM23 3LU

Pupils: 1,193 • Ages: 11–18 • Sixth form: 379 (121 girls)

Tel: 01279 868686
Email: office@tbshs.org
Website: www.tbshs.org

Headmaster: Since 2014, Mr Dale Reeve, previously deputy head of Leventhorpe School, and a maths specialist. He attended a state comprehensive in Harlow, after which he did a maths degree at Essex University and a PGCE at Leicester University. This is the sixth school he's worked at.

Lives locally with his wife and two young children and comes across as an affable and traditional family man, who is firm but fair. Certainly never one to keep students at arm's length, often getting stuck right in with their activities. 'It's brilliant that he coaches. My son is a very shy boy and he connected with him straight away,' says one parent. Other remarks from parents include, 'He has a great manner with the boys and parents' and 'Everyone likes and respects him.'

He takes an 'If it aint broke, don't fix it' attitude to leadership. Word on the street (well, at the school gates, anyway) is that he watches quietly, including sitting in on classes, rather than bringing in changes for the sake of it. 'One shift I am making is on discipline, though,' he says. 'Discipline is good here, but it could be even better. So we are focusing on things like low level distraction.'

Academic matters: There have been peaks and troughs over time' when it comes to GCSE results, says the head, but on the whole it's positive. In 2016, 80 per cent 5+ A*-C grades including English and maths (28 per cent A*/A). At A level 24 per cent A*/A grades and 58 per cent A*/B. Chemistry, English language, theatre studies, PE and history are particularly strong.

Class sizes hover just under 30 in the early years, falling to 13-22 for A level. Expect fast-tracking of able students from year 7 in maths. ICT is a cornerstone of the school, with lots of great facilities across all subjects, and maths is the clear stand-out subject when it comes to success, with around eight Maths Challenge gold winners annually.

The school is heavily research-based, with one member of staff dedicated entirely to encouraging teachers in the area of research and development, with the ultimate aim of innovating their teaching. One pupil said, 'We are encouraged to be creative and challenge, which makes for lively classes,' whilst another reported, 'There's no spoon-feeding here.'

There are 97 students with SEN and they tend to do well, as do the less academic, despite the school's above-average ability intake. Parents and pupils are particularly keen on the so-called clinics at break and lunch times, aimed at pupils who struggle in specific subjects. 'These have saved my child,' said one parent. 'It's great that the children get a chance to speak to the teacher about what they're not grasping, with the aim that the teacher can hone in on that area in the next class,' said another. A third said, 'Certainly no need for tutoring, even if your child isn't as clever as others.'

'Enabling the less able is an area we have really focused on improving,' explains the head. But don't bother applying for sixth form unless academic – anyone seeking below level 3 should look elsewhere. Usual subjects offered at this level, plus philosophy, film and Latin. Speakers who have come to the school include Lord Rowan Williams, Alistair Campbell and Boris Johnson.

Games, options, the arts: It's hard to think of an extracurricular activity that isn't offered here, with everything from the normal (and highly successful) rugby, football and cricket fixtures (pupils regularly play against top private schools) through to go-carting, student-led charity groups and even a pupil-led class in IT skills for senior citizens. In fact, it's not uncommon to see large numbers of students still at school at 6pm, with many also coming into school early in the mornings. 'If there's a club that isn't offered that a few of us want, we pretty much know it will be brought in,' explained one pupil. Expect weekends to be taken up too. Saturday morning rugby training is 'expected but not compulsory' for year 7s, for example, with parents watching from the sidelines.

Music and performing arts are both strong, with imaginative and inspiring staff. Facilities, including recording studio and impressive music technology, enable the school to double up as a Saturday morning venue for budding musicians, whilst the orchestra pit allows for live productions and the impressive-looking drama hall encourages professionalism. Concerts and festivals happen all year round, not just at Christmas, and art is also taken seriously, with pupils regularly encouraged to apply for national competitions. School trips are often cited as the best parents have ever heard of, with recent examples including a rugby tour to Australia and a geography trip to Iceland. 'They're not cheap and that can be hard,' said one parent. 'But they're worth it.'

Background and atmosphere: There are some sports facilities, including a large sports hall that's thronging with basketball players at lunchtimes, but it's the extensive playing fields and an excellent sports ground (35 acres) some three miles away that students and parents rave about. Main school was built in the 1950s for a lot fewer students and although there have been many add-ons since, the school is bursting the seams in places, especially in sixth form centre. 'In the winter, the boiler can be weak and children have been known to have to stay at home if it's been on the blink, but that is rare,' said one parent. Some areas lack displays and need a paint job, but others are spot on and all have a strong welcoming vibe. The school claims to have a strong Christian ethos, with Jerusalem as the school hymn and close links with nearby St Michael's Church, but the emphasis is by no means in-your-face, with plenty of room for other religions and non-believers.

Pastoral care, well-being and discipline: 'There's no room for silly haircuts, trainers or shirts hanging out here,' summed up one parent. She's not wrong – these boys look super-smart all the time, thanks to the high standards of dress, including compulsory blazers, which are expected from the pupils. 'So embedded is the level of formality around dress that my son even keeps his blazer on until after he's done his homework!' laughed one parent.

There's a similar attitude towards behaviour, which the head sees as closely related: 'If we let these small things slip, then everything slides,' he explains. Should any boys fall foul of the clearly set-out disciplinary procedures, they find themselves in a small isolation room with plenty of posters of the school rules to remind them while they're there. But few spend more than a day or so in isolation and critically, the school's excellent counsellor (also available for staff) is based just outside the room and is well-known for supporting any boys who find it hard to conform.

Indeed, this is by no means a school ruled by fear, with boys seeming as positive as they are polite. Tellingly, they look adults in the eye when speaking and seem to be as at much ease chatting to the teachers as amongst themselves. Parents and pupils alike put it down to a structured pastoral set-up, mutual respect between staff and pupils and a bottom-up approach that enables pupils' suggestions to be listened to and acted upon – mainly through the school council. 'A while back, they put in a bully box and it just made the bullies tease you even more if you were seen putting a note in there,' said one pupil. 'But as soon as we explained that, alternatives were looked into.'

Year 7s may struggle, due to the culture shock. 'They really crack down on them straight away, with an instant no-nonsense and zero tolerance attitude,' said one parent. 'It can be quite hard on some of the children at that age, particularly the sensitive ones.' Pupils of this age say some teachers can get a bit too caught up in the discipline side of things and fail to praise enough. But again, it's generally agreed that this is balanced by an open-door attitude among staff. 'One of my friends had a son who loathed a particular subject and had nightmares about it. He went to see the head of year and he was completely understanding, and they came to an agreement about a solution. Ultimately, you feel they want the kids to be happy.'

Pupils and parents: This school is in an affluent part of town and the parental mix echoes this. Parents see this as a cheap alternative to independent education and by and large remain satisfied throughout. 'If you say your children go to this school, the normal reaction is, 'Oh aren't you lucky?' and that's pretty much how we feel,' says one parent. Sociable parents are kept happy – there's a PSA (Parent Sports Association) and PTFA (Parent, Teacher and Friends Association), both of which plan regular events including bingo nights, candle-lit suppers etc and raise serious funds. Even outspoken parents are generally content. 'There's a minority who are not afraid to speak up, but we don't shy away from them,' explains the head. 'We're all for parental involvement.' Former pupils include Ben Skirving (rugby) and Greg James (Radio1 DJ). The 130 girls in the 350-strong sixth form bring balance and breath, as well as maturity.

Entrance: This is the kind of school that people move to the area for and even then, many boys don't get in. Places are awarded firstly on the basis of compelling medical reasons, secondly by sibling link. Ten per cent of places are also allocated 'to pupils with a proven aptitude in music or sport,' although with 170 boys recently applying for eight places on the back of their sport and 135 for seven places on the back of their music, there's stiff competition to prove yourself. The rest of the places are based on where pupils live (there's a traditional catchment area, defined by postcodes) and primary school attended.

The co-ed sixth form has 100 places open to pupils who have not attended the lower school – good results with minimum grade B in subjects chosen for AS/A2, essential.

Exit: Around a third leave after GCSEs for local colleges or to pursue vocational courses; a minority go directly into employment. Nearly all sixth formers move on to university, around a third to Russell Group institutions. None to Oxbridge in 2016. Some students gain apprenticeship contracts.

Remarks: There are five secondary schools in the town, all rated by Ofsted as good or outstanding. Parents who opt for this school tend to do so because of the emphasis on respect and working hard, as well as the plethora of extracurricular activities. And despite the reputation that it has for serving the more naturally academic, we found the less able are also encouraged to shine, thanks to the drive to maintain standards and provide outstanding support for all.

Bloxham School

Banbury Road, Bloxham, Near Banbury, Oxfordshire OX15 4PE

Pupils: 430; 200 full, weekly and flexi boarders • Ages: 11–18 • Sixth form: 150

Fees: Day £17,385 – £24,630; Boarding £23,235 – £32,445 pa

Tel: 01295 720301
Email: admissions@bloxhamschool.com
Website: www.bloxhamschool.com

Headmaster: Since 2013, Mr Paul Sanderson (40s) previously a deputy head and director of curriculum at Gordonstoun. Originally from Northern Ireland, he was educated at Banbridge Academy before studying evolutionary biology and genetics at St Andrews University. Postgrad qualifications from Oxford (PGCE) and Cambridge (MPhil). Taught at Lancaster Royal Grammar, Oundle and Carr Hill High before joining Gordonstoun as housemaster.

Drawn to the school's modest size (around 430 pupils), where children are 'less likely to disappear', he described his first year as a 'rollercoaster', and has made great strides in raising the academic profile of the school. Ambitious and determined, with a refreshing heart-on-his-sleeve honesty (a few watery-eyed moments when recounting the achievements of his pupils), Mr Sanderson's mission is to redefine what makes a Bloxham education.

A rugby enthusiast, with a passion for ice climbing and skiing. Runs a climbing wall class and recently took a group of students alpine climbing. Married with three young children.

Academic matters: In 2016, 65 per cent A*-B at A level (35 per cent A*/A); small numbers taking most subjects but business studies and maths top the popularity polls. Forty-six per cent A*/A at GCSE in 2016. No plans to introduce the IB. IGCSEs currently offered in English, geography and sciences.

Management restructure has introduced new deputy and five new heads of department and there's a definite sense that the bar has been raised when it comes to teaching standards. Staff:pupil ratio average is 8:1 and progress is measured across the year through a challenge grade system. Length of lessons has recently been increased from 35 minutes to an hour and music and drama have been shifted to the afternoon in response to latest research that children become more creative as the day goes on.

While Bloxham is quick to point out that it is not a special needs school, it does have a good reputation for nurturing able pupils with mild to moderate dyslexia who have become demoralised in more competitive arenas. A specialist dyslexia course is offered for up to six pupils a year in the third, fourth and fifth forms, focused on improving their reading speed and accuracy, spelling and study skills.

The Eunoia Society (ancient Greek for 'beautiful learning') provides an intellectual 'stretching' beyond the academic curriculum. As well as offering prep for Oxbridge entrance, it boasts an impressive programme of events, with trips to exhibitions, opera and ballet, and recent visiting speakers have included an art historian, a US diplomat, a professor of biophysics and a senior civil servant.

Games, options, the arts: While there's been some rebalancing of a historic bias towards sport, the school still takes great pride in its achievements. Rugby and hockey are particular strengths (girls reigning county hockey champions at time of visit). Regular rivals include Stowe, Warwick, Marlborough and Wellington and competition is taken seriously. Coaches use iPads to record games for post-match analysis.

Facilities are excellent. In addition to two all-weather pitches, the school boasts extensive playing fields, two squash courts, two fives courts, six outdoor netball courts (doubling up as tennis courts during the summer) and a 23m indoor swimming pool. The Dewey Sports Hall has a well-equipped fitness suite with yoga and an assortment of classes also on offer. Sailing takes place on a nearby reservoir. Recent national successes in both clay pigeon shooting and equestrian competitions (twice national schools eventing champions). No stabling at school but pupils may arrange to bring their own mounts for twice-weekly tuition. Those who don't own their own horses can arrange to hire from local stables.

Bloxham is fast gaining a reputation for its drama programme. Since his appointment in 2013, the director of drama has increased the number of productions from one to eight a year and all pupils are expected to take part, either front of stage or behind the scenes. The school recently staged its first original production (about Bloxham boys who fought and perished in the Great War), selling out all four performances to rave reviews: 'as good as the West End', commented one enthusiastic parent. The Great Hall stages the major productions, with the rest at the Wesley Theatre (a former Wesleyan Chapel).

The music department is housed in the Sam Kahn Music School and there's a new orchestra – quite an achievement given the size of the school's population. Fifty per cent split across music and music tech subjects. We dropped in on a lesson about film scores and learned of an impending visit from an old boy who now works as a film composer in Hollywood – such 'value-added' is much in evidence. Lots of rehearsal rooms support a busy performance schedule and there's the added bonus of a school radio station, run by pupils. Art provision is equally impressive. Sixth form students benefit from dedicated personal workspaces in a charming room that resembles an artists' garret, complete with sloping eaves.

'We want kids who are hungry and ambitious inside and outside the classroom', says Mr Sanderson and Bloxham's enrichment programme is extensive. As well as the Eunoia Soc (see above), pupils can choose from clubs ranging from astronomy to knitting as well as a wine society for sixth formers. Animal club is offered once a week for pupils keen to help look after the school's resident lizards, snakes, hermit crabs and beetles.

Boarding: First and foremost a boarding school; day pupils (known as day boarders) make up half the population and can stay until 10pm, and the school is opening a new day house in September 2017. There's also the option of flexi-boarding (pay per night). One local parent said her son doesn't want to come home for fear of 'missing out on the fun'. This flexibility was a big draw for a number of the parents to whom we spoke.

Seven boarding houses are clean and bright with large communal areas – a bit dated in places but a rolling programme of refurbishment is under way. Weekly and flexi boarding in years 7 and 8, with own lower school boarding house. Full boarding from year 9. Thirteen per cent of boarders from overseas. Maximum of three beds to a room, full boarders have their own room from year 10. Opening a new day house in 2017

Background and atmosphere: With its picture-book cluster of buildings in honey-coloured Horton stone, manicured lawns and homely atmosphere the school blends harmoniously with beautiful Bloxham village. The lower school (Exham House) is actually situated in the former village pub.

Originally known as All Saints School, Bloxham was founded in 1860 by The Reverend Philip Reginald Egerton who wanted to establish a school that embodied the high church values of the Oxford Movement. In 1897 it joined the Woodard Foundation, the group of schools founded by Canon Woodard to promote education in an actively Christian environment.

Food excellent (we took full advantage of visiting on Curry Thursday). Great choice and emphasis on healthy eating. Sociable lunchtimes with teachers sitting happily alongside pupils.

Pastoral care, well-being and discipline: Self-proclaimed 'gold standard' of pastoral care is justified. Multiple systems in place to ensure children's emotional welfare, including a team of 'peer listeners' – sixth form student volunteers with formal counselling training. Small size of school promotes healthy mixing and solid friendships between girls/boys and different year groups. Head meets daily with head boy and girl, helping to keep abreast of any grumbles or issues. School refreshingly honest about (infrequent) incidents of bullying; intervention swift and effective, according to parents. Keen sensitivity about emotional needs of pupils: 'let's face it, the teenage years are difficult', says head.

Holy communion for all once a week. School doesn't shy away from talking about the importance of spiritual development in education but head recognises need for religion to 'translate into the 21st century'. It's less about doctrine and more about getting children to think about their place in the world, 'To be a giver, rather than a taker'.

This ethos is reflected in service initiatives such as Reading Club, where older pupils help children from local primary schools with reading difficulties. According to head this has inspired at least one student to go on and train as a primary teacher.

Pupils and parents: Bloxham has long been a popular local option and is now increasingly so for London refugees looking for a smaller, more 'gentle' boarding school. Recent push to improve parent-school communications has been warmly welcomed. Very informative parents' handbook published annually; newly established parents' association. Saturday matches are well attended and there are plenty of opportunities for parents to get involved if desired. Former pupils include impressive numbers of high ranks from all three forces plus novelist Tom Sharpe and journalist John Sergeant.

Entrance: Candidates for lower school (age 11) via school's own exam (maths, English and verbal reasoning) and interview; CE for 13+ entry. Sixth form requires minimum six GCSEs at grades A*-C, with at least a B in chosen A level subjects (A grade required for maths and physics). Lower school intake is from state primaries or independents such as Carrdus; at 13+ pupils from preps including Ashfold School, Beachborough, Bilton Grange, Swanbourne House and Winchester House.

Exit: Small leakage (around 10 per cent) after GCSEs. Post-A level, varied subjects and destinations; Bristol, Nottingham and Loughborough currently popular. Two medics in 2016.

Money matters: Parents say flexi-boarding option and late stay for day pupils represent value for money. Scholarships (20 per cent fee reduction) for academics, sport, DT music and drama. Means-tested bursaries can be combined with scholarships; limited number of full-fee bursaries.

Remarks: Successfully combines academic challenge with plenty of sport, service and practical life skills. A perfect environment for happy all-rounders.

Box Hill School

Mickleham, Dorking, Surrey RH5 6EA

Pupils: 420; 133 full, 20 weekly boarders • Ages: 11–19 • Sixth form: 124

Fees: Day £16,710 – £18,300; Boarding £25,500 – £31,050 pa

Tel: 01372 373382
Email: enquiries@boxhillschool.com
Website: www.boxhillschool.com

Headmaster: Since 2014, Mr Corydon Lowde BSc, MEd, NPQH (40s), previously school's deputy head who took over following sudden departure of predecessor. Before that, nearly three years' handy overseas experience in similar role at British International School of Boston, preceded by seven-year stint at Hampshire Collegiate School, starting career at large state comprehensive.

'Has a vision he wants to share' and 'never tires of talking about what we're doing.' Hours he's putting in (lots of them) paying off, thought insider. 'School is going up.' Was 'gutted' that had to speak on the phone (in hospital having wonky knee put right on day of visit) as meeting best way of 'understanding where all that energy is coming from and where the school is going.'

Felt to be doing as good a job as anyone could manage in difficult circumstances, style reserved but friendly, reviews

B

cautious but generally positive. 'It's new thing but I feel that Cory is on the right track,' thought one parent, speaking for pretty much everyone. Overwhelming desire is that he keeps school atmosphere just the way it is. Nobody is hungry for change.

A teacher from the off (management, part of his degree, was the career that got away), he comes across as quiet, mild-mannered and slightly quirky with self-deprecating Brit humour (honed, no doubt, during own schooldays at Dragon and Frensham Heights) that must make international parents want to take him home gift-wrapped in a Burberry bag. (Should really be Duchamp, says Mr Lowde, a loyal fan of their ties, socks and, indeed, 'pochettes'.)

Goal is school that reflects the world when it comes to nationalities (they have around 30 but no monocultures) and ability range. Would like more Brits – 'who wouldn't?' he says – and is hoping rising tide of Londoners is high enough to lap against admissions desk.

When not headmastering, follows sport. Was British Karate Champion in the 1990s (not an Olympic sport – down to international wrangling). We had visions of desk being reduced to matchwood after one emphatic gesture too many but, no, it's all neat and splinter-free.

Karate, he says firmly, is all about 'turning search for perfection into your own personal journey – not about aggressive confrontation,' – a nothing-to-prove message that's not million miles away from how would like school to see itself.

Academic matters: That increasingly rare sighting in them thar Surrey hills – senior school that has continued to welcome the all and sundries who, these hard-nosed, results-driven days, wouldn't necessarily gain a place elsewhere. In circumstances, nearly 25 per cent A*/A, 43 per cent A*-B at A level in 2016; IB diploma average of 33; and 82 per cent of pupils getting 5+ A*-C GCSE grades (27 per cent A*-A grades) a tribute to quality of teaching.

While near neighbours have sought solid A grade glory, here they've carried on with broader ability range (many are around the national average). But school's frequent self-referencing as 'non-selective' needs grain of salt. Minimally selective, yes, but everyone accepted as 'greenies' (blazer colour worn to year 11) needs to be capable of passing eight or nine GCSEs.

Able pupils who do deliver top grades (parents pinching themselves at children's better than predicted results aren't hard to come by) won't, however, be held up as only aspirational model worth pursuing. 'Am great believer that competition crushes one's self-esteem,' says head (though not when it comes to sport, where all-out drive to win is 'about character'...).

Academically, it's about 'my growth, learning and success [being] made greater by your learning,' sentiments that do him credit, as does desire for kind, empathetic colleagues. They're well up to the job, say pupils, and palpably keen to get everyone involved. Maths department gets X Factor squared award for pupil recruitment, department head 'a genius.'

Similar stories elsewhere. Even visitors may find themselves dredging up rusty French and Spanish greetings, courtesy of bustling, friendly language teachers who won't take non for an answer, while we assume whiteboard spelling of 'clergimen' [sic] in otherwise pacey English lesson was designed to test pupils' eye for detail.

Ethos derives in part from membership of Round Square group of schools, linked to ideals of eccentric but hugely influential educationalist Kurt Hahn, who stressed compassion coupled with 'just do it' mentality. (We quizzed tour guides who, impressively, were able to cite every one of key principles – and swore they hadn't mugged up in advance...).

Extreme cleverness catered for but also support 150 pupils with SEN, from mild dyslexia to school refusers – 'though we're not special school,' says head and pupils must be able to access curriculum. Helped by lowish pupil to teacher ratio (nine to one) and small class sizes (average 15 to 18 up to year 11, as few as two pupils in EAL and ISC lessons). Support includes one-to-one specialist help (normal maximum of an hour a week, mostly maths or literacy focused) and multi-sensory teaching. Will also try to help those (often with high functioning Asperger's) struggling with social communication.

About 70 of 110 EAL pupils follow mainstream syllabus, 50 in sixth form, English studied at range of levels, from IB diploma level to IGCSE, ESOL and IELTS. Others are found among 40 plus pupils at International Study Centre who can chose from four courses aimed at 14-16ish age range, most popular the one-year intensive GCSE programme (also marketed as pre-IB).

Some ISC pupils start a year or so behind peers, about half eventually joining 'mainstream' pupils (school's words, not ours). All 'fully integrated into school life...' says glossy literature (repeated several times for added emphasis) though some national groups stick together and school pupils can feel onus is on them to make first contact and bridge the cultural gap.

School's best recent curriculum decision has been reintroduction of A levels, reducing at a stroke post-16 departures of the IB-averse who 'want to stay but don't want to take six subjects,' says head, though they're encouraged to opt for extras such as IB Theory of Knowledge, extra maths and creativity, action and service – and some do (one keen A level student was even doing IB Spanish module out of love for the subject, though skipping the exam). Staff, insouciant about extra workload involved, see dual system as best way of boosting numbers studying top subjects at top unis, particularly maths and straight sciences.

Games, options, the arts: With practice rooms open all hours (7 in the morning till 9 at night) and free instrumental taster lessons, no shortage of opportunities for 100 or so budding musicians who hone skills, some to diploma level – one so impressive that visiting top musician offered tuition on the spot.

Other hands-on subjects housed in range of (mainly original) buildings including small, cobble-paved stables minimally converted to create atmospheric and fitting home for DT, every tool's home marked by penciled outline on wall behind – very Patrick Caulfield. Visual arts headed by practising artist, who, paintbrush in hand, was adding final touches to own masterpiece as pupils worked around him, inspiring similarly accomplished work (our favourite among many featuring off-duty angels enjoying an off-duty cig).

Sport key to 'holistic' approach, though girls enjoy pinker-shaded version – holassism, perhaps? – and do netball and rounders (rugby and cricket for boys) with hockey and football in common, though pupils confident that if school would happily accommodate changes if demand was there. Frank acknowledgement that team sports 'not for all'; new sports hall construction pencilled in to finish in mid-2018. Room to improve, thought parent, as not viewed as top priority, perceptions rubbing off on potential staff recruits (lure not yet sufficiently great to attract top talent). Results, which tend to align with levels of each intake's innate talent, can fluctuate fairly widely from year to year. That said, manifest advantages for the keen who, with minimal numbers of school teams, can get their fill of matches, though accepted that anyone requiring high quality sporting fix and nothing but will probably end up elsewhere.

Sensible decision to offer individual fitness from year 10 when 'almost anything is possible,' says school, the more so as sport happens twice a week, Tuesdays and Thursdays being reserved for school activities including magic club, sign language and – a rare treat – corsetry and dressmaking class which teaches traditional panelling and boning skills and is run by passionate devotee, enthusiasm largely responsible, as with fashion and textiles GCSE, for bringing in impressive numbers of boys.

Boarding: With large numbers of full boarders (around two-thirds boys), spending priority is six boarding houses, four in the grounds, two across the (quiet) village road. House names, though full of meaning to school, have certain random quality for outsiders, Constantine named after eponymous Greek king – school patron; Ralph apparently commemorating past VIP (though sounds like rakish English take on IKEA furniture policy).

Plenty to help boarders take mind off décor difficulties. After prep on Saturdays, seniors can travel into London. Must be back by '2230' [sic] (time rather than century, we assume), shopping trumping culture every time. Excellent range of trips including 'experiences' (Jamie Oliver and Harry Potter). One houseparent (male) runs regular pizza making sessions ('leave dough to rise during the day, cook in the evening.') 'Never a dull moment' insists school, firmly. Boarders agree. 'Can be almost too much going on,' said one.

Background and atmosphere: Word du jour, judged to pack a punch in terms of punter appeal, is 'inspiring', writ large throughout new school video, overlaying jolly images of suitably fired up pupils fencing on the school lawn (a summer term reality, not just camera-friendly set up) or putting up tents at summit of Box Hill, buffeted by gale force winds.

There's also much talk of holistic approach, though 'mindfulness', other all-purpose buzz word of choice, appears to be the meme that got away – so far. 'Not sure why aren't using it,' says member of staff.

'Stunning' is other obvious candidate, given village setting in Mickleham, between Dorking and Leatherhead and about 20 miles from London. As pretty as they come, main building once private gothic revival Victorian house with aspirations to grandeur, full of delightful stained glass biblical scenes and window seat epidemic (even modern boarding houses are rotten with them). Newer wings tacked on at the back sufficiently sympathetic to keep the charm intact though some more elderly stand-alones have their work cut out. 'Has the smell of an experienced building,' says one of tour guides of modern languages block.

Original grandeur belies school's relative youth, founded only in 1959 by Gordonstoun housemaster on principles inspired by inspirational educationalist Kurt Hahn, with much emphasis on whole pupil development (and plenty of non-Hahn inspired beatings for those failing to progress along right lines, according to one rueful 1970s-vintage OB). Now, pupils 'will all excel at something,' reckons school, while extending talent range to include high profile qualities such as friendship and general good egg-dom, which are 'acknowledged though not in OTT way,' says member of staff.

In any case, it's Hahn-lite (don't set them loose in all weathers on high seas: land-locked setting on Surrey Downs is against them) but ticks off must-dos: democracy, environment, adventure, leadership and service – with whole school activity week in September with camping, canoeing and rock climbing for all in Wales or New Forest. D of E – closely linked in ethos – from year 9 and just about everyone takes bronze. 'No reason not to,' says school, though silver and gold recruited on opt-in basis. Star attraction is trip to Philippolis, South Africa, where pupils have helped add new buildings including crèche and classrooms. 'Proof of faith in school,' said mother, whose son, just turned 13, had spent a month there.

Luxury goods on offer to counteract struggle with elements – 90 inch TV in new sixth form common room used for films and for pupils to 'enjoy live streams from the Royal Shakespeare Company,' trumpets prospectus. We're sure they do little else (sotto voce giggling when we asked undoubtedly down to recollection of Bard's many bon mots...). And when Titus Andronicus palls, there's always fun of watching vast tame rodents (gerbils not rats, despite unnerving tails) rolling around in exercise balls.

Overall impression is of well-tended school with little evidence of slight messiness reported by a couple of visiting parents – nothing to do, we're sure, with sign reading 'GSG visit [today]. Rooms have to be very tidy...' And so what if it's not immaculate? 'Don't send son to school for the décor,' commented mother.

Grounds undiluted gorgeousness (impressive mown stripes of grass that continued either side of small pond on back lawn giving unnerving impression that Jerry – the groundsman, and noted duck whisperer; pupils say he's followed by family of mallards each year – can walk, or at least ride, on water).

Golden glow set to spread as governor-sanctioned spending spree continues, aided by canny bursar who 'always has six months of staff salaries in the bank,' and is clearly a dab hand at curbing any headmasterly dash over cash tendencies. 'We're strong and robust – though hate that word, makes me sound like politician,' says head.

Now well on the way to transforming slightly dismal befores to far nicer afters. Rooms where clutter of tables and beds currently fight yellowing paint for supremacy slowly but surely transformed by attractive furniture, much of it custom created 'by our own maintenance team' and essential as most non-standard alcoves aren't compatible with off the peg designs.

'Work in progress,' says head. Will be followed by new sports hall (biggest current absence) – local council currently dragging heels – and more space for creative arts ('absolutely not forgotten,' says head). Some Portakabins – some exteriors slightly shabby, interiors as well as can be expected and could be far worse – will remain.

Pastoral care, well-being and discipline: 'Willing to cherish the children for what they are – don't treat them as a commodity,' thought feeder school registrar. 'Very open and honest, don't sweep things under the carpet,' agreed parent. Example is alcohol policy. If over 18, boarders can purchase but 'carefully monitored' – to ensure any headaches are admin, not consumption, related.

Quality of communications only widespread complaint, described with single-word pithiness by several parents fed up with night-before notifications of matches and recent music event. (Though full marks to music staff for re-running one child's performance so late arriving mother didn't miss out).

Other parents, however, reckoned that greater attention to termly calendars and school website would iron out most of the difficulties. New fortnightly newsletter from head also generally going down well, while more text alerts and email updates should take uncertainty out of nitty gritty-ness of who is doing what and when.

Nurturing element otherwise practically perfect, attended to with care and sensitivity. One pupil, bullied elsewhere and finding settling in hard, was cajoled out of foyer into class by head of year, now thriving. 'Helped him become accustomed to school until he was able to let go of that helping hand for a day or two.' Unpleasantness does happen but quickly and effectively dealt with, think parents whose children have been on receiving end. School's 'expose and eradicate,' approach includes ambassadors – 'our eyes and ears,' says head – who report any hint of transgression, backed up by anonymous online whistleblowing.

Boarders send two reps from each of the six houses to discuss issues – often food related, with school headed by 13-strong syndicate who supervise breaks, administer tellings off for minor uniform infringements and are led by head boy and girl, known as Guardians, superhero connotations a highly successful recruitment tool. Handover speech to successors an annual tear jerker, with one post-holder 'talking to her parents through the speech and saying how grateful she was,' said mother, welling up all over again at the memory.

Unlike other top dogs we've encountered, not shy about using superpowers and will impose detentions, though not often and mainly for repeated rudeness. 'Know when someone's just being cheeky.' Given incumbents' nicknames (President Nice and Madame Fuhrer) we thought they showed commendable forbearance, though all pupil behaviour witnessed, in and out of lessons, was universally immaculate.

Pupils and parents: Parents range from diverse international community to ecstatic locals, often first time buyers, thrilled about what school has done for their children. All aware that school still seen as second choice. 'Wrong postcode for some Reigate mums,' said one. General sense that won't last, though nobody's in a hurry to add more competitive feel to a place felt to run on happiness. Boy numbers (outnumber girls two to one) and international element (around 84 per cent of boarders) also put others off, though seeing real life consequences of world events played out – one parent cited falling out of former best friends from different war zones – provides 'amazing' insights.

Monthly Friday teas for parents when school provides the cakes but 'doesn't overpower with teachers,' said mum. Later life reunions all over the place – Hong Kong the latest when checked bustling Facebook page (as well-tended as the grounds) though plenty of alumni stay don't move far away, careers covering eclectic range from surveyors to musicians and authors.

Entrance: Officially take into years 7 (40 places), 9 (20 places) and 12 (variable) but if there's space, will take at other times.

Majority of pupils from 10-mile radius though extending, Kingston and Horsham (as well as thriving metropolis of Nork) all now within reach thanks to extensive bus network (6.45am start for furthest flung locations). Micklefield, Downsend, Reigate St Mary's, Chinthurst, Aberdour, Priory Prep and Kingswood House among preps sending pupils, though no official feeders. Local primaries also well represented.

Exit: Many schools have much-trumpeted cohort who leave post-16, recognise error of ways and stage tearful prodigal son (and daughter) return, accepted with nary a 'we told you so'. Here, parent confirms it's the real McCoy with mother phoning Mr Lowde to ask if could have place back. 'Missed it so much.'

Other post-16 losses, often to local sixth form colleges, partially staunched but trickle will continue, think parents, as pupils cast off 360 degree care for grittier experiences elsewhere. 'Not a criticism of the school but tribute to confidence-building,' pointed out mother.

Of the 50 or so percent who stay on, university entrance for most, over 80 per cent to first choice, no Oxbridge currently but aiming for one or two a year – no special department as 'we're small enough to personalise timetable where needed.'

Unis of Exeter, Royal Holloway, Queen Mary and Portsmouth currently popular. Subjects include business, management and economics, regular contingent each year to art and music colleges including Central St Martins and Northern Royal College.

Money matters: Generous support for deserving families whose income range isn't cosily clustered at top end of £ dial. Warmth of welcome and matter-of-fact help with bursary application process felt to speak volumes about school's ethos.

Remarks: Warm-hearted, encouraging school that's easily overlooked in favour of guarantees of undiluted top grades elsewhere. 'Not right for families who want everything in neat and tidy boxes,' thought mother. 'It's not draconian here. You're doing it because it's what you need to succeed.'

Bradfield College

Bradfield, Berkshire RG7 6AU

Pupils: 773 (473 boys, 300 girls); 696 boarders • Ages: 13–18 • Sixth form: 328 • C of E

Fees: Day £28,224; Boarding £35,280 pa

Tel: 01189 644516
Email: admissions@bradfieldcollege.org.uk
Website: www.bradfieldcollege.org.uk

Headmaster: Since 2015, Dr Chris Stevens MA DPhil (v early 50s). Previously second master at Marlborough College (from 2011), he started his career in prep schools as a (very) young man. Brambletye, briefly as a gap student, and then Ashdown House as a young master where he split the year in half, six months at Ashdown (where a lot of the time was spent establishing the Ashdown château in France) and half the year studying for his doctorate. He finally firmly established himself in the boarding senior school world in 1997 when he started at Uppingham where he was master-in-charge of cricket and housemaster for nine years. Educated in an all boys' environment at Tonbridge School, Dr Stevens read modern and medieval languages at Caius College, Cambridge and researched Italian literature for a DPhil at Oxford. This is where he met Helen, now associate professor of English at Corpus Christi, Oxford. They have school age daughters.

A highly intelligent man; sometimes you have to run to keep up with Dr Stevens in conversation. He thinks fast and talks fast, everything spoken in a mellifluous voice, however, and everything considered and thoughtful. He made the decision to work in schools rather than devote himself to academia largely because, despite his intellect, he loves the rough and tumble of life in a boarding school. Thoroughly unpretentious, he scoffs at the hierarchies that can divide the prep and senior school worlds and values the time he spent with much younger children and the very different challenges that are found in prep schools. Both he and his wife missed the boarding house atmosphere while they were at Marlborough and both are relishing being back in the fray and at the heart of things. They are still in the process of getting to know all the pupils, which he is determined to do. Sixth formers are regularly invited to dinner at their house, and a privileged few in lower years are also invited to dine with him and his wife. Otherwise it's at breakfast in the dining hall that he seizes the opportunity to eat with the more junior pupils and get to know their views on life at Bradfield and beyond. 'Best insight into who are the best teachers are too', he confides.

The 'beyond' is something that he holds very important. An outward looking man, he celebrates the influence of families from different cultural backgrounds – often each parent from a different country, and shudders at what the landscape may hold post-Brexit. An international outlook and mindset he considers to be essential, particularly in the face of how easy it could be to reflect a pocket of little England, given the picturesque, chocolate boxy location of the school.

An inclusive man, he has changed the staff photo so that it genuinely incorporates the whole staff, not just the teaching staff. Everyone is invited for hog roast and ice cream in his garden. He is passionate about avoiding pretension and a sense of entitlement. While keen to maintain the sense that Bradfield is a warm, relaxed and caring environment, he is concerned that this should not be mistaken for a lack of ambition. Students here are to be challenged without becoming stressed. Stretched in order to be stimulated, alive and curious. Parents approve, while noticing a shift towards heightening the academic standards. 'Fabulous,' said one; ' very sensible,' another.

Academic matters: A school that is, without question, on the up. A real contender now, academically, and firmly on the radar of aspirational parents as well as those who have always wanted a rounded and broad education for their children. At A level in 2016, 73 per cent A*-B, with 39 per cent A*/A. Third IB cohort got an average of 34 points (out of a maximum of 45). Pupils normally take 10 GCSEs; in 2016, 59 per cent A*/A grades. Economics – the most popular and successful A level subject in 2016 – business studies, film studies, textiles and photography all offered alongside the traditional subjects. Not one person did Latin or Greek A level in 2016 (though a small number take the Latin certificate at GCSE, and an even smaller number do Greek) but one did Chinese, and three took Russian A levels. Eighteen chose to do the IB in 2016, with 15 achieving over 30 points. In 2017 there will be 50 taking the IB. Sixty pupils taking EPQ in 2016, wide range of projects from 'Aid or trade in Africa, which is better for development?'; to 'To what extent is diversification the main reason for Apple's success?'; and 'Was the Lance Armstrong scandal beneficial for the sport of cycling?' Results over 50 per cent A*/A.

The Blackburn science centre is a hugely impressive. As well as being eco-friendly and thoroughly up to speed with technology, it is beautiful to look at and ergonomic. Ten classrooms and laboratories, spaciously spread out on each of the two floors. What goes on inside is also impressive. Parents regard it as one of the stronger subjects. 'Fantastic,' they said. The library, on the other hand, is reassuringly old school. Constructed of the local flint and brick with diamond paned windows, it is properly stocked with books as well as decorated with looming portraits of former heads and wardens. Not a high tech environment, but a refreshingly studious atmosphere prevails, young men and women working and collaborating in here. Comfortable areas filled with smiley faced emojis to escape to with a good book.

Large study skills and support department (SSSD – SEN to you and me). About 150 receive support; caters for everyone from those who require minimal support to those who need a reasonable level, but no specialist unit to cater for extreme needs. Would not automatically turn away someone with specific difficulties but will always ask the question, 'will they be happy here?' says head. Vast majority who use the SSSD have had a history of provision in their previous schools, but teachers can refer individuals, initially to houseparent.

Help given across the board at key pressure points. 'Extra lessons to help with GCSEs have been phenomenal,' said a seasoned parent with children at other schools. However if a child is not responding to being pushed, then the pressure drops. 'You have to want to do well, and what is brilliant is that it's cool to work hard and to get good results,' confirmed another parent. Grades given each side of half term. Reassuring to parents who like to feel on top of how hard their child is working.

Games, options, the arts: Bradfield is a football school, no rugby here at all. They are good – and known to be good. A recent captain of the first XI played for England in an international match against Scotland, we were told by our proud sixth form guide (who was a water polo aficionado himself). 'If you're good,' he said, 'opportunities open up for you at international level, but if you just love to play you can play at any standard that suits.' A wide range of teams means everyone can take part but a competitive edge survives. Boys' major summer sport is cricket, for girls it's lacrosse (there is also mixed lacrosse, and girls can play in boys' teams) and netball in the winter, tennis in the Summer. Hockey and swimming are also major sports for both boys and girls. 'There is a team for everyone who wants to play and the B and C teams will get the same rewards as the A team. No elitism,' said a parent. Lush facilities from acres of green sports fields as far as the eye can see, to splendid indoor tennis courts, as well as outdoor courts, dotted around the grounds. Lots of sports tours to as far afield as Sri Lanka (cricket) and Singapore and Malaysia (hockey).

One of the most enticing range of minor sports we've seen. The school website reads like a highly exclusive action-packed adventure camp. From clay pigeon and rifle shooting (school has its own ranges for both) to zumba and yoga, with fives, real tennis, dodgeball, sailing, canoeing and polo as well as water polo and golf. A nine hole golf course is nestled towards the end of the games pitches. Water polo takes place in the glistening 25 metre pool that forms part of the swanky sports complex. CCF compulsory for year 10; Duke of Edinburgh also has a high uptake – our guide had just achieved gold. Standards are high here – both in the quality of provision, the teaching as well as facilities, and in the quality of commitment and enthusiasm from the pupils.

A Bradfield flagship is its Greek theatre, Greeker, as it's known. Recent performances include Antigone (in the ancient Greek). Theatre has been carefully restored and is sheltered in a shady bower. It is well used, whether it be for Shakespeare (Midsummer Night's Dream), a rock concert, or the whole school prize giving, which involves the famous handshaking ceremony ('a chance to test my knowledge of each child,' winks the head).

Music thriving, as is the art. Music is housed in a spacious building with two large classrooms, a concert hall and plenty of practice rooms. 'I'm enjoying coming here to play and practice,' enthused one sixth former; 'everyone is so friendly here.' A plethora of groups and choirs, jazz and classical, some pupil led, some staff led. We watched year 9s having rowdy noisy fun with steel drums, shakers and tambourines. The art rooms are tucked away on the other side of a brook in a delightfully separate, rustic cottage-like building. Everything is tidy and organised here but without losing a sense of spontaneous creativity. Well-thumbed art books are scattered amongst the workstations. A welcome relief to see them here rather than neatly stacked and barely touched in the library. Art is popular; students like the teachers as well as the subject. We saw monochrome butterflies on wire in the textiles department and an oil painted elephant on newspaper. Photography, sculpture and screen painting all in interconnecting rooms. One particular talented student had their work exhibited at the Tate Modern.

A plethora of societies from the religious (Swinbank) to philospy, debating, drama and feminist (Neska).

With so much available you would have thought some students might become overwhelmed and not do anything at all. Not possible here. The Bradfield Diploma, a qualification pursued in years 10 and 11, involves pupils being assessed according to their co-curricular pursuits, and quite apart from that, affirmed one student, 'the Bradfield ethos is about getting involved; it is a family community and you get out what you put in.'

Boarding: Let there be no mistake, Bradfield is a boarding school. There are only 80 day pupils. However, with most families living within a 50 mile radius, only about 150 out of 750 pupils will be in on a Saturday night. 'We only have them home from Saturday tea time until Sunday evening, but it's a much needed chance to recover,' said one mother; 'it's so full on during the week.' Pupils will make the effort to stay in for a particular event, like the famous Michaelmas Goose weekend – a weekend packed with an interhouse riot of a competition which includes 'total wipeout' style water and inflatables obstacle course as well as dodgeball, debating, dancing and singing ('very raucous, and loud,' warned a student). The summer term sees more people opting to stay, and the further up the school they are the more they choose to enjoy the freedom to finish work and socialise with friends. Year group dinners are organised for Saturday nights and the unschooly feel to the place helps attract pupils into staying. Blundells Bar plays a large part in this, open in the evenings for sixth formers on Saturday nights (as well as two weekday evenings), this is the real deal with comfortable leather armchairs and pool table, doubling as a café in the day time for all year groups with proper coffee machines and muffins. With its decked terrace overlooking the cricket pitch, it's perfect for long summer evenings.

Faulkners – the mixed house for the whole of year 9 – is a Bradfield triumph. Not many schools do this, but the idea is to weld the year group together so that as they branch off to their different (single sex) houses in year 10 (all of which have been selected before they even arrive at the school), everyone will know each other and there will be less scope for cliquishness. There is the added advantage, suggested the super impressive and engaging housemaster and housemistress of Falkners, that the young 13-14 year olds don't have to navigate what can be an intimidating hierarchy of older boys and girls. Most parents remarked on how much their children's confidence grew throughout the year, although inevitably we heard the odd case of difficult relationships, particularly among the girls. The building itself is modern, functional but attractive. Neat little drawers with names attached for mobile phones to go to bed in at the end of the day, very comfortable and tasteful common rooms on each boys' and girls' side, and a place in the centre where they can all gather to play games and hang out.

First class boarding accommodation – some of the most comfortable we've seen. Many of the study bedrooms have ensuite bathrooms, two or three to a room, there is a kitchen on every floor, and the comfortable common rooms are not the tatty stinky ones of olden days. Well upholstered sofas, pool tables and table football in good condition with all the pieces still intact, and best of all, when we visited at least, a lovely fresh smell of clean laundry.

Attempts are made to avoid houses becoming stereotyped – 'the sporty one', 'the nerdy one', although those trends can creep in without some social engineering.

Background and atmosphere: Founded in the 1850s by Thomas Stevens, lord of the manor and local rector, as a choir school for his church, Bradfield may not have a long sweeping drive, a grand central building, miles away in the middle of nowhere, but it is nonetheless a rural school. A picturesque one to boot, with its flint and brick buildings and sloping roofs. The village and the school are one and the same. There is no bank, post office or pub, but a fabulous arts and crafts manor house with stunning quadrangle and beautiful gardens, complete with astronomy hut for stargazing as well as the school chapel at the heart of the site. Here children have a chance to be children for longer, and there is not much to distract them from all that is available to do at school. Lots of walking to and from lessons, and that enticing sixth form bar is quite a hike. Faulkners eat in their house with some senior pupils. Others eat in the main dining room.

Plenty of quirky old fashioned public school traditions, including the many nicknames for things (glossaries are distributed on arrival arrive at Faulkners). Kitchens are Brewers, prefects, Beaks, Rux is the outdoor space near your house where you can kick a football around. The headmaster is the headman.

Day pupils fully integrated – sometimes leaving as late as 10 in the evening. They can leave at pm but are encouraged to do their prep at school. In the sixth form they can get permission to drive themselves to school. All day pupils have a desk in a dormitory. Flexi-boarding arrangement is available, but not encouraged and not many take it up.

One housemaster (and ex-BBC sports commentator) observed that the fact that Bradfield is a football school, rather than a rugby school, allows it to lend itself more readily to a healthy, collaborative co-education environment. He may have a point. Relationships between the genders here certainly seem to be positive. Neither wary nor subservient but natural and enjoyable.

A strong community spirit, manifest in its educational partnership with Theale Green Academy, a local school which has gone from being in special measures to 'improving' and, 'we hope, to good,' says head. Pupils from Theale Green can come and learn science in the splendid labs here, but largely it's about sharing knowledge and expertise and providing support for their teachers. Continues to nurture the more than 100 year old relationship with Bradfield Club, a youth club in Peckham.

Pastoral care, well-being and discipline: Dr Stevens has a broadminded and sensitive approach to punishment. Highly experienced (chief disciplinarian was one of his major roles as second master at Marlborough), he recognises the difference between 'naughtiness' and 'nastiness'. As much of a concern as drugs now, in all schools, is the abuse of social media. While you need clear boundaries on the former, 'if you had zero tolerance with regard to social media you could empty a school,' he observes. One bad post may amount to stupidity, however three may well amount to bullying. Dr Stevens encourages an approach that helps pupils learn from their mistakes.

Faulkners students hand in their phones at night (quite apart from the threat to well-being caused by social media, the use of phones affects sleep, which is an even greater threat, he points out). Policies on phones and screens vary from house to house for year 10 upwards, but a heightened awareness of the effect – positive and negative – of screens is universal. 'The only criticism I have of the school is that they don't remove the phones of all pupils at the end of the day,' remarked one parent. Clear lines are drawn on intimate sexual relations as well as on using drugs in school – it's automatic expulsion. 'We don't have open season'.

Effective mentoring and support system between the sixth formers and newbies. Sixth formers eat lunch with year 9 in Faulkners and monitor their homework time. Complicated system of appointing head girl and boy, prefects, heads of house. Not all parents and pupils are fans, not least as some teachers can be indiscreet and partisan. It involves applications with references, an interview process, with some selection by the head boy and girl and some by the teachers. Within each house pupils are appointed to particular roles – head of academic, head of media for example, not difficult for the odd person to slip through the net and find themselves without a role.

Well-being is part of the curriculum for years 9 -11. This takes place in the Well-being Centre, a comfortable place among the roof beams where pupils can sit on beanbags, in chairs around a circle or at a large table to talk about difficult issues. A recent discussion was 'what does cancer mean to you?' They also do yoga, mindfulness and relaxation. The cynic may detect the influence of their grander neighbour up the road, but well-being is – or should be – firmly on the map in all good schools and this is just another indicator that Bradfield is keeping up with the times.

Tutors (all teachers also act as a tutor), attached to the houses, are assigned eight students. They will mentor, support and keep an eye on their progress – including their study skills and prep. Keen to strengthen and capitalise on this personal, focused support, Dr Stevens has freed up more time for tutors to meet their tutees so that as well as keeping a watching brief, they can take a more active, inspirational role. Some parents observed that their child had had four tutors since they started. Delicate balance struck between sticking with a tutor to form a solid relationship and moving on when the dynamic is not working.

We heard some reports that a high turnover of staff, particularly housemistresses and masters in the past, meant that not all holes were plugged soon enough when they appeared; however, it would seem that things are settling down now, and the atmosphere we experienced was purposeful, collaborative and stimulating.

On the whole a tolerant, unpressurised environment. 'You're always busy at Bradfield,' said a sixth former. 'If you're not doing something then something's wrong.'

Pupils and parents: Large London and local – Reading-Windsor-Ascot – contingent. About 10 per cent international families, based overseas. 'We keep an eye on numbers of particular nationalities, just to avoid cliques,' says head, but there is no quota at all, no missions to the East (or anywhere else) to recruit. Some Europeans – Spanish, Danish etc – but a more English flavour to it than many boarding schools. Certainly not flashy nor grand. Families here are pretty comfortable in their skin and with their lot. 'Impossible to pigeonhole,' commented one parent. 'There are foreign royalty, the odd celebrity, some very ordinary English folk and a few on full bursaries, a well-rounded community.' Boys still outnumber girls, about 62 per cent boys, but number of girls continues to grow.

Within those parameters, the pupils too are diverse. This is not a sausage factory. Dr Stevens values what he describes as 'the integrity of difference – one of the great strengths of a boarding education.' Pupils come from 60 different prep schools. No one school ever sends as many as 20. Among the prep schools that send numbers in double figures are Cheam, St Andrews, Lambrook, Northcote Lodge and Broomwood. Siblings are welcomed and their assessment looked at favourably: 'it would be wrong to turn them away on the basis that they scored a few percent less than they should have,' says head. Bradfield remains a broad church and under the current leadership will continue to do so.

Former pupils include politicians, Lord David Owen and Sir John Nott, authors Louis de Bernieres and Richard Adams, cricketer and broadcaster Mark Nicholas, actor Claudia Harrison and astronomer Sir Martin Ryle.

Entrance: Main entrance point is into year 9. Selection criteria are 'attitude, character and potential for happiness,' says head. School increasingly selective as demand for places has shot up in recent years. CE pass mark is 55 per cent (no slippage). Introduction of a pre-test in year 7. School considers prep school heads' reports and on the basis of that invites pupils for assessment in years 6 and 7. All candidates interviewed and tested. School works closely with prep school head with borderline candidates especially. The main aim is to find candidates who will be 'net givers' to the school.

First step is to see the school. Tours every Saturday morning and head makes himself available for personal meetings at other times. Occasional places do arise in year 10 and between 50 and 60 places in the sixth form. English and maths tests plus two interviews in November before year of entry into year 12. Minimum of six B grades with at least Cs in English and maths GCSEs.

Exit: About 10 per cent leave after GCSE to sixth form colleges and day schools. Practically all sixth formers go on to university. Current popular ones include Bristol, Exeter, Leeds, Manchester, Newcastle, Bath and Oxford Brookes. Increasing numbers head for US universities and European ones. A very few (though school feels this is likely to increase) go straight into employment or on apprenticeship schemes.

Money matters: Although lots of scholarships awarded – including academic, sport and music – a fee reduction is only available with means-testing. The school is a charitable trust and provides bursary support, from anything from 100 per cent of fees to one per cent.

Remarks: Thoroughly unpretentious yet with lots to boast about, Bradfield is a heavenly place to learn and to grow. Very difficult to imagine who would not thrive here. There's something for everyone and lots for all.

B

Brambletye School

Lewes Road, East Grinstead, West Sussex RH19 3PD

Pupils: 275; 96 boarders • Ages: 2½ -13 (boarding from 7) • C of E

Fees: Day £9,105 – £19,635; Boarding: £23,400 – £23,940 pa

Tel: 01342 321004
Email: registrar@brambletye.com
Website: www.brambletye.co.uk

Headmaster: Since 2015, William Brooks, previously deputy head at Port Regis school. Studied combined arts at Durham; also has a PGCE and an MBA in educational leadership. Has also been deputy head at Bruern Abbey and Sunningdale. At Port Regis, he taught maths and coached sport – he is a keen sportsman and plays cricket and golf in his spare time. Wife Amelia plays a leading role at Brambletye; their three children have joined the school.

Entrance: No assessment for pre-prep but likes to see previous school reports. Consciously broad intake, but has introduced an assessment morning and reasoning tests and a chat for the prep school. About half come up from pre-prep and the rest from elsewhere. Will only turn a child away if it is felt they would not be able to cope with common entrance. A handful join for the last two years.

Exit: To a huge range of schools – Tonbridge, Benenden, Brighton College, Charterhouse, Lancing, Ardingly, Stowe, Eton, Millfield and Winchester among the more popular. Not a feeder to anywhere in particular and three children going to the same school in one year is considered a lot. In 2016, 22 scholarships – academic, art, music, DT, all-rounder and sport. Virtually all stay on until 13, but girls occasionally leave at 11. No specific preparation for 11+ but children well prepared in verbal and non-verbal reasoning and current affairs for pre-tests.

Remarks: Founded at Sidcup Place, Kent in 1919, it moved to its current site in 1933 along with the chapel which was moved brick by brick from Sidcup. The original building is an old hunting lodge set in 140 acres up a long drive a mile from East Grinstead and 20 minutes from Gatwick Airport. Glorious views in all directions, and children can look out of their dormitory windows across the terrace and playing fields to the reservoir in the distance with not another house in sight, yet only 30 miles from London. Everything you could wish for here: sports hall, purpose-built theatre, indoor swimming pool and award-winning classroom block complete with its own weather station, and even a red letter box outside the front door; not to mention dens, zip wires and an assault course. Wonderful panelled hall and rambling passages adorned with sports trophies and portraits of previous headmasters. Brambletye's signature pink and grey colours everywhere from the uniform

B

to the rugby posts, and even the ponies in the show jumping team have pink saddle cloths.

The 1960s prospectus stated that 'our main aim is for our boys to do what is right because they choose and not because they have been told to do so'. Although so much else has changed about the school in the intervening years (including girls since 1999), these core aims still hold true. Children are encouraged to develop a set of values and to appreciate what they have got and what they can do for others – 'community, co-operation and team spirit'. They are expected to 'do the right thing and hold a conversation with confidence'.

Specialist subject teachers for older children – good balance of youth and experience, with several recently appointed heads of department. 'It's the teachers who make the difference' – all are very supportive and committed and about 80 per cent live on site. Setting in maths, English and science from year 4 and in other subjects where possible, and all learn Latin from year 5. Scholarship stream for the last three years.

Good learning support with a specialist teacher, mainly for mild to moderate dyslexia. Each child has an individual education plan with appropriate targets and is given one-to-one and in-class support and allowed to use a laptop in exams. Everyone subtly tested for learning difficulties via reading and spelling age tests and CAT tests. 'Teachers' instincts are crucial'.

Boys play football, rugby and cricket and girls netball, hockey and rounders. Athletics for all in the summer. A myriad of other sports also offered: canoeing, taekwondo, fencing, judo, golf, squash, riding and clay pigeon shooting to name a few – and has recently introduced sailing on the local reservoir. 'Great emphasis is placed on good sportsmanship, on winning in a sporting manner and losing with grace'. Football and netball trips to Madrid and cricket to Kenya as well as mini tours in the UK. Inspired heads of art and DT – you can feel the buzz as you walk in the door, and school gets about 10 art and DT scholarships a year. Artist in residence and local sculptor, and art students come in at weekends and work alongside the children – many children spend a lot of their free time here. Annual exhibition of pupils' work at local Arts Centre in East Grinstead.

Music increasingly vibrant and you hear the sound of music all round the school. About 85 per cent learn at least one instrument, some to grade 8. Newish director of music and team of peripatetic teachers have 'made music fun and everyone wants to be in a band'. Orchestra, chamber group and other instrumental groups, kettle and African drum ensembles and three choirs. Production each term in 250 seat theatre as well as drama in form assemblies. Big musical for top two years like Oliver! and South Pacific with professional musicians and microphones and often hired stage sets.

Children help choose a different charity each year and have raised over £100,000 in last 10 years – some recently visited a school in Kenya for which they had raised £14,000.

Most children board for the last two years – about 60 boarders in on Saturday nights; weekly boarding not an option at this stage but exeats every two weeks. Boarders in year 6 and below can go home every weekend after matches. Recently introduced fixed-night boarding has proved popular and most beds now full. Bright, light dorms gradually being refurbished and beds laden with teddy bears and walls covered in posters – Harry Stiles and One Direction much in evidence in the girls' dorms. Visiting speakers on Saturday nights and for chapel on Sunday mornings. Some trips and treats on Sundays but most activities on site – the banning of hand-held games consoles has been surprisingly well received by the children: 'Now I have more people to play with,' said one. Good food – homemade cookies for break and plenty of choice at lunch and supper, and even Weetabix before bed for anyone who is still hungry. Staff eat at tables with children and much emphasis placed on manners and good behaviour.

Parents involved and welcomed. Mainly London commuters, many of whom have boarded themselves – very few first time buyers. About 17 international children from a wide range of countries; strong links with Spain and Thailand – no EAL offered but do offer curriculum support. No parents' group as such but lots of events involve parents – focus on charitable fundraising and the 4x4 challenge a major feature of the social calendar. Doesn't have to be a Range Rover, the old farm Land Rover will do just fine. 'The school produces lovely, all round, grounded children, well prepared for the next stage,' said one mother. 'Whenever I call in during free time the place is always filled with laughter, and I love to see the children just mucking around in the garden,' said another. The most famous old boy is probably Benedict Cumberbatch.

Pre-prep and nursery run by the much-loved 'progressive and welcoming' Dawn Atkinson; 'She sold me the school,' said one happy mother. The 85 children aged 3-7 housed in purpose-built octagonal building adjacent to the prep school with its own entrance and car park. Central hall and lots of space indoors and out, with two playgrounds and fencing made to look like brightly coloured pencils decorated with wellington boots planted with flowers. Big focus on rewards, and children earn crystals and gems for good work and behaviour. They learn music from year 2 and have own practice room. Big on drama and dance, and children encouraged to take part in assemblies, concerts and the Christmas production. Use the prep school's theatre, sports hall, swimming pool and games pitches,and come over to the dining room for lunch. Teachers from the prep come over to teach ICT, and netbooks and iPads used in lessons. Children allowed to go at their own pace, and booster groups offered for the very bright and those who struggle.

New weekly baby and toddler group gives families a glimpse of what Brambletye has to offer.

Brentwood School

Middleton Hall Lane, Brentwood, Essex CM15 8EE

Pupils: 1,541; 41 boys, 23 girls board • Ages: 3–18 • Sixth form: 291

Fees: Day £13,380 – £17,400; Boarding £34,135 pa

Tel: 01277 243243
Email: headmaster@brentwood.essex.sch.uk
Website: www.brentwoodschool.co.uk

Headmaster: Since September 2004, Mr Ian Davies PGCE MA (50s), theology degrees from Oxford and Cambridge. Previously head of St Dunstan's College. Taught religious studies at Sackville School and became head of year and head of RE at The Latymer, Edmonton. An ISI inspector, member of D of E National Advisory Council, and helped select naval officers for training at Dartmouth for the Admiralty Interview Board. Very approachable – once volunteered as a guinea pig for a nitrogen experiment during science lesson where his hands were set alight. 'It didn't hurt at all, as it burnt above my hand, and the children loved it.' He sees the school as 'educationally... more sophisticated than most' thanks to its diamond structure, educating boys and girls in separate gender classes from age 11 to 16, but together at other ages. 'We all learn in different ways and I think there are gender differences and also gender stereotypes which need to be cracked.' So the school employs all 'the benefits of single sex education' while enabling pupils to 'also get the social benefits of choir, orchestra, combined cadets' and more 'as part of a co-educational environment'. He adds, 'Nothing pleases me more than having a girl who is great at maths and physics go off to university to do engineering.' Considers himself 'very lucky' in his career, having 'worked with great people all the way through' and being mentored by some 'great heads' in the past.

Preparatory school head: Since 2011, Mr Jason Whiskerd BA PGCE. Previously head of Aldenham Preparatory School in Elstree, Hertfordshire and deputy head of the King's School (junior) in Chester. Read history and politics at Trinity College, Carmarthen (University of Wales) and serves as an ISI Inspector of other preparatory schools. He is also an active member of the Independent Association of Prep Schools (IAPS).

Mr Whiskerd is a keen sportsman, having played cricket and rugby at regional level and, as testament to his Welsh roots (he attended Llandovery College as a boy), Welsh rugby and Swansea City are his passion. He is married to a junior school teacher and has three daughters attending the prep and senior school. A friendly man: extended a hearty welcome and warm handshake when we visited.

Academic matters: They start learning oral French from year 1 'since this is a time when they are most receptive to learning a new language'. Verbal reasoning is taught from year 4 and Latin from year 6. There is emphasis on 'learning habits for life' so lots of push to get children to think for themselves, ask questions and 'look at things in detail'. From year 3 they are introduced to a house system so they can build relationships with older pupils. By the time they get to year 6 pupils take on roles as prefects, house captains, council representatives and more. Plenty of preparation for the move to senior school including a Q&A session with year 7s. Able children also well catered for with plenty of challenging extension opportunities. We know of at least one boy who showed aptitude for maths and was given the chance to sit his maths GCSE at age 9. A couple of parents described similar experiences where their children had been labelled as 'slow' and 'easily distracted' at previous schools, only to move them to Brentwood and discover that the real problem was that their children had been bored, under-stimulated and capable of more.

GCSE results in 2016 were slightly down on the previous year's: 58 per cent graded A*/A. Alongside critical and creative thinking and the core subjects, they study French and Latin in year 7, and choose from German, ancient Greek or Spanish in year 8. IGCSE in several subjects; head sees it as 'a stepping stone to the IB'.

At A level in 2016, 39 per cent A*/A grades and 76 per cent A*-B. School offers 26 curriculum subjects, plus other activities such as law, cooking at university, Italian, peer mentoring training and sports leadership. IB scores averaged 37 points.

School encourages creative and critical thinking across all subjects, whether improving goal-scoring in sport, performing West Side Story in German, or applying maths in the composition of music. The school 'teaches you to think for yourself and how it is up to you to determine whether you succeed or not,' said a pupil. The syllabus is 'flexibly adapted to suit all pupils' needs' and 'able pupils do not get bored here', says the school. Parents agree with this, saying that although children are set early in year 7 in French and maths, these groups are not set in concrete and support is available if needed. 'I think it really is important that the children are not stuck with a label of being really clever or really daft,' said a parent. 'That doesn't happen at all. It is very, very flexible.'

EAL support provided to 35 pupils, largely through teachers that have lived and worked abroad. The learning and development team also provides support to around 50 students with special educational needs. This includes an Independent Education Plan, one-to-one tuition, subject support and lunchtime drop in sessions. The department is very successful – some who receive additional support make such 'good and exceptional progress' that they 'sometimes outperform their peers', noted the ISI.

Games, options, the arts: There is a long sporting tradition here. This was one of three independent schools selected as an official Olympic training venue and it made world headlines when it opened up its doors to rescue an African Paralympic team left stranded at the airport with neither host nor facilities after a funding promise failed to materialise.

Sport is one of the scholarships offered; football, cricket, hockey, rugby and netball coaches often successful sportspeople. Pupils have played at national and international level in fencing, water polo, cricket, football, squash, tennis and netball. School has won the Public Schools Fencing Competition 'more than 30 times since 1962'. Both girls' athletics teams have made it to the English schools' track and field national finals. One England Under-19 cricketer has been offered a contract with Essex. At any one time around 400 pupils are out representing the school in a whole variety of sports. Alongside sports hall, pool, gym and dance studio, there are glass-backed squash courts, fitness suite and a fencing salle, plus extensive playing fields and a full-size running track.

Art, music and drama are also well catered for. Many pupils' works are exhibited at the annual art exhibition and school also tries to instil appreciation for art whether pupils 'consider themselves to be "arty" or not'. Various competitions include the popular water colour competition and the head's sculpting competition. DT and ICT are taught with art and food tech in the Hardy Amies Design Centre, equipped with its own library and computers. Recently a group of students scooped the top prize in an international design award with their life-saving 'glow' glove. The six, led by a student who 'a year ago wouldn't have said boo to a goose', took first prize in the annual Virtual Ventura competition against opposition from 300 teams. 'We thought about different things and narrowed it down to safety as during the dark people don't see cyclists very well.' Their winning design went on display at the Design Museum in London.

Music and drama are taught in a separate building equipped with rehearsal studios and 14 practice rooms. We witnessed one group using Sibelius to compose 'an answer in response to a melody' in preparation for their GCSE creative task: 'We have to pick the right melody chords to make it work. The answer must relate to it but not repeat it'. Many students get involved in the school symphony orchestra, big band (which creates its own CDs), choir or choral society, and the regular musicals and house music concerts. A number of ex-pupils are exhibitioners at London music colleges or hold organ scholarships at university; there are two organs in the school, one in the music hall and another in the chapel. Prep school has two orchestras and a junior choir that rehearses weekly and has performed at the royal Albert Hall. On the day of our visit many of the prep school classrooms were empty – our guide seemed baffled by this and was somewhat relieved when we happened upon a very noisy music lesson where children were exploring how to synchronise sound for a silent film. They were clearly having fun with flute, cymbals, drums, voice and more, but we got the feeling that the cover teacher may have pulled the short straw.

Similar story with drama: three major annual productions covering every genre from musicals to comedy to classics. Examples include Macbeth featuring video clips showing the war in the Middle East; Antigone performed with modern ballet choreographed by a student; a third year production of Arabian Nights; and West Side Story in German, all performed in the school's 400-seat auditorium. Mainly girls, but a few boys too, take part in dance showcases including tap, jazz and street.

Too many extracurricular activities to name: Trivial Pursuits, cross-country, table tennis, chess, Duke of Edinburgh Award, Cine & Literatura, a Spanish film club, public speaking. 'You have to choose at least three; it's compulsory now,' we heard a year 7 pupil tell a sixth former. The Sir Antony Browne Society invites guest speakers on a wide range of current political, financial and medical topics. One of the most popular activities at the school is the 152-year-old Combined Cadet Force (CCF), one of the largest in the country, which has been enlisted by the DfE to help set up branches at other schools. It really creates a buzz in the atmosphere on Fridays when its 500-odd members come to school dressed in combat gear, ready for the afternoon and weekend activities. These include map reading, camp craft, basic first aid, hill walking, canoeing, flying and skydiving. 'CCF is a big thing here,' said one pupil. 'It opens you up to a lot of things you might not have been able to do', and at very low cost. Other pupils join the Community Service Unit and help raise thousands for charities in the local area and abroad. With so many competitions there is no excuse for not finding something you like, although one student did complain about the lack of a house dance competition.

Boarding: The two boarding houses are a 'home from home' for the small boarding community of some 23 girls and 41 boys, 60 per cent of whom are from overseas. Both are situated off campus, 'so you don't feel that you're there all day'. They are run like a 'well-oiled machine,' say the husband and wife houseparents, with regular routines (for homework, bedtimes and activities) and good links between houseparents, teachers and parents. As well as email, the 'children are Skyping every single night and we are Skyping with parents almost on a daily basis. I go into the rooms and they say, "Say hello to my mum".'

Background and atmosphere: The story behind the school's foundation is a history lesson in itself. During the English reformation a 19-year-old Protestant was burnt on order of Sir Antony Browne, then acting as a magistrate on behalf of Queen Mary. He purchased Weald Hall and land for the school in 1557 as an act of penance. The school received its motto in 1622 from the pen of John Donne, Dean of St Paul's. It also has its own prayer and song. Was a boys' grammar school, principally boarding, for many years. Admitted girls into the sixth form in the mid 1970s and into the main school in 1988.

The prep school was established in 1892 and moved to its present site at Middleton Hall in 1949; became co-educational in 1999. Pre-prep (ages 3 to 7) opened in 1995 and has its own grounds and buildings. In 2013, the pre-prep and the prep were amalgamated under the one headship of Mr Whiskerd, providing a seamless progression from 3 to 11. There is a strong sense of the traditional alongside the modern – bright and lively classrooms, decorated with pupil's work, are housed in both 19th and 16th century buildings. In the gorgeous chapel (1868), pupils listen to biblical stories with a modern twist, for example, an account from one of the gospels about the danger of judging others, delivered alongside a screening of the Susan Boyle audition on Britain's Got Talent. Art and science is taught in an old stable block and Middleton Hall itself features stained glass windows and stucco ceilings. On the wall in the reception area is a large, colourful picture illustrating what it means to live by the Brentwood School motto of Virtue, Learning and Manners: 'We teach our children that the opportunities we create are best enjoyed when others benefit from them too'.

Set in the heart of the Essex town of Brentwood, across the road from the cathedral, the school stands on a 72-acre site. Not much is left of the Weald Hall save a few ruins. The Old Big School, built in 1568, still has the original front door and is used for lectures, meetings and discussions. There is a beautiful Victorian chapel built in 1868, with arches, beams and stained glass windows detailing the narratives of Moses, Elijah and other biblical prophets, as well as patron saints of the Great War. It seats 320, so cannot contain the whole school at once, but the six year groups take it in turn to have a fortnightly service there.

More recent buildings include the science block, opened by the Queen in 1957, the 1986 Courage Hall sports centre, and the 1999 Hardy Amies design building. The refurbished sixth form block which houses the 400 seat auditorium has distinctively Victorian style arched roofs. The Bean Academic Centre, 'the intellectual heart of the school', includes a lecture theatre, café, social and study spaces. The main grounds resemble a university campus quadrangle and seem to run as far as the eye can see: beyond the rugby posts is Mill House, the girls' boarding house, Hough House, the boys' boarding house, the prep school and then the running tracks and fields.

Pastoral care, well-being and discipline: Parents say 'pastoral care here is excellent' and that 'the older pupils help the younger pupils'. They value the peer mentoring room where sixth formers make hot chocolate for younger pupils, who can sit and talk if they have a problem. Year 6 pupils are trained in peer mediation and this helps 'pupils to resolve their own problems in the playground'. Bullying is rare, and the few 'misunderstandings' that do arise are 'nipped in the bud by the school very quickly,' say parents. One, whose daughter had been home educated and found the first few weeks a little daunting, commented on how well she had been helped to settle in.

Pupils have good relationships with their form tutors and teachers – 'everyone is helpful here', said a year 7 pupil. 'The teachers do tend to treat the children as adults,' said a parent. 'They communicate openly with them, so the children are not frightened to say, "I want to speak to you about something".'

The house system fosters a sense of belonging and there is good support from a careers service, with an annual careers convention. Parents report that initial concerns are likely to involve ensuring children can cope with homework alongside the large numbers of extracurricular opportunities. 'One of the things we were told at a meeting before starting is that you've got to be organised. My son comes into school early to get homework done because he wants to do swimming and football after school.'

Plenty of contact with parents through subject, house and tutor reports and parents' evenings, but parents also appreciate in particular the introductory meeting held for parents of new year 7s. The school is 'really on the ball like that,' said a parent who has two daughters in the school, one in the sixth form and another in year 9. 'Whatever topic it might be, you get the information in time to talk about it.'

Pupils and parents: Parents are mostly professional. There is a mix of backgrounds, races and religions here, with the majority being white English. 'Although we are a Christian school we welcome pupils of all faiths,' says the school. Many pupils move from the prep to the senior, others come from local independent and state schools. The school also has a number of international students (about 60 per cent of boarders, plus a few day pupils) from the Ukraine, Russia and other Eastern European countries, Central Europe and the Far East including China.

A number of notable former pupils including Douglas Adams, author of the Hitchhiker's Guide to the Galaxy, Sir Hardy Amies, couturier and dressmaker (he designed the school uniform), Lord Black of Brentwood, executive director of The Telegraph, Frank Lampard, footballer, Jack Straw, former lord chancellor and secretary of state for justice, and many more.

Entrance: Pupils assessed on language and dexterity skills for entry into the early years (about 40 places). Twenty places are available for external year 3 entry (age 7) and candidates sit an entrance test in English and maths in January. 'They [the questions] are on the national curriculum for the child's age so

I needn't have worried,' said a parent. 'They make the children feel at ease too.'

Year 7 entry by maths, English and verbal reasoning exams examination and an interview to 'assess a pupil's intellectual curiosity, potential and flair for learning'. Sixth form entrance is by interview and successful GCSE results (generally at least six B grades).

Exit: Over three-quarters of prep school pupils go on to senior school (86 per cent in 2016). They sit the same 11+ exam as external applicants and are prepared well (parents are warned a year or so in advance if the school perceives any problems). All candidates are interviewed if they do very well (for an academic scholarship) or if they have struggled on the day (have not quite achieved the standard). A few pupils go on to local grammar schools in the Chelmsford area.

Most – about 80 per cent – of senior school pupils stay on to sixth form and most proceed to university. In 2016, two to Oxbridge and over half to other top 20 universities such as Bristol and Edinburgh, or further afield to Harvard. Record number of medics, dentists and vets – nine in 2016. The school also helps those students who want to go straight into work through the alumni association and network of ex-pupils.

Money matters: A good variety of scholarships, of up to 50 per cent, on offer to top academic scorers in the entrance exam or those with specialist talents in art, drama, music, choral and sport. There are also means-tested bursaries of up to 100 per cent. Sixth form scholarships valued at between £500 and £1000, offered via a two-hour critical thinking paper.

Remarks: Strong on values and has all the facilities and opportunities needed to provide a child with a rounded education. Very impressive.

Brighton and Hove High School

Montpelier Road, Brighton, East Sussex BN1 3AT

Pupils: 615 • Ages: 3–18 • Sixth form: 54

Fees: £6,750 – £13,530 pa

Tel: 01273 280280
Email: enquiries@bhhs.gdst.net
Website: www.bhhs.gdst.net

Head: Since 2012, Jennifer Smith MA, MEd (50s), aims to be in post for the long haul after a series of two-to-three year predecessors. An engaging and sensible Glaswegian, she spent the previous 10 years rising to deputy head at Wilson's, a state funded selective all boys school in Sutton. She still commutes south from there, her husband goes north to his headship in London and their daughter is at Sutton High (one of the 28 other members of the Girls' Day School Trust). It was the vision of the CEO of the GDST, and the way she engages with political debate in a non-stuffy way, that really attracted Ms Smith to her first headship. 'It's about building resilience in girls' learning and confidence, while also very important to give value for money. My main aim is for each girl to know that we care for her and about her progress.'

Earlier challenges include five years as a head of English at an all boys grammar in her late 20s (and the first years of GCSEs) and a vital role in the turnaround of the ranking of Wilson's results. She uses her daily train journey to Brighton to blog for the school website – part of the 'technical explosion' she spearheaded in her first year, with a new online portal and online reporting. She doesn't teach the timetable at present, but does cover lessons, watches teaching and does duty in the canteen, using that time to hear suggestions from the students – and act on them eg new transparency in the behaviour system and a consistent 'tariff of discipline'.

Prep school head: Since 2011, the sparky yet realistic Mrs Sian Cattaneo BA (Sussex) Cert Ed (50s). Came from over nine years as head of St Ives School, Haslemere, before that 16 years in Nairobi at the Banda School. Her son and daughter are now in their 20s. She was attracted to the Girls' Day School Trust by the attitude and dynamism of the chief executive and now 'I'll never go and work in a mixed school again!'

Parents say she 'has a heart of gold and cares deeply about every child' and that she works very closely with her deputy, creating 'a family atmosphere with kindness and grace'. She sees herself as a 'green hat' thinker (Edward de Bono's Six Thinking Hats) while her team puts her creativity into practice. Her office is set up with space for parents and children to come in and talk – she's gathered opinions on what is felt is important about the school and worked hard to reinforce and build on them.

Academic matters: Prep staff seen as the lifeblood of the school – and their friendliness and understanding of the need for flexibility given parental challenges is really appreciated by the parents. All teachers have email addresses for parent contact, there's a weekly newsletter, virtual learning platform for curriculum enrichment and source of information for parents and the nursery and reception have interactive learning diaries that can be added to by parents online.

Two classes per year all the way up the prep school. Reception has free flow to extensive outside space with an outdoor classroom. From year 3 the girls are taught by specialist teachers in specialist rooms – accustoms them to independence. We saw Victorian washing strung across the classroom, butterflies in remembrance of the suffragettes, all these part of the creative curriculum. Head is keen to ensure pupils are not too cosy; instead they are put in situations where they have to make their own decisions.

Year 5 and 6 use individual iPads for each pupil – staff are hot on training to ensure pupils use them to create presentations, share ideas and carry out research rather than just delight in the flick of the technology.

SENCo's 'learning differences' focus is about supporting girls with an empathetic approach and regular training for staff. There's a full time learning support assistant and she is used for individual and small group support.

Academic results excellent with 84 per cent A*-B grades at A level, 55 per cent A*/A, and 55 per cent A*/A grades at GCSE in 2016; dedicated staff passionate about their subjects. Bright, stimulating, independently minded, confident girls – a description approved by parents, staff and the local general public. Pupils are very conscientious and pile the pressure on themselves, but are encouraged to progress as individuals. Parents wonder at the results without overt peer rivalry – they feel it is extremely supportive, all of BHHS want everyone to succeed.

Touchscreens or interactive whiteboards in practically every classroom, both of which enable and encourage pupils to share centre stage with teachers. Pupils say the use of these and the online portal with past papers and learning tools really simplify catching up on classes and revision. Assessments for dyslexia and dyscalculia provided by the school and support for moderate cases via the SENCo team. Online reporting should now ensure that a diagnosis of dyslexia is attached to pupils through all subjects; in the past communication about the need for extra support has broken down.

Science is very popular, young and dynamic rather than geeky- the worktops in the revamped labs wouldn't look out of place in a kitchen showroom in Hove. Each sixth former has her own tray of instruments and test-tubes, encouraging responsibility and continuity. Latin is taught all the way through, along with a choice of French or Spanish, while maths and English are also strong with great use of external resources, whether it is a Cipher Challenge, guest author or theatre visit. The combined alumni of the GDST help to encourage aspirational and concrete links with world outside lessons, the pupils are busy and keen on learning, aware that their choice of single-sex education may already have given them a leg up.

Careers programme impressive with close links with the local careers service and employers, free psychometric testing in year 11 and the school organises work experience at the end of that year too. There are enterprise activities in all years, the Temple Project Qualification (the school's version of an Extended Project Qualification) and an intensive programme of visiting speakers, all of which apparently makes writing your personal statement for university application easy, although it may take you until then to realise that all these experiences are rounding out your character...

Sixth form has the biggest space in the whole school – although the numbers are small at present. This means very focused teaching and a real family atmosphere for those that stay, with plenty of experience coaching and mentoring the younger girls. Traditionally over 50 per cent leave, many to the range of great (free) six form colleges around Brighton where there are more A level choices on offer externally eg media studies and vocational ones. Many BHHS girls have been there since the age of 3 or 4, so are keen to spread their social wings and learn with boys, although some regret leaving when their A level results are not so impressive as those who remain. Ex-students, with their male friends, can pop (and sign) in to visit the sixth form centre from the nearest college, BHASVIC.

Games, options, the arts: Great modern sports hall with disabled access and the normal rainbow of court lines, layered nets and trampolines, also two outdoor netball courts and Astroturf at the junior school. Netball and athletics are the most successful teams, but the track record is spread like the matches between independent and state sector opponents. Sport is good but it wouldn't be the reason to come to this school. The pleasant walk to the courts in St Ann's Well Garden is enjoyed by tennis players, girls are minibussed to Brighton Swimming Centre to swim, and the fitness studio is hugely popular – especially with the sixth form. However, the dance studio next to it appeals across all years, with one mirrored and one glass wall and all dancers with their eyes on the highlight of the year, a performance in a central Brighton venue. Drama also well taught in dedicated studio with professional lights and mixing desk, which doubles as make up and dressing room in the whole school productions. Attitude to games in the prep more focused now with new head of sport (previously taught PE by class teacher) and 60-80 external fixtures a term; netball, athletics, hockey, running, swimming, gym. PE hall (also assembly), new Astroturf, netball and tennis courts. Head of dance comes in to teach from senior school – this is very popular.

Art department is beloved and productive – a microcosm of the ideal atmosphere of the school where teachers listen to individuals and then encourage each one to stretch themselves beyond their own expectations. 'It doesn't feel like a lesson, the teachers let you decide.' Officially it occupies two floors in a separate building with a darkroom and a Mac for photography (at A level) but the students' work is placed all over the school, is changed regularly and entices visitors to follow it to the source. Design technology also impressive with great use of acrylics and projects that range from concept to marketing. Likewise, home economics' projects are all-encompassing eg tasty biscuits in enticing packaging and a level 2 food hygiene award – very useful for a summer job in a café.

Some great art on the prep school walls and in process – ranging from Mexican Day of the Dead inspired foil skulls to precise drawings of the back view of the hairstyle of a friend in your class. Also examples of business enterprise eg creating the marketing, organisation and fundraising for Children in Need. As in other GDST schools, great outreach to local charities through visits to community, Guild Collections and music performances. Currently one of only two independent schools in Sussex that have the green flag of an eco-school, takes energy saving, Fairtrade, bio-diversity (raised beds in garden and allotment off site) and bikeability very seriously.

The music house has been revamped. Full range of peripatetics, three choirs, two orchestras and a jazz band – as well as a biennial school musical – and packed performances. Also hosts Springboard, the Brighton and Hove Performing Arts festival. Music is fabulously taught in the prep with three school choirs, a ukulele group, orchestra and 70 per cent of years 1 to 6 learning at least one instrument. Performances of all kinds in assembly, old people's homes and whole school shows and strong emphasis on music technology.

Background and atmosphere: The original building (the Temple) became part of the GDST schools in 1880 – still central to the site, with pillars said to represent inverted cannons. Cluster of contemporary extensions spread out from this, wonderful height and light in the science block, other subjects spread between new and old buildings. Year 9 has a separate block near the netball courts and the sixth form centre and canteen are over a (narrow) public road from the main house – Brighton's youth mayor is in the sixth form at present, so she aims to present a case for a pelican crossing, a typical example of a BHHS girl's can-do attitude. Main hall, used for two assemblies each week and performances, has retractable seating – when we visited, a vicar had just given a thoughtful address; apparently she has to be good since there are a fair few sceptics in the student body. The canteen is a smaller area; children eat in sittings with a good choice of hot and cold and a snack bar where crisps and sandwiches can be bought with fingerprint activated pocket money. Staff eat in the sixth form centre canteen.

Main library is peaceful, with high ceilings – sixth formers can work there or in their own centre, computer access to the online portal as well as shelves of books. Sixth formers are allowed phones but the younger ones are not allowed to use theirs during the day – it is a busy site, so there wouldn't be much chance in the five minutes when the girls flood the corridors and stairs between lessons, racing back to the basement locker room to get more books or their sports kit. Uniform for the younger years, with small earrings and no bracelets – sixth formers can wear what they like.

A strong ethos of charitable giving with a 'Guild' collection every Wednesday, where pennies are collected by reps in each form room. This all adds up and is given to two chosen charities per year. The charities are pitched by the girls at an assembly, so almost always have a personal motivation behind them, and the students use all their initiative to raise funds through other events eg a fashion show.

School council is also influential, with suggestions and complaints fed up through reps in each form. The same system operates in the GDST as a whole, so a case for change in BHHS would be pitched by a student rep to the Trust governors. Food is locally sourced and now cooked in house, salad option and no packed lunches.

Pastoral care, well-being and discipline: Strong pastoral support system with form teachers and sixth form tutors and year heads – set up for easy communication and accessibility. A mentoring service for younger girls – BLOBs – is an old acronym for Best Listeners of Brighton Schools. This really works, and is made easy by the amount of inter-year, inter-house contact through drama, sport competitions and end-of-year entertainment. Imaginative PSHE – we have encountered this in other Trust schools: the special events and whole days given over to topical issues all help to raise awareness and assist pupils with self-expression on current affairs.

School nurse on site, at the heart of the school near the basement locker room – parents and girls really value that common sense support; it eliminates the drama from long-term health conditions. Families really appreciate the frequent personal letters home from the head celebrating individual achievements. At the other end of the spectrum, some parents talk of bullying not dealt with swiftly enough in the past; however, the head appears to be a fresh broom.

Students see themselves as a recognisable type, 'a BHHS girl through and through' – plenty of room for spirited girls but everyone is aware of the opportunities that the school gives them, so they are ambitious, organised and self-motivated. The head girl team is an example of the way cooperation and communication is fostered within the school – and links to organisations outside it.

Pupils and parents: Probably 70 per cent from Hove with the rest from Brighton, Pulborough, Eastbourne, Worthing, etc. Buses from Patcham, Worthing and Lewes. A real social and ethnic mix – artists, creative industries, investment bankers, local vicar, teachers – and, due to competitive fees, a good economic mix. Busy parents, both normally working to afford the fees, or taking some help from grandparents.

OGs Karen Pickering MBE, Olympic swimming gold medallist, Claire Hicks MBE, director of Impact Foundation, businesswoman Heidi Cooper, Beth Cordingley from The Bill, several recent University Challenge competitors.

Entrance: Prep school entry by tests and observation. Eighty per cent are referred by current and former parents.

AT 11+ from a wide range of local maintained and independent schools and also the junior school. A recent 23 per cent rise in the intake at year 7 is hoped to swell the sixth form numbers. GDST entrance assessment for the main school – selective, but not super selective. Entry at sixth form requires five GCSEs at C grade or above, with A or B in subjects to be taken at A level; girls come from The Towers, Warden Park, Shoreham College.

Exit: In 2016, 70 per cent of prep school girls to the senior school after entrance exam. Rest to other independents such as Roedean or Brighton College (where parents say academic teeth are bared) or to local state schools.

Some 60-70 per cent leave post-GCSE, often for the sixth form college (less than half a mile away) BHASVIC – the very wide of subjects and boys in the classes are enticing and often it is a financial decision for the families. Latest university destinations include Durham, Oxford (one in 2016), LSE, Exeter and LAMDA.

Money matters: Means-tested bursaries at year 7 normally awarded in rank order of performance in the entrance exam (50-100 per cent of fees); academic and music scholarships (10 per cent of fees) also available, plus Temple scholarships for all-round performance. More bursaries at year 12 and also another eight scholarships (10 to 30 per cent discount).

Remarks: Parents say it produces empowered, confident, clever girls – but not cocky ones – 'education rather than status'. Has suffered in the past through comparison to its noisy neighbour, Brighton College, both by staff and onlookers – now hopefully in an era where it is certain of its own value and ethos, with individual encouragement producing fantastic results and grounded girls.

B

Brighton College Prep and Pre-Prep School

Linked with Brighton College, Handcross Park School

Walpole Lodge, Walpole Road, Brighton, East Sussex BN2 0EU

Pupils: 505 • Ages: 3-13

Fees: £9,420 – £18,210 pa

Tel: 01273 704343
Email: prepadmissions@brightoncollege.net
Website: www.brightoncollege.net

Head: Since 2013, Harry Hastings (40s), came from eight years at Cumnor House, where he was assistant head, head of history, director of sport and plays. Energetic, enthusiastic and entrepreneurial, in his last year there, he created Harry Hastings' History Heroes, a cross between Top Trumps and Trivial Pursuit, sparked by a quiz played to occupy kids on history trips. He's sold it now, relieved to be once more focussed on his school full time – but it's a good example of his skill at coming up with creative solutions and ensuring they stick. His introduction to teaching was through gapping at his old prep, and his path to this first headship has led him through Exeter and Oxford Universities, a prep in Devon, Peponi House in Kenya and the Dragon School. Has a good support network of other teachers he's befriended along the way (now heads themselves) and has grounded himself with sport, both playing (Greyhounds at Oxford) and supporting. Passionate about rugby and athletics (always seen at the national championships with clipboard, stopwatch, radio and English Schools tie) and loves golf ('18 handicap ... in summer holidays').

Kate, his wife, is a consultant anaesthetist at the county hospital down the road, and they have three children, two at the prep school and one at the pre-prep. They commute in seven miles from near Lewes – at present by car, but he intends to cycle or run eventually. Is a great believer in finding space for peace and reflection in a busy life; one of his first actions as the new head of BCPS was to ensure the prep school kids are in silence as they snake in single file across the road to the main college. Initially, they thought they were being punished but the head feels being reflective is the unofficial 10th item in the BCPS code of conduct.

He feels very supported and privileged to be the headmaster of such 'extraordinary, brilliant and different children – beautifully mannered, fun, bright, interested and interesting, all wanting the best for each other.' They certainly greeted him charmingly and creatively; the responses to his request for a postcard over the summer are plastered over the hall walls, some in different languages, one with a 'postage stamp' made from a photo of the senior school's head. He knows all 300 children by name, greets them outside each morning, rain or shine, and teaches year 7 history, three times a week.

Pre-prep head since 2010 is Jo Williams, previously head of year 2 at Tanglin Trust School in Singapore. Alumna of University of Plymouth, head of early years foundation stage and then PE and girls' games at Oakwood School. Meets with head of prep weekly, phone calls and emails in between, he attends pre-prep open mornings and their staff share INSET days.

Entrance: Into pre-prep at 3+ (nursery) and 6+ (when third form is added, year 2 entry). Into prep at 8+ by assessment in maths, English and verbal reasoning plus observation (internal pupils have to sit English and maths exams). Special arrangements for dyslexic pupils, with recent educational psychologist's report. There's a waiting list. Pupils come from the state sector and private schools (lots of the girls from single sex schools) and the staff also have experience of both. Some 98 per cent of those that leave the pre-prep school come through to the prep. Travel via the same buses that serve the senior school – a third of the prep school children live in town, a third from Hove and the rest come from Lewes, Worthing, Shoreham, Hassocks etc.

Exit: Some 80+ per cent to Brighton College, although they have to take CE on a par with outsiders, with a pass mark of 55 per cent in maths and English and 60 per cent in all other subjects. The rest mostly to St Bede's, Roedean, Hurst, Lancing or Worth. If your child seems like they're not going to make the CE pass mark for the senior school then form teachers/head may well encourage going for another school rather than taking a punt on good luck on the day – so as to avoid a feeling of failure, About four children each academic year leave early, 50 per cent financial reasons, 50 per cent deciding to settle into a school that is not so academically ambitious, with advice from BCPS. We have reports of the year 3 prep school assessment assuming increasing importance, with many pupils having a tutor; parents of children struggling academically – many of whom chose the school because of its excellent learning support – will be warned in year 2 that the prep school might not be suitable.

Remarks: Compact busy campus, just one block to the east of the senior school and the two are very closely linked – the little ones walk across in reflective silence for lunch, chapel and games; both schools have the same shape of the day. The children are focused and engaged, polite and sparky – the eldest ones very aware of regular exams and what hangs on them (including those to graduate from the pre-prep to the prep). 'Why are we doing this when it has nothing to do with CE?' asked one, when being taught some tools for writing an essay. The head uses a metaphor for twice yearly exams as series of little hurdles rather than the Grand National. The achievement grades have been rejigged recently, aiming for more transparency in the comparison of these and common entrance percentages; it may feel a bit bumpy initially for the kids who are struggling to hit the marks necessary for entry to the senior school, but the head is convinced of the importance of clear communication and welcomes meetings with parents as soon as they have any concerns.

They do have an enormous amount of fun too; the teaching is inspiring and embellished with plenty of non-curriculum activities – from sleeping overnight on the Golden Hinde II in London to dancing with Kenyan Maasai. The children are taught by class teachers initially, working up to being setted in year 6. Three forms per year, each with 20-22 pupils – no physical room for any more. A buddy system makes for good cross-year peer support, also there are lots of siblings, reading groups with the pre-prep and the prefects cover wet break in classrooms for the little ones. Normally they are outside on two playgrounds (now Astroturfed), kicking balls and shrieking about – although lunches are also used to squeeze in a mime class (60 per cent of the school do LAMDA), or to catch up on some work in the ICT room.

Four houses compete in sport, drama, debating etc. Pastoral care is well organised, with spreadsheets covering achievements, pastoral concerns and public recognition, ensuring that every child gets an acknowledgement – whether it is the star of the week trophy for the little ones or a Headmaster's Show up in the Pelican Post weekly newsletter. Some parents feel the flip side of this effective documentation is a need to pigeonhole or label kids, whether as dyslexic, dyspraxic, having a processing problem or as a scholar. All of whom are well catered for here – there is a smaller dyslexia centre and two full time SENCos as well as strong connections to the main one in the senior school. A maximum of nine pulled out for each SEN group, with 12 or so students left in the English or French lesson in the third set, so both clusters benefit from the more focused attention of the teacher. Humour is used to tackle awareness of dyslexia too eg a great assembly by a couple of older boys playing on hot grills/ girls.

The children begin their days with assembly in the main hall four out of five mornings a week, sitting on the wooden parquet floor. It is also used for rehearsals, art displays and, when we visited, storing the Christmas shoeboxes for communities in Eastern Europe as well as local hospices. Music is marvellous here – from the accomplished chamber choir rehearsal we heard in the main hall to the junior wind group squeaking their way through Jingle Bells. Recent choir trips were to Disneyland and Barcelona.

The very youngest children (3-7 year olds, at the pre-prep) have their own purpose designed building (ex-St Mary's Hall, ex-Roedean Junior). Gorgeous light classrooms, well-stocked library and IT room, a big playing field as well as a playground out the back and all look jolly in their sweatshirts for nursery, smart uniforms for reception and upwards. Specialist teaching includes music, PE, art, Mandarin and French. Weekly swimming after reception, competitive matches for the top year and a huge variety of clubs run by outside coaches and teachers. Among the school council's achievements has been the idea for three new after-school clubs (Horrible History, singing, and calligraphy) and adding chicken curry and treacle pudding to the lunch menu.

The little ones at the prep do projects every three weeks, getting passionate about making a video on volcanos erupting or designing a tooth hygiene poster. The library is a converted chapel, bright and well used, as an alternative ICT room and for English lessons, reading on the bean bags in the corner (as long as you write a book report...) The oldest years get to use email, only with their @brightoncollege.net address. One of the two science labs has a veritable menagerie of pets – from snakes to rabbits. The pet club love to take some home at the weekend and there are tablets for each child to use for individual research during science lessons.

There's a wonderful home economics room, with tasty ingredients laid out and recipes published in the weekly Pelican Post – as ever, the most popular is pizza. This is compulsory up until year 6 and then the separate sciences take over that slot in the timetable. Latin is done in year 7 and 8 for those in the first set in English.

The art and DT departments are also impressive, the shelves stacked with class projects and a couple of big ones like a clock for the playground and a sign for the revamped Brighton train station (the children wrote a letter and got shown around). There's a newish head of art whose intention is to move away from what has been described in the past by parents as a contained feeling, as opposed to the freedom of creativity. The work produced looks fabulous and the kids seem to love it – they are aware they may get an art or DT scholarship if they put together a portfolio and hand it in.

There is a clear scale of minus and misconduct marks leading up to the normal worst case scenario, a headmaster's detention, for which the miscreant will have to fill out a TAL form (Trigger, Action, Learning) – head commented, 'children need to be taught the right, the wrong and the way to get it right'.

Sport is spread all over the town but minibuses nip back and forth and there is a huge range of team abilities – one main sport for boys and girls each term but always clubs on offer, with boys recently joining in with the girls playing hockey on the Astroturf. New climbing wall. The director of sport organises several football tournaments and athletics matches each year for local primary schools including a separate girls' one. You couldn't possibly try everything that is available, since the buses leave at 4.45pm each day. Homework is restricted to two subjects for 30 minutes each for years 7 and 8 (less for the other year groups), with one additional Latin prep at the weekend. A prep diary ensures that this is documented for parents and teachers – it also helps the children learn self-organisation.

Brighton College

Linked with Brighton College Prep and Pre-Prep School, Handcross Park School

Eastern Rd, Brighton, East Sussex BN2 0AL

Pupils: 995; 365 boarders • Ages: 11–18 • Sixth form: 413 • C of E

Fees: Day: £15,780– £22,800; Boarding: £31,290– £40,590 pa

Tel: 01273 704200
Email: registrar@brightoncollege.net
Website: www.brightoncollege.net

Head Master: Since 2006, Mr Richard Cairns MA (40s). Oxford history first. His path to Brighton was via a law firm in Australia, a Palestinian refugee camp, Stewart's Melville in Edinburgh, The Oratory in Reading and the deputy headship of Magdalen College School, Oxford. Staggering list of achievements/ accolades includes the opening of Brighton College, Abu Dhabi; a rise from 147th to top 20 in the UK academic rankings; doubling boarding numbers; trebling applications; a huge new building programme; the acquisition of Roedean Junior and Handcross Park Prep Schools; ISI inspection report with outstanding in every category; The Sunday Times Independent School of the Year.

Keen not to take sole credit for this, he has built a teaching and management structure to ensure that ideas and initiatives can be sparked and grown – inside and outside the student body. This attitude is magnetic – for pupils, parents and staff. He sees himself and the college as a mix of tradition and modern – that was the design brief for the decorating team that were part of the recent revamp but it goes much deeper than the furnishings. 'I want every pupil to be who they want to be – as I say to them in assembly [pupils agree he does, and they remember it ...] "If I try to be him, who will be me?".'

Plenty of other schools try to tempt him away – the governors recently agreed a 10 week international trip, he says, 'to give me thinking time for the next seven years'. It was a global reconnaissance mission, visiting universities in the US and Canada as well as potential twin schools in Finland, Sweden, Singapore, Ontario and Hungary. Such symbiotic connections are characteristic of this head – and they appear to stem from a dedication to improving education wherever he can use his influence or initiative. He kicked off his tenure with compulsory Mandarin lessons but also connected with Kingsford, an East London school that was doing the same. Out of this link grew the London Academy of Excellence (LAE) in Stratford, East London, the first new sixth form free school academy in the country, helping children from disadvantaged backgrounds to get into university by making sure they pass the right A levels – with a powerful independent school sponsoring one of each of the major subjects eg Brighton College sponsors economics, Eton does English, Highgate does maths etc.

Has high expectations for his pupils, wanting them to be excited in the classroom. Teaches history to the fourth form. They report creative punishments from him for inattention eg writing a whole story about a turtle, or a poem about the girl the note was being passed to. Less formally, he has breakfast with the prefects and invites sixth formers to dinner. The pupils love getting to know the head in this way (one of seven children, he certainly knows how to cope with a large dinner table) and they discuss everything from divorce to cricket. He's not shy of involving the pupils in practicalities – from how much the new boarding developments cost to how much he would need to be sponsored to run the Big Balls relay for charity.

Academic matters: Shining results: In 2016, 92 per cent A*/A at GCSE, 97 per cent A*-B and 79 per cent A*/A at A level; this is up with the best in London too. One of top value-added schools. Twenty-six subjects offered at A level. A 60/40 split arts/ science at A level; biology, chemistry, economics and maths are particularly popular (the latter taken by about two-thirds of the pupils). About a quarter take four A levels. Outside speakers (John Major, Boris Johnson, Viv Richards, David Dimbleby, David Starkey, Jeremy Paxman, Michael Gove, Matt Prior..) visit in a Wednesday afternoon slot. Each department runs both a course-specific and a general Oxbridge activity, which obviously pays off, with a record number of pupils heading up to Oxford or Cambridge.

Staff are sparky and motivated – attracted by the charms of 'London by the sea' and being part of a school that's going up and up. An appraisal system is at the heart of the classroom: pupils fill in an online questionnaire on each teacher which gets fed back to the head of department, who in turn gives a summary to the director of studies. Quirky and effective teaching is respected by the pupils – whether it is their Mandarin teacher throat singing on YouTube or a video of a worked through past paper available for maths A level revision. The Story of Our Land course combines history, geography, philosophy and religion for the third form who, when talking about an invasion force coming over the cliff, study the geography of that cliff or debate the merits of the Muslim or Christian standpoint while looking at the Crusades.

Languages popular, not just through the Mandarin innovation – compulsory in the pre-prep since 2007 and now a GCSE option (mostly A* grades so far), with graduate students from Chinese universities to assist – but also Latin, French, Spanish, Russian, Italian, German and Greek. The burgeoning Mandarin option is a USP, with the school being awarded Confucius Institute status by the Chinese Government as a centre of excellence for the teaching of the language – the first such honour for a UK school. The school-wide recommendation of only nine academic GCSEs (with at least one other being artistic or creative) encourages a good balance between academic and extracurricular – as does lesson time between 8.30am and 4pm being sacrosanct, enabling an extra five hours a week for music, sport or dance.

All new pupils attend a literacy class and the dyslexia centre is nationally famous, specifically helping around five per cent of

B

pupils. English is taught within the centre (instead of a second modern language) for years 7-11 in small groups, individual help available in sixth form. Taking complete control of English makes a huge difference, removing embarrassment and stress. School actively seeks out and welcomes the bright child with dyslexia, dyspraxia or dyscalculia. Entry based on recent education plan report, CE assessment morning (observed in groups) and interviews by head and excellent head of centre. Approximately 50 taught in centre, also supports the prep school students. Group work means that children become fantastically supportive of one another, concentration on remediation with younger ones and study skills with older. Time to finish tasks is not an issue – a good end product motivates students.

The bright library has a mezzanine level used for quiet working space for the sixth form frees. Dedicated sixth form centre also has computers but is generally more social. Comprehensive intranet with update alerts sent by email and text. Saturday morning revision classes on offer in the holidays, mostly to boost confidence before exams. Class sizes average 18 up to GCSE; after GCSE, the average is eight.

Games, options, the arts: Year groups of 150 and everyone has to do dance, PE and drama. House drama, house song and up to 15 different productions a year (including visiting companies, A level and GCSE performances and Commedia dell'Arte). Dance achieves nearly 100 per cent A*/A at A level and at GCSE happens in performing arts studio completed in 2000 (outside classes offered to the community). Six-strong faculty teaches over 70 dance classes a week. Examinations in ballet, modern, tap and jazz, and the school boasts boys' street dance, modern and tap groups from junior to senior level. The Montague studio is two minutes' walk away.

New music school. Half of the pupils have individual music lessons, from more than 40 visiting music teachers; 22 music groups: choirs, orchestra, rock groups, concert band and various chamber groups, with participation in the National Chamber Music Competition as well as tours to Prague and Moscow. Ex-parents miss going to the performances.

Two hugely popular and innovative sixth form house competitions stem from the entrepreneurship programme and Strictly Come Dancing. The former gets academics and creatives developing a business plan together, each team competing to win £3,000 to commercialise their idea – previous winners have been a parking app and a device to stop babies knocking hot tea over. Strictly ensures boys are valued for more than just sport – the biggest applause in Monday morning assemblies goes to most unconventional achievements.

Purpose-built spaces for art, photography and DT make for beautiful art and design – there are still some lessons when the pupils watch a video for low maintenance inspiration but the proof of the art is hanging on walls around the campus.

Sport is enormously important here, all pupils taking part in games twice a week – rounders, netball, tennis, cricket, swimming and rugby possible on campus, otherwise it's a minibus to the college's Jubilee Ground, with six rugby pitches or two cricket grounds, further floodlit netball courts, a pavilion and three hockey Astroturfs nearby. Withdean's athletics stadium also hosts fixtures; each weekend sees some 300-400 children involved in competitive matches. National trophies in rugby (1st XV has particularly strong record of victories in Sussex) and netball (Sussex champions and national finalists), and leads the county in athletics. Cricket for both sexes a great strength – three former pupils play have gone on to play for England women's team.

Community service a vital part of school life: pupils visit elderly people and help disabled children or teach pensioners how to use a computer; Make a Difference Day (MADD) sees every member of the college serving the community in more than 100 different activities, from cleaning beaches and clearing scrub to sorting clothes for charity. School raises money for local charities (including Whitehawk Inn, Rockinghorse, Chestnut Tree House) and those further afield (Romania, Kenya, Sri Lanka, India).

Boarding: Weekly boarding extremely popular – no Saturday school; many go straight home after Saturday morning matches. Full-time boarders can avoid the school curfew at the weekend if they stay with local families who take responsibility. Pupils can return from home by 9.30pm on a Sunday night or on a Monday morning – buses to outlying towns.

Five boarding houses for years 9-13 – two for girls and three for boys – plus a junior boarding house for 11-13 year olds at Handcross Prep. Plenty of inter-house competitions, plus lectures, debates, music evenings, quizzes etc, and the after-school use of all facilities eg swimming pool and art department.

Background and atmosphere: Compact campus in Kemp Town, just four blocks from the sea front. Imposing buildings purpose-built in 1840s by Gilbert Scott (designer of St Pancras Station and the Albert Memorial). The school has spent £35 million in the past five years on an award-winning School of Design and Technology and teaching block for English, language suites, two boarding houses, two sports pavilions and an award winning Smith Café, where boarders can meet in the evening, health centre and staff common room. The most popular part of this are the places where the boys and girls get to hang out casually together instead of signing in and out of each other's boarding houses.

Sited to the east of the landmark pier and pavilion, the school succeeds in being fashionable, practical and innovative – no Saturday morning school means that everyone has a full weekend and the chance to be part of the town instead of just being educated within it. This could put some parents off, since Brighton and Hove, like many seaside cities, has its fair share of addicts, drunks and loons. However, we've heard no disturbing reports and most sensible local parents realise that their children are going to come to Brighton at the weekend anyway and it is far better that they feel comfortable in their favourite cafés, bars and shops rather than loitering round Churchill Square.. Officially, there is a square patch of Kemp Town streets where pupils can stroll for 20 minutes of an afternoon, in a group, as long as they sign out. However, some definitely sneak a walk to the beach – they feel it's their right considering the prospectus proudly features pupils enjoying this out of bounds place.

Pupils are thoughtful and articulate – we visited on the day of Margaret Thatcher's funeral and got into a discussion with a group of 13 year olds about whether people would dislike her so much if she had been a man who had implemented the same policies. The head picks an individual each Monday to share a random act of kindness in assembly – this type of awareness is at root of the school's ethos which goes a fair way to balancing the social mix here. As in all schools, cliques could be found if you looked for them but the most popular are not necessarily the richest or prettiest; difference is respected and often admired. The pupils are aware that they are privileged. Has now scrapped its uniform code for 11-16 year olds in favour of a 'skirt uniform' and 'trouser uniform', with either sex able to wear either. The sixth form wear smart business-like clothes with some restrictions that are flouted when girls fancy tottering on high heels. They can drive themselves into school but must use street parking – high council charges are unpopular, with parents driving to attend chapel as well.

School benefits from a sense of the outside world, whether through exchanges with schools in Russia, Africa, America and Australia, the perspective offered by pupils from an inner-city school or the opportunity to twist their tongues round a year's worth of Mandarin Chinese. Link with Kingsford Community School in Newham, East London, beginning with heads' shared desire to make Mandarin mandatory, has grown into an HSBC sponsorship of three Newham pupils' education in Brighton for a year. Sixth formers buddy up with pupils at the London Academy of Excellence and share study tips via Facebook (boarders allowed 10 minute slots) and email.

The chapel, just big enough for the whole school, used three or four times a week for secular and multi-faith assemblies as well as Christian ones. Tradition still holds firm here (the oldest public school in Sussex) with the heads of school taking it in turns to sit alone in a pew, yet the chaplain is entertaining and eccentric – a new hymnal was an opportunity to get each house to prepare a song and belt it out in competition.

Pastoral care, well-being and discipline: As the head comments, this is 'a town school that is part of the real world, not apart from it'. At the beginning of every term he reiterates the ground rules on theft, bullying and beyond: expulsion and no second chances is the line on drugs and the security at the school gates is tight, yet cheery.

Report emailed home every three weeks and there are parent meetings – although some parents report not much time for parent feedback. Those needing the most help definitely get it – those who are motivated enough to dance between options will attract it too.

Head of lower school and the headmaster meet every registered pupil in their own school before they enter Brighton College. This reduces the fear of attending a new school and gives the pastoral staff a heads-up on what house and friendship group might suit a newbie. The little ones arrive three days before the rest of school and go on a treasure hunt to help them get their bearings. The transition to the upper school is another focus point for the empathetic head of lower school – moving from being one of 40 to one of 150 under the shared care of tutors and houseparents.

One lower school house and 13 others when the post-common entrance cohort enter, 325 boarding and 650 day – about 70 children in each so a good chance to develop cross year relationships. All of the youngest year in each senior school house share a tutor – as pupils grow they are matched with another for GCSEs and then A levels. Majority of housemasters and housemistresses are married and parents report incredible empathy for the fallout from tricky family and financial situations. Pupils learn how to iron a shirt, sew on a button and hold their own at a dinner party through house activities – really useful preparation for university admission and beyond.

Any bullying is dealt with speedily and with emotional intelligence – no homophobia or racism, some teasing but real respect for individuality. Two options at meals and dishes containing wheat are labelled, the school is nut free. Food is also available in the Smith Café and Café de Paris below the dance studio – and the houses all have kitchens for an emergency stack of toast for a starving teenage boy.

Pupils and parents: A great social mix from the children of butchers to highbrow TV presenters, successful entrepreneurs and a smattering of Conservative MPs; 33 per cent boarding, most weekly but seven per cent overseas (five per cent Asian). Lower school just under 50 per cent from Brighton state schools, also many from London schools that stop at 11. Head ensures that useful parent contacts are wound into life of school in way that benefits both – from Leon providing soup recipes for sidelines at matches to a stylist helping with a fashion show. No Saturday school (weekly boarders can leave Friday 4pm, return Monday am) is popular with parents. School buses from towns ranging from Crowborough to Eastbourne with express services for weekly boarders Friday evening and Monday morning from Tunbridge Wells and Chichester. Pupils are cheerful, enthusiastic, friendly and polite and have an easy, relaxed relationship with teachers – at the top end of the school they feel part of a wider community; again, good preparation for life outside.

Entrance: Eleven plus entry via maths, English and verbal reasoning tests. Dynamic head of lower school has worked hard to build brilliant enrichment days for Gifted and Talented at local primaries – practical lessons in science labs, language work and unique experience of a senior school. All of this very attractive alternative to Brighton state school ballots.

Pre-test assessment for 13+ entry; CE pass mark now 60 per cent – whether from coming from prep school or externally – with a minimum of 55 per cent in English and maths. Emotional intelligence used in assessment of intake for Brighton College Prep so a maximum of five out of 60 each year do not go through to the college – they must be the bright side of average or they will not be happy here – and those who disrupt the learning of others won't fit in either. Around 45 from the prep join 40 already in the lower school. Seventy more from 54 other preps including St Christopher's, Hove and Handcross (now run by Brighton College).

Around 70 new pupils at sixth form (B+ grades at GCSE are essential), mostly from Burgess Hill, Brighton and Hove High School, Eastbourne, Hurst and Lancing.

Exit: A handful after GCSEs to local sixth form colleges, almost always for financial reasons. One hundred per cent of A level leavers to university. Thirty-nine to Oxbridge in 2016, and 11 medics; UCL, KCL, Bristol, Imperial, Durham, Manchester, Exeter and Leeds all popular. Famous Old Brightonians, including Peter Mayle (writer), Lord Alexander of Weedon (lawyer and banker), Lord Skidelsky (historian and politician), Laurie Penny (writer), David Nash (sculptor), Matt Prior and Holly Colvin (cricketers), Sir John Chilcot (chairman of the Iraq Inquiry), Sir Michael Hordern (actor) and Jonathan Palmer (racing driver), testify to range of successful careers which may ensue.

Money matters: At a recent open morning, parents were wondering about what extras Brighton College might offer to justify its fees being higher than rival local schools' despite its limited campus space – half an hour later they were totally sold, having been treated to a Commedia dell'Arte take on the drama, a taste of Strictly Come Dancing by sixth formers and the heads of schools speaking about the high quality lessons. Many parents struggle to pay the fees but bursaries and up to 20 academic awards (5-50 per cent off basic fees), five music scholarships (up to 30 per cent off), art, drama, dance, sport, chess and all-rounder awards (up to 25 per cent off) and a DT scholarship (up to 15 per cent off) are available.

Registration fee and hefty deposits for accepting an offered place, into five figures for overseas boarders. Only refundable if pupils don't pass the entrance exam. Deposits retained to cover extras charged in arrears, balance refunded on exit from the school.

Extras include dyslexia support and EAL tuition.

Remarks: Happy, broad-minded town school for children and families who are keen on learning – producing fantastic results and sparkling individual success stories. Pupils are encouraged to achieve as much as they can, so you'd never be bored, but you could end up with too much on. Bold ideas fostered in student, staff and parent body, all the while anchoring the opportunities enabled by the fees in real world experience. Detractors of the school (often parents of ex-pupils at the prep or pre-prep) see it as too results focused, with some families turning to outside tutoring to enable their children to get into the college. Raising of CE pass mark to 60 per cent fuel for the fire of those who judge the school to be top-slicing to climb the results ladder, explained transparently by the school as a tool to manage the high volume of applications.

B

Brighton Hove and Sussex Sixth Form College

205 Dyke Road, Hove, East Sussex BN3 6EG

Pupils: 2,500 • Ages: 16–18

Tel: 01273 552 200
Email: admissions@bhasvic.ac.uk
Website: www.bhasvic.ac.uk

Principal: Since September 2016, William Baldwin, previously assistant principal and psychology teacher at Godalming College.

Academic matters: Results are very good for a lightly-selective provider: 62 per cent A*-B, 33 per cent A*-A at A level in 2016; 88 per cent distinction/distinction* at BTec. One of the largest centres for EPQ, with 339 students last year, two-thirds of those getting A*-B. Not quite the bulky numbers of high achievers you might find in a highly selective school, you might be thinking, but read on: stats from the Higher Education Statistics Agency show that BHASVIC students go on to get more first or high second class degrees than other sixth form providers; including independent schools. In the long term, BHASVIC equips students better to succeed at university, and, they might argue, in life.

Not an intellectual hothouse, but very academic, says college. Lessons plunge in straight away – the immediate start could be as simple as addressing the problem on the board as soon as you come into the room, which, students say, puts them in the mindset to work: 'Everyone is motivated to work, it's a habit'.

Students here need to be independent, one saying 'it's all on you – it's your responsibility'; but not in a manner which suggested this caused any anxiety; rather some level of pride. 'We'll do better at university', she added confidently. Another said, 'you do need to do more work, and there are fewer contact hours than school. But if you're struggling, support is there'. There are subject extensions (help clinics) available every day, which some students choose to attend, while others are instructed to do so; in which case, non-attendance could result in an action plan to ensure students are hitting targets. If students need more help than this, they will need to source it themselves.

No spoon feeding here – 'flipped learning' means students cover basic content in preparation before lessons (ranging from research to short videos on the VLE), so they come to lessons ready to discuss, evaluate and analyse at more skilled level than would otherwise be possible. A physics student told us how helpful she found it to know the aim of a practical experiment before she attempted it herself; in sociology, failure to prepare means you will be sent to the library to catch up: it's just not possible to play an active part in the lesson without it. 'It makes me feel more invested', said a student thoughtfully.

A wide range of subjects available, from traditional to not (such as performing arts, or health and social care). Sciences and history are popular, with many students achieving highly.

Maths is outstanding, most students achieving A*or A. 'They expect a lot at the beginning', said one student; 'maths is infamous for being the most demanding', said another. Students describe a teacher who gives out his home phone number in the first lesson (for those maths crisis moments); a classroom with the walls all whiteboards, each pair getting a bit of whiteboard to work on – 'works really well'. BHASVIC maths is even on YouTube, and has apparently rescued many a maths student; and not just those from BHASVIC. 'Great', said a parent, 'the best teacher my daughter has ever had'.

A radical improvement in the fortunes of English literature, after previous head suggested English was being over-taught, and proposed fewer assignments, less marking and more learning. 'Nobel prize, not Olympic medal': the idea being that students are not leaping through a hoop in an act of one-off brilliance (as in the Olympics), but engaging thoroughly with a subject, and this being recognised – as it might be by a Nobel prize.

Doesn't matter how individual teachers teach, but how the students learn, and what teachers do to help this. They set about it in whatever ways they please: one history teacher puts history to songs – the classic 'I marked a book' is well known here.

Class sizes are large compared to what are usually seen as the desirably small classes in independent schools: numbers range from 18-25. And everyone, from principal to teachers to students, thinks it is a good thing. Lots of learning takes place between pupils, explains college; so a big class will generate more discussion, ideas and buzz than a tiny class could hope to. Classes are often seated in small groups, which helps shyer students participate; and in history, a student is appointed head of group, whose job is to draw in those who are quieter. Students say 'classes are not too big to get attention'; and this large sixth form college attracts many specialist teachers.

Classes are mixed ability and taught at a basic level, with able students getting further tasks. BHASVIC is one of the best providers of value added at A level (tracked by A Level Performance Service) showing the less able learn positive behaviours from being in mixed classes, and that the larger the cohort, the better the results.

There are issues: boys underperform compared to girls, and some subjects are gender dominated: hardly any girls do physics (they're trying to make the subject more attractive to girls, and have replaced boy-friendly astronomy with medical physics); equally, boys are less likely to take arts. But, said a teacher, the die is often cast by the second year of secondary school, long before pupils reach sixth form.

The level of independence expected here is difficult for some students and parents to cope with: one parent, disappointed that her daughter didn't achieve an expected AS result, said she and her daughter felt unsupported by the college. They wanted someone to go through the paper, and identify where things went wrong; and in fact the student's paper was remarked, and went up a grade; but it was not the level of support and care that this parent (used to independent schools) expected. The college points out that students are made aware of support available in tutorials, and in communications from the exams office, which are also emailed to parents; though tutors will always attempt to resolve concerns with a student before contacting parents. If students do fail, the college will examine data carefully to try to identify one-off disasters, or trends.

Each student is part of a tutor group of around 20, students being placed into the relevant tutor group: university, medicine; Oxbridge; or employment. The Oxbridge group follows a tailor-made programme including practice interviews, which has a phenomenal success rate – 34 last year. Getting to Oxbridge here has become something quite normal.

Will flex the timetable for the needs of students if they can, or at least make arrangements for students to catch up; so one student was able to pursue his modelling career alongside his science A levels; and another found time to play the viola with the London Symphony Orchestra.

More computers and space to work please, say students; although there are computers and places to work in the library and the café in the sports hall, and space to work in the canteen, the hall and refectory. Others praised the hire a laptop scheme, and students are encouraged to bring their own devices to reduce demand on college equipment. Available work space varies through the day – we observed the college at capacity, with students working in every possible space; and later, with plenty of space available. The college is listening to the student union representations on study needs, and doing its best to provide for them.

Well-equipped library, with a large range of hard copies of journals, accompanied by a large range of e-resources, from online newspapers to specialist academic journals. A small budget to get extra texts for EPQ; but more importantly, access to Sussex University library on a reference basis.

A super SEN suite across the floor of the new building, one large room which can be subdivided, well supplied with computers, and high backed and sided comfy seats for students who need to feel private and safe. Do they cater for severe needs? 'Yes, absolutely', (a rare response indeed). A student with Asperger's and threatening behaviour was supported: staff were given special training to cope, and the student was always accompanied to lessons. A disability-friendly college, from extensive learning support, to the fitting of ramps and lifts wherever possible, and a braille direction to the college website on the back of the prospectus.

Games, options, the arts: The student union runs a raft of societies, from the popular feminist society to Amnesty, the socialist society and the transgender/gender questioning support group. Providing minimum numbers are satisfied, students can set up whatever they want. The staff runs a more traditional-looking list which includes various music ensembles, drama and first aid.

Open access to extracurricular, but there's no pressure to join in. It's generally unnecessary: students know they are going to have a personal statement to write. 'But if you do too much extracurricular, you can get in trouble', said one student feelingly. 'If your grades slip, they'll talk to you about it'.

Largest centre for gold D of E in Sussex. Students have taken part in the PM's global fellowship programme.

A lively media and performing arts department; a big drama production every couple of years; an NCFE interactive media qualification for those into multimedia and web design– the college even has a YouTube channel – BHASVICtv.

Art is outstanding, says college – light high ceilinged studios filled with colour and application. Students here do very well, and have gone on to St Martins, and, holy grail, Chelsea. Parents spoke warmly of fantastic facilities and good teaching.

Music is a small room in the bottom of a building, walls lined with books and manuscript, flanked by four practice rooms. 'Not good', says college, hoping to raise the money for a purpose built music block – and a Steinway in the hall.

Sports teams have many county and national successes, and field competitive teams in basketball, netball, rugby and football (male and female); also teams for the keen and not able, but on an ad hoc basis. All students can play recreational sport at lunchtime, 'no ability needed', including basketball, futsal (indoor football), table tennis and volleyball. A well-equipped sports hall, and shares fields with a nearby secondary school.

Background and atmosphere: BHASVIC feels more like university than school: own clothes, first names for all; not pupils but students. As a stand-alone sixth form, students feel they have to take a deliberate step to come here; and this filter seems to result in a very motivated body of students, keen to break away from school and childish things; ready to start taking responsibility for themselves and their learning.

A democracy in miniature, with an open consultative style of leadership which listens to issues put forward by the student council. 'We are held to account for the benefit of students', say staff passionately; and it means a lot here.

BHASVIC democracy seems to work a great deal better than the one outside, with most of the students actually participating, and relishing doing so. But students are not obliged to take part. The college is a facilitator: opportunities and support are here, and those who succeed here will be the ones who take advantage of them. For some, perhaps particularly those from smaller private schools, BHASVIC might be too much of a leap: one parent felt there was too much independent learning, and not enough social opportunities – 'they need to be ready for a high level of independence'; another described it as 'a steep learning curve from school' – his daughter was ready for it, but he was not sure if his less organised son would have coped. But for the right sort of student, this feels like liberation: 'It's so different from [my last school]. We're not told what to do'. One student said of pupils at her former independent school, 'they're still secondary school children, being told what to do at school from 8-5'.

This college is very large – 2,500 students; but for some students, this was the pull – 'I was attracted by the big mix of people from different schools'; 'a little bit intimidating – but I was looking for it'. Students say it's easy to just go up and meet people when you get here, knowing that it's very likely that they too have left all their friends at school – 'you rarely see people on their own; unless they're working'.

As we walked around with the principal, students smiled, and sometimes greeted; but no independent school jump to attention. During our visit, there was a fire alarm. Everyone trooped to the netball courts, and when safe, head put two fingers in his mouth and whistled loudly – 'you can go back in now'. Must seem like light relief to students after some school regimes.

Food looked rather pastry dominated, although there is a small salad bar; and students say the nachos and chill are really, really nice. But with the freedom to come and go as they please, many go to nearby Tesco for a meal deal. Students appreciate the fact that breakfast is available from 8.30am to just before lunch: porridge, sausages and beans.

Pastoral care, well-being and discipline: 'At this stage they need as much freedom as they can have, with support in place to catch them', says college, and support here is provided by the student service centre, which provides advice from finances and careers, well-being and counselling, to sexual health and substance misuse. Students say plenty of people use the services, and that you can just send a text to ask for help. Second year students can become peer supporters to first year students, and receive additional training in psychology, sociology or health and social care, which they use to make awareness-raising presentations during tutorials. One parent, whose daughter received regular support from her peer supporter, said the meetings were very helpful.

Students see tutors in groups, with a home-designed curriculum to ensure kids get all the messages – careers, UCAS, pastoral care etc; but students can also opt to see their tutor once a week on their own. A parent told us how supportive his daughter had found her tutor in assisting with the transition from school to college; and that the tutor had also emailed them to say that the door was always open if they wanted to talk about anything.

As for high pressure working environments, it's rather different to those in schools, where the pressure comes from a school keen to keep its reputation as a high performer. One student told us how differently she felt about pressure she decided to put on herself to work at college, compared to the stress of being ordered to do so by her old school. 'We don't drive a work ethic as an end in itself', say staff, who feel this is where schools are going wrong; although 'anxiety can show in all sorts of different ways; and it's difficult to expect young people to work hard without the shadow of it..But if they have a problem, it's going to show': evident in poor attendance (someone rings around if students don't show up) and poor work. For incidences of self-harm and anorexia, they will suggest counselling; and are extremely careful what is divulged to parents. Teachers and tutors are trained to know that they are duty bound to divulge and report pastoral problems with students. With this, and peer group support, it is unlikely anyone would slip through the net.

Students say that being late or disruptive, or failing to attend, could mean parents are called; it feels like the ultimate sanction in this college, where students are treated as far as possible like adults.

There's a smoking shelter here, which isn't packed. Sex at a college event off campus was treated seriously and resulted in suspension. 'Exclusion has limited deterrent value, and it's important to work with people'; or, as a parent said, 'they're realistic, and they have to be'. Drug use would and has resulted in suspension, could end up in exclusion, and would involve parents. The question always: is the behaviour so serious that it puts an obstacle in the way of learning? 'The supreme value here is individual student well-being; not the institution's reputation'.

Bullying is rare, says the college, and we couldn't find a student or parent with any experience of it. There were a couple of incidences of cyber-bulling, resulting in suspension; but since they have started to tweet as a college, this sort of threatening behaviour has retreated.

Pupils and parents: Many from local state schools, with some from those further afield (as far as Crawley and Eastbourne) and a scattering from independent schools.

A good mixture of parents, wealthy and not, including those relieved that they don't have to sell their soul to the devil or get a second mortgage to send their child to an excellent sixth form. No PTA, two parent governors. Only a few pushy parents.

Entrance: By application form, priority being given to students who apply by the relevant date in early December, and to those who live in the area. An interview ensures students are enrolling on the correct course for them. Lightly selective, although selection is not the ethos: entrance is at a level which should guarantee someone will succeed: six GCSEs at A*-C to do three A levels, seven GCSEs at A*-C to do four. Budget constraints mean most students no longer have the luxury of starting with four A levels, and dropping their least favourite subject after the first year; but students who have a good reason to take four, such as taking double maths, can still do so. Students who didn't get a C in English and maths GCSE must retake.

Although word on the independent school street is that pupils would be lucky to get into BHASVIC, this college works exceptionally hard to turn no-one away, fiddling with timetables and taking on board extra teachers if a course is particularly in demand, so that as many students as possible can be accommodated.

Exit: The great majority to university, many to Russell group, and 36 to Oxbridge in 2016, from law and medicine to experimental psychology and human, social and political sciences.

Money matters: Basically free; but can charge for trips, visits and consumables in art.

The welfare co-ordinator advises students on financial support available, including means tested-bursaries, of which 321 were awarded last year, each worth £1,200. Student discount schemes for bus and train.

Remarks: An excellent sixth form, where those ready for independence will thrive and be well prepared to continue to do so at university. One parent described it as being about 'hard work, having fun, getting good results, being independent and learning to be a young adult'.

Brockhurst and Marlston House Schools

Marlston Road, Hermitage, Newbury, Berkshire RG18 9UL

Pupils: 320; 20 full, 90 flexi boarders • Ages: 3-13 (boys at Brockhurst, girls at Marlston House; pre-prep and years 7 and 8 mixed) • C of E

Fees: Day £9,834 – £16,470; Boarding £22,119 pa

Tel: 01635 200293
Email: registrar@brockmarl.org
Website: www.brockmarl.org.uk

Heads: Brockhurst head since 2000, Mr David Fleming MA MSc (50s); himself educated at Brockhurst, then Radley College followed by natural sciences at Trinity College, Oxford. A member of the family which owns the school, he projects an air of relaxed authority. Clearly in a very secure position, but doesn't rest on his laurels. Parents like the fact that they are 'talking to the decision-maker.' Aims to 'preserve schools' family feel' whilst maintaining high academic standards and improving existing facilities. Married with two daughters; wife has high flying job outside the school. 'She's the clever one!'

Marlston House operates in tandem with Brockhurst and has own head. Appointed 1999, Caroline Riley MA BEd Cert Ed (50s) works alongside Mr Fleming and has free rein to run the girls' school as she sees fit. Educated at a West Country girls' school and Southampton University, she is former head of a mixed school in Hazelgrove and has taught in both single sex and mixed schools. Allows headmaster to do most of the talking, but they make a good double act: her contributions are quietly efficient, focused and informed. Teaches RS and history in upper school (headmaster teaches geography). Husband is retired and they have two grown-up children.

Entrance: Children join Ridge House (pre-prep) following their third birthday. Youngest children get used to school by attending swimming lessons on Wednesday mornings and free toddler and parent sessions. Boys and girls educated together up to the age of 6, after which they join Brockhurst (boys) or Marlston House (girls). Occasional vacancies for older children after age 9; school says, 'Special help can be given [to boys and girls] to catch up where necessary.' There is an informal interview and assessment for anyone seeking a scholarship or bursary.

Exit: Academic scholarships in 2016 from Downe House, Abingdon, Bradfield and Pangbourne; music awards from Oxford High, Downe House and Pangbourne; drama and sports awards from Pangbourne; and all-rounder from Radley.

Remarks: Founded in 1884 in Shropshire as a boys' prep school, Brockhurst moved to its present home – a mock-Jacobean listed mansion set in 60 acres just outside Newbury – in 1945. Marlston

House opened its doors to girls in 1995 and is located in a separate (also listed) building on the same site. Main building boasts imposing façade of deep red brick and stone, with baronial windows, turrets and heavy oak main door opening into wood-panelled passages and spacious Great Hall. Heads gave their interviews in a large room with impressive views over school's extensive grounds – would make a good backdrop for filming period drama. The rest of the school's buildings, although modern, sit comfortably alongside older ones and blend in thanks to clever architecture and landscaping.

Two schools join forces to marry the best of co-ed with single-sex education; boys and girls are educated separately between the ages of 6 and 11, only coming together for art, music and drama. Classes merge in the final two years of 'senior school', in order to prepare pupils for academic scholarships and common entrance exams on an equal footing. Quirky 'back-to-front' year groups mean those leaving reception begin in year 8 and finish in year 1.

Evidence of modern, quality teaching and good effort from pupils – however, some parents say it is patchy. Able children streamed into scholarship sets as soon as they are ready, usually in year 5. Some children 'accelerated' ie moved up a year. Maths tuition caters for a wide range of ability and pupils take common entrance at all three levels. Scholars take level 3 maths in year 7 and then focus on scholarship papers. English teaching excellent; pupils are encouraged to read widely and develop critical skills. CE syllabus completed by year 7 and scholarship set extends pupils' knowledge in final year. Good provision for languages, especially French, which is taught from age 4. Château Robert near Biarritz is school property and all 11 and 12-year-olds spend two weeks every year studying the language intensively and exploring the area. Latin from year 4 to both CE and scholarship levels; those taking scholarship Latin also learn Greek. Pupils begin German in the last two years and have taster sessions in Russian and Spanish once exams are over.

Usual range of subjects elsewhere on the timetable; we observed a lively practical science lesson in which pupils spoke confidently about extracting chlorophyll. History is clearly good fun; walls of history room festooned with pictures of students getting into the spirit of ancient times on Celtic Day (ably assisted by those 60 acres). Knights of the Sealed Knot have visited to perform re-enactments of medieval battles. Plenty of school trips, eg to Hampton Court. Good ICT facilities and library. Parents praise school communications and particularly news section of website. 'They get it right 90 per cent of the time.' Progress reports issued two or three times every half term. 'Children are treated as individuals, with stars, effort points and lots of praise for good work ... the sheer scope of opportunities seem boundless.' Saturday school from year 2 up, so schools run clubs in the morning for younger siblings.

Learning development centre (LDC) goes well beyond usual remit of dyslexia, eg developing comprehension and study skills and exam revision techniques. LDC helps gifted and talented to extend knowledge, supports EAL students and even adults from the local community with dyslexia. Also helps pre-prep pupils who don't pick up on phonics first time around. However, not the place for behavioural challenges.

Music is clearly in good health, with around 80 per cent receiving individual tuition on one or more instruments. There are senior and junior orchestras and choirs, plus a chamber choir and string quartet. Swing and R+B bands, guitar, flute and recorder groups provide other opportunities to make music. Class music includes use of composition suite. Heads keen to point out that schools are very flexible and 'will adjust timetable to suit individual talents such as music.' Art and DT block ranges over two floors which provide plenty of space for painting, drawing and pottery; not as well-equipped for practical DT as some other preps we've seen, although facilities for art and pottery are excellent. Standard of work on display is high and the most talented pupils are coached for art awards. Trips to galleries and museums organised post CE.

Schools' extensive grounds are a boon to sports staff; all major sports are on offer in addition to minor sports such as golf, judo, shooting and fishing in school's lake. Soccer, rugby, cross-country running and cricket for boys; hockey, netball, rounders and tennis for girls – all do athletics and swimming in 25m indoor pool and boys can play hockey too. Sport is timetabled every day and there are A, B and C teams for major sports. A big draw for girls is the equestrian centre, where pupils can stable their own pony or learn to ride on schools' horses. Heads are proud of sporting record of their pupils, which have included winning national judo championships, IAPS swimming gold and athletics at county level. Keen to build more tennis courts; at present there is one indoor and three all-weather courts. Joint drama productions take place in new performing arts centre.

Family ethos encourages good pastoral care; we met a very dedicated housemaster who clearly poured heart and soul into the job. There is zero tolerance for bullying and parents report that issues are sorted immediately. One parent commented, 'The headmaster took time out from a school inspection [to deal with my concerns].' All pupils belong to a house and school council meets once a month. Full-time boarding is encouraged, but flexi-boarders must spend a minimum of two nights a week in school. Boys' dorms are much less pretty than girls' dorms, as is the norm. Corridors kept tidy and routines well organised. Lots of posters on walls to reinforce anti-bullying ethos; full boarders can have mobile phones and iPads and their use is managed by boarding house staff. Overseas boarders have access to Skype in a specially designated room.

Multiple evening clubs and activities on offer (day pupils can join in) and all staff give up one or two evenings a week to run these. Lots of sporting activities but a couple of unusual options include geo-caching and barbeque club. School fireworks display is an annual highlight. Everyone takes part – children hold torches and process with their parents to the bonfire, which is lit traditionally by the youngest child in the school. Three sittings for lunch ensure that all pupils sit on a 'family table' with a member of staff present. Food a bit plain on the day we visited, but not in short supply and plenty of fresh fruit, cheese and other choices for pudding. School runs daily bus services to local towns and there is good after-school care for working families.

Children come from a wide variety of backgrounds, eg South Africa and the US, but are polite, articulate and unassuming without hiding their light under a bushel; they state (honestly) that there is nothing about the schools that they would change. Centenary and Foundation Scholarships are worth up to one third of fees, but headmistress keen to point out that 'a talented child can come here on a full scholarship.'

Twin schools offer a unique blend of co-ed and single-sex education. Blessed with a rich endowment, they are free to indulge mild idiosyncrasies such as different holiday and half-term dates. Clear moral steer and family values keep students, staff and parents on side. Obviously hard working – the school motto is 'no reward without effort' – but a happy place as well.

B

Brockwood Park School

Brockwood Park, Bramdean, Hampshire SO24 0LQ

Pupils: 56; all boarders • Ages: 14 -19 • Sixth form: 34

Fees: Boarding £20,790 pa

Tel: 01962 771744
Email: enquiry@brockwood.org.uk
Website: www.brockwood.org.uk

Co-principals: Since 2013, Dr Gopal Krishnamurthy and since September 2015, Mr Antonio Autor. Dr Gopal has spent most of his life, since the age of 4, as a student and teacher at Krishnamurti's schools in India, the UK and the USA. He was a student, mature student and staff member at Brockwood and teaches physics and maths as well as being co-principal. He has a PhD in education, MAs in education and philosophy and a BA in physics.

Antonio Autor has a degree from the Bilbao School of Business Studies and was a professional footballer for nearly 10 years. After that, he studied English in Cardiff, Brighton and London, and joined Brockwood Park in 1987. He has been head gardener here, sports organiser, pastoral coordinator, business studies teacher and adult study centre coordinator. He lives with his partner and daughter.

Why two principals? 'We'd like to avoid the notion of the heroic head.' They both, in common with all residential staff, are committed to the teachings of Jiddu Krishnamurti, inspirational writer and speaker on philosophical and spiritual subjects.

Academic matters: Exams 'are not our main thrust', says school, with understatement, 'but are seen in perspective alongside things like yoga, working in the garden, and care of rooms' (all compulsory). Now offers IGCSEs (25 per cent A*/A grades in 2016, but NB 'we offer only maths as a taught subject'). The school uses Cambridge International Exams for A levels, and mixed results are achieved – in 2016, 15 per cent A*/A and 30 per cent A*/B grades (hard to draw out any trends from such a tiny number of students). Some retakes taken at local sixth form college and many pupils will be returning to their home countries for higher education, so British exams not the be all and end all but do need to be recognized in Europe.

No fixed academic timetables into which pupils must slot – each programme is created afresh for each child with plenty of scope to concentrate on a single passion. An 18-year-old musician we met had secured two free days a week to spend on intensive piano work. Another had dropped all academic subjects to study only art, yoga and pottery. Others were focused on more traditional subjects.

No pressure; no punishments if homework is not done; lots of one-on-one teaching. SEN support offered on individual basis – one weekly session is partially covered by the fees, further help is charged for. ESL for overseas students who need it. Computers discouraged but permitted. 'K Class' compulsory once a week to study Krishnamurti, held in soothing white carpeted room with scatter cushions. Lots of sitting on floors here. 'Inquiry time', when the whole school gets together to discuss a theme – eg why are we vegetarians?; why do we value silence? – a core part of education.

Staff comprised of renaissance men and women, most teaching two or three subjects at any given time. So some teaching inspired, while some a bit patchy, 'and teachers can suddenly head off on sabbatical or stop offering a subject,' said a parent. Non-residential specialist teachers are brought in to fill gaps.

Games, options, the arts: Health and fitness, yes – games, no. Some sort of exercise is scheduled twice a week (gym with fitness equipment). Not keen on competition, no prizes. Has been known to play football against another school, but never in anger. Music inspiring and given space to flourish, with two concerts a year and a variety of instrumental lessons offered. 'It's not about excelling,' a teacher told us. 'It's about a feeling of enjoyment.' Five pianos, a drum kit and a recording studio on hand – pupils can record their own albums. Art barn, designed by Keith Critchlow in the arts and crafts Cottage style, is the fine art centre. Dance, drama, photography, pottery – all the arts – thriving.

Boarding: Boys' rooms, 'the Cloisters', surrounding small pond – exceptionally nice, like a boutique hotel (though boys speak of noise reverberating through the thin partition walls and single glazing). Seven new and beautiful interconnected boarding pavilions now provide extra accommodation.

Originally set up to be international, fully boarding (no day pupils, and pupils may stay over half terms) and small, and has remained so to this day, 'But we could get a bit larger,' says school. Has softened its early ascetic, socialistic ethos, when staff were discouraged from having children of their own, yet remains curiously spartan – no TV, 'except news and football' on one aged set 'that receives three channels'! No cleaning or kitchen staff – all members of the community, including teachers, do their own laundry and help clean/clear tables/wash up meals.

Background and atmosphere: Founded by Krishnamurti in 1969 with a gift of £40,000. This was meant to be his retirement fund – instead he bought Brockwood Park and 40 acres of inspiring, serene grounds within South Downs National Park. Still has the same gentle feel he would have liked, with the main building housing admin, classrooms and girls' dorms. Beautiful octagonal assembly hall used for silent meditation before breakfast, whole school meetings (twice a week) and concerts. A huge rambling and impressive library with interesting selection of books, eg on alternative medicine.

Kitchen fully vegetarian and mainly organic. Smaller 'eco-kitchen' available to the students. Garden and greenhouses lovingly tended by all, produces everything from pumpkins to sweetcorn – all eaten at the school. Seeds are gathered for the following year. Twenty chickens provide eggs. Care for the environment a priority and recycling given its own room. Roughly 10 'mature students' (early 20s) an important cog in the Brockwood wheel – they do the cooking and some other work within the community in exchange for room, board and the opportunity to study and bask in Brockwoodian tranquility.

Pastoral care, well-being and discipline: No school rules – instead pupils and parents sign an 'open letter', a group of agreements including meat-free diet, attending morning meeting, staying in rooms after 10pm and no smoking, alcohol or drugs. No automatic punishments for anything – everything open for discussion. 'Fear is a destructive force in education. Take away fear and authority and pupils can be creative, willing to try things. It's important to discover what they love to do.' Relationships, getting along in a community, solving problems are key. Drinking a big no-no, whatever a pupil's age: this may be the first school we have visited where drinking and smoking are highly uncool. All that said, does have to expel the odd pupil, for the usual reasons, and can be tension between providing structure for younger pupils and freedom for the 18 and 19 year olds.

Some 30 members of staff, plus the mature students, live on the campus and students work and live alongside them, the school's greatest strength – or a weakness, depending on how you look at it. Telephone numbers of school's 'independent listener' and Childline prominently displayed around the school.

Pupils and parents: International – around 15 out of 78 from the UK, none local. Others Spanish, French, German, Dutch, Danish, and then from literally everywhere. Everyone looks quite normal – not much inclined to purple hair or facial piercings – and impressively verbal, eloquent and softly spoken. Most pupils come from families with an interest in Krishnamurti. Others find it on the web (key words vegetarian, holistic or alternative). Some parents consider Brockwood Park alongside other alternative schools, eg Bedales, Frensham Heights, St Christopher's, the Steiners (especially Michael Hall), Summerhill (A S Neill got some of his educational ideas from Krishnamurti). A few come from Inwoods, the 'small school' within Brockwood Park grounds educating 30 children age 4-11 (started as a school for staff children). Estimates that around 1,400 men and women have now been educated at Brockwood Park and keen to involve them more in the school through workshops, fundraising etc.

Entrance: Same process for prospective pupils and for staff – a trial week followed by a meeting of the school community to share impressions of the visitor. Up to a third of applicants are turned away. Maturity is the essential qualification according to the pupils – 'We won't take someone who ruins the community'. Despite unorthodox ethos, most definitely not a magnet for alienated teenagers. 'We're low profile, and don't want to be a sink school for problem kids.'

Exit: Students leave equipped for life, though not necessarily for higher education in the UK. However most students will go to university, either straight away or eventually – frequently overseas, especially the USA.

Money matters: Fees kept low. All residential staff are paid the same (frugal) salary so are, in effect, subsidising the running of the school. One third of pupils receive some level of bursary.

Remarks: Uplifting and unique school with the modest aim of completely transforming consciousness and creating a new human being. 'The bar is set high,' said one member of staff. 'Feels a bit like an academic retreat,' said a student trying to sum up the school's ethos. Or a kibbutz. The sort of school that changes lives. Intellectual curiosity will flourish here – but exam results may be elusive.

Brookham School

Linked with Highfield School

Highfield Lane, Liphook, Hampshire GU30 7LQ

Pupils: 192 • Ages: 3–7 • C of E

Fees: Day £10,500 – £13,950 pa

Tel: 01428 722005
Email: headteacher@brookhamschool.co.uk
Website: www.brookhamschool.co.uk

Headmistress: Since 2015, Sophie Baber BA PGCE postgraduate diploma in psychology, who previously taught at Marlborough College Malaysia.

Entrance: Most families within a 25 minute drive, Haslemere, Liphook, Liss and Petersfield the norm, Midhurst and Farnham at a stretch. Some dyed in the wool locals; growing numbers of 'view starved' Londoners and expats.

First come, first served until year 2 when school is 'sightly more cautious, as we need to ensure we can support pupils.' That said, there's not much that can't be handled in the way of learning needs, including one pupil statemented and fully LA funded – very much not the norm; school's deep regret that school is a postcode's throw from special needs switched on Hampshire.

Most commonly school can cope with mild to moderate dyslexia, dyspraxia and dyscalculia, speech and language, auditory and sensory processing difficulties, fine and gross motor skills, Asperger's and mild ASD.

Support, through Highfield team, one full time plus assorted specialists – ranges from study skills to specific help with literacy and maths. Seen as part and parcel of daily life by pupils – 'helps you write and read if you are having a problem,' reckoned one – support is regularly reviewed and, in the case of one rapidly progressing pupil with ADD, withdrawn altogether.

Access all pupils largely down to owner says yes approach. Grandson of the founder, he has children at the school and what appears to be fairly substantial behind the scenes presence. 'When I first arrived, I asked, "Do you want me to be very tough in who we take on?" He said, "I want you to take them on and make a difference",' said previous head.

Exit: Almost everyone to Highfield. Only two pupils in recent years have been advised to look elsewhere, learning needs requiring specialist help.

Move is viewed as an exciting prospect by year 3s. 'It feels you can be free, because you get to walk around by yourself without a teacher following and there's much more playing area,' said one.

Remarks: Layout on Venn diagram lines, pre-prep largely self-sufficient but overlapping with prep when it comes to music, art and some sport, especially for older children. Cosily named nursery classes, Little Bears and Big Bears, lead a more self-contained existence, with attractive classrooms and separate, secluded and well-equipped play area. Integration starts early through treehouse families, small groups that span the age range and meet to share worries or good news, enjoyable sessions in forest school for all, and mealtimes, with older bruins having lunch in Highfield dining hall (Little Bears bring packed lunches instead), fajitas much enjoyed, 'salty' ham one of few dishes that wasn't.

Reception pupils start off in similar seclusion, though by the end of their first year, they're enjoying substantial tumbling about green space featuring gorgeous (though rather ignored) outdoor xylophone, as well as more conventional but attractive equipment, mad galloping in tentative sunshine seemingly the main amusement, though with behind the scenes staff presence to suggest games. Space gorgeous, only drawback ease of mislaying possessions: 'That sports jumper was there yesterday,' said pupil, with interest.

Inside, every inch of relatively compact and modern building is used to maximum effect. New and grandly named research area (library with computers – touch typing is taught in reception) was recently added, entrance area come assembly hall occupied by high flying and wonderful woven willow dragon spouting red velvet fire. Onesie design, though highly efficient, means some areas, such as nursery/reception music, are also through routes to somewhere else. Not a problem as remains '...a nice quiet place though sometimes people go through it,' said pupil.

Everywhere is extremely neat with not an inch wasted and loads to see and do, including rocket in reception class, less final frontier than cosy den, though strange lifeforms, courtesy of tank o'tadpoles, had already been discovered. Classrooms for older children, all interesting spaces and angles, were big on colourful, extensive and up to the minute displays (including some gorgeous monster poems).

Parents rate academics. 'We want our kids to have been pushed to the level where they can achieve either common entrance or scholarship to one of the major public schools,' said one. Achieved with no setting to speak of until year 3, maths the sole exception. 'If we have a big enough spread, might do it in year 2.' Anything but laissez faire, however, with lots of monitoring and no automatic move up between years, those who would benefit from 'spending extra time at a stage' as it's diplomatically phrased, doing just that. School also has a fair few of the extravagantly bright, who get fair share of extra support and encouragement – including peer socialisation (occasionally tricky for those punching above their weight conversationally).

Big thing is the creative curriculum, introduced some four years ago as a way of avoiding national curriculum ennui by adding all round oomph. Takes a theme such as 'Day at the sea', 'Knight in the castle' (pun intended), launches it with wow factor event (Sir Teach-a-lot knocking thunderously on pre-prep door to invite pupils to visit castle for a spot of princess rescuing) and ends similarly, with parents invited to share the fun by coming to medieval banquet or turning school into Brookham-sur-Mer, complete with donkeys and sand.

Subjects are knitted in en route, some national curriculum must-dos covered off-piste. While not everything can be shoehorned in (many science discoveries, for example, having inconveniently post-dated Round Table days) it's amazing how many dots can be joined. Would an exciting display of ultra-tactile rocks in year 3 classroom be followed by a snazzy volcanic eruption? Of course it would.

Huge staff enthusiasm provides a welcome outlet for pent-up creativity and they are encouraged to give full rein to creative instincts. Children are pretty sold on the idea (even if you did get the impression that overlaying a narrative element was even more popular with staff than their pupils) with activities, many hands on, doing wonders for confidence, one dyslexic child 'growing about three feet' after trebuchet improvement tip dramatically improved its destructive powers during siege weapon-making session.

With or without fun element, lessons are generally enjoyed, science for strong practical dimension, art at least in part because of resident dog, asleep in corner, music for charismatic teacher, whole-school favourite. Spanish, taught from year 3, seemed to be the only laggard – 'I just don't get it,' said pupil.

Everyone, however, undoubtedly 'gets' sport. Previously dreary sports day (little tension, less enjoyment, said parents, following children from non-event to non-event like zombies) ditched for something with a bit more gladiatorial oomph. Officially, 'we aim to teach pupils that it's all about taking part.' However, 'Life is competitive.' And while prospectus may highlight 'development of fine and gross motor skills', pupils, organised on mainly traditional lines (cricket, football and rugby for boys, rounders and hockey for girls, swimming for all in decent pool) are in no doubt that purpose is to form ace teams and slaughter the opposition. 'We've only lost one match this year,' say 7 and 8 year-old football and rugby stars.

Big programme of optional Saturday sports undoubtedly helps, as do popular after-school clubs (majority sign up for at least one) judo, gymnastics and orienteering amongst the options, street dance, pottery and chess ringing the changes and 60 per cent of pupils also learning an instrument. Animated children also encouraged to look outside immediate surroundings, worthy swapsies with London multi-cultural Catholic school – a valuable eye-opener for all. 'I suddenly realised that there's all these other people like me,' said one of only non-white pupils.

In an area that groans with educational choice, best recruiting tool is stamp of approval from dinner party set. This one is definitely on the menu.

Burford School

Cheltenham Road, Burford, Oxfordshire OX18 4PL

Pupils: 1,166; 551 boys, 615 girls; 90 boarders • Ages: 11–18 • Sixth form: 167

Fees: Boarding £9,900 pa (tuition free)

Tel: 01993 823303
Email: head.4040@burford.oxon.sch.uk
Website: www.burford.oxon.sch.uk

Headteacher: Since 2008, Mrs Kathy Haig BA MEd (40s). Educated at Burford School herself (her family lived at nearby Shipton-under-Wychwood), followed by Leeds University, where she studied food science and nutrition. Taught at schools in Hull, Keighley and Preston before moving to Ellesmere Port Catholic High School in Cheshire. Spent 12 years there, rising to be deputy head. Made a point of focusing on teaching and learning from the minute she arrived at Burford. When it comes to making decisions she always asks 'does it improve the teaching and learning?' If it doesn't, the school doesn't do it. Her approach has paid dividends. GCSE and A level results have risen year on year over the last seven years and the school received a letter of congratulations from the schools minister on being in the top 90 secondary schools in England for sustained improvement.

Outgoing, full of ideas and a good listener, she says that 'the culture of inclusivity and mutual respect' is key to the school's ethos. Parents told us that she is 'very down-to-earth,' 'easy to approach' and knows every pupil by name (no mean feat in a school this size). Her open-door policy means that if her door is open pupils can stop by and chat. When a group of boys mentioned that they'd like to play chess at lunchtimes she immediately put the idea into action. Now there's a chess league four times a week and Burford competes against other schools.

Head still teaches five hours a fortnight (child development GCSE to year 11 pupils). 'I love teaching and I think that it does the staff good to see that the head still has to do reports,' she says. Married to management consultant and has two teenage children, both at Burford.

Academic matters: A large, rural comprehensive that takes boarders (it's one of only 30 or so state boarding schools in the country). Offers wide range of subjects to wide ability intake but expects everyone to work hard and fulfil their potential – in line with head's belief that if you have high expectations then 'children will live up to what you expect of them.' Curriculum is mainly academic, with a small number of vocational qualifications. Most pupils take nine or 10 GCSEs and homework plays integral part, with parents asked to sign children's student record books once a week up to GCSE.

Exam results are very good – 68 per cent of pupils gained at least five GCSEs at grades A*-C including English and maths in 2016, with 24 per cent at A*/A grades. At A level, 35 per cent at A*/A and 63 per cent A*-B. Thirty A level and BTec subjects on offer at A level – all the usual, plus economics, psychology, media studies and photography. EPQ and AS critical thinking also available.

Lessons are largely taught in form groups, apart from maths and French, which are set according to ability. Class sizes of 26 up to GCSE (20 for practical subjects) and average of 12 to 14 in the sixth form. Languages compulsory at key stage 3. All students do French in years 7 to 9 and can add a second language in years 8 and 9.

Learning support is housed in own block – The Learning Zone – and deals with a wide range of needs, including speech, language and communication difficulties, autistic spectrum conditions, dyslexia, dyspraxia and dyscalculia and social, emotional and mental health needs. Help given to children who arrive with lower than average literacy and numeracy as well as those with EAL requirements and the gifted and talented. There's also an inclusion room called The Bridge for students who temporarily need to study away from the main classroom. A mother whose daughter had to undergo spinal surgery was full of praise for it. 'Lessons were brought to her there,' she said. 'Potentially she could have had four months being home-schooled but thanks to The Bridge she only missed two or three weeks of school.'

In keeping with its rural setting, school has an outdoor classroom called The Acre. As well as being a base for GCSE course in environmental land based studies it has chickens, ducks, rabbits, two miniature donkeys and a vegetable patch.

Games, options, the arts: With acres of green space for pupils to run around in, Burford is very sporty. PE and games are compulsory – sports offered include hockey, football, rugby, netball, tennis, athletics, keep fit and dance. As well as games fields (including a cricket square and pavilion), school has a gym and sports hall, netball and tennis courts. Loads of matches with local state and independent schools (rugby, hockey and netball teams particularly successful). Burford also hosts schools from Argentina and Australia every year for rugby, hockey, netball and cricket. School has its own equestrian team and runs an inter-house riding competition in the grounds every summer – everything from best turned-out pony to show-jumping and dressage. If there's a sport pupils want to do, 'we will try and put in on,' says the deputy head, citing girls' cricket and volleyball as recent examples.

Music is fantastic. Around 300 pupils have instrumental lessons – 'you name it, we play it,' said one of our sixth form guides. Wide range of orchestras, string ensemble, wind band, jazz band and rock school plus a music residential for 100 pupils in North Wales in the summer. School hopes to build its own concert hall and recently became music hub for the area, offering workshops by visiting specialists, the chance to play in professional concerts and master classes at St Anne's College, Oxford. School stages musical every two years – they'd just done Sunshine on Leith when we visited – and a drama production in the intervening years. 'We try and involve everyone,' said the assistant head.

Well equipped art block, with different areas for art, design, photography, textiles, plus computers, scanners, colour printers and digital cameras that professional studios would give their eye-teeth for. Loads of voluntary extracurricular activities – during lunch breaks and after school on Monday, Tuesday and Thursday (late buses put on so everyone can attend).

D of E and Young Enterprise on offer and lots of trips to foreign climes. The school is rightfully proud of its 20-year tie with a school in Uganda. The first group visited Uganda in 1995 and since then an annual exchange has taken place. Burford pupils visit partner students in Uganda one year, then host them in Burford the next. Along the way Burford has raised money for everything from a library and computer room for its partner school to two cows.

Boarding: The head says she could fill boarding places twice over and we're not in the least surprised. Parents pay for children's accommodation but their education is free. 'State boarding schools show that you can have it all, but at a fraction of the price of independent schools,' the mother of a sixth form boarder told us. 'We loved the feel of the place from the start. There's no keeping up with the Joneses. It's very diverse and there are people from all walks of life.'

The 90 boarders (half of them boys, half girls) live in Lenthall House, a listed building in Burford itself and a 10 minute walk from the main school (uphill on the way there, downhill on the way back). As we said last time, it's a bit of a Tardis – a maze of interconnecting buildings with bright, newly refurbished rooms and excellent facilities. The school has created a flat within the boarding house for five sixth form girls – to help them prepare for the university years. Boarders come from all over, from down the road in Oxfordshire to Hong Kong and China. Most are full boarders (a couple of weekly boarders when we visited) and staff put on loads of evening and weekend activities. Everything from go karting and ice skating to theatre trips and craft sessions. Supervised prep every night and in-house structured revision during GCSE and A level study leave.

Pupils eat breakfast (full English on Saturdays and croissants on Sundays) and tea at the boarding house – food cooked by own catering staff – and lunch at the main school. Boarders can invite day pupils to tea and there's a formal dinner at Christmas, plus monthly lunches for local OAPs. Six live-in staff, including head of boarding and his wife. Boarding head moved to Burford from the independent sector and says: 'There is more drive and purpose among the boarders here. They are keener to do well and to take advantage of all the opportunities we offer.'

Application form on school website for boarding places. School asks for reference from children's current school and prospective pupils are invited to attend a taster day during term time. Students from overseas (30 per cent of total number of boarders) welcome as long as they have a relative or host family living in the UK.

Background and atmosphere: Founded as a grammar school for boys by charter in 1571 and still celebrates Charter Day in October each year. Main school is situated on the busy A40 on edge of beautiful Cotswold town of Burford (just over an hour away from London in reasonable traffic). Moved to its present 36-acre site in 1960, with boarders moving into the original grammar school at the bottom of the high street. An academy since 2012.

School still maintains many old grammar school traditions, including house system, prefects and smart uniform (blazer and house tie) for all but the sixth form (who wear their own clothes but are expected to dress appropriately – no ripped jeans or Ugg boots). This year's first XV rugby team have opted to wear smart suits when they travel to matches – a custom they reckon will continue.

Sixth formers have their own block, with common room, study area and more freedom. Year 13s are allowed off-site at lunchtime and if they don't have lessons. Some drive to school. 'We get treated like grown-ups,' an appreciative youngster told us. The only grumble we heard was that they'd like more parking places. Students keen to be head girl or head boy write their own manifestos, take part in hustings and are voted for by staff and fellow sixth formers.

Like the pupils themselves, the atmosphere here is busy and purposeful. Ofsted's 2014 report judged students' behaviour to be outstanding and when we visited we were impressed by pupils' politeness, charm and enthusiasm for the school.

Pastoral care, well-being and discipline: Well-defined rules set out in excellent student record book – smart hardback given to each pupil at the start of the year, with ruler and whiteboard they can hold up for plenary sessions in class. Contains everything from equipment needed for school to spelling lists and what to do if the school bus is late.

School's core tenet is that 'everyone will act with care and consideration to others at all times,' and it clearly works. School governor told us that Burford is 'very caring' and 'takes great pride in how we look after our youngsters.' There's a strong Team Burford ethos, with students keeping in touch for years after they leave.

Excellent induction programme for new pupils. Year 7s are mentored by trained year 13s and also get a three-day residential trip early in first term to help them settle in. Year groups are divided into seven or eight forms, each with own tutor, who's also responsible for registration and PHSE. All pupils belong to one of four houses named after school founders and benefactors – Falkland, Heylin, Warwick and Wysdom. Houses are fiercely competitive, with lots of competitions, from rugby and netball to art and even forensics. School council with four reps from each year group. Pupils have assembly twice a week – once for the whole school and once for their year group.

Pupils say the food has improved a lot and offers a daily choice of hot meals, pasta, salad bar, vegetarian options and baguettes. Cashless canteen – biometric system reads students' thumbprints.

Pupils and parents: A real mix. Pupils come from a wide variety of backgrounds, from disadvantaged to quite posh. Some have lived in the area for years, others have parents who commute to Oxford or London every day. Relatively few from the town of Burford itself – steep house prices mean properties tend to be owned by older residents and second-homers. School gives financial support 'very discreetly' to pupils whose families can't afford to pay for school trips.

Old pupils include Gilbert Jessop (cricketer), Simon West (film director) and Alice Freeman (rower).

Entrance: Children living in the catchment area and attending one of Burford's nine partner schools are virtually guaranteed a place. Thirty-five to 40 per cent of pupils come from outside the catchment area, from as far afield as Hook Norton, Faringdon and Bourton-on-the-Water, with priority given to those with siblings already at the school. Additional pupils arrive in year 9, including up to 30 a year from local private schools. 'We've had to put in an extra year 9 form,' says the head.

Up to 20 new pupils a year join the 220-strong sixth form (minimum of two Bs and four Cs at GCSE required by all, plus some subject-specific requirements).

Exit: Around 40-50 per cent leave after GCSE – for vocational courses at local FE colleges (including Cirencester, Abingdon and Witney and City of Oxford), apprenticeships and employment.

Three-quarters head to university after A levels – to study everything from biomedical science to fine art. Four to Oxbridge in 2016, and two medics; others to eg Edinburgh, Durham, Cardiff and Exeter. School has a full-time careers adviser – professionally qualified and very experienced – who organises higher education and apprenticeships evenings, mock interviews, a careers convention and work experience (for year 10s and year 12s) and sees students one-to-one. School is creating strong links with local businesses too.

Remarks: A happy and successful comprehensive school with an impressive 'can-do' attitude. Pupils are keen to succeed and rise to the challenge admirably.

Burgess Hill Girls

Keymer Road, Burgess Hill, West Sussex RH15 0EG

Pupils: 590; 55 boarders • Ages: 2–18 • Sixth form: 88

Fees: Day £7,350 – £16,950; Boarding £27,300 – £30,450 pa

Tel: 01444 241050
Email: registrar@burgesshillgirls.com
Website: www.burgesshillgirls.com

Head: Since 2014, Kathryn Bell. Vigorous, friendly and energetic – would be the last woman standing against battalions of establishment men; and in fact was the only female head ever appointed at her last post at Ackworth school. Previously second deputy head at Ardingly, and earlier teaching posts at Burgess Hill Girls, Brighton and Hove High, Hazelwick and St Michael's Burton Park. Has four grown up children, one of whom has had some educational and health problems, which means she has particular empathy with parents struggling with SEN.

Determined to dispel the myth of girls' schools being fluffy and pink, and Burgess Hill Girls has undergone a recent rebrand to stamp out all traces. Girls need 'to punch above weight in all disciplines', says the head, who has no time for female quotas. 'If you were shipwrecked, Burgess Hill girls would be those helping others to survive'. Wants her girls 'not to apologise for being who they are. They are not pretentious; but can stand up boldly and show what they have achieved and what they can offer'. Enjoys a 'good meaty discussion'.

Both pupils and parents approve; described by parents as 'amazing','proactive and approachable' and 'frequently with the children'; and on one occasion 'covered in mud', added a pleased mum. Pupils like the fact she spends time with them, and is 'really interested'.

Head of junior school: Since 2011, Heather Cavanagh, previously head teacher of Dover College Junior School. Popular with pupils – 'nice and really kind', 'always listens to you'. Good relationship with parents, who says she's approachable, and always with the children.

A hanging on Mrs Cavanagh's wall says THINK. She clearly does, a great deal. The head encourages her staff to always deal with pupils and parents with thoughtfulness and compassion, explaining that if you build trust and faith in parents, this works better if the road gets bumpy; and parents really appreciate being sent handwritten notes capturing moments of significance to children.

Academic matters: Happy junior school girls take academic work very much in their stride. Mostly single classes of around 13; years 3, 4 and 6 are currently double classes. The head says, 'If they don't get it [academically], that is our responsibility, not theirs. Girls should not feel it is their fault that they don't understand'. And they don't. One pupil told us 'I'm not good at spelling – they help me, and not in a mean way'. The school take a wholehearted responsibility for pupils' academic development – a parent told us about her concern that her daughter just wasn't engaged with school work, particularly maths; and her relief at their response – don't worry, we will deal with it. They managed to engage the girl with maths – took her into the garden to count seeds, mum said vaguely – and it worked.

Outside activities are taken into account by school: three tasks to be completed over the course of each week, so prep can fit in with a child's out of school activities. Optional prep club available every day – teachers always help if you need it, and then you get tea and toast. 'My mum really likes it...'

Great focus on SEND, spotted both though baseline assessment and other data, but also through constant discussion between staff. In-class support, and dyslexia and dispraxic specialists. One-to-one charged as extra. Also booster groups for things any student might be struggling with, such as cursive writing. They're aware that the most able sometimes need help – 'if they feel they need to succeed all the time, girls can avoid doing things differently, or taking risks'– so aim to build resilience in all their girls.

Consistently excellent results averaging over 80 per cent A*-B grades at A level for last 13 years (80 per cent in 2016, with 61 per cent A*-A). Parents are very satisfied with their children's progress. Similar consistent achievement at GCSE, with 66 per cent A*/A in 2016.

GCSE maths and IGCSE science are high performers, alongside success in English, humanities and the arts. A good variety of mostly traditional subjects, with plenty of languages, both ancient and modern. Lovely language suite built in 2013, with laptops which rise from the desk lid when required. A pupil was awarded a gold medal at the International Linguistics Olympiad, which included a four hour challenge translating the Universal Declaration of Human Rights from Armenian into English.

Small class sizes in sixth form (3-12) mean the girls have plenty of attention in class. Around 40 per cent of entries at A level are in science, maths and technology, and girls achieve excellent results in these subjects, with plenty of experience in using them: 'engineering experience day made me realise that engineering is not just about fixing things but about being creative and making a difference'. There's also an engineering education scheme, in which lower sixth pupils have a seven month project working alongside a company.

Very good results in many other areas, including PE, media studies and textiles, and although one parent commented that the range of subjects on offer at A level is not extensive, she was satisfied that the it was best for her daughter to concentrate on 'bread and butter' subjects now: she could always specialise at university. 'Traditional values and methods here,' she added. Traditional values clearly do matter here; but this school comes across as modern and engaged. Value added is carefully monitored using CEM, which shows that GCSE performance is on average one grade higher than of children of a similar ability: girls certainly thrive academically here.

There's a good mix of male and female staff, and the dedication of these teachers is, parents say, extraordinary. Extra clinics and one-on-one support means no one falls behind – one parent described how her daughter received extra help in science, running over things whilst others were at registration. Pupils say it's easy to ask for help.

There's a new focus on SEND, until recently ad hoc in different rooms, but now in a dedicated room. Parents who have used the SEND provision say it very good, and are pleased that the support in small group sessions (in English, maths and science) is free of charge. (One-one is charged as an extra, as it uses outside support.)

A beguilingly named head of futures advises on A levels, university and careers, and will go over personal statements umpteen times until just right. There's lots of careers advice, and parents are encouraged to participate in 'take your daughter to work day' – all part of the head's drive to get the girls out there.

Decent size library, open 8.30am-18.05pm. Super computers sunk into the desks, screens visible through transparent desk top, key boards pulled out for use as required.

Games, options, the arts: School minibuses take junior pupils to Ardingly reservoir for water sports, and to the Triangle for swimming: the juniors had just returned on the day of our visit, and hair dryers buzzed from each classroom – 'so they're not actually dripping down the chairs'. Girls play tag rugby and football, alongside all the usual sports. Extracurricular is led by girls' interests – scrabble and dance are popular, as are sports clubs, orchestra, and quilting bee. Seniors run drama club and textiles club for juniors, which are enjoyed by both age groups.

Both curriculum sports and clubs available to all in senior school, regardless of ability, with fixtures at all levels. There's one field on site for athletics and rounders, lovely pavilion, five floodlit hard netball courts, also used for tennis, and floodlit Astroturf. The gym is old, but light and well kept. Facilities are not quite as extensive as parents might like, but on site expansion limited by site. Size of facilitates is no predictor of success: teams here do very well, girls saying being a small school means that they get more time from coaches. The girls excel at netball, hockey, athletics, rounders and horse riding.

Girls enthuse about extracurricular sports for all ethos at lunchtime, with clubs in badminton, ultimate frisbee, and fitness and dance. If there's demand of an activity, the school will do its best to provide: polo club started recently. School buses pupils to Ardingly reservoir for water sports and uses excellent local facilities for swimming and hockey.

Rare weekend fixtures means girls have the time to join local clubs, and girls like the fact that those busy with competitions have ring-fenced time to catch up with their academic work.

Creative arts events for all to enjoy – 'they don't chose the in your face confident girls to do everything here', said a parent approvingly. Busy drama and music departments, with regular productions ranging from Euripedes to Playhouse Creatures (a play about the struggles of actresses in a men's world). A big musical every year, last year The Shot Heard Round the World – written, composed and directed by three girls in upper sixth (one of the girls is now at Berkeley USA studying music and song writing). Croft II Drama was built onto the hall in 2013, a circular soundproof room with good acoustics which serves as a drama studio, recital room and place for parents to mingle during the interval of events held in the hall. The hall was refurbished at the same time, the (underused) stage removed and replaced with removal flooring, and stadium seating for 300 installed, which can fold back into a huge wooden wall.

Art is housed in a prefab block with a flat roof (bane of the bursar's life), surprisingly light around the edges, with a dedicated room for sixth formers, who can leave work undisturbed. The darker, but well lit space towards the centre of the building houses the exhibition of excellent A level and GCSE work.

Textiles are taken seriously here, and it's a very successful department. Material here is used for anything and everything, from the practical making of device cases for laptops, to a handbag styled like a pocket watch, with an opening clock face (the maker winning national handbag designer of the year 2014 aged just 15).

Plenty of extracurricular, from law society and public speaking to D of E and Young Enterprise. But, the girls say, if don't want to be busy, that's fine. OMG here (not the expletive – Only Motivated Girls), but 'in our own particular little ways'.

Boarding: Boarders live in one of the two elegant Edwardian boarding houses, which house girls of mixed ages. Alongside full and weekly boarding, there are two flexi boarding spaces (£45 a night). Boarding available from year 7 upwards, occasionally year 6 depending on the maturity of the child.

Most boarders are from overseas (Hong Kong and China), with around eight nationalities in total (no wish to increase overseas numbers, says the head). One parent told us he would prefer boarding to be less of an overseas service; but it has meant his daughter has a best friend from Madrid and a desire to learn Mandarin.

Describes as a day school with boarding, and this felt like the case. The boarding house we visited felt quiet: the girls don't return to houses during the day, so there's not the busy to and through evident in many big boarding schools. But boarders are very happy here, and call the houses home. One parent told us, 'The care and attention from the staff is exemplary. I feel my daughter is extremely well looked after'; another, that 'boarding has had a huge and positive effect'.

Inviting trellis covers the entrance to a boarding house; inside, a comfortable common room with TV, table football, books and games; kitchen with fruit and cereal always available. Games room, with a church pew to perch on – makes lingering games seem unlikely – and large screen in front, also used for dancing with the Wii. One of the messiest rooms we have ever seen, but we are told this is unusual, and a reward scheme is in place to encourage tidiness. Fresh decoration, with bathrooms recently redecorated and deep cleaned.

If parents are late picking up day girls, they simply go over to the boarding house. Burgess Hill Girls is well situated in town, so if boarders haven't got a club, they may go into town in small groups after school. Supervised prep, then down time in the boarding house until bedtime, with years 7-9 handing in electronic devices before lights out at 10pm. Wifi is turned off at midnight and comes back on at 6am. Boarders contact home via Skype or internet phone, with the office phone or computer available as back up.

Activities organised for each weekend, both trips and on site activities, compulsory for year 7-10. Ideas for activities come from the girls. There is a suggestion box, a weekly discussion between pupils and catering; and although parents told us the quality of evening meals is not the same as lunches, the school say suggestions for changes to food are acted on immediately.

Background and atmosphere: Set back from the road in a leafy suburb of large houses and big old trees; we had to peer up driveway to be sure it was the right place – planning permission is being sought for an 'illuminated totem' (a bright sign you can see from the road) and new entrance railing. Buildings are a mixture of old Victorian villas and modern, with a slightly colonial feel; beautifully kept grounds, encircled by trees gives an immediate sense of safety and seclusion. But the girls here are not cosseted; Mrs Bell feels the most important thing is to 'get the girls out there' –and they are out there a lot.

Entry through glass doors, a large navy sign fronted with gold chairs, and a vertical radiator. Everything about the entrance says up to date. Parents describe the buildings as 'clean, crisp and fresh.' Decor inside varies from swish purpose built to elderly, with recently refurbished areas in blue and gold; a blue stripy carpet that makes you feel as if you are in a mathematical game with lines which sway and lift your path. Traditional moments though: portraits of heads decorate an old staircase, much like 10 Downing St.

The food is tasty, agree the girls, and the chef takes on board suggestions from the box in the dining hall. There are old fashioned school desks filled with fruit (described in several languages), a spoon and fork clock, and a good selection of food, to which soup is added midway through the autumn term. In the annual poverty lunch, pupils lunch on soup, with one piece of bread and a piece of fruit: a reminder of how fortunate they are.

Most of the parents we spoke to were not specifically looking for a single sex school, but chose Burgess Hill Girls because it was school they liked most –'it felt the most authentic', said one; 'plain speaking', said another. The head believes being away from boys allows girls room to develop, to be themselves – and the necessary strength, resilience and broad shoulders to cope and be the best in a male dominated world. The girls we spoke to agreed; one girl who came from a mixed sex school said she was not afraid to shine here – 'boys interrupt,' she added. Parents feel girls here don't get shouted down or belittled by boys; and although one admitted her daughter did find life at university a bit of a shock, she added that the sixth formers are well prepared, and have workshops on everything... including boys.

Girls here are encouraged to step out of their comfort zones: on Roche days, twice a year, pupils spend a day pushing their boundaries – we saw a group learning to plaster, patiently working their way up four columns planted in the lawn (no chance of contamination, with hooded plastic space suits and plastic goggles). Roche day ends listening to motivational businesswomen, encouraging the girls to take risks to succeed.

Other activities are designed to practise business rapport, and networking breakfasts are organised by the girls. There are plenty of trips out, from Greece to the Old Bailey; and the lower sixth annual challenge to race the sun, setting off at sunset to walk across the downs to reach Beachy Head by sunrise, dressed up for the occasion as nuns, football players and pirates; the nuns, appropriately, treating everyone to highlights from the Sound of Music on the way.

The navy and stripe uniform is about to change, with pupil and parent views being sought; although it might have been less controversial to move the school to the Bahamas, says the head wryly. Sixth formers currently wear their own clothes, with the requirement to be smart (although jeans are allowed). Teachers apparently have different views of what's smart, and what's acceptable to some isn't smart enough for others, say the girls. Suits are being considered.

I am, I can, I ought, I will are the words of the school motto, and they pop up all over the place. There is a strong moral tone about this non-denominational school, with a focused time to reflect on moral messages during a period of silence on arrival and departure from assembly, and healthy links with the local community. This is one of the few schools we have visited which views community service as an essential part of life balance, alongside academic work and play, rather than an optional extra, and it appears in many areas of life at Burgess Hill: from raising money for local charities, to holding an annual pamper day for local carers, and helping children with their reading at a local primary school. Sixth formers raised money for a local nursery and helped set up its Facebook page, while year 10 held a workshop to make bags for hospice patients to hold medication. The whole school take part in the Sports Relief

Mile, and on an international level, the school supports Plan – a charity to raise the profile of girls across the world who do not have access to education.

Pastoral care, well-being and discipline: Burgess Hill is a school with academic focus, so it is no surprise that most girls move seamlessly from the junior school to the rigours of senior school. But to parents, this is not what they appreciate most about the junior school: 'they support confidence and emotional well-being first, before moving on to the complexities of work', said a parent; and this certainly seemed true. The girls were happy and relaxed – 'I love being with my friends', 'everyone is so kind', 'people always help you'. Parents emphasised the thoughtful and detailed approach to care of their children, one describing how the school worked with her daughter, who had a stammer, for 10 months for free before she even started at the school; and how once she was there, she received extra care and work, with a daily update to the parent.

Another described her daughter's anxiety at going on a school trip away in year 4. The teacher chatted with child before the trip, and worked out a bedtime strategy: if the girl became anxious she would move her soft toy to certain position on the bed so teacher would know she was worried without her having to say anything. Pupils felt confident who they would go to for help: form teacher, TA in the playground, a sixth former – 'if there's no one else around'. Girls choose a member of staff to be their mentor, with meetings weekly, but daily if needed.

Their approach to bullying is to always first listen to kids and parents until they have talked themselves out. Most incidents turn out to be friendship issues, rather than systematic and sustained behaviour, says the head, and we need to ask why a child is lashing out.

Senior school parents say the staff work 24/7 for the girls 'above and beyond the call of duty'. 'If you send an email saying you're worried about something, you'll be at school at 8am the next morning chatting about it'. The school is excellent at keeping in touch, and parents emphasis the all round care – one described how she was chatting to a teacher about her worries about her daughter's anxiety, and the next day received a handwritten card through the post suggesting websites that might help. Girls agreed that they all knew who they would go to with a problem, from the head to favourite teachers, or the nurse (much loved by all). Sixth form mentors help younger girls, and all girls meet their teacher mentor every fortnight, to discuss work and anything else.

Bullying is dealt with straight on, and rapidly, said a parent. Both parties received counselling, and, most importantly to the parent, her daughter was taught strategies for dealing with bullies.

The honesty of this school is much appreciated by parents, who feel that problems here are dealt with head on: they are very engaged with the problems that can assail girls, and often make their appearance in years 9 and 10 – for example, obsession with image and being skinny, and rare instances of self harm. 'They are right on it', said a parent. A comprehensive drugs policy exists, with every girl treated as an individual and every situation independently assessed before decisions are made.

This feels like a place where a high standard of behaviour is expected, and by and large adhered to by the girls. Parents felt that poor conduct is very unlikely and would be much more of an issue here than poor performance.

A lively house system; though a little strange, you might think, for a modern girls' school to name its houses after dead male poets. A little bit of left over tradition, says the head. Lots of inter-house competition throughout the year, from public speaking, chess and sports, to performing arts day.

Pupils and parents: Parents are a mix of wealthy and not: city professionals, businesspeople, and working several jobs to keep their girls at Burgess Hill. Some are competitive – 'keen to ensure their daughters are achieving and being seen to achieve'.

Parents receive a grade sheet for attainment and attitude to learning every half term. Year 10s upwards receive working at and working towards grades as well. Two parents' evenings and one full report per year.

The school bus service is popular – a year 6 girl described her bus driver as one of the nicest things about school. It covers eight routes around Sussex every morning, children coming from as far afield as Horsham, Crawley and Uckfield. Season ticket is £400 a term, each route being offered in the morning and twice after school, with an early bus at 4.00pm and a late bus at 6.15pm. Drop off is a bit tricky; cars can drive in, through, and out, but it gets congested, and many parents drop off at the road outside. School is three minutes walk from Burgess Hill station, and just 45 minutes by train from London.

Communication with parents is excellent, and there's no prolonged email back and forth with parents: the head encourages teachers to invite parents with a concern or issue to come in, or pick up the phone. Junior school parents feel very involved with school life, and are invited to Friday assembly every week. All superstars go up and describe their piece of work – excellent for building confidence, say parents.

Notable former pupils include Holly Willoughby, television presenter, Kim Sears (Mrs Andy Murray) and Caroline Atkins, former international cricketer.

Entrance: Non-selective entry for nursery. Reception to year 2 assessed informally by spending part of the day at school. For year 3 upwards girls sit written papers and the school likes to see any current school reports, but looks beyond just academic ability. A few scholarships for academic and musical ability. They will admit mid-year if there are places available.

Most senior school entrants (80 per cent last year) come from the junior school, though this is not automatic. A good number also from local state primaries and preps in the south east and London. Skype interviews for overseas students.

Exit: Almost all juniors go on to the senior school; automatic entry unless headmistress feels any girl may not cope with the workload.

No one has had to leave in the last few years due to poor GCSE results. This school emphasises personalised education, and will create a programme to suit the needs of a pupil who got weak grades at GCSE, to include resitting key GCSEs, and close monitoring of progress.

Two to Oxbridge in 2016 – both to read languages – and two medics, with the majority going to Russell Group, and others to art schools. Vast majority gain places at first choice universities, for mostly traditional subjects.

Money matters: No charge for pre and after-school care, from 8am-6pm, including breakfast. Academic, music, art, sport and drama scholarships, up to 40 per cent of fees, awarded at 11+,13+ and 16+. A number of significant bursaries (which do not take account of academic standard). Great value for money, say parents. 'The John Lewis of education,' says the head.

Remarks: This nurturing school puts time and thought into finding the best in each girl. Its excellent academic standards do not make it intellectually exclusive – parents felt it would suit all sorts, one saying that it suited both her very academic daughter, and the one whose talents were more middle of the road.

C

Caldicott School

Crown Lane, Farnham Royal, Slough SL2 3SL

Pupils: 289; 114 boarders • Ages: 7-13

Fees: Day £15,984 – £17,196; Boarding £25,353 pa

Tel: 01753 649300
Email: registrar@caldicott.com
Website: www.caldicott.com

Headmaster: Since 1998, Mr Simon Doggart BA (50s), educated at Winchester and read history at Cambridge. School-mastering is in his blood – his father was a legendary figure at Winchester for many years – and he previously taught history at Eton, where he also ran the cricket. Friendly, relaxed even, he is nevertheless utterly professional and we doubt he's ever off duty. Parents describe him as 'charismatic' and 'very genuine, not corporate' and, 'best head ever.' He knows every inch of his school, is proud of its thoughtful developments and is greeted cheerfully by the boys as we pass by. 'He's outside the school every morning at 8, welcoming the boys in, he's an amazing figurehead,' said one very impressed mother. Maximum praise and affection also for his wife, Antonia. She hosts 'girlie' lunches for mothers, birthday teas (complete with parlour games) for the boys and, we are sure, attends to the innumerable duties that a head's spouse is heir to. 'Food, pastoral, I notice things,' she says, with classic understatement. The Doggarts have three children, two at university and one at Wellington, and a working cocker spaniel.

The last few years must have been very difficult as historic abuse made headlines (with the unrelated juice of Caldicott being Nick Clegg's old school). Mr Doggart's remedy has been 'light and windows', both metaphorically and literally. Every parent we spoke to wanted to put on record how well the school handled the court case and attendant revelations. They say that the head kept them informed in advance at every stage and that he was always available to answer questions.

Glancing round his comfortable study, it was hardly necessary to ask Mr Doggart about his interests; the Wisdens and history books did the talking. He remembers being inspired by Gary Sobers' autobiography as a child and these days enjoys reading Robert Harris. School holidays find the Doggarts beside the seaside in the Witterings.

Entrance: Two form entry in year 3 is joined by another two form entry in year 4 (legacy of Bucks middle school system). There is a short formal academic assessment plus an opportunity to meet other pupils and teachers. Mr Doggart likes to show prospective parents round (several said they felt they were under as much scrutiny as their sons) and there is an open day in June.

Exit: Nearly all at 13, mainly to trad boys' boarding. Harrow gets the lion's share followed by Eton, Radley, Wellington, St Edward's, Winchester and Stowe. Good clutch of scholarships most years (ten in 2016), mostly sport, art and all-rounders. Definitely not a school for those with eyes on the Bucks grammars at 11.

Remarks: Caldicott sits on top of a wooded escarpment with views down to Windsor; 40 acres of prime Bucks real estate adjoining beautiful Burnham Beeches. The school was founded in 1904 by Heald Jenkins who named it after his new bride, a Miss Theodora Caldicott Ingram. The school and its wonderful Harrison Harrison organ (recently restored and residing in the chapel) moved from Hitchin to Farnham Royal in 1938.

Perfect pitches extend as far as the eye can see, busy with grounds staff rolling and mowing grass that already looks like a billiard table. We defer to one of our guides who observed, 'I can't think of a prep school with better pitches.' Cricket and rugby are a big deal here with up to eight teams (is there really an 'H' team?) ready to take on all comers at all levels. Oxford's Dragon School, as its name suggests, is their fiercest opponent. And what about that H team? Do its duckers and triers really get the same standard of coaching as the Olympians in the As? Certainly, says Mr D. 'We want everybody to take part, the coaches aren't baby-minding. The challenge can be finding other schools ready to field as many opposing teams.' When it comes to sport for all, noble aims such as these are often at odds with the grass roots actualities. Not so at Caldicott. Parents of unsporty boys do not find them swinging round the corner posts while the A team triumphs on a distant pitch. 'If the A team is playing then so are the Bs, Cs and Ds.' And it's the same with other things, drama for instance, lots of groups (teams) at all levels to 'keep everyone improving'.

A jarring note in the song of praise for Caldicott seems to be the standard of its music. Memorably described to us as 'joyless', music seems to occupy a lower profile than in similar schools so this may not be the place for your mini Mozart. No shortage of practice rooms and lots of music tech equipment, but something's missing. There are a few chamber groups but no orchestra, the chapel choir is, well, just that and the repertoire of the junior and senior choirs has been, to paraphrase several parents politely, 'underwhelming.' However, things may be on the up. A recent whole school performance of Captain Noah at St Paul's Knightsbridge was a triumph, joyfully received by boys and parents.

Half the pupils are local, the other half come in from the capital on the 7.30am Caldicott express. Mr D says school 'invented' busing in from west London – we hope the other busing Bucks preps pay a copyright fee. 'The service is incredibly efficient, the buses run like clockwork, they're travelling against the traffic,' we were told. Youngest go home at 4.30pm but rest stay until 6pm – it's a long, active day, but at least there's no homework 'apart from a few spellings or a bit of reading,' until the last two years (and the boys are all boarding then). Saturday school is 'proper' with lessons until 12.30 for all and matches in the afternoon for the older boys. London parents just as visible on sidelines as locals. Is there a divide between the local and London boys, we asked? 'Not at all, the boys don't even notice,' said one mother, although she conceded that the London chaps seemed 'a bit more polished and prepared' when they joined.

All boys in years 7 and 8 board; it's an integral part of their preparation for senior schools such as Harrow, Eton, Radley and Winchester. Dorms are upstairs in the main school building – clean, bright with home duvets, photos and posters. Evenings and weekends are busy with dedicated clubs including fly tying and model making, and competitions and activities such as fondue nights (boys have to go and buy the cheese as well as cook it) and a Caldicott Bake-off. New boarders are given an 'uncle', an experienced boarder in the same dorm who will help him settle in. Senior houseparents live on site with their family and all full-time staff do boarding duty. Our sixth form (year 8) guides, almost ready to leave for senior school, were waxing nostalgic, 'There's so many people around, it's a community,' said one. What would they remember, we asked? 'Summer evening cross-country runs through Burnham Beeches; after-school swims in the outdoor pool; the boarders' Christmas party with carol singing around the huge tree.' Sigh.

Teachers are called 'sir' and 'ma'am' but that apart, education is firmly in the 21st century with bright classrooms, smartboards, well-equipped labs and lots of techy stuff. We loved the screens outside the DT studio flashing up individual photos of every boy proudly holding his finished work. Mr D was not in his happy place when we asked him about programming and mighty relieved to bump into a physics teacher who could tell Raspberry Pie from Python. Back in his comfort zone, the head proudly showed us the new wedge-shaped ('cheesy') library, built on the site of a 'horrendous 60s pre-fab' that the 'whole school watched being demolished'.

One way in which Caldicott is untraditional is its neatness – it's the tidiest prep we've ever visited. In fact it was a relief to see some naughty geranium cuttings sprawled muddily beneath a windowsill in the biology lab. Even the art room, usually reliable as a haven of creative chaos, was ship-shape. Parents describe the Doggarts as 'incredibly well organised' and it really does seem that no corner of the school escapes their attention to detail. Very reassuring.

Boys are 'loosely' set in maths from the start and in other subjects later on. According to the head there's 'much less setting than of yore', but several parents commented that the system wasn't clear and didn't seem that flexible. Average class size is 16, there's a good mix of staff – old and new – and about a third of teachers are women. The lessons we peeped into were lively and interactive, boys bursting with ideas and eager to contribute. Some grumbles in the recent past that school was slow to pick up SEN but this no longer seems to be the case; several new parents said teachers had been very quick to act on potential problems.

Monitoring is generally regarded as good and communication as excellent, 'Teachers are all contactable by email and usually reply within a couple of hours.' Pastoral care and school counsellor came in for high praise; wobbly new boarders are ably helped through those tricky first few weeks. Several parents remarked how thoughtfully boys in different year groups (so often tribal) related to each other.

Boys say food is 'so much better'. Chicken Kiev is top choice, closely followed by the Thursday roast and cooked breakfast. We were, however, told to 'avoid Saturday lunch at all costs.' We couldn't find out exactly why, but you have been warned. On the wall of the school dining room we were shown the honours boards and there he was, Nicholas Clegg, the only head boy in the school's history to hold the post jointly. The Caldicott coalition – you couldn't make it up.

The word we keep reaching for is 'traditional', but in its best, unstuffy, sense. Parents who choose Caldicott told us they do so because it has secure values: courtesy, fair play, loyalty, regard for others. 'When the boys leave they are young gentlemen,' one said. All in all, this is a cracking prep that will play more than fair by any boy lucky enough to get a place.

Carrdus School

Overthorpe Hall, Blacklocks Hill, Banbury, Oxfordshire OX17 2BS

Pupils: 111, including 15 boys • Ages: 3-11 (girls); 3-8 (boys)

Fees: £9,900 – £10,725 pa

Tel: 01295 263733
Email: office@carrdusschool.co.uk
Website: www.carrdusschool.co.uk

Headmaster: Since 2012, Edward Way BSc (40s). Educated at Radley College and UCL, where he read geology. PGCE at University of Bath, followed by posts at Cothill, Chandlings, Cheam School and Lambrook School, then 10 years as head at Great Tew Primary School, 12 miles away.

Entrance: Junior school is currently full to bursting – tribute, says school, to the amazing staff. No entrance test – 'It's first come, first served'. Very broad intake. Majority of pupils come from Banbury and surrounding villages, with parents registering children up to three years in advance. Most common entry points are nursery, reception and year 3, but it's worth trying in between too. No scholarships offered but means-tested bursaries sometimes available.

C

Exit: About a third of girls to 'big sister' Tudor Hall. Rest to a wide range eg King's High Warwick, Rugby, Oundle, St Mary's Ascot, Bloxham, Headington. Boys head at 7 or 8 to preps eg Cothill, Warwick Junior, The Dragon and Winchester House.

Remarks: School started in 1952 and moved to its present site in 1970 when founder Kathleen Carrdus bought Overthorpe Hall for the princely sum of £22,500. Has always had strong links with Tudor Hall, which bought school in 2011. Union seems to have worked well and Carrdus staff say they consider Tudor Hall their 'big sister'. Main building a rambling 1880 hunting lodge set in 11 acres of grounds.

Friendly teachers pride themselves on making children feel happy and secure in 'informal yet stimulating' environment. Lots of fresh air, smiley faces, muddy knees and heaps of praise. Despite relaxed ambience, pupils work hard and school's academic record is impressive. School says: 'We set high standards and help children achieve them.' Hugely experienced staff, with good mix of ages. One class per year group, with an average of 20 per class and maximum of 24. No setting, but the most able get the chance to move faster in 'sparkle sessions'. French from reception and Latin for last two terms of year 6. No scholarship stream – school prides itself on giving everyone the chance to shine. Homework for all. Reception children take reading books home while year 6 pupils get 30 minutes' homework a night. Thousands of books, all colour-coded for different reading abilities.

A number of pupils with mild dyslexia, developmental coordination disorder (dyspraxia) and/or learning difficulties. One-to-one help available from three-strong learning support team or in small groups, often at start or end of school day.

Arts strong, with all pupils encouraged to play instruments, speak confidently in public and take part in concerts. Children's work on display everywhere you look. When we visited, year 5s were busy making glorious pink Mother's Day cards, while a group of jolly year 4s were rehearsing for their forthcoming medieval Britain's Got Talent assembly. Music terrific – everyone learns recorder from 7 upwards and at least half the pupils learn piano, violin, guitar, saxophone, flute, cello or drums. Orchestra, choirs and bands galore.

School day starts at 8.50am and finishes at 3.40pm, but to help working parents children can arrive from 8.15am and stay on for (paid-for) Teatimers sessions after school till 5.30pm. All children attend at least two clubs a week – everything from art and craft to roller skating. Daily assembly, as well as weekly hymn practice and bible story. Delightful (and short) list of school rules advises pupils: 'No sticks, no stones', 'Only climb as high as your friend's head' and 'It's only fun if everybody is enjoying it'.

No school uniform, apart from games kit. Dress code is 'not smart, not scruffy', with parents advised to send children to school in comfy, machine-washable clothes. No jeans, bare midriffs, nail varnish, jewellery, mobile phones or chewing gum. Children are encouraged to be children, not mini-adults. Pupils are well-behaved and discipline is not an issue. As school points out: 'Children like boundaries, as long as they are fair and they can see the point of them.'

C

Sport is compulsory for all. Children do hockey, netball, athletics, tennis, gymnastics, dance, cycling proficiency and swimming in a heated outdoor pool set in pretty walled garden. Cross-country a particular strength. All year groups get two trips a term – to places like Stratford-upon-Avon, Oxford's Ashmolean Museum, Warwick Castle and the Roald Dahl Museum. Year 6 pupils have annual expedition to Normandy – French speaking only the minute the coach leaves the school gates.

Nutritious, wholesome lunches cooked on-site and served by friendly dinner ladies who know all the children's names. Extensive salad bar and more choice than before. At breaktime youngsters help themselves to cheese, crispbread, raw vegetables and fruit (they can bring in their own snacks on Fridays – no chocolate, though) before racing off to play outside in all weathers. Carrdus is one of the only schools we know that keeps spare wellies for visitors. Lovely grounds boast four friendly guinea fowl, outdoor tuning bars and lots of hidey-holes. Latest addition is the stunning Diamond Wall, built to celebrate school's 60th anniversary. Names of old pupils and staff inscribed across wall, along with touching plaudits like 'a joy to teach here', 'always a Carrdus girl' and 'Carrdus = happiness'.

Parents are hugely supportive of the school. 'They embrace individuality here,' one mother told us. 'Pupils aren't machined out. The teachers totally bring out the best in each child.' Another parent commented: 'My children are really happy here. It's fun, but competitive when it needs to be.' Very active PTA, with activities ranging from new parents' breakfasts to annual bonfire party, Christmas fair and spring sale. Instead of standing in the car park, parents arriving to collect their children gather in the entrance hall, complete with huge, welcoming sofas and, in winter, a roaring log fire. Twenty years ago, way ahead of its time, the school launched annual At Work day, giving mums and dads the chance to work alongside their children in lessons.

Children have a whale of a time here, while achieving good results along the way. Devoted pupils (boys as well as girls) stay in touch for years after they leave, ringing for advice about everything from university entrance to career choices. 'They come back and back and back,' says the school. 'It's not simply nostalgia. It's all about revisiting a place they enjoyed'.

Caterham School

Harestone Valley Road, Caterham, Surrey CR3 6YA

Pupils: 1,166; 164 boarders • Ages: 3–18 • Sixth form: 304

Fees: Day £5,454 – £17,478; Boarding £31,185 – £32,613 pa

Tel: 01883 343028
Email: admissions@caterhamschool.co.uk
Website: www.caterhamschool.co.uk

Headmaster: Since 2015, Mr Ceri Jones, previously second master at Tonbridge School. Read history at Fitzwilliam College Cambridge and an MEd in educational leadership. He is a former head of history at Caterham and returned after 10 years at Tonbridge. In 2012, in collaboration with The Sutton Trust, Fitzwilliam College and a number of Kent independent schools, he launched an access programme for disadvantaged but academically bright year 9 students at state comprehensives in Kent. In 2013 he was seconded as executive principal to the Marsh Academy in New Romney, which is a state school that Tonbridge School co-sponsors. He is married to Kay Moxon and they have two daughters.

Prep school head: Since 2005, Mr Howard Tuckett MA (Ed) HDE (50s). Born in Epping, but educated in South Africa where he began his career in various prep schools, arriving back in the UK, via a stint in Botswana, in 1995 as deputy head at Kings Hawford Prep School in Worcester. Then headmaster at St Joseph's College Prep School in Ipswich for five years before coming to Caterham. Not the obvious oppo to Julian Thomas (head of Caterham snr school), but in fact they share an educational philosophy and get on well. 'Nice', 'approachable' and 'a lovely man,' say parents, who feel the school has improved since his arrival. Popular with the children, to whom he appears something of a gentle giant. Self-deprecating and not afraid to muck in (was off to the pool with one class after our visit), fits in some teaching, mainly history, where he is said to do 'hilarious impressions of Winston Churchill' and Latin – 'I'm a page ahead of them', he jokes. Married with two children, keen on fishing and gardening, plays guitar and is involved with the church.

Academic matters: Lessons are pacey in the prep; a broad curriculum with plenty of cross-curricular activity. Interactive whiteboards in every room. Strong emphasis on children being heard to read, not just while they are learning, but right up to age 11. 'The school really makes time for everyone,' said one mother. Subject teaching by year 4. Mr Tuckett pleased that he has flexibility here, nothing set in stone, so he may have one year working in three sets and another in four, depending on the particular need. 'Nothing is hide-bound,' he says. 'We don't expect the cohort to adapt to fit our system – we will do what is best for them.' School aims to teach children 'to create their own success', in acknowledgement of the fact that they may grow up to work in industries that don't exist yet.

Now among the UK's top independent schools, outperforming many of its more famous rivals, yet strangely still just under the radar. At GCSE in 2016, nearly 79 per cent A*/A. At A level, one of the top 50 independent schools in the country – 85 per cent A*-B and 57 per cent A*/A.

Maths and science are stand out subjects here (triple science the norm). The biology and physics departments have received a several GSG awards for A level results over the past few years. French, German, Spanish, Latin and Greek offered to GCSE and A level. The school has introduced iPads so that, eventually, each pupil will have their own mobile device. There are 800 computers throughout the school, all networked and with email and internet access.

However, school quick to stress that academic success must not be the pupils' only achievement – watchwords are 'An education for life'. Parents agree that the school gets the best out of all the children – not just the super-academic. Also on the curriculum are study skills such as speed-reading, research techniques, typing, all designed to give students the edge out in the real world. The first independent school to be awarded Thinking School status by Dr Edward de Bono – too detailed to explain here, but it involves planning thinking processes using coloured hats. Children we met understood it perfectly; school offers courses to enlighten confused parents. No plans to introduce IB, but IGCSE offered in English, maths, sciences.

First class teaching team works hard to engender a passion for learning. Parents describe it as dynamic, dedicated and (again) youthful. Lessons are enjoyable and lively, not all chalk and talk. Great head of science, wearing a bright pink overall when we saw him, and pupil guides proudly announced he had new labs designed to his specification. Lots of ongoing staff training and opportunities mean turnover is low. Class sizes in first three years average 20-24, dropping to 15-20 for GCSE teaching and usually eight to 12 for sixth form. All the facilities, resources, bells and whistles you would expect for the money. Oozes prestige.

Not huge call for SEN provision (a handful) but around 90 pupils have learning difficulties and disabilities. A TA for the visually impaired and some one-to-one teaching. A dyslexia specialist is available. Inclusive system of study buddies sees older students passing on their experience to the younger years – anything from straightforward subject help to other issues like time-management. Eighty or so pupils receive EAL support.

Games, options, the arts: All strong, in keeping with school's aims to develop all-rounders. Sparkling achievements on the sports field are just as impressive as the academic results. Priority sports are rugby, hockey, cricket, lacrosse and netball, with many teams winning regional awards, but lots of others on offer, from athletics to taekwondo. Sport is taken seriously but not just for the elite – everyone encouraged to have a go. Prep just as sporty as you would expect – again good preparation for the active senior school – but don't be concerned if your child is usually a less than keen participant. 'There is no such thing as a non-sporty child,' asserts Mr Tuckett, confident he can enthuse anybody. 'They just need to be taught properly.' So children see a lot of the great outdoors – plenty of space and facilities here – and everyone will get match practice: they'll put up a D team if necessary. Such endeavours paying off now, with particular success in football and netball; lacrosse popular too.

Drama has a fairly high profile and is improving. Impressive performance space but no dedicated studio. Music next on list for development. Years 3 and 4 learn the recorder and years 5 and 6 take up guitar – their first lesson is usually Deep Purple's Smoke on the Water, which sorts them out. Up to 30 per cent of senior pupils currently learn a musical instrument (exams can be taken) and plenty of opportunities to perform. But although lots get involved in high standard school and house productions and concerts, only handfuls take music and drama at GCSE and A level. Better take-up of art and design, with pottery, textiles and photography offered.

Both the Duke of Edinburgh Award Scheme and the Combined Cadet Force are thriving – pupils regularly win armed forces scholarships. All told, around 35 clubs and societies, from chess to debating, kit car challenge popular. 'Put us up against any school and we'd win for sheer range of activities on offer.'

Boarding: Boarding facilities recently upgraded. Years 7-9 in good sized, four-bed rooms, thinning out as they rise through the ranks to qualify for single, ensuite accommodation by upper sixth. Ofsted pronounced the boarding offering as 'outstanding' – in fact some university halls may be a come-down. Homely atmosphere – lots of staff live in and build up good relationships with their charges. Growing requirement for flexi-boarding acknowledged and accommodated wherever possible. More space now for rising numbers of weekly boarders. Boarders (100 boys, 64 girls and around a fifth overseas) do really well here where their life is fun, but well-structured. Prep every night under controlled conditions and then checked – boarders get great results. Staff delighted as TVs and computer games gather dust – too much else on offer: loads of sport and special events.

Background and atmosphere: Situated in 200 acres of loveliness in a wooded valley of the North Downs, south of London, just inside the M25. Approach is via a quiet residential road of substantial houses. Main school building is an attractive, Victorian, red-brick building looking out onto its own impressive playing fields, hills beyond. Inside a preponderance of tiling and brick – looks nicer than that might sound. Modern science block and sixth from centre.

Located along the valley past the main school, the prep and pre-prep buildings nestle in sweet seclusion in a natural dead end, making for a peaceful and completely traffic free zone. Share many of the main school's top notch facilities, although prep's own buildings are two former mansion houses, so not so modern and sparkling as others you may see. New woodland outdoor learning centre shared with senior school.

Not the place for a slacker – one mother felt strongly it was all work and no (or not enough) play. Although a two-hour lunch break, it can be fairly chocka with music and games practice and other clubs and activities. Certainly not surprising if pupils have to up their game as popularity of senior school increases. Around 20 children in each class – air of industry around the place as purposeful children get stuck into all on offer. School encourages everyone to get involved with everything. Uniform reflects the active buzz of this place, including sensible and smart anoraks for the outdoor stuff.

All the senior pupils smartly turned out, business suits for sixth formers. A happy, vibrant place, where students are enjoying, rather than enduring, their days. Nice easy atmosphere – always visitors around, parents welcome, teachers used to having their classroom doors opened mid-lesson.

Pastoral care, well-being and discipline: Standards of behaviour are high ('exemplary,' says ISI) and pastoral care is top-notch, based on the principle of mutual respect. Any problems dealt with quick time and would never punish a significant misdemeanour without getting to the root cause – a holistic approach. School conscious that young people get a maelstrom of mixed messages in today's media and can get caught up in a 'cool to be cruel' culture. School sees itself as the counterbalance to that – 'we want to show the pupils that kindness and courtesy matter'. Staff set the tone, aiming to turn out 'nice people that parents and school can be proud of'. Need we add zero-tolerance of bullying, drugs and drink – all non-starters? Minor demeanours dealt with by way of warnings and gating – practical things like litter duty, rising to detention. Suspension and expulsion obviously the end game – but both are rare events. Pupils generally have good relationships with teachers and other staff. School linked to URC, but it's a light touch, no Christian exertion, all welcome.

Pupils and parents: As in the senior school, links between parents and prep school are strong and communications friendly and informative. Lots of opportunities to help, from thriving PTA to running the library. 'I sometimes joke that I've given up my life to this school,' said one busy mother, who evidently wouldn't have it any other way. A boon to working parents is the after-school care – available up until 6pm and including a supervised homework session.

Parents are really supportive of this place – it's not unusual for 500 spectators to support Saturday fixtures. Largely a local school – 70 per cent travel less than five miles to school – but other day pupils from up to 30 miles away (plenty of school buses and good transport links with mainline BR just a 15 minute walk). Boarders from 25 different countries, including UK, but significant numbers from East Asia and Eastern European countries.

Parents from a wide mix of professions and businesses. Successful and productive parents' association has a good time raising significant sums for the school. Old Cats (boys so far, as school only fully co-ed since 1995) include Geraint Jones (organist, conductor); Angus Deayton (television presenter); Sir Alan Moncrieff (first Nuffield professor of child health); Sir Arthur James (Court of Appeal) and recently cricketers Ali Brown, David Sales and James Benning. Old Cats a big feature – turn up at all the events, plays, fixtures, magazine launches, giving the current pupils a real sense of their school's history and traditions.

Entrance: First come, first served at junior level – most pupils join in nursery or reception classes in the order in which they applied, with no formal entry requirements, other than an informal assessment to exclude those with any significant learning or behavioural difficulties. Both nursery and reception are oversubscribed, nursery typically 60 applications for 20 places, then another 20 join at reception (taken from the nursery waiting list). Entry at other years – up until 11+ as the occasional space comes up. At this stage applicants will be assessed during a full day spent as part of a class at the school.

Senior school academically selective, mainly at 11, 13 and 16. Own exam used (English, maths and verbal and numerical reasoning) plus interview and report from current school (common entrance for setting at age 13). For sixth form entry, six GCSEs at grade A (grade B for existing pupils moving up).

No special skills or religious requirements; school has URC affiliation but pupils of many faiths within it. Thirty per cent of intake from state schools (plus 10 per cent to sixth form).

School's main feeder is Caterham Preparatory School, which provides around 40 pupils in year 7. Others are The Hawthorns, Hazelwood, Oakhyrst Grange, St Mary's C of E Junior School, Sevenoaks Preparatory School, New Beacon School and Copthorne School.

Exit: Vast majority of juniors to senior school. Plenty of warning for anyone not expected to make the grade, although apparently 'not many'. However, as senior school gets increasingly popular and academic, it may become more of a struggle for some to make the transition than in the past. Others to eg Woldingham, Lingfield, Notre Dame, Millfield.

Around 10 per cent leave after GCSE, generally because eg drama or art specialists, or for financial reasons. All sixth form leavers to university, 14 to Oxbridge in 2016, most of rest to other top tier destinations. Exeter, Southampton, Birmingham, York and Bath.

Money matters: About a third of pupils receive either scholarships or bursaries. Scholarships and exhibitions awarded at 11 and 13 (academic, art, music, performing arts, sports and all-rounder). At 16 academic, art, music, sport, science and drama are available. Most represent 25 per cent of fees with academic scholarships of up to 50 per cent. Boarding/international scholarships are also available. All 11+ and 13+ day pupil candidates are automatically considered for academic scholarships, but specific application forms are required for other scholarships. The number offered varies each year, but essentially funds are available equivalent to 10 school places.

School also has a bursaries scheme for children of United Reformed Church clergy, for families in the Forces or those on a low income. There is a new, fully funded sixth form bursary named in honour of slavery abolitionist William Wilberforce, who was a friend of the school's founder and a subscriber to the school, giving Caterham 10 guineas a year.

Remarks: A classic independent school – great results, large, leafy grounds, good facilities, strict discipline, polite, charming and well-informed pupils. You can see what you are paying for here. It's on the up and pulling ahead of the pack now.

Chandlings

Linked with Cothill House

Bagley Wood, Kennington, Oxford, Oxfordshire OX1 5ND

Pupils: 425 • Ages: 2-11

Fees: £11,370 – £14,970 pa

Tel: 01865 730771
Email: office@chandlings.org.uk
Website: www.chandlings.org.uk

Head: Since 2015, Mrs Catherine Bufton-Green, previously head of Surbiton High Junior Girls and Boys Prep. After five years teaching in junior and middle schools in Somerset, she moved to Bute House Prep, where she spent five more years before arriving at Surbiton. Outside school she is a keen musician (she plays trumpet) and is also very sporty (played rugby for Wales in her time), enjoying netball and triathlons. Married with two young children, who are at the school.

Entrance: Children may join at any time, providing there are spaces. Nursery (from 2 years), reception (age 4/5) and year 3 most common. Parents put children's names down early. First come first served for the nursery. Reception children have an informal assessment, thereafter it is by competitive assessment. 'We are gently selective,' says school. Behaviour is important too; school is reluctant to take a pupil who would spoil family atmosphere. Neatly positioned just off the A34, pupils travel in from Henley, Newbury and Woodstock, as well as out of Oxford, thereby missing the daily crush.

Exit: Complicated. Chandlings is very much a day school. Chaps aiming for the trad public schools are encouraged either to board at Cothill, or, if they want to stay day, The Dragon is the answer, but alas inevitable if they are destined to the increasing number of schools which pre-examine age 9/10 for entry at 13. Pupils leaving age 11 head into the big Oxfordshire day schools: St Helen and St Katharine, Oxford High, Headington for girls; Magdalen College School, Our Lady's Abingdon and Abingdon for boys. On the boarding front, Wycombe Abbey, St Mary's Ascot and Calne, Cheltenham Ladies', Tudor Hall and Downe House are popular for girls. The Oratory features in the boy rankings. Both to Bloxham, Cokethorpe, d'Overbroeck's, Pangbourne. Goodly number of scholarships won every year.

Remarks: Stunning. A Lewis Carroll of a school; the whole place could have been a film set (apart from work on the pond at the front). We felt like Alice: previous head said she thought she had found the gingerbread house when she first arrived. A country prep school with 'all the facilities of a boarding school in a day school setting,' was her description. And so it is. We consulted our local educational expert, a former don, who lives almost next door. 'Ducky little school', he said, 'deservedly useful and popular'. Ducky, certainly, but little it ain't.

Think Tardis: despite outward appearances, this is not a small school: parallel classes (ie 64 boys and girls) at reception, four parallel classes age 5 and 6. Main complaint from parents is lack of car parking spaces – full during our visit, but there was an international food fair in the new hall – we had jolly good Sri Lankan delicacies. The build-up to the harvest festival was in full swing, plus a newbies' parents/staff coffee morning in the entrance hall. This is a busy, buzzy school; we parked in the bus park. Mad Hatter comes to mind.

This is an expanded and, frankly, not v grand former manor house, set in 60 acres of manicured countryside on the outskirts of Oxford, with woodlands, ponds, ponies; extensive playing fields (cunning double sized goal posts, with picnic tables pour encourager parental support), indoor and kidney shaped outdoor swimming pool (new indoor pool in the offing), as well as a nine hole golf course, ticks all the boxes. Certain amount of not so recent hoo-ha via Mumsnet gives vent to some of the most vicious and irrelevant comments we have read for a long time. This is not North Oxford, 'nor does the school cater for the polo set' (that having been said, some of the polo wives/ groupies leave FWAGS at the starting post: though perhaps not the Kirtlington crew); in reality most of the comments seem to come from the hacked off Yummy Mummy mob (aka the car park mafia).

Founded in 1994, part of the Cothill Educational Trust (CET). Cothill (four miles down the road) is a trad boys' prep with an overflow of 50 13 year old boarders who sleep only in dorms at the top of Chandlings. 'They make no impact on the school.'

Cothill, an early exponent of the French experience, owns a mini château at Sauveterre near Toulouse; charm itself, now much tarted up (with central heating) and available to all in the Cothill empire by rote. CET recently bought the adjacent La Chaumière de Sauveterre where 9 year olds get a short taster, with the option of spending une trimestre en régime Francaise for their last term at Chandlings (age 11, year 6) in the château itself. The whole of year 6 decamps to Picardie for a short 'cultural experience': no doubt with a handful of battlefields thrown in. French proper from age 4: labels in French on everything from nursery up, native speakers from age 2.

Crèche filled with sleeping babies and trained nursery nurses when we visited (five cots); proper nursery from age 2, vouchers ok, 60 max at any one time, operates term time only. Tiny classes, no more than 12 in each, variable sessions, currently 30 pre-school full time. Min two sessions a week, fully flexible: two trained teachers per class, reading from age 3. Safe room for temper tantrums and yoga for all – 'Tatty Bumpkins'. Older children, both boys and girls, help in the nursery – particularly with reading.

School is inclusive with extended support for the challenged at both ends of the spectrum: brace of learning support rooms (no problems with the dys-strata, nor with the milder ADHD, Asperger's stream, epileptics, diabetics, ok Ritalin – full time nurse on site, one profoundly deaf child has one-to-one assistance), qualified staff as you would expect; ed psych's reports: parental consultation all along the way; will say if school can't cope. One-to-one at extra cost. Extended learning on tap for the brightest. EAL, open to all, in the heart of the school. Number of 'real' foreigners (Abingdon is rich in innovative engineering and IT companies); young tend to need less need formal help with transition to a new school and culture than their parents. Osmosis is good. All set for reading, writing and 'rithmetic on entry: five phonics groups (but any other system that works). Spelling Bees. Chandlings prides itself on being 'rigorously academic'.

Fab pre-prep in the heart of the school, complete with sandpits (rather damp during our visit) and splendid ride-on JCBs. Each class room is hosed down at lunch time (to cope with the sand and other essential child inspired detritus). Woodland (as opposed to forest) school, with boys and girls getting to grips with the real world, mock battles if and when needed.

Latin option from age 8/9 or classics and philosophy. Parents get a maths crib before any new addition to the syllabus, maths drop in clinic on Tuesday and Thursday. Specialist teachers from reception for music, ICT, sport, PE, music, ballet, drama et al.

Interactive whiteboards throughout; one formal IT lesson a week, otherwise computers used as a learning tool, with touch-typing for all at 9 (criminal not to be mandatory in all schools). Wonderful doubledecker library. Proper science labs – science teaching focuses on the practical, like building electronic circuits and writing intergalactic postcards. Lower years IB a possibility in the future. New build seems to have been constructed round modules, with carefully delineated play areas for each year group. At no time did we feel we were in a whopping great prep school. Yet it is. Latest Ofsted report enthusiastic.

Huge emphasis on sport: the usual suspects: netball, hockey and rounders for girls; footie, rugby and cricket for chaps, with individual representations all over the shop. Programmed swimming up to age 9, plus snorkelling, lifesaving as well as golf, riding (collection of coated equines: 80 riders a week), short archery, fencing, croquet and myriad of clubs: everything from Spanish through to (organic) gardening and orienteering. Film making popular, music technology, recording, verse and public speaking, Mandarin, puppet making, Inuit throat signing and debating. The list would make many senior schools weep with shame.

Music strong: majority learn a musical instrument ('everything but the pipes'); individual lessons cost extra. Guitar ensemble. Three choirs and choir for all, 'squeaks and all'. Concerts and musicals galore in a new school hall. Wonderful art on display throughout school, plus DT, textiles and pottery. This is a grown up happening school; we found little groups happily reading all over, with formal reading for every child four times a week. Home economics popular, special low cookers and sinks. School food 'wholesome' and organic produce used as much as possible, but not kosher or halal. Vegetarian option throughout, the young have a say in future menus. Three sittings for lunch in the ginormous dining room; member of staff sits at end of each table to reinforce good table manners and chat. Curry was on the menu during our visit: we had serious discussions with a variety of pupils. Did they prefer the strong or the milder curry? Empty plates all round, and at the end of lunch the whole assembly rose to their feet singing 'thank you Father' to the tune of Frère Jacques – with such a strong French influence in the school, we were rather surprised they didn't do it in the round.

Eight am drop off, prep club free till 5.00pm, costs extra till 6.00pm. Parents a mixed bunch: collection of first time buyers plus the ever increasing two-parent earners, one or two trad parents plus more modern combos. All parents belong to PACH, impressive charity fundraising with serious input into Nakuru, a village in Kenya. Six per cent ethnic mix (we thought it might be more). Cothill is a C of E foundation and Chandlings shares their chaplin, but song rather than hymn practice; assemblies are inclusive, school welcomes pupils of all faiths and none. Trips to mosques, synagogues and temples where possible. Other faiths acknowledged.

Pastoral care important here. Children encouraged to be courteous, helpful and responsible, and they are. Pupils have also written their own Chandlings' code of conduct (tenets include caring for others, doing what is right and being a good friend; latest addition, is that children should be courageous). Revamped house system: pupils play snakes and ladders with house points according to achievement or wickedness. Discipline not a problem; child asked to explain poor behaviour and discuss ways to improve it rather than getting a reprimand. 'If you behave, you can stay'. Trips abroad for all (Paris for 8 year olds); skiing – no parents allowed – 8 to 11 year olds only.

Recent increase in numbers, ditto classrooms. This is an active, happy school. As one parent said, 'There is never a day when my children are not happy to go to school'.

Charterhouse

Admissions Office, Godalming, Surrey GU7 2DX

Pupils: 815; 770 full, 30 day boarders • Ages: 13–18 • Sixth form: 430: 276 boys, 154 girls

Fees: Day £30,387; Boarding £36,774 pa

Tel: 01483 291501
Email: admissions@charterhouse.org.uk
Website: www.charterhouse.org.uk

Acting Headmaster: Andrew Turner is holding the fort until a new head is appointed to replace previous head Richard Pleming MA, who took over in January 2014. First a chorister at Canterbury Cathedral, thence to King's School, Canterbury (became captain of school) thereafter to Pembroke, Cambridge where he took a first in English. After a year as marketing officer for Scottish Opera, he spent five at Schroders and 3i. Saw the light (and a massive salary drop) in 1990 and began teaching at St Paul's, London, then at Eton. Housemaster and head of English at St Edward's, Oxford and then head of Wrekin College for two and a half years. Married to Rachel Crowther, a doctor and novelist; they have five children.

We took to him at once. However, others didn't. There was a campaign against him from the outset and things have run less than smoothly since, in some respects. He stood down as head in December 2016 but will stay at the school until the summer 2017, working on 'a number of strategic projects for the governors'. A top job for someone.

Academic matters: Most take either the Cambridge Pre-U or the IB diploma. A levels survive in four subjects, the most popular of which is government & politics. The Pre-U still seen as controversial among parents, who worry unnecessarily that universities are bemused by it. IGCSEs taken in preference to GCSEs in most subjects. But Mr Pleming – who was new to the Pre-U – was a convert and made no plans to change the current arrangements while, as he said, A levels are 'in flux'. Whether his successor agrees, remains to be seen.

The mix of curricula here make judgements about exceptional performance in specific subjects difficult. Maths, history and economics are the stand-outs in terms of sixth form popularity. Art does well and many minority subjects shine. IGCSEs sparkle and demonstrate the value added by good teaching and individual attention. 2016 results saw 76 per cent of IGCSEs A*/A; 92 per cent of Pre-U exams achieved distinction or merit (A*-B equivalent) and 58 per cent distinction (A*/A equivalent). Average IB point score 37. This has to be impressive for a school which requires only 60 per cent at CE.

'Not frighteningly academic if you've come from a pushy London day school,' we were told by one parent, while another said, 'It's far more academically rigorous than we'd expected.' A third felt that, 'A lot of the seriously bright chaps are the international students.' However, 'There's a culture of trying hard and achieving,' another observed. Mr Pleming introduced an 'academic tie' ('It's a rather attractive apple green,' he avered) for under school boys, to match the one for senior school boys and girls. We deeply approve of the first year's geography and history syllabus being largely focused on the rich history of the school. Not here do you meet pupils with no idea of the key figures and moments in the story of their alma mater. Careers provision and university preparation, having been described as 'needing a kick' by several parents, now rapidly improving, and school is building on Old Carthusian networks and willingness to support current leavers.

System of 'Calling Over' – boys get praised for effort or pulled up for lack of it publicly in class four times a term – is controversial. 'It's brutal,' complained one parent while acknowledging that 'it does mean they are doing something if a boy isn't pulling his weight.' Mr Pleming admitted he was uncertain about it at first but then saw it as a useful tool to help monitor progress, and assured us that 'the more difficult conversations are held one-to-one'.

Very few with recognised or serious SEN of any kind. No withdrawal from classes for individual support. 'We subscribe to the idea enshrined in current legislation that all teachers must be teachers of special educational needs. The best person to support a pupil's needs is his or her subject teacher. All teachers receive regular training in supporting pupils' individual needs. We individualise learning as much as we can.'

Games, options, the arts: Everything done with vigour, dedication and enthusiasm. Ben Travers Theatre – opened by the great farceur himself in 1980 (at 93) – now looking a little tired, but still an excellent performing space with a cosy foyer. Lots of productions. Surprisingly small proportion learn an instrument – only 280 of the 800 pupils – but the standard of those who do, and the intensity of participation in multiple performance opportunities of all kinds, is exemplary. Very lively and creative art and DT ('someone made a motorbike') – each sixth form artist has their own space and we admired the flair and scope of work. Super ceramics, collage and painting, especially. Two new 3D printers.

Enormous sports complex with everything you'd expect and used, out of lesson time, by the general public. All-weather pitches, courts, fields and tracks in all directions plus a nine hole golf course. A famous football school – Spurs 'Legend' directs the game – with seven teams in each year and masses of matches for all. Sporting opportunities and achievements here of all kinds and hard to better. 'And if there's something you want to do which they don't offer they will try and set it up for you,' we were told. Also a famous CCF and formidable pioneering expeditions to all kinds of high up and far away places.

Boarding: Old houses and new houses and everyone has an opinion on each and on the system as a whole. The new houses – 'architecturally weird and further away from everything' – are preferred by some as more functional, better resourced and nearer to sports facilities. Eating in the new houses is communal, so 'You can't go down in your pyjamas – such a shame,' thought one parent. Four girls' 'hostels' but they study in the boys' houses until 10pm when they trot demurely home. Boys not allowed anywhere near girls' hostels – ever. Sixth form facilities being extended at time of our visit to add a further 30 or so boarding places.

Girls' hostels felt to be better – all rooms have en-suite bathrooms, are very cosy and their rooms are only for sleeping. Accommodation in the older houses is not up to that offered in many top schools these days. En suites are scarce, some rooms are tiny, though no-one shares a room with more than one other. Arcane systems of swapping rooms and girls changing hostels every term – we won't try to explain here; you need to ask – but all is aimed at integrating people and fostering community.

Background and atmosphere: Lincolnshire man, Thomas Sutton (1532–1611), discovered coal on two estates he had leased near Newcastle-on-Tyne and made his fortune. He endowed a hospital on the site of the London Charterhouse and left a legacy to maintain a chapel, almshouse and school. After much legal wrangling, a foundation was set up to run a home for 80 pensioners (gentlemen by descent and in poverty, soldiers that have borne arms by sea or land, merchants decayed by piracy or shipwreck, or servants in household to the King or Queens Majesty), and to educate 40 boys.

The school moved to its present home in stockbroker-Surrey in 1872. The main school building, a substantial gothic statement of purpose, cannot fail to awe. Its post-WW1 chapel – the largest war memorial in the country – is vast, stark and sombre; no mistaking the genuine horror and grief at the nearly 700 lost Carthusians which inspired it. Many more buildings – some of less obvious architectural merit – have since accrued, some having been opened by impressive visitors eg HM the Queen and – the MFL building – by Javier Perez de Cuellar in 2007. Super library – subdued lighting, comfortable sofas, tables with laptop points and exemplary stock; a library that has been nurtured and loved.

The site has grown to 250 acres with fields and pitches stretching away into the landscape. Trees, little gardens and courtyards humanise it and pathways meander about to give the impression of a sizeable and complex school 'village'. And some people definitely drive too fast down the main thoroughfares!

The advent of sixth form girls into what many still feel is a very male establishment is a source of joy for most. 'The boys love it when the girls arrive,' one seasoned father of boys told us. 'It gives them the best of both worlds.' One sixth form lad told us the only thing that would make the school better would be more girls. Others concur, though stress, 'it takes a certain type of girl – they have to be confident and not stand any nonsense.' Sporty girls go down particularly well, it seems. And, inevitably, 'They do rank us on prettiness so you have to be robust'. School getting better at integrating the girls. A two-day get-to-know-you pre-term event introduced in head's first year has done much.

A Christian school and a school in which this is still overt – for all its inclusiveness. A school with its own argot – yes, teachers are 'beaks' here. Parents comment on that old-fashioned thing, the school 'spirit'. 'There's a strong sense of loyalty. They engender it very quickly. Loyalty to both house and school.' A seriousness about the place reflected in its publications, its sending of expert teachers to support the teaching of individual subjects in local state schools and in the appointment of a likeable 'director of social responsibility'. We like this.

Most weekends, pupils may go home after sports fixtures on Saturday afternoons and return for chapel on Sunday evening. For those pupils who remain in school overnight on Saturday (around 20 per cent), a full programme of weekend activities. This was a Pleming innovation – 'There used to be absolutely nothing to do at weekends,' a sixth former told us. 'Now there's loads.' So not, as some parents fear, a lure to keep boys from going home – though it might work that way with some. Most staff live on site – many in a strange tower, nine floors of a highly eccentric 1970s folly – and all live within a mile of school. Some school officers allowed bikes to get around. We wonder whether this privilege could, without imperiling safety or hierarchy, be extended to others on such a large campus?

Pastoral care, well-being and discipline: Vertical tutor system described as 'brilliant!' – one tutor for two boys from each year. Tutor sees each tutee at least once weekly and parents feel 'My son's tutor is on his side – we can't fault the system'. Very much a school for joiners-in. 'They do their best to make them try out everything. So even lazy boys get really pushed to try things.' Pupils are polite and charming and discipline is good, though parents tell us of the odd drink smuggling escapade. 'It's really not a problem here' though, affirm sixth formers. Junior boys wear tweedy jackets, older boys wear blue blazers and girls seem uniformly to have long hair and short black skirts. No pushing at boundaries to be seen anywhere.

Most housemasters accorded warm praise, though one or two houses described by parents as 'out of control'. School assures us this is being tackled – and we gather there have been several recent changes in the pastoral team. Boarders are 'very well supervised,' in their leisure time and 'the school is very sensible about absences and so on,' assert parents. Matron is especially highly praised. Most teachers described as 'incredibly kind' and as being a good mix of 'nice young ones – sharp-witted and impressive – and safer, older pairs of hands'. 'Kindness' was a word we heard a lot from parents – this being valued highly in the school community as a whole. School seen by almost all as collaborative and encouraging mutual respect between staff and pupils.

Pupils and parents: About 80 per cent from London or the home counties, and currently many go home after Saturday sports at weekends. Vast majority boards and all boarders have to be back for Sunday night chapel. Twenty per cent made up of around 37 nationalities – a few have some EAL support but this is not the norm. Presence of overseas pupils is not new: Charterhouse has a relationship with Hong Kong going back 200 years and has long valued its international reach and reputation. The IB seen as reflecting the school's long-held international perspective. Some sense that being sporty is valued more highly than being arty, and some creative but left-footed types take a while to feel at home.

Immense list of notable Old Carthusians includes poets Richards Crashaw and Lovelace, writers Joseph Addison, Richard Steele, WM Thackeray, Max Beerbohm, Ben Travers, Robert Graves, Simon Raven, Frederick Raphael, publisher John Murray, classicist Henry Liddell, actor-manager Johnston Forbes-Robertson, founder of the scouts, Robert Baden-Powell, cartoonist and wit Osbert Lancaster, composer Ralph Vaughan-Williams, historian Hugh Trevor-Roper, sculptor Anthony Caro, politicos and journalists James Prior, William Rees-Mogg, Dick Taverne, the Dimblebys, Jeremy Hunt, Duncan Carswell, philosopher Don Cupitt, pop impresario Jonathan King, the rock group Genesis, composer Rachel Portman and innumerable venerable ecclesiasts (among them, John Wesley) and redoubtable military men of high renown.

Entrance: Register early. School very popular and lists can close three years before entry, so don't hang about. Year 6 interview and prep school reports – which carry much weight. Houses matter here. Parents and boys visit two or three houses, meet housemaster and staff and boys and have a good poke about. All are interviewed in the first house they visit – a record is kept for other housemasters to see if necessary. Parents then choose their preferred house – but they don't always get it.

For those entering from September 2018, entrance arrangements will change. Candidates will sit the ISEB common pre-test in year 6 at their current school. School assures parents that boys will still be invited for interview and close contact will be maintained with prep schools. Some consternation among parents who wish that the school had 'stuck to its guns'. School insists it will continue to take note of any major discrepancies between the pre-test results and the picture created of an individual by the interview and school report and consult prep heads where necessary. A few places not dependent on pre-testing will remain for late applicants and exceptional cases.

Most are offered conditional places plus places in their first or second choice house. Parents pay an initial deposit to confirm place and are asked whether Charterhouse is their first choice. Boys not offered house places are placed on the general list, as are those who are accepted after general list interviews. They are invited to choose a house after meeting housemasters during the spring of year 8. In the autumn of year 8, preps send updated reports – this can result in some boys being asked to withdraw.

About 125 places in year 9. CE pass mark of 60 per cent expected. They don't over-offer which is refreshing.

At sixth form, 75 girls and 30 boys come, most as boarders and a few as day pupils. Admission by competitive examination, school reports and interview. Offers of places are unconditional but high proportion of GCSE A*s and As are expected. Little choice of houses.

A few places reserved in years 9 and 12 for overseas candidates. Quite diverse admissions systems, depending on where you are from. 'It doesn't suffer from being too fashionable,' one wise parent ventured. 'It is good at choosing the boys who will suit it.'

Exit: Eighteen to Oxbridge in 2016. Large numbers to Bristol, Edinburgh, Durham, Exeter, Manchester, Nottingham, Newcastle, London unis and, increasingly, to prestigious colleges in the US – Chicago, NYU, California, Berkeley. No narrow range of subjects studied but a bent towards economics, politics, business and management perhaps. No silly subjects pursued by anyone.

Money matters: Not a rich school. Most fee assistance now in the form of bursarial help rather than scholarships. Scholarships – whether at 13+ or 16+, exhibitions, academic, art and music scholarships, more for glory than dosh. However, can be topped up by mean-tested bursaries up to the value of full fees in cases of proven need.

Remarks: An all-round impressive school – confident of what it does and doing it well. Pupils genuinely value what they are given here. As one, thoughtfully, expressed it, 'You feel you're part of something that should continue'. Obviously, now experiencing a bump and a hiccup and we await news of new appointment with much interest.

Charters School

Charters Road, Sunningdale, Ascot, Berkshire SL5 9QY

Pupils: 1,617 • Ages: 11–18 • Sixth form: 420

Tel: 01344 624826
Email: charters@chartersschool.org.uk
Website: www.chartersschool.org.uk

Co-Headteachers: Since 2009, Mr Martyn Parker and Mr Richard Pilgrim (50s). Appointed as deputy heads at Charters in 2000, they worked together so well that when the previous head, Dame Marcia Twelftree, retired, they decided to apply for the headship as a team. The result is a highly successful partnership, liked and respected by pupils and parents alike, who describe them as 'involved, approachable, very supportive'.

Richard Pilgrim, who also teaches physics here, has been at Charters 29 years and proudly declares, 'I can honestly say the school has never been as good as it is now.' Married with three teenage children, likes reading and the outdoors and describes himself as 'a lapsed French horn player'. ('He's very talented!' puts in his colleague.) Martyn Parker is married with two grown-up children, and worked briefly in local government before coming into teaching 29 years ago. An English teacher, who also still teaches here, he signed up for a science GCSE last year 'because I realised how much I don't know' and taught himself. ('He got an A!' adds Pilgrim.) A very well-matched couple, who even finish each other's sentences.

Academic matters: Extremely good, and getting better all the time. GCSE and A level results consistently put them in the top 20 per cent of state schools nationally, and that includes the grammars. In 2016, 58 per cent of A level grades were A*/B and 26 per cent A*/A; 78 per cent of pupils got 5+ A*/C grades at GCSE including English and maths and 35 per cent of GCSE grades were A*/A. All the more creditable, given the non-selective intake: children with a reading age of 6 rub shoulders with potential Oxbridge candidates, but, say heads, 'it's really important for us that we cater for all abilities; the school is comprehensive and will remain so.' Curriculum is therefore very broad. Traditional GCSEs and A levels still very popular, but are offered alongside BTecs and NVQs, with the less academic KS4 pupils able to study off-site subjects such as motor vehicle technology and construction. French and Spanish are both taught to years 7-9, and we liked the way that all signage in the school was trilingual. Latin offered to G&T students.

Facilities in all teaching spaces are up to date, with both Macs and PCs available for students to use. Really excellent library and sixth form study area, accessible to students from 8am to 6pm, and guarded by the thoroughly lovely Miss MacDonnell, who, our guides assured us, was the reason that 'it's always this quiet.' Everyone we spoke to lauded the staff as enthusiastic and knowledgeable, with one boy falling over himself to give praise: 'The teachers here are really up for giving everyone and everything a go.' He went on to describe how one of the English teachers, who happened to be a law graduate, was teaching him and his friend GCSE law as an extracurricular, simply because they'd asked if they could do it. Parents confirmed that 'studious children are accepted and congratulated by other children.' A sixth former commented, 'The school doesn't put you in a bubble; they emphasise independent learning here.'

Games, options, the arts: Charters became a sports college in 2002 as part of the specialist schools programme, which entitled it to receive extra funding for sports-specific teaching and facilities, provided this was used to drive the whole school forward. The coalition axed the programme in 2010, but sport remains central to Charters' success and their facilities are excellent: seven tennis courts, full-sized hockey pitch, two Astroturf pitches, and two sports halls including basketball court and weight-training facilities. Every year group has 10 hours of sport per fortnight, and out of 70+ extracurricular activities offered each week, 40+ are sports and dance related. As well as the more traditional football, netball etc, sports such as golf, trampolining and skiiing are all available to do off-site. Although the school scores some impressive successes on track and field, much of what's on offer is intended to be fun rather than competitive, so that all pupils are catered for. It clearly works. As one satisfied parent observed, 'My daughter loves the sports. She's never home from school!' Both heads very positive about the value of sport to education as a whole, adding 'We don't have an obesity problem here!' And we could see, as we walked about, that they really didn't.

Annual drama productions in purpose-built drama studio are popular, and music is strong too, with choirs, orchestras and a broad range of instrumental lessons. Extremely varied programme of trips, both day and residential: the school jointly owns Tirabad Outdoor Educational Centre in rural Wales, and sends parties there throughout the school year. All the pupils waxed lyrical about the good times they'd had at Tirabad, with several calling it the best thing they'd done at Charters. Other destinations have included Spain, the USA, Sri Lanka, Beijing, Rome and Paris. Strong D of E programme, and lots of clubs – science, creative writing, debating, chess, etc.

Background and atmosphere: Established in 1958 as a secondary modern with 400 children, Charters became comprehensive in the 1960s to cope with increased demand and remains committed to comprehensive ideals. Became an academy in 2012, say heads, 'because of the benefits of self-determination. We're less subject to the whims of education.' Since its beginning, the school has occupied the same site in an affluent, leafy suburb of Ascot. The uniform is sensible and unfussy, the modern(ish) buildings clean and businesslike, and there are a number of very pleasant green spaces in which pupils can sit and chat. Highly regarded by locals throughout its history, the school exudes purpose, cordiality and calm. All the students we spoke to said that they'd made plenty of friends here and that it was a very welcoming place. 'The people are open and friendly here'; 'The teachers help you get to know people'; 'My son has had a good time at Charters'; 'My children love all their teachers and find them very approachable,' were typical comments.

Pastoral care, well-being and discipline: Outstanding on many levels. The Maine Centre offers on-site support for any child with medical, social, bereavement or emotional issues and is fully staffed throughout the school week. Any pupil can drop in there with or without an appointment; students praised it as 'fantastic'. The school has also been a centre for physically handicapped pupils since 1981, and is fully equipped with ramps, lifts, etc. It works closely with a nearby autistic school, and provision for its high number of statemented children is excellent. Horizontal tutoring system, with tutors remaining with their charges from year 7 through to year 11 wherever possible. School has been nationally recognised for the leadership opportunities it provides for its students. Incidents of bullying are 'quite rare', according to the pupils, who also said that such occurrences were dealt with 'very well, very quickly and with an iron fist'. 'I've never, ever felt unsafe at this school,' added a year 9 girl. Year 11 prefects are all encouraged to take pastoral responsibility and, say parents, develop into mature and thoughtful young adults. A concern about discipline in their child's tutor group was raised in one quarter, but this appears to be exceptional: sixth formers we spoke to emphatically denied that there had ever been such issues during their time at the school and seemed genuinely shocked to hear otherwise.

Pupils and parents: Very much a product of the locality, with about 87 per cent of students from white British families, but high employment in the area has meant that families from all ethnic backgrounds are moving here in increasing numbers. Very broad social diversity, with deprived Bracknell pupils being bussed in alongside those from advantaged Ascot. Very strong parent support for the school.

Entrance: With 500 applicants for 270 places, the school is heavily over-subscribed. As an academy, Charters is now its own admissions authority, but it buys in admissions admin procedure from local authority and the usual criteria apply: statemented children, proximity, siblings, etc.

Exit: After year 11, up to 40 per cent per cent to local colleges or to employment. The rest continue into the Charters sixth form, where 90-95 per cent go on to a wide range of universities, including Russell Group ones. Several Oxbridge successes each year – four in 2016, plus two medics.

Money matters: Government bursaries available to disadvantaged post-16 students who would otherwise be unable to continue their education.

Remarks: An admirable and humane school, with some of the sparkiest, brightest, most articulate and most delightful students it's been our pleasure to meet. Successfully holds its own against its glossy independent neighbours, and is preferred to same by many parents. If we hadn't lived in Crystal Palace, we would have sent our own children here.

Cheam School

C

Headley, Newbury, Berkshire RG19 8LD

Pupils: 420; 140 flexi boarders • Ages: 3–13 • C of E

Fees: Day £11,415 – £19,965; Boarding £26,985 pa

Tel: 01635 268242
Email: office@cheamschool.co.uk
Website: www.cheamschool.com

Head: Since September 2016, Mr Martin Harris BSc PGCE (40s), prevously head of Sandroyd School. Educated at The Skinners' School and read geography at Loughborough University. Began his teaching career at Ashdown House in East Sussex; after a stint as deputy head at King's School, Rochester, he returned to Ashdown House as deputy head (acting head for one year). A keen sportsman, he plays cricket, golf and tennis. Wife, Catherine, is a chartered physiotherapist. They have two young sons.

Entrance: Non-selective into the nursery and pre-prep. Higher up, the headmaster sees all children for a familiarisation day to ascertain their suitability for entry. This is not just based on academic data but rather an assessment of the whole child, games, musical ability, character etc.

Exit: A main feeder to Marlborough but also regularly sends pupils to St Edward's Oxford plus eg Bradfield, Eton, Radley, Wellington, Sherborne, Downe House, St Mary's Ascot and St Mary's Calne. The transition to mainly boarding public schools appears to be reasonably easy, according to one parent of girls who loved the place so much she returned to work in the bursar's office when her children moved on. However, we were told by others that some boys seem to find it hard moving into a less protected environment.

Remarks: A school for active, busy children. As one parent said, 'it's incredibly beautiful'. Set in 100 acres of glorious countryside, it is the perfect place for sporty, outdoor loving, energetic types to spend their early school days. Anybody who remembers it, as we do, as the rather stuffy, unexciting royal school of the early '90s, would be amazed to walk round it today. One current father, ex-Cheamite, who refused to even look at it until his children went there, is now one of its greatest fans. The focus here is not totally on academia and they get so much more than just lessons. The outcome is a band of happy, confident, well-balanced children who generally get into their chosen school, often with scholarships.

A broad curriculum from the start in preparation for common entrance to top schools. All children setted for maths and French. Scholarship forms for two top years with Greek introduced to the brightest. Young teachers (average age 35 to 40) have easy, relaxed relationship with pupils. Some bachelor staff accommodation in grounds, Cheamville, so fewer geographical restrictions. Small classes, max 18, often fewer. Books regarded as an essential part of their lives. Silent reading, or 'digest', is timetabled in for half an hour after lunch each day and, for boarders, every evening. Weekly general knowledge quiz encourages them to look things up.

Light, bright classrooms with interactive white boards throughout. Good IT, art, science facilities. New art and design centre. Parents say 'music and drama very strong' and they put on 'excellent productions'. One major play or musical each year. Lots of choirs and several orchestras including a jazz band. Most learn an instrument with lessons timetabled differently each week and practice sessions set up for boarders. Anything from beginners to grade 6. Masses of art and photographs on display everywhere. Internal news and information computer screens in main halls. Loads of field trips, expeditions and excursions, home and overseas. These really are privileged children.

Perhaps it's sport that's the most impressive and they all love it. Everything is on offer from football, rugby, tennis, hockey and cricket to polo, judo, fencing and golf on their own course. Games every afternoon with matches on Wednesdays and Saturdays. National polo champions, national cross-country champions and cricket and rounders teams reached the National Jet finals in Oxford. Lots of matches against other schools and overseas cricket and hockey tours. The trophy cabinet is proof of their achievements. Despite this, one parent told us 'even non-sporty children are well catered for. One boy even got a scholarship to the Royal Ballet School'.

A long list of extracurricular activities. There is even a climbing place called Cheam Tops in the grounds. Indoor sports hall ingeniously provides courts for different games as well as all necessary gymnastic equipment and great changing rooms. Everything has been well thought out. Only parental complaint: 'Why do they have to be sexist? Why can't girls play football?'

Excellent pastoral care and learning support where needed. This will be one or two sessions a week with a specialist teacher on a rotating basis if in lesson time. About 10 per cent have processing problems, there is the occasional statement but nothing seriously major. Gap year students help with games when needed. Gentle counsellor is always there to listen. Believes very much in the importance of building self-esteem, which she feels is definitely one of the school's assets. Specialist EFL help given, often one-to-one in class. Believe it's absolutely essential to keep parents involved. 'Our children do not have difficulties, they have differences'. G&T register currently being reformed. PSHE is strong, each child has a tutor and anything verging on bullying (probably not the right word) is quickly and sensitively dealt with. 'We want everyone to be happy'. Timetables rigorously watched, so the whereabouts of any child at any time is always known.

Parents have nothing but praise. 'A very happy school', 'sussed out our daughter very fast and gave us excellent advice on her next school', 'children are easy-going, sensitive and supportive of each other', 'very good at involving parents', 'the kids have such fun'. One even told us, 'we brought our children over from South Africa where they were a good year behind academically and the system was totally different. Nevertheless, our 11-year-old was quickly assimilated into the system, booked himself into boarding after one term and achieved an all-rounder scholarship to Radley'. A happy parent indeed.

Boarding is either weekly or flexi. Children can do just two nights a week if they like. We were assured that this is not at all unsettling and that they seem to love it, opting in and out as and when. The majority of the top year weekly board in preparation for their next school. They go home after games on Saturday afternoon and return in time for lessons on Monday morning. Most come from within a 15 mile radius of the school although there is a largish London contingent. Dorms are upstairs in the main building, boys on one floor and girls on another. Homely, welcoming rooms with a variety of duvet covers and lots of teddies. Always one or two older pupils in with the younger ones. Smart modern bathrooms, not at all as we used to know them. Great pile of bags on the landings waiting to be collected by flexis at the end of the day. Recent 'outstanding' boarding certificate from Ofsted. We asked a pupil what she felt about weekly boarding. She replied, 'I love it. It's so great to be at home with my brothers on Sundays and to see my horse but it's also good to be at school with my friends'. Bedtime routine pretty regimented with time for reading and talking before lights out but after that, silence reigns.

Quite a large amount of charitable stuff going on. Support for a school in Zambia, a rural school in Johannesburg, the Red Cross children's hospital in Cape Town and the children's wards in the Royal Hampshire Hospital. Hands-on partnership with local primary schools who can apply for funding and use their facilities for free. Some scholarships and bursaries and a fund for suddenly needy children.

Perhaps the oldest prep school in the country, with its origins in the 17th century, there is an interesting archive room containing mementos of past headmasters and pupils. Apart from HRH the Duke of Edinburgh and HRH the Prince of Wales, William Pitt the Younger, Lord Randolph Churchill, Ivo Bligh, 8th Earl of Darnley and Jake Meyer also spent their formative years at Cheam.

A school full of happy, open, confident, polite, exceptionally busy children who are used to living to a rigid timetable and to keeping their shoes done up and their shirts tucked in. One slightly wonders how they will manage to cope with the rebellious, disorganised world outside.

Chelmsford County High School for Girls

Broomfield Road, Chelmsford, Essex CM1 1RW

Pupils: 893 • Ages: 11–18 • Sixth form: 233

Tel: 01245 352592
Email: office@cchs.essex.sch.uk
Website: www.cchs.co.uk

Headteacher: Since 2007, Mrs Nicole Chapman (50s). Brought up in Burgundy, France, but says she feels 'like a local girl', having relocated to Essex soon after gaining her licence ès lettres (BA honours equivalent) in English with Spanish and French at university in Tours. Further qualifications gained since her time the UK include PGCE, NPQH and MBA (Leicester). She has a son and two stepchildren and joined CCHS after six years as head of a girls' grammar school in Gravesend, Kent – prior to which, she worked at a mixture of challenging and high-achieving grant maintained and foundation schools – both mixed and girls'.

Perspicacious, dedicated and single-minded, she is certainly a safe pair of hands for Chelmsford's stellar girls' grammar and is revered for her tough stance on standards ('Girls here are delightful, but they will take advantage if you let them'), inspiring them to greatness ('Being the leaders of tomorrow is something of a mantra here.') She tirelessly scours the state's coffers to make sure that her super-bright girls have access to the best possible facilities and resources, and has a long wish list for what she wants next (a new sports hall is at the top). Doesn't teach – 'I did do it one year, but my job is so big and I only have a small senior leadership team,' she explains. 'Plus it's not fair on the girls to teach without being entirely committed to all that goes with a teaching role.' But girls say she is a visible presence – taking assemblies, observing lessons and inviting selected girls to join her for drinks and biscuits to congratulate them on hard work. Parents describe her as '101 per cent committed,' 'exacting' and 'driven,' although some feel she could relax slightly with the girls over more pedantic matters, such as make-up. That said, she has been praised for bringing in a more relaxed uniform in suffragette colours.

Keeps fit through tennis, and loves reading and theatre, along with holidaying in France, where she has a house. Lives in Brentwood.

Academic matters: A real star of the league tables, twinkling brightly among the UK's top 10 state girls' schools – and outshining all but the most hefty-fee-ed of the public schools. 'We benchmark our practice with the 19 girls' grammars around the country with similar intake to ours – and this year we came fifth,' says the head. Indeed, the academic achievement is famously sky high, with 11 A*s at GCSE common and regular achievers of four As at A level. In 2016, 89 per cent A*/A grades at GCSE. At A level, 85 per cent of grades were A*/B and 56 per cent A*/A. Results strong across the board, with no one subject area standing out.

Students praise the high quality teaching – all of which is done by subject specialists, who are passionate about their subject, as well as being acutely aware of how girls learn. 'There is no didactic approach to teaching here – it's a real mixture of styles including interactive, more formal presentations and encouraging independent learning,' says the head, who herself recruited the vast majority of teaching staff. 'It's very much my school, in that way,' she says. Teachers are as accessible outside lessons as in them, say students, offering workshops for those who run into difficulties, as well as 'access lessons' for sixth formers who struggle in any one area of a subject. Targets for girls are minutely detailed, so there's no slipping through nets, and girls also cite the single-sex environment as a factor in their willingness to throw themselves into the more traditionally male technological pursuits, without fear of opprobrium. 'The only thing I'd say is that there's too much homework,' one student told us, while another said 'I do feel the tests are too close together.'

No setting – 'there's no point with a range of ability so narrow,' says the head. Languages are taken seriously, with a fabulous new foreign languages block, complete with cutting-edge language lab, a great source of pride for the girls. 'It's pretty incredible, isn't it?' smiled one. French and German compulsory from years 7 to 9, with girls then picking up Latin from years 8-9. Spanish is an option from year 10 – and Mandarin is offered as an after-school option from year 9. Italian and Russian available in sixth-form. All girls have to take at least one language for GCSE, plus English, Maths, three sciences, a humanity and a creative 'to give their academic studies balance,' says the head.

Very small number of SEN – only eight when we visited, all of whom are supported in the classroom for their mild to moderate needs. 'Staff are aware of their needs and use specific strategies,' says head. 'The public profile of the school is quite scary, so we weren't sure it would be right for our daughter – but actually they've been amazing, with every teacher in completely in tune with her needs and the smallness of the school meaning that she never feels lost,' said one parent of a child with SEN. Wheelchair access throughout, although no students with mobility issues when we visited.

Twenty-three A levels on offer – mainly traditional, but with a few more unusual ones, including philosophy and classical civilisation. IB introduced in 2009, but low take-up and reduction in Government funding means they're phasing it out. 'I'm disappointed,' admits the head. 'I understand the reasons – it's perceived as harder than A levels and students are put off having to carry on with subjects they want to give up. But I see carrying these on as a good thing. If you want to be a scientist, you need to know how to make speeches. If you want to be a lawyer, you have to understand science as you never know what you'll come up against. The girls who did the IB thrived, but we can't continue it with such low numbers.' It's not all doom and gloom, though – it's changed the way CCHS teach, claims the head, with sixth-formers now increasingly challenged to question what they're learning, with no danger of any girl being spoon-fed.

Games, options, the arts: Despite the academically-biased two-week timetable, less bookish pursuits are also encouraged at CCHS, with a cross-curricular enrichment day every half term seeing students off timetable, working on an extended project or activity, often off site. Examples include year 7s teambuilding at Mersea Island; year 8s being shown how an enigma machine works at Bletchley Park (an old girl worked there during WW2); a Holocaust survivor giving a talk to year 11s; and year 10s visiting Cambridge.

The list of lunchtime and after-school clubs is long and well taken-up – every department makes a contribution. French film club, football, netball, musical theatre, hockey, cross-country, netball, junior choir, history society, henna club and debating (particularly big here) are just a fraction. Student-led societies for future doctors, lawyers and the like are also evident. Lunchtime is nearly an hour so plenty of time for a 30-40 minute activity and then food, though girls often combine to save time. 'If you want to join a club that's not aimed at your year group, they'll still let you come if they think you're committed,' one girl told us.

PE is compulsory all the way to the top – years 7-11s have two one-hour lessons a week and sixth formers do sports for one afternoon a fortnight, either in or outside the school grounds. At least one sporty club every lunchtime and every day after school including gymnastics, fencing, table tennis and trampolining, alongside the team games. Tennis, netball, hockey and athletics are particular strengths – collects trophies from national and district competitions, and many do less traditionally girly options including tag rugby, cricket and football. 'We get a lot of individual successes too – one girl recently reached international level in taekwondo, and another in pentathlon,' says head. All-weather hockey pitch and playing fields, plus refurbished swimming pool, although everyone agrees there's a desperate need for a sports hall. 'The gym was built for a school of 450 girls and we now have twice as many – we've got the plans all passed to turn into a learning resource centre and build the new sports hall – now all we need is the money,' says the head.

A quarter of the school learns a musical instrument – the orchestras, choirs and ensembles are of a frighteningly high standard, with girls regularly reaching finals of competitions such as Music for Youth. A welcoming music block – packed with instruments galore (from drums to glockenspiel) – is home to two large classrooms, practice rooms and recording studio. 'At Christmas, all the year 8s recorded a version of Do They Know it's Christmas?' our guides told us, with great excitement. The performing arts block is a real asset with a large drama space – we saw girls doing mesmerising solo performances to their peers in here. Annual whole school performances alternate between more serious literary productions and fun musicals, such as Jesus Christ Superstar. 'You audition for the main parts, but anyone can be in the chorus,' a student explained. Art is also pursued with enthusiasm and amazing talent, with some gifted paintings on show throughout the school – although the two art rooms don't provide the space the girls really need.

CCF is available – run by King Edward VI Grammar School down the road, although we were surprised the two schools don't team up over more school activities (there is a disco, but apparently the girls tend to dance, while boys stand on the other side sipping coke). Long and commendable tradition of community service, with almost all sixth formers involved and girls forming strong bonds with local special schools and retirement homes, often giving up their free time to continue beyond the prescribed sessions. Links with a school in Uganda, which a group of sixth formers visits every two years to do building work and teach classes. Other regular trips and visits include Latin students to Bath, geography students to Wales, plus French, German and Italian exchanges, just to name a few.

Background and atmosphere: A traditional red-brick Edwardian grammar school on one of the main roads into the county town of Essex, which will bring back memories for any grammar school girl of the last century. Opened in 1907, it has remained largely unchanged since, save for some tacked-on additions and the impressive music centre, languages centre and performing arts block. Sixth formers have their own house – including a very pink common room downstairs, and quiet study area upstairs. A café has been set up to encourage girls to eat food cooked on site, and the school serves decent enough food – we enjoyed a lovely roast – although students told us 'the eating area is too small and can get a bit squashed.'

The atmosphere is, as you might expect, ordered, focused and disciplined, but it's also lively, uplifting and supportive – lots of smiles and laughter in lessons and at lunchtime when we visited, there was a great raucous in the main hall as the girls performed dances for the annual house karaoke competitions. 'We make sure girls get lots of opportunities to let their hair down,' explains the head.

Not a school for girls who can't keep up with a fast pace of learning – although students insist all personalities fit in, including the very shy. 'I remember one particular girl who wouldn't say boo to a goose when she started here – she went onto be a medic at Cambridge and is a great public speaker now. And that's the thing here – it doesn't matter if you arrive without confidence because that's the bit we will transform,' says head. Debating clubs, Model UN and an internal programme called 'Find Your Voice' all help. 'It's gradual – you start by being encouraged to speak out in class, building right up to giving assemblies in front of whole school,' explained one student.

Pastoral care, well-being and discipline: In a close-knit community of fewer than 900 girls – who feel extremely grateful to be here – discipline is hardly an issue. 'Very rarely do I have to be stern – girls here are trained to be very well-behaved, caring and respectful, although I'm tough when I need to be,' says the head. Girls showed us the green cards they have to carry about – with black marks given for infringements such as chewing gum or wearing too much make up. Three infringements equals an after-school detention, but not many get them. 'They're held once a week, and the maximum we get is half a dozen,' says the head.

Stress, however, is an issue for some. 'It's not necessarily the school. Many of the parents have very high expectations, as do the girls themselves – and there will be times when they find it all too much,' says the head. No wonder the pastoral programme has been heavily invested in during the last decade, with the girls we spoke to knowing what teachers they can turn to for support, and there's a visiting counsellor and nurse too. Peer mentoring has been trialled, but isn't really taken up. Head also points to their growing emphasis on close monitoring, confidence-building and occasionally making adjustments to individual curricula. 'We have to make sure that the girls enjoy being here and do well. They need to cope with being among very bright girls, so we sometimes have to work hard to build self-esteem,' says the head.

Unusually, both the head and the girls are adamant that bullying is not an issue. 'The girls are very supportive of each other, with new sixth formers often commenting on the lack of unkindness in this school. Of course some girls are nicer than others, but we watch them carefully and intervene where necessary,' says the head. 'Very occasionally, a girl has posted something not very nice on Instagram, but we stamp anything like that out very quickly, taking the approach of "How would you feel?"'

Pupils and parents: Hard working and very able girls come from supportive homes – although 'supportive' is perhaps too soft a word for some of the most demanding parents. 'Sometimes at a parents evening, you'll hear these parents saying, "But shouldn't my daughter be doing more work at home?" to which the teachers respond, "No! They do enough. Let them have some downtime,' one parent told us.

Around half the girls are white British. The next most dominant ethnicity is Indian, while the remainder are a real mix. The school is crystal clear on the characteristics the girls should leave the school with – articulate, principled, knowledgeable, enquiring, resilient, reflective and creative – and girls are encouraged to look for opportunities in areas where they are weaker. We'd say these descriptions are pretty fitting for the girls we met.

Entrance: Admission is no longer by the CSSE 11+ exam, but instead by tests 'designed to measure comprehension, vocabulary, verbal reasoning, non-verbal reasoning and numerical reasoning skills', prepared by Durham University's Centre for Evaluation and Monitoring, and intended to be tutor-proof (no practice papers available, although there is a familiarisation paper on the school website). 'I adamantly disagree with tutoring,' says the head. 'If you're tutored to pass a test, you may well pass it – but you won't have the depth of understanding to get on in the school, and that makes for a miserable life.'

Tests held in September, with initial results in October. Places are offered through the local authority on national offer day in March to the 150 girls who have performed best in the selection tests and not been offered a place at a higher preference school. A waiting list stays open all year. Occasional vacancies further up the school are filled by inviting all girls on the waiting list to sit a test ('to see where they are in their foundation subjects,' says the head).

The result of all this is that more girls come in from the state sector (there are now less than a quarter from preps – much lower than previously), as well as from more deprived areas of Essex – and the ability range has also gone up. 'All this is as it should be – grammar schools exist to provide an education for the very brightest, whatever their background,' says the head.

Another new admission rule is that 80 per cent of the year 7 intake must now live within 12.5 miles of the school (which takes you up to the M11 and down to the M25). The remaining 20 per cent can come from anywhere. 'We were finding that some girls were travelling up to three hours a day and this was having an impact on extracurricular life, with many rushing out of school for the coach. We've now seen a marked difference, particularly with music, sport and school productions,' she says. In fact, so strongly does she feel about the travelling aspect that parents whose daughters get offered a place can also expect a letter asking them to think very carefully about it over the next seven years. 'It's a killer to have to spend hours a day travelling at 11-years-old.'

Vacancies in the sixth form – of which there are always 30, plus extra to replace any girls that leave after their GCSEs – are readily filled. These girls need an average score of 6.4 in their best eight GCSEs (see school website for details on how to work this out), and at least an A in the subjects they want to study at A level (except in humanities, where you can get away with a B).

Exit: Generally, around a dozen girls are tempted away after GCSEs by mixed sixth forms (although that number became uncharacteristically higher when the IB was brought in – head expects it to drop again, now that the IB is being phased out). 'We do advise against girls leaving for this reason, however, as anecdotally we know that the time it takes to adapt to the new environment doesn't do anything to help with their final results,' she says.

Vast majority go on to higher education. In 2016, 15 to Oxbridge, plus 24 medics or medical-related course. Nottingham, Southampton, Durham, Exeter, Bristol, Warwick and London unis also popular. A wide range of subjects are studied, with popular ones including languages, sciences, engineering, economics and business.

Old girls worthy of particular note include the United Nations' first woman under-secretary general, the late Dame Margaret Anstee, Dragons' Den dragon Rachel Elnaugh, sculptor Catharni Stern, Bletchley Park's Mary Kenyon and BBC correspondent Emma-Jane Kirby.

Remarks: An intellectually stimulating environment that gives a flying start to the brightest of girls. There's room to let your hair down, which seems to lead to few instances of teenage rebellion – certainly within the school gates – but there can be pressure, meaning it's not for the faint-hearted.

The Cherwell School

Marston Ferry Road, Oxford, Oxfordshire OX2 7EE

Pupils: 1,858 • Ages: 11–18 • Sixth form: 515

Tel: 01865 558719
Email: head@cherwell.oxon.sch.uk
Website: www.cherwell.oxon.sch.uk

Head: Since September 2016, Chris Price. Appointed as an NQT in 1992, he is a rare example of someone who has progressed through to headship from within. Formerly deputy headteacher and head of school, he is married, with three children at state schools locally. He is a former captain of Oxford Harlequins Rugby Club.

Academic matters: Cherwell has maintained its place as one of the best state secondary schools in the county, oversubscribed and building on its impressive sixth form reputation. It offers a breadth of subjects at GCSE, both academic and practical, from dance to product design. The science specialist status attracts large numbers who pursue physics and further maths in sixth form. History and English are popular and all take citizenship at GCSE. German or Spanish and French are supplemented by trips abroad. Maths is set in year 7, but other subjects are mixed ability. In 2016, 71 per cent got 5+ A*-C grades, including English and maths. Post-GCSE there is an extremely wide selection of A level and vocational courses, including health and social care, science in society and BTecs in sports and engineering plus EPQ. A*-B pass rate has risen over last few years to 65 per cent (37 per cent A*/A) in 2016. As the head says, 'You can't come here and be bored'.

Nearly 75 per cent of students go on to sixth form, the other places being eagerly taken up by locals from nearby maintained and independent schools. Strong results and Oxbridge places as well as interesting subject range attract fierce competition for places.

Very inclusive school: dynamic learning support department manages fluctuating numbers on SEN register, can be as many as 300. Two resource bases run within the school: hearing impairment and communication and interaction, which are filled from county-wide referrals, with over 20 specialist teachers and clinicians. Hearing-impaired students attend mainstream classes, some in sound-proofed classrooms, with additional support, such as laptops, to access curriculum. Resource bases integrate children into mainstream where possible so the students are 'very used to children dropping in and out of their classes'. In addition, The Base provides specialist support for students with behavioural difficulties and 'fragile' students at specific times, although not on a permanent basis. Vulnerable students have access to behaviour management professionals and counselling, as well as a range of activities and courses. Bases are valued by all, which 'enhances the inclusive nature of the school'. Empathy and support for peers are qualities specified in The Cherwell Code, displayed round the school. Students with identified needs are visited at primary schools and benefit from a programme of transition into the secondary site, above and beyond the taster day for prospective year 7s. Word on the street, however, is critical of the level of dyslexia support within the school. The 23 per cent of accelerated learners have access to their own gifted and talented officer.

Games, options, the arts: The school spreads over two sites, each with access to games fields, netball and basketball areas and tennis courts, as well as three gyms between them. In addition, the local Ferry sports centre and rugby club are a stone's throw away, resulting in strong rugby teams for both men and women, football and indoor racquet sports. Under 15s are national basketball champions. Parent grumbles that the school has a 'chip on shoulderish' attitude to cricket, given that there are so many pitches and teams to play with locally. Wheels are the thing here, however. The school boasts first place in the 'cycling to school' league, with an advisor on hand to new entrants to advise on bike routes. The lively Cycle Club enjoys links with national cycle associations, and offers bike polo, grasstrack and BMX training, as well as bike maintenance courses open to the whole school. Not surprising to find a professional skateboarder among the alumnae. Sadly, with a pool next door, the school has not the funds to offer swimming lessons, which is a shortcoming in a city sited on a river.

Art, music and drama are taken by all year 7s, and offered as choices at GCSE and beyond. Extracurricular music is popular, with a choice of gospel choir, chamber choir and a guys-only barbershop for singers, several bands and a full orchestra which performs impressively in local churches. One year 12 boy recently conducted the orchestra in his own trumpet arrangement. Scratched corridors are livened up with exciting art work (a tea-bag evening gown greets you in reception) and artwork spreads out over the ground, literally, with a pavement drawing project. The younger years take advantage of Oxford's rich museum, gallery and library treasures, while older years also visit London exhibitions as part of the GCSE or BTec courses. The Chicken Project combines business studies with a charity fundraising venture bringing agriculture to a South African village; proceeds go towards education. This was also embraced by the science department, which hosted a cross-curriculum research study into chickens' colour preferences. After-school clubs are popular, to inspire the students in anything from rowing to chess (old boy is an International Chess Master).

Background and atmosphere: Outshone by the architectural beauty of nearby independents, this is a diamond in the rough school. An organic collection of modern buildings, some dating from 1963, when the school was founded, make up the North Side (years 10-13) while a more homogeneous building for the younger years sits across a busy road, connected by a frescoed tunnel. Wide fields and the meadows of Marston surround the students, and direct access to a long bicycle boulevard protects them from the traffic. Once you have located the main entrance in the smart sixth form block, the welcome is warm and genuine.

What started out in the 60s as a small secondary modern is now an academy and a leader in the Oxfordshire partnerships drive, with an active programme to share expertise with local secondary schools and raise standards in primary ones.

Pastoral care, well-being and discipline: Discipline, in particular absenteeism, has seen the greatest change. There is now a clear rewards policy familiar to all students, which has been effective in reducing exclusions and keeping standards of behaviour high. All the students we met seemed motivated by the Amazon vouchers they earn for success, academic and non-academic; and happily none seemed to have had experience at the other end of the scale: solely problems with equipment and lateness. Parents of students joining at sixth form reported a 'sink or swim' culture, which teaches students to 'run their life a bit'. Those that can, do well; those that can't are now monitored closely by a full-time inclusion and attendance officer. Recent change to written reports system means they are sent home rather than entrusted to the students. Each year group has both a teaching and non-teaching head, for day-to-day worries, as well as a mentor system using teachers and people from local community; the head sees individual cases himself. Bilingual buddies are assigned to new starters from overseas who have language support needs, and peer monitoring is also used. As one parent said, 'It is very good if your children are keen and get on with it; if you are easily distracted, you're distracted'.

Pupils and parents: Around the school, you hear the healthy hum of discussion, as students move between the sites and nearby Summertown shops, where the older ones hang out at lunch. Others use the popular canteen or take advantage of the multi-gym. Students span a wide range of social, academic and socio-economic backgrounds, with above average numbers of English as second language speakers. Catchment families range from university members, medics and white-collar professionals to Oxford's more vulnerable families; but all benefit from the active parents' groups raising money both for school building projects and charity. The United Nations feel is reinforced by the lack of uniform. There is a three Bs rule for girls (decent covering of body parts beginning with B) and a 'no low slung pants' rule for boys, but otherwise anything goes. The by-product of this informality, according to the school, is a strengthening of staff/student relations. Interchanges we overheard were spirited and challenging but this side of respectful. Famous alumnae include Rachel Seiffert (writer); Tom Poster (winner of BBC Young Keyboard Musician of the Year) and Yasmin le Bon (model).

Entrance: Oversubscribed from a dozen or so local primaries within Oxfordshire LA, except for the two resource bases which take students with statements/EHC plans and by referral. Sixth form causes a stir in the local community by attracting students from excellent independent schools, persuaded by wider range of options, perhaps funkier than they have been used to as well as greater independence. One parent remarked, 'They get more of a taste here for what is to come at university'.

Exit: Some 60 per cent move up to the sixth form. Fourteen to Oxbridge and eight medics in 2016. Dazzling range of subjects taken at university, reflecting vibrant mix of sixth form, but science subjects are popular, as well as history and maths. Careers counselling starts early and guidance to popular vocational courses; a few go directly to employment.

Money matters: School welcomed the recent academy status as 'protection from the difficult financial climate', though this protection is unlikely to last. Large sums raised by PTA, when needed, including helping to fund a library in SE Asia by taking advantage of school's links with the Bodleian.

Remarks: The Cherwell fulfils its slogan, 'A Centre for Opportunity', a contender in the competition for Oxford's brightest children. It offers an exciting range of subjects and activities geared to the real world; a lively melting pot of students who span the social spectrum and staff who know how to get the most out of this diversity. The result is articulate and worldly leavers, many of whom achieve good results. Those who can't ignore disruption do less well.

Chesham Grammar School

White Hill, Chesham, Buckinghamshire HP5 1BA

Pupils: 1,260 • Ages: 11–18 • Sixth form: 390

Tel: 01494 782854
Email: office@cheshamgrammar.org
Website: www.cheshamgrammar.org

Head: Since 2015 Miss Annmarie McNaney (50) BA PGCE. Educated in Coventry and at the University of Bristol where she read theology and sociology. Having sworn never to follow her mother's footsteps into teaching, she nonetheless stayed in Bristol to do a PGCE 'just to fall back on.' Bitten hard by the bug the first time she stepped into a classroom and turned down graduate traineeships with the NHS and M&S to take up first teaching post at Backwell School – 'a fantastic place to cut my teeth' – where she was promoted to assistant head of sixth form. Joined CGS 20 years ago to the day we visited, as head of sixth form – a job she planned to do 'for five years'. Promotion to assistant head and then deputy head within the school followed, with the 'do or die' moment for her coming in 2015 when she decided to apply for headship to fill the gargantuan shoes of local superhead Philip Wayne, now at RGSHW. Part of team that moved the school from a satisfactory Ofsted rating in 2005, via good in 2009 to outstanding in 2014. 'Expectations weren't high enough – but we could all see the potential'.

What next? 'Outstanding doesn't mean perfect,' she says. 'Now we need to move the school from outstanding to exceptional – it's not just about ticking Ofsted boxes'. Down to earth and popular with pupils and parents (her window ledge is stacked with thank you cards from departing year 13s – one of whom writes she hopes to send her children to CGS), still teaches critical thinking to year 7 and A level sociology – says 'I'll always be a teacher first'.

Lives in Berkhamsted with husband and two sons, one at CGS ('I'm constantly asking myself how I perceive things as a parent, not just as head,' she says) and the other at a local prep. Loves France and watching her boys play sport.

Academic matters: With many parents considering CGS in the fortunate position of being in catchment for more than one grammar school, competition's stiff on the academic front and with its tech college past, school has had to work hard to shake off its 'also ran' status. What's crystal clear, though, is while others ride high on the power and heritage of their brand, complacency is not a word in Chesham's vocabulary and it's steadily inching up the academic league tables, sitting comfortably now within the top 100 state schools. 'Once upon a time the school was happy with 44 per cent of GCSEs at A or A*,' says head, 'but now we want the main point of difference between us and our competitors to be whether parents want single sex or co-ed'.

And, thanks to a shift in focus 'from teaching to learning', things are moving forward apace, with 61 per cent of GCSEs graded A*/A in 2016. History, geography, English and maths top performers with social sciences doing 'fantastically well' at A level. Similarly solid A level results: 6

A*/A grades. 46 per cent A*/A and 76 per cent A*/B in 2016. Ten GCSEs the norm, with majority taking four AS levels and three to A2, plus around 30 pupils taking the EPQ.

Broad curriculum with focus on a mix of traditional subjects (hoorah for the recent reintroduction of Latin) plus others including photography, politics, sociology and psychology at A level plus, unusually, economics at GCSE as well as at A level. All take French and Latin in year 7 plus either German or Spanish in year 8, with pupils allowed to state a preference for which they would prefer. Setting in year 8 for maths only. Triple science for all but a few at GCSE. The onerously named 'more able and talented programme', which uses pupil data and teacher recommendation to identify potential superstars, aims to provide activities to benefit not just the top few but the whole cohort. Initiatives run across all year groups, from aspiration days where former pupils share careers advice with year 7s, to Elevate sessions – six hours of training on exam preparation and technique delivered by external speakers over the course of years 12 and 13.

Superb SENCo supports pupils needing additional help – currently seven statemented children and approximately 100 on SEN register, mainly due to dyslexia or processing issues. Also equipped to work with children with ASD and because of the broadly flat site, school's a feasible option for pupils with physical disabilities. Aim is to keep pupils in the classroom, but one-to-one and small group work provided when necessary.

Games, options, the arts: It's rugby, football and cricket for boys and girls luck out with the same three on their sporting curriculum, plus rounders and netball, with games compulsory to year 12. There are also options for basketball, athletics, lacrosse and tennis plus zumba, which takes place at the community leisure centre that conveniently opens onto school grounds, providing school with its gym and sports hall facility. Sport for all ethos seems genuine – our guide assured us that sports staff were 'very inclusive' and that trials for teams took place each term – no shoo-ins. Limited fixtures, although school puts out A and B teams for most matches and a C team wherever possible: 'you're more likely to get a match if you turn up to training religiously than if you're talented but not committed', pupils told us. Parents too seemed satisfied that their keen but average sportsmen and women were getting a fair bite of the cherry when it came to turning out for the school. Several elite athletes also pursue their sports as extracurriculars (currently fencing, shooting and swimming to name a few) and are supported wherever possible with time off etc allowed by school. Sports staff highly focused on excellence and there's plenty of silverware in the school trophy cabinet to prove it, despite the fact that there are fewer pupils to make up teams due to co-ed factor. Most recently year 9 were district basketball winners; year 10 smashed the County Cup basketball finals to a degree where they stopped keeping score; the U13 girls' footie team won the county championships and school has held the Chiltern District Athletics Championships title since 2012.

Music reported by parents to be 'amazing' with performances aplenty (major productions Easter and Christmas), plus chances for everyone to get involved with a general choir and 'men's choir' (we assume for tenors), orchestra and house performing arts, encompassing drama, choir, solo performances and musical theatre. Perhaps not the broad spread of groups and ensembles found in some schools but we are told that the standard is 'exceptional'. Sixth form produces an all-school annual play, most recently The Tempest, run with parallel casts to increase the options for participation. Drama on curriculum in years 7 to 9, taught in a superb and very well-equipped studio space.

Fabulous art department run by 'inspirational' departmental head according to our guide. We were blown away by the standard of A level work on show in the art mezzanine – and, although there's plenty of IT in evidence around the school, the good old DT labs still survive in their original form: saws and lathes aplenty and home to subjects including food technology, engineering, textiles, electronics, product design and systems control.

Loads of extracurricular for keen participants in every mainstream sport from badminton to riding (school owns five ponies) – and academic help sessions, societies and catch-ups for just about every subject going. Other options are limited (although mindfulness about to be introduced) and occasional grumbles from parents that clubs are cancelled 'a bit too often'. Plenty of trips and tours, both curriculum linked and for enrichment. World Challenge has a noticeable presence around school and has taken students to Madagascar, Cambodia and Czech Republic in recent years. Also link schools in Ghana and China, exchanges to Italy, France and Germany, not forgetting departmental trips to eg USA (politics), Vietnam (history) Iceland (geography) and Netherlands (art).

Background and atmosphere: What's in a name? Rather a lot, apparently. Founded in 1947 as the all boys' Chesham Technical School, later becoming Chesham Technical High School, then Chesham High School when it went co-ed in the 1970s. Finally cemented place as a credible player in the South Bucks grammar school scene with yet another – its final – change of name in 2010. Buildings wouldn't win any architectural awards – and decorators clearly had a job lot of drab, grey paint to use up – but the collection of low rise red-brick buildings hang together as a functional whole and school doesn't have the overpopulated, cramped feel of many local grammars. The jewel in the crown is the wonderfully bright and modern sixth form centre (2015) with its floor to ceiling architectural glazing and fair trade coffee shop and snack bar: an aspirational space for sixth formers to start to spread their wings. Canteen also gets the thumbs up: an appealing area, designed by students as another modern, social space offering hot food and healthy salads as well as all the usual pizzas and sandwiches.

Pastoral care, well-being and discipline: Head describes school's pastoral ethos as 'unique' and parents generally concur. Bullying – even 'friendship issues' – almost unheard of, as are exclusions, and heavy handed discipline rarely required. Vertical tutor groups enable pupils to build relationships with others from all year groups, meeting daily for 20 minutes to catch up on timetable changes and forthcoming exams, share revision tips and achievements, as well as home-made cakes and Haribos. Everyone from year 7 upwards gets a voice and the youngest tutees speak confidently in front of the most senior. Pupils uniformly clear that they can 'be who they want to be' and head reports that tolerance of all differences and preferences is extremely high, with 'nothing considered a big deal by the end of year 7'. Plenty of leadership opportunities falling out of strong house system – heads of house, senior prefects, learning leaders and, since 2009, head boy and girl are elected by peers and teachers.

Pupils and parents: Around 15-20 per cent from local independents, mainly Chesham Prep, The Beacon, Berkhamsted Prep and Heatherton House, with the majority from a host of state primaries. Still gets a minority vote from those in catchment for the Challoner's schools but increasing numbers giving it serious consideration thanks to its nurturing, less pressurised vibe. Ethnic mix reflects local community with around 15 per cent non-Caucasian, mainly of second or third generation Indian origin. Pupils we met were perfect ambassadors for school – quietly confident, understatedly charming and not remotely precocious. One mother we spoke to had recently hosted a party for 80 CGS sixth formers and couldn't express strongly enough how well behaved and at ease they were with one another – something we noticed all around the school.

Entrance: Selective. Prospective pupils sit the Buckinghamshire Transfer Test – usually at their primary school – in early September of year 6 (register during May/June of year 5). Those who pass (usually around 30 per cent of candidates) are entitled to a grammar school place. CGS doesn't fill from catchment most years so hopefuls from across the Bucks/Herts borders usually find themselves in luck on allocation day, with non-catchment pupils travelling on a fleet of coaches from Berkhamsted, Hemel Hempstead, Tring and Bovingdon plus down to the Chalfonts and Gerrards Cross in the other direction. Ones and twos from as far afield as Harrow thanks to proximity to Metropolitan Line.

Around fifty additional places in year 12 makes for a buzzing sixth form of around 400 pupils. About 100 applicants for these, from a variety of state maintained schools and small – mainly single sex – independents (regular applicants from Thorpe House, Claire's Court, Piper's Corner). 46 points or an average of eight Bs required.

Exit: Around 85 per cent stay on for sixth form very small number leaving at end of year 12. Vast majority to higher education, most to their first choice destination. Around two-thirds to Russell Group (Birmingham, Bristol and Nottingham all popular). 'Several' to study medicine and veterinary science and a very respectable 12 to Oxbridge in 2016. Applications supported by a dedicated team, praised by pupils and parents. Small handful to degree apprenticeship programmes with eg PwC, Deloitte, again well supported with their applications by school.

Remarks: In the south Bucks microcosm of pushy parents, competitive children and a focus on academic excellence at any cost, here you will also find an overwhelmingly kind, nurturing and in many ways relaxed school, coupled with a clear focus on excellence and getting pupils to achieve their very best. Steadily climbing the local academic ladder without having to jeopardise its pupils' happiness – in the words of one parent: 'I decided I wanted my daughter to come out of school with her mental health intact. That's why we chose Chesham.'

Chigwell School

High Road, Chigwell, Essex IG7 6QF

Pupils: 932; 30 sixth form boarders • Ages: 4–18 • Sixth form: 187 • C of E

Fees: Day £11,850 – £16,500; Boarding £27,930 pa

Tel: 020 8501 5700
Email: hm@chigwell-school.org
Website: www.chigwell-school.org

Headmaster: Since 2007, Mr Michael Punt MA MSc PGCE (40s), a physicist who lives on site with his wife Gill and their three sons, all of whom attend the school – a fact that many parents say 'keeps him in tune with pupils' and parents' experiences of Chigwell.' His calm and positive influence is palpable throughout the school, with parents describing him as 'approachable,' 'well-liked' and 'respected.' In fact, many were swayed against the local competition purely on the basis of meeting him. 'He doesn't just talk at you in some grand hall – he chats with you in a relaxed way and seems to know exactly what you want to know,' said one.

Pupils also speak enthusiastically about him. 'He knows every one of us, as well as taking an interest in us,' one pupil told us. Not for him a chief executive type headship, but rather a personal touch that's helped by the size of the school and the fact that he and colleagues interview every child that comes here. Mainly, though, it seems to be down to his hands-on approach – he teaches pupils, does a lot of mock interviews and is often seen around the school. The week before our visit, he'd had all the prefects round for a meal and he eats regularly with the boarders.

Having grown up in nearby Brentwood, he did his degree at Oxford and his masters at Imperial, then worked at St Dunstan's College as a physics teacher, working his way up to head of year and head of physics, after which he did a stint at The Perse School, Cambridge, as deputy head (academic) where he continued to climb the ranks until moving to Chigwell.

Head of junior school: Since September 2016, Mr Andrew Stubbs BA PGCE, previously deputy head of junior school, who joined the school in 2005.

Head of pre-prep is Mrs Evelyn Gibbs PA, PARICS, PGCE. Previously acting head in St Mary's Catholic Primary School, Chingford. Did her degree in history, then became a chartered surveyor, retraining as a teacher, after which she worked in the state sector, teaching year 6s and under, before moving into educational leadership. A friendly and softly-spoken woman, she doesn't have an obvious air of leadership, but make no mistake – she is largely responsible for the pre-prep having hit the ground running and staff, pupils and parents praise her for achieving the 'perfect balance of making the children feel nurtured, whilst also getting them academically ready for the junior school.' There was quite a bit of parental anxiety, a few parents told us, that with automatic entry into the junior school (rather than the usual rigorous assessment at age 7) that standards would subsequently drop in juniors. Also known for her enthusiasm and constant push on innovation, and other staff told us she's never short on great ideas. 'The pre-prep is her baby and she seems to love it with the same level of passion,' said one parent. Lives locally with her husband, and has two grown-up children.

Academic matters: The biggest recent challenge for the junior school has been linking with the school's newish pre-prep, which took its first intake of 4-year-olds in 2012. 'We want to ensure all the year 2 pupils come in seamlessly, so there's a lot of work on getting them to come in for assemblies, playtimes and lunches and talking to parents about the transition,' explains school, saying (and parents concur) that it's going well. 'Despite pre-prep being separate, Mrs Gibbs works very hard to make sure it is part of the bigger school, bringing juniors over to read to the children, organising joint assemblies and events and running a buddy-system, just to name a few initiatives,' added one parent. This pre-prep, which takes 4 to 7 year-olds, is set in a stunning, state-of-the-art, purpose built building a few minutes' walk from the junior school. The pre-prep curriculum is creative, including forest school type events, and highly practical. French from reception. Plenty of specialist music provision, along with an emphasis on art and drama, including two musical concerts per year. 'We're big on language and communication, so all children do presentations,' says head. Two hours of sport every week, including by specialist coaches. Close monitoring of pupils, with results shared with parents.

Back in the junior school, expect academic rigour at the core, so that children leave well-equipped at 13 to go into the senior school, but with an emphasis on fun in learning, with interactive, interesting lessons by well-qualified teachers that the pupils describe as 'firm but fair'. Enrichment includes the likes of day trips, visitors running workshops, presentations and taking part in regional and national competitions, whilst clubs range from animation and astronomy to debating, gardening clubs and BBC School reporting – plus all the usual academic and sporting clubs you'd expect. Plenty of opportunities to take part in activities in partnership with the seniors, and there are visiting speakers for year 6s and over. 'We want children to seize opportunities and really find and develop their interests.' This means that whilst the school day starts at 8.20am, with a staggered finish time from 3.05 to 4pm, many end up staying on – and there's also after-school care until 6pm for an extra cost (and a breakfast facility from 8am). 'Literally, whatever you're interested in, there's a club,' said one pupil, although one parent pointed out the clubs can be a victim of their own success, with disappointment felt due to many of them inevitably clashing. Plenty of school trips, mainly day trips into London, but some residentials further up the school.

National curriculum is followed. Languages strong, with French from pre-prep right through, and Latin from year 7; pupils are offered a choice of either German or Spanish from year 7. Mandarin offered as extracurricular. Setting in maths from year 5 and French from year 7. Pupils taught mainly by their form teachers in year 3, but they have a growing amount of specialist teaching as they move up the juniors, and all lessons are with subject specialist teachers from year 7. Latest Sats results when we visited put the school 22nd in the prep school list in the Sunday Times. 'If you need an extra session with the teacher, that's always fine,' said one pupil.

SEN provision across both pre-prep and junior schools involves one full-time SENCo on hand to help children cope with the academic pace here. Dyslexia is screened for on entry, and any necessary mechanisms in place for this and any other issues, such as ADHD, autism or dyspraxia (although none statemented when we visited). TAs help too, with most help classroom based. Plenty of provision for gifted and talented, both in the classroom, and via (for juniors) literary or science workshops, links with the senior school and trips open to the Scholars' Group to places like the Royal Courts of Justice and Royal Observatory. For pre-preps, extra provision is regularly provided for any speech issues.

Excellent results, which have risen steadily since 2007 – 69 per cent of GCSE grades were A*/A in 2016. Head puts this down to pupils' positive and conscientious attitude to learning and an excellent relationship with teachers, both points which the latest ISI inspection praised. 'Teachers are dedicated, both in and out of the classroom, and they very rarely shout,' one pupil told us. 'I was amazed when my son emailed teachers about his essay during half term and got detailed feedback the same day, but that's how it is here,' said a parent. The tone of the communication seems to be spot on, too. 'In many schools, it's either too matey or terribly stand-offish, but they seem to have got the balance just right here,' said one parent. Lessons interactive and busy, with plenty of IT embedded across all subjects – and a pilot of tablet-embedded learning going on in years 9 and 12 when we visited. 'We'll see how it goes and may well expand it in future,' the head told us.

Low turnover of around 6-7 per cent a year for teaching staff, with applicants for replacements of a high calibre, and they must be willing to teach beyond their subject, with the school following the somewhat old-fashioned model of all teachers getting involved in an extracurricular activity. 'It's not unusual to see maths staff getting stuck into games or English teachers helping to run chess clubs here,' says the head. 'It's the Chigwell way, this family-type approach.' Head regularly observes all teaching staff and has implemented a rigorous structure that ensures constant reflection, whilst the Teaching Skills Group means staff regularly share good practice. Tracking is big here – both pastorally and academically, with the aim of the two working closely together.

On entry, four classes of 22 maximum, although class sizes drop considerably for at GCSE level and to around a dozen at A level. Latin and French taught to all year 7s, and all try German and Spanish in year 8. In year 9, all pupils continue French and select one or more of the other three languages, with all pupils doing at least one modern language for GCSE. Mandarin also taught as extracurricular from junior school upwards. Setting in French and maths from year 7 and some in German from year 9. English and sciences setted from year 10. Regular testing means there can be movement between sets to start with, although this is uncommon later on. Homework taken seriously, although it's never set for the following day.

At GCSE, all students take maths, both English subjects, one modern language and the vast majority do the three sciences. Other popular options include geography, history, RE, with a strong interest also seen in other languages, drama, DT and music. 'We don't have option blocks – we make the timetable work around the pupils' choices,' says head, who adds that there are no early GCSEs taken here, although the top maths set in year 11 take additional maths.

Wide choice of subjects at A levels. Economics, maths, sciences, geography and English are strong, but psychology, drama and DT are on the rise too, enforcing Chigwell's reputation as a place for the all-rounder. In 2016, 80 per cent A*-B and 52 per cent A*/A at A level.

Plenty of extension opportunities, including EPQ and HPQ (latter at GCSE level), essay competitions and Olympiads. Enrichment programme impressive and includes subject-specific groups, such as law groups, medics' groups, social sciences groups etc. University preparation stunningly good, with guidance for UCAS applications starting in the February of the lower sixth, with plenty of targeted guidance and support, and mock interviews aplenty.

Junior school pupils screened on entry for SEN, with further testing in the senior school. Learning support provided throughout the school as necessary either inside or outside the classroom. Not a school for severe learning disabilities, however, with only one statemented when we visited.

Games, options, the arts: mass participation in sport does what it says on the tin here, with the possible exception of football, which one parent told us is all about the A team. Core boys' sports include football (first term), hockey (second term) and cricket and athletics (third term). For girls, it's hockey (first term), netball (send term) and rounders and athletics (third term), along with some football and cricket also in the summer term. Other sports include golf (played at nearby club), swimming, basketball and badminton. School punches above its weight in competitions, regularly getting through to regional finals, along with national finals for football and hockey. Junior school also does well in competitions, with the under 11 football team reaching national finals for independent schools, and regular appearances from teams across all sports at regional finals.

Outdoor facilities are vast, with 100 acres of playing fields, including Astroturf, surrounding this small school, and indoor facilities are being steadily improved through an ambitious development plan. Pupils particularly keen to have an indoor pool, rather than just the small outdoor pool they currently have, and many want to see the unfancy sports centre updated – both projects under consideration.

The drama centre is an eye-catching red-brick building with impressively professional facilities – foyer big enough for pre-theatre drinks receptions; 170-seat theatre designed for use by the whole school community; green room; rehearsal and teaching spaces; and dressing rooms. All children use it for weekly drama up until the end of year 9 and it's also a popular GSCE option, with around a dozen taking drama at A level with great success. All pupils have weekly drama lessons up to year 8, with a biannual play performed to parents, with cast of over 100. Junior drama club particularly popular and around 100 pupils take LAMDA, with 100 per cent pass rate, and plenty of distinctions. Related subject areas, such as theatre make-up and costume design, also taken seriously here, and the centre is used for public speaking, debating and LAMDA too. Numerous productions take place throughout the year. 'It would be rare to find a child who isn't somehow involved in drama,' says the head.

Weekly music lessons for all up to year 8 and every other pupil learns an instrument, making for an impressive sounding 40-strong junior school orchestra, which regularly performs concerts. Year group concerts for everyone else. The Primary School Music Festival is a big event here, in which over 100 pupils learn three pieces to participate. Music very inclusive in senior school too, with every other pupil learning an instrument (over 300 lessons per week from 23 visiting music teachers), some of whom play to incredibly high standards (usually one a year to Oxbridge as a choral music scholar). Plenty of opportunities to perform in ensembles, with a wide range of musical tastes catered from swing bands to string bands, as well as rock and pop. The chapel choir, an elite choir for 40 odd students, performs regularly in the likes of Westminster Abbey, Canterbury Cathedral and Yorkminster, and there are plenty of other choirs too. 'Every aspect of music is amazing here, from the singing right through to every instrument you can think of, along with many you didn't even know existed,' said one parent.

Art and DT work closely together in the spacious and hi-tech facilities, with graphics offered as a GCSE option and many pupils going onto study architecture and fine art when they leave. Phenomenally good artwork displayed throughout the school, much of it in 3D.

Huge choice of extracurricular activities, from D of E and scouts to art exhibitions and the inspiring and thought-provoking talks on everything from evolution to restorative justice for schools, which are run as part of the Williams Project, named after philosopher and Chigwell alumnus, Bernard Williams. 'The amount of opportunities here is immense and you'd frankly be seen as a bit daft if you didn't utilise it,' said one student. 'I haven't had a free afternoon in the last three years – but in a good way,' laughed another. A seemingly infinite amount of trips available too, including French and Spanish homestays, hockey tour to South Africa, scout trip to Switzerland, annual ski trip to France, along with smaller scale trips including activity weekends in the likes of Wales and the Lake District. 'We are conscious that there is a broad mix of wealth and make sure we do not offer all five star trips,' says head.

Boarding: Sixth-form only boarders, of whom there are 30 living across four equal-sized boarding houses, either on the school site or just across the road. Hailing from around 16 countries – mostly central and Eastern Europe and China – the boarders are almost all international, and no two boarders who share a language share a room. Everyone agrees they bring a lot to school life, in terms of the insights they provide into other cultures and a more worldly ethos overall – all helped by the fact that they are encouraged to give talks on the issues affecting their homelands. 'The boarders help give the school a homely feel,' added one student.

Boarding houses are inviting and not the least bit institutional. Rooms mostly twin, although the odd one has three beds, and boarders told us 'there's a good balance between houseparents letting you get on with it, and providing clear boundaries.' Each houseparent, who lives in with their family, is a big part of daily life and seen as a major figure in boarders' lives. 'In our house, the parents have children aged 4 and 6 and we always love hanging out with them,' said one pupil. Curfews are 10.30pm on weekdays; 11.30pm at weekends. Daily study time between 7-9pm during weekdays – 'Even if you don't have work to do, you have to respect that others have and be quiet,' one boarder told us.

No shortage of events – the week we visited, they'd just had Divali weekend celebrations and a film night – which day pupils also join in, but boarders welcome the opportunity to be allowed to be self-reliant too. Boarders told us they'd formed close friendships with both other boarders and day pupils and already felt sad about the prospect of leaving the school.

Background and atmosphere: Founded in 1629 by the Reverend Samuel Harsnett, the local vicar, who became Archbishop of York and Chancellor of Cambridge University. Today the original red-brick schoolhouse, which is located on the approach road to the historic high street, forms the centrepiece to this pretty village of neat buildings, punctuated by gardens, blooms and trees. The surrounding playing fields stretch towards Epping Forest and give a rural aspect to the school and some lovely views from the windows of the attractive, low-rise teaching blocks. None of the facilities are more than an easy and pleasant stroll apart, with the junior and senior schools just steps away from one another and the stunning new pre-prep a few minutes' walk away. Buildings all kept up to date, with a nice combination of traditional and contemporary, and new building works always in the pipeline. In 2010, for instance, there were two new boarding houses and catering facilities, along with a sixth form coffee shop, whilst 2013 saw the new pre-prep and science labs. New sixth form centre, with a dining hall extension, new sports hall and indoor swimming pool next on the agenda.

Of particular note is the 1920s chapel, which was built in tribute to fallen alumni and is a mainstay of life here. Pupils usually attend at least once a week for a service (and another weekly service at the local church), but there's plenty of room for all the beliefs represented at this multicultural school, with speech day services including a passage from each of the six major world faiths.

All have lunch in the Harry Potter-esque dining hall (where teachers eat on the stage) and students can have tea at 4pm for no extra cost, as well as breakfast, for which they can bring parents and siblings. 'Every Thursday, our whole family has breakfast here – we love it,' said one parent. Food is plentiful and very good (we tried it ourselves), with healthy options and popular themed days. The uniform is smart and sober – kilts or plain trousers with a navy blazer, though the sixth formers wear office attire.

No need for intrusive bells here to mark the change of lessons, with pupils making their way around the school in an ordered fashion, and newbies of any age wear a plain tie so they can be spotted and helped when in need. 'This is a harmonious school, with really lovely young people who, in the majority of cases, you'd be proud to have as your own children,' says the head. Indeed, 'happy' was a word used a lot by the pupils we talked to, with several referring to it as one big family. Life really does seem to just flow very smoothly, with laughter never far from earshot. Even communication systems – homework submitted electronically and an electronic noticeboard system, among them – seem to work effortlessly. No wonder old Chigwellians feel such a sense of loyalty, with growing numbers willing to come into do talks, mock interviews and offer work experience.

The school council doesn't seem to have achieved a great deal more than the usual increase in number of water fountains, although they do meet regularly. There's a strong charitable culture, with a committee consisting of staff and pupils who choose the charities to support and raise in excess of £30,000 a year. 'We want to understand the charities we support, we do a lot of promotion around that part too,' says the head, who adds that the school is very much part of the local community, which often joins in with fundraising events.

Pastoral care, well-being and discipline: Pastoral care is taken seriously in the junior school, with each form tutor knowing their pupils well. School counsellor also available, and there's lots of regular contact with parents, who know they can email any time. The junior school has its own house system, with house points and competitions, whilst opportunities for leadership include heads of house, prefects, librarians and catering committee. House points aside, pupils' stand-out behaviour and work is also rewarded via Chigwellian of the Year award and a golden time system. Meanwhile, bad behaviour (mostly forgotten homework and escalating misbehaviour) results in lunchtime detentions. 'We like discipline, but it's more a case of high expectations than lots of rules.' Temporary exclusions have happened (for example, for misuse of social media), but no permanent exclusions recently.

'We're pretty lucky when it comes to bullying. We keep a behaviour log and track any patterns that are emerging. Children also know who they can talk to if they feel anyone is being unkind.' But most of all, there's a culture of kindness and looking out for each other, so the main work is preventative, not troubleshooting. School council meets fortnightly to thrash out issues pupils feel strongly about, such as catering issues and the rewards system, and each form has a rep who contributes to this.

Homework only given 'if it has a clear purpose and links with learning,' with a maximum of one hour a night, and there are plenty of open-ended homework tasks given to encourage independent learning. Children learning about the Tudors, for example, might get to choose a Tudor portrait and write a story around it.

Over in the pre-prep, which is located behind a coded gate, life is rather more lively, as you might imagine. But the extremely well-thought-of head keeps the 40 pupils in each of the three years (two forms in each) in check in a manner that the rest of the teaching staff mirror – that is, never shouting and with a nurturing and soothing manner, but with clear boundaries and expectations. The children seemed at ease with all teachers when we visited, and overall the atmosphere is described by parents and pupils alike as 'happy' and 'family like.' 'I love coming to school. It's nearly as good as being at home,' one pupil said.

Pastoral care is as strong in the pre-prep as in the rest of the school. 'This is a small, family community and we work very closely with parents,' says head and parents agree, praising the way friendships are encouraged among parents, as well as pupils. 'We're invited to a lot of things like assemblies and lunches, which is lovely,' said one parent.

The transition from junior to senior school is gentle, with parents praising the 'seamless process.' A strong four-house system, and staff who 'really know their pupils', according to the head, mean students are comfortable in the knowledge that they are being 'looked out for'. 'There are lots of personalities among the teachers here, but we all have someone we know we could speak to – a teacher that really stands out for us,' said one pupil, with many of the younger pupils talking about how friendly the older ones are. The school counsellor, employed for two days a week, is also on hand, and works with families where necessary. School promotes a society in which everyone takes responsibility for each other and the wider environment.

Discipline system highly structured, with detentions the most common sanctions, typically for late homework, missing chapel and being late. 'They're not given out willy nilly, so you take it seriously when you get one,' said one pupil. 'The pupils aren't saintly, and they've got a twinkle in their eye, but they're also hard working and really nice. We don't have many behavioural problems,' says the head. Indeed, current head has only made one permanent exclusion, although occasionally there are temporary ones, for instances such as smoking and repeated misbehaviour. Bullying rare, with pupils pointing out the 'confide' button on every school computer, where you can report issues anonymously at any time, or talk to a staff member confidentially.

Pupils and parents: This leafy suburb is spoilt for choice education-wise, with several good fee-paying schools on the doorstep and some of the best grammars in the country a short hop on the train away. Even Old Chigwellians admit to investigating the competition before signing up their offspring, but the school still wins people over with its ability to develop not just academic success, but confident, well-rounded people. 'One of the things that swung it for me was the way pupils talk to adults in a sophisticated way, but not without respect,' said one.

The parents – around two-thirds of whom are middle-class white British, with the remaining third mostly British Asian – seem to love the sense of community that the school has. 'My children have always said they felt they belong to something here – so much so that my daughter felt a real sense of loss when she left, and the same can be said for many parents,' said one. Most live within a five mile radius, although there's a growth in the number coming in from East London. Mainly affluent parents, although not exclusively. 'I was worried it would be full of rich kids and Landrover-driving parents, but although you do get that, there's a reassuring number of hard-working professional couples who make sacrifices to send their kids here,' said one parent.

There's a good 50:50 split of boys and girls, who we found to be relaxed, confident, articulate and helpful, as well as having a great sense of humour. Parents, meanwhile, particularly welcome the many opportunities to speak informally with staff about their children's progress and well-being at breakfast get-togethers and afternoon teas, as well as the programme of social events put on by the 'Friends of Chigwell' PA which also raises significant funds for things like new canoes and stage lighting. Five school minibuses available for pupils, with others using public transport, notably the tube or bus, whilst many get dropped off by car.

The list of distinguished alumni includes William Penn, Sir Arthur Grimble, Sir Austin Bradford Hill, Sir Richard Dales, Col Bob Stewart and Sir Bernard Williams.

Entrance: Competition is fierce. For entry into the pre-prep at 4, around 140 applicants for the 40 places, with young candidates evaluated via an assessment based on the EYFS curriculum and is primarily play based. 'They come from around 26 nurseries,' says Mrs Gibbs. Meanwhile, entry for 7-year-olds to the junior school sees eight times as many applicants as places, with all applicants going through an assessment, interview, classroom experience and report from their previous school.

Most junior school pupils move up to the senior school, forming about half of the year 7 entry, with the other half from a wide variety of local prep and primaries. 'It's very welcoming, so my children took to it like a duck to water, despite not coming from the junior school,' said one parent. Around 300 apply for these 40-odd places; assessment by interview (separate ones for pupils and parents), and English, maths and verbal reasoning papers. Small number of vacancies at 13 (English, maths and a modern foreign language exam). At 16, those moving up within the school are joined by around 10 local entrants as well as around 14 overseas boarders. Entrants to the sixth form are expected to have achieved at least four As and two Bs or in six GCSE subjects and A*/A in their A level choices.

Exit: Most parents send their children here hoping they won't leave until after sixth form, and indeed only a handful choose to send their child to another junior or secondary school, though all are reassessed at 11.

Hardly any post-16 leavers and 95 per cent of those who leave after sixth form move on to a degree course at university, or music and other specialist colleges. In 2016, six to study medicine and seven to Oxbridge; some 70 per cent to Russell Group universities, notably Exeter, Nottingham, Bristol, Leeds

C

and LSE. Popular degree subjects include economics, English and humanities.

Money matters: Academic scholarships available at 11 and 13 years; scholarships for art, drama and music offered at 16. Increasing number of means-tested bursaries available. 'I visit every family we are considering for bursaries,' says the head.

Remarks: A happy, nurturing and busy school with a genuinely family feel and an emphasis on creating caring all-rounders. Academically, pupils are put through their paces, but it all seems to be done in such a civilised and pleasant manner that you're far more likely to hear pupils talk about opportunities and prospects than pressure and stress. 'Anyone that wants to do well will do well here,' said one student, 'and I can't think of a nicer place to succeed.'

Christ Church Cathedral School

3 Brewer Street, Oxford, Oxfordshire OX1 1QW

Pupils: 169; 20 chorister boarders; co-ed nursery • Ages: 3-13 (chorister boarding from year 4) • C of E

Fees: Day £7,191 – £15,177; Boarding choristers £9,564 – £10,578 pa

Tel: 01865 242561
Email: registrar@cccs.org.uk
Website: www.cccs.org.uk

Headmaster: Since 2014, Richard Murray BA MA (Durham), previously a housemaster and English teacher at St Edward's School in Oxford.

Entrance: Most day boys are from the Oxford or Bucks area, and enter at nursery or reception; the single class grows as more boys join in year 3 and the majority stays until common entrance. A few girls in nursery only. Assessment is by participation in class for the younger boys and informal academic tests for the older boys. Four chorister places are available each year from year 4, selected by voice trial. Choristers come from further afield, board and receive a two-thirds fee reduction in a bursary established by royal appointment in 16th century. School benefits from recommendations by old boys, siblings and music teachers. The Cardinal's Scholarship is a new introduction, for up to three year 3s, who are expected to achieve well academically throughout the school. Parents of choristers are a particularly music-focused sub-set; others are local professionals, medics and academics

Exit: To a range of schools: in 2016, Magdalen College, Winchester, Abingdon, Our Lady's Abingdon, St Edward's, The Oratory, Leighton Park, Bloxham, Plenty of music scholarships and exhibitions, as one would expect – nine in 2016 plus one sports and two academic awards.

Remarks: Described by one parent as 'the secret of Oxford', it is hidden in a historic corner of the town in the shadow of Christ Church Cathedral. Every available inch has been transformed, embracing the original Tudor residence of Cardinal Wolsey, a Victorian parsonage-type house commissioned by Dean Liddell, father of Alice in Wonderland, and a bright new block to commemorate old boy William Walton. The net effect is a warren of classrooms, labs and play areas combining traditional and modern. Henry VIII's charter of 1546 established the education of eight boy choristers and a master for Christ Church Cathedral. Shame it didn't stipulate a few parking spaces too, as staff parking on the playground is an issue, according to one parent.

Music permeates through the school, from music-stands among the pyjamas to treble clef murals in the corridors. The cathedral choristers' day kicks off at 7.30am to fit in their three hours of choir practice and daily services. In addition they all learn the piano and one other instrument. There are celebratory services throughout the year, including Easter and Christmas Day, as well as singing tours, recently as far afield as China, performing in the world's largest concert hall. The rest of the school has caught the bug too: with pianos in every corner and 140 individual music lessons per week, there are informal concerts which start with the smallest to encourage confidence, 'even if it's a recorder and they play the same note 10 times,' laughs one parent. However, having heard the choir sing like angels at evensong, we were struck by the skill and professionalism of even the youngest. Parents are welcome to watch the weekly service in the cathedral and some day boys are chosen for Worcester College choir. 'They see that older boys are doing it and it's fun'.

These are not just pretty voices: under the surplices there is an academic rigour to the school, starting with the tiny tots in the Montessori nursery. The historic cardinal's house now holds a climbing frame and zoo animal frescoes in the garden. Small class sizes in the pre-prep, approximately 16, rising to a maximum of 20 when choristers join in year 4. The pre-prep enjoys recently refurbished classrooms with play areas, music corners and piano. French classes in year 2. There is a conscious promotion to the prep, a separate building, a more formal uniform, and a more exacting curriculum, in which subjects are taught by specialists from year 5 and maths is set in year 6. We witnessed a vibrant Latin class and were invited to help judge the Roman legionary cut-out doll competition – it was a tough decision, but the joy of learning in the classroom was infectious. IT resources have multiplied and are used, among other things, for workshops on Sibelius (musicians' software, not the chap). Head sees all parents in year 6 to discuss future schools and makes prefects of all the final year boys. Teachers include alumnae of the college.

The school makes good provision for a surprising variety of SEN children, with one full-time and two part-time staff. 'Some schools attract a uniform product and this is a school which attracts eccentrics'. One parent reported that a boy who was severely dyslexic won a top place in the annual poetry competition. 'That's part of the school's draw: it treats everyone with a lot of respect'. Oxford's fluid population means that there is often a handful of EAL children, which our guide appeared to relish as contributing to the school's rich tapestry.

Picture the most idyllic cricket field you can imagine – these boys play on it, overlooked by the dreaming spires of Magdalen and Christ Church, the sound of rare breed cows lowing by the river; a timber cabin of a cricket pavilion, now with modern additions, electricity and a loo. One parent criticised the school's outdoor areas – 'Boys don't have far to run in the playground' – but Merton field over the road more than makes up for it (there's also new Woodland School in Christ Church Meadow). No wonder the fixtures in rugby, football, cricket and athletics are successful and many boys make the renowned A teams in their next schools. Parents enjoy a summer fair here on sports day, a scene which is eagerly photographed by tourists, looking for a snap of old England. 'I've never seen so many cakes,' gasped a parent. The school is conscientious about all boys representing the school in sport at some stage – school also offers an autumn half term course with Premiership footballers. Inflatable sharks and papier mâché snakes in the art room testify that the creative child is catered for. Art and poetry are celebrated on Arts Day, by visiting professionals who run workshops in photography, fine art, music and poetry. This year's cartoonist helped produce some lively portraits of composers, one of whom looked suspiciously like the bursar.

Named after the cathedral's organists, including John Taverner, the boarders' rooms in the main building are decked with photos and teddies from home; the largest dorm sleeps eight cosily. The bright and tidy shower room confirmed our suspicions that these are no ordinary boys. 'We try to make it their home,' said our guide. The choristers' common room is in cardinal red, like their cassocks, and houses a computer to email home,TV and, of course, ivories to tinkle upon. Our noses led us enticingly to the dining room, lined with scholars' and house point boards – houses are named after dignitaries associated with the school: (Lewis) Carroll; (Cardinal) Wolsey and (Dorothy L) Sayers, who lived next door and whose father was headmaster. There's a traditional tie for the winners of the merit awards to wear each term; another system for poor behaviour culminates in a mild punishment of sitting outside the staff room. Good discipline is inherent in a musical training: 'It's not external discipline we're after, it's a means to self-discipline'. Lots of clubs after school, from knitting to furniture-making to amuse the boys, while parents fight with the city traffic: 'Bit of a pain to get to at 5.30 at night,' said a parent. Free after-school prep club until 6pm pleases working parents. However, not really set up as a boarding school; reports of choristers at school at weekends kicking their heels with no organised activities, and sometimes missing meals.

The school is proud of its reputation for good manners, and rightly so. Boys stand when visitors enter the classrooms, address teachers as 'sir' and learn to hold the door open at an early age. It is a conscious emphasis on courtesy which comes across as old-fashioned. As one parent remarked, 'I think we are paying for the education I received'. Parents are happy with the contact from teachers: 'They speak to you, and really listen to what you say'; office staff got particular praise, 'even with difficult parents they are very diplomatic'. It is no coincidence that in premises seeped in history the school play should be Old Father Time. He has certainly instilled character and sound traditional values here, from the daily Latin quotation in the head's study to the boys' charming Thomas More-style hats. The honest traditions are summed up by the bursar: 'Snowballing? Of course we allow it. I think being a boy nowadays is not as exciting as it should be'.

Christ's Hospital

Horsham, West Sussex RH13 0YP

Pupils: 861; 814 boarders • Ages: 11–18 • Sixth form: 317 • C of E

Fees: Day £16,290 – £20,490; Boarding £31,500 pa

Tel: 01403 211293
Email: enquiries@christs-hospital.org.uk
Website: www.christs-hospital.org.uk

Head Master: Since 2007, Mr John Franklin BA Dip Teaching MEd admin (60s), came from nine years of headship at Ardingly. Born in Australia and is quietly-spoken yet firm. His experience is spread across both hemispheres – six years as a deputy at St Peter's Adelaide, the oldest continuous school in mainland Australia, prior to that an English teacher and acting housemaster at Marlborough for three and a half years. Wife, Kim, teaches English part-time. His ambition to teach again has been leapfrogged in the past nine years by his role in the modernisation of the school and foundation's joint governance structure.

Likes to tinker with cars and compares Christ's Hospital on his arrival to an E-type Jaguar that was terminally rusty and had two drivers fighting for the wheel – the clerk of the foundation and the headmaster. Now the vintage car has been lovingly restored, is running soundly and the head is comfortable in the driving seat; a whimsical metaphor for what has been a gargantuan and sometimes Machiavellian struggle from a £4.5 million deficit to more than half a million net profit from holiday lettings, and an ISI inspection giving the school an excellent across the board rating. The division of governance is now clear and functional and the school is being marketed for the first time in its life – 'a school like no other.'

Sets clear expectations and they are firmly applied, so pupils respect him. Temperature testing of the school is done via the Senior Grecians (head boy/girl and prefects) and by walking the school and sports pitches (with or without his dogs). Understated in his pride of 'the bright and talented pupils who otherwise would not have had these opportunities; and what they achieve, year on year.' Aware that the archaic uniform erases all trappings of family circumstances and passionate about diversifying the pupil population with fee-paying families without eroding the school's unique ethos. Thoughtful and perceptive, he'll be retiring to his cottage in Storrington in July 2017.

His successor will be Simon Reid BA (50s), currently principal of Gordonstoun, who was housemaster here for six years earlier in his career. A South African who read English at the University of Witwatersrand. Came to Britain in 1985 because he 'wanted to teach English literature in the country where it was written'. Was previously deputy head of Worksop College, having started his UK teaching career at Brentwood School, thence Stowe. His wife, Michele, is French, the family bilingual. Two grown up young.

Academic matters: Junior class sizes up to 25, 20 in core subjects at GCSE and fewer in option groups, 10 or 11 for A level or IB. Latin compulsory for first two years, second foreign language for one. GCSE subjects chosen at end of year 8 – one modern language and one humanities subject must be included in the four options outside the core curriculum. Pupils say staff try exceptionally hard to incorporate exams in unusual first languages. The first cohort of IB diploma finished in 2013. Take up was slow initially (28 in first year but now rising), partly because pupils are very concerned about getting it right (most have no family money to fall back on if exams don't work out). In 2016, 64 per cent A*/A grades at GCSE, 32 per cent at A level; IB average 36 points.

Campus arranged by subject blocks, all with high ceilings and plenty of space and equipment, including science and language labs. The ugly sister IT department (was known as Grange Hill by the students), replaced 2015 with a new classroom block and resource centre. One main library, with a 16th century painting (cut to size in the move from Newgate a century ago; unfortunately the signature was a casualty) and a mezzanine level with extra computers. Scheduled to be redone as a sixth form centre with a focus on careers and vocations – the thinking is that Old Blues can provide enough mentoring and connections for some pupils to enter a profession in the City without going to university. Art and humanities have their own specialised libraries (open for evening work, as are all academic departments, providing support).

C

The SEN unit has one part-time and two full-time SENCos – support ranges from mild to a tailored IEP if SEN is profound. Everyone with SEND gets a laptop. The whole campus has Wifi and all the IB pupils and upper sixth are offered a laptop too – these can be taken home. Parents appreciate 'equality of provision and equality of access to provision.'

Weekly chapel and tutorial periods; upper sixth get weekly lectures on topics ranging from photo-journalism, through medicine, dentistry and accountancy to Tom Avery's experience as a polar explorer. There is a huge amount on offer here and as pupils grow older they tend towards the management of their own studies, as they would at university, an enormously important piece of preparation for life after CH. Houseparents and staff who supervise prep periods play a great role in advising children on study choices as well as pastoral issues.

Games, options, the arts: Main sports are hockey, netball, football, rugby, cricket and tennis, with a decent fixture list against local co-ed schools, winning about 60 per cent. Blue Coats sports centre – 25m pool, double-sized sports hall, six squash courts, spin bikes, split-level fitness suite, vending machines and a café – is used by the public 60 per cent of the time, although the school has its own changing rooms. More esoteric sports such as fives also on offer. D of E and CCF very popular. Scout hut now converted to a multifunction theatre seating 200.

A 500-seat theatre, modelled on Shakespeare's Globe, with padded red benches instead of the standing yard, is used by travelling drama companies too (contemporary dance as well as curriculum-relevant plays). Open access attitude for these performances endears the school still more to Horsham residents. The debating society and the Model United Nations give student speakers more confidence in competition in and outside school.

The music department is a popular target for donations such as harps, bassoons, French horns. Listen to, play or sing in any one of the 43 ensembles, inside or outside the school, and the joyful noise is gorgeous. Chapel choir is now restricted to a maximum of 150, the gospel choir has around 80 members as does the Big (jazz) Band, the junior choir 50, 150 in the symphony. Most pupils love to sing and the cathartic feeling of their voices joined together, soaring past the frescoes in the chapel is one of the moments they squirrel away in their hearts – the BBC was hugely impressed that it could record them in just one take. Lots of Macs enable bedroom producers to hone their skills with music technology at A level.

Energetic art department, successful and focused on working on pupils' own ideas, which produces an enormous range of work – exhibiting at the train station and a theatre in Horsham grants a wider audience. Three floors of bright and naturally-lit space, an artist in residence, art historian, two full-time staff, sewing room, computer suite (although the primary source of each project is drawing, digital images are always involved) and a library full of glossy books – all open from 7.15am to 10pm. DT department occupies almost as large a space and is just as well equipped with computers, AutoCAD, laser cutter, graphics area etc. and admirable focus on SMART objectives for each project. One pupil not only achieved the top Pre-U art mark nationally recently, but also won the sculpture category of the new HMC schools' art competition with his remarkable recreation of a Brazilian favella.

Boarding: Eighteen boarding houses – 16 single sex ones along The Avenue and two upper sixth co-eds built in 2000. Nearly all are looked after by a married couple (most of the 110 staff live on site, often with their own families), so every child gets a taste of parental and sibling relationships that may well be lacking in their own home. A recent revamp has left these boarding facilities sparkling – no junior shares a room with more than three others, big common rooms with ping-pong and snooker, bright kitchens, a phone room (for the first two years everyone hands in their mobile until 2pm). Every new arrival gets a nursemaid in the year above – they write letters to the new students the summer before they arrive – and this relationship produces a family tree stretching across year groups. Ingenious support where need arises – matrons giving hugs, cleaning staff joshing the dedicated student and the head of learning support teaching a tai chi course, an innovative balance to the busyness of student days.

The two Senior Grecian houses (the nomenclature comes from the sixth form historically having to study classics) would be the envy of any university student. Often more space than the children might have to themselves at home – big windows, a sink in each (senior's) room, double-height communal spaces, bowls of fruit, kitchens shared between eight, a BBQ on the deck, a little library area with a piano and students' art displayed. A quarter of the Grecians might be in long-term (more than a year) relationships with each other but no peer pressure to do this. The proximity of co-ed living space means that sex could be a problem, but the co-ed nature of the full school normalises boy/girl relationships. Lovely story of a Valentine's Day charity fundraiser, pay a penny for a snuggle – really inclusive.

Matches on Saturday afternoons while Saturday evenings feel good with discos, theme nights or just a fun time in each house – watching football, a film or playing a game devised by the seniors with a slapstick pie in the face for those who mess up.

CH runs in three-week blocks before a leave weekend – some children don't want to or can't go home; they can stay in or get matched with a friend and spend the weekend with their family. 'There's no one way to be a CH pupil,' we were told. This diversity is the school's strength – whatever obstacles or advantages your home life might present, everyone is equal as soon as they tie on the bands of their uniform. The new 'deps' (deputy Grecians, lower sixth) probably find the acclimatisation most difficult. Pupils learn within the first year to live with a huge range of personalities, which stands them in good stead in later life.

Background and atmosphere: School was given its Royal Charter by Edward VI in 1553 to help orphan children of London. In 1902 the boys moved to the current purpose-built campus in Horsham (designed by Sir Aston Webb, also responsible for the façade of Buckingham Palace and King's College, Cambridge). The girls, who had stayed at a site in Hertford, joined in 1985 to make it co-ed once again. Nowadays the demographic is much more mixed, but the uniform is still resolutely Tudor – mustard coloured socks and long blue coats. The pupils love the warm 'Houseys' and although the younger ones choose their 'civvies' carefully after lessons are over, the older ones default to school tracksuits – a refreshing lack of emphasis on trainers as a signifier of social tribe.

Progress supports the heritage showcased by the plaque-studded cloisters – from the plasma screen with BBC news and current school photos in the reception to the skylight-lit food hall. Six days a week, barring rain, the entire school marches to lunch from the quadrangle, house by house, to the accompaniment of the parade band. Parents and pupils say 'butterflies in the tummy' are caused by this sharing of 'music, ambience, exhilaration, aesthetic, ceremony, tradition and spirit' on a daily basis.

The food (delicious and varied) is cooked by team headed by a chef who has turned down offers from Michelin starred restaurants, and is eaten under the longest oil on canvas in Christendom. This mingling of tradition and technology is characteristic of the school. It may appear incongruous yet, in truth, it is inspirational.

The pupils are proud of their uniform, don't mind being taunted as Harry Potter lookalikes on trains (they prefer references to The Matrix), are delighted to be recognised by Old Blues on the tube and smile wryly when confessing to smelling like wet dogs after marching in a rainy Lord Mayor's Show. They pour through the cloisters between their lessons, some holding the lead of a master's dog for a treat. One of the best bits of the school is reported to be the spread at breakfast. They need that as fuel to get them around the huge campus – by the upper sixth you earn the privilege of a bike.

The whole school meets in the chapel on Sunday morning – seats 1,000, 140 in the gallery. Stained glass windows (some Victorian and a couple of 14th century Flemish) came from the earlier campuses, but the Sir Frank Brangwyn frescos were commissioned for the Horsham site. Whole school assembly is conducted every three weeks by the head in Big School, under the largest unsupported wooden ceiling in the country.

Pastoral care, well-being and discipline: Chapel services are important, not least because it is a space big enough for all the pupils to gather on Tuesdays and Sundays. The school was founded partly in response to a sermon preached by the Bishop of London and sermons are still powerful today; even if every pupil is not touched, they definitely pay attention. Lots of children here whose parents or carers are ill or struggling, so faith can be a real touchstone. School council is very thoughtful, student-run although spearheaded by an English teacher. Recent topics include racism, considering the effect close groups of international students (Hong Kong Chinese) can have in a community – empathetic research came up with how tiring it was to speak in your second language all day long, therefore what a retreat your own culture could be.

Minor misdemeanours mean getting up for 7.15am and a dress parade. Mini-detentions on Sunday am, the big one is on Saturday night, and a card system which restricts free time by having to sign in (for smoking, bullying, drinking alcohol.)

Internet access is not restricted very much (you often can't get onto useful sites with blanket bans) but it is monitored – a 14-year-old looking at porn will lose his/her laptop and school email account. 'Swearing at the staff is unacceptable' (suspension) and continued difficulties will result in a behaviour contract between the pupil, parents and school – a line drawn in the sand. Drugs – class A or supplying – mean immediate expulsion with the involvement of the police; for cannabis there will be one chance, after which the ongoing drug testing policy is implemented. Family circumstances are always taken into account. Parents really appreciate consistent and accessible staff. Email conversations may continue long after they have been sparked during parents' evenings.

Pupils and parents: The pupils know they're lucky to be here. For every student who gets in, four or five are turned away. Accepts pupils from all over the UK, in reality about 30 per cent from London (Hackney, Tower Hamlets, Islington, Acton), 30 per cent from Sussex, 30 per cent south west and home counties, rest from Scotland, Wales, north of England (most from further afield enter at sixth form, but only if they have some extended family in the south east). Historical links with Richmond, Newbury, Reading and Twickenham – the towns on the route of John and Francis West (17th-century scriveners) to Christ's Hospital.

Eleven per cent international pupils – mostly Europe (three and a half per cent) or the Far East (five per cent). Lots of second and third generation Nigerians and Gambians, Hong Kong Chinese are particularly attracted by CH's status as The Royal Mathematical School and German anglophiles love the school's excellence and tradition while valuing the fact that it is not an enclave of privilege. Since 2011, five per cent each from the UK, Europe and the rest of the world pay full fees – these are families who have made a conscious choice to pay for an egalitarian ethos. It has not been easy to change the pupil profile. A small number of international pupils were admitted initially with great care taken to see what they and their families needed. Now students appreciate the still wider diversity. It's easier to chat in German with a friend who is a native speaker or swipe some Asian cooking tips in the house kitchen.

Only 42 per cent of pupils have both parents resident at home and lots of aspiring middle class and freelancers. Houseparents encourage communication between parents when new pupils arrive (forums and blogs online help this). Pupils are drawn from all walks of life and the majority enjoy some form of means-tested bursary. If CH does its job, then former pupils will be ineligible to send their children to their alma mater, unless they pay the full fees.

Notable Old Blues (the dead ones have boarding houses named after them) include Coleridge, Middleton, Peele, Barnes Wallis, the cricketer John Snow, comedians Mark Thomas and Holly Walsh, the academic Alan Ryan, conductor Sir Colin Davis, Martin Linton MP, England Rugby Union second row Joe Launchbury, Baroness Ruth Deech, Lord Simon, former Chairman of BP, and General Sir Garry Johnson MC, strategic adviser to the MOD.

Entrance: Most at 11+, 25 to 30 at 13+ and 45 to 50 after GCSE. No feeder schools, but a very good relationship with south of England primaries and preps. Fifty heads came to a recent open day so they can see what type of child will thrive at CH.

Not on the public school radar, so not much cachet on the dinner party circuit. The initial application form elicits lots of information about family circumstances and finances – from previous school, local church, social services. The staff in the admissions office are at the end of the phone to answer questions and baffled or swamped parents really value this.

Exit: Some 10 per cent leave after GCSE for vocational courses. More than 90 per cent of sixth formers to university – the Upper Grecian houses are a real stepping-stone to life there. In 2016, six to Oxbridge and five medics. UCL, Durham, Bristol, York, Manchester, Leeds, Birmingham and KCL popular; medicine, engineering, archaeology, classics, law, music, maths degrees. Artists seem to take it in turns to go in posses to Camberwell, Falmouth and Central St Martins.

Money matters: Currently 14 per cent pay nothing, 34 per cent pay less than 10 per cent of full fees, 72 per cent per cent receive some level of bursary support and 19 per cent pay the full boarding fee. Of the £301 million allocated to means-tested bursaries by ISC schools last year, £15.5 million of that was at Christ's Hospital alone.

Parental contributions are assessed on the total family income of the home in which the child resides, interest and dividend payments plus a percentage of any financial and other assets above £25,000. Most DSS benefits are included, but not housing benefit, disability allowance and carer's allowance. Reviewed each year. Discounts for siblings within school. Tudor-style uniform is free. Extras include £20 pocket money per term, music contributions (means-tested again), a dictionary and a bible. CH has a big endowment but, like every other school, lives beyond its means.

Curriculum-based trips are partially funded by the foundation (means testing applies). Old Blues provide travel grants for gap years etc.

Remarks: Well-adjusted, confident and accepting children who look forward to coming to school. This is the only independent school that escapes the state school prejudice when attracting principled teachers. The Old Blues are incredibly loyal and you can see why – with 75 per cent of them in the top quartile of income in their later life, CH turns many lives around in an unpretentious and joyful manner. Admirable work.

Churcher's College

C

Ramshill, Petersfield, Hampshire GU31 4AS

Pupils: 1,101 • Ages: 2+-18 • Sixth form: 219

Fees: £9,060 – £14,220 pa

Tel: 01730 263033
Email: enquiries@churcherscollege.com
Website: www.churcherscollege.com

Head: Since 2004, Mr Simon Williams BSc (biology, Durham) PGCE Cambridge, MA education management (40s). Previously deputy head of Warwick School, he started his career teaching biology and rugby at King's College School, Wimbledon, where he was also assistant housemaster, followed by a stint as head of science at Newcastle-under-Lyme School. Married to Alison, an accountant, who is a strong supporter of all the school events; they have three children, two at university and one a pupil at the senior school.

Full of energy, he remains very much a hands-on head – once a week he fulfils the role of a classroom assistant at the junior school, teaches PHSE to year 7, getting to know everybody in the new intake, and general studies to older pupils. He has an eclectic range of interests in the arts, carpentry and, of course, sport, having been a keen rugby player and worked as an outdoor pursuits instructor. At weekends he can be found refereeing school matches or simply spectating and cheering on various sporting events.

Head of junior school: Since September 2016, Ffion Robinson, previously head of junior department at The Lady Eleanor Holles School and before that deputy head at King's House, Richmond.

Academic matters: Very much a user friendly junior school, with new nursery, where children learn at their own pace in a cosy and comfortable environment. Academically well structured, with younger pupils in mixed ability classes involving lots of activity-based learning in eg the new infant play area. Additional intake arrives at 7+ and thereafter two forms per year group, setting for maths and English. There's a brand new seven-classroom teaching block for years 1-4 plus a library and ICT suite, as well as a VLE, and iPads and Chromebooks are used in classrooms across the school. The teaching of modern foreign languages is exceptional for a junior school – the children are introduced to German in year 4, Spanish in year 5 and French in year 6. Year 6s are taken on a residential trip to France and the school employs German gap year students. Children who need additional support are identified and can attend small group classes or have specialist one-to-one teaching. Everybody brings their wellies to get stuck into the school gardens and greenhouse – much of their work is linked to the science curriculum and should produce some budding naturalists. A new sensory garden has just opened, part of evolving outdoor learning environment that's a big feature here.

Academic results produced 57 per cent A*/A at A level, 83 per cent A*-B, in 2016. At GCSE, 64 per cent A*/A. Traditional school offering lots of added value; equal importance is given to each area of the curriculum and pupils appear to be flourishing. Everybody's progress is regularly monitored; from year 8 pupils move into ability-related sets for some subjects. Maths teaching is notably good and pupils say it's a subject they really enjoy – quite a rare comment from schoolchildren. Young mathematicians have great successes in both local and national competitions and Olympiads, and the most able can take GCSE and AS early. Pupils study separate sciences; four new science labs, bringing the total to 12. All study at least one modern language with good grades being achieved in Spanish, French and German.

Sixth formers have a good selection of choices at A level, along with general studies and life skills programme. Students benefit from classes in cookery, first aid, self defence and the ever important personal finance, the aim being the young people will go on to university well-equipped for coping with life as well as their studies.

Humanities have an admirable reputation amongst pupils, offering some interesting and unusual trips to enhance educational experiences, bringing events and prose to reality. Up-to-date technology throughout the school includes a digital photography studio; pupils can access school computers system from home, so no excuses for not doing your homework.

Small SEN department run by two members of staff, both with specialist qualifications, who work with colleagues to assist them in differentiating lessons to meet pupil needs. One-to-one literacy support and study skills available, also hearing loop. All year 7s are taught study skills and touch typing classes are on offer.

Games, options, the arts: Boys' two main winter sports are rugby and hockey with cricket in the summer; girls' main sports are netball and hockey and in the summer it's rounders. That said, oodles of other minor sports and options – anything from tennis or golf to horse riding. Over 20 acres of playing fields; on-site facilities include Astroturf and indoor swimming pool. Certainly an outdoorsy school – superb range of expeditions and sports tours: younger pupils start with camping trips in the UK, moving on to mountaineering in Montenegro or possibly trekking and canoeing in South America. Large numbers of pupils take advantage of the D of E scheme, CCF and World and First Challenges; younger pupils can join the school's own outdoor activities club, OSCA.

Personal fitness is a high priority in the junior school, taught by dedicated PE teachers – pupils have access to a great range of sporting activities such as the Astroturf pitch, school adventure weekends and camping trips. In addition to sports, the school offers an equally good range of musical, dance and hobby-based clubs, alongside an early bird drop-off and after-school prep club, always a bonus for working parents. This hive of activity is brought together by the school's Guild Awards – the scheme allows the children to demonstrate their interests and strengths, in fitness, awareness of others and the environment and a new skill, at three levels of competence.

Orchestras and ensembles galore run for all abilities of young musicians; jazz and blues bands, string quartets and various choirs have an impressive local reputation and tour both here and abroad. Lots of class music lessons; the music centre is visited by over 20 music teachers each week offering tuition on more or less any instrument from the harp to the piccolo. Big open-air summer concert is of a very high standard and a popular annual event.

Upbeat drama department encourages students to write, acting and direct their own plays, junior and senior drama club members can get involved with everything to do with a production. Cooperation between artists, musicians and theatrical types makes for a great combination of set designs, costumes and acoustics, leading to very professional performances. Good number take a range of LAMDA examinations. Nice light art studios, fine arts and design and technology look stimulating, the next artist in residence is a sculptor. Huge design and technology studios, large enough to accommodate students wanting to build their own racing cars and bikes. Extensive selection of clubs and societies both at lunchtimes and after school.

Gold Artsmark for junior school – all arts are expertly entwined across the curriculum, giving the pupils a wide and creative education alongside all the traditional subjects. Attractive well-stocked music studio, most pupils learn an instrument and ABRSM exam results are impressive for young children. Drama is taught as a separate subject, pupils learn to communicate through plays and workshops and explore social and ethical issues in literature. Plays and concerts abound all year round; every pupil from reception to year 6 is involved. Professional artists and bands join with parents and pupils to perform at Churchfest, an annual social event. Top notch art and design – the dedicated art room is very well resourced, with DT of a particularly high standard for a junior school.

Background and atmosphere: Founded in 1722 by Richard Churcher for Hampshire boys, so they could be educated and apprenticed to masters of ships sailing for the East Indies. Continues its tradition of rowing, sailing and things military – every year they send a team on the Ten Tors expeditions to Dartmoor, a test of endurance, navigation and survival skills. Naval heroes' names are all given to school houses.

During most of the 20th century was the local grammar, until the local authority withdrew support and it became an independent fee-paying school. Pioneers of co-educational establishment – the first girls arrived in the sixth form in 1980 and they became fully co-ed in 1988. Comfortable atmosphere boosting the can-do attitude – pupils definitely understand meaning of 'nothing ventured, nothing gained'. Staff, parents and pupils contribute to some lovely, colourful garden areas including a butterfly garden, which go towards promoting positive feelings to work and play. Sixth form centre with its own pool room, conservatory and garden to relax in. No uniform, but expected to dress appropriately, smart jacket and trousers/skirt or suits.

The junior school, with attached nursery, is located on a lovely rural green site approximately 12 miles from the senior school. Hard work and the enthusiasm of the staff and pupils beam through – the Guild Awards, the gardens and the wonderful photographic displays lining the corridors that record the children's numerous achievements and events.

Pastoral care, well-being and discipline: Junior school pupils are invited to take on responsibilities as they mature and have their own school council – children can run for election once they enter year 3. The council meets with senior staff and discusses all sorts of issues that they wish to develop or perhaps change, including catering, equipment needed for the playground and ideas for clubs.

Senior school pupils are split between five houses. House captains and sixth formers act as peer mentors to younger members of their house. Form tutors are always available to pupils and their parents for day-to-day matters. Pastoral care system is eager to develop each young person's sense of responsibility for themselves and others. The buoyant extracurricular programme sees sixth formers getting involved with and encouraging younger children to try out new things and develop many different skills.The school's aim is always to work in partnership with parents and develop good relationships between staff, parents and pupils. PHSE programs are regularly reviewed and staff say they find student feedback invaluable. Confidential email helpline for students who want to contact pastoral staff.

Pupils and parents: Mostly local and fairly well-heeled; pupils come from an approximate 25 mile radius around Petersfield; lots of pick-up points for the school coaches around Hampshire, Surrey and West Sussex. Parents have the opportunity to become deeply involved in school activities; they can train as volunteers to help with countless outdoor pursuits events and Duke of Edinburgh – a committed and enthusiastic bunch. Fortuitously, lots of arty types as well, who help out with theatre productions, costume making and concerts, even joining in as instrumentalists. Very definitely a family based and community school. Buckets of highly successful fundraising for charitable projects all over the world. Green Day helps staff and parents promote awareness amongst pupils of wider international and environmental issues. Old Churcherians society produces quarterly news magazine. Good few actors, journalists, England rugby union players and businesspeople, eg Tiny Rowland, are amongst the alumni.

C

Entrance: Non-selective into nursery at rising 3 and reception at 4+; from 7+ pupils are invited to an assessment morning. Main entry to the senior 11+ and 16+, a few places available at 13+. At 11+ and 13+ entrance exam in Maths, English and verbal reasoning, followed by an interview with the Headmaster and references from current school. At 16+: interview, reference and candidates' GCSE results.

Exit: At 11+ the vast majority (90 per cent plus) of juniors go on to the senior school. A small number choose to move to eg RGS Guildford, Lord Wandsworth, Seaford, The Royal School and Bedales. At 16+ around 20-30 per cent move to state sixth form colleges. At 18+ all to university or art college – Exeter, Durham, York, Leeds and Bath all popular; one or two to Oxbridge (eight in 2016, plus five medics and two vets).

Money matters: Scholarships are awarded on the basis of performance in the entrance exam, usually between 10 and 25 per cent of the fees. Music scholarships and a number of music exhibitions to cover instrumental tuition fees. Sixth form scholarships for academic excellence and exhibitions for excellence outside the classroom. Bursaries of up to 100 per cent are means tested and reviewed every one or two years to ensure they are awarded to those most in need of financial assistance.

Remarks: Very successful all-rounder school which understands how to balance its curriculum to bring out the best in all its pupils, be it physical, musical, artistic, dramatic or academic. Exceptional value for money, for an action packed service.

City of London Freemen's School

Ashtead Park, Ashtead, Surrey KT21 1ET

Pupils: 896; 50 boarders • Ages: 7–18 • Sixth form: 210

Fees: Day £12,687 – £17,196; Boarding £24,837 – £27,867 pa

Tel: 01372 277933
Email: admissions@clfs.surrey.sch.uk
Website: www.clfs.surrey.sch.uk

Headmaster: Since 2015, Mr Roland Martin, previously head of Rendcomb College in Gloucestershire. Read English at York; Newcastle-under-Lyme School for six years followed by 13 at Eton, where he taught English and drama, was head of year 11 and a housemaster. Friendly, but not effusive, he has a rather charming, understated intensity. Married to Kerri, also an English teacher; they have two children. He loves 18th century novels, particularly Tristram Shandy and, in no particular order, is a huge fan of Simon Armitage, cricket and Italy – above all Venice.

Junior school head: Since 2014, Matthew Robinson (40s), previously deputy head. BA from Plymouth, MA from Surrey, QTS from Institute of Education, currently studying for an MEd at Buckingham. Has also taught (English, Latin and humanities) at Cranleigh Prep, King's College Wimbledon and, mostly recently, at Junior King's School Canterbury. Evidently not a man to let grass grow under his feet: has been boarding tutor and coached football, rugby, hockey, cricket and golf as well as directing various school plays and editing school magazines. Married to Victoria, also a teacher; they have four children while also finding time to go to the theatre, walk, play golf and squash and listen to music.

Academic matters: Class sizes start at around 12 at 7 years, rising towards a maximum of 20 by age 11. Three forms per year, increasing to four in the final two years of the junior school, when a further intake of pupils. Setting in maths from year 4 and English from year 7 has recently been introduced: 'School is flexible and big enough to do whatever suits the cohort. It may be different for different years'. Watch this space as the experience develops. French, German and Spanish are taught as a 'taster' for a term each in years 3 and 4. In year 5, pupils select one language to learn exclusively and then add a second choice in year 7.

Very good results year on year at both GCSE and A level – in 2016, 83 per cent A*/A at the former, with 55 per cent A*/A, for the latter.

Not a pressured academic hothouse. Parents are universally complimentary about the teaching, singling out physics, English, politics and business studies – 'Teachers fabulous, with lots of them there a long time'; 'Teaching is excellent and without high pressure'. Superb teaching facilities housed in the Haywood Centre (named after the previous, long-serving and very popular head). This hub of the senior school is an airy and attractive, well-equipped block of classrooms, IT and multimedia rooms plus a large library open until 6pm for individual study.

Not a first choice school for a pupil with significant SEN, and ask lots of questions for a child with mild SEN just to make sure the school can help. SEN support is limited – very few pupils with statements. School would ask parents to consider whether this is the right academic environment for their child – it 'may not be suitable for pupils with formal SEN statements'. A parent of a mildly dyslexic pupil reinforces this view saying, 'There is little specialist help, but teachers are kind and supportive and do the necessary such as extra time in exams; maybe it wouldn't be suitable for a child who is quite dyslexic.' A head of learning support provides help within the curriculum for mild needs, such as a slow reader, and support classes are available for children who are struggling in English. A parent of a pupil accessing this help praised it, saying, 'The kids call it the remedial class, but they have a very positive attitude towards it.' They have had hearing impaired children and wheelchair users and the issue is, 'Can we enable a youngster with special needs to access the curriculum?'

Games, options, the arts: The stunning facilities are not aged and beautiful but very much contribute to an environment which cannot fail to impress a pupil (or perhaps even more their parents). Sports facilities are outstanding and would compete easily with the best of the public school fraternity. Glorious and extensive grass pitches, huge Astro pitch for tennis, football and hockey, a vast sports hall, an enviable 25-metre indoor swimming pool, two squash courts and a multi-activity room for table tennis and aerobics. Sport is well and truly part of life here – parents report a 'massively active programme but it's not forced' and sport is 'made fun not a chore'. Very much a 'come and try' atmosphere, rather than a 'team place or else' school. For the seriously sporty, A and B teams are fielded in the more popular sports. Most fixtures are scheduled on Saturday mornings and squad members are required to attend.

The junior school really benefits from sharing the extensive sports grounds and top-notch sports facilities with the seniors.

Drama occupies as central a position as sport, both within the curriculum and in extracurricular clubs. A hugely enthusiastic head of drama (who maintains a dedicated drama website for the school), plus more terrific facilities including a professionally equipped theatre, mean plenty of productions. Good GCSE and A level results and some impressive acting alumni. Music is encouraged, with plenty of choirs, ensembles and an orchestra putting on about 30 performances and concerts; new music school. Musical theatre productions performed to sell-out audiences in a nearby 800-seater public venue are described as 'great' and 'the highlight of the musical year'. Students' artwork of a high standard is displayed around the school and the art and design technology facilities, like others, really are top class.

A huge range of lunchtime and after-school clubs cater for all tastes and interests. Senior pupils run some and can even start them on their own initiative. Trips out of school include an annual whole school visit to the City of London to celebrate the school's close ties with the City, plus many regular field trips both locally, within the UK and abroad – the list of destinations is long.

Boarding: Boarding is part of the school's statute and must be provided. (To this day a small number of 'foundationer' places – they have their fees, be it boarding or day, met in full.) However, boarders are almost exclusively pupils from abroad (vast majority are sixth form entrants). The boy boarders are from Hong Kong and Russia, apart from seven English pupils. All the girl boarders are from Hong Kong or the Far East. The girls' housemistress said she had to make them 'stop working sometimes and go out for a walk' – they are under immense personal and family pressure to succeed. With their very strong work ethic and extremely high standards, the boarders are often culturally different from the local day students.

The girls' accommodation in the main house is by no means trendy and high tech – in fact, quite the opposite: rather old fashioned and fusty. Boys' boarding house is a rather uninspiring building due to be completely renewed; new co-ed boarding house. Potential for boarding numbers to increase to 80; junior boarding from 2017.

Background and atmosphere: Founded to educate orphaned children of the Freemen of the City of London and owned by the Corporation of London. Support staff are employed by the City of London and governors are largely from the Court of Common Council (ie City officialdom). The Corporation provides financial support for capital projects, which helps to keep fees to a minimum. HR, planning and management all operated by the City, which leaves the head and school free to run and manage the education – the Corporation was described as 'forward looking with a long term view, also traditional and a little bureaucratic'. 'A little bureaucratic' may be something of an understatement – all our interaction with the school was slow and slightly difficult. The admin side worked like an old fashioned office, hierarchical and by the book – one gets the impression the whole school probably works like that, as everyone ultimately refers to a more senior authority.

The junior school is housed in the purpose-built, modernish Kemp House. It is acceptable, but couldn't be called inspiring. Painted breeze block walls (which are covered with artwork). Buzzing with well-occupied children, some classrooms can be tight and crowded in use. A couple of newer ones are more spacious and well-equipped with IT. Impressive art room and lovely, decorative and inspiring artwork displays all over the school.

It is the outside space which is the very, very, big plus – fantastic, a definite 'wow factor'. The rolling parkland of grassy embankments, shady trees and crested iron railings are shared with the seniors, although juniors have broadly their own area beside Kemp House – it is not sectioned off. A large fenced and well-equipped adventure playground is used exclusively by the juniors during supervised breaks.

Ashtead Park's 57 acres are owned by the City of London Corporation and the grounds are subject to open spaces regulations. Expansive, formal and well kept, with zebra crossings and double yellow lines, the City of London coat of arms on railings and bins really do make it feel like a London park. The feel is of a campus with pupils moving between various buildings. Parents particularly appreciate the 'beautiful setting' and 'great atmosphere to work in'. The 'mansion house', in grand country house style, houses music practice rooms and the dining room (rather small and old fashioned) plus reception rooms, offices and girls' boarding.

All pupils and staff are in one of the three houses – good opportunities for positive relationships between age groups. Each house holds a weekly assembly and accumulates merits through music, sporting and other achievements and good work to win the annual house competition. The sixth form has its own centre and is run 'almost like a separate school'.

Pastoral care, well-being and discipline: Parents are positive, describing pastoral care as 'excellent' and 'second to none'. Pupils have a daily tutor group and parents are encouraged to get in touch if they have any issues – they feel 'It's made clear who is responsible' and they 'always have somewhere to go – staff have an open door policy'. The spirit of the school is respectful and listening and pupils are encouraged to be kind and helpful. Parents and staff describe it as 'a family school with lots of siblings across it', the environment is 'caring and very friendly', 'Boys and girls mix well' and 'They grow up to be rounded on gender issues'. Pupils report that 'staff treat them with respect', which sets a good example and gives them self-confidence. Senior pupils mentor juniors and volunteer as class prefects and to run extracurricular clubs.

Discipline is laid down in clear policy and stuck to firmly; bullying is not tolerated. Incoming pupils sometimes find the regime initially rigorous as they learn the rules, but it is seen as fair. Parents say 'no bolt out of the blue – problems are flagged up early' and it's the 'right balance'.

The junior and senior schools are managed as one – each has its own staff, but it feels very much one school. The top two years of the juniors (ages 11 and 12) use some senior classroom facilities and are taught by some senior school staff. Parents report, 'They are so familiar with everything there is no huge transition when moving into the senior school.' Senior school pupils trained as listeners visit the junior school daily to provide an informal point of contact to help pupils with personal or school issues. Seniors also run some of the huge range of lunchtime and after-school clubs.

Pupils and parents: Pupils neither scruffy nor especially tidy – just nicely ordinary. Despite our request to be shown round by a pupil, we were, unlike at most schools, put firmly in the hands of the marketing manager. Both boys and girls we met en passant were communicative and pleasant when asked questions. Pupils predominantly from surrounding Surrey towns of Ashtead, Epsom, Banstead, Leatherhead, Esher and Cobham, but some travel down from south west London and even a couple from north London. School transport from most of these local areas plus a shuttle bus to Ashtead Station help parents avoid the school run.

CLFS has a solid, non-elitist, family feel, but lacks a certain pizzazz. This does not worry the CLFS faithful, for whom the real draw is the through education – once in the junior school, worries about future school choices and entry exams are a thing of the past. It is straight through to 18 – and a family can have all their children at the same place if they are 7 or 17, boy or girl. A big headache solved for time-poor working parents. 'Going through from age 7 takes away the stresses of 11+ and CE,' said one parent. Another added, 'With progression through the school, you don't notice any pressure at any particular point and don't realise the high levels children have achieved, as they've got there slowly and steadily.'

Families from a wide range of backgrounds – plenty with both parents working. Parents say this 'adds to the rounded normal feel of the school'. Many find the variety comfortable, with lots of ordinary families. Definitely not posh, does not even try to compete with its neighbour Epsom College. Some parents we spoke to were positively anti 'the four wheel drives and mothers dressed for tennis one upmanship' of some other local schools. 'Everyone is friendly', parents can get involved if they want and regular parent and family socials.

Entrance: Selective entry to junior school at 7 and 11 and at other ages as and when available. The tests in English, maths and non-verbal reasoning are the 'first filter'. Results are considered together with feeder school report, with an eye for consistency. All candidates are interviewed, looking out for 'a positive attitude to learning, evidence of interests and attributes to contribute to school life or just a spark of something'.

Juniors can move up to the senior school at 13+ with no entry tests – seen as a major advantage by parents. A further 25-30 are added from local preps including Downsend, Danes Hill, Cranmore and Lanesborough. Entry is competitive with screening tests at 11 and 12 confirmed by entrance exam or common entrance at 13. Head is pleased to add a little variety from other schools to 'leaven the mix'. Sixth form entry on predicted GCSE grades, school report and interview – about 20 join, including overseas boarders.

Exit: The overwhelming majority of juniors move up to the senior school. About 20 per cent leave after GCSE to taste life in a sixth form college or another school. Those who stay expect to go to university and do, mostly to Russell Group; nine to Oxbridge in 2016, plus six medics; other current favourites Birmingham, Bournmouth, Durham, Warwick, Bath, UCL and York.

Money matters: Generally perceived by parents to be excellent value for money and cheaper than other comparable schools in the area. Academic and music awards at 13 and sixth form available to current pupils and incomers. Means-tested bursary awards, sponsored by the City Livery Companies and often tied to certain professions. A very small number of children of Freemen who have lost one 'family breadwinner' parent attend completely free as Foundationers.

Remarks: A good, solid school, not quirky or elitist, in fact quite the opposite. It does what it says on the tin: genuinely providing pupils with wide opportunities and an all-round education including consistently good academic results, without a hothouse atmosphere.

Cobham Hall

C

Cobham, Brewers Road, Gravesend, Kent DA12 3BL

Pupils: 180; 89 full, 7 weekly boarders • Ages: 11-18 • Sixth form: 70

Fees: Day £16,713 – £21,156; Boarding £25,248 – £31,821 pa

Tel: 01474 823371
Email: enquiries@cobhamhall.com
Website: www.cobhamhall.com

Headmaster: Since 2008, Mr Paul Mitchell BSc (50s). Read maths and completed his PGCE at Newcastle University and started his teaching career at a state school before moving into the independent sector. He taught at Radley and Godolphin before becoming head of maths at Tettenhall College and the The Royal High School Bath, and then deputy head of St Mary's Cambridge for three years before moving to Cobham as headmaster. He represented GB for 10 years as part of the modern pentathlon team and managed to combine this with part-time teaching – he is still a keen one day eventer. He and his partner live in a house in the grounds; she works for a law firm in London. He is a passionate advocate of both the Round Square and the IB and this is what drew him to Cobham. 'The IB is the best preparation for the next stage of the girls' lives..The Round Square ethos of all round development of the individual through adventurous challenges and service works well at Cobham and fits well with the IB..It offers a holistic education and is all about fulfilling potential – it is about what is right for each girl..The Round Square ideals of internationalism, democracy, environmentalism, adventure, leadership and service are central to what we do'. He was struck by the friendliness of the place when he was interviewed – the Guardian (head girl) and house captains were part of the interview panels and they sold it to him. He is a 'calm and caring man and a good communicator who has surrounded himself with a very effective senior management team,' said a parent. 'The headmaster is very kind; he always remembers the girls' names and makes them feel special,' said another.

Academic matters: The IB was introduced in 2009 and A levels phased out at the same time. The results reflect the wide range of abilities within the school. The average diploma points in 2016 was 31, with best ever GCSE results: 50 per cent A*/A and 75 per cent A*-B. All girls take at least eight GCSEs and most do 10. Girls setted in maths, English and science from year 7 and sometimes in other subjects depending on the size of the year group. Sixth form curriculum tailored to each girl and some take IB certificates rather than the full diploma. 'Girls generally do better than expected,' says the headmaster. Class sizes up to 20 in the lower years with an average of 12 and no more than 12 per class (and some much smaller) in sixth form. One parent said that she was concerned about the small classes before her daughter started but added: 'the brightest girls are stretched and encouraged'. The teachers are a 'good combination of the homely and the vibrant and dynamic' – about half are male.

French, Spanish and Latin offered at GCSE and at standard and higher level in the IB. German offered as a first language to native speakers in IB. Chinese offered as first or second language in the IB and can be taken ab initio at standard level – taught by a native speaker. Science is popular and most take three separate sciences at GCSE although dual award is available – 'girls are braver about sciences in a single sex school,' says the head. Good range of subjects offered in the IB including theatre, psychology, music and computing science at the higher level and sport and exercise science and health and environmental systems and societies at standard level. The small size of the school means that they can be 'reactive to demand and flexible with the timetable'.

Cobham offers a pre-IB course and girls joining this for the year have the option of sitting up to five GCSEs. Many join for only one or two terms to brush up their English or as preparation for the IB at Cobham. They are taught separately in most subjects but may join the school's GCSE students for sport. They live in Main Hall with the other GCSE students.

About 60 girls need help with English and the EFL programme is tailored for each girl. Girls joining in years 10 and 12 need good English and will generally study the English B qualification (English for non-native speakers). The school is a registered centre for ESOL (English for Speakers of other Languages) exams but not IELTS (International English Language Test System).

The school is CReSTeD registered – about 20 need some sort of learning support. Much emphasis on inclusivity; girls offered one-to-one support to develop strategies and there is good support for teachers in the classroom to enable them to get the best out of students. Occasionally have to turn a girl away if the school feels they cannot meet her needs.

Girls offered careers advice from early on: via PSHE in the lower years and are then help with interview technique before work experience in year 10. They take part in the Big Business Pitch, a two day event where girls learn about starting and marketing their own business. Year 12s attend a higher education fair and an Oxbridge conference. Plenty of help with personal statement and university choices. The school also belongs to the ISCO which, for a fee, offers girls individual interviews and career profiling until the age of 23 – most sign up to this.

Games, options, the arts: Sport has come on by leaps and bounds in recent years; 'it was at the egg and spoon race stage when I arrived,' says the head. 'Now we have girls trialling for the England U18 hockey team, the Kent County Schools show jumping champion, a girl in the South of England eventing team, finalists in the National Biathlon Championships and an Elder (old girl) is heading for Rio with the modern pentathlon team.' Good links with local hockey club – some county hockey and netball players and a girl training with the girls' U16 West Ham football team. All girls up until year 11 have to take part in team sports two or three times a week and sixth form have to take some exercise – zumba and yoga are popular. Indoor heated swimming pool with swimming coaching twice a week. Duke of Edinburgh compulsory in year 9 – most do bronze and a good number do silver, some start gold at school but complete it at university.

Impressive artwork displayed around the school reflects the internationalism of the pupils. Photography popular and school has its own darkroom as well as a suite of Apple Macs for digital work. One photography student invited to exhibit at the Royal Academy. Ceramics and sculpture particularly dynamic under the tutelage of the 'legendary clay man'.

The school has a fully-equipped drama studio, but the magnificent Gilt Hall is often used for productions and everyone has to take part in the inter-house drama competitions. One whole school play a year and girls do well in LAMDA exams.

The school fosters a spirit of adventure and leadership – girls encouraged to take assemblies and stand up in public, and about 20-30 attend the Model United Nations each year. Trips and expeditions all over the world as part of the Round Square – conferences and exchanges, usually for three to four weeks but sometimes for a whole term, and involvement in international projects working with students from other Round Square schools.

Ambitious head of music who previously worked in Barbados 'pushes the boundaries and has got the choirs going'. The school has links with Rochester Choral Society and the chamber choir has recently returned from a trip to Poland. About half the school takes individual music lessons in the music wing with nine practice rooms, a recording studio and digital music suite. 'It's a small, lively department – not that many do music, but those who do are very good and into it,' according to one girl.

Boarding: About 50 per cent board, mostly full with about 10 weekly boarders, and most of the rest do some flexi-boarding – school is very accommodating but likes 24 hours' notice unless there is an emergency, and charges accordingly. The younger girls sleep in Main Hall in bright light dorms of two to five. Two sixth form houses – Bligh and Brooke – with single and double rooms, many ensuite. All boarding houses have kitchens and common rooms with large televisions.

Sixth form boarders can eat breakfast and cook supper in their houses – they have a weekly visit to supermarket and are taught about food hygiene. 'We have a lot of fun in the boarding houses and boarding makes you learn how to rub along with people,' said one girl. Girls have genuine friends in different year groups and it really does seem to be a 'home from home'.

No Saturday school, but day girls have to come in on some Saturdays for activities, project work, and some school trips. 'My daughter sometimes asks to stay in for the weekend as the boarders have such fun, especially if there is a tip to Bluewater shopping centre,' said a mother. Cookery club runs on Saturdays: girls cook a meal and eat together in the evening

Background and atmosphere: The school is housed in a grade 1 listed Tudor mansion complete with turrets and chimneys and set in 150 acres of parkland between Gravesend and Rochester, about 30 miles from London and 10 minutes from Ebbsfleet station, with Eurostar connections to mainland Europe. Built for the 10th Baron Cobham in the 16th century and sold to the earls of Darnley in the 18th, it remained their family home until 1957. Often used as a film set, including for the Hetty Feather BBC series by Jacqueline Wilson and feature film Tulip Fever, as well as weddings and conferences. The school was opened in 1962 by Mrs Bee Mansell as an international boarding school for girls where they could enjoy the same education as boys. Cobham joined the Round Square in the early 1970s and was the first girls' school to do so. The name comes from the Round Square building at Gordonstoun, one of the original member schools where the first RS conference took place in 1967. Everyone given a map on arrival but girls quickly get used to their stunning surroundings – the ornate fireplaces and plasterwork ceilings and the glorious Gilt Hall complete with an 18th century organ soon get taken for granted.

Pastoral care, well-being and discipline: The Round Square philosophy 'There is more to you than you think' and 'education through experience' underpins everything the school does. 'It is only when girls step out of their comfort zone that they truly discover themselves,' says the headmaster. Girls given a lot of autonomy and encouraged to use opportunities and 'they seem genuinely to care about the Round Square programme,' said one mother. 'Girls want to do well and we put so much pressure on ourselves – it is important to make time for yourself,' said our guide. Girls are trained and expected to take part in the running of the school and all staff and girls vote for the Guardian (head girl).

Older girls very supportive of younger ones and everyone is given a 'big sister' when they arrive; the mixed aged tutor groups in each house means there is good mixing between year groups. 'Everyone is very kind and my daughter and I both felt part of the Cobham family from the start,' said a mother. Years 7-11 have their own common rooms with kitchens, which encourages mixing between day girls and boarders. Weekly 'family lunch' when girls sit in tutor groups and practise their conversation skills. Bullying rare but nipped in the bud and restorative justice applied. Automatic suspension for drugs or alcohol – not that it is an issue here – and repeat offenders would be asked to leave.

The CAS (community, action, service) element of the IB has been extended to the middle school and there is a dedicated member of staff who gives half her time to this – anything from visiting old people's homes and collecting food for food banks to helping out in local primary schools and youth clubs. There is a Christian Union group within the school and those of other faiths are encouraged to worship locally – there is a Sikh temple, mosque and synagogue nearby. Good communication between staff means any problems are picked up quickly

Pupils and parents: About 40 per cent of pupils are foreign nationals, rising to about 60 per cent in the sixth form, with increasing numbers of Europeans. No one nationality dominates; 'girls really do mix' and integration taken seriously – no two girls of the same nationality are allowed to share a bedroom and there are 'small sanctions, like kitchen duty, if you are caught speaking your native language during the day,' said our guide. Day girls come from as far afield as south east London. The school turns out girls who are 'confident and worldly-wise, who are keen to get involved and tend to be quite adventurous,' says the headmaster. 'The girls don't grow up too quickly and there is no need to yank up your skirt or slap on the make up as no one is going to see..They are more likely to be seen chatting in Lady Darnley's garden or swinging on "the branch".' 'Turns out confident and beautifully eloquent girls,' said one mother. The girls all see themselves as global citizens and have no fear of travel – 'the Round Square network means they have friends all over the world,' said a parent.

Elders, as the old girls are known at Cobham, are hugely loyal to the school and include Mishal Husain, news presenter, Olivia Graham, archdeacon of Berkshire, journalist Alex Crawford, Francesca Amfitiahtrof, creative director at Tiffany's, Princess Antonia, Duchess of Wellington and Kate French, who was part of the modern pentathlon team at Rio.

Entrance: Entry into years 7, 8, 9, 10 and sixth form via tests in English and maths and an interview with the headmaster in the autumn before entry. International students can either take the school's own tests or apply via UKiset. A taster afternoon and sleepover can be arranged at any time and parents are also given the opportunity to get to know each other. Main feeder schools are Steephill and St Joseph's at Gravesend, Pointers in Blackheath and south east London preps and local state primaries – the school runs a minibus service as far as Sevenoaks.

Some 10-20 join from abroad for the increasingly popular pre-IB course.

Exit: Around half leave after GCSEs, mainly to larger co-ed schools, local grammars and sixth form colleges. For those who stay on for the sixth form, great trouble is taken to choose a course and university that is right for each girl. Around a fifth to Russell Group universities (the occasional one to Oxbridge); art foundation and business courses popular as are eg criminology and biomedical sciences. Growing expertise in helping girls with the process of applying to foreign universities including Australia and the US – the school is able to help with SATs.

Money matters: Art, drama, music, sport and Round Square scholarships by application, and general (academic) scholarship by invitation only – identified through the entrance assessments. Means-tested bursaries are available for up to 100 per cent of fees.

Remarks: A small, truly international school which turns out compassionate and adventurous global citizens.

C

Cokethorpe School

Witney, Oxfordshire OX29 7PU

Pupils: 660 • Ages: 4–18 • Sixth form: 146

Fees: £12,150 – £17,850 pa

Tel: 01993 703921
Email: admissions@cokethorpe.org
Website: www.cokethorpe.org.uk

Headmaster: Since 2002, Mr Damian Ettinger BA MA PGCE (40s). Educated St Joseph's College (Beulah Hill), Universities of Manchester and Surrey (theology and philosophy). Previously head of theology and housemaster at Downside and before that at Prior Park College, Bath. Teaches theology up to GCSE and philosophy in the sixth form. Voluble and delightfully opinionated, his passion for Cokethorpe and all it can do for its pupils is undimmed since our last visit. We searched high and low for evidence of squashed laurels in Mr Ettinger's wood-clad study but found none.

We cannot recall touring a school and hearing the head's name mentioned so frequently: 'They were Mr Ettinger's idea – some people didn't get them at first but now everyone loves them' (of the delightful metal animal and bird sculptures that pop up on lawns, walls and roofs) or, of the excellent termly newsletter, The Ocellus, 'Mr Ettinger set that up'. The Trafalgar-inspired fourth plinth in the courtyard? You guessed it – Mr Ettinger and his ideas again. It is this vision and energy that have driven the renaissance of Cokethorpe, making it now a first choice school for many. He is pretty frank about the changes he made when appointed: 'Learning support was dictating the culture of the school'; LS now at roughly 10 per cent and, as a result, 'is much more effective'. He wants Cokethorpe pupils 'to exhibit the old-fashioned virtues of kindness and decency' and challenge the current trend of laddishness in both boys and girls. Big on manner, he restored proper plates, cutlery and glasses to the dining hall against advice and, guess what, the sky didn't fall in.

Among the buzzier bees in Mr Ettinger's bonnet is the question of 'why kids lose enthusiasm for science' – one way of tackling this at Cokethorpe is links with nearby Rutherford labs so that teachers can go and play with the latest equipment and bring their renewed enthusiasm back to pupils. His pipedream is an 'interdisciplinary science park approach to teaching'; also on his wish list are a new theatre, music school and dedicated examination hall.

Mr Ettinger is something of a jazz buff and reviews for Jazz Journal. When asked what he would do if he were not headmaster, he claims he would like to run a garage (he owns three classic cars and has recently done a welding course), but we think something of the architect manqué there too. He's big on 'sightlines', and the extensive (and expensive) building programme has been managed with real vision – new and old flow together in productive harmony. He pays tribute to his second in command and the 'hands on' governors and is grateful not to be 'shackled by internal politics'.

Mr Ettinger, who describes himself as a 'Roman Catholic of the English variety', is married with five children; his wife teaches IT at a nearby FE college – 'The fact that she isn't involved in the day-to-day running of the school allows me to go home and be a typical family man'. When asked what car he would be he points to a model on his desk – 'That one, a brown Ford Cortina Mk 3'.

Head of junior school: Since 2006 is Christine Cook. Educated Westminster College, Oxford, Brockenhurst Sixth Form College. Formerly director of studies at Chandlings School, teaching houseparent at The Dragon School, head of year at The Oxford Academy (formerly Peers School), Oxford.

Academic matters: National curriculum is followed but with plenty of extras such as French in the junior school. There is specialist teaching for music, art, drama, French and games – apparently this last is a real favourite as mini-Cokethorpeans are put through their paces by the senior school sports coaches. Latin is taught in years 5 and 6 but this is not continued in the senior school, although there are plans to do so. Small class numbers (average 16) in big high-ceilinged rooms, yet everything is friendly and child-centred. We watched as children in bright yellow polo shirts sat in a circle on the floor devising 'smart questions' about shapes. The pace of this hands-on lesson was just right, with plenty of time for all to think things through. The children's concentration was so intense that you could almost hear those youthful synapses fizzing and popping as they made connections and worked things out. We were momentarily distracted by a wall covered in delightful paintings of the things to be found in the Quangle Wangle's hat – Bisky Bats and all. Classes are mixed ability with setting for maths and spelling from year 3.

Solid results – in 2016, 47 per cent A*/A at GCSE, 42 per cent A*/A and 64 per cent A*-B at A level. The long-term concerted effort to instil academic rigour is clearly paying dividends, but the head is by no means complacent, claiming that although he doesn't want to depart entirely from Cokethorpe's valued reputation as an inclusive, family school, room for 'nudging' things up.

School is changing to IGCSEs for most subjects, but IB has been considered and rejected. Instead, Mr Ettinger's sights are on widening what is currently a trickle into a regular stream of pupils heading for Oxbridge and leading American universities. Most popular A level subject choices are currently the Oxbridge-unfriendly PE, business studies and psychology, but geography, maths and science not far behind. Relatively small numbers taking languages and English.

One of the first schools to introduce Cambridge pre-U for history (with excellent results) and same for other subjects (English, modern languages, economics and philosophy) arriving shortly. Impressive general studies programme of visiting lecturers and other extension activities for sixth form, including English Literature recitals where staff hold forth on matters of literary interest.

Lessons we observed were, on the whole, pacy and inclusive – small classes (average 14, max 20) should mean nowhere to hide, but perhaps muttering at the back will always be with us. Work we saw was very helpfully marked with positive comments and constructive criticism.

About 10 per cent, mainly pupils with dyslexia or dyspraxia, receive specialist individual support (up to three hours per fortnight) and liaison between teaching staff and the LS department ensures pupils' needs are met in lessons.

Games, options, the arts: Cokethorpe is indeed fortunate in its spacious grounds, and maximum use is made of these for all sports that require acreage – rugby, football, hockey, cricket and even golf. Strong inter-house competition in addition to matches with other schools means that all get a chance to participate at some level. County champions in rugby and hockey, and county and national representatives in athletics, cricket, tennis, netball and cross-country. Particularly strong record of national successes in clay pigeon shooting and kayaking. Climbing wall but no swimming pool – 'Everybody thinks it should be on my wish list but it isn't,' declares the head, so wet stuff takes place at Brize Norton. Standard issue large echoing sports hall with gallery gym – our guides described this (and practically everything else Cokethorpean) as 'amazing', but we thought the gym rather macho. It is, they conceded 'mainly for the rugby players', but girls' only sessions too. An hour at the end of each day and extended Friday lunchtimes are for over 50 'AOB' activities such as salsa dancing, bird-watching – surely pretty rewarding, given the sylvan setting – poker, touch-typing and archery.

DT and art benefit from spacious well-appointed workshops – some great examples of student work on display including beautifully turned and decorated paddles. Art, photography and textiles are offered at GCSE and A level. Music for all and to a very high standard – we liked the way it is unavoidable even for those who do not play or sing: pupils give lunchtime music recitals, madrigals on May Day, a singing category for all in the inter-house competition, and the choir sings grace from the gallery to dining pupils below every Wednesday. An award-winning school jazz band and termly gig nights are a very popular platform for the less classically minded. Drama offered both as part of the curriculum (theatre studies) and as an AOB option; two main school productions a year including a summer Shakespeare and plenty of house plays keep Cokethorpe's thespians busy.

Days are long – buses leave at 5pm for what can be an hour's journey home – and an enormous amount going on. Add to this field trips, workshops, charity fundraising, competitions, homework, weekend matches and Saturday morning performing arts academy – it's no wonder parents tell us some pupils can fall behind.

Background and atmosphere: Founded in 1957 with 14 pupils, the school occupies a Queen Anne mansion surrounded by 150 acres of serene, manicured parkland complete with ha-ha and ancient trees – recently reduced by 10, thanks to a tornado that ripped through (fortunately on a bank holiday). The Vanbrugh-style mansion, where the first Viscount Harcourt entertained literary fellows Swift, Dryden and Pope, is now home to admin, head's study and the junior department. Entrance hall and public areas uncluttered and notably free of pupils' artistic endeavours (an absence more than made up for in rest of school), all the better to appreciate the original Georgian lines perhaps.

Juniors are taught in the Georgian splendour of the Mansion, sharing the 150 acres of parkland, sporting and academic facilities (science labs, IT suites etc) with their senior comrades. Juniors also eat in the splendid new dining hall.

Behind the mansion in its cobbled mews is, wonder of wonders, The Grove, a Costa Coffee outlet serving free drinks and snacks (fruit, biscuits etc) to sixth formers. This venue also used as 'philosophy café' hosting talks and seminars. Our guides were immaculate in the sixth form 'business dress'; what manner of business some of the other Costa denizens aspired to we can only speculate, but the head prefers a degree of individuality to abandoning the dress code altogether. Teaching and learning for the seniors is in new-build academic departments arranged round a quad, a fab library and luxurious sixth form centre – lots of glass and metal successfully merging modern with the mellow Cotswold stone.

Another architectural triumph is the double-height dining hall – the head fought planning, not to mention health and safety, to get the huge baronial fireplace installed; it must be quite a sight at Christmas. We stood in the gallery and looked down on refectory tables and benches beautifully designed in plain solid wood and thought of all the cabbagey subterranean school watering holes we have had the misfortune to visit. In fact the food does also appear to be 'amazing'. Lucky, lucky Cokethorpe.

Smart pin-striped trousers and skirts, navy jumpers with gold trim – it's a challenge for the determined fashionista to tweak a uniform like this but, bless 'em, they do. Perhaps, like a wise parent, the school picks its battles, and rather than being too stuffy about minor infringements, sets its sights on encouraging the major virtues such as tolerance and respect for others. Interestingly, the head might prefer pupils to channel their rebel spirits into 'underground magazines and the like'; he expressed a nostalgic regret for the absence of such.

Pastoral care, well-being and discipline: Cokethorpe is a joint Roman Catholic and Church of England foundation and pastoral care has long been seen as a strength of the school; pupils to whom we spoke endorse this – 'It's a real community – everyone knows everyone else and looks out for each other'. Rules and useful information including school policies on bullying helpfully set out in the pocket-sized Blue Book issued to all pupils. Head keen to maintain family feel and will 'bend a little' to accommodate siblings of varied abilities. Having pupils aged 4 to 18 on the same site certainly seems to foster an atmosphere of mutual support and it's hard to imagine any child passing through anonymously.

Pupils and parents: Subsidised buses pick up 70 per cent of pupils from 22 routes encompassing Swindon, Oxford, Brize Norton and Didcot. School population not ethnically diverse – reflects local demographic (any episode of Midsomer Murders will give you the idea) and parents are the usual mix of professionals and first time buyers. Pupils seem to be a sparky bunch.

Entrance: Reception to year 2: visit with assessment in maths and literacy. Years 3-6: assessment day in January plus report from previous school. Cokethorpe juniors must pass same assessments as external candidates for entry to senior school. Increasingly popular, not just because independent co-ed options in Oxfordshire are pretty limited – roughly two candidates for every place.

Senior school (age 11): interview, tests and observed activities. Candidates for 13+ offered provisional place on basis of pre-test, conditional on satisfactory performance in CE. Sixth form requires A* to C in maths, English and science plus 'good' grades in subjects to be studied at A level.

Main feeders are local state primaries and independents such as The Manor, Chandlings, St Hugh's, The Dragon, New College School, Abingdon Prep. Cokethorpe has an 'association' with nearby Westfield House Nursery School, from where a number of children enter the reception class every year.

Exit: Virtually all juniors to senior school. During year 5, parents of junior school pupils unlikely to make it into the senior school are helped to look elsewhere. A fifth leave post GCSE. At 18, to a wide range of universities, including Durham, Chichester, Hull, Birmingham, Manchester, Cardiff, Bristol and Nottingham, to read anything from marketing to medicine.

Money matters: Lots of means-tested scholarships/bursaries of all kinds – academic, art, music, sports, drama, classics, modern langs and all-rounder. Minor schols for two years from 11. All gauged on exam performance and interview with head.

Remarks: Cokethorpe is an interesting study in just how long the tail of a school's former reputation can be – even now, in the second decade from Mr Ettinger's year zero, one still occasionally hears it referred to as a 'soft option' (but this is Oxfordshire, where 'soft' is a relative concept). Prep school heads know different and the days of, 'Never mind – there's always Cokethorpe,' are long gone. This is a thriving, energetic school; several parents mentioned they liked it because it is a less stuffy, more grounded place to learn than some of the competition. As a relative newcomer, Cokethorpe has been able to cherry-pick some of the more appealing traditions of older establishments and make them its own, forging ahead with all the positive benefits of modern co-education in a classical English setting.

C

Colchester County High School for Girls

Norman Way, Colchester, Essex CO3 3US

Pupils: 931 • Ages: 11–18 • Sixth form: 247

Tel: 01206 576973
Email: office@colchestergirls.essex.sch.uk
Website: www.cchsg.com

Headteacher: Since 2010, Mrs Gillian Marshall MSc BSc (biochemistry) PGCE NPQH. Previously deputy head at the mixed comprehensive Notley High School, Braintree, for 11 years. Prior to that teaching posts at Bishop's Stortford High School for Boys, Townley Girls' Grammar School in Bexley Heath and Davenant Foundation Christian Ecumenical School in Loughton. A biology and chemistry specialist, she says she has 'always loved teaching and never considered doing anything else'. Keen on all sport, particularly running. Mrs Marshall has three children. Her arrival at CCHSG, after the long tenure of the previous headteacher, inevitably led to some changes, and a newly invigorated SLT is now on a mission to take the school 'beyond outstanding', by 're-evaluating its vision' and making sure that its precious cargo of some of the country's brightest students are instilled with a 'world-class education', and the self-belief and resilience to use it to make a real difference.

Academic matters: A regular feature in the UK's top 10 high-achievers, CCHSG attracts the cream of the crop with ease. These bright girls have fought their way through the rigorous consortium of selective schools in Essex 11+ exam and are veritable sponges for the stimulating, thought-provoking, multi-faceted education that awaits them. French and German are begun in year 7 and Latin kicks in in year 8. Pupils must take at least one of French or German to GCSE. Sciences are taught separately from year 7 and are popular A level options – reflecting CCHSG's status as a specialist college for both science and languages. Technology lessons for years 7, 8 and 9 are run in conjunction with Essex University where the girls learn a variety of skills in state-of-the-art facilities.

Taking 11 GCSEs is the norm – 88 per cent A*/A, 2016. A level results are impressive across the board – 51 per cent A*/A and 82 per cent A*/B. Maths regularly delivers at least an A grade for 90 per cent of those taking it. Everyone studies creative and critical thinking, and takes the AS exam during years 10 – 11. Last year three students sat GCSE maths in year 9. Sixth formers mentor the younger ones.

Such stellar achievement in all areas may cause a few anxieties, but parents applaud the school's ability 'to achieve excellent exam results without the girls being stressed' and the 'serene atmosphere'. The quiet expectation is that girls will be independent, organised and, adds a parent, 'achieve high grades from year 7 onwards'. Indeed the most recent Ofsted report was tantamount to flawless. 'Girls here enjoy being successful and achieving,' explains the headteacher. Lessons encourage the deeper exploration of knowledge through lively debate, challenge and innovation. Ever-present is the necessity for all learning to have a real-world application.

Only four pupils are on the school's SEND register and a variety of needs are represented. An assistant headteacher takes on the additional role of SENCo and support is generally offered on an individual basis – no in-class assistance as the school does not have the requirement for teaching assistants. However, staff themselves are constantly updated on individual students' needs, and the school works closely with students, parents, and external agencies, if need be.

Games, options, the arts: The headteacher's drive for 'excellence in everything' really does extend to everything. Numerous musical groups, ensembles and choirs, many instigated by the girls themselves, all of exceptional quality. Drama traditionally strong, although some parents and pupils lament a decline in opportunities in recent years, perhaps due to the proliferation of newer extracurricular activities, including dance. Art shows great depth of sensitivity, maturity and complexity for students of such relative youth and – typical of the CCHSG approach – projects are seen as an opportunity for general education as well as refinement of artistic technique. Works are displayed in galleries and exhibitions across the region and in London, including the RA Summer Show, on a regular basis. 'Creativity should be in every lesson' says head. Artsmark award.

CCHSG girls have dominated Colchester Blackwater School Sports Partnerships competitions of all kinds – netball, hockey, basketball, athletics in particular – for the past 25 years, and more recently students have reached national finals in fencing and junior biathlon. Gym and dance is on the PE curriculum for all year groups. Elite athletes are picked and trained in squads, but those with more enthusiasm than talent have many active clubs to choose from, including very popular before, during and after-school swimming in the recently roofed pool. Most clubs run by senior pupils; staff are generous with their time and encouragement. D of E is thriving and now run in-house – last year, 77 year 10s achieved bronze and 20 year 11s silver. Plans afoot to add gold. Involvement in European Youth Parliament and Young Enterprise (recent shower timer product still on sale in local stores). Inspirational speakers (eg first British woman to reach the top of Everest, Rebecca Stephens, and Olympian Sally Gunnell) emphasise the 'I can do anything' ethos that pervades all aspects of the school.

Background and atmosphere: Founded at the turn of the century but relocated to its current site, a campus setting on a quiet road a mile from the centre of Colchester, in 1957. Aims to be the 'new generation of grammar school' – free of the shackles of traditional Victorian architecture and atmosphere that pervades some of our longest established state selective schools. Exterior thankfully very much upgraded since our last visit. Biggest impact made by replacement of the once rattly metal framed windows of the main teaching block with fresh energy efficient panes and painted panels. Brings the campus into the 21st century. More than a million pounds have been spent on upgrading the facilities here (including science labs) to ensure that they do justice to the quality of teaching and learning at one of the UK's very highest achieving schools. Half of the funds – secured by canny bidding – spent on the windows and the rest spread judiciously throughout the school for maximum benefit.

Catherine Bullen Centre named after a former pupil, who passed away working as a medic in Africa; in her memory, her parents established a medical foundation in Uganda. Includes a superb new dance studio complete with professional sprung floor and full length mirrors added in 2012 and used for all sorts of cross-curricular activities (including practice for the staff's revue number). New changing rooms are a welcome improvement and now offer disabled access as per many of the recently refurbished areas of the school (including loos, designed by pupils and partly paid for by the PTA's 'Flushed with Success' fundraiser).

Showcase high-tech i-lab is used by all for timetabled lessons – students scrawl their thoughts on the wall and then recall them at a later date for further study. Recently reorganised sixth form common room now has a work area, banks of computers and seating for the 230 girls; next door is a dedicated resources room hanging with computers. All blocks are now accessible by swiping personal ID cards. A further bid for funds for a new teaching block to replace a community of tired portakabins and add new lecture theatre is still pending.

Playing fields on site, and green spaces between the teaching blocks have been much improved with fencing and picnic benches for girls to gather on at breaks.

Girls rave about the food – a one-man band buys fresh ingredients every day and even tries out recipes suggested by the girls. Bright dining space – recently expanded – serves hot and cold food, and girls who have lunchtime clubs can request food to be speedily collected and eaten wherever is most convenient. Payment is via a biometric system (fingerprint recognition). Breakfast club has been relaunched due to popular demand – porridge galore.

Pastoral care, well-being and discipline: With so much talent in a relatively small space, CCHSG could be something of a pressure cooker environment; however, the strategy is to use PE and PSHE lessons to teach coping skills, approaches to revision and even breathing exercises at crucial times. Girls themselves say they feel well supported by form tutors, who move up through the years with their charges as far as year 11. Very many opportunities for girls to act as role models – year 10 Literacy Leaders run sessions on eg the proper use of the apostrophe and give literacy lessons to local primary pupils, Junior Sports Leaders and Youth Health Champions offer lifestyle workshops. Charity work is intrinsic – girls choose good causes to support through cake sales, non-uniform days etc and raise around £6,000 a year. Recently a focused effort meant a whopping £10,000 was raised for a school in Uganda. Girls appear to get along happily together and self-discipline is exemplary – detention rarely resorted to. Students recently prompted an overhaul of the rewards system – merits in years 7 and 8 and now 'R awards' in year 9, with the names of those receiving them entered into a raffle for a tasty prize (recently an iPad), plus pens, pencils and Amazon or book vouchers along the way. Years 10 and 11 receive commendations. Every half term each member of staff recognises a pupil for achievement and another for endeavour with a congratulatory letter home – seniority of staff member signing denotes the magnitude. Also rewards for attendance, community service and many Jack Petchey. Grade for 'attitude to learning' now replaces 'effort' in reports.

Pupils and parents: 'Self-awareness, self-esteem and self-discipline' are key attributes here, and girls grow up in a supportive environment that nurtures confidence, maturity and the belief in oneself necessary to achieve any chosen goal. Joining CCHSG from around 65 different primary schools across central and north Essex and south Suffolk, girls are from varying home backgrounds, a handful with English as a second language (although their fluency has enabled them to get through the entrance exam).

Keeping in touch with parents is not easy, given the geography, but there's a monthly e-newsletter celebrating the many achievements and weekly bulletin to parents (also published on website); parents are largely supportive of school events. Within the school, a creative arts e-magazine is on the drawing board, while a welcome guide for new year 7s is prepared by older students who identified a need.

Old Girls include plantswoman, garden designer and author Beth Chatto OBE, Olympic gold medal-winning sailor Saskia Clark and MP Stella Creasy.

Entrance: One of the top-performing schools in the UK, it's no surprise that places are highly sought-after. Entrance is granted to those 140 girls who perform best in the notorious consortium of selective schools in Essex 11+ exam – maths and English. For all students joining the sixth form, minimum entry requirement is four As and two Bs, including English language and mathematics and grade A/A* in the subjects to be taken at A level. Many travel from far and wide, some lodging in Colchester for convenience.

Exit: Around 30 per cent left post-GCSEs in 2016 – mostly to co-ed sixth forms eg Colchester Royal Grammar or The Sixth Form College – and just under five per cent at the end of year 12. Only one or two choose not to go on to university. In 2016, five to Oxbridge, six to study medicine and just over half to Russell Group unis, vast majority to first choice destinations. York, UAE, UCL, Sheffield and Bath recent popular choices. Law, medicine and academia established career paths.

Remarks: A place of education that is not just a beacon nationally, but also internationally, delivering a world-class education to girls equipped with the drive, intelligence and integrity to take the lead in any chosen field and to make a rich contribution in life.

Colchester Royal Grammar School

6 Lexden Road, Colchester, Essex CO3 3ND

Pupils: 904; 30 boarders (sixth form boys only) • Ages: 11-18 • Sixth form: 361 (including 109 girls)

Fees: Boarding £13,200 pa; Day: free

Tel: 01206 509100
Email: info@crgs.co.uk
Website: www.crgs.co.uk

Headmaster: Since 2015, Mr John Russell BSc MA ARCS, previously deputy head of Cranbrook School. Physics degree from Imperial College; first job in a Loughton comprehensive school before becoming head of physics at Ilford County High.

Gracious, unintimidating and refreshingly honest and transparent, he is a hands-on head, who teaches physics to at least one year group every year, and has plans to do more. Students regularly pop into his office unannounced, usually to tell of their successes. 'If I grant them a leave of absence – which I sometimes do for competitions as far away as Poland – the criteria is that they have to tell me how it went afterwards.' We noticed he pays the same level of respect to students as they give to him in conversations – it's all very mutual, with no draconian rules around standing up when he walks into a classroom etc. 'He's not like a headmaster – he's one of the team and the students love him for it,' a parent told us. He has a weekly drop-in session for parents and staff say he is highly supportive and consultative.

He lives five minutes' walk away with his wife, Michelle, a chemistry teacher, and their three children, two of whom are at the school. Describes himself as an enthusiastic sportsman if not a very accomplished one, with a particular enjoyment of football and racket sports. Also has a passion for music.

Academic matters: Extremely high academic standards, with the school's A level results nearly 70 per cent A*/A and 90 per cent A*-B in 2016 – having made them number one in the government league tables for nine out of the last 10 years. 'One student recently got nine A*s and 2 As, and that was at A level,' says the head. For GCSE, 76 per cent A*/A grades, including maths and English, and 15 per cent achieved at least 10 A* grades.

No setting in years 7 or 8, French and maths setted from year 9 – 'but this is only a question of pace,' says school. 'Set 4 pupils will still be expected to achieve A* at GCSE.' French and Latin in year 7, plus additional choice of German or Greek in year 8. One of the very few state schools to offer Greek to A level – for a state school, an above average number go on to study classics at university. No areas of weakness to speak of at either GCSE or A level, with particularly outstanding results in humanities, maths, sciences, D&T and economics. 'We have lots of further maths students,' says head. If the school doesn't teach a subject that a student desperately wants to do, they'll try to provide one lecture a week if the student agrees to self-teach the rest. 'We've done this with government and politics, Mandarin and a number of other subjects in the past,' says head.

So what's the secret of their success? One word – teaching. Students rave about the teachers here, notably their commitment to keeping every single pupil intellectually stretched and on track to meet their targets, providing extra support and revision clubs as necessary, and being available out-of-hours via email. 'There's lots of talk about where you should be at and how to achieve it.' Then there's the sheer quality of teaching. 'They keep it imaginative, fresh and innovative at all times.' 'They're not afraid to throw the textbooks aside.' 'You are never bored in a lesson.' 'Their enthusiasm is contagious.' Etc. Not a single inattentive expression spotted during our visit – these youngsters are hungry to learn and the teaching is a feast, in every sense. 'It's made very clear that it's ok to fail – that's how you learn – and my son has thrived because of it,' said one parent. 'It's not just intellectually rigorous and stimulating, it's relevant too – showing boys how what they're learning fits into today's world,' said another. 'It's more than about getting these youngsters to pass exams – it's about where this learning is going to take them in life.' Homework levels are, according to students, 'reasonable – and if you haven't been able to do it, there's a culture of support, rather than an immediate sanction.' Maximum of 30 in a class lower down; 25 at GCSE; and 20 in sixth-form.

Some SEND pupils with physical disabilities, including visual impairments, and a fair number of Asperger's, plus a few dyslexic. Support is mainly classroom-based, and parents could not praise it more highly. 'With our son, they have taken a difficult autistic boy and grown him into a wonderful young man – coping with his complexities and outbursts in their stride, and celebrating every minor success. The staff should be getting an OBE, in my opinion,' one parent told us. Any EAL pupil will have had a high enough standard of English to pass the selection tests.

Games, options, the arts: Cricket and rugby strong. Regular fixtures against state and independent schools, with some representation at national level. Increasing strength in athletics. Netball, and now rugby, for sixth form girls. 'That's the one thing I'd change – I really think there could be more on offer for girls,' one told us. Other sports available as extracurricular activities, including sailing and weight-training. Also plenty of non-sporting activities. 'Sport here is inclusive – it's not all about the top players,' parents assured us. Extensive playing fields five minutes' walk away – 'less than ideal, but that's the way it is,' says head. Within the school, there's tarmacked playground, which is regularly used for sport, plus a heated outdoor pool.

Exciting music department, which takes up a whole (onsite) three-story house, with loads of opportunities for any pupil with any musical ambitions. 'Our son is musical, but I didn't know what to expect with this school because it's better known for the academia, but the opportunities for learning and performing have massively impressed us,' said one parent. No shortage of instruments (many donated by old boys) and break-out rooms. Live music in every assembly; choirs and school orchestra; ensembles and bands, many student led; and 200 learn an instrument with a peripatetic teacher. 'I came here with no musical experience whatsoever and I'm now much more confident and enjoying the piano,' one boy told us.

Drama only offered as extracurricular, but popular, with a much-talked-about annual performance, with examples including Fame and West Side Story. Rehearsals for a French play when we visited, as part of French lessons, highlighting their commitment to cross-curricular teaching. Spacious and light art block boasts a kiln, dark room, printing press etc and although there is some seriously talented artwork on the walls, the more average work is equally celebrated. 'If I'm honest, art is not my son's strongest subject, but he still wanted to do it for GCSE and he's been encouraged at every turn – the school understands that the benefits of art aren't just for those who are brilliant at it,' said one parent. Around 12 do art GCSE art, and similar figures for A level. DT rooms also spacious, and clearly well-used and loved.

Big on extracurricular, with lots of clubs and societies held during breaks, lunchtimes and after school, many of which are student-led eg sixth-formers run the law and medical societies. Very strong public speaking society, which regularly competes. 'You should see them – watching one of the boys talk is like watching Tony Blair,' says the head. Lots of sport and music themes among the clubs, plus the likes of BBC Young Reporters' Club, right through to more obscure ones such as Rubik's cube club, Swedish club and even a colouring club. 'Our philosophy is that we value our students excelling in anything – and that includes things like sport and Rubik's cube club,' says head. Students enter so many competitions that even the head loses track, although he's now got himself a 'little black book' to record them in. Day trips to London for cultural days out and year 7s were at Colchester Zoo the day we visited. Plus residentials eg classics trip to Italy; languages trips to Germany; sports tours to Italy. 'We do bonding trips too, including taking all year 7s to the cinema at the end of the first term, and we recently took year 12s on a bowling night,' says the head. Plenty of charity work, including an award-winning mental health charity, Time to Talk, which was set up by students themselves.

Boarding: Two boarding houses – one directly opposite the library in the main old building; the other a self-contained building behind the sixth form block – both with a mixture of single and double bedrooms (generally, you share in year 12 and get your own room in year 13). There are cooking facilities and a communal area in each house, and four resident staff members for the 30 boarders. These boarders – all sixth form boys – are mainly those who would have too far to travel to school each day and pupils from abroad; particularly popular in Hong Kong, where a member of staff visits each year to interview potential sixth formers, with these students now making up around half of all boarders. Head is a big supporter of boarding – 'it contributes to the school environment and the international element. I'd like to expand numbers,' he says.

After school finishes at 3.40pm, there's free time, followed by dinner at 6pm and study time from 7-9pm. Lights out at 10.30pm on weekdays and 11pm on weekends. Plenty of freedom to go into town, albeit with a strict signing in and out system.

'Some go into London too, as well as to stay with local friends, although we need permission from their parents for that,' the housemaster told us. Organised trips out include cycling and visiting Cambridge. But, for the most part, they seem content to hang around school, where they are permitted to use school sports and music facilities during evenings and weekends. The gym – which had unfortunately flooded when we visited – is also popular. 'Staying here also gives us a chance for a weekend lie-in,' one boarder smiled.

'It's all pretty relaxed,' more than one boarder told us – and with bedrooms not quite as tidy as in many schools we visit, we weren't surprised when we were told by the housemaster that 'we do guidelines, rather than rules. These are young men, and we treat them as such – but with the pastoral structure very firmly in the background,' he explains. Lots of transition work, especially for the Hong Kong contingent, where boys get to meet each other before they arrive and are given plenty of information to help them prepare. The result of all this is a very happy bunch of boarders, who are in no way seen as separate from the rest of the students. In fact, our only criticism was that some of the rooms could do with a bit of TLC, but then again this is state boarding.

Background and atmosphere: Directly descended from a Colchester town school that existed in 1206 and was granted royal charters by Henry VIII in 1539 and Elizabeth I in 1584. Set in an affluent residential area of Colchester, the main buildings date back to the late 19th century. These are home to some classic grammar school classrooms, with big windows overlooking the shiny floored corridors, plus a very traditional, well-stocked library, complete with oil paintings of old headmasters on the wall, and additional silent room at the side.

Newer additions – which include blocks for science and engineering, computing and art and renovated music and drama facilities – fit well with the attractive old school buildings. The new George Young Building serves as a concert hall, performance studio and lecture theatre, while the even newer Jenkinson Building boasts state-of-the-art science labs (with air-con – a godsend on the hot day we visited), and ICT suites. Wonderful to see sixth-form engineering students hard at work on imaginative projects (top secret, we were warned when we busily scribbled down the details – but all proper real world stuff that could potentially change lives). 'Students looking to study engineering can cut their teeth on it here, while others can explore if it is really right for them,' a teacher explained.

The sixth-form centre is home to a lively common room, with a large, all-school, cashless refectory to the side, serving a wide variety of food that nobody had any complaints about. Lovely, well-tended gardens of a standard unusual in a state school, featuring quiet and private sitting areas for students – in full use when we visited. The only thing the head said he'd like to add to facilities is 'more room for sixth form private study, but I think we're lucky with everything else.'

Despite the emphasis on academic brilliance, the atmosphere here is supportive, caring and – according to some students, 'almost family-like.' 'Everyone assumes it's a hothouse, but it's really not. And we have such a diverse range of people – some are natural brainboxes; others have to work really hard to get on.' The common denominator, they say, is that everyone is a self-starter and highly motivated. 'If you're inclined to slack off, it's probably not school for you.' We encountered lots of laughter and fun banter, including with teachers. At sixth-form, there's a particularly cohesive unit of students, 'which makes for a much tighter knit group than you'd get at sixth-form college. It's lovely.' 'There's something very special about the ethos here that quite a few of us parents get quite emotional about,' one parent said.

Everyone welcomes the addition of girls at sixth form. 'They settle in very quickly and tend to be very sociable, bringing the boys out of their shell,' explains the head, who points out that this year's school captain is a girl. Uniform includes a vivid purple blazer, and for sixth formers, it's smart dress. Loud, old-fashioned bell system that's a bit of a bone-shaker until you get used to it, but it certainly gets kids moving swiftly from one class to the next.

C

Pastoral care, well-being and discipline: Excellent standard of conduct and not many discipline problems, yet nobody describes this as a 'strict' school. 'There's nothing onerous about the discipline here. In fact, there's plenty of space to make mistakes and learn from them,' said one parent. 'They have this gentle, reward-based, quite soft culture that brings out the best in everyone,' said another. Punishments, when they do happen, include loss of privileges and lunchtime and after-school detentions. No permanent expulsions in the head's time at the school, although around three temporary ones. Zero tolerance of drugs – possession leads to expulsion – with no cases in recent years.

Lots of staff leadership roles, which helps create a strong pastoral system. Beneath the deputy head is the head of lower school, head of sixth form and heads of year. Big focus on promoting mental health and healthy lifestyles. Buddy schemes; part-time school counsellor; plenty of emphasis on transition to make sure year 7s and new year 12s settle in well. Minimal bullying. 'My first school assembly of the academic year is on how we celebrate difference in this school,' says head – and pupils concur that there's an atmosphere of supporting and looking after each other. 'I can't imagine anyone bullying here,' said one student, incredulous at the thought. Inevitably, there's stress, particularly around exam time – but there's support. 'My son had a wobble due to the pressures of work and the school dealt with it very compassionately, gathering together the relevant teachers to support him and keep us informed.' Students enjoy their leadership roles too, although they said other prefects got to do little more 'than wear a different tie – there definitely needs some changes there.'

Pupils and parents: Years 7-11 mainly from Colchester and surrounding area, but students travel up to an hour each way each day, including from Ipswich and even east London. Students come from a complete mix of families, both ethnically (including international, especially in the sixth form boarders contingent) and in terms of wealth and class. All feel extremely grateful – rarely have we come across such an appreciative bunch. Very active parents' association (called CRGSA), which raises funds for the school – there had just been an Autumn Fair before our visit – and they're always present at parents' evenings and social events too.

Old boys include Telegraph columnist Giles Smith, economics commentator Tim Congdon, costume designer and double Oscar winner Jim Acheson, founder of Freeserve, John Pluthero and former BBC education correspondent Mike Baker. 'Our alumni are very supportive,' says the head. 'If we have a big project on the go, they always try to help and they are very keen to support anyone who is in a financially vulnerable position – those who would otherwise miss out on an opportunity. They are also supportive when it comes to careers, helping sixth formers move on, offering internships, interview advice and networking.'

Entrance: Highly competitive September 11+ exam, made up of English (including verbal reasoning) and maths papers. Places are awarded in rank order to the top 120 boys who have named Colchester Royal Grammar School as a preference (the school is expanding, so while there used to be 850 students, they're increasing that figure to 1,000). The exam is set by

C

the consortium of selective schools in Essex, which has 12 members, and is held in September at the school. Candidates do not have to live in Essex. Around 450 apply. Head discourages tutoring your way in, but is sensible enough to know he can't eradicate the practice and is therefore trying to offer more support to able local primary school students who can't afford it. No preference for those on pupil premium.

Minimum of four A and two B grade GCSEs for entry into sixth form for internal and external candidates. 'But because places are awarded in rank order, in reality they'll need a lot of A*s,' says the head. Around 450 external entrants apply for the 100 or so places (half of them girls), who also require a school report and must satisfy the school's academic requirements. Candidates for sixth form boarding places must meet the academic requirements first. Overseas boarders must be British or EU passport holders.

Exit: Some 95 per cent stay onto sixth form – 'the five or so boys who leave usually do so because we aren't offering the courses they want,' says head. Sixth formers virtually all to university, mostly to Russell Group including Imperial, LSE, Durham, Bath, Bristol and increasingly, St Andrews. Average of 35 to Oxbridge most years (30 in 2016) and 20+ to medical school. Popular courses include sciences, economics, history, English and languages.

Remarks: 'This is the best education that money can't buy,' was a favourite expression of the head's predecessor – and we think that's still the case. One of the country's top selective boys' state schools, which rivals many independents, but without the hard edges that schools of this calibre can have. 'It's exceeded our expectations,' was the most common phrase we heard from parents. Any academically able and hard-working boy (and sixth form girl) should thrive here.

Cothill House

Linked with Chandlings

Cothill, Abingdon, Oxfordshire OX13 6JL

Pupils: 220; all boarders • Ages: 8–13 • C of E

Fees: £26,220 pa

Tel: 01865 390800
Email: jane@cothill.net
Website: www.cothill.net

Headmaster: Since 2011, Mr Duncan Bailey (30s). Educated at Cothill, followed by Eton and a gap year in West Africa, then Manchester University (French) and Vienna University (German). Bitten by teaching bug during his year abroad but harboured ambitions to nurture his passion for sport, particularly tennis (he was a contemporary of Tim Henman) and moved into sports management. 'Fell into teaching' after being asked to stand in for the head of modern languages at Eton, where he spent two years. Prior to taking headship at Cothill ran Sauveterre, the Cothill Trust's French outpost, for eight years.

Married to Maria (his 'secret weapon' according to parents), lives at heart of school with his two young daughters, currently schooled at nearby Chandlings. A hands-on head couple, the Baileys are in true loco parentis – head says he is 'a parent above all things' – taking full responsibility for the four year groups housed in the main school building. Maria 'does everything,' from rolling up her sleeves to help with cooking, cleaning, teaching and running the school if required, right down to marching boys back to the salad bar if they don't have enough veggies on their plates.

Relaxed and approachable, with the chameleonic ability to switch between the persona of favourite uncle and respected leader, and not adverse to taking pupils on at table tennis or joining in with an after-hours skateboarding session, head says he 'likes boys to be happy, expects them to be busy and insists they are polite.' Parents consider him 'very dynamic, involved and committed to the school' and the few that were 'worried he might be a bit green' when appointed have climbed firmly back into their boxes.

Entrance: Recruits about 20 boys with a 'fairly broad brush' into year 4, with intakes in both September and April and numbers swelling to between 25 and 30 by end of year. Parents and boys interviewed together ('we choose the whole family') to establish fit rather academic ability. Boys assessed rather than tested, in English and maths. Majority at this point from London prep schools with just a few local boys in the mix. Good number of Forces children and between 10 and 15 per cent international (mainly Spanish and Russian with a few Chinese and Thai) although head insists on fluent English and no EAL on offer ('they have to be able to survive in the boarding environment').

Oversubscribed from year 5, with head looking for 'boys who are prepared to roll up their sleeves and get stuck in' above all else. Drop-out rate of less than one a year. A number join in summer term of year 5 to settle in before real focus on destination schools starts in year 6.

Exit: As in previous years, 20 to 25 per cent each to Eton, Radley and Harrow in 2016. Smaller numbers to Winchester, Marlborough and Wellington, plus Sherborne, Stowe, St Edward's and Malvern for less starry academic achievers. No fall-out to day schools. Huge focus on 'negotiating' places with destination schools with evidence of heart and soul going into making sure boys land in the best places. 'A good handful' of scholarships most years, most notably in art and music.

Remarks: Steadfastly traditional, Cothill is so discreet you could almost miss it altogether in its picturesque village setting. No grand buildings or flashy reception. Visitors arrive directly into the heart of the school (the dining room) – giving the first clue to school's substance over style ethos. Main building is a large country house with several later additions nestled in 26 acres of grounds, playing fields and woodland. Sports and leisure facilities include a super 15 metre indoor pool, six all-weather tennis courts, a nine-hole golf course, a somewhat shabby, albeit well used squash court cum table tennis room and a fleet of shiny BMXs for tearing around the woods. Equally appreciated by pupils is the wealth of retreats where they can spend as much free time as they like indulging creative passions such as woodwork (a real favourite with boys, guided by former police officer known as 'PC'), pottery and art. There's also a large, modern library and gleaming ICT suite for, amongst other things, Skyping home, although a handwritten letter once a week is compulsory.

No common rooms to speak of, bar a pool room, and no significant evidence of televisions (junior movie nights and major sporting events only are hosted in head's sitting room) or other passive distractions. Parents report boys roaring around on scooters in their pyjamas before bedtime rather than gluing themselves to screens. And therein lies the magic of the place. Macs and iPads do have a home here but what Cothill really offers is a Swallows and Amazons approach to education. It's a school where boys can 'have a childhood,' say parents. Boys can build dens or bird boxes, go pond dipping or interpret Notre Dame Cathedral in clay to their hearts' content. Parents and boys also firmly supportive of full boarding ethos (two exeats per term), which makes for fun-filled weekends jam packed with activities for all, not just those who live too far from school to make a weekly journey home. Broad geographical spread, from Scottish Highlands to Norfolk as well as overseas, makes for a collegiate bunch.

Majority of parents from upper echelons, most of whom have gone 'through the system' (read Eton, Harrow etc), with titles aplenty. Car park generally occupied by ancient mud splattered 4x4s rather than gleaming Maseratis on match days and supporters, who are encouraged and welcomed to visit twice a week, tend to be of the green welly variety, with the odd royal godparent thrown in for good measure. In the words of one mother, 'definitely not the facelift and white Range Rover crowd.' That said, head reports increasing numbers of professional, middle class London parents, keen to escape the hothouse London day school scene and allow their boys the space and roundedness offered by a country prep. One such parent reported that without exception the children are just from 'incredibly nice families who want the very best education.' Boys confident, smiley and polite with no sign of entitlement or arrogance and, with shirts untucked and ties askew, the slightest hint of Just William.

Strong artsy feel around the place with examples of boys' excellent work festooning every spare wall and surface. Music, art and DT highly praised by parents and boys alike and head's bet with us that 'about 70 per cent' of boys would say their favourite subject was history appeared to be bang on the money. A visit to the history room demonstrated what teaching at Cothill is all about – getting boys out of their seats and experiencing things firsthand. A mini Battle of Trafalgar was laid out across pushed together tables, complete with tablecloth sea and stacks of wide, slim drawers opened to reveal other famous (mostly French) battlefields to enable boys to visualise and act out events. Another recent highlight for history department was the re-enactment of the Dambusters raid on the school field. No wonder it's top dog, although this kind of thing is apparently all in a day's work for most departments here, with teachers across the board described as 'inspiring' and often 'quirky – in a good way.'

The star draw though, has to be Sauveterre, Cothill's unique French chateau outpost near Toulouse where all year 7 boys spend a whole term immersing themselves in French language, culture, food and sunshine. Parents evangelise about the benefits of this, not only where tipping the balance at CE is concerned but in terms of an unforgettable life experience.

Boys 'loosely set' from the outset for all subjects with maths more tightly so, but flexible according to exam results. Class sizes between 10 and 15 at the bottom of the school, gradually shrinking to seven or eight from year 7 onwards, consistent with head's belief that 'success at common entrance comes from small classes at the top of the school.' Each subject teacher reports to head on every boy on a weekly basis, resulting in a score out of 10 read out in Friday's assembly. High running totals at the end of term lead to treats and trips. Although school not equipped to deal with serious SEN, superb support in place for those who need a bit of extra help with a highly experienced, passionate SENCo who spends time with every boy before they join the school.

'Spectacular' drama, with frequent plays and shows, including My Fair Lady, Mary Poppins and original works written by Cothill teachers. And yes, boys do take on the female roles ('mainly with enthusiasm,' they told us). Around 80 per cent of cohort plays a musical instrument and there are bands and choirs galore for them to showcase their talents. Sport every day, with a focus on health, fitness and everyone getting a go at representing the school. Lower teams celebrated as vigorously as superstars – a recent fixture saw the bottom football team allowed to wear the first team strip as a reward for thrashing the opposition in their previous match.

Parents moving 'overeducated' children out of London preps shouldn't be surprised if boys cruise a bit academically initially. Year 4 is all about getting to grips with boarding to set the foundations for future success and happiness. Tidy, basic dorms for about eight boys, adorned with all the usual football paraphanalia, house years 4, 6 and 7 in the main school and year 5s are split between here and 'the bungalow' – a cosy outpost across the games field where according to parents boys feel 'terribly grown up.' Action-packed weekends mean boys eventually become wistful when they are at home, missing the mix of organised activities – an optional trip out every week and free time on their rollerblades, Ripsticks or exploring the woods.

All year 8s minibussed out after supper each evening to sleep at nearby Chandlings School, which looks disastrous on paper but in reality 'works brilliantly' according to parents and boys we spoke to and gives boys 'the space to be pre-teenagers.' Weekends also spent there, in the care of an 'extraordinary' house couple, with boys given their own activities and free run of Chandlings' facilities. Formerly sceptical parents now evangelise and are insistent that this part of Cothill life should 'never change.'

Unsurprisingly top notch pastoral care with parents reporting that school 'celebrates high spirits' and 'really understands each boy's potential and how to get him to reach it,' with more than one parent telling us their son had been 'turned around.' Very impressive, albeit informal, daily staff meeting where issues or concerns are raised (from which boys need to be reminded to wear their spectacles to who is struggling with the pressure of scholarship exams) leads to holistic care for every pupil. Boys know they can confide in whomever they wish, whether it's their tutor or junior matrons (usually gap year girls). Parents report boys returning to school 'without a backward glance' – and our guides themselves encapsulated the spirit of the school by telling us that the only kind of boy they could imagine not liking Cothill would be 'an iPad lover.'

Cottesmore School

Buchan Hill, Pease Pottage, West Sussex RH11 9AU

Pupils: 150 (100 boys, 50 girls); 120 full boarders • Ages: 4–13 • C of E

Fees: Day £9,144 – £17,124 ; Boarding £23,406 pa

Tel: 01293 520648
Email: office@cottesmoreschool.com
Website: www.cottesmoreschool.com

Headmaster: Since 2008, Tom Rogerson, married to Lottie, with two small sons, Wilf and Bear. Cottesmore runs in the family (grandad and dad were heads before him) – 'I've been quietly planning to take over since I was 17', said the head. Routed via other schools (Ludgrove, Eaton House and Broomwood); his dad wouldn't let him take the headship too early. Quite right, dad.

Articulate and thoughtful, focuses on each pupil and knows them all – they chatter away happily with him. A strong team with Lottie, who provides ballast for the head's lively energy.

Parents like him – 'He's a warm guy, easy to talk to, and always there when I pick up and drop off from exeats'. Another: 'A school derives its culture from the head – and I like its culture. It places emphasis on traditional Christian values: kindness, courtesy, honour and fair play.'

Entrance: Pre-prep: taster day, during which prospective pupils will do a piece of work assessing English and maths. Prep: English and maths tests, interview (children need to be 'interested and interesting') and head's report from previous school.

Exit: To many of the more magnificent public schools: Eton, Harrow, Cheltenham Ladies' College, and other varieties too. Twelve academic scholarships in recent round – nearly half the year.

Remarks: Approach the school past towering rhododendrons, lawns mowed to velvety smoothness, golf flags, the fragrance of flowers and hedges. Cottesmore is a stately Victorian pile – enter through the heavy wooden door carved with mischievous sprites. Wood panelled walls, stately hall with minstrels' gallery; fishing rods leaning casually against the wall in a corridor. Things here are orderly, but it's not an institutional tidiness: there's a feeling of a home, where places for things arise organically and become established through habit.

Grounds which beg to be played in: climbable trees everywhere, from 'the monkeys' – a cave of under rhododendron/ tree branches – to the hollow oak: climb its ancient trunk in a circular direction (teacher present, and only up to a certain height). Bamboo for forts and den making – so popular here that it occasionally has official activity status. A parent described his son, who had fallen out of a tree, limping towards his wife on the last exeat – 'he's having a childhood and that's wonderful.'

Children here are bubbling, confident and eager, so keen to tell us about their school that we hardly needed to ask questions. They happily fill their own skin: we've rarely met a group of children so content to be themselves. Some bounced up to say hello and give their views; easily said, in front of their head, what they didn't like about school (the chairs are too low and they want new showers).

We met too, quieter introverts, busy with the library and their model railway in the basement. They've started their own after-supper library lecture series ('tea' was exceedingly popular). Not so likely to bubble eagerly about the things they love; but no hesitation in expressing their views, and total confidence in their value. Geekiness is certainly not frowned upon – 'they're lauded for loving the library', said Lottie.

The head said, 'we're a family school', then chuckled; whether this is a good thing clearly depends on how dysfunctional the family. Certainly the warmth and care seen here must exceed what many families experience at Christmas. Home to 150 pupils ('beautifully small', said a mum).

Broad church here – which means chapel isn't optional. Cultural Christianity, whose values informally underpin the community, but 'we go about it quietly'.

An academically rigorous school – 'rigour balanced with fun', said the head. A flamboyant fashion designer to be is celebrated; but 'he has to be good at maths by the time he leaves'. Lack of endeavour here would be a problem – 'that's not an option'.

'Not a pressure cooker', said a parent who has experienced the hothouse of London preps, '[and] notches up in balanced and useful lives'. Relative to other preps in the area, it's doing extremely well: another parent we spoke to was very happy with the academic side, describing it as 'pretty strong and rigorous', with parents getting regular feedback – every three weeks. (His son had just got a place at Harrow – he was an extremely happy dad.)

Small classes, no bigger than 14. Single form entry until year 4, then double form entry, finally splitting in three in the final year. Pupils are streamed (but not labelled) and set within those streams. Academic subjects take place around the quad, the fountain in the middle providing restful accompaniment to those getting their heads down. Lively walls showing work, but order and method evident – displays are exceedingly neat. This school does extremely well at enthusing its pupils: they showed a keen interest in Latin, eagerly pointing out Latin in the roots of words, and telling us their favourite myths.

Maths lessons have been transformed by new IT (iPads, Chromebooks and a Raspberry Pis). Pupils were whizzing through tables on iPads – less time marking means more time teaching; or 'connecting', as the head likes to say. Excelling at maths is something this school particularly prides itself on: the head has increased the number of maths teachers and seen CE scores soar.

A geography teacher was enthusiastically making geography pertinent to the real world: 'What are the pros and cons of building a Tesco in the Cottesmore grounds?' (The head's smile became a little fixed at this point...) Making ant homes was cited by one excited little girl as the best geography lesson ever. Parents are happy that the computer room is well policed: no chatrooms or other elicit YouTube pleasures; no own devices in school (other than for travelling).

Achievement is celebrated through stars (house points), show ups and stay ups. Show ups for extremely good work or behaviour; stay up for a jolly if you come top in an assessment or effort, or when teams have an unbeaten day – popcorn, movie and games. A popular treat.

Learning support helps students who have mild dyslexia, dyspraxia and dyscalculia, also those with speech and language difficulties. Ten to 20 per cent of pupils receive one-to-one help, and in-class assistance (charged as an extra). The fact a child has SEN doesn't make any difference to attainment here, says the head.

Behind a glass panelled door is pre-prep, the colour and liveliness evident through the glass panels. Coloured cellophane hung from the ceiling in strips – 'we're doing under the sea at the moment'. Single form entry, around 10 per class, children seated at round tables, doors in each class opening onto the lawn: a much more relaxed, crazy colour atmosphere than on the other side of the door, but a similarly high standard evident from the written work in displays. The rather extraordinary cubed times tables produced by a boy in year 1 caused adults in the area to look at each other blankly, each hoping one of the others might know if he'd got them right. A parent told us that Cottesmore was the only school they visited which was more interested in the child than the parents: Lottie got right down to her daughter's level – 'so, do you like spiders?' And off they went to find one.

A large array of sports on offer: 33, including all the usual major sports, as well as the less usual: archery, shooting and billiards. Pupils of all abilities play in matches, and even the C and D teams play a good number of fixtures. They win plenty of matches (the Colts As and Bs recently unbeaten in any sport for seven months) and get plenty of support – Danish housekeeping team take great joy in waving their pompoms in support of the third X1.'It is competitive – they care a lot for sport, but they know they have all types, and encourage and get the best out of everyone.'

Houses here are called sets, and there's plenty of friendly inter-set competition. A parent, commenting on the set dash, said 'The whole school cheer each other, particularly the useless ones...To be very kind, is to be very Cottesmore', he added.

Indoor heated pool and Astroturf large enough for three tennis courts; three grass courts too, with some boys racing in from playing tennis at break. The 'gravel' – an open sided, covered Astroturf – is so popular that ripping it down was out of the question: the roof has been replaced.

Plenty of clubs, from real tennis to fishing for carp in the pond – 'the film club is just the best', said one girl. Chess compulsory for two years – it's taken very seriously here (under 11 girls champs).

Music is strong, with 80-90 per cent learning instruments; there are three choirs, including the chapel choir, which often tours abroad. The head of music is also head of drama, so every play tends to be a musical, said a parent: Oliver! the last, described by another parent as 'excellent – my quite shy son volunteered for it...'

Everyone in the prep has a bed and boards to some extent: 80 per cent full time, everyone else up to four nights a week (must stick to chosen nights). In this small school, there are no separate boarding houses: everyone just troops upstairs to bed, the matron's flat situated between the boys' and girls' dorms.

Large dormitories for 8, three per room for older pupils, the usual is six. Pupils wake to music – the latest charts.

'Palatial since my day', said a parent; but actually they're mid renovation – decoration of some rooms is a bit tired. Some new loos, one landing with a squidgy new carpet, and couple of lovely lampshades, one in white feathers, another rose shape (both in response to pupil request). Pine bunk beds, well used. Showers and basins clean, but a bit elderly – nice old taps though; 'it's all going', said the head briskly; although the parents we spoke to were happy with it as it is.

Matrons and nurse (who is an angel, we were repeatedly told) reside in nearby rooms on every corridor: if pupils are poorly in the night, they wake the dormitory monitor who gets matron. Lovely bright sick bay, complete with bears and TV.

Year groups take it in turn to occupy the drawing room in evenings (music, piano, chess, Wi dance), other year groups spilling out into hall, library and ICT room, playing ping pong or snooker. Children here flow everywhere – no feeling of being penned into a particular area.

Lots of activities at the weekends: Saturday morning school, then matches; trips on Sundays – children talked with great joy of a trip to Brighton Pier, when older pupils were allowed to go off in groups of four, and told us how much they love the independence – 'at my last school they never stopped watching us', said one, impatiently. 'Here, they trust us'.

Children keep in touch by email 'asking for things', Sunday letter writing, Skype and can phone if they want to.

Each class sends a rep to the school council and food committee – a food committee board in a class room simply stated 'BETTER BURGER'; but they don't have much to complain about: they've won awards for their food, which a parent described as 'brilliant' – the custard (with stewed apple) was clearly not just tipped from a tin of Ambrosia.

The children's happiness is testament to how well they are cared for – and indeed the school Happiness Charter is on the wall of every room. A parent described the school as 'gentle'; they chose Cottesmore for its rounded, happy pupils, and nurturing environment. Easy for pupils to speak to staff here – they're all out in the hall at break time, accompanied by their coffee trolley.

Certainly the best mannered children we've met at a prep, leaping to their feet if we so much as glanced over, opening doors, shaking hands. Watching the children, it seemed evident that the respectful environment influences how they treat each other.

Time out area on a wooden chest in front of the study – pupils who've been a bit rowdy perch there until they've calmed down. A clear bullying policy: pupils and staff are expected to bring forward if they see it. The one incident a parent described to us was 'clamped down on quickly'.

Pupils from London, home counties, and abroad, including expats and diplomats. Lots of London parents, but not the competitive ones (school reckons that leavers' list suggests some parents are competitive). A parent from London told us he looked at 20 prep schools, and Cottesmore had the best combination of options one could get: 'A* in all the things that really matter in life'.

C

Coworth Flexlands School

Chertsey Road, Chobham, Woking, Surrey GU24 8TE

Pupils: 130 • Ages: Girls 3-11, boys 3-7

Fees: £8,250 – £12,825 pa

Tel: 01276 855707
Email: registrar@coworthflexlands.co.uk
Website: www.coworthflexlands.co.uk

Head: Since 2010, Mrs Anne Sweeney MA, DipEd (50s), an Aberdeen maths graduate married to a globe-trotting management consultant who's also a dab hand in proffering career advice to his forbearing wife, making it a condition of their engagement – 'with a twinkle in his eye,' she insists – that she become a teacher, to be around for their own putative offspring (obviously worked, as has a doctor, budding social worker, lecturer and IT specialist to show for it, plus a grandchild). Not that she needed much persuading. Family legend has it that she threw all the dolls out of her toy pram, lovingly pushing books round instead. Add games of school where she was always the teacher – 'I don't know how my friends tolerated it' – and her subsequent career, after a brief teenage flirtation with fashion design (nipped in the bud, this time by her father) seems a forgone conclusion.

Quietly pragmatic – otherwise immaculate office has boxes of toys for visiting toddlers – she's effectively had two teaching careers, starting out as a maths specialist in Scottish and English secondary schools and colleges and moving down the age range to pre-school and primaries/preps, after taking a 10 year break to raise her children and finding senior school posts rarer than hen's teeth. Previous post was as deputy head at Maltman's Green, a flourishing prep school in Gerrard's Cross.

Mrs Sweeney has won approval from parents with cracking academic results and speedy, sensitive problem-solving. 'My child told her class she'd got a boyfriend on the internet – she'd absolutely made it up, of course – and she handled it really well,' said one.

This is education on a miniature scale and all the better for it. Pupils get a say in everything from sets (English and maths from year 3) to scholarship streams, and small isn't just beautiful but the key to her approach. 'If someone doesn't fit the mould it can make for a miserable childhood, so we modify whatever we can,' she says.

Her approach, low on pressure, high on imagination and big on community spirit, with parents closely involved, is cutting the results mustard, with nearly all, including substantial percentage with special needs, securing safe passage to their senior school of choice. 'Academically, she's done so much,' said one mother.

Head sees size as school's biggest asset. 'We say it's an education as individual as your child,' she says. Parents wouldn't disagree.

Entrance: Single form entry all the way through, with official maximum class size of 22, though far lower in practice and completely non-selective. That goes for special needs, which cover the full spectrum through to physical disabilities. Severe behavioural difficulties might be a sticking point, though even here school would do its best to help. 'If you're in the door, you're in,' confirms head.

No official feeders as school mainly grows its own through co-ed Skylark Nursery, then girls only to year 6 (boys may stay till end of year 2). Reception and year 3 are other main entry points, with small but steady flow in and out in other years, inevitable, given upwardly and geographically mobile M25 corridor location.

Exit: Wide range of independent day or boarding schools for the majority include Wycombe Abbey, Lady Eleanor Holles, St George's Ascot, St Mary's Ascot, St Teresa's, Sir William Perkins's, Downe House, Farnborough Hill, Queen Anne's, Caversham, Tormead, LVA and The Marist, Sunninghill. Around a third of year 6s secure awards. A few to state schools including Gordon's School, Woking (non-selective boarding).

Head especially proud of success achieved by children with special needs – 'When they're off to different senior schools and you look at who's had learning support, you wouldn't be able to tell which is which, so that's our end point'.

When it comes to deciding on 11 plus options, little sense of 'school knows best', assumption being that families, equipped with enough information, will make the right choice. Invariably they do, says head. It's subtly done – head could teach government a thing or two about nudge psychology. Innovative two-tier clubs allow the seriously arty, musical, sporty or academic to hone their skills potentially to scholarship level; the merely interested do the same subjects but just for fun – no pressure either way. 'If you find the going tough, then you tend to deselect yourself,' says head. Add conversations about possible senior schools from year 4 onwards, 'open book' sessions every half term so parents can see progress being made and senior school sample papers set as homework, and the upshot is no nasty surprises, school tempering any unrealistic expectations with gentle guidance. 'I've yet to meet a parent who hates a child so much that they would put them through utter misery,' says head.

Remarks: Tucked away down a tiny, tree-fringed lane and with easy-to-miss signage (imposed by council restrictions rather than a shy and retiring corporate disposition), the school is unlikely to attract much in the way of window shoppers, a possible plus point for privacy-conscious royals and celebs (the Princesses Beatrice and Eugenie of York are former pupils). With Old Windsor, Ascot, Virginia and Chobham all within comfortable commuting distance, location is less golden triangle then titanium polygon.

If the convenience hasn't already got to you the place, a bijou red-brick country house probably will, even without this reviewer's early morning, atmosphere-enhancing demonstration of community spirit, with approachable welly-wearing bursar clearing the snow in the drive and cheerful parent governor photographing the winter wonderland for posterity.

Main building features enough tradition – big, airy classrooms, some with old-fashioned desks, almost all with panoramic views over grounds (youngest two classes now have conservatories attached) – to fuel a midnight nostalgia-fest. Even the occasional faint but authentic whiff of damp, legacy of a leaking roof, now replaced.

Tucked tidily to one side, a recently completed extension houses busy, happy nursery, much praised by Ofsted and ISI inspectors, assembly/dining hall (nice touches include bowls of freshly chopped cucumber/carrot on each table as amuse-gueules for the ravenous, and home-made biscuits and yogurt, though menu overall did elicit a few quickly suppressed grimaces) and additional well-equipped form, language, science and ICT rooms. To the other, a block devoted to performing arts, very strong here and recognised as such by award of hard to come by Artsmark Gold, with prize-winning chamber choir, much-praised productions and even youngest pupils belting out songs and speeches to parents with huge panache during class assembly.

Sport, once effectively non-existent, now taken off, says school, citing netball, hockey and rounders teams winning against tough local opposition. Claims to be 'leading the revolution in girls' football in prep schools' (we applaud), with passion nurtured by sport director who is current county football player, and Berks U9-U11 team largely made up of CF girls. Judo club also producing successful competitors.

Pupils not just courteous but look visitors in the eye and even smile – shouldn't be unusual, but for this age group, often is. They're thoughtful and wildly enthusiastic, encouraging visitors to experience every detail from a ride in the disabled lift to animal tracks identification (robin and rabbit were best guesses) in the grounds. Staff are introduced with great pride and full biographies – obvious respect and liking on both sides. Witnessing the quirky, absorbing lessons, many taught by specialists – year 1 girls counting with rising excitement in French as a wind up caterpillar squirms across the table; a window packed with bagged up bread for mould-growing research in science – you can see why. 'When a teacher leaves, you'd think someone had died,' said one mother.

It's not just the teaching that sparkles. Standard dull but worthy educational ideas are dusted off and reinvented with a sprinkling of fairy dust. Pupil targets become cuddly YETIs – 'I don't know it YET': achieve all six and you're presented with a certificate sporting the eponymous shaggy beast in assembly, while good behaviour is rewarded with prize draw – winner takes Muffin the (toy) dog home for weekend and writes up his adventures for posterity.

Even transport can be scaled down – 'Mrs Sweeney took six of us in her car, dropped us off with Mrs Dawe and went to get the rest of year 5,' says account of school trip to Chobham Common in (beautifully produced) school magazine (parents' committee has apparently now funded a minibus).

Given brisk turnover of pupils, school rightly makes it a priority to settle in newbie families pronto. Bustling parent-run social committee issues first coffee morning and play date invitations almost before ink dries on acceptance forms. School also has own Brownies and Rainbows packs and a highly evolved house system that brings all ages together for meals (year 6s set, clear and wipe tables for younger children four days a week) and creative whole-school projects (if you've ever wanted to see a frog's life-cycle communicated through the medium of dance, this is the place to be).

Philosophy also colours approach to learning support, tackled with great flair and sensitivity, so that every child plays full part in life of school, from productions to target setting. Even central location of room rather than a small, apologetic broom cupboard in bowels of school sends clear message about belonging. 'Children are never made to feel odd,' confirmed parent. 'It's just an ordinary part of school life.'

Caring, yes, precious, no. Thirteen glorious acres include a peace garden for older girls (with disconcertingly realistic sleeping faun), games fields, tennis courts and well-equipped side-by-side playgrounds, while a play advisor suggests games for the needy or bored. School is also in touch with its inner rufty-tufty side, offering term time timetabled forest school sessions for all (apparently a favourite trip for year 6 last year was a morning watching Skylarks in their habitats) and popular daytime forest camps in the holidays – children produce impressive leaf-decorated head dresses while teachers are noted for legendary storm kettle superpowers. Other idyllic back-to-nature add-ons include new pitches, wildflower meadows and even allotments to follow, if canny freebie deal with a local firm keen to off-load excess topsoil goes ahead (school is reassuringly candid about finances which, following 2004 merger with Flexlands School and sale of site, are in good order).

Not yet the place for the highly competitive – school captains exhort their teams, in capitals, to 'HAVE FUN' – and playing fields wouldn't currently make Duke of Wellington's long list for future Waterloo fodder. Rapidly changing, however, and sports scholarships could well start cropping up in the leavers' lists. In the meantime, the arty, musical and, increasingly, academic are well catered for in successful, embracing small school where standard ideas are so imaginatively cut down to size.

Cranbrook School

Waterloo Road, Cranbrook, Kent TN17 3JD

Pupils: 745; 240 boarders • Ages: 13–18 (11–18 from 2017) • Sixth form: 290

Fees: Boarding £12,120 – £13,020 pa; Day free

Tel: 01580 711804
Email: registrar@cranbrook.kent.sch.uk
Website: www.cranbrookschool.co.uk

Headmaster: Since 2012, Dr John Weeds MA MPhil EdD (50s). Read classics at Pembroke College, Cambridge and his academic studies have long been part of his life. He jokes that he didn't want to be outdone by his talented micro-biologist wife, but the letters after his name attest to a driven and committed educationalist.

His most recent thesis was on the subject of the gifted and talented, which will come in useful here. But having consciously chosen to work in the state sector, he is very concerned with equality of opportunity too. He has an eye on re-balancing Cranbrook's increasingly independent school intake; he has ensured there are some less financially demanding school trips and wants to see the girls at Cranbrook given more of a voice too.

We visited a year after his arrival, following what has been described to us by the tactful as 'a difficult period of adjustment' and by the more forthright as a 'baptism of fire.' The head heartily agrees with the latter, clearly enjoying the calm for now – although the thought of having to tackle performance related pay next makes his hair stand on end.

He found the school somewhat laid back, and hasn't been afraid to grapple with it – 'some traditions I'm prepared to take on,' he told us. One of the contentious changes was suits for sixth formers five days a week. 'It's created a different feel – more business-like and focused,' he says. Understanding that parents 'really do want best grades,' he aims to deliver consistency of performance and to retain the focus on the academic. 'I don't want to lose sight of the diverse extracurricular offer, but we need more balance,' he says.

The parents we spoke to are right behind him. One told us: 'He is not a slick performer but the benefit is that I believe he listens and engages with both students and parents.' Another said: 'I feel his quest to raise results is to be praised and supported.'

He has three university-age sons.

Academic matters: A level results generally on upward curve in 2016 – 73 per cent A*-B, 39 per cent A*/A grades. There have been tweaks all round, including a new approach to mock exams. Pupils know what is expected of them and are fired up to achieve it.

Some subjects notably out-perform others by a mile, namely the large cohort of talented mathematicians. The school has been a specialist science school for years and has a new observatory equipped with telescopes. A third of pupils take science A levels, with chemistry particularly popular with the girls, and almost all taking single sciences at GCSE. Strong humanities, but English seems to be a weak spot. Head says the new assessment framework is challenging. Numbers taking languages fall off at A level, to only 10 per cent. Most seem pretty focused on traditional curriculum subjects but a sixth form enrichment programme offers additional choices such as astronomy, sports leadership and psychology.

At GCSE in 2016, nearly 56 per cent A*/A grades. Pupils study 11 or more (mainly academic) subjects at GCSE, excelling at maths, physics, Latin, IT, French and art. Maths and RE are out of the way a year early. A third of maths whizzes currently take home an IGCSE too, with year 9 and 10 students winning a clutch of gold medals in national maths challenges. Languages on offer are French and Spanish, with Chinese for native speakers.

More than a third of teachers have been at the school for longer than 10 years. The head assured us that only two staff left last year but parents are less concerned about turnover. They approve of the new focus on performance and are keen on removing the few 'dead wood.' One told us: 'There are a handful of teachers who struggle to control the class and some who could explain their teaching and homework better.' Other teachers singled out as inspirational. The pupils we spoke to said teachers will stay behind to explain things if they don't understand something, while RS and physics teachers were praised for their revision guides and pre-university preparation. The brilliance of the maths results is due quite simply, says the head, to 'the best maths teacher in Kent.'

Parents seem split between those who think the amount of homework is about right and those who think there should be more, particularly in the holidays. A pupil said: 'Teachers will always give you more if you ask for it' – clearly a loophole for the less inclined, but there don't seem to be many of those here. The online parent portal keeps parents up-to-date with progress and there are half-termly assessment records for effort and attainment.

Two full-time student support assistants offer additional support for specific difficulties (outside the classroom). SENCo is a dyslexia specialist and admin assistant is also listed as having mentoring skills. Between 10 or 20 pupils each year with special educational needs (whether or not recorded by the local authority as such).

Head told us with feeling: 'We're very committed to supporting those with particular needs. We will do just about everything we can.' If pupils need a laptop they don't necessarily need to bring one – the school will find one. Pupils won't slip under the radar here, he said, and added: 'We will pick up those who can become hard on themselves and down, and won't forget other children who can achieve great things.' A handful with EAL needs – EAL tuition is offered free of charge for anyone who needs it.

Games, options, the arts: School has a strong sports tradition. Fifty acres of sports fields and everyone participates. High-calibre cricket and rugby teams, with a growing fixtures list. One pupil told us he'd left a prestigious local grammar specifically to join the Cranbrook rugby first XV (he'd played against the team and admired it). Some pretty glamorous sporting tours – South Africa for cricket, Fiji and New Zealand for rugby. A team of under-15 girls recently became British fencing champions. Facilities include an outdoor heated pool, squash courts, Astroturf, plus sports hall with dance studio (currently offering Bollywood classes), climbing wall and gym (popular in the evenings with sporty boys).

Not much consensus about music here. Head claims it's the 'story of the year' but some parents not so ecstatic. One told us: 'One concern is that the extracurricular music programme is not as strong as it could be. There are great facilities and talent but this is not always harnessed effectively.' It's certainly a well-resourced and vibrant part of school life, with several choirs, an orchestra, jazz and rock bands, folk, string, sax and brass groups, charity concerts and community carol services. Total of 150 students take individual instrument lessons, with many learning more than one and working on higher grades. Lots of pupils trying an instrument for the first time. Live music at every assembly and whilst pupils still seemed a little wrapped up in their early morning fugs we saw teachers toe-tapping along to a jazz band which could easily take a turn at Ronnie Scott's. However, no longer offers music GCSE or A level.

The more artistic may be in the minority – only a handful taking art A level. Having tackled exam performance as her first priority, art teacher is encouraging boys into the classroom (now one third of pupils). Art room is open all hours and cool graffiti art pop-ups grab the attention of everyone as they move around the school. Large, well-used facilities for DT and food technology.

The Queen's Hall is the home of the drama department and is a fully equipped and recently refurbished theatre – largely run by the pupils, but also used by outside touring companies. Annual house plays as well as junior, senior and whole school productions.

What Cranbrook does well is encourage pupils to be self-reliant and take responsibility, whether that is through CCF or D of E, fundraising for the charities they care passionately about – no standard Sports Relief here – or being given the freedom to set up any clubs they're interested in (40 at the last count, including curling club which promptly won a county-wide competition).

Annual trip to Tanzania to work on health and education projects is a stand-out opportunity. Pupils compete for a place and work hard to raise the money themselves. 'It was the best thing I have done in my life,' said the head girl. There's also an exchange partnership with a school in Kerala for two weeks at the end of the autumn term. All richly eye-opening, and no doubt contributed to the school's International Schools Award from the British Council.

Enrichment programme for years 9 and 10 means pupils go off timetable for two weeks. 'We take them out of their comfort zone,' said the head. 'They have to research and do presentations on what they've learned. This year they met everyone from a policeman to a prisoner. It gets youngsters who are bright to think.'

Boarding: Boarding houses are a bit of a lottery architecturally – some old, some modern. The year 10 dorms we visited in one house were more like tiny ships' cabins, with multi-tasking bunk-beds/desks, but as pupils get older they often get more space. There's a rolling programme of new carpets, curtains and bathrooms and we were impressed by the accommodation – squishy sofas, polished wood, no institutional paint colours (tasteful greys). Washing gets turned around in 24 hours – setting the bar quite high for when pupils return home – and there wasn't the slightest whiff of a less than fresh sock. Boarding pupils can invite day pupils over after school and it's easy to see how self-sufficient youngsters can be here, without the need of the rural parental taxi service.

Background and atmosphere: Founded in 1518 and given a Royal Charter by Elizabeth I in 1574. School's buildings straddle the main road into the pretty Kent town of Cranbrook and are a jumble of every architectural style, from 1970s accommodation blocks to a fine Georgian mansion. Local church of St Dunstan's is in the middle of the campus – very much part of the community.

The fact that Cranbrook is a selective state school with a large boarding contingent gives the place a unique feel. The alumni society is awash with hugging groups from reunited houses. Total of 12 houses – seven for boys and five for girls. Day pupils are grouped geographically to start with to help out of school socialising.

A parent told us that the school offers 'a balance of high academic achievement and extracurricular activities that is the equal to many public schools.' Another described Cranbrook as 'a very intriguing mix of competitive and laid-back.' They added that 'it places responsibility on the students rather than spoon-feeding them, which means that students need to step up.' Pupils want to go places here – it's not uncool to be clever.

Pastoral care, well-being and discipline: Pastoral care is highly praised. On arrival each child is allocated a tutor who will monitor their academic and activities programme, social progress and work with their head of house. As one parent pointed out, the houses and tutor groups are something of a haven. Pupils return to their houses regularly throughout the day – which helps to prevent the build-up of any bullying.

Mentoring is a word that crops up a lot (peer to peer, sixth form to younger pupils, staff to pupils). There is a smart new medical centre (like a mini hospital, with beds for sick boarding pupils), and counsellors offer appointments four times a week. Head has tightened up on discipline and believes the behaviour of pupils is now excellent (a view backed up by parents). Good liaison with parents, plus contracts for good behaviour.

Pupils and parents: Head says that youngsters who are 'particularly interested in learning' and have 'a real spirit of enterprise and adventure' will thrive here. Parents reckon school is ideal for self-motivated, well-rounded pupils who have capabilities beyond the academic, and are organised, not overly sensitive or under confident – or 'the engaged, interested and aspirational'. The place 'may not be suited to students expecting to be hand held,' although quieter children have found their niche too. Independence is held in exceptionally high esteem.

Parents tend to be less the super-rich and more middle class professionals with increasingly high expectations. Definitely a varied bunch, suggesting there's a good chance of finding like minds. Some parents are reputedly stirred up and vocal about the recent changes, whilst every other parent we spoke to was quick to say they liked to be 'hands off.' Head cites strong relationships with parents and a tradition for supportive involvement, particularly with careers teaching.

Notable alumni include Es Devlin, superstar stage and costume designer of the 2012 Olympic closing ceremony, Tim Smit, founder of the Eden Project, astronaut Dr Piers Sellers, comedian Harry Hill, designer Ptolemy Mann, journalist Sir Charles Wheeler and sports commentators Peter West, Brian Moore and Barry Davis, plus many high up in the Forces.

Entrance: Selective, catering for the top 20-25 per cent of the academic ability range. Has historically started at 13, but has first 11+ intake, of day pupils only, in 2017. This will gradually increase, from 30 places in 2017 to 90 places from 2021 (all day pupils), whilst the 13+ places decrease (from 162 to 72, including 52 boarders).

There is an 8.5 km preferred catchment, pushing up house prices even further nearby (inaccurate addresses taken very seriously). Applicants previously often came from the Cranbrook state secondary, The High Weald Academy. Now the competition has shifted up a gear – a strong intake from prep schools such as Marlborough House, Dulwich Prep and St Ronan's. Boarders mostly come from just outside the catchment area – most within

generally well received: lessons are now 50 minutes instead of 35 ('gives pupils more time to think and encourages problem solving', he says) and there's a drive to get pupils going with independent learning skills from the prep school up. His mission to 'ensure we are current' has lead to the appointment of a head of contemporary music to support 'non-traditional' musicians. Art provision has had a makeover and the new head of DT is a robotics specialist. What makes Mr R's heart sink is 'constant measuring'. He fears 'the enriching cultural experience' that lies at the heart of a good education is in danger of being sacrificed on the academic altar. 'It is possible to do both and be successful,' he says.

Head feels school needs to 'burst the Surrey bubble' and to that end has encouraged the 'Beyond Cranleigh' programme. Pupils help the local community, litter picking, working in local schools and staging joint concerts. He is developing an exchange with a Chinese school and building on longstanding links with a community primary school in Zambia. His wife, Amanda, who is head of careers, is also very involved with this project. The Readers have a son at the prep and a daughter in the senior school.

Outside school Mr Reader enjoys cooking and he also preaches in the local church. He's a trustee of the Hawk and Owl Trust and hopes to encourage barn owls to nest on campus (maybe he should offer a barn owl bursary...). Favourite book? 'Crime and Punishment. It's got everything – violence, love, tragedy, morality.' No owls though. When asked to sum up the Cranleigh ethos he says, 'It's a competitive school. We love to compete but we play for the shirt, not individual glory.'

Academic matters: One competition school doesn't enter is the race for exam league table glory – the Cranleigh way is educational breadth rather than narrow academic focus. Nevertheless, the healthy spread of exam grades from A* to Cs and Ds, not to mention a good handful of Oxbridge places every year, confirms that teaching covers the spectrum of ability. In 2016, very creditable 67 per cent A*/A at GCSE; at A level it was 40 per cent A*/A (75 per cent A*-B). General feeling is that Mr Reader will tighten academics where necessary. The newly-appointed director of teaching, learning and innovation (who also teaches physics) told us about plans to build up the EPQ and a school-wide drive to embed independent learning and thinking skills.

We sat in on a fourth year art lesson where not everybody was as engaged as they might have been, but it was just before lunch. Fair to say this is not a school where you will find silent concentration behind every classroom door – we got the feeling that while most eyes were on the board, more hearts were outside on the pitch. A level options pretty standard but also include geology and Greek (as two-year AS courses) and, unsurprisingly, PE. English, history and economics are the most popular subjects at A level, followed by maths and sciences. Very small numbers for music and languages – as elsewhere. Pre-U so far only for maths and further maths. Cranleigh also runs its own specially designed EPQ courses.

Around 100 pupils with SEN, mostly mild dyslexia etc. Some receive one-to-one tuition (extra cost) but most are supported in class. Parents were keen to tell us how well their very different children have done, 'Pupils are treated as individuals academically,' and 'There are lots of subject clinics and if a child needs some hand-holding they'll get it.' One mother said that the teaching at Cranleigh had 'absolutely been the making' of her daughter. Longer lesson times took a while to bed in, 'My children complained at first but they appreciate them now.'

Games, options, the arts: Cranleigh has 31 sports pitches and appears to be outstanding on all of them. This success is all the more impressive considering that the school is half the size of its closest rivals, 'We have to play big schools to get all our teams matches,' the deputy head told us. He added, 'Sport here is about participation, not just about the elite. Everyone is expected to be involved, staff as well as pupils.' Recent silverware includes National Rugby 7s schoolboy champions, Finegold Cup (riding), under 16 girls' indoor and outdoor hockey champions and Devizes to Westminster (international kayaking challenge) title holders. There will undoubtedly have been more wins since so best see school website for latest. Average of 29 teams playing on match Saturdays which doesn't leave many to cheer from the sidelines. More than 20 sports are on offer, there's a nine hole golf course – golf mainly played for relaxation pupils told us, but that doesn't stop the golf team winning inter-school tournaments – several Astros and a conditioning room. Two physios, a sports doctor and strength and conditioning coaches on hand to tailor individual fitness and nutrition programmes. Equestrian centre has two all-weather arenas and 60 acres of grazing and riding land. Pupils may bring their own ponies; those without learn on the school ponies.

Music and drama are tackled with typical gusto. According to the school's handy infographic, Cranleigh in Numbers, there are nine plays and 70 concerts (home-grown and visiting talent) a year. The arts certainly aren't a competition-free zone with keenly fought contests for house dance, singing and drama. Strings and woodwind also compete (separately), as do poets and creative writers. Speech Hall is the largest performance venue, seating up to 500 and there are two smaller studio theatres. When we visited one of these was being very creatively fitted out for a junior production of Treasure Island. The Merriman Music School (named after first headmaster) has a 100 seat auditorium and 14 practice rooms. School bands can practice in the fully soundproofed 'rock room'. New head of contemporary music adds another, possibly louder, string to school's bow. 'Spine-tingling' congregational singing is more than fully supported by splendid three manual-pipe Mander organ in chapel. Organist in residence gives lunchtime recitals and organ lessons are available. Much participation at all levels, but as elsewhere, small uptake for music and drama A levels.

Plenty of extracurricular options, including visiting speakers and lecture programme for A level students. Timetabling genius ensures CCF and DofE don't clash. There's so much going on it's hard to see how pupils fit everything in; little wonder day pupils stay until 9pm several nights a week. Might it all be too much for some, we asked one mother. She thought not: 'Yes, it's full-on but the children are so happy and if they're happy, they perform better.'

To conclude, Cranleigh is a very sporty school but, as parents and staff were at pains to tell us, it's not just a sporty school. Message received. Even so, perhaps not the confirmed ball dodger's first choice.

Boarding: Four boys' and two girls' houses at present; another girls' house will open in 2017. No flexi boarding, day pupils are fully part of boarding houses and have a cabin desk in boarders' rooms – it's their 'centre of gravity' within the school where they do prep, get changed for sport, make toast and drinks and take part in house activities. Day pupils can sleep over occasionally if activities such as school plays or trips finish very late and 'we will always scoop up in an emergency.' All do prep in their rooms 'with doors open and prefects in corridors.' 'We expect proper, disciplined work,' said housemaster. Tutors are on hand to inspect and any slackers can expect a short sharp spell at one of the 'naughty boy desks'.

Boys' houses are, inevitably, older and, though clean and bright, looked pretty worn out. Grubby polystyrene ceiling tiles rarely enhance a room and walls looked as though they'd been crashed into by generations of schoolboys – probably because they have. Common areas very lived in; walls decorated with team photos and vintage style black and white shots of heroes: Mohammed Ali, Steve McQueen, James Dean. Dorms of up to four for first years, single study bedrooms for sixth formers. Very few personal touches (artistic arrangements of massive shoes don't count), but that's boys' boarding for you. Sixth formers' single study bedrooms looked better – more in the way of photos and posters. Matron's room is the focal point on the ground floor from where she keeps an eye on comings and goings. Nice big garden for kickabouts and barbecues. All upper sixth formers are prefects – 'they're positive role models' – and year groups are mixed (not segregated by corridor). The housemaster stressed how 'integrated' the year groups were and how seriously his sixth form prefects took their house responsibilities. 'We have a beer and a chat with the prefects, they're quick to notice if things are getting a bit scratchy.'

All in all one feels that the concept of gender fluid has yet to find a foothold in Surrey. Girls' houses are modern, done out in pinks and purples and considerably better provided for on the soft furnishing front. Perhaps they could loan a few beanbags or pom-poms to the boys? Matron ('She knows everything,' our guides said) resides in a room just like a family kitchen, with sofas, throws and lots of photos. Girls can make drinks and snacks and talk over the day's events in comfort. Study bedrooms (most are doubles, some ensuite) are tidy and colourful, bedecked with bunting and fairy lights. Housemistress told us that the new girls' boarding house will provide a bit of 'breathing space' – not that the current accommodation is overcrowded, but it's felt that three smaller houses would be a better arrangement. Girls are 'affiliated' to boys' houses – 'it fosters co-ed spirit', we were told – and join them for activities such as plays, music and themed socials (wine and cheese, jazz).

Staff reassured us that houses are competitive 'but not tribal' and that the school works very hard to mix pupils up, especially important when so many come from the prep across the road.

Background and atmosphere: Founded in 1865 by George Cubitt, MP for West Surrey, and Rev John Sapte, who decided that what Victorian Surrey needed was 'a public school for the education of the middle classes.' The school was to 'provide a sound and plain education ... for the sons of farmers and others engaged in commercial pursuits.' The 'Surrey County School', funded by public appeals, was built on eight acres at the top of a hill just outside the village of Cranleigh. As the school grew to its present 280 acres, neighbouring farms were gradually acquired, remembered only in names such as The Butts (a sixth form café). If the original red-brick buildings embody the school's founding ideals: 'sound and plain', their elevated position at the top of a short avenue lends a certain aspirational grandeur. Most recent addition, the Emms Centre, houses modern foreign languages, science labs and IT, its double height atrium, flooded with natural light, was being well used by pupils revising for exams when we visited. A new humanities teaching block with dedicated business and careers centre is next, but definitely not last, in line.

Transition to co-ed, which started in the 1970s, was finally realised in 1999, but numerical equality of boys and girls is not on the cards. A ratio of 60:40 in favour of the chaps is the desired aim and the third girls' boarding house should help achieve it. No plans for significant increase in pupil numbers and parents certainly think school is 'just the right size'.

Parents told us they felt Cranleigh's reputation as a school that was just good for sport was always unfair and has, finally, been laid to rest. 'The school itself hasn't changed but the mindset of some people has', one told us. In our last review we noted that Cranleigh had become 'fashionable'. The school is undoubtedly still fashionable but its enduring popularity owes more to highly satisfied pupils and parents than any transient modishness. A 'sister' school, Cranleigh Abu Dhabi, was opened in 2014.

Pastoral care, well-being and discipline: 'Houses are everything' at Cranleigh, both academically and pastorally. 'Returning to your house should be like coming through a family door,' we were told. Each is almost like a mini-school but they 'aren't empires' and are run on consistent lines. House parents have a detailed overview of every aspect of a pupil's school career and tutors, teachers and prefects form 'layers' to catch problems. The parents we spoke to were very positive about all aspects of pastoral care, several commented on how well the school had dealt with 'difficult' teenage moments. 'They're so supportive, whatever the problem,' said one parent. Another told us, 'they expect the pupils to be independent but they know exactly when to step in.' Tutors are very quick to pick up on and let parents know about missed homework deadlines – whether the child is a boarder or day pupil, 'they want to work with parents'.

Pupils told us that their opinions were listened to although the democratic triumphs we heard about were small and mainly food based: Weetabix is now served every morning, spaghetti hoops are on the Wednesday menu and pepper is back on the tables (we couldn't find out why it disappeared). More significantly, after some wrangling, a termly teaching feedback survey will be implemented. 'It will improve communication', our guides said. Teachers weren't available for comment.

We heard several observations to the effect that expectations were higher for girls and that it was possibly bit easier being a boy at Cranleigh. These weren't criticisms, consensus is that school is right to make allowances for chaps' 'rough and tumble', although the interior décor of their boarding houses might disagree. Relationships between pupils are 'few' but 'managed extremely well'; the rules are crystal clear and it's not the Cranleigh way to break them – apparently 'you just wouldn't do that.'

Pupils and parents: Very much a local (home counties and London) boarding school – nearly all parents live within a two hour drive and matches, plays and concerts are very well supported as a consequence. 'I love the fact that my children get a great education and also have local friends', a mother told us. While school didn't seem to us as high end as its popular reputation suggests, a quick count of the Range Rovers doing Sunday night drop off will give you the superficial demographic. That 'Surrey bubble' may be in Mr Reader's sights but perhaps he's going to need a bigger pin.

Pupils are relaxed, confident and friendly, 'not overly sophisticated', said one mother, approvingly. There appears to be some leeway when it comes to hair and uniform (especially skirts below the knee rule) and many of the boys looked like they'd be much more comfortable in sports gear than suits. Very small number of international students, mainly from Russia and Poland. Former pupils include numbers of successful sportspeople, fair few military types plus Patrick Marber (actor, director, screenwriter); actors Julia Ormond, Laurence Naismith and Michael Cochrane; historian Andrew Roberts and former editor of the Guardian, Alan Rusbridger.

Entrance: About half come at 13+ from Cranleigh prep. Also Feltonfleet, Aldro, Danes Hill, Godstowe, Amesbury and Windlesham House. From 2019 the majority of places will be offered at 11+ for a 13+ start. Applicants are invited for an assessment day with a short test in English and maths and an interview to make 'an informal assessment of their interests and abilities.' Conditional offers made on the basis of this and reference from current school. Offer dependent on performance in CE or other assessments. School says it is looking for children who will thrive academically but also those who will make the most of the many opportunities on offer. All schools say this but oversubscribed Cranleigh means it and can afford to be choosy.

A few places are available at 16+ but competition is strong. Candidates should be predicted A*/A grades at I/GCSE and must sit verbal and non-verbal reasoning papers and submit an essay. Interview and reference also required.

Exit: A few leave post-GCSE, mostly to pursue courses not offered at school. University destinations and courses of those who stay on are as diverse as one might imagine. Lots to Bath, Birmingham, Bristol, Exeter, Durham, Newcastle and York. Handful to Europe and North America. Four to Oxbridge in 2016.

Money matters: Fees broadly in line with similar schools. Day fees towards the upper end of the scale but you are paying for six long days a week. Variety of scholarships on offer (music, sports, all-rounder) and these can be supplemented by means-tested bursaries.

Remarks: Cranleigh's motto, 'Ex cultu robur' (From culture comes strength), is a potent and timely reminder that education is about so much more than just exam results. This is a school where the team is defined as much by its fellowship as its success, although it helps that team Cranleigh does win quite a lot of the time. Mr Reader has distilled the famous Cranleigh ethos into five words: wholeness, time, family, love and hope. We think he's got it about right.

Cranmore School

73

Epsom Road, West Horsley, Surrey KT24 6AT

Pupils: 475 • Ages: 2.5-13 (boys); 2.5-7 (girls) • RC

Fees: £11,385 – £13,650 pa

Tel: 01483 280340
Email: admissions@cranmoreprep.co.uk
Website: www.cranmoreprep.co.uk

Headmaster: Since 2006, Mr Michael Connolly BSc BA MA MEd (50s). Scottish, quietly confident, straight bat, no nonsense. Years of experience as teacher, housemaster and head in a number of HMC senior and prep schools. He keeps active with squash, tennis and dog walking; reads something philosophical or theological most days (his arts subjects) and enjoys a broad musical taste. Mrs Connolly is a qualified teacher who also works in the school in the marketing department and shows prospective parents around. They have three sons, all in their 20s.

Parents tell us he was initially single minded in developing Cranmore; subsequently he has consulted and communicated with pupils and parents, taking account of their opinions; ultimately he knows where he is taking the school. Thoughtful and considered, he tackles difficult topics up front and head on. Parents describe him as 'reliable', 'straight talking', 'unassuming' and 'trustworthy'. Under his leadership, Cranmore is widely inclusive while maintaining high academic and social standards, with many opportunities for individual children to succeed.

He has limited contact with junior pupils (this is left to Miss Margaret Kieran, the very experienced head of the junior department), increasing as children progress through the school. In their final two years he teaches weekly lessons and gets to know them really well.

Entrance: Not selective and proud to be so. Prospective pupils spend a session in class and are assessed to ensure they would be happy and successful. Assessment definitely not competitive; head reassures that 'the average child will be fine', so long as they are prepared to 'get stuck in and have a go'. Places allocated first come first served, waiting list occasionally for some year groups.

Co-ed Bright Stars Nursery (2 +), reception and year 1 classes; girls can now join year 3 and the school will gradually become totally co-ed. Academic, music and sports scholarships awarded for entry at 7+. Also, means-tested financially assisted places potentially provide, at most, a free place.

Entry into Bright Stars Nursery means you are coming to Cranmore; Mr Connolly explains, 'It's not a stand-alone nursery, it's an investment by the school'. Two terms notice for term-time only nursery children and six months notice for all-year-rounders.

Exit: Pupils move on to a wide variety of senior schools, reflecting the non-selective intake: Brighton College, Charterhouse, City of London Freemen's, Cranleigh, Epsom, King's College Wimbledon, Lancing, Millfield, Reigate Grammar, Royal Grammar School Guildford, Reeds, Sherborne, St George's, St John's, Tonbridge, Wellington, Winchester, Worth.

Around third to half leave at 11, mainly to avoid stressful pre-testing and/or common entrance. Of those who leave at 13 around a quarter win scholarships, awards or exhibitions.

Remarks: Cranmore is genuinely an all round school, maintaining academic standards, terrific sports and much-praised music. Parents feel 'it's very balanced between academics, sport and music' and 'ticks boxes in lots of different areas'.

Located deep in Surrey's green commuter belt, on a large site; the original Victorian building tucked away around the back is used as the nursery, plus a few classrooms upstairs. The rest of the buildings are modern, spacious and purpose built. Nursery, junior and senior share all facilities but at different times, so they are usually separate, and it is not overwhelming for the youngest.

The school has high expectations of its pupils, and for the most part the children 'surprise themselves' with their achievements. Mr Connolly aims to limit the inevitable academic pressure; he is 'not a big fan of homework' and believes 'if pupils come to school fresh and get engaged while at school that should be enough to realise their abilities'. A long-standing Cranmore mum explains, 'He tries to educate the Surrey parent not to get too worked up about academic success'.

Parents are confident of the academic standards, telling us Cranmore 'turns out pupils who want to learn', that their children have been 'well challenged and tutored' by 'talented teachers' who 'know what buttons to push'. They feel 'the school sticks by all the pupils throughout and has great belief in the mix of abilities', and their children are 'monitored and assessed so there are no surprises'. Mr Connolly meets every parent during year 5 to discuss aspirations and manage expectations for suitable senior schools.

Broad range of subjects taught, although recently Latin has been dropped from the CE syllabus, a pragmatic decision by Mr Connolly which has stirred strong sentiments both for and against. He reassures that Latin is not compulsory for the majority of senior schools, and says those few parents for whom it matters will use a tutor. He teaches senior pupils on a carousel of (non-examined) Latin, Greek and philosophy, two terms of each over the final two years. Pupils are set in English and maths from year 4; for the final two years they are streamed into either a scholarship class or one of two CE classes. Teaching facilities are spacious and impressive, particularly the science labs and IT classrooms.

Post-CE programme is 'fantastic, every day is jam packed,' say parents, who are pleased their children stayed on to enjoy final two prep years with smaller teaching groups, prefect responsibility, exclusive blazers and a common room with PlayStation, pool table, air hockey and table football.

Sport is the 'wow' factor which attracts lively, active types to Cranmore. The facilities are 'amazing' and coaching is 'totally professional' with a 'squeaky clean, gentlemanly sporting ethos'. Exposure to variety is a big positive: by the time pupils leave they will have had the opportunity to try over 20 sports, including climbing, rowing and skiing (with ski club lessons at Sandown Park for pupils and families). There are plenty of clean, flat pitches, including all-weather pitches, sports hall with squash courts and fitness room, gym with climbing walls (laid out for lunchtime judo club when we visited), a 25 metre indoor swimming pool (in which all pupils have timetabled lessons) and newly refurbished changing rooms. There's enough indoor sporting space to accommodate all, so rain never stops play. Huge number of teams are fielded for matches so all get some opportunity to play, however those less successful or uninterested in sport may not feel entirely comfortable in this super-active environment.

Outdoor areas include spacious equipped playground areas for nursery and, separately, for juniors and, a new addition, a forest school tucked away beside the playing fields.

Music is strong, valued and highly praised by parents; 'incredible facilities' coupled with an 'exceptionally good head of music'. Music forms part of every day in assemblies, performances and curriculum, plus most senior boys learn an individual instrument, lots at the lower grades and a handful up to grade 6-8. Over 250 timetabled individual instrumental or singing lessons each week.

Catholic ethos runs through the school; head explains: 'It's a Catholic community and everyone does everything, it's fundamental to the school. If you want to come to Cranmore you accept this'. Having said that, the majority of families are not Catholic, and feel perfectly comfortable with daily prayer, half-termly mass and Catholic RE syllabus. Pupils are 'not indoctrinated' and parents recognise solid, Christian values that 'do pupils quite a bit of good'. They feel school focus is on 'confident, well-rounded children, who care about each other and are allowed to be individuals'.

Pupils see their form teachers twice a day for registration plus five minutes at the end of each day to 'gather their thoughts'. On the whole, they work calmly within clear, tight boundaries and are well motivated to please, earning merit points for their house. Junior children have weekly Marvellous Merit award based on Golden Rules code of conduct, kindness, honesty etc. Much parental praise for the deputy head, Mrs Sue Walker, who deals with occasional episodes of bullying. Pupils are helped with coping strategies and parents are involved. Discipline is about learning and moving on with 'no labels for bad children'; the aim is to educate children to make the right choices via drip feed over a long period.

Mr Connolly is onto the dangers of cyber-bullying: his approach is zero tolerance to any cyber-messaging he deems inappropriate, and he has suspended pupils. Not a fan of children having mobiles, he encourages parents to monitor their children's online and phone activities. Feels there have to be boundaries, clear guidelines and standards.

Cranmore families are hard working, busy, 'definitely Surrey people'. Most can comfortably afford fees, a few making financial sacrifices. Plenty of stay-at-home mums picking up or watching matches in muddy Hunter wellies. Active parents' association provides friendly socials and fundraising. Pupils' classes are changed around each year so children, and parents, get to know all in their year group.

An all-round school maintaining high standards and impressive results from a non-selective intake, with so much on offer that every child can find something in which to succeed.

Cumnor House Sussex

Danehill, Haywards Heath, West Sussex RH17 7HT

Pupils: 385; 30 full, 45 flexi boarders • Ages: 2–13 (boarding from 7) • C of E

Fees: Day £9,945 – £18,795; Boarding £22,365 pa

Tel: 01825 790347
Email: registrar@cumnor.co.uk
Website: www.cumnor.co.uk

Headmaster: Since 2001, Christian Heinrich BA PGCE (40s). Degrees from Kent and Oxford. Previously housemaster, then deputy head, at Summer Fields. ISI Inspector, IAPS appraiser of fellow heads, and chairman of the Boarding Schools Association in 2013, so plenty of insight into schools at all levels. Confident, and very sure of his approach to childhood and education: 'If a child is happy, education takes care of itself.' Described by pupils as fair, fun and someone who 'doesn't get unreasonably cross.' Most important quality for pupils to achieve in their time at Cumnor House: consideration. Loves films, skiing and wine: takes great joy in picking the bottles for post-parents' evening jollies.

Parents are very enthusiastic about him: 'Incredibly kind and supportive of kids – particularly those who struggle'; 'Easy to see when you want to'. 'Radical and brave...in that he works for the kids and not the parents,' added one parent thoughtfully, giving the example of his support for strong story lines in year 8 film making: a recent film told of a child desperate to win a swimming gala who practises all night and drowns. It was felt parents might not be able to stomach this ending, and a parent version was filmed in which the child comes up for a breath. Parents might find it difficult to accept the extraordinary level of pressure to succeed that can be absorbed by children – but the head and pupils here are fully cognisant, and the head does what he can to relieve the pressure.

Married to Belinda, who teaches French in the pre-prep; they have four children.

Entrance: Non-selective in early years; thereafter selection of those most likely to be fully involved in school life. Prospective pupils join in for a day to be observed for fit, with interviews for the occasional candidate for year 6 or above. Most join in nursery or year 3, but there's a healthy smattering in other years up to year 5. No waiting list as such; but they'll only show you around if there's a space. Two full bursary places for local children.

Exit: To a large variety of senior schools (30+), including Benenden, Brighton College, Bryanston, Cranbrook, Cranleigh, Eton, Harrow, Hurstpierpoint, King's Canterbury, Radley, Sevenoaks, Tonbridge, Wellington, Winchester, Worth. In directing children towards schools, considers not just whether they can meet the academic requirements, but also whether they're sufficiently emotionally robust to cope with life at the school in question.

Remarks: Beautiful setting in the Sussex countryside overlooking the downs. Buildings range from the charming to the unremarkable, in a village-like cluster. The core of the school was once a farmhouse, and some feel of this remains, with the carcass of a barn, formerly a splendid all-weather outdoor area, recently revamped into 'music HQ', and a new science, technology, engineering and maths centre called The Peake. Lush green grounds, and large pond to row over in the Cumnor boat, or swing over on a rope (it's drained and cleaned and carefully tested for any virulent bacteria first, assured the head's wife).

Main entrance is slightly scuffed country house hotel – parquet floor and log fire, and a few Famous Five books on a window sill by a sofa. Lego table and 70s sweets jigsaw on the go. 'Another genius from Cumnor' cushions – to reassure existing parents, or perhaps tempt prospective ones?

Common room with a log fire, couple of pool tables and newspapers (including Times and Independent) – not read at the time of our tour, but perhaps flicking through the papers comes later in the day. Award-winning art work on the walls, and a long piece of paper where pupils had drawn self-portraits in the style of Quentin Blake to celebrate World Book Day. A new iibrary area provides a welcome space for peace and calm.

Pre-prep is a cosy separate entity that particularly attracted one mum, who remembers fondly the special mothers' day celebration in reception, children presenting mums with handpicked flowers wrapped in foil, then escorting them into school for special cakes and poems – 'very simple and lovely.'

'Academic, but not pushy academic,' says the head. Certainly a school which achieves a goodly number of scholarships, but not, in atmosphere or method, like a prep with an eye on the prize for the duration. Many parents fresh from pressurised London preps may struggle initially with the comparatively relaxed Cumnor environment – 'you don't know at what level everyone else's child is reading,' said one startled mum. Take a deep breath, parents: your kids are not going to be constantly tested, so you won't receive that reassuring stream of test results as evidence that they are progressing nicely towards the senior school of choice. I have to tell them to trust us, says the head –- 'children are meant to be enjoying themselves and having fun.'

So things don't get really serious until years 7 and 8, when a scholarship set comes into being. The focus shifts somewhat towards achieving the desirable scholarships, and others start preparing for common entrance.

Usual range of subjects, with children being put into sets from year 5. Just French and Latin on the languages front – Latin is the basis of European languages, says the head, and teaches logic which can apply to other subjects, giving a derisive snort in passing to other schools' cosmetic glance at Mandarin. Careful consideration of the timetable, which is broken up so kids are not using their brains in the same way for long periods of time – pre-prep dance outside before each maths lesson. No one model fits all – so if there is good reason for the usual school curriculum not to apply to a child, then an exception will be made.

Not much prep until year 7: just vocab and spelling, which could be learnt in the bath or around the dinner table, and reading, occasionally left undone – 'I don't read on Friday nights as mummy and daddy have gin and tonic,' said a child in year 1.

Year 7 and 8s all have iPads for use during lessons, purchased by parents in an optional scheme ('you didn't have to sign up, but if everyone else was going to have one...'). No social media or unsuitable apps.

Learning support is excellent, and not only provides support to (around 30) pupils with special needs, but also to those who just need a bit of extra help now and then. There's an educational psychologist on the staff, who observes classes, and deals with any emotional problems suffered by pupils which may be exacerbated by school, from separation anxiety to bereavement. No extra charge for counselling or one-to-one learning support. Additional charges for extras such as speech therapy.

Saturday school on alternate weekends, which children seem happy with (though some parents would prefer a lie in, and more family time).

School motto – 'be kind' permeates everything, said one parent: apparently the head boy's job is to make sure everyone is happy at break time, and no one is being left out; so it comes as no surprise that the pastoral care is very thorough: regular full staff pastoral care meetings where every child's name is read out, and their welfare considered. Form teachers are the first port of call for difficulties until year 5, after which each child has a tutor whom they meet twice once a week to talk about everything and anything. School policy on bullying is to make sure children understand what bullying behaviour is, and ask them to blow the whistle: senior children attend the ABC committee (Anti-Bullying Committee) every week to report on anyone they are worried about. One parent whose child experienced bullying behaviour said it was dealt with quickly and efficiently, and also praised the presence of 'gappers' (gap year students), who she said could pick up on things teachers might not get to hear.

C of E, but not evangelically so. Exposure to the most valuable tenets of faith with a bohemian touch: daily prayers described by head as also a school silence – a time for a loud school to be silent and consider things (there is a cheery noise as kids move around here, but children are friendly and well mannered).

The school shares facilities in the local community, and links with a local primary each year. The head is setting up the Cumnor certificate (own brand D of E), which will involve years 7 and 8 working in the local community, and being part of drama workshops with younger pupils from local primaries.

Food is 'amazing' say kids – apparently there are no adjectives which can do justice to the wraps. In-house custard creams and jammy dodgers bulge with cream and jam and were startlingly yummy to those of us used to the pedestrian version (they've got an award winning pastry chef). Well, if the cushions didn't do it for you...

Occupations, as clubs are called at Cumnor, range from boules to calligraphy, and vary each term. Cinematography described in detail by enthusiastic kids – 'it makes you look at films in a completely different way.' There's a waiting list for cooking, but everyone gets a turn eventually. Year 8 learn to cook a three course meal as a post-exam treat.

The 'co-curriculum' (sports and arts) is given equal rather than ornamental value here ('they find out what every child has going for them,' said a parent).

Sport is for awareness, commitment and health – and everyone: a poor enthusiastic player will be in teams all the way through, playing matches most weeks. 'It's nice to win,' said a pupil; but it's not the only or main purpose of sport here. No A, B or C teams until year 7: teams change from week to week, and the make-up of teams depends on whom they are playing. Lots of it – up to seven sessions a week, including swimming. Ample playing fields and courts with views over the rolling downs, and a new Olympic size Astroturf. Swish indoor swimming pool, old chilly outdoor version.

Art is 'exceptional,' said one parent. Housed in a barn-like room with high beams, glass doors and space to hang strange colourful objects. Secured the two top prizes in the Royal College of Art Young Art Exhibition last year.

All learn a musical instrument –- it can be dropped in year 7 to make way for the demands of common entrance and scholarships, though many continue. Eight instrumental groups, from orchestra to the sort-of-samba group.

Each year from year 3 upwards does an annual production, Shakespeare being the year 8 remit (one heavyweight, one adapted comedy for those with less Olivier inclinations) to be performed in the mossy green outdoor theatre. Everything from Snow White to Oh! What a Lovely War in the years below.

The uniform and sports kit is good quality but expensive – one parent complained indignantly at the cost of school sweatshirts; but there's some second hand provision in the uniform shop. Sports kit is laundered by the school, much to the joy of parents.

Boarding is possible from year 7: 30+ full timers (although all go home every other weekend), and up to 50 flexi boarders, who spend a few nights every week at school. 'They are completely flexible,' said one grateful parent. Tremendously popular with pupils, several of whom commented on their difficulty persuading their mums they were old enough – 'but it's so fun.' Lots of activities: preparations for Dragons' Den were under way, not to mention Marlborough Murders, Friday night is magic night and day trips at the weekends. So much going on that on just one night in the summer term did boarders watch anything on TV. Gappers help make the boarding experience really fun, said one parent: they're always there to play a game and provide an injection of energy and enthusiasm.

Rooms are for five, and cosy: four beds at ground level, and one bunk. Bathrooms are clean and up to date. Parents like the proximity of houseparents (described by parents as 'warm and welcoming' and 'extremely efficient'), and the easy access pupils have to gappers, who have rooms on each corridor, and are the first point of call in the night.

Current common room is the one used during the day, transformed for boarders with an additional rug and sofa (the new block will free up space for boarders to have a dedicated room). Fruit is always available, and there's a pantry where boarders can make tea, toast and hot drinks (with gappers' help). Obligatory weekly letter writing, and phones available for making calls in the evening or at break time – parents and pupils were happy this was sufficient. No Skype, iPads or mobiles allowed ('they get technology soon enough,' said one parent). Useful experience for those who move onto boarding senior schools. Currently no overseas boarders.

Parents around 30 per cent London, the rest local, mostly professionals or city types. Not cliquey, said one parent, outgoing and sociable, inclusive of newcomers, with an imminent buddy system to match new parents with old. Parents are encouraged to use the swimming pool and join the zumba class –- 'not a drop and go school.' Indeed coffee and croissants are available every morning in the dining room after drop off. 'Parents should certainly not worry about being lonely in the country.'

One full bursary at the moment, but the Cumnor Foundation is about to be launched, with the aim of providing two assisted places in every year by 2020.

Dame Alice Owen's School

Dugdale Hill Lane, Potters Bar, Hertfordshire EN6 2DU

Pupils: 1,465 • Ages: 11–18 • Sixth form: 430

Tel: 01707 643441
Email: admin@damealiceowens.herts.sch.uk
Website: www.damealiceowens.herts.sch.uk

Headteacher: Since September 2016, Hannah Nemko, previously senior deputy. She joined the school in September 2015 from Yavneh College, where she was deputy head and helped to set up the college. French degree from Nottingham and MA equivalent from Strasbourg. Has taught in a variety of school including the Royal Grammar, High Wycombe, where she was head of year.

Academic matters: Dame Alice Owen's has high expectations of its pupils – and they rise to the challenge. Almost 40 per cent of youngsters are selected by academic ability or musical talent and results and facilities are more than a match for local independent schools. In 2016, 55 per cent A*/A grades at A level, and 82 per cent A*/B grades. Wide range of academic A levels, with maths the most popular, followed by chemistry. Some students choose to do the EPQ too.

At GCSE 68 per cent A*/A grades in 2016. School specialises in science, music and languages and pupils either take triple science or core and additional science. All take a language from year 7, then add a second in year 8. Most do two languages at GCSE. French, German and Spanish on offer and for keen linguists Italian, Mandarin, Japanese, Russian and Latin can be arranged too. Regular trips abroad, including staying with host families in year 9 and study trips in year 12.

Parents say their children are encouraged academically and given lots of homework, though there's plenty of help and support in place. Most recent Ofsted report commented that staff were 'willing to go that extra mile' and it seemed that way to us. Sixth formers, for instance, were full of praise for the support they get with UCAS forms. Each student is assigned a UCAS tutor and they meet at least once a week to discuss university applications. Philosophy teacher is pioneer of revision methods and several pupils said they'd been encouraged to learn what worked for them individually – everything from mind maps to spiral learning. Very few behaviour issues, say the teachers. 'The children are very motivated and focused,' said one. 'You can really teach your subject here. You don't have to dwell on managing behaviour.'

Maximum class sizes in years 7 to 11 are 32, with seven or eight groups per year. In years 7 and 8, mainly mixed ability, apart from maths. From year 9 English and languages are set. In the sixth form, class sizes range between 12 and 20. Approximately 100 pupils on the SEN register – learning support team works alongside them in lessons. Sixth formers encouraged to offer additional support once a week too.

Games, options, the arts: A very sporty school, with a huge expanse of games pitches, large sports hall and floodlit Astroturf. Boys play football (the year 9 team won the national final a few years back), rugby, hockey, cricket, athletics, gym, badminton and basketball while girls do football, netball, hockey, badminton, athletics, tennis, rounders and cricket. School produces lots of talented cross-country runners – perhaps not surprising with 35 acres of grounds to run around in. County and national representatives in many sports.

Superlative music. The school marked its 400th anniversary in 2013 by hosting a sell-out concert at the Royal Albert Hall. There was also a service of thanksgiving at St Paul's Cathedral – 'the whole school got the train and we walked from Moorgate to St Paul's,' said a sixth form girl. 'I don't think I'll ever forget it.' Approximately 400 pupils learn an instrument and there's all manner of orchestras and groups to join, from flute ensembles and chamber choirs to jazz quartets and soul bands. School boasts a host of grade 8 musicians and several play in the National Youth Orchestra.

Art is popular, with about 80 pupils a year taking it at GCSE, 25 at AS and 15 at A2. Four large studios filled with easels, tables and work filling every inch of the walls. Regular drama productions, including lower school play for years 7 to 9 and upper school production for years 10 to 13, all performed in fabulous Edward Guinness Hall. Plenty of other extracurricular activities to choose from – 147 at the last count, so something for everyone, including D of E and World Challenge. Recently a dynamic group of budding engineers designed, constructed and raced their own miniature Formula One car and went on to win the national F1 in Schools competition. They topped that by becoming runners up in the world finals in Abu Dhabi. Lots of photographs of their triumphs on display.

Background and atmosphere: School was founded in 1613 by Dame Alice Owen. Born Alice Wilkes, she narrowly missed being struck by a wayward arrow when she was young and vowed that as soon as she was rich enough she would do something for posterity as a mark of gratitude. Fifty years on and thrice widowed, she used her wealth to establish a school for 30 boy scholars from Islington. She entrusted its running to the Worshipful Company of Brewers, which for the last four centuries has supported and encouraged the school.

A girls' school was added in 1886 and in the late 60s, a search was made for a new location. The school moved to its present site on the edge of Potters Bar in 1973. To this day Dame Alice Owen's takes immense pride in its history. All year 7s receive a crown (now a £5 commemorative coin) at a ceremony at the Brewers Hall in the City of London. Older pupils receive annual 'beer money' till they leave (£1 for year 8s, rising to £6 for year 13s). Dame Alice originally instructed the governors to visit the school annually to inspect the pupils' progress and this still forms part of the annual open day and prize giving. In the early days the scholars collected flowers to make buttonholes; today pupils in years 7 to 11 wear white carnations while sixth formers sport red carnations.

School is modern and purpose-built, surrounded by woods, fields and a lake. Lots of new buildings in recent years, including the concert hall, maths, art and DT centre and cricket pavilion. When we visited new science building well underway. Atmosphere everywhere is purposeful, busy and friendly. Effective school council (which has its own Twitter account) has achieved a myriad of changes, from more water fountains to a café where older pupils can buy sandwiches and paninis (a sort of mini Subway). Food gets the thumbs-up – hot food, vegetarian options, salad bar, jacket potatoes, sandwiches and chips served once a week. Pupils pay via fingerprint scanners and can sit where they like in a large, airy dining room which boasts a life size model of Dame Alice Owen (sculpted by Sir George Frampton, best known for his statue of Peter Pan in Kensington Gardens) in one corner.

Pastoral care, well-being and discipline: Pupils say they feel at ease and able to be themselves. They see their form tutors for 20 minutes every morning, with sessions ranging from checking homework diaries to discussing risk-taking, the use of the internet and bullying ('not a massive issue here.') Tutors hold regular progress reviews with their tutees. Reports sent home twice a year plus parents' consultation evening once a year. If pupils have done particularly well at something a 'well done' postcard is sent home.

Fairly nondescript black and grey uniform though girls get to wear jaunty red jumpers. School rules stipulate 'no jewellery, piercings or ornamentation of any kind' and we didn't spot any. Sixth formers, clad in smart office wear, are enthusiastic about their outfits. 'The novelty of wearing a suit hasn't worn off yet,' grinned a year 12 boy in a stylish floral tie.

School gives sixth formers a greater degree of independence, with five study periods a week for year 12s and ten for year 13s. 'We're encouraged not to waste them,' said a sixth form boy. 'Actually, it's nice to be in an environment where people work hard. There is a real work ethos here.' Sixth formers have their own sixth form centre, with common room, kitchen and SALC (student access learning centre). Head boy, head girl and four deputies meet the head every week and there's a raft of school and form prefects.

Pupils and parents: Pupils travel from far and wide – not just from Potters Bar but also from Enfield, Barnet, Hatfield, South Mimms and Islington. The youngsters we met seemed industrious, grounded and as keen as mustard. One boy told us: 'When you look forward to coming to school you know it's good.' Another remarked: 'It's a very positive atmosphere. The teachers are very enthusiastic about their subjects they are teaching and you can't help but fit into that pattern. Everyone works hard and feels very proud to be here.' Lots of distinguished former pupils, including Gary Kemp (and three other members of Spandau Ballet), Madness guitarist Chris Foreman, Sir Alan Parker, Dame Beryl Grey and Joss Ackland. A framed letter from Gary Kemp on the wall in reception declares he's 'proud to be an Old Owenian.' Spandau Ballet gave its first performance in the school hall and a commemorative plaque is planned.

Parents are an eclectic mix – media types and factory workers to company directors and teachers. They are hugely supportive (hosting fundraising events, quiz nights and a summer ball) and all keen on the idea of an academic, non-exclusive school.

D

Entrance: Unusual admission rules. School is semi-selective and vastly oversubscribed – around 1,300 children compete for 200 places each year. Special needs and looked after children take priority, then 22 who live closest to the school and siblings of pupils already at Dame Alice Owen's. Ten places for musical aptitude, 65 awarded on academic ability (tests in English, maths and verbal reasoning), 20 places for children living in or attending school in Islington, then staff children and other children nearest to the school. Children taking the entrance exam and music tests must live in one of the school's designated local priority areas.

Around 500 compete for around 30 additional places in the sixth form. Applicants come from local state and independent schools and need in the region of six A*s at GCSE. Slightly more girls than boys in sixth form.

Exit: Around 5-10 per cent leave after GCSEs. After A levels virtually all to higher education. Eighty per cent to Russell Group universities. Fourteen to Oxbridge in 2016 and six medics. Lots to UCL, Imperial, Bristol and Durham. All manner of subjects – from medicine and engineering (nearly half go on to study science) to economics and politics. 'Our students are eclectic in their interests.'

Money matters: Funded by government as an academy but also gets money from the Dame Alice Owen Foundation (The Worshipful Company of Brewers is the trustee), fundraising events and donations.

Remarks: 'Positive, energetic and progressive' – that's how one of the teachers summed up Dame Alice Owen's and we agree. This is a gem of a school, where teachers can teach, pupils work hard and parental support really makes a difference.

Dame Bradbury's School

Linked with Stephen Perse Pre-Prep and Junior Schools, Stephen Perse Senior School, Stephen Perse 6th Form

Ashdon Road, Saffron Walden, Essex CB10 2AL

Pupils: 220 • Ages: 3-11

Fees: £10,380 – £12,825 pa

Tel: 01799 522348
Email: admissions@damebradburys.com
Website: www.damebradburys.com

Head: Since January 2015, Tracy Handford, previously head of St Hilda's Prep in Bushey. Educated at Lancaster Girls' Grammar School and the University of Leeds, where she read applied biology. Followed this with an MA in curriculum studies from the Institute of Education, University of London. Began career as a boarding tutor at Taverham Hall School, Norwich, then Holmwood House, Colchester. Moved to become head of year and head of science at Bishop's Stortford College Junior School before becoming director of studies at St Faith's School, Cambridge. Status as ISI inspector should mean she has her eye on the competitive ball and her experience means she is au fait with the Cambridge school scene. Likeable, down to earth, 'professional and knowledgeable,' say parents. Committed to providing her pupils with 'more than a set of qualifications'. Lives in rural Cambridgeshire with her husband and daughter.

D

Entrance: Waiting list with sibling preference. For the kindergarten and reception, informal visit with head of early years. Later entrants, depending on age: chat/observation in the classroom/tests in age appropriate core skills of maths and English. School purports to be non-selective, but says children are accepted on the basis that they can access the learning – gives school some wiggle room.

Exit: School starts talking to parents about next school when their children are in year 4. Over 90 per cent get their first choice. Stephen Perse Foundation senior school a favourite – helped by tempting early offer process which removes the need for entrance testing and SPF going co-ed in September 2017. By no means the only option though, with large numbers boarding the so-called Hogwarts Express daily from Saffron Walden to schools in Cambridge (Perse Upper, The Leys, St Mary's Cambridge, as well as SPF) and others to board further afield (Cheltenham, Oakham, King's Ely, Oundle, Cheltenham Ladies). Academic, music, art and sport scholarships frequently awarded. A handful to Saffron Walden and Linton state schools

Remarks: Dame Johane Bradbury is named after its founder – the sister of an early 16th century rector of Saffron Walden. Today the school is situated in a quiet suburban street not far from the town centre. Slightly dour late Victorian edifice belies the modernity inside – all white walls and funky accent colours since becoming part of the Stephen Perse Foundation in 2013 and the arrival of Mrs Handford. Parents have appreciated the step change and note improvements to the facilities, administration and academic rigour. 'Being part of a bigger foundation results in a scrutiny that previously did not exist apart from ISI inspections, and I feel much more comfortable knowing that the future of the school is secure as part of Stephen Perse,' commented one. Foundation offers CPD opportunities for staff and central administration, giving more time for teachers to teach and to develop curriculum approaches.

Mrs Handford is credited with 'taking the school forward', boosting academic standards through specialist teaching, IT and creativity across the board. Commitment to instilling values, developing integrity and personal qualities continues with added oomph. 'Children are encouraged to make good choices in their learning and behaviour,' says head and this is quite strategic, with classroom displays focusing as much on 'learning habits' and 'what makes a good monitor' as examples of (extremely) good work. Useful, according to our guide, when you're struggling in a maths test and catch sight of the word 'determination' writ large on the wall behind your teacher's head. Every pupil holds a position of responsibility at some point and super 'YAK' accreditation for those identified as 'being yourself, aiming high and being kind' – school's key aims in a nutshell – while the house system 'gives a real sense of pride,' exclaims our guide.

'Hard to find children sitting down at a desk – they're outside dragging a branch or using technology,' says head, and indeed a sparky and innovative approach to learning when we visited with pupils actively engaged in purposeful activities – from 'office' role play in kindergarten, to learning Spanish while studying Miro, to a soundtrack of the Gypsy Kings in year 4. Says head, 'investigation is integral' to the curriculum, which is devised by SPF and reviewed regularly. Thematic learning is the key with a four year theme cycle in pre-prep and two years in the juniors to keep things fresh. 'We're moving away from the curriculum being driven by content and instead taking a skills based approach,' head explains. Much use of digital technologies with Macs and iPads all around – ideal for in-class support as well as extension. Google classroom for years 5 and 6. Homework only in English, maths and science – parents encouraged to take their children out instead, 'to satisfy intellectual curiosity'.

Collaboration across the foundation gives scope for enrichment activities (recently pre-prep multicultural day in Cambridge on understanding diversity, World War Two workshop for upper juniors). Specialist teaching for music, science and languages – French and Spanish for all, and Latin from year 5. Learning support has made great strides – the focus is on inclusion, ensuring pupils are supported within the classroom. Room and capacity for increased roll but 'space is a benefit,' says head. Two form entry with pre-prep classes of up to 16 and the rest to 20. Kindergarten for around 22 rising 3 to 4s, awash with wellies and sharing 'big gym and little gym' outdoor play and learning area with the two reception classes and all of the school's facilities. Large kindergarten classrooms have plenty of corners for creative play – on the list for refurbishment. Parents invited in to watch lessons including music, languages and weekly forest school. Year 6s help as buddies.

Fab new brightly coloured art room is an inspiring work space. Innovative library with lit, carpeted shelves, dominated by central 'reading tree' with nooks and crannies filled with books and places to sit. Graphs of most popular reading and pupils' own reviews. Very tempting. Rainey Hall opened in 2013 by Earl of Wessex, indoor sports facility presided over by no fewer than eight PE trained members of staff (a record for this size of school?) offering rugby and netball, athletics and cricket (two girls' teams wiping the floor in local fixtures). Outside 184m track and Astro as well as playing fields. Also a teaching garden complete with pond for dipping.

School's own theatre is the venue for assemblies – raked seating for privileged year 6 – and annual productions for every year group from kindergarten and reception nativity to year 5 shortened Shakespeare and year 6 musical. Also houses lively music department where year 2 up learn the recorder and year 5 the ukulele. Thriving orchestra open to all when ready.

'The provision of extracurricular activities is second to none,' asserts a parent, and certainly the wide choice of clubs runs the gamut from STEAM (STEM plus arts), to iPad photography and ceilidh band. Sports clubs change every term (all welcome unless squad training). Residential trips much anticipated building from four days in York for year 4 to five day trips in year 5 (Cornwall) and year 6 (Snowdonia). Different years take on different projects – last year's Snowdon visitors produced an iBook.

Fresh fruit and a carbohydrate are the usual breaktime snacks supplied by the kitchens and there's a choice at lunch of the cooked meal, vegetarian option or salad, followed by a hot pudding or yogurt plus fruit. Breakfast club is popular for the hot chocolate. Dining hall doubles as an arena for critical thinking – enormous green board invites mind maps and the articulation of thoughts and ideas.

Any type of child is suited here, says head. All we met presented as enthusiastic learners with a solid work ethic and an appreciation of worthwhile personal qualities and values. Refreshing. 'You can be a great learner but you need to know how to use what you've learnt to get the most out of life,' says head. Pupils are assessed on their engagement with learning and all make good progress, she adds.

Parent profile has changed somewhat in recent years due to the establishment of local science parks and greater commuting to London or Cambridge. Invited in to school often, including to help with clubs. Working parents booked in in advance. Parental trust in the school runs high.

An exciting and enormously positive prep school which inspires children to learn independently and enthusiastically and to develop the skills and qualities to apply their learning in life. Quite likely the shape of prep education to come.

Dane Court Grammar School

Broadstairs Road, Broadstairs, Kent CT10 2RT

Pupils: 1,196 • Ages: 11–18 • Sixth form: 318

Tel: 01843 864941
Email: admin@danecourt.kent.sch.uk
Website: www.danecourt.kent.sch.uk

Head of School: Since 2014, Mr Andrew Fowler, previously assistant head (curriculum) at Queen Elizabeth Grammar School, Penrith. Read music at Exeter and worked as an accountant for seven years, whilst also completing an MA in 17th century music at Durham. Retrained as a teacher at Durham (PGCE in music and maths), then worked in comprehensives in Warwickshire and County Durham, as well as as Reading Blue Coat School. Completed an MSc in education assessment at Durham and is an expert on musical education and assessment. He has been a member of several cathedral choirs, tutors early music groups and has published Tudor choral music. Married to Linda, formerly a lecturer in religious education at Durham University.

Mr Fowler oversees the day-to-day running of the school, while Mr Paul Luxmoore is executive headteacher of this and King Ethelbert, both members of the Dane Court and King Ethelbert Trust. The school is a member of the Coastal Academies Trust, a small group of local primary and secondary schools dedicated to working together to improve the educational chances of all children in Thanet.

Academic matters: The school converted entirely to the IB in September 2012, 'because A levels have proved not fit for purpose, and students with an IB are more likely to gain a place at the best universities'. Students can choose between the more academically focused diploma or the careers certificate, which is a vocational version and offers courses such as applied business, sports science, and health and social care, alongside the core subjects.

It's an intense programme but school says: 'Busier students get better grades. They will only have two to three free study periods per week, but once they get into the rhythm of working at that pace they really enjoy it.'

Not all parents are happy about this change. One commented: 'It feels as though the sixth form has suddenly gone comprehensive, offering vocational courses as well and I feel our children are ill prepared for the IB through our style of education which is not European style. They have been narrowing their studies and heading towards specialisation since year 9.'

English, science and maths departments are strong, and sixth formers rate the history and politics departments. Parents say languages are an area of concern, and school agrees, calling that a 'fledgling' department. A newly appointed languages head and staff are charged with turning the department around. French, German, Spanish, Italian and Japanese are on offer. For years 7-11, there's a new skills and character-based curriculum, called ICE (Independent Cultural Enrichment) and reduction in GCSEs taken – now 9 or 10 GCSEs rather than 11.

D

Results 'reflect the community'. In the Thanet area, there are around 40 more grammar places than children reaching the required standard each year. 'You would expect to see 100 per cent A* to C at GCSE in a grammar, but that is almost impossible to achieve in our community.' Some pupils have not in fact passed the Kent test.

Given that context, the school delivers well – 2016 results show over 99 per cent of pupils achieving 5+ A* to Cs at GCSE (including English and maths), with 45 per cent of GCSEs at A* or A. Sixth formers take their studies seriously – 'You're expected to work hard here', they say – and a couple make it to Oxbridge most years. In 2016, average IB point score of 33.

Games, options, the arts: Arts are a real strength, reflecting a community where many musicians and artists make their home. There is exceptional art on display, and photographs outside the theatre show professionally costumed and staged productions of Grease, Annie, and Midsummer Night's dream.

Broadstairs has a big reputation for folk music, hosting an annual festival and performances in its pubs every night. There are a lot of musicians among the parent body which in turn encourages the children – lessons on a wide range of instruments are provided. 'The equipment is well respected, the doors aren't locked,' says school.

Overseas tours include a 10 day trip to teach in Namibia for the sixth form, a pastoral trip to Bonn for year 8s, skiing, and departmental trips to Valencia, Iceland, Ypres, Paris, and New York.

Sporting teams do the school proud – both girls' and boys' football teams regularly reach the Kent Cup final. Girls came ninth in the country at the National Rugby finals at Twickenham, and the school table tennis team are national champions. Those who aren't selected to play for the school have an opportunity to compete in house sporting events. Those who aren't enticed by team games can take part in extracurricular sports such as rowing, rock climbing, orienteering and mountain biking.

Parental reports on sports provision are all good, and one mother of two pupils comments: 'The sports department is outstanding; it has been really good both for my child who isn't good at sport and the one who excels at it, they've both been encouraged and it has built their confidence.'

Background and atmosphere: One of the lucky few to see renovation under the Building Schools for the Future programme, before it was scrapped by the coalition. A £20 million rebuild and refurbishment completed in 2011 has created a spacious and natural light-filled campus, which appears at once industrious and serene. It's the kind of building you walk into as a parent and immediately cross your fingers and hope everything else is right.

The aim of the programme was to create inspirational buildings to make pupils feel valued and worthwhile – and in this case it works. Walking into the central atrium, it looks more like the offices of a prosperous technology company, and it's not hard to see how this motivates children more than the grimly oppressive Victorian architecture of many schools.

At break time we saw students milling around the big central space or queuing at the coffee bar, sitting in comfortable chairs chatting in groups, looking over their notes prior to exams.

D

There's no regimentation, and they look more like university students.

There are six open plazas, each hosting a house base. Each plaza or hub is also a curriculum area base, and has labs or classrooms leading off from a large central study space. The plazas are open at break for their house to eat lunch in, play games, or do homework.

The sixth form has a distinct area in each house plaza and in the central atrium, but there's been a deliberate decision to integrate them more with the rest of the school. School wanted to move away from having a sixth form common room, now they help with supervision across the school. 'Everyone mingles more now,' agree the students.

One plaza houses a computer room with 80 machines which is open at lunchtime, before and after school for homework or general use.

Pastoral care, well-being and discipline: There's no uniform for the sixth form – depending on the day, a mixture of 'smart business wear' and jeans and shorts can be in evidence. Younger pupils are in uniform, with a simple 'black, white and gold' theme: white shirts (sometimes hanging out) for all, tartan skirt (sometimes hitched up) for girls and black trousers for boys. Black and gold ties are optional for girls, and black blazers with a gold badge are worn by all. 'Our students are not always the neatest, but they're happier for it.'

Recently established house system is used to entrench a sense of community, and the first thing pupils see as they walk through the front doors is a screen displaying live house point totals. A house cup and book tokens are awarded to top performers.

Students who cross the line are dealt with by a restorative justice system. 'It's not a punitive approach, we urge people to do the right thing. We talk to them, and we listen to them'. Lots of the students have had training in peer mentoring and they will meet with the pupil concerned, he or she will also hear from other children what their actions felt like to them. One student who has transferred to the sixth form from another school finds the atmosphere very different. 'Everyone here is a lot nicer, and there's a lot more respect,' she says.

Pastoral care is delivered through a mentoring system that is popular with both students and parents. 'I really like mentoring, it allows us to have time with our form tutor and if you have a problem you can go to them about it,' says one girl. A parent with two children at the school concurs. 'The pastoral care is excellent, they are supported really well,' she says. Another parent wishes more detail was conveyed home, saying: 'I don't feel we get enough information. There were plans for a computer system, where parents would be able to see for example if their child had been late for a lesson, or got a house point, which looked like it was going to be good but it never got off the ground.' School says this system will be introduced in September. But one mother has found staff 'very accommodating' when she has needed to discuss anything, saying: 'It's a real advantage that you can ring up and a teacher will call you back or see you to sort out any problems.'

Pupils and parents: The deprivation in the area and scarcity of jobs – 3,500 applied for 180 jobs at Primark – means that students see no future for themselves, and 'we have to do a lot of work on confidence building'. These social problems are compounded by London boroughs buying up cheap housing in the area in which to place their overflow social housing tenants, and clusters of Eastern European immigrants settling in the area 'which causes some tension and resentment. We have to do a lot of work with students on equality and understanding'.

Mixed parent body, with some finding themselves in challenging circumstances, the vast majority are supportive. In surveys, 98 per cent of parents said it is a good school and they are happy with the education their child is getting. A parent we spoke to commented: 'I work in a junior school and I always recommend it to parents there'. Pupils agree that it's a pleasant environment. 'It's a nice community, everyone is happy and friendly,' says one.

Entrance: There are two grammars in Thanet – this is considered the better one and is oversubscribed. Students come from more than 30 feeder primaries.

School is currently over planned admission numbers in every year group, so joining mid-way depends on a place coming up. Pupils can join in the sixth form, and need six Bs and two Cs at GCSE to do the IB diploma, and three Bs and two Cs to do the IB Careers Certificate.

Exit: Around 25 per cent leave after GCSEs and four per cent or so after year 12. Three quarters of sixth form students went on to university in 2016 – was 80 to 90 per cent but numbers have dropped since the increase in fees. In 2016, two to Oxbridge, nine to study medicine or medically-related courses, same number taking biomedical sciences or biochemistry. Some to Russell Group universities, over half to top 25, including Bath, Bristol, Durham, Exeter, Kent, KCL, Loughborough, Nottingham, Reading, Southampton and York. Others to Canterbury so can live at home. 'There's a lot of support to help them make university choices,' says a parent.

Remarks: This would be a great fit for the child who doesn't respond well to authoritarian, old school regimes. Everything about the school speaks of treating the pupils respectfully, on the assumption that they will behave maturely.

Children are not publicly bawled out for misdemeanours, instead they talk through their actions with their peers. Expensive equipment isn't locked away – why should it be, there's no assumption that the kids will damage it. And the physical space looks more like a university, which in turn creates the expectation that this is a place for serious learning.

Danes Hill School

Leatherhead Road, Oxshott, Surrey KT22 0JG

Pupils: 880 • Ages: 3–13

Fees: £6,405 – £17,745 pa

Tel: 01372 842509
Email: registrar@daneshill.surrey.sch.uk
Website: www.daneshillschool.co.uk

Head: Since 2007, Mr Willie Murdock (50s), BA PGCE, both from Queen's University, Belfast where studied Latin. Previously deputy head who stepped into the breach following sudden death of charismatic predecessor. CV short to extinction. Arrived at school as Latin teacher after qualifying in 1980s, loved it and simply never left. Though not one for introspection, career choice just might, he thinks, be down to desire to rework deficiencies in own education in N Ireland state system – rigour first class, teacher empathy rather less so.

Wife teaches here (one of several married couples at the school) and all three of offspring went through, again common practice. Would send out worrisome message about the school if shunned by own staff, he says. Decent discounts help, as does staff-only early morning crèche down at the pre-prep, a 10 minute drive away, but universal staff enthusiasm for school (and regret from teachers whose older children missed the boat) would disarm all but most hard-bitten of cynics. Though a stayer himself, supportive of wanderlust in others. Funds training and, if can't provide appropriate hike in responsibilities (though often can) gives blessing to search for more senior roles elsewhere, five or so deputy heads and heads amongst them.

Size may make this an empire worth having, but job is no sinecure. 'Think of him as being administrator rather than educator,' reckoned one parent. Something he's definitely good at and given school this size, way with spreadsheets an essential core competency. Ditto ability to engage talented staff – interviews will seek to weed out any 'two-dimensional characters' and will always ask how they fill leisure hours (he admits to love for shooting and fishing, assisted by German shepherd 'who thinks she's a labrador').

Though has a lighter side, takes some digging to uncover. While won't ever make heads' year book as most likely to 'roll his sleeves up and josh with the kids,' reckons one parent, he is 'jovial and approachable' – as well as running very popular camp for year 8 leavers in his own garden. Those who ski will see a fair amount of him. Also teaches Latin and 'definitely knows us,' reckoned older pupils, though they felt that form tutors would be place to go for problems (head of pastoral care runs regular surgeries for those with less run of the mill issues).

Relaxed about partial knowledge of parents. 'May not know every name but know a teacher who does,' he says. Deals effectively with battalions of challenging mums, described by one local as 'the Marbella mob' and by a current parent as 'the black Range-Rover brigade' (certainly well represented in car park). Perhaps, theorised one mother, has made sensible decision to resist demands to set up PTA, so can 'bat parents away one at a time', rather than cope with a whole classroom of opinionated and occasionally disgruntled customers. No, he says firmly. 'PTAs can create conflicts of interest' – so trustees say 'no', though Friends of Danes Hill 'organise social and charitable events,' stresses school.

Unlikely to make drastic changes. With excellence the order of the day, results excellent and pupil numbers at capacity, why rock the boat?

Entrance: Highly popular, all 880 places filled and then some. Particularly oversubscribed in year 2. Anyone joining in nursery or reception will go straight through, year 1 and 2 hopefuls observed, taster sessions with literacy and numeracy tests for year 3 and above, though stressed that 'we are looking at the whole child.'

Billed as virtually non-selective and inclusivity is the name of the game, range of mild to moderate needs catered for in and out of class courtesy of well-staffed SEN team. A busy bunch with 90 children alone who have SpLD. School takes it seriously with SENCo part of senior leadership team, plenty of training to ensure good, school-wide understanding of SEN – a real strength. No-go area, predictably, behaviour so challenging that would disrupt learning of others.

Increasing numbers now coming through pre-prep (Bevendean). Has recently added new mornings-only class for children turning 3 in academic year but too young for kindergarten (follows pleading from parents keen to avoid multiple morning nursery drop offs) and ends at year 1, numerous visits to main school minimising worries about move to year 2.

Priority in all year groups given to returning families (fair few start, are posted abroad, and then move back again) and siblings. Feeders range from local primaries and preps to city centre establishments. No waiting list – easier to give straight yes or no decision, says registrar, who is now so attuned to London school stress that can identify family location by tones of desperation alone. Inroads into SW London reflected in extensive bus route services (everywhere from Leatherhead to Wimbledon, Weybridge and Richmond).

Trad families remain but now equalled by influx of new blood, much from City, plus other assorted sources of wealth (several well-known footballers are current parents, though 'don't big themselves up, you don't know they're there,' said relieved parent) while growing international component felt to add welcome richness and variety to school community.

Exit: You name it, they send someone there. Guildford High, Sevenoaks, RGS all feature together with local faves (Epsom College, St John's Leatherhead). Around 50+ scholarships a year; 66 in 2016 including King's scholarship to Eton (results in glut of honours boards overflowing into dining hall, another couple in hall foyer, would make for entertaining I Spy game). Good on school, too, for praising hard work of scholarship candidates 'who did their best and came so close' (which would also include the children diplomatically referred to in prospectus as 'yet to find their talents...')

Once rather reluctant to prepare pupils for year 6 exams – inevitable given siren call of 11 plus – school now phlegmatic about manning up to slight loss. Stresses (quite hard) that 'we do not have a big drop-off' with around 90 out of the possible 100 year 8 seats filled and that runs 'established programme that produces a great success rate [in year 6]'.

Remarks: Not a school that hides its light under a bushel. 'Practically perfect in every way' screams banner outside (well, almost – we paraphrase), greeting motorists on the main Oxshott to Leatherhead drag. Given the early morning queues caused, according to one local, entirely by fleets of parents blocking the only through road, they'll certainly have time to digest every syllable.

What school is trumpeting (could do so literally, what with 300 plus pupils learning instruments and the 13 ensembles available for them to showcase talents, from chunky orchestra to assorted string, wind and brass groups) is recent all-outstanding inspection. Given just how much of the school there is, pride understandable.

While site, at 55 acres, may not be the biggest in the area (though lavish by London escapee standards), it's pupil numbers – larger for a fair few than the senior schools many will eventually go on that cause jaw to drop. 'Dread it when it's first question parents ask,' says registrar.

Even inspection team was giant-sized – needed to be, what with viewing 100 lessons in two days. Biggest prep in the country, thinks school. Would have been bigger still had previous head realised dream of ramping up to 1,000 pupils and extending leaving age to 16. No longer. School size just right, thanks, says head, ditto leaving age – school not temperamentally equipped to handle fallout from any heavy duty teenage angst. Why so big? Undoubtedly makes good financial sense – economies of scale are 'awesome' but main benefit is creation of 'a senior school for little people,' says senior teacher.

Some may balk at notion of teenies mustered into maturity beyond their years but, with exception of very early GCSEs taken by year 8 scholars for fun – not our idea of jollity but takes all sorts – it's not about hothousing but giving primary aged children access to range of opportunities and subjects that come with giant-sized staff roster. Means more esoteric languages can be taught, vast range of school trips organised, recently including visits to Liverpool to watch tide washing over Gormley figures, all courtesy of staff pool, deep and talented enough to resource the lot.

Pupil largesse does come with inevitable logistical problems. 'You'll ask one child if he knows another and because he's in a different class, he'll never have heard of them,' says local. 'Can be hard to find your friends at break,' agreed pupil. And while we loved the school mag (who wouldn't, given lookie-likey resemblance to iPad, all gloss and cleverness?), with under a handful of entries from each year group (three for year 4, for example – four if you count pictures as well) we couldn't help wondering if there were times when opting for quantity over quality would improve otherwise microscopic chances of being one of the favoured few to be featured.

Newer parents are more accepting of the scale. Some, with several children and longer term experiences that span rise and rise of pupil numbers, are less sure. 'They can feel it's not the school they signed up to,' said one. Biggest question mark was how well school managed the invisible middles. 'Can go unnoticed,' thought parents. Difficult for any school, accepts Mr Murdock, well behaved average pupils with talent for inconspicuous survival all too easily camouflaged when flanked to one side by the troublesome, to the other by the super able.

But however thick the bushel and deeply buried the light, school adamant that will be discovered, even if it takes years. There's even special group, Big Foot Club, that acts like living pending file, where simmering potential gets extra encouragement to come to the boil – one pupil went from hating sport to captain of rowing.

Other secret weapons include delightful librarian. 'Knew she was right for the job as soon as walked into the room' says head. No wonder. 'Job means I have fun all day,' she says and clearly means it, running parent and child reading-and-hot-chocolate sessions (sports-mad dads and sons make up sizeable chunk of regulars) relegating useful reference books to lower shelves and making fiction the star of the show, array of colourful spines as appetising as they come.

Very littlest also well catered for in pre-prep, popularity enhanced by jolly staff, imaginative outdoor learning with wonderful dipping pond (part of main school grounds) and thoughtfully expanded site featuring swimming pool, jigsaw-shaped mural, seasonal chickens (one recently – and usefully – completing circle of life by going from egg to extinction) and cheerful long, low building, each window adorned with different coloured shutters.

For the keen, able or talented anywhere in school, finding niche unlikely to be a problem. 'If you have a child who is very good at something, they will fly,' says mother. For one, joining from tiny school, 'It was like he'd always been there,' agreed another. Cracking organisation is glue that holds the fabric together, courtesy of terrific, friendly backroom team, says parents, with admin staff who 'do a fabulous job,' says one. 'Because it's so well managed, you just don't feel it is such an enormous school,' felt another.

Effective split into lower, middle and upper schools, who eat, play and leave together, means that though it is huge, 'they manage the size extremely well,' said mother. So small are many of the classes, the result of setting (starts year 2 with English and maths, more subjects added each year) or splitting (half will take DT, half drama, for example) that it's a rare class with more than 10 or so pupils (official class averages are between 16 and 20, maximum 22, with overall teacher to pupil ratio of one to eight). Teaching praised for overall quality across the board, small amount of slightly dull lessons compensated for by the many that aren't.

Level of light-touch but effective behind the scenes management reinforced by relaxed-looking pupils with impressive manners and well-controlled volume (enjoyable impromptu version of 'Let it go' from Frozen in the distance was as loud as it got).

Site structure also helps, varying gradients working in school's favour as without resorting to aerial view, it's just about impossible to see the entire place in one go. Only time you get sense of scale is at lunchtime, as one third of pupils, swapping places with the next, tumble out of dining hall to enjoy masses of well-supervised activities outside, from zip wire and small climbing frame, rota ensuring fair use by all, to ball games and den building in woodland or, in case of two small girls, madly rushing round in circles on the path.

Strong house system (points accrued for academic and sporting success, flag of current leader displayed in school hall) and masses of loyalty-building competitions also do wonders for sense of togetherness, enhanced by involvement through school council which petitions for changes. Some, such as marine biology club and more water fountains by sports pitches 'where we really get thirsty,' points out year 8 pupil, successful. Others, notably own common room for year 8 pupils, mentioned by at least 10 of the children (appeal of own area in the woodlands understandably sags in winter months) are pending, though Mr Murdock seemed to be giving off buying signals.

In general, however, facilities are so good that parents touring future senior schools prone to regular 'is that all there is' moments. Upgrading required here and there, notably sports hall (adequate but lacking in appropriate bells and whistles) and indoor swimming pool (current version achieves all-weather status by virtue of marquee topping during winter months. 'So English,' says member of staff.)

School stresses opportunities – no mountain too high, no valley too deep, expanding exponentially in line with numbers. Thus curriculum can be broader, specialist staff more numerous, speech, music, art and drama more ambitious in scope. Summer concert is 'highlight of the year,' reckoned mum, with 'energy rolling off the children as they perform,' while even the kinetically challenged have gentler option of tea time concerts, beginner performers welcomed with enthusiasm.

No doubt that list of can-dos is impressive, sport taken very seriously with pitches to make spectators pinch themselves – 'feeling of space when you're watching a match is unbelievable' – nearing 20 different sports, games grouped by ability A-F squads from year 2 (those losing their places in teams 'will have reasons explained to them' says literature) parents similarly invited to keep comments about the ref to themselves – children ditto, and should be thanked after the match, urges literature. Extra tuition on offer for the keen, while, from year 6, pupils can ditch ball games altogether for something completely different, such as rowing.

Staff roster even runs to full time head of swimming. Individual sporting successes impressive. Same names tend to crop up across the sporting range 'to the point where it's tedious,' thought one parent – three of four names cited for tennis brilliance all belonged to the same boy, for example. 'Maybe games staff are under the cosh for timing but sometimes would be good if looked beyond the obvious,' thought parent.

Large (predictably) amounts of team triumph (boys score with county football, girls currently ahead on national honours in IAPS hockey, netball and skiing, both sharing honours for indoor rowing).

All adds up to pupils who, says school, 'often lead the way'. Less charitable might think that on probability alone, given numbers, so you'd hope. Children themselves, however, many who had ended up here following bad experiences at smaller but palpably less nurturing schools, were clearly having a whale of a time. 'You don't need to be any sort of character to succeed here,' said one year 8 pupil. 'They'll help you find your strengths. You can just be yourself.'

You might not have to top the ebullience charts to be happy here, but an excess of confidence certainly isn't going to hold you back. Inspectors noted school's aim of turning out 'well-rounded and self-assured individuals who enjoy succeeding.' Locals can be a bit (but not much) blunter. 'Occasional whiff of arrogance,' reckoned one.

Those braving it are buying into largesse of opportunity doled out to bouillabaisse-like mix of abilities. Few subjects come without some added buzz, from geography department's new weather station to DT's 'outdoor kitchen' – in everyday parlance, a garden – where grow things and then cook them.

You go in expecting to be confronted by pupil-rearing on an industrial scale and leave with senses nicely stimulated rather than overwhelmed. Though a big, bouncy, confident school that won't appeal to everyone, worth leaving preconceptions at the gate (along with the traffic jam). Despite yourself, you're likely to end up being charmed.

Dolphin School

Waltham Road, Hurst, Reading, Berkshire RG10 0FR

Pupils: 223 • Ages: 3–13

Fees: £9,540 – £13,215 pa

Tel: 01189 341277
Email: registrar@dolphinschool.com
Website: www.dolphinschool.com

Head: Since January 2015, Tom Lewis (30s), previously head of a prep school in Seoul, Korea. He grew up partly in Hong Kong, moving to Oxford for his school years, then read classics at King's College London. He worked in the City for several years before joining Papplewick as a teacher and stayed for eight years, becoming head of classics and deputy head, then worked for the Eaton Square Schools Group (now Minerva Education) before heading abroad.

An affable man with a calming influence, who is clearly passionate about the progressive approach of the school. But perhaps inevitably, given the quirkiness of the school, there were concerns when he arrived that he would 'move the school more towards a classic prep school feel,' as one parent put it. Staff too got a bit twitchy when he brought in traditional measures. But actually, there's a consensus that he's added clearer structures where required, without over-conventionalising.

Married to Catherine, who was a teacher before moving to an NGO and who has some involvement in the school. For instance, they co-wrote the school's new earth studies course, which they teach to years 6, 7 and 8. They have two young children, both of whom attend the school. Interests include classical music and he still travels extensively with his family during school holidays.

Entrance: The vision of the founder, who started this alternative (then Montessori) school in 1970 from the gardener's shed in the grounds of her house (which remains adjacent to the school and where she still lives), was for Dolphin to cater for the more academically able. And whilst the school is still well suited to brighter children (and the Montessori approach still shapes nursery and reception learning), the pupil demographic has changed, particularly since the recession, with Dolphin now welcoming a wider mix of ability. Indeed, it's non-selective for entry into nursery and reception, although pupils entering from age 5 upwards are informally assessed during a day of tests, including for maths and English. Traditionally, parents have been largely academics, visiting Europeans and artists who are attracted to the school's free-thinking ethos, but equally expect their children to gain places, if not awards, at top independent and grammar schools. Today, though, they're just as likely to work for IT companies in the Thames corridor. If parents entering the school higher up have concerns around their more traditionally educated offspring settling in, there's really no need. 'There hasn't been a settling in process,' laughed one parent. 'Thanks to the welcoming, informal atmosphere, caring teachers, smaller classes and buddy system, almost immediately it felt like my son had been there forever.'

Exit: Roughly a quarter of pupils leave at 11 for local state and independent schools, the rest stay on until 13 for common entrance. The vast majority, according to the school, gain places at their first choice schools, which include Abingdon, Queen Anne's, Wellington College, Reading Grammar, The Abbey, Gillotts, Leighton Park, Sir William Borlase, Reading Blue Coat, Pangbourne College, Headington, Holyport, Luckley House, Shiplake College, Rugby and The Piggott Academy. 'There's no snobbery here about secondary school choices,' reported one parent, who was opting for one of the many good local state schools. 'Our options have been treated with the same respect and dignity as any fancier private school.'

Remarks: You don't have to spend more than about 10 minutes in this school to realise it's unique, yet defining exactly what its magic ingredient is remains a challenge even the head teacher can't rise to. 'There's something intangible that's special about this place, but I'll admit I can't quite put my finger on it,' he says.

The first thing you'll notice is the lack of school uniform, with staff also casually dressed and most addressed by their first names – both approaches that provide a taster into the broad-mindedness and rejection of rigid educational ideology that mark this school out. 'We take the view that at the centre of our job is providing an environment that feels comfortable because if children are comfortable, they're much more likely to be engaged and confident,' explains the head.

And engaged and confident these youngsters certainly are – no doubt helped by the fact that throughout the school is a total immersion approach to learning, the polar opposite of spoon-feeding pre-chewed lumps of facts that can characterise the national curriculum at its worst. In every classroom we visited, children were engaged – no, engrossed – as well as hands-on and busy, with teachers (of whom, by the way, there's a good gender mix) dedicated to enabling and encouraging independent thought and learning, with no subject ever dumbed down. 'In every science lesson this term, we've done an experiment,' one year 5 pupil told us, whilst a younger one told us about geography being taught almost entirely outside. 'It means that even if you don't like a subject – I didn't like maths, for instance – you get to like it because it's never repetitive or mundane,' said one pupil.

Also key to the school's approach is the fact that subject specialists teach in dedicated rooms from year 3 upwards, with pupils so adept at making their way from lesson to lesson that the level of independence and organisation among Dolphinians is noted by senior schools they go onto. 'There are other benefits to having subject specialists,' says the head, 'not least that we are exposing children to people who are really passionate about their subjects.'

Within these lessons, pupils are encouraged to take the scenic route down their own 'avenues of thought', with learning regularly going well beyond the usual boundaries. 'If that means going off on a tangent for a whole lesson, so be it,' says the head. It's the children who take the lead here, asking questions and discussing their ideas in a forum that gives them space to really be themselves. One can't help feeling teaching here must be all-consuming, but incredibly rewarding too. In fact, several members of staff who have joined from other schools enthused, saying it had restored their faith in their vocation.

If you're worrying that this means subjects are inevitably taught in silos, don't be. Far from it; the cross-curricular approach to learning knocks the socks off most primary schools. 'For instance, we were learning Mary, Mary Quite Contrary in Latin, then being taught what it's all about in history,' said one pupil. 'My son loves how everything is gelled together to create the big picture,' said a parent.

The upshot of all this is that school life can seem, to the onlooker, somewhat chaotic and disordered. 'But,' as one parent pointed out, 'it's a misconception, because everyone knows exactly where they're supposed to be and what they're supposed to be doing. Whilst at my daughters' previous school, they learned how to toe the line and do what they're told – which is what you expect to see in a school – here they have the space to figure out who they are and what they're interested in.'

Besides the usual range of subjects, there's French from nursery and classics from year 3, which becomes Latin from year 4. Spanish and Greek are available from year 7, with other extra subjects including architecture, astronomy and – most recently – earth studies. 'We are a humanist school, so there is no divinity or RE on the curriculum, but what earth studies does is incorporate philosophy and morality with current affairs to explore big questions like, Why are we here? Why is there so much suffering in the world? What can be done about the situation in the Middle East?' explains the head.

Although this is not a hugely techy school (staff are more interested in getting children outside in muddy fields than getting them to tap away on iPads in classrooms), there's a good IT suite and – joy of joys – touch-typing is taught from year 3. The head also points out that programming has become the most popular after-school club. Maths is a stand-out subject and juniors and seniors regularly arrive home counting awards won in the UK Maths Challenge. Reading is another big focus, with 15-25 minutes a day dedicated to heads in books for children and staff alike. 'Reading and literacy is your passport to accessing the curriculum, so we take it very seriously,' says the head, who adds that homework is set weekly, with pupils expected to do four to six hours of homework per week by year 8. Exams are held off until the end of year 5.

Drama is big, with pupils often gaining drama scholarships to their senior schools. Almost every year group is involved in some kind of annual performance, and there's great excitement among pupils about the annual production put on by years 7 and 8 at the Edinburgh Fringe Festival. Many of the plays are written by the drama teacher and they're often thought-provoking, with one recent example being These Fragments, a poignant production about refugees. Around 10 peripatetic staff teach the usual range of musical instruments and there's a school choir, ukulele band and various ensembles, with children regularly performing during assemblies, house music competitions and a concert in summer.

Then there's the school trips. Not for these pupils a day's outing to a museum, after which they're told it's now back to business as usual. Trips here – of which there are at least three a term from nursery upwards – are business as usual, with the whopping 120 of them per year forming the very cornerstone to the school's unwavering approach to experiential learning.

A highlight of the school trips happens in year 8, when pupils embark on an eight-day hike through the Alps, although in order to reach these heights, children must warm up with a trek on the South Downs in year 4 and ascend year by year through the likes of the Brecon Beacons, Lake District and Snowdon, each trip a day or two longer than the last. For the field trips, children begin with a three-day trip to Sussex in year 3, followed by a four-day trip to Dorset in year 4. Year 5s get a four-day trip to Ironbridge; year 6s get a five-day trip to North Wales; year 7s get a six-day trip to Northumbria or Normandy, finishing with a nine-day trip to Italy in year 8. These visits are 'threaded' into every subject and a wall of photos in the assembly hall provides encouragement along the way. All trips except foreign ones (where parents pay about half) are included in the fees, with the occasional contribution to food requested on top.

In terms of SEN, the school is relatively inclusive, taking on the usual range of dys spectrums, plus mild ADD, ADHD and ASD, although it's honest about what it can't cope with and does turn children away if it feels they won't keep up. Pupils and parents praise the diagnostic abilities of the SENCo, as well as the one-to-one support provided in break-out classrooms, which is used to supplement what goes on in the classroom. Meanwhile, the gifted and talented are helped by a variety of methods including tailoring work, setting in maths and French from year 5 upwards and English from year 7 upwards, and extracurricular activities such as scholarship science club and debating club, which particularly (although not exclusively) attracts the more intelligent.

Sport is more about cooperation than competition. That said – and despite Dolphin's numbers – it competes successfully against some much larger schools, and some children achieve regional and national representation. Boys mainly play football, rugby and cricket, whilst girls focus on netball, hockey and rounders, using the two on-site tennis courts and three grass pitches, as well as the school hall and Hurst Cricket Ground, a two-minute mini-bus ride away. Tennis is a particular strength too. Twenty after-school clubs supplement the timetabled sport along with the gentler exertions of yoga, ballet and dance.

Don't expect wonders when it comes to facilities, which – with the exception of a shiny new science lab – are pretty average, with some on the shabby side. There are some space issues too, including the tiny (but well-stocked and well-run) library and small (but charming) art room. Children eat packed lunches in the classroom – an ongoing bugbear of parents that the head is looking into. The swimming pool is just about indoors but only used in the warmer weather because it lacks changing rooms – not even these intrepid children fancy a bathing suited dash across the tarmac in February. But none of this seems to impinge on the quality of teaching or learning, which just goes to show that in the end it's about the teaching, not the facilities.

Parents are also unflashy, with only a sprinkling of the big black 4x4s that you get at many local preps – many work their socks off to get their children an education here. For those who want to be involved with school life, there's no shortage of opportunity to volunteer on the school trips, even driving the minibus, as well as getting stuck into fundraising via events such as curry nights and the annual summer fair.

Pastoral care is highly praised by pupils and parents alike, with the school appearing to achieve that tricky balance of being nurturing, yet also encouraging maturity and independence. In addition to the form teacher, who is seen as the primary conduit for pastoral care, pupils in year 6 upwards have a mentor – someone who, ideally, isn't their form teacher and who doesn't teach them at all, whom they meet every other week informally over lunch. It also helps that the school is small – with two classes per year, with an average of 12 children in each (although one class had 19 when we visited) – meaning children know the names of pretty much everyone else. This, together with a buddy system, leads to cross-year friendships, as well as helping to prevent bullying, which is quickly nipped in the bud on the rare occasion it does happen. The school's charitable focus, meanwhile, helps prevent the school being a bubble of privilege, with children regularly encouraged to think about others around the world. There are clear warning systems for poor behaviour – of which the worst tends to be around missing homework, being rude or unkind and not putting in enough work – which culminate in breaktime detentions.

No wonder the pupils we talked to – all of whom were eloquent, chatty, sharp and witty, without a shred of arrogance – were familiar both with the word 'kinaesthetic' and its meaning. The very ethos of the school is to provide a learning environment that's all about moving around and working manually with ideas. Sitting still in class and just listening simply doesn't happen here – underlying everything that happens is the principle that the more activity you experience while doing a skill, the better you learn it. This, along with a genuinely cross-curricular approach to learning that's coupled with traditional academic rigour, is what seems to set this school apart, the result of which are 250 self-motivated children with a love of learning and an enquiring mind.

Also no wonder that so many parents are evangelical about this school, with many moving to the area solely to get the kids in. 'My son was unhappy at the state village school, yet the self-belief he has now is wonderful,' said one parent. 'We have two very different children – one who prospers in challenging environments and the other who is far more sensitive and gentle, and we struggled to find any school that could accommodate them both. But here, they're both flourishing. It's hard to exaggerate how much it has transformed both their lives,' commented another.

It's not for everyone, with one parent describing the school as having the 'Marmite' effect. 'If you're after the established, traditional prep school experience, you'll walk away thinking, "No way!" as one friend of mine did,' she said. Another pointed out that children who thrive on routine and take comfort in the security of the same classroom might struggle here. But if you like the concept of a school that never straightjackets children, enabling them to take the lead and work at their own pace within a context of high expectations and indeed aspirations, this is a school with a wow factor.

All schools say that they treat every child as an individual but this school actually does it, producing cheerful, humane, confident, mature and thoughtful children with a life-long love of learning ahead of them. As one parent put it, 'They bring education alive.' 'If schools got stars for children's engagement and happiness,' said another, 'they'd be off the scale.'

Dorset House School

The Manor, Bury, Pulborough, West Sussex RH20 1PB

Pupils: 140; 45 weekly/flexi boarders • Ages: 4–13 (boarding from 9)

Fees: Day £7,875 – £16,875 pa; Boarding £90 per week

Tel: 01798 831456
Email: info@dorsethouseschool.com
Website: www.dorsethouseschool.com

Headmaster: Since September 2016, Mr Matt Thomas, previously deputy head (academic) at Moulsford Prep. Degree in PE, geography and education studies from St Luke's Exeter; recently completed a master's in educational leadership. Has had a wide variety of roles including teaching GCSE and A level at state schools, being a lead teacher for two education authorities and various positions in independent schools. A fellow of the Royal Geographical Society, he likes to attend Monday evening lectures there. Enjoys trekking in the Himalayas and has climbed Kilimanjaro; runs marathons and ultra-marathons. Married to Julie and they have two children, both at the school.

Entrance: Children can join at any time so long as spaces, subject to informal tests in English and maths, a report from their current school and, ideally, a taster day. Parents are made aware of what the school is able to offer and that the ultimate goal is CE.

Exit: To a wide range of senior schools, including Hurst, Brighton College, Lancing, Ardingly, Christ's Hospital, Winchester, Marlborough. Most children stay until CE at 13+, but will prepare for 11+ entry to senior schools and also for pre-selection tests. Scholarships won every year for the past few years – mixture of academic, music, sport and all-rounder.

Remarks: Founded in 1784 as Totteridge Park School in Hertfordshire. After various incarnations it became Dorset House in 1905 and moved to its present site in 1964. Housed in a 12th century manor house, with medieval great barn, modern teaching blocks and separate junior school building. Set in 16 acres of grounds at the end of a quiet country lane, next door to the church and with magnificent views in all directions. Children allowed to build camps and dens in the woods and play in the adventure playground. 'No one minds about mud – you just fling on your wellies,' said one boy. Children spend as much time as possible outside – pre-prep has two hour forest school session each week – and some of the younger children often drink their break-time hot chocolate on a log in the woods. Small amphitheatre in the garden used for speech day and house drama competition.

One-form entry, with a maximum of 20 per year group – nearly full in years 4 to 8 and waiting lists further down. Numbers have now reached 140 (maximum capacity of 160). The 45 boarding places for flexi and weekly boarders are now over-subscribed on some nights – often suits families who live in London and have a weekend cottage nearby. Warren of dorms under the eaves reached by a spiral stone staircase are warm and cosy, with old fashioned iron bedsteads and lots of teddies. Real family atmosphere – feels more like someone's elegant country house than a school – the children take their breakfast and tea on the terrace during the summer. Everything immaculate with not a weed in sight and fresh paint everywhere. School sees itself as 'traditional but forward looking.'

Streaming for maths, English and science from year 5, depending on the class size and the ability range within the group. Scholarship children kept within their year group and offered extension classes at break and lunchtimes.

A dynamic team of staff with a good mix of age and experience. Charismatic science teacher who brings the subject to life – he teaches through experimentation and investigation like testing the efficacy of indigestion remedies. Bright, light and airy science lab where 'we love blowing up jelly babies in the fume cupboard,' says one budding young scientist. Recently won Green Link award which funded the boardwalk around the pond. Children do particularly well in science at CE, often achieving top grades, and many go on to study it at university. Very enthusiastic young geography teacher is also the director of sport – geography trips to the Isle of Wight and the Jurassic Coast; the flood plain of the river Arun just beyond the garden makes a wonderful outdoor classroom. French taught by a native speaker. Latin or classical civilisation introduced in year 5; Greek taught to bright year 8s.

Light, cosy library with comfortable sofas where children can curl up with a book. Prep done at school and supervised by members of staff. Three full-time SEN teachers, mainly for mild dyslexia and dyspraxia. Bright yellow room for the junior SENCo where the motto is 'learning with laughter.' Children not routinely tested but any problems picked up quickly in such a small environment.

Magnificent medieval barn acts as the school hall and is big enough to fit everyone in – also doubles up as the sports hall and is hired out for weddings. Inner barn is used for plays and assemblies. New head of art has revitalised the art department.

Art and DT are linked and the kit car club built a car and raced it at Goodwood as part of the Greenpower project. Photography very popular – each child is given their own memory card from year 3 to take photographs around the school and taught to use Photoshop. Photographs of the children displayed around the school and dining room doubles as an art gallery. Brightly coloured totem poles made from recycled materials dotted around the garden.

D

Young director of music (Dorset House old boy) also acts as a houseparent with his wife (who also teaches reception) and dog Mylo – has made music 'cool and fun' and now lots of informal concerts, ensembles and whole school concerts. The choir sings at services in the church next door and at the Christmas carol service at Arundel. Music timetabled from the early years and every child learns to read music through learning the recorder – about 60 per cent learn a musical instrument. Is apparently the first prep school in the country to have JamClassHD system which is linked by JamPod technology (no, we don't know what that means either). Senior play each year, plus one or two for juniors as well as the house drama competition. Annual poetry reciting competition and children have to read out match reports and prayers – all great for building self-confidence.

Heavyweight sporting success: under-9 rugby team recently unbeaten in Sussex. Almost all the boys and girls in a year group are required to make up a team and often children who did not consider themselves sporty step up to the plate. All children in years 3 to 8 play in at least three matches a term – everyone has a go. Now enough girls to put together netball and hockey teams to play other schools. Ballet and gymnastics particularly popular and girls can take exams in these. Riding a popular extra and team takes part in regional competitions.

Other extras include drama, pottery, Mandarin, cookery and football coaching (with pros from Chelsea). Chess taught by outside specialists. Recently formed cub group with children from local primaries and some from Dorset House meets in the barn every week during term time.

Leadership and taking responsibility promoted from a young age through leadership programme – 'Children learn how to work together as a team and to listen to one another.' Leadership training once a week before school for year 8s – they take part in the decision making of the school as elected representatives of the school council and act as positive role models. More opportunities to take a position of responsibility in a small school – children start as lunch helpers and book monitors and progress through outdoor adventures and camping trip (including one to the top of Mount Snowdon). Grand finale is an adventure training week in north Devon after CE.

Small nurturing school with a family atmosphere produces open, chatty children where everyone knows everyone and each child is given the chance to find their niche. 'It's a lovely, friendly school where children have a proper country childhood and don't grow up before their time,' one happy mother told us. School is run on Christian principles and the parish church next door is central to the life of the school – Monday morning assembles in the church and parents often come to the special Friday service. The vicar is a part time member of staff and teaches RE. New pre-school for 2+ on site.

Recently introduced house system means lots of crossover between year groups and as one parent said, 'The older children are sweet to the younger ones'. Firm policy on bullying. Many young members of staff live on site and in the manor house, which contributes to the family feel. Board games round the library fire in the evenings for boarders and a dedicated games room.

Most children live within a 20-mile radius and the school is increasingly popular with families moving out of London – 'a good antidote to the pushy London day schools,' according to one new arrival. Active parents' association raised £25,000 at the summer ball for an Astroturf (in a school with 140 pupils). Also organises bonfire night party, quiz and welcomes new parents to the school. A fathers' cricket team meets regularly. Famous old boys include former Gordonstoun head Mark Pyper, comedian Harry Enfield and actor Ed Speleers (of Eragon fame).

If you are looking for an all-singing, all-dancing school with facilities galore, this school might not be for you, but if you are looking for somewhere that achieves good academic results, is small and nurturing and where every child gets a chance and is expected to do their bit – take a closer look.

Dover College

Effingham Crescent, Dover, Kent CT17 9RH

Pupils: 294; 102 boarders • Ages: 3–18 (boarding from 11) • Sixth form: 63 • C of E

Fees: Day £7,005 – £15,225; Boarding £19,590 – £28,920 pa

Tel: 01304 205969
Email: admin@dovercollege.org.uk
Website: www.dovercollege.org.uk

Headmaster: Since January 2015, Gareth Doodes, previously (briefly) head of George Heriot's School in Edinburgh, and before that head of Milton Abbey School in Dorset. Read history at St Andrews; PGCE from Cambridge; worked at Taunton school then at Oakham for seven years, two as master of scholars and five as a housemaster, before joining Milton Abbey.

Academic matters: One class per year group in the junior school and class sizes limited by the size of the classrooms – usually 10 to 12 but up to 16 at key stage 2. Non-selective so a wide range of abilities. Spanish taught from year 1 and French from year 3. Pupils take annual NFER tests in maths and English, with CATs (cognitive ability tests) from year 4. Optional Sats from year 2 onwards.

Specialist junior school teachers for sport, music and languages. Juniors have their own laptop room but also use the senior school's ICT facilities – ICT taught across the curriculum by ICT savvy staff and early years children have touch screen computers. All classrooms have either an interactive whiteboard or projector.

A broad ability range – 51 per cent A*/B and 44 per cent A*/A grades at A level and around a quarter of GCSE grades A*/A in 2016. Sciences taught separately for the dual award. Good range of subjects offered in sixth form. The introduction of BTecs in sport and PE, travel and tourism and health and social care has meant that more are staying on for sixth form. Apart from the usual subjects, GCSEs offered in health and social care, PE and business studies.

About 12 per cent need some sort of SEN – lots of help available, from help with study skills to more intensive one-to-one help. All pupils screened for dyslexia and other potential problems every year. Two individual needs teachers in senior school and one part time in junior – sometimes children go over to senior school or teachers come to them, either one-to-one or in small groups and mainly help with maths and reading. A very dedicated team of teachers who 'go the extra mile' for the children and focus on individual learning styles. 'I could not believe how much trouble the teachers took with my son,' said one mother. Small classes – 12 to 14 for GCSE and sometimes only six for A level.

Has welcomed international students since 1957 and the International Study Centre opened in 2001 – total immersion in English plus lessons with peer group in maths, ICT, DT and sport. Depending on the level of English, pupils prepared for Cambridge Preliminary English Test (PET), IGCSE or IELTS. All international pupils are integrated into the main school. Some start in International Study Centre and move over when ready. Others join the main school on arrival. About 50 pupils need some sort of EAL support.

Games, options, the arts: The usual sports – football, hockey, netball etc. Cross-country popular and successful (Dover College hosts a big inter-school event each year). Aerobics, basketball, sailing with Dover Sailing Club, swimming at a local pool. Everyone given a chance to shine and 'teachers are always trying out new people for sports and giving people a chance to showcase their talents'. Some matches for under 9s and lots for under 11s, with most children getting a chance to play in a team. Strong swimming team – two inter-school swimming galas a year held at a nearby leisure centre as well as a junior school gala. Sport compulsory up to sixth form and most carry on after that. Most girls continue with sport but fitness classes, dance and yoga also popular. Not a school with acres of rolling fields but has its own pitches as well as an Astroturf, sports hall, dance and fitness suites and a basketball court. 'Some of the sports facilities could do with a bit of a makeover,' say some parents. Link with Canterbury Christ Church University's sports department ensures a steady supply of recently qualified sports teachers who 'refresh the department and bring new ideas'.

Lots of music, including chamber orchestra and ensembles. Members of the local community often play in the orchestra and the choir sometimes sings evensong in Canterbury Cathedral. Tallis Music School has been relocated and refurbished and now provides soundproof pods, a recital room and teaching rooms. Informal junior concerts twice a term in the Tallis Music School as well as a summer concert, carol concert and junior school Christmas play. School also takes part in Young Voices concert at the O2.

Strong arts. Textiles, art and photography offered at A level. Particularly good photography – annual photographic competition also open to parents and fabulous photos displayed around the school.

Huge range of activities – from belly dancing and debating to madrigals and horse-riding. Leadership activities, including D of E Award (up to eight gold awards a year) and Young Enterprise, all designed to build self-confidence. Junior school has listened to parents and worked on the outdoor curriculum – a discovery garden recently opened and street dance and taekwondo added to the long list of clubs.

Strong emphasis on community and charity work. Senior pupils can get involved in the Ukraine project. A group raises money for the charity and then spends two weeks in the Ukraine refurbishing an old people's home, running a sports camp for disadvantaged children and chopping logs for the elderly. One parent described it as 'a life changing experience for my son, who realised for the first time what true hardship is'.

Boarding: Vast majority (86) are full boarders, with just a few weekly and flexi. Roughly two-thirds are boys. Year 7 and 8 day pupils are housed separately in Priory House, which ensures a gentle introduction to the senior school. All the other houses mix day and boarding so everyone gets to know everyone. 'It's nice to mix with different years because then you get to make more friends', a pupil told us, although another said 'some nationalities still stick together and keep themselves to themselves'. There is 'major house loyalty' and lots of inter-house events – music, sport, drama and the keenly fought house conker competition. All boarders have supper together at the weekends. Entertainment, theatre and shopping trips organised although many are happy 'just chilling with their friends' and catching up with schoolwork.

Background and atmosphere: Founded in 1871 by a group of local businessmen who wanted Dover to have its own public school. Housed in the grounds of the 12th century Benedictine St Martin's Priory, an oasis of green in the middle of Dover with wonderful views of Dover Castle and nestling behind the famous white cliffs. Went co-ed in 1974 (one of the first boys' schools to do so) and now almost 50:50. Although much of the original priory was destroyed by Henry VIII, there is still a feeling of history. This is despite the hotchpotch of buildings added over the years, from late Victorian houses to the uninspiring modern. The school has the only Norman refectory in Britain – still used for its original purpose and doubles as a concert hall and theatre too. Junior school opened in 2001 and occupies two houses in the grounds. Light and airy classrooms decorated with cheerful artwork.

Dover College is a small local school with an international dimension and a strong sense of community 'where everyone knows everyone'. We heard comments like 'it's not overly posh but perfect for where it is' and 'it's a local school with a kind and caring environment which understands the kids' needs and gets the best out of each pupil'.

Christian foundation. Chapel is physically and spiritually at the heart of the college but all faiths and none are made to feel welcome. Three services a week, including Friday afternoon chapel.

Pastoral care, well-being and discipline: 'Because confidence matters' is the motto of the school and huge emphasis is placed on personal development and building pupils' confidence. 'I am confident that the school has the control of my children's well-being and promotes good social skills and ethics,' a parent told us. 'I am very proud when people comment on how well-mannered my children are'. Well-developed tutorial system, and house staff and prefects have finely tuned antennae for drugs and alcohol. School likes to bring together the students and the non-teaching staff. For example, the kitchen chef is also linesman for the first XI football team, a minibus driver is the referee and the estates manager runs D of E.

Strong family atmosphere and parents invited to Friday chapel, a highlight of the week when children's achievements and birthdays are celebrated and house points awarded. Head of senior school hands out awards in his flowing red St Andrew's gown. Parents like to feel involved. One mother told us that her children 'are treated in a caring and understanding way and I can talk to the teachers whenever I want'. School has worked hard to develop lines of communication with parents and sees the relationship as a partnership overseeing the children's education. Parents kept up to date with events via parent portal and social media sites.

Pupils and parents: Day children tend to be fairly local and many are ferried to school via a network of minibuses. About 30 per cent from abroad (30 nationalities), 10 per cent service families (including a number of Nepalese families who serve locally with the Gurkhas). About 10 per cent of local children choose to board 'because it's fun'.

Huge range of abilities – some children very bright whilst others struggle to get five good GCSEs. 'A lot of the kids are not that academic but the school brings out the best in them', said a parent. The emphasis on building confidence produces comfortable, well-adjusted children who are happy to strike up a conversation with anyone. Life is full on here and as one pupil said, 'sometimes we are just too busy as every teacher wants you to do their thing'. Even so, they seem to love every minute of it.

Prefects given lots of responsibility and say that 'it is important to act as role models to the rest of the school'. They apply in writing and are then interviewed by a panel chaired by the head. Lower sixth enrichment week takes the pupils well out of their comfort zone and often a few previously hidden talents come to the fore. Pupils have to stage a senior management meeting, role play a crisis, take part in an Apprentice-style marketing project and film a debate – all in one day.

No typical Old Doverian, although many are entrepreneurs who have made their own way in the world. They tend to keep in touch. Former pupils include composer Dai Fujikura, choreographer Sir Frederick Ashton, X Factor supremo Simon Cowell, film producer Guy East and various ambassadors and military figures.

Entrance: School takes children from 3 and most start in the nursery. Some join in year 6 and then move up to the senior school. Non-selective and will only reject a child if school feels that it can't meet a child's needs. Happy to take children who might fail elsewhere and build their confidence. All children strongly encouraged to attend a taster day before they join. Senior school has its own 11+ test in November before entry for setting purposes only and everyone interviewed. Will take children who might fail elsewhere and give them the confidence to succeed. Only turns children away if they won't be able to cope. Most join at 11+ from the junior school and local primaries. A few come in at 13+ from prep schools like Northbourne Park, Spring Grove and Wellesley House. About 25 students join the sixth form – mainly from abroad. Pupils can join at any time if there are spaces, except into year 11.

Exit: Most juniors progress to the senior school, but numbers vary from year to year. Good record in the Kent Test – mainly to Dover Grammar and the Folkestone grammars. School helps children with practice tests but parents sometimes get outside tutoring as well. No entrance exam as such for senior school but all children take the academic scholarship. Smooth transition.

About 25 per cent leave after GCSEs, mostly to the state system. Sixth formers head to a range of universities for a wide variety of courses – recent choices include business at City University, sports science at Canterbury Christ Church, pharmacology at Bristol, business at Surrey, engineering at Nottingham, computer technology at Portsmouth. Lots of help with UCAS – careers adviser knows pupils well and 'keeps expectations realistic'. Not many take a gap year.

Money matters: Range of awards offered, including11+ scholarships in English and maths, 13+ scholarship awarded on strength of CE and 16+ scholarship on strength of GCSEs. Academic, art, music, sport and all rounder scholarships on offer. About a third of local pupils on some sort of scholarship or bursary. Not a rich school and bursaries come from fee income but school does what it can for those who encounter unexpected financial difficulties whilst at the school.

Remarks: Not hugely academic and nor does it pretend to be, but this is a happy, relaxed place where the building of self confidence underpins everything the school does. It's high praise indeed when a sixth form pupil said, 'I have been very happy here and can't fault it'.

d'Overbroeck's Oxford

The Swan Building, 111 Banbury Road, Oxford, Oxfordshire OX2 6JX

Pupils: 336; 141 boarders • Ages: 11–18 (boarding in sixth form) • Sixth form: 260

Fees: Day £16,065 – £22,350; Boarding an additional £7,050 – £12,675 pa

Tel: 01865 310000
Email: mail@doverbroecks.com
Website: www.doverbroecks.com

Principal: Since 1996, Mr Sami Cohen BSc (50s). Educated in Baghdad, then moved to London at the age of 17 to do his A levels. Read chemistry and French at Leeds University – the course was created for him and sparked a lifelong passion for 'breadth' in education. Followed in the footsteps of his mother and aunt, who were both teachers, and began his own teaching career at d'Overbroeck's in 1979 – two years after sixth form was founded. Moved to Paris in 1992 before being invited to return to d'Overbroeck's as principal four years later.

Charismatic, focused and approachable, he is particularly proud of opening the college's 11-16 arm in 2005, transforming d'Overbroeck's from a sixth form college into an all-through 11-18 school. 'We are able to offer each age group an environment that suits that particular age group,' he explains. 'We are open to a reasonably wide range of abilities and we value people with interests and enthusiasms. We want everyone to have a well-rounded, lively education, to be able to laugh a lot, to make great friendships and to feel that they have personally grown, developed and flourished.'

A keen linguist (he speaks French, Italian and Arabic), he no longer has time to teach these days – 'which saddens me.' Knows all the students well and is a familiar presence around the school's two sites, constantly stopping to chat. Pupils address teachers by their first names at d'Overbroeck's so he is 'Sami' to all. 'I'm totally immersed in the life of this place,' he says. 'There's a lot more I feel I can contribute.' Wife Emily is an EFL specialist and they have three daughters. The elder two both attended d'Overbroeck's before going on to undergraduate degrees at Oxford and UCL.

Retiring in July 2017. His successor will be Emma-Kate Henry, currently principal of Hampshire Collegiate School. Read English literature and African & Caribbean studies at Kent after a gap year teaching in Jamaica, which inspired her to do a PGCE at the Institute of Education after a year in IT recruitment. She has taught in state and private schools, including Surbiton High and St Christopher, where she was deputy head. She is married to Tony, a qualified athletics coach, and they have a young son, who will join the school.

Academic matters: Sixth form offers 35 subjects at A level (all the usual, plus others like film studies, history of art, philosophy, sociology and photography). Unlike some schools (and thanks to nifty timetabling) students can choose virtually any mix of A levels. 'The key to students' success is getting the subjects right,' says the principal, who encourages students to choose the subjects they'll enjoy and do well at. 'There is no subject combination that we rule out,' says the head of sixth form. Alongside their A levels some sixth formers do an Extended Project Qualification (EPQ). In 2016, 85 per cent A*-B and 55 per cent A*/A grades.

The principal says the school appoints teachers 'who know their subjects inside out,' are enthusiastic and care deeply about teaching. Lessons are relatively informal, while being highly engaging and interactive, with teachers constantly checking that everyone has 'got it' before moving on. The students we met were unanimous in singing their teachers' praises. 'You won't find better teaching anywhere,' one girl told us appreciatively. 'I switched to economics quite late and my teacher stayed behind for an hour every week to help me catch up, from the day I started till the week my AS exams began. I've never found teachers who care this much.' Another said: 'The teachers want the best for you and it makes you want the best for yourself.'

GCSE results are good too. Fifty-nine per cent A*-A grades in 2016, with maths, biology, chemistry, physics and drama particularly notable. Most pupils take 10 GCSEs, including three separate sciences and at least one language. French, Spanish, Latin and classical civilisation are on offer but school can organise German, Italian, Japanese, Mandarin and Russian if required (the benefits of having the dreaming spires of Oxford close by).

Academic ethos is the same in both sections of the school. 'We are an academic school,' Mark Olejnik, the genial head of years 7-11, told us, 'but we want children to enjoy their learning. Happiness is the very essence of what we do here.' Learning support offered for mild dyslexia and dyspraxia at no additional charge. Sixth form teachers have been known to spot issues that have been missed by previous schools and target appropriate help for students. Class sizes are small – no more than 15 up to GCSE and up to 10 at A level. There's an emphasis on discussion and confidence-building throughout, with pupils encouraged to offer their views.

Games, options, the arts: The school has worked hard to offer a broad range of sports and activities. Sport isn't compulsory for sixth formers but students are expected to do at least one extracurricular activity in the lower sixth – everything from hockey, rugby and netball to film club, yoga and first aid, plus Young Enterprise and D of E. Lower sixth students also have a compulsory enrichment programme – a variety of outside speakers, from university professors and admissions tutors to writers, scientists and entrepreneurs.

d'Overbroeck's doesn't have its own playing fields but makes the most of the extensive facilities across Oxford. This seems to work well, with students being ferried by minibus to a number of excellent sporting venues including Oxford Brookes (which has an Astroturf, fully equipped sports hall, fitness gym, squash, badminton and basketball courts, climbing wall and more). Year 7 and 8 pupils get three hours of games a week while those in years 9, 10 and 11 have two hours and 20 minutes of timetabled sport.

Drama is a delight, with younger pupils teaming up with sixth formers to stage major productions like Les Misérables and Peter Pan. In years 7, 8 and 9 pupils have a double lesson of art and a double lesson of music each week. When we visited, a group of year 8s were studying 'impossible architecture,' designing fantastical creations that would give our most eminent architects a run for their money. Many go on to study art in the sixth form and one parent told us: 'I am an artist myself and can say that my daughter has been brilliantly taught.' Eighty students take individual music lessons – all levels (beginners to grade 8) and everything from the violin to electric guitar. Recitals by pupils are often held at the Jacqueline du Pré auditorium at St Hilda's College, as well as regular concerts for students of all ages in the school hall. Music and music tech are popular at A level too.

Debating and public speaking are hugely popular. A couple of years ago, a team of year 9 pupils reached the national final of the Youth Speaks public speaking event. 'Opportunities are thrust on you here,' one of the team told us. 'It really makes you want to participate.' Loads of school trips, including recent summer expeditions to Namibia, Iceland and China for year 10 to 13 youngsters, annual ski trips and visits to theatre productions in London and Stratford-upon-Avon, science visits to the Rutherford Appleton Laboratory, one of the UK's national scientific research centres, and much else besides.

Boarding: Most lower sixth boarders live in one of two co-ed boarding houses close by (20 places at 106 Banbury Road and 18 places at Hayfield House). Double rooms with en-suite bathrooms at '106', singles with shared bathrooms at Hayfield. Girls and boys live in separate 'zones', but meet up in communal areas for meals and socialising. Houseparents cook supper, lend a friendly ear to boarders, oversee the 7pm to 9pm study periods and make sure everyone is in by the 10.30pm curfew (11.30pm on Fridays and Saturdays). Upper sixth boarders live with host families, all carefully vetted and regularly inspected. There's also a small girls' boarding house – Benson's.

Background and atmosphere: d'Overbroeck's is 'a mushroom-shaped school' – the place gets bigger as it progresses up the age range. It started out as a sixth form college, founded in 1977 by French and Spanish teacher Malcolm van Biervliet, who was head of languages till he retired in 2007. Invited to speak about the school's ethos he said: 'Friendship is a cornerstone in the d'Overbroeck's structure, contributing to the happiness of staff and students alike, and thus making the process of teaching and learning a more enjoyable and symbiotic experience.' Staff and students agree that his vision still holds true today. Was purchased in 2014 by the Oxford International Education Group.

Sixth form is housed in two large Victorian villas in leafy north Oxford, complete with stained glass windows, tessellated floors, classrooms, library, student common room, admin offices and a large garden at the back. Students doing science A levels walk up to Ewert Place in Summertown while the performing arts department is based round the corner in Leckford Place. Lessons are 65 minutes long and sixth formers get 15 minutes in between to get to their next class.

School is currently building a new sixth form centre on Banbury Road, due to open in September 2017, which it says will 'transform our sixth form facilities', bringing them onto one site and including science labs, a 180 seater auditorium, performing arts suites, library and common rooms. A new sixth form boarding house rises apace across the road.

There's a real buzz everywhere you turn – lots of lively chatter, teachers and pupils on first name terms and an informal and energetic atmosphere throughout. No dining room but a local caterer, Taylors, sets up shop in the common room to sell sandwiches, paninis and drinks at lunchtime. Lots of students stroll up to M&S or Taylors in Summertown to buy lunch – they're spoiled for choice. 'This is a relatively informal environment,' says the principal. 'We don't stand on ceremony but there are clear boundaries and we have high expectations of the students.' Youngsters heartily approve. 'It's not stuffy here at all,' a girl told us.

d'Overbroeck's opened its lower school in 2005, snapping up a Victorian building in nearby Leckford Road previously occupied by Phil and Jim's, a local state primary. A 10-minute walk from the sixth form, the years 7-11 site is compact but makes the most of every inch of space. The lower school now boasts an ingeniously designed main building, with a galleried library resembling the upper deck of a ship, light and airy classrooms and a social area with a vivid pink wall, café tables and glossy blue lockers. The original school hall next door is used for lunch (wholesome meals dished up by nearby St Hugh's College), assemblies and theatrical productions. Numbers in years 7-11 are now pretty much on capacity at around 175, with two forms in years 7 and 8 and three from year 9.

No uniform for sixth form but year 7 to 11 pupils wear smart navy polo shirt or jumper with school logo. 'Apart from that they can wear their own clothes,' says the head of years 7-11. 'As long as they are reasonable. No purple hair, hoodies, hats or nose piercings.' He admits that being called by his first name took a bit of getting used to though the principal and students reckon it enables everyone to be themselves.

Pastoral care, well-being and discipline: Pastoral care is widely praised. Sixth form students are assigned their own director of studies (universally known as a DoS) – usually one of their subject teachers. Youngsters talk to them about academic and pastoral matters, with academic progress, attendance, punctuality, work rate and general well-being closely monitored. 'I see my DoS every day,' one boy told us. Parents get a progress report by email every six weeks. Pupils can also talk to a trained school counsellor if they prefer and many turn to the school's dynamic young social organiser – a huge asset to the school, who organises everything from film nights to barbecues. 'We are strict about the things that we need to be strict on,' says the principal, and students and parents concur with his words.

Firm rules on alcohol, drugs and smoking. No drugs tolerated – offenders asked to leave immediately. Students say bullying 'just doesn't happen here' and that unlike many other schools 'there is no sense of being considered cool or not cool.' 'Everyone is included,' a sixth former told us. 'It's a really friendly place.'

Sixth formers say that d'Overbroeck's has got its priorities right and appreciate the fact that it doesn't impose pointless rules and regulations. 'If you want a school that makes you go to chapel and has an army of prefects this probably isn't the right school for you,' one boy remarked. The school is firm about pupils being prompt for lessons and handing work in on time. Students who are 10 minutes late aren't allowed into the class at all and an email is immediately sent to their parents. The only gripe we heard from sixth formers was the lack of lockers – a perennial whinge.

Form teachers are the first port of call in years 7-11, with tutor groups meeting every day and staff holding a meeting every week to discuss pastoral issues. The head of years 7-11 stands at the school gate every morning to greet pupils – 'even in the pouring rain,' said one girl. 'It makes you feel really welcome.' Younger pupils we spoke to praised everything about the school, from the small class sizes, 'fair' rules and chocolate cake ('it's not overcooked') to being able to email teachers for help and getting answers back in double-quick time. 'You rarely have anyone in a bad mood here,' said another pupil. 'And I'm not just saying that.' The school has its own car-themed house system – Cooper, Morris and Austin – but unlike more traditional establishments, these focus on environmental matters and fundraising for charity as well as competitions and sport.

Pupils and parents: Pupils are an eclectic mix of high achievers and grafters. Year 7 pupils generally arrive from local primary schools while year 9 entrants tend to come from Oxford preps like Christ Church, the Dragon and New College. No boarding at 11-16 – most live in Oxford and surrounding villages, but some travel from as far afield as Wantage, Faringdon, Swindon and even Warwick. More boys than girls in lower years, but a few more girls than boys in the sixth form. Post-16, equal numbers of day pupils and boarders. UK students come from a vast range of schools (both state and independent) while international students fly in from more than 30 different countries, including Italy, Spain, Russia and China. A handful of very clever Thai government scholars every year too.

The school makes a big effort to keep parents in the loop. Parents we spoke to appreciated its 'modern, unstuffy approach,' 'family atmosphere' and 'emphasis on the important things.' 'My son never enjoyed school until he came to d'Overbroeck's,' one mother told us. 'But he has thrived and been happy here right from the start. He'll be very sad to leave.'

Entrance: The school is selective but its principal emphasises that pupils should have 'a reasonably wide range of abilities.' Alongside the academic requirements staff are looking for students 'who will enjoy the environment and make the most of it.'

Main entry points are year 7, year 9 and sixth form. At 11 and 13 applicants take internal assessment tests in English, maths and non-verbal reasoning, plus a short interview and reference from current school. 'We are looking for potential,' says the head.

At 16 prospective students have an informal interview (they can also sit in on a few lessons if they wish) and need eight A*-C grades at GCSE, including maths and English. the school also stipulates that pupils need at least a B in subjects being taken at A level while those doing maths need at least an A at GCSE (further maths needs an A*). International students sit written English language test (and maths test, where appropriate) and their level of English must be strong enough for the courses they want to do.

Exit: At 16, around two-thirds of year 11 pupils progress through to the sixth form (a few head to local state schools like Cherwell and Cheney and in recent years a few girls have moved to Magdalen College School's co-ed sixth form). At 18, virtually all go to university – two to Oxbridge in 2016, plus two medics and a vet; Birmingham, Bristol and Manchester all popular, with some to eg Imperial, LSE and Royal Holloway.

Money matters: A range of academic, art and performing arts scholarships for pupils entering years 7 and 9 (up to 20 per cent of tuition fees). Academic, art and performing arts scholarships available at sixth form level (up to 40 per cent of fees).

Remarks: d'Overbroeck's has made its mark in Oxford as an exciting and forward-thinking place to be, with a lively, happy environment that fizzes with energy and ideas. Along with top-notch teaching and rigorous academic standards the school helps students to achieve impressive results and make lifelong friends along the way.

Downe House School

Cold Ash, Thatcham, Berkshire RG18 9JJ

Pupils: 587; 569 full boarders • Ages: 11–18 • Sixth form: 185

Fees: Day £25,440; Boarding £35,160 pa

Tel: 01635 200286
Email: registry@downehouse.net
Website: www.downehouse.net

Headmistress: Since 1997, Mrs Emma McKendrick BA PGCE FRSA (40s). Educated at Bedford High and at the universities of Liverpool and Birmingham (German and Dutch). Previously at The Royal School, Bath, where she had been i/c careers and sixth form, a housemistress and deputy head before becoming head in 1994. Remarkably young when appointed to her first headship – that this was so is to the credit of the school's governors. She is soft-spoken, stylish, somehow very grown up, calm and relaxed. Her office and the room in which she receives visitors is a joy – windows on three sides so she can 'see everything', bright, light and tasteful. Parents – who tend to be deeply passionate about the school and many of whom are old girls – sigh with pleasure: 'She is excellent, on top of everything'; 'She is miraculous – I can say nothing against her. She is so professional, warm, and has a sense of humour. One cannot but be in awe of her, but you love her too'.

Academic matters: Had opted for Pre-U in preference to A levels in all but a few arts subjects – 'It really has made a difference to my upper sixth,' said the head. 'They are forced to be more independent. They are far better served by the Pre-U in terms of coping with what they will get at university.' However, with demise of ASs, now returning to A levels for most subjects.

In 2016, just over 70 per cent A*/A at A level or DI/MI at Pre-U. Maths very popular, with biology and English close behind. Good numbers for Latin and the odd taker for Greek. Politics, photography and economics offered along with history of art, plus all the trad subjects. Wide range of languages including support for home ones. Eighty-six per cent A*/A at GCSE in 2016. Blissfully small classes – this is nurturing indeed.

Most teachers highly praised, many seen as 'inspiring'. Learning skills support given to those with mild dys-strata plus those who need extra help with organising themselves or time management. Also stretching help for the most able. Hopeless site for anyone in a wheelchair – the buildings are too scattered and the site is too up and down for this to be possible. EAL support given where needed – 35 in receipt of individual help when we visited.

Games, options, the arts: That the extracurricular life of the school is run from its own sizeable woodland cabin in the heart of the site with designated staff tells you everything. Every kind of opportunity is offered here – from trips to The Royal Opera House to playing lacrosse for Berkshire, to preparing soup for hungry people in South Africa from sackfuls of bones fresh from a slaughterhouse during a trip to a link school there. Lots of visits from outside speakers, who clearly inspire and motivate. Much lively and imaginative charitable activity – often with the boys from Radley. Excellent drama – again, often with Radley – generously supported by old girl Geraldine James, who opened the performing arts centre and has been known to take aspiring actresses under her wing. Two recent successful auditions for the National Youth Theatre. Successful and popular debating.

Sports are many and varied and include, for older girls, pilates, fencing and golf. Several girls are England lacrosse players – lax taken more seriously here than other sports. Internal competition between houses seemingly counting more than fixtures against other schools. Art is lively, though housed in the least attractive building on site – great range of activities: we loved the individuality of work in textiles, ceramics and woodwork, along with truly impressive painting. Ballet, modern dance, tap and hip hop on offer and around half the girls take speech and drama. Practically all of them learn at least one instrument. 'They all do so much extra,' a parent told us, half-admiring, half-concerned. 'They do whack on the pressure – the girls themselves, that is.'

Houses clearly of immense importance here – friendly but significant rivalry in all areas of school life. Lots of trips at home and abroad – all with sound educational or charitable purposes. Most exciting, memorable and generally aaaahed over is the term spent during year 8 at the school's own converted farm in the heart of Perigord. Those who join the school in year 9 seem to spend the next five years biting their lip at having missed an unforgettable experience. A seasoned sixth former told us – as if it were obvious – 'Oh, we never stop talking about it.' It's about French and French life, cuisine, charity work, community and living ensemble.

Boarding: All but a handful of local day girls are full boarders. One boarding school veteran told us that the boarding staff were much the best she'd ever come across. The boarding houses themselves are much loved. We relished the dressing up boxes in the junior houses.

New lower school house for all year 7 and 8 girls, providing a sheltered introduction to boarding life. Older girls are in mixed age houses – dorms are mostly spacious; singles and doubles for the older girls are homely and attractive. Everywhere is properly carpeted and curtained. Fresh flowers abound – no sense here that 'nice' areas are just for show – this is home and it feels like it. All houses either wireless or with network points.

Sixth form houses are exceptionally well designed and furnished. Pigeonholes for girls' post and newspapers; sofas, careers areas, meeting rooms, kitchens. Girls can be independent here, if they wish – no wonder so few leave after GCSEs. All have a personal safe in their rooms. Further extension to and enhancement of the boarding facilities planned.

Lessons until 12pm on Saturdays are followed by sports, so everyone signs up to the full boarding life. Saturday evenings are spent in rehearsal, at concerts, trips to theatres, cinemas etc. Sundays include trips, D of E activities and chillin'.

Background and atmosphere: Founded in 1907 by Olive Willis, its first headmistress, as an all-girls' boarding school. Its first home was Down House in the village of Downe, Kent – formerly the home of Charles Darwin. The school outgrew the house so Miss Willis bought The Cloisters in Berkshire – its present home – on a high ridge which provides occasional views over distant downs. The Cloisters – still at the heart of the school – comes as a surprise. Built by Maclaren Ross for an order of Spanish nuns, who named it The School of Silence, it has an arched walkway linking most of the classrooms which – with its white walls, arches and terracotta pantiles – is incongruously Moorish in the heart of Berkshire.

However, the school has grown many newer buildings – boarding houses, specialist blocks etc – around the main building and the site is now extensive – many buildings nestling amongst trees, woody areas and neatly planted beds. All maintained by 'little green men' who hover around the site on electric car-lets. No architectural gems here – nor any monsters – though a few blocks lack charm. The whole has a sense of modest purposefulness – described by one mother as 'almost spiritual'.

The uniform is standard school green skirt, shirt and jumper, though the sixth form still cling to their floor length black skirts – 'They wear them so they can keep their pyjamas on underneath,' one mum told us.

Pastoral care, well-being and discipline: 'Completely faultless,' a mother said of the pastoral care. 'The house staff are very responsive and email you back at once.' 'When people complain, things do get done,' another vouchsafed. 'We've been bowled over by the pastoral care,' said yet another. 'The attention to detail is extraordinary – almost obsessive. Nothing is too much trouble.'

The loveliest school dining room we have seen in over 100 schools – proper tablecloths on round tables seating six to encourage time over meals. Food – 'We make all our own bread and sausages and buy in the absolute minimum' – which occasions rhapsodies in the girls.

Some sense that the sixth form centre separates older from younger girls and work still to be done on integrating those who arrive after the first year, but this is tricky in girls' schools everywhere. Very few discipline problems – smoking sighed over as 'an occasional safe rebellion which one wishes they wouldn't do', and illicit drinking looked upon as a threat to a girl's personal safety – 'You need to be safe, to look after yourself and to preserve your dignity,' the head reminds them. No drugs incidents within memory and the very rare girl who 'cannot stop being unkind has to go'.

D

Pupils and parents: Girls from all over the UK and beyond; increasing numbers of daughters of alumnae. Seven per cent from overseas – mostly from the Far East but also the US, Nigeria, Kazakhstan. Parents solid middle class, usually with boarding backgrounds.

Exceptionally impressive list of notable alumnae includes: chemist and educator Rosemary Murray, Geraldine James, Clare Balding, Mary Midgley, Elizabeth Bowen, Priscilla Napier, Anne Ridler, Audrey Richards, Sophie Conran, Lulu Guinness, Fru Hazlitt, wildly different comics Miranda Hart and Laura Solon, Hannah Wright – pioneering barrister, Jenifer Hart – pioneering civil servant and Oxford don and Aileen Fox – pioneering archaeologist. Oh – and Kate Middleton. A rare degree of loyalty amongst alumnae – few schools excite more affection, it seems, and many keep in touch. Mrs McKendrick fosters this in imaginative ways, enlisting old girls to support newbies in their professions, eg an established barrister mentoring a recent alumna in her pupillage. A considerable attraction to potential parents.

Entrance: Lists close at 110 applicants and head interviews all those over four days, during which all are tested in maths, English and reasoning. They also participate in drama and sports activities et al to see whether they're happy and likely to fit in with boarding life. Eighty then invited to sit CE for the 60 available places. At 13, around 65 are assessed similarly for the 35-odd places. Girls from 180+ preps/primaries have joined Downe in recent years – from all over the UK.

At 16, it depends on how many are leaving but usually around 8-10 places for the 'huge' number who apply. Applicants sit the school's own papers and the strongest are then interviewed, the best offered conditional places. Seven I/GCSEs at B or above expected including A*/As in sixth form subject choices.

Exit: Some 10 per cent leave after GCSEs, often for co-ed sixth forms. Most to top universities, eg Bristol, London, Warwick, Exeter, Leeds, Edinburgh; six to Oxbridge in 2016. Some to universities in the US. Popular subjects include science/medicine, psychology, history of art, MFL, economics, politics, RS, business related degrees plus music and creative arts.

Money matters: Scholarships for sports, arts and academics more of an honour than a significant contribution to fees. Bursaries up to 100 per cent of fees plus additional help available for the right applicant.

Remarks: Archetypal traditional girls' full boarding school turning out delightful, principled, courteous and able girls who go on to make a significant contribution to the world. As one parent said, 'We couldn't be more thrilled.'

Downsend School

1 Leatherhead Road, Leatherhead, Surrey KT22 8TJ

Pupils: 433 • Ages: 2-13

Fees: £11,535- £13,965 pa

Tel: 01372 372197
Email: admissions@downsend.co.uk
Website: www.downsend.co.uk

Headmaster: Since 2013, Mr Ian Thorpe BA MA (40s). Previously four years as headmaster at Chinthurst School and before that head of junior school at City of London Freemen's, preceded by stints all over the place, from Caterham Prep, where he was deputy head, to Witham Hall (deputy head and housemaster).

Married to 'very patient' wife, a teacher at Caterham, attended by two sons. A former grammar school boy, he's bright, jovial and energetic (looks exactly like sportsman he is, PE his main degree subject at Exeter). Refreshingly candid about strengths. He's a 'good all-rounder,' he says, with knack of getting what he wants – likely to come in handy for persuading 'supportive' bosses at Cognita, school's owner, to declare corporate wallet open.

Trilingual in French and Dutch (expat upbringing in Belgium) – results in excellent conversion rates for overseas families delighted to find head able to talk the talk in own language. Works wonders with Brits who have only to hear strains of unknown tongue (all but their own, generally) to assume 'you're really clever.'

Parental niggles leave him unfazed – most logged and being sorted, including pressing need to visit senior schools further afield to plug the knowledge gaps. 'Want more than helicopter perspective,' says a father. Just as well he's dynamic and good at disseminating the corporate message, think parents. While some 'see his style as slightly in your face,' supporters praise energy levels and hours worked. 'He's always there,' says one.

And while not necessarily quite such a details man as his predecessor (reckoned he knows about two-thirds of pupils' names though had 100 per cent strike rate during our visit) his verve and vision felt by others to be just the ticket. 'Has shaken things up (in a good way),' reckoned a mother.

Easily bored, and enjoys a challenge. Just as well, what with numbers declining slightly in recent years following big rise about five years ago which saw school creaking at the seams, leading to some parents who bemoaned lack of intimacy voting with their feet.

Decision by St John's Leatherhead and Epsom College to offer 11+ as well as 13+ entry from 2016 means he has a fight on his hands to hold on to pupils in top two years. Currently loses a third after year 6 and, if parents desert wholesale, thinks Mr Thorpe, area as a whole could be the poorer, smaller preps taking only to year 6, only a few larger schools, this one included, able to finance the CE years.

Officially, it's stiff upper lips as usual, helped by increased pupil numbers and a big drive to proselytise benefits of the traditional prep school model, though behind the scenes furrowing of brows likely to be the in look for foreseeable future. Efforts to increase year 7 recruitment and build better links with traditional public schools (Wellington is starting to appear on parents' wish lists) continue apace.

Thus far, head has tended to stay four years in each post before moving on. His clear relish for fight to demonstrate, in the face of substantial reasons not to, why it's worth staying for the whole prep school experience, means that he's unlikely to be getting itchy feet for some time to come.

Entrance: Mixed ability and proud of it, declining to offer places only if child's behaviour or learning difficulty outside school's ability to cope. Otherwise, possession of place in nursery or reception usually leads to automatic passage through the school. Informal assessment for entry in year 2, tests in English and maths in year 3, ditto for other occasional places, may also be interview with the head. Pill can be considerably sweetened by interspersing exams with a spot of art or sport. Scholarships on offer in year 3, sibling discounts up to 15 per cent.

Prep packs them in from assorted points close to school locations, many local. Recent decision to provide return buses as well as inward bound ones a boon to growing numbers of working and longer distance families. Many originally from London, dual-income professionals increasingly the norm, making school's early morning, after school and holiday care between 8.00am and 5.30pm (and even later during term time) even more a boon. We really only close over Christmas,' says staff member.

Exit: Very rare that pupils don't make it from pre-prep into year 2 though occasionally happens if felt that won't manage the pace. Some parents take it badly, others are more pragmatic. Better the conversation now and support to find another school than 'drifting through, hitting year 6 and not have a place,' thought one mother.

Big senior school menu features occasional guest appearances by Hampton, Harrow and Guildford High but most senior schools – like many of delicious school lunch ingredients – are locally sourced, St John's heading destinations, Epsom College entrants dipping slightly, Reigate Grammar increasingly popular. Scholarships – around a quarter academic – steadily increasing.

Remarks: Founded in 1891 and fully co-ed since 2001. Snapped up by Cognita in early noughties and with around 470 pupils, slightly more boys than girls (though equal numbers of girls the aim, think parents). One of the largest schools in the group.

A mini-brand all on its own, extending tentacles (albeit embracing ones) into other regions of Surrey, courtesy of three additional pre-prep outposts, nearest just a few doors down from the prep. Were called lodges, name ditched after school sensibly worked out that associations with retirement homes, hunting and freemasonry rather than exuberant education of the very young were very possibly unhelpful. Though size and layout varies (Leatherhead, most generously endowed with space, has delightful tree and topiary-edged field off to side, so able to host own sports day rather than holding it at prep). Each offers small-scale cosiness, Ashtead notable for tiny reception classes of no more than 10, lunch fresh-cooked each day on all three sites, regular visits by minibus to prep for concerts, swimming and sport (including matches between the three), ensuring fear-free transition in year 2.

Parents tend to choose pre-prep that's an easy buggy stroll away, confident that curriculum and ethos will be pretty much identical in each. Some variation in specialist teachers and ways of doing things, though parents feel convergence of management styles is on the way in.

Pre-prep heads also bring stamp of individuality while sharing honours when it comes to warmth – we liked Ashtead's entrance featuring a beribboned tree next to weeny placards, each announcing birth of a new baby.

Pre-prep numbers on way up, Ashtead full, Leatherhead close. Epsom, the outlier (it's about five miles from mother ship) and located at end of private road close to well regarded state primary, currently siphoning off a fair few pupils in reception, has more work to do. If new wildlife and woodwork-mad head, bursting with ideas, from bringing chick from home on first day of autumn term to transforming part of playground into woodland paradise, we suspect they'll be hanging on to many more.

As for the prep, it's seen as the well-balanced option for those searching for something in between colossus and boutique establishment – neither over wood-panelled nor fetishistically au courant.

In an area bristling with good schools this one stands out as happy medium in terms of ethos, achievements and family background. 'More balanced than other schools – some parents aren't short of a penny, others are scraping the kitty to pay the fees,' thought one father. Balance applies equally to look and feel of the place. While there's an attractive square, original Victorian house looking out over 'sacred lawn' (where pupils walk at their peril) and fringed with modern(ish) add-ons, a predominance of beige and inoffensive low ceilings elsewhere avoids anything smacking of ostentation.

School has willingness to accommodate those whose interests don't follow those of the common herd. You don't have to love rugby, for example – table tennis or badminton enthusiasts are catered for with equal dedication, while one upper school basketball fanatic dreamed of dedicated hoops that 'didn't wobble.'

Hard to argue with sporting success that regularly makes local headlines – it's a rare year when school doesn't secure national title somewhere along the line, swimming the biggest strength. 'Can't remember the last time they lost a match,' says father. Girls' sport as strong as boys – revved up following slightly lukewarm comments in last inspection.

Generally good, too, with SEN pupils – over 150 receiving some form of support in slightly bleak room slightly apart from main drag, though help is limited to mild difficulties only. Parents praise openness to new ideas such as allowing laptops for those with SpLD, though one mother felt had needed to push to ensure that SEN awareness and approaches make it into collectiveness staff consciousness. Head, who agrees, is bumping up admin team so SENCo can spend more time working with class teachers.

The school isn't right for everyone. 'A bit of a hothouse,' thought local senior school insider, though tutors hired to plug specific gaps rather than as a permanent accessory, as elsewhere. Parents a motivated bunch and it's a rare child who isn't read to at night, thinks mother. Teachers an impressive bunch, too – though these days unlikely to hang around for long if they're not, think parents. Though the head couldn't possibly comment, he has made expectations clear. 'I've used the words "uncompromising standards..."' Also rejigging structure, appointing heads of lower (years 2 to 5) and upper school (years 6 to 8), both impressively fast-talking enthusiasts.

Well-structured curriculum, where academic focus, though sharp, isn't allowed to blot out cookery and sewing, both on offer all the way to year 8. Enjoyable lessons include junior pupils writing letters to favourite authors in English and upper school science lesson practical comparing exhaust fumes of (teacher's) Jaguar (good) with school minibus emissions (sootier). Lots of praise from pupils, all mentioning 'happy' teachers who 'have lots of friends' (always nice to hear). They tell terrible jokes too, to relieve entrance exam pressure – 'so bad that they're funny,' say pupils.

Teaching staff donate minimum of an hour a week to run lunchtime or after school club (includes green-fingered nurse and science technician who recruit helpers to tend idyllic garden haven). Fab range of activities, now free of charge.

'Hats off to school for exam preparation,' said mother, child in proud possession of several excellent offers. Results aren't trumpeted perhaps as much as they might be elsewhere, despite goodly number of scholarships, though new, modernistic honours boards may help.

As with youngest pupils, attention to detail is good, from homework – 'just enough to stretch you,' says year 7 pupil – to carrot-focused discipline, detentions possible but rarely necessary, credits and house points the norm (with highly desirable trip to Guildford Spectrum for the winners).

Successful occupation of middle ground makes for very happy pupils, think parents. Possibly too much so, reckons head, who has found school's oft-published desire to produce 'children who enjoy life' a bit much to bear, especially when proffered as excuse for iffy behaviour and appearance, something he's cracking down on (two message-bearing boys, both barefoot after PE, were swiftly returned to sender).'It's like saying we're a school for children who breathe air,' he says. While head may want to tweak the recipe, no doubting parents' happiness with the basic ingredients. 'It's about having fun,' says mother. 'Sounds a bit twee but that's the core of what they do.'

Dr Challoner's Grammar School

Chesham Road, Amersham, Buckinghamshire HP6 5HA

Pupils: 1,331 • Ages: 11–18 • Sixth form: 407

Tel: 01494 787500
Email: admin@challoners.com
Website: www.challoners.com

Headmaster: Since September 2016, David Atkinson, previously deputy head. Geography degree from Oxford; has taught here ever since, becoming head of geography and director of sixth form on his way up. A chartered geographer, appointed to the Royal Geographical Society in recognition of his work in geographical education, including texts on geomorphology. Has worked to promote wider access to higher education, especially in STEM subjects; leads the Astra Learning Alliance, which provides training and development for teachers in Bucks and Herts.

Academic matters: Unrivalled as Buckinghamshire's top performing boys' grammar school, the Challoner's brand is synonymous far and wide with academic excellence, regularly appearing in the top 20 state schools nationally. Parents and boys unanimous, however, that undue pressure is not the norm, although it is taken as read that underperformance is not acceptable, with one boy earnestly saying, 'we're all generally disappointed with a B'.

Ten GCSEs the norm, with IGCSEs on offer in English, history, geography and the three sciences – 'great for differentiating at the top of the academic spectrum,' says head. Strong focus on school teaching only subjects in which it can invest and excel – hence recent discontinuation of business studies ('very little take up at A level') and no obvious weak areas. In 2016, 73 per cent of GCSE grades were A*/A; with 59 per cent of A levels graded A*/A, 82 per cent A*-B and around two-thirds of cohort taking four. Success attributed to school's 'emphasis on learning habits and skills other than mere academics,' as well as largely excellent staff: classes are engaging, lively and interactive with a good number of young innovators in the staff mix.

Traditional-ish curriculum focuses on the solid, academic subjects required by Oxbridge and Russell Group universities with no media studies and not an 'ology' in sight. Specialist status in science with results to match and maths also described by parents as a 'stand-out' subject. History department described as 'really, really strong.' An unusual in-curriculum offering of electronics adds to school's scientific feel, with languages – although well taught and compulsory at GCSE – 'a little bit second fiddle – there's definitely a scientific bent,' according to some parents. French, German and Spanish on offer but no Latin or more unusual offerings such as Mandarin, Japanese or Russian. That said, parents and boys praise the language exchange programme from the rooftops. Sixth formers describe support around university applications as 'stringent,' with all boys 'absolutely' receiving the same level of input from school regardless of where they have applied.

Not the obvious school for DT fanatics or really arty types. The saws and lathes of yesteryear have gone by the wayside and been replaced with a super whizz-bang graphic design suite, equipped with state of the art kit, leading to boys producing outstanding work and many leaving to head down this avenue in higher education. Two art rooms are somewhat run of the mill, although work on display was of good technical quality. Some super examples of boys' artwork showcased in school magazine and website, if not so much around the school itself.

Thirty to a class standard for the first two years with setting from year 9 in maths, year 10 in science and at GCSE in English – 'cleverly done,' said one parent. 'The top and bottom sets are kept very small – sometimes as few as 12 to a class.' Class sizes shrink uniformly to around 20 at GCSE and 15 at A level, depending on subject.

School has invested in excellent Wifi rather than fixed IT equipment, and study areas are awash with boys using smart laptops. All year 8 and 9 boys have iPads, supplied by parents, a predictably popular move with pupils but something the parents 'grapple with,' according to head. Cookery on curriculum in years 8 and 10 as part of PSHCE, taking place in a gleaming kitchen space, complete with flat screen televisions to walk boys through recipes. We sampled delicious oatcakes – 'great for giving us energy for sport,' chirped one enthusiastic young chef.

Games, options, the arts: Hugely improved sports programme. What parents describe as a 'formerly elitist approach' to team sports has been given a full makeover in recent years, thanks to a strong partnership between the school and a group of passionate parents, with opportunities to represent the school now for every child who wants to 'as long as they show commitment to training.' When asked how many make the cut, 'there is no cut,' insisted head of games. Top-notch sportsmen (of which there are plenty – 15 county cricketers in one year alone) of course play to win at weekly fixtures – and there are A to C teams for all major sports – but the school is now focused on making sure every boy gets a chance to stride out for Challoner's – and head of games keeps a list to make sure they do so at least once a term. Cross-country competitions open to all comers, with this inclusivity underscored by the introduction of sports including fencing and mountain biking.

Unlike local rival RGS, boys can choose from three major winter sports (rugby, football or hockey) with strong cricket in the summer term. Although lacking the sprawling grounds of its privately funded rivals, school makes effective use of the fields it does have and boasts a super climbing wall, spacious sports hall and, new in 2015, two new championship tennis courts and a multi-use Astroturf.

Plenty of sporty squads, training and teams for boys to throw themselves into at lunchtimes and after school, although from year 9 onwards other extracurricular seems a bit thin on the ground – perhaps to keep all eyes on the academic prize. One boy we spoke to racked his brains for a while, then came up with debating as the only option. However, music and drama ('huge,' say boys) flourish, often in conjunction with sister school Challoner's High, with bands and choirs aplenty performing to exceptionally high standards – the jazz and swing bands received high praise from parents, as did joint school productions, most recently musical The Boy Friend. Lots of discos, balls and other social events provide further opportunities to socialise with the girls.

Huge range of trips and tours, for both academic and enrichment purposes, ranging from a popular ski trip ('if it's oversubscribed, we try to offer places to the less obviously sporty boys first') to Iceland (geographers) and Washington DC (historians) as well as the golden ticket – the biannual Caribbean cricket tour.

Background and atmosphere: Founded 1624 under the will of Dr Robert Chaloner (sic), former rector of Amersham and Canon of Windsor. Moved to present site on the edge of Amersham High Street in 1905, when it became co-ed. Due to expanding numbers, girls got their own premises a few miles away in Little Chalfont in 1962. The original fascia lends the school a reasonably attractive frontage – particularly in comparison with the majority of grammars thrown up in the decades that taste forgot – and the campus, although now a smorgasbord of architectural styles spanning the decades, feels spacious, well-organised and accessible. The jewel in the crown is the spectacular newish three tier sixth form centre which caters for all the boys' needs: a casual lounging area and Café Africa run by a local not-for-profit organisation on the ground floor, a group study area on the first level and the cherry on top: a stunning, airy library with small break-out rooms for silent study. Pre-sixth form, boys lunch in an equally gleaming dining hall with good food and plenty of wholesome, healthy options to keep energy high.

Remarkably pristine fabric of school with no obvious tatty corners – and even some very smart ones – is matched by an equally smart student body. Uniform of blazer and tie is worn with pride (frequent reminders from head to keep shirts tucked in) until sixth form when boys can wear their own suit and tie. At this point, boys given considerable responsibility and freedom. Morning attendance is compulsory then free to go if no timetabled lessons. A young, dynamic staff keeps things fresh with around 30 per cent female teachers to dilute the testosterone.

Pastoral care, well-being and discipline: 'Extraordinary' pastoral care, according to parents. Boys get off to a great start with the thoroughly affable head of year 7 visiting each and every one at their primary school. A well-attended summer sports camp before they join gives those joining in ones and twos from village schools a chance to make friends before term starts. Huge number of official roles higher up the school with up to 80 elected prefects, house captains and head boys give older boys a sense of responsibility. Six houses drive the school's competitive spirit, fighting it out throughout the year at 'virtually anything you can name.' Tons of fun boy-initiated fundraisers – both for charities and school – range from 'peg the teacher' to teacher/student penalty shoot-outs or designing and selling Challoner's beany hats.

A 'fantastic' student development team provides counselling, support and SEN wherever required. School recognises that boys these days 'have to manage a lot of challenges'; Challoner's boys know the school is 'on their side.' On the whole, a pretty well-behaved bunch by all accounts, with little need for intervention, and even deep digging in the locality didn't unearth any noteworthy behaviour other than minor misdemeanours. Plenty of friendly interaction between year groups fosters a collegiate atmosphere: sixth formers apply to be mentors to year 7s, visiting their classrooms with fun activities up their sleeves or just to chat and listen. Year 10s pulled in to advise year 9 pupils on their GCSE choices and pupils drew up the anti-bullying charter, displayed in every classroom. Issues raised by parents in relation to teaching staff are reportedly dealt with head on and with full transparency. Would a boy ever be allowed to just drift at Challoner's, we asked? 'Absolutely not,' came back the unequivocal parental reply.

Pupils and parents: Predictably, solidly affluent middle class, many of whom, were it not for the god of catchment areas smiling on them on school allocation day, could ably pay for their sons' schooling. Around a third of boys join from local preps (mainly The Beacon or Gayhurst with a few from Davenies and Chesham Prep) but these are indistinguishable from their peers who join from state primaries in leafy commuter villages. Small number from ethnic groups (around 15 per cent) with a minute number on free school meals. Coaches bus boys in from all directions.

With their easy confidence and erudite chatter, most boys could have been airlifted from any public school and dropped on the Challoner's campus. School buzzes with the drive of a cohort who are definitely there with their minds on achieving great things – where other grammars have whole programmes dedicated to convincing boys that they are good enough to try for Oxbridge, Challoner's boys feel (and some grumble) that's just what's expected of them – nice problem to have. One sixth former we happened across couldn't wait to update head on progress with his latest must-have invention (we were sworn to secrecy – but seriously impressed).

Entrance: Selective. Prospective pupils sit the Buckinghamshire Transfer Test – usually at their primary school – in early September of year 6. Those who pass (usually around 30 per cent of candidates) are entitled to a grammar school place. Challoner's widely perceived to be the hot ticket and as such massively oversubscribed, so selection then comes strictly down to distance from candidate's home to front door of school. And don't be fooled into thinking that living in catchment (which stretches as far as eight miles in one direction) will entitle you to a place. Offers can extend to about six miles from school, but this varies from year to year. And no more can savvy north London parents rent a flat in Amersham for application purposes, hoping to pop their little darling on the Metropolitan Line each day – you need to have lived at your home address for two years before applying to the school. And yes, they do check...

Occasional late entry places (post year 7) do crop up, and at this stage, catchment goes out the window and the place goes to the child with the highest score in the entrance exam. Around 25 new places open up in year 12 and are offered to the candidates with the best GCSE results, mainly from local non-selective state schools, occasionally defectors from the private sector. Sixth form now co-ed.

Exit: Consistently impressive list of destination universities. Twenty-one to Oxbridge in 2016 ('usually around 10 per cent') with a host of Russell Group universities for the rest – Nottingham, Birmingham and Warwick the most popular recently – and seven medics. Very few leavers after GCSE.

Money matters: Like all grammars in this part of the world, neglected by state funds in favour of schools in run down areas, so more or less kept afloat by the generosity of parents. The active 'friends' association raises in excess of £30K a year with its various fundraisers. Regular parental contributions are 'solidly reliable,' raising around £100K each year according to head – although parents are not press-ganged, just 'gently encouraged' into making these.

Remarks: The pinnacle of state funded education. Many Challoner's parents may argue that they're indirectly paying for their son's first class education with their hefty upper middle income taxes and house price premiums, but staff describes the school as 'the best education money can't buy' and we can't argue with that. Think ahead, buy up as close to the school as you can and get that 11+ supertutor booked. You can save your money for the Oxford tuition fees...

Dr Challoner's High School

Cokes Lane, Little Chalfont, Buckinghamshire HP7 9QB

Pupils: 1,075 • Ages: 11–18 • Sixth form: 320

Tel: 01494 763296
Email: office@challonershigh.com
Website: www.challonershigh.com

Head: Since September 2015, Alan Roe, previously a member of the senior team at Chesham Grammar School, which he helped towards its outstanding Ofsted rating in 2014. A geographer, he initially taught at the Downs School in west Berkshire, and became head of humanities at Dr Challoner's Grammar School, where he worked for nine years before joining Chesham Grammar in 2011. Teaches geography to year 11s and mainly sees students by appointment and for informal chats around the school – as well as offering birthday teas to year 10 girls in his office (in small groups).

Fairly reserved and not a man to waste words, he is nonetheless engaging and utterly passionate about the school, particularly its mission going forward. In fact, he kicked off his tenure by working with some parents (management consultants, working with the likes of Costa and BA) for six months to create a one-page vision – no mean feat for a school that 'was traditionally unable to describe itself very well. Now, it can.' Parents describe him as a 'strong and visible leader,' 'a man with real presence' and 'someone with huge emotional intelligence.' 'He recognises and respects in a very public way the contribution of all stakeholders to the school,' adds another parent. Students applaud how he celebrates individual successes and say he is 'clear on expectations' and 'very approachable.'

Lives near Aylesbury with his wife and two daughters, both of whom are primary school age.

Academic matters: DCHS regularly hovers around the top of regional and national state school league tables. In 2016, 73 per cent A*/A at GCSE, with 36 per cent A*s. At A level, 51 per cent A*/A and 82 per cent A*-B. Six classes of 30 in each year group (phasing out the old intake of five classes), with setting from year 9 in maths – although it's purely about pace, as one student explained: 'I was in the bottom set for maths GCSE, but still got an A. Most of us did.' Indeed, maths is one of the greatest academic strengths of the school at all levels, with the number of year 12s choosing to take further maths testament to this. 'This department is a machine – maths is easily our most popular A level,' says the head – although one parent said he'd like to see girls competing in more inter-school competitions.

DCHS is also super-strong in languages. Unusually, pupils take three in year 7 – French, German and Spanish – and not just as taster courses, with 1.5 hours per week dedicated to each language. From year 8, they pick two of them, as well as taking up Latin. Parents say it 'takes away the difficult decision about which two to go for when girls join the school.'

Good breadth of subjects available at GSCE, with most popular non-core subjects including RE, geography and history. An impressive 25 subjects are taught at A level, with the most popular including biology, chemistry, English literature, geography and history – plus, of course, maths and languages. Less traditional offerings at A level include Latin, classics, psychology, graphics and textiles. No gender stereotypes – with around 30+ typically doing GCSE computing and 20-30 doing physics A level. 'It's part of the joy of being an all-girls school. They just find their passion and get on with it,' says the head.

Recruiting and retaining good, experienced teachers is prioritised within the school's budget, leading to an 'expensive, but stable and outstanding 70-strong team', according to the head – with a healthy staff turnover of five or six leaving per year, while others stay as long as 30 years. 'Our philosophy is that the best schools have the best teachers.' Parents praise the 'extremely supportive' relationship between teachers and pupils, which 'involves lots of mentoring and coaching.' Students describe teaching as 'collaborative' and 'inspirational.' 'You sometimes get teachers standing at the front of the class, but equally often, it's interactive – and this means we support and learn from each other too.' The school is widely praised for its depth of learning – girls here don't just learn about the subject itself – they drill down deeper, making links with other subjects and doing their own investigations. Target setting is high on the agenda, with formal monitoring every term. 'These teachers know your precise strengths and weaknesses and how to overcome the latter – it's astonishing,' one pupil told us. There are a few bad apples, parents told us – 'my daughter is damning of a few of her teachers, but you get that anywhere.' Homework typical for a Bucks grammar – an hour a night in year 7, reaching up to two-three hours a night by year 13.

Dedicated SEN team includes an experienced SENCo, who (significantly) is the deputy head. This team supports pupils with a wide range of needs ('not just mild and moderate,' says head – although only two statemented when we visited), both in and outside the classroom. No wheelchair access, however.

Head keen to point out that despite the school's strong academic reputation, 'this is an A*-C school. So while the majority of our grades are A* and A, our staff battle hard for the girls in their best, worst and middling subjects. In fact, their eyes often gleam the brightest for those hard-sought Cs.' 'The teachers really went the extra mile to help my daughter in her weaker subjects,' one parent confirmed.

Games, options, the arts: PE mandatory from years 7-11, with 20 sports taught to a high standard by enthusiastic staff – netball, hockey, athletics and cross-country at the core. Sport popular off curriculum too, with a sports leadership programme in place for those competing at country, national or international level – which involves DCHS girls having worked with over 2,000 primary school children. DCHS successfully competes at a high level across the board, including more marginal activities like fencing, basketball and rowing in its armoury. Cricket is on the up, and there are non-competitive exercise options including pilates, yoga and boot camp. Majority of sports clubs are free, with just a handful (such as rowing and fencing) charged as an extra. 'While there's lots in place to ensure the elite thrive here, sports at DCHS is also about participation, with a staggering 110 year 7 girls doing after-school netball this year,' one parent told us – although another pointed out, 'There's no full-size hockey field – you can't deny that's a weakness.'

Huge range of music, drama and art-based extracurricular activities on offer (again, mostly free), with 370 girls involved with one of the many ensembles, orchestras and choirs when we visited. Choirs alone range from the all-school, 60-strong junior and senior choirs through to the elite 12-strong Con Brio choir.

A favourite is the swing band, which tours with the boys' school biennially – just one of many opportunities for musically-able girls to perform publically. Some 500 girls learn an instrument with a peripatetic teacher – a huge number for a school of this size. And music lessons are also built into the curriculum up to year 9, after which it is optional. Decent numbers take it as GCSE.

Budding actors are also in for a treat here, with two main school productions performed joint with the boys' school every year – one senior production; the other open to all. 'Normally, one of these is student led,' says the head. 'Last year, year 10 wrote Lady of the Flies, which was phenomenally good.' In addition, girls can apply to be in the boys' school performances, so ultra-keen thespians at DCHS can potentially perform in four plays across both schools. Opportunities for girls to learn technical sound, lighting and set building.

Strong arts and technology faculty, with quality work festooning the immediately surrounding area, although it's a pity this doesn't make its way further into the school. Also a shame the spacious art studios don't have more natural light, but that's all set to change with the forthcoming upgrade. 'There will be a gallery area, plus specialist classrooms – important as art continues to grow in popularity,' says the head.

Other extracurricular options of note (most of which take place at lunchtimes or after school) include Mandarin from year 12; D of E; the fiercely contested debating, with regular trips to the Oxford Union; and the economics society, which attracts external lecturers from the worlds of business and government. Many of the clubs and societies are student led – and some are run joint with the boys' school, including the English society and the award-winning Young Enterprise. In short, something for everyone, although some parents told us they'd like to see the girls pushed to do more. 'That's improving, but not fast enough,' said a parent.

Unbelievably long list of school trips for all year groups, from curriculum based and language exchanges to an activities break for year 7 and a visit to Tanzania for year 12 (with girls expected to raise funds to travel and work for charity). There's a year 9 residential enrichment week, with a choice of 5+ options including to Iceland and Germany, and plenty of one-off trips, such as music and sports tours. Start saving your pennies, though – these trips 'cost anything from £200 to over £1,000,' says the head.

Background and atmosphere: Founded in 1624 by Dr Robert Chaloner (sic), becoming co-ed in 1906. Girls hived off to Little Chalfont in 1962 (the boys' school, Dr Challoner's Grammar School, is a few miles away in Amersham). Tucked away amongst prime South Bucks real estate, visitors may feel transported back to the 1960s as they drive in, although the mix of tired-looking, no-frills buildings from this era includes some smarter additions from the 1990s. Plus points include the feeling of spaciousness – although not by any means a vast campus, the school is surrounded by mature woodland. We also like the outdoor amphitheatre, used for summer term performances, and new courtyard café, where students can socialise and study. There's an impressive number of multi-purpose spaces including a large, modern sports hall, assembly hall, gymnasium and sound-proofed drama studio, all excellent for the school's large and active performing arts community.

And while the fabric of DCHS lacks many of the gleaming facilities one might expect in a leading school, it's worth noting that the school is in the midst of a five-year premises plan, which includes a new sixth form common room and study rooms (already complete) and two cutting-edge science labs and general improvements throughout the school. Noticeboards in corridors generally used to inform, rather than displaying pupils' work – we particularly liked the photos of recent leavers, with details of the course and university they've gone onto. 'It's great for us to see as it shows how many different courses and universities there are out there.' Food is good, say students, albeit served in a rather overcrowded dining room.

Despite fierce competition for places at this hard-working school, there is an informal vibe. Pupils look happy and relatively care-free – although the consensus is that unmotivated souls might struggle. 'If you are not a self-starter or naturally curious, I think you could feel uncomfortable here,' one parent told us. Pupils say they are given 'a lot of freedom' and there is a feeling of trust and ownership around the school, with girls given free rein of the buildings – including the computer labs – at break times. 'There's not constant supervision – we know they won't start trashing classrooms,' smiles the head.

D

Parents of younger girls generally agree that the 'whole child is nurtured' – and there's certainly lots of work on transition, with every pupil visited in their primary school and every girl given a mentor. Pressure ramps up from year 10, though, when girls are expected to sing for their supper, according to parents we spoke to.

Pastoral care, well-being and discipline: The school day – which runs from 8.40am-3.35pm to fit in five one-hour lessons – includes tutor time both at the start and end of the morning. 'We wanted to make sure there are two key points of contact for the girls every day – important from a pastoral perspective,' says the head. Other key features of the excellent pastoral system here include the strong relationships between the teachers and girls; the fact that girls generally have the same academic tutor from year 7-11 at the school; the non-teacher student support officer, who is available at all times for both academic and emotional support; the two part-time school counsellors; and full-time matron. There are also befriending schemes between year groups and a 'big sister, little sister' initiative, with older girls able to mentor junior sports squads or tutor younger ones if they are struggling academically. 'My daughter had some anxiety problems, which became quite serious, and they were brilliant at dealing with it quickly and well.'

Hugely successful house system encourages mixing and co-operation between year groups. A head girl team is elected each year, with one head girl and 11 deputies, each looking after a specific aspect of the school ranging from innovation and student voice to press and PR. Very professional glossy school magazine, put together by pupils, showcases girls' talent in writing features, poetry and short stories as well as photography and artwork. Popular termly discos with the boys' school enable them to let their hair down in a safe environment.

Bullying 'practically non-existent,' according to the girls. 'It's not like my last school – it's so friendly,' is a phrase you'll hear over and over again. 'It's unbelievably tolerant and if bullying does happen, it's dealt with swiftly,' says the head. In fact, incidents of any poor behaviour are generally 'very rare', says head – with girls getting the odd detention, but generally no more than one or two during their entire school careers. 'I've never seen anything like it – the behaviour is ridiculously good,' says the head. 'The girls police themselves – there isn't a need to be heavy handed,' said one parent. No permanent exclusions in living memory and no temporary exclusions during the current head's time.

Teacher/parent communication has 'greatly improved', with parents now able to email individual teachers via the school office. Parents also praise the weekly newsletter.

Pupils and parents: Families mostly middle-class, with around a quarter of girls joining from local prep schools and a negligible number eligible for free school meals. Furthest distance that girls can come from changes annually, dependent on number of applications and how many make it through the 11 plus, but most live within six miles and the furthest currently come from 10.5 miles away. Excellent bus service from surrounding areas morning and afternoon, but parents need to be on hand to collect after later activities. 'Increasingly, girls use the Met line, with Little Chalfont tube station only a seven or eight minute walk away,' adds the head. 'It's particularly popular with our sixth formers.' Good ethnic mix for the area – typically 67 per cent white British, with a wide variety of ethnicities represented among the remaining girls.

We found the girls polite, well-turned out (the school cuts no slack around the uniform looking smart) and confident. 'When you meet girls at the open day, you can't help but think, "I want one of those!"' said one parent. 'My daughter is quirky and that quirkiness is fully embraced,' added another.

Parents are a sociable bunch, compared to many state schools, while a very active parents' association helps out with regular fundraisers, as well as organising events for the girls, particularly before they join eg bbq/bowling. Parental expertise highly welcomed. 'We currently have two architects helping us, as well as financial and legal support, just to name a few – we're very lucky,' says the head.

Alumni include Amal Alamuddin, international human rights barrister (married to George Clooney); Olympian, Clare Cunningham; television presenter Fern Britton; actress Carey Mulligan; editor Lisa Markwell; and Lucy Winkett, canon at St Paul's Cathedral (first female).

Entrance: Highly selective, with entry dependent on success at 11 plus, administered by a conglomeration of the county's grammar schools following collective achievement of academy status. As you might expect, there's no shortage of tutoring (often for years in advance) by hopeful year 6 parents for those 180 coveted places. The two largest feeder schools are Little Chalfont Primary School and Maltman's Green School in Gerrard's Cross, after which there's around 50 different feeders, with many girls joining in ones or twos from their junior schools, forcing them to integrate and make new friends quickly. Even the largest feeders only send between 10 and 15. After looked after girls, preference to those living in the catchment area, then those on free school meals, then siblings, then medical or social need.

The vast majority stay on to the sixth form ('the ones who leave either want to study different courses or the tight-knit community isn't for them,' sixth formers told us), with around 40 additional places open up in year 12, attracting girls to apply direct from other grammars, independents and the brightest from the upper schools. This is oversubscribed and girls are selected on GCSE results (minimum of two As and four Bs required, with As or Bs in chosen A level subjects).

Exit: Ninety-six per cent on to higher education – around three-quarters of them to Russell Group universities; 10 to Oxbridge in 2016. No one course is particularly popular, and only six or seven go to any one university. 'Our girls head off in every single direction under the sun – and we are very proud of that,' says the head.

Money matters: State maintained. Parents invited to make a voluntary contribution per year to the Challoner's Girls' Foundation to enable the school to fund a variety of initiatives such as pupil laptops.

Remarks: Full of bright-eyed go-getters who give their private school peers a real run for their parents' money. The Challoner's brand continues to live up to expectations for parents lucky enough to have both 11 plus results and the moveable feast of distance in their favour, although those who have been pushed through the 11 plus may face a tough challenge. An outward-looking school that supports and inspires, stretches and challenges, and frees up bright minds.

Dragon School

Bardwell Road, Oxford, Oxfordshire OX2 6SS

Pupils: 621: 378 boys, 243 girls; 238 boarders • Ages: 4–13 (boarding from 8)

Fees: Day £11,250 – £19,860; Boarding £28,590 pa

Tel: 01865 315405
Email: admissions@dragonschool.org
Website: www.dragonschool.org

Headmaster: Since 2002, Mr John Baugh (50s), BEd. Born in Uganda, educated at Aldenham School and St Luke's, Exeter. Previously head at Solefield School, Sevenoaks and Edge Grove, Hertfordshire. Believes in breadth of education and being child-centric – the relationship between staff and pupils is paramount. Teaches RS occasionally, observes each and every teacher once a year in the classroom and would not appoint a member of staff who was not willing to adapt to the needs of the child. His mantra to the children is 'be kind, be kind, be kind'. 'This is a school that never stops,' he says, 'it hums like an ocean liner'. Parents comment that he plays a straight bat and is good for PR.

Married to Wendy who teaches at the school and has two grown-up daughters, one of whom also teaches at the school – 'not appointed by me,' he is quick to point out. Says the school is his passion but enjoys escaping to his house in France in the holidays. A former sportsman, he once played for Exeter City, and continues to enjoy sports, especially cycling.

Retiring in July 2017. His successor will be Mr Crispin Hyde-Dunn MA (Oxon) PGCE MA(Ed) NPQH (30s), currently head of Abingdon Prep. Read history at Oxford. Previously deputy head of King's College School, Cambridge; was head of history at New College School in Oxford. He lives with his wife, Lucy, a medical research fellow at Oxford, in the school house just down the road.

Entrance: Register early – as early as you like post-conception. The school is full and there are waiting lists at all stages but head is keen not to put off potential pupils as spaces can occur at any time. Backed up by parents who confirm places appear all the time despite horror stories to the contrary. Potentially easier to get in as a boarder but it depends on the year group. Non-selective entry although the school does assess maths and English to check that a child will be able to cope. Five 100 per cent bursaries at year 4 for five years – means-tested and not based on academic merit – head maintains they 'start with need', but the school has to be sure the family is able and willing to commit to the Dragon way of life – Saturday morning school, extracurricular commitments etc. Scholarships up to 50 per cent fees based on academic merit and non-means-tested. Weathering current economic climate.

Exit: Frequent destinations include Abingdon School, Cheltenham Ladies' College, Eton College, Harrow School, Magdalen College School, Marlborough College, Radley College, Rugby School, Stowe School, St Edward's School, Wellington College, Winchester College and Wycombe Abbey. No favourite school, but 'we have a strong working relationship with St Edward's', as the two schools have similar ethos and are co-ed day and boarding (13 places in 2016). Pupils are not prepped for pre-test at 11 or entrance exams at 11 – no hothousing for local academic day schools. Head would not want a child to get into a school on the basis of excessive prepping. Deputy agrees that schools take note of the Dragon's reports and trusts their judgement but this isn't a school whose priority is to get children into the most academic local seniors. Bucket-loads of scholarships won – 35 to 40 per year (40+ in 2016). Famous Old Dragons include Sir John Betjeman, Leonard Cheshire VC, John Mortimer, Antonia Fraser, Alain de Botton, Rageh Omaar, Hugh Laurie and Tim Henman to name but a few.

Remarks: The Dragon, so named after an early school football team called 'dragons', is as sought-after as ever. Originally founded as the Oxford Preparatory School by a group of dons who wanted a progressive, liberal school for their sons where learning would be fun. Once avant-garde, education and society have caught up with these principles so that today the Dragon can only aspire to unconventionality. It has resisted formality and retains the ethos of ordered disorderliness – a charmingly unpretentious, relaxed atmosphere.The head confesses they are relaxed about petty issues – untucked shirts, scruffy uniform and clutter – while concentrating on the things that matter, such as learning. He likens the school to an upturned swan – feet paddling busily on the surface whilst the underlying systems of the school are serene and quiet. Unconventionality, or 'colouring outside the lines', has always been and still is encouraged, although head admits it is 'a balancing act' between risk-taking in schoolwork, striving for imagination and curiosity on one side, and discipline and toeing the line on the other. The Dragon aims for and encourages both.

Broad curriculum with a huge extracurricular programme including languages such as Mandarin, Japanese, Arabic and bilingual French as well as 'toast and translation' (a Latin club), music and drama etc. Most subjects are setted with scholarship classes at the top of the ability range. Learning support needs are screened in year 2 or on intake and help is available at extra cost. Dedicated learning support unit with five full- and three part-time members of staff who advise and update colleagues and draw up IEPs. Additional groups provided at no extra cost for handwriting, reading comprehension and social skills.

Breadth is key at the Dragon with excellence across the board – outstanding sport with fantastic facilities and accolades too numerous to mention. Non-sporty children can find refuge in music – equally successful and receiving high praise from parents. Over two-thirds of pupils take individual music lessons. Fantastic art work in light airy art rooms and space in the Forum for the annual art exhibition – check out the school magazine – worthy of any secondary school. Facilities in general match those at many senior schools with science labs, impressive library (look out for dragons etched on the glass fronted mezzanine), 25m swimming pool and playing fields stretching down to the river and boat house. A mini-campus with happy free-range children roaming around, unrestricted by petty rules and health and safety, having a jolly time; play by the river still possible as long as a child can swim two lengths of the pool fully clothed. Traditions such as this survive along with others – female teachers are called Ma, Bun Break at mid-morning and tea in the afternoon. The blue cords of yesteryear have stood the test of time – shorts in summer, longs in winter plus polo shirt and jumper; for girls, a kilt and bright yellow shirt, summer plaid dresses.

The Dragon is large (640) plus pre-prep Lynams, a mile or so up the road. Boys outnumber girls two to one. Some grumbles about middle of the road children lost in the masses and unable to find a niche if not sporty or musical. Head says that the children are separated into smaller units within the school so that they operate within age-related spheres at any one time without being overwhelmed. Good pastoral care – children are discussed weekly and communication is paramount. The school takes its privileges with responsibility and is committed to raising money for charity through entrepreneurship which starts with the concept of the 'little society' and the teaching of philanthropy to children, and extends to ventures such as the locally renowned Dragon Sale which raises tens of thousands of pounds. School is lead sponsor of a new multi-academy trust which includes three Blackbird Leys primary schools, The primaries can use the school's science, art, music and sporting facilities, while Dragon teaching staff are developing initiatives within the new academies. The Café Dragón brand of ethically-sourced coffee is sold at school events.

Boarding houses, separated by sex and age, run by married couples with a homely atmosphere and individuality. Bun breaks and tea in the houses with supper in the dining hall. Children can pop in and out of their house during the day. Day pupils often invited back. Full boarding means that the boarders are 'the heartbeat of the school', says the head. Weekends are packed with activities and many day pupils opt to board – one boarder walked from his boarding house past his family home every day. Day pupils easily fielded until 6pm, playing with boarders or participating in the huge number of extracurricular activities.

Once established for dons, they have largely been priced out of the market (in line with all independent schools, points out head). Lots of London money and business parents buying up north Oxford but professions also in evidence – many medics, lawyers, as well as a few academics (wealthy ones or few children). Lots of OD children. The Dragon remains the choice for the social elite of Oxford – if you want to be invited to the smartest dinner parties, this is your school. Head says there is still plenty of mix and parents agree that everyone can find their level and this is not necessarily a school full of nannies in the playground. Boarders local and international, with no particular country in predominance. Currently 30 pupils have EAL lessons.

The Dragon is still the prep school in Oxford, in sound heart as ever, chosen by parents for breadth of education, good old-fashioned freedom and encouraging a 'can do' attitude. Lifelong friends and contacts start here.

Dulwich Preparatory School Cranbrook

Coursehorn, Cranbrook, Kent TN17 3NP

Pupils: 540; 100 flexi boarders • Ages: 3–13 (boarding from 9)

Fees: Day £10,365 – £16,605 pa; Boarding £42.50 per night

Tel: 01580 712179
Email: registrar@dcpskent.org
Website: www.dcpskent.org

Headmaster: Since 2010, Mr Paul David BEd (40s). Married, with two children at the school. Grew up in Cornwall and read maths and education at St Luke's, Exeter University, where he played rugby. Started his career at the City of London Freemen's School, where he taught maths and games, was head of cricket and became a housemaster aged 28. Moved on to Colet Court, where he spent four years as deputy head and taught rugby across all ages and maths to the senior boys at St Paul's School. He then spent eight years as headmaster of Eaton Square School, a mixed ability London prep.

Energetic and dapper, and requires his surroundings to be dapper too – everywhere is immaculate with not a weed or piece of litter in sight (pounces on any he spots). Spiders with any sense of self-preservation have long since picked up their webs and gone elsewhere. Lots of fresh paint on the walls and vases of flowers all over the place. A very visible presence around the school, attends assemblies at Nash House and Little Stream each week and teaches maths and games in Upper School.

Came into the school after a period of disorganisation had rather unsettled parents. Tightened everything up from manners and pastoral care to redesigning the uniform. Each class now has a weekly greeter who will welcome any visitors and engage them in conversation – head very keen that children should know how to talk to adults and look them in the eye. Parents delighted, teachers too, as far as we can judge (they clearly were made to feel part of the process). Children seem at ease with him. This editor was struck, above all, by how this big, beautiful but soulless school had at long last a feeling of character and style about it.

Not everybody's cup of tea – the Guide and Mr David never hit it off in his previous incarnation – but appears perfectly suited to Dulwich Prep, and vice versa.

Entrance: Priority for siblings, but otherwise on a first come, first served basis. Non-competitive assessment tests from age 7+ – very rare for a child to fail but school doesn't want to take someone who can't cope. Intakes in nursery, reception, years 3 and 5 (and in between, if space). Another intake in year 7, when some children leave for the grammar schools and others come from local primary schools to prepare for Cranbrook entrance at 13+.

Exit: The raison d'être for many for going to Dulwich Prep is to get into Cranbrook at 13, and about half do just that. Fifteen per cent leave for the grammars at 11 – the school takes a positive attitude and is happy to help, but this is not grammar school country (the good ones are quite distant). Otherwise the most popular schools are Tonbridge, Benenden, Sutton Valence, Sevenoaks and Bethany, with a few going further afield to, eg, Charterhouse, Bedales and Winchester. Good selection of academic, art, music, sports and drama scholarships, particularly to Sutton Valance.

Remarks: Established as a war evacuation camp for Dulwich College Preparatory School (now Dulwich Prep London) in the orchard of the then headmaster's father-in-law's land at Coursehorn, and allowed to survive as an independent, unconnected entity when the war was over. Set in 50 acres of grounds, it has a campus-like feel.

The school is divided into three self-contained sections: Nash House (3-5 year olds), Little Stream (5-9 year olds) and Upper School (9-13 year olds). Children from the age of 6 are split into four Tribes: Chippeways, Deerfeet, Mohicans and Ojibwas – lots of inter-tribe competitions and activities.

Nash House and Little Stream (both recently rebuilt; all classrooms opening onto the garden and outdoor retractable roof – light and airy with lots of space) are set away from the main school in interconnecting buildings. Lots of computers and interactive stuff – Mr David a fan, but school has been well stocked for years. Own swimming pool. Superb library, IT and facilities generally in Upper School.

Structured but relaxed atmosphere in Little Stream with lots of theme days. Children are awarded brightly coloured ribbons for good work. Great emphasis on building children's social confidence and they are encouraged to stand up in front of an audience on a regular basis, whether it be relating their news in assembly, taking part in form plays or participating in class 'showing times'. Structured mornings and child initiated afternoons; children spend as much time as possible outside. Outings, talks and workshop days a major part of the curriculum, particularly in history and geography. Specialist teachers for PE, French, science (taught in a lab) and music.

Gets more serious in upper school. Children setted (where possible) for academic subjects, apart from a separate scholarship form in the final year. Average class size 18, maximum 20. Latin for all from year 6 and about 50 per cent take it at common entrance. Authors visit every term, also library competitions and twice yearly book fairs. Educational outings a major feature of school life.

Learning support for maths and English offered as part of the package – either in class, withdrawn in small groups or one-to-one, or as instruction for parents in how to help at home. 'Special needs department on hand to give extra help where necessary.' What this all amounts to is unstinting and unshaming help for (about 20 per cent of) children to get into Cranbrook etc.

Music strong – fab Little Stream music suite decorated with semiquavers; all learn the recorder from year 2 (we feel a wave of sympathy for tortured parents whenever we read this, but violins would be worse) and can learn other instruments from year 3. All children can read music by the time they leave Little Stream; Upper School has a music director and three full-time music specialists. All children have two or three class music lessons a week, and almost all learn an instrument with one of the 19 peripatetic teachers. Lots of extracurricular groups including an orchestra, two wind bands, six choirs, a jazz band, pop groups plus a number of smaller chamber groups. Music tours in Italy, Germany, Holland, Paris and Austria.

Separate Stream House art room with an artist in residence – very creative team – with children's artwork everywhere (ditto Upper School). Art clubs after school, plus extra tuition for those taking art scholarships (usually wins a couple of these each year). When we visited the children were designing beautiful play houses which were going to be made up in India (no crumbling shelves for those parents). Art room open every lunchtime – jewellery to Scalextric model making. Jewellery making so popular that an evening class was laid on for the parents.

Upper School drama timetabled, with clubs and ESB exams for the enthusiasts. Wonderful John Leakey Hall.

Good sports facilities – well-equipped sports hall for upper school. Large outdoor swimming pool, tennis courts/all weather hockey pitches, eight-lane athletics track etc. Strong tradition of cross-country running for boys and girls. All the usual sports with teams in most: as many children as possible are included – up to four teams per year group and the school tries to have regular inter-school or 'tribe' fixtures. Opportunities to have trials and play for Kent teams.

Parent friendly. Nursery is very flexible and children can build up attendance sessions during the year. Parents welcome at any time to come in and see how their children are learning, and in particular to the Friday morning assembly, when the headmaster celebrates children's achievements and offers coffee afterwards. Even homework clubs and drop in clinics for parents.

Very strong pastoral care and children encouraged to be aware of each others' feelings and friendships issues. They can enter their own and each other's acts of kindness on the good deeds chart. Older pupils choose a member of staff to keep an eye on their academic progress and general well-being. No prefects or head boy or girl, but every year 8 pupil is a 'senior' with a specific area of responsibility.

Food praised by all with some quite adventurous choices – pigeon pie, monkfish wrapped in prosciutto – and proper puddings still on the menu. Children encouraged to try new foods – not British, you may feel.

Flexi boarding popular, with boys at The Lodge and girls at The Manor. School very accommodating (when they have room) if parents need to go away for a few days or on holiday. School day for boarders ends at the same time as for day children, and the boarding houses are very much 'homes from home'.

Most children live within about 15 miles of the school. No Saturday school, but optional Saturday morning academic clinics three or four mornings each term for pupils in year 8 preparing for exams. Lots of parents new to independent education, but great loyalty amongst old boys and girls (Old Coursehornians, after the original house on the site) and many children in the school are second or third generation.

Big. Superb facilities. Produces confident children who are happy and do well, and particularly suits those who are up front, determined and capable – quite a competitive environment. School has high expectations of everyone, but gives them a huge breadth of opportunity to succeed.

Eagle House School

Linked with Wellington College

Sandhurst, Berkshire GU47 8PH

Pupils: 390; 10 full, 40 weekly, 50 flexi boarders • Ages: 3–13 (boarding from year 3) • C of E

Fees: Day £10,905 – £17,070; Boarding £22,920 pa

Tel: 01344 772134
Email: info@eaglehouseschool.com
Website: www.eaglehouseschool.com

Headmaster: Since 2006, Mr Andrew Barnard BA (40s). Educated at Christ's Hospital, thence to Sheffield for a degree in archaeology (claims he 'still gets excited by a pile of earth'). 'Dabbled' in the restaurant business but was diverted to a PGCE via a stint helping out in various prep schools. Started at Eagle House as head of history and English teacher, then housemaster and head of English and drama at Heath Mount School, deputy head at Winchester House and then back to Eagle House as head. He loves poetry, especially the Liverpool poets. Favourite author? Julian Barnes. Married to Sarah, who comes from a dynasty of teachers – no doubt it is from them that she has learned to embody grace under pressure: serving lunch to the nursery children, shepherding excited girls as they mass to play a rounders match against her old school, teaching French and EAL, taking care of front of house. They have three children, all at Wellington.

The Barnards have steered Eagle House successfully though some big changes. Their initial challenge was the move to co-ed and they admit that increasing the number of girls at the top end was, initially, 'hard to crack'. Intake is now 'robust' at about 40 per cent, with the few who leave at age 11 replaced and then some by girls joining for the last two years. Next item on the list? Building. The Golden Eagle Centre, a splendid sport and performing arts centre, opened in 2013 and there's yet more construction under way: new homes for DT and art, another science lab and a food tech room.

Current rather daunting project is bidding to run a new primary academy, a younger sibling to Wellington's. Why, we wondered, does Mr Barnard want to take this on? He says he has, 'already learnt from the process', which has, 'opened his eyes'. The mutual benefits he cites are professional development for staff and 'enrichment of diversity' for pupils at both establishments. There's a gleam in his eye when he talks of these plans; he recently returned to his alma mater, Christ's Hospital, and this has further strengthened his faith in the positive impact of bridging social and educational divides.

Living on site means the boundaries between home and work are pretty porous though the Barnards say that they and their children love every minute. This notwithstanding, sanctuary is a house in the Loire and all things French.

Entrance: Parents are advised to visit and register 12 months before their child is due to start. Pre-prep: trial day and usually automatic progression to prep. Prep: trial day, copies of reports and a reference from current head. Prep is relatively non-selective but pupils are 'expected to be able to cope with the school's academic course'. Year 7 entrants are tested in English, maths and reasoning.

Exit: Up to 80 per cent to Wellington – this is, after all, part of the deal. Bradfield scoops up most of the rest; singles to eg Marlborough, Cranleigh, Millfield.

Remarks: Set in woods and heathland between Crowthorne and Sandhurst, Eagle House was founded in Hammersmith in 1820 and has been on its current 30-acre site since 1886. Owned by near neighbour Wellington College (the two schools share a boundary) and head says that these days, 'links are much better defined'. Being part of 'brand Wellington' includes teaching exchanges (each member of Eagle House staff is twinned with one from Wellington) as well as a definite trickle down (or up) of innovative approaches to education. For the past two years staff have attended life coaching courses at Wellington, there is a life skills club for prep pupils and now parents are snapping up taster sessions. We were particularly struck by how teachers of all ages were fired up by new ideas, welcoming change and educational debate – Eagle House clearly no place for moss gatherers.

Lessons are an hour long and those we saw were well-paced and active, pupils using hands as well as heads. Although Eagle House is not an official forest school, increasing use is being made of the grounds with lessons from science to English taking place outside. History comes to life in the Tudor House, a thatched replica where children dress up and learn about the past through workshops and activity days. Creativity is boosted by evening writing workshops and there are plans for another school literary festival after the success of the first one. Setting from year 3 in English and maths, and then for French and Latin in year 6. Latin for all from year 5, Greek for scholars. Four SEN staff support pupils individually with dyslexia, dyspraxia, mild ADHD (extra charge). EAL also offered.

We hear that as pressure to gain coveted places at Wellington builds a few parents are paying for extra tuition in years 5 and 6 to prepare for pre-testing in year 7, though when exactly their children fit this in is unclear. Not a reflection on the prep's teaching, rather more indicative of the holy grail a Wellington education has become. School is alert to this, saying that a few parents have unrealistic expectations, wanting their children to be 'brilliant at everything'. Some grumbles that the scholarship class (years 7 and 8) is 'divisive', citing detrimental effects on friendships. Scholarship exams are in February and March so the children in this class are 'off on trips' while the rest are studying for CE until June.

Eagle House differs with Wellington on one thing at least: books. The clean lines of big brother's splendid new library may not be spoilt by shelves and their dusty contents but for now at least, eaglets are still encouraged to curl up on squashy sofas with a good book. 'Over my dead body' were the young librarian's words when we asked if there were plans to defect to e-readers. Long may she reign.

In keeping with the school's 'learning for life' ethos, the Golden Eagle programme of activities introduces pupils to a rich mix of experiences intended to challenge and develop interests. Clubs such as golf, orienteering and Scalextrics run in the extended lunch break – a good example of making a virtue out of a necessity since limited size of the otherwise charming wood-panelled dining room means that it takes two hours to feed everyone. A conservatory-style extension is on head's list but the courtyard memorial garden will have to relocate. Years 3 and 4 can do optional Saturday morning activities and older children also have timetabled Golden Eagle session once a week.

The Eagle House journey starts, naturally enough, in The Nest. Here in the nursery little ones (many of whom have older siblings in the prep) begin to learn through play. They are introduced to the big school and its curriculum via weekly sessions of swimming dance, music and IT. Delightful inside and outside spaces full of tempting toys, sand and water.

Pre-prep pupils gradually begin to explore the subjects that they will be taught once they move up, with specialist teachers for French, music, art and drama. Head of the pre-prep wants her pupils to have a 'happy start to school life, develop confidence and a love of learning' – we thought the kinaesthetic approach to numbers via 'maths stories' looked like a great idea. Literacy is taught using Read Write Inc phonics and the pre-prep is a model school for this scheme. No male class teachers, but music and football are taught by chaps borrowed from the prep. Dance is a popular activity and we enjoyed watching 5-year-olds' imaginative evocations of tarantulas – all part of the term's rain forest topic. Apparently playing medieval games in the Tudor house and visits from a 'real, live knight' are highlights.

A trio of energetic eaglets treated us to an access all areas tour. The dorms are on the first floor of the original mock Tudor house, rooms have large windows and high ceilings. The boys' (blue) rooms were predictably unadorned but the girls' (pink) rooms were as homely and sparkly as anyone could wish. Isn't this blue/pink cliché rather at odds with the progressive educational ethos of brand Wellington, we wondered? The eaglets told us gleefully that the showers and changing rooms in the new sports centre were similarly gendered, right down to the colour of the soap. Bathrooms, corridors and common room are clean and fresh, if towards the make do and mend end of the homely spectrum. The 15 or so pupils in over the weekend (or rather Saturday evening to Sunday evening) amount to, as Mrs Barnard pointed out, a 'minibus full'. Each member of staff does a Sunday stint so we imagine that minibus must go on a very interesting range of trips.

According to our guides, hockey and football are the main sports and nearby Cranleigh is the arch rival. The trophy cabinets show that boys do well at county level hockey and cricket but it's the girls' silverware that fills the shelves. Most recently the under 13s were national champions in hockey and the under 12s in netball. Such success is certainly celebrated but the Eagle House philosophy is not 'win at all costs' and the children we spoke to got huge enjoyment from their daily sport – whatever the result. Facilities are pretty good, with standard issue multi-purpose gym and an indoor swimming pool. Outside there's Astroturf and all-weather pitches for hockey, netball and tennis, though boys told us they would like separate cricket and athletic fields. There's a lot of beautiful green space around the school but much of it belongs to venerable trees bearing preservation orders so, in the absence of a hurricane, cricketers and athletes will be sharing for many summers to come.

Music department resides in a deceptively spacious Portakabin though once inside listening to a superb impromptu performance of a Schumann Polonaise we wouldn't have cared if we were in a coal bunker. 'Brilliant' was the adjective most often used by parents to describe music at the school. Trial lessons and plenty of opportunities to develop talents great and small; lunchtime concerts allow new players to have their first experience of performing in a 'non-judgemental' environment. As we admired the beautifully decorated small organ in the charming chapel, choirmaster told us that organ lessons were just being established.

School may not have its own theatre (major productions are staged in Bracknell) but drama is big here. In the new performing arts studio we saw year 3 and 4 pupils belting out a song for their forthcoming show, not a single reluctant soul mouthing the words. On the walls of the foyer are larger than life photo canvases of past theatrical triumphs. So much for the stars, what about the tremblers in the wings? Everyone gets a chance to shine, school said; parents, while praising the 'wonderful' productions, weren't quite so sure.

Art and DT departments may be eagerly anticipating move to their new premises but no sign of a reduction in creativity. In art pupils were busy learning the patient craft of stop motion animation using 'indestructible' iPads and in DT they were dreaming up designs for boats. Work of a very high standard was on display everywhere.

Pastoral care generally praised and children we spoke to had a clear understanding of anti-bullying policies and what to do if they had a problem. Every child now has their own tutor from year 5 (prior to this form teachers are first point of contact) and the new system is intended to be more 'open and flexible', involving all members of staff in pastoral roles.

Most pupils are from 15-20 mile radius but increasing numbers from London. Handful from abroad, no dominant country. Small contingent of Spanish children come for a year or two – it's not an organised thing, more 'word of mouth', according to the head. Parents, the usual Thames valley mix of management and high-tech industry professionals, like the boarding ethos even if their children are day pupils. We're not surprised, pupils can stay until 6pm and by then prep has usually been done (older children may have to finish theirs at home). For most though it's the Wellington connection that makes this a first choice school and leavers' destinations over the last few years bear this out. Several parents told us they thought the school had changed, describing it as much more 'under Wellington's thumb'. However another said, 'We initially chose Eagle House because of its links with Wellington but now realise that's only one aspect. It's a great start, wherever your child goes on to'.

Eagle House is a happy, creative school. The atmosphere is eager and unstuffy – honouring the best of prep school tradition; nimbly assimilating 21st century educational thinking. Eaglets headed for Wellington and other eyries will find this a great place to learn to fly.

Eastbourne College

Old Wish Road, Eastbourne, East Sussex BN21 4JX

Pupils: 638; 50 per cent full boarders • Ages: 13–18 • Sixth form: 282 • C of E

Fees: Day £21,390 – £21,750; Boarding £32,625 – £33,000 pa

Tel: 01323 452323
Email: admissions@eastbourne-college.co.uk
Website: www.eastbourne-college.co.uk

Head: Since September 2016, Thomas Lawson (40s), previously deputy head at Christ's Hospital. PPE degree from Oxford; taught economics and humanities at Winchester for 15 years, where he was also a housemaster, and under master for two years. His wife, Jessica, is also a teacher, and they have two young children.

Academic matters: Everyone starts with a wide sweep of subjects, tasting everything until they settle down to GCSE choices; can take a selection of French, German, Spanish, Latin and Greek. Parents say not the place for the brightest of the bright but meets the needs of the very smart ones (and stretches – one ex-London prep pupil went up a set in most subjects after first year) while the value added in the classroom and out is excellent – as the school says, 'what really counts is how you work with people'. Lovely large science labs, six ICT suites, fibre optic network, three theatres, library with silent, chatty and headphone screen-watching areas – also an amazing three floor design technology centre.

Four assistant heads, one dedicated solely to the curriculum, mean that each pupil can have a bespoke timetable according to their choices. Mind boggling yet liberating, since 'you only get children achieving their best if they are doing what they want to do'. And they do – whether sciences and languages or textiles, woodwork and product design: in 2016, 59 per cent of GCSE grades were A*/A. School day from 8am to 8pm means that parents have their day children home with no homework when they finally arrive – there is a 6pm bus for those who have nailed all their commitments for the day and commute from further afield (Rye or Tunbridge Wells). Houseparents and the co-curricular assistant head juggling sports, clubs and preps help synchronise multi-talented kids and single-minded staff and ensure 'whatever happens, the kids don't feel the pressure'.

Not a huge breadth of A level subjects – no psychology, sociology, politics. If demand is timely then senior management team will make it happen – RS has become an examination subject with intelligent wide-ranging debate. Maths, science and humanities most popular; EPQ and scholarship/leadership courses now offered. In 2016, 44 per cent A*/A grades overall.

Entire jigsaw is monitored with the slick electronic report card which culminates in the tutor sitting down with the pupil and focusing on the past, present and what needs to be done. Input far more supportive than reflective as the houseparent adds their comments before a pdf report is emailed home at least twice a term. Parents are relieved by challenge grades rather than predictive ones (much more motivational). Continuous opportunities for parent or staff to monitor and add input when the issues arise and overseas parents particularly enjoy this access (10 per cent of pupil body). Ramps up staff's accountability to parents and Duke of Edinburgh, Oxbridge or scholar reports can be added for those interested. This transparent system was created by a full-time software developer, who continues to mine the data and present it to the staff via web-based platform, winding in pastoral incidents and academic progress, enabling a holistic view of the pupil when considering discipline or going up or down a set. Parents appreciate standardised teaching that makes it easy for a pupil to move between sets even mid-term.

Informative 'white book' provides a structure that the new pupils follow, empowering them to such an effect that a parent recently just sat back and observed as the parents' evening went on between the pupil and their tutor. School aims to include all SEN pupils where possible, but specific provision for mild dyslexia, G&T and EAL. One full-time and one busy part-time teacher. All children are screened on entry. Individual SEN lessons are charged for. No separate cost for the G&T provision, however, which is department specific.

Games, options, the arts: Activities and sport sandwiched between morning and afternoon of classroom learning suits the youngest ones especially. Myriad teams so that 95 per cent of the pupils take their turn to win or lose together against another school, and with elite talent emerging, there are Olympic or international professionals coaching in tennis, hockey, netball, rugby and cricket; major sports tours for these too. The manicured rugby pitch dominates the front of the school but the main sports fields are a five minute drive away – the girls in particular enjoy the walk for the warm up and catch up it provides. The range of sports currently on offer stretches from basketball to equestrian events (a bit more parental input) and there's zumba classes if team sport really doesn't appeal, or space to chat and listen to music. All full-time sports staff teach academic subjects and are tutors as well, meaning that badminton, table tennis and jujitsu have emerged from clubs to potential fixtures by encouraging children's initiatives.

Development (to be completed 2017, one and a half acres in the centre of the site) will revolutionise the on site facilities, with a small hiatus for swimmers while they splash in other local facilities. This sharing of resources and experiences with the wider Eastbourne community is a pattern that is demonstrated by the architecture of the Birley Centre (public entrance on Carlisle Road) and the school values. The school's creative arts centre (next to the Towner Art Gallery and Congress Theatre) is a part of the town's artistic centre, with musicians from the school busking to raise money for St Wilfred's Hospice, professional artists coming in to run masterclasses in creative barter for the foyer exhibition space and a resident from the Rambert Dance company running courses for local state and private schools and the rugby team. Pupils are involved in all of these initiatives, as well as working with adults with learning needs and teaching pensioners to surf the internet.

Interlocking array of different sized lockers and muted practice rooms is testament to the orchestral music tuition (three choirs, a concert band and two orchestras) while Battle of the Bands is a highlight of the musical year, with a recording studio enabling music technology as an A level option. The art studios are light and bright with examples of excellent student work dotted around the school (routinely 100 per cent A*/A at A level and over 92 per cent at GCSE), plenty of Macs for digital editing and two kilns for firing experimentally glazed ceramics – all anchored by visits from artists making a living in the outside world. Paths to the commercial acting world also well trodden, a whole school production annually, while all year 9 put on a play in their first term and house concerts are really enjoyed – sometimes end up on YouTube.

Boarding: Separate day and boarding houses, so no day pupils feel they miss out on dorm time horsing about, and 6pm and 8pm buses give them the chance to 'organise their work, co-curricular activities and family life most effectively for them and their families'. All pupils are registered in the common room of their house, assemblies, announcements here too; good facilities, each with their own garden; junior boarders share three to five to a dorm, reducing up to the sixth form, where they have large single rooms – the more modern girls' ones with en suite bathrooms. Real retreats, managed by the houseparents and matrons, with touches that appeal, whether a pupil-run tuck shop with entrepreneurial offers or a mirrored dance studio, girls plaiting each other's hair and boys kicking about on floodlit Astroturf. New development promises more open social space for boys and girls to mix (now mostly the atmospheric cloisters), with no dark corners and the staff common room next door. Majority of sixth form don't have boy or girlfriends at school; boarders get town leave on Saturday night; they hang out with each other in the holidays too. Younger boarders explore restaurants in Eastbourne too and petition their parents to come and take them (and all their friends) out for lunch.

Background and atmosphere: Founded in 1867 with the seventh Duke of Devonshire allotting 12 acres to the new enterprise, the current Duke is president of the Eastbourne College council along with influential Eastbourne residents. Main school is an imposing red-brick building, amid an aesthetically pleasing mix of others, old and sympathetically new and ensconced

E

in the heart of Eastbourne, with five-storey Victorian houses, retirement homes and boarding and day houses all cheek by jowl. Parents see three main communities in this part of Eastbourne, the old people, the young people and those who serve those two communities – many staff live on site or very near; 'kids walk around old people with respect and the old people are safe in the knowledge they won't be mugged!'

Close to the railway and next to Devonshire Park, home to the pre-Wimbledon men's and ladies' tennis tournament; constant traffic of hearty pupils hurrying to lessons; friendly, happy and confident teenagers, who all belong to a single sex day or boarding house. This is their home from home, but they can invite others to come and knock about between preps. In the lower years this means mostly single sex hanging out when not in lessons or activities (whether on comfy sofas or around a pool table). Everyone eats as a school (new dining hall on the horizon); good food with an excellent range of choices.

New sixth formers are welcomed, those from local state schools make new friends and keep their old ones too, broadening the sixth form across all backgrounds and outside the college. Some drive themselves in from more rural homes, others keep younger ones company on the train commute. Chapel every Sunday for boarders and visitors, otherwise one weekly service – with alternative arrangements possible for other faiths – a spiritual basis but nowadays more about a collective act, with thoughts about the wider community.

Pastoral care, well-being and discipline: Very, very strong indeed, with excellent and insightful communication; the first thing all happy parents say is 'they really know our kids'. Probably why it is so successful at reaching all abilities and improving the confidence of many. Housemasters and housemistresses are first point of contact, for day pupil parents on drop off or pick up, for those further afield on email and phone. Often issues have a plan to sort or are sorted before a parent even learns about them, within a school day. 'Families' in girls' houses, with a mother in the sixth form, a cousin in year 10 and peer listeners. Support in boys' houses is organised less metaphorically but the same relationships develop – older ones sit in on prep; not a chore to help with studies, this opens conduit for buddy support and cross-year friendships. A recent charity bike-a-thon had girls and tutors staying up and eating pizza and supporting the 24 hours of pedalling.

We heard concrete examples of issues dealt with empathetically, tactfully and effectively, whether they stemmed from a staff or a pupil incident, with the children's welfare held at the centre. House and school prefects are in the upper sixth; head says, 'not a position for privilege but for service'. Drinking and drugs stamped on hard (although supportive testing if drug use happens out of term), deputy and assistant head of pastoral are fully aware of the range of misdemeanours, from shaving a head, roughing up playing football, through to sexting – and the electronic system enables rapid staff communication on spotting patterns or a change of routine.

Pupils and parents: Varied social mix, with children that are spread across all four quartiles. On one side you have the Sussex Downs and the rolling Sussex countryside, the other side the deep blue sea. Fifty-fifty day to (no flexible or weekly) boarding, farming families who have been coming for generations, more recent locals who also have horses, London boarders and the international contingent (10 per cent) of Chinese, German, Russian, Italian, Spanish and Nigerian. Only 90 minutes by train from London; boarders have exeats every three weeks but Saturday school does cut the weekend short. Parents don't mix much away from the touchline or horse events, unless they know each other from prep schools, although more social functions are being organised.

Entrance: Overseas pupils are accepted provided their level of English is proficient. Candidates for year 9 entry sit CE or the college's scholarship papers. The hurdle for sixth form is B grades or better at GCSE. About 35 pupils enter for sixth form from surrounding state or private schools.

Exit: Very small number leave post-GCSE (15 per cent or so). At 18, mainly to a mix of redbrick, Russell group and vocational colleges; seven to Oxbridge in 2016, and three medics; some 25 per cent take a gap year; Durham, Exeter, Leeds, Manchester, Newcastle and Nottingham popular over the last few years. Old Eastbournians come back to talk about being a pilot, farmer, doctor or graphic designer at the careers fair, just one of over 50 events organised by The Eastbournian Society for alumni, parents, staff and current pupils.

Money matters: Scholarships available for most subject areas (five to 20 per cent) and means-tested bursaries for up to 60 per cent of the fees. The registrar is very switched on, candid and efficient – his practical approach much appreciated by parents, especially if their financial circumstances change. Foundation director oversees the fundraising and bursary fund. He is aiming to build a pot by contributions from parents and staff to allow financial help to the struggling. All staff contribute the price of a pint per week to the fund. This equates to approx £250 a week and thus £15,000 a year. This philanthropic pint fund consequently translates to a) a full bursary for a fortunate and worthy pupil and b) a thirsty staffroom!

Remarks: A school for families who take joy in what their kids become rather than pride in what they've made of them. Bespoke timetables backed up by outstanding pastoral care make for happy and stimulated kids who work and play hard.

Edgbarrow School

Grant Road, Crowthorne, Berkshire RG45 7HZ

Pupils: 1,467 • Ages: 11–18 • Sixth form: 387

Tel: 01344 772658
Email: secretary@edgbarrowschool.co.uk
Website: www.edgbarrowschool.co.uk

Headteacher: Since 1999, Mr Robert (Bob) Elsey BA (50s), following 10 years at wildly successful Charters School, Ascot, as head of faculty, assistant head and deputy head. Trained as DT teacher (and still takes some classes), first post at Haydon School, Pinner where rapidly promoted to head of year before taking advisory role for Barnet education authority.

He's 'big hearted, community spirited, a true bloke who tries to do a lot because knows what it's like to be at the tough end,' says father. Even by Mr Elsey's own standards he's currently exceptionally busy, juggling headship here with turnround role at Brakenhale School – now coming to an end with appointment of Mr Elsey's number two as head there (fourth to move into top slot elsewhere).

Might bring slight reduction in working week (60 hours plus currently the norm for senior management). Will certainly bring relief to charming admin team trying to carve out space in diary – visitors have sense of ever-lengthening but patient queue forming behind them – though clearly adore working with him. 'Very inclusive – we all feel part of it and if it went wrong would have a huge effect on us.' 'Big man, big character,' thought a parent. 'Very able so can juggle – not hard for him to run two schools.'

Confidence reciprocated – he can zoom in and out (occasionally escaping through his office's back door), secure in knowledge that not much will go drastically wrong in his absence – though one mother felt some more disruptive pupils 'knew he wasn't there and pushed the boundaries,' during a prolonged spell at Brakenhale. 'When he was back it all fell back into place.' Style – officially dad-like (has four grown up children of his own). 'Won't tolerate inappropriate behaviour, or not being on time,' thought one parent. 'Children know not to mess with him but can go to him if there's an issue.' Mr Elsey agrees. 'I want to care for the children in same way as my own, so if they need a bit of a telling off, they get it, but if they need to be looked after and cared for and understood and listened to, they get it. They could get both of them in the same day, in the same moment.'

Hugely endearing. Scrawls pencilled notes directly onto office table, to slight consternation of colleagues – it's felt to send wrong message to children – but it's 'how I learn.' Has a becoming modesty – believes in keeping ego, like boys' shirts, well tucked in and doesn't really take to interviews (has been approached and turned down every other request – we're honoured).

While delighted when dead certs get their top A level grades, biggest satisfaction is seeing the outliers make it in life, 'someone who's not that confident but takes on double BTecs, get starred distinctions, was never going to university – that was always for other people to do – and now they're going, not in droves but in 10s and 20s.' Equally responsive to parental concerns and big on personal touch – parents who help out on regular painting and gardening days are individually thanked. 'Takes time and trouble to put pen to paper,' said parent.

Though there's much praise for his colleagues, parents are in no doubt that he's at heart of school's success. Fortunately, stresses that this is 'one and only headship' – as long as continues to enjoy it. Sees complacency as the enemy of success. 'You must always be striving a little bit because it's another set of children, it's their time, their opportunity – you can't live off the back of how good things were three years ago. The time to look back and think we did OK is when you stop.' With plenty he'd like to happen here (upping quality of teaching areas a priority) has no plans to seek out fresh challenges. There's plenty to sort out right here.

Academic matters: Plenty of top teachers (staff to pupil ratio is around one to 16, average class size of 21) to ensure that those capable of it get the grades. Impressive A level results with 39 per cent of grades at A*-A and 63 per cent A*-B in 2016. GCSEs also very respectable with 35 per cent of all grades at A*-A, and impressive 92 per cent of pupils achieving five A*-C passes including English and maths (including GCSE equivalent level 2 exams).

Pupils put in an intensive day to get there, with four one-hour lessons every morning – worth it for easier afternoons, reckoned pupils, just one lesson taking place after late lunch that starts at 1.30pm. 'Friends ask if we get hungry, but you get used to it,' said year 8 tour guide, who praised well-ordered lessons, manageable homework and sensible deadlines.

No subject laggards, with languages, geography and history all extolled, while maths, biggest subject at A level, is 'pushed', thought one parent – though in good way. 'Gave my child some extra lessons to bring her up (before GCSEs) and is now storming on.' RE, however, gets the most praise, with colourful lessons (discussion about avatars well under way on day of visit), enticing display cabinet stuffed with crucifixes and figures of Buddha and Durga and provocative quotes on walls '...of all the things which have been permitted, divorce is the most hated by Allah...'

Setting starts early, three weeks into year 7 for science, maths, English and languages ('lets you get to know your form first,' said year 8 pupil) but will take individual aspirations into account – optional Latin taught by Wellington College staff member (several send own children here) and we heard of one budding scientist with borderline grades given lots of support so could take triple rather than dual science at GCSE.

Much praise for attention to detail – pace noticeably quicker in top groups but, said one pupil, 'priority is to make sure we understand.' Out of lesson meetings encouraged if pupil needs help, rapid response to parent queries. 'Sometimes disagree with comments on homework reports. Teacher will email straight back to arrange meeting,' said father.

One parent wondered if chilled-out coasters sometimes get away with it, citing bright child guaranteed Cs and not particularly inclined to push for greater grade glory. Head points (literally) to pinboards lining wall-and-a-bit in office, filled with postcard-sized pictures and predicted grades of all year 11 pupils, who also get a copy. Goal is to move as many could-do-betters as possible along wall till hit five A*-Cs with English and maths or better section. Not all will manage it, but won't be for want of trying.

For the 80 plus SEN pupils (100 have EAL) there's progress department which caters for moderate learning needs including SpLD, BESD and language and communications difficulties. May be withdrawn from languages (bottom sets in any case will often take one rather than two), instead receiving literacy, numeracy or social support. School praised for speed in picking up undiagnosed needs and fighting for support, thought parent, even to extent of matching child and key SEN staff member. 'If don't feel the connection, will find you someone else.'

Little to complain of bar need to upgrade IT – currently not possible to access homework online and at least one parent's wish list priority – together with plea with more diplomatic names for sets. 'Not keen on calling them top and bottom group,' says parent. 'Even adults like to be told they're good at something, so why not choose colour or French fruit instead with no connotations?'

Games, options, the arts: Mr Elsey, who turned down Bristol Rovers FC contract for teaching career, beams with pride over sports success. Talented well catered for (several subject teachers are qualified coaches/referees), kind but determined staff also determined to ensure that those whose natural roosting spot is spectator side of the touchline don't miss out either. 'Daughter doesn't like games but is never left alone or pushed aside,' thought one mother. Masses to do after school, too, from trampolining to badminton.

Parents aware of living in shadow of Wellington College where 'if you're good, get into England and under 18s squads,' said one; Mr Elsey welcomes collaboration – both schools are part of local trust which funds deserving students – but clear that 'we're not in competition.' Mild – very mild – grumbles aside (one over academic support being timetabled during PE – now changed; other relating to difficulties for working parents with 4.00pm match timing) contentment is again the norm.

Similarly the case with music. Helps if brass is your thing, with touring swing band a star attraction, though numbers are currently down and cooler guitars attract more interest. 'Would be nice if had own group,' thought parent. Once approved by teacher, enthusiasts have open access to practice rooms. 'Incredible and brilliant – if are going to turn into good adults, need to be trusted,' said mother.

Bustling activity programme includes D of E – no limit on numbers (around 55 do bronze, 10 sixth formers working on gold) – language trips to Germany, France and Spain, though proposed US skiing trip for year 8 children cancelled – without fuss – when families told school that was a continent and financial commitment too far.

Background and atmosphere: Huge friendliness of the place is a hallmark: if there were any jobsworths, they've been weeded out, judging by knowledge of how the school works and alacrity with which we were put through to right person – and no automated switchboard, either. This is a school tangibly operated by real people for the benefit of real students – to extent of putting end-of-term lost property on hangers for easier identification and retrieval (worlds better than slightly sordid looking – and smelling – lucky dip boxes elsewhere). 'Even if reception is busy, they'll welcome you with a smile,' said mother.

Setting, just outside small village of Crowthorne, more unobtrusive than pupil numbers might suggest, many buildings – mostly low rise in compact group – as well as can be expected, all immaculately tidy (staff pick up stray bits of litter, forms take turns to carry out more extensive sweep).

Grounds extend to new, lovingly tended Astroturf (funding provided on condition that, like sports centre, is open to public out of school hours), two large fields – shortly to be drained and relevelled – bordered by woodland. Dog walkers are most frequently spotted wildlife, though deer and red kites have occasional walk/fly on roles (assertive seagulls, automatically reset to British Summer Time, form orderly rooftop queue at lunchtime). Low-key security balances protection and sense of independence. 'Mr Elsey says he doesn't want us to feel trapped,' said pupil.

Wonders done with limited resources: long, potentially dingy corridor transformed with artwork (picture of girl meditatively demolishing gingerbread man one of many attention grabbers), lines of lockers sprouting clutch of fanciful ceramics.

School's wish list inevitably huge – including makeover for wonky paved areas in year 7 pupils' break time area (all KS3 pupils have own space). Funding on the way to pay for new classrooms as pupil numbers increase. Attractive sixth form centre with vast atrium area shows what can be done – member of staff there 'conscious of how lucky I am compared with colleagues.' Focus for much study and limited loafing – 'if we see someone who's been sitting around doing nothing for ages, will remind them to get out books.' (They do, too – and it works).

Other top areas singled out by parents include canteen (meals served in hall used also for drama, assembly and exams) where, boon to working parents, can pre-order family evening meal for four (giant pizza a bargain £8), all boxed up ready to come home with child. Few complaints about menu offerings. One parent thought could ease up on the carbs but tour guides quick to explain that even the Slushies (bright blue) 'now made with much healthier ingredients...'

Pastoral care, well-being and discipline: Traditional-sounding sixth form organisation, with head boy and girls, five deputies and six captains for customary sport and performing arts to fundraising and debating. Also a tuck shop manager and two freshers reps. Total of 30 posts – with more to come as create subject ambassadors.

Bullying, virtual and otherwise, not felt to be huge issue – many parents unaware of any problems, those who were praised school's efforts to reduce incidence: running pupil talks, sending regular updates on new, potentially worrying apps. 'I probably get three emails a week,' said father. Families realistic about technology-related difficulties. 'Peer pressure very different from when we were at school – cyber-bullying did spoil child's enjoyment of school,' felt parent. Student support, well known as place to go for the sad or troubled, offers counselling, mentoring and, in one instance, special notebook for 'timid' pupil to record concerns.

Numerous chances to shine, not just academically but through SPEAK awards, which recognise sterling all-round qualities – the A stands for 'Above and beyond'. Correspondingly brisk sanctions policy, with failure to get homework diary signed or being late for lessons (there's latitude for new year 7s) resulting in warnings and detentions, Friday break the one to avoid, said one pupil, as 'teachers have cake and you have to watch them eating it.'

School's excellent online behaviour policy uses pictures and simple language to spell out exactly what each rule means in practice and they're felt to be fair, nothing heavy handed or draconian about application – pupils even respond with occasional touch of humour. 'Get to know your teachers and find out how lenient they are,' features on display of pupils' year 9 survival tips. Eases off in sixth form (no uniform as would require policing and 'they've had bellyful in lower school,' said sympathetic member of staff).

Care over smallest things felt to be exceptionally good. After child had nasty but accidental spill on stairs, family received several calls (unprompted) outlining efforts to check cause. Girls' friendship issues imaginatively tackled – Mr Elsey encouraging self-help, one child ostracised by reigning queen bee enfolded by willing alternative group.

Ethos helps even the shy to flourish – no mean feat for the many swapping from minute primary schools for seven form entry. Some use as opportunity to reinvent themselves. One child, formerly known as 'the shy one', has become dynamic form rep – revelling in chance to ditch preconceptions, courtesy of encouraging tutor. 'Got behind her and really brought her on,' said approving parent.

Pupils and parents: Catchment area that spans mansions to mid-terraces, ladies who lunch to nine to fivers, results in varied social mix, seen mostly as desirable melting pot – 'kids count the person more than the money,' thought one mother – though one father reckoned could lead to occasional awkwardness. 'One of child's friends asked me, "Do you always drive old cars?"'

Entrance: Via LEA (Bracknell); is its most oversubscribed secondary – around 600 apply for 210 year 7 places. Priority for looked after children and those with medical or social needs followed by those in catchment area, siblings and linked primary school. Distances 'calculated using Pythagoras' Theorem,' says LEA website, with 'measurement in metres is then multiplied by 0.000621317 to convert this measurement to miles.' Impressive stuff. We're sure parents would settle for nothing less.

Exit: Around 20 per cent leave after GCSEs. More careers guidance would be appreciated – though felt to be good support for helping sixth formers prepare for world of work. Two to Oxford in 2016 (one turned down her offer in favour of Bristol), while Russell Group is well represented. Southampton, Cardiff, Edinburgh and Surrey popular destinations. Sciences dominate with sprinkling of arts and humanities (history, English) though also plenty of excellent artists coming up through school, many aiming for foundation courses at nearby highly rated Farnborough.

Money matters: Help for those in difficulty felt to be well handed, with all school trip notification letters urging parents to come forward if will struggle with finance. For 16-19s, bursary scheme offers maximum of £1,200pa. Shame similar option not open to school itself, which has (reluctantly) asked families for optional financial payment of five pounds a month to keep things ticking over. Some parental unhappiness, directed not at school but at government decision to solve sixth form colleges' financial woes by cutting schools' budgets to match, leading to permanent million pound hangover. 'You've got Wellington costing £8,000 a term yet we've got to pay money to our school just to help it out,' says father.

Remarks: Big school, individual approach, stemming from can do everything, open all hours headship style. 'Your school is successful because it is very well led,' says succinct Ofsted report. RE excellence no doubt helps lend power of prayer to parental hopes that like Mr T******r (partly redacted by way of apology as he's emphatically not a fan) Mr Elsey will go on and on...and on.

Edge Grove Preparatory School

Edge Grove School, Aldenham Village, Hertfordshire WD25 8NL

Pupils: 450; 45 flexi and weekly boarders • Ages: 3–13 (boarding from 7)

Fees: Day £11,835 – £15,825; Boarding +£4,170 – £5,970 pa

Tel: 01923 855724
Email: admissions@edgegrove.com
Website: www.edgegrove.com

Headmaster: Since 2012, Ben Evans (40s). A Devon lad (mother still breeds Dartmoor ponies there) with a love of all things country. Head boy at Bramdean School before heading to Exeter University to read history and archaeology. Returned, armed with his degree and PGCE, to Bramdean where he 'learned to teach,' before taking up the post of head of history at Brighton College, later returning as deputy head to his alma mater.

Had a 'now or never' moment before hot footing it to Sri Lanka to teach at the junior school of the British School in Colombo, Sri Lanka, where he served a total of six years, the final four as head. Returned to the UK following the birth of his first child and found love at first sight with Edge Grove – 'exactly what I wanted,' he says. Laughingly says wealthy Sri Lankan parents provided good grounding for dealing with those of the ambitious north London variety, although parents say it is clear he is not trying to turn school into 'a typical north London hothouse.'

Lives in head's house at school with wife Alex – 'an absolute gem,' according to parents. Described as dynamic, likeable and no nonsense, she regularly rolls up her sleeves and gets stuck in in the boarding house, sorting things out 'with a deft hand,' says one mother.

Huge sighs of relief breathed by staff and parents alike at the end of Evans' first year in tenure as he appears to be there to stay, having scrapped Saturday lessons, made dramatic changes to the school day and really 'upped the ante' on the academic front. One parent said Evans had achieved more over the summer holidays (new adventure playground, gleaming home economics room and upgrades to textiles facilities) than they'd seen over the last three years. Just what Edge Grove needed after an unsettled patch with a revolving door of head teachers.

Entrance: Gently selective, with relaxed assessments and parental interview – 'we want parents to have chosen us for the right reasons,' says head. Little ones at 3+ and 4+ come for a short session where staff engage them in an activity and observe their skills in, for example, sharing and socialising. Currently oversubscribed for nursery and reception. Entrants at 7+ attend an assessment day and take verbal/non-verbal reasoning tests before spending a day in class to see how they fit in. 'We want the kind of children who will take advantage of all the things we have to offer,' says head.

No bursaries in the lower part of the school apart from those offered to military families. New scholarships introduced for existing pupils in years 7 and 8 to 'acknowledge their contribution to the school.'

Exit: Majority of girls leave at 11; others and most boys leave at 13. Girls to St Albans High School for Girls, Haberdashers' Aske's School for Girls, Abbot's Hill and Downe House, with St Albans Boys, Merchant Taylors' School and Harrow popular for boys; plus both to a range of co-ed schools including Rugby, Haileybury, Uppingham, Berkhamsted and Aldenham. A good handful of scholarships achieved annually, ranging from academic to sport and music. Conversations about next schools start with parents in years 5 and 6.

Remarks: When you arrive at this idyllic country prep it's hard to believe that it's just a stone's throw from north London and that the background hum is the M25. Set in grassy parkland with the requisite cows grazing next to the drive, Edge Grove – formerly the home of JP Morgan – is a world apart from many of its concrete-clad urban rivals.

Smiling boys and girls (school is now 50/50 and 'firmly co-educational,' according to head) in woolly red sweaters cheerfully and proactively greet you as you walk around, giving the impression of a happy, down to earth and confident cohort. Not surprising when you see the space they have to occupy – campus feels as if it could accommodate twice the number, with a huge open space for the nursery alone and separate science and art school buildings for older ones. Lovely manners abound, with classroom doors hardly opened before children leap to their feet.

Pupils and parents 'a really good mix,' according to head. About 20 per cent London based with the rest from around Radlett, St Albans, Elstree and Borehamwood and some Forces, based at Northwood. Ethnically diverse, reflecting the local area: 'wonderful,' say parents. Some discreet old money, others more flash and plenty of hard-working dual income first time buyers.

New school day structure popular with parents who say 'it just makes sense' to teach core subjects in the mornings when the children are most receptive. Activities take place either between 4 and 5pm or 5 and 6pm depending on year group and children can also stay for prep and supper, helping working parents or those further afield manage the pick-up. Saturday school abolished by current head in 2012 and replaced with voluntary Saturday attendance to take part in fun activities like music and drama or the Edge Grove Award (like a mini D of E) and stay for lunch if they wish – 'the quality of what we offer is much better now,' he says. Fleet of new iPads introduced for year 3 and up in 2013, kicking the school firmly into the 'progressive' bracket as far as technology is concerned. Class sizes capped at 20 in the pre-prep and 18 in the prep school.

Head 'aiming for excellence in all subjects.' International Primary Curriculum taught in pre-prep, which also has a forest school curriculum. French taught from reception and classics from year 5 with setting starting in year 3 for English and maths, then for French and science from year 5. New virtual language lab. Years 7 and 8 see pupils split into a scholarship set and two other common entrance sets. Parents talk about the 'academic rigour' being teased out of pupils on current head's watch and report a welcome increase in homework for younger ones. Mandarin, Spanish and Italian offered as after-school clubs for budding linguists.

Parents praise staff mix: 'some really old school, some young and dynamic,' although concede that 'some are better than others.' Communication between parents and teaching staff is reportedly 'excellent' in the main: parents are able to email class teachers direct and, with occasional exceptions, receive prompt, useful replies. Even throw-away comments in the car park are taken seriously and actioned, said one. Whole school communication 'getting better,' according to parents, with recent introduction of weekly email letting parents know of all forthcoming fixtures and trips to help pupils be better prepared. Head, keen to iron out any bad habits inherited from predecessors, has introduced weekly staff training sessions to ensure consistent quality across the board. SEN and EAL limited to offering learning support to children with mild difficulties and no plans to increase provision.

E

Outstanding art taught in inspirational atelier style space with first class work in genres ranging from cubism to pupils' favourite, street art, on display. Host of shiny new sewing machines will no doubt add to pupils' textiles capabilities; home economics also on the curriculum. Classrooms alive with sound of music: head wants 'music to be happening all the time,' and is getting his wish with over 180 peripatetic lessons each week ('brilliantly timetabled,' say parents) and a new director of music (ex Haileybury) driving musical excellence in all its forms. Choral music is 'very strong,' says head and a lucky few get to try their hand in the school rock band – recently kitted out with four electric guitars, a drum kit and, most importantly, a soundproofed practice room. Plenty for budding thespians too – year 5 recently performed A Midsummer Night's Dream in the school's grounds, with a production of Bugsy Malone another success.

Sport taken seriously for both genders with a total of around 800 fixtures a year and specialist teaching from reception. Girls benefit from the guidance of an ex-England netball coach and the school has strong links with Radlett Cricket Club. U13 six-a-side football team current national IAPS champions, with other pupils reaching county standard for cricket, archery and squash and recent introduction of international tours for top teams. For less starry types, there are plenty of inter-house matches and tournaments which are fiercely contested, so everyone gets a go. Weekly swimming lessons and galas take place in the immaculate heated outdoor pool on the site of a former beautifully walled garden, mirrored on the other side by impressively sized, albeit slightly tired, tennis courts.

Around 25 full and weekly boarders, just under 10 per cent international, many Forces children, with a total of 50 beds to accommodate flexi-boarding. Newly appointed non-teaching head of boarding has made a 'huge difference,' to what was formerly a fairly chaotic boarding function according to parents, although many agreed that there is still some way to go in terms of organisation: very little wardrobe space (one wardrobe for seven girls) and no lockers lead to lost clothes, with one parent reporting having lost up to 20 pairs of socks and others on-going problems with lost sports kit. Occasional issues with bullying and bad behaviour are 'not dealt with badly,' for the most part but parents have high hopes the 'new broom' will step up discipline and eliminate these issues altogether, to create a calmer and more nurturing boarding environment.

Bright, newly decorated dorms sleep up to eight pupils, with seniors (years 7 and 8) having their lounging and TV area incorporated into the dorm. There's also a games room in an annexe with snooker, table tennis and table football. Head, determined to avoid 'sleepover culture,' insists that boarders stay for a minimum of three nights a week from year 5, although they can stay for one in years 3 and 4, and all year 3 pupils are expected to board for at least one night during expedition week when years 4 to 8 head off site. Popular fun themed weekends twice yearly give all pupils a chance to taste boarding on a first come, first served basis.

Clubs galore – many of which are included in fees – from gardening and chess to taekwondo and war gaming. These are integrated well into the long school day and parents happily describe their children as 'very busy.' Two minibus services ferry years 3 to 8 to school if they choose, along routes covering Hemel Hempstead, St Albans, How Wood, Totteridge, Whetstone, Barnet, Brookmans Park and Shenley.

Elstree School

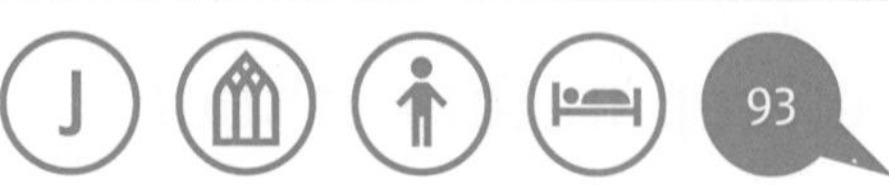

Woolhampton, Reading, Berkshire RG7 5TD

Pupils: 260; 110 boarders: 15 full, rest weekly/flexi • Ages: 3–13 • C of E

Fees: Day £10,908 – £19,605; Boarding £21,114 – £25,152 pa

Tel: 01189 713302
Email: registrar@elstreeschool.org.uk
Website: www.elstreeschool.org.uk

Headmaster: Since 2013, Mr Sid Inglis BA (40s), previously headmaster at Ludgrove. Uncertain as to career until taught English in Chile (where met wife Olivia) and realised that as professions go 'there is no finer job.' Appointed at exciting if nerve-wracking time following wobbles in leadership, parent confidence and pupil numbers. It's now all go again, with school at capacity, no need even to contemplate going fully co-ed (girls leave at 8), scholarships back to full honours-board levels – and all right in world.

Mr Inglis's first name is unusual and, even more unusually, shared with last head but two. Would be karma except that real name is Andrew. All the other more predictable essentials are also in place: labrador ('though had her before we arrived,' says equally charming Mrs Inglis), three cherubic offspring (two still at the school) and website must-have – photograph capturing whole shebang smilingly disporting themselves on well-positioned, sunlight-drenched bench if human (and beside it if not).

Would take a mean-spirited reviewer to deny that Mr Inglis exudes winning headmasterly qualities of authority and personability. Out and about like nobody's business. 'Very much a figurehead,' said parent. 'I don't know how he can be in so many different places all the time. He and his wife go around like a pair and are very supportive of one another.'

Even slots in weekly story-reading session to different pre-prep class each week (we encountered him en route with book, wondering if would require 'funny voices'). While parent approval can reach adoration levels, pupils' response more down to earth. 'Lets us get on with life as long as we're sensible,' said one. 'Doesn't feel special – acts just like a normal teacher.'

Relaxed, too – when this reviewer turned up at the very last minute for an open day visit, he (and all colleagues) were genuinely welcoming (if there were any less positive feelings, were fathoms deep).

He thinks it's part and parcel of the ethos that made this a dream job. Does a spot of teaching (RS, his degree subject, has yielded to classics here) and loves it. Aim, as laid out in prospectus, is to discover 'how a child is intelligent rather than how intelligent a child is' – while still preparing them for range of senior schools.

Translated, means that 'don't want academic success at the expense of muddy knees,' he says. 'If a child is confident and happy in their own little shell, academics will follow.' School, he says, isn't for chest-beating alpha males, jostling for position (or females, either). Will have a few who struggle academically but exude sense of purpose elsewhere, shining on sports field or stage. Combination of variety, straight-talking pupils and enjoyable challenge of (successfully) giving school boost it needed makes this a role he relishes. 'Love being busy.'

He is passionate about sport, particularly rugby and cricket, and enjoys playing golf and fishing. He took over after the school spent a year under an acting head, after the abrupt and unexplained resignation of the previous head, and brought with him parental hopes for stability after troubled times.

Head of Home Farm School (the pre-prep), Mrs Kay Markides, arrived 2009. Graduated in science, married with a family (including a son who attended Elstree) before deciding to train for teaching young ones. Taught for a while at another school nearby. Thrilled to be involved with Elstree, and it shows. Warm and at ease with the children ('I love them') she is clearly not only very competent but also exudes calm dependability. Presides over a talented young staff who clearly relish the company of their young charges, patiently explaining things and then rushing around with them in the grounds of the prep school.

Entrance: Non-selective in Home Farm, the pre-prep (nursery to year 2), whose 60 pupils are accommodated in next door farmhouse and converted outbuildings, with own separate entrance and playgrounds but overlapping grounds. Co-ed but boy-dominated as 'people are signing up for the whole school,' points out amiable pre-prep head and former parent Mrs Kay Markides. No girls in current year 2 and a cheerful minority over in the prep for year 3.

Open to learning needs including ADHD. Key is ability to keep up academically and impress with right attitude: prospectus stresses that 'effort is king'. Growth of waiting lists (in almost every year group) means that while ability range is wide, 'we have become gently selective,' says Mr Inglis.

While teachers sometimes sorely tried, rare that won't make a go of it, helped by much-praised learning needs department. Will, though, review progress in years 4 and 6 when long-term compatibility of child and school will be weighed up, says headmaster. Thus far, nobody has been asked to leave.

Exit: Good links with Bradfield (former head, now at Eton, sent all his brood here), most of first rank southern staples represented. Eton, Harrow, Winchester, Radley, Bradfield and Stowe have all featured recently.

Year 3 girls to St Andrew's Pangbourne, Cheam, St Gabriel's, Marlston House and the Manor, Abingdon.

Remarks: School that likes life in duplicate. Pre-prep's 60 pupils have large magical woodland area (annexed from prep), paths canopied with intertwined branches or bordered with wild grasses (there's even a troll bridge) – and a second mini wilderness for everyday, star attraction a palatial roofed sandpit big enough for whole class to enjoy. Even Mrs Markides shares year 2 teaching duties with colleague (though second best rule undoubtedly doesn't apply).

Appearance, in pairs or otherwise, is winningly green and traditional. School's 150 acres include two lakes, one used for Elstree Award activities (like D of E but bespoke), croquet lawn with wire sculpture of (Lewis Carroll inspired?) flamingo, courts and pitches (including full-sized Astro), dog-walking parents and staff adding homely touch.

Though vibe is venerable (pre-prep uniform list specifies named napkin ring), mood is progressive. 'Lots of tradition and trust, but we're well aware it's a modern world,' says Mrs Inglis. Mr I stresses importance of charitable activities that open pupils' eyes 'to the wide world away from idyllic leafy confines.' Perhaps accounts for staff list hedging its bets – some male teachers are Esq, some are Mr, while headmaster, straddling both worlds, is bereft of any salutation at all.

'Pushes children hard but pleasantly so,' thought prospective parent. 'It's not "you will learn 10 verses by Tuesday".' By way of proof, there's combined staff and pupil YouTube version of 'Happy' to mark departure of recent batch of girl leavers, treat for dad dancing (or teacher equivalent) connoisseurs and anyone needing lesson in chutzpah.

Full boarding the only traditional element that isn't faring so well, hanging on but only just. Now a minority occupation for 15 out of the 100 or so boarders, mainly overseas (Russians, sprinkling of Spanish) plus odd Londoner, though most stay for at least three nights a week. They 'get used to it,' thought pupil. Not most ringing of endorsements, even backed by run of grounds at weekend.

However when it comes to flexi or weekly stays, 'boys are clamouring to board,' the head told us firmly, reeling off vast list of evening activities on offer when they do – from bridge to fantasy football, debating and improvisation. School now so 'full to bursting' from Monday to Friday that it's a case of joining the queue with waiting list in operation. No quibbles with boarding logistics, which work a treat, year 4 to 6 dorms to the side – we liked their emergency cuddly toy cubby hole to keep homesickness at bay – while years 7 and year 8 have separate quarters in main building.

Dorms on large side – eight to 10 not uncommon – but with spacious, pleasant rooms and friendly, uncrowded feel. Décor variable, one room a shrine to Shoot! magazine, plastered floor to ceiling with pictures of footballers, another, the former ballroom, featuring stucco storks looking down from ceiling in gentle amazement at year 8 pupils' beds in formation on parquet floor. Possible setting for new reality TV show, 'Come boarding,' perhaps?

If full boarding continues to decline and parent vibe suggests it will – 'strong majority who like the day aspect,' thought one – Big Weekends could be the future, with 40 or so other pupils piling in for fun and games including Laser Tag and exciting Indoor Lions, inside version of Stuck in the Mud played in the dark for added thrills.

Extremely popular (currently free of charge, so no wonder) and means 'full boarders have more company,' says school. Also an organisational cinch as Saturday school – a full day with lessons and afternoon games – is in full force from year 4. Can be shock to the system (as is late weekday finish) for those coming from state sector, though 'only do easy subjects then,' said tour guide. Well, maybe – if you consider French and maths a bit of light weekend banter, though heavy-duty exercises are interspersed with the odd quiz, which helps. And without Saturday school, 'weekends are too long,' thought pupil.

Best teaching (and there's lots of it) combines humour and memorability. One English teacher (a school favourite) known for quick draw funny pictures – enthusiastic year 7 boys (like all other pupils smilingly standing up for adults) praising memorable stick person imagery that instantly conjured up poetic protagonist 'swimming against tide with heart sinking...'.

Impressively inclusive, say parents, with children's confidence boosted by lessons cannily pitched at challenging rather than daunting. 'My son thinks he's brilliant because they've given him the work that's appropriate,' said mother. Even less inspirational teachers – maths felt to be slightly variable – usually get the results in the end. 'If you get something right, you get a point. Didn't like it but it does work,' thought one pupil.

Heroic efforts elsewhere, with year 7 pupil in DT class who had elected to make sundial out of seasoned oak and, equipped with bow saw, was two-thirds of way through chunky tree trunk. 'Has taken an hour already,' was weary comment.

Pre-prep pupils similarly keen on lessons and given undiluted praise from parents – staff 'can't do enough, there morning, noon and night, so happy and 100 per cent involved with the children' – no wonder. One small maths fan was full of praise for 'hard sums', another extolled virtues of recent pirate topic because 'they kill people' – before being gently shepherded into more wholesome approach by teacher. 'Our pirates wouldn't do things like that.' (He didn't look totally convinced).

Music 'absolutely thriving,' says head, with 200 individual lessons timetabled each week, top performers reaching grade 8, two recent scholarships (Radley and Charterhouse) and department 'always full of boys.' Prep choir (one of three) is 30-deep, recent delights including choral evensong at Bath Abbey.

E

Encouraged by many means, including piano located somewhat unusually on first bend of main staircase in prep school for impromptu concerts – one boy at a time, ban on James Bond theme tune (popularity led to aural repetitive strain injury risk for admin staff nearby).

Drama similarly successful with boys happy to take female roles and lack of self-consciousness that comes with single-sex environment. Parents thrilled with gentle encouragement that sees the formerly un-keen blossoming into performers. Talent search starts early with violin (free lessons for all in year 1) and recorder (year 2) – parents apparently thrilled with results, performers shining in end of year concert.

Sport equally strong and inclusive (goes down to E teams and sixth XIs). Fine summer evenings an enthusiast's delight, with croquet on front lawn. Lots more – from swimming to shooting, golf and judo, as well as school staples – athletics, football, rugby, hockey, cricket (coach, current Berkshire captain, also teaches pre-prep pupils, one mightily impressed to find his teacher known to Lord's).

Plenty of informal activities, too; one tree full of roosting boys, like giant navy blue rooks. Though staff presence seemed to us to be relatively hands-off, some parents and pupils feel free time can be over-supervised. 'Always a teacher walking round.' Reasons for adult presence well understood – 'it's so someone doesn't get hurt,' and by year 8, said pupil, things improve. 'They accept you need some time alone.'

Greta Garbo tendencies no doubt forgotten in excitement of table football matches and hotly contested corridor cricket. Boys very keen, though one thought teachers possibly less so when caught in path of oncoming cricket ball during evening rounds.

Gentle pace gets up speed through the school, senior school entrance exam pressure an inevitable fact of life for year 8 pupils, though teachers do best to defuse the tension, felt boys. Weekly form time used to air difficulties; friendly gap students a more informal source of support, comfort food – evening bowls of cereal – provided for boarders.

Pastoral care generally felt to be good, from daily staff briefings to half hour catch up sessions at lunchtime. Pupils urged to use common sense if someone is feeling left out of activities – 'they expect us to find something that fits,' said pupil. Bullying clearly well managed. 'Issues dealt with very quickly with children pulled in. If you overstep the mark there's a punishment and everyone knows that,' said parent. Pre-prep opts for circle time and golden rules. Staff had slight struggle to remember them but do appear to work, parents full of praise at absence of problems in any age group.

Highly organised parents notable for efficiency and ability sweep up newcomers – 'integration' events include lunches for the mums and curry nights for dads (or vice versa one progressive day?). Praise, bar mutterings about over influential queen bees from former parent, was universal, school community the icing on the cake. Attracts London exiles as well as locals, drawn by welcoming culture and lots to keep sporty and arty happy.

'Son has been pushed where would like to be pushed and pushed along where needed to be. An amazingly efficient school that continues to surprise me,' said mother.

Epsom College

College Road, Epsom, Surrey KT17 4JQ

Pupils: 800: 510 boys, 290 girls; 171 full, 206 weekly boarders • Ages: 11–18 • Sixth form: 326: 208 boys, 118 girls • C of E

Fees: Day 17,100 – £23,472; Boarding £23,520– £34,617 pa

Tel: 01372 821234
Email: admissions@epsomcollege.org.uk
Website: www.epsomcollege.org.uk

Headmaster: Since 2012, Mr Jay Piggot, BA MA PGCE (50s). Previously headmaster at alma mater Campbell College, Belfast between 2006 and 2012, and, before that, put in 17 years at Eton (clearly a hard place to leave) starting as assistant master in 1989 and becoming house master 10 years later. Not bad going given that it was only his second teaching job: his first, immediately after completing his MA in English Renaissance literature at Liverpool, was at Millfield, where he taught A level/ Oxbridge English.

Career success undoubtedly assisted by personality and appearance – quietly dashing, though doesn't overdo the leading man business. Gimlet vision, too – noticed and swiftly dealt with errant piece of rubbish – a very small plastic wrapper, only one in otherwise immaculate grounds.

Lordy, lordy, what a popular man he is. Pupils – 'a joy,' he says – say he makes an effort to know names, comes to matches and makes with the social chit chat. Biggest vote winner, however, are the birthday cards – otherwise sophisticated international pupil clearly thrilled with his, particularly handwritten signature – cynic had checked authenticity with damp finger just to be sure. Parents also like what they see. Innovations all welcomed. 'Very proactive behind the scenes and has pushed through some sensible changes,' says one. Definitely a step up from predecessor. 'School ran well but didn't have the personality.'

College was already known to him before the headhunters came a-callling, and found vision, ethos and commitment very much to his taste. Younger son, a keen golfer, moved with him (older brother is going great guns at Eton).

'Would love' to teach again and might when has got through current to-do list, which is lengthy. Getting shorter by the minute, though. 'Some heads would take a while to work out what they were going to do,' says teacher. 'He's made lots of changes already.' Popular changes include axing of seasonal timetables, originally to make most of winter light, but cause of mega all-round confusion to all.

High profile reintroduction of matrons into the houses was an Eton-inspired development that's brought a caring, maternal touch (thus far, all women) to details such as tracking down missing shirts and sewing as well as control of rowdy element. Of even greater significance has been academic shake up, still ongoing, starting with observation of every member of staff since he arrived, followed with ISI-style feedback. 'A privilege,' he says. (We're sure they feel the same). Many stay for years. No wonder, with perks headed (for many, though not all) by housing either on-site or within a few minutes' walk. 'My wife told me we're not going to move,' said one. Given Epsom property prices, you can't blame her.

In addition to the introduction of heads of year, designed to add missing link identified in recent inspection, he's also not going to stand in path of old-timers who could be moving on to greater things elsewhere, while rejigging weak spots including A level languages and biology and GCSE English literature. Dynamic incomers, including former Uppingham head of modern foreign languages – similar developments in science – are being brought in together with fledgling new generation of bright young things adding oomph to lessons (occasional dullness one of few inferred criticisms in last inspection report).

Still more shaking up to come, however, essential given school's previous sleepiness and 'red-hot' competition – Wellington, Cranleigh and Charterhouse as well as St John's Leatherhead and Reed's School. Bumping up interior life of school is part of the process, with Eton's dawn to dusk (and beyond) intellect-boosting programme the inspiration for mind-expanding programme – expect more pupil-organised drama, musical and debating activities (medical, history and politics societies are already on the go) sparking impassioned discussions that ramp up the intellectual temperature from tepid to mercury-busting.

Mark of success? Would like popularity of places to increase to the point where competition for boarding places as strong as for day hopefuls.

Academic matters: One of formerly mid-ranking schools to have substantially upped game in recent years. Fun lessons got pupils on the go, literally so, with movement minus the music, A level students standing up for miracles (theology) and marginal cost (economics) – everything, in fact, but their rights.

Parents, while agreeing with head that some teachers are 'past their best', think generally offset by vast majority who are 'engaging, personable and, most importantly, able to motivate. They appear to love their subjects and to enjoy teaching and the company of the children – none of these are a given, in my experience.' Megawatt enthusiasm often a game-changer, especially at sixth form level. Sciences score particularly high conversion rates. 'Was my dream to be a translator – now it's chemistry,' said pupil.

Ability to devote time to all (an impressive 55 hours contact time a week) means that 'there are no lost causes,' says head. Plentiful tracking and feedback means pupils know where they are and how they can improve, feedback seamlessly integrated in lessons. 'We put down our comments when we've had a test and it gives teachers a good idea of where we are,' said sixth former.

Though class sizes aren't teeny tiny – average 20 for GCSE (maximum 23) and between 10 and 12 at A level (15 max), with pupil to full time teacher ratio of 8.4 – school is consistently good when it comes to added value, setting in maths, banding in languages and sciences (where small group of less able students might do GCSE dual sciences rather than IGCSE triple). No-one takes 'silly' numbers of GCSEs, says senior teacher – aim is to ensure good grades in manageable quantities.

Currently, results generally very good given relatively mixed intake, with 70 per cent A*/A grades at GCSE; 85 per cent of A level entries graded A*/B and 61 per cent A*/A in 2016.

Good, largely traditional subject range, almost ology-free – 'nothing against psychology but it just isn't us,' says teacher – though language options now include GCSE Mandarin, originally for overseas students but now open to all. However, MFLs not the strongest suit, with few takers at A level – maths and economics much the most popular.

Hugely dynamic head of DT is also bumping up recruitment, particularly amongst girls, by ensuring that environment, full of technological marvels – though it's pupils' superb mortice and tenon joints and chamfering skills that help pull in the A* grades – is also tidy ('was grubby and fragmented') with plenty of wood-turning (apparently the secret of cross-gender appeal).

Big feature is Extended Project Qualification (EPQ), a mini-dissertation that, at best, combines originality and staying power (recent topics include carcinogens in food and madness in Henry VIII's court – separately). Worth the effort. One pupil, down an A level grade and out of university course, called department head and used hers to talk her way back in again. No doubt that attracts the very able – one pupil, exile from leading girls' school, delighted to be somewhere that praised good work rather than training spotlight on pupils only when failed to deliver top grades – though one parent queried its suitability for the truly brilliant. 'Might be a bit too comfortable,' she thought. 'It's a broad church and some kids are too bright [and] shouldn't be there.'

Extra scaffolding where needed, with clinics all the way through the school in all key subjects and teachers not just present (many live in) but in many cases 'always available.' That said, school isn't geared up to cope with anyone with more than mild learning difficulties. Of the 100 or so pupils with SEN, none is currently statemented, SpLD the overwhelmingly dominant need, though have coped with (mild) ADHD as well.

Plenty of emails home and 'progress reports every three weeks,' ensure that everyone knows what's going on, while lengthy school day (finishing 6.00pm) incorporates sufficient free periods for the organised to sock it to the homework.

And though initially gentle pace startling to alumni of non-stop pushy preps, school gets praise for stress-appropriate levels of pushing tailored to each child. 'They know which way to push,' says mum of recent leaver. 'The teacher told my child that she "might get an A in biology GCSE, but I don't think so".' Nettled, daughter was spurred on to do just that.

Games, options, the arts: Sport success plentiful – boys' and girls' rugby VIIs regular regional winners, lots of post-school success, too (five OEs play for Harlequins), ditto hockey (mixed seniors won Surrey U18 competition), as do minors with recent captain of golf driving his way to Stanford Golf Scholarship (first European for over 10 years, says school) and shooting. Facilities generous – including swimming pool – and, in case of one of two sports halls, close to giant-size (even better when new sports pavilion up and running), two cracking sports halls, one giant sized, six squash courts, a swimming pool and a fencing salle, No partridge in pear tree (but would undoubtedly be doing a few press ups if there were).

Outside, timetable pushes variety – first years will have both outdoor and inside sports in an afternoon and, further up the school, non-standard sports can be done off site – riding, for example and climbing, until school got its own climbing wall. Range ensures that 'you're not penalised if you're not sporty,' thought a mother, with matches for all. 'Sport is very important, whether you're A team or D/E/F team material,' agreed another parent. Sports captains, rated by the rank and file – 'positions are well earned,' thought one – have a real say in team structure. 'You can discuss team composition with the coach and that's good,' thought pupils. Termly activity sheet encourages pupils to experiences shock of the new. One boy, initially dreading jive dance, discovered instead that he was 'that sort of person' – and loved it.

Plenty head for D of E, room for all (can add more staff if demand is high). CCF feather in school cap – one of oldest and biggest in country, teeming with facilities, (we liked esteem-heavy 'confidence' rather than assault course). Wears success lightly – numerous impressive sports cups casually behind bars with the guns).

Arts also attacked with relish. Music felt to be 'on the ascendant,' thought teacher, with lots of instrumental lessons – drums, singing, electric guitar and piano the biggest sellers, some reaching diploma level; challenging, performance opportunities ranging from low stress impromptu recitals to high quality productions including The Cunning Little Vixen and excellent chapel choir, masses lining up to audition – a macho-free area, reckoned year 9 and 10 pupils. Those not making the grade can 'let voices develop' in non-selective Glee Club instead.

Visual arts, recently upgraded, feature confident, instantly recognisable year 9 pictures of Kew Gardens – one of many trips. Everybody gets out a lot, DT excursions to real factories (Brompton bikes to Henry vacuum cleaners) so popular that school staff sign their Sundays away, too, school chef enjoying outing to Cadbury's as much as pupils.

Boarding: Similar numbers for full boarding and weekly. Boarding houses, dotted round the site, now all done up to the nines – matching up to head's aspirations to equal best in Britain – with decking and glass snazzy-ness. Sensible trouble-preventing measures include half-termly dorm swaps and plenty of weekend activities for full boarders, from trips to Thorpe Park to house evenings and bowling. 'Never lonely because lots going on,' said sixth former.

Buddy system helps combat homesickness (most reckoned that worst was over within first week), one house even creating own surrogate family, one year group per generation and organising popular old fashioned sports day as an ice-breaker. Here, too, matrons, add much appreciated extra tea and sympathy layer (housemistresses – always academic staff – can 'sometimes be more of figure of authority,' thought sixth formers).

Background and atmosphere: Altogether a civilised place to be, starting with laid-back parking regime, permitted along one side of the one way road that winds round the lush green campus (new upper sixth drivers are vetted by the head), imposing chapel at its heart. Though patron is HM the Queen, not a high-society institution. Started life as the Royal Medical Benevolent College, a charitable Good Thing, helping the relics of deceased impoverished medics. Strongly Victorian in spirit and execution – most buildings completed between 1850s and 1920s. School wasn't welcomed by all, overt charitable status 'distasteful' to recipients, reckoned contemporary letter to Lancet.

Took only boys for the first 120 years or so (sisters presumably expected to marry their way to economic success); girls added 1996 largely as emergency recession-busting tactic (local area had suffered heavily and pupil numbers had plummeted). Now, of course, school wouldn't be without them and they're on almost equal terms in the sixth form, though minority partners in other years. Desired ratio is 60:40 is, thinks head, about right, ensuring girls have the same options as boys, particularly when it comes to games. 'All get the chance to contribute,' he adds, firmly. No complaints from girls themselves, or parents, so seems to be working. Added a lower school – years 7 and 8 – in 2016.

Though it's all 19th and early 20th century authenticity from the front with 'real wow factor,' thought parent, sold on first visit, tasteful modern extensions stretch back a considerable distance to the rear (current bursar, a woman, was a former architect, and it shows). Behind public face is 'pupil world', the second sweep of buildings where most of the teaching takes place. Modern additions – humanities building particularly palatable – don't jar (though some areas, like maths and theology blocks, could be nicer, and almost certainly will be when funds permit).

When it comes to décor, different departments exhibit endearing idiosyncrasies – from pot plants in chemistry lab (and sign announcing 'nudisme interdite au delà de cette limite') to blue-painted English rooms (also notable for friendly clutter of framed posters and attractive display boards already filling up nicely in second week of term) while modern languages is all-purple (even down to lampshades). Black wall in one of physics labs, however, is for sensitive experiments and 'not because we're pandering to goths,' explains larger than life department head.

Technology warmly embraced with Wifi throughout (and 'extreme' internet safety settings triggered by word 'Middlesex') and the Hub, new high tech room where lessons can be recorded for posterity. Tradition equally enjoyed but not pointlessly so – most of original medical artefacts and stuffed animals that once dominated science rooms have gone. 'Antiques dealer took the rest,' says teacher, cheerfully.

Pastoral care, well-being and discipline: Seniors a strong force (and will be even more so once head succeeds in replacing current sixth form block with something altogether spiffier). Take turns to lead assemblies that are so far removed from commonplace fare that we had to double check that searingly articulate reflections on 9/11 were being delivered by sixth form girls. It appears effortless. No wonder – it's been in rehearsal since June, points out the friendly chaplain. Older pupils keen to stress that 'hierarchical system associated with traditional English boarding school, pitting year group against year group' is 'a terrible idea' and will pitch in to take sides if older boys show signs of picking on younger ones. 'It's part of our role and it works.'

Little in the way of serious misbehaviour, however, with just two pupils 'withdrawn by parents' (expulsion by face-saving euphemism) in senior teacher's 15 years. Drugs issues in both cases, though it's very rarely the end, behind the scenes second chances often possible. Day to day, class silliness and late homework the main issues, reckoned pupils, with escalating sanctions – lines, notification of tutors, warnings, departmental then school detentions – rattled off by all.

Lots of rewards, too – from pizza or chocolate for work-related merits and distinctions to privileges of seniority – sixth form day girls cited joy of leaving sports kit on shelves in study rooms instead of trekking, when younger, to go to separate storage area.

And though house system (separate for day and boarding pupils) engenders ferocious sense of competition (choir contest in particular), it isn't carried over into lessons, 'which stops it becoming tribal,' reckoned parent.

Pupils and parents: Predominantly local intake with vast majority of pupils, including 95 per cent of UK boarders, living within 10 to 15 miles. School keen to expand the range but, meantimes, results in happy fusion of streetwise Londoner with leafy Surrey-ite, reckoned teacher – cool without the ennui.

Many staff have own children here (has peaked at 40 or so). One parent we spoke to who'd opted for local alternative thought numbers were excessive – though appeared to be a lone voice. Working mums – far more these days – were something of a feature to the point where socialising tends to feature nights out to ensure 'you don't feel out of the loop,' thought career-driven mother.

Cosmopolitan feel added by international component (largeish at 20 per cent) drawn from Hong Kong, Malaysia, Russia and Korea, though many more from western Europe. For the 10 per cent who are non-native English speakers there is a structured EAL programme in place, but they're fully integrated into the curriculum says the school, 'right from day one'.

Malaysian numbers probably not affected by opening of sister school in Kuala Lumpur in 2014 – first foray into pastures new, as 'there will always be pupils who want a UK education,' reckons school.

Entrance: School is after all-rounders with several strings to their bow and 'fair share of the bright pupils'. Once a second choice regular, increasingly a bill-topper, recruiting from over 40 preps and state schools, likely to increase as it extends reach (Danes Hill and Downsend, Shrewsbury House, Aberdour and Feltonfleet feature prominently though no official feeders). Full-on charm offensive attracting south west London schools.

New 11+ intake via maths, English and VR tests plus interview in January of year 6. Second intake into year 9, with January pre-test in year 6 (VR – scores of around 118-120 the norm – NVR, English and numerical skill plus interview), same again (minus NVR) for non-prep candidates in January of year 8.

Once 'day pupils were brighter and more studious' than boarding pupils, thought one insider. No longer the case.

If no joy at 13+, small number of places at 14+ (three to five only, English, maths and NVR tests). Second biggest influx is post-GCSE with 45 to 50 joining the sixth form, following VR, NVR and numerical skills tests plus interview. Push to up state school numbers (currently around 20 per cent of the total) as a way of 'supplementing the ratios'. Some haggling after year 12 for a handful of pupils whose progress gives cause for concern. Repeating year not an option, dropping a subject can be the solution.

Exit: No shortage of ambition, most achieving first choice unis; Exeter, Bristol, LSE, Loughborough, Nottingham, Warwick, Durham, Edinburgh, SOAS, Manchester, Oxford Brookes and Queen's Belfast are top 10 university destinations; four to Oxbridge in 2016. Economics and finance followed by business, geography and sociology popular though, despite high quality art as A level option – and photography just added – it's currently not being pursued as a degree option.

Money matters: Annual bursary spend close to £750,000 on up to 100 per cent of fees. Possible additional financial support for families with medical connections through the Royal Medical Foundation, based at the school, though since 2000 a separate legal entity. Lots of scholarships on offer, academic and Headmaster's (for 'a wide range of disciplines' from drama to chess) at 11+ and 13+, sports and music at 16+ too.

Remarks: With demographics and parent power going his way, head's boarding aspirations could well be realised. 'A brilliant school for my son,' said mother. Another commented that school had got 'everything there was to get' out of her child. 'You really can't ask much more than that'.

Eton College

Eton, Windsor, Berkshire SL4 6DW

Pupils: 1,320 boys (all boarding) • Ages: 13–18 • Sixth form: 520 • C of E

Fees: Boarding £37,062 pa

Tel: 01753 370611
Email: admissions@etoncollege.org.uk
Website: www.etoncollege.com

Head Master: Since 2015, Mr Simon Henderson MA PGCE (an extremely youthful looking late 30s; possibly Eton's youngest ever head), previously head of Bradfield College. Educated at Winchester College, followed by Brasenose College, Oxford, where he read history. Teaching career started at Windsor Boys' School, moving to Eton College in 2001, where he was a deputy housemaster and head of history, and on to Sherborne School in 2009 as deputy head (academic). Straight-talking, unpretentious – more technocrat than autocrat, Merkel than Berlusconi, Bill Gates than Donald Trump. Married to Ali (a civil servant) with four children under the age of 5.

Academic matters: First class all round. In 2016, 79 per cent A*/A at A level and nearly 80 per cent D1-3 at Pre-U. Tutor for admissions told us that it's seen as 'cool' to be academically successful at Eton. Majority of boys take A levels, but Pre-U offered in a growing number of subjects too. Maths is most popular subject at A level, followed by history, RS, physics and economics. School doesn't have plans to offer IB – 'The advantage of the IB is breadth,' a master told us, 'but we feel that the boys get that breadth anyway through the options on offer.' As well as their main subjects, sixth formers choose two additional options – a wealth of choice, from philosophy to Portuguese.

At GCSE, most boys take 11 subjects, including at least two of the three sciences. In 2016, 95 per cent A*/A grades. IGSCEs taken in sciences, languages, maths, history, music and DT. Fabulous languages department – nine languages taught, including Arabic, Japanese, Mandarin and Russian (department will soon move to new £20 million quadrangle, complete with 22 classrooms, two language labs and a library). Younger boys in classes of 20 to 22 (setted from ability from their first year and up to 14 sets per year group), with smaller class sizes as they get older. Total of 35 lessons (called schools at Eton) a week, but most boys have some free periods. Pupils have internal school exams in Michaelmas and summer terms. Youngest boys get an hour of prep a night, and two to two and a half hours as they progress up the school.

Full-time teaching staff numbers 150 – a good mix of old and new, and more women teachers than before. School is keen to encourage boys to be independent learners and boys get sessions on time management, study skills and exam technique. Rather than instructing pupils, 'You must do it like this,' school asks boys, 'How do you think we could do this better?' All pupils have a tutor and they meet once a week in small groups (maximum of six) at their tutor's house. Same tutor for first three years, then boys choose their own sixth form tutor. The new Tony Little Centre for Innovation and Research in Learning aims to transform teaching methods.

Has invested heavily in SEN support – an educational psychologist spent a year setting up and coordinating the SEN unit and training staff. Around 50 to 60 boys receive regular learning support for mild to moderate dyslexia, dyspraxia, dysgraphia – either one-to-one or in small groups. All boys assessed during their first term and any whose results give cause for concern get extra help.

School reports are meticulous. All subject masters write reports for every boy they teach. These are sent to tutors, who add their own reports, then to housemasters and finally to parents. 'You get a pretty good idea of how your child is doing,' says one appreciative mother.

Games, options, the arts: Excellent – every extracurricular activity on offer, including cookery lessons from top chef (and provost's wife) Caroline Waldegrave. 'The opportunities are phenomenal,' a father told us wistfully. 'I only wish I'd gone there.' Sport remains superb, with facilities (and results) second to none. Boys must commit to a main sport every term – football or rugby in Michaelmas term, hockey, rowing or the Field Game in the Lent term and athletics, cricket, rowing or tennis in the summer. A raft of minor sports on offer – from Eton's own Wall Game to beagling. Unlike some schools, boys encouraged to continue with sports through exam terms.

E

Dazzling art department (the Drawing Schools), with marvellous open aspect over playing fields – one of the best we've seen. Remarkable and challenging work, beautifully executed and displayed. When we visited, eight boys were off to do art foundation courses after A levels. Paintings by the likes of Anthony Frost and Patrick Heron hanging on walls, collection of ceramics donated by an old boy, art library, CAD suite, two 3D printers – the place definitely has the wow factor. Music is brilliant too. Department attracts the brightest and best in the country via its music scholarships. Around 1,300 instrumental lessons a week and regular and very polished concerts held in concert hall.

Not surprisingly, with starry alumnae like Hugh Laurie, Damian Lewis, Dominic West, Eddie Redmayne and Tom Hiddleston, takes drama very seriously indeed. The drama department has its own full-time designer, carpenter and manager, plus a part-time wardrobe mistress, and puts on a plethora of school and house plays, some led by teachers, some by boys. When we visited, eclectic forthcoming productions ranged from Cyrano de Bergerac to Flames over New Jersey, a play co-written by a pupil and member of staff.

Huge number of outings, visits and field trips, and good provision for pupils post exams. CCF very popular – army is the biggest single employer of Old Etonians (including ex-soldier Prince Harry, of course). Vast number of clubs and societies, with top-notch speakers, often launched and run by the boys themselves. 'We give boys confidence in themselves,' says one beak. 'We treat them as adults and they get a lot of responsibility quite young.' Recent activities range from a charity cycle ride to raise money in memory of Horatio Chapple, the Eton pupil who died in tragic circumstances in Norway, to a spectacular fashion show (attended by Dame Vivienne Westwood, no less) staged by a boy with ambitions to be a fashion designer. 'I would have worn one of his ballgowns,' an impressed mother told us.

Boarding: Twenty-five boarding houses, including College (for King's Scholars). Single study bedsits for all from day one. Huge variety of rooms and décor. The rooms we saw were pretty salubrious – one housemaster we met drew the line at 'floor-drobes'. Sanctions imposed for messy rooms range from laundry duty to black-bagging, where boys' possessions get stuffed in a bin bag and the culprit must pay a fine to get them back. All rooms networked and school endeavours to teach boys about responsible computer use. Boarding houses scattered either side of the High Street and beyond. Houses are known by the names of the housemasters in charge. They are in post for 13 years, so the names of the houses change with them.

In the boarding houses dames keep a weather eye on the boys, stay in contact with parents and run domestic matters. 'They are the co-runners of the houses,' a housemaster told us. 'They're not emergency first aid SWAT teams.' Older pupils volunteer to mentor new boys and answer questions like how to cope with the volume of work or what to do on Sunday mornings. House common rooms equipped with table football, pool table and TV. Lots of inter-house competitions.

Half the houses offer in-house catering while boys in the others eat breakfast, lunch and supper in a large central dining hall. Lunch is a formal, if speedy, affair, with grace said at the start and finish. 'The houses are like little schools within a house,' a father told us. 'Everyone says their own house is the best.'

Background and atmosphere: Founded in 1440 by Henry VI (sister college of King's College, Cambridge, which was founded a year later). Seventy King's Scholars still live in the original buildings (most elegant dining hall and ancient classroom with original benches and graffiti). Buildings of mellow old red brick, medieval courtyards, grounds running down to the Thames, boys in tailcoats and white bow ties hurrying to lessons – the whole place looks like a film set. Magnificent chapel built by Henry VI and a second chapel for Lower Boys. Has appointed an imam and RC chaplain, Jewish and Hindu tutors on the staff too.

Boys wear tailcoats and stiff collars – apart from office bearers, who wear proper wing collars and white ties. Brilliant for posture, as boys stuff pockets in their tailcoats with essential school kit, pulling even the most round-shouldered teenagers straight. School uniform not as expensive as you might think – good second-hand trade, both boy-inspired and via the school tailors in the High Street. Fancy waistcoats worn by the school prefects, or to give them their proper title, the Eton Society ('Pop'). Pupils don't wear tails across the bridge to Windsor any longer – much informal changing and half-changing (putting on a jacket rather than tails) after lessons. Teaching staff mostly live within 600 yards of the school, which creates a 'good sense of community'.

Lively atmosphere. Every day is structured and active, with boys and beaks constantly on the go. Beaks wear gowns for their three-line whip coffee break – Chambers – when one beak will attract the attention of another by tugging at his gown. Has its own traditional (and ever-evolving) school language: terms are 'halves', weekly tutor sessions are 'private business' and boys who aren't King's Scholars are Oppidans – luckily, a helpful glossary on the school website to explain all. Excellent school mags (The Chronicle, The Junior Chronicle) which are sold on high days and holidays for commission. All boys now have mobile phones and discount-available laptops.

Pastoral care, well-being and discipline: Still the traditional school it always was, but broad-minded, outward-looking and liberal in principle. Boys who get into trouble are given lots of support. Clear policies on drugs, alcohol and cigarettes. Any boy caught using, selling or possessing drugs 'will go,' says school firmly. But if a suspicion that a pupil may be dabbling with drugs and is prepared to talk about it, school takes 'a different route' – parents are informed and both they and the boy are asked to sign a contract, offered counselling and subjected to lectures and random drugs testing. Alcohol less of a problem now ('tiny numbers,' says school) but smoking is still there – though less than in co-ed schools, apparently. For first offences, smokers pay fines to cancer charity and will 'go on the bill' – Eton-speak for when a boy misbehaves and is sent to the headmaster or lower master. Boys have limited (but increasing with age) rights to go into Windsor and further afield – but only with their parents' permission.

Pupils and parents: 'There isn't a typical Etonian,' the tutor for admissions told us. 'It's a very big school but it isn't one homogenous block. It's a school that is vastly more socially and culturally diverse than it's ever been.' He reckons that the boys who thrive are those who are 'curious, prepared to try out new things, have a love of learning and a deep-seated desire to get on'. Around 20 boys a year from state schools and 12 per cent from overseas – Hong Kong, China, Russia, Germany, France, Italy, Nigeria and the US.

The boys we met were a sparky bunch who cited the sports facilities and the friendly atmosphere as the best things about the place. Boys say they aren't bothered by being at a single-sex school – girls from St Mary's Ascot, Wycombe Abbey and St George's Ascot team up for some drama productions and, as one chirpy pupil told us, 'We can meet girls in the holidays'. Asked whether you have to be a boffin, gifted sportsman or one of the lads to get the most out of the school, Eton insists not. 'A boy who wouldn't say boo to a goose when he arrived got really involved in theatre lighting and sound while he was here,' a master said. 'By the time he got to 17 he was so respected that he was cheered admiringly every time his name came up at the end of performances.' A mother said that even though boys need to be 'self-starters and able to keep up with the work', the school suits different types – super-bright, sporty, quirky, you name it – and boys don't have to be utterly brilliant. 'My three sons are all quite different,' she told us. 'But they have all been very happy there and done well.' Another parent described it as 'an extraordinary school, with amazing opportunities', though, given its size, 'perhaps not the place for wilting violets'.

The fourth of June (aka school speech day) is as buzzy as ever, but the mass of royal watchers have gone. A huge mix of families – 'We have boys whose families live in castles and boys whose families live on inner-city estates,' says school. Lots of first-time buyers, along with sons of Old Etonians.

Notable old boys listed on school website – illustrious roll includes Hubert Parry, David Cameron and 18 more previous prime ministers, loads of politicians (Eton provost William Waldegrave, Nicholas Soames, Douglas Hurd, Boris Johnson), Captain Oates, the poets Gray and Shelley, Princes William and Harry, a clutch of journalists (Charles Moore, Nicholas Coleridge, Craig Brown), plus chef Hugh Fearnley-Whittingstall, rower Matthew Pinsent, counter-tenor Michael Chance and Edward Gardner, musical director of the English National Opera.

Entrance: Around 1,000 candidates for 250 places – from more than 100 different schools. Entry procedure appears to be working well (the traditional 'put his name down at birth' regime was abolished in 2001) and the parents we spoke to expressed firm approval of its thoroughness. Pupils must be bright enough to cope with the academic demands of the school, but Eton is also looking for boys with spark, flair and potential who will thrive in a boarding environment.

All prospective applicants assessed in year 6 – ultra-detailed assessment includes verbal reasoning, numeracy, perceptual potential, interview and school report. Five-strong committee spends two days assessing the candidates, and out of 1,000 boys assessed at the age of 11, 250 will be offered places (conditional on passing CE or, for boys at state schools, Eton's own exam in year 8). Another 80 are placed on the waiting list. School recognises that by assessing in year 6, system may penalise late developers, so stays in touch with school heads and gets feedback on near-miss candidates. Successful candidates visit four boarding houses and list their choices – 80 per cent get one of their top two preferences.

Scholarships are a central part of the school – around 20 per cent of boys receive some form of financial support. Scholarship boys include 14 King's Scholars (decided on academic merit alone), plus New Foundation scholars (boys joining Eton from state schools) and many more.

To progress into the sixth form boys need a minimum of six A grades at GCSE, although in reality this is easily exceeded by all of them. Twelve sixth form scholarships offered a year – only for boys from state sector or independent schools lacking sixth form provision.

Exit: Sometimes loses one or two after GCSE – mainly those who opt for co-ed or day schools. At 18, virtually all progress to higher education. PPE, PPS, philosophy and theology the most popular subjects, followed by history/history of art, science and engineering. School says between 60-80 a year to Oxbridge, but refuses to give numbers for 2016; others to Russell Group and increasing numbers to American universities, the majority Ivy League.

Money matters: Pots of money and assets. Stunning setting means school has a popular sideline from films (The Madness of King George etc). Can afford to (and does) have everything of the best. Pays its staff very well indeed. Aim is that finances shouldn't be an obstacle to any boy who is offered a scholarship and a large number of bursaries for parents who can't afford the fees or have fallen on hard times. Regular subsidised summer schools – rowing a popular option for prep school wannabes.

Masses of public activity – the rowing lake at Dorney is used nationally for training international rowers (and for the London 2012 Olympic rowing and kayak events), and the athletics hall and swimming pools (indoor and outdoor) are much in demand by locals out of term time. Currently on a mission to raise £50 million to fund further bursaries – has raised more than half so far.

Remarks: Still the number one boys' public school. With teaching and facilities that are second to none, Eton produces bright, purposeful, articulate young men with a sense of ambition and self-worth. School is far more forward-thinking and outward-looking than many realise and really does encourage boys to make the most of the dazzling array of opportunities on offer.

Farleigh School

Red Rice, Andover, Hampshire SP11 7PW

Pupils: 430; 75 full/weekly, 33 flexi boarders • Ages: 3–13 (boarding from year 3) • RC

Fees: Day £5,055 – £18,405; Boarding £21,585 – £23,955 pa (HMF Boarding £20,355)

Tel: 01264 710766
Email: office@farleighschool.com
Website: www.farleighschool.com

Headmaster: Since 2004, Father Simon Everson BA Cert in theology (50s). Educated at Caterham School, studied theology at Leeds Collegiate and Ripon College, followed by three year certificate in theology awarded by Oxford University. An Anglican curate and vicar in London for 14 years, he moved to Hurstpierpoint College as senior chaplain in 1996. Following his conversion to Catholicism, he was appointed as chaplain and teacher at Farleigh in 1999, then head five years later.

A modest, softly spoken and self-effacing man, he doesn't engage his inner salesman straight away – prospective parents take note and beware of making snap judgements. Current parents and pupils were falling over themselves to tell us how highly they rate him (one mother phoned three times) and that he is an outstanding head. Whilst watching over every aspect of his charges' development – spiritual, social, moral and academic – he endeavours to dispatch children to their senior schools as educated, fair, kind and generous human beings. Still teaches half the school each week and leads by example, setting high expectations for manners and behaviour. Positively lights up around his pupils. Firmly believes that the school is there for the whole family and encourages wholesale parental and sibling participation.

Head's wife, Gail, is involved at all levels – a qualified nurse, she works as a learning support teacher in the pre-prep, helps in the nursery, teaches swimming and organises school flowers. They have two daughters, both at senior school.

Entrance: Not selective, pupils join at all stages. In pre-prep, the majority join aged 3; a few more at 5 (mostly from local nurseries), leaving occasional places in years 1 and 2. No formal assessment in pre-prep. Most transfer to the prep, but entry is not automatic (parents are kept well informed). From year

3, pupils come from local primaries or London schools, eg Broomwood Hall, Thomas's, Newton Prep, Fulham Prep and Finton House. One-to-one assessments in reading, writing, spelling, vocabulary and maths ('get to know the child' sessions) and report from current school required.

Numbers capped at 425, therefore priority given to practising Catholics, boarders and siblings, plus children of past pupils. Usually oversubscribed. Means-tested bursaries at head's discretion, 15 per cent discount to boarding children of Forces families.

Exit: Most at 13 – more than a third leave with scholarships and exhibitions: a good tally across the board, with sport and art featuring strongly, plus a healthy scattering of academic, all-rounder and music awards. Catholic schools are obviously popular, eg Downside, Ampleforth, St Mary's Ascot and St Mary's Shaftesbury, although a good number opt for local choices, eg Sherborne, Sherborne Girls', Marlborough College, King Edward VI, Winchester College and Cheltenham Ladies'. A few boys go to Eton, Radley and Harrow each year. A small number (fewer than five) leave at 11, mostly to senior girls' boarding schools, eg Downe House, St Swithun's and Godolphin.

Remarks: Founded in 1953 by Jocelyn Trappes-Lomax as a prep school for Catholic boys, initially based at Farleigh House, residence of the Earl of Portsmouth. Moved to its present home in 1982, a magnificent 19th century Georgian house built by General Webb. Set in 60 tranquil acres of sweeping parkland and has a landscaped arboretum (for history buffs, trees were planted in the troop formation of the Battle of Malplaquet in 1709). It's hard to believe that the A303 threads its way past just five minutes' drive from the school gates (handy for London parents).

The house has been sympathetically adapted to school life and some of its original charm remains in the elegant drawing room, used by the whole school as a common room in the evenings. Elsewhere the focus is on the modern and practical, both within the main house and without. All new buildings – including new science and food tech building – have been added to one side of the school, thereby preserving swathes of parkland on the other side and woodland to the rear.

Parents are full of praise for academic approach and achievement. One told us, 'Farleigh fulfils parents' ambitions and then some.' Children are taught by subject specialists from year 5 (French from year 2). Small class sizes – average 15. We observed plenty of sound teaching in core subjects. Maths is set from year 4 (for all other academic subjects from year 6) and parents say teaching is 'exceptional'. Able mathematicians given extra work and compete against other schools (a pupil in year 8 was current maths champion at Dauntsey's). English is also good – 'The teacher is wonderful, really old school' – and clearly effective, as a year 7 pupil won Marlborough's poetry competition. French good and looked like huge fun. Latin taught from year 6 and plenty of it, so those needing higher levels in CE can get there. Whole school follows a course known as The Way, The Truth, The Life in RS (not limited to Catholicism).

Exam preparation for scholarships is excellent. We noticed lots of extra coaching sessions squeezed in for individual year 8 pupils in most subjects (some voluntary). Scholars also have taster sessions in Spanish and Greek. Gifted and talented group meets several times a week for extra activities, eg debating (school has won Marlborough's prep school debating competition several times). All are helped to discover how they learn best. 'Teachers go the extra mile for the children – if a child expresses an interest in something they'll use breaks to teach it,' said one parent. Another told us: 'A work ethic is instilled in year 7 and there are grades every four weeks, so any problems are picked up early.' ICT provision is quirkily good, with a room full of computers and iPads for classroom use. Well-stocked library is run by hugely enthusiastic librarian and pupils can borrow Kindles as well as books, newspapers and magazines.

Exceptional, free SEN provision provided by four members of staff with impressive qualifications (69 pupils on the register when we visited). A few Spanish nationals receive EAL tuition. No surprise that more than a dozen teachers have stayed at Farleigh for more than 10 years – 'Father Simon has created a very happy stable ...The school has a satisfied customer feel'.

Sport takes place on wide expanse of playing fields bordering the front drive of the main house. Games on four afternoons a week and matches on Wednesday and Saturday afternoons. All the usual prep school sports on offer and staff put together three or four teams at the top of the school for boys' rugby, football and cricket and girls' hockey and rounders, with many more lower down the school. 'Everyone gets a chance at sport,' says the school. Annual rugby tour to France for boys in years 7 and 8; senior girls go on hockey and netball tours. Pre-season training is free of charge. Consistently good athletics results, with around 10 children each year representing the school at the National Athletics Championships. Unusual amount of competitive tennis on the calendar, eg house tennis, internal tournaments and matches against other schools. Pupils play tennis all year, with 80 per cent having coaching in the prep school. LTA Mini Tennis Awards scheme followed to year 6 and colours also awarded.

A good range of minor extracurricular sport played on two afternoons a week, eg girls' football, golf, squash, badminton, riding and fishing. Boys who don't enjoy rugby matches can choose to play hockey. School has a large gym and full size indoor swimming pool – boarders have access all week for free swimming. The best are invited to join swim squad; also weekly aqua fit and water polo sessions. Outdoor pool amongst the trees is used in summer.

The arts are thriving – modern, bright art block (two large rooms with high ceilings for painting, ceramics etc) doubtless contributes to the healthy number of art scholarships gained by pupils, who can use it whenever they like in free time. Well-equipped DT room next door.

Music block is somewhat less spacious – rooms for individual tuition and practice either side of a single corridor, with space for ensemble rehearsals on entry. Some 300 pupils have private music lessons, with over 60 learning more than one instrument. Singing is a popular choice and nearly 80 have voice lessons (we noticed good exam results here, with half the total number of distinctions awarded for voice). Lots of singing on the timetable, eg daily in chapel, weekly hymn practice and in class music lessons. Chapel choir is auditioned and occasionally tours abroad. Individual music lessons rotate through the timetable (year 8 pupils don't miss academic lessons) and practice timetabled for all. All the usual instruments on offer, as well as harp and bagpipes. Two further choirs, a school orchestra and rock academy, plus around 20 ensembles which rehearse weekly and perform music from jazz to chamber repertoire. Senior jazz band, The Thundering Herd, has played twice at the Edinburgh Festival. School musicians give seven big annual concerts, including a jazz dinner night. Music theory is offered as an extracurricular activity. Father Simon even makes music part of his morning assemblies, eg listening to Maria Callas.

School theatre is well equipped, with semi-professional lighting and sound and tiered seating (a good view of the stage at last). Two annual school productions include a year 8 musical (The Sound of Music, Bugsy Malone) and alternate productions by years 3 and 4 (Alice in Wonderland) or years 5 and 6 (Annie). LAMDA speech and drama lessons available and pupils can take exams if they wish. Optional creative activities include ballroom dancing, pottery and toy making.

Approximately one-third of the school boards, with flexi boarding available from year 3 up to the summer term of year 7, when families choose between day and full boarding. The majority choose to board in preparation for senior school. About 30 children stay in school every weekend and the full complement on the four 'all in' weekends every year.

Boarding provision is well organised (junior and senior dorms for boys and girls) and the house parents are 'brilliant at instilling spiritual values and manners'. Bigger rooms with more beds for the younger ones, shrinking to doubles for older children, and quite the cleanest and most orderly bathrooms we've yet to see, with a place for everything and everything in its place (possibly for our benefit, but suspect probably not). A really lovely touch is that some single rooms available for exam candidates, so they get a good night's sleep before a big day. Not a lot of room for storing personal possessions in dorms, so most clothing is stored in communal (and very tidy) cupboards and drawers, which lead into large senior common rooms with lots of home comforts, eg computers, TV, squashy sofas and toasters (healthy bowls of fruit here too).

School food is excellent, served cafeteria style in a bright, welcoming dining room. Even though we were slightly late for lunch, still plenty of choice and the food was very good, with fresh fruit on offer for pudding daily. School chef is a bit of a local hero, we gather, not least because he treats boarders to Dinner Night twice a term – pupils dress up and sit down to a themed dinner, which can be anything from Indian to Spanish. Junior boarders get the chance to cook every Friday, when they become kitchen sous chefs and prepare supper for the whole school.

Masses to do during evenings and weekends (including for day children staying late), from cub scouts, zumba and tennis to band practice and street dance. Acres of space to play in outside, either at Fortress Farleigh (traditional play area on the edge of the woods) or deeper into the trees, where pupils are free to roam, build dens etc.

Pastoral care praised time and time again by parents, as was inclusive ethos – 'The school includes my family in their big family,' a parent said. Staff too are welcomed into the fold – all staff members (not just teachers) belong to a house. As well as fostering community spirit, head cares passionately about behaviour and standards – 'Father Simon instils good moral values..The children become self-regulating'. Pupils confirmed zero tolerance of bullying and that kindness to others is prized above intellectual prowess. Everyone is encouraged to 'look beyond themselves' by helping others, eg hosting children with severe learning difficulties in school each week, helping at a local food bank and actively supporting a charity for street children in Colombia – 'It keeps hearts large,' said a parent.

The Catholic faith is at the school's core and Sunday mass is open to all. As well as preparing for first communion and confirmation, children can go on (short) religious retreats; an annual gathering for Patronal Feast Day. Head aims to keep faith both enjoyable and contemporary, eg interpreting the book of Genesis through Holst's The Planets. Members of other churches stress they 'never feel discriminated against for not being Catholic' and 'there is no default setting to send children to Catholic schools'. Perhaps most important is that the school's caring side ensures 'every child will leave with the sense that they have a strength ... not always the usual – it could be something unusual'.

Pre-prep housed in a super building on the fringes of the main campus and is 'beautifully run and thoughtfully managed'. Kindergarten off to one side, away from the hurly-burly. Children looked happy and engaged. Head of pre-prep made us smile by wishing aloud for more room – in fact the building is positively spacious, with four classrooms for years 1 and 2, another for reception, its own library and four separate play areas, not to mention masses of storage space for wellies, bookbags, coats and trainers.

Children in pre-prep walk to the main school for lunch and use other facilities, including the swimming pool and tennis courts. Swimming lessons and ballet timetabled for everyone all year; tennis coaching and football from year 1. After-school clubs include football, cricket, hockey, rounders and woodland games. A free violin taster group each term. French taught from year 2. Staff put on an annual summer concert, spring term production and Christmas show. Father Simon takes assembly one day a week to present children with 'good worker' certificates.

Parents are a harmonious mix of Londoners, locals and some Forces – 'There is a real mixture of people, some Sloaney and some not so; the Forces families are taken very seriously'. Lots of siblings, a few Spanish nationals and overseas British complete the mix. School escorts London-based pupils on the train to and from town on exeats and at half-term. Overseas boarders often stay with local families on exeat weekends (matrons help to coordinate arrangements). Pupils are open, honest, thoroughly genuine young people who clearly love their school and have respect and regard for each other. The fact that the Farleigh Society (old boys and girls) publishes a 25-page newsletter every year is proof that strong bonds are forged here; these often continue on through senior school and beyond.

Former pupils include Lord Stafford, Marquis of Bute, journalist Craig Brown, actor Rupert Everett, rugby player Hugh Vyvyan, TV presenter Hugh Cordey and climber Tarka l'Herpinière.

Every so often, we visit a school which is enjoying a real purple patch and getting most things right. Parental plaudits say it more succinctly than we could – 'It hasn't sacrificed values for academic successes,' and 'They are unwavering in their advice, honest and direct.' When it comes to the head, parents can verge on the evangelical, such as, 'Father Simon is absolutely extraordinary ... on a pedestal with so many parents'. We'll let them off – were we parents here, we rather think we would say the same. Not perhaps for anyone unwilling to buy into school's ethos, but clearly most see the light, and we suspect that this outstanding prep school will become even more sought after than it already is.

Felsted Preparatory School

Linked with Felsted School

Braintree Road, Felsted, Essex CM6 3JL

Pupils: 503; 10 full time, 44 weekly/flexi boarders • Ages: 4–13 (boarding from 9)

Fees: Day £8,775 – £16,650; Boarding £21,585 – £22,620 pa

Tel: 01371 822610
Email: rmw@felstedprep.org
Website: www.felsted.org

Head: Since September 2016, Mr Simon James BA PGCE (40s), whose degree is in history. He moved from Chigwell Junior School, where he was also head, before which he was head of Rossall School, Lancashire. Prior to that, he was director of studies at Kings School, Chester, a post he took up following various teaching posts at key stage 2.

He's relaxed, easy-going and chatty – definitely more of a 'carrot' than a 'stick' man, and with an open door policy for children, parents and staff alike. But don't be fooled – despite his warm and cuddly exterior, this is a head that kids don't want to disappoint and who is not afraid of being proactive when it comes to improving school processes and strategies. 'He's out and about every morning at the school gates, which is a really nice touch,' one parent told us, and he teaches games and history 'to keep in touch with pupils.'

He lives a 10-minute drive away with his wife, Jill – who joined Felsted as a teacher four years prior to him – and their two daughters, who joined the school when their mum did. 'It made this a very easy move for me,' he smiles. A keen cricketer and ex-rugby player, he enjoys cooking and travelling with his family during school holidays.

F

Entrance: Various entry points including 4+ and 7+, with big intake at 11+ when prospective pupils submit a confidential report from their previous school and undergo interview and assessments in English, maths, non-verbal and verbal reasoning. 'Entrance isn't overly selective, but it is rigorous when it comes to the process involved,' one parent sums up. Entry lower down is less stringent, although interview and taster day still a must (and a school report, if they're moving from another school). Academic scholarships are available, covering up to 20 per cent of fees. There's also the Mary Skills award (a convenient surname, if ever we heard one) for talent in subjects including music, sport, art, design, technology and engineering, which covers up to £2,000 of fees. Some open bursaries are also on offer. Unlike many other preps, classes continue up to the end of year 8.

Exit: More than 90 per cent proceed to the senior school, often to join older siblings. 'Caters for all types, so why look elsewhere?' The remainder head mainly to other boarding schools (one to Eton in 2016) and local 11+ grammar schools.

Remarks: The prep school is made up of a hodgepodge of buildings (some beautiful; some less so) directly across the road from its big sister, the senior school. With a few exceptions, these buildings are divided into four separate areas – each home to the school's four 'phases,' which move the pupils on towards greater self-reliance, focus and specialisation. Each phase has its own head, who – together with the director of learning and deputy head – make up the senior leadership team. Stewart House – home to reception, year 1 and 2 – is a contemporary, purpose-built two-storey building with lots of sunlight and stunning views, not to mention a huge, cuddly 'FelsTed' in the reception area. The colourful classrooms are spacious and colourful, with plenty of imaginative artwork adorning the walls, and there's a library, multi-purpose hall and wide, bright play spaces instead of corridors. Years 3 and 4 are based in Ffrome Court – a series of prefab buildings, where pupils can use the dedicated contained playground or venture out into the bigger green space, shared with the older children. At this age, children start to be mainly taught by subject specialist teachers. Years 5 and 6 move up to Cloisters – based in (you guessed it) the old cloistered part of the school, and finally, there's Courtauld House for years 7 and 8, which includes a sociable common room. All share the new and shiny science labs, spacious ICT suite, Ross Hall (for assemblies, performances and some games) and art block as part of their impressive facilities.

As with the senior school, parents here recoil at the thought of increased pressure and favour greater focus on individual educational plans, with the aim of ensuring maximum academic success – but not at the expense of other activities. Every pupil and parent we spoke to believes the balance is just right and we were impressed with the school's commitment to that overused term, 'holistic education.' Indeed, Felsted claims one of the biggest co-curricular programmes in the country, with LAMDA, golf, riding, cooking, gardening, Mandarin and judo just a few of the wealth of opportunities on offer for these lucky young things. There are also lots of trips – including overseas sports trips and a year 8 leadership weekend to Wales – and the head was about to introduce a bushcraft trip for year 6 when we visited. Day trips to support the curriculum include Colchester Zoo (pre-preps) and parliament for year 8s, and the five houses – known as leagues – bring some friendly competition to sports, music and drama. Plus, each league does its own charity work. 'It's a 24/7 school, so if you're not prepared to sign up to it, it's not the school for you,' warned one parent, but those who live it, love it.

The three classes per year group are kept to a maximum of 18 students up to year 3, which then rises to 20, and there's setting in languages, English, maths and science – usually with five tutor groups per year, with some exceptions (eg there are four groups for maths in years 6 and 7). There is plenty of personalised learning on offer for SEN, usually outside the classroom and for half-an-hour lessons – as many as necessary per week. 'Welcome to my box,' laughed the head of SEN when we met her. But although her office is indeed compact, there are two other dedicated learning support rooms upstairs and children seem to like the environment – definitely no stigma attached. As for the very able, extension lessons are available for subjects where students have particular strengths, as part of the VAPs (Very Able Pupils) programme. For year 8s, this programme involves one-and-a-half-hour Saturday morning sessions available with a sixth form mentor. 'I've got a very intelligent child, who is also very strong-minded, and they've dealt with him brilliantly,' one parent told us. 'For example, they wanted him to learn Greek and he was adamant he didn't want to, so they agreed that if he translated all the Harry Potter spells from Latin into English, they'd let him off – and he did! They stood by their word.'

Languages are strong, with all pupils learning Spanish, to which they add either French or German from year 6. The brightest kids also take Latin from year 7. Homework is given twice a week from year 5 and three times a week from year 7 and woe betide anyone who hands it in late. 'They cut you no slack,' one student told us, despite the long school day. Indeed, while year 2s and under finish at 3.30pm, year 3s start to be introduced to lengthier days that, by year 8, last from 8.20am-5.55pm – that's longer than a lot of adults spend at work in a full-time job. 'At least, there's Saturday school,' a couple of students said – which is optional for years 5 and 6 (with around 60 per cent take-up) and compulsory for years 7 and 8. Confused? 'Saturday school includes homework time,' they explain. In fact, the consensus was unanimously (and perhaps surprisingly) positive towards Saturday school among students and parents alike. 'You get to do activities like forest school and golf,' one student explained. Lots of development opportunities for teachers – one told us about 'a kind of speed dating event, where we had to share best practice in speed time, working our way round the room – it was really fun, and very useful.'

Drama is taught to all students weekly, with many choosing to take it as an extracurricular option on top. The result is a much-talked-about all-school performance every year, plus extra ones from some individual years. Ditto with music – as in all students do it, and many do extra, including belonging to the orchestra, chapel choir or one of the many bands and ensembles ranging from the jazz band to steel drum group. Plus, around 60 per cent learn an instrument via peripatetic lessons. We particularly love the two art rooms – an Aladin's cave of opportunity for budding young artists, who can try their hand at everything from textiles to pottery. 'The children particularly like getting involved in making props for the school plays,' the art teacher told us, and there is no shortage of proof – the huge elephant's head from the Lion King performance probably the most prominent.

Sport – of which the core for boys are rugby and hockey, while for girls, it's netball and hockey (and cricket for both in the summer) – seems to strike the right balance between healthy competition and inclusiveness, with regular fixtures for A-G teams in many sports. 'We like our A teams to do well, but we also like everyone to play because sport is such a central part of school life here,' says the head, and parents concur. 'My son is not naturally good at sport, but he enjoys it,' said one parent. That said, with players reaching county level in cricket and rugby – plus national finalists for hockey, netball and horse riding – there's plenty or silverware to keep the school cabinets glistening. Facilities are great, including five rugby pitches, three cricket squares and four tennis courts. There's also an outdoor swimming pool and sports hall. In addition, there are two all-weather Astroturf pitches, numerous netball and tennis courts (grass and hard) and indoor swimming pool (which needs updating) that they use over in the senior school.

Boarding is a major part of school life here, with Felsted Prep boasting its own – very uninstitutional – boarding house for year 6s upwards, which has a capacity for 64 students: one floor for boys, the other for girls. In reality, an average of 54 use it, which includes 10 full-time boarders, who tend to be international (mostly from China, Spain and expat families when we visited), while the rest are weekly or part-time boarders, where parents commit to three specific days a week. One weekend in three is full boarding, one is optional and the third is an exeat, so the most a child would be continuously at school is likely to be three weeks, which we think is right for children at this age and a good preparation for senior boarding schools. Bedrooms have between two and eight beds, with children encouraged to personalise their space, and each floor has its own common room. Just as we were noting that the house could do with a lick of paint here and there, we were introduced to a flamboyant woman who was painting not just plain walls, but some lively and modern murals. Meanwhile, the 1970s-esque pine beds are being updated with more contemporary oak veneer ones – also a much needed move.

The boarding day begins at 7.45am for breakfast, while evenings include homework time, activities ranging from ICT to football (with different choices each night), and weekends include trips out ranging from cinema to the beach. The house is heavily staffed (with very low staff turnover) by a set of houseparents, a second set of deputy house parents (both have families, adding to the family feel), plus house tutors, resident matron and four gap year students who live onsite in their own apartment. Even the so-called 'domestic fairies' get stuck into the community feel, with lots of friendly notes from students to them, and vice versa, left on doors. Communication with parents is encouraged, with animated videos regularly sent home and unlimited phone calls allowed during sociable hours. 'We now have a boarding house administrator to help manage this communication,' the housemistress – a delightful, bubbly woman – told us. The children we spoke to enthused about boarding, while the parents rave about the pastoral support.

Pastoral care is a key strength back in the daytime part of school too, with each head of phase tasked with ensuring the children are happy, while a tutor system for the older children means those in years 6, 7 and 8 have their own personal tutor for three years, who acts as a single point of contact for parents and with whom the children have a weekly individual meeting. We think this is an excellent model to ensure no one slips through the pastoral net. 'These tutors know us well and make sure we feel comfortable talking to them,' one student told us. 'It's a talking community anyway,' piped in another. 'So if you didn't want to talk to your tutor for any reason, there's always an older pupil available via the peer support system. And I know my mum likes the fact that she often gets emails telling her if I've done well in something like spellings or maths. It's just very, very open.' There's a matron available too, as well as mindfulness classes. Bullying is rare, not just for these reasons, but also the fact that they do talks on what it is and how to recognise it, and students told us it is dealt with quickly and humanely when it does occur. The school is keen on giving the children responsibilities and has created many leadership roles, and it doesn't just pay lip service to student voice, with the head meeting the pupil council weekly. There's a charity committee and global gang too.

While rewards are seen as being more effective than punishments to keep kids on the straight and narrow, misdemeanours are certainly not overlooked. Indeed, each child carries round two cards in their pocket, reminiscent of an old train ticket from the 1960s – green for good deeds and cream for bad ones. Teachers sign them when either happens (holding doors open might be a good one, while running in a corridor a bad one) and three signatures equals a house point or, conversely, a detention, either on a weekday – or for serious transgressions, a Saturday one with the headteacher.

F

Many of the weekend activities, which the children tell us they adore and are keenly anticipated, are open to parents and the grounds are fully used on a daily basis. The children have built an outdoor pizza oven, there are outdoor classrooms and mini Duke of Edinburgh style award activities outdoors one afternoon a week. There are clear rules about where in the grounds children can explore but plenty of space for climbing trees and building dams. The head is keen to introduce even more challenge to the outdoor education programmes.

Food is good – we tasted it – although the dining space options aren't great for the younger ones. It's taken to pre-preps; years 3 to 6 eat onsite in a small hall; and years 7 and 8 in senior school – to our mind, a great policy that helps older ones feel more independent and on their way to the senior school. In fact links with the senior school are increasing generally. 'In the past, it was seen as a separate school, but we're trying to make it a more seamless transition for the vast majority of students who go onto study there,' says the head – and that includes joint academic ventures, such as years 7 and 8 working with seniors on science projects and use of sports facilities.

Despite the school being located in rural Essex, it feels part of a much bigger world rather than existing as a primary school bubble – no doubt helped by things like their 'global centre,' complete with a Skype wall, which enables pupils to communicate with a school they support in India. Families – who are a mixture of traditional farming families, the super-wealthy, entrepreneurs, middle-class professionals and no shortage of dual-income families – can't get enough of it. 'Felsted is more of a way of life than a school,' one parent told us. 'And it's one the children know they are very lucky to have.'

Many schools claim to be child-centred, focusing on each individual across a wide ability range, but not all achieve it. Felsted does, providing a busy, bustling and largely fun environment, where the ethos is all about doing the very best you can and finding your key strengths. This early growth mind-set has many of the youngsters believing everything is possible – great preparation for the senior school, where an all-round education is taken to a whole new level. 'This is a school that brings out the best in everyone,' sums up a parent. 'It's education to fit the individual child, not the other way round.'

Felsted School

Linked with Felsted Preparatory School

98

Felsted, Great Dunmow, Essex CM6 3LL

Pupils: 542; 254 full/weekly, 237 flexi boarders • Ages: 13–18 • Sixth form: 246 • C of E

Fees: Day £22,125 Boarding £27,585 – £32,985pa

Tel: 01371 822605
Email: admissions@felsted.org
Website: www.felsted.org

Headmaster: Since 2015, Chris Townsend BA PGCE (40s), previously deputy head. Classics degree from Oxford, where he was an exhibitioner and won three cricket blues. First teaching post at alma mater Dean Close, then housemaster and head of boarding at Stowe, then to Felsted in 2010 as deputy head.

Students and parents alike revel in recounting the story of the moment his appointment as head was announced. 'The whole school – including staff and pupils – erupted into applause, which lasted for about 10 minutes!' we were told, with all parents, staff and pupils we spoke to enthusing about how 'excellent,' 'inspirational' and 'nurturing' he is. 'He has a huge amount of respect from everyone and knows every child,' one parent told us. 'He is absolutely committed to making education well-rounded so that every child's strengths are valued and nurtured,' said another. 'He leads by example and gets really stuck into school life,' a student told us, with evident pride. Indeed, he teaches when he can (Greek and Latin), plays piano at school concerts, referees some of the rugby, as well as doing the corridor rounds and attending some school trips, including one to Uganda and Malawi in the summer holidays. But despite his larger-than-life reputation, he is not extrovert, loud, opinionated or loquacious. Conversely, we found him mild-mannered, quiet and unassuming – just the kind of chap you'd feel safe leaving shy, petrified little Johnny with on first day of boarding school. Not that he's afraid to discipline, as any student will confirm.

He couldn't live closer if he tried, with a door behind his office desk leading straight to home, where he resides with his wife Melanie (assistant head at another local school), their two children (both at Felsted) and a red setter.

Academic matters: Not overly selective, but each year a solid cohort achieves top grades across the board in both GCSEs and A levels: in 2016, 46 per cent A*/A at GCSE and 30 per cent at A level. The broad ability range is big pull to many parents, including one who told us, 'My son got into a top grammar school, but I didn't want him in a highly pressurised, "work-work-work" environment – Felsted still gets good results, but it's more fun, offers a more holistic education and has a mix of people that better reflects real life.'

At GCSE, the strongest subjects are maths, English, sciences, RE and languages, with other popular options including geography and history. There's also a good creative uptake, with decent numbers of students and grades in DT, music and drama. At A level, students do particularly well in psychology, geography, RE and history – and, increasingly, maths and science. Other popular options include business studies and economics. 'This part of the world is known for its entrepreneurial buzz,' points out the head. More generally, the school has a reputation of bringing out the best in all and IB is taking off even among quite conservative local families – currently about a third of the sixth form opts for it: 35 average point score in 2016.

Year 9s all learn Spanish (the core language here), plus French, German or Latin, then in year 10 they can take up to three languages, with other options including Italian. Other languages also on offer as part of the IB, where they can be self-taught, with past students having done just that with Japanese, Russian and Mandarin. Parents praise the 'native speaking language teachers and high number of classroom assistants to make sure everyone stays on track.'

Setting (up to six sets per year) in maths, English, sciences and languages and class sizes are kept small, between 15-20 up to GCSE, and often considerably smaller in sixth form. Staff development encouraged, with both peers and pupils invited to provide feedback on selected lessons and suggest what constitutes good or outstanding teaching – all part of the collaborative ethos of the school. Projects with other schools also exist, with a view to sharing best practice. Teachers – all of whom are involved in pastoral care and who really get to know the children – are known for being a thoroughly committed bunch, with a positive and engaged staff common room.

Homework isn't for the faint-hearted, although for the younger ones, homework sessions are built into the school day – a welcome relief, say parents, given that the school day lasts from 8.15am to 6pm and there's also Saturday school. IT is embedded into learning, with pupils encouraged to use Chromebooks, Google Classroom and even smartphones in some lessons (more of which, later).

SEN pupils, of whom there are many (albeit at the mild to moderate end – mainly dyslexia, dyspraxia, ADHD and autistic spectrum), have personalised support from the learning department, which has no stigma attached, not least because it's open to everyone, offering everything from intensive one-to-one tuition to drop-in sessions to help with prep. 'Why wouldn't you want extra support to help you do your best?' one student asked, rhetorically. 'My son has dyslexia and he wound up with As and A*s, thanks to the personalised support he got behind the scenes,' said one parent. EAL teachers also on hand, also in a specialist department.

Games, options, the arts: Traditionally sporty, with the school producing some outstanding cricketers and Olympic athletes, and there were three boys signed to professional rugby teams when we visited. In fact, hockey, rugby, netball and cricket (including for girls, now that it's replaced rounders) are all strong, with regular success at regional and national championships. Partnerships with professional clubs such as Saracens Rugby, Essex Cricket and Blue Hornets Hockey. But fear not if your child doesn't make the teams as the emphasis is very much on participation. 'Neither of my children are hugely sporty, but they still play in matches, which is great,' one parent said. Lots of other alternatives to keep you fit and occupied, including swimming, badminton, squash, show jumping, water polo and tennis, to name a few. Games fields and facilities stretch as far as the eye can see across the school's 80 acres and includes 12 pitches, nine cricket squares, two floodlit AstroTurf fields, 10 hardcourts, squash courts, gym, weight training – and the rather less impressive and tired-looking sports hall and indoor swimming pool, the latter of which was mentioned by almost every parent we spoke to as the 'main downside of the school.'

Pupils are all expected to have a crack at music, in one form or another – and few complain, with lots of pride around the many choirs (including the elite chapel choir that sings at main services) and orchestras. The House Shout singing competition is a favourite event, and all students sing in chapel. Quite a few learn an instrument via a peripatetic teacher and there's an emphasis on percussion, including marimba players (a marimba was donated to the school by Dame Evelyn Glennie, who performed here). Regular opportunities for overseas tours – the choir was going to Italy at Eastertime during the academic year we visited.

Everyone does drama in year 9, then it's an option – but a popular one, with a few students going onto study it at university. Easily the best school play posters we've ever seen displayed on the walls – including Jesus Christ Superstar (which around 120 pupils took part in) and Joseph. Parents rave about the quality. 'My daughter has the most wonderful experience, when it comes to acting – she's got involved in absolutely everything and loved every minute,' one parent told us. Every two years, the school takes a production to America, including a past performance in a maximum security women's prison.

The art school, which is based in the old school laundry, is fabulously quirky and practical, with plenty of great facilities (although no dark room, we noticed) and an authentic feel. Popular at GCSE, IB and A level, with history of art and art options available. Extracurricular possibilities are plentiful, including weekly life drawing sessions. Evidence of some serious talent.

Foreign exchanges to a wealth of countries and residentials to practically everywhere you can think of. Biologists and geographers go to Bali; tennis players to Portugal; business studies students to New York; sports tours to Australia etc etc. Back in the UK, geography field trip to rather less glamorous Swanage and plenty of cultural trips to the likes of Cambridge and London. Charity volunteers to Uganda, their partner school in Ethiopia and a former pupil's Magic Bus, which supports children in the slums of Mumbai – and there are links with Royal Docks Community School in the East End, which pupils regularly visit.

You won't find many schools with a longer list of extracurricular options – we felt exhausted just looking at the 50+ options including academic society, charity projects, amateur radio club, astronomy club, beekeeping, bridge, Greek club, life skills, Model United Nations, Science film club. Huge take up of D of E – at the last count no fewer than 12 gold awards in the upper sixth – and 237 enrolled in CCF. Very much accords with Round Square school promoting IDEALS – internationalism, democracy, care for the environment, adventurous pursuits, leadership and service. Felsted has been a global member since 2010. And because students queue up for opportunities to break the 'Felsted bubble,' it all makes for very full days and busy weekends. No wonder it was pointed out to us time and again by pupils and parents that this school is not for the retiring, ill-organised or easily-wearied type.

Boarding: Some 80 per cent board, taking up one of these three options: full-time (mostly international and expat families, with a sprinkling in the UK), weekly (usually, when both parents work) or three-nights-a-week (mainly local families – some even in the village itself). 'We live in the village, but I asked my mum and dad if I could board as you get the best of both worlds,' one student told us. 'There's always a waiting list – the boarders are really happy,' said a parent. 'They love the camaraderie and really enjoy the relationships with the houseparents, matron and the ladies who help with cleaning and ironing. There's a real sense of community, a great atmosphere and they form strong bonds,' said another.

Two day and eight boarding houses, five for boys and five for girls – plus co-ed boarding in the prep school from 9 years upwards. Separate upper sixth form boarding houses. Here, students get their own room and more freedoms – seen as good preparation for university. Each house has its own unique feel and ranges from being in the main building of the old school (traditional rooms – almost an Oxbridge feel) to the brand new, open-plan girls' boarding house. Ongoing investment means that a seven-figure sum was also about to be spent on upgrading one of the boys' houses when we visited. Every boarding house has an emphasis on homeliness and sociability, but also allows the children personal space – with dorms ranging from singles up to eight beds. 'They're pretty strict on tidiness, but it's more a case of matron having a quiet word, rather than draconian room inspections,' a student told us. 'Bedtimes feel fair – year 9s have lights out at 9.45pm, which goes up to 10.30pm in upper sixth,' said another, who adds that mobile phones are handed in overnight.

While the boarding timetable is highly structured (in evenings, it's supper in main school, back to your house for prep, then quiet time, while weekends have a full activity programme, with chapel on Sundays), there's also 'lots of chances to catch your breath,' as the head puts it. Boarders particularly like the independence – for example, being able to walk to the local shop or getting a Chinese take-away from the village – which is well balanced by the feeling that this is a really supportive environment, with many of the houseparents having young families. There are no restrictions on parental visits and robust measures in place to help new and international students settle in. And although many local boarders disappear at the weekends, the stayers-in are rarely short of invitations to stay with local families, outings or on-site activities to fill their time. Likewise, there's no need for day pupils to feel left out, with one parent commenting, 'Both of my kids are day students and they were at school until 10pm three evenings last week. They often stay on for a house BBQ or pizza evening – it's all very inclusive.'

Background and atmosphere: Traditional, yet progressive, it feeds off its history but is not hidebound by it. Founded in 1564 by Richard, Lord Riche, Lord Chancellor of England, the school's original Guild Hall is still in use with other, later, attractive grade I and II listed buildings scattered throughout the village, interspersed with well-tended lawns and sports fields and cut through by the quiet Dunmow to Braintree road. Most recent additions include the music school and the sixth form centre – a great space to hang out, play pool or enjoy regular social events where the odd glass of wine is permitted. Pupils particularly like the coffee shop – open to all in recreational times, although only sixth formers are allowed to work in there. Some areas could do with an upgrade, notably the swimming pool and sports hall – and we'd hoped for more of a wow factor in the library. 'My husband went to Felsted and much of it doesn't feel look like it's changed from 30 years ago – but then again, it's not the facilities that make a great school,' said one parent. We can vouch for the fact that the food is good (new caterers had just been brought in, thanks to the student food committee, when we visited), and parents praised the fact that youngsters can now go up for unlimited helpings. 'My son is a strapping lad, so he needs it!' said one. As a C of E school, the chapel is at its heart and Felsted is one of only two remaining independent schools to have its own mission church in the East End of London, with links to the church and the young people in the surrounding area.

Overall impression of being a happy, happening place with parents content to be swept along for the ride. 'I'd be amazed if you found a Felstedian that wakes up and think, "I don't want to go to school today",' said one student.

Pastoral care, well-being and discipline: 'We have very well behaved children at all times,' says the head and although he's teasing, there's no doubt the balance of rewards and sanctions sets a high standard. This is a school with big expectations around behaviour and uniform, which seem to be unanimously welcomed by parents and local businesses – and even the children agree it's 'all pretty fair.' 'You're as likely to get rewarded for good behaviour as you are punished for misdemeanours,' one told us, explaining the school's card system, which involves each pupil carrying two small cards in their pocket – one for good deeds to be instantly recorded by teachers ('If we carry books for a teacher, for example') and one for transgressions ('If our uniform is really scruffy or we talk in class, for instance'). 'The principle is that any incident is dealt with at source,' explains the head, explaining that a full 'good' card gets you housepoints, while a full 'bad' one lands you in detention, of which there are various levels – Saturday ones being considered the gravest. Around a dozen temporary exclusions in the year we visited, mainly for serious bad language, bullying and alcohol abuse.

All this is balanced with some surprisingly lenient policies, including around mobile phones, which pupils are allowed to have throughout the day. 'Mobile phones are part of modern living. So there seems nothing to be gained by denying their existence, and much more to be gained by embracing them and it's for this reason that we sometimes ask students who have one to produce them during a lesson and use them to assist with learning,' one teacher told us. And because the school called on the student council to help write up the code of conduct around the use of mobile phones (students aren't allowed to walk around using them, for instance), the rules are respected and followed, say pupils – adding that this is a reflection of the seriousness with which student voice is taken at Felsted.

Pastoral care highly praised and attributed to a range of factors, including an atmosphere of openness and purpose; the house system that 'means everyone is close – and not just with people in their year,' said a student; peer counselling; and prefects being trained in child protection. Bullying minimal, doubtless for all the same reasons – and when it happens, it's dealt with swiftly on both sides. A life coach and a counsellor are on hand.

Pupils and parents: Felsted produces self-starting, entrepreneurial and independent spirits – characteristics that are immediately evident among the ambitious, self-motivated and self-aware pupils, who have some of the healthiest can-do attitudes we've seen. The mix of students – who range from the highly-driven and academically-oriented to the more fun-loving and easy-going – is a breath of fresh air. And they are all pretty down to earth. Parents (many of whom went to the school themselves) love that this is no academic hothouse, yet their offspring still do very well, and they champion the provision of holistic education. 'If you're the kind of young person who just wants your head in a book the whole time, your parents would probably be wasting their money on Felsted because of the ridiculous number of opportunities on offer,' one student told us and parents concur.

'But if you think a lot is expected of the kids at Felsted, wait until you hear about the parents,' laughed one mother we spoke to. 'We're only into the second week of term and already we've had harvest festival and a charity event – and that's not including Saturdays spent watching sport.' But nobody says it with an ounce of irritation. 'I love it – we all do.'

Long list of notable OFs includes English test cricketer John Stephenson and General Sir Richard Dannatt, until recently chief of the general staff. Huge diversity of talent is reflected in the senior positions and success OFs have achieved in science and medicine, the military, politics and public service, academia, business, sports and the media.

While most live within a couple of hours of the school, it is increasingly attracting London-based families. Taking advantage of its proximity to Stansted Airport, international students make up some 18 per cent of pupils – getting towards the high end amongst schools in this guide. Lots of Germans, Spanish and Italians do IB and a similar number of students from Middle East and all round the world.

Entrance: A hundred pupils – split across three classes – come in at year 9: around 70 come up from the prep (having passed a transfer exam), with the remaining 30 from feeder schools including Holmwood House, Heathmount, Orwell Park and Edge Grove. Those taking CE are required to obtain 50 per cent in each paper. Others take a verbal reasoning test, interview and submit a confidential report from their current school. They may also take tests in maths, French and English for setting purposes. The same is true at 14+ entry. At 16+ (when the year group increases from 100 to 125), there is a similar entry procedure and pupils are required to obtain five GCSEs at grade B or better including B grades in the subjects being pursued. Pupils who do not have English as their first language will be assessed by the head of EAL.

Exit: Around 90 per cent stay on to the sixth form. After A level, most to good universities such as Exeter, Brighton, Leeds, Newcastle, Birmingham and the top London universities. Two to Oxbridge in 2016. Business-related subjects, medicine, humanities, law and the sciences popular.

Money matters: Academic, music, sport, art, design and technology or drama and all-rounder scholarships offering up to 20 per cent off the fees are available at 13+ and 16+. There are some assisted places up to 100 per cent on a means-tested basis or via open bursaries.

Remarks: At one time, the focus on catering for a wide ability range meant this school's reputation in the academic stakes wasn't as high as it could have been. Not so now, with a renewed focus on academic performance striking just the right balance with valuing individualism and quirkiness. No wonder there's such a sense of excitement as this school becomes increasingly recognised as a leading independent boarding and day school.

Feltonfleet School

Byfleet Road, Cobham, Surrey KT11 1DR

Pupils: 400; 48 weekly and flexi boarders • Ages: 3–13 (boarding from age 7) • C of E

Fees: Day £11,115 – £16,335; Weekly boarding £22,470 pa

Tel: 01932 862264
Email: office@feltonfleet.co.uk
Website: www.feltonfleet.co.uk

Headmaster: Since 2012, Mr Alastair G Morrison BA PGCE (40s). Follows 12 years as deputy head and director of sport at Fettes College Preparatory School. Before that, three years as class teacher of Edinburgh Academy Junior School.

Bitten by education bug when shared a house with two teachers at Durham, saw them in action and was won over by variety and fulfilment.

Instant appeal of school took trauma out of first foray south. 'Love being here,' he says on the website. Family immersion is total, what with smiley wife Lizzie, arts and ICT whizz, now 'fully supportive HM's wife' and three daughters all attending the school. Even dog gets own portrait on the 'Who we are' notice board. (Bursar, not an animal lover, isn't keen but as 'doesn't like humans either,' jokes school insider, it's staying.)

Zest, opportunity and confidence, 'the benefit that boys and girls reap from learning' (always good in a school) are some of fab reasons that, says head, puts this establishment 'in the front rank.'

Slightly stiff-sounding formality in print is in marked contrast to relaxed affability in the flesh. Parents unanimously keen. 'Approachable and friendly, cheerful and bubbly,' says one. 'You just want to eat him and take him home,' drooled another.

Officially 'doesn't take himself at all seriously,' proof provided by skills with the dressing up box. Has delighted all by appearing as the Pink Panther. 'Took everyone by surprise,' says parent. More conventionally, donned kilt for Foreign Countries day (in suit and tie during morning of visit, but we're sure he has suitably patriotic knees).

We'd lay odds, however, on necessary layer of igneous rock lying just underneath charm and soft accent, essential when there's law to be laid down and assertive parents to be tackled. 'Definitely strong enough to deal with that – no pushover,' thought mother.

Considered a breath of fresh air to point where parents wonder if hasn't got some of local schools running scared. A little over-stated, reckons Mr Morrison, though is unquestionably ambitious, sights set on making school first choice all the way through rather than acceptable reserve.

Mr Morrison is also charged by governors with bumping up boarding, turning it from current niche add-on – despite considerable perks including extra subject tuition as well as, says school, 'super' choice of fun stuff – to over-subscribed wanna do (expect heavy duty puns round theme of Feltonfleet Knights). With Sir William Wallace, St Joan of Arc and St George all likely to feature, could make for entertaining Saints vs Sirs tournaments...

Though extensive transport links suggest bit of own goal (why board if you can bus daily from Wimbledon?) school won't go the day-only cop-out route. Irreplaceable depth and richness added by boarding makes it a non-negotiable.

What won't change is school-wide emphasis on importance of treating others as you wish to be treated. Signs promoting head's motto: 'Be kind, be kind, be kind,' started by predecessor and dotted round the school, show every sign of going strong, from refusal by pre-prep staff to hand out party invitations unless whole class invited (we wish it happened everywhere) to prompt quelling of pitch-side bad behaviour, parental support now so low key that Mr Morrison is having to put out message that small, selective outbreaks of cheering are perfectly OK. Useful particularly when, as referee, is on business end of choice abuse from opposing teams.

Anxious parents should feel reassured. 'Sounds corny but there's something intangible here which is very warm and special,' says Mr Morrison. 'My predecessor has handed me a lovely school and we're not going to change in too much of a hurry but keep pushing in the same direction.'

Entrance: Though no longer as non-selective as it used to be, exam success still 'not the be all and end all,' thought one mother.

First come, first served nursery entry means, says Mr Morrison, that 'broad range of ability inevitably comes through.' Parents well advised to be fleet of foot, successful bagging one of just 20 places achieved by registering at (or possibly during) birth.

Competition for 35 external year 3 places less of an extreme sport, though popularity growing so fast that border controls in form of maths and English assessment plus interview 'to search out character and enthusiasm for learning' are now in place. (Own year 2 children aren't tested). No official feeders, though The Rowans, Wimbledon College Prep, Lion House, The Merlin, Weston Green and Glenesk all feature on suppliers' list.

Lots of behind the scenes liaison to ensure smooth transition to prep, extra support formalised in year 5 (English and maths), setting introduced for most subjects in year 7 – in class and one-to-one support for 11 EAL and 80 or so SEN pupils a fixture on the menu, head's desire to ensure barriers posed by learning difficulties are surmounted tempered with realities of what can be achieved. While classroom disruption, if severe, point at which school says no, parents praise thoroughness of approach. 'They did assessments and have been all over it – definitely worth it,' said one whose child has mild difficulties.

Occasional places also crop up, year 7 next biggest entry point following some post 11+ departures at end of year 6.

Judging by children we met, school's character-judging abilities are first rate, pupils to a boy or girl displaying a maturity, vivacity and sense of fun that made them outstanding tour guides (and some of the hottest – blazer-clad, through choice, on boiling June day).

F

Exit: Good guidance on future schools. St John's, Epsom and Reed's remain the obvious destinations in 2015 (and prominent fixtures on scholarship list) though most of big names (Eton, Wellington, King's Wimbledon, Hampton, Brighton College) put in occasional appearances.

School has right connections, reckon parents, head cultivating contacts, scholarships hovering round 16 mark (around two academic, very successful for sport).

Some year 6 departures inevitable, says Mr Morrison, 'mainly those who parents perceive would struggle with CE.' Makes equal boy/girl split in each year group commendable, though with year 7 places easily filled, virtue pays off.

Remarks: 'Really lovely,' say parents, who warn against being over-influenced by either location (side turn off fast road makes for 'hairy' arrivals and departures, says one mother) or building work (new performing arts centre, now open, was under construction on date of visit).

Occasional cement mixing aside, charm is order of day. Calvi, the separate building for nursery to year 2 pupils, winningly equipped, from own hall to shaded play areas (trees a feature everywhere) with big sandpit and marked out scooter track, library that doubles as ICT room (now re-christened Digital Learning Facility – good tinies' tongue-twister, we'd have thought), double-banked computers forming orderly row down the middle.

Sensible child and parent-friendly touches, from box packed with named bottles of sun cream by door on sunny days to big, smiley puppets adding comforting touch to office. Plentiful wildlife, too, some real (popular guinea pigs, available for cuddles, and tadpoles, who aren't) others artistic creations (we liked jellyfish hung at optimum viewing height for the under-7s; adults compelled to peer through forest of dangling paper fronds, Sir David Attenborough-fashion).

Homely domesticity extends to main prep building (mid-19th century Victorian gothic), which opens out into sweep of green, stretching away down gentle slope towards grass pitch, idyllically bounded by woods, dipping pond much used by all year groups, boarders given exclusive romping rights once day children have gone home. 'Wouldn't even guess space was there,' says parent. 'Like a little hidden pocket.' Weekly and flexi plus day boarding options – latter can include a full boarding day without the sleepover.

Here, as elsewhere, essential to shut ears to competing clamour of A3 that borders one side of site, though pupils oblivious, head ditto, despite home so close to slow lane that recently extending kitchen has brought them within number plate spotting distance (governors are considering acoustic barrier – we hope they get it).

Head's study, essay in dignified blues, gets best of panoramic views, where life 'is all happening in front of you,' says parent, from matches to pleasant end of day tradition of biscuit distribution, children flocking in from all over grounds in response to telepathic signal beamed out by biggest box of bourbons we've ever seen, like navy-clad pigeons.

Plenty of idiosyncratic charm throughout, from recently revamped junior block (years 3 and 4) classrooms with winning cosiness, colour and light to seniors' French classroom with miniature shop and restaurant, complete with groceries and chalk 'specials' board, much used for role play.

We'd also recommend viewing astonishing Latin room, folders block-banked by colour like giant Rubik cube, walls ringed with sturdy supermarket bags – one per child – for instant decluttering before tests, and even back-office, Perspex towers of meticulously labelled stationary boxes soaring to the ceiling, the whole like prayer to Roman god of organisation (if one existed).

F

Teaching styles similarly varied, shock and awe a science speciality, with prospectus (helpfully written in nice big typeface – boon for older first time parents) featuring open-mouthed wonder as Bunsen burner shoots impressive flames across lab. Most staff are 'lovely', says pupil. 'My son randomly said, "Mummy, I've got the best teacher in the whole world, because she's really kind",' confirms pre-prep parent.

Best, judging by quick-fire exchange with prep pupils in English lesson to tease out clues in short story, are also brilliant, though zeal not yet universal, thought parents. 'Some are not as motivated as I think they should be,' reckoned a mum.

Years 1 and 2 stick broadly to national curriculum (as was) with specialist teaching for French, PE, swimming and music and get shot at DT, too – as well as input from grand-sounding and popular director of digital learning who sweeps in to 'enhance use of computer' – visits nursery and reception, too. Options grow with age, array of tempting additions bulked up in prep, judo to trampolining all good, food tech so sought after that canniest book up in winter, the longest term.

Surprise subject addition all way through from year 1 is positive living, new(ish) big hitter on PSHE timetable, stopping in year 7 (when perhaps pupils are so positive expectations need to be hoicked down slightly).'Love it,' says pupil. 'It's about living a happy and good life.'

Useful antidote to emphasis on emotional resilience made much of elsewhere. 'Saddens me that it's seen as necessary,' says Mr Morrison.

Maximum class sizes of 18, optimum size for lively classroom atmosphere, reckons Mr Morrison, and overall teacher ratio is around half that (one to just over nine) ensuring help for any waifs and strays (almost universally true, save for one child whiling away whole class reading session by reconfiguring contents of pencil case, apparently unobserved).

Parents generally delighted with academic running, bar desire for a little more in the way of help both with exam preparation – 'Child didn't even know how to revise,' thought one – and additional feedback outside formal parent teacher meetings. 'Have to assume no news is good news,' says prep parent. Mr Morrison is on the case with 'eye on the reporting structure,' he says, also stressing staff responsiveness to parental concerns whenever and however expressed.

A few will relate to sport. Strong range on offer (netball, hockey, rounders and lacrosse basic range for girls, football, rugby, hockey and cricket for boys, swimming, cross-country and athletics for both). Fab facilities, too, indoor swimming pool, all-weather Astroturf and 'suite' of cricket nets most recent to be added to 25-acre site which already accommodates yodelling-quality sports hall, hard surface tennis courts and two rifle ranges (air and.22) on top of scenic sports fields. All tucked in neatly, consistency of design making additions easy on the eye.

School recognises not just talent but wholesome attitudes by awarding internal sports scholarships to year 7 pupils (does same with drama and music). Strategy is to seek out challenge, everyone representing the school regardless of talent, plenty of tolerance for the rugby-averse – not the case elsewhere. 'Often the nicest boys who do hockey,' said year 7 pupil.

Mega results in shooting – teams beat everyone everywhere, including older siblings in senior schools (Wellington and Epsom College). Coach, who travels here from Wales 'because he likes us' secret weapon. Success not always replicated elsewhere, felt parent. Enviably good sportsmanship comes at a price – teams losing when, says Mr Morrison 'I know that if they had wanted it a bit more, they could have done it.' Delicate balancing act, thinks parent, who reckons top layer of loveliness needs to be scraped away and long-buried competitive instincts excavated so sport can take off. 'Winning matters, that's how life is, you get the job or you don't get the job. School needs to teach pupils that should love to win but that it's OK to lose.'

Performing arts popular and wide-ranging, one year 3 boy renowned for tap dancing, budding actor in year 6 making West End début. Drama high in pupil approval ratings for raising serious issues (bullying, gender wars) but not neglecting humour. 'Emotional but funny – what you'd find in everyday life,' said year 7 pupil of recent production.

Music draws in many, courtesy of good peripatetics ('nicest school I work in,' said one) almost half learning instruments, talented hitting grade 5 and up, occasional prodigy whistling through to diploma stage, orchestra supplemented by different single-instrument ensembles (flute and wind) as well as choirs (junior and senior), rotating timetables made easy with yellow badge reminders distributed daily. 'You're not going to forget with this hanging off you,' says pupil.

Something of a sanctuary for with those arriving from nearby little prince (and princess) establishments, often breathing big sigh of relief at low tiara factor (or gender neutral equivalent). That said, parental attitudes, though NFS (Normal For Surrey) can prove unwelcoming for incomers. Fine for those in at the start – 'joined in nursery and our friends will be friends for life,' said one mother – but can translate to 'cliques and Queen Bees,' according to parent who joined further up the school and felt Mr Morrison might usefully beam 'be kind' message into minds of some adults, too. 'Am hoping [his] influence will trickle down.'

Ditto consideration. Some irritation over parking habits of minority who cope with what one parent describes as 'wholly inadequate' spaces by routinely usurping slots reserved for minibus. 'Seem to feel that so special or busy those normal rules don't apply,' says another parent. Other (minor) niggles include lost property black hole which can suck in objects for months, then mysteriously spit them out again – whereabouts in the meantime a mystery. Recruitment of year 8 prefects to scan changing rooms reducing the problem, reckoned pupils, though excessive spoon feeding should be curbed, thought mother. 'Kids have to learn the responsibility for keeping their own things in check.'

Amongst all parents we spoke to, biggest gripe was reserved for uniform. Tons of it, some sensible or suitably traditional (woolly blazers, nice looking and sufficiently robust to stand repeated use as ad hoc goalposts, a case in point), others tending towards overkill/slightly bonkers, headed by summer only fleece. And don't get parents started on the ankle socks, dark blue with – go faster?- stripes. Justifiable in summer, with khaki shorts, less so in winter with long trousers 'when can't see them anyway.' 'Needs a cull, or at least a rethink,' thought parent. Good news, courtesy of Mrs Morrison, who feels exactly the same way, is that it's getting one.

With the Morrisons running the show, atmospheric school seems set for still better things to come in years ahead. As long as the kindness that really does emanate from delightful pupils remains, it's a gem heading for disco ball sparkle (but without corresponding tackiness). Expect more bullseyes – and not just in shooting.

The Folkestone School for Girls

Coolinge Lane, Folkestone, Kent CT20 3RB

Pupils: 1,098 • Ages: 11–18 • Sixth form: 237

Tel: 01303 251125
Email: headteacher@folkestonegirls.kent.sch.uk
Website: www.folkestonegirls.kent.sch.uk

Principal: Since 2004, Mrs Tracy Luke. First joined the school as deputy head in 2001. A 30-year career in teaching has taken her from a school in inner city Manchester where one child murdered another in the playground, to one of Kent's best performing schools. She has also taught overseas (at the King's School for service children in Gutersloh, Germany) and at Welbeck College.

Her tenure has included a five-year concurrent appointment as executive head at Marsh Academy, a school in difficulties. She has been back full-time at Folkestone School for Girls since 2012.

She's warm and smiley and the girls seem at ease in her presence. But she's also ruthless when it comes to ensuring the highest standards from her teaching staff. She has a likeable honesty – just as ready to tell us where she still needs to make improvements as to talk about successes. Definitely on top of her brief.

Academic matters: In 2016, 48 per cent of GCSE grades A*/A. 'Each year we have a group of at least five girls who in other schools would not get their GCSEs,' said the head. 'We make sure they do.'

The school operates an online learning gateway, which teaches parents how to help with their children's education. It lists what children will be studying and how parents can complement this with exhibitions to visit, websites to look at and topics to debate. There are also video tutorials on topics like how to solve maths problems, so parents can learn for themselves or go over it with their children. All new parents are invited in for evening sessions in groups of 30 to learn how to use the system effectively.

Head is passionate about creating equal opportunities for children from less advantaged backgrounds – from using the school's own entry test alongside the Kent test in an attempt to weed out raw talent rather than coached performance through to providing this group with extra resources. It troubles her that the value added score is lower for pupils in receipt of free school meals. Again, this is far higher than national averages but the head thinks it isn't acceptable. 'We have to do the best we can for all kids,' she says. 'We have identified a small gap in progress between those receiving free school meals and other students. We have paid for individual tuition in English, maths and science for every underachieving free school meals child and we pay for revision guides. We try to do the bits a middle class parent does – that is, buy books for their children, pay for tuition if they are behind, take them out to places.'

The other reason behind the great progress is a determination to ensure that all teaching is excellent. Teachers carry a lanyard around their neck with the school's four tenets for outstanding lessons: engagement, challenge, independent learning, and feedback. 'We have training sessions around those four things,' says the head. A teacher who fails in any of these areas gets six weeks of coaching and if they are not at the right standard after that 'we would start to move them out of school.'

The result is 'the best education in the area,' parents told us, with some 'charismatic and inspirational' teaching. In 2016, 54 per cent of A level entries were A*/B, around 19 per cent A*/A. Most popular subjects at A level are English, maths and psychology.

Maths is the strongest department. Children are set from year 7 (seven sets). 'It's a mistake to mix ability,' says the head. 'You need to teach at pace and you can't do that if half the kids haven't got it.' Girls do maths GCSE a year early, then do further maths or statistics in year 11. Science and English set from year 9.

All have to do the EBacc (taking science, maths, English, a language, plus history or geography to GCSE). Students pick two languages from French, German and Spanish in year 7, then can keep both going in year 8 or drop one. The head identified languages as a failing department 18 months ago and after focusing on this area the results are changing now. We witnessed one French lesson where the energy almost visibly burst through the door. Girls were singing a French song using karaoke equipment – lots of hilarity, but the notes on the board showed that they were learning to conjugate verbs. A parent told us this was a regular event, with verb tables on one occasion set to a One Direction song.

In other classrooms the atmosphere was quiet and studious, with desks in rows. The students say that 80 to 90 per cent of the teaching is good – they were able to reel off the names of teachers whose lessons they enjoyed, including a history teacher who often performs in costume from his dressing up box and is, one said, 'the most passionate teacher I've ever come across.'

Games, options, the arts: We didn't get a sense of this being a very sporty school. Vast playing fields, but indoor facilities are meagre and the gyms look untouched in 30 years, save the addition of a lonely exercise bike. Girls are often bussed up to the sports centre in town for better facilities. 'Sport hasn't particularly impressed me,' said a parent. 'A lot of parents don't see it as a priority and often clubs don't run because no-one turns up.' However, school has now upgraded tennis courts – now a multi use games area, and has added new fitness suite packed with everything from treadmills to cross trainers plus kettlebells, medicine balls, dumbells and stability balls.

The head confirms that the first priority is academic but also says other schools in the area put up little competition, with Folkestone girls winning all their matches. One parent wishes the school would raise its sights and play more competitive teams in Canterbury and Ashford. Sports day is apparently a highlight though – a relaxed event with the head of history providing hilarious commentary.

Music is 'a great department', according to one pupil – regular concerts and musical productions and girls can qualify for a BTec by managing their own production (from fundraising to selling tickets and overseeing lighting and sound). Art department has a darkroom and green room and studio with sea views. Last year 15 pupils went on to art colleges to do fine art, fashion and photography.

Overseas trips include a biennial four-week expedition for years 11 to 13, with a focus on volunteering and environmental studies. Destinations include Borneo and Ecuador. Girls undertake projects such as building bridges and converting buildings into a nursery or village hall, as well as activities like scuba diving. During year 11 girls do internships, where they spend one day a week throughout the year in an industry related to their career aspirations.

Background and atmosphere: School feels like a happy ship; staff passing in the corridors greet each other by first names – no stiff hierarchy here. Head and her vice principal have worked as a team since 2001 and clearly rub along well. 'The leadership team is confident,' a parent told us. 'They are in a comfortable place because they have done well, so they are not trying to put in knee-jerk policies or react to inspections. They can take a considered approach.'

Girls seem very relaxed – they turn out the results but somehow don't have that glassy eyed look of industry we've seen in some schools. None of the parents we spoke to thought it was an overly pressured or competitive environment. Social skills are good too – the girls we talked to gave a confident account of what they were doing, and why.

The school is set along a leafy road in the posh part of Folkestone, a stone's throw from the sea. Sixth form has its own cliffside terrace off the common room, with views to France on a clear day. It's considered the best school in the area, although it faces competition from Canterbury grammars. Unjustly so, says one parent. 'At our village school the playground talk was that Canterbury was the place to go, but those of us whose children went to Folkestone are all delighted with it.'

Current campus was created when the Victorian girls' grammar merged with the next door technical school, so there are now double-sized areas of playing fields and two school halls. The Victorian part has had recent facelift and benefits from wood panelling and curved staircases, giving it a hint of grandeur. The modern half has the dated and knocked about décor sported by most of the county's grammars.

Pastoral care, well-being and discipline: No behaviour problems according to the girls – 'no one would dare,' says one. The head disagrees, saying the school encounters the usual range of rebellion and personal problems, all dealt with through support and sanctions. Each of the school's four houses is headed by a student development leader who has no teaching commitments and whose role is to oversee the well-being and academic progress of girls in the house (and is also the first point of contact for parents with any concerns).

There are quite a few luscious lashes and blushed cheeks in evidence – staff say they take a pragmatic approach to this. 'They are not supposed to have a lot of make-up, but we're moderately relaxed about it,' says vice-principal. 'What's going on in lessons is much more important.' Sixth form dress is liberal – jeans and trainers allowed, but a bare midriff might result in girls being sent home to change.

Pupils and parents: Broad mix of backgrounds, with 20 per cent of pupils receiving free school meals. Number of pupils from non-British backgrounds, including several Nepalese girls whose parents are stationed at the nearby Gurkha regiment barracks. Around half of parents have been in higher education. The head desperately wants to change perceptions among some local parents who don't have this background. 'Parents think it's snooty and not for them,' she says. 'They put limits on their children and lots don't do the Kent test who are capable of passing.' Even with newspaper headlines proclaiming that the school was first in the county for GCSE results recently, there were still empty places at first round offers in March.

Entrance: You get two shots at it. Girls can either enter with a pass in the Kent 11+ test or through success in the school's own exam. The latter comprises verbal and non-verbal reasoning, English and maths. It's not uncommon for girls to pass one and fail the other, head says. It's a lot easier to get in here than in other parts of the county – head says that only 15 per cent of the local children will pass the Kent test, compared to 38 per cent in the pushy parent enclaves in the west of the county. Entry at sixth form requires six GCSEs at A*-C, with at least four Bs.

Exit: Most girls stay on for the sixth form, with about 10 each year moving on to vocational courses. After A levels more than 90 per cent progress to higher education (one or two to Oxbridge most years, and around 25 per cent to Russell Group).The school regularly invites back old girls who are now in professions like law, medicine and banking to develop pupils' ambitions.

Remarks: You can't argue with the results – or with the school's zeal to ensure that every girl gets the results she is capable of. What's particularly good is that they seem to achieve this without the girls feeling under great pressure. Yes, they know they have to work hard, but not to the extent that parents worry about them overdoing it. It's 'quite rounded and balanced,' one mother told us. We like the head's determination to weed out poor teaching too – it's something a lot of schools would be all the better for.

Forres Sandle Manor School

Sandle Manor, Fordingbridge, Hampshire SP6 1NS

Pupils: 220; 75 full, 25 weekly boarders • Ages: 3–13 (boarding from 7) • C of E

Fees: Day £13,755 – £16,905; Boarding £18,940 – £23,085 pa

Tel: 01425 653181
Email: office@fsmschool.com
Website: www.fsmschool.com

Headmaster: Since 2010, Mr Mark Hartley (40s), previously deputy head at Winchester House, Brackley, and before that housemaster at Mount House School, Tavistock. Studied biological sciences, now teaches PSHE to older ones and maths tutors those who struggle. Started his working life as an insurance underwriter, met wife Beth at a 21st birthday party and shortly afterwards discovered his true vocation – teaching. Three children later, Beth has returned to her former stomping ground with responsibility for marketing and promoting FSM – though we hear bottles of champagne, sent to parents, for recruiting newbies, are a thing of the past. Described as fresh, fun and funny by youngsters, Mr Hartley is something of an action man, enjoying hockey, cycling, kayaking and climbing. Inheriting a school that required fine tuning rather than wholesale overhaul, he has tinkered at the edges: tightening up reporting procedures, smartening the kids, introducing a parent portal and encouraging more competition via house events. So far so good on the parental front, 'He's livened things up, smartened up the children but not pushed things too far'.

Entrance: Most at age 3 or 8, boarders from 7. Non-selective but works from premise of 'Will a child be happy here?' Stomping grounds include New Forest, Avon Valley and environs of Cranborne. Predominantly white British with a handful of short-stay pupils from Norway and Spain. Boarders a 50-50 mix of expats, mostly Forces, and locals. Around half are first time buyers. Start when you like, if room (pressure on boarding places – must pay for full even if weekly board). Means-tested bursaries and discount for Forces.

Exit: Over 25 different schools in the last four years, including Canford, Bryanston, Clayesmore, King's College Taunton, the Sherborne schools, Eton, Winchester, Marlborough, Stowe and Uppingham. Over half won scholarships in 2016. Eminent old boys: Michael Foot (Forres), Alec Guinness (Sandle Manor).

Remarks: Set in child-friendly grounds, centred around an elegant Jacobean manor, a stone's throw from the New Forest. It's hard to imagine a more captivating environment for the tweenager. Delightful pre-prep with inspirational head who ensures learning is child-led, fun but pacey. Super pirate ship playground and forest school ensure year round fresh air and plenty of boisterous play.

All 6 year olds screened for reading delay – those found in need are given booster sessions till back on track. 'We never guarantee a child will improve but are yet to have one that doesn't.' Fans of Ruth Miskin's Read Write Inc, which promises every child a reader by age 6. Imaginative teaching and learning captivates the spellbound youngsters. We especially liked the 'naughty bus' that hides on a daily basis and had been found encased in ice on our visit. Even an errant bus can't compete with the excitement of making stinky, brown poo – a simulated investigation which begins with crushing of digestive biscuits (to mirror crunching of teeth), mixed with water (replacing saliva), washing up liquid and vinegar added (enzyme and stomach acid), then squeezed through grandma's stocking, simulating the intestine and final movement: learning at its gory, imaginative, and experiential best.

Fairly relaxed approach to learning in the prep school – not a soft option, but perhaps uniquely, youngsters say they'd like more prep sooner, 'The year 8 workload is a shock and we could be better prepared for it'. Gifted children pepped up via PACE activities; some, such as Green Giant, an eco project examining biodiversity and recycling with hands-on fun – chopping bamboo, mixing smoothies and making wool – open to all.

Learning support encompasses wide range of cognitive ability. 'We have children who cannot read/decode but are L4 and L5 national curriculum in some subjects, so we have to help and support'. Parents enthuse, 'My child struggled at his previous school, but since he came to FSM and got the support he needed, he has never stopped smiling.' Another added, 'It's a long day yet my child is never tired. Somehow they work it just right.'

Most teachers deliver multi-sensory lessons geared to active learning. English, drama and science top the popularity polls; 'Our science teacher respects us – he's not patronising, we do lots of experiments, it's fun and there is practically no writing,' cooed one boy. History, geography and RE depart from confines of CE, a conscious decision to develop skills of enquiry and investigation. Testing topics include Smuggling in Fordingbridge. Senior schools approve and see some seriously good work – not that fun doesn't come into it: we spotted a wall of history jokes, our favourite, 'Who built the Ark? I have Noah idea!' Post CE youngsters hone their practical and problem-solving skills – changing a tyre, wiring a plug, ironing shirts or finding the scariest ride at Thorpe Park.

Most lessons take place in The Barn with scattering of specialist buildings for art (we loved the bronze Olympian action sculpture), DT and music. Sports hall and climbing wall on wish list, but grounds contain heated outdoor swimming pool, courts for netball and tennis plus myriad of pitches. Ennui not an option – daily sport and afternoon activities as diverse as scuba diving, golf (even for the tinies) and banana boating, alongside annual trips and tours to everywhere from Iceland to Africa. Project week and cub-camp, with Boy's Own firelighting, knife-skills, cooking and camp craft, perennially popular. All lower school do ballet (a good way to spot potential dancers and dyspraxics) – optional classes for seniors. We listened to the fledgling Exterminators jamming and spotted imaginatively named groups, eg Flute Pastilles, and fabulous fiddlers. School has a competitive edge: thrice finalists in the Junior Memory Championships and recent debut as finalists in Kids' Lit quiz.

Seemingly parents equally competitive when it comes to teams, with boarder parents saying, 'Local parents seem to have everything sewn up – it can be difficult for the boarding fraternity to get a look in, especially for parent fixtures,' adding, 'Communication could be better – they're great at reporting on the kids but not on activities: we need time to schedule and plan'. Parents kept busy with quiz nights, football, hockey, plus 'maths for mums and dads', courtesy of Friends of FSM – hardly surprising they jest that an in-school Costa Coffee concession is on their wish list.

Meals are table served in one of two dining rooms, the mantra to always try a little, including experimental offerings such as beetroot brownies and soup concoctions dreamed up by the youngsters. Sports teas are legendary and, as we flicked the last melt-in-the-mouth crumbs from our lips, could only nod in heartfelt agreement as our trusty guide declared them 'outstanding!'

A boarding school that welcomes day children – 'It's a family-friendly community, flexible when we need it'. Fairly healthy weekend boarding numbers though parents of full boarders (75, compared with some 25 weekly) say to check the age and gender of those who stay, if this is important to you. Cheery boarding accommodation with ongoing renovations – though we were a tad overwhelmed by the swathes of bubble-gum pink adorning the girls' dorms. We loved the 'getting better bay' with healthy doses of TLC for the homesick and panaceas for the poorly. Seemingly all want to try boarding, so expect up to 11 per dorm and the odd grumble that it can be difficult to escape, 'Sometimes you need time or space but they can be hard to find'. Nothing too heavy-handed on discipline front: naughty boarders are red-carded and miss the coveted Wednesday special boarding night or put on dreaded laundry duty, sorting socks, folding shirts. Matrons praised, 'You can tell them things because they have seen it all before and know what to do', ground-staff lauded as cheery and fun, 'They have a nickname for everyone'.

Focuses on developing happy, confident children. Takes a broad range, delivers the goods, 'One minute you are watching a really talented child, the next someone who is just keen to join in'. Children are respected and 'feel part of the gang,' say parents. Children candid, 'It can be a bit difficult for those who are naturally loners or need quiet space.' Not posh or pushy. A happy, homely school with a sunny disposition, going from strength to strength. Turns out friendly, confident, quietly ambitious youngsters.

F

Frensham Heights

Rowledge, Farnham, Surrey GU10 4EA

Pupils: 499; 54 full, 36 weekly, 9 flexi boarders • Ages: 3-18 • Sixth form: 90

Fees: Day £6,525 – £18,210; Boarding £23,775 – £28,785 pa

Tel: 01252 792561
Email: admissions@frensham-heights.org.uk
Website: www.frensham-heights.org.uk

Headmaster: Since 2004, Mr Andrew Fisher BA MA DipEd (50s). A relaxed, breezy and natural educator. It's in the genes – his grandfather headed Repton and became a bishop, his father was head of Geelong Grammar, a brother heads an international school in Belgium and other relations have run schools both here and in Australia. Mr Fisher – 'Andrew' (everyone is on first name terms at Frensham) – still sounds Aussie, despite 20 years in the UK – the first 10 spent at Wrekin College, where he became head of English and, finally, deputy head (pastoral), and you can immediately see why – the pastoral aspect, that is.

This is a practical, hands-on head and one of the roundest pegs in the most circular hole we've met. He's a motivator and a believer in people. Parents pay tribute to, especially, his skills as a communicator: 'He is a complete star and inspiring,' 'he can speak equally well to parents and children,' 'extremely human and talks to everyone as individuals,' 'he keeps you in touch, even on minor matters' and so on. Wife, Catherine, is deputy head at one of the local large sixth form colleges attended by one of his daughters, the other a pupil at a local comprehensive at time of our visit. A likeable, unpretentious head – we queued for lunch along with everyone else – no way he'd jump to the head of the queue – and he clearly values highly his relationships with the pupils: 'They treat me with great respect but it's not based on traditional school values. I can laugh at myself.'

Junior school head: Since 2005 is Mr Nic Hoskins BA (40s) who also acts as assistant boys' housemaster in the senior boarding house. Previously deputy head at Willington Prep, Wimbledon. Cheery, energetic Cockney, Nic's degree was in primary music, art and drama and he has 'a passion for the arts'. His weekly newsletter to parents is, as you'd expect, reflective, creative and very much in keeping with the 'thinking' ethos of the school. He clearly loves his job and seems as thrilled now to have it as when he first arrived. Nic teaches music to children from nursery through to year 3 and IT from years 3-6. 'How can you mould children if you don't know them?' Quite!

Academic matters: Not 'selective' as normally understood – this school is more concerned that you join them for the right reasons than because you will help them soar to league-table-topping prominence. A smallish school, so not the hugest range of subject options at GCSE or A level. Very high pupil:teacher ratio makes for lots of small group and one-one support. Impressive results in Eng Lit; the three sciences, when taken separately, also impress though most take IGCSE double award. Blissfully small classes for eg RE, ICT (computing GCSE, computer science A level). No Latin, no Greek. Photography taken – spectacularly – as an extracurricular GCSE with huge numbers and great success – see below. All A level subjects taught in small groups – much appreciated by students. English, maths, geography, history, art most popular. Only a few take langs, including some native speakers. Sixth form seen by some as being less rigorous academically than it might but the newish head of sixth is 'driving up standards,' we were assured. And 'we are upping our game in stretching the gifted and talented'. Parents concur. 'Not hothousing doesn't mean they can't achieve highly,' affirmed one. In 2016, 40 per cent A*/A at GCSE and 25 per cent A*/A grades at A level (53 per cent A*-B). Disappointing library which doubles as café and place to sprawl in breaks with little evidence of its books being used. Recent expansion of science block to create six separate labs.

Loads of support – eg maths clinic each lunchtime. Not great for wheelchair users as the site is huge, bumpy and has steps. Main House not wheelchair-friendly at all. But school will try to take anyone they feel will benefit – mild SEN are catered for with enthusiasm and dedication and some families shared between Frensham and nearby More House for those with greater needs. 'My daughter had one-to-one for her reading and her reading age jumped two years in a term.' SEN support is careful and threaded through the school; junior school has its own SENCo who gives small group support where needed (known, appealingly, as 'clubs') and one-to-one (charged extra) if necessary. 'We could take anyone whose presence wouldn't be detrimental to the rest of the class,' says Nic..

Games, options, the arts: Think, Create, Explore is inscribed around the school and the vast menu of extracurricular options should tempt the most sluggish teenager to do just that. Bike maintenance, American football, boules, tap dancing, barbershop and various dance forms – before, during and after school and at weekends. Excellent new music block; around half learn at least one musical instrument in school – 'Frensham bends over backwards to find teachers if you want to learn some different instrument,' a budding soloist enthused. Masses of bands, orchestras, ensembles, choirs and performance courses through the veins of the school. Dance much praised and popular. Drama is well-provided for and central to the school. The theatre is a wonderful asset – it has everything and does everything – and is well used, as are the two drama studios and the little wooden outdoor theatre on the front lawn. Performance values are high with a healthy, pervasive culture of it being OK to perform. Creative drama team under innovative long-serving head of dept.

Outstanding photography under even longer-serving, inspirational leadership and now with unique facilities for techniques old and new. Brilliant, diverse and poly-faceted artwork – we were truly struck by the rigour and values underpinning the skills and the freedom pupils were given to develop as they needed. Witty ceramics, clever textiles, wood and resistant materials productions with mind-opening themes explored with structure and solidity. 'Art and drama must challenge me,' says Andrew. Arguably, the most impressively led art dept in the country.

Sports are enthusiastic, various and 'improving', according to parents, though some feel they could and should be better. School points out that they are now competing against much bigger schools and taking part in various national cup competitions. We enjoyed junior boys and girls playing football together and harmoniously – not a common sight. 'Outdoor education' is important – there is forest school, the outdoor Terrace Theatre, the swimming pool in the walled garden and loads of activities to develop outdoor skills – D of E gold award taken here and the whole school breathes in its own glorious 'outdoors'. Facilities – indoor and out – are certainly conducive to performance but one senses that real energies go into creativity rather than goal-scoring.

Boarding: Boarding arrangements changed in 2014 to become co-ed throughout the school. Hamilton House accommodates the 11-13 year-old boarders – boys and girls housed on different floors. They share a breakfast room/kitchen and a large garden. Main House houses the older boarders – girls and boys in opposite wings and with entry codes. Roberts House, the sixth form centre – co-educational from its inception – is unchanged and is everyone's base all day: day pupils share studies and workspace. We knocked at a random door and found two lads in hoodies actually working and blinking at the disturbance. Whole school on fibre-optic broadband and Facebook etc blocked till tea-time. Boarding is good – decent sized rooms in the main though some singles are tightish; nice bright shower rooms and good kitchens. Exceptionally welcoming sitting rooms – especially 'The Sit', which looks like home. Food – very good, we tried it – served in big dining room with tables and banquettes and everyone eats ensemble. Around a third stay in at weekend and are busy – see note about extracurricular above. Powerful cleaning fluid smells almost knocked us over in several buildings.

Background and atmosphere: Charles Charrington, the brewer, acquired Fir Grove House on the edge of Rowledge village, overlooking a panorama of Surrey woods and hills and transformed it into Frensham Heights – an imposing gothic red-brick residence with turrets, leaded lights and stained glass, splendid Georgian-style interiors, cornices, architraves, fireplaces – the lot – in 1902, as a would-be ancestral pile. Alas, the First World War intervened and the house became a military hospital and, as the old order changed, was reinvented as a school by three redoubtable women – Edith Douglas-Hamilton and joint headmistresses, Beatrice Ensor and Isabel King. Ensor, an early proponent of Montessori education, was a theosophist, a vegetarian and an anti-vivisectionist. Fascinatingly, one of the teachers at the school in those early years was Krishna Menon. But the school's progressive credentials, being coeducational and liberal, were integral to its ethos from the first. Strangely, every head since its pioneers has been male.

Set in extensive woodlands and the older children trail 10 minutes through the woods to the village with its supermarket and sweetshop. Immense and meticulously kept grounds – Andrew pays tribute to the excellence of the financial management and, indeed, it is admirable that the place is so well maintained with so small a population of fee-payers. Newer buildings nestle in trees and witty sculptures sprawl on the lawns and in foyers – we loved the slumbrous wire rabbit ('the little kids curl up in its ears') and the jokey wax mushrooms, as well as the huge black panther.

Junior school in two buildings: nursery to year 3 in sunken single storey, red-roofed accommodation with attractive, good-sized classrooms full of attentive, relaxed looking tots and really interesting activities going on. Light, airy rooms and space to explore and breathe. 'Flottage' (apparently a contraction of 'The Flat Over the Cottage' – but irrelevant now) houses the upper years and sees that time as very much preparatory for the senior school. One form in each year. Rooms arranged very intimately – though teachers have free rein over this – but we liked the shell-like arrangement with little tables in a curl around the teacher's desk in one year 4 room. Senior pupils love coming back on visits and have fond memories of what they learned where and with whom. 'It was magic.'

No uniform – so everyone bar a few in uniform of hoody, leggings/jeans, sweatshirts, boots/trainers. It looks relaxed and sane – enhanced by the amount of linked arms and hugging we saw – more like a bunch of French children, we thought. Central to the ethos is personal maturity: 'They are given real responsibility,' one parent told us, 'and can take the initiative – the school's approach to that is excellent.' This extends to falling in and out of love, which, of course, they do, but we were impressed by the compassion and mutual respect with which this is handled. 'It does happen but anything more than a hug or kiss in public is frowned on and people are respectful of what others want to see.. if people break up, we look after each other,' a wise mid-teen averred. 'It's not for everyone,' said another. 'If you need real structure and routine it's not for you.' 'Conventional parents need to look beyond the informality and recognise that the pupils respect the teachers because of the way they treat them rather than because of the rules,' a less conventional parent asserted.

Pastoral care, well-being and discipline: Everyone agrees about the staff: 'It's almost personal tutoring – they know how I learn so they explain it to me how they know I can understand,' a bright sixth former told us. 'They encourage pupils to excel in music, art, sport – whatever they're good at,' said a parent. Also a sense of a recent tightening of discipline – especially on illicit fags and booze. 'Some people were getting cocky – they've cracked down on it now,' we were advised. But pastoral care universally praised: 'They're not heavy-handed over minor transgressions – they see them in a learning context but if you cross a line you'll be suspended.' And another parent: 'If you've got that much freedom you need the support to go with it.' A strong sense that mutual respect and mutual support is central to the ethos of the place.

Pupils and parents: Around 75 per cent day pupils who come from a radius of about 40 miles – Petersfield, Goldalming, Farnham. Boarders are weekly eg from London or from overseas and school has wise policy of not taking more than four pupils who speak any one language into any senior year. So penny nos from eg Russia, Germany, Croatia, Spain. Intensive EAL available though needed by very few. Notable Old Frenshamians include performers Bill and Jon Pertwee, Jamie Glover, David Berglas, Rufus Hound, Hattie Morahan; also Sir Claus Moser, Noah Bulkin (Merrill Lynch, Lazard, now entrepreneur) and Uber-fraudster, Edward Davenport.

Entrance: Entry to nursery in the term of 3rd birthday for 16 places or the following year to reception – assessment done by informal observation during a visit. Years 1-6 take a few more – roughly two apply for each place (years 5 and 6 now expanded to two classes each). Candidates spend a day with peer group and are assessed in reading, spelling, maths – while having a fun day.

All candidates for years 7-9 are interviewed. Exams a week or so later – 11+ take tests in reading, writing, spelling, maths and non-verbal reasoning. Same plus a science test for 13+ candidates. Similar for occasional places which do occur. Sixth form places require six GCSEs at A*-C, ideally with Bs in A level subjects, 'but we're flexible,' says Andrew. School also sets its own papers for sixth form entry. Oversubscribed by 4:1 at this stage.

G

Exit: Vast majority of juniors move on to senior school and why on earth wouldn't you? Around 50 per cent leave at 16 – mostly to the several large state (free) sixth form colleges round about, some few for the IB or for subjects not on offer here. Nearly all who stay get to their first choice university which suggests good guidance and realistic applications. To one of the widest range of tertiary education establishments we have seen. Many to creative courses – arts, design, music – but also the odd Oxbridge entrant (three in 2016) and others to study everything from architecture at Nottingham to geography at King's, London. Different, diverse, distinctive.

Money matters: Sibling discounts for third and subsequent children of 10 per cent. Scholarships and exhibitions in academics, performing arts, creative arts and sport up to £750 pa – so glory rather than gold. Means-tested bursaries in case of need but school has no endowments so not plentiful.

Remarks: A place to grow up in. Every kind of opportunity to become the person you are meant to be and to learn about others while you're at it. Civilised, liberal values with wraparound care and support. We loved it.

Gayhurst School

Bull Lane, Gerrards Cross, Buckinghamshire SL9 8RJ

Pupils: 341 • Ages: 3–11 • C of E

Fees: £11,460 to £14,550 pa

Tel: 01753 882690
Email: enquiries@gayhurstschool.co.uk
Website: www.gayhurstschool.co.uk

Headmaster: Since September 2016, Gareth Davies, previously head of Alleyn Court School in Essex. A mathematician, he has a BA and PGCE from Welsh universities, MEd from Cambridge, is an ISI inspector and has always worked in prep schools. A rugby enthusiast, he is married to Lisa, and they have two young daughters.

Entrance: Non-selective up until year 2, after which there are tests for reading and maths and a 'gentle' interview. Nursery has 24 pupils, reception has 34. There are two classes of 20 in year 2 and year 3 upwards is now four classes of 16 per year, with space being made available by the phasing out of year 7s and 8s altogether by 2018. Originally a boys' school, it became co-ed in 2008. 'I'd say it's a prep school for boys that girls can go to rather than being truly co-ed yet,' said one parent. 'My daughter is just one of five girls in reception, but every new intake attracts more females, so it is changing,' pointed out another. The school has certainly made efforts to adapt areas like sports and library books. Waiting lists in younger years, but 20 per cent movement in the local area (mainly due to job relocation) means spaces often appear higher up the school. There's a means-tested bursary for one fully-funded place every year for a child going into year 3.

Exit: Half leave age 11, which helps explain why the school is phasing out years 7 and 8 altogether by 2018. The majority go onto local grammar schools, including Dr Challoners Boys, Dr Challoners High, John Hampden, RGS High Wycombe, Beaconsfield High, with other popular schools include Berkhamsted, Royal Masonic, Pipers Corner, St Clement Danes, Eton, Merchant Taylors', Radley College, Shiplake and Westminster School.

Remarks: Don't expect to be wowed by a grand entrance and reception area that you get in many independent prep schools. For one thing, there's not much of the original school, which was relocated to the present site in 1930, left (only the bottom part of the main building). And for another, the entrance is tucked round the corner and takes you straight into the school office.

But once inside the five acre site, the large, well-kept field and pretty woodland behind provides a stunning view and indeed the centrepiece for the whole school. In front of the field lies the all-weather Astroturf, where children were enjoying tennis when we visited, whilst behind the woodland (which is also home to an adventure playground) lie three large rugby fields The newest of the school's buildings is the traditional-style wooden cricket pavilion, which turns into the heart of the school during sporting events.

The nursery, junior and senior departments feel quite separate here, although the junior school does share some of the facilities of the senior school. Nursery, which has 24 places, has light and airy classrooms, with a reasonable sized outdoor area. Because the school is set in a residential area, expansion can involve buying up actual houses and for the junior school, the upshot is a feeling of a small village, complete with signposts, which is actually rather quaint. Meanwhile, senior school – whose classrooms are in the Georgian-style main building – has a secondary school structure, whereby children have entirely specialist subject teaching. Whilst some parents feel it's a 'bit young to be keeping a timetable and packing a bag', others feel it 'prepares them well for secondary school.' Also dotted around the school are dedicated IT, art, science and music facilities, all of which are well-equipped and welcoming.

The sport hall, which is also home to many after-school activities (some of which cost extra) is adequate, although nothing special. But the sports teaching, which involves sports specialists from reception upwards, is seen as a big plus point and sport really is for all, with main sports including rugby, football, cricket, athletics, cross-country, hockey, netball and rounders – for which they are matches most weekends for all abilities. There are strong skiing teams and swimming takes place nearby Maltman's School weekly for one term a year, although swimming clubs are available weekly.

Music is strong, with a lovely big music room, four practice rooms and a dynamic head of music. Nearly half of children are given individual instrumental or choral lessons, for which they are taken out of normal lessons on a rotational basis. The only auditioned choirs are the chamber choirs and vocal groups. There's a big passion for art here too – everything from textile art to intricate paintings were displayed when we visited. School trips often combine both subjects, including a recent choir and art trip to Rome for years 6 to 8. Plenty of other residential trips too, including skiing (with parents and teachers so that all years can go), adventure camps and a trip to the battlefields as part of history in year 7 and 8. 'We're lucky to be near London, so we utilise the museums and galleries regularly too.' Drama is big too, with every child in the school being involved in at least one drama production annually. Recent productions include Oliver! and Bugsy Malone.

Academically, the school is 'no pressure cooker. But we do send children onto highly selective schools, so even the most able are challenged.' Many win scholarships, both academically and for music and sport. National curriculum is followed, with extras such as dedicated weeks to science and arts. Subjects including science, French, IT, music and PE taught by subject specialists while all class teachers teach English and maths. French and Latin from year 4 and Spanish from year 7. Sets from year 4 upwards for maths and English and streaming in years 7 and 8 for all subjects. 'We're somewhere in the middle where homework is concerned, that is, there's not loads but there's more than a little.' Extracurricular activities are wide-ranging, including chess, cooking, science and masses of sport.

An SEN co-ordinator works in small groups at no extra charge for anyone with any extra needs, no matter how small. Some parents believe this has hasn't been up to scratch, although one parent was quick to really sing its praises. The co-coordinator also runs the gifted and talented programme, which works in conjunction with other local schools, including extra workshops and trips and suchlike.

'Teachers are kind, but firm,' said one pupil of the 53-strong teaching staff, summing up the views of others too. 'You know what is expected of you, which really helps,' said another. Staff turnover small but annual, almost exclusively due to retirement or promotion.

Pastoral care said to be the cornerstone of the school. 'Part of our mission statement is to produce happy, confident children and the form teachers are heavily involved in ensuring this is the case.' No denial of bullying, 'but we have a zero tolerance and clear policies' and parents we spoke to who had experienced any difficulties between their child and others said the matter was dealt with promptly and extremely well.

Pupils are mainly English and white, with 20 per cent non-white students and around six per cent from overseas. Mainly local families, but some travel 10 or so miles from places including Amersham, Uxbridge, Penn and Stoke Poges.

Food is self-service, under two sittings, in the dining room, and considered excellent. 'My son loves it so much that he asked if the caterers could do the food for his 13th birthday!' one parent said.

The school day runs from 8.40am (although children can be dropped off from 8am at no extra cost) and the end of the day is staggered according to year groups, with the oldest ones finishing at 4.20pm, although there's plenty of opportunity to extend the day with activities and after-school care.

School council is surprisingly new (2013), but they've managed to get more water fountains and more play equipment outside including skipping ropes and giant Connect 4.

Pupils were polite, not arrogant, and there was a definite feeling that they have fun, without being raucous, with a resulting buzz around the school. There's a strong sense of being a part of the whole here too, so it's not surprising that houses are important, with heads selected in senior school. There's also a huge push on responsibility, with every pupil given responsibility at some time in their school career, from reception upwards, whether as a form leader, librarian, leader of the orchestra, dining room or class helper. 'You get a real feeling of team work here and all that involves,' summed up one pupil.

Active parents' association, with all the usual charitable events. Parents say historically, new joiners have often felt left to settle in with the help of other parents rather than the school itself, but that's changing, with new joiners teams, for instance. As for settling in new pupils, parents say this is excellent. Parents say communication has been lacking in the past too, but is improving.

This is a school of mixed ability, which is good at finding children's strengths and building on them, as well as enabling children to enjoy things they may not excel in. 'So if, like me, you have one who's academic and one who's not, they both shine,' said one parent. 'That goes for sport too,' said another. 'One of my sons is in the A team every time; another is more likely in the C team, but both are equally enthusiastic about school sports.' Above all, it has a family feel, rather than anything too institutional, and pupils are happy, ambitious and well-challenged.

George Abbot School

Woodruff Avenue, Guildford, Surrey GU1 1XX

Pupils: 1,941 • Ages: 11–19 • Sixth form: 445

Tel: 01483 888000
Email: office@georgeabbot.surrey.sch.uk
Website: www.georgeabbot.surrey.sch.uk

Headteacher: Since September 2016, Mrs Kate Carriett, previously principal of Kings College Guildford, which is part of the same multi-academy trust. Studied music at Royal Holloway and Bedford New College and trained as a secondary music and English teacher at Birmingham. Was head of music in Warwickshire and Staffordshire before moving south to become head of year in Surrey. Her first headship was at Kings College.

Academic matters: In 2016, 60 per cent of A level entries received A*-B grades and 34 per cent A*/A. The school also sits in the top five per cent in the ALPS A level value-added ranking. They achieve this through rigorous attention to the quality of teaching, and no hiding place for the weak. 'The way that we quality assure individual staff and departments is so stringent there is no escape here. Our reputation means that we employ the best teachers and we have good candidate fields in the vast majority of subjects. We run faculty reviews biannually, look at data, and do lots of lesson observations and drop-ins. Where a performance issue with a teacher is picked up, they quickly improve or leave.'

Each year around 38 A level courses are offered, as well as four BTecs/diplomas. The most popular A levels are maths and sciences. Almost half of the sixth form is taking maths, and options in this subject include further maths and STEP (which uses questions similar to undergraduate level maths, and is used by Cambridge for conditional offers). Next comes biology, with 100 currently on this course, and other popular options are English literature, photography and psychology. There are BTecs in sport, science, creative media and business studies. All year 11 students are interviewed individually to look in depth at their sixth form choices.

GCSE results are tremendous for a comprehensive – in 2016, 78 per cent of pupils got 5+ including English and maths at A*-C, and 30 per cent of grades were A*/A. There is setting for maths from year 7, science and languages from year 8, and English from year 10 – everything else is mixed ability. One mother said her child sometimes finds mixed ability sets frustrating, when they struggle to get through a lesson because someone is playing up, but she says he has also grown to realise 'that's life'. In KS4, less academic students can go to college one day a week to study vocational courses.

Children with additional needs are very well catered for, according to parents – we heard numerous rave reviews and tales of extraordinary achievement. One parent spoke movingly of examination results day 'when my son who was not expected to succeed achieved eight GCSEs', and another parent of a dyslexic boy was overjoyed by his grade A in English GCSE.

Changes are under way in language teaching – older pupils studied both a choice of French and German, plus either Spanish or Latin, but it was found that middle ability students were diluting their chances of getting a good grade by trying to do two, so now most students will study one language, with just the able linguists picking up a second in year 8.

Games, options, the arts: Sport has had a new lease of life at the school with additional facilities this year including an Astroturf pitch, sports hall with two full sized basketball pitches, and performing arts centre with mirrored walls for dance teaching. 'We now have a PE curriculum to suit all children. Before it was team game biased but now it's more varied.' Internal matches are 'all quite friendly', with not too much jeering at the non-sporty, said one such boy, and there's a big programme of fixtures for the keen. Commitment to sports and clubs is rewarded with half colours after two years, and full colours after four years.

Creative subjects are strong, with more than 90 per cent of entries gaining an A*-C in all visual arts subjects. Large textiles work hangs around the school, produced with their silk screen printing facility. We saw a textiles group working on costumes inspired by Tim Burton films. Pupils and parents praise the photography and fine art provision. 'It produces excellent art work and fantastic exhibitions every year,' said one.

In a music lesson students were composing film scores on Macs, using Garage Band and Sibelius 7, which is the best music software, according to our music-nut guide.

There are fashion shows, dance shows, and big drama performances – pictures of last year's Les Misérables production show near-West End quality staging and costumes. The chamber choir and rock choir tour frequently, with the rock choir booked for three performances in Paris this year.

Parents praise excellent clubs, extracurricular activities and trips. 'These really do enrich the curriculum. My children have been on several trips including year 8 residential to PGL, ski trips, theatre trips, maths trips and French exchange,' said one mother.

The school has a partnership with various overseas schools in China, Canada, Tanzania, South Africa and India, and reciprocal visits are arranged.

Background and atmosphere: The school was built in 1976, and looks like a typical 1970s comp. Nothing to write home about then, and the most appealing part is the sixth form common room, which has a café area designed in the same way as the Coffee Republic high street brand, and lots of space for lounging.

It is in partnership with Kings College Guildford, Boxgrove Primary and Sandfield Junior, the four now known as the Guildford Education Partnership.

It's big, with 10 forms to a year, but still manages to tend to the individual, parents told us. 'Students who are gifted in a particular subject are encouraged and stretched. Students who have specific learning difficulties are also supported well including students with disabilities,' said one. 'The school I feel promotes the individual. All students are encouraged to do their best academically but also to develop other interests such as music, drama, visual art, sport etc,' said another.

Prize-giving used to feature a local vicar or primary head handing out the prizes, but now they bring back former pupils who have done well. 'They come back as role models, and it's one of the best things we've done.'

The school undertakes a Kirkland Rowell survey every three years to investigate areas of concern for students, parents and staff. A recent one highlighted a priority to improve staff morale, bludgeoned by constant changes to Ofsted and mounting workload, while students and parents want to see more consistent rewards and sanctions, and consistency in setting homework. And it's not just a PR strategy – these will now be the next areas of focus for the leadership team.

G

Pastoral care, well-being and discipline: Those trembling at the idea of letting loose their sweet 11 year-old into a community of 2000 will be especially cheered by year 7 arrangements. They are cocooned in their own block, with their own toilets, they have their own area in the playground, and eat lunch separately. Two heads of year are dedicated to year 7. After this they are passed on to another pair of heads of year (academic and pastoral) who will stay with them through years 8 to 11. 'They move up the school with the students and therefore they know their students very well by the end of year 11. My daughter has a strong relationship with her pastoral HOY and would be very happy going to talk to her about any issue,' said one parent.

Pastoral care – and strict monitoring – continues in the sixth form. 'We'll pick up quickly if they are not in lessons, and we have as much contact if not more with parents at this stage. It's a disciplined environment, we don't allow year 12s off site during the school day, if they have a gap between lessons they can go off to private study and they will be registered there. In year 13 they are only allowed out if they can show they are keeping on top of their study.' Some may feel this is too strict and restrictive, but school argues that the students invariably find that friends who have transferred to more liberal environments do not cope well with too much freedom in the sixth form, and their own students then see they are meeting their potential better.

By all accounts, the school excels at special needs. It has its own unit for 15 visually impaired students, including two who are braillists. They have their own base building, and support assistants to work with them. We saw one girl happily and confidently moving about the school with her white stick, chatting away to friends. Students who come with significant special needs and find it difficult to cope with a secondary set up are educated to begin with in a transition room. Here around 10-12 pupils will spend 70 per cent of their timetable, and will receive intensive lessons in literacy and numeracy, before gradually moving into the main classes by the end of year 8.

There are also dedicated members of staff overseeing gifted and talented pupils, who get masterclasses in subjects such as forensics, hieroglyphics and tessilations, and are encouraged to enter national competitions.

Parents say access to staff is very good, with problems always sorted out quickly, and one related that parents of a child with emotional problems feel particularly well supported by the school.

One parent criticised reports as 'very unsatisfactory – mostly comment banks and tick boxes' – but the school does better than the average secondary school parent evening experience of five minutes per year. There are three days per year known as progress monitoring, when parents come in with the child to look at data monitoring sheets, set targets, and have one-to-ones with tutors or subject teachers.

Youngsters are turned out in a tidy way, no missing blazers, ties are notched up to the top button, and neat hair. Many have blazers festooned with badges where they have gained colours for sporting clubs or voluntary work.

Much is made of leadership opportunities, and ensuring these aren't restricted to the sixth form. Student ambassadors are appointed from year 10 – they get two days leadership training, including learning how to do presentations and lead tours. There will be 30 ambassadors appointed at any time, and other pupils can volunteer to be prefects.

Pupils and parents: 'Skewed towards the able and motivated,' says school. It's a predominantly wealthy area, and some parents choose to send children here who could afford independent education. 'It's not overly competitive, but there's a good attitude to study, ie kids are not embarrassed to be keen to achieve,' said one parent.

No skiving for mums and dads – 96 per cent of parents attend parents' evening, 'and if they don't, we phone them.'

The PTA is unusually strong for a secondary school, parents say, and another added: 'Although there are 2000 students and a large staff, it is very friendly community.'

Entrance: Places are fiercely fought over; nearly 1,000 applicants for 300 places. Places are allocated first to looked after children, on exceptional need, and to siblings, and then on proximity, which for a first round offer means you are likely to need to live within two miles of the school. Attending primaries within the GEP will not have any advantage in admission. An average year sees around 10 appeals lodged, of which one-third may be successful.

Students wanting to stay on or join the sixth form will need five A*-C grades at GCSE to study A levels. A maximum of 50 sixth form places are available for external candidates each year, and a significant number of new joiners come from the independent sector, often attracted by the wide range of courses on offer. Requirements are lower for existing pupils wishing to follow one year BTec or diploma courses, or a foundation year leading to A levels.

Exit: The majority – around three-quarters – stays on into the sixth form. Some 60 per cent to Russell Group universities. A dedicated higher education advisor processes every UCAS application to ensure it goes off without mistakes. Nine to Oxbridge in 2016, and eight medics/vets.

Remarks: Utopia made flesh – the kind of school successive education ministers, and parents, have dreamed of, but which rarely comes to fruition. A school which delivers a baker's dozen of Oxbridge offers in a year, but also offers great support for students with special needs, and and excellent 5+ A*-C pass rates. Leadership team manages to be both down to earth and statesmanlike according to parent reports. The downside – trying to find a house within its two mile bull's eye.

Godalming College

Tuesley Lane, Godalming, Surrey GU7 1RS

Pupils: 2,200 • Ages: 16–18+

Tel: 01483 423526
Email: college@godalming.ac.uk
Website: www.godalming.ac.uk

Principal: Since September 2016, Emma Young, who is also CEO, and was previously deputy principal at Esher College. A firm believer in sixth form college education, has spent her entire career working in the sector. She started her career as a geography teacher at The Sixth Form College, Farnborough. In 2005, she joined Esher College as assistant principal, curriculum and staff development and was then promoted to deputy principal in 2010.

Academic matters: Students flock here from state and private schools for the teaching quality and results. Open access means just that. Five GCSE C grades theoretically opens the door to the 40 A level subjects on offer (including BTec equivalents), though Bs and above are required for maths and sciences and 'the better the grades, the easier the transition,' says college.

Half way house courses such as AS use of mathematics offer a way in to an otherwise out of reach subject, while access courses for anyone not achieving entry grades first time round provide second chance GCSE essentials including English, maths and science, together with BTec starter courses. Add one year express language courses and a good range of not-to-be-sniffed-at BTec national diplomas – lots of distinctions and merits, new subjects regularly added to the roster, most recently hospitality and entertainment – and there really is something for just about everybody.

Results very good, given such a wide range of courses and aspirations; in 2016, 31 per cent A*/A and 61 per cent A*-B grades at A level and 86 per cent starred distinction to merit grades for BTec. Most take four AS and three A levels, some more, with a compulsory second year add-on, generally themed to your main subjects and ranging from EPQ to hip-sounding rock school award.

Compared with the general run of schools, the humanities are notably popular. English literature heads the pack, followed by history (more girls than boys opt for 16th century, vice versa for modern variant; relative size and excitement of modern ordnance plus the Philippa Gregory factor could be at work). Sciences a little below average in popularity but still strong, with a budding biologist one of four British Olympiad winners, and physics, though boy-dominated ('they often see the maths so easily,' says tutor) inspiring a few girls to enrol on engineering courses afterwards.

Good languages, French most popular. Enticements include a week's work experience abroad, though German students have yet to bite. 'I offer every year but...' says slightly doleful tutor. Good spread of the more modish subjects (world development, media and film studies courses) – one classroom converts into bijou cinema for home-grown film screenings.

Overall, though, the arts have it, performing or static, from textiles (a largely though not exclusively female enclave) to dance, art, drama, and theatre studies, all exuding top grades (in some cases, nothing but). 'Imagine being able to dance for A level. It's amazing!' enthuses parent. Quality is taken as read – one art student is a BP portrait award entrant – and jaw-dropping displays of talent abound, off the walls when it comes to dance and drama; on them elsewhere. Inspirational tutors who talk to each other as well as the students (blindingly obvious, you'd think, but very definitely doesn't happen everywhere) and are universally praised for going beyond the call of duty.

Unsurprisingly, special educational needs – all sorts – are enthusiastically welcomed as are physical disabilities and far more than lip service is paid, with specialist support for everything from Asperger's to ADHD and cerebral palsy. Lots of lifts, while one learning support room is deep in heart of English block (a big 'welcome' sign drives the message home). Independent learning centre (aka library, but with reams of added features) houses drop in centre catering for anyone requiring a bit of tlc. Add some in class and individual support together with smallish teaching groups (average of 15 to one, though there's considerable subject variation) and the bottom line is that the lost are unlikely to stray too far without being brought back into the fold.

G

Games, options, the arts: 'If all you're doing is thinking about exams, you're not going to get an all-round education,' says college. Timetabled enrichment activities and a choice of 20 or so extracurricular activities from Amnesty International to zumba. D of E notably popular. Sport lives up to the colossal gorgeousness of facilities (sports hall is the size of a small school all on its own) with strong swimming, football and rugby squads and national championship-winning netball team.

Arts won't disappoint either. Two theatres in frequent use by dance and drama companies, noted for high octane, large scale productions, often involving local school and community groups. There's a host of talented musicians, too.

Background and atmosphere: Twelve acre campus that's truly handsome and everything the most demanding parent could ask for. Large but easy to navigate. The main building, all recessed lights and colourful but restrained carpets set against pristine white, is a delight to walk through. Just about every subject is now housed in luxury.

'Big but tight knit,' says the college. Not for anyone who wants the 'more custodial setting' of a smaller scale school environment. Much talk of recreating yourself, resulting in enjoyable stylistic differences between the philosophy set (highly articulate, sitting cross-legged, guru-like, on their desks during open day) and the buzzy drama and music crowd (big on hand gestures and hair flickage).

'It's a place of serious study. One student turned up late for lessons just to be noticeable. In her old school, everybody would giggle. Here, everybody rolls their eyes. They're not impressed,' said parent.

Pastoral care, well-being and discipline: Personal tutors, the first port of call for help, are seen weekly and are expected to know their charges well. Supplemented with regular one-to-one sessions with subject specialists. Relationships generally are excellent.

There's a clear three strikes and you're out policy, though few go off the rails and exclusions are rare. 'You are expected to mature and we will be on your case if it doesn't happen.' 'When my child was falling behind I got a pretty swift email saying she needed to hand in her work,' said a parent. 'The problem was dealt very quickly once I was made aware of it.'

Pupils and parents: Intake reflects the affluent, middle class demographics of the area.

Old boys and girls are an extrovert bunch, including comedians Ben Elton (who opened the new performing arts centre) and Rufus Hound, together with actresses, Drop the Dead Donkey's Ingrid Lacey among them. Current generation of funny, articulate pupils seem to be carrying on the tradition, though attempts to shock by the small group on Godalming Station, identifiable by orange 'can I help you?' badges from open day, noisily speculating on the quality of mathematicians' love lives (limited, they felt) left surrounding bourgeoisie anything but épaté.

Entrance: Guaranteed places for linked Waverley federation schools Broadwater, Glebelands, Gosden House, Rodborough and Woolmer Hill, no matter when they apply. For others, used to be a first come, first served scrum until admissions policy was changed, making prospects of a place nearly as good for those attending Bohunt School, Fullbrook School, Midhurst Rother College and Weydon School, as long as they submit applications towards the end of the September preceding year of entry.

For all other applicants, distance from college is the deciding factor, though things aren't as gloomy as they might sound. 'In the past, though not this year, we have been oversubscribed.' Students can come from as far away as Clapham.

Exit: Around a third of A level students to UK's top universities, while some 70 per cent go on to higher education in some way, shape or form. Some subjects excel: 60 per cent of chemistry students, for example, make it to Russell Group universities, Oxbridge (nine in 2016, and six medics) or the Royal Veterinary College. Often ranks in the top 10 of sixth form colleges in the country.

Vocational courses feed through nicely as well, on the whole, though universities, blowing hot and cold, don't help – two were havering over whether to continue accepting diploma in childcare and education as an entry qualification after experiencing a high drop out rates amongst students recruited elsewhere. College was limbering up to make forceful case against. 'We'd argue that our higher levels of pastoral care make it very unlikely,' says tutor.

Remarks: Modern surroundings, excellent results, committed tutors and enthusiastic, ebullient students. One student was worried about going on to university not through fears about demanding course but because 'it might not live up to the standards here.'

Godstowe Preparatory School

Shrubbery Road, High Wycombe, Buckinghamshire HP13 6PR

Pupils: 440; 100 full and flexi boarders • Ages: 3–13 (girls), 3–7 (boys); (boarding from 7)

Fees: Day £10,005 – £15,381; Boarding + £7,218 pa

Tel: 01494 529273
Email: registrar@godstowe.org
Website: www.godstowe.org

Headmaster: Since 2006, Mr David Gainer (50s). Educated at Claires Court, Maidenhead and Belmont Abbey in Herefordshire, followed by St Mary's University College, Twickenham, where he studied maths and drama. Began career at Llanarth Court Prep in South Wales then returned to alma mater Belmont Abbey as housemaster, followed by three years at Forest Grange Prep in Horsham as deputy head, before taking up first headship at Belmont Prep near Dorking in 1991.

Lives in the thick of it in the main school building with wife Cathy, the school registrar. According to one parent, 'if you could choose a headmaster for your son or daughter, it would be Mr Gainer.' Girls and parents alike comment on his energy, enthusiasm and hands-on presence around the school (he attends all sports matches and eats dinner with the boarders every night) – and they're not the only ones: he was recently named best head of a prep school by Tatler. Praise indeed. Commands respect yet obvious affection from pupils – appears truly in loco parentis. Parents are 'hooked' as soon as they meet him – and no wonder: he lets them have his home telephone number.

Passionate about the benefits of years 7 and 8, the head describes these years as 'dynamic bubble wrap' – keeping the girls in a nurturing environment while they mature, yet allowing them genuine responsibility, freedom and leadership opportunities at the top of the school. Highly focused on personal development and believes that academic success depends on it. According to the head, Godstowe encourages 'everyone to aim high, whatever their ability and potential.'

Pioneered a system of deferred senior school places, 'brokering deals' to secure girls' places at 11 to transfer at 13. Strong relationships with senior schools borne out by the fact that 25 schools choose to send their head as representative to Godstowe's biannual senior school fair.

Leaving in July 2017. His successor will be Sophie Green, currently head of Herries School in Cookham. She has also been director of studies at St George's Windsor Castle, where she prepared pupils for scholarships and was involved in the demanding boarding life of the choristers. She is also an ISI Inspector.

Entrance: Despite Godstowe's growing popularity, head is adamant that it will remain a 'first come first served', non-selective school. Majority intake (about 80 per cent) at 7 from its own pre-prep, The Lodge, with girls joining all the way through to year 6 from a variety of local prep and state schools, and boarders joining from further afield in the upper years. Boarding can be full time or flexible with many day girls choosing to try it in years 7 and 8 as a taster for senior school.

Exit: Not a specific feeder, with alumni most years heading off to some 20 different senior schools notably Wycombe Abbey, Cheltenham Ladies, Queen Anne's and Downe House; others to eg St George's Ascot, Rugby, Wellington, Stowe, Haileybury, Tudor Hall, Oundle, Uppingham, Pipers Corner, St Edward's, Bradfield, Millfield, Headington and Marlborough. A handful leave for local grammars at 11.

Remarks: England's first girls' boarding prep school and Enid Blyton's inspiration (though not the only contender) for Malory Towers, purpose built in 1900. The grounds make excellent use of a hilly, if a little blustery, site overlooking High Wycombe, with the original pretty Virginia creeper-clad buildings now housing years 3 to 8, plus The Lodge and nursery buildings. The few boys in pre-prep, mostly siblings, move on at the age of 7.

The airy new double height reception building (buzzing at pick-up and drop-off times) is a modern addition to the more rustic Victorian buildings and has a gallery-like atmosphere, setting the tone for the rather artsy feel of the whole school. Other recent revamps include the dining room (we highly recommend the lasagne), early years centre, art room and food technology centre, opened in 2007 by Raymond Blanc. There's also a new £2m sports hall for eg indoor tennis, hockey and lacrosse plus dance and gymnnastics to compensate for the antiquated and somewhat uninviting swimming pool building, chilly water and all. The school says it has made significant investments in this in recent years but it is far from being its star attraction.

Definitely not a school placing importance on hushed tones, although good manners are notably present. Girls dash about chatting noisily between lessons, picking up considerable speed when heading to the dining room for lunch. Posters all over the school that indoctrinate pupils to be happy, confident and successful are clearly doing the trick.

Non-selective it may be, but success is in the air here. Minority (about 15 per cent) peel off at 11 to local schools (parents have to 'opt in' to 11+), but unlike many prep schools in the area which hothouse pupils for the sought-after Bucks grammars, this is a true 3-13 establishment, feeding its post-CE alumni into a heady mix of top day and boarding indies, many with scholarships. Which are pretty abundant, by the way, with the current record for one year standing at 26, to 17 different schools. Head puts this down to 'quality teaching' and the fact that girls are 'led rather than pushed through the curriculum'. He is proud not to share the pushy reputation of some of his competition.

French is taught from reception, Latin and Spanish from year 5 in creatively themed classrooms. Classes in pre-prep school 'subtly' streamed, with a maximum class size of 18. Formal streaming from year 6 for English, maths and French. Girls stay in form rooms for lessons in years 3 and 4, after which they start to move around the school for individual subjects.

General acceptance that everyone learns differently and SEN is all in a day's work rather than marginalised. Two dedicated SEN staff in place and an excellent EAL programme – mostly for those boarders from the Far East, Spain and Nigeria, with girls' needs assessed upon entry to the school and timetabled to meet their specific requirements. Boarders' prep takes place from 4.30pm to 6.30pm, although an hour of this is often taken up with an enrichment activity. Day girls report homework levels to be acceptable.

Creative pursuits are well catered for, with a dedicated sewing room in CDT where girls knock up the odd wedding gown for the year 8 fashion show. Some 300 girls learn musical instruments and practise daily in bright, well-equipped studios. Pupils' artistic endeavours are displayed throughout the school – and with good reason. They look more like GSCE work, thanks to the inspirational head of art, who specialises in 3D work.

The art department, with its gleaming new extension, has the wow factor in terms of space and light, as does the work on show there, from glazed pottery meals on plates to life-size papier mâché humans – not a still life fruit bowl in sight. Taught by specialists from the word go, senior girls win art scholarships every year, but importantly parents report that a passion for creativity has been bred into the core of the school and latent talent is eeked out of those who didn't know they had it.

Parents say the standard of music is 'incredible', with one slipping in that the girls' achievements and public performances by far outstrip those at their brothers' schools. All pupils are encouraged to participate from the age of 3 in regular recitals and choir is compulsory in years 3 to 6. Revamped JK Theatre is used for music concerts, after-school clubs, art exhibitions, assemblies and parents' evenings.

Sports lessons are four times a week, with the usual suspects (netball, lacrosse and hockey) taking centre pitch – all to a high competitive standard. Athletics, rounders and swimming are also on offer, as are ballet, gymnastics and dance. Parents of children in larger year groups occasionally grumble that the A and B teams are a bit exclusive, with not everyone getting a go, but the head is keen to introduce more teams and by and large most girls are able to compete at some level, often with winning results.

Boarding facilities have a real home from home feel, with bedrooms (sleeping between four and eight) rather than dorms, cosy sitting rooms and homely kitchens. All have their own large gardens, with swings and other outdoor equipment. Housemistresses are non-teaching staff, leaving them free to focus on girls' pastoral care. Pupils are charming and poised without a hint of precociousness and describe their typical peer as 'kind and happy'. Early drop-off plus breakfast (7.30am) and late pick-up plus supper (6.30pm) is available for day girls at low cost.

The mobile phone arms race was stopped by the clever acquisition of 100 bog standard phones (yes, these do still exist) into which girls can insert their own SIM cards to call home. Thursdays are 'no go gadget' evenings in the boarding houses to further encourage those old fashioned skills, reading, conversation and game playing. Girls say the best thing about Godstowe is 'everyone is happy all the time' – future careers in PR await.

The 'enrichment curriculum' – that's after-school clubs in old money – offers up to 50 free options for two hours a day from 4.30pm. These range from the traditional sports, LAMDA and wind band to the more diverse knitting, prop-making and cross-stitch, with up to 100 girls staying for these. Boarders benefit from a buzzing spectrum of activities at weekends too (rarely fewer than 50 girls in), many of which take place off site (bowling, skating, theatre, cinema etc).

Post CE, year 8s are given a lifestyle crash course to prepare them for a less cosseted existence. Includes classes in self-defence, internet safety and relationships, charitable works, trips out, visiting lecturers and, in a surprisingly retro twist, a hair and beauty day, which seems a little old fashioned but, hey ho, girls will be girls.

G

Gordon's School

West End, Woking, Surrey GU24 9PT

Pupils: 790; 128 full, 74 weekly boarders • Ages: 11–18 • Sixth form: 208

Fees: Day free; Boarding £7,143 – £16,167 pa

Tel: 01276 858084
Email: registrar@gordons.surrey.sch.uk
Website: www.gordons.surrey.sch.uk

Head Teacher: Since 2010, Mr Andrew Moss BA MEd NPQH (40s). Started teaching in 1992 and has worked in a variety of boarding and day schools, including most recently a headship in a Cognita independent school. Before that he was a deputy head in Hampshire, and deputy, director of studies and housemaster at Wymondham College (also a state boarding school). 'He's a breath of fresh air,' said one in the know, 'bringing the school forward, without losing the best parts.'

He's less of a father figure than his predecessor, who transformed Gordon's from plodding to premier league, but is equally enthusiastic about this rather unusual school. 'I'm in the best of both worlds,' he says. 'We have the sort of heritage and behaviour you'll typically see in an independent, but with more grounded, authentic people around, people from all walks of life.'

Every parent we spoke to described him as 'professional', then variously as 'dynamic', 'pleasant' and 'ambitious', although some admitted they did not know him very well yet. 'He speaks well at meetings, seems a good manager and has a very business-like manner,' said one, 'but he hasn't put himself out to get to know people'. Yet all agree he has a good handle on the school and is well-respected by pupils, from whom he'll take no nonsense. 'If he told my children to jump, they would simply ask "How high, Sir?"' said one. Interviewed by pupils in the school magazine, they said of him, 'His signature stern, tough chapel talks have become synonymous with his presence itself'.

He's undoubtedly got strong ideas, but does use staff and parents as a sounding board and talks about 'empowering people' and 'decentralisation'. 'You can't build capacity all by yourself,' he says. 'You need good people to get involved and play a role in ideas and delivery'. Wasted no time in making his presence felt – investing in several projects including building new and revamping existing facilities, improving reporting systems and assessment methods and sorting out better communications with parents.

Keeps a finger on the pulse by taking PSHE lessons on economics and finance once a week. Has two children of his own (both at the school) and is a keen skier in his spare time.

Academic matters: Among the very best state offerings in the country, with an academically rigorous curriculum. It is an all-ability school, for which pupils are not selected via entrance exams, yet its results are top notch. In 2016, 97 per cent of pupils achieved five or more GCSE A*-C grades, including English and maths, with 47 per cent A*/A grades. At A level in 2016, 48 per cent A*/A and 80 per cent A*-B grades.

Its secret? Head puts it down to school's balance of traditional and modern methods – everything from reading out loud and spelling tests, through to use of peer assessment and mini whiteboards. Parents like its size (small), the emphasis on setting (rather than mixed-ability teaching) and its boarding school ethos.

Although two-thirds of its pupils live at home, the school is structured as a boarding school, with these 'day boarders' (as they are known) organised the same way as the wholly residential boarders in an extended school day. So everyone is in a house, with houseparents, and following the same programme, including supervised homework, until 7.30pm.

Everyone is set for English, maths and science (out of four) and also for languages in years 7 and 8 – a language is compulsory at GCSE; either German, French or Spanish. Lowish requirements for additional support; some seven per cent have one-to-one EAL help and four per cent have statements/EHC plans, led by full-time SENCo and delivered in small groups and individually. 'Although it's a regimented place, the school does adapt well to individuals', said one mother. 'They are very good at saying, this person has issues, let's sort him out – and I've seen some children really blossom here'.

They plough through the work, books filled at a pace, and there are plenty of practice papers and timed tests to make sure everyone is well prepared for GCSE. 'The new linear exams will suit us,' says AM. 'In fact we will gain as our work ethic is all about keeping it together to the end'. School has never been keen on the 'retakes' culture which fuelled much of the GCSE discontent.

Parents praise a strong and disciplined teaching team with high expectations that pupils will be self-disciplined to work hard and be courteous at all times. Good systems in place ensure that nobody slips through the net. 'Monitoring is really good', said one parent. 'If someone isn't working at the expected level they will be pulled into a clinic to get them up to scratch'. One of AM's tasks has been to improve the process still further, with more informative, more frequent reporting, particularly for key stage 4/5. On top of an effort grade, pupils now receive target and working grades and every half term they receive significant feedback on what they need to do next. Lessons are fairly formal, there's an atmosphere of calm, but pupils are fully involved. Word on the street is that supply teachers find covering lessons at Gordon's a pleasure – they do not get ripped to shreds as in some state schools.

Homework is 'reasonable' – homework diaries are an important part of keeping on top of everything, really well used, signed every week by parents and school. 'They have to have it with them at all times and it's great for day to day communications, gets them organised and responsible,' said a parent. 'It's almost like the children are on report at all times,' said another. 'But it's for good comments too – they can get a stamp (like a gold star) and sometimes we'll get a note from a head of department or a housemaster if they've done something wonderful'. Evidently the regime can be stressful for some. 'My son cried for half an hour when he lost his homework once,' one mother said.

Around 180 at sixth form take 'facilitating' A levels (serious subjects that will win students places at Russell Group and other leading universities). No vocational qualifications on offer. 'We retain those for whom the sixth form is suitable,' says AM. Parents like it that sixth formers are not allowed off-site during teaching hours, so are more likely to work during their free periods – school calls them 'study periods, there are no frees'.

Ofsted rated school as 'outstanding'; its glowing report is littered with superlatives like 'exceptional' and 'beyond excellent'.

Games, options, the arts: It's all going on, both during the school day and as extracurricular options. After what would be the end of the school day at most state schools, the extended day here begins with 'period 6' – anything from sport to cooking, calligraphy to mountain biking or ultimate frisbee. It's compulsory, and costs some £7,143 a year, although if pupils have a bona fide after hours activity not available at the school there will be a dispensation.

Masses of sport on offer, with good facilities on site – more than 40 acres of playing fields, and all the usual football, rugby and hockey pitches, to the less usual (for a state school) shooting range, Astroturf and indoor heated swimming pool. Gordon's teams are happy to take on the toughest opponents and often play independent schools. Next on AM's wish list is a new sports hall – you don't doubt he will get one. 'Sport is a great release for everyone here,' said one mother. 'There's so much for them to do so that it's not all about pure academia. It's more of a lifestyle, there's a total mix of ages on the parade square after school and always someone around to kick a ball with'. 'I love that my son's outside instead of on his Xbox,' said another. 'The amount of physical activity is great.'

There's a huge emphasis on Duke of Edinburgh, with some 90 pupils achieving awards every year and lots of it at the much tougher gold end of things. 'Bronze is one thing, but getting stuck into a trip to Borneo is quite different from working in a charity shop for an hour a week,' said AM. 'It's quite striking how many golds we get, in fact we have organised 40 overseas trips in the past 10 years'. And all three Forces are represented in Gordon's combined cadet force – quite a feat to manage a naval unit in landlocked Surrey.

Great tradition of hard-fought inter-house competition gets everyone involved, regardless of ability; not just in sport but also in art, music and drama, with specialist facilities for all – an outdoor theatre is the latest addition. There are two annual art exhibitions and two full scale productions every year. Music very big, as well as an orchestra, choir and concert band, there's a pipe and drum band which, together with marching practice, is a major focus of the school.

Boarding: There are five day houses and four residential houses – all well used by both day and full boarders, who mix well. Boys and girls are allowed freely in each other's houses, but no boy is allowed upstairs in the girls' boarding houses and vice versa. Boys' houses with pool and table tennis tables, girls' centred more around comfy sofas and bean bags. Full boarding houses include common rooms, study areas and dormitories with study/bed units – all homely and understandably more relaxed and not as tidy and regimented as other parts of the school. Ofsted's inspection of boarding facilities pronounced them 'outstanding' in every respect. One boarder said that he doesn't 'go home' in the holidays, saying that he and his parents considered the school to be his main home.

Background and atmosphere: Ceremony and discipline is in the DNA of Gordon's, which was founded in 1885, at the behest of Queen Victoria, as a national memorial to General Gordon who was killed at Khartoum. The reigning monarch has been the school's patron ever since.

Every pupil learns to march and takes part in every one of the eight parades and chapel services held each year, accompanied by the previously mentioned pipes and drums marching band. There is marching practice every Friday, and once a year pupils go to London and literally stop the traffic when they march down Whitehall to the Cenotaph, ending up at the bronze statue of General Gordon on the Embankment. Although right up the street of the keen musicians in the band, it can be rather a chore for the others. 'I wouldn't say the marching is universally popular, but they get used to it – it's just what they do, everybody does it, it's part of Gordon's,' said a parent. 'And in fact after they have left school I think that trip along Whitehall will be a really special memory for them.'

Day to day things are rather less regimented, but all very orderly – AM likes to describe the atmosphere as 'purposeful calm'. The school is built around a large quadrangle, quite bare and military in feel, with the odd bench here and there, where the students hang out during break and lunch if they are not in their houses. Alongside the original Victorian buildings are some less pretty 1960s additions, and (much better) 21st century facilities, including the new music and drama centre, science block and sixth form centre. Classrooms are large, light and spacious, in both the older and newer buildings, and well resourced. Stunning chapel, built in 1894, which houses numerous school treasures, including a book which lists the names of all the Gordon's boys killed in the two world wars. Pupils are never for a moment in any doubt about their school's heritage.

Pastoral care, well-being and discipline: A very disciplined place; 'Without good order there can be no learning in the classroom,' says school. Generally not much allowance for anyone stepping out of line, but for those obedient souls happy to stay within the set boundaries there are plenty of rewards and responsibilities on offer. Pupils quickly pick up on what's expected of them at Gordon's – they get it and are generally hardworking and appreciative of what's on offer. 'It's brilliant fun' and 'not one horrible teacher', our tour guides told us. They don't even seem to mind their 'boarders' duties' – vacuuming and emptying the bins.

School terribly keen on simple good manners, insists that pupils are courteous and considerate of others. Similarly picky about uniform. If a girl's skirt is deemed too short (and we didn't see any) she will be given a week's grace to get a new one. Everyone attends the chapel twice a week. Very close companionship among pupils who say they trust each other. New peer mentoring system working well. Need we mention zero tolerance of bullying, alcohol, drugs and associated misdemeanours? Strong culture of 'telling' to house parents and tutors is encouraged from the off. One longstanding parent convinced it's the combined support from house parents, tutors and teachers that underpins the academic success here.

Pupils and parents: Although it's a state school, most parents have money, certainly parents of boarders who have to cover the boarding fees. Parents of day boarders must be able to afford the £7100+ day boarding fees and will be in a certain socio-economic demographic to live in the catchment; of necessity they must live practically next door and some will move house to get this education for their children. 'We may have spent time and effort moving so close, but we saved on tutoring for entrance to a selective school and are continuing to save a fortune in comparison to the level of fees we'd pay for an independent school now,' said one. Aside from these locals, parents are a huge mix of professional, diplomatic and Forces. Weekly boarders typically live within an hour's drive, full boarders come from all over the UK, with about 15 per cent from overseas.

Pupils seem friendly, happy and very proud of their school; all regular young people, not quiet and cowed by the rules and regulations, but confident and ambitious types who seem to thrive in the order of everything.

Parent/school communications have improved – still a way to go, but would have been more of a criticism a few years ago. Text messaging system, emails, more frequent newsletters and bulletins are all AM innovations and remodelling of website is next on his 'to do' list.

G

Entrance: Tough. There are typically 400 applications for the 108 year 7 places on offer (76 day boarders – around 300 applicants – and 32 full/weekly boarders) and around half of these are generally swallowed up by siblings. Non-selective, so no entrance exams. Full or weekly boarder places prioritised by 'need to board'. This usually means children from Forces families from the UK and overseas – the school foresees increasing numbers of such children following recent changes to legislation.

For admission as a 'day boarder' think purely of location. Catchment varies but typically you'll need to live no further than 600m from the school. Mother of a baby was enquiring when we visited and local estate agents are well used to dealing with desperate parents who've left it rather later, but want to move next door. A small number of places allocated each year to children with statements of special educational needs.

Some additional places are available for the sixth form, where the entry requirement for both existing and new pupils is five GCSEs A*-C (including English and maths) with Bs for subjects to be taken at A level.

Exit: Around 40 per cent leave after GCSEs, some to more vocational courses at nearby Brooklands College. Most sixth formers on to university; around half to Russell Group. Two to Oxbridge in 2016 and four medics.

Money matters: The education is free, but parents pay for the boarding, and even parents of day pupils ('day boarders') must pay for the compulsory post 3.30pm element of the day, house system, Saturday school, lunches and teas. Some bursaries available.

Remarks: A very different state offering – more like a private school without the price tag and elitism. Committed to traditional values, high standards, good discipline – doesn't share its 'semper fidelis' motto with the US marine corps for nothing. Those happy with the 'heads down and work' ethos are rewarded with an all-round, top notch education, pastoral care par excellence and enviable opportunities for sport. Suits focused, self-directed types, rather than a rebel who would be exhausted by the discipline. It's a school for achievers – a child with no oomph or aspirations would be lost among these go-getters.

Guildford High School

London Road, Guildford, Surrey GU1 1SJ

Pupils: 700 • Ages: 4–18 • Sixth form: 189 • C of E

Fees: £9,879 – £16,032 pa

Tel: 01483 543853
Email: Guildford-Admissions@guildfordhigh.co.uk
Website: www.guildfordhigh.surrey.sch.uk

G

Headmistress: Since 2002, Mrs Fiona Boulton BSc PGCE NPQH MA. Previously deputy headmistress and, before GHS, teacher and housemistress at Stowe and Marlborough. Mother of three school-age children, Mrs Boulton is very keen on work/life balance and carefully keeps her own work and home lives separate. However, she obviously thrives on spinning many plates at once, finds the challenges 'enormous fun' and describes the vibe in the staff room as of 'friendship and mutual support'. She has picked her staff to work together and expects the same commitment and plate-spinning knack from them too. Over the 10 years she has been at the helm she has 'aimed to make GHS outstanding in every area with no weak links', seeing this as the best way to compete with the wealth of other local girls' schools. She hates the suggestion that GHS might be considered an academic hothouse and is certain that is not the experience of any of her pupils, citing the sheer range of activities on offer here. Girls are very fond of her, whilst also being 'slightly scared'; she can silence the full school hall by just walking in. Parents value her honesty about the pressures to expect for their daughters in each year.

Head of junior school: Since January 2016, Michael Gibb, previously deputy head. BA in economics and social policy from Royal Holloway, then went to the royal Military Academy and spent seven years in the army before doing a PGCE at Canterbury Christ Church and joining Westbourne House School, where he became senior teacher and head of boarding. Moved to Guildford High Junior as deputy head in 2011.

Academic matters: Teaching in the junior school is a combination of traditional and innovative, practical work and academic rigour. Girls feel 'it's cool to learn' and the head feels they 'make accelerated progress due to the sense of nurture and fun.' Extra help is readily available, whether for catch up or in a challenge group. The girls showed us a quiet corner set aside for one-to-one help; they felt anyone might need it – or ask for it – without stigma. But these are bright girls and we can't help feeling they wouldn't want to be catching up for long.

The breadth and depth of the curriculum sets GH junior school apart: 14 subjects are taught including Spanish from age 5, French from age 7, drama, DT, food tech and IT (from touch typing to how a computer actually works). Up to year 5 there are separate English lessons for grammar and spelling (including the origins of words). Exams focus on the core subjects of maths, English and science; without the pressures of application to the next school there is no need to teach to or sit 11+ exams. Key stage 2 results are outstanding, and expected to be so, with over 90 per cent at level 5 in every subject most years, up to 100 per cent in science.

Senior school academically outstanding: results-focused culture plus a strong and empowering sense of expectation in the girls leads to top performance at GCSE and A level, permanently in the upper echelons of national league tables. In 2016, over 96 per cent of GCSE grades A*/A and 83 per cent of A levels (A*/B 96 per cent). Predicted grades are tracked throughout senior school and show an average increase of 1+.

Mrs Boulton describes her pupils as 'some exceptional girls, but the vast majority are bright and enjoying life', and puts their success down to 'fabulous staff, supportive parents and it's cool to be clever'. Younger pupils echo her describing 'great teachers, you can ask them anything, nothing is seen as stupid to ask', whilst sixth formers tell us 'teachers will spend as long as you need to explain anything', describing one-to-one sessions fathoming some tricky maths or English dilemma. The girls are taught how to learn, think and debate rather than what to learn.

At 11 girls choose two of French, Spanish or German; all girls have three years of Latin and separate sciences are studied throughout school. Additionally philosophy, Mandarin, touch-typing, Adobe Photoshop and current affairs are covered on a rotational basis throughout the first three years. Innovative information booklets give a complete insight for parents and pupils as to expectations and curriculum in each school year, including guidelines for parents on how to help at home; these booklets are typical of the professionalism and clarity of everything at GHS. Parents describe the culture as 'driven' and 'focused'; they feel it's taken for granted that girls will cope academically.

The first three years involve less homework (Mrs B recommends using a timer) and more fun trips out; the pace steps up at the start of GCSE courses in year 10. Girls need to be motivated and organised to take it all in their stride; one parent felt 'you could sink quite quickly', although there are few casualties. No homework is given over the holidays, allowing a complete break mentally to 'create balance and perspective'; parents, pupils and staff really appreciate this.

A tiny number of girls have SEN, but the pace here suits only the most able and provision for SEN is simply to ensure 'staff take into account specific learning needs'. The few for whom English is an additional language are sufficiently fluent not to require additional support.

Sixth form is a breed apart: girls say they feel different, are treated differently and have a different experience – all important to keep the interest levels up for pupils who may have been at GHS for 10 years already. The sixth formers have their own house, with teaching rooms, a quiet study room and a large, funkily furnished common room complete with kitchen for lunch or snack-making. Really buzzing with clever, confident, animated young women concerned with everything from the latest heels to the meaning of life.

Games, options, the arts: Junior school works hard to ensure that sport, music and art all hold similar status within the school. Sportswise there are some pretty high standards and sensational achievements in swimming and netball. The juniors have use of the netball courts and fab swimming pool in the GHS sports centre, rounders is played on nearby Stoke Park. Teams are fielded from A to F and participation in extracurricular squad training is strongly encouraged.

Sport is a significant part of senior school life; although it doesn't capture all the girls, there is genuinely something for everyone. Main sports are lacrosse and netball, though many more are timetabled – swimming, gymnastics, athletics, rounders, football, badminton, yoga, dance. Standards are incredibly high in the top school teams (county or national) and girls who are not at these hugely committed levels may lose interest in the main sports by the time they are 15 or so. Mrs Boulton tells us 'we create lots of opportunities for sport' and there is an enormous array of unusual fitness options, taekwondo, fencing, indoor climbing and, the latest addition, zumba. Indoor rowing was started a couple years ago, became very popular and in true GHS fashion they won two golds and a silver at the National Indoor Rowing Championships. About 100 metres up the road and overlooking Stoke Park is the newish sports centre. Home to a fab pool with electronic touch timing, it also houses an sports hall (within indoor netball court, so no freezing evening training sessions), a fitness centre for the 16+, and a large social area for comfortable match teas, meetings and sixth form parties with the boys from the Royal Grammar School (half a mile away).

Music is another big part of school life with hundreds of individual lessons taught weekly by specialist teachers. There are plenty of opportunities for performance with the many choirs, ensembles, bands and orchestras, including some at very high standards. A joint choir and orchestra with RGS boys toured Italy, performing in Verona and Venice. All junior girls participate in drama and music, everyone takes a part in a drama production and almost everyone plays a musical instrument (or two) and performs in a group or orchestra.

Opportunities for drama in the senior school include the annual panto written and directed by lower sixth and performed by year 7. Girls from year 10 up may audition for the two main productions a year (one with the RGS boys), whilst years 8 and 9 take part in a Shakespeare Festival – each form puts on a play with girls directing and acting, eight plays in all over two hectic days.

Parents marvel at the commitment required of their daughters to take part in so many activities, at such high standards, 'some girls do everything – but it's difficult'.

The list of junior extracurricular activities and clubs would exhaust many senior schoolchildren. Lots do incur extra costs and a few, for catch-up or enhancement, are by invitation only. Every year group has a programme of trips, days out at museums, the ballet, theatre, science events, and longer visits abroad to immerse in foreign culture and language. Enormous array of clubs in the senior school too. On the first Friday of each term girls sign up for clubs and groups in music, sports, creative arts, science, cooking, language, maths, cartoon, reading, board games, textiles; just about everything is covered and girls can do something extra every day.

Background and atmosphere: GHS is the jewel in the crown of United Learning, which owns 11 independent schools and sponsors 17 academies in the maintained sector. The school is run by Mrs Boulton and her team rather than centrally, but with the advantages of a wide group of other United Learning heads, teachers and managers to consult over best practice, as well as a central budget to draw from for major projects.

The school is located where Guildford town centre meets leafy Victorian suburbia. Buildings are a mix of old and new, though all very well maintained. There's always something being added or improved: the sports centre a few years ago, then an attractive large house next door was purchased and converted to provide sixth form teaching rooms as well as some welcome garden space, and the latest is a music block housing a recording studio and teaching studios, with a recital hall for lectures as well as concerts.

Junior school in a clean and well-kept modern building slotted into the middle of the GHS campus. Every corner well used and the bigger rooms, the library, art room and science lab, feel quite spacious. Outdoor space is at a bit of a premium; girls can play on a variety of colourful equipment including a wooden adventure playground in a grassy garden.

GH junior school 'nurtures a joy of being at school'; this was certainly borne out by our 10 year old hosts who covered every aspect of school life with huge enthusiasm and pride as well as considerate praise for others' different achievements. They showed us beautifully neat exercise books, colourfully vibrant text books and personal planners chock full of activities and reminders. There's something interesting at every turn – a large, light stairwell with a fantastic mural spiralling through centuries of monarchs, wars and historical happenings; the library's Challenge Corner with demanding books to try out; classrooms equipped with Activexpression handsets enabling the whole class to participate fully in lessons; the online virtual learning environment so girls can access their work at home.

Hugely positive attitude to school and academic work throughout the place. Pupils value their abilities and want to make the most of themselves; their mission is to work hard and get good results. Respect for each other is evident in the way girls interact and the general lack of nastiness. Parents describe GHS as 'an exciting and buzzy place to be' and say 'if you have an ability the school will find it', and everyone celebrates all success without resentment. No-one treats others differently if they're in lower sets, but make no mistake, this place is not for the faint-hearted, over-sensitive or needy; it would not be comfortable to just scrape in and bump along the bottom. Pupils need to be robust to make the most of everything on offer.

Pastoral care, well-being and discipline: Pastoral care is the number one priority. Junior girls describe how 'teachers hear both sides' in arguments; form rooms have a worry box where girls can leave messages for their form teacher about anything that may be worrying or upsetting them. Kindness and consideration for others are genuinely apparent in the girls' behaviour and talk. School is proud of the high levels of individual care, including for girls who may need extra support in the short or long term.

Senior girls' first port of call for help and advice is their form tutor, followed by their head of year and the deputy head. However, pastoral care is seen as the shared responsibility of all staff and girls know they can talk to any of them. Importantly, there are clear procedures for communication amongst staff including regular updates, pupils' records and a 'TLC list' in the staff room for any special situations. Mrs Boulton is particularly proud of the individual care, especially in unusual and tragic circumstances.

The atmosphere amongst the girls themselves is genuinely supportive and respectful. Parents say there's little of the nasty bitching often associated with girls' schools. Inevitably there is a bit, but the school deals with any quickly and works hard to prevent it. Occasional fall-outs amongst these strident and feisty individuals, but no out-and-out bullying.

School rules, listed on the website, are pretty sparse; maybe these pupils are just too busy to be rebellious. Very few detentions seem to be given; when we visited our young hosts hadn't heard of any girl getting a detention and were quite shocked at the thought of it.

Drugs, drinking, legal highs – Mrs Boulton tells us there have been no issues during her time here, though she recognises that as a day school she is not involved with the girls' weekend activities. She explains girls are taught 'decision making, how to extract yourself from difficult situations and how to act' so they may look after themselves.

Seventy per cent of the girls arrive by public transport, mostly train, which parents find 'fantastic and convenient' even for later leaving times with after-school activities. A 'buddy system' links new girls with existing pupils who travel from the same home rail station; the buddy accompanies their charge to the school door for as long as is required until they are confident.

Pupils and parents: Families from a wide catchment both geographically and socially, though the majority are solid middle class with both parents working; not flashy, more grounded with plenty of common sense and less touchy-feely than some of the other Surrey girls' options – not many with ponies! Parents are very on-board with the work hard, play hard ethos to achieve top results.

There is no specific type of girl for GHS, says Mrs Boulton, 'there's an eclectic mix of personalities'; the emphasis is on respecting each other's differences, 'it's OK to be yourself'. She feels any type can find a niche here whether sporty, musical, an all-rounder or a quiet bookish girl. The parents we spoke to had a variety of daughters and concurred they all fit in; the rider was they needed to be focussed, motivated and pretty robust. When we looked around the girls were a confident, ebullient lot, comfortable in their own skins and with the business of learning; not show-offish but definitely proud of their school and achievements.

Little or no evidence of customising uniform or wearing make-up or nail varnish. Girls all neat and tidy in their practical, rather than lovely, uniforms. Sixth formers in own clothes but still workaday and no eye-boggling fashions.

Notable old girls a surprisingly arty lot – portrait artist Jane Allison, playwrights Ella Hicks and Lucy Prebble, actress Celia Imrie and TV presenter Louise Roe.

H

Entrance: Selective entry by assessment and interview. At 4+ girls are assessed using games and puzzles to spot skills (language, number, cognitive, physical and social). At 7+ girls complete papers in English and maths, a computerised reasoning test and reading aloud. Competition is undoubtedly stiff with 60 to 100 sitting for 32 places in reception and only eight to 10 places in year 3. School is looking for an ability to learn rather than IQ, and for girls who will enjoy GHS. The latter is key as the pace and commitment required from both pupils and parents is substantial and could make life rather miserable if the girl and her family did not enjoy it.

GHS describe itself as 'an all-through school with natural progression junior to senior', thus girls from the junior school take around 40 per cent of senior school places at 11. For the others, entrance assessment is over one full day early in the Lent term comprising an exam based on the national curriculum, one hour of English, creative writing plus comprehension, and one hour of maths, from addition and multiplication through to problem-solving. Candidates are interviewed by the headmistress or other senior teacher. No trick questions; Mrs Boulton describes it as 'a friendly chat about yourself'. The process is very transparent with the aim of creating a level playing field for entrants of all backgrounds, looking for individual's skills not previous teaching standards. About three applicants for each of the 60 available places, and competition is tough as the school's reputation puts off unlikely candidates. Big range of feeders, with almost a quarter of girls entering from the state sector. Independents include Rowan, Hoe Bridge, St Ives and Halstead; state juniors include Cleves, St Paul's, South Farnham, Pyrford, Horsell, Holy Trinity and Bushy Hill.

In the lower sixth there's a maximum of 10 places available. Girls sit three one hour papers from a choice of subjects plus a general paper and an interview. Entrants are expected to have at least eight good GCSEs with A*/A in their chosen A level subjects.

Exit: Once in the reception year there is a place for girls right through to the sixth form of the senior school – a 'natural transfer' which nearly all the girls make. This goes some way to explain the fervour to get into the junior school since a GHS education is something of a Holy Grail for bright girls across Surrey.

Small fall-out after GCSEs – around 10 per cent. High aspirations plus lots of school support – including a dedicated higher education advisor – means girls generally get what and where they want. Each year around 20 per cent go to Oxbridge (17 places in 2016); Durham most popular destination followed by a long and varied list of good UK universities headed by Bristol, Birmingham and Exeter plus eg Harvard. Most popular courses are medicine and languages of all sorts, but there's an enormous range including chemical engineering, psychology, art, politics and veterinary medicine.

Money matters: Scholarships worth up to a third of fees. Assisted places available at 11+, bursaries for daughters of the clergy and for any sixth formers, all assessed on financial need. Small sibling discounts of five and 10 per cent.

Academic scholarships equally available to incomers and existing pupils; all sit the 11+ or 16+ entrance exams if they wish to apply. So although girls may move from junior to senior and into sixth form without taking any exams, if they wish to have a go at scholarship they do need to sit the entrance exams alongside the external candidates. In reality only the few truly shining stars do so.

Music scholarships similarly available to internal and external candidates. Girls at 11+ must be at least grade 4 on an orchestral instrument and on piano and at 16+ grade 8 on two instruments or one plus singing at chamber choir standard. Lots of clear and encouraging information available, but only worth it with a real musical talent and dedication.

Remarks: Outstanding at every turn, providing a superb education, not just fantastic exam results but a whole positive and enquiring approach to life, the universe and everything. Girls need to be very bright and hard working to make the most of the opportunities. In return the school will uncover all talents, make the most of every iota and send girls off with confidence and a fistful of accomplishments.

Haberdashers' Aske's Prep and Pre-Prep

Linked with The Haberdashers' Aske's Boys' School

Butterfly Lane, Elstree, Hertfordshire WD6 3AF

Pupils: 257 • Ages: 5–11 • C of E

Fees: £13,914 – £18,456 pa

Tel: 020 8266 1700
Email: admissions@habsboys.org.uk
Website: www.habsboys.org.uk

Headteacher: Since 1997, Ms Yvonne Mercer BEd Adv Dip Applied Educational Studies, who heads the prep and pre-prep. Trained as a PE teacher and then went on to become deputy head of Ashton Church of England Middle School for seven years, and continues to be a governor. It was at this school, she says, that her future was 'implanted'.

Assertive but with a twinkle in her eye, her 16 years as the head of the prep and pre-prep schools have done nothing to dampen her enthusiasm for the job. On the contrary, she hates the word complacency and says, 'There's always something you can improve on.' We got the distinct impression that she lives for her job: 'I was ill during the holidays, but completely fine once I returned to work', and revels in all the achievements of her boys, whether she's standing on the sidelines spurring her pupils on in their various sports fixtures, or watching proudly as they excel in exams. While academia is important here, she also acknowledges that kids have to be kids and therefore will not overload them with homework. 'My philosophy is, enjoy a working day at school, but then enjoy some leisure and chilling time afterwards to maintain a healthy balance.'

She is a hands-on head, and to get to know her pupils continues to teach religious studies, 'although not as much as I would like any more.' She believes there is a huge advantage to educating boys in a single sex school: 'It gives them the freedom to participate in some of the subject areas where, if girls were around, they would perhaps not be quite so open.'

Very much of the opinion that boys should be aware of their privileges, so fundraising events are a priority. The biggest challenge of her teaching career to date was a recent two month sabbatical to South Africa to work at The Sparrow School in Johannesburg, where 60 per cent of pupils are orphans, primarily as a result of HIV. 'It was an amazing and humbling experience, and wonderful to see how the money our school has raised has been used to house some of these orphans and provide textbooks.' Her experience was filmed and shown to the students on her return.

She is a popular and approachable head, and as one parent said, 'She has a profound concern for the children and their education. She is the sort of person who goes that extra mile.'

Entrance: Selective entry at 5+ and 7+. Pre-prep: first round of assessments in age bands; tasks aim to 'identify potential'. Those called back for second round have individual 45 minute assessments; parents interviewed by head. There are 36 places. Prep: around 120 take reading, writing, maths and verbal reasoning tests, competing for 18 7+ places; some 48 invited back for further assessments and interview. No sibling policy as such but having a sibling in the boys' or girls' school, or being the son of an Old Haberdasher, may help in a tie break.

Exit: Automatic entry from pre-prep to prep. Most, if not all of the prep school students continue on to the main school, although all have to sit the 11+ exam.

Remarks: Driving through the impressive gates off Butterfly Lane in leafy Hertfordshire and up the winding, immaculate drive, we felt as if we were about to embark on an exclusive spa break rather than arrive at a school campus.

The prep and senior school share 100 acres of parkland with the adjoining girls' school, separated by a fence lovingly nicknamed 'the passion gate'. In the heart of the grounds (once the rival of Kew Gardens), stands Aldenham House, a grade 2 listed building dating from the 17th century and home to the senior school. The prep school is situated in a less impressive 1980s purpose-built block a short walk away, with bright, airy, well-equipped rooms.

The prep school building has 12 classrooms with around 18 pupils in each class and three classes per year group. There is a specialist science lab, an art and design room, a large multi-functional hall and sports changing facilities. None of the old familiar school smells down these corridors: there are pristine, shiny floors, immaculately presented pupils' work adorning the walls, displays of historical facts, various celebratory events and stories written in handwriting a secondary school pupil would be proud of. Outside the door of the small, but extremely well-stocked library (which one parent mentioned needs 'updating'), there is a panel with newspaper cuttings of major recent news events – in this case, the death of Margaret Thatcher.

Sats results are consistently outstanding. Standards and expectations are high and 'no one will leave you to flounder', said one father. Slackers need not apply. Twice winner of the Sunday Times' Independent Preparatory School of the Year, and the only boys' school to have won at all.

Little on first impression to suggest that individuality or anything remotely left of centre is high on the agenda at this school. We almost expected to be confronted by a bunch of sullen-looking Stepford boys, in military uniform (bearing the school crest and motto 'serve and obey'), filing past. However, we met spirited boys, all of them extremely well mannered, and seemingly relaxed and happy, although one 8-year-old pupil did mention that he would 'like less homework.'

Academia is undoubtedly high priority at this school, but one parent said she resented the word 'hothousing' to describe their academic ethos. 'Don't get me wrong, it's not a holiday camp, but they only push children to an extent they are comfortable with. I have no issue with it being a high achieving school – eventually they'll be up against it in the real world.'

Dedicated language teachers, and all teaching by subject specialists in years 5 and 6. There is also a practising artist on staff. One parent told us, 'The teaching is consistently good. There are no substandard teachers.' He also said that it is the parents who put pressure on their children, not the teachers.

The boys are encouraged to think creatively. Stimulating lessons can involve making motorised cars in design technology, and flying hand-made helicopters from the hall balcony when learning about weight and force; younger boys design and produce their own version of Mr Men books with their own characters. An initiative to teach more lessons outside is currently under way. The head says, 'Some children learn better outside the confines of a classroom. It makes them less inhibited.' (Very Dead Poet's Society).

Happy to accommodate children with mild learning difficulties eg dyslexia or dyspraxia, and will give some one-to-one specialist help if necessary at no extra cost. However, the school says 'All pupils must thrive and we make sure the pupil is in the best place for this to happen', so greater difficulties may entail a move elsewhere.

Plentiful opportunities outside the classroom, with clubs ranging from judo, which attracts a quarter of pupils, to scuba diving, table tennis, basketball and chess (judo and chess at an extra cost). The school has won the English primary schools chess title three times in the last eight years, and many boys have been selected for the England squad.

More than half the prep school pupils have music lessons and all boys in year 5 learn to play an instrument. Throughout their four years they get a flavour of different sports, from football and rugby to cricket, rounders and softball. Exercise plays a major role in the boys' week, and one parent admitted that 'even if your boy doesn't stand out in maths, there's plenty of opportunity to do so in sport.'

In their last report, inspectors highlighted the quality of pastoral care, and as the head says, 'We take pride in ensuring the children are happy because they will then make progress.' The prep shares an all-weather pitch, athletics track, chapel, extensive playing fields, new sports hall with covered swimming pool, tennis courts and theatre with the senior school.

The almost legendary coach system (mentioned in former pupil William Sutcliffe's book New Boy) will transport any child from the age of 7 from as far as Welywn Garden City and is shared by both the boys' and girls' schools. One parent called it a 'dating agency' for the older students. The school has a large cultural mix, with some 20-30 per cent each of Jewish and Asian families, and students are actively encouraged to learn about other faiths.

Our tour ended in the dining hall at lunchtime. Hogwarts springs to mind and we almost expected a counter overflowing with every flavour beans. The puddings are not far off – an assortment of brightly coloured jellies and blancmanges, accompany tempting fruit, as well as patisserie-style fairy cakes and muffins. Not a whiff of lumpy custard in sight.

'The pre-prep looks a bit like a scout hut,' the head told us almost apologetically, before we embarked on the six mile journey from the main Haberdashers' campus to the pre-prep site. The school, situated at the bottom of a residential street (a nightmare to find), does indeed, on first appearance, bear resemblance to some sort of make-shift, high spec Portakabin. However, we were immediately drawn to the large playground, with an adventure climbing area surrounded by beautiful woodland.

Within this little prefab, there are four bright and colourful classrooms, a multi-purpose hall, a kitchen and a catering team who provide a hot meal for every boy each day. The boys, known as Kingfishers, play weekly games at the prep school, and have sports events and cross-country there at least once a term. They also use the prep school hall for concerts and productions.

One teacher told us that they like to integrate the pre-prep students slowly into the main school so it doesn't come as quite such a shock when they leave their little safe environment to enter a large campus at 7 years old. They are bright, highly-motivated boys. As a teacher said bluntly, 'We are lucky in that we can pick and choose who we want'. Impressive art work was on display in one of the classrooms. No stuck-on pieces of pasta here, but replications of Van Gogh's Sunflowers.

'The pre-prep is a lovely, very protective little school,' one mother said. 'Standards are high, which permeates throughout the school. It's a nice way to ease them in to the Habs system.' And a prep school parent told her boys, 'If you're not happy here, you won't be happy anywhere.'

H

The Haberdashers' Aske's Boys' School

Linked with Haberdashers' Aske's Prep and Pre-Prep

Butterfly Lane, Elstree, Hertfordshire WD6 3AF

Pupils: 1,418 • Ages: 11–18 • Sixth form: 314

Fees: £18,456 pa

Tel: 020 8266 1700
Email: office@habsboys.org.uk
Website: www.habsboys.org.uk

Headmaster: Since 2002, Peter Hamilton, MA. Educated at King Edward VI Grammar School, Southampton and Christ Church College, Oxford, where he read modern languages (French and German). Taught at Radley before becoming housemaster and head of languages at Westminster. Then to King Edward VI Southampton, as head. Still teaches regularly: 'You need to keep your hand in' – a philosophy he clearly applies to learning as well, as he spent a recent sabbatical in Morocco studying Arabic: 'It's a fascinating language'. When not expanding his linguistic range, he likes riding and hill walking, windsurfing and fast motorbikes – 'I have a death wish,' he jokes (confirmed, perhaps, by his support of Southampton FC). Like his pupils, business-like, energetic and intelligent. Feels his contribution has been to 'reinvigorate' an already high-octane offering (a viewpoint clearly shared by the Independent School Inspectors, who recently found the school provided 'an outstanding educational experience'). French wife, Sylvie, is an osteopath; two daughters.

Academic matters: This is a top-of-the-league-table school and no one has ever been heard to voice the opinion: 'Exams aren't the most important thing'. Exam success is a priority – to the school, pupils and parents (who occasionally sneak off and get their children to sit extra exams elsewhere). 'Grades matter,' says the head, 'because they let parents know that most doors will be open to their sons.' And there are certainly few that aren't flung wide on the basis of these consistently high results – in 2016, 78 per cent of A levels A*/A, 98 per cent A*/B. GCSEs are seen merely as 'a hurdle to get over' (boys soar over the bar, with 95 per cent of GCSEs A*/A in 2016). Quality not quantity, however, is the head's guiding principle – exam numbers are kept to a manageable nine or 10 at GCSE, three at A2. ('Unless you're taking further maths, they discourage you from doing four,' said one sixth former.)

The head is also a traditionalist as far as the curriculum is concerned, undistracted by the IB, the Pre-U or the EPQ: 'We don't muck around. A levels serve boys very well'. That said, he feels the A* has not really solved concerns about 'stretch and challenge', an issue addressed at Habs by teachers taking pupils well beyond the specifications – 'We really ramp it up at A level'. Both pupils and parents are appreciative of the effort – 'Nearly every teacher is a good teacher,' said one recently departed student. 'Some are truly exceptional and inspiring. You hardly ever see a bad teacher.' Parents agree: 'My two sons have had consistently good teaching,' said one. Independent study projects in year 9 and year 12.

Though maths and economics are by far the most popular A level choices, sciences and arts are equally strong. A language carousel is offered in year 7, with four taster tongues (Latin, German, Spanish and French). Italian, Russian and Arabic are added for GCSE, with Japanese, Dutch, Mandarin available as tasters in the sixth form. Some subjects set on ability from year 9 – a good thing, say parents: 'There are boys here who are just light years ahead'. At A level, something of a cultural divide, with the sciences dominated by Asian pupils. Year 7 can be tricky for those not already in training for the school's intensive regime and those from homework-free primary schools can sometimes feel daunted. They soon learn, however, to take it in their stride.

Games, options, the arts: Whatever boys do here they do well – as strong an emphasis on the extracurricular as the academic – 'It's a work-hard, play-hard place,' said one parent. Sport is played energetically and competitively – excels at cricket and water polo (national champions). As well as the usual team effort (a rugby and hockey school), individualists can enjoy athletics, orienteering, badminton, shooting and golf. New sports centre used by whole school.

Two-thirds play a musical instrument – music and drama have always been taken seriously, with a demanding choice of work (think Brecht, Arthur Miller and Shakespeare, rather than High School Musical) and a high calibre of performance. Excellent facilities include one of the country's few operational fly towers and a well-used drama studio. (The school has a notable history of creative talent – recent alumnae include Matt Lucas, Sacha Baron Cohen, David Baddiel and Booker nominee, A D Miller.) Some adventurous art work, too, with a series of individually painted cow sculptures dotted round the site.

Characteristically, the more intellectually demanding pastimes also attract a high turn out, so plenty of chess champions and debating-cup winners. 'Our boys can talk for England,' says the head. Wide range of activities, mostly at lunchtimes, with a fair number of brain-stretchers, including crosswords and Scrabble. Community service is given a strong emphasis – 'We try to make them realise that being gifted brings the responsibility to put something back into society,' says the head.

Background and atmosphere: Opened in 1690, endowed by wealthy merchant haberdasher, Robert Aske, for the benefit of less fortunate members of his profession. Founded in Hoxton, it moved to Hampstead in the early 20th century and then, in 1961, to its current spacious 100-acre site in the grounds of Aldenham House in Hertfordshire. The attractive 17th-century red-brick mansion, once the residence of banker and influential botanist Vicary Gibbs, remains the focal point of the school. As well as the undoubted delights of its rolling rural expanses (the house and grounds served as the backdrop for '60s television series, The Avengers), notably well-equipped, with a medley of well-planned and well-laid out buildings – 'The facilities are superb,' said one parent. The newly-extended library is perhaps one of the most attractive features – spacious, bright and busy, with enthusiastic and knowledgeable staff.

One of the school's advantages (and sometimes disadvantages) is its secluded location, giving the feel of a country boarding school (or 'outer space,' as one pupil put it tartly). With the exception of a few sixth former drivers, most boys arrive in the morning and stay firmly put until they are ferried home by parents or coaches at 4 or 5pm. The house system is strong here, particularly in the lower school, where boys are taught by house, and remains a focus of exertion throughout. (This is a competitive school, particularly early on, when who beat whom at what is a regular conversational gambit.)

'Diversity' is a word the school could have invented. The entire spectrum of belief is celebrated weekly with 12 individual assemblies covering everything from Hindu, Buddhist and Jain, to Jewish, C of E and secular. Most are led by the boys themselves and all pupils, whatever their persuasion, are welcome to attend whichever they choose. Most try out at least one alternative to their own faith (bagels seem to be a big selling point in attracting custom for Jewish assembly). 'The school is very good on multicultural,' said one parent, 'with strong friendships across all the ethnic and religious groups.' Extensive network of prefects in the sixth form, elected by the boys. Food generally considered 'very good', with a new 'grab-and-go' area and sixth formers able to stock up in their own common room.

Pastoral care, well-being and discipline: These are bright, well-behaved, motivated boys – disciplinary issues are seldom a concern. A ferocious work ethic is necessary to survive happily at this school and the push from parents, particularly of the Tiger variety, tends to be as strong as that from teachers – 'We don't have arguments about homework here,' says the head. Parents agree: 'Boys work very, very hard'. Discipline is firm, however, with detention for minor misdemeanours (like forgetting your swimming costume), and prep not done to a satisfactory standard. 'Boys like to have boundaries,' says the head. 'I see myself as a benign despot.' Problems regularly seen elsewhere are not really part of the culture – 'People make mistakes, of course, but we rarely see anything malicious'. London's usual temptations tend to remain safely outside the gates – 'If they're brought in, there's zero tolerance. The boys know what's expected'.

Pupils and parents: Primarily the affluent and aspiring professional classes, reflective of the north London/Hertfordshire borders in which the school sits. (An extensive network of coaches with 110 stops imports boys from a 30 mile radius, from St John's Wood to Luton, Harpenden to Ruislip.) The school has traditionally had a significant Jewish core, who still represent about 30 per cent. This has more recently been overtaken by Asian families, who now make up about 30/40 per cent of the intake. Whatever their ethnic origins, these are families where the mantra 'education, education, education' is not simply spin. 'They know education is important to the future of their children and are full square behind them,' says the head. Some feel this can lead to a view that the only set to be in is the top set. Boys don't generally wilt under the pressure and come out positive and polite, self-assured without being self-regarding. The list of illustrious old boys is long and includes Simon Schama, Sir Nicholas Serota, Sir Martin Sorrell, Damon Hill and Brian Sewell.

Entrance: The main intake is at 11, when the school sets its own exams in English, maths and reasoning. About 600 apply for 100 places (in addition to those coming up from the prep school); 300 recalled for interview, which takes place in groups and individually. 'We don't mind crooked profiles,' says the head. 'If someone is outstanding at maths, we can cope with the fact that they're less good at English.' That said, a school where a high percentage of successful candidates will already be at, or near, the top of their class. NB part of a group of independent co-ed/boys' schools that coordinate 11+ results, but forbid those who have accepted a place at one school from taking up a subsequent waiting list offer from another. At 13 plus, 70-80 apply for 20 further places, with exams in English, maths, science, French, humanities and an optional Latin paper. At 16 maybe a handful of places to cover gaps left by leavers – entry by interview, a general essay and – for those wishing to study maths – a maths paper; minimum of six As or above required at GCSE.

Exit: Many to top universities – eg 2016: 33 to Oxbridge; Imperial, Bristol and Birmingham all popular. Large numbers into the professions – medics (15 in 2016), law, vets and dentists. 'Parents want practical careers for their boys,' said one father.

Money matters: Fees not outrageous by any means, but money tends to be dealt with penny by penny and extras are added regularly to the bill. Some 200 boys are on scholarships of between 10-30 per cent of fees. Bursary help also available, ranging from 5 to 100 per cent.

Remarks: A school which prides itself on identifying talent and building on it. Not the place for free spirits or those who want to muck around, but an outstanding offering for the bright-eyed and directed.

H

Haberdashers' Aske's Junior School for Girls

Linked with Haberdashers' Aske's School for Girls

Aldenham Road, Elstree, Hertfordshire WD6 3BT

Pupils: 326 • Ages: 4-11

Fees: £14,446 pa

Tel: 020 8266 2400
Email: juniors@habsgirls.org.uk
Website: www.habsgirls.org.uk

Executive Head of Junior School: Since November 2015, Mr Robert James-Robbins, who is also senior deputy head of the whole school. He was previously interim head of the junior school for 18 months, and has also worked at JAGS, as English teacher and senior teacher. He has an English degree from King's College London and a PGCE from the Institute of Education.

Entrance: Now taking in two reception classes (rather than one at 5+); selection is a careful process and girls have to demonstrate their 'Habs-ability' to win one of the most coveted school places in the area, if not the country. At 4+, girls are observed and chatted to within small groups of children with similar birth dates. Of some 250 who apply, the parents of about 80 will be invited to meet senior staff to talk about their daughters and why they might suit the school.

School is looking primarily for 'personality, teachability and sociability,' as well as 'some evidence that the girl is more advanced than usual' and 'chatting to parents is useful.' To weed out the pushy, we wonder? No comment. Come year 3, around 100 girls compete for six places, taking papers in maths and English as well as a group exercise and that all-important parent interview.

Exit: Vast majority to the senior school with just a handful each year moving to pastures new, mainly for financial reasons (local grammars beckoning) or to boarding school, with girls very occasionally advised in year 5 that they may not flourish in the fast-paced environment that is the senior school. All girls sit the same entrance exams as potential newcomers and are encouraged to take them seriously with a set of mocks ('harder than the real thing,' according to girls), despite places being almost guaranteed.

H

Remarks: A wonderfully modern, spacious building attached by a corridor to its equally stunning big sister school. No sense of it being a waiting room for the real thing – this school is special in its own right. Easily navigable even for its youngest pupils, with large classrooms displaying uniformly excellent work. Super art room displaying some outstanding work, plus own gym, music room, a cheerful library which can be used by girls at break from year 3 up and state of the art ICT suite. Fabulous adventure playground, used by year groups on rotation. New play area under construction, funded substantially by PTA.

Readers sceptical that such an academically successful school can also be fun should think again. Habs girls are down to earth, noisy and animated and clearly love every minute of the school day. Although many parents naturally reassess whether to move on to the senior school at 11+ or look elsewhere, they uniformly give a clear message that their daughters would never speak to them again if they were moved. Rather than pushing girls, school aims to 'nurture a love of learning' and focuses on 'resilience, self-esteem and risk-taking' as keys to success, noting that 'very able children put enough pressure on themselves.' Girls say school is 'five out of 10 for strictness'. At 25, classes are quite large compared to other preps but parents say it's not a problem as school attracts girls who want to learn. Girls add: 'We know that if we're sensible, everyone has a nice time.' Enough said.

Families generally from surrounding area as there's no school transport until year 3, with the odd girl travelling from as far afield as St Albans. Demographic reflects diverse local area with large Jewish and Asian contingents, although 'cliques don't divide on cultural grounds,' according to interim head. Plenty of wealth, but also a strong contingent of parents making sacrifices to offer their girls this top opportunity, and parents say school is sensitive to families' differing situations.

Alas since 2014 Japanese lessons are no more, but French taught from year 3 and a 'wholesale review' of languages is under way. Watch this space. Specialist music and PE teachers from reception and for science from year 3, when girls start to move around the school for different subjects. Setting in maths from year 4. Individual music lessons on offer from year 3 with around 40 per cent taking up an instrument. School 'wants music and sport to be for everybody,' and girls agree that they are. A and B teams compete in all the main sports (including football) against other schools, but less starry enthusiasts can follow their sporting passions at a recreational level if they don't make the team.

Part time SENCo works with girls needing extra help due to mild dyslexia or dyscalculia and routine screening introduced for the first time in 2014.

Good pastoral approach, with school 'keen to hear children's voices' – one girl per class elected by classmates as representative on student forum. Bullying has to be dealt with on 'a very occasional basis,' and school places a particular emphasis on educating girls on how to avoid cyber issues. All year 6 girls are prefects, with two elected captain for each of four teams (houses) which compete – although not fiercely, according to parents – throughout the year for team points, with the prize of a mufti day in the summer term.

Overall, a best in class girls' prep and first step on the ladder to reaping all that the Habs brand has to offer. With this start, these girls are undoubtedly on course to be the movers and shakers of tomorrow.

Haberdashers' Aske's School for Girls

Linked with Haberdashers' Aske's Junior School for Girls

Aldenham Road, Elstree, Hertfordshire WD6 3BT

Pupils: 865 • Ages: 11–18 • Sixth form: 235

Fees: £16,446 pa

Tel: 020 8266 2300
Email: admissions@habsgirls.org.uk
Website: www.habsgirls.org.uk

Headmistress: Since 2011, Ms Biddie O'Connor MA (50s). Educated at St Helena School, Chesterfield followed by St Hugh's College, Oxford (classics) and Sidney Sussex Cambridge (PGCE). A doyenne of girls' education, she cut her teeth teaching classics at Francis Holland before moving to Old Palace School, Croydon as head of department. Joined Haberdashers' Aske's School for Girls as head of classics and sixth form before becoming deputy head, then taking up the headship at Loughborough High School, where she spent nine years before, as one parent put it, 'coming home.'

Inheriting a flourishing, massively oversubscribed school when she joined Habs' as head, she was 'able to take time to assess the changes needed,' before putting in place a 15 to 20 year plan to improve the site. Wonderfully grounded with 'boundless energy,' according to parents, recognises that these days her main competitors are the state grammars, and is focused on outperforming them not just in the classroom but by 'building resilience,' and turning out 'happy, adaptable girls,' ready to take their careers and lives 'global.' Parents describe her as 'thoroughly sensible,' saying she 'works hard to tone down the panic' that can arise (mainly amongst parents) in highly academic environments.

Academic matters: School continuously shows its gleaming metal, flying amongst the top schools in the UK in all league tables with year after year of outstanding results. In 2016, 97 per cent of A levels were graded A*-B with 83 per cent A*/A. GCSEs equally impressive with 94 per cent A*/A. Five forms of 25 girls per year group with class sizes shrinking to 15 for GCSE and sometimes just five or six for A level. Ten GCSEs taken as standard with four full A levels commonplace.

Balanced curriculum with no particular bias – in popularity or results – although strong take-up of sciences at A level as well as English, history, maths and economics. Although eyes are firmly on the academic prize, a good number take art at both GCSE and A level, and the quality of work on display around the school is staggering. Girls report 'quite a bit' of homework, with about an hour and a half a night by year 10, but say the deadlines are long and some subjects are heavier than others. They claim that school discourages homework on weekends and are lenient if pupils are feeling the pressure. School keen to maintain balance between strong academics and nurturing a love of learning and doesn't constantly test girls.

Recent appointment of new ICT co-ordinator aims to push school towards the 'progressive' bracket by moving towards technology becoming part of day-to-day lessons rather than a specialised subject.

All girls assessed for SEN on entry to senior school, with mild dyslexia the most common issue but school also experienced in dealing with profound visual and hearing problems. Two SENCos cater for individuals' specific needs with customised learning plans, and 'lost sheep,' albeit a rarity here, are dealt with empathetically. Exceptionally gifted girls are nurtured in a 'very low key' manner, according to head, monitored 'by sleight of hand' through cosy chats with heads of department, and scholars are, in the main, anonymous. Roundedness is the name of the game with school ensuring that even top brainboxes participate in a broad spectrum of extracurricular activities.

Games, options, the arts: High octane sports programme 'to cater for all tastes and abilities' according to girls and parents, with five star facilities across the board. Seven new tennis courts and one of the best swimming pools we've seen where girls can train to become lifeguards or join the synchronised swimming squad. Super fitness suite, well used by years 12 and 13 in free periods, great sports hall and separate gym with the only notable absence a dedicated dance studio. Sporting prowess in abundance for those with a competitive streak – lacrosse is the main winter sport, accompanied by all the usual suspects – but it's not the school's sole raison d'être and girls preferring more artsy or academic pastimes are equally well catered for: 'we want sport to be for everybody, not just the elite,' says head, and those not making the teams have plenty of opportunities to indulge their sporting passions recreationally.

'Outstanding' music, perceived across the board to be 'just as cool as sport' with the vast majority of girls learning at least one instrument, and so many reaching grade 8 that nobody turns a hair when they do. Choirs, elite as well as non-selective, cater for all abilities and there are opportunities to perform aplenty in bands, ensembles and orchestras covering all tastes and abilities. The 50-strong symphony orchestra is the cherry on top, performing not just at school but on international tours and at prestigious venues such as the Barbican, often in conjunction with the next door boys' school, with parents declaring the standard of performances 'phenomenal'.

Art, led by a 'charming' departmental head, according to parents, is equally impressive, with walls throughout the school festooned with work of an exceptionally high standard and some outstanding three dimensional projects displayed in a wonderful atrium. DT also alive and kicking and a surprisingly popular exam choice, even amongst the most academic girls. A full programme of drama completes the set with a major play each term (most recently a joint production of Guys and Dolls with the boys' school) and opportunities for everyone to get involved, whether on stage or behind the scenes. Proof in the pudding that roundedness is a genuine ethos at Habs'.

Background and atmosphere: Founded following the bequeathment of £20,000 in 1698 by Robert Aske, Master of the Worshipful Company of Haberdashers, to found a school and almshouses in east London. Moved to its current site in the early 70s to join the boys who had taken over Lord Aldenham's – rather grander – estate a few years earlier. The happy co-existence of two single sex schools provides the best of both worlds for many, although parents uniformly agree that the cultures of the two schools are totally different – each catering perfectly for the specific needs of its single sex cohort. Pupils love the fact that they can collaborate and socialise together (including informally at lunchtimes) but learn totally separately.

Set amongst vast grounds just minutes from the roar of the M1, the Habs' campuses offer the unique balance of a leafy country feel for the London set and something a bit edgier for those hailing from the comfy home counties. A reasonably uninspiring exterior compared to the grandeur of the neighbouring boys' school, but functionality is top notch and the interior of the school feels light, clean and wonderfully spacious. The atmosphere is nicely cool for such an academic powerhouse. Girls move cheerfully and noisily from class to class with not a bluestocking among them. In many ways the feel of the school – first class facilities aside – is that of a top notch grammar rather than an elitist girls' school, testament to infiltration of a down to earth and no-nonsense approach of the head and her staff, determined to prepare their charges for success in the modern world. Year 13 girls said that with all the new developments planned for the coming years, they wished they could have their time all over again.

Pastoral care, well-being and discipline: Staff and parents agree that school is 'happy and supportive' and girls concur, describing the cohort as 'really friendly' and appreciating the fact that they 'can always talk to girls in other years.' Girls in year 8 are 'amigas' to year 7 newbies, a relationship that starts with a personal letter sent to each new girl's home during the summer before she joins, offering helpful tips on settling in. Girls claim that 'the whole atmosphere is relaxed' and staff say they aim to 'inspire not push.'

Rare incidents of bullying taken seriously with form prefects the first port of call in helping to deal with friendship issues, but teachers fast to mediate ('always with a box of tissues,' said one) should the need arise. Older girls help educate their younger peers on bullying, with a recent year 9 drama production focusing on the issue. Parents happy with pastoral care, which includes a counsellor available on appointment, with girls saying 'there's always someone for you to talk to.'

Lots of pupil-led charity initiatives with girls showing their wit and putting their creativity to the test to put on shows for the school, including panto assemblies starring the head girl, teachers' dance competitions and, recently, tongue in cheek 'Made in Elstree' T shirts for sale.

Pupils and parents: The vast coach network ferrying girls in from far and wide makes for a truly diverse and varied cohort with pupils travelling to school from across north/north-west London and Hertfordshire. School caters for the spiritual needs of all religions with weekly Jewish, Hindu/Jain/Sikh, Muslim, Humanist and Christian assemblies – with girls given the freedom to attend whichever one they choose regardless of their own faith. No place for the cocksure or work-shy – parents say they are 'paying for the peer group' – it's cool to study and hit top grades and the girls drive each other on to achieve great things. Girls need to be 'energetic not timorous,' according to head, to cope with the long school day followed by 'loads of activities.' Old girls include BBC's Charlotte Green, Vanessa Feltz and shoe designer L K Bennet.

Entrance: Ferociously competitive. Fifty move up from junior school, and applications for the remaining year 7 places come from approximately 50 per cent state primaries and 50 per cent prep schools, with feeders including Manor Lodge, Radlett Prep, Orley Farm and Beechwood Park. Over 600 girls take the exams, with a new format seeing girls tested in English (including reading for understanding), maths and verbal reasoning. Applicants spend a whole day in school and are looked after by older pupils.

About half of these will then be interviewed by a member of the senior leadership team; they are looking for about 80 girls who can 'think on their feet.' All prospective parents meet the head and although the school 'likes' to take siblings, above all they want parents to treat their children as individuals and 'won't break the rules' if they think a girl won't fit. Girls coming in ones from state primaries benefit from an extra induction day where they can get to know others in the same boat.

Between 10 and 20 join in year 12 from a range of state and independent schools, largely to benefit from the support around higher education applications. School equally scrupulous in selection at this stage: 'girls are jumping on board a moving bus,' says head. About three applicants for each sixth form place; head says there's no quota but that school is 'looking for a good social fit.'

Exit: Very few leavers after GCSEs (some 15 per cent) – Habs' girls know when they are onto a good thing. Dedicated head of careers and higher education oversees every university application, with the department also boasting an Oxbridge tutor, interview tuition ('although we don't want universities to criticise us for over-preparing candidates') and guidance in international applications. The process starts in year 11 when girls are exposed to the choices on offer to them with a programme of organised careers events (some organised by old girls) and university visits. School supports and encourages 'meaningful gap years' and offers hands-on guidance with girls' UCAS applications when they return.

H

About a quarter to Oxbridge (29 in 2016) with the remainder mostly to top universities. Bristol, UCL, Durham, Warwick, Nottingham, Birmingham and King's College London popular destinations. Medicine currently most popular subject (eight in 2016, plus one dentist) followed by economics, history and English. Usually one or two to drama or art colleges.

Money matters: Up to £6,000 a year means-tested financial assistance for a limited number of pupils, including full bursaries. Academic and music scholarships for up to half fees.

Remarks: Undoubtedly best in class girls' education. Turning out super accomplished, confident and thoroughly likeable young women with their feet on the ground and their eyes on the prize, the Habs' brand continues to go from strength to strength. School recognises that its charges' careers and lives are going to be global, and directs its charges accordingly towards excellence across the board – not just in academia. Parents concur that 'what makes Habs is the range of opportunities on offer.'

Haileybury

113

Hertford, Hertfordshire SG13 7NU

Pupils: 796; 493 boarders • Ages: 11-18 • Sixth form: 322 • C of E

Fees: Day £15,822 – £23,802; Boarding £20,094 – £31,674 pa

Tel: 01992 706353
Email: registrar@haileybury.com
Website: www.haileybury.com

Master: Since 2009, Joe Davies MA (Cantab) PGCE (50s). Educated at Christ College, Brecon, then St John's College, Cambridge, where he read history. After graduating, he worked in the City for a year but 'hated every second,' so returned to Cardiff (where his father was an academic) to do a PGCE. 'I'd wanted to be a teacher from the age of 14, but thought it was too drippy to go straight back to school.' Teaching clearly in the blood, since two brothers and three of his four grown children are also in the profession.

Taught at Tonbridge, where he became a housemaster, then deputy head of St John's School, Leatherhead, before taking on his first headship at Sutton Valence. Stills teaches history to the higher level IB. He feels his achievement at Haileybury has been to increase the emphasis on academic performance, while placing ever more significance on the extracurricular. Sets a good example. A keen cyclist and marathon runner (who recently completed the Venice marathon with his wife and two of his children), he also enjoys cryptic crosswords and reading history.

Retiring in July 2017. His successor will be Martin Collier MA, currently head of St John's School Leatherhead. He read modern history at St John's College Oxford, followed by PGCE from London University. His first 10 years of teaching were in the maintained sector, at the 'fantastic' Thomas Tallis in south London and the 'tough' Weavers School in Wellingborough. He then moved into the independent sector and Oundle School, where he worked through roles of head of history, director of studies and second master. He also has many years' experience as an examiner with different boards, has been involved with the Qualifications and Curriculum Development Agency and has appeared as an examinations expert before the House of Commons select committee on education. In short, he has a broad experience and detailed knowledge of all things educational. Married with three older children.

Academic matters: A famous name in public school education, Haileybury has in recent years become equally well known for its enthusiastic participation in the IB. 'We began in 1998 because it promised a broader curriculum and a boost to boarding, but we're now totally idealist,' says the head. Today about 110 sixth formers follow the diploma programme, with about 40 arriving each year specifically to do so. A levels, however, are still very much on offer and the school does very well in both sets of exams, with 37 average IB points in 2016, and pleasing results at A level (45 per cent A*/A in 2016). Biology, chemistry and history notably strong. Though not the easiest thing to run a school with a dual set of qualifications, this is managed by highly-qualified staff (including a hefty sprinkling of doctorates), who generally teach across both systems. The ISI commended the 'often outstanding' teaching.

Lower down, IGCSEs in just about everything, with 66 per cent A*/As in 2016. Here, all do a compulsory core of maths, English language, science and RS ('because of its philosophical and ethical bent'). Languages include Italian, French, Spanish, Latin and classical Greek, with German also taught to the 15 or 20 native speakers taking the IB. New IGCSEs are computer science and positive psychology. Pupils are set in maths and languages from year 7, science and English from year 9. Reasonable numbers who require some type of learning support (typically 50-80), with two teachers to address their needs, one a specialist in language, the other in maths. A small number, too, have extra help with English as a second language. Overall high aspirations, with sane expectations. 'They work hard, but it's very unpressured,' said a parent. 'They expect you to try your very, very best.' Relationships with staff particularly good, both in and outside of the classroom.

Games, options, the arts: Co-curricular activities are very much part of Haileybury's raison d'etre and the school has an outstanding reputation for both sport and choral music. Sport compulsory for all throughout, with games afternoons twice a week and matches on Saturday. Plenty of teams too, often from A-D, so everyone gets a chance to show their mettle. Those who aren't fans of the playing field can do 'something less taxing,' with options including aerobics, badminton, trampolining, rowing, rackets, golf and sailing (which currently boasts one girl who sails for Great Britain). Though boys triumph in hockey and football (where the school plays in the Boodles Cup) and girls in tennis, hockey, netball and lacrosse (competing at county and national level), rugby (boys only) and cricket (mostly boys) remain the 'communal sports.' 'Boys' rugby is the main thing,' said a girl, and the whole school turns out to cheer on rugby matches played on the front field. Facilities can only be described as superb, with a bright, modern pool, two Astroturf pitches and a professionally operated tennis club in the grounds. The rackets court is also considered one of the finest in the world and plays host to the world rackets championship. High Performance Programme (including training and lectures) aims to help talented sportspeople raise their game.

The school has a 30-year tradition of exceptional choral singing and won the BBC Songs of Praise School Choir of the Year some years back (it has reached the semifinal twice since then too). 'One of the things I enjoy most about the school,' said one parent, 'is the Christmas concert. It's just magnificent.' Chamber choir of about 30 ('very intense,' said one member) plus larger chapel choir of about 90. Wide range of other musical opportunities, from jazz bands to concerts and musical theatre. Twenty peripatetic music staff. 'You potentially can do any instrument,' said a teacher. 'We currently have pupils studying the steelpans, jazz piano and the organ.' New 'associated composer' will compose music for school events and lead class projects. The stand-alone music building, which already enjoys a charming beamed concert hall, has recently undergone a £1m refurbishment.

Art taught in its own large, light, purpose-built building, which not only caters for those doing GCSE or A level, but for leisure enthusiasts, seven days a week and in the evenings. Offers 2D and 3D, print, ceramics, photography and textiles, with exams tailored to individual interests. Dance lessons on offer for about 100 keen participants in jazz, ballet, street and tap, plus an annual dance show. 'Fantastic drama,' said a pupil, listing an energetic range from house drama to full-school musicals, which take place in the well-equipped studio theatre.

An abundance of trips. Sport (South Africa) and music (Slovenia, Prague and Venice), plus charity and subject specific (Uganda, Tanzania, Vietnam, and Sinai), as well as more modest outings to battlefields and cultural events.

Wednesday afternoons are devoted to community service, D of E and CCF for years 9 to 11, broadening out in the sixth form to take in activities like photography and web design. One extended weekend each term devoted exclusively to D of E and CCF (which flourish in equal numbers). Plenty of societies and lectures. Model United Nations particularly popular and the school recently played host to a world conference with 800 delegates. The head, who feels strongly that co-curricular activities build up life skills, has devised a specific year 9 programme which includes such fundamentals as outdoor pursuits skills and life saving.

Certainly you wouldn't enjoy the school if you weren't happy with a busy life. 'Everyone encourages everyone else and invites them to get involved. It's very full on,' said one pupil. 'You do have to learn to plan your time to fit in all your commitments, but you go to bed feeling fulfilled.'

Boarding: From year 9, about 70 per cent of pupils board, with a sizeable chunk of weekly boarders who leave late on Saturday and return on Sunday evening (except for five or six weekends annually, when all remain). Boarding ethos even for day pupils, who stay till 6.30pm and have their own beds at school. Seven boys' houses, five girls'. Four recently built, with light, bright rooms, the rest older but updated. All sit amongst pleasant greenery and house 55 boarders, overseen by a housemaster or mistress, plus a resident tutor. In the early years, eight to 10 pupils share a large, subdivided space; from year 11, single or shared rooms.

Girls do their own laundry, boys have theirs done for them. 'They think girls prefer that arrangement,' justified one pupil. Active inter-house social life and plenty of weekend activities for full-time boarders, with Saturday film nights and Sunday trips. Plus 'a lot of people have flats in London' or visit local pupils (with beneficent parents). Parents ('my son's housemaster is just wonderful – warm, jolly, intelligent, everything you could hope for in a male role model') and pupils ('my housemistress is the most reasonable woman') praise the boarding care.

Background and atmosphere: The school was designed in 1806 for the East India Company by William Wilkins (also responsible for the National Gallery and Downing College, Cambridge) as a training college for civil servants bound for India. In 1862, after the closure of the college, it was taken over by Haileybury, to be transformed into a public school for families in the professions and services, amalgamating, in 1942, with the Imperial Service College. The first girls were admitted in 1973. Today the school continues to occupy an impressive 550 acres of rural Hertfordshire, complete with magnificent neo-classical university-like buildings constructed round a traditional quadrangle. Later additions are sympathetic and well designed, with most subjects benefiting from purpose-built space. Beautiful, well-stocked and well-used library. 'If they don't have a book, they will get it for you.'

The school remains a Christian foundation with an Anglican chaplain who officiates in a domed chapel of cathedral-like proportions. Though Haileybury is ethnically and religiously diverse (with a fair number of Muslims, Jews and Hindus) everyone must attend services four or five times a week. 'It's here they learn the values that hold the school together,' says the head.

Charity work is taken seriously and the Haileybury Youth Trust, first set up in the East End in 1890 by old boy Clement Attlee, has been working with impoverished Ugandans since 2006. It has been commended by the UN as a model of a small-scale charity, patenting a brick now used for buildings schools, kitchens and water towers.

Two further Haileybury branches now operate in Kazakhstan, the first British public schools to be opened in Central Asia. These help underwrite bursaries for UK-based students.

Pastoral care, well-being and discipline: The school essentially operates as two schools, a more-or-less self-contained lower school, running as a day prep from 11 to 13; and an upper school, from 13 to 18, which is very much a boarding school, with a full day of lessons and sport on Saturday.

Not a grand school in atmosphere. 'It's cosy and terribly, terribly happy,' says one parent. 'You could not think of a better place to have your teenager running around.' Food comes highly commended. 'It's one of the things people rave about,' said a sixth former. Three compulsory meals a day (plus an optional snack on games days), but with plenty of choice. The new Costa Coffee, a latter-day tuck shop, is 'the' place to congregate. Manners are formal (new pupils jump to attention, teachers are addressed as Sir) but not stiff. All pupils wear uniform, tartan skirts and blazers in the junior school, plain navy suits in the sixth form.

Discipline runs the usual gamut from detention to permanent exclusion. Drugs dealt with firmly. First offenders are suspended for a week, and regularly drugs tested thereafter, second-time offenders are expelled – though the head 'can't remember excluding someone.' Strong prefect system, with 30 to 40 college prefects given additional responsibilities and privileges (more flexibility in uniform, better rooms, pub visits).

Pupils and parents: Largely from the surrounding counties – Hertfordshire, Essex, Buckinghamshire, Cambridgeshire. In general parents are 'City folk, business people, successful professionals' and as most live reasonably nearby, more involved than usual at boarding schools. Large numbers from Europe for the sixth form, particularly Germans and Italians; a trickle from Haileybury's sister schools in Kazakhstan. Pupils seem happy, confident, friendly and balanced.

Entrance: Fifty in year 7, a further 60 in year 9. Unusually, also a healthy intake (10 to 20) in year 10. Typically 50 new pupils enter the sixth form, including about 40 from overseas. At this juncture the school is heavily oversubscribed, with about three applicants for every place. Entrance tests at all levels in maths, English, verbal and non-verbal reasoning. Year 9 entry pre-tested by negotiation with the prep school 12 or 24 months in advance and CE used for setting. 'We are looking for somebody who wants to do their best, is B+ to A* academically and will throw themselves into the co-curricular,' says the head. Wide range of feeders includes Heath Mount, Edge Grove, Lochinver House and Keble.

H

Exit: About 10 to 20 leave after GCSEs, often for local day schools. Post A levels and IB, it's mainly to Russell Group universities (most popular choices include UCL, Warwick, Durham, Nottingham, Leeds, Bristol and King's College London), and increasingly, to Europe and the US. Three to Oxbridge in 2016 and seven medics. Good range of specialist advisers, for Oxbridge, medical school and North American universities. Three or four to art college.

Money matters: Music, sport, art, and all-rounder scholarships of up to 30 per cent of fees, plus a range of (generous) means-tested bursaries.

Remarks: A dynamic and energetic school, with a long established, successful IB diploma programme. Haileybury actually achieves what many boast about, a well-rounded education. Great fun for those who want to be involved in everything it has to offer.

Hall Grove School

London Road, Bagshot, Surrey GU19 5HZ

Pupils: 438 • Ages: 3-13

Fees: £5,715 – £13,335 p.a.

Tel: 01276 473059
Email: office@hallgrove.co.uk
Website: www.hallgrove.co.uk/

Headmaster: Since 1981, Alastair Graham (early 60s), son of the founder, who took over soon after his father died. He started his own education with the shortest of school runs (just down the stairs), continuing at Bradfield (the Greek theatre there may explain his enthusiasm for drama and for the classics) and then to Reading University. After obtaining a degree in estate management he set off for the great outdoors, an experience that has clearly influenced his approach to developing the Hall Grove ethos.

More country squire with Tattersall shirt and cords than gowned academic, pastoral care was always top of his agenda and he worked as a shepherd in both Scotland and New Zealand before exchanging his flock of sheep for a classroom of children. The external difference is that he swapped collies for labradors, the internal one that he sees himself more pater familias than farmer.

He says that he felt like a 'prodigal son' returning from the other side of the world to take over the school after his father's unexpected death, but now feels 'blessed that he was given such an opportunity' to develop Hall Grove, overseeing on his watch a fairly stratospheric rise in pupils from 130 to nearly 450. Although this number would have astonished his parents facing their original class of six, they would, surely, have felt that his decision to move out of the fields and into the schoolroom was a sound one. Whilst keen to say that he is 'not a one man band', he tries not to have too many administrative staff: 'we are not a bureaucracy'. With no governors, the school is still very much his baby and he sees it as an extended family for which he is responsible, although one parent said he was finding this more difficult now that the school has expanded.

Passionately keen on 'taking learning outdoors,' he hosts a conference on bolstering happiness and academic learning with a greater knowledge of the natural world. This concept is explored in theory and practice throughout the school and enforces his individual approach to the prep school experience. His love of the wild has even led him to become a Conservative candidate in the Highlands, where Tory voters tend to be badly outnumbered by sheep. Married to Catriona, four children – all Hall Grove pupils,

Entrance: The Barn (early years), which opened in 2013, offers places after seeing parents and discussing the child's current development. There is a main intake at 3+, although this is a non-selective school at this stage and also embraces a sibling policy. The children from pre-school get first crack and now make up over 50 per cent of the reception class, which, according to Catriona, leads to the newbies settling down very quickly. In year 3, the expansion to three forms allows room for an additional 20 children, who take tests in maths and English at the school. At the beginning of year 7 the upper school replaces any leavers (mainly girls going to a school where the intake is at 11+). At this stage, potential pupils spend a day at the school and are assessed to help confirm that they will fit in with their peer group.

Exit: Girls tend to leave mainly at 11 and boys mainly at 13, though some girls do stay on, usually heading to co-ed senior schools. Wellington and Hampton appear the first choice for more academic pupils, probably partly on proximity grounds, but children also go to a wide range of both private and state schools, often fairly local. These include Bradfield, Bryanston, Eton, Gordon's, St George's College, Weybridge and St Mary's Ascot. The head or the head of the upper school starts a dialogue with parents about senior schools in year 5 or 6, but encourage parents not to close doors by making a final decision too early. They have an excellent record of matching children to schools and can only remember 'one or two in the last 13 years' who failed to get into their first choice. The children in year 8 were confident that they had been prepared properly and spoke highly of the support given. An above average number of scholarships are won, particularly in music, sport and all rounder categories.

Remarks: Despite London being just down the road, this is more Wind in the Willows than Wandsworth. Forget the tarmac drive, cause of a twice daily logjam, 'complete mayhem and madness': this is in every sense a country school, complete with cheerful rosy-cheeked children.

Bought by the head's parents in the 1950s, Hall Grove, once a small estate set in Surrey countryside, has grown somewhat organically from an unpretentious Georgian house into an educational hub, and although the ice house is fenced off (not a health and safety winner), the gardens, grounds and stables (moved but fully inhabited) are still there. Forty acres of land, still displaying a hint of an agricultural past, now includes the old walled garden being busily restored to its former glory. The wish to stock it with pigs as ambulatory waste disposers may not go down too well with modern regulations, but if porkers don't make it there are plenty of plump ponies, serenading cockerels and labrador puppies to ensure that the atmosphere belies its slightly suburban situation.

The original house, home to both the Graham family and the flexi-boarders, has a hall dominated by a fine 'school of Thomas Lawrence' painting, portraying a Byronic figure staring into the distance, presumably not sure what to make of the current inhabitants. The four boarders' rooms (mainly used on a one night basis but available for longer stays if necessary) are bright and cheerful, with a funky communal space under the roof and smart new showers; but, inevitably, the traffic of so many feet leads to more well-worn carpet than shiny new floors – no sign of a trendy decorator's hand here. The academic side of life is scattered in rather random fashion through converted outbuildings and log cabins, disparaged by a few parents but clearly enjoyed by the children. All the classrooms have fresh displays of work in progress, there is a huge adaptable space for IT, separate rooms for art, pottery and DT and generous space for the thriving music department. It may not be the tidiest of lay-outs but the various components all appear loved and well cared for, in particular the new(ish), imaginative building for the early years.

Two classes at reception increase to three from year 3 to year 7; in the final year there are two sets plus a scholarship stream. The last is not universally popular with parents, who say that it can lead to divisions in the year group, but the head of the upper school points out that the scholarship exam requires a different syllabus. All children fill in a daily diary charting progress, open to staff and parents and monitored in the beginning by the form teacher and after year 5 by the child's study tutor, basically a liaison officer. There has been a report of holes in this system, in particular with children in the middle school who might need additional help, but the head says that further training is being given to teachers and there is evidence of one-on-one tutorials to tackle the problem. The school has a SENCo, is open to children who have mild educational problems and tries hard to help them. However, it does not appear to have the back-up to manage any child who has serious problems in keeping up, and one parent was not entirely happy with the support given. Although 'not an academic sweatshop', the upper school succeeds in hitting a high mark on a regular annual basis.

Sport is taken seriously: 'mens sana in corpore sano' definitely features amongst the head's axioms along with 'the busier they are, the better they do'. This can result in sending them out to run through the snow if the games pitches are unplayable, a practice one parent thoroughly approved of. 'Sport for all' is not just a slogan and the less talented receive equal encouragement from young enthusiastic staff and gappers, often past pupils. Lots of trophies line the sideboard and both sexes punch above their weight in several conventional sports, such as rugby, hockey and tennis, as well as the more unlikely golf and judo. On an ambitious note they are aiming high and have built up relationships with Chelsea Football Club and Harlequins to help spot and nurture future stars.

An annual art exhibition proves that attention is not only focussed on the games field and the children's artwork, including desirable pottery, is visible all over the school. Drama and dance fill the seats regularly and the smiley faces of the casts speak for themselves. The head believes that 'music helps brain development' and music scholarships to senior schools are won almost every year. Over 200 individual lessons are given each week, leading to both classical success outside the school and the formation of a popular jazz band. Singing, a highly praised choir and composing, using music technology, also rate positive feedback from pupils. After-school clubs satisfy most interests, ranging from Lego (for littlies) to Lab Rats (for the scientifically mad) via Pony Grove (for the horse mad).

The majority of parents have a business background, so aware of the fairly common need for two salaries, maybe partly to pay the school fees, Hall Grove tries to help by offering not only a bed for the night but also early breakfast and late tea: 'can be a godsend,' siad one over-stretched mother. Finally, the star turn for the children, even above the highly competitive Masterchef competition, is the annual outing by year 4 upwards to the school house and farm on the Devon coast. It's universally loved by pupils, who describe it as 'the best thing'; teachers also rate it highly, saying that it can help flag up hidden talents which might slip under the radar in the classroom, but often show up in the lambing shed or when paddling a canoe.

Halliford School

Russell Road, Shepperton TW17 9HX

Pupils: 398 • Ages: 11–18 • Sixth form: 76: 69 boys/7 girls

Fees: £14,700 pa

Tel: 01932 223593
Email: registrar@halliford.net
Website: www.hallifordschool.co.uk

Headmaster: Since 2015, Simon Wilson, previously deputy head at The Leys School. Educated at City of London School and Royal Holloway College (maths degree), has also been head of maths at Latymer Upper and head of year 9 at RGS Guildford.

Academic matters: Not the local academic top stream, but very much a place where an academic boy, suited to a smaller, broader school, can flourish. 'My son was allowed to be smart, punctual and bright, and was not teased much.' Entry requirements having been pushed up a few years ago, exam results have now reached respectable levels: 49 per cent A*/A at GCSE in 2016; at A level, 48 per cent of grades A*/B, 17 per cent A*/A.

Value added looks good, too. 'There was one boy who did not quite pass our entry exam, but I gave him a place as he was a brother and there was also something about him. I warned the parents there was a distinct possibility that he might not do very well at GCSE (I still have the letter I wrote). He achieved nine A*/A grades at GCSE. It was all about confidence and late development.'

All take Latin in the early years, and all are expected to emerge from GCSE with a pass in a modern foreign language. A good range of subjects at A level, with less of an emphasis on the sciences than is usual in a boys' school.

Generally focused on bringing out the best in each child, with a great deal of personal attention when they falter in their progress. Immediate, easy and deep support for everyone with specialist support being extended with the recent appointment of a full time special needs teacher. Online assessment on arrival to confirm, diagnose and update. Plans organised for those who need it: for most this means making staff aware, for those who really need it specific support from the new specialist teacher. We spoke to one parent who was fizzing with pleasure at having her dyslexic boy looking forward to a maths exam.

Games, options, the arts: Every boy leaves here as an initiate of the national male religion of sport, and many with an eye on the priesthood. Rugby and rowing have the largest temples, but a wide range of minor gods, all well provided for. Sport binds this community together and gives the boys confidence and comradeship. Much excellence, but it is participation that counts, and parents report that even those with no noticeable sporting talent or bent join in, enjoy the experience and feel comfortable. Sixth form girls get to enjoy the sporting atmosphere, but not, unfortunately, to participate in much of the competition.

Drama way out of the ordinary. Excellently resourced, with a fine small theatre. Highly regarded by the boys (several of the sporting champions are keen participants), wide enjoyment of participation, a strong tradition of technical theatre, easy integration with academic subjects, eg Shakespeare, superb exam results and many going on to take theatre-related subjects at university level.

Music and art both very strong and engagingly taught. Several parents commented on the strength of support for their son's musical talents and the school's willingness to allow practice to infringe on lesson time. Expanded facilities in a pleasingly designed new building. By no means all boys' schools have this dual enjoyment of sport and the arts – it has always appeared to us to be a great strength in readying boys for the world. Lots of other extracurricular activities, with a strong emphasis on human engagement.

Background and atmosphere: A Georgian house, looking across a busy road to the Thames, surrounded by classrooms and other school buildings in a pleasing and coherent style. Lots of sports fields behind, much used.

'A happy, disciplined family'; a very pleasing collection of young men, relaxed, easy to be around, but clearly accustomed to hard work; 'Individuality respected, not ground down'. Everybody, particularly staff, expected to look out for others and to deal with, or find someone to deal with, problems when they find them. 'Will give a boy a chance to turn around and will bring the shy out of themselves.' A number of parents told us that their son's confidence had been really boosted after just a few months at the school – 'He was encouraged to give his all, given responsibility'.

Not, in practice, a perfect system – 'It happens with some teachers, not others; sometimes you have to chase', but the impetus from the centre makes sure that it happens in the end. The school is probably around its maximum size if this approach, reliant on human interactions rather than numbers and systems, is to work – but it is excellent while it does.

Those girls who arrive for sixth form seem happy and successful: well worth a look if you think your daughter might enjoy the company of a very civilised and respectful gathering of boys.

Staff enthusiastic, 'happy to join in with pupils' activities, really know the boys well'; 'approachable and not at all stuffy, and really seem to get the balance right so that things are not regimented, more relaxed but respectful'. Good communications with parents; yearly questionnaire gets a good response. Staff eat (the passable) lunch with pupils in newly refurbished Riverside Bistro.

Pastoral care, well-being and discipline: All wound up in the general structure of support and expectations, with excellent results. 'Bullying quickly dealt with.'

Pupils and parents: Parents largely local, hard-working. Pupils bright-eyed, engaging, unstressed, but get the work done. 'Confident, but not cocky. Self-assured, but not in a mean way,' said a parent, and that's the way they appeared to us too. Girls very much at home. Not a place that would suit someone who does not want to join in or who loves mucking around.

Entrance: Has upped pass mark to 50 per cent, with a noticeable effect on results, but will still take brothers who miss the grade if the school thinks they have a reasonable chance of keeping up with the pace. Cares more for the interview than the marks alone. Half come in from state primary schools: some practice in verbal and non-verbal reasoning recommended.

Exit: Quite a flow after GCSE to local colleges for more vocational provision, the odd one to more selective schools' sixth forms, but those (50 per cent or so) who stay on almost all go to university, with a notable interest in drama, media studies, engineering and sciences. A few to grand universities eg Warwick and Nottingham; others to eg Bournmouth or LCCM (London College of Creative Media).

Money matters: Sensible fees, plus some scholarships and bursaries.

Remarks: A sporting, harmonious school, comfortable in its role as part of the local Championship, doing very well for the boys (and sixth form girls) that it suits.

Halstead Preparatory School

Woodham Rise, Woking, Surrey GU21 4EE

Pupils: 214 • Ages: 3–11

Fees: £6,945 – £13,053 pa

Tel: 01483 772682
Email: info@halstead-school.org.uk
Website: www.halstead-school.org.uk

Headmistress: Since 2013, Mrs Penny Austin BA. Age not disclosed so we'll hazard 40s. Previously head of Walthamstow Hall Junior School, which she joined in January 2004 after working for 10 years at Ardingly College Prep School, starting off as class teacher and promoted to deputy headship in 2002, when also became an independent schools inspector. Musical training – was a professional singer – took her into schools where was willingly subsumed into world of education. Led inexorably to a PGCE followed by two years as class teacher in state primaries in Brighton and East Sussex before move to independent sector.

Whether in academic dress for special occasion assemblies or – admirably – working as a teaching assistant with all year groups (ensures she knows pupils and staff inside out), style is 'me being me,' she says. These days leaves the school music to others, though still runs chamber choir with husband close to Sussex home. Certainly works for parents, who rate her as approachable and aeons away from previous twinset and pearls approach to leadership (though we can testify that she's peerlessly smart). 'She's brought a warmth to the school,' said a mother.

Bar a few instant, unilateral changes when first arrived, like ditching the compulsory school napkins ('didn't get washed very often'), approach is consensus-based. Involve everyone and listen to ideas, she says, and changes will be faster and happier. With new uniform, building, lunch menu and timetable all under her belt in first two years, clearly knows what she's about.

Girls think she's 'amazing'. Older pupils may come to her office for help with reading, tinies can confide problems to the big, friendly teddy there. Either way, 'You don't ever feel uncomfortable,' said year 6 pupil. Firmly committed to single sex education for girls, is working hard to ensure that niminy piminy aspects kept under control – she's aware of dangers of school being seen as pocket of beribboned niceness.

Sweet it may be, but it's the sort on the golden syrup tins, deriving from strength rather than sickliness. Thus new mission statement namechecks self-belief and love of learning and reins back the references to homely, caring feel. Football and judo enjoyed as much as origami and cake decorating, she says – important that everyone realises it.

Entrance: Most families within 10 mile radius of Woking, just under three-quarters white British, around 10 per cent Asian. A small number (currently seven) have EAL requirements, just over 30 multilingual.

Message that proudly non-selective is changing because it isn't, really. Though largely come as you are in nursery (from age 2), still need to attend taster session, while year 3 must be up to reasonable speed in maths and English assessments – 'or show potential,' says school.

Unusually, offer academic and music scholarships, sat by all current year 2 pupils as well as by external candidates and worth around 10 per cent of the fees. No public announcement of winners and successful families 'asked to be discreet,' says head, keen to mute the competitive parent rumour mill. (Most are.) Sound financial management and some tough decisions (no sibling discount, for example, though do have priority in the applications process if oversubscribed) also enables schools to offer means-tested bursaries (up to 100 per cent) for new and existing families. Real hardship has to be demonstrated, stresses literature. Frequent or expensive holidays and luxury cars and a second home are among lifestyle choices unlikely to give you a head start in the applications process (criteria still come as an occasional surprise to some, says head).

Caters for 15 pupils with SEN, three with statement or EHC plan, one receiving intensive one-to-one support and LEA funded, some with more than one disability. Can manage specific learning difficulties to processing and speech and language, ADD/ADHD (as long as no severe behavioural difficulties) and other conditions including epilepsy and physical difficulties.

Exit: Most nursery joiners stay all the way to year 6, when leavers almost exclusively head for single sex senior schools. Good years (and most are) see significant (high single numbers at least) to GHS and St Catherine's, Bramley as well as Sir William Perkins' School. Tormead, Prior's Field plus selection of Catholic schools (St Teresa's, Farnborough Hill, Notre Dame) also feature. Occasional (one a year) to St George's Weybridge. In 2016, seven academic scholarships and one exhibition plus a sports and an art scholarship. But don't get impression that fuss is reserved for high flyers. All abilities enjoy same levels of care. 'Staff told me that they'd get her into the right school for her – and they did. I trusted them and was right to,' said mother.

Currently no word on future career success ('none known' says school) though it's busy attempting to fill in the gaps.

Remarks: Founded as boarding school in Kent in 1927, evacuated to Wiltshire in WW2 before popping up in 1947 on current site as a day school. Became a charitable trust in 1970s with what's described as 'Christian, non denom ethos...' (sensibly hedging bets, perhaps) for next phase in almost 90 year history.

Site, in quiet residential road a mile from Woking, is the perfect size – Goldilocks would have a ball. With just under 220 pupils (numbers impressively constant, even during worst of recession), it's small enough to 'know where everyone is,' says head but big enough for pitches, lots of greenery, delightful enclosed nursery and reception playgrounds packed with fun and educational goodies (they can't get enough of junk music kit, sounds of rhythmic bashing carrying beautifully all the way up the road).

Has even managed to buy extra land from neighbours to create secret garden, one half green and tranquil, the other featuring blinding white gravel and diamond, L-shaped and triangular wooden planters at different angles, less Frances Hodgson Burnett than a non-verbal reasoning problem reimagined by Alan Titchmarsh. 'Maths teacher did have an input,' says head.

Older part of school, the original Edwardian house, is home to well-stocked library on top floor, cosy SEN room – 'wanted it in centre of school,' says head – and older pupils, top years somewhat compressed, though clearly very happily so, into compact classrooms.

H

Easy on the eye new wood-clad building, nicely slotted in without jarring, is spacious in looks and feel – showpiece vast first floor picture window, adjoining and apparently inaccessible windowsill that runs above steep staircase used as display area and crammed with delightful ceramic pots with paper flowers. 'Teacher pushes them along with extra long ruler,' explains pupil.

Small size really matters to pupils and parents. 'Came from school with 30 in the class,' said pupil. 'Nothing was a challenge – now everything is.' There are just 33 in the biggest year group and 21 in smallest (tinier still for Chicks and Ducks, the two nursery classes). Means lots of delightful family touches that include stirring of school Christmas pud by every child in the school in assembly.

Clearly good at ingredients in general, given end result – girls who are a credit to their parents and teachers – even more so following Mrs Austin's directive that all shall stand up for visitors (a few parents were initially unsure but now won round, and we admired year 5 group placidly carrying on with needlework while waiting to be told to sit down again).

But though show up at senior schools as 'nice, polite, well-behaved little girls,' says one registrar, don't get the impression that only the instantly compliant are welcome, stresses Mrs Austin. 'Strong characters learn that there's a time and place for everybody.'

They're smart, too, even more so following uniform redesign, feisty triumphing over fusty, drab brown blazers and skirts consigned to great secondhand uniform shop in the sky and replaced by smart toning blues (new tartan even features on cushions in reception, no doubt an effective aide-memoire). It's example of Mrs Austin's ability to steer canny line between the new and outré. There may be a new games skort (great favourite with pupils) but there are still three Alice bands on the uniform list and compulsory panama hats continue to line the cloakroom shelves, brim up (and huge on 'aaah' factor when worn by nursery children on visit to local farm).

Similar balance struck elsewhere. Handbell rung by senior pupils (a favourite duty) marks the end of lessons that may feature iPads, used tactically, never slavishly, or handwritten work (pen licences are much coveted). Even the parents' association has changed name from 'Ways and Means' (suggests stay at home sewing circles) to the altogether more businesslike Halstead Preparatory School PTA. It's far more in keeping with growing numbers of dual income parents – and school looks after them with excellent value out of hours care (7.30-8.00am, including breakfast, for under a fiver) and reassurance.

'If someone's stuck on a train and can't collect on time, will always manage,' they say.

It's all achieved, say parents, by team of happy, well led teachers with enough time for every pupil. No compromise on recruitment, says Mrs Austin, who'll advertise as often as it takes to get top quality candidates through the doors. While academic ability is generally above average on arrival, school boosts pupils' appetite for learning – inspectors highlight progress made by both SEN and G&T pupils is impressive.

Class size maximum of 16 to year 2 and 18 for other years. Staff ratios are generous (one for each 10 pupils) without being lavish, overwhelmingly female – just two blokes including head of pre-prep, four if you count the bursar and IT expert and seven if you get desperate and add in the peripatetics. Cosy, long term team – average age mid 40s, nine staff who've been here for over 10 years.

Plenty of specialist staff (PE, drama, dance and music from nursery with art, DT and food tech, ICT and French added from reception and year 1). Maths and English specialists introduced in year 5 when both subjects are set. Academic support either in class or one-to-one provided as needed.

H

There's no shallow end stuff here – topics are in depth, with cross curricular weeks for years 1 and 2 (The Circus, Under the Sea), recent food-themed special offering chance to make own vegetable character (politicians presumably off limits).

Results, given range of ability, extremely impressive, from year 6 pupil-designed science experiments – one feeding snails different diets and mapping preferences, another swabbing different areas of the school for bacteria – to group recital of poetry, diction, sound effects and sophisticated choreography all created without any input from teachers.

Throughout, fear-free originality is a real feature – easy to understand why recent latest inspectors went positively gaga about educational wonders that had come their way. 'Genuinely inclusive,' felt a parent. 'Celebrate success without quietly stressing the girls out.'

Hallmark was enthusiasm for all pupils for maths – including those happy to admit they struggled. Voted a top favourite courtesy of buzzy teachers who stop at nothing to help, from motivating 3D stickers and Percy Pigs – 'We go mad for them...' – to personalised revision material. One keen young cook even had term's worth of problems recast as numbers to be fed and cost of ingredients. 'Was so touched,' said mother. 'Made her realise why she needed to do maths and it changed her.'

Numerous – and largely voluntary – opportunities to shine range from Owl Awards against the clock times table competitions (three minutes, perfect answers or no award), to celebration assemblies where good work means house points, as do out of school triumphs – even budding dog trainer had moment of glory. And once given, points are for keeps, say pupils. 'Nothing can be taken away because you've [already] earned it.'

Encouragement to try new things extends to delicious food (chef busily but largely unsuccessfully encouraging pupils to essay an asparagus spear on day of visit) and residential trips – not just for leavers, who head for France, but for years 4 and 5 who enjoy UK-based residential stays. There's equal sense of adventure closer to home. Over half the girls learning an instrument, some to grade 4, encouraged by timetabled taster sessions on different instruments – no faffing about with recorders, either, with girls lugging trombone cases round the place (tips on knee-bashing avoidance covered in first lesson, says teacher). Enthusiasts, some beginners, others 'incredible,' said mother, can perform at tea time concerts – and then graduate to orchestra, run as a club, as are the four choirs.

For the sporty, plenty on offer, from athletics and rounders to football, matches achieving variable success, upside the number of ABC teams and guarantee that 'your daughter does get to play in matches no matter how appalling she is,' said parent.

While pupils pride themselves on good sporting manners – 'We're not sore losers,' said one. 'We just say 'OK, we tried our hardest' – one parent reckoned that needed occasional prompt from school when 'can see that not very pleased the other team have won.' Particularly true on sports day, when house rivalries reach fever pitch. 'If cheer other houses because they've lost, teacher will say "that's not very Halstead, is it?"' said mother. 'They're encouraged to support everyone, and I like that.'

For a very few parents and pupils in need of broader canvas, can feel slightly too compact. For most, combination of imaginative teaching across the ability range and confidence-building delivered in an atmosphere that's cosy rather than cloying is hard to beat.

Mrs Austin stresses that this isn't a school full of 'frightened little rabbits – we don't want to be the sweet little girls' school but the excellent girls' school where they grow up into confident young ladies ready for the next step.' Year 5 pupil, diligently putting final touches to delightful Father's Day specs case, very definitely no Cottontail. 'I'll expect something in return,' she said. 'This has taken all year.'

Handcross Park School

Linked with Brighton College Prep and Pre-Prep School, Brighton College

Handcross, Haywards Heath, West Sussex RH17 6HF

Pupils: 378; 22 full, 27 weekly boarders • Ages: 2–13 (boarding from 7) • C of E

Fees: Day £9,180 – £18,120; Boarding £15,270 – £23,160 pa

Tel: 01444 400526
Email: registrar@handxpark.com
Website: www.handcrossparkschool.co.uk

Headmaster: Since September 2016, Mr Richard Brown MA PGCE (40s), previously head of Dorset House. Educated at Magdalen College School, Oxford and at Oxford Brookes, where he read English and law. After five and a half years as an officer in the Royal Dragoon Guards, he took an MA in English and education at Reading University and a PGCE at Roehampton. Then spent three years teaching English at the Edinburgh Academy, where he was also a boarding tutor and games teacher. This was followed by eight years as a housemaster and English teacher at Pangbourne. Divorced with two sons. In his spare time loves mountaineering and trekking in remote places.

Entrance: By one or two-day taster experience including English, maths and reasoning assessments and interview, plus reports and references from previous school. Remote assessments and Skype interviews possible for overseas applicants. Pupils come from local nurseries and preps, but with expansion of boarding the catchment area is widening to Brighton, Crawley, Haywards Heath and London. Boarders (30 per cent) mainly from London, Forces families, a few from Europe.

Exit: Pupils move to a variety of schools, including Brighton College (around 40 per cent), Wellington, Hurst College, Ardingly, Charterhouse, Worth, Stowe, Epsom College, Sevenoaks, Bedes, Eastbourne College, Christ's Hospital and

Lancing. A number gain scholarships – academic, sport, drama, art, music and dance.

Remarks: School founded in 1887 as a boys' boarding establishment and after various changes of name and identity moved to Handcross Park in 1968, became co-educational and took day pupils. Merger means that Brighton College has gained a country boarding prep with acres of playing fields just 10 minutes from Gatwick; Handcross Park has gained from joining the hugely successful Brighton College family of schools with strong leadership, sound financial backing and support from experienced governors and staff.

The visitor is treated to a breathtaking approach down a long, roped track through extensive parkland and pitches before coming face to face with red-brick mix of Tudor and Elizabethan.

Claims to be one of the first prep schools in the country where all pupils learn the world's top three languages: English, Spanish from age 2 and Mandarin from age 4, plus French and Latin from year 6. The aim is fluency in at least one major European language. 'The workplace is becoming increasingly global and competitive; it will give them the edge in the job market,' says school. The director of studies explains they work on the philosophy of 'anti pressure but pro challenge', and some new parents commented how motivated their children had become since joining the school. 'The staff are a happy bunch and passionate about teaching,' said a head of maths.

Progress in English and maths monitored via verbal and non-verbal reasoning tests, spelling ages, NFER assessments etc. Active tracking procedures considered rigorous enough to avoid any pupil slipping through the net. The school identifies and caters well for special needs from the outset – 'My child was seen to be struggling in nursery, received informal extra help and progressed to more formal support in the main school'. Learning support takes place in the 'dairy rooms' and staff are, apparently, 'great communicators... parents are kept in the loop throughout'. Others speak of the academic and social advances their children have made within this unit and how confidence building it has proved to be. 'We are never complacent and have been to other good schools to view similar departments, but concluded that none could be offering anything better,' said another parent. A high ability programme – some attend masterclasses at Brighton University. The English department is exceptional, say the pupils, and geography, maths, sport and art also got the popular vote.

Masses of art of all standards on display and pupils have the chance to extend interests via clubs (textiles, sketching, crafts). Music lively with junior choir for all and voluntary senior choir, plus orchestra, jazz, rock and recorder groups. Head of music and performing arts favours a balance of traditional and contemporary music. A drama production held each term with every child taking part in at least one production a year. Plans are afoot for a new theatre in time.

Everything from the usual hockey, netball, rugby and cricket to ballet, riding, street dance and cross-country on offer, supported by a team of young and energetic sports staff. Glorious pitches, huge sports hall and Scandinavian design swimming pool, plus new Astro pitch. School believes kindness should be the underlying ethos, but what about on the games field, we asked? Sports staff on message, 'It is not just about winning (although that's nice sometimes) but about sportsmanship.' Parents and visiting teams are greeted by courteous pupils who hand out programmes with a map and a sporting 'code of conduct' just in case...

The pre-prep department is surrounded by high walls enclosing an enchanting 'secret garden' complete with mud kitchen and pigs – its head told us that days there were 'all about exploring, challenging, listening, before they go on to learning more formally. We love to take the curriculum outdoors, offering anything but a sedentary education'. Music plays a big part in curriculum. Lots of clubs on offer, some at extra cost, eg cookery, swimming, multisport, choir. Weekly 'wow' moments celebrate effort and achievements and a buddy system eases transition to main school. Forest school and outdoor classroom.

Boarding house has had a makeover and been extended, offering full or weekly boarding (minibus service from south London) but no prospect of flexi option, considered 'bad for continuity'. The rooms, fresh and light with views over the grounds, are almost hotel spic and span – not many personal touches. Are children really that tidy? Food considered excellent and boarders have input into choices and themed menus. Weekend activity programme; full boarders encouraged to invite their day friends for sleepovers.

Handcross Park may once have been described as 'coasting' but it is now sailing full steam ahead. With Brighton College's support, the school's future is set fair on all fronts.

Headington School

H

Headington Road, Oxford, Oxfordshire OX3 7TD

Pupils: 1,044; 218 full and weekly boarders • Ages: 3-18 (boarding from 11) • Sixth form: 275 • C of E

Fees: Day £8,640 – £17,970; Boarding £22,410 – £35,250 pa

Tel: 01865 759113
Email: admissions@headington.org
Website: www.headington.org

Head: Since 2011, Mrs Caroline Jordan (50s). A local girl, she was educated at St Helen and St Katharine in Abingdon, read geology at Oxford and did her PGCE (science) at Manchester. Previously head of St George's Ascot and before that spent 10 years at Wycombe Abbey where she was head of sixth form and deputy senior housemistress. Lives on site; married to Richard, a company director, one adult son, two border collies. Currently president of the Girls' Schools Association.

Before going into teaching Mrs Jordan ran her own business. She says that heads 'need those skills'; they do, and indeed we could imagine her as one of the dragons on Dragons' Den – not that she's scary, but she is direct and, well, businesslike. As one parent said, 'definitely not fluffy'. She's forward thinking and ambitious, hyper alert to social and educational change and ready for whatever the future holds in these areas. Parents describe her as 'really on the ball' and 'ahead of the game' and are mostly in favour of the changes she's making. 'She's mad about rowing,' we were told; 'you should hear her shouting from the riverbank when her crew are racing!' Another was impressed by Mrs J's energetic networking when she accompanied crews to a competition in the US. 'She took the girls round as many universities as she could, making contacts.' We anticipate US college scholarship offers rolling in for Headington rowers.

Parts of the school are being seriously revamped – not just bricks and mortar but also Headington's Achilles' heel (rowing excepted): sport. Mrs Jordan is frank about this; historically lack of opportunities and support meant that girls had to join outside clubs to progress in team games such as hockey. A complete overhaul of facilities and teaching will see the 'inspirational' head of rowing become director of sport, no doubt expected to do his magic in other departments.

Favourite childhood reads were Dorothy Dunnett's Scottish historical novels but these days Mrs J enjoys quick crime thrillers on her Kindle. Down time is spent 'mixing concrete' – she and her husband are restoring a 500-year-old house in France.

Head of junior school: Since 2014, Mrs Jane Crouch BA MA (40s). Studied French and geography at Keele. Her masters, in educational management and administration, is from the University of London. Was previously head of Dame Bradbury's School, Saffron Walden and before that head of Ashford School, Kent and deputy head of Great Walstead, West Sussex. It was early days when we visited but Mrs Crouch had the confidence of parents we spoke to and her easy, friendly relationship with the girls already seemed well established. Tempting though the calm of her study must be, she told us that she 'loves getting into the classroom' and was 'determined to fit some teaching in'.

All possible building work having been done, we wondered whether Mrs Crouch wanted to redevelop any other aspect of the school. While not hatching plans for revolution, she told us that she hopes to set up a breakfast club, extend the range of after school activities and has her sights set on the prep becoming an 'eco' school. She's also keen to up the involvement of sixth formers from the senior school, 'helping with assemblies and other activities'.

Mrs Crouch and her husband are keen coastal walkers but, since coastline is in short supply in Oxfordshire, they are enjoying new vistas in the Chilterns. As if running a school wasn't enough she enjoys zumba, spin and step classes and visiting art galleries. On her Kindle you'll find Swedish crime fiction.

Academic matters: Small classes (average 16) allow junior school pupils to develop at their own pace, as do 'flexible' maths groups in the older years. Years 4, 5 and 6 get two hours of science a week in a proper lab; 'We do as much hands on stuff as we can.' In the grounds there's a greenhouse, pond and plots for growing plants and vegetables. Girls also enjoy visits to the Oxford University farm at Wytham where they learn about agriculture on a larger scale.

In 2016, 80 per cent A*/A at GCSE. At A level, 64 per cent A*/A. Maths, economics, sciences, fine art and English literature notably successful. Languages don't seem to attract many (as is so often the case).

More than respectable IB average of 39 in 2016. Take-up for IB roughly 20 per cent and growing – Mrs J certainly thinks it is a more secure option at a time when 'A levels are up in the air.' She's particularly keen on the IB theory of knowledge course and this is now being offered lower down the school. We're sure the girls benefit but it's also a canny and not so subliminal bit of IB marketing.

Gone are the days when girls ploughed through up to 13 GCSEs; it's 10 now with increasing number of IGCSEs. Choice of one language from French, Spanish and German; surprisingly there's no Mandarin GCSE although it's offered as an after-school club, as is ancient Greek. All do Latin in first two years.

Twenty-nine subjects to chose from at A level including fine art, photography, computing, law, psychology and government and politics. EPQ encouraged but there's 'not much time' in term and research and writing during the summer holidays post year 12 can be a big ask. Oxbridge, medicine and veterinary hopefuls get application support and so do girls applying for architecture. The latter receive specialist lectures and help with portfolio preparation – must account for the unusually high number of Headington girls accepted to study this oversubscribed subject.

Special mention here for ICT – girls learn to code in Python and apply this and other skills to robotics. Not content with winning 'best rookies' and 'first moves' prizes at recent Student Robotics Competition, the Headington team (one of just two all girl teams) designed, built and programmed an autonomous robot from scratch to become champions. 'It sent a real buzz through the whole school,' the head girl told us proudly.

School says it makes 'reasonable adjustments' for girls with mild SEN including one-to-one weekly support for girls in the lower school and drop-in sessions for the middle school and sixth form. EAL tuition also provided.

Games, options, the arts: The 'inspirational' leadership of Headington's South African head of rowing has brought the school national and international success on the water (most recently the J8 crew won the Henley women's regatta). Girls start training in the summer term of year 7 and some parents think this is too young (boys generally don't begin until age 13); school says the programme is run in conjunction with Oxford Brookes and everything is very carefully monitored. Compared to the riverside facilities enjoyed by other notable Oxfordshire rowing schools such as Abingdon, Headington has it tough – they row out of a couple of portakabins shared with St Edward's School. 'Our success is all down to inspiration,' says Mrs Jordan.

School boasts over 30 different sporting activities (many are lunchtime or after-school clubs) including fencing, synchronised swimming, dance and cheerleading. It's also pretty horsey, despite the urban setting. 'It's a side branch of the Pony Club,' we were told. What if you don't have a horse? We asked. 'Oh, someone will lend you one,' came the airy reply. Girls compete in blue Headington silks and bring back plenty of rosettes.

Mrs J acknowledges that there's still work to do when it comes to 'sport for all'. 'Every girl should have her own regime to stay fit and healthy, whether or not that includes competitive sport. We should expect these things from a school.' She wants team sport to be 'for everybody', not just the chosen few. With this determination and the new facilities taking shape in the grounds, Mrs Jordan's ideal of 'scholar athletes' may soon be realised.

Prep school sport came in for particular praise (has a Sport England Activemark gold award); all girls get the chance to represent their school and extracurricular activitites include cricket, dance, fencing, trampolining and cross-country. Older girls use the senior school all-weather pitch for hockey and netball.

Musicianship starts young – reception and year 1 learn how to read music and play the keyboard. Singing and orchestral days are a great way for older players to workshop and develop ensemble skills. Budding artists, actors and musicians are spoilt for choice – facilities include a 240 seat theatre complete with box office and professional backstage team. The seriously well-equipped music school, opened by Brian Eno, a former parent, provides ample teaching, practice and recording space. Girls must participate in some musical activity during their first two senior school years – the emphasis is on taking part and most choirs, orchestras and ensembles are audition free. Music for all is the message with break and lunchtime concerts and, recently, a Garsington opera workshop.

Pupils' paintings of a very high standard are proudly displayed all over the school, including the head's office. A level results for fine art should also be put in a frame – almost every candidate is awarded A*. As we marvelled at the work in the splendid double height art building our guide confessed that it was 'a bit overwhelming for those who can't draw.' So pristine was the remodelled junior school that we were beginning to wonder whether the girls felt able to let rip, but an art room full of plaster and paint be-smattered girls enthusiastically constructing props for a forthcoming play dispelled our concerns.

CCF (from year 10 upwards) is 'huge' and girls love the camps – whether in Dartmoor, Scotland or the school grounds. D of E attracts good numbers too. Tempting range of trips from geography in the Alps and diving in the Red Sea to expeditions and charity work in Ethiopia, Kenya and Zanzibar.

Boarding: About a third of pupils board, either full time or weekly. Head is not a fan of flexi boarding (describes it as 'bed blocking') but school may accommodate pupils for one offs (plays, trips) or family emergencies. Year group boarding houses are cheerful with plenty of home comforts. Most have double study bedrooms with good storage and room mates are swapped around each term (sixth form can choose). For those who don't go home on Fridays there seems to be plenty on offer – we saw sign up sheets for strawberry picking, a day trip to Brighton and a make up workshop. Sixth form boarders have kitchens and may cook for themselves as long as they ask in advance – enables house parents to be sure girls aren't missing meals. They can also go to parties and stay over with school friends – parents are emailed for permission.

Background and atmosphere: Founded in 1915 by a group of evangelical Christians to provide a 'sound education for girls to fit them for the demands and opportunities likely to arise after the war.' Occupied various houses in the area, trading up as it grew from 18 to today's 1,000 (including 280 in prep school). Present main school was built in the 1930s in a sharp-edged, no frills style described (rather kindly) as neo-Georgian. Set in 23 acres just off Oxford's busy London Road, it's right next to the hospitals and ambulance sirens lend it an extra urban edge. Despite its town site there's a sense of space, and plenty of greenery remains undeveloped. Newer buildings are very well appointed, especially the Diamond Jubilee Building – home to large, modern teaching rooms, ICT and that award-winning robot.

Lessons we observed were challenging but not intimidating, girls were contributing enthusiastically and seemed keen to have a go and share opinions. In an A level English 'taster' class we were impressed by how quickly students got to grips with new ideas. A brief introduction to the principles of critical theory and they were off, producing Marxist and feminist readings of Where the Wild Things Are. The library is all you could ask for and dedicated librarians also provide a cuttings service – filing cabinets hold the latest journal or newspaper material for over 250 subjects. This resource, hand in hand with Google, introduces girls – particularly sixth formers tackling the EPQ – to university style research techniques. 'They know everything here', said our guides.

The prep is based just over the road in a large Edwardian house with generous gardens. Stunning curved glass atrium is the impressive culmination of several years' refurbishment work to build what is, in effect, 'a new school inside an old building'. On a large board just inside the entrance photos of girls were displayed alongside their 'hopes and dreams'. If all goes to plan these mini Headingtonians in their smart blue pinafores will become the film directors, nurses, actors, civil engineers and prime ministers of years to come. Nor do we need to worry about a shortage of ice cream shop owners or cup cake bakers.

It must have tested the architect's ingenuity to fit everything in but these lucky girls now have a brand new dining room, the floor of which depicts a river and meadows (could this be a ploy to get them thinking about rowing?). Apparently the food has improved along with the accommodation. There's also a gym, dance studio, music rooms and, drum roll, a proper theatre with retractable seating.

We've seen some forest schools in our time and it has to be said that this is one where the word 'forest' is stretched rather thinly. Nothing daunted, Headington Prep is officially so designed. Mrs Crouch is a fan. 'It increases their independence and helps develop a genuine interest in nature.' She wants her pupils to 'have time to play, make mud kitchens, just be in the woodland.'

Pastoral care, well-being and discipline: Parents and girls we spoke to were generally very positive about pastoral care, but the senior school is large and busy and we did wonder how quickly a quiet or unhappy child would be noticed. This is where the sixth form prefects come in. Each class of around 20 is allocated two prefects, whose job is not only to be a friendly non-teacher face, but also to get to know the girls and alert staff if they suspect a girl is struggling socially or in any other way. There is also a drop-in counsellor. Prefects are elected by peers and candidates for head girl and deputies have to make speeches at hustings before those on the chosen short list go before senior staff for final interviews. Win or lose, it's all very good experience. Sixth form common room was looking rather forlorn when we visited, but it's since had a make over and is now, apparently, much more inviting.

Some concerns expressed about the lunch arrangements – feeding 800 girls in an hour and a half must be quite a challenge. Sittings are by year group, but with only five minutes in between, one pupil acknowledged that lunch break was 'a bit of a mosh.' Staff 'bouncers' are positioned outside for crowd control and 'when it's raining you push.' All good fun when you're used to it but 'quite intimidating' for newbies. Once you're in, though, food is seriously good, varied and plentiful. We enjoyed a delicious meal in the large, modern dining hall decorated with huge canvases of old school photos – all the food is serve yourself and girls help themselves to as much as they like of everything.

Pupils and parents: 'Not too posh' – nice, swishy-haired girls who don't seem to kick too hard against uniform, skirt length and make up regulations. Most families from Oxford's private and public sector employers – medics, lawyers, academics, IT professionals. Head says, 'girls understand that parents are making an investment'. Growing cohort of weekly boarders commute from London on the Oxford tube (stops outside). International students from 47 countries – IB and rowing reputation are attracting more Europeans. Zealous overseas recruitment in the past led to large groups of one nationality (evident when we visited the sixth form Costa café). Parents say that this has been 'a big issue' and they would like to see better integration. Head acknowledges these concerns and says things are now being managed. OGs include Baroness Young, Julia Somerville, Lady Longford, Christina Onassis, Emma Watson and Lily van den Broecke

Entrance: From age 3. Register at least a year in advance; offers made strictly in date of registration order with priority to siblings. Those applying for 7+ places are tested in maths, creative writing, reading, comprehension and spelling.

Several applicants for every senior school place (but bear in mind that girls will be sitting for other schools too). For entry at 11+ girls sit papers in English, maths and non-verbal reasoning and have an interview. Prep school candidates (13+ entry) come for an interview and taster day after the pre-test. Sixth form entrants sit exams at Headington in the November before their proposed entry.

Exit: Nearly all prep girls move up to the senior school, with parent given plenty of warning if a girl looks unlikely to pass the entrance exam. Senior school looks at applicants in the round, so a talent for music, sport or drama may boost chances.

Inevitably some girls depart post-GCSE, lured to local co-ed sixth forms, although we hear that it's not uncommon for there to be a return to the fold after a few weeks. Nearly all sixth form leavers go on to university, including usually several to Oxbridge (12 in 2016); LSE, UCL, Durham, Bristol, Bath, Brimingham trending currently.

Money matters: Academic, music, art, drama and sports scholarships (£300 per year). Means-tested bursaries of up to 100 per cent of fees plus help for Forces and clergy. Of course there are extras but parents told us that these weren't unreasonable;

they also said that they approved of the sensible and inexpensive uniform.

Remarks: This dynamic school is going from strength to strength. True to its founders' aims, nearly a century on it is still sending out girls ready and able to tackle whatever the future has to hold.

Heathfield School

    119

London Road, Ascot, Berkshire SL5 8BQ

Pupils: 190; 5 day pupils • Ages: 11–18 • Sixth form: 60 • C of E

Fees: Boarding: £32,400 – £33,300; Day: £22,680 – £23,310 pa

Tel: 01344 898343
Email: registrar@heathfieldschool.net
Website: www.heathfieldschool.net

H

Headmistress: Since September 2016, Mrs Marina Gardiner Legge, previously director of studies here. MA in English literature from Oxford and PGCE from the University of Hong Kong, where she started her teaching career. Head of year and assistant head at Rutlish School, a boys' comprehensive in south London, before joining Heathfield in 2013.

Academic matters: Best known for nurturing BRIT style talent in the arts, bolstered by partnership with London College of Fashion, which guarantees interview and careers advice to interested sixth formers. Not hard to see why, given quality of work in progress, including striking coat (part of GCSE project) themed to bullying, part red (for anger) and black (for depression) and with a big collar 'for protection,' says creator.

But aims high across the subject range, say parents. 'Upping its game because in this day and age you have to,' thought parent. 'Results do matter – everyone works hard and pays a fortune.'

Top line results good overall. In 2016, 42 per cent A*/A grades at A level (75 per cent A*/B). Spikier profile for individual subjects – brilliant art and design results but sprinkling of D grades in facilitating subjects. Slightly mixed at GCSE, too, though achieve healthy percentage of A*/A grades (47 per cent in 2016). Parents get money's worth with impressive added value (Durham University research puts school in top 20 for pupil progress) and generous staffing levels – one to every four pupils – resulting in small class sizes with a maximum of 19, average around 13 to 15, often single figures in sixth form.

Teachers, average age 47, a fifth into second decade, praised for ability to capture interest (candle in one of English rooms with sign: 'Poetry is life – light and discuss'). Also adept at dispelling clouds of confusion – crystal clear maths lessons came in for particular praise. 'Standards have gone up a lot,' says sixth former. 'They recruit people you want to listen to.'

Current push is – unsurprisingly – on sciences, off to high profile start with Lord Winston opening new STEM building, boosted by lively lessons (year 10 biology lesson debating best way of killing locusts – 'Die if you pull their heads off.'). Goal is bigger take up of sciences – very limited at A level in previous years – and it's starting to happen. Hanging on to quality teachers (extra staff accommodation in the pipeline) could make all the difference.

SEN well-resourced through Spectrum centre – name intended to evoke rainbow shades of pupil diversity rather than autism, and widely used as drop-in service for walking worried as well as those with identified need (headed by dyslexia). Pupils must be able to follow the curriculum and cope socially and nobody misses lessons, with some in-class support from higher level teaching assistant as well as group or one-to-one sessions, some after school.

Reversing 'Heathfieldisms' (pupil speak for bright girls horribly crushed by one bad grade – school prefers 'resilience') a whole school priory – 'they bring out charts to show that they are just blips,' says sixth former. High flyer awards similarly showcase budding stars in photography (well resourced with two staff and a dark room for recently rediscovered 35mm film) as well as normal academic suspects. 'Awarded for things you wouldn't think you'd be recognised for,' said sixth former.

Games, options, the arts: 'Can get involved in so much more than in a big school,' said one parent. Good at knowing who'd rather take a back seat, though nobody escapes altogether, with termly chapel reading for all, even the shyest accepting it as the norm. Gentle encouragement from school results in what parent describes as 'nice confidence'.

Mind-broadening opportunities for anyone who wants them, from ambitious performing arts – swathes of girls mastered tap dancing in a term for whole school production – to extensive team sports, matches often twice a week, staff and parents in regular attendance, with some of sportiest playing across several year groups – only drawback the minnow vs shark issue if facing opponents from far larger schools.

Lacrosse popular, no doubt helped by decent tours – USA, Canada in pipeline – and pupil success (regular selection for county and regional squads and one girl picked for great glory with England's development squad).

Strong equestrian resources coordinated by briskly efficient full-time staff member, adept at finding good livery stables and organising dashing events (like military riding with swords) though don't expect ponies on the front lawn – all off site. Successes include one girl selected for national riding development programme, another a cup winner at 2014 Horse of the Year Show.

Plenty of opportunities for the musical, from audition entry chapel choir to choice of bands including orchestra and flute ensemble for instrumentalists. Visual art is particular strength, with quality work dotting the walls and talent bursting out in all directions – some of most colourful from pupil who would only draw in black when first arrived. Works range from Psycho-inspired bloodbath, not seen but very vividly described, ingredients courtesy of local butcher (bucket of liver and lights for £5), to extraordinary junk-model heating system, radiator a row of cans, cistern formed from flower pot, boiler a biscuit tin with row of lighters underneath.

Extensive clubs range from academic support (include dissection – possible use for any left over locusts) and cookery, with five-week sixth form course leading to Leith's Certificate in Food and Wine. Why leave for uni knowing how to boil an egg when you could have mastered the intricacies of gelatin use and know how to pair wine with food? (We bet they're the ones everyone wants to houseshare with.)

School open to ideas for other pupil-run clubs but no pushover. 'You have to show your angle and prove it – a good life lesson,' said founder of Athena Club dedicated, appropriately, to cultivation of wisdom.

Might all come across as living in a bubble, but extensive outreach ensures it's one with a permeable membrane. If asking girls to plan £5 meal for struggling family could feel like presenting deprivation as useful educational aid, school points out that it's a huge improvement on Harvest Festival donations of 'out of date pickled walnuts' which 'are of no use to man or beast' (and even at their peak, never were).

Boarding: Like giant Von Trapp family, everyone heads upstairs at bedtime, each year group in own small corner of the main building, bonus if corridor is close to laundry chute. 'Want them to feel they're going home after school' – hence limited use of houses: not boarding related and feature only occasionally to whip up short lived sense of rivalry on sports day and for assorted competitions.

Levels of off-duty shrieking suggested that good times were demonstrably had by all, though 'not like a sleepover all the time,' we were told firmly by pupil. (As one dorm is directly above head's study, probably just as well...)

Homeliness personified – 'No beds in a line,' enthused one pupil though another, slightly fed up that corridor was through route for other years, felt could be slightly too cosy. Lots of little touches like teddy bears on tap as extra comforters for the youngest, while gizmo a year policy (kettle and toaster added in year 10, dishwasher and sandwich maker year later) adds to the fun. 'So exciting – talk about it in the summer holidays,' says sixth former.

It's all expertly managed by housemistresses, majority – deliberately – with solid child care (team includes childminders, nannies or youth workers) rather than academic background. They're brilliant, say pupils, at dealing with homesickness that's felt to be as transient as it's inevitable and knowing whether hot chocolate and cuddle or 'on your feet, soldier' pep talk is required.

Two closed weekends a term, otherwise first two years who want to can go home after Saturday sport (one mother had nagging sense that daughter would have preferred to stay on), returning Sunday evening – similar freedom of choice for sixth formers. Has just introduced weekly boarding.

Plenty to do for those who stay on – no idle hands in lower years. Sports dominate (swimming pool, tennis courts and the sports hall 'in constant use,' says school literature), but also dance and music, craft, cookery and discos, bands, quizzes and competitions in the evenings. Outings as well (naturally, like every other school in the area, featuring Laser quest...) trips to cinema and teeming metropolis of nearby Reading heading faves list.

Drive to pack spare time with activities eases off towards top of the school, licensed lazing about time much relished as are socials with local boys' schools (solitary tangerine on a table in year 11 common room sole reminder of previous weekend's black tie event with Radley).

Background and atmosphere: Were any proto revolutionaries to maraud through Ascot, might have a hard job choosing between targets, Heathfield being just one of a number of tiny, gorgeous girls' schools in the area that, to the untrained eye, can seem pretty much indistinguishable. What makes this one different?

What sets it apart is particularly happy and homelike feel with a dash of top school trimmings. There's not a hair out of place (and if there were, it would be cashmere). Pupils wear their uniforms with pride, despite slight love/hate feelings for ties (plain for most, striped for prefects, red for outstanding achievement, scholarship version under discussion). 'Have grown to love mine,' said one.

It's as if someone has carefully curated a best of boarding school experience, from the tiny, bow-fronted tuck shop where, says sixth former, 'hordes of first formers run to get strawbs and ice cream and eat them in little groups on the pitches,' to the occasional water fight and spontaneous dancing, both popular exam pressure relievers. 'Gets the ants out,' thought pupil.

Originally founded in London by Victorian educational mover and shaker Eleanor Beatrice Wyatt for the disadvantaged of South Ken (doubtless a more substantial group in 1882 than today), school moved to current site in 1899 when she decided to concentrate on training future educators in greener surroundings.

In 2006, gained pupils and financial boost after merger with St Mary's Wantage, commemorated in attractive performing arts centre, old honours boards displayed in foyer.

Eleanor Wyatt, meanwhile, would have no problem recognising the school today, down to high church accoutrements that include a termly candlelit mass once a term (white dresses on the uniform list) in tiny chapel, pews bearing names of all leavers and heads.

Has avoided educational sprawl, everything neatly tucked into compact and well designed 36-acre site, common rooms all leading off old assembly hall, playing field invitingly handy for groups of friends to congregate in summer. Dominant corridor colour may be cool mint green – for 'calmness', reckoned pupils, and an unobtrusive backdrop for smart, up to date displays, but no doubting warmth of welcome, with catering staff pressing you to sample wares (bring a doggy bag for the home made cake).

Though firmly anchored to the real world, its ruderies seem comfortingly far away. No wonder many parents are such regular visitors that one – who hadn't been a pupil here – asked to join the old girls' association.

Pastoral care, well-being and discipline: Careful pupil selection the key to keeping school a happy place, friendships formed here generally for life. 'When you first arrive, everyone rushes up and asks if you're all right,' said pupil. Outsize personalities probably better suited to larger school. 'One to two disruptive children could ruin a whole year group,' said parent. Small size means that tends to function as a family, thought parent with pupils 'like sisters, which obviously entails the odd sibling row.'

Behaviour policy prioritises praise over punishment – ratio of 3:1 or better makes for a happier school, apparently. And, yes, they do record it. Similarly, Christian ethos – particularly 'forgiving and redemptive nature of the community should be evident' – demonstrably put into practice when pupils sent out St Trinian's style spoof letter to parents back in 2011. Head exercised considerable forbearance, describing girls as showing 'unusually poor judgement'. Now that's what we call squashing with style.

School reckoned to be big on emotional intelligence, knowing just how to handle family difficulties in unobtrusive and helpful way. One pupil who'd been unwell thrilled when whole year group dropped in for tea, parking coach outside her house.

Little left to chance. Notably strict phone policy – only allowed own from year 8 (can use only after 4.00pm), first years using school phone for calls, parents able to reach them by arrangement with housemistress. Safeguarding, though, creates its own paradox – youngest pupils might struggle to speak to say, Childline, in confidence. Here, as elsewhere, no easy answers when keeping children safe clashes with need for privacy.

Pupils and parents: Plentiful parent-to-parent socialising (massed pub lunches before exeats) and strong school loyalty. Plenty of old money keeps on rolling down the generations as satisfied customers send on their daughters and granddaughters. Balance is firmly in favour of 'British girls' (just under 80 per cent of total, a fifth from expat families, international pupils largely from Europe, Russia and Far East. Old girls include designer Nina Campbell, actor Sienna Miller, polar explorer Rosie Stancer and the late Isabella Blow. Current pupils feature Emilies, Kathies, Charlottes, Daisies and Roses in abundance – a roll call of reassurance.

So many famous names that aren't so much dropped as infused into school literature. When you've so many celebs that 'Mrs Le Bon' judging the school fashion show merits only a (large) postage stamp-sized picture in the school mag, you've got nothing to prove about your connections.

Entrance: Post registration 'invitation' day – potential-judging workshops and activities to suss girls who 'would cope with life in this exciting, full-boarding environment...' Communication, teamwork and creative skills definitely wanted en voyage (school also stresses 'verve and vigour' and 'awe and wonder' so come prepared to demonstrate these as well).

Will turn away those who wouldn't cope (say on balance around two applications per place) and offers are conditional on passing 11+ (18-20 places) or 13+ (16-18 places) – can take school's own entrance papers at current school. Handful of places in the sixth form – interview plus minimum five A*/C GCSEs with Bs in A level subjects.

Majority of pupils within 50-mile radius, many from West London with Finton House, Fulham Prep, Eaton Square, Pembridge Hall, Garden House, Broomwood Hall and the Thomas's trio – Clapham, Fulham, Battersea – the biggest feeders. Others from Surrey, Sussex and nearer bits of Hampshire (Ashdowne House, Cottesmore, Daneshill, Farleigh, Godstowe, Wellesley House). A few from East Anglia, Yorkshire, Scotland. Bright locals interested in day places also encouraged to get in touch.

Exit: Small numbers go post-GCSE (under a handful). Mostly family's decision – school erring on side of compassion in few cases where hard working but less able pupil is desperate to stay on.

Currently, sciences and maths popular – two medics, one at Oxford, in 2016. Over 70 per cent of UK places at Russell Group, with Edinburgh the most popular uni in 2016.

Money matters: Discounts of 10 per cent for children from diplomatic, 20 per cent for armed forces families (five children max in each case) down to five per cent for siblings (flat rate).

Music, drama art and sport scholarships offered at 11+, 13+ and in sixth form. Also academic, by invitation – top 40 per cent of entrants sit extra tests. Confer lots of glory but, at £750 a year, little in the way of spondoolies. Also means-tested bursaries covering up to half the fees (though not extras). Helping hand extended to existing pupils if family finances hit a crisis.

Remarks: 'You could sit in chapel and know everyone's name and what they're about,' says sixth former. Delightful and quintessentially British boarding experience – though working hard to ensure that cutting edge never tips into cutesie.

Heathside School (Weybridge)

Brooklands Lane, Weybridge, Surrey KT13 8UZ

Pupils: 1,051 • Ages: 11–18 • Sixth form: 226

Tel: 01932 846162
Email: sburoni@heathside.surrey.sch.uk
Website: www.heathside.surrey.sch.uk

Principal: Since 2009, Mrs Anne Cullum BA in English, PGCE NPQH (50s). Previously in Shropshire and Staffordshire and moved to Surrey in 2001. Head of sixth form at George Abbot, Guildford, before joining Heathside as vice principal. At the school for a year before taking over as acting principal, encouraged to apply for headship proper and won the job ahead of external candidates. She's no nonsense, working hard to move the school forward, strategic, but recognises and is respectful of the school's history. While the previous long-standing head was a tough act to follow, Ms Cullum rattles through a long list of initiatives and projects, which reflects some feeling that school had rested on its laurels for a while. She stresses the work on curriculum changes and that the school is now a real mover and groover within the county. Sits on several education and policy committees and councils. Consensus among parents is that she is doing a grand job and is good for the school. 'She's a fantastic head,' said one mother.

Of course in a place of this size many parents who have not had personal dealings with her and have only heard her speak in public, where she does not shine – she's better one-to-one. School expresses surprise at this and says she loves doing assemblies etc. 'She's not a huge personality,' said one mother. But another reported that her son and his friends described her as 'a legend' after spending time with her on a school ski trip. Parents also appreciate little things she has done, like improving home/school communications and tightening up on uniform standards. Married and has two children (in further and higher ed). Outside of school she spends time with her family and enjoys reading and sports, particularly skiing and aerobics.

Academic matters: Gets very good academic results which put it up with top-performing comprehensives nationally. From a non-selective intake, 78 per cent of pupils gained five or more A*- C passes including maths and English in 2016, 32 per cent at A* and A. At A level, 60 per cent of the grades were A*-B and 28 per cent A*/A.

Heathside is a technology and modern languages college, so pupils now buck the trend and all take Spanish, French or German at GCSE. Two language assistants, native speakers. Huge emphasis on English and maths, which are seen as absolutely core – some subjects are more equal than others. Anyone who joins sixth form without maths or English GCSE will have to add it to their timetable – 'They do it until they pass it,' is school's attitude. Good take up of solid traditional subjects like history, geography and single sciences. 'We encourage them to choose subjects that have credibility,' says Ms Cullum. Lots of specialist teachers, even in physics where a national shortage. Parents feel very confident that Heathside will deliver for their children.

School received 'good' grading in latest Ofsted inspection (down from 'outstanding' previously) with the sixth form rated outstanding. Head has revised the curriculum radically and first fruits of this appear in Ofsted comment about 'some outstanding' English teaching. Similar drive now being applied to monitoring and improvements in other subject areas. 'I am always asking "how good is the learning?" and I want to look at any weaker subjects and develop them so that every area is outstanding,' said Ms Cullum. Staff are skilled up, valued and consulted, and generally only leave to take up promotion or if moving aboard. Parents pleased that teaching is consistently good, homework always marked, and describe staff as 'enthusiastic' and 'great'.

Some complain about the number of GCSEs – as many as 12 – school insists on: a GCSE in technology is compulsory (either graphics, textiles, resistant materials, electronics or food technology) and very time-consuming. Students are grouped with others of broadly similar ability and setted for maths. Reorganised and re-setted in year 9 in readiness for GCSEs. 'It seems to be streamed for everything,' said one parent. 'Great if your child is clever, but I do worry that the less bright ones will find themselves in a class with the disruptive pupils.'

Sixth form is up against strong local competition, but has a reputation for high-quality teaching – most stay on and do well. Great take up of science at A level, politics, only English lit, no English language, critical thinking to AS. Pupils in search of vocational courses head next door to Brooklands College – the sixth form offers 'academic' A levels only. Dedicated sixth form block, newer than the main building, ground floor shared with main school but, as you go upstairs to sixth form proper, you are greeted by leavers' desirable destinations posted up on the walls to inspire others.

EFL provision as needed (not much – it's hardly multicultural) and a special needs facility on site within the learning resource centre, though most support is classroom-based. School says it teaches all its students in a 'multi-sensory way, responding to specific learning difficulties by offering different learning styles'. The SEN area supports students further by offering clinics to sort out subject-based learning needs. No specific testing on entry. Teaching assistants and higher level teaching assistants help in classrooms, with over 30 pupils receiving one-to-one assistance. Can cater for most needs, including visual and hearing impairment – some classrooms equipped with induction loops. Access for the physically disabled, including a shower and treatment room, dedicated loos and lift, ramps everywhere – aiming to make whole school accessible.

Games, options, the arts: All valued and well executed. Sport and music strong and locally renowned. Very sporty place, success in rugby has come out of nowhere – year 11 boys have won rugby scholarships to Rugby and Millfield, one plays for Harlequins. Runners up in U15 boys' national squash competition. Plenty of football and cricket. Netball is main sport for the girls. Lots of other activities on offer – from athletics to volleyball – though one moan that, despite the long list of offerings, effort is concentrated on rugby players.

Drama department beefed up by addition of a second specialist teacher. Music very good – hundreds of students get involved, everything from individual lessons to school orchestras and choirs, productions and after-school clubs. Duke of Edinburgh very strong and completion rate good. Fantastic trips, sports tours in Europe, footballers to David Beckham Academy, gifted and talented regularly off to special events. Always loads going on and students encouraged to give it all a go – 'The opportunities here are second to none,' said one parent. Everyone does some community work, eg in a retirement home, other school, or hospice.

Mrs Cullum says, hand on heart, Heathside has the best links with industry and business she's ever known – certainly the effort is huge here: for example Glaxo Smith Kline helps with science and BP sends over 30 staff for a work experience day, conducting mock interviews with students, mentoring and giving help with CVs etc. Lots of (Ofsted highly praised) governors drawn from local businesses. Geographically fortunate, also has links with local businesses like Mercedes, Honda, McLaren.

Background and atmosphere: A happy school where staff are committed and students generally enthusiastic. Despite large numbers, not a scary place for a tiny year 7 – friendly and caring, though overcrowded: most of the buildings date from 1966, when the school was built for just 500 students (students are rather buffeted along the corridors). It's a bit grotty in places, but recently completed a £6.5 million building programme.

School tries to cope with high numbers by a system of dual break times and having just a short lunch break ('Helps keep order,' agreed one mother) and some teaching is done in the hall. The school's situation is better, down a quiet lane, opposite a cemetery and playing fields, surrounded by trees. No access down the lane for drivers at school start and finish times – parents are asked to drop at the top. Fifteen minutes from station, lots walk – the lane is awash with a sea of students in their cobalt blue blazers at the start and finish of the day.

A good feeling of community around the place – echoes of a primary school atmosphere where key staff know the students and really engage with them. 'The children must believe they can do what they want to do,' says Ms Cullum. 'We tell them they can achieve whatever they want.'

Pastoral care, well-being and discipline: All good and recently revised. Dedicated, non-teaching student support staff on hand for administration in this area, eg contact with parents, monitoring attendance and dealing with emotional issues. Parents happy that school is responsive and proactive about any issues raised.

As everywhere, a few difficult pupils, but not huge numbers and the school has a reputation for trying hard with them. It's strict but fair and sanctions are explicit. Full-time exclusions have halved in the last couple of years – it's taken seriously. For example, students in isolation were previously based in a room on a main corridor, attracting too much of a buzz – they've now been moved right out of the way and have no chance to revel in their notoriety. The school's code of conduct, 'Give respect/gain respect', is well known to all. The 10-strong senior leadership team is seen around the place, not remote.

Generally pupils' behaviour and attitude to learning are good – it's OK, even cool, to be clever here. School repays that with ethos of 'listening to the student voice'. Head girl and boy, prefects and house system all recently introduced. Successful mentoring programme. Pupils fairly smart – no uniform in sixth form.

Pupils and parents: Middle class, reflecting local area. Lots could afford to send their children privately but choose Heathside instead – whole families go through. Equal numbers of boys and girls – a friendly bunch, motivated to achieve. Engagement from parents is good, for example 60 plus to a presentation on introduction of house system, and in a parent/governor election, there were six applicants for one vacancy. The five unelected candidates all went on to ask how they could help the school in other ways, prompting Mrs Cullum to think about developing an area where parents can offer support somewhere between governors and Friends of Heathside, the PTA. Parents raise a huge amount of money for the school, at the same time PTA offers an enjoyable social aspect with usual mix of quiz nights, parties, murder mystery events and so on. Recently their funds paid for refurbishment of reception and new projectors in classrooms. Nearly all now have interactive whiteboards.

Entrance: A real scrum to get in here from Weybridge, Walton and Hersham area. Parents prepared to go down the private route will try their luck here before shelling out fees. Average of 700 plus applications for 210 places. At 11+ students join from up to 20 primaries, but predominantly from Ashley C of E (Aided), Cleves School, St James C of E. Strong links with its primary feeders – employs staff to go into them on a weekly basis. Otherwise usual sibling and distance criteria in operation. Reduced from eight to seven form entry in an effort to sort out overcrowding, but numbers back up in 2016, as the current primary school bulge reached it. No longer selects a percentage by aptitude.

To join the sixth form, students need five A* to C GCSEs, including at least a B in subjects for A level – recently some 25 external applications.

Exit: Up to half leave after GCSEs. Sixth form leavers to a range of universities. In 2016 one to Oxbridge and one medic; others to eg Exeter, Warwick, Southampton, Birmingham, Nottingham, Leeds, Bristol, Cardiff, Sheffield, Edinburgh.

H

Remarks: A happy school with high standards, now with academy status. Unpretentious, offering its students a good all-round experience. Winning combination of committed staff and eager students – state education as it should be.

The Hertfordshire & Essex High School and Science College

Warwick Road, Bishop's Stortford, Hertfordshire CM23 5NJ

Pupils: 1,225 • Ages: 11–18 • Sixth form: 373, including 96 boys

Tel: 01279 654127
Email: admin@hertsandessex.herts.sch.uk
Website: www.hertsandessex.herts.sch.uk

H

Headteacher: Since 2009, Mrs Cathy Tooze MEd (Cantab), previously head of Hadleigh High School in Suffolk. Positive and authoritative, her manner is relaxed, though you feel she can be firm when the situation demands. Instantly likable, and both interesting and interested, pupils wax lyrical about her approachability, fairness and commitment to not letting a single student slip through the net. 'She'll always give you a smile, and if she's strict about something, you know there's a good reason for it,' said one student. A National Leader of Education and Ofsted inspector, she is often away from the school, but has created a strong leadership team to ensure she's not indispensable. 'I'm not a massively hands-on type of head anyway,' she says, pointing out that she doesn't teach much (an hour a week of maths to years 8 and 9 when we visited) and she doesn't pretend to know all the students by name. That said, she eats with students in the dining hall daily, as well as taking assemblies and regularly visiting classrooms. 'Students often pop into my office unannounced,' she adds, 'asking anything from "Can we do a cake sale for charity?" to "Can we tell you about something we did today?"' Parents describe her as ambitious, aspirational and sincere. 'She's a really good role model for the girls because she's so driven, but also such a nice person, and she absolutely practises what she preaches,' said one.

Academic matters: A very successful school, a particular feat given the fact that it is totally non-selective. In 2016, 92 per cent got 5+ A*-C at GCSE, including English and maths; 45 per cent A*/A grades. Head puts it down to 'exceptional standards of teaching and learning' and the very positive work ethic, along with ensuring the school is not a mere exam factory. 'We realise that the greatest gift we can give our students is a fantastic CV, but you can't do that if they're not happy and enriched,' she says.

Certainly no glazed eyes or yawning in classes when we visited, with enthusiastic and animated teachers ensuring lessons are fun, inspired and challenging. Chalk and talk is out; hands-on, interactive teaching is in. The curriculum itself is traditional, with modern aspects, including technology, with one computer to every three students, although iPads only regularly used in sixth form.

First two weeks in year 7 are spent rigorously but pleasantly assessing students, then setting them individual and detailed targets, with progress tracked three times a year thereafter. Targets regularly notched up to help raise expectations, although they never come down, with students provided with peer mentor and/or one-to-one catch-up teaching to get them back on course if they stray. 'I've had three daughters at the school and they're all quite different academically, but have all thrived,' said one parent.

Generously staffed (80 teaching staff when we visited) and good admin support allows teachers to spend more time in the classroom and less on pen-pushing. All teach their degree subject, which, the head says, means they are focused, committed and keen to broaden the students' experiences through a huge variety of trips and extracurricular activities. Regular out-of-hours email communication between staff and students and relatively little staff turnover. 'All the teachers are involved in research into pedagogy,' adds head. 'You can't just tell children things and expect them to remember it, so we focus heavily on developing interesting techniques to make memorable experiences of learning.' School has a partnership with Cambridge University for the Initial Teacher Training Programme, and are experienced providers of placements for trainees. Also works with other local secondary schools (Leventhorpe, The Bishop's Stortford High School, and Presdales) to deliver its professional studies programme, which develops trainees' understanding of research and pedagogy.

As a science specialist college, it's no surprise that many students take triple science, which stands them in good stead for A levels. School has been chosen as one of 34 Maths Hubs across England and leads a number of workgroups across Essex and Herts to develop outstanding practice in maths teaching, making this another strong subject. Languages growing in popularity. French and Spanish compulsory until year 9, and Mandarin and German have recently been introduced. For many, the technologies are a good contrast to the more academic classes, and there are some unexpected GSCE subjects including astronomy. Setting for languages, maths and English from year 7, although head says 'the setting is not particularly tight, with lots of moving around.' Top sets can number as many as 28, but the lower classes are often much smaller.

Very wide choice of subjects at A level – all the traditional academic options, plus more unusual ones including Latin, photography and government and politics. Also offers further maths. In 2016, 68 per cent A*-B and nearly 31 per cent A*/A grades. Sixth formers have a half-day of enrichment on Wednesday, which includes D of E, extra languages and sport, and also listen to struggling readers in year 7. Cambridge Pre-U global perspectives and research course gets intellectually bright students studying hard and thinking outside the box, and stands them in particularly good stead if applying for Oxbridge.

Able, gifted and talented students are identified early on, in addition to those who will benefit from individual learning plans, including SEN (66 when we visited). With students arriving from around 40 primary schools, head points out that the number of students requiring such help is often quite large, especially at the beginning. Among these are the average of five students in every year 7 who require some catch-up time with the school's visiting primary school teacher on areas like phonics. The cognitive ability tests in year 7 can also highlight issues like dyslexia that may not have previously been identified. Other students have particular needs such as visual impairment and cerebral palsy, which can require learning materials being adapted accordingly and staff training put in place so that they can continue to ensure these students fully access the curriculum. 'The main thing is that nobody is held back unnecessarily,' says the head, who points to one student with severe dyslexia, who had achieved seven A*s at GSCE and was offered a place to study economics at Leicester.

The base for all this is The Lodge, an on-site converted house with living rooms and bedrooms that have been transformed into welcoming looking breakout rooms, although help is classroom based where possible. Impressive amount of staff, including five teaching assistants timetabled to offer both in-class support and some small group literacy sessions, SEN learning manager, two learning coaches and one counsellor. Ground floor access is good throughout the site. Where some of the school buildings are inaccessible to wheelchairs above ground level, rooming considerations are taken into account when timetabling.

Games, options, the arts: Netball and cricket are the strongest sports, with the school boasting county champions in both. Tag rugby, basketball, volleyball, trampolining, water polo, futsal and judo are also popular, with plenty of gold, silver and bronze medals from the Herts County School Games, and indoor rowing is an unusual forte. Facilities good, although tired in places, including hard courts for tennis, netball and basketball, four rounders pitches plus a football pitch on site, as well as a 25m indoor pool and dance studio. Has its own large playing fields with hockey pitches and a grass running track five minutes' walk away. 'The school is crying out for a big sports hall,' said one parent – and it has just secured funding for a brand new sports hall complex complete with floodlist Astro and six netball/tennis courts. Plenty of extracurricular sporting opportunities (19 extracurricular clubs every day and 30 different clubs throughout the year), with sixth formers continuing an interest in sports, at which point the boys compete well on the football and rugby fields. Links with the Jacqui Ison School of Dance, Bishop's Stortford Volleyball Club and Hertfordshire Cricket to bring coaches into school and develop school-club links. 'It doesn't matter if you're not sporty, though, as they're inclusive, but not pushy,' said one student.

Art and DT taken seriously, with students inspired to produce work that is original, skilful and personal. Facilities excellent and welcoming, including industrial laser cutter and 3D printer. Makes use of the Rhodes Centre in the town for exhibitions, raising the school's local profile. Exceptional work displayed in public places throughout the school too. Large numbers attend art clubs and workshops and regular visits to art galleries, particularly in London and Cambridge. A level options in art, art and design and fine art printmaking.

The music block across the road is a hive of activity, with the two big teaching rooms and several break-out rooms all in full use when we visited (one small group performed a Coldplay song for us, having only practised for about half-an-hour). One of four local schools to give entry to eight pupils who show exceptional musical aptitude at age 11 – 'It's about an innate aptitude for music, not experience,' says the head. Plenty of other students with musical ability entering through usual channels, though – 10 per cent learn an instrument. Concerts described as 'breathtaking.' Several choirs, an orchestra (for students with grade 5 minimum and includes a harpist) and ensembles for regular playing practice, including junior strings, jazz band among others. Combines with drama for whole school performances, with recent examples including Hairspray. 'This year, we're doing Annie and 53 auditioned to be Annie, with 200 applying for the parts of the six orphans,' says head.

School has the British Council International Schools Award and, as such, has a genuine focus on global citizenship. Close links with Eden High School in Uganda for over a decade (teacher exchanges and an annual trip for year 12s and 13s, where they build a house, work in a nursery and teach English) and a science exchange programme with a school in Germany. Other trips include Cambodia and the school had just established a partnership with a school in China when we visited. Interact Club for young Rotarians run in sixth form, which had raised £13,500 for charity the year we visited (overall, the school had raised £17,000).

Background and atmosphere: The original buildings, which date back to 1909, have the look and feel of a grammar school in a leafy and private residential road a mile or so from the town centre (it's a dead end so hardly any traffic). In fact, The Bishop's Stortford Secondary School for Girls was initially founded to prepare girls for a career in teaching for a fee of £3 a term. In 1944 fees were waived and the school was granted self-governing status by King George V, who presented a portrait of himself that still hangs in the impressively panelled school hall.

New teaching blocks have been added in the intervening years, all of which have generously sized classrooms and other teaching spaces (no bursting at the seams here) and a house over the road was acquired to make an impressive music school. Two large school halls (although whole school can't fit into either all at one time, which means assemblies are split). Large, although not particularly inspiring, dining hall, with no complaints about the food. 'I'm vegan and have never had any problems,' said one student. Decent sized science labs and a well-used library, open from 8am-5pm, with a 40-strong book club and 26 active student librarians. 'It's not a geeky library, but a really lively hub,' said one student.

Plenty of clubs, including astronomy club, media club and jazz, so although the school day is officially 8.40am-3.40pm, many students arrive earlier and leave later (although generally not beyond 5pm). Sixth formers can leave the school for one hour at lunchtimes, with many driving into town or having a driving lesson. 'But as the food is so good, many stay,' said one.

A student reception, run by years 7 and 8, gives students a chance to learn valuable skills, whilst visitors get greeted by the girls themselves. Run on a rota, the students are given work to do when there are no visitors. Atmosphere around the school is laid back, yet purposeful, with students appearing happy, stimulated and motivated.

Strong links with local primary schools, with every faculty in the school having a primary ambassador, which culminates in plenty of clubs whereby younger children benefit from the school's facilities and students.

Pastoral care, well-being and discipline: Coaching and mentoring are big here, with trained coaches offering one-to-one coaching sessions and sixth formers trained as peer mentors who support pupils lower down the school by acting as 'buddies'. Leadership also strong, with a head boy and girl as well as a swathe of prefects and a school council, who have achieved such things as improved student toilets and better cooking facilities in the sixth form common room. 'I couldn't tell five people what to do before coming here, but now feel confident being a tour guide for visitors and leading whole teams of students when the need arises,' said one boy.

Form teachers send postcards home to parents if students do particularly good work, go out of their way to help another student etc, with five postcards resulting in a letter home. No real discipline problems, with less than a handful of students, if that, attending Friday afternoon detentions, mostly for uniform infringements (four of these gets you a detention), chewing gum or forgetting homework three times in a row. An immediate one-day exclusion rule for use of bad language, and head says she would exclude for bullying, but in reality everyone is so disapproving of it (students looked aghast when we asked if there was any) that any problems are nipped in the bud. In an effort to keep cyberbullying at bay, phones are to be kept in lockers all day and there are regular talks on e-safety. School awarded a Stonewall School Champions Bronze Award – given to those with good policies to tackle homophobic and transphobic bullying.

A form per year for each of the five houses, with half-termly competitions in sport, music and others such as best hamper for Harvest Festival. 'The house points system creates healthy competition,' says head.

Pastoral care second-to-none, according to the parents we spoke to, one of whom has a daughter who's suffered extreme mental health problems, including the need for an ambulance at school. 'They could not have been more amazing with her, with staff putting in a lot of time and effort to help and providing a complete open-door policy, as well as special measures and contacts where necessary.'

Pupils and parents: A half-an-hour's drive is the maximum distance that students tend to travel, with the majority much closer. On paper, local competition is hot, with parents spoilt for choice amidst excellent state secondaries in Bishop's Stortford, but the traditional approach to education and single-sex environment makes this school particularly popular for parents of girls (and boys at sixth form). Indeed, it is often picked ahead of the local fee-paying institutions. 'This means we are very fortunate in having many families that have the same vision of education as us, which makes for an easy partnership,' says head.

'Students here are keen to learn,' says head and they immediately come across as being determined, sensible and savvy learners. Boys enter at sixth form, which head says works well for the girls because the mixed experience helps prepare them for university, whilst the boys benefit from the good teaching. 'It was so easy to fit in,' one sixth-form boy told us. 'I'd never spoken to anyone here and worried the girls would have entrenched friendship groups, but they were really welcoming.'

Active PTA, a proactive governing body and a parental forum, which has real input into changes of direction and provides feedback. 'This consultative forum is a great arena for us to bounce ideas such as a new report system,' says head. Parents are kept in touch with weekly news updates and newsletters roughly once every half term; requests to see the head are usually granted for the next day.

Entrance: Non-selective, except for five per cent of places, which are reserved for students with an aptitude for music, and another five per cent for sports. Amounting to eight students in each discipline, these places are highly sought-after, with around 200 students applying to do the test, which takes place on a Saturday morning. Regularly three times as many applicants as year 7 places, with children in the looked after system/SEN prioritised, followed by siblings and staff children, then it comes down to where you live. All students are visited in their primary school prior to joining the school.

Not many pupils leave, so very few spots open up in other year groups. New sixth formers occasionally bring a younger sibling with them. Any gaps that do materialise are filled from the 'continuing interest' list, in accordance with the admissions arrangements, with those with siblings already in the school jumping to the top.

Around 450 applications into sixth form for 190 places. Five Bs or over, with a minimum of C in English and maths, to succeed – plus A in selected A level subject (if Latin, languages, sciences and maths) and B in any other chosen A level topic. Existing students who meet this criteria are prioritised. Each year, around 70 students who have achieved seven As or A*s at GCSE are supported towards an Oxbridge or Russell Group destination, with courses including the Cambridge Pre-U global perspectives and research course.

Applications from boys for year 12 are increasing and they currently make up a third of the sixth form. The offer of government and politics, economics, philosophy and ethics, Latin, media studies and film studies combined and the science specialism draws them in, and many transfer from the local Anglo-European school, which only offers IB.

Exit: Around 40 per cent leave after GCSE, primarily to do a BTec, performing arts qualification or vocational qualification. Of those who stay on, 99 per cent go onto university. One to Cambridge (classics) in 2016 and one vet. Many to Russell Group universities; East Anglia, Kent, Nottingham and Reading the most popular destinations this year; several off to study psychology, with others doing eg physics with theoretical astrophysics, ancient history, midwifery and automotive engineering.

Remarks: Like its head, this school manages a clever combination of being laid-back and fun, whilst at the same time focused and resolute in striving for the best. Coupled with the school's astonishing attention to detail in the assessing, motivating and monitoring of each and every student, it's no wonder that there really isn't a type of character or learner that won't fit in here – and more than that, has every possible chance of flourishing, with the school regularly appearing in the top three of the comprehensive school league tables. An exceptionally well-oiled machine, this school embraces new attitudes towards education whilst holding onto strong traditional values and, in doing so, provides a dazzling learning environment for hard-working pupils.

Highfield School

Linked with Brookham School

Highfield Lane, Liphook, Hampshire GU30 7LQ

Pupils: 265; 120 full, 45 weekly boarders • Ages: 8-13 • C of E

Fees: Day £10,500- £20,295; Boarding £22,410 – £24,600 pa

Tel: 01428 728000
Email: admissions@highfieldschool.org.uk
Website: www.highfieldschool.org.uk

Head: Since 1999, Mr Phillip Evitt, MA (Cambridge) and previously head of history at Dulwich College (50s). Brainy, articulate and a dead ringer for Tony Blair in his glory days, reckon a fair few parents (particularly the mums), some staff and probably pupils too, if able to connect with dim and distant political past.

Personable (head, that is – we can't comment on T Blair) with smile, voice, animation and epic hand gestures to the fore, but very much his own man. Attractively self-deprecating – 'It's very sweet of you,' he says when complimented. Emphatically not a spin doctor, he's 'totally genuine' thought a parent (coal-effect gas fire in his study was only non-authentic accessory).

He's good with the 'pushy, intelligent, successful parents,' says a dad and even better at cultivating highly effective relationships with senior school heads, securing places through 'amazing contacts to enable you to get what you want. If school's operating well, that's really what you need at the end.'

Leads a happy band of teachers who have 'a strong sense of unity – they're all good mates,' thought one, though it's taking a few turns of the wheel to secure uniform quality across the subject range. Maths and sciences 'excellent' but 'weaker in languages,' reckoned one parent, though 'not borne out in the sets the children are placed in at senior school,' says school.

Lyrical about post, for which he was head(master)hunted despite having no plans to go to the country and prepare for government. 'I never aspired to headship.'

Drove down 'on a profoundly unpromising late April day' battling new baby sleeplessness (last of four children, all – impressively – home births, now aged from teens to their twenties, who came through the school), and was instantly captivated by pupil élan as future charges played in the rain with evident enjoyment. 'I thought "how intriguing." These were children who felt comfortable being children, they didn't have that world weariness of the south London streetwise 13 or 14 year old.'

Modestly assumed he wouldn't suit. Of course, he did, and still does. Now well into his second decade, he's sixth head since school's foundation in Southampton in 1892, though far from being its longest serving (number two, member of family that still owns the school and responsible for move to purpose-built accommodation in 1907, clocked up a staggering 49 years).

Not much given to imposing his own world view, he lets school success (and its originators) speak for itself (we particularly liked school's weekly parish-style newsletters, featuring ads from local business amidst the reports of sporting and musical successes).

Relishes all that school has to offer in the way of tradition but is careful to keep the pace of innovation ticking over. Years 7 and 8 pupils have iPads which talk to school whiteboards and can store and file homework. May sound fancy but well in keeping with school's reputation for doing things earlier than most (it's been co-ed, and taken day pupils, since the 1970s).

He's taken difficult decisions from the off, starting by axing the 'madness' of compulsory boarding which was putting off many a parent who loved everything else about the school. To traditionalists, 'I was the hunter who'd shot Bambi's mother.' Many others approved and ultimately it proved a vote-winner. Now it's boarding because you want to, not because you have to – and, combined with sterling exam success, school is packing in the numbers, helped by increasingly popular pre-prep incubating the next generation.

Feels it's vital to listen to parents. Schools were 'conceited and arrogant' for too long, the experts in education who kept their customers at arms' length. These days, with successful, highly educated parents, 'you ignore what people have to say at your peril'.

Suiting action to the word may make him 'possibly too accessible,' thought a parent. 'Does well to keep himself slightly aloof because otherwise, he'd end up having to get involved in every single micro issue that every parent had.'

Radiates clearly heartfelt belief in role of schools in providing not just rigour but also 'joy and wonder, enchantment, delight, challenge, excitement, fun.' Collect the set and learning becomes 'something you get out of bed to do, like turning a page in a book and wanting to move on to the next page.'

Despite rumours that he was considering his options as he approached his 10th anniversary, we weren't picking up any sense that he was off to scribe his memoirs (or indeed, set up a Peace Foundation). Just as well, then, that there's no Gordon Brown figure lurking on the premises.

Best bit about the top slot? 'Genuinely, I want to make things better.' We feel a song coming on. Could it be D:Ream circa 1997? We think it could.

Entrance: Non-selective-ish, most from Brookham, school's in-house pre-prep, though parents think number told they may not make the cut is rising (there's also no automatic rite of passage for siblings.) 'Definitely raising the standards,' reckoned one parent. 'When we first started, you had to have a severe problem not to get in.'

Families, broadly local, are augmented with influx of well-heeled Londoners, offspring increasingly the products of Thomas's and similar ultra-smart establishments.

Atmosphere is changing too. Once 'a bit chaotic and very friendly', it's now 'much slicker' – bemoaned by some though 'not necessarily a bad thing,' thought one mother. Though on the rise, the pushy, assertive contingent ('mums who wear hats at matches,' according to a local – we're keeping a watching brief on this one) is small enough 'to be squashed' by fellow parents. Tutoring, so far at least, remains a minority out of hours occupation 'and only if your child is really struggling.'

Though parent felt that SEN support could be even better, it's generally still felt, however, that full time SENCo, five other therapists and positive attitude from owner, a brilliant and dyslexic businessman (sister was a highly-rated teacher here until recently) creates haven for those with mainly mild learning needs. Children are 'never made to feel persecuted' and '...one of the great glories of the place in that we are a very broad church,' says head. Especially good with late developers, giving them the confidence to bloom in senior school – and many do.

Exit: School has opted for laissez-faire approach to departure age, loosening the ties by offering preparation for 11 plus (and even 12 plus) as well as common entrance. It's proved a smart move, parental freedom of choice coming down strongly in favour of staying the course, with what head describes as 'a small attrition rate' – as few as four leaving at end of year 6 and senior boarding for most. Widespread destinations, from Eton and Winchester, to Bradfield and Cranleigh, reflects ability range, Canford, Wellington and Marlborough amongst the perennial favourites. Scholarships, being pushed hard, thought parents, are going great guns.

Other local schools, wrestling the will they, won't they stay on beyond year 6 conundrum, must envy top years stability here. Though a few do leave early (some, reluctantly, because of financial pressures) seniors-only delights lure vast majority, headed by wonderful trips – voluntary year 7 trip to remote Scottish island to build own camp (look, no adults) one of the most memorable.

Parents feel breadth of talent and characters in top years something to celebrate. 'You've got people who are going to Eton, people who are struggling ...but who might be the best at sport or the best at music, and they can accommodate that,' says parent.

Remarks: Approached through prosperous Liphook, school looks a treat on a sunny spring day. Picturesque brickwork casts early morning shadows on a sea of green, pitches everywhere, side order of bluebell-carpeted woodland (provides fuel for new biomass boiler as well as home for achingly on-trend forest classroom), all 175 acres well-used by mothers who 'turn up in their lycra and go running with their labradors,' says former parent who also bemoaned the fact that 'it's easy to start feeling a bit smug.'

Top-up scenery fix every Wednesday when there's post-match 'car park time', families enjoying picnics together (courtesy of Messrs J Sainsbury – branch a short 4x4 schlep away), invitations to international boarders from local families ensuring nobody is left out.

Interiors are corridor heavy, twists and turns best tackled with an expert guide – star turns include attractive, solemn (but not sombre) chapel (nearby plaque commemorating school's founder must be touched if passed – brings luck, say older girls), nice, bright main music room (with a second for composition); excellent library, walls stuffed with reading lists, each personalised with jacket illustrations as effective aide-memoires – a time-consuming but worthwhile labour of love that ensures everyone broadens literacy horizons, say staff –

H

and one of the small details that shows just why, academically, the school shines.

'What we do – I'm sure all schools say this – is absolutely aim to add value,' says head, disarmingly. Boasts 'unbroken record in getting everyone to first choice senior school'. Trickier these days because of the rise of pre-assessments, think parents, which has pushed up academic standards, and a tribute to what one described as 'fantastic' teaching across the ability range.

So far, no sense of pressures feeding through to pupils, let alone creating the 'pale, wan' types that one parent reported seeing at other, more academically-focused hothouses closer to the capital. Indeed, this bunch were notable for good cheer (and delightful manners, too) though some parents felt that a few families have increasingly to be restrained from ramping up the anxiety levels at home.

Pupils, though reassuringly relaxed, have no doubts as to expectations, though lead-in is gentle, usually (though not invariably) mixed ability teaching for everything in year 4, maths set in year 5, when there's across the board specialist teaching, academics ramped up several notches in year 6 with three sets for everything, strengths in English, maths and science determining who you're with for everything else, including music and sport.

H

Fourth set is added in year 7, and scholars identified. 'They try to give them other names,' say pupils 'but we know exactly which group we're in.' (School, which sticks to 'obvious' one to four numbering, was slightly baffled by this).

Staff, reckons one of their number, are 'lifers, not bolters' who '...all like children, and that's not always the case with some teachers,' says head (laughing, but we don't think he's joking).

This lot include many clearly in love with their subject – head of maths was happy to deliver short tutorial on iPad geometry apps, their habits and haunts to this reviewer (only flaw the occasional unintentional transmission of scrawled notes to mothership whiteboard in classroom, visible to all).

Year 8 pupils, with impressive maturity, were quick to acknowledge that though some teachers were clearly more down with the kids than others (sports teachers and witty head of music particular favourites) even those with a less obviously child-pleasing style 'could turn a good pupil into an excellent one,' said one – and had the scholarship to prove it.

With increasing numbers testimony to school's appeal there's the inevitable fraying at the edges. It's all change, however, with new sports hall planned, together with major surgery to senior teaching block including two additional science labs.

Parents, while praising efforts, keen to see replacement of 'old fashioned' kitchens which, though good for terrific range of break time snacks and 'lovely' lunchtime fajitas as well as recently introduced salad bar, can be slightly over-reliant on stodge for afters. May improve when attractive dining hall refurb, allowing whole-school reunion for meals (older pupils currently have meals separately) is completed.

Boarding has also had a fairly substantial shake up following period when lack of feedback made parents feel uncertain about pastoral care. New houseparents have 'definitely breathed new life and energy into our boarding.' Parents agree. Now 'hand on heart I'd say boarding is excellent whereas before I wouldn't have been able to recommend it,' thinks one.

Stalwart adult presence reassures – you're never more than two dorms away from a houseparent – as does good communication including separate boarding email updates and mobiles 'strapped to us' says houseparent, whose cosy office becomes an informal meeting place for 'tea and gossip' and who has custody of special huggable piggy which 'slots round stomach' and is loaned out to ward off homesickness blues. Approachable matron, meanwhile, full-on mending session under way when we visited, is 'always here at breaktime for chats and spare clothes.'

There's considerable smartening up (showers in reds and pinks, girls' dorms very fetching – Tom Daley pin ups adding final touch) with more to come. Loss of linen room, imminent, will be mourned by the heat-starved Spanish boarders who 'go in to soak up the warmth,' says houseparent. Biggest casualty, though, will be boys' shower golf, fondly imagined to be a secret from staff, ball propelled round vast, old-fashioned, Carry on Camping style washroom course, bonus points awarded for sinking hole in one into tooth mug.

Has all made boarding wildly popular. Pupils plead to start – 'mine were supposed to be day,' says one mother, resignedly – and is almost universal in top years. Who can blame them when evening cricket calls (there's always a summer term surge in numbers) and lures include guinea pigs and climbing frame in juniors' cosy cottage garden, as well as dress down Sunday morning breakfasts and highly rated cook your own supper sessions for years 7 and 8, run by Mrs Evitt who, though a vegetarian, gamely tackles hard core red meat dishes including 'delicious' burgers stuffed with mozzarella.

Day pupils, however, get fair share of the action, staff interests swiftly channelled by head into delightful range of clubs. School boasts of 'enough to experience something different every day of the week' – probably an understatement, given range extending from recently introduced 'Hyperdrive' after school talks (history of flight the ambitious inaugural topic) to the remote control club which races model boats across smart swimming pool), as well as Bushcraft group (one for the Bear Grylls wannabees, if ways with newly defunct wild rabbits anything to judge by).

Bonds are further strengthened by compulsory Saturday school, well tolerated by all (marginally later starting time sweetens the pill – just – for sleep-starved parents), as allows five clear afternoons of sport a week, Thursdays reserved for Highfield Keys – school's own D of E equivalent with 'spectrum' of activities ranging from 'charity outreach to outdoor pursuits.'

House on house whomping is a big thing (not for nothing do their names commemorate famous English victories). Ranges from the big set piece pomp and ceremony of sports day, where knights set forth from separate marquees to do battle, to Bonfire Night guy contest, Lady Gaga a recent winner (Bradley Wiggins would have been a strong contender but 'his head fell off' – rarely a recommended tactic). If there's no house to duff up, 'we can turn anything into a competition,' says year 8 pupil, citing tidiest dorm, cleanest teeth and best veg plot by way of proof.

Matches are, naturally, played to win with staff who are proud that their own teams regularly trounce those of other schools setting high class example. School says that it's emphatically not out 'to win at all costs' and stresses that all pupils shall have team games and represent the school in matches, whether endowed with athletic superpowers or not. Good sportsmanship comes with the territory and 'full respect is given to other teams in defeat and in victory. It's not personal.'

Parents agree that victory never comes shorn of good manners, which are emphasised throughout the school, year 8 monitors supervising younger pupils at break and lunchtime.

School, as a result, is a breeding ground for 'amiable killers,' says one parent, with netball stars known for pausing as they streak to victory to voice tender concern for opponents after collision. 'My daughter stops to say, "are you OK?" if she treads on someone's feet,' said mother. Boys' sport is 'excellent – I would say they win three-quarters of their matches,' reckoned dad. One parent felt girls' sport was a bit undernourished compared with boys'. Absolutely not so, says school, which puts it down to perceptions that girls currently 'don't win as many of their hockey matches because they are less experienced on

Astroturf than other schools' teams,' though will all change when they get their own.

All in all, a super school that radiates enthusiasm and good cheer. Head says it's the happiest place he's ever worked in, felt previous GSG description 'tradition with a twist' summed it up to a tee. Aim is for greater cultural variety in the future, particularly in the top years, 'because it's good and healthy for the children.' Track record of all round success makes it a safe bet that it will add extra flavour to the mix.

Hockerill Anglo-European College

Dunmow Road, Bishop's Stortford, Hertfordshire CM23 5HX

Pupils: 834; 179 full, 17 weekly boarders • Ages: 11-19 • Sixth form: 260

Fees: Day Boarder £ 6,216; Boarding £11,670 – £15,789 pa

Tel: 01279 658451
Email: admin@hockerill.com
Website: www.hockerill.herts.sch.uk

Principal: Since September 2013, Mr Richard Markham MA. An Oxford historian and former international hockey player who represented Wales, he began his teaching career at Marlborough College in 1994, where a variety of roles (including teacher of history and history of art, deputy housemaster, master in charge of hockey and IB coordinator) culminated in director of studies for his last four years. Insists the differences between Marlborough and Hockerill are 'not as pronounced as most people think', with key similarities including boarding and academic rigour. Whilst he inherited a school that was by no means complacent about its continued success, staff and students agree that he has pushed for a rounder education than his predecessor, believing that 'exam results are important, but a good education is about so much more.'

Relaxed but self-assured, he manages that winning headteacher combo of putting people immediately at ease, whilst still retaining a clear air of leadership. Staff clearly feel valued, able to explore innovative teaching techniques, and are never micro-managed, but woe betide any who go to him with a problem rather than a solution. Regularly dines with groups of students to seek their feedback, pointing out that with 92 per cent of day students eating lunch on site, the refectory is 'a good place to keep your finger on the pulse.' Meanwhile, year 12 students in his history class are taught at the conference table in his magnificent, spacious office.

Married with two children, he lives on site; interests include reading history, as well as playing and watching most sports, notably cycling, golf and hockey, the latter of which he coaches at Hockerill. Favours the term principal over head.

Academic matters: One of the most successful comprehensives in the country. In 2016, 41 per cent A*/A grades at GCSE. Also top non-selective state school post-16, with an average IB point core of 35 in 2016 (and 16 per cent obtained 40 plus points) – excellent by any standard.

Part of the DNA of the school is to bookend GCSEs with the IB, with an IB middle years programme that means all pupils continue with a language, arts and technology. Class sizes average around 24, dropping to 18 at sixth form. Setting in English and maths from year 7 and science from year 9. Students expect to (and largely do) work hard and study hard, with Saturday morning school compulsory and plenty of prep (two hours a night by year 10). But this isn't just a school for the academically gifted; it has a wide mix of ability. 'You're not pressurised to get good grades, but you are expected to do your best,' said one student. Another, who has now left to study A levels at an independent school, said, 'Unlike my current school, which is all about teaching you how to get top marks, learning exam techniques, and basically being an alpha student, Hockerill's ethos is that education should be much broader, and I love that I left with so much more than a bunch of qualifications.'

Head claims the biggest change for him was 'coming to a school with a curriculum model I had not seen anywhere else.' Indeed, even in the gilded private sector, you'll be hard pushed to find a school where years 8, 9 and 10 are taught geography and history in either French or German – a programme with 80 per cent participation and which really sets the pace for this truly international school, where languages are genuinely embedded in the curriculum. Seven languages as separate subjects also currently on offer, including Japanese and Mandarin, with less than a handful of students doing fewer than two languages.

Truth be told, nothing here is taught in siloes, with students expected to link humanities with languages, languages with art etc. Lots of self-appraisals of work are encouraged throughout the school, especially at sixth form, and teachers are particularly praised for making subjects exciting and offering careers support in their topic area. 'There's a real passion among teachers about preparing us for both university and life beyond university,' said one student.

The college had 15 children with a statement of SEN when we visited, including one wheelchair user, extreme dyslexia and Asperger's, all of whom are dealt with by the SEN co-ordinator, both in and outside the classroom. 'The transition in year 7 was faultless, with the school knowing all about our daughter and her needs before she'd even started,' said one parent, who added, 'The reviews are excellent, the head of SEN is accessible and there's a great emphasis on any extra help being made to be enjoyable.' Meanwhile, the EAL co-ordinator helps the international students who need assistance with language and settling into a different way of teaching. 'We keep abreast of teaching styles in the countries these students come from,' explains head.

Games, options, the arts: The IB requires a mood of involvement and pupils here lap this up, with over 70 popular clubs which run on weekdays from 4-5pm, including fencing, public speaking, knitting and dance. 'Younger students really get stuck in, trying new things out before they find where their interests lie,' said one student. Sport is strong, with girls playing mainly hockey, netball, rounders and athletics, whilst boys are largely drawn to rugby, cricket and football. Fixtures against both state and private schools in all these sports, with the school pulling above its weight, and there's some exceptional individual talent too, with national champions in golf and karate, among others. Facilities are good, with two outdoor courts, a full-size Astroturf pitch, two rugby pitches, two training pitches and a rather tired indoor hall (although there are plans in motion for a new sports hall).

Music, drama and art part of the curriculum until year 10, with music including music technology, and 388 individual musical instrument lessons a week, including the organ (the director of music is an organ scholar). Regular performances from the popular orchestras and choirs, with a good balance of classical and modern, of which one parent said: 'You always go away with goosebumps because they're just so good.' There's a rotating pattern for drama performances – one year, there's a whole school production; the next, there's a dance show; and the next there's an art-based competition. Art and DT boast good facilities and interlinked rooms.

Given the global theme of the school, it will come as no surprise that there are some impressive international trips, including to India and Uganda, as well as language exchanges in years 8, 9, 10 and 12, whilst in school pastimes include Amnesty International and Model United Nations.

Boarding: There are 196 residential boarders, of whom 17 are weekly (from Monday morning to Saturday lunchtimes) and 179 are full-time (seven days a week). Also on offer is a day boarding pupil option, which enables pupils to be dropped off at 7.15am and picked up post-prep at 9pm, a great asset for those living a distance away or working long hours. 'You do everything the boarders do, except actually sleep here,' explained one student.

Year 7s start off in Winchester (girls) and Canterbury (boys). At 13, boys move onto Durham, and at 15, girls move onto Rochester. Rochester takes girls aged 15-16, whilst Roding is for girls aged 15-18 and then there's the pupils' favourite boarding house, Thames, for boys aged 15-18. All the boarding houses (where the teachers also have flats) are world class – bright, well-maintained and welcoming, with all pupils having a study bedroom, sharing until year 12, then winning their own private space in their final year. Regular room inspections ensure pupils keep their belongings tidy, with downstairs reception rooms in Thames boasting polished floors, leather Chesterfields, beautiful fireplaces and large windows, whilst the other more modern boarding houses including comfortable and homely reception rooms.

All boarders are cared for in relaxed manner by housemaster (male or female), some with own family. All meals are in the refectory. Supervised prep sessions for all boarders, as well as plenty of opportunities for clubs and organised activities, events and trips. In fact, boarders enjoy the vibrant lifestyle so much that many choose to hang around even on exeat weekends. School prides itself on constantly evolving its boarding offering according to student feedback, and there are several forums (eg entertainment committee and food committee). Pastoral care praised. 'My eldest was horrendously homesick for a very long time, and the school was brilliant,' said one parent. 'They make sure there's a real sense of community among the boarders,' said another.

Background and atmosphere: Compact and leafy site close to Bishop's Stortford town centre with an attractive mix of arts and crafts, 1930s and contemporary buildings, including a new boarding house. Boarding schools are a relatively rarity in the state system, but this is very much first and foremost a boarding school, with two large senior boarding houses pre-GCSE and another for those entering the sixth form. (Teachers have flats within the boarding houses.) The school's calendar is similar to a conventional independent boarding school, with longer holidays to allow boarders to return home for two weeks at October half term, three weeks at Christmas and nine weeks in the summer. Pupils make good use of the extra time – 'It allowed me to go to China,' said one. Boarding houses are bright and well maintained and all pupils have a study bedroom, sharing till year 12, then winning their own private space in their final year. Classrooms are quiet, teachers politely addressed. Very strong community feel, with everyone getting involved. 'Not just a place to be – a place where you grow up,' said one remarkably mature young man. Strong sense of mutual respect between teachers and pupils: 'Teachers give a lot. We want the knowledge and the teachers help us to learn'.

Pastoral care, well-being and discipline: A traditional but non-denominational school, where teachers are called Sir or Ma'am and everyone has sensible haircuts and wears uniform (blue in the lower school, black and white in the sixth form). Not excessive on school rules, though, with more of an emphasis on expectations of politeness, kindness and punctuality. 'If you set the right tone, you avoid major issues,' says the head, with low level prep-related detentions about as harsh as it has to get on the discipline front. Attendance problems and defiance non-existent, which students attribute to being well aware there are 10 applications for every place. 'There's an ethos that we are fortunate, and with that comes responsibility,' explained one. Incidents of bullying extremely rare, with incidents of unkindness dealt with quickly. Pastoral care is praised.

Pupils and parents: The latest school photo shows mainly white faces, but by no means exclusively, and even those are by no means all English. Indeed, 40 per cent of boarders (who are required to hold an EU passport) come from overseas, with significant numbers from mainland Europe eg Spain, Germany, Italy and France. Twenty-four nationalities altogether. Weekly boarders generally from 1.5 hours travelling radius, whilst day students tend to be local families. Pupils are articulate, mature, friendly and confident, appearing genuinely to enjoy interaction with adults. 'I walk into school, knowing I'll be stopped and asked how I am and that they really mean it,' says head. Certainly no signs of teenage diffidence, where students avoid eye contact. Parents are grateful. Hockerill Parents and Friends Association, which includes both current and former parents, is an active fundraising and social community responsible for changes such as refurbishment of the library and chapel, and which runs staff bids in the summer term which have resulted in eg 3D printers and a camera for sixth form.

Entrance: Eight hundred plus applications from over 60 primary schools for 120 places in year 7. Hertfordshire residents are allowed four choices at year 7, and you can use two of these to apply for both a day and boarding place. Places are allocated on the basis of siblings, language and music aptitude tests, children of staff and distance. For boarders, priority is given to Forces and diplomatic personnel plus boarding need. Those looking to board are interviewed – away from their parents – to assess how well they would adapt to life away from home. Boarders pay for board and lodgings, but all academic provision is covered by the government. About half of the 130 year 12 places are reserved for boarders.

Exit: Around 40 per cent leave post-GCSE, some because they prefer A levels, some because they don't meet the entrance criteria and some because they fancy moving to a sixth form college or other local school. Post IB, over 90 per cent get first choice of university, with around three-quarters to Russell Group universities (Nottingham, Exeter and Leeds are particularly popular) including four to Oxbridge in 2016. Quite a few to a range of overseas universities, including Bocconi, Hokkaido, Madrid, Milan, Maastrich, Paris, Barcelona and Zaragoza. 'We get lots of help to apply for universities, both here and overseas,' said one student. Very wide range of subjects – languages, humanities and medics (four in 2016), disproving the myth that IB makes it harder to get into medical school. Pupils would like to see more alumni involvement, and the school and sixth form are working on it.

Money matters: Boarding fees far cheaper than a conventional independent boarding school, roughly between £11,000 – £16,000 pa, with a day boarding option at £6,000+.

Remarks: 'There is no such thing as a typical Hockerill student,' the head girl wrote in a speech she was about to deliver when we visited, and you really do feel variety is the spice of life at this extremely well-run school, where students are encouraged to gain a genuinely holistic education, but with enough opportunity to follow real passions. For students who are willing to knuckle down (and this doesn't necessarily mean they have to be highly academic), this is an exciting and dynamic place to learn and grow up, knocking the socks off many fee-paying sc hools.

Holmewood House School

Barrow Lane, Langton Green, Tunbridge Wells, Kent TN3 0EB

Pupils: 445; 44 weekly/flexi boarders (full also possible)
• Ages: 3-13 (boarding from 6)

Fees: Day £8,130 – £17,805; Boarding £21,060 pa

Tel: 01892 860006
Email: welcome@holmewoodhouse.co.uk
Website: www.holmewoodhouse.co.uk

Headmaster: Since 2010, Mr James Marjoribanks (pronounced Marchbanks). Education is in the blood, as his father was head at Sandle Manor, although he's made it his business to be less remote in the role. 'Children won't freeze if I walk down the corridor,' he says. Nevertheless he believes they should be respectful to adults. 'Eyes up, heads up, hands out of pockets, move aside for adults,' is the expectation.

His specialism is French (Exeter University), and the interest in languages is clear in the school – even the nursery has a specialist French teacher. Better brush up – he's been known to deliver addresses to parents in French. Career has included spells as head of French at Forres and head of modern languages at Cothill, followed by leadership posts as deputy head of Terra Nova School in Cheshire and head of Chesham Prep School in Buckinghamshire.

He has aimed to make the school more relaxed and family oriented. But his management of pupils, staff and parents alike is robust. 'I'm a benevolent dictator, a school is not a democracy, I consult with colleagues but I have to be firm,' he says.

Our moles told us that he has a tough gig with a particularly forceful parent body, and he is unafraid of holding his ground, which inevitably ruffles some feathers. 'I give the parents what they need, not what they want. We are the education professionals, we know best. A couple of parents didn't agree with a decision last year, but if it is right for school, it has to happen,' he says.

He has his fans too, with one parent saying: 'I really like Mr Marjoribanks. He is very charismatic and approachable. He is a visible character at the school and the children love him. My son had Mr Marjoribanks for French one year and found him a very good teacher too.'

Retiring in July 2017. His successor will be Scott Carnochan, currently head of Sedbergh Prep in Cumbria. Degree from Heriot-Watt University and postgrad from Nottingham. Has taught at Hillcrest Prep in Nairobi, been housemaster at St John's College School, Cambridge and head of boarding at Repton Prep. He played 1st XI cricket at school, was captain of rugby at school and county level and played international rugby, representing Scotland at U18 and student level. He and Kate have two young children.

Entrance: For nursery and reception it's first come first served, and entry into the pre-prep is non-selective, although informal assessments will ensure the child can keep up. Around 15 children join at year 3, and for this stage onwards prospective pupils take tests in maths, reading and spelling, plus there's an interview, and reports from the previous school are considered. Academic scholarships, which can be topped up with bursaries, are available from year 3.

Exit: Has previously had a reputation for not supporting children aiming to take the 11+ and for frowning on departures before 13. However that was a thorny issue indeed in the grammar school hotbed of Tunbridge Wells, and policy changed in 2015. School now says it welcomes children intending to leave at 11, and although it does not provide bespoke 11+ tuition, the preparation all children receive for secondary school entrance and common entrance pre-tests will be relevant. It's likely to take a while for this change of heart to filter through both in local reputation, and through a cohort which entered before this policy was in place. Not that it was ever impossible to move to a grammar – parents have previously organised their own tuition, and the last few years have seen many pupils move on to grammars.

At 13+ the school has a reputation for harvesting a good crop of scholarships. In 2016, 21 scholarships and awards (academic, music, drama, sport and art). Mr Marjoribanks has been instrumental in broadening the range of schools children go on to – it used to be Tonbridge for boys, Sevenoaks for girls, but in 2016, other senior schools included Mayfield, Brighton College, Eastbourne, Walthamstow Hall, King's Canterbury, Woldingham, Hurstpierpoint, Lancing, Eton, Cranbook, Kent College and Wycombe Abbey. A roadshow with 20 senior schools is held every two years to help families decide.

Remarks: No doubt about it, the facilities are fantastic and will be even more so once £4.5 million building project is complete, adding among other goodies new classrooms, science labs, learning hub, digital library, enrichment centre as well as a modern cloister.

It's one of very few prep schools with its own 20 metre rifle range – and the pupils are champion shooters among English schools. There's also a 25m indoor pool, squash courts, a climbing wall, and a snazzy sports hall. Lots of sporting success at county and national level. But we like the fact that the non-sporty don't get it rammed down their throats as much as in some other prep schools – there are two afternoons of compulsory team games, but on the other three they can choose drama, music or craft activities, or individual sports instead.

There's a 350 seat theatre and lots of big productions – and treading these boards launched the careers of old boys actors Dan Stevens of Downton Abbey and actor Tristan Gemmell (Casualty and Coronation Street). More remarkably, perhaps, Shane McGowan of The Pogues was also here.

All this, alongside what the head claims is a high staff to pupil ratio (1:9), and the number of specialist teachers, comes at a cost. You know what you're in for when one of the FAQs on the website is 'Why are your fees relatively high?' Mr Marjoribanks says he has deliberately narrowed the fee gap between the school and neighbouring preps, but it's still about £1,000 a term higher than others in the locality. We heard talk of school gate grumbles about fees funding large numbers of bursaries; whether you applaud that or not will be a matter of personal conviction.

They do a great deal to ease the way for working parents. There are minibuses at 4.30pm and 6pm to accommodate different finishing times through the school, and children can be looked after until 7pm. There is also a health centre staffed by nurses between 8am and 7pm every day. It means they can manage complicated medical regimes, but also look after a child who just needs to rest for half an hour before bouncing back, rather than having to call parents to collect them.

Saturday morning school and afternoon matches means that parents don't have to take off a working day to watch

H

a fixture, and can often schedule school meetings at the weekend. But this is another bone of contention. From year 5 the children are required to attend lessons on Saturdays from 8.50am to 12.50pm, and often also games until teatime. On top of a school day of 8am to 6pm by year 6, it means the children get exhausted, some parents say.

The head says Saturdays account for 125 lessons per year, and 'we would have to dilute our offering if we didn't have it'. He believes parents dislike it more than children do. But he has recently introduced exeats and a two week half term holiday in October to provide some breathing space.

The full-on timetable is part of Mr Marjoribanks' aim to be the top academic prep school, and to ensure that children in common entrance forms (year 6 to 8 have two of these and one scholarship form) are well prepared enough to get into their chosen school without any doubt. 'The last thing we want is them sitting the common entrance exam with everything crossed,' he says.

He has put back creating the scholarship class to the start of year 6, believing they can better identify the children suited to this class after they have had a year working with subject specialist teachers, which begins in year 5. 'It's not a designer accessory. It's hard work and the last thing I want is a child in there who is struggling. Parents perceived that they got the best teachers, but I have deconstructed the idea that you get a better deal in the scholarship class. Now I get children or parents who turn it down because they don't want to be put under increased pressure, and scholarships are not worth much financially these days.'

From year 5 there are two periods a week of Latin, and scholars can also do ancient Greek. There's also Mandarin philosophy in year 8, a Spanish option from year 6, and French from nursery.

The seniors get Christmas and summer term exams in every subject, although for year 5 this has now been cut down to just English, maths and science exams in the Christmas term. Teaching is generally very good; the children learn a lot and are pushed quite hard, parents told us.

There are two full-time specialists and three part-time learning support assistants, and parents reported being very impressed with this input. It was highly visible on our visit, when a number of children were receiving individual or small group tuition.

In the junior school, years 3 and 4 are classroom-based with a form teacher, although they go to music, art, DT and science in dedicated classrooms. There are three proper science labs, complete with a skeleton, and the art department has specialist equipment for etching and a kiln for pottery work. Interesting work on display included flint knapping and cave art.

The pre-prep curriculum includes timetabled IT, and everyone starts an instrument in year 1. This, along with a specialist music teacher just for the pre-prep, enables them amazingly to have a pre-prep orchestra. Reception, year 1 and year 2 have a separate block with their own dining room. Posters around the building ask: 'Do you have good manners?' They're big here, even illness isn't an excuse, as another poster in the health centre asks children whether they have said please and thank you.

Boarding is available to children from the age of 6, either weekly or on a flexi basis. There are currently seven weekly and 34 flexi boarders, but Mr Marjoribanks aims to bring the weekly ratio up to half. Boarding accommodation has just undergone refurbishment, and there is scope to increase the places to 50. Dorms are six-bedded and there's a combined games room. It's loved by the children – the two houseparents are 'really kind', they say, and they enjoy activities such as playing It, having a pizza party, or playing outside on skateboards.

There's a new energy about the place as Mr Marjoribanks' reforms are working their way through. 'I have deconstructed the atmosphere of elitism generated by a very competitive scholarship stream and attitude to sport; it is wholly inclusive and there is no-one outside looking in,' he says. Whether your child is a scholar or needs extra support, a sporting whizz or an arty type, they'll find their place here.

H

Holmwood House School

Chitts Hill, Lexden, Colchester, Essex CO3 9ST

Pupils: 305; 65 flexi boarders • Ages: 3-13 (flexi-boarding from 9)

Fees: Day £9,450 – £16,695 pa; Boarding £33 per night

Tel: 01206 574305
Email: headmaster@holmwood.house
Website: www.holmwood.essex.sch.uk

Headmaster: Alexander Mitchell, 40s. Originally from Perthshire, though he worries the burr is fading, having spent more of his life down south than north of the border (not to Essex ears, it isn't). Educated at Napier in Edinburgh, with a degree in music from Colchester and PGCE from Reading. Has taught in the state and public, single-sex and co-ed, day and boarding sectors, most recently for three years as head of the music school at Loughborough Endowed Schools and 10 years as director of music at Haberdashers' Aske's School for Girls. ISI inspector for 10 years. He's only the fifth Holmwood head in its 90-year history and the first ever not to have any past association with the school. 'Underneath his friendly, easy-going exterior there is a respected, efficient, deep-thinking workaholic,' notes a perceptive parent. Lives on-site ('handy for fire drills,' approves a pupil) with his wife Helen – head of PSHCE – and their three children, all in the school and ranging from reception to year 5. Conducting was his love, but he says he doesn't miss the music – 'I have plenty to be getting on with here as headmaster and our head of music and drama is outstanding; I'm very lucky to be doing what I feel I was meant to be doing, it's the best job in the world.' Still finds time to play bass guitar in the school's jazz band. 'Happiness is the key to progress,' he says. 'I can't promise a perfect school but I can promise a happy one.' Chimes with Holmwood's Latin motto, which translates as 'I was glad'.

Entrance: A third from the school's own nursery, which takes 53 children from 6 months and is set in an attractive rural building a few miles from the main school. The rest go off to good local primaries. Usual entry point to the main school is at age 4, straight into the dedicated reception, which takes two classes of 18 in each year. A handful more pupils arrive at throughout each year. Boys in the majority.

Exit: Year 8 children largely depart for Felsted, Framlingham, Ipswich and Oundle. One or two to Uppingham and Rugby and a similar number to Royal Hospital School, Culford, New Hall and Greshams. School proud of range of scholarships won. Occasional places at eg Eton, Harrow, King's Canterbury, Benenden, Ampleforth, Brighton College, Millfield, Stowe.

Remarks: The principles of the school have remained the same since it was founded on this very site, two miles from Colchester, in 1922 by a Mr and Mrs Duggan, whose aim was 'to develop the individuality and abilities of each child, to make him self-reliant and adaptable and to help him face reality.' A collection of semi-rural buildings punctuated by courtyards and outside spaces that cleverly maximise the opportunities for outdoor education (we've never seen so many woodland classrooms, play areas and nature trails in one prep school). Garden Block arranged around a tranquil garden in memory of a former pupil and treated by all with respect.

The Holmwood day is divided into lessons until tea at 4pm and then prep and activities until supper for boarders and more activities until lights-out. Flexi-boarding – minimum one night – is popular and most take advantage by year 8 ('I tell parents their children will let them know when they want to board,' says head). Houses are named after the elements and there are competitions and challenges all year round. Intriguing range of reward systems – golden leaves, superstars, as well as 'showups' and 'showdowns' for older pupils with the requisite number of showdowns leading to a detention ('I had one once,' confessed our guide. 'I'm not getting another one'). There's 'a week for everything' – recent Citizenship Week brought in speakers from the Red Cross and local charities, and when we visited a celebrated scientist was setting up ready to give a demonstration as part of Science Week.

Reception children have their own little world, across a path from the main school. Cavernous for the two classes of 18 in the early years department – with airy classrooms and intriguing corners tailored to computer play and dress-up – it also has a lovely outside play area with a patch of age-appropriate, safe woodland to explore. The main pre-prep department houses years 1, 2 and 3 in spacious, modern, purpose-built accommodation. Moving into the prep, pupils are arranged by ability in English, maths, French and science and in years 7 and 8 into a scholarship and three further sets. A few new arrivals, but the head points out 'as the year group gets larger, the sets get smaller'. The scholarship set is made up not just of the brightest but those who have the 'emotional maturity to cope with the stretch and challenge'. Pupils from year 4 begin to move to specialist classrooms – 'you're exhausted for the first few days but you soon get used to it,' reassured our guides. Year 6s learn Latin, or study skills for those not suited. French from reception. A few drift off into the strong local state selective system at 11+ but the vast majority press on to CE at 13.

Music and drama is 'about to explode' under the direction of the new head of department, predicts Mr Mitchell. Matilda being rehearsed with years 6 and 7 throughout our visit and, recently Pirates of the Curry Bean. Art room described (accurately) as 'humongous' by our guide, and full of unusual projects including animation installations by year 8s, who all received a still turned into a souvenir picture. DT is offered as an activity in a fully-equipped studio. Sport every day for those who want it. Rugby, hockey and cricket are major for boys, while girls play netball, hockey and rounders. Some 20 acres of the 34 are given over to sport, plus a vast newish sports hall and indoor swimming pool. On-site Lexden Rackets Club – financed by compulsory purchase of school land for the A12 decades ago – is heaving with fit young retirees on a dreary Wednesday morning, but also a superb resource for the school at other times. School has its own tennis and squash coaches.

Library with 12,000 books and an intriguing colour-coded filing system, presided over by the school librarian. Red sofas for the exclusive use of year 8 are as close as they come to a common room. Science labs in converted stables. Jubilee Hall with tiered seating for nearly 200, backed by professional-looking exhibition space – self-portraits when we visited. Dyslexia unit recently renamed learning support (although the sign-maker hasn't yet caught up). Excellent provision for SEN. 'We make progress here,' says the head. 'That might be a scholarship for one child, or an improvement in reading for another. We nurture strengths and support weaknesses and develop young people who are confident, and above all comfortable with whom they are.'

Boarding house open from Monday evenings to Saturday mornings – no full boarding. As well as using school sports, art, music and cooking facilities, boarders have a games room with pool, table football, table tennis etc in the main building cellar for evening recreation.

Courtesy and respect are still ingrained at an early age and children here are at ease with anyone (the head swears by the 'train to Norwich test' – in a parallel universe as the proprietor of his own company, he would be sufficiently confident to put any Holmwood pupil on a two-hour train journey with his best client). 'Every child is well mannered and friendly,' agrees a parent. 'Even on the sporting field – win or lose, the children are always gracious.'

Surrounded by its own playing fields, Holmwood has the feel of a much larger school, but at its heart it's a small community of some 300 pupils which extends to embrace their families too.

Horris Hill School

Newtown, Newbury, Berkshire RG20 9DJ

Pupils: 120; 103 full boarders • Ages: 7–13 • C of E

Fees: Day £19,170; Boarding £25,830 pa

Tel: 01635 40594
Email: registrar@horrishill.com
Website: www.horrishill.com

Headmaster: Since 2011, Mr Giles Tollit BA (40s). Tall and lean, reminded us a little of Bryan Ferry in his salad days. Seems reserved at first but soon unbends and shows a nice, dry sense of humour. Educated at Holmewood House in Kent and then Sevenoaks, where he was an academic scholar. Initially destined for a career in the military, he studied classics at Bristol on an army bursary. Took gap year job at a prep where he was expecting to teach Latin in a fairly junior capacity, but before term started found himself head of classics. Such a fiery baptism would have been enough to turn a lesser chap off teaching, but it had the opposite effect on Mr Tollit, and Sandhurst's loss turned out to be preps' gain. Ten years at Caldicott and thence to Bilton Grange as deputy head. He's 'delighted to be back in an all boys boarding school' (he loved his own time at prep) and certain about the positive benefits of a sector he believes suffers from outdated stereotypes. Not that he has to sell boarding to the parents he meets; they've all done it themselves. Describes school, memorably, as being 'not dissimilar to a cruise ship; doors close at the start of each term and off we go.'

Mr Tollit teaches Latin and Greek and helps the scholars polish their skills in debating, logic and philosophy, he 'mucks in' as necessary and takes year 8 camping at his house in North Wales after exams. Describes HH as a 'seven day a week' school and is unconvinced by flexi-boarding, which he feels is sometimes the worst of both worlds. A former UK shot, he has introduced clay pigeon shooting and a rifle range is planned. He's also a keen photographer and, because 26 miles just isn't enough of a challenge, an ultramarathon runner.

Married to Molly, also a classicist, whom he met at university. It seems that three young sons aren't enough for Molly, who has turned her energies to transforming part of a field in the school grounds into a thriving kitchen garden. Establishing one at their former school, Bilton Grange, taught her 'what works and what doesn't' and HH is reaping the rewards. Chickens, an orchard and a dog (standard issue black lab?) are next on the list.

Parents think the Tollits have brought new energy to the school and like the fact they have their own young family. They have total faith in Mr Tollit, think he knows their boys incredibly well and praise his (and rest of staff's) swift response to calls and emails. Boys think head needs to be 'a bit more relaxed' but like the fact he's introduced clay pigeon shooting.

Entrance: From age 7. No exam 'as such'. Head meets all prospective parents. Boys have informal interview with the head, simple maths and English assessment and spend a day, a year before entry for those pre-registered. Mr Tollit says he's 'not looking for superstars'; boys are observed to see how they interact and whether they are comfortable being 'in the academic spotlight' of such small classes. Years 3-6 can be day or boarding; years 7-8 boarding only (does not take new entrants to year 8).

Exit: Nearly all to senior boarding schools. Recently: Winchester, Radley, Eton, Harrow, Sherborne, Marlborough.

Remarks: Founded in 1888 to prepare boys for entry to Winchester, Horris Hill is set in 80 acres of wooded heathland on the borders of Berkshire and Hampshire. You'll need your satnav first time round so as not to miss the quaint wooden signpost directing you down an unpromisingly narrow lane; it's almost as though only those who need to will find their way here.

One of Horris Hill's idiosyncrasies is that it doesn't do year groups, it does 'termly remove'. Boys are placed in small classes (average 12) according to the progress they are making and remain there until they have mastered all their subjects to the requisite level. It might sound like a nightmare to organise but head says the maximum discrepancy between similar age boys is 'a couple of terms either way'. A boy's performance is reviewed via 'form order' (mark, position and effort grade) every three weeks, and at the end of term he stays or moves up accordingly. It's an unusual (possibly unique) system and only feasible in a school of this size (max 130) and age group. Besides accommodating summer birthdays, advantages are no B stream, no individual subject setting and ongoing challenges for both brightest and less able. According to Mr Tollit, it's as close as you can get to an education that is customised to each boy's needs. Arrangement is only for academic work; boys are grouped by age for sport, dorms etc. Parents all in favour, say it's great both for confidence and humility as boys are usually towards the lower end during first term and nearer the top in the second. The consensus is that the system works, even if one or two parents admitted they didn't entirely understand it.

Lessons we observed were fun, inclusive and challenging – a hard trio to achieve but less so with a class of 10, perhaps. Subject classrooms are named after senior schools: Winchester, Harrow, Eton, Radley etc. It took a bit of getting used to seeing such an age range, but the boys' enthusiasm and rapport with teachers was inspiring. In geography, impressive answers to quick fire questions were rewarded with chocolate; in the next classroom we thought we'd come across boys being punished but discovered that immersion in French pop music is a great way to practise listening and vocab. In the DT workshop, small boys in enormous aprons were busy sanding and drilling – some with more finesse than others. Was there anything, we asked, that they would like to change at their school? Extra free time was one suggestion, as was getting rid of second prep (senior boys do this after supper). Most popular idea was being able to bring small pets to school, something we mentioned to Mr Tollit, who promised to consider the proposal. Few boys with SEN – dyslexia, dyspraxia – receive support but this isn't the place for those with more than mild problems.

The no mobiles, laptops, iPads (basically, no screens) rule is, as far as we could tell, no big deal and so much easier than trying to control limited access. Boys write weekly letters and may email/Skype from the house computer. As a teacher observed, if the no screens policy were to change, 'it would mean more rules.' Boys accept the policy and parents love it. They're not quite so keen when, for instance, CE results come out and they can't talk to their sons because the boarding house telephone is engaged – surely room for a little more 21st century communication technology here? This is a school where 'live' notice boards mean that someone changes the pictures and display on the wall in the dining hall corridor several times a day. There aren't smartboards in every classroom, although those we saw were being creatively employed; boys treasure the one or two teachers who spurn their use. Science labs, art and DT rooms have all the necessaries in a charmingly scruffy, no-frills style. By contrast, a high-tech rooftop weather station relays the prevailing conditions to a screen outside the geography room.

Sensible uniform features navy blue cords – either trousers or shorts, boys can decide. Apparently 'some boys wear shorts even when it snows.' Sartorial democracy extends to choice of tie as well. Long morning and lunch breaks allow plenty of time to work in the kitchen garden, ride bikes (boys can bring own), play outside in the meadows, make dens and have adventures in their own bosky dominion (known as 'Spain' because it's roughly the same shape). Nowhere is out of bounds but pupils mustn't go off alone. Camping out and cooking in the woods is one of the ultimate post-CE treats. Juniors have their own wood, 'too tame for us,' said our super-confident year 8 guides. One of the characteristics of HH is the amount of personal freedom pupils enjoy, finely balanced by the equivalent expectation of personal responsibility. Boys organise their own activities (or Sign Up), recording where they are on a notice board so that everybody knows.

Youngest boarders (age 7-9) have lovely rooms in the 'Private Side' above the head's family quarters, with teddies on beds and lots of posters. Evening activities include silent reading, film nights with popcorn, board games and even shoe polishing (try suggesting that at home...). Numbers are small so things are flexible; if it's hot they can have a swim, if everyone's exhausted they go to bed early. Gappies 'bridge the gap' between boys and staff and are, as always, very popular. What about the homesick, we ask? Of course it happens, but staff are vigilant and boys support each other, telling tutors if they're worried about someone. 'You feel awkward at first,' our guides said, 'but it only lasts a week.'

Lots of younger teachers with families live on site, married couples head up the boarding houses, but after the junior forms most of the teaching staff are men. This notwithstanding, the traditional boys' own atmosphere prevails and is what many, especially army families, treasure. There are a few local day boys who are 'building up to boarding', rest may go home after matches on Saturday until Sunday evening (except first and last weekend of term) but most stay, 'or you miss too much fun.' That fun includes cross-country cycling, tree running, kite flying and ghost stories round the campfire. A parent praised the 'pater' system that pairs new boys with older boys and said that these cross-age friendships are kept up throughout school. Older boys move on to one of two Edwardian houses a short walk across the playing fields. Four-bed rooms are very comfortably furnished with home duvets, posters, beanbags and lovely soft carpet. Fruit bowl and toaster fill the gaps between meals, all of which are eaten in school dining room. Everyone, staff and pupils, sits down together at large tables, boys serve the food. Head v keen on benefits of 'interaction across a table'.

Spacious and well-designed music school can accommodate all for studio theatre or concert performances. Twenty-six practice rooms means there's no excuse for not getting down to scales and arpeggios after breakfast. Parts for all in 'fantastic' music and plays. Main venue for drama, assemblies etc is rather tired windowless sports hall, not enhanced by pervasive whiffy trainer smell, but never fear, Mr Tollit is on the case and this part of the school is undergoing complete refurbishment. As he says, 'HH is not a flash school', but a shooting range, climbing wall and upgraded squash courts are on the way. Interestingly, it seemed to us that there was less of an obsession with organised sport and winning here than at other similar schools. Plenty of options: usuals plus hockey, squash, tennis, sailing, golf, fencing. Boys think cricket and football are what they're best at and all get to represent school in something. Parents come and watch matches, although it's a long round trip if you live in London. Swimming pool is outdoors (very) with wooden changing huts – all a bit basic but doubtless character building. One of the school's 'quite old fashioned secret things' is the modelling and train room, a glue and paint besmattered garret where Warhammer enthusiasts create their miniature worlds and model railway buffs of all ages can operate trains and signals.

With a maximum of 130 pupils, quite a few who are siblings, the parent body is small, self-selecting and fiercely supportive. Although it's in a wealthy part of the country, HH is definitely not (outwardly at least), a smart school. Parents are welcomed to plays, concerts, matches and Sunday evening chapel and there are social events such as fathers' and sons' cricket matches and mothers' and sons' tennis, but there's no PTA, sports day or speech day. One father, who had considered London day schools for his sons, spoke of the way in which HH 'preserves innocence' – not just by absence of personal technology but also because full boarding means boys develop a camaraderie that is not influenced by each others' possessions or houses. On a more practical level, parents love the fact that all sports kit is provided, washed and maintained by the school.

Horris Hill is such a distinctive school it's unlikely you could choose it by mistake; proud to be different, it epitomises the very best prep school traditions without being pompous or rigid. HH boys are confident but not precocious; they think for themselves but aren't arrogant. There's room for big characters but a shy child won't be trampled underfoot; academic success is important but not to the exclusion of other talents. As another happy parent told us, 'it's a hidden gem.'

Howard of Effingham School

Lower Road, Effingham, Leatherhead, Surrey KT24 5JR

Pupils: 1,545 • Ages: 11–18 • Sixth form: 330

Tel: 01372 453694
Email: Howard@thehoward.org
Website: www.thehoward.org

Executive head: Since 1999, the school has been overseen by Rhona Barnfield MA BSc CBE (for services to education). She is CEO of the Howard Partnership Trust – a not-for-profit, multi-academy trust made up of nine local primary and secondary schools, including Thomas Knyvett College in Ashford and Oxted School. She chairs assorted education-related committees in Surrey, and is a member of the Regional Headteacher Board, a group elected by professionals who support the regional schools commissioner in his work in overseeing the performance of academies in south London and south east England. She is 'more of a figurehead than anything else now,' as one mother puts it, rarely even attending events at the school.

Day-to-day management is the remit of Mrs Helen Pennington BSc NPQH, the former deputy head, who has been the head of school since 2012. A hands-on presence, Mrs Pennington heads up the senior team. A long-serving teacher with more than a decade's experience at the school, year-long absence in 2009 to 2010 on secondment to Ofsted, followed by troubleshooting support at assorted struggling schools has given her a breadth of experience. We found her chirpy, down-to-earth and no-nonsense, while parents who know her (not all parents that we spoke to did) describe her as 'a positive force,' 'a good listener' and 'easy to talk to.' While she doesn't teach (except on an ad hoc basis when necessary), students told us she's a visible presence in the school.

Academic matters: Long-held reputation for excellence, managing consistently good results against stiffish local competition, including from independents. In 2016, 78 per cent of year 11 pupils passed five or more GCSEs at A*-C including English and maths, with 34 per cent A*/A grades. At A level, 59 per cent of grades were A*/B and 30 per cent A*/A.

H

School takes considerable pains to choose high quality teaching staff who are not just subject specialists, but passionate advocates for their subjects. 'They make sure every child reaches their full potential, no matter what it takes,' one parent told us. We wondered if the first class we passed – in which excitable, but immaculately behaved students were thoroughly engaged in a fun subject quiz – would be a one-off; but it wasn't, with every teacher we saw using imaginative techniques. 'You'll rarely see a science lab without a practical going on,' one student told us, while another added, 'The teachers are so supportive – you never feel you're getting in the way if you knock on their office door and they'll think nothing of spending an extra half hour with you if it's needed.' Strong academic results also helped by 'the fact that we've worked so hard on behaviour and attitudes,' believes the head. 'It means teaching can be a real joy here, with extremely positive relationships with students.'

There's constant feedback, with students kept informed about where they stand and what they should be capable of, while parents get three reports a year. If any student's work slips, they're given a mentor and strategies are put in place – whether that's a revision course or one-to-one support. Teacher training is superb, with inset days maximised – for example via a 'best practice festival,' in which teachers showcase examples in under two, four or six minutes. 'We create a video and blog so teachers can go back to it. It's inspirational seeing the techniques,' says the head, who adds that there's also a lot of sharing of best practice with other schools in the Howard Partnership Trust.

Academically strong across all GCSEs, with stand-out results in English, maths, science, history, technology and drama (which are also the popular options, with the addition of PE). Practical GCSE options include food preparation and nutrition, and there's also a good range of vocational qualifications offered either by the school (or at local college for one day a week) as GCSE alternatives/additions, including BTecs in science, business studies, sport and vehicle maintenance. Everyone takes at least one modern foreign language GCSE – with language teaching beginning in year 7, when almost all students take two languages out of French, Spanish and German. 'In year 9, the ones who appear to have the least aptitude for languages drop one,' says the head, who adds that they also offer 'express languages' to students who show the most aptitude. Latin available as an enrichment option for the most academically able from year 9. With early setting (for maths and languages in year 7 first term and humanities, English and science added in year 8) the aim is for each to receive according to need.

An impressive 37 A levels available, with maths, sciences, social sciences and humanities attracting the highest numbers of students – while the strongest results are in maths, sciences, psychology, media studies, history, geography, geology, product design and graphics. Languages have a relatively low take-up, but they do run here. Dance is increasingly popular. School listens and will add new subjects if demand and resources are there.

Not a high proportion of SEN, but there's the full range of mild, moderate and severe – who are helped both inside and outside the classroom with tailored help. 'The SENCo is extraordinary – she and her very caring team work really hard with the children,' said one parent. 'I was advised that my son should go to a specialist school because of his needs, but he wanted to come here because all his friends were – and it was absolutely the right decision. He's loved it and passed all his GCSES, which I would never in a million years have thought possible,' said another. 'You wouldn't know the difference between students with and without SEN in this school – and that's the way we like it,' says the head.

Games, options, the arts: Two hours a week devoted to PE. In winter, the core sports are netball, hockey, rugby and football, while in summer, it's tennis, athletics, cricket and rounders – but there's plenty more variety besides, including gymnastics, badminton, trampolining and dance. Extracurricular sport is high on the agenda, and there are regular tours, for instance for rugby and football – plus, the school supports individuals whose talents lie in more unusual sports, such as ice skating, rowing, sailing etc. Lots to brag about when it comes to sporting successes, both from individual students and school teams – and indeed the school does just that every week on the PE faculty's twitter feed. 'To my great delight, we hold up well against our fee paying neighbours,' smiles the head.

Students reassured us that sport isn't just for the elite: 'I'm actually not that good at sport, but I enjoy it and have had no shortage of opportunities here,' one sixth-former told us. Parents not so sure, with one saying, 'Some of the PE teachers do seem to have their favourites, who get picked for everything.' Another believes the issue is more the lack of PE staff, 'which means they can only run an A team and sometimes a B team.' Facilities include a big sports hall (which doubles as a dance studio), plus a gym. Outside, there are hard-ground courts and a field, but as it's not the best quality, the school also rents the King George V Playing Fields, just a minute's walk away.

Slick annual productions from the drama department – one for key stage 3 pupils and one open to the whole school, which is held in Leatherhead Theatre. 'Nobody is turned away who wants to be involved, so this often means very big casts,' says the head. 'The last production, Evita, was amazing – they put so much work into it,' a parent told us. Drama is increasingly popular as a sixth form option (boys as well as girls).

Richness of offerings inside art and DT departments reflect willingness to invest in pupil creativity. Students can choose from GCSE options of art and design, fine art, textiles, product design, graphics and food preparation and nutrition – while at A level, there's art, textiles, fine art and photography in the art department and graphics and product design in DT. Some stunning work is displayed throughout the school, as well as some more average work – always a good sign that art is recognised as beneficial to all, not just the extremely talented.

Music is a major part of school life, with a whole school orchestra, chamber orchestra, jazz bands and various choirs including a pop choir. Some of the performances (eg rock and pop concerts) are co-managed by the students – while other regulars include summer and winter concerts, an annual music festival with a local primary school and students going out to sing in local old folks' homes at Christmas. Peripatetic teachers come in to teach over 100 children everything from drums to trumpet.

Masses of trips. Natural History Museum, Kew Gardens and Barton-on-Sea are just a few of the day trips on offer. Language exchanges, including to Switzerland (which covers French and German). 'One recent exchange trip involved 90 children flying out to Spain,' says the head. Sports tours to various countries. Even Disneyland Paris is a potential destination for students here, while sixth formers studying science are invited to expeditions to the likes of Honduras or Mexico, where they do real research work. Sixth formers are speedily drawn into a range of other CV-friendly activities that don't involve travelling. These include working with year 7 and 8 pupils and getting involved in busy student committee which runs everything from Christmas ball to sale of Valentine's Day carnations. Extracurricular options – besides the sport, music, drama and art already mentioned – include more unusual offerings such as Top Trumps and Rubik's cubing.

Background and atmosphere: Set in the east of the village of Effingham, the school first opened in 1940, when it was built for 240 pupils. It's a good job facilities have since expanded (including a sports centre, purpose-built sixth-form block, new senior canteen and some specialist science facilities) as the school now has in excess of 1,500 students. 'You do feel the squeeze in some departments, such as drama, and in some corridors,' one student told us – although sixth formers say there's no lack of private study areas, which is the most common complaint around physical limitations in secondary schools. Nor is there any shortage of outside green space, certainly at the front (lots of grass and a playing field) – although tarmac prevails round the back, including a bleak-looking netball court, albeit with a fair few mature trees dotted around.

There's no frills when it comes to facilities – and many look tired and run-down. We were particularly disappointed to see two half-eaten apples on the floor of one corridor – and they had clearly been there for some time, even though there was a bin just a few metres away. What's more, nobody picked them up as they passed. That said, we saw very little litter in other areas and it is, by-and-large, kept tidy. It's also worth noting that this school is proof that outer appearances do not have to be a guide to inner beauty, with students clearly bursting with pride about their school, which seems to strike just the right balance between a pervading sense of order and a feeling of overall cheeriness. In all classrooms we visited, engaged students looked absorbed in their study, and with smiles on their faces, while the overall atmosphere is calm and purposeful. And it's not as if the students are particularly interested in having shiny, new state-of-the-art buildings. 'What we have serves us well,' one told us. 'More than once, I've said to my children, "Surely you'd like newer buildings and more space?" but they defend it to the hilt,' one parent told us. The library is lovely – a large, open-plan space that includes a library garden, while the computer suites are plentiful and well-stocked. Art – including DT – also spacious and well-equipped. Two separate canteens serve different age groups, with students reporting positively on the standard of the food.

Pastoral care, well-being and discipline: Highly rated by parents. 'My child had the same form tutor from year 7 right up to her GCSEs, and she was wonderful,' said one parent. Year 7s are eased in very gently, with support from trained-up year 9 mentors, their own area at break time and earlier lunchtime to give them a few minutes' head start on the mêlée. Refreshingly, there's also lots of work on resilience in these earlier years – the theory being that students may encounter fewer problems if they are more resilient. At the other end of the age range, sixth formers start by having to be in at the same time as younger pupils, though later on, after demonstration of requisite commitment, they may enjoy a lie-in if they don't have early lessons. They wear own clothes and can melt away into own common room for R and R, bizarrely furnished with railway platform style slatted metal benches on one side, soft seating on the other.

Strong pastoral structure means there are 'lots of different channels you can go down,' say parents. 'The first point of call would be the form teacher, then you've got head of year, head of subject, deputy head and then the head.' Pupils, too, praised staff accessibility – felt to be good throughout the school and exceptional in the sixth form. 'You can go to anyone,' says one. 'They're very sympathetic.' Flexible, too. And there are part-time counsellors.

Parents says it's a kindly place, with plenty of rewards for effort – including house points, postcards home, green cards, headteacher's commendations and achievement assemblies. But the school is no pushover, with high expectations, particularly around good manners, uniform and deadlines. 'The big step change with good behaviour was us deciding that if we modelled it – treating the students in exactly the same way we would want to be treated – then it might be copied, and it has been,' says the head. 'Behaviour here has improved dramatically,' agree parents.

Students are crystal clear on the rewards and sanctions ladder system – which include B1-5 cards (1 for low-level behaviour like talking in class, while 5 is for serious stuff like bad language) – although we found it quite complicated. 'Students tend to get the most detentions in the earlier years, students told us – and even these are tiered, with the two-hour Friday headteacher' s detention the most shameful. Fixed-term exclusions have declined dramatically within the last five years, although unusually the school refused to provide any figures. No permanent exclusions at all – although very occasionally (again, they won't provide figures), students are referred to off-site provision (mainly for physical violence, although it would be unfair to suggest this is a problem here. Nor is drugs – there have been no issues at all in recent years).

Not bullying free, but trained student anti-bullying ambassadors and the promise of prompt response to any issues all help. 'We take robust action when any issues come to light,' says head and parents concur. 'My daughter was on the receiving end of some nasty behaviour and it was stopped immediately.' Another told us, 'I've had a couple of issues, but I emailed teachers on a Sunday night and got a phone call back on the Sunday night. They are keen to nip things in the bud.'

Student voice reasonably strong, with students having brought about change in the usual areas like food and uniform, while the head boy and girl also chair a primary school confederation council made up of representatives from the main feeder schools.

Pupils and parents: Huge numbers attend Wednesday morning guided tours in the first half of the autumn term. Lots of affluence (local property prices have gone up, largely thanks to this school), with some having used the independent sector for the primary years, but this is by no means the case for all. 'In fact, one of the reasons I love this school is because it's socially varied and not all one type,' one parent told us. The furthest come from 10 miles away, with most pupils getting one of the seven contract coaches, while others get public buses, cycle or walk. 'A few are dropped off by car, but not many,' says the head. Families are 90 per cent white British – a reflection of the area.

Great sense of community for such a large school, and most families that send their eldest here also send subsequent children, even if they have wildly different personalities and strengths. 'I have three very different children at the school – including one with special needs – and they've all flourished. I couldn't have asked for more.'

Notable alumni include Tom Felton (played Draco Malfoy), Tom Shanklin (rugby union), Emelia Gorecka (athlete) and Dan Gallgher (footballer).

Entrance: Predictably over-subscribed for 240-place year 7 entry, with over three applicants for every one place. The seven-tiered local authority entry criteria is pretty standard and basically means that anyone living in Horsley (East and West) is in; ditto Howard-facing Fetcham inhabitants. Those with siblings at the school are in with a stronger chance, though priority status is given to those living within catchment area. Combination of proximity and attendance at feeder primaries (Oakfield, Eastwick, St Lawrence, The Raleigh, The Dawnay and The Royal Kent, among others) is the next best bet.

For sixth form – which sees between 20-30 students joining from other schools – net is cast a bit wider. School welcomes applicants from a range of private and state sector – and gets them. 'Normally, we expect the equivalent of five Cs at GCSE and at least a B in the chosen subjects,' says the head.

Exit: Around 25-30 per cent leave at 16, many for sixth form colleges – although interestingly, a number of these students (some years, as many as 10) return to the school during the academic year. Of those who leave after sixth form, over 95 per cent stay in education. Assortment of subjects studied, including STEM, psychology, geography, business and economics. Destinations also varied, with current popular ones including Nottingham, Southampton, Bristol and Exeter. In 2016, 19 to Oxbridge – 13 to study science, maths or engineering.

Remarks: High-quality education from a serious-minded and effective school. Minute attention to detail and inspired teaching ensures that, for a large school, nobody slips through the net, with strong results in both absolute and value-added terms. A well-oiled machine that students are rightfully very proud of.

Hurst Lodge School

Bagshot Road, Ascot, Berkshire SL5 9JU

Pupils: 183; 34 weekly and flexi boarders • Ages: 3–18 (boarding from 9) • Sixth form: 14

Fees: Day £5,040 – £25,200; Boarding £13,835 – £34,005 pa

Tel: 01344 622154
Email: admissions@hurstlodgesch.co.uk
Website: www.hurstlodge.co.uk

Principal: Since 2013, Miss Victoria (Vicky) Smit BSc (40s). Had an earlier stint as head between 1998 and 2011. But, concerned about the propriety of being both co-owner and head (her brother, Sir Tim Smit, started the Eden Project and the school belonged to their mother), she appointed another head in her place for a brief period. It didn't work and Miss Smit is once again head.

This former Hurst Lodge girl, who 'has been 23 years in the place,' bounced into our meeting in rather fetching wellies, waterproof trousers and trackie top. She had been helping out at Hurst Lodge's forest school and was clutching a wet teddy – which she handed to her assistant with the comment that 'he needs to have his bum dried.'

Previously worked with the army and a team of agricultural management consultants but helped her mother move the school in 1999 and never left. A forest school leader (younger Hurst Lodge pupils learn how to take risks in the real world), she has undertaken 'multi-discipline training' (which sounds a bit like being qualified in common sense). A joy – rather like the best possible Girl Guide, favourite aunt or big sister. She bubbled with enthusiasm, giggled and waxed lyrical and we positively skipped round the school, hopping up the odd staircase to avoid being mown down by busy children. (Our notes actually say: 'bubbly, bouncy, loving'.)

Academic matters: Not a Russell Group route. School is non-selective and mixed ability. One third are on the SEN register – the majority are on the dys-spectrum: dyslexia, dyspraxia, dyscalculia, plus Asperger's, high functioning autism, ADD, ADHD, epilepsy, diabetes. Mild Tourette's, but no pupil who 'would disrupt the balance of the class' is accepted. All children with SEN are assessed prior to entry. Taster for all, sometimes two or three tasters (and usually after the third, the answer is no). Two SENCos, eight staff with 'SEN commitment,' tiny caring classes (10 the norm for GCSE, max 18).

H

Children are withdrawn for support from mainstream classes – between one and five lessons per week (charged as extra, same as individual music lessons). Some statemented children have learning support assistants in class and a number of students attend sessions with the speech therapist. Timetables are adaptable, nothing is written in stone. Gifted children either work with the class above or attend special extension classes. EFL support on tap. The odd GCSE module taken early. Parents and guardians invited along to relevant assessment meetings with ed psychs and SENs, co-training sessions and open discussion with and by all concerned with any particular pupil's problems. Regular reports home and school hopes that parents will be upfront about concerns and vice versa. School both small enough to care and big enough to pull punches.

Spanish from 2+; French from 12. Baby science room and tremendous playroom and studio theatre.

At GCSE a full range of subjects on offer. Double science, triple science, interactive white boards, computers, everything you might expect from a mainstream school. Students take an average of 11 GCSEs each, 'as in 10.5 GCSEs each, of which seven are academic and three and a half arty.' Wide range of traditional academic subjects alongside more vocational stuff – dance and performing arts. BTec in childcare, in-house nursery and placements available (next step perhaps to follow Norland into self-defence?)

In 2016, 24 per cent A*/A GCSE grades. Difficult to quantify results from such a tiny cohort. Some subjects offered as IGCSE or BTec, which school says gears 'subject delivery to individual need.' For most, each exam passed, at whatever level, is the result of a massive joint pupil/parent/teacher input and a huge boost to self esteem and morale.

Academic change is in the air and new enhanced sixth form programme began in September 2014. This has 'a slightly different focus' and subjects offered include business studies, English, history of art, Spanish, French, environmental studies, art, textiles, photography, drama, and music. In 2016, 54 per cent A*-B and 25 per cent A*/A grades (from a tiny cohort).

Pupils say that teachers go out of their way to explain things and really take time. 'We get lots of attention; our teachers are amazing,' we were told. School practises a total immersion approach – if, for instance, the history project is the Tudors, then it is Tudor in the art room, Tudor exploration in geography, Shakespeare, Marlowe and probably lampreys for all at lunch time.

The most recent ISI inspection found the school to be 'excellent.' So did we, and we loved the idea that the principal would happily cancel all lessons to have a gigantic snowball fight. Or get the entire school to make kites and fly them one windy day, while the music department blasted 'Let's go fly a kite' on mega-megaphones.

Games, options, the arts: Terrific. Halfway to a stage school, with all students studying performing art (including ballet and modern tap) until the age of 14 – boys too. Hair workshop (dancers' buns – natch) and make-up lessons. Some pupils combine school with performing in the West End, while others take part for the hell of it. Two amazing (odd floor surface – slightly bungey) dance studios which link up to provide the most impressive performance space. Huge LAMDA take-up. Large numbers go on to further dance, ballet, modern, tap and jazz, ditto drama. Southern circuit national drama heats held here. Principal is the Independent Schools' Association National Arts Co-ordinator and in charge of national drama, art and essay competitions. Eighty per cent of pupils learn a musical instrument and most take voice lessons. Recording studio on site.

Mind-blowing creative arts, undoubtedly amongst the best fabric/art portfolios we have seen in any school. Outstanding. We were seriously impressed by a quilted memory box with fabric detail of professional standard. Artwork round the school wasn't that bad either and sewing machines and cookers vied for space in the art/craft room. Life class, computer aided art, Photoshop. Practical cookery lessons preferred to the more theoretical food tech – optional at 15 and compulsory for sixth formers. Ceramics, sculpture and animation (there's also a wowser YouTube video online of Buff Orpington eggs hatching as part of school's eco project).

International sportsmen/women (and an Olympian or two) are allowed two weeks off for competitions during the year. Swimming important – school has open air 25m pool, surrounded by child-inspired gardens. Lifesaving, tennis, footie with the local village club on Saturday, riding Tuesdays, polo Thursdays, netball, hockey, rounders, karate and athletics, judo.

Pupils grow veggies in a polytunnel, and a nearby pen is full of weird and wonderful ducks and chooks (their eggs currently off the agenda until six weeks after worming). This is a hands-on smallholding and we were constantly interrupted during our tour by little people asking 'if they could help feed the hens.' The head replied: 'tomorrow we have to put cream on them. Do you think you could hold them?' Bees – and school makes own honey. For many pupils, this hands-on approach to life beyond the classroom or their (sub)urban roots is their first taste of how the other half lives.

Forest school is important at Hurst Lodge, with younger pupils (kindergarten to 11 year olds) all enjoying role play and exploration. In the real Hurst Lodge world (a bit like Enid Blyton's if that's not a dirty word), pupils learn how to take risks and set their own boundaries. They may not wave sticks about but they climb trees ('they mustn't climb higher than they can get down from,' says the head), build shelters, light fires and make their own seesaws with real saws, branches and logs. They fabric besoms, build forts from wood and burn them down – 'a practical lesson in why wood gave way to stone in ancient times as a building material.' This is idyllic childhood stuff. The young learn to work as a team and have survival days in all weathers. Parents occasionally complain about the lack of homework and are assured that their young have learned how to negotiate, use their imagination and identify various trees by bark and by leaf. This is grown up stuff – serious companies call it bonding and charge heaps.

Learning for life classes important throughout, but particularly at the top end where pupils are prepared for the world outside. Strong links with the Eden Project started by Tim Smit, and work experience there, as well as on the school's own smallholding. This is sustainability education at its best.

Pupils are taught interview techniques (and what to wear), public speaking, sex education, first aid, flower arranging (well, you never know), deportment, proper etiquette, how to lay a table, which glasses to use for what wine and how to reply to formal invitations (might be quite clever to offer a level 2 food hygiene certificate so the little darlings could get proper paid holiday jobs). Staff brainstormed to come up with a list of skills that proved most useful in later life and this programme is the result.

Mega collection of after-school clubs. School estimates that only about 20 per cent of pupils go straight home after school – all the others (usually fortified with a cake and drink from the canteen) stay to do extra activities. Dance of all descriptions, ballet, tap, jazz, modern. Pupils can take a GCSE after hours, if they can't fit it into their timetable, plus all the usual sport, arts and crafts, gardening, electronics, public speaking, and polo. Staff stay on too; mathematical challenge popular plus knitting, touch typing...

Boarding: Small boarding house upstairs in school proper, max 38. Students can board from the age of 9. Weekly or flexi boarding or odd night. Small size means the students have friends of all ages and it's run like a large family, with students and staff sitting down to breakfast and supper together. Ofsted reckoned the boarding provision to be 'outstanding.'

Three/four to a room (the most recent conversion still smelled of paint during our visit, having been subdivided the previous week) and a third boy joined the other couple of boarders three weeks into term. Pupils can start at any time assuming there's space available and with the taster caveat previously mentioned. We much enjoyed a short chat with the (married) housemistress who tries to make life as homelike as possible, organising trips to the cinema, board games, bread making, barbies and 'going off-site.' In-house wickedness equals discussion, followed by 'house chores'. Buddy system of the same age for new boarders. Girls have a splendid dolls' house and Wendy house and boys their own common room. Waiting list for boarders at some ages.

Background and atmosphere: Founded as a dance school in London in 1942 by Doris Stainer, a formidable woman with a cane. The school has grown and moved several times since then – to its current 22-acre site on the outskirts of Ascot in 1997. Main school building is nostalgically Victorian with extensive add-ons, including kindergarten, classrooms and studio block. Jolly modern nursery for tinies from the age of 3 to 6. Boys are wriggling their way up the school. The tiny chapel – now used for choir practice – has rather fun stained glass and a very low door to ensure that one slightly bolshy incumbent actually made obeisance to the altar.

Children deeply involved in the food they eat and catering staff happily join them at mealtimes to discuss future menus and their respective nutritive values. This is an all-embracing outlook on education, celebrating every achievement and keen to boost self confidence. Supervised homework, limited access to the internet and constant advice regarding social media and cyber-bullying.

The recent addition of boys is gradually having an effect. It started when one boy – a sibling – was taken on to help a family in need and snowballed from there. A third of pupils are boys, most of whom, to be honest, are in the junior school. But as co-ed credentials fairly recent, numbers growing. Three boy boarders as we write. School ain't for all boys though. Unsurprisingly, it's the fathers who have the biggest problem with hearing their sons may be dancing (optional for boys as they may choose an alternative such as sport or technical lighting), but could suit some gentler souls who might flounder in a large, male-dominated environment.

Pastoral care, well-being and discipline: Ofsted found pastoral care to be 'exceptional.' Not many rules – they are summed up as 'accept everyone.' Pupils have a good relationship with staff – friendly but respectful. One of the worst sanctions is apparently that head is 'disappointed.' Polite pupils stand up when teachers and visitors enter a room.

Non-denom, 'global mix'; church for Christmas, synagogues visited, comparative religion taught (though veggie not kosher). Proper wrap-around care, from brekky at 7.45am to supper at 5.45pm. Assembly for all on Tuesdays, plus the odd parent. Neat tartan pinafores and tweed hacking jackets for all.

Pupils and parents: Locals from a 30-mile radius. Boarders from Birmingham, Cornwall, plus a fair sprinkling from overseas, Korea, Japan, Africa. Working parents appreciate the good before and after-school care provided. Boon for all: 'There's so much laid on here that I don't need to run myself ragged taking them to activities outside,' one told us. 'They can even have some tea here and then do their homework. It's a real help.' Number of first time buyers, plus old girls' children. Notable old girls include Duchess of York, actresses Juliet Stevenson and Claudie Blakley and TV presenter Emma Forbes.

H

Entrance: More or less at any time into any age group. Non-selective, but 'pupils need to fit in to the class without altering its dynamic significantly,' says principal. Twelve-year-old would-be pupils spend a day here, with papers in English, maths and reasoning – more of a placement test than entrance exam. At all other times, they spend a taster day (or two or three: ditto those with SEN hiccups) at the school, during which they will be assessed 'to ensure that they can access the school's curriculum.' Special needs children are assessed by the learning support team who need a copy of their last ed psych report or EHC plan. No place offered if the school reckons they can't offer the right kind of support.

New pupils welcome at any time throughout the year assuming there's space available (often from the state sector in the run-up to Christmas or in instances where 8/9-year-olds are overwhelmed by transition to independent preps).

Exit: Chaps sometimes leave at 11 for trad preps, including Woodcote House, Hall Grove and Papplewick. Nearly all junior girls move up to senior school. Around two-thirds leave after GCSEs, many for art college or performing arts courses, leaving a tiny sixth form.

Money matters: Academic, dance, drama, music and art scholarships on offer. Be warned that there are extras to pay – LAMDA exams, special needs support, after-school care etc. Discounts for siblings and Forces families. 'Lost a few' in the recent recession, but numbers are stable, with rather more refugees from the state system.

Remarks: It is not often that this long-time Good Schools Guide editor comes out of a school with a happy buzz that lasted all the way back to London, and even now, when faced with the computer, still feels that all can be right with the world. A happy mainstream school that's not afraid of a special need or two. And it doesn't have to be anything major – also good for helping pupils who just need a little bit extra individual attention to help them succeed, whatever their talents. Unusually strong performing arts programme. No amazing sparkly facilities, just spoonfuls of common sense and human kindness.

Hurstpierpoint College

College Lane, Hurstpierpoint, West Sussex BN6 9JS

Pupils: 1,109; 374 boarders, majority flexi • Ages: 4-18 • Sixth form: 320 • C of E

Fees: Day: £8,535 – £22,425; Boarding: £26,235 – £32,970 pa

Tel: 01273 833636
Email: registrar@hppc.co.uk
Website: www.hppc.co.uk

H

Headmaster: Since 2005, Mr Tim Manly BA MSc (40s). Educated at St Edward's Oxford followed by Oriel College, Oxford, where he read classics. He had always wanted to go into the teaching profession and after six years as a headhunter in the City and an MSc in industrial relations from the LSE, he went to Cambridge to do his PGCE at the age of 30. Says it was the best decision he every made and has never looked back. Spent six years at Sevenoaks, where he became head of classics and housemaster, before moving to Oakham as deputy head. Married to Henny; they have four children in the school.

He arrived when Hurst was treading water and has taken it from strength to strength and increased the numbers from 630 to 1,030 (for all three schools). He has raised the intellectual atmosphere, but 'feels that academic achievement is not an end in itself but a key to future success – life is about personal bests and engaging with opportunities'. Manners, civility and courtesy are his personal crusades, and pupils are strongly encouraged to write thank you letters and reply to invitations. He is a man of extraordinary energy who does not believe in down time, apart from the odd brief escape to his cottage in Wales. Feels there is no room for complacency as things can slip very quickly. The staff room has been revitalised, and about 70 per cent of teaching staff have joined since he took over. One pupil said, 'The headmaster makes people want to do well for him'. His door is always open and he knows children and parents by name.

Prep school head: Since September 2013, Mr Ian Pattison, previously a housemaster at the senior school.

Academic matters: In 2016, nearly 52 per cent A*/A at A level, 77 per cent A*/B. At GCSE, 68 per cent A*/A. Strong sciences and maths at A level. Pupils can do A level in their native language eg Dutch and Polish. IB offered since September 2011 – average point score 38 in 2016. The school offers the A1 language paper in German. The head would like to see the IB embedded as a viable alternative to A levels and would like about 40 to choose IB each year whilst 100 do A levels. About 30 per cent of A level students take the extended project qualification. Need to get an A or A* in GCSE in subjects to be studied at A Level or IB.

Challenge grades are particularly popular with parents. Based on IQ tests, an ambitious but, with hard work, achievable grade is set at the beginning of each academic year. Children are assessed through challenge grade reviews every three to four weeks and these, accompanied by teacher comments and a graph to plot progress, are emailed directly to parents. 'Problems are picked up as soon as they arise and there are no nasty surprises,' says one happy parent. Children meet their tutors each week to discuss academic progress. There is a strong work ethic throughout the school; children are set extra work during the holidays and half term and are encouraged to take initiative and responsibility in all aspects of their lives.

As with the senior school, prep has upped the academic ante and offers a fairly academic but rounded education – plenty of help for bright dyslexics but those with low general ability might struggle. Expectations are high and children are set in maths and English from year 3 and in all subjects for years 7 and 8. They are well prepared for the scholarship exams, and although there is a level playing field with those coming from outside, they get about half the awards and do particularly well in drama, music and sport. As in the senior school, it is all about aiming high and fulfilling potential. The top two years are housed in the academic quad of the senior school, which makes transition easier. iPads have been introduced for years 7 and 8 (and put on the bill) and have transformed learning eg nth term formula can be taught in 10 minutes. Digital tasks bring together a range of subjects and make learning more exciting and fun.

Good SEN department with three full-time and four part-time teachers – about 15 per cent of pupils need some support, mainly for mild dyslexia and dyspraxia; this is charged for.

Foreign nationals who want to join the sixth form are screened for English before arrival. EAL compulsory for anyone who needs it and is included in full boarding fee for international students. Although there is a well-stocked library, the use of text books is diminishing in favour of electronic media; increasingly, work is done on subsidised iPads, and the academic block bristles with Apple Macs. Plenty of careers guidance – sixth formers are given interview skills coaching and help with writing cvs. Parents and pupils can attend presentations on UCAS and there are gap year fairs and seminars. All are encouraged to take part in Young Enterprise initiative where pupils have the opportunity to create and run their own business – they were the local prize winners for best company recently. OJ Club of former pupils very supportive of the careers programme and many come back to make careers presentations and offer executive shadowing schemes.

Games, options, the arts: Prep considered locally as quite a sporty school, with particularly strong rugby – the school recently won the Sussex Cup and Sussex rugby sevens. Encourages a 'can do' attitude and no one is left on the bench if they want to play in a team. No stigma if you are not the athletic type as long as you do something – kayaking and orienteering popular with those who hate team sports.

Games are compulsory in the first year of seniors but after that, those who hate team sports can do something else eg outdoor pursuits or health-related fitness programme monitored by the school. Lots of enthusiastic teachers mean that most people find something they enjoy – biking, surfing, kayaking, sailing etc. Everyone has to do at least three exercise sessions a week, reducing to two in the sixth form, and most keep going with sport. Minor sports include fencing golf, shooting, triathlon, power-walking and riding – Hurst sponsors the annual schools' competition at Hickstead. House and inter-school competitions in the major sports and many minor sports eg water polo and cross-country running. 'Everyone has a chance to play in a team if they want to – the school will put together a team and find a fixture.' Everyone encouraged to have a go and 'you don't have to be good but just have fun' – it is hoped pupils will find a sport they want to continue after they leave. Lots of sport played at county level and occasionally pupils are selected to represent their country.

Lots of music in the prep and about half learn an instrument – big orchestra plus smaller bands and choirs, and the chapel choir is particularly popular. Lots of drama, with four plays a year, plus one for talented actors in year 8. LAMDA, public speaking competitions, poetry recitals and assemblies all good for building confidence. Vibrant music department in the seniors too with orchestra, jazz band and wind band as well as various ensembles and quartets; some 140 in the choir. Class music compulsory in Shell (year 9) and the whole school is involved in some way in the annual house music competition.

Huge range of activities from car racing to rock climbing and all Remove (year 10) do silver Duke of Edinburgh award through the CCF. The school has set up a farming project in conjunction with Plumpton College with pigs (one of the pigs is used for the Boar's Head Feast), chickens, fruit trees and a conservation group where children can learn countryside skills like hedge-laying. The aim is that they discover what they enjoy and develop life-long hobbies and interests.

Art room open to all – not just those studying for public exams. Photography, textiles, ceramics, sculpture, graphics as well as drawing and painting. Drama is offered at GCSE and A level as well as an extracurricular activity. There is a Shakespeare play each year and a musical most years as well as lots of small productions in the drama studio – often student directed. There is a playwright in residence with weekly workshops for those who want to write for theatre.

Dance compulsory for Shell (year 9) and is also offered at GCSE and A level. Increasingly popular with boys and girls – contemporary dance, breakdancing, hip hop, street dance all offered. Trips all over the world – community expedition to Malawi, cultural exchange to China, plus subject trips to eg Italy, Barcelona, Iceland.

Boarding: Just under half of the seniors board to some degree – mostly flexi (equal numbers of girls and boys), often three nights a week, but nearly 90 weekly boarders. Full boarding not offered until sixth form and tends to be for foreign nationals. There are 10 houses up to lower sixth divided into day and flexi-boarding – with a strong system of pastoral care and communal responsibility and a tradition of inter-house competition.

Background and atmosphere: Founded in Shoreham in 1849 by the educational pioneer Nathaniel Woodard. It moved to its present purpose-built site in 1853 and the chapel was finished in 1865 – a beacon of Victorian muscular Christianity. Set in 140 acres, with views to the South Downs and surrounded by playing fields. From a distance it could be mistaken for a monastic community, but this first impression belies a vibrant and forward-looking school. Constant updating and refurbishment – the science and DT blocks were refurbished, the new academic quad was unveiled, second Astroturf completed a few years ago and new digital library underway.

The mantra 'achieving your personal best' permeates all aspects of school life, not just academic but also participation in sport and clubs, activities and social relationships. When the school was founded in the 19th century, 'ancient' ceremonies were introduced to give it a feeling of tradition and history. There are banner ceremonies and on Ascension Day, everyone climbs the nearby Wolstonbury Hill for a special service, and the headmaster distributes 'Lowe's Dole', money left by the first headmaster for the choir. The Boar's Head procession and Feast at the end of the Michaelmas term, when a boar's head is carried through the cloisters accompanied by the choir singing a 16th century hymn, is one of the highlights of the school year.

Pastoral care, well-being and discipline: There is a robust anti-bullying policy, a representative from each year group in each house sits on the school council, and house guardians are chosen for their approachability to discuss any social issues within the house. The lower sixth act as prefects, mentor the younger children, are responsible for the day-to-day running of the houses and supervise prep and lights out. Sniffer dogs and random drugs testing from time to time – all sounds a bit alarming but Hurst does not have a drugs problem.

Upper sixth has its own house, St John's, which is set apart from the main school buildings and is more like a hall of residence where everyone has their own study bedroom. Co-ed, with girls and boys in separate wings, which are alarmed at night. Students have their own common room, kitchen, computer room and laundry room. They run their own lives, but are not cut off from the rest of the school, and organise school functions and charity events; all the sixth form have to do some form of community service.

Hurst is a Christian school and the chaplain plays a major part in school life, but Christianity is not imposed on anyone. Pupils encouraged to recognise spiritual dimension and to develop a strong moral compass and sense of duty. Compulsory Friday evening chapel marks the end of the school week. No Saturday school, just sport, activities and play rehearsals.

Pupils and parents: Around 95 per cent live within about 45-50 minute drive. Head wants to keep the school local with an international dimension. Tweeded landed gentry, city commuters, medics and local farmers and businesspeople. Good network of school minibuses run morning and evening from as far away as Hove, Copthorne, Lewes, Seaford, Forest Row and Horsham. 'Very parent friendly, and school bends over backwards to make life easy for parents,' said one working mother – the weekly and flexi-boarding option and no Saturday school particularly popular. Parents particularly praise the very good communication via emails and newsletters and the regular parent-teacher meetings Active parents' association runs social events – coffee mornings, barbecues, inter-house quizzes and the Christmas fair.

Famous former pupils include Admiral Sir Michael Boyce, chief of the defence staff in the Gulf War, various MPs and ambassadors, former general secretary of the National Association of Head Teachers, Sir David Hart, actor Michael York and film director Ronald Neame.

Entrance: Most prep entrants into reception, year 3 and year 7 but spaces occasionally available in other year groups. Reception applicants spend an hour or so on group activities and games in current reception class. Year 3 applicants spend a day at the school that includes reasoning, maths and English tests as well as fun activities and games. Year 7 applicants sit the ISEB pre-test in verbal and non-verbal reasoning, maths and English plus an interview. They are looking for children who are prepared to 'have a go' and take advantage of the opportunities. Not super selective, but they need to be of at least average ability; school wants all children to be able to move on to the senior school if they wish. The senior school entry exams and scholarships are towards the end of the summer term, so there is none of the usual slacking after common entrance. A number come in from other prep schools and local primary schools at 11+ and most of those who enter in year 3 come up from the pre-prep.

Senior school not hugely selective, with ISEB common pre-test in year 7, offers subject to 55 per cent pass rate at common entrance in maths, English and science, 50 per cent in other subjects. Keeping a fairly broad church becomes increasingly difficult as the waiting list grows. School's own exams in English, science and maths for those coming from schools which do not prepare for CE. Doesn't cull after GCSEs. Many come up from Hurst's own prep school; others come from local prep schools, eg Windlesham House, Great Ballard, Dorset House, Great Walstead, Pennthorpe, St Aubyns, Westbourne House and Handcross Park. Some from local primaries and a few from London day schools. Some 40-50 join in sixth form. Need an A* or A in subjects to be studied plus a minimum of a C in maths and English or the equivalent in home country. Occasionally spaces in year 10 at start of GCSE course – entry by school's own tests. Almost at capacity, with waiting lists in some years – does not want to get much bigger as will grow out of the chapel – already building a gallery.

Exit: Very few leave at 11+. Nearly all move on to the college at 13+ but a few leave, either because it is decided that they would not be able to keep up or want to go elsewhere. Will prepare children for entry and scholarships to other schools.

About 20-25 per cent leave after GCSEs, often to go to sixth form colleges – do not lose any to competitor schools. Send to a wide range of universities (most to Russell Group and 1994 Group), including several to Oxbridge each year (eight in 2016, plus two medics). Others to a good range of universities – Loughborough, Birmingham, Exeter and Bristol popular. About half take a gap year.

Money matters: Means-tested bursaries, sibling discounts and special bursaries to help children of former pupils. Range of awards at 13+ and for the sixth form – academic, art, sport, drama and IT worth up to £1,600 per term – can be topped up by means-tested bursaries. Also means-tested bursaries to take a child to the next stage if parents experience financial hardship.

H

Remarks: A school which is going from strength to strength under the strong leadership of its dynamic headmaster. It is now the first choice for many parents who would traditionally have sent their children further afield. We tried hard to elicit negatives from parents, but everyone was universal in their praise. Fantastic value added, where each child is tracked and challenged to reach their full potential in all areas of their lives, and where they are encouraged to push themselves beyond their comfort zone.

Hurtwood House School

Holmbury St Mary, Dorking, Surrey RH5 6NU

Pupils: 340; mainly boarders. • Ages: 15–18 • Sixth form: 340

Fees: Day £27,225; Boarding £40,839 pa

Tel: 01483 279000
Email: info@hurtwood.net
Website: www.hurtwoodhouse.com

Joint Headmasters: Mr Richard Jackson MA (70s), originally an English teacher, is the founding head. Richard's (we are all on first name terms here) soft-spoken and understated manner belies the weighty and imposing presence of a man who has lived and is still living a remarkable dream, a dream he and his team bring about daily for their privileged students.

Mr Cosmo Jackson BEd (40s) and son of Richard was appointed 2004 to do the main day-to-day running of the school. An alumnus of Charterhouse, Cosmo spent two years at Bristol University not enjoying economics and thence to the University of the West of England to do his – perhaps inevitable – BEd. He was, in all senses, to the manner born, as were the majority of his siblings, their spouses and, quite possibly, ultimately, their offspring as Hurtwood is, triumphantly, a family concern and four other Jacksons are on the staff. Parents seem a little bemused. 'He's very charming but the students don't see much of him once they're in. He doesn't teach anyone.' A pity as he is easy to talk to, smilingly enthusiastic and loves his job.

Academic matters: Contrary to popular opinion, this is not just a school for arty/media types. Sciences are strong and the results across the whole range of subjects are uniformly starry. A levels offered include all three sciences, economics and sociology. Some students yearn for more eg philosophy. Most popular are, unsurprisingly, drama, media, English, maths and psychology. Fine art and textiles an astonishing stand-out success.

Average class size is between eight and 12, often smaller. Teaching is, according to parents, 'pretty excellent' and the students we spoke to were extravagant in their praise, admiration and, in some cases, hero-worship of teachers. The Jackson philosophy is all about bringing in the best and assiduously monitoring both staff and students to ensure that no slacking, laurel-resting or coasting occur. Parents know what they are paying for: 'They're spoon-fed to a terrible degree,' said one, 'but that's why the fees are so enormous.'

According to the Jacksons, success depends on kindness and monitoring. 'Socially and pastorally we are the friendliest school in the world but we're strict when it comes to work.' Cosmo says, 'We have the cosy feel and intimacy of a prep with the academic rigour and maturity of a university.' Weekly staff meetings to check on anyone whose performance causes concern. Everyone graded A1-U5 and staff swift to pick up on anyone not meeting expectations. In 2016, 83 per cent A*-B and 57 per cent A*/A at A level.

No SEN dept – Richard talks of 'enthusiastic amateur support' and acknowledges that among such creative people, the 'dyses' are bound to be common. But, he feels, 'they should, by now, have learned the strategies and techniques to manage their difficulties'.

Games, options, the arts: The glory of Hurtwood and at the heart of its ethos. Arts and media all to professional standards – largely because the teachers are West End/media pros absolutely on top of their game and all the latest in production. And this is the great attraction. We spoke to numerous academically-minded students who had come to Hurtwood because their previous schools offered the chance of one or two productions each year in which they might, or might not, get a part. Here, productions, films, videos of all kinds and sizes roll off the blocks constantly and, if you are of a mind to, you can be constantly engaged in them. Acting 'company', a film 'academy' and a dance 'company' are elite groups restricted to a dozen or so devotees.

No glitzy performing arts centre such as are now routinely found in 'top' schools. The theatre is good, of professional quality and seats 180 though with little backstage or flyroom/ wing space. The students learn the design and building of sets not by doing, but by seeing it done by the pros, very expensively, brought in. This a positive policy decision of the Jacksons. They do learn lighting though, again, lighting pros brought in to do the actual biz in the 'jaw-droppingly good' concerts and shows, as parents concur. 'They walk out of here and could manage a BBC studio,' one thought, 'and those who go on to media courses find they know pretty much everything they do in the first year, at least.' New TV studio complex and edit suite the envy of many strapped production companies.

Around a quarter learn an instrument. A further quarter take singing lessons and a sixth take dance. Music tech is, inevitably, a big deal here with two tech rooms plus recording studio. Art is rich and varied – impressive and imaginative portfolios emerge from the small studio down the track through the woods. Costume design makes practical use of textiles skills and the results are stunning. Monthly newsletter produced in-house and largely by students is a slick, cool number.

Games an also-ran. It's just not why you come. 'If you want to do a sport, you're pretty much in the team,' we were told by an enthusiast who gave up his place in his elite's school's elite first XI to come here. There's a football pitch, all weather-hockey/

basket ball pitches, two tennis courts, a new sports pavilion, so it's there if you want it. Pool and table tennis around the place as well.

Boarding: Around 50 boarders live in the upper floors of the main building. Not over-roomy or over-appointed but perfectly adequate and with inspiring views. The rest in houses within a short bus ride – school keeps a fleet of buses which shuttle to and fro. All boarding houses are attractive and interesting architecturally though the loveliness of the interiors varies according, as much as anything, to taste. But most parents agree, 'it doesn't worry the pupils,' and 'the house staff are lovely.' Assuredly, here are not the dinky study bedrooms with en suites and all mod cons found elsewhere. As one parent opined, 'They haven't chucked money at the accommodation, but I'd rather have good teaching than smart bedrooms.'

Background and atmosphere: Richard Jackson conceived his school way back in the late 1960s and it bears the stamp of those idealistic, anything-is-possible, heady and experimental days. Hurtwood's first incarnation was in a building rented from the National Trust and he looked for three years until he lighted on this lovely house in its perfect spot. It was always to be a 16-19 school, GCSEs being, for Richard, 'the absolute natural breaking point.' And so it has proved.

Set in 25 acres of stunning Surrey rural idyll, the house is a 1900s late arts and crafts, genteel mock Tudor fantasy, beautifully sited on the hills overlooking the North Downs. Getting here is a challenge as the road darkens and narrows, winding though and over the wooded hillsides – reminding one just how rural Surrey can still be, though each bend has a gated entrance with entryphone – this ain't your hill-farming sticks. The place is beautifully kept and the car park must have one of the most privileged views in the country. Downstairs is lovely – a huge and inviting drawing room with coffered ceiling, grand fireplace, sink-into sofas and lots of warm limed oak. Similarly, the library has a wondrous ceiling and, when you look down, a jolly good stock of books, periodicals etc. Dead posh loos too. Less artistically pleasing outbuildings house various subjects and classes, common rooms etc.

Food is 'out of this world'. One parent marvelled at 'the amount they must invest in the kitchen. It's all cooked there – nothing is brought in.' Another enthused, 'I turned up one day out of the blue and there was a dressed salmon!' Breakfasts apparently so good, superlatives fail. Much-loved ice cream machine and barbeque bar.

Pastoral care, well-being and discipline: Pupils and staff on first name terms – works fine although those who come from stiff public schools never quite get used to not saying 'Sir'. Parents praise the 'very secure environment'. Residential 24/7 but students are free to go home at the weekends with permission and around 75 per cent do. No rich programme of activities over the weekends as elsewhere because those who do remain – or come in especially – have rehearsals, projects etc they just can't put down. Occasional weekend activities include hiking, camping in Snowdonia, paragliding, powerboating, high ropes courses and paintballing. School runs buses into Guildford and Cranleigh for shopping etc.

Very strict regs on smoking, drink and drugs. On our trail down to the arts block we met the 'smoking teacher' ready to ambush those having a sneaky drag but, although some parents sighed over these perennial problems, most felt it happened at weekends out of school and school is absolutely resolute against all such folly. Lots of counselling given when needed; random testing for drugs. Mixed boarding houses though sexes on separate floors or wings and 'very-strict no-go areas'. Girls wear black leggings, ankle boots and hoodies and boys wear skinny jeans, trainers and hoodies. Very little self-expression via 'see-me' garb. Sensible attitudes seemed pervasive. If there are any worried parents, we did not find them.

Pupils and parents: Approximately two-thirds are British, mostly from London and the home counties. Rest from, well, everywhere – nationals from 33 countries at the time of our visit. Sixty with EAL needs supported by specialist department. We did hear knots of students talking Chinese but mixing is better than at many schools – largely because productions bring people together. No distinction made or felt between day and boarding students, those who drip wealth and those on scholarships. 'There is,' a clear-eyed student told us, 'an ever-present sense of being part of an elite, but most people are very grounded and it's only with some of those from overseas where you really sense loadsamoney.' Everyone says how well everyone mixes.

Parents also a good mix – many in the arts. School/home links not touchy-feely. One parent said, 'They don't do parents' evenings – such a relief as we're not hands-on parents.' On the other hand, another said that they'd like the teachers to be around when they pick up on Friday evenings and a third echoed the feeling that she didn't get a chance to know her son's teachers.

Notable former pupils include Nikki Amuka-Bird, Emily Beecham, Phoebe Boswell, Emily Blunt, Amelia Brightman, Ben Chaplin, Amelia Curtis, William El-Gardi, Edward Fox, Aidan Gillen, Sam Harrison, Jack Huston, Tom Mison, Leah Wood, Hans Zimmer, Hannah Herzsprung.

Entrance: There are 150-170 vacancies each year (55 per cent girls and 45 per cent boys). No open days, it's much more personal here. School says, 'We are looking for students who are going to make a positive contribution to our community. Character, personality, willingness, cheerfulness, liveliness, helpfulness, maturity, a sense of responsibility and a strong sense of purpose are all qualities that we are looking for.' Admissions criteria like these – in all their triumphantly civilised vagueness – are not found everywhere.

Parents and prospective pupil are seen by the head and the interview usually lasts over an hour. Then, if you are still keen, you register and apply. What matters is whether you will fit in and make the most of the opportunities on offer. Some turned down at that point, a few, obviously outstanding, applicants are offered an immediate place, subject to reference, at that stage; the rest are put in a 'pool' for selection later in the year. Oversubscribed and currently a waiting list of around 50-60, entirely acceptable, hopeful would-bes. Places not dependent on GCSE results (except for eg the sciences and maths).

Exit: To a surprisingly mixed bunch of courses at a very wide range of unis from Oxbridge (four in 2016) to California eg LSE, Durham, Bristol, King's College London, Warwick, Imperial. Music, art (13 in 2016), drama (11) and film courses, as you'd expect but maybe fewer than you'd expect. Quite a few engineering and business management degrees. School runs its own agency, now headed by Emily Blunt.

Money matters: Famously and unashamedly expensive. Until you get here and sense the quality it's hard to gauge quite why. Two performing arts scholarships on offer annually worth 50 per cent of fees; two more at 25 per cent. Jacksons use their discretion to support those who deserve it and need it. Definitely worth trying, especially if you are local and utterly determined to succeed.

Remarks: Unique and impossible to label or compare. If you're talented, hard-working, collaborative, appreciative of opportunities and in love with performance and production, you'll have a stunning time.

Immanuel College

Elstree Road, Bushey Heath, Bushey, Hertfordshire WD23 4EB

Pupils: 638 • Ages: 4–18 • Sixth form: 126 • Jewish

Fees: £9,390 – £16,500 pa

Tel: 020 8950 0604
Email: admissions@immanuel.herts.sch.uk
Website: www.immanuelcollege.co.uk

Head Master: Since 2012, Mr Charles Dormer MA (40s). Born in New York into a third generation Jewish-American family, and initially educated there, but had most of his formative education in the UK – has dual American and British citizenship. He studied English at Magdalene College Cambridge at the age of 17 and had arranged to continue his PGCE at Cambridge, but was offered the opportunity to teach at St Dunstan's College. Went on to launch media studies at Colfe's School, leaving there to work in the preparatory sector: 'I was keen to discover what made literacy work for young people.' In 2002, he became head of English and then director of studies and deputy head at Westcliff High School for Boys, rapidly turning round English results: 'I did the job which I was told couldn't be done.' First headship at the King's School, Grantham (Sir Isaac Newton's school); came back south when the opportunity of being head of Immanuel College arose.

We heard Mr Dormer before we saw him – large voice and somewhat imposing character. We entered his office with some trepidation, but our worries were unfounded. This is one witty head teacher. Razor sharp, acerbic and an amazing raconteur. (If Stephen Fry ever retires from public life..) One staff member told us that it was not unusual for her and other staff members to be in stitches, during staff meetings. However, he takes his job of being head of the school very seriously – a position he feels privileged to have; 'The minute I walked into this school, I felt like I had come home.'

This is no mean feat for someone who had a very transient early life. His father died when he was 8 years old, and he was sent from New York to live in London with his aunt and attend an independent school there: 'School was everything to me, my teachers were my role models and education became my life.' He admits that he would've given anything to have been offered the opportunity to study at a school like Immanuel, as being a Jewish boy in Leyton in the 1970s 'wasn't a bundle of laughs.' Immanuel, he says, is a 'school where everyone is treated with genuine respect – we rarely have to be authoritative.' Mr Dormer embraces the challenge of working in an independent school set up to give Jewish children a British public school education: 'In the state sector, people are often trodden down by politics and it is very hard to maintain a social and moral spiritual line.'

Rarely does this head allow himself any down time (12 hour days are commonplace), but when he does, he enjoys cooking, reading, walking and swimming. However, he calls his job 'a labour of love', and says that if you are doing the job properly, there really is no proper holiday time: 'You can't be off duty, especially in a Jewish school.'

Prep school head: Since 2012, Mrs Alexis Gaffin BEd (Cantab). Educated at Haberdashers' Aske's School for Girls, South Hampstead High School and Homerton College, Cambridge, where she read education and religious studies. Worked in state primaries in Manchester, before spending three years in Israel. Took some time out when her four children (now aged 14 to 21) were young, before returning to Noam Primary in Wembley, where she went from 'very part-time' to 'very full-time' as deputy head. An Ashdown Fellowship raised her sights to 'team leadership', and a subsequent visit to Immanuel changed her life: 'I said I've found my job...Thankfully they found me, too.' An early years specialist, she continues to take all children for PSHE: 'I may not know everyone's reading level, but I know their personality, know who needs support.' Judaism is fundamental to her educational world view. 'I am as Jewish doing maths as when saying my prayers.' Competent, clear-sighted, caring and efficient, she believes the school is very much an extension of the family: 'A postage stamp of my philosophy: build whole, happy people'. Parents praise her highly: 'She cares passionately and gets things done.' Married to a teacher at Hasmonean, in her (limited) free time, she loves to read, cook and bake and 'spend time with my family'.

Academic matters: Prep school teaching largely follows the national curriculum. 'You don't have to reinvent the wheel,' says the head, 'but you shouldn't see it as straight jacket either.' The academic emphasis is on 'structured learning', with a mixture of 'teacher-led' and 'self-initiated' activity. During our visit, activity of the self-initiated sort seemed purposeful and enthusiastic, with two keen 5 year olds rushing to play 'spot the matching words', while, over in the 'vet's corner' a busy crowd was tending its stuffed animals. A further pair tested the sands of time with the help of the head. 'Shake the glass harder. Is the sand going faster?'

The school provides a 'modern Jewish orthodox' education and, as well as a class teacher and teaching assistant, each year group has a designated rabbi to help develop understanding of Jewish customs and practice, as well as an appreciation of biblical and rabbinical texts and love of Israel. Daily morning prayers, plus weekly Sabbath assembly. Specialist teaching, too, in modern Hebrew from year 1, expanding to three full periods of modern foreign languages (two of French, one of Hebrew) in year 3. The head is also contemplating an after-school club in Mandarin (learning herself in order to test-drive the experience).

A part-time SENCo helps provide 'structured intervention' where necessary: 'If we can, we support pupils and provide for their needs,' says the head. More complex matters are addressed by external specialists (at an additional cost).

'We specialise in those pupils who don't believe in themselves as robustly as other children. Anyone can take in A* kids and get A* kids at the end. We spend a significant amount of time in the value added band', says the senior school head. And yet despite this, and the school's historical reputation as being for the wealthy but less able, several years of good, solid results mean that Immanuel can sit proudly alongside its competitors. 2016 saw 64 per cent A*/A grades at GCSE and 70 per cent A*/A at A level. Though it is selective at 11, the academic range is reasonably broad, albeit skewed to the more able. Small class sizes, sometimes as few as 10 in a class, depending on set, means the teachers really have the chance to get to know pupils as individuals. School probably works best for the child who needs close care and attention, rather than the one who needs academic extension. That said, one parent told us: 'One of my children is very academic, the other has mild dyspraxia. The school caters amazingly well for both.' Another parent said: 'What is so nice about the school is that pupils can naturally achieve their potential. There is no sense from the school that you are a failure.'

An independent learning project in year 8 develops research and study skills. Years 10 and 11 setted and top two sets (of four) take IGCSE in English, maths, history, music, and triple science.

Jewish studies forms a fundamental part of the curriculum. Modern Hebrew is taught in years 7, 8 and 9 and students have the option to study biblical Hebrew as well as textual Jewish learning. There are three religious options for sixth formers: A level RE with Judaism and ethics; preparation for Jewish life and an intensive textual course (some pupils go on to study at Yeshiva and seminary); or a course about Jewish wisdom for life called Chochma. Secular A level options include sociology, theatre studies, PE, maths and psychology. A kosher bar/bat mitzvah is a condition of college membership.

'Relationships between staff and pupils are excellent' (ISI), and teaching has been much praised by parents as being very nurturing, caring and aiding in emotional development: 'I've had follow-up calls from teachers to my home', one parent told us. Once appointed, teachers (half of whom are not Jewish) tend to stay. Good and caring special needs provisions for both physical and learning difficulties are another reason why parents choose this school. Despite the upstairs-downstairs site, a specially adapted lift makes all things possible. Outstanding and specialised support and individual learning plans are used as necessary.

Games, options, the arts: Art is a biggie here and for many the reason they chose this school above others – good numbers of sixth form pupils awarded places at St Martins School of Art, or other high profile art institutions. The art we saw was imaginative and innovative, with students enthusiastically explaining to us the thought process behind their work. A few art scholarships for 11+ entry.

A vibrant drama department produces two productions a year, and students excel in their musical theatre examinations. The chief examiner of the London College of Music was 'blown away' by the talent and application of the entire cohort, we are told. Music is part of the core curriculum, but only a handful take it at GCSE. There are three concerts a year.

'We're not hugely well known for our contact sports..but that might be because our children like to keep their teeth!' So says the head. This is not a school where parents prioritise sport, and high level competition is certainly not part of the creed, although in the last five years 'increasing success has been earned by a dedicated and skilled PE department'. Older pupils have access to a small but well-equipped gym, and football, basketball, tennis and netball are played with enthusiasm and success. 2014 saw the first Immanuel Sports Award evening and district trophies were awarded for all the afore-mentioned sports. Football, basketball, tennis, athletics, cricket, badminton and trampolining all available, plus netball and dance (very strong) for girls. One mother told us: 'Because of the class sizes, my daughter gets exposure to all sports which perhaps she might not get in a larger school where she wouldn't necessarily make the team.' The college has adequate rather than inspiring facilities; prettily positioned running track, well used tennis courts.

There is a strong and enthusiastic following for debating, and indeed when we visited, the debating society (versus Mr Dormer) were about to discuss the motion 'why homework should be scrapped.' (Sadly, we couldn't hang around to see the outcome). There is full participation in awards schemes such as Young Enterprise and Duke of Edinburgh awards, and the students are exceptionally ambitious and entrepreneurial: three recent ex-pupils have appeared successfully Dragons' Den, and another is currently working with a winner of The Apprentice. 'We have a phrase here called Tottenham Chutzpah,' said the head, 'and it means that an Immanuel pupil really punches above their weight.'

Plenty on offer at the prep beyond the school day, with clubs in arts and crafts, chess, choir, football, board games, gardening and drama. Individual music lessons, too, in guitar, violin and piano from Year 1, and LAMDA qualifications from year 3. Whole school 'musical extravaganza' held annually, and school play now in the pipeline.

School trips are definitely a strength – the whole of year 9 to Israel for four weeks, the entire year 12 to Poland. One student wrote of his experience to Auschwitz: 'It was a truly powerful moment and helped us to begin to comprehend the scale of our people's tragedy.' Suffice to say, these trips are life-long bonding experiences between the pupils.

Background and atmosphere: Founded in 1991 by the then chief rabbi, Immanuel Jacobovits, who wanted to establish a religious school to rival some of north London's most famous academic names. The core of the building is a magnificent, turreted Victorian pile (formerly a convent school) described by Pevsner as sitting atop its 11 acres of Hertfordshire green belt like a 'Harrogate Hotel'. Plenty of later additions, including the recently opened Bet Knesset (synagogue), funded by one of the parents, which means pupils now have a place to worship on site as well as facilitating those who are shortly about to undertake their bar or batmitzvah. When we visited the school, the new science block was due to be unveiled in the next couple of weeks – a large, sparse space with functional classrooms (not yet decorated with pupils' work). 'Apologies for the industrial look of the new block', the head said: 'This is what comes with having to be bomb-proof, bullet-proof, earthquake-proof.. everything proof.'

Sadly, these added security measures were perhaps never more pertinent then during our visit, which followed a spate of antisemitic attacks in France and the threat of more local ones. We noticed a heavy security presence patrolling the entrance of the school, where parents are no longer allowed to park their cars or loiter. We were told that a new, heavy duty gate was in the process of being built. One parent told us: 'You do worry that sending your child to a Jewish school can potentially put them in a dangerous situation. But the school is doing everything they can to make it as safe as possible like doing regular drills, and parents are kept well informed.'

Once you get past security and enter the school, you are confronted with a bit of a mish-mash – rather like a comfortably shambolic family house. This is definitely no pristine show home like some of its private school contemporaries, and whilst this arguably lends itself to the homely vibe, we couldn't help but feel that a fresh lick of paint, or a few more displays of students' work (particularly the wonderful art), would work wonders to brighten up the place. Clearly, it is not the school's priority, but we wondered if parents were concerned about this at all. After all, this school is still as costly as many of its private contemporaries. One parent told us: 'The building is a bit tatty, but it was the grounds I was impressed with.' Another said: 'It's not something that really bothers me or my daughter at all. It's the privilege of having very small classes with individual attention that we're paying for.'

The students we spoke to seemed to agree. One told us: 'I got offered a place at Haberdashers' and City of London, but chose this school because class sizes were so small and it felt very welcoming.' Another said: 'This school really seems to have the ability to get the best out of us and it caters for everyone.' The pupils we met were a very astute, friendly and well-mannered bunch. 'Happy' was the word banded around from head, to parents, to pupils themselves. 'Because of the size, it has a real family feel,' said one parent.

The prep school shares the senior school's leafy, well-equipped and well-protected campus, but has its own light and spacious new building with a separate playground. Generously-scaled classrooms provide ample accommodation for 20-22 (max) in each year group. Founded in 2011, the prep school is increasing classes yearly. The gaps are filled in as younger ones progress upwards.

Unlike some of its orthodox state school competitors, Immanuel has a relatively modern approach to the faith: 'This school, after all, was founded on the belief that girls should have the same chance as boys', said the head. The school aims to turn out young people who are 'kind and confident, know themselves and help others. They understand where they are going, have a loyalty to being Jewish and a relationship with their faith that is going to continue.' Food is kosher, healthy and appetising (schnitzels on the day we visited). Staff share pupils' dining rooms which, from what we witnessed, are places of eager conversation and thoughtful dialogue.

School does a very good job of involving parents. Every couple of years a trip, solely for parents is organised to Auschwitz, which, as one parent told us 'bonds us completely.' Regular coffee mornings and quizs also organised. Programme of social action in Jewish and wider community a high priority, and a long list of funded charities.

Pastoral care, well-being and discipline: Second to none at this school, and the reason most parents we spoke to chose it above others. One parent told us: 'My son was quite badly bullied in his former school, so we removed him and chose Immanuel because we had heard it was a very nurturing school. He's a completely different boy now and is very happy.' Others said that Immanuel has a reputation of being a 'safe haven', with children joining at random times if they don't get on at their current school.

Two co-heads of year plus four tutors in year 7; designated pastoral leaders in years 8 and 9. Deputy heads constantly available to pupils and parents. Prefects are self-elected – those who are keen to take on the responsibility apply for the post and are interviewed. Once appointed, they play a large part in the life of the school, helping younger people to read Hebrew, organising social events and charity fairs. Jewish identity and prayer is very much part of the ethos. Boys are expected to wear a kippah (head covering) at all times, and years 7-11 have compulsory prayers before class. For sixth formers, prayer is primarily voluntary, but compulsory before the major festivals. It's not a problem for the pupils, the head told us; 'This is a school where it is cool to be observant, but by the same token, nobody makes anyone else feel embarrassed if they are less observant.'

Discipline not particularly high on the agenda, although uniform rules becoming stricter, primarily for religious reasons; 'If a female pupil has her skirt rolled up, she is told to roll it down straight away', one parent told us. However, another parent bemoaned the lack of discipline in other areas, particularly the fact that her daughter seems to be allowed to chew gum in class, or certainly during school hours, 'which amazes me, and I'm not sure why.' No serious concerns about drugs: 'this is an amazingly innocent place, and although we are not blind to it, we have never had to worry about drugs being an issue. Pupils who have a bit more money would prefer to spend it on FIFA World Cup tickets.' Exclusions are virtually non-existent; only three pupils have been suspended in three years, and those were due to 'technology related issues.'

Pupils and parents: Applicants must complete the standard certificate of religious practice form designed by the office of the chief rabbi, but after that the school takes in the full spectrum, from the seriously observant to those who don't attend synagogue, but have an attachment to the Jewish way of life. Immanuel is particularly popular with Sephardic Jews. Pupils tend to be 'very friendly, welcoming, and self assured.' (ISI). While there are many affluent, professional parents from a broad sweep of north London and Hertfordshire, there are also a large number of families assisted by scholarships and bursaries, and modesty, respect and consideration of others are the watchwords. One parented commented that 'you really don't get the feeling here that these kids have it all.' A coach service available, which brings pupils from as far as St John's Wood.

The school prides itself on its family atmosphere and communication with parents is excellent. 'We always feel we know exactly what's going on,' said one. A weekly newsletter keeps them posted on what's happened in class and regular invites are sent out to celebrate religious festivals. Working parents, too, can avail themselves of the before- and after-school clubs.

Entrance: From small beginnings, Immanuel Prep has quickly become oversubscribed and selective. 'We've grown from a few little people and some adults to a highly sought-after school,' says the head. She is, however, still very much looking for a mixed-ability intake. Most new entrants arrive from nursery school, an increasing numbers of siblings among them. The admissions procedure aims to establish 'school readiness': 'We want to see how sociable they are, whether they can listen to instructions.' Not every small child, of course, can, and the head is happy to be flexible. 'They may just be nervous. I'm willing to visit them in their own setting.' Children transferring into existing classes have formal interviews and tests in maths and English. Year 6 applicants are jointly assessed by staff of the senior school. Siblings are given priority throughout, though not guaranteed entry. 'We're not doing a favour to the family if we don't have the facilities to help the child reach their potential.' Some scholarship and bursary funding available.

Selective entry to the senior school, but not overly so – prospective pupils have to sit the college's own 11+ exam, with scholarship papers available in Jewish studies and science, and the school is looking for pupils who can pass GCSE at grade C or above. However, the head says: 'We don't always take students who score highly in exams. We take on board other factors, and in that respect we're no different from Eton.' There is small external intake into the sixth form.

Exit: The vast majority of parents her are looking for a reception-to-sixth-form education and most pupils will proceed seamlessly to the senior school, but not without first demonstrating their capacity to 'access the curriculum'. The head is firm that preparation for senior schools elsewhere is not on offer. 'I'd like everyone to go all through.' That said, each child is given a firm grounding. 'Are we facilitating the child to fulfil their potential? Yes. Are we giving them practice papers? No.'

Good preparation for university – series of seminars, plus tailored individual advice. 'No stone is left unturned. We find courses that suit pupils' strengths'. Also prepares students for any additional tests required for medicine or law. Birmingham tends to be much the most popular university followed by Nottingham; others to a range from Imperial to Reading. Occasional Oxbridge place (one in 2016, and one medic). Many do a gap year in Israel.

Money matters: Not a rich or well endowed school, largely because any extra money raised or donated contributes towards scholarships and the four week trip to Israel, which some pupils can't afford: 'We currently offer nearly 25 per cent of students scholarships in some form or other, either in full or part payment, but we are constantly striving to offer more,' the school told us.

Remarks: Produces confident and well-qualified young people with a deep understanding of their faith.

International School of London in Surrey

Old Woking Road, Woking, Surrey GU22 8HY

Pupils: 204 (currently 72 seniors) • Ages: 2–11 (2–18 until July 2017)

Fees: £18,200– £19,750 pa

Tel: 01483 750409
Email: admissions@islsurrey.org
Website: www.islsurrey.org

Head: Since 2015, Richard Parker (50s); started working in a law firm in the City, which may have been the inevitable job choice for a Cambridge graduate in history, but he left law and went to the Institute of Education, London, trained as a secondary school teacher and taught at several state London schools before he and his wife moved to teach in international schools in Spain, Argentina, Hong Kong, Portugal and Brunei. He knows what it is to be an expat and this experience of different cultures and systems brings a wealth of understanding to the development of International School of London in the Surrey countryside. Married with two children (one of whom attended the school), he lives very locally and is clearly committed to making the school not only a friendly place for families coming in, but also innovative and open in the widest sense. He wants the school to have at its bedrock a 'sense of community' and encourages this with Buddy Parents (who settle new parents in), a transitional programme (allowing for easy entrance and exit for pupils) and the fact that every child has language lessons in their mother tongue, thus valuing each student's own culture. He loves art and weekends are spent in galleries as a restorative relaxation.

Entrance: Admissions officer looks at previous school reports, interviews prospective pupils and their parents and tries to match the needs of the child with the school's resources. Tours of the school available throughout the year and because of the large expat numbers, entrance and exit is flexible, with places coming up mid year sometimes. Expect to meet the head, who likes to know all pupils and is very active in admissions too.

All the staff and parents we spoke to made it clear that the school was genuinely inclusive – parents believed that the inclusive nature of the school enhanced the children's education and added to 'the soft stuff that you can't put your finger on like the warm atmosphere'. Children with learning differences are accepted wherever the school could meet those needs – experience of cerebral palsy pupils, speech and communication difficulties, dyspraxia and dyslexia. Fees are all inclusive – no extra charges for the mother tongue language lessons, learning support, day outings, most clubs.

Exit: As with all international schools, pupils are often moving country. The life of a Third Culture Kid almost inevitably involves moving school before the end of the school life. The junior school tends to keep pupils right through unless the family is relocated. Very few have previously left after primary school, and most continued to senior school whilst that was in place – the senior section at the Surrey branch of ISL will close at the end of the summer term 2017.

Remarks: Modern low level buildings set in wooded area of suburban Woking. Large playing fields and woods around the school with new building projects all round – new theatre, community café and music room, new outside common room, portacabins that will one day be changed no doubt as this school grows from its tiny beginnings to current 204 pupils and longer term plans for doubling those numbers. Airy and modern inside, with very practical spaces – almost all wheelchair accessible. Clearly in need of more organisational systems to deal with the increasing numbers of pupils and staff, but for the moment still very informal and open, no uniform and everyone on first name terms. The relaxed approach can unnerve some parents who have tight schedules and expect super efficiency, but was seen by one parent as a school that tests and improves systems and they liked the idea that 'it is a growing school and our kids are growing with it'.

Privately owned by the Lebanese family who started the International School of London, bought up the Surrey school and now also run an international school in Doha, Qatar. The Makarem family members are still on the board, have weekly updates and visit regularly.

Tiny early years department set up originally for siblings, but growing as a viable alternative to local nurseries thanks perhaps to its extensive outdoor play area. Some questions about whether the nursery will remain in place, however. In the garden space for early years they are gradually exchanging all their plastic equipment for more sustainable materials – we loved the play kitchen with copper, steel and wooden utensils and pots. The first indoor sandpit we have ever seen – very well used, not just for decoration.

Primary classes round an airy atrium with access for each class to an outside play/study area. Small classes with teachers and assistants as well as specialist teachers coming in for music, PE, performance, language acquisition and mother tongue language learning. All classes have a bank of iPads that we saw being used in several of the classes as children typed out work they had previously written and edited. English of varying levels depending on child's level of fluency on arrival with the emphasis on language development and vocabulary followed by more phonic-based work. Maths at a good level and other subjects taught using the International Primary Curriculum – topic-based work covering history, geography, technology, science and art and as many other subjects as can be included. Rainforest corners in several classrooms when we visited, with children preparing a jungle performance, learning songs from the Jungle Book, and fabulous 3D constructions of four levels of the jungle ecosystem. Education through as many styles and strategies as possible – outdoor work, experimentation, technology, performance, debate. This multi-sensory type of learning ideal for a school where children join from so many different countries. Parents spoke of having chosen this school for its ethos of embedding learning 'in a real world context' and 'the creative approach to teaching and the flexible curriculum'.

The work on the walls clearly reflected the way what they learn in class is part of wider world issues – they call it 'enquiry based learning'. 'Kids feel they are developing not being pushed,' according to one parent. 'They are academically stretched but in a nurturing way'.

Pupils say that the strength of the school is teaching them to be individuals and in preparing them to be able to study independently. The fact that each child will bring their own language and culture is acknowledged in a basic tenet of 'individualised learning' whereby each has their own starting point and goals. Eventually the aim is for each – not only special needs pupils – to have their own learning profile, as each pupil has their own learning aims. There are individualised learning coordinators junior who support children with individual lessons where needed but mostly by giving in-class support plus giving teachers strategies for differentiated teaching.

Exciting artwork considering it is a small school with not a huge amount of space, developed by teachers who are clearly motivated and passionate. Emphasis on ideas and self-initiated work in all the arts, and options as well as in the academic area of school.

Sports with specialist PE teachers in the large 'field' outside the school. Swimming weekly at local baths. Netball, football, basketball, a few tournaments with local schools as well as more unusual bubble football, circus skills, dance. A badminton team was set up one year when a child who arrived at the school with no English was found to have great badminton skills – his English soon improved. However, this is not a very sporty school and it was suggested that more inter-school sporting events should be a goal of the PE department. As well as sport, there are generous amounts of outside learning – twice weekly timetabled play in the forested area for the primary students.

Music teacher with passion and commitment bringing more music into the school and a large new music room in construction when we visited has now been finished – school choir and a band plays in assembly as well as during shows and performances that are whole school affairs of some importance. Timetabled twice weekly class music lessons. Individual instrument lessons possible.

Pupils we spoke to said that there were not as many extracurricular options as in a larger school but that 'you were involved' and that 'the school has a family feeling'. There is an award-winning 'transitional programme' which helps support on entrance and exit, especially for expat families. Value placed on moral education and wider learning seen with awards being given for, amongst others, adaptability, resilience, co-operation, morality and thoughtfulness.

Student voice heard loud and clear through student government with reps from all classes and several subcommittees for culture, sport, events etc. Much debating in student government, then voted on in school assembly, then taken to senior management who say their job is to make these decisions reality.

Pupils said the school was 'nice and caring' and the family atmosphere they spoke of was apparent in the way mixed ages were seen outside playing together and looking out for each other. Students appreciated that 'you learned in lots of different ways – not just writing' and that what you learned was related and 'everything fits together'. Confident and socially aware pupils spoke of the school helping them understand 'what I am good at'. Pupils said there was no bullying or unkindness, but the school has an anti-bullying policy so they are not oblivious to the possibility. A full-time school counsellor with an open door available for pupils, parents and teachers. Well-used resource especially among the teenagers and around exam time. Also an art teacher, she uses art therapy as one of several resources.

Very international school but with a growing number of local students who come for the small classes, language learning and innovative style of learning. Largest proportion of students are from the Netherlands (partly because it used to be a Dutch school for children of Shell employees). But wide number of other countries represented – Arabic mother tongue speakers, some Russian, Spanish speakers, German speakers. Parents very involved in the school and use it as a start to their integration in the UK and a social hub. Regular talks on bilingualism and TKC (Third Culture Kids). Parents appreciate the relaxed approach and the emphasis on education in its broadest sense, and rather than being pressurised with teaching to exams some had chosen the school because it made their children 'enquirers' and gave them 'skills of how to learn'.

Invicta Grammar School

Huntsman Lane, Maidstone, Kent ME14 5DR

Pupils: 1,380 • Ages: 11-18 • Sixth form: 317 (including 32 boys)

Tel: 01622 755856
Email: office@invicta.kent.sch.uk
Website: www.invicta.kent.sch.uk

Headteacher: Since 2009, Mrs Julie Derrick (50s). Not a hair out of place in an immaculate bob, not a chip in her nail polish, well-cut clothes on a tiny frame. Very few papers on her desk, and these are all neatly squared to their neighbour. According to her deputy, she's a stickler for attention to detail. Ask her any fact about the school, and a spreadsheet or printout is there in a flash. But she's no ice queen – she's warm, chatty, curious. And under the serious side there's a lover of musicals and Bridget Jones novels.

Parents say she's highly visible and involved in everything at school, and girls say she's 'really nice' – they respect her, but aren't scared of her, they say.

She joined the school as head of business and enterprise, being promoted to deputy en route to the headship, and is now also joint CEO of the Valley Invicta Academies Trust. She began her career in management consultancy, working for Holiday Inns, before training as a teacher in her late 20s. Early postings took her through a series of comprehensives in deprived areas of London, including Sir John Cass and Catford Girls' School, 'a tough introduction to what education and social mobility is all about'; and Aylesford Sports College in Kent.

There's shop talk at home, as her husband is vice principal at a high school, and the elder of her two daughters is in teacher training – the younger is at university, and was formerly a pupil here. And Derrick herself is an ex-pupil of the school.

Academic matters: Recent results put the school as the best in Maidstone, with 68 per cent A*/B and 11 per cent A*/A grades at A level and 72 per cent A*/A grades at GCSE in 2016. 'We're giving as good an education as the super-selectives, but the delivery is far more creative, it has to be as we have a broader ability range, so our curriculum offer is far more exciting,' says Derrick.

We were impressed with the rigorous attention to quality of teaching. Staff have regular inspections to ensure they are up to scratch, with the deputy head observing the 'pace, variety and challenge' of lessons, and grading them as outstanding, good or requiring improvement. It's all part of an accountability they call Metal (monitoring and evaluation of teaching and learning) – which also includes student interviews, parental surveys, and interviewing other staff. The result – parents say the girls never complain they've had a boring day. 'There's lots of hat wearing and role playing, for example they did Lenin's funeral in history and they all had to wear something black. And my daughter loved it when they put a mobile phone in a microwave to see the waves in science. Every lesson has a creative and a serious element,' said one mother.

Derrick makes no apologies for doing her best to ape the independents. 'If we can give as near to a private education as possible without the parents paying for it then I'll be very happy,' says Derrick. As indeed will the parents, we suspect.

The majority of sixth formers take the AQA Baccalaureate (which comprises three A levels, an Extended Project Qualification, work experience and community service). Maths, biology, politics, and history are popular choices. A level results in 2015 put the school in the top 50 in the country by average point score per pupil, but the sixth form here is no place for slackers; those lacking in work ethic, or top grades ability, advised to move elsewhere. The requirement of minimum C in every subject at AS to progress into year 13 is rigorously applied, and results in relatively high levels of departure at the end of year 12 (14% of the year group in 2016). 'Superb for coasters who need spurring on, and at getting pupils to perform to the best of their ability, but you have to be able to run with the pack,' said one parent.

It's rare for a pupil to become disaffected or disengaged with the curriculum, says Derrick, but in the odd case where this has happened the school has devised a package for that pupil where they do fewer GCSEs, put in place work experience, and develop their leadership skills to prepare them for employment.

The classrooms are informally arranged, and most are buzzing with chatter. There's lots of discussion, and you're allowed to help each other, the girls say. Sets are based on learning style. 'They never have a feeling that they are not good at something, because the school does psychometric testing and divides them into learning styles, so they might say you are a visual learner, and we'll put you in a set with similar learner types,' said a parent.

All of the pupils study Thinking Skills and Habits for Success – 16 characteristics shared by successful people, such as persistence, thinking flexibly, communicating clearly and taking responsible risks. Business and enterprise is timetabled from year 7. 'I felt strongly that we should be giving this to everybody: no matter what you do you will be in the world of business,' says Derrick. There's also an hour per fortnight on 'academic discipline', which includes some literacy, Latin, topical issues, and memory techniques.

In languages, year 7s are allowed to make their own choice from French, German and Spanish, with a second choice introduced in year 8.

Homework is given in three categories: must, should, and could. Most want to do all three, we're told, but it means they can choose how to spend their time, and if they attend a club one evening they won't be punished for dropping the optional homework.

Games, options, the arts: There's a big choice of interesting clubs and societies – beekeeping, equine, debating, astronomy, boxing, pre-med, and Moda fashion magazine are just a flavour. Music is growing: 'They got rid of the whole music department and brought in a new one about two years, ago; since then the choir has really taken off,' said a parent. There's a big school production every year and the school says that everyone who auditions gets a part. Those not in the production get involved through enrichment days, designing costumes or making goodies to sell in food tech.

Art is well resourced, with a huge, light filled studio and a broad range of options including art and design, photography, fine art, graphics, and textiles, which has enabled students to gain places at art colleges without the need for a foundation year.

It's not a sporty school. 'I don't get the impression there is very much focus on sport; it doesn't seem to feature,' says a mother. Derrick says it is under development: 'Sport is not as high profile as in other grammars, but we recruited a new head of PE last year to improve competitive sports. For the first time this year 40 students went on a sports tour of Spain.' Indeed, there is a brand new all-weather pitch, eight tennis/netball courts and cricket facilities.

Background and atmosphere: There's some clever use of budgets going on here. It looks very swish indeed compared with the majority of old-fashioned and crumbling grammars in the region. In what could reflect Derrick's early years in hotel industry, reception wouldn't be out of place in a mid-range hotel chain, and there's more idea about branding than we usually see in schools. The girls' maroon blazers are reflected in a lighter shade in the carpet, while a deeper shade on the walls sets off huge oil canvases highlighted with pinpoint lighting.

The artwork looks professional, but has all been produced by the pupils. There's a strong creative bent here – the walls also showcase impressive textiles work the girls have produced for school fashion shows. There are well-used noticeboards everywhere, with all the posters neatly aligned and current. Everywhere is very clean. 'Even at 3.30pm the toilets are immaculate,' said a mother.

You almost expect to see a housekeeping trolley down the corridor, and it's all deliberate. 'The learning environment is key – we keep it as fresh and modern as we can within the confines of a school budget,' says Derrick.

The school converted to an academy in 2011, and picked up an Outstanding from Ofsted in 2012. It previously had a pressure cooker reputation, which Derrick is keen to dispel, and we're convinced this is more than just lip service. 'When I took over we had an accelerated curriculum, and they took all their GCSEs at the end of year 10, it was a one size fits all, and could be criticised as very much an exam factory. Now they are on individual programmes, and they will all take GCSEs at the end of year 11 with some acceleration where it is right for them,' she says.

Talking to parents, we'd say the culture change is more apparent to those with children lower down the school, with more time under the new broom. 'The head's changes are making a difference, the atmosphere has changed,' said one parent. But another is sending her second daughter elsewhere. 'It's a very good school for the academic child. It's very efficient. My elder daughter has been happy, it has served her well and she is staying on at A level. My younger daughter is more middling, and I don't have that warm, fuzzy feeling about it for her, although if I had another like my elder daughter I would send her to Invicta,' she said.

Another mother judges the balance is right. 'They are quite pushy, they want to get results, but there's extra support for the girls where they need it. It's not over the top,' she said.

One parent particularly liked the fact that when her daughter was struggling with maths, part of the package of support included a mentor from the year above who helped her twice a week.

Pupils say they are encouraged to do lots of clubs and develop a broad range of interests. And pushing an all-round education extends out of hours. 'One thing I really like, they do expanding horizons trips – to the theatre, ballet, art exhibitions – which are open to whole family. They hire a bus and you have an opportunity to go to the West End at reasonable prices,' said a parent.

There are regular Women in Profile days, attended by businesswomen in everything from finance to personal bodyguarding, who hold workshops and encourage girls to realise they can do these jobs. 'Invicta is great for the businesswomen of tomorrow. I expect a few power brokers will come out of it,' said a mother.

Pastoral care, well-being and discipline: This school has the best approach to transition we've come across, which puts to shame the half-day in July preparation for the big bad world of secondary school more commonly offered. It begins in year 5, when prospective pupils are invited in for maths and English workshops, and subject-based days such as performing arts, business studies, geography, or team building. Once girls have a confirmed place in March of year 6, they will take part in a series of events over the next six months, including a languages day when they will choose their first to study, and receptions where they can get to know each other. 'It means they start in September knowing where the toilet and the medical room is, how the dining hall works, and they hit the ground running,' says Derrick.

'Transition was amazing,' confirms one year 7 parent. 'My daughter went to so many workshops, meetings, and events, from the start of the summer holidays she was an Invicta girl, and she settled in incredibly well.'

Early into year 7 they have a one-to-one meeting for staff to find out about them, their hobbies, whether anything is worrying them. 'They get to know your child phenomenally well. There is a huge amount of tailoring to your child,' one parent commented.

Parents say that Mrs Derrick knows every child personally, and one parent whose children have also been in the independent sector says: 'My children have been at four different schools and I would say on pastoral care, this school is in a league of its own.'

Derrick was at pains to tell us that she places an equal amount of importance on the care as the academic results the school delivers. 'I look for a certain type of staff; their care has got to be as good as their qualifications,' she says.

Parents reeled off examples of the school responding quickly to parental wishes and concerns. 'We weren't happy with the long bus journey to school,' says one. 'So Mrs Derrick called in the bus company. We managed to reroute the bus, so the journey time has now been reduced from 80 to 40 minutes.'

Another added, 'They had a medical club for year 10 onwards. We asked why there wasn't one for younger pupils, and within three weeks they had set one up for the lower school.'

Girls say there isn't much in the way of discipline because they don't get a lot of bad behaviour; teachers are strictest about uniform, they say, with the usual groans about restrictions on earrings and make up. There are lots of reward trips to Thorpe Park, Disneyland, the cinema, they report.

Pupils and parents: The pupil body is predominantly white middle class, but there are 126 pupils whose first language isn't English, including Nepalese pupils whose parents are stationed with the Gurkha regiment at Maidstone's barracks. Girls come from a wide catchment extending to Hawkhurst, Ashford, Sevenoaks and Tunbridge Wells, and from around 70 feeder primaries.

Entrance: Girls must pass the Kent 11+ in order to apply. In case of oversubscription, priority goes to those with siblings in the school and then those living nearest, not to those scoring highest in the exam. For entry at sixth form, pupils must have six GCSEs at A* to C. Around 40-50 students, including some boys, join the sixth form each year.

Exit: Around 10-20 per cent leave after GCSEs, further 14 per cent departed end year 12 in 2016. On average, 90 per cent go on to university, and nearly half to top 25 universities (a fifth to Russell Group). The University of Kent, Canterbury Christ Church and the London universities are all popular destinations, as they enable students to economise by living at home. But some are going much further – the school has developed links with Harvard and Yale, which deliver presentations to pupils each year, and an increasing number of the school's pupils are applying to them.

Remarks: Strikes us as a place for the more serious-minded and less worldly-wise girl – as one mother put it: 'If you've got a girl who is into boys, ahead of her years, gobby, with a rolled up skirt, she'll go to one of the other schools.' And we'd pinpoint it for the creative rather than the sporty – the work on show points to some seriously good art and textiles teaching. Its importance in the life of the school is clear, from the hardback books of pupils' work available to browse in reception to the properly lit and displayed work throughout the school. Head is on the ball, so we'd say it's a safe bet as long as she's there.

J

John Hampden Grammar School

Marlow Hill, High Wycombe, Buckinghamshire HP11 1SZ

Pupils: 1,083 • Ages: 11–18 • Sixth form: 317

Tel: 01494 529589
Email: office@jhgs.bucks.sch.uk
Website: www.jhgs.bucks.sch.uk/

Head: Since September 2016, Tracey Hartley, previously deputy and interim head of Nonsuch High, where she worked for 10 years. Has also been head of history and head of sixth form in various co-ed schools. Originally from Canada, she started out at Mr Kipling delivering cakes around the country, with her first job being in south Bucks, before turning to history teaching. Sport and the arts fill her spare time: having lived in Scotland and Manchester, she has spent Saturdays at Murrayfield and Old Trafford.

Academic matters: Don't be fooled by hard data which doesn't place JHGS at top of local league tables – this can be skewed partly by those of mixed sex cohorts, boosted by girls' results, and partly by more affluent catchments. School is now competing ably against its closest rivals and, importantly, value-added measure is the highest of Bucks grammars and amongst the highest nationally.

Solid and constantly improving academics should help doubters sit up and take notice, with 57 per cent of all GCSEs taken in 2016 achieving A*/A. A level results also consistently robust in recent years – now just about neck and neck with the nearby rival RGS, with 78 per cent at A*/B in 2016, 47 per cent A*/A. Boys take between nine and 11 GCSEs (some 70 per cent take 10) with about 17 per cent taking four or more subjects at A2 level.

Pre academy status (2011), school held specialisms in design technology and science, sport and art and modern languages, with these still strong suits. School says maths is a 'stand out subject', with humanities also 'consistently strong.' Boys take French, German and Spanish in year 7, electing to continue with two of these from year 8 onwards. Latin as a club from year 9, leading to a GCSE for those who want it. IGSCEs offered in a number of subjects and EPQ classes offered all through lower school to develop the necessary skills for later success. Up to 30 per cent continue with this in years 12 and 13.

Progressive new digital learning programme with iPads standard issue for all boys from year 7 to use in class and at home (parents can buy or lease from school at preferential rate). 'Not a gimmick,' according to school – iPads widely used in almost every class across the curriculum. We watched boys in the quad using them to write a script and film their acting as part of a year 8 English class. Wifi extends as far as sports fields ('coaches can film pupils and show them how to correct themselves') and there's Apple TV in every classroom so pupils can instantaneously share their work with the class. All classes have two digital leaders and an 'i-genius' to help other less techy pupils maximise benefit. Slight eye-rolling from parents who can't get boys off their gadgets at home.

Form sizes between 30 and 32 with most GCSE classes capped at 24, although some grumbles from boys that occasionally class sizes exceed this by far, with one IGCSE maths set comprising around 50 boys having to be taught in the lecture theatre. Boys set from year 7 for maths and year 8 for English. Setting for languages if the need arises. Form groups shuffled annually helps keep things fresh – 'and iron out any friendship issues,' say parents.

Expected grades set at the beginning of each year and monitored digitally to make sure boys stay on track. Half termly reports to parents report on pupils' achievements and attitudes to learning, with school stepping in quickly if performance or motivation starts to slip. Catch-up classes in all subjects at lunch times and after school keep standards high – 'intervention is huge,' says school. 'Gifted and talented' outlawed as label, with school preferring 'high achievers,' to place a higher emphasis on hard work ('we try not to jump on government bandwagons'). Boys with highest GCSE grades now set in their own 'high achievers' form in year 12 – part of school's efforts to up weight entry into top universities – although some we spoke to failed to see advantage of this, uncomfortable with their own elitism.

Lots of young, male teachers are 'great role models for boys,' say parents and school 'constantly tries to recognise achievement,' with honours for everything from sport or academic achievement to community work. 'Awesome' learning support department, according to school, with a number of specialised staff on hand to help those who need it with personalised learning plans. 'If anyone doesn't cut it here, we've failed them.'

Games, options, the arts: Lots of sport played at competitive level and fixtures far and wide, with good opportunities to get into teams for those who may not quite have passed muster at schools recruiting more heavily from the independent sector. Four football teams in county cup finals and footie team usually reaches final rounds in the schools' FA cup. National U15 squash champions, and at least three international tours annually (eg Australia/NZ and USA) for top players with an ethos of 'selecting not just the best players but those with the best attitudes,' according to school. Boys' achievements inside school and out applauded.

Over 30 county and national standard pupils displayed proudly in hall of fame, showing prowess in everything from cricket and cross-country to basketball and golf, and recently a contender in the GB taekwondo squad. Lovely sports hall used for indoor cricket, badminton, basketball and hockey training, plus an older hall packed with table tennis equipment and a newish climbing wall. Recently renovated cricket pavilion and immense new Astroturf – a shared project with the neighbouring community sports centre – bound to be the envy of the competition.

Plenty to choose from on and off the sports pitches on the extracurricular schedule too, with clubs galore at lunch times and after school, although parents say that it's 'very much up to the boys to motivate themselves to sign up,' right from day one – a criticism being that boys are 'left to their own devices' in this respect. 'Huge' emphasis on leadership according to school, with plenty of opportunities for boys to participate in weekends away and international expeditions from year 9. Cadet corps popular, with one parent saying it 'transformed' her formerly shy and retiring son. Debating and public speaking also important with one or two senior boys debating at national level.

Evidence of 'phenomenal' musical prowess strong throughout the school ('we could put out about 10 jazz bands') with both music and music technology available and popular at A level. Professional standard recording studio where boys can cut their own tracks, and year 9s get to plan a European tour for their own rock band as part of the curriculum. Musical production staged annually, most recently Return to the Forbidden Planet, following in the footsteps of We Will Rock You and Phantom of the Opera, which JHGS was first school to perform. Uniquely, school allows only pupils to play instruments in productions – professionals, parents and staff strictly banned – and performance and backstage roles are open to the whole school. Top musicians are recognised each year at an awards ceremony with prizes for both excellence and improvement.

High performing art department. Not the most inspirational atelier we've seen, but outstanding work on display and school boasts several former pupils who have moved on to study art at top establishments including Central St Martins. Factory-esque DT lab a hive of activity and enthusiasm, and the gleaming food technology lab hosts cookery lessons for years 7 and 8 that are extremely popular with boys (and no doubt parents).

Background and atmosphere: Founded in the early 1890s as an art and technical school to support children of High Wycombe's traditional craftsmen and known as High Wycombe Technical High School, before achieving grammar status in 1984. Boasts an eclectic list of alumni ranging from chef Heston Blumenthal to author Terry Pratchett, both of whom maintain relationships with the school, as well as a number of sportsmen including mountaineer Kenton Cool and swimmer Simon Burnett.

Fabric of school has little of the polish of its nearby competitors, with buildings in the main very scruffy and crying out for licks of paint and a good sweep. The 'new corridor,' dining room and stunning library and sixth form centre ('not sexy, but important') are the exceptions, and beneficiaries of major fundraising schemes.

Overall vibe remarkably calm and relaxed for an all-male environment. Boys uniformly talk about school's 'friendly atmosphere,' adding that it's 'neither overly strict nor pressurised.' Pupils appreciate the weight of the school council which 'really gets things done' – the renovated pavilion and new cardiovascular room were both driven by the student voice.

Pastoral care, well-being and discipline: Bullying 'remarkably rare,' says school, and parents concur that any incidents are dealt with proactively and quickly. Boys have access to welfare officer to deal with non-academic problems – 'especially useful when our son had problems settling in,' said one parent. School has worked hard to combat inappropriate use of homophobic language, recently sending a group of ambassadors to an external conference run by the Stonewall charity, with attendees then presenting back to classmates. Zero tolerance of drugs and alcohol – 'we always intervene even if we hear of incidents outside of school,' and cyber mentions of school are tracked and dealt with as necessary.

Unusually, no house system in place, but 'achievement points' motivate individuals, with 'behaviour points' also there to keep them on the straight and narrow. 'The school doesn't take any nonsense,' said one parent. Sixth formers act as mentors to younger boys, another contributor to the school's friendly vibe. Lots of opportunities for leadership at this stage, with positions from prefect or librarian to the school's own dinner jacketed PR team, known as the 'men in black', up for grabs.

Pupils and parents: Pupils from some 40 feeder schools across the county spanning High Wycombe, Marlow, Bourne End and as far afield as Denham and Farnham Common. Buses run from far and wide offering a good service, although parents complain they are 'very tatty.'

Vast majority join from state maintained primaries, with just nine per cent joining from local preps. Broad range of socio-demographics, but in the main more grounded than neighbouring grammars, with families hailing from urban High Wycombe as well as leafy South Bucks villages, and around 22 per cent of the cohort from ethnic groups (mainly Pakistani). Tiny minority eligible for free school meals. Boys come across as serious and focused, diamonds but as yet mostly unpolished – a down to earth, respectful and well-mannered bunch.

Entrance: Selective. Applicants must have passed the Buckinghamshire 11+, taken in the October of year 6, with a pass mark of 121 and top mark of 141. Government's most recent prior attainment figures placed school's current year 7 slightly above their peers at the desirable Dr Challoner's Grammar School, demonstrating shifts in intake demographic. School's average entry score over past three years is 126. New 11+ format, introduced in 2013, aims to identify potential and weed out heavily tutored candidates. School not filled within catchment so definitely worth an application if your heart's set on a grammar and you're outside the stipulated area.

Exit: Vast majority (some 80 per cent) enter sixth form, with those leaving at the end of year 11 heading to a range of destinations from vocational courses to boarding schools. Some 95 per cent to higher education at the end of year 13, with around 50 per cent to Russell Group universities. Oxbridge entry is 'an issue,' admits school, with just a small handful of successful applicants annually, but a new initiative is in place to address this head on and build an 'Oxbridge culture' with realistic targets in place which, if successful, should make prospective parents sit up and take notice (four to Oxbridge in 2016, and one medic). Joint programmes with girls' schools such as RMS, Wycombe Abbey and Wycombe High School aim to encourage and develop ambitious university aspirations. Boys speak highly of careers advice on offer ('they really show us what's out there') and enjoy frequent visits from professions as well as lunch time seminars with university admissions tutors. Those in the 'high achievers' group benefit from extra tuition in interview skills.

Money matters: Ongoing fundraising via PTA events – some better attended than others.

Remarks: A purposeful boys' grammar school where pupils can be themselves and achieve personal bests in a focused but supportive and friendly environment. Gradually moving above the radar to become a genuine consideration for middle class parents, despite lacking the private school vibe of the local competition. Not overly macho, celebrates pupils for a range of achievements from sport to debating and has close working and social relationships with Wycombe High. Beats the other grammars hands down on value-added, with ambitious targets in place to upweight successful entry to top universities.

The Judd School

Brook Street, Tonbridge, Kent TN9 2PN

Pupils: 1,097 • Ages: 11–18 • Sixth form: 249 (including 82 girls)

Tel: 01732 770880
Email: enquiries@judd.kent.sch.uk
Website: www.judd.kent.sch.uk

Headmaster: Since 2004, Mr Robert Masters BSc maths (first class from Reading University) and PGCE (maths with games from Bristol); 50s. Previously taught at two boys' grammars in Gravesend and Torquay (where he was deputy head). Looks as if he could still keep up on the hockey pitch but prefers cryptic crosswords and jogging these days. Parents can find him somewhat aloof and, while some speak of the encouragement he's given their bright lad, others wonder if he would know them. We suspect he keeps closer tabs than he lets on – he smirks as he points to the glass bookcase in which he can observe unnoticed their comings and goings. He is praised for attracting substantial resources and has robustly and controversially protected the school's lack of catchment area – now introduced. His personal commitment to his ideals is also apparent. 'Our pupils should leave able and willing to change the world with intelligence, good morals and ethics.' Married with three children.

Moving on in July 2017. His successor will be Jon Wood, currently deputy head.

Academic matters: With a high entry standard at 11+ and excellent GCSE results (81 per cent A*/A in 2016), there's no doubt that this is the domain of the fiercely able. 'It does them no favours to tutor them to death to get in. Once there they'll struggle,' say parents, with peer pressure and the workload pretty relentless (snow closures no respite). Nothing most boys can't cope with and they generally thrive on the challenge. It's a place where you're expected to take the initiative and focus on the job at hand and, though closely monitored in the early years – teachers are praised for gaining a good understanding of individuals' strengths and weaknesses – later on some might be allowed to slip behind. Parents of the more applied enthuse about the support received from the high calibre and dedicated staff. Pupils too. 'I only half mentioned I was interested in a book and the teacher had ordered it for the library.' Its specialist status in science, maths, music and English also helps make it an exciting place with doors opened to local primaries and others.

Success is celebrated but the benchmark set high. The talented are singled out through a one to watch section in the school magazine and those attaining the top GCSE results receive a letter welcoming them to the sixth form. Says one parent, 'By any external measure, on academics and in other fields, pupils outperform, but some fail to get a sense of just how good they are and lack confidence'.

Unlike other local grammars, has stuck with a fairly traditional curriculum. German is obligatory in year 8, other standard language offerings being French and Latin. Says the head, 'We want to make sure that everything we do, we do well'. There's streaming in maths and some get the GCSE out of the way early, freeing up additional time to pursue wider interests, which all are expected to maintain. Alongside GCSEs all study a non-examined subject – forensic science and philosophy being just two of the subjects on offer. In the sixth form four or five AS, and three to five A levels is the norm with 58 per cent A*/A and 86 per cent A*-B in 2016. At the end of year 11 the school loses one or two wanting to do IB, but the head has no plans to introduce it, championing A levels as an opportunity to specialise and considering the A* grade challenge enough. Lots of free study periods and self-discipline required in the upper sixth, which is well ingrained in most by then. Some parents wish for a little more hand-holding as university options are considered.

Individual and group support is available to those not up to scratch in English at lunchtime and in other subjects too, for example through mentoring. The school is increasingly experienced in SEN and integrates dyslexic pupils, other mild SENs and the exceptionally gifted and talented within the classroom. It also caters well for those with physical disabilities.

Games, options, the arts: Most boys love their sport and there's no excuse in the younger years, when the school fields several teams in each sport and anyone turning up is guaranteed a game. Later it can prove difficult to carry on and, in some parents' views, pupils are given insufficient encouragement. Lots of rivalry with county grammars and independent schools, it holds its own in rugby, cricket and positively excels in athletics, cross-country and rugby 7s – it's one of the top state schools in the country. Pupils also receive national recognition in other sports – rowing, sailing, swimming, table tennis, judo and taekwondo being but some examples. At lunchtime any thought that shirts can be kept tucked in and uniform neat are dispelled, as you witness hordes of boys kicking around a football or doggedly defending a basketball net.

Music is another area of real strength. 'I think my son's sometimes overwhelmed by the opportunities to get involved and perform and I have been simply spellbound by the standard of the choirs and orchestras.' The school gives about 30 concerts each year with pupils also involved behind the scenes, using the technology lab in the well-equipped music block. Individual lessons are scheduled to ensure pupils rarely miss the same lesson twice. Drama is less prominent and not offered at A level, although sixth formers do stage productions regularly, doubtless made easier by the influx of girls to take on female parts. Annually more than 100 pupils pursue D of E bronze award with 20 or so going on to attain gold. Many also distinguish themselves in the CCF while others partake in the school's well-developed outreach programme in maths, science, music and sports.

Background and atmosphere: The school retains strong links with the Worshipful Company of Skinners, which established the school in 1888 to provide an affordable alternative to Tonbridge School. It moved to its current site in 1896 and is a 10 minute walk or so from the railway station, on the southern outskirts of the town, near other schools and colleges with its sports fields bordered by housing estates. It's a hotch-potch of buildings, dating from the late 1800s and 1920s, and interspersed with recent additions, with a somewhat scruffy, collegiate feel, not without charm. The Atwell building, housing geography and maths, was completed in 2009 and, together with additional labs, modern music block, sports hall and additional pitches, one all-weather, offer some compensation for the irritation of long lunch queues due to lack of space – hopefully now eased by completion of new dining hall. Moving around, there's a fairly relaxed feel, with boys huddled in groups and bags strewn about.

Pastoral care, well-being and discipline: Early on boys are left in no doubt that they are expected to work hard. If you don't do well enough, you take the test again and work handed in late lands you a detention. Most soon get used to it and toe the line.

Socially, early days can also be a little tough as boys settle in with their peers from a wide range of schools. The mixing up of classes after a year is also sometimes a challenge for the shy, but different tutors are allocated to look after pupils as they progress through the school and parents find them and other staff responsive to concerns raised.

Minor infringements on uniform and the like tend to be played down, the embarrassment factor of clearing lunchtime tables often being all that's required by way of punishment. Parents are expected, and generally do, take the lead on issues such as drink, smoking or drugs and, on the rare occasion they feature, parents say they are dealt with swiftly and conclusively.

Girls are jokingly said to be a civilising influence in the sixth form and are briefed on what to expect in a predominantly male environment. They seem to hold their own and soon integrate, judging by the smiles and buzz of purposeful activity in the sixth form common room. Prefects and heads of houses are appointed and older pupils act as mentors to the younger years, some wearing 'listener' badges or manning a room where pupils can go during lunch to play board games or to discuss problems. The house system is also designed to promote cross-year contact and a sense of community.

Pupils and parents: Parents tend to aspire high for their offspring and to be active supporters of their efforts, in whatever field. Pupils are keenly aware of the academic credentials that accrue when they get into the school, but this rarely spills over into arrogance. Most are open, friendly, direct, supportive of each other and keen to engage, the reticent or disorganised generally being those who make less of their time there.

The parents' association is active and organises regular events including coffee mornings, a popular football fiesta in the summer term and well-attended bi-annual ball.

OJs include Terence Lewin, former Chief of Defence Staff and Admiral of the Fleet, rugby player Martin Purdy, Cecil Frank Powell, Nobel Prize winner for physics and Humphrey Burton, music presenter and broadcaster.

Entrance: Competition for the 155 places in year 7 is very stiff. There are usually more than 500 applications. Now has catchment area: inner area (135 places) covers large parts of west Kent, including Tunbridge Wells and Sevenoaks; outer area (20 places) covers the rest of the country. Selects by rank order in the Kent 11+.

About 70 external candidates come in at sixth form; many are girls from local grammars, with a requirement of 60 'Judd' points. In practice, two-thirds of entrants have got five A*s or above. Again, places are much sought after and may become more so as nearby schools switch to the IB.

Exit: Some 85 – 90 per cent stay on to the sixth form. Rare that a pupil does not go to university either directly or after a gap year, 75 per cent to Russell Group, ten to study medicine in 2016. Approximately 50 apply to Oxbridge each year; 13 places in 2016.

Money matters: Many parents and former pupils contribute readily and generously to the Development Fund, contributing half of the £2.4m cost of the Atwell Building. There is a quiet presumption of affluence which at times results in grumbles over fundraising requests, and the cost of trips: 'Could they not ski in Europe?' There is a Hardship Fund but pride deters some from making requests.

Remarks: Offers an exceptionally good education for the unashamedly bright and motivated. The opportunities to shine are there for those who want to take them but no mollycoddling for those who don't. Said one sixth form prefect with a brother at a nearby independent school, 'My parents still can't quite believe they've got all this for free'.

Kent College

Old Church Road, Pembury, Tunbridge Wells, Kent TN2 4AX

Pupils: 640; 70 boarders • Ages: 3–18 (boarding from 10) • Sixth form: 130

Fees: Day £8,829 – £20,700; Boarding £24,000 – £30,600 pa

Tel: 01892 822006
Email: admissions@kentcollege.kent.sch.uk
Website: www.kent-college.co.uk

Headmistress: Since January 2016, Julie Lodrick, previously head of The Mount School in York. (40s), BA music and

K

related arts (University College, Chichester), PGCE (Kingston University), MA education, leadership and management (OU), professional practice certificate in boarding (BSA), national professional qualification for headship (NCSL). Wide experience in educational management; deputy head of Farlington School, West Sussex for four years. Also a tutor and lecturer for the Boarding Schools Association. Five years as housemistress at Queenswood School, and as head of music at St Margaret's Senior School, West Sussex before that. Talented singer and pianist, performing when opportunity (has classical music softly playing in study). Believes in healthy lifestyle, runs and swims in school pool daily, completed York marathon in 2013, raising funds for school charity.

Head of prep: Since September 2016, Nik Pears, prevously head of pre-prep at Sevenoaks Prep. Degree from Cambridge; founded and managed a company comprising a small record label, publishing company and 'sessions' agency, providing professional musicians for events, recordings and tours before turning to teaching. He has been sports coach and head of music as well as class teacher and senior form tutor. He is married to Emma, a professional musician and qualified teacher, and they have two children.

Academic matters: Great emphasis on play in the early years and a play therapist comes in once a week to help build girls' self-confidence and interpersonal skills. One-to-one learning support offered at no extra charge – mainly for mild dyslexia and dyspraxia. French taught from nursery to year 6.

K

Apart from the usual subjects, film studies, product design (textiles), food technology, drama and theatre studies, psychology and PE are offered at A level. In 2016, 73 per cent A*/B grades and 42 per cent A*/A grades. GCSEs: 57 per cent A*/A grades. Option to take all three sciences separately or as a dual award. Inspirational textiles teacher has taken the subject to new heights. Science is strong and a pupil recently won bronze in the International Chemistry Olympiad.

RE taught to all up to the sixth form and all younger girls take food technology. Healthy eating is covered in PSHE. The careers department is proactive and helpful and sixth form attend a higher education preparation programme with weekly sessions on interview technique, gap year planning, money management etc. Due to the recent increase in pupil numbers, several new teachers have joined, so a healthy mix of new younger teachers and others who have been in the school for many years. Plenty of male teachers and housemasters. Good support for minor learning difficulties and good communication between learning support and mainstream teachers.

Games, options, the arts: Sport features strongly in junior school – dance, gymnastics, netball and swimming in lessons and clubs. U11 netball team recently the runner up in a national tournament for prep schools. All the usual senior school sports – girls have competed at national level at swimming, hockey and gymnastics and are recent U13 south east area cross-country champions. A gymnastics academy is also open to outsiders on Saturdays. A fitness suite with gym equipment was added in 2012 and planning has been granted for a new all-weather pitch and extension to existing sports hall. Outdoor activities seen as important and the school has appointed a head of outdoor education who oversees the Duke of Edinburgh programme and various adventure trips at home and abroad. A 'confidence course' has been built in the grounds which includes a scramble net, a 12ft wall and a 30ft abseil tree – school officers in sixth form have a team-building weekend using the course. Sixth formers are required to take part in sport for one double period a week but this could be trampolining, aerobics, aquarobics, Salsa or more mainstream team sports. Everyone encouraged to get involved.

Lots of clubs before and after school and at lunchtime, from tae kwon-do to public speaking lessons and clay pigeon shooting, and girls are encouraged to initiate activities and start clubs, eg a street dance club and gospel choir. Astonishing that they can fit so much into a day. They are even good at beekeeping – the school's honey was commended at the National Honey Show.

Top two years have enrichment programme where they work in a small team on a project of their choice to gain a Record of Achievement by the Open College of the North West. This could be producing the school magazine or a cooking course leading to Leith's certificate in food and wine, an extended essay and community service. Young Enterprise scheme where they can run their own business for six months, working in mixed groups with other local schools. Charity Committee organises fundraising events. Plenty of opportunities to hone public speaking skills and look at the bigger picture in World AIMS (Action in Methodist Schools) Weekend, where such issues as the arms trade, climate change and development are debated, and at the Global Students Forum and model United Nations events in Tunbridge Wells and Bath. Women in Leadership conferences are held annually with outside inspirational speakers; girls also debate subjects such as 'Are women taking over the world?' – lots of thought-provoking and challenging stuff. Dan Snow, Sandi Toksvig and Miriam Margolyes were recent visitors.

Drama impressive with whole school productions in the purpose-built Countess of Wessex theatre – 'The school has very high expectations of the girls and they always seem to step up to the plate'. Their highly acclaimed theatrical productions, musicals and operas are very ambitious and rival the West End. Music on the up with a modern music centre and Apple Mac computer suite where girls can compose. LAMDA and English Speaking Board exams and every girl will speak in at least one assembly a year.

Boarding: Small boarding community, 20 per cent from overseas, eg Nigeria, China, Russia, Thailand and mainland Europe, but nationalities carefully balanced and trouble taken to prevent cliques forming. Another 20 per cent of boarders from Forces families. Only four full junior boarders at the time of our visit but they seemed happily integrated. Flexi-boarding from the age of 10 a popular option with local children. Modern and well-designed junior and senior boarding houses cluster around original baronial style Victorian house and everywhere has a light and airy feel. Usual evening and weekend activities such as shopping trips, skating, cinema and sport. Day girls are allowed in the social areas of boarding houses and encouraged to try flexi-boarding, and older girls help supervise younger ones at bed time.

Background and atmosphere: Founded in 1886 in Folkestone and moved to its present site in Pembury, just outside Tunbridge Wells, during World War II. Managed by the Methodist Independent Education Trust's board – but with a very light touch. Also has its own governing body, half of whom are members of the Methodist Church or members of a Christian church. Methodists state that their schools aim to be 'caring, family communities committed to the development and full potential of each individual, having regard for their personal attributes as well as their academic aspirations'. Kent College certainly does this and caring for the individual is central to the ethos of the school – each girl's well-being is paramount.

Huge amount of refurbishment and number of building projects with fitness suite, science labs and IT suites completed, plus expansion of sixth form centre. £4 million art and library centre, including café, studios and exhibition space, opened in 2013. Junior school has own purpose built teaching block on the same site as the senior school and with the use of the senior school facilities – science labs, computer suite, sports facilities, music block and theatre.

Pastoral care, well-being and discipline: The school has a warm and welcoming atmosphere and girls are happy and relaxed while leading incredibly busy lives. A strong Christian ethos is a subtle part of the routine – girls are expected to take part in assemblies but the celebration of other religious festivals is an integral part of school life. A spirit of tolerance and respect is part of the ethos, with great emphasis on kindness, respect and emotional well-being and a strong sense of community that encompasses everyone. Relaxed and comfortable girl/staff relationships. The tutor system ensures any problems are picked up early – mentors are allocated to girls who struggle; also a school counsellor. Girls are supportive of each other across the year groups and the house system means that different year groups pull together in sporting competitions and charity work. New girls are integrated quickly and attend an induction programme which includes an overnight camp in the school's orchard. Discos, socials and joint productions with local boys' schools are popular.

Pupils and parents: The school seems to breed great enthusiasm and loyalty, seeing itself as a small global community. No typical Kent College girl, but they do have a great zest for life and want to try everything, are extraordinarily confident with a 'can do' attitude and are encouraged to surpass their expectations and believe that they can be anything they want to be – yet no hint of arrogance. They come from as far as Bromley and Tenterden – good network of school buses. Wide variety of parents from all walks of life – great tolerance of difference – but mostly from business and professional families. Famous old girls include the Countess of Wessex and Sarah Sands, editor of the London Evening Standard. Good links with parents, who feel involved at every step. Active parents' association who organise social events throughout the year – a ball, coffee mornings, new parents' social evenings and a pamper evening. Also a thriving old girls' association and active Friends of Kent College Association, which includes ex staff, parents and governors.

Entrance: Not overly competitive – broad intake and can cope with a wide range of abilities as lots of individualised care. From the age of 3. If spaces, girls may join at any time and are encouraged to come for a taster day beforehand. Entrance tests in English and maths taken from year 3. Most enter senior school at 11+ and attend the entrance day in the November before entry, when they are interviewed and sit the school's own exams in English, maths and verbal reasoning. The school also requires a letter from the girl's current head. Entry at 12+ and 13+ with exams in the January before, when they are also tested in science and French. A taster day and overnight stay are strongly encouraged. Those who come up from the prep school also have to take the test. Sixth form entrants need six GCSEs at C or above and A*, A or B grades in the subjects they wish to study at A level. Children come from a wide range of local prep schools and primaries including Holmewood House, Rose Hill, Sevenoaks and St Michael's, Otford.

Exit: In 2016, 60 per cent of juniors made the transition to the senior school at 11+, with the majority of the rest going on to the grammars. The school has a good track record in the Kent Test and also prepares girls for the entrance exams to other independent schools and runs a revision course during the summer holidays. Girls coming up from the prep have to sit the entrance test to the senior school in English, maths and verbal reasoning. A requirement of the senior school is that girls must be able to sit nine GCSEs and three A levels, so occasionally it is decided that the senior school might not suit a particular girl. Parents are always kept closely informed of their daughter's progress, so this is always very much a joint decision.

Up to 20 per cent leave after GCSEs, usually for co-ed independents or grammars. Sometimes girls come back and have been known to repeat the lower sixth year rather than stay somewhere else. Most go on to some form of higher education in the UK (mainly Russell Group) or overseas (Boston, Netherlands, Sydney). In 2016, eight students to Oxbridge. Lots of help with UCAS forms and personal statements. Oxbridge preparation lessons include interview practice with a local boys' school.

Money matters: Academic, music, drama, music, art and sport scholarships offered at up to 10 per cent of fees. Means-tested bursaries also available.

Remarks: Has improved hugely over past few years – numbers up, recent glowing report from the Independent Inspectorate. Girls leave with great self-confidence and strong sense of purpose.

King Edward VI Grammar School, Chelmsford

K

Broomfield Road, Chelmsford, Essex CM1 3SX

Pupils: 978 • Ages: 11–18 • Sixth form: 364 (including 115 girls)

Tel: 01245 353510
Email: office@kegs.org.uk
Website: www.kegs.org.uk

Headteacher: Since 2014, Thomas Carter MA PGCE NPQH (40s), previously deputy head and associate head. He read maths at Clare College, Cambridge and worked in management consultancy and strategic development before changing to a career in teaching. He also has an MBA from Warwick and a PGCE from the Institute of Education and holds a diploma in French language and literature. Before coming to KEGS in 2001, he spent five years at Westcliff High School for Boys.

Affable and frank, he is also ultra-efficient. Says his three key principles are excellence, equality and compassion – and students agree: 'He achieves very high standards within a culture where everyone is treated with dignity and respect.' He's big on leading by leading by example too. 'He speaks to us in the same way he expects us to speak to him and he is as quick to pick up a litter as we are.'

Teaches far more than most heads – around an hour a day of maths to the upper school. 'It's partly to connect with students – I don't want to be too remote. And I think teaching is important if I'm to have credibility among the staff.' Impressively, he tries (and succeeds, according to the students we spoke to) to get individual time with all 150 year 7s, if only for a few minutes. 'He's very fair – he'll always stand back and listen to your side of the story,' we were also told. Parents describe him as 'approachable,' 'enthusiastic' and 'quietly authoritative.' 'He's just perfect for the school.'

He is married with two sons, both of whom are at KEGS. His wife has two careers – a professional singer and a garden designer. He has a serious interest in music (violin, piano, singing) and enjoys learning languages and skiing.

Academic matters: In terms of academic achievement, one of the top 10 state grammars. In 2016, 81 per cent A*/A grades at GCSE and 69 per cent A*/A at A level (not including general studies, which is taken by the majority of students). Outstanding commitment from staff who, according to a parent, 'go a thousand miles beyond the call of duty and don't just stick to the curriculum. They give a proper education.' 'Teaching isn't obsessively focused towards exams,' and a love of learning is engendered right from the word go. 'I just spent an hour with one of my teachers, who is known for giving up pretty much every lunch hour to help students – and that's not unusual among staff here,' one student told us. Younger boys enjoy creative lessons – Blackadder used to illustrate a point and volcanoes made from bicarb of soda – and all are stretched and challenged, with target setting and monitoring all busily happening behind the scenes. 'There's almost a university ethos in terms of levels of enquiry and intellectual curiosity – but with a safety net if any boy struggles,' said one parent. Lots of CPD for staff, with younger ones supported to do extra qualifications. 'There's a lot of research on how people learn best – and just as doctors are expected to be up-to-date with medical advances, we ensure our teachers are kept up-to-date with these,' says the head.

Known for sciences, although GCSE results are also particularly strong in maths, Latin, geography and history. Languages popular. At A level, art, chemistry, English, geography and geology do particularly well, while maths is also popular (many do further maths). History and English at Pre U, with very successful results for English. Some sixth-form classes feel a bit too big, say students – 'hovering at around 20' – and some would like a wider A level curriculum, perhaps with less traditional subjects such as psychology and business studies. 'But the teaching at this level is phenomenon.'

K

Setting from maths in year 8, 'but it's fairly fluid and boys are never far from the top set,' says head. Year 7s all take French or German, which they learn at a fast pace – then they take their GCSE in that subject in year 9. In year 8, all boys also take up Latin, which they can continue for GCSE if they choose, and they pick up a second modern foreign language in year 9 too – either the one they didn't do in year 7, or Russian or Mandarin. 'All language teachers only speak in that language, which is daunting at first, but a great way to learn,' say students. Head explains, 'Learning a language isn't just about passing the exam here – we want students to leave knowing how to converse in a second language because that should be a normal thing to do.'

IT embedded in all subject areas. Awards for those who tot up the most effort marks. Homework starts at around 1.5 hours a night in year 7, then builds up slowly, peaking in middle school at around two hours a night. 'It is intense and if you don't like homework, this is not the school for you,' says the head. 'We hope by the sixth form that students have learned to plan and manage their own time.'

A few have special educational needs – a SENCo oversees these students, who generally have visual impairment, dyslexia, dyspraxia or Asperger's syndrome. 'Understanding, inclusive approach,' according to parents, whilst students told us the pupil support unit is 'discreet.' 'There's not a stigma, but you don't shout about going there,' one said. That said, there's great support for those at the more severe end of SEN, 'with real cheers in assemblies when they are singled out for achievements.' 'This department worked with our son's care team – they really did everything they could to make sure he could reach his full potential. I can't praise them enough.'

Games, options, the arts: Not known for its sporting prowess, 'but it should be,' believe many parents. Rugby fares well and full range of fixtures in all major sports. Students also win competitions in basketball, badminton, table tennis and tennis. Sport is compulsory up to end of year 12, and optional in year 13. Sixth-formers get the chance to play squash or swim at the local sports centre. Lots of house competitions – particularly popular among those who aren't so good at sport. 'It's fine if you're not that great as you play other people who aren't that great,' said one student. 'There's definitely a have-a-go culture, rather than just focusing on the elite.' Most sports take place at Bedford Fields, an impressive 30-acre site four miles down the road, although the main school site does have some tennis courts, a playing field – albeit a bit tired. There's a new sports hall on the way, due to be completed in 2018.

Welcoming, modern art department is veritable Aladdin's cave (albeit with a lot of natural light) rammed with lively work, especially by the younger ones. Music block is also new and there's plenty to write home about from this department, not least the commitment for 30 year 7s to learn an instrument free of charge in lessons of three. 'It's partly to build our orchestras of the future, but also because learning an instrument isn't always affordable,' says the head. Ten peripatetic teachers on hand to teach instruments to other students, for a fee. Three orchestras, wind band, jazz band and various choirs, with concerts every term and lots of participation (40 for the wind band alone when we visited). Plenty of music tours. 'My goodness, the music opportunities are fantastic – there is literally something for everyone,' one parent gushed.

The students also take great pride in their drama department, with one big production taking place every year – usually a musical one year, then a straight play the next. 'The standard is breath-taking,' one parent told us. 'I was one of the 150 students involved in Les Mis and it really helped me build friendships, as well as allowing me to experience a high quality production,' one student said. Smaller scale productions – with some of the plays written by students – run throughout the year.

D of E, CCF and good selection of clubs enrich beyond the curriculum – including sport, music, drama, chess, maths clubs, three debating clubs, computing clubs, young engineers, school newspaper, just to name a few. Many win national competitions and most are student-led – the newspaper, for example, has no input from staff whatsoever. Most take place at lunchtimes – some boys fit two in their lunch-hour, although a few told us it can be a squeeze to fit one in, 'especially if it involves changing clothes.' Medical society particularly popular – 83-strong when we visited. Charity work managed by the student-led charities committee (again, student-led). 'Extra-curricular life here is so diverse – you can be anything from a young engineer to a keen actor to a maths mentor – or, more likely, all three. The added extras beyond the academics is a huge pull of the school.' 'A lot of these very bright boys could easily be one-dimensional, but the school ensures that never happens. I don't know anyone who doesn't do anything extra.'

Trips to just about everywhere you can think of – Alsace. Boulogne, Iceland, New York, China, Rome, Paris, Barcelona and Kenya are all visited most years, with KEGS Foundation and school funds available to help those who can't afford it.

Background and atmosphere: Founded in 1551, nearly 350 years before it settled on the present site close to the town centre. Last 100 years have seen numbers increase eight-fold and buildings, permanent and 'temporary,' added behind the original low-key red-brick frontage. Absolutely no frills and some students said they can 'feel a bit cramped indoors,' but there are impressive features, including the grand, stain-glass-windowed and well-stocked library, housed in the school's first hall; and the Darwin Centre – sixth form centre – which is a three storey state-of-the-art building containing a spacious study area oozing natural light, a classroom and colourful and roomy sixth form social area on the top floor. The fabulous new art centre is 'a joy to work in,' according to students, and we also like the Oxbridge-esque feel of the outside cloistered quad areas that sit within the figure-of-eight shaped original buildings. Science labs could do with a face-lift, but surprisingly this doesn't seem to bother students one iota – 'It doesn't impact on our learning,' they told us, and the results speak for themselves.

Despite the ferocious competition for places and intensive pace of study, students are clearly happy. Parents agree: 'this is no exam factory', 'with a real emphasis on creating a positive environment,' although everyone we spoke to said boys who are over-tutored to pass their 11+ can struggle once they get in. 'It seems a shame as you can tell another learning environment might be better for them.' Strong sense of community where the acquisition and sharing of knowledge exude from every pore, and where the atmosphere is generally calm and concentrated. Uniform is standard white shirts, ties and black blazers, customised with a bright red stripe round collar – and it's an instant detention for any top button undone. Plain blazers for boys and girls in the sixth with a free choice of shirt colours.

Pastoral care, well-being and discipline: Counsellor on hand if help is needed, although some students we spoke to had no idea about this, and the ones who did weren't aware of where you'd find her. 'But the fact that we haven't needed to see her could be seen as telling in itself,' pointed out one student, with all parents agreeing that the school is generally nurturing and that teaching staff are on hand to help iron out any problems. 'Any difficulties are identified early on and strategies are given to help,' say parents. 'This is a school that really listens and they act quickly.' The pastoral structure is certainly strong, starting with form tutor and rising up five levels to the head, although many students told us that in reality, 'you just find the staff member that you've most bonded with if you need someone to talk to.' 'The fact that many of the older children mentor the younger ones is also relevant, say students – 'you can confide in them if you've got any worries you don't want to talk to staff about.'

Slightest sniff of bullying is instantly investigated – but it's rare. 'It's ok to be quirky or different here – I don't know anyone who feels they can't be themselves,' said one student. Strict on mobile phones (where and when you can have them – they're not actually banned) and uniform, but it's not a school brimming with rules and an active school council encourages a high level of civilized co-existence. A new-ish strike system means that if you get four strikes in less than five weeks in any one of the three areas of equipment, homework and behaviour, and you get a detention. 'It's not unusual to get a detention at some point in your school career, but lots of boys get no more than that,' says the head. High expectations of conduct in the classroom – full engagement and no chit-chat at all in the ones we saw. No permanent exclusions in the current head's time – although he has 'helped move one student to another school, following an incident' – and there are a handful of temporary exclusions each year, usually as a result of physical violence.

Pupils and parents: Pupils from as far afield as some London boroughs, but most much closer – with students mainly travelling in by train, bus or on foot, a few cycling or dropped off in the car. Diverse parent body – range of occupations and backgrounds. Good ethnic mix – around half white British, while the rest include Asian, black, Eastern European and more – 'a glorious mix,' says the head. Old boys include Lord Fowler, Simon Heffer, Grayson Perry and Alex Dowsett. A lively PA and parents tell us there's good communication from the school.

Entrance: Hugely competitive. In recent years, over 1,000 of the brightest examined for the 150 places. Lots of tutoring goes on to help smooth the process, although the school has got rid of verbal reasoning in the 11+ in an attempt to create a fairer playing field – and it's true that there are small, but growing, numbers on pupil premium: four per cent of years 7 and 8 when we visited. Wide catchment area with over 60 feeder schools – prep and primary – but 80 per cent of places are reserved for those living within 12.5 miles.

Almost all stay onto sixth form. Minimum of five As and three Bs to do so, with at least an A in the subjects to be studied. 'In reality, lots have seven or eight A*s or more,' says the head. External applications (who include girls – increasing numbers of them) come from a mix of other grammars (including the girls' grammar across the road), private and comps.

Exit: Virtually all to university – 15 to Oxbridge in 2016 ('there was one more offer successfully met, but he turned down his place,' says head) and around three-quarters of the remainder to Russell Group universities, with a sprinkling doing gap years or apprenticeships. Good spread of locations and courses, with Warwick, Exeter, Bath, UCL, Kings and Imperial among the favourites. Lots of medics – 27 in 2016.

Remarks: Inspired approach towards teaching and while it's clearly an intensive environment in which to learn, the pastoral care is outstanding and students are generally a very happy bunch. Staff are passionate about their subjects and students thrive in an atmosphere where it's cool to study. Beware of over-tutoring to get your child in, however – they could struggle to keep up.

King Edward VI School (Southampton)

Wilton Road, Southampton SO15 5UQ

Pupils: 975 • Ages: 11–18 • Sixth form: 250

Fees: £14,985 pa

Tel: 023 8070 4561
Email: registrar@kes.hants.sch.uk
Website: www.kes.hants.sch.uk

Head: Since 2002, Mr Julian Thould MA – Pembroke College, Oxford (50s). Surprisingly, for this overtly scientific school, his subject is history with a passion for medieval castles, evidenced by some detailed scale models in his office, including an intricate one in chocolate, that he was judging for a year 7 competition. Worked in industry before a teaching career in some top schools, Westminster, Cranleigh and King's Worcester, until appointed to his first headship at King Edward VI. Impressively well organised but definitely approachable, he believes children do best when they are happily occupied. Hence the exciting co-curricular programme, which not only attracts some to the school but also encourages enthusiasm, enjoyment and ambition that spills over into academic work.

Parents say he runs a tight ship and nothing is too much trouble. During his 10-year tenure he has had the whole of the inside of the school refurbished. Everything gleams, from the highly polished blue lino in the wide corridors to the cream paint, which looks universally new. Prolonged search could only find some chipped paint in the music department (all those bulky instrument cases) and shabby props in drama. The governors have bought much-needed space in form of the Wellington sports grounds on the edge of the city. Also new is a residential outdoor centre on Dartmoor, used as much for reading and study groups as for adventure activities. PHSE has been another priority, plus more facilities both for pupils needing extra support and for the unusually gifted, with a fully-

K

qualified team of special needs teachers and a care team of three nurses, counsellor and chaplain.

As a dedicated educator and a parent himself, with one child still in school, and three at uni – medicine, history and earth science – he feels himself identifying with parents' concerns and in touch with their children. Even his personal interests veer towards the educative. As a Francophile, his enthusiasm takes the form of accompanying the summer trip to Normandy. Though he cites keeping fit by cycling and walking as his personal interests, books and reading are central, exemplified by his insistence that all pupils share this and spend an hour's reading time each week in the library – appreciated by most students, though one 'real reader' said it was infuriating since whatever he really wanted to read was always at home.

Over the past 10 years the school has grown, with just under 40 per cent girls – there are some whizzy girls-only schools in the area. The head is especially keen on the extensive projects in science, reading, languages etc which staff and pupils run with local state primaries. It encourages links, and there are good bursaries for the less privileged. He still has plenty of plans up his sleeve: upgrading of art department, theatre and music rooms is planned in the immediate future.

Academic matters: 'All our pupils are bright enough to do three sciences and a language,' says the head, and certainly exam results speak for themselves. The swathes of A* s at GCSE are in maths and the sciences (76 per cent A*/A grades overall in 2016), with maths also multi-starred at A level, but there is a fair sprinkling at all levels in every subject in the wide and demanding curriculum (nearly 85 per cent A*/B grades and 55 per cent A*/A in 2016). In the lower school everyone has a go at two mod langs and Latin and carries on with one modern plus at least one other (either modern, Latin or Greek) until the end of third year. At GCSE everyone takes RS early (a bit reluctantly at present, though with tip top results – this is due for a change). All do three sciences and a language with the option of three further subjects, adding up together with maths and English subjects to a total of 10.

There are routes to either three or four A Levels in sixth form with everyone doing 'foundation studies' as well. Pupils can do subjects not taken at GCSE, except of course in maths, science and languages, where knowledge is cumulative. Despite the excellence of the arts and humanities, most choose maths and science. In one group of 10 pupils, all but one claimed maths a favourite subject and, incidentally, RS as the least. 'You can get maths done and either you understand it or you don't.' Work ethic is strong with pupils saying 'it's great if you do well but no one is afraid to ask if they're struggling with something'. Possibly science and maths are so popular because there are so many medical/scientific families, and it's what the school is known for. But the head says, 'Look at the results. There's a better success ratio.'

Sixth formers clearly have high expectations and are appreciative of the support the school gives them. The classes we saw had a quiet buzz of interested discussion and pupils talked about their work with serious enthusiasm.

Games, options, the arts: Art is exciting with masses of multi-media, sculpture, abstract, photography flourishing and expanding with the advent of a new head of art with an impressive photographic career. Some really good art going on; also some frustration within the department that comparatively few take it beyond GCSE.

Music certainly lively and enthusiastic. A very impressive a capella choir organised by the sixth formers was rehearsing during our visit as well as the strings boning up on Prokofiev for an orchestral concert. Lots of pop and light music as well, and students doing music technology on equipment resembling aircraft consoles. A few get to National Youth Orchestra standard and there are lots of tours, concerts, festival triumphs, high-powered workshops and masterclasses etc. Drama also popular with several performances annually, musical and other. Some are in the lofty great hall with its airy but formal atmosphere and acres of honours boards and some, such as a recent History Boys, in an intimate theatre in the round, professionally lit and equipped and due for expansion soon.

The importance of sport is emphasised by the school being fronted by sports fields, both grassy and green Astroturfed. The cavernous sports hall is flanked by a new dance studio much used by the girls, though even the boys do a dance module in the third year. Some of the girls' games, compulsory for all, are really fun and a chance to unwind from a tough curriculum, but for many it's serious business. Fantastic record in netball (girls), hockey (both girls and boys) and cricket at county and regional level. Rugby is less strong, 'but a keen coach'. Masses of individuals achieve in fencing, sailing, rowing, swimming etc and there's strong support for athletes of all varieties. Double Olympic sailing gold medallist Iain Percy was here, also Keith Wiseman (past chairman of the Football Association), John and Simon Francis (county cricketers), Dudley Kemp (England rugby cap and past president of the RFU) and Rob Moore (hockey Olympian). Parents like the Saturday fixtures – they keep 'em out of town.

Fifty-plus clubs, many as intellectual as the most academic parent might hope, but some with a distinctive King Edward's twist to them: the Byron Society, the German Magazine Club, the Scamp Club (concerned it seems with codes and code-breaking). The Green Team is busy planting veg and its work has now been crowned by the award of a Green Eco Flag. The recent appointment of an assistant head of co-curricular to coordinate it all demonstrates both how important this aspect is to the school and how incredibly well organised – essential if pupils are to fit it all in.

Real training for social awareness too, with masses raised for charities by the 'charity commission' – £25,000 plus per annum in a huge variety of enjoyable ways – and pupils enjoy the contact they have through educational programmes with local primary schools: 'It's a real pleasure to be able to help someone with reading or science'. Lots of D of E – gold awards – and a plethora of trips enthusiastically promoted by staff. 'Good staff – good at their job,' a parent commented.

Background and atmosphere: A historic foundation funded by William Capon for the poor scholars of Southampton, under royal charter from the boy king, it opened a year after his death in 1554. The present buildings date from its return from evacuation in Poole during WW2. From the outside it still looks like a post-war grammar school, despite acres of grass and smart blue railings all round – a recent really efficient security and check-in system is in place. Inside, it feels distinctly sophisticated and academic, with the acres of polished lino and slightly institutional coat of arms set into the front hall floor. Everything is geared to a comfortable, work-friendly environment. The atmosphere in the attractive sixth form centre, with its elegant metal arches, break-time snack bar and constantly manned careers offices, positively invites hard work. 'You can get more done here in an hour than in a whole evening at home,' an upper sixth boy commented.

Lots of recent refurbishment in the science zone part funded by the Abraham Trust. No shortage of money, so a new all singing and dancing technology centre and of course appropriate IT everywhere – iPads just coming in for the art department.

Recently acquired the Stroud School in Romsey, one of its main feeders, now known as Stroud, the King Edward VI Preparatory School.

Pastoral care, well-being and discipline: Terrific rapport between pupils and staff, especially amongst sixth formers. Prefects, known as Prepositors, and heads of houses patently feel part of the team running the school, and the head boy talks as eloquently as the head in the video clips on the website. Collaboration is key, with school council having a say in major decisions and undertaking research into pupils' needs. They take credit for the streamlined but inviting dining arrangements. Good healthy fare with svelte sixth formers tucking into old-fashioned nursery puddings – too busily occupied to put on weight. Rules on uniform etc are strictly observed, keeping the confrontation points at a superficial level. It must work since they look pretty smart, including the non-uniformed, 'dress for work' sixth form. Pastoral care run through tutor groups drawn from one or two years depending on age and stage. PHSE stresses intelligent responsibility. Lots of drugs education. Head more concerned about 'legal highs' – alcohol etc – and pupils' awareness of what they are doing to themselves. Sanctions range from detention for minor infringements of rules to expulsion, short suspension and investigation, testing for drugs. All staff get pretty extensive pastoral training and meeting times to coordinate concerns. The school assumes an intelligent attitude from pupils, and all rules and policies are clearly laid out with relevant explanation in the student diaries.

Pupils and parents: It's efficient and serves the large proportion of local medical and academic families, with very small ethnic minority proportion. The huge catchment area is right up to Andover and Winchester to the north and edging Portsmouth and Bournemouth east and west. Seventeen bus routes, all energy-savingly full, with major routes doing a second evening run for after-school activities. Locals, including the head, use bikes. Lots of community-minded parents run a PTA (the KESSoc) with second hand shop, social stuff etc. Most can't find anything but good to say of it.

Recent old Old Edwardians range from Hugh Whitemore (playwright and dramatist) and Michel Vickers (pop group Manfred Mann) to Michael Langrish (Bishop of Exeter), Ian Bruce (ex-president of the RNIB) and Sir Edward Abraham FRS (Oxford academic – ground-breaking work on penicillin and synthetic antibiotics). Also His Honour Judge David McCarraher, Sir Michael Bichard and Her Majesty's Ambassador Richard Kinchen MVO.

Entrance: Known to be hard enough to put off unrealistic would-bes but still about two try for every place. Exams in maths, English and reasoning plus interview and report from previous school. Half from state primaries, and around 25 local independents. Sixth form entry asks for six GCSEs at grade B including English and maths but possibly getting a bit more competitive after a bumper crop of super bright applicants. Pupils from the newly acquired Stroud prep school compete on equal terms with the other entrants – no special preference.

Exit: About 70 per cent go through to sixth form. Almost all to Russell Group universities – the cream. Around 10 per cent to Oxbridge.

Money matters: Bursaries, means-tested, 100 per cent remission for the most deserving. Scholarships, academic (up to 10 per cent) and creative arts (up to five per cent) of the fee. Entry at 11, 13 and sixth form. A tight budgeting school with a policy of never borrowing to build. Always has enough cash in hand to cope with any eventuality

Remarks: At first sight a juggernaut of a school, but definitely more upmarket than its grammar schoolish image. Everything done thoroughly and well, as its confident, lively and hard-working pupils attest. Certainly worth the commute from Andover.

King's Rochester

Satis House, Boley Hill, Rochester, Kent ME1 1TE

Pupils: 482 • Ages: 3–18 (boarding from 11) • Sixth form: 106 • C of E

Fees: Day £9,570 – £18,210; Boarding £20,580 – £29,580 pa

Tel: 01634 888590
Email: admissions@kings-rochester.co.uk
Website: www.kings-rochester.co.uk

Principal of King's Rochester and head of the senior school: Since 2012, Mr Jeremy Walker MA (Oxon) (40s). Previously head of sixth form and senior manager at Berkhamsted School, Hertfordshire. Educated at Sherborne School and read theology at Oxford before taking an MA in educational leadership and management at the Institute of Education, University of London. Started his career at Bishop Stopford School, a state secondary in Kettering, and became head of department after a year. Then moved to Ardingly, where he was head of religious studies and of theory of knowledge, and housemaster. He does not have time to teach here but is involved with Oxbridge preparation and interview technique and lateral thinking skills. His main objectives have been to improve academic performance, sports and careers and he has already negotiated the acquisition of a local sports centre and had it refurbished, introduced sports scholarships and been involved in setting up an effective careers network.

He says that he has 'built on the strengths of the school but has not shied away from areas which needed attention'. He is proud of the wide ability intake and believes in a broad curriculum and personalised education and, most importantly, that school should be fun. 'You get the best of both worlds here – a day school with a boarding school ethos.' He is 'sticking with King's traditions but making them relevant' and encourages parents to come to services in the cathedral. Parents full of praise: 'He is very disciplined and hard working, and that is the message he gives to the pupils'; 'A very efficient, caring man who knows the kids well and drops into lessons and chats to them; 'Very enthusiastic and has brought new vigour to the school'; 'Kids love him'. He is tightening up on everything including the uniform and has introduced zero tolerance on alcohol.

Met his wife, Harriet, when they were both at Sherborne; they have two children in the school and she teaches in the nursery and is involved with the Friends' Committee (parents' association). The school is their home and family life is very important to them, and they are keen to put down roots in the area. Mr Walker sits on the Cathedral Business Guild and a local cultural partnership to promote Rochester, and has strong links with the local military – the Royal Engineers.

Headmaster of the prep school: Since 2001, Mr Roger Overend BA FTCL ARCM (60s), a musician, educated at Trinity College of Music and previously head of Westminster Abbey Choir School. Married with three children, one of whom is in the prep school. An experienced headmaster who is very well regarded by parents. 'He has an air of authority – the kids respect him and know where they stand but are not afraid to ask questions'. 'Open approachable, understanding and thoughtful'. 'The kids are happy to ask for help – he makes them feel valued'. 'He's always there and knows where everyone is.' 'He listens to

K

parents and always replies promptly to emails, even over the weekends'. He teaches music theory to the choristers.

Headmistress of pre-prep and nursery since 2009 Mrs Sarah Skillern MA BA NPQH (late 30s). She works closely with Mr Overend and both heads sit on the school's executive board with Mr Jeremy Walker, principal of the senior school, although both heads are largely autonomous.

Academic matters: Children streamed from year 6 and setted in some subjects. French introduced in year 5, PSHE taught from year 6 and Latin and DT from year 7. All three sciences taught separately in year 8, and can use the senior school labs. 'Kids gradually prepared for senior school and are encouraged to take responsibility for themselves'. About a quarter of lessons taught by senior school teachers in the last year, some in the senior school, and top two years can play in the senior school symphony orchestra. German introduced in the nursery via fun-based activities with songs and puppets, and continues into the senior school – taught by a native speaker. Years 7 and 8 do an exchange with a school in Munich every other year. New head of IT 'very forward thinking' and IT is integrated into all lessons and taught as a subject throughout the prep school. The library is the centre of the school and younger children are taught how to use it – a bright light space.

Good learning support – one full time and three part time SEN teachers. Offers mostly in-class support, mainly for mild to moderate dyslexia and mild behavioural issues, and has a 'joined up approach'. Staff often go into English lessons to look for issues. The school no longer has CReSTeD status. Light touch EAL when required.

K

Caters for a wide range of academic ability from 'Oxbridge to average'. In 2016, 37 per cent A*/A at GCSE and 28 per cent at A level (58 per cent A*-B). Pretty impressive for an almost non-selective school in grammar school country – in fact they often outperform grammars in exam results. Offers double and triple award science and all do RS and ICT at GCSE. PE, music, classical Greek, Russian and German are among other subjects offered. Business studies, government and politics and history of art amongst 24 A level offerings. Will run an A level class for as few as three pupils and 'will go to great lengths to tailor the timetable to suit the children'. Extended Project Qualification also offered alongside A levels – another feather in your cap for university entrance.

An extraordinarily dedicated team of teachers – a good combination of some who have been in the school for many years and bright, young, newly qualified staff, and Mr Walker has brought in some new blood since his arrival, including a dynamic new head of ICT. 'The levels of devotion are extraordinary – they even ran revision classes on Easter Monday,' said one parent. 'The teachers really seem to care how we do,' said a pupil. Dedicated careers department – 'school has beefed up advice for university and beyond,' said a parent. An old boy has set up Jobs Network to provide advice and work experience to current and former pupils and help with interview practice and technique. Current and former parents encouraged to offer help with work experience or as a mentor. All upper sixth have mock job interviews with feedback and lower sixth have cv writing clinics.

Team of qualified SEN teachers – mainly for mild dyslexia, although school happily accommodates those with greater needs where possible. Pupils assisted in class, through withdrawals and with IEPs.

Games, options, the arts: Sport on the up helped by the introduction of sports scholarships and the new facilities. School has recently taken over the Stirling Sports Centre and adjoining Holcombe Hockey Club from Medway Council, now refurbished and renamed the King's Rochester Sports Centre, a 10 minute walk or short minibus ride from the school. Olympic standard Astroturfs and new outdoor tennis and netball courts plus indoor hockey, badminton and cricket nets and a fitness suite. Free membership for King's parents and open to the general public too. Some team sports still played on the pitches within the school grounds. On site netball means the girls now get match teas – has made the 'netball mums' very happy. Rowing from the school's own boathouse on the Medway near Maidstone – 18 rowing boats and five large canoes. School very supportive of outside achievements eg national level pentathlon plus sailing and skating, and several pupils play cricket, rugby or hockey at county level. Strong tradition of fencing – fencing master was involved with organising Olympic competition. Duke of Edinburgh popular and 10-15 do gold each year. CCF offered in all three services – compulsory for the first two years and many keep going. Our guide had learnt how to fly a plane with the RAF division.

Impressive music – the prep is a cathedral school so the choristers (boys only 8-13) are part of the school and the chapel is Rochester Cathedral. Choir trips all over the place and they make recordings for Radio 3. Several choirs, orchestras and ensembles, a wind and jazz group and inspirational and 'brilliant' director of music. About 50 per cent learn at least one instrument with several reaching grade 8 each year, and a number go on to study music, often with organ or choral scholarships; pupils recently won scholarships to the Royal College and Royal Academy of Music. On a lighter note, the annual house music competition and popular termly 'Open Mic' night gives pupils an opportunity to perform in public. Termly junior concerts in the school hall and a celebration of the performing arts in the summer term. All children in the pre-prep have the chance to perform in a concert. One lavish theatre production each year and plenty of opportunities to perform in public; poetry festival, LAMDA exams and informal concerts as well as visiting theatre groups and drama workshops.

Busy art department with photography, sculpture and fine art offered – product design particularly popular and pupils often go on to art college. Three major drama productions a year, numerous theatre and opera trips to London, and visiting theatre groups organise drama workshop within the school.

Numerous after-school clubs and societies with 'something for everyone' including bell ringing, debating, ICT and chess. Ballet popular throughout the school: some up to grade 8, and a handful keep going into sixth form. Lots of trips and outings – choir to Vatican and China, Physics to CERN, maths to NASA and World Challenge to Northern India.

Boarding: Up to 70 boarders, about half from overseas – 14 different nationalities and school works hard on integration. Boys' boarding house for 43 and girls' for 25. Start off in small dorms, and sixth form and most of fifth form have their own room with ensuite bathroom. Always something organised at weekends and children are expected to take part.

Background and atmosphere: Part of the Foundation of Rochester Cathedral, the school was founded in 606AD at the same time as the cathedral and re-founded under Henry VIII in 1541 when the monastery at Rochester was dissolved. It is the second oldest school in the UK after King's Canterbury. Prefects wear a gown and carry a cane but the school is certainly not old fashioned and inward-looking. A great sense of history here with the buildings clustered round the cathedral and next to the Norman castle; Charles II spent his first night in England at Restoration House on his return in 1660 and Queen Elizabeth I is rumoured to have stayed at Satis House (now the school administration building). A range of buildings from the medieval cathedral to Georgian, Victorian and 21st century, with Watling Street running down the high street. An unexpected and peaceful oasis in the middle of the bustling Medway towns.

Prep and pre-prep very much part of the whole King's School. They are all part of the strong Christian community with the cathedral at its centre, but all faiths made to feel welcome. Prep and pre-prep are both self-contained but use the senior school facilities including the swimming pool, art and DT room, games pitches and sports centre. Purpose built pre-prep has bright and colourful classrooms and its own play area. Prep school is a cluster of modern buildings surrounding the paddock (used for rugby and cricket) and shares a large hall with the pre-prep. Light and airy with photographs all over the place. One of the few co-ed independent schools in Kent which offers a seamless education from 3-18 years.

Pastoral care, well-being and discipline: Strong Christian ethos; the cathedral is the centre of school life and the service held four mornings a week is a period of quiet reflection before the day begins. All faiths and backgrounds welcomed. All are expected to come to the services in the cathedral but do not have to participate. All new prep school children have a buddy who contacts them in the holidays and looks after them when they arrive. A tangible sense of community where everyone knows each other well and it is 'a very family oriented school where there are genuine friendships across year groups and kids look after each other,' said one happy mother. 'It is a close knit community that produces confident, self-reliant children who are not cocky,' said another, and 'It really does try to cater for all, and they are very personal in the way they deal with the kids'. 'My son has at last found a school where he is happy – it offers the best pastoral care I have come across. Most schools say they treat every child as an individual but King's Rochester really does,' said a father. School takes a firm line on drugs and runs a programme of drug awareness through PHSE but has not had any issues.

Pupils and parents: Big range from traditional to first time buyers and some who make genuine sacrifices to send their children here. Some come from the Medway towns and villages, some from 25 miles away and some come down on the train from SE London, Bromley and Blackheath. Extensive minibus service from as far away as Tonbridge and Sevenoaks. Children generally 'down to earth and engaging – they exude confidence and are compassionate, sociable and great fun to be with'.

Former pupils known as Old Roffensians and are hugely supportive with a great sense of loyalty to the school, and tend to keep in touch. They go on to follow a variety of careers and include surgeons, musicians, authors, artists and poets. Alumni include Prof Sir Derek Barton, who won the Nobel Prize for Chemistry, John Gummer, former Conservative cabinet minister, Pete Tong, Radio 1 DJ and Matthew Walker, professional cricketer.

Good communication with parents who say they feel involved. Moodle, a virtual learning environment where children can access classwork, homework and notes is proving popular with parents, who can keep an eye on what is going on.

Entrance: Most join in the nursery at age 3+ and move on to the pre-prep the following year. Places allocated on a first come first served basis. Entry into the prep is via an interview with both parents and the child and a report from the child's current school – most join at 8+ and 11+ but will take children at any time if there are spaces. Large intake at 11+, particularly from primary schools and independent schools which finish at this age – testing in English, maths and non-verbal reasoning; this also guarantees them a place in the senior school. Will only not offer a place if a child needs more help than the school can offer – mild to moderate dyslexia no problem. Choristers (boys only) admitted via a series of musical and academic tests and join in year 4, and are offered music scholarships worth 30 per cent of fees which can be topped up with a bursary if necessary and 30 per cent off (compulsory) music lessons.

Broad ability intake to senior school but children are expected to be able to take 9/10 GCSEs and 3/4 A levels. Summer exams for those coming up from junior school are used for setting purposes and very few fail; and school will give plenty of warning if this is likely to happen. Entry from other schools at 13+ via common entrance or school's own tests. Occasionally spaces in year 10. Very few leave after GCSEs. Another 20 per cent join in sixth form and are expected to get at least five GCSEs at grade C or above and As or Bs in subjects to be studied at A level.

Exit: Most juniors move on to the senior school. About six a year to local grammar schools. Support and help with maths and non-verbal reasoning but do not coach for the Kent Test. Very few leave after GCSEs. None to Oxford in 2016, one to Michigan and one to RADA. Exeter, Royal Holloway and Southampton popular destinations.

Money matters: Offers sports, academic, all-rounder and music (including organ) scholarships worth up to 30 per cent of fees which can be topped up with means-tested bursaries up to 75 per cent of fees. Choral scholarships offered in the prep school. Discounts for clergy, Forces families and siblings.

Remarks: A warm and caring family school with some of the best pastoral care around where children can grow up in the shadow of the cathedral. A wide ability range but all made to feel valued and the brightest get into the best universities. Going from strength to strength under the dynamic newish head.

Kings' School (Winchester)

Romsey Road, Winchester, Hampshire SO22 5PN

Pupils: 1,680 • Ages: 11–16

Tel: 01962 861161
Email: kings.school@kings-winchester.hants.sch.uk
Website: www.kings-winchester.hants.sch.uk

Headteacher: Since 2013, Matthew Leeming. Educated at Westminster School and St John's College, Durham. He taught geography at schools in Liverpool, Lincolnshire and Peterborough before moving to Hampshire. After spending six years as deputy headteacher at Brookfield Community School, he was appointed headteacher of Crofton School in Stubbington. Married, with two children, Mr Leeming lives in Chichester, which has a similar school system and his family experience confirms his view that secondary 11-16 school followed by sixth form college is a very beneficial arrangement for pupils. Friendly, unpretentious and easy to talk to, he evidently loves Kings'. Describing himself as 'the cat that got the cream,' he believes it is an exceptional school and seeks to maintain its outstanding academic standards and well-ordered discipline, perhaps 'softening it a little to make it a more nurturing atmosphere for 11 year olds'. He exudes pride in the school, and this attitude is shared by many of the staff (there are an exceptionally high number of staff children in school), and this clearly rubs off on the confidence and motivation of his pupils. Under his guidance Kings' has become the lead school in the Winchester Teaching School Alliance, which includes all the

Winchester schools and the university. It has resisted academy status, regarding Hampshire as a very education friendly local authority.

Academic matters: Results rival those of grammar schools, which is impressive for a school with a totally comprehensive admission, and one which accepts a high number of disabled and special needs pupils. In 2016, 83 per cent of pupils got 5+ A*-C at GCSE including maths and English and 38 per cent of grades were A*/A, an achievement which would be considered gratifying for upper streams elsewhere. Business studies, which moved to a new business suite in late 2016, is key to the curriculum and is added to the GCSE core of maths, English and science (plus PE and PHSEE) for all. Since all the staffing concentrates on only five year groups with 336 in each, Kings' is able to offer and a bigger and more flexible group of options than most. Pupils are divided into bands for two groups of subjects – maths/science and English/humanities. Other subjects are taught in mixed-ability groups. This gives a combination of setting and streaming which allows all pupils to be in appropriate groups even if they happen to be brilliant at one subject but struggle with others.

All but one humanities group are encouraged to take at least one modern foreign language and some encouraged to take two, so the languages are better served than in many schools, with French, German, Spanish and Italian on offer from first year. Pupils who request a particular language normally get it, and can add a second language from the second year. Native speakers of other languages are given help to tackle GCSE in their own language and get consistently high results. No Greek at present but Mr Leeming wonders if they are missing a trick there, as Latin is popular – so watch this space. Science can be taken as a double GCSE or three separate subjects depending on the pupil's band and science, English and maths are sometimes taught in single sex groups depending on the needs of each group.

Results for the separate sciences demonstrate quite how well Kings' does for able students: A* and A grades are achieved consistently by about 60 per cent of biology and chemistry students, and over 70 per cent in physics, with a regular 100 per cent A*-C in all three. Single subject Science results (all three sciences as one subject) offered to those with less scientific interest or aptitude. More than 40 option choices including child development, photography and a BTec in PE among the less common.

Since the school is a centre for access for physically disabled pupils there is a huge allocation of 30 or more staff, who provide extra help in class for a variety of needs. SEN pupils can have up to three hours individual support teaching or get support in lessons, and every assistance is given so that only in exceptional cases are pupils excluded from a subject of particular difficulty. Both the SENCo and pupil support teachers ensure that all aspects of pupils' needs are met including sport for physically disabled pupils.

Some parents worry that Kings' may not develop academic strugglers as well as high fliers, but as one parent pointed out, 'outcomes for lower streams are exceptional' – and the figures certainly confirm this view.

Games, options, the arts: Art, music and drama all do respectably as exam subjects with good sized groups. Music is immensely well served as an activity with choirs, orchestra and groups for classical and popular music, and there are annual drama productions and performance nights – The Crucible was in rehearsal at the time of our visit. Kings' now incorporates the Tower Arts Centre with theatre and dance space so has use of some professional facilities.

Sport is definitely a key feature with lots of post-school and lunchtime extra sport – cricket nets, tennis etc and boys' and girls' teams for major sports. Stopping at 16 means they don't get the national accolade that some all-through schools manage, but the girls proudly announced that they had been second nationally in U16 girls' football recently 'and it was all decided in a penalty shoot-out at the end. Half the school went up to Manchester to watch'. One sporting publication judged them as best comprehensive school for sport. Teams do pretty well locally with a star player nominated by the school after each match, and there are regular tours abroad for netball and football. The impressive sports hall and pool are a shared with the local community and there is generous provision of Astroturf and other playing facilities.

Though there is not the huge diverse range of activities that some independent schools offer there is definitely something for most interests, with maths, science and other subjects running teams in national challenges. (Maths does particularly well.) Activities are mainly in the lunch hour and before 4.30pm with a second fleet of buses provided for those who stay on. Homework club offers a chance to get it done before going home with a bit on help on hand, and there is a catch-up homework session in the lunch hour. Theatre visits bound plus exchanges to Spain, Germany, France and Italy, and subject related-trips to Iceland, Germany and even New York.

Background and atmosphere: The spacious green site originally harboured a girls' school and a boys' school – both rather rocky. Their visionary amalgamation into an 11-16 mixed school over 25 years ago created an exceptionally well-organised and thus academically fruitful academic atmosphere. The buildings are harmoniously set round courtyard spaces amid green pitches and park-like grounds. It feels like an independent school, except that Hampshire manages to maintain the grounds as fit for purpose but not to manicured garden standard.

Wheelchairs and walking frames cause no comment and there is a special wheelchair-friendly space in the dining room. On our visit the dining room was functioning as the floor of the stock exchange in a noisy and extremely enthusiastic business studies day, but was miraculously restored to function in time for lunch. Pupils say food is OK and appreciate the summer ice cream and winter hot drinks stalls run as business enterprises by senior pupils. Work experience is compulsory for everyone in year 10, while younger pupils have activities week.

Pastoral care, well-being and discipline: Uniform is pretty smart on the whole with very few ties at half mast. A parent commented that this is a place where it is definitely OK to do well. Pupils say there are few rebels and hard working responsible behaviour is so much the norm that it is definitely 'uncool' to flout the rules. This was very evident on our visit when an unscheduled fire alarm had 1,700 pupils standing in perfect silence for 10 minutes while well-oiled procedures checked the buildings. Everyone was accounted for within eight minutes – quite a feat in the middle of lunch break in so large school with so many wheelchairs in evidence and some groups miles away on the games field!.The support team was noticeably watchful for anyone who might have problems standing long in the sun and everyone had an extra bit of time off to make up for missed lunch break.

Pastoral care is mainly through tutor groups of about 30. Discipline is traditional and strict, though Mr Leeming is very aware that children also need kindness and a bit of freedom, so there is a distinct and possibly necessary softening of atmosphere in favour of really good pastoral care. Pupils said there was little or no bullying and Mr Leeming said that the inevitable few issues were quickly pinched in the bud.

There is strong leadership from the year 11s, who considered they had a good social life and were looking forward to their leavers' prom. They told us that they enjoy the disciplined atmosphere and consider the rules sensible, saying that very few pupils don't really buy in to the Kings' mindset.

Pupils and parents: Catchment includes some outlying villages but mainly local housing which has quite a wide social mix; some quite downmarket as well as the academic shady suburbs. Pupils are friendly and articulate. The prefect layer gains from responsibility earlier than in an 11-18 school, so that they are confident and definitely proud of their school.

Until recently there was a small boarding house mostly for pupils from abroad. There are still a few pupils who lodge in the town to attend Kings' but the emphasis is now on children from the locality.

Alumni include comedian Jack Dee, actor Colin Firth and footballer Wayne Bridge, though the first two date from before the current amalgamation.

Entrance: After looked after children and those with medical needs, priority to siblings, those in the catchment area (mostly south and west of the school), those from linked primary schools, children of staff.

Exit: The vast majority (about 70 per cent) go to Peter Symonds, with the others spread between Barton Peveril, Sparsholt and Eastleigh Colleges for sixth form. A few go to vocational courses. In 2016, nine Kings' pupils who went on to Peter Symonds College made it to Oxbridge.

Remarks: An exceptional school. One parent told us that she and her children were proud and privileged to belong to such a great school – and all for free. Definitely Kings' has all the characteristics of a good school, whether maintained or independent: academic excellence, strong leadership, sound and enlightened discipline and wonderful facilities. No wonder some parents are prepared to pay by accepting Winchester house prices.

The King's School Canterbury

25 The Precincts, Canterbury, Kent CT1 2ES

Pupils: 1,235; 636 full boarders • Ages: 3–18 (boarding from year 6) • Sixth form: 381

Fees: Day £10,500 – £26,700; Boarding £24,240 – £35,295 pa

Tel: 01227 595579
Email: admissions@kings-school.co.uk
Website: www.kings-school.co.uk

Headmaster: Since 2011, Mr Peter Roberts MA PGCE (50s), previously head of Bradfield College for eight years. He was educated at Tiffin Boys and read history at Merton College, Oxford where he got a first, followed by a PGCE at London Institute of Education. Started teaching career at Winchester as head of history, then also as master in college. Always immaculately dressed – 'sometimes a vision in tweed and sometimes besuited'. He is super brainy and regarded as 'quirky and eccentric but with a good sense of humour and perfect for the job – we would not want anyone who was run of the mill,' said a happy parent. A thoughtful academic 'who works unbelievably hard and is always out and about with his dog.' He attends every play, recital and concert and even attends the matrons' meeting; describing his job as 'vastly enjoyable.' Teaches the Shells (year 9) 'when he can'. Says he was struck by everyone's enthusiasm about the school when he first arrived and 'listened to the constituent parts'; he has now set out his vision for the future and what he considers to be the 'essence' of King's. Major projects include the acquisition of the Malthouse, which will be converted into a performing and visual arts centre, and a Victorian primary school, which houses a new girls' boarding house.

The headmaster describes the ethos of the school as 'interactive osmosis'. 'It is the richness, the diversity and range of our lives here that makes it distinct and special.' He feels the school 'gives a strong sense of belonging, a realisation that King's helped to make them (the pupils) what they are' and 'this creates the wish to give something back in return' and sees the atmosphere of the school as 'like a massive confidence-building machine'. Expects very high standards from the children at every level and has tightened up on discipline, manners and presentation. Each week the Robertses invite 15 different pupils, one from each house, to lunch in their private dining room. Much expected too from staff and light being shed on the few pockets of less than good teaching.

Married to Marie, an elegant and accomplished Frenchwoman who was head of department at two large state schools and, in addition to teaching French and German, is also a harpist. They have three daughters. Enjoys spending time in France where he sails, practises calligraphy and paints watercolours.

Head of junior school since 2000, Mr Peter Wells BEd. Educated at Eltham College and Exeter University where he studied art and design. Before coming to Junior King's he was headmaster of Liverpool College Prep and St Hugh's School in Lincolnshire and previously a housemaster at Dulwich College and head of art and design at Cheltenham College Junior School. Teaches art when he can and likes to get involved with clubs and activities. He is an ISI inspector and a member of the IAPS education committee, as well as being a member of the King's senior management team. A headmaster 'at the top of his game', he is married to Vivienne, who is the registrar and an ISI boarding inspector, and together they make an effective and dynamic team. They live in a cottage in the grounds and escape to Cornwall during the holidays. They have three adult children. Peter is passionate about the school and has a keen eye for detail and is always looking for ways to make improvements. Has recruited 'top notch' senior management and teachers. Respected by children and parents alike and knows all the children by name.

Academic matters: Average class size 15-16, max 18 in junior school. Three parallel forms with setting in maths from year 5, English, maths and languages from year 6 and science in year 8 – very flexible and all about challenge and support. Separate scholarship class in year 8. Children start learning French in reception and Spanish and Latin taught from year 5. Greek offered to scholars. Special provision for French, Spanish and Chinese bilingual children. Separate sciences taught in specialist laboratories from year 7. ICT incorporated into most subjects and also taught as a specialist subject from year 1 and children learn programming skills eg making computer games as well as spread sheets, presentations and website design. 'Everyone is expected to participate in class and it is a fast-paced academic school which does not suit everyone'. Very occasionally, it is suggested tactfully that a child might do better elsewhere.

Bright, sunny library central to main junior school with 14,000 books and run by a part-time librarian – the most widely-read children are appointed to 'The Most Honourable Order of the Book'. Pre-prep and year 3 have their own libraries. Experienced staff of 'inspiring and dedicated teachers' as well as talented young graduate assistants who come to work for a year before going to train as teachers. Much more attention given to SEN in recent years, about 10 per cent with some sort of learning support, either withdrawal or in-class help – system of monitoring and referrals means problems picked up early. Two dyslexia teachers, one full-time, one part-time plus a graphologist. EAL support if required.

The pursuit of academic excellence is at the heart of everything the school does but co-curricular activities given equal weight and pupils have a 'rich' day. The brightest take some GCSEs early, allowing a head start on A level subjects; the less academic may drop a subject at GCSE. Pupils encouraged to take a creative subject like art, drama IT or music alongside academic subjects. In 2016, 55 per cent A*/A at A level. Seventy-five per cent A*/A at GCSE (IGCSEs for most subjects). Strong across the board and languages particularly good – mainly taught by native speakers and housed in the Old Palace. Sciences popular – female head of science and five out of the seven physics teachers are women. Most subject combinations can be accommodated even if some have to be taught outside the timetable. School always looking at ways to stretch the most able and curriculum constantly adapted. Currently 27 subjects to chose from at A level (including geology) and advanced extension awards in most. Astronomy offered as a GCSE along with Italian, Russian and Mandarin GCSE ab initio in sixth form. Strong work ethic and 'Children do not seem to realise how much they cram into the day, it is just normal for them,' said one mother.

Pupils encouraged to think about their broader academic profile and alongside A levels there are enrichment subjects such as critical thinking, perspectives on aesthetics, globalisation and science and the extended project. Careers advice starts in the first year on a drop-in basis and fifth form have timetabled careers periods to help with A level choices and beyond.

Stunning William Butterfield designed library (1848) is centre of academic life with a hushed and studious atmosphere and combining the best of the old and new with 30,000 books and a range of periodicals and European newspapers as well as DVDs and online reference sources. It is a great source of pride and always staffed and open every day until 10pm and at weekends. Somerset Maugham and Sir Hugh Walpole both left their personal libraries to King's.

About six per cent need extra help, mainly for mild dyslexia, and any pupil can ask for help with study skills. Probably would not suit anyone with bigger difficulties and some parental concerns that children do not get as much support as they need. EAL for a handful of pupils but all must be fluent on arrival. No plans to introduce the IB.

Games, options, the arts: Acres of playing fields about 15 minutes' walk away as well as a modern sports centre incorporating pool, indoor courts, climbing wall, café and gym – more akin to the smartest private leisure centre than the school sports department. Huge choice of sports – girls' hockey thriving with 15 girls in the English hockey training system. Cricket and rugby going from strength to strength and several boys have been selected to play for Kent U18s; school has also produced several international fencers. Rowing on the up for boys and girls after a period in the doldrums and old boy Tom Ransley won gold at Rio 2016. Sports coaches include England cricketer Mark Ealham and Olympic hockey player Jennifer Wilson. Not everyone represents the school in matches but still play sport for 'fitness, health and fun' and most people find something they enjoy. Everyone is expected to get involved and participation is everything – 'you don't have to be brilliant but just give it a go and have fun.' Sporting trips all over the world – rugby in Argentina, cricket in Grenada and netball in South Africa.

Long tradition of excellent drama and music and anyone involved is definitely awarded 'cool status.' Fab new junior music school opening early 2016 – over half the pupils learn at least one instrument. Symphony orchestra plus numerous bands and ensembles; the pupil-run jazz club is particularly popular. Plenty of choral groups, from the Crypt Choir which tours annually, most recently to China, to the choral society which is open to anyone who enjoys singing, including parents and staff. 'Wherever you go around the school there is always music coming from somewhere'. Masses of drama both on and off the curriculum – house plays, GCSE and A level productions, drama competitions, fashion shows, full school plays – 'Wherever there is a quiet corner, you will find a rehearsal going on,' as well as regular theatre trips to London. Busy art department housed in 12th-century priory has a different artist in residence each year. New photographic studio and pottery centre opened by old boy Edmund de Waal.

Huge range of activities continues into sixth form – anything from academic societies with visiting speakers to mountain biking, cryptic crosswords, debating and the Model United Nations. CCF once again a popular option. Community work and volunteering are central to school life and are often part of Duke of Edinburgh Award and include teaching science in local primary schools, riding for the disabled and help with swimming for handicapped children.

The famous King's week at the end of the summer term is the highlight of the year for pupils and parents alike and is a festival of music, drama and dance with events being staged in all corners of the school every day for a week – parents and friends come bearing picnics and it is a major social event culminating in Commem Day and the leavers' ball. 'The quality and variety are phenomenal' and there is everything from Shakespeare, classical concerts and jazz as well as a lighter touch provided by the house harmonies. Those not involved do not feel excluded and have as much fun as those taking part.

Sport taken seriously in the junior school and the school likes to win; pupils consistently encouraged to make the most of everything. Superb facilities and children can go to King's for anything not available at Junior King's. Rowing an option from year 7 in conjunction with senior King's plus a cricket pro and winter coaching and squash offered at King's. Floodlit Astro (funded by a parent) opened in 2013 means hockey now a major sport for boys and girls. Girls have been IAPS champions three times in recent years. Huge galleried sports hall and 14 tennis courts. LTA tennis coach recently appointed and school usually sends a team to the national IAPS tournament at Queenswood. Heated outdoor pool for fun but serious swimming taught at the King's recreation centre. Fencing particularly strong and a number of international fencers started at Junior King's. Few parental grumbles about children not getting picked for teams or getting into school plays but school aware of this and tries to address it. Inter-house competitions give everyone a chance to take part and new talents often emerge at the summer sports day when a huge variety of sports are contested.

Performing arts take place in the Tithe Barn, recently insulated and refurbished thanks to another very generous parent. Music is central to the life of the school with class music from reception upwards, over 60 per cent learn at least one instrument and the choir is a special part of school life. New purpose-built music school opened in January 2016. Range of bands, choirs and ensembles cater for every age and ability and with at least one big concert each term, 'music is never far from your ears.' Advent carol service and sung evensong at the end of the summer term are held in the cathedral and there are music scholarships to King's Senior most years. Drama part of the curriculum from year 3 and just about everyone has a chance to get up on stage at least once a year.

Busy art department – photography, film making, art history, graphic design, pottery, textiles – the sort of opportunities you would expect to find at a senior school and children can use the facilities at King's as well. DT from year 3 includes racing car design when children build and race a car in the Kent championships, jewellery making and T shirt design and a Dragons' Den type competition when children form teams to solve problems.

Annual Spanish exchange, skiing, weekend in Normandy, post-scholarship trip to Greece, the much looked forward to post-CE jaunt to Cornwall, rugby to Paris, hockey to Holland, cricket and choir tours to Brussels – European destinations which do not put too much strain on parental pockets.

Activities most afternoons and evenings, dozens to choose from (some charged for), everything from animation, circus skills and bushcraft to debating, gardening, jazz dance, riding and photography (digital and dark room).

Boarding: Six boys' and five girls' senior boarding houses (latest, Kingsdown House, for girls, opened September 2015). Half the houses clustered round the cathedral and the other half across the road on the St Augustine site where they have their own dining hall. Pupils equally happy to be in houses in either location, most popular houses booked up years in advance. Boarding houses friendly and welcoming with areas where pupils can make their own snacks and relax. Small dormitories for younger children and individual study bedrooms for sixth form. Large and popular social centre open for the whole school during the day and for sixth formers in the evening.

Full-time and weekly Junior King's boarders (mainly from year 6+) cared for in two immaculate houses: Kipling (boys) and Juckes (girls). Local children often ask to board for the last year and one mother commented slightly wistfully, 'my daughter wants to be at school more than she wants to be at home'. Lots of evening and weekend activities plus Saturday school with lessons in the morning and sport in the afternoon means there is no time to get bored or homesick. Around 45 per cent boarders are overseas.

Background and atmosphere: Set in the shadow of Canterbury Cathedral and part of a World Heritage Site, this has to be one of the most inspiring settings for a school. Founded in 597 when St Augustine arrived in Canterbury and then re-founded as The King's School during the reign of Henry VIII after the dissolution of the monasteries – not many schools can produce a list of headmasters going back to 1259. Beautiful ancient buildings and cloisters and immaculate gardens with the busy city life going on just beyond the gates. Pupils enjoy the contrast and the fact that the city with its shops and cafés is on the doorstep and say, 'it makes us feel part of the real world'. The headmaster says the combination of the cathedral and a vibrant student city 'grounds the children in a wider reality'. The school sponsors the Folkestone Academy and lends its facilities to the wider community.

Took girls into sixth form in 1970s and went fully co-ed in 1990. Boarding houses plus thee day houses and a smaller sixth form girls' house in a variety of architectural styles from the 13th century Meister Omers to 21st century Grange. A close knit community, 'it's got everything, the spiritual dimension from the cathedral and a sense of beauty and history'. Former pupil Michael Morpurgo said, 'King's is like a university designed for younger people.'

Junior King's founded in 1879 as the prep school for The King's School, Canterbury and spent its first 50 years in the precincts of the cathedral. Boys were known as 'parrots' because of the noise they made and houses are still named after parrots. Moved to current site in 1929 when Lady Milner gave Sturry Court, an Elizabethan manor house, together with the Tithe Barn, in memory of her husband. It was opened by their friend Rudyard Kipling. Two miles from the centre of Canterbury, it is set in 80 acres of grounds and playing fields with the River Stour running through the middle. Along with King's, it is part of the Canterbury Cathedral Foundation, shares a governing body with King's and has a committee of four governors closely linked to the junior school.

Junior school has a reputation for being quite competitive and according to the prospectus 'endeavour and success are held in the highest regard'; however, the number one Golden Rule is 'Do be kind, gentle, helpful, respectful and polite' and there is great emphasis on good manners, tolerance and friendliness. Parents full of praise for the school: 'My children are all very different and have all been happy – you don't have to be very sporty to have fun here'. 'The competitive environment has brought my daughter out of herself and given her confidence.' All agree that this school is 'best for children who are good at something' and that 'there is a very nice balance between academia and other things so children can build confidence in different areas'.

Pre-prep housed in the Oast House with own hall and library. Seven classrooms with up-to-date ICT provide a colourful and stimulating environment. Children learn PE, French, dance and music from reception onwards and use the prep school facilities – sports hall, Tithe Barn, sports fields and dining hall. Accredited forest school in the grounds where children learn about nature and risk-taking in a safe environment – they were making nettle pancakes over a camp fire on the day we visited. Nursery now housed in newly built Swiss-style chalet known as Little Barn with all the mod cons and under floor heating – a busy happy place with guinea pigs and fish tanks.

Pastoral care, well-being and discipline: Relationships with staff relaxed but respectful in Junior King's and there is always someone to talk to – year 5 onwards have two class teachers, one male, one female. 'The teachers seem interested in developing my child as a human being not just on an academic level,' said one happy parent. Bullying rare and dealt with swiftly via detailed anti-bullying policy. Good healthy food with lots of choice and staff make sure children eat a balanced meal.

Smart uniform worn throughout the school, pinstripes, wing collars and a jacket – and a brooch for the girls. All look very professional and businesslike; monitors wear purple gowns and are, unsurprisingly, known as 'Purples'. Astonishingly busy day – one of the first lessons the children learn is how to plan their time – but there is still room for lots of fun. Strict rules and punishments regarding drugs, alcohol and parties and children know where they stand. Strong Christian tradition and moral values. The main school services held in the cathedral but different religious and cultural backgrounds recognised and valued.

Children have a healthy respect for each other and are generally self-regulating regarding bullying and other misdemeanours, and honesty and integrity are highly valued. Pastoral care comes in for particular praise from the inspectors. Big effort to address everyone's happiness with several staff/pupil committees to ensure all have their say.

Regular communication with parents especially through housemasters and house mistresses. Good interaction between year groups facilitated by mixed age tutor groups and mentoring from older pupils. New 'Shells' have a top year mentor. Day children and boarders mix well and 'you can't tell the difference,' according to one pupil.

Pupils and parents: A good mix socially and culturally with a wide catchment area – popular with locals, London and county sets and Foreign Office families and increasing numbers from abroad. About 20 per cent foreign nationals. Doesn't really produce a type but pupils are articulate, well rounded and very supportive of each other, appearing genuinely to celebrate each other's achievements. 'The finished product is amazing,' according to one mother. 'The boys and girls are charming, personable, not shy or arrogant and have a great sense of fun but are still ambitious'.

The recently formed King's Society, a cultural, social and educational society for parents and friends, now comprises over 300 families. Members organise lectures, music recitals, tours of the cathedral with the dean and social events. Old boys and girls include potter and writer Edmund de Waal, astronaut Michael Foale, Patrick Leigh-Fermor, Christopher Marlowe and William Somerset Maugham, supermodel Jacquetta Wheeler, Olympic silver medallist and world champion rower Frances Houghton and Anthony Worrall-Thompson.

Entrance: Most join in nursery and reception but major intakes into year 5 and year 7 when extra classes are added and occasionally into year 8 for common entrance if going on to King's. Younger children have a taster day and informal assessments and from year 5 children tested in English, maths and non-verbal reasoning.

At 13+ by common entrance. School's own exam and an interview for those who have not been prepared for CE. Occasionally spaces in year 10. About a third come from Junior King's but they still have to take the same exams as everyone else rest from a range of Kent and Sussex prep schools and London day schools. Pass mark has recently been raised to 60 per cent but school likes to keep families together and takes an enlightened view if someone is borderline. It is also possible for pupils to take an entrance exam to Junior King's at 11+ which would guarantee entry to the senior school – they would still have to take CE for setting purposes. About 30 join in the sixth form with entrance by competitive exam and interview in Nov before entry with minimum of seven Bs or equivalent at GCSE. Seven Bs required to move into sixth form.

Exit: About 75 per cent of juniors go on to the senior school. Others to destinations including Tonbridge, St Edmund's, Eton and Battle Abbey. A few leave for the grammar schools at 11+ – some after-school coaching provided but parents usually get their own as well. Scholarships to senior school every year plus recent academic scholarships to Sevenoaks, Wycombe Abbey and Tonbridge and art and sports scholarships to Tonbridge and music and sport to Benenden. Two recent sports scholarships to Millfield. Those considered borderline for King's required to sit a pre-test and parents are given plenty of advice if it is thought a child might not pass common entrance to their chosen school.

Those who leave after GCSEs (very few), usually go to local schools or London day schools. Vast majority of sixth formers depart to top universities – 23 to Oxbridge in 2016, with Exeter, Edinburgh, Durham, York, Imperial and Warwick all popular. Increasing numbers to American universities (12 in 2016). Languages, sciences and economics/business management most popular degree subjects recently. Between 10 and 15 to medical school each year.

Money matters: Means-tested bursaries available from year 7 for up to 100 per cent of the boarding fee. Academic scholarships offered at 11+ for new joiners and children already in the junior school – worth a max of five per cent of fees. Additional bursary support available. Up to 20 King's Scholarships and exhibitions as well as music and sports and art scholarships, all with a rigorous selection process and worth up to 10 per cent of fees. Three or four sixth form scholarships awarded for outstanding performance in the sixth form entrance exam. Greater emphasis on bursaries – the King's foundation has been set up to fund both scholarships and bursaries and allocated over £1 million a year. Parents means-tested annually and can receive up to 100 per cent of full boarding fee.

Remarks: Thriving academic school with highly motivated pupils. 'The children never stop – I do not know they fit everything into their day and still have time for a busy social life,' said one parent. Not a heavily religious school but the Benedictine tradition of care for body, mind and spirit is very much in evidence.

L

Lambrook School

Winkfield Row, Nr Ascot, Berkshire RG42 6LU

Pupils: 530; 30–40 flexi boarders • Ages: 3–13 • C of E

Fees: Day £10,578 – £18,588; Boarding £20,778 – £22,251 pa

Tel: 01344 882717
Email: info@lambrookschool.co.uk
Website: www.lambrookschool.co.uk

Headmaster: Since 2010, Mr Jonathan Perry, previously head of Kingsmead School in Hoylake. Wife Jenny is a clinical pharmacist who works part-time at a nearby hospital but also has a pastoral role at the school. She has an eye for interior decoration too: the fresh flowers front of house and general spruced up air are thanks to her. The Perrys' son and daughter attended the school (have since progressed to Wellington and Downe House) and were described by one parent as 'a perfect fit'. Mr Perry is the son of a bishop, his degree is in religious studies and history, but there are teachers in his family as well as members of the clergy – certainly a strong tradition of public service. Although he teaches no timetabled lessons, he runs current affairs sessions in his study for the older pupils. He told us modestly that he 'helps out' with sport, but parents love the fact he's so visible – greeting children every morning, present at all the matches – and is always available. He has revitalised Saturdays and added a lecture programme (parents welcome to attend these) to the extended learning sessions. Saturday school compulsory for years 6 and above. Another thing we learned about Mr Perry during our visit is that he really does seem to know every pupil, and not just by name either.

School is increasingly popular but headmaster has no plans to expand; he is 'happy with the size' and concentrating instead on improving facilities. The Performing Arts Centre was opened by HRH the Earl of Wessex and has stimulated and inspired a love of the arts across the school. It would be fair to say that not all parents saw this project as a necessity, but they have now been very much won over. There is no doubt Lambrook's many musicians and performers have enjoyed treading its boards providing an excellent space for rehearsing for drama performances at the Edinburgh Fringe and choral performances in Notre Dame. A new cedar clad 25 metre indoor swimming pool came to fruition in February 2015. Also in the pipeline is a plan to build new art and tech studios. Managing these projects must be taking up a fair bit of Mr Perry's time, but he is determined to ensure that the results will respect the school's tradition and surroundings and has changed architectural details to this end. 'Parents like to see things happen in their time,' he says. The coffee table in the head's study is made from the trunk of an oak from the grounds, its rings marked with events from the school's 150 year history – must help put things in perspective. A keen sportsman, Mr Perry enjoys golf, tennis and cricket, but more often these days from the sidelines. Favourite book? Sebastian Faulks' Birdsong. Cornwall is where the family go to get away from it all – sea being practically the only thing lacking in Winkfield Row.

Entrance: Mostly at 3, 4 and 7 years. School meets all prospective pre-prep families to ensure they can best meet the family's needs. Followed by a formal assessment day for entrance to the prep, up to a year before prospective entry. Assessment criteria include academic ability, wider interests, character and behaviour. School reports growing waiting list and advises parents to put names down several years before desired date of entry.

Increasingly favoured by West London parents, word-of-mouth is also attracting families from beyond Ascot, Windsor and Maidenhead to villages across Berkshire, Buckinghamshire and Surrey. Some girls join in year 7, mainly those aiming for Wellington or Downe House. Parents a mix of traditional and first time buyers.

Exit: All, many with scholarships, to first choice senior schools including Wellington, Bradfield, Eton, St Mary's Ascot, Downe House, Harrow, Marlborough, Charterhouse, Radley and Stowe. In 2016, 22 awards – academic, all-rounder, sport, music and drama – to all these schools and others, too.

Remarks: On the glorious early summer day of our visit Lambrook could not have looked finer. The school's 52 acres of Berkshire's lushest prime estate were at their peak of green and pleasantness; children played under venerable trees, the cricket pitch was like velvet as was the nine hole golf course – and birdsong was nearly winning against the noise coming from the construction site (now the performing arts centre). Inside the main building the newly extended library, with its gothic wood panels and shelves, seems timelessly bookish but was originally the dining room. Here, as elsewhere, are historic photographs of past pupils – teams, plays etc – part of the fabric rather than separated into an archive. Founded in 1860, Lambrook is alma mater of, among others, Lord Alfred Douglas (Oscar Wilde's downfall), Queen Victoria's grandsons Prince Christian Victor and Prince Albert, W C Sellar and R J Yeatman, authors of 1066 and all that. More recent alumni include actor Alex Petyffer and rugby internationals Max and Thom Evans.

The fine chapel with its gleaming brass and polished pews can no longer accommodate everyone, so whole school assemblies and inter-house competitions (singing etc) take place in the the performing arts auditorium. The boy:girl ratio is 60:40 overall but despite this the feel is thoroughly inclusive and co-ed. Children with SEN and/or physical disabilities 'welcome' so long as the school can meet their specific needs.

In addition to the aforementioned birdsong and building, another noise we heard as we toured the school was laughter. Lambrook lessons seem to be good fun, with relaxed but respectful relations between pupils and staff, many of whom live on site. Parents told us they like the balance of male and female teachers and the mix of quirky 'old school' and new blood teaching styles. Thumbs up too for the enthusiastic gappies from pupils and parents alike. We saw heads in books in English and quick fire questions and answers in science too – it was just a few weeks before CE, after all. Our year 8 guides (scholarships in the bag) already sounded nostalgic about their Lambrook years. Music is exceptional; over 80 per cent of children learn at least one instrument up to and including grade 8 (370 performing arts lessons each week) and play in school bands and ensembles, not to mention a full symphony orchestra. The choir had recently sung evensong at St George's Chapel, Windsor and had obviously been given the royal seal of approval because they've been asked to return. Have also performed at Notre Dame Cathedral and Disneyland – and set up new inter-school choral competitions to celebrate singing talent in the area. Newish performing arts centre with theatre, peripatetic teaching rooms, green room and dance studio. In recent years Lambrook has provided actors, dancers and singers for professional productions including The Sound of Music, Oliver!, Matilda and Billy Elliott and has even performed at the Edinburgh Fringe. In the wonderful, creatively messy art room (school has plans for new wing for art, design and technology), pupils were singing along to music and screen-printing their own designs onto sports day t-shirts.

It must be tough to do justice to the perfection of the pitches (or, apparently, the match teas) but boys' and girls' teams are bringing home gold and silverware in rugby, hockey, trampolining, tennis, skiing and basketball, played at county and national levels. Plenty of joint activities, but girls get separate PE, hockey, and netball. Everybody loves winners, but we were encouraged to hear of children who were never going to make the team being included and given important non-playing roles. Choice of clubs and after-school options described by one parent as 'ridiculously diverse' and so it is – from creative writing to diving (new swimming pool), sailing and polo (well, this is Ascot).

We visited the nursery, separate from but close to the main school, just before lunch (meals on wheels from main school kitchen). Tinies sitting on the floor were engrossed in a story. At age 4 children move on to the pre-prep, not a huge step geographically but parents praised the way the staff prepare children for this transition. This is the time when educational needs may show themselves, and the pre-prep SENCo observes and identifies any potential learning, speech and language problems. For those who need a little more time to consolidate the basics there is extra phonics and 'maths crew', activity-based small group work to reinforce knowledge. School has also invested in outdoor classroom with tepees and a sensory walk. Pre-prep has its own hall, used for before (from 8.15am) and after (until 6pm) school care – a bonus for parents, especially if they have older children at the main school. Lively notice boards give parents all they need to know about what's going on, lesson topics and other key information. Expansion of nursery provision has not been without collateral damage – in this case the pre-prep library. Wider than average though it may be, a corridor doth not a library make. Something else for Mr Perry to add to his grand plans.

The girls' dorms are up three flights of stairs in the eaves of the main house, charming rooms looking out over the grounds painted in contemporary colours and full of homely touches such as beanbags. The boarders' kitchen was large and sunny with gingham oilcloth on the table and fresh flowers. Every effort has been made to keep things as uninstitutional as possible. Flexi-boarding is particularly popular at the end of the week – parents certainly appreciate it – and most of the older day pupils have tried (and, apparently, enjoyed) it at one time or another.

Lambrook is a lively and unstuffy prep school in an idyllic pastoral setting where boys and girls are educated to the best of their potential without excessive pressure. Several parents said to us that although they rather liked the fact it was a 'well-kept secret', the school deserved to be better known. We agree. To quote from old boys Sellar and Yeatman's classic, 1066 and all that, Lambrook is 'a Good Thing'.

L

Lancing College Preparatory School at Hove

Linked with Lancing College

The Droveway, Hove, East Sussex BN3 6LU

Pupils: 253 • Ages: 3–13 • C of E

Fees: £8,610 – £15,186 pa

Tel: 01273 503452
Email: hove@lancing.org.uk
Website: www.lancingcollege.co.uk

Head: Since September 2016, Kirsty Keep, previously head of lower school at Downsend School. She has also taught at Edge

Grove Prep. She is married to Edward, also a teacher, and they have a daughter; they are keen skiers.

Entrance: Non-selective. Taster day 'allows us to assess whether we shall be able to meet the child's educational needs'. For year 1 upwards, current school report also requested. Means-tested scholarships (up to 50 per cent of fees) available from 11+. Prospective scholarship pupils are tested on progress in English, progress in maths and non-verbal reasoning.

Exit: Most to Lancing College, where they need to get 50 per cent in CE. A handful to other schools – St Bede's, Brighton College, Bryanston, Lewes Grammar, Ardingly and Purcell School.

Remarks: Main building has an old school feel, with a wood-panelled hall lined with ancient school photographs. Hall morphs into a dining room in the middle of the day. 'It's my third best pudding today,' sighed one pupil about the rice pudding on offer (apparently not much can compete with the apple cobbler). Food was delicious and disappeared rapidly. Tables are mixed between year groups, with year 8s serving. Pupils undertake a different job each week, one piling up leftovers and stacking plates with business-like resignation. 'Stacking is the worst job,' he confided.

Classrooms of all shapes and sizes, larger rooms for the pre-prep where there is more emphasis on practical work, packed with colour and displays. Smaller rooms are a snug fit for the 20 pupils who generally make up the prep classes. Lovely library in the old school with bean bags and cushions in a comfy area. A bit of ducking and diving outside to reach other classrooms: science lab (modern), art room (some fabulous work – a strong department) and gym (small and old). Lovely outdoor classroom for sunny days with benches set in a semi-circle. Easy access to Lancing College facilities – children are bussed up to the college to swim, for DT, and to visit the farm – every child in pre-prep has seen a ewe give birth.

L

All the usual national curriculum subjects, but with a particular emphasis on music and sport. Whole of top floor is given over to music. When we visited, year 3 children's Punjabi song echoed through the corridors. More than 80 per cent play instruments and vast range of groups to perform in, including ensembles, orchestra (from grade 5) and contemporary music group. Multimedia used a lot in music – year 6s were all plugged in, happily writing soundtracks. Prep share a drama teacher with the senior school and rehearsals were well under way for Bugsy Malone. 'Nearly everyone's in it,' a pupil told us.

French is the only language on offer: the school would like to increase language provision, but can't think how to fit another language into the packed curriculum. Homework is kept to a minimum for the pre-prep (reading), rising to around 40 minutes for each exam subject per week for those at the top of the prep school – certainly not an amount that the pupils find irksome. Occasionally parents seeking a more challenging academic regime will look elsewhere, but 'our academic scholarship results will stand comparison with any'. Lessons are lively and relaxed.

Staff feel school suits quirky children and it's easy to see those who don't run with the pack finding a home here. School has a Christian ethos but place feels like a broad church. No statemented pupils. SEN support given where necessary in the form of one-to-one support in and out of lessons (where support is given out of class, there is a separate fee). School is proud of being mixed ability – lessons are planned for individuals, SEN and mainstream alike. Sometimes holds a struggling pupil back a year, so a summer baby who was the youngest in the year becomes the oldest, which often sorts out problems. Equally, an able pupil can be accelerated to the next year and may spend a second year in year 8 as a scholarship pupil.

Plenty of sports here (hockey is big at the moment), and lots of opportunities for those who want to play to a high level – competitive sport is a big part of this school. A-D teams, so the school can seem practically deserted when they are all playing. Of course many players are particularly interested in the match tea, says the head.

Any bullying is dealt with promptly, and (generally) at a low level – 'it usually amounts to name calling,' says the school. The approach is that the bully needs help too, and while a bully may lose their lunch play, they will do an activity based on bullying scenarios to try and reform their thinking. Pupils are encouraged to whistleblow and look out for each other. A variety of people on offer to talk to, from year 8 mentors to teachers and the head.

Day ends at 4.30pm, but most don't go home then. Activities last until 5.30pm, and range from the usual homework club, sports, and musical activities to Lego club, Welsh club and the eco garden club. Dance has recently started, and covers a range from modern to jazz to Strictly Come Lancing last year. Year 7 and 8s can also opt to visit the local residential home – many do. Clubs are included in the fees at prep age, and are paid as extras at pre-prep age.

Portakabins cluster round the back of the school, again rather on the cosy size. Plans are afoot to sweep the whole lot away and build something swish to house two classes a year (a double nursery intake inhabits recently-acquired next door bungalow).

There is a drop off problem – the council won't play ball with a drive through system, and it can be difficult to park, but the school opens the back gate so pupils can walk in across Hove park; finishing times are staggered at the end of the day too (although most opt to stay until 5.30pm). Pupils can come to school by school bus, which comes from all over, and works specific routes according to need. There is also a shuttle between Lancing Prep and the college to help parents with children at both schools.

Prep seems to do a good job at focusing on an individual's strengths. When asked at what the school excels, one pupil said, 'It's really good at music and sports, particularly hockey'; another indignantly responded, 'But it's a very academic school – the best things are extra science and maths.'

School feels like a very green and pleasant land. There is tangible warmth and friendliness here. 'I was a bit lonely at my old school, but everyone here is friendly,' a pupil told us. 'It's a family. I know everyone.' Our pupil guides were greeted by all and sundry on our tour, the little ones in nursery racing up to say hello. Family ethos includes all staff – school photo includes cleaners and chef (who's very popular and gets mentioned a lot).

Parents say pupils relate well to each other across the years, and that older ones look out for the younger ones. One questioned whether increasing numbers would have an effect on the family experience. Our enthusiastic pupil guides indulged in much nostalgic remembrance of things past, but were also very excited about their imminent move to the senior school. When asked if there was anything they would change about the prep, there was a long contemplative pause. 'I wouldn't change much – it feels right as it is,' said one.

Lancing College

Linked with Lancing College Preparatory School at Hove

Lancing, West Sussex BN15 0RW

Pupils: 580 • Ages: 13–18 • Sixth form: 260 • C of E

Fees: Day £23,850; Boarding £33,915 pa

Tel: 01273 452213
Email: admissions@lancing.org.uk
Website: www.lancingcollege.co.uk

Head Master: Since 2014, Dominic Oliver MPhil, who left an academic career at Oxford to teach in schools, starting out at the Royal Grammar in Worcester, then moving to head of English at Malvern College, before becoming deputy head of Bedales schools. Married to Lydia, with a child at Lancing College and another at Lancing Prep.

Clearly feels comfortably at home at Lancing, which he describes as 'recognisable public schooling with a unique combination of warmth and vigour'; more subtle than Bedales 'self consciously liberal' approach, but perhaps no less radical under its new leader. As a head who enjoys the work of old boy David Hare and other establishment rebels, he wants to hear his pupils' voices: school council will soon come into being and Mr Oliver teaches the third form debating – he enjoys provoking argument. It takes a certainty and confidence in both self and school to allow dissent and a bit of cheekiness; and quite some nerve to put a big wheel and carousel outside that grimly beautiful sinners and hellfire chapel on founder's day.

Mr Oliver brings a new culture of reflective education, with a greater emphasis on enrichment, and more students than ever doing the EPQ. They're tightening up on entrance standards – there must be evident sparks of intellect, and the very best grades will be needed for entrance and expected as outcomes (although they should be a natural outcome of the new intellectual regime).

Mr Oliver's most desirable quality for pupils is to be illuminated (a word which suggests a glowing sort of enlightenment).

Academic matters: Very good, consistent performance at GCSE and A level: 59 per cent A*/A grades at GCSE in 2016; at A level, 53 per cent A*/A grades, 77 per cent A*/B: great results from a virtually mixed ability school. Not top grades at all costs: pupils are set a target appropriate to them, and there is celebration if the target is met; whether that target be a C or A*. 'Not an exam factory, so doesn't attract those sort of parents', and one parent commented that they opted for Lancing over a more academically pressurising competitor. Tremendous value added at Lancing – pupils achieve exam grades they wouldn't have dreamed of.

Core subjects are always streamed, others usually so (where numbers allow). Class sizes around 18 in years 9-11, down to a maximum of 15 in the sixth form. Maths is outstanding, popular with pupils and excellent results – a triple maths A level student enthused about the teaching, and useful weekly drop in sessions. Pupils give good reports of history too. Super science labs, remodelled in last few years, although science results not outstanding. Great well-stocked library with mezzanine level of computers. There are plenty of languages on offer: French, German, Spanish, Italian, Greek, Latin – pupils start with two languages in year 9, and must continue with one until GCSE. German and Chinese strong. A jolly year 9 German class showed off their iPads (now standard issue), which come into their own when teaching languages: teachers can set oral homework, and iPads will correct pronunciation; no more lost homework since pupils are emailed assignments.

Two reports during each term with grades for each subject, and a full written report at the end of term. Early remedial action if someone is falling behind – 'no one falls through the net'. A learning support department supports around 80 pupils with mild to moderate learning difficulties (mostly mild dyslexia), of whom 35 require continuous one-to-one support (at extra cost). Recent significant increase of in-class support via two full time and one part time learning support teachers who assist small groups within curriculum areas.

Games, options, the arts: School week covers six days, so four afternoon sessions for options – pupils here like to keep very busy. One afternoon a week students choose between CCF or community service. Drama is popular, even with non-actors – some of the academic hard core work backstage for light relief. Theatre seats 180, retractable seating means it's possible to play in the round, and make an orchestra pit in part of the old swimming pool on which the theatre was built. Drama GCSE, but not enough takers for A level, though LAMDA available. About 15 productions a year – recently full-scale musical Oliver! and risque 'Tis Pity She's a Whore. Also an open air theatre.

Plenty of games sessions (down to twice a week for sixth formers), with lots of choice – focus on football, hockey, netball, cricket and tennis, but lots of other options, even for the not keen – 'I get by on yoga,' said one. One boy said he came to Lancing because it's a football school – other public schools generally favour rugby. Extensive playing fields, tennis courts, Astroturf pitch and swimming pool. And for those who love animals, farm is a sports/activities option – a sport hater/animal lover could exist blissfully at Lancing. The farm has really developed in recent years, particularly on the conservation front, and includes rare pigs, alpacas, lamas, turkeys, chickens, geese and goats, and lots of cuddly smalls and sheep – kids can get permission to stay out late and help with lambing. Meat and eggs from the farm have started feeding the school this year, and they are experimenting with a market garden with the aim of supplying veg too. Opportunities for five years' worth of vet experience as well as links with local agricultural colleges and primary schools and, via the school's Young Enterprise programme, for the marketing of college produce and wood supplies.

The music department is housed in standard 60s fare, but is staffed by teachers full of love for their subject and incredibly enthusiastic about sharing that love with pupils. Their scruffy studies overflow with sheet music; one, curiously, with a child's layout mat on the floor and a dog in the corner – who has apparently won over many recruits to music. 'They are mad,' said one pupil kindly, 'but we have a great time.' Plenty of practice rooms, which only get too busy at Associated Board exam times. Drum kit handy for those who want to pop in for a jam. Glorious choir (lovely CD – Surrexit), and numerous orchestras and bands. Lunchtime concerts most weeks, and a big concert every half term. Many continue to patronise the music block even if they don't take the subject, and around 300 learn instruments, some multiple instruments. A fine tradition of composition and of producing organ scholars to Oxbridge colleges.'It's all about joy in music making,' said one teacher – there is certainly much delight taken in music here. One parent, who encouraged her reluctant son to join the choir, says he enjoys it more than he ever (as a teenager) would admit – 'It's a very special thing to be part of.'

Art is a strong area: housed in a contemporary purpose-built centre, full of light, with eager students keen to show off their amazing work: everything from oils to an installation of hanging clingfilm, called 'Urban' – clay room and kiln, printing, etching, photography and fine art – 'Waterfront was our first topic this term, so we went to Venice' – where else? Older pupils have their own areas, so don't have to clear up paintings under way – the spacious rooms feel full of many little studios. Weekly drop-in art sessions for those who have never lifted a brush, or keen artists who just haven't got enough time to follow an art course. Art at every turn throughout the school – one house has turned the curve at the bottom of a stairwell into Venice.

Great DT centre, with examples of GCSE and A level work which wouldn't look out of place in a designer furniture store, along with a few quirky ideas – for dog owners who feel all that bend and throw is just a bit too energetic, how about an automatic dog ball launcher? Again, those who don't continue with this option can nevertheless return to pursue DT as a hobby.

Boarding: Over two-thirds of pupils at Lancing are boarders, around 330 full and 70 flexi (more boys than girls). Certainly boarders seem very happy and enjoy having a wealth of activity available on their doorsteps. Modern, comfortable accommodation, with a rolling programme of refurbishment, although you won't find the gold taps one parent was hoping for. Years 9 and 10, two to four in a room, from year 11, single study bedrooms. Shared rooms are filled to capacity with beds and desks, but the pupils don't object to cosy conditions: one sixth former told me how much she missed sharing a room with friends – 'I've been with them since I was 13 – they are like my sisters.' Day pupils can board for a night free if they are at school after 9 pm on school business, such as play rehearsals, which pleases parents.

Friends can visit house communal areas – although pupils often go and chat out on the quads after dinner. Houses have common rooms (with Sky +), squashy sofas and views over rolling countryside, and kitchens with daily deliveries of bread, spreads, and fruit for any time consumption. Each house has Wifi throughout; one house has a sweet shop open in the evenings. Sixth formers have their own common room and houses have a number of kitchens for different year groups – 'It's the best thing about the house.' School café opens at break, in the afternoons and evening for hungry pupils after prep.

Flexible boarding structure, with no differentiation between full and weekly boarders, who pay the same fees and can stay at weekends if they wish. Day pupils can pay by the night for flexi-boarding if they have evening activities.

Background and atmosphere: Grand old buildings of Sussex flint, dating from 1848, with elegant quads and huge chapel standing on the hill overlooking the rolling Downs. In this beautiful setting, it feels distinctly public school, but it's not as cut glass as all that. Clearly impresses parents – 'They're experiencing things to do with heritage and a sense of history which seep into their experience and become something they value.'

A Woodard school, it has a strong Christian tradition, still very much in evidence. No skipping weekly chapel here, for conscientious objectors or other faiths – 'It might not be something they carry on with later in life, but at least they have been exposed to it – like maths,' said a teacher. Although a Christian school, they are not out to convert you – pupils of all faiths or no faith are welcome here. It's more about the values of Christianity, and in particular caring for each other. The service is a wonderful thing to experience – inside, the chapel is glorious and the voices of the choir soar – only St Paul's Cathedral has a higher ceiling. High church with plenty of bells and smells and the accompanying pageantry. Pupils seem to attend quite happily though, girls wrapped in 19th century style cloaks of house colours; boys just cold. Most troop up for communion or a blessing. Pupils assure us that a fair number attend voluntary chapel – held in the crypt daily before breakfast or in the evenings in houses. One parent said she felt doing the communal thing is very important – apparently leavers most miss their time in chapel. New television screens mean that, on high days and holidays, when the place is packed with parents and former pupils, all can see and be involved in the services.

There is a rather splendid dining hall – could almost be a back up chapel should something happen to the other one, with long wooden tables and new wooden chairs. Wide range of food available, nice, but not remarkable on the day of our visit – one pupil said it 'goes up and down a bit.' Sixth formers can skip breakfast in the dining hall and cook their own.

The sixth form is not for those who want to scruff around in jeans and tee shirts for a couple of years – smart business wear is expected here, with more responsibility as prefects or house captains, and more independence, in organising time in and out of school: year 11 and sixth formers can go into Brighton, and they're considering allowing the sixth up to London. In common with the rest of the school, some fabulous trips on offer: the travel section of the school magazine resembles a highly desirable travel brochure.

Pastoral care, well-being and discipline: Parents say it is 'like being part of a community with a strong family atmosphere.' Well-defined house system with a network of people taking care of pupils. As well as housemasters/mistresses (the first point of call for parents), there is a matron on hand, year 10 'uncles' and 'aunts' for new year 9s, and the peer support system provided by sixth formers. If all this fails, 'there is always a teacher you get on with particularly well'. Pupils admit to feeling a bit homesick for a few weeks, but say it quickly wears off. At break time, kids troop back to their house common room for squash and biscuits: some kids pop in and straight out again, others sit and chat to matron and other house staff. It is a moment away from work – like having a break with your mum. Matron – 'We are their family here.'

Parents feel discipline is 'not in your face'. Seems to work, but quite gently done. Approach 'firm but fair'. One mum says the balance must be right, because the kids are so relaxed about going to school. Bullying, drug and alcohol abuse not generally a problem, but will be dealt with severely. The one pupil who could recall an episode of bullying was clearly startled by how strictly it had been dealt with.

Communication is good where a parent has a concern – email or telephone contact will lead to a rapid and thorough response; new Parent Portal. Parents say school is very welcoming and encourages parents to feel involved; plenty of social events – plays, concerts, matches, lectures, informative talks, dinners and a healthy Parents' Association. There is some small tension between the parent who felt that parents of day pupils require more communication (than those of boarders), and the staff feeling that 'occasionally helicopter parents need to be told to buzz off in the interests of their child.' This does feel like a school where parents should be prepared to step back a bit, and let their child develop responsibility for themselves.

Pupils and parents: Fits oddballs – we met some pupils who were strongly individual but seemed very happy at Lancing. 'Not for the inert,' said one teacher, 'nor for one-dimensional academic types,' said another. Pupils from Lancing's two preps and other prep schools in the area. Parents generally middle class professionals, city types, and around 25 per cent of boarders from overseas. School runs its own buses, routes to suit need from the surrounding area, and shuttle between Lancing College and the preps.

Former pupils include playwrights Sir David Hare, Christopher Hampton and Giles Cooper, lyricist Sir Tim Rice, novelists Tom Sharpe and Evelyn Waugh, Shakespeare scholar and writer John Dover Wilson, singer Sir Peter Pears,

Archbishop Trevor Huddleston, TV presenter Jamie Theakston, Sir Christopher Meyer, Charles Anson, Dr Rana Mitter, Sir Roy Calne, Stephen Green (Baron Green of Hurstpierpoint) and Alex Horne.

Entrance: Gently selective – mid 50 per cent pass rate at CE, with separate assessment for those from the state sector. For the sixth form, need good GCSEs and school reference, interviews and tests.

A few places in year 10; some 30-35 places for girls at sixth form, 10-15 for boys.

Exit: Around 15 per cent leave after GCSEs. Five to Oxbridge in 2016, several to North American universities. UCL, LSE and other London colleges popular alongside Exeter, Warwick and Bristol. Broad mix of subjects ranging from engineering and economics to zoology and theology.

Money matters: At 13, academic, music, art, drama, sports and all-rounder scholarships, up to half of fees, which can be augmented depending on family circumstances. Sixth form awards – academic, music and art, up to a third of fees.

Remarks: A friendly and beautiful place to grow up. Pupils are happy, and unselfconsciously themselves. This is a place where individuals will flourish, and there is evidently great care and attention to ensure this is so. Not for those who like to take things easy – a culture of keeping busy.

Lanesborough School

Linked with Royal Grammar School (Guildford)

Maori Road, Guildford, Surrey GU1 2EL

Pupils: 350 • Ages: 3–13 • C of E

Fees: £10,047 – £14,082 pa

Tel: 01483 880650
Email: secretary@lanesborough.surrey.sch.uk
Website: www.lanesborough.surrey.sch.uk

Head: Since 2007, Mrs Clare Turnbull, previously deputy head for three years, but after a decade here she has no itchy feet, she assures us. 'I have no desire to move on to another headship. Here I can still teach, and that matters, and every year I have done new things,' she says. It was always her ambition to work in a cathedral choir school, following a childhood in which she was immersed in Canterbury Cathedral, where her father is a retired honorary canon. Mrs Turnbull is herself a lay canon at Guildford Cathedral. Previous posts include director of studies and head of French at Maidwell Hall School in Northamptonshire.

Outside the school gates most evenings, having informal chats with parents and boys, we're told. Plain speaking, and wants to know about it if parents have an issue. 'If they've got an anxiety, let's talk it through, or it will bubble through to the boy,' she says. Not that an issue is likely to pass her by, according to parents. 'We find it incredible that she knows in such depth what our sons are doing well at or are struggling with – her attention to detail is astonishing,' said one.

'Very enthusiastic and clearly born to teach. She communicates well, is highly visible around the school, and accessible,' is another parent's verdict.

Entrance: Focus on the key entry points (nursery, reception and year 3) to give yourself the best chance of a place. The school is currently full with a waiting list, so otherwise you are relying on someone leaving.

Mrs Turnbull describes the school as 'unashamedly selective' – and more than half of the boys each year go on to the Royal Grammar School (RGS) Guildford, which is one of the top performing boys' schools in the country. So you'll want to be sure your boy can keep up. 'Is your boy going to love it academically, and thrive?' Mrs Turnbull asks.

For nursery and Shell (the school's name for reception), selection involves a boy coming in for an hour as part of a little group, doing activities, games and reasoning. The school will look at how he responds to these tasks, and his social skills. For entry into year 3 boys will first come for a familiarisation afternoon of sport, music, team building and social activities. Academic tests will follow, mainly taken on a computer, and featuring maths, reading comprehension, writing and IQ type tests. 'We are looking for a boy who loves learning, who asks questions: why, how is that happening?' says Mrs Turnbull. 'It's not necessarily about levels. You might get a wonderfully quirky boy who may not get level 4 writing but will get level 6 maths, but one would think carefully, are his issues in English going to stop him loving the whole curriculum?'

Exit: Strap in for the long haul financially. It's rare for a boy to go on to a state school (one every few years). Around 55 per cent go on to the RGS, where they form up to one-fifth of the pupil cohort. In 2016, others to St John's Leatherhead, City of London Freemen's, Reigate Grammar and Reed's. Of those going on to RGS, about one-third will go at 11, the rest at 13, but this varies from year to year.

Remarks: A common thread in parents' comments is that the school really 'gets' boys, and structures its approach accordingly, in aspects such as boredom thresholds and length of breaks.

Parents say it's first and foremost an academic school, and one best suited to boys who are willing to knuckle down. 'There is fierce competition among able students,' one parent told us. 'Boys are definitely stretched academically, and I am pleased that there is often extension work particularly in maths and English,' said another.

Nevertheless, parents say it is a nurturing environment. 'It is competitive, and the work load is pretty high, but allowance and time is made for those who find it more of a challenge; they will be split into a smaller group and helped,' one told us. Another insider said: 'I know several parents of boys who are not academic and who would still be very positive about the academic training that the school has provided, so I think it is fair to say that it caters for boys of all abilities.'

There is setting for maths from year 4, and other subjects in years 7 and 8, but there is no scholarship stream bagging every place in the top set, allowing boys to be placed according to strengths in individual subjects.

The style is fairly traditional – most of the classrooms are organised with desks in rows, although the atmosphere is lively within. We saw year 8s enjoying a debate on whether RE should be taught in schools; the fact that the 'yes' camp won may be testament to the school's RE teaching. Science teacher Mrs MacDonald sometimes brings in her snake and duck, the latter waddling happily around the lab. Boys are taught from the age of 8 in a proper science lab. 'The boys often come home full of chatter about a lesson or activity during their day,' a parent said.

Children study three languages from year 5 – French, Spanish and Latin – although occasionally boys with dyslexia, or who are struggling, drop Latin. Pupils with dyslexia or other difficulties can have one lesson per week with a specialist at no extra charge.

From year 5 all teaching is by subject specialists, and this year also sees the introduction of school exams. 'We spend a lot of time teaching them how to learn, and getting them ready for the mental and emotional side of life and exams,' Mrs Turnbull says. Parents praise the preparation for senior school entrance exams, as one says: 'The head engages in an extensive one-to-one meeting with parents before the run up to entrance exams. The school prepares boys very well for these examinations with additional work and mock exams.'

DT is taught from year 3, and the artwork and ceramics on display point to some inspired teaching.

The school is easily accessed from the A3 with no winding country lanes to negotiate – the corollary to this is that it doesn't have the easy parking and rolling fields of the preps deeper in the country. Hence the two parent gripes (pretty much the only ones we heard) are over the lack of sports facilities and the nightmare parking. With two other independent schools in close proximity it's havoc at drop off and pick up times, and can be scary watching boys trying to cross the road, parents say. The school does its best to ease this. It arranged restricted parking with the council to prevent commuter parking, and school run times can be staggered – there's a one hour window for morning drop off between 7.30 and 8.30am, with a breakfast club for early arrivals, and children of all ages can stay until 6.30pm.

The pre-prep department is based in another Edwardian house in a parallel road, headed by Mrs Heath-Taylor (in post since 2010). It has attractive play areas, including an outdoor classroom called Boyzone. This has its own bird hide, wooden staged seating for drama, and playground toys. The main playground has wooden trains and boats to play in, a covered cave area, and a planting area for the popular gardening club. The pre-prep has its own dining room, and everyone from reception up is expected to scrape their own plates.

Lessons showed high levels of engagement on our visit. In a year 1 maths class a boy told us solemnly, 'We are learning to use a ruler, follow instructions, and make predictions'. Another group was studying Scott of the Antarctic. 'Conditions were very bad, and they ran out of food,' one boy told us.

The pre-prep curriculum includes French from reception, and swimming from year 1. All learn the ocarina (three-noted recorder) and children can take the violin from year 1, and piano from year 2. The school provides the choristers for Guildford Cathedral (boys are invited to join at age 7 in year 3, and receive a bursary which reduces their fees). Hence Paul Provost, the sub-organist from the cathedral, works with and talent spots from the year 2 chamber choir.

Bursaries are available up to 100 per cent from 7+. The head is assiduous about keeping these confidential. Nobody besides herself and the financial director know who is on a bursary. And Mrs Turnbull is acutely aware that some parents will be stretching themselves to pay the fees, so she gives you the reassurance that there will be no slips in the book bag asking you for more money. 'We promise there will be nothing over the compulsory extras; everything is very transparent,' she says. Costs for summer term residentials are split across the year to help parents budget, with one additional amount payable each term covering this and all other extras (ranging from £21 to £270 per term as the boys move up the school).

The 18 choristers aside, it's a musical school. There are 100 boys in the school choir, 60 in the chamber choir, and more than 70 per cent learn an instrument. All boys in year 4 play a violin or cello provided by the school.

The town centre location meant boys had to go off site for some games – no longer, with new sports hall for 2016. The current hall is being converted to a performance space opening 2017 – there are large senior productions every two years with every boy in years 7 and 8 and most of year 6 involved, plus annual drama opportunities for every boy in years 3 – 6.

In sports 'we win more than we lose,' says Mrs Turnbull, but it's not elitist: 'Having a go is avidly encouraged, and B/C/D teams get plenty of matches,' parents told us. There is some feeling that sports staff are overstretched as a result of this and the amount of options on offer.

There are around 50 extracurricular clubs. Favourites among the big boys includes an astronomy club, which even enables them to take a GCSE in the subject after one year; baseball club; and senior classics, based around a computer programme designed by a member of staff, in which they take control of a Roman state and lead armies through randomly generated scenarios. Airfix club is a top pick among younger boys.

There is lots of promotion of responsibility. Year 2 boys each have a buddy in Shell, and they take them out at playtime and keep an eye on them, and read to them. They all get some sort of leadership role, such as house captain or playground supervisor. Year 8 boys are all assigned a younger form, and they take morning registration once a week, and help with that form. There's lots of interaction between different ages in the school – we saw year 5s working on their own version of an Aesop fable which they were later going to read to the year 1 and 2 children. 'What I particularly like is that the senior boys go into pre-prep and read to the younger ones, making a great connection between the two ends of the school,' said one mother. This rids any sense of scary big boys – as we toured the school the younger boys called out delightedly to our year 8 guides.

And the parent body is friendly too, we're told. There's a good number who have moved out from London, and one parent told us: 'Having arrived in Guildford knowing no-one, we found the parents very friendly and welcoming, helping us all to settle in to our new town.'

Langley Grammar School

Reddington Drive, Langley, Slough, Berkshire SL3 7QS

Pupils: 1,070 • Ages: 11–18 • Sixth form: 320

Tel: 01753 598300
Email: school@lgs.slough.sch.uk
Website: www.lgs.slough.sch.uk

Head: Since 2010, Mr John Constable BSc (50s), an affable man who has lived and breathed the grammar school system for most of his life. Having attended one himself as a boy in Suffolk, he then had physics teaching posts at Aylesbury, Watford and Sir William Borlase (Marlow), before becoming deputy head of Wycombe High School. This wasn't Plan A, he admits, which was to work as an engineer at Unilever for 10 years after graduating from his degree in engineering science and management in Durham. 'I wanted to work as an engineer for a decade before doing teacher training. But I didn't enjoy it and probably wasn't very good at it, so I moved the teaching plan forward and did my PGCE after two years,' he says. Was told that choosing the grammar system would mean he 'wouldn't get very far', but he happily proved them wrong.

Not the kind of man to beat around the bush, he says it how it is, but does so with both warmth and charm. Known for being a consultative leader, although directive when required, with the main changes under his reign including a greater focus on the well-being and mental health of pupils; more systematic monitoring and tracking of students' individual progress; and ensuring students are better supported to achieve the grades they are capable of ('before, they were rather left to get on with it in many subject areas,' he says). Pupils say he's 'often seen in corridors' and is 'very approachable'. 'Children respect him, but are not intimidated by him – a difficult balance to get as a head,' sums up one parent. Seen as a perfectionist who strives for the best in everything, pupils overwhelmingly agree that the ethos of the school comes directly from him.

Lives in nearby Herts, with his wife and their teenage son and daughter. Sails, and is a qualified dinghy instructor, as well as enjoying hill walking and photography.

Academic matters: Among the top state grammars in the country and a beacon of pride locally, this is a school where expectations are high and students are serious about their studies (we saw heads down or hands up in every classroom we visited, bar none). Fifty-seven per cent A*/A grades at GCSE in 2016 and 37 per cent A*/A at A level.

A former specialist maths and computing school, there remains an emphasis in the curriculum on acceleration in ICT/computing and enrichment with additional year 11 qualifications in maths. Science also strong, with students expected to take three separate sciences at GCSE. In recent years, English has also come into its own, thanks to a fresh, more dynamic approach. 'Parents nearly always value maths and sciences, but arguably not always English to the same extent, so this has been a challenge,' admits head. French and German taught from year 7 (one of which all students take at GSCE), along with basic Latin, and classical civilisation is an option for GCSE and AS level. All the usual suspects when it comes to A level choices, with popular options including maths, sciences, geography, psychology, economics, history and English, with uptake of languages at A level small, reflecting national trends. Sixth form boasts a broad enrichment programme, including a LAMDA public speaking qualification taught by the head and head of drama. Independent learning encouraged, particularly in sixth form. 'Even in the first two weeks of term, they treat the year 11s differently, which is great,' said one parent.

Class sizes are 30-31 (dropping to mid 20s for GCSE subjects), although these large numbers seem to pose no challenge to learning. Setting from year 9 in maths and year 10 for English, maths and science. Mutually respectful relationships between staff and students, particularly noticeable in sixth form, although a few pupils told us they feel the custom of standing up when a teacher walks into the classroom is 'outdated and disruptive.' Oodles of admiration for teachers' willingness to go beyond the call of duty. 'Nothing is ever too much trouble in helping you reach your potential and that includes giving up lunchtimes to help you get the grades you want,' said one pupil. Parents agree. 'Students have access to teachers by email and they often answer late into the evening or during the holidays,' said one.

Frequent linking of lessons to the world of work, whilst students also praise the cross-curricular links. 'If you go from an English lesson into a history one, there's an expectation you'll link the two and build on what you just learned,' explained one. 'We had one science class in which we studied butterflies, then an art class where we turned them into detailed posters,' said another.

Huge success in the use of iPad technology in lessons – with year 8s the latest to join the school's rolling programme, which already involves years 9, 10 and 11 regularly making use of them in school. 'We disagree with the government that mobile technologies are disruptive,' says head, and pupils concur that it encourages innovative ways to enhance learning. 'We're not exactly pioneers because we learn from others, but we are considered a leader in the field,' says head.

Small number (22 when we visited) on the SEN register, mainly due to dyslexia, learning impairment and Asperger's. Support is provided by an individual needs co-ordinator (SENCo qualification, as well as being a psychology teacher), who also helps with wider issues like disorganisation and lack of social skills, mainly outside the classroom (working in conjunction with the school's learning mentor and the school counsellor.) Parents largely impressed with the 'proactive approach'. 'The school has made lots of suggestions and facilitated everything my son has needed. We haven't had to push for anything,' said one. 'Our son has been well supported all the way through,' said another. On entry to the school, around 50 per cent of students speak English as a second language, although intervention work in English (especially in essay writing skills) goes a long way to addressing this.

Plenty of school trips, including short residential trips for year 7s upwards. Pupils speak particularly highly of the language trips to France and Germany, whilst geography field trips have included visits to Slapton, Northern Ireland, Sicily and Iceland, and classic civilisation students visited Pompeii. Older pupils can also get involved in expeditions to the likes of Morocco, Jordon, Ghana and Zambia.

Games, options, the arts: Despite the school's hard-working ethos, there's no shortage of encouragement for pupils to take up less academic subjects. Good sports facilities, notably a main four-court sports hall that can accommodate the whole school (and which the community also uses), several outdoor courts and a floodlit, all-weather pitch. There's access to the park next door, too, and there's also an old gym to complement the new sports hall. The sheer variety of sport rules it out of being known as 'a rugby school,' 'a hockey school' etc, but this is considered a positive. 'There's something for everyone,' explained one pupil. Two hours of timetabled sport a week is strengthened by plenty of lunchtime and after-school activities and matches, with particular successes against private and other state schools in cricket and basketball (including girls' basketball). Retaining interest in sport higher up the school can be a challenge, however.

Music a growth area, with over 250 individual music lessons taking place each week, plus weekly lessons for years 7, 8 and 9. All the usual orchestras and choirs, plus some student-led groups, which include a lot of girls with guitars. Plenty of opportunity to showcase talent in assemblies, concerts and productions, with recent examples including Beauty and the Beast (juniors) and Blood Brothers (seniors). Drama (for which there's a spacious purpose-built studio) part of the curriculum up to year 10 and a popular GCSE choice, although interest fluctuates year-on-year as an A level option. Art is encouraged, sometimes even pushed, and includes plenty of visits to galleries. Some impressive artwork adorns the corridors and head's office (interestingly, we noticed no work from other subjects prominently displayed around the school, with the exception of canvas photography prints showcasing pupils doing different activities across subject areas).

Background and atmosphere: Nestled among quiet residential streets of red-brick semis, this isn't an aesthetically pleasing school from the outside, with the core block a giant box-like construction, typical of 1950s Brutalist architecture. That said, it has softened with age and paint and it is surrounded by plenty of green space and more attractive modern buildings (some of which were financed by selling off a 'redundant' strip at the edge of the site about 10 years ago). Moreover, it's kept scrupulously clean and well-maintained, both outside and in, with areas of note in the old block including the colourful and welcoming dining hall and the well-stocked and spacious library. In fact, given that this main block has suffered some serious structural problems (which has meant erecting some unsightly pillars throughout the interior), the school has done very well to keep it looking as neat, tidy and welcoming as it does. Only the science labs stand out as being particularly tired, and the pupils certainly have no beef with their facilities.

Alas, structural issues continue, however, which is one of the reasons that the announcement was made in 2015 that the main core will be demolished and rebuilt over the next few years, as part of the Priority Schools Building Programme. 'As far back as 1966, the HM Inspectorate acknowledged that whilst the school was built to an experimental design, it had not been entirely successful,' points out the head, with a raised eyebrow. The second reason is that Slough Borough Council wants to support the expansion of the intake by an extra 30 pupils in response to pupil numbers rising in Slough.

The purpose-built sixth form building, on the other hand, is light, spacious and welcoming, with facilities including a well-used 220-seat lecture theatre and several airy sixth form classrooms and common room. Built in 2007 to have a university feel, it has stood the test of time. Meanwhile, the not-very-imaginatively named '1996 building' has decent sized, airy classrooms and is home to music, drama, English, history and maths. Other separate blocks include the sports hall and single story building for food tech and textiles.

If there's one overriding atmosphere in the school, it is one of calm. There are no bells, no boisterousness (even at break times) and between lessons, students walk purposefully and quickly to their next lesson, chatting in groups. Green blazers with the school insignia for boys, green jackets for girls, traditional enamel badges for positions of responsibility worn proudly.

Pastoral care, well-being and discipline: Exceptional transition programme for year 7s, largely because pupils enter from over 80 primary schools across a wide geographical area and across varied cultural backgrounds. 'Around half of the students come here knowing nobody,' explains head. 'Not that this is a disadvantage as we find it means they make a real effort to make friends and build relationships.' Pupils agree, with older students fondly remembering the efforts the school made to settle them in. When we visited, one corridor displayed post-it notes that new year 7s had posed anonymous questions on, ranging from 'What if you're late?' to 'How do you know where you have to be?' which teachers had answered in pen underneath.

Pastoral care offered mainly from form teachers, phase leaders and school counsellor. Religion(s) a key part of school life, with lots of visiting speakers and everyone taking RE at GSCE (typically 65 per cent or more get A* or A, which head sees as proof that students enjoy it and take it seriously).

Anti-bullying initiatives considered successful, including a telling atmosphere, trained anti-bullying mentors, restorative justice, a school counsellor and a clear no-tolerance policy. Pupils say diversity also helps. 'I think it's because we're all so different that we learn to respect differences early on,' explained one. Lots of cross year friendships, helped by the wide range of after-school clubs.

Traditional house system, which provides the framework for all manner of competitions, ranging from music to sport, with the annual sports day held at Thames Valley Athletics Stadium, an event that causes great excitement.

A clear set of expectations, rather than school rules, with the usual range of sanctions for those who break them. The head rarely has to implement them, though, and even mobile phones are allowed to be used in school, provided they're not used in lessons or with headphones.

Pupils and parents: Pupils enter from as far as west London boroughs (although entrance criteria now focuses on being more local) and typically from over 80 primary schools. Students (of whom 94 per cent are minority ethnic and two-thirds are from Asian/British-Indian backgrounds) are articulate, respectful and polite, although some are quite passive, with staff having to work hard to encourage more lively participation. Currently no PA and parents rarely get together, except at school events, although attendance for these is high. No school bus, with pupils arriving by train into Langley, by public bus, car share scheme, cycling or walking.

Entrance: Slough is not a fully selective authority, so parents must opt in for their children to take the test (CEM – Centre for Evaluation & Monitoring – 11+) set by the four Slough grammars acting as a consortium. This test is taken in September. Places have historically been allocated according to rank order of performance. But now pupils in the three Langley postcode areas who achieve 111 or above in the test get priority, plus those on pupil premium/free school meals. New oversubscription criteria also favour musical talent (five per cent of intake) and those on free school meals. Intake increasing from 150 (plus a few on appeal) in year 7, spread across 5 classes, to 180 over six classes in 2017. Head is under no illusion about the prevalence of tutoring, but does point out that CEM was selected over the previous GL Assessment on the basis that they are more guarded about the information in the public domain and won't release practice papers. Minimum of 20, and maximum of 45, sixth form places for external candidates, with admission on the basis of general standard of GCSE grades and some specific criteria for A level subjects selected.

Exit: Russell Group universities, along with the London colleges, are favoured, with three pupils into Oxbridge in 2016. Popular subjects include maths, science, engineering, medicine and business, accounting and finance – nothing remotely fluffy. Support for pupils continues after they leave, especially if they delay university entrance, although gap years aren't common.

Remarks: This is a school that takes the top 30 per cent of ability range, so rather than being super selective, it's built on the noble ideal of the Bucks/Kent grammar school model (it was a Bucks grammar school until the 1970s when the local authority boundaries changed). And perhaps because of its location, it manages to avoid sharp-elbowed parents after a private education on the state. But make no mistake, this is a serious-minded school, where students are hungry to learn and highly focused. 'You never go home at the end of the day without feeling you've learned a lot,' said one student. 'Nothing is ever stagnant and no one is ever lazy,' agreed another. But whilst you feel some of the students could do with giving themselves a bit more downtime, this school could never be accused of being an education hothouse, with staff doing all they can to encourage a holistic education and produce rounded individuals.

Leighton Park School

Shinfield Road, Reading RG2 7EE

Pupils: 463; 97 full, 34 weekly, 16 flexi boarders (roughly two-thirds boys). • Ages: 11-18 • Sixth form: 151

Fees: Boarding £22,749- £33,174; Day £16,689 – £21,570pa

Tel: 01189 879600
Email: admissions@leightonpark.com
Website: www.leightonpark.com

Head: Since 2013, Mr Nigel Williams BA MA PGCE (known here – as are all staff – by his first name). Educated at Monmouth

School, Nigel read history at Bristol and then a masters in Victorian Studies at University of London. Began career at St Albans, where he became head of general studies. Joined Leighton Park in 1994 as head of history and became, successively, housemaster, director of studies, deputy head: academic, deputy head: pastoral and then, with nowhere else to go – head. An unusual trajectory and represents a terrific vote of confidence from the school governors and community. Plus a recourse to stability and continuity. His tenure followed the lengthy reign of a highly-regarded predecessor with a brief hiccup in between when another appointee rapidly came and went. No scandal but a mismatch and no hard feelings thereafter, in a way that is characteristic of the school as a community.

Nigel – whose delight and surprise at his assumption of the headship is touching and genuine – is larger than life, colourful, smiley, warm and an easy man to talk to. He embodies his school and its values but is more than a safe pair of hands, having learned the place all through and having sound and sensible ideas of his own. This was a wise appointment. Leighton Park, already in stout heart, will be the better for it.

Academic matters: Academic work is taken seriously and pupils strive for success – as they should – although not, thankfully, a results-driven school. In 2016, 45 per cent A*/A at GCSE. A level and IB offered though IB numbers not yet on a par with A level takers. In 2016, 41 per cent of A levels gained A*/A. Overall IB average 35. IB retained partly because 'its values are so much those of the school,' explains Nigel. Useful cross-fertilisation – IB and A level languages often taught together in year 12 and all take an Extended Project Qualification for its educational value. Good languages. Very good teacher:pupil ratio at 7.5 pupils to one full-time teacher and some sixth form classes with only one or two students. Small but well-stocked library and much praise for the range of visiting outside speakers. Interesting displays of work – we were moved by the WW1 montage of Old LPs fallen in battle which made it all pathetically real.

Parents, for the most part, praise the teaching – 'my son is enthused by everything – especially the Mandarin', while there is some sense that a little more rigour, vigour and initiative might not come amiss here and there. Probably not a school for workaholics, but then, they probably wouldn't come. Very much a school for joiners-in and those with breadth and brain.

EAL classes for small number of students who need them and school prepares them for FCE and IELTS exams. They don't take an additional language and use one of the class English lessons to boost their language skills. Some 15 per cent on the SEND register – surprisingly few for a school with such a good reputation for supporting those with an educational special need. Individual learning centre and all staff involved in support. No in-class assistants unless provided by the pupil's LA. Helpful and flexible approach, as parents attest, and 'they are quite relaxed about Ritalin, they take it in their stride'. A sense that the large and highly-regarded SEN team are there to make themselves less and less needed.

Games, options, the arts: Large and beautiful site, with fields, pitches, courts and tracks which positively set your muscles aquiver. 'My son is not sporty but they have really got him to love it,' a mother marvelled. Music is big here and no other house activity compares with the annual House Music, which is taken very seriously – 'almost too seriously,' we were told, 'as everyone gets really into it and the noise is louder than at a football match'. Good number learn an instrument in school and remarkable cohort of fine musicians – ie beyond grade 8 – practise here. Art exceptionally varied and imaginative. We loved the year 10 work on 'Surfaces, facades and veneers' and the sixth form studio was full of mind-stretching, clever creativity, alongside examples of the crucial skills of drawing and painting. Pottery, photography, textiles and DT work provide evidence of novel, individual ideas being fostered. DT provision newly enhanced by laser cutter, CNC router and 3D printer. Drama also lively – big productions, mostly musicals, in attractive, flexible theatre, its regular seating arranged, interestingly, in the guise of a Meeting. Also small drama studio in stand-alone brick building, formerly a squash court.

Lots to do. And lots of encouragement to try things out. Huge range of clubs and activities and masses of space for them all. Young Enterprise, D of E, trips of all kinds but no CCF, of course.

Boarding: School would not claim that boarding accommodation is up-to-the minute. Rooms are spacious enough. Most younger years share in 3s and 4s. Sixth formers in singles but not an en-suite or even a bedroom with basin anywhere on site – yet. All houses well-provided with table games, TVs and sofas – they feel like home only with more fun. Meals now eaten in Oakview rather than in houses and pyjamas – to the regret of some. Many day pupils stay until 7.00pm or even 9.00pm, thus getting the best of two worlds.

Many staff live on site and have boarding duties. Head's modest house, also on site, all adds to the sense of community and pupils love that 'our tutors are in the boarding houses after school and we can just chat to them'.

Background and atmosphere: Situated in the centre of 'the park' – an apt name for this spacious, meadowed site with hundreds of mature trees, garden areas, large reedy pond, generous planting and low-rise blocks – is the main building, an elegant 1850s white house. It was bought by an earlier incarnation of the school in the 1880s and more land was donated by the Reckitt family – the aim being to educate Quaker children for Oxbridge. It remains a Quaker-run school as the majority of governors are Quakers and, although no member of the Friends remains on the staff and only penny numbers of pupils are Quakers, the school lives by and exudes those gentle, civilised and socially responsible values. Few who leave here take nothing of those with them, and many see them as a guide for a healthy life. A palpable sense of calm pervades the place – you feel it as you drive in and your shoulders drop as you step out of your car and breathe out.

This is not just another school and it is best not to approach it as such. Nor is it 'alternative', though the pupils and teachers being on first name terms can deceive you into thinking so. The Quaker philosophy is central and, although it is never pushed at you, its calm wisdom steals gently into one's consciousness. 'When you're in year 9, you don't really get the meaning of it,' one soon-to-be-leaver told us, 'but, by the end, especially when life is hectic, you really appreciate it. It helps you find quiet time to clear your thoughts.' Weekly Meeting for Worship and monthly Meeting are the overt Quaker practices but, in the diverse mix of today's population, no particular faith dominates and everyone brings to the sessions what they wish. In practice, this approach changes relationships. 'Calling teachers by their first names makes you treat them as people – you don't have to be on your best behaviour and it makes you more inclined to learn,' we were advised. And, of pupil:pupil dynamics – 'If we fall out we tend just to fix it and hug it out.' The 2015 Peace Pole – an extraordinary carved wooden column visible from most parts of the school – enshrines these principles, as do the many examples of pupil creativity – benches, tables etc carved from fallen trees on the site – around the place. Very much a school for joiners-in and those with breadth and brain.

Lots of buildings of all eras, little of startling architectural merit though the recent Oakview restaurant is cleverly designed and a popular addition. We were very impressed by the food – its freshness and variety – and deeply regretted not being able to stay to sample it. 'Theatre Special is when they cook it in front of you – like a performance; pork baguette is a thing of beauty,' apparently.

Some splendid individual rooms, especially in the main building. We were repeatedly struck by the good order of the site – not an instance of peeling paint, a shabby carpet or a stained wall met our eye and, over an extensive tour, we saw not a shred of litter. Signing is useful and not municipal in style.

Houses, named after notable Quakers, matter but not too much – except at House Music. But the traditions and values of the place inspire spontaneous, unaffected loyalty.

Pastoral care, well-being and discipline: Discipline maintained with a light touch and some incomers given refuge after mishaps elsewhere become model citizens here. A great place for deserving second-chancers – 'The only people to get kicked out are complete idiots as they'll have had several warnings'. So – very occasional permanent exclusions, usually of those with more money than sense. A parent told us that 'they encourage them to become self-reliant and independent' and 'unlike at other schools, they can pick up their own clothes and make their own supper'. 'They are good at integrating kids who've been fish-out-of-water at their previous schools.' More rules than you might expect – no eating while walking around, no use of mobiles during the school day – but all designed to consider others and to maintain the peace. And Nigel is subtly stiffening the teacher-pupil dynamic to remind all that, in the classroom, work is what matters and discipline is there to protect that principle.

Pupils and parents: Day pupils outnumber boarders 3:1. Full boarders outnumber flexis by 4:1. And boys outnumber girls – as in most co-ed schools – by more than 2:1. Some 72 per cent are UK nationals, the rest from everywhere – 29 nationalities at time of our visit, so no cliques and enclaves. Vast majority of UK students are local or local-ish. Healthy 75 per cent of boarders in school at weekends. Old Leightonians: Sir David Lean, Sir Richard Rodney Bennett, Jim Broadbent, Laura Marling, Eliza Bennett, Michael Foot, Lord Caradon, Lord Frederick Seebohm and a fair clutch of MPs plus Rowntrees, Cadburys, Clarks, Reckitts, Morlands and Frys.

L

Entrance: Online entrance tests in English comprehension and maths, plus creative writing exercise and short interview in the January preceding entry for years 7-10. Entry to sixth form conditional on GCSE or equivalent results, plus interview. At 11+, 95 apply for 40 places; at 13+, 35 apply for 15-20 places. At year 10, 20 apply for 10-15 places. Year 11 is a 'pre-sixth' year for overseas students. There are six applicants for each of the 20-30 places in the sixth form. Second language speakers sit an EAL test.

Exit: Around a third leave after year 11. Most who leave after sixth form go to a range of courses at respectable universities but, as one parent enthused, 'we liked the fact that alongside the leavers who read medicine at Oxford they celebrate those who go and learn circus skills'. Most, however, to eg Sheffield or Exeter to read eg engineering or philosophy. One to Oxbridge in 2016 and one medic; others to Birmingham, Exeter and Swansea.

Money matters: Not an immensely rich school but a decent amount of money available for bursaries. Emphasis on enabling those whose financial situation would not allow them to attend, to do so, so most recipients on awards of 50 per cent or more. Robust mean-testing and assessment of income/commitments/assets etc. Six on 100 per cent bursaries at time of our visit. Scholarships mostly worth 10 per cent.

Remarks: A school in which to grow. Not for hustlers, bustlers and takers but great for thinkers, makers, givers, be-ers.

Leventhorpe School

Cambridge Road, Sawbridgeworth, Hertfordshire CM21 9BY

Pupils: 1,200 • Ages: 11–19 • Sixth form: 290

Tel: 01279 836633
Email: education@leventhorpe.net
Website: www.leventhorpe.net

Head: Since 2008, Mr Jon Locke (40s) BA PGCE. Read maths – and played international rugby – at Cardiff which led to him being recruited to play for the varsity team at Cambridge, where he completed his PGCE. Grew up in Harlow with both parents in the teaching profession (father was a head – and fellow rugby enthusiast), as are his brother and wife. Quips: 'It makes it easy that we can all have our holidays together'. Cut teeth teaching maths at Newport Grammar School at a time where he was also playing for Saracens first team and relished opportunity 'to be a role model to boys' as games coach. From there, joined Richard Hale in Hertford as assistant head before moving to Sir John Law in Harpenden as deputy head, working as part of an 'inspirational' team responsible for driving school to Ofsted Outstanding status. Returned to Harlow to be close to family and joined Leventhorpe at a time when 'it needed a fresh perspective'. Despite passion for competitive sport has never been drawn to independent sector, fiercely believing that a good state maintained school should offer 'the best of both worlds' to its pupils. Strong believer in 'freedom and authority' for staff, 'growing our own future leaders', as well as collaboration with local primary and other secondary schools. Led effort to achieve Training School status in 2009, propelled school to Ofsted Outstanding in 2012 and most recently has worked to set up a multi-academy trust with the vision of outstanding educational provision for local children from 4 to 18. So what next? 'There are always new challenges,' he says. 2015 saw a dip in GCSE results that he has been working closely with staff to 'put right' – small improvement in 2016 – and with around half of his heads of department new appointments, consolidation is high on the near term agenda.

An all-round good guy. Self-deprecating, speaks freely from the heart – no spin, no script – you'd be happy to bump into him at the pub (and so, probably, would the sixth formers). Places strong emphasis on interpersonal skills: 'I teach pupils to shake hands and look people in the eye.' Highly visible around school: seen on the touchline every Saturday, front of house a few mornings a week and throws himself into parent quiz nights and other social events. Lives locally with wife, a teacher at Birchwood High School in Bishop's Stortford and his two children – a son who attends Leventhorpe and a younger daughter. Coaches Harlow U13 rugby team and, when time allows, enjoys cycling and climbing.

Academic matters: Traditional timetable caters for mixed ability cohort, who join as six form entry in year 7 and are set for maths from their Sats results. Setting flexible and parents 'really impressed with levels of communication' when pupils moved up or down. Results respectable, with 24 per cent A*/A grades at GCSE in 2016. At A level, 47 per cent of grades were A*/B and 25 per cent A*/A. Head reports star subjects to be English and social sciences, plus 'spectacular' results at both GCSE and A level for technology (students also uniformly declare this department 'inspirational') and maths, where parents report 'variable quality of teaching', reportedly 'on its way up'.

Science has, he admits, been 'a weakness to date' but a new departmental head is on track to boost results by 10 to 15 per cent in this year's round of exams alone – so watch this space. It's French and Spanish for all in years 7 and 8, and compulsory to continue with one (or both) in year 9. Parents praise teaching of languages, which incorporates creative methods such as film and music rather than just text books. 'Student choice comes first,' says head, so no compulsory language at GCSE: 'If a student is able to choose subjects they like as their options, they are more likely to do well in these, hence their confidence and self-esteem will benefit and they'll do better all round.' Financial literacy qualification offered as enrichment subject alongside GCSE and A levels is popular with brightest pupils.

Majority of pupils take 10 GCSEs, with brightest adding one more if they take triple science. Less traditional routes on offer for those of a non-academic disposition, with students able to choose fewer than four GCSE options to lighten the load and – where appropriate – day release to attend vocational college courses. Recent increase in SEN provision – now a full time SENCo, one higher level TA and eight TAs to offer support to those on the register. Focus on early intervention for students falling behind in literacy and numeracy in years 7 to 11, with withdrawal from other subjects for special booster sessions run with the aim of getting them back on track and able to keep up with the cohort. No fixed approach to nurturing pupils at the top of the academic spectrum – 'we teach a growth mindset,' says head. 'Anyone can achieve if they work hard – that's the philosophy of the school.' This reflected in the replacement of an elitist speech day with 'achievement awards' – 25 per year group up for grabs at the end of each year to celebrate endeavour as much as – if not more than – results.

Games, options, the arts: Compulsory sport to year 12, with four periods per fortnight. Unsurprisingly, school is 'more rugby than football' and is, he says, 'coming on' in competitive fixtures with year 7 finalists and year 8 recently winning the district plate. Keen competitors are selected for an A or B team, and head says that 'everyone who turns up regularly to training will get a match,' even relative beginners if they are keen, according to parents. Football popular with both sexes too, although with more talent to choose from it tends to be harder for hopefuls to make the squad. Strong cricket, thanks to an arrangement with Sawbridgeworth Cricket Club, and netball and hockey for girls. A and B teams for girls' rugby, football and cricket on top of trad sports, with increasing competitive success at district level

Sports tours moving up the agenda, with a rugby tour for 60 boys aged 13 to 15 to New York – the first of its kind for Leventhorpe – in 2017. Cleverly partially funded by a combination of parent fundraising, local businesses sponsoring kit and negotiation through contacts on the ground of free accommodation with families, cost has been made feasible for majority of families, with any boys on pupil premium receiving full funding. Plenty of other trips tick the academic and enrichment boxes: skiing in Fiesch, a girls' hockey and netball tour to Cyprus, exchange trips to Canada, battlefields trip to France and philosophy and ethics to Rome, to name a few.

Drama, newly on curriculum for years 7 to 9, and run by a former head girl, thrives with strong results at GCSE and productions aplenty for budding thespians of all ages. Shows tend to be more Oliver! than Othello and in recent years have included The Wizard of Oz, Grease and West Side Story. Parents report ethos to be 'very inclusive' and quality to be high – and our musical tour guides said that playing in the orchestra pit would be their overriding best memory of their Leventhorpe years. Lack of swanky music centre more than compensated for by wildly enthusiastic and talented teaching staff ('fantastic' say parents). Grant funded free instrumental lessons for all year 7 and 8 pupils requesting them – with funding continuing to year 13 if pupils choose music as GCSE or A level option. Lower and upper choirs, orchestra, folk band and even an accordion ensemble (the only one we know of in the area) all strut their stuff at termly concerts, with beginners and improvers given the opportunity to show what they have learned at termly chamber concerts. Annual tour to Paris for choir and instrumentalists places cherry on top of this active department.

Background and atmosphere: Although your heart may sink when you pull up outside the drab low level 1960s blocks that front the main road through Sawbridgeworth, the moment you step into the recently refurbed reception area, all high ceilings, glass and colourful displays of artwork and textiles, you get an inkling that there's something special beyond. And although the majority of classrooms tick the 'tatty' box, in the main they are large and light – and we've never seen so many computers. The wow factor really hits you when you step into the learning resource centre and library (2013) – an airy, double height space, flooded with light and punctuated by bright colours, beanbags, plus a beautiful mezzanine study area for exclusive use by years 12 and 13 (complete with yet more IT). By the time you walk across the piazza to the fabulous, architecturally stunning leisure centre (2012), you'll have forgotten that the 1960s ever happened. Equipped with everything from trampolines to cricket nets and a state of the art dance studio and gym that's open to pupils before and after school, plus an outside viewing balcony overlooking a vast Astroturf, playing fields and beyond as far as the eye can see across farmland. All that's missing is a swimming pool. But that's just next door.

The artsy side's well catered for too, with a superb drama studio and buzzy art rooms displaying huge canvases and pottery designs. Super food technology facility, with equally appealing textiles room showcasing high quality creations from fleece hats, shorts and dresses. And with pupils telling us 'there are just so many' clubs and societies to choose from, we're not surprised school is becoming so popular.

L

Pastoral care, well-being and discipline: Head says 'mutual respect' is the driving force behind a culture of good behaviour in school, with little need for heavy handed discipline beyond 20 minute lunch time detentions and a weekly after school detention which rarely sees more than 15 pupils in attendance. Recognises that 'mental health is a growing concern' amongst young people and is making it a key priority for next three years, with a 'mental health first aid' programme aimed at educating pupils and parents of warning signs. Differences of race or sexual orientation are reportedly well tolerated. 'Students feel safe here to be who they are,' says head. 'It's genuinely not an issue'. 'We like to give pupils the chance to let us know about bullying if it occurs,' he says. Trained 'active listeners' in years 10 and 11 are on hand to address concerns raised by their younger peers and school works closely with parents on current issues, eg cyber bullying, with 'eye opening' seminars and briefings. Pupils describe school as 'really friendly – we all really look out for each other' and parents say bullying is 'taken very seriously' and 'jumped on quickly' when it occurs.

House system pervades all and is manifested through house ties for boys and coloured blazer badges. Pastoral care channelled through heads of house, with year group heads now taking responsibility for academic progress and parents have an email address for every teacher – and, importantly, report receiving fast replies – making communication simple. Inter-house competitions for absolutely everything, plus house points as rewards for endeavour and achievement in the classroom.

Pupils and parents: School's geographical location – wedged between middle class Bishop's Stortford and less affluent Harlow – makes for a totally mixed parent demographic, from city workers to manual labourers, 'which is why I chose it for my son', says head. An aspirational choice for Harlow parents, and an increasing favourite with the Bishop's Stortford crowd if they're looking for co-ed. The melting pot seems to work – school has a friendly, stress free vibe and pupils we met were a delightful combination of articulate, inquisitive and quietly confident. Because of musical aptitude entrance criteria, there's a fair bit of talent knocking about too (anyone who has attempted to learn piano will understand our awe at our tour guide modestly saying he was 'struggling' with grade 4 having been learning for just a year. That on top of grade 8 violin) which adds to the generally diverse and convivial feel to the school.

Entrance: Priority given to pupils attending one of eight feeder schools in surrounding villages and their siblings. School has filled from these in recent years. Eighteen places held back in each year group for applicants not at these feeders showing exceptional musical aptitude, with test taken in consortium with two other local secondaries.

Exit: Around 70 per cent stay on after year 12. Thereafter 'the landscape is changing', according to head, with increasing numbers of pupils – around a third – choosing straightforward or degree apprenticeships or management training schemes with companies ranging from M&S to HSBC, Deloitte and PwC, rather than the traditional university path. Of those heading to university, popular destinations are London colleges and Nottingham with large numbers also stay closer to home, heading to Anglia Ruskin University – up to 20 in some years. Two or three to Oxbridge most years, notably Robinson College Cambridge, which has taken at least one pupil a year for the last few.

L

Remarks: In a survey carried out recently by school, over 95 per cent of parents said that they would recommend Leventhorpe, with its super facilities, community spirit and strong discipline all top reasons. With a young, purposeful head who parents say 'never lets things stand still' as its driving force we predict it will go from strength to strength, giving pupils of all abilities abundant all round opportunity and positive attitude towards learning. In the words of one parent: 'They celebrate success, whether it's 10 A stars at GCSE or a pupil who has simply exceeded their expectations; it's just what they do.'

Lochinver House School

Heath Road, Little Heath, Potters Bar, Hertfordshire EN6 1LW

Pupils: 350 • Ages: 3–13

Fees: £10,320– £13,575 pa

Tel: 01707 653064
Email: registrar@lochinverhouse.com
Website: www.lochinverhouse.herts.com

Headmaster: Since 2011, Mr Ben Walker BA PGCE CELTA. Educated at Lochinver House (head boy in 1977, badges proudly displayed in his office on a cut off blazer lapel), St Albans School and Reading University where he read English. A teacher by vocation, followed a non-conventional path to his current position, joining retail group C&A as a management trainee after university. Realised after a year that the commercial world was 'not really for me' and took a PGCE at the Institute of Education. Spent 13 years in inner city state secondary schools, rising through the ranks, before he and his wife decided in 2002 to sell up and move the family to Kenya to carry out development work. They spent three years there starting a school, coordinating health care projects and working as Church Mission Society partners. Towards the end of that time, took a post at St Andrews, Turi, a prep school for expats and wealthy nationals, which led him on his return to the UK in 2005 to the role of deputy head at Swanbourne House in Buckinghamshire. Came full circle and joined Lochinver House as head six years later.

Calm, engaging and a natural communicator. Married to Jill, deputy head at Glendower School in Kensington, with three children. Feels he inherited 'a good school with a few challenges,' the largest of which was to 'encourage celebration of the 13+ journey.' Promptly surveyed heads of top schools including St Albans School, Merchant Taylors' and Eton on the matter to strengthen his case, and has set about communicating to parents the merits of prep school until 13 from thereon.

Governors say he has made the school calmer, achieving 'stronger achievement of values' and giving it a 'stronger sense of spirituality.' Parents agree and add that he has also given the school a 'more academic feel.' Popular with pupils, perhaps because of his qualities as an educator, or perhaps because of 'headmaster's hot chocolate', a weekly Friday event for those who have received the most house credits for their efforts that week, or 'head's pub lunch,' a termly treat for one deserving boy chosen from each of the three houses.

Entrance: Currently oversubscribed and 'gently' selective. Candidates at 3 and 4 assessed informally in small groups ('a fun day,' say parents) to check suitability and potential. Boys entering higher up the school, some from state primaries and some new to area, spend a day at the school with a 'buddy' and are tested in numeracy and literacy, with competition often stiff for these occasional places. Maximum class size 21.

Exit: Around 80 per cent stay to year 8, with the usually less academic remainder taking different 11+ paths to avoid the Common Entrance hurdle ('they can benefit from a longer run in to GCSEs,' says head) or leaving for financial reasons. A few to selective state schools. Majority to day schools (22 in last 10 years) including Aldenham, Habs, Haileybury, Mill Hill and St Albans, occasional one to Westminster, with 'a handful' on to boarding schools in ones and twos including, recently, Bedford, Oakham, Oundle, Radley and Uppingham.

Remarks: Tucked away in residential suburbia, Lochinver House won't seduce you with its good looks, but in true ugly duckling style it could well win you over with the functionality of its bijoux eight acre site, a warren of practical facilities, all aimed at squeezing excellence out of its young charges.

Pre-prep block unlikely to win any beauty contests but has its own small library and the walls are cheered with loads of art and written work by its young residents, as well as a 'giving tree', which gives a clue to the supportive nature of the school, with kind deeds posted as leaves on a daily basis. Also has its own garden – a haven in the north London urban jungle – where the youngest pupils grow vegetables, build, dig and have story time when weather permits. Play times are spent in the enclosed adventure playground (made less alluring by proximity to car park) or, for reception, in their dedicated outdoor play area away from the rough and tumble of older boys.

The star attraction from the boys' perspective is undoubtedly the huge Astroturf that multi-tasks as play area, sports field and cricket pitch (although not for A and B teams for fear of nearby windows). Sports fields are split between the main site and additional space across the road, offering plenty of options for matches and games practice. For older pupils, there's a lovely eco garden, complete with bug hotel and swamp-like pond, home to 'loads of newts and snails,' according to boys. Other stand out facilities include a theatre, used for assemblies and the many school productions and recitals, a light and bright dining room and modern, well-equipped science labs. The senior music room recently benefited from an injection of cash, now boasting a suite of gleaming keyboards for aspiring musicians to get their tech fix.

Parents and pupils largely local with intake reflecting the north London multi-cultural mix and the majority professional, often dual income, families – 'very grounded.' A small proportion have English as an additional language but generally do not require additional support. Fees considered excellent value. Not only are they amongst the lowest in the area, but also include almost all trips and excursions, moderate learning support requirements and many after-school clubs. Extremely active PTA organises the usual fundraisers – balls, fêtes, bazaars and quiz nights – and parents say this gives the school a really family orientated feel, 'one of the school's greatest strengths.'

'Very strong' language offering according to head, with French from year 3, Latin from year 5, a two year Spanish course in years 5 and 6 and Russian offered as an extension subject for the brightest in years 5 and 6. St Albans school reportedly considers Lochinver boys amongst its best linguists and has created an accelerated class almost exclusively for them when they arrive in year 9. IT, music and games taught by specialists from reception up. Setting from year 3 for maths, year 5 for French and from year 7 for sciences. School retains two form entry format to the end of year 6, with years 7 and 8 splitting into three smaller classes, including an accelerated group. Staff described by head as 'a perfect mix of experience and youthfulness,' with a great balance of male and female staff. Parents generally agree that 'the teaching staff really make the school,' with just the odd grumble about a job share in the junior school having an impact on teacher/pupil relationships. Majority of classes held in form rooms until year 5, when boys start to move around school for specialist teaching in all subjects – 'brilliant preparation for my next school,' said one. Good scholarship output with around 7 most years to a variety of next schools.

No statemented children but a number supported in various ways by a 'highly qualified' full time SEN coordinator plus team. Head is proud of the level of support they give as a primarily academic school to lost sheep. Special adjustments also made for gifted pupils with those in senior years encouraged to undertake independent project work to stretch their abilities – 'children's specific needs are met,' according to parents, although some muttered about lack of recognition for less academic boys: 'all the awards go to the clever ones.'

Musical pursuits 'very popular,' says head, with two thirds of all pupils learning an instrument and half of that number learning two. Compulsory recorder in year 2 and between six and eight musical recitals every year – 'We try to create a balance,' says head. 'Parents want breadth.' Plenty of opportunities for the thespian community to shine too, with performances for all year groups and a major production each year, recently Wacky Soap, with almost everyone getting involved either on stage or behind the scenes.

Head also proud of school's sporting prowess: 'we punch way above our weight.' In addition to the usual competitive suspects (rugby, football and cricket), boys are also able to sample the likes of sailing, golf and taekwondo and report that sports day is 'very competitive.' A-C teams throughout the school for major sports, so 'almost everyone gets a chance to play,' say parents. A plethora of after-school clubs on offer from year 5 upwards, such as horror film making, debating, model making and, for prospective new age men, cookery and touch typing.

Good happy vibe ('it feels like my family,' said one year 8 boy). Boys in years 3 to 8 are reading buddies to little ones in reception and year 1 and the popular house buddy system from year 3 up galvanises vertical relationships up and down the school, with other initiatives such as the pupil-run ABC (Anti-Bullying Council) in place to deal with the usual friendship issues and playground problems. Parents 'feel supported' when problems arise and report that they are generally dealt with proactively and in collusion with home.

Morning assemblies complimented by house tutor group sessions for boys in years 6 to 8 with daily discussions covering topics such as self-awareness, British values, democracy and friendship, aiming to prepare them for the world at large and strengthen inter-year relationships at the top of the school. Two head boys elected by teachers and supported by house and vice house captains (one for each house). Immense leadership opportunities on offer for elected prefects, with the head boys' charities (chosen from a selection in a whole-school ballot) raising up to £20,000 each year for good causes.

Head sees wrap-around care as 'an important part of what we do,' and offers a free early morning club from 7.45am, tea time club running to 5.30pm (including tea for those that want it) and homework club (both charged as extras) for older boys, in addition to the array of extracurricular activities that keep boys at school after hours. School minibuses ferry children from Finchley, Southgate, Totteridge, Hadley Wood and Barnet directions for a small daily charge, mornings only.

Lockers Park School

Lockers Park Lane, Hemel Hempstead, Hertfordshire HP1 1TL

Pupils: 153 (including 3 girls); 20 full, 50 flexi-boarders • Ages: 4-13 (boys), 4-7 (girls) (boarding from 7) • C of E

Fees: Day £10,050 – £16,530; Boarding £23,160 pa

Tel: 01442 251712
Email: secretary@lockerspark.herts.sch.uk
Website: www.lockerspark.herts.sch.uk

Headmaster: Since 2013, Chris Wilson BSc, PGCE Cantab (30s). Educated at Winchester House in Northamptonshire, where he boarded from the age of 6, and Oundle. Read rural economics at Newcastle before moving to Cambridge to take a conversion course to enable him to teach maths to A level, followed by his PGCE at Homerton College.

Returned to alma mater Winchester House for first teaching role, where he spent 11 years teaching maths and running first XI cricket and colts rugby, heading the boarding house for 10 of them. Moved to Lockers in 2012 as deputy head, drawn by its rigorous sporting culture, boarding heritage ('boarding is infused through the school,' he says) and pastoral approach, as well as its superb musical offering (although he cheerfully describes himself as 'woefully inadequate' in this respect). Headship came after a period which was, according to parents 'turbulent', with three heads of school in six years. He has reportedly 'steadied the ship brilliantly' and restored confidence to staff, with parents describing the change in mood after his appointment as 'palpable'.

Still teaches years 7 and 8 maths and revels in being able to 'physically see the path of the boys' development' in a prep school and having 'involvement in all spheres' of their lives. Parents describe him as a 'fantastic communicator' and say that he has returned a focus on academic achievement which had formerly been 'slightly lost'. A cricket fanatic, he likens the patience and thoughtfulness required for the game to his role as head. Intent that his charges will remember the fun side of school, believes in 'freedom within boundaries' and aims to 'fly in the face' of pushy parents to 'ensure Lockers boys have a childhood'.

Engaging and likeable with a relaxed persona, and ably supported by wife, Hayley, who fulfils a traditional head's spouse role as well as caring for their two young daughters.

Entrance: New pre-prep school housed in a purpose designed building welcomes girls as well as boys. From here, most girls likely to move to local girls' school, Abbot's Hill School, whilst boys move into the 'steadfastly single sex' year 3.

Not currently oversubscribed, although at highest ever numbers. Main intake into year 3 with a 'low key' assessment day including tests in verbal reasoning and maths. Scholarship day in February with applicants also observed in music, sport and a fun activity such as a treasure hunt. Head says they are 'not only looking for academic strength' but for children who can bring 'that certain something' to the school.

Pupils join mainly from state primaries, occasionally other preps (a large influx recently from Berkhamsted Prep), within a 20 to 30 minute radius of the school. Approximately half the cohort are day boys, with the rest doing 'some form' of boarding (two nights minimum). Twenty full time boarders with about 50 per cent of these overseas pupils (typically Russian or Chinese) and some Forces plus some 55 flexi boarders.

Exit: The small number of pupils means they tend to leave in ones and twos to a broad variety of schools. In recent years, good numbers to Harrow plus Bedford, Stowe and Bradfield. Day boys to Merchant Taylors', St Albans or Berkhamsted, with the occasional one to state maintained grammars at 11+, although this is 'definitely not encouraged,' says head. Three or four scholarships achieved each year. Head deliberates carefully over choosing of senior schools 'on a very individual basis.'

L

Remarks: Adamantly traditional in its fabric but with a subtly modern feel (thanks to a rolling programme of improvements), Lockers was purpose-built in 1874, based on Mitchell House at Rugby School, and sits atop 25 glorious acres of woodland – a Boys' Own oasis in a drab Hemel suburb. The heart of the school is undoubtedly the stunning, light-flooded panelled dining hall, which typifies Lockers' success in juxtaposing the modern with the school's rich history, the names of alumni etched on its walls. Everything about the school is focused on bringing out the best in boys – from the 40 minute morning break where they can tear around fields and woodlands with just enough time for a bit of den-building before the bell calls them to lessons, to the pristine well-structured classrooms (if there was a GSG award for the cleanest prep, Lockers would be in with a good chance) and predominantly male staff. Staff know all the boys and are '100 per cent accessible,' say parents – 'clearly visible and just a phone call or an email away.'

The spacious, well-stocked library has a cosy feel, with armchairs and banks of computers, and the chapel can house the whole school at a squeeze. Art room large and airy with its own kiln, although feels suspiciously tidy – and whole school could benefit from more artwork on display, especially as standards are high enough to win a senior school art scholarship most years. DT recently rehomed into a modern block with two super rooms – one for design and one for work. A comfortable boarders' common room is supplemented by the 'boys' hall' and the old gym, home to table tennis and pool tables for boys to use in their free time. Engine enthusiasts will adore the 'train room' – a dedicated space for a huge model railway for boys to tinker with. Pianists practise on a baby grand situated in a very public space rather than tucked away in a practice room – 'great for getting them used to performing,' says head.

Tousled boys bomb happily around between classes with plenty of cheery greetings for staff and visitors. The uniform – or lack thereof – comprising a check shirt of the boys' choice and a pair of navy cords, sums up the collegiate learning environment where boys can be boys and the endgame is reached via a path punctuated with a lot of good, wholesome fun as well as academic rigour. 'Best' is when the jackets and ties come out – again the boys' own choice of jacket – reserved for school outings, concerts and away matches. School committed to small class sizes with between 10 and 15 in most forms – parents feel that school's bijoux size is its 'true strength'.

Long days – sometimes up to 11 hours for older boys – with all allowed to arrive at school from 7am and stay for breakfast and supper at no extra charge and with no prior arrangement, all of which helps to cement the seamless boarding vibe – parents say it's like 'one big family.' Boarding house is part of main school, with boys split over two floors according to age and presided over by a housemaster who is supported by a team of live-in matrons.

Bright, functional dorms housing four to six boarders slightly lack the personal touch, although boys can bring their own duvet covers. Clothes kept in the laundry room and matrons lay out boy's outfits each day. Exeats every third weekend, unusually from Friday lunch time until Monday evening, with Saturday morning school still going strong on non-exeat weekends, optional for pre-prep.

Setting from year 7 in preparation for CE with specialist teaching across all subjects from year 5. Modern languages exceptionally strong, with head describing French as school's 'stand out' subject and parents adding history and geography to the list. A brief audience with the head of modern languages certainly confirmed his passion for language and inspirational teaching techniques. Latin and ancient Greek also on the menu, although not considered by parents to be school's strongest suit. Maths and English 'on the up,' says head, due to recent staff changes.

Music 'firing on all cylinders', according to head, led by the 'most dynamic, committed' head of music who secures a music scholarship for at least one boy each year. Violin for all from year 3 and at least 96 per cent of boys continue with an instrument, some playing two or three. Choirs, ensembles and bands galore with an invitation to join the 'intensely serious' main choir considered a real accolade (dare we say cool?) and with parents saying it's 'totally normal for boys to be singing' at Lockers. Drama on curriculum from years 3 to 5 (replaced by Latin in year 6), with opportunities galore for budding thespians to perform in plays, poetry competitions, debating etc.

Sport not the school's raison d'être but a good ethos in place – head laments the demise at some fixtures of the traditional post-match tea in other schools ('a bag of crisps and box of juice – just not the same') – and places huge emphasis on fair play and sportsmanship, fielding A-E teams whenever possible so everyone gets a trip on the bus whatever their ability. Sports department has taken a hit in recent years, tragically losing its two sports coaches to cancer in a short space of time, but is striding on and making the most of its not inconsiderable facilities, including cricket nets, a renovated outdoor pool, tennis courts, and putting green. Sport every afternoon for all boys, with the timetable adjusted seasonally to allow for more light for outdoor fun. Occasional parental grumbles that less sporty boys are 'labelled' in the early years and don't get the same coaching opportunities as their more able peers. Tons of extracurricular from chess club to year-round skiing at the nearby snow dome. Lockers' own cub and scout packs thrive, and boys who take part generally stay the night afterwards.

Chapel every morning takes a 'general studies' approach and acts as a 'reflective, calming exercise' to start the day. Boarders' fun nights well attended by day boys and the anti-health and safety 'Dark Tower' night, an unlit night time treasure hunt around the school, hugely popular. In summer, day boys stay over after evening barbecues and are 'swept along' with boarding activities throughout the year, some parents saying their boys never want to come home. Action-packed weekends for full-timers with activities split three ways between the cultural, educational and purely fun. All prep done in school – a popular move with boys and parents. School even has its own vernacular – with quirks so numerous that newcomers are issued with a handbook to decipher it all. Parents report that any incidents of bullying or upset are dealt with effectively in a 'supportive and understanding' way.

In all, a small but perfectly formed school which gives boys all the tools they need to continue on to top public schools. Lockers offers the best of both worlds – boarding for those who want it, with all the benefits plus their own beds at home for those who don't. In the words of one happy parent who moved two boys from another prep: 'boys are known and valued at Lockers, rather than unknown and undervalued'. Newish head has much to build on.

Long Crendon School

Chilton Road, Long Crendon, Aylesbury, Buckinghamshire HP18 9BZ

Pupils: 210 • Ages: 4–11

Tel: 01844 208225
Email: office@longcrendon.bucks.sch.uk
Website: www.longcrendon.bucks.sch.uk

Headteacher: Since 2010, Mrs Sue Stamp BA (60s). After completing her degree in English Lit at Westfield College, London, she gained her teaching qualifications from the now defunct Philippa Fawcett Teacher Training College. 'I didn't go into teaching straight away because I was offered a place on the Selfridges training programme – where I stayed until I had my first child in the late 70s,' she says. When she did finally take the plunge, she had an interesting array of teaching jobs, including in international schools in Africa for 10 years, where she climbed the ranks to middle management. She then began teaching in Bucks in 2003 (also becoming SENCo) and from there, became assistant head into Bearbrook School, Aylesbury, then deputy head at Waddesdon School, before moving here.

Any staff member who's been at this school longer than Mrs Stamp will tell you that it has been on 'quite a journey' since her arrival – priorities are clearer, staff work more collaboratively and outdoor learning (more of which later) is integral to the curriculum. She doesn't teach regularly, but she does get stuck in if required, and she has a clear open door policy ('actually a closed door doesn't stop the pupils here!' she laughs), with children popping in to tell her anything from a new idea for an after-school club to concerns around friendship issues. We found her dedicated, no-nonsense and perceptive. 'She's not touchy-feeling, although she is approachable,' one parent told us. 'She is not a big, gregarious character that you rally behind, but I think it's great we have someone who is more interested in pushing children forward, than herself.' Others describe her as 'no pushover,' 'disciplined but fair' and 'unbelievably supportive, when you need her behind you.' Pupils describe her as 'strict, but nice at the same time.'

Lives locally, and hobbies include reading, walking and making the most of her National Trust membership.

Entrance: Admission by means of the local authority criteria – which means that, in order of priority, it's looked after children, SEND, living as in catchment and siblings of children already at the school. In practice, that means the vast majority of families live in the village, no more than half-a-mile away and many year groups (of which there is single entry in each one) are oversubscribed. 'If you're on the outskirts of the village, there's a chance you won't get in,' admits the head.

Exit: Grammar schools in Bucks are popular – notably Aylesbury High, Aylesbury Grammar and Sir Henry Floyd – and many parents tutor their offspring in preparation of the 11+. Lord Williams's School, Thame, is the nearest comprehensive – 'it's a great school and many of our children go there,' says the head. Occasionally, children move into the private sector, usually in the Oxford area.

Remarks: This is a true village school, with a community vibe, and it is regularly described as 'unique' and 'special.' Parents attribute this to a variety of reasons: 'I've never come across a school that is so focused on values, ranging from kindness to resilience.' 'This is a school that believes in setting children up for life – it doesn't just tick boxes.' 'The teachers don't just go the extra mile – they go an extra 100 miles.' And so on.

Then there's the staggering commitment to outdoor learning, which has had a direct impact on academic results. It all started when foundation teacher Simon Poote, who won the 2015 award for Best LOtC Innovator, worked with the children to create a special outside space from a neglected area of the school site. The children helped him to build hills and landscapes, sow wild flowers, build a veg plot, add ropes, pulleys and water channels, create a fire pit, bird hide, camp out tent and even a mud kitchen. There's a wooden outdoor learning lodge, plus wet weather gear for the whole school, and the school has also formed a strong link with a neighbouring teaching farm, where the children spend time looking after animals, collecting produce and cooking the food they harvest. 'Writing results from the foundation stage children dramatically improved as the children are desperate to write about what they are experiencing,' reports the head, who adds that children are also 'much less likely to give up and more likely to undertake challenges across the curriculum as they have experienced what hard work can achieve.' 'You're always out and about here,' one child told us, with others pitching in with example upon example – 'We get to make jam!' 'The bug hunting is awesome.' 'We did apple pressing!' 'Look at all our trowels – we get to really dig and build.' 'We made reindeers out of twigs.'

The school – which was originally built as a secondary school in the 1960s and then became a primary in 1972 – certainly has no shortage of outside space, including a huge sports field, tarmacked playground, plus the outdoor learning spaces. Inside, there are big, light and airy classrooms galore – with one class getting two classrooms all to themselves – with a sliding door between them. Downstairs is home to foundation, year 1, 2 and 3, while upstairs there's years 4, 5 and 6, as well as a spacious art room – which is strangely devoid of artwork on the walls, perhaps simply because it's already been pinned to every other school wall. Indeed, rarely have we seen such imaginative, colourful and spectacular wall displays – a real showcase for the school's creative side. Also downstairs is a huge sports/assembly hall, with a lovely big stage; a canteen, which isn't very big, but pupils simply have their lunch in rotas; ICT suite, which disappointingly only has 16 computers (although the head says tablets are regularly used in lessons); a large, instrument-packed music room; and conservatory for any extra lessons needed for individuals or small groups. The library is split in two – fiction in the foyer; non-fiction in a closed off room. There's no doubt the facilities could do with an upgrade in places, but we've seen a lot worse, and what they lose in aesthetical décor, they gain in sheer space. Indeed, there's still room left for the school to rent out space out to a private onsite nursery and charity pre-school.

Teaching staff are praised for being 'fun' and 'engaging' and are given freedom to try out new and innovative methods – although some parents said they wish there were more male staff. Every classroom, bar none, that we visited, were full of pupils who were thoroughly absorbed, with single arms so enthusiastically held up in the air that you felt they might burst through the ceiling. And that enthusiasm only gets stronger outside. One child, for example, excitedly explained that when they studied the Great Fire of London, the pupils all made miniature replica houses, then took them outside and laid them out in streets and burned them to recreate the feeling. 'Every bit of learning seems to be brought to life,' said one parent.

French from year 3 and Spanish for year 5 only. No setting – 'A rising tide raises all ships,' explains the head, who adds that leading on from their decision to eradicate ideas about where children sit on the continuum is their emphasis on a growth mind-set. 'We don't talk about children being "good" or "clever". Instead, we encourage them to select a type of challenge – from hard, harder, hardest and Herculean – in each lesson. They're all individually explained, and none of which is presented as easy. The result has been that the more able ones feel able to admit it when they can't do something – which had been a problem – and the less able ones have started to challenge themselves more,' says the head. 'The children are really encouraged to have a go at things – they're never afraid of failure,' said a parent. School strong on CPD for teachers, helped by the fact that they're part of a federation of schools (local comp, plus eight primaries), who share best practice, training days etc and have strong networking links.

L

The school has a history of turning out children who excel in reading, grammar and punctuation – head puts it down to a combination of children regularly visiting the school and local libraries; guided reading all the way up the school; plus plenty of stories read by teachers. Homework in key stage one is all about number bonds and daily reading, while in key stage 2 there's a gradual increase, with all assignments based on whatever they're learning that week. 'Nobody's expected to do hours and hours – it's all kept to a minimum,' says the head.

No statemented children when we visited, but that's not to say they don't get children on the more severe end of special needs from time to time. Around 10 per cent have more mild to moderate SEN at any one time – dyslexia, dyspraxia, ADHD and autistic spectrum, in the main. All get class-room based help, while some get extra help in small groups in the conservatory.

Sport has become more competitive under the current head's leadership ('Parents told me this was top of their wishlist when I joined,' she says), with Friday afternoons now dedicated to house sports, overseen by the specialist sports teacher. Football, rugby, netball, cricket, hockey and basketball are all played with gusto – and the school does well competing against other schools. There's plenty of sports-based extracurricular clubs and no shortage of facilities including three football pitches and an outdoor swimming pool that's used from May to the end of September. 'All classes swim twice a week – we don't have any children leaving this school unable to swim,' says the head.

Music also has a specialist teacher, with singing and instruments a big part of life for everyone here – with a school band (The Brass Snakes), which plays at events. Seven peripatetic teachers also come in to teach trumpet, piano, guitar, flute, drumming and more from year 3 upwards. Drama – which is taught in the main hall – is a firm favourite among pupils, with annual productions for year 6 leavers (The Porridge Pot the year we visited) and separate key stage 1 and 2 concerts at Christmas. Meanwhile, art seeps into practically every subject. Pupils regularly exhibit at the Roald Dahl Festival in Aylesbury, making puppets and suchlike. Extracurricular clubs include all these areas, plus the likes of dance, comic club (requested by pupils) and science club. All children go on a school outing once a term, determined by their topic – Oxford Castle, Living Rain Forest etc – and there are also small forays into local community, including village library, farm and tennis courts. Residentials for year 4 upwards – they have one night in Frontier Centre, Northampton; year 5s have two nights in New Barn, Dorset; and year 6s have a week in the Isle of Wight.

Parents say this is a nurturing and friendly school, where teachers really get to know the children and one of the teaching assistants is a trained counsellor. 'She is particularly good at picking up on issues,' a parent told us. One child had struggled with going to school for over a year, and it was this school that turned him around. 'They could not have been more supportive,' said the parent. Pupils feel comfortable approaching the head and there are robust rewards systems – dominated by house points system and the much-loved Smartie Awards, in which pupils or staff can nominate a child for effort in anything at all. The children pull out two entries from the Smartie box every Monday and that child gets a certificate, sticker and sits on the special chair in assembly. 'There's a Special Smartie award too – for consistently modelling the values of the school. Generally, these are the kinds of children who sit quietly and get on, but who can so easily get missed when it comes to praise,' explains the head.

Selected pupils are trained as play leaders, who organise a different sport for all each lunchtime. Plus, foundation children are buddied up with a year 6 student. 'The older ones take this responsibility very seriously – my son is adamant that the person he buddies is always happy,' one parent told us. Perhaps most impressive is the commitment to values – all schools say they have them, but this one lives and breathes them, and they keep them fresh by changing them every half-term, as well as getting the youngsters to really think about what they mean and how they can integrate them into their lives. When we visited, they were resilience and determination – and we saw pupils get oodles of praise when they showcased them in their work, play or behaviour. 'It really matters to the children that these values shine through in their daily life – they talk about them nearly every day,' said one parent. Bullying rare, and dealt with quickly. 'We get the parents in straight away,' says the head.

Student council is a big deal – they decide on how to raise charitable funds; they get a budget to spend on the playground; and they're involved with policies around things like behaviour policy and sanctions – which probably helps explain why there's so much pupil buy-in. Sanctions for transgressions – such as talking in class or being unkind – mainly including missing some of playtime, seeing the head teacher or having a letter written home to their parent. 'It can be a strict school – but it's fair,' one pupil told us.

Parents mainly middle class – many dual income (grateful for the optional before and after-school care). They're a sociable bunch, and very supportive, with a strong PTA and no shortage of offers to help out with guided reading, accompany children to the farm, help with forest school and going on school trips. Reflecting the local village's ethnicity, the vast majority are white British.

This is the kind of friendly, values-driven community primary that families move to the area for – and they're not disappointed. The dedicated teaching staff are focused on the whole child, rather than ticking boxes, and there seems to be no end to the lengths they'll go to in order to bring teaching alive. 'My children skip to school – who could ask for more?' summed up one parent.

Lord Wandsworth College

Long Sutton, Hook, Hampshire RG29 1TB

Pupils: 540; 85 full, 71 weekly, 152 flexi boarders (roughly two-thirds boys) • Ages: 11–18 • Sixth form: 169

Fees: Day £19,290- £21,750; Boarding £22,950- £30,870pa

Tel: 01256 862201
Email: admissions@lordwandsworth.org
Website: www.lordwandsworth.org

Headmaster: Since September 2015, Adam Williams (40s). Born Down Under, he went to Bradfield then Durham University. Previous job was deputy head of Glasgow Academy; has also been head of geography at Bradfield and Oakham. A neat man with an open face and the hint of a twinkle, he honed impressive cricketing and golfing skills, making it into national teams at schoolboy and university level. Out of school he still keeps his skills up to scratch, preferably on some windswept Scottish course more easily reached from his last job. His Australian start may have led to his love of travel and he rather endearingly admits to having used his geography classes as an excuse to bring out the holiday snaps.

Feeling that his first task on taking over was to thoroughly understand the school staff from groundsmen to departmental heads, he shed the suit and successfully donned the overalls. He was also pretty sharp over his pupil homework: one leaver last year was 'bowled over that he knew my name the first time he met me'. Described as an 'absolute legend' (a term more usually handed to brilliant steeplechasers), he plans to set this down-to-earth, country school firmly in the educational firmament, an approach that is steadily gaining appeal with local parents and is endorsed by his regular, witty, self-deprecating letters about life as a headmaster.

Married to Karen, a busy medic who tries hard to be on tap as much as possible; three children – the eldest offspring is soon to join LWC.

Academic matters: They work hard at the three Rs and it clearly pays off with GCSE results (46 per cent A*/A) ranking in the top 250 on the Guardian independent schools list in 2016. The results at A level were also solid but not stellar by independent school standards, 35 per cent A*-A and 60 per cent A*-B. However, bright children feel sufficiently stretched: for some Oxbridge is a definite possibility not a dream and the remainder speak confidently about reaching the next step, whatever it may be.

The 60:40 boy:girl split may partly account for maths and science having tended to be the school's forte, and the new building for the former backs up the quality of the teaching. One sixth former said he was so well taught that he'd moved from a doubtful pass at GCSE to a predicted A* at A level. A concerted move to change this bias is in progress and parents report that arts-orientated children are flourishing.

All pupils take one or two languages at GCSE and a new outing to France takes place 'pour encourager les autres'. Latin is compulsory for the first two years and either this or classical civilisation is taken by 35 per cent at GCSE. Language numbers at A level are quite small (19 last year) but in a French oral class a valiant attempt to explain why the French are so French was being combined with politics in the shape of Marine Le Pen.

Screening for dyslexia takes place in the first and third years and again in the lower sixth. All teachers are aware if there is a problem and the nine per cent who need it have weekly one-to-one sessions. Strong encouragement to hand in original work and not to succumb to the temptation of Wikipaedia is given to pupils and parents. There is also a popular tutorial system ('they become friends when you're in the sixth form and even stay friends after you've left').

Across the board the staff training budget has been doubled and the slight tendency to have brilliant sportsmen/women who can teach a bit is being reversed by sourcing teachers who are also sporty.

Games, options, the arts: Famously strong at rugby, they don't just pay lip service to a wide range of other sports but are winning prizes, particularly at girls' hockey and cricket. As well as providing several club and county level players on the turf, they have even managed to switch surfaces and pull an international ice hockey player out of the bag. There are plenty of teams across the sporting spectrum for the less starry, who can also choose anything from yoga to rock-climbing or riding. The system works well, parents happily reporting that they 'run them ragged on the sports field'.

There are chances to give almost anything a go at the beginning: 'All schools say that they try and bring out your strengths, but here they really do it'. Saturday morning clubs, including options for the arty, sporty and those keen to fill academic gaps, are so popular – particularly the destruction and reconstruction of electronic or electrical objects – that parents are prepared to make sure day children don't miss out. 'He might even be able to mend the Hoover at the end of it so it's well worth the drive.'

Lots of takers for D of E, and the possibility of taking to the sky in a glider is a strong card for the CCF, with the added draw of yomping in the wilderness far from tidy, cultivated Hampshire.

Art is important, both visibly around the school ('he tends to claim any empty space,' said a teacher wryly) and because it is a favoured subject for exams (nine taking A level last year) as well as a good fun co-curricular activity.

The new teaching centre topped by a mirrored dance studio for zumba fans and Strictly wannabes is run by a head full of energy and ideas, attracting an increasing number of students from senior scholars to shy first termers. Choirs cater for all abilities, 'even the tone deaf are encouraged to give it a go', an admirable if slightly worrying thought. The practice rooms are full all week and the department head 'beams with pride', not only at the mastering of Scriabin but also at the squeaky rendering of an Abba tune.

The drama department is flat out all year round, tackling everything from Sheridan to Lloyd Webber, plus clubs, technical workshops and sorties into the outside world. The only negative is the lack of a dedicated auditorium, richly deserved, according to parents.

Boarding: Enormous flexibility is the key, a policy very popular with hard-working parents whose life is made easier by the ability of the school to scoop up their children when necessary, rescue only an email away. The eight boarding houses, one co-ed for the first two years, three for girls and four for boys, are run by multi-tasking house parents. A rigorously enforced tracking system prevents chaos and assures parents that their offspring's whereabouts are known at all times.

Background and atmosphere: The century-long transformation from farming orphanage to present day public school began in 1912 with the bequest of Sydney Stern (the one and only Lord Wandsworth), a wealthy playboy turned Liberal politician. For the son of a Victorian banker buried in the Balls Pond Road it was rather an odd choice as a memorial, but due to the financial ability of the foundation trustees it turns out to have been a wise one. The school motto, 'perseverantia vincit', was taken most literally by the redoubtable Scot Sandy Henderson, headmaster from 1943-1968 (25 years of perseverance), who inspired the metamorphosis from agriculture to academics.

Still surrounded by the original farm, the school may have a rustic setting, but once through a surprisingly pompous, arched entrance there is a view of neat brick buildings and a shiny tarmac drive bordered by expectant playing fields. This is not a school with architectural pretensions, and one of the boarding houses was described as a 1960's disaster. However, a flight of fancy that one might have stumbled onto a low budget film set is swiftly squashed at the sight of lively teenagers purposefully swopping classrooms. No slacking here, as one day pupil put it; in fact the only negative point she could raise was how tired they were at the end of a packed day.

There is now a firm, securely financed, 10 year plan for change in place, including the completion of all brand new classrooms over the next five years as part of a concerted effort to modernise the school. Part of the regeneration, the new maths block – kitted out with wickedly clever whiteboards – and an assembly hall are finished, and the creaking science block is next on the agenda. The junior boarding house has girly curtains and rows of cuddly toys in the dormitories, and although the senior houses seem a little bland, long on new bath and shower rooms but low on cosy clutter and smelly socks, reliable information reveals that they can also look as if 'regularly burgled'. Maybe it's all squashed into the huge cupboards when the GSG comes round?

The newish head is determined to stop it being pigeonholed as a rugby crèche (all the fault of poor Jonny Wilkinson, who heads a list of high flying alumni so long that it seems as if LWC rugby has seen more dramatic conversions than the road to Damascus).

L

Pastoral care, well-being and discipline: One parent described the pastoral care as 'second to none', a claim backed up by ubiquitous signs in a boarding house reading 'I am available 24 hours a day, in or out of term'.

Hot on bullying in every form with notices everywhere, and all pupils have to carry a laminated card with examples on one side and how to get help on the reverse. Practical emails about cyber-bullying and internet dangers are sent to parents, giving detailed instructions that even confirmed Luddites can follow.

The rules don't come to parents as a surprise but are applied on a fair, case-by-case basis and not necessarily sticking entirely to the book. No outward evidence of teenage rebellion – these are not students likely to sport green hair or facial piercings. Some parents have a minor niggle that the younger ones can look pretty scruffy, particularly in comparison to the exceptionally tidy sixth formers.

A strong impression is created that most (not too wacky) ideas from the pupils will be seriously listened to, and that the head's statement 'their ideas and views are at the heart of the school development and planning' is no vain promise.

Pupils and parents: The distinction between day and boarding students is blurry as they seem to morph from one to the other pretty seamlessly, and lots of supposedly day pupils stay on to work or play long after the academic stuff is finished. Up to five per cent international students and the head plans to recruit more into the senior school. The Sternians' Association with its deliberately rustic (covered in tractors) website encourages parents to muck in and even make fools of themselves at the Santa Dash, a charity run started by the new head.

Entrance: Almost all from prep schools including Yateley Manor, Eagle House, St Neot's and Hall Grove, with a few from local primaries. Selection at 11 through school's own tests in English, maths and reasoning, aiming to identify a bit above average pupils who will fit into this tight community. Thirteen plus candidates need 50 per cent at CE; mid-range GCSEs, a school report and an interview to join the 6th form. 'All along we are looking for pupils who will get stuck in and put their hand up.'

Exit: About 20 per cent leave after GCSE to go to one of several excellent state sixth form colleges in Hampshire, usually for budget reasons. Three to Oxbridge in 2016; the school is rightly proud that the remainder have left for destinations as varied as Aberdeen, York, Camberwell Art College, LSE and the Royal Agricultural College to read everything from archaeology to civil engineering via law and theatre studies. Good next step communication with students, who say that the well-informed careers advisor 'will always find out if she doesn't know the answer'.

Money matters: Eight per cent of pupils are supported by The Foundation; means-tested awards restricted to British children who have lost the support of one or both parents through death, divorce or separation, and whose surviving parent (if there is one) has not formed a new relationship. The order of priority is: 'children who have an identifiable boarding need, the need for pastoral care and support, the need for stability and security in a structured environment, the candidate's home and family situation, the ability to cope academically, integrate socially and contribute to the college community, the family's financial circumstances'.

Remarks: Until recently a bit under the radar but worth watching this spot. An impressive head, smarter buildings, improving results and a firm set of values should encourage more potential parents to key this postcode into their Sat Navs.

Lord Williams's School

Oxford Road, Thame, Oxfordshire OX9 2AQ

Pupils: 2,100 • Ages: 11–18 • Sixth form: 511

Tel: 01844 210510
Email: office.4580@lordwilliams.oxon.sch.uk
Website: www.lordwilliams.oxon.sch.uk

Headteacher: Since 2005, Mr David Wybron MA (50s). Previously, deputy of lower school, then deputy head overall before becoming acting head. He joined in 1991 as head of humanities and still teaches a history GCSE class. Read history at Swansea University and taught in Cambridgeshire and Great Missenden, Bucks, before arriving in Thame. He exudes a serious-minded confidence and dependability that comes from long experience as a head. Married to a secondary school head of department with a son at LSE and a daughter training with a London law firm. He is rightly proud of his school's good reputation and has ambitions to continue at the current high standards, whether in winning university places or fitting a 16 year old for a good apprenticeship. 'I'm pleased the school is judged to be outstanding; the next challenge is to keep it there'.

Academic matters: In 2016, 78 per cent of pupils got 5+ A*-C GCSE grades including maths and English, and 25 per cent of results were A*/A. Additional science, art and design, English and history are popular choices at GCSE; French, German and Spanish languages as well as a range of tech options from electronics to food – we found a disembowelled car engine in one of the work rooms. A levels saw 46 per cent A*-B and 18 per cent A*/A grades in 2016. Wide range of subjects at all levels, taking advantage of the partnership programmes with other schools to offer anything from academic subjects, strong in sciences and maths, to practical alternatives dance, sport/PE and health and social care. Class sizes don't exceed 30. If there was a weakness, one mum felt, it was that a child would achieve what they expected, but not more.

Some 60-70 per cent of students go on to sixth form (boasts biggest sixth form in Oxon) joined by students from other local schools including Bucks grammar schools, who are attracted by the size, range of courses and good reputation. There were reservations by one parent about the intake at sixth form. 'Some kids didn't really want to be there... and were a bit of a distraction.' However, head felt it was evidence of a supportive and inclusive school – 'we don't make children move if they are not getting A/B grades.'

Teaching staff turn over at a healthy rate, but are organised and professional, according to one parent, and 'make you feel proud of the teaching profession'. Energetic both in and out of school day, some taking adventurous trips abroad or answering emails in the evening and at weekends. Parents felt they showed a refreshing and realistic attitude about the qualifications needed for life rather than for the top university places. 'It's easy when you throw money at it or have a swanky headmistress, but here they are working with budgets that are incredibly challenging'. Slight regret that this meant library wasn't open every day after school.

Comprehensive in the best sense. There is a hefty learning support department, with 400+ on SEN register and over 30 specialist teaching assistants. The ambition is to encourage students to independent working both academic and social, so teaching assistants are rotated throughout the school week. The reputation for learning support is widespread, with families known to have moved to the area to make the most of the specialist provision. The department can be accessed voluntarily by students wishing to catch up with classwork. In addition, there is a resource base for ASD, with separate admission requirements, and visiting clinicians. Integration into mainstream classes is tailored to the individual, but students we met were very comfortable with inclusion, to the extent of barely noticing it.

Games, options, the arts: Sports specialism status remains, although now not of any financial advantage – one parent remarked, 'sports college doesn't appear to be that organised' – more to highlight the healthy mind, healthy body ethos. Acres of green and pleasant fields, supplemented by three new Astroturf pitches, athletics track and rugby pitch make up the site; students also pop into Thame Leisure Centre next door in their lunch hour and for year 7 swimming lessons. More unusual options include handball and girls' football. Head delighted that it is the only state school to play an annual cricket match with the MCC. Old boys lists number a professional footballers and rugby players among them.

Dance and drama is also popular, and has picked up Artsmark awards. There's a snappy new performance studio for concerts and plays and a versatile exhibition area for art installations. Our guides were enthusiastic about their clubs and surgeries in the lunch hour, even 'catch-up' clubs, as well as debating and gymnastics. Musicians take individual instrument lessons on a rotation scheme, but numbers who take up an instrument are not great. There is an annual 'singer of the year' competition for the lower years and musical ensembles for the older students. The Duke of Edinburgh would be tickled pink to hear how many Tamensians attend his award courses (about 200) and the head rolls up his sleeves to muck in on the residential weekends: 'You've got to be different things at different times'.

The exciting World Challenge displays the school's breadth of vision, offering the chance for the older students to experience a cultural trip overseas, including India, Africa and Far East, to the envy of the parents. One week at the end of the school year is Ace week, given over to extracurricular activities, which may be anything from car maintenance to camping and water sports.

Background and atmosphere: One glaring inconvenience: the school occupies two sites, a couple of miles apart. The older site on Oxford Road is for key stage 4 and sixth form and the newer site at the other end of the charming market town for key stage 3. Commuting is done by staff, not students, and timetabled, although one parent griped that the split site caused a few delays in classes. Head's vision for the school is to bring it all into one camp, after some horse-trading with the local authority.

Wandering through the leafy grounds of the upper site, you wouldn't guess you were in such a large school. The stately old schoolhouse with sunken lawn, now the sixth form centre, is surrounded by low-level newer buildings in a variety of styles, like a university campus. Currently busy refurbishing science labs and various classrooms. The school was established in 1559 by Lord Williams of Thame with connections to New College Oxford. Portraits of the venerable old headmasters still peer out from the walls of the old building, and antique scholars' boards add a sense of heritage. The history is kept alive by the famously active alumnae, The Old Tamensians, who meet regularly at the annual founder's weekend, 'more like in independent schools,' says the head. We saw present-day students, visibly engaged in their work and pastimes, intent on study but with a healthy hum of discussion; all but sixth form tidily presented in their popular maroon polo shirts and hoodies.

L

Pastoral care, well-being and discipline: Head projects confidence about dealing with bullying and problem behaviours, 'I don't duck things', and happy that he has a strong team for pastoral issues, including support officers and home/school link workers. One parent commented the system of reporting was superior to other schools, another that there was a 'high level of responsiveness' that had been missing at her child's previous grammar school. As well as face-to-face parents' evenings, tutors keep in touch by email, and one parent was chuffed to have received a postcard for her child's outstanding work. Head was savvy about new technology, defining it as a new challenge to schools: 'There is always a surprise; this job is never boring'. Students were familiar with straightforward points system for rewards and discipline. Good behaviour is rewarded by watching a film or a paintballing jolly. Poor behaviour, after a series of warnings and detention, could incur a short period of 'solitary', but as our student guides said, 'if you do it once, you don't want to do it again'. Parents agreed that the process worked and kept the school's standards high. Transition into the school at year 7 is managed by taster days for all, extra visits for SEN children, and a week-long summer school of fun activities to taste it and see.

Pupils and parents: Varied social backgrounds: some academic, some rural and some from more deprived areas, but real sense that it reflects the local community. Statistically, lower than average numbers on free school meals and ethnic minority students but higher numbers of SEN, due to the Resource Base. At the time of our visit, and rather surprisingly, there were no children requiring EAL support. One of the first schools to recognise 'young carers' and set up support system for them. Students are agreeably confident, articulate and appeared attentive and focused in the lessons, 'always so courteous and pleasant,' said a parent. They are proud of the links with a twin school in The Gambia, which involves cross-curricula expeditions and cultural visits. New parents are encouraged to join the Lord Williams's Association, and get to know one another and the head at the meetings. Alumni include Restoration dramatist, Etherege, a clutch of poets and composer, Howard Goodall.

Entrance: Oversubscribed from local primaries within Thame and Chinnor; also takes Buckinghamshire applicants from over the county border. The Resource Base is filled by students with statements and by referral. Separate sixth form entrants take a range of routes, some from independent schools.

Exit: Some 60-70 per cent go on to sixth form. Others follow courses at FE college or start apprenticeships. About two-thirds of sixth form leavers go to university, with about a quarter off to Russell Group unis; two to Oxbridge in 2015. One parent was delighted at the broad-minded attitude of the senior staff to university destinations: 'If you don't get in (to Russell Group university) it's not the end of the world'. Careers counselling starts in year 10 and students are encouraged to make an appointment at any time after that, if needed.

Money matters: Head hopes academy status will go some way to protecting from the cuts in funding all secondary schools face. Lord Williams's Association (parent-led) helps with fundraising and the students themselves raved about class competitions to collect for the Gambia school.

Remarks: 'Lord Bill's' is a modern comprehensive with traditional roots. An experienced and egalitarian head runs a tight ship over two sites, maintaining steady standards whilst keeping an eye out for trouble. The school is 'a broad church' – academic success, alongside a healthy mix of sports and arts, as well as insightful pastoral support. Said a parent, 'A caring, community school that turns out decent people'. Quite definitely a competitor to the independents and grammar schools over the tracks.

Ludgrove

Wokingham, Berkshire RG40 3AB

Pupils: 192; all full boarders • Ages: 8–13

Fees: £25,950 pa

Tel: 01189 789881
Email: registrar@ludgroveschool.co.uk
Website: www.ludgrove.net

Headmaster: Since 2008 Mr Simon Barber BA (40s) following six years as a teacher here and, before that, at Ashdown House. Mr Barber, who grew up here (and has fond memories of watching cows being milked in what is now the art and carpentry block), completed teacher training at robust state school Cranford Community College with aplomb, tweed jacket and Eton education no barrier to pupil acceptance – when asked where he was at school 'I said, "down the road, just south of Slough".' Spell teaching geography at LVS Ascot was followed by short digression 'as junior squit' in corporate finance – quickly realised not for him.

Headship shared until 2013 when joint incumbent moved on to school of his own. After initial parental nerviness, Barbers now universally reckoned to be bit of all right, having grown into role. Mr Barber teaches Latin, PSHE and Greek myths – 'so important, you can see their little minds buzz.' He's nice but strict if necessary, thought pupil – 'if people are talking after lights out.'

Mrs Barber ('Sophie' to all) sorts domestics – 'kitchens, matrons, nurse, cleaners' – as well as being first point of contact 'for mothers' worries' and prepping boys for first phone calls home. '[Mr Barber] likes children, enjoys their company and knows how to make them feel good about themselves,' said one parent. 'As a team, they are superb,' agreed another.

Barbers' immersion in school life is almost total (though Mrs Barber does get short daily break to collect youngest child – they have two daughters and a son – from local school). Instead of separate house have own (though separate) quarters in the main building, but appear miraculously claustrophobia-free. Mr Barber, in particular, can go for days without leaving the building. 'I love walking round the school and thinking about creating an environment that is fun, safe and full of opportunities,' he says.

Entrance: Takes 30 in year 4 when it's completely non-selective – unless you count speed of registration as competitive sport. 'Don't believe in testing boys at 8,' says school. After initial enquiry (at birth) parents receive letter from head (handwritten) with registration form (printed). Two years before joining, there's a fun day for boys with confirmed places, followed by final make-your-mind-up time.

For occasional places (around eight in year 5, four in year 6 and even a couple in year 7 – generous bursary scheme helps bright boys fill gap between state primary and common entrance), hopefuls sit English and maths tests 'to be sure they can slot in easily.' Duvet changing and tie-knotting practice before start of first term also urged.

No official feeders, but road here well trodden by families moulded in traditional cast (plenty of second generation pupils or better). Around 40 per cent from well-connected pre-preps (Finton House, Thomas's Fulham, Eaton House, Knightsbridge and Broomwood Hall in London, Pinewood and Farleigh outside), many escaping competitive inferno of London school entrance.

Around half of places to country dwellers, most within two-hour commute (Wiltshire, Hampshire, Berkshire, Northants). A few from further away (East Anglia, Scotland). Remaining 10 per cent overseas, split about equally between expats (FO, MOD) and international pupils from all over – India, Thailand, Ukraine, Russia, Spain, China, Nigeria, Korea. A few arrive for year's immersion in penultimate year then head for home. DBS-cleared drivers (ideally same one both ways) on tap to do the airport run.

Exit: Given diverse input, rightly proud of output – reckon to get around three-quarters, sometimes more, into Eton, Harrow and Radley. Mr Barber's expert knowledge of all three won't mean special treatment at CE, though word dropped in admission tutor's shell-like can't go amiss if results an unexpected disaster. Others to eg Marlborough and Tonbridge.

Best-known OBs are Prince William, Prince Harry and Bear Grylls (who recently waxed lyrical about his experiences in print). Very occasionally head may suggest specialist school. One dyslexic pupil has recently gone to Bruern Abbey, though 'welcome back at any time,' says Mr Barber.

Remarks: Mood is determinedly upbeat...'a belief that one should always look on the bright side of life,' says prospectus and reflection of Mr Barber's philosophy. May not sing the Monty Python song but lives it. 'The eternal optimist,' says Mrs Barber.

So at their best, teams 'are a match for anyone.' School trips – a range, from Devon (leavers and geographers) to Sauze D'Oulx (skiers) – return having learned that 'a sense of humour can see you through most tricky situations'. Torrential rain makes sports day 'a memorable occasion.' Breakages in Roman-themed pottery session 'added to the authenticity.' Boys ward off looming homesickness by 'thinking of funny things and looking forward to the next lunch,' said one.

Upbeat approach translates into academics. Teachers are 'amazing,' say parents, talking round subjects and knowing their pupils. 'They work you hard but within your ability,' thought pupil. 'I wasn't clever when I arrived – now I am.' 'Never gave up on my son...and he flew,' said parent.

Small classes (average 12, maximum 15, minimum eight) undoubtedly help. So does overall staff to pupil ratio of just under one to seven (and that's not including the nurse and six matrons; all live-in). Streaming in English and maths from the beginning, lessons lively – new boys attacking Venn diagram in geography with enthusiasm; ditto 11 year olds discussing perils of 16th century religious affiliation. (Can read on in cheerful, traditional library, popular titles enticingly face up in long rows, pupils trained in old-fashioned referencing using real encyclopaedias).

Boys go through order papers with division master (form tutor) so clear on how to improve. Ups and downs caused by small class sizes and narrow range of marks (can shoot from second to eighth place) can cause occasional jitters among success-focused parents who need lots of reassurance. 'Boys pick up on their hopes and fears,' says Mr Barber. While coming top is well and good, the message that endeavour counts is received loud and clear. 'Trying hard is better,' said top year boy firmly. Workload in and out of lessons bearable, adjusted if necessary. No shame in saying you're struggling – teachers will set less and help with catch up, thought boys.

Individual excellence (good work) commended by head and rewarded with sweets. Plus marks also awarded, best performing house rewarded with special (and, needless to say, 'delicious') tea. The naughty get minus marks – occasional detentions. Boarding runs its own rewards system, giving angels, however dirty their downstairs wings, a second chance at redemption

Parents get emails summarising life in and out of the classroom and can phone child's class during a 40 minute slot at lunchtime to speak to son. Resulting free-for-all generally works (a bit of muttering about parents who go beyond allotted five minutes) though substantial redialling sometimes required. Alternative – giving boys mobile phones – felt by all to be far worse. Some – 'particularly sweet boys who want to make sure their parents are all right,' said mother – also send emails.

Daily staff meetings, attended by boarding nurse, ensure whole-school awareness of any issues. Wobbles impressively dealt with. 'Support without throttling,' said parent. 'Nurtured from the start but guided towards independence as they get older.'

Solid assistance for pupils with learning needs – around 30 or so in the school – includes academic support (booster groups for spelling, maths, reading) as well as help with handwriting, one-to-one EAL lessons and esteem and confidence-building sessions – we liked King of the Shelves award for better organisation skills. Four specialist teachers develop programmes for pupils with more complex needs – speech and language or specific learning difficulties – and ensure that subject teachers know how to implement it. 'Have been called a Rottweiler,' says jolly but firm head of learning support. Younger pupils have support sessions during art, drama and music while older pupils can opt to miss occasional rest period or break so don't lose out on favourite subject.

Merely mastering school's year group numbering system must be considerable source of pride. 'Sixes are year 4; fours year 5, threes year 6, twos year 7 and top year is year 8,' says school handbook. And those missing fives? 'Not a year group but a game with a small ball and leather gloves,' it adds, helpfully.

Uniform options similarly quirky. In addition to giddy whirl of jacket choices (a tweed spotter's dream), school jumpers offered not just in navy, but rather more exotic pink and green, adding welcome flash of colour to massed gatherings.

Great outdoors spread over 130 acres includes usual playing fields as well as nine-hole golf course and plenty of space for building camps. Every parent commented approvingly on boys being out in all weathers. 'All is underlined and bold and caps,' said one. Sports rampant and not just for current pupils, either. Most recent alumni calendar featured five matches and just one drinks party.

However, quantity doled out can be varied to taste. Everyone, talented or otherwise, gets shot at glory of minibus trip and match tea. How much glory is a tad confusing to decipher, what with online match reports dating back to 2013 with tendency to linger on the glories of game well played rather than the score.

Deadline for posting team lists is 7.00pm the night before, seemed a bit tight in giving parents sufficient time to change all arrangements and rush up to watch their son score the winning try/goal/run – but felt largely to work as most teams, once settled, there for the duration. Parents in broad agreement, biggest issue we encountered relating to yawning gap between the keen and talented – who get lion's share of training and interest – and keen but less so, who don't and can be completely overlooked. More matches on the cards for every shade of ability, says school, while swimming notable for squad training that's open to all.

The less athletic joyfully opt for extra art, pottery or, top favourite, carpentry/DT, where Portuguese fishing dinghy, owl nesting box as well as enough chairs and tables to equip several classrooms are among impressive projects to have helped school to several DT scholarships in recent years.

Music busy, with choirs, open access music block, numerous ensembles and vast majority (85 per cent) playing at least one instrument (bagpipes, tuba and bassoon adding interesting new timbre to conventional choices). Not as busy as drama, however, now in impressive new theatre (none of that 'performing arts centre' nonsense here...) where according to prospectus, boys 'have been on stage non-stop...' Crumbs. Our visit clearly took place during one of brief periods of non-occupancy. (Drama teacher was having lunch at the time, explained school later, keen to ensure nobody got the wrong end of the stick, and theatre 'has had a tremendous impact on provision of music and drama'). No wonder exeats billed as a time to relax. Happen every fortnight, so not too punishing for the youngest recruits.

Attractive 19th century building was purpose-built as school and it shows. Dorms, all south-facing with attractive big windows and same gorgeous view over greenery as from head's study but a floor up, hold four to 10 pupils from single year group, some in bunk beds, each with top year monitor, honoured with different coloured laundry basket (vibrant pink in one case). Every pillow adorned with loved, often dilapidated soft toy, resident seamstress ('crucially important,' says Mrs Barber) on hand to work miracles when teddies' arms come adrift or eyes go missing – 'upsetting but it's the smell they like...' Matrons much praised. 'Never shout if you do something wrong,' said pupil. 'Say it doesn't matter, don't worry.' Occasional accidents sensitively sorted – boys squeeze matron's arm when woken up, signal for sheets to be unobtrusively washed and replaced.

Dedicated maintenance posse roams school, killing at least 99.9 per cent of all known germs dead and rounding up errant possessions. Basins, loos, baths in communal washroom all radiant; boys' clothes and towels a tribute to precision folding, cloakroom a thing of wonder, coats and shoes lined up as if on parade – a daily, 90 minute task undertaken with pride.

Not a job for the boys, though perhaps it should be, joining list of well-organised activities carefully balanced to ensure that everyone is just busy enough and thus avoiding too much time for introspection, particularly for newbies (who have dedicated matron and allocated 'shadow' to help them settle in), but ensuring 'can flop if they want to,' says school.

Saturday is the faster-paced weekend day, with lessons till lunch, matches afterwards followed by free time, film screenings and a spot of X-Factor if in season. Sunday has fixed slots: chapel and assembly to announce the day's happenings. Otherwise less structure, with activity staples (swimming, art, films) and specials (visiting climbing wall, circus workshop and – occasionally – ice cream van) but also potential for spontaneity – boys will organise own games of cricket, five-a-side football or make camps. Less official dorm raids and stair run (down one, up the other at night without being caught) also happen but 'I know nothing about it...' says Mr Barber.

For youngest, there's comfort zone story time with Mrs Barber, 'special half hour when they're piled like puppies on the sofas and all over the floor.' Tuck, in the form of sweets, isn't allowed. Instead, school suggests packing 'useful and fun' – but inedible – items such as bluetac, string, stickers and playing cards.

School-supplied treats appeared attractive replacements for missing goodies, particularly birthday ice cream cake with choice of five flavours, multi-coloured remnants being solemnly enjoyed by small break time group on day of visit. Similarly colourful foodfests celebrate pupil nationalities (Ireland with mandarin, whipped cream and lime jelly...). Match teas a more restrained mix of sandwiches and cakes (parents) with doughnuts, crisps and juice for boys. Pupil committee gets unpopular dishes pulled and replaced (fish pie with scampi).

L

Other trad preps can feel as if saturated in own past. Here, though pride in history is evident, it's not overwhelming, with few pictures of ancient OBs. Instead, names of new boys are added to the honours board within a few weeks of start of first term – simple but effective way of generating pride and self-confidence and looking ahead.

'You've got to look at what you're doing – and how to do it better,' says Mr Barber. 'It's amazing,' said one parent. 'The camaraderie amongst the boys is one of the key things and they leave with lifelong friends. I couldn't fault it at all.'

LVS Ascot (Licensed Victuallers' School)

London Road, Ascot, Berkshire SL5 8DR

Pupils: 642: 405 boys, 237 girls; 195 boarders • Ages: 4–18 (boarders from 7) • Sixth form: 160: 103 boys, 57 girls

Fees: Day £9,528 – £18,261; Boarding £24,384 – £32,085 pa

Tel: 01344 882770
Email: registrar@lvs.ascot.sch.uk
Website: www.lvs.ascot.sch.uk

Headmistress: Since 2010, Christine Cunniffe BA MMus MBA. Three children, all at the school (husband goes to the parents' evenings). Personable, open, quietly assured and one of what seems like growing number (or should that be band?) of musicians to forsake lieder for leadership. Other careers have beckoned. After university, had close brush with the law (professionally speaking, that is) securing postgraduate traineeship with Slough-based legal practice only to succumb to alternative role as pianist to fashionistas and London high society (think white baby grands and late nights in plush hotels). Four years in, realised that though 'loved life, not what I wanted to do when I was getting older'. Putting aside renewed yearnings for law when husband-to-be pointed out years of study ahead, she tried her hand at teaching and loved it from the off, going straight in as head of music, first at a Stevenage school, then St Bernard's, a selective co-ed grammar school in Slough. Joined LVS Ascot as ambitious director of music in 2003 (school, which had no choir when she arrived, was performing Vivaldi's Gloria at Eton College Chapel just two terms later).

Overcame crisis of confidence in first year as head when numbers dipped (they're now on the rise again), confessing all in school magazine – unusual if not unprecedented openness for a head – which, she feels, sends useful message to pupils. 'You have self-doubt. I thought, the children are going to face problems in life, so why pretend it doesn't happen?'

Is considered by parents to be doing a good job though some would like a greater presence and more speechifying at major school events. 'She needs to be seen and heard a bit more... you've got to be the front runner, Ursain Bolt-ish and get up there if you're a head with over 1,000 pupils and fee-paying parents,' said one. Pretty visible during the school day though, the more so as job comes with house in grounds (she also has west London bolthole for change of scene). 'I'm not one of those people who hides behind a closed door; there's no point.' Doesn't teach but asks boarders to choose lessons for her to observe every week, and on day of visit was in gym encouraging sixth formers flagging half way through 56-mile sponsored row for charity. 'I said, "I'll be your Mrs Motivator".'

All parents have her email address, a useful barometer as 'they'll only bring something to me directly if they are really upset,' and doesn't shy away from taking criticism on the chin. 'I don't want people to tell me what they think I want to hear but to be honest.' Pleased, she insists, to get lots of 'forthright' comments when recently invited parent group in for dinner and presentation on proposed introduction of heads of year to help raise academic bar through better tracking and target setting.

Own experiences make her sympathetic to late developers. 'I experienced problems at about 13 and it's made me passionate about not giving up on a child until we have exhausted all areas,' though firm when line has to be drawn – handful of children have been asked to leave during headship. 'The boundaries are like an elastic band – you have to know when it's going to break.'

Like Mary Poppins, will go when mission is accomplished. 'I'm a realist. If, after five years, I think my job's done, I'm not going to stay around.' Not necessarily to another headship, either. 'I might just become a lawyer after all,' she says.

Academic matters: Though tolerant, school isn't the place for skivers. 'The school's a hard runner... and they want the exams. Non-selective doesn't mean an easy ride,' said a parent.

Mission in junior school is to ensure that no child is left to languish in educational no man's land; regular meetings picking out those 'falling below or zooming ahead'. Children give a high rating to all subjects, particular favourites being literacy (popular library-based reading scheme, which carries on into main school, tests comprehension rather than merely rewarding headlong dash for the last page) and science in year 6 – where, joy of joys, 'you get to light the Bunsen burner'. They're also unexpectedly appreciative of small teaching groups (average is about 12). 'In state schools you have 60 in a class,' said one horror-struck year 6 guide.

There's minimal setting (maths from year 3) and a pick and mix approach to national curriculum – used or modified where it works, ditched if it doesn't (children's progress well ahead of national averages). Everything is seasoned with welcome dash of carpe diem flexibility so teachers can go off piste if not-to-be-missed educational opportunities present themselves; recent stick collection and den-building exercise for reception was a case in point. Lots of popular outings, too, including the inevitable trip to Swanage.

Exam results compare well with local competition – GCSEs in 2016 26 per cent A*/A, reasonable for non-selective school, let alone one so large. Ten the norm though whittled down to nine for some students with learning difficulties who fill the time with extra English and maths support. Choice of around 20 subjects, nothing showy (there's no Latin or classics, for example). English, maths, French or Spanish and science/environmental science all compulsory with options including German, humanities, all the sciences, media/business studies, art and PE.

Sixth form options broad and getting broader, with law and psychology recently added to the roster of around 30 courses. Students will need GCSE B grades or better in chosen subjects though vocational courses such as ICT and sport also available for those of a more practical mindset. In 2016, 43 per cent A*-B and 20 per cent A*/A grades at A level.

Head on mission to ensure that ability is unearthed and nurtured earlier through advanced data crunching and addition of heads of year to management team. 'We haven't even scratched the surface with gifted and talented children,' she says (something also picked up in recent inspection). School's strength thus far has centred on bringing low achievers up to snuff (several heart-warming stories of pupils helped up the academic ladder to top exam grades) and parents like the approach, big on encouragement, small on class sizes – average teacher to pupil ratio of 12 to one – and low on hothouse forcing (definitely not the school's style).

Games, options, the arts: School's philosophy is that there's something for everyone and brave attempts are made (with help of extensive range of activities, all bar four included in the fees) to keep participation rates high all the way through the school. A dip in current year 10 and 11 girls' teams reflects lack of numbers rather than interest.

Approach, strong on inclusion and optimism – sports honours board runs to 2023 – is recognised by award of Sportsmark Gold and helped by cracking facilities including two games halls, the larger with climbing wall and cricket nets, the smaller with cushioned floor for happier landings in judo and high impact sports. Enticing heated pool is well used, offering all-ability training at 6.30am three times a week, while thumping pop music from upstairs broadcasts presence of well-equipped fitness suite, predictably popular with older boys. Has recently set up elite golf academy for sixth formers which combines coaching at a nearby club with a BTec in sports science.

With recent wins in judo, swimming and rugby, achievement counts but so does nurturing, for B as much as A teams so not seen as also rans. Felt by some parents to handicap the single-minded. 'Everyone gets a game which is to be encouraged but [can be] a drawback if you really want to excel at one sport,' said one.

Head would like greater take up of outdoor activities and has appointed ex-marine who 'doesn't sleep and likes to live in tents' to make it so. With rejigged timetable incorporating two additional sessions a week for all (year 9 upwards can do as part of D of E, open to as many as are interested) expect substantial increase in fresh air intake.

Vibrant artistic life is similarly wide ranging (though indoor-based) with ringing endorsement from award of Artsmark Gold to prove it and enthusiastic support from (literally) all-singing, all-dancing staff who aren't averse to taking to the boards as hoofers in zingy, highly regarded productions like Hairspray and Bugsy Malone. (By all accounts do a mean version of 'Teacher, leave them kids alone' too).

Year 3 teachers (and their classes) break into spontaneous song about Mothers' Day. 'It happens a lot here,' says one, who's also, as it turns out, responsible for junior school's huge, ambitious productions with 100-strong cast (all 'proper' parts: 'People don't want to be a third tree') and special effects including ultraviolet bubbles and even an exploding shark – 'every gizmo I can get into it'. Every other summer there's a Dance for Fitness workshop instead – fun and worthy, no doubt (and considered sufficiently cool for embarrassment-free participation by older boys) though you sense teacher's regret that it can't be waterfalls of lights and smoke effects every year.

With five choirs, numerous ensembles including rock school, and around a third of pupils learning instruments, some to diploma standard, performance is shifting from niche activity to sizeable minority occupation. Possible that numerous pianos lurking in school nooks and crannies (some boarding houses have several) are conveying subliminal positive message; whizzy music tech studio probably better recruitment ad. Admittedly, boys in years 10 and 11 remain somewhat shy and retiring – 'Music's not a cool thing to do,' says pupil – but some at least are drawn in again to at sixth form (though the need to pep up UCAS forms with wholesome balance of activities is, they confess, also a factor).

Boarding: Four boarding houses – co-ed junior house, one each for senior boys and girls and co-ed sixth form house – are now plushness personified with full-size beds and colour-matched walls, carpets and curtains chosen by pupils. Palettes err towards predictable blues in boys' boarding house though biggest difference is in communal areas where girls arrange smart leather sofas close together to maximise eye contact and conviviality, boys in contrast opting for side by side seating for maximum cheering-on potential during pool matches.

Boarding house staff, particularly those with experience of compromise Victorian conversions, are enthusiastic. 'A breeze to run,' comments one. Experienced houseparents are experts at sidestepping homesickness and ditching superfluities like complex laundry rules – 'I'd much rather you were clean than worried about what day you need to put your washing in,' says one.

It's all about fine-tuning to achieve delicate balance between homely family feel (thoughtful inclusion of year 8 boarders with juniors for extra cosseting) and early detection of transgressions. Morning lethargy beyond normal teen parameters can signal OTT late night laptop/mobile use (enormous phone bills arriving at parental home the other tell-tale sign). Controlled independence, such as giving year 11s separate kitchen and TV 'so they don't have to watch the same thing as year 8s,' explains teacher, is carefully cultivated.

Keeping idle hands (and brains) busy is the priority. 'We don't want boarders sitting around, twiddling their thumbs,' says pastoral head. Steady but not relentless stream of activities from house talent shows to relaxed Saturday breakfasts in pjs. Weekend minibuses, booked by the hour, swap returning sports teams for boarders off on assorted excursions (shopping, films and bowling all popular) with departures and arrivals as precisely coordinated as flight control at Heathrow.

Background and atmosphere: Site was formerly home to Heatherdown, an ultra-traditional prep school for chaps and David Cameron's pre-Eton alma mater, with own miniature steam railway. It was demolished in 1982 after Licensed Trade Charity (LTC) – which runs school, founded 200 years ago to support drinks trade employees – made such an advantageous sale of previous premises in Slough to well-known supermarket chain that could fund construction of what prospectus claims is the 'most modern boarding school in the UK'.

It comes complete with LVS branded drainpipes and school houses named, delightfully, after major drinks brands, leading to such pleasing sentences as 'this year saw the introduction of many new staff and students to Guinness,' in school magazine.

And yes, lovers of mellow brickwork may need to recalibrate their aesthetic sensibilities when it comes to the exterior (think sheltered housing designer meets Etch a Sketch addict – prospectus sensibly avoids any full-on shots of the facade). However, it's well worth the effort as school lacks neither charm nor character and is stuffed with quirky touches from the formal (two back-to-back reception desks, one glitzy for corporate visitors to charity HQ, the other, smart but workmanlike, for school traffic) to the relaxed (skeleton of dolphin in science lab, Garfield soft toy clasped lovingly between jaws). There's tradition, too – the 25 acres of grounds with rustic bridge spanning small but perfectly formed lake prove the point – but exists primarily to serve a purpose (lesson bell all but abolished after it broke five years ago, ending mid-sentence rush for the door and making teachers so happy that was never reintroduced).

Thoughtful layout now past 30th birthday may no longer be at cutting edge of school design but fundamentals still apply, noticeably the way space-intensive subjects like performing arts get the room they need in central location rather than being consigned to outer reaches of site, while related subjects are housed together making navigation a breeze – at least if you're a pupil. 'It's the adults who struggle,' says passing teacher.

It's all well cared for, too – maths display board with cracked plastic cover is rare exception ('Children pick at it without realising they're doing it,' explains staff member) and nicely spruced up where required.

L

Add lively art room with wall-to-wall high quality work (intriguing bronze-effect sculpture floats above plinth), busy, popular DT department with more saws than you could shake a freshly trimmed stick at and fabulous learning resource centre; light, airy and staffed by team of affable universal aunt and uncle types who always have a giant jigsaw on the go and live for research – 'You need a bit up here and to love finding things out,' says one – and easy to see why purpose-built practicality gets parental thumbs up. 'Some private schools try to make the best of the [space] they happen to have, such as a former chambermaid's room being used as a biology class room, [whereas] LVS have great classrooms built to deliver good lessons,' said a father.

Junior school has good-sized infants' play area with buddy bench (hardly used, though, insist pupils 'because there's a bare minimum of people who feel sad') and lots of sturdy wooden equipment to climb and balance on. Year 3s and up enjoy scaled up versions in adjoining area, separated by unmarked but universally recognised boundary line. Reception also has smart new outdoor classroom and cheerful playhouse, starting point for innumerable let's pretend games. Eagerly awaited musical train complete with three carriages and bells (if no whistles) currently being built by senior school sixth former as part of DT A level is arriving soon.

Pastoral care, well-being and discipline: Highly regarded focus of pastoral care is the tutor group system with same teacher responsible for child's well-being throughout school career. Works well given high percentage of old-timers (figuratively speaking) on staff – 40 out of 340 have been there over 10 years – and is liked by parents and pupils. 'They have a vested interest in you as a person, you're more than just a pupil,' said 17-year old.

In contrast, tribal yin to sensitive tutor group yang is a house system that's far more than convenient administrative format. Pitting combined boarders – normally four houses strong – against teams of day pupils, it's a focal point of school life, with fiercely contested matches generating 'as much rivalry amongst the [teachers] as pupils,' says member of staff.

Not as daunting as it sounds, however, given universal insistence that loyalties do not cross into lessons nor escalate beyond friendly rivalry ('It's just banter,' confirmed sixth former). Day pupils can also cross to other side by signing up for occasional one-off boarding sessions and there's added flexibility with extended day, including meal and the run of learning resource centre, popular with working parents.

School works hard to raise aspirations without upping the pressure, particularly at junior school level. Parental feedback – 'not sure what a hothouse is,' said parent, when questioned – suggests it's working.

Pupils and parents: A nice, un-showy and straightforward bunch, pupils are thoughtful rather than introspective, articulate but not glib, and fond of school (in touch with emotions, too – one burley and soon to be ex-sixth former admitted to welling up when contemplating imminent departure). Start of term, said one, 'feels like you're going home rather than just going back.' There's affectionate tolerance for teachers who, they say with preternatural (but approving) gravitas, 'want to have fun but in a sensible way'.

As in other schools, pupils on show to visitors usually the top dogs. Here, cheeringly, they may only recently have had greatness thrust on them and reformed Horrid Henries stand as much chance as card-carrying Perfect Peters of getting their day in the sun. 'Prefects aren't just the "right" people,' explained one of the current glorious band of brothers (and sisters).

Families cover socially and economically broad spectrum from royalty to socially deprived (borne out by range of parental cars at drop off – five and six figure off-roaders rubbing fenders with elderly mid-range saloons). Mix of working parents/career mothers, but either way are generally friendly and polite, though won't hesitate to come forward if there's a problem, though occasional hothouse impulses 'are squashed quite quickly by the school,' said approving mother.

Entrance: Most children arrive at junior school in reception (single form to year 2) or year 3 (two forms to year 5). At 11+ majority from school's own junior department with assorted state and private schools supplying the rest. Also small but significant international component, with 30 overseas students from as far afield as China, Russia and Korea and 40 or so from expat families, many in Forces.

Once settled, pupils tend to stick around. 'We were never going to take the boys out unless we needed to,' says mother. Locals form large proportion of the clientèle and, while job mobility means some degree of coming and going each year, there's not as much as you might suppose. Around 50 per cent of pupils stay on into sixth form ('places will only be offered where deemed appropriate by the head of sixth form, director of studies and head,' says admissions policy) with incomers, including first time boarders from local day schools, plugging the gaps. 'In my [elder] son's year, I'd say that 80 per cent went all the way through,' said parent.

Catchment area extends 15-20 mile radius or so to Reading in west and Maidenhead up north, compass points ably covered by seven school bus routes (some oversubscribed, so worth checking). Head is on a mission to spread the word elsewhere so expect increasing numbers of refuseniks from super-selective London fringes, deepest Berks and Bucks

Exit: As you'd expect given breadth of intake, pupils take corresponding range of university courses from the solidly academic – medicine, law, economics – to the more vocational, including photography and journalism. Many secure first rank uni places including occasional Oxbridge place. In 2016, 25 per cent to Russell Group unis. Old boys and girls end up as community stalwarts, many as successful entrepreneurs or 'something in the City'. Few facts and figures to back this up though with-it marketing manager is making good the omission with 'where are they now?' campaign.

Money matters: Ten per cent discount for siblings (but only third onwards and then only while all three attend school), 15 per cent off for MOD and diplomatic service employees, including five per cent early payment discount and a 20 per cent reduction for anyone who has worked in the licensed drinks trade for five years or more.

Families are attracted by all-through co-education, cracking facilities, local reputation and complete absence of entrance exams unless you're after a scholarship, academic worth a not-to-be-sniffed-at 50 per cent off fees; music, art, drama and sport a slightly less headline-grabbing £1,000 a year, in which case standard hurdles apply.

School tries to keep budgeting simple with many senior school clubs and activities included in the fees – rowing, riding, sailing and ballet plus individual instrumental lessons and one-to-one language or learning support are the main extras. Means headline fees are just that, with minimum of extras buried in the frequently expensive small print.

Remarks: All-comers welcomed in this well-equipped, friendly and unpretentious school that combines non-traditional exterior with timeless values and makes non-selectivity the starting point for success rather than a justification for its absence.

Magdalen College School

Cowley Place, Oxford, Oxfordshire OX4 1DZ

Pupils: 896 • Ages: 7–18 • Sixth form: 306 (including 108 girls) • C of E

Fees: £16,485 – £17,115 pa

Tel: 01865 242191
Email: registrar@mcsoxford.org
Website: www.mcsoxford.org

Master: Since September 2016, Helen Pike MA (x 3), previously head of South Hampstead High. Formerly a teacher of history/politics with a pedigree to intimidate all-comers – her previous schools include St Paul's Boys (head of politics), Westminster (history) and City of London Boys (dep head of sixth). She is a novelist (The Harlot's Press – a Georgian, political bodice-ripper which, of course, all the South Hampstead girls rushed to read) and an academic editor. Her stepsons studied at Magdalen College School and her partner is Professor George Garnett, the senior proctor at Oxford – so with this move she can, indeed, spend more time with her family. She is a very modern, dynamic head.

Head of junior school: Since September 2012, Tim Skipwith, previously head of the middle school (years 9-11), a biology teacher who has been at the school for over a decade. He is 'a wonderful guide for parents on the 11+ process' and is reputedly very hot on pastoral issues. As the third head in a short space of time, we hope his tenure will be a long and stable one.

Academic matters: The academic pace at the junior school can be a shock to those coming in from more relaxed establishments, especially as the 11+ exam looms. They learn French from year 3 and can go to Spanish and German clubs. Everyone is assessed in year 5 for special educational needs and can have one-to-one help as necessary.

'This is a school full of A*s,' and its results are undoubtedly up there in the firmament – 94 per cent A*/A at GCSE, and 88 per cent A*/A at A level in 2016. This can, commented a parent, make a child feel that getting an A is an abject failure. However, another recounted how kind and helpful the school had been when her son achieved (relatively) duff GCSE results – 'They were very positive and he felt they were on his side'.

A strongly traditional school in many ways. It was founded as 'a school of the university and within the university' and is focused accordingly. Everyone does three sciences (though one parent commented that 'actually my son would have preferred to have been able to do another humanity instead') and classics is a given – 'they take it for granted as a way of training the mind'. A narrow range of subjects – philosophy, politics, further maths and economics are the extra A level options.

However, 'our curriculum is on the other hand quite liberal.' One afternoon a week in the lower sixth is spent on Waynflete studies (the school was founded by William of Waynflete), which involves a series of talks by experts in their fields on anything from world economics to swine flu. Pupils then choose their research topic (generally, but not always, closely linked to their likely university subject) and are taught initially by lectures and seminars at school, then in individual or paired tutorials by university academics. Thinking skills programme also introduced.

By common consent very high teaching standards – 'my son finds virtually all the teaching exciting and the staff are very interesting and helpful'; 'You have a real sense that they are on the boys' side. My son says, "The masters are really cool – you feel that they love their subjects".' Hard work is expected – 'It's not for the academically idle' – and certainly the school has been hauled up through the league tables. 'Lots of the boys have sisters at Oxford High, and their parents felt that they should be achieving the same high grades,' said a parent. Most parents agree that their children are not hothoused – 'they don't feel that their noses are to the grindstone' – but they are expected to buckle down and work long hours at home. However, the mother of a talented sportsman was impressed by how flexible the school was prepared to be over his training schedule – 'there was a good symbiotic relationship, and he didn't let them down'.

M

Games, options, the arts: Compact site, which includes a sports hall with a multi-gym and floodlit tennis courts. The 13 acre school field is just over the Cherwell – rowers can launch straight from the school – and it also has access to a range of college and university sports grounds, hockey pitches, athletics tracks and swimming pool. Support for sports is excellent, with a number of high flying sports professionals on the staff, eg Philip DeFreitas (England) for cricket; Grant Seely (England 7s, Northampton Saints) for rugby; Todd Williams (Australia) and Andy Watts (England A and Reading) for hockey; and Sadie Lapper (England) for netball. The main team sports are rugby, hockey and cricket. Sixth form girls play hockey, netball and tennis – with sailing, rowing and badminton also popular. Pupils have competed in national teams at hockey, shooting, rowing and sailing, and many school teams are county champions. The school has had exceptional successes at sailing – recently they won the National and International Schools' Team Racing Championships, RYA National Youth Team Racing Championships and National School Sailing Association's single-handed team racing championships.

The junior school recruits the 16 Magdalen College choristers and music is an integral part of life in the senior school too. Singing is particularly strong, as one would expect, with several choral societies and choirs. Choristers sing from the top of Magdalen Tower on May Day morning, Madrigals Society sings from punts on the river, the Oxford Sixth choir sings in a variety of venues in Oxford. Also orchestras, bands and ensembles. 'The standards are fantastic. A lot of pupils are incredibly talented,' said a parent.

Sixth form drama scholarships were introduced in 2013, but drama is still not a GCSE or A level option – 'We don't have the facilities. But we will have'. The school hall doubles as a chapel and theatre, with an altar and stained glass windows at one end and a stage at the other. Has a collaborative project with Oxford Playhouse. Performs large-scale musicals – including Sondheim's Sweeney Todd and the world premiere of a sung Lord of the Flies – as well as works by playwrights as diverse as Pinter and Shakespeare.

An annual Arts Festival has been running since 2009 with speakers including Baroness Sue Campbell, Rupert Everett and children's author Julia Golding. There are also concerts, lectures, theatre, tours, films, workshops and an art show – 'We want to liberate all the creative forces around us'.

Bright-eyed, bushy-tailed junior school boys perform in productions of Oliver and Noye's Fludde, win national chess competitions, compete in house music events, play football, cricket and tag rugby. Refreshingly, sufficient teams and fixtures to give almost everyone a chance to play for their school.

Background and atmosphere: Founded in 1480 by William Waynflete to educate choristers and prepare other boys for Magdalen College. Former masters include Cardinal Wolsey, former pupils St Thomas More and William Tyndale. It moved in 1890 from its original location in Magdalen College to its present site just the other side of the bridge, opposite St Hilda's. Buildings of a variety of pedigrees, from the School House, built in 1893 and now housing the junior school, to the 2008 New Building, which includes the swish canteen (serving rather tasty lunches), up to date ICT centre and fabulous top floor art and design rooms with views to die for.

M

Like other former direct grant schools, it has the feeling of a city grammar rather than a public school, with a relaxed approach to uniform and heaps of schoolbags in random corners – 'We're a little Byzantium, situated where east meets west, where Cowley meets Oxford, very multi-faceted and multi-ethnic'. An overtly Christian school, with non-denominational services in chapel every morning. Pupils can opt out, but very few do. 'I like going to chapel,' said a sixth former. 'The whole school gets together, and people enjoy singing.' Pupils are relaxed and friendly – 'They don't have that public school arrogance,' said a parent. 'A typical Magdalen pupil is high achieving but modest.' 'Most pupils can find a niche here,' said another. 'There's such a mix: bookish, geeky ones, sporty extroverts – they're not clones. It's fine to be eccentric.'

Pastoral care, well-being and discipline: Pastoral care is 'a speciality. It is the part of the school of which we are most proud, and we sense it has been fantastic for a long time. We have a light touch – we're disciplined and liberal simultaneously. Lessons can go from quite chatty to silent concentration when necessary.' The pastoral system is based round the six houses, which are organised by home location and compete at sports, singing, debating etc for the house cup. Expulsion (rare) for theft, systematic anti-social behaviour or involvement with drugs. A parent commented: 'When we've raised any issues they've been prompt and sympathetic. They're worldly-wise about what teenagers get up to.' 'They run a tight ship,' said another, 'but pupils do need boundaries.'

Pupils and parents: Mostly academic and professional families, including some who are scarily high-powered on the academic front and quite a few who struggle to afford the fees. 'You're not up against much "big money",' said a parent. Many Oxford pupils, but private buses serve far-flung areas such as Abingdon, Wantage and Banbury. OBs include (amongst many) Ivor Novello, Sam Mendes, Misha Glenny and Ben Goldacre.

Entrance: Two-class entry from year 3 upwards. At 7+ entrance is by maths and English papers plus a half day of group activities. 'Attention is paid to each child's co-operation, enthusiasm, self-discipline and ability to concentrate.' At 8+ and 9+ by maths, English and verbal reasoning papers plus interview. Junior school pupils all take the same 11+ exam as outside applicants to the senior school, and almost all pass. Auditions for choristers in October and January. Also run pre-assessments giving feedback on suitability.

At 11 by maths, English and verbal reasoning tests and an interview. At 13 by common entrance for prep school boys, after pre-test in year 6. By school exam for state school and other secondary school boys at 13 – maths, English, verbal reasoning and French. For the sixth form, by verbal reasoning test and interviews. Pupils are expected to get A* GCSE grades in their chosen A-level subjects; incomers – mostly girls – generally have at least six A* grades.

Exit: Nearly all juniors move up to the senior school, with occasional families advised to look elsewhere. A few (perhaps 5-10 per cent) leave after GCSEs, mostly for local state sixth forms. Forty-two to Oxford and Cambridge in 2016 (preparation apparently 'super-delux'), plus 14 medics; nearly all to top universities, including Bristol, Durham, Imperial, Warwick, KCL, Nottingham, Leeds, UCL, Newcastle, Birmingham, Exeter, Edinburgh, Manchester, St Andrews, Bath and LSE. Two to the US and two to Europe (Sciences Po and Amsterdam University College) in 2016. Sciences probably more popular than humanities, anything from aeronautical engineering to cognitive neuroscience.

Money matters: Scholarships and exhibitions for academic and extracurricular excellence – modest amounts, but can be topped up by means-tested bursaries. Will generally try to help families who fall on hard times.

Remarks: Up there with the top of the academic high-fliers. Uses its Oxford connections – intellectual, sporting and creative – to the best advantage, creating a niche where sports stars and geeky bookworms are equally at home. 'I feel the school is in safe hands,' said a parent. 'It's a very impressive place.'

Maidstone Grammar School

Barton Road, Maidstone, Kent ME15 7BT

Pupils: 1,237 • Ages: 11–18 • Sixth form: 349 (62 girls)

Tel: 01622 752 101
Email: school@mgs-kent.org.uk
Website: www.mgs.kent.sch.uk

Head: Since 2012, Mark Tomkins BSc NPQH PGCE (40s). Grew up in Cheltenham, where he was educated at Arle Comprehensive and Pate's Grammar. Read maths at Birmingham University and went home to Cheltenham to do his PGCE. Has spent almost all his working life in Kent boys' grammar schools, the first nine years at Dartford Grammar and latterly six years as deputy head at The Judd, Tonbridge. Says he knew MGS well before he applied for the job and felt part of the school within a couple of weeks. Tall and enthusiastic, he feels that the headship is the 'best job in teaching – it is such an honour and a privilege to be able make a difference in a big way'.

Highly regarded by everyone we spoke to, he is 'friendly, welcoming and approachable and will stop and have a chat,' said one pupil, but 'he has an air of authority when he walks into a room'. 'He talks to the kids as young adults and asks what people think and listens to their views – an absolute inspiration, who has re-energised the school,' said one mother. He says it is 'not just about raising expectations but also giving children the knowledge and skills to succeed', and he wants pupils 'to be interesting and interested, self-assured and with a strong work ethic'. He is also an inspiring maths teacher.

He took up rowing about 10 years ago and it has become his passion. He has twice competed at Henley Regatta and is a member of Maidstone Invicta Rowing Club, where the school keeps seven boats. He coaches when he can and rows with the boys, and has recently rowed the length of the Thames. He loves travel, especially if it is rowing related.

Academic matters: In 2016, 34 per cent A*/A at A level (62 per cent A*-B) and 47 per cent A*/A (75 per cent A*-B) at GCSE. Only 98 per cent generally get 5+ GCSEs at A*-C – English usually the stumbling block and head trying to address this; he has also raised the bar to get into sixth form. All take 10 GCSEs – top two sets take maths a year early and then take further maths GCSE the following year. All pupils study at least one modern foreign language and can choose from French, German, Mandarin and Spanish, taught in well-equipped language labs. Latin also offered. Sciences offered as separate subjects or dual award. Media studies available at GCSE and A level and all have to do courses in religious studies, personal development, careers and citizenship. The school offered IB for a while; no plans to reintroduce it, but does offer enrichment sessions similar to CAS element of IB. Group work and individual research encouraged in homework. Years 7 and 8 take part in applied learning days where they learn teamwork and project management skills. Well-used library with 15,000 books, 10 networked computers, newspapers, magazines and journals as well as the careers library.

Careers guidance praised in recent parental survey – careers education in tutor periods and pupils encouraged to listen to guest speakers and informal lunchtime talks; all have a careers interview and are supported in their subject choices at GCSE and A level. Everyone is expected to find work experience at the end of year 12 – school will help with contacts if someone is struggling. Old Maidstonians offer mentoring scheme for sixth formers and guidance on job opportunities and university selection as well as help with contacts for specific careers. School keen to promote Oxbridge. 'I thought it was only for private school kids,' said one boy, 'but the school took us to the open days and gave us lots of support and encouragement and six of us got offers at Cambridge.'

A good balance of age and experience amongst teachers, but most in their 40s. 'Teachers are approachable and genuinely seem to care,' said one girl, who had recently arrived from another school and was pleasantly surprised by the good rapport with teachers.

Some 45 students have some SEN, mainly mild dyslexia. All staff dyslexia trained and track children and a team of teaching assistants available to give in class help – no withdrawal from lessons. No official Gifted and Talented programme but all stretched and challenged, and Ofsted, which considers the school to be outstanding in all areas, said that 'students thrive on the high expectations'.

Games, options, the arts: Sport taken seriously, especially rugby; the school has won the Kent Cup two years running and when we visited the rugby team had recently returned from a training trip to Portugal. Cupboards of silverware proudly displayed around the school. Girls' rugby team also popular and successful. Sport compulsory in lower years – year 7 fields C and D teams, although further up the school there are the usual grumblings that it is always the same boys who are picked. Extensive extracurricular programme for sport with inter-house, club and team practices at lunchtime and after school six days a week. Good facilities with refurbished sports hall, gym and weight training room and indoor and outdoor cricket nets, tennis courts and sports pavilion. Pupils also use Maidstone Leisure Centre and Cobdown sports centre. Some sports fields on site but no floodlights (neighbours) so rugby and hockey teams train off-site in the winter. Rowing also popular on the Medway at Invicta rowing club.

CCF a big part of the school culture – about 250 take part in army, navy and air force, learn about 'camaraderie, service and leadership' and are given the chance to do adventurous things like abseiling, climbing and sailing. The RAF section offers flying scholarships and the opportunity to train for a private pilot's licence. Most of year 10 takes bronze D of E but popularity of CCF does not leave much time to take it further.

'The music scene is buzzing,' said our guide, and there is a wide repertoire. Instruments and ensembles for beginners to advanced: full orchestra, symphonic wind band, teachers' bands and students' bands which play alongside each other, four-part choir and pupils encouraged to form their own ensembles and pop groups. All have the chance to perform in concerts locally and further afield, including regular lunchtime concerts and at least one major concert each term to which parents are invited.

The school play has been re-launched under the direction of an inspirational English teacher and the school has recently staged Oh What a Lovely War! and Oliver! – large cast plays which draw from all year groups. Pupils can get involved with stage management, sound and lighting as well as acting. Shakespeare Day and workshops for year 8s to encourage younger boys into acting, and regular theatre trips to London, especially the Globe Theatre.

Impressive array of artwork in a range of media, techniques and styles and annual art exhibition coincides with summer concert, a 'cultural extravaganza' when parents can come and picnic.

Extended Learning Week takes place in the summer term for years 7-10, when children can follow their own interests for a week – anything from foreign residential trips and educational visits to putting on a pantomime for local primary school children. The aim is to extend cultural and social experiences through teamwork and interaction between year groups. Very popular and particularly praised by parents. The school recently sent a group of pupils to take part in the Model United Nations in New York and Harvard.

Background and atmosphere: The school was granted its first charter in 1549 and has had an unbroken existence since, apart from a temporary closure in 1554-8 due to Maidstone's connection with Sir Thomas Wyatt's Rebellion against Queen Mary. A second charter was granted under Queen Elizabeth in 1559. It was founded to teach the boys of Maidstone and in 1818 had 10 day boys and 15 boarders; by 1914 there were 139 boys, and now there are 1,237 pupils. It moved to its current, purpose built site off a quiet street on the edge of Maidstone in 1930. Eclectic mix of architectural styles from mock-Tudor quad – used for concerts and speech days, cloisters and assembly hall; and imposing gatehouse – 'the most iconic part of the school,' said our guide – to some less beautiful 1960s structure. These are gradually being replaced by well-designed 21st century buildings including the applied learning centre (2010) and the sixth form and food technology centre (2011). Sixth form block a social space with computers where students can work, make snacks or just chill – has good views of the playing fields so a popular place for watching matches. (Some sixth formers complain that they do not have anywhere quiet for private study.)

Strong sense of history and tradition here and the school motto can be translated as 'One day it will be a joy to look back and remember'. All former pupils become Old Maidstonians (OMs) when they leave and 'the allegiance is incredible, the strongest I have ever seen in a school,' says the headmaster. OMs hold open evenings for year 7s and sixth formers to talk about the motto and being a Maidstonian. Pupils value the traditions and woe betide anyone who tries to stop them: there was outrage when a previous headmaster stopped ringing the big bell for assemblies – it was immediately reinstated. The school song, written in 1908, is still sung in Latin on speech days and the beginning and end of term. When the headmaster arrived he asked the pupils and teachers to help design a 'word cloud' depicting the core values of the school, like enthusiasm, achievement, integrity, community, but at the centre of the poster in the largest letters is 'tradition'. This has been turned into a poster and displayed around the school, lest anyone forget.

Pastoral care, well-being and discipline: 'Pastoral care the best I have seen,' says the head, and the school is a 'community within a community'. Full-time student services department, described as 'fabulous' by one parent, where students can go for advice and guidance, but all teachers have pastoral responsibility. Pupils have the same form tutor for the first five years, which gives consistency of care in a big bustling school. Parents encouraged to contact school as soon as there is a problem. Bullying issues taken seriously and punishments are severe, but school want bullies to learn from mistakes. They are made to write a letter of apology and to try to understand what effect their behaviour has had. 'Parents want a firm line on discipline,' says the head, and he will excluded pupils permanently if necessary. 'I do not apologise for this – boys know there is a line they cannot cross'. Having said this, exclusions have gone down year on year since his arrival.

M

House system reintroduced in 2007 with pupils choosing the names of the six houses, which include Hurricane, Endeavour and Invincible, all suitably galvanising, each with its own identity and all arranged vertically to enable pupils to get to know different year groups.

Younger boys wear black trousers and jacket with the school badge and white shirt with the house tie. Sixth formers are expected to dress in a businesslike way and to set high standards, with a jacket and collared shirt for both boys and girls, and a beady eye is kept on skirt length – not that many seem to want to push the boundaries. Everyone expected to show respect for all members of the school and wider community, and sense of pride pervades. Over 20 senior prefects and a captain and vice-captain help run the school, and all wear their badges with pride. All have to apply for positions of responsibility and are interviewed by current prefects and the senior teachers.

Good food served in the new refectory run by an independent catering company, but still about half bring in pack lunches.

Pupils and parents: All sorts, but mainly white middle class, with majority from professions. School founded to teach the 'boys of Maidstone' and doesn't want to move far from this ideal. Most from local primaries and small handful from prep schools. Some from Maidstone housing estates, others from prosperous surrounding villages. All seem to have a strong allegiance to the school and are incredibly proud to be there, and are generally a well behaved and polite bunch. Does not produce a type – stress on boys being comfortable in their own skins and not having to fit into a mould. Only a small proportion receive the pupil premium and a handful need EAL help.

Parents generally very supportive and are made to feel welcome from the start: head has reintroduced well-organised parents' evenings and open mornings – previously many parents never met their child's teachers. Parents kept informed via the parent portal where they can check subject and tutor reports, attendance record and the timetable. They receive a full school report once a year and two academic progress summaries. All parents automatically made members of the parents' association and are asked to contribute £30 per pupil per year into the amenities fund to raise money for activities. They also raise money via social events for school improvement projects.

About 40 girls join the sixth form each year, often for the wider choice of subjects, and settle in quickly. 'My daughter was pleasantly surprised how easily she settled in and felt part of the school from the start – the best decision she ever made. The more laid back approach and increased freedom encourages the kids to work hard'. 'It felt quite daunting, but also exciting. The boys involved us from the start, but you do need to be the sort of girl who puts herself forward; it would not suit someone who was very shy'. Plenty of opportunities for girls to take on positions of responsibility, and one was recently appointed vice captain of the school.

Entrance: Via the Kent Test in September of year 6. Not super-selective, but a complicated oversubscription arrangement for boys living in named parishes as school wants to be able to continue to draw from the villages it served originally. Oversubscribed, and very few appeals successful, but they do run a siblings policy.

To enter or join sixth form pupils must gain at least 45 GCSE points including at least a C in English and maths. About 40 girls and 10 boys join in sixth form, mainly from Invicta Grammar, Maidstone Girls' Grammar and a handful from the high schools.

Exit: Some 10-15 per cent leave after GCSEs – some to move to local girls' grammars which take boys in sixth form, others to colleges or work. A small number fails to get the required grades to stay on. All bar about 10 per year who stay until year 13 go on to a wide range of universities – a lot of trouble is taken to get the course and the university right. A handful to Oxbridge each year – six in 2015. About a quarter to Russell Group universities, the rest all over the place including one or two to the US and Europe. History, engineering, economics and maths always popular, but range of subjects includes medicine and music, and some study more vocational courses like property development, event management and police sciences.

Remarks: School now back on track and is again healthily oversubscribed under the inspirational newish headmaster. Strong sense of tradition, and extraordinary allegiance and loyalty among its pupils and alumni, make this a very special school.

Maidstone Grammar School for Girls

Buckland Road, Maidstone, Kent ME16 0SF

Pupils: 1,225 • Ages: 11–18 • Sixth form: 360

Tel: 01622 752103
Email: central@mggs.org
Website: www.mggs.org

Head: Since 2015, Miss Deborah Stanley BSc ARCS, educated at Highworth Grammar School in Ashford, as was her mother before her. She made up her mind to become a teacher aged 6 when she realised that she would be much better at getting the children to sing in assembly than the grown up in charge. Her ambition had always been to teach in the Kent grammar schools so, following a maths degree at Imperial College and a PGCE at Christchurch Canterbury, she did her teaching placement at The Norton Knatchbull boys grammar in Ashford and ended up spending eight years there. She then spent five years as head of maths at Simon Langton Girls' Grammar before moving to Rainham Mark Grammar as assistant head. Joined MGGS as deputy head in 2007, and when the previous head left unexpectedly in 2015 after a bumpy year, she stepped into her shoes.

She is well liked and respected, very cool, calm and caring and dedicated to the school, but also 'full of creative ideas', as well as approachable – her door is always open to staff and pupils. She is 'quiet but does not miss a thing and is also financially astute and on top of the budget'. Very involved with her local church – particularly with young people, where there is frequent banter about her being a head teacher. She loves gardening and walking holidays along the south coast – especially walks involving tea shops. Has taught maths to boys and girls and says maths and science need to be taught differently for each: 'girls need to be taught to believe they can do it. We have high expectations and set high standards, and work hard to build self-confidence and leadership skills'.

She still teaches and is highly regarded by the pupils. She has restructured the leadership team since her appointment and takes huge trouble over recruitment – she would prefer to manage without than take someone whom she did not consider up to scratch. Does not shy away from discipline but is very perceptive and aware of children's backgrounds, and adapts pastoral care accordingly.

Academic matters: Thirty subjects offered at A level, the most popular being English Literature and maths, followed by psychology, sociology and media studies but wide range including, computing, PE and drama. 'Economics A level popular with the boys and encourages them to come,' said one of the girls. In 2016, 30 per cent A*/A and 66 per cent A*-B at A level.

Girls are not afraid of science nor mathematics and school takes these subjects seriously. Girls are streamed in maths and most take three separate sciences at GCSE. 'There are often more girls doing physics than at local boys' schools,' said a parent, but school offers a broad curriculum including food technology, business studies, drama, music and PE. All study two foreign languages from year 7 and French, German and Spanish offered at GCSE – French taught by a native speaker. A French exchange with families in Perpignan has been started. In 2016, 53 per cent A*/A grades overall at GCSE.

Annual STEM week dedicated to science, technology, engineering and maths – anything from a visit to Kew Gardens and science careers guidance to the Big Reptile show which generates enthusiasm in the lower years. Annual inter-house maths and science competitions, mathematics days and science themed assemblies. 'We are committed to nurturing the scientists of the future,' says the school. 'We do masses of practical work which helps you remember the theory,' said one girl and 'we get lots of extra support with maths,' said another.

Plenty to stretch the gifted and talented who have their own co-ordinator. An increasing numbers take the Extended Project Qualification (EPQ) 'which challenges the girls to make sure they know what they are talking about', says the head. Debating competitions with other schools are popular and the most able work independently with a mentor on Oxford University degree modules. The school has its own observatory and about 20 of the brightest girls study for an astronomy GCSE – completed in one year with lessons outside the timetable.

One of the school's stated aims is to develop a lifelong love of learning and there is an emphasis on fun eg games for literacy and numeracy: WOW (word of the week) and POW (puzzle of the week). 'English teaching is outstanding,' said our guide. 'The teachers recommend lots of books and it is important we enjoy literature'. 'All the teachers are incredibly supportive and we can email them at any time'. 'The sixth form office is always open and you can talk to anyone – we get lots of support from subject teachers but we are not spoon fed. You are on your own at uni and the sixth form is a bridge.'

Enrichment courses in sixth form include personal finance and spoken English. Community sports leadership course popular with those wishing to develop leadership skills and is especially useful for potential teachers.

MGGS is an accredited Advanced Thinking School and pupils are taught to ask perceptive questions and think laterally. Full time careers and higher education co-ordinator and a well-used careers library. Pupils have careers interviews in years 9,11 and 12 as well as talks by outside speakers, including local engineering firm BAe Systems and a recent visit to King Digital Entertainment (of Candy Crush fame) to find out about jobs in creative digital industries and computer science. Interview prior to sixth form application to make sure subjects match career plans and great trouble taken with timetable to try and enable pupils to take the combination they want. All year 11s are expected to do work experience after GCSEs, with help from an outside agency if necessary, and workplace shadowing offered in year 12.

A small number need EAL assistance but usually for technical language. Some 60-70 need some additional support, mainly for mild dyslexia and dyspraxia, and one-to-one support given outside lessons. Good mix of teachers, some of whom have been at the school over 30 years, but also take on three or four NQTs per year – one boy who joined for sixth form returned as a teacher after reading history at university

Games, options, the arts: 'The holistic approach to educations helps pupils see the bigger picture and there is a focus on fun', said a parent. Fab new sports hall opened in April 2016 and named after Molly Tipples, chairman of the governors, who had been instrumental in the fundraising; used for volleyball, badminton, indoor football, etc. Netball the most popular sport – the school has five courts (also used for tennis), girls play at district and county level and school is currently U19 Kent champion. Indoor rowing in the gym – they take part in national rowing championships and can also row on the Medway at Maidstone rowing club. Boys play full-side football outside and 5-a-side football indoors and also get involved in tennis and rounders clubs.

All year 9 expected to take part in bronze Duke of Edinburgh Award with an 'if not why not' approach. About 20 achieve gold each year. Vibrant music department and MGGS has set up Kent initiative to get pupils started with small group music lessons to share the cost, and has instruments available to borrow. Two music studios with editing suites and individual practice rooms. Lots of music clubs including year 7 band, wind band, samba band, brass band and clarinet choir as well as numerous other choirs – pupils and staff sing together in the chamber choir. Pupils perform at assemblies, at lunchtime charity concerts and other concerts throughout the year – the carol service being the highlight. Not forgetting the year 9 Oxjam concert which raises money for Oxfam. One student read music at Oxford in 2015.

Dance particularly popular and school has on site dance and drama studios but no theatre. The main hall, equipped with a new lighting system, is used for the annual dance show and whole school production – recent plays have included Daisy Pulls it Off and Oh! What a Lovely War. A member of the support staff is Latin and ballroom European champion.

The house arts day in the autumn term has been going since at least the 1930s – totally student organised on a three year rotation between music, drama and art – 'phenonemal,' said a parent; 'I was wowed'. 'I love the school get togethers like house arts and assemblies – it gives you such a sense of belonging,' said a year 9 pupil.

Artwork all over the school rotated fortnightly with a wonderful display in the reception area. Textiles particularly impressive – when we visited the theme was Titania, using recycled fabric. 'Sewing is a skill for life,' said our guide, 'and I now make a lot of my own clothes' Fine art and graphic design offered at A level, but ceramics and photography not an option, which is a disappointment to some. Regular subject-based trips including geography trip to Iceland and psychology trip to Auschwitz.

Background and atmosphere: Founded in 1887 with funds from the Wardens of Rochester Bridge, the school opened in 1888 in Albion Place with 18 pupils and moved to its present site in Great Buckland in 1938. It is up on the hill above Maidstone set in 16 acres and surrounded by woodland and grassland, but within walking distance of the town centre and two mainline train stations. Eclectic mix of buildings: Buckland House, opened in 2012, houses the main teaching block and sixth form centre and has wide, bright corridors and a hushed and studious atmosphere with a self-contained area for the sixth form with a café and private study area. Then there is the T (for temporary) building which is the science block, put up in the 1950s and still standing – although the actual labs have been refurbished in the meantime. 'No frills – you get what you see – but it is still a school that shines,' said a parent. Two lovely courtyards filled with roses, refurbished with money raised by the parents' association and with much input from the students, great places to sit and revise. It is still possible to visit the tunnels where the girls sheltered and had their lessons during air raids in World War II.

M

Brown uniform not the most flattering, but has been the same for 100 years and girls like the continuity: 'At least it's not going to affect your adult wardrobe,' said one girl. School is 'hot on uniform transgressions'. Sixth formers allowed to wear own clothes but are expected to dress decently – may wear jeans but no bare shoulders, sandals or crop tops and girls respect this: 'It's more like uni – we can express our personalities; the school trusts us and it works well'. School keeps a stash of suitably modest tops in case a girl arrives at school indecently clad.

Charity fundraising embedded in the culture; each year group holds one event a year and can choose the charity – can be anything from dressing up, to cake stalls, to 'crazy sporting events'. Last year the school raised £19,000. Close links with two schools in Nepal, sends old computers to them and pupils keep in touch via Skype. Longstanding tradition of Rag Week held just before Christmas, which raises at least £4,000 per year for charity. Entirely organised by the four head students, it includes lunchtime performances, fancy dress day and a rag ball. 'It is very hard work but lots of fun', said one senior girl. Strong links with local primary schools, with pupils coming in for masterclasses in maths, English and PE, and senior girls helping with French and reading.

The house system, with six houses and including all staff, is about community values – strong house loyalty, and old girls always remember which house they were in. Girls encouraged to develop leadership skills – each house has three house leaders and pupils have to put themselves forward and make a case for election and are then given a mentor if they need one – 'this creates and brings leaders to the fore', says the head.

Pastoral care, well-being and discipline: High levels of discipline 'but not in a shouty way' – eg mobile phones confiscated for a day if pupils caught using them without permission. Girls stand up when a teacher comes into the room and are taught self-discipline and respect. The senor leadership team is highly visible – all teach and there is always someone at the school gate at going home time. Teachers are good role models and have high standards and expectations of pupils. It is a school which is proud of itself. Pupils mostly well behaved – transgressions generally dealt with by 'direct and redirect', but depends on the scale – occasionally have to be sent home for the day but exclusions are rare.

The school motto is 'non sibi sed omnibus' (not for oneself but for all) and pupils encouraged to be aware of others – kindness awards are announced at speech day. Strong pastoral system – form tutors the key source of support from year 7 upwards, student leadership team is responsible for each year group and sixth form management team offers academic and pastoral support.

'My daughter knows she can go to anyone for help if she needs it and feels someone always has tabs on her, teachers are honest with her and only give praise where it is due but she always feels she matters'. 'There is a limit on the amount of homework set in the lower years and exam pressures are well managed; my daughter has never felt overwhelmed'. Parents given information and advice about how to support their children. 'As a parent I have always felt included – before my daughter went into sixth form we were invited to hear about the syllabus and I always felt part of the learner's journey'.

Pupils and parents: Parents are from a wide range of backgrounds, with many in professional jobs either locally or in London – the high speed train has changed the area. Generally loyal and supportive, and active fundraisers through the parents' association. About seven per cent are on pupil premium, and although pupils are still mostly white British, the increasing ethnic mix reflects the Maidstone area and the school has strong links with the local Gurkha community. Girls are 'hard working and want to do well and are concerned for their friends and peers', says the head, and they go on to a huge range of careers. Old girls are very loyal to the school and many come back for speech day. They include: Lizzie Yarnold, winter Olympic gold medallist; Josh Zare, X Factor contestant; Carol Goble, professor of computer science at the University of Manchester; Dame Karen Dunnell, national statistician and registrar general at the Office for National Statistics; Mia McKenna-Bruce, actress (Penny Branning in EastEnders).

New pupils who join for sixth form made to feel welcome, and one became head student. ' Everybody has been so lovely and welcoming and I have had no problems settling in', said one. 'Moving into the sixth form is such a change and the boys diffuse the girls,' said another. Boys usually come from other selective schools, either because they want a change of scene or because of the subjects offered. 'The boys integrate well and the girls love having them around', said a parent, and they are in great demand for plays and drama groups.

'The bit I valued most about MGGS', said one old girl, 'was the strong sense of community: it's like one massive family and you really get to know other years – all normal, lovely, funny people.' Strong sense of tradition amongst the pupils and the leavers' celebration is always a children's party with pass the parcel and ice cream – and also a prom at Leeds Castle.

Entrance: Year 7 entrance via the Kent Test taken in the September before entry, which involves tests in English, maths, verbal and non-verbal reasoning. Almost all come from primary schools with only about five a year from prep schools – partly because there are very few prep schools in the immediate area. Tight catchment area and those in villages outside Maidstone vulnerable to boundary changes. Occasional places in years 8 and 9 – tests for these year groups taken at the school.

Some 50-60 join the sixth form, mainly from other grammars and high schools, and include about 25 boys. New applicants and current students have to fill in online application forms and places are awarded purely on academic merit. Internal and external entrance criteria exactly the same – six GCSEs at C or above including English and maths and including at least four Bs, and at a least a B in subjects to be studied at A level.

Exit: Only about 25 per cent to Russell Group universities and still a bit 'Kent in aspiration' – the head says that pupils get the grades but are reluctant to move too far away from home, and London is very expensive. Keen to promote Oxbridge – about 10 per cent apply and about one or two per year usually go (one in 2015, three the previous year, though none in 2016). One to study veterinary science. Around a fifth leave post-GCSEs: some leave for the boys' grammars, some go straight to art foundation courses or into work.

Money matters: Government funded bursary fund is available for sixth formers in the greatest need. Old Girls' Society gives annual £50 prize to the pupil the school considers has contributed the most to school life and also makes donations to the cost of various activities.

Remarks: A compassionate and caring school with a strong community feel and good academic results.

Maltman's Green School

Maltmans Lane, Gerrards Cross, Buckinghamshire SL9 8RR

Pupils: 415 • Ages: 3–11

Fees: £10,410 – £14,040 pa

Tel: 01753 883022
Email: registrar@maltmansgreen.com
Website: www.maltmansgreen.com

Headmistress: Since 2005, Mrs Joanna Pardon MA BSc PGCE (50s). Educated mainly in France, with A levels at Folkestone Grammar School, followed by London University, then a masters in environmental studies (still her passion – Maltman's is a leading eco school) at Wye College. Has had a varied career teaching in schools including Riddlesworth Hall, Norfolk (history, technology and director of studies), Ashford School, Kent and, prior to landing at Maltman's, Gateways Prep in Leeds, where she held her first headship. If there's such a thing as a headmistress aura, Mrs Pardon has it in spades, oozing something of the 'old school' surrounded by a halo of calm, coupled with healthy dollops of common sense and a purposefulness only found in truly vocational teachers.

Understands her audience to a tee and refuses to be drawn into conversations about pushy local parents. 'The flip side of an ambitious parent is that they are totally supportive of the school,' she quips. And in this most aspirational of suburbs she is, in the main, keeping parents very happy by 'producing girls that senior schools want.' Revered by the majority, who describe her as 'very approachable, if not overly hands on', with just occasional mutterings from some that too much air time is given to the most demanding parent voices. Head says she is more than happy to stand her ground – and frequently has to. Even those who vent frustrations with the school (mostly in relation to relentlessly driven helicopter parents dominating the scene) concur that Maltman's has been the making of their daughter.

Strongly rebuts local rumblings of staff jumping ship, saying although a number of senior staff have left of late, these were almost exclusively retirements. A number of new staff appointments include a new deputy head, head of junior school and, a new position, head of professional development – 'crucial', she says.

Presides over her domain from a splendid drawing room, littered with personal effects giving clues to her role as doting aunt and keen fell walker, and dominated by Malty, an enormous old English sheepdog rug sprawled in front of the fireplace. From here she tutors hopeful scholars, holds lunches for year 6 girls and heads off on her various duties around the school, stepping in for absent staff members whenever necessary. Lives on site with husband and spends school holidays walking in Devon, where she also has a home.

Entrance: Non-selective and generally not oversubscribed for entry into nursery or reception. A maximum of 32 into nursery at 3+ (compulsory five mornings a week) with an additional 22 into reception, rising to a maximum of 16 spread across four classes in years 3 to 6. From January 2017 the school will admit pupils at 2+ into new pre-school. Occasional places higher up the school dependent upon year group – definitely worth a call if you're moving into the area.

Exit: Careful placement at senior school a huge strength, with conversations starting with parents in year 4. About a third to local grammars, mainly Dr Challoner's High or Beaconsfield High, depending on the current catchment lottery.

On the independent front, feeds a large number of girls to The Royal Masonic School, Piper's Corner and Berkhamsted, with several to Wycombe Abbey and others off in twos and threes to eg Queen Anne's Caversham and St Mary's Gerrards Cross.

Remarks: Situated in the leafy super-affluent enclave of Gerrards Cross, somewhat unexpectedly down a residential lane lined with prime South Bucks real estate. The original house dates back some 300 years and is now a very attractive combination of arts and crafts and art nouveau with modern additions. From the moment you set foot on the highly polished tiles in the entrance hall, dazzled by the silverware displayed in the entrance's trophy cabinet, you know that what will follow can't fail to impress. A private house until 1918, the school was founded for young ladies from Yorkshire and had boarders until the mid-1990s. Nowadays it's attended by immaculately turned out stockbroker belt girls – noticeable by their purple wool coats, impressive array of hats for all occasions and unwavering eye contact.

Super facilities abound from the charming and spacious nursery, housed in a former stable block, upwards. Large, brightly decorated classrooms proudly display girls' work with barely a centimetre of bare wall on show – a theme continued throughout the school, which is festooned from top to bottom with high quality artistic endeavours from screen prints and puppets to hand-made pop-up books. Two inviting, well-stocked libraries, gleaming new labs, a pottery room and kiln, lovely art room and DT lab, used by the whole school. The jewel in the crown is currently the stunning indoor swimming pool complex (the grapevine tells us the water's a bit chilly but our guides, ever on-message, disputed this), possibly soon to be matched, if not eclipsed, by the multi-purpose gym and performance space under construction. Not the most spacious prep school campus we've seen, but grounds well utilised with separate, well-equipped playgrounds for junior and senior girls, a discovery garden (part of head's eco push) and decent playing fields.

Given the non-academically selective nature of Maltman's, its results speak volumes about a school rich in educational and extracurricular opportunities ('our outcomes are those of a selective school', says head). Feeding an array of senior schools across the academic spectrum from the lofty heights of Wycombe Abbey down, girls are taught by specialists for all subjects from year 4 and parents praise the quality of teaching at all levels, as well as an extracurricular programme that spans the usual sporty and artsy suspects as well as opportunities such as RSPB Club (run by head) and woodland detectives. School's reputation for pushiness precedes it but parents aren't complaining – 'my daughter has loved every minute,' said one – particularly not when the secondary school offer letters drop on the mat en masse.

Roundedness may be the official Maltman's mantra, but parents and girls say sport is still top dog, with Maltman's girls – or those of them that make the rather exclusive A or B teams anyway – regularly trouncing the competition in everything from netball to gymnastics. A coveted place in the gym squad is akin to membership to an exclusive club. Taking on all-comers in national competitions, the 'Maltman's Army' as it's known by parents, only slightly tongue in cheek, is drilled and rehearsed to within an inch of its life – an ethos which pervades the school. Parental ambition appears to be a major contributor to this excellence, and although parents say the girls are 'driven to win', it can be an exhausting regime for those who are putting in up to nine hours training a week outside of school to keep their place in the squad, although school says they do not encourage this. Head says she is tirelessly focused on 'balancing excellence with participation', although it seems that the former still often trumps the latter. That said, sports day is reportedly only 'quite' competitive, according to girls, with everyone able to take part and some fun races as well for those not in the elite athlete bracket.

Girls' voices heard loud and clear, evidenced in the wonderful 'Malty's News' newsletter, brainchild of a year 3 pupil and written exclusively by pupils for pupils. Another suggested an 'act of kindness week' which was duly implemented. Girl power at its best. Pupils also elected to sit on the school council and the eco-council.

Music another strong suit with around 50 per cent of girls playing a musical instrument and choirs, bands and ensembles galore. Parents with boys at many a nearby school sigh that their sons just can't compete with their sisters' school performances. Drama on curriculum and, in true Maltman's style, productions are exceptional – a recent rendition of Bugsy Malone was close to professional standard. In addition to this, there are four nativities for staff to put on at Christmas, plus carol service, lots of LAMDA and numerous other opportunities for budding thespians to strut their stuff. Lapraik Hall now boasts latest lighting and sound equipment plus retractable seats. Notably, at prize giving, six girls are selected to speak, with head saying she makes an effort to choose those who don't always get the opportunity to shine.

Quality rather than quantity in the languages department, with French from year 1 but no Latin on curriculum. Mandarin, Spanish and German on offer as clubs or for private tuition and girls say top subjects are science and maths. Three classes of up to 18 stay together from reception to year 2, at which point there's a reshuffle into 4 classes of max 16 with occasional movement thereafter if the need arises. Setting for maths and English (two sets, politically correctly coined 'regular' and 'upper') in year 5. Eagle eyes are peeled for SEN and a robust approach is taken to providing appropriate help with one-to-one support taking place in an inspiring dedicated room. Head of learning support is qualified educational psychologist and is supported by a specialist literacy teacher and team of support staff who tackle girls' needs at no extra charge.

Very few discipline problems and head empathises that when things go awry it's often because 'something else has gone wrong,' hence a light touch employed in most cases ('I'm not into retribution,' she says). Despite the competitive ethos fostered less in school than in some of the families, the atmosphere is purposeful and friendly. A few question marks over how effectively 'friendship issues' are dealt with, particularly in the lower part of the school where parents feel the school could do more to foster kindness in the playground.

Good work and high achievement praised at all levels. Exceptional work rewarded with a 'Malty's Favourite' certificate, prized by girls of all ages, and headmistress commendations given out for 'really special work'. As well as external awards for regional and national excellence in all things, the trophy cabinet shows how school values and rewards girls for everything from academic progress (not just achievement – we approve) to consideration, enthusiasm and love of learning.

Head says 'we will do our girls proud' and of this there is no doubt. Shrinking violets should proceed with caution – and some do head off for gentler pastures along the way – but send your daughter to Maltman's and watch her sing, dance and cartwheel her way towards secondary school success...and quite possibly, with her eyes fixed determinedly on the prize, world domination.

Manor House School

Manor House Lane, Bookham, Surrey KT23 4EN

Pupils: 291 • Ages: 2-16

Fees: £8,970 – £16,341 pa

Tel: 01372 457077
Email: admissions@manorhouseschool.org
Website: www.manorhouseschool.org

Headteacher: Since September 2016, Tracey Fantham BA MA NPQH, previously headteacher of Blenheim High School in Epsom, one of Surrey's leading state schools.

Academic matters: The range of abilities is genuinely broad, from high flyers who want to work without pressure to those who struggle with academia. GCSE results are excellent from such a spectrum, pitching the school well against the local competition – 38 per cent A*/A grades. Most popular GCSE subjects are art, Spanish, French, geography and science – around half do triple science. High flyers in English can take GCSE a year early. Nice to see plenty of vocational options at GCSE – food and nutrition, child development, art, music, PE and drama.

Parents feel confident in the teaching, saying, 'The lines of communication are very open,' and, 'They cover the spectrum by extending classroom work for the brighter girls'. They agree good academic results are gained by small classes and the small scale of the school, telling us, 'The girls are a bit spoon-fed,' but the work ethic is positive and 'being clever is OK, not geeky'. Teachers instil a sense of security and growing independence in the girls, whilst making lessons fun and interesting. One pupil described enthusiastically how fractions had been taught by cutting up and eating a large cake.

The school feels all abilities are catered for 'because we teach in small groups and have stable staff who know the girls well'. Many of the teachers have been there more than 10 years – a few taught current pupils' mothers and clearly have great affection for both the school and the pupils. One teacher we spoke to had been at the school for many years, and was so wildly passionate about the place, she would probably have talked all day about the joys of Manor House had the bell not rung when it did. Some staff movement; as the school only has pupils to 16, young ambitious teachers would have to move on if they want to teach A level.

The full-time head of academic advancement provides help to girls throughout the school (junior and senior), individually or in small groups. No SEN assessment on entry, however all families are asked to detail any learning support being received, and all year 7s are screened for symptoms of dyslexia as a matter of course. Any pupils requiring more than a couple of learning support sessions are charged extra. Girls have a positive view of the help they are given at all levels.

Games, options, the arts: Sports are developing under the new head – all the usuals and matches most afternoons for A through to C teams whenever possible, so most gain match experience, much appreciated by parents and girls. Games teaching widely praised, 'The PE staff work incredibly hard'. Some girls very involved and with excellent results. On-site outdoor facilities (including pool) and sports hall good; changing rooms for each year dotted around school, but no showers, which can be a problem for the older girls.

Music, art and drama all enjoyed as part of the fun, have-a-go ethos. Busy, inspirational art room buzzing with girls and their pretty and impressive artworks. Drama is praised by parents as very strong with a 'wonderful teaching team' – girls of all ages take part in productions both on stage and backstage. Director of music is 'young and full of enthusiasm'. Individual music lessons taught by a variety of peripatetic teachers; standards range from beginner to grade 5, with plenty of opportunities for performance in school.

Background and atmosphere: Housed in a classically beautiful Queen Anne house set in formal gardens and parkland, tucked away in a surprisingly quiet and leafy Surrey lane close to the busy A3 and M25. The house can be hired as a wedding venue via a completely separate events company. The lovely gardens, sweeping lawns, as well as the 'safe feeling' location, are much appreciated by parents and many of the girls. Inside, the house feels as much like a rather grand home as a school, with a central staircase leading up to classrooms on the upper floors. Behind the main house are a number of newer blocks housing the art room, school hall (doubling as a theatre and gym) and classrooms for the oldest girls. Purpose-built nursery facilities sit alongside the prep classrooms and share an extensive outdoor play area. Junior classrooms are located in the very beautiful main house and girls play outside in the lovely grounds. The whole place has a quiet, country feel and parents feel strongly that their daughters will be safe here. Unusually, a well-equipped home economics department – girls are taught nutrition and diet as well as child development and textiles.

Truly a through school – little, if any, separation between early years, juniors and seniors: it is one community, a major USP the school uses to differentiate itself from the competition. Although the juniors and seniors do have some separate playing areas, they are involved in each other's school lives on a daily basis, with most of the senior girls having a role – prep and subject prefects, house and sports captains – with responsibilities across the whole school. They are greeted with excitement, hugs and kisses by the juniors, who love the seniors to bits. 'A small, friendly, nurturing school where everyone is known'. Parents generally like the small size, especially at the younger end, feeling, 'It's a good choice for a quiet child,' but sometimes find that 'in such a small environment one girl can upset the applecart'. Delightful website (in fact one of the best school websites we have seen) with loads of pictures of happy smiling girls, gives a real flavour of the place.

Pastoral care, well-being and discipline: 'An individual approach to academic success' is the school motto. The girls we met on our visit were charming, polite and confident without a hint of precociousness. Huge praise from every parent we spoke to for the pastoral care – 'second to none'. Parents describe the caring environment as 'cosseted' and 'like being wrapped in cotton-wool', acknowledging that a few find it too much so in their latter years.

A counsellor visits for one day each week, providing confidential advice and support for both girls and staff. Issues of potential teen angst – alcohol, drugs, eating disorders, cyber-bullying, self-esteem – are covered in class. The school reports very few problems, explaining they work 'with clear policies and consistent boundaries' and discuss bad behaviour and its effect. Parents tell us, 'Girls who have been particularly unpleasant are taken for a chat'.

Pupils and parents: Parents choose it to avoid the academic pressure and competition of the 'Surrey schools mafia' – they are a varied and non-judgmental lot who mix comfortably. They feel Manor House suits 'girly girls', 'quiet girls' and families who are 'not too pushy' and like the 'innocence, warmth and friendliness'. Plenty with family ties, mothers who are old girls, as well as lots of sisters. Girls look fresh faced and tidy, with swinging pony-tails and sensible skirt lengths. Not for the wild child, the rebel or rule breaker: she would stick out like a sore thumb.

Pupils come from around a 15 mile radius from Epsom to Guildford to Wimbledon. School minibuses run in the mornings and afternoons with a minibus running to Effingham Station before and after school.

Entrance: Baby and toddler group once a week helps ease children (boys and girls) into Manor House before they can remember anything else. Nursery, also co-ed, starts from age 2. School proper, with uniforms and for girls only, at age 4 in the prep, moving through into the juniors at age 7. Entry assessment for juniors on a 'taster day' – English, maths and interview with a teacher – plus school report and reference.

Most girls move seamlessly through from the junior to senior school here; the largest external intake is at reception, 7 and 11, with pupils coming from a scattering of local state and independent schools. An entry testing day is held in January prior to entry in September for 11+ – SPaG, English and maths – plus science for 2018 onwards – and an informal interview with head/deputy head; they're looking for girls 'who want to be here' and the school accepts a wide range of abilities, from the very academic to those whose interests are in other areas of school life.

Exit: All girls leave after GCSE, mostly to study for A levels, at eg Reed School, Hurtwood House, King's College Wimbledon, Epsom College, Esher College, Godalming College, Howard of Effingham, Hurtwood House, Prior's Field, St John's and Tormead. A few jump ship at age 13 – particularly girls who have been at Manor House all through nursery and juniors.

Money matters: Two new academic 50 per cent scholarships plus one sports and one creative and expressive arts, both at 30 per cent of fees. Annual means-tested bursaries are available, in line with the school's charitable status, for new and existing pupils, theoretically covering up to 100 per cent of fees, though the school is keen to manage expectations. Applications for bursaries need to be made by December for the following September.

Remarks: A charming, small, friendly school, ideal for girls who need a caring environment to reach their full potential, be they very academic or otherwise. Wholesome unpretentious girls mix with other 'nice' girls (no fears they would lead each other astray). Pupils work hard, play hard and form friendships for life

– a school, which though fully embracing the new, harks back to a wonderful bygone era. Think Enid Blyton's Malory Towers (without the boarding) – in the nicest possible way (think, but do not say: the school takes huge exception to the comparison).

Manor Lodge School

Rectory Lane, Ridge Hill, Shenley, Hertfordshire WD7 9BG

Pupils: 424 • Ages: 4–11

Fees: £9,645 – £11,535 pa

Tel: 01707 642424
Email: enquiries@manorlodgeschool.com
Website: www.manorlodgeschool.com

Headmaster: Since 2011 Mr Gil Dunn Cert Ed (60s). Educated at Brooklands School, Leighton Buzzard and Milton Keynes College of Education. Understated, sincere and popular with pupils ('he's really funny but can be strict') and parents, who say he is 'totally dedicated to the children.' Describes himself as an 'accidental headmaster,' having been persuaded into the role by governors after 10 years as deputy, following the sudden departure of the short-lived former head. A keen cricketer and former tennis coach, started his career at Burnham Secondary ('tough but great fun,') with a one-year stint teaching PE, rising to head of department. Moved as director of sport to Wakeman School in Shrewsbury before joining Frensham Heights School as housemaster. Took first deputy headship at Beisham Mae Jewish School in east London then moved into the prep world with his appointment as head of PE and Games at Lochinver House, Potters Bar.

Joined Manor Lodge in 1994 as head of year 6, senior English teacher and sports coach. Moonlighted throughout career as counsellor and later director of a USA summer camp but gave this up when appointed deputy head in 2001. Says it was always his calling to work with children and keeps his hand well in teaching year 6 English and handling the secondary transfer process. 'An excellent communicator,' according to parents, he says it's important 'not to be remote,' and although he doesn't see himself a typical charismatic prep school head, says he has his 'own style,' and is oft seen pressing the parental flesh at sporting fixtures and both ends of the day.

Die-hard Chelsea fan and published author of children's fiction and historical western novels, he also writes the lyrics and scripts for all year 6 school productions. Stands apart from majority of prep heads in his belief that 11 is the right age for children to move to secondary school, partly to avoid 'the pressure of common entrance' and partly due to belief that some children can 'go stale' in the last two years of prep. Sees the most important factor as having given his charges 'a joy of learning,' and producing independent thinkers who 'investigate rather than just learning facts.'

Entrance: Selective 'to a certain extent' at 4, with more than three applicants for every place. Assessment takes about an hour, and is equal in importance to interview with candidate and parents: 'We're looking for children with character and parents who recognise the importance of partnership with school for 11+ success,' says head. Automatic entry for siblings, with around 25 per cent from the sibling-only nursery on site. Waiting lists for every year group, with those entering post-reception, mainly from state sector or due to relocations, invited to spend a morning in school and tested in maths and English.

Exit: Strong record of feeding to the south Herts/north London plethora of academic powerhouses including Habs Boys and Girls, St Albans Boys and Girls and North London Collegiate. Those not reaching such dizzy academic heights well catered for too, with movement to St Columba's, Aldenham, Haileybury, Queenswood and St Margaret's. Hardly any to boarding and an average of five per cent to state schools, including Dame Alice Owen's. Outstanding scholarship record.

Remarks: Nestled at the end of a country lane in a rural setting of fields housing the local pony population, the only clue to the urban environs of Manor Lodge is the M25 sign just visible on the horizon. Excellent use has been made of the grounds surrounding the 300 year old former country house, which has a colourful history as health spa, film set (notably A Clockwork Orange) and the private home of double agent Eddie Chapman. Wonderful grassy outdoor spaces include two adventure playgrounds, one of these exclusively for reception children, two sports fields and a large wildlife garden ('a great privilege to visit,' say children), often used for science lessons and complete with well-populated swamp and observation hut.

The main building provides an impressive façade for the school but the classrooms, which include a dedicated dojo for martial arts, don't quite live up to the grandeur of the exterior, although there is a quaint charm to the winding staircases and narrow panelled corridors. Thankfully the 'new block' (2003) with its brightly painted corridors bedecked with fruits of the children's labours and large airy form rooms, delivers light, bright classrooms with a more modern feel. The Grand Designs style dining room added in 2008 plays a starring architectural role and multi-tasks as dance and gymnastics studio. New sports hall/theatre (2015) with rooms for music and drama, plus all-weather multi use games area.

Head constantly refers to Manor Lodge as a 'family school' and it benefits in atmosphere from its co-ed pupil body which gives off a friendly, relaxed vibe. Boys and girls mix freely and provide 'healthy competition' for one another in the classroom, according to parents, and pupils say that although the school has high standards, it is 'not super strict.' School community, from the north London/south Herts environs, is 'very demanding' in its expectations according to head, although children come over as earnest and serious, many articulate beyond their years but not precocious. Very few super-affluent families, with the majority hard working middle class and many first time buyers. Diverse ethnic and religious mix representative of the local area.

Quality rather than quantity in the language department, with French from reception and Spanish from year 5. No Latin or classics but specialist teaching for music, art, CDT, IT, PE, drama and languages from the word go. Around 25 per cent of teachers are male (including one in infant department) lending a healthy dose of testosterone to the mix. Pupils continuously assessed using PIPS scheme – 'it gives us a constant flow of information,' says head. At the top of the school, children benefit from a tutorial system 'almost like university,' where they are given instant feedback on all work, with 'some responses from teachers almost as long as the child's essay,' according to head. All year 5 and 6 pupils receive a mini report every four weeks to track progress and constantly reassess targets. 'Thorough preparation' for 11+ is the name of the Manor Lodge game, with all year 6 pupils receiving interview technique coaching from a former top senior school admissions tutor.

Pupils mixed mainly according to geographical location in reception 'to minimise pressure on parents,' says head and classes are shuffled in year 3. Setting in maths from year 2 and English from year 5, when children start to move around the school for individual subjects. Head cautiously picks out English as the school's 'greatest strength' but quickly adds that most scholarships achieved are all-rounders. Parents say that children 'hardly know they're learning' lower down the school and that pressure 'steps up just a little bit each year.' More than lip service paid to focus on independent thinking, with all pupils working towards completion of their 'thinking skills passports,' focusing on creativity, independence, collaboration and persistence. Extremely close bonds in evidence between staff and children, with teachers referring to the 'sheer joy in learning' they hope to give their young charges and even reception staff showing clear affection for pupils.

Not much in the way of heavy duty SEN, but that said there is very little call for it – just a handful of pupils per year group receive extra help from the part-time SENCo to iron out minor issues. Maths and English specialists join classrooms to provide support to those who need it, and those with specific talents, either academically or in music or art, receive accelerated tuition outside classroom time.

Art room on the basic side but one of the most orderly we've seen – 'you can't create in chaos,' according to the art teacher – and pupils enthuse about the teaching in this area, with evidence of their work displayed around the school. DT also a firm favourite with both sexes, with pupils describing their teacher as 'passionate,' although facilities in this area are not the star attraction. Music lessons take place in a room with spectacular views across the countryside and are very popular, with 50 per cent of junior pupils taking peripatetic lessons and a host of bands and choirs on offer for budding performers to display their wares. Head says 'nobody leaves Manor Lodge without being a performer,' with frequent recitals on all scales, ranging from class assemblies, which 'quietly teach confidence,' according to parents, to musical productions, most recently Charlie and the Chocolate Factory. Year 6s bow out of the school each year with a major production at the Radlett Centre.

The trophy cabinet in reception tells visitors all they need to know about the sporting culture of the school which has, according to parents, 'hugely improved,' in recent years. Two dedicated sports staff (one male, one female) run the show and have helped school inch its way up league tables and earn its place in a competitive local fixtures list. A-D teams are put out wherever possible with cricket and netball being standout sports – teams in both finished the season unbeaten recently. Girls' football on the up and cricket also popular with the female cohort, although no fixtures – yet. Trophies and accolades also up for grabs for less sporty ones, with annual awards for everything from maths and handwriting to reading – and even one for 'good egg.'

Hugely popular (and competitive) house system and pupil body vociferous in school matters with the school council, introduced in 2012. Two councillors elected from every year in the school attend monthly meetings to put forward ideas and suggestions for improvements. School introduced badges for those on school teams, choir or bands and holding responsibilities such as librarian as a result of council discussions –many pupils now proudly weighed down with these. School presidents from each gender are elected by the pupil body ('they always get it right,' says head) and lead council meetings. Pupils proud of school's Green Flag status and boasts an eco team, recycling club and bird watching amongst its enrichment programme. No specific anti-bullying measures in place but head says that 'children know they can talk to any adult,' adding that incidents of unpleasant behaviour are 'pretty rare.'

The Manor Preparatory School

Faringdon Road, Shippon, Abingdon, Oxfordshire OX13 6LN

Pupils: 385: 58 boys/327 girls • Ages: 2-11 (girls), 2-7 (boys) • C of E

Fees: £8,571 – £14,400 pa

Tel: 01235 858458
Email: admissons@manorprep.org
Website: www.manorprep.org

Head: Since 2006, Mr Piers Heyworth MA PGCE (50s). Educated at Papplewick, Marlborough and Christ Church, Oxford where he read English. Started his teaching career at Latymer Upper School, became head of English at James Allen's Girls' School and then head of James Allen's Prep for 14 years. Mr Heyworth is married with two children; his wife also teaches at the school, dividing her legendary talents between the SEN and art departments. Mr Heyworth is a man in his element; he radiates joie de vivre and one feels that what he enjoys most about his job is seeing the world afresh through his pupils' eyes. He teaches drama from year 3 upwards using his large study as a performance space. 'We move the furniture back and improvise... everyone gets to act, the children get to see me make a fool of myself and I get to know them.' It's not just the pupils who act: most years in January there is a surprise staff panto that begins with the head introducing a deliberately deadly assembly – for example on the colour grey – which is then hijacked, much to the pupils' delight.

Over hot chocolate and pastries at 'birthday break', Mr Heyworth and his wife chat amiably with those whose birthdays fell in the preceding week, from the tiniest pre-prep boy to the confident year 6 girls. Talk with him about his school and you will hear no educational newspeak, no bureaucratic terminology; he is fluent and engaging and raids his literary education for apposite quotations (Browning and Desmond Morris!) without pretension. Now while we are certain that nothing as harsh and unyielding as an iron fist is hiding in Mr Heyworth's jolly velvet glove, no school is judged 'outstanding' in every aspect (ISI 2011) without a huge amount of rigorous management and scrupulous attention to detail going on behind the scenes. He generously ascribes much of the school's success to its staff, who are expected to 'jump through a lot of hoops' before being appointed. 'We are looking for that extra edge; not just solid teaching but candidates who are clever enough to inspire and give that special Manor warmth, openness and candour.' Try as we might we couldn't find a parent who was less than dewy-eyed about the place, the teaching, the way their sons and daughters had flourished.

Relaxation is golf (clearly passion rather than pastime: it featured in assembly), which he plays at nearby Frilford with his wife. He has 'revived' his piano playing and takes lessons out of school. And is The Manor bearing up in these uncertain times? Expansion of the over-subscribed pre-nursery provision and building plans – a two-storey block to replace some perfectly respectable temporary classrooms – would say a confident yes. 'Numbers are up. Our governors take the view that quality is recession proof.'

Entrance: 'Virtually non-selective'. Informal visit with parents for youngest, trial day for pupils entering years 1 to 6.

Exit: No formal links to any senior schools but pretty seamless progression of girls trailing scholarships and awards – majority (around half) to St Helen and St Katharine; Headington also popular, some also to Oxford High.

Boys leave at 7, most to Abingdon Prep where they have a 'reserved' but definitely not 'guaranteed' place, also The Dragon and Magdalen College.

Remarks: Approach via the educational super-highway that is the Faringdon Road in Abingdon and just when you think there can't be another school, take a sharp turn into The Manor. We arrived at drop off time and bravely nosed the modest GSG-mobile between the juggernauts of the Oxfordshire school run. One of the sensible benefits of the Abingdon4Education partnership (or 'soft federation', as the head calls it) is a joint bus service that ferries children in from all points of the compass (Henley the latest to be added) and serves Abingdon, St Helen and St Katharine, The Manor and thence (by minibus) Abingdon Prep. According to Mr Heyworth, even The Manor's tiniest will soon have their own dedicated bus with age-appropriate booster seats and school staff to accompany them on their travels – this should ease car park congestion.

Our visit began with assembly and a rousing blast of Land of Hope and Glory from the small but perfectly pitched orchestra, segueing into Dancing Queen – a fine start to anyone's day. Mr Heyworth's inspiring talk on heroic failure was illustrated not only with famous examples (Eddie the Eagle) but also anecdotes from staff and pupils. The most frequently cited experiences were riding and skiing challenges – doubtless a reflection of the school's demographic, but one brave soul claimed to have 'weeded the garden in the rain'.

The friendly, relaxed but orderly atmosphere of assembly set the tone for the work and play we observed. Manor Cottage is the first stop on the 'chronological horseshoe' ground plan of The Manor estate, the charming home of the pre-nursery Manorites, brightened outside with little pots and wellington boots full of pansies. Up to 16 boys and girls come here for anything between one morning and five full days from the age of 2. Play, gardening, stories, cookery – children make their own snacks once a week – this is very much a home from home.

The nursery block has an enclosed garden with space to ride bikes; 'we do as much learning outside as we can'. Eager beavers in smart bottle green sweatshirts were having break when we visited, excited about making jam tarts after break – part of the term's jubilee theme. For nursery children who do a full day a mezzanine area allows a soft space, if not for sleep, then quiet rest according to parents' requirements. We thoroughly approved of the 'Ask me about...' whiteboard at the entrance to the building – staff write up some of the day's key events so that parents can ask their forgetful darlings leading questions and maybe even receive answers.

More formal teaching begins in reception and, as in other schools, hard stuff goes on in the morning. In every classroom we visited busy hands were doing: in one class pupils were sitting on the floor with little whiteboards practising writing numbers; in another fractions were being explored by folding sheets of paper. Lessons start with a mental maths warm up, move on to practical work and finish with 'recording'. In each room thinking skills boards pose problem-solving challenges. 'What we don't do is spoon feed.' Indeed, independent learning and 'risk taking' are built into the teaching programme right from the start. Pupils are set from year 2 in maths; an extra set means that each gets exactly the support or extension work they need. All the requisite technology is in place and IT lessons are once a week; screens are mostly in dedicated areas, actively used for research but not dominating classrooms. The hands-on approach to learning persists in the science lab: we saw enthusiastic year 6 girls pile in from the grounds brandishing newly captured mini beasts in magnifying jars, ready to be drawn, described and then released...until next time. Library just a little less splendid than the rest of what we saw – tidy and well stocked but rather spartan. It is, we were told, awaiting refurbishment and may thus become the kind of place one would want to curl up with a book.

The learning support department is at the centre of things, in the manor house from which the school gets its name. 'We can cope with anything, from a pupil needing a bit of extra help with maths and reading, to severe dyslexia.' Parents we spoke to endorse this, describing the learning support team as 'fantastic', 'working wonders.' Three dedicated teachers assess all children and offer support individually, in small groups or in class; this is free up to the end of year 1. According to one parent whose child needed significant support, 'costs can escalate but the school advised us what to expect so at least we didn't get any nasty surprises.' A private speech therapist is also available and the school has accommodated children with hearing and sight problems. Support is tailored to the individual: 'we are flexible according to need'. EAL also on offer and pupils often go from speaking no English to fluency in an astonishingly short time. Impressive gifted and talented programme also in place.

And now to sport. Lucky Manor sports staff (all specialists) are based in a splendid stone barn. There's plenty of green space for running around; additional specialist netball and tennis take place at the nearby White Horse Leisure Centre and swimmers get to use the splendid pool at Abingdon School. When asked about Manor sport, the head suffered a temporary modesty lapse, 'We win everything!' Can this be true? We checked: from cross-country to equestrian, tennis to biathlon, Manor girls leave others standing and compete at county and national levels. Part of the secret of the school's success could be the fact that one member of staff is employed solely to coordinate matches and ensure that all clubs, sporting or otherwise, run and run smoothly. If The Manor says it offers a club, it really does; 'we're not half-hearted', says the head (as if).

Mainstream offerings are free, specialist options such as Spanish or Mandarin are charged and pupils can pursue interests from golf to face painting, chess and touch-typing. Instrumental lessons (including harp) are supported by before and after-school music clubs including guitar, chamber group, singing and wind band. The dreaded music practice is encouraged by an awards scheme; teachers set weekly goals and give practice tips. Our charming guides were looking forward to the year 6 Stratford visit (a post-entrance exam treat) which includes a trip on the river, a play and the chance to romp through the Bard's home town in Elizabethan costume and duelling scars (courtesy of a former head of wigs and make-up at the theatre). Other excursions include camping on the Ridgeway, outdoor pursuit adventures on the Isle of Wight and a week in Normandy.

Some of the parents to whom we spoke described how The Manor had 'rescued' their children from unhappy schooling elsewhere and 'returned the smiles to their faces.' Others praised home/school communication, saying that queries were always answered promptly and parents felt that dialogue with teaching staff was genuinely encouraged. A few had concerns about how the pace accelerates in year 5 in advance of entrance exams but said that their daughters, having been 'thoroughly manored', took this in their stride.

So, what manner of magic goes on here? Does the studious atmosphere of those high-octane senior schools waft along the road? Perhaps, but that doesn't quite account for the enviable results achieved by this happy, unpressurised, non-selective school. The head defines it thus, 'We want to cultivate bright-eyed enthusiasm, to say "let's go for it and play with heart"; learning should be linked to the fun of life.'

Marlborough House School

Hawkhurst, Cranbrook, Kent TN18 4PY

Pupils: 320; 40 flexi-boarders. • Ages: 3–13 • C of E

Fees: Day £8,190 – £16,935; Boarding £30 per night

Tel: 01580 753555
Email: registrar@marlboroughhouseschool.co.uk
Website: www.marlboroughhouseschool.co.uk

Headmaster: Since 2013, Martyn Ward, married with two girls at Marlborough House School (MHS). Went to Westminster College Oxford, then taught at The Hall and Cothill House, before becoming deputy, then acting head of Eastbourne College Prep.

Warm and personable, much liked by pupils – 'he's fun, and interested in us' – and parents – 'he's a breath of fresh air'; 'always around when you want to speak to him'; 'knows the children and is genuinely interested in them' (he sends birthday cards to all the children, which is much appreciated).

Entrance: 'No type it wouldn't suit', says the head. Broadly first come, first served, with taster days and soft touch testing so they know where pupils are and can monitor development. Wouldn't accept a child who would feel exposed in a year group, academically or socially, which would be unfair on the child. A parent thought that it wouldn't suit children who don't recognise discipline – pupils here need to be respectful of all ages.

'Took a long time to get in', said a parent who waited two years to get a place for her daughter, but it's evidently worth the wait. 'Our experience is overwhelmingly good at many different levels...'.

Exit: Large number to Cranbrook (which is starting 11+ entry in 2017, which may affect numbers at MHS); Eastbourne College, King's Canterbury, Benenden and Tonbridge are also popular. A few to Eton, Harrow et al.

Remarks: Some children really do skip between lessons here; it's a very buoyant place. Elegant buildings, beautifully kept. Gravel crunches under foot. Mature trees (no climbing); but under the rhododendrons at break time, flashes of uniform and scrambling limbs. A plastic cow peers around the edge of the bushes, a school jumper draped around its head.

'When education looks [this] good and learning is [this] inspiring, how can you not choose it for your children?' said a parent. When the head arrived, he replaced some of the old guard with a young, lively staff which transformed the school academically – 'fun and active lessons'; 'inspiring', say the children (yes, the children). 'The staff the head brought in are utterly amazing', said a parent, 'and anything you might wince at occasionally is overwhelmed by their reinvention of lessons'. One teacher blows a bugle of brilliance if he reads something fabulous in class; another gives top gun award for great work: aviator shades and a moustache for the day. 'They enthral the children', said another parent, in awe. Dull or mediocre will not be tolerated from teaching staff here; an assistant head's role is continuous assessment and improvement of all teaching staff (360 appraisal is coming, and these articulate pupils will welcome the opportunity to make their views known).

The curriculum in year 5 starts to prepare pupils for both CE and 11+, the focus being on maths and literacy – 'this is what gets pupils into senior schools', says an assistant head. Commenting on the atmosphere, a parent said ' it's not wholly laid back; but [doing] the best you can do is perfect'. Both the very able and those towards the middle of the pack thrive here, bright pupils being stretched with extension work.

The SEN unit is open door to anyone, including those who just want a chat and some reassurance. One pupil with difficulties at home knows that they can go at any point to the unit, to sit quietly, or as a safe quiet place to work. They help those with a variety of needs, including severe dyslexia, and one parent described how her daughter's English has come on in leaps and bounds. Most support is offered in groups of up to six (the dynamic is better in small groups, they say, and it's more fun for pupils). One-to-one help is also offered, and is charged as an extra.

The school is divided into nursery, pre-prep, middle and upper school, with separate buildings for pre-prep and nursery. A jolly nursery, with children learning to care for rabbits, guinea pigs and giant snails. A quiet area behind ribbons, for snuggling down for a nap or quiet time.

MHS is often chosen by parents and children for the happy comfortable atmosphere that pervades the school, one parent adding that it is 'neither as clinical or feral as other independent options in the area'. Another was attracted by the respectful interaction between staff and children, and described the role modelling by staff as 'exceptional'. 'It does feel like a special greenhouse environment', said one parent who worries a bit that her children won't be able to cope in the real gritty world, and would like more integration into the local community – 'but they learn great values [and] they have found [my son's] areas of potential and fanned them'.

MHS promotes British values, says the ISI (tolerance and respect, in case you were wondering). Officially non-denominational with a Christian ethos; it actually feels distinctly Christian, with a sung grace (lovely chime-like responses), and chapel twice a week. One parent said, 'I like the fact that it's not afraid to have a Christian ethos: in word and genuinely in spirit it is a kind school'.

The uniform is moving from navy to grey tweed, 'curiously old fashioned', said a parent: the school listened to pupils and parents about the faults of the current uniform (itchy jumpers and tricky tracksuit bottom linings), but parents don't feel they were sufficiently consulted over the new design. Pupils do feed back their views on school through the class rep to the pupil forum twice a term, but these very vocal pupils were clear that they would like a greater voice, particularly to make suggestions about food: puddings are excellent, first courses variable, and some outrage that only year 8 get to visit the salad bar. More outrage that burgers and doughnuts have disappeared (quiet hurrahs from the parents), and disgust at the courgette buns and beetroot brownies which have appeared in their place. Thank goodness for much loved fishy Fridays.

Sport every afternoon from year 6 upwards (three times a week for younger pupils), with lots of pupils saying that sport is their favourite thing about MHS. They excel in many areas, often achieving national level: quite something for a small sized prep. But for a school that fields excellence, there is a pleasing emphasis on sport for all, with an approach that highlights enjoyment, inclusion and effort: coaches focus on the bottom teams, with most parents and pupils saying that everyone gets a regular chance to represent the school in matches.

Superb outdoor facilities (although one parent said the outside pool is the 'size of a pond' and 'the team is not strong as a result'. It looked a fairly standard school pool to us, and there are individual successes who supplement their training outside school at swimming clubs). Decent sized indoor sports hall.

There is the traditional sports gender divide along cricket and rounders lines, which causes a little parent discord -'as a progressive prep, they should have girls' football'. The school is not averse to girls playing boys' sports, but it can be hard to find other preps for them to play against.

Forest school for pupils up to middle school, and it's very popular – a big door at the edge of the woods with Forest School across the top gives a feeling of welcome to the jungle: camp fire; mud slide; dragon (felled horse chestnut); tarpaulins and hides when it's raining. A magical place to learn – 'you can see the kids' shoulders going down', said a teacher.

Music is really lovely – pupils benefit from a comprehensive programme, which evidently fosters a real love for music: an ad hoc group was singing a pop song at break, accompanied by the year 5 music scholar on the piano (blimey), while pupils passing the room in the corridor outside joined in with the odd phrase as they went past. Various instrument and vocal coaches from illustrious stables such as the ENO and the Globe. Busy programme of concerts, from informal at home events, to chamber choir at the Wealden Times Fair, and Junior choir with the Cranbrook Choral society. Parents particularly like the informal concerts, one describing with pleasure one held in the local pub.

Pupils here love drama, and would just like to do more of it (a play a term in pre-prep, but only in year 6 and sometimes year 8 in the rest of the school, say parents; school insists that there are annual plays for all middle school children and more informal plays and recitations higher up).

A wealth of clubs, including philosophy in the forest and theatre make up. Must be one of the only schools with a permanent indoor maypole, children learning that the important thing is to keep smiling merrily, even if the ribbons are getting in a frightful tangle.

'Good manners cost nothing but mean a lot', says a notice on a door. 'Are you looking as smart as you could be?' says another. Respecting self and others is the theme which runs through this school from nursery to year 8, with much of the system of rewards and sanctions being tied in to this ethos. Bad marks may well land you in the reflection room to consider the impact of your behaviour and what you might do differently in the future.

Most pupils said that they would go to their form tutor if they had a problem, one shyer pupil saying he would rather use an independent listener box so he wouldn't have to talk in front of others. 'It's a very caring school', confirmed a parent whose daughter needed a lot of support after her father died: the school made sure there was a safe person to go to if she was upset, and weekly meetings at SEN to talk about her dad. A parent whose son experienced bullying at his previous school said he was 'brought back to life' by MHS. There have been one or two incidents at MHS which caused concern, but the school sat the boys down together and talked things through – 'it was dealt with thoroughly and communicated well', said the parent. 'I have the odd issue with friendship or inappropriate behaviour', said another parent, 'but it's dealt with straightaway and properly: questions, small or large, get a response the same day'.

'The best club is boarding', said one boy, who has finally persuaded his mother that he should have one night a week at school. Fifty-five boarders over the course of a week, around 17 a night on Tuesdays and Wednesdays, and 26 on Thursdays (a bit of party atmosphere was suggested by one parent.) Last minute requests for boarding will be accommodated if there's a space. Pupils can board from year 4, but most are older. Some pupils drop in and out of boarding to get used to being away from home, one parent praising the support given to her nervous son who has gradually built up to boarding two nights a week, and loves it.

Comfortable common room with sofas, TV and table football. Evening activities are popular – laser guns and throwing marshmallows into a bucket are recent hits, and pupils enjoy roaming the grounds. A nice supper for boarders – 'pitta bread things, and hot chocolate or milkshakes', said one boy with enthusiasm (no kitchen for snacks at present).

Rooms with bunk beds, mostly for six; cosy, but not cramped. Ample bathroom facilities in good condition. Blue sheets for boys, pink for girls; but white provided to older girls who asked. Boys' dorms named for sport, mostly skiing, with the black run stairs (roped for safety) down from their top floor dorms; girls' dorms named after flowers and bubbles (pupils chose dormitory names a few years back). An evening matron comes in for bedtime and stays overnight, and both she and the head of boarding are available to pupils who need help during the night. Matron's rooms is conveniently situated for knocks and injuries.

Parents are diverse: city, professionals and business, old money, and 'just working hard to get them through school'. A very parent-friendly school – coffee and nibbles in school every morning after drop off, and clubs including yoga, football and bootcamp; even a special breakfast for fathers and daughters. The friendly parent group quickly scoop up newcomers.

Mayfield School

The Old Palace, High Street, Mayfield, East Sussex TN20 6PH

Pupils: 354; 148 full, 67 flexi boarders • Ages: 11–18 • Sixth form: 120 • RC

Fees: Day £19,650; Boarding £31,800 pa

Tel: 01435 874600
Email: registrar@mayfieldgirls.org
Website: www.mayfieldgirls.org

Headmistress: Since 2008, Miss Antonia Beary, previously deputy head here, and before that at New Hall, Ampleforth and The Leys. Read English at Cambridge. Devoted to the school and its pupils, and determined to inspire her girls to do anything: 'they don't have to be something safe or obvious [in their careers]'. Hear hear.

In assembly, challenges Britain's Got Talent as lamentably failing to model good behaviour or taste; in fact, encourages the girls to challenge lots of things on a regular basis. Parents are confident that she handles the school well, and impressed at her knowledge of every child. 'Delightful head...very professional', said one; 'slightly eccentric...has helped us so much', said another. 'Girls like her, but have a healthy respect for her', said a dad, adding that his daughter is happy to write or speak to the head if things go wrong.

Academic matters: 'Some absolutely amazing teachers', said a parent, who told us about staff who have 'engaged and enthused' her daughter in subjects she didn't like. 'I feel that teachers really know my children', added another. A good number of top end results at this gently selective school – 45 per cent A*/A at A level, 68 per cent A*/A at GCSE in 2016. The highest marks in the country for Pre-U ceramics. The school is in the top 20 per cent of value added schools, adding at least one grade onto pupils' scores.

Maths, chemistry and biology are very popular here, determinedly bucking the trend for girls to choose more humanities. The head says it is important to create an environment where girls can make mistakes, and the approach to learning maths at Mayfield is based on this: 'Maths is brilliant', confirmed a parent. Geography is also a favourite – 'we're evangelical about geography...' A delighted group of girls were departing on a field trip to Morocco on the day of our visit. RS is 'very lively', say the girls, and a parent who described herself as a committed atheist said how much her children enjoy this subject: plenty of challenge and discussion.

Lessons of quiet, determined concentration; though an excited physics teacher showed us a burst of air pinging out of a bucket, to the slight embarrassment of our guides.

Most pupils take 11 GCSEs, which must include a language: pupils choose from French, Spanish or Latin. Class numbers in lower school are up to 15, with up to 12 in A level classes.

Pupils here happily mix subjects, splitting their time between sciences and arts, for instance, and the school prides itself on not labelling pupils and persuading them to choose options accordingly. One parent felt that that girls should be guided towards studying their strengths, though the school was very supportive when her daughter needed to change her A levels. But other parents like the open choice at A level – 'I knew the girls would struggle to choose, but it was important it was their choice'. We love the idea of the subject fair, with teachers pitching their subjects to girls. A wonderful way of keeping teachers on their toes. (As is their habit of getting girls to help interview new staff.)

One parent said she was 'worried they wouldn't push kids enough', but they have been 'brilliant at handling different levels of maths, and pushing them where necessary'. Subject clinics are open door and well attended, and pupils can email teachers direct. Pupils described teachers willing to put in extra time, one saying how her physics teacher came in early to go through work she hadn't understood.

Small library with age-appropriate books in the lower school (much liked by the younger girls, who felt that the upheaval of changing schools was much helped by having their own safe area away from the rest of the school), and a well-stocked main library for years 9 upwards (New Scientist, Psychology Review, Pharmaceutical Tech and The Tablet).

Swish new sixth form centre, complete with kitchen and 'friends' common room'. Lovely views over the countryside, study rooms with designated desks, and intimate classrooms – a full-size cardboard David Cameron in the politics room. Own clothes for sixth formers, but no jeans or leggings. A small room overlooking the chapel with beanbags and candles for quiet moments of reflection.

Around 40 pupils receive SEN help, which in this school can be anything from assistance with a particular problem, to help for dyslexic pupils or extra work for gifted and talented. 'No extra time in the real world', says the head, and the unit aims to give pupils strategies to deal with and make the most of their talents. A parent whose friend's daughter attended the unit raved about it: 'They have a very practical way of helping with difficulties'.

'No negativity smudge', said a parent; 'so many use [the unit] one way or another'. Help is usually on a one-to-one basis out of class, although it is occasionally one-to-two, or in-class help. Help is charged as an extra. Dyslexic pupils achieve at the same rate as other pupils.

Games, options, the arts: Sports are extremely popular, and there's everything imaginable here, though some, such as football, are extracurricular options rather than mainstream. Pupils have PE three times a week, the usual compulsory sports in years 7, 8 and 9, with free choice after that (pilates, fitness room and zumba become options at this stage). Girls decided they wanted to learn kickboxing, and a couple of months later it was up and running – 'an incredibly responsive school', said a parent. Riding is immensely popular: pupils can bring their own horse to school, or take part in a horse share. Fabulous equestrian facilities on campus include an indoor and outdoor school – pupils ride at national level. All have a chance to represent the school in matches if want they to, and netball is popular even with the girls who find it difficult. One parent described how her daughter was awarded a muffin when she scored in netball – 'her ball skills were so abysmal', she cheerfully explained, 'they didn't think it would happen again'.

Plenty of trips, an imminent one to Cambodia to teach children English – 'an extraordinary initiative', said a parent, with teachers managing to fit teaching TEFL to pupils into the school day. 'I was gobsmacked', said a parent, who said the trip has led on to so many things, such as designing a t-shirt, and a video workshop so that pupils can compile video libraries while away.

Two-thirds of pupils here learn an instrument, and many play them in the orchestra. Several choirs, the more selective ones singing at illustrious venues, such as Westminster Abbey. Regular school productions, and both LAMDA and GCSE drama are popular, though there are fewer takers at A level.

A vast range of options available, with activity sessions built into each school day – compulsory down time. There's even a pig club – though the last residents have just been eaten.

Food and nutrition is 'quite splendid,' said a parent, and compulsory in years 7-9, on the basis that however brilliant your mind, you can't function in life without a healthy body. There's a session every Saturday morning for boarders, and it is part of the life skills course for sixth formers – how to eat well on a budget (roux sauce and making bread – no white slice at uni for Mayfield girls).

Exceptionally beautiful artwork on display around the school, with some lovely ceramics: a pot modelled on church architecture captures the feeling of a soaring church roof, and butterflies fly from the edges of a ceramic gold fish bowl. A parent said 'we've got ceramics dotted all over the house, they're fantastic, so professional...' One student recently got the highest marks in the country for Pre-U ceramics. A dress inspired by WW1 is made of teabags and luggage labels; a half decomposed shirt shows the stress and texture of the material. Shelf after shelf of coloured fabrics and shining silks: such riches would tempt even those who can't sew.

Despite these glories, these subjects are less popular as exam subjects than academic options; but really it's about pressure of time. The girls love them, but want to do other things more – and anyway can keep up an element of artistic work during activities. Often art or ceramics will complement a science or maths A level.

Boarding: Over 50 per cent of pupils are boarders, divided into four houses by age. 'The school is ultra flexible about adding extra nights', said an appreciative parent. We saw Leeds, the junior house, and St Dunstan's, the sixth form house. Leeds has comfortably sized rooms for two, three and four, with beds for anyone who boards more than two nights a week, bunkbeds for the odd night flexi boarder. All rooms have basins. Common room of colourful squashy sofas, Wii and TV; lovely to see a dressing up box.

Plenty going on: a crammed notice board includes details of a trip to the Harry Potter studios and an animal rescue centre, and Pride and Prejudice catch up night; two-thirds of boarders are around at weekends to enjoy activities. Fruit, toast and cereal are always available in the kitchen, where a map of the world – 'where do you come from?' – shows a wide spread of flags.

All girls have their own laptops, but can't access certain sites, and devices are handed in at 8.45pm, though pupils can reach parents on school phones if need to. Trusted to keep them from year 11.

'Rooms are quite nice,' said a parent, 'but it's the personalities that make [the boarding experience]', describing his daughter's slightly eccentric housemistress who enjoys extreme sport –

'a great role model', he said with enthusiasm. 'They love and respect her in equal measure'.

Sixth form boarding, in St Dunstan's, is spread across the top floor of the old school in four areas, with around 20 pupils in each. Sixty-six sixth form boarders, of whom 52 are full time. (Anything over three nights is full time, because this encourages pupils to stay for the weekend, which makes a better atmosphere.) Good-sized individual study bedrooms. Considerable freedom and responsibility for sixth formers, who are allowed up to London at weekends, and into Tunbridge Wells by bus.

No work on Friday night – movies, popcorn and mocktails... 'food is important to these girls', said the housemistress. Brunch in house on Sundays: pupils turn up in their pyjamas for waffles and eggs of all sorts.

Laundry is done for younger ones, with pupils gradually assuming more responsibility, until they are doing their own in sixth form.

An overseas parent was full of praise for the care her homesick daughter received from the housemistress: she was confident that the school would email her straight away with any problems, and they respond immediately to any emails from her. Her daughter keeps in touch by telephone and Skype (mobile signal comes and goes). Transport home is arranged well.

Background and atmosphere: One parent said that the moment her girls walked into the site they loved it: 'They saw the school in action and were enchanted by it'. It offered something to both her girls, the more academic and the less so. Another said that the surroundings and small size of the school attracted them – 'everyone knows each other'.

M

The religious backbone of this Catholic school underpins the supportive, caring atmosphere. Pupils are of any or no faith, but they do have to attend liturgy (some think it's boring; some like the space to be quiet and think), and boarders must go to mass on Sundays. But the Catholic ethos is applied gently, and often with cake – the history teacher described attending mass at a church in France on a school trip, and the delight of going to the patisserie next door for cream cakes afterwards.

Community service, in the Actions not Words programme, is scheduled into the day: 'A fundamental part of who we are', says the head. This sees girls working at a local primary school or an old people's home, and helping with riding for the disabled. 'I think they benefit more from doing it than the people they help', said a member of staff thoughtfully, explaining how important it is for girls to look beyond themselves.

Most parents are happy with the single sex environment, one saying that she felt girls don't want to appear cleverer than boys – 'I don't want them to have to bother to look after male egos...' The head says the girls value the space to be themselves, and of boys – 'we bring them in when we want them, then put them away...' (Tonbridge or Skinners boys come in for parties). But it's not exclusively female here: there are male teachers in nearly every department.

Plenty of smiles and good manners from pupils. 'They develop the whole person', said a parent, who felt that girls from other schools are not as well rounded or comfortable with themselves and adults; another that 'they look after every aspect of the girls and every aspect is equally represented'. 'They are good academically, but there is not too much pressure', said another. Girls here are competitive, and there is certainly vigorous competition between the houses, but 'resilient, not bloodthirsty', said a member of staff.

Food is good: since the new chef arrived 'they come home raving about it'. Changes are made in response to suggestions in the food comment books: the request for savoury snacks at break time resulted in the delights of cheese scones and sausage rolls.

Beautiful buildings and grounds, once a palace for an archbishop, discovered by the school's founder when she took her girls on a picnic from the school, then situated in St Leonards. The chapel is ancient, movingly plain and unadorned. At Christmas, the village cluster in for the live crib – baby, donkey and all, the angel Gabriel singing from a balcony. The Hub (café) is the centre of the school, and many pupils' favourite place (for good reason: deluxe hot chocolate, doughnuts, and blue raspberry slush, with healthy snacks besides).

The school puts itself out for parents – one parent said that when they were unable to make the last parents' day, the school gathered all the teachers for an tailor-made alternative meeting. Another confirmed that 'if we're unhappy about anything, an email or phone call gets an immediate response'; but 'occasionally they make changes to something without fully socialising the changes amongst the parents...' referring to the extension of the day from 4.30pm to 6.00pm, adding in more extracurricular. The school says there were focus groups and letters home before the change, and this certainly was a move popular amongst many parents (a fuller school for longer is also great for boarders). The overall impression is of a listening school: 'They are constantly trying to make it a better experience for parents and girls', confirmed a parent.

Pastoral care, well-being and discipline: Pastoral care is the particular responsibility of the deputy head, who is quick to point out that actually it is a responsibility of each teacher here. This works, emails shooting around between teachers, boarding mistresses and parents so that any problems are quickly picked up. There are plenty of people for pupils to talk to: tutors, the head of pastoral care, the school counsellor, the chaplin – and two members of staff additionally trained in counselling, one in CBT, the other a humanist. 'Care of pupils here gives stability. I feel teachers will listen to any problems they have', said a parent.

Tutor groups in the middle school stay the same for three years, which means the eight girls get to know each other really well. Girls are good at looking out for each other, one teacher telling us that some girls came to see her, anxious that one of their friends was skipping meals. This school is extremely aware of the various conditions which can affect teenage girls, and staff are ever vigilant.

The head is keen to teach girls coping skills – 'in the real world they are going to meet difficult and dominating people...if they're wrapped in cotton wool, they won't be able to cope'. True to this, a parent said bullying behaviour is often 'cut off at source by the girls'. But systems are also in place to capture anything untoward, from general unhappiness onwards – 'they're very vigilant', said a parent, who described a conflict between girls, efficiently sorted out by the housemistress.

Disciplinary measures are rarely needed here, though accumulated bad marks would result in detention, where you sit in silence and consider the implications of your crime. No one has been excluded in the past year, though persistent disruptive behaviour could lead to a mutual conclusion that a girl would be better placed elsewhere. Selling drugs would result in immediate exclusion; a contrite drug user would probably be given a second chance. Behaviour out of school must be as responsible as in, and things that happen out of school will have implications inside.

Pupils and parents: 'You won't find old girls on the cover of Hello', said the head. 'They will be influential, but this is not the cult of the celebrity'. The large variety of families at this school is reflected in the mixed entry, with 50 per cent from state primaries and the rest from local preps, with a small number from overseas.

Entrance: At 11+, 13+ and 16+. Gently selective, but largely on the basis of fit: pupils attend a two day assessment, which includes papers in English, maths and verbal reasoning, and fun activities.

Less good performance in one area can be compensated for by excelling in others.

For sixth form entry, pupils take exams in three of the subjects they wish to study at A level, and a general paper. Pupils must get at least nine GCSEs at A*-C, with A*/A in the subjects they wish to study at A level.

Exit: One to Oxford in 2016 (law), others to Bath, Edinburgh, Exeter, Durham and Oxford Brookes, amongst others. Two medics and a vet in 2016; other subjects range from fashion to neuroscience.

Money matters: Encourages prospective pupils to do the assessment, then ask if a bursary is available. Seven full bursaries, one in each year group, and scholarships worth 10-20 per cent of fees.

Remarks: A great all-round school with high academic standards, extensive extracurricular and the outward-looking expectation that its pupils will enrich the lives of others, both at school and beyond. A parent said: 'They get so much right. Would recommend to anyone. Sheer awe...'

Mayville High School

165

35–37 St Simon's Road, Southsea, Hampshire PO5 2PE

Pupils: 451 • Ages: 2–16 • C of E

Fees: £7,080 – £10,410 pa

Tel: 023 9273 4847
Email: enquiries@mayvillehighschool.net
Website: www.mayvillehighschool.com

Headteacher: Since 2014, Mrs Rebecca Parkyn MA French and German MA Phil PGCE MCIL. Educated at Mayville High School and The Portsmouth Grammar School, then read modern languages at St Hilda's College, Oxford. After that she pursued her interest in continental philosophy and read for a second MA at UCL. Teaching career started at St Benedict's School, Ealing, following PGCE at the Institute of Education, London.

Career led her to Bedales, where she held various management positions. Most recently she worked for five years as head of faculty at King Edward VI School, Southampton. A member of the Chartered Institute of Linguists and Chartered Institute of Educational Assessors, she has a proven track record in the strategic management of the curriculum, academic resourcing, staff development and raising the standards in teaching and learning.

Academic matters: Boys and girls are taught separately for main subjects and the school's two-form entry means there's a boys' class and girls' class in each year group. Wide ability range, with mild to moderate dyslexia a speciality – the school has four highly trained dyslexia teachers. Lots of bright sparks too, but many who have wilted in more bracing environments respond well to the nurturing of a small friendly school. Mayville allows children to prove they are good at things. Not too much testing and no KS2 Sats as some children have fled here from all that.

Classes small – maximum of 24 in senior school, with some groups in single figures. History, geography, plus some drama, dance and music in mixed groups, but core of English, maths and sciences separate – 'because boys and girls learn differently'. Very keen on individual learning styles and giving homework differentiated for varying abilities. School achieves sound results for able children and has an impressive success rate in subjects taken by all – maths and Eng language and literature. Good mathematicians do statistics as well, with considerable success. Nearly half do three separate sciences, the remainder doing dual award. Low-ish take up of languages (some dyslexic pupils drop French at KS3) but French and Spanish offered. Technology popular and well-equipped and plenty of IT and interactive whiteboards etc. Choices for GCSE tailored to fit each needs of each group. In 2016, 33 per cent A*-A grades at GCSE.

SEN is exceptional: well staffed and impressively organised. Provision made for the gifted and talented. Sensibly, Mayville only undertakes what it can do well, so very severely educationally challenged are not accepted.

Parents report that children's achievement and confidence improves – 'beyond our wildest dreams,' one told us. Highly qualified teachers do all the right polysyllabic things – multi-sensory, kinaesthetic etc, but above all they make the children feel they are achieving. A further six teaching assistants give classroom support. One parent commented of his son: 'He thought he was an idiot, but now he's ready to take on the world.' The combination of small classes, one-to-one teaching, kind, helpful teachers, setting and achieving their own targets and more time in school (a longer day with shorter breaks and more learning time) seems to work wonders for both the strugglers and the bright sparks.

Games, options, the arts: Sport four times a week, lots of fixtures with other schools, masses of enthusiastic teams. Only one netball court on site (used by one year group after another in staggered break times) but a massive playing field eight minutes away by minibus. Mayville is also a major user of the local authority sports centre just behind the school, so facilities are surprisingly plentiful.

Drama and performance skills something of a speciality. Dance for all, including specialist lifting classes which get the boys on board. All pupils can take part in anything, with everyone fully engaged and 'needed as part of the team.' Music block looks tiny but was purpose built and has whole class space and three practice rooms. It was locked on the day we visited 'because it wasn't the music teachers' day' and is crammed into what looks like a garage space, but there is now an orchestra (masses of flutes but a bit short on strings), choirs, jazz group and rock bands. All juniors are given experience of recorder, a brass instrument and violin and many of them go on to take up instruments. Biggish list of after-school clubs – St John's Ambulance, sport, digital photography etc are all well attended – plus supervised homework. Open from 8am till 6pm, 50 weeks a year, with holiday clubs for Mayville pupils only.

Background and atmosphere: Almost 500 pupils from 2 to 16 are crammed into five town houses and a bungalow – conversion of a bungalow into six classrooms underway – but even so, the place doesn't seem squashed. All four to 11-year-olds are now in purpose-built classrooms. Airy all-purpose hall, largish classrooms, new library, design technology area and SEN centre.

The rest of the accommodation is well used – even a bit battered in places – but neither parents nor pupils mind. Parents know they get excellent value and children respond to kindness and good teaching by trusting the staff and each other. The school has been in this collection of seaside villas, two streets from the sea, since before 1900. Has been through periods of being girls only but boys finally arrived to stay in 1995. Boys use the reception building as their form bases while girls have one of the houses. Classrooms are hidden away up twisting staircases, the art room (very bright and modern when you get there) is perched in the attic and the much-used library takes up most of the main ground floor.

Pastoral care, well-being and discipline: Firm guidelines, but this is a happy and friendly school. A parent who accompanied a football tour commented on how considerate the children are to each other and how well mannered. Smart uniform with neat, trimmed blazers, pink gingham shirts (no ties) for girls and pink and navy ties for boys; girls obviously like their scarlet games kit. Tinies – known as Cygnets, Swans and Kestrels – have practical all-in-one overalls for their weekly outings.

A sense of security is key. Asked what they value about the school, one parent told us: 'It's how they make my children feel.' Good behaviour is taken for granted and underlined by the notices about respect, consideration etc that appear at strategic points all over the school. Parents we spoke to said bullying is seldom a problem here, rules are very clear and the school gives very good guidance and education on issues such as the internet. They added that nothing is too much trouble and teachers always get back to them when they ring.

Pupils and parents: Most pupils are local, though the minibus routes include the Isle of Wight and Hayling ferry terminals. Down-to-earth, unsnobby PTA.

Entrance: No academic hurdle, just an interview. They recruit for balance, so where SENs are concerned they do turn away 'the one too many.' Dyslexia, dyspraxia, mild ADHD and ASD no problem, equally physical disabilities, but no emotional and behavioural disorders. 'There's only so much we can do.'

Exit: Havant and South Downs colleges popular, plus Peter Symonds College in Winchester. Some go to local sixth form colleges and academic independent sixth forms and a few straight on to BTecs etc. Lots of pupils progress to university afterwards.

M

Money matters: Fees are modest for what is provided and parents say it's well worth overtime and sacrifices. After-school care (tea included) is extra. Academic, creative arts and sports scholarships worth 50 per cent of fees. Some means-tested bursaries of up to 100 per cent.

Remarks: A real find for parents with children who need a little extra support. Friendly, business-like and affordable, it provides a wraparound care that identifies and develops children's individual talents. Whatever they are good at – academic, sporting or unusual skills like fire-eating or juggling – the school will find it and showcase.

Michael Hall School

166

Kidbrooke Park, Forest Row, East Sussex RH18 5JA

Pupils: 484 • Ages: 0–19 • Sixth form: 53

Fees: Day £4,675 – £12,180; Boarding + £7,650 pa

Tel: 01342 822275
Email: adele.yeoman@michaelhall.co.uk
Website: www.michaelhall.co.uk

Chair of the College of Teachers: No head, instead a senior management team currently consisting of six: one college chair, one upper school faculty, two lower school faculty chairs, the kindergarten chair and the resources manager. All but the latter on a 2.5 year stint. UK Steiner Waldorf schools are strengthening (or implementing) their management structure partly in response to government-led policies. Some parents would like to go the whole hog and have a head teacher, one that was freed from the teaching load to manage and concentrate on staff development and appraisal – and to deal with tricky parents. Someone who was totally supportive of the school but would take ultimate responsibility for issues that arose and ensure they were dealt with quickly. As yet, this is a step too far for a system that was originally designed to avoid hierarchy.

Parents used to find the lack of direct accountability disturbing, especially when faced with the substitution of specialist staff and/or the management of high-spirited children. Hence more teacher assessment and faculty reflection than previously – a gifted and talented list considered in relation to the national curriculum. Growing percentage of the staff come from mainstream private or state schools and say the varied educational changes that are going on externally give the Steiner faculties more confidence in their own stable approach. Weekly faculty class teachers meetings to look afresh at the curriculum, gain advice from peers and share research. School reception well-ordered and professional with a cupboard marked PE kit for sale – no sign of the ubiquitous Steiner font on that door.

A charity, with its only trustee a company called Michael Hall School Ltd; the trustees and directors (council of management) are split between parents, teachers and independents – all elected by members of The Michael Hall Association. Independents contribute a range of perspectives from Forest Row, mainstream schools and retired Steiner teachers. As the oldest (90th birthday in 2015) and largest Steiner school in the UK, best practice and more mundane admin are shared with the rest of the Steiner Waldorf school fellowship, while city Steiner school kids in particular are welcomed to share the fantastic grounds.

Academic matters: Kindergarten feels like a farmhouse kitchen, homey and calm. Earthy rather than bright colours are used in the decoration, pictures are taken home rather than being put up on the walls – children are encouraged to find their own level of creative play and imitate the adults with plenty of repetition and ritual. Each of the six classes (age range 3 to 6.5) has access to its own garden (and a bread oven, built by the older students), where apples are peeled, crushed and juiced in the autumn – a strong seasonal rhythm. Books on the window sill; children can take one down if they are interested but stories are told and not read, pictures are used to feed imaginations. Same principle applies to toys – all unformed with no detail.

Ideally the same class teacher from 3 to 7 and then 7 until 14. In reality, staff's modern personal lives mean that this post held by one teacher 50 per cent of the time; recent council consideration to reduce the length of these sole class teacher years but current consensus against. Range of ability is huge – one parent complained that are all taught at the pace of the slowest pupil, resulting in bored bright ones, while another delighted that her bilingual children get to expand their language skills creatively while less fluent children are coached. This variety of experience must stem from the skill of the teacher, which used to be a bit of a lottery, less so nowadays with tighter appraisals and continuous training; new teachers also have mentors.

By age 13 some specialist teachers for maths, English and languages (French and German from 7, Spanish from 12). Parents have reservations about size of teaching body, sometimes only enabling one specialist teacher per subject. Class size about 18 with a traditional layout, a rolling blackboard, games and music used in lessons. Children taught to write before they read (7 or 8 – usual in mainland Europe, startling in the UK); they learn manually and are encouraged to do before they understand. Never just sitting at a desk, instead alternating with the left and the right side of the brain, encouraging both intellect (singing times tables) and body (crochet and knitting) nimbleness. Parents take great joy in the students' 'whole body grace'.

Not suitable for a child with serious learning challenges for whom a group learning experience would be difficult. Staff say it is tricky for a child to get a statement here since it is privately funded and council prefers to provide support in a mainstream school where staff skill set can be shared with a group of SEN pupils. However, three SENCos teach in small groups or one-to-one with word processors, a reader and scribes available for exams. Square pegs thrive within a huge range of different language and abilities – kids who would have been eggheads elsewhere are running, skipping and hopping and grounded within their bodies. Overtly intellectual kids will not be pushed to excel in one area, aiming to round out the individual rather than just concentrate on documented strengths.

Mnemonic power of free-ranging discussions and holistic links cannot be underestimated – walking from Forest Row to the seaside during geography main lesson, through landscape showing signs of smelting, charcoal burning and shipbuilding; chemistry experiment allowing a child to explore tens of different types of mould on own initiative. However, when the children get to GCSEs (first external targets or tests), they are doing the work for these exams in 50 per cent of the time that their mainstream peers get. Extra main lessons on practical numeracy and literacy. Whether a child stays for A levels or not depends mostly on their strengths and the family's finances – one parent says no dilemma for creative child, but another that is interested in all things mechanical may need more technical resources to explore her passion eg at present laser cutting done out of school through teacher's contacts.

Such organic schooling relies on a three-way partnership between the child, the teacher and the parent – communication between these is vital for success. End of year reports are ramped up to come out twice a year in the upper school. Some parents have been frustrated during parents' meetings (once a term) by the lack of focus on individual children – now scheduled time for each child common in upper school parent evenings, spreading to lower school as well. Lower school teachers frequently do home visits to enable a good dialogue to take place between parents and teacher about the child. Staff see themselves as meeting their children's developmental needs as opposed to mainstream schools which they see as swimming apart from them eg post-GCSE work experience at Plaw Hatch Farm, midsummer play and talks about e-safety and drugs awareness to balance teens' tendency to look inwards.

Upper school (14-19) now in the main mansion (feels more like a traditional sixth form transition); maths is streamed while A level choices mean more select groups, even though the main lessons can be in a community of around 30. These operate concurrently with A level choices – each one lasts a shorter time than they did in the lower school, but the curriculum still covers a huge range of topics (eg ecology, meteorology, economics, gym, drama). Subject cross-pollination is ubiquitous. Product design is fabulous – mat that responds to heat of food, nautilus shell light – coming out of well-led department with 10 PCs with AutoCad and Google sketch up, technology here is a mere facilitator and not ubiquitous. The purpose-built library (non-computer catalogue) is well stocked with old Steiner favourites and eight computers available for project work during the middle and upper school, the ICT department has 24, the art and photography department have four. Wifi in two rooms in the mansion, phones and Macbooks can be used, five school laptops in a cupboard, five desktops and a printer. Students say lack of computers is due to school finance rather than Steiner restrictions.

The breadth of education is really appreciated by the upper school – they feel it is one of Michael Hall's USPs. They also comment one of the few areas kept unexplored is the Steiner Waldorf philosophy itself – upper school wait until the year 12 conference for the big reveal of the education theory – some feel they could cope with that knowledge earlier. One suggested filming a nature documentary on the relationship between staff and pupils but at present no video cameras available for that. A relatively traditional range of A level choices on offer, no media, film, technology or textiles – 'quality rather than quantity,' say teachers. Exams certainly not the be-all-and-end-all but in 2016 impressive 89 per cent of pupils got 5+ A*-C grades at GCSE including English and maths; 50 per cent of grades were A*/A. Less impressive at A level: 56 per cent A*-B grades and 26 per cent A*/A grades.

Games, options, the arts: Balance between practical and academic disciplines is the aim, constantly linked into physical changes of a growing child: each class of 12-14 year olds has a chance to cultivate a bed in the two and a half acre walled biodynamic garden, literally grounding an emotional wobble with earth. Seasons run through the timetable too: whole school assemblies mark natural festivals as well as the end of term – Michaelmas, Advent. Initially, class teacher on stage with little ones, snapping fingers, clasping legs, stamping feet and singing rounds, soon poems are learned by rote and recited, costumes, lighting and sets designed for productions in the theatre. Pupils don't choose drama over sport or art or vice versa, everything is a whole class activity which bonds them socially. Midsummer play is a great example of this, post-GCSE kids put together costumes, dialogue, music and staging for a performance in a just one week – The Tempest, the Conference of the Birds.

No competitive games until middle school and then only ones that use the hands – three outside tennis/netball/basketball courts and a multi-purpose gym with lots of imaginary narratives to link different disciplines together – balancing, climbing, skipping, trampolining, trapezing, rock climbing, athletics, gymnastics, archery. Swimming only for the upper school during a three week rotation at a local sports centre, also squash. External matches in basketball, netball and volleyball with both private and state schools; 'we win more than we lose'. No football since the Waldorf Steiner development philosophy encourages upright throwing of a ball rather than kicking and heading – but one talented boy who plays for Brighton gets day release to train there.

At age 11 (apparently the peak of athletic fitness before puberty and lumbering teenage years), everyone takes part in the Olympic Games (this coincides with the study of ancient civilisations in the curriculum). Steiner schools from all over the UK and Europe come and camp and compete – but with enough categories to ensure everyone receives a medal. The GCSE years are bookended by an earth stewardship apprenticeship camp (bushcraft, tracking, a woodland sauna) at the beginning and, after the exams, external work experience work projects that benefit the school (bread ovens, boat climbing frame, environmental classroom).

Everyone learns woodwork and bookbinding as well as to knit and sew, moving from a gym bag to their own shirt. Impressive pottery, drawing is integrated into all topics – eg, while studying the Renaissance, everyone will draw a room with perspective. Initially art has a uniform 'Steiner look' – this stems from wet on wet painting and colour being the essence of the work until the age of 15, when a period when only black and white is used – to link in with the 'I love this, I hate this' period of development. However, individual styles, talents and mediums are breathtaking by GCSE and the older ones return to help the younger pupils post-exams before a trip to Italy where they sing in churches and look at art.

Finally eurythmy – described by Rudolf Steiner as 'visible speech and music'. At first glance it looks like a bunch of kids clanking metal pipes to the accompaniment of a piano, kept in check by a softly spoken lady. However, no denying that it aids the development of rhythm, teamwork and coordination – and it's fun. Nowadays there are two terms of ballroom dancing (more circle dances than cha-cha-cha) which probably coincides with when the children get fed up with it, but by the upper school they appreciate the measured left brain exercise during peaky adolescence – and the cheeky ability to spell out insults in dance to non-Steiners.

Background and atmosphere: In 1919 the Austrian philosopher and scientist, Rudolf Steiner, began a school in Stuttgart for children of the workers at the Waldorf-Astoria cigarette factory, using a curriculum based on nurturing emotional and cognitive intelligence. Today 1,000 schools and 2,000 early years centres in over 60 countries now use this holistic approach, making it the fastest growing independent education system in the world. Their curriculum is unique and, in the lower school, all teaching is done 'through the teacher and not via text books'. Michael Hall, founded in 1925, is the longest established of the 35 UK Steiner schools to offer national curriculum exams. NB do bone up on Steiner philosophy of Anthroposophy before signing up.

Many families move to Forest Row so their children can attend, as local estate agents well know. This makes for a community feel with school buses to Tunbridge Wells, Lewes, and Brighton and East Grinstead train stations, allowing children to come from far and wide – you can walk down the hill (the estate consists of 60 acres of parkland) from the A22, along the Cow Path, to the main building (Georgian listed). An ongoing plan for site development, many of the buildings are modern and distinctive, eg the kindergarten (Hobbitshire-like – the Waldorf Steiner font on all signage begs more Elvish references), the gym, the theatre. Pupils build climbing frames, edge a path and help to maintain the garden – this produces food for the kitchens (hearty and healthy), sells to the community and feeds a compost dragon each year.

M

The site and school do feel magical and slightly removed from reality – gloriously green – classroom blocks with art on walls and stained glass (created by a former parent) lit stairs encircle natural play areas. Some families see it as a refuge from mainstream education where children are 'criticised and their self-esteem damaged', 'like workers in an intellectual factory'. A few Forest Row residents call it 'Sandal City' (a lot of the villagers own a pair of Birkenstocks too), full of 'Michael Hooligans', although the monthly mansion market, school performances and Christmas fair go some way to demystifying the school community with outreach. The small number of detractors 'feel sorry' for the children who, if their parents cannot afford the fees any more, end up at the local state school 'unable to read or write' and see the children as unruly and hippy rather than confident and open. Upper school might kick off their shoes in summer (not policy) but they also hold open doors and give polite directions and make sure they don't call the play ship a 'pirate ship' in the little ones' hearing, keeping it open for their imaginations. Pupils say that outside reactions include 'oh, the special needs school' and 'you don't do any work' – they do think they can spot other Steiner pupils at 50 paces though, 'a bit rainbow hippy, a bit knitted'.

Pastoral care, well-being and discipline: Class teacher is first point of contact in the concerns procedure, followed by the chair of faculty. Each upper school child also has a class guardian and a tutor – he or she can request a particular teacher for this latter role, choosing one to suit a particular subject choice or emotional support. Ideally the one class teacher for eight years in the lower school should be a constant, could well see you through your parents' divorce, puberty, your gran's death. Obviously character clashes – children go through love and hatred of parents and class teachers – and this system teaches you to confront the things you don't like, instead of turning away from them. If open and honest conversation fails, the child may move into the parallel class (in the lower school) or leave. Peers also learn to provide support: when a best friend going abroad left one child lonely, the other class mates took turns to play with her, since she found it hard within a large group; when a stammerer was teased by a parallel class, his classmates fetched the teacher to help sort it out.

Three parent evenings a year and a year end report written by the class teacher; no ranking within the class, instead a good understanding of how they thrive. Education is matched to the development stages of the children to avoid unnecessary friction. A pastoral care team helps with techniques, even the capacity for an extra teacher for a limited period to support the social aspect of the class – less experienced class teachers have permanent mentors, which reassures parents. An Anthroposophical doctor sees the children for pedagogical related issues but a qualified nurse manages day-to-day medicines and conditions.

Kindergarten parents are impressed by the self-possession and responsibility of upper school kids; they look out for the little ones both in and out of organised school. Any smoking is done outside the grounds, there isn't really any underage drinking and the norm is to be single although there are some couples. No phones for youngest children, progressing up the school to having them switched off in a bag, then not being used in spaces were the little ones can see. Pedagogical stories are used a lot in the younger years – remarkably effective (obviously this does not work so well in mid-teens). A system in upper school for behavioural, alcohol or drug incidents – resulting in anything from detention through a behavioural contract and finally to exclusion.

Pupils and parents: Practically all local families – some as far as Lewes, Tunbridge Wells, Nutley and London. Twenty-five per cent non-UK born, around five with EAL and nine boarding with local families (Ofsted outstanding). Can be roughly divided into three groups – the New Age-ers (instinctively want their children to have as much of a childhood as possible before being forced into tests and bombarded by materialism), the Anthropops (done a lot of reading on the Waldorf Steiner philosophy) and the cosmopolitans (moved from a country where their children attended a Steiner school or kindergarten). Lots of Steiner pupils send their children to a Steiner school and many return to teach or volunteer, to help 'create innovators'.

Lots of small to medium sized business owners, educated parents making an educated choice – natural risk-takers, musicians, feng shui consultants, architects, lawyers, teachers, equity analysts, bankers. Self-selecting one income families since the slow build up to a full school day means one parent must be around for pick ups and drop offs for years – school is well aware that this restricts part-time working and now starting three long days by age 9. Expensive holidays are often sacrificed for this Steiner education, in practically all families a measured and happy decision; parents thrill in children's ability to entertain themselves with their imagination, pen and paper, no recourse to an iPad.

Those parents who are frustrated with the unconventional way the school is run are those who are least involved. Parents organise advent fair, mansion markets, donate their expertise – 'most of us parents have the equivalent of a masters in event management by the upper school' – craft mornings, gardening and building a new bread oven. The community surrounding this school looks after its own – but the outside world can be a bit of a shock for some pupils. By upper school many non-Steiner friends have fallen away. A girl who left to go to Lewes Sixth Form College wanted to return after three weeks – no exercise, she missed mixing with a wide peer age-group and she didn't like the regimented way subjects were taught.

Past pupils: Oliver Tobias, Sean Yates (international cyclist), Bella Freud, Esther Freud, Marty Boysens (mountaineer), Prof John Pearce (author and professor of child psychiatry at Nottingham University), Stuart Korth (Osteopathic Centre for

Children), Frank Dillane (actor), Oliver Chris (actor), Rowan Harrington (DJ and producer).

Entrance: At no specific age – 'the younger the better'; natural breaks in the Steiner curriculum occur at 6 and 14 years old. Non-selective in academic sense, although much effort to ensure class communities mesh. Mild dyslexia and dyspraxia fine (often diagnosed and always supported by learning support department) – more severe conditions sometimes OK as long as children are in system from kindergarten and their needs do not detract from quality of whole class education. Class teacher will interview potential parents/pupils – previous experience of French or German and music an advantage. Brighton Steiner and Waldorf School of south West London are main feeders at age 14. Sixth form entry by interview.

Exit: Up to 15 per cent leave at age of 12/13 to enter public schools. Fifty per cent after GCSE for sixth form college in order to take more vocational A levels. Sixty per cent of upper schoolers go on to degree courses at eg York or Bath; many European universities take Steiner pupils without external qualification. One to Oxford (music) in 2016. Other subjects include architecture, history, psychology, drama and art foundation. Some take gap years to improve language skills and cultural appreciation.

Money matters: School runs a bursary scheme through which families on lower incomes are able to pay lower tuition charges. To qualify, a detailed statement of income has to be provided to the school. Discounts on fees for siblings. Extras: organic two-course hot lunch, charged for each day of the week it is eaten, individual music lesson and instrument hire.

Remarks: A gentle school which aims to keep children from rushing into adulthood before they're ready and parents value for 'creating innovators'. This education will not work for every child, nor every parent – both would need to be tremendously involved in the educative process. Very difficult to explain a Steiner school without direct experience or attending an open morning – hippy stereotypes abound and you might find a compost bucket resting on a photocopier – yet this school is a beacon of professionalism among UK Steiner schools and the children who emerge are confident, articulate, international, open-minded and grounded. Lucky them.

Milbourne Lodge School

43 Arbrook Lane, Esher, Surrey KT10 9EG

Pupils: 235; roughly two-thirds boys • Ages: 4-13 • C of E

Fees: £11,325 – £14,085 pa

Tel: 01372 462737
Email: registrar@milbournelodge.co.uk
Website: www.milbournelodge.co.uk

Head: Since January 2016, Judy Waite, previously deputy head. She has been at the school since 2010, originally teaching history and English; her two sons attended the school.

Entrance: Entry to pre-prep is on a first come first serve basis. From September 2016, two form entry (32 pupils) through the school. Children feed through to the prep, with new entrants joining in year 3 via maths and English test and an interview with the head.

Exit: The wooden board in the school's main hall shows an impressive array of leavers' destinations – for boys. St Paul's and Westminster feature regularly, with King's College, Wimbledon a recent favourite. Regular places at Charterhouse, Epsom, Eton, Hampton, St Paul's, Tormead, Wellington and Winchester, though confusingly there also appear to be scholarships to Godolphin & Latymer and Uppingham. One current parent thinks that the school relies on its past reputation. 'Very few students get scholarships to Eton any more,' we were told (school responds: 'We have had seven since 2010' – the last was in 2013). Some girls end up at equally prestigious destinations such as Wycombe Abbey and Benenden. But there are also complaints about the links with London girls' day schools. 'The school has always done well in finding good schools for boys but now they need concentrate on doing the same for the girls,' explained one mother. Quite a few girls leave at eg 7+ – few stay till year 8.

Remarks: Founded in 1912, Milbourne Lodge built up its academic reputation under the classicist Norman Hale, who was owner and head from 1948 to 1998. In 2007 the school was sold to Cognita, which owns and manages a growing group of independent schools across the country. The school underwent a turbulent few years while management changes were under way but the most recent Ofsted report (2010) said 'significant improvements have taken place' and the latest ISI report is complimentary.

Main building is a converted, gothic-style house, with office, kitchen, entrance hall and dining room downstairs. Upstairs are classrooms and offices, with art and IT rooms in the attic. Four classrooms in what are essentially wooden huts in the garden – rather basic but fit for purpose, light and airy. Pre-prep is housed in the old headmaster's house. Previous head lived in upstairs flat during the week but successor won't be on site and pre-prep building now being extended and adjacent prefab demolished. Four new classrooms and science lab (for pre prep and prep pupils) already completed – more space for extra numbers.

School offers a traditional, classical education for bright, motivated and energetic pupils in pursuit of excellence. 'It's a great example of the fact that you don't need technology, but great teachers,' said a parent. 'The teachers are amazing.' Milbourne Lodge doesn't follow the national curriculum, instead adhering to the requirements of CE and the passions of the staff. In addition to the main subjects, Latin for all (from year 4) and Greek for the scholarship stream. Pupils are streamed from year 4 into A and B – scholarship stream and CE stream – but movement between the two as necessary. 'Individuality is celebrated,' the head told us. Inside the classrooms children work hard and quietly. Reference books may have seen better days but beautiful and neat work can be seen. Children stand up politely as visitors enter – all very smart in blazers and ties.

Speech and drama offered as an extra activity. Art and music are real strengths, with pupils regularly winning music scholarships. Two choirs. Large music room; tuition of all sorts is available, with opportunities to play in various groups.

School grounds are beautiful and include an award-winning garden and outdoor (heated) swimming pool. School is very keen on the great outdoors – 'healthy body, healthy mind,' explained the head. Fabulous playing field incorporating football, rugby and cricket pitches, as well as an eight-lane athletics track. Older boys and girls do cross-country runs; younger ones play a wonderful 'ambush' game in the woods (unique to the school; invented 40 years ago by a teacher and just as popular today). No mollycoddling on the curriculum – a happy Milbourne child will generally be a robust character and a very bright, sporty type who doesn't feel the cold. Compulsory outside sport every afternoon, rain or shine, plus necessary moving around between buildings.

Although girls were first admitted in 1982 (usually sisters of boys at the school) it still feels like a boys' school. 'It's a masculine school,' explained the head. Girls need to like the outdoors and feisty girls do well. 'My daughter loves it,' one parent told us. 'It's very rough and tumble.'

Moira House Girls School

Upper Carlisle Road, Eastbourne, East Sussex BN20 7TE

Pupils: 328; 60 full,15 weekly/flexi boarders • Ages: 1–18 (boarding from year 5) • Sixth form: 61

Fees: Day £8,940 – £17,280; Boarding £22,515 – £31,065 pa

Tel: 01323 644144
Email: admissions@moirahouse.co.uk
Website: www.moirahouse.co.uk

Principal: Since 2013, James Sheridan BSc MA. Grew up in Scotland and read mathematical sciences at university, followed by teacher training, postgraduate certificate in school leadership and MA in education. Taught in both day and boarding schools and spent more than 10 years teaching in the Middle East. Also an ISI Inspector.

Married to Elizabeth (head of maths at a local school) and they have three grown-up daughters, all teachers. He's a classic car enthusiast, plays golf and tennis and as a keen Celtic supporter, tries to get up to Glasgow when he can.

M

Academic matters: No setting or streaming in junior school and all classes are mixed ability – occasionally subjects are taught in mixed age groups.

French taken seriously and immediately: taught from nursery by a native speaker, and each year the hall is transformed into the French town of Moiraville where the girls are given Euros to spend at the café and market stalls and in the boulangerie, and can send postcards from the post office. Mandarin is offered as an after school option.

Particular emphasis on reading and the pleasure it can bring – regular book weeks when the girls can read to each other and share their favourite books and dress up as fictional characters. Citizenship is taught as a separate subject and involves discussion about social justice, diversity, human rights and sustainable development.

All girls are assessed for learning difficulties on arrival and are then offered extra help as required – mainly for mild dyslexia and dyspraxia. No specialist unit, children given a mixture of help in class or in small groups or individually. All have individual learning plans, parents kept closely involved. EAL also available for those who need it.

A broad church in the senior school too, with non-selective entry and a good reputation for value added. In 2016, 41 per cent A*/A and 74 per cent A*/B at A level. Maths and the sciences popular, followed by business studies and psychology. Inspirational science teaching; trips all over the world including one to NASA. Indeed, our strong impression is that the general standard of teaching here is good. The science labs are well equipped but quite small so girls taught in very small groups.

Drama, PE and photography offered. Mandarin and Japanese as extracurricular subjects. GCSEs: 51 per cent A*/A in 2016 with IGCSEs in English, maths and science. Over 20 subjects to choose from including ICT, PE, German and Spanish. Separate sciences available. Year 7 and 8 girls are introduced to five languages within the curriculum – French, Latin, Spanish, German and Mandarin, with numerous trips and exchanges arranged.

Results generally pretty good for non-selective entry and all girls are allowed to sit exams irrespective of ability – no one is turned away because they are not expected to get the 'right' grades.

The senior school learning support department consists of one full time SENCo, mainly for mild dyslexia and dyspraxia. All those from overseas with English as a second language are given a language assessment on arrival and, if necessary, have to complete a one year foundation course in intensive English and are expected to take the English IGCSE.

Good careers advice. Girls encouraged to think about their long term future from early on, and careers interviews start in year 9. Compulsory Friday afternoon lectures for sixth form – former students often come back to talk about life at university and beyond.

Welcoming, well-used library with enthusiastic librarian, assisted by student librarians. Girls encouraged to read books for pleasure and then discuss them at the MoHo Bookworms book club and book chat groups. Lots of trips and visits to bring the subjects to life – Hampton Court Palace, Imperial war Museum etc. French exchange programme, annual Spanish trip and Latin trips to Bath, St Alban's and Fishbourne.

Games, options, the arts: Vibrant music department with various ensembles, a chamber choir – 38 girls recently went to Barcelona to sing at Montserrat. Newly refurbished music studio and a recording studio. The school will go to great lengths to make it possible for a girl to learn any instrument. Drama productions every term for the senior, middle and junior schools. Biennial performing arts tour: music and drama productions at link schools around the world. In recent years they have performed in St Petersburg, San Francisco, Hong Kong and Dubai. Despite this, not heavy on or particularly successful at arts-based exams. In 2015 launched a school of music and performing arts: evening and weekend dance, drama and music workshops and lessons (at extra cost) plus trips to professional productions and the opportunity to take part in national competitions.

The usual sports – hockey, netball etc and also cricket, which is on the curriculum from year 7 – Moira House was one of the first girls' schools to introduce cricket and has several county players. Everyone does a bit of everything each week up until year 10 and tends to keep going – it is considered quite cool to continue with sport. Extraordinary variety of minor sports, including sailing, windsurfing and canoeing in the sea. The school is very flexible about outside events eg training for an international eventer in the U21 Italian team. A number of keen and highly competent golfers, a GB archer, some county level athletes and particularly strong swimmers – Swimming particularly strong – girls have swimming lessons all year in the school's own indoor heated pool and keen swimmers can opt for extra training before school – many swim for local clubs and some at national level. Very fortunate to have their own playing fields across the road. Has recently opened an equestrian centre and has a partnership with local stables.

The principal is keen that girls are involved at a local level and that the school works with the local community. The sports hall and swimming pool are used by pupils at neighbouring schools, and they also come in for Mandarin lessons and masterclasses as well as dance and drama. Moira House girls take part in the Eastbourne Festival of Music and Drama every February. Girls and staff play in the local netball league and girls also play in the Eastbourne Hockey Club teams. The older girls visit local old people's homes and the disabled and get involved with local charities.

Boarding: A few weekly and flexi-boarders, but mostly from overseas, from year 5 up, but majority in the sixth form. No Saturday school but plenty of matches – never a problem getting girls to come in for these.

Always something going on for the boarders at weekends – visits to art galleries, ancient buildings, bowling, ice skating, cinema etc. Boarding houses for years 5-9, 10-11 and Boston House for the sixth form, which serves as a bridge between school and university; girls are given increasing independence and are expected to manage their own time.

Background and atmosphere: Founded in 1875 by Charles Ingham and Mona Swann – pioneers of female education who were determined to give girls the chance of a good start in life. Charles Ingham's philosophy of 'Respect for self and for others and a sense of duty and responsibility' lives on in the school today.

A step back in time, at least for Londoners. A jumbled, flamboyant late Victorian house complete with turrets and towers in the semi-rural outskirts of Eastbourne. Comfortably scruffy in places with a welcoming and homely atmosphere. The two head girls are known as Knights and the prefects as Standard Bearers, others with positions of responsibility are called Pages and Squires.

Much of the teaching in 1960s blocks in the garden – not architecturally inspiring, to speak unreasonably kindly of them, but no one seems to mind. The grounds open directly onto the South Downs and there are views of the sea from the upstairs windows.

Junior school is a self-contained unit within the senior school and has the use of many of its facilities. Light and airy classrooms all recently refurbished with their own ICT suite and outdoor playground and play area. Includes a nursery, also known as Mini MoHo, for 0-5 year olds (takes boys, open for 50 weeks a year).

Pastoral care, well-being and discipline: Tutorial-based lessons with tutors acting as mentors and guides. Good relationships with teachers – very natural and relaxed. As one girl put it, the MoHo spirit is 'about respect and friendship with teachers when you are lower down the school, and the other way round when you are in the sixth form' 'A very nurturing school – not just of the girls but the parents as well,' says one happy mother.

Parents particularly struck by the 'unpressured family atmosphere and the fact that girls are given the space to think for themselves and the freedom to learn from mistakes'. Lots of involvement with the local community – girls take part in the Proms concert at Seaford and have even read extracts from their history project work on Eastbourne Youth Radio.

Pupils and parents: Boarders from a huge range of countries (27 different nationalities), the biggest proportion coming from Asia – plenty of cross-pollination between cultures. Locals generally down-to-earth business people who like the small classes and the all girls environment. 'Popular with parents who want a bit more than the state can offer,' according to one mother. Most of the day children live within a 20 mile radius, with a fleet of nine minibuses bringing them in from as far away as Hastings, Battle and Brighton. The two groups of children get on well, and parents are clearly very happy with the school.

Active parents' association ensure all new parents feel welcomed, host new parents lunch as well as organise summer ball and various social and sporting events. 'It is a very nurturing school to us as well as the girls,' according to one new parent.

Pupils thoroughly nice, charming in fact. Welcoming. Entrepreneurial. Old Girls include Prunella Scales, Susannah Corbett (actor Harry's daughter), author Rumer Godden, explorer Virginia Fiennes, whistleblower Katharine Gunn who founded the Truth Telling Commission. Katie Gibbons was the first girl to win the Top Gun award at NASA and was awarded an air force flying scholarship – she flew jets for the RAF and is now a pilot with Cathay Pacific She first discovered her love of flying whilst on a school trip to NASA.

If we were to single out one quality of this school it would be the calm, not at all brassy, self-confidence of the older girls: 'I can do it', 'I'll give it a go'. Unusual, and most heart-warming to see.

Entrance: Students can and do join every term as long as there are spaces – some international students come on a short stay for perhaps a week, a term or a year – very flexible. Lots of Spanish in the autumn term and French, Germans and Italians in the summer – all integrated within their year group. Accept girls with a wide range of abilities, but they must be able to follow the GCSE course. No entrance tests – really non-selective – everyone comes for a taster day, including girls joining in years 5 and 6 from local primary schools, and those coming in at 11+ from outside are assessed by interview and on their school reports. Automatic transfer from junior to senior school, but girls can apply for academic scholarships and art, music and drama awards.

Exit: Nearly all junior girls move up to the senior school. Up to two-thirds leave after GCSE – tend to go to sixth form colleges for more vocational courses. To a variety of universities, some to Russell Group and art foundation courses. Some to former polys to read everything from veterinary science, politics, history and biomedicine to product design and fashion photography. Four medics in 2016. Very few take a gap year.

Money matters: Two academic scholarships worth up to 35 per cent of fees are awarded each year. Can be topped up by means-tested bursaries. Exhibitions up to 10 to 20 per cent of fees in drama, music, art and sport, can also be topped up with a bursary.

Remarks: A traditional English girls' school with a 'cosmopolitan and international flavour and a global perspective'. Does not look for UK pupils beyond its local catchment, but for the right girl will be the perfect school wherever she comes from.

Moulsford Preparatory School

Moulsford, Wallingford, Oxfordshire OX10 9HR

Pupils: 336; up to 50 weekly or flexi boarders. • Ages: 4-13 (boarding from 10)

Fees: Day £10,650 – £15,900; Boarding £19,950 pa

Tel: 01491 651438
Email: pa.registrar@moulsford.com
Website: www.moulsford.com

Headmaster: Since 2014, Mr Ben Beardmore-Gray (40s). Educated at Ludgrove (where his father taught) and Ampleforth. After history degree at Newcastle he trained as a lawyer and worked in the City, but the lure of the family business was too much for him and he succumbed to teaching. Back he went to Ludgrove where he gained his QTS, thence to Farleigh Prep as deputy head followed by seven years as head of Mowden Hall School in Northumberland.

Mr B-G is a huge fan of boarding. He and his wife, Sarah, have done a stint as houseparents and he also ran boarding at Farleigh. While the majority of pupils at Moulsford may be day boys, the small Monday to Friday boarding community is 'key to the school's ethos,' he says. He sees weekly boarding as 'dynamic' and 'forward thinking' and believes it could well be the future for schools like his.

Boarding also 'draws staff' who are enabled, courtesy of the school's staff flats and houses, to live in what could otherwise be a prohibitively expensive part of the country.

By all accounts Mr B-G had a job of work to do in his first headship at Mowden Hall, so he must have been glad to find his next school in such rude health. He pays tribute to his predecessor (who retired after 20 years) and says, with some relief, that he inherited a 'cracking school' that was 'running very nicely' and 'fantastic' staff. He also seems to have been bowled over by the support and dynamism of the parent community.

Having 'spent his first year observing' and consulting parents, Mr B-G has exciting plans for Moulsford's future. The school already has a deservedly strong reputation for sport; Mr B-G wants to raise its profile in other areas, particularly the performing arts. Hence forthcoming redevelopment of the theatre and music school – cue more plays, ensembles and concerts. He wants Moulsford boys to enjoy breadth of opportunity in as many different areas as possible. All this, we were assured, will not come at the expense of sporting excellence. Some parents we spoke to hoped that leadership change would also herald ethos change in this area. While no one wanted the school to be less successful on the sports field, quite a few wanted more opportunities for chaps who are never going to make the A teams.

Mr and Mrs Beardmore-Gray, who met at university, both hail from this part of the world. The couple have three children – one at Radley, one at Cheam and one at Moulsford – plus the standard issue black lab. Down time is for cricket, golf, tennis and cycling.

Entrance: Main entry points are reception (for pre-prep) and year 3 (for prep). One pre-prep class; expands to three in year 3 when boys join from schools such as Rupert House (Henley), Cranford House (just across the road), The Manor (Abingdon) and Harriet House (Frilsham), which all kick boys out after year 2.

Entry to reception is first come, first served. Assessment day in October for following September's year 3 applicants. School says it's not 'overtly academically selective' but paucity of boys' prep options in Henley area means a scramble for places.

Exit: Abingdon takes the lion's share of day boys followed by Readley, Pangbourne, Bradfield, Shiplake, Marlborough, The Oratory and Magdalen College School. Boarders to Radley, St Edward's Oxford, Marlborough, Wellington, Stowe, Harrow and Eton. In 2016, 13 scholarships (to Abingdon, Radley, Wellington and Bradfield).

Remarks: Moulsford and its eponymous village sit on the banks of the Thames just outside Wallingford in South Oxfordshire. Fast rail links to the capital make this picturesque area attractive to London escapees with young families (and deep pockets). The school has always been popular with locals; its distinctive red blazers and caps give chaps a retro Just William charm and make for great free PR in Waitrose. The strange dearth of boys' preps in and around Henley is Moulsford's gain – about a third of the school's pupils come in from there by coach (about half an hour each way).

Before Moulsford took up residence in 1961 the Victorian red-brick building at its centre was a private house and subsequently the boarding accommodation for Cranford, the girls' school across the road. It sits, high and dry, on top of a steep bank overlooking the Thames. Lush water meadows at the foot of the bank do their job if the river floods and the rest of the time accommodate a fire-pit, camps and the school's fleet of river craft.

Head's study and front of house admin are downstairs and boarding accommodation is upstairs. The library occupies what must have been a delightful drawing room with bay windows overlooking the river. Room and contents have been completely refurbished and there's a new librarian to go with the new reading material.

No Saturday lessons but extensive programme of matches demands attendance. Boarding starts at age 10 and is Monday to Friday only. Flexi boarding parents must commit termly in advance to minimum of two nights a week. 'Day boarders' can stay until 8pm. Dorms sleep up to 13 and were, at the time of our visit, looking rather down at heel. We're pleased to report that these have now been refurbished from top to toe, including new mattresses (the latter were previously source of some parental grumbles). As we looked through the dorm windows we wondered if the occupants were inured by familiarity to the priceless view of river and water meadows so charmingly framed by Virginia creeper. We hope these lucky boys remain blithely ignorant for as long as possible of the hours they would have to slave in order to open the curtains onto such a vista as adults.

About 35 boys board at any one time and those we met were keen to tell us how much they enjoyed the experience. 'There's so much freedom. After prep and supper you can kayak or go in the pool and in winter there's movies'. Food – especially fish and chips – got the thumbs up apart from 'something like couscous'. We certainly enjoyed sharing the boys' riverside barbecue lunch.

General consensus from parents is that teaching is 'brilliant'. First on our tour was an inter-house maths challenge in the multipurpose hall with stage, retractable seating and very impressive lighting gantry. Small groups of boys, the 'top two or three from each house', were tackling maths problems in a relay. Later on the whole school (including staff) gets involved. Apparently it's very entertaining although we remain to be convinced by the dramatic potential of equations.

Next stop was a year 6 class in the rather swish ICT suite. Boys were learning how to select and export images for use in the picture books they were designing for young children. By way of contrast we also saw little year 2s who were learning to tell the time in a reassuringly hands on and low tech style.

Top set French was a hoot. An inspiring teacher, a bag of props and imaginative use of the interactive whiteboard kept everyone on their toes. No 12-year-old boy should be without the ability to say 'There is a stain on the pillow' or 'The mini bar is empty' and these chaps (according to our notes they were all called Henry or Monty) could bandy such useful phrases with Gallic gusto.

Science labs and art rooms are in good shape and we loved the new stand-alone classroom, all cedar and glass, topped by a living roof – it's been commandeered by geography, which considering the riparian views, seems fair enough. Music and drama are tackled with typical enthusiasm. There are currently two choirs and an orchestra; parents said that music had improved 'hugely' in recent years and all supported head's plans to raise the status of the performing arts.

Currently after-school clubs are limited to optional 'Hobbies', twice a week. This is something parents felt needed addressing, pointing out that compared to other preps the day is relatively short and they'd like a much wider range of after-school activities. Mr B-G says the 'structure of the whole school day is under review, including activities and the range on offer.' To that end a new 'head of activities' has been appointed.

We mostly heard praise for Moulsford's approach to SEN though there were one or two grumbles about cost and how out of class support timings didn't always fit in sensibly with lessons. 'Little and often' is the mantra and whether it's help with motor skills, speech and language or handwriting the school will provide support from in-house or external experts. 'Come and talk to us' if you're worried, the head of SEN tells parents.

And so to sport – acknowledged by everyone to be Moulsford's forté. Cricket, rugby, football, hockey, tennis – courts and pitches are tip-top. 'Rugby is our best sport,' boys told us, but added that the school isn't 'just about rugby'. School says all teams get expert coaching and plenty of matches against rivals such as the Oratory Prep, The Dragon and Caldicott. Some parents say this isn't the case for the boys in teams C-F and felt boys who weren't natural athletes not encouraged enough to try different sports such as hockey or tennis. Moulsford is also a top judo school (came joint first in 2015 IAPS championships) and offers trampolining, fencing, gymnastics, a climbing wall and 'wonderful match teas'.

Canoes, kayaks and dinghies are launched from the school's own creek for expeditions upriver to 'Goose Poo Island'. Forest school, camping in the tepee, bows and arrows, fire building and whittling – plenty of opportunities to make the most of school's dampest asset. Not quite Swallows and Amazons though – participation is limited by the number of craft so not everyone gets a go. Nevertheless, by the time they leave boys should be pretty handy around boats of all kinds – great for those heading to rowing schools such as Abingdon, Eton or Harrow.

The legendary post-CE tradition of throwing each other in the river, beloved by former pupils (known as Old Moles), was retired with the last head. Now boys can enjoy multiple goes at hurling themselves down a huge water slide while parents drink champagne and try not to watch. We imagine most are secretly relieved that their sons are in no danger of a ritual ducking in the Thames

What did they think of the new head, we asked a group of boys enjoying their riverside barbecue? 'He's lively,' we were told. And what should he do for the school? 'Make it more famous, not enough people have heard of it.' Other boys were keen to add to Mr B-G's to-do list with requests for a retractable roof for the outdoor pool (parents echo this one) and loos on the far pitches. The cricket nets are, apparently, fine for fast bowlers but too low for spinners. Several boys were very keen to see fishing re-introduced as a hobby. Greatest consensus was over the inverse relation between the expense and quality of the special school socks. 'Six pounds a pair and look!' (They fall down.)

With a loyal crew and new captain at the helm the good ship Moulsford is steaming ahead. Yes, things will change but from what we heard the head's plans are in harmony with parental consensus. Mr B-G told us his favourite book is The Great Gatsby but parents can be confident that under his leadership Moulsford will most definitely not be 'borne back ceaselessly into the past.'

The New Beacon School

Brittains Lane, Sevenoaks, Kent TN13 2PB

Pupils: 400; 16 flexi boarders • Ages: 4–13 (boarders from Year 5)

Fees: £10,905 – £14,745 pa

Tel: 01732 452131
Email: admin@newbeacon.org.uk
Website: www.newbeacon.org.uk

Headmaster: Since 2008, Mike Piercy BA (40s). Educated at Gresham's and the University of Leicester where he read English. An experienced headmaster who held two headships before this one – seven years at Moor Park Prep in Ludlow and at Dunhurst (Bedales Prep) where he loved the liberal, progressive ethos. Previously deputy headmaster at Forres Sandle Manor. He met his wife Lucy, an Oxford music scholar who teaches senior music, when he joined the school. They live in a house in the grounds and have four children between them. He teaches English to all year 5s and runs a weekly drama activity group, 'a natural teache,' said one parent. He believes that self-discipline is very important and life is unfair, so boys need the mechanisms to cope and must be given as many opportunities as possible. He says that managing parental expectations is a major part of the job – something which he does extremely well. 'He is very approachable and personable,' said one parent, 'but he is tough when he needs to be and knows what he wants.' 'He is relaxed and well in control, popular, fair and a good speaker,' said another, and is 'passionate about the arts and good at the big picture'. He is 'adept at managing high achieving parents with opinions and quietly sticks to his guns in a non-confrontational way'.

N

Entrance: Most join in reception where entrance is non-selective and on a first come first served basis; tends to be oversubscribed so worth registering boys as soon as possible – occasionally a third reception class can be added if there is space. About 60 per cent of boys do the full 9 years. Selective entry from year 3 with testing in reading, reasoning and maths. Those entering in year 5 are expected to commit to stay until 13+.

Exit: Send to a wider range of schools than in the past, but Tonbridge then Sevenoaks are still the most popular, with increasing numbers to Caterham and a few each year to King's Canterbury, Sutton Valence and Eastbourne. About 20 per cent leave at 11+, mainly to the grammars and a few to Sevenoaks. 'The teachers are very good at talking to parents and choosing schools and take great trouble to get the school right,' said one parent. Impressive list of scholarships including academic, sport and music scholarships to Tonbridge for the last couple of years – all displayed on the boards in the dining room.

Remarks: Founded in 1863 at St John's Road, Sevenoaks and moved in January 1900 to its present purpose built site in 21 acres on the outskirts of Sevenoaks. It stayed put during the war and even admitted girls for a while. The school was ahead of its time in many ways and introduced a pre-prep department and science, languages and maths laboratories as well as a parent-teacher association long before other schools in the area.

Everywhere well maintained with a rolling programme of refurbishment. The school makes good use of its relatively small site and the latest addition, a swanky new sports, arts and media centre for sports with auditorium, gallery, activity studio and technology zone, is already under way and due to open in the autumn of 2016. The chapel, built in 1912, only holds 100 boys, and Friday evening service is compulsory for years 7 and 8 and includes a talk from a visiting speaker, often a from a senior school.

The school is proud of its academic tradition and has high standards and expectations. 'We ask boys to strive for personal excellence,' says the headmaster, but the school 'caters for all and boys are taught at the level they need,' said a parent. Boys don't feel 'over-pushed,' said another. 'They get used to working hard and playing hard but they never feel under pressure; the school is very good at tailoring to an individual boy's needs'. Parents say it is 'very annoying' that the school has a reputation in the area for being a 'bit of a hothouse' as it is 'simply not true and there is a very good level of emotional and academic support'. The school works hard to develop confidence and self-belief and is good at spotting potential – 'my son would not get on the stage when he joined but now has the main part in the school play', said a mother.

Pre-pre and reception housed in bright, airy purpose-built block with their own Astroturf playground. Some14-16 per class and two members of staff – around half of all teachers are male. Specialist teachers in music, ICT, swimming and games. High expectations and firm boundaries and boys taught to respect each other's opinions from an early age. Taught health and hygiene and given a sticker for eating their veg. Good communications with staff mean parents feel they know how their children are progressing. Early years highly praised by the inspectors, who say all teachers have a good understanding of how young children learn.

The prep school is divided into three distinct sections: the junior school for years 3 and 4 with its own building, the middle school for years 5 and 6 and the senior school for the top two years. Usually about 45 boys per year group with an average class size of 15, but sometimes up to 20. Streaming from year 5, but flexible approach and movement between streams if required. A scholarship class is added in year 8 and the high achieving common entrance boys are streamed, with the other two classes being mixed ability. Boys have specialist teachers from year 4 and are given increased independence from year 5, when they start moving classrooms for lessons. ICT ties in with all subjects and 'it's fun,' said a boy. French introduced in year 5 and the brightest start Latin in year 6. Classical Greek offered as an after-school club from year 6. Although some of the language teaching further down the school can be 'a bit hit and miss', according to one parent, most do very well at common entrance, with over 90 per cent getting an A. Sciences taught separately in well-equipped labs from year 5. The headmaster appointed three new heads of department soon after he arrived, and a female deputy head, and the staff are a good mix of age and experience. The teachers know the boys well, said a parent, and the reports are very 'insightful'. 'The teachers are very open', said a boy. 'We can ask questions and they don't bite your head off if you get it wrong'. 'I like the fact there are no girls around – it is more relaxing and it means the teachers focus on you'.

Well-used and well-stocked library in what was a 23 bed dormitory, headed by a librarian and assisted by a team of pupil librarians. Boys are encouraged to do their prep at school. Wide range of outings, including history trip to the National Portrait Gallery and Canterbury Cathedral, geography trips for all year groups and the year 8 trip to France includes visits to Agincourt, Crécy and the Somme battlefields.

One full-time SEN teacher and two part-timers a well as EAL and maths specialists, and others brought in as required. About 60 boys need some sort of help, and emphasis is on identification and support in the lower years – all are tested for dyslexia in year 2. A handful has one-to-one support in year 5 and above.

N

Sport taken seriously with the usual rugby, football and cricket and the recent introduction of hockey on the new floodlit Astroturf (also used by the local community). Inevitably more focus on team than individual sports, although school trying to address this with some recent additions to the fixtures including inter-school swimming. Specialist teachers brought in for minor sports like judo and fencing, and sailing offered at a local reservoir. School works hard to find fixtures for the lower teams so everyone has the opportunity to play in a match. Loyal and enthusiastic bunch of parent and staff supporters. Sporting etiquette taken seriously and woe betide any boy who argues with the referee. 'The facilities are not the best in the area due to the limited space', said a father, 'but the boys still win most of their matches', as is demonstrated by the abundance of silverware on display in the entrance hall.

Mike Piercy's particular interests are music and drama and these have come on in leaps and bounds since his arrival in 2008, but not at the expense of sport. The school aims to develop a love of music in the boys, most learn an instrument and all sing – 'it is part of the culture; there is always something musical going on,' said a parent. Two lessons a week starting with the recorder in year 3 and the ukulele in year 6, and boys can learn to compose their own music from year 5. Purpose-built music and arts centre with space for whole class teaching and smaller rooms for individual lessons and rehearsals. Wide range of ensembles including woodwind quintets, percussion groups and string quartets as well as the big band – boys get the chance to perform in all three parts of the school, with informal concerts most weeks and three big ones a year. Two choirs in the middle school, one inclusive and one selective, and year 6 and above can audition for the chapel choir. Choir trip every other year – boys have sung in St Mark's Venice and at St Peter's, Rome. Two music scholarships to King's Canterbury in 2016. Each part of the school puts on a production once a year with everyone involved. Lots of opportunities for standing up in public, including poetry recitations and debates, and the senior boys hold a Question Time.

Busy art department with its own kiln and opportunities for litho and screen printing. Artwork displayed around the school includes some impressive Dale Chihuly-esque installations in the dining room, made from recycled plastic bottles and painted in the house colours. The art room is well used and always open at lunchtimes. Well-equipped DT room including a laser cutter. Recent DT and engineering scholarship to Tonbridge.

Varied extracurricular activities mean there is something for everyone and include chess taught by a grand master, model making, photography, shooting and athletics. 'It is not all about spor,' said a parent, and 'helps boys appreciate and respect different talents'. Strong sense of community and boys appear to genuinely celebrate each others' gifts. Bullying is rare and is dealt with quickly and effectively and boys know who to turn to if they need support.

Boarding offered from Monday to Thursday with space for 18 boarders – about 40 boys flexi-board throughout the week, with a handful staying the full four nights. 'It's so civilized,' said a boy. 'It's just like home'. The boarding master runs a tight ship and boys do prep and music practice in the evenings and take part in a well-structured evening activity programme. 'My son gets much more done than he does at home', said one mother.

Many parents 'high achieving, aspirational professionals who drive large 4x4s'. They choose New Beacon because it is clear about its mission of high expectations and academic tradition – there are very few unhappy parents here. About 30-40 foreign national children, mostly of City workers who have been posted to the UK. About 50 speak English as a second language and a handful need EAL assistance.

Early morning club from 8am to help working parents and after-school club until 5.25pm.

Active parents' association puts on two or three events a year, including a summer ball, which give parents the opportunity to get to know each other. Old boys include high court judge Sir Guy Newey, ambassador Sir Sherard Cowper-Coles, England cricketer Sam Billings, Siegfried Sassoon and Vice Admiral Sir Tim Laurence.

New College School

Savile Road, off Mansfield Road, Oxford, Oxfordshire OX1 3UA

Pupils: 158 • Ages: 4–13 • C of E

Fees: £9,246- £14,679; Choristers £5,319 pa

Tel: 01865 285560
Email: office@newcollegeschool.org
Website: www.newcollegeschool.org

Headmaster: Since 2008, Mr Robert Gullifer MA Cantab (50s). Educated at Bristol Grammar School, followed by a choral exhibition at St Catharine's College, Cambridge (English). Previously head of English and under master at KCS Wimbledon, deputy head at The Dragon and deputy head at Bristol Grammar School. Was delighted to be appointed and is 'extremely proud of the school and its boys'. Said of his formidable predecessor, 'I have a different style': clearly one that's an improvement and has proved popular with parents. Enthusiastically moving the school forward – has developed Saturday morning music, improved pastoral care, broadened extracurricular activities – 'so important for the boys to develop lifelong interests' – and introduced a weekly short service in New College chapel for the school plus parents. Teaches RS to the scholarship class, ie philosophy for those tricky questions, and leads story time with the pre-prep.

Married to an Oxford law don and has two daughters, both just finished at Cambridge. Still sings regularly with the Oxford Bach Ensemble and loves drama – directs the year 7-8 play: Richard III last year. Aims to affirm New College as an academic school within a small, caring environment. Popular with parents and staff. 'Listens,' say parents – a universal comment. Stands at school gates every morning and is available for any concern – 'If a boy's cat dies, we need to know so that we can fully understand that boy on that day'.

Entrance: Put your child's name down by 1 to 2 years for the pre-prep (entry of 16). Boys invited in for a session of play to check that they will be happy. At 7, a further four to six join – 'gentle assessments' in maths, creative writing, reasoning and reading aloud to head. Sympathetic to relocaters where places available – vital in a place like Oxford. Not super-selective, but would refuse a boy they thought would struggle to keep up or who would not be happy.

Choristerships – voice trials for 6 to 7 year olds held in January preceding the year of entry by college organist (director of music). 'Very simple assessment – he can immediately hear a boy's potential'. Roughly two-thirds fee remission for choristers.

Exit: The odd one at 11, though most parents keep their sons here until 13 to reap the rewards of being senior boys. Good liaison between the head and heads of senior schools. Admissions evenings held when senior school representatives can chat to parents. Advice is given to parents on suitable choices for their son and the vast majority grateful to receive this. Majority to Magdalen College School, Abingdon School and St Edward's. Others to places like Cokethorpe, Radley and Warwick. Lots of scholarships.

Remarks: School was founded in 1379 to provide an education for the choristers of New College and is governed by its warden and fellows. Tucked away in a quiet corner of central Oxford, it is described by a parent as 'a rare gem of a school'. A programme of development has ensured growth and provision of facilities including a fabulous new sports hall with a climbing wall. Light and airy, it houses a new art room, music room and technology suite on the upper level and received an Oxford Preservation Trust Award. Otherwise the usual motley collection of school buildings – original, '60s and modern, cheek by jowl on the tiny site, but the school is able to spill into New College for use of the chapel and for special events.

Class size is small – average 16 in pre-prep, 18 in prep with max of 20. Pre-prep classes bright, buzzing and cheerful. Years 3 and 4 taught mostly by class teachers, years 5-8 by specialist teachers. French from reception, Latin from year 5, optional Greek in years 7 and 8. SEN tends to be picked up in the pre-prep by experienced teachers. Parents are advised if further assessments are needed and extra tuition is provided at a cost. EAL (one boy at present) also catered for through learning enrichment department. Classrooms are mainly small and traditional but with data projectors in every room. Multi-purpose science lab with interactive whiteboard, IT room with enough terminals for all, DT room, pottery room, library and media room, etc. Head always keen to introduce new blood into the staff-room as well as new ideas – iPads and VLE in 2014. Staff encouraged to take opportunities to visit other schools and import fresh approaches.

Music 'phenomenal,' said one prospective parent. This is a musical school and it's taken seriously – 91 per cent of boys play an instrument, 50 per cent two. Some older pupils reach grade 7. Choristers learn two instruments – the piano and one other. Many practice rooms, ensemble rooms, music technology room etc. Saturday morning music for instrumentalists so that more time can be devoted to playing without the restriction of a school timetable – optional for boys in year 5 and above, compulsory for choristers.

Twenty-four choristers in school have a schedule not quite as gruelling as some other choir schools – choir practice four times a week at lunchtimes and after school, evensong five times week including Sat and Sun evenings but, surprisingly, no Sun morning commitment. Ditto Christmas or Easter. The choir is world-renowned and frequently tours worldwide. Won the Gramophone award for Ludford recording. Head encourages choristers to share their musical experience with the other boys and bring the music into the school.

Extracurricular opportunities encouraged at lunchtime – fencing, archery, table tennis. Drama specialist after school for LAMDA awards and many school productions, including annual French play.

School uses the playing fields of New College for sports, including tennis courts. Not known for its sporting prowess, though it holds its own on the local circuit. Boys say it's difficult to win when the team is chosen from so few – keen, though, to point out that some have, on occasion, won sports scholarships. Wide participation – all can have a go. Wet afternoons on playing fields (this head's schoolboy memory) now a thing of the past, courtesy of the new gym.

Revamp of pastoral care system under Mr Gullifer. Recent inspection report, excellent in every aspect, commented on outstanding pastoral support. Head has implemented clear guidelines on rewards and sanctions – feels rewards are hugely important but boys also need clear boundaries on behaviour. Series of warnings – in reality only one to two headmaster's detentions in a year. Any concerns with any boys are discussed at head's weekly meeting with staff – 'can discuss every single boy if necessary'. No evidence of poor behaviour on our visit, indeed the boys were happy and industrious. Articulate and delightful guides extolled virtues of school. What's the best thing about this school? 'Absolutely everything,' came the answer. Favourite teacher? 'All of them!' – clearly experts in diplomacy as well as model pupils. An 'OK' for food.

Majority of parents academic, medical, business. A few with more limited financial means have been able to send their sons with a choral scholarship. Head points out that the link with New College brings university into contact with many parents who may be otherwise excluded – bridges town/gown divide. Huge parental expertise, as one would expect in Oxford, from which pupils profit, as parents are generous with their time. Parents choose the school for its warmth, family feel and academic reputation. Say head has opened the door to parents – now has parents' committee, parents' choir one evening a week and views are taken seriously. We were treated to the short weekly service in the chapel (New College organ scholar provides music) with presentation of achievements and coffee for parents afterwards – 'Love to be able to see my son in the school setting,' says one; 'A time for quiet reflection during a busy week,' says another. Some prospective parents fear the school is too Christian – 'Not at all,' says a current parent. 'It's pretty low key.'

Others put off by small size, but if you're looking for an intimate, family, nurturing school with a good academic reputation and lots of music, this is ideal.

New Hall School

172

The Avenue, Boreham, Chelmsford, Essex CM3 3HS

Pupils: 1,503; 119 full, 88 weekly, 30 flexi boarders. • Ages: 3–18 (boarding from 7) • Sixth form: 219 • RC

Fees: Day £9,087 – £18,729 pa; Boarding £18,342 – £28,755 pa

Tel: 01245 467 588
Email: registrar@newhallschool.co.uk
Website: www.newhallschool.co.uk

Principal: Since 2001, Mrs Katherine Jeffrey MA PGCE MA (EdMg) NPQH. Previously an RE teacher at St Mary's School, Shaftesbury, head of RE at Woldingham School, deputy head at The Marist School, Ascot before coming to New Hall as its first ever lay principal and teacher of theology. Awarded the Institute of Directors' East of England Businesswoman of the Year Award, followed by a national Independent Schools Award for Outstanding Strategic Initiative. Since 2010 she has been a committee member of the Catholic Independent Schools' Conference. Mrs Jeffrey is married with four daughters – all educated at New Hall School.

Making the change from dyed-in-the-wool Catholic convent girls' boarding school of variable academic results to one of the UK's foremost successful pioneers of the 'diamond model' (co-educational prep school, single-sex teaching for ages 11 to 16, returning to co-education for the sixth form) took Mrs Jeffrey a speedy five years. Presumably also nerves of steel, which we don't doubt pulse beneath her polished exterior. 'She oozes confidence and enthusiasm,' swooned one impressed parent, and many laud her 'efficiency'. Indeed, the school comfortably met all the targets it had set itself when adopting the 'diamond model', notably a student body of exactly half girls and half boys. When we visited, New Hall had recently trounced Harrow at rugby and Eton at tennis – to the transparent delight of Mrs Jeffrey. However, amid all this blatant success, at its heart – and its principal's – New Hall remains a Catholic foundation Christian community with core moral values to impart. 'My aim is to shape the adults of the future, form their characters as people of integrity and kindness,' says Mrs Jeffrey. 'We are a community – no-one is here in isolation.'

Preparatory school headteacher: Since September 2015 is Mrs Carole Goodwin BEd MEd, previously vice principal and head of lower school at Colchester High.

Academic matters: All aspects of the curriculum start in pre-reception – science, maths, English, music, PE, performing arts, ICT etc. All learn French from a specialist. At KS2 English and maths are divided into ability sets of around 13 pupils to allow the delivery of a more detailed and bespoke curriculum. Latin once a week in year 6; Latin club open to all in years 3 to 6. Educational visits, workshops, residential trip for year 6, bring classroom learning to life. 'Consistent high quality teaching with a vibrant, engaging, relevant curriculum ensures that our children exceed all expectations, develop a wide range of knowledge, skills and understanding and build a firm foundation for future success.'

A well-stocked and meticulously organised library is arranged with corners for each age group – colourful stools for little ones to perch on while reading – and a suggestion book for titles the librarian said she would be happy to 'investigate' before stocking. No plans to move to e-readers as yet – 'you can't beat the feel of a book,' says librarian, who has a band of year 6 volunteers to help scan in and out.

'At the preparatory school, we aim to prepare our pupils for the future world; to be independent learners, able to adapt to different situations and of course literate in ICT in order to prepare them for the technological age in which they live.'

In 2016, 48 per cent of A level grades were A*/A and 78 per cent A*-B. Similarly impressive results at GCSE – 50 per cent A*-A. Interestingly, the genders at New Hall are on a par results-wise at GCSE, bucking the national trend for boys to fall behind by 10 per cent. More grist to the mill of the 'diamond model', allowing the teaching between 11 and 16 to be tailored to gender-specific learning styles, with co-ed lessons in the prep and sixth form.

French and Spanish are taught from year 7. Theology is compulsory up to year 11. In year 9, classics, Latin and critical thinking are introduced. GCSE students have timetabled religious studies, English, maths, science and a choice of modern language. Head of science has the final say in who takes separate sciences and head of languages gives the 'oui or non' or 'si or no', to students opting for two languages. Most students take 10 or 11 subjects, a few more or a few less according to ability. Each student in years 10 and 11 follows a tutorial programme including 'life skills' and careers education. Games afternoon once a week, with team sports and individual options. Staff reputedly bend over backwards to make sure students shoehorn in their favourite subjects – one parent reported the head of PE giving up his lunch for individual lessons with her son whose GCSE timetable was already full to bursting.

Gifted and talented is taken seriously with accelerated and differentiated learning in lessons and encouragement to take part in enrichment opportunities. The DELTA club promotes scholarly habits (including 'challenge', 'persistence and big picture thinking', 'intellectual courage' and 'metathinking'), and the OMEGA club is for the several each year with sights set on Oxbridge.

Games, options, the arts: 'Our co-curricular programme is not an add-on,' emphasises principal. Sport in particular is taken very seriously. Income has been ploughed into facilities – sleek, purpose-built gymnasium block stuffed with cardio machines and weights overlooks a sweep of sports pitches, 10 courts for netball or tennis (full-time tennis pro nurtures future stars), 400-metre cinder running track and chlorine-free pool in its own block with changing room facilities (also used by the Essex swim squad). A former equestrian arena is now an indoor sports hall with state-of-the-art flooring, while the many horse-related activities take place off-site. County and national athletes in many disciplines, including UK independent school golf and equestrian champions, not to mention star swimmers, cricketers, tennis, hockey and rugby players. A New Hallian athlete competed in the Commonwealth Games in 2014. Prep has its own games teachers but these are bolstered on games afternoons by specialists from the senior school who coach pupils in specific sports, with great success in local derbies.

More than half of the prep school pupils learn an instrument and there's a 35-strong, full prep school orchestra. Top musicians get to grade 5 with distinction by end of year 6. Lots of performance opportunities (recently at the O2 and the Royal Albert Hall) and three choirs – infant, junior and chamber (chamber choir has won the Stratford and East London Music Festival for nine years running; junior choir recently won its category too). Impressive. The first time we've come across a choir that's compulsory – year 7 boys and girls enjoy or endure a year before being given the option to remain. 'We have discovered some great voices that way – people who wouldn't have put themselves forward,' says head of music. Choice of choirs for those inclined, including 'Voces' for the broken-voiced, plus instrumental ensembles of all kinds and the occasional rock and pop band. Organ lessons on the restored Norman & Beard organ in the school chapel. Many informal as well as the formal performances. Despite a good take-up at GCSE, a small handful study A level music and the odd one or two each year progress to conservatoires.

There are regular – and by all accounts, spectacular – drama productions all year round and involving all ages, and the Walkfares Centre is the venue for all performing arts. Annual dance show is a highlight and dance A level popular. Own dance company takes students from year 10 upwards and crosses over with the local community. ESB and LAMDA thrive. Around 30 a year take art A level – working away in a warren of atelier-style studios – and about a third continue beyond, though architecture tends to win out over fine art.

In keeping with the school's focus on community and charity, all pupils are heavily involved with the New Hall Voluntary Service, which for many becomes a way of life. One pupil recently received the Princess Diana award – for swimming the Channel to benefit Great Ormond Street Hospital – but all make a contribution of some kind.

Eight houses – unrelated to the boarding houses – contest in competitions of all hues.

Boarding: Cream sofas? Cushions? Can this be a boys' boarding house? For 7-13 year olds? Indeed it is at New Hall. Quite apart from Earle House's jaw-droppingly ornate cornicing and mouldings worthy of a royal palace, the place is spotless in the face of a most unforgiving neutrally toned décor – not a muddy rugby sock nor a mouldering trainer to be seen. Either the staff deserve a medal or this is a new breed of boy. The usual entertainment – large-screen TV, Xbox etc – but arranged in such civilised, convivial surroundings that one could happily invite one's grandmother for a spot of GTA. The dorms too are a revelation – again tidy beyond belief with all belongings stowed neatly into storage compartments hiding behind the ladder treads of ingenious high-sleeper beds, designed by the former New Hallian director of boarding and incorporating a study space underneath. Magdalen House, for girls in years 3-8, is more the usual fayre – though rooms for ones and twos rather than the multiples for boys (full boarders usually roomed with the flexi-boarders) – and a comfortable lived-in look with cheery décor chosen by the girls themselves. Four other houses – two for boys and two for girls as they progress through the year groups – accommodating the 33 per cent who board on a flexi, weekly or full-time basis. Up to 16 reserved places for junior (full and weekly) boarders from year 3 onwards.

Background and atmosphere: The original Palace of Beaulieu, ancestral home of the Boleyn family and thought to represent much of the attraction to King Henry VIII of his second wife (beheaded), perhaps with good reason. Henry expanded the existing building to create a most imposing and gargantuan edifice, with eight courtyards behind a 550-foot wide red-brick frontage and two enormous gatehouse towers. Channel 4's Time Team dug up evidence of the foundations of what appears to have been a nursery for Henry's first-born, Princess Mary. Having passed through a few hands (including those of Oliver Cromwell) after Henry's demise, in 1799 the palace became occupied by the Canonesses of the Holy Sepulchre, one of the most ancient orders in the Catholic church, established in Europe long before the English Religious Community was founded in 1642. Forced out of their home in the Low Countries by the French Revolutionary Wars, the Canonesses brought their school to the Palace of Beaulieu with the intention of offering a Catholic education to girls denied this in England in the Post-Reformation period. Thus, New Hall is the oldest Catholic girls' school in England.

Today's New Hall is (in terms of footprint at least) but a fraction of Henry's pile, but breathtaking nonetheless and approached via a mile-long avenue at the end of which one fully expects a National Trust ticket booth to appear. Perhaps one of the most impressive interiors is the chapel, with its original solid wood door and Henry VIII's coat of arms over the main entrance.

Behind the long façade of the main building, which houses an impressive entrance hall with waiting room, the chapel, classrooms and a boarding house, there is a dedicated arts block incorporating two large studio spaces (which host the school's popular Saturday dance and drama schools as well as lessons throughout the week). The Eaton Theatre seats 210 and is used for productions as well as lectures and year meetings. Large library with study area for all-comers and hanging with Apple Macs. Eight science labs. Spacious refectory reminiscent of the restaurant in an upmarket London department store with a choice of three hot options (the traditional fish and chips on the Friday we visited), plus a salad bar and other cold choices.

Sixth form is a tight-knit community of 250, presided over by staff other than those that continuing pupils will have met in their junior years. Sixth formers have their own wing of the arts block, with study space and chill-out zone including snack kitchen.

The prep shares the sweeping mile-long avenue approach to the main school, with a quick swerve to the left to reveal its self-contained wing. A more functional building than its palatial neighbour, the prep school is an elongated brick-built edifice with a central corridor on both floors, with spacious classrooms leading off either side, all with large windows drinking in the surrounding acreage.

Indeed, no sooner had we stepped across the threshold of the prep school than a display case fairly brimming with gleaming cups drew our eye, and our young guides were more than happy to rattle off the most recent accomplishments – many county and national – of young New Hall academics and athletes. A member of the school council was in our midst and, on passing a board featuring his own beaming face and those of fellow councillors, he explained that the school is on the face of it run by the head and the teaching staff but that the school council also in fact has quite a say in what goes on around there. He did, however, lament the veto of a recent request to reinstate crisps as a breaktime snack. 'Worth a try,' he shrugged, philosophically. Yet more cups proved the point that the house system (houses Matthew, Mark, Luke and John) provides scope for countless annual competitions and opportunities to rack up hotly contested house points, including house singing, book week (poetry recitals etc), swimming galas, general knowledge quizzes and sports days. Every Friday, the week's house points are awarded to the house captains during the whole prep school assembly. Annual house cup presented at prize giving. Serious stuff.

New Hall hit the education sector headlines when it became the first independent school in the country to enter a partnership with a struggling state primary school. The school now lends its expertise and guidance to Messing Primary School, 15 miles away – management input, plus New Hall pupil-run events, such as an international day and community carol service.

On Mrs Jeffrey's wishlist is a new science centre and a large auditorium with the capacity to seat the whole school together, but these she admits have fallen victim to the more pressing need to keep fees 'reasonable' for parents (minimal increases and none at all in one recent year; flexi-boarding rates have actually been reduced).

Pastoral care, well-being and discipline: 'Parents remark on the smiles here – on the faces of pupils and staff alike,' says Mrs Jeffrey and this does appear to be a rather serene community. Personal qualities, kindness in particular, are recognised and drawn out, and pupils we met were certainly happy in their own skin. This is a Catholic school and although those of all faiths and none are welcome, Christian values are at its core. Support and care for others, both in school and outside it, are fundamental to life here for even the smallest New Hall pupils. New Good Hope café donates proceeds to For Jimmy charity.

Parents too are comfortable in the fold. 'The school has always encouraged parents to give feedback and support the development of the site, by running parent forums and questionnaires,' says one satisfied parent.

Pupils and parents: One clearly in touch with her target market, Mrs Jeffrey appreciates the fact that her school is surrounded by a changing profile of local parents – from the traditional farmers and professionals to city commuters and the grammar school educated. 'Some have attended the historic Catholic schools such as Stonyhurst and Worth themselves and are now looking to us for their children,' she says. Being Catholic is not a prerequisite, but engagement with the religious life of the school very much is. 'If you come here you sign up to the whole package,' says Mrs Jeffrey. 'I would hope that our pupils would leave here well-informed on matters of faith, and that they would have absorbed our core moral and spiritual values.'

Buses zero in on the school from a myriad directions daily and boarders come from all over the south east, many from London thanks to the fast and frequent commuter train service – 35 minutes from Liverpool Street to Chelmsford, four miles away. The rumour is of a proposed new mainline station right at the end of the New Hall drive (no prizes for guessing Mrs Jeffrey's preferred name for it). Long a favourite with overseas pupils, about 45 per cent of boarders, who represent more than 30 countries.

Entrance: Earliest joining point is at 3+ into the pre-reception class. Assessment is by nursery reports, parent interviews and trial sessions, but the school also carries out home visits and nursery visits, 'so that we can build strong relationships with our families and ensure that a child's start at New Hall is as smooth as possible'.

Year 7 has 120 places – usually three times over-subscribed. Around 40 pupils come up from New Hall's own year 6, although they too must go through the same entry procedure as external applicants – papers in English, maths and verbal reasoning plus a three-minute presentation to members of the senior school SLT. Lengthy admissions preamble – families have usually visited for at least one open day as well as a group tour including the opportunity to ask questions of the senior leadership team before beginning the formal application. Lower sixth has 150 places, with new entrants needing two As and four Bs at GCSE to be in with a whiff. 'Our A level classes are very fast-paced,' says principal, 'with pupils aiming for A* to B grades.'

Exit: Some 70 per cent move up from year 6 to the senior school; the rest waylaid by the chart-topping state selective schools in Chelmsford and Colchester, one or two to other independents, and a very few to other state secondaries. Even New Hall Prep children must take the year 7 entry exam in English, maths and verbal reasoning and give a three-minute presentation to members of the senior school SLT to secure their transfer.

Some 40 per cent leave after GCSEs. Two to Oxbridge in 2016 (law and human, social and political sciences), others mostly to their first choice of a range of universities to study subjects in all realms.

Former pupils are automatic members of the Old Fishes' Association (being rebranded as New Hallians) and this association numbers many notables, including international fashion designer Anya Hindmarch, CNN international correspondent Christiane Amanpour, artist and novelist Leonora Carrington, opera singer Stefanie Kemball-Read and Horrid Henry actor Theo Stevenson.

Money matters: Scholarships for Catholics, academic, music, all rounder, sport (general) and tennis, plus means-tested bursaries.

Remarks: There is the feeling that New Hall is much more than the sum of its parts, with personal qualities and integrity as central to the ethos as an application to study and success.

Northbourne Park School

Betteshanger, Deal, Kent CT14 0NW

Pupils: 140; 37 full boarders • Ages: 3–13 (boarders from age 7) • C of E

Fees: Day £8,598- 16,005; Boarding £18,789 – £23,040 pa

Tel: 01304 611215
Email: office@northbournepark.com
Website: www.northbournepark.com

Headmaster: Since September 2015, Sebastian Rees, previously head of Seaford College Prep in Sussex. He has also been assistant head at neighbouring Northbourne Primary School and director of studies at Junior King's School, Canterbury. Studied French at UCL; is also fluent in Spanish and worked in two Spanish schools earlier in his career. Coaches football, cricket and rugby.

Entrance: Taster day and tests in English and maths. The head likes to meet the whole family where possible. Almost non-selective – can adapt the curriculum to suit a child with learning difficulties as long as they are not too severe. They look for children who will be happy at Northbourne and most children are of at least average ability. Usually spaces in most year groups.

Exit: Most children go on to King's Canterbury and St Edmund's in Canterbury. One or two a year to Benenden and Kent College and one or two to Sevenoaks, Tonbridge, Dover College, Cranbrook. Occasionally a couple go further afield. Three or four each year leave at 11 to go to the grammars – the school will prepare children for the Kent Test but doesn't offer one-to-one coaching. Good range and number of scholarships each year – academic, music and sport.

Remarks: Set in 100 acres of parkland and woods on the Betteshanger Estate near Deal, formerly the home of the Northbourne family. Large, rambling Victorian house – a much-loved, happy place. Traditional values, a strong work ethic and a belief in and encouragement of service to the community. Not a grand school – great sense of informality and freedom with a cosy, family feel. Children are encouraged to climb trees, and each year group has a designated area of woodland where they are allowed to play. Some classrooms housed in very well-appointed outdoor classrooms in the garden erected by the Canadians during the war, which somehow got listed along with the rest of the house. Lord Northbourne, whose family used to live in the house, is still involved with the school and likes to take the top year to tea in the House of Lords.

A broadly Christian foundation, with great emphasis on instilling a sense of care and respect for the needs of others both within and outside the school. Boarders attend the local church in the grounds on Sundays. One class per year of about 15 children with a maximum of 19. The brighter children are extended and the less able are nurtured and encouraged. Some setting in the last two years; the scholarship children are taught within the class. Well-equipped new computer room and increasing use of ICT in curriculum. New girls' boarding house with bright airy dormitories; boys' dormitories all recently refurbished.

The French and Spanish programme is unique among prep schools. Two full-time classes of French and French-speaking Spanish children – the equivalent of an extra year 7 and 8, known as the Sixième and Cinquième. This programme is not actively marketed but is spread by word of mouth amongst families in France and Spain whose children come to learn English for one or two years. The smart French children are often from top Parisian schools. The Spanish children tend to be already attending a Lycées in France and might then opt for British or American schools abroad – tend to be very European-minded. The French and Spanish children are taught separately by French staff and follow the French national curriculum in history, geography, French and maths – the exams are ratified by the Lycée in London and monitored by the CNED in France. The deputy head is French. Children come together outside lessons for all other activities and sport (including cricket), art etc. Charming to hear echoes of French and Spanish voices along the corridors. Inevitable benefits to English children who also spend a few days with an exchange school in Lille and with families in Spain. The children interact well, lots of close friendships are forged here and there is 'much to-ing and fro-ing across the Channel during the holidays,' said one happy mother, whose daughter has been invited to France several times. 'What makes Northbourne really special is the interaction between the English, French and Spanish children. It gave my son a real head start in languages,' said another.

Excellent pastoral care – 'Happiness is at the core of everything they do,' said one mother – and much emphasis on children becoming good citizens. Active school forum for children to develop their own ideas on eg break-time rules and expectations around manners, and an increasing emphasis on the role of the prefects. Girls sometimes have special 'girls' nights in' when matron administers 'beauty treatments' and does their hair. Currently 37 full boarders in the school (mainly the French and Spanish) with some flexi and weekly boarding. Wednesday and Saturday film nights in the old drawing room.

Good food prepared on site and served on a cafeteria system. The school regularly gains the National Heartbeat Food Award – two sittings for lunch and staff sit amongst children to supervise table manners and encourage conversation.

Dynamic director of sport, a Kent county cricket coach, has re-energised sport and breathed new life into the game, and there are now increasing fixtures against other schools – although some parents feel that there could be still more. Quite a small pool to choose from which means everyone has a chance to play in a team, and often children who might be overlooked in a bigger school find they have a sporting bent. Usual range of sports including rugby, plus cross-country, triathlon, tennis, badminton, fencing, clay pigeon shooting and archery – something for everyone. Outdoor heated pool – they go to Duke of York's School or Dover Leisure Centre for triathlon training during the winter.

Gets at least two or three music scholarships each year – recently to Benenden, King's Canterbury, Kent College and St Edmund's. About 70 per cent of children learn at least one instrument, some up to grade 8. Music tech also taught and iMacs used for composition. Lots of collaboration with the local community, and a number of children play in the Betteshanger band and join the Saturday music club. The director of music is an old girl of the school. Lots of encouragement and music lessons from pre-prep upwards. Several opportunities to play in informal concerts – children are encouraged to have a go. Plenty of opportunities to stand up in public too. One junior and one senior play each year – usually a musical. Public speaking competition and occasional debates. In-school clubs include electronics, art, pottery, computers, cookery and the popular and productive gardening club in the old walled garden. After-school academic societies include The Sophists, a literary discussion group open to all and held in the head's study, bilingual society, Greek, Latin, new science, maths, geography and history societies. Senior children and especially scholars are encouraged to attend.

Busy art department – head of art works for the Canterbury Festival and produces vast three-dimensional pieces so likes big projects eg remarkable (authorised!) graffiti in the changing rooms, and won the prize for the best giant scarecrow at the Hampton Court Flower Show. The children love getting involved even if they are not very artistic. Lots of art competitions, Christmas card competition, pavement art on MDF. Local artists invited to workshops. Pottery housed in the dairy, which still has the Victorian tiles and marble slabs intact.

Good learning support – one full-time and two part-time teachers – mainly dyslexia, dyspraxia and ADHD. Problems identified early and support given either individually or in small groups, in or out of the classroom, each with an individual education plan reviewed by teachers and parents each term (extra charge for the support programmes). The few children in the school with mild Asperger's are carefully selected and assessed. School will take statemented/EHC plan children but not more than one per class. Wants to attract bright dyslexics.

The school day finishes at 5pm, but about half the children stay on for prep until 6pm. The pre-prep children can be looked after until their older siblings are ready to go home. School every other Saturday from year 4 – as well as lessons and games, a leadership course which has been going for years and is a particular feature of the school – like a mini Duke of Edinburgh scheme with lots of den-building and campfires in the woods. Very popular with the children – gives confidence and fosters team-building and leadership skills. Lots of gutsy stuff; children are encouraged but not made to take part. They are put into teams and challenged to build camps in groups – they learn how to make a camp fire and are allowed to use penknives. They then spend the night in their camps, are given luxury ration packs and can turn rabbit and pheasant into a stew if they choose. This often develops a life-long love of the outdoors. Year 8 children go on an adventure holiday to the Ardêche as part of their leadership programme.

The recently-introduced Lord Northbourne Award Scheme also recognises life beyond academia – sport, music, expeditions, drama; children complete this at different levels in their own time. They have to visit the Mountain of Sport, the River of Adventure, The Temple of Learning and the Forest of Beauty and complete challenges in these areas. It culminates in a overseas expedition.

Close links with the French Lycée in London, which sends a group down for a weekend each summer – sleeping outside in the camps can be a bit of a revelation for some of them. Northbourne children do a return day trip to London.

The pre-prep school is housed in the recently-refurbished Old Rectory about 10 minutes walk away, and caters for 3 to 7 year olds. They eat separately – food prepared in main school. The head takes assembly once a week and gets to know the children, who are taught French by French nationals every day from nursery upwards. Hall for assemblies and PE. Directors of music and sport come over from the prep; lots of team sports. Seamless transition to prep school with year 2 going over once per week for science, games lessons and swimming.

Parents mainly local farmers and businessmen as well as a few from London. Lots of first time buyers and working mothers – quite a cross-section of parents, many of whom have made great sacrifices to send their children here. Loyal and enthusiastic team of staff – some old hands and new young teachers including new heads of maths, science and English. Governing body reinvigorated by new chairman with a clear sense of purpose and direction. Friends of Northbourne Park a welcoming and sociable group. Lots of social and fundraising events – wine tasting, quiz, Christmas fair, a major summer event and a ball every other year.

Old boys include writer Giles Brandreth, composer Sir Richard Rodney Bennett, concert pianist Freddie Kempf and reporter Giles Dilnot.

N

Notre Dame School

174

Burwood House, Convent Lane, Cobham, Surrey KT11 1HA

Pupils: 710 • Ages: 2–18 • Sixth form: 37 • RC

Fees: £9,975 – £15,615 pa

Tel: 01932 869990
Email: admissions@notredame.co.uk
Website: www.notredame.co.uk

Headteacher: Since September 2015, Mrs Anna King MEd MA, previously vice principal and head of senior school. A Cambridge geography graduate and Fellow of the Royal Geographical Society, Mrs King has 20 years' experience of secondary education. She has also written for Oxford University Press secondary geography publications department.

Head of prep: Since 2012, Merinda D'Aprano. Masters in education management; has been a senior leader at Notre Dame for over 17 years. She is a writer, composer, musician, choral singer and enthusiastic gardener, cook and wine maker.

Academic matters: The average class size is 15-20 in the prep. Lessons are pacey. The whole curriculum has been overhauled to keep it 'fit for purpose, fresh and valuable,' as school describes it. Called TASK, it stands for Thinking and discerning, Active participation, Skills for learning and Knowledge with understanding – these girls really won't get away with simply printing out internet 'research' they have not really read or understood. Spanish just introduced from nursery. Good IT throughout the school and girls taught to touch type; a library in every alcove. Parents all mention 'good' teaching from a 'settled' staff.

Around 50 prep school children have English as an additional language, but 35 of those are actually bi- and trilingual, so school sees that as an asset not a problem. Two staff lead SEN, supported by outside tutors for which parents pay extra. School is happy to take girls with all sorts of needs, as long as they can cope with the curriculum.

On the up with good value added. At GCSE 51 per cent A*/A grades in 2016. Theology – not religious studies mark you – is compulsory and most pass with A*-A grades. Latin is an option but only a handful takes it. Similarly lowish take up of music and drama, despite lots of girls involved in this in extracurricular time. Art and design preferred and done well. History another popular and successful subject.

At A level, 35 per cent A*/A grades and 71 per cent A*/B in 2016. Five new subjects are offered for 16+ students – psychology, sociology, business studies, classical civilisation and economics – and there is now a group taking AS drama. Low sixth form numbers mean just a handful in many classes. Most popular subjects are biology, chemistry, history, maths – only one physicist of late.

Average senior class size is between 12-14. In year 7 the girls are taught in three groups, apart from maths where they are set in four. Then from year 8 they are set in all subjects apart from PE, technology and art. They can take up to 11 GCSEs; most take nine or 10. Fairly hefty amounts of homework – two hours a night ('more than my friends at Tiffin,' said one girl) and parents feel their daughters are pushed. Holiday homework not routine, but was set this summer for girls staying at the sixth form. 'Nothing too onerous, but kept her brain in gear', said one mother. 'I really feel they have got all the basics covered,' said another mother.

School has put a strong focus on science recently and beat 1,300 other entrants to win the School's Chemistry Challenge final at Imperial College – 'I jumped out of my seat,' said the delighted previous head. 'It was the result of years of hard work and investment'. The school's 10-year development programme included investment in science and there are now plans to put the same effort into raising the profile of maths.

Parental praise for teaching staff who 'go the extra mile', although we did encounter one parent who felt strongly that some areas could be tightened up – 'Her [daughter's] class barely finished the syllabus in time.' In an otherwise wholly positive interim report, ISI did recommend more consistent monitoring of teaching quality and use of pupil progress data. Worth asking a question when you look around.

Some seriously impressive facilities include the learning resources and sixth form study centre – a shame that more students don't stay on to take advantage of it. 'I'm very impressed by the sixth form', said one mother. 'They get so much more out of it than purely their A levels, with masses of opportunity to get involved throughout the school, mentoring and helping younger girls with their sport and studies. And career suggestions have come flying thick and fast.' School says average size of sixth form fluctuates, but is usually between 50-55, although only 37 currently.

Parents feel it's a plus that a straight A* daughter and her significantly less academic sibling could both thrive in the same school – there's a good mix of girls of differing abilities. School has around 80 pupils with learning difficulties or disabilities, of whom 40 receive specialist support, and 30 with EAL requirements, although most are actually fluent in English.

Games, options, the arts: Lucky prep pupils share the senior school sports facilities, which pays off – recent IAPS swimming champion was a Notre Dame girl, doubtless helped by her practice in the school's fabulous indoor pool. Prep has also opened up some less traditional options for girls by adding golf and football to the curriculum. School ski trip is hugely oversubscribed. Keen to get girls out of the classroom more often – and quite understandably, given the school's beautiful grounds – head is now developing a forest school and a putting green, along with 'green' initiatives like beekeeping and a school allotment.

Sport is popular in the senior school too. Top notch swimming and netball. There are compulsory swimming lessons for years 7 and 8 in on-site indoor heated swimming pool (recently retiled and refurbished) resulting in competition success. For netball, there are 14 teams so that 120 girls represent the school at various competitions from U12 to U16 and older girls head for Tobago for a tour. Cross-country success at county and national level, also plenty of gymnastics, badminton and even football and a little lacrosse.

But several parents mention that, given the seductive grounds the school enjoys, there is potential for further development of sporting facilities. Biggest bugbear is that there is no hockey – 'A big omission', said one mother, mystified as to why there is no all-weather hockey pitch and peeved to hear that the school's new Montaigne theatre was a £3 million plus project. 'Why not have spent some of that on sport?' she said. (It's next on the list, says school, and indeed planning permission has just been granted).

But that said, what a bonus – a 370 seat Elizabethan-style theatre, nonagon shaped, best for acoustics so picks up even the tiniest voice from a nervous performer. Its first production, the musical history of St Jeanne's life and her Order, was streamed live across the world to the Company of Mary Our Lady schools, colleges and convents. Parents have come to expect polished productions from Notre Dame, where drama and music are very popular – 38 per cent take external LAMDA exams and 33 per cent take extracurricular music lessons, and merits and distinctions abound. Music is not left to the older girls either – there's a choir and orchestra for infants too so that girls are into it from the off.

Standout GCSE results in art and design, with all students gaining A* for fourth year running. Students work displayed around the school includes mosaics, sculpture and paintings.

Background and atmosphere: Opened on its present 17 acre site just outside Cobham in 1937, the school is part of the Company of Mary our Lady, a worldwide educational foundation and the oldest recognised order for teaching girls in the world. It was founded in Bordeaux in 1607 and current pupils, staff and governors still pilgrimage there today. The vision of the order's founder, Saint Jeanne de Lestonnac, is embodied in the school's mission statement – you will be in no doubt that your daughter is at a Catholic school.

Set in parkland on the banks of the River Mole, the school buildings comprise the rather splendid Georgian Burwood House, home to the prep with a maze of modern buildings running off it. All is tidy, well-maintained and resourced with plenty of space. An air of calm pervades.

All starts with 80 children, including 12 boys in the Bluebelles nursery, which has just been refurbished and is bright and welcoming. Parents particularly like wrap-around care on offer – Early Birds and Owls breakfast and tea clubs can provide care from 8.15am to 5.30pm. Like the whole school – the rest of which is of course girls only – it is well resourced and the children look busy and happy.

Transport has to be a consideration as the school is tucked away at the end of a long narrow lane with access by car or school coach only. Rapped knuckles for parents attempting to drop their daughters off to take a walk or cycle up to school – deemed unsafe. There is a minibus to take sixth formers into the town at lunchtime. But generally day to day, girls have to rely on coaches or lifts from parents; 'Doesn't do much to foster their independence,' laughed one rueful mother/chauffeur. And those at after-school clubs miss the last coach and have to be collected.

But this slightly out of the way location is actually very appealing to some parents, especially those with daughters joining at 11 and looking for a nice transition from a protected primary school environment. The school feels safe, with its pretty setting, away from it all. And the strong Catholic ethos furthers the nurturing feel of the place. Even though a significant percentage of families are not actually Catholic, they sign up for the school as if they were – accepting that the belief system is very much part of the set-up here. Parents need to feel comfortable about their daughters attending masses, studying theology and undertaking days of reflection. On the school's 'reflection day', pupils and staff take a break from 'hectic and eventful lives'. It includes bible discussions, prayers and meditation, with soft melodic music playing in the background. 'Pupils and staff come back to work with a fresh mind. Young people don't generally have enough proper quiet time – there's always a red light bleeping at them from a phone or computer even as they go to sleep'.

No plans for expansion. 'I know there's a tendency to think bigger is better, but if you get too big I don't think your young people can still feel as special and important,' said the previous head.

Pastoral care, well-being and discipline: Girls are well looked after – this place is very strong pastorally with gospel values at its core – 'respect, honesty, forgiveness, kindness, patience,' says school. Lots of peer mentoring and 'big sister' schemes, while praise and reminders about 'desirable behaviour' are drip fed by staff. 'My daughter feels valued and recognised; she is not a number,' says one parent. There's a 'telling' culture and school says any necessary action will be swift. 'I think of the school as a loving envelope around our girls,' said the previous head.

Tradition of pupils helping with a pilgrimage for sick people to Lourdes and sixth formers working in a local home for the elderly and contributing to a project for disadvantaged students in Albania. Even girls with no Catholic belief get involved with this. There are still a few nuns with a pastoral role at the school. 'I think Notre Dame is very good at sorting out girls who don't fit into a standard mould,' said a long-standing parent. 'It's not a very big school, so nobody gets lost and issues get picked up'. Another parent felt that the school was well organised so that the girls all got to know each other and were 'well aired – they are in different groups, for registration, sets, teaching groups and houses so that they are not continually with the same group of girls. I think that helps avoid a lot of issues'.

It's not an intense place and generally speaking parents feel the girls get on well. 'My daughter and her friends all feel happy and valued,' said one. 'So I think bullying and bitching are less likely to happen then. And I feel confident the school would deal with it if I ever went in with an issue.'

Pupils and parents: A supportive bunch of largely local professional and business families, including a scattering of celebrities among the parents and actress Ruth Wilson and hairdresser Sacha Mascolo-Tarbuck among the old girls.

Many reminders that this is a Catholic school, with lots of 'special places,' say our young guides, including the chapel, which can take the whole prep school, and the La Mothe prayer garden. Polite pupils saying good morning and thank you to their teachers, courteous, holding doors open for each other, no pushing or charging about.

Girls we saw were a neat and tidy bunch – and it's hard to roll up a kilt. Sixth formers in business wear. Some grumbles that day to day communication with the school is a bit hit and miss and could be better for the everyday enquiry and message. 'I don't get the speed of response I'd like,' said one parent. Parents' association, Friends of Notre Dame, is busy and well supported, organising plenty of events – all the usual from quiz nights to golf days.

Entrance: Juniors from 2+ (early years) 4+ (reception) and 7+ (prep). Occasional places at other times – worth asking. The children attend an observation/assessment day at the school before offers are made – 'We look for a competent grasp of basic skills at a level appropriate to their age,' says school. 'Not ruthless, but working with parents to help them make the right choice.'

At 11, entrance assessment in English, maths and non-verbal reasoning. 'It's all humane and not hard-edged like some of the London schools we considered', said one mother. School says it is looking for talents that already exist that they can foster. Fifty per cent of places go to girls moving up from the prep school. The rest from all over, including St Charles Borromeo, Weybridge; Cardinal Newman, Hersham; Our Lady of Lourdes, Thames Ditton; Rowan, Claygate; Rydes Hill, Guildford; Halstead, Woking; Holy Cross, Kingston; Westwood, Walton on Thames; and Greenfield, Woking. Dedicated to Catholic faith, but welcomes those from other faiths or none provided they are 'sympathetic' to the school's ethos. 'Not all Catholic by any means, judging by the numbers taking communion,' said one mother. 'But Catholicism clearly underpins life here'.

Exit: The majority of prep school girls (80 to 90 per cent) stay for the seamless transition to the senior school. It's not automatic – girls retain their place through assessment of their progress during years 4 and 5. Those wishing to apply for an academic scholarship are still required to sit the entrance exam. At 18+ most to first choice universities, over 80 per cent to Russell Group – and always one or two to Oxbridge (one in 2016 – medicine). School stresses that admission tutors report back that the quality of the students' personal and school statements is frequently the deciding factor for choosing a Notre Dame student over another.

Money matters: Bursaries and scholarships for year 7 and the sixth form. Parents warn of a few extras to include when budgeting – 'There are always trips to pay for, plus lunches and the coaches are quite expensive'.

Remarks: Solid, good all-round, ecumenical. 'My only gripe would be that Notre Dame does not sell itself,' said one. 'While some come from out of London, it's not on the radar at all from Guildford, where no-one seems to have heard of it – it's a hidden gem'. Does a good job of keeping its girls busy and focused.

Oratory Preparatory School

Linked with The Oratory School

Goring Heath, Reading, Oxfordshire RG8 7SF

Pupils: 440: 285 boys, 155 girls; 21 full, 12 weekly boarders • Ages: 2–13 (flexi boarding from year 3, full and weekly from year 6) • RC

Fees: Day £9,435 – £15,135; Boarding £19,500 – £22,620 pa

Tel: 01189 844511
Email: registrar@oratoryprep.co.uk
Website: www.oratoryprep.co.uk

Headmaster: Since January 2017, Robert Stewart, previously housemaster and master in charge of Roman Catholics at Eton. Theology degree from Durham and PGCE from Cambridge, then taught for five years at Ampleforth, moving to Eton in 2001. During his stint there he has been head of the divinity department and taken a masters in education management at King's College London. He is a keen sportsman who has played and coached rugby and cricket, and he loves running marathons. He enjoys watching Chelsea play football, and listening to the music of Bruce Springsteen. Rob is married to Sam, a GP. Sam was born in South Africa where she became a national qualified swimmer. She qualified as a GP in London, and currently works in Windsor. Sam and Rob love using their holiday time to travel as a family. They have three children, who will join the school.

Entrance: No academic selection for prep, assessment morning and report from previous school. Observed visit for pre-prep entrants or else head of pre-prep visits them at current nursery.

Exit: At age 11 – handful of girls plus one or two boys. Rest leave at age 13. Around a quarter of boys to The Oratory, girls to Queen Anne's School, Caversham, St Mary's Ascot, St Helen and St Katharine. Others to Abingdon, Bradfield, Canford, Marlborough, Uppingham. Good number of scholarships to The Oratory, Bradfield, Wellington, Headington and Abingdon.

Remarks: Approach is down a quiet lane and through a riot of rhododendrons. The 65 acres of grounds are a real feature of this school with beautifully kempt topiary, sunken lawns ideal for croquet or a marquee (recently hosted 300 for dinner and ball) and, when we visited, sculpture by a visiting artist. One parent commented that it's by no means a 'ritzy' school; this may be true but it's certainly easy on the eye. Looking out over another perfect view one couldn't help wondering whether the imperfections of the real world come as a shock to departing pupils.

Our year 8 guides (who were remarkably composed considering they received their CE results during our visit) started the tour in the chapel. Although neither was Catholic, both knelt respectfully and spoke warmly of the school's inclusive and welcoming attitude to non-Catholics. When we asked what their stand-out memories of prep school were, for one it was 'all the hands-on science stuff and experiments'; for the other it was performing in the annual Shakespeare festival. The learning support department got a special mention, as did fish and chips and chocolate cake and custard.

Average class size 16. Latin from year 6, no Greek. We sat in on a year 7 maths class, impressed by the pupils' teamwork as they explored different methods of solving what seemed to us pretty challenging algebra. In history we enjoyed an enthusiastic and knowledgeable debate on arms escalation in the First World War – serious stuff enlivened by role playing and hammy French and German accents. Parents were full of praise for staff, from dinner ladies to teachers, particularly 'old hands' who might seem a bit old fashioned but were 'loved by children' and 'brilliant'. Smallish library is welcoming and well stocked, there's a library lesson once a week and, according to our guides, 'always lots of new books'. Around 30 pupils with SEN, mainly mild to moderate dyslexia, dyspraxia etc. School approach focuses on developing necessary skills and self-confidence via one-to-one lessons with specialist staff (extra charge).

Extensive games fields plus one Astroturf for hockey and three tennis/hockey pitches. As at 'the big O', sport, above all rugby, is central with local and national successes. More than one parent commented to the effect that a non-sporty child would not get the most out of the place. Creditably, we heard no grumbles that girls' sport comes second, nor that the keen but less good were overlooked. The rather swish 25m swimming pool plus separate learners' pool is a real bonus. Decent sports hall but boys' locker rooms must be bit of a bear garden at peak times – our guides thought they ought to go on head's improvement list. Seven music practice rooms plus a recording studio; large numbers of singers and instrumentalists have gained grade 5 or above by the time they depart. Serious choir (for mass) plus orchestras, ensembles etc – we were treated to a blast from the excellent jazz band as they rehearsed for forthcoming annual trip to Torquay.

The children we met were polite and sociable. Four houses, named after the school's previous locations, compete for the usual glory and silverware. What about bullying, we asked, in front of a notice board showing work done during recent anti-bullying week. Our guides were confident: 'You can tell any teacher and if you tell them it will stop.' School's extremely useful parents' handbook covers policies about this and pretty much everything else.

Our visit coincided with CE results day and was punctuated by relieved, happy year 8s clutching mark sheets and being warmly congratulated by their teachers. Some concerns expressed that smaller numbers of girls in years 7 and 8 meant that fallings out were harder to weather, but on the plus side there are plentiful opportunities for positions of leadership and responsibility. And, as a parent observed, girls who stay on don't seem to grow up quite as fast.

Boarding described by one parent as 'fantastic'. Lovely quirky dorms at top of main building, various size rooms with maximum 10 beds. Boarding most popular in the last year with pupils keen to gain experience for senior school. Regular influx of Spanish boarders who stay for a few terms.

Jolly common rooms with properly comfortable sofas and cushions for film nights, quizzes and meetings. Four bed san with nurse on site. Matron, houseparents and family live in, staff augmented by gappies. Flexi and occasional boarding possible if there's room and school will always 'scoop up anyone' in emergency. Working parents praise 'huge support' from matrons who will, for instance, review and acquire necessary uniform items and kit on their behalf. Likewise weekly newsletter that keeps all informed about what's going on.

Day pupils come from within a 30 minute drive: Henley, Reading, Watlington, Didcot and closer villages, vast majority are white British. Families, 60 per cent of whom are not practising Catholics, choose school for its strong faith-based values. Overseas boarders (about two-thirds of total) mainly from Spain. Active parents' association (FOPS) organises coffee mornings, fundraisers and class reps.

Pre-prep housed in delightful chalet-style wooden buildings (were old stables) with verandas and bright hanging baskets. Top of the range outdoor facilities include a good size kitchen garden, 'jungle' (wooded) and covered play areas and athletics track. Majority of staff female, balance redressed somewhat by gap chaps who looked as enthusiastic about the games set up for a pretend fête as the excited children. Yellow curtained classrooms are plastered in colourful posters and children's work. Multi-sensory approach to learning includes lots of work outdoors and exploring in adjoining fields and ponds. Weekly baking, art and all other messy stuff happen in a stand-alone room so no need to clear up ongoing projects. In core subjects (maths and English at this stage), a teacher plus a TA cover one topic but pupils (max 18) divided according to learning style and ability to tackle the work in different ways. RE (Catholic syllabus) once a week, pre-prep mass once a term. Lovely old barn for assemblies and after-school clubs (include Mandarin, music, dance, Lego) that run from 4-6pm starting with tea. Small charge for activities goes towards buying new equipment – head of pre-prep ensures after school toys and equipment are 'not the same as those used during lessons'.

New Little Oaks nursery now open. One or two parents commented that they hoped there would also be investment at the top end.

The Oratory Prep is a vibrant, welcoming community, just the place for your sporty all rounder – boy or girl – and now the 'little O' experience is available to their younger siblings. We were told that someone described the school as a 'sleeping giant', and while we're not sure about the slightly scary part of that simile, we agree that it has been a little under the radar – undeservedly so in our opinion.

The Oratory School

Linked with Oratory Preparatory School

Woodcote, Nr Reading, South Oxfordshire RG8 0PJ

Pupils: 300; 150 boarders • Ages: 11–18 • Sixth form: 114 • RC

Fees: Day: £16,050 – £23,700; Boarding: £21,540 – £32,595 pa

Tel: 01491 683500
Email: enquiries@oratory.co.uk
Website: www.oratory.co.uk

Head Master: Since September 2016, Mr Joseph Smith BA PGCE MEd (40s), head of the Oratory Prep since 2010, who took over after the very brief tenure of Adrian Wyles. Son of a farmer, educated at Catholic primary school and then the local comp in King's Lynn where he says he 'achieved despite the poor education he received'. Admits he was 'rather lazy' and believes that sometimes children 'need to be compelled' to learn. (Parents say, approvingly, that he won't let pupils coast, even post CE.) He 'didn't start working until university' (studied English at Liverpool) but then something clicked and he graduated with a first. After PGCE at Brunel his first post was at Colfe's School in London, then 12 years at Monkton Combe, Bath where he was head of English and housemaster.

Likes to communicate face to face with colleagues and parents, not 'hide behind emails' – a 21st century interpretation of Cardinal Newman's motto, 'heart speaking to heart', perhaps. Parents give him the thumbs up – they say he's very visible and 'understands children'. He also seems to understand parents and endeared himself to many a father at the prep school by introducing beer to match teas.

Since moving to Oxfordshire he says he is returning to the country pursuits he was brought up with. When time allows he enjoys shooting and cooking the results. Loves dogs, has acquired a black lab (wry smile, he knows it's a headmaster cliché) and plays cricket for the village. His wife, Debbie, is the registrar and they have three children at the school. Favourite books? Sir Gawain and the Green Knight and Byron's Don Juan (well, he is an English graduate...).

Academic matters: School describes academic results as 'inching up', although this is perhaps a little too incremental for some parents. Relatively non-selective intake yields solid results at GCSE (IGCSEs now in English language and literature, French, Spanish, three sciences). In 2016, 40 per cent A*/A grades at I/GCSE. Wide choice of subjects at A level and school will accommodate single students who wish to study, for instance, Dutch, Latin, Italian. All take RI GCSE (Catholic syllabus) and subject remains compulsory in the sixth form, although it is not a public examination subject. As for A level results, leaving aside art (see below), majority achieve A to C but there's clearly still work to do on the A* front (36 per cent A*/A grades in 2016; 53 per cent A*/B). Time spent talking to the director of studies about the school's 'value added' results will add some colour and detail to the statistics. Academic high flyers certainly not held back as Russell Group and Oxbridge success attests. Sixth formers are encouraged to do the extended project qualification and have tackled subjects as diverse as military law, hotel management and Greek tragedy. There's a new head of SEN and for boys who need it there is the option of taking nine, rather than 10, GCSEs, the remaining timetable being reserved for curriculum support – thus improving final outcomes. A system of reports (quarterlies) means that any academic problems/ homework issues are not allowed to slide too far. Parents we spoke to were on the whole pretty positive about this provision and felt that it would be hard for a boy to fall down any cracks. 'Our son feels secure, that the school is on his side.'

Lessons we observed were in good order: challenging, information-rich chalk and talk in A2 classical civilisation, sparky and good humoured quick-fire thinking challenges in first year English. Science labs have been refurbed but we were delighted to find boys and Bunsen burners at the original wooden benches with old burns and battle scars still visible beneath the new varnish. Usual technology seemed to be present but not dominant in labs and classrooms; library peacefully free from such modern menaces but is, apparently, soon to be networked into the 21st century.

The area is hardly undersupplied with high-achieving academic schools but these are not for everyone. Parents we spoke to had chosen The Oratory because it offered their boys an academic environment that is individually challenging without being overly competitive – along with lashings of unashamedly competitive sport. School acknowledges that the timetable might seem a little old fashioned and some parents observed that there is a certain amount of 'wasted time' post games that could be put to more profitable use. Dr GSG tentatively wonders if shaving just one or two hours a week from the time spent on corpore sano might not improve the mens sana still further.

Games, options, the arts: Let there be no mistake, this is not a school for boys who don't enjoy running around or those who raise a cynical eyebrow at competitive sport (such boys do exist). Sport is big here, pitches seemingly endless and there's nowhere to hide. Cricket is played on a glorious sward with views over the Chilterns and Thames valley and, apparently, 'the best match teas.' New £5m sports centre with 25m pool. Morning lessons and lunch are followed by two and a half hours of rugby, football, cricket, rowing, real tennis, shooting, swimming, golf and the rest (delete as appropriate according to preference/season). Sport happens every day, apart from Thursdays when it's CCF, compulsory until fifth year after which the less military minded can take part in conservation work or community service. No wonder The Oratory was crowned Sports School of the Year in recent Education Business Awards (this in addition to similar accolades in previous years). The yellow and black-hooped Oratorian rugby players are formidable foes for many opposing teams drawn from larger schools. Celebrations for the school's 150th anniversary were heightened by the 1st XV declaring an unbeaten season, as did the junior colts A and B teams. No sloping off for sixth formers either. Sport may be big, but it's also inclusive and everyone gets to play in matches whether representing school or house. We asked a number of boys what they thought about this during our visit but were met with rather blank responses. 'If you don't like rugby you can do shooting.' And boys who don't want to do rugby or shooting? 'It's probably not the right school for them,' we were told but got the impression that such boys were beyond the imagination of Oratory chaps.

And so to art. Some schools have art rooms, others may boast art departments; the Oratory says it has an art department but what it really has is a kingdom. Results in art and design subjects, both at GCSE, A level, Pre-U and foundation (yes, foundation) are in a league of their own. School has won GSG top boys' school for A level art award many times. All those taking Pre-U art and design got at least D3 (A equivalent) in 2016 and everyone who took art A level got A*. Wonderful facilities (printmaking, etching, ceramics, DT, sculpture) arranged around a gallery corridor with tomes on plinths open at pertinent pages. A professional painter gives drawing lessons or, as he describes it, 'lessons in how to look,' and boys work standing (no chairs allowed) at easels. There's a dark room too; in these days of ubiquitous cameras and instant images, all boys learn the ancient art of developing photographic prints.

Culture more than holds its own alongside sport. Plenty of music, Schola Cantorum sings at masses, vespers and school functions and there's a variety of bands, orchestras and ensembles. Popular programme of visiting speakers. The Hopkins society (named after poet Gerard Manley Hopkins who was a master at The Oratory School under Cardinal Newman in the 1860s) oversees cultural activities such as trips to the theatre and also runs a bookshop. Sixth formers debate and deliver papers on a range of topics at Windhover Society meetings (named after Hopkins' poem – nice to see the old chap getting a double look in). Drama is a popular after school option, girls are borrowed from nearby Our Lady's Abingdon or St Anne's Caversham, but as an academic subject it is perhaps more Cinderella than Fame. The new 200 seat theatre complete with the latest sound and lighting technology may inspire future thespians.

Boarding: Boarding houses we saw were in pretty good nick; there are two brand new and three refurbished. Seniors have single study bedrooms, younger boys are four to a room and occupants are mixed up every half term. Just under 10 per cent of boarders are from overseas.

St Philip house is for junior boys (11-13) and they have separate recreation, social and teaching areas as well as their own sports teams and clubs. Day boys have a locker room (and we do mean just lockers, nary a chair or poster) in each house, but perhaps they are not intended to linger here. Resident house parents, live-in tutors plus a day housemother and gappies oversee proceedings. In senior houses boys are responsible for washing and ironing their own clothes – with some assistance at first; great training for future domestic harmony we thought, but limited evidence of ironing (although the Spanish boys are apparently exemplary at this task).

Background and atmosphere: The Oratory School was founded in 1859 by Cardinal John Henry Newman. Newman, who was beatified in 2010, was a Christian thinker and educational pioneer and the school was intended as a boarding school along the lines of the English public schools ('Eton minus its wickedness') serving England's Catholic community. Newman's personal motto is also the school's: 'Cor ad cor loquitur' (Heart speaking to heart). While it remains a proudly Catholic institution the school welcomes boys of all faiths and none; the doctrine of valuing the special gifts of every individual makes The Oratory an accepting and welcoming community.

The school may be only 20 minutes' drive from Reading but enjoys, to quote Hopkins out of context (but not out of county), a 'sweet especial rural scene.' Visitors ascend a drive flanked by red maples and velvety playing fields leading to the Queen Anne style manor house, home to the school since its move from Birmingham in 1942. Grounds, all 400 acres of them, are immaculately maintained. Front of house is impressive with echoing marble foyer and arresting 'black room' (black and gold are Papal colours) used for concerts and teas. Business areas the usual confusion of scuffed corridors and unremarkable teaching rooms. Pace art department, school not lavishly decorated with boys' efforts, rather restrained, formal atmosphere prevails – but our visit was at the start of term.

Pastoral care, well-being and discipline: Sensible rules re use of laptops, mobiles, social networking sites. Junior chapel is in a rather charming former tithe barn, senior chapel is a slightly less inspiring modernish building. Daily prayers in houses, weekly assembly for all; Sunday evening mass for all boarders, optional for day boys. Non-Catholic parents we spoke to seemed to have different perceptions of the religion's role in school life. One thought it was a dominant (dominating) feature; another didn't think it impinged too much on their boy's school day. All participate in the spiritual life of the school and Catholic and non-Catholic boys serve at mass.

Not much in the way of transgression: one imagines exhaustion may be a contributory factor (the school's mantra is 'a busy boy is a happy boy'); three hours of games every day plus weekend matches and evening activities such as circuit training must take the edge off boyish over-exuberance. In those cases where it doesn't, standard regime of detentions is called into play. Exonerated in a recent case where a housemistress sued the school for unfair dismissal – though the case did reveal some extremely unsavoury behaviour amongst one or two boys. After matches on Saturday boarders can go into Reading; some parents felt older boys left a little too much to their own devices on these trips. Houses have cinema and steak nights, pool competitions etc and there are socials with girls from Queen Anne's Caversham and St George's Ascot as well as ballroom dancing for the lower sixth – culminating in a ball held at Queen Anne's.

Our guides thought the food was 'excellent'. 'There's loads of it. It's boy food,' they said. So, anyone for seconds of slugs, snails and puppy dogs' tails? Breakfasts came in for especial praise: 'you can have cereal and then the works, every day'. Boarders can supplement with toast, pot noodles etc from the kitchens on each floor. Newly formed food council has managed to get Cocoa Pops onto the breakfast menu but on the whole one feels that the school is closer to benign dictatorship than democracy. The school day officially ends at 7pm after prep but day boys may question the logic of going home; some live up to an hour's drive away and there's no bus service. Parents advise packing provisions for pick up at 7pm because supper is not provided for day boys (although those staying on for other activities get supper and it's not billed). Boys can stay overnight if they are involved in evening activities but we have also heard that some GCSE options necessitate staying in school until 9pm. Boarding numbers certainly increase in the upper years, pragmatism triumphing over home comforts perhaps.

Pupils and parents: The old fashioned certainties are all present and correct here. Boys are confident, smart, polite and look you in the eye. RC and non-RC – all religions welcome. Day and flexi-boarding pupils come from Reading and South Oxfordshire villages. Boarding is a cosmopolitan mix of UK boys, those from European Catholic families (Spain in particular, some for just one year) and Russians; fewer Chinese boys than at other places. No parents' association but plenty of opportunities for fraternisation at matches etc.

Entrance: At 11 by English, maths and non-verbal reasoning exams plus informal interview; at 13, CE pass at around 55 per cent required plus head's report from previous school and interview. Numbers from nearly Oratory Prep. Special consideration will be given to brothers of boys already in school and the sons of old boys. Five C grades at GCSE minimum entry to sixth form.

Exit: In 2016 destinations ranged from chemical engineering at Bath to classics at Durham.

Money matters: Scholarships and exhibitions up to half fees available: academic, art, music, sport and all-rounder. Generous bursaries. Extra charges for specialist sports coaching eg golf, real tennis, books, trips, laundry and haircuts.

Remarks: One of a kind. Go and explore, meet the head, chat to the boys – we doubt you will be undecided by the end of your visit. If you have an exuberant, energetic boy with an artistic bent this could be the perfect match.

Our Lady's Abingdon

O

Radley Road, Abingdon, Oxfordshire OX14 3PS

Pupils: 488 • Ages: 3–18 • Sixth form: 86 • RC

Fees: £8,079 – £14,355 pa

Tel: 01235 524658
Email: office@olab.org.uk
Website: www.olab.org.uk

Principal: Since 2012, Mr Stephen Oliver BA MLitt PGCE (50s), previously deputy head of St Benedict's, Ealing. Educated at the universities of Birmingham (Latin with Greek), Cambridge (PGCE) and St Andrews (ancient history) and has taught at Stonyhurst, the Royal Grammar School, Guildford, Uppingham and Haberdashers' Aske's School.

Was a novice monk at Downside Abbey for a year and a half in his 30s in between teaching posts. Enjoys cricket, jazz and writing – has published Smoke in the Sanctuary, a comic novel set in a Catholic parish in the west of England, and is currently writing his second novel. Frequent, erudite blogs on the school website clearly demonstrate his literary leanings.

This is his first headship, and he says that he was drawn to OLA's 'calm atmosphere' and 'nurturing quality'. He enjoys the variety of the job, keeps his hand in teaching Latin and is 'never bored for a second.' Although business-smart with impeccable dress-sense and manners, he fervently denounces the 'creeping corporate culture' increasingly apparent in many of today's independent schools. Married to Caroline; three young children, all at the junior school.

Head of junior school: Since September 2016 Ms Erika Kirwan, previously a member of the senior leadership team at St Mary's Catholic Primary School in Hornchurch, Essex. Before this she was acting deputy head of New Hall Preparatory School in Chelmsford. She has also taught in countries including Egypt, Poland and Portugal. Classics degree from Cambridge, PGCE in primary education and masters from the Institute of Education.

Academic matters: The school motto is 'Age quod agis' (Whatever you do, do well) and while grades are strong, emphasis is on cultivating confident, well-balanced members of society rather than Nobel Prize winners. Teaching in the junior school loosely follows the national curriculum: 'we adapt it to our needs'. In the classes we visited, we didn't see a single teacher behind a desk but instead often huddled down at eye-level with the children, friendly enthusiasm combined with focused attention. Older children were quietly sitting down, hands up and no-nonsense.

Students take an average of 10 GCSEs, with 50 per cent of grades A*/A in 2016. The school follows the AQA syllabus for science and additional science with further enrichment and practical assessments helping ensure that over half the students take one or more science subjects at A level – with solid results.

At A level, 28 per cent A*/A grades in 2016 and 57 per cent A*-B. As more boys filter through to sixth form (the school turned co-ed in 2009), the range of subjects on offer is evolving to reflect this demographic shift. For instance, product design has just been added at A level to run alongside food and textiles design and technology subjects. Now offers EPQ. As you might expect at a Catholic school, religious studies is a core subject and all pupils take it at GCSE – they've got a new suite of classrooms together with the PE department, as well as a new science lab.

Touring the classrooms, obvious efforts are made to inject imagination and fun into learning. One year 8 Latin class in the middle of learning about Pompeii had just scattered outside to start building volcanoes. As one student remarked, 'The teachers work hard to make sure lessons aren't boring'.

Games, options, the arts: Colourful artwork adorns the corridors and walls of the junior school and we eavesdropped on a delightful class guided reading of Ted Hughes' The Iron Man. We had a fright upon discovering a full-size coffin laid out in one room, only for the drama teacher to pop up and explain its presence as a prop for the summer performance of Oliver!. 'One of the dads is an undertaker – very handy!' she exclaimed with glee. The senior school has a long-held reputation for the quality of its art, design and technology, and as you enter through its light and lofty Mall, walls are adorned with quite breathtaking artwork. There is good take-up of art and DT at GCSE and A level.

OLA has its own drama studio, equipped with Wifi, audio-visual equipment and professional video cameras. Regular drama performances take place in the school auditorium, which has a seating capacity of 400. On the day we visited, pupils were rehearsing in glorious sunshine for an upcoming outdoor production of Wind in the Willows. Music provision is also strong, with five rehearsal rooms and an ICT suite equipped with the latest music-writing software. The whole school takes part in the annual house singing competition, and carol services often take place at Dorchester Abbey.

The roomy and well-stocked Ratcliffe Library also incorporates a sixth form study centre. Recently renamed to commemorate former pupil, first world war veteran and military cross recipient, Bertram Ratcliffe, the library is also at the heart of the school's very successful annual Festival of Reading.

The school has an impressive 25m pool located between the junior and senior schools. Tennis and netball courts are on the main school site, while playing fields and athletics facilities are just down the road at Barton Field. Hockey is played at nearby Tilsley Park, recently taken over by Abingdon School. However, as parent of a year 9 boy pointed out, the school is perhaps best suited to 'boys who have other interests than playing rugby every five minutes'. Junior school sees itself as an 'all-round' school, although perhaps not for the super-sporty. 'We don't shine at sports', especially when pitted against the many local preps. 'We often come away bruised but happy'.

The extracurricular offering is impressive. Students are expected to get involved in at least three lunchtime and after-school clubs every term, with choices ranging from chess to judo to Young Enterprise and justice and peace group. Duke of Edinburgh is particularly strong. Trips outside school are an important part of the educational experience and expeditions have included climbing Mount Kenya and working in an orphanage in Patagonia. Forest school is a big hit with junior pupils, and recent junior school trips included Marwell Zoo and Sulgrave Manor. At the time of our visit, year 2 children had just spent the night in the school gym to prepare them for their first residential. The sixth form was in the middle of its annual enrichment week, and we witnessed clouds of icing sugar in the auditorium during some enthusiastic cake decorating, while other students were preparing to embark on a treasure hunt to Oxford.

Background and atmosphere: The school was founded in 1860 by Sister Clare Moore, a nun from the order of the Sisters of Mercy who worked closely with Florence Nightingale in the Crimean War. The Sisters are still represented on the board of governors and visit on various occasions during the school year.

The junior school incorporates the original convent buildings and the charming nursery is housed in the nuns' old laundry room. Red brick, leaded windows and giant arch doorways lend an atmosphere of quaint gothic. The senior school is much more modern with work ongoing to improve and extend the space. Highlights include the new DT centre, emblazoned with signs declaring 'Visioneering' and 'Imagineering', and a smart new cafe open to years 10 and above with hot pressed panini, pastrami salad and tuna niçoise on the menu. GSG's guided tour didn't include the dining hall, perhaps unsurprisingly as it was mentioned by some parents as desperately needing a facelift (although GSG heard only praise from students and parents about the food). School says that work to improve the space is planned.

The school went co-ed in 2009, largely due to demand from parents at the co-ed junior school who wanted their sons to stay on past year 6. To reflect its evolving character, the school has recently undergone a brand makeover. A new logo with a greater emphasis on the acronym 'OLA' and an altogether fresher, more contemporary feel, reveals the school's desire to move away from a convent girl image while still celebrating its Catholic heritage.

A centrepiece of the school is the 1907 chapel, where solemn carvings and sacred adornments co-exist with brightly-coloured prayer cards and hand-made paper flowers that dangle in strings from the balcony. It's an image that sums up the essence of this school – a happy and nurturing place built upon strong historic and moral foundations.

Pastoral care, well-being and discipline: A focus on pastoral care is obvious throughout, underpinned by the school's Catholic ethos. Junior pupils spoke enthusiastically about the annual 'animal blessing', where children bring their pets in to be blessed. 'We had horses in the gym!' shrieked one. Around a third of the senior school intake is from Catholic junior schools, and the school welcomes children from all or no faiths. Senior school masses are held at regular points during the year and on particular feast days – 'We want the link to the Catholic school tradition to be explicit but in an inclusive way,' explains the principal. 'For most people, the Catholic ethos is an attractive feature of the school.' This was generally echoed by the parents The Guide spoke to, who were impressed by the school's emphasis on moral education.

The head of year 7 doubles up as the induction tutor, making sure that all new students settle in well, and small class sizes help to cultivate a distinctive family feel. Bullying is 'minor and infrequent'; 'we nip things in the bud'. Pupils we spoke to agreed, saying any bullying is stamped out pretty quickly. The school has been 'building up' its special needs provision and a designated head of learning support leads a team of five. One parent of a dyslexic son described the learning support as 'absolutely fantastic'.

Pupils and parents: Nearly 500 children on roll, with room to increase numbers at sixth form but no desire to grow too big. Not an ethnically diverse mix, but reflective of the area's wider community. Gradually increasing proportion of boys. During a sunny lunch break, this reviewer observed a fevered game of footie in the playground, with a solitary girl in goal, while an impromptu game of basketball saw a mixed gathering of girls and boys from different age groups.

A recent survey conducted by the senior school showed that parents felt communication could be improved, an observation repeated to us. One parent felt that children were entrusted with too much information to relay home, while another commented that 'there isn't a great deal of social interaction between the school and parents.' But overall, parents were full of praise for the school, approving of its small size and a 'family' atmosphere between staff and pupils.

Parent-teacher communication excellent in junior school, however. 'The teachers are kind, responsive and open at all times', said one parent. Every class teacher writes to parents at the beginning of each term, and in the morning the school operates an 'open-door policy', where children can be dropped from 8am and parents chat with teachers. As a result, parents are very engaged, the PA is thriving and a number of parents run after-school clubs.

Entrance: Children are accepted into the school's nursery class at any point after the beginning of the term in which the children reach their third birthday. Flexible about entry at other stages. From years 4 and above children are given short written assessments to determine their academic ability.

Roughly 25-30 per cent of senior school entrants from local Catholic schools (eg St Edmund's and St Amand's), some from as far away as Newbury and Swindon. Around 80 per cent of the OLA junior school leavers move up to the senior school. Main intake at age 11, following exam and interview and at sixth form minimum of five GCSEs at B or above. One parent of an existing OLA pupil who failed to make the grades for sixth form felt the admission policy was 'confused', with the school initially refusing entry but then changing their minds and offering a place.

Exit: Usually 80-90 per cent of year 6 goes on to the senior school. The two head teachers meet every week and there are shared facilities with senior school for science and DT and shared staff for PE. But an element of distance between the two schools is encouraged to create 'a nice balance between familiarity and mystery' for children moving up. One parent of a pupil with learning difficulties spoke with high praise of the 'smooth transition' from junior to senior school, with the senior school learning support team receiving a 'thorough briefing' about her daughter's needs.

Approximately half stay on for the sixth form (47 per cent left after GCSEs in 2016). The size of the school means that A level students benefit from very small classes with plenty of individual attention and advice. Leavers to a range of universities, with Swansea currently popular, others to eg medicine at UCL and English at King's College London. Usually several to art foundation courses.

Money matters: Fees are on a par with the other local independents. Lunches are extra. Academic scholarships and bursaries are available for entry to years 7, 9 and 12, providing up to a 60 per cent reduction in school fees. Special consideration for bursary funding is given to children whose parents are practising Catholics and who attended Catholic primary schools.

Exhibitions are also awarded in art, drama, music and sport, providing some financial assistance with purchasing relevant kit, equipment and materials.

Remarks: This is a school that treats education as an exciting journeyn not just a means to an end. Parents of academic high-flyers or sporting champs will probably look elsewhere, but worth serious consideration if you want your child to experience a well-rounded education and the freedom and encouragement to develop their strengths, whatever they might be. Its Catholic ethos has helped create a happy, nurturing school where pupils' spiritual and emotional needs are valued as much as their academic ones.

Oxford High School

Belbroughton Road, Oxford, Oxfordshire OX2 6XA

Pupils: 880 • Ages: 4-18 • Sixth form: 135

Fees: £9,873 – £14,424 pa

Tel: 01865 559888
Email: oxfordhigh@oxf.gdst.net
Website: www.oxfordhigh.gdst.net

Head: Since 2010, Mrs Judith Carlisle BA (50s). Educated in a 'small Kent convent.' Studied English and drama at Bristol then worked in theatre in education for a few years followed by a PGCE at Goldsmiths. Previously deputy head at King Edward VII School, Norfolk and then head of Dover Girls' Grammar. Oxford High is her first post in the independent sector but so far she has found that the similarities between the grammar and independents more than outweigh any differences – committed pupils and parents with high expectations in both. She says that working in the state sector has given her a 'sense of perspective, the ability to see the whole picture of education and where our young people sit.' Very friendly, genuine and refreshingly informal; her style is smart bohemian – good camouflage for forays into Summertown and beyond.

Oxford High's previous head, Felicity Lusk, left things pretty ship-shape when she decamped to Abingdon, so 'what next?' we asked Mrs Carlisle. 'OHS doesn't need fixing, it's a fabulous school. Part of my task is to make sure that we respond to what girls need, running with change but standing firm with the school's values and ethos.' Her plans are for increasing bursary provision and developing community links, including possibly becoming educational partners with a free school in East Oxford. She is also keen to help the girls develop what she calls 'good habits', such as 'steadiness and thoughtfulness.' 'We want girls to have strong core values, to value relationships as well as careers.' Mrs Carlisle has no truck with the 'factory model' of education and believes that 'the added twinkle in OHS results comes from pleasure, from very bright girls being encouraged to go one step further.'

Mrs Carlisle's husband also works in education and both enjoy outdoor pursuits, especially walking, cycling and cross-country skiing – Norfolk is a favourite destination. She recently went trekking in Nepal with some of her pupils. 'I'm so glad I went, mountains make you feel small and that's a good corrective for a head!'

Moving on in July 2017.

Head of junior school: Since January 2016, Mrs Kate Gater, previously deputy head of Edgbaston High Prep School.

Academic matters: Early years and national curriculum followed in junior school but with plenty more added in. Specialist teachers for science, art, music, PE, ICT and foreign languages. School hopes to supplement the ICT provision with iPads – much more mobile and versatile than desktop terminals. Parents we spoke to were all pretty happy with facilities, even more so the teaching and staff. There was a lovely display of photos showing mums and dads sitting at tiny tables trying out some of the activities their children got up to in a normal day. SEN identified early and teaching then 'goes at the pace of the child.' Peripatetic SEN specialists provide one-to-one support as necessary but fewer than 20 at any one time receive extra help. School can (and does) accommodate bright girls with eg Asperger's, but 'parents send their girls with a view to them entering the senior school so they must be able to cope.'

Girls study for 10 GCSEs (none taken early) and in 2016 an impressive 92 per cent of grades were A*/A. Dual award science, but subjects are taught separately and enhanced with a tailored science enrichment course that is, apparently, 'better preparation for A level.' IGCSEs currently in maths, modern foreign languages, English language and literature, science. Decisions on syllabus are devolved to department heads and 'always under review.' Responsive and flexible when it comes to A level choices; girls choose from 26 subjects and staff timetable around them, running courses even for three or four only (including Greek, Latin, Mandarin and Russian). School says that most take three A2s and a few do four. One girl we met was doing five and she probably wasn't unique. In 2016, 67 per cent of grades at A level were A*/A. Very strong science, plenty go on to study medicine and up to 30 per cent in any year head for Oxbridge.

Teaching is taken 'beyond the curriculum' and staff enjoy the opportunity to lead (or possibly follow) girls off piste academically. All sixth formers do critical thinking as part of their general studies programme and many opt to take this as an AS level. Also available is the extended project qualification (EPQ) and ACPA baccalaureate. The 360 programme encourages a broader outlook with leadership opportunities, lectures and elective courses. No Pre-U as yet but it's not ruled out for the future. Lessons we saw were a teacher's dream – bright, curious girls excited by their subjects and full of questions and ideas. And what of the perennial problem, girls' reluctance to take risks and get things wrong; how does the school encourage courage? Mrs Carlisle is on the case. 'We want to help girls develop a core, an inner strength, a sense of self.' She speaks of a drive to foster bravery, of setting the bar higher and higher, either literally in PE, or metaphorically. 'We get girls to talk about the fear, to confront the worst that could happen.'

Games, options, the arts: We were astonished by the ambition and quality of the pieces made in what used to be called woodwork but is now known as resistant materials. A wonderful chicken coop (it was, in fact, a chicken gypsy caravan) with heart-shaped shutters; a beautifully designed desk; an elegant console table. Impressive welding too. DT facilities are extensive, more like a small industrial unit, and girls can come and work on projects outside timetabled lessons. In years 7 to 9 girls sample creative subjects such as textiles, DT, ceramics etc via a 'circus' system that gives them a term of each. Inspiringly messy art room with very high quality work on display, likewise textile creations of an impressive standard – OHS girls have gone on to the Ruskin and the Royal Academy. Sixth formers can opt to take an AS in art or textiles over two years as an extra subject; this creative outlet is apparently popular with girls intending to study medicine. How do they fit it all in? Staff say that girls enjoy being able to draw on their other subjects such as psychology and history to inform their art. We're sure they do but it still doesn't quite answer our question..

Masses of musicians, as one might expect, with choirs, orchestras, ensembles and bands for all levels of ability. Girls benefit from Oxford's cultural venues and OHS performs in the Sheldonian and various college chapels. Music and drama enthusiastically and successfully pursued as extracurricular subjects but penny numbers taking them at GCSE and A level – not quite academic enough, perhaps.

Clubs are, with exceptions such as bridge, CCF and knitting, subject or sport based. Thus: engineering club, dissection club(!), biomedical club – all serving to extend studies beyond the syllabus. But lest you think OHS girls are living up to the school's bluestocking reputation by being worthy but dull, take a look at the school magazine: it's one of the most witty, affectionate yet wickedly irreverent we've read (and we've read a few...). The rules from 'Top 10 secret tips for writing articles about school trips' should be carved into the desks of all school magazine editors: 'Thou shalt not murder... us with boredom,' being the first.

We have heard mixed reports about sport, some feeling that it doesn't quite match up to the standard of academics (rather a tall order) but girls have represented their county and country in a range of events, notably hockey – under 16 and 18 county champions – swimming and cross-country. Indeed, swimmers from OHS were selected for British Olympic and Paralympic trials. Girls pursing individual sports at national and international level are fully supported eg exam timetables adjusted to avoid clashes. Sixth formers may take a sports leadership course. Super swimming pool, standard issue sports hall, but on a 10 acre town site space is pretty limited – use is made of the playing fields at the nearby Dragon School (although this is not mentioned in the prospectus). Partnership with Oxford Hawks hockey club means girls get specialist coaching and use of their pitches. Fair to say, we think, that sport gets A-, rather than an A*.

Background and atmosphere: Tucked away unexpectedly behind dons' grand Victorian villas (school is somewhat at odds with local vernacular), the site has undergone considerable renovation to the tune of £9,000,000 and now almost works as a coherent, if constrained, campus. Bold metal sunflower centrepiece outside reception is an effective focal point and is illuminated at night, thus delivering school's motto 'Ad lucem' (To the light) at all times. Founded in 1895 with just 29 pupils, the school has moved between various North Oxford venues and settled in Betjeman's 'bonny Belbroughton Road' in 1957. Was a direct grant school and head is committed to continuing the meritocratic tradition by beefing up bursary coffers.

The new senior dining hall is a bright and welcoming space with glass walls overlooking outdoor space for al fresco lunch, but with its determinedly jolly coloured plastic chairs looks as though it was designed by adults to be 'down with the kids'. Ditto the reception area in grey and lime green: it's smart now but we hope it will stand the test of time and not look dated in a few years. Sixth form cyber café with laptops open all day. Girls say that the food has improved and all usual options – baked potatoes, pasta, salad bar, etc served up. We were surprised to see beanbags lining the walls of the corridor outside the dining room. 'What are these for?' we asked, imagining perhaps wearyingly long queues for baked potatoes. They are, apparently, a relaxation area for sixth formers, rather popular and thus much hijacked by other years. Since we were not invited into their common-room – it was 'undergoing renovation', and 'not even the teachers want to go in there,' one can only hope that conditions will become a little more salubrious. School says that sixth formers are project managing the revamp, including the budget, themselves so the end result should meet their needs.

Junior school reception and year 1 are in Woodstock Road and years 2-6 at Bardwell Road – both within walking distance of big sister. School believes that girls benefit from being taught in a single sex environment because they are usually ready to engage with academic study more quickly than boys. Not, thank goodness, that we saw tinies doing anything too academic in their characterful Victorian house on the busy Woodstock Road (which even boasts a parent café). Jolly outside space with canopied play area and 'nomow' turf. Youngest start on ground floor and ascend as they grow. Infants now get a hot lunch; other parents must provide packed lunches. Rather neglected feeling library and music room on top floor plus multi-purpose space – one of the benefits that came from the school's decision to close small nursery dept. Another is that reception children now have improved ground floor facilities with more access to the outdoors.

We were shown around the Bardwell Road site (years 2-6) by two very self-assured year 6 girls in smart kilts. Lower years wear pleasingly timeless navy blue tunics. Everywhere we looked girls were busy, busy, busy: happily creating delicious-looking Plasticine cupcakes in the big messy art room; doing cartwheels in the gym (it's a red letter day when the wall bars are pulled out apparently, but 'it only happens once or twice a term'), learning about mad Tudor instruments in music; doing 'lots' of experiments in the science labs. The site – another, larger, Victorian villa – seemed rather confusing to this (easily disoriented) editor, with dim corridors and back stairs, all in need of a lick of paint (about to happen apparently). System of different staircases operates to avoid rush hour chaos at lesson change-over. General air of make do and mend; nothing at all wrong with that although the library (doubles as venue for music lessons), seems to be in a corridor, with a few uninvitingly deflated beanbags for seating. Hardly the place for those OHJS voracious readers to curl up in bookish quiet. School says that big plans are afoot, 'parents, girls and governors have been consulted about how to make best use of the sites and develop them for 21st century learning.' Our unfailingly diplomatic guides said the food was 'sometimes nice, sometimes nasty', but appreciated the option to have a jacket potato on the nasty days (who doesn't?).

Inevitably, given its central Oxford location, OHS has a reputation for being the bluestocking school. And what's wrong with that? It's hardly an insult to be linked to a movement that championed women's education and no one could accuse OHS girls of being dull or frumpy. The uniform is comfortable and low key with sunflower logos on navy blue sweatshirts. Sixth formers wear their own clothes and do not, thank goodness, have to adhere to the style black hole that is 'business dress.' No token nod to democracy here: the OHS school council is an effective and well-supported body that has a real influence over school policy – part of what the head refers to as the school's 'yes culture.'

Pastoral care, well-being and discipline: There doesn't seem to be an OHS 'type'; several parents told us they were surprised to find 'a real mixed bunch.' Mrs Carlisle says that it is important for OHS not to have a 'house style'; she wants all pupils to find someone to whom they can relate and we can report that the phrase most often used to describe the girls is 'really friendly'.

Parents praise the way in which staff treat pupils as individuals, giving positive encouragement to the less confident and helping to bring out the best in every girl. Particularly important at a school where there is bound to be a vocal 'hands up' team in every class. Discipline low key, bullying or other friendship group problems headed off at pass or dealt with promptly. Usual range of sanctions for smoking, alcohol (short-term exclusion), drugs (exclusion).

Pupils and parents: Broad international mix of cultures, especially for a day school; some families are connected to Oxford University or the nearby hospitals. Not snobby; Mrs Carlisle is keenly aware that parents make significant sacrifices to send their daughters here. They've probably seen the list of former pupils. Deep breath: Dame Maggie Smith (actress); Sian Edwards (conductor); Elizabeth Jennings (poet); Emma Bridgewater (potter); Ursula Buchan (journalist); Sophie Grigson (cookery TV/writer); Louise Williams (violinist); Dame Josephine Barnes (first woman president BMA); Miriam Margolyes (actress); Dame Rose Macaulay (novelist); Anne Pasternak-Slater (academic); Julia Hollander (director); Harriet Hunt (international chess Grand Master); Joanne van Heningen (architect); Cressida Dick (Metropolitan Police); Martha Lane Fox (lastminute.com); Gemma Mortensen (executive director, Crisis Action), Sarah-Jayne Blakemore (Royal Society University research fellow and professor in cognitive neuroscience at University College London). OHS girls are most definitely not highly-strung thoroughbreds – these tend to be stabled elsewhere.

Entrance: First come first served into reception, then selective; year 3 other main junior entry point. For entry to years 1- 6 girls spend an observed assessment day with tests in maths, English, reading and spelling. External candidates can apply at any age to junior school. School says it tries to give positive individual feedback to parents of girls whose applications are unsuccessful.

Main senior school entry at 11 and 16. Year 7: own assessments in maths, English, reasoning and interview. Parents say that the entrance test is a good filter and doesn't disadvantage bright girls from state primaries, but don't imagine that these children aren't given a little coaching. For sixth form entry, admissions interviews and at least grade A in most GCSEs, and certainly for chosen subjects. Academic potential and ability looked for.

Exit: Vast majority of juniors go on to senior school with offers now made in year 5. Will advise parents in good time if senior school not appropriate and help find alternative. Ten to 15 per cent decamp elsewhere (local co-eds) post-GCSE. All sixth formers to higher education; eight to Oxbridge in 2016, plus six medics; two off to the US; otherwise to a range of mostly Russell Group unis.

Money matters: As other GDST schools, regarded as good value for money. Fees include day trips and ISCO test in year 10 (many other schools charge this as an extra). Variable number of scholarships worth 10 per cent of fees awarded at 11 (academic, music and head's scholarship). Scholarships (worth 15 per cent of fees) also awarded at 16 (academic, head's, art, sport, music and drama). Bursaries, up to 100 per cent of fees (based on financial need), available at age 11 and 16.

Remarks: Oxford High manages the seemingly impossible task of turning out confident girls with exemplary academic results without turning up the pressure. Serious matters are certainly taken seriously but there seems to be time for plenty of fun. As Mrs Carlisle says, 'When the time comes we want them to be ready to burst out of the doors but we want them to look back with a tear in their eye.'

Pangbourne College

Pangbourne, Reading, Berkshire RG8 8LA

Pupils: 410 (270 boys, 140 girls); 100 full, 125 part boarders • Ages: 11-19 • Sixth form: 145 (95 boys, 50 girls)

Fees: Day £16,479 – £23,223; Boarding £20,685 – £32,847 pa

Tel: 01189 842101
Email: registrar@pangbourne.com
Website: www.pangbourne.com

Headmaster: Since 2005, Mr Thomas Garnier BSc PGCE (40s). Educated at Sandroyd and Radley, read physics at Bristol and was a seaman officer in the Royal Navy for seven years. He left the Navy 'for love' after meeting his wife Alexandra and trained as a teacher. Did PGCE at Oxford, followed by first teaching job at King Alfred's, high performing state school in Wantage, Oxfordshire. Spent 10 years at Abingdon School, where he progressed to housemaster and then head of boarding.

Dedicated, energetic and keen to listen to pupils' views, he still manages to fit in some physics teaching and runs the naval section of Pangbourne's CCF. He describes Pangbourne pupils as 'good, solid citizens who are prepared to work hard and willing to participate.' Makes a point of being out and about in school and meets the two chief cadet captains (head boy and head girl) for 10 minutes every morning. 'We suit active children who like being busy,' he says.

Head's wife is very involved in school life and they have two sons. They live in a house attached to the main school building, with panoramic views stretching 20 miles across the Berkshire countryside. In his spare time (not that there's much of it) he enjoys rowing, running and music. A firm believer in 'lifelong learning,' he recently took up the flute again after a 25 year gap, passed his grade 8 with ease and plays in the school orchestra. He is keen to start piano lessons too. 'Someone said to me "you can always find 15 minutes a day and if you do that it adds up to 90 hours a year".'

P

Academic matters: School takes children across a broad range of ability. Head agrees that Pangbourne is sometimes perceived as being 'for the less able' but says they do a very good job for academic children (there's a gifted and talented programme for the most able). In 2016, 48 per cent of A level grades were A*/B and 20 per cent A*/A. The school told us: 'While the top students gained their straight A grades, some of the most heartening performances were to be found in the middle ground, among those who worked tremendously hard to secure Bs and Cs. We take real pride in these.' Some sixth formers, particularly those considering careers in the Forces, take public service BTec as well as their A levels.

Most pupils take 11 GCSEs, including IGSE English and maths. French, German and Spanish taught and music, art, DT, drama, business studies and PE on offer at GCSE. In 2016, 33 per cent A*/A grades. New timetable has introduced one-hour lessons. Pupils are setted for maths, English, science and languages – four sets in years 9 and 10 and five sets in year 11.

Teaching staff (two-thirds male and a third female) are a healthy mix of experienced and newly qualified teachers (school has links with teacher training departments at universities of Buckingham, Reading and Oxford Brookes). Half the teachers live on site. Staff hold regular academic clinics for youngsters who need help (pupils can also email their teachers). Learning support available for pupils with minor learning difficulties – individual lessons on offer at extra cost. Tutor system – in senior school pupils stay with same tutor for year 9, then change for years 10 and 11 and again for the sixth form.

Games, options, the arts: A very sporty school. Teachers and pupils alike told us that 'Pangbourne punches above its weight' when it comes to sport, and its impressive results bear this out. School regularly beats far larger schools, particularly at rugby and rowing. Pangbourne boathouse is a mile from the school, on the scenic banks of the Thames, and school has won the Princess Elizabeth Challenge Cup at Henley four times.

Unlike some schools, where pupils drop sport in the sixth form, everyone does sport here. School's size means that virtually all get the chance to represent Pangbourne. Main boys' sports are rugby, hockey, rowing and cricket while girls do netball, hockey, rugby, rowing and tennis. Open-air pool (keen swimmers get bussed to indoor pools at Bradfield, Reading and Newbury). Lots of equestrian enthusiasts – riding and polo are popular.

Stunning new music school houses recital hall, recording suite and 10 practice and teaching rooms, as well as four prized Steinway grand pianos. Around a third of pupils take individual music lessons, with brass, drums, guitar and singing leading the pack. Loads of musical groups to join, including orchestra, jazz band, choirs and a marching band. Art and DT departments thriving, with healthy numbers taking subjects at GCSE and A level. Performing arts are on the up with a variety of college productions, theatre trips and drama workshops. Three drama studios and pupils encouraged to take LAMDA exams. Everyone does CCF for at least a year and D of E is compulsory in year 9.

Boarding: Four boys' houses and two (ultra-modern) girls' houses. Just over half of the pupils board – more than 100 are full boarders while the others ('part boarders') board four nights a week (Monday, Tuesday, Thursday and Friday). Boarding grows in popularity as the pupils move up the school – by sixth form 75 per cent are boarders. 'We don't actively push boarding,' one teacher told us. 'It's a natural phenomenon.' No flexi-boarding, although school offers parents chance to buy 15 extra boarding nights a year per pupil. Girls' houses are stylish and bright – 'I want to make it like home from home,' a housemistress told us. Pupils eat breakfast, lunch and supper in the central mess hall.

The youngest pupils (years 7 and 8) are housed in Dunbar, a detached red-brick house with its own garden (loads of space to play football, jump about on the trampoline and catch up with friends). Lower school lessons take place in the main school but the rest of the time pupils trot back to the cosy environs of Dunbar. Dynamic housemaster of Dunbar ('he's strict, but huge fun,' one parent told us) also teaches DT and memorably described his subject as 'making a noise and making a mess.' Dunbar pupils have their own head boy and head girl and all pupils are divided into four 'watches,' (Port, Starboard, Forward and Aft), each with their own 'watch captains.' Currently more boys than girls in this age group, but numbers vary from year to year.

Background and atmosphere: School is set in 230 acres, in an area of outstanding natural beauty. Founded in 1917, Pangbourne's aim was to prepare boys for service in the Merchant Navy and Royal Navy. In 1969, however, the school was established as a charity, with a similar curriculum to other schools, and these days only two or three leavers a year join the Forces. Even so, Pangbourne prides itself on maintaining many of its original traditions and is the only school in the UK where pupils wear Royal Navy officer cadet uniform every day.

Pupils parade in their number one (ceremonial) uniforms every third Sunday. Uniforms have to be immaculate and shoes polished. A guest of honour inspects the whole school on the vast parade ground and takes the salute as pupils march past. Head says Pangbourne's parades are an integral part of school life and help to develop self-discipline (pupils have to stand still for 15 to 20 minutes, often with a biting wind whistling across the parade ground), confidence, teamwork, leadership and a community spirit as well as attention to detail. When we visited pupils told us that the parades 'bring us together' as a school, while parents are hugely supportive (many turn up to watch every parade). 'It is very impressive,' a mother told us. 'It seems to give them great pride in what they do.' But despite the emphasis on teamwork, the school encourages youngsters to be individuals. 'We certainly aren't trying to put everyone in a mould,' one teacher told us.

Pangbourne has its own distinctive vocabulary, much of it nautical. Study bedrooms are cabins, house common rooms are gunrooms, the dining hall is the mess hall and casual clothes are always referred to as scruff. When the head arrived he introduced 'flag values' – kindness, integrity, industry, moral courage, selflessness, resilience and initiative. He sees these as the school's core values and pupils are urged to display them throughout their time at the school. Firm Christian ethos. Chapel is a key part of Pangbourne life, from 'congers' (congregational practice) to Saturday evensong for boarders. Many services are held in the Falkland Islands Memorial Chapel, opened by the Queen.

School has been fully co-ed since 1996 (it's now two-thirds boys and a third girls).

School is keen on student voice and pupils sit on food committee and pastoral welfare committee. Very inclusive 'Team Pangbourne' feel to the place and pupils are fiercely loyal to their school. Sixth formers can apply to train as peer mentors, helping others to cope with everything from time management and exam preparation to friendship issues and internet safety. Raft of prefects – called cadet captains – chosen by head and senior staff. Lower sixth pupils take leadership course in readiness for their responsibilities in the upper sixth and head reckons this has reaped dividends.

Pastoral care, well-being and discipline: Head says school's policies on drugs, alcohol, cigarettes and knives are 'crystal clear.' Any pupil caught using, selling or possessing drugs 'can expect to be expelled,' he says, though 'every case is treated on its merits.' School devotes a lot of time to PHSCE and is strict about boy-girl relationships – PDAs banned. Sixth formers have their own bar (Medway), which is open for soft drinks on Thursday evenings and pizzas and beer/lager (strictly limited) on Saturday nights. Pupils are allowed mobile phones but firm rules on when they can be used. If phones go off in lessons, for instance, they get confiscated for 24 hours.

Staff believe that the school's strict uniform policy is a 'great leveller.' Pupils must need hefty trunks to pack all their kit though – list includes number one uniform (jacket, trousers/shirt and cap with badge for Sundays and ceremonies), number two uniform for every day (trousers/skirt, navy jersey, epaulettes, beret and Dr Martens shoes), and recreational rig (known as 'rec rig') for social occasions and away matches. And that's before they even think of throwing in games kit and weekend clothes.

Pupils say that Pangbourne is 'a caring, friendly school' and that it's easy to settle in. One boy told us that wearing the distinctive uniform had given him 'a sense of discipline' and that most pupils see it as 'really cool.' Asked whether it's a snooty school, sixth formers said 'definitely not.' Other pupil comments during our visit included 'people come out of their shells here,' 'it makes you really independent' and 'it prepares you for life outside.'

Pupils and parents: Fleet of minibuses brings day pupils in from as far afield as Basingstoke, Newbury and Highclere. Majority of boarders live within an hour's drive. Around eight per cent from overseas (including the Far East, Kenya and Germany). Despite school's naval associations, only 20 youngsters from Forces families. Former pupils include the late film director Ken Russell, Olympic gold and silver medallist sailor Andrew (Bart) Simpson (a sailing foundation was set up in his name after he drowned whilst training for the America's Cup), motorcycle racer Mike Hailwood, hedge fund founder David Harding, former Second Sea Lord Admiral Sir Michael Layard and Dazed & Confused founder and journalist Jefferson Hack.

Pangbourne prides itself on taking pupils 'from a broad spectrum of ability.' A parent told us: 'Pangbourne isn't known for being an academic school but the opportunities are there for academic children and they do really well. At the same time the school brings out the best in those for whom studying isn't so easy. Every child seems to have their chance in the sun.' School says it selects as much on character and suitability as academic criteria and is looking for youngsters who will throw themselves into Pangbourne life and make a difference. The only children the school might turn away, says the head, are those whose learning difficulties are 'too profound for us to cope with' or youngsters with 'behaviour issues.'

Entrance: Pupils come from a host of state and prep schools, including Brockhurst, Moulsford, Thorngrove, St Andrew's, Pangbourne and many more. Main entry points are at 11, 13 and 16. At 11 and 13, admission is by school's own entrance exam or CE (interview and head's report taken into account too). Pupils joining sixth form (up to 20 a year) must have at least five GCSE passes, including English and maths.

Exit: Around three per cent left after GCSEs, mainly to do subjects not offered by Pangbourne, or as one pupil told us wryly, 'because they want more free time.' Around 90 per cent to university and sometimes one or two a year to Oxbridge. Popular destinations in 2016 included Bristol, Exeter and London (King's College and UCL). The rest start full-time work (one boy recently went straight to aviation college to do his commercial pilot's training), with a handful going into the Forces.

Money matters: 'We're not a rich school,' the bursar told us, although with its centenary coming up in 2017 the school is busy upgrading many buildings. Means-tested bursaries available (from 10 per cent to 100 per cent) and a variety of scholarships (including academic, music and sport) at each entry point.

Remarks: A small and distinctive school that puts huge emphasis on self-discipline, teamwork and leadership. Caring and supportive, Pangbourne buzzes with activity and encourages every pupil to have a go and get involved.

Papplewick School

Windsor Road, Ascot, Berkshire SL5 7LH

Pupils: 204; 128 full and flexi boarders • Ages: 6-13 (boarders from 8) • C of E

Fees: Day £15,435 – £21,435; Boarding £27,915 pa

Tel: 01344 621488
Email: registrar@papplewick.org.uk
Website: www.papplewick.org.uk

Headmaster: Since 2004, Mr Tom Bunbury BA PGCE, (40s). Educated at nearby Woodcote Prep and then Millfield, read law at Durham but turned his back on the legal profession to return first to Woodcote, then Homerton College Cambridge for a PGCE followed by Papplewick, where he has remained since 1993. He was head of maths, a housemaster and then deputy before taking over as head. It was, he says, a chance to lead a great team and make it stronger. He is modest and quietly confident, with a charming absence of ego. Parents appreciate the fact that he has guarded the traditions of Papplewick while moving with the times on issues such as demand for flexi-boarding.

He lives on site with his wife, Sallie, and four children. Sallie oversees the matrons and catering – each week she organises a 'tasty table' at which 12 boys picked at random on their way in to the dining room get to try a new meal and give it the thumbs up. Or down. The head places great emphasis on the school's 'real family atmosphere', two-thirds of staff live on site and many have families; the boys enjoy playing with the younger children, teaching them to ride bikes and explore. Parents endorsed this, seeing it as a real strength of the school. Living at one's place of work may be convenient but you need an escape route, and whenever time allows the Bunburys pack buckets and spades and head off to their bolt-hole on the Isle of Wight.

P

Entrance: Entry from age 6, first come, first served. Day boys from local preps in Berks, Bucks and Surrey but increasing numbers now coming in from west London. Parents have cottoned on to the fact that just 40 minutes on the Papplewick express will enable their boys to escape the capital's overheated prep rat-race. Several we spoke to described Papplewick as 'a blessed relief' from the intense competitiveness of the capital's schools, adding that their boys still got to the senior schools of their choice but at their own pace. According to the head, there's no 'Papplewick type', families have 'broad horizons' and the atmosphere is tolerant and undliquey; parents say much the same. About 10 per cent from outside UK, no dominant country, some expats, EFL available. Handful of academic and all-rounder awards available annually, can be worth up to 50 per cent of fees.

Exit: Most popular choices are Eton, Harrow, Wellington, Marlborough and Charterhouse. Impressive scholarship record, including to eg Eton, Harrow, Wellington and Winchester.

Remarks: Papplewick may be across the road from Ascot racecourse but it's not going to give the new grandstand (or indeed the old one) a run for its money in the architectural stakes. Parents say a few may be disappointed by the absence of grandeur but 'the boys don't notice'. Recent building works have transformed what was a rather jumbled site; the new entrance hall is particularly impressive – it seems to pull everything together as well providing a light and modern space for exhibitions and receptions. Plans have been drawn up for an art, DT and ICT block as well as a stand-alone year 8 boarding house. As for the inside, take a boy of your acquaintance, multiply him by 200, imagine the toll this cohort might take on the interior of any building and you will be ready for Papplewick. There is a Just William charm about this place and its delightful pupils – unaffected, exuberant boys in their element. Uniform is blue shorts and blue shirts, open necked in the summer or fastened with one of the huge number of ties that declare an individual's allegiance to house, sporting or other pursuits.

Our year 8 guides were quite the best PR team we've had the pleasure to be escorted by. When we ventured that the absence of poolside changing might make winter bathing a little frosty we were told that it was 'very character building.' Asked whether they thought other schools were better equipped, they conceded that this might possibly be the case but claimed that they just 'deviated around any lack of facilities.' To be fair, all the prerequisites of 21st century schooling are present and correct – plenty of computers including a suite of Macs in the music tech room, smartboards and such like. Chapel is a dog-leg off the main hall, demarcated on our visit by a truly impressive display of art – some by boys who had just won scholarships. Two imperious (if slightly moth-eaten) stags' heads, whence the school emblem, oversee proceedings – if only they could talk! Electronic screen in the hall shows live feed of house points, great for motivation; weekly winners get to choose Friday night supper – usually chicken and chips.

Average class size is 12. Flexible setting and streaming – boys moved up and down as necessary. Cambridge Latin course for all, Greek for scholars. In the classes we observed there was a palpable rapport between staff and pupils; one felt that boys knew exactly how far they could go with their sparky banter and wouldn't push it any further. Likewise, the teachers responded to the boys as individual characters, enjoying their company. And all the time minds were developing, being guided and challenged.

There are some younger boarders, 'I was a bit shy to start with but I soon got used to it,' and some flexi boarders (around 15), but most start when it becomes compulsory in the summer term of year 6. As one boy told us, 'You can have fun with your friends all day, you don't have to worry about rushing because mum wants to go somewhere.' The year 6 French class we chatted to were very keen to tell us about their favourite activities – extra DT where you can 'make what you like', drama, clay pigeon and rifle shooting three times a week, golf and polo. All games (apart from polo) played on site; football, rugby and cricket are tackled with gusto and everybody gets a game. Most unusual and tremendously popular is Herpetology or Snake Club; this is the first time a Good Schools Guide reviewer has conducted interviews with a bearded lizard on her shoulder. As with many of the activities, including a game of football we saw, Snake Club is for all ages – boys buy their reptiles, now all bred in house, for a modest £10 and learn about the creature's habitat and how to care for it. Any offspring are sold back to the club for the same price. The club was founded by the charismatic science master who joined from a school in South Africa, having 'discovered' Papplewick via a visiting rugby team. Some 10 years on and he's still 'loving' it; his wife is in charge of life upstairs in the dorms.

Each year group has its own den (common room) with friezes painted by a member of the art department (these also adorn the dorms), and a mixture of pool tables and tiered benches for watching films. Dorms are no-frills but they're tidy and boys expected to change their own sheets; pin boards were fairly empty when we visited but there is, we were told, a hotly contested prize for the best decorated. There are televisions and beanbags in the dorms and boys can watch after 4pm; mobile phones are allowed but for talking only – no moving images. Parents are mainly contacted via Skype or mobile. Year 8 can use Facebook under supervision. The boys we met were very clear about the rules and seemed to take them in good part, understanding the necessity. Posters visible in strategic places detailing where to go for help; boys can take problems to their tutor or, if preferred, can phone and speak confidentially to the 'private listener' who will give advice.

Head keen to point out that while the idea of a boarding prep may strike some as old fashioned, Papplewick has evolved along with modern family life. Parents are welcome to drop in whenever they like; Saturdays are particularly popular – those who come to watch matches stay and listen to the sublime four-part choir ('full of first XV rugby players') at a short chapel service and then eat lunch with staff and boys. The 40 or so boys who are in school for the weekend enjoy camp outs, trips to local restaurants and socials (bit of a Lynx fest apparently) with Wycombe Abbey, Heathfield and St Mary's.

According to the head, relocation to a larger site was considered a few years ago but decided against – would it have broken the spell? Who knows. There's certainly a whiff of magic about Papplewick that seems to inspire fierce loyalty in staff, parents and boys. We think perhaps Mr Bunbury should bottle it and build that new boarding house.

Parkside School

The Manor, Stoke D'Abernon, Cobham, Surrey KT11 3PX

Pupils: 300 (including 26 girls in co-ed nursery) • Ages: 2-13

Fees: £11,835 – £15,840 pa

Tel: 01932 862749
Email: enquiries@parkside-school.co.uk
Website: www.parkside-school.co.uk

Head Master: Since 2014, Mark Beach (50s), previously head of the junior school at City of London Freemen's School. He has also been head of Longacre Prep in Shamley Green. History degree from the University College of Wales and MA in education, management and leadership from the Open University.

Easy-going, cheerful and good-humoured, but as efficient as they come, with parents and staff enthusing about how he's turned the school around with his 'businesslike approach' – staff now have their own budgets; there are more action plans; staff are regularly appraised etc. Teaches PSHE and boys say 'he shakes every single boy's hand on the way into assembly.' Embraces the traditions of the school, but is also forward-looking. 'This generation will have to jump through more hoops than we did for the careers they want and I see it as my role to provide a foundation that sets these boys up for that.' Described as 'a breath of fresh air' by pupils and parents alike.

Lives half-an-hour an hour down the road with his wife, Louise, an English teacher, and their three children. Avid moor walker and skier; recently gave up rugby.

Entrance: Boys in the co-ed nursery get an automatic place in the pre-prep reception; likewise, boys in pre-prep seamlessly move into the school proper, aged 7. Entrance at pre-prep and 7+ for external applicants is dependent on an assessment day held in November, which includes being tested in English and maths. Any SEN issues will be taken up then too. 'We are looking for whether a boy can access the curriculum, cope with common entrance and fit into the Parkside ethos, which is basically being able to throw yourself into the wider aspects of school life,' says head. Perhaps less choosy than some of its rivals, but if boys are rude and disrespectful on assessment day – 'some are,' admits the head – then they will be turned away.

Boys join from a wide local radius including Wimbledon, Kinsgston, Esher, Claygate, Weybridge, Oxshott, Byfleet, Cobham, Stoke d'Abernon, Fetcham and Leatherhead. Mainly English, some Korean, Russian, American, South African and Australian. Most year groups full, but there are sometimes gaps higher up the school – always worth a phone call – and if there is a place, it is dependent on maths and English tests, plus spending time with the head to check 'fitablity'. Limited number of means-tested bursaries available, covering up to 80 per cent of fees.

Exit: From nursery, 70 per cent of boys move on to pre-prep – others to the state system (Royal Kent, St Matthews) or co-ed preps such as Danes Hill and Feltonfleet. School not geared towards pupils leaving at 11 and very few do. At 13+ boys depart to an increasingly wide range of senior schools – 17 different ones in 2016 including Reeds, St John's Leatherhead, Millfield, Sherborne, Stowe, Charterhouse, Epsom College and Lancing. Occasionally to Eton and Harrow. School well practised at matching each boy to the right school – it's all handled gently and kindly and the school works hard to provide firm links with schools across the south east and south west, as well as providing an annual senior school exhibition, boarding school evening etc. Six scholarships in 2016.

Remarks: This is a happy school, set in stunning grounds, which is strong academically, but without the pressure-cooker ethos of some other schools in this moneyed area of Surrey. 'There's no doubt my sons are challenged in the classroom and reach their full potential, but it's no hothouse,' one parent told us. Head keen to point out that some boys 'do need that extra push' – and as such, he has made the top set (of which there are three from age 9 in maths and English) exclusive to scholarship applicants from year 7. Setting in lower years is reasonably fluid, and as one boy pointed out, 'We do the same stuff, just at different speeds.' French from nursery and Latin from year 5. Two classes of 20 per year, but with the setted subjects, the average teaching group is nearer 12.

Teaching staff (a good proportion, male) are a healthy mix of NQTs ('they bring fantastic ideas straight from college,' says head); those with two or three years teaching experience ('they bring new ideas, plus a bit of experience); those from industry ('they bring great experience') and longstanding staff ('they bring continuity'). Big push on professional development being more targeted and the head is refreshingly focused on succession planning. There's clear target setting for each boy and, according to pupils, 'Teachers always offer extra support if you don't understand something – nothing is ever too much trouble.' A few parents feel the school may not be right for the super-bright, 'but that's not to say the boys don't do really well,' said one.

Boys have a lot to fit in their day, with a pacey 10 lessons a day timetable – each lesson a short sharp 35 minutes to keep boys focused and ensure the school day is not too long. It's not quite as frenetic as it sounds, though, with some double periods (and even triple for art and sports). Homework kept to just one or two 35-minute assignments a week (term time only) and there's no Saturday school. General subject teachers in pre-prep, then subject specialists in French and music from year 3, after which they pick up more and more so that by the time they're in year 5, they are taught entirely by subject specialists.

Good provision from quite a large SEN department – 19 per cent of boys SEN when we visited, albeit at the mild to moderate end. These boys receive varying levels of support, including up to two one-to-one support lessons a week if they need it, plus extra support from a classroom assistant – and any necessary classroom adaptations eg wobble seats for pupils with dyspraxia. Learning support centre accessible to other pupils too eg to improve handwriting or deal with anxiety issues.

IT embedded into learning and two IT suites regularly used – we particularly liked the main one, where groups of four computers set around single pods are favoured over the usual rows of desks – so much more appealing. Coding, programming, touch-typing all part of everyday life here.

Music strong, with weekly classes praised by boys as being 'really exciting.' Plenty of extracurricular opportunities too, including choir, big band, rock group and ensembles. A third of pupils learn an instrument with a peripatetic teacher. Facilities for music particularly impressive, including an appealing and well-equipped main music studio, some practice areas and a hall dedicated to music performance (but which also doubles up for assembly and sports). Drums, guitar, brass and piano have traditionally dominated in terms of instruments, but there's a push on strings to be taken up by more boys. Pupils regularly perform at music festivals.

Art is outstanding – a fact that is immediately apparent when you enter the delightful studio, packed with talented paintings, textiles, pottery etc. DT also impressive, with facilities including a 3D printer. Boys were busy making scaled-down bedrooms, complete with furniture, when we visited – enchanting.

Historically, drama has not been a strong point. Not so now, with a new teacher – 'she used to be an actress,' we were told in awe by one boy – brought in to shake things up. So far so good – many boys now do LAMDA, and annual productions will now be performed by most year groups with a review show from year 8.

It's a famously sporty school, well used to picking up county and national trophies in U11 and U13 competitions. Core sports are football, cricket and hockey, the latter being extremely popular and successful. Rugby an option in years 7 and 8, with other key sports on offer including athletics and swimming. Super sports facilities set in school's 45 acres of parkland include a 20m swimming pool, a splendid cricket academy, tennis courts and even a river (the Mole runs through school grounds) used for kayaking. 'There are some really good coaches,' pupils told us. More than one parent we spoke to felt sport here could be more inclusive, but head insistent that, 'as a school one of the things we have put a lot of effort into in the past two years is to achieve a fair chance for all levels.'

At the centre of the striking grounds is the historic manor house, with decorative ceilings, pillars and panelling, which houses the head, staff rooms, boys' dining room and a magnificent salon, complete with Rococo fireplace, used for school assemblies and functions. The classroom block, the Crescent, is a newish well-designed and airy space. A 100 seat performing arts hall, lecture room and art block have been added since, plus a superb library for the prep school (pre-prep and nursery have their own libraries). This has become rather the hub of the school, hosting talks by visiting authors and there are fun competitions held here too, including the 'Who can read the most words in a term?' We spoke to the current winner, who managed a whopping two million. Separate languages block, which houses two classrooms. The nursery building, a converted barn, is really appealing, colourful and brimming with activity – all safely cordoned off from the bigger boys. Parents really appreciate the after-school care available at the nursery and pre-prep. Picturesque church (and hall) on site, which the boys attend for a service every half term.

As you would hope in a smallish operation like this, pastoral care is first class. There's a head of pastoral care and staff are friendly and approachable. Boys in the top year wear white shirts so that the younger boys (in grey) know who to ask for help and advice, and teachers know the boys well so they can often spot any problems before they escalate. Plus, there's a worry box. 'My son has had a few rocky terms on and off and when he's struggled, they've noticed and really supported him,' one parent told us. Boys seem proud of their school and loyal and kind to each other and there's lots of cross-year friendships. If a bullying ever occurs, staff will immediately talk to the bully and his parents, tackling it quickly and firmly – there was one temporary exclusion for it the year we visited. Strong student council.

There's a well understood framework of discipline, but not masses of rules, and parents approve of the way any bad behaviour is dealt with. 'There's no naming or shaming,' says one. Good and bad marks awarded as carrots and sticks, nothing heavier than that really necessary (six strikes during a half term equals a detention, but they're rare – the system is really for the school to monitor any patterns of poor behaviour before they become a real problem).

We usually ask the pupils we talk to what they would change if they were headteacher for the day and we got the best answer ever from this school – 'We do get to be headteacher for the day!' Indeed, one boy gets picked every term to spend the day doing some of the things the head would do – sitting at his desk, inviting people to lunch in his office, reading out awards in assembly etc. 'It's amazing – everyone loves it,' one boy told us. Other fun regulars include a class rota for hot chocolate break.

En route to the school, we passed flash cars galore, yummy mummies and houses belonging to Chelsea footballers (the school backs on to the club's training grounds). But Parkside aims to play down this aspect of the area and some families choose the school precisely for this reason. 'People are surprised by the range of backgrounds, with lawyers and bankers, electricians and plumbers,' says one. There's a good sense of community among the parents, with 'Friends of Parkside' (the PA) holding regular socials.

School fees include books and lunch and most of the after-school clubs. The only additional charges are for extracurricular activities provided by outside companies, such as judo and music. Lots of clubs and activities on offer (eg fencing, cooking, chess, golf, skiing and Sandown and supervised prep) with everything finished by 5pm. Nursery outings include farm, Santa's grotto, park and reptile centre; pre-prep outings include fire station, zoo, museum and Pizza Express; prep boys get day trips to the likes of the farm and theatre, plus residentials to Guernsey (hockey tour), Jersey (football and hockey tour), Caribbean (sports tour) etc.

Several parents told us there's something very special about this school that you can't quite put your finger on. 'Bigger schools – and some other smaller ones – just don't get the friendliness and warmth of this one,' summed up one. Parents also praise the single-sex aspect. 'When I went to look round the school, I sat at the back of the classroom and the teacher suddenly got all the boys up exercising round the classroom for a fun few minutes. I asked her afterwards if that was a formal break. "No," she told me. "Didn't you notice their energy was starting to dip? I wanted to get them re-focused." And that's the thing about this school – they understand boys because their speciality is boys.'

A good traditional prep school, where boys enjoy an all-round education and are friendly, polite and confident.

Parmiter's School

High Elms Lane, Garston, Watford, Hertfordshire WD25 0UU

Pupils: 1,419 • Ages: 11–18 • Sixth form: 375

Tel: 01923 671424
Email: admin@parmiters.herts.sch.uk
Website: www.parmiters.herts.sch.uk

Headmaster: Since 2010, Mr Nick Daymond MA Cantab PGCE NPQH (40s), previously head of Roundwood Park School in Harpenden. He went from St Paul's School to Queens' College, Cambridge to read modern languages, but changed to theology in his third year. He did a PGCE out of pragmatism rather than vocation, but had an 'inspirational' PGCE language tutor, and found Goffs School, where he had a placement, 'a stimulating place to be'.

Married with two children, he is popular with parents and pupils, who comment that he is 'very approachable' and 'always around at school events, often with his family'. They are appreciative that he did not leap in to make immediate changes 'just to make his mark', and that he evidently values the traditions of the school.

Academic matters: The ability range is undoubtedly skewed towards the more able, with 25 per cent chosen by academic ability, and 10 per cent for musical aptitude – 'Musicians tend to be good at maths and languages too'. Plus their siblings, of course. However, says the head, 'It's more mixed than you would imagine.' Everyone is in all ability form groups for the first three years, with setting and a variety of other groupings in subjects such as maths, science, languages and music. 'It seems to work really well,' said a parent. 'My son really likes working with people at the same level as him.' The school has specialisms in technology, music and languages, and everyone takes a language to GCSE, starting French in year 7 and taking up Spanish or German in year 8.

Maths, English and sciences are much the most popular A level subjects, but most other A level subjects are well supported too. In 2016, 91 per cent of pupils got 5+ A*-C GCSE grades, including maths and English, with 51 per cent of these grades being A*/A; 75 per cent of A level grades were A*/B and 45 per cent A*/A. Very high value-added scores.

The school works with Villiers Park Educational Trust to develop independent learning in sixth formers and encourage high aspirations. 'I want to ensure that we're not just an exam factory, but end up with well-rounded students.' Groups of teachers and year 12 pupils have jointly explored how they can improve teaching and learning and research skills. 'It's very powerful having students talk to you about what works and what doesn't work.'

Games, options, the arts: The 60 rolling acres of playing fields have a public school feel. Also an Astroturf, sports hall with fitness suite and dance studio plus floodlit tennis and netball courts. Plenty of inter-school matches and tournaments in all the usual sports, including boys' rugby and basketball and girls' football, with teams often reaching county finals. 'It's good that there are B and C teams too,' said a pupil, 'so everyone can have a go.' PE popular at GCSE and A level. Music places given for aptitude rather than ability, so not all recipients are hugely experienced, but plenty going on, with many instrumental and choral groups performing in 'fabulous' concerts and going on European tours. Lavish school productions of, eg, Jesus Christ Superstar, featuring actors and musicians. DT and art both popular and high quality, with a high proportion of GCSE art entrants getting A*. Vibrant art studios jammed with photographs, ceramics and silk screen printing as well as interesting paintings.

Lots of language exchanges, as one would expect, plus physics trips to Switzerland, geography trips to Iceland, history trips to the Somme. Refreshingly, the visits are designed to be affordable – eg Normandy rather than Quebec – though students spend a long time raising funds for the sixth form trip to Tanzania, 'the experience of a lifetime'. Huge numbers take part in D of E.

House system provides lots of opportunities for competing in, eg the golf tournament, short story competition, ironman challenge and ICT design competition. Colours awarded for dedication to and achievement in extracurricular activities.

Raises large amounts for charity – 'I've been very struck by the amount of charity work we do. So many students are actively involved outside school as well as inside, and it is a good opportunity for them to initiate things'.

Background and atmosphere: Founded in 1681 in Bethnal Green with funds left by wealthy East London silk merchant Thomas Parmiter in his will. Became a boys' grammar school, but turned comprehensive and co-ed when it moved to Hertfordshire in 1977. Still has links with Bethnal Green: the Old Parmiterians' Society, with many members from the East End grammar school, is very active, and each year some 60 or 70 east London pensioners travel up for lunch and entertainments. The head is educational adviser to the Bethnal Green Educational Fund – 'It is a very important part of the school and brings a different dimension to our lives'.

The school looks like a classic '70s comprehensive from the outside, but has a traditional grammar school feel on the inside, with portraits of former head teachers and honours boards. Parents and staff evidently value the combination of traditional values and progressive outlook and the head comments: 'It was the traditions and ethos that appealed to me'.

Pastoral care, well-being and discipline: 'I've had very little to do in terms of behaviour,' says the head. Most upsets are related to 'the usual bits of nastiness, such as friendship issues and routine run-of-the-mill problems, such as late homework'. A parent commented that staff are 'very supportive, really approachable. They have been fantastic in helping with the settling in issues we've had (and these have been very few).' Another said, 'I always find the children well-behaved, walking along after school chatting and smiling in friendly groups.'

Pupils and parents: It may be 'more mixed than you would imagine', but pupils are largely from nice Hertfordshire families from the surrounding postcodes. Runs buses from Shenley, St Albans, Bushey, Harrow, Radlett and Hemel Hempstead. Former pupils include ambassadors Sir Terence Clarke, Emrys Davies and Alper Mehmet, Nick Leeson of Barings Bank fame, footballer Jordan Parkes and TV gardener Tommy Walsh.

Entrance: Looked after children get first priority; then 10 per cent of places to those living closest; then siblings; then compelling medical reasons; then 25 per cent academic, via verbal reasoning and maths tests; then 10 per cent musical aptitude (test and audition); then children of staff who have been there at least two years; then remaining places by proximity (generally not much further than a kilometre). Nearly all the medical, academic and music places are allocated to children from surrounding WD, AL and HP post codes; however, 'Applications will be welcomed from the Ancient Parish of St Matthew, Bethnal Green'. Consistently the most over-subscribed school in Hertfordshire, with more than seven applicants for each place.

Students going into the sixth form – internally or externally – need at least six GCSEs with mostly B grades or above.

Exit: Between 10 and 30 per cent leave after GCSEs, mostly for FE colleges. Nearly all sixth formers go to university – a wide spread – studying anything from physics at Imperial College to biblical studies at Sheffield. Twelve to Oxbridge in 2016, five medics, a dentist and a vet.

Money matters: Parents' Association very active and raises large sums from, eg Three Peaks' Challenge, craft fair and Bollywood evening. Also gets funds from the Parmiter's Foundation charity, which has helped with considerable redevelopment: new languages, music, sixth form and drama centres have been built over the past few years and a new maths block is at planning stage.

Remarks: Extremely successful, semi-selective state school with public school facilities and grammar school traditions, in enviable green surroundings.

Peter Symonds College

Owens Road, Winchester, Hampshire SO22 6RX

Pupils: 4,000; 67 full boarders • Ages: 16–18

Fees: Day free; Boarding £12,675 – £13,620 pa

Tel: 01962 852764
Email: psc@psc.ac.uk
Website: www.psc.ac.uk

P

Principal: Since 2013, Mr Stephen Carville. Joined Peter Symonds in 2002 as assistant principal and was promoted to vice principal two years later. Prior to joining Symonds he was an HMI inspector for Ofsted, leading college and area inspections nationally and before that, worked at Barton Peveril College as curriculum manager for business, economics and modern languages. He has been a manager and teacher in other sixth form, tertiary and general FE colleges.

Academic matters: Everything is here, both in terms of subject matter and the full range of human ability, from the star student who became head of the Cambridge Union last year to those who bump along at the bottom with a string of Ds and Es. A level performance on a mega-roll, improving year after year. Exam results outshine many independent schools – 'and we send more students to Oxbridge!' In 2016, 61 per cent A*/B grades and 34 per cent A*/As. The usual wide array of courses one finds at sixth form colleges, includes, eg, photography, film studies and environmental science. Everyone takes general studies ('It strengthens university applications') and quite a few go for other non-subjects like critical thinking (very good results) and citizenship. A few subjects beam particularly brightly: maths, art, textiles, music, media studies. Some courses are 'victims of their own success' and students have reported that they could not study their first choices. Candidates may have to audition for dance or performing arts.

Numbers are huge – 21 sets for biology. No streaming. Largish class sizes with 15-19 average – sounds overwhelming in theory but seems to work in practice. Less academic students (about 100 of the total) can pursue vocational courses – level 2 BTecs or OCR Nationals in, eg, health and social care or business and finance: 'Much more useful than re-sitting GCSEs and struggling with A levels'. A few GCSEs on offer for retakes, and good linguists may pick up Italian or Spanish from scratch, taking GCSE on the way to A level in just two years. Those aiming for Oxbridge or competitive courses such as medicine or vet science get additional guidance (with governors roped in to provide interview practice).

Fifteen per cent benefit from some form of learning support including essay planning and self-organisation. Wheelchair access to much of the site ('We don't do badly for a sloping site'). Corridor to learning support centre lined with pictures of successful and famous dyslexics. Lunchtime workshops for those needing extra tuition – at both the top and the bottom ends of the achievement spectrum. Students report all the help they need if they ask for it – but they have to ask for it. Organisational ability is important here – 'it's like going to uni,' said a girl – and indeed PS has now been authorised to offer university courses for those who cannot tear themselves away from the place.

Latest Ofsted report gushingly rated Symonds 'outstanding' across the board.

Games, options, the arts: Strong teams because of its size. Sports hall funded by 'Mercers' money' (loosely part of the Mercers 'cluster' alongside, eg, St Paul's and Abingdon). Lots of grass about the place but the principal dreams of an Astro; however, new sports pavilion now open. Drama strong and an A level in performing arts is offered. A performing arts centre also on the principal's wish list. Brilliant results in art – course said to be very broad: 'almost like a foundation course'. Former fives court enjoying a second life as a photo studio. DT wedged into one large workshop. Students take part in an extracurricular programme (two hours a week) with activities chosen from long list (50+) ranging from Amnesty International to creating the high quality American-style yearbook; knitting particularly hot at the mo. Some of these are accredited, such as the Community Sports Leader award and the Duke of Edinburgh award. Lots of fundraising and local community work.

Fabulous, unique Hampshire specialist music course curiously low profile. Around 12 students a year are selected and study two instruments (free of charge) to a high standard, alongside academic music and two or three further A levels. 'Costs a fortune – we spend three times as much on the music specialists as we do on the other students.' The course gives the college a solid core of talent, but music spills out over its edges:140 students are studying music and/or music technology A level. Other music students receive free tuition on their main instrument and can play in a variety of bands, orchestras and choirs.

Boarding: Two boarding houses (girls one floor, boys the other, electric door between). School House is a handsome Victorian building in which students share two to four bedded rooms. Falkland Lodge was opened in 1998: single or twin rooms, all en suite, but it costs more. Feel almost, but not quite, like university halls of residence, with an air of independence, eg boarders do their own laundry, aside from bedding. Boarding inspection reports rated it 'outstanding'.

Boarders (from 16) may use college's LRC until 8.30pm and the sports facilities are also open three evenings a week. Boarding 'events' take place once every half term but there's not a huge programme of activities. Boarders are given quite a bit of freedom to manage their own time but are expected to be back in their rooms by 10.20pm (11pm weekends); they may stay with friends or have people to stay by prior arrangement.

Background and atmosphere: Peter Symonds founded Christes Hospital (no relation to the Horsham school – it was a 'trendy name' at the time) in the 17th century to look after aged brethren, assist two divinity students and educate four poor boys. Sale of land during the expansion of the railways enabled a boys' grammar school to be built on the current site in 1897, operating first as a boys' independent, then a grammar and finally becoming a co-ed sixth form college in the early 70s. Heads arrive and proceed to make the place their life's work: only six since 1897.

An intense conurbation perched on a hilly spot overlooking the suburbs of Winchester. Original late Victorian building now completely surrounded by dedicated buildings purpose-built in the last 10 years, including newish cavernous learning and resources centre (library plus). Everything being used to full capacity – jam-packed with strapping youths. Students socialise in giant departure lounge style common-room and sunbathe like seals on Hopkin's Hump, a little knoll named after former head, Neil Hopkins. Large canteen plus satellites provide cheap and plentiful food. No uniform (style leans to grungy rather than trendy), teachers called by their first names, 55 minute lessons, no bells: really a halfway house between school and university.

Pastoral care, well-being and discipline: Sanctions minimal, although a zero tolerance policy on drugs and alcohol on site and smoking is not permitted except in one small fenced off area outdoors. 'Six or seven' students expelled most years – more common for them to leave 'by mutual consent'. Most common reason is 'laziness'; the occasional drugs bust. Full time counsellors available for personal matters.

Pupils and parents: Fifty per cent from the three Winchester 11-16 schools – Kings, Westgate and Henry Beaufort. Perins in Alresford tops the long list of other feeder schools. A further 15-20 per cent from independent schools and the rest from far and wide – Reading, Salisbury and the Isle of Wight included. Student social profile directly reflects Winchester skew towards ambitious middle classes – one teacher remarked, 'Nothing as formidable as a Winchester mother protecting her young'. Former pupils include comedian Jack Dee, Olympic gold medallists Ben Ainsley and Iain Percy, Coldplay drummer William Champion, 'Page 3 girl' Lucy Pinder.

Entrance: Some 1,600 pupils pile into the school at 16. Deadline for application is December. Non-selective, but requirement for A level courses is at least five grade Cs at GCSE level, 'ideally' including maths and English. Maths and science are exceptions – you need a B. Every applicant is interviewed. Vastly oversubscribed – local pupils automatically get in; beyond that pupils are accepted geographically in concentric circles radiating out from Winchester. Exceptions made for musicians, boarders and students from a windswept corner of the South Atlantic (has the honour of being the official sixth form of the Falkland Islands – construction of Falkland Lodge boarding house was partly funded by the Falklands government). Candidates for the Hampshire specialist music course audition in February/March on two instruments, one of which should be at grade 7/8 standard.

Exit: Some 85 per cent to universities of all descriptions. Thirty-eight to Oxbridge in 2016 and over a third to Russell Group. Students on the music course frequently move on to the top music colleges.

Invited by Cambridge University to act as a regional hub as part of its HE+ initiative. This involves providing extension classes for its own and other local sixth formers and helping with applications to the most selective universities.

Money matters: Sixth form colleges receive less money per pupil than normal schools so the management employs meticulous budgeting, plus a dash of sorcery, to keep the whole shebang on the road. Hardship fund available. Students compete for several bursaries each year for gap year projects.

Remarks: A huge, friendly metropolis which falls neatly between school and university in approach. Most people would be happy here, but not those who need spoon-feeding.

The Pilgrims' School

3 The Close, Winchester, Hampshire SO23 9LT

Pupils: 250; 87 full boarders • Ages: 4-13 (boarders from year 4) • C of E

Fees: Day £10,425 – £18,135; Boarding £22,890; Choral scholars £13,734 pa

Tel: 01962 854189
Email: admissions@pilgrims-school.co.uk
Website: www.thepilgrims-school.co.uk

Head: Since January 2015, Tom Burden (40s), previously head of Hereward House School in London. He grew up on the Isle of Wight, where he was educated at local schools before proceeding to Oxford (with a scholarship) to study theology. After graduating, he started teaching as a bit of fresh air before settling down to something earnest, but was soon gripped. Five years at Alleyn Court School, Southend, then a further five at boarding prep Lockers Park, Hertfordshire, where he headed the English department and ran the scholarship set, while still managing plenty of sports coaching. 'I loved every minute and took away the idea that boys should be boyish, enjoy their childhood and be trusted to have responsibilities.' A sports fan and regular at Lords, he relaxes by playing football, bowls and cricket. His boy's own enthusiasms include Bletchley Park, the Underground, the gothic Revival and the London sewer system. He's also 'hugely interested' in politics, philosophy and religion.

Entrance: Boys are assessed at all main entry stages and tests vary depending on age. Reception entry via 'fun activity morning'. School offers around 10 extra places at 7+ and 8+ – assessment during individual taster day. Around six more join the school in year 7 to prepare for 13+ entry to senior schools. Those interested can get a taste of boarding life (from age 8) by spending a few nights in school. Places in other years are occasionally available. School states that it is 'selective in the broadest sense' but clearly has an academic focus.

Auditions for the two choral foundations are in November, with most new choristers (who sing in Winchester Cathedral) and quiristers (who sing in Winchester College Chapel) joining in year 4 and 5. Voice trials include singing a prepared piece, aural tests and an academic assessment.

Boys come from all over to be a Pilgrim, moving from local nurseries, state primaries, independent pre-preps and London schools. Overseas parents choose the school as a route into Winchester College.

Exit: Around 40 per cent of leavers to Winchester College and Eton in any given year, many with music scholarships and exhibitions and a few with academic or double awards.

Steady trickle to Harrow, Radley, Charterhouse, Wellington, Canford, Bradfield, Sherborne, Bryanston etc, many with music, academic and all-rounder awards. One or two may leave at 11+ for independent day schools.

Remarks: School can probably trace its origins back to the early song schools associated with Winchester Cathedral in Saxon times. Current school was founded in 1931 in former priory (thought to have been redesigned by Sir Christopher Wren) when non-singing 'commoners' joined the choristers for their education. Quiristers, boys who have sung Winchester College chapel services since 1382, moved from the college to Pilgrims' in 1966. Cathedral and remains of Wolvesey Castle form an imposing backdrop to main school building, which sits in a far corner of The Close. Once inside, there's more space than the outer façade suggests; two inner quadrangles flanked by octagonal concert hall and modern classrooms rub shoulders with ancient medieval hall and converted Priory stable block. School escapes feeling cramped thanks to extensive playing fields in front of Bishop's Palace and design of newer buildings.

We got the feeling that this school does lots of things well, and parents confirm that academic standards are good. Form tutors and academic tutors (years 6-8) keep tabs on individual study via daily meetings with their charges and are 'very honest about progress.' Director of studies 'seems to know the capabilities of all the boys and school reports are extremely thorough, accurate and personal.' Maths set from year 4, English from year 5 and there is further division from year 7 into Winchester entry, scholarship and CE sets (depending on destination schools). Separate sciences taught from year 5, Latin from year 6 and French from year 3 (senior French classroom had piles of shiny new textbooks and posters of complex tenses on walls). Enthusiastic head of English encourages creative writing at every opportunity; clearly has a love for poetry, and boys produce some really imaginative work inspired by anything from Pilgrim's Progress to a letter from the Queen. Rest of curriculum is as expected and music is clearly strong. The three groups – choristers, quiristers and commoners (non-scholars, the majority) – are all mixed together in lessons and socially. The school is geared up for boys with lots of what it describes as 'strong male role models'. At the time of our visit, 15 students had SEN reports (dyslexia, dyspraxia) and two learning support specialists were giving individual and group lessons to around 30 pupils. Class numbers are capped throughout at 20; numbers in year 7 and 8 classes are smaller and determined by 'next schools.'

P

Housed in converted medieval stables, music department is very accomplished, active and busy, with around 235 individual music lessons taught each week by 27 visiting music teachers. 'Almost everyone plays an instrument,' noted a parent; singers usually learn two. Every boy is assessed for musical potential on entry to the school. Children in year 2 have strings and woodwind taster sessions and usually begin formal instrumental lessons in year 3. Bands, orchestras and choirs abound. Main prep school orchestra tackles repertoire such as finale of Beethoven 5 and Mahler 1 (arranged by director of music) with weekly sectional rehearsals. Big band, woodwind and baroque ensembles also practise weekly; music staff 'team boys up into [chamber music] groups that work.' Junior strings and band sometimes join seniors for concerts. Four other choirs besides the two professional choirs give everyone a chance to sing. Music lessons rotate through the timetable and aim to miss the same subject no more than once every six weeks. Practice sessions for boarders (four per instrument per week) are timetabled and supervised; 25 pupils can practise simultaneously, including a few day boys. Music theory lessons for all and acres of space for music technology and composition suites. School organises two full days of ABRSM music exams every term, routinely passed with distinctions and merits. Music department has access to Winchester College for larger concerts and uses hall and the Octagon for smaller affairs. Cathedral (chorister) and College Chapel (quirister) choirs sing to professional standards and parents say there is no difference in kudos between the two. Parents (and boys) can choose at audition whether they wish to be considered for one or both. Daily singing for all, although quiristers sing fewer services, practise more secular repertoire and have no holiday commitments (a bonus for some families). Both choirs make recordings and go on tours. 'It's fantastic to go to a school where there is music going on, it's just part of life ... even if you don't know you're learning, you are.'

Despite being renowned for music, Pilgrims' manages to field an impressive 11 teams for football, 12 for rugby, nine for cricket and a first hockey team. Parents say results are respectable, even though one laughed, 'The boys are so polite that they're more likely to say "after you" on the football pitch.' Usual range of sports and games timetabled daily; less mainstream activities include fives, golf, fencing, rounders, judo, martial arts, squash, water polo and sailing. All-weather court floodlit for use on darker evenings. Sporting successes include U13 1500m national prep schools champion and cricket at Hampshire county level. Heated outdoor pool – affectionately dubbed 'the puddle' – for swimming in warmer months, although boys use 25m indoor pool at the college next door for serious swimming, eg lessons, swim squad and galas. Large art room, smaller DT room, ICT suite and library dotted around the quads. Parents say that drama is very good lower down the school, with a 'fantastic junior production each year,' but add that they would like to see more for older pupils. School says, 'We have a senior production every year, the last was an outdoor Shakespeare.' Productions staged in atmospheric, medieval Pilgrims' Hall, in purpose-built Octagon theatre, outdoors in the Quad or in the cathedral.

Two boarding houses have space for 82 beds, all fully occupied when we visited. Lovely couple in charge stress that all boarders are treated equally and there is a clear division between the school day and boarding. Senior quiristers board in Q-school, a few minutes' walk away. Dorms homely and comfortable; each has a year 8 dorm monitor in charge of waking boys up etc. Breakfast served on family tables, after which boys go off to choir, instrumental practice or have free time. Extracurricular activities (known as 'Commoners' as singers have choir practice) happen after school on four afternoons a week. These include lots of sport, but unusual pursuits like fishing, bell ringing and Mandarin caught our eye. Boarders come back to the house after evening prep; houseparents keep a close eye on any missed homework and help singers cope at busy times. Laundry done in-house and parents say belongings are checked regularly. No flexi boarding, but commoners can go home at weekends and choristers occasionally; around a dozen boys are in school regularly on Sundays. Lots of trips and activities arranged on weekends and during 'choir time', when choristers board over Christmas, Easter and a week in summer.

Parents are happy with pastoral care and school's attitude towards misdemeanours, bullying etc. 'Issues are dealt with proactively and nobody brushes anything under the carpet.' In spite of the fact that boys wear distinctive sweaters depending on whether they are choristers (red), quiristers (blue) or commoners (green), we didn't sense any social divisions. Boys are mixed up when allocated to one of five 'Sets' (houses) on entry to the school, and we observed different coloured jumpers dotted all over at lunch tables. Although the two choirs spend a lot of time together, close bonds are also formed on the football field. Parents of commoners say their sons couldn't care less about the name and feel 'just as important as anyone in a red jumper or a blue jumper.' The only quibble was that there are too few phones in the boarding house, although any urgent messages are unfailingly delivered by staff on duty. School says, 'Several mobile phones are handed out each evening and there are ample landlines to use.'

Super little pre-prep has its own hall for assemblies (youngest children have lunch here) and plenty of outdoor space. Outdoor learning in forest school every Monday and there is an outdoor play area and garden. Pre-prep holds special assembly in the cathedral every fortnight and parents are welcome. Has its own choir and music teacher (director of music also takes lessons) and there are two clubs just for the under-7s. Lots of non-fiction in library encourages boys to enjoy reading.

Pilgrims' attracts a broad mix of families – overseas nationals hail from Hong Kong and China; a few others come from Russia and Switzerland. Some overseas British based in Brazil, France and Russia. Boys are lively, but generally well-behaved, courteous and very natural. Not a Sloane Ranger in sight. Choral foundation provides scholarships worth 40 per cent to all choristers and quiristers and free music tuition on one instrument. Means-tested bursaries worth up to 100 per cent are available for all. Over 20 boys had additional funding when we visited. Any boy awarded a bursary also receives his first set of uniform free. Former pupils include Jon Snow, Jack Dee, Patrick Gale, Ollie Baines and Jules Knight (members of Blake), Nick Glennie-Smith (film composer) and Anthony Smith (sculptor).

A fine school in which the musical, the sporty and the clever boy will positively flourish. Atmosphere is now less formal and the school has a good work/life balance.

The Portsmouth Grammar Junior School

Linked with The Portsmouth Grammar School

High Street, Portsmouth P01 2LN

Pupils: 422 • Ages: 2.5-11

Fees: £9,510 – £10,545 pa

Tel: 023 9236 4219
Email: jsadmissions@pgs.org.uk
Website: www.pgs.org.uk

Head: Since 2010, Mr Peter Hopkinson. Read communication studies at Sheffield, and was previously head of the junior department at Abbey Gate College, Chester, and Arnold Junior School, Blackpool.

Parents say he's very visible, and they wouldn't hesitate to go to him with a problem: 'Very approachable and friendly'; 'an able leader'.

The head does circle time with all the children over the year – 'a really good way to get to know all the kids,' he says, discussing themes such as awareness of world with the little ones (a teddy also attends), and developing philosophical thinking skills with older pupils.

Mr Hopkinson is a head with a clear vision for his school, and the energy and determination to effect change. It took persistence and determination to persuade everyone that the 11+ was unnecessary, but he has been vindicated by the transformation: children and parents are no longer stressed by the exam ('it's nice they don't have to feel those nerves any more', said a parent, reminiscing about a boy who threw up from anxiety before the exam); the curriculum is freed up for other learning, and the senior school has all the information it needs on pupils from the school's programme of continuous assessment. So everyone's happy.

Married to Michaela, a TA here, with two children, who also attend the school: it's a family affair.

Entrance: Most pupils join in nursery, others in reception, year 3 and increasingly year 5. Three classes per year increases to four classes in year 5. Entry to nursery through observed play; 5-10+, by assessments in maths, English, non-verbal reasoning, and spending time with peer group to observe sociability.

Exit: No 11+ to progress to senior school for pupils already in-house. Very few in each year don't make it on to the senior school, usually those with severe SEN.

Remarks: 'I don't believe in private school', said one devoted PGS parent, who feels that the advantages of PGS weigh decidedly in its favour against even outstanding state primary schools in the area, commenting on the combination of welcome, friendliness, mixed demographic and outstanding resources which make PGS unique: 'I stopped looking for houses back home up north...' Summed up succinctly by another: 'What you get for your dollar is incredible...'

Community is strongly encouraged here, both at school and outside the school gates. 'What we picked up on when we visited was its feeling of happiness, [a] feeling of cohesion and working together...', said a parent. Democracy gets things done here, pupil council members seeking suggestions to write in their special notebooks: successes include a new junior school playground (including a hobbit house); refurbishment of the boys' and girls' loos; and packed lunchers shedding their isolation and being able to sit with those having school dinners. Outside school there's a termly beach clean, and the brass band and strings orchestra perform frequently. 'Not for someone not keen to be involved', said a parent.

Parents too, have their say: the parent forum deals with whole school issues – 'parents really feel like stakeholders', said one, describing how they were instrumental in changing the layout of canteen for juniors, so they have to queue past little pots of crudités and fruit. The kids like their smallness; take and eat: parents are happier.

Achievement assembly recognises academic achievement, effort and being a good friend, and pupils can acquire a wealth of blazer decoration: under one scheme, the House Badge Award, pupils annually complete a list of tasks under various headings, such as charity, creative writing, sports and ICT. Completion of all challenges results in a stripe for your blazer, a different colour each year.

On the disciplinary side, after two warnings for misdemeanours, pupils must stand by the wall at break time for 5/10 mins. The next level up is a supervision at lunchtime, moving on to a 'red card' and then detention.'That's very rare,' said our guide, gravely.

Small classes (from 12 in reception, triple entry, to 15-20 from year 2 onwards) and fast paced learning, though the deputy head was quick to point out that those who can't cope with this can get help from learning support. 'You don't need to be academically gifted, but average plus, and need to work hard, or you'll struggle with the pace', said a parent.

Nursery to year 4 are situated on the main school site. Years 5 and 6 are housed over the road in the original Victorian school, where classrooms conditions are a bit tighter, but pupils benefit from their own set of specialist classrooms, including DT, drama studios and cookery. The walls are full of neat displays of work, and photos of school trips: happy memories described in some affectionate detail by our guides. School trips range from year 3's recent trip to Ufton Court to experience life as Anglo Saxons, complete with Saxon banquet and stories from Beowulf, to the ski trip – fabulous skiing, bum boarding in the evening and 'a hotel with a bar and everything' said a year 6 guide enthusiastically, to the nervous laughter of a teacher – 'they had great hot chocolate,' he added, slightly bewildered. Residential school trips get going in year 2, and a worried parent told us how much she appreciated the teachers tweeting photos – 'I couldn't speak to [my daughter], but I could see she was happy!'

There was a lively buzz in most lessons we saw, hands springing up to answer questions – 'What's the opposite of a synonym?' 'A cinnamon bun?' suggested one bright spark, to the chuckles of her classmates.

Education in the junior school is based on the PGS Connected Curriculum, the head's brainchild: a model of thematic topic-based learning, which interconnects disciplines to encourage transferable and flexible skills. It's similar to Primary Years IB, but 'avoids its wooliness', said the head: not every subject fits every topic, but connections will be made where they are relevant, and enhance learning. Year 4's current connected curriculum topic is Mighty Mountains, the topic launched with learning survival skills in the wooded area behind the playing fields. As far as possible, year 4 will be learning across the subject range through this topic.

As part of the Connected Curriculum, pupils study a quality text, with all lessons being based around that text, from Monkey Puzzle in year 2, to Northern Lights in year 6, pupils' chalk pastel drawings capturing beautifully the eerie northern lights.

Pupils are set for maths from year 4, but are otherwise in mixed ability groups. iPads are in frequent use for all years, and regular lessons in the computer room, with its coloured keyboards, ensures everyone can type by the time they get to year 6.

Pupils are continually appraised, and if problems arise, are assessed pastorally, first by talking to the pupil, then to their family, and by conducting SEN assessments if necessary. Around 34 of the junior school receive learning support, mostly in small groups out of class, but also through in class support by TAs.

The creative curriculum covers food tech, DT, drama, music and textiles, the textiles room piled high with coloured cloths and wool, one of our guides pointing out the beauty of the colours in the sunlight pouring in from the window. This room is the base for the sewing machine club, which make clothes to send to PGS's connected school in Uganda.

P

Music is important here, and most pupils learn an instrument, with a flying start from the school: in year 3, each pupil gets a term's free tuition on a string instrument, then on a brass instrument. Junior school music week saw the school alive with the beat of Indian dancing and drumming workshops. PGS is the cathedral choir school, and pupils can audition for the boys' or girls' choirs: boys from year 3, girls from year 5. Drama is popular too, with LAMDA available from year 1, and an annual production each year from year 2. The year 6 production is a big affair, costumes and backdrops designed and made by teachers, the score composed in-house for the instruments played by year 6.

A big nursery, in spacious purpose built classrooms, with between 40-60 children and lots of staff: 15 working at a time means they are always well staffed. Trips to the beach (PGS has beach school status), yoga and dance, and a role play room which transforms into pet shop, cafe or realm of snow and ice, depending on the theme. A darkened room with a tower of glowing lights for sleeping or calming down. Joint ventures with reception make the transition to school easy. It has an excellent reputation locally, and is oversubscribed, one parent putting her son down for a place when he was 6 weeks old.

The sporting year starts with a talk by head of sport about the school's philosophy of sport: inclusivity, and being happy putting your trainers on. Ask if they enjoyed the match, not who won, exhorts the school (the newsletter no longer includes results). 'One or two of the parents are...enthusiastic...' on the touchlines, said a parent – teachers will have a quiet word. 'We have done some work with parents to make sure their expectations meet our expectations...', said the deputy head.

'It's really splendid,' said parent, 'because everyone is in teams from the beginning, everyone is good enough to play, no one inadequate'. In this school, membership of teams depends on sportsmanship, not just performance on the pitch. The usual gender divide in sports: rugby and football for boys, netball for girls, but girls here also play football, and are starting cricket this summer. The PGJS cheerleading squad is southern champion.

One parent commented on the great use of twitter by PGS – if a match is cancelled at the last minute, the school will tweet. 'Communication is excellent, sometimes too much!'

A thorough pastoral system, with each child's well being regularly assessed by teachers, including consideration of what's going on for a child at home. The pastoral team includes two counsellors, who provide individual counselling for pupils, but who also do circle time with all the children at some point, and run special groups. All counselling services are included in the fees.

'Great pastoral care', said a parent, extolling the care given to pupils following a parent death, adding that teachers always email back quickly to queries, and it's easy to have quiet word at end of the day.

One parent described how carefully the school look out for one of her children who is 'painfully shy', and was very upset by a mild telling off from a teacher which resulted in panic attacks. The school took this very seriously, and has now included dealing with anxiety as part of PSHE.

Pupils are encouraged to look out for each other, and to spot and report bullying behaviour. Playground pals (special friends in lower years), mean that those who have no one to play with can go to the friendship bus stop, where special friends will scoop them up. Bullying is dealt with 'very carefully', said a parent, whose daughter was on the receiving end of some of the subtler forms of emotional bullying often particular to girls. The teacher started with general conversations with the whole form about friendship and kindness, moving on to specific conversations with the girls concerned, which resolved matters. '[My daughter] wasn't belittled or made to feel it wasn't important. She really trusts her teachers'.

The Portsmouth Grammar School

Linked with The Portsmouth Grammar Junior School

High Street, Portsmouth PO1 2LN

Pupils: 1,113 • Ages: 11–18 • Sixth form: 335

Fees: £14,817 pa

Tel: 023 9236 0036
Email: admissions@pgs.org.uk
Website: www.pgs.org.uk

Headmaster: Since, 2008, James Priory, married with three children, all three of whom attended or is attending Portsmouth Grammar School (PGS). Read English at Oxford, before his first teaching post at Bradford Grammar School, moving on to PGS in 2000 as head of English. Mr Priory has remained loyal to PGS since, taking on posts as head of English, senior teacher, and assistant head of the sixth form before becoming head. A nice line in self deprecatory humour: standing proudly surveying the playground on his first day as head, he overheard some very small juniors talking to each other – 'I know who that is...it's the new headmistress'. A friendly and energetic head, who has an infectious enthusiasm for PGS and its pupils – it was easy to understand a pupil's statement that Mr Priory was for him the decisive factor in choosing PGS over another public school – 'he was interested in me'.

Loves the poetry of Edward Thomas, the Downs, choral music and Portsmouth: Believes in the importance exploring local heritage, space and place, and teaches a short course on Sherlock Holmes to all year 7s as part of the school's Portsmouth curriculum.

Parents love him, describing him variously as 'wonderful' ; 'funny'; 'very human'; 'thoroughly decent and cares very much', to 'adorable' and 'as good as he looks' (like chocolate cake?).

The head's most important quality for pupils: to develop to be confident and secure in themselves; and in fact the head's Valentine's day blog told pupils that learning to love themselves and say so to the world was one of the most important things they could do.

Academic matters: Most parents are attracted first by PGS's stellar academic reputation, and results are consistently excellent: in 2016, 81 per cent A*-B, 57 per cent A*/A at A level, an average of nearly 39 points at IB. At GCSE, 70 per cent A*/A. Maths and sciences are particularly high performers, but excellence across the board here. The line locally is that it is terribly selective; but one parent said, 'not as much as all that', and the parents we spoke to agreed that average or better would thrive here. Pupils describe a strict working environment, where you are encouraged to work hard. 'That's how we want it to be', one added seriously.

Pupils and parents appreciate the availability of both IB and A level, although A levels are a great deal more popular: around 50 do IB, 250 A levels. The IB is seen as more challenging and rigorous ('definitely harder', said a parent), and A levels as a safer option. But those who take IB are glad they did: 'a global and outward looking course,' said a parent, while a pupil described how easy it had been to move to the IB from the US system. Another described the IB as 'pressured, but valuable', adding that her 'daughter got a tremendous amount out of it'.

PGS Extend takes place over the summer break between lower and upper sixth, similar to the EPQ, but this in-house version allowing greater flexibility of approach – recent entrants included a presentation on the Tanzanian health care system, a composition based on musical styles from around the world, and the creation of an animatronic hand.

The school produces a rough guide to sensible subject combinations to help pupils take the right subjects for particular career paths, keen to help pupils consider not just which university to attend, but where they will be at 25.

Both pupils and parents commented on the calibre of teaching and commitment of staff: 'I've experienced no better', said one pupil who had arrived for sixth form; 'It's incredible how hard the teachers work', said a parent; 'the quality of teaching is amazing'. This is a school which invests in its staff, and has developed a bespoke leadership course with the university. There's around a 10 per cent staff turnover annually, which is probably right amount for new blood and vitality, thinks the head.

A wide range of subjects from ancient to modern: 'we are committed to providing minority subjects', said the head, and those who take Greek do extremely well; though there is appetite for even more, one pupil suggesting that the curriculum could benefit from the inclusion of Mandarin. RS here comes with a P – philosophy -'It really encourages kids to consider ethical conundrums of modern life', said a parent. Maths and sciences are very popular, pupils relishing the smart new science labs. Pupils from year 9 upwards use mobile devices, which are particularly useful for collaborative work in lessons, and homework is often set in google classroom. Every break time there are clinics for the struggling, and pupils are comfortable emailing teachers if they need extra help.

Lessons have recently got longer, and the six 50 minute lessons have apparently lead to a calmer pace of day, much praised by a sixth former – 'It allows you time to get into a subject'.

Once a year the timetable is suspended for enrichment week, this year's curriculum enhancing activities including a mini Apprentice style competition to market a new drink for year 9 money management pupils, and a year 8 trip to a theme park to design and programme a new ride, combining business, ICT and physics.

Years 7 and 8 have much less to worry about than their peers at prep school, who are busy preparing for the CE. The focus in middle school here is on learning how to be independent: working out strategies for learning, and taking responsibility for themselves, and a reasonable amount of communication home to parents. One parent commented that her year 7 son initially struggled to fit in rugby matches, rugby training and all his homework, but as year went on, he worked out better how to organise himself.

The SEN unit assists pupils with mild to moderate dyslexia, although it is possible they could meet the needs of a pupil with severe dyslexia. No extra charge for SEN help, including one-to-one. There has been a lot of work done to ensure access arrangements for exams meet individual requirements.

Games, options, the arts: Pupils are bused to the Hilsea playing fields for most of their outdoor sport, around four miles from school. 'Bit of a trek', said a parent, 'but it's an inner city school'. The legendary Hilsea match teas take the edge of the drive ('I don't have lunch on match tea days', confided a parent.) One pupil wistfully told us how much he would love a pool on site (the school uses the local Navy pool); but it is likely that the school will benefit from any new university facilities in the vicinity.

Plenty of competitive teams, PGS particularly excelling in athletics, cricket, hockey, and netball. In year 7, every pupil represents the school at hockey, netball, or cricket, so all get match experience. Not a football school: there are a couple of club options, but serious football players play outside school. Boys at this school play rounders as well as cricket – a rare thing. For those less keen on teams, beach running is available. The indoor sports centre includes squash courts, gym, a climbing wall, and a bar. For parents.

The sports department start the year with a talk to parents about sportsmanship and touchline etiquette, which is mostly effective, though there remain a few who are 'very keen to win at sports', as one parent delicately put it. Teachers are sometimes strategically placed on touchlines...

'Grades open doors', said the head, 'but often pupils are more inspired by their co-curricular activities'. Pupils are encouraged to join at least two clubs in middle school, and keep up their extra curricular until they leave. Options range from the stock market club to Pride, with over 50 activities to chose from.

Music is a focus at this school, with an array of ensembles and orchestras. 'Children are taken very seriously as musicians', said a parent; 'the first violin is always introduced at concerts'. They will find a teacher for whatever instrument your child wants to learn, and the music school has ample practice rooms and a beautiful wooden ceiling rotunda. PGS forms partnerships with other musicians, composer Alexander Campkin challenging the choir with high notes and close intervals in his new work World of Merriment, while the London Mozart players do masterclasses for pupils. PGS is the choir school for St Thomas's cathedral, with separate boys' and girls' cathedral choirs, and a range of other school choirs, from selective to all-comers, the combined choirs taking part in the BBC's Festival of Remembrance at the Albert Hall. The cathedral is used for assemblies, concerts, and the house music competition: 'The most fabulous evening', said a parent. 'Young people doing what they love to do. Sheer joy in making music together, of an incredibly high standard'.

Annual drama productions are immensely popular with pupils, around 60 pupils from middle school taking part in their last production, Lion King, the use of puppetry meaning that even those less confident took part. Performances often take place in Portsmouth theatres, giving productions a professional edge, a parent commenting how much her daughter relished being part of the tech crew in productions.

A sculpted plaster head with a lollypop in its mouth stands near the door door of the art studios. Art is not splashed all over at this school, but there's an impressive array in the art department. We watched year 10s drawing dead things, Death in Venice playing in the background to get them in the mood. Art GCSE is heavily dominated by girls – 'boys don't quite get its purpose,' said art teacher; although the A level class is more balanced. Teachers are introducing more graphic design at GCSE, which they say boys relate to better.

Background and atmosphere: The energy and friendliness of PGS are what strike you first: 'It's a buzzy vibrant place', said parent, another adding that 'it's a big school, but doesn't feel like it, with small tutor groups helping pupils feel secure, and always plenty of people around that you know'. The strong feeling of community was mentioned by several parents, and indeed it was one of the few schools we have visited where one of our guides intervened with some younger pupils' misbehaviour. There is nothing lax about this school.

Pupils dress in different combinations of the school colours of black and red, depending on their house and seniority, the blazers black with red piping (somehow avoiding the feeling of public school precious that often accompanies piping). Even sixth formers wear some uniform here, the girls apparently loving the sixth form tie (which they can pair with any smart jacket). In a piece of open discrimination, sixth form boys have to wear a blazer.

P

The house system is very lively here, the 'healthy rivalry' reaching its peak in the house croquet tournament, with other competitions throughout the year, and each house having its own base within the school.

'C of E, but not pushily so', said a parent. There are services at the cathedral a couple of times a term, but 'it's more about decency, and a moral framework', nowhere more evident than in the enormously popular club PGS Pride, busy changing minds in the three years since its inception: now 69 per cent of pupils think it would be easy for a pupil to come out (just 47 per cent in 2013). Pride has hosted speakers on living with HIV; being Muslim, gay and a drag queen; and being gay, a priest and a dad. 'It's had a tangible impact on self worth', says the head, and is embraced school wide, the canteen even producing rainbow cup cakes. Diversity is accepted here: a parent happily describing her three very different children who were, or are, all very happy at PGS.

Food is excellent – not a single criticism to be found. Pupils can pay by card or thumbprint, which impresses everyone, the system also recording what kids choose to eat for the benefit of parents. Breakfast is available from 7.45 every morning.

Splendid old buildings mingle with the modern (though the one time barracks are a little foreboding from the street). The new sixth form centre is the glassy jewel in the crown, with sixth formers enjoying their own café, library, and a glass bridge which connects to the rest of school, so the sixth can keep their gadgets dry while the rest of the school scurry across the playground in the rain. There are plenty of places to work, from the project room designed for collaborative work, its walls lined with research books, to the senior library, and strictly no talking Memorial library, pin drop silent, sixth form and teachers only – or with special permission. Well cared for interiors, everything spic and span. PGS is home to the first twinned toilet we have ever visited, its sibling a remote latrine in Uganda.

PGS plays an active role in the Portsmouth community: it runs the Portsmouth arts festival with a range of local partners; organises a community beach clean every term; its ensembles play out and about; and it connects with local state schools – a number of sixth form pupils join PGS on bursaries every year, and they exchange staff to develop experience and expertise. The PGS gap year programme attracts applicants from across the country, gappers combining teaching with singing daily services at the cathedral.

Pastoral care, well-being and discipline: 'It's known as an academic school', said a parent, 'but it's the pastoral care and extracurricular which make [it]'; 'it doesn't sacrifice children's well-being for the need to do well academically', said another. Parents are pleased at the new emphasis on PHSE as a specialist lesson, not just a chunk of tutor time (whose quality depended on the skills of your tutor).

Tutors have big role in pastoral care, and are likely to be the starting point for a child with a problem: 'I feel they really "got" my kids', said a parent. 'There's always someone looking out for them, usually their tutor', said another, commenting how the school made sure things ran smoothly for her children when she was unwell.

Pupils can also talk to a peer listener (selected and trained sixth formers, who attach to tutor groups between years 7-9), or a counsellor (two part-time counsellors provide full week coverage). Counsellors are well known to children from circle time and clubs, such as the one for kids whose parents are separating. Children can be referred, or refer themselves by email or telephone. Counsellors can meet with families if this would be helpful and will deal with any issue which effects a child: we heard how helpful they had been to a pupil coping with bereavement, and a sixth former struggling with anxiety. There is also a medical centre with a doctor and three nurses.

Pupils said they would go to their tutor with any concerns about bullying behaviour, and parents feel that any problems are dealt with promptly. Incidences of bullying, both homophobic and other, have fallen since PGS Pride came into being: it has helped foster an atmosphere of tolerance and equality – for instance, pupils are clear that saying 'don't be such a girl' is not acceptable. Lots of people go to Pride who aren't gay, a parent told me, her son telling her 'it's part of being a well-rounded person'. One, whose daughter decided to come out, was very impressed with the support both she and her daughter had from the pastoral team – 'it's a very tolerant school'.

Minor offences are usually punished by tray duty, litter duty, or helping canteen staff, severe offences by after school detention. Pupils are expected to behave properly out of school, particularly when they are in uniform. Behaviour out of school will inform treatment in school.

Drug related problems are rare. They will test if necessary, but haven't had to for a few years. If perpetrators show remorse, respond and learn from their mistakes, they will probably be given a second chance. Parents think that bad behaviour and don't give a damn will be asked to leave, and indeed the only recent (temporary) exclusions have been for antisocial behaviour.

Pupils and parents: Traditional types, said one parent, with lots of hardworking professionals. Plenty of opportunities to be involved at PGS if you want to be, with the parent forum, community choir and guest lecturers.

Stations are 15 minutes walk from school, and pupils travel in from all over the south coast, from Petersfield, Haselmere, Guildford, the Isle of Wight and Chichester. A private coach service brings pupils to the door.

Communication from school is good, say parents, and although information coming via children has a less reliable arrival rate, but there's always plenty of warning by direct methods about trips and concerts.

Entrance: Most pupils at the junior school progress to the senior school, without exams, and make up around 50 per cent of year 7. The rest come from state primaries and local independent schools.

For external candidates, at 11+, assessments in English, maths, comprehension and non verbal reasoning and interview. At 13+, as above, with additional assessment in a modern foreign language.

For entrance to sixth form, at least six GCSEs at grades A*-B, to include A*/A in the subjects to be studied at A level or IB higher level, and at least B grades in subjects to be studied at IB standard level. External candidates also sit papers in non-verbal reasoning and comprehension.

Exit: A handful leave in year 11, mostly to sixth form colleges. Most leave after sixth form, with 18 to Oxbridge in 2016, others to Russell Group, and a range of other destinations including RADA, Royal Holloway and the Royal Agricultural College University.

Money matters: Means-tested bursaries may be awarded to those with outstanding academic potential, and may be up to 100 per cent of fees. Scholarships are typically 3-6 per cent of fees, but more significant awards are made on a discretionary basis, depending in the level of achievement.

A parent told us, 'You can really see where your money is going – on things which directly benefit the children, like quality teaching and food'.

Remarks: 'Come here for the variety', said a pupil, and those who like to be involved would certainly thrive at this busy school, which succeeds across the board, excelling academically, and in sports, music and drama. But more than this: PGS is a school where diversity and tolerance are part of its lifeblood, not just a tag line. As one parent said – 'The school makes its claims, as they all do, but here they are all true'.

Portsmouth High School

25 Kent Road, Southsea, Hampshire PO5 3EQ

Pupils: 492 • Ages: 2-18 • Sixth form: 72

Fees: £7,890 – £13,188 pa

Tel: 023 9282 6714
Email: admissions@por.gdst.net
Website: www.portsmouthhigh.co.uk

Headmistress: Since 2011, Mrs Jane Prescott BSc PGCE NPQH. Was deputy head of Leicester High School, then deputy head of Loughborough High School, with a background in the army. Energetic and engaging, she is liked and admired by parents and pupils alike. Very focused on the well-being of her charges (she feels that the girls' well-being is the most accurate indicator of the school's success).

She is 'very hands on', one parent told us, and has open door to pupils, staff and parents (apparently fully used). 'She is very approachable and comes to everything,' said one pupil approvingly.

A devoted advocate for single sex education, she sent her two sons and daughter to single sex schools. 'Boys shuffle for the top of the pack while girls tend to take a back seat', she told us. 'Girls feel the benefit here – there is no subject stereotyping'. Her aim is for her pupils to emerge as confident learners and resilient young women who will rise to the challenges of the world of work.

Head of junior school: Since January 2014, Paul Marshallsay; studied physical education at Exeter University. Joined the school as deputy head in 2011 and became acting head in 2013. He started his teaching career at Victoria College in Jersey before becoming head of department at Burgoyne Middle School in Bedfordshire, followed by deputy head at Yorston Lodge School in Cheshire. Has taught all age groups from reception to sixth form, specialising in a variety of subjects including physical education, mathematics, geography and computing. He is married with one daughter.

Academic matters: An enquiry-led curriculum in the junior school. Year 2 children returned to school at start of term to find 'an alien called Zapper' had arrived on the classroom ceiling, complete with a letter of introduction saying that the creature only appeared at night. They were encouraged to ask questions – so they wrote to the head of ICT to request a camera to record Zapper's night-time activities. No flies on year 2. In a maths in motion project girls run a virtual Formula 1 car, measuring the angles and length of the track and checking tyre pressure and gradients.

Results are good. At A level, 43 per cent A*/A grades in 2016 (80 per cent A*/B) while at GCSE, 70 per cent A*/A. Overall GCSE results from 2007 to 2010 showed a steady decline, but soared when the current head arrived. Head says the school was on a complacent 'OK plateau'. The girls were very well behaved and the focus was purely academic (ironically, given the falling results), which was 'just not good enough'. 'Pastoral care was nowhere', she told us. 'I switched it around'. Invigorated staff and pupils now aim for outstanding, and the school's results reflect this.

Pupils report a surprising lack of pressure to get those A*s. 'It's very caring', said one girl. 'I got a D in my mocks, and they said, "let's work out what went wrong". I got an A in the actual exam – but there wasn't pressure to get an A'. Parents talk of nurture and 'support without pressure'. One said that a D grade would be celebrated as much as an A grade if that was the best a girl could achieve. 'The competition is for the girl, not the school'. Parents say the school is less fiercely competitive than the nearby grammar and that there's no pressure here to retake disappointing grades to tweak those league tables. 'Move on', says the head firmly. 'All things are explainable'. (Even if the explanation might be laziness and recent reformation of character.)

A smaller selection of subjects on offer than at larger schools, but staff will do their best to accommodate a girl's urge to learn something in particular. A parent whose daughter spoke good French asked if she could learn Spanish instead. The school did better than that, and she now learns Spanish as well as having a weekly one-to-one French session. Most girls take a language up to GCSE, but a few struggling with the basics can drop their language to focus on maths instead. School offers French, Spanish, Latin, Mandarin and Russian. Pupils who arrive with little English are supported to learn the language – only a basic ability in English required before joining the school.

More than half of pupils take maths at A level – lack of stereotyping means girls don't avoid maths and sciences. Subjects offered at A level include government and politics, drama, psychology and Latin (provision shared with St John's College in Portsmouth).

RS is popular – we observed a lively GCSE class doing some bartering (a slight relief to hear the noise after the sheer concentrated effort of most classes observed). The topic was economic trading with ethical dimensions. 'They are trying to solve world poverty', explained the teacher. 'They haven't done it yet,' she added dryly.

Spacious labs, which after the £1.2 million refurbishment (amongst other things) allow pupils to use the data feed from solar panels on roof. When we visited, upper sixth pupils were just off to hear Lord Winston speak. 'We try to give the girls all the opportunities we can – as much extracurricular as possible to make science relevant to the rest of life', says the school. No more ICT – computer science has taken over. Bookable sets of iPads for pupils, particularly used for language lessons. Much focus on trying to encourage independent thought. Analytical, philosophical, ethical and political skills lessons have the aim of diffusing these skills through the curriculum.

Constant data collection on performance, so those falling behind are quickly spotted. Immediate redress, starting with a chat to pupil and parents. Annual parents' evening, half-termly report cards and one full report a year.

All pupils are screened for SEN, but just a handful with special needs. SENCo for the whole school and special individual and group sessions where necessary. One pupil has been given an iPad of her own to assist her learning.

Games, options, the arts: Sport taken seriously and despite small urban site, school offers almost everything. If there is a criticism from the girls, it is that they don't get enough games lessons (although most years have five sessions a week). Sport England standard sports hall and school uses fleet of minibuses to reach the naval sports ground and pool and Portsmouth University's multi-use games area and synthetic turf pitch (co-owned with the school). Nearby common is used for rounders and tennis. Games range from pop lacrosse to Pilates, with everything in-between (including football and tag rugby – no sex discrimination here). Sports trips for netball and hockey.

Wide enrichment programme offered. Before school trampolining is popular, as is sailing club cookery club, chess, debating, pupil-led Christian society, and Amnesty group. Girl-led initiatives are encouraged. Big take-up for D of E.

Strong music department, with individual instruments encouraged from year 7. Plenty of public performance, overseas tours, recent choral performance at Royal Festival Hall. Big musical every other year. Drama studio, plus larger stage in the hall next door. Girls have performed at Portsmouth's Theatre Royal, and Edinburgh Festival.

Lovely art space – central atrium flooded with light from glass ceiling. Art courses cover ceramics, textiles, photography and fine art, with girls dictating the content as they get older. DT room packed with exciting equipment and a Tiggerish devotee of DT for a teacher. Rows of tiny models lined the shelves when we visited – a mini-me project for year 7s. DT lunchtime club very popular too.

Music is strong in the junior school too, with 90 per cent learning an instrument. Art room packed with papier mâché heads, gauzy fish and skydiving figures. Lots of clubs – 'always something going on,' say parents. Gardening club, football, trampolining, dance, strings and athletics – and are winners of the U11 Wessex Netball League. Year 4 do swimming and there's sailing from year 4 up.

Background and atmosphere: Junior school is located in elegant house, five minutes' walk from senior school. Slight feeling of other worldliness, perhaps engendered in part by being a single sex school, with an emphasis on old-fashioned good manners, perhaps because the entrance is so non-institutional – a high ceilinged white entrance hall, full of light, with white frescos dancing around the top of the walls. Brightly coloured seating and papier mâché hens, along with a suggestions box.

One parent told us that she walked through the door and knew it was the right school for her daughter. Girls are articulate and charming, and a real tribute to their school. The previous head felt that the school's focus on speech and drama helps to develop confidence, and certainly the girls we met, from reception upwards, were keen to share their thoughts about their school. They like an awful lot of things, from fraction Fridays (a chocolate or fruit cake is divided into fractions before consumption) to their favourite teachers. Most of the girls' criticisms concerned lack of space and décor. 'The paintwork in the hall is wearing away', said one. 'It gives it an old sort of feel'.

School buildings are a combination of styles, including the lovely main building, a purpose-built pre-prep and what was a rather down-at-heel, converted Victorian house with squashed classrooms for years 3 to 6. Girls, parents and school alike keen to gut and redo this building. 'It's a bit crowded and it's difficult to focus when the window rattles sometimes', said one girl. Although the walls were painted in bright colours, displays were rather limited in this part of the school. School has now invested in new KS2 building with three classrooms and PE changing room.

Lovely outside space with topiary teddies, mini gardens, allotment, beast areas and a chick house with a webcam so pupils can see the eggs hatch. Also an area known as the Dell (looks like a miniature assault course – it's not all so ladylike).

Senior school buildings are a hodge-podge of styles. Old buildings are lovely, particularly the sixth form house, though some of the new buildings look a bit like Tesco. Interior is mostly well cared for. New catering manager has improved food dramatically. Eating in the dining room compulsory for year 7 (tables laid and waiting), but optional from year 8 onwards, so many opt for the school café. Parents astonished that their daughters choose to sit next to a teacher and chat at lunch time.

'You are known for who you are here', said one girl, adding that she felt 'anonymous' at the local grammar. Class sizes of around 20 for years 7 and 8, 15 to 20 at GCSE. A level classes vary in size. Parents feel that school's small size is its strength – girls can't get lost, literally or otherwise. Numbers on school roll are down – head reckons this reflects economic climate but bewildered parents suggest more marketing might work. School wouldn't want to be larger than 500 though, says the head. Small numbers mean staff and girls know each other well, and the curriculum can be tailored to individuals.

School is calm – difficult to imagine extremes of behaviour here. The pupils are confident and friendly. One parent told us that girls have 'confidence without cockiness', while another commented that her shy daughter was transformed after a couple of years here.

'It's nicer without boys – boys are disruptive', said a year 8 girl firmly. This seemed to be the prevailing view of pupils, and the school attracts a few disillusioned escapees from the local grammar. One parent who worried about single-sex education before she sent her daughter here said: 'I thought they would be, you know, bitchy, but they are almost too nice to each other. They are very caring.' With two boys' schools nearby, girls have plenty of opportunity to socialise on the way to and from school and during activities like the cathedral choir. Sixth formers share a few lessons with boys from St John's, too. Parents happy with communication – email update every week and email queries to school get prompt response.

The sixth form centre is part of the school, but sixth form girls get far more independence. Head girl and senior prefects (elected by peers) have lots of responsibility. School has tried to create a college atmosphere for the sixth form, and succeeded. Sixth formers attend house meetings and assemblies first thing, then come and go as they please. If they abuse the system, they have to stay in school, but this is very rare. No uniform, but smart dress with the silver Portsmouth High badge – no jeans. They are self assured, polite and friendly. The sixth form house has a white seating area, very tidy kitchen (with its own dishwasher) peaceful study rooms, small library, computer room and conservatory. 'When things are stressful at home, I just want to get to school and be in the sixth form centre', a sixth former said.

Officially it's a non-denominational school but in practice it's mildly Christian. Morality is a general approach, not religion-led. Lots of community activities too. Girls contribute to local charities, volunteer at the local food bank and at beach clean ups and are part of the British Council's Connecting Classrooms project.

The senior and junior schools are increasingly close. Parents told us that the junior school is more under the senior umbrella since arrival of current senior head. Most junior girls progress to the senior school. Great care taken in the transition from junior to senior, with taster sessions from year 5, year 6 pupils doing some science lessons at the senior school and teachers travelling between the two sites.

Day ends at 3.40pm but pupils can stay until 6pm and use the library, which is well-stocked with books, online periodicals, computers and iPads.

Pastoral care, well-being and discipline: Junior school girls are encouraged to take care of each other's feelings, and older children are very solicitous of younger pupils. A newcomer told us: 'I don't know why, but I don't fall out so much with my friends (here)'. Everyone we spoke to was happy to be at an all-girls school. Why? Because 'boys are annoying, loud and noisy'. Girls are very well behaved. Extraordinarily quiet line of nursery pupils were waiting for instruction in their ballet lesson – girls have clearly absorbed the adage that manners maketh (wo)man, and apply it fully. Meanwhile year 6 pupils applied lively energy to their science lesson, responding to the question about 'upthrust' by saying in a delighted chorus – 'that means you can pick up Daddy in a swimming pool'.

New emphasis on pastoral care under current senior school head. Girls feel that they can talk to the head, that they will be listened to and that their efforts are appreciated. 'You get a handwritten card the day after you are in something – a proper one, not just one of those ink print things'. If something is wrong, the girls had no doubt to whom they would turn – 'the deputy head ... she's like a mother hen'. School also has a welfare officer.

Bullying very rare. Girls supported through any friendship problems by deputy head. Pupils can become peer supporters in year 9 and receive training in confidentiality. 'You have to fill out a proper application, like a job', a pupil gravely assured us. Great care taken in smoothing the transition from junior to senior school for year 7s. Girls appear to have good relations with teachers – 'not invasive, but caring', said a sixth former. Another girl told us: 'If you are struggling (with work), it's caring... how can we work together, how can we sort this out?' This is certainly not a rap over the knuckles, must do better, sort of place. Head is a firm believer in pupil voice and school has a code of conduct that all are expected to maintain.

Pupils and parents: Famous old girls include Dame Mary Donaldson, the first woman Lord Mayor of London, Dr Jane Collins, chief executive of Marie Curie Cancer Care, author and broadcaster Jane Hill, MP Meg Hillier, TV presenter Charlotte Jackson, Dr Katharine Vincent, an expert on sustainability and climate change, Dr Frances Saunders, president of the Institute of Physics and actress Denise Black.

Pupils travel in by school minibus, public transport, hovercraft from the Isle of Wight, by bike and on foot. Parents are a broad church. 'I thought it would be all Boden mums, but it really isn't', one mother told us. Parents say it's for those who value education and are prepared to invest. 'We don't go on holiday much,' said another.

Entrance: Prospective junior school pupils are informally assessed in maths, literacy, English and non-verbal reasoning. There's also an informal interview with the head.

Most girls start senior school in year 7, but pupils can join in any year. Standard entrance exam in English and maths. Seven or eight pupils join at sixth form level.

Exit: Ninety-three per cent of juniors to senior school (automatic entry, but may sit entrance tests if they want to try for scholarship/prizes). Around 30 per cent leave after GCSEs, many going to local sixth form colleges, and a further five per cent at end of year 12. Most sixth form leavers to top universities. One to Oxbridge in 2016 plus one medic. Recent destinations include Sussex, Bath, Cardiff, Durham, Bristol, Exeter, Kent, UCL, Portsmouth, Aberdeen, Birmingham, Manchester, East Anglia, Surrey and the Central School of Speech and Drama.

Money matters: Much cheaper than most schools of its ilk – great value for money. A number of small scholarships and bursaries (a couple of which pay the fees in full).

Remarks: A super no-frills choice. School is big enough to appeal to almost any girl, but not at the expense of the personal touch. Pupils and parents agree that all girls would thrive here and that it's a place where timid souls will flourish. Prestigious local reputation and a member of the GDST sisterhood.

The Prebendal School

P

52–55 West Street, Chichester, West Sussex PO19 1RP

Pupils: 175; 27 full/flexi boarders • Ages: 3–13 (boarders from 7) • C of E

Fees: Day £7,695 – £14,610; Full Boarding £20,100; Choristers £10,050 pa

Tel: 01243 772220
Email: office@prebendalschool.org.uk
Website: www.prebendalschool.org.uk

Head Master: Since 2005, Mr Tim Cannell, MA BEd (50s). Educated at Chigwell School and Davies College, followed by Winchester (formerly known as King Alfred's College). Read theology and has a masters degree in education management. Taught maths and RS in several prep schools – Bialla International School, Papua New Guinea, and Eagle House and Moor Park in the UK – where he was variously day master, housemaster and director of studies. A friendly, approachable man who knows his school, pupils (and probably parents!) very well and has thought carefully about how to achieve the best educational balance for both choristers and other students, he was clearly in the throes of planning the amalgamation of the whole school on one site at the time of our visit. A keen cricketer, he also enjoys playing squash and listening to music. Member of IAPS and CSA; has two grown-up children, one a Cambridge graduate and another still studying there.

Entrance: Parents can register for entry to the nursery at 3, but otherwise at any stage; those entering up to year 2 are informally assessed, while those in year 3 up may be tested in English, reading and maths. Current school report is required from year 1. Voice trials for chorister places – boys only – take place in November and February each year, usually for entry the following September, but sometimes sooner. Choir hopefuls are also assessed in verbal reasoning, English and maths to ensure that they can cope with the extra demands of chorister life. Choral scholarships (at least 50 per cent, sometimes more) are awarded by the cathedral chapter and include free piano tuition. Bursaries and academic scholarships (both means-tested) worth up to 50 per cent of school fees are awarded at head's discretion; sibling bursaries offered in increments of five per cent (10 per cent for a third child). Music scholarships (also up to 50 per cent) include free tuition on one instrument. All candidates going into year 7 may apply for two awards in three areas (sport, art, academic) worth up to 15 per cent of day fees. There's also a Forces bursary (maximum award is 15 per cent fees remission).

Exit: Most leave at 13 to a range of senior schools, many with music, academic, all-round, sport or art scholarships. Music scholarships abound here naturally, but there is a healthy scattering of academic awards too and art scholarships are on the up. More than half of year 8 leavers have gained a scholarship since 2006 and the tally is rising. Parents full of praise for head's ability to steer children in the right direction. Popular destinations include Portsmouth Grammar School and Lancing College as well as Eton, Seaford College, Bedales, Worth, Ardingly College, Bryanston, Cranleigh, Clayesmore & Canford. Few leave at end of year 6.

Remarks: Dating back to the foundation of Chichester Cathedral in the 11th century, when it would have been a 'song school' to educate the choristers, the school is the oldest in Sussex. Re-founded as a grammar school in 1497 by the then Bishop of Chichester, it was attached to the Prebend of Highleigh, hence its name. School now occupies a range of buildings dating from the original 14th century song school to the modern Highleigh building.

P

Separated from the beautiful edifice that is Chichester Cathedral by a stone wall and an iron gate, there is little physical division between the two buildings and this is reflected in the spiritual ties that link church and school. The cathedral is the venue for major concerts and services, eg Founder's Day, and school assemblies take place in the nave twice a week. Next to the splendour of the cathedral, some parents remark that interior of main school building is 'dated and needs modernising ... a bit like a rabbit warren with lots of staircases', but school's expansion into the building next door in 2012 provided more space for classrooms and a more user-friendly layout. The children probably don't mind their surroundings and doubtless learn their way around quickly.

Classwork is based on the national curriculum up to year 6, followed by a focus on CE and independent school scholarships in years 7 and 8. Pupils are taught as a class up to year 4 and then by subject specialist teachers from year 5. Average class size is 13, rising to a maximum of 16 (14 in pre-prep). Head has adjusted the academic timetable, increasing lesson length to 45 minutes, 'so less time is wasted between lessons.' Outdoor learning has also started to feature on the curriculum – school also has Beach School status. We observed sound teaching in year 5 maths (regular revision throughout the year) and a lively French lesson, which is taught from the age of three. CE syllabus in core subjects is completed by the summer of year 7 to allow for scholarship preparation and exam practice. Maths is set in years 7 and 8 to stretch the able. 'Prebendal really gears up for the scholars,' commented one mother, adding that leavers are usually ahead of their peers in year 9. Latin for all from year 5 is taught by a member of the cathedral clergy and set from years 6 to 8; as a result Latin scholars gain a very good grounding. School monitors the gifted and talented as well as the less able. Academic clubs support classwork after school and on Saturday mornings, eg science revision, maths and French at CE and scholarship levels, geography, history and homework clubs. 'Brilliant' learning support teacher coaches around 20 children; others with special needs are supervised by teachers and a learning support assistant.

Good-sized art and DT studio at the top of the building (up the inevitable long flight of stairs) gets plenty of light; artists enter local school competitions (and win) and gain scholarships to senior schools. There is a well-equipped ICT suite and modern science laboratory. Classrooms opening off narrow corridors aren't especially spacious, but are not overcrowded. Assembly hall doubles up as a performance space for drama and music – year 6s were reading poetry to the whole school on the day of our visit. Another large, if rather cold and damp, older room used for orchestra and ensemble rehearsals; head says a new music block is part of the current expansion plans and will house music technology facilities and a small performance space. Modern Highleigh building, home to the nursery plus all of pre-prep, has light, airy, spacious classrooms and a small separate playground. Charming walled garden provides a quiet outdoor area close to the cathedral gate.

As expected, music is at the heart of school life, although it is by no means the sole preserve of the cathedral choristers. 'Music for all' is the school's philosophy and most parents and pupils buy in with enthusiasm (only six were not learning an instrument at the time of our visit). Peripatetic musicians teach some 280 instrumental lessons each week; there are also two orchestras, two concert bands and five choirs in which over 200 children sing. School choir sings evensong in the cathedral once a term. In addition to the big concerts twice each year, there are regular informal concerts, a house singing competition and a week-long music festival. At the two weekly cathedral assemblies, junior and senior pupils take turns to perform solo, one of the school choirs sings the anthem and a pupil from year 8 does the bible reading. A parent commented that she 'cannot put a price on how much the children gain from performing music and reading in the cathedral.' The pre-prep sings the last anthem of term and has its own music coordinator, orchestra, choir and recorder ensembles. Every chorister receives free piano tuition and usually plays a second instrument; many other students also learn more than one. Although some music lessons are fixed, most rotate through the timetable and parents say the system works well and appears to have little impact on academic work (there is an edict not to miss games). One parent said, 'Music exams make all other aspects of life easy, like French aurals,' and results support this. A child doesn't have to be musical to thrive here, however, as 'the school is good enough at other things, like sport and academic work.'

Although head has sacrificed one weekly games session, there are still three afternoons largely devoted to games – soccer, rugby, hockey and netball in the winter terms and cricket, athletics, rounders and tennis in the summer. School has its own outdoor, heated pool for swimming lessons in the summer term. As well as the usual grass pitches and courts, there is an all-weather cricket pitch and all-weather cricket nets; the school also has access to Chichester College Astroturf. Everyone is encouraged to represent the school in sport; the less sporty are rotated through the B teams so that they are able to play a match at least once a term. First hockey, cricket and netball teams regularly do well as does the girls' soccer team.

Fencing and gymnastics clubs, plus cross-country running, offer alternatives to main school sports.

School has a friendly feel and children lining up for lunch looked happy (meals are provided by outside caterers and appeared reasonable). Literature states that individual happiness is important, and this was certainly evident during our visit when one young man seemed distressed during a lesson changeover. Whilst we talked to the (hugely enthusiastic) children about their work, head immediately took the time to speak with the teacher. Two heads of pastoral care (years 3 to 5 and years 6 to 8) lead a regular weekly assembly and are responsible for any serious issues. Parents confirm that discipline is fair and that school is 'very good at dealing with energetic young boys; what happens in school, stays in school' commented one. The chorister tutor sees the 18 choristers and probationers every day to sort out any issues, check prep and manage their busy lives.

The cathedral choir is the mainstay of the boarding community as boys remain in school to sing weekend services. They are joined by a small number of weekly and flexi-boarders and occasionally by children attending Wednesday or Friday 'theme nights', eg LAMDA performance evening, Canadian evening – even water fights! All pupils are English speaking; a few of the school's pupils speak other languages (Romanian, Polish, Chinese, Japanese). Many of the local medics choose to send their children here. Main dorm has an unusual vaulted ceiling and comparisons with Hogwarts are irresistible – the likeness ends there, however, as boarder parents speak very highly of the matrons. In practice, the choristers are the only boarders in school after lunchtime on Saturday, although they have the opportunity to go home on most Wednesday and Saturday evenings (chorister parents are welcome for Sunday brunch). One mother felt that lunchtime supervision could be better to ensure that younger children are eating well; there are also no mid-morning snacks provided beyond pre-prep for day children.

Extracurricular activities take place every day after school and on Saturday mornings (no Saturday school) and are open to all. Activities range from ICT and music theory to rugby, knitting and stamp clubs. Choristers can join Saturday morning clubs after music practice, eg tennis, rugby and cricket. There are also supervised prep and revision sessions and voluntary maths coaching on Saturdays. Day pupils can come in if they wish; some clubs incur a charge (eg fencing) but most are free. School trips have included residential trips to Normandy, France, youth hostelling in North Wales and a week in Rome. Very active PTA raises funds for anything from loos on the sports field to whiteboards and car park resurfacing. 'There is a good social network here if parents want it.'

Actively sought out by local parents for its strong Christian ethos, this is a friendly, 'softer round the edges' place than some cathedral schools. It is agile enough to meet the academic, social and spiritual needs of the whole student body without sacrificing the particular requirements of a small number of choristers. The unification of the entire school on one site can only benefit pupils, improve internal communications and continue to foster a family atmosphere.

Prior's Field

Priorsfield Road, Godalming, Surrey GU7 2RH

Pupils: 440; 107 full/weekly/flexi boarders • Ages: 11–18 • Sixth form: 80

Fees: Day £17,100; Boarding £27,300- £29,100pa

Tel: 01483 810551
Email: admissions@priorsfieldschool.com
Website: www.priorsfieldschool.com

Head: Since September 2015, Mrs Tracy Kirnig MA PGCE, previously deputy (and for one term acting) head of Caterham School. She has taught religious studies in co-educational and girls' boarding and day schools in the maintained and independent sectors. She studied religious studies and philosophy at UCW Aberystwyth, followed by an MA in education at King's College, London and a PGCE at St Martin's, Lancaster.

Academic matters: Not the top academic school in the county but possibly the most rounded and least competitive. The school does not totally agree with this, saying it's more that 'Prior's Field girls are not unhealthily competitive. They can be when they need to be, as in sport and when winning the Surrey Schools' Problem Solving Competition'. School says they are now attracting more girls at the top end of the ability range and parents are confident that they are capable of dealing with all sorts. Certainly their results are more than acceptable, and the fact that it 'does not feel like a pressure cooker' enables girls to learn and develop at their own speed. Set in maths, English, languages and the sciences from day one, but this is flexible and not definitive. In 2016, 33 per cent A*/A grades at A level and 55 per cent A*/A at GCSE

High quality teaching with average age of staff at 42, around a quarter of whom have been at the school for over 10 years. Average class size 15, never more than 22. Pupil:teacher ratio approximately 8:1. A parent said, 'their main strength is that they focus on an all-round education'. That is certainly born out by the range of subjects they can study, plenty of extras and a huge variety of clubs and activities. Just reading the possibilities is mind boggling – especially in such a relatively small school.

Each girl is treated as an individual and, because the school is not overly selective, the focus is not solely on her intellectual achievement but also on finding the best path for her to follow to develop her personality and confidence. This also encourages most of them to stay on for sixth form, where a girl can pursue pretty well any course or combination of courses that she likes. We met one, on her own, doing AS level food technology, thrilled at the individual help she was being given.

Flexible and inclusive approach to SEN. Anything beyond mild unlikely to be catered for. Prefers to do as much as possible within the classroom situation; anything more may involve individual or group support lessons, charged for as an extra. G and T also treated within the classroom, with an extension programme for scholars. EAL tuition also available.

Games, options, the arts: Good space within the school grounds and sports hall for all the usual activities, especially since recent addition of large all weather pitch. Only small covered swimming pool, so girls taken to Surrey Sports Park for lessons. About 45 per cent take part in some type of competitive sport during the year – either extracurricular or inter-house matches. Some 35 winter and 21 summer teams compete locally and regionally against other schools. Several pupils also reach national level, or higher – one of their tennis players reached number 90 in the under 14 English ranking and others have represented their country in riding, kayaking and skiing. The seniors can choose their own sports, whether they be competitively physical or more along the yoga/pilates line.

Wonderful art on display, the standard appearing exceptionally high. Plenty of opportunities to follow various courses and techniques. Talent abounds; several go on to do degree courses using their well nurtured creative ability. When we visited the textiles department, some sixth form girls were creating extraordinarily complicated designs for an A level millinery project. It really would seem that this school is able to cater for anything anyone wants to learn.

Music also important. Around half of the girls play, ranging from grade 1 to diploma level, on a variety of instruments. They can try orchestral, pop and rock music and learn music theory. Singing also important, with several choirs.

And, of course, there is drama: a whole school production – usually a musical – each year and a lower school play. Everyone is involved in something – on or off stage. Other smaller plays and productions as time and curriculum dictate. Several girls follow the LAMDA courses, and RADA lessons are also offered. Some even go on to drama school and a stage career.

Plenty of outings and expeditions, and after-school clubs cover a wide range of interests. D of E programme which included a trip to Norway for the gold recently, and some girls also follow the national Sports Leaders programme. Then there are trips to France, Spain and further afield. Lucky were those who went to Malaysia as part of the World Challenge.

Boarding: Sixth form building is very grown up with own café and common room, and self-decorated, individual bedrooms for all. The overseas pupils get slightly bigger quarters – 'they have more stuff to store'. All looked great fun. Good boarding facilities for 11-15s. The younger children share double rooms, the older ones have single rooms but can choose to share if they prefer. Lighter supervision as girls go through the school – older pupils complete prep in bedrooms to help foster independent learning skills. Bathrooms look a bit shabby but, we gathered, there are refurbishment plans. A couple of common rooms for them to relax in after school is over. Happiness is paramount.

P

Plenty of flexibility with weekly boarders (most popular option) leaving school Friday night or Saturday morning and returning Sunday or Monday morning – though welcome to join weekend activities. Will also do best to fit in day girls wanting one off stays at school. Each year group has different activities – boarders also meet for themed suppers. Trips include ice-skating, bowling, theme parks, London museums and galleries, theatre visits, meals out, concerts and (naturally) shopping.

Background and atmosphere: Founded in 1902 by Julia Huxley, the granddaughter of Thomas Arnold of Rugby and mother of Aldous, the only boy ever to have attended the school. The main school building was designed by Charles Voysey and, externally, provides an interesting contrast to the extremely modern facilities that have been created inside over the last 10 years. All very well done, his oak hall and staircase remain, as well as his quirky motifs, and the Gertrude Jekyll rose garden is still there for the girls to run round.

The first stop on our tour of the school was the main hall, where all the juniors were seated on the ground in circles drawing small falcons perched amongst them. We had arrived on a cross-curricular day involving problem-solving in mathematics, feathers, flying and sketching, encouraging enthusiasm and the desire to find out and discover. This appeared to typify the general adventurousness of the school, the imagination brought to engaging the pupils and the importance they put on cross-curricular learning.

No uniform; supposedly some limitations but looked pretty relaxed to us. Black suits and jackets for formal occasions. Open, relaxed pupils perfectly happy with the all girls' situation. They said they have 'good relationship with teachers'. Small classes, average eight, some just two to four pupils.

Same buzzy atmosphere throughout the rest of the school. State-of-the-art facilities everywhere. New science, music and technology centre. New creative arts section, everything to stretch imaginations. Music corridor including composition room full of computers. Everything bright and airy. Incredible DT room, where one pupil was working on her GCSE project – a very modern-looking circular rocking chair. Some other wonderful small creations, and the beginning of an idea for a hovercraft – 'that will take at least two years to put together'. Their last such major engineering project, a solar powered car, has qualified for the national final at Goodwood each year since. Here was a teacher positively brimming with enthusiasm. The old biology lab, now relocated to the science wing, has become a food technology room suitable for MasterChef. And the library, possibly the lightest one we've seen in many trips round schools, is well equipped and resourced. School is acceptably proud of it.

Pastoral care, well-being and discipline: Sympathetic, positive head of sixth has been there for many years and never had a problem with drugs, drink or smokers. Says girls give each other lots of support and the vibrant PSHE programme really does seem to work. Appears to be true throughout the whole school, where it is incorporated into daily routine. Sixth form have one-to-one sessions with their tutor each week, and form tutors meet all girls regularly. We were told 'there is a real yes culture', 'staff do seem to care about their students'. Small school, so really does become 'one big community' where every one cares for everyone else. Nobody should slip through the net.

Pupils and parents: Wide range, local and further afield; day girls, weekly, flexi and full time boarders. Not so much social Surrey, more those looking for value, but not a hothouse. All wanting an all-round education and an unthreatening atmosphere for their daughters, that, even so, pushes them to their full potential. Generally a friendly, relaxed lot.

Approximately 10 per cent from overseas, four per cent Oriental, the rest from all over. Good bus service for day girls. Interesting former pupils: Sam Cam's great grandmother, author of National Velvet, Enid Bagnold; Baroness Mary Warnock, educationalist and philosopher; Lily James, actress; and prominent editor and stylist Grace Lamb.

Entrance: Preview day in November: a taster day 'for us to get to know each girls and for them to get to know us'. Individual interviews and 'various fun departmental activities'. Girls return in January to take maths and English exams. Places then offered to approximately one in three. 'Meet the head' coffee mornings each term.

Exit: All over. Some leave at 16+ on the hunt for mixed sixth forms but the majority stay on and leave after A level for an exceptionally wide range of higher education establishments – including Bath, Liverpool and the Royal Veterinary College – to study courses as varied as architectural engineering, Arabic and adult nursing.

Money matters: Several scholarships available at all entry points, worth up to 20 per cent of fees; exhibitions worth 10 per cent. Quite a few bursaries which could be worth 100 per cent. Some means-tested sixth form bursaries for locals who will need top GCSE grades in chosen subjects. Forces children eligible for 20 per cent discount and daughters of old girls get 10 per cent. A school, ready and willing to help.

Remarks: If you are looking for a school that will provide a broad education, excellent facilities and get the best out of your daughter in an unpressurised environment, then this could be it. In this high flying, girls'-school-rich corner of Surrey, it provides a refreshing change, nurturing rather than hothousing, unearthing each girl's strengths and teaching her to use them.

Priory School

Bolters Lane, Banstead, Surrey SM7 2AJ

Pupils: 200 • Ages: 2–11

Fees: £9,675 – £12,330 pa

Tel: 01737 366920
Email: office@prioryprep.co.uk
Website: www.prioryprep.co.uk/

Headmaster: Since 2000, Mr Graham Malcolm B Ed MA, 50s. Decided to become a teacher whilst still at school himself, when a PE teacher with a knee injury asked him to cover some lessons. Taught at Winchester House in Sevenoaks, Newland House in Twickenham and was deputy head at St Michael's in Otford before taking up the headship of Priory, and after 16 years clearly relishes the job as much as ever. A down-to-earth, self-made man, and an ardent sportsman who still gets down and muddy with the boys on the rugby pitch and whose pleasant, oak-panelled study is dotted with trophies. Held in the highest regard by pupils and parents alike. 'Mr Malcolm is a teacher I really, really like!' 'He doesn't sit in his office all the time, he's really involved,' were typical comments from the boys, and parents concurred: 'Approachable, always willing to hear parents' views'; 'He understands the boys and he's very supportive of his teachers'; 'He has a wonderful manner, and I can see how boys would try their best for him.' Married to Jenny, also a teacher, with a grown up son and daughter.

Loves his work, and works tirelessly at it. Takes the job of managing the boys' school careers very seriously, actively forging and maintaining links with senior schools and negotiating future opportunities for his pupils from the moment they join the school. ('He is being terrifically ambitious about secondary schools for our son,' reported a satisfied parent,) In his scanty leisure time, relaxes with a pleasantly 1950s-style combination of interests: golf, football, reading, news, DIY and family holidays.

Entrance: Non-selective at reception, with an informal taster day the only assessment. Two-form entry, with a maximum of 16 places per class, around half of which go to boys coming up from their own nursery. A further four places available at year 3, when the class size increases to 18: applicants at this stage are tested on their maths and English and will have a chat with the head. Bursary available at this entry point, plus academic scholarships of 5-10 per cent. Occasional places do arise from time to time as families move about – always worth checking.

Exit: Destinations in 2016 include Epsom College, Whitgift, St John's Leatherhead, KCS and Ewell Castle. Also Aberdour, The Cedars, Cheam, City of London Freemen's and Dunottar. Usually several scholarships and success at local grammars: Sutton, Wallington and Wilson's.

Following the decision of St John's Leatherhead and Epsom College to admit pupils from 11+, Priory is phasing out its top two forms: the current year 7 and year 8 cohorts, already noticeably smaller than the other year groups, are the last in the school. 'I'll be sorry to see them go,' admitted the head, 'but it was the right thing to do.' Deputy head was optimistic about the change: 'We've been successfully preparing boys for the 11+ for years, so this gives us the opportunity to streamline everything.'

Remarks: Founded in 1921 on the site of a former priory in Sydenham, the school came to The Red House in Banstead in 1936 and has remained there ever since, despite being hit by an incendiary bomb in 1940 (lessons simply relocated to the cellar). Originally surrounded by fields and open countryside, Priory still has a village-like, homely feel to it, and we weren't surprised to learn that several parents and grandparents of the present boys went to school here. Indeed, one of the most engaging aspects of this little school is the way it manages to combine being thoroughly up to date with an old-world charm that we haven't quite seen anywhere else: think of a multicultural Jennings and Darbyshire bringing their iPads to school and you won't be far wrong.

The nursery and pre-prep are housed in the school's light and airy new building, where the inter-connecting classrooms all have soundproofed doors and the feel is modern yet cosy. Thoughtfully-equipped rooms hosted lively lessons – we saw the reception boys donning silver spacesuits and foil-covered colanders for helmets to celebrate Major Tim's spacewalk – and the standard of work on display was excellent. Reading scheme is personalized to the school and geared towards boys – 'Lots of non-fiction,' explained the head of prep-prep; 'boys like bursts of information.' Attractive play area with sandpit and all the etceteras, plus a delightful little garden and potting shed, and even a pint-sized washing line complete with smalls. As a woodland school, Priory sets aside a day a week for outdoor activities, and both staff and pupils show a genuine love of fresh air and exercise.

Years 4 to 8 are taught in the old Red House, where classrooms are smaller and, according to one parent, spartan, albeit equipped with interactive whiteboards and everything needful for the present age. The science lab, where white-coated year 8 boys were busily using charcoal to extract copper, smelt nostalgically of Bunsen burners and hydrochloric acid, and the temperature in the sports hall was a good old-fashioned freezing. But we found we didn't give two hoots, because what really impressed were the pupils and the staff. Priory boys are enthusiastic, sparky, articulate, smartly turned out, impeccably well-mannered, and very proud of their school. What goes on in the lessons here is clearly outstanding and parents declared themselves delighted with it: 'The teaching is wonderful, absolutely excellent'; 'They really know and understand each pupil'; 'The teaching staff have been fantastic'; 'The staff motivate the pupils and engage their imaginations'; 'Academically stretching lessons but fun and hands-on.' One mother whose children recently moved to Priory wrote, 'The best part about the school for me is how excited my sons seem about lessons. Some days they come home just lit up about a topic in history or science, or a computer science exercise, or a debate in religious studies.'

Music provision includes choirs, orchestra, and lots of opportunities to learn instruments and/or singing, and was highly-rated by everyone we spoke to. Plenty of public speaking and performance too – the result, according to one parent, is 'confident boys who will happily stand up in front of the school, something I couldn't have done at their age.' Art is highly creative and innovative – a real strength of the school, according to parents. Wide range of clubs – cookery, gardening, science, chess, drama, Spanish, electronics, and many more.

SEN is well catered for, and the school has a good track record in early diagnosis and support for mild dyslexia, dyspraxia and dyscalculia. One mother of a very bright lad with Asperger's expressed great satisfaction at the way the school was helping her child. That said, school was anxious to stress that, whilst it goes to great lengths to support boys with SEN, it is not a special needs school, and pupils need to fit in with its ethos of hard work, good behaviour and team spirit.

Sports at Priory are particularly strong. The main team games here are rugby, football and cricket, led from the front by the head and taken up eagerly by just about everyone. Off the playing fields, boys can do gymnastics, basketball, athletics, swimming, tennis, badminton, cross-country, fencing, kayaking and judo, 'plus target rifle shooting,' added the head cheerfully, 'and hockey for the less sporty.' The school is proud of its success in local and national competitions, but its policy is one of Sport for All and aimed at giving all boys maximum possible enjoyment. 'They've managed to get some amazing things out of my son on the playing fields,' wrote the parent of a non-sporty child, 'and I do think playing team sports has been an overall positive experience for him.' 'I wasn't too keen on football in year 3, but now I really enjoy it,' said one child we spoke to, and another added, 'When I was new here in year 4 I didn't know anything about rugby, but then I tackled someone and my confidence grew.' 'The sport is really good fun here!' was a universal sentiment. Annual sports trip to Jersey is enjoyed by everyone, the boys insist, and we believe them.

And yet, unlike some boys' preps we've visited, this school didn't strike us as either uncomfortably boysie or too comfortably-off. Families come from a wide range of backgrounds, both ethnically and socially, and the overwhelming impression we got was of everyone working hard to make life at school happy and successful on all fronts. The boys are willing to have a go at anything – they've won handwriting competitions in the past – and their sisters happily attend Priory's popular breakfast and after-school clubs. Indeed, the school believes in being a good neighbour generally, offering its facilities when it can to local groups and initiatives. 'Every now and then I have to go and measure marrows for the Banstead Horticultural Society,' observed the head, giving us once again that pleasing sensation of having walked into an Anthony Buckeridge story. Only for a moment, though. This is a hidden gem of a school, traditional but forward-looking, and turning out confident, likeable, happy and well-informed young men.

P

The Purcell School

Aldenham Road, Bushey, Hertfordshire WD23 2TS

Pupils: 182 (60 per cent girls); 143 boarders. • Ages: 8–18 • Sixth form: 79

Fees: Day £25,452; Boarding £32,499 pa

Tel: 01923 331100
Email: info@purcell-school.org
Website: www.purcell-school.org

Headmaster: Since January 2016, Stephen Yeo BMus LTCL NPQH (50s), previously head of Exeter Cathedral School. A chorister at The Cathedral School, Llandaff prior to music scholarship at King's College, Taunton. Studied music at Sheffield, then at Trinity College, London. Unusual career path took him first to top-notch senior schools in Ireland. Later became head of music and creative arts at selective King Edward VI, Handsworth, followed by three years at Bedales as director of studies. Joined Exeter Cathedral School after five years as head of Lyndhurst School in Camberley, Surrey. Married to Catherine, a languages graduate, registered nurse and midwife; they have four grown up sons. They both enjoy walking and cycling in Ireland and Wales, where they have a home.

Academic matters: Academic results variable. In 2016, 26 per cent of A level results A*/A and 59 per cent A*-B. However, music, art and English lit the only subjects with candidates in double figures; history next in line with seven takers (six for music tech German and five for maths and French). Negligible numbers studying sciences. Hardly any A*s, even for music. All of this is a sharp change from the fairly recent past when the school routinely featured high in the independent school A level league tables. The school is working hard to 'sort out the academic side'. In 2016, 56 per cent of GCSE grades were A*/A.

Years 5 and 6 taught as one group; thereafter pupils taught within their year groups. Setting for maths starts in year 9. Everyone in the GCSE years takes music, maths, English lang and science but generally take no more than seven or eight subjects. Small classes for everything. New music library and IT has been upgraded throughout. Much individual help and support, especially for musical prodigies who arrive playing perfect Paganini but with little English. SEN well supported.

Games, options, the arts: Sport surprisingly good for a school that doesn't really offer any. 'My son never liked sport until he came here,' enthused one mum who reeled off the games he was now involved in: badminton, volleyball, football. One competitive football match each year against fellow music geeks at the Yehudi Menuhin School. Currently one PE lesson per week; plans perpetually afoot to offer more physical activity. Lots of ad hoc activity, from kicking a ball about the enormous playing fields to a bit of netball and off-site swimming. Art and drama enthusiastically pursued, and drama has recently been formally added to the curriculum (art already there).

Music provision is, of course, superb. The musical day begins at 7.20am with pre-breakfast morning practice and continues, interspersed through the day, until bedtime. Practice supervisors support the under-13s. Choir compulsory for all – though resented by some as an intrusion into their practice time. That said, the senior chamber choir was described by a parent at 'simply the finest and most exciting youth choir I have EVER heard'. Most of the staff teach at the RCM or RAM and all are of that professional standard – they have to be. Professional accompanists work with the pupils – a real and special privilege. No shortage of performing opportunities. Last year there were 71 public concerts, 15 'outreach' concerts and upwards of 150 lunchtime concerts. Composing very strong and one girl was one of five winners of the BBC Young Composers' Competition recently.

The mint green music centre features a stunning recital room, teaching rooms, a recording studio, dozens of practice rooms, from which concert quality playing seeps, and nice little architectural touches everywhere. Music tech covers all aspects of creative studio work including multi-track recording, electro-acoustic music, arranging, studio engineering, producing and composition for film. A large new percussion suite. The multi-purpose school hall is still used for most concerts.

Boarding: Boarding accommodation, formerly poor, now tickety-boo. Sunley House, upstairs in the main school building, provides accommodation for 50 girls plus resident staff. New co-ed boarding house very popular – with a boys' wing and a, larger, girls' wing. The recently refurbished junior boarding house makes a cheerful home to around 20 (mostly) girls and (a few) boys ages 8-12, all in double rooms (a few singles), though with such small numbers friendships can be hard to form. Sixth form pianists have a piano in their rooms.

Pupils enthuse about their fantastic camaraderie – 'We all encourage each other – everyone is so supportive of everyone else,' and you feel this as you see them greet each other in the corridors. A few girls mentioned feeling (geographically) divided by the current split of girl boarders between Sunley, in the main school, and the new co-ed boarding house. Would make more sense to put all the girls in the new house and whack the boys into Sunley. Most boarders go home on Friday nights and return 48 hours later, but there are always around 50 in on weekends, many from abroad.

Background and atmosphere: An interesting history. Founded as recently as 1962 by Rosemary Rapaport and Irene Forster – but nonetheless the UK's oldest specialist music school. It began life as The Central Tutorial School for Young Musicians, at Conway Hall, then resided for a while in Morley College, from where it moved to Hampstead. In 1973, it was renamed The Purcell School – perhaps reflecting the new enthusiasm for 'earlyish' British music – and, in 1998, relocated to the site of the former Royal Caledonian School in fairly dismal Bushey, Hertfordshire. The main building is an attractive low-rise Edwardian pile with wide corridors, good-sized concert hall, assorted classrooms, smartened up canteen (food now provided by outside caterers and has improved no end) and new girls' boarding accommodation.

Staff and pupil morale knocked in the spring of 2013 by the redundancy of the school's well-liked head of music who conducted the school orchestra. Redundancy, after 25 years at the school, left bad feeling, with pupils melodramatically taking to wearing green ribbons to protest his removal. 'It makes us feel like music is less important now,' said one pupil. 'It's like the nerve centre has been ripped from the school', said another. School governors have had a much-needed shake-out and the average age of staff has plummeted by around 20 years. Rapid through-put of heads does not help stability. All the specialist music schools are going through a period of introspection and Purcell is no exception.

Pastoral care, well-being and discipline: Pupils given more leeway than at most schools and chafe when their freedoms are reigned in. Much friction over rules eg about when children are allowed out to visit shops and which shops they may visit. A few expulsions for use of alcohol or cannabis.

Pupils and parents: All sorts, from every economic, academic, national and social background, all united by a love of music. Some 17 per cent of boarders from overseas: nine per cent Korean, five per cent Singaporean and rest from all over. No quotas or limits on nationalities joining. A healthy slab of local children make up the day contingent who lead a very different existence to the boarders. Children can attend from age 8, though numbers are so low at that end of the school that we can't recommend boarding here quite that young. Big intake of (mainly) boarders at sixth form. Former pupils include Oliver Knussen (composer and conductor), Nicholas Daniel (oboist and first winner of the BBC Young Musician competition), Catrin Finch (former harpist to the Prince of Wales), Lara Melda (winner of 2010 BBC Young Musician), Janice Graham (leader, ENO Orchestra), and Yiruma (Korean pianist and composer).

Entrance: Pupils are selected by musical audition, supported by interviews and reasoning test. Auditions take place every week from September to March. Children come for a preliminary audition and then a majority return for a more thorough going over. Musical standard for admission is very high but not ridiculous. No academic threshold, but school must be 'able to cater for them'. No set numbers for entry at any particular age, and more coming and going here than at most schools. About 20 musicians enter at sixth form.

Exit: Mostly to The Royal Academy of Music, The Royal College of Music or The Guildhall, many with scholarships – 15 in 2016. The rest mostly to other music courses hither and yon; a few to university to read other subjects. Two to Oxbridge in 2016, both to study music. Most pupils end up with careers in music – whether teaching, production, business or performing.

Money matters: Fees have been frozen for four years. Which cannot be said of any other independent school in the United Kingdom. Indeed, fees now significantly less than many public schools, if you factor in the cost of music lessons which are included here. Meanwhile, most pupils receive some kind of financial support – under the government's music and dance assisted places scheme, school bursary or scholarship. An amazing opportunity for the brilliant but broke – many pay nothing.

Remarks: Buffeted, but not bowed – still providing a unique education to some of the world's most talented youngsters.

Queen Anne's School

6 Henley Road, Caversham, Reading, Berkshire RG4 6DX

Pupils: 450; 220 boarders • Ages: 11–18 • Sixth form: 119 • C of E

Fees: Day £22,125; Boarding £32,610 pa

Tel: 01189 187300
Email: admissions@qas.org.uk
Website: www.qas.org.uk

Headmistress: Since 2006, Julia Harrington BA, NPQH (50s), previously deputy head at Prior's Field School. Mrs H comes from a family of teachers, was educated at a grammar school in Lydney and studied history and politics at Exeter. Worked in the media and then decided to train as a teacher and psychodynamic counsellor. As a child she 'wanted to be a vet' but was told that 'girls didn't do jobs like that'. You don't need a qualification in counselling to see that this experience might have shaped her as an adult.

Mrs Harrington is a head who doesn't just sit back and let the same old tried and trusted methods do their best. She keeps up with the latest neuroscience research into how people learn, working with university psychology departments at Reading and Oxford. It's certainly heady stuff; never before have we heard the word 'amygdala' used so many times in one conversation. She stresses the importance of environment and mindset, 'Instead of saying, "I can't do this", we want girls to say, "Why not me?"' To this end she is working with preps so that girls don't come into senior school already thinking, for instance, that they're 'rubbish at maths.'

Let us say with admiration that the teenage brain is, apparently, not a mystery to this head. 'I tell the girls, the reason you want to keep checking your phones or Facebook is for the dopamine hit. If you understand the brain then you can give a reason for behaviour. Girls on the social front are hardwired to conform and it's this that can lead to behaviour like saving seats

Q

or being unkind. We challenge this by making girls aware of what they're doing and why.' Mrs H has the zeal of the convert and her enthusiasm is infectious, but before we got too carried away on the crest of a cortex we wanted to know whether she was in danger of treating her school like a laboratory. 'Not at all. I always ask, so what? How can this research help our girls?'

Mrs Harrington enjoys running but 'doesn't find it easy', and is learning Mandarin at Saturday morning classes alongside QA parents. Lives on site with her husband, who works in IT for a cancer research charity, and has three adult children (doctor, barrister, nuclear scientist. Yes, really). Favourite book would be, we assumed, some weighty work of neuroscience. It's not, well not quite. The Little Book of Thunks is a compendium of brain challenging questions that she likes to use in assembly. Favourite childhood read is good old Enid B's Five at Finneston Farm.

Academic matters: In 2016, 64 per cent A*/A at GCSE. Very good results in individual sciences and IGCSE maths but languages are trailing a bit. At A level, 34 per cent A*/A, 64 per cent A*-B, and again the sciences and maths are strongest with French still in dernier place. New head of modern foreign languages appointed.

Teaching methods are developed through the school's Life and Learning programme and staff are encouraged to apply their knowledge of the teenage brain to develop 'brain friendly lessons'. Such educational initiatives notwithstanding, teaching we observed was reassuringly similar to what we see in good schools everywhere – small classes, attentive pupils, smartboards, plenty of Q and A. The World Cup based maths lesson we witnessed was described by the teacher as 'light relief' after summer exams and looked like a lot of fun. As Mrs Harrington explained, 'by providing a complex real world mathematical challenge but framing it as an ethical conundrum,' girls are 'encouraged to take risks suggesting competing solutions to find the most ethical outcome.' In the smart and very well equipped biology lab we were impressed by the lack of squeamish squeaking as scalpel wielding as pupils prepared to dissect hearts. Girls are set in core subjects following the first half term in year 7. Lessons are 40 minutes long, doubles for eg languages, maths and science.

Our year 9 guides had obviously been paying attention to the head and were keen to tell us that 'striving' was very important at their school. 'We're not put under pressure but teachers help us strive to achieve our very best.' One or two parents mutter that they would like their daughters to be pushed to strive a bit harder, but general consensus is that school has balance about right.

Heaps of praise for excellent individual attention, subject support and UCAS advice in the sixth form but we hear that girls who don't want to go to university feel rather sidelined. School says that recent pupils who haven't gone on to university have taken up places at RADA, Central St Martins and the Deliotte Undergraduate Training Programme.

SEN support mostly provided in class; individual sessions also available if necessary. EAL taught in place of modern foreign languages or Latin; all international pupils take English language and literature GCSE.

Games, options, the arts: At the time of our visit, the performing arts centre was being fitted out for the lower school production of Peter Pan (flying scenes to be done with puppets) and we enjoyed chatting to some very excited cast members. What would they do with a million pounds to spend on their school, we asked? 'We'd build a theatre like the one in Glee!' they cried. These young actors felt the school would benefit from bigger, better performing arts facilities but, though smallish, their current theatre lacked for nothing as far as we could see.

Plenty of options for the musical – choirs, ensembles, swing band and orchestras plus an exciting programme of visiting professionals, not only from the world of the arts but also science and business, all part of a programme called World Class in Class. The head is keen for girls to 'see and know excellence' and also to demystify it. 'They meet these talented people and discover that they are also ordinary human beings who work very hard.'

Sloping games field is apparently a bit of an uphill struggle in lacrosse matches (it's the C team that gets to play on the steepest bit) but such hardships are obviously character building since QA lax is pretty fierce and successful. Main rival is Downe House. Excellent sports facilities, including 25m pool, fitness suite, dance studio, climbing wall plus loads of tennis and netball courts mean that there's something for everyone – even ballroom dancing with The Oratory boys. Plenty of horsey stuff, too, including riding and polo clubs and the annual Queen Anne's Grass Roots and Inter-Schools' Show Jumping Competition.

Boarding: All seven boarding houses are tip top – these are the bases for day girls as well – and quite the smartest we've seen. Purpose built, modern and (very) brightly furnished (pink and blue chenille sofas and bucket chairs) and carpeted in house colours. Student artworks decorate the walls and common rooms, as does an abundance of bunting. No poky kitchenettes here; huge kitchens with all the kit are a great social hub. The large fridges are filled with Waitrose bags – older girls may go down the road to this and other local emporia in groups. International students love to cook up a taste of home, and luckily Ocado delivers any esoteric ingredients not to be had for ready money in Caversham. Girls are challenged to produce meals on a budget, they bake cakes for charity sales and teach each other favourite dishes. They also host dinner parties and invite chaps from nearby schools.

Regular socials with nearby schools – mainly The Oratory and Shiplake. Parents say that there's not much to persuade older girls to stay at the weekend and most prefer to head for home.

Upper sixth day and boarding girls are based in Michell, a house that is separate from the main cluster of buildings, affording privacy and a degree of independence. Many older day girls drive in and can park on site.

Background and atmosphere: Built on 34 acres of primest Caversham (or 'Caversham actually,' as it's known by residents. It may be just over the bridge from Reading but mix the two up at your peril). Handsome Victorian brick pile set in immaculate lawns with, at the time of our visit, groups of girls dotted decoratively about, reading in the sunshine. Reception hall and offices are elegant, rather in the smart country hotel style; vibrant contemporary stained glass panels in the front door are the first hint that this school may be traditional, but with a modern twist.

Atmospheric galleried chapel now only accommodates everyone when upper years are on study leave. Chapel services for lower and upper school several times a week and regular hymn practice; female chaplain recently appointed. Brand new sixth form centre, The Space, also includes a digital library, a restaurant for staff and pupils and Kirstoff's at Café 6. Meal times are staggered and those who need to be at clubs and activities get packed lunches or can collect a deli-style lunchbox, and the food got a moderate thumbs up. Apparently breakfasts are fantastic and fish and chips on Friday is top lunch. Sixth formers have their own rather cool café in an old hall (former gymnasium); other years can get lunch there on Saturdays – much friendlier than having to eat in a half empty dining room.

Queen Anne's is part of the Grey Coat Hospital Foundation (other schools include Grey Coat Hospital, Emanuel, Sutton

Valence and Westminster City School) and was established on its current site in 1894. Historic links with Westminster and the Abbey remain.

Website and marketing material are big on warm and fuzzy but rather low on boring old facts such as exam results by subject. We don't want to come over all Gradgrind but sometimes facts are necessary. Especially when parents or grandparents are making expensive decisions. The prospectus declares that the school is 'full of bubbly, smiley and enthusiastic people'. While we can't argue with that (actually, we might pick a fight with 'bubbly': it's usually an adjective of last resort and rarely applied to an intellectual equal), one can't help pondering whether all the buzz words – resilience; empowerment; brain plasticity; synthesis – might put off those who just want to know exactly what you get for boarding fees of over 10 grand a term. Stick with it, we say, it's all here and a bit more too.

Pastoral care, well-being and discipline: Day girls have a desk and often a bed and can stay over at short notice – flexi and weekly boarding options much appreciated by parents. It's a long day (home at 6.30pm) but prep is done under supervision in houses and tea is provided. After 4.30pm it's clubs and, if necessary, subject clinics; girls choose a minimum of three clubs from an enticing range of sporting and cultural options.

Parents told us that pastoral care is excellent, and our guides loved the strong inter-year group relations; the older girls 'are like big sisters'. Girls told us that there are no cliques and that everybody gets a chance to shine in drama, sport and music. Sixth formers have smart single en-suite study bedrooms. As we observed and several parents confirmed, university accommodation is sometimes a let down after this.

Recent drive to spruce up uniform not entirely popular with older pupils but has gone down well with younger pupils and parents. Sleeveless red V neck pullovers, white shirts, blazers and, according to our guides, socks, not tights, even in winter, 'In the snow!' Perhaps there was a bit of dramatic licence here, since school says it isn't the case. Staff are 'very' vigilant about skirt lengths, apparently. Sixth formers wear the dreaded 'smart business' mufti. Distinctive red hooded cloaks are no longer mandatory but still used at biennial service of thanksgiving at Westminster Abbey, carol services and other special occasions. They're also rather photogenic, especially in the snow, and as a result are more frequently seen in marketing material than in real life. Girls we spoke to thought the school rules were 'strict but fair. Apart from the socks.'

Pupils and parents: Generally rather well-heeled. Majority local, boarders mostly live around an hour away. Increasing numbers from London who see it as a positive and also convenient (only 25 mins to Paddington) alternative to metropolitan school rat race. International students from over 15 countries seem to integrate well and UK girls get invitations to plenty of exotic sleepovers. Famous old girls include Posy Simmonds, Jenny Seagrove and the real Joan Hunter Dunn, immortalised by John Betjeman.

Entrance: Prospective pupils (from wide range of local preps and state primaries) are encouraged to attend a taster day and overnight stay. Assessment for entry at 11+ consists of tests in maths, English, verbal and non-verbal reasoning and a group interview. For entry to the sixth form students sit an exam and will need a minimum of six GCSEs at grade C or above (including English and maths) and B in subjects to be studied at A level

Exit: Some 25 per cent depart after GCSEs to local colleges or co-ed sixth forms. Those who stay for A levels go on to respectable universities including Bristol, St Andrews, Nottingham (medic) and Leeds. Wide range of subjects (law, medicine, engineering, art and drama) testament to strengths in all areas. One to Oxford in 2016 to study music with a choral scholarship.

Money matters: Boarding fees broadly in line with home counties compatriots. Day fees are good value considering girls get extended school day and thus some of the boarding perks. Art, music, drama, sports and all-rounder scholarships at 11+ and 13+. Will help in cases of hardship.

Remarks: A welcoming, dynamic and forward-thinking school. Delivers academically but there's much more than that to an education at Queen Anne's. Who would it suit? We leave the answer to Mrs Harrington: 'When parents ask what kind of girl is a Queen Anne's girl, I answer that I hope there never is one, they are all individuals.'

Queenswood

Shepherd's Way, Brookmans Park, Hatfield, Hertfordshire AL9 6NS

Pupils: 430; 184 full/weekly boarders • Ages: 11–18 • Sixth form: 132

Fees: Day £20,925 – £24,825; Boarding £30,450 – £33,750 pa

Tel: 01707 602500
Email: admissions@queenswood.org
Website: www.queenswood.org

Principal: Since September 2016, Joanna Cameron, previously deputy head of Ipswich High. Degree in environmental science from Surrey; she has taught science at St Mary's Wantage and was a member of the senior leadership team at St Gabriel's in Newbury. A keen sportswoman, with a passion for running, hockey and equestrianism, she is married to David and they have two sons.

Academic matters: A level/Pre-U results strong. In 2016, 73 per cent of grades were A*-B in the 23 subjects offered and 51 per cent A*/A. Forty per cent of students gained at least three A*/A grades, while over 20 per cent of all grades achieved were A* – the highest ever tally for the school. Broad intake, coupled with commendable performance, places school at pinnacle of Hertfordshire's value-added tables. Languages are hot here, with most girls taking two at GCSE and one to A level. Japanese really gaining momentum from year 8 up, thanks to enthusiastic teaching and a cultural visit to Japan (alternative for those staying at home is a week of Japanese visitors and activities). Latin from year 7 and the recommendation is that pupils either continue with it or switch to classical civilisation from year 8. Italian and Spanish also on the menu and girls encouraged to continue studies in their own native languages.

No one is refused a go at a GCSE – 'they're keen to push the academic students as much as possible, but are also prepared to coach and encourage those who are less academic and need a different approach,' noted a parent. In 2016, 64 per cent A*/A grades. Teaching is mainly traditional with ICT increasingly used by all – every girl has a laptop. Sets for maths, French, English and science; class sizes not larger than 24, many smaller (DT scheduled against ICT in year 7 and textiles in year 8 to allow for smaller groups, for example). Pre-U English and history of art going great guns and EPQ alongside A levels (no IB here and no plans). RE growing in popularity with a dozen taking A level and one or two per year to study theology or philosophy at uni (often Cambridge). Government and politics a popular newcomer. Academic scholars have a staff mentor.

About 15 per cent have EAL needs. Support available for those with moderate dyslexia or other, mild SEN. Some 90 on register, many monitored and some receive one-to-one (max two lessons a week) from helpful and enthusiastic learning support co-ordinator. Most have SpLD type difficulties but a few with mild ADD, ADHD or ASD. School earnestly insists that parents matter. 'They're the ones who know the girls, what makes them tick, what causes them to crumble, so we're always keen to discuss issues, strategies and ways forward.'

Games, options, the arts: A school for budding international sports stars – 'We love watching sports and it's a joy to be part of a school that wins'. Lots of successes at regional and national finals. National hockey players include members of the England junior squad and one recent leaver is now a promising player on the international tennis circuit, another a world-class rower. School is a national LTA clay court centre and hosts the annual national schools' championships. School's tennis team were silver medallists at recent World Schools Tennis Championships and the Lawn Tennis Association recommends it for would-be tennis stars. With 27 courts in all – 12 clay, 13 all-weather and two indoors – 'you can play tennis at any level,' and at almost any time. One pupil is a national and international wheelchair tennis star. Budding stars in all disciplines are carefully mentored – help given with diet, fitness (fitness coach onsite who devises individual programmes), training, fixtures etc. Masses of inter-school competitions ensure sport for all. Facilities include large, modern indoor swimming pool, Astroturf hockey pitch, fully equipped fitness suite, aerobics room, professional dance studio and huge sports hall.

More than half learn a musical instrument and many at least two. Ensembles for everything and very enthusiastic teaching – a lively percussion session was in full swing when we visited. School rock band. One pupil a BBC Young Chorister of the Year finalist recently. Meanwhile drama thrives, with half taking LAMDA lessons and awards for actors and public speakers. Lower and upper school productions every year, plus one for GCSE and A level students and scholar plays in between. Rehearsals for Sweeney Todd in the rehearsal space when we visited – great gusto on display. Dramatists visit Edinburgh Fringe. Celebrated its 120th anniversary in style with a music, drama and dance extravaganza at the Barbican Hall in London.

Thriving 3D art department with its own kiln. Around 10 a year continue to A level (upper sixth students have individual atelier workspaces) and a few move on to art school, while architecture is also popular. Artists are inspired on trips to Milan and Florence.

One of only 20 schools to run the elite Leith's cookery course in preference to food tech – taught right from the beginning (even including lessons on choosing the right wine to accompany). When we visited girls were whipping up macaroni cheese or rack of lamb with a herb crust, depending on ability. Timetabled lessons for years 7 and 8 and a club thereafter. Each student issued with her own set of Sabatier knives, uniform and Leith's 'bible' to keep. Leith's teacher was formerly a chef in the school's own kitchens.

Dance unsurprisingly popular and the school has its own dance team (puts on an annual spectacular and contributes to other school shows too). Model United Nations, Young Enterprise, debating society, plus charity works. Thriving D of E – 25 working on gold, 45 recently achieved bronze. School awarded silver level eco-school status.

Trips galore, especially with London on the doorstep (museums, galleries, Wimbledon etc). Year 9 girls have the opportunity to study for a term overseas, usually Australia or New Zealand. Language visits to Spain and Japan. Sports teams tour all over the world – all 'help the girls to develop independence, work as a team and cope when things don't go right'. Acknowledgement of the global community though exchange schools in Australia, New Zealand, South Africa, Canada, Japan. Girls work on education projects with schools in Malawi and Zambia. Closer to home, community work in local primary schools and with the elderly – developing 'generosity of spirit and the importance of giving, to counteract the materialism communicated by the media'.

Boarding: Cosy houses with contemporary interior design to please even the pickiest of teenage girls integrate day and boarding pupils – one for years 7 and 8, four for years 9, 10 and 11, plus sixth form houses. Day girls have the flexibility to board when they wish if a bed is free and this is encouraged. Some fixed 'in school' and 'home weekends,' otherwise boarders can spend full weekend at home with choice of Sunday evening or Monday morning return. A few traditionalists would prefer a return to full boarding, but most appreciate this is a move to meet 21st century family needs and preserve the boarding ethos.

Background and atmosphere: Founded in Clapham Park in 1894 and moved to purpose-built neo-Tudor building in 1925 (masses of later additions). Splendid grounds – glorious gardens open to the public at end of May and 120 acres of sports fields and woodland. Two miles from the M25, a 'commutable hour' from London. First-rate Audrey Butler Centre (aka the ABC) houses lecture theatre, language labs and masses of classrooms. Impressive new theatre and associated facilities a jewel in the crown. Science labs recently refurbed. School is 'quietly fundraising' for a Queenswood Hall as an alternative to chapel.

Sixth formers have their own comfortable pad – known as the Pizza Hut, originally thanks to its reminiscent shape and roof, but latterly more for the number of Domino's orders. Beautifully decorated common room – very girl suitable, with squishy leather sofas, large flat-screen TV, chic bar tables and stools and pool tables. Quiet area equipped with computers for studiers, plus kitchen corner for break-time snacks.

Girls are smart in grey and purple – 'unfussy and not ridiculously expensive,' approved a parent – with sixth formers in office-style apparel.

Pastoral care, well-being and discipline: There is a Queenswood way of doing things, which begins up high and 'permeates its way through the rest of the school,' comments a perspicacious parent. Certainly the school day reflects the level-headedness that typifies the school's approach to everything. The day starts with boarders' breakfast at 7.30am, then chapel (school is Methodist foundation but services are non-denom) twice a week at 8.15am and lessons from 8.45am until lunch, with a mid-morning break. Year 7s have a study hour incorporated in their day and all girls participate in their chosen activities – crafts, sport and other clubs – after formal lessons finish at 4.20pm. 'Balance is key,' says the school.

School's approach is to encourage girls to adapt and assimilate change – 'We applaud having a go. We tell them that failure is a part of learning and challenging themselves.' A secure support and pastoral network through housemistresses, tutors and friendly faces. The overwhelmed or anxious are free to confide in any member of staff with whom they feel comfortable. All keep an eye out in particular for girls who are stretching themselves thinly to take advantage of all Queenswood has to offer.

Houses are run by teaching housemistresses, with assistants and a team of academic tutors (around 10 tutees each). Pupil-teacher and parent-teacher relationships relaxed but respectful – 'we work in partnership with parents; we want them to take an active interest in the school and their daughter's education.'

Now a large prefect team with specialist responsibilities. Girls who put themselves forward for head girl must present on stage to the whole school and everyone votes for the speech they found most compelling. Principal's choice from then on.

Range of visiting speakers use personal experiences to raise awareness of hard-hitting issues such as drugs, sex, HIV and alcoholism. Girls taking drugs 'lose their right to be a member of the school.' Rewards and sanctions system aims to reward girls for contributions to school life and help them overcome any problems they may have with that. Postcards of praise, gold badges and stars reward pupils; demerits and detentions aim to deter miscreants. Parents involved at early stages.

Food is 'delicious,' enthuses a self-confessed foodie year 8. Serving area a top hotel would crow about, even with its own showcase area where food is cooked to order. Option of outdoor eating in new picnic/BBQ area when weather permits.

Perhaps acknowledging the reason some girls opt to leave for sixth form, school now hosts joint projects with Bedford and Radley but school says Q girls never have a problem integrating in a mixed environment when they go to university – 'that's just a myth.'

Pupils and parents: 'The girls are self-confident and very resourceful,' says school, though adds that there's no particular type. 'They're real individuals, not moulded.' Nearly 50 per cent boarders. Twenty per cent from abroad – fair proportion from Hong Kong and mainland China, with some expats. All continents represented. EAL taken seriously. Scholars are well recognised around the school – 'there's no envy,' said our eloquent sixth former guide. 'Everyone is inspired by them and shares in their success.'

Very much a 'sleeves rolled up' school for community-minded doers who are happy to get stuck in. Refreshing to find pre-teen girls as excited by camping out and playing hide and seek as they are by beauty and make-up sessions. Sixth formers articulate, poised, feisty but sensible.

Lots of first-time buyers, with both partners working. Masses from London. Drawn by Q's 'warmth and positive energy,' explains one. Strong parents' association much involved with social activities throughout the year and generous contributions to school development projects.

Old Queenswoodians' Association is arguably one of the largest, with more than 4,000 members and branches around the world, ready to befriend and advance Queenswood girls in all sorts of careers and all sorts of places. OQs include Sky Sports presenter Georgie Thompson, actress Helen McCrory, Professor Dame Alison Richard (former vice-chancellor of Cambridge University), journalist Carol Thatcher, tennis player Naomi Cavaday and GB athlete Jodie Williams.

Entrance: Early registration advised, but entry into most years if vacancies permit, either by CE or own entrance exam. Visits welcome by appointment, pupils act as tour guides. Broad ability intake but should be capable of gaining good grades at GCSE. Strong sixth form intake – candidates must get six GCSEs at B or above, with As in the subjects they want to study at A level. Pupils join from a number of schools, including Stormont, St Mary's (NW3), Lyonsdown, Beechwood Park, St Hilda's (Harpenden), Heath Mount, Maltman's Green, Duncombe, Edge Grove and Palmers Green High.

Exit: Up to 25 per cent leave at 16, usually lured by co-ed. Some come back. At 18 majority to wide range of universities eg London unis, Birmingham, Bristol, Loughborough, Warwick, York. One to Cambridge in 2016. Many gap years – school offers support with planning.

Money matters: Majority of scholarships are honorary, bringing glory and support rather than cash, though bursaries available in cases of need. Very much looking at what they can offer that will foster girls' talents rather than offering financial sweetener. Music (including organ scholarship), drama, art, tennis and sport scholarships. Occasional bursaries – means-tested. Discount for Forces families.

Remarks: A modern girls' school to which others should aspire. A winning combination of traditional values with a broad, forward-looking education to equip bright young women with the integrity and self-belief to make a difference in the world of the future.

Radley College

Radley, Abingdon, Oxfordshire OX14 2HR

Pupils: 688; all board • Ages: 13–18 • Sixth form: 273 • C of E

Fees: £35,490 pa

Tel: 01235 543000
Email: admissions@radley.org.uk
Website: www.radley.org.uk

Warden: Since 2014, John Moule MA (40s), previously head of Bedford School. Educated at a Telford comprehensive and sixth form college, he won a history scholarship to Lady Margaret Hall, Oxford and left with a first. Refreshingly atypical background for a post like this. Taught history and politics at Dean Close, Cheltenham, moved to Stowe as head of history and became housemaster, then senior housemaster. Perhaps it's Radley's proximity to Oxford but we thought Mr Moule had a little of Laurence Fox's (aka Sgt Hathaway in Lewis) lean, pale intensity. This impression only somewhat dampened when we learnt that pallor was a result of his 'feeling under the weather'.

He seems to have made a very favourable impression and was described to us as a 'brilliant' speaker, able to hold an audience of parents and boys simultaneously. 'He's very visible and really involved' one mother told us, 'He drops into Socials (Radley-speak for boarding house) and plays chess with the boys.'

Married with three children, his eldest daughter is a veterinary student, his son is finishing A levels at Bedford School and the youngest is at a girls' day school nearby. Having worked in medical research his wife completed a second degree in maths and now divides her time between the many and varied duties of a head's spouse and teaching at a school in Oxford.

Like so many heads Mr Moule claims to have 'fallen' into teaching. (Watch out, there must be a huge and cunningly disguised hole somewhere designed for just this purpose.) It goes like this. He was all set to study for a PhD in 16th century English theological history but the grant-awarding bodies had other plans and chose this moment to withdraw the financial support that had hitherto been awarded to arts students with first class degrees, 'You could say that I was saved by lack of funds'. At a loose end in Oxford, someone inevitably suggested he try teaching. 'I'd never set foot in an independent school but after two weeks I knew it was right.'

Of course Mr Moule is convinced of the benefits of a full boarding school. 'It fosters strength of character and independence'. He goes on, 'The 24 hour culture is hugely creative, it allows teachers to develop boys' genuine interests beyond the classroom.' He describes the 'powerful' triangle formed by the school, the parents and the boy, 'all have to buy into it', he says. For fee paying parents that is both metaphorically and literally the case.

Since becoming warden Mr Moule has done a great deal of observing. Not only has he dropped unannounced into lessons and watched every don (Radley-speak) teach, he also shadowed pupils throughout their day (including late afternoon and evening) to learn more about their experience as well as the school's 'flow'. And what were his conclusions? He was seriously impressed by the variety he found but felt some lessons were rather too teacher led. We imagine it can be hard to avoid in a school full of bright boys who for the most part will arrive having had eight or more years' listening and learning in prep school. We saw some young hopefuls during our visit, serious little chaps wearing polished brogues and tweed jackets – just like the fathers accompanying them.

He wants to do more to raise boys' awareness of the world beyond Radley's 800 prime Oxfordshire acres and has also told parents, and boys, that he intends to 'wage war on teenage apathy'. While acknowledging that every day should still contain a little time for creative boredom, he says boys have a tendency to do 'just enough' and feels this should be challenged. When he's sorted that one out perhaps he could let us know.

His plans for the school itself are well underway. The website has already been improved beyond recognition – it's now (fanfare) welcoming and informative – and the college's famously esoteric ('mystical' was how the warden described it) entry procedure has been revised. It used to be the case that if you had to ask Radley how to apply then you were probably too late. The process is now more open, in line with other, similar schools, though the 'List' remains and is an advantage for those who want to sign up early. Increased bursarial support is another target, as is 'careful' recruitment of applicants from beyond (even far beyond) the home counties.

Mr Moule's strong Christian faith means Radley's timeless tradition of whole school chapel four times a week is in safe hands. Boys 'love' chapel he told us, 'especially as they get older', and indeed this was borne out by those we spoke to. Of course it's important to the 'sincerely spiritual' but it's also valued by chaps who just want a bit of peace and quiet, or 'separated space' as the warden puts it. It may not be as fashionable, but perhaps this is mindfulness, Radley style.

When not wardening Mr Moule says he is an 'avid' armchair sportsman and enjoys a spot of golf or real tennis. Reading is, naturally, another recreation and favourite books include Wilkie Collins' The Woman in White and P G Wodehouse's classic, The Mating Season. Box sets are also high up on this warden's list, especially The West Wing and the US version of The Office. And if he hadn't so carelessly 'fallen' into teaching? Journalism, the law and the church are all the poorer for his stumble.

Academic matters: Even with the recent changes to its entrance procedure Radley is not a school that selects solely on academic ability; excellent GCSE and A level results stem from fine teaching and staff who don't think their job is done when the lesson finishes. Recent reintroduction of the linear, two year A level has proved that Radley wasn't so maverick after all when it held out against AS levels being taken at the end of the first year sixth. We did detect a certain quiet satisfaction that the rest of the country has finally come into line. Sixth formers sit three or four A levels, a fourth subject is generally one that contrasts with the other three. All will also do an extended project.

In 2016 84 per cent A*/A at IGCSE/GCSE; particularly strong results in, well everything, but also some Cs, Ds, even a few Es. At A level 72 per cent A*/A, most popular subjects history, maths and English literature followed by sciences. Notable proportion of A* in art and English lit. Nice to see decent numbers taking classics, languages and geology too. While maths and further maths are very popular, Radley has always stood apart from the overwhelming science/maths dominance so commonly found in boys' schools and we're glad to see this remains the case.

Teaching in the lessons we observed was of the tried and tested sort – a fast pace and lots of quick fire questions kept everyone on their toes. Very clearly exam focused. However, despite adding a distinctly scholarly air, gowns didn't seem to make Radleians any more elevated or less prone to muttering at the back than their non-gowned counterparts at other schools.

Latest ISI report called learning support 'exceptional' and parents are in agreement. All boys have to meet the entrance criteria to get into the school but once there SEN support is extensive and lacks stigma. Individual and small group sessions are arranged according to need. Some take place during what is known as 'central hour' (1.30-2.30 daily), time set aside for relaxing, working, music lessons, extracurricular activities etc.

We met some really amusing and inspiring dons who just seemed to love their jobs (less jobs, more way of life, we thought) and the very stones of the place. Good mix of ages and lots of women among teaching staff. Dogs seemed to be part of the package too – that explained the water bowls we'd wondered about in some of the classrooms. All dons and their families live on site.

Much talk of efforts to 'learn from other schools and widen diversity'. Strong links with local primaries and a Maidenhead secondary school; some exchange of teaching staff but latter a little too far away for frequent activities. Closer to home the warden hopes to further develop joint academic extension activities for A level subjects such as music, English and geography with Headington School. There are links for the scholars with St Helen and St Katharine's and plans for 'ambitious extension days' with Oxford High School. Lest we get too carried away by all this talk of diversity, at Radley take your dog to work day is unlikely to be joined by enrol your daughter day any time soon.

Games, options, the arts: All rather civilised. Manages to maintain a creditable sporting reputation without the ruthlessly competitive atmosphere than can prevail at boys' schools. We got the impression that the disinclined to run are not regarded as also rans. Rugby is main game of Michaelmas term – around 20 separate teams do battle every Saturday.

When it warms up the 'wet bobs' row; 'dry bobs' play hockey, fives, cricket or tennis in the summer term. Boat house on the Thames is 10 minutes away and those wet bobs are usually up there with near neighbours Abingdon and rivals Eton and St Edward's during the Henley Regatta and head of the river competitions.

Twice weekly so-called 'minor sports' include swimming, golf (there's a course on site), fives, squash, real tennis, cross-country, rackets, tennis, badminton. Those who wish to can do a spot of beagling. Alternative sports programme (ASP), is a circus of different sports for boys (remove upwards) who don't take to rugby. Sixth formers can choose which sport they want to play.

Art school, complete with rather cool gallery space, is in Clocktower Court. Pupils' work, paintings, ceramics and photography, not confined to here, it's all over the school – eerily lifelike papier mâché boys peer down from beams in the library. Ambitious projects undertaken in DT include surfboards and a rather spectacular trebuchet. Once again, facilities lack for nothing and are open late into the evening and at weekends. Nine or 10 boys take art or DT at A2 with creditable results.

Large chapel choir with trebles from local primary schools and preps sings at services and evensong in chapel and elsewhere, including Oxford colleges. Weekly concerts in the school coffee shop, house and college concerts give boys as many solo and ensemble performing opportunities as possible. The music school is open until 10.15pm and boys are expected to organise their own practice although a member of staff is on hand to help. Just one or two doing music at A level despite high profile of music in the school – theatre studies more popular option.

Inter-house competitions and endowed prizes are great motivators and boys take to the stage for such keenly fought contests as the part song competition, debating, declaiming, battle of the bands, piano and percussion trophies. The legendary Piano Extravaganza featured, most recently, 91 players from age 6 upwards (under 13s are dons' children) playing on eight pianos. The Silk Hall is school's premier music venue and next door is the theatre where college and year group plays are performed as well as A2 drama devised pieces. Parents rave about the drama at Radley; even shy boys take to the stage. No reluctance from boys to take on female roles but every so often school puts a 'Girls wanted' advert in the local paper if the production requires the genuine article. Warden told us he directed several plays at his former school and might be tempted again.

CCF compulsory for removes, fifth form do community service and sixth formers can choose enrichment activities such as opera, film or cooking. Couple of parents thought a few more 'life skills' wouldn't go amiss at this stage. Seriously impressive calendar of visiting speakers including WW2 RAF hero, Auschwitz survivor, scientists, authors, journalists, MPs and members of the clergy. Vast array of trips – theatre in London, art in Florence and music tours (singers and instrumentalists) to America. Energetic fundraising for variety of good causes including partner school in Tanzania and Christian Aid.

Boarding: Boarding houses at Radley are known as 'Socials' and Socials are distinguished by letters of the alphabet (A Social, B Social and so on). First years ('shell') have curtained 'cubs' or cubicles with a sink and cabin bed. Apparently Radley was the instigator of this arrangement that affords pupils some degree of privacy within a dormitory. It caught on and can still be seen in many prep and senior boarding schools. From removes (second year) on it's single study bedrooms. In typical boarding boy fashion these were all rather tidy, noticeboards generally unadorned by photos, posters and the like. Our guides told us they liked the busy, structured days at school and appreciated the relative freedom of home life all the more for it. 'We probably take Radley for granted,' one added.

Boys may buy uniform, stationery, tuck etc in school's shop (known, wait for it, as 'Shop'). Card system for purchases in Shop or coffee shop; 'jam account' (upper limit of £60 per term) for tuck. One parent thought it was a shame there was no opportunity to buy secondhand uniform, sports kit etc.

'Oxford leave' allows boys (mostly sixth formers) to travel into Oxford (by bus or taxi). Upper sixth chaps may spend Saturday evenings there as long as they're back in Social by 10.30pm. Quite a restricted regime for boys of this age, although exeats and privis allow a few slightly longer Saturday nights out elsewhere.

Background and atmosphere: In the quartet of boys' full boarding schools (first violin Eton, second violin Winchester, cello Harrow), Radley would be the viola – less frequently played ('mystical' entrance requirements), smallish solo repertoire (690 boys), confident, necessary, but unflashy (low profile) and so on. It's also the newcomer, having been founded by Oxford movement devotees, The Revs Sewell and Singleton, in 1847 to 'provide a public school education on the principles of the Church of England.'

The founding Revs organised their school along the lines of colleges at the University of Oxford, hence some of the nomenclature: warden, dons etc. Indeed, Radley still has that slightly separate feel of an Oxford college, enhanced by the sight of boys rushing to and fro, gowns billowing behind. Last vote saw proposal to do away with gowns defeated by 95 per cent. Daily choral services were, and remain, a key aspect of the school.

It was believed boys' minds and souls would be improved by learning in a beautiful rural setting and well-designed environment. Shades of William Morris perhaps. School motto is the succinct, Sicut Serpentes, Sicut Columbae ('Be ye wise as serpents, and harmless as doves'), and these creatures appear on the coat of arms – with the cross keys of St Peter, to whom the college is dedicated, safely between them.

Radley College is neither overwhelmingly grand nor intimidating. Reception is small and unpretentious, seating would indicate that they do not expect more than three people to arrive at any one time. Reception staff friendly but appeared to be fighting a losing battle to stop the office becoming overwhelmed by online delivery packages. 'Radley boys keep Amazon in business,' said a long-suffering voice from behind a pile of boxes.

School originally occupied the Mansion, an 18th century house that belonged to the Stonehouse, then Bowyer families. This rather elegant building with grand panelled reception rooms is now home to admin and the warden's offices. Other parts are usual mix of charming and slightly less charming additions. Wide vistas, generous lawns and paths are another great advantage of a large, rural site. The grounds were by laid out by Capability Brown and some features of his design remain visible. Many trees, looking especially lovely on the golden autumn day of our visit. Immaculate pitches (delightful cricket pavilion) stretch into the distance.

Queen's Court (aka the Doughnut), opened by Her Majesty in 1997, may dominate aerial views of the college but we were rather taken with the inside, which seems to have stood the test of time. It's home to maths, economics, biology, geography and geology and the communal space outside the classrooms is full of fascinating natural history specimens and large tanks containing turtles, scorpions and cockroaches. Members of the animal society come here to get up close with reptiles and snakes, if not doves.

Pastoral care, well-being and discipline: The tutor (housemaster) is the key figure in a boy's life at Radley. He oversees the boys in his Social along with sub-tutors and pastoral housemistresses (PHMs) – the latter come in for particular praise from mothers of younger boys. Form masters monitor academic progress. Boys in the first two years also have a lower sixth mentor. Cocoa at 9pm every night is a chance for all the boys in a Social to meet up and chat about the day; this and other activities help blur year group hierarchies. Boys are expected to help with the running of their Social: shell do chores such as collecting post; sixth form house prefects supervise prep and bedtimes. Parents all praise dedication of Social staff and say that any enquiries are dealt with 'by return', they also like the regular progress reports.

Two exeat weekends per term and boys earn 'privis' or privilege weekends for good behaviour, work etc. On 'Sunday outs' boys can go out with parents or a friend after chapel for the day. One mother lamented, 'My son doesn't take his privis, there's too much going on at school to miss.' Rather sweet little handbook sent to boys before they join includes useful advice such as, 'Bring more tuck. Most don't bring enough,' and, 'If you are lost, confused or unhappy don't be afraid to ask for help.' Information about who to ask (both in and outside college) and how to do this is also included.

School places great emphasis on tolerance, kindness and manners. Biggest crime, according to new boys' handbook is, 'to be rude to a cleaner, a member of catering staff, the ladies who help you in Shop or any other member of the College staff.' This is not intended in a de haut en bas way – as the Warden says, 'we discourage any sense of entitlement or arrogance.'

School is keen to enhance the quality of social activities with girls' schools. Shell still get the chance to disco with the likes of Wycombe Abbey, but older boys now join girls from St Mary's

Calne, Tudor Hall, Headington and St Helen and Katharine for dinner and discussion or joint theatre trips.

Pupils and parents: The warden describes a Radleian as 'civilised, friendly and engaging, in short, good company' and all the boys we met lived up to his definition. He also debunks a commonly held myth (that may stem from former entrance procedure) that most boys are sons of former pupils. 'It's 15 per cent', he told us. Seems that the lower sixth drama group we had spoken to where all but a couple were second or third generation Radleians was just a blip. 'Most people find out about us through word of mouth,' continued the warden. 'They've met and liked a Radleian at work or university and think of us as a possible school for their own son.'

Even so the hour has arrived to tweak what school describes carefully as its 'cultural variety'. Don't expect a revolution, or a rainbow nation – it'll be a while before the grain of truth packs its bags and departs from school's nickname, 'Ra Ra' Radley. Change will happen, carefully, in Radley's own time, and it will most certainly be for the (even) better.

Former pupils (ORs) include Andrew Motion, poet; Sir Clive Stafford Smith, human rights lawyer; Lord Wilson of Dinton, former cabinet secretary; Peter Cook, comedian; Sandy Nairne, former director of the National Portrait Gallery; Christopher Hibbert, Historian; Ted Dexter, Andrew Strauss and Jamie Dalrymple, England cricketers; Sir Charlie Mayfield, chairman of John Lewis; Lord Wolfson, CEO of Next. And many other actors, writers, lawyers, engineers, sportsmen, clergymen and public servants of all kinds.

Entrance: Still the forward planner's choice. Radley remains loyal to those who register early and 'conditional' offers are made three years in advance to boys on 'Provisional' and waiting lists. Subject to interview and ISEB common pre-test results, they will get firm offers on 1 March of year 6. No open days, individually arranged visits all through the year. Friendly and approachable admissions staff will explain system.

Admissions procedure is changing but up until 2018 boys not already registered may apply for one of around 40 'Warden's List' places. Radley puts 'much emphasis' on candidate's performance at interview and head's report when assessing applicants for these. From 2019 onwards, after offers are made to boys on the 'Provisional' list, there is an open entry system whereby all interested candidates are first asked to sit the ISEB common pre-test in year 6 and send a school report; interviews will be offered to shortlisted candidates and offers made in June of year 6.

Few (around eight) places at 16 + but on the whole this is a settled community and there's not much movement.

R

Exit: Bristol, Durham, Edinburgh, Exeter, Leeds, Manchester, Newcastle and UCL hoover up most of Radley's leavers. Regular 15–20 boys to Oxbridge every year (15 in 2016, plus three medics) – mock interview exchange scheme with nearby Abingdon School seems to benefit both sides. School's university entrance team recently expanded to integrate expertise in applying to universities in North America, Europe and beyond.

Money matters: Cheapest of the quartet (no viola jokes please) but there's barely a gnat's crotchet between them. Uniform requirements less painful on the purse – parents told us that suits, shirts etc can be bought from high street. Gowns aren't expensive and, look on the bright side, might save on jacket dry cleaning bills (and they cover books if it's raining, boys told us). Sports kit will cost you but then it does everywhere. Lack of coffee shops (or indeed any shops) in immediate vicinity looks promising but remember the Amazon overwhelmed reception desk ...

Scholarships of up to 10 per cent off fees awarded annually at 13+ and can be topped up to 100 per cent with means-tested bursaries. Foundation awards enable boys from state system to attend a prep school for two years before admission. Armed Forces Fund provides assistance to boys from Forces families. All very clearly explained on school website.

Remarks: In our last review we said that Radley was the connoisseurs' choice; this remains the case. Yes, it's traditional, but it's utterly unstuffy. Like the serpent and the dove in the coat of arms, respect for tradition lives harmoniously with tolerance, intellectual curiosity, humour and humanity. Radley provides boys with an immersive education of the highest quality and a strong moral and spiritual core.

Reading Blue Coat School

Holme Park, Sonning Lane, Reading, Berkshire RG4 6SU

Pupils: 740 • Ages: 11–18 • Sixth form: 273 (86 girls) • C of E

Fees: £15,660 pa

Tel: 01189 441005
Email: admissions@rbcs.org.uk
Website: www.rbcs.org.uk

Headmaster: Since September 2016, Jesse Elzinga, previously director of studies at Harrow. BA in comparative religion from Harvard and MSt (as a Rotary Ambassadorial Scholar) from Oxford. The only student ever to go from his Detroit state school to Harvard, he captained varsity lightweight rowing there, twice winning the national championship in the eight. His first job was teaching theology and philosophy at Whitgift, later becoming assistant head of sixth form, before moving to St Edward's Oxford as head of RS, later becoming director of studies. He and his wife Elaina have two young daughters.

Academic matters: All the usual subjects plus a few unusual are taught here with results that are going from strength to strength. In 2016, 69 per cent A*/A grades at I/GCSE. Currently IGCSEs in maths and English, but geography is next and science set to follow. Sciences, maths and economics most popular A2 choices and leaver destinations reflect this, but the takers of English, art, history of art and languages are equally successful, though fewer in number. In 2016, 79 per cent A*/B and 45 per cent A*/A grades at A level. Enrichment opportunities in the sixth form include Mandarin, visiting speakers and the school's own PLUS course, which covers giving a presentation, writing an extended essay and effective note-taking as well as careers, personal statements, finance etc. Lessons are a boy-friendly 35 minutes, Latin is compulsory until year 9 and all take RS and IT short courses. We were delighted to open a door off the library (very quietly) and see a whole class of boys relaxed on beanbags reading. Once a week for the first two years all boys read books of their choice in these peaceful surroundings.

The world of geology has much to thank Reading Blue Coat for – the serendipitous result of a former teacher's passion for rocks is a dedicated lab full of fascinating specimens in the new geology and psychology centre. Boys take a taster course in year 9 and many go on to study geology (via a Welsh exam board) for GCSE and beyond. Variations on the usual theme in the sixth form are classical civilisation, DT, government and politics, performance studies, sports and physical education and psychology.

The beautifully produced 'creative arts' publication, The Whetstone, is a delight to read and contains writing and art of exceptional quality. In fact pupils' artistic endeavours are on display all over the school – a particular talent for portraiture, with over-sized faces to be seen everywhere. The huge canvases that decorate the dining room are really impressive and a wonderful papier-mâché giant's head greets visitors in reception.

All are screened at 11 and 16, learning support department provides assistance for those with mild SEN (dyslexia mainly) and pupils who require it are given extra time in the entrance exam.

Games, options, the arts: Given its wonderful Thames-side location and fine new boathouse, one might expect trophy cabinets bursting with rowing glory but, so far, Abingdon and Eton are beating them to it. Instead Reading Blue Coat's sporting successes take place on the soccer, rugby, hockey and cricket fields with a number of boys also playing at county and national level. Oh, and the synchronised swimming – a sixth form girl is in the UK squad, but while the school gives her every support and is proud of her success, it's not on the sporting timetable (although photos of the squad of sixth form boys she trained to perform for a charity fundraiser were rather fetching).

CCF is very strong here and popular with boys and girls – much orderly drilling was taking place outside during our visit and cadets have represented the whole movement at national remembrance events. Impressive public speaking record – junior and senior teams have orated their way to become local, national and world champions in recent years. Music is at the heart of the school – all boys are auditioned for the choir and learn a musical instrument for the first two years. Musicians perform at the popular 'Swing into Summertime' concert for parents who picnic on the lawns and listen to the latest talent; also a chance for school bands to play, 'if they're good enough'. Riding, shooting, archery, politics, Young Enterprise, D of E, fencing, scuba diving, creative writing, journalism and technology are on offer alongside drama productions and sports activities. Sixth formers help in local primary schools and with sports coaching as part of the Sports Leadership Award. As the head put it, 'We want every pupil to find their niche'; as a pupil put it, 'There's a ridiculous amount of things to do here'.

Background and atmosphere: 'Reading' may be in the name, but put whatever mental picture it engenders aside and think instead of Wind in the Willows or Three Men in a Boat. Better now? Reading Blue Coat is in the delightful riparian village of Sonning-on-Thames – ancient bridges, half-timbered and thatched houses, tea shops and, at certain times of the day, gridlock in its narrow roads. Founded in 1646 by local merchant Richard Aldworth to offer education for the poor children of Reading, the school moved to its current site 300 years later. The traditional uniform of long blue coat (hence the school's name), breeches, yellow stockings and buckled shoes is now only worn on high days by prefects – girls and boys.

The school sits amid cricket and rugby pitches (yet more across the road), and wooded grounds roll down to the Thames and the new boathouse. The classical proportions of the Regency mansion that once stood here (a picture in the head's study) fell victim to a serious case of Victorian mock gothicism and sprouted towers and mullions. Not at all sinister on a bright spring day but could be rather a brooding presence on a winter's afternoon. Nevertheless a striking building, and the brick and flint exterior is more in keeping with the local vernacular. In the entrance hall polished panelling, huge display of fresh flowers and honours boards full of names, just as one would expect. The charming 'buttery', formerly the boarders' dining room, overlooks the gardens and is the venue for many musical events including jazz concerts. Above is a confusion of back staircases and half landings, and every so often a delightful teaching room complete with oversized stone fireplace and arched windows framing ancient trees. A slightly makeshift feel to this part of the school at the time of our visit, not surprising as a number of departments were camping here during building works. New IT and DT centres now open.

Considerable effort (signs indicating a one-way system?) has been made to achieve what interior designers call 'flow' – but as the bell went during our visit it was more of a tidal surge, as busy boys channelled to their next lesson. Staff and pupils stoic about this – the new building, now open, worth the temporary disruption. It has 23 new classrooms for several departments and a middle school common room.

Two separate receptions (one for visitors, one for pupils) and a scattering of rather functional teaching blocks must make the first few weeks rather confusing for new boys (and girls). 'I couldn't understand how everyone got to the lessons before me,' said our guide, 'until I discovered the short cuts.'

Pastoral care, well-being and discipline: The recent ISI report is enthusiastic in its praise for pastoral care, an opinion endorsed by parents and the pupils we spoke to. The school has active and well thought through policies to foster vertical as well as horizontal bonding and pupils were keen to endorse the fact that these work in practice as well as in theory – 'You don't feel so small as a first year,' one said. Four houses, named after the school's founders and benefactors, are the focus for competitive sport, music – house singing – and charity fundraising. Tutor groups comprise two years so, for instance, new boys mix with those from the year above. One guide, who had come to RBC from a local primary, remembers how thrilled he was to receive a letter from his future tutor group in the term before he joined. Girls coming into the sixth form have at least three taster days and get to meet their subject teachers and fellow pupils. Our guide felt that the school had made every effort to ease her transition from a small girls' independent and relations between sixth form boys and their new classmates seem mature and appreciative.

Pupils and parents: From roughly a 30 mile radius, taking in Reading, Maidenhead, Wokingham, Camberley, Wallingford, Fleet, Twyford and villages between. A fair few first-time buyers. The split of boys coming in from state primaries and local preps, such as Crosfields and St Edwards (Reading) and Holme Grange (Wokingham), is pretty equal and bodes well for balanced, un-cliquey year groups. Girls come from schools with no sixth form such as Cranford or for a change from single sex education. Fees roughly a couple of thousand per annum lower than local competition, but this is regarded as a nice bonus rather than a deciding factor for most parents. Former pupils (Old Blues) include television presenters Jeremy Kyle and Matt Allwright (Rogue Traders), Reading West MP Alok Sharma, round-the-world yachtsman Mike Golding OBE and the actress Natalie Dormer (Casanova, The Tudors).

Entrance: Just under three applicants for every place at 11 and two at 16. Interview with headmaster or senior colleague, entrance examination in January comprising English, maths and verbal reasoning plus reference from current school. A further competitive intake at 16+: around 30 girls and five boys enter the lower sixth each year. Entry at this age requires verbal and non-verbal reasoning tests plus a minimum of seven GCSEs grade C and above, with at least Bs in the subjects to be studied at A level.

Exit: About 90 per cent go through to sixth form. Nearly all to first choice university (Bristol, Cardiff, Loughborough, Leeds, Birmingham...), most, but not all, to study heavy duty subjects such as aeronautical engineering, dentistry, maths, modern langs and physics. Sports science and, not surprisingly, geology also popular. In 2016, four to Oxbridge and two medics.

Money matters: Cheap-ish, as Basil Fawlty would say – fees lower than at a few prep schools in the area. Scholarships for art, music, academics – up to 25 per cent of fees – and a number of means-tested bursaries of up to 100 per cent. Two foundation scholarships awarded annually on merit and means-tested (up to 100 per cent of fees).

Remarks: No shortage of other good schools to choose from in this area, state and independent, so why do parents opt for Reading Blue Coat? 'It's down to earth', 'friendly and approachable', 'genuinely interested in developing my son's talents'. Maybe small is beautiful or perhaps it's the civilising influence of the sixth form girls, but this school is not inclined to spar with the big beasts in the Berks/Oxon independent jungle. Yet Reading Blue Coat wears its laurels lightly and remains true to its founding principles; it continues to put all its efforts into providing a first class all-round education for the boys and girls fortunate enough to go there.

Reeds School

196

Sandy Lane, Cobham, Surrey KT11 2ES

Pupils: 704; 85 full/weekly boarders • Ages: 11-18 • Sixth form: 260 (including 69 girls) • C of E

Fees: Day £18,615- £23,265; Boarding £24,810 – £29,985 pa

Tel: 01932 869001
Email: admissions@reeds.surrey.sch.uk
Website: www.reeds.surrey.sch.uk

Head: Since 2014, Mark Hoskins BA MA MSc (50s). Previously second master (senior deputy head in modern currency) at RGS Guildford between 2005-2014. Before that, spent eight years at Whitgift, starting as head of economics and business studies in 1997 and then becoming head of middle school. First posts were in highly regarded maintained schools – two years apiece at Rosebery (comp, girls) and Wilson's (selective grammar, boys). Mixed sixth form here first foray so far into co-education.

Praise from parents comes thick and fast. 'Impressive'; 'A lovely guy'; 'Has accelerated the academic side without losing the breadth.' Ditto for wife Sharon, whose diligent attendance at events has been approvingly clocked. Has two children, son (at the school) and daughter (distinctly miffed she isn't as too young).

Though an able sportsman (coached soccer in US during gap years), Mr Hoskins talks down his successes – becoming modesty a given, he says, when working in schools with world-class pros on the staff. Nobody, though, likely to call him out on academic qualifications, what with two masters, a second in economics from the University of London, accomplished post-marriage with small children and combined with full-time teaching. 'When you're teaching bright pupils, they push you and so you want to push yourself.' Still fits in some teaching currently economics to upper sixth, switching effortlessly between different roles – father to head – without breaking step, with son's friends at ease within minutes.

Parents who already know (or have heard tell) of previous achievements at RGS are quickly converting others. He's taking the school by stealth (as well as charm) and doing the evolution not revolution thing. Latest inspection praises democratic, light touch management style, with teachers regularly observed but encouraged rather than censured while management structure is being reworked to give more opportunities to the talented.

He's forceful where necessary. 'Don't ever want to be on his bad side,' says pupil. Not out of fear but because 'wouldn't want him to lose his respect for you.' Not a hacker and slasher, think parents, whose perception is of new talent being grafted on to the staff team (average age early 40s) and tired areas jazzed up with a bit of extra colour – new chaplain, impressively also a maths teacher and rugby coach, a case in point. School was 'ripe for a shake up,' said one mother. Mr Hoskins seen as the person to administer it.

State educated himself and with a strong moral purpose, he'd like to up numbers of foundation places for disadvantaged pupils.

Academic matters: Edging ever closer to nearby powerhouses like Hampton and RGS as locals wake up to educational excellence on their doorstep and, in small but growing numbers, start to make this their first choice. Elsewhere, pupils' brilliance polished till it shines but personalities remain unchanged. Here, parents feel pupils' characters have room to grow, too.

Pupils, particularly those living some distance away and involved in matches, clubs and events will, however, need to arrive with a few ready-to-wear sterling qualities, headed by keenness and motivation. Disorganised types can end up trailing home to face sizeable quantities of homework ('they do get quite a lot,' said mother) and a few, say parents, may not last the course. School disagrees. 'No-one has left due to being disorganised,' says Mr Hoskins.

Won't be for want of numerous helping hands from the school, reflection of high staff to pupil ratios – just over one to eight – and reasonable class sizes (17 up to year 11, 10 in sixth form). Following substantial makeover, there's more setting, regular testing and additional feedback on academic attainment with boys awarded bronze, silver and gold grades for effort as well as achievement. 'Have no worries about where son is going academically – am more than comfortable,' said parent.

School is notable for quality of support – currently offered to around 80 pupils, vast majority with assorted dys difficulties, and very small numbers with ADD, ADHD, ASD, visual or speech and language issues. Just under 20 with EAL are supported individually or in small groups.

Regardless of need, pupils must be able to thrive in relatively (but not ridiculously) fast-paced environment. 'If they need so much support that it would be difficult to access, this wouldn't be the right place because your confidence takes an absolute hammering,' says Mr Hoskins. If make the grade, progress is often exceptional, helped by well thought out support including ADR (assess, do and review) programme.

While overall pass rates remain pretty consistent (62 per cent of GCSE grades in 2016 were at A*/A; at A level, A*/A grades 46 per cent, 75 per cent A*/B, all similar to previous year) subject popularity ebbs and flows. A few more girls taking A level physics would be good (numbers are very small) though those we spoke to felt were well supported whatever their interests.

Subject choices are fairly standard up to GCSE (electronics is about as outré as it gets), though there's a research project for year 9s. Post-16, there's an extended project for all and impressive 27 A level options include graphics, taken by around 10 each year. Will also keep subjects going for very tiny numbers (one or two year each year taking computing, for example, slightly more taking art).

It's reinforced by boundless staff enthusiasm. Every subject gets own write up – 'It's been another bumper year in the world of physics,' burbles school mag – as well as appetite-whetting extras such as recently-formed medical society where would-be doctors justify career choice to peers. Most mentioned by parents, however, is fabulous Futuretech programme – DT reimagined to give free rein to 'what if' projects linking STEM subjects. DIY model wind turbines created by second years and visit from TESLA among the many highlights.

Games, options, the arts: Old Reedonians' website may convey message that life without sport is one wasted ('injury, marriage or the arrival of children...' quoted as distinct inconveniences) but school these days is natural home for those eager to improve pen or bow hold as well as racket grip. Head, with consummate diplomacy, felt by parents to avoid any suggestion of sports vs the rest, drama and music sharing equal place on the rostrum. Agreed, says teacher. 'You just don't win world titles for them.' (Just as well given that sports trophies take up almost enough space to host own open day).

Ham-fisted, two-left feet or otherwise, everyone will have talent, however limited, coaxed out of them. Parents and pupils stress effectiveness of school's approach – a fine balance between compulsion and encouragement. 'Do something whether you like it or not – and you mostly do,' said sixth former. Activities – 75 plus, ranging from archery to golf and judo to silk painting – cater for dabblers as well as enthusiasts. Sixth form boys – who have fourth X1 fixtures – organise 'not very good' gentleman's hockey team just for the fun of it. 'We just want to play,' said one.

There's also popular D of E (with strong philanthropic dimension) and CCF. Don't neglect social skills either, with everything from debating club (so can participate in discussion) to Toastmasters for older pupils (where discover how to lead it). Many new sixth formers, compelled to try previously hated activities (two a week in years 11, 12 and 13; three to year 10) converted into fans. Brilliant for bonding even if not, thought pupil.

Strength of arts, performing and visual, particularly impressive, from scale of ambition to levels of investment and numbers involved (over 200 individual music lessons each week and a fifth of all pupils taking part in recent concert). Sixth form technicians, recently rewarded with two RADA technical course places, work into small hours to put final touches to lighting for major productions (created a big top – inside – from scratch for The Impresario), while music scholar who complained about piano quality wasn't just listened to but flown to Germany to help choose brand new Steinway.

Whatever your specialist interest, facilities excellent, packed in on relatively compact site. Trees know their place – confined largely to the perimeter so space can be given over to cricket, rugby (big and little pitches), two Astros and tennis courts. Whole shebang has accolade of being accredited by Tim Henman Foundation as model primary school outreach programme for others to follow.

Inevitably, sport remains biggest selling point for some families. 'Why we chose the school,' said mother. Biggest lure for the ultra-talented are three academies (golf, tennis and skiing) offering elite coaching (every major sport comes with own professional), flexible timetable and extra training (before or after school and – in case of skiiers – sent off to the snow), plus osteo clinic and sports injury rehabilitation. Youngest sports scholars enjoy substantial perk of all day trackies to avoid frequent changes of clothes, school adamant that no wizard/muggle divisions exist. No swollen heads either – 'they've lovely boys,' said parent. Individual successes at national and county level are copious across range of age groups and sports (including 26 for hockey). Ditto stonking team triumphs (tennis – three consecutive wins in World Schools' Championship; golf – regular national finalists).

System relies on, and gets, happy cooperation between academic and sports staff, particularly in sixth form with pupils allowed to devote some private study time to sport ('a privilege and must be able to invest time to catch up on work,' stresses school). Significant weapon is sizeable number of teachers so blessed with charm that can even make punishments a laugh a minute. 'If we forget our kit, coach makes us run and touch all the lines on the pitch – there are about 500,' said junior pupil, chortling at the very memory. 'Makes it so funny.' You probably had to be there.

Smaller numbers mean fewer limits, thought one mother. 'At other schools you have to make choices early on, here they can do anything.' One originally sports-centric boy was also singing and acting at every opportunity – slightly to his own surprise, as well as that of parents. 'Confidence has gone through the roof.'

Boarding: Though only 15 per cent board, juniors in The Close, seniors in School House, sixth formers upstairs in own courtyard block complete with lecture theatre, they're a happy clan, with a strong and oft-(very oft) mentioned sense of community. Sixth form girl boarders, a particularly minuscule group (under a handful in upper sixth), flock together and take pleasure in niche status, downstairs common room a homely oasis of papers and possessions. Offers full, weekly or occasional B&B – a boon to any child with a late finishing match or parents with work commitments. Despite low numbers, school rarely feels empty, say pupils.

Accommodation is spick and span, white and magnolia the prevailing signature décor, eye-catching touches headed by world's reddest kitchen in School House, neon signs and slinky bar-style seating for its 36 year 9-11 boarders. Elsewhere, communal areas are businesslike rather than breathtaking, though as long as there's space enough to pack in the crowds for must-watch TV (usually matches, we'd assume), pupils clearly don't mind.

Tempo of life is exceedingly brisk and a marvel of logistics, junior boarders showered and powered into breakfast in just 30 minutes – even faster when bacon's on the menu (food – bar some evening meals – generally excellent) – while all-action weekends for everyone are filled with (more) sport, mixed age cinema trips, shopping (in groups of three, one phone compulsory) and doughnutting (descending Sandown Park's dry ski slope in rubber ring).

Pace accounts for absence of personal touches. Some pinboards stay empty because there's just no time to unpack. 'Too much to do,' said pupil, who'd had initial reservations about absence of down time. No longer. 'Now realise that being busy is perfect.'

Cheerful matrons keep everything ticking over, washing machines permanently on spin cycle (18 loads of laundry in one day a personal best), aided and abetted by thoughtful, compassionate houseparents proffering small hours hot chocolate and DVDs when homesickness strikes and with welcome ability to tread the fine line between firmness and latitude. 'With boarding you try to make it like a family,' says one. 'When someone's done something wrong you try to think if they'd be in trouble for something similar at home and separate something that's annoying – like being too loud or watching TV too late – from something that merits a detention.'

Background and atmosphere: Founded in 1813 by Andrew Reed, social reformer, minister and serial setter upper of charitable institutions (and upsetter of fellow trustees), but the only school to survive intact, discounting change of name (originally the London Orphan Asylum), location (arrived here via Clapton,

Watford and – briefly during WW2 evacuation – Totnes), and financing (fee-paying pupils first admitted 1950s, though charitable focus on foundationers has never changed).

Handy for M25 and with Gatwick and Heathrow just a 30-minute drive away, it's a cinch to get to, as long as you avoid rush hour and don't take address too literally (says Cobham but actually in Oxshott – it's a postal area thing).

Heart of the school is restored arts and crafts building, home – among other areas – to attractive chapel and library, surrounded by separate music school, labs, classrooms and airy sixth form block with lecture theatre which doubles as venue for film screenings. Packs a lot on to 40-acre site – including mysterious amounts of lost property, despite school's comprehensive naming service. 'Usually get it back but can take a very long time,' said mother. 'In my experience, much better than other schools on this,' says Mr Hoskins.

Overcoming pupil/space dilemma by corralling outside areas and roofing them over – small courtyard is now a conservatory-style dining hall extension while The Close boasts an impressive stretch reception, 100 or so tennis balls trapped on the roof a happy reminder of previous incarnation as impromptu sports pitch.

With master plan now agreed, there's plenty of future development on the way. Likely to be equally imaginative and ambitious, says Mr Hoskins, though won't put up buildings all over the place and ramp up pupil numbers as 'would ruin what we have.' Includes indoor cricket centre (due for completion 2017) as well as redevelopment of sixth form centre.

Pastoral care, well-being and discipline: Cordial relations between staff and pupils ensure that lines are clearly drawn, usually toed and rarely crossed, mild eccentricities tolerated while not actively encouraged. Year 11 boy, dealing with exam tension in his own way by sporting a rolled up trouser leg, was clocked by adult tour guide – 'High spirits' – then left to own (if rather more self-conscious) devices. Headmaster has flexed disciplinary muscles for serious breaches (as with other schools, drink and drugs the main culprits) – offenders likely to be asked to leave.

Everyone very much at home here, much emphasis on age-appropriate three-day induction programme. For year 7s includes on-site camping and games of chubby bunnies ('See how many marshmallows you can get in your mouth and still say "chubby bunnies",' said pupil – well, of course). Activities for new sixth form girls include rather more sophisticated (and confectionary-free) meal out in Kingston.

For first two years, The Close, a separate building, is a world in miniature. 'Opportunity to settle very well without being overwhelmed – a home away from home,' said parent. Have own houses, games, activities and responsibilities, plus quality pastoral back up from sixth form mentors, a high profile and popular presence, who dispense quiz questions and chocolate brownies, organise house drama and deal with acts of minor unkindness.

System works exceptionally well, houseparents keeping a close eye on charges, say parents, but not exclusively so. 'Everyone needs to have an idea of collective responsibilities,' said pupil. 'If they're not willing to put in the effort, they wouldn't be suitable.' For the majority who are, individual record books – an initiative from the chaplain (he's buzzing with them) – will be a chance to list golden deeds of compassion and virtue as well as mere academic success.

Pupils and parents: With just a handful of expats and around 12-15 international students, 80 per cent from Hong Kong, most families are UK-based Brits living maximum of an hour's travel time away, network of school bus routes reading like estate agent's bumper book of desirable destinations (Putney, Richmond, Wimbledon and Guildford).

Foundationers, some with traumatising early life experiences, are painlessly absorbed. 'Ensures other children don't live in a bubble,' says school. Parents agree, though one warned against excessive hikes in school fees. 'Run the risk that end up with two categories, those who can afford it and foundationers, with a gap in the middle.' Mr Hoskins points out that 'in the last two years, fee increases were less than many of our competitors.'

End product includes plenty of high-grade sportspeople (Tim Henman most glorious example), though crop of musicians, actors and entertainers is almost as substantial. One 1980s batch (they organise alumni by decade here) yielded two opera singers, an art dealer and a Jordanian prince. Plenty of somethings in the City as well.

Sports, arts or royalty, Old Reedonians stay in touch. 'Keep caring and giving to family long after graduation,' said one. 'Once a Reedonian, always a Reedonian.' Partners, we were told, like to swap notes, finding ORs nicer and gentler than the common herd.

Judging by today's happy mixed age lunchtime throng, pupils impressively (and unusually) relaxed about talking about their feelings, oldest pupils encouraging the youngest to speak, everyone giving strong impression of liking everyone else, nothing much has changed.

Entrance: At 11+ English and maths tests plus VR, all (normally) taken at school in January for entry in September. For 13+, register a good three years in advance, pre-test in year 6, CE in June if at prep school. Other candidates sit English, maths, science, modern language and VR papers. Sixth form hopefuls have observed lesson to judge teamwork and two subject-based exams – superior ability mentioned by inspectors.

Foundation pupils – some referred by own school or children's charity – have range of difficulties, from financial hardship to loss of a parent or seriously ill sibling. Need to sit entrance exams and will also have home visit.

While greater competition inevitably means more able applicants achieving well beyond pass mark, head doesn't go by grades alone. Good relationships with prep heads essential for CE so can consult 'if they bomb because of real pastoral issues,' and may still take, with academic support to fill in gaps.

Children of former pupils urged to identify themselves at registration. Won't give you edge over competition, says Mr Hoskins – but bad news is more likely to be accompanied by a phone call.

Exit: About 15 per cent exit post-16 – fewer each year – freedom offered by local sixth form colleges ('longer hair and earrings,' says Mr Hoskins) the main lure. If shy of required GCSE grades (official minimum 16 points – equates to around eight B grades) school will help if possible, though substitute subjects may be imposed (DT rather than physics, say). Also possible to repeat years.

Translates into gamut of places: Nottingham, Leeds, Southampton, Loughborough, the London lot (UCL, King's Brunel, Royal Holloway), plus hot favourites like Bristol, Exeter, Durham feature most years. Courses ditto – modelmaking to nutrition, speech and language to quantity surveying and design in every permutation. Several taking medicine though geography currently having a moment in sunshine; 2016 best ever for Oxbridge places (four – natural sciences, engineering, music and economics).

Money matters: Bursaries for foundationers up to 110 per cent of fees. Also range of scholarships – DT and drama at 13+ and in the sixth form – also open to existing pupils, plus headmaster's award for able but not quite scholarship level candidates at 11+ and CE; additional scholarships awarded to existing pupils during school career if merited. Fees steep but include majority

R

of extras – meals to choir tours so 'looks more expensive than it is,' said mother.

Remarks: One parent equated school to post-privatisation Jaguar – took a while for shift in quality to be recognised. 'Took years for prices to catch up, but they did.' With Mr Hoskins in the driving seat, this revamped model is definitely proving an all terrain winner.

Reigate St Mary's School

Linked with Reigate Grammar School

Chart Lane, Reigate, Surrey RH2 7RN

Pupils: 342 • Ages: 3–11

Fees: £11,220 – £13,860 pa

Tel: 01737 244880
Email: office@reigatestmarys.org
Website: www.reigatestmarys.org

Head: Since 2005, Mr Marcus Culverwell (40s). Previously deputy head (joined school in 2003). Before that, head of science, then director of studies, then deputy head at Lancing College Junior. A local boy, he was educated first at Caterham, then Archbishop Tenison's sixth form after squeeze on family finances. Sporty, science-y and spiritual. 'Very Christian,' says a parent.

Teenage years dominated by dreams of joining Aviation Mission Fellowship – dashed when failed final stage of commercial pilot training. Studied aeronautical engineering at Hertford followed by MA at Brunel. With dearth of jobs in industry, teaching was originally intended as stopgap career but rapidly became something far more. He realised that he wanted to work with younger children when, while combining teacher training with spell on staff at Cardiff FE college, he was unable to comfort weeping student encountered in corridor.

Personable, child-friendly (has three of his own, two at the senior school, one here) and pupils rush to talk to him, clearly confident of sympathetic hearing. No wonder, given approach to playground duties (takes guitar and sings – though 'not a musician') as well as breaking out into the occasional assembly rap. Keeps staff on their toes and though 'we never sit still', potentially exhausting pace is tempered with generous dollops of non-teaching time to regroup for the next big think (eyes down for eco-flag green school status next).

It's a work in progress that started with Mr Culverwell's first inspection, five weeks into the job, when he produced rationale of planned curriculum development, now on overhaul number three, each marked by progressively closer ties to senior school.

Desire to make a difference is manifest – has just completed book on educating children for social responsibility, teachers and pupils encouraged to explore 'the big questions' and commit to making a difference. Parents acknowledge value of approach but aren't always receptive to newsletter homilies exhorting them to 'down tools and cuddle the children – hard when you're trying to pay the school fees,' said one.)

Academic robe on one side of study, Captain Considerate outfit (worn by pupils to deliver hi-tech homilies on behaviour) on the other sums up approach – relaxed gravitas. Ultimately perception is that it's Mr Fenton down at the big school who rules the roost and makes the big decisions. Thumbs up, however, for being well intentioned – and, overall, 'a nice man.'

Entrance: Non-selective at 3 – first come first served and increasingly over-booked, almost reaching London frenzy levels (including occasional pre-pregnant enquiries). Sympathetic attitude to SEN, permeating from knowledgeable head and increasing resources – SENCo, until recently an add-on responsibility for class teacher, now a separate post. Covers the works, including EBSD, ASD, ADHD, severe dyslexia and those with physical disabilities – rated 'brilliant' by senior school specialist on recent visit.

Gets our vote for recently revised curriculum and brilliantly humane transitions between stages. 'Our ethos is that happy children learn,' says nursery manager. One and 2-year-olds have regular playdates with parents, getting to know big, bright nursery up to two years before they start.

Atmosphere 'moves from buzzing to calm classroom by end of reception so ready for change in pace in year 1,' says staff member. Class sizes rise from maximum 15 in reception and below to maximum 20 in years 1-6.

Choristers, original reason for school's foundation, have voice trials at 6 or 7 and, if successful, become probationers. Boys only – for now, though growing parental rumblings could well see girls involved in the future.

Exit: Vast majority to senior school, but not all. Other destinations include Box Hill, Dunottar, Ardingly and Worth. Parental anxiety following decision to offer firm places to many in year 5 considerable but misplaced, thinks school, as around three-quarters will end up going on to the senior school while those without guarantee can still sit the exam in year 6 and take chances with other outsiders. Much better this way as avoids previous misery of sitting and failing entrance exam, says school, when children can be guided to a better place instead. Some playground gossip means pupils aren't as blissfully unaware as parents would want and 'if you're just one of a handful not to go through to the senior school it can be hard on the individual,' thought one.

Remarks: Originally founded as choir school by Godfrey Searle, canny chartered stockbroker and musician who calculated (accurately) that selling off small area to council for municipal bowls green would avert desire to run bypass through grounds.

Unusually, a cathedral choir without portfolio, though makes up for it with regular appearances at Chichester and occasional visits to St Paul's, tradition starting in the Second World War when regular choir was evacuated. Commercially in demand, too, for Disney amongst others. Choristers' robes line corridor, atmospheric practice room, low-tech shelves bursting with music-stuffed folders, fruit and biscuits laid out for after-school rehearsal – a bit like a time capsule (laptop apologetically to one side the only modern note).

Acquisition by senior school in 2005 was a relative no-brainer, once established that decline in pupil numbers was reversible. Now healthy enough to justify recent £4.5 million investment on impressive glass and brick main teaching block for years 1 to 3, which rears up behind original building, partially concealed on far side by man-made hill, demanded by planners to avoid upsetting locals' sensibilities and incorporating splendiferous downstairs sports hall. Years 4 to 6 are quartered in less plush but perfectly acceptable older-style block. Bright kindergarten (corridor a cheerful clutter of wellies) taking up the ground floor.

Hard-surfaced games area close to school. Attractive, undulating grounds beyond, partially wooded (lots of den building in warmer months) and with beautifully planted memorial garden where head boy and girl lay wreaths in front of school. Assorted pitches (four football, two multi-surface) plus athletics track and cricket pavilion are attractively set in the greenery, all well used and supplemented with additional sessions at senior school and trips to playing fields a short coach ride away.

Though there's some parental moaning if children don't make top teams, school makes efforts to secure fixtures for Bs and Cs as well 'so there are games for all.' Sport broadly split along trad gender lines, but it's permeable – current year 5 rugby and football star player is a girl (while zumba and gymnastics clubs also attract small numbers of boys).

Staff work hard, lessons supported by what head describes as 'phenomenal' planning. All expected to run a popular club two terms in three (free unless run by outside experts). Start in modest way from year 1 (reception parents clamour for share but 'they've had a busy day and need to go home,' thinks head). Really gets going in year 3 with waiting lists 'for everything' and impressively wide ranging, from programming (involves sending delightful little robots on search and rescue missions) to Living World (plenty of pond dipping). Good range of popular trips, too, from bushcraft – a current fave rave – to even more rugged Snowdonia and Mont Blanc.

Ever closer links with senior school sees growing number of specialist teachers (maths the most recent addition, as well as music, games, art, IT) making short walk over. Curriculum consistency between two schools means not just singing from same song sheet but with barber shop harmonies, too.

Impressive signs of expansion in scope and success, with non-selective intake making excellent progress – Sats scores, internally assessed, put 100 per cent of pupils at level 4 and above, 30 per cent hitting a level 6.

Academic focus on continuous assessment is seen as quite intense by parents – though doesn't necessarily permeate through to children – with charismatic staff implementing sensible rewards system (golden time is king) that helps to produce confident, courteous children. 'I hope you have a lovely afternoon,' was heard from one 6-year-old. Smart too – dress code is nostalgic (caps and trad hats for younger pupils, grime-management grey shirts for boys).

Innovative language teaching keeps French as the big one with Spanish and German each taught for a term in year 6. Though maths only subject with formal sets, year 1 has informal streaming, while differentiation is 'part and parcel of lessons' aided by excellent staffing ratios – younger children have full time TA as well as teacher. Classes notably calm though not at expense of fun, reception children listening, rapt, to end of day story, year 1 pupils falling over themselves to show delights of science lessons – leaves 'that were crispy and brown if didn't have enough water,' flowers with ink-dyed petals. Favourite subject? 'It is now,' said one.

R

Big on purposeful technology – WiFi up and running, iPads on the way for all pupils – 'a tool we'll use everywhere,' thinks head; deliberate mix of Macs and PCs 'so children bi-lingual' and Kodu so widely used that 'should be official foreign language.'

Lots of pride in past and at least one eye on the future. Parents of the vast majority of RSM pupils (not just the dead certs) will find passage to senior school eased. For a small number aim is managed and failure-free exit elsewhere. Being a pupil here 'makes it much easier to get to the grammar school, not for the few but, in the future, for almost every St Mary's child,' says school. Means you know what you're buying into. 'You have to live with it or move on,' says parent.

Reigate Grammar School

Linked with Reigate St Mary's School

Reigate Road, Reigate, Surrey RH2 0QS

Pupils: 970 • Ages: 11–18 • Sixth form: 268

Fees: £17,460 pa

Tel: 01737 222231
Email: info@reigategrammar.org
Website: www.reigategrammar.org

Headmaster: Since 2012, Mr Shaun Fenton MA PGCE Med NPQH (50s). Formerly head of Pate's and founded and chaired National Grammar Schools Association. Educated at Haberdashers' Aske's, then PPE at Oxford. Started and ditched City career for education, first in west London comprehensive until drawn by challenge of The Ridings School in Halifax, labelled worst in Britain in TV documentary. Exhilarated by challenge of working with one of the first superheads, who achieved rags to riches magic, forged in hotbed of innovation. 'If something worked here, would work anywhere.'

Much in demand to repeat the process, quickly promoted to first deputy headship in Hertfordshire, followed by spell as troubleshooter injecting aspiration into other troubled schools that had shed senior management following inspection failures. Tough, energetic, enthusiastic and 'comes up with about 1,000 ideas a week,' said member of staff. 'A very nice young chap,' reckoned a paternalistic local.

His arrival has had a mixed reaction from parents, who seem to be holding back while they gauge the measure of the man. They love his God particle-like ability to be in several places at once (one had recently come across him at a hockey umpiring class – his latest qualification) and the way he's handed out his email address and positively implored parents to get in touch – no issue too small. 'I love to hear from them,' he says (he also likes to use them to gauge temperature of public feeling – the words 'focus group' crop up, in other contexts, more than once).

Particularly good at unpicking existing school practices and refashioning with more stuffing. Sixth form mentors don't just talk to pupils but are also charged with speaking to their families. Scholars are challenged from day one, with a programme designed to shape talents into Oxbridge-friendly material if academic and all-weather leadership fabric (sport) with captaincy a managed exercise in building relationships, helping develop struggling teams and nurturing individuals. 'No point just getting them to play matches – it's about the psychology.' Lots of praise, too, for innovations to date, notably reintroduction of house system.

Parents worry that new system of offers to some prep pupils as early as year 5 could reduce numbers making it through to senior school. But though one parent felt it had 'put the cat among the pigeons', head was clear that 'it means offers for the vast majority of Reigate St Mary students and not just the high performers'. Overall, 'admission at age 11 is approximately half from excellent local state primary schools and half from prep schools.'

Conundrum for some might be why, with solid A* career, he has opted for first time move into independent sector instead of carrying on down the path to government darling roles as a superhead's superhead, advising the great, good and better on how to do it. But it's simple. As at Pate's, he can educate society's leaders himself and cut out the middleman. As to why here – it 'was the only school that stood out for its ambition to make a real difference.'

Nervous to start with (he says), he certainly isn't now. Has been charged by the governors with providing education 'the way it should be, with no short cuts.' Slow cook approach lets top grades rise from teaching that lets pupils live their subjects – converting hall into mini Parliament to explore legislative process, for example. 'This could not be further away from a hothouse approach but can deliver stunning, authentic learning,' says head.

Wants to make school one 'you drive past others to come to'. And, yes, he does want to get results up, though refused to be drawn on any specific targets, or schools he'd measure himself against (Caterham is the long term rival at the moment). He also wants staff asking 'what excellence looks like... what are the best teachers and schools in the world and doing? What does it mean to us?' Too many schools coast, he thinks, relying on showy but shallow academic gimmicks, where pupils, drilled to the test, fetch up as 'charlatans, not historians.' As to 'outstanding' inspection ratings, pretty much waved aside as something that for any really good school is the starting point.

Will know he is hitting the sweet spot when shared language of excellence permeates the building and crosses the departments. No wonder 'some staff feel they have been hit by a tsunami – need to hold on tight,' thought insider.

Pupils, meanwhile, see a lot of him as he beams out from airy office overlooking playground. He somehow manages to pack in a bit of teaching, too. An RE teacher originally, he takes 1675 (school's foundation date) as starting point for philosophical debate about pupils' place in the world. Lively charm makes him a winner. Jolly, determined and, through previous posts, has seen it, done it and got the results to prove it, leaving no doubt that this head will make his mark on every area of the school without, despite recent appearance in full Darth Vader regalia, necessitating a walk on the dark side.

Married – wife Anna works part-time at the school – with two sons at linked prep.

Academic matters: 'Not a hothouse, but academic,' is the view of one prospective parent who, like others, reckons head has been charged with ramping up results. Sciences and maths top the popularity chart, history close runners up, geography, government and politics and RS leading second wave, while marginals include music and Latin (13 taking music A level a couple of years ago was 'exceptional', says department director, who is happy with small exam numbers and big involvement).

Much that's good, little bad and nothing ugly, with GCSE and A level grades both onwards and upwards. In 2016, 83 per cent of GCSEs and nearly two-thirds of A levels A*/A grades. Expect best feet to be put forward and pips squeaked, all, however, without imposing undue stress. Direction of travel is gladdening head's heart.

Ten subjects taken by most, with IGCSEs for sciences, Eng lang and maths, where very able whizz through a year early. Maths is only formally set subject apart from languages, grouped to allow later starters (often from state primaries) to catch up with early adopters.

Following tried and tested approach at Pate's, where A* grades shot up from the merely very, very good to the stratospheric, head is rethinking time taken to cover GCSE ground, covering foundation stage in two years, then taking three years (years 9 to 11) to cover the rest.

Teaching of a fairly formal nature (and some classrooms plain rather than purl when it came to display) but judging by interest levels – front-facing, engaged pupils clearly absorbed in subjects – it's quality stuff. 'Not every single teacher is brilliant,' felt parent, though praised the many who were. 'There's lots of laughter and interaction.' And while teenagers 'might moan, they do get on with lessons.' Plenty of oohs and ahs in year 8 chemistry class, as teacher created solid. 'I love chemistry – teaching is brilliant,' said Oxbridge hopeful. Computing another winner – first year pupils animatedly creating crests and GCSE candidates' amazing robotic creations proudly on show (A*s the norm).

Relaxed pupils clearly weren't feeling the strain. Big benefit – plenty of time for non-examined goodies on offer during the normally exam-dominated GCSE years of fourth and fifth form as electives ensure there's no lull in the pace of learning. Result is sense of open house, with teachers welcoming followers in and out of lesson time, subject loyalties very keenly felt and endearingly expressed. 'It's my third home,' said year 9 enthusiast of computing. 'Music's my second.'

Games, options, the arts: Something for everyone, even down to flourishing forensic club (DNA testing one of covetable skills covered) with music, drama and sport taking joint curtain call in neatly blended annual summer festival featuring show-stopping goodies like fashion catwalk, school v MCC match and assorted productions and concerts.

Extracurricular, indeed, is 'the heartbeat of the school,' says head (who should know, what with taking games lessons on a Wednesday afternoon and being brains of the enterprise). D of E, CCF and many, many trips – 'more than we need,' thought one parent (but in a good way). Clubs and activities get a brochure of their own, writers' enthusiasms waxing and waning. Much made of indulging pupils' 'love of numbers' and 'passion for writing' in writing/maths clubs – trickling down to lower key 'interest' in arts clubs, while medical discussion club can muster only the quiet decorum of 'relevance.'

Sport big but not bloated (offers 'the opportunity to play both winter sports simultaneously' – now that's what we call co-ordination), and gets unusually modest showing in school literature. Success, though substantial (fourth form rugby team stuffed with county players) isn't a front, back and middle pages splash.

The talented are well catered for, girls too (their sixth form rugby team 'popular,' reckon pupils), as well as enthusiastic triers. 'My son had a fixture practically every Saturday, daughter hardly at all,' thought parent – now approaching equality for both. Particularly strong in athletics (dogged too – one national biathlon finalist swam and ran in below zero temperatures) as well as cricket (impressive wins against strong schools).

On site facilities stretch not just to sports hall but very snazzy swimming pool (open to parents every Sunday). Focus for games is 32-acre site (stonking but chilly, 'about four degrees colder than everywhere else,' thought staff member'), just 'five to 10' minutes away (15 in rush hour – we tried it) and worth a Saturday visit for the bacon butties alone.

Arts, performing and visual, cast equally long shadow. Supercharged head of drama reaches across age and interest range. Pulsating productions including puppet play, Animal Farm and A Winter's Tale complete with revolving clock – 'bonkers but really good,' thought pupil. Breathtaking in both scope and ambition, with talented individuals scoring places in national youth ensembles of every type, including largely undergraduate-level festival.

With strong singing (many prep choristers move up to senior school), you'd expect super music and you get it. 'Jaw-dropping,' said parent. Around 50 per cent have individual music lessons, some reaching diploma standard. Once a year giant orchestra (participants numerous rather than Goliath-proportioned) scoops up local junior school performers. Normal sized version for daily use plus concert band, intermediate versions too, for those en route to grade greatness but not there yet. Add free theory/aural classes, five choirs, most audition-free, one open to staff and parents, new house music competition and evening soirées in head's garden, and it's a wonder the director of music isn't fraying at the edges. 'Music is so relaxing,' he says, however, smilingly picking way round percussion break-out sessions in attractive (and tactically soundproofed) building.

Background and atmosphere: Despite 17th century foundations, it's the 19th century that dominates, with up to the minute additions nicely accommodated (delivered via smart new Ballance building with change in floor covering only hint to seamless welding to existing block). New £4m learning and resource centre provides (inter alia) a library and sixth form centre surrounded by landscaped gardens.

Close to centre of Reigate, market town made good thanks to commuter-friendly train connections (and very slow level crossing). Canny land acquisition almost allows stroll into town to be accomplished entirely on school land. School has personable, unintimidating, family-centric feel. Its two sites are mere yards apart, quickest walk along the front restricted to sixth formers because of thunder and fury of non-stop A25 traffic (teachers stand guard by pedestrian crossing at end of school day to block off-piste excursions). Other ranks, like earlier generations, commute between buildings along peaceful path behind the school that runs along perimeter of St Mary's Churchyard (venue for year group assemblies, four times a year whole school get-togethers in extendable concert hall).

Atmosphere nicely inclusive, and not just for pupils – support and academic teachers, who share common room, all muck in, clearly feeling both wanted and involved. They include head of IT, former City type, running lunchtime talk on morality of banking and head of catering heavily involved in ICT. Until recently, 'was nice but a bit sleepy,' thought school insider. 'Not any more – there's something new happening every week.'

Pastoral care, well-being and discipline: Pupil happiness and pastoral care is the priority and carries all before it, says head. Get it right and you 'can light the touch paper of success in all other areas of their life.' Parents confirm school's fleet-footedness in troubleshooting and what mother described as 'open door feeling' to problems. One girl's friendship issues reported to teacher who 'sorted it' effectively. 'Unique' staff lend an ear with problems, with form tutors (who move up with pupils) as well as sixth form mentors and listening service run by chaplaincy.

Poor behaviour a minority interest, serious problems almost unknown, reckoned pupils we talked to. Detentions 'for cheekiness' and late work, rewards via on-line credit system.

Pupils and parents: Mixes 'indigenous Surrey with incomers,' says local. Lots from south west London. Some grew up here, went off to work and then came back, says local estate agent. 'I know lots of families.' As to children? 'A credit to the town,' he reckoned. Most famous old boy is David Walliams, who was recently doing a spot of filming at the school. Other alumni include Trevor Kavanagh, Keir Starmer, Susan Gritton and Ray Mears.

R

Entrance: School proud of flexible approach, despite applications at record levels since arrival of current head. For the right candidate, computer doesn't invariably say no, even out of season. 'Come and talk to me,' says head.

Entrance isn't 'just about testing and measuring,' he adds. Teacher feedback and reports count too. He's after children 'who will make the world a better place,' especially when 'parents would want them to be their child's best friend.' Choristers, though welcome, subject to same criteria as the rest. Now pre-tests for 13+ entry in year 6 (maths, English and reasoning).

For sixth form, A grades at GCSE in subjects to be studied at A level and an overall tally of at least four As, four Bs and no grade lower than a C. Some parents worried that entry requirements were being toughened up but school again works on case-by-case basis resulting in 'a number without the full requirement coming back,' says head. 'I see any individual leaving because they are without the grades or even grades close enough as really sad,' – and where possible, 'will waive the requirements'. If it isn't possible, 'they are a very, very small minority.'

Also notably brilliant at resolving year 12 nightmares. Head 'hugely supportive' when things go wrong, agreed parents and pupils, moving mountains to keep pupils at the school, sometimes repeating year or dropping a subject.

Exit: Some 80 per cent stay on to the sixth form. Six medics, two dentists, one vet and three lawyers in 2016; one medic to Cambridge and one engineer to Oxford. Highly rated for quality of HE destinations by Sutton Trust which placed school in top two per cent of all UK co-eds – Exeter, Southampton, Bath, Durham and Warwick most popular destinations currently. Saturday morning help sessions for leavers needing help with deferred entry post A level a real boon.

Money matters: A scholarship programme (about 150 awards across the school), with awards of 30 per cent, potentially 'significantly more' at head's discretion. Also head's scholarship – for children bringing a je ne sais quoi activity or interest which offers 'value to the school community – scholars are expected to give back.' And, a nice touch, all those with straight A*s at GCSE automatically get £1,000 off the sixth form fees (parent to child bribe chats, you'd imagine, are rife as a result).

Remarks: Hothouse ethos not on the agenda but, given the head's success at Pate's, where similar approach had transformational approach on results, we'd predict similar marvels here. Definitely one to watch.

The Rochester Grammar School

Maidstone Road, Rochester, Kent ME1 3BY

Pupils: 1,213 (boys in sixth form) • Ages: 11–18 • Sixth form: 333

Tel: 01634 843049
Email: office@rochestergrammar.medway.sch.uk
Website: www.rochestergrammar.medway.sch.uk

Interim head of school: Since September 2016, Mr I Macaulay, previously deputy principal.

Executive principal is Mr G Bassan BA NPQH. CEO is Mr S Gardener.

Academic matters: In 2016, 71 per cent of GCSE entries were graded A*/A. At A level, 81 per cent of grades were A* to B and 44 per cent A*/A, and IB the average total point score was 38. The school has specialist status for maths, ICT and music; history, English and science are all strong departments. Modern foreign languages haven't matched up so new language teaching methods introduced. Students in years 7 and 8 learn languages through drama workshops and role play with no written work, with the aim to build their vocabulary and confidence before moving to the next level. 'The brain is wired to learn languages orally first. The worst that will happen is that students will get Bs, but they will be able to order sandwiches confidently and catch a train using that language. Language teaching hasn't worked for so long. We have watched children dumbstruck in France and Germany, asking "do you speak English?" in

English. If we see a problem we get to the bottom of it and we're prepared to take a bold step to make a difference.' The school also offers Latin, which unusually is oversubscribed. One parent explained why her daughter loves it: 'They also cover the civilisation, history and literature. It's a good option if you're not a good linguist'.

As we walk the corridors there's a hubbub coming from all the classrooms. Pupils are animated, some half on their feet. Tables aren't arranged in serried ranks, but in blocks or U-shapes and there's much collaborative work and discussion going on. 'There's lots of guided discovery. We are told a limited amount, and we are supposed to find out the rest, we're not spoon-fed', say the girls. Thinking and memory skills are big buzzwords in the school, or, as the students explained it to us, 'We focus on how to learn, not just what to learn'. They all know what type of learner they are, and how they work best. 'I'm a logical thinker', said one. 'I can't understand diagrams', said another, 'so the teacher gives me an explanation in words'.

Sixth formers speak of an individuality in teaching styles that makes lessons lively and interesting. 'History and politics are fantastic, the grades are consistently amazing and the teacher has such a passion for the subject he turns bright red when we're having a debate', said one. Another, who transferred from a different school, said the gap in expectations between the two is huge. 'It's very demanding; the school expects you to be on top of your game'.

No teaching slackness tolerated. 'If a member of staff, after appropriate support, is unable to demonstrate an ability to improve, they move on. It's the same with supply teachers covering sickness absence: we might have two or three supply teachers in quick succession which concerns parents, but it's important to get the right one.' You can't argue with the success of this strategy.

One parent calls the school 'a jewel in Rochester'. But the other side of the coin is that the pace is fast and your daughter will have to be prepared to work hard. The school follows a two year compressed KS3 to enable some accelerated students to sit English, maths and science GCSEs in year 10 and AS courses in year 11. One parent related that when her child took three GCSEs in year 9, 'She got three As which she wasn't happy with, so she retook them to get A*s'. The pace and quantity of work can impact on family life too, as one parent explained: 'Some parents find it quite hard to accept the amount of work their child has got to do'. Her daughter worked a couple of hours a night in year 7/8, and all evening in year 9, but willingly, she said. The school expects around 14 hours of homework per week to be completed in the sixth form, but many students go beyond this of their own volition. Parents report one or two girls who have left because this environment didn't suit them. But they stress that children are not left to flounder. 'There are lots of support clubs, they don't just write them off,' said one.

Speaking to sixth formers, it's apparent that the vast majority develop a self-belief that they are capable of anything, rather than being flattened by the expectations. 'It does get to the stage that you think a B is not good enough. But that's how life is', one told us. 'When I got a B in a mock I was distraught, I didn't deserve a B. Then I think, if they're getting A, why can't I? If she can do it, I can, and I ask other students how they are doing it.' Another girl told us, 'I don't want to go to Cambridge, but I know that if I did, the school would enable me to get th ere.'

Games, options, the arts: Lack of green fields equals lack of serious sporting provision. Football and athletics are the school's main areas of competitive success. An old girl made the GB synchronised swimming squad, another's an international skier.

The school has the largest girls' D of E centre in the country and opportunities include a three week trek in China. Takes part in the Comenius project, promoting European culture. Individual trips encouraged to develop the girls' personal interests and career intentions. One girl is going to the student UN in Geneva, with the school matching her fundraising, another has been to CERN for an extended project.

'Join the choir, see the world', they say – anyone can be in the choir, which has taken them to the Vatican City and the USA. Music concerts on a termly basis, international musicians brought in to perform in the school's Thorndike Arts Centre. Two governors' places for musicians – students get bursaries to spend on music lessons, in return they give back to the whole school by running extracurricular activities – one girl runs two choirs, another a quartet.

Language exchanges to France, Germany, and Spain. 'We believe in exchanges and immersion, spending a week with a host family, we do not believe in day trips.'

Background and atmosphere: No dreaming spires, it's a functional building, but it's modern and in a good state of repair by the standards of state grammars. 'A bit soulless,' said a parent.

The school moved to this new building in 1990, having opened in 1888 with a then progressive aim to educate young ladies. Became an 'academy of excellence' in 2011. The school is a combined mathematics/ICT and music specialist school, a Thinking Foundation school, and the first'Memory school accredited by Exeter University – teaching students how to learn and memorise is a priority.

It's a powerhouse for women. Houses are named after an eclectic group of women such as Jane Tomlinson, Eva Cassidy, Ella Fitzgerald, and Hildegard (of Bingen). Corridors are lined with posters detailing the most powerful women in the UK today, as well as the illustrations of ex-pupil Evelyn Dunbar, held up as a beacon for forging her way into the entirely male dominated theatre of war when she became the only female commissioned war artist during World War II.

Work is under way on developing an old girls' network. 'In public schools the former students associations can be very powerful; we want to give our students that same advantage. There are still some industries where it matters who you know, and we would like our young ladies to look after each other.' Its young alumni group, now 100 strong and growing, brings back former pupils to help current students see themselves five years down the line, and to give them contacts to go to for advice.

Everything reinforces a message to be the best, which concerned one parent, who said: 'One thing I didn't like when we looked around, there were so many lovely displays and all the work was excellent; other schools had things up which weren't quite as good, but where people had done their best. I wondered, if you weren't quite up there, how would you feel?'

R

Pastoral care, well-being and discipline: Discipline? There's quite a pause before the sixth formers respond, 'People don't really go out of line here'. It usually only comes into play for uniform infringements, for which the girls have to do community service, helping out the teachers.

Pastoral care thrives on teachers knowing their pupils very well indeed. Girls have the same head of house and the same form tutor for six years, which means problems are spotted and interventions organised early. There are vertical form groups, with years 7 to 12 mixed together, and family groups of five or six within each form. Younger girls like this because they can ask senior students for help with their homework, or advice on which options to choose, and it means they don't find the big girls so intimidating. All new girls are mentored by a girl a year older. For year 13 they are put in subject specialism forms – those headed for medicine in one, musicians in another, for example.

Parents speak highly of the school's rapid identification of and solutions for any learning difficulties. One recalled: 'Soon after she started the school, her CAT tests showed a big discrepancy. The school arranged further testing and we found she was dyslexic with processing difficulties. I was astonished because this had never been suspected before. They've given her a range of strategies to help her cope, and it's not holding her back in any way.' School is 'very proud of the special educational needs provision at this school; we find a lot of students have SEN which wasn't identified before'.

To deal with the pressures they are under, the school has introduced a Sumo initiative, to develop 'bounce-back ability'. 'It's about developing their resilience to take the knocks when they occur'. It takes students through a series of responses, such as: How can I change this situation? What can I learn from it? Is there anything positive about it? Am I responding appropriately? and how important will this be in six months' time?

Pupils and parents: No question about the added value here. From a school community where just 25 per cent of parents are graduates, it delivers one in three pupils to a top 10 university.

The pupil body is a true social mix. Some parents are not working and are in difficult circumstances, some are doctors and lawyers. Some children live in public housing, around 10 per cent were privately educated at primary school. One in 10 pupils are from non-white backgrounds. What they have in common, say pupils, is that, 'everyone really wants to do well'.

The pupils feel it's an extremely supportive community. 'There isn't a person who won't help you', said one. Another said she has experienced 'overwhelming kindness' from fellow students. A third needed to raise funds for a work experience placement at the United Nations and was humbled that with fellow pupils' help, she managed this in one week.

Entrance: There's no catchment – entry is entirely based on scores in the local 11+, the Medway test. The pass mark for this fluctuates around 509 and last year students needed 514 or higher for a place at Rochester Grammar. There are two music scholarships and five places are held for appeals. 'Some of our greatest successes didn't pass the test.'

Around 30-40 places become available in the sixth form, when entry also opens up to boys. Some 12-18 boys join the sixth form each year as the school achieves better results than any other in the area. Minimum entry requirements are 5+ A*-C grades at GCSE, with B grades in all courses to be studied at A level or IB except maths and the sciences, which require an A grade.

R

Exit: Around 80 to 90 per cent stay on into the sixth form when they can opt to take either A levels or the IB. There's a tailored programme for students wishing to apply for Oxbridge or medical school (one place in 2016). All are expected to go on to university and the school does a great deal of work on guiding pupils' choices; many of them will be the first in their family to take a degree. A virtual university week is held in year 12, when pupils are taught in university format and given advice on UCAS applications and accessing bursaries.

Pupils looking at wackier courses are likely to be discouraged. 'We engage in a lot of research with the students, looking at where that course is likely to take them, and the value of investing in their education. A student might say "I want to do X course at Y university, I like the tutor, and the facilities are really nice." We unpick that. Where do people from that course go to post-university? What percentage gets full-time employment at a certain level of money? We make them understand, it's not just the next three years, make the wrong choice now and you play catch up for the rest of your life.'

The result is that nearly one-third of pupils go to a top 10 university, one-half to a top 20, and 80 per cent to a top 40.

Remarks: The poise, focus and articulacy of sixth formers here is incredible – it's like talking to young graduate professionals rather than a bunch of schoolgirls. So is their work ethic. 'I want to stay in and study on Friday nights, I'm not forced to,' said one, as the others nodded in agreement. The school is determined that the girls will make the best use of their intelligence and take their rightful place at the high table of professional life. You'll be hard pressed to find a school more likely to steer your daughter on to great things. But you need to be sure she'll cope with the pressure.

Rochester Independent College

Star Hill, Rochester, Kent ME1 1XF

Pupils: 290; 60 boarders • Ages: 11-19 (boarding from 16) • Sixth form: 180

Fees: Tuition £12,000 – £17,400; Boarding + £11,400 – £13,200 pa

Tel: 01634 828115
Email: admissions@rochester-college.org
Website: www.rochester-college.org

Co-principals: There are three co-principals: Brian (Pain), Alistair (Brownlow), and Pauline (Bailey) – it's all first names here. The three heads say they work in a collegiate way, sharing responsibilities. The kids tell you Brian is the big chief, and the one they're a bit scared of. Brian is as far from a typical public school head as you can imagine. He has a passion for sailing barges, and he walks into the meeting as if he has just stepped off one – clad in a T-shirt, hair looking like it's been in a force eight, and hands he needs to wash before shaking as he's just been scrubbing blackboards. He tells it like it is, including telling kids who aren't putting in any effort that they are not staying to waste their parents' money. Alistair's the great communicator, bouncing with enthusiasm like Tigger, and expressing the school's beliefs and methods with an articulacy which backs up his reputation as an ace English teacher. Pauline has a background in management and is the one who ensures they are meeting regulations and dotting the 'I's. She oversees all boarders and the year 7-10s.

It's a stable ship – Brian set up the school with a co-founder in 1984; Alistair joined as a new graduate in 1997, while Pauline was once a pupil here, joined the staff in 1989, and has sent her own two children here. All three still teach, 'so we don't lose sight of what we're here for'. It started as an A level college, and extended to take pupils from year 7 in 2007. Bought by Dukes Education in 2016.

Academic matters: There's no uniform or dress code, and the teachers are just as likely as pupils to be wearing a hoody. Everyone goes by their first name. So far so hippy – until you walk around the building during lessons. Hush has descended, and opening a classroom door reveals silent pupils, and desks in rows. Alistair says: 'People try to place us in the progressive/alternative mould, but we're not. It's common sense; small classes, good teaching, and an informal but ordered and respectful atmosphere.'

The next surprise comes in the teaching methods. 'We teach-test-teach-test,' says Alistair. The idea that testing thwarts children gets short shrift here. 'A lot of schools don't do enough regular testing. At A level we do a test every week in each subject. If we're going to put something right we need a rigorous diagnosis of what is wrong,' Alistair says. There's no objection to this degree of testing from pupils – in fact the students seem to welcome it. 'Testing means you can't get delusions, you really know where you are at any point,' said one. Another, who was told by her grammar school that she needed to 'lower her sights', said: 'The teaching style is completely different, we are tested all the time and my grades have gone up consistently.'

There is a firm concentration on exam technique, but still the school isn't seen as an exam factory. One sixth form pupil said: 'The focus is on exams, but it is still enriching. We get a two hour lesson for everything which means the teachers can drift off topic which helps a lot with general knowledge and essay subjects.'

Teachers are 'very passionate about their subjects,' say parents, and another pupil, comparing the teaching to that at his former grammar school, said: 'The teaching is of a better quality and the teachers know their subject to a greater depth.' And a pupil at the lower end of the school said: 'You don't get to the end of one lesson without doing something fun.'

Many students transfer here after poor progress at AS or A level and the effect can be dramatic. One pupil told us he was predicted to get Ds and Es at AS; he moved from his grammar to the college in February, and in July he achieved three As at AS and an A at A level. Another student moved after getting a U at AS, and she said, 'In my first two weeks here I learned more than I had in the whole previous year.'

There are three pathways through the sixth form, mainly set in different teaching groups. There are those doing a two year A level course through the school; students who have transferred here for year 13 after a disappointing year 12; and those who have done two years elsewhere and are doing retakes. The A level programme is flexible with no option blocks, and students can do speed courses in a new subject to complement retakes. Results for 2016 A levels show 29 per cent of entries achieving A*/A and 60 per cente A*-B. Maths is the biggest A level subject. English literature and film studies are also strong departments, both having received Good Schools Guide awards in recent years.

At GCSE, biology, chemistry and physics are taught at International GCSE level for those aiming to study sciences at A level, and students also take the IGCSE in English and English literature. Languages on offer include German, French and Spanish, but it is not compulsory to take a language. Pupils can also take subjects such as astronomy, film studies and photography at GCSE. In 2016, 12 per cent of GCSEs were A*/A and 38 per cent were A*-B.

And it would be hard to find better provision for an artist. GCSEs are offered in six disciplines – fine art, graphics, photography, textiles, ceramics and 3D. Some students take three of these to A level, which enables them to bypass a foundation year. There is terrific work on display. Two students have won places on the prestigious fine art degree course at UCL's The Slade School. Dominik Klimowski, former BBC online picture editor, teaches photography, and local artist Billy Childish is a visiting lecturer.

Parents especially appreciate the efforts made to ensure each pupil gains the best possible grade. One said: 'There are a lot of extra lessons before exams, in the holidays and so on. They will do as much as they can if they think you can improve your grade.'

Another praised the fact that they don't charge for extra tuition in the evenings and holidays, adding: 'I was concerned about my son's maths and suggested getting him some tuition. They said it was their responsibility, and I should not be looking for tutors. They did some extra work with him and he got an A, so I was ecstatic.'

Classrooms are named after Brian's beloved Thames sailing barges; 2014 saw this interest taken a step further, with the introduction of an apprenticeship course in boatbuilding, enabling students to gain City and Guilds qualifications up to NVQ level 3.

Games, options, the arts: Sport is growing, but the school doesn't have the infrastructure to provide serious provision. There's a newly created rugby team for year 11 to 13s, which uses the facilities of a local rugby club and is coached by a player from England's women's team. It also supports those playing at higher levels – one sixth former is training with a London football club, and the school enables him to fit lessons around his sporting commitments. Another sixth former is hoping to compete as a sprinter in the next Paralympics. But as one student points out, it is not the type of school which tends to attract the sporty, and so PE provision tends to be more activity based, like ice skating, sailing, self-defence and climbing.

Lower down the school the students play in mixed teams, so boys say games have to be less rough.

There's a rich cultural programme – a drama theatre hosts visiting theatre companies and art shows, and the school's on-site cinema regularly hosts the National Schools' Film week.

Boarding: Boarding is only available to students of 16+. Virtually all students have single rooms. Some have a very small 'pod' ensuite, otherwise it's shared bathrooms. Furnishings are basic but the Georgian high ceilings and big windows add light and space, and all rooms have a phone and internet point. There's a big common room with a pool table and comfy chairs, and a study for quiet work.

Currently 60 out of 290 students are boarders – 40 per cent of these are from the UK, 11 per cent from Europe, and the remainder from countries including Canada, USA, Thailand, China, Russia, Nigeria, and South Africa.

Background and atmosphere: The campus is as unique as the school. It started as one terraced house, but as the school expanded, it gradually bought up 13 properties in adjoining roads, including a Georgian terrace which houses the boarding accommodation. What would once have been the back gardens to these houses now form the grounds with ancient apple trees and wild garden areas, paths to secret nooks and crannies, a viewing platform to climb – and an oversized garden shed where Brian likes to hold his maths classes. Students work on garden projects such as the allotment as part of their D of E award, and the gardens have won a Kent Wildlife Trust Gold Award.

Mid-career, Brian took time out of teaching to become an architect, and the campus reflects this interest. The theatre in the grounds is known as the Womble building – the theatre space is under ground, whilst over the top there's an outdoor seating area which can be used as an open-air auditorium.

An igloo-like structure in the garden is used as an outdoor classroom, shelter, and quiet space. Intended to inspire and motivate, it has a central roof opening for cloud watching.

When we visited the school was awaiting delivery of some steel sculptural musical gates – an art installation created by Henry Dagg, who plays with Icelandic pop star Bjork, and has transformed his garden fence into a glockenspiel. You will be able to play three octaves on these gates, sufficient to pass your music A level, according to Brian. Reflecting on the £100,000 price tag of these gates, Brian says, 'I'm committed to culture'.

Pastoral care, well-being and discipline: A level students have one-to-one meetings with a personal tutor every couple of weeks, more frequently if they wish, and pupils lower down the school have individual meetings every half term.

Parents receive formal reports once a month, which are 'meaningful, not full of euphemisms, and not from a software package'. Younger pupils have a parents' evening, but in the sixth form tutors deal directly with the students as young adults, and reports only go home which they have seen first. 'We promise there will be no surprises through that feedback,' says Alistair.

A number of the pupils have been labelled as bad apples or having limited prospects in previous settings, but have quickly turned things around at the college, where they are free from discipline based on minutiae. One such pupil, previously at a girls' independent, said: 'I was constantly getting picked on by teachers and getting detentions for stupid things, like going to the toilet'.

The principals say they are strict about homework and behaviour, but removing petty rules means the rapport between pupils and teachers is much better. Or, as one pupil put it, 'The only thing to rebel against here is education itself'.

Other pupils have come from grammars where they felt under too much pressure, or from large schools where they felt overwhelmed, and all say they are learning better and enjoying school more here. 'I worried a lot at my old school, here it's a better environment,' said one. 'At my old school if you improved, they didn't notice,' said another.

Parents all speak highly of the pastoral care, and the growth in confidence they have witnessed in their children. One has three children at the school and she says: 'They are all very different but they are spot on about all of their weaknesses and strengths.'

Pupils and parents: Local pupils form 70 per cent of the cohort and come from a wide catchment – there are minibuses from towns including Tonbridge, Tunbridge Wells, Maidstone, Ashford and Sevenoaks, and the train station opposite brings pupils from Bromley and London. A further 15 per cent come from elsewhere in the UK, and 15 per cent from overseas, including Thai government scholars (who tend to be very high performers, often ending up at Oxbridge).

Numbers lower down the school are small. It starts with around 10 pupils in year 7, who have deliberately opted for a small and different type of school. These are added to over the years, generally by pupils who have been disaffected or haven't thrived in other schools, to numbers in the mid-20s for GCSE years. By sixth form it grows to 50 in year 12, and 130 in Year 13/14. This is something to consider in the younger year groups, especially as currently two girls are each the only girl in their years. The flipside is it makes for more natural relationships between the boys and girls and less of the gender division that you see in big schools – they are clearly relaxed in each other's company. None of the pupils or parents we spoke to saw the small year groups as a problem – there's much more mixing between years, and pupils keep up with other friends in their neighbourhood – and many see this as a plus.

The students are a strikingly nice bunch. It's a place for individuals, and there's a lovely air of tolerance and warmth between the pupils – many of whom seem relieved to have found a home among other square pegs. 'They look after each other, and if someone does well they are pleased about this,' said a parent. Those whose strengths lie outside the traditionally alpha areas of academic or sporting have their own kudos. 'There is a lot more respect for art and creativity,' said one pupil.

Students say it is not competitive, and that there's a huge range in academic ability and ambition. 'If you work your hardest and get an E that's fine,' said one. 'Stronger people help the weaker people; no-one's struggling because everyone helps each other,' said another.

Parents love the lack of school gate competitiveness: 'That playground talk, everyone wanting their child to be in the top set, you don't have that here,' said one relieved mother.

About 50 per cent of pupils have been previously in the independent sector, but a lot of pupils come from families with no tradition of private education.

Entrance: It's non-selective in that there's no entrance exam for children joining at 11 or 13, and there's no minimum GCSE grade requirements for sixth form entry. But every prospective student is interviewed, and the principals say they do turn some away.

Direct entry into any year group at any point in the academic year is possible, and places can be secured in the short gap between exam results and the start of a new term. Around 60 students join each year, either to retake their A levels having completed two years of A levels elsewhere, or directly into year 13 after disappointing results in year 12 elsewhere.

Exit: The courses students go on to reflect the broad range of abilities and interests catered for: some go on to read law, maths, medicine or classics; others have taken up courses in animal behaviour, film studies, marketing, photography or midwifery. Five to Oxbridge in 2016 (four of them Thai government scholars, plus a Brit off to read medicine); three other medics; other destinations range from Edinburgh (astrophysics) to Instituto Marangoni, Milan (fashion design) to Cumbria (accounting and finance)

Money matters: Around £100,000 per year goes into means-tested bursaries, which are awarded not on academic ability, but 'if we think they'll make a good contribution'. Scholarships include the Ralph Steadman Art Scholarship, which offers a two year full scholarship for A levels.

The school has a policy to keep extras to the minimum – music lessons, buses and exam fees are extra, but extracurricular trips are kept deliberately modest. 'We don't take for granted that parents have bottomless pits of money,' says Alistair.

Remarks: This won't be one that sits on your shortlist and you can't make up your mind about. You'll either love or hate this place. Your money won't buy the trappings of a public school – no mahogany-rich headmaster's study, certainly no suave head in a handmade suit. No pupils with collars and lips firmly buttoned. No PTA committees or fundraising balls. For some that will be a blessed relief.

You'll get that warm buzz in your heart when you recognise your kid in the personalities here – or not. That might be one of several types we saw – the quirky one, condemned to be picked on in an average school; the fiercely intelligent, who has rubbed teachers up the wrong way by being too smart for his own good in other settings; the kid whose education got derailed by too much focus on petty rules and discipline.

It won't suit sporting jocks – facilities are meagre, and there are rarely enough pupils of the right age and inclination to make a team.

But it's a great option for the cash-strapped; many parents with only enough gold in the pot to fund a couple of years in the independent sector buy in for the last year of GCSEs, for the A level course, or for retakes. And it's a sound investment – most improve considerably on expectations at their previous school.

Roedean School

Roedean Way, Brighton, East Sussex BN2 5RQ

Pupils: 492; 230 full, 33 weekly/flexi boarders • Ages: 11–18 • Sixth form: 159 • C of E

Fees: Day £15,495 – £20,160; Boarding £22,170 – £36,180 pa

Tel: 01273 667500
Email: enquiries@roedean.co.uk
Website: www.roedean.co.uk

Headmaster: Since 2013, Mr Oliver Blond (40s). Previously head at Henrietta Barnett School, one of top selective state girls' schools in the UK, for seven year stint – perfect for seeing through a generation of pupils without starting to repeat himself, he says. Before that, deputy head, North London Collegiate, so something of an expert in all-girls education. Not certain post here was natural fit until visited, when was instantly won over by school's charisma. So far, the feeling seems to be mutual. 'Aspirational, sweet and delightful,' says old girl.

Busy, busy, busy – as well as teaching (English, drama, philosophy) also academic director of the Princes' Teaching Institute charity, as well as raising two young children with wife Helen, teacher turned successful children's author. Highly articulate (goes with the headship territory), he's also soft-voiced and a great listener (both rarer commodities). Forthright mothers, old girls and especially pupils who 'know everything that I took six months to learn': he listens to the lot.

Formerly forbidding mood amongst tight-knit school community, including a few who were a tad suspicious to find bloke in charge, now one of almost palpable relief, with rave reviews for speed with which Mr Blond has tackled perma-complacency that dominated teaching and attitudes. School is going back to roots – academic, all-round school for British girls with a smaller percentage of international students, though with many more day students and total numbers increasing to around 500, building on an already healthy surplus.

While working on amplifying siren call to Londoners, even contemplating lowering weekly boarding prices so a closer match for day school fees in the Capital, he's also ensuring locals start to see school not as impenetrable posh fortress but accessible Sussex place offering warm welcome on the cliff tops. They're coming round, brand starting to feature on trendy Brighton ravers' educational wish lists, with admissions team fielding 300 per cent increase in enquiries from locals and over 170 families attending recent open day (one of three).

Integration by stealth should help. Girls and boys from local schools now involved in co-ed go-karting to hip-hop curriculum enrichment, while sixth form Wednesday afternoon community service includes sessions in local primaries. School is also pushing bursaries for state schools in the area. And, yes, though previous attempts have been made to bring in bright but financially challenged, with slightly sporadic results, we'd back Mr Blond to make it happen.

Longer term, would like a third of places offered to UK pupils on needs-blind basis (school already offers some support to similar proportion of existing pupils). Will only work, though, if pupils and families, with or without scholarships, have evidence of change. 'A school that's waiting to be different just isn't enough,' he says. 'That's why we've gone at it really quite quickly.'

Presciently, Mr Blond's first choice career was, apparently, Spiderman. Scaling the heights and accomplishing the impossible? No wonder he's proving so successful.

Academic matters: Formidable competition from other local independents including Brighton College and Lancing, and any number of London options, has made school necessarily self-critical about results. Things now very definitely on the up, with 74 per cent of GCSE grades coming in at A* and A in 2016.

At A level, English, humanities (with exception of history) and languages currently minority interests, and of the star subjects, maths is outstanding year in, year out. Further maths also highly successful. Almost the cue for spot of subtle back-patting, A*/A grade percentage at A level rocketing up to 62 in 2016, 83 per cent A*-B.

Parents are hugely relieved that school's previous shortcomings have been addressed. The fear had been that essence and iconic status as landmark British girls' boarding school were in danger of ebbing away, with rise in international pupils and non-negotiable format – full boarding or nothing – putting off many potential customers. And while nothing wrong with cultural diversity – 'you get a huge level of tolerance for other people and ideas,' thought insider – proportion of international pupils had caused sense of alienation, numbers of OGs sending own children dropping like a stone.

One of Mr Blond's first acts was to undertake wholesale lesson observation. Though he 'didn't wave a big stick,' thought school insider, a third of staff and half the heads of department left during his first year, many taking arrival as cue to retire. Parents' perspective distinctly un-nuanced. 'About time somebody put a bomb up them,' said mother. 'If I'm paying £35,000 a year, I don't want my daughter to be told to read page 46 if she doesn't understand.'

Focus since has been to seek out 'dynamic, inspirational and energetic staff with new ideas and teaching methods,' he says. The ones we saw in action certainly lived up to their star billing, with head of drama scoring bonus marks from pupils for wearing 'Vans with a suit' (must play well in Brighton). Parents approve of youth and energy. Girls agree. 'They make you feel you can do anything,' said one.

School is also recruiting master teachers, heroic role and a half involving mentoring, studying for extra qualifications and doing a spot of original research on top of normal teaching duties – and quite possibly summoned by shining silhouette of MA gown into night sky.

More is accomplished with less, school day finishing earlier (and no longer at different time each day), some assemblies moved from afternoon to morning slots, lunch break increased and lessons shortened by five minutes. Parents approve, especially day families – under older regime many pupils were simply 'too tired,' thought one, to take advantage of the benefits of plugging into 24/7 boarding school culture.

Rethink of mixed ability teaching also under way following parental concerns about sluggish pace in English lessons. Those needing additional English help in sixth form able to take pre-A level course to bring them up to scratch, parallel streams operating in earlier years.

School also offers strong support for pupils with learning difficulties, staffing recently bumped up with appointment of new head of English with extensive experience of dyslexia. 'They push the message that dyslexic children are taken on the same basis as everybody else,' said parent. Engagement in lessons the only line that must be toed, says Mr Blond. Otherwise, school will do best to help, working with parents to put extra support – as needed – in place.

Million dollar question is how much can be achieved without recruiting more able pupils. Parents like current mix. 'Varied – not just full of professionals' kids who all want to go to Oxbridge,' says one. Mr Blond adamant that most important point is that 'girls at all levels will thrive here, though standard of entry is rising already with increased interest in the school.' Aspirational, yes, but 'won't become some hothouse and wasn't the case in last school.' Get encouragement and self-confidence right, with school 'a platform for women to go out and feel that anything is possible,' and good exam results will be the by-product with no need to go out and trawl for straight A grade students.

Key to success, he believes, is ensuring that pupils are listened to – he's very hot on fatalistic tendency of girls to see low grade as final judgment. Wants teachers to say less, listen more and help pupils articulate sometimes hidden ambitions so can be helped to achieve them.

Creation of more shared meeting areas – teachers' own dining hall has been sacrificed to the cause; common room with outstanding sea views is on its way out – will mean better communication. School, though, already good at 'finding people's strengths and helping them patch the weaknesses,' reckoned insider. 'Their drive is to make bring out the best in everybody, no matter what it is.' Girls all – unconsciously – smile when asked about life at school. Endorsement doesn't come much more authentic.

Games, options, the arts: A place that allows unforced blossoming amongst kindred spirits. 'Whether you're a singer, guitar player or sports player, it's very good to have social identity around the stuff you're interested in,' says mother.

No them and us divisions between sport and arts, and 'not too binary,' reckoned parent. Pupils full of praise for school's desire to cater for budding polymaths, from rescheduling some after-school events, to offering subsidised or free overnight stays to ensure music or sports enthusiasts have the after-school opportunities they need, to new co-curricular programme for pupils in years 7 to 9, which offers two afternoons a week physical and intellectual stretch (car mechanics to Russian literature). Can result in unexpected blooming – only girls' team to reach national finals of programming competition, for example. Head's push for more community involvement is also building Brighton connection. 'The girls want to pitch in and go and visit old ladies in the sixth form, so there's very much a sense of community,' says OG.

Sports increasingly busy and competitive – 'come back in three years and we'll be winning everything,' reckoned girls, grounds at the front pitch-perfect with all the trimmings and added sea views, fixtures lists, previously on the empty side, busily being filled (and such a priority that features in new sports teacher's title), teams running to D in some sports. As elsewhere, nothing appears too much trouble for highly motivated staff, from developing tempting options for the less enthusiastic (zumba, synchronized swimming) to encouraging links with outside clubs, planning training programmes with external coaches for some of the sports scholars, even finding assessor for pupil working towards umpiring qualification.

Creativity, arts and music consistently good, even through leaner academic times. Art winds way into much of life there, with works on display as beautiful as design of original art room, partially glassed roof letting in northern light – 'the best' says teacher – tiles with scenes of 1930s school life and, our favourite, a stove featuring heaven (gates and kettle stand), purgatory (oven) and hell (fiery flames), which broke in 1960s and hasn't (sadly) been used since.

Performing arts a particular strength, vibrant new drama team shaking things up, replacing previous worthy performance choices, all bang on syllabus but distinctly lacking in clapalong appeal, with a few more popular options. 'Was Chekhov before,' thought distinctly envious sixth form tour guides, watching infectiously toe-tapping rehearsal for open day, featuring selection from Hairspray.

Encouragement a feature of the process, with talented instrumentalists working with others who can't read music, for example. 'The degree to which they are supportive of one another is very striking. Has nice moral effect,' thought parent. Latent talent encouraged by trumpet, clarinet or violin lessons for all in first two years and around half the pupils have individual music lessons in school.

School trips extensive, masses abroad.

Boarding: Boarding – four houses each named for a colour and decorated to match – is wonderfully homely, rooms prettily proportioned and furnished, teapot lights hanging cosily down over breakfast bar to add domesticity to giant-height ceilings.

Boarders enjoy busy weekend activities such as visits to Buckingham Palace and local animal sanctuary, which day pupils can also sign up for. That said, with tunnel down to the sea (much enjoyed) and stile onto the South Downs (blank looks when mentioned to pupils, despite mention in school literature), staying put isn't half an attractive option.

Background and atmosphere: Founded by pioneering Lawrence sisters in 1885, heavy financial lifting courtesy of bunch of Midlands industrialists and friends, brilliant connections including artist Sir George Watts. Apart from brief reincarnation as HMS Vernon during the war, when was filled with Royal Navy electrical specialists while school was evacuated to Keswick, has been making stand for girls' education here for well over 100 years.

Like Eton, name has entered national consciousness as shorthand for certain type of education (school is commonly – though not uniquely – thought to be inspiration for Enid Blyton's Malory Towers series). Reality is 'consistent' finished product, thought parent: 'Articulate people who think for themselves and are conscious of the community.'

School now reacquiring spring in step, as increasing numbers of parents discount siren call of nearby co-eds whose idea of success is founded on 'noisy alpha male over-achiever,' said parent. Like others, finds this a less stressful enclave for her 'un-pushy' child. 'My daughter's not one who'll walk in and want to take over socially, but she's managed to have very strong identity here.'

Ditto school itself. 'Looking outward, aiming high,' says sixth form prospectus, with literal accuracy, dainty Oxbridge-style mini cloisters conveying – perhaps – subtle message about founders' higher education aspirations for pupils. Cosy-looking it ain't, at least from the front, with cliff top, slab-like buildings (think turreted Kendal mint cake) menacing coast road to Brighton, 45-acre site on permanent collision course with the elements, salt spray countered by special rations for plants, bracing winds the stuff of nostalgia for past pupils and, we were told by pupils, sea breezes, on one occasion, so strong that minibuses had to be used on-site to prevent accidental Mary Poppins-style departures. (Slightly overstated, thinks school, pointing out that 'we are a sunny seaside location, too.')

Odd Portakabin aside (wall of one is top party joint for local daddy long legs population), much to enjoy, including cheery dining halls (youngest two years have small scale version of their own, formerly staff area, table cloths in cupcake pinks and reds) while Horizons café, small box of lettuce aside, concentrates on essential sugar-rich snacks. Now developing a school farm (16 sheep and lambs arrived recently).

Inside, makeovers are transforming the place. Pupils have also been refurbished, with eccentric uniform policy (comfy in the week, smart only on Sundays) now reversed. Most now reconciled to house tie (initially a sticking point for a few) but all like smart, tailored blazers, badges crammed onto lapels recording sunny hours of school lives.

Pastoral care, well-being and discipline: You want it, they've got it, from excellent health centre taking range of difficulties such as diabetes in its stride to happy relationships between pupils and staff, hot chocolate and chats available for as long as needed to help boarders settle in.

School listens and responds to problems. 'Has been really easy to get help,' says parent. Bullying isn't tolerated – will expel – while effective peer listening programme, backed with proper training so sixth formers know when adult assistance should be sought, stops anyone suffering in silence. 'If someone is sitting alone in the dining hall, you'll tell them "you're going to sit with me – you're not going to be on your own",' says sixth former.

Big feature of success is open door policy that sees day girls on the premises, with school's blessing, well past advertised hours every evening and welcomed back at weekends.

'They are very clear that you are part of the school whether a day girl or boarder,' said mother. Integration something school has always done well. 'In my day, we were from very different backgrounds and just mulched along together and I'd be very surprised if there was a huge amount of perceived difference between day and boarding pupils now,' agrees OG.

Pupils and parents: 'Sweet, polite girls,' was one comment, though OG pointed out that niceness often comes with 'let's have a pop at it' attitude. 'Makes you more robust so perhaps you do a few more things you wouldn't have done.' Certainly borne out by career choice dilemmas faced by pupils, one agonising over whether to opt for being a barrister or singer, a second torn between primatology and acting...

Pupils feel liberated by school's approach. 'When I came here I was quite a pessimistic, glass half empty person. Here, you feel you've got another chance to get things right if they go wrong, without feeling judged,' thought one.

Once part of the place, it doesn't let go easily, old girls busily spreading the word, enthusiasts one and all – and 'a mighty source of strength,' according to school literature. Old Roedeanians see school days as 'catalyst' for happiness and success in later life and very special part of lives. 'Felt I should be at the back giggling with my mates,' said one OG, who'd been back for recent visit.

While 'it's always been quite an international school,' points out one (ample proof in OGs' website, with thriving communities all over the place), increasing recruitment of London and local families is creating a balance everyone is happy with. Mix and match in every sense 'and I like that.'

Entrance: Numbers rising, with additional year 7 form introduced from 2014 and intake now likely to be around 60. Majority from local schools, state and independent. Further 20 to 25 pupils join year 9, up to 60 admitted in sixth form.

Exit: Post-GCSE exodus now substantially slowed after massive confidence-boosting exercise to reassure pupils that school can deliver the results. 'Retentions will improve as soon as our A levels improve.'

Turns out girls with 'a bit of purpose in life,' thought OG. 'We're very good at being able to slightly reinvent ourselves and get on with just about anybody.' Strong on medicine (reflected in pupil base) – four in 2016, with three to Oxbridge – and good showing in all the best places, UCL heading list of destinations, closely followed by Bristol, King's College, Loughborough – and Hong Kong. Medicine, maths, engineering, and science-related degrees mop up around a third of degrees. History, economics, politics and business also popular.

Money matters: With £10 million foundation endowment, able to offer considerable help and scholarships worth up to 40 per cent of the fees, bright locals, in particular, should be making a beeline for the place. Brighthelm awards at 11+ and sixth form of up to 100 per cent for extremely bright girls from local state schools, who must be nominated by their current head.

Remarks: No danger of sun setting gently on past glories. This is a school that's going places. Sixth formers leaving as the tide turns would gladly do it all over again. 'Wish my daughter was starting there now,' says mother. 'It's a fabulous place.'

Rowan Preparatory School

6 Fitzalan Road, Claygate, Surrey KT10 0LX

Pupils: 314 • Ages: 3–11

Fees: £10,551 – £13,998 pa

Tel: 01372 462627
Email: school.registrar@rowanprepschool.co.uk
Website: www.rowanprepschool.co.uk

Headmistress: Since 2014, Mrs Susan Clarke BEd NPQH. Joined the school in 2012 as deputy head; was previously head of West Acton Primary School. Educated at the University of Southern Queensland (BEd in primary and psychology).

Entrance: Non-selective throughout, save a very low key assessment for girls joining the prep at 7+. The nursery takes from age 2 and these girls get priority for joining kindergarten – other places on first-come-first-served basis, usually from local nurseries. Then automatic transfer from kindergarten to pre-prep at 4+ and to prep department at 7+. Usually also a small outside intake at 7+ (around a dozen). Feeders at 7+ include Emberhurst, Glenesk, Weston Green, Shrewsbury Lodge, Denmead, Jack & Jill and Thames Ditton Infants. Draws from the up-market local area of Claygate, Esher, Surbiton, Wimbledon, Molesey, Walton, Weybridge, Cobham, Epsom and Oxshott. School says it is keen to help parents not otherwise able to afford it and supportive of those who may fall on hard times – worth asking.

Exit: Most popular destinations Guildford High School and Surbiton High School (both fellow UCST schools) as well as St Teresa's, Effingham. Other independent girls' schools, from Tormead, Notre Dame and St Catherine's Bramley to Lady Eleanor Holles also feature. A few move on to co-ed, a few to board, usually Benenden, and consistently one or two to highly-sought-after state grammar, Tiffin Girls in Kingston. Always a handful (or two) of scholarships.

Remarks: A happy, vibrant school which gets the best out of its non-selected intake, smoothing their path to an impressive list of senior school destinations.

Tucked away in a leafy residential village, 16 miles from central London, the school is split physically and administratively into two – Rowan Brae, the pre-prep and Rowan Hill, the prep, both under the aegis of Mrs Clarke from her office at 'the Hill'. Just a few minutes' walk apart, both premises are converted Edwardian red-brick houses that blend seamlessly with surrounding imposing properties – hence a combination of slightly odd-shaped classrooms in the original buildings, with more spacious later additions.

Rowan Brae, which houses the nursery to year 2 (ages 3 to 7) is overseen by its own head, Miss Carolyn Sharps, in post since September 2011 when she was promoted from her previous position as head of Early Years Foundation Stage (EYFS). She is chatty and enthusiastic, and seemingly just as excited about school as the children themselves – everything is 'fantastic', 'wonderful' and 'excellent'. 'I'm getting used to being talked to as if I am also 7,' joked one mother. 'But in fact like everyone here she is very sweet and most forthcoming if you ask a question. She's very responsive, happy to have you in class and explain all about what work they are doing.' Each child has an individual 'Learning Journey' folder accessible by parents at any time.

It's quite a tight site and, with nursery and kindergarten children sharing an entrance, it can be rather a scrum as everyone arrives, but things quickly settle down. Classrooms are lovely, bright and airy. Lots of it is purpose-built, so the layout really works and rooms have their own direct access to the playground. Latest addition, the Millar Rooms, has added seven classrooms plus a new library and kitchen. In common with the Hill, the place is extremely well-resourced; cupboards are brimming with goodies – from glue sticks to musical instruments, these girls want for nothing. And the 7/1 EYFS pupil/staff ratio means they get plenty of support and attention. Rowan is very strong on presentation and handwriting – school regularly wins prizes for this – and everything is clean and colourful. Imaginative topics and artwork abound.

At the end of year 2, the girls take KS1 Sats, with 100 per cent achieving the required level 2 and 60 per cent getting a level 3 in speaking and listening/reading, writing and maths. The latest ISI inspection described Brae's EYFS as 'outstanding'. Communication between the Hill and Brae has improved a lot in recent years and Hill staff visit regularly, particularly during year 2, to give the little ones an appetite for moving up to the Hill.

Once the girls reach Rowan Hill, things hot up rather as more pressure kicks in. Instead of being form-room-based, the girls move around the school to be taught in excellently equipped, bright classrooms with evidence of much hard work and inspired teaching adorning walls and corridors. Each term takes a theme – recently 'perseverance' and 'creativity'. All the children on task and eager to join in; hands shoot up and bottoms are bounced upon as they vie to answer teachers' questions.

Learning outcomes are excellent across the board, with gifted and talented girls and those with learning difficulties equally well supported. Currently around 15 girls receive support with English as their additional language and school also works with any parents whose own English may be weak. All pupils are screened for dyslexia in year 1. There are currently 16 girls with special educational needs of some variety, typically visual and hearing impediments, dyslexia etc. School is not set up for wheelchair access. Generally all strengths and weaknesses are addressed through small group intervention work with such support (school calls it enrichment) at no additional cost to parents. One mother suggested such provision could be more joined up, so keep on top of school if you are concerned.

Specialist teachers for music, PE, French, ballet and swimming. Latin from year 5 and Spanish and German available as clubs. All the girls get a free cello or violin lesson in year 1 and years 2 to 5 have a timetabled recorder lesson – 65 per cent of them go on to learn an instrument and take grade exams. Standards high enough for some to win senior school music scholarships. Performances of music and drama always polished – 'I've been blown away by some faultless productions,' said one parent. 'They work so hard.' Sports provision is also good, given fairly limited on-site facilities.

Class sizes a little larger than some parents would like – averaging around 18 but can be up to 22 – with a pupil teacher ratio of round 10/1 at the Hill.

It's all very charming and at first glance appears quite traditional, but the curriculum is actually rather creative and the school works hard to make learning fun and inspire the girls to branch out and think for themselves. It's a very rich learning environment; all is bright and beautiful – and it's not just for show; staff feel equally well resourced and supported in their work with the girls. 'Education can never be about complacency. We are always looking for ways to make things more interesting.' A new outdoor area is a good example of this, incorporating an eco-area, outdoor classroom, mini amphitheatre and, in response to pupil input, a 'fairy grotto'.

Plenty to do in the playground, from the organised Twister and Jenga games to the more imaginative provision of brightly coloured sticks which the girls use for all sorts of improvised games from hobby horses to fencing. There's a gazebo area for the exclusive use of 'grown up' year 6 girls. Breakfast club each day from 8-8.45am. Plenty of extracurricular clubs from art to yoga, (Chess club was packed when we looked in, while only a few girls in jazz/pop singing) and all the day and residential trips you would expect.

Local parents who by-pass this place for their daughters say they imagine it to be a bit precious, girly and old-fashioned. Certainly the sight of pupils neatly turned out in their uber-cute cherry-red tartan uniforms, topped off by blazers and boaters (of which more later) does nothing to assuage this impression. But although it is 'girly' by virtue of the fact there are no boys and they all take ballet, everything is actually much more contemporary than might first appear. We saw nascent engineers designing wheeled vehicles, maths is strong, a pilot had visited recently to talk about future careers and staff work hard to embrace all the virtues of a single-sex education.

'I've sent my two very different daughters through the school and it's been great for both of them,' said one mother. 'One adored the "can do" attitude and threw herself into it all with gusto. The other is much more introspective, but they make sure she's always involved in everything and I know she'll get to a good senior school'. That said, there seems to be a general understanding among parents that Rowan prefers its girls to 'fit the mould' – for which read be enthusiastic, well-behaved, reasonably academic and sporty. 'You always hear the same names mentioned in despatches,' said one. 'And you see the same faces representing the school. Not sour grapes because it's not my daughter, just a fact of life here. You need to be confident and assured to really shine'.

Girls we spoke to were generally confident, even perky, articulate, polite and friendly and really seemed to feel a sense of belonging. They positively ache to win a trophy or two, or, even better, a head's commendation. Generally keen to please, eager to learn little girls, so discipline is a minor issue here. By all accounts the primary sanction of losing a bonus mark is treated very seriously by one's peers. Doesn't sound much, but means a lot. 'You have to stand up and explain to the rest of the house what has happened', explained one pupil. Friendship issues feature large for little girls and this and other pastoral issues addressed through 'hidden curriculum of understanding, truthfulness and integrity, which is embedded into the whole school'.

Since our last visit Rowan has joined the United Church Schools Trust – a family of a dozen or so independent schools across the UK including Guildford High and Surbiton High, where Rowan has traditionally sent sizeable numbers of its pupils. But school stresses that it retains its independence and is still entirely free to send its pupils to the full range of schools it currently feeds. Rowan does however benefit from UCST's extensive educational resources, training opportunities and facilities, including shared sports pitches about a mile away.

Home/school communication is good, at the classroom door, via emails and texts, weekly Friday Notes and curriculum information evenings; it all combines to ensure parents are up to speed with what's going on. Parents in these parts can be a demanding lot, so the currently increasing numbers coming into EYFS attests to Rowan's success in meeting their high expectations. In return, Rowan parents are a committed bunch, happy to help in school and support the parents' association, Friends of Rowan, which provides a nice social side and raises hefty cash sums.

Grumbles about this place are few and far between, but several parents mentioned the 'excessive' uniform. 'I'm sure it's fine for the super-rich, but for those of us who find school fees more of a stretch it's a huge outlay,' said one. 'Do they really need a winter coat, raincoat and blazer? And piping on the blouses means I can't get away with a supermarket pack!' Similarly short notice requests of the 'please bring in a bean sprout cake tomorrow' variety don't help working mothers – though we should add that lots of Rowan's 'at home' mums seem to love this sort of thing and get stuck in with relish. 'You should have seen the creations in the Easter bonnet parade,' confided one (bitter?) working mother.

It's a premium school and more adventurous than you might imagine. Suits tenacious types; tryers keen to do their best.

Rowledge C of E Primary School

School Road, Rowledge, Farnham, Surrey GU10 4BW

Pupils: 210 boys and girls • Ages: 4–11 • C of E

Tel: 01252 792346
Email: admin@rowledge.hants.sch.uk
Website: www.rowledge.hants.sch.uk/

Headteacher: Since September 2015, Ms Sarah Oliver, previously head of Woodpecker Hall Primary Academy and before that deputy head of Cuckoo Hall Academy.

Entrance: Thirty in reception, most from the village's two nursery schools. Single form entry and only occasional places in other years means the waiting list hovers at around 10. Tight catchment area – the efficient admin team field frequent boundary queries from disbelieving parents.

Exit: Almost all to local (excellent) secondaries – Eggar's School in Alton, Hampshire, or its Surrey counterpart, Weydon School in Farnham. A few each year to local independents such as the Royal Grammar School in Guildford, Churcher's College in Petersfield, Alton Convent and Prior's Field School in Godalming.

Remarks: Imagine a small country school in an idyllic village setting, complete with traditional butcher, house names like Serendipity and even a parent-operated one-way system to alleviate school-run trauma, and this is it. With its red-tiled roofs, arched windows and generous playground – three acres including a field running the length of its low-rise buildings – the school oozes charm. Reception children start with separate, secure play area (complete with cosy if weather-beaten playhouses), then, as confidence grows, join the main, well-supervised melée at break time where there's football, pretend pony lunging (well, this is home counties borderland) and piles of old tyres to spark the imagination.

Goldilocks would approve. The main building is cosy, not cramped, with staggered exits to avoid playtime chaos. Tidiness is encouraged. Children look smart (ties worn from year 3 up) and are generally polite. Good academic results. Lots of class sports, including gymnastics, athletics, team games and dance, to keep them busy in school hours and netball and cross-country (netball team undefeated league and tournament champions recently), amongst others, out of them. Good range of other extracurricular activities that vary each term and range from a thriving newspaper club to board games and textiles. There's an underlying, not over-bearing, spiritual dimension, with regular church-based worship, a leavers' assembly in Guildford Cathedral 15 miles away and a values week where balloons, filled with prayers, are released. Every child, refreshingly, gets to be a young governor and has a say in decisions like what colour to paint revamped toilets.

Staff turnover is 'refreshingly regular rather than cripplingly constant', with teachers, typically in mid-30s, averaging around four years before moving on. They're good at subtle discipline. 'She just gives us a look that says we can't do it,' one child told us. Parents appreciate the school's academic success but above all praise the atmosphere. 'The children all look out for each other,' said a mother. Four year olds rush to greet older children with hugs and even party invitations.

Valuing everyone seems hardwired into Rowledge's DNA. House system and rewards for good behaviour, including the chance to ring the school's traditional bell on a rope for morning lessons. Projects, completed with minimal parental involvement, make children think for themselves and favour the tenacious – one girl cut and stitched a Roman toga from scratch. Lots of thought is given to those needing most encouragement, with achievements great and small listed on a special board and teaching that plays to the children's strengths. 'Just because you find times tables difficult doesn't mean you're hopeless at talking about shapes, so it's not helpful to confine the same child to the same group,' says the school.

The school ethos is reinforced when it comes to special needs. The Sunshine and Sparkle SEN teams (six children have statements, while four receive additional support) are in charge of four kudos-adding hens, writing idiosyncratic dos and don'ts lists for holiday carers and – with enormous pride – collecting the eggs. Parental niggles are thin on the ground. 'My children are very different and it's catered for them both – it's very nurturing,' one parent told us, while another said 'they send out questionnaires asking "what can we do better?" I've never been able to think of anything.' Truly a small school with a big heart.

Royal Grammar School (Guildford)

Linked with Lanesborough School

R

High Street, Guildford, Surrey GU1 3BB

Pupils: 940 • Ages: 11–18 • Sixth form: 286

Fees: £16,935 pa

Tel: 01483 880600
Email: admissions@rgs-guildford.co.uk
Website: www.rgs-guildford.co.uk

Headmaster: Since 2007, Dr Jon Cox BSc PhD (40s). Educated at St Mary's College, Southampton, then studied physiology and biochemistry at Southampton University. Postgrad course at Royal College of Music (French horn is his instrument) and toyed with becoming a professional musician before deciding on a career in teaching. Joined Whitgift School in Croydon as a biology teacher in 1992 and stayed for 14 years, rising through the ranks to become deputy head before his appointment to the RGS in 2005 as headmaster in waiting.

Hasn't frightened the horses with wholesale changes to what was already a very successful operation, but neither has he rested on the school's considerable laurels. He began with a long 'to-do' list, which he still runs today. 'Every time I cross off a job done, I add something new to the bottom. It's just like a house, something always needs doing,' he says, brandishing another long list of 40+ points he's jotted down to mention during our interview. It covers all sorts – everything from academic innovations, creation of new staff roles, building programmes, community links; the list literally goes on – he's a man on a mission.

Affable, down to earth, buzzing, you sense his delight at having what he calls 'the best job in the country – fantastic boys, inspirational staff, parents on side and appreciative'.

RGS is very much his show and he's great at managing parents – they don't run this school. 'He's very much in control and you don't get the impression he would welcome a waste of his time,' said one mother. 'But equally he's approachable and I wouldn't hesitate to speak to him if necessary'. 'He's very at ease in his role and really cares about the school,' said another. 'A fabulous figurehead for RGS,' agreed a third. 'I've heard him talk to prospective and current parents many times and he's a good speaker, witty and easy to listen to, he handles all that side of things very well'.

Pupils like and respect him – 'he's a nice guy' and 'smart' they say – and seems to know what they are about; writes a comment on every boy's report. 'He never talks down to them,' said one parent.

While absolutely mindful of his school's many strengths, not least its academic prowess, Dr Cox says he takes most pride in the fact that RGS is 'a wonderful community. Mostly you'll ask your son if he has had a good day, not for details about his maths test,' he says. 'There's a great, supportive atmosphere here that really enriches the boys in all aspects of their lives'.

With his own son having recently joined the school, he understands the anxiety parents feel around the admissions process. 'I was out of school when my son did his test and interview, but it was agony nevertheless, so I do empathise with parents.'

He's working hard to overcome the school's elitist tag and dispel two main myths about RGS – that it's a hothouse and not for the sporty; 'Neither are remotely true,' he says. 'I want people to recognise that we are a school for bright children, irrespective of their backgrounds'. To this end the school entertains children from local primary schools every Monday to do Tudor project work (buildings reflect school's Tudor origins and Dr Cox's office includes a Chained Library) and runs Saturday master classes and a summer school. Service to the local community is a big theme at RGS.

He is married with three children, still plays the French horn and is a keen amateur magician. Also a governor of a school in Watford.

R

Academic matters: Outstanding in all respects and very much the academic school for boys in the area. RGS features in top 10 or 20 of league tables of all variety. Pupils are selected from the top ability band, working far above the national average. Maths and science very popular and two-thirds take maths a year early. Maths is also the most popular option at A level, followed by physics, economics and chemistry. Pre-U offered in chemistry and the school has great success with this subject – at recent Chemistry Olympiad RGS achieved five gold, 10 silver and seven bronze awards. English and humanities give equally good accounts of themselves; philosophy and theology a new Pre-U offering. Modern languages (French or Spanish from 11+ or German at 13+) compulsory to GCSE. Arabic, Chinese, Russian and Japanese also available. Latin a popular option and Greek also on offer. Positively dizzying success in exams overall – in 2016, 96 per cent of grades at GCSE were A*/A while at A level 78 per cent of grades were A*/A (nearly 95 per cent A*-B).

Head has conducted an enormous push on teaching and learning, including lowering the pupil/staff ratio. We've heard nothing but huge parental praise for 'exceptionally good' teaching staff. 'Teaching is inspirational – absolutely no dead wood,' they say. The boys are encouraged to be self-motivated, independent learners, and the lessons are intensive and conducted at a brisk pace. It's cool to be bright at the RGS and the boys set themselves high standards as they jostle for position. 'My son was surprised to find himself towards the bottom of the class having been top dog at his old school,' said one parent. 'I really wouldn't coach a boy to come here as it would be no fun if you were struggling', said another, more seasoned parent. 'These boys are a competitive bunch and frankly anything less than an A* is a disaster for them. But that's really not because it's a hothouse – it isn't – it's simply that they do so well on their own abilities'.

It's a can-do culture – the school talks of 'strengths' and 'development areas' rather than 'weaknesses'. Extra work on offer to help anyone falling behind. 'I know they keep a watch on grades and are absolutely on top of everything,' said one mother whose son had slipped a little. 'He got all the help he needed to get back on track'.

On average two to three homework assignments an evening of around 30 minutes each – 'nothing too onerous,' parents feel. Support available for the handful of boys with a learning difficulty or disability.

Games, options, the arts: A broad and balanced offering. DT a popular subject choice (a pupil proudly showed us a 3D laser cutter, and the new John Brown building – linked to the main school by a stunning, architecturally distinctive glass bridge – provides inter alia a purpose-built DT centre). No PE or drama taken at GCSE (though a handful take theatre studies at AS and Dr Cox is now promoting drama lower down the school). Not huge numbers doing art either, but what there is is remarkably good.

Most sport is off site at Bradstone Brook, the school's 20-acre playing field and pavilion a few miles away. School rails against its reputation for being less sporty than some of its heavyweight public school neighbours in the area and can in fact hold its own. Rugby, hockey and cricket on offer, but football is lacking. 'Such a shame good footballers cannot represent the school,' moaned one miffed mother. But lots do play at break on the Astroturf and Dr Cox points out that 'We do run football very successfully in the sixth form with A to D teams'. Shooting range is popular. Facilities not whizzy – no swimming pool for example, so boys troop down to the local Spectrum swimming pool (a bit down market for some) and to Guildford Lido for the annual gala. 'Actually the boys love getting off site for this,' said a mother. 'It's only 10 minutes away and the walk warms them up – plus they get to run past Guildford High (School for Girls)!'

Music now has the space it deserves –a fab new music centre, including a recording studio and rehearsal space.

There's an extensive timetabled programme of extracurricular activities, known as Period 8, which includes all sorts of clubs and societies, house competitions in an array of sports, plays and musical performances, CCF, DofE and even a scout group. It's a school where things happen, lots going on, often until about 7pm.

Background and atmosphere: Historically a grammar school and still a grammar school at heart. The school was founded in 1509 under the will of Robert Beckingham, and became 'Royal' in 1552 by charter of King Edward VI. Was run as a state school for 30 years after the war, but returned to the independent sector in 1977 rather than become non-selective. Charming tall, white 450 year old building on one side of Guildford High Street (includes

Chained Library and various public rooms) while on the other side of the street the school buildings date mostly from the 20th century, although pleasing facades mean there's no horrid 60s look to them. The site is a little cramped, but fortunately RGS boys have manners and respect, otherwise it could be mayhem. Pupils are respectful of staff, hold doors open for each other and parents say they relish knowing where the boundaries are and settle into what is expected of them. 'The school understands them, how they learn and gets through to them in a way that switches them on and makes them responsible for their own studies,' said one parent. 'They really play to their strengths.'

Pastoral care, well-being and discipline: Although a non-denominational school, its ethos is firmly based on sound Christian principles. Parents describe the school as very supportive. Senior staff operate a pastoral data base and a 'care list' of boys to keep a special eye on. Parents feel their sons form good relationships with each other and across the year groups. 'They bond really well', one parent told us. 'And it's a joy to see'.

Dr Cox claims to have improved the behaviour of many a 'scallywag' – 'I'll give them some responsibility, that generally turns them around'. In the grand scheme of things any bad behaviour is of the mild variety. These are regular boys, school appears very on top of things and is quick to clamp down on anything untoward with the occasional incident of the argy bargy variety firmly and quickly stamped on. Nothing serious enough to warrant exclusion in the last few years. A benevolent atmosphere, with no hint of a heavy hand. 'I think we do a good job of selecting them in first place and sussing out their attitude to work', says Dr Cox, who for all his bonhomie, is no soft touch – 'They really don't want to come to me for a telling off,' he acknowledges. 'But I think they know I am basically on their side. These are impressionable young men, finding their feet in the world. I see our job as being to correct their behaviour. I'd rather they made their mistakes here, before going off into the world'.

Pupils and parents: School's town centre, close-to-station location means it attracts families from some distance away, involving a few quite complicated train journeys. Some parents are really discerning (there are plenty of good independent schools in the area, although no other single sex boys' day schools). For others RGS is their only independent option and if their sons don't pass the exam, they will stay in the state system.

Latest parental survey attests to parents being happy with their choice. 'There's a pretty good mix of boys here, with the extremes probably drawn to the centre by the camaraderie and sense of "we are grammar school boys with a shared identity",' said a long-standing parent. 'No outlandish types among boys or parents' – although some quite quirky, dare we say eccentric, boys find a happy home at RGS. Generally a nice broad spectrum of society, all bright, but a mix quite reflective of life generally. 'The longer he's there the more I am happy,' a parent told us. 'The school seems to have had a very insidious effect that has turned him into a lovely young man. They're not swotty and snobby, but a down-to-earth, nice group of lads'. Boys we came across were very courteous, not super smart, just regular teenage types, but seemed friendly and happy as they milled around.

Parents pleased that they don't have to crack the whip at home; it seems that the school sorts their sons out to be completely self-sufficient. 'These boys are the real thing from an academic point of view – they are not arrogant and don't grow up believing the world owes them a living,' says Dr Cox.

Entrance: Tough – has one of the highest academic hurdles in Surrey. On average there are 350-400 applications from boys from almost 100 local schools for 140 places. All sit exams in English, maths and verbal reasoning plus an interview: 'We're looking for potential,' school says. Advice from everyone we spoke to is 'don't coach, other than a little exam practice'. 'You'd be miserable here if you'd just scraped in,' summed up one parent, speaking for many. 'Even a bright boy who was absolutely top dog at his old school might well find himself 25th in the class here'.

By and large the school is happy that they get admissions 'spot on'. Dr Cox can only recall one or two boys who subsequently couldn't cope with the academic rigour of the place. At age 11 the majority come from the state sector, reflecting the relationships built up with local schools. Then at 13+ another 45/50 boys join from prep schools, with Lanesborough the major feeder school, sending around 30 boys a year.

Don't expect red carpet treatment when you visit. 'Everyone is very nice and it's well-organised, but they don't have to try very hard', one mother said. 'We visited other schools where we got more special treatment because they really need to fight to get families to choose them – RGS are in a strong position because they don't have local competition.' Dr Cox sees all prospective parents himself – can be 20 or so a week – and unsurprisingly he has a great conversion rate. NB After an interregnum of a couple of years when no sports scholarships were awarded, RGS reintroduced scholarships for sport.

Exit: Almost all to their first choice of university. Thirty-one Oxbridge places in 2016, and four medics. Many to Imperial and Durham (which can be harder, Dr Cox points out) and the rest as you would expect to other Russell Group heavyweights including notably Exeter, Nottingham, Bristol, Bath and Warwick.

Money matters: Lower than average fees, with the school working to keep them low. Appeals to parents who don't have the funds for more expensive schools. 'Proper' bursaries include money for uniform, sports kit and books, 'There's no point otherwise,' says Dr Cox. A few years ago RGS could not give bursary money away, but now there's a good take up following the establishment of better links with other schools.

Remarks: One of Surrey's most highly regarded and sought after schools. Cutting edge and working hard to keep its top spot as the best school for boys in the area. It's an environment where boys spark off each other and learn at a fast pace, so it's not for a worrier or a 'scraper-in'. A school for bright boys, who don't have to have been overly prepped or privately educated at primary level.

The Royal Grammar School, High Wycombe

Amersham Road, High Wycombe, Buckinghamshire HP13 6QT

Pupils: 1,370; 14 full, 40 weekly boarders • Ages: 11–18 • Sixth form: 360

Fees: Boarding £12,576 – £14,172 pa

Tel: 01494 524955
Email: admin@rgshw.com
Website: www.rgshw.com

Headmaster: Since September 2015, Philip Wayne, previously head of Chesham Grammar. He studied at Manchester University and the Royal Northern College of Music. Following a number of years as a freelance organist, pianist, conductor and lecturer, he qualified as a teacher and held several leadership posts in the Midlands. He moved to Buckinghamshire in 2004 as deputy head of John Hampden Grammar and became head of CGS in 2007. He is married with twins.

Academic matters: Consistently delivers a good showing in national league tables for academics, although still snaps at the heels of the area's top performing grammar when it comes to hard exam data. Local competition is very stiff but school proves itself a real all-rounder at GCSE with 65 per cent of GCSEs graded A/A* in 2016. Seventy-three per cent of A levels achieved grades A*-B and 48 per cent A*/A in 2016.

Boys take an average of 10 or 11 GCSEs, with about 60 per cent taking four subjects at A2 level. Brainboxes can take more (one boy took seven a few years ago, achieving A* in all of them) but the school only encourages this in exceptional circumstances. Good range of subjects on offer at GCSE, including Latin and Greek, with French compulsory and a large take-up of geography, history, Spanish and German. Sciences, economics and maths highly popular at A level. Languages 'really excellent' according to pupils and parents, with Italian, Mandarin and Japanese all available either on or off curriculum.

Six classes of 32 in each year group with setting in maths and French starting from year 9. School 'goes in heavy with homework from the word go', according to parents, with at least three 30 minute pieces per night, but boys seem to take this in their stride – as they do the rigorous tests they take after every topic. The minority of pupils joining from prep schools (about 25 per cent) 'can coast a bit' in year 7 say parents, and the uplift in recent years in children from non-English speaking homes presents some challenges for teachers initially, but by the time the heat is turned up in year 10 things are reportedly pretty equal across the board.

Cutting edge technology not widely used across the board of subjects, although iPads are starting to creep in, but parents say the VLE is 'great – and genuinely useful', particularly when it comes to revision. Geography department is trialling virtual lessons to be taken at home over the VLE then followed up with practical discussion and development in class.

Games, options, the arts: Sport, sport and more sport for those so inclined, with rugby leading the charge as a year-round occupation. When the rugby league season finishes, top players continue to play rugby union – and to a very high standard, with the under 12 rugby league team going to Wembley to compete in the finals of the Carnegie Champion Schools tournament recently. No football ('we get used to it quickly', say boys), but hockey and cricket are main sports and taught to a high standard by the 'inspirational' games teachers, although a few parents grumble they don't get the same quality fixtures or kudos as the rugby teams. Sighs of relief from some non-rugby parents though as it's a 'major commitment' with training five times a week and fixtures most weekends in season.

A-D teams in junior school take on – and frequently beat – schools such as Wellington, Marlborough and Harrow as well as their local grammar peers and recently vanquished Charterhouse at Eton fives, despite only having played the sport for two years. Although parents consistently equate sports here with rugby, there really is something for everyone, whether it's rowing, fencing, swimming or tennis. Just don't expect the same hero status in the playground.

Thursday afternoon activities (TAA) allow boys to choose from a vast array of sporting or academic enrichment activities ranging from Japanese or Mandarin to eco army. This is in addition to after-school activities and indulges boys' passions for more marginal activities like climbing (the school boasts an impressive 40ft climbing wall in main sports hall) and astronomy or endeavours like the 'Caterham project', which sees year 13s building a car from scratch. CCF is also extremely popular from year 10 and 'offers huge leadership opportunities', says head.

Music 'really, really strong', according to parents. A quarter of boys learn one or more instruments – 'they all play about three these days', according to head – and about 180 turning up on a weekly basis to participate in various choirs, bands and orchestras. The school's big band is currently run by the BBC big band leader and the director of music is 'highly charismatic', say parents. The performing arts community is also thriving with high quality productions put on annually, most recently a 'stunning' performance of Les Misérables in conjunction with local girls' schools. Check it out on YouTube for instant goosebumps. Plenty of opportunities to get involved for non-performers too, with the school's stage lighting and sound team proving hugely popular.

Trips, tours and exchanges galore. World Challenge scheme starts in year 7 then branches out globally higher up the school, with destinations in recent years including China, Vietnam and Belize. Lots of other opportunities for boys to get out and about to enhance the curriculum, enrich their cultural experience or just for fun.

Boarding: The bright, modern boarding house (1999) sits in the heart of the school campus and is home to some 54 boarders, albeit 'an important 54,' insists school. Boarding offers great value for money, with full boarding costing less than most day school fees. Boarders say they 'feel really at home' and the boarding house has a relaxed, happy feel, partly dictated by the energetic and approachable head of boarding who seems almost like one of the boys, and partly by the way older boys mentor the younger ones. Each academic subject has a pupil champion that younger boys can approach if they need guidance with any part of their studies and the pupil food and boarding council electorate voices collective opinions about how the boarding house is run.

Younger boys are housed in spacious four-man dorms, decorated with personal effects to varying degrees. Years 12 and 13 are in cabin-like single rooms with en-suite shower rooms and the communal areas are peppered with boy toys like pool tables, table tennis and air hockey tables and flat screen TVs. No wonder most years are oversubscribed.

Boys return to the boarding house after school to get the blood sugar levels back up with a snack then participate in organised group activities on two or three afternoons a week. All meals are taken in the boarders' own canteen ('better food than in the main school', agree pupils) and prep takes place after supper from 7.30 to 9pm. Major advantages according to boarders' parents are that 'masters are on tap' to help with tricky homework and they have the 'luxury of not wasting time commuting to school', instead playing touch rugby or football with friends while others sit on the bus for up to 45 minutes each way. Some 10 or so 'day boarders' come for breakfast and stay for supper and prep each day at a cost of £4,500 pa.

The majority go home at weekends, with around 15 – mainly international pupils – staying. The schedule at the weekend is 'pretty relaxed' and boys are allowed into town in groups of two or three. There is a major trip organised every half term – paintballing and Thorpe Park recent highlights. Mobile phones are allowed until bedtime when prefects collect them from the younger boys. Older boarders are given lots of responsibility to mentor and guide their younger housemates, with one describing the self-discipline and independence he has gained during his time at the school as 'great preparation for uni'.

Background and atmosphere: Founded in the 12th century and given a royal charter in 1562. Centred round an attractive red-brick Queen Anne style building, with the usual ubiquitous additions bolted on from the 60s onwards. An interesting mix of ancient (the oldest classrooms are just approaching their 100th birthdays) and modern, the school has recently been the beneficiary of large grants from the Academies Capital

Maintenance Fund and now boasts gleaming new facilities including a bright, modern canteen, cookery suite (all boys do one term of cooking 'to prepare them for real life'), multi gym plus outdoor terrace with panoramic views of the sports fields and new changing facilities for the sports hall and swimming pool. There's also a lovely pool with retractable roof which, despite its 40-year vintage, still knocks spots off many we've seen, three lofty art rooms displaying an array of boys' superb work (pity some of this hasn't made its way into the rest of the school, though) and a large, airy library with plenty of space for quiet study. Sixth formers lack a common room, although measures in place to fundraise for one, but do have two study mezzanines to cram for those all-important exams in free periods. Size of the vast music block gives away the school's collective passion for music, driven by the 'inspirational' director of music, and is home to a drumming suite ('as far away from head's office as possible', say staff) and a music technology centre.

Overall vibe of the school is traditional with a modern, multi-cultural twist. Despite its mixed socio-demographic and ethnic profile, with its boarding house, chaplain and expectation for formal manners (all staff are 'sir' or 'ma'am' to boys) place feels like a 'natural step from prep school' and, say parents, 'offers the roundedness of public school'. The majority join from state primaries, however, and all are polite, fun and talk with genuine enthusiasm about their school. A true camaraderie between year groups is immediately visible in the playground and boarding house.

Pastoral care, well-being and discipline: School 'doesn't put up with any rubbish,' according to parents and pulls boys back into line quick smart if they step out. Few major disciplinary issues, but severe punishments administered for smoking, although 'apparently all the sixth form do,' sighed one parent. Boys dismissive of bullying question and it's clearly not a regular feature of school life here, with reports of just occasional issues in the Twittersphere. School is active in social media and carries out periodic checks to ensure no pupils are breaching the online code of conduct – acting swiftly if they do. Full care for boarders from matron, housemasters and tutors.

Pupils and parents: Diversity at its best with all-comers ranging from those hailing from leafy south Bucks villages to boys from the less affluent local towns. Ethnic mix changing rapidly and school is now about 30 per cent non-Caucasian (higher in lower years), reflecting the local community. Intellect is the common denominator and school sees social mix as 'one of our great strengths; if we're preparing future leaders of the world, we have to be fully appreciative of other backgrounds and races'. Parents of boarders lean towards the middle classes, often professional dual income families, and internationals. About half a dozen girls join for specific lessons (Greek, classics) in year 13.

A plethora of high profile alumni from the sporting, political and showbiz worlds England rugby players Matt Dawson, Nick Beal and Tom Rees; GB hockey captain and Olympian Jonathan Wyatt; professional golfer Luke Donald and, representing the artsy crowd, pop stars Howard Jones and the late Ian Dury and comedian Jimmy Carr.

Entrance: Ferocious competition for places. Selection subject to success at 11+ exam and Buckinghamshire criteria, including the ever-moveable feast of catchment. School's own procedure adopted as and when places become available higher up the school. Some places available in year 10 when a few boys each year choose to move, largely to independent schools, and again in year 12 when around 25 new places are up for grabs, about half of these in the boarding house.

Worth considering boarding at 11 if a day place looks unlikely and candidate has a high 11+ score. Forces families and boys in care are prioritised and these are mixed with some overseas pupils (although they must have a British passport) and locals keen for the boarding experience.

Exit: Some 90 per cent stay on to sixth form. Majority straight into higher education with between 15 and 20 into Oxbridge most years – 15 in 2016 – and strong numbers to other top universities – Durham, Exeter, Birmingham and Southampton popular. Good university advisory provision in place, with specialist support for those hoping for entry to international universities.

Money matters: Rolling renovation plan funded by a number of external sources. Ongoing fundraising by highly active parents' association who run well-attended events, including family quiz nights, wine-tasting (parents only!) and good old-fashioned school discos. Old boys also generous donors and current parents are asked to make annual voluntary contributions to be channelled towards music, transport, the school as a whole or all of the above – and many do.

Remarks: Don't believe the hype pitching The Royal Grammar School as a hotbed of rugger boys. Yes, they play rugby (and 18 other sports from Eton fives and racketball to fencing) to an exceptionally high level, but there's also outstanding music, drama and academics all wrapped up in a supportive, friendly package. Parents at other local grammars might consider it 'a bit God and country' but the traditional values that have the school competing ably with its independent and state maintained neighbours – and thrashing many top public schools on the sports field – mean boys (and their parents) benefit from a private school ethos without the hefty price tag.

Royal Masonic School for Girls

Rickmansworth Park, Chorleywood Road, Rickmansworth, Hertfordshire WD3 4HF

Pupils: 931; 105 full/weekly boarders • Ages: 4–19 (boarding from 7) • Sixth form: 195

Fees: Day £10,455 – £15,915; Boarding £18,345 – £28,140 pa

Tel: 01923 773168
Email: enquiries@royalmasonic.herts.sch.uk
Website: www.royalmasonic.herts.sch.uk

Head: Since January 2017, Kevin Carson, previously co-interim head at The Grammar School at Leeds. His teaching career began in a single-sex girls' school, following which he headed up the English and drama departments at Cheltenham College and subsequently Abingdon School, also taking on the role of resident tutor in boarding houses in both schools. He particularly championed equal opportunities for his female tutees within Cheltenham's co-educational environment.

Married to Sarah, they have two young daughters who Sarah is currently caring for at home, having previously worked as an equal opportunities officer for both Oxford University and the police. Outside of school, the family pursues a wide range of sporting and cultural interests.

Head of the junior school, Cadogan House: Since September 2014, Mr Ian Connors BA PGCE TEFL MBA (in education management) NPQH (40s), previously head of primary at Harrow International School, Bangkok. Degree in English and American history and literature. Has also been director of studies at King Edward's School, Bath and head of a Cambridgeshire primary school. Keen sportsman – Arsenal supporter – and loves walking, cycling and travelling abroad with his family. Married to Ingrid, a teacher who runs her own phonics company; they have three daughters at RMS.

Academic matters: Strong languages – Spanish from reception and French from year 3, extracurricular Spanish club also on offer. Robust academics across the board. 'Gentle' setting in English and maths from the word go, with this formalised for maths in year 5. Classes are mixed up at the end of years 2 and 4 and girls get a taste of senior school life by starting to move around the school for some lessons from year 4. Years 5 and 6 see this step up a notch with them heading to the senior school for specialised teaching in textiles and design technology.

Full time SEN co-ordinator in junior school plus three part-time assistants on hand for those in need of help. Statemented children are rare here but minor problems are ironed out with a creative, friendly approach; materials such as board games sent home to get parents involved in the process.

Turning formerly dismissive heads and winning more and more parental votes with persistently improving results. In 2016, 50 per cent A*/A grades at A level and 56 per cent at GCSE. Small class sizes (maximum 20) across the board and setting from year 7 in maths and French, with fewer than 10 in some lower sets. More setting (English, science) from year 9 but these are totally flexible, with one parent delighted that her child moved from the bottom to top of six sets for maths in the space of a year. Must be the 'outstanding teaching' that theschool is so proud of. Teachers 'go the extra mile', say parents and pupils, and are happy to tutor any stragglers in their free time. Enrichment programmes and extra work for the gifted and lots of clinics to make sure nobody slips through the gaps.

Parents say it's a 'good all round school' where their children can have a go at 'absolutely anything'. They like the fact that the brightest children are made to feel so in this mixed ability environment rather than bumping along feeling average in a class packed with boffins, as they might in more selective schools. Geography and history most popular subjects at GCSE with sciences and maths coming to the fore at A level.

Both highly academic parents with children to match and those with less intellectual offspring feel that the school has the 'right balance' regarding achievement. Girls can choose to do between nine and 11 GCSEs depending on ability and those staying on in the sixth form to take two A levels in photography or art are treated with as much care as mathematicians and scientists taking four. To keep everyone happy, academic girls wishing to take arty subjects can take A2 exams in these in year 12, freeing them up to concentrate on their academic subjects thereafter. EPQ results are also impressive, with 25 per cent choosing to enter and all of these achieving grades A*-B. Strong languages on offer, with girls able to choose two plus Latin at GCSE; Mandarin on offer for the most gifted linguists from year 8.

Girls put on a 'carousel' of arty subjects in years 8 and 9, dipping into subjects from ceramics and 3D design to home economics and DT. All taught by specialists in purpose designed (albeit a bit tired) facilities.

Good SEN, with individual lessons on offer to girls needing support. All pupils screened to detect literacy or numeracy difficulties on entry. Specialist EAL teaching for overseas pupils, charged as extra.

Games, options, the arts: Impressive sports facilities. Gymnastics, trampolining, dance et al take place in a jawdropping double sports hall that would give most public sports centres a run for their money. Four squash courts and a multigym, available for the girls' use whenever they wish, also housed in the complex. Swimming pool is poor relation to the rest, functional at best. Acres of playing fields, great for cross-country and adventure training, and new all-weather pitch.

Lots of competitive sport with trophies galore of late – the school recently claimed the independent girls' schools golf championship title and the gymnastics team has just been placed nationally. Occasional grumbles from parents, however, that the school needs to work harder to engage more of the less obviously sporty girls in physical activities that are in tune with their lifestyles, claiming that some older girls get away with doing, 'hardly any or no sport at all', although school disagrees: 'They have all sorts of options from year 10 including zumba, pilates and yoga.' Recent injection of young sports teachers has opened up more opportunities, including football and rugby.

School has strong artsy feel, offering a well-used photography studio and dark room, drama studio and 'loads and loads' of musical and theatrical productions throughout the year, according to girls. Music 'improving all the time', say parents, with 300 girls learning an instrument and plenty of opportunities to show their skills in concerts and shows. 'Very strong' performing arts, say junior school parents, with girls clamouring for parts in the annual (usually musical) production. Take-up of instruments is high, with the ukulele played by all in year 3 (collective sighs of relief from parents when the school decided to drop violin for all), about 60 per cent of girls choosing another instrument, and a thriving prep orchestra and choir.

Competitive sport from year 4, with a host of extracurricular clubs and activities to choose from for the physically inclined, including skipping, kick boxing, maypole dancing and fencing. Plenty for less sporty types too with other clubs ranging from meditation and doodling to rummikub. Occasional grumbles from parents that there could be more clubs for younger girls as most start from year 3. Annual residential trips from year 4 onwards allow pupils to spread their wings outside the campus bubble.

Senior school trips and tours of all sorts, for sports teams, choirs, curriculum and just for the fun of it. Vast array of extracurricular activities including very popular D of E and cadets means the school continues to buzz after lessons are over. Girls enthuse over chess and Chinese clubs as much as astronomy (in school's own planetarium) and taekwondo. Plenty of charitable works too, with prefects nominating a charity for the school to support each year. Others such as the Royal Hospital in Chelsea and schools in far flung places (Ghana, Japan) also benefit from visits and performances.

Boarding: Around 100 boarders in the senior school live in three boarding houses. Boarding most popular in years 10 to 12 with a mix of weekly, flexi and full time. Around 40 per cent from overseas – Europe, the Far East and, increasingly, Russia. Traditionally very popular with Forces families but this is in decline due to MOD cuts. Boarders are treated to an outing every Saturday (bowling, cinema, theatre, London attractions). Older girls allowed to London in groups for shopping and lunch and in years 12 and 13 to the cinema in the evenings. A renovation programme of boarding houses is under way. We visited the most newly refurbished which, like the rest of the school, was extremely spacious, clean and well-equipped with a pool table, DVDs and Wii in its large common room. Not as cosy and homely as many boarding houses we've seen but certainly not lacking in mod cons. Light, bright and modern dining room, where boarders and day girls take all their meals, feels like a hub of chatter at lunch time, with girls seated at sociably round tables, enjoying freshly cooked meals which are, by all accounts, 'outstanding'.

Ten or so full-time boarders among over 200 junior school children, with a handful more taking advantage of flexi- or ad hoc boarding. About a third of full-timers are international (from Asia and Russia) with a handful of Forces families in the mix. Junior boarding house is home from home to girls from years 3 to 7 and has good facilities and plenty of space, although parents are hoping for a refurb soon. All meals apart from weekend breakfast, when girls can pad downstairs in their pyjamas, are taken in the senior school. Food is reportedly 'outstanding'. Boarders take advantage of the full array of after-school activities, plus games, in-house events and an extensive DVD collection. Weekends see them participate in creative activities (tie-dying was named a top recent favourite) and head off on outings such as local bowling, shows and rollerblading or further afield to the seaside.

Background and atmosphere: Founded in 1788 to educate the children of masons who had fallen on hard times, the current 150 acre site, built in the 1930s, is the school's fourth home. A vast campus (NB visiting parents – wear flat shoes, if not trainers, for your tour), more akin to a redbrick university than a suburban girls' school, with smart, identikit buildings surrounding two quadrangles ('teeming with girls chatting in the summer term,' said one), and the longest teaching corridor in Britain. Became an independent school, open to all, in 1978 while continuing to fulfil its charitable obligation and still offering full bursaries to some 50 children in need of financial support at any time, although most staff don't know who they are.

Sharing the same campus as the senior school, Cadogan House opened in 2011 as the gleaming newly refurbished home for the pre-prep and prep. An enviably spacious facility (so serene you sometimes wonder where all the children are), nestling in its own lush grounds, it mirrors the grandeur of its big sister but maintains a safe and nurturing vibe. Benefits from a few shared facilities with the senior school (dining hall, swimming pool and breathtaking sports hall), which also gives girls a natural and very comfortable transition into year 7. Own art and DT rooms, ICT suite, a well-stocked library and brand new hall that was built as part of the renovation, providing an excellent light and bright space for assemblies, dance and PE lessons.

Classrooms and corridors are proudly adorned with artistic endeavours and handwritten work; regular themes run through the whole school enabling all year groups to display their creative wares side by side. Outside is an enticing new adventure playground, large grassy play area, wild flower garden and beyond that a new outside learning facility, part of the forest school initiative, 'great for bringing children out of their shells'. Boaters and tidy plaits abound among these confident, down-to-earth girls who were super keen during our visit – arms stretched out of sockets – to answer questions about a recent school field trip (quite something as it was to Watford). Younger ones engage in lively chat as they crocodile back from lunch in the senior school. Plenty of room for growth in its new home gives the school a quiet, studious air rather than the chaotic clatter of many prep schools.

New sixth form centre where all year 12 and 13 girls take the majority of their lessons. Fabulous common room, interior designed by pupils, complete with hot pink walls and matching sofas. All whistles and bells, with girls able to borrow laptops from the library, or bring their own, and log onto the centre's Wifi network. A senior team of 20 drawn from year 13, plus a head girl and eight deputies, elected by girls and teachers. Girls describe guidance at this stage of their education as 'excellent', with teachers giving up free time to help with personal statements and a dedicated Oxbridge co-ordinator on hand for brainboxes. Lovely rotunda library, one of the nicest we've seen: fingerprint withdrawal technology and plenty of space for quiet study.

Parents say the school is 'very into tradition' and this feeling permeates its very fabric. RMS is the only school in the country still to do 'drill': a spectacle of pinafored girls with pinned back hair performing something akin to synchronised swimming but without the water. Places in the squad are highly sought after, with dozens volunteering even for the reserves.

Pastoral care, well-being and discipline: Nurturing feel in prep consolidated by presence of peer mentors in year 6 to act as 'big sisters' to the younger ones. Trained by the school counsellor, they are on hand to support and guide through any minor personal or friendship issues. Girls' concerns can also be anonymously posted into a 'worry box' and are then addressed in the appropriate manner by the relevant form teacher. PSHE extends to parents, who are brought in for seminars on subjects ranging from internet safety (all girls are given a school email address from reception) to coping with bereavement or avoiding 'helicopter' parenting.

Senior school head is 'anti-clique' and works hard to minimise the inevitable girly issues. Sixth formers are trained as peer mentors by the school counsellor, with year 9 girls taking on 'big sister' roles to new year 7s when they join the school.

Serious disciplinary problems are few but parents say school has never been afraid to 'take a hard line' when necessary and has even been known to call in police to educate girls on the outcomes of certain scenarios if they rear their ugly heads – as in a recent inappropriate staff/pupil relationship. School claims alcohol is 'not an issue' and persistent bullying is dealt with by permanent exclusion. In a recent Ofsted boarding inspection, 92 per cent of girls interviewed said they had never seen or experienced bullying; 'an exceptional figure', says school, compared to most boarding environments. Year 13 girls are well prepared for the real world with a range of seminars offering advice on subjects from budgeting at uni and car maintenance, to getting the most out of gap years.

Chapel once a week, plus Sundays for boarders, taken by the school's full time chaplain. Boarders of other faiths do not have to attend Sunday communion, although many choose to. The whole school crams into this impressive space at Christmas for the traditional carol service.

Pupils and parents: Unlock your sons. RMS girls seem much younger and fresher than their more streetwise grammar peers and are just the kind you would love your boys to bring home for dinner. Confident and articulate without arrogance, they seem a genuinely grounded bunch. Good ethnic mix, reflecting the school's position on the London borders, with the vast majority taking full advantage of all the extras the school has to offer. 'Lots of bat mitzvahs to go to at weekends', said one parent.

Parents from all walks of life from the well-heeled to hard working, dual income, first time buyers. Some expats and international parents, largely of overseas boarders. Many from across the Chilterns and Hertfordshire, with an increasing North London crowd. The school provides an excellent coach service from all these areas, with the London brigade able to take advantage of the shuttle bus from the tube station. Parents of girls at smaller prep schools reported a bit of a culture shock when their daughters joined this vast establishment, but added that they felt totally at home 'after just a few weeks'.

Entrance: Entry at 4 currently oversubscribed, enabling selection of those the school thinks will best fit its culture and, ultimately, that of the senior school. Academic ability is 'just a part' of the selection criteria, with the way candidates approach tasks and interact with other girls held in equal regard. Prospective students come for a half a day assessment which is so gentle that according to one parent, 'they hardly know it's happening'.

There is another small intake of about half a dozen into year 3 but girls can and do join at any point, with class sizes growing gradually to a maximum of 24 in year 6. Those joining post-reception come from both state and independent sectors and are asked to attend a full day assessment where they join in whatever existing pupils are doing and also take assessments in English, maths and reasoning.

About 50 per cent transfer into reception from the on-site co-ed pre-school, Ruspini House – although places are not guaranteed to children coming up through this route – with the rest joining from a variety of other, mostly local, pre-schools.

Senior school increasingly selective, now parents are seeing RMS as a desirable option in an area of excellent independent and maintained schools. Majority join at 11+ but some places are also available for girls to join up to 14+. Candidates spend a full day during which they take the University of Durham online test to assess skills in English, maths and reasoning. The test is designed to accurately gauge girls' natural ability and – pushy parents be warned – cannot be tutored for. There's also a creative writing exercise, group activity and group interview. School is keen to find space for girls with 'something else to offer' and looks closely at report from current school as well as test results. Candidates for entry in later years sit tests in English, maths and non-verbal reasoning.

Around 170 girls compete for approximately 40 places with successful ones, about half from state primaries, guaranteed a place in all future stages. Good sibling policy too, a relief if younger ones aren't as starry as big sister. Approximately 50 per cent join from Cadogan House (these girls are guaranteed entry, making for a mixed bag academically). Around 25 new places are available in year 12, with girls being selected on GCSE results and extracurricular achievements.

In line with its charitable ethos, school has an ongoing social mission to offer a limited number of assisted boarding places to disadvantaged children from London boroughs of Hillingdon and Tower Hamlets, and Norfolk. Head says that integration of these girls, and that of the mainly international boarders, is 'fantastic'.

Exit: Cadogan House girls are guaranteed a place at the Royal Masonic School and about 85 per cent take it, making it the clear choice for parents looking for a one stop shop. Those that do move go mostly to local grammars for the obvious financial reasons. Hardly any to other independents.

Majority of sixth formers to Russell Group universities, Birmingham, Nottingham, Leeds and Exeter all popular; one medic in 2016. Worth bearing in mind that as school's academic reputation continues to improve, Oxbridge places likely to increase as fresh talent filters through. A small exodus – around 20 per cent – at 16, recently to local grammar schools; perhaps girls wanting a somewhat more worldly environment, although head says all were for financial reasons.

Money matters: Capital expenditure is underpinned by an endowment set up by the masons and the school is a tenant of the site. Multitude of scholarships and exhibitions available at 11+ (academic, all-rounder, art, music and sport), and sixth form (adding performing arts to the list) offering a maximum 25 per cent discount on fees. Five per cent discount for siblings and 10 per cent for Forces families. Means-tested bursaries available.

Remarks: A school where girls can be girls and sing, act and run their way to well-roundedness in a safe and nurturing environment. Steadily improving academics over a number of years mean RMS has now secured its position as a serious contender in the competitive local market, and first class facilities help turn out real all-rounders.

A school that aims to draw the best out of everyone, whatever their abilities and turns out confident, rounded young ladies. Parents 'never mind writing the cheque to RMS', according to one. Eggheads and pushy parents might prefer some of the surrounding competition, though.

Rudolf Steiner School (Kings Langley)

Langley Hill, Kings Langley, Hertfordshire WD4 9HG

Pupils: 370 • Ages: 3–19 • Sixth form: 34

Fees: £5,356 – £9,520 pa

Tel: 01923 262505
Email: tours@rsskl.org
Website: www.rsskl.org

College of Teachers: Like Steiner schools the world over, does not have a head but a non-hierarchical College of Teachers which spins off to form mandate groups dealing with different areas of running the school. First point of contact doesn't give the slickest of first impressions when compared to other independents. Absence of figurehead permeates culture, giving school an ergonomic, somewhat free-wheeling vibe and there's certainly no risk of being blindsided by flashy marketing.

Academic matters: One of just three Steiner schools in the UK that carry pupils through – in one class per year group of around 30 – from the age of 3 to 19, culminating in GCSEs and A levels. These are taken a year later than in conventional schools in line with the Steiner philosophy of 'not too soon, not too late,' underscoring the method of organising the curriculum according to Steiner's philosophy of child development.

Parents considering a Steiner education might want to Google Anthroposophy before signing up to what at first glance can appear to be an idealistic approach to education. The educational model recognises three key developmental stages: birth to the age of 6 or 7 (the kindergarten years), where the focus is on developing curiosity; 7 to 14 when it is deemed that children are ready for a more formal education and pupils move into the lower and middle schools, then 14 to 19 years when they enter the upper school and finally focus on intellectual pursuits. Parents believe this approach leads to 'greater academic rigour ultimately, because it hasn't been forced.'

Don't expect Biff, Chip et al to make an appearance until your child is at least 7, when Steiner pupils are first introduced to phonic sounds. Until this point they are in mixed age groups in a house on the school campus, enjoying the freedom to explore 'earthly pursuits' like baking and modelling. Lots of time spent outside with all playthings supposed to be made of natural materials (although we did spy a few plastic spades scattered around the garden). Books don't feature until class 2 (year 3), in line with the Steiner belief that if children engage with intellectual properties too soon it can affect their emotional development.

From entry to the lower school at the age of 6 or 7, pupils ideally have the same class teacher for the next eight years, which parents say leads to 'outstanding synchronicity' (they describe the teacher as 'like a captain steering a ship'). At this point, feelings and, contrary to current educational trends, memory are key approaches to learning and subjects are presented not as conceptual but experiential, for example learning history through drama. French and German taught from class 1 (year 2), with numbers, days of the week and other useful vocab taught through movement, song and repetition. Mornings dominated by 'the main lesson,' where a specific topic or theme is studied for two or three weeks, with all aspects of learning (reading, writing, history etc) linked to this theme, often culminating in a dramatic performance.

At the age of 14 pupils move into the more academic 'thinking' phase of learning, with specialist teachers for each subject, and begin preparation for their nine GCSEs in a limited set of subjects (current exclusions include geography, RE and music). At this point they are split into two or three streams according to ability. Bearing in mind that no testing takes place until this point, results are respectable (42 per cent A*/A and 72 per cent A*-B grades in 2016) and slightly better than some local schools although lagging some way behind nearby state sector high performers. Pupils say they are not loaded down with homework, but claim to be highly self-motivated to carry out additional studies without need for either carrot or stick.

Small number of exam candidates makes for great student/teacher ratios. Lots of artsy options for those that way inclined, ranging from photography and graphics to history of art. At A level the subject range is even more limited and has had heavy arts bias. Tiny teaching groups – some with a single candidate and many just two or three. In 2016, 37 per cent A*/A and 63 per cent A*-B grades. Students sometimes outsourced to other schools to pursue specific minority subjects.

Around 30 per cent of cohort falls into SEN category, although only a tiny number statemented, possibly as Steiner's emphasis on the practical and creative appeals to those who are failing to thrive in more conventional schools. School geared up to cope with mild dyslexia, dyscalculia and dyspraxia but recently closed its specialist Tobias class as 'the goal is always integration.' Several specialist SEN teachers now use dedicated classrooms to offer one-to-one help to those needing it on a weekly basis. Mild autism dealt with to a certain point but school 'cannot offer a sufficiently structured environment,' as the daily routines vary and with class sizes at around 30 teachers are not able to dedicate sufficient time to those with greater needs.

Games, options, the arts: Sports facilities modest compared to other independent schools, although recently resurfaced sports hall is more than adequate for school's largely non-competitive sporting ethos. Physical activity is for health and fitness (spiritual as well as physical) rather than an outlet for aggression and competition, and football is not allowed until class 9. Volleyball and basketball very popular with older children however, and teams compete very successfully in these.

Younger children play non-competitive sports and there's an additional focus on gardening, digging and building. Eurythmy, a dance-like art form (more Googling required), is uniquely practised – and oft performed – by all in the school for the benefit of mind, body and spirit.

Enviable arts and crafts facilities, with separate workshops for fine arts, woodwork, metalwork and pottery, plus a photography studio and dark room. In addition, pupils participate in biodynamic gardening from year 1 up, with older children tending the school's allotment with an enthusiasm unlikely to be found in any other school. Huge, well-used 450 seat theatre multitasks as assembly hall (anthrophilosphical, natch) and production space, with two major upper school productions each year and many more for lower years.

Music forms backbone of school, with all pupils taking recorder and singing lessons from class 1, although no opportunity to learn instruments during school time. Further opportunities to perform, however, with orchestra from class 5, culminating in an exchange for more senior pupils with the Steiner school in Ottersberg, Germany, where members of the respective orchestras perform at each other's schools and stay with their German counterparts.

Background and atmosphere: Situated amongst 10 acres of grounds on the site of a 13th century royal palace – which makes it sound grander than it actually is. As a visitor you feel a bit like you've been transported back to a time before polished, hothoused children existed and whiteboards, fleets of iPads and Astroturfs were par for the course. The fabric of the school needs some serious updating, although it functions adequately in its somewhat tired buildings, with pupils coming across as happy, relaxed and very individual. There's no uniform or apparent dress code (bar a ban on logos), let alone dictates regarding length of hair (on heads or chins). Definitely no 'them and us' where parental relationships with school are concerned – this is a true community, with family involvement key to the running of the school in anything from fundraising (the annual advent fair has around 3,000 visitors) to decorating classrooms.

True to Steiner's beliefs, there is no Christian or other secular ethos to the school, but a daily prayer-like verse is recited each morning and a non-religious grace to show respect for food said before each meal. Unfortunately the latter takes place mainly over packed lunches at pupils' desks as there is no dining room or provision for collective school meals, just a small café serving snacks and drinks. Festivals such as the solstices and May Day are celebrated, and are a huge part of school life, but 'rooted in tradition' rather than religion.

Pastoral care, well-being and discipline: Parents and pupils evangelise about the level of pastoral care, describing school as 'a sacred place,' with a 'sense of honesty, realness and love.' Steiner teachers are trained to think about the challenges facing each child in their charge before they go to sleep every night and shake hands with every child at the beginning and end of each day, reinforcing the strong morals and principles of the ethos. 'School is respected at all costs,' according to parents, who add that children are treated totally individually, with teachers effectively forming a team with parents to guide the child to adulthood.

Very little bullying and no cliques reported (perhaps due to tiny size of school) and posters around the school remind children to be kind to one another. Two peer mentors assigned to each child from year 3 to act as sounding boards for any problems arising.

Ofsted visited to check safeguarding concerns, most recently in November 2016; management (deliberately not a Steiner strongpoint) appears to be a complete mess in this area, and not getting better fast enough, though we understand that the school is intending to bring in someone to get them up to speed. Parents we have spoken to remain supportive and committed – but do make sure you understand where things have got to.

Pupils and parents: Many Steiner educated parents – and their friends – move to Kings Langley to be near the school, and others commute from a radius incorporating London, Chesham, Milton Keynes and St Albans, where there are Steiner primary schools. Parents typically have spiritual or creative outlook, many from artistic or healing professions. Lots of international families from countries where Steiner schools are more common – Germany, France, Holland. Pupils not your typical sophisticated, on-message public school bunch; they communicate in a noticeably more animated, less reserved way to their more conventional counterparts. Many refugees from other schools and the school puts its success with these pupils down to 'not shaping them but allowing them to express their nature.' Lots of spontaneous hugging going on amongst pupils – somewhat disarming for visitors but makes for a very supportive vibe where 'people feel they can be themselves,' say parents.

Pupils possibly a somewhat insular group, with the majority having spent their whole education on the same campus, and some we talked to indicating they didn't really have many friends outside the Steiner community. That said, one top year pupil described herself as 'fully cooked,' confident that she was ready – and well prepared – to face the outside world.

Entrance: School encourages full participation in Steiner ethos from the word go and runs its own pre-school parent and child group, from where little ones more or less automatically move to kindergarten at the age of 3.

School isn't oversubscribed but priority is given to siblings and children from other Steiner schools, then local families. No formal test or assessment for entry thereafter. Applicants asked to provide a report from their existing school and bring some examples of their work before spending some time with the class teacher. A handful of new joiners into class 13 (year 12), mainly from international Steiner schools. School says that children joining from conventional schools 'love it, and embrace the freedom.'

Exit: An exodus of around half after GCSEs, with reasons cited varying from a desire for a shorter commute to wanting more sport or seeking subjects not offered by the school. The remaining few enjoy a very hands-on support with their university or college applications, a process which 'seems to work well,' according to parents.

Good mix of higher education destinations for those who choose that path, with one to Oxbridge in 2016 and London popular in recent years (UCL, King's, Birkbeck, Imperial, Goldsmiths), plus Sheffield and Bristol amongst others.

Money matters: Not a wealthy school. Fees around 20 per cent lower than other independents, with many parents benefiting from means-tested bursaries.

Remarks: A unique school delivering a niche offering to families either already familiar with the Steiner ethos or those seeking refuge from results-driven mainstream exam factories.

Parents not clued up about Steiner should do their homework very carefully before embarking on this educational journey. Not everyone's cup of tea, but it's practically impossible to get a negative remark out of its fans, with parents who have experienced both mainstream and Steiner schools claiming alumni of the latter are 'more centred, aware, self-assured and sensitive, with a wider vision of life than those who have been through conventional education.'

Ryde School with Upper Chine

Queen's Road, Ryde, Isle of Wight PO33 3BE

Pupils: 960; 55 full, 1 weekly, 2 flexi boarders • Ages: 3–18 • Sixth form: 130 • C of E

Fees: Day £6,450 – £12,375; Boarding + £9,405 – £14,880 pa

Tel: 01983 562229
Email: school.office@rydeschool.net
Website: www.rydeschool.org.uk

Headmaster: Since 2013, Mark Waldron. Previously head of the English College in Prague, deputy head of Sherborne, and taught at The Leys School and Radley College. Eager for a new challenge, returned from Prague to run Ryde – and for the joys of Waitrose. Mr Waldron's experience in Prague has given him a different perspective and he feels well placed to make a difference at Ryde: he emphasises the importance of preparing pupils to compete internationally, and has shaken up language provision to support this. Parents find the head approachable, are impressed by his change in priorities, and say the school is friendlier now he's in residence.

The head encourages his teachers to think about the potential for creative and independent thought when planning their lessons: could the lesson take place without the pupils? Mr Waldron teaches maths – always the bottom set, so he knows the lowest common denominator. Regularly turns cakes into fractions; and what are the chances of getting that elusive blue in a tube of smarties?

He is learning to sail, and currently classes himself as incompetent crew; is a politics junkie and devotee of the races. Just finished reading Solar by Ian McEwan, and is about to embark on a book about Gordon Brown's spin doctor – feels a bit guilty when reading fiction. Likes pub quizzes. You can see how he might.

Head of junior school: Since September 2015, Mrs Linda Dennis, previously deputy head at St Faith's School, Cambridge, where she held many roles over 25 years, including curriculum co-ordinator, deputy head (pastoral), head of drama and head of languages. She is an ISI inspector.

Winchester-born Mrs Dennis grew up on her parents' dairy farm, near Andover, before attending La Retraite School, in Salisbury, and graduating with a BEd from Southampton University. She began her teaching career in Dorset before moving to Cambridge in 1990. Her husband, Philip, is a history teacher and she has two sons. Paul is a housemaster at Wellingborough Prep School and Joe is reading anthropology at Oxford Brookes.

Academic matters: Two or three classes a year in the junior school, size 14-18. Set for maths and English from year 4. There's the usual love/hate split for maths, but even the haters say the teachers are really nice and helpful if you don't get it. And for those who love it – 'we have maths challenges as well as sports fixtures', said one boy proudly.

There was a huge basin of conkers in the science lab: year 3s were finding out whether size and shape have an impact on strength in a very joyful conkers experiment. New focus on languages, with Spanish becoming the second language, and Mandarin or Latin being taught from year 6. A nice emphasis on creativity – not always the case in through schools with an eye on the end results: year 4 write a story or poem every week, and after their trip to the Amazon World, wrote stories about the Amazon in geography. Plenty of monitoring and the school will do everything and anything to help children falling behind.

Children from nursery to year 2 are at Fiveways, a separate campus across the road, run since 1988 by Sally Davies. Mixed ability classes, although teachers will hand out work of differing levels within classes. Children work in quiet deep concentration, slightly startling in children so young. Classes of 14-16. Pupils read with a teacher or teaching assistant every day. For all that, a surprisingly small library. Mandarin and Spanish from age 4, two lessons in each language every week.

Good solid academic results for a non-selective school. In 2016, 68 per cent A*-B at A level, 35 per cent A*/A. At GCSE, 48 per cent A*/A. IGCSE also available, and the head has introduced the vocational IB (IBCP). Ryde is chosen by some parents for its consistently good results, which give a 'degree of assurance': it is in the privileged position of being virtually the only independent mainstream school on the Island (the other is very small), and it is fair to say that Island state secondary schools do not rank highly in the league tables. One parent said that he feels his children 'have the chance to excel and achieve their full potential'.

Class sizes at A level 8-14, a maximum of 22 at GCSE. Lessons are now 55 mins instead of 35 mins – an improvement, pupils and parents agree. There's a five min break between lesson times to ensure that no one is late – or 'that's the intention,' said one pupil, cautiously. There is a strong work ethic at Ryde – the classes we saw were almost universally heads down, working hard, the concentrated effort almost palpable. Pupils who have come from other schools comment on the fact that it is ok to work hard at Ryde – 'It's not something that you get teased for: it's actually cool to be clever.'

Maths and science are popular – due in part, says the head, to the large number of doctor parents; and illustrated by year 10 turning the whole periodic table into cupcakes in the school bake off. Victoria sponge...or periodic table...They must like it.

The head has come from a school where students were studying in their third or fourth language, and firmly subscribes to the saying 'if you only speak one language then you can only live one life': he is determined that everyone shall learn at least one other language. Spanish is the new second language at Ryde – it's also easier for dyslexics to learn. Mandarin and Latin are also finding a place in the curriculum.

With Mr Waldron has come a new emphasis on the sixth form, which now blossoms in a new sixth form block on the main campus. The sixth are pleased that the previous nod towards career planning, apparently only really useful if you wanted to be an engineer, has been replaced by something really helpful; and lifelong learning has been introduced in a personal development lesson every Monday. It's about destinations, says Mr Waldron: pupils needs to understand where they want to go, and how to get there. IB students know what they are doing and why; not always the case for those studying A levels. So at Ryde even A level pupils will do the theory of knowledge core of the IB, so they 'get an idea of what it means to think.'

The sixth formers we met were polite and articulate, although they didn't quite have the spit and polish you might encounter in some mainland independent schools: perhaps this is because the Island and school constitute a secure and rather more laid back environment. Mr Waldron is well aware that his domestic pupils might lack some of the edge which is evident in his international students, particularly those from the eastern block, who are well aware of the privilege of attending Ryde and of the international stage on which they will be competing. This is something he is clearly determined to address.

Parents receive mini monthly report cards detailing effort and progress, until GCSE, when this turns into attainment, and predicted and target grades – to flag up any problems with work. Focus on praising effort: merit badges worn on blazers, like awards for courage under fire, are awarded entirely for effort. When the school as a whole has achieved 2,000 efforts there's a mufti day.

Strong SEN provision: around 15 per cent of pupils here have special needs, and the school makes provision for up to moderate dyslexia. Aim for SEN pupils: to make all capable of independent learning.

Games, options, the arts: Music is super here – our tour guides, neither of whom were taking music A level, said their happiest hours at school were spent in the music block. The teaching inspires a real love of music, and as well as junior, chamber and concert orchestras, there is a student-led ukulele orchestra. Pupils relish the joys of the annual Global Rock – an international dance competition. Students put together routines and costumes themselves: parents describe the results as 'incredible'. The summer musical and winter production are popular with parents and locals alike, and lots of pupils are keen to take part.

Not a school, says the head, for a top sportsman or woman: two pupils left at 16 to attend schools with more focus on hockey and rugby. The provision is decent; but a parent commented that it's difficult to get good mainland schools to come and play on the Island because of the travel expenses involved; another said that although sports teaching and facilities are good, Ryde is a small school, so there's a limited choice of pupils for teams. But the compensation is that those good at sport get to be a big fish in a small pond and can become team captains – positions they might not occupy at larger schools.

Senior pupils say there is not sufficient emphasis on sport: because their standard is much higher than that of the other schools on the Island, they easily win local matches, but can struggle with matches against schools on the mainland, who tend to play at a higher level – 'we don't lose all our matches,' said one sixth former (actually, this is a bit harsh – most sports have a respectable showing). But sailing, recently started at the school, is thriving (as might be expected at an island school where so many children sail regularly with their parents). More alternative options for sixth formers include yoga and mindfulness.

The three junior school houses compete vigorously, not just on the sports field, but also in the sailing challenge and the inter-house sandcastle challenge – you would expect no less from an island school. The usual range of clubs, plus ASC (Adventure Service Challenge) which is like a mini Duke of Edinburgh for years 5 and 6.

Grand DT room in the predominantly glass block built three years ago to house art and DT. 'If I get them in year 7, they stay,' said the DT teacher with a smile; and indeed both our guides expressed huge enthusiasm for the subject, and remembered with affection their first task of designing an insect in year 7. Roof terrace with lovely view out over the sea – it's made full use of for parties – and a few beds of weeds which apparently have an eco purpose. The art rooms have the hushed atmosphere of a cathedral: any talking is done is whispers, pupils concentrate hard. Here, clearly, there is no sense that art is a light option: it is afforded proper respect. Pupils commented on the dedication of those taking art A level; and GCSE students are apparently rarely out of the art department, spending all their lunch times perfecting work. The new building contains a large IT suite just for DT and art – apparently the other IT space can get crowded, and it isn't quiet enough for the artists here. Lower sixth reached the regional finals of a young enterprise competition last year selling luxury gift items, cards and gift wrap and such, and won a Kenko competition for designing a logo. Design is clearly a thriving area.

Although there didn't in general appear to be a distinction drawn between girls' and boys' activities in the junior school, the club set up has some divisions: Rainbows is a Brownie group for the girls (arts and crafts, cooking etc), Only Boys Allowed for boys – where they do things like make codes, modelling and camping, and sign in with a thumbprint: sounds super, and possibly quite a few girls might think so too? Though questionable whether many boys would fancy joining Rainbows...

Both CCF and D of E are popular here; a parent commented that it is the good provision for music, arts and extracurricular that give children here such a good level of confidence.

Boarding: The boarding campus is some 10 miles from the school, but there's a daily bus service and the school pass can also be used to obtain free travel on public transport on the Island. The boarding houses are beautiful arts and crafts buildings, sensitively restored and converted. Admiring the lower gallery, a long elegant sitting room with squashy sofas, packed bookshelves and piano, you might think you are being shown around a rather lovely National Trust property. Then you would spot the drum kit and TV and know you're not. The upper gallery above has been turned into double bedrooms surrounding a living area for year 10 girls – an idyllic set up, flooded with light from the long windows. Sixth formers get single rooms, unless they request to share. Others are usually in rooms for two. Two house parents resident overnight so pupils have someone who they can contact if ill. There's also a sixth form boarding house in Ryde within walking distance of the school for those who want to live more independently.

Ryde chosen by one parent for the strong sense of family in the boarding houses, compared to other schools where boarding provision seemed like 'housing for battery chickens.' His children are happy; any minor issues arising have been dealt with successfully, and he has 'absolute confidence in the boarding set up'. Some boarders' parents fall in love with the Island when they visit their children here: one Tunisian mum even decided she would rather retire to the Island than to the south of France.

The large site is shared with an activity centre, so there are plenty of outdoor facilities for boarders to enjoy – anyone for after-school caving? Indoors there's a room with pool, table tennis and table football. Pupils say the boarding experience is sold on the basis of lots of activities, but really some of them rarely happen: quad biking, for instance, only happens during the first week of term. (There is, perhaps, a particular push on special activities at the beginning of terms to help new kids to bond.)

Boarders can roam the 100 acre grounds more or less as they please, providing they sign out first. Must keep in sight of the drive on dark winter days, and need to seek permission to go the beach, which is off campus. The youngest boarder is currently year 6 – there isn't an age restriction, but the head of boarding likes there to be boarders of a similar age to keep each other company.

Pupils comment that the food in the boarding house is 'awful' (in comparison, food at the school is 'gourmet'). School is well aware of the problem, which is tricky to rectify since the catering facilities at the boarding house are shared with the activity centre. But there is a gorgeous mural in the dining room of animals waiting to board Noah's ark, a pair of black cats, tails held jauntily high, leading the way. The mural remains unfinished: the painter pupil didn't return from the First World War to finish it off; but it must be lovely to look at while wading through the substandard grub.

Boarders set up their own clubs – cheesy Tuesdays (the cheese on toast club) and the Coco Pops club – foodie clubs popular for obvious reasons. They make good use of the kitchen facilities, and can cook as they please – there's plenty of fruit and cereal available at all times, and a Tesco run every Friday night (no Red Bull allowed).

Boarders have plenty of opportunities to make their views heard, with a suggestion box, weekly house meetings and an open door policy for the head of boarding (and yes, they have mentioned the food).

R

Background and atmosphere: A school surrounded by stunning scenery – how lovely to sit in the library and stare out at the picture postcard view over the sea. Venerable main building with nondescript (but well cared for) adjuncts; swish new glass DT and art centre.

The advantages of attending school on the Island are clear: it is safe, secure and beautiful. The counter to this is perhaps an element of complacency born of isolation: the head is keen for pupils to look beyond the Solent – pupils must not be limited by the stretch of water: they will need to be able to compete nationally and internationally. Mr Waldron intends to ensure they can.

Pupils are friendly and polite (although this is not a leap to your feet place) and pupils clearly enjoy being at school – a pupil who transferred to Ryde from a local school commented how good it is to be at a school where he actually wants to stay and do activities; just because it's nice to be there. One parent said the best thing about Ryde are its pupils: 'grounded, mature; and nice kids to be around.'

Feels like a traditional environment – although surprisingly pupils are allowed to use mobile phones in class for task-related research: one parent commented that he is not happy with a rule so open to abuse. C of E but with a light touch – prayers at the end of assembly, because that's just what happens; much like a full stop at the end of a sentence. But Mr Waldron is keen for religion to play a larger part, and has introduced compulsory church as a fortnightly event. Sixth formers are unimpressed: they've been told that this is reflection time, but don't quite see why it should have to take place in church.

Parents are happy with communication levels, and reaction to complaints (which are rare): when one did have a problem and raised the issue with the head, it was dealt with swiftly and well.

School council of pupil representatives who have been feeling a bit disenchanted with the slow reaction to their views and requests: for instance, the school council requested a shelter outside the canteen, so that pupils waiting in the lunch queue on rainy days didn't get wet. A sensible request – but it took a couple of years to happen. The head says this has been addressed: democracy has come to Ryde, and the school council is operating under a new pupil-run system.

End of year trip to somewhere theme parkish has been replaced by an activity week focusing on life skills. This has not been uniformly welcomed by pupils, the majority lingering on the side of 'not fair.' Lower sixth, in particular, felt they might have had more fun on a roller coaster than learning to tidy and clean – although there must have been a number of grateful parents, and those changing a tyre skills may well come in handy. Year 7 spent their week building a secret garden, which some love; another year group were camping on the games field with team building exercises – apparently a bit too local to be considered fun.

Uniform is the usual fare, but some parents, apparently, are obsessed with wanting a 'trendy exclusive uniform' – think black blazers with yellow trim; although one parent we spoke to observed dryly that 'Ryde kids don't actually want to stand out on the bus.' Quite.

Pastoral care, well-being and discipline: Parents view the pastoral care at Ryde as exceptional – 'they do a terrific job' – and describe the advantages of a small school where staff know all the pupils and their families. Parents like the strong community atmosphere at school, and comment on the extraordinary level of support and counselling from the school following the tragic death of a pupil, both to the immediate family, and to other pupils; another parent was similarly appreciative of how supportive the school were after a family death: 'wonderful' and 'very caring'.

The head is keen for his pupils to achieve a balance in life, and there is new emphasis on life skills and mindfulness to emphasis the importance of enjoying and experiencing the present (involves controlled breathing – even those who were sceptical beforehand were happy to admit that this was super – one admitted to taking relaxation as far as sleep). This does not feel like the sort of school where grades will be achieved at the expense of well-being; indeed the head muses on whether the Norland nanny in last year's batch of sixth formers, who worked hard to achieve her two A levels, will be happier than the Cambridge mathematician.

Disciplinary system of minus points and detentions run on Friday and Saturday mornings (Saturdays are relatively rare). Drug taking can and has led to expulsion.

Pupils confident that there would be a teacher or form tutor they could talk to if they had a problem. There is a move to involve sixth formers more with younger years, and prefects now wear listener badges, so kids have an obvious person to go to if they want to talk to someone other than a teacher.

Any bullying occurs is dealt with properly – 'sensitively and appropriately' said a parent.

Parents praise the detailed and thorough communication from Fiveways: the Fiveways flyer comes out every Friday; parents receive emails and texts, and the flipchart in the foyer makes sure that parents are kept informed about everything including the menu for the day. If they know their child is going to loathe everything, they can sign up their child for a sandwich or a bowl of plain pasta.

The most notable thing about this part of the school is the detailed thought and attention given to the pastoral care of each child. Mrs Davies understands all the nuances of bullying; how it differs between the sexes; and how, for little girls, this could amount to a look passed during a lesson (the seat plan would be varied accordingly). A similar level of detailed consideration would be given to get to root of bad behaviour, in order to resolve the problem – 'we will do whatever is necessary, even if it means involving an educational psychologist'. One parent commented on how well her child's learning difficulty was spotted and dealt with. SEN provision is excellent. No stigma here – everyone is happy to visit the SEN teacher.

As you would expect in a school this nurturing, parents are encouraged to come up to classrooms in the junior school – 'it's important to know if the hamster has died'. Community and family are important words here. Constantly in contact with parents by text and email, and there is very little that they rely on children to tell parents; although parents who are used to the gold standard communication at Fiveways infants section sometimes find the move to a bit less information challenging – apparently a Facebook group has been set up, and parents remind each other of things they need to remember for school trips.

Pupils and parents: Large number of parents scrimp and save to get their kids to Ryde – the state schools on the Island are famously poor. Around 80 per cent of boarders are international; also pupils from all over the Island, DFLs, and those from Portsmouth who commute over on the ferry. More pupils arriving across years 9/10/11 since Island middle school closure. Parents range from fish and chip shop owners to medics. Not a snobby school, although one parent commented that 'a few parents are'.

Former pupils include: Seb Clover (sailor), Donald Gordon (cricketer), Philip Norman (author), Lucy Emmerson (academic) and Arthur Venables (cyclist).

Entrance: Non-selective. Tested in English, maths and non-verbal reasoning higher up for placing purposes. IQ test for those for whom English is not first language. The closure of state middle schools on the Island has resulted in a steady stream of pupils into years 3, 4, 5, and 6, although there has not been a marked increase in overall numbers. Interview with head for all prospective pupils. Most pupils stay through to the sixth form.

Exit: Typically 95 per cent of juniors go through to the senior school with rest going to Island state schools or occasionally an independent school on the mainland. The majority of sixth formers to a range of universities, particularly King's College London, Southampton and Loughborough. One to Oxbridge in 2016 and three medics; others to eg Courtauld for history of art, fashion design in Paris, psychology at Leiden.

Money matters: Wants to keep fees affordable for Islanders. Three IB scholarships of 50 per cent which are advertised on the island. Bursaries of up to 90 per cent of fees, available on a needs basis, the number available depending on the amount of the bursaries already paid. A number of small scholarships of around 10 per cent, which may soon be combined into fewer more meaningful scholarships, possibly in sailing. Pupils feel current absence of scholarships in sports or music suggests that these subjects are perceived by the school as less important, and this is something the head is keen to address. Around 30 per cent of pupils have discounted fees. Four 100 per cent HMC scholars from eastern Europe.

Remarks: A school distinguished by its strong community, set in beautiful surroundings with solid academic provision. Not somewhere you are likely to encounter much unscheduled exuberance, but vitality is likely to increase with Mr Waldron at the helm. Clearly the best option for many Islanders.

Rye St Antony School

Pullen's Lane, Oxford OX3 0BY

Pupils: 350; 50 full, weekly and flexi boarders • Ages: 3-11 (boys; day only), 3-19 (girls; boarding from year 5) • Sixth form: 55 • RC

Fees: Day £9,360 – £14,175; Boarding £19,410 – £23,985 pa

Tel: 01865 762802
Email: info@ryestantony.co.uk
Website: www.ryestantony.co.uk

Headmistress: Since 1990, Miss Alison Jones BA (apparently early 60s although her skin says 20 years younger). Read English at York followed by PGCE from Oxford from whence she cut her teeth teaching English at St Mary's School, Cambridge, ultimately rising to head of sixth form. More chairperson than CEO, a figurehead and embodiment of Rye's value system, ably supported by a dynamic senior management team comprising some impressive young blood. Which is not to say Miss Jones is old fashioned – quite the contrary. Despite her tenure and the fact that she is only the fourth headmistress since Rye's foundation in 1930 she comes across as open minded and progressive ('very straight talking', according to parents), speaks with passion about overturning gender stereotypes and is bang up to speed when it comes to modern day issues affecting young people. 'Confiscate all technology?' she scoffs, 'No! Teach them how to keep themselves and their friends safe. And educate the parents.' Right you are.

Reportedly the only head in the area that speaks directly to the girls rather than their parents when she meets families. Acts as conduit between old girls past and present who may be able to help each other, or simply just get along well. Trusted and revered by girls, perhaps because she consults with them about, well, everything. It's not just about the school council at Rye – girls are appointed to committees aplenty covering site development, scholarships and plain old disciplinary issues which, according to head, fills them with an all-important 'sense of duty and community.' Knows every pupil and family by name and pays no heed to league tables or competing in the uber Oxford education scene: 'rank and order in league tables doesn't mirror rank in real life', she quips.

The pre-prep and prep departments are headed by Mrs Emma Coode, a relative newcomer who joined the school in 2012. The inclusive philosophy of Rye starts from the get-go: 'everyone here is valued for who they are', she says.

Academic matters: You won't see Rye hovering around the top of the league tables alongside the plethora of academic superpowers that populate the local school scene – but that's just fine with them. And with their pupils' families, for that matter. 'We value the mix of ability', said one earnest sixth former; 'it's not judgmental and we all help each other'. 'Very nurturing', say parents. 'What you see is what you get and it's all about what's good for the pupils not about what they can do for the school.' Head steadfastly allows school to steer its own course – 'we are unique in a different way', she says. As focused on instilling 'a sense of duty and community' in its pupils as sending them off in the right direction when it comes to higher education – which incidentally covers anything from Oxbridge to secretarial college in any given year group. 'Parents want a school that can look after all their girls, whatever their academic aptitude', says head. To this end, school is constantly seeking ways to enhance and expand opportunities with options such as a BTec in business option for sixth formers from September 2017 or the Leiths Food and Wine course, on curriculum for years 12 and 13. Parents (many of them academics) of the brightest girls 'choose Rye with every confidence it can deliver on the academic front' but are also attracted by the unique quality of 'valuing the idea that happy people are the most successful.'

Public examination results bear out the soundness of this approach with some consistently solid outcomes; in 2016, 36 per cent of A levels were graded A*/A with 65 per cent grade A*/B. At GCSE in 2016, 28 per cent were graded A*/A and 47 per cent A*/B. Pretty respectable given the thoroughly broad church intake. Breadth of subjects on offer also impressive given school's size, with maths and history top A level choices. All the usual suspects on offer at GCSE, plus food and nutrition, drama and Latin. At A level, girls can include Chinese, classical civilisation or government and politics in their choices should they be so inclined. Timetable almost entirely – and uniquely – flexible, again a benefit of school's size, with girls able to combine any mix of subjects without the restrictions of fixed 'blocks'. A level classes tend to be tiny – just four girls were studying French and two religious studies when we visited – and it's no sweat if just one wants to take any given subject at A level – 'we just make it work', says head.

Class sizes in the senior school up to GCSE average 16 and with a pupil to teacher ratio of 1:5 there's little chance of any strugglers slipping through the net. When it comes to SEN, 'we have catered for the needs of the extreme and the mainstream', says head. Those needing the most support are given the flexibility to complete their schooling in the most appropriate way and emerge with a skill set that equips them for life. Learning support (charged as extra) is available to any pupil who needs it but outside of formal intervention little touches such as the fact that there are four maths sets help iron out any minor issues without a fuss. Strong links with several European countries – as well as boarding pupils joining from eg China and Russia means that specialist teachers support a significant number of pupils with EAL, with outstanding results – 'sometimes after a couple of terms you can't tell they're not English', enthused one pupil of her international peers.

Games, options, the arts: 'When it comes to games, we're never going to win all the trophies', says head, 'But we're enthusiastic and inclusive and that's what counts'. It's a traditional roster of netball, hockey and athletics at Rye plus a super range of clubs including badminton, fitness and rounders in the senior school. An outdoor heated pool provides a popular summer term lunch time club for pupils from year 3 up. Some success in fixtures – occasionally against much larger schools – but winning at any cost is not Rye's raison d'etre, which is better described as by one pupil as 'competitive and fun'. Parents say girls are always – charmingly – a bit surprised when they win a fixture. School has grounds rather than acres of showy playing fields, but as with everything here, it does the trick and a large, multi-purpose sports centre, well-equipped gym and respectable tennis courts provide ample facilities for pupils to get sporty. School boasts 'serious' rowers and horsewomen amongst its cohort and celebrates victories won outside of school in assemblies. In fact, parents say school 'celebrates everything'.

Punches way above its weight when it comes to extracurricular activities with a good array on offer for all ages. Books feature widely, with A Book A Month and Carnegie Medal Shadowing Club building on the fantastic foundations laid in the junior school by Rye's devoted librarian (when we visited she was outside with some of the youngest children drinking pumpkin soup and reading Halloween stories). For prep pupils there's forest school, indoor climbing, small animal care and even a festive decorations club (Christmas is huge at Rye, but more of that later). Seniors throw themselves into everything from dissection, mindfulness and Minecraft to psychology, Duke of Edinburgh and Young Enterprise. There are choirs aplenty (happily, almost all non-selective) as well as an orchestra and chamber music group. Additional optional activities for boarders cover baking, power walking and climbing and there are further opportunities to join external clubs such as the Oxford Fencing Club and Oxford Isis Korfball Club. No wonder school feels the need to produce such a beautiful booklet to showcase its plethora of activities.

Arts taken seriously and 'very strong' according to head. Drama on curriculum from reception, LAMDA and ABRSM results alike are very good and there's no shortage of opportunities for pupils to flex their performing muscles. From termly teatime concerts for novices to drama festivals (when we visited the sixth formers were preparing to perform a musical with script and score both written by pupils), the halls of Rye are certainly alive with the sound of music. And it's not just local performances on the agenda – notice boards in the smart music block advertise past and future musical tours to far flung regions including Paris and Venice.

Lovely drama studio gives girls all the space they need for performances with the light and bright art studio, festooned with high quality paintings, 3D work and textiles, the cherry on top of the arts offering.

Boarding: Boarding officially available for girls from year 5, although when we visited the youngest were in year 7. The idyllic Croft, boarding house for girls up to year 10, is straight out of Enid Blyton with its parquet floors, sweeping staircase and spacious dorms. Communal areas are vast and beautifully furnished, years 7 to 9 are in mixed age dorms and the eldest girls aspire to quirky attic rooms, up endless flights of stairs, sleeping just two or three and with panoramic views of the grounds. Years 11 and up are housed in The Cottage – also home to the sixth form centre – in single study bedrooms with a halls of residence feel, perfect preparation for uni. Maximum 65 boarders at any one time and there's full, flexi or weekly boarding on offer – even occasional nights if beds are available. Good chunk (70 per cent) of boarders are from overseas – lots of South East Asian names on study doors, particularly in the upper year groups, but also a few Europeans (mainly Spanish) – three or four per year. Girls really value the opportunity to build international relationships: 'it makes for the best friendships', they told us. Breakfast and lunch are taken in houses, with dinner for all boarders in the main school dining hall. On top of special boarders' after school clubs, which include anything from pumpkin carving to climbing, good provision over weekends with school making the most of proximity to London and Oxford, plus sports, art and drama, film or cinema nights. Each year kicks off with a team building weekend away and girls can venture into Oxford in groups from year 10 upwards.

Background and atmosphere: One parent told us 'there's a little bit of magic at Rye', and we definitely sensed a special and unique 'girls own' atmosphere – an inexplicable feeling of sisterhood that can clearly be traced back to the founder and very first headmistress, Elizabeth Rendall, of whom a wonderfully atmospheric photographic portrait (complete with packet of cigarettes in foreground) presides over the entrance hall. She and Ivy King started the school in a house on the Woodstock Road in 1930, moving to its current site, a house formerly owned by Henry, curator of the Pitt Rivers Museum, in 1939. King's mother and sister moved into the new school and many saw out the war here, growing fruit and veg in the gardens and taking fire warden duties at night. Girls learned to scull on the Cherwell and swimming was taught at Dame's Delight (ladies' counterpart to Parson's Pleasure). Miss King took over the helm on Miss Rendall's retirement, succeeded by Miss Sumpter, from whom Miss Jones took the reins in 1990. It is from these formidable females that the school still takes its lead and the bravery and progressiveness of the founders – who were as competent in site maintenance as teaching Latin, all whilst persuading parents to allow their daughters to go to university – lives on in Miss Jones. It's no wonder that Old Ryes are so dedicated to their alma mater to the point that there are, at time of writing, five on staff.

Oft described as a 'hidden gem', you stumble across the school at the end of a residential cul-de-sac just off London Road. Very different to the first impressions made by the heavy hitting schools in the area, and initially it feels a bit like entering via the tradesman's entrance, but this is where books by covers should never be judged, as past this little car park with its modern attachments lies a charming, leafy – albeit bijoux – campus. The main school building is a fine example of late Victorian splendour with immaculate modern additions nestled amongst beautifully tended gardens and ancient trees. Signs of investment and updates abound. A lovely new reception area (2016) provides a warm welcome to the main school building with its tall ceilings and wide, light corridors, bedecked with works of art and colourful notices. The modern library (2012), among the most inviting we've seen, is well stocked and furnished with a mix of cosy beanbags and more formal tables and, presided over by a dedicated (and dare we say dynamic) librarian, is hub to the many literary activities (author visits, creative writing workshops, bookclubs, trips to Oxfordshire Author Awards) on offer. Plus the views across the lawns are to die for. Other new additions such as the sports hall and stunning sixth form centre, with its own dining room and boarding quarters for most senior pupils, have been skilfully integrated, delivering the necessary facilities without ruining the quaint original architecture. There's a super new food tech centre (2014) too. Hopefully next up for some attention are the rather basic science labs.

School has a genuine 'all-through' feel, with juniors and seniors taught in a collection of equally charming buildings separated by just a winding path. The nursery is housed in King House, in quirky, rambling classrooms up in the eaves that can't help but inspire young imaginations. Nursery open from 7.30am to 6.30pm – useful for the working parents that largely make up the Rye cohort. Juniors housed in Langley Lodge, part of the original collection of school buildings that retains its Victorian charm with winding staircases (complete with colourful giant papier mâché giraffe at the bottom), giant sash windows, fireplaces and high ceilings, yet with all the requisite classroom technology present and correct. Prep will be a member of IAPS from 2017.

Pastoral care, well-being and discipline: School has a lay Catholic ethos, meaning that while Catholicism is integral, it is outward looking and inclusive of all religions (or none) and cultures, and focused on spirituality rather than doctrine. Indeed, staff reported one Muslim girl 'gaining the confidence to wear the full hijab' in sixth form, thanks to her supportive experience at Rye. In this vein, pupils are expected to understand and observe certain principles of tolerance and consideration to prepare them for adult life. There are no frocked clergy or nuns on the teaching staff and the lovely little chapel is an understated stand-alone building open throughout the week and used in particular for the weekly Sunday mass.

A more contented cohort you couldn't hope to find. Absent are signs of pressure, stress and ferocious competition, and instead smiles abound. There's a genuine feeling of girls looking after each other, but the support infrastructure is built upon a friendly and down to earth (largely, from what we saw young-ish) staff room: 'the support we get from teachers is amazing', said one pupil. Patricians (senior prefects) are trained in basic child protection and advise staff and governors as well as organising a mentoring system for all new pupils which involves each girl being allocated a 'housemother' – an older pupil – to help her to adapt to school life and answer any questions or concerns. And for when things do go wrong, there's an 'independent listener' – a retired teacher at the end of the phone – to help put things in perspective.

Girls say they know every other pupil at least by sight, if not name, and talk about the school's 'family atmosphere'. 'We love it when the whole school comes together', they say. Which, as promised, brings us on to Christmas. As with any family, it's the unrivalled highlight of the calendar, and even on a dull day in early November, enthusiasm effuses from staff and pupils at the mere mention. Girls say they're 'hoarse by the end of term' with all the singing that goes on, from the staff panto (male teachers in drag an apparent highlight), the Christmas lunch, classroom décor competition, traditional 'tangerine party' and carol service. Much enthusiasm too for the house system ('house points really matter,' according to one earnest year 7) with its many year-round competitions from charities day to sports day with the top house winning a house barbecue.

Discipline takes a magnanimous approach with head often consulting with offenders' peers to 'get an insight into family matters' and 'steadily unpick the issues to find the reason'. Open discussions are key and resolution rarely involves suspension or harsh sanctions. Even detentions are unheard of.

Pupils and parents: 'Representative of local fluid population', says head. Happy mix of locals and overseas pupils with many parents working at nearby BMW, the university or John Radcliffe Hospital. Largely down to earth, dual income – plenty of first time buyers mixed in with old farming money and the children of old girls. Strong links with European countries (Italy, Spain, France and Germany), with pupils visiting from these countries for part of the summer term most years.

Entrance: For entry into all year groups, parents and prospective pupils are interviewed together by head who always tries 'not to turn girls away'. It would be 'hypocritical and silly' not to admit all girls from the prep school. So parents can happily buy into Rye safe in the knowledge that it is a genuine all-through offering. About two-thirds of girls of the 30 or so moving into year 7 join from a mix of local state and independent schools – no particular feeder. Parents and prospective pupils are interviewed together by head who always tries 'not to turn girls away'. Candidates asked to bring a portfolio of their work and attend an assessment day which is 'diagnostic rather than selective'.

Exit: Boys now peel off at 11 (rather than 8 – a recent change made due to parental demand) to a variety of local preps and secondary schools with almost all junior girls moving seamlessly up to the senior school. A handful of departures post-GCSE and, due to the broadest church of intakes, impossible to identify trends when it comes to higher education which runs the gauntlet from Oxbridge colleges and Russell Group Universities to secretarial college, art schools or performing arts colleges.

Money matters: Fees comparative with nearby 'league table' girls' schools with all their gleaming facilities might raise eyebrows from some. Scholarships and some means-tested bursaries available at 11+, 13+ and 16+. Pupils can apply for a King Award for up to £300 to enable them to further an interest or learn a new skill.

Remarks: Above all, a most civilised and humane school which achieves good individual outcomes for its girls wherever they sit on the academic spectrum. Although not an obvious choice if your girls are all high academic flyers, parents select Rye for all the girls in their family, safe in the knowledge that their daughters will have their individual potential developed whatever their ability. In the words of one happy sixth former: 'Rye accommodates everybody. We all have a chance to shine.'

Saffron Walden County High School

Audley End Road, Saffron Walden, Essex CB11 4UH

Pupils: 2,035 • Ages: 11–18 • Sixth form: 560

Tel: 01799 513030
Email: info@swchs.net
Website: www.swchs.net

Headteacher: Since January 2016, Caroline Derbyshire MA (in English Lit from Cambridge). Previously executive principal of the Chilford Hundred Education Trust for 10 years, and before that deputy head at Saffron Walden for six years. Although she is executive head of the Saffron Academy Trust, which includes three other local schools, students very much see her as 'their' headteacher and this is where she spends most of her time. Known for being both strategically astute and working closely with students and staff, she feels strongly that 'I don't want to be a faceless or nameless figure' – and students concur that she's not one to hide away in her office. 'As a headteacher, I believe you have a significant influence as a role model and in the tone you set and optimism that emanates from you,' she told us. We certainly found her cheeriness infectious, and she's fantastically easy to get on with too – down-to-earth, warm and amiable. 'What's not to like?' said one student, while others describe her as 'bouncy,' 'inspirational' and 'very visible.' Parents say she's 'friendly' and 'never makes you feel like it's a them-and-us experience. It's more like talking to a friend.' Make no mistake – she runs a tight ship, but she achieves it with more carrot than stick.

S

Lives locally with her husband and two teenage children, and interests include reading, theatre, musical concerts and playing tennis.

Academic matters: Rigorous setting across all core subjects, with 10 sets per year group. Pupils set for maths and English from year 7, for languages (all study French and German from year 7; Spanish from year 9) from year 8 and for sciences from year 9. Tracking is as thorough as it gets, with one parent reporting, 'The best thing about this process is how much they engage the students, with the result that they own their own targets, as opposed to having them imposed on them. It makes such a difference in them being determined to meet them.' A graders felt to be A* students get just as much attention as D students who are believed to be capable of Bs and every department is kept on its toes. 'It's pretty forensic,' says the head – and nobody slips through the net here, agree students.

GCSE results excellent. In 2016, 83 per cent got 5+ A*-C grades including English and maths and 42 per cent of grades were A*/A. Students choose their options (usually eight or nine subjects) in year 8 and then start their courses in year 9, rather than the usual year 10. Everyone takes English and English literature, and a very high proportion choose triple science, while other popular subjects include history and geography. Results strong across all subjects, with particularly outstanding results in humanities, DT, classics, languages (especially German), drama, PE and computer science. Unusually for a state school, County High (as everyone calls it) offers Latin to more able linguists at GCSE as well as A level. A few take BTecs in vocational subjects, such as hospitality and health and social care – but, says school, 'as part of a balanced academic curriculum.'

Sixth formers follow one of three routes – one for the most academically able and requiring at least five GCSEs at A*-B (including maths and English) and at least Bs in chosen A level subjects, another for those with five GCSEs at A*-C and a third for those with five GCSEs at D or above. Students choose from a vast array of subjects – all the usuals, while classical civilisation, media studies, philosophy, PE, psychology, criminology, film studies, music technology, government and politics and sociology among the less obvious. 'There's plenty of guidance about which ones to choose,' one student told us. A level results impressive, with 41 per cent A*/A grades and 75 per cent A*/B grades in 2016 – and the sixth-form is in the top one per cent in the country for A level value-added performance (ie progress made from GCSE to A level).

Dedicated teaching staff of 140, with good mix of ages. Strong links with Cambridge University's education faculty, and every subject department has at least one trainee teacher. There is a culture of professional development and staff are keen to enhance their skills, with many taking education masters degrees in their spare time. School leads a teaching group alliance too, which involves providing support for teaching across other schools, among other things. 'Bottom line is staff here are incredibly focused on reflecting on their own practice,' head told us. 'Teachers are always trying out innovative new techniques, and their passion for their subject really shines through,' one student told us, while others gave examples about how staff go 'above and beyond to make sure we keep up – whether that's in lunchtime, after school or even in holidays.' Communication with both students and parents is excellent – via email, student planners, yearly reports and parent evenings. 'It's not just seen as acceptable to contact teachers directly – it's encouraged,' one parent said. In fact, the only thing students could criticise about lessons here is the lack of use of phones – 'I know other schools incorporate them and I do think there's a place for it in today's teaching,' said one.

SEN team of 22 offers one-to-one support and in groups to pupils needing extra help. Additional challenges provided for gifted and talented. 'Our daughter, who has special needs, has gone from a quiet, shy girl to someone who puts her hand up in class and feels confident. I can't speak highly enough of the learning support team,' one parent told us, clearly delighted.

Games, options, the arts: The music department is the beating heart of this school, boasting two orchestras, a concert band, jazz band and a myriad of choirs and ensembles – all performing to an exceptionally high standard, with around six sell-out concerts a year. 'Students perform at various levels, but the result is astonishingly good – honestly, it's amazing to hear,' one parent told us. More than 400 pupils have individual music lessons in school and the multi-million pound Saffron Hall concert hall has become an acclaimed international venue with artists specialising in everything from classical music to jazz regularly visiting to play alongside the students, as well as providing music masterclasses. 'This term, the National Youth Jazz Orchestra played alongside our jazz band, with our students performing solos in their concerts – you can imagine how much our students learned,' the head enthused. The school has also launched a post-16 music academy, 'which attracts talented young musicians from the local area'.

Art is also strong, evidenced by the sheer volume of students' artwork displayed throughout the corridors – including everything from giant 3D creations to finely detailed textiles. Literally every art room was a hive of excited activity when we visited – from students getting messy with clay to youngsters experimenting with pastels for fine art. A large proportion of the students who take A level art (there are three to pick from) gain A*s.

Drama was also in full swing on our visit, with all three drama practising areas (the two school halls and blackened 'Pit') revealing some clear talent and a great deal of fun. Popular at both GCSE and A level. Film studies also an A level option, and the school runs the Gordos, an annual short film competition for budding Steven Spielbergs. School productions taken seriously (Twelfth Night and Goodnight Mr Tom were performed the year we visited – plus a bespoke opera written for the school entitled The Glass Knight, based on local legend). 'The productions here are very slick, both thanks to the hard work the students and staff put in and the professional-quality production facilities,' one parent told us.

Lots of clubs at lunchtime and after school – debating, sport, chess, film club, LGBT group etc – and trips galore, ranging from cultural visits to China and Africa to exchanges to France, Spain, Germany and Chicago. Strong emphasis on green issues and charity work, with sixth formers running an annual charities week every December, raising money for global, national and local causes chosen by them.

The array of silverware on display in the hi-tech sports centre is testament to the sporting prowess of this school, whose Saturday morning fixtures include frequent wins (to the head's delight) against independent schools. All students play sport up to 16 – mainly the usual suspects of rugby, hockey, netball, cricket, tennis and athletics. Outdoor facilities include huge fields, grass cricket square, pavilion, tennis courts and Astroturf – impressive for a secondary state school.

Background and atmosphere: Located on the edge of the pretty market town of Saffron Walden, in north east Essex. Extensive grounds, including own farm with cattle and sheep (and a highly successful farm club), and plenty of trees. In springtime pupils can see lambs gambolling in the paddock from the rugby and hockey pitches. Main building dates back to the 1950s with plenty of modern add-ons since – all kept in pristine condition. Classrooms mainly bright and airy, with lovely wide corridors, and stand-out facilities include Saffron Hall, a truly world-class venue, and the Hartley Learning Centre, an uber-modern library of the likes we've never seen. Pupils fiercely (and understandably) proud of the school, with the students we spoke to unable to think of a single facility they are left wanting.

Extremely strict on uniform ('I don't think there's any point in having one unless it's going to be worn properly,' says head) – blazers, black trousers and ties for boys and blazers and tartan kilts for girls, up to the age of 16. Sixth formers can wear what they like, within reason, and get their own block, with study centre (silence during lessons) and common room (the only disappointing room we came across – roomy, yes, but homely, no). Over half the students have school dinners in the cashless cafeteria or on the hoof from the other café – while the rest bring in packed lunches.

Pastoral care, well-being and discipline: 'One of the things that has astonished us about this school is the quality of the pastoral provision,' was reflective of several parent comments we heard. 'You're never short of someone to talk to if you have a problem here, either academically or around well-being – and no matter how small it is,' a student concurred. Each year group divided into 10 tutor groups and children stay with the same tutor up to GCSEs. And as well as their tutors and heads of year ('both of whom really get to know you,' say students), youngsters can talk to one of the school's full-time counsellors, who are trained in areas including cognitive behaviour therapy. Students say it's easy to settle in too – thanks to a special induction programme for newbies, maps and mentoring from older students. Bullying rare and quickly nipped in the bud, with preventive work including a recent focus on celebrating student 'acts of kindness.' 'We wanted more emphasis on the positive, less on the negative,' explains the head – there's that carrot again.

Instead of having a head boy and head girl, there's a team of 10 head students – each one tasked with an area such as fundraising or student council. Year 11s are appointed prefects and encouraged to mentor year 7s and 8s. School also keen on 'student voice,' which is split into three areas (green voice team, well-being team and teaching and learning team). Recent successes include a campaign for a better outdoor eating area and improving the way electricity is used in the school.

Not the kind of school with traditional rules, not least because the head dislikes both words. 'I prefer "code of conduct" because I think it encourages self-discipline, and I don't think a lot of people know what "traditional" really means in this context. So I'd say instead that we have high expectations around good manners, as well as about being positive and community minded,' she says. It clearly works because run amuck these students do not, with exemplary behaviour throughout. Many students go through the entire school without a detention, and there tend to be less than handful of fixed term exclusions each year, with no permanent exclusions at all under current headship. Drugs, smoking or alcohol are all met with zero tolerance (and no excuses), but again there have been no problems for years. 'We recently delved deep into year 10s' behaviour in class and given that age 14 can be the most colourful of the teenage years and that some of our students have complex needs, we were delighted to find that not one student was off-task in any lesson,' says head.

Pupils and parents: Pupils come from a mix of rural and urban backgrounds, with more than ever from Saffron Walden itself since the town's expansion, including extensive new housing. Many walk or bike in, while others travel by bus from surrounding villages. Ethnicity reflective of the area, with a whopping 88 per cent of families white British – and the majority are middle-class, with only a small proportion from disadvantaged families. Parents and pupils feel a lucky lot. 'Whenever I meet a parent, the first thing they say is how delighted they are to have a child at the school – in fact, even when they are objecting to something, that's their opening gambit,' says the head. Students, meanwhile, are engaged, motivated learners – and we were struck by their high aspirations and articulate and engaging conversation. 'They're a joy to teach,' smiles the head. Ex-pupil Ben Maher was part of the gold medal winning GB show jumping team in the 2012 Olympics and also rode at Rio 2016.

Entrance: Heavily over-subscribed, with over 600 parents fighting for 290 year 7 places. Siblings get priority, followed by residents of 12 listed parishes. Further three criteria, but the vast majority of places are offered on the first two, so if you don't live in catchment, forget it. No feeder primary schools as such – that's not how Essex entry criteria works. More than three-quarters stay on for sixth form, when they are joined by 100 newcomers a year, making for a mammoth 630-strong sixth-form, which many locals see as a kind of sixth-form college in its own right – and a popular one at that, with many more applications than places. 'We get a lot of children who don't get a year 7 place going off to other local state schools and independent schools, then coming back to reapply to do their A levels here,' says head.

Exit: About a quarter leave after GCSEs, mainly to do vocational courses or apprenticeships at local colleges including Hills Road Sixth Form College and Harlow College. 'We don't lose many who want to study academically,' says the head. Around 85 per cent of sixth formers go on to higher education; the rest are 'supported by the school with their progression into employment or other educational opportunities'. Six to Oxbridge in 2016, others mainly to Russell Group universities including Durham, Bristol and Exeter, and five to study medicine or veterinary science. Students get loads of one-to-one help to guide them through the complex UCAS maze and parents and pupils alike rave about the Oxbridge preparation course. 'You hear reports that state schools don't prepare kids for Oxbridge – well, this one does. They do everything imaginable to help them,' one parent told us. The year we visited, 40 had applied to Oxbridge for 2017, 35 of whom had secured interviews. Popular courses include sciences, classics, history, English, law, psychology and medicine.

Remarks: A vibrant, fast-moving local school of outstanding quality, with innovation in teaching and great facilities. It buzzes with activity from dawn till dusk – ideal for children who want to work hard and play hard. Even though it's a big place (with all the advantages of the breadth of opportunity that brings), students say it feels small, thanks to every child being treated as an individual. If anywhere will make a high achiever of your child without undue pressure, this is it.

St Albans Girls' School

Sandridgebury Lane, St Albans, Hertfordshire AL3 6DB

Pupils: 1,215 • Ages: 11–18 • Sixth form: 250 (including 7 boys)

Tel: 01727 853134
Email: admin@stags.herts.sch.uk
Website: www.stags.herts.sch.uk

S

Headteacher: Since 2010, Mrs Margaret Chapman BSc, NPQH (40s). Educated at the University of Wales, Aberystwyth before teaching geography, geology and ICT and ultimately becoming deputy head at Mill Hill County High School. Moved as deputy head to The Priory School, Hitchin. Parents say she's 'business like, but with a sense of humour,' pupils 'strict, but in a good way,' and staff describe her as 'highly driven,' saying she has infected them with her determination to 'never stand still.' A definite contender for hardest working head award, should one exist, she can often be tracked down to her office at 9pm. Lives locally with husband and teenage children, a daughter at Leeds University and a son at Verulam School. A geologist at heart, is the proud owner of a large rock collection and loves the outdoors, particularly the sea.

Indefatigable on the subject of STAGS, brimming with opinions on all things educational and extremely proud of the changes she has made since her appointment. Sets high standards of behaviour and work for staff and pupils alike: 'if you follow it through and keep on message you get the right result.' Believes in teaching staff taking ownership of student pastoral care rather than just academic success and has aimed to empower all members of the school community – including support staff – to create a dynamic, democratic environment. 'Highly energetic,' according to parents, holds a monthly surgery for them to keep channels of communication open on subjects from academic progress to frustrating behaviour at home. Keeps her hand in teaching A level economics and geography to year 8. Focused on turning out 'articulate and confident women who are ready for society and the world of work.'

Academic matters: Robust results, particularly given school's non-selective intake and broad range of abilities. In 2016, 45 per cent A*/A grades at GCSE. Smallish take-up of EPQ but good results.

Form groups of 28-29 girls, with some GCSE classes as small as 15 and up to six sets for most popular A levels to keep groups as tight as possible. Girls benefit from a bespoke learning progamme, enabling them to take between eight and 13 GCSEs depending on ability. For those who struggle with the challenges of academia, the school offers specialised programmes to help with life skills and build self-esteem and confidence. Consortium and partnership arrangements with other local schools and colleges enables a few girls to take vocational courses such as hair and beauty from year 10 during school hours.

Quality not quantity is the order of the day in languages, with French and Spanish on offer from year 7. Languages and history popular at GCSE with a good showing in sciences and maths for A level. Dance, media studies, food technology and textiles available for those looking for diversity in their GCSE choices. Some 'ologies' very popular at A level, as are government and politics, media studies and English lit. In 2016, 27 per cent A*/A and 60 per cent A*-B grades. Setting from year 7 in maths and languages, with sciences and English streamed from year 9 and languages from year 10.

VLE offering expanded from a formerly piecemeal approach to having a whole school focus, 'aiming to create a seamless link between home and school learning,' says head. School keen to use it to encourage greater parent engagement too and 'flipped' lessons being trialled, where pupils take online lesson at home, followed by discussion in classroom time.

SEN all in a day's work for the 12 per cent of school requiring additional help, with policy of 'inclusion' into classrooms. Four full-time SENCo teaching assistants cover one-to-one classroom support – head considers this 'an area of outstanding provision.' School well equipped to deal with its significant proportion (around 20 per cent) of EAL requirements – the product of a 'huge array of backgrounds' from around 60 feeder primary schools – and ensure that it remains a language issue rather than a barrier to academic achievement. Strong gifted and talented programme touches 22 per cent of pupils, with all staff now required to plan enrichment exercises into lessons to benefit everyone, encouraging them to think creatively and lead, preventing a 'more of the same' approach for bright sparks. Mutterings from parents that reporting system is 'a bit impersonal,' but most concede that it is 'getting better.'

Games, options, the arts: Head adamant that pupils 'don't miss opportunities to develop talent and roundedness,' and school is well equipped for sporting excellence, with nine tennis courts, three hockey pitches, a cricket square, athletics track, outdoor pool (heated to tropical temperature) and purpose built sports hall complete with multi-gym for staff and pupil use. STAGS families can buy summer membership to use pool in evenings and weekends for the princely sum of £40 and many do, although the odd parent grumbles it's not used enough for timetabled swimming lessons.

Teams successful at district, county and national level (packed trophy cabinets adorn the school entrance), although we only noticed fixture lists for A and B teams. Particular strengths in swimming and athletics, with year 7 recently being crowned district football champions and the addition of a new Astroturf bound to help secure this specialism. Girls' accolades out of school also celebrated, with press coverage of Olympian alumni and a current national judo champion proudly festooning the reception area.

Dance and gymnastics very popular and school has recently renovated a mobile unit to accommodate enthusiasts in these areas. Not the most appealing dance studio we've seen but head says girls 'really appreciate it' and the quality of the biennial production, part choreographed by the girls, is 'exceptional,' say parents. School is 'a hotbed of creativity,' according to staff, with drama and music both 'excellent' and around 16 per cent of girls taking individual music lessons in school. Two well-used (and rather well-worn) drama studios, with girls constantly preparing for performances, often transporting their talents to competitions and events such as the Shakespeare Schools Festival. Large, inspiring art department with an impressive and diverse array of work on show, to a notably high standard, throughout the school.

Good range of extracurricular from year 7 up, ranging from the intriguingly named Spitfire and Battle of Britain club, to more predictable drama, textiles and sports activities, with girls rewarded for regular attendance and parents happy that they are 'actively encouraged to do at least one.' After school academic support in the form of spelling, reading and English clubs for younger girls, with the likes of history 'stretch those brains' seminars for A level students. D of E taken very seriously as a means of gearing up to higher education and broadening horizons. Trips and tours galore, from London Fashion Week to the Himalayas. Charity work is 'an enormous focus' for the girls, says the school; 'they really get their teeth into it,' raising on average £18,000 each year for their selected chosen charities.

Background and atmosphere: Founded in 1920 as a girls' grammar, STAGS shrugged off its selective mantle some time ago in favour of status as a business and enterprise college. Occupying a ubiquitous low level 1960s warren of buildings in the north of the city, the uninspiring fabric of the school belies the fact that behind its façade lies a buzzing hub of enthusiastic, independent learners turning out commendable academic results. These, by the way, are consistently on the up with girls also benefiting from a culture which helps them develop employment skills through its 'leadership passport', a bespoke programme that from year 7 instils in them the skills they need to be successful in the world of work.

Few whistles and bells where facilities are concerned but those that matter are functional and well-equipped. Sixth form centre is a star attraction, with a bright (and unusually tidy) common room and two large study rooms; one unsupervised (chatting allowed) and one for silent study with a member of staff on duty. The well-stocked, fully computerised library provides more space for quiet study and handy types should be impressed by the superbly equipped DT lab. Seven purpose built ICT suites benefit from a rolling renewal programme, with Wifi across the school.

A rolling technology upgrade programme has heralded the arrival of iPads and iMacs in the new Innovation Centre to allow girls to access high level technology, not just in the context of ICT but across all subjects. This is all part of the school's reshaping of its strategic vision – to bring a 21st century learning experience to its pupils, not just through IT but also through awareness of relevant developments in the employment market. With its state maintained budgets, the school has to 'tread carefully' with expenditure and technological improvements must 'enhance learning rather than distract pupils,' says head.

Grounds and buildings generally in fine fettle (staff are militant about tidiness and order), with thoughtful touches such as covered picnic areas and plenty of outdoor seating, to ensure the girls have somewhere to loll during break times. Dining room spotless and ruthlessly efficient, with fingerprint technology payment scheme, and a 'snack shack' for those preferring to grab something on the hoof.

Staff 'not allowed to sit still,' according to one. Strong measures in place to ensure a 'critical mass of outstanding teaching,' ranging from staff 'coaching triads', enabling teachers to share good practice, to personal development programmes including staff book groups. About 20 per cent of teachers are male, lending a healthy dose of testosterone to the school.

Pastoral care, well-being and discipline: Directors of learning for each year group ensure that girls are kept on track academically, socially and emotionally. Hugely successful house system, with seven houses named after influential women. Good work and behaviour rewarded with house points, with girls working hard to keep 'consequences' (that's minus marks in old money) to a minimum for the greater good of their housemates. Heaps of events to build house spirit, from competitions, plays and challenges to a plethora of fundraising efforts, with each house choosing its own charity – almost daily cake sales attack the staff's waistlines with ruthless efficiency. Leadership is a 'big deal' here, says head, with girls offered opportunities to show their metal at all stages; there are two heads of house per year group from year 7, captains of everything, from games to charities and over 100 year 10s working towards their bronze Duke of Edinburgh award.

A team of empathetic year 12 and 13 girls run a 'hear 4 u' group to mentor younger pupils through school related personal or academic problems, an initiative that won the school a Diana anti-bullying award. Trained by the school counsellor, they run frequent drop-in clinics and have a dedicated email address for those too shy to approach them directly. Anti-bullying ambassadors in each year group to keep awareness up: 'the more you know about it, the more resilient you become,' says head. Alcohol, drugs and smoking are 'not an issue', with staff describing the girls' behaviour as 'generally immaculate'. Exclusions extremely rare but staff ensure an 'on the table' conversation before offenders return, offering them holistic support and guidance to make sure they feel part of the school community again.

Pupils and parents: Fresh faced, pony-tailed and immaculately turned out pupils more akin to convent girls than those from a large comprehensive move calmly around the corridors. School in general has the feel of a traditional grammar about it, perhaps a legacy of its history, more likely rigorous standards put in place by current head. Deputy head says he has 'never come across a more focused cohort of students'. A few boys filter into year 12, looking for 'an enhanced educational offering', and integrate well with the girls according to staff.

Majority from St Albans and surrounding towns, with just a few from further afield. Broad socio-demographic, ranging from affluent families choosing STAGS over fee-paying alternatives to less well-off but aspirational families, seeking a traditional yet forward thinking education for their girls. Head says she is happy – and has been known – to knock on doors to engage the few parents who are 'scared to aspire.' About eight per cent qualify for free school meals but staff say they are 'hard to spot' even in this middle class setting. STAGS girls are described by teachers as 'well presented, serious about their studies and very pro school.' About 27 per cent from ethnic minorities.

Regular PTA meetings with the school's senior team ensure parental voices are heard and that, in line with the ethos of the school, things keep moving forward. This is replicated by the 'vociferous' pupils via the student leadership team ('the student voice is huge,' say staff), giving the impression of real partnership between school and its community.

Entrance: Parents 'move heaven and earth' (not to mention house) to get into STAGS and it is non-selective, with admissions still administered by the local authority despite academy status, and no plans to change this. Majority join at 11 from a wide range of local primary schools, although some from as far afield as Borehamwood and Hitchin. Any admissions post year 7 are dealt with by lottery if there is more than one applicant for the place. Extra places available in year 12, with applicants required to achieve a minimum of 5 grades A*-C at GCSE and B grades or higher in their chose A level subjects.

Exit: Around 30 per cent leave at 16 as mixed gender environments beckon, or to pursue more vocational courses, with the odd one seeking out subjects, such as classics, not on offer at STAGS. Majority (about 90 per cent) leaving at the end of year 13 go straight on to higher education, with one to Cambridge in 2016 (psychological and behavioural sciences) and others to eg law at Brunel, film and TV studies at Nottingham, maths at Warwick and veterinary physiotherapy at Writtle College. Huge amount of advice given to guide girls down right paths right from year 7, from frequent work experience opportunities to Oxbridge days in year 10. Parents say school 'has got it all covered.'

Money matters: State maintained. PTA is 'very involved – and then some', says head, raising around £40,000 a year for the school with various events. Funds have significantly enhanced the sixth form centre, dining hall and the next target for these formidable parents is the library. Around 10 per cent of parents make a voluntary contribution to bolster coffers towards rolling improvement programme.

Remarks: Whether your daughter wants to sing, dance or swot her way through school, there's something for everyone from the top of the academic pile down. In the words of the head, 'everyone can shine at STAGS.'

St Albans High School for Girls

S

Townsend Avenue, St Albans, Hertfordshire AL1 3SJ

Pupils: 903 • Ages: 4–18 • Sixth form: 160 • C of E

Fees: £13,215 – £16,800 pa

Tel: 01727 853800
Email: admissions@stahs.org.uk
Website: www.stahs.org.uk

Headmistress: Since 2014, Mrs Jenny Brown, previously director of senior school (head of sixth) at St Paul's Girls. English degree from Oxford; spent two years in publishing but found it 'a pretty soulless, thankless experience'; the move into English teaching at Cranleigh 'felt like coming home'. To Highgate, South Hampstead High and then Channing, as head of English. Lives in north London with her playwright husband and two teenage children; the house has a distinctly literary flavour. Feels that 'results matter, but ideas matter much more'; she wants to lead a school full of girls with 'broad horizons and broad shoulders' who can carve their way in life with charm, wit and intellectual confidence.

Clearly happy in meetings: she sits on the advisory board of the New College of the Humanities, the membership committee of HMC and professional development committee of the GSA. Any leisure hours are full of John Donne, George Eliot, Jane Austen, editing her husband's plays, swimming in very cold water and enjoying the company of her two teenaged children.

One of what is probably the GSG's first set of identical twin heads: her sister, Jane Lunnon, took over as head of Wimbledon High in September 2014.

Head of prep school: Since September 2015, Mrs Judy Rowe BEd. Educated at North London Collegiate School and Durham University. Taught in Zambia and South Africa and was previously head of Lower School at Belmont, Mill Hill Preparatory School.

Academic matters: Prep school head says the school covers much of the national curriculum but goes 'broader and deeper.' Teachers are highly committed and keen on using new technologies, encouraging girls to develop thinking skills, independent learning and skills for life. Girls write their own blogs, do lots of video conferencing with museums and galleries and the school has its own carefully managed Twitter account to keep parents and locals up to date with what's going on. Parents say the school sets high standards –'but if anyone is struggling, they are on it.' 'The emphasis is very much on the individual,' a mother says. 'Yes, it's very academic but the school prepares them very well and it's a very happy school. The girls are very motivated and thrilled to be there.'

French is taught from reception, with extracurricular clubs for Italian, Spanish, Mandarin, Japanese and Latin. As head points out: 'We are already selective and the last thing we want is for a child to feel they aren't doing well.' Science, ICT, French, Mandarin, music and PE are all taught by subject specialists. Science is very hands-on – new science lab, lots of practical experiments and school is one of the few preps to take part in The Big Bang, a national event for schools celebrating science, technology, engineering and maths. All girls get an hour of ICT a week – everything from creating postcards and Viking fact sheets to filming in the grounds.

Class sizes range from 20 in reception to 24 in years 3 to 6. All girls are screened for literacy difficulties at the start of year 3; one-to-one lessons for specific learning needs such dyslexia and dyspraxia are offered.

Senior school prides itself on achieving stellar results in 'a very caring environment.' Results are certainly impressive. Seventy-three per cent A*/A grades at A level in 2016. Twenty-two subjects on offer at A level – all the usual, plus others like classical civilisation, drama and theatre studies, economics, food technology, government and politics, PE and product design. Sixth form curriculum also includes a range of independent study programmes, courses and lectures.

At GCSE in 2016, 92 per cent A*/A grades. Double and triple science on offer and all girls take at least one language (French, German or Spanish). IGCSEs taken in all core subjects, as well as in history and modern foreign languages. No early exams these days – 'we want the girls to have time to extend and enrich themselves,' says the deputy head. Most pupils take a creative GCSE, whether it's textiles, art, DT, drama or music.

All girls are screened for literacy difficulties at the start of year 7. One-to-one 'additional curricular education' lessons (ACE for short) for specific learning needs like dyslexia and dyspraxia available at an additional charge. Currently 46 girls with SEND. Class sizes of up to 24 in years 7 to 9, average of 18 in years 10 and 11 and maximum of 16 in sixth form, though in practice often smaller.

Lots of guidance given when it comes to university choices, UCAS forms, personal statements and work placements. Girls are encouraged to use the careers room (which has a vivid pink wall and scores of university guides and resources) from an early age.

School recently introduced a two-week timetable (five one-hour lessons a day) and girls get five minutes to move from one lesson to the next. The teaching we saw was engaging and interactive, from a year 11 Spanish class on pronouns to a year 8 geography class where the girls had written and recorded their own songs about global warming. 'We try and be as innovative as we can,' the enthusiastic head of geography told us. Girls say that the teaching is top notch and teachers are hugely supportive. 'If I hadn't been at this school I would never have come out with A*s and As at GCSE,' a sixth former told us. 'This school makes you want to do well. You learn how to revise and you feel really well prepared.'

Games, options, the arts: Even though the games pitches are a five to 10-minute walk away, sport is big here, with six PE staff and teams trailing clouds of glory in netball, lacrosse, swimming, gym – the whole gamut really. Dynamic head of PE and sport says that in a highly academic environment 'it's important for the girls to let off a bit of steam' and girls jump at the chance to take part in every sport under the sun. Facilities also include new sports pavilion, dance studio, netball courts, lacrosse pitches and 25m swimming pool. Unlike some schools, sixth formers carry on with sport, though they can opt for activities like keep fit and yoga instead of traditional sports if they prefer. 'We try and get girls to find something they like,' says head of PE. 'It's brilliant to see them enjoying sport so much.' Matches (often four teams per year group) virtually every night of the week, plus Saturdays too. Sports hall boasts cabinets bulging with silverware and wall of fame highlighting girls' very varied sporting triumphs. When we visited these included an England U19 netball and lacrosse player, a British dressage rider and a national level Irish dancer. Sport is an important part of the prep school curriculum too, with girls doing netball, football, lacrosse, gym, dance and athletics. A sailing duo recently came fifth in the national IAPS championships. All year groups swim for a term, using the senior school's pool.

Drama is a key activity, whether it's year 13s studying political theatre in an A level class or everyone throwing themselves into the annual house drama competition. The houses are given a theme (last year's was 'horrors' so Sweeney Todd and Dracula featured heavily) and girls must choose a play, adapt it, choose a cast and direct it. Jubilee Hall, the school's new theatre space, can accommodate 350 and is used for shows, concerts and public exams (it has retractable seating). Music impressive, with around 520 instrumental lessons a week across the prep and senior schools. A host of choirs (chamber to gospel), bands and four orchestras.

Light and airy art studios (one specifically for A level students, with electric windows, northern light and huge ceilings). Lots of work on display, including a set of acrylic sheets sculpted into flowers by a former A level art student and worthy of a top London gallery. 'She was so prolific that she worked her way along the corridor, filling up every inch of space,' the girls told us. Art is a delight in the prep school. Pictures on display everywhere – including vibrant, multi-coloured artwork inspired by Andy Warhol's Campbell's Soup Cans on the walls of the head's office. 'They're photocopies, so the children can take their originals home,' she says thoughtfully. Some innovative work in DT, with reception girls designing their own flip-flops and making their own miniature boats to race.

Sixth formers get the chance to do Young Enterprise, D of E and Model United Nations and also have an enrichment programme – including AS critical thinking, GCSE Italian or astronomy and the Extended Project Qualification (EPQ). Recent trips to China, Nepal, Iceland and Washington.

Background and atmosphere: Founded in 1889, the school moved from its original location to its current site half a mile from the city centre in 1908. It maintains close links with the diocese of St Albans through the bishop and the dean. Locals call it the High School to distinguish it from St Albans Girls' School.

School entrance looks traditional, with wooden floors and long corridors, but behind the front façade tradition gives way to modernity, with new, bright reception area, glass panelled meeting room with student artwork on the walls, new performing arts centre and swish art and technology block.

Pupils aged 11 to 16 wear smart uniform of striped navy blazers, skirts and blouses. Sixth formers are allowed to wear their own clothes, just so long as they are 'appropriate.' Jeans allowed but 'no shoulders, no shorts,' no wildly coloured hair and no heavy make-up. On formal occasions, such as for the carol service and founder's day (when girls walk through St Albans to the abbey), sixth formers wear 'official navy' – smart blouse, skirt and school blazer. Sixth form block has its own library, with copies of all A level books, newspapers and an eclectic selection of magazines (everything from History Today to Marie Claire), plus kitchen and common room. When we visited during morning break the place was festooned with balloons, party poppers and birthday cake. 'We go overboard for 18th birthdays,' laughed our sixth form guide. She also confided, 'I'm dreading leaving. I'm going to miss my teachers.' Praise indeed.

Main school library has more than 16,000 resources and is well used. Librarian has introduced the 'whole school read,' which involves buying more than 600 copies of the same book, asking the girls to read it and then posting their reviews on the school's VLE. The most recent choice, Wonder by RJ Palacio, got the firm thumbs-up.

Most girls have school dinners (a specially-themed pirate menu on the day we visited) and tuck shop serves up flapjacks, sandwiches and cheese on toast at break. The school even has its own Starbucks (sixth formers can use it any time, year 11 at specified times and anyone after school).

Prep school is located in the pretty village of Wheathampstead, a four-mile drive through country lanes from its St Albans-based big sister. Moved to its current home (former HQ of Polaroid UK) in 2003 and the place has since been transformed into a lively prep, complete with 18 glorious acres, extensive woods, adventure playgrounds, outdoor learning classroom and a meadow. Lots of emphasis on outdoor activities (younger girls keep wellies at the ready in school).

Pastoral care, well-being and discipline: 'The girls have an inbuilt sense of how to behave towards each other,' says the deputy head and pupils have written their own eight-point code of conduct, including tenets like treating others 'as we would like to be treated ourselves' and giving 'encouragement and support in times of success and disappointment.' New school mission of fostering scholarship and integrity, developing a lifelong love of learning and respect for others.

Atmosphere is focused and busy, with many commenting on the good rapport between staff and pupils. 'The school is very upbeat,' a mother told us. 'They encourage the girls to work hard and they are brilliant at developing the girls' self confidence.' House system is integral to the school. All girls belong to one of four houses – Julian, Mandeville, Paris or Verulam – and housemistresses play key role in pastoral care. Raft of school officers and house officers all voted in by girls and staff (including head girl, three deputies and games captain). School takes a lot of care in settling new year 7s in. No homework for first two weeks and year 8 pupils act as buddies to new girls, writing them a letter of welcome in the summer holidays before they start.

Prep has same house system as the senior school, with girls learning to work as part of a team and develop leadership skills right from the start. Form captains and vice captains from year 3 and year 6 girls take on house responsibilities. The environment is nurturing and caring, with the oldest pupils setting up games for the youngest and helping them to make friends. Effective buddy system and buddy families. Like the senior school, the prep sets great store by the three aims – scholarship, adventure and integrity.

Sixth formers get more freedom. They still have to be in school first thing, even if they have don't have a lesson during first period, but are allowed to go home once they have finished in the afternoons.

Pupils and parents: Many girls live in St Albans but others travel from as far afield as Luton and Potters Bar to London suburbs like Winchmore Hill and Mill Hill. Parents admire the school's ethos. 'The teachers are very good at instilling the importance of learning and of the girls getting their heads down and getting on with it,' one mother told us. 'But it's not all about results. There are so many extracurricular activities, for girls of all abilities too.'

The girls are smiley, polite and brimming with enthusiasm, without being in the least bit arrogant or showy. They leap to their feet when visitors enter the class and when teachers ask questions a dozen eager hands shoot into the air. 'I love my school so much,' a year 6 girl told us, and her friends all concurred. 'They seem to teach the girls to want to learn,' an impressed mother told us.

Well-known old girls include the late Dame Anna Neagle, TV weather presenter Isobel Lang and Selfridges MD Anne Pitcher.

Entrance: Academically selective. Main prep school entry points are 4 and 7 but vacancies occasionally crop up in other years. For entry into reception girls come in for an informal 90-minute multi-activity session. Older girls have assessments in English, maths and reasoning.

Senior school heavily oversubscribed (up to 300 applicants for the 96 year 7 places available each year). Girls selected by means of school's own English and maths exams, group interview and school report. Up to half the year 7 entry comes from school's own prep, four miles down the road at Wheathampstead. Others arrive from local state primaries and preps. New sixth form entrants need at least five A*/A at GCSE (regardless of whether they are already at the school or not).

Exit: Vast majority progress from the prep to the senior school, although the occasional one or two opt for boarding or local state schools. Discussion with parents if staff feel senior school may not be the right school for their daughter and families are helped to explore suitable alternatives.

A handful (some 22 per cent) leave at 16, primarily for boarding, co-ed schools or simply a change of scene. At 18 all progress to higher education. Ten to Oxbridge in 2016, plus five medics and two vets; popular destinations including Leeds, Bristol, Durham, Exeter and Nottingham.

Money matters: School offers a number of means-tested bursaries (up to 100 per cent). There are also academic and music scholarships from year 7 and academic, art/DT, PE and drama scholarships for sixth formers.

Remarks: A happy and high achieving school that turns out confident, down-to-earth pupils who feel nurtured, supported and well prepared for university and beyond. For girls with ambition it could be just the ticket.

S

St Albans School

Abbey Gateway, St Albans, Hertfordshire AL3 4HB

Pupils: 844 • Ages: 11-19 • Sixth form: 303 (including 79 girls)

Fees: £17,238 pa

Tel: 01727 855521
Email: hm@st-albans-school.org.uk
Website: www.st-albans.herts.sch.uk

Headteacher: Since September 2014, Jonathan Gillespie, previously head of Lancing College for eight years. Read modern and mediaeval languages and did a PGCE at Cambridge; taught at Highgate School and Fettes College before joining Lancing. Doesn't teach pupils on timetabled basis ('the demands of a head mean I couldn't give it my all'), but gets stuck into Oxbridge trial interviews, assemblies, giving out weekly commendations etc. A more consultative leader than his predecessor (brought in the first parental questionnaire the school has ever seen), but believes in 'evolution not revolution' in terms of making changes. Pupils describe him as 'approachable' and say that whilst no pupil dared to step out of line with his predecessor, 'the reason you don't step out of line with Mr Gillespie is because you don't want to let him down.' We found him amiable, chatty and excitable, but also traditional and authoritative. Keen sports coach, especially hockey (he umpires at national level), and has been involved in CCF. Other interests include hill walking and golf, and he celebrates family's Scottish roots by playing the highland bagpipes. Married to Caroline, former civil servant, with whom they have two sons, one at university and one in sc hool.

Academic matters: In 2016, 77 per cent of GCSE grades A*/A, placing the school in upper echelons of league tables with no weaknesses at either GCSE or A level. Home grown sixth formers average an impressive points score equivalent of nine A*s at GCSE. Top performing subjects are English, maths, history, music, design technology, sciences and classics. IGCSEs in maths, sciences, languages, history, music and English. In 2016, 66 per cent of A levels were graded A*/A. Maths popular and successful, with strong showings in sciences, art, classics, geography, drama, economics, DT, RS, history, ancient history and English. Languages less popular but interest increasing. French, German and Latin are on an equal footing in year 7; top sets take French in year 10 and international O level in year 11. Setting from second term in the first year in maths and from the start of year 9 in other core subjects, which pupils are comfortable with. 'A bottom set here is still well above average,' says head.

Many take an extended project qualification (EPQ) in the lower sixth, which facilitates independent study and research. 'We've rejigged it so that pupils crack on with it as quickly as possible, then use it as part of their university application,' says head. Typical titles include 'Is the creation of Chimeras ethical?' and 'Was Cicero as influential an orator as he thought?'

Traditional, didactic lessons, although plenty of room for interaction and work in small groups, as well as creative ways of learning, with proof of this adorning many of the school corridors (one exceptionally well presented science display was complete with flashing lights). 'My son comes home itching to research more about the subjects he's taught,' said one parent. Drop-in subject clinics at GCSE and A level for most subjects at least once a week. Teaching staff highly praised, with the latest inspection report noting that they are an 'inspirational force in and beyond the classroom.' 'You can email them at any time and they get back to you promptly,' said one parent. Homework taken seriously, with at least one hour a night in first form, moving up to two hours a day in sixth-form. 'It doesn't feel like an add-on, though, but an integral part of everything they teach,' said a parent.

Tablets (not iPads) used in some lessons, although by no means embedded into the curriculum. No room for complacency or coasting. 'There's a strong expectation that you do your best and nothing less,' one pupil told us. 'Average, borderline or overly-tutored children would struggle, as would children who only feel comfortable when they get things right,' added a parent. 'Teaching is all about constantly challenging the children, who have to be prepared to learn through failing sometimes.'

Not the best place for heavyweight SEN, but the learning support unit (which is located centre school) employs good, competent staff (an extra one just appointed when we visited, allowing for more individual help) who cheerfully and successfully handle bright pupils with processing or other difficulties. 'Our admissions process is good at finding those who will thrive here, so it's generally a smooth process getting them the help they need once they join,' says the head. Parents concur. 'We knew our son was dyslexic, and whilst it was not really recognised by his primary school, this school picked it up in a single test at the application stage and has been fantastic in ensuring he gets all the support he needs now he's a pupil, including special lessons in the school day.' Mostly dyslexia, dyspraxia and Asperger's, and although relatively few enter with SEN, regular monitoring usually means that the one or two per cent reach four or five per cent by third form. Speaks of the 'gift of dyslexia' and how it enables the world to be accessed in a different way. Learning support also organises mentoring for those struggling to maximise their potential, as well as help around resilience, relieving stress, facilitating study skills etc.

Careers guidance starts in the fourth year, peaking in the sixth form. Similarly detailed help with university applications in sixth form, with any pupil aiming for Oxbridge or any of medicine, dentistry or veterinary science given no shortage of special assistance. 'This starts early and is incredibly detailed and individual,' said one parent. But the rarefied approach to academia here means careers are not regularly discussed in the classroom. 'We are not providing a vocational education,' says head. 'Our view is that the more academic our pupils are, the stronger they perform at university and the more doors will open for them. In any case, many pupils will wind up doing jobs that haven't even been invented yet.'

Games, options, the arts: Sport has such a strong reputation here that there's a myth that non-sporty types won't get on. Pupils, parents and the school assure us this isn't the case, with one pupil telling us, 'Everyone has to take part in sport because it keeps you fit and healthy, but there's no ethos of "You will enjoy sport, no matter what!"'

Excels in rugby (D teams in most year groups), hockey, cricket and cross-country for boys and netball, lacrosse and tennis for girls. International reputation in cross-country. Other major games also on offer, along with sailing, squash, badminton, aerobics, golf, athletics, climbing and table tennis. School owns a 400 acre farm – Woollams – about a 10 minute drive away, with 75 acres dedicated to world-class, jaw-droppingly impressive pitches (including Astroturf) and courts, plus a spacious and modern pavilion, where pupils who do commit to sport are expected to spend most Saturdays. These dazzling outdoor facilities are complemented by a state-of-the-art sports centre on site, with good-sized climbing wall, fitness centre, dance studio, sports hall, gym, swimming pool (where sixth-formers can train to be lifeguards and then get a job at the pool in the summer) and even an endless pool with motion-capture technology to analyse style, strength, conditioning etc (the sports hall also has cameras throughout for analysis of sports play).

Outstanding coaching, and national and international sporting honours, plus numerous school representatives in county teams, across many sports. In the English Schools AA national cross-country championships, half the county senior team come from St Albans and the intermediate team are current national champions. School are 10 times winners of the King Henry VIII relays and recently notched up fourth place in the world cross-country championships. But whilst the school enjoys its winning, head insists this is not at all costs and fixture list constructed to ensure a balance of easier and more challenging matches.

Music on the up, with 185 lessons taught by peripatetic teachers every week and many pupils play to a very high standard. Now a Steinway school, it's no wonder that piano is increasingly popular. Inclusive school choir (which includes some teachers) performs at the abbey twice a week, and there are plenty of bands, ranging from jazz to rock. Drama collaborates with music department for some impressive whole school performances, whilst the drama department (located opposite the school) puts on regular smaller plays. Art and DT boast some real talent, with excellent facilities to fuel passions, although some pupils express disappointment that there is no food technology. Outdoor team-work fostered through robust and popular CCF and D of E, who work in a spirit of camaraderie and cooperation not competition. Army and air options available, though parents say RAF wing plays second fiddle to Coldstream Guards – despite the former offering opportunities to take off and fly!

Extracurricular clubs mean the school day is regularly stretched beyond the official 8.35am-4pm. 'There are so many clubs and everyone feels really encouraged to try them out,' said a pupil. 'Special transport is provided, so nobody misses out and they often lay on food for them,' added a parent. Trips could hardly be more diverse, including to Pen Arthur, a rugged farmhouse in rural Wales, which is owned by the school and used for various activities and field work. Triennial charity visits to an orphanage in Tanzania (one of many charitable ventures), whilst sporting trips to the likes of Sri Lanka (cricket) and southern hemisphere (rugby). 'You name somewhere, we'll go,' says a smiling head, although he quickly adds he's aware of potentially mounting costs for parents and so they're always optional and plenty within the UK.

Background and atmosphere: There's a real buzz here, with a purposeful, dynamic and friendly vibe, where students are hungry to learn but don't take themselves too seriously. Originally founded in 948, this is one of the oldest extant schools in the country (so ancient that the first pupils did not speak English) and this sense of history is a great source of pride to pupils. Adjacent to the abbey, the school has some extraordinary rooms and nooks with gothic windows and yard-thick walls. One such is home to the school's small museum. In contrast, there's the light, contemporary Aquis Court building (former home to KPMG), which the school has acquired and uses for art, with five studios including ceramics and kiln, sixth form centre with private study area and classrooms, with other buildings nestling among well-maintained gardens. Facilities are all outstanding, with some particularly well-equipped science labs and a spacious junior and senior libraries.

From fifth year, pupils can go into town for lunch (although the privilege is quickly removed if they're not impeccably behaved), keeping the school from feeling remote and elite. That said, the on site cashless refectory serves an excellent array of food (some of the best we've seen) keeping younger ones happy. Breaktimes usually spent in class common room and outside in the abbey orchard (with teachers on duty) at lunchtimes.

Boarding went in the 1950s, direct grant in the 1970s – girls arrived (mainly from local independents and states) in the sixth in 1991. 'It's a wonderful co-ed school for girls to enter from a single-sex school because all the girls are new together,' said one parent. 'I don't know any of the girls who don't love it here,' said one female pupil, although it's generally agreed that girly-girls may struggle amid the testosterone. Boys say the presence of girls 'makes us more mature.'

Lots of outreach work (school motto is translated from Latin as 'Born not for ourselves'), involving pupils going into care homes, working with children with learning disabilities etc. Children from local state schools enjoy some of the facilities, including pool and science labs. In fact, exceptionally strong links exist with local state schools, with sixth formers mentoring primary school children and together with staff providing masterclasses in maths, sciences and drama. Student voice traditionally weak, but improving, with recently formed student council having brought about more water fountains and refurbished toilets. 'I think they're really working on this area, but there's still some way to go to ensure pupils are instrumental to what goes on in the school,' said one parent. Despite the obvious links with the abbey, pupils say religion is low-key.

Pastoral care, well-being and discipline: Horizontal tutorial system, plus prefects, full-time school nurses, school counsellor, chaplain, two heads of sixth-form and lots of senior staff with pastoral roles reflect the emphasis on pupil support. 'My son says you can ask the prefects anything and that you never feel silly,' said one parent. 'Initially when my son started, he was a little bit quiet but his confidence has really grown, all thanks to the pastoral care,' said another. Traditional when it comes to discipline, boundaries and order, although there's room for boys to learn from their mistakes and we witnessed usual boisterousness at break. Entrance into sixth form earns a whole new level of respect and grown-up facilities, including an on-site Starbucks (not surprisingly, also used by staff).

Bullying? 'Yes,' says head, 'because every school does. But if you're asking me if it's persistent, then no.' This, he puts down to both strong sanctions and encouraging pupils and parents to report any unpleasantness early on. 'I always think youngsters are like pebbles on a beach – when the tide comes in, they inevitably bump and give each other a polish. But we have to make sure that's all it is.' Legal highs had just been added to the list of drugs for which pupils are expelled, when we visited.

Pupils and parents: Over 70 per cent of pupils from local Herts area and about half of those from St Albans itself. The rest, including quite a few Jewish pupils, from north London, mostly from Enfield. Smaller number from other ethnic minorities or families where the first language is not English. Boys come into the first year bright-eyed, bushy-tailed and in the main, grow into interested, sharp, articulate young people who are, on the whole, grounded, not pompous. School works hard to integrate girls but it remains steadfastly a male environment, attracting resilient and robust girls into the sixth form. Eight school bus routes bring the majority of children to school, whilst others walk or get the train.

Parents are ambitious – mostly professional, many first-time buyers, plus a handful whose children would otherwise qualify for free school meals. Good sense of community among parents, if that's what you want, but easy enough to opt out of the events and parent get-togethers if you don't. Some parents say the school could be better at communication with them, particularly electronically. 'As it is, I have to get my son to take a picture with his phone of the fixtures information,' said one parent. Very strong Old Albanians, many of whom send their sons here and, later, their daughters. Only 13 schools have produced more Fellows of the British Academy and Royal Society. Notable former pupils go back to the year dot but recent ones include Sir Tim Rice, archaeologist Lord Renfrew, film producer Mike Newell, General Sir Richard Lawson and Prof Stephen Hawking.

Entrance: 'Unashamedly a selective school, but not ultra-selective,' insists head, although it is seriously over-subscribed, with more than three applicants per place. IQ of 125+ at 11+ and 127+ at 13+ (say discrepancy is due to tutoring, not innate ability). At 11, tests in English, maths and VR and interviews, all on the same day. NB part of a group of independent co-ed/boys' schools that coordinate 11+ results. At 13, apply early, conditional offers made following assessments in Y7; late-comers compete for the few remaining places. Tests as at 11+: three interviews and entry dependent on CE results. Around 100 applicants for 40+ places at 16 – with minimum grade A required in A level subjects and a grade average of 6.6 or over (with an A giving 7 points and a B giving 6) at GCSE for both external applicants and those moving through from GCSEs.

Exit: A laudable 80 per cent go onto Russell Group universities, notably Durham, Nottingham, Birmingham, and Exeter, with popular subjects including history, economics, maths, engineering, the sciences and law. Regular success with medicine and veterinary science applications (eight in 2016) and 14 to Oxbridge.

Money matters: Academic scholarships, for absolute excellence, worth five per cent of fees awarded on the basis of performance in the entrance tests at 11 and by separate exam at 13 and 16. Choral scholarships by audition at 11+. Art, music and sport scholarships at 13+. Currently 42 bursaries, 20 full-fees remission. Bursary funds equivalent to five full fees pa allocated by combination of need and merit so if top three pupils require 100 per cent bursary there will be little left for anyone else, but school usually manages to offer something to almost all who need it.

Remarks: Hovering towards the top of the league tables, this is a friendly, outward-looking county school where academia comes first, and sport a close second. Fear not if your son (or sixth form daughter) isn't sporty, however, as the 'work hard, play hard' ethos of the school can (and frequently does) mean pupils are drawn more towards drama, art or music than sports, in addition to their more intellectual studies. Traditional, disciplined and highly structured, this school demands high standards from all, but its emphasis on a rounded education means it is not the academic pressure-cooker that so many London schools are.

St Andrew's School

Buckhold, Pangbourne, Reading, Berkshire RG8 8QA

Pupils: 286 • Ages: 3-13

Fees: Day £10,110 – £16,830 pa; Flexi boarding + £3,048 pa

Tel: 0118 974 4276
Email: registrar@standrewspangbourne.co.uk
Website: www.standrewspangbourne.co.uk

Headmaster: Since 2015, Mr Jonathan Bartlett (40s), previously head of Moor Park School in Shropshire for seven years. Read PE and history at Brunel University. The youngest of seven children he grew up on a pig farm but also 'loved' his time at a boys' boarding school in Wiltshire, so much so that his first job after university was at Papplewick, one of the boysiest of boys' boarding preps. Took off on a round the world trip which included setting up an online education company in America, where he also met his wife. All very entrepreneurial and exciting but he still missed Papplewick, eventually returning there and becoming deputy head.

When we met he was beaming with pride at pupils' CE results ('I can take very little credit for these'). Given school's size and non-selective admissions policy 15 scholarships is certainly worth smiling about. Says he was drawn to St Andrew's because of its 'country prep values' and 'relaxed, informal feel'. He has plans, of course, but there's no revolution on the cards (and none necessary). Somewhat overdue improvements to sport and drama facilities are underway and longer term he's keen to 'build boarding'. On the academic front he has appointed a new head of learning and re-introduced Latin (year 6 upwards).

Mr Bartlett, who says he 'hates being behind a desk,' takes year 8 scholars for Problem Solving and Reasoning. His wife, a linguist with a Master's in health education, also teaches. Favourite books? Animal Farm (unsurprisingly) and A Prayer for Owen Meany.

He describes the school's demographic as 'quite diverse' (emphasis on 'quite' we think) and definitely 'not stuffy'. And what do parents think about the Bartletts? 'It's so exciting, they're absolutely fantastic for the school' said one. 'Mrs Bartlett is really involved and easy to talk to' said another, who thought Mrs B's being American was a 'breath of fresh air'. Several others commented that they felt the head was genuinely listening to parents' ideas and had a clear vision of what needs to be done. Children were won over almost at once by the zip wire and new climbing frame that were installed at the same time as their new head.

The Bartletts live on site and have three children (one at Moor Park, one at Malvern and one at St Andrew's) plus two of the obligatory prep school head Labradors – 'heads have them because they're bombproof' countered Mr B. Down time is for sport (cricket and golf) and family bolthole in Pembrokeshire.

Entrance: Mainly from local nurseries and primary schools or families relocating from London. Admissions ethos couldn't be simpler, St Andrew's is 'a family school which offers places to children who will be happy and thrive academically'. That all sounds lovely but remember, it's also a popular school that receives many more applications than it has places. Main points of entry are at ages 3, 4 and 7 although places may become available in other years. Younger children invited to spend a day or half day in the school; older children sit 'short' tests and year 7 candidates are assessed formally. Priority given to siblings and children of former pupils.

Exit: Mainly all over (the home counties). Co-eds Bradfield College and Pangbourne scoop up the majority; one or two each year to Wellington and Marlborough. Fair few boys head to Abingdon, Magdalen College School and Radley; girls to Downe House, Tudor Hall and Queen Ann's Caversham. Head says they lose 'a few' girls to day schools at age 11 but can sometimes arrange 'deferred places.' Good spread of academic, sport and music scholarships – an impressive 15 in 2016.

Remarks: St Andrew's motto is 'Altiora Petimus' (we seek higher things) and this is certainly the case as one ascends the steep hills of the Thames valley in search of the small village of Buckhold. School occupies a rather delicious gothic revival pile designed for Herbert Watney (of the brewing family) by Alfred Waterhouse, better known as architect of the National History Museum. Not all parts of the school building are by him – no prizes for guessing those in which he didn't have a hand. Lawns roll down to meadows and woodland, in total 54 acres of greenest Berkshire, where Buckhold birds do their best to drown out the persistent hum of the M4 – a reminder that less pastoral regions (Reading and Newbury) are close by.

Not a school with ancient lineage, it opened in 1934 under joint heads. Two heads may be better than one but this was somewhat over specified considering the inaugural page of the register runs to eight boys. First girls were admitted in 1971. At just under 290 pupils it's comfortably full and while head acknowledges it 'could expand', he says there are no plans to stretch numbers beyond 300. Parents will be relieved, several told us that they chose the school for its size. 'We looked at bigger preps but felt that our child might get lost.'

Our visit started with a walk through the dining room, worth a visit if Royal Doulton tiled panels are your thing (they are ours). Then it was out and over to the cluster of modern buildings housing nursery and pre-prep. Up to year 2 children are taught by stage, not age, we were told as we tiptoed past a group working hard on their phonics. Adaptable multi-purpose conservatory with small cookery area was lovely and bright (though we wondered if it didn't get a little warm in summer). Specialist teachers for French, music, PE and swimming. Parents told us that pre-prep was 'on top' of the basics such as reading, spelling and times tables and aimed to get these 'out of the way' before move to prep.

Some parts of the pre-prep looked in need of a revamp – outside areas in particular were a bit scruffy and didn't appear to make best use of extensive space available. Staff acknowledged things could do with 'sprucing up' and told us that future plans include opening up the reception class and extending the indoor/outdoor space with a canopy.

Some of the Forest Schools we've seen are a challenge to the conventional meaning of the word 'forest', but with 50 bosky acres St Andrew's isn't one of them. Actually it isn't officially a Forest School yet, but staff are being trained. Accredited status may be pending but outdoor activities, rain or shine, have always been a big part of the school day – whether it's collecting bundles of 10 sticks for maths or going on a 'shape hunt'. Each child plants a tree on arrival and sees it grow as they move through the school. All-in-one waterproofs and wellies hang in the cloakroom and get a lot of use. 'We love the fact that children can play and explore in the grounds. They're encouraged to be bold and enjoy the freedom.'

Independence is the aim and even the youngest are expected to dress themselves, use knives and forks and pour their own milk or juice at break; some parents take a little convincing, especially if they have to wash the aftermath. We loved the noticeboard in the nursery cloakroom which had a filthy shirt pinned to it with labels pointing to each stain reading, 'I'm sorry that my uniform got dirty today but this shows that I have been learning x.'

After-school provision has been beefed up for all age groups. Pupils enjoy use of the outdoor pool in summer (a cover is on head's to-do list) but after school swimming club and lessons take place at nearby Bradfield College. Equestrian skills are honed at the next door stables. The summer bike ride club has been a huge success, 'We weren't sure if parents would want to bring their children's bikes into school, but they love it.' (Preponderance of 4x4s may be a factor.) Pupils learn cycling safety via the 'bikeability' scheme and the course culminates in an Enid Blyton style group ride and picnic.

We came across a group of pupils (according to our notes they were all called Daisy, Harriet or Freddie, but surely that can't be right) enjoying their morning break 'squash and bs (biscuits)' outside and conducted a quick vox pop. What did they like about their school? 'We have two breaks every day and you can climb trees, it's just amazing.' 'Everyone can be in a team; no one is left out. And everybody cheers.' And what about their new head? 'He's SO nice and really friendly. He chats to us about football during supper.' 'He's strict, but not mean strict.

He's only strict to keep us in order.' 'We've got more freedom to climb trees, as long as you do it in threes so that if someone hurts themselves there's one person to tell the teacher and one person to calm them down if they're upset.' So, all good – especially on the tree climbing front.

Next stop was year 5 history and pupils arrived, sorted out their seats and were ready to work in double quick time. It was an enjoyable, pacey lesson based around interpreting portraits and every pupil got to contribute their ideas. Teaching style seems to be fun – hands on with lots of activities and trips – but also rigorous. None of the parents we spoke to thought it was an academically pushy school, instead they used words like 'intense' and 'thorough.' Science labs are pretty trad, with specimens in glass cases and stuffed alligators; pupils told us that they really enjoyed all the practical work.

Learning skills (no longer known as learning support, 'everybody decided on the name change') steps in quickly if necessary, whether for short-term confidence building or extended help for pupils with mild SEN such as dyslexia. Focus is on individual, rather than group, work and the approach is holistic – children are taught relaxation techniques and staff are vigilant for signs of stress. Parents say homework 'not excessive, just a bit of reading or spelling until year 6, unless there's a test coming up'.

'We're quite sporty' a pupil told us, modestly. In fact St Andrew's, though small, is a big player. Hockey was described to us by one parent as 'phenomenal' – recent achievements include girls' team getting to the national finals and boys' team winning the county championships. School orienteering team are also national champions. Swimming, tennis, lacrosse and equestrian also enthusiastically and successfully pursued. One of our guides was glad she could now play cricket instead of rounders but thought that girls should also get a chance to play rugby (not yet on the cards). Both guides wished the planned new sports centre could arrive quicker (it's due for completion in the autumn of 2017).

Drama lessons take place in the rather small studio – lots of lighting equipment but no actual stage. After school drama club is popular and there are regular productions (performed in sports hall) but head and parents acknowledge that the subject has been something of a Cinderella. New specialist teaching has already improved matters and plans for a proper stage and better facilities are afoot. Pupils may work towards the LAMDA grades and several have won drama scholarships to senior school.

While drama may be playing catch up, music at St Andrews is in a class (in fact a music block) of its own. Head told us he was 'blown away' by the high standard. A quick look at the noticeboards revealed three recent grade 8s and even a diploma, not to mention a range of individual instrumental lessons that started with bagpipes and, for all we know, ends with Xylophone. Three choirs (plus one in pre-prep) a full orchestra, a string orchestra, big band, jazz band and concert band and any number of ensembles. Parents of musical children are delighted with the provision but we did hear one or two mutterings about (almost inevitable) music/sport timetable clashes. The sporty and musical child might be stretched rather thin here, given the predominance of both.

S

Boarding (no weekends) increasingly popular. Accommodation is up in the eaves of the main house (boys at one end, girls at the other and a sensor alarm between!) and preponderance of beams and wood give the space rather an alpine feel. Small numbers make for comfortable and homely arrangements, dorms spotless but not at all institutional. Boarders love the experience – hot chocolate and toast in the common room, summer evenings playing tennis, swimming or 'just lying on the grass talking'.

No house system, school has 'sections' distinguished by colour (red, blue, green etc). 'It's a bit boring but that's the way it's been since the beginning', we were told. Parents confident that pastoral care system would pick up any problems early on and also praised home-school communication, 'Teachers respond very quickly'. Chapel (can just about seat whole school) three times a week, 'it's a buzz when everyone is singing' said our guide; Christmas carol service is held at Bradfield College. When asked about food the pupils were very keen to share: curry Mondays and chicken in barbecue sauce are firm favourites; rocky road and chocolate brownies are top puddings. Opinion sharply divided as to whether macaroni cheese was best or worst.

Families live within 45 minutes' drive and are mostly long-term local or London escapees. Parents, many both working, appreciate the improved after-school care. Very active parents' association, FOSA (Friends of St Andrew's) arranges social events such as pub nights and charity fundraisers. 'It's not a cliquey school' we were told, 'there's a really good mix'. While this is undoubtedly true, it's worth bearing in mind that the 'mix' doesn't have that many different ingredients ... Former pupils include author David Cornwell (aka John le Carré); broadcaster Adam Hart Davis; artist Sir Howard Hodgkin; actress Emily Bevan and, wait for it, James and Pippa Middleton and their sister, Catherine, Duchess of Cambridge. Apparently it was at a hockey match on the fields of St Andrew's that Prince William, then a pupil at Ludgrove, first saw his future wife. All credit to the school for not overplaying this particular connection.

Many of the parents we spoke to had looked at larger or better-known schools before choosing St Andrew's. 'It's a little gem,' was a phrase we kept on hearing. The fact that it has been below the radar appeals to some, rather like that favourite, 'unspoilt' holiday destination. One mother said, 'I don't really want to tell my friends [about St Andrew's], it won't be so unique and special.' Er, sorry about that. School's relative youth means that some founding old boys from the 1930s are still on the mailing list. The registrar told us of one chap who, at nearly 90, loves to come back and visit. And his verdict? 'Yes it's changed, but the magic is still here'.

St Catherine's School

Station Road, Bramley, Guildford, Surrey GU5 0DF

Pupils: 652; 136 boarders • Ages: 4-18 • Sixth form: 171 • C of E

Fees: Day £8,580 – £17,550; Boarding £28,905 pa

Tel: 01483 899609
Email: admissions@stcatherines.info
Website: www.stcatherines.info

Headmistress: Since 2000, Mrs Alice Phillips MA Cantab (50s). First teaching post was at the Royal Masonic School, Rickmansworth, where she rose to being head of English. Thence to deputy headship at Tormead in 1993. Mrs Philips is president of the Girls' Schools' Association. She impresses at once as being full of brisk common sense, good humour and get-up-and go. But she is also super-bright, super-articulate and super-focused on the highest of standards for her staff, her charges and herself. 'She is utterly determined for her girls,' one mother told us. And this blazes forth in her dedication to the job of equipping girls for the future – 'girls need to be in an environment which demonstrates that there's nothing you can't do'.

Mrs Phillips relishes the process of turning her 'rough-cut GCSE diamonds into highly polished gems' – and the process needs the St Cat's sixth form to be complete. 'We hit the wall of hormones together,' she says, 'I love the wall of hormones,' which she sees as an essential stage in becoming an adult. And she is not interested in turning out demure young ladies. 'We teach them to challenge every darn thing.' Neither is she a petty disciplinarian; 'you pick your fights with teenage girls. If you pick on something trivial and make a fuss about it they will hate you forever.' Parents are universally impressed – 'Her speeches are very entertaining and she devotes her whole life to the school.' 'She is very fair and very good at sorting things out.' A few parents – and girls – can find the intensity of her commitment 'scary', but one's impression is that her uncompromising concern is for the 'whole' of each girl. When her pastoral care is praised, she responds, 'but we do also seek to get the girls into the best possible universities and to do that you have to get them to aim high and target improvements all the time'. One awe-struck mother summed her up: 'She is amazing.'

Head of prep: Since 2012, Miss Naomi Bartholomew MA BEd Cantab (30s) who was educated at Portsmouth High School and went on to read English and education at Homerton College, Cambridge. She spent two years in South West China with the VSO, then taught in state and independent primary schools. Five years as head of English at Yateley Manor was followed by the deputy headship at St Catherine's in 2009. Miss Bartholomew's appointment to the headship was as much as anything by public acclamation. 'Some don't know her so well yet but those of us who do value her highly,' one mother told us. 'She is very calm, clever and warm.' Miss Bartholomew is plainly thrilled to be in charge and has a lovely smiley relationship with both girls and staff. Not remotely a dragon – more of a gentle but firm and very professional fairy princess.

Academic matters: Prep stimulating and orderly. Specialist teachers for most subjects including French; some setting in maths. Residential trips for all years; sensible mixing up of friendship groups, good library and IT room. Lively art – and years 5 and 6 use the senior school for DT – we enjoyed the really scary papier mâché masks. Emphasis on using the internet and other IT with discernment and discrimination rather than as an end in itself. Good learning support – 'academic mentoring' here – lots of monitoring, working with parents and use of two support teachers for as and when.

IGCSEs in almost all subjects now. Success relies on traditional good teaching alongside the best that modern IT can offer – so keen to keep abreast of all that is innovative and helpful. 'The apps for learning languages are fantastic,' enthuses Mrs Phillips, who tells us that her classics department has always led the way when it comes to embracing good new IT. So iPods/iPads allowed in class with an emphasis on 'learning to discriminate' between reliable web info and the rest – we applaud; in fact all girls up to year 10 now required to have iPads. We saw nothing but quiet and attentive classes and teachers who kept order by being interesting rather than via sanctions. Results excellent across the board – no weak areas. Ninety-two per cent of subjects taken at A level in 2016 were graded A*-B, 68 per cent A*/A. Good to see Greek and German surviving alongside business, economics, history of art and photography. At IGCSE in 2016, 92 per cent A*/A grades. It cometh not much better than this. Lots of options, lots of opportunities – real education takes place here.

Disquiet among some parents and girls on the subject of 'SCAGS' (St Catherine's Assessment Grades) – the St Cat's method of assessing and tracking progress. It's designed to support girls in the pursuit of improvement in their different subjects but some are confused or unconvinced. Mrs Phillips – an ardent believer – concedes, 'we are mindful that it is complex and try to inform parents as best we can.' She is lightning quick to react when we report concerns raised with us – 'it is not the St Catherine's way not to listen to parents – we will expand the explanation and make it more user friendly.' And recent results support school's contention that the scheme works – the first group of girls brought up this way achieved 17 per cent more A* grades than their predecessors.

Library open all hours and well-stocked – the only one we have so far seen with a section on 'feminism'. Sensible system of sixth form subject mentors: you're 12 and struggling with physics? – find the sixth former who understands! Overall, the best of trad with the slickest of innovative in matters academic.

Girls with only mild dyses likely to be able to stand the heat. 'We pride ourselves on our tracking system,' says head, 'and on spotting any late-emerging problems' and monitoring, academic mentoring and clinics are more the way here than a busy special needs set-up.

Games, options, the arts: Lively art in many media – photography especially strong but ceramics, DT, life-drawing – all thrive and all run clubs for those who aren't taking them as curricular subjects. A sense of vibrant life and colour about the studios. 'The drama in the senior school is really good,' we were told and the new building has given drama and the technical side of production an immense boost. Music also lively and productive – just as you'd expect with this calibre of girls and encouragement. Music in the prep is highly praised too. Some sense that more drama productions would be welcome and the hope is that the stimulus given to the subject in the senior school will filter down.

Excellent sports facilities and sport now seen as more inclusive – lots of opportunities for those less than Olympian in their prowess. 'My daughter is in C and D teams', said one mother, 'and she has lots of matches.' The Olympians regularly reach the heights – county and national finals places in several sports and stellar showings in swimming, lacrosse and tennis. Range of sports on offer. Riding club run by parents. D of E thrives and everyone is productively busy all the time. Excellent outside speaker programme, sixth form lectures – and PTA lectures – and lots of stimulating trips.

Boarding: Fifty per cent of boarders from overseas. Bedrooms and dorms are spacious enough, welcoming and homely. Most in two-bedders, often with a third bed for flexi-boarders. Even sixth formers mostly share: they in their own separate and much-appreciated block with common rooms – possibly the messiest we have seen – most refreshing. Most full boarders – normally between 50 and 70 girls – remain in school each weekend and are offered a 'full and varied programme of activities'.

Background and atmosphere: Established in 1885, this is a school with a proud tradition and, unusually, has grown and developed all on the one site. Located 10 minutes south of Guildford in a quiet leafy village, it is unremarkable architecturally apart from its striking conference room plus arts 'n' crafts fireplace, its memorable gothic style chapel – splendid stained glass windows celebrating notable female saints, fabulous rose window and Willis organ. Boarding and most of the school areas are functional, a little tired in places (upgrading in process), with the emphasis on practicality rather than opulence. Useful 'chat-rooms' for one to-one sessions – a good idea but the one we nosed into was freezing.

Now boasts a 'fantastic' £15 million complex – the '125th Anniversary Halls' arts and sports building with an unrivalled auditorium (seats 300 and has 'better acoustics than the Barbican') plus other studios and backed by the sports hall, gyms, dance studios etc. All carefully, thoughtfully and skilfully integrated and an exceptional new resource with which the girls are clearly thrilled. School buildings mostly abut big central area used for car parking though pitches and courts stretch away on the perimeter. Latest addition is 'university style' sixth form study centre, designed with input from the girls, plus refurbished lecture theatre that now hosts chamber music recitals, talks, presentations etc.

Immensely strong house system – everything done in the six houses to which loyalty is unflinching – underpins virtually all school activities. Strong ethical dimension to energetic charity work – extends to water vending machine which supports pumping system in Africa. Food seen as improved – salads particularly praised – though 'it can get a bit monotonous for boarders,' we were told. The day we visited the choices included 'deep fried battered pangasius' and 'oven roasted pangasius'. (We had to look it up too – it's a type of catfish.)

Over the road from the senior school, the pre-prep and prep have separate buildings but share much including many facilities with the senior school – a real plus. Pre-prep is delightful – has its own outside space along with what it shares with the prep and senior schools. Peaceful 'cottage garden'. Charming little library, each classroom is chocker with interesting displays and stimuli but all is orderly and reassuring. 'Senses Den' in each room – very exciting. Lovely artwork – we loved the pasta palaces and the various penguin habitats. Top-notch loos with Mickey Mouse taps.

Pastoral care, well-being and discipline: Parents are universally grateful that their girls are here. 'They pace it beautifully,' one told us. 'Eight year-old girls behave like 8 year-olds – they are not pushed to be older than they are.' 'Everyone is busy but calm – there are lots of clubs and nice quirky things.' 'The teachers are warm, friendly and approachable. They don't overdo assessment – they just tell you whether they're in the top, middle or lowest third in a subject'.

'Lovely dedicated staff,' universally praised. A sense that all girls can fit in and do well here – whatever their aptitudes, enthusiasms, personality – something to which all parents we spoke to attested. 'It can be a bit full-on for some of them,' one parent admitted – and others agreed: 'the girls themselves push themselves to the limit – the atmosphere makes them want to be the best of the best.' 'They do the best they can,' another said, 'but they do it while looking after each other.' 'They are very supportive of each other's differences,' another agreed. School divides the girls into houses, sets, classes – lots of mixing up to encourage friendship and to discourage cliqueyness – and it works. Strong sense of an equitable and kind community. 'They don't favour the bright ones – my two very different girls feel equally welcome and valued.' 'Every single child gets a well-thought-out prize at prize giving – for best results or for kindness – everyone walks out feeling valued for what they are.'

Serious misdemeanours off the radar. Preventative and common sense approach. 'We do some very robust woman-to-woman talking with the girls about our expectations and what is and is not acceptable,' says Mrs Phillips and a sense of friendliness, mutual support is tangible. Some of the most approachable staff we know.

Pupils and parents: St Cat's 'Association' founded in 2004 – now a 3,000 strong membership of alumnae, parents, former staff – makes a real community of the school, past and present. Head's PA one of around a dozen alumnae now on the staff. Lots of parental involvement and unquenchable enthusiasm. Mostly local-ish families. Lots of old girls' daughters. Middle class and comfortable backgrounds, in the main. Notable old girls include Francine Stock, Juliet Stevenson, Elizabeth Beresford, Zena Skinner, Davina McCall, Fay Maschler, Joan Greenwood, UA Fanthorpe, Dorothy Tutin, Elinor Goodman, two ambassadors and legions of academics and other high flyers.

Entrance: Around 50 applicants for 32 places at 4+ and immensely worthwhile nabbing one of them if you can. Tots come in for a morning of fun and observation in groups – heavy staff:tot ratio to allow for lots of encouragement and stimulation – and discreet assessment. They look for children who are 'curious, engaged and absorbed in what they are doing'. At 7+, around 15 apply for 4-5 places – similar approach plus testing in English, maths and verbal reasoning with 'an emphasis on show us what you can do'. 'We're a pacey school – we look for girls who will thrive here'.

Entry to senior school by academic selection, using St Catherine's own assessment. Eleven plus candidates take papers in English, maths, science and verbal reasoning. Few places at 12+, 13+ or 14+ – papers in English, maths and reasoning. Reports from existing schools. Sixth form general paper, verbal reasoning and predicted GCSE grades – As expected in A level subjects. Interview for potential sixth formers. Roughly 1.3 applicants for each 11+ place – so not too daunting for a bright girl; for those who try for places in higher years, date of registration is important so register as early as you can. Around 70 apply for the 10 or so annual places in the sixth – they can afford to be very choosy. School flexible and helpful – happy to interview via Skype if you're abroad. Locals come from everywhere but mostly the school's own prep and from Haslemere, Midhurst, Farnham, Guildford, Godalming, Cranleigh, Woking, Esher, Oxshott, SW London. Overseas pupils predominantly English with some EU nationals. Full boarders from Turkey, Moldova, Nigeria, Japan, Hong Kong, Russia, Ukraine, Malaysia, Korea and Singapore. Not a school for anyone with less than fluent English.

Exit: Most prep school girls to the senior school, some to board at other top schools (some on scholarships) or to other local schools. Lots of strong, local competition in the area.

Around 10-20 per cent leaves after GCSEs – mostly to co-ed sixths or to have a change. Sixth form leavers to top unis – three to Oxbridge in 2016 (including one vet off to Cambridge) and four medics. Exeter, Cardiff, Birmingham, Leeds, Warwick and UCL popular – aeronautical engineering and chemical engineering two choices. Unusual number of geographers. Good number of medics. All do proper subjects.

Money matters: Small number of scholarships – some open and some internal – most worth up to 20 per cent of fees. Music and art awards. Bursaries for the bright broke at 11+ and sixth. Usual means-testing and disclosures required but up to 100 per cent of fees on offer.

Remarks: If you want convincing that girls only education is the right and modern way for your bright and motivated daughter, go and look. This is as good as it gets.

St Christopher School

Barrington Road, Letchworth Garden City, Hertfordshire SG6 3JZ

Pupils: 358: 236 boys, 122 girls; 32 boarders • Ages: 3–18 (boarding from 11) • Sixth form: 96

Fees: Day £10,470 – £17,355; Boarding £18,960 – £29,670 pa

Tel: 01462 650850
Email: admissions@stchris.co.uk
Website: www.stchris.co.uk

Head: Since 2007, Richard Palmer (50s), who first went to St Christopher as a gap student and then went on to get a first in education at Nottingham. He taught science, drama and design technology at several schools, eventually becoming head of DT and housemaster at St John's College School, Cambridge before finding his way back to St Christopher. He became head of the junior school in 2004 and has been head of the whole school since 2007.

Previously chair, now on the committee of the Society of Heads, he is also a school inspector with the Independent Schools Inspectorate, giving him an opportunity to see other schools in action. His office is full of mechanical toys and old cameras – a man who loves design and technology still managing to teach it to all in year 7.

Described by parents as well respected, level headed, genuine and a little shy. He does not overwhelm with charisma or charm but is clearly confident in his decision making and that clear decisiveness feeds down to the school. He allows for things to be liberal without being in the least slack. He wants the school to 'remain distinctive' with a breadth of education and for 'pupils to be able to work and live with difference'. He has some freedom to do this since pupils do not do Sats and they follow the national curriculum only loosely. He wants to create more dynamic middle school years and allow topic work and individual work to continue in those years before exams set in. He is keen to find ways to bring drama and philosophy earlier on in the school. So far from a complacent head, but one with vision and goals.

Academic matters: Not narrowly academically selective, yet clearly a school with an expectation that each child be hungry to learn and participate. Independent learning is encouraged throughout the school by teachers who are enthusiastic, energetic and creative.

Nursery has more space than usual with plenty of outside play areas – grassed, soft surfaced and a covered 'outside classroom' with lots of equipment clearly being well used for learning. Historically Montessori, so lots of practical learning, playing and making but now following the EYFS curriculum with clear evidence of more formal phonic learning and number work. Children seen in wellingtons in the garden as well as in wonderful fairy dressing up clothes. Children change into indoor shoes on re-entering school. Reception children well prepared for reading and writing when they are ready and lots of trips to the junior school in preparation for year 1 transfer.

In the junior school, topic based learning and much creative planning seems to allow students to develop and research ideas, which allows for more independent learning than usually seen in a junior school. Topic learning across all subjects very much in evidence – stretching the topic to music and maths not just in humanities. Small classes – 20 is the average – with a teacher and teaching assistant in each airy classroom. Desks grouped – a sign of collaborative learning with lots of space for carpets, beanbags, making and creating. Early introduction to democracy with class rules and ethos very much child instigated. The junior library is extremely well and widely resourced – a joy in this technology based era – with pupils and parents encouraged to take books out at any time even if the enthusiastic dedicated junior school librarian not available. Interesting to see extension maths in this non-selective school, allowing for more challenging work. Learning support staff (two) in the junior school take pupils out of class but pupils also given in class support.

Five one hour lessons each day in the senior school so no rushing between lessons with bags full of books, and as a result much less tension all round. Extra impressive therefore that they manage to give such a breadth of subjects (though no Latin or RS). Spanish and French expected for all students, where appropriate. Language exchange trips considered a rite of passage and something to look forward to in year 10. Geography trips also popular as is the history war graves trip to Northern France. The trips get more exotic as the students move up the school – Rajasthan one of the most original we have seen. Creative English learning involving role play, drama, filming, and journalism work. Setting in maths from year 7 then more subject setting in year 9. Separate sciences from year 9.

Art, music and drama not considered soft options but very valued subjects. Sciences and maths get particularly good GCSE results as do English, arts and crafts and DT. Parents and students appreciate being able to choose whatever combination of 18 GCSE subjects they want with no timetable limitations or restrictions. Subjects include film studies, additional science, PE and Spanish. At A level there are even more subjects to choose from with the arts and sciences getting particularly impressive results. Career evenings and seminars to help students from Year 11 onwards with choices for further education. Extension classes for Oxbridge candidates and extended project qualification for those with particular interests. In 2016, 35 per cent A*/A grades at GCSE and 23 per cent at A level, with 57 per cent A*-B grades.

Dedicated learning support staff in both junior and senior parts of the school take students out of classes for extra (paid for) lessons as well as supporting in class. Touch typing taught before school if desirable from year 5 onwards and we saw several students with laptops as well as having amanuensis (teaching assistant writing for them – particularly useful in exams). The school takes some 25 per cent pupils with special needs, though these places fill early with cognitively bright dyslexic pupils and a few with autism spectrum disorders or ADD. Pre-screening for children with special needs, so apply by November in order to make sure the school has enough provision in place for individual needs.

Games, options, the arts: St Chris is often chosen is for its wider curriculum offerings. A very lively music department with practice rooms for individual instrument learning as well as much music creation in music technology suite. Bands and groups abound – some students we spoke to were very delighted to go to a gig in North London pub and see one of their school bands on stage. Plenty of opportunities to perform at weekly Morning Talks. More jazz and rock and small ensembles than classic orchestras, although these too exist. Junior school choir and some singing.

A large theatre building ideal for drama classes and huge annual musical productions. All the school involved in these extravaganzas, and if you don't like to be in the limelight, lots of opportunities backstage, in production and stage management.

This school is well known for its visual art department which is marvellously well resourced – sewing machines, pottery studio, printing room, woodwork, metalwork, fine art in very mixed media. A whole room dedicated to displays of their work – and one rather wonderfully designed piece of woodwork even ended up in a shop window to display shoes.

The forest school site is generous and gloriously muddy and wooded and well used.

Despite the non-competitive ethos, successful sports teams despite that definitely punch above their weight for such a small school. Everyone is involved and the theory is that this brings up the weaker sportspeople – evidently it works. Matches against local teams and county games. Netball, rugby, football, tennis, volleyball etc. Swimming pool used from early years up – for swimming lessons and fun swim club as well as squad training. It is also an opportunity for older students to obtain a lifeguard certificate so they can work at school or outside in the holidays. Heaven to find a pool with a very civilised and warm temperature of 28 degrees. More sports in lunchtime clubs and after school – rambling, cross-country, cycling, jogging, dance, canoeing, trampolining, athletics and fitness training. Their spacious green fields much in use when we visited for an inter-school football competition with five games going on at a time.

An impressive climbing wall up the whole of one side of a classroom block. But there are also trees in the grounds that are specifically 'climbing trees' – any child welcome to climb in break time if they think they can get up and down. Such a joy to see kids climbing trees in these health and safety conscious days. Plenty of fruit trees and others growing in the extensive grounds. The apple trees are picked and juiced in October by the students who get a bottle to take home. Other growing areas including a wormery from which compost is made and sold locally or used here. Nothing wasted from vegetarian school lunches. A garden shed designed and built by students made from recycled plastic bottles and bamboo sticks provides a good greenhouse for seeds and plants before planting out. And the role of food is not only evident in the growing and composting, but of course in the cookery suite. The Vege Centre is a serious part of the school curriculum where students are taught to make meals not just bake scones. The enthusiasm for all these extracurricular activities was brought home, according to one mother whose son came home eager to show off his cooking skills one day and another time wanting to make a board game.

Once a week there is an enrichment programme allowing students to choose an activity to explore – film making, jewellery, yoga, tai chi, philosophy, dependent on the interests and skills of current staff, supplemented where necessary by external tutors. These are across the age groups so give an opportunity for different years to get to know each other and perhaps explains the familial atmosphere.

Boarding: Extremely flexible boarding available from year 7 upwards. Where there is space and availability, pupils can choose between 'day boarding' between 7.30am-7.30pm and includes breakfast, supper and supervised homework, flexi boarding just for the odd night, weekly boarding from Sunday evening to Friday afternoon or full boarding. Inevitably more full boarders as the students move up the school, especially for international students. Three boarding areas according to the age of the student, with some 20 year 13 pupils in a separate house on the school grounds, year 11 and 12 students in a very modern and light extension, and younger years in cosy traditional rooms in the heart of the school. Many of the rooms are single ones – privacy being part of the respectful ethos of the school. Kind houseparents and gap students involved in weekend activities, and each teacher also responsible for one Saturday activity a year. Weekly evening activities available include movie night, cookery, games nights. Weekend activities almost always involve a trip away from school. Cooking facilities for snacks available to students, though older students have a good kitchen and cook for a weekly supper club. Meat meals are available for boarders after the vegetarian only daytime school canteen. Despite separate boarding areas, it felt very family-like, with older students and younger all hanging out together. We liked the rule that phones were taken away and charged overnight and only returned in the morning once beds were made (something to start in all homes perhaps?).

Background and atmosphere: Founded during the First World War, this school aims to treat children as individuals, to be non-judgemental and to encourage independence. The Quaker origins of one of the first heads are reflected in Morning Talk three times a week that always involves a period of silence. This opportunity for silence was also seen when we visited: in the middle of a lively lunch, one student rang a bell, the hall fell silent for a moment, and the pupil thanked the hall and the day continued. The right to ring the bell is clearly a privilege allowing for a moment of calm.

Large grounds and airy classrooms with plenty of space also add to the atmosphere of calm. Set in a quiet road in Letchworth, and based around an arts and crafts building with wood panelled rooms, several newer buildings and extensions: a slightly ramshackle group of buildings, with plenty of opportunity to walk outside between classes. Immaculate grounds and planting and freshly painted and very clean rooms despite the fact that many of the buildings are old. The school exudes clean orderliness, which is surprising in view of the reputation it has for being liberal. Students wear their own clothes, call teachers by their first names, are all doing projects and exploring ideas, and there are no bells between lessons, little noise and a great sense of purpose. Teachers appear passionate and engaged, as do pupils. The friendly and efficient catering staff, ground staff and administrators all spoke of loving their jobs. One doesn't sense hierarchy here at any level. Parents said that they appreciate that the school concentrates on things other than uniform and it was one less thing to pay for and worry about. A parent said the school 'has fantastic facilities, is not selective and is all inclusive. What's not to like?'

Pastoral care, well-being and discipline: You wouldn't choose this school if you wanted a safe route or wanted to impose on your child, said one parent, but it really works if you trust your child to make their own choices and the school to nurture and empower them. Parents described it as 'non-pushy and non-selective but allows the child to pursue what they most want to do'. The pupils do choose – their subjects, the direction they want to take and how they work best. Classrooms were busy with students carrying out their own projects and working at their own pace. This is possible because the teachers work hard and there is so much mutual respect. First name terms with teachers – we saw pupils open doors for teachers and teachers waiting for pupils in the lunch queue. No pushing and shoving. Older pupils making allowances for younger pupils and sitting together at lunch. More like a family rather than exclusive year groups.

Dedicated head of pastoral care who liaises with heads of year, who in turn meet with advisors or tutors. The fact that students meet their advisors every day means that issues are fed back quickly up the school, and students and parents feel that they always have someone to speak to. Parents we talked to all knew exactly who they could speak to or email with questions or complaints or concerns.

Self-government (a way of introducing democracy and ensuring students are totally engaged in the school) is an important feature of St Chris according to students we met. Anyone can attend the school council, at which student representatives can vote. Any proposals that get passed by the school council go up to a meeting of the entire senior school where each student can vote. Resolutions passed by the school are enacted unless vetoed by the head (which almost never happens). Pupils we met loved the fact that even the youngest child in the senior school could make large things happen – like the building of the cookery Vege Centre.

Pupils and parents: Quite a large proportion commute from north London thanks to trains from Finsbury Park and school buses. Also some from Cambridge, and more who are either local or move to be near the school. A growing number of international students, especially higher up the school, who tend to be boarders. This is not a narrowly academically selective school and students and parents really reflect this – some making sacrifices to have their children at St Chris, some second generation St Chris families, some bursary students, some with quite significant special needs, some with multiple strengths and huge academic ability. Ideal for a family with several children of mixed interests and abilities – how rare to find a school to suit both the artistic child and the mathematician, the reader and the doer, and to value them all equally. Parents said they are 'encouraged to be involved' and 'can pop in at any time to ask questions'.

Entrance: The school has wonderfully popular open days (the head thinks the free lunch helps keep everyone cheerful for the day) and many parents visit several times to get a feel of the school. Applications are followed up with an interview – both of parents and, separately, the child – to make sure that expectations match. All applicants over year 4 are given cognitive ability assessment which is age related. They aim to accept 25 per cent with special needs if the school can match child's needs to school resources. Since all applicants are interviewed, the school looks for a match of school's ability to match the child's needs. Mild dyslexia well supported with extra individual lessons, high functioning verbal pupils with autism spectrum disorder seem to do well, and especially good for anxious children. The head says that 'some children need to be here', and they may well be given a place even if they don't meet the requirement that 'all prospective students need to show cognitive ability of at least 100 standardised score'. Oversubscribed senior school, and years 5 and 6 generally full too. Children with individual needs must apply by November for the following year.

Exit: All early years move onto junior school, and almost all move from junior to senior school. Some movement at 16 as London students get weary of the commute and move to sixth form colleges in the big smoke, and some are just ready for a change or move to technical colleges. Some years as many as 40 per cent leave.

As for further education, interesting split between the large number who go on to do art and those who do engineering, science and maths. The art teacher was very proud to show that every single child who applied to art college got places at every college they applied to (including Parsons in New York, Bournemouth College, London University of the Arts). Some even applied for foundation art courses but were offered the art degree course directly since they were so well prepared by St Chris. A good range of universities – including many from the Russell Group – art schools and one or two some years to Oxbridge or to read medicine. A special extension group prepares sixth formers for entry into the most demanding courses.

Money matters: This school is built on solid foundations with good transparent governance provisions in place. Financially stable and well supported. The facilities show recent and regular investment and maintenance. Despite having to pay for extras like music lessons and individual learning support lessons, parents say that the school does its level best to keep costs to parents down as much as possible. There are some 100 per cent bursaries and small allowances (10 per cent fee remission) for art and academic scholarships for pupils at years 7, 9 and 12.

Remarks: Calm and orderly, busy without feeling hectic. Palpable sense of mutual respect between pupils and teachers, between pupils and other pupils and a sense of confident self-respect in the pupils themselves. Passionate, quietly self-confident and articulate students suggested that this was because everyone felt empowered thanks to their role in the school council and self governance. The ethos of respect included the school buildings – extremely well cared for with interesting wall displays, spotless toilets and no sign of writing on desks or chewing gum under desks. The pupils are given a voice at this school so there is no need for graffiti.

St Clare's, Oxford

139 Banbury Road, Oxford, Oxfordshire OX2 7AL

Pupils: 279; 250 full, 2 weekly boarders • Ages: 15–19

Fees: Day £17,995; Boarding £37,080 pa

Tel: 01865 552031
Email: admissions@stclares.ac.uk
Website: www.stclares.ac.uk/ib

Principal: Since January 2017, Andrew Rattue MA PGCE, previously head of King's College, the British School of Madrid. English degree from Oxford; taught at Mill Hill and Haberdashers' Aske's, head of English at Highgate, second master at RGS Guildford and head of RGS Worcester. He was a Fulbright Exchange Teacher in Dallas, Texas and also worked in Thailand after leaving university so internationalism is very much in his blood. Four children; his interests include drama, music, film, all sports, the Victorians and other cultures and languages.

Academic matters: They come from the four corners of the globe to study here for the two-year IB diploma. The school was a proud pioneer in offering the IB, now has over 35 years' experience, and achieves consistently high results. IB is no walk in the park, six subjects: three at standard level, three at higher, including home language and English, a humanities subject, science, and maths, not forgetting the compulsory theory of knowledge course; extended essay and community, action and service (CAS) programme. School describes it as an 'outstanding qualification in terms of the breadth and depth it offers'. Parents happy with the diversity of subjects: 'My daughter had no clear idea of what to do, therefore keeping it broad in range of topics rather than specialising too early was one of the things that attracted us to the IB'. Others with children who had attended a range of different schools abroad felt the IB was the only option: 'It would have been difficult for him to settle into a traditional English school, with uniform and rules'. St Clare's claims that it has the edge over other IB schools in that it doesn't attempt to teach A levels at the same time. Recent leavers' results put St Clare's regularly top of the Oxfordshire sixth form tables. Average score of 36 in 2016, with nearly a quarter of students getting 40+ points.

Students too young to sit the IB course, or whose English needs practice, take the Pre-IB course. This is flexible in length (up to one year) and can be joined at any time, to prepare English and core subjects for diploma level.

All tuition is in English and class sizes average nine, some even smaller. All students study the literature of their home language so individual tutors are often recruited from the university for more exotic tongues, anything from Ukrainian to Farsi. Classrooms, in a number of nearby houses, are abuzz with IT equipment – students encouraged to bring their own laptops. Informal teaching style from a multi-lingual staff; 'if you can't enjoy teaching at St Clare's, I don't know where you will enjoy teaching'. Parents impressed by calibre of staff: 'They simply ooze experience' said one. 'None of this fluffy "your son is such a nice boy" stuff'. A new teaching block, with four new science labs and classrooms, co-ordinates with local architecture. Cosmopolitan lab technicians and librarians can juggle Dostoyevsky in English or Harry Potter in Cyrillic. Art takes place in a charming converted chapel, where the high ceilings and gallery provide a serene light for painting. There's a dark room, complete with leering skeleton, for photography.

Apart from the display of retro propaganda posters from various nations, the classroom was more like a modern boardroom, throbbing with discussion about European current affairs; 'It brings history and economics to life,' said a student. Watching these 16 year olds unpick global economics certainly gave us hope for the Euro crisis.

There is no SEN department. Profound learning difficulties are not provided for, but the college has had students with dyslexia, ADHD and hearing impairment.

Games, options, the arts: As a mandatory part of the IB programme, students take CAS (Creativity, Action and Service) over the two years to develop personal skills of planning, team work and conscientious thinking. A minimum number of points is needed in these areas, preventing any of the students becoming too bookish. In reality, the plethora of activities from art to zumba make up the social life of the school and run into the weekends and evenings. A mass of notices about clubs, classes and overseas projects draws students to the 'covered way', a busy corridor between classes and café. One family chose the school for the efforts it made to accommodate their son's ice hockey talents; 'I didn't want to go to a school where everybody rowed or played rugby'. The creative part involves a wide range of arts, music, writing, debating, Model United Nations, dance and drama. Behind the guitars, drums and piano in the music room is a full-time music teacher, and Sibelius music software is available for the budding composer. Concerts take place throughout the year, but the hot ticket is the international day concert in which students and some staff stage their own gig, with singing, dancing and jokes. Theatre productions by each year group were remembered fondly by senior staff, even if they had a senior moment remembering the titles.

The school has no playing fields. All students are given membership of the local sports centre and swimming pool; other facilities are a short minibus ride away at local schools or at Oxford Brookes University. Football and rugby teams use Astroturf pitches at Oxford City grounds. Parents forgive the lack of facilities: 'St Clare's does a great deal with very little'. Girls' volleyball is a particular strength. The CAS programme also involves community service (not the punitive kind), which takes the form of charity work in local shops, visiting the elderly or helping at local schools. A personal tutor is on hand every week to monitor progress and offer advice. The programme is open to Pre-IB and IB students and changes every term.

Students make full use of the cultural life of Oxford University, as well as the local shops and cafés of nearby Summerstown. There are organised excursions to places of interest in half terms, plus D of E field trips. Students are encouraged to go home in the holidays to recharge, but foreign excursions and tours to more remote parts of the British Isles are arranged for those who want them. Each year's leavers celebrate by cruising on the Thames in a party boat.

Boarding: St Clare's boarding houses are all within a five-minute stroll. First years share rooms with someone of a different nationality; 'arguments are rare,' we are told, and language learning rapid. 'Suddenly she had a massive range of friends from other backgrounds,' chimed a dad. Second years can have a single room or join with a friend in a double. All are comfortably furnished, most with own shower, hairdryer, strongbox and Wifi. Fraternising takes place in the common room, over the TV and kitchen area. A warden, in loco parentis, handles general well-being of the youngsters and counts them all in before the strict curfew. Day students are allocated a house and can stop over one night a week. Our impression when stepping out into the raked gravel drive was less of having visited a typical teenager's bedroom and more of a comfortable hotel.

Background and atmosphere: The school motto, 'To advance international education and understanding', stems from the principles of the visionary founder, Anne Dreydel, who despite being confined to a wheelchair by a bomb during the blitz, established exchange programmes for German students in her drawing room. Rightly recognised with an OBE and the German equivalent, her cultural olive branch towards international peace has grown into a thriving sixth form for 260 students. A collection of fine Victorian villas (27 buildings in total) along the cherry blossomed streets of genteel north Oxford provides boarding accommodation and classrooms. 'The buildings do not look as smart and luxurious as those of most boarding schools', commented one parent. To the rear, gardens dotted with the quirky addition of red telephone boxes have been joined and landscaped to allow the students some green space to eat, work or chill, but no loud music, smoking or ball games allowed.

Students can take three meals a day in the canteen, which serves up a suitably international menu. Predictably, none of the students rated the dish from their own country but were positive about the others. Stylish refectory tables encourage mingling and English chat out of the classroom. The Sugar House (refreshingly un PC name) offering a continuous temptation of snacks, pizzas and lattes, was doing good business when we visited.

Pastoral care, well-being and discipline: With so many youngsters far away from home discipline could be a problem, but isn't, thanks to the school's clear code of actions and 'consequences' – a portentous term that is famously effective at deflecting trouble, we are told. A strict curfew is respected, 11pm during the week, midnight at weekends. Alcohol is not tolerated, drugs result in an immediate suspension and we couldn't see any bike sheds for the usual teenage experiments: smoking and sex. The system works on trust; 'It's a very powerful glue,' says the school. The students are given a reasonable degree of freedom in return for responsible behaviour. 'When my son transgressed (in a very minor fashion), they were immediately on to him', said a parent. Lateness or poor behaviour results in loss of free time, confinement to the library or the house for varying spells, at worst for a term. 'It's rare someone will transgress twice', smiles the vice principal, eloquently.

A weekly session with a personal tutor, on first name terms, covers pastoral and academic issues. Rather than homesickness, the students complained that home life now seemed quiet; 'I miss people around me'. Student council, elected democratically, is first experience of democracy for some of these youngsters. Councillors hold office from January to December so as not to interfere with serious study, and meet with senior staff once a week to pow-wow: coffee machines, laundry problems and swivel chairs were the order of the day when we visited. 'It's easier to deal with a small problem than let it grow', says the school pragmatically. Parents have email addresses of teachers and tutors as well as official parents' days at the beginning and end of terms. 'There isn't the tradition of parents' evenings as in a normal school', said a parent, but in practice, there is an open invitation to visit whenever in the UK. Reports and test results can be viewed electronically via the parent portal, explained a parent, and 'we can see when he's been late!'

The students grow noticeably in confidence over the first term, and parents report that after seven weeks a different person has come home – 'the levels of motivation are astonishing' – confident in English and more self-reliant. 'At the start of the year people looked for comfort in their own national group, but not now', chorused a bunch of students. 'The more you get to know about each other, the more relaxed you are'. Despite the school's name, there was no sight of any religious bias, rather an emphasis on internationalism, learning about culture and diversity from each other. 'People think differently here...you learn a lot of stuff about the world. It's eye-opening', said one student. 'Awesome,' said another.

Pupils and parents: Forty-six different nationalities with almost as many different languages; biggest groups are German and Italian, but Russian is also common. Some 85 per cent of boarders are from overseas. Students criticised the size of some of the national groups. Eight per cent are British, who join from international schools abroad or are UK youngsters with an interest in the IB. Ten per cent are day children, with parents working in Oxford at the university, BMW or similar businesses. Round a table, they are an impressively mature, articulate and dynamic bunch, redolent of a UN delegation. School says, 'students bring each other on'. Perhaps they were hiding the mumbling, moody teenagers, but we didn't meet any. Instead, the break time discussion was open-minded and lively, peppered with a dose of multi-cultural joshing. Hugely purposeful about the work; 'Studying in the UK gives international prestige and broadens your interests', said one girl. The standard of English was astounding – rivalling many native schools – and the dress sense a positive improvement.

Entrance: Students are drawn to St Clare's by word of mouth or siblings' experience. No entrance test (except for scholarships), but highly dependent on two years of reports and references from previous school. The 'personal and intense' selection process won over one family who had initially looked for a public school. Interview in UK is compulsory, at which students are sized up for their enthusiasm for the IB programme. 'This is not a place for people to try to escape from their existing school'; St Clare's is full to capacity. Test for maths at interview determines which IB maths course students can tackle. There is a four day induction programme for newcomers, supported by senior students.

Exit: Majority go to university, 75 per cent to UK (LSE, Bath, Exeter and UCL are recurring choices) some to US or European universities and business schools eg Sciences Po, McGill, Bocconi, Medical University of Warsaw. Three to Oxford in 2016. Popular courses are engineering, medicine, law, economics and, not surprisingly, international relations. Staff proud that St Clare's has equipped them well for it; 'our students do not drop out of university'. An award-winning careers adviser offers one-to-one advice on applications and CV with seminars to prepare for UK and USA applications in the final year. 'Within a month... he was suddenly seriously considering his future and deciding what he should do', revealed a shocked mum. An education day of visiting speakers from business was under way when we visited, with groups of students carrying out Alan Sugar-style challenges, the kind of thing most of us first experienced at job interviews. These global citizens are ahead of the game; 'they are more willing to look abroad for opportunities in education and for work', says the careers adviser.

Money matters: Fifteen students each year receive scholarships or means-tested bursaries based on previous academic performance and scholarship exam; February deadline. Registrar called the fees 'reassuringly expensive, good value for Oxford'.

Remarks: Academically and pastorally mid way between school and university: 'University life with safety nets'. St Clare's attracts ambitious students from around the world, with an eye to a global career via a UK, US or European university. 'In some ways St Clare's is not a boarding school', said one mum, 'but rather a pre-university college'. The diverse student population is savvy; already aware that the world is a shrinking place and that the motivation to do well comes from within. Restores your faith in world peace.

St Clement Danes School

Chenies Road, Chorleywood, Rickmansworth, Hertfordshire WD3 6EW

Pupils: 1,394 • Ages: 11–18 • Sixth form: 338

Tel: 01923 284169
Email: enquiries@stclementdanes.org.uk
Website: www.stclementdanes.org.uk

Head: Since 1998, Josephine Valentine BSc PhD, previously deputy head from 1995. Originally from Manchester, she gained her BSc in microbiology and PhD in oral histopathology from Liverpool University. Later took a PGCE to fill a study gap, but wound up 'falling in love with teaching' and taught biology at St John the Baptist School, Woking and Beaconsfield High, where she worked her way up the ranks.

Outgoing and friendly, with a good sense of humour, she has one of the plushest offices we've seen in a comprehensive school (which also doubles up as a meeting room). Staff say she's a nurturing leader, as well as being decisive and unwavering in her vision for constantly moving the school forward. On the whole, parents like her too. 'She can chat away on a normal level, but she can rule with a rod of iron when she needs to and is hugely visionary. She's great,' says one. There's a feeling among some that she's 'untouchable,' with claims that it's virtually impossible to meet with her to express concerns, but she says going straight to the top isn't always the solution, with other staff often better placed to deal with any parental concerns. Pupils say she's a visible presence around the school, although her growing list of responsibilities means she stopped teaching in 2011. The biggest addition to this list happened in 2013, when she was approached by Herts County Council to open a free school in nearby Croxley Green in 2017. 'There's a phenomenal demographic need, with a real bulge in the population coming through,' she explains, although is insistent that St Clement Danes won't be left behind. 'If the children don't continue to get the results here, it would have been for nought and I'm very mindful of that,' she says.

Has two grown-up children, both of whom attended the school, and lives locally with her husband, where her hobbies include walking.

Academic matters: Consistently impressive results at all levels and Ofsted outstanding. In 2016, 87 per cent got 5+ A*-C at GCSE, including English and maths; 50 per cent A*/A grades. At A level, 37 per cent A*/A and 70 per cent A*-B, which the head is quick to point out are the same as the famously good nearby Bucks grammar schools. Rigorous attention to detail in the tracking of all students means personalisation at student level is strong. This kicks off in year 7 with cognitive ability tests, among others, which give the school a flavour of the type of learner each pupil is – 'essential as we're an all-ability school,' explains the head. 'The targets are just right- stretching but not stressful,' says one parent. Good results also attributed to the purposeful, 'can do' culture. Indeed, we found classrooms full of happy, attentive learners and dynamic teachers, although a few parents told us they feel middle-of-the-road pupils can fall off the radar a bit. 'You'll breeze through if you're bright and quick, but it can be more tricky if you're average, below average or lazy,' said one, although others disagree. 'I'd never have thought my daughter would go onto A levels and university, but she excelled in her GCSEs and A levels and is now at a great university.'

High calibre teachers and good staff retention, both helped by the fact that this is a National Support School, which leads the Herts & Bucks Teaching School Alliance – a group of over 20 schools, universities and local authority learning trusts who collaborate to promote exceptional standards of education. 'The alliance has a massive role in helping us to keep our talent, because staff get training opportunities well beyond the school itself,' explains the head, adding that it also enables the school to remain at the forefront of research and development. In the English department, when we visited, there were three ex-heads of English teaching, two of whom are specialist leaders in education. 'You come away from parents' evening buzzing from how passionate the teachers are about what they do,' said one parent. 'I think the kids feel that too and it inspires them to go above and beyond.' School also known for strong cross-fertilisation of teaching.

No specialist subjects at this school. 'We aim for excellence across all subjects,' says head. French from year 7 and German or Spanish from year 8. Italian had just been dropped when we visited, to the disappointment of some pupils. 'I wish they'd add in another language in its place,' said one. Most popular GCSEs tend to be the humanities. Setting for languages, maths, English and science from year 7, although there's plenty of movement. Subject clinics across all subjects, as well as study sessions during the Easter holidays for pupils with upcoming exams. Technology embedded into lessons, although head insists on there being good reasons for it, rather than 'for the sake of it.' Pilot scheme of iPads being used in year 7 when we visited.

Majority of pupils stay on in sixth form, choosing from 26 A levels, the most popular of which are science, maths, English, economics and business studies. Plenty of help in transitioning from GCSE, as well as lots of monitoring and assessment to keep students on track throughout the two years. Comprehensive guidance for university applications including Oxbridge, as well as job applications, and an impressive programme of external speakers. 'This year, these have included people from Warner Brothers, RAF and people talking about how to set up your own business and go into football management,' said one pupil. Extended Project Qualification increasingly popular, with 50-60 pupils doing it per year on average.

Students who are identified as gifted and talented go on the 'Exceptional Performance' programme for the duration of their time at the school, which involves being given a mentor (staff member) to champion their needs. Meanwhile, SEN (seven statemented when we visited) mainly includes dyslexia, autism and ADHD, all of whom receive mostly classroom based help. 'We look at every child on a case-by-case basis and are very honest about how we can help and where we'd struggle,' says head, who adds that although they've never turned anyone away, some parents do decide to go elsewhere – for example, although the school has accommodated three wheelchair users in the past, they might struggle with some of the narrow corridors in a school which was originally built for 821 students and now serves 1,400.

S

Games, options, the arts: Rugby, football, tennis and athletics are the strongest sports, with teams regularly competing at a high level, including against independent schools and Bucks grammar schools. District and county champions in athletics, with particularly talented students getting their picture framed on the school's honours wall (seen as a majorly big deal among pupils). Facilities include an all-weather flood-lit pitch, hard courts, gym and sports hall – all more than adequate. The annual Gym and Dance display is a highlight of the year. Hockey is weak, according to some parents, and there's no swimming, although the school supports the swim teams that practise outside school. In fact, they had just made the national finals when we visited.

Swish new art facilities about to be built when we visited. Evidence of some strong artistic talent – mainly fine-arts based, with photography also becoming increasingly popular. DT and food tech facilities impressive. Two areas for drama practice, with whole school performances and junior school productions put on alternative years. Examples include Macbeth, Les Misérables and Joseph.

Music flourishes here, with well-equipped facilities and no shortage of enthusiasm among both students and staff. Ensembles include two orchestras (around 70 in the main one and 60 in the junior one), two choirs and a jazz band, which provide opportunities for beginners through to National Orchestra members. Regular concerts, including the prestigious annual Commemoration Service in St Clement Danes Church in London, are described by parents as 'stirring stuff.' Student-led music groups regularly set up, including flute, folk, guitar and brass groups. 'I'm in the gospel choir, chamber choir and first orchestra and I love them all,' one pupil told us.

Extracurricular clubs plentiful and although some parents say they're mainly sports based, the school is clearly open to new ideas, including student-led clubs. 'A mother wrote in asking if we did a pony club – we didn't, so we set one up,' says the head. Sixth formers expected to get involved in community service – anything from working in a local charity shop to running a brownie pack.

Over 70 national and international trips per year, including London museums and galleries; annual activities week to Bude for year 7s; music tours to Paris and Barcelona; annual athletics training camp in Lanzarote; football tours to USA; language exchanges to Lyon, Bilbao and Potsdam; art trips to New York and Venice; and World Challenge expeditions to Cambodia, Vietnam, South America and Africa. Because the school receives the support and financial backing of the St Clement Danes Holborn Estate Charity (established in 1552 to support the education of the children of the parish of St Clement Danes Church in England), pupils rarely miss out on relevant activities, even if affordability is an issue.

Background and atmosphere: Founded in 1862 as a boys' grammar school in Houghton Street, London. Relocated to Hammersmith in 1928, before transferring again in 1975 to its present location in Chorleywood, where it became an all-ability, co-educational school. Its reputation has since gone from strength to strength and it's largely responsible for soaring house prices in the area. Became an Academy Trust in 2011.

All the original 1970s buildings remain, mostly in surprisingly good nick, with other buildings – including the maths and languages blocks, Barbirolli Hall and Carey Sixth-Form Centre – added more recently. Barbirolli Hall (named after Sir John Barbirolli, an Old Dane who went onto conduct the Halle Orchestra in Manchester for over three decades) given a facelift in 2014, with £20,000 of the funds raised by the pupils themselves. 'They were each given £10 and told to invest it in fundraising,' explains the head. Meanwhile, the Carey Sixth Form Centre, was due to be expanded when we visited, ready for an extra 30 students in the 2016 intake. With the feel of a halfway house between school and university, it has well-equipped classrooms and three types of self-study areas – café; quiet study area; and silent area. A £5.7m grant will also enable the school to rebuild maths and art areas (including a gallery area for permanent art displays), remodel the original centre of the school (currently cramped) and increase the number of study areas and sports facilities. 'There's always plans for the future, although beyond the hall is an area of natural outstanding beauty, which can limit our building aspirations,' admits head.

Each block has shared study areas in addition to the classrooms, with the English block boasting a central, roomy IT room. Some classrooms and walkways could be bigger, but clever timetabling and classroom allocating, along with a strictly enforced one-way walking system, helps prevent any overcrowding. Library disappointingly tired, but pupils assured us it's a lively and popular hub. Some parents feel the food could be more nutritious, and many take in packed lunches. Not a single piece of litter in sight during our visit, with everywhere spotless. 'You have to love your learning environment,' says the head. We found the atmosphere calm and structured, with a reassuring amount of liveliness at break times. Pupils articulate, confident, curious and happy.

Leadership opportunities include a prefect system, peer mentoring, Franklin Scholars and a strong student council, with five subgroups ranging from fundraising to student welfare. 'Sixth formers help the younger years a lot – there's no feeling of them being cut off in any way,' one pupil told us. Eight houses, with plenty of inter-house events throughout the year, culminating in Sports Day.

Celebrating success is literally centre-stage at this school – with prize-giving ceremonies, a sea of silver trophies adorning the long cabinets outside the head's office, along with the honours wall. Also a house point system and plenty of daily praising of students in various forms.

Pastoral care, well-being and discipline: Pastoral care has always been notable here, even in the 1970s, with every student supported by form tutors, pastoral leaders and the senior management team, in addition to a full-time matron who doubles up as a school counsellor and part-time welfare worker who goes out to families when necessary. School also leads pastoral care for the South West Herts group of schools to share good practice. Particularly big on transition, with every pupil visited in their primary school and a huge focus on settling new pupils in.

On the strict side, with clear expectations around behaviour and detentions for things like regularly disrupting class or persistently failing to hand in homework for no good reason. That said, the head insists they allow for grey areas. 'Take bad language, for example. A pupil using it when they're not expecting a teacher to hear is very different from someone swearing at a teacher, for instance – although both would be punished.' There has to be room to make mistakes, she adds. 'If you can't learn from your mistakes as a teenager, when can you?' No mobile phone policy, except in sixth form.

'Oh yes,' was the head's answer when we asked if there was bullying. 'Every school has it,' she says, but a restorative justice programme called Learning Together, which is led by the deputy head, and clear anti-bullying policies and e-safety evenings for parents all helps prevent it, she says. Most parents we spoke to hadn't encountered any bullying, although one parent we spoke to felt that in her case, it wasn't taken seriously enough.

Suspension rate generally low, with some peaks and troughs. Very low exclusion rate, with head preferring to work with other schools to provide a student with 'a fresh start' if needs be – with no more than one case per year on average. 'We also take in children from other schools on this basis from time to time,' she adds.

Pupils and parents: Most families from within a five-mile radius – mainly Chorleywood and Rickmansworth. Most pupils walk, many across Chorleywood common or through residential areas, whilst those from further afield generally get the bus. Some sixth formers drive, but few parents drop their children off, not least because parking can be a nightmare.

'People see this is a very middle-class school, but in fact there's a big range,' says head. When we visited, 24 pupils were on free school meals. Seventy-eight per cent white British students, the rest a wide range of other nationalities and ethnic backgrounds.

Parents talk of feeling 'privileged' their children got into the school and many are very involved in their children's education, with 100 per cent attendance at parents' evening. Active PTA, with a small band of very dedicated parents (mostly mums) fundraising and organising social events, such as comedy evenings and wine and nibbles evenings.

Entrance: Heavily oversubscribed, with 940 applicants for 208 places in 2015. Non-selective, except for 20 per cent of places, which are reserved for students with an aptitude for music (10 per cent) and academic ability (10 per cent). The furthest these students tend to come from is Watford or Pinner, although the places are highly sought-after. For the remaining 80 per cent of places, children in the looked after system/those with a Statement of SEN/EHC plan which names the school are prioritised (following the admissions code), followed by siblings (usually amounting to half the cohort every year) and children of staff (around 2-3 pupils every year), then it's down to distance, with priority given to a WD3 postcode.

Not many pupils leave, so very few spots open up in other year groups. Around 80-85 per cent of pupils stay on for sixth-form, although they need to get B or above in the GCSE of the subjects they choose at A level, which some parents complain is too strict and excludes pupils who'd really like to stay on. An additional 35 places are opened up for external applicants, usually attracting around 160 applicants who are assessed on their GCSE average points score.

Exit: Around a quarter leave after GCSE, most for BTech courses, performing arts or vocational qualifications. Of those who stay for the sixth form nearly all go onto university including Durham, Nottingham, Bristol, Southampton, Leeds, Imperial and UEA. Popular subjects include English, history, maths, physics and psychology. Seven to Oxbridge in 2016; two to medicine/dentistry courses. Around 10 per cent go into high level apprenticeships or directly into employment.

Remarks: This is a school that aims to be good at everything, refusing to pigeon-hole itself into excelling in certain areas over others, making it a great place to study for pupils, no matter where their strengths lie. Embracing new innovations in teaching, it is also a school that feels progressive, whilst still retaining traditional values. Above all, it stands out for being a place where most children are happy and, in the main, reaching their full potential. No wonder it's a school that parents move to the area for.

St Edmund's College

Old Hall Green, Ware, Hertfordshire SG11 1DS

Pupils: 829; 130 boarders • Ages: 3–19 • Sixth form: 142 • RC

Fees: Day £8,940 – £16,560; Boarding £21,825 – £28,110 pa

Tel: 01920 824247
Email: admissions@stedmundscollege.org
Website: www.stedmundscollege.org

Headmaster: Since 2012, Mr Paulo Durán BA MA (London). Educated at the London Oratory, King's College London and Heythrop College. Married to Alice, a teacher, with one daughter at St Edmund's. After spells at South Hampstead and

Alleyn's, he took up a post as head of modern languages at Mill Hill School where he stayed for six years, before moving to St Edmund's as deputy head in 2009. After three years he was offered the headship, and, he says, would like to stop here. Parents hope so too. 'A very warm, very charismatic man and a very strong leader,' said one mother. 'Please don't leave!'

Prep school head: Since 2013, Mr Steven Cartwright BSc. Joined the school in 2009 as deputy head and became acting head before taking up the post of headmaster. Married with two daughters, one at St Edmund's. Interests include squash, climbing, running, 'my family, my school!' Popular with parents, who describe him as 'lovely'. 'He's such a nice man, very approachable,' said one. 'He's really good with the children,' said another. An enthusiast who wants the best for his students. 'I am passionate about this school. I do sincerely believe that we strive for the best, and we've got a very nice community.'

Academic matters: Broad curriculum in the prep, including French, with a learning support manager to provide help for those who need it; we liked the learning support room, which was welcoming and cheerful. At the other end of the scale, a child who was particularly gifted in French attended lessons over in the senior college, and all the children go there for science. 'The teachers always encourage the children not just to learn, but to understand and ask questions,' said one satisfied parent.

Generally a sound performance with top grades consistently accounting for around a third of results. 2016 figures, for instance were 35 per cent A*-A at I/GCSE and 46 per cent A*-A at A level, which percentages are broadly on a par with the previous few years. 'Results are very good, and I want them to improve,' says head, but aims to achieve same 'without changing the children or the school. It's about moving up those league tables the hard way.' One big change has come, however. Since September 2014, the school has offered the IB alongside A levels. This is in response to parental demand, says school, as well as to a growing awareness that, as an international school, it's the right route to take. 'Catholic means universal, so we're already part of an international network.' In 2016, average point score was 33.

Broad curriculum comprises all the usual arts, humanities and sciences, with maths being a particular favourite. 'I like maths, purely for the fact that the teachers are so willing to help you,' said one boy, and his friends agreed. French, Spanish, German, Latin and Italian are on offer. All students learn French in year 7 and study an additional language throughout year 8 and 9. As you'd expect in a school of this ethos, religious education has a high profile, and RE is compulsory up to and including GCSE. The pupils aren't bothered by this, because 'the RE teachers are really good!' Bang-up-to-date ICT suites, and well-resourced classrooms and science labs. Food tech a popular option, and the children were proud of their achievements in the school bake-off. Lots of good quality work on the wall displays, and we were pleased with the standard of writing and spelling. The handsome library is surprisingly small for a school this size, but was lively and welcoming and regularly hosts visits from the likes of Kevin Crossley-Holland and Dave Cousins.

Our young tour guides were upbeat about lessons and about the amount of individual attention they got from teachers; the average class size is 21 (14 in sixth form). Parents described the teaching staff as 'really fantastic' and 'always there for the pupils', and praised the unwearying help given, in any subject, to students who needed it. 'If you're in the top set, you're pushed just as hard as you would be in a top academic school,' commented one sixth former. But a broad range of abilities is catered for here. The school currently has 105 children on its Learning Difficulties and Disabilities register, and pupils with SEN requirements are well-supported, both in class and at homework club, which happens four afternoons a week. EAL is also important here, because of the school's international intake. IGCSE second language English is offered to overseas students where appropriate.

The intake is only gently selective, which may account for the odd unexpected hiccup in student knowledge here and there. Talking to us about the school's history, a year 9 pupil told me, 'France wasn't Catholic back then, which is why the school moved here.' But the school's history is quite long and involved, and we were impressed by the pride with which the children talked about it. Everyone we spoke to was adamant that the school fostered a strong work ethic and helped all students to achieve their best.

Games, options, the arts: One happy parent, a musician herself, described the music as 'fantastic', and we certainly liked what we saw. The school's top choir, Schola Cantorum, regularly gigs at the likes of Canterbury and Westminster Cathedrals; chapel choir sings on Sundays during term time, and the chamber choir is much in demand for more secular school functions, such as weddings and dances. Lots of ensembles including an orchestra and jazz band, ably supported by a 21-strong team of peripatetic music teachers who get the children up to scratch on voice, strings, brass, woodwind, percussion, piano, guitar, harpsichord and organ (there's a magnificent organ in the school chapel). The school is particularly keen to build on choral scholarships 'and to see where that takes us.' There's a musical production every year; Our House by Madness is a recent example, and the curtain will shortly rise on Half A Sixpence at the nearby Broxbourne Civic Hall. 'They're a lot of work and a big commitment but they're absolutely wonderful!' enthused one student. Drama is also popular, with lots taking LAMDA exams, and student-directed productions such as – amazingly – One Man, Two Guvnors.

The last period of every school day (which finishes at 4.30pm) is given over to extracurricular activities, so all pupils participate in something. An extremely wide range of arts, crafts and other interests are offered, including CCF, D of E and Model United Nations. There are also some pretty special opportunities for travel. 'The trip to Thailand was one of the most amazing things I've ever done,' said one girl, and other pupils were starry-eyed about their experiences in India, America and Barcelona.

Wonderfully spacious campus means lots of playing fields plus tennis courts and Astro. Girls' sport is strong and includes hockey, netball and football. The boys' provision for traditional team games appears to be something of an issue. 'I'd like to see more organised compulsory training for the top teams,' said one boy, diplomatically. Parents (eager in their praise of all other areas of the school) were more forthright, criticising what they claimed was a 'lazy' lack of coaching for school teams who then had to 'go out and get slaughtered every week against better-trained sides.' Students confirmed that rugby/football practices were sometimes scheduled after the school buses had left, so that pupils, who travel in from an unusually wide geographical area, had no choice but to miss the sessions if they wanted to get home. The school counters by saying that the after-school clubs, targeted at mass participation, were scheduled at the request of parents, who had seemed happy to collect their children themselves. A sports academy focuses on the development of elite players in years 7 and 8. The less traditional sports – table tennis, golf, badminton, aerobics – are all flourishing, and there can't be many schools which can offer their students fishing (in the school pond) as an option.

Plenty of extracurricular activities at the prep too, with music and drama flourishing, and lots of sports (football is particularly successful). 'This is a very sporty school!' said one little boy, enthusiastically. Children can use the senior school's sports facilities.

Boarding: Boarders (full, weekly and flexi) are very well looked-after, with lots of staff living on site, and the school counsellor is always on hand. 'Bullying here is mercifully rare, and we set the bar low,' said head, firmly. One boys' and one girls' boarding house (twin or single rooms), with a communal common room where they can socialise together after prep. The usual weekend theatre, cinema and shopping trips for boarders, who include pupils from 20 different countries; activities include themed cultural evenings.

Background and atmosphere: Founded in France in 1568 as a seminary for English Catholics when the Reformation's prohibition of Catholic education forced Cardinal William Allen to decamp to Douai in Flanders. A couple of hundred years later in 1793, the French Revolution had professors and scholars packing their bags once again and moving to the village of Old Hall Green just north of Ware, where a small (and very secret) Catholic school had formerly acted as a 'feeder' for the Douai seminary. On 16 November 1793 – the feast of St Edmund – the school was created. It weathered various changes of fortune during the 19th century, but celebrated its quarter centenary in 1968, admitted girls to the sixth form in 1974 and has been fully co-educational since 1986. The school lists 20 canonised saints and 133 martyrs amongst its alumni, and is proud of its history, which it commemorates throughout the building in drawings, paintings and artefacts. Now occupying the whole of the village of Old Hall Green, the site is spacious (440 acres), wooded, and stunningly beautiful.

If Catholic iconography makes you uneasy, this ain't the place for you. Pictures of popes, archbishops, cardinals and saints are everywhere, along with statues, shrines, relics, holy paintings, and even a graveyard, containing, said an earnest pupil, 'people who died for the school'. It was something to see students lining up, in their own free time at their own volition, to use the Scofield Chantry for a few moments of candle-lit private prayer. The prevailing mood throughout the school, even at its liveliest times, was one of calm benevolence and order. 'We pride ourselves on the way we talk to our students and the way they talk to each other,' said the head, and all the young people we spoke to were in agreement. 'Everybody is nice, everybody respects each other,' 'I love it here, all my friends are nice,' 'The atmosphere is lovely,' were typical comments. Prayers are said before every lesson, 'And some of the prayers are really nice!' cried a pupil, who then recited one for me with great affection, adding 'You don't have to join in, but everyone respects it.' The school's Pugin chapel is lofty and awe-inspiring, and is used for weddings, funerals and baptisms as well as for school services. It's flanked by the smaller shrine chapel, built to hold St Edmund's left fibula that was presented by Cardinal Wiseman in 1863.

The college is overseen not by a specific order but by the Archdiocese of Westminster, and the Roman Catholic ethos is completely central to the life of the school. Even the year groups are named after Catholic principles: Elements, Rudiments, Grammar, Syntax, Poetry, Rhetoric I and Rhetoric II. 'We're proudly and unashamedly Catholic,' as the head put it, but added, 'We're also proud of being inclusive.'

Located on the same beautiful campus as its big brother, the junior school benefits from an enviable degree of space and wooded tranquility. Whereas the main senior school building is grand and imposing, the prep is a smaller, cosier affair, housed in a former family home designed by Pugin and containing many of his hallmark features. The prep children have their own very appealing little chapel, which is in daily use, plus an outdoor amphitheatre.

Pastoral care, well-being and discipline: Everyone we spoke to was especially warm in their praise of this aspect of the school. 'It's really good, very strong,' 'The school is very nurturing,' 'A very, very welcoming place, my child settled in straight away,' were some of the comments, and the last ISI inspection report praised the pupils' spiritual and personal development as outstanding. The house system is the main source of pastoral care with each pupil having a tutor and head of house.

The prep school children we met were relaxed, happy, well-mannered and fond of their school. 'They're really kind here, and I've made a lot of friends,' 'I prefer this school to my old one, there's so much to do,' were typical comments. As one parent added, 'There's a very nice atmosphere within the school. We're really pleased, no complaints at all.'

A number of pupils and parents commented on the lunch queues, which, they alleged, were not always well-managed. Some children spoke of having to miss lunch if they needed to attend clubs, or even if the queue just was too long. 'She loves the meals, but doesn't always get to eat them!' said one mother, 'I can't understand why they haven't nailed that problem.' (School admits that the situation needs addressing, and says it is working on ways to improve things.) On the plus side, the boarding means that all pupils can stay for supper at the school when they need to – when there are concerts or parents' evenings, for instance – and generally students seemed cared for and contented, moving with calm purpose about the school; uniform was worn tidily and behaviour everywhere was good. The spacious, well-kept and eye-pleasing buildings themselves seemed to help create a relaxed and happy community of individuals, quirky and otherwise, with a refreshing range of life-aspirations: one student hopes to set up a museum dedicated to vacuum cleaner parts.

Pupils and parents: Day pupils make up the majority of students, and are bused in from all over Hertfordshire and beyond via a network of 17 different routes. Excellent scholarships and bursaries ensure wide social diversity. Significant community of international students, many of them from eastern Europe, Africa and Asia. About 40 per cent of pupils are from Catholic families. The rest are from other Christian denominations, and from 'all other faiths and from none'. ('We have a fantastic Diwali celebration every year,' the head told me.) Notable alumni include William Scholl the sandal designer, perfumiers James and Robert Floris, and Ralph Richardson.

Entrance: Entrance to nursery from the term following children's third birthday. Further admissions at 4 and at 7 by interview ('crucial,' says head) and informal assessment. Up to 20 children per class; the school prefers to keep them small. Around a third of the children are from Catholic families, the rest from all faiths and from none. Scholarships available at 7+ based on academic merit – applicants sit an exam in January. The school's popularity is rising, and they recently went to two form entry from year 3 in response to demand.

About 20 a year of the senior school entry come from the prep, for whom entry is automatic, provided they joined in year 4 or below. The rest, who come from a wide range of preps and primaries, sit entrance exams in maths, English and non-verbal reasoning. However, the report from the child's previous school is just as important, along with the St Edmund's interview. 'We interview everyone for at least 30 minutes, and for as long as it takes, really,' says head, who puts great emphasis on getting to know what the children are like. The school's popularity continues to rise and they are now oversubscribed, with around 220 applicants for the 80 available places. Small additional intake at 13+. Some join the school at 16+, for which they need five A*-B grades at GCSE with at least B in their chosen A level subjects.

Exit: Nearly all prep school pupils move up to the senior school. At 16+, around 30 per cent to state sixth form colleges, or, very occasionally, to other independents (one boy found he'd grown away from the Catholic ethos and wanted a change). The rest stay on for sixth form here. At 18+ mostly to university: Manchester current front runner, with Hertfordshire Uni another favourite, alongside several London universities. One medic to Oxford in 2016 and one GlaxoSmithKline apprenticeship in cell and gene therapy

Money matters: Academic scholarships at 11+ and 13+, awarded on performance in the entrance exam. Music, art, sport and all-rounder scholarships also available, often in combination with academic awards. Total awards can be extremely generous – we heard from one parent whose child's scholarship was worth 90 per cent of the annual fees. A few sixth form scholarships. Limited number of means-tested bursaries, covering up to full fees.

Remarks: A successful, flourishing, dependable school with real spiritual heart. Well worth considering.

St Edmund's School

St Thomas Hill, Canterbury, Kent CT2 8HU

Pupils: 580; 143 boarders • Ages: 3–18 (chorister boarders from 8) • Sixth form: 115 • C of E

Fees: Day £9,027 – £19,671; Boarding £20,202 – £31,716; Choristers £21,249 pa

Tel: 01227 475601
Email: admissions@stedmunds.org.uk
Website: www.stedmunds.org.uk

Head of school: Since 2011, Mrs Louise Moelwyn-Hughes (40s). Previously senior deputy head of The Perse in Cambridge, and spent 13 years in various roles from year head to housemistress at Marlborough College, following a degree in classics at Cambridge. Now immediately dismiss the picture you've formed, because she's far from the Cambridge to Perse public school head you're imagining. Still has the accent from her humble but bookish Belfast background, and says she didn't really know what Cambridge was when a teacher suggested that her schoolgirl love of ancient Greek could be a ticket there.

Utterly comfortable in her own skin, seems to enjoy being different to the pack. 'I do things my own way, I call a spade a spade,' she says. No airs, no grandstanding, just that type of quiet authority which can bring a room to silence just by sitting still. 'A quiet powerhouse,' said a parent. 'She attends many events, but never seeks to take glory from those who organise – so at a chapel service, she may be sitting in the back pew while the lovely chaplain does his bit; same at junior school concerts, there to show support and cheer them on, but lets the master give the thanks and praise. Very respectful, but she watches everything, and seems to know everything.'

S

She's been responsible for some record-breaking results, and a 20 per cent increase in pupil numbers in the last three years. Parents describe the school as 'better in every element', and the transformation as 'quite extreme'. 'I can't speak highly enough of her,' said one. 'She has turned the school around, and changed the whole ethos, and it's clear teachers have a lot of respect for her.'

Another said: 'It is always quite obvious to me that she knows the students individually, as is the tremendous respect both students and staff members all have for her. I have met very few people in life who display such grace and level of consciousness in their dealings with others.'

Remarkably she has also transformed her home life, with two children produced during her time in post, and these toddlers are now curbing her hobbies of squash, running, walking and reading.

Academic matters: There is now an ex-Perse triumvirate at the top. Deputy head Ed O'Connor joined in 2013 from head of sixth form at Perse, and 2015 saw Matthew Jelley, previously deputy head of Perse's Prep school, becoming head of St Edmund's junior school. The pre-prep is also under a newish broom – Julia Exley joined as head in 2013 from Northbourne Park School.

Three leaders from this academic heavyweight is bound to have an impact, and the head makes no bones about the fact that she is stepping up expectations. 'Perse is in the top 10 academically, St Edmund's will never be that, but I am looking to raise the bar so that people feel tested,' she says. Rebranding means the school is no longer marketing itself as a music and drama school, and no longer describing itself as non-selective.

But while all the families we spoke to were aware of the change, none felt that a more academic bent was at the expense of less able pupils, or non-academic activities. 'I think this is an additional benefit to the school. The music and drama department is just as excellent as it was,' says one parent. 'It's a great turn around, without losing the school's comprehensive ethos,' said another. 'There is no feeling that you can settle for what you get – if you are predicted a C you have to try to get a B or higher.' Sixth formers told us that they would be heartily congratulated for a C grade if that was the best of their ability. 'Everyone has their own target grade which they are pushed to exceed,' said one.

We heard particularly strong praise from parents of dyslexic children. 'They are very good at identifying but not labelling,' said one. Another described a child who was struggling with the GCSE curriculum, but through what was described as 'learning tailor-made to him' went on to win a place at Cambridge. Moelwyn Hughes says she expects higher academic standards to result in more pupils with special needs, as it will encompass more students with Asperger's, many of whom are in the highest academic band nationally.

Should your child fall behind, it won't be seen as your problem. In this instance, the head says they find out what is behind it and put in a lot of pastoral and academic support. 'We don't say to parents you are going to have to supervise this, we make it our business to turn things around,' she says.

When some pupils were struggling in French, her response was 'Let's throw Arabic at it'. These pupils took a Cambridge Certificate in Arabic and Middle East studies instead. 'Four kids got distinctions. It's a Perse way to take something which looks higher end and give it to kids who are struggling, it builds confidence,' she says. It might also be testament to her teaching, as the children studied with her. She dismisses her own mastery of Arabic with an 'oh that' wave of the hand.

As well as Arabic other new subjects the head has introduced are economics, politics and Greek. At A level there are 26 subjects to choose from, the EPQ and an option to do the AQA Baccalaureate. The most popular A levels are biology, history and photography. Maths and theatre studies are also strong departments. In 2016, 33 per cent of A level entries achieved A*/A grades; at GCSE, 28 per cent of entries were A*/A.

There's no hiding place for teachers. 'If a parent complains about staff performance, I call the teacher in immediately and tell them and I deal with it,' the head says. Teachers are left to their own styles, as long as it works. Music teaching is said to be 'inspirational' and the head of junior school music was running a lively class investigating scores from Bond films when we visited. A sixth form economics class was studying the cement market, and the teacher was relaxed about some having earphones plugged in as they worked, as he said they were all turning in A*/B grade work.

'There are some fabulous teachers, and there have been some teachers whose tenure has been short because they just weren't up to the job. That's what we call progress. They use different techniques for different children – above all it's not a one size fits all school,' said a parent.

The junior school has its own bright and cosy classrooms, and the curriculum includes swimming, music, dance and French from the earliest years. In years 3 to 5 subjects are extended to include geography, history, IT and Latin. There is some streaming – we saw year 5 maths groups tackling number problems on paper in one set, while another was learning weights and ratios through making biscuits. The artwork on display in a variety of media is notably good.

In the upper half of the junior school – years 6, 7 and 8 – lessons are taught in a separate block in the upper school, where they can use the senior's science, art and design technology rooms, and all lessons are taught by subject specialists.

Games, options, the arts: Go in with your eyes open. It's a small school so you can't expect to have top flight teams. Some parents mourn the lack of rugby – the school plays football and hockey instead, which works better in a mixed year group of just 65. 'There's lots of sport there if you want to do it, but you have to be realistic, they are not going to beat the massive teams,' said one parent. For the top level players it can be frustrating, but a parent of one of these is pragmatic about it, saying, 'Even in big schools they are only going to get one or two county level players. And they are doing a lot to improve, such as getting in professional coaches.'

Music is strong, as you might expect in the school which educates the choristers of Canterbury Cathedral. There's a purpose-built music school with a recording studio. It's big on theatre too, with theatre studies well subscribed, and a full size theatre with five wings and a green room to perform in.

Some parents would like to see more trips, though one reeled off an impressive list her children had taken part in – skiing in Italy, drama trip to New York, music/language trip and watersports to Spain, Rua Fiola survival adventure, Christmas trip to Lille, language trip to Switzerland, and history trips to Portsmouth.

Saturday morning school is now optional. It's not charged for, pupils don't have to wear uniform, and the activities are the likes of international cuisine, technology, art, film making, sport, and music. One-third of day pupils come in for it.

Boarding: There are 140+ boarders, over half of whom are from overseas. There are flexi, weekly, and full boarding options. Junior boarders (11-13) live in School House, a wing of the main school building. Senior boarders live in the main school building or in the nearby Clare, Sunfield and Gorsefield Houses. Boys' dormitories have views over the fields to the cathedral, through arched mullioned windows. Girls overlook the changing rooms. Boys have ensuites, girls don't. The boarding rooms are fairly cramped, but there's a big common room/kitchen and sixth formers have separate studies shared between three or four people. After optional morning school on a Saturday, afternoons are free, and Sundays see outings to London museums, Bluewater, ice skating and so on. The 26 choristers (boys only) live separately in Choir House within the cathedral precincts, with a timetable which includes 20 hours singing, attending evensong six days a week, and recordings.

Background and atmosphere: The school is centred around a High Victorian building with its own chapel. The exterior is grand, and there are commanding views across the fields to Canterbury Cathedral. But the senior school interior has stained carpets, holes gouged out of plaster, some cramped classrooms shoved into unlikely parts of the old building, and is frankly scruffy. If you're doing the circuit its shabbiness will be evident among the more glitzy schools; but current parents don't notice it and see it as all part of the warm, family atmosphere. The head has made staffing and small class sizes a priority, and says increased pupil numbers in the last two years will now fund refurbishment.

It's a school with a smile on its face, a great sense of ease and happiness pervades. 'It's as friendly and warm as a prep school. Every single teacher knows me and you just feel welcome,' said one parent.

Will you fit in? One parent describes it thus: 'It's not a competitive school. If you want to be told that your child is number one at everything, don't come here. If you get your kicks from being told you're better than everyone else, it's not for you. If you are a show off, don't come here. There's no pride in being better than someone else here – it's about being better than your own expectations and about being part of the school.'

Pastoral care, well-being and discipline: Praise for the pastoral care from parents was overwhelming. One child missed several months of school owing to health problems in his GCSE year, and he was given one-to-one teaching on his return to enable him to catch up. We also heard about a teenager who had derailed; the response, as the parent described, 'Spending days after talking, planning, resetting goals and wiping the slate clean for a new start. At all times protecting his dignity and his self-esteem. Within days all teaching staff adopted a completely different set of rules for him, and never mentioned earlier failings.' Moelwyn Hughes says: 'I'm a big fan of meeting with parents and the pupil and deciding what we're going to do.'

Another family had to deal with bereavement, and the parent said: 'I can categorically say that had it not been for the pastoral care and time and attention Louise Moelwyn-Hughes and her housemaster provided to him, and what he gets out of the school community, his world would be a far worse place than it is today. I am eternally indebted to Louise Moelwyn-Hughes and St Edmund's School.'

And lots of parents told us that the head will always seek out children and congratulate them individually on a big achievement in their own sphere. 'It's the little touches you don't normally get in a senior school,' said a parent.

Pupils and parents: People tend to stick with the school. At transition last year, 52 out of 54 came up from the junior to senior school last year, and around 10 new pupils join at this point.

International students represent 28 nationalities – there are larger groups from China and Germany, but kept no bigger than 15 students – and also students from Thailand, The Congo, Kazakhstan, Russia, Nigeria, Poland, Belgium and France.

It's not a school where you need designer clobber for the school run. One parent described the parent body as 'trying to do the best for their children. Very mixed finances, not all necessarily finding the school fees that easy, and not doing it for the social cachet of being an old boy. Very few pushy parents, certainly not seeking advance for their own child at the expense of another.'

Another described the school gate as 'friendly, warm, no parents whinging in your ear "my child wasn't the shining star ..."'

Entrance: Usual entry points (3+, 7+, 11+, 13+ and 16+) plus other year groups when places available. Junior school entry is based on assessments on a taster day to gauge academic levels; nearly all juniors move up to the senior school with no entrance test. At 11+ entry for outsiders (a few join at this stage) there are formal entrance tests (verbal and non-verbal reasoning) and consideration is given to Kent Test results. Year 9 entry involves tests in maths and English, and a guideline requirement would be common entrance marks of around 60 per cent or above (although you don't have to pass common entrance). Sixth formers need A*/B at GCSE in the subjects they wish to study. On top of that, head says personality and character is part of it. 'It matters the mix you have. I take the opportunity to meet every kid so they recognise that I chose them,' she says.

Exit: Nearly all juniors join the senior school. All sixth formers go to higher education including conservatoires and drama schools, and popular university destinations are Manchester, Reading, Exeter, King's College, Royal Holloway, UCL, Durham, Bristol and Canterbury. Two to Cambridge and one to Yale in 2016.

Money matters: Scholarships from 10 per cent to 50 per cent of the tuition fees for both day and boarding pupils are awarded in academic, music, sport, art and drama categories, and occasionally to all-rounders. These can be topped up by means-tested bursaries for those currently at the school. Discounts offered to children of clergy, members of the armed forces, and third and subsequent children.

Remarks: Which of the effusive quotes to use? We've seldom seen such overwhelming praise for a head, and for pastoral care, from parents. Nor such a sense of a cohesive parent body without factions. Not for you if you want a school high on social cachet and entry to society by school tie, or smart teas after thrilling wins against top flight teams. But if you want a school which is going to take great care of your child, and get the best out of him/her, whether s/he's a Cambridge or C grade student, definitely one for the shortlist.

St Edward's Oxford

Woodstock Road, Oxford, Oxfordshire OX2 7NN

Pupils: 680; 567 boarders • Ages: 13–18 • Sixth form: 296 • C of E

Fees: Day £28,545; Boarding £35,940 pa

Tel: 01865 319200
Email: registrar@stedwardsoxford.org
Website: www.stedwardsoxford.org

Warden: Since 2011, Mr Stephen Jones MSc MLitt (50s), previously head of Dover College. Educated at both Hurstpierpoint and Lord Wandsworth Colleges. Erudite, a man of many degrees, went to Durham to read maths and physics but graduated with a rare first in philosophy, then read maths before embarking on research in philosophy of maths. Was an assistant housemaster at Cheltenham College, head of maths at Berkhamsted School and a social tutor at Radley before his appointment at Dover. Married to the delightful Katie, who has her own successful career in the church – no mean feat alongside being a headmaster's wife. They have three children, two of whom have flown the nest.

We're told he is a good sportsman, keen on staying in shape, enjoys fives and sailing and has a keen sense of humour, 'His student house was dubbed Front, so he could talk about going back to Front'. An accomplished mathematician, he loves poring over the figures and has a brain that specialises in pure logic, in whatever discipline. Parents say, 'Youngsters respect him, he is easy to talk to.' When we meet he is chatty, relaxed, enthusiastic – 'I don't have all the answers, what head does?' – but stresses that 'I want to engender a culture of academic excitement, sharpen things, raise expectations tempered with understanding of what the world is really like'. He is realistic too and under no illusion that keeping St Edward's on top of its game and rubbing shoulders with competitors will demand toughness and vision.

Academic matters: Most take nine or 10 subjects at IGCSE/GCSE, all the usual plus Latin or classical civilisation and Greek alongside PE, DT and drama. In 2016, 63 per cent of GCSE papers were graded A*/A. Philosophy/ethics/political literacy courses for lower school pupils and all sixth formers study for an EPQ or equivalent: 'Great preparation for independent study at university and beyond,' says warden. In 2016, 70 per cent of A level grades were A*/B (42 per cent A*/A) and the IB average was a creditable 35. Scholars' societies – OX2 for lower school and The Woodstock Group for seniors – stretch the able. Parents say science teaching is variable: 'Joint offering of IB and A level has resulted in good teachers being stretched too thinly' – school aware and say they are working hard to redress. At A level biology and art & design popular and successful.

Good for self-esteem: those who can, will, those who can't will be helped to. Currently 15 per cent of pupils receive learning support, mainly for mild dyslexia – timetabled and free: 'We are an inclusive school so subject support is offered'. Learning support concentrates on strategies, including use of smartphone and ICT. 'If they are disaffected we look closely at what is going on. They can't hide here.'

Has a reputation for being gentler on the old grey matter – both entry and exit – than many of its near competitors yet, in these league table propelled days, parents may seek a school that is 'forgiving' on entry but don't want an apology on exit – nor do they get one. Teddies (as it is affectionately known) has been shimmying up the league tables: not via hothousing – 'There are enough schools in the locality doing that,' says school – nor by upping the entry ante (though scholarships have been expanded and a new girls' house, Jubilee, helpfully nudges boy-girl ratio close to 3-2); rather the main thrust has been to eke more out of everyone, think good breezy airing, rather than squeezed through the wringer. Pupils write A* and keep in their pockets; IGCSEs introduced; IB has been extended ('Oversold,' say parents, school says not the case, adding, 'Pupils are choosing it in increasing numbers'). A levels remain, though no Pre-U, the tougher alternative to A levels; 'Not really the thing for our cohort', said warden.

However the biggest buzz (and buzz-word) is meta cognition ('know about knowing,' said our young informant). Warden wanted children to develop intellect, to reason, question and enquire. 'Some children arrive browbeaten through CE; we have to rebuild their confidence, inspire and invigorate them'. Working on the youngsters meant developing staff. 'I appointed a new academic director who encourages staff to share good practice, go off-piste, explore and enjoy their subject,' says warden. A move that appears to be working: 'Teachers love the curve ball question but some had lost their nerve, teaching only to pass an exam rather than exploring their subject,' says academic director. 'That is changing'. Dead Poets Society this isn't, there is still a generous nod to the syllabus and ticking boxes – plenty of routine revision, past papers, chalk and talk during our spring visit, but our guides said they're treated to discussion-based, interactive, active lessons. Parents approve: 'It's a happy, friendly common room with a great vibe that rubs off on kids'. Academic push still a work in progress but generally all things learned are looking up and bucking up.

Games, options, the arts: Fabulous facilities – 100 acres of prime north Oxford; outdoor courts, cricket pitches, a new cricket pavilion (Gloucestershire Cricket Club runs a satellite academy at the school for pupils and local juniors), a nine hole golf course, boathouse. Indoors there is a superbly equipped, sparkly leisure centre – the hub of middle class Oxford mummies working off their lunches – shared with, and leased from, the school, providing a fantastic gym, indoor and outdoor pools, indoor tennis courts and fitness and dance studios. Pupils win accolades – cricket team undefeated, have their fastest first eight ever, runners up at National Schools' and Henley; several GB junior oarsmen and county cricketers; girls' senior hockey team have been county champions seven years in a row – currently county champions at U14, U16 and U18. Rugby less robust: 'We take a few hits,' confess boys, though school hopeful tide turning. New director of sport is working hard to tempt talent of tomorrow to Teddies – with an array of special events. Not that those who wince at the thought of catching a ball should worry: 'They will find a sport you can not only do but do so proficiently; it's all about building confidence. Staff get involved too – it's lovely to see their commitment – it rubs off on the youngsters.' Only moan is expense of sports kit: 'Always something else on the bill; they must be in-league with the supplier,' joked one parent.

Art good with results to match, especially at A level with facilities for jewellery making, ceramics, sculpture and large fine art displays. The North Wall Arts Centre (enjoyed by the local community – hosts visiting artists and theatre groups) boasts exhibition galleries, drama studios and a cosy 250 seat theatre. Parents say dance has come on in 'leaps and bounds' and music is on the up (new music school features, inter alia, recital and rock rooms plus a recording studio), with something for everyone regardless of where you sit in the talent pool. 'Kids try hard, there's a huge number of bands, plus excellent choirs including one for parents and the community.' Excellent extracurricular provision including ever popular Duke of Edinburgh and CCF.

Boarding: Boarding houses have own identity – quad or field side: choose quad for a disorganised child, field for those who relish open space. New girls' house, Jubilee, is, according to warden, 'more like an upmarket hotel than a traditional school house'. For most of the rest, including odd Cinderella house ('about to improve,' say school) it is standard, homely rooms – shared save for the older years, with an assortment of communal facilities.

Cohesive boarding houses provide welcome support and foster inter-year friendships. Good food, all dine centrally, pupils say it's fun to mix with friends from other houses, parents rue table manners: 'They're noticeably very much "bolt-food" variety.' Safari suppers, ice-skating and discos are a sample of the many weekend jollies.

'Lots of boarders go home on Sunday after chapel, leaving school feeling somewhat empty and unloved for those forced to stay in,' said one parent, but another added, 'I like that they can come home on Sundays; we relish the family time.'

Background and atmosphere: Situated in leafy north Oxford, the setting is privileged indeed. Much akin to an Oxford college, the main buildings surround a lawned quad. Recent additions include an eco-inspired life sciences building – solar powered with 'more technology than you could wish for'. School isn't the grandest we've seen, it may lack the edge of some of its established upper-crusty rivals, but it has enough of everything, is polished and looks good. Simple peaceful chapel, compulsory on Sundays for boarders, C of E but all faiths welcome. Day pupils stay until 9pm (ad hoc early finish at 6pm on request), all can have a bed in the boarding houses and sleep over if they're too spent to go home.

Pastoral care, well-being and discipline: Parents say pastoral care is excellent, only caveat, 'We'd love our child to have the same tutor throughout, someone who can help and support when pressure builds or child overloaded, overwhelmed or overwrought'; school counters, 'structured tutor system for continuity of tutoring in lower school and in sixth form is ideal for a boarding school'. Still has its fair share of rich kids, some with arguably too much pocket money at their disposal.

Tough on drugs; warden says, 'If we suspect, we test; if positive, save the most exceptional circumstances and I can't think of any of those, they're out.' Punishments for smoking, parents say booze handled brilliantly for the child. 'Quite a number drink and smoke in younger years (same everywhere?), they push boundaries but school pushes back.' Local pubs policed, those aged 18 get a pub pass but other savvy sixth formers sneak off to Summertown for their Saturday night tipple. 'If they get caught they get bust but it doesn't stop them,' said our mole, adding, 'You must be able to say a lucid goodnight to your HM, otherwise it's a night in the san and the ignominy of being woken every 30 minutes.' School adds, 'All have cheese and biscuits and spend an hour with HM when they return; it's great fun for HM and means we get to keep a friendly eye.' Despite tolerance, some parents feel school needs to be more trusting, offer more privileges to older ones, with a long rein tugged hard for those who rail against.

Pupils and parents: Parents a mix of academics, professionals and business. Twenty per cent of boarders from overseas, from a huge variety of countries. Most of rest from Oxford or the home counties. Has a local reputation of privilege and at times pushing the boundaries – Teddies' girls in particular – yet the pupils we met were grounded, down to earth and friendly, a view shared by others we spoke to. 'They're clubbable, they've had to live with people in close confinement, they learn how to get the most out of others,' says warden, with a student adding, 'My parents gave me The Good Schools Guide and I chose Teddies; it has lived up to all in the review but especially on the friendship and friendliness front.' Notable former pupils include Kenneth Grahame, Laurence Olivier, Douglas Bader, Guy Gibson, Jon Snow, Emilia Clarke and Sam Waley-Cohen.

Entrance: From a range of prep schools, majority of day from Dragon. Skype interviews possible for those based overseas. Gently academic 55 per cent at CE, non CE candidates take the school's own exam. A handful sit an exam at 11+ to guarantee a place. Runs an academic challenge day for local year 6 pupils, with diet of philosophy, Arabic, economics, architecture and politics, to spot scholarship potential and encourage applications.

Exit: Handful (some 10 per cent) leave post-16 to pursue courses not offered here or to save on fees. One to Oxbridge in 2016, rest to eg London, Exeter, Bristol, Edinburgh, Newcastle, the US (UCLA, Northeastern), Canada and Europe. One medic and one vet in 2016; other popular subjects include geography, biomedical sciences, engineering, maths, modern languages and history. Inspiringly, St Edward's doesn't view the path to university as job well done: 'We look to the bigger picture, the young employable 25-year-old making strides in business, commerce, enterprise and academia. Understanding the cut and thrust of the world beyond university is paramount.'

Money matters: New scholarships introduced – academic, music, sport and all-rounder can be means-tested to a maximum of 100 per cent. Sizeable number on bursaries: 'Often the most able,' says warden. 'Attracting bright pupils is good for the school, good for the teachers and good for results.' All are considered annually for an honorary scholarship. Minor scholarships available for drama, art and dance.

Remarks: For those uncomfortable with ultra prestige, the trappings of the old and bold, or the sheen of highly-polished academia, St Edward's offers an established, acceptable, dependable alternative. Those who seek out Teddies will either be judging it against day school rivals or other co-ed boarding schools; it doesn't sit at the top of either pile but it holds its own, taps on elbows and keeps them on their toes. All-round broad education with plenty of nurturing, perceptibly raising expectations and results while maintaining its discernible cheer and friendliness. A busy school with a rosy outlook, ideal for a broad range of academic abilities, the late bloomer, the all-rounder and the high-flyer who doesn't wish to be a mere pebble, fighting for survival, in the tidal wave of Oxford's academic powerhouses.

St George's College, Weybridge

Weybridge Road, Addlestone, Surrey KT15 2QS

Pupils: 1,590 • Ages: 3–18 • Sixth form: 264 • RC

Fees: £8,160 – £17,745 pa

Tel: 01932 839300
Email: contact@stgeorgesweybridge.com
Website: www.stgeorgesweybridge.com

Head: Since September 2016, Mrs Rachel Owens, MA PGCE NPQH (40s), previously headmistress of St George's School Ascot. Previously vice principal at New Hall School and, before that, head of history at Prior Park College, Bath, following spell in career-nourishing environment of North London Collegiate School. Married to Tom, who teaches at RGS.

State educated (former grammar turned comp), Oxford history graduate who started reading for the bar, realised wasn't for her and instantly got teaching job near home town of Bolton, in part to alleviate guilt towards perennially-supportive parents. Hasn't looked back since. poised and super bright, radiates quintessential head qualities, said parents at previous school. Highly energetic, and as mother of primary age twin sons, undoubtedly needs to be. Needle-sharp efficiency too – completed Open University PGCE while teaching full time. Turstee of an HMC scheme that brings talented Eastern European sixth formers to British schools.

Head of junior school: Since 2003, Mr Antony Hudson MA PGCE NPQH (50s). Previously deputy head at Prior's Field. Before that, worked at assorted independents, all secondary and in Surrey or close, bar a three-year stint as housemaster and sixth form head in deepest Derbyshire to get taste for rural lifestyle out of system.

The first layman in the post, head is understandably relieved to have joined after the dust had settled and blood-letting had been accomplished (teachers had to reapply for jobs – all very traumatic). 'A lovely man,' one mother told us. Doesn't dissemble – you'll get the truth from him, even if it hurts, say parents, and, fittingly, his office alone would win awards for transparency, with doors or windows on three sides. Two doors ajar is the 'surgery is open' sign for parents who want a quick chat. Office filled with assorted artefacts – books, photographs, guitar, even a Toy Story character – that tell his life story, illuminated by the warm glow of five desk lamps ('not very environmentally friendly but I can't bear a central light').

Like office, like man: he's engagingly frank about his life to date. A couple of years into teaching career he was within a whisker of following in footsteps of an older brother (he has four) and entering the priesthood, when doubts set in. Instead of taking his vows, he opted for marriage and a family. Very much to the community's benefit as he and his wife Helen (a teacher at St Hilary's in Godalming) play a huge part in church life. Their two sons are both at St George's College.

To the slight bafflement of some colleagues, head enjoys local celebrity and recognition (shopping expeditions can resemble a royal tour, he says). This despite a period when he feared he would become a local hate figure amongst well to do mummies after he changed admissions criteria, reduced numbers with learning difficulties and some pupils were asked to leave. 'I thought they'd be burning me in effigy on the high street.' But, Piaf-like, it's a case of 'je ne regrette rien' – school needs to keep numbers feeding through to college at age 11, so it's not fair on anyone if he's taking students who won't make it and diverting too many resources away from the able ones who will. 'We'll never achieve 100 per cent but we aim to come close,' he says.

Teaches all reception pupils music, splitting the workload with a colleague, so gets to know children well from the beginning and is an extrovert type who's happy to dress up in the line of duty. 'Togas can be dangerous when everyone is wearing shorts,' he says of his recent appearance at school fête. Not averse to direct action, once taking to the streets to urge poorly parked parents to mend their ways (with a follow up number plates of shame section in school newsletter).

Academic matters: Junior school not the place to go for educational fads and fancies. Focus is always on keeping in step with the senior school (their staff visit regularly – more so now, you get the impression, than used to be the case). The result is that parents are never in doubt, for good or ill, about how pupils are doing. Maths set from year 3, English from year 5 and regular assessments for all.

Teachers, who span the experience/age spectrum, win pupil approval – especially as 'there aren't any shouty ones now,' said one pupil – and come across as unflappable. In classroom-based subjects, lots of traditional teaching from the front (lidded desks still the norm, too) though plenty of hands-on involvement elsewhere. Textbook-only lessons 'a rarity,' said a science teacher as, with evident relish, year 6 girls applied a Bunsen burner to magnesium and iron filings in well-equipped lab.

Once a haven for those with learning difficulties, things are very different now. Informal quota agreed with governors limits numbers to around 25, though 'nobody's going to die in a ditch if we have two extra,' says head. However, unlikely to be the right place for anything more severe than mild dyslexia, well catered for by learning support team either in lessons or through withdrawal.

As with the senior school, no shortage of things to do. Science and art rooms (there's even a kiln) are open at break-time and large, inviting 14,000-volume library (librarian would make world a Kindle-free zone if she could) welcomes little readers in. Everyone, from tinies upwards, has minimum of one library session a week.

School radiates confidence. There's a sense of having arrived and pausing to take stock. Yes, pupil numbers have doubled and standards have risen steadily, but though there's natural enthusiasm for further upwards striving, isn't 'remorselessly trying to make this more and more academic.' Parents back this up. 'It's not force feeding,' says one.

Results good – 67 per cent A*-A grades at GCSE in 2016. Similar story for A levels with 81 per cent A*-B and 49 per cent graded A*-A in 2016, something that puts them among area's stronger performers (and local competition, state and private, is fierce).

How's it done? Enthusiasm comes as standard with teachers not just on emergency call out in exam season but still working to timetable when pupils are on study leave (though they request emails to avoid teaching to empty rooms). Attitude filters down – year 8 pupil, unprompted, rushes over to visitors during drama class to extol delights of rehearsing Pardoner's Tale for performance. 'A head girl in the making,' said the incumbent.

Overall, there's sense of constant nudging to bring everything on that bit quicker and better, less hothouse, though, than prize winning allotment (all quality produce – think asparagus rather than bog standard giant marrows).

You see it in imaginative projects for gifted and talented cohort (year 10 poets clad scale models of London landmarks with photographs and words) and English language IGCSE taken a year early by everyone, sensible as capitalises on three years of timetabled library sessions where 'we can direct pupils' reading,' says head of English, who's clearly good at inspiring a love of books further up the school. 'Reading is all I do in my spare time,' said sixth form boy. Recent library extension and roof replacement have no doubt helped, literally shedding extra light on the experience.

Unusually, no fast track maths (top number crunchers take additional maths GCSE by way of compensation) though a flair for languages can find pupils sailing through AS exam before they reach sixth form (here as elsewhere, language take up falls off sharply post-GCSE, something school is keen to reverse).

Don't, however, expect subject choices to extend beyond tried and tested varieties. Unlike Maureen Lipman of BT ad fame, staff not a fans of the 'ologies' (technology is the exception), feeling that A level psychology and sociology don't carry the same clout as traditional 'hard currency' subjects. Budding girl rocket scientists should also consider the gender fault line that runs through the school at A level – and elsewhere, of course – with biology a largely xx chromosome subject and chemistry and, overwhelmingly, physics dominated by the xy brigade. 'It just tends to be a boy's science,' said pupil (girls' only schools, however, would almost certainly not agree).

When things go wrong, school does best to help. Policy is emphatically not to throw weakest to the wolves but catch problems early. May be the option to repeat a year. First port of call is often the academic support unit which also helps those with specific learning difficulties (dyslexia, affecting 50 or pupils, by far the most common, handful of pupils have ADHD, ADD and ASD, only two statemented; around 20 with English as an additional language). Attendance at its supervised study periods, used to hone study rather than subject skills, is very strongly hinted at, though not compulsory, and parents are kept in the loop. 'It's not a draconian approach, more "if we don't feel that you're achieving this ... we'll all get together and try to work it out",' said a mother. 'You're not allowed to slip but it's not done in an unpleasant way.'

Games, options, the arts: Would be criminal if games results didn't live up to glorious facilities (so many pitches, courts and nets that you could play somewhere different just about every week of the academic year). Fortunately they do, successfully, with whacking great double-fronted trophy cabinet stuffed with silverware – a challenge to even a posse of cat burglars – as proof.

It's all set in 100 acres, vast for home counties, let alone within M25 – property developers must salivate every time they drive past – and comes with a delightful 19th century cricket pavilion, a boathouse on the Thames and even a brace of rivers running through the grounds (why stop at one?).

Natty ultra-traditional cricket and rowing blazers confer huge cachet on wearers, though the new is also embraced with basketball, currently being beta tested with series of successful friendlies and just about to go live. Overall, lots to cheer on and about with rugby a particular star and many other teams regularly reaching national finals. A few heroic near misses, too. 'The boys' first XI only lost three matches [...] unfortunately two were in the semi-finals...' begins wry hockey report in school mag.

Triple-colour awards are a regular phenomenon, as are small but steady numbers of rowers, cricketers and netball players cherry-picked for regional and national squads. Keenness as well as talent is rewarded – turn up to under 12 boys' hockey training and you're guaranteed at least one go in school team.

The only fly in ointment is felt to be strength of mind required for those joining at 13, where 'it's a hard effort to get included in teams,' said parent. Not deliberate, she added, 'it's just human nature'. 'Of course it's going to be tough,' added another, more forthright mother, 'but there again it depends on how determined you are.' With school offering 100 timetabled activities every week, vast majority included in fees, no shortage of opportunities to find your inner sporting hero – or indeed cook, artist or musician. Volunteering ethos very strong and often with religious dimension. Highlight for many is oversubscribed week in Lourdes where lower sixth volunteers become full-time carers for disabled children – 'life-changing' says one. Standard fare of D of E and slightly more glamorous International Challenge also on offer.

Feel, though not macho, is equally far from precious. Music, highly successful (school won prestigious BBC Songs of Praise Senior School Choir of the Year the first time it entered) balances highly selective with audition-free: whole school choir, open to all comers, tackles demanding choral works with panache. Energetic department director is unfussed by smallish numbers taking GCSE or A level music, refreshing in an age when there's increasing sense that if you can't measure it in exam results it's scarcely worth doing. 'I'd rather have a full orchestra and big choirs than massive exam sets,' she says. She also relishes large amount of informal music making that goes on out of hours in first come first served practice rooms. Sound of pupil playing the grand piano in the chapel, not for an audience but just, apparently, for the pleasure of it, underpinned her words.

The sporty (and competitive) are well catered for at the junior school too with excellent facilities – heated outdoor swimming pool (complete with ring of safety steel fencing to Fort Knox standards), two tennis courts and all weather surfaces for hockey and tennis and results to match. Many near misses in quarter and semi-finals and some impressive county and regional championship wins (boys' tennis and girls' mini hockey particularly strong).

If sport doesn't appeal (and even if it does) you can go à la carte with a 45-strong menu of clubs and activities, ranging from puppet making to country dancing (recently introduced and popular enough for school 'to have requisitioned a maypole'). Lots of music and as school owns 80 violins, all year 2 parents have precious gift of squeaky open strings alternating with taster recorder sessions. Works, though, with 60 per cent playing instruments in year 3 (numbers fall off in further up school as some 'can't cope' with commitment required, says the head of music, and orchestra, just 19-strong, is due a bit of a re-think. New performing arts centre no doubt an incentive. Sensible timetabling of instrument lessons avoids clashes with vital academic subjects. Two big junior choirs – all comers welcome, including 'lots of boys,' say year 6 girls with distinct froideur, who 'get a house point for joining which we don't.' Sewing, however, remains a solidly girls-only (and housepoint-free) zone.

Background and atmosphere: 'You won't see a macho school.' Instead, you'll hear a good deal of the phrase 'politesse and douceur'. Hard to pin down but think Arthurian knightly values (the good ones) given a 21st century co-educational makeover and you're probably not far off.

May sound a bit highfalutin but clearly goes in: pupils don't just behave exceptionally well in school (doors routinely held open a good 40 feet in advance in longest of corridors) but out of it, too – a test with far higher ecological validity. Watching small group of unsupervised 11-year-old boys in local country club restaurant eating and chatting quietly 'ignited the spark' for parent who hadn't previously considered the school for her children and ended up sending both there.

Ethos stems from Josephites, a small Belgian Catholic order dating from early 19th century, who founded school in 1869. Though declining in Europe, order is vibrant in the Congo and blessedly scandal-free everywhere (only hint of controversy is at US school run by similarly named though unrelated order which is fighting, with strong parental backing, to retain corporal punishment).

As the UK mother house, the school is home to elderly priests who, like everyone else, must relish the space at their disposal. For vista-starved visitors from London it's a breath of fresh air (quite literally) with many pretty buildings, some Victorian, others a slight mish-mash of periods, and the widespread use of gorgeous unifying and beautifully tended greenery to bind everything together.

There's a green and pleasant quad for the youngest pupils accessorised with what sounds like the loudest blackbird in Surrey and, amongst many other areas, a sixth form garden – though if the school put its mind to it, pupils could all have their own plot and you'd scarcely notice.

Many of the classrooms have been refurbished, and with the exception of the occasional beige carpet tile moment, overall effect is smart and welcoming – music floor with cream and blue walls is particularly inviting as is dining hall, all light wood and toning shades of school burgundy. (Well-trained guides dutifully intone virtues of appealing and varied meals though there's widespread ditching once they cease to be compulsory.)

Tradition looms large, from new stained glass chapel windows, some inspired by words from school prayer to an almost subliminal appearance of the school crest all over the place, etched into windows, in undertones on walls and even face-painted on to pupils, featured in the magazine. Corridors, too, pack a momento mori frisson. One is adorned with team photos, many pre-dating the Great War, with fresh-faced youths staring, unknowing, into the camera ('We sometimes try to work out which of us they look like,' said sixth former); the next stuffed with GCSE and A level artworks, all thoroughly of the moment, though, reassuringly, prevalence of tortured-looking figures tearing at faces signals response to exam themes rather than profound inner torment, say pupils.

Recently completed Henderson Centre, however, is very much of the moment. All soft curve loveliness, it's the best incentive for staying on at a school post-GCSE that this reviewer has so far encountered. Sixth formers, recently granted new study rooms on top of everything else, also have café-style common room complete with balcony, mood lighting and instant boiling water (kettles – so old hat). Keep out signs warn off incursions by younger pupils – 'they get The Stare if they come in,' said prefect. Also home to sixth form only subjects like economics, plus humanities (geography and history, previously housed in less than glamorous huts, got first dibs on best seats in the house by way of compensation).

S

One parent described St George's Junior as 'a well-rounded education that's hard to get elsewhere,' and only real fly in the ointment has been fabric of the building, definitely more shabby than chic. 'It needs reinvigoration,' says the deputy head, with masterly understatement. It's getting it with new lower years building, The Ark, just opened, with refurbed nursery following soon.

In the meantime, it's nice to see priority given to small things that make a difference, like the de luxe refurbishment of girls' and boys' toilets on every landing in main four-storey block that houses years 2 to 6. Credit must also go to school's groundsmen, who are responsible for some of the most successful floral camouflage in the business – beautifully maintained greenery and hanging baskets that distract the eye as you brave the long walkway that runs between two rows of Portakabins.

'We're in a position to build for the next 50 years,' the head told us. 'I'd love to be here till I'm 65.' On the evidence of pupil numbers and parent positivity, there are plenty who won't have a problem if he is. Other school bursars must look at the rising numbers and weep. Big site is well organised and unified by strong emphasis on belonging. Even majority of nursery children, housed in their own separate block, wear uniform and everyone in junior school plays in at least one proper match regardless of ability. Wearing the school badge 'means something' (after that, selection is down to talent and commitment to turning up to after hours training).

School's sense of tradition is inescapable but not overweighty and inextricably bound up with religious dimension, centred on imposing chapel with a weekly mass conducted by Josephite priest. In a nod to the sensibilities of the softer 21st century child, though, there's an element of sugar coating, with some crucifixes round the school depicting cheerful Holy Family rather than the agony of Christ.

Pastoral care, well-being and discipline: 'A very nurturing school,' say parents. Four-house system provides the focus for inter-school competitions but caring role is down to much praised heads of year. They win accolades for their light touch but effective approach to bullying – 'once I'd pinpointed it, they were quick to make sure it was not going to happen again, and didn't involve the children so they never knew anything about it,' said a mother – and in theory stay with a year group as they move up through school. It's not bombproof and promotion or maternity leave are, as elsewhere, the enemies of continuity, though in the (rare) event that you don't get on, 'it can be a good idea to have a change because then you've only got to tolerate it for one year,' said a parent.

For minor misdemeanours, there's 'lots of nipping in the bud,' says school, with parents called in for meetings. Next come Friday detentions followed by suspension for repeated offences. Removal or expulsion 'a very rare occurrence' ('school doesn't like to wash its dirty linen in public so it's hard to know how many,' said parent) but would normally be automatic for drugs. Drink possibly ditto, though might be commuted to a warning or suspension instead.

Any bad or even slightly dubious lots would have to undergo a very public Damascene-type conversion to be considered as prefects. Informal talent spotting starts well down the school. Once appointed (towards end of lower sixth), powers include the ability to impose instant detentions on everyone, theoretically extending to year above, 'though staff and pupils counsel against it,' said one (wisely so, it's reckoned, to avoid detention at dawn showdowns).

Would-be head boys and girls, meanwhile, put their names forward, deliver make or break 'I could be so good for you' speeches, followed by a one pupil one teacher vote and 'almost perfect concordance' on the winners. Judging by bonhomie in the corridors, they're liked, not feared, by younger pupils, something that should stand current head girl in good stead if plans to introduce informal 'doctor is in' drop in sessions for the troubled and needy come to fruition.

Junior school parents, prospective and existing, comment on exceptional pupil manners on and off the premises. Lots of (almost) unprompted standing up whenever a teacher enters the room, though observance of the no running outside rule is more of a lip service job with pupils executing a quick, slow, quick manoeuvre, decelerating as they draw level with teachers before picking up speed again once past.

It's down in part, school would say, to the 'douceur and politesse' factor – Josephite-inspired attitude of mind that permeates school life. There's a sizeable staff presence in the welcoming and well decorated dining room for example. All food is cooked from scratch, with year 6 pupils allowed the almost unspeakable sophistication of sandwiches – 'as we have more responsibilities,' one pupil told us.

Pupils and parents: Sensible and cheerful children with exquisite manners with more socialising and less friendship exclusivity the higher up the school you go. Families cover more of a social mix than the area might suggest, with a predictable number of marble hall dwellers, but plenty who don't need to plug in Satnav to borrow cup of sugar from neighbours. Anecdotally reckoned that there's a growing number of families where both parents work. Though parents, like children, can find it hard to fit in if they join the school after common entrance, everyone rubs along. Lots of social events help (even second hand uniform shop has termly coffee morning). 'I just think it's got a good balance of people, there are some very wealthy, there are some not very wealthy, but you don't feel it too much,' said mother.

Entrance: Junior and senior school combined dominate independent education locally, with 90 per cent coming from within 10 mile radius, subsidised coach services doubling the distance for remainder (school open to suggestions for new routes if there's sufficient demand) and convenient rail links making commuting a doddle.

Entrance is selective all the way through, with behaviour and social skills assessed for nursery places and academic tests added at appropriate levels from reception onwards. School officially welcomes parents who sign up in nursery for a mere 15 hours a week (the maximum that is government funded) and are exempt from stumping up the £500 deposit that is otherwise payable (and non-refundable if they take up a reception place elsewhere). However, they will have to reapply if they want child to carry on through the school, automatic for the majority whose children put in longer hours from the off (school likes evidence of commitment).

While it's not essential to be a Catholic, sympathy with the belief system undoubtedly helps, as does realisation that while the Josephites who founded the school have a child-centred and kind approach to education (rare in 19th century circles), it doesn't preclude weeding out the under-achievers. 'We call them late developers,' said one mother, who approves, as do others, of the tough but honest approach. 'It's a cruel to be kind thing.'

The academically able get unconditional offers of senior school places as early as year 2, though everyone takes senior school entrance exams for scholarship and setting purposes and it's far from being a licence to take it easy, as school 're-evaluates' if performance slips. You haven't necessarily missed the boat if you join in year 3 or above, as there are a few more secure golden tickets each Easter term up to year 5. Others compete with pupils from outside and remaining old timers, though hard-working mid-roaders usually end up with places. 'It's never going to be a hothouse,' a parent told us.

Large numbers of places – 110 on offer at 11+ – sounds good on paper but at least half (and rising) are collared by own junior school pupils – standard scholarships with some, like art and drama, available only at 13 + and in sixth form).

Additional 44 places at 13+ are in equally hot demand, especially since schools like Kingston Grammar, one of the few other selective co-eds in the area, ditched common entrance. School has no plans to follow suit. It's about giving the children who wouldn't be ready for school at 11 an extra two years to mature, though they will need to sit 11+ or, if unsuccessful, 12+ pre-test to stand chance of a place. Parents and teachers in school's 30 or so feeder preps, Bishopsgate, Cranmore, Feltonfleet, Hall Grove and Hoebridge among them, others as far away as Kingston/Twickenham and southern side of Guildford, can breathe a sigh of relief.

Decent GCSEs needed to join at A level – entry 'dependent on maturity and academic profile,' says school. Further down the school exam success is just one of the factors. 'We want the vast majority of our junior school children to get through, though we take in children who academically will not be as strong as the others.' Siblings, too, will be accommodated wherever possible. For aspiring newcomers, demonstrating strength of commitment is advisable – high profile attendance at open days and strongly articulated desire to be part of school community won't go amiss.

Exit: Lots in to junior school (usually some every term) and lots out, too, with around 30 (five per cent) of pupils leaving before their time is officially up – most commonly because of relocation, some because of money issues and three or so each year after being tipped the wink that academics aren't up to snuff. However, school won't cast them off into outer educational space, say parents, and efforts are made to help find alternatives.

For those who stay on into year 6, approaching 80 per cent transfer to the senior school, with the additional incentive of range of scholarships not available to external candidates. Of the remainder, most head off to other independents – Hampton, SWPS, RGS, Reed's, Kingston Grammar and Surbiton amongst them.

Having taken in some borderline candidates at the start, senior school does spit out a few along the way, some post-GCSE (around 15 per cent), a very few at the end of first year of sixth form. It's 'tragic' if it happens and 'extremely rare', compared with a few years ago when veteran parents talk of small scale but regular culls as school fought its way to better grades. 'I couldn't understand how it squared with the Josephite ethos,' said one. However, while the order may have coined its own version of 'every child matters' philosophy well over a century before UK government advisors saw the light, they were always clear about where to draw the line. 'It is always better that one be abandoned rather than the good of several be destroyed,' said 19th century founder, firmly.

For the vast majority who make it through, university places are the norm. Steady numbers to Oxbridge (two in 2016 – sprinkling of choral scholarships too, often, and lots of support) and around three-quarters secure Russell Group places. Range of subjects, geography and history well represented as are business and management, but almost everything from law (four in 2016) and medicine to architecture featuring somewhere; psychology too. Careers followed later are just as diverse – apart from respectable numbers of first grade sports stars amongst the old boys and girls, impressive list also numbers Sir Clive Sinclair and Lisa Tarbuck.

S

Money matters: Scholarships, capped at 25 per cent of the fees, won't do much to plug financial gaps but there are also assisted places and some nifty behind the scenes footwork to help struggling families in 'torrid times'.

Remarks: Unlike some other confident schools, avoids tipping over into either arrogance or complacency, instead exuding bonhomie and a sense of being happy in its own skin, something that it transmits successfully to bright, motivated pupils (the few slackers who fail to get the message may not necessarily stay the course). Add nurturing atmosphere and wraparound pastoral care and it's no wonder it can be a hard place to leave. 'I've never been outside the St George's bubble,' said one sixth former. You have to hope it doesn't come as too much of a shock when they do.

St George's School (Ascot)

Wells Lane, Ascot, Berkshire SL5 7DZ

Pupils: 273; 110 boarders • Ages: 11–18 • Sixth form: 86 • C of E

Fees: Day £21,120; Boarding £31,170 – £33,060 pa

Tel: 01344 629920
Email: admissions@stgeorges-ascot.org.uk
Website: www.stgeorges-ascot.org.uk

Headmistress: Since September 2016, Elizabeth Hewer, previously deputy head at St Mary's Ascot. Geography degree and PGCE from Cambridge, where she captained the women's hockey team and got two half blues for cricket. She has taught geography, coached hockey, netball and tennis, sung in choirs and led outdoor activities at Bedford School, Marlborough College and the Royal Grammar School in Guildford. She joined St Mary's Ascot in 2006 and was housemistress and director of studies as well as deputy head. She and her husband, Jim, have two children and a Hungarian Vizsla dog, Laszlo. Outside St George's, she's a governor of a co-ed boarding and day school in Sussex, and a boarding inspector with the ISI.

Academic matters: School is 'deliberately small' says the blurb. Titchy, really, with just 35 pupils per year in years 7 and 8, another 14 added in year 9, class sizes pre-GCSE capped at 20 though average 14 in first three years, 10 for GCSE studies and just eight in sixth form (and often rather smaller).

Teachers jolly, chatty and exude contentment with their lot (we got the impression that those who didn't had been encouraged to find temperamental niche elsewhere), average age 40 and a quarter or so around for 10 years or over. Bar (rare) worries from minority of parents about some favouritism, imperfectly concealed, there's nothing but praise for staff, with some incredulity at maths team's uncanny knack of inspiring the previously un-keen – one unwell child insisting on attending lesson. 'Asked if they'd got the right girl,' said stunned father.

However, 'not a hothouse' says school, though parental perception is that temperature likely to rise to at least balmy levels. As it is, school ladles on the added value (GCSEs average a grade higher than entry levels would suggest), impressive given mixed entry. In 2016, 50 per cent of GCSEs graded A*/A in 2016. At A level, 37 per cent of entries were A*/A and 74 A*/B.

Lots of stress on growth as individual, being best you can be – if not, won't be for want of trying, with staff on call during study leave, pep talks blended with reassurance, changes frequently rung – 20-questions-style quiz, past papers and spider diagram creation simultaneously under way in one notably calm GCSE history class. Lower down the school, there's help of a more basic nature. 'Don't use "of" as a verb' is tip in first year pupil's English folder.

With nine lessons a day (extra pre-lunch bonus session for sixth form), 8.15am start and 6.15pm or later finish ('terrific value for money,' school points out) no shortage of opportunities to be inspired and, in case of most able, sufficiently challenged. 'Could give them textbook, tell them to learn it and would still get an A* – it's about giving them something extra that goes beyond confines of syllabus,' says deputy head.

Hence introduction of EPQ for all year 12s, studied alongside two A levels. Extended essays, one top-graded effort exploring finer points of depleted uranium ('at least at undergraduate level,' reckons school) have also featured as component of AQA Baccalaureate, a calorie controlled version of IB diploma.

Pre-16, 10 GCSEs the norm for most, business and communication systems the only deviation from the norm, though curriculum has been expanding, Spanish now on offer as a second language from year 9 together with more 'exotic' options such as Chinese and Japanese (agreed) and ... German (who knew?).

Learning needs similarly well planned, around 50 girls receiving support, overwhelmingly for specific learning difficulties (teachers from Helen Arkell Institute, one of UK's top dyslexia centres, visit regularly) similar numbers speaking English as an additional language. Sensible aids to diagnosis – those struggling in exams swap to different coloured ink when into extra time. 'Sister's grades have improved so much,' says year 10 pupil. 'Dyslexic girls do as well or better than those who aren't because they get fantastic study skills,' says school insider.

Support, not spoon feeding, self-discipline encouraged, freedom doled out in ever increasing amounts as girls go up the school (trips to high street allowed from year 3 – though one parent queried wisdom of arranging GCSE geography field trip there during Ascot Week to ask harassed shopkeepers if they were busier than usual...) tempered with emphasis on cultivation of desirable learning habits via timetabled study skills sessions for first years, regular subject clinics and even sessions with subject tutors as one of the Saturday morning activity options.

Thoughtful touches make it easy to get the work and play balance right, prep setting making home a largely work free zone. Study areas in communal rooms, though generous, often off to one side. 'Work but not to excess,' seems to be the message, underpinned by separate fiction library, tiniest of three (all pending major redevelopment elsewhere) stuffed with sofas and smelling (mysteriously) of roses, urging the prep-weary to tarry awhile, an antidote to the pleasant but business-like atmosphere of non-fiction section on the other side of the wall.

Games, options, the arts: The works, website giving equal prominence to lively productions as well as range of sports (U14 championship success) and economics (serious talk from think tank expert) by way of proof.

Arts, performing and otherwise, very strong, ranging from seriously good acting talent (judging by mesmerising final rehearsal of A level drama monologue) to audition-only chapel choir (occasional HRH in audience no doubt adds to appeal) and head of art who is 'just fantastic at getting the most out of everybody,' said parent, art room filled with natural light and quality produce including delightful silk snakes threading their way through ceramic hoops and exuding (just resisted) strokability. Some parents harder to win over when comes to carrying on to A level. 'Want daughters to do subjects leading to a good job,' says member of staff.

Outside world also fully embraced. If Australian exchange scheme for two year 9 pupils doesn't bring home sense of good fortune, plentiful additional reminders driven home via community service both near (help for Slough homeless and socially excluded) plus carol singing and visits to the elderly, and far (fundraising for READS Indo International School in Rajasthan).

Energetic equally well catered for indoors (vast fitness suite, soon-to-be replaced swimming pool and good sized sports hall) and out, with lots of convertible spaces (netball to tennis; lacrosse to athletics). Something for everyone, polo amongst team sports on offer, paid add-ons including tennis, zumba and..polo again (well, Ascot race course is but an anvil's throw away).

While not the most seriously sporty school, manages steady supply of county lacrosse players, work sometimes trouncing play, mainly timetabled after 4.00pm and on Saturdays when replaced by compulsory prep for anyone not selected for matches. Tone, running from rugged to dauntless, set by head of sport, former women's army champion, with timetabled events running through exam season, enabling welcome sublimation of nervous tension through exercise, pupils 'staying on to unwind,' said one, sixth former grimly tackling treadmill by way of demonstration. Plenty for also-rans, felt do best in junior years when A to D teams and a bit of dedication can take you a long way. 'Turn up to training and you'll be in a match,' said pupil.

Some good results, though a bit of parental grumbling about occasional stonking defeats by lesser schools. Later on, when team options smaller (As and Bs only) it's less about taking part, more about winning, with girls who 'care so much that cry when they lose,' said parent. Sensitive souls pulled in several different directions at once can find it all too much (some parental niggles about early morning detentions handed out for missing practice sessions). Confident, multi-talented high flyers lap it up, however. Will be tired but, 'it's a good tired,' said mother.

Boarding: Well thought-out boarding houses. Larger scale to start with – up to eight to a room, daily tidiness vetting (termly winners treated to pizza). Sensibly, say older girls, as 'you want to be with as many people as possible,' particularly when homesickness strikes. 'Helps as there's so much going on.'

Looks range from the jolly for younger pupils (bright pink patches above beds for personalisation, custom made centralised storage) to cleaner feel later on, single Hokaido-style plants straining sinuously round corners for year 4 sophisticates, who also enjoy sombre shades of common room. 'Not one for bright colours,' said one. Bar the odd slightly dim and grey-ish corridor – school does its best to add natural light where architecture permits – boarding is thoroughly welcoming with clear demarcation between work and relaxation that's appreciated by girls. 'Really homely,' says one. 'Makes you feel the day is done.'

Terrific activities sandwiching army assault course between film nights and ice skating. Spontaneous family treat times also encouraged. 'Really smart about how boarders need to have a hot chocolate with their mums sometimes, whereas with other schools, absolutely not,' said parent.

Unsurprising that boarding is highly popular, day girls enticed in with free trial sessions (space availability permitting) that let them experience the joys of home cooking (most go no further than popcorn and toast), though experiment with separate penthouse enabling sixth formers to try out independent living wasn't a hit with girls and has since been abandoned.

Background and atmosphere: Approached off high street down side road, tranquillity temporarily duffed up into submission by roar of builders' lorries (this is prime mansionville), parking a perennial problem. Winding lane opens up, unexpectedly, into vista of open spaces and tree tops, school perched attractively on hilltop. Steep descent to car park apparently irresistible in snowy weather – 'we go down it on tea trays – and so do the staff,' say pupils.

School's motto 'Vincent Qui Se Vincunt' or 'They Will Conquer Who Overcome Themselves' could usefully have been adopted by original founders, who went bust in 1904. School, which had up till then been a boys' prep attended by the very young Winston Churchill, and was lavishly equipped with the very latest in educational fixtures and fittings including electric light, was also notable for flogging-mad head.

Reincarnated as a girls' finishing school in 1904, school took off in 1920s with arrival of new owner rich in academic as well as social aspirations for pupils. Stayed put through Second World War (courtesy of air raid shelters in the grounds). Further 'structural metamorphosis' aka major building splurge added chapel, labs, music and sixth form space and assorted classrooms in 1980s, art and technology block and sports complex in 90s, performing arts block in 2002. Small footprint should, and mainly does, make navigation easy despite moments when split level construction and multiple entrances would make Escher feel right at home.

Pioneering spirit much in evidence from the start with girls prepared for college entrance from the 1920s. Has continued unabated – school had first wireless network up and running in early noughties, while nimby-ism certainly not an issue, with some original buildings and land sacrificed to make way for the new, though we admired grotto-like construction, once key decorative feature that formed part of extravagant water course.

Excellence of food could well damp down culinary aspirations. Food outstanding – menu, in conspicuous contrast to many others we've seen, was as delicious in reality as on paper (first time drooling has ever threatened effective note-taking).

Domestic bursar's Mafia-like tentacles (probably marinated, though he's ex-Forces rather than Sealife) extend to nationwide quayside contacts, fish 'caught yesterday,' everything cooked fresh in six at a time batches. 'Always enough of the nice things,' said pupil, approvingly. Only complaint – a minute steak that was 30 seconds late – was something we could probably learn to live with.

Pastoral care, well-being and discipline: Framework as sturdy as they come, school endeavouring to set girls' own moral compasses pointing in right direction for life. Friendships wide-ranging, helped by shake-up when new intake starts in year 9 (or 3, in school parlance) ensuring absence of them v us as new and old faces are thoroughly mixed in class and dorms. Helped by house system that promotes togetherness without overdoing the aggressive loyalty, together with pervasive sense of encouragement – we liked big screen and website beaming messages of support for GCSE students about to embark on exam performances, like cheering onlookers at a regatta.

A bit of soul-searching appears to have taken place when it comes to behaviour, initiation rites banned (not that they happened anyway, says school, putting presence in policy down to excessive 't' crossing and 'i' dotting by conscientious back office team, ditto online posting of 'incorrect, inappropriate or inflammatory material' verboten 'without permission' – rarely granted, we'd suspect).

Requirement for bullies and victims to 'understand each other's feelings and points of view' (victims often understand bullies' perspective all too well in our experience...) appears to work, remaining an occasional blight, largely dying out when GCSE preparation becomes uniting factor, say pupils, bar very occasional unhappy story of social isolation (not the experience of the vast majority, however).

Overall, however, school 'knows which battles to pick,' said approving parent, who with others praised quick, decisive action on rare occasions when girls have been asked to leave. Down in part to sensible rules – pupils in year 9 and above can hang on to phones and tablets overnight, though excessive tiredness can lead to privilege being withdrawn – together with top-down nurturing, prefects watching out for younger girls, sympatico gap students (one highly skilled at plaiting hair) and highly effective form tutor system.

We heard lavish compliments for, amongst others, head of music – 'the heart of the school' and 'big teddy bear' from pupils and 'heaven, has made being in a choir cool,' from parent – together with head of sixth form who 'really listens and explains, takes our side,' said pupil, gist is that for each girl, there's a kindred spirit to talk to on the staff. Styles vary, though brisk member of pastoral team who 'believes in school of hard knocks,' thought parent, is countered by wonder matron, on hand for tea (or hot chocolate) and sympathy, running popular sessions on everything from skin care to pre-exam stress busting. 'A really nice woman,' said one pupil.

Pupils and parents: Haven for the blue blooded with Princess Beatrice of York, Lady Davina Lewis and Lady Rose Gilman amongst the OGs, together with assorted actors and assorted presenters, DJs and the occasional personality.

Somewhere between 10 and 20 per cent per cent are international boarders, China (mainland and Hong Kong) and Russia by far biggest nationalities represented (plus, currently, a couple of Ukrainians).

While locals are well represented, numbers of weekly boarders from London are also healthy, meanwhile (handy bus service collects Chiswick/South Ken Sunday, drops Friday), though locals still rule OK (literally so, given proximity to Windsor Castle).

Inclusive, active Parents' Association – 'like meeting up with friends,' said mother – with annual meet and greet event for new parents and decent array of suitably social/fundraising events of a reassuringly trad nature, recently including get together at – where else? – Guards Polo Club.

Entrance: Popular and getting more so (candidate numbers up 60 per cent in a year), most desirable entrants those capable of bringing something unique to school which, in practice (and excluding own one of a kind DNA), means nothing too outré. 'We're looking for a girl whose eyes sparkle.' Around 20 feeders, many local (Coworth-Flexlands, Upton House School and St George's, Windsor Castle) others in London (Garden House).

Following appetite-whetting taster sessions for 8 to 10 year olds, consisting of lessons plus overnight stay, would-be year 7 pupils sit English, maths, VR papers plus interview, no Sats equivalent – pass rate around the 65 per cent mark. Not as academic as some but 'still need to be able to work towards 10 or 11 GCSEs'.

Second smaller intake at 13, successful candidates spending day with class to be and invited to school events. Occasional vacancies in other years (though won't accept pupils once GCSEs under way). For (large) sixth form, not desperately demanding – minimum six A*-C GCSEs with at least B grades in A level subjects.

Exit: Used to lose fair few post-GCSE, single sex blues and desire for larger-scale environment almost universal reason. Fewer now (12 per cent in 2016). While some seepage inevitable as 'we're not getting bigger and we're not providing boys,' sixth formers extol benefits.

Higher education advisors help sixth formers whittle down higher education options, leavers heading to broad spread of unis and courses, everywhere from Durham to Southampton to Central St Martins, subjects ranging from molecular biology to social policy and criminology, creative arts well represented. One place at ULC to study medicine in 2016. Usually several to Oxbridge or Ivy League each year – school good at securing interviews, less good at closing the deal so far, reckon parents.

Money matters: Range of 11 + scholarships available. Standard range (academic, music, art, sport) gratefully received – though one parent felt varying levels of participation by scholars (music scholars, for example, not obliged to join choir) meant their gain was sometimes school's loss. Same again, plus drama, at 13, open also to internal candidates, as are sixth form scholarships. Maximum reduction 10 per cent but means-tested bursaries available. Though not HMC school, part of their scholarship programme, offering 100 per cent funded boarding place each year to super bright East European whose family has income of £25,000 or under.

Remarks: Though accurate, website pictures of girls seated on balustrades dreamily overlooking tons of top-quality swathes of Berkshire countryside tell only part of the story. Change in style, from quirky 'traditionally English school' to ambitious and aspirational pleases almost all, though parent who joined under previous tenure felt had 'bought into one thing and you're existing in another.'

The many who approve feel children are offered not a retreat from life but a well planned introduction to its realities. Princesses on board? Though they can come (sometimes literally) with the territory, they should – together with other pupils – end up as princesses with attitude. 'Am still waiting for the bubble to burst but each year is as good as the last,' said one mother.

St George's School (Harpenden)

Sun Lane, Harpenden, Hertfordshire AL5 4EY

Pupils: 1,329; 115 full boarders. • Ages: 11–18 • Sixth form: 383

Fees: Boarding £11,400 pa; Day – free

Tel: 01582 765477
Email: admin@stgeorges.herts.sch.uk
Website: www.stgeorges.herts.sch.uk

Headmaster: Since 2013, Raymond McGovern MA (early 50s). Educated at St Thomas Aquinas School, Glasgow. Came to teaching via, in his words, 'a circumvented route.' Left school at 16 to take up engineering apprenticeship at British Leyland, then fulfilled his childhood dream, born from his time in the ATC whilst at school ('it gave me a real sense of community') of joining the RAF where he spent nine years, including a stint in Germany. In his early 30s, landed role as lecturer in engineering and aerospace technology at HE college in Hounslow before undertaking two years' training whilst teaching DT at Charles Darwin School in Kent. Promoted to deputy head of sixth form before moving on to Christ's College, Brecon as head of DT then boarding housemaster. Bitten hard by boarding bug, moved to state boarding school, Sexey's School, firstly to run boarding and pastoral care, rising to head after seven years.

Inherited school in top five per cent of non-selective schools nationally, so clear vision to 'ensure quality remains stable.' Team comprises many 'very professional', longstanding teaching staff who, despite tenure, were 'hungry for change' in some areas of school. Reporting systems previously paper based and overly bureaucratic so major investment in bringing them up to date – now all done online. Head's vision is to make school 'as paperless as possible', as well as enabling parents to access information 'as and when they need it rather than when we choose to release it.'

Likeable, sincere and grounded, head has the aura of a vocational teacher and leader. Senior pupils reminisce about looking up at vaulted chapel ceiling with McGovern when they joined and him pointing out 'it's like a boat, and we're in all in it together.' Not all parents have met him, but describe his weekly newsletter as 'informative and amusing' and uniformly seem impressed, albeit sometimes from afar. Lives locally with wife Rachel and three children – two boys in their 20s who are working and at university respectively and a daughter who is at St George's.

Academic matters: As a totally non-selective school regularly delivering high results, parents can bank on St George's knocking it out of the park when it comes to value-added, with a vast majority of students (90 per cent in 2016) leaving with at least five A*- C grades at GCSE; 35 per cent of grades A*/A. Head is clear to point out, however, that this is not just in the realm of academia, but also in 'confidence, values and esprit de corps' that his students outperform expectations, acclaiming his staff's 'ability to instil a sense of can-do' in its charges. Top A level grades are similarly commonplace. In 2016, 66 per cent A*-B at A level.

Ten to 11 GCSEs are the norm, with compulsory RE amongst them, leading, unusually, to a full class at A level. Parents appreciate flexible approach to timetabling at GCSE. Maths, 'without reservation,' says head, is the jewel in St George's crown and the most popular A level choice by both sexes – 'it's phenomenal to see how much they enjoy it.' Art also outstanding with school boasting the highest percentage of top grades in county at both art GCSE and A level. Setting in maths and science from end of year 7, with English set for GCSE.

French from year 7, German and Spanish from year 8 and all on offer at GCSE but, disappointingly, only French at A level. Mandarin available to all, although not examined, and school is one of just 45 'Confucius Classrooms' across the UK, meaning that it has Chinese firmly embedded in its own curriculum and strong links with China, including a popular exchange programme. Also has International School status.

SEN all in a day's work for the full time SENCo and seven teaching assistants on staff. Plenty of experience dealing with statemented children, and learning support ranges from helping with a few extra spellings to an individually planned timetable. Large percentage of cohort identified as gifted and talented, with extension work provided accordingly both on and off curriculum with Science Olympiads and Maths Challenges.

Games, options, the arts: Sport taken seriously but 'not elitist', according to head, with all abilities trained together. Rugby and cricket are main boys' sports, with A-C teams playing competitive fixtures most weeks in all year groups. It's lacrosse for the girls – St George's is the only state maintained school in the south of England to play, so all fixtures are against independents, hence often at weekends. Other popular options are netball, rounders, basketball, tennis, athletics and, to a limited extent, dance. Compulsory participation to year 13, with more casual mixed classes in sixth form that encompass table tennis, badminton and trampolining. Indoor games take place in the impressive newish sports centre, also home to an attractive and well-equipped gym and weights room.

Possibly the best art department of any school for miles around – 'the pride of the school,' say pupils. Every inch of the art corridor walls and ceilings festooned with breathtakingly creative and technically exemplary work also spilling over to cover most walls throughout school. Huge (four foot) three dimensional papier mâché masks welcome visitors into this showcase area, and from that point on it's hard to know where to look, as outstanding paintings, drawings, sculptures and installations – no two the same – assault the senses. Creative facilities also superb, with three huge DT labs – again with some wonderfully turned work on display – and two huge art rooms provide yet more exhibition space for pupils' superb creative endeavours. Textiles, photography, sculpture and graphic design all on offer.

Music provides St George's heartbeat. Choirs, orchestras and bands galore and so much talent to display that annual house music competition now takes place in Watford Colosseum. One major annual drama production – Scrooge, Fame and Hairspray in recent years – in which all year groups can participate as well as smaller shows throughout the year.

Plenty of extracurricular activities from sewing and gardening to chess or curriculum based classes take place before and after school – excellent for boarders and day pupils alike. Well-attended ATC as well as World Challenge expeditions to far flung destinations from Argentina to Mongolia. School's connection with Gansu Province, China, has yielded exchange trips and a small team led by head to lecture at University of Beijing. Other trips include educational expeditions to Washington (politics), Space Camp (maths) and a popular biennial ski trip.

Boarding: Despite the small number of boarders (maximum capacity 135, with anything between five and 15 each of boys and girls in any given year group), they are very well integrated into the school. Friendships between day and boarding pupils flourish and visits to day pupils' homes encouraged. Far from feeling like a minority group, boarders take pride in their status to the point of having requested their own, slightly different, tie. Relationships between year groups are forged through fun activities such as 'speed dating' – an in house way of getting to know newcomers.

Boarding houses have friendly family feel, thanks in no small part to the young (40s), bubbly director of boarding who lives on campus and oversees the pastoral welfare of her charges full time. 'She really understands what makes teenagers tick,' said one happy parent. Girls from years 7 to 12 are housed in the old school building – safely tucked away up what seems like 15 flights of stairs – in dorms which sleep anything from two to six: 'we tailor it according to intake from year to year and girls' individual needs,' says director of boarding. Year 13 girls have the run of a swish new house with single rooms and en suite bathrooms. Boys are in a stand-alone block with a less cosy, more practical feel – though we are assured that the sparse decorations in dorms and common room are purely by choice ('it's not cool to have posters up,' said one of our guides). Both houses have tons of communal space – massive common rooms furnished with plenty of squashy sofas and other nooks and crannies around the house with beanbags, armchairs and computers for boys and girls to congregate outside of school hours. Both houses have well-equipped kitchen areas for boarders to make themselves snacks – and there are baskets of goodies out to keep them going after school.

Boys and girls are allowed to visit each other but only in common rooms – although apparently romantic liaisons are incredibly rare: 'There is a strong sibling-like feel amongst the boarders,' say pupils. The terms 'flexi' and 'weekly' are not used and, although some boarders go home more frequently than others, all pay the same fees (less by some stretch than most private day schools) and have the same status. Around half stay for weekends (more boys than girls), with all meals apart from weekend breakfasts taken in the main school dining room. Pupils from year 9 allowed into Harpenden with permission in twos and many attend classes such as yoga or dance in the village. Pupils grumble that school is too strict about them leaving the premises – parents breathe secret sighs of relief.

Channels of communication to home left wide open with boarders allowed phones, handed in at bedtime, although they are trusted to keep iPads and laptops 'to keep it as much like home life as possible.' Weekends bring Friday night football club, competitive matches for many on Saturdays, cinema trips and one big trip each term (paintballing, Thorpe Park, Brighton have featured recently). Boarders also have their own formal dinner or ball each term, organised by senior pupils. Younger pupils have a fixed programme of after school activities including boarding skills – learning how cook, do their laundry, make jam etc.

Background and atmosphere: Feels more like a private school than some private schools we know – and certainly wins the prize for smartest comprehensive school uniform with its green Harris Tweed blazers for the boys and pleated kilts for the girls. Situated a stone's throw from Harpenden High Street, school was founded in 1907 by the Rev Cecil Grant as a non-denominational Christian foundation with its own Anglican chaplain and weekly Sunday chapel service, which occasionally hosts up to 400 members of the school community and their families. One of the longest established fully co-educational boarding schools in England, the school retains many of its historic traditions, with pupils taking great pride in their house competitions, formality of chapel, speech days and all the different ties awarded.

The original Victorian gothic-style building still provides the heart of the school – and girls' boarding house – with various additions and extensions which run the full gauntlet from occasionally gleaming (sports hall, language block) to downright shabby (most of the rest). Despite its somewhat down at heel sum of the parts, however, the whole hangs together with a feel of purposefulness and functionality and is actually part of the school's overall charm. Sixth form common room and study areas in dire need of a refurb, but nobody seems to mind – the overall feel of the school is welcoming and contented – 'children can grow up at their own pace,' say parents. A new link with nearby Batchwood Tennis Academy hopes to attract talented players from all over the country to boarding houses.

Pastoral care, well-being and discipline: Very little need for strong discipline – hard to believe that 'chewing gum' is the worst that happens but that was all our guides would confess to. Occasionally pupils 'don't work out' on the boarding side but in the main 'they feel very lucky to be here – there's no sense of entitlement,' says director of boarding. 'Traditional values and caring ethos,' makes school tick, according to head with strong support from parents. Pupils rewarded for demonstrating school's core values of courtesy, integrity, manners and discipline. Head has passport sized photo of every child in school on his study wall – split by the four houses that give school its shape. Houses presided over by a head of house, assistant and team of tutors. The arrangement of tutor groups gives pupils very little room for manoeuvre when it comes to bad behaviour. An 'excellent' student services department supports children with welfare or emotional needs with its qualified counsellor, to whom pupils can self-refer, and a pastoral support worker.

Pupils and parents: Affluent Harpenden and its surrounding villages provide the vast majority of day pupils with boarders coming mainly from further afield, and around 55 per cent of these from overseas. Cohort is hence naturally inclined towards hard work and success upon which school can build. A highly involved and vocal parent body turns out in droves for matches, concerts and shows and the Sunday service in chapel is very well attended. Alumni include philosopher and political theorist Michael Oakeshott, classicist and writer Rex Warner, actress Laura Haddock and rugby player Owen Farrell.

Entrance: The most oversubscribed of Harpenden's three secondary schools, with a complex admissions process run by school. No academic selection but a series of priorities including catchment (currently extending to around 800 metres from school), regular church attendance for at least two years (minister's letter required), and siblings receiving priority. Genuine devoutness not put to the test – local parents can cynically choose to pray rather than pay as long as they think ahead and accept that their child will have to attend chapel at school on at least three Sundays a term. A handful each year from local prep schools join in year 7.

Boarders must be EU resident or hold British passport and are interviewed by head and director of boarding to assess suitability, as well as provide a good reference from their previous school. 'Need' also comes into play – for example children with both parents working or in the Forces, with occasional children switching from day to boarding places to save time on the daily commute. Applications should be in a year in advance, although boarding places not currently oversubscribed. Very occasional charitable places but no bursaries offered.

Exit: Around three-quarters stay on into sixth form after GCSEs – leavers generally move to other schools and colleges. More than two-thirds to Russell Group/other top universities, with six Oxbridge places in 2016.

Money matters: As a voluntary aided school, St George's buildings are owned by the school's Foundation, which has to find 10 per cent of the cost of all capital projects and on-going building maintenance from very limited funds. 'There is a lot of do-it-yourself work here'; school enlists the assistance of its active parents' association for fundraising support throughout the year.

Remarks: A real gem of a local secondary school with plenty to offer pupils whether they want to paint, study or play their way to success. Riding high as one of the top non-selective state schools in the country, St George's can boast a secure, Christian community as well as top notch results.

St Helen and St Katharine

Faringdon Road, Abingdon, Oxfordshire OX14 1BE

Pupils: 719 • Ages: 9–18 • Sixth form: 177

Fees: £14,745 pa

Tel: 01235 520173
Email: info@shsk.org.uk
Website: www.shsk.org.uk

Head: Since 2015, Mrs Rebecca Dougall BA MA (40s), previously head of the Royal High School, Bath. She has also taught at Wycombe Abbey and Oxford High, where she was deputy head. An English literature specialist, she is chic, sprightly, youthful and dynamic, as well as being passionate about single sex schools, having attended one herself. Doesn't teach, but certainly not a chief executive type head and is known among pupils for being personable and approachable, regularly popping into lessons and having an open-door policy. 'She doesn't just know our names – she knows what our interests are, often stopping us to ask us about them,' said one pupil, with another adding that she gives 'great thought-provoking assemblies that we genuinely look forward to'. Parents also impressed. 'She has her finger on the pulse and you absolutely feel you can trust your daughter to do her very best in her care,' said one. Impassioned about the school without being dewy eyed about it, one feels she could wax lyrical all day about the girls' achievements and aspirations, whilst also being very mindful of the practical steps and vision that's needed to make this possible. No dramatic changes in her early reign, although she fairly quickly changed the language offering and introduced computer science ('At last!' said one parent). Lives locally with her husband, who teaches history. Extracurricular interests include medieval literature, design, property, travel and absorbing other cultures – in style.

Academic matters: Unapologetically selective and academic. In 2016, 94 per cent A*/A grades at I/GCSE, and while the girls would probably be too modest to say out loud that 'St Helen's girls don't get Bs', this perfectly respectable grade doesn't seem to see much light of day here. Head puts this down to the traditional recipe of good teaching, hard work and high expectations. There's a fizz and energy about learning here, along with a refreshing lack of cynicism, which was palpable in every classroom we visited and among every conversation we had with pupils. 'It's cool to learn here and that comes across very quickly,' said one parent. Teachers, too, have a fire in their eye, with pupils referring to 'their first rate subject knowledge' and dedication, which often involves them putting in a lot of extra hours.

Most girls do 10 subjects and choices include DT, drama, Latin, Greek and computer science. Spanish is the lead language from year 7; then in year 8, pupils add a second language of French, German or Mandarin. Additional language options at GCSE include Mandarin and there's an Arabic course for sixth formers. Take up for separate and dual award sciences roughly equal. A level results also fairly lofty (67 per cent A* or A grades in 2016) with sciences, maths and English the most popular choices closely followed by geography, history, art, and religious studies. Some subjects (government & politics and theatre studies) are taught jointly with Abingdon boys. Small junior department (years 5 and 6), which is by no means a 'light' version of the senior school, but rather its own operation with dedicated teachers, but which accesses many of the senior school facilities.

School wants girls to develop as 'active, independent learners, able to think for themselves and prepared to take risks' and to take a 'broad and balanced approach' to their education, says the head. 'We're not grade hunters,' she insists, although there are lots of tests and exams. Lessons we observed were indeed stimulating and interactive, with plenty of questions and debate – no sign of young brains being crammed with facts. 'Flipped classroom learning – currently all the rage – is what we've been doing here for years,' explains the head. Indeed, pre-reading and extra resources being provided to students to study at home before the class session, which then is devoted to exercises, projects and discussions, appears to be business as usual here. Sixth form teaching, in particular, goes above and beyond the syllabus requirements, providing a depth of learning that gives girls a real edge. EPQ a significant feature of sixth form life; coding recently introduced.

The learning support co-ordinator is praised by parents for excellence in diagnostic testing and support for the few girls with mild dyslexia/dyspraxia or who are on the autistic spectrum, with the head ensuring that every staff member is on board when it comes to any special needs, along with extra pastoral care, which she firmly believes should be at the heart of any SEN provision. 'What's particularly impressed me is the effort that all staff have gone to, whilst keeping it all very low-key so as to prevent my daughter feeling fussed over or stigmatised,' said one parent.

Games, options, the arts: Art and DT facilities are bright, spacious and well-equipped – the former comprising of sky-lit, atelier-like studios in the old building, the latter housed in the new 3D design centre. Some innovative results are displayed throughout the school, with a particularly striking ceramics display when we visited, although one parent with experience of other local schools told us, 'I don't think there's as much opportunity for keen artists as Headington and Oxford High.'

Plenty of ambitious music and drama productions, with examples including Anything Goes (senior school), Alice in Wonderland (middle school) and The Lion King (lower school) – all of which boast big audiences. These are often in conjunction with the Abingdon thespians, with singers and orchestral support drawn from the combined, deep talent pool of both schools. Performance spaces are the intimate, round studio theatre, a larger stage in YPH and Abingdon School's Amey Theatre. The annual playwriting competition creates quite a buzz, with the winner directing her own piece.

The practice rooms in the music department are in constant use for singing and instrumental lessons (450 per week) and, unsurprisingly, school musicians do well in local and national competitions. There are four orchestras, eight choirs, two wind bands, a big band and more than 20 smaller ensembles, Large and successful uptake for D of E and Young Enterprise. 'My daughter didn't go down the exam route for music, but has been given a love of music that I think will last her for life,' enthused one parent.

Sport facilities never stand still here. That was literally the case when six outside courts were moved from one side of the playing fields to the other so that they could be floodlit (houses overlooking the old spot weren't keen). There's an extra 12 acres of sports fields just across the road and the brand new large modern sports centre include a large sports hall (able to host international competitions), improved gym, indoor rowing facilities and dance studio. For swimming facilities, climbing wall and more courts, girls use Abingdon School.

Although we saw for ourselves fixture lists with A, B and C teams – and the head vouches for the fact that she's stood and watched C teams competing – a recurring grumble is that less attention is paid to the B and C teams. Girls who start school keen to have a go at, say, lacrosse (the only school in Oxfordshire to offer this sport) or play in netball matches can feel sidelined if they don't make the As, according to some parents. 'My daughter loves sport, but isn't that good, and at one time she was told she couldn't even do the after-school netball club,' said one parent 'But, to be fair, as soon as I mentioned it, the school set up after-school netball provision for those not in the top teams. I honestly think the school is trying to be more inclusive.' Regional, national and even international representation across several sports, particularly among equestrian performers, with great excitement about the netball team having reached national level for the first time when we visited. Among the less predictable activities on offer in lessons or as after-school or lunch clubs are football, rugby, trampolining, cheerleading, Frisbee, sailing and golf, and there's a recognition by the head that as girls get older, they are often more keen on the idea of fitness than wet pitches, with a consequent emphasis on the likes of gym and dance.

Plenty of other extracurricular activities, ranging from knit chic to Christian club, and every department runs subject-based clubs, some of which are student-led. School trips aplenty, including an annual ski trip for lower and middle school and residential team-building trip to Somerset for year 7s, plus lots of foreign exchange trips to France and Germany. Other recent one-off examples of trips include a geography trip to Iceland, history trip to Berlin, art trip to Cornwall and there's a sports tour every three years for lacrosse players to the USA.

Background and atmosphere: The distinctive main red-brick building is original to the school's 1903 foundation by nuns of the Community of St Mary the Virgin, who wished to provide a 'liberal and advanced' education to the young ladies of Abingdon. Behind reception, the central atrium, once the dining room, is now used for little more than lunchtime cake sales and provides the walkway through the junior department to the shiny new palace of science – a striking facility with 12 spacious, state-of-the-art, colour-co-ordinated science labs (where we saw girls enthusiastically dissecting pigs' hearts in biology), a hall/theatre complete with stylish break-out areas, as well as contemporary kitchen and dining facilities.

Thanks to a very generous private donor, study facilities are superb throughout this school, including the stunning library in the Jean Duffield building. Bookcases are curved and arranged spaciously in circular sections, seating is comfortable, walls boast Farrow & Ball tones and glass walls and doors lead into silent study areas, including the dedicated area for sixth form study, complete with banks of computers. 'I love studying here – even more so than at home because the dedication to study is infectious,' one pupil told us. Natural light is amplified by a central well and a winding staircase leads to a ground-floor fiction section that itself leads through to a university-style 120-seated lecture theatre and café with opening hours to cater for early birds or girls staying on for the numerous clubs and after-school activities. Other facilities of note include the spacious, well-equipped IT suites, modern (and reassuringly chaotic) sixth form common room, and delightful chapel.

The atmosphere is calm and purposeful until the bell goes for break or lunch, when there's a refreshing amount of clamour and excitement. We saw girls running eagerly to lunch ('Food here is the best!' one exclaimed, and we agree it's outstanding), with others chatting cheerfully in huddles. While there's no prevailing type of girl here, there's a core spirit of endeavour and enthusiasm.

As you might expect, tradition is big, with plenty of rituals, such as 'the bonkers school hymn' (head's words) and the 2p race on St Kate's Day, whereby girls, in their year groups, compete to line up 2p coins on the tennis courts for a chosen charity.

The school day begins at 8.30am, with eight lessons kicking off at 9.10am, including a decent stretch for lunch and finishing at 4.15pm – unless girls stay on for clubs. A joint bus service with various local schools delivers from as far as Reading, Oxford, Thame and Faringdon in the morning. Separate ride home at the end of the day, including for those staying on at 5.20pm.

Pastoral care, well-being and discipline: 'We talk a lot here – pupils and teachers, teachers and the rest of the staff, staff and parents, all of us really,' reports the head, claiming that this – above all else – means problems are generally prevented or nipped in the bud. 'There are no hidden corners where someone stays worried and festers. This is a culture based on dialogue and sharing.' Pupils concur, although we were reassured that nobody is resting on their laurels. 'No head should think they've cracked pastoral care. It should always be developing,' says the head.

At the centre of the current pastoral care system are the form tutors and heads of section, and there's also a full-time chaplain, health centre staff and part-time counsellor (with the head considering employing a second when we visited because 'it's good practice to have an alternative approach'). Friendship fall-outs are tackled quickly, thereby helping to prevent bullying, with the other main issues pupils facing including problems at home and balancing aspirations of parents with those of the children. Then there's the pressure academically. While girls are trained to handle it well, there are inevitably moments when it all gets on top of them, and molehills can become mountains, particularly around exam time. 'Emotional support here isn't just for the pupils,' insists the head. 'It's for the whole family if they want it.' Parents agree, with several reporting that the support is 'phenomenal' and communication more generally is excellent too.

All the usual responsibilities for students, including prefects (who proudly adorn boaters and blazers for big occasions), house captains (there was a new house system when we visited as the previous one wasn't encouraging enough cross-year bonding), school council and mentors – along with plenty more besides. In lower sixth, every single girl has a role of responsibility, such as charity or sports rep.

Discipline requires a light touch. The expression of disappointment by a highly regarded teacher goes a long way here, along with a firm set of rules that mean everyone knows what's expected of them in the first place. 'I'm not saying I haven't had girls here on a Saturday morning, for instance for misuse of mobile phones, but discipline really is a nominal part of my job,' says the head.

The school's founding Christian values remain central to its ethos, and the school continues to mark key moments in the Christian calendar, as well as requiring girls to attend chapel once a week – although school life itself is becoming increasingly secular. Girls are enthusiastic and aware charity fundraisers, busy with lunchtime cake sales and other enterprises; many serve in the school chapel as sacristans, readers or choristers. 'There are lots of ways to get involved with the chapel here – not just religious ones,' adds the head, who says the weekly chapel visit is synonymous with what other schools call 'mindfulness'.

Pupils and parents: Bright ambitious girls. Ditto parents. About half come from local primaries and the rest from feeder preps – around 25 in total. 'There's a sweetness about the girls here,' adds the head, while parents are, she says, 'level-headed and interested'. There's a lively PA, which does fundraising for charity and the school, as well as fostering friendships among parents. Almost all white British, reflecting this part of Oxfordshire, although there is a sprinkling of African-Caribbean, Indian, Sri Lankan, Turkish, Chinese and Japanese, among others. Former pupils include Samantha Cameron and her sister, deputy editor of Vogue, Emily Sheffield (both decamped to sixth form boarding at Marlborough), Alice Thomson (leader writer the Times), Belinda Bucknall QC, Lindsey Russell (Blue Peter presenter) and Becky Wait (author).

Entrance: Entry at 9, 10, 11, 13 and 16, though the majority come in at 11. Maths and English tests and informal interviews for 9+ and 10+ candidates, who get automatic admission to senior school, though they take a transfer test for the school's records and possible scholarships. Exam at 11 (maths and English) plus observed 'taster days' and informal interview with head; roughly three candidates for every place. 'We take a long time over admissions,' reports the head, who says she's looking for potential, not overly coached children, as well as a 'confidence hook.' 'If they're passionate and brilliant a particular subject, or they love singing in the choir, for example, we know that can boost their confidence at times when it may fall in other areas.' Girls who get a place go into one of four classes per year, each with 22 or 23 places (maximum 24).

Existing pupils gain entry to sixth form even if they have wobbled at GCSE – there's no weeding out to 'bump up' A level results (not that this seems necessary). Candidates from other schools – of which there are usually anywhere between 15 and 20 each year, and who come from both the state and independent sector – chosen via pastoral and academic interviews and verbal reasoning test. They will need good I/GCSEs (at least five A*/A grades, including in subjects to be studied) and a positive reference.

Exit: Around 10-20 per cent leave post-GCSE, and roughly the same number join, but most stay on – no uniform and shared teaching with Abingdon boys does no harm to retention figures. Six to Oxbridge in 2016, the rest mainly to first choice Russell group institutions, Bristol, Exeter and Warwick being favourites. No significant subject bias, though 15 medics in 2016; we can look forward to Helkat doctors, lawyers, engineers, vets, musicians and psychologists in years to come.

Money matters: Fees relatively low, with the school featuring in the Telegraph's top 10 schools offering value for money, but extras (including lunch) can soon mount up. A small number of academic scholarships are awarded according to performance in entrance exam and, at 13+ interview. Music scholarships (free tuition on one or two instruments) offered on basis of audition, and also small in number. 'We keep them small and moderate on purpose as we don't want to create a point of contention around affordability and we are mindful that some girls might lose their interest in music later on and we wouldn't want pressure to be put on them if that happened,' says the head. In all, approximately 10 per cent of students are currently in receipt of financial support. There are also hardship funds available to support families whose financial circumstances change suddenly mid-year.

Remarks: This is a school whose outstanding teaching, go-getting culture and breathtaking facilities and opportunities produce confident, spirited girls with fine minds, but who aren't afraid to roll their sleeves up to get things done. The pacey environment – and the school really does move at a brisk speed – isn't for everyone, but the fastidious emphasis on admissions and ongoing support and encouragement for the girls means that they keep up, with few, if any, wilting. We found the girls fiercely proud of their school, as well as being acutely aware of how fortunate they are. If your daughter is bright and curious, then this school could be the golden ticket to Oxbridge and beyond.

St Hilary's School

Holloway Hill, Godalming, Surrey GU7 1RZ

Pupils: 202: 171 girls, 31 boys • Ages: Girls 2–11, boys 2–7

Fees: £9,705 – £14,280 pa

Tel: 01483 416551
Email: registrar@sthilarysschool.com
Website: www.sthilarysschool.com

Headmistress: Since 2012, Mrs Jane Whittingham (early 50s), previously deputy at nearby Rowan Prep in Esher, with particular interest and qualification in dyslexia. Mother of four (teens and 20s), came somewhat late to her first headship due to time spent with her own family. She prefers the prep school model (as opposed to a through school) 'where pupils prepare for their future, as well as their next school, and move on to a new landscape at 11'. Mrs W is bursting with new ideas, 'I have one idea a day while driving up and down the A3', covering every aspect of school life and made many changes in her first year at St Hilary's, tweaking teaching standards upwards, introducing head girl, house captains and positions of responsibility for every year 6 pupil, creating a plethora of awards. Her open door policy includes almost daily visits from groups of pupils for TLC and encouragement dressed up in fun sessions such as reading with Ronnie (her pet dog), Ludo and lemonade, dodgers (jammie) and dominoes. Groups of year 6 girls are regularly invited to lunch in her study, with table cloths, wine glasses (of juice) and 'posh cutlery'. Parents tell us their girls 'love going to visit Mrs Whittingham in her office' and say that Mrs W is doing good things and moving St Hilary's on without losing the happy, unpressurised vibe.

Entrance: Entry to nursery at age 2 allows unfettered progression throughout school; others join into reception year or at age 7. Quite a few join from local state infants' schools. No academic selection, prospective pupils and their parents meet the head and the child spends a morning in school so staff can benchmark their current attainment and give them a taste of life at St Hilary's.

Handful of scholarships up to 30 per cent. Means-tested bursaries available, mostly 10 to 50 per cent, including very occasional full bursary. Scholarships at year 3 entry, in-house scholarship tests for girls already at St Hilary's; 'they write a story and do a maths paper during a lesson and don't really realise so there's no pressure'. Current pupils can apply for academic, art, sports, music or drama scholarships.

Parents describe the whole entry and scholarship process as very low key and are comfortable with the range of academic ability.

Exit: Boys leave aged 7, two-thirds to nearby Aldro, a couple each to Lanesborough and Cranleigh Prep. The vast majority of girls leave at 11. Prior's Field, Guildford High and St Catherine's most popular recently. Also occasional one or two to Churcher's College, King Edward's, Tormead, Amesbury, Frensham Heights, Farnborough Hill, St Edmund's, St Teresa's and Wycombe Abbey.

Parents appreciate the help given with entry exams for senior schools, noting how work ramps up at the start of year 6 with a focus on English, maths and science, plus recently introduced verbal and non-verbal reasoning. They are comfortable that 'girls are very well prepared for their next step'.

Remarks: The ethos of St Hilary's, repeated by staff and parents alike, is an encouraging but unpressured prep school education. Parents feel the school is 'very happy' and pupils are 'allowed to be themselves', it's a 'buzzy place' with something for everyone and 'makes the best of each child without pressure'. This unpressurised aura sets St Hilary's apart from some of the other local girls' schools and really appeals to the relaxed parents of St Hilary's pupils. Typically, a mother told us, 'homework is not a big deal, it doesn't get in the way of family life.'

The lack of pressure doesn't mean lack of academic success. While intake and classes are 'completely mixed ability', parents feel St Hilary's 'seems to cater for all' and 'gets results with quality teaching'. There's plenty of praise for teachers, many of whom are relatively new, including a good few mentions for the 'dynamic deputy head' credited with improving standards. There's a sense that 'nobody fails, because it becomes clear which senior school they're heading for'. Mrs W meets all boys in year 1 and girls in year 5, individually with their parents, to discuss choices for next schools, telling us she 'works with parents to find a senior school which fits'. Parents are confident that St Hilary's is 'good at placing girls and preparing them for the right senior school'.

On our visit we saw small classes, some of only 8 to 10, with quiet, attentive pupils. Classrooms, science lab, music and art rooms were interesting and colourful, inter-linked with lots of open doors in the younger age groups. Nothing stupendously modern, but all thoroughly fit for purpose. Buildings are a mix, from Victorian with additions throughout the 20th century. Internally a bit of a warren, but our pupil guides were totally confident of their routes and eager to show us everywhere. The nursery section, taking boys and girls from age 2, is bright, fun, well organised and with a newly kitted out, spacious, TeleTubbyland-esque outdoor area. Older pupils can come here for half an hour before school and have breakfast (as an extra); staff say young and older children enjoy each other's company.

Kindness is another recurring theme: parents mention how children are aware of each other and the need to be kind. Mothers explain, 'kindness is noted, recognised and rewarded,' saying 'girls are kind, inclusive and celebrate friends' achievements' and 'everybody looks out for each other'. One of Mrs W's newly introduced awards is a True Friend wrist band awarded to pupils who have been particularly kind and helpful to others. Girls are not the sort to be bothered by fashions and fads; they are 'not worried about what they're wearing or having the latest rubber or pencil'. One girl who had moved on to a popular local girls' senior school noticed the difference between her St Hilary's friends and louder, more assertive girls from other schools.

Parents report that music, art and drama are strengths, citing the 'very enthusiastic head of music'. They like the availability of 'taster instruments', their girls 'love being involved in music'. Another parent enthused over the variety of musical clubs, groups and orchestra her 'very musical daughter' enjoys, while being delighted that 'this is all included in the fees'.

Sport has been given a recent boost by the new, 'young and bubbly' head of sport, a British gymnast who the girls love to Google and watch on YouTube. Usual netball and hockey, with football and cricket for boys, on offer and everyone does everything. Pupils of all abilities attend practice sessions during lunch break or after school and everyone who wants to has a good chance of playing matches in a team. New sports recently added just for fun include girls' football, tag-rugby and pop-lacrosse.

Families tend to be classic middle class professionals, although a little more laid back and less demanding than the Surrey stereotype. Many with both parents working but lots of stay at home mums too, some first time buyers and all pretty local. Families are undoubtedly comfortably off; the car park is populated with new four by fours, but few are flashy or brash. Some recent relocations from London wanting less city life for their children, but parents and teachers alike say this has not changed the local, Godalming and villages vibe of the school. St Hilary's PTA is active with lots of social events, all the usuals, plus others such as a family camping weekend in the grounds.

Overall, happy, charming and a little bit old fashioned; academically successful and, above all, unpressurised.

St Hilda's Preparatory School for Girls

High Street, Bushey, Watford, Hertfordshire WD23 3DA

Pupils: 184 (including co-ed nursery) • Ages: 2-11

Fees: £11,052 – £11,883 pa

Tel: 020 8950 1751
Email: secretary@sthildasbushey.co.uk
Website: www.sthildasbushey.com/

Headmistress: Since 2015, Sarah Jane Styles, previously head of Francis Holland (Sloane Square) Junior School. BA, QTS in theology and MA in philosophy of education. Previously director of studies at Wheathampstead House. Was a member of the royal navy and now a member of the royal naval reserve at weekends and in school holidays. Seen by Francis Holland parents as being 'approachable', 'sweet' and 'fair'. Likes cycling, walking and being on the go.

Entrance: About 50 per cent of the potential 18 reception places are filled from the school's co-ed Bluebird nursery. Not academically selective but all potential newcomers are assessed to ensure good fit with the school and places are not a given. Girls join other year groups from a mix of local state schools and pre-preps, with the occasional joiner from competing preps as parents start to see St Hilda's as 'more academic.'

Exit: Despite recent alliance with the Aldenham Foundation, not a feeder to any particular school, with girls leaving at 11 to the enviable range of the top independent and selective maintained schools that populate the area, with the occasional one off to board. In 2016, girls headed off to St Margaret's, North London Collegiate, Aldenham, Royal Masonic, St Albans, Watford Grammar, City of London, Edgbaston and St Helen's. Multiple offers and several scholarships the norm most years.

Boys leave the Bluebird at 4 for nearby schools including Northwood Prep and St John's.

Remarks: Dr Who springs to mind when describing St Hilda's buildings. Set at the end of Bushey High Street in an unassuming Victorian house (originally the home of artist Hubert von Herkomer), with a number of more modern add-ons crammed into the site, it has a compact, urban feel, more akin to a London school than a leafy suburban prep.

In architectural terms it certainly wouldn't give the glossy Bushey Academy down the road a run for its money, but step inside and the Tardis effect takes over. Classrooms are bright and inspiring, full of examples of the girls' work. The hard-working hall does an adequate job share as dining room (head chef knows all the girls by name and delivers crowd pleasing lunches every day), rehearsal space and assembly hall. More surprises lie behind the façade of the swimming pool building – recently rebuilt – which somehow hides a good sized, indoor heated pool, and the Whitby Hall, an uninspiring 80s construction which houses a well-equipped gymnasium.

The acres of fields boasted by many preps are sadly lacking, but there are creatively used grounds with hard and grass play areas, a woodland spinney and a spanking new adventure playground recently paid for out of PTA coffers. Sports fixtures requiring more space now take place at Aldenham School, just a 10 minute minibus ride away and well worth the journey. These boast a 400m running track, sports hall and long-jump pit. And they've thrown in the use of their minibuses too.

There's a quiet energy rather than a buzz around the school, generated by a loyal staff, some of whom have taught at St Hilda's for 15 years or more. The more senior teachers we observed had a spark many young guns would envy and a range of creative approaches up their sleeves to cater for their pupils' individual foibles – a tangible benefit of tiny class sizes. The exuberant deputy head, well into her 50s and sleeves firmly rolled up in the classroom, is a passionate advocate of ensuring girls are literate across the full range of media and has recently completed a PhD in developing an online learning community with 10 year olds.

Girls seem studious and sensible – not a hint of precociousness – probably because most parents are from the hard-working middle class, many stretching themselves for their daughters' education. Lots of first time buyers and a variety of ethnicities, reflecting the local area. Religious affiliation – or lack thereof – means school also has to be sensitive to this mix, although grace is said at lunch and there are prayers in assembly.

St Hilda's punches well above its tiny weight when it comes to academics, ably competing with its neighbouring hothouses. Girls are encouraged to be all-rounders, 'to give something back to their school'. Ferocious London parents be warned – 11+ tutoring outside school is not encouraged. After-school homework club, supervised by teaching staff, means that girls and parents can indulge in family time – great when everyone's working hard. Recent scholarships (from all-rounder and

S

academic to sport and music) are the proof in the pudding that good things can come in small packages.

It's not all work and no play, though. Parents found it refreshing that the school encouraged 'children to be children' on snow days and allowed them to play outside rather than kowtowing to health and safety, and felt this to be an accurate reflection of the school's home-like culture.

Specialist teaching in all subjects in years 4-6 is a unique feature amongst local schools, as is a recent focus on languages, which has seen the school forge links with others in five European countries.

Light homework is set from nursery; 10-15 minutes a night from year 3, rising to 40 minutes in year 5. School doesn't believe in setting pupils, believing it's important to allow for a child's different capabilities within a subject – average class sizes of 16-20 allow this utopian ideal to be a reality. A strong belief in accountability saw school registered for key stage 2 Sats for first time in 2013. In 2015, nearly everyone got level 5 in English (plus a few level 6s), and 30 per cent got level 6 for maths (plus another 30 per cent at level 5).

The school's size also means that SEN can generally be mainstreamed into the classroom, but a range of friendly-sounding 'clubs' for areas such as spelling and language enrichment allow pupils who need it to receive extra help without feeling marginalised.

Flashy facilities for art and music are less in evidence than at many other girls' preps but provision is fair for the size of the school, with peripatetic lessons on offer in violin from year 1, and 60 per cent of upper school learning an individual instrument across the range of strings, wind and piano. An annual production – usually musical – is a focus for girls in years 5 and 6, with many girls citing drama as their favourite extracurricular activity, inspired (again) by their deputy head who runs the show.

The Aldenham Alliance means that sport is 'really getting there' now, according to both staff and parents. Netball and athletics, with girls representing the borough in the latter, are flagship sports, with supporting roles from rounders, gymnastics and dance, and year-round weekly swimming for all from nursery up. More competitive fixtures than previously and the provision of Aldenham's minibuses has made this previously prohibitively expensive exercise feasible, resulting in a more sporty outlook.

Parents can sleep easy knowing what's coming on the bill as extracurricular activities are listed on two separate menus – one for free activities and the other for paid-fors. Freebies range from art, Spanish and ICT to football and the more quirky Orff Ensemble – an opportunity for lower school girls (read non-musicians) to play percussion and recorder pieces in a variety of musical styles, with others such as ballet and short tennis on offer at the going rate.

Busy families also benefit from the new Bluebird nursery which offers wrap-around care 50 weeks a year. Parents of nursery age children can select term-time, state school or St Hilda's school terms to fit in with their situations and deliver flexible childcare. This ethos also spreads up the school with reasonably priced breakfast club (from 7.30am), free early drop off (from 8am) and late pick-up, including tea (up to 6.30pm), available for 'a few pounds'.

St Hugh's School, Oxfordshire

Carswell Manor, Faringdon, Oxfordshire SN7 8PT

Pupils: 340; 19 weekly, 96 flexi boarders • Ages: 3-13 (boarders from 7) • C of E

Fees: Day £10,995 – £18,675; Weekly Boarding + £3,675 pa

Tel: 01367 870700
Email: registrar@st-hughs.co.uk
Website: www.st-hughs.co.uk

Headmaster: Since 2006, Mr Andrew Nott BA (early 50s). Son of a bishop, educated at The Beacon Prep and King's, Taunton. Studied history at the University of Wales, PGCE Westminster College, Oxford. Worked for the Church Commissioners where he met his wife, Sarah. First teaching post at St Andrew's School, Eastbourne, rose to deputy head. Thence to Davenies for his first headship prior to St Hugh's. Parents describe him as 'amazing' (adjective also frequently applied to Sarah) on a personal level; one or two said they found him a little shy on more public occasions.

Mr Nott is proud of his scholars' achievements but he is also a true champion of the strugglers and late bloomers who are inevitably part of the cohort of a non-selective school. He told us that he had thoroughly enjoyed his time at prep and it is this 'carefree' existence that he wants children at St Hugh's to experience. He loves sport, especially cricket (he is a member of MCC and had a bookcase dedicated to copies of Wisden) and is determined that all the children at St Hugh's get a match, including the E and F teams. He vividly remembers 'the boys who weren't in the A team picking daisies on the boundary' during his prep school cricket matches, and though St Hugh's may be a traditional school in many ways, this is one bit of history Mr Nott does not want to repeat. His mantra is 'excellence and inclusion' and he's also a big champion of kindness, a 'hugely important virtue' that he believes is undervalued these days.

School has acquired five acres of adjoining land for additional games fields, but although the roll is full there are no plans to increase numbers of pupils significantly. Mr Nott says, 'We could be a lot bigger but I want to keep the character of the school, to know every child.' Sounds pretty definite to us but a few parents expressed worries about the school getting bigger. Development on this beautiful rural site is no doubt a planning nightmare, but the newish Cannon Building – named like other parts of the school after a former head – is a superb facility housing science, art and DT. The heads of these departments worked with architects to design their ideal rooms and are still purring contentedly.

Mr Nott and his wife Sarah have five children; four attended St Hugh's and the two youngest are still there. Sarah is responsible, among many other things, for the tastefully low-key marketing and excellent newsletter. The Notts live just over the lane from school; it's not much of a boundary but just far enough to allow time to switch off and enable the head to enjoy planning the family's next trip abroad and practising creative cookery. Though usually pretty competent, he admits to a recent disaster courtesy of Heston Blumenthal (who doesn't't?). He's also fascinated by the academic side of leadership. Favourite childhood reads? Tintin and the Willard Price series of adventure stories.

Entrance: Non-selective, non-competitive, it's first come, first served. Mr Nott likes to meet parents as well as children. Prospective pupils spend a day; those entering year 3 or above have assessments in English and maths. Main entry is into reception (up to 26 places), year 3 (up to six places), year 5 (up to eight places). Nursery takes up to 25 a year.

Exit: To schools all over home counties. Many to board eg Cheltenham College, Cheltenham Ladies', Harrow, Radley, Eton, Marlborough, St Edward's Oxford, St Mary's Calne, Wellington. Rest to local day schools including Abingdon, Headington, Magdalen College School and St Helen's and St Katharine's. Over ninety-five per cent of girls stay on until age 13; apparently this is very popular with parents – perhaps because their girls stay children for that little bit longer.

Remarks: We arrived on a perfect English summer's day and Carswell Manor, which looks like a bijou country house hotel, seemed to glow with the golden warmth of Cotswold stone. On closer inspection much of façade is pebbledashed but somehow still pretty classy. The Manor was once home to the Niven family and it seems fitting that David Niven, the quintessential English gentleman, was born here – the old place even gets a mention in his autobiography. St Hugh's is without doubt the tidiest school we've ever visited and it's not just the buildings and grounds that are polished and groomed, the teachers too were quite remarkably elegant – not a baggy cardigan or tatty sandal in sight.

Founded 1906 in Chislehurst with three pupils and co-ed since 1977, St Hugh's is now very much a family school – nursery was established in response to parent demand and the minute it opened was 'immediately full with younger siblings.' Mothers walk their dogs in the grounds after morning drop off. Indeed dogs are a bit of a feature: they kept trotting by or popping out from under tables during our visit – all glossy coated and impeccably behaved, of course. Though we saw no ponies we hear that they also loom large here – jodhpurs (very much not pyjamas) are what the busy St Hugh's mother wears first thing in the morning.

Small classes (average 13), spacious modern facilities and glorious surroundings are enough to inspire any child to reach their full potential, and while not all will be scholars and high flyers, everyone is encouraged to find their talent. Much is expected of these children and sometimes Mr Nott's role is to manage expectations; by their second or third child old hands know they can relax and put their trust in the school. Parents we spoke to felt that Mr Nott's advice about senior schools was excellent and absolutely right for their child; the broad spectrum of schools St Hugh's sends to bears this out.

Maths and English set from year 3, French from year 6; rest of subjects taught in mixed ability groups but this can and does vary from year to year according to cohort. French and Latin for all, optional extracurricular Spanish and Mandarin. Greek for scholars. Middle school pupils (years 3 and 4) have their own teaching block and activities such as drama, choir, sports day etc – a nice way to let the youngest take centre stage. Low turnover of staff apart from gappies (usually old boys and girls) who stay for a year. In lessons we observed pupils were quiet, engaged, working hard individually and in pairs. Small class sizes mean teacher can tailor tasks according to ability; they also make it hard to mess around at the back (not that there seemed to be any such tendency). Parents describe SEN support as 'brilliant'; the head of the service told us that the aim is for it to be 'flexible and fluid', to give pupils a boost when needed and then 'launch them back, even if they need to be picked up again later.' Support is either individual or in booster groups and is not charged as an extra. Pastoral care also came in for high praise – merest whiff of bullying is dealt with at lightning speed.

A school tradition and one of the highlights of year 8 is a week's post-exam adventure trip to Wales, during which Mr Nott gives the children their CE results over fish and chips on the beach. Once back in Oxfordshire as part of an extensive leavers' programme, pupils are initiated into important life skills such as how to tie a bow tie, polish shoes and iron shirts; they also create and stage a fashion show for a local children's charity.

Excellent sporting facilities both inside and out host sport for all, every day. All main ones plus squash, basketball, tennis and introduction to lacrosse. Head confirms that every child gets to represent the school in matches. Notable recent success in riding, tennis (and real tennis) and cross-country. Large number of sports scholarships awarded to St Hugh's pupils every year. Music and drama are also inclusive with enough plays, choirs, bands and ensembles to accommodate the full range of abilities and a new music block. Outdoor production of A Midsummer Night's Dream staged around atmospheric ivy-clad 'temple' in the grounds. St Hugh's seems to produce thinkers and listeners (as opposed to shouters) and recognition for this comes in the form of a clutch of top awards for debating and public speaking. Art and DT thriving in their new building – art room boasts a large walk-in kiln, ready to receive the most ambitious ceramic creations and electric windows that can be controlled to provide optimum natural light conditions.

Pre-prep is housed in the old stable block with classrooms round a flexible central space that can be divided up and used for small group work. Rooms are carefully decorated with colourful posters and children's work and, as in the main school, the atmosphere seemed to be one of gently restrained exuberance. Or so we thought until we came across a monsieur from the big school delighting the pre-prep pupils with his all-singing and dancing weekly French lesson. Literacy taught via Read Write Inc phonics programme and for this children are grouped by their stage of development, not age. Official forest school: pupils from nursery to year 6 get to do lots of messy learning in the woods (last two years have bushcraft). As one member of staff remarked, 'Some children come to life outside, and it's not just the boys.' Parents promised us that pupils really are allowed to get muddy.

Youngest (age 3 upwards) start in The Cottage nursery, a charming house that originally belonged to the groundsman (he is happily accommodated elsewhere). On our visit we saw determined excavation in the large sandpit that is, fortunately, six feet deep. Children sign in for their sessions on the interactive whiteboard and there is an ICT suite upstairs along with a rest room for pupils who still need a nap. Same phonics programme as pre-prep used to introduce letter sounds etc. Specialist teaching for music, dance, ICT. Introduction to French is via croissants and chocolat chaud.

Flexi and weekly boarding – parents pre-select boarding options at the start of term. Those wanting a full week get priority, those who want a couple of days are most likely to get them if they are consecutive. As a rule can't do sleepover style occasional boarding but will work something out in an emergency. Boarding is very often 'children driven', it's the parents who need persuading. Comfortable, characterful dorms up in the eaves, all very civilised – common room with original John Piper on wall (sigh). Matrons inspect every morning to ensure that boarders live up to the St Hugh's standard of tidiness. Day pupils can stay until 7.30pm for prep and supper (no extra charge) and about a third do. No Saturday school. Wednesday evenings are reserved for 'fun' things and there's no prep. Parents pre-select home time but emergencies and late changes accommodated. Sensible uniform and termly bill low on the dreaded 'extras'. Fees include all trips (including trips abroad) and SEN support. Means-tested bursaries of up to full fees available.

S

So, what's the demographic? Put on your deerstalker and consider these clues: nearly all the pupils are children of privately-educated parents; a school bus scheme was discontinued after a couple of terms because no one used it (private lift sharing arrangements more popular); mussels are a favourite on the scrumptious lunch menu. So far, so county, but though the social profile be small, parents say it's neither snobbish nor exclusive and the children we met were down to earth, funny, normal kids.

St Hugh's is seemingly a school with nothing to prove. It doesn't advertise and prospective parents are not bombarded with glossy anythings. For a flavour of the place, ask to see a copy of the beautifully produced half-termly magazine, St Hugh's News. Such understatement, coupled with fees that are higher than local average (but are all-inclusive and considered 'good value' by the parents we spoke to), might seem counter-intuitive in an area that is not under-served with preps, but St Hugh's is always full courtesy of the low-tech marketing marvel money can't buy: word of mouth. Happy parents, happy children, happy dogs – what could be better?

St James Senior Boys' School

Linked with St James Junior School, St James Senior Girls' School

Church Road, Ashford, Surrey TW15 3DZ

Pupils: 390 • Ages: 11–18 • Sixth form: 64

Fees: £17,280 pa

Tel: 01784 266930
Email: admissions@stjamesboys.co.uk
Website: www.stjamesboys.co.uk

Headmaster: Since 2013, Mr David Brazier BA MSc PGCE. Studied English and American literature at the University of Kent and has an MSc from Reading University. He joined St James from six years as head of Long Close School, Slough, where application numbers tripled during his reign (and which some boys left to follow him to St James). Prior to this, he was head of English and drama at Crosfields School in Reading and assistant headmaster at Davenies in Beaconsfield, Bucks.

Chatty, warm and amiable, but not a man who's afraid to big himself up, he makes no secret of his clear intention to dramatically advance the school, particularly academically. 'The previous head was Margaret Thatcher's speechwriter, so he wasn't an educator, whereas my background is in school improvement,' he says. So far, so good – within just three years, applications for year 7 rose from 80 to 160 boys and there is a waiting list for the first time in the school's history. It's no coincidence, he believes, that he's the first head with no connection with School of Economic Science (SES), the philosophy that the school was founded on. It's not that he isn't spiritual, he insists. 'I was using mindfulness as a drama teacher years ago and have meditated for years,' he says. 'In fact, it was when I saw that the school wanted someone with a background in both meditation and school improvement that I decided to apply. The ethos fits me perfectly.' What he's done, agree parents and staff, is taken the founding principles and 'sharpened them up for the modern world.' 'His arrival felt a breath of fresh air,' said one parent. 'He's progressive and outward looking, but has kept everything that's important about the school.'

A hands-on head who knows every boy by name, he teaches philosophy to year 9s, including a course he has written on 'Love, relationships and sexuality,' and drama periodically across all year groups. 'You get the feeling he's a teacher at heart,' said a parent. Has an abiding love of the performing arts (especially Shakespeare) and he has written three plays that have been performed in schools. Having played for Berkshire Schools and Hurst in the Thames Valley League, he is also passionate about cricket and is a qualified coach, which the boys benefit from. Has plans to live on site with his wife, Lizzie, a leadership and management consultant. Has two grown-up children, one a maths teacher.

Academic matters: Despite the selective entrance criteria, academic promise has never been the be-all-and-end-all here, with the school favouring a well-rounded education in which boys' strengths are valued, wherever they may lie. And although the emphasis on academia has been much greater in recent years, this is still not a school for parents who want to push their children to their absolute limits. Indeed, all subject teaching is underpinned by a philosophical and spiritual ethos that means boys are encouraged to constantly focus on wholeness ('not being stressed and managing your energies well,' explains the head) and harmony ('ensuring you get on with others and are at one with your environment'). In practice, this involves a big push on mindfulness (which boys are taught from year 7) and meditation and quiet time, which is a major feature at the start and end of every day.

In 2016, 44 per cent A*/A grades at GCSE. At A level, 20 per cent A*/A grades (61 per cent A*-B), with similar subjects topping the list, with the addition of chemistry and economics. Traditional range of subjects on offer at both levels, with the addition of business studies BTec for sixth formers. Allows pupils to specialise early, following their individual bents. Spanish, German and French introduced from year 7 and everyone takes one of these modern languages for GCSE. Unusually (uniquely, believes the school), Sanskrit – the Indo-Germanic language pre-dating even Greek and Latin – is introduced to year 7s and continues for those who can manage it until year 9, becoming an option thereafter. 'Sanskrit used to be seen as the language to do if you wanted to be spiritually enlightened,' explains the head. 'But we've taken the mystical mumbo jumbo out of it, with a university-based teacher coming in to teach it.' Heartening to see Greek and Latin as relatively popular GCSE options, though few continue classical or any other language to A level. Year 7s are set in maths and Sanskrit; year 8s in maths, French, Latin and Sanskrit; and by year 9, boys can expect to be in one of four sets in these subjects, the weakest of which has around 10 pupils. Homework in abundance (one-and-a-half hours a night in year 7, up to 4 hours a night in sixth form) and if it's not up to scratch, boys can expect a detention.

Notable mutual respect between boys and their teachers, both of whom describe each other as 'enthusiastic'. No talking down to pupils whatsoever during our visit, although some parents told us that whilst there are plenty of stars among the staff, a handful are old-school 'and not so well-liked.' This is brushed off quickly enough, though – 'it's inevitable,' shrugged one. Help instantly and easily available, with the option to email teachers when on study leave, or come in for support. They respond readily to parental emails too. The school is aiming for teachers newly employed under current headship to have a masters or PhD and all now use a rigorous monitoring system to ensure all boys are on track, as well as undergoing weekly teacher training themselves.

SEN (which includes the usual remit of dyslexia, ADHD, autistic spectrum etc) pupils have historically been so numerous and well-supported here that the school started to get a reputation as being a special needs school – something the head is keen to change. 'When I joined, we had a third SEN, now it's a quarter, with far fewer statements,' he says. It's not that he's any less dedicated to the school's 'lovely bespoke SEN department, with the caring ladies that run it,' he says. 'But whereas before SEN seemed like an add-on, with boys doing their lessons, then going off to the department – an approach that to my mind was 20 years out-of-date – most of the extra assistance from the SEN department now happens in the classroom itself, embedded into the lessons. That makes us much more mainstream.' Parents say it works well, praising the extra courses put on for boys struggling to keep up.

All boys work towards a St James Baccalaureate, recognising the breadth of education as well as academic success.

Games, options, the arts: At the risk of sounding gooey and romantic, hearing some of the younger boys sing in the chapel stopped us in our tracks. Singing is, in fact, so established here that when we asked some of the boys if they enjoyed it, they looked confused. 'It's part of daily life,' they answered, as if we'd asked them if they enjoy getting dressed. In the old days, it was strictly classical, but nowadays boys are just as likely to sing gospel or pop – a welcome change, they say. There are all the usual school choirs, school orchestra and various ensembles and bands – and besides the music lessons for all, 85 boys (around a fifth) learn an instrument with a peripatetic teacher in one of the (newly refurbished when we visited) private practice rooms. Electric guitar and drums particularly popular, although head is pushing for less gender stereotyping (which basically means more strings). Opportunities to perform publically, including the much talked-about annual concert in Hammersmith Town Hall.

Drama mainly takes place in the studio called The Empty Space after Peter Brooke gave his support for it (a deliberately minimalistic rendering of 'creative space'), although we also saw boys performing Shakespeare (well) in the roomy school reception area on our arrival – a joy to watch. Performance is important, as is speech itself. 'If you have not mastered speech by the time you leave here, then those who have will master you,' is a maxim quoted at the boys. 'Makes them talk and engage in conversations,' say parents. Serious annual productions in collaboration with the girls' school in Olympia, with everyone making light of the considerable amount of inter-school ferrying this involves.

Art facilities decent enough, with two roomy, well-lit studios, although we'd like to have seen more examples of pupil work around the school. DT facilities impressive, shiny and well-equipped with new workshop and computer lab – an increasingly popular GSCE option and now also offered at A level.

Sport is pushed hard here, with facilities including lake, tennis courts, rugby pitches (two more recently added), cricket squares (now plus one), AstroTurf and football pitches – practically all in full use on the sun-drenched day we visited. Kept beautifully (not a weed in sight), these form a striking backdrop to the main school building and can be seen from most classrooms. Inside sports facilities less notable. Rugby, hockey, cricket and cross-country are the big sports here, with football on the up, although not quickly enough for some boys we spoke to. Plenty of minor sports and opportunities too – everything from martial arts to kayaking or open swimming in the school lake and climbing (particularly popular). 'It means that if you don't like sport, you'll find something fitness related to love instead,' said one boy, although some feel there's still too much emphasis on rugby. 'If you don't like rugby, where do you go?' said one, as if he hoped we might actually have an answer. School punches above its weight in sporting competitions, particularly in rugby, where it regularly reaches the Surrey cup finals and plays some seriously big schools. 'Boys regularly go on to get sports scholarships,' adds the head.

S

Wednesday afternoons are dedicated to clubs run by a mixture of staff and sixth-formers, ranging from the likes of magic club and comic club to military history club. 'Boys suggest a club and we make it happen,' says the head; pupils concur. Then there's the before and after-school programme of activities – everything from sports clubs to philosophy club. Around a quarter enthusiastically takes up the cadet force, doing all the adventurous things that that offers. A popular D of E scheme attracts others. Around three-quarters of the school takes up one or other of these outdoor options. Some charitable and social activity, but less than we had expected to find.

Plenty of leadership and team-building days on offer. For example, in year 8, students are visited by Steve Cunningham, a world-record breaking blind man, who assists them in writing personal, meaningful targets. In year 8, they have a service day in which they assist the groundsmen with practical tasks like fence-building and gardening, whilst in year 9, a 'Stepping into Manhood' formal dinner allows the boys to experience formal dining with an inspirational after-dinner speaker. A trip to Lucca, Italy, presents a scenic opportunity to year 10s to develop a wide range of personal skills and there are lots of other school trips besides. 'My exchange programme in Montpellier was one of the best experiences of my life,' one boy told us. On offer to all boys are twice-yearly lectures at the RSA given by everyone from eminent physicians to ambassadors. The Ficino Society is a programme of academic talks designed to foster and care for potential Oxbridge candidates, which adds to the intellectual life of the school and thus meets its requirement to nurture the gifted and talented.

Background and atmosphere: The school was founded in the 1970s within the bosom of SES, which itself was founded in 1937 as a means of exploring through the study of the world's great religions and philosophies what it is to be fully human in a spiritual way and, in so doing, what goes to make a spiritually healthy and prosperous community. But whilst the SES flame burned high back then, it has attracted increasing controversy over the decades, with some even calling it a 'cult'. Particularly since the current head's appointment, the school has distanced itself from the movement, now describing itself as 'a philosophically inspired school whose roots are in the SES, but which has grown and evolved, with the philosophy and ethos made available to all.'

Originally based in Twickenham, the school moved west in 2010, now occupying a truly beautiful site in the West London Lake District, in stunning buildings erected by The Society of Ancient Britons in 1857 to house the Welsh Girls' School. They have been well renovated to make a spacious and light environment, although facilities are not quite as glossy as at some neighbouring schools.

Pastoral care, well-being and discipline: The boys' form tutors are at the heart of pastoral care here and it's a role they take tremendously seriously. 'I've never experienced such understanding and support from a teacher,' said one parent, whilst a boy told us, 'I had some issues at home and my teacher really helped.' Buddying system between sixth formers and year 7s popular and a school counsellor was about to be employed on a part-time basis when we visited. 'It's ok to admit vulnerability here,' said one pupil.

Misbehaviour and anti-social behaviour not tolerated and a yellow and red card system culminating in after-school detentions, along with high presence of staff including head in corridors between lessons and in breaks, ensures it stays that way. School particularly strict on uniform, with staff regularly uttering the words 'Shine your shoes' on the gate in the mornings, whereby boys are sent to the dedicated shoe-shining room. Bullying a bit of a problem in the past, but current head claims to have cut it by half, having 'moved a few pupils on' early in his role and introduced new, stricter-than-ever policies around it. Drugs a non-issue to date.

Lots of leadership opportunities, thanks to the prefect system, class representation on the school council and the sixth-form run clubs, among others. 'Manhood', 'character' and 'character-building' are terms much in evidence here. 'Gets teenage boys, all noise and go and fast paced, to meditate in silence,' said one parent.

School food is vegetarian (those SES foundations again) and we enjoyed a mean vegetable lasagne and salad. Some boys love it; others are less keen. But one thing's for sure, says the head – they don't get that weighed down feeling after lunch and there won't be any cases of food poisoning here.

Boarding, which was weekly only, closed in July 2016.

Pupils and parents: All but one pupil came west when the school moved, and the catchment area still stretches far to the east, with school run buses helping to keep it that way. The rest use public transport, with three-quarters arriving by train (the station is opposite the school) or public buses, which stop right outside. Hardly anyone dropped off by car. Ethnic and social mix is typical of the area – that is, predominantly white, with some Asian, African-Caribbean and Chinese, among others. A mixture of different faiths, notably those (Hinduism, Buddhism) on which the SES drew heavily. SES a non-issue among parents these days, though, with only a couple of members left. Parents range from the super-rich to those working all hours in modest jobs to get their boys in. Lively and sociable PTA, including annual ball, quiz nights etc. 'They want the parents to be part of the school,' said a parent.

Boys are lively, creative and sparky, but well-mannered and disciplined when they need to be, with lots of heads down in the classes we observed. No talking over each other among the boys we spoke to, with respectfulness and listening skills clearly deep-rooted. 'Boys here are kind, generous and determined – it's the reason I chose the school,' said one parent. Plenty of confidence, but not a shred of arrogance in the boys we met. 'My son has blossomed. No more hunched shoulders. He walks square,' said a parent. Emerging very much as young men, not youths, the boys told us there is 'a spirit of looking out for each other – it's very supportive, almost like a big family.' Not for the kind of child who thinks they can do it all on their own, this is a school for those who are willing to ask for help.

Entrance: Around 160 applicants for 70 places in year 7. Selection on the basis of entrance tests in English, maths and verbal reasoning plus interview with the head. In fact, the interview can outweigh the entrance test if it is felt the boy has 'character' or other gifts which the school feels would benefit from its distinctive educational approach. 'We're looking for a renaissance man vibe – boys who like singing, sport, leading, speaking confidently and valuing what others say too,' says the head. From 2016, pre-tests required for 13+ entry.

Entry into the sixth form requires a minimum of six B grades at GCSE plus interview with the head of sixth form and headmaster. This requirement extends to the boys already in the school and some are encouraged to look elsewhere or helped into more vocational areas if the school feels that A levels are not appropriate.

Exit: Between a third and a half leaves after GCSEs for a clutch of comfortable reasons – access to the IB, wanting more practical courses, or just having been there since age 4. Majority who leave go on to colleges or co-ed school sixth-forms. None to Oxbridge in 2016. Courses wide-ranging. In 2016, ranged from anthropology at Durham and neuroscience at Nottingham to philosophy at London as well as one to music college. Other destinations include SOAS, Edinburgh and Brunel. As in previous years, several to study medicine.

Money matters: Not a rich school, with lower-than-average fees. But whilst the pot for scholarships and bursaries has historically been correspondingly small, it is growing, with five academic and sports scholarships in the year we visited. School aims to support with means-tested bursaries those who could otherwise not come or who have financial problems once accepted.

Remarks: Although not as distinctive and different as it was in the SES-focused days of old, this relatively small school is still set apart from the norm, with spiritual principles influencing every aspect of curricular and extracurricular life. That's not to say it isn't academic – the current head makes sure of it – but, as one parent put it, 'It's not a school that makes boys who don't have academic excellence feel any less of a person.' In short, it's all about the individual, helping boys grow into the best adult men they can be, both spiritually and intellectually. Two pieces of advice for parents – first, acquaint yourself thoroughly with the ethos and second, take note that the head, who has brought about sweeping changes, sees the school as being very much on a journey. 'Come back in a few years and I think you'll find something really magical,' he told us. We think he could be right.

St John's Beaumont School

Priest Hill, Old Windsor, Berkshire SL4 2JN

Pupils: 300; 25 full, 28 weekly boarders • Ages: 3–13 (boarders from 7) • RC

Fees: Day £9,018 – £17,253; Boarding £20,853 – £26,175 pa

Tel: 01784 432428
Email: admissions@sjb.email
Website: www.sjb.community

Headmaster: Since 2006, Mr Giles Delaney (40s). Educated at Hereford Cathedral School, studied music and psychology at Cardiff (instruments are the not-at-all-easy French horn and organ). PGCE at Cambridge and thence to St John's Beaumont. Became deputy head three years later before being catapulted at a very young age to headship on sudden death of his predecessor. He seems so at one with the school, staff and boys that we wonder if it was always his plan to stay at the old place for so long; his answer is a wry smile.

St John's Beaumont, like other RC schools, has a reputation for being pretty disciplined, although Mr Delaney is anything but a martinet. He sees no reason why boys can't be expected to give their very best in a caring and nurturing environment. He's extremely interested in research on how boys learn, especially the importance of pupils' relations with staff: 'boys don't learn subjects, they learn teachers.' In a boys' school 'everyone will have a go at orchestra, choir, dance. They will give everything a shot and smile if it doesn't work.' Certainly when it comes to the importance of context, relating academic subjects to the real world, it seems that Jesuit schools were there long before the educationalists.

Mr Delaney, who looks a bit like a young Colin Firth, is modest and charming. He told us that he had taught 'most stuff', still teaches year 5 ('getting them ready for pre-tests surreptitiously') and is looking forward to a new challenge: introducing the pre-prep boys to music. We weren't taken in by his self-deprecating answers. Boys and parents say his teaching is 'absolutely brilliant', 'fantastic', 'the best'. Loves preparing assemblies and shares a keen interest in medieval history with his wife, Katie, who teaches in a school in north London. He is currently studying for an MSc in education at Oxford. They have four daughters – must be something of an antidote to life at SJB. And if he hadn't gone into teaching? A conductor, he thinks, or a graphic designer, 'something not in an office.' Favourite book? Solzhenitsyn's One day in the life of Ivan Denisovich: 'It's about endurance, valuing the smallest things.'

Entrance: There's a waiting list so plan ahead. Most boys enter at age 4 after attending a taster session to assess suitability. Parents and children interviewed. Further small intake at year 3 (dependent on performance in school's own assessment and reference from current head). Priority given to practising Roman Catholic families, siblings and applicants with connections to St John's or a Jesuit education

Exit: To all the big beasts and all the more impressive given non-selective intake: Eton, Harrow, Tonbridge, Winchester, Wellington, Charterhouse, Ampleforth, Downside, Stonyhurst, Hampton. Notable record of academic, sport and all-rounder scholarships.

Remarks: St John's Beaumont sits in red-brick gothic grandeur on a hill overlooking Old Windsor, surrounded by 70 acres of grounds and playing fields next door to Windsor Great Park. Designed by John Francis Bentley (also responsible for Westminster Cathedral) and opened in 1888, it was the first purpose-built prep school in England. Tucked behind the Victorian edifice are recent additions: a fine sports centre with vertigo-inducing climbing wall, music, science and art departments, a theatre and the pre-prep block, all on a rather more human scale. The huge reception hall, hung with portraits of old boys and next door neighbour Her Majesty the Queen, sets a rather formal tone. Classical music playing discreetly in the background only just takes the edge off what could be an intimidating first impression for some prospective parents and their boys.

Our visit started in one of the original high ceilinged classrooms with a year 8 maths lesson. Considering it was nearly the end of term and these boys had done CE (many had won scholarships), their quiet concentration was remarkable. Working in pairs, they applied themselves to bisecting a line so that they would 'impress maths teachers at their next schools'. In accordance with the principles of Jesuit education, they then discussed context, suggesting where this technique could be applied in real life. Maths is a particular strength of SJB and the best take part in national competitions and maths challenges, winning medals at all levels. Three finalists recently gained distinctions in Junior Maths Olympiad. Science very hands-on; boys told us that a highlight was 'setting custard powder on fire' and went on to explain the theory behind the conflagration. Latin from year 6, Greek for scholars.

Having learnt (and swiftly forgotten) how to bisect a line it was off to year 6 history in a slightly less lofty Portakabin. After the maturity of the mathematicians we were relieved to find a sparky class tackling the causes of the First World War. Their presentation skills may have been a work in progress but there was no doubting their enthusiasm and depth of knowledge. Here, context was relating 1914 alliances to the current situation in Afghanistan. Distracting them from the task in hand, we asked what one thing would improve their school. The answer was unanimous: girls! Apparently girls would 'make the place tidier' and 'help with questions'. Dream on, chaps.

Golf, cycling, climbing, sailing, skiing – SJB boys pursue and excel at all kinds of sport, but rugby rules. They regularly field 16 teams and successfully play David to some much bigger Goliaths. Most recently the 1st XV was undefeated in all but one match. Usual parental grumbles that it's not much fun in the lesser teams who don't get any of the specialist coaching. Football gets a proper look in, too. There's an impressive swimming pool and a climbing wall in addition to all the usual facilities. Proximity to the Thames doesn't always guarantee a commitment to rowing but in this case it does and there are 50 boys in the squad netting a haul of medals in regional and national championships. For years 6, 7 and 8 it's sport every day plus matches on Saturday. It's a long day too: years 4 and 5 finish at 5pm, for older boys it's 6pm or later if they're doing extra activities. One of our guides said he thought parents should know that 'it's quite tiring'. Music, art and drama don't seem to be overshadowed by the sports behemoth; that long day means there's time for both.

Sixty or so boys board (one junior and one senior dorm) and according to one parent, it's 'proper boarding, not flexi.' Full weekend programme of activities, many chosen by boys on the boarding committee, includes paintballing, tank driving and trips to Windsor Castle and the Science Museum. Weekly boarding also an option. Interesting animal themed house system engenders keen rivalry for 'TYE' points (Tiger, Yak and Emu). Junior uniform (navy blue Bermudas until year 6) looks smart but several parents still reeling from eye-watering cost of anything crested, including jumpers and shirts.

Approximately 60 per cent of boys come from RC families but don't imagine this leads to monoculture – a peek into any classroom will dispel doubts on that score. Parents unanimously praised the pastoral care and the way the school welcomed diversity. One who was not Catholic said that religion was 'not an issue' but described the RE curriculum as 'very truly Catholic, up to and including creationism', so SJB unlikely to be destination of choice for Dawkins minor. School's view is that they welcome boys of any faith or none but those who join, 'join a community', and must play their part, including attendance at mass. Admissions process wise to parents who are only interested in the school for its CE results. The scholarship boards provide a record of the school's evolution. Thirty years ago practically all went on to Catholic schools such as Stonyhurst, The Oratory, Ampleforth; today's scholars are just as likely to be bound for Eton, Winchester and Wellington.

Mr Bentley the architect obviously believed in giving boys lots of space and air, hence the wide corridors and high ceilinged classrooms, and the generosity of his design, while unmistakably Victorian, stands up pretty well to the demands of the 21st century. His intimate and beautifully decorated chapel, bearing the scars of wartime bombs, only seats 60, and at Christmas there are several services so that all parents can enjoy the special atmosphere and 'magical music'. Whole school events take place in the somewhat less atmospheric sports hall. Part of the Jesuit educational ethos is that a child should be 'well rounded and worldly wise' and to that end SJB boys go far and wide; not only history and sports trips to France and Italy but also swimming the Midmar Mile in South Africa to raise money for charity. They're also stretched by the school's impressive Magis programme; senior boys have weekly lectures from visiting speakers, parents and members of staff and are also encouraged to present talks themselves. Recent subjects include deafness and language acquisition, Battersea Dogs' Home and space exploration. Lots of fundraising to support a sister school, St Rupert's, in Zimbawe.

Day boys come in from a 10 mile radius (bus service operates from Chiswick and Maidenhead). Parents a mix of trad Windsor and glossy Middletonshire (or as someone put it, those who have Wentworth membership and those who don't). Their sons are commendably oblivious to such pigeonholing and there's a great sense of camaraderie; boys are proud of their school and its traditions. Mr Delaney describes St John's Beaumont as a community that asks its members, 'What can you give?' It expects the very best but also give boys the confidence to try new things and learn from mistakes. As a parent remarked, 'It can appear prescriptive but the boys don't see it like that, they thrive on structure and clear rules. My son loves going to school.'

St John's School (Leatherhead)

Epsom Road, Leatherhead, Surrey KT22 8SP

Pupils: 715; 235 boarders, all weekly/flexi • Ages: 11–18 • Sixth form: 258

Fees: Day £17,850 – £22,920; Boarding £23,880 – £28,950 pa

Tel: 01372 373000
Email: admissions@stjohns.surrey.sch.uk
Website: www.stjohnsleatherhead.co.uk

Headmaster: Since 2011, Martin Collier MA, married with three older children. He read modern history at St John's College Oxford, followed by PGCE from London University. His first 10 years of teaching were in the maintained sector, at the 'fantastic' Thomas Tallis in south London and the 'tough' Weavers School in Wellingborough. He then moved into the independent sector and Oundle School, where he worked through roles of head of history, director of studies and second master. He also has many years' experience as an examiner with different boards, has been involved with the Qualifications and Curriculum Development Agency and has appeared as an examinations expert before the House of Commons select committee on education. In short, he has a broad experience and detailed knowledge of all things educational. We found him to be a quiet, almost unassuming man, a strategic thinker who was looking five years ahead in planning for St John's and has launched some very major changes at the school.

In addition to his responsibilities for the school's strategic management and teaching standards, Mr Collier also covers the outward facing aspects of St John's, which includes meeting all prospective parents and visiting local prep schools. Mr Collier has been rather an unknown to some parents, although they are aware that he has been hard at work behind the scenes developing the significant and progressive changes now taking shape at St John's.

Moving on in July 2017 to head Haileybury. His successor will be Rowena Cole BSc PGCE MBA, currently head of Dunottar School in Reigate. Biology degree from Exeter; taught biology at Howard of Effingham and City of London Freemen's before deputy headship at Guildford High. Married to Alistair; they have two young children.

Academic matters: St John's has been gradually on the up academically over the last few years and is aiming still higher. Exam results in 2016 were 66 per cent A*/A grades at GCSE, and 50 per cent A*/A at A level. It has been considered as a school which provides a good education but not a high pressure one – a suitable place for a child who would not be happy or comfortable in an academically high-flying school. Parents here certainly want their children to do as well as they can academically, but are also looking for an all-round education including social values and leadership.

Mr Collier believes improving academic results goes hand in hand with improving pastoral care and, unsurprisingly, higher levels of academic selection at entry. It's not rocket science, and the effects of changes taking place now should be seen over the next few years. There has been somewhat of a range of teaching styles and standards at the school including one or two described by parents as 'rather unimpressive', but they are reassured by the new broom and improving exam results. The head tells us he has made important new appointments to improve the quality of teaching, introduced new staff performance assessment and a new management structure with a focus on academia – he's obviously on the case and wants to 'increase fizz in the classroom'.

This big academic push has still to filter through to all pupils; parents tell us that hard work and academic success is not universally seen as cool. Although pupils do work hard and want success, sometimes they keep it rather quiet. Mr Collier notes that girls' academic work and success helps to pull the boys along, although by the sixth form they are equal. In his extensive experience, he has found that boys and girls have different needs and pace at different ages, their operation and processing is different, girls gain confidence and maturity earlier than boys. The range of academic ability is catered for by setting in all subjects based on the pace at which pupils learn.

All pupils are tested on entry to identify their 'learning profile', which also identifies any SEN. School tells us that learning support is available to all pupils at all ages, ranging from study skills and time management to specialist tuition for specific learning difficulties. Around 10 per cent of pupils currently have SEN and they are catered for by staff in the classroom, by extra small group sessions and, where necessary, by individual one-to-one support. Parents praise the 'excellent' SENCo. The small number of pupils with EAL have flexible, small group provision alongside support from tutors.

Games, options, the arts: All extras and additions to the academic curriculum are taken very seriously at St John's. They are well taught and valued by pupils and their families; school is very keen on leadership development and believes that sport, drama and music are of equal value to academics in developing a rounded and balanced individual.

Sport is pretty well at the centre of life at St John's and is compulsory, daily and at all ages. There are lots of options and the facilities are very good, with spacious pitches and sports centre. Essentially boys play rugby and football, girls play netball and rounders and both boys and girls play hockey, cricket, tennis and do athletics, cross-country and swimming. There's also a whole array of less usual sports and activities available. Saturdays are match days and older pupils tell us they watch and support their school teams. Rugby is at the top of the sports pecking order; the girls' housemistress is a top women's player and she referees matches – much to the surprise of visiting teams.

All this sporting activity brings a deal of success: in rugby St John's boys recently Surrey U16 county VIIs champions and in football won the national independent schools league. The girls have recently won an U16 county hockey trophy and, over the last two years, have been runners up in the county netball championships.

Music is another big part of St John's life, a third of pupils learn an instrument (up to diploma standard) and choral singing is also very strong – pupils win choral awards to universities and are involved in the National Youth Choir and other top external choral groups.

Drama is well represented with lots of opportunities for aspiring actors in many and varied school productions. St John's recently won a number of awards at the local Leatherhead Drama Festival.

Art and DT facilities are superb, housed in a gleaming new classroom block and equipped with everything the most dedicated artists and design technology students could want. The standard of work is correspondingly high, with displays of impressive and inspiring art and functional DT projects. The brainy (and charming) sixth former who showed us round was combining maths, physics and DT at A level and heading confidently towards an engineering degree.

Other activities include CCF (compulsory for four terms), community service and D of E, all involving challenging activities and trips. There are also lots of school activities going on in the evenings: concerts, plays, rehearsals and talks, all of which pupils are routinely involved in. It can be very demanding of pupils' time, particularly if they are not boarders, but it suits families who are busy and those who like their children to be fully occupied with school activities.

Boarding: Although the majority are day pupils, boarding is flourishing. Parents say flexi-boarding, two or three nights a week, has been a real winner and many pupils love it. Mr Collier has further long term plans for boarding: he describes it as 'currently in the foothills of change; it needs to lose its old-fashioned connotations and become fluid, social and involve parents in order to thrive'.

Care in the boarding houses is practical and pragmatic, although the nail polish remover in the entrance hall of a girl's house had obviously been ignored by one young lady we spotted unashamedly sporting fuchsia nails. The accommodation itself varies from neat, modern twin rooms with small en suite loo and shower to somewhat institutional six or eight person dorms with loos down a chilly corridor.

Background and atmosphere: St John's is very much a local school – most pupils come from within a 15 mile radius – with a strong sense of its own community. Essentially it's a traditional environment providing a 'values based education'; school says that parents here are interested in much more than academics, they want a well rounded, emotionally intelligent education for their children so they leave school able to interact well with others.

However, there is no doubt at all that St John's is currently going through some major changes, as previously mentioned regarding academic matters. These changes are also apparent in other areas and are leading to something of a culture shift, from an ultra-trad boys' boarding school into something much more 21st century, while still holding on to the values of an all-round schooling which are popular with parents. Since 2012, girls in every year throughout the school, albeit in the minority, Saturday lessons disappeared a few years ago with the arrival of the younger girls, though St John's is very definitely a six day a week school. Lower school for years 7 and 8 opened in 2016 with 54 pupils. Boarding is 'family-friendly' and flexible; no full time, seven days a week any more. New buildings have popped up to accommodate the 50 per cent-ish increase in pupil numbers over the last few years, entry requirements have just been hiked to a new high, lesson lengths and timetable arrangements have all been changed and a new tutor system introduced. It's not exactly a case of being dragged kicking and screaming but there's a lot happening and there may well be die-hards who need to be convinced. All this change has been brought about by a consultative process, Mr Collier reassures that 'everyone has had their say' – but it's early days and, like everyone else, we can only wait and see.

Some things remain the same – notably the school's structure around houses, 'important in engendering loyalty and belonging in pupils'. School life revolves around pupils' houses, the day starts and ends there, their tutor is to be found there, studying and socialising takes place there. The culture of each house differs depending on the master, but they are not quirky.

The look of the place reflects its character. It comprises a splendid Victorian building with cloisters running around a central quad and an imposing panelled dining room used by everyone for all meals (and once rumoured to be a potential set for Hogwarts). Just beyond the quad are other newer buildings including the terrific classroom, art and DT block and a very attractive modern new boys' house plus a new boarding house for girls.

On one side of the quad is the modern chapel which is a crucially important part of the school. St John's has a Christian foundation which forms the basis of daily life. Pupils are required to attend daily chapel as well as Sunday evening services with their house around once a month. Parents also attend these house services and go on to drinks in the houses.

Pastoral care, well-being and discipline: Pastoral care is yet another aspect undergoing a revamp at St John's. The tutor system has been reorganised so that every staff member is a tutor to a small group of pupils and every pupil has their own tutor for support and monitoring. Mr Collier describes the tutor as 'the pupil's champion and mentor'; tutor's role is as the point of reference for those pupils under their care and the individual who oversees all aspects of a pupil's school life.

Discipline is much in evidence; bad behaviour in class is not tolerated with detentions for minor infringements. There are clear punishments for drinking and smoking, fines and detentions – it does happen; the housemistress pointed out that pupils are easy to spot around town and do get pulled up. Mr Collier expressed his zero tolerance policy towards drugs – any offence and a pupil would be 'straight out'; he feels education of pupils and parents is the key and more is on the cards.

Pupils and parents: Currently the gender mix is around two-thirds boys to one third girls, but the school is aiming for a 50:50 mix. School says the differing styles of boys and girls are beginning to rub off on each other; most girls here are 'outgoing and get stuck in,' and it's all about 'a values-based education, for privileged children who learn the responsibility of service'. Families here are well-heeled, middle class professionals but less flashy and more down to earth than many other parents at Surrey boarding schools.

Pupils who enjoy St John's are those who can cope with the pace – academic plus everything else, who want to get involved in school life and enjoy the long day. This all-encompassing style of full-on days, Saturday sport and Sunday chapel would be a godsend for families with two working parents who need their children to be kept busy. However, pupils wanting to run a social or sporting life outside school may find the time commitments of school demanding.

We found the pupils to be sparky, friendly, chatty and well-mannered. On the sports field boys are competitive but very decent; rugby is their number one sport and many display its characteristic discipline alongside fun laddishness. Girls are mostly boisterous, sporty, outgoing and comfortable with the boys' banter. On our visit a group of girls were snuggled up chatting on the sofas in their house, while another group in a different house were catching up on work together. Much time is spent in pupils' single sex houses, whether day or boarding, and pupils mainly socialise with others in their own house, so boys and girls tend to socialise separately; a recently opened mixed common room may help them all normalise a bit more in each other's company.

Notable OJs include the architect Lord Richard Rogers and the senior BBC broadcaster Gavin Hewitt.

Entrance: St John's is a popular local option and has around three applicants for each place. Opened a lower school (year 7 and 8) in 2016: entry to year 7 by maths, English and abilities assessment plus informal interview. Selection at 13+ is on the basis of pupil's current head's recommendation and a pre-assessment taken in the January of year 6; parents report that lately some applicants are being turned away at this stage. The common entrance entry standard is now 55 per cent across the board and Mr Collier feels 'maths is the key to selection'. St John's has its own entrance assessment in maths and English for any applicants who are not taking CE. Consideration of the pupil's strengths in sport, music or drama is also important. At 13 most pupils come from a range of local preps, particularly Danes Hill and Downsend.

For entry to the sixth form, applicants sit an assessment and interview in November of year 11, plus report from current school; places are confirmed by GCSE results. 'Co-curricular strengths are taken into account.' At 16, lots of girls come from nearby Manor House, and a few boys wanting a change from local state schools or other independents.

Exit: Pupils exit to a huge range of universities, no clear favourites due to the broad academic range here. One to Oxbridge in 2016; others to eg Birmingham, Nottingham, Loughborough and Exeter. Parental and pupil expectation is certainly for university and hopes are pinned on Russell Group places.

Careers and university guidance is built into the curriculum from the lower fifth (year 10) onwards and there is regular contact with army, navy and RAF careers officers.

Money matters: Scholarships available in music, drama, art, design and technology, sport, academic and all-rounder, at 11+, 13+ and sixth form entry, worth 5-10 per cent. Means-tested bursaries and grants available, including up to 100 per cent of fees for children of Anglican clergy – Foundationers, reflecting the school's foundation. Also two free places available per year – Albany Awards for children from disadvantaged backgrounds. Discounts for siblings are 10 per cent and for children of Old Johnians are five per cent.

Remarks: A local, newly fully co-ed school currently undergoing quite a lot of change and expansion. Excellent facilities and a well-deserved reputation for an all-round education. Straightforward middle class pupils and parents enjoying a busy school with days full of activity.

St Lawrence College

College Road, Ramsgate, Kent CT11 7AE

Pupils: 614; 180 boarders • Ages: 3–18 (boarding from 7) • Sixth form: 108

Fees: Day £7,800 – £17,995; Boarding £23,640 – £32,985 pa

Tel: 01843 572931
Email: admissions@slcuk.com
Website: www.slcuk.com

Principal: Since 2013 Mr Antony Spencer MA (Oxon) ACA (early 40s). Educated at Chesterfield Boys' School and Oxford, where he read PPE. Previously spent five years as academic deputy head at Clifton College and before that director of studies at Denstone College in Staffordshire. Offered numerous jobs when he left Oxford, including a place on the police graduate scheme, a place at Sandhurst and the civil service fast stream but chose to train as an accountant at Ernst and Young. The draw of teaching was always there, and after seven years in the City he answered an ad for a job at Eastbourne and has never looked back.

Enthusiastic, energetic and very chatty and easy to talk to, he 'lives and breathes the education system'. He has 'added a bit of contemporary oomph and is just what the school needed,' according to one parent, and is looking at new ways of doing things. He says he has arrived at an exciting time when the school is poised for growth, and it has grown by 10 per cent in his first year and is now nearing capacity. He is raising the profile of the school, has upped the marketing locally and internationally and redesigned the website. He feels the 'great strength of the school is its size – the optimum size for a close community', small enough to have strong links between year groups but large enough to be able to afford good facilities.

A number of recent retirements – something he knew about before he took the job – has meant that he has been able to appoint his own team, including two deputy heads and various heads of department. Well-liked by the children, who say 'he is friendly and makes us feel comfortable, and understands what we are talking about and listens to what we say'. They are particularly pleased that he has moved boarders' Sunday chapel to the evening, which means they can have brunch and a lie-in on Sunday mornings. Married to Suzanne, who he met at Oxford, they have four children who have all settled happily into the school. She previously taught history but is now training to be an EAL teacher. They live in a house in the grounds and spend much of the holidays at their house in France.

Head of junior school: Since September 2016, Ellen Rowe BA PGCE, previously head of Haddon Dene Prep in Broadstairs. Geography degree from Sheffield; worked for her local authority then for Shelter before turning to teaching. Has taught at state secondary and independent prep schools, including as director of sport at Spring Grove Prep in Wye. Married to Adam; they have twins who are both at St Lawrence.

Academic matters: In 2016, 17 per cent A*/A and 44 per cent A*-B grades at A level. At GCSE 91 per cent achieved 5+ A*-C grades including English and maths (33 per cent A*/A) – not bad for a non-selective school with quite a few EAL pupils, and good value added. As well as the usual subjects, psychology, music and music technology, PE, ICT and theatre studies offered at A level – 24 subjects in all. AS photography proving very popular. German A level available for native speakers. Pupils do particularly well in history, maths, economics and psychology. No plans to introduce the IB. Science offered as dual or triple award at GCSE and taught by young and enthusiastic team in old-fashioned but redecorated science labs across the road, complete with small science lecture theatre. Popular science and engineering week and science lecture in conjunction with the Royal Society of Chemistry. Maths and science clinics for anyone who is struggling. Non examined RS course for all. A number of foreign trips including geographers to Iceland and physicists to CERN.

About 10 per cent need some SEN help, one-to-one coaching as well as support alongside lessons and some small group teaching with focus on inclusion to make sure pupils do not feel pigeonholed. Head of department a mainstream teacher who has specialised in SEN plus two part-timers. School has CReSTeD status. About 60 pupils receive some EAL support with a determined focus upon integration; now offers intensive EAL course for lower sixth entry. Lots of support tailored to individual needs, most take English GCSE and a few do ESOL. IELTS offered for university entrance.

Careers centre open every afternoon; careers programmes for years 9 and 11 and sixth form – seminars, lectures and group sessions and one-to-one advice about higher education.

Saturday lessons and afternoon sport from year 9 upwards, with years 7 and 8 doing activities on Saturday mornings. Years 7 and 8 taught separately in Kirby House but by senior school teachers, and can use the other specialist facilities. One lesson a week of thinking and study skills and ICT incorporated into core lessons.

Games, options, the arts: Wide range of sports offered and both boys' and girls' hockey particularly strong. Cliftonville hockey club has its home at St Lawrence and a number of old Lawrentians are in the team. The principal is a keen player and trains with the local side when possible. School brings in additional outside coaches and runs a cricket and netball academy during the winter, and several pupils train with the Kent squad – 'sports coaching is exceptional,' said a parent. The school is now the shirt sponsor for the local rugby club and the main sponsor for Kent girls' cricket. Growing sporting reputation is attracting more local families. No-one made to take part in team sports, but everyone has to do some sort of exercise – the mirrored dance studio is popular with the less sportily inclined. Keen to encourage an ethos of sporting achievement and a healthy lifestyle beyond school. 'They like to keep you fit and active,' says one boy, and many day children stay on to exercise in the evenings. Duke of Edinburgh popular and several gain gold each year. CCF compulsory for boys and girls in year 9 and many carry on. Juniors can use the sports centre and theatre, indoor heated pool, Astroturf and games pitches and have plenty of sport and fixtures against other local schools.

Music part of the curriculum for years 7 and 8 and also offered at GCSE and A level. A number of bands and ensembles including rock, jazz, samba and concert band as well as various sixth form bands outside school, and school has its own recording studio. Regular music trips at home and abroad and school has invested in instruments for children to borrow.

Has a 500 seat multi-purpose theatre with specialist lighting and sound equipment, with seats that can be covered so it doubles as the examination hall; everyone has a chance to take part in major productions, either on stage or behind the scenes. Drama part of curriculum until year 9 and also offered at GCSE and at A level. Enthusiastic head of drama gets everyone involved.

DT taught by inspired teacher and pupils undertake projects for real clients – we saw a fine chair which had been designed and made for the local council. A number go on to study product design at university. The school has recently bought a 3D printer.

Good range of activities including maths and science club, chess, musical theatre, various minor sports and debating society. Extended school day available for juniors, from 8am to 5pm, at extra charge. After-school activities for reception to year 2, whilst years 3-6 can take part in optional Saturday morning activities – these are popular with the children and can range from scuba diving to computing to play rehearsals.

Boarding: Two boys' and one girls' boarding house all with common room, kitchen and tuck shop. House kitchens closed at lunchtimes to make sure pupils eat a proper meal. Year 7 and 8 boarders and day children live and learn in Kirby House, a light, modernist building with a glass atrium and a library which is housed in what looks like a large blue pottery chimney – inspired. All junior school boarders sleep here too. Large bright common room area with sofas, table tennis, a piano and a large television and 10 five-bed dorms with en-suite bathrooms and two flats for resident staff. Pupils allowed into Ramsgate at the weekends and some activities organised.

Background and atmosphere: Founded in 1879 as a boys' boarding school with the purpose of combining 'careful religious training with a sound, liberal education'. The college was incorporated as a public school in 1892 and went fully co-ed in 1983. It is set in 45 acres of walled grounds in the middle of Ramsgate and within walking distance of the sea. The Virginia creeper clad main building, complete with towers and turrets, is a monument to muscular Christianity. Inside it is all panelled corridors and sweeping staircases. The chapel, with its beautiful stained glass windows and fine organ, was built to commemorate the lives of over 130 Old Lawrentians who died in the First World War. Impressive 19th century dining hall decorated with portraits, shields and silverware. Major investment in building projects in recent years including the theatre and a new girls' house, Bellerby, which is light and bright with comfy sitting area, galleried atrium and en-suite bathrooms. Sports hall with fitness centre and dance studio, squash courts and climbing wall and a floodlit Astroturf.

Pastoral care, well-being and discipline: The strong Christian ethos of the school underpins its religious and spiritual life. Chapel services three or four times a week and on Sundays for boarders help maintain an ethos of consideration for others and moral values – one of the stated aims of the school is to encourage 'a sense of serving others as a source of personal satisfaction'. The popular chaplain, often with iPad in hand, 'makes the services interesting', according to the children. All major world faiths are represented within the school; Jewish pupils can attend the synagogue in Ramsgate and Muslims can observe Ramadan.

Strong house loyalty and plenty of friendly inter-house rivalry – plays, matches and singing competitions. All houses have live-in house parents and a resident tutor. School takes firm line on bullying – principal believes in restorative justice and likes to get to the root of the problem. Instant expulsion for the supply of drugs – children know where they stand.

Good food with plenty of choice including a salad bar and can cater for special diets and allergies. Food committee made up of pupils and staff and meets regularly to make recommendations. Coffee shop open at break time, evenings and weekends – also popular with parents at drop-off time. Lots of interaction with the local community – children from nearby schools invited to watch plays and the Chemical Magic show and take part in the annual science and engineering challenge.

Pupils and parents: A big range: traditional families from local prep and primary schools, a number of first time buyers and first generation immigrants who are aspirational and ambitious for their children. Popular with the arty crowd moving down from London – new high speed railway means it is just over an hour to St Pancras. School prides itself on its internationalism and 30 per cent of pupils are foreign nationals from 27 countries including a sizeable contingent of Nepalis from the Gurkha barracks in Folkestone. Strong Nigerian connection and particularly popular with the Germans in sixth form. Children generally integrate well, although some say there could be more interaction between boarders and day pupils.

'Relaxed yet respectful' relationships between pupils and teachers. 'I love the way the children are treated like young adults,' says one parent. 'Everyone is respectful of everyone else, it is a very caring and supportive school.' 'My son joined for the sixth form and felt welcome from the start – sending him there was the best thing we ever did'. A very loyal team of former pupils – successful businesspeople and entrepreneurs who help with work experience. Pupils are 'natural and friendly and unpretentious' and very supportive of each other. Lots of mixing between year groups, helped by the house system. Parents encouraged to get involved, and are pleased with principal's improvements in communication, particularly the parent portal where they can view their children's marks, teachers' notes and homework.

Entrance: Just about non-selective but need to ascertain that a child would be able to cope with the curriculum, and international students tested in English and maths. Entry to junior school via meeting with head for parents and child plus taster day and report from child's current school, and sometimes an assessment if there is concern a child might not be able to cope. Very few take common entrance – usually just reports from a child's current school and an interview. Will take children at any stage including occasionally into year 11. About 50 per cent of senior school entrants come up from the junior school, others from a range of state and independent schools – they have a big primary school engagement programme. Some transfers from local grammars. Around 15-20 join in sixth form – assessed on GCSE performance (normally five passes) and must have adequate English.

Exit: Automatic transition from junior to senior school and some three-quarters stay on – the rest mainly to grammars and non-selective state schools. Preparation for the Kent Test is part of school life, but some parents still get outside coaching. Scholarship and a discount in fees for those who pass Kent Test but choose to stay on at St Lawrence. Around a quarter leave after GCSEs, either for financial reasons or to take vocational courses. Most go on to university, with Bristol, Warwick, York and London particularly popular. Others to a wide range of careers: one recently went on to train as a yachtmaster and another to join the band of the Royal Marines. One to Oxbridge in 2016.

School looking into ways of getting those not interested in university onto apprenticeships. Some parents say they would like a bit more information and be more involved in their children's university choices

Money matters: All rounder, academic, sporting and music scholarships offered at 11+ and 13+ – worth up to 50 per cent of fees. Sixth form scholarships for up to 50 per cent of fees for academic, arts, music and sport. Also means-tested bursaries, and special bursaries for Forces families who qualify for the Continuity of Education Allowance. Generous sibling discounts.

Remarks: A school on the up with a new energy and buzz since our last visit, all helped by the raising of standards in all areas, especially sport, and the influx of London commuters taking advantage of property bargains. 'The school has so much potential and is just beginning to realise this,' said one parent.

St Mary's Catholic School

233

Windhill, Bishop's Stortford, Hertfordshire CM23 2NQ

Pupils: 950 • Ages: 11–18 • Sixth form: 175 • RC

Tel: 01279 654901
Email: info@stmarys.net
Website: www.stmarys.net

Headteacher: Since 2015, Mr Andrew Celano BSc MEd, previously deputy head at Sir John Lawes School in Harpenden and a past pupil at St Mary's. He has also been assistant head at St Edmund's School.

Academic matters: Pupils are taught in mixed ability groups in year 7, with setting only for maths, additional setting later. GCSE results are good with year on year improvements; 73 per cent gained five A*-C including maths and English in 2016. At A level, 50 per cent A*-B grades in 2016; sociology, film studies and English literature popular options. Alternatives to traditional A levels include applied courses, BTec performing arts and NVQ business.

SEN well looked after with successes celebrated via a 'caring to achieve' board. Nine children have statements, plus others on SEN register. Range of SENs catered for including children with ASD, SpLD, medical needs, MLD and VI; have technicians and support staff to help as required. Work on self-esteem through circle of support programme etc. Some grumbles from pupils that they don't always get individual attention, particularly in larger classes. School says, 'In part, our drive to increase standards has raised the demands and aspirations of our pupils, but as 90 per cent gain five good GCSEs and all pupils leave with at least five qualifications we feel we meet all needs'. In addition, the school has identified differentiation within classrooms as a key priority. Sixth formers happy – 'we have small teaching groups, it makes a real difference, you get to know the staff really well and they, you.'

Games, options, the arts: Plenty of trips to theatres, exhibitions and places of interest and opportunities for travel abroad including Space Camp to USA, football to Holland, history to Berlin and separately to Flanders, rugby to Italy and netball to Jersey and skiing to Spain. Wide-ranging extracurricular activities include D of E and plenty of sport including Gaelic Football and girls' rugby and football teams. Regular music and drama performances in a dedicated theatre involving large numbers of pupils in everything from Cabaret to Coldplay liturgies. Have choirs, orchestra, recorder group etc. First class newish sports centre complete with under-floor heating, cricket nets, new kit etc. Pupils are encouraged to help in the community through various activities, from free heart screening with the CRY charity to volunteering at the St Mary's Motor Show. Head stresses importance of interacting with the community, including non-faith and multi-faith.

Background and atmosphere: Established by an order of nuns in 1896 as a girls' convent but co-ed since 1976. Situated near the centre of Bishop's Stortford on a large and pleasant site. Ofsted said 'The School's motto "achieving excellence for all" has become a reality at this outstanding school'. Near to bus routes but about a 15-minute walk from the rail station. A mixture of traditional and new. The new includes a modern library, theatre, and sports hall plus recently built sixth form centre offering plenty of space for both study and relaxation. The old is being refurbished, for example four new toilet blocks; there is a big current building/refurb programme, aiming for first class facilities, and although new buildings are coming on stream all the time, eg new six classroom block, there is still more to do.

Pastoral care, well-being and discipline: Praise from all quarters. Pupils say school is incredibly caring and any problems are swiftly and effectively dealt with. Discipline straightforward, firm. Staff have high expectations; recognise they have a duty to educate pupils to be the citizens of tomorrow. Work hard to keep and support students but not afraid to exclude temporarily or permanently when needs must. Recent innovations include peer mentors trained by Childline and an inclusion unit to prevent exclusion. Prospective sixth-formers have a team building/induction week with taster lessons at end of year 11. Very strong Catholic ethos. There are regular lunch-time masses and residential retreats; chapel always open.

Pupils and parents: Predominantly white Catholic families. St Mary's serves the Lea Valley Deanery, which stretches from Bishop's Stortford to Hoddesdon, Cheshunt and Waltham Cross and many pupils travel significant distances across Hertfordshire and Essex. Unlike some local schools, St Mary's does not practise backdoor selection so has, the head stresses, a truly comprehensive intake. Serves a fairly affluent area so pupils tend to have relatively few social problems. Very enthusiastic support and fundraising from parents through the PTA especially through its innovative St Mary's Motor Show each year, bringing together car dealerships and classic cars all on its site.

Entrance: Has expanded to five form entry. Heavily oversubscribed – even practising Catholics may miss out on a place. First priority goes to Catholic children with a brother or sister in the school. Next in line are Catholic applicants with no sibling connection. Places are awarded according to where applicants live, with 40 per cent going to children in Bishop's Stortford and Sawbridgeworth, 40 per cent going to children in other parts of the Lea Valley Deanery and 20 per cent to those living in another five surrounding Essex parishes. Next come any other Catholic applicants who don't fit the above criteria. Criterion four offers places to those with a non-Catholic sibling in the school. Contact the school for full admissions information.

Entrance to sixth form is dependent on GCSE grades. 'If students are not able to sustain the level, we ensure that they leave that course and take up alternative provision.'

Exit: A few pupils leave after GCSEs to move to other sixth forms in the area, a few go straight to work. The majority of those leaving the sixth form go on to further education, with a quarter going directly to employment. Regular places at top universities including one or two most years to Oxbridge, but the head hopes to see this figure increase with the introduction of a new year 12 extension studies programme and a dedicated Oxbridge programme.

Remarks: Aims to produce well-rounded youngsters with values they can defend. Ideal for Catholic parents who are keen to have their children educated in their faith, in a happy, pleasant and academically successful environment.

St Mary's School (Gerrards Cross)

Packhorse Road, Gerrards Cross, Buckinghamshire SL9 8JQ

Pupils: 302 • Ages: 4–18 • Sixth form: 44

Fees: £7,476 – £15,696 pa

S

Tel: 01753 883370
Email: registrar@st-marys.bucks.sch.uk
Website: www.stmarysschool.co.uk

Head: Since 2010, Mrs Jean Ross BA NPQH (50s). Educated at Manchester University (French) followed by an interpreting course. Took an unusual route to headship: founded business with husband manufacturing Swarovski crystal animals which they grew to 150 people. Maintained a burning desire to teach, however, which finally got the better of her once eldest daughter entered sixth form, when she started her PGCE. Taught French at large comprehensive in Dunstable for five years before joining St Albans High School, where she spent nine years and was head of modern languages and ultimately deputy head. Says it was love at first sight with St Mary's ('I knew instantly this was my school') and the love affair continues: 'I can't believe I get paid to be here,' she says.

Parents say 'she has a plan – and it's working.' Formerly sniffy locals certainly starting to sit up and take notice and school tripled its applications for entry into year 7 in 2013. Educational philosophy focuses on 'children being happy' and believes that '...to improve the education of the girls' should be the suffix to every statement of intent. A business-like figure with no sign of ego or ambitious career plan, she appears focused on academic robustness and roundedness, although insists 'the caring ethos will never change.'

Head of Prep: Since 2013, Mairead Carney BA DipHE (late 40s). Educated at University College Galway where she read English and French, followed by a higher diploma in education. Afterwards worked with disadvantaged local children before moving to London to pursue a career in investment banking. Had calling to teach after 11 years in business, so volunteered at Manor House School in Ealing, where she spent six years as a year 2 teacher, followed by another six at St Helen's Hillingdon. Joined St Mary's (as did her daughter, now in the senior school) as a form teacher in 2009 before becoming head of prep department following her predecessor's retirement.

Warm, direct and ambitious for her charges. Keen to raise expectations of parents and 'give girls tools to cope in a fast changing world.' Focused on raising levels of independent thinking and feels fortunate that school is sufficiently small to be able to appreciate and cater for all different learning styles. Like head teacher Mrs Ross, fell in love with St Mary's at first sight.

Academic matters: 'Good teaching across the board,' according to prep school parents. French from year 1 and Mandarin club on offer at lunchtimes for all year groups. Maths department 'vibrant' and 'becoming more challenging' according to head, with a weekly 'I can do maths' initiative in place which sees pupils split by ability rather than year group. No setting, but innovative approaches – such as stacking 'traffic light' cups on pupils' desks to let the teacher know how they are feeling about the work – means everyone can go at their own pace.

Results solid and mostly improving. In 2016, 67 per cent of GCSE entries graded A*-B with 38 per cent A*/A grades. At A level, 63 per cent A*-B, 26 per cent A*/A, and while this falls short of starry stats from other (albeit highly selective) schools in the area, it's commendable given the gentle selection criteria and proportion of girls gaining automatic entry from the preparatory department. Worth noting that with increased demand for places, results bound to continue on an upward trajectory as these girls work their way through the school. Also, unlike most other schools, St Mary's bijoux stature (30 to 40 girls per year group) enables it to cater for the broadest of academic spectrums, from Oxbridge types all the way down. Some take Bucks 11+, although even those who pass tend to stay put in the main.

All the usual subjects offered at A level, as well as theatre studies, PE, media studies, health and social care and most recently government and politics. French from year 7, with German or Spanish as options in year 8 and free choice of language at GCSE. Latin recently discontinued on curriculum (although available as a club) and replaced with thinking skills to help girls move away from rote and towards independent learning – study skills also offered in year 7. Setting in maths from mid year 7, for French from year 8 and science from year 9, when girls make an early start on their GCSE course. Science department 'amazing', according to head, with 'really exceptional' teaching. Girls report great teaching all round.

Excellent SEN, holistically incorporated into curriculum by head of learning support appointed. Girls speak openly about their (usually mild) dyslexia or dyscalculia, thanks to an overwhelmingly friendly and supportive school ethos – and possibly the clever 'cake club' where extra help is administered over home baked patisseries.

Games, options, the arts: Prep school seems more artsy than sporty in general with ballet on curriculum from nursery and LAMDA a popular option from year 1. Each key stage performs an annual drama production and there's a strong take-up of music, with around 50 per cent of the cohort taking advantage of peripatetic lessons. Art classes take place in a dedicated room and DT – covering everything from sewing to mechanics – follows the design process used in industry, according to a parent who designs aircraft. Wonderful works of girls' art festoon the corridors and shown in art exhibition.

'Amazing' head of senior creative arts faculty appointed 2011 'transformed art department,' according to parents, getting to the nitty gritty of what kind of work inspires girls. Superb fashion drawings recently led to a show with girls modelling recycled or upcycled garments made with their own fair hands. Wonderful works of all genres are displayed on every spare inch of wall around the school, and the overall feeling is of a culture that truly values creativity and artistic endeavour. Head admits that music and drama 'needed a boost' when she joined, and to this end 2013 saw school's first ever Christmas Extravaganza, with girls singing, acting and dancing their way through a packed programme. Other recent performances have included Mary Poppins and Romeo and Juliet, and head reports that 'legions' of peripatetic music lessons take place each week as well as 'good quality' efforts from the choir, chamber choir and orchestra.

Plenty of sport going on, although it's definitely not school's raison d'être. Occasional competitive fixtures come into play in years 5 and 6 with prep school turning out A and B teams for netball matches, but sometimes it's 'a bit of a challenge to get a team together as the school's so small,' according to parents. PE taught four times weekly, though, so girls are no couch potatoes, with swimming at the local sports centre for one term each year. Sport lovers craving more can sign up for dance, gymnastics or various sports clubs at lunchtimes or after school, many of which are covered by fees.

Senior school fixtures for netball, rounders and tennis, and head says 'every child competes if they want to,' although it's a struggle to get enough girls together for a hockey team. Numerous individual sports on offer from fencing to badminton, with dance a very popular option now, thanks to new state of the art sports hall, leading to a biennial gym and dance show in which the whole school participates. Flexibility and support offered for those with talents which require time out of school.

Senior head launched 'mission to take girls out of themselves' on arrival, introducing the 'St Mary's Challenge,' requiring compulsory participation in at least one extracurricular activity. Now happily reports that formerly quiet girls have discovered debating, others football or rugby, and girls agree that the new approach is paying off as they enthusiastically reel off lists of clubs to which they now belong.

Background and atmosphere: Founded in Paddington in 1872 as a school for girls, run by Anglican nuns; moved to current premises in 1938. Senior school housed in an Elizabethan manor house, feels more like a cosy prep than a senior school – until you spot the purposeful teenagers moving between classes. Closure of nursery has given more space to reception and a new library; pre-prep now has its own centre, Paddington House. Small numbers of keen learners able to flourish in classes the girls uniformly describe as 'fun.' No whistles and bells when it comes to facilities, and the fabric of the school is all rather higgledy piggledy, but somehow it all just works and even little ones talk about the school community as being 'like a family.' Very much a school where staff and girls are known to each other (most know every other girl in school by name) and girls of all ages describe the cohort as 'like a family.' Newcomers say they are made to feel one of the gang within days and that there are absolutely 'no cliques.' School uniformly described by pupils as 'unique', and girls quick to dismiss questions from friends at other schools about how it feels to go to such a small school. Facilities nothing to write home about, but somehow it all pulls together nicely – sixth formers proud of their new centre complete with common room.

Pastoral care, well-being and discipline: Refreshingly un-pushy compared with many in the area. Nurturing not pressurised, focused on gentle encouragement towards the best outcomes for individuals rather than mass league table glory. That's not to say school doesn't give girls a bit of oomph when it's needed though, with ambitious targets set across the board for all. Very little goes unnoticed ('the joy of a small school,' says head) and reputation for caring well-earned in the locality and responsible for luring many a parent through its doors. Worry box present but rarely used, and each class has a sixth form prefect, trained to advise in the event of minor difficulties. School council, made up of two girls per form and chaired by head girl, has drawn up charter against bullying.

Astoundingly happy prep pupils skip (literally) around the school, with some saying they never want to go home and many resisting parents' suggestions of taking the 11+ as they 'never want to leave St Mary's.' Size of prep school means that very little passes by unnoticed, and although there are initiatives such as buddy systems to help keep harmony in the playground, the compact critical mass makes being friendly easy, and girls say they know the name of every other pupil in the school. Bijoux size also enables sharing facilities (the science teacher cited the school skeleton as an example) with the senior school a straightforward process.

Senior head praised by parents for zero tolerance approach to negative aspects of social media, with active monitoring of Facebook, Twitter et al and parents and girls educated to give it a wide berth for as long as possible. School's size makes it easy for such messages to hit home, and although electronic devices are sometimes allowed for correct usage, they're not compulsory – 'we're not ready to go there yet,' says head.

Strong 'mysteriously named' house system rewards girls for everything from academic excellence to kindness, ensuring all feel valued, and frequent competitions from the swimming gala to the house quiz, where the pupils 'raise the roof', offer an element of non-threatening competition.

Pupils and parents: A diverse social mix, given affluent environs, with most very local – often within walking distance – but a smattering from surrounding areas including Bourne End, Farnham Common and Denham. Ethnic mix reflective of local area with around 25 per cent non-Caucasion, mostly Indian. Parents want 'challenge but not pressure' for their daughters, says head. Many girls a bit unpolished in their appearance with lots of un-brushed heads of hair and the odd pair of ripped tights in evidence – very different to some of their pristine local competitors – but somehow this all adds to the unpretentious charm of the place. Very active parents' association welcomes all-comers and head describes active social scene as 'a real community.'

Entrance: Entry into reception at 4+ by visit to class to 'assess their suitability'. Class sizes remain very small in the lower years (some as low as nine), growing as girls move up, where by years 5 and 6 they generally reach – or are close to – capacity. Girls joining post reception, typically either new to the area or refugees from either the state system or other pushier preps, are gently assessed in English, maths and – from 7+ – non-verbal reasoning.

Senior school entry by assessment and interview. Vast majority join year 7 from prep department, with head commenting that the fact that there's 'no cut off point at the end of year 6' is key benefit to the school – girls sail seamlessly into senior school with no hiatus. New joiners at 11 are gently selected and come from a range of local state and independent schools into one of two classes of no more than 16. Form groups capped at 20 in sixth form, with maximum class sizes fixed at 12.

Exit: Around 70 per cent of prep pupils move up to the senior school, with a few off to local grammar schools. Around a fifth head to new pastures post-GCSE (mainly grammar or co-ed boarding schools) but most into year 12 to benefit from small class sizes and individual attention (some A level classes are as small as five or six). All to higher education to read a variety of subjects, around half to Russell Group universities and the occasional one to Oxbridge. Wide range in 2016 took in Sussex, Bournemouth, Loughborough, Liverpool, Royal Holloway, Bristol, Coventry and Exeter.

Money matters: No bursaries in prep department, with scholarships of up to 30 per cent of fees up to year 6 available for up to three girls entering year 3 demonstrating all round academic excellence. This is available either to existing or new pupils and may be split if more than three prove their mettle. Not a rich school but academic scholarships available at 11 and 16 to existing and new pupils, plus a music scholarship at 11. Small number of means-tested bursaries available in senior school.

Remarks: A safe bet for parents who don't believe that bigger is necessarily better and are keen to avoid the trials and tribulations of the year 6 examination frenzy. Not the natural choice for alpha females or those who thrive on competitive sport, and doesn't offer the bewildering breadth of extracurricular or gleaming facilities of larger schools, but a happier school you couldn't hope to find, and academics are robust given the broad church intake.

St Mary's School Ascot

St Mary's Road, Ascot, Berkshire SL5 9JF

Pupils: 393; 375 boarders • Ages: 11–18 • Sixth form: 124 • RC

Fees: Day £25,170; Boarding £35,370 pa

Tel: 01344 296600
Email: admissions@st-marys-ascot.co.uk
Website: www.st-marys-ascot.co.uk

Headmistress: Since 1999, Mrs Mary Breen BSc MSc (40s). Married, no children. Previously spent seven-year stint at Eton, where she ended up as head of physics. Before that, taught science at The Abbey School Reading.

Her career was kick-started by head at Wellington who, having appointed her husband to a teaching post, saw Mrs Breen's useful physics degree lying fallow and suggested putting it to practical use. 'A few months later, my first class was 22 Wellingtonians. I discovered I could do it and loved it,' she says. The rest, as they say, is history or, in her case, science.

The school's first lay head, she has commendably piloted St Mary's through the choppy waters of changing educational fashions without once changing course. The result is a school that has remained totally true to itself – and unapologetically so. 'We're not trying to be all things to all people', she says, 'but we've got a coherence that works'.

Smart, with a hint of va va voom (and no doubt requiring every ounce of it at times), she relishes the job and is reassuringly in control without anything of the martinet about her. Her genuine and purposeful charm is particularly effective when directed at parents. 'I say "we're Catholic. We're all girls. We're full boarding. We're a good medium size, with just under 400 and no plans to get any bigger or smaller. And we're very proud of our academic reputation. If that's a match for your daughters, let's take it further".' Most do.

Head is no slouch when it comes to heading off potential defection higher up the school. 'Having seen them grow up as teenagers, you want them as your gorgeous sixth form', she says. Plenty of official endorsement too. School recently breezed through visits from Ofsted and ISI (who decided to pop in at the same time) and scored glowing reviews from both.

Parents are universally full of praise, highlighting head's professionalism and nous. One father told us she should have a 'sainthood'. 'All you could ask for in a head', said another parent. 'She's the right person at the top to build the right team round her'. Admiration extends to 'excellent' communication following a one-off resignation of a member of staff found with inappropriate images on computer in an incident which was, the head is at pains to point out, 'unrelated to school'. Equal enthusiasm from pupils. 'She knows everyone's name and is personable, efficient and approachable', said one. Felt to be particularly good with family-related issues requiring delicate handling.

Wears regular questions about whether she's thinking of moving on with slight (and understandable) weariness. Her answer? Until she wakes up thinking she doesn't want to do this job, she has no intention of moving on, though she wouldn't be averse to a bit of industry-spokesperson duties on the side were the opportunities to come her way. Our advice to suitable bodies? Snap her up while stocks last. A natural in front of a crowd, she'd be jolly good at it too.

Academic matters: All round excellence, helped by well-stocked staff room (overall pupil-teacher ratio of six to one). Class sizes average 16 up to year 9, 15 for GCSE years and seven at A level. Three in a class not uncommon for more rarefied subjects such as further maths.

At A level, 71 per cent A*/A grades and 89 per cent A*/B in 2016. GCSE results similarly classy – 87 per cent A*/A grades in 2016. Head is keen to dispel the suggestion that results are easily come by or a foregone conclusion. While they may suggest highly academic intake at 11+, with the vast majority at the top end of spectrum, behind the scenes number crunching (school uses MIDYIS) tells a very different story. Pupils span just about everything from the mid-range and below to the giddy super-bright heights.

A well-managed process steers a careful line between encouragement and pressure. The universally cheerful and confident demeanour of sixth formers about to enter final preparation for A2 exams indicated that it was working. Pupils rated supportive ethos – 'It's cool to work', said one – and extensive out of hours access to staff. 'So many of the teachers stay late that it's easy to meet up with them', confirmed another. Well-structured lessons where peers, as well as staff, assist with problem areas are a boon, too, say pupils.

Transformation of geese to high-flying swans isn't lost on parents, who talk of being 'staggered' by strings of GCSE top grades achieved. It's something that the head, to her credit, doesn't care to over-stress, given that it's unlikely to do much in the way of improving pupil confidence.

Subject range, though not vast, is well chosen and augmented only after considerable deliberation. Religious studies a non-negotiable core subject at GCSE. Latin (taught like French from year 7) taken by around half the year group at GCSE, well ahead of Spanish, German, Italian (added year 8) and Greek (year 9).

Three cheers for science, a particular strength, with five well-equipped labs and surging physics numbers post-16 (head takes some classes) on a par with biology and chemistry. Around 10 (not far short of 20 per cent) take it to A level and the numbers are about to double as a particularly science-oriented group works its way through the school.

Maths also has consistent numbers of fans, though broad sweep of subject popularity (English literature, politics and French all make an appearance in the top five most years) means most tastes are well catered for. 'There's no subject that's a no-go area. When people ask me, I'm really proud to say what I'm doing,' said a further maths and science star.

Games, options, the arts: 'We're academic but with lots of extracurricular activities', a pupil told us. 'The school encourages you to thrive'. And how. Being not just good but 'brilliant' at everything, including sport, drama and music, is the goal, though not easy in such a small school stresses the head. If anything holds them back, it won't be resources, with sports facilities positively glistening with new honed and toned additions. In addition to swimming pool, the Orchard Centre has a big sports hall, two squash courts and a dance studio. One of few girls' schools to have own 400-metre running track, green instead of customary red. Polo available, courtesy of local stables.

While there's a steady crop of outstanding individuals and teams at county level and above (tennis a particular strength), any lingering perception that the keen but hopeless are left to languish is out of date, says the head. All shall have matches (if not prizes). Team sport ceases to be compulsory post 16 but there's enough to inspire even the most sedentary-minded to stay happily active. Body conditioning, universally (though to official disapproval) known by girls as LBT (legs, bums and tums) particularly popular.

As with sport, the arts boast range of spaces that would be outstanding in a school with double the numbers. With its studio, full-size theatre, enormous green room (partitioned for girl/boy casts), bar and extensive costume room, the Rose Theatre is a budding thespian's dream. Many work towards LAMDA exams, gaining the full set by the time they leave. Productions every term, some girls-only, others involving other schools. Production of The History Boys featured an all-girl cast, apart from the French mistress, who was played by an Etonian. A sixth form group took its own play to Edinburgh Festival, gaining good reviews into the bargain.

Art, housed with textiles (DT, though not a GCSE option, is taught as a carousel subject in years 8 and 9) is terrific. In some schools, head of department's hand often all too visible in strikingly similar interpretations of GCSE/A level coursework theme: here, variety (including burqa-clad, slogan adorned figures in entrance) suggests pupils really do think for themselves. Quality is so impressive that you almost forget where you are and start peering for red spots. Portraiture wonderful – not surprising as school, in one of many go-ahead moments, offers life drawing. Here as elsewhere, school's decision to go its own way has left it ahead of the game. 'We stick to traditions worth sticking to', a senior teacher told us.

Music is a high-profile affair. Well-equipped recital room, numerous practice rooms (including one, doubly soundproofed, for drums), concerts also in the chapel to capitalise on 'wonderful' acoustics. Head of music who grows her own compositions is now inundated with requests for new works following première of spine-tingling Easter Story and also plans to up numbers taking subject at GCSE and A level (scant handful currently).

Activities provide outlet for girl power in every form. For younger pupils, few delights trump pet club housed in mish-mash of cages and runs. Hamsters and rabbits dominate. with talent shows featuring animals in natty little homemade outfits. Animal friendliness is a big thing generally and mercy dashes aren't unknown. 'Only this school would put a damaged pigeon in a taxi and send it to the only vet open on a Sunday,' said a member of staff.

Wide range of clubs and societies, from the mind-expanding (human rights, music appreciation, current affairs) to D of E, London theatre trips and upscale wine-tasting (upper sixth only). Born movers and shakers (and there are many) can hone their organising skills in assorted forums, from influential school council ('what we recommend gets done', say girls) to range of committees. Old girls regularly pop up to widen careers horizons as part of a programme that kicks in from year 9.

Boarding: Modernising elsewhere in the school has seen large-scale abolition of big dorms (mostly no more than five to a room). Top favourite, however, was blast from the past curtain-partitioned 'cubies' in year 8 dorm, voted the best fun, with last night of term midnight feasts.

Sixth form privileges include no uniform (pupils were delighted by this, some parents less so), permission to queue-barge at meal times and annual ball. Biggest perk is separate living quarters, away from main school hurly burly, circle of little homes corralled around own courtyard. Decent kitchens are well used (fruit and veg high on request list, adding to menu staples of toast, pasta – and chocolate crispie cakes). Entertaining is encouraged, with guests treated to more elaborate fare (visiting Etonians haven't thus far reciprocated in kind. 'They don't have the same facilities,' say the girls).

Multitude of house-organised weekend activities helps to dispel any boarding blues. Staples include mass pizza ordering as well as rare forays into deepest girly territory (nail decoration a favourite) and specials like St Patrick's Day marked with cookery (Irish potato scones) and crafts (shamrock felt jewellery).

Background and atmosphere: School was founded in 1885 by the Institute of the Blessed Virgin Mary (IBVM), a religious order begun by Mary Ward (1585-1645). Her dreams of founding a Jesuit-inspired apostolic women's order (she even crossed the Alps on foot to put her case to the Pope) came to nothing in her lifetime. Undaunted, followers continued to plead her cause, though it was 2009 before her 'heroic virtue' was recognised by Rome.

Catholicism defines the school, sweeping in the committed and the less so. Morning chapel compulsory for all while regular weekday masses are optional, attracting anything from a dozen to 60 just before exams. Houses take it in turns to organise mass and pick the hymns, the more rousing the better. Recent election of Pontiff greeted with huge excitement. 'Someone started screaming "white smoke!" – I had coursework to do but the Pope comes first', a sixth former told us.

School makes the most of its 55-acre site. Main buildings, some on gothic revival lines, go up rather than out, with long but not unfriendly corridors, helped by warm terracotta and mosaic tiles and a riot of gleaming staircases (some now adorned with essential if unattractive anti-slip edging).

We were the first outsiders to experience the gorgeousness of school's former concert hall, now transformed into a terrific new senior library (juniors separately and snazzily catered for). Nicer than many universities, say pupils. No wonder, with its curvy window seats, acres of bookcases and wonderful first floor curved ceiling. Café, complete with morning papers, coming soon. No learning resource centre faffage here. Pupils can take in iPads and laptops but the printed word is definitely the star of the show. 'Books betoken silence', says head firmly.

Pastoral care, well-being and discipline: A little light rule-bending aside, few serious offences on this head's watch. Sanctions, when they do occur, are now consistent from house to house (just about the only minor imperfection found after recent inspections). Internet misuse would lead to merit-cancelling red ticket. Drink and smoking, almost unheard of, would result in suspension and 'you'd be out' for drugs.

Day to day, six heads of house have the biggest pastoral responsibility. They're considered mainly excellent. Praise too, for boarding. Inevitable beginner homesickness well handled with the help of older buddies and kindly boarding staff, vast majority of whom don't teach. 'They're lovely and very sympathetic if you say you have too much work,' said sixth former. Residential chaplain is mentioned by almost everyone as inspirational force for good and a multi-tasker to boot.

There's a fair bit of moving around which stems from a sensible desire to head off anything that could lead to cliques forming. Sleeping arrangements changed at least once a term and occasionally twice to mix and match the personalities. As a result, happiness tends to rule, and on the rare occasions it doesn't, there's a swift resolution of problems. Sixth form exceptionally strong, with friendships that often endure for life.

Pupils and parents: Around a third from London, a third within an hour's travel, a fifth from overseas (half non British) and the remainder from elsewhere in the UK.

Before head's arrival, vibe was a bit 'Frost in May', with slight sense that the very grandest of old Catholic families had a more exalted cachet than others. Now, though they're still represented, and anyone paying full fees needs to be 'mega rich' to afford them, there's a more egalitarian spirit abroad.

Increasing numbers are funded by bursaries, and though there's lots of emphasis on socialising with other top notch schools (Eton the top favourite) there's careful control of the trappings of excess. Nickames, amongst them Biggles, Squeaky and Booey, are plentiful and once bestowed are generally there for life.

Parents are a happy bunch. Not hard to see why, given the St Mary's effect, resulting in girls who emerge ready to subdue the world with charm, intelligence, confidence and poise. 'I think anyone in my year could stand up quite happily in front of 500 people and speak,' one former pupil told us.

Entrance: Selective but not awesomely so. Siblings, while favourably viewed, need good dose of what it takes to secure a place. School gives preference to girls who are Roman Catholic (nearly all pupils are). Many from bilingual backgrounds, though no formal support offered. Learning support geared towards those with 'generally mild' dyslexia and dyspraxia, with weekly, external support from Dyslexia Action.

Main entrance points are 11 (English, maths and general knowledge/intelligence tests) and 13 (English, maths, science, religious studies, history or geography, MFL, Latin). Feeder schools many and various (300 preps and maintained primaries); so oversubscribed that process can be 'an exercise in disappointment' says head.

For the unsuccessful, there's another chance in the sixth form (test in proposed A level subjects plus general paper). Chances of success are diminutive though. The maximum new intake is just five, though in reality often fewer.

Exit: Virtually no fall-out after GCSEs. Seven to Oxbridge in 2016, plus five off to the US/Canada and two medics. Bristol, Edinburgh and Exeter also popular. Subjects range from sciences to languages, law to art. Numbers going into performing arts are increasing – one old girl is currently working with Steven Spielberg.

Money matters: Standard range of scholarships at 11, 13 and 16 on offer (five per cent reduction on the fees). Music scholarships include free tuition on up to two instruments.

Remarks: Catholic education at its best. So popular that when it comes to getting a place, faith may not be enough.

S

St Michael's Preparatory School

Otford Court, Otford, Sevenoaks, Kent TN14 5SA

Pupils: 451 • Ages: 2–13

Fees: £11,169 – £13,587 pa

Tel: 01959 522137
Email: jthornton@stmichaels.kent.sch.uk
Website: www.stmichaels.kent.sch.uk

Headteacher: Since 2013, Jill Aisher BA PGCE MCIL (50s). Read modern languages at Oxford. With 25 years of teaching experience, her career falls into two parts – working in a selective state grammar as a teacher of Latin, French, Spanish and English, followed by senior leadership in the independent sector. Deputy head at Newton Prep for six years, then three years as head at St Nicholas Prep, Hyde Park, prior to taking up a Kent headship (fulfilling a long-held plan to return to where her husband grew up and her children went to school).

Says she was drawn to the 'strong sense of emotional well-being' at St Michael's, as well as its stable population, where she can prove herself. Pupils tend to stay from 2+ to year 8. Now installed in her palatial office, with splendid views and a Hogwarts-type turret for her desk, she couldn't be more delighted.

Warm and friendly, a fast-thinker and talker, highly articulate in her vision for the school. Priorities will be a more outward-looking view – both injecting a global perspective into the curriculum, often via ICT and connecting locally, and enabling children to master learning by understanding their own learning style and giving children more of a voice, as equals. Myriad ways for children to do just that – take part in the newly energised school council, put a note for head in her red postbox, put themselves forwards to be head boy or girl, librarian, or prefect, or most radically, helping the head interview new staff.

Parents say that head is 'very efficient and pro-active.' 'My children say she is strict, but also sometimes very funny,' one told us, while another said: 'She's made a strong, convincing start.'

Married for 30 years to Johnny, a senior employee of our nation's favourite department store, with three children. One son is studying for a second masters at the RCM, another a music producer and her youngest daughter is at King's Canterbury.

Entrance: The majority (intake of 40) enter the pre-prep at 2+, with 14 additional places at transition to the prep at year 3. Prospective parents need to get on the waiting list as early as possible. Some sibling priority and an informal assessment day, but entry is not selective and places are offered to those heading the list in the June, 15 months prior to entry. The majority of pupils come from within a seven-mile radius.

Entry at 7+ is via a standard maths test, together with a school reading and English test. Entry into year 7 is via maths and English test and being observed participating in a normal school day. Bursaries from year 3 and scholarships and bursaries for year 7 entry.

Exit: Head stresses that school prepares children for either the 11+ or CE. Parents agree. 'I have total confidence in preparation for their next school,' one told us. Of those who exit at 11+, almost all will be successful in achieving their first (guided) choice of school. It's a strong list of destinations, headed by

Tonbridge Grammar, then The Judd, Skinners' and Sevenoaks, with others dispersed across the long list of local grammars and independents. 'We have all abilities,' says the head. 'We set out to prepare for a broad range of schools that will encourage and affirm. For some a slower pace is appropriate.' Between 40 and 60 per cent continue into years 7 and 8. Popular destinations at 13+ include Sevenoaks, Tonbridge, Caterham, King's Rochester, and Sutton Valence. A handful or so of scholarships each year – often sporting, some academic.

Remarks: St Michael's was founded in 1872 as a school and home for orphaned boys. In the 1980s the pre-prep was added and girls welcomed, and in the 1990s it became a day rather than boarding school. Prep is housed in a large red-brick Victorian gothic mansion, with an adjoining sports building. Inside, modern, bright spaces, smart purpose-built science labs and dining hall mix in a homely jumble with the chipped paint, gothic panelling and stained glass of the old building.

This isn't the prettiest part of Kent, cheek by jowl with the M25, but the gain is swift commuting to central London. Less than four miles to Sevenoaks and once you have arrived at the school, the 90 acres of grounds, which swoop up and down before the main house are stunning. Wooded hills for bushcraft, camping and fitness runs, plus games fields and pitches.

The curriculum does not surprise, but ticks every box. The head singles out science and English, sport and art as particularly strong – and parents agree. In the modern science labs we watched white-coated children experiment with the boiling point of water and our enthusiastic guides ('science is really fun here') were keen to tell us all about explosions, trips and their participation in the national CREST competition (they designed a games console).

Despite the head's modern languages background, nothing too 'bold' on the horizon for languages. Focus is on consolidating current provision, with a Mandarin club set up in response to parental requests. A wonderful moment as the French teacher invited one of the boys to share his work with this editor – they were discussing which school subjects they preferred. 'Je déteste le Français,' he had written in immaculate French.

Nearly a third of staff have been at the school for more than 10 years. Parents say they are 'very caring and accommodating' and that there are 'some outstanding teachers,' though a couple would like more of an open door policy. Maximum class size is 20 in pre-prep and 18 in prep and setting is gradually introduced – for English, maths, science and French by year 7. One pupil we met told us the 'teachers are really supportive,' describing how they always have time to sit down with pupils if they don't understand something. Another parent said of her child: 'She's gone from feeling unnoticed and swimming in knowledge gaps from her last school experience to feeling totally included and valued in class.'

School says there are plenty of opportunities for gifted children to excel. Full-time SENCo, known as head of learning development here, who provides in-class and one-to-one support. Thirteen per cent with SEN and 13 pupils with EAL needs. Laptops can be used in classrooms. 'My son is still struggling with literacy, reading and spelling but he feels supported and not alone in his battles,' a parent told us.

Head is keen on the power of technology to 'transform and personalise learning,' so tablets and mobile devices are on their way. As always, the debate on homework rages but there is a feeling that it is quite intense in the upper years, with up to two hours a night by year 6. But a parent told us: 'When I feel that they are overloaded and not managing, the school immediately reviewed and reduced their homework.'

School has a strong reputation for its sporting talent and success. On the day we visited the school gates were being painted gold in honour of the school's golden girl, former head girl Lizzy Yarnold, team GB skeleton Olympic gold medallist. Swimmers compete in IAPS national finals, rugby teams punch above their weight against bigger preps, netball teams compete well and a year 8 pupil recently represented the UK at wakeboarding. Two games afternoons a week – all of the usual things on offer. One parent praised the excellent standard of coaching, another pointed out that if children are interested in something more unusual they will still need to find it elsewhere.

All pupils are given the opportunity to represent the school in major games every term. This seems transformative, at least to the children who had recently joined the school and described themselves as not particularly sporty. One said: 'I feel I can try my best, and I don't get shouted at.' Sports day is enjoyed as much for sitting around on blankets with friends between races as the competition itself. 'The school has a happy atmosphere, not too laid back but certainly not fiercely competitive,' said a parent.

Every pupil has a class music lesson every week. Around half receive individual instrument tuition, with pupils currently studying 11 different instruments. If a child has a musical whim ('anything other than the bagpipes') the school will strive to find a good teacher. Four choirs, two concerts per term, instrumental groups. Children also take part in the Sevenoaks and Royal Tunbridge Wells International Music Festival. New head of music taking things up another notch.

Much high quality art and design work on show – children had just completed their own take on Keith Haring canvases and were keen to show us their post-it note animation to rap music. Parents agree that drama is a relatively weak spot. No dedicated theatre, but new head of drama has big plans.

A wealth of arty, sporty, and musical pre- and post-school clubs including extreme collage, golf, Lego, dance and scratch programming. Currently consulting parents about their thoughts on extending the school day to support working parents.

Pre-prep is housed in a spacious, light, purpose-built building, entered via a suspended walkway. Parents with a love of Grand Designs will adore it. Every class has outdoor access, wellies hang in little wooden houses ready for muddy play, Astroturf for wet weather and bulb-planting just getting under way. Maximum class size is 20, with two staff. Far higher ratios in the nursery and kindergarten years.

Whilst the children are meticulously prepared for every new experience, parents may need a little hand-holding in their transition to the (as yet) less swankily designed prep. As, one satisfied parent put it: 'The pre-prep is second to none.'

Parents speak very highly of pastoral care. Bullying not unheard of, but staff very quick to take action and empower children to handle it themselves. The children we met said they found the school 'cosy' and that they knew everyone because it wasn't too large. Many schools talk of 'the individual child' but St Michael's truly delivers on this. At every turn parents and pupils fell over themselves to paint a picture of inclusivity. One said: 'We've had four children at the school at various times over the past four years – all very different in abilities and personalities. The school has suited them all.' Parents said the school suits 'self-starters, those with special needs, the academic and less academic.' 'It is quite a big, bouncy school,' one added, 'but the staff take care of the less confident ones and help them come out of their shell.'

A huge mix of families. Parents with children higher up the school likely to be Kent families, but new families coming up the school comprise working parents, relocators (from London and internationally). Car of choice in the car park very definitely a shiny black Range Rover. Particularly glowing reviews from those arriving from or returning from abroad who remark on the warm welcome from other parents. Such are their numbers that they've recently set up their own international club (sounds a bit 'gin-slings and elephant polo' but is more about helping each other to settle into Kent life).

St Paul's Catholic Primary School, Thames Ditton

Hampton Court Way, Thames Ditton, Surrey KT7 0LP

Pupils: 389 • Ages: 4–11 • RC

Tel: 020 8398 6791
Email: info@stpauls-thamesditton.surrey.sch.uk
Website: www.stpauls-thamesditton.surrey.sch.uk

Head Teacher: Since 1990, Mrs Fionnuala Johnson, BEd (late 40s), married with two children. Garners huge respect from parents, who regard her as the architect of the school's (and their children's) success. Descriptions of her vary along the spectrum from 'strong, impressive leader', through 'powerful personality' to 'formidable' (we'll vouch for that) – but most also mention her caring side. 'The children adore her – tempered by due reverence,' said one mother. 'I've seen children run across the playground to hug her,' said another.

Has plenty to say about the school – of which she is fiercely proud – and is full of plans and ideas for the future. She knows all the children by name – and promises to keep this up even when the school has doubled in size. As it is, parents wonder at her grasp of all the smallest details of their lives, and the praise continues – 'she's fantastic – the school is as good as it is because of her. She talks to the children quietly and they all listen – she never needs to raise her voice. They want to please her, and if ever they are in trouble and sent to see her they are not frightened but sorry they have incurred her disapproval'.

Entrance: Heavy over-subscription has allowed funding for expansion from single to two-form entry. School accepts 60 children per year and the pressure has eased up a little – but Catholic families whose children have been baptised (and you need the certificates to prove it) still take 99 per cent of the places. The school serves the parishes of Cobham, Esher and Thames Ditton, a mostly white, middle-class lot. It is non-selective academically – regular church attendance will get you a long way.

Exit: Where to go next is the most vexing question for parents. 'I just wish this school had a secondary equivalent,' sighed one mother, echoing the view of many. St Paul's pupils are guaranteed entry to the RC Salesian School in Chertsey, and vast majority go there. Some to eg Holy Cross, Royal Grammar, Claremont.

Remarks: An academically strong school with a solid Catholic ethos. Set back from a busy dual carriageway, in functional rather than beautiful accommodation, purpose-built in the mid-1960s. There is plenty of space, including a large playground and a grass playing field. The smart new block built to provide the necessary seven extra classrooms does make the older classrooms look a little tired, but good art displays line the walls and lift the spirits. A well-resourced school, with a shiny IT suite and three well-stocked libraries. All classrooms are spacious and light; and each is named after a saint – reflecting the importance of Catholic teaching at the school.

The Catholic Church schools' 'Search for Excellence' theme is seen as key here – both in the spiritual and academic development of the children. Academic standards are high. At key stage 2, there are more level 5s than 4s in all three subject areas. Many parents tell us that this is a school for academic girls rather than non-academic boys. Even parents who are not quite so dogmatic believe the environment is more suited to the academically inclined. 'It is not a hothouse, but there is just a general expectation of achievement,' said one mother. Mrs Johnson disagrees strongly – so does Ofsted, which also singles out the SEN teaching for praise. The number with SEN is below the national average but those with SEN do as well as their peers. There is an SEN teacher with teaching assistants on hand and the school also brings in outside specialists.

High praise from parents for an able and effective teaching staff. 'Every time we change classes we say we wish we could have that teacher again – and then the next one is just another delight,' said a mother who has had children at the school for many years. 'Discipline is strong, the children know their boundaries and understand them,' said another. There is plenty of praise and reward, with a system of highly-prized stickers and certificates, not just for academic work but also for helpfulness, cheerfulness and so on. Prayers are said at the end of each day, and children attend mass regularly. The religious teaching really kicks in at year 3 as the children are preparing for holy communion.

All the parents we spoke to agree their children are happy at the school, which they describe time and time again as 'very caring'. Pupils are respectful and polite – and also extremely smart – with even the reception children wearing neat ties. 'The fact they can get a 4-year-old to tie a tie says a lot about this school,' enthused one mother. Mixed feelings abound over sports provision, with some parents feeling it is not a particular strength, especially among the boys – though the school does well in the borough in netball and cross-country and the girls recently won the local football league.

A real sense of community, which staff and parents are keen to maintain as the school expands. Some parents have expressed concerns that the strong sense of community they have enjoyed may be eroded as the school grows. However, the niggles are few and far between, and overall the positive comments far outweigh the negatives. It is still a first choice for parents seeking a good education for their child in a distinctively Catholic environment.

Saint Ronan's School

Water Lane, Hawkhurst, Kent TN18 5DJ

Pupils: 432; 84 flexi boarders • Ages: 3–13 (boarders from year 4) • C of E

Fees: £9,876 – £16,923 pa; Boarding +£35 per night

Tel: 01580 752271
Email: info@saintronans.co.uk
Website: www.saintronans.co.uk

Headmaster: Since 2003, Mr William Trelawny-Vernon (40s). Very much a joint enterprise with wife Emma (she's the Trelawny, he's the Vernon) – who is both registrar and head of history. Known as Mr and Mrs TV to pupils and parents alike. The couple met at Exeter, where Mr TV read biology. Previously at Stowe School for 12 years, including posts as a biology teacher and seven years as housemaster of Chatham House. 'Universally loved', according to parents.

The business is in the blood – his father was head of Hordle House (now Walhampton) in Hampshire. Four children – the youngest at the prep, the other three have moved on to King's Canterbury. The family left the head's accommodation to move off site in 2005 and they eschew the parental dinner party circuit, believing it's important to maintain a distance. Parents think they get it right, as one commented: 'One of the areas in which the school excels is in managing very successfully the line between parental involvement and keeping parents distanced when necessary.'

Both grew up in a four-child family, and with their own gang of four have that deep respect for fairness and equality of treatment which comes from big families. 'Neither of us likes the concept of the alpha child,' says Mr TV.

School and family is everything to Mr TV – time off finds him socialising with the wider family, and stress relief comes by sitting on his tractor and mowing the grass, or researching the history of the two families. Both are content with home and hearth, or as Emma puts it, 'We're like labradors sitting in front of the fire'. Holidays take them to the West Country, home of Emma's ancestral seat (her brother John inherited the Salusbury-Trelawny Baronetcy).

Entrance: All children attend a taster day, and children seeking places in year 3 and above are assessed by the class teacher and take verbal and non-verbal reasoning tests. Intake covers wide-ranging abilities, but all are expected to pass common entrance or the Cranbrook grammar tests, so 'There will be a couple of children where we will have an honest dialogue with the parents and tell them that their child's needs are not going to be met here,' says Mr TV.

Scholarships are available for academic, music, art and sporting talents, and there are strictly monitored means-tested bursaries. Minibuses bring children in from Staplehurst, High Halden, Burwash, Wittersham, and the villages en route.

Exit: It's not the place to come if you have your sights on the West Kent grammars – despite these being within travelling distance, the school doesn't encourage exit at 11. Only one or two children per year sit the Kent 11+, so it'll be a lonely experience and you'll have to find a tutor.

The majority of parents are buying into private education for the duration, although around 30-40 per cent of pupils have previously gone to Cranbrook grammar at 13. Key destinations include Benenden, King's Canterbury, Battle Abbey and Sutton Valence. Others go further afield – recently to Stowe. 'Since I've been head we have fed into 52 different schools,' says Mr TV. Parents say they are very good at helping you choose the next school – the TVs visit a clutch of senior schools together each term so they are well informed, and were freshly back from visits to Sherborne, Bryanston and Milton Abbey when we visited.

Generally a good number of scholarships, and one or two parents admit to feeling some playground one-upmanship from other parents about places and scholarships secured. 'There is competition from some of the parents, which can make you feel uncomfortable if you let it, though not between the children,' said one.

Its quirkiness ensures there is no Saint Ronan's product – and the roll of past pupils is stuffed with the great and good. 'Just look at the alumni to see how successful it is in producing movers and shakers and Boy's Own heroes,' said one parent. Indeed the list reads like a fantasy dinner party guest list: BBC security correspondent Frank Gardner, spy Donald Maclean, MP Airey Neave, Olympic rower Matthew Parrish, and the late Mark Shand, travel writer (and brother of Camilla, Duchess of Cornwall) are just a few.

Remarks: It's a what's-not-to-love campus. Gorgeous grounds with ancient, spreading trees, inspiring views, a fishing lake, and its own 100 acre wood. And there's even a farm with pigs, alpacas, and chickens – newborn piglets greeted our visit. The emphasis is on old-fashioned, wholesome fun, making every use of this natural playground. 'It's idyllic, they get to dam streams and play with pigs and chickens,' said one parent. Everything is named for Boy's Own adventures – there's the Gulch, an area around a stream ideal for making mud pies, the Saltmines, an overgrown area with secret pathways, and even the pitches have names, such as Timbuktoo (because it's a long journey to reach it). A new classroom on the edge of the woods is the Hobbit House. As one parent put it, 'If Enid Blyton was still around, Saint Ronan's would be exactly the sort of school she would be writing about. We are buying a truly magical childhood experience, not just a superb all-round education.'

All this romping is made easier by probably the most relaxed and colourful uniform we've seen – corduroy trousers, skirts or pinafores in sensible colours, topped with school sweatshirts in a choice of colours – pink, green, red, purple, light blue and navy. There's a formal uniform which is worn on Fridays, key days and for trips out.

The pre-prep is in a separate bright and modern building (where a corridor poster advises on 20 things to do before leaving pre-prep, such as dam a stream, make a mud pie, and hold an animal). There's also a cosy kindergarten in the former headmaster's house.

Moving up to prep brings the grandeur of Tongswood House, a Victorian mansion built by an Oxo magnate. The original features are well-maintained – including a sprung floor ballroom, now used for performances and gatherings, where frescoes of semi-naked nymphs on the ceiling liven up assembly for the older boys.

There's wood panelling and grand staircases aplenty, and classrooms are eccentrically named, such as Old Bailey, 10 Downing Street, Lombard Street (because that's where the safe was), and Windsor Castle (once a lavatory). Children scrape to their feet as you enter – standing up for grown-ups is something the teachers are strictest about, say the pupils, along with manners, being kind, and being honest.

Kindness is the rule for staff too. 'If we heard a teacher shouting at a child, they would have to come into the office and explain why,' says Mrs TV. 'We like to treat them in the same way as our own children. I don't want to be head monster,' says Mr TV. Prefects are elected by the children in a secret ballot 'which means they go for someone who is kind and gentle, not necessarily just one of the first XV,' says Mr TV.

In reception you're greeted by a wood fire burning in the hearth – where parents come to warm up for post-match teas – and a basket of free range eggs for sale. You can also pick up school produced pork and apple juice. The head's secretary is Mrs TV's sister, known as Aunty Amanda. Parents love the reportedly eccentric ways of school admin. They talk of things being done in a Saint Ronan's way, one of 'happy chaos', which 'wouldn't suit parents who want everything done in a completely perfect planned-out way'. It looks disorganised, but it works, they say. 'We do slightly chaotic and quirky with great aplomb,' said one mother proudly.

Whilst it delivers on results (100 per cent success rate in the Cranbrook Grammar and the common entrance exam many years) it does so in a thoroughly gentle way. Prizes are given for contribution as well as achievement, and one parent said, 'although they are encouraged to achieve, this is not done in an over-competitive manner'. And pupils say that the teachers discourage any jostling for position. 'When we get exam results the teachers encourage us not to ask each other what we got, but if you get a bad mark people still always say you've done really well, or tell you what to do to improve. I once got 27 per cent but the others just said I was unlucky,' said one boy.

Setting for subjects begins in year 4, with streaming in year 8. Latin is taught from year 6.

Parents praise the efforts made to find and develop talents, which may not be academic. There are 16 peripatetic music teachers, and a DT building which develops practical skills – it's equipped with laser cutters and scroll saws, and children take woodwork from year 3, making everything from working pens to cars for drag racing. 'We are so impressed that every child has something they will achieve in. For my kids it has been music for my daughter and sport for my boys,' said a mother.

Sport has developed as the school has doubled in size in the last 10 years, 'so we can now play decent schools,' says Mr TV. There's an impressive new sports hall, an Astroturf and an outdoor pool, and a great range of sports on offer – an extras programme one afternoon per week offers archery, fencing, golf, sailing and lacrosse. The school's sailing team has been prep school champions, and one girl has made the GB under-15 team for fencing. There's other options on extras afternoon for the non-sporty, such as farming, funky dance, fishing, beekeeping and touch typing.

Much is made by the head and parents about keeping the pupils children as long as possible, and they are clearly successful at cocooning them. The year 8s seem younger than their peers we meet in secondary schools – no less articulate, but definitely less worldly. Parents report no divide between age groups, saying: 'You constantly see older children encouraging and playing with the younger ones, and children in year 3 aren't scared of the year 8s.'

Parents predominantly work in the City of London; others are doctors at the nearby hospital, or farmers. 'It is very inclusive and friendly with no social divides, and parents are always ready to help one another out,' said a mother. There are fitness groups for parents to join including zumba, Nordic walking and joggy-doggy.

The only gripe you'll hear from parents – and that's a mild one – is that they find it a long day for the prep school children (8.30am to 5.15pm, with prep afterwards at home or at school from year 5 until 6.30pm). A lot of children take up the flexible boarding option – 'really fun,' the pupils agree; around one-third of children stay for up to four nights per week. Rooms are up in the eaves, and again you wouldn't be surprised to find the Famous Five up there having lashings of hot chocolate. Boarders do supervised prep for one hour, then after supper, the options include swimming, singing, and playing outside. Matron Julie is reportedly 'nice to cuddle with'.

St Swithun's School

S

Alresford Road, Winchester, Hampshire SO21 1HA

Pupils: 713 (4 boys); 109 full, 118 weekly boarders • Ages: 3-18 (boys 3-7); boarding from 11 • Sixth form: 128 • C of E

Fees: Day £9,930 – £19,575; Boarding £31,368 pa

Tel: 01962 835700
Email: admissions@stswithuns.com
Website: www.stswithuns.com

Headmistress: Since 2010, the contained and cogent Ms Jane Gandee MA (40s). Read French and Spanish at Girton College, Cambridge, then a local government accountant until she went into teaching (OU PGSE) at Lord Wandsworth College, Oakham, Queenswood and finally director of studies at City of London School for Girls. The stamina and thoughtful tactics that make her a successful athlete (represented Cambridge at athletics and cross-country, captained the women's football team) are combined with a rigorous passion in her stewardship of the girls here.

Her retired husband manages the logistics of shuttling their three kids to school (St Swithun's Junior and Kings' School Winchester) enabling her to teach Spanish in the lead up to GCSEs and speak at two out of the five assemblies each week, finding raw material in books ranging from Freakanomics to Daphne du Maurier novels.

Proud of the expanded co-curricular and sport options ('she's got the place buzzing'), determined to open the pupils' eyes to a real range of issues via external speakers (John Humphries, Germaine Greer, Polly Toynbee) so they can make their own decisions. Committed to developing girls' resilience and confidence – they once took the mickey out of her for her frequent championing of feminism, but now they join in.

Junior school head: Since April 2017, Rebecca Lyons, previously deputy head at Stroud, King Edward VI Preparatory School, since 2013. Degree from Northumbria University, a PGCE and an MBA from UCL. She was director of studies at West Hill Park School from 2011 to 2013, and head of English at Stroud from 2007 to 2011. Before that, she taught across the primary age range in both the state sector and internationally from 1997.

She lives with her partner Trevor, a consultant gastroenterologist, and her two stepsons.

Academic matters: ICT in junior school grows from bugs for simple coding in nursery to podcasts for a humanities project on natural disasters. Topic-based curriculum feels exciting (war artists' sketches, air raid shelters in DT and war poetry in English) with off curriculum science days, one offering an insight into the trades of electrician, architect, project manager, all linked to the new building which opened in 2015. Spanish and German for the youngest, a trip to a château in France on offer for older girls.

Brilliant exam results, up in the dizzying thin air at the top of the league tables. How a relatively unselective school like this one manages it is mysterious and must drive the London hothouses – with their exacting entry testing of pupils from the age of 4 – around the bend. Parents say 'they don't cream off the top of their applicants; they help girls reach their potential'. Famed for its hotshot sciences (three floors of dedicated labs) and maths; English is just as impressive, even if pursued by fewer girls – pupils say teachers are great, 'no duffs'.

Food tech, psychology and art history offered at A level (though take-up is low for food – cookery not seen as a golden ticket into Oxbridge). Compulsory GCSE subjects are English, maths, PE plus a foreign language and at least two sciences. Setting in maths and modern languages – with support (one full-time SENCo, part time assistants and outside support if necessary) an SEN child can still access the curriculum. French and German both studied to the end of year 9 when Spanish enters as an option. Most take (only) 10 GCSEs, and just French taken early – a strategy that produces few results below a B. In 2016, 85 per cent A*/A grades at GCSE. At A level, 66 per cent A*/A.

Parents report that teachers expect a lot and the girls push themselves, which means that confidence must be built elsewhere if not academically strong. The whole of the lower school enters the Maths Challenge, which encourages different ways of thinking. The Stretch programme helps put academia in perspective – a compulsory hour per week of a loosely cerebral activity for every pupil eg film clubs, music composition, chess, Amnesty international.

The timetable is in half hour units but most lessons are an hour; each A level choice has an hour of each subject per day for balance and to mitigate risk when missing a day. The light and warm library is used for study periods mostly by the sixth form, although whole classes can book out the IT area. In the upper sixth both day and boarding girls can return to their one dedicated house to study and hang out.

Careers fair annually in Harvey Hall with parents and old girls and speakers ranging from architects to philosophy teachers. Families report that careers advice strong on well-trodden paths such as medicine and Russell Group universities, yet quirky directions need more research initiative from home.

Games, options, the arts: Lacrosse is the strongest sport with a fixture every Saturday in both the two terms it is played, attendance at the nationals and amazing international tour (Niagara Falls is on one itinerary) a highlight. Conscious effort to broaden the range of sports – netball and tennis are on the up in terms of competition; also swimming, archery, golf, fencing, squash, scuba diving, badminton, cheerleading, football, polo, skiing, pilates. Some of these are only on offer as one of the 30 or so co-curricular choices, others have emerged into the fixture list. The pool is 25m with an Olympic standard diving board (Winchester residents use it too), stables are 10 minutes away and the sailing squad heads off most Sundays. Location in South Downs National Park means limited permanent floodlighting for sports pitches but play continues regardless through temporary arrangements. Gym cards track over- or under-zealous exercisers (early morning swimming popular until studying gets really serious in sixth form) and equipment has been recently updated so apparently girls watch The Big Bang Theory while running.

In the lower years there is an hour of art, drama and food tech each week, all housed in the same block. Very enthusiastic art team with a regular life model, Rosa Verloop inspired sculptures (stuffed tights), nominated desks and eventually cubby holes for A level students – DT floor just as sparky with electronics, laser cutter and Green Power car (has to be fast, green and involve good team) racing every year at Goodwood, but no A level take up at present. Amazing aromas sandwiched on the floor between the other choices, cooked up in the professional tech kitchen. Textiles popular too with A level newly on offer.

Performing arts centre provides a lively hub for music and drama in the school (and doubles as the venue for morning assembly). Drama studio backs on to the main stage and is used for lessons (no A level at present). Girls do plays on their own initiative too, inviting Winchester boys in for male parts (and vice versa) eg Alan Ayckbourn's Bedroom Farce. Parents would like more academic links to Winchester College, but it plays quite hard to get; lots of local girls' schools would like to be partnered with it more closely. Enormously popular fame academy just for junior school ends with a recording in a studio off site: the girls write a song together, perform it (eg dulcimer, drums, piano), entries whittled down by peer votes and creative teams grow as the field shrinks. Drama ranges from Shakespeare to the West Side Story with four performances a year, roles are auditioned for and Pilgrims' boys are asked in if needed.

Great range of orchestras, bands, ensembles and choirs – chamber, gospel and a capella – some open to all, others more selective. Music school houses practice rooms and an IT suite with Sibelius for composition, basic Cubase skills for recording performances. Around 55 per cent of pupils learn a musical instrument and some 145 candidates are entered for external music exams each year. Senior choir sings evensong each term in the cathedral and tours overseas every other year.

Boarding: Separate boarding and day houses until a single combined one for upper sixth; the latter are the only ones allowed to go back to their house to work during the day. The seniors do prep duty for the younger ones and there are clusters with a 'mother' in the sixth form and younger 'sisters' or 'cousins' in other years, a 'family' that looks out for each other. A race back to day houses for a hot chocolate made for the girls at break – and letter delivery for the boarding girls; day and boarding girls become less separate as they move up the school. Different nationalities are more likely to hang out with their own at the weekend – the balance is well set between cultural comfort and integration.

Initially Toblerone shaped dorms with equal sections under Velux windows, flexible boarding and school bed linen for the youngest, privacy growing through curtains to a single room at GCSE with a hand basin, useful essay quotes and posters on the wall. Each house has thoughtful inclusive touches that soften the necessary (safeguarding) communality – word of the week board for little ones, movie night, pool table, Wii, piano – as well as the vital drudge of learning to do laundry. Everyone sits around the breakfast bar at the weekend in their pyjamas and the houseparents make sure that full boarders keep busy with three activities during week nights and three at weekends eg a trip to the zoo, decorating your mobile phone cover, making gingerbread men, skating or music practice.

Background and atmosphere: Founded as Winchester High School in 1884 by Anna Bramston, daughter of the Dean of Winchester, who remained as school secretary for over 40 years – the dean, the headmaster of Winchester College and the mayor are still part of the governing body. Changed its name to St Swithun's in 1927 and moved to the present 45 acre site in 1931. Vast, intimidating, red-brick, Queen Anne style building with blonde parquet flooring, large windows and long corridors – girls learn to look up and smile as they pass each other rather than hold/avoid gaze as they approach from either end.

New junior school building (2015) is gorgeous, light and bright (huge argon-filled double glazing) with Ethernet, Wifi, Chromebooks, underfloor heating, 21 square-metres of photovoltaics on the roof, a lift (school council requested music and a mirror!) and a separate external entrance for the nursery. The building is designed to reflect the school's teaching rather than the other way around with the science room opening out into the shelter belt and nature trail, an open plan library at the entrance and all classrooms and staff training rooms with windows onto the internal corridors, transparency for all.

Daily assembly (separate for the nursery and the pre-prep), the nursery has outside free flow, the older ones help out at break. At lunch the littlest are served by the teachers and the older ones, while year 3 and above help themselves – cookery lessons and clubs enjoyed. New uniform takes its orange from the so successful senior school lacrosse team, shorts in the summer instead of dresses are great for climbing trees.

Senior school a tight community of supportive girls with a culture of 'go for it' rather than 'too cool' to join in eg minority of girls remain in normal clothes on dress up days. Flip side of this is the pressure for good results that they can exert on each other. Boarders and day pupils retreat to different houses for break but all eat together at lunch, and head girl team blogs, runs the school forum and instigates a school wide and term long game of tag. This has everyone searching for their targets, who in turn dye their hair, swap uniforms and even hide in cupboards – all for glory, chocolate and side effect of integration. Pupils give regular assemblies and topics range from Beyoncé to the Khmer Rouge, while the school forum has input to subjects as disparate as the air con in the gym and more tenor timbre in the hymns. Fundraising Friday is another equaliser, as money is raised for the voted annual charities, and some girls do EdClub, a worldwide initiative that uses Skype to encourage disadvantaged children (many in slums) to learn using broadband.

Winchester the town is important for the freedom it offers only 15 minutes' walk away – and usually a cab ride back up hill. Provides an opportunity to meet up with Winchester boys; the seniors can eat out or go to a play. The outgoing ones say it is very relaxed, no-one puts on make-up, they are all just a group of friends with about 20 per cent in relationships and many of the day girls knowing the boys from local life; the less confident ones mention a pressure to add the boys as friends on Facebook as soon as they return – yet all monitored (some girls reckon too closely) by the housemistresses and house assistants. The latter have a non-teaching role so that they can concentrate on the emotional temperature in each house – there is a health centre staffed 24 hours on site and a clinical psychologist offers discrete appointments in the old chapel; the whole school benefits from her years of experience of the lives and issues of teenage girls. The leavers' ball is usually just for the girls alone (their choice, no Winchester boys); that, and the singing of Jerusalem, is guaranteed to cause some tears to be shed.

Pastoral care, well-being and discipline: The ethos in the junior school is to have fun and make mistakes, no spoon feeding – it feels a very happy school, with the kids joking and teasing confidently with the adults and each other without overstepping the mark. Form teachers are on top of the ins and outs of friendships.

Houseparents are first point of contact in the senior school for issues from homesickness through bullying to A level choices – although a form tutor is vital for the latter too. Parents feel everything is dealt with swiftly and sensibly; avoiding a before bed phone call can give both parent and child a less weepy night. Phones are used for email nowadays, particularly useful for older girls looking at timetables and emailing essays, restricted for the younger ones.

An art project of smiles photographed around the school has found a permanent home on the wall of the modern (2013) chapel – all full boarders and staff attend every Sunday, optional for the upper sixth. Over-indulging in alcohol the most common serious disciplinary issue – and that not very, if girls' shock at relaxed attitude observed in their visits to boys' or co-ed schools is anything to go by.

New Thrive programme for all years 'aims to inculcate the habits of good mental and physical health, and to prepare students for the world outside the school gates'. Lessons designed around 'real world' experiences have included year 7s trying out setting up a new community after a plane crash on a desert island, year 10s practising empathetic listening through role-play and year 13s taking part in a student survival programme including cooking and cycling.

Pupils and parents: Down to earth parents who value education; armed forces, businesspeople, diplomats, lawyers, doctors and bright children with parents working in less lucrative professions; four wheel drives rather than Bentleys. Over half are day pupils – school bus services are getting better after unflattering comparison with King Edward. Twenty (and rising) per cent of boarders from London, often with more local weekend houses – weekly boarders make up 15 per cent of the school. Heathrow is less than an hour away and Southampton airport only 20 minutes, so 15 per cent of boarders from overseas, range of 20 countries. Occasional international guest pupils come for a term from France, Germany, Spain, Czechoslovakia – must be fluent in English. Alumni range from actor Emma Chambers (Alice in the Vicar of Dibley) to journalist and radio presenter Fi Glover.

Entrance: Junior school non-selective with a waiting list that should shrink now it has two form entry (since 2015). Mostly girls (fewer than 10 boys – though nursery numbers are rising) although officially co-ed until year 3. When The Pilgrims' School (choir school of Winchester Cathedral) opened a prep department in 2008 there was a natural single sex split between these two schools.

Main intake into senior school at 11 with pre-test, January 11+ and CE. Places offered on pre-test and reference from current head – no longer in order of registration. Everyone must pass CE, whether from state, private, or school's own junior school. The latter provides about a third of the intake, others from London day schools and local preps. About 20 more enter at age 13 with a pre-test 18 months before (can be taken overseas) and then a firm offer; if there is a crisis and they don't make the necessary 60 per cent at common entrance then there is leeway – occasional places further up the school. About 20 join the sixth form with own entry and test in November; a summer year 10 report is necessary before registration – very competitive.

Exit: Around 30 girls go from the junior to the senior school, although entrance not guaranteed – others to Downe House, Godolphin, or King Edward VI. The girls say that some try the other schools and then come back. Boys go on at 7 to local prep schools eg The Pilgrims' School, Twyford, Farleigh.

Around 20 per cent leave after GCSEs, bound for the local sixth form college or for other co-ed sixth forms. Almost all the others go on to university, mostly the old-established ones, with Oxbridge (five in 2016), London, Edinburgh, York and Durham being favourite destinations, sciences unsurprisingly popular (three medics in 2016, plus some biomedics and neuroscientists).

Money matters: One in six pupils have a means-tested bursary, an academic scholarship, sports scholarship or a music award (available at 11, 13 and 16). All scholarships are for up to 20 per cent of fees and based on the calibre of the applicant, rather than need. Bursaries are means-tested and available for 50 to 100 per cent of the fees. Music awards include free music lessons.

Remarks: Academic powerhouse with bluestocking reputation now widened into great co-curricular and sports options; pupil assemblies range from the Beyoncé to the Khmer Rouge. Girls egg each other on to great results and fun too.

St Teresa's Effingham School

Effingham, Surrey RH5 6ST

Pupils: 605; 80 boarders • Ages: 2–18 (boarding from year 6) • Sixth form: 65 • RC

Fees: Day £8,385 – £16,515; Boarding £22,500 – £28,410 pa

Tel: 01372 452037
Email: a.charles@st-teresas.com
Website: www.st-teresas.com

Headmaster: Since 2012, Mr Mike Farmer (50s). First teaching job was as a sailing instructor, spending three years post-graduation in Greece and Turkey. He met his future wife Mary-Ann in Greece and looming marriage and family took him to a job in the real world at Godolphin School, Salisbury, where he taught economics, business and ICT. The head there, Hilary Fender, took him with her to be assistant head at Headington, Oxford in 1997. First headship was at Kilgraston in Perthshire (2003), where he achieved the gong of UK Independent School of the Year in 2011 and turned around a school that had been dubbed 'the Marie Celeste' to achieve the highest growth rate in its sector.

He has a sound business head, the confidence of his governors and a clear sight of what he needs to do to ensure the school flourishes in a wealthy and highly competitive area for independent schools. Comes across as self-effacing and unassuming but what lies beneath is steel. Has taken bold risks to finance capital projects in order to boost the roll and scythed staff where necessary. Educated at a large comprehensive himself and not at all stuffy. 'He's a very humble man – he doesn't have that ego you see in some heads,' a parent told us.

Career paths of his children show that he pays more than lip service to developing individual talents – one is a theoretical physicist, one a theatrical agent.

Head of prep: Since September 2015, Mrs Sarah Conrad, previously head of New Hall Prep School in Chelmsford. Having graduated with a BA in English, German and theology from the University of Durham and completed her PGCE, began her career in primary education teaching in a variety of schools including a four-year post in the renowned British International School, Tanglin Trust School, in Singapore. Returning to the UK, worked as director of music at top preparatory St Cedd's School in Chelmsford before moving to New Hall. Married with two daughters.

Academic matters: Prep school parents are impressed with the care and the quality of teaching. 'Our daughters bounce into school every day,' one told us. Another said: 'Our daughter had struggled at her last school. We felt she had slipped through the net and not progressed at all in years 4 and 5. We were concerned about how far behind she was when she entered in year 6. The prep school teachers were amazing. She caught up without feeling stressed or pushed at any point in the year.' Setting for English, maths and science. Pupils taught by specialists in some subjects from year 3. Science lab for the younger children within the prep and from year 5 pupils are timetabled to use the science labs in the senior school. Computer science including coding and robotics taught from year 1.

School is non-selective – head's aim is to boost its academic reputation, but not make it a hothouse. 'We have got to make sure we can stretch the top end,' he says. To this end, he has brought in a new assistant head (academic) who runs the Oxbridge enrichment society and the gifted and talented programme. She is like a glamorous Miss Jean Brodie, brainy and geeky but with spiky heels and stylish clothes. Just the job to have teenage girls hanging on her every word and parents love her weekly 'All geek to me' emails, with their suggestions of enriching books, radio programmes, exhibitions etc. She also runs academic seminar evenings, where girls present findings in front of their peers, and brings in visiting speakers – recently a talk from the Nuffield Foundation on the ethics of treating dementia.

Most popular A level subjects are English, maths and science. Head has overseen the introduction of new A levels, including classics, classical civilisation, Latin, government and politics and music technology. In 2016, 75 per cent of entries achieved A*/B and 50 per cent A*/A at A level; at GCSE, 41 per cent A*/A.

Languages include French, German, Spanish and Latin, with Mandarin and Russian as after-school options. Double and triple award science on offer and there are visiting speakers of the calibre of Sir Robert Winston. The school is considered a specialist for art, especially in the overseas market, and each year pupils progress to fashion design and art foundation courses. We saw some fantastic textiles work and sixth formers deeply engrossed in their work in the art room.

Pupils talk of the individualism of teaching, so there is not one particular style. We saw a key stage 4 class dissecting a poem and noted the pupils' confidence in voicing their individual interpretation; nearly all had something to say and they were unabashed in front of visitor. Loads of praise for the English department from parents – indeed, for most of the teaching – although one told us: 'There are still a couple of old retainers who some of us feel should be sent down the hill, but generally Mr Farmer has got a grip on what he expects from his staff.'

Games, options, the arts: Lots to appeal to tennis players or riders. Newly formed St Teresa's Tennis Academy is headed by former Wimbledon player Lee Childs. Four hard courts and nine artificial grass courts. Recently opened equestrian centre stables around a dozen horses and riding is offered as an after-school option. Head says it's an unashamed way to draw in new pupils and differentiate the school from the competition.

Sports hall has been redeveloped and a coach brought in to run a swimming academy. Negotiations are under way to become the Surrey hub for Pentathlon GB, which will give the school access to Olympic coaches. 'We will become a very sporty school,' says the head. Meanwhile a parent told us: 'Negative comments have been made about sport (or lack of it) by many parents but this has been addressed by Mr Farmer and a much more efficient PE timetable is now in place.'

Director of music effused enthusiasm as he showed us round the music department. A professional French horn player, he has performed with the most prestigious orchestras but is just as keen on bringing in local rock bands for the girls to produce in their own sound recording studio, or using digital technology. We saw one class composing on computers using serialism, a method often used to produce discordant film music. His contacts enable him to bring in professionals as peripatetic music teachers – cello teacher works at the Royal Opera House, flute teacher is in the BBC orchestra. Notice-boards are crammed with flyers for music events and pictures from overseas choir tours (girls have had the opportunity to perform in venues like Notre Dame Cathedral). School also hosts the Surrey Hills Music Festival, as well as numerous recitals.

Thesps can take LAMDA courses in public speaking, musical theatre and acting. Three achieved gold medals last year and some have gained up to 200 UCAS points from these qualifications. New arts centre on the way – old art rooms will be converted into an new sixth form study facility.

Week night activities for boarders range from pudding club to ice skating to picnics, with Saturday afternoon outings to theme parks, theatre, paintballing, bowling. On site activities include falconry and circus skills. Plus tennis, riding and other sports.

Boarding: Some 60 per cent of boarders are international students though school has set maximum of 10 per cent in school as a whole. Boarding accommodation recently refurbished, decorated in light neutral colours and homely touches. Rooms range from singles for the sixth form to dorms for three to six girls for the younger pupils.

Background and atmosphere: St Teresa's was founded in 1928 by the Religious Order of Christian Instruction, and the main house now forms the centre of the senior school. Other buildings have been tacked on over the years, and the former nuns' accommodation has been converted to classrooms. The prep school was newly built in 2009 (it moved here from another site) – new prep classrooms being added. There's nothing to set an architecture fan's pulse racing, but the classrooms are bright and functional. The campus is a lovely 48-acre parkland with ancient trees, set in an area of outstanding natural beauty. Very secluded – it would be nigh on impossible for girls to sneak out for a night on the town.

When the head arrived he made wide-ranging changes straight away in order to turn around the school's fortunes. Rebranding meant changing the school's name, modernising the school's newsletter and bringing in a new uniform. It was out with the old and in with the new in key staff appointments – 'there was some staff movement,' he told us diplomatically. In 2013 he brought in a new head of prep, head of science, head of boarding and assistant head (academic).

It's been well received by parents. As one told us: 'I have yet to hear a negative comment about Mr Farmer. I think we are all astonished at how he has managed to turn the school around and increase the numbers in such a short time.' Another said: 'He has transformed it from a good to an amazing school. The children's view of the school and their pride in it has changed a lot.'

There's a buzz about the staff – they are clearly rejuvenated by the changes. And word is spreading. 'I was at a coffee morning for new parents and the vibe was amazing. People were saying it was their number one choice and were queuing up to get in – well, that's new,' said one mother. Year 7 intake doubled to four forms.

School's Catholicism comes in the gentlest form – as an ethos of kindness, supporting the weaker, and strong pastoral care. Around a quarter of the pupils are Catholic and there's no requirement for staff other than the head to be Catholic. Although certain feast days are celebrated, the school recently celebrated Diwali, led by an Indian member of staff. mass on Sundays is compulsory for Catholics and all boarders attend twice a term. The chapel is modern, with some stained glass and soothing music throughout the day – a place to wander into for peaceful repose. The priest is reportedly young and trendy. There's nothing to frighten off those not of the faith, said one parent. 'The school isn't overly Catholic but it has a Christian way about it, which is a good thing. I know people are put off by it, which is a shame because it makes the school a more nurturing place to be.'

Pastoral care, well-being and discipline: In school, younger girls' well-being is monitored through a buddy system – sixth formers meet their charges once a week. Girls feel able to raise issues and know they will be listened to. "We can make suggestions and we will be heard and acknowledged,' said one girl. 'We weren't happy with the school food so we surveyed pupils and presented the findings and it has improved a lot since.' Head plans to introduce Big Brother style video diaries (which he previously ran at Kilgraston), where girls can raise any concerns.

Pupils and parents: Girls are wholesome looking – all pony-tails and make up-free faces. Wide range of nationalities – 15 per cent of students are international boarders from countries like China, Hong Kong, Mexico, Spain, Russia and Nigeria. Locals bus in from a radius extending to Guildford, Reigate and south London.

S

Most parents who choose the school haven't put academic reputation as their top priority. This means there's a blessed lack of competitive parent syndrome, we're told. Some very wealthy parents, but a mix of economic backgrounds. 'Those with limited funds will certainly not feel intimidated, although the arrival of the tennis academy and equestrian centre could change this,' said one mother. 'One prospective parent did ask me if a horse was going to be an option on the kit list.'

Entrance: Entry into the co-ed nursery is from the age of 2. Entry into the prep is by report and informal assessment during a welcome day, as well as references from previous school. The main criterion is whether the child is likely to cope in the senior school. In practice this only rules out those receiving high levels of learning support.

Senior school currently has a waiting list for the first time in many years. More top end girls have been applying, which means the academic standard for entry at 11 is now similar to an 11+ pass or level 5 in national curriculum tests. Canny parents who think their child may miss this mark are putting girls in the prep in year 5 or 6 as this gives automatic entry. However other talents can tip it. 'A girl may be very good at sport, art or music – we won't go just on the exam,' says the head. There's a big influx at senior entry – year 7 currently has 25 pupils from the prep and 35 newcomers. Virtually all year 6s progress to the senior school, many with scholarships.

When it comes to the sixth form, all current pupils are accepted 'as long as we can offer them a programme,' while incomers need six Bs and an A at GCSE.

Although the school is Catholic, there is no requirement to be Catholic. Children raised in the faith do not get priority, although it may be a deciding factor.

Exit: Vast majority of prep school girls move on to the senior school, with automatic entry, and usually several with scholarships. Recent higher education destinations include medicine at Leeds, human sciences at Oxford, accounting at Durham and Manchester, art foundation at Central St Martin's and youth and community studies at Winchester. Two to Oxbridge and two medics in 2016, with nearly half going to Russell Group universities.

Money matters: Scholarships are awarded for academic excellence, art, drama, music and sport.

Remarks: Moves afoot to ramp up school's educational attainment by pushing the brightest, but not at the expense of the middling. We reckon that this is a school that truly can cater for wide ranging abilities. There's a lovely, gentle atmosphere – we saw no cliques of glossy haired alpha girls. A good fit for girls who want to take their time to grow up or those who need to know it's OK to be geeky.

The Schools at Somerhill

Somerhill, Tonbridge, Kent TN11 0NJ

Pupils: 592 • Ages: 3–13

Fees: £6,942 – £14,730 pa

Tel: 01732 352124
Email: Admissions@somerhill.org
Website: www.somerhill.org

Heads: Headmaster of Yardley Court and principal of The Schools at Somerhill since 1998, John Coakley BA MA PGCE (50s). Educated at Bishop Wordsworth's Grammar School in Salisbury, read English at York, followed by a PGCE at Oxford and an MA in English at New Brunswick University, Canada. Previously headmaster of Ryde School on the Isle of Wight and of Saltus Grammar School in Bermuda.

He is warm and welcoming, straight-talking and fizzing with enthusiasm. Known affectionately as Mr C by children and parents, his modest office in the eaves suggests a deliberate lack of grandeur. He lives in a house in the grounds, with his chocolate labrador, Stanley, and holidays in France.

A pupil describes him to us with genuine enthusiasm as 'fantastic, he's always there to help us' and a parent sums him up: 'First class – he knows the names and characters of every boy within Yardley Court. He is highly visible, attends (and coaches) sports matches, runs clubs and the boys hold him in extremely high regard'. His aim for the school begins with the happy child: 'If they are happy, everything else falls into place'.

He will retire as head of Yardley Court in July 2017, remaining as principal of The Schools at Somerhill until July 2018. His successor will be Duncan Sinclair MA HDE, currently head of Taunton Prep. Born in Zimbabwe, he moved to South Africa at the age of 7. Read English and environmental science at the University of Cape Town before completing a higher diploma in education. Began his teaching career in Cape Town, also coaching cricket, rugby and athletics. At the same time, he enjoyed a secondary career as a semi-professional rugby player representing Western Province as a second row forward. Moved to St Michael's Preparatory School, Kent, in 2002 where he was year 4 teacher, head of geography and PSHE and deputy head and completed his MA in educational leadership and management. In addition to taking part in competitive cricket and hockey, he plays the clarinet, trombone and tuba and is a keen chorister. Married to Georgina, a primary teacher with a PE specialisation; they have three young sons.

Headteacher of Derwent Lodge since September 2016, Helen Hoffman, BA MA Lit PGCE, previously director of studies at Vinehall. In her mid 40s, Helen has worked in independent education for over 15 years and in management roles for over nine. Creative and dynamic, she is a literacy specialist with a passion for developing a growth mindset in those she teaches.

Head of Somerhill Pre-Prep since September 2014, Miss Zoë Humm BA Ed from Goldsmith's; previously taught KS1 and KS2 in south east London state primary schools; was year 2 and ICT coordinator at JAPPS; deputy head at DUCKS.

Entrance: The schools describe themselves as mixed ability and the majority of children join Somerhill via the co-educational pre-prep (main entry points at pre-school and reception). Transfer to Yardley Court (boys) and Derwent Lodge (girls) is automatic at year 3. Those wishing to squeeze in at 7+ may sit a brief assessment. Prospective parents could get lucky with a place beyond year 3, but the numbers say if this is the school for you, you'd be wise to get in early. The principal pragmatically supports some applicants in the final pre-exam years, space permitting. Discounts for siblings: five per cent for a second child, 10 per cent for three or more.

Exit: Girls are prepared to leave at 11+ for Tonbridge Grammar, Tunbridge Wells Girls' Grammar, Walthamstow Hall and Kent College. High number of boys, around 40 per cent, also exit at this stage for the Kent grammars, principally The Judd and Skinners. Principal is clear that Somerhill is 'not an 11+ factory', neatly illustrated by the pupil we met who was unfazed by having sat the exam the previous day. Nonetheless, results are strong with a 90 per cent success rate. Tutoring does go on – a sore point – but both heads see it as unnecessary and generally to be discouraged. Of the rest who stay on for common entrance, most go to Tonbridge, Sutton Valence or Cranbrook, many with scholarships and exhibitions (22 in 2016).

Remarks: Traditional curriculum with plenty of active learning eg times table shoot-outs for the boys. At Yardley Court maths is particularly strong and the most successful subject at CE. English comes in for praise too: 'teaching has made the boys truly love this subject.' Latin from year 5.

For the girls in Derwent Lodge maths setting based on pace not ability starts in year 3 (it's from year 4 for the boys) and extends to English and sometimes science by year 5. Memorable highlights for the girls are cross-curricular theme days such as outdoor learning when every lesson takes place outside.

Plenty of long-serving staff and both heads have made new appointments, with young male teachers significantly visible at Yardley Court. The principal expects all to go the extra mile, such as those we saw on the day of our visit, cheerily preparing to take part in a school camp out. Parents describe the quality of teaching as excellent, with the inevitable few exceptions. Reports graded for effort as well as achievement, individual targets identified and timed so that parents have an opportunity to follow up quickly at consultations – not always a given.

Just over 10 per cent identified with special educational needs, mainly dyspraxia and dyslexia. Two full-time and three part-time staff across both preps, offering mostly in-class support. Dyslexic children using laptops during lessons were less visible on our visit than in some preps, but the principal assured us that this is supported where beneficial.

Somerhill is a terrifically sporty school, with over 500 fixtures annually. Hardly surprising given the sport-loving heads and extensive parkland that enables it to host large-scale events. 'Provision is great if you're into it, not so good for the non-sporty', said one parent, meaning there's little escape and regular compulsory Saturday fixtures from year 5 for the boys. But it's not just about the A and B teams – boys and girls play in at least one inter-school match a term, whatever their ability. The school is particularly strong in athletics, notably cross-country, winning a haul of medals at the Kent IAPS, and bounced its way to gold-medal success in the British national schools finals in trampolining. As befits the locale, the school has a new equestrian team for pupils who compete on their own ponies. Inspirational sporting figures pop by – Rebecca Stephens, mountaineer and the first British woman to reach the summit of Everest, recently talked to Derwent Lodge pupils. Paralympian swimmers Stephanie Millward and Claire Cashmore have visited, while Yardley Court pupils heard from Kenton Cool, who has scaled Everest 11 times.

There is weekly homework in years 3 and year 4, moving to 40 minutes per night from year 5 – a slower ramp up than in many other schools. Holiday homework can be bothersome, sometimes requiring advanced levels of skill and organisation – as one parent observed, it 'appears to be a project for parents'.

Music teaching is singled out for praise, as inspirational, inclusive and fun (new music centre) The summer concert involves more than 300 pupils in both junior and senior choirs, as likely to include pop songs as the classics and recently featuring songs from Les Misérables. Pupils can choose from more than 22 instruments for individual tuition and roughly two thirds do. In year 5 Yardley Court boys can take choral auditions for Tonbridge School's Chapel Choir.

The two preps share good size art facilities, high up in the attics, including two new pottery kilns. Art on display is of a very high standard. 'Some amazing work produced,' said one parent and we agree – we saw year 6 pupils animatedly discussing with their teacher how they were to build a life-size wire animal sculpture.

Clubs are squeezed into every moment. For the girls, active options include ballet, tennis, hockey and netball, or they might try knitting, ceramics, jazz and modern art. Boys can start the day with a spot of Samba Band, and end it with sport of every kind or, for the non-sporty, camp-building, gardening, or Cubs. Creative minds can try camera, animation or cookery clubs. We wondered whether the girls might like a few more of the boys' outside larks? The school assures us there are plenty of outdoor clubs for girls over the year, though apparently no camp-building.

All three parts of the school are housed in a large Jacobean stone mansion – formerly a boarding school – set in 150 acres: part manicured lawns, part playing fields and extensive woodland. The school perches at the highest point, giving it great views over the Kent countryside. With the Derwent Lodge houses named after the Lake District, a dipping pond, den-building and sledging on snowy days and not one but two proper adventure playgrounds (which will sell the school in an instant to children) there is a definite whiff of Swallows and Amazons. Inside is a confusing maze of staircases and classrooms, some rather utilitarian, others all stained glass windows and polished wood. And, while there is a bit of chipped paint like any lived-in family home (the family feel is frequently mentioned by old boys and girls), the wood gleams and there's not a leaf out of place.

The preps seem right for parents and children wanting a single-sex environment – there are very different uniforms and separate play-times in addition to tailored teaching – but there is also a bit of mixing. Shared activities include taekwando and indoor athletics, choirs, cake sales, orchestras, theme days and trips such as ski-ing and sailing. Some parents would like the boys and girls to mix more; it's a balance the principal strives to get right. Parents agree the school is hot on anti-bullying.

Somerhill seems particularly well-suited to the working parent. Not only does the single site mean a life-saving single drop off for most families, but the school day begins at 8am, and pupils can remain in school until 6pm. After-school clubs run until 5.30pm (some additional fees) and then co-ordinate with tea if necessary and late supervision (small fee). Younger children can be supervised for free as they wait for their siblings.

Highly popular pre-prep: more than 250 children, with three classes (20 max) in most of the years. It neatly slots into the former coach-houses, providing spacious classrooms with plenty of natural light. Younger children play in the soft-surface central courtyard, but also benefit from their own adventure playground and time in the grounds. The atmosphere is warm, calm and caring and there's a team of plentiful, long-serving staff. The twin focus on both academic achievement (SEN assistance where needed) and teaching of good behaviour was in evidence during our visit when children worked diligently in small groups, greeting us politely.

Pupils travel from Sevenoaks, Tunbridge Wells and Tonbridge and surrounding villages. A school minibus service operates most usefully from Tunbridge Wells and Tonbridge both morning and afternoon, with mornings only from a range of other localities. Mostly children with English as their first language, with no EAL requirements. Parents come here from all walks of life but are a well-heeled bunch in the main – plenty of takers for a £1,000 school trip to Bermuda in year 8, for instance. They describe their peers as friendly and supportive, 'very, very rare to hear any school gate carping'.

What kind of child would thrive at Somerhill? According to the principal, there is 'No set mould, you don't have to be a certain type, or to conform. A child who is happy in his or her own skin'. Parents say the school doesn't wrap children up in cotton wool, and while 'sporty kids would be in their element, it's also good for wallflowers ... the art room is open for all at break times as is the library'.

Seaford College

S

Lavington Park, Petworth, West Sussex GU28 0NB

Pupils: 516; 46 full, 98 weekly, 22 flexi boarders • Ages: 13–18 • Sixth form: 160

Fees: Day £9,660 – £20,160; Boarding £20,100 – £31,185 pa

Tel: 01798 867392
Email: jmackay@seaford.org
Website: www.seaford.org

Headmaster: Since 2013, John Green. Background in professional rugby – he teaches the first team, donning wellies with suit. Taught previously at Barry Boys' School, Ardingly College and Hurstpierpoint, before becoming deputy at Seaford. Married to Sîan with three children, two of whom are still at Seaford.

Tiggerish energy, staunch and unapologetic supporter of the underdog, with a clear vision of how he wants Seaford to be. Works hard to install a sense of value and self worth in all his pupils: A* pupils at Seaford now consider Oxford; BTec pupils are told 'you could be employing those A* pupils in a few years time'. Quality he most desires for his pupils: pride in self.

Academic matters: In 2016, good solid results: 56 per cent A*-B, 30 per cent A*-A, at GCSE; 34 per cent A*-A at A level. Judged on its place in a league table – unremarkable. But the remarkable exists within these figures at this non-selective school. The most able are achieving the high grades you would expect; but so are a good number of those of more average abilities, and as an overall picture, they are generally adding at least one grade to pupils' attainment.

New pupils at Seaford all have a data interview: a detailed meeting showing parents and the pupil their CAT scores and the national picture of attainment for someone of their abilities. 'Children in the middle can achieve highly and shouldn't put a ceiling on expectations'. For some, it makes top grades suddenly seem like something attainable: one parent told us about her son, told by his previous school that he was a no hoper. His confidence has soared at Seaford: he's predicted good grades at A level, and led Young Enterprise last year. When he went up on speech day for an academic prize, 'it was worth every penny'.

'Seaford was seen as a school for dunces,' said a parent who was initially dubious about the school, thinking it was a 'too relaxed environment.' On meeting the head, the parent quickly felt that things had changed. Rigour is now a word which could apply to Seaford. One parent described how her son did a mock paper which went wrong: 'they were all over it and him, in a supportive, but thorough way'.

There's a new focus on high flyers here: a head of enrichment now guides the Oxford application process, gently steering candidates away from inserting an academic joke into every sentence at interview. An enrichment programme is under way (in its infancy at present) which aims to select high performers in each subject and add a layer on top of syllabus stuff – masterclasses in maths this term with lectures on chaos and infinity. The aim is to develop the most able, but in true Seaford style, lecture doors will be open to anyone truly interested, while trying to exclude crafty prep dodgers.

The head has made several staff changes, to the relief of parents: 'The dead wood's gone', said one briskly. There was a lot of praise for the effort put in by teachers: 'what makes this school special is its staff'; 'the commitment of staff is extraordinary'; 'teachers go above and beyond to help failing pupils... three extra sessions a week to help my son get a pass'; 'she [a maths teacher] turns her life over to help them'.

An extremely active tutor system, with a weekly meeting of an hour, and daily catch up of five to 10 minutes every morning. Pupils are also part of vertical tutor groups spanning year groups.

Homework is marked with comments, not grades – 'if pupils get a grade, they immediately want to know what their friend got'. Grades are only communicated to pupils in conversation with teachers. Effort grades have been abandoned – 'only pupils really know how much effort they've put in', says the head. Instead, effort and attainment have been absorbed into the Challenge Grade system: grades set are a indication of potential – what a pupil could achieve if they work hard. Different colours indicate how well they are progressing towards their challenge grades, from significantly underachieving red, through amber, green and gold to extremely high-achieving platinum. Challenge grades are set with tutors and can be upped by pupils if they feel the challenge is not sufficient (hollow laughs from the students seated next to me).

A good array of subjects on offer at both GCSE and A level, plus BTecs. Pre-university courses, as well as EPQ. A minimum of 45 points is required to go on to sixth form for A levels (A* = 8 points, A = 7 points and so on). Most subjects have a spread of attainment in grade terms, English, history and maths with clusters towards the top end.

Learning support here is done extremely well by a staff of nine specialist teachers, five full-time, four part-time. Seaford proudly locates learning support in the centre of the campus, 'not the usual broom cupboard under the stairs', said a parent wryly. 'There's always a correlation to where the learning support department is, and how much the school embrace it', she added.

Nearly half the pupils at the school use the unit at some point, by teacher or self-referral. Parents like its size and focus, and the fact that the unit is part of a school which excels in many ways – 'you don't have to feel [your child is] attending a second rate school because they support dyslexic children'.

'I've been to a lot of schools who say they are good at SEN', said a weary mum, 'but here it isn't just a soundbite'. The unit describes an approach that involves nurturing and developing individual potential, working hard to increase confidence, by not pointing out what's wrong, but what's right, and how to improve. Even mindfulness is included for some pupils, to support a positive approach to school. High degree of joined-up thinking to enable dyslexics to access the curriculum: the unit meets with teachers monthly, and some departments regularly: someone from learning support attends the weekly English department meetings.

And their approach yields results. A parent spoke of her son's confidence soaring; another described how her severely dyslexic son 'changed overnight' here. Having been told at his prep that he wouldn't be able to sit GCSEs, he is now at the school of architecture in Oxford, having left Seaford with three A levels and an EPQ. If things weren't working, Seaford always looked for alternatives which fitted him better, she explained.

Mild to moderate dyslexic pupils in general, though the door is not closed to those at the severe end of the spectrum if they have a high IQ or good underlying ability; but they need to be able to access the mainstream curriculum with the help available. Some 220 of unit users are dyslexic,15 of these severe,190 moderate and 20 mild. The unit assists 44 pupils with dyspraxia and 13 with speech and language problems. Others using the unit might have slow processing speeds or memory problems which mean they would not perform up to their ability level without help. Would consider mild Asperger's, but not the place for autism. Help also given for ADHD (experienced but not specialists in this).

There is one guaranteed one-to-one session a week (which is charged as an extra). Some end up with more than one session: we spoke to a parent whose son has three sessions a week. She believes he couldn't manage with less and that the level of help is an important factor in his success. Extra sessions are offered to pupils if they become available, on the basis of need. There is a little in-class support.

Challenge grades for those with dyslexia are set according to a pupil's ability, as with any other pupil. They're expected to achieve as well as anybody else, but 'it might just take them longer to get there, and they might get there in a different way', said the head of the unit diplomatically. They have had a number of high-achieving dyslexics, one achieving his eight As and one B at GCSE with the help of a scribe; another part of the current small group of high flyers trying for Oxford.

Games, options, the arts: A new focus on games with the rugby-playing head: hockey's always been strong here (county winners); now rugby's just as good. Girls were languishing behind the boys a year or so ago, but head has given girls' sport a new emphasis: more matches, and they're working hard to get them as good as the boys: hockey and netball are flourishing.

Pupils have six lessons a week (in two triple sessions). Teams for all, the best playing every week, less able around six times a term. Specialist coaching for all ability levels here; and it's not just the top performers who get the accolades: recent team of the term was the under 14 hockey C team.

Cricket and tennis for both girls and boys are taking off. There's a full golf course and lots of other sports on offer, from polo to clay pigeon shooting. New sports centre includes a gym and dance studio. Swimming not currently competitive, but with a glass retractable roof soon to be built over the outside pool, this is an area about to develop.

Some notable individual success, including a national triathlete, national paddle board champion, and a player for the national first XI hockey under 18s.

Music at Seaford is glorious. At a year 9 lunchtime concert, treats included spine-tingling singing of a Mozart aria. Singing is outstanding here – the head of voice is also head of voice at junior Royal Academy in London. The head soloist describes 'music coming up through my toes' – it's no surprise that she and the choir were selected to support Gary Barlow on the last night of his tour. The music block is all white paint and new wood – smooth, calm surroundings to complement the mellifluous sounds. Kids enjoy the 'incredible vibes' at Seafordstock every summer, and the head was keen to ensure that every year has a rock band.

Not as great an emphasis on drama as music ('not enough,' said one parent bluntly) – the arts calendar is dominated by music events. But drama is now part of the year 9 carousel, some pupils do LAMDA, and there's a main school production and senior production each year: Dr Faustus the last, a dyslexic pupil taking the lead part, learning his lines by drawing pictures. They don't shirk the big stuff here.

Compulsory CCF in year 10 – pupils think the parades are rather dull, but 'once you get past standing and marching for half an hour, you get to the woods and the fun stuff'. Both our guides said CCF camp was a favourite memory. D of E also available.

Art here is superb, with a big range on offer, from fine art to creative media production. Exam work was on display in room after room of glories: dresses of balloons and feathers; curvy wooden speakers and fabric stags' heads (they look so much better in tartan). Ghoulish sci-fi heads in the animation area; a fabric prawn (Shaun), life-like and eerily huge, hung casually from the ceiling. Sixth form art students almost live in the block – there's even a kitchen so they can brew – 'we look after them', said the head of art, comfortably. Students depart for art colleges across the country, including Central St Martins, Kingston and the London College of Fashion.

Boarding: It's really particularly nice here, and one of the nicest things is its lack of uniformity. The boarding houses are all different, but each with a strong sense of home. Around 180 boarders spread between four houses: most are weekly, with the greater number of full timers being international (10 per cent of boarders are from overseas). Flexi-boarding is also available, and it's usually possible to get a room at the last minute (£42), by emailing houseparents. Prep school boarders have rooms for seven or eight in the Mansion.

Boys (years 9-12) are in a crisp new building (which parents love), run by houseparents with fluent ease. Basket drawers for shoes as soon as boys come through the door – they generally remember: it's nice to walk around in socks with underfloor heating. If they don't – hoover duty that night. Rooms for two, with temperature gauges in each room and a sofa which can turn into another bed. New wood furniture, built in above bed lights. Rooms compact, but not tight. Worth getting the big jobs – head of house gets a comfy chair and ensuite, TV and fridge (wow).

Wifi throughout (indeed, throughout the campus), and a system so house parents can see if pupils are online when they shouldn't be (after 11.30pm); younger pupils hand in tech at bedtime. Comfortable common room, kitchen for snacks, fruit and toaster. Homework is supervised, house parents pleased that their only niggle ('haven't got any homework sir') has been resolved by internet site which makes it clear what everyone's got. A house mum bakes pancakes and fudge crumpets for movie night. Houseparent dogs bounce into the common room in the evening. The kids love it.

Girls in years 9-12 are housed in the Mansion: rooms of all shapes and sizes for one or two, some extremely spacious – elegant windows, dreamy views. Graceful spiral staircase up to the boarding floor. In various states of paint, just done and needs doing ('needs to be modern and fresher', said a parent). Good quality wood furniture, comfortable furniture, the usual kitchen provision.

Sixth form boys housed in what parent and pupils refer to as 'the youth hostel' (aka Hedon Hall); 'but the boys are all happy in there and love the housemaster'. The fabric is old, and inside it is painted lime green (gulp); but the furniture in bedrooms and common room is smart and new, bathrooms are clean, and the common room is decorated with sports paraphernalia, donated by past and present sixth formers. Residents have a fierce affection for the house and apparently feel no deficiencies.

The pupil who randomly assumed the job of showing us around, was polite, articulate and engagingly straightforward. The usual kitchen, and not just for brews: they competed in Hedon masterchef –'felt sorry for the people who had to try it', said our guide. Head of house is popular with the boys, and from his side, a staunch supporter of them. He enforces an hour's leisure reading every afternoon in the winter term (proper books, not magazines), having found out that dyslexic commuters do better because they read on the train.

Sixth form girls live in a bungalow, well-mown lawn with gnomes and assorted companions in front, patio with BBQ around the back. Some feeling of arriving in antipodean suburbia. Scottish giant of a house dad, casually consuming his Magnum, showed us a bright pink sitting room, golden buddha in the fire place: hippy girl power – felt like a teenage heaven. Kitchen and seated area – they can go to the dining hall for breakfast, but most prefer to eat 'healthy girly breakfasts' in house. Cosy rooms, with the usual high quality fittings. A warm friendly relationship between pupils and houseparents.

Plenty going on for boarders at weekends, with the Sainsbury's trip on Friday evening, sports and shopping trips on Saturday, and trips to places of interest on Sunday.

S

Background and atmosphere: A long driveway, past golf flags waving the in the breeze and ancient trees with improbably massive trunks up to the mansion house: stately home turned school. Seaford College sits at the foot of the downs, wooded hills rising immediately behind it, mists caught in the trees on the drizzly day of our visit – brewers' dubbin, said the head of English dreamily, clearly finding considerably more satisfaction in the rainy day than most of his fellows. A beautiful flint chapel nestles in the grass behind the school. Compulsory weekly service, but all beliefs welcome.

Stately elegance mixes with old cottages and swish new build. A few tatty Portakabins, due to be ripped down soon. Most parents we spoke to would like things to be a bit smarter –'there shouldn't be peeling paintwork – it needs a bit more polish'; but the head is working hard to spruce up buildings as well as pupils. Some pupils have been less than keen to polish their shoes, but most look smart: just a few shirt tails still hanging out. Manners are of the old-fashioned variety, and include standing up for visitors and handwritten letters of thanks. A taxi driver described pupils as very polite; then added, 'but they could do with mending the drive'.

There's an emphasis here on giving something back: community service activities every week, and community action day once a year, which includes activity programmes with local primary school children, or clearing beaches.

It would not suit a child who was full on academic with no other interests, said a parent. 'Very intelligent children will thrive there if they do other things...it could be a very lonely place for those just absorbed by maths and physics. Everyone's outside at the end of the day – you need to be able to mix and be a bit independent'.

Pastoral care, well-being and discipline: Pastoral care at Seaford is 'unbelievable,' said a parent, as she described the extraordinary level of kindness and understanding from the school when facing family tragedy. And they're very aware of the pressures of growing up. Staff in the Pink House provide a listening ear at any time – pupils can even ask to be excused in a lesson, and staff will email the Pink House to say a pupil is on the way. It's staffed by one full-time director of care and welfare, a part-time safeguarding officer, the rev, a counsellor and Poppy the dog (who is particularly busy in September helping homesick pupils). At least 10 pupils turn up at the Pink House every day, but problems can be also be picked up by phone, tutors or peer mentors. Any bullying is dealt with promptly, confirm parents. One described how her daughter would pop in to the Pink House to get some perspective on school squabbles – so and so's being a bit nasty, I'll go the Pink House and see what they think.

In discipline terms, rules are firmly based on traditional good manners and strict enforcement of standards. No more easy-going Seaford: the new head is ensuring the school is up to the mark, from looking smart to the top 10 rules: break them and you risk exclusion (interestingly, dishonesty is ranked outside the top 10 as a less serious offence, alongside chewing gum...). No second chances for sex or drugs (although first time joint users might get a managed reprieve, depending on the circumstances). And to make sure no one flouts the rules, sniffer dogs (a crazy spaniel and a labrador) check the lunch queue. They're much loved by kids – and have never actually found anything. Two exclusions in the last year: for persistent disruption, and bullying. No surprise, in this caring school, that those suspended or excluded can go the Pink House for a chat with support workers 'to feel the love.'

Delicious lunch served for us in the head's study – is it always this nice? 'It doesn't look quite like this', said the head boy carefully, regarding a swirl of purée, 'but it tastes good'.

Pupils and parents: Posh, and not, here – 'I know someone with a jet, and others working three jobs to get their kids through'. Lots of weekly boarders from London, and school buses serve the surrounding area.

Fewer girls than boys (around a third), but the head is keen to attract more, and ran an everywoman conference to provide aspirational role models for girls.

Parents are happy with a good level of communication, with frequent emails from school, and teachers letting parents know if there's a problem – 'in the past we'd have had to work this out for ourselves'.

Notable former pupils include: Hugh Bentall, pioneer of open-heart surgery; Sir Louis Blom-Cooper, lawyer; Anthony Buckeridge, children's author; Val Guest, film director; David Purley, Formula One driver; Matthew Rose, opera singer; Toby Stephens, actor and Tom Odell, musician.

Entrance: Fifty per cent of year 9 from Seaford Prep, the rest from a range of preps and local primaries. Non-selective until GCSE; thereafter need 45 points to enter sixth form. Screening for SEN on entry.

Exit: Around 35 per cent leave to go to local sixth form colleges, usually for financial reasons. After sixth form, a good number head off to Russell group universities; Plymouth and Oxford Brookes are also popular. None to Oxbridge in the last year or two but one medic in 2016 and one off to be a cyberspace communications specialist in the RAF.

Money matters: Fees good value for money, said a parent; but she wouldn't want them to be any more. Extra for SEN and counselling. Means-tested bursaries.

Remarks: A happy, exceptionally caring school, which strive to do well by all who cross the threshold, whatever their ability.

Sevenoaks Preparatory School

Godden Green, Sevenoaks, Kent TN15 0JU

Pupils: 385 • Ages: 2.5-13

Fees: £9,480 – £13,335 pa

Tel: 01732 762 336
Email: admissions@theprep.org.uk
Website: www.theprep.org.uk

Headmaster: Since 2012 Mr Luke Harrison BA PGCE IAPS. Early 40s. An old boy of the school (along with three other members of staff), he was educated at Tonbridge and St Mary's College, Twickenham (University of Surrey) where he read English and drama. Did his PGCE at St Luke's, Exeter with his first job at the Weald of Kent Girls' Grammar, where he met his wife. He then taught English and theatre studies up to A level at Kingston Grammar. Joined Sevenoaks Prep in 2001, as he wanted the opportunity to get involved with all aspects of school life and had a brief to get drama back on track.

Married to Clare, a trained teacher who, among her many roles, is assistant head, in charge of admissions and teaches history to years 7 and 8 – 'they work well together and are a very effective team,' according to one mother. They have two daughters in the school. Considers the strong family and inclusive ethos a particular strength of the school and is always available to parents – prefers face to face meetings rather than emails – and will visit families at home if there are problems. High praise from parents, who say he 'is a good communicator who is highly visible and approachable, and seems to care and understands what parents are looking for, and is open to new ideas'. 'He knows the kids well and they respect him'. Parents also say he has a 'great approach' and they like his philosophy: 'If a child is happy, everything else follows' and 'Kids need resilience, and while success is always celebrated, they must take risks and learn to fail'. 'He has tightened things up and is on top of things,' said one mother, but he feels that any changes are 'evolution rather than revolution'.

Entrance: Non-selective means a diverse group. Nursery takes children from 2 years with intakes in Sept and Jan and build up sessions through kindergarten to be ready for full-time school in reception. Four children join in year 3 after a taster day and assessment in English and maths and an hour with the head of learning support. Another intake in year 7, mainly from local primary schools or those returning from overseas. Very rarely are there spaces at other times. Many children's names put down at birth and there are only places in reception if someone leaves. Most from nursery are guaranteed a place as long as the school feels they can cope with the curriculum. The emphasis is very much on ensuring that the school is the right setting for the child. No open days and parents always shown round by pupils 'so they can see school as it is'. School wants happy parents and families always encouraged to look at other schools in the area before making their decision.

Exit: Up to half leave at 11+, mainly to the grammars and some to Sevenoaks School. No specific tutoring for 11+ (Kent imposes strict rules against this) but, as well as ongoing maths and English lessons, there is a focus on reasoning skills in year 5. Many get outside tutoring as well. Sends to a widening range of schools at 13+ including Tonbridge, Sevenoaks, Walthamstow Hall, Brighton College, Kent College, Sutton Valence, King's Canterbury, Bethany, Hurst, Caterham, Cranbrook and Lingfield Notre Dame, and parents encouraged to look further afield. All are CAT tested and, as one parent commented, 'the head is very good at helping parents with the choice of senior schools – it is always about what is best for the child'. A good handful of academic and music scholarships each year, including to Tonbridge and Sevenoaks, as well as the occasional art and drama scholarship

Remarks: Founded 1919 with six boys who were too young to attend Sevenoaks Grammar (now Sevenoaks School), the school moved to its present site in the 1960s and went co-ed in 1991. The original building is an old farmhouse just outside Sevenoaks, set in 20 acres of playing fields and backing on to the 1,000 acre Knole Park, which is used for nature walks and cross-country running. No grand central building but well-designed additions over the years including a large sports hall, also used for plays and assemblies, new classroom blocks and the architect-designed light and airy Oakery dining hall with drama and music upstairs.

Pre-prep school is a self-contained unit with a warm friendly atmosphere a few minutes' walk from the prep school and with its own hall, dining room and four new classrooms opened. All teachers and assistants are specialists in early years' education and work in partnership with parents. One particularly charming touch is the twilight nativity play with live animals.

Children move from the pre-prep into the prep school in year 3 and are taught in year group blocks with their own classrooms; years 3 and 4 have their own playground. Class teaching for core subjects and specialist teaching for drama, languages, music, PE, ICT and games. Specialist teachers for all subjects from year 6, when children start to move classrooms for lessons. French taught from nursery and Spanish from year 6. Normally 20 per class but smaller groups in top two years. Informal setting in class from year 3, setting in maths from year 4 and setting in all subjects from year 7. Potential scholars in years 7 and 8, and those who need stretching, offered special sessions before and after school. 'The school is very inclusive,' said one parent, 'and particularly supportive of high flyers and underachievers'.

Low staff turnover but enough to 'freshen things up' – good combination of consistency and new blood, most in their 30s and 40s; most who teach at the top end of the school are secondary-trained subject specialists. School has introduced Singapore Maths with an emphasis on mental arithmetic. 'It gives the children a deep understanding and is not just about learning by heart,' says the very enthusiastic maths teacher who gave us a demonstration. Maths Challenges popular and school does well in inter-school competitions. Geography quizzes each week and children are expected to keep up to date with news and know what is happening in the world. Recently refurbished science lab used by years 6-8 – masses of practical work, and we saw some fine models of energy-saving houses and watched some splendid erupting volcanoes. Emphasis on creativity and fun (but no games) in ICT lessons and children taught coding and programming.

One full-time and one part-time SEN teacher, mainly for mild dyslexia and dyspraxia; support in lessons or small groups and some one-to-one help, but 'don't want to make children feel different'. Teachers always on look-out for problems and children screened from reception upwards. EAL offered – children mainly taken out of class and are encouraged to celebrate their own culture and background.

Sport for all and puts out as many teams as possible – rotates players in Cs and Ds to make sure everyone can play in a match. The usual sports: football, rugby, cricket for boys and netball, hockey and rounders for the girls. Judo and fencing also popular and archery offered in years 7 and 8. Gymnastics club recently set up and lots of children are members of sports clubs outside school. 'It's not too competitive, kids want to do well and be part of a team but it's not all about the glory,' said one mother.

One hour a week of music for all and most try out an instrument, even if only the recorder or triangle. Vibrant music department with lots going on: rock band, orchestras, string quartet, brass groups and the 80 strong choir. Drama part of the curriculum, annual plays for each year group and all children encouraged to take part.

Good range of lunchtime and after-school clubs include judo, tennis, gymnastics, street dance, fencing and archery. Lots of outings and visits to help bring learning to life with an emphasis on learning through experience – some local and some further afield eg history trip to Bayeaux and the WW1 battlefields and a moving memorial service at Ypres.

Bushcraft course at beginning of year 8 when children spend several days camping in the woods. Staff on the look-out for leadership qualities and heads of school and prefects are announced afterwards. Children taught that they are part of a wider community and pupils' charity committee an important part of school life – 'it's not just about raising money; kids spent some time at Age UK drop in centre'. Social entrepreneurship project after common entrance when children are given £10 by the Rotary Club to set up their own business and turn it into £100 or more. They have to design spreadsheets and a business plan.

Strong pastoral support aims to help parents and children alike and all treated with 'empathy and understanding,' said one mother. 'The school is very nurturing and really looks after the kids'. Good food with plenty of choice served in the Oakery dining hall, which was opened by Gary Rhodes and which our guide referred to as the 'restaurant'. Children sit in year groups with teachers and kitchen staff keeping an eye on healthy eating. Healthy lifestyles encouraged and discussed in lessons and reinforced by helpful messages on the dining room wall.

S

Top two years help run the school and have different uniforms with badges and ties for positions of responsibility. All year 8s become a prefect at some stage but have to earn their position. Coveted Oak Award given to those who play a particularly active role in the school community. Our guides felt that 'friendship issues were sorted out quickly' and they were 'given more freedom than at other schools and that 'personal responsibility makes people more organised'. School finishes at 4pm but many opt to stay till 6pm and do supervised prep.

Most families live within about 15 minutes of the school and are mainly commuters, local professionals and medics – some very wealthy, others who require bursaries. Most are incredibly supportive of the school. Increasing number of double income families but also some stay at home dads. About eight per cent foreign nationals. Headmaster says he tries to 'get away from the elitist feel, and it is the broad spectrum which attracts parents'. 'A real mixed bag,' said one parent; 'all abilities, walks of life and family dynamics.'

Social events committee, with reps from each class, organise coffee mornings and nights out for parents as well as the Christmas bazaar, summer ball and family day – some purely for fun, some to raise money for charity. 'The school is very supportive of parents and it is a great way to make new friends – we are allowed to picnic in the grounds and use the tennis courts and treat the school as an extension of home.' Notable alumni include Ian Walker (yachtsman), Mike Conway (racing driver) and Daniel Collings (journalist).

Sevenoaks School

High Street, Sevenoaks, Kent TN13 1HU

Pupils: 1,069; 352 full boarders • Ages: 11–18 • Sixth form: 437

Fees: Day £21,591 – £24,516; Boarding £34,479 – £37,404 pa

Tel: 01732 455133
Email: admin@sevenoaksschool.org
Website: www.sevenoaksschool.org

Head: Since 2002, Dr Katy Ricks, 50s. Previously deputy head at Highgate School and before that posts at other top flight schools – St Edward's Oxford, where was head of English, Latymer Upper and King Edward's, Birmingham. Career choice clinched by first teaching role at St Paul's School for Girls where became clear that that 'talking to young people about literature' was going to give her more satisfaction than research.

Elegant with penchant for vivid colours, she lays claim to purple handbag, and pink and grey study described in previous review as 'minimalist' (no change there). Married to academic (at King's College London) and of course vastly intelligent (first from Balliol). Conversation is scattered with quotes – we were treated to Keats and Dr Johnson.

The first woman head in school's history, has made this the place to be if you're after consistently top, top IB results (GCSEs are equally amazing). Fiercely proud of the school and bursting with ideas, she's engaging and charming – and disarmingly open about mugging up on previous Good Schools Guide's description of her 'infectious enthusiasm' and ensuring it came across just as strongly this time round. It did.

Headship is 'brilliant', biggest perk being in charge and 'making things happen,' she says. Point of education is about 'letting people feel free to be themselves in the best way that they can,' and giving them means of creating robust moral and intellectual framework for themselves – qualities enshrined in IB learner profile. Some parents see her as a CEO type rather than a hands on head but pigeonholes are unhelpful, she says. 'I'm simply myself.' They describe her as impressive, something she's aware of though feels 'completely un-terrifying'.

Pupils, particularly in senior years, say she's both inspiring and approachable. 'Barrier is still there but you feel comfortable to talk,' thought one. Another praised seamless transition from 'extremely personable' English teacher to school figurehead as required, though she's not heavy on the small talk – it's straight down to business.

Does she feel it's lonely at the top? Never. 'In fact,' she says, 'bring on the loneliness.' As to role models? 'I'm my role model.'

No plans to move – she attributes rumours of itchy feet to sabbatical taken to finish PhD. Here for the foreseeable future – 'A mover who became a lifer.' After all, why waste all that accumulated experience? 'You want to use it, that's what it's for ... and make it beneficial for everyone else.'

The school feels smiley – and she is a very smiley head. Her pride and excitement in the school permeates the place. We felt it in everyone we met.

Academic matters: Not so much a case of getting down with these kids but scrabbling up to their level. Regardless of mother tongue, notable for gift of gab and desire to avoid muscular Christianity (or contortionist's pantheism) in favour of secular education that builds curiosity, creativity and critical thinking. They leave, says school with 'enlarged capacity for independent thought' – and without, as far as we could see, acquiring swollen heads on the way out. This despite evident brightness starting early, year 7 packed with top of their year types – no surprise given school's entry criteria: grammar school level or better (possibly a bit OTT, thinks Dr Ricks). 'Other girls took five lessons to learn something; I took one,' says typically bright 11 year old. Most pupils find flocking with similar high fliers an easy transition, though brilliance of plumage can be dazzling. 'It was hard at first,' said one recent leaver.

Being on the ball essential, what with just 45 minutes for breakfast and dinner (lunch is a more leisurely 90 minutes – though you'll be packing an activity in as well) and not a place for the vague, thought parents: something that this reviewer, who'd never been whistled round a school with such friendly but single-minded efficiency, or written notes faster, can confirm. Unquenchable sense of purpose the norm. 'A lot of people had very strong opinions about where they'd be in life in the next five or 10 years time,' said ex-pupil. (And you can probably assume they aren't thinking middle rank pootling with safe pension in Basildon).

But while spreading a little zappiness throughout, school doesn't ramp it up to mind-blowing levels. Don't sit exams early – why spoil the pleasure of discovery? Staff lay on homework with a light touch rather than trowel – if not necessary, won't set. While around 10 per cent of pupils have some form of learning need, it's mild only for dyslexia, dyspraxia, dysgraphia, ADHD, Asperger's Syndrome and visual impairment. Only exception is hearing impairment.

Curriculum – naturally – is robust. Three sciences from the off, second language added in year 8. Most teaching is mixed ability – maths and languages the exceptions – sometimes adjusted instead for gender balance. For years 10 and 11, formulaic in the sense that these very bright children have only to be shown the way to strings of A*/A grades at GCSE and it happens (92 per cent in 2016). Norm is 10, school teaching own English lit course to avoid dreary staples. ('Nobody wants to do Lord of the Flies,' said mother). Ditto for art, music, drama, history of art and technology and critical perspectives course. By sixth form, IB is natural extension of school's way of thinking, most pupils revelling in mind-stretching approach that's been their lot so far. It's about 'developing brain muscle so can frame an argument,' said upper sixth English teacher leading typically lively, interactive lesson. Intellectual weightlifting produced 39.8 IB average in 2016.

Maximum class sizes sound large (24 to GCSE, 15 in the sixth form), but average is far lower (16 to age 16, and between eight and 10 in final years), with overall teacher to pupil ratio of one to nine.

Credit to Dr Ricks for staff team so strong that (unusually) parents and pupils couldn't name a single weak area (inspection accolades agree). 'Can go away and think about it,' offered recent leaver. Stable core of middle management reflected in average staff age of 41, with 55 notching up 10 years plus. Inevitable turnover of younger mob to more senior positions elsewhere (around 10 to headships in recent years). Not an issue, think parents, as quality replacements are lining up to take their places (final year Oxbridge undergrad sitting bolt upright in waiting room on day of visit).

Dr Ricks shortlists all staff applications herself, exercising football manager's eye for talent. Down to being 'a curious, observant person if you put it nicely or, if you put it nastily, a nosey parker.' Stand out staff quality she's after? Personable brilliance. 'If child was on a bus with this person for two hours, would they enjoy their company and be sparked by it?'

Games, options, the arts: Visitors might find numbers of events and activities almost overwhelming. Not so pupils, busily adding more, from coding to Middle Eastern Society, at a rate of knots. Others enter – and win – high profile competitions, one group snaffling £15,000 prize after developing app for autistic children. Overdoing things isn't an issue, they say. Can mean hard choices – some pupils (reluctantly) give up drama in the sixth form, and school keeps watchful eye on the ultra-active, though approach, ladling on the encouragement rather than activating the brakes, is distinctly hands off. 'If you feel you can cope, you probably will,' says pupil. Latest initiatives are three institutes – teaching and learning, service and entrepreneurship and higher education and professional insight.

Lavish facilities the norm. For sporty, substantial outside spaces supplemented by great indoors of Sennocke Centre – just lapping its three tennis courts, pool and giant sports hall probably enough to meet daily exercise requirements. With some international pupils completely new to team sports, hasn't been high profile area in the past, though recent successes – U14 hockey and U16 netball teams making national finals – could signal a change, achievements recognised by must-read authority, School Sport Magazine. Individual sports generally more popular – sailing especially so. However, numerous parents and pupils testified to star ratings for CCF, available from year 10, khaki-clad mob milling prior to drilling, rugged in tee shirts despite below zero temperatures on day of visit.

Performing arts impressively housed in The Space, with vast, acoustically advanced theatre that takes staging challenges in stride (pop up orchestra pit for Les Mis a doddle) and umpteen practice rooms for 750 weekly individual lessons. Very talented flourish (conductor Andrew Gourlay is a former pupil) with symphony orchestra, jazz band, gospel choir and song writing groups among many ensembles on offer, though 'have a go' spirit sees all abilities from virtuoso to enthusiast rapturously received when take to the stage.

Boarding: Until eighth boarding house completed, sensible to book your place early – not easy to change to boarding later on and even sixth formers (house captains excepted) share rooms. Not that pupils mind, enjoying companionship and, according to one sixth former, preferring in any case to study in three-level, attractively nook-filled library, which like Sennocke Centre and practice rooms is open late. 'Less distraction as you don't have your stuff round you.'

Cleanliness comes as standard (a spot of stuffiness in one bedroom was nothing that open window or two wouldn't solve), ditto entertainment (TV/DVD, Sky, snooker or table tennis, Wifi) and bulk deliveries of bread, fruit and milk (sensible refrigerated dispensers).

Considerable variation otherwise. Sixth formers have International Centre (boys) and International House (girls). Then there's Lambardes, vintage low rise 1960s and home to around 20 year 7 and 8 pupils who board only if have older siblings at the school or live just out of comfortable commuting range. In contrast, there's gorgeous Johnson's, one of four houses for year 9 to upper sixths, hall all early 20th century Agatha Christie-whodunnit-style fixtures and fittings.

Some non-negotiables. No solo travel to more distant boarding houses regardless of age and, if late, with accompanying teacher. Youngest pupils have phones removed at night to begin with – and at any age if used after lights out (parents predictably thrilled that off this particular hook).

Otherwise, trust and flexibility dominate, from lockers (unlocked) to negotiated later bedtimes for older pupils if vital world events like US election intervene. 'About compromise,' says warm houseparent, who teaches ironing and cooking as university preparation, though washing happens, magically, off stage. House rivalry low key to point of invisibility – 'Children have to compete with the outside world, they don't need to compete with each other,' is parent's take on school's philosophy.

No them and us between day and boarder, local or international pupils – 'seamless,' said pupil of integration between the two (national groups split up, factions/combatants eg Russia/Ukraine brought together). House events include Valentine's meal (partners can be blind date, same sex, day or boarding pupils – one boy invited his best friend).

Around three-quarters of sixth form boarders stay on at weekends (it's half or so in other years). Home clothes allowed though if inappropriate will be 'sent home at the boarder's own expense...' (not a regular occurrence).

Sunday excursions enjoyable if not cutting edge (a liking for Lazer quest definitely useful), but a welcome change from frantic pace of life in the week. School prefers parties for younger pupils when hosted out of school to be alcohol-free – and provides useful hints and tips including checking water bottles for vodka – though sensibly stops short of laying down law (impossible to enforce, we'd have thought).

Background and atmosphere: Given awe-inspiring prospectus – fabulously well written, slightly tongue in cheek self praise in vignette form – school could have work cut out just living up to it. For the most part, succeeds – triumphantly, even if tiny imperfections (like smeary bin in visitor's loo) are the more jarring by comparison. And though it comes with over 500 years of history – was one of the earliest secular school foundations in the country – and literary references in works by everyone from Daniel Defoe to Charlie Higson, isn't weighed down by it, with plenty of space, physical and philosophical, to let in plenty of fresh thinking and the odd bit of quirkiness.

'Wonderfully happy location,' thought pupil. Good for the area, too – Sevenoaks's biggest employer, owning substantial chunks of the high street (all pupils must use underpass – severe sanctions if they don't). Waitrose – appropriately – marks the boundary line. Most of 100-acre site, which backs on to Knole House, isn't visible from the road, though year 7s and 8s initially operate on a smaller scale for registration and break while are finding their way round the school's '...30 buildings, 107 classrooms, 14 sports pitches, 12 lawns, six ponds and thousands of trees.' Latest planned additions to bump up the numbers will science and technology and IB Global Study centre.

S

Each modern language merits own room off long corridor, the world in miniature, while English scores paved courtyard with baby olive trees and silver birch – a grove in the making – just needs own Muse. In the meantime, plenty of inspiration from works of art dotted around, many by teachers and former pupils. One orange sculpture is featured in nuts and bolts parent handbook, together with similarly toned handbag. Possible reimagining of lost property cupboard? 'Probably to give sense of scale,' thought sensible guide.

All well worth a look given that one talented sixth form artist (product of satisfyingly messy art room, complete with artist in residence and pile of larger than life-size clay busts) recently flogged one of own works for £1,000...

Pastoral care, well-being and discipline: Copers will thrive. 'You shape up pretty quickly,' said parent. Big on nurture in year 7 but given pace of life here, in other years best to get with the programme pronto. Plenty of help around. Daily meetings with tutors reckoned to be a good safety net, staff normally quick to respond to parent queries. Counsellor also well used – sometimes making appointments difficult but school is planning more.

Robust but not unkind sanctions – suspended 40 pupils in 2014 for misuse of alcohol on school trip. For drug use, possible that might be allowed back but would have to agree to random testing for remainder of school career.

Commonsense advice issued on everything from pocket money allowance (keep it sensibly low to avoid 'over-reliance on material goods' – nice thought though we can't help wondering if that boat has already sailed – even recent lower school cake sales raised over £1,000) to cases of bullying – rare, according to school surveys, but acknowledged to rear head now and again.

School sensibly quotes examples of nastiness: 'You've got no friends, you're fat/gay...' and urges telling at all times. One parent agreed that unkindness happens but room to escape the tormentors helps. 'You can breathe here,' thought pupil. Minor problems tend to work themselves out, school on the whole reserving its energies for coping with more serious problems – has fair share of mental illness including eating disorders and self-harm. 'Very on the ball,' thought mother.

Parents are also expected to behave. Don't expect leave to remove children in term time without a very good reason (weddings or funerals might just about hack it but little else). And as for taking unilateral decisions to run holiday of lifetime into first few days of term? No way. 'School holidays are fixed at the absolute maximum consistent with good learning,' says school. In contrast, an empty school is the goal at exeat weekends though pupils 'in real need' can stay.

One parent felt that a bit more approachability 'would make it a better place for parents and allow better communications.' Emails felt by several to be a bit too abundant (about 10 a week, more at start of term, thought parent) and hard to prioritise. Rethink is underway, says school.

Pupils and parents: Has always been cosmopolitan, first international pupil arriving in the 18th century. Currently international 175 pupils from Australia to Azerbaijan, Serbia to Singapore, Malaysia to Moldova – greater proportion further up the school, plus 70 expat families. Walls of vast dining hall serving quality food that even Italian tour guide, initially sceptical, was happy to endorse, decorated in a sea of flags representing every pupil nationality.

Sizeable numbers of local-ish families (Kent, Sussex and accessible bits of Surrey plus some Londoners). Can join popular parents' choir. Friends' organisation, recent innovation, going great guns with monthly drinks and cultural excursions.

Some parents reckon that small proportion of pupils – Londoners in particular – afflicted by sense of entitlement. Absolutely not, we were told, indignantly. 'We're grounded, also there's so much cultural diversity.' School's down-to-earth outreach programme (two pupils diligently sorting stock in local charity shop, medics putting in time at local school for the disabled) doubtless helps.

Entrance: At 11+, 80 places, same number again at 13+. For year 7 place, entrance tests in maths, English and VR, references, interviews and reports. Numerous feeders including Granville School, St Michael's School, Sevenoaks Prep, Holmewood House, Solefield School, Walthamstow Hall Junior School, New Beacon, Russell House, Amherst Junior School, Derwent Lodge, Blackheath Prep, Hazelwood, Hilden Grange, Yardley Court, Dulwich (DPSC), Cumnor House and Vinehall. Rumour that state school entrants may be favoured if tie break for a place.

Applicants for 13+ entry take maths, English and VR tests in year 7, plus 40 minute group interview and reference. Unconditional offers made in June of year 7; high-fliers invited to take scholarship exam in May of year 8. Those at prep schools asked to aim for 70 per cent at common entrance (used for setting purposes). For sixth form entrance, when another 75-80 pupils taken in, tested in three proposed IB higher level subjects plus maths and English if not native language (high levels of fluency essential though can offer a session a week to 10 pupils needing short term boosters).

Exit: Vast majority (over 95 per cent) stay on into sixth form. Count down to UCAS form completion handled extremely well with teachers pitching their own degree subjects. Also 'how to' personal statement talks, coaching for US SAT tests and support if predicted grades don't work out quite as planned – school has talked near misses on to foundation places at desired uni.

Many offers from highly prestigious unis here, there and everywhere – 10 to 15 per cent to US, Canada currently very popular, few to anything other than Russell Group or top international equivalents. 'Work really hard to support them, in the end it's what you pay them for,' said parent. As a result, destination list tends to resemble a global best of higher education list, 29 Oxbridge places in 2016 plus Ivy League, McGill (Canada), Chinese University of Hong Kong, University of Hong Kong, ETH Zurich, University of St Gallen, Charité–Universitätsmedizin Berlin, teamed with list of solid gold subjects (sciences in abundance, 14 medicine and vet science places in 2016).

Money matters: At least five full bursaries at 11+ (may trickle up to year 9 if funds permit), some partial bursaries and offer of temporary support if difficult times strike existing pupils. Scholarships of up to 10 per cent.

Remarks: Exhilarating, immersive education that's ideal for intellectually voracious, organised, go-getting types. Less so for those in search of a more gentle voyage of self-discovery.

Shiplake College

Shiplake Court, Shiplake, Henley-on-Thames, Oxfordshire RG9 4BW

Pupils: 458; 177 full/weekly boarders • Ages: 11–18 (boarding from 13) • Sixth form: 171 (including 47 girls) • C of E

Fees: Day £16,650 – £20,850; Boarding £19,650 – £30,900 pa

Tel: 01189 402455
Email: registrar@shiplake.org.uk
Website: www.shiplake.org.uk

Headmaster: Since 2004, Gregg Davies BSc Cert Mgmt (mid 50s). Married to Alison, who works in learning development here, and to whom he frequently refers in conversation. They have a daughter, who is an Old Viking (former deputy head of college), now at university. Mr Davies, a reporting inspector for ISI ('the best CPD I do') is, at once, intimidating and benign, humorous and serious, mischievous and earnest. His luxury is the speedboat he keeps moored just below the front lawn. He is direct, looks you straight in the eye, but has a light touch. Immediately likeable, he not only has a twinkle and warmth, but is the kind of man you would be pleased for your son (and daughter) to have as a role model.

Passionate about 'growth mindset' – 'I grew up dreaming of playing rugby for Wales or Scotland and at 36 I played for Scottish veterans – that's an example of growth mindset.' He coins words/phrases for the year. Last year it was 'yet', this term it's 'just try'. Mr Davies, with his two great bearded collies that share his office, is a man you could work with in a crisis. Parents describe him as 'very extrovert', 'going the extra mile', refer to his 'refreshing, individual approach' and a noticeably 'thoughtful, non-judgmental attitude but unafraid to say what he thinks.'

He started his career at Haberdashers' Aske's boys where he taught biology (his degree was in physiology), and moved on to Fettes where he relished the role of housemaster. As a young boy at a local comprehensive, he was spotted by one of the masters at Shrewsbury school, who recognised his commitment and potential. Mr Davies still regards Eric Anderson, his headmaster at Shrewsbury at the time, as a mentor.

While proud of the 'all ability' nature of Shiplake – 'students here go into people jobs,' he says – he is still keen to impress upon us the steady improvement of results. 2016 was the first year that they achieved 100 per cent pass rate at A level. Pupils perform outstandingly in BTec too. He is determined that no one leaves the sixth form feeling they've failed.

Davies is a headmaster who genuinely knows his pupils. By name, sight as well as by their dreams and fears. He enjoys randomly summoning them, whether to talk to us, to discuss their state of dress or praise a recent achievement. The same applies to his staff. No-one escapes any encounter without some sort of remark, observation or comment. They in turn appear to feel great affection for him. He succeeds in treading the delicate line between being everyone's friend and confidante and that of esteemed and highly respected headmaster.

Academic matters: Very small class sizes, maximum 16 in a class, allowing each child to get individual attention and creating strong value added scores. Boys take eight or nine GCSEs, enabling them to concentrate on maths, English and sciences. Maths offered as an IGCSE now as well as a GCSE; English, French and Spanish are all IGCSEs too. For science it's either double or triple science award (even when small numbers choose the triple option, the school will support it) and exceptions will be made if a boy arrives late and wants to continue with his, say, two chosen science subjects. The modern language options are French and Spanish (but will facilitate the teaching of other languages such as Mandarin for an additional fee). No Latin, Greek or Arabic. Successful in performing arts and solid but not quite so glowing in ICT, music and PE. Percentage of A*s and As at GCSE firmly in the mid 20 per cent bracket for the last three years: 23 per cent in 2016.

BTecs in business, travel/tourism, music and sports studies, the two latter available as A levels too. Proving to be popular as well as successful – particularly business. Computing, ICT, media studies, drama, philosophy, photography and psychology are also options. Results have improved enormously over the past few years; 41 per cent A*/A grades at A level in 2016, 87 per cent A*-C, and no-one fell short of an E.

A school that celebrates its 'all ability' intake, Shiplake is creative and innovative in how it instils a healthy learning attitude in it pupils. The 'Shiplake Seven' is a mantra engraved in the breast pocket of every maroon, black and gold striped blazer (curious, open-minded, motivated, reflective, determined, creative, independent). This is enforced and reinforced throughout the academic, as well as the co-curricula. In addition there is a highly developed programme of 'flipped learning'. Students are expected to have researched a topic before a lesson – frequently teachers will have created video presentations for the pupils to watch before the lesson begins – so that the lesson itself can be used for more in-depth exploration of the issues and themes. Mindfulness is an option as an activity, but if you want your child to be educated in Happiness this is not the school for you. 'My aim is to create an environment where happiness is not taught but a by-product,' says Mr Davies.

The Thinking Space – what we would usually call the library – is modern and high-tech, but only two small neon shelves with books – this library is online. Brightly painted telephone boxes contain periodicals and store laptops. A canary yellow pod filled with cushions is where, one imagines, you might find a student or two curled up with a book (if there were many to choose from). Moving seamlessly through to The Quiet Space or Flow Room, a cool blue and white area, designed to represent the Henley regatta and the Thames. This is where students can tap away at their essays in silence and calm tranquillity.

Shiplake has long had a strong reputation for excellent provision for those with special educational needs, a reputation that Mr Davies regards with wry scepticism. Quite apart from the fact that he likes to regard each child as having a special educational need, with their own unique learning style, he feels that reputation was undeserved when he arrived here over 10 years ago. Now, however, the support provided by the learning development department is exceptional. There is a definite drive, nonetheless, to diminish the understanding that SEN is Shiplake's strength. No one in years 7 or 8 will be offered support from the learning development department. Anyone who needs that kind of support applying in those years will be told that this is not the right school. The story is different from year 9 upwards. Parents pay extra, but their sons can receive up to four 50 minute lessons per week (always replacing a modern language lesson). Seven dedicated teachers as well as two support workers give a wide range of support from small seminar subject tutoring to one-to-one help as well as assisting with organisation and study skills. We witnessed years 12 and 13 benefitting from 'guided study', given help with structuring essays and proof reading. On average about 15 per cent of pupils have access to the LDD, with a range of conditions – most commonly dyslexia and dyspraxia but also a smattering of ADD as well as Asperger's and ASD.

Games, options, the arts: The focus on sport here is evident from the number of teachers who have some kind of physical education qualification and/or interest. There is tremendous enthusiasm for sport throughout the school and this is the arena where many of the students grow their confidence and self-esteem.

Rowing is excellent. The boathouse nestles below the main building and grassy slope right on the bank of a bend in the river Thames. The Lynch, the island beyond owned by the school, makes this area ideal for adventure, rafting and camping exercises. This isn't a large school, and yet the boys who row, do very well, and it is a growing sport for girls. Three Vikings represented Great Britain in the European and World Championships last summer, winning four gold medals. A lot of enthusiastic rugby, football, cricket, netball, hockey and tennis players too. Games sessions are timetabled and there is an emphasis on inclusivity. Students who might not get a chance to play in matches in some schools will definitely get a chance if they're keen here. Plenty of pitches as well as an Astroturf, a well-equipped gym (especially for the rowers), with squash courts, charming outside pool and rather tired sports hall (scheduled to have a new roof and refresh in 2017). Enthusiastic and popular D of E, community service and CCF.

Art housed in spacious beamed roof space in the eaves at the top of one of the modern buildings. Photography in the adjoining space. Lots on display around the school. About 11 pupils do art A level each year. Busy ceramics department, a stunning life-size ram made out of chicken wire and fur ushered us there. Large DT space, four rooms with capacious work stations. DT compulsory in years 7, 8 and 9 about 28 choose it as a GCSE. Large lecture theatre where the full orchestra practises and performs. Chamber choir and auditioned-for First VIII a capella group, as well as an HM choir for those who can't sing but want to, although it sounds pretty painful. Another example of Mr Davies' natural ability to muck in. One parent cringed at the idea of performing badly on stage – the headmaster's choir embrace it and work on the motto 'choice, risk, consequence' that permeates so much of life here. Plenty of jazz groups and string groups. Winter, spring and summer concerts give them a chance to perform. Music technology with all the gear – Macs and keyboards – takes place in the comfortable, new John Turner building. Lots of individual practice rooms and all overseen by an energetic and inspiring head of music. Recent drama productions include Curious Incident of the Dog in the Nighttime (years 9 to 11) and The Jungle Book (years 7-9). Atmospheric theatre in the Old Tithe Barn area. Painted black, with black wooden floorboards and black stone walls, complete with old wood smell. We witnessed a red nosed group of year 8 boys bringing colour and humour to the place with their improvisations about the Olympics.

'One of the exceptional things about the school,' observed a parent, 'is the ability to find something in which a boy or girl can shine.' Singers emerge who never knew they could sing, and the same applies to drama, dance and all areas of school life. 'A lot of this is down to Mr Davies's influence,' commented a father. 'He knows the children so well and he learns what their needs are, how they can be motivated and inspired.'

Boarding: Five core houses from years 9-12, mixing day and boarders (though full boarders predominately live in Burr House). In addition there is a sixth form girls' house (Gilson), as well as a house dedicated to the year 13 boys (College House). Years 7 and 8 join Olympians or Titans, and attend the majority of their lessons in their house group.

Boarding comes in all varieties here and is tailor made to meet the demands of the families. The smallest number is still the full boarding pupils. 'We haven't done a full marketing push to attract overseas families,' says the school's communications director. The school feels relatively local. Flexi-boarding is popular and attractive to busy families where both parents work but can have quality time with their children at weekends. Some senior girls lucky enough to have ensuite bathrooms. Younger boys normally share their room with two or three others.

Not a lot of pupils stay at school at the weekends, but a dedicated team of housemasters and teachers as well as matrons make sure that there is plenty to do for the few who are in. We were told of a particularly popular trip to Liquid Leisure in Slough, as well as enjoyable nights out at the local curry house. Each house is comfortably (and remarkably tastefully) equipped with sofas, kitchens and games rooms with, when we visited, a delicious smell of clean laundry, and the lubricated sense of being well run.

Background and atmosphere: Situated in the luxurious Oxfordshire countryside, on the banks of the Thames only a couple of miles from Henley, but far enough from the bustle of Reading to feel secluded and remote, Shiplake Court began its existence in 1895 as family home and farm. In 1959 it became a boarding school, and it has always been smaller and a more nurturing environment than many schools of similar ilk. The site has been very tastefully developed through the years, modern buildings and windows, blending with the old, and the red brick and flint atmosphere here is calm and well kempt. Church services are a short walk away in St Peter and St Paul. Daily services are short but an important part of the routine in keeping students focused, on message, and well clad – Mr Davies will pull anyone up for scruffy attire, let alone poorly polished shoes.

Mr Davies runs a tight ship. Staff are wholly committed and everyone rows together to achieve the best possible outcome for each student. He has recently bravely tackled the modern bane – mobile phones. Now every student has to hand their phone in at the beginning the day, to be returned in the evening. Reluctant to do this initially as he regards technology as an important element in their learning, he was driven to do it after observing that young people 'rarely talk to each other any more'. The benefit has been palpable as chattering can be heard again over break and while walking down the numerous pathways.

Parents praise the communication. It's frequent, inclusive and inescapable, from everyone – the receptionist to the head – and covering everything from discipline to rewards and merits. Not a school for a fire-and-forget parent.

Sports fixtures happen on a Saturday morning – if Jack isn't in a team then he can find another programme to keep him busy (art club, LAMDA, for example). There are no Saturday lessons, allowing more family time at the weekend for day pupils and weekly boarders.

Pastoral care, well-being and discipline: Shiplake's reputation as having an exceptional standard of pastoral care is justified (we couldn't find anyone to disagree). This is founded on high teacher to pupil ratio (roughly 1:6), a highly effective school chaplain, the Rev, who doesn't teach but is the pivot of the pastoral system. Parents even go to him with their troubles ('He is your Rev too, I tell them,' says Davies). A strong system of tutors (primarily assigned to individual pupils for academic support and normally house-based, but sometimes work across houses for older students), as well as houseparent, matron and various support staff within the house. Parents warmly praise the extent to which the staff get to know their students and understand any difficulties. The school GP is excellent and is proactive about communicating with any external specialists. There is cross communication throughout the departments and houses and through to the head, and in turn excellent communication with parents. Pupils feel safe here. The structures are there to keep them so.

Quite apart from the structures, however, there is also a strong set of principles running from the top downwards. From growth mindset, the Shiplake Seven and the annual key words and phrases to mindfulness clubs and good old-fashioned exercise and fresh air, constant care and attention is given to the well-being of the students. The food is delicious – and there is plenty of it (one parent was delighted that her son eats six sausages for breakfast) with properly cooked meals, and a wide choice in the wood panelled gothic great hall plus piles of toasts back at the house. Mentoring – responsibility taken by the sixth formers for the new year 9s – is both popular with the students, and an effective way to break down hierarchies. Bad behaviour not tolerated – from drugs to bullying – and the school will not accept children with behavioural difficulties. However, Mr Davies is remarkably open minded about young boys who come to him with a chequered past, always prepared to recognise potential and give people a second chance.

Pupils and parents: Set in the heart of shiny Range Rover well-heeled territory with sky high property prices, Shiplake has plenty of parents who live up to their environment. Most parents work, a lot are in business. Some are demanding and discerning, some completely hands off, and school prefers the former. Most parents share a balanced view about exam results, and while they want their children to flourish are not obsessively competitive about how they are performing academically. Not a smart or fashionable school ('no fancy airs and graces,' said one former pupil), parents here are grounded and practical, with sound middle class values and concerned more about the right fit for their children than brand. A few Forces children, but mostly local families (the majority live close enough to be day or flexi boarders). Only five per cent of families from overseas, school looking to increase that number.

Most of the catchment is east of Reading (navigating Reading during rush hour puts a lot of people off).

Pupils here are allowed to be individuals. They are taught to be practical and hands on. Encouraged to roll up their sleeves and get a Sunday job. Work experience ideally is work in a builders' yard (no holding onto to mummy and daddy's coat tails in a law firm here). The broadness of selection helps to contribute a colourful mix of ability and personality. They come in all shapes and sizes with a range of skills, from the uber rower, to a committed oboist, with no doubt some future actors, designers and entrepreneurs in between. We were pleased to meet Will Satch, Olympic gold and bronze medallist and old Viking, who was visiting his old school. Mr Davies, clearly proud of Will's rowing achievements, was equally full of praise for his communication skills (Will is regularly wheeled out to deal with the media). Other notable alumni include Nick Jones, Soho house proprietor, Alex Pettyfer, actor, Chris Standring, jazz musician and Jonty Hearnden, antiques expert.

Entrance: Assessment is thorough, takes a day and enables school to see 'the whole picture'. A maximum of 20 pupils are assessed on any one day. Numeracy and literacy is just one part of the jigsaw. Candidates participate in a group activity during the afternoon, they are interviewed by the houseparent and deputy and finish the day with a sports activity. The question staff ask themselves is would this child be happy here – the long days, the exercise (even for day pupils there is a strong boarding ethos) – and what will they contribute to school life? A mix of 11+ prep and state primary pupils enter at year 7; the main intake, however, is at year 9. The number of girls in the sixth form has doubled, now at 47. Incomers require 5+ GCSEs (with at least a C in English and maths) though they make exceptions for those they feel will fit in. 'We will let our own boys stay on if we can find something useful and enjoyable for them to do.' Will rescue those burnt out from (or shot out of) Thames valley swot-houses.

Exit: Nearly all to first or second choice university. 'We got the pupils onto the right courses,' says head, 'played to their strengths.' A huge range of universities. Popular in 2016 were University of the West of England, Bath Spa and Oxford Brookes. Russell Group destinations included Sussex, Exeter and UCL. Applications are starting to be made to US universities. Equally wide range of courses from law and mathematics to sports development, television production and maritime business and logistics. Around 20 per cent leave after GCSE but are replaced.

Money matters: Art, drama, music and sports scholarships awarded but more for prestige than pounds. Sixth form schols depend on general aptitude test, plus test results in two subjects to be studied at A level. Means-tested bursaries awarded at the school's discretion with small pot to assist existing pupils, should financial hiccups occur.

Remarks: Perhaps the only child Shiplake would not suit is the super clever nerd. Possibly the only parents not suited are those for whom brand comes before substance. In Gregg Davies, Shiplake has found a head who perfectly reflects and holds dear those values that have made it stand out as a uniquely nurturing school for half a century and more. It is highly unlikely that anyone will leave here with a feeling of having failed; some will shine more than others but no one will be made to feel less valued. The key to success, however, is a wholehearted commitment to contributing to the community – in whatever way suits.

Sibford School

Sibford Ferris, Banbury, Oxfordshire OX15 5QL

Pupils: 413; 40 full, 26 weekly/flexi boarders • Ages: 3–18 • Sixth form: 77: 50 boys, 27 girls

Fees: Day £8,688 – £13,950; Boarding £24,747 – £27,105 pa

Tel: 01295 781200
Email: admissions@sibfordschool.co.uk
Website: www.sibfordschool.co.uk

Head: Since September 2016, Mr Toby Spence, who was previously head of Greensteds, an all-through, co-educational, British curriculum, international day and boarding school in Kenya. Born in Newcastle upon Tyne, Toby was brought up as a Quaker. He attended the King's School in Tynemouth and went on to study history and PE at Sheffield before beginning his teaching career in 1992. Five years as head of history at Bootham, a Quaker school in York, and in 2007 was appointed director of learning at Yarm School in Stockton-on-Tees. In 2011, 24 years after leaving its sixth form, Toby returned to his old school, King's, as deputy head. He began his headship in Kenya in 2013.

Toby is married to Jill and they have three young children, who are all excited about their move to join the Sibford community.

Away from work, Toby is a great outdoor enthusiast and enjoys combining this with a love of travel – a passion that has led him to paddling a sea-kayak with killer whales off Vancouver Island, making a number of first ascents of mountains in South America and sailing Tall Ships around the coast of Australia. More recently he has also taken up mountain triathlons, which he enjoys more for the views than the physical exertion.

Academic matters: Generally good facilities, including a smart, bright, well-stocked school library with plans afoot to upgrade those few areas in need of TLC. Mainly class taught in junior school with sets for the basics and specialist subject teaching for music and PE. Plenty of help and good range of programmes for those with SpLD including reading recovery.

Senior school classes are small and set independently, so it's possible to be in high group for maths, middle for science, low set for English etc – whatever works for the child. A third take triple science, usually those thinking of studying science at A level, with rest taking 21st century science. 'The course applies science, to everyday life which stimulates interest in a subject when otherwise it might not have been there,' say science staff. Enlightened approach to English setting, look at the whole child and at their ability to understand, analyse and interpret English. 'We have children in top sets who use Dragon software. Sometimes the mechanics of reading or spelling may not be there but they may be incredibly insightful with a high verbal IQ. We have to stretch them, not constantly criticise every spelling mistake or punctuation error.' In 2016, 15 per cent of GCSE grades A*/A.

Range of activities for those identified as gifted, talented or able (which includes some 40 per cent also identified as dyslexic). Sixth form pupils make guided subject choices. 'I like the freedom within subjects, the support from teachers when you need it and small classes mean lots of attention'. For the 20 per cent or so who need additional support, learning is tailored to the individual. 'We wanted a school where our son mattered as a person. He slipped under the radar in his previous school. He deserved more, so we looked for a school that would make him feel special and found that in abundance at Sibford.' Full support consists of five 35 minute lessons per week plus in-class support if needed, and consists of any combination of literacy, numeracy, fine motor and speech and language input. Super revision library display board sets the tone, with handy hints such as 'use a timetable', 'record questions and quotations onto your iPod' etc. Lunchtime activities include popular trampoline and swim sessions for those with gross motor difficulties. Regular internal audit process includes pupil interviews to ensure staff are supporting youngsters in a helpful and constructive way so they can learn to articulate their difficulties and accept that it is permissible to be dyslexic. Parents say support is impressive. 'There is no stigma, my child's self-esteem has rocketed; I cannot believe how chatty and confident he is; Sibford has transformed him.' Not a school that worries about league tables; it stands by and encourages pupils.

Music/music technology and textiles currently in vogue, with girls generally performing better than boys, especially in the sciences and maths. Good value added, though typically fewer than 50 per cent A*-B grades at A level (48 per cent in 2016, with 18 per cent A*/A grades); grades must be seen in context of intake and school's policy of allowing pupils to pursue subjects that interest them, not what shows the school in the best light. As pleased with a child who struggles and achieves four or five GCSEs at grade C as they are with the most able who achieve their fistfuls of A stars. 'We take great store by the journey to get there and the effort a child makes'. Wonderful collegiate approach means if a child hasn't understood something with one teacher, it is fine to seek extra help later, either from their teacher or from a different one. If a strength is identified, or child has a passion, staff will do all they can to encourage that. Working to embed independent learning, allows youngsters to fail then succeed. Striving for excellence, candid about where they are, 'We've climbed the mountain and can see the summit, but like a diet, it's the last push that is the hardest to achieve.'

Games, options, the arts: Something for everyone: proud of music facilities, practice rooms, recording studio, music tech and bright, light ensemble room. Plenty of bands, orchestras and ensembles – with opportunity to perform publicly, regardless of grade. Super art with atmospheric lessons; we dropped in on an introduction to pop art via the psychedelia of Sgt Pepper tracks – fun, and saw impressive displays of pottery, textiles and sculpture. All usual sports: rugby, football, cricket, hockey, netball, rounders plus squash (own courts), riding at local stables and swimming in own swish, 25-metre pool with rowing and a multi-gym on wish list. Clubs galore with youngest expected to participate in at least three lunch offerings; huge variety: knitting, science awards, board games, origami and more. Range of inter-house challenges include musicals for the creative, quiz nights for the cerebral and construction challenges for the practical. Lots of activities and entertainment including philosophy club for juniors, looking at 'how to think' not just 'what to think.'

Pièce de résistance, guided by enterprising head of environmental science and horticulture, is outdoor education; whether through science, history, gardening club or just as a hobby. Mud, mud, glorious mud, with wellies and bright red boiler suits for juniors lending a touch of the 'heigh-hos' as off to joyful work the youngsters go. Ideal for the active, inquisitive child who learns by doing, listening. Daily junior outdoor sessions, come rain or shine, bring the environment to life, while reinforcing the basics of numeracy, literacy and social skills. Senior lessons stretch beyond those of ecology, horticulture and the environment, to the economic, with plants marketed and sold to fund future ventures. The fantastic themed beds, ranging from sensory and historical (World War 2 utility garden and rotating allotment) to a sprinkling of the whacky and experimental, sit alongside a sturdy reconstruction of a Celtic roundhouse and wattle fence. We admired the student-designed prototype greenhouse built from recycled plastic bottles; very much epitomises the school's approach to learning: expect pupils to think up ideas, create designs, lay foundations, construct, kit-out, appraise, refine and improve. Has embarked on BTec countryside management and animal husbandry: expect to see pigs, sheep and cows among the throng.

Boarding: Only around 40 full boarders (do check age and gender mix) so weekends operate on a cosy, home from home basis with brunch rather than breakfast, a trip out – 'Trips are great fun, they encourage you to mix across the years' – and emphasis on relaxation and rest: no Saturday school or matches. Food much improved but not yet cordon bleu (school says 'excellent' – 'the local council's Eat Well in Cherwell scheme graded us as Platinum') and surprisingly, no-one objects to technology/gadget free lunchtimes. Houseparents mainly get huge thumbs up: 'They listen, are fun and there for us'. Around 60 per cent of boarding community is from overseas.

Three boarding houses – one each for 11-16 year old boys and girls, plus co-ed sixth form house – all refurbed over recent years and include laundry, games rooms and quiet areas. Praise for the atmosphere, camaraderie and care.

Most recent ISI inspection report described boarding provision and houseparents as 'excellent'.

Background and atmosphere: Sibford Ferris isn't a manicured Cotswold weekend retreat for city slickers playing at country life but a pretty, homely, much-loved village and community, with the school central to that. Sibford was founded as a co-ed boarding school by the Quakers in 1842. Originally housed in a splendid Cotswold stone manor house, in the 1930s it expanded into a hotchpotch of buildings known as The Hill. In recent times, the manor was sold and the proceeds astutely ploughed back into purpose-built music and art blocks, with new sixth form centre following a couple of years later. Extensive, idyllic, 50-acre grounds, include an orchard, woodland, pond and even picnic benches for students. All new year 7 pupils (and new staff) mark their arrival at the school by planting either a tree or bush.

A school with a family feel, attention to detail and few places to hide, it was a heartbeat from failing when previous head arrived. 'I could see the potential but lots had to change. The location is wonderful, I pinch myself that I am here, but the school was looking unloved and uncared for.' He wasted no time appointing a financial director and together they worked out an investment/development plan. Resuscitation was needed, but recognising it is all too easy to pour money into schools, then watch them haemorrhage, they went for the full face lift, rather than sticking plaster approach. Tough decisions were taken. School changed from boarding to a day school with boarding; a sustained and sustainable refurbishment programme began in earnest and some staff departed, not all wholly voluntarily. 'We had become the school of second choice, but thanks to our development programme and marketing initiatives we are now a conscious first choice. People understand what we are about; we focus on the child, take them as our starting point, and that is what our families buy into. The school has a wonderful local feel so we consciously restrict international boarding to 10 per cent. We'd like a few more boarders but not at any cost'.

Pastoral care, well-being and discipline: Excellent pastoral care is a given. 'It is crucial we consider long term mental health, so we start with values and relationships, not academic excellence.' Aim to develop emotional fortitude so pupils leave with emotional robustness. 'We help them balance social life and work so they don't burn out.' Daily staff briefing ensures all aware of potential pupil issues. Parents say pastoral staff never leave problems until the following day, 'They spend an inordinate amount of time dealing with issues, nip things in the bud, give time to parents, explore avenues and work out how to proceed; with child's interests at heart.' Has a deserved reputation for being nurturing and is very much the place where 'you go if dyslexic', but the perception that it is just for dyslexics no longer holds. 'They really do find the best in every single child,' say parents, adding, 'to feel special and to be good at something is incredibly important for self-esteem; our children go from strength to strength. It isn't an easy or soft option, they just have the knack of getting all children to really want to do well.' Staff know children well: 'There is no place for my child to hide, not that he'd want to,' said one enthusiastic parent, adding, 'The children are confident, they feel secure, so it's especially ideal for those who tend to be shy or insecure; it really brings them out of their shell.'

Pupils and parents: Not a 'stand aside, call me Sir' school; equitable outlook extends beyond the classroom, so expect to find staff queuing and eating with children. 'Can do, will do' attitude means there's never a lack of volunteers, even if they're not quite sure what they are volunteering for. Happy to get their hands dirty and rise to any challenge. Emphasis on team work. Lack of overt competitive edge means some parents feel it isn't a great place for those aiming for top tier sport, but conversely believe it is ideal for the bright boffin who may either struggle to fit in elsewhere or who finds the social aspects of school life a challenge. Huge praise from parents. 'It's a fantastic school. If I had known how good it was I would have sent all my children here, safe in the knowledge that all would have done extremely well. Teachers have time for individual pupils so different characters can grow and flourish.' No typical pupils but tolerance is in the blood. 'My child has a huge variety of amazing friends, some slightly weird, some terribly normal.' Few families (or staff) are practising Quakers but all buy into the ethos, with tolerance to the fore. 'My child is geeky but he fits in and is accepted.' Goes beyond the bounds to support and encourage ambition; expect to find budding artists, thespians, entrepreneurs, eco-warriers et al. A school where tomorrow's doctor will be helped and encouraged, not just to gain a place at medical school but to think fully about career paths – surgery, Africa, professorship, though always with emphasis on the importance of all team contributors, whether cleaner, technician or top-dog.

Parents from a wide range of backgrounds and income brackets, including a number of first time buyers; many very involved in school. Not a school for the pushy brigade; most choose Sibford precisely because they do want their children to achieve and do well, but that means prioritising mental health and well-being above exams and grades. Notable old Sibfordians include the late Paul Eddington, Guy Ritchie and Charlie Boorman.

Entrance: Into junior school at any time between the ages of 3 and 10. Parents of 3 and 4-year-olds can choose to enrol their child on a full-time or flexi-session basis. Into senior school at 11 and 13 with entry at other times if places are available. Pretty broad brush intake: 10 per cent gifted, 10 per cent who might struggle at hotter-houses. Look for youngsters who want to be at the school and will benefit from their time there. Good at second chances and helping those who have struggled elsewhere; Sibford picks up the pieces, stands by its brood, when other schools surrender. Often second choice school but not second best; it isn't unusual for parents to visit just to tick the boxes, then become enamoured. 'They think they want fancy facilities, labels or names but end up buying into the Quaker values and ethos; those of respect, nurturing, care and quiet ambition.'

Exit: Some 85 per cent of juniors move on to the senior school. Up to half leave after GCSEs, mostly for further education colleges, independent schools offering different subjects at A level, apprenticeships or training. Majority to university but school conscious that uni is not right for everyone; three off to study film production in 2016, with physiotherapy and engineering also popular. Unis include Southampton Solent, Cardiff, Warwick and Oxford Brookes.

Money matters: Not a rich school but offers a number of academic, music and art scholarships, plus means-tested bursaries to both Quaker and non-Quaker families. Sound financial management means the school continues to improve buildings and facilities.

Remarks: In the words of one youngster, 'It just gels; they make you feel important, believe in yourself and want to do well.' No boxes or moulds. A school with a comprehensive intake, universal outlook and concentration on the individual; not fine or fanciful but fun and fair with a flair for finding, and focusing on, talents.

Sir Roger Manwood's School

Manwood Road, Sandwich, Kent CT13 9JX

Pupils: 796: up to 56 boarders • Ages: 11–18 • Sixth form: 272: 124 boys, 148 girls

Fees: Boarding £11,385 pa; Day – Free

Tel: 01304 613286
Email: info@srms.kent.sch.uk
Website: www.manwoods.co.uk

Headteacher: Since 2013, Mr Lee Hunter, previously deputy head of Tiffin Girls' Grammar School in Surrey. A biochemist (read natural sciences at Cambridge), he first joined Tiffin Girls' as head of science in 1997. His career also includes stints as a science teacher at the Royal Grammar School in High Wycombe, the Sir James Henderson British School of Milan and Framwellgate Moor School in Durham.

Some of Mr Hunter's proudest school moments have included leading expeditions to the Indian Himalayas and introducing the Duke of Edinburgh award. Living on the Kent coast enables him to enjoy his hobbies of running, walking and cycling, as well as travelling frequently to France.

S

Academic matters: In 2016, 32 per cent A*/A and 66 per cent A*/B at A level, and 43 per cent A/A* at GCSE. A quarter take history to A level. Maths is also a popular choice with more than a third of students taking A level and others taking further maths. The school has a resident maths genius who competed last year in the International Mathematics Olympiad and was placed 30th out of 548 of the world's best mathematicians. All three sciences also strongly represented at A level. The school is designated a high performing language college, and languages offered include French, German, Spanish and Mandarin Chinese (fortnightly lessons help year 7s decide whether to take it on as second language in year 8), plus Italian as a sixth form option.

If there's a weak department, it would appear to be ICT. Given that the school has computing as a specialism, it's surprising that very few candidates take it to A level. 'It's the way the lessons are taught, it needs changing,' complain sixth-formers. This cohort were among the first to take a compulsory GCSE in business and communications systems, which has appeared to turn many off computing (although it may well be a qualification they appreciate more when they are drawing up CVs). There are plans to introduce ICT courses which students will find more stimulating and relevant, following a government review of the ICT curriculum. Student requests led to A levels being introduced in film studies, psychology and sports studies, although head says that some universities' preference for traditional academic subjects seems to be turning the tide away from these newcomers.

Pupils feel they are largely taught well, 'There are one or two teachers I wouldn't employ myself, but many are the best you could get,' said one student. It's a competitive environment, but not harshly so. 'People who arrive here for the sixth form say they are pushed harder here than at other schools, but teachers work with you, they help people who are not doing so well,' one student said.

In the sixth form group, the brainy boy off to do medicine at Cambridge comes in for as much gentle joshing as the one who has found the going harder and will be reading sports sciences. 'I was one of the people who got extra help, but it didn't make me feel that everyone else was better than me,' says the latter. Another related how effective the teaching support was. 'It was spotted that I was weak at French and I got extra help. Well, then I got an A* in my French GCSE,' he said.

SEN department caters for students with dyspraxia, dyslexia and autism and provides individual support for a pupil with visual impairment.

Games, options, the arts: Sporting whizzes will be right at home here. The head reels off a long list of current and former pupils who are competing at the highest levels. 'We're very good at tennis, we've got the under-14 number two in the country. We've allowed him to reduce his timetable and take time off school. One girl is representing the country in the under-19 MCC ladies' cricket team. Two girls represent England in the ISF World Cross Country Under-18 championship. One girl competed in the National Youth Swimming championships, and the school has produced an international hockey player who has represented GB at two Olympic games, and a member of the England ladies' cricket team.' Such high levels of sporting success gave one parent of a boy out of this league cause for concern, but she said, 'He is not sporty and I worried about him fitting in, but he quickly found friends through the CCF and music groups.'

About 120 pupils get involved with the CCF, going on annual camps, shooting days and field weekends, and D of E awards are also popular. One parent wished there was more kudos for the musicians. 'Music is tiny within the life of the school, sports and languages get much more attention,' she said. However, the school counters that music has a very high profile with lots of students learning to play an instrument, and many opportunities to play music in the orchestra, various bands, choirs and concerts. Orchestral tours have recently taken pupils to Sicily and Istanbul, and the school is 'very good for musicals' according to the sixth formers. The annual big production is open to all. 'Obviously some singers are better than others, but you can still get a part if you're mediocre,' said a student.

An internationalist approach is a big part of the school's ethos, and this sees children offered exchange visits to China, India and Germany. There are language tours to Barcelona, Madrid, Paris and Berlin, a politics trip to Washington, and a visit to the Gambia every Easter, where sixth formers work at the village school.

Boarding: It's a spacious campus with lots of green space and the two boarding houses are a stone's throw from the teaching blocks. Boys have the grander accommodation with oak floors, ornate staircases and mullioned windows (33 spaces). The girls' house (23 spaces) is nondescript but cosy. All but two bedrooms are shared. Rooms have high sleepers with desks underneath and look like every teenage girls' bedroom with mates' pictures on the walls and hair straighteners lying across the beds. The housemates are 'like a family', said a boarder. The menu pinned up featured school meal standards – the food is 'bad', lamented a boarder, although the school argues that it has been rated good by Ofsted.

Boarders' weekends are filled with a mixture of organised outings and pursuing individual interests – students can, for example, take riding lessons or go for sleepovers at friends' houses. More staff are now on duty at weekends to organise a wider range of activities for the increasing numbers of younger boarders.

Background and atmosphere: Tucked down a quiet and leafy residential street, the school is an appealing jumble of historic buildings with modern day additions such as an IT resource centre, science blocks and Astroturf. It was founded 450 years ago by Sir Roger Manwood to bring learning to the townspeople of Sandwich. Academy status has given the school more autonomy and extra funding which has so far financed building refurbishments and an extension to the sixth form common room.

Pastoral care, well-being and discipline: Asked who is most approachable on the staff, the students rattle off a long list of names – clearly it's the majority rather than the odd one. Relationships with the staff seem unusually warm. 'The teachers are friendly, they really care and they know you on a personal level,' said one pupil. 'They care about us so much, and help us so much,' echoed another. And it would seem that treating students with kindness and respect filters down through the school. The sixth formers looked genuinely surprised when we asked about any tendency for the big kids to put the younger ones in their place, and said that would never happen. A parent concurred: 'There is no rough and tumble, there's no bullying, our child has been happy all the way through'. Another parent was worried about her child making the transition from a small independent school, but she said: 'He fitted into a family incredibly quickly.'

Pupils and parents: There's an uncommon gentleness about the school, which makes it an absolute find for parents who are concerned about how their child will deal with the hurly-burly of secondary school. A few minutes in the company of these young people is all it takes for pro-single sex school arguments to crumble. There's a warmth and naturalness between the students – no macho posturing from the boys or cliquey ring-fencing from the girls. 'Our year gets on really well,' the year 13s agree.

Sandwich regarded as posher than many of its neighbouring towns on the depressed East Kent coast and free school meal numbers lower than at nearby schools. Recently the town has been hit hard by the withdrawal of pharmaceutical giant Pfizer and the loss of 2,500 jobs, although the local council is offering enticements to businesses with the aim of creating a life sciences hub on the site. The commute to London is a slow trundle stopping at all stations; parents tend to be employed locally or stay in town for the working week.

Around half of boarders are from overseas; pupils from Nigeria, Nepal, Hong Kong, Estonia and Germany bring a healthy melée of cultures and backgrounds to the pupil mix.

Entrance: Pupils must pass the local 11+, the Kent test. Children with British or EU passports are entitled to a free education here. Out of 120 places in year 7, six are reserved for boarders. The boarding places are not usually over-subscribed, but day places are. Each year around 30 cases go to appeal, with around a further six places being awarded after appeals.

Pupils come from more than 30 feeder primary schools and the catchment is just below five miles, with the majority of pupils living in Deal, Walmer and Sandwich.

Entrance from year 8 onwards via a test administered by the school. Vast majority stays on for the sixth form; new pupils need six GCSEs at A* to C, and at least a B grade in chosen subjects.

Exit: Around 15 per cent leaves after GCSEs, either for college or apprenticeships. Two to Oxbridge in 2016, others to the old guard of eg Imperial, KCL, Durham and Bristol. Creative types headed for courses in advertising, footwear design, sports journalism, dance, and musical theatre. Each year a few go on to study medicine (three in 2016), encouraged by the Claringbold scholarship from an old Manwoodian which provides an income of £1,000 per year during their studies.

Remarks: If you're seeking a school to move house for, this should be on your list. With a full hand of grade 1s from Ofsted it's unquestionably a good school, and the town of Sandwich offers a gorgeous beach, a golf course which regularly plays host to the Open Championship, creekside walks, and some of the best preserved mediaeval architecture in the country. Plus, unusually, it's a mixed sex grammar, so you can educate sons and daughters together.

If you don't want to move house, there's also the option of boarding at state school prices. Parents fighting whitened tooth and manicured nail over places in the West Kent grammars may be missing a trick here. You can get a top flight education paying only the boarding fee, a snip compared to independent day school prices in the south east.

Sir William Borlase's Grammar School

248

West Street, Marlow, Buckinghamshire SL7 2BR

Pupils: 1,081 • Ages: 11–18 • Sixth form: 419 • C of E

Tel: 01628 816500
Email: enquiries@swbgs.com
Website: www.swbgs.com

Headteacher: Since 1997, Dr Peter Holding MA BA MA (Ed), studied in both the United States and back in the United Kingdom. Highly ambitious and determined leader, who has a very clear understanding of what 'great' looks like in the grammar school sector. Achieving and maintaining Ofsted outstanding quickly became his holy grail and that remains the case.

Not the warmest, but certainly approachable, and big on celebrating individual achievement, as well as seizing opportunities to develop young people in the wider community, with a particular emphasis encouraging his pupils to mentor children in local primary schools. Values international links, with pictures of smiling pupils on recent overseas trips adorning the walls of his large and smart office, where his friendly golden retriever Henry is usually found lying in front of the open fire.

'He's a bit invisible,' reports one parent, who regularly helps out in the school. 'The people you tend to see are his deputies, whereas we'd like to see him walking around the school more,' says another, although Holding points out that's because he spends so much time in meetings, interviewing prospective students and mentoring.

Academic matters: Selective intake and consistent performance well above average across all subject areas, with the most dramatic hike seen in STEM subjects, where there is a big push to ensure girls are also on board. Although teachers can give plenty of examples of IT being embedded into core subjects, some pupils complain that computer technology as a subject in its own right is in danger of falling behind.

Historically, the school has been criticised as being an elitist, academic hothouse, but there is overwhelming agreement that is no longer true, with staff being pushy, but by not overly so. Less able students are well looked after, with parents of children of mixed abilities feeling satisfied. Less than a handful of SEN pupils, but significant resources and effort poured into ensuring they reach maximum potential.

Some mixed, but strong, views about homework, with a school survey showing that a third of parents think there's too much, a third think there's too little and a third think it's just right. 'Arguably, they are all right because each child's learning needs are different,' reports the headteacher, who believes it is further proof that the school's focus on personal learning programmes is critical.

References to some outstanding teaching and a robust learning mentor programme, in which staff and sixth formers ensure everyone is on track and sufficiently challenged. Big emphasis on student-led study, with the library dedicating significant space to entirely student-led societies in subjects such as medicine, English and physics. Great excitement from both students and staff about the evidenced impact on their learning and the fact that students from these societies have persuaded the likes of author Simon Singh and the chairman of the Institute of Physics to provide lectures. These societies also regularly persuade major companies to let them visit. Overseas trips are plentiful and open to all students, with recent examples including Uganda, Greenland and Iceland.

Independent learning is a major focus from an early age, which culminates in undergraduate level research carried out at sixth form, where dissertation titles include 'Is music therapy useful in the treatment of Alzheimer's?' And 'Do the laws of physics prevent the operation of time machines?' Meanwhile, events like Take A Risk Day, in which children do anything from cook something new to learn a new language, form part of the emphasis on encouraging students and teachers regularly move out of their comfort zone. 'One of the challenges of a grammar is that many children have never got stuck or failed and it's really important for all children – but especially these – to develop resilience,' explains the headteacher.

Most pupils take 10 GCSEs and in 2016, 70 per cent of grades were A*/A. At A level in 2016, 46 per cent A*/A, 77 per cent A*-B.

Games, options, the arts: The school earned a specialist status in performing arts in 2005 and although the specialist school programme has since disappeared, the school's drive in this subject area hasn't, with very little resistance to it being compulsory from years 7 to 9. 'The reason we went for performing arts was to counter perceptions that we are purely academic and because we strongly believe that creativity helps students think laterally,' explains the headteacher. Big push for boys in drama and dance, which has been helped by a recent Strictly event and a popular all-boys dance club.

Impressive amenities, including a top-notch dance studio, theatre and cutting-edge recording studio, facilitate an innovative arts programme, where everything from 'Roctober' to an annual 'Boscars' (complete with red carpet and bronze statuettes) are the source of considerable excitement and pride. Regular productions of the likes of Kiss Me Kate, Forbidden Planet and Les Misérables involve pupils from all years, always with an eye to reinforcing different aspects of the curriculum and individual achievement. Students are particularly proud of a stirring play about World War I, which moved around the whole school and ended in a commemorative silence. Musical talent abounds and gets due recognition within the school and local press, with no less than 10 choirs, all conducted by students, not to mention the bands ranging from rock to jazz.

Strongest sporting activities by far are rowing and hockey, with two full international girl rowers and 40-50 county hockey players. But the school offers much more than that on the sporting front, with around 20 at any one time forming the Borlase Elite Sports Team (BEST). Extra clubs and competitions exist in pretty much every sport you can think of, including cheerleading, dance, table-tennis and girls' rugby. In fact, so popular are sports and performing arts that many students wind up overstretching themselves, with the school increasingly focusing on teaching time management. But there's no on-site swimming pool and students complain the gym is on the small side.

Background and atmosphere: The fact that the Hand and Flowers (the only UK pub to be awarded two stars in the Michelin guide) is right next door speaks volumes about the affluence and charm of the area, and the school's striking 17th century brick and flint buildings do not look out of place. Inside the school grounds, expect pretty cloisters, gardens and a feeling of space, with the more modern buildings towards the back of the school. A much-loved (but overstretched) café and outdoor areas are populated by relaxed and happy-looking pupils and the school is proud of the lack of corridors and the hustle and bustle that goes with them, instead providing lots of areas where pupils can be calm and quiet. It seems to pay off – even when the bell goes for lunchtime, students walk around relatively serenely.

On the downside, the school currently has capacity for 950, but actually contains over 1,000, which means there are buildings that bursting at the seams, notably sixth-form facilities. That said, the school has plans to build a three-story development. Also disappointing is the lack of ethnic diversity, although that reflects the local area.

Pastoral care, well-being and discipline: Evidence of an ordered and respectful attitude when walking around, with rooms containing expensive equipment left open and low levels of bullying and other troubles. The school puts it down to a strong commitment to developing student voice, leadership and team skills, particularly among prefects, as well as a lot of both formal and informal mentoring. Vertical tutoring, a system of organising students into small pastoral tutor groups made up of pupils from different year groups, is highly praised by pupils and teachers alike. There are also regular surveys checking that students feel supported and have at least one main person within the school to confide in about any existing or potential difficulties.

Teachers on the strict side, particularly when it comes to uniform and homework deadlines, but with consistent and well-laid-out expectations, although low level disruption is an ongoing issue. There's a big drive on dealing with the behaviour not the child, with one sixth former reporting, 'One of the boys who was naughtiest in years 7 and 8 has just got an offer at Oxford, which I think says it all about the lack of labelling of students among both teachers and students.'

There's a sense that you can be who you really are at this school. 'There's room for every type of person,' confirmed one student. Parents agree. 'Whether you're in the nerdy academic bunch, the sporty lot or the performing arts bunch – or in no particular bunch at all – you are seen as equal,' said one.

Pupils and parents: Virtually non-existent parking ('I feel sorry for the Hand and Flowers pub!' said one parent) means parents don't feature at the school gates much, but many are very active when it comes to helping out with sport, music and drama. There's a good parent rep system that is particularly valued by parents in the first few weeks of joining, where quiz nights and other social events ensure those who want to socialise can do so, although there's no pressure. Communication between the school and parents can be hit and miss, according to some parents, but the new and improved website has helped. Pupils are respected in the community for being a well-behaved and polite bunch, and their aspirations tend to reflect their moneyed and ambitious parents.

Entrance: Catchment area shrank considerably in the late 90s and has remained relatively small, but the school is still heavily over-subscribed at 11+, with entrance by school exam. The admissions policy allows for 45 external sixth form spaces, but they normally accept 80, some from as far as Ealing. Selection on GCSE results and the school's assessment of commitment to their chosen subjects.

Exit: Some 10 per cent leave after GCSEs. Students are introduced to a wide range of professions and careers through presentations and workshops. Many go on to top level universities and colleges, with nine Oxbridge places in 2016, five medics and two vets. Other popular destinations include London, Durham, Warwick, Exeter and Bristol, across a wide range of subjects. No shortage of support for students in everything from completing UCAS personal statements to ensuring leadership, presentation and interview skills. So much so that some students complain of preparation overkill.

Money matters: This is the third lowest funded of the 1,800 or so academies in the country when it comes to money per pupil. But because lack of funding not always immediately obvious, some parents complain of getting fed of being asked to do yet more fundraising. That said, 'Build a Better Borlase' has a strong history of mobilising financial and other support from current and past parents and pupils, resulting in great facilities.

Remarks: This is the kind of school that many of the parents wish they'd been to and that pupils are very proud of. Yes, there are niggles, but they are relatively minor and the focus on creating and celebrating confident and responsible, respectful individuals who do well in their subjects is abundantly clear throughout the school. Very much part of community life and yet it feels like something of a haven from many of the typical problems that beset teenagers.

Sir William Perkins's School

Guildford Road, Chertsey, Surrey KT16 9BN

Pupils: 625 • Ages: 11–18 • Sixth form: 150

Fees: £14,358 pa

Tel: 01932 574900
Email: office@swps.org.uk
Website: www.swps.org.uk

Head: Since 2014, Mr Chris Muller BA (40s), promoted to the top slot five years after joining school as deputy head. Before that, at Kingston Grammar as head of classics for nine years, with six as head of sixth form. Preceded by identical pairing one level down (classics teacher/deputy sixth form head) at RGS Guildford, with first teaching post at St Dunstan's. BA from UCL.

Parents very happy with his appointment and approach – forward thinking that stops well short of the revolutionary, a moderate who'll keep the new buildings coming but the essential values the same and won't 'be too comfortable – or frightened of addressing challenges,' felt a mother. Packs a lot into his weeks – working an 11-hour day undoubtedly helps. Attends every event going ('girls like it that you're there'), teaches classics-related subjects to all year 7s, some year 9s and lower sixth and still manages the time for frequent, and much appreciated, corridor chats with pupils.

A bibliophile and burgeoning public speaker, managed to combine both interests in recorded online TEDx talk on the need to read, garnering 629 views (close to school numbers) but a solitary comment – 'Woo, go, Daddy' – (our punctuation) posted by a certain 'Got Mullered' (one of his two teenage children, who'll be 'thrilled' to be in print). Current affairs are another interest (he's a member of 1964 Club for Epsom and Ewell locals who 'share common values and objectives with the Conservative Party and wish to see them elected.') Currently a happy man, then. Dr Who is another interest (Peter Capaldi for prime minister?), family skiing trips his escape.

Also, like other heads, writes blog which, again traditionally, is completely comment free ('Got Mullered' clearly needs to be pressed into action again) though one parent recently told him that 'it's the first thing I look at on Saturday.' (We're delighted for him).

Sees good pastoral care as the starting point for success. Have fun, enjoy your lessons and learning without tears will follow – and is at pains to point out to parents that perfection isn't all it's cracked up to be. 'Things go wrong and that's fine – it's working out what you've learned from that missed step, that's the important part of the experience.' Lives the message – won't ask anyone to leave post-GCSEs. 'If you come here, we're committed to you for life – not going to cull anyone at the end of year 11.' Approach has community-wide benefits, he says. 'The really bright pupils see that you're looking at girls as individuals with needs and realise that "that could be my daughter one day," and they're quite reassured by that.'

Academic matters: School's correct if bloodless aims are to 'maintain high academic standards and encourage the enjoyment of learning and good habits of work'. But behind the prim words is corporate warm heart as well as big aspirations. Yes, school pulls in the grades – 82 per cent A*/A grades at GCSE in 2016 and 50 per cent of A levels (85 per cent A*/B). But achievements come without sense that they're the be all and end all of anyone's existence.

Parents are clear about who school is for – local bright, conscientious girls who'd wilt in heat radiating from area's famous all girls' academic sizzlers. 'Not about results to the exclusion of everything else,' said one. 'It's academics plus drama and dance.' One mother shook her head over friend busily cramming daughter for entrance exams elsewhere 'so could be stretched.' Challenge not lacking here but 'didn't want daughter to feel she had to run every day in class.' Another praised sensible approach to illness. If missed a few days of school 'don't feel that world will come crashing down around their ears or that have to struggle in with a temperature.'

All about 'aiming for excellence, not perfection,' stresses Mr Muller in op-ed for school magazine – something worth restating in big letters over every classroom. 'We want them to like the challenge but not create such a pressurised environment that it almost paralyses them.' Lessons notable for easy rapport between staff and pupils, from year 10 girls leaping to their feet in enthusiasm to come and explain their approach to algebra problems on the whiteboard, to selection of biology class year 10 'victims' to help label a heart. 'It's easy,' enthuses teacher. 'You say that...' replies pupil, grinning.

Reports of SEN support via parents were encouraging. Learning support coordinator (appointed to address previous shortcomings identified in last inspection) qualified to diagnose SEN and is gentle but persistent in ensuring all staff see learning needs (mainly mild) as everyone's concern. 'Kills with kindness,' says school. Currently school supports 50 or so girls, two with mild physical difficulties (hearing impairment/juvenile arthritis). May be by withdrawal from lessons (usually a language), extra help with organisation for others.

As with SEN, academic performance is a whole school issue, staff presented with results across subjects so can see struggles, strengths and anomalies – expect to add at least a grade at GCSE over baseline assessments, traffic light system used to flag up sudden dips in performance – A grade students scoring B in a test will flash red. 'Might be issues, parental or personal, so don't use as be all and end all but it's a piece in the jigsaw,' says head. Results in spot on grasp of pupils' abilities and weak points. 'Got the absolute maximum from my daughter,' said one. 'They've been right on the button with [exam] predictions.'

Won't shirk from hard-to-hear stuff – if predicted GCSE grades aren't good enough to carry on with sciences to A level (they reckon As needed to bridge difficulty gap), you'll be told. A few parents don't like the plain speaking and move schools post-16 – with mixed success elsewhere. 'Changing your school to hear what you want isn't the answer,' said parent.

Bar occasional member of staff or form tutor who doesn't quite gell and tends to move on pronto, teaching gets good all round ratings. Class sizes hit 22, maximum 25 in years 7 to 9 then drop rapidly to maximum of 12 in years 10 and 11 and to as low as one for sixth form (maximum 14, depending on subject) with overall pupil to ratio of just under 10 to one.

Maths (like French, set from year 7 – though plenty of movement as natural ability becomes evident) a particular strength. Ditto science where heads of biology and psychology hold doctorates. 'Fantastic,' said parent. 'Good, solid and organised.' Borne out in results, bar recent A level physics blip, with two D grades out of just seven entries. A one-off that shouldn't be repeated, says head.

Post-GCSE, almost infinitely flexible course options in the sixth form with core programme in lower sixth (three A levels plus life skills, leadership and PE/lectures) and assorted options, ranging from further maths to extended project or an additional AS or GCSE). More of the same in final year – six week student grub cookery course inevitably popular. If subject blend doesn't quite work for everyone first time round, school will keep on rejigging until it does.

For whole school horizon widening, there's also large, trad looking library. Oasis of calm (though 'don't want everyone sunk into stupor,' says librarian, who runs it on trust – no barriers should come between girls and reading). Little to complain of, bar one parent's sense that marginal ratcheting up of aspirations for top achievers wouldn't go amiss. 'Interesting,' said head, diplomatically, pointing to current results (eight per cent to Oxbridge) as proof that it's a far from neglected area. Academic pupils get 'stretch and challenge...to ensure fulfill undoubted potential.' Whole animal dissection is the big advertised treat for budding medics. Wouldn't do it for this reviewer but, 'we've done a rat and a squid,' beams animated sixth former. Who could ask for more?

S

Games, options, the arts: Impressive numbers learning instruments (500 or so within school), with mega spring concert the powerhouse performance of the year – though low profile among families who aren't directly involved.

Art far harder to miss, vast, high quality canvases dotting walls everywhere. Pupils' accomplished depiction of withers-wringing emotions – stigmata-studded arms; a tear-stained child draped in Union Jack; supplicant girl, holding out cup and saucer at entrance to dining hall – a tribute to benefits of catharsis, given cheery, turmoil-free public faces of their creators – at least, those we talked to.

Sport dominated by rowing with many and varied successes – regular medallists in national schools rowing championships. Currently 180 girls involved. 'The largest female rowing programme in the country,' says school, with brand new boat club on Laleham Reach. School's other highlighted achievements all individual ones – badminton, sailing, ballet – which could also do with a tad more chronology, while netball and hockey are considered by pupils and parents to be the pick of the team sports.

Incentives include natty sportswear range (duvet coats for extra swaddling on match days) and stickers – far cry from olden times silver and gold stars. Instead, there's unicorn for creativity ('don't hand out many,' says games teacher, wistfully); pearl for grit and determination, dog (sociability), bee (organisation) and tree (reflection). Just needs addition of pulsating brain symbol for staff who successfully commit the range to memory...

Usual mutterings about time and effort lavished on top teams at expense of everyone else. 'If not in the A or B team, don't bother getting out of bed,' thought one disappointed mother. 'Turn up to practice and you're going to get a match,' insists Mr Muller, while acknowledging challenge of increasingly elite nature of sport as pupils progress up the school. 'Want them to enjoy camaraderie as well as enjoying sport, but finding fixtures for them is quite tough.'

We also heard reports of staff driving to local fitness centre and enjoying a coffee while senior pupils (who had walked there) were busy exercising – a 'do as I say, not as I do' approach that could benefit from a rethink, felt one parent. School points out that car needed in case of accidents to repatriate injured pupils.

Considerable energy, in contrast, expended in organising range of trips that includes alternate years visit to Ghana – longstanding link with school there, themes woven into range of lessons (numbers of pupils with malaria nets in geography, for example) and generally impressive head-on approach to the big issues. Problems faced by LBGT community addressed in recent newsletter – school also runs weekly Stonewall group for over 16s.

Inspectors couldn't, meanwhile, get enough of Duke of Edinburgh, which garnered more separate and adulatory references than just about any other aspect of school life. Decent cohort off to Buck House each year for gold medal presentations. Run largely by devoted parents, some now qualified trainers, and the scheme's single biggest asset.

Background and atmosphere: Known informally by all parents we spoke to as Willie Perks (but to pupils by universal and unendearing acronym SWPS) it's a jolly sort of place that presents the journey to adulthood as something that, while challenging, holds the promise of being really rather fun, rather than lifelong Duke of Edinburgh expedition, shinning up increasingly sheer granite cliffs in the rain.

So, yes, there's a serious entrance exam, but experience is sweetened with bowls of chocolates dotted around. Sixth formers mastermind dazzling expositions of drama talent, writing and directing junior drama competition plays, but also create eagerly awaited Christmas pantomime, lampooning the staff so effectively that several teachers requested urgent staff meetings with previous head's doppelganger.

One parent wondered if Christian ethos that originally defined school had been getting a bit blurry round the edges and mourned passing of traditional hymn singing – 'good for the soul.' Mourn no longer. Never really went away and is undergoing a resurrection, says Mr Muller, who's also a fan.

Boys had first dibs on education when school was founded in the 18th century by successful merchant keen to give something back. Daringly co-ed from 1736 before move to present 12-acre site in 1819, and was a successful girls' grammar from 1940s until the changing political climate led it into independent sector in 1970s, where has remained ever since.

Completely rebuilt in 1914 and no problem getting to grips with school layout – just think of a figure of eight on its side. Got it? No, nor did we, but girls clearly don't take long to master logical layout. Outside are two inviting little quads, both with greenery, one with a pond. Inside, subjects sensibly housed together (only anomalies are art next to science – airy windows the reason – and DT, which gets own little building, the former gym). Corridor displays bloom like well tended gardens, from beautiful handmade fabric books created to mark year 7 trip to Southall to physics corridor (hearteningly, work that may not have the highest mark but 'show(s) good practice') and biology (colourful paper flowers).

Additional thoughtful details, from info on train times and events courtesy of 'Muller TV' (was a Mr M innovation) to sensible location of year 7s (own corridor bounded by admin at one end, staff room at the other, for easy wobble containment) make this brilliant place to grow up – and grow out of, girls loving time there but raring to go by the end. Just what you'd want, it could be argued. 'I did enjoy SWPS, but equally I was quite happy to leave when I did,' says former pupil. 'It's a lovely school, but I found it got a bit small and familiar by the time I was in sixth form.'

Top two years shortly moving into purpose built accommodation which will also house drama and music. Should stop school bulging slightly at the seams – pretty much at capacity currently – and may at least postpone ennui for future generations.

Pastoral care, well-being and discipline: School, like others, is picking up slack as government-funded services struggle. 'Difficult for teenage girl to walk into CAMHS and ask for help, so schools do need these services,' says Mr Muller. And it's not just girls who are helped. Parents are increasingly calling in for support, with school's blessing. 'We've realised that the more information we give them about the road bumps in the way of their daughter's journey at school, the more they realise it's not the end of the world.'

Former matron now relaunched as full time counsellor, though still known to all by previous title, despite school's efforts to update it 'as term doesn't capture what she does,' says head. Doesn't sweat the small stuff (sore finger, said sixth former, greeted with a brisk 'what do you want me to do about it?') but brilliant with the big issues, regular sessions scheduled as required. Felt to be particularly good at developing rapport with vulnerable pupils, including those with eating disorders. 'Daughter will go to her if a bit wound up or needs some help,' said mother.

Teachers, particularly form tutors, also felt to do a pretty neat job in pastoral care. Pupils enthused about emailed reminders to take multi-vitamins, another teacher de-thorned roses at desk as a Valentine's Day treat. 'Just like a mum at school...'

Pupils also fully involved, from school-wide mentoring, new year 7s by year 11s, who in turn have teacher to support them through horrors of GCSE preparation to sixth formers who take turns to run a listening room so younger girls can air problems. Seems to work, with bullying felt by pupils and parents to be a rare thing, friendship issues the normal bugbear. Inevitably, incidents can happen out of range of teachers but will be followed up if raised. 'I feel they do have people they can talk to,' said parent.

While supportive of the needy, zero tolerance of the naughty, with detailed behaviour policy that would make any would-be transgressor think twice, and that includes parents, who'll find their children excluded not just for drugs, violence and tampering with fire extinguishers (among other crimes) but also if fail to pay fees or are unreasonably snippy with staff. Sensible sanctions include carrying out 'useful tasks' for minor misdeeds (such as include eating food in classrooms or naughty use of make up, phones, cameras...).

Girls, in the meantime, able to be thoroughly themselves – one head girl praised for concentrated effort made in everything 'including wholeheartedly singing the wrong tune to a hymn in assembly'. Teachers, too, have a happy time here. One, formerly at tough-ish school, 'thrilled that can walk home thinking about physics equations rather than "why did the boy jump out of the window?"' enthuses head.

Pupils and parents: In contrast to other establishments notable for girls with glamorous hairdos 'sculptured into tousled creations,' thought mother, here you don't dress to impress. 'Not a lot of peer pressure on looks.'

Some parental sighing over lack of sixth form uniform and what one described as 'sloppier' all round appearance – as well as reduction in desirable role models for younger pupils. Head and pupils united in vociferous disagreement. 'Easier to learn in comfortable clothes – and it's good for us,' said sixth former. Girls look smart when need to, says head, but 'worrying about what's in their heads rather than how they look is really important – and I'm happy to argue with anyone who doesn't think so.'

Families geographically homogenous (most live within 15 miles of the school), culturally, too, affluent white Surrey dwellers and suburbanites the overwhelming majority.

Old girls in search of proper name – SWPSies? – meet up for annual catch-up and cream buns session and also help mentor current pupils. Careers impressively varied – one landing job at Network Rail following degree in ancient history (possibly researching origins of first BR sandwich...). Masses of science, too – again with welcome touch of levity – astrophysicist and BBC science broadcaster owning up in school magazine to intense boredom of PhD topic.

Active Friends of...hosts sell-out events and pulls in the donations – current target is £40,000. School also sends out leaflet with contact details for parent ambassadors, a great idea though not currently a well-used service. 'You're only call I've ever had,' said one.

Entrance: Has 100 feeder schools, state and independent (Staines Prep and Halstead both regulars), and currently running at about two candidates to every place.

Entrance exam in English and maths taken in year 6 in January. Fine with EAL pupils (currently 31) though don't normally need to offer support. Most pupils start year 7 (normally between 90 – 96) but school also offers deferred 13+ entry places.

S

Exit: Big on science and maths subjects – five medics and a vet in 2016, with Durham, Bristol and Exeter all popular. Four Oxbridge in 2016.

Sports and arts scholars presumably account for the decent showing in related courses though music scholars seem to have changed path along the way – with few currently going on to study subject at uni. A large number of sixth formers were happily undecided about what to do and praised lack of pressure to make a decision – and unlimited support along the way. 'Wasn't a case of "don't be ridiculous" but "what can we do to help?"' said parent whose daughter went on to pilot school.

Money matters: Academic, music and art scholarships on offer in year 7 and in sixth form where sports scholarship also added. Reward achievement and potential and worth between five and 25 per cent of fees. Music (at least grade 4 for year 7 and grade

7 to 8 for sixth form) comes with warning to 'consider girl's ability..to avoid unnecessary disappointment...' (We're sensing a few Mrs Worthington experiences here...) Foundation bursaries cover up to 100 per cent of fees.

Remarks: Excellent results achieved with a big dollop of humour, humanity and freedom of thought. 'If you don't excel at something, you're not going to feel that you can't achieve in other areas,' thought parent.

Would soon-to-qualify pilot daughter be tempted to complete victory roll over Chertsey on maiden flight out of nearby Heathrow out of sheer joie de vivre? 'Wouldn't put it past her,' said mother.

The Sixth Form College Colchester

North Hill, Colchester, Essex CO1 1SN

Pupils: 3,110 • Ages: 16-19+

Tel: 01206 500700
Email: enquiries@colchsfc.ac.uk
Website: https://www.colchsfc.ac.uk/

Principal: Since 1997, Ian MacNaughton BA (50s), read economics and social sciences at UEA. Previously taught at Brighton, Hove and Sussex Sixth Form College and Brockenhurst College. Also worked in a Hampshire County Council residential boarding house for 11-18 year-olds.

With his office based smack in the middle of the main college building, he is a visible presence around college, which is also helped by the fact that he usually teaches economics (although didn't the year we visited due to management and strategic demands). Students and parents describe him as 'approachable,' although inevitably in an educational institution of this size, many have no experience of dealing with him personally. Passionate about not just the college itself, but the wider FE sector – although we noticed he can be better at talking than listening when he gets going on a subject.

Interests include sports (tennis, football, cricket, running), current affairs and travel.

Academic matters: Achieves consistently strong academic results, especially given the context that Colchester has two super-selective 11-18 grammar schools that cream off the local top talent (that said, approximately 20 per cent of students from those two schools choose to transfer to the college for sixth form). In 2016, 25 per of A level grades were A*/A and 50 per cent A*-B. But the real boon here is the value added – with the college having, for many years, achieved the best value-added scores for any sixth form in the country, with students' package of A level results regularly streets above their package of GCSEs achieved prior to entry.

A whopping 55 options on offer – English, psychology, maths and biology among the most popular. Sciences and humanities do particularly well in absolute terms, while subjects that shine from a value-added perspective include English and biology. Art related subjects are both popular and get great results. Four languages on offer – French, German, Spanish and Italian, along with introductory courses in Japanese, Mandarin, Greek and Latin. No subject combination is rejected – 'as long as you get the entry requirements, we find a way' – and if you do pick the wrong course, staff help you switch. 'Both my children made alterations to their courses and they felt senior tutors were both accessible and prompt in dealing with their concerns.'

The extended project programme does well, as does IB – an average of 33 points in 2016, including one student with the maximum 45 points. Students are also able to do a variety of courses leading to GCSE (usually retakes), including a one-year 'improvement' (Advanced Foundation) programme. Special programme available for those wishing to apply to Oxbridge, medical schools and other competitive career areas. 'My daughter wants to do medicine and the college could not have helped her more. She feels very prepared.'

Plenty of praise for the high quality and accessible teachers. 'If my daughter is worried about something over the weekend, she'll email her teacher and 99 per cent of the time, they'll email her back. Support seems to be around the clock.' 'They spend lots of extra time with students individually in college time to make sure they are on track.' Students told us, 'they don't force you to work like they do in schools – they gently motivate you through engaging teaching and high expectations.' 'At school, you do the work because you know you'll get told off by the teacher if you don't – here, you do it because you want to. It's a totally different mindset – and one that really prepares us for uni.' Classes are lively and engaging – with students giving regular presentations in English lessons; lots of experiments in science; plays in history; debating in politics etc. 'You never get lessons where the teacher just talks from a textbook and you take notes.'

The fact that teachers only teach this level and age group is a major benefit to students as they are completely specialist and don't have to worry about younger year groups or other syllabuses, points out the principal, who adds that plenty of resources are made available to students to read around their subjects. 'Two of my teachers have a PhD,' said one student. Some students quibble that classes can feel a bit big at 20, but other classes have only a handful – with an average number per class of 17.5, according to the principal.

All students have access to one of 120 personal tutors, who are in turn supported by senior tutors, with other specialists on hand for individual counselling, careers and HE information. All students get a regular (termly) review of their academic progress. There's also a student mentor programme, run in most departments. 'This is brilliant if you want someone to explain something to you in a different way to the teacher,' a student told us.

The learning support centre takes up a whole on-site house, where a team of 17 staff provide support for those with learning difficulties including dyslexia and dyspraxia, as well as physical disabilities or health (including mental health) needs. 'Some of our students have really quite high care needs,' says the head. Others use the centre for help with study skills, with regular workshops on issues ranging from coping with anxiety to creative writing. 'I came here to get help with handwriting – they were brilliant,' said one student. The buildings and outside areas are 99 per cent adapted for those with physical disabilities, and one student with complex medical needs told us, 'the college could not have been more accommodating with my regular hospital appointments and need to use the lift when in college.'

Games, options, the arts: Students are expected to embrace at least a few of the 100 extracurricular opportunities, which range from sign language to Shakespeare club. 'If you just want to study qualifications, this is not the college for you,' says the principal, although two parents we spoke to told us their children hadn't embraced this side of college life. For those do like the idea of a more rounded education, there's D of E, Amnesty International and plenty of outside speakers, in addition to the clubs. There's also a pre-teaching programme, which involves around 90 students going out for two-hour placements on a weekly basis. There's an active college council, with six main committees (social, arts, charities, sport, environment and international), and students can also apply to be student ambassadors and peer mentors.

No shortage of sports on offer both on and off the curriculum (with around 200 doing sport and PE at A and AS level), with facilities including an onsite sports hall and all-weather courts, in addition to which the students have access to a range of facilities around town – including Colchester Rugby Club, a local leisure centre pool and local squash, football and tennis clubs. Core sports are soccer and basketball, with a growth in volleyball, with the college regularly doing well all three at competition level – while the more unusual sports include boxing and tchoukball. 'We have a big push on getting girls more involved in sport, including in rugby, football, basketball, netball and hockey,' says the principal. Lots of sports programmes eg of team squads, community sports leaders awards etc.

Atmospheric art department, with a fabulous art school feel, including lots of natural light and impressive works on display. 'I just come in here to hang out sometimes – it's so relaxing and reminds you what else is going on around the college,' one science student told us. Courses include photography, art history, graphics, textiles and sculpture – all of which are also on offer off as extracurricular. Drama and art also popular, with courses including music, music tech, dance and performing arts – the latter of which is a popular option at university. 'I'd love to have a big auditorium for 1,000 people, but we have a very good drama studio for 300,' says the head. Students rave about the Shakespeare drama club, among others.

Long list of day trips and residentials, ranging from day trips to Stratford, Colchester Zoo and local nature reserves to history tours to Berlin, Holocaust memorial trips to Poland and a regular German exchange. There's also the opportunity to undertake voluntary work abroad, including to South India with the Russ Foundation to work with orphan children and blind women. The students raise funds to take over – often to the tune of £10,000, and even have a shop on site for this purpose.

Background and atmosphere: Located on a historic town centre site, right on top of Roman ruins – 'a boon for archaeology students.' A school occupied the site until 1987, using the original building which dates from 1912 – then the college took over, giving it a significant face-lift and large new extension, with a maze of newer buildings having been added onto the site in the years since. Now, the feeling is largely of a purpose-built college, with plenty of natural light and spacious classrooms and study areas – and generally well-equipped facilities. The most recent additions are the Pavilion facility, a uber-modern building dedicated to student study and social areas, and 58 North Hill – an house that was adjacent to the college, but which is now on site and has been converted into the learning support centre.

'There's a feeling that the facilities are really invested in, and that the site is constantly being updated, whether that's new desks or fans right through to whole new buildings,' said one student. Most departments have a glass-walled staff room by the entrance, so you can see who's in and who isn't and there's a noticeboard in each faculty, with named photos of all staff, 'which really helps when you're new.' The two refectories serve hot and cold food, although lots of students also head into town for lunch or to Starbucks, Costa etc when they have a free period. Well-stocked library, with an upstairs silent study area.

The atmosphere is relaxed and informal – with students wearing their own clothes and on first name terms with teachers. Inside classrooms, they're attentive and enthusiastic and during recreational time – when corridors and outside areas can get a bit congested – they're chatty and jovial, but not unruly. 'It's not uncool to want to work and be involved,' one student told us. 'There's a strong sense of community,' said another, who pointed out that students are expected to be in college five days a week.

Pastoral care, well-being and discipline: Not all 16-year-olds are self-motivated, natural self-starters – but if your child is, there is no reason they shouldn't thrive here, even if they have the odd wobble. 'If you have a problem, your personal tutor is always on hand and they sort things out quickly,' a student told us, adding that there is a very high level of individual guidance, 'which can help stop things escalating in the first place.' Also ensuring a strong pastoral system is a team of counsellors (some staff; some voluntary), a health worker, the study support centre and peer mentoring. And as staff only work with this limited age group, they come to know the kinds of issues they face, says the principal. 'We are very big on progression for students – and I think that helps too,' he adds. 'If students have a clear sense of where things are going for them over the next two to five years, it can help enormously with meeting short-term targets.' The main challenge pastorally is mental health, he says. 'It's a growing problem everywhere.'

Transition is well thought out, with new students eased into this more adult world with an induction day in the summer before they start. Meanwhile, the extracurricular focus helps them build friendships beyond their courses. 'Students tend to bring friendships from their previous school, but make many more during their time here,' says principal.

'They're strict on punctuality and deadlines, but that's about it,' said one student. 'Even then, they don't tell you off or chase you. They just make it clear that if you don't put the effort in, they can't help you and that, really, there's no point in you being there.' Principal claims to have 'virtually zero' discipline problems. 'This is voluntary education – people choose to come here and we make sure they're committed before we take them on,' he explains, adding that permanent exclusions are non-existent and temporary exclusions very rare. 'When they do happen, it tends to be for not complying with work, rather than any behavioural issues,' he says. 'But generally, we tend to resolve those issues well before they reach the "You're not coming in, so what's the point of you being here?" point.' There are good frameworks in place to counter bullying which is, again, very rare.

Pupils and parents: 'There's a real mix of personalities and backgrounds here,' say students, and there's a higher ethnic intake than you might expect from the location, albeit still small – 12 per cent non-white compared to six per cent for the whole area. All come from with a 12 mile radius, mostly by bus or train if they live any distance. We found them a mature and dynamic bunch – and clearly happy. 'They are keen to do well – they enjoy learning.' Past students include Dermot O'Leary (TV) and Joe Twyman (co-founder of YouGov).

Parents feel involved via parents' evenings, reports, 'and we know we can call the teachers or principal too.' 'Not much of a sense of community among the parents – but you wouldn't expect that at a sixth form college,' said a parent.

Entrance: Students wishing to do A or AS levels – who form the majority of the 3,000 students – generally need a minimum of two Bs and three Cs, 'but there's flexibility when it comes to individual courses,' says the principal. 'So you might have three Bs and not get on a course or one B and four Cs and get to do three A levels.' 'On paper, I needed a higher grade in art GCSE than I actually got because I missed my art exams, but they agreed to look at my portfolio and accepted me off the back of that,' said one student. For IB, students specifically need a minimum of three Bs from GCSEs in maths, English, a foreign language and a science. Vocational options vary but criteria is generally lower.

Applications available from the time of the open evening in October until the closing deadline in January. All candidates must be between 16 and 18 when starting at the college and all are interviewed face-to-face. College also requests previous school report. Fear not if you're worried about picking the wrong course – there's plenty of help on offer, with many of the interviews overlapping into careers advice, and you can always change later if it really doesn't work out.

Around eight per cent from independent sector. Currently only fractionally oversubscribed, largely thanks to the college having expanded dramatically, although the principal expects this to change when the area comes out of its five-year demographic dip. 'Colchester is a popular growth town, with the biggest percentage rise in Britain,' he adds.

Exit: Over 80 per cent to university (some after a gap year or art foundation course), to a wide range of destinations. London universities, UEA, Leicester, Sussex and Southampton particularly popular. Most popular subject choices include sciences, law, architecture, economics, English, history, philosophy, art and creative arts. Twenty medics in 2016, and eight to Oxbridge.

Money matters: Parents are asked for £30 contribution for the two-year stint – towards facilities and insurance for school trips. A £20 refundable deposit also required for text books.

Remarks: An upbeat, hard-working, can-do culture exudes from every nook and cranny of this college. Not for students who expect to breeze through, but a fantastic option for motivated young people. We were left in no doubt about how well they respond to the high expectations of the college, which are well supported by a brilliant tutorial system and plenty of individual guidance and support. A highly recommended bridge between school and university.

The Skinners' School

St John's Road, Tunbridge Wells, Kent TN4 9PG

Pupils: 978 • Ages: 11–18 • Sixth form: 250

Tel: 01892 520732
Email: enquiries@skinners-school.org.uk
Website: www.skinners-school.co.uk

S

Head: Since 2013, Mr Edward Wesson MA (early 50s). Educated at Tonbridge, where he was head boy, and at Cambridge, where he read law. 'Dabbled in journalism' and worked on the Sevenoaks Chronicle before training as a teacher. 'I became a teacher because I knew it would be a lot of fun,' he was overheard telling a pupil. Taught at New Beacon, Sevenoaks and Wellington School, Somerset, followed by 12 years at Hampton, where he became head of sixth form and master in charge of cricket. Was deputy head of Reigate Grammar for four years and then head of King's Tynemouth for three years before moving into the state sector as headmaster of Skinners' – although he says Skinners' also has 'the DNA of an independent school'. He teaches history and politics and is married to Susie, also a teacher; they have two young daughters. He is a keen sportsman and still loves his cricket, and goes to the theatre whenever he can. Approachable and easy to talk to, although boys say he is 'quite low profile' and they don't really know him. 'He does not shirk discipline and is strict but fair,' said a parent. He presides over the weekly whole school assembly and attends matches and concerts, and 'he comes across well and makes a good speech and really cares about the school'. He attends the teenage forum (school council) and is heading a drive to limit the amount of time boys spend staring at screens. He is a governor at Skinners' Kent Academy which Skinners' sponsors and says both schools benefit from the cross pollination.

Academic matters: Most pupils take 11 GCSEs, with 66 per cent of grades at A*/A at GCSE, 60 per cent A*/A and 88 per cent A*/B at A level in 2016. There are no current plans to introduce the IB. Specialist status in science and maths with best results in these subjects at GCSE, especially physics and maths, with maths, physics and geography being the most popular at A level, along with English and history. Sciences taken as three separate iGCSEs and some take maths early.

Works with a local school to increase the range of subjects, especially in sixth form. TWGGS (Tunbridge Wells Girls' Grammar) girls come over for German and PE and boys can go to TWGGS for Spanish and psychology. Dedicated languages building and all study French and German in Year 7; boys can do either or both for GCSE. French trips to the Loire, exchanges with schools in Vannes and Avignon, and a German exchange with a school in Bonn. Latin has been reintroduced at KS3.

RS GCSE for all with an emphasis on philosophy and ethics leads to some interesting discussions. Skinners' own tailor made course on thinking theories, techniques of problem-solving and evaluating ideas for all of years 7 and 8. Civics programme in sixth form involves critical thinking and gives space to discuss challenging ethical questions via lectures and visits from outside speakers. ICT and computing offered up to GCSE including website design and data handling, all in well-equipped IT suites, and there is a strong focus on internet safety in the lower years.

Well-resourced careers library with careers co-ordinator. Careers advice through PSHE in lower years and boys encouraged to find work experience after GCSEs. Sixth formers offered talks from visiting speakers and presentations on student finance, studying abroad and the UCAS form. Own biennial careers fair and all are offered a careers planning meeting with an external advisor.

Teachers hardly ever leave but attend regular courses to keep up to date; there has been a recent influx of new young teachers due to retirements and nearly half are now women – boys always address them as Sir or Miss.

Full time SENCo and a qualified assessor for dyslexia, dyspraxia and other difficulties– about 60 boys need some support; a few on autistic spectrum and currently two statemented children. Help tailored to individual needs with either one-to-one or small group work. A counsellor comes in weekly. Most able given extension work within the classroom and are stretched and challenged through a wide range of societies but otherwise no special treatment.

'Although the school is super selective, it is not a pressured environment, and individual targets are set for each child; boys never feel inadequate and streaming is very sensitively done,' said one parent. Another thought that 'the ethos of hard work and achievement can be quite daunting for some, and the emphasis on independent study can be difficult at the start', although 'we don't get tons of homework,' said our guide approvingly.

Games, options, the arts: Sports grounds at Southborough, 15 minutes' walk away with five rugby pitches and a football/cricket pitch and running track. Big emphasis on rugby, which is taken seriously, and good parental support at matches with teas provided by parent volunteers. Recent leaver playing for Harlequins and others go on to represent their county or region. Fierce rivalry with The Judd grammar school at Tonbridge. While some parents say that rugby is still a major focus of school life, another said, 'There is much more on offer now for non-rugby players' and there is a 'conscious effort to accommodate boys not into major sports', who are allowed to give it up after the first term. 'If a boy is not mega-sporty it is not an issue, as there are plenty like him,' said the mother of a boy who does not enjoy rugby. 'The school is putting more focus on the creative and sensitive aspects of being a boy and not just rugby'. All have to do a minimum of three hours of sport a week and there is something for everyone – the school is becoming increasingly good at badminton and basketball, in new sports hall with its own climbing wall and winter cricket nets. Good range of sports clubs, including tennis on own on-site courts, and shooting. Strong cross-country running – much of it done through local clubs. Football lower profile, and keen footballers tend to belong to local clubs. Hockey training at Tunbridge Wells Girls' Grammar and a local hockey club. Boys tend to be health and fitness conscious, said our guide, and the fitness suite is 'sixth form heaven' with weights and a cardiovascular section.

CCF, with its emphasis on self-reliance, teamwork and leadership skills, is popular and enables the school to offer outdoor adventures with the army's support. D of E recently established with huge take-up. Active music scene with about 60 per cent learning an instrument and a music room, bristling with computers, which is open all the time. 'Music is fantastic with a huge number of clubs,' said one parent. 'If a boy is musical he will be catered for'. Two orchestras, choirs, swing bands, big band, jazz band and chamber orchestra with regular concerts. Music offered at GCSE and A level and one boy doing grade 8 saxophone. Drama increasingly popular with three performances per year including a senior production in on-site multi-purpose theatre. They also team up with TWGGS for drama.

Art compulsory for the first three years and housed in a light, bright space with a wide range of media offered including installations, film, graphics, sculpture and photography. Parents' Association helped fit out the junior art room with digital cameras, a projector and a sewing machine. Art popular at GCSE with a high proportion getting A*s, and a handful take art A level – sixth formers have their own art room and recent trips have included visits to Berlin and Amsterdam. Impressive GCSE and A Level art shows, art displayed around the school and art students also involved with stage painting.

Good range of lunchtime and after-school clubs including sports, music, debating and baking as well as academic societies, and year 7s are given tasters in their first term. Year 10 takes part in the BBC School Report at the Tunbridge Wells studio, and a sixth form group recently returned from a 10 day Model United Nations trip to Harvard and New York, and came within the top five internationally. Recent history trip to Krakow and Auschwitz. Others have included Morocco, Iceland, Madagascar and Ladakh.

Background and atmosphere: Founded in 1888 by the Worshipful Company of Skinners with 53 pupils. The burghers of Tonbridge were not happy that Tunbridge Wells had been chosen for the site of the new grammar school, and this led to the foundation of The Judd the following year; and so a fierce rivalry was born. The school still occupies its original site in Tunbridge Wells. Even in the 1930s space was at a premium, and there were plans to move to Southborough, but World War II got in the way and only some foundations were laid – still visible in the corner of the playing fields. Most of the architectural styles of the last 130 years are represented somewhere in the school. Main school is the original Victorian building, and there have been many additions over the years. The stark, concrete 1960s block still known as the New Wing houses refurbished science labs (new lab recently completed) and the dining hall, where whole school Monday morning assemblies take place. Then there is the 1980s Knox Wing classroom block and the 1990s Leopard Building, which houses maths and ICT. Byng Hall, an ex-Victorian church institute acquired in 2002, used for music and the performing arts, won an award for its sensitive conversion. The Cecil Beeby Building houses modern languages, and fine sports hall was opened in 2012. Planning permission has recently been granted to turn the little-used old gym into an art and literature building, new sixth form centre and library, but school is still hoping for funding, and it will be at least two years away.

Strong sense of purpose about the school; 'Boys are proud to be here and proud of what it stands for as part of the community,' says the headmaster. The school is proud of its green credentials and holds the eco-schools green flag for sustainability.

Pastoral care, well-being and discipline: Instant expulsion for transgressions beyond the pale eg supplying drugs. Our guide said he 'could not imagine anyone being caught with drugs'. Effective team of heads of year, tutor groups and teachers means that there are prompt interventions, and bullying dealt with quickly and effectively. Pastoral care consistently praised by parents: 'My son has thrived there and he has been really looked after,' said a mother. 'They focus on the child as a whole and embrace them for who they are. I always feel I can email or phone if I am worried and I feel I am listened to'. Others commented: 'The pastoral support is outstanding – if a boy needs help there is always someone to talk to'. 'It is a very inclusive school and the older boys look out for the younger ones'.

Sixth formers have a new common room with study area, and sixth form prefects act as mentors to years 7 and 8 and assist in the running of tutor groups. Senior boys have to apply for these positions and attend an interview and are then given support and training. They help year 7 settle in and explain to them what is on offer.

All look well turned out in smart uniform with blazers with the school emblem of the leopard and edged in the school colours, each slightly different to signify the house, school tie in house colours and dark trousers. Sixth formers wear a suit with collar and tie.

Four houses with strong house loyalty; inter-house competitions like sport and debating. The food is good with plenty of choice and a salad bar and there are often international themes. 'My kids love the school dinners and it's reasonably priced – very few bring in a packed lunch,' said a mother.

New boys are given plenty of support settling in – the head of year 7 visits as many boys as possible in their primary schools, induction afternoons and a parents' evening are held in the term before entry, and boys are likely to travel to school together are put in the same form. Year 7s start school a day early so they can learn how the school day works before everyone else returns.

Pupils and parents: Largely middle class parents with very few children eligible for free school meals – school is trying to redress this on entry. Parents generally very supportive as they are 'happy their kids are here and support the ethos'. 'Boys are spirited and happy in an unforced way, and loyal to the school and to each other,' says the headmaster. 'There are some real scholars but most enjoy school just as much for friends and the extracurricular activities as the academics.'

Famous old boys include Christopher Hogwood (classical musician), Nick Knowles (TV presenter), Bob Woolmer (England cricketer), Jamie Spence (golfer), Tony Eldridge (war hero – the 'human torpedo').

Entrance: Entry via the Kent Test, or more formally the Kent Assessment Procedure, in the September before entry – those with the highest scores offered places first and then those who live closest to the school. Five pupils on free school meals admitted as priority if they have sufficient test scores. Oversubscribed many times over – four applicants per place.

Some 85 per cent come from 75 different primary schools, with St John's being the biggest feeder, and the rest from local prep schools, especially Rosehill in Tunbridge Wells. The other 15 per cent come from up to 20 miles away. No siblings policy. 'The Kent test is now much more difficult to coach for but it doesn't stop people doing it,' says the headmaster. About 20 boys join the sixth form from other schools and need an average of 48 GCSE points (between A and B) from their best eight GCSEs. This also applies to those already in the school, and most progress to sixth form – priority is given to current pupils.

Exit: Hardly any leave after GCSEs (five per cent or so) and just one per cent at the end of year 12. A handful go straight into work after A levels but most go on to university. Sixteen to Oxbridge in 2016; six for medicine, nearly all to top 30 universities. Exeter and Nottingham currently very popular; biggest subjects, engineering, English and economics. Extra Oxbridge help and interview practice. One or two to art college most years. Most join the Old Skinners' Society when they leave and become 'Leopards'.

Remarks: A consistently high performing grammar school where boys are happy and well supported – they come out with good grades and go to good universities, from whence there is a well-trodden path into the professions and the City.

South Farnham School

Menin Way, Farnham, Surrey GU9 8DY

Pupils: 788 • Ages: 4-11

Tel: 01252 716155
Email: info@south-farnham.surrey.sch.uk
Website: www.south-farnham.surrey.sch.uk

S

Headteacher: Since 1988, Sir Andrew Carter OBE BEd, maths specialist (60s). 'A complete character who runs a very tight ship and expects a lot from his staff,' says one mother, though 'Doesn't expect to be called "Sir",' says another. Small screen star of BBC 2 head swap series and numerous educational programmes. Twinkly, avuncular, chatty and hands on. Fast on feet, moves in mysterious ways, one moment arranging chairs for assembly, the next shifting toilet blockage. Enjoys being out and about rather than confined to pin-neat, pleasant office. Approachable, all parents have home phone number – 'Never misused'. Abolished answerphone, lines manned 8am to 6pm. 'Why let children agonise about problems which can be sorted out quickly?' Oozes understated authority from every pore, living embodiment of the word 'dapper' though trad exterior – sports jacket/parade gloss shoes combo – disguises voracious appetite for change: infant department takeover and academy status completed just months apart. Lives locally, wife Mary also teaches there, grown up children attended. Sees inevitable high profile as part and parcel of school's central community role and relishes it. No plans to hand over reins any time soon. 'This notion of retiring is a funny business. Why would you do that?' Gleeful at abolition of compulsory retirement age, cites Churchill's third age achievements. Dreams of day South Farnham named in same breath as iconic public schools, nationally recognised shorthand for educational excellence.

Entrance: Non-selective, over-subscribed, sense of fabulous sweetshop surrounded by disappointed parents pressing noses to glass. Now 90 places at 4+, two more classes added at 7+, many from four feeder infant schools. After standard queue jump priorities – looked after children, siblings – success hinges on home to school distance. Dozens of families, turned away outright, don't even get that far. No wonder local estate agent pays for website link.

Exit: Majority to highly thought of Weydon School; significant minority to leading independents including Salesian, Royal Grammar School Guildford.

Remarks: Currently one of the nation's top performing primary with 135 plus children – that's four classes' worth – regularly hitting Sats level 4 or better at KS2 – KS1 results excellent as well. Puts boot in commonly held belief that with primaries, small equals beautiful, with consistent year in, year out demonstration that bigger substantially better.

Detractors might point to affluent locale as significant unfair advantage – annual fundraising total of both parents' associations, separate for infants and juniors, now closing on £30,000, is a pointer. Surroundings undeniably attractive. Infants – sensitively modernised Victoriana – cheerful interiors, disabled lift. Tardis-like, appears tiny at front, opens up to reveal idyllic wooded valley setting and generous running around space, veg garden producing harvest soup for all, sensory garden and – a rarity – heated outdoor pool.

Juniors, spacious with enviable facilities '... better than some secondary schools, ' said parent. Architecture – best-quality 1930s municipal, topiary-fronted, much improved and deceptively square-shaped – 'It took me two terms to find my way round,' said year 6 guide. Grandfather clock and scholarship board residual reminders of pre-1970s incarnation as girls' grammar, Joanna Trollope rumoured former teacher.

Outside, seven acres of space with grass, Astroturf – school regularly does well in matches – dipping pond and attractive courtyard area complete with looming model heron. Inside, two floors of vibrant corridors with eye-catching displays – letters from linked Japanese school, all 42 Unicef Children's Articles, year 6s cover one a week – link classrooms, five libraries and six art rooms – some large, others bijou – well-equipped ICT suite that children – ultimate praise – vote better than home PCs. Jewel in the crown is the two dance/drama studios, gym, hall and practice rooms all much in use for large-scale, multi-cast Christmas/summer shows, plus spring concerts. New music block added in 2015.

But while it's lush, especially with surroundings, all pitch perfect winding lanes, detached homes (frequently bordered with vaguely intimidating noli me tangere high hedges) pupils come with normal range of needs – currently 147 with some form of learning difficulty, 87 with EAL needs. 'We take whatever the community gives us,' says head.

Educational community flocks to touch hems of these particular academic gowns – it's an elite National Support / National Teaching School – and no wonder, given way staff work with raw material, spinning it into results gold. Lesson quality outstanding but tip of the iceberg – it's the 90 per cent under the surface preparation that's magic weapon, achieved by talented, well-led staff, average late 20s, mostly women, cohesive, happy, talkative, incredibly hard-working – who are the true ingredient X. Inevitably many are high-flyers on way to greater things elsewhere – 'We've had people leaving here after three years to become deputy heads,' says head – so high(ish) turnover. For occasional few the intensity, though undoubtedly rewarding, simply too much. No shortage of talented replacements, however, with first-class internal training programme helping many teaching assistants qualify as teachers.

Adds up to environment where no child in need of a helping hand allowed to slip through net. Junior class size of 35 headline figure but misleading. Emphasis is on differentiated learning, with 30 teaching assistants – all in training, many teachers in waiting – and seven personalised learning specialists making it happen and true child/adult ratio of 13:1. Is piloting super-size classes of 60, with experienced teacher backed up by two newly qualified teachers and two teaching assistants. Able pupils stretched – members of National Association for Able Children in Education while from year 1, rigorous monitoring identifies any literacy/numeracy stragglers, 'Often the ones at back of class, not putting up their hands,' says teacher. They'll have separate sessions – up to five a day by year 6 in small focus groups, covering same work as higher ability group, nuanced to iron out any difficulties en route.

Forensic attention to detail sounds dry but translates into enthralling, nth-degree planned lessons. Even usually drab spelling notebooks burst with colourful doodles as children encouraged to create own aide-memoires for tricky words. Chalk and talk clearly discarded long ago in favour of lessons where individual work prefaced by engrossing group activity – 'soundscape' recreating Dickensian London for year 6 pupils, teacher stomping round room as plausibly crabby Scrooge – in costume, too, children in character as cringing street urchins – so riveted that, unusually, not a single head turns for visitors, though could have something to do with sheer volume of traffic as everyone from VIPs to visiting teachers beats path to this educational nirvana.

Other comprehensively scotched myth is that big means noisy. Lack of volume takes some getting used to – you almost welcome (rare) sight of child pushing ahead through doorway – though reassuringly less Midwich Cuckoo than well-tuned powerful car. Teachers uniformly soft-voiced, children ditto. Seeing them en masse, a blue-jumpered sea of tranquillity in assembly a revelation to anyone assuming that little eddies of fidgeting/chat, countered with mild adult irritation were an educational fact of life.

Inspirational teaching must help. Hand in hand with this is top-down faith in the children. Year 3s taste responsibility from word go as message bearers. 'We don't get that many notes home and it's left to the children to tell you,' says slightly shell-shocked mother.

There's unsupervised break time access to practice rooms – conflicting rhythms, keys and styles fight for supremacy in the corridors. Children get say in casting decisions for many large-scale, multi-cast plays that are highlight of school calendar. Also decide when to have lunch – delicious, freshly cooked, at least two mains and puddings, fresh bread on the side, unobtrusive wastage/veg consumption checks, standing invitation to parents to eat with child – late bell reminds latecomers to get a move on.

Instead of convoluted rewards vs sanctions system common elsewhere, trust is the big motivator. No house points, no 'honour of the school' sticks or carrots – indeed, children politely puzzled by notion. Significant that exceptional good – or bad – deeds yield the same result, chat with head, who does his best to tease out mitigating circumstances in cases of problem behaviour and tries to resolve with child before escalating to contact-the-parents stage.

Result is children with quiet confidence of people who know what they're about, behave and do well because of 360 degree assumption that they'll want to. Tangible sense of purpose and pride in accomplishment. 'I don't know anybody in the school who isn't interested in something,' says year 6 boy.

Parental niggles minimal with exception of parking. Infant school has parent-assisted 'stop and drop' system. 'They get your child out and you can drive on. If they had something like that [at the junior school] it would be amazing,' says one mother.

So is this a one-off establishment or something others could replicate? 'Every school could be [as good],' says head. 'There's many as good or better. When we work with other schools, the key element is the striving for success and the total belief that it can happen...You've got to have an ambition.'

Sees job as sacred trust. 'When you grow up, you need to be stimulated intellectually, spiritually, emotionally, physically – all of those things. If any one of those is diminished, the rest are diminished as well.'

In the meantime, this remains a jewel in educational crown, demonstrably good at what it does, fortunate in its focused, dedicated staff and making a virtue of its size, producing happy children whose quiet confidence and pride in their many achievements is a pleasure to witness. Head says, half jokingly, 'I'll be here till I die.' Parents even now probably organising whip round for Elixir of Life.

Steyning Grammar School

Shooting Field, Steyning, West Sussex BN44 3RX

Pupils: 1,946; 125 full boarders • Ages: 11–18 • Sixth form: 495 • C of E

Fees: Day free; Boarding £9,060 – £10,725 pa

Tel: 01903 814555
Email: sgs@sgs.uk.net
Website: www.sgs.uk.net/

Head: Since 2013, the energetic and insightful Nick Wergan (40s). He began his career in investment banking before retraining as an English teacher in 2004; then rose rapidly after being dubbed Outstanding New Teacher of the Year (2007) by the National Teaching Awards, through posts as head of English (Sackville School, East Grinstead) and deputy head (Blatchington Mill, Hove). He's resourceful and decisive, empowers his teaching team to lead and role model leadership for the pupils, and this delegation means he can also turn his powerful brain to looking at business partnerships to help with the funding crisis that dogs state schools, no matter which party sits in power in Westminster.

He has a house on site in the Elizabethan part of the school, but also owns and lives on a vineyard nearby with his family – producing award-winning sparkling wine. This pragmatic mix of localism and global business is at the heart of his tenure. He looks to local secondaries (through Challenge Partners network) to keep Steyning Grammar striving to be its best, trumpets the school's 400 year tradition to make new legacy connections, has a conference phone on the table in one of his two offices to enable frequent management communication across two sites, and tweets and blogs avidly. He teaches English to year 7 once a week, and students say he pops in and out of classes, corridors and the canteen, working closely with the head boys and girls to take the temperature of the school too.

Academic matters: Reflections on learning are intrinsic to the school success – whether that is implicit in weekly year group assemblies (hall only holds 350); explicit in the title of the school's newsletter; or sustained through what has been created through the IB learner profile, even though the qualification is no longer on offer here. (Few state schools in the UK can afford it financially now after funding cuts.) The size of the school means that over 30 A levels and just as many GCSEs are on offer, class sizes normally 24 with 16 (restriction in practical subjects) to 20 at A level. In 2016, 22 per cent A*/A at GCSE and 75 per cent got 5+ A*-C including English and maths. At A level, 31 per cent A*/A and 50 per cent A*-B.

Years 7 and 8 are in the Church Street site, so their atmospheric classrooms have parquet floors and a maze of doorways leading to subject-based areas. Learning is far from low tech, though; there are banks of computers and we saw a fizzy drink can that had been rigged to record sound. At the other end of the tech spectrum, a class loved building the rock cycle using plasticine. The library was buzzy with authors visiting and pupil volunteers, and an enterprise day involved a pitch to businessman Lord Sugar. However, by the time they have made their GCSE choices pupils are panting to get the open corridors and swell of new students in the Shooting Fields Site. The latter is dominated by the huge and successful A level specialist sixth form, which feels more like a college but with the pastoral support of a school – a real draw for the third of students who join for GCSE.

Tutorials are one-to-one and a curriculum reform back in 2013 means pupils now do fewer topics but more richly. Project-based learning is electric here; the pupils love it and the opportunities it provides to anchor their academic subjects in the practical and take the experience back into the classroom: a trip to the European Organization for Nuclear Research in Cern; Kimmeridge for biology and geology; the Globe Theatre; Oviedo for Spanish.

The learning resource centre is not just about books – a remote access system means students can log on at home and avoid emailing documents back and forth. The mezzanine level is the sixth form domain and students congregate here even in break time, a sure sign of their commitment to learning – they also gather in the canteen and a learning zone behind that.

A trial period of the 'show my homework' app pleases parents as well; they like to log in and see what needs to/has been done and by when. Kahoot gamifies learning in conjuction with an interactive whiteboard; apparently a warm up to a class can get pretty heated.

Engaging teachers make for the most popular A level subjects, maths, politics and chemistry at present – science labs have loads of space for practicals, which might have 16 in each class compared to 20 in extended subjects. The school is a member of 250 Challenge Partners, in a hub with three Brighton secondaries sharing constructive collaboration and challenge to improve practice and so the education of their children – the leadership team finds it a really valuable to have such critical friends. During the GCSE years the pupils become responsible for booking their parents' appointments and act as their guides on the parents' evening itself – family feedback is that this independence works well.

The Cuthman Centre is a separate building that acts as a haven for the more vulnerable students (category 3 SEN), eight at present with specific learning difficulties; they have roll-call or more casual tea and toast there when needed, and there are NHS nurses, a counselling programme funding by pupil premium and enabled by GP referrals. In-class SEN support with learning support mentors is targeted and the impact evaluated: it ranges from laptops in exams for those with illegible writing to an SEN passport created with parent and carers. The gifted and talented (now More Able) are supported outside lesson time with book clubs and an Oxbridge programme.

S

Games, options, the arts: Competitive sports are netball, rugby, football, rounders and cricket, with fixtures against both independent and state schools across the county – and the Marylebone Cricket Club. The site itself has two rugby pitches and a football one hidden behind a line of trees, while sixth formers have free access to the town leisure centre adjoining the school – they can use facilities such as the pool, squash courts and dance studio (external reputation for good boys' dance). They also love the chaos of the sixth form sports day with its wheelbarrow races and Fairy Liquid slide. The equestrian team (pupil-owned horses) trains at Hickstead. We saw a game of rounders being planned using the computer suite below the boarding house – a wet weather PE lesson. If PE is not a GCSE choice, then pupils have non-competitive sport a couple of times a week.

The music department is thriving with ticketed performances each season and 20 A level students, but would love more space (who wouldn't). Logic is used for composition on Macs, there are opportunities for mixing with the use of the live room. Plenty of individual practitioners eg a boy playing the violin, guitar, piano; a ukulele and keyboard in a shared room in the boarding house.

Art and technology is exhibited throughout the halls of the school – and the drama hall is open to the public. The whole school competition is Steyning's Got Talent – some kids think it is profoundly uncool, others use it as a springboard to more public performances across the county. Full school performances such as The Wedding Singer might involve 300 people in the six-night production – set, backstage, make-up as well as performers.

The 50th school anniversary trip to the Norfolk Broads had just passed when we visited and all were proud that they are the only school still doing it, despite Health and Safety hobbling. Jailbreak is another riot of a challenge where the whole of year 13 is locked up and has to escape from the science department windows, source vehicles, collect permits and get to Horsham for their recapture. This, and other initiatives such as Macmillan coffee mornings, Pink Day, Comic and Sport Relief, all add up to raising around £15,000 each year for charity.

Wilton Park is nearby, the only branch of the Foreign Office outside London, and interns from there come to work with the More Able – this gives rise to a foreign affairs discussion group, tackling topics such as Syria and Ebola. For prospective medics and vets there are established links with Brighton University and timetabled prep. There are opportunities for students to become equalities, digital or eco-commissioners, do Duke of Edinburgh award and Young Enterprise, as well as lunchtime enrichment activities and independent learning working across year groups.

Boarding: On the State Boarding Schools Association committee and in the second tier of state boarding in terms of numbers. The first state boarding school to be judged outstanding by Ofsted under the new framework – in every category, with no recommendations to make. Since the school cannot make a profit, there is a limited return to invest in the boarding; the major advantage of the provision is the diversity of students. The boarders take enormous joy in their international mix, while grounding themselves by earning money on shifts in the canteen and volunteering.

Four boarding houses, two adapted and two purpose built, all with live-in houseparents. The pupils share rooms in the younger years, and are really joyful about the different cultural traditions that they get to experience, from jollof rice on Nigerian Independence Day to Chinese New Year; they promote their differences yet all order takeaways together. In the most modern house the year 13 pupils have a wet-room shower/ toilet ensuite; they prop their doors open to their shared corridors and apparently are very responsive when told to turn their music down – 10.30pm curfew in the week and 11pm at weekends. The (mostly) boys watch the Premier League on their laptops; they have an ironing board and a kettle in their shared kitchen; when fending for themselves they eat toasties and pizza since Health and Safety dictates there is no proper oven. The houseparents lend their kitchen when a bake-a-thon is organised for charity and a list of suppliers is amended weekly to taste eg Marmite, jam, squash, milk, biscuits, bread.

The girls have photos as well as their names up on their doors – the images are taken by a photography student, whose work also features on the achievement board; this is the most obvious sign of a real sense of supportive celebration of peers. One girls' common room is huge and more homely, with desks for quiet study places too, since this is a realistic experience away from home, with scheduled time for work, although laundry returned to your cubby within a day would be unusual at home...

Facebook photos posted (eg rocket club with powder paint ejected from a parachute) and well dones handed out by the houseparents for being tidy and general good, with prizes drawn at the end of term – once it was a helicopter ride! There is chance to pitch to a 'houseparents' dragon's den' for a new piece of equipment, whether a freezer or a pool table. As elsewhere, technology is used to facilitate rather than trumpeted for its own sake: Skype interviews for prospective boarders; applications scanned and emailed in; Wifi or ethernet with hotspots means that Skyping home via an iPad is easy; WhatsApp is used to tackle awkward time differences.

Background and atmosphere: Founded in 1614, turned co-ed in 1953 and now spread over two sites in the small Sussex town of Steyning with architectural styles ranging from chocolate box Elizabethan black and white, through classic 50s secondary modern school architecture, to the super functional and crisp boarding house, not yet a decade old. It was boys only before the turn of the millennium; now it is equally co-ed and non-selective (apart from the 125 boarders), and the leading school in the country on character-based learning. The latter is now at the centre of the curriculum – teaching, assessing and reporting home on learning characteristics like grit, growth mindset, curiosity and zest.

The 'Steyning family' is made up of children who are encouraged to take risks so that they are not afraid of failure, and staff who are set on preparing the next generation to take over – 'the sooner the better!' says the head. The ethos of the school is printed large on boards in both sites, and the children are resilient and well-supported through exam and everyday academic pressure. The infrastructure for boarding, with the 125 teaching staff and 150 support staff, helps to produce excellent outcomes for disadvantaged students in particular. The staff tenure is traditionally long (30 years is not that unusual), since it is a big school with plenty of space to develop and enough room for children to escape a parent/teacher's shadow. The results are above national average, so it is really the staff's continuing challenge to find the hook to secure each student into a love of learning, demonstrate stickiness in all relationships and make sure they discover how to apply all this both in and outside the exam hall.

There are plenty of huts that deal with the overflow of lessons from this huge school; however, the head is collaborating with local industry to scratch backs and improve the school's facilities, and make those research links even stronger – funding has just been won to demolish the huts and replace them with a new classroom block.

Pupils bus in from local villages (two-thirds), are dropped off by their parents, or walk if they are lucky enough to live that close. Far from an inner city urban intake, but everyone is aware of where they stand in the wider society – boarders from the Caribbean come across occasional piercings and extensive LGBT support, the local village kids taste cultures from Barbados to Spain, and parents say, 'it opens up everyone's minds'.

Busy, big and teeming with children at break time – especially in wet weather, when they head to the gym, eat lunch in the classrooms or the school canteen. No hall large enough for a whole school gathering, but the split site means that the pupils have a real sense of progression and responsibility, from getting a key to their own locker in year 7 to wearing their own clothes in the sixth form, and using the canteen as a study space as well as one to eat in. Those with food intolerances struggle to enjoy mass meals produced within a tight budget, and the low maintenance cashless system means some parents worry about students selecting from a tempting array of sugary snacks instead of some of the healthier fruit.

Independence is highly valued here, and pupils often ask teachers for help on what suits them best in terms of learning as an individual. The staff are committed and respond swiftly and with initiative; the 400 year heritage adds gravitas when looking for aspirational connections. Ofsted, the State Boarding School Association and C of E status are all three seen as important benchmarks, but by no means the most important measure of the school's success.

Pastoral care, well-being and discipline: Both school and year councils provide feedback on issues such as uniform, the colour of leavers' hoodies, the learning resource centre, internet access to YouTube research etc. Prospective head boys and girls write a letter of application, then the school participates in an online survey, meaning year 13s get some input even though they are leaving – then they must pitch with a speech to the whole of the boarding cohort.

Horizontal pastoral system through year head and form tutor; the tutors have 12 students each and the learning mentors 10. Their aim is to personalise the school – whether that is via checking in at the Cuthman Centre and munching a piece of toast or through Pizza and Paragraphs for English Support. Growing confidence is vital, and the classes of 24 are a practical maximum to enable that.

More casually, there is supported (by the heads of year) revision in the dual purpose school canteen – peer mentors enable paired reading and might meet for breakfast in Bøltons (one of the boarding houses).

No truancy, no smoking on site and no drinking. If a kid impacts the learning in a classroom then they are removed from that classroom. The student could end up in the Cuthman Centre, then a follow up and reintegration. Blazers must be worn in the corridors and using of phones in classes is at teacher discretion. The range and policy of sanctions is reportedly reassuring for kids who have been beating at the boundaries at other schools; 'It's different here, you know what to expect'. The documentation and communication of the next steps is vital for everyone involved. Academic, social or emotional barriers are identified and everyone gets analysing, understanding and working together – parents and grandparents included – with reflection and using principles of restorative justice. Head says, 'we see the best of the students' behaviour at school...'

Pupils and parents: Local, rural and coastal catchment area encompasses a huge range of parental employment – multinational companies, small business owners, teachers; families will relocate and buy within the area to ensure they can get access to such a good state secondary education. A state boarding school can be a niche choice for many students – from Northern Ireland, Antigua, Denmark, to name just three.

The live Twitter feed on school trips is much more reassuring for smartphone equipped parents than interesting for the pupils back at school – likewise the Facebook page. Pupils arrange their own social lives, which is part of the independence that the school aims to build, and since so many walk, ride or bus into the school there is very little chance to of casual school gate friendships between parents.

Entrance: Strong relationships with primary schools such as Steyning Primary, Upper Beeding, Ashurst, Jolesfield in Horsham, Henfield. Catchment is 200 square kilometres encompassing Henfield to Rydon, from schools such as The Towers Covent, Shoreham College, St Andrew's High School, and Durrington High School. The local authority handles the year 7 and year 9 intake. Only boarding is selective, and that is about balancing fit and gender in a year group, aiming for 50 per cent of each sex. The sixth form is amongst the largest in the south east of England and only started marketing in 2013; before that it was just word of mouth. As a level 3 course provider (A level and equivalents), the admission is usually a B or above in the subject of choice.

Exit: Up to half leave after GCSEs. After the year 13 leavers' celebration – they get into limos and head off to a club in Worthing, thrilled there is no room on site for something more low key – 70 per cent head off to higher education. Destinations and subjects range from Guildford School of Acting to history at Exeter; six to Oxbridge in 2016 and two to study medicine; others attracted to the reduced fees in Holland or by the established link with Harvard in the US.

Money matters: No fees for tuition, just for boarding; discounts available for up to three siblings.

Remarks: A grammar school by name only, non-selective with a huge sixth form and all the curriculum choices that size enables. Diversity of boarding provision enables the broadening of everyone's minds – from Sussex villagers to Caribbean islanders.

Stowe School

Stowe, Buckingham MK18 5EH

Pupils: 796: 684 boarders • Ages: 13–18 • Sixth form: 350 • C of E

Fees: Day £24,780; Boarding £34,470 pa

Tel: 01280 818323
Email: admissions@stowe.co.uk
Website: www.stowe.co.uk

S

Headmaster: Since 2003, Dr Anthony Wallersteiner MA PhD (40s), Cambridge history scholar and art historian, married to Valerie, three children. Previous two posts were at the academic powerhouses of St Paul's and Tonbridge, but in Stowe he has discovered his nirvana. Charming, impressive, a maverick with a keen sense of fun; on arrival we said, 'Think sired by Stephen Fry out of Nelson's Column with a trace of HRH the P of W and Boris Johnson somewhere under the blanket. He is frank, relaxed, confident, charming and unstoppably chatty.' Plus ça change plus c'est la même chose. 'He is inspirational, lacks ego, delegates,' say staff; pupils add, 'Dr Wallersteiner is friendly, funny and fun; he gets involved, chats to us, knows our results and how we are doing but doesn't pigeonhole.' Parents equally enamoured: 'Simply magnificent. Not an intellectual snob: he just gets the best out of all in the most charming way.'

Dr Wallersteiner's appointment was no accident. Stowe was in the doldrums, needed lifeblood and direction but, with a dictum of academic excellence, nervous onlookers twitched; would this erudite polymath try to morph Stowe into another A* and Oxbridge hothouse with selection limited to the bright and bookish? Or, would his vision be the panacea? 'I wanted to return Stowe to the glory days, to its founding principles, but with a 21st century twist. We used to stand shoulder to shoulder with the great public schools: Eton, Rugby, Harrow; Stowe was renowned for being idiosyncratic, for looking after the individual, encouraging them to pursue interests with enthusiasm, allowing characters to emerge – Leonard Cheshire, David Niven – Stoics with an innate sense of confidence. Branson in the 60s probably typifies what it is to be a Stoic and that's what I wanted to inject into the place. Old Stoics have set the world alight; I want that to continue'.

A perfect fit for the school, precisely because he didn't always fit at school: a boy whose prep school reports tell only of a time waster, a lazy boy who would never amount to anything. Yet his final school report dazzled; a cerebral scholar heading for Cambridge. Inspirational teachers unlocked both talent and a desire to learn; masters lit the flame, he uncovered a universe. 'You can't underestimate the power of a teacher in transforming lives. I want the pupils to find their passion and drive, to be inspired and to inspire, to love learning, to appreciate the beauty of life, to be creative, to find their Utopia. You have to be so careful with children: they remember the time they were told they were thick or stupid, it sticks. If you say they will never amount to anything that one line can define their experiences, motivation and determination. A teacher should stand up, perform and remember that the hundredth time for them is still the first time for a child.'

Academic matters: Dr Wallersteiner has moved academic rigour centre stage: 'I didn't want people to apologise for coming to Stowe'. Pupils are motivated to achieve, some aiming for traditional paths, medicine, economics, others for courses we had never heard of – lots keen on the environment with study to match. Head passionately believes if one path is blocked others should be tried, so good teaching and openness to new ideas, delivered in a supportive environment, are the priority. 'I watch some staff teach and feel so humble: many are masters of their craft, they are inspiring and motivating.' He pleads the fifth amendment when we quiz him about weaker departments and staff, but concedes not all are centres of excellence, though says the pockets are getting bigger. Drive to improve teaching and learning has included time spent looking at how all individuals learn, not just those with a recognised need. Teaching has new blood, greater monitoring and evening clinics for everything; if you don't get it first time round, there is always a second chance: 'A child's brain has to be unblocked with sympathy and care'. We met dyslexics who enthused about help not just from support staff but across the board.

Value added is excellent and confidence high; results fine given the comprehensive intake. A level results generally on the up (nearly 29 per cent A*/A in 2016), and 49 per cent A*/A at GCSE in 2016. Latin and Greek remain, chemistry and religious studies popular options, DT – the Cinderella when it comes to provision – as favoured and successful as ever. Head wants the school to embrace the estate and hopes to offer farm-orientated courses in the future.

Games, options, the arts: Heart and soul spring to mind – whether trout fishing or trotting, beagling or bugling, singing or shooting, running or reading. All do CCF or D of E with push towards community work. Sport strong, with national representation in rowing, cricket, rugby, lacrosse, golf, fencing and equestrian events. Teams draped in accolades too – top the National Schools' League Table for cricket, first division lacrosse champions, with similar levels of success for polo, hockey and rugby. Superb facilities: playing fields, assault course, a new golf course, courts, sports hall, climbing wall, fencing salle, fives courts, and pool. Latest offerings include a scrambling track (shiny motor bikes) and brand new equestrian centre with 20 stables. Bring your own horse or ride one of the rescue ones. Key winter sports of rugby, hockey and lacrosse cede to summer offerings of leather on willow, athletics and tennis, with polo, rowing, sailing, clay pigeon shooting and golf just some of the country-club offerings.

Strong art and arts – several to art school – annual arts festival encompasses science, sport, dance, music, art, drama. Music popular, plentiful, oft polished with weekly, summer al-fresco performances the perfect backdrop for picnicking parents. New music school. Stowe also boasts its own radio station with resident DJs plus weekend nightclub (kitted out from the remnants of Crazy Larry's in London) hosting high-octane party nights, ranging from themed skiing to bungee runs and magic.

Boarding: Twelve boarding houses in total, all comfortable with kitchens and communal rooms. Boys envious of newish, purpose-built accommodation for the girls (en-suite rooms) which boasts in-house gym, pool room etc. Care is delivered in abundance with everyone from cleaners and caretakers, housemistresses and academic staff on hand to help, plus close liaison with parents, as befits a proper full boarding school.

Background and atmosphere: Breathtaking, such stuff as dreams are made on; so resplendent that romance, not tragedy, be inspired; imagine Isolde sailing into the sunset with Tristan, Anthony falling not on his sword but into the arms of Cleopatra, Romeo living happily ever after with Juliet. Youngsters adore the place: 'Once you get here you never want to leave; when it snows, it looks more magical than Narnia.' The 750 acres of parkland and sublime landscape gardens are widely regarded as most significant in Europe and the embodiment of 18th century enlightenment. They include exquisite woods and waters, temples and gardens.

Campus is surprisingly compact with boarding houses, courts and other facilities nestled cosily in sylvan wilderness. The main building – 'the mansion' – is a splendid, neo-classical palace, largely modelled by Robert Adam in the mid-18th century and benefiting from the respective geniuses of Sir Johns Vanbrugh and Soane, William Kent and Capability Brown among others, and became a school only in 1923. Buildings have had massive numbers of facelifts, so few blots remain. We were in awe of the library with its magnificent ceiling (part of an £8.8m restoration) but less enamoured by the 1960s science block – now, however, refurbished with six new labs and a sixth form study centre.

In 1989 house and gardens passed to the National Trust and opened to visitors – much restored, Plug Street, named after the village of Ploegsteert south of Ypres, at the southern end of a famous series of long tunnels, is home to the school's nerve centre. This stone-flagged, below-stairs administrative centre includes the head's breathtaking study – 'Sir John Soane in gothic fantasy mode' – a mini replica of Henry VII's chapel in Westminster Abbey with fabulous fan vaulting, lead canopies, brass screens and tracery. Grandeur yes, but if London and the bustle of the city set your child's heart racing or, when visiting, they see fields not dreams, Stowe may be a county too far. 'It is a tight-knit place, but can be too claustrophobic for some,' say pupils.

Pastoral care, well-being and discipline: All eat together in super dining hall overlooked by three Knellers. 'Food is simple but tasty with plenty of variety,' say pupils. Head sees every child on their birthday. 'It's a good opportunity to chat to them, find out what works, what doesn't.' We quizzed the pupils on vices and sins: drink and drugs? 'Compulsory and random testing. Second chances may be possible but never a given'. Bar for sixth form but random breathalyser catches those who transgress. Eating disorders? 'Careful monitoring and being there for friends,' with a comforting 'putting friend before confidentiality and informing staff', if things look serious. Cyber bullying? 'Fairly recent exclusions, discussed openly and frankly in both assemblies and pastoral time so all informed and understood.' Not that there are many transgressions these days, but the press hounds round at the merest whiff of a wrongdoing. Google the craft knife incident if you must but remember virtually all schools have skeletons somewhere; Stowe's are in the open not the closet.

Pupils and parents: Eclectic accepting place where cultures and languages mix. Attracts the solid and the decent plus oddballs and those who might be overlooked elsewhere. Blend of high flyers and spiky IQs: 'We like those', confided the head. Pupils, formal in approach, are polite, grounded and know how to behave and interact. 'They are confident and entertaining, the sort of person you want to sit next to at a dinner party,' say staff. Parents a mix of entrepreneurs, academics, old money (lots), new money (handful), country, creative and celebrity. 'Stowe may look posh but most of us aren't,' say pupils; parents add, 'A few are from wealthy backgrounds but equally some live in modest semis with parents who struggle to find the fees'.

Entrance: Handful from state schools, rest from a range of preps, including Winchester House, The Dragon, Summer Fields, Ashdown House, Papplewick, Sunningdale and Windlesham. School is no longer the 'back-up plan' but a conscious first choice. Pre-tests in year 6 or 7; looking for 50 per cent plus at CE and happy to take a chrysalis and nurture until a butterfly emerges. 'When I interview prospective pupils it is not high grades that are important, though they are welcome, but there must be a spark, something we can ignite. I look for success – however small. Plane spotters, stamp collectors, ferreters, budding astronauts, entrepreneurs, the imagined destination less important than the drive and journey.'

Exit: Majority to a broad spread of universities – usually a couple to Oxbridge (two in 2016, plus three medics and dentists) and others to the Courtauld, SOAS, Bristol, Edinburgh, Exeter, Newcastle, Warwick, Manchester, York and UCL. One or two to US. Business-related courses popular. A considerable number to good art schools, with some going to highly-acclaimed music or drama schools.

Money matters: Range of means-tested scholarships (more about honour than finance). Means-tested bursaries available, a small number of fully-funded places for exceptional candidates with proven financial need. Additionally, Roxburgh schols (named after Stowe's revered founding headmaster) awarded to outstanding all-rounders nominated by the heads of their previous schools. Stephan schols available for bright day pupils from the state sector – worth up to 25 per cent of fees, with further support from bursaries as with other scholarships.

Remarks: 'My son loves it, there is so much to do, he is flourishing, has great friends – boys and girls – like a huge extended family.' Captivating from first glimpse to last breath, something for everyone. Mixes the erudite with the sporty and studious, with space reserved for the eclectic and maverick. Ideal for those keen to learn within, and beyond, the bounds of the classroom; but if your sights are firmly set on bright lights, league tables and brags about academia, Stowe is ready for you but you're probably not yet ready for Stowe.

Summer Fields

Mayfield Road, Oxford, Oxfordshire OX2 7EN

Pupils: 237; 204 full boarders • Ages: 8–13 • C of E

Fees: Day £21,738; Boarding £28,071 pa

Tel: 01865 454433
Email: office@summerfields.com
Website: www.summerfields.com

Headmaster: Since 2010, Mr David Faber MA Oxon (50s); came to Summer Fields as old boy; former parent and governor, as well as grandson of illustrious alumnus, Harold Macmillan PM. After Eton and Balliol, became a Conservative MP from 1992-2001, including Opposition spokesman foreign affairs (recently secured schools minister as a speaker for a meeting of prep and public school heads). A keen cricketer (sits on MCC committee) and has introduced new cricket nets to the fields; also referees boys' football matches.

Interesting appointment as not originally from a teaching background. Urbane and reserved in manner until on the subject of the boys' achievements – fond collector of past medals; 'sporting caps' and historical mementoes of the school. Uses his experience as a historian and author (two books on modern history) in teaching history to the older years and lecturing on 'Appeasement and the Munich Crisis' to public school history societies. Popular with parents ('dream headmaster'), who have seen him institute 'a lot of changes for the better, one thing at a time'. Makes himself available to the parents and appears to know the boys by name and character. Married to Sophie, not on school staff, with two school-aged daughters and a son at Oxford University.

Entrance: Boys are selected by assessment day, which includes written tasks (English, maths and non verbal reasoning) and informal interview, along with an all-important report from current school. Early registration necessary, but occasional late entry places and mid-year starters also accepted. Special assessment day for the Maclaren Scholarship – up to 100 per cent bursary for a year 6/7 boarder given to a high-flyer, usually from a state primary. Academic and music scholarships at 8. Head refers to it as a 'national' prep school, with most coming from within an hour's drive of Oxford; some overseas and regular group of Old Summerfieldian sons. Previously thought of as upper-crust, and hasn't entirely shaken off the image. Head disagrees, but one parent regretted the narrow social compass. No plans to take girls or to increase much in size – emphasis on keeping a tight-knit community, especially in chapel and dining room.

S

Exit: About 60 per cent to Eton, Harrow, Radley and Winchester. In 2016 20 scholarships were offered to 17 boys by Eton, Harrow, Bedales, Wellington, Radley, Harrow and Oundle. They covered academic, art, sports and outstanding talent. Head maintains, 'Proof of the pudding is that the less academically able boys still get into public schools'. Parents like the fact that it doesn't feel like a 'feeder' but still gets great results.

Remarks: Set in over 70 acres of stunning grounds in the heart of North Oxford, the school is unremarkable from the front, but boasts a stately bow-fronted building with fields, woods and river at the rear. Founded by Victorian educationalist husband and wife team, Maclarens, in 1864 and still conscious of its Christian traditions with Victorian chapel and oak-panelled hall. However, there are more modern additions of several smaller houses along adjoining road; two pools (indoor and outdoor); a sports complex, Eton fives courts, a climbing wall, new all-weather tennis and Astroturf courts, as well as golf course and cricket nets and new very large sports pavilion.

Very long day for both boarders and day boys, starts with whole school convening for chapel or assembly. Lessons in small classes (10-17) and early setting promote strong academic results at CE. Scholarship class in last two years given Greek, and Latin and French learnt by all. New DT and ICT suite and science labs, where boys encouraged to 'design your own experiments and make things pop', as well as large, busy library. Boys genuinely motivated by trips to Oxford museums and field trips, including to France. Teaching staff visible round school, as most live in, some of long-standing (30+ years); 'most staff leave to become a headmaster somewhere else'. Academic success earns boys personal and house points which can be enjoyed by tangible rewards in the school shop ('Buzzer') and a house feast. A staff of six for learning support, with some experience in EP support and statements. One parent felt that it was particularly good for boys who aren't particularly socially confident and so may experience difficulties elsewhere.

Lodges (boarding houses) for boys of same year group; run by husband and wife team and kept apart from the teaching rooms (no homework or dining in lodge). Remarkably neat dorms, sleep 4-6, with effective in-house incentives for boys to change own sheets, polish shoes and tidy up. One parent commented, 'What I like is that Summer Fields doesn't smell like a school'. Generous but confusing system of 'credits' allows boarders extra weekends out above normal exeats. Pastoral care is managed with a three-tier 'belt and braces' approach. Lodge parent claims, 'Homesickness is more of a problem for the mums' than the boys, who are kept busy in the evenings with board games, computers and giant chess sets. Parent of a young boarder was hugely relieved how easily the youngest were settled in. Discipline maintained by healthy competition and withdrawing privileges rather than anything more gruelling. Boys appear to appreciate this.

Music is a strength, with a dedicated music block and theatre. Three choirs, one with adult voices, sing in Oxford colleges and on tour (Rome recently). Specialist music staff allow boys to take up to three instruments (we heard of a 10 year old playing four), ranging from conventional to electric guitar, even quirky. They recently hunted down a Marimba (eastern xylophone) teacher in Oxford for a lad from the Far East. Drama productions for different year groups from Twelve Angry Men to We Will Rock You, open to all those who risk taking time from their scholarship clubs. Sport is plentiful and all-inclusive; parents like the fact that all boys make the teams, which play twice a week. Football has recently had its best season since 1937; rugby and hockey also strong, with some players in county cricket and rugby teams. Prolific art and ceramics studio, obviously not PC – fantasy coats of arms and big game trophies made from papier mâché adorn the walls.

Boys emerge from lessons brightly but quietly. They are articulate and confident, although suspiciously neat and clean in brightly coloured shirts and sweaters. Parental niggle that boys were 'a bit too polished'. However, children appear kind and supportive – 'when you are in the third year you know everyone's names' – and a nice touch that both staff and children refer to the school as 'We...'. Boys don't seem fazed by formality or overt competition – academic progress bulletins are posted on the board every two weeks for all to read – but seem to enjoy it as 'healthy rivalry'. There is a wealth of extra-mural activities, spanning spiritual (Time for God group), sporting (fencing, shooting, polo) and more earthy interests (cookery and Adventure Quest – bushcraft-style camps – for handy skills in lighting the campfire and skinning a rabbit).

An appreciation of the school's history is encouraged with scholars' boards lining the walls of the hall; and a moving remembrance day service, when choral speakers read out names of the fallen alumnae. Boys follow this up with a trip to the Somme. Old Summerfieldians include generous helpings of baronets, colonial civil servants and military leaders as well as Dick Francis, who set one of his detective novels at the school. Active old boy links suggest happy memories.

A small and cosy school, in a serene and beautiful setting, successfully eases a boy in to a boarding career. It provides a breathtaking array of sports and music facilities as well as being reliable in placing boys in top public schools. Sense that boys work hard/play hard and turn out to be happy, considerate and polite, if slightly formal. Not for Just Williams.

Sunningdale School

Dry Arch Road, Sunningdale, Ascot, Berkshire SL5 9PY

Pupils: 110; 100 boarders • Ages: 7–13

Fees: Day £18,180; Boarding £23,400 pa

Tel: 01344 620159
Email: headmaster@sunningdaleschool.co.uk
Website: www.sunningdaleschool.co.uk

Headmaster: Since 2005, Mr Tom Dawson MA PGCE – and recent distinction in grade 1 piano (40s). Previously taught at Harrow before taking over the shop (school is fully owned by the Dawson family) inheriting headship 'because I'm the boy,' he jokes (slightly).

Family-run is understatement and a half. Wife Elisabeth, fellow modern languages graduate, is highly organised director of studies, garnering almost as much praise as husband. 'Lovely' 'kind' and their ilk crop up in conversation with parents with Swiss railway regularity.

Amy, a jolly Dawson sister, one of three (others educationally occupied elsewhere) runs high quality art department and masterminds school productions, more fulfilling than previous career as mural painter (only so many David Beckhams you can glorify on child's bedroom wall without spot of existentialist angst).

Also living and working on site are Mr Dawson's own parents and uncle, who acquired school as going concern in 1960s and are a genial background presence, mother putting final touch to colossal flower arrangements, father waving from ride-on roller. 'Keeps them going,' says their son.

We wondered about sotto voce presence of school parents, who don't, currently, have own association. 'Don't need one,' says Mr Dawson, who points to numerous 'meet the Dawsons' opportunities at well-attended matches, concerts and exhibitions. Parents, professing ardent faith in his leadership, fall over themselves to deliver several carillons' worth of ringing endorsement apiece. 'Exudes incredible values,' 'outstanding personality' two among many.

Mr Dawson, while amiable, is reckoned to miss nothing and parents felt that wouldn't shirk from tough decisions. 'If there's one super naughty boy in the school then I guess somebody has to be expelled, as in all schools,' thought one. Impressive networking skills don't go amiss either. 'I know a lot of people,' he says, and what a useful crowd they are. Barnaby Lenon, former Harrow head, extols virtues of pupils and school at length on school website. Mr D cultivates contacts through cricket – a predictable passion. Another – repairing pre-digital Roberts radios (impressive range neatly arranged in his study) – possibly less of an obvious social asset.

Entrance: Register at birth for one of 22 places, waiting list if full (as, increasingly, it is). Mr Dawson understandably hates putting up 'no vacancies' sign – 'don't want to be known for it,' – but is currently 'turning down a lot. It's a cosy, happy place and I don't want to get any bigger.'

While has plenty of high flyers, entrance requirements aren't stratospheric. School expects fluent reading and writing and grasp of basic arithmetic. May ask for report from current school and very occasional pupil is directed elsewhere.

Prospective pupils spend day at the school year before they join when sit short papers in maths, English and VR. Also attend music, art and sport workshops. Main purpose is to work out forms ('we don't really operate in year groups,' says school). Some scholarships available as well as means-tested bursaries. Also takes maximum of 10 day boys through the school, all locals, inherited by Mr Dawson who has 'just stuck with them.'

If you miss the boat, there's a diminutive chance of place or two in year 7 – 'incredibly rare for anyone to leave,' says Mr Dawson – offered after cognitive ability tests (though non-academic strengths also taken into account).

No linked feeders; elite London mob – Garden House, Thomas's, Eaton House – increasingly feature, as do old boys' offspring – at 10 per cent and rising, says school, which stresses that fees 'are kept as low as possible.'

Gaps increasingly filled by international families – one boy we met saw family only three times a year – though school has recently started live feeds for concerts. Otherwise, pupils come from all over the country 'except Cornwall'. We were hoping for some ancient West Country vs home counties blood feud. Disappointingly, down merely to poor transport links.

Exit: Mr Dawson not a fan of serial entrance exams and suggests maximum of three senior schools, two aspirational, one 'a safer bet'. To most of major, trad names in south-east. Harrow often features prominently. Other usual (and desirable) suspects include Winchester (two academic scholarships in 2016), Eton, Rugby, Charterhouse, Uppingham, Oundle, Radley, Stowe, Tonbridge and Marlborough.

Remarks: Long the place where old money arrived as small change. Cricket commentator Henry Blofeld, Duke of Westminster, horse trainer Sir Henry Cecil – list of old boys says it all. All it takes is names of first two heads – Girdlestone and Crabtree – to know you're in the presence of Tradition, with capital (and gold-embossed, gothic-lettered) T. Would make a fine detective series title as well. Additional helpful pointers come by way of slightly fly-blown pictures of Victorian worthies in visitors' loos – OBs Duke of Marlborough 1893; Lieutenant the Honorable FHS Roberts VC, killed Colence SA 1899,

Scratch the surface and you'll find...more tradition, bookcase packed with Biggles, Worrals and even a Henty or two (remnants of old library) adorning the morning room – or, more prosaically to those of less gentle birth, the school office. Makes statement architecture of curved library – first building visitors see and the newest – the more startling by comparison. Accoutrements – refectory table and two sternly positioned sofas – are set off by glow-in-the-dark bright blue carpet (also a dormitory feature), bare walls crying out for some splendiferously mustachioed OBs, picture windows giving vistas not of bosky woods or slumbrous streams but cars approaching up the drive.

Shelves reassuringly weighted in favour of fiction, wooden blocks with school number marking borrowings, one per boy.

And if you want to borrow two books? 'Two?' asked Mr Dawson, experiencing mild Beadle-like moment. 'Why would anyone want to read more than one at a time?' It's the hallmark of a school with a strong sense of its own place in the world, conventional yet not in thrall to crowd mentality. Summer half term, for example, happens a week later than normal. Trade off, with school taking strain of final revision for CE exams, worth hassle of arranging two sets of holiday activities for offspring elsewhere, reckoned parents.

Class structure, average size 12, also takes a bit of getting used to. Ability rather than age-based, so while nobody is ever moved down, brighter boys will go up a year, sometimes two, never more. In top years, carefully planned scholarship work ensures there's no 'here's one I made earlier' duplication.

From animated debate on how to stop extinction of coral reef in science – 'tries to make it as visual as possible,' said star pupil – to year 6 pupils reading (beautifully) extracts from end of year English exam, a 'do-able' past CE paper, impression was of willing learners enthusiastically taught. Bright, super-engaged staff, majority male and with average age of 39, includes several of distinctly young fogey-ish disposition and bouffant charm – Boris Johnston recast with auburn and brunette tresses.

Impressive commitment to pupils with SEN. One, with ASD, initially reluctant to attend lessons, supported with one-to-one help, funded by parents, 'fully integrated,' says Mr Dawson. More usual needs (mild dyslexia) respond – miraculously so, thought one parent – to small classes and skilled teaching without intervention. Head 'isn't a big believer in throwing tons of time and money at extra tuition,' said one parent. 'Because the classes are so small, and teaching so good, you don't really need it.'

Staff praised not just for ability to inspire love of learning – 'never did we expect such commitment,' said mother – but for reinforcing universally wonderful manners and behaviour. One parent thrilled when master told son to 'stand up and show the way for your mother.' Compliments, convertible to house points, awarded for the dutiful, complaints doled out for the untidy or overly chatty lead to writing out code of conduct.

Had been very slight relaxation in discipline, now checked, thought one pupil (like peers, a charming lunchtime host) and all to the corporate benefit. 'Wasn't working so well before – now good for the school but bad for the individual.'

Minor transgressors write out school code of conduct; serial offenders lose 'privs' for a week, part of plentiful school jargon that includes 'going across' – signals need for comfort break rather than deepening interest in spiritualism – 'grub' (sweets) – and 'lemonade', a generic term covering hot chocolate, juice and even cake.

Parents universally thrilled by restricted presence of i-anythings out of lessons, and tactical use within. Rather than mass breaktime retreat into solitary cyber universe, pupils here whizz energetically about in real time with friends. 'Really important because children become so addicted to these games that they don't interact with their peers,' said relieved mother.

Plenty for them to enjoy, from lovingly tended plots with courgette flowers and tomatoes to three Gloucester Old Spots, sensibly not named, bees ditto – though for logistical rather than emotional reasons. Other tucked away treats include shaded mini-adventure playground for first years and personable wood-paneled and about to be extended colonial-style chapel, consecrated 1880 after arriving in kit form (so many identical labradors on site that you start to wonder if assembled in similar way).

While academic success is all well and good (and often very well and very good), school also does best to find ubiquitous spark. Music a strength, with 80 boys learning at least one instrument, variety of ensembles to play them. Many cheering examples of mild reprobates transformed by gift for singing (there's a queue to join the choir, say parents).

But whichever formerly dark area of the curriculum light of budding talent might illuminate, helps to have at least nascent interest in sport. Not for everyone, one OB recently describing it as 'an acquired taste', but for most, it's a way of inculcating right values, particularly as school size ensures participation by all. 'Perfect because even the boys who are mediocre at sports all get to make the teams – nobody gets left out,' said parent. Year to year results vary considerably – inevitable consequence of small size. One cricket and rugby team had been undefeated all season; others with less enthusiastic cohort won't do half as well.

In addition to big three (football, rugby, cricket), tennis, Eton fives (since 1892), golf and swimming are all provided on site. Five pitches (four multi-use) appear to stretch away into far distance, courtesy of clever landscaping that makes the most of stand out planting, including massed rhododendrons (Mr Dawson has sole pruning rights over favourite). Provides effective masking of more functional buildings including vast sports hall (for basketball, fencing, air rifle shooting and much more) and gives 25-acre grounds feel of something much bigger.

Sport, inevitably, dominates the summer term after school activities list, replaced in winter by idiosyncratic range that currently includes Warhammer and fly-tying (teachers, all required to take at least one sport or activity, encouraged to indulge own enthusiasms). All adds to the fun, as do the 'endless' activities (now that's what we call organisation). Being on the go essential (particularly for new boys) in helping to acclimatise to full boarding lifestyle – weekly an option in the first two years, though 'half full board from the word go,' says school.

In addition to two long weekends (Friday to Monday evening), a couple of bonus Sundays and half term, there's much anticipated treat of year group excursions to school/family-owned house in France. Icing on the cake (almost literally) is first class food prepared by Mrs Dawson Snr. One boy 'asked why I can't cook like that,' said mother.

School points out that boarding for all hurts parents far more than the boys – 'always rather sad for the mother,' agreed one, 'but we just knew they'd be so happy.' Also ensures a full house at weekends for Saturday film nights (no lonely minority waiting for life to start again on Sunday evenings) when all but first years, who have own small scale version, pile into theatre with pillows and duvets.

All happens within or next to main building, dorms six to eight-bedders, comfortable rather than haut couture ('they're nice, cute, small, humble,' said parent), possessions neatly arranged, pinboards sometimes rather sparsely filled. Bathrooms and loos clean, fragrant and hygienic – bar single cracked tile surround in need of repair. Most pupils in top two years enjoy additional privacy of individual cubicles (new arrivals will start off in dorm). Buddies take settling in duties seriously – 'boys were all waiting and had his bed made,' said parent, leaving son for taster weekend.

For the very youngest there are separate quarters with common room (reassuringly compact) and playroom (ditto – Hide and Seek games a non-starter) and own live-in matron, one of five, three full time, notable for reassuring names (Miss Turnball and Miss Foynes – yet another detective team, surely?) and a guaranteed presence on the touchline at matches.

Education here is all about bestowing resilience, self-awareness, realism and courage (fairy godmothers might blench). 'Finally and most importantly, pupils must learn to love life...' says website. If they don't while they're here, won't be for want of trying.

Parents are in no doubt they succeed. 'We put our trust in Mr Dawson,' says mother. 'We've been so incredibly impressed with the results.'

Sutton Valence School

North Street, Sutton Valence, Kent ME17 3HL

Pupils: 886; 135 boarders • Ages: 3–18 (boarding from 11) • Sixth form: 182 • C of E

Fees: Day £8,880 – £20,175; Boarding £20,685 – £31,425 pa

Tel: 01622 845200
Email: enquiries@svs.org.uk
Website: www.svs.org.uk

Headmaster: Since 2009, Mr Bruce Grindlay MA Cantab (organ scholar) MusB FRCO (mid-40s). Came from Christ's Hospital School, Horsham where he was director of music for eight years. Previously boarding housemaster and head of chapel music at Bedford School. Came in with desire to up the ante on discipline and academics and has succeeded in taking pupils and parents with him. Parents find him calm, personable and articulate, with his nose to the ground and swift to take action when needed. Pupils frequently pop by his office for advice or to tell of an achievement. Expectations are set high and all are challenged to do their best. 'I'm not slow to remind pupils, or staff for that matter, that termly fees are the cost of a small Caribbean holiday.' His wife teaches English in the sixth form and is completing a PhD. Two children, one here, the other a chorister at Westminster Abbey Choir School.

Head of prep: Since January 2017, Claire M Corkran, previously deputy head. Degree in education and RE from Homerton College Cambridge and an MEd in educational management and leadership from the Open University. Has been head of history at JAPS, senior teacher at the British School of Houston and assessment coordinator at Copthorne Prep before joining Sutton Valence in 2010.

Academic matters: In 2016, 91 per cent gained five A*-C grades including English and maths at GCSE (32 per cent A*/A). At A level 67 per cent A*/B and 41 per cent A*/A. Parents bridle slightly at the notion that it's a school for the less academic. 'The strong ethos that there's a lot more to school life than exam results in no way means the bright aren't stretched.' The head highlights solid value-added scores; school moved into the top 15 per cent nationally for adding value at A level last year, equating to half to one grade better for each child than initial predictions, per subject. He emphasises that a pupil moving a D to a C is every bit as significant as another getting an A* and that its main focus is on producing confident all-rounders. Small class sizes and a caring, individual approach draw many.

ESL and other learning support staff commended for their kindness, patience and dedication with highly-rated SEN support in lessons and, by arrangement, during extra sessions, at times in place of non-core subjects. 'Staff always happy to go the extra mile to help my son and, with such a broad intake, he's never felt different or out of place.' Popular subjects include geography, maths, business studies, art and design.

A few grumbles that problem areas, either in relation to particular subjects or pupils, come to light slowly, but once issues are identified, most agree action is swift and effective. The e-newsletter, information evenings and other recent initiatives are welcomed. 'More of the same please. It's great to now know when and what homework is being set and to be able to get more involved.'

Games, options, the arts: It's easy to see why sport forms a major part of life at Sutton Valence. Playing fields stretch as far as the eye can see, there's a track used by Olympic athletes, Astroturf hockey pitch, sports hall and hugely inviting indoor pool. The socialising that goes on around regular after-school practices and fixtures also tempts even the least sporty to have a go. The school fields several teams in hockey, cricket, netball and rugby. Some parents comment that inclusion comes at the expense of developing real excellence and that pupils would benefit from more specialist coaches, but several pupils play at county level and above in hockey, rugby and cricket and the website is brimming with team sport successes. Pupils excel in more unusual endeavours too – roller dance, small bore shooting, ballroom dancing, fly fishing and race walking being just some examples.

So much part of life here are CCF and D of E that there's no great fanfare when pupils routinely go onto the higher levels, though their contribution to individual development and community spirit is emphasised. With his musical background, the head was always sure to encourage that side of things, though music has long been considered strong. Noticeboards are crammed with news of rehearsals and performances and the schedule of clubs and, along with, we're told, truly excellent drama productions in the plush Baughan Theatre, you're left wondering how pupils, parents and staff fit everything in. Little wonder flexi-boarding is such a popular option.

Boarding: Around 50 full boarders with twice as many weekly or flexi boarders; around nine per cent from overseas. Lots of space, friendly faces and homely touches. 'Often think my children would prefer to live there, and on the various occasions when it suits us too the school has always done its best to accommodate,' said one parent.

One of the boarding house matrons in no way resembles the dragon poster she pins on boys' dorms to remind them to tidy up. Not sure that a dragon would have such a keen interest in every child's welfare either. Day, full, flexi or occasional boarders, it's clear staff keep tabs on pupils and do their best to develop a joint approach to overcome homesickness or other issues, most of which are minor. Visits to local preps to put future pupils' fears at bay are also not unknown.

Background and atmosphere: At the core of a small village in Kent, in beautifully kept grounds, gracious old buildings house pleasant and at times grand communal areas and well-equipped classrooms. On a clear day, though, there's a danger it's all overshadowed by the breathtaking view of the Weald to the south. Main site separated by a short distance from the prep school (and junior mixed boarding house). Most staff live on site or nearby. 'A happy and relaxed local community – what better place for my child to learn and grow?'

Perhaps that accounts for its longevity. It's one of the country's oldest established schools, founded by William Lambe in 1576. In 2010 over 1000 attended a ceremony in Westminster Abbey, a fitting location given the school's strong Christian ethos, to mark the centenary of becoming part of the United Westminster Schools Foundation.

Pastoral care, well-being and discipline: Head has impressive recall of pupil names and goings-on and has got the prefects, parents and pupils almost universally on side in introducing somewhat tougher discipline. Nothing too draconian, 'tough love' is its basis. Correct uniform, orderly lunchtime queuing/ clearing up and, at the prefects' initiative, the use of pleases and thank yous are all in hand. Head also sweetened pupils up with a fresh system of rewards to acknowledge even small individual contributions and achievements.

Pupils and parents: Other than real non-conformists, most likely to feel at home here. 'No one thing defines you. I'm not a bit like my siblings but we've all found things to get our teeth into here.' Pupils are described as nice, normal and confident without arrogance. Many parents both work and are a mix of local businessmen/entrepreneurs, farmers and city workers. Foreign students – mostly from Germany and Asia – do not exceed nine per cent of the total and on the whole settle in well, though for some life in rural England is somewhat of a culture shock. Head would like to see a more vibrant PA but, even though most UK families are based in the south east, he may face an uphill battle as many travel quite a distance to get to the school. This can be an issue, especially in bad weather, and makes flexi and occasional boarding popular options (which younger full-time boarders can find unsettling). The school runs buses and a few sixth formers drive – some in rather flash cars.

Alumni include journalists Robert Fisk and Ben Brown, Ashley Jackson, GB hockey player, opera performer Kathryn Choonara and Sir Rustam Feroze, gynaecologist.

Entrance: Entry into nursery to year 2 is non-selective. For entry to years 3 to 6, assessment with the director of studies involving reading, spelling, maths and non-verbal reasoning to ascertain the child's academic levels.

Senior school entrants come up from the prep school and an assortment of other local preps and primary schools. At 11 the school sets its own entrance exam. There's usually a waiting list but a number drop off having secured places at local grammars. Smaller intake at 13 when a CE mark of approximately 55 per cent is required. State school applicants must pass the school's exam. The 25 or so students entering sixth form from outside need at least five GCSE passes at B grade or above. Most international students come in the sixth form and also sit a language exam.

Exit: Some 60 per cent of prep school pupils to the senior school, 30 per cent to local grammar school and rest to other local schools. About 10 per cent leave after GCSEs, most going to local grammars. Almost all sixth formers go on to higher education – popular destinations include Loughborough, Oxford Brookes, Exeter, Bournemouth, Nottingham, Reading and Bath. One medic and one to Oxbridge in 2016.

Money matters: Academic (11+ and 13+), art, DT, music, sports and drama (at 11+, 13+ and 16+) scholarships and the Westminster scholarship (to those obtaining five GCSEs at A*) available. Worth up to a maximum of 20 per cent of either boarding or day fees. Also offers bursaries and reductions for Forces families.

Remarks: Friendly and relaxed atmosphere and solid all-round confidence-building credentials. Its idyllic setting and enviable sports and other facilities make it a popular alternative to more academically demanding senior schools in the south east. Can suffer perhaps from being labelled the non-academic alternative. 'That old chestnut,' says one parent. 'Obviously needs to market itself better. Put all your kids there. It's got lots to offer any child.'

T

Tonbridge Grammar School

Deakin Leas, Tonbridge, Kent TN9 2JR

Pupils: 1,144 • Ages: 11–18 • Sixth form: 274 (including 33 boys)

Tel: 01732 365125
Email: office@tgs.kent.sch.uk
Website: www.tgs.kent.sch.uk

Head Teacher: Since 2005, Mrs Rosemary Joyce BA MA PGCE NPQH (40s). Read religious studies and history at Stirling, followed by a PGCE and MA at London. Previously deputy head of Nonsuch High School for Girls, Cheam; senior teacher at Clarendon School, Trowbridge; head of religious studies at Aylesbury High. A highly effective administrator who managed to get funding and organise the rebuilding of large parts of the school in record time. She is charming and businesslike and considers her role to be a privilege rather than a job, saying that 'education should be about transforming people's lives'. Teaches philosophy to the sixth form and takes assemblies, but some pupils and parents feel she cuts a slightly remote figure and they don't really know her. She has twin daughters in the school.

Academic matters: High achieving selective grammar with academy status and specialisms in maths, computing and languages. Has received the British Council's award for internationalism each year since the introduction of the IB in 2004 and has been top IB state school in the UK for five consecutive years. Ran IB and A levels side by side for a number of years and exclusively the IB from 2012 – caused a bit of a fuss at the time as some families felt they had not been given any choice. However, this has settled down and school and teachers are fully committed to the IB; students who want to do A levels move elsewhere after GCSEs. The head stresses that the IB has not meant a change in direction and the ethos of the school remains the same; Academy status means the school is free from the constraints of the national curriculum, 'we are now in charge of our own destiny'. In 2016, average IB points 37. About 10 per cent get 40 points or more and usually a couple a year get the maximum 45 points. Languages and sciences particularly strong with German, French, Italian and Spanish offered and regular foreign exchanges. Latin also offered. Wide choice of subjects maintained under IB but sometimes a subject doesn't run if not enough takers. 'Natural sciences a more natural fit than than sports science' but film and theatre studies popular.

At GCSE, 89 per cent A*/A in 2016. School works within the principles of the IB Middle Years Programme (MYP) but is not accredited and will continue with IGCSEs and GCSEs.

Co-ed sixth form since 2000 with about 20 boys in each year who appear to integrate well and 'add a new energy to the classroom'. Good support for Oxbridge and more pupils being encouraged to apply – help with choice of college and preparation for tests, Oxbridge tutors invited to talk to students. Reciprocal arrangements with local schools for interview practice. Medical and vet students come back to talk about the application process.

Good balance and age range of staff (respectable number of male teachers), from very experienced to newly qualified – extraordinarily dedicated team who give up their time to run clubs and sporting fixtures. Maths and chemistry teachers are old girls of the school. Class sizes no more than 30 or 25 for practical subjects with setting from year 8 for maths and

French and ICT integrated into every subject. Ofsted considers the teaching to be 'outstanding'. Study skills programme and regular assessments through practical projects, online assessments and presentations. Progress reports sent to parents and pupils are 'given the freedom to learn from their mistakes'. Form time every day and sixth form have daily contact with their learning mentor – three tutor reviews with learning mentor per year to review progress and set targets. House points awarded for good work.

Curriculum designed to stretch the gifted and talented – maths challenge in Holland and a national level language Olympiad held at school. Enrichment programmes include debating society and subject-led clinics at lunchtimes to stretch and support pupils. School sends a team to the Model United Nations and recent study trips to Iceland, Singapore and Swaziland. Good SEN support, mainly for mild dyslexia, either individual or small groups. Everyone screened on arrival and new entrants to sixth form also screened; teachers alert for other difficulties. About one per cent need some sort of EAL help – families who speak another language at home or those who move into the area to join school for IB in sixth form. Increasing number from abroad who stay with local families.

Games, options, the arts: Music particularly strong and caters for all ages and levels of talent; facilities recent refurbished. About 300 pupils learn at least one musical instrument. Masses of group music and individuals can shine at house musical events. Three formal concerts a year, array of ensembles, swing bands and orchestras, often student run eg the ukelele orchestra. Three choirs, classical and contemporary – Motet choir won Barnardo's National Choir competition which led to an invitation to sing at the Royal Albert Hall, and were runners up in Songs of Praise Choir of the Year competition. Concerts at St John's Smith Square and at the Cadogan Hall with London Chamber Orchestra. Music offered as a Higher in the IB.

Active drama department with lunchtime and after-school clubs and drama is part of the curriculum in the lower school. Whole school production every other year with annual smaller productions as well as some joint drama with Tonbridge School. Theatre studies is offered as part of the IB. New drama and dance studios. Creativity encouraged at all levels. Vibrant art displayed around the school taught by 'enthusiastic and friendly teachers'. Art taken early with excellent results – textiles popular.

Team sport compulsory until sixth form and many continue as it forms part of the CAS element of the IB, but can be 'a bit patchy' according to the girls. 'There are not enough matches and sporty girls join outside clubs,' said one. Netball, tennis and hockey are the main sports; some hockey coaching on site and at Tonbridge School. Basketball popular with boys and girls in sixth form and boys have their own football team and many play for local clubs. School's own pool has seen better days and swimming now done elsewhere, but school says plans are afoot for 'an exciting new development project' on the site. Fab new sports hall and netball/tennis courts recently resurfaced. Clubs and activities at lunchtime and 'Action!' on Wednesday afternoons for years 7 and 8 – something for everyone – anything from sports, first aid and glass painting to Indian head massage but clubs 'peter out further up the school', according to some pupils. Some run by sixth form as part of the CAS element of the IB. Pupils also take part in the Young Enterprise scheme and run their own radio station, Radio TGS. They are involved in a community project in Africa – recently a group of about 20 raised money and built a library for a school in Swaziland – 'they lived in fairly basic conditions and it was a life changing experience for my daughter,' said one mother.

Background and atmosphere: Founded in 1905 on the top floor of Tonbridge Library with 19 girls and the motto 'Courage and Honour'. In 1913, when it outgrew the library, moved to current site, 14 acres on a hill in south Tonbridge with great views in all directions. £10 million Hands Building opened in late 2009 with a large glass atrium and 43 new classrooms – some with moveable walls, a drama and dance studio and sports hall. £850,000 raised from loyal band of parents and former pupils and helped by a land exchange with a house builder. Science labs refurbished with help from a grant from the Wolfson Foundation in 2012. In 2015, opened new sixth form study and social centre, IBarn.

Strong sense of community with compulsory service activity once a week – younger children do something within the school, older pupils might help in a primary school or volunteer in an old people's home and sixth form do community service as part of the IB. 'We like to take pupils out of their comfort zone where they flourish and it helps them see themselves as part of a broader picture', says the head. In a recent project some senior pupils worked with children from a pupil referral unit using the photography and IT facilities at the school.

Pastoral care, well-being and discipline: Pastoral care seen as a whole school responsibility; 'we want to get the support right so pupils can be as successful as they can be,' says head. Programme of monitoring, tracking, support and interventions. Learning and peer mentors offer support to girls at form time, and 'there is always someone to talk to and the school wants us to be happy,' said one pupil. Dedicated student manager oversees the transition from primary school and provides a crucial link between home and school; children are put into forms with similar postcodes so they can make friends with girls who live near them. Years 7, 8 and 9 have registration together so they can get to know other year groups, and sixth form has mixed year tutor groups. Year 7s have a bushcraft camping week in nearby woods and new sixth formers invited for a bonding weekend at the University of East Anglia in the summer before they join.

Pupils and parents: A fairly middle class group whose parents take an interest in their education – under 20 children on free school meals. Loyal alumni who come back and speak to pupils and often send their daughters here. 'Well rounded, grounded children who are highly motivated with a good work ethic – we cannot believe our luck,' said one delighted mother. 'Our daughter is interested and happy and loving every minute'. 'The school has high expectations and the children have so many experiences and opportunities,' said another. The pupils have a 'privileged education but are not necessarily privileged; they push themselves in all areas and have a strong sense of being part of the wider community,' says the head.

Attractive uniform with blue jerseys and straight check skirts, and dress code for sixth form of dark matching suits with skirts as short as they can get away with. Alumni include Victoria Hislop (novelist and travel writer); Rebecca Stephens MBE (first British woman to climb Everest and the seven summits); Lynn Wallis (artistic director of the Royal Academy of Dance); Angie Sage (author of Septimus Heap series); Felicity Aston and Jo Vellino (polar explorers). Active and committed PTA involved with fundraising and social events.

Entrance: Entrance via the Kent Test at 11+ in verbal, non-verbal reasoning and maths administered by Kent County Council, and places are hard fought. No allowance made for siblings. No catchment area but most fairly local and proximity to the school taken into account where there are two girls of equal ability. A minimum of 35 'Governors' places' reserved for able pupils from outside the area but same criteria apply as for Kent selection.

Sixth form entry (including boys) based solely on academic results with a minimum of three As and three Bs at GCSE or equivalent and guidance meetings offered at the school to discuss subject choices. Mainly from other grammars for the IB and East Sussex schools which finish at 16+. Occasionally spaces in other years – entry via school's own test.

Exit: Historically very few left after GCSEs but numbers have increased as those wishing to do A levels move elsewhere. Over 95 per cent to higher education and a huge range of universities, 80 per cent Russell Group or med school/dentistry (12 places in 2016). Durham, Exeter, Leeds, Southampton and Bristol current favourites. Eleven to Oxbridge in 2016.

Money matters: Music bursaries available and awards in sixth form. Tradition of helping families where money is tight. Pitchford Fund set up by PTA in 1950s and enables those in immediate financial need to take part in activities.

Remarks: A remarkable school, and anyone who gets in here is very fortunate. Considered to be one of the most academic schools in the area, but pupils wear their learning lightly and have time for so much else. Everyone we met was self-confident and ambitious but down to earth and very much aware of the wider world beyond the school gates.

Tonbridge School

High Street, Tonbridge, Kent TN9 1JP

Pupils: 788; 460 full boarders • Ages: 13–18 • Sixth form: 317

Fees: Day £28,158; Boarding £37,539 pa

Tel: 01732 365555
Email: hmsec@tonbridge-school.org
Website: www.tonbridge-school.co.uk

Headmaster: Since 2005, Mr Tim Haynes BA PGCE (50s). Educated at Shrewsbury, where he is now a governor, he read history at Reading University and after a couple of years as a stockbroker in the City, he took his PGCE at Pembroke College, Cambridge and began his teaching career at Hampton School where he taught history. He then spent 13 years at St Paul's in London leaving as surmaster (deputy head) and 10 years as headmaster of Monmouth School before taking over the post at Tonbridge. He lives in a house on the edge of the grounds and has two sons.

He is a great enthusiast and is considered very approachable. 'You can always see him in an emergency, and he is measured and helpful.' 'He talks to everyone and is not a headmaster in a gilded tower.' 'The sort of person you would like to sit next to at a dinner party.' He can always be seen bicycling round the pitches during matches on Saturdays. Highly regarded by the boys, he knows all the novi's (new boys) names within the first few weeks. He describes Tonbridge as a 'high octane, high achieving school on so many levels. There is real ambition amongst the boys and a co-curricular breadth and a special quality of relations between boys and their teachers – informal, relaxed, respectful and purposeful'. He describes Tonbridge as a school where 'respect for tradition and an openness to innovation are equally valued'. He meets all prospective families – 300-400 per year.

Academic matters: Very impressive. In 2016, 75 per cent A*/A at A level. Twenty-four subjects offered at A level and, apart from the usual, include Mandarin, PE, theatre studies, business studies and government and politics. Most popular are maths, economics and history, followed by physics and English – particularly good results in maths, English and economics. Boys still find time for further academic work – three presented their scientific research to an international conference in China and another has published a GCSE French text book.

Most take 10 GCSEs (mostly the more rigorous IGCSEs). In 2016, 90 per cent A*/A – among the best results in the country. Science offered as dual award or individually – particularly good showing in individual sciences. All have to take a language at GCSE and a good range offered including French, Spanish, Chinese, Italian and German. Our guide singled out history and French for being especially well taught – 'the head of French is inspired'. Art GCSE offered as fine art or photography. All do non-examined course in divinity, which is largely discussion based and includes critical thinking. Everyone takes digital creativity (ICT) in three fab digital creativity labs. Voluntary Extended Project offered in upper sixth year.

Good liaison between teaching departments – very dedicated team of teachers 'who really seem to care and will go the extra mile for us,' say the boys. 'Bright young teachers [mostly male although there are now 15 female teachers] who are great role models for the boys.' Academic staff also involved with coaching sport and are 'passionate about opportunities available to the boys'.

Boys need to be organised and there is an emphasis on independence from the start, and all encouraged to find their own learning style. All boys screened for learning difficulties on arrival (mainly mild dyslexia and dyspraxia) and all are offered help with study and revision skills and note taking, essay writing, memory and organisational skills – boys often self-refer for drop in sessions or targeted help. Learning mentor training programme so boys can help each other. Novi (first year) dyslexic pupils trained as dyslexic specialist mentors and can help in partner primary schools. Two part-time EAL teachers mainly offer help with technical and scientific language.

Games, options, the arts: Huge range of opportunities help develop self-reliance and leadership skills. Long tradition of sporting excellence but ethos of participation by all, and everyone has the chance to play in a team. Truly superb sports facilities, and was a training venue for the London 2012 Olympics. A hundred acres of playing fields, all immaculately groomed, three Astroturfs, clay tennis courts and an all-weather athletics pitch. Sports centre with cricket nets, 25 metre swimming pool and climbing wall and a fitness suite to rival the swankiest of London health clubs. Membership open to general public. School has hockey, rugby and cricket academies, has produced county and international cricketers and has one of the best rugby sides in south east; recent leavers play for Harlequins and Saracens. Every imaginable sport including fives, ultimate frisbee, fencing and water polo and sailing – novi (first year) encouraged to try lots of sports so every boy should find something he enjoys. Weekly house leagues sports for those not in the top teams.

Increasing numbers involved in music, with about five boys taking music A level each year and over 50 per cent of all boys learning one of a huge range of instruments, including the Marcussen chapel organ, one of the best in the country. All Steinway status means top quality pianos in every practice room. Director of music a professional conductor. Wide range of orchestras, bands and ensemble groups for all musical styles including flourishing jazz and pop groups and thriving choral music. Numerous concerts and recitals, including the Octagon concerts, which feature a different instrument each week. Excellent facilities include two recital halls, a suite of teaching practice rooms, music library, soundproof room for jazz and percussion, and a state of the art recording studio. Often team up with musicians outside school eg a concert with Benenden at St Martin in the Fields and South Bank Sinfonia at the Royal Festival Hall; and choir has sung at St George's Chapel, Windsor and Chichester Cathedral, and deputised at St Paul's when the cathedral choir was away.

Drama also thriving, with about eight major productions a year in 400 seat EM Forster theatre (complete with orchestra pit and studio theatre), including three major school plays, with girls from local schools taking part in most productions. Boys get involved with all aspects of production including set design, stage management and lighting. Regular drama competitions and house plays, which are put together by the boys with drama staff acting as mentors, as well as other small scale productions and plays in Spanish, French and German.

Arts workshops by visiting professionals include street dance, masks, puppetry and film making and upper sixth boys invited to take a play to Edinburgh Fringe via the Hogshead Theatre Company. Boys also take part in the National Theatre's play writing competition. Varied programme of lectures by visiting speakers, and boys can choose from a huge range of societies: cultural, political, scientific and sporting, anything from bee-keeping, astronomy and wine appreciation to sub aqua and robotics.

Seminar programme in GCSE and lower sixth years encourages boys to questions their assumptions and see things from a different perspective – eg sustainability in business or organ transplants. About 200 boys take part in CCF across all three services. Duke of Edinburgh Award also popular with about 20 achieving gold each year. Not forgetting numerous foreign visits and exchange trips during the holidays.

Boarding: There are seven boarding houses and younger boys start in small dorms of up to six. Older boys have their own rooms. Strong system of pastoral care. Housemasters seen as 'father figures' who get to know boys and their families very well. Aided by assistant housemaster and five tutors per house – boys have regular meetings with their tutors. During the week all boys eat in their houses but at weekends boarders eat together in the Orchard Centre. Most boys go home after games on Saturday, but have to be back in time for Sunday evening chapel. Although trips and outings are organised, it can be quite lonely for those who stay in.

Background and atmosphere: Founded by Sir Andrew Judde in 1553, the school still has close links with the Worshipful Company of Skinners, and Skinners' Day is celebrated each year at the end of the summer term. The school grew rapidly in the 19th century and has been rebuilt twice on the original site. Dominated by the fine rebuilt Edwardian chapel (it was gutted by fire in 1988) the school is set in 150 acres of immaculately kept grounds behind the not-so-glamorous Tonbridge High Street on the northern edge of the town, stretching down to the river and the railway line. The imposing Victorian buildings with tasteful, modern additions manage to combine a respect for tradition with the most up-to-date facilities. The Vere Lodge Centre for DT and art, with its spiral staircase and light-filled space for private views and exhibitions, is particularly impressive. Well-used library – built in 1962 and recently extended and refurbished – with 23,000 books, a number of which date from the 17th century, as well as the 1479 Jensen Bible – although boys seem to get most of their information online, and there's plenty of digital technology here too.

Pastoral care, well-being and discipline: Seven boarding and five day houses situated on the edge of the playing fields and along the high street (most recently refurbished) each with about 60 boys. Strong sense of belonging in houses helped by range of inter-house competitions in art, music, film, sport plus house plays and concerts, and close friendships are formed. School aims for as wide a mix as possible in each house and tries to split up boys from the same prep school to stop cliques forming. Good food – all eat in their houses, with grace before lunch.

Boys 'very driven – it's cool to work and there are not many problems on the behaviour front – the boys know they are there to work and are expected to work hard – the pace can be quite challenging for some,' said a parent. Mindfulness meditation is taught as part of PSHE to all boys in year 10 and is increasingly popular as an activity. Boys are taught to focus on the present and not worry about the past or the future – a skill for life which helps them cope with stress. There is an emotional literacy programme for senior boys and an on-site school counsellor.

All boys are expected to attend weekday chapel services four mornings a week, and other faiths encouraged to attend their own places of worship for special religious festivals. School is increasingly connected with the local community and there is a growing sense of social responsibility, with large numbers of boys involved with Tonbridge Community Action – boys help in local primary schools and hospitals and develop the skills and confidence to do things which make a difference. Local primary school children come to use the labs on Wednesday afternoons and hold inter-school sports days at Tonbridge. Recently, 150 boys spent the night under cardboard boxes and raised £5,000 for a homeless charity. Tonbridge has close links with The Marsh Academy at New Romney and is one of its sponsors – Tonbridge boys act as e-mentors and provide help and support to Marsh students, and Marsh students come to Tonbridge for practical science work in the labs. Gap year boys can also work at Marsh Academy for a term.

Pupils and parents: Most boys live within about an hour and a half of the school and it is becoming increasingly popular with London families. The headmaster describes the typical Tonbridge parent as 'understated and low-key' and the boys as having a quiet self-assurance – 'great team players who get on in all settings'. Alpha males thrive here and sport still dominant, but boys also admired for other things and music and culture increasingly important; it is 'a much more tolerant and a kinder place than it was some years ago'.

About 10 per cent foreign nationals from 33 countries, who are generally well integrated. Each house twinned with a house at Benenden for socials, restaurant outings and quizzes. Parents encouraged to get involved, and there is always strong support for Saturday matches. Most parents are members of the Parents' Arts Society, which organises cultural and social events each term, everything from private views at art galleries, theatre trips, wine tastings and lectures to weekend trips to Europe. 'It is such a fun way to get to know the other parents,' said one mother. There doesn't seem to be a typical Tonbridgian – some sporty, some less so, some musical, some not – but all seem to enjoy themselves, and the key seems to be to take part in everything. They have a keen sense of fun, demonstrated at the annual Pink Day when all boys dress up in pink in support of breast cancer charities with some very imaginative and outrageous outfits.

A long list of famous old boys includes EM Forster, Frederick Forsyth, all members of the band Keane, Vikram Seth, Patrick Mayhew, several generations of the Cowdrey cricketing dynasty, Dan Stevens of Downton Abbey fame, Tim Waterstone and Kit Hesketh-Harvey.

Entrance: Most join at 13+ from 50-60 prep schools. Computer based pre-assessment and interview in year 6 followed by common entrance (pass mark about 65 per cent) or the school's own exams in English and maths. School operates a reserve list and keeps in close contact with prep schools. A handful joins in year 10 and about 20 join in lower sixth. Sixth form entry via tests in subjects to be studied at A level.

Exit: In 2016, 31 to Oxbridge and one medic. Other popular destinations are the usual suspects: Durham, Bristol, Exeter, Bath, London unis and Nottingham, mostly to read hard academic subjects, but not all follow the herd – other destinations include film production at Bournemouth, golf management at Birmingham, land management at Cirencester and popular music performance at the Royal Northern College of Music. Full-time university and careers advisor widely praised, plus guidance and support from housemasters and other specialist staff. University and careers offices open all day – careers and higher education programme starts at end of first year. Good relationships with European and American universities and provide on-site training for SAT exams. Boys have recently gone to Harvard, Berkeley, New York, Queen's University Canada, Trinity College Dublin and Maastricht.

Money matters: A well-endowed school which offers numerous awards. Up to 45 scholarships offered at 13+ – academic, music, art, drama, technology and sport. Academic and music scholarships offered in sixth form. Top academic scholarship worth 50 per cent and all others 10 per cent, which can be topped up with a means-tested bursary. About 15 boys on full fee remission and a further 15 on 80 per cent fee remission. Means-tested foundation awards given to boys to help fund years 7 and 8 at prep school followed by a guaranteed place at Tonbridge.

Remarks: The prospectus says that 'Tonbridge seeks to excel in everything it does' and it certainly lives up to its aim. 'We have been delighted with the school and our boys have been happy and done well here, but you sometimes wonder if the next stage of their lives can live up to this amazing start', said one parent.

Tormead School

27 Cranley Road, Guildford, Surrey GU1 2JD

Pupils: 722 • Ages: 4–18 • Sixth form: 84

Fees: £7,581 – £14,454 pa

Tel: 01483 575101
Email: registrar@tormeadschool.org.uk
Website: www.tormeadschool.org.uk

Head: Since 2010, Mrs Christina Foord BA MPhil PGCE (40s), previously deputy head and head of boarding at St Catherine's, Bramley. Prior to this she taught English and history in a number of schools including The Queen's School, Chester. She takes a keen interest in music and sport of all sorts and is eager to provide her girls with opportunities to showcase their talents. Known throughout the school as being 'up for a challenge', she recently abseiled down the tower of Guildford Cathedral in aid of charity. Married, with two senior-school aged children and two dogs. Staff remark in admiration that she's ready to get 'stuck in', and when the new climbing wall was inaugurated, she was one of the first to scale it.

Junior school head: Since 2014 is Mrs Louise Salmond Smith BA MMus PGCE MBA (late 30s). Read music at University of East Anglia (emphasis on performance – recorder – and electroacoustic composition) then MMus in performance and educational composition at Hull University. A PGCE from Gloucestershire soon followed, as well as an MBA from Keele. Currently doing an MA in ICT and education at Leeds. Experience in education ranges from being a gap student in a boarding school to working on large-scale educational projects for a Lincolnshire music charity. Five years as director of music at The Grange School, Santiago; a stint in the maintained sector; then director of music at Hall Grove. Also loves teaching ICT and English, and has run photography and podcasting clubs as well as musical activities. Always a keen volunteer on school trips that are likely to involve mud, rain and jumping into lakes; encourages girls to challenge themselves by venturing off piste. Plays the recorder at art festivals round the country.

Husband Andrew is head of Wellington College International Junior School, Shanghai; they have two teenage daughters.

Academic matters: The junior school manages to be both happy and academic, and its wide curriculum very much reflects the priorities of the senior school across the road. In reception, literacy and numeracy are taught in the mornings, when the little ones are fresh, with content reflecting the national curriculum and the primary frameworks for English and maths, but teaching designed to extend well beyond. Core English, maths, science and ICT, plus French from year 2 and Latin from year 5. Girls are gradually prepped for the entrance exam to the senior school, although everyone is keen to stress the lack of pressure – pupils included.

Progressive changes in the curriculum over the past several years, with much closer tracking of children, internal Tormead exams in years 3, 4 and 5, plus standardized tests every summer term. No setting or streaming in the lower school, until year 6 when the girls are set for maths and English.

Much focus on thinking skills, learning attitudes, and encouraging the girls to take risks, both academically and physically. Ethos geared toward helping them to have confidence in their work and in their lives. Much effort to create a culture of thinking outside the box, exemplified in the Out of the Box Project in which pupils invent a 360 degree art project or answer questions such as 'What's inside Paddington Bear's suitcase?' or 'What's Leonardo's next invention?'

One of the high fliers in Surrey (and way beyond). Excellent academic results across a wide range of subjects – 2016 GCSE results were 80 per cent at A*/A; A level results 90 per cent A*-B and just under two-thirds A*/A. 'Does really well even by less academic students,' says a parent. Plenty of scope for choice in languages at GCSE and A levels including Spanish, German, and Greek.

Ten GCSEs is the norm. Refreshing to see that risk-talking is also encouraged – pupils who are keen to pursue a subject which may not be their academic forte are still encouraged to follow their dreams. Pupils do not feel unduly under pressure academically ('not as pushy as other schools,' said a parent), and any worries about exams are sensitively handled by the school. Grade sheet system introduced where pupils are marked for effort as well as attainment throughout the school year, so the less academic still get plenty of credit for trying hard and 'you feel on top of how your daughter is really doing,' said a parent.

SEN provision recently upgraded from peripatetic support to a full-blown department, including a full-time member of staff in the junior school, offering not only dyslexia support but also study skills, maths clinics and acknowledgement of different learning styles. 'Brilliant,' say pupils, 'Extremely good at helping you out,' and no stigma here for anyone having extra help. Personal attention pays off. Pupils with dyslexia credit their teachers with helping them flourish – dyslexic pupils have achieved A*s and served as head girl.

Games, options, the arts: A school known for its gymnasts ('we're hot on gymnastics here,' said one pupil, proudly); there's an excellent complex with sports hall, specialist gymnasts' training hall with sprung floor, strategy area with teachers' rooms leading off and viewing gallery. All sport is played keenly and to a high standard – including hockey, netball, rounders, swimming and tennis. Enthusiastic uptake of a new system of 'development squads' for the keen but less naturally able players. Increased number of fixtures for the B and C teams after parental complaints that the A teams were stealing the show.

It's a small campus and space is at a premium, but on-site facilities are supplemented by use of formidable local ones, such as the Surrey Sports Park at the University of Surrey – the school has an agreement that lets the hockey team use it as their home pitch, allowing the introduction of junior hockey; other sports include spinning, zumba, a climbing wall and squash. Tennis is on two on-site all-weather tennis courts. Tormead has sporting success at county level and nationally, especially in swimming, gymnastics, biathlon and sports acrobatics – a lack of on-site facilities isn't holding them back.

From reception upwards, games and gymnastics weekly with specialist teachers, with swimming added in year 2. Junior extracurricular sports offerings impressive – netball, hockey, swimming, dance, gymnastics, tag rugby, athletics and tennis – and timetabled so that anyone can join, either in the 'all welcome' meetings or in selective teams.

Music strong but school is looking to improve. The 'have a go' approach applies to music in the junior school, so that there are musical opportunities for 'kids who can play three notes and those who can play at grade 4'. Two music lessons per week until year 2, then three weekly lessons thereafter. Loads of private lessons taken up, plus choir, chamber choir, two orchestras, jazz band and more. The majority of girls play a musical instrument or are part of the choir.

Music mandatory until year 9, enthusiastic participation afterwards. Some 275 individual music lessons a week, plus two senior school orchestras, a jazz band (which tours Europe biennially), numerous ensembles and choirs. Lots of performance opportunities for budding musicians, including lunchtime concerts on campus and in town. A programme of events throughout the year, including the inter-house music competition in which every girl takes part. The performing arts centre provides a modern and vibrant venue, with a proscenium stage and professional lighting and sound. LAMDA speech and drama awards are a popular extracurricular option and several girls each year get gold medals. Art is exceptionally strong here – wonderful examples are on display around the school and new art suite recently opened.

Much buzz around other extracurriculars, including additional sporting, language, film, art and craft activities, plus fencing, movie club, cake decorating, origami and debating (another school success story). Sports and music clubs can be selective, but there is something for everyone and there is a definite 'have a go' attitude. Students regularly achieve recognition in D of E Award Scheme (multiple gold awards achieved each year), the Wings of Hope Achievement Awards, and others. School is one of only a handful nationally to have been awarded Star status by the British Schools Exploring Society. Past sixth form destinations have included Vietnam and Zambia, with plans for Ecuador and Galapagos and a partnership in Nepal.

Background and atmosphere: Founded in 1905, the school has made do in the past with a hodge-podge of classrooms and Hogwarts-style corridors tacked onto the original Victorian building ('Frankenstein's building,' quips Foord), but ambitious modernisation and expansion has seen addition of new pupil entrance with drop-off zone to ease congestion on the residential street in front of the school, enlarged atrium-style dining (allowing longer lunches and mid-day activities), wider corridors and even breakout areas – plus 22 large classrooms and full disabled access to senior school. The main junior school building is in a large, charming, if somewhat care-worn old house, with a snug little library off the main hall.

Goal is not to increase size of the student body, but to 'improve the experience of those already there.' Grounds are relatively small, befitting Tormead's practically urban status within Guildford. It feels quite intimate and is divided into four sections; heads of year report to pastoral deputy head.

Numerous and well-equipped science labs (sciences very strong here), plus a dedicated sixth form physics room with a white board, computers, etc. An impressive art department and design and technology room. The library which is new with sixth form area. Library resources accessible from home. Food described as 'pretty good for school food,' with an array of hot and cold selections – salad and pasta bar, jacket potatoes, etc. Increasing uptake of the early morning breakfast club, which starts at 7:50am. IT provision good, with plenty of computers and internet connections, WiFi soon available to the whole school, but closely monitored, as school is still considering how to integrate technology into school life without opening the floodgates to Facebook and Twitter on campus.

The sixth formers have their own department (revered and envied by the younger girls), no uniform, and recently refurbished lair complete with kitchen facilities, groovy furniture and a clock designed by the DT teacher. Sixth form girls love their freedom and love being treated as equals, compliment the school on letting them organize charity events, discos, etc themselves. They are visibly proud of their achievements in maths and science and comment on how much extra time teachers will spend to help students understand the material. Popular socials with local boys' schools – RGS, Lanesborough, Cranmore – plus quite the social life with other Guildford schools via the daily train journeys.

Pastoral care, well-being and discipline: A strength of the school is its nurturing environment. 'Good at taking the timid and shy and making them blossom,' said a parent. In addition to emphasizing girls' independence and strengths, the junior school has a very proactive policy on creating a positive atmosphere and combating bullying in any form. It works this magic by focusing on the small things, whether it's a pencil case or an unkind comment, because for girls of this age, 'that's their reality'. Junior staff are trained to ensure that if girls come to them with an issue, no matter how small, it is dealt with promptly. If it becomes bigger, the school looks at both sides and actively monitors the girls on a daily basis to ensure that the issue remains resolved. In school's view, girls should not have to go home with unresolved issues; at the very least they should know someone is aware of the problem and will deal with it on the morrow. Expectations of pupils' behaviour are made clear to all, and serious breaches might mean a call into head's office, followed by a conversation with parents straight away.

The school has embraced the ethos that girls need to be happy in order to learn, work and enjoy school. Various problem-solving options start with the form tutor and a trained counsellor is on hand. System of 'aunts' whereby every new girl in the senior school has another girl assigned to her to help through the first few weeks. New full-time staff member for university counselling and professional development, keen to refocus pupils not only on university entrance but also 'what they will be like when they're 35 and beyond.' 'Oxbridge teas' to link past and present pupils, higher education evening for lower sixth, even support for SAT tests for those pupils considering university in the US.

Pastoral care programme unanimously praised by parents as superb, for some the deciding factor in choosing the school. 'My daughter comes off the bus happy all the time. Nothing seems to overwhelm her,' says one parent. Another notes, 'Mine doesn't compare herself to others, but she used to in her old school. Academics used to be very hard, now she just takes it in her stride.' Less confident girls benefit from the caring and positive ethos; girls leave the school with self-confidence, good social skills and a dash of worldliness.

Parents 'have no hesitation' in getting in touch with the school. Any issues are dealt with promptly. PSHE lessons start in the junior school and extend, by the time they reach the sixth form, to discussions about substance abuse, personal safety, relationships and childcare. Assembly an important beginning to the school day, emphasis on care, respect and highlighting the six 'core values' of the school, which cover topics such as respect, academic excellence, a varied curriculum, and bringing out the best in the girls in preparation for life beyond school. Tough line on all transgressions – drugs possession a cause for instant expulsion, similar stance on persistent smoking or misbehaviour. Both pupils and parents say bullying is confronted openly and with great success.

Pupils and parents: Pupils are bubbly and enthusiastic, self-confident and friendly. They appreciate their all-girl campus ('You can come to school ugly!') and have a strong sense of their good fortune in being there. Neatly dressed in blue blazers (new rules for wearing them), no ties but occasional personalised uniform in evidence. Happy chatter in the hallways between classes.

Parents' association encompasses the whole school, with a co-chair for the junior school and the senior school. Class reps are part of the parents' committee, and they serve as point of contact for new parents. Parents have very much bought into the ethos and enhance the community of the school.

Parents mostly English or foreign nationals raised in the area, with a mixture of backgrounds – old girls, professionals, London-bound commuters, first-time buyers. Excellent bus service extends all the way to Esher and Haslemere (and beyond); parents and offspring alike sing its praises. Old girls include comedian Sandy Toksvig and Claudia Parsons, the first woman to circumnavigate the world by car.

Entrance: Selective at 4 (by a 'party' where girls are observed by staff members) and at 7 by maths, English and reasoning tests.

Entrance exam at 11, with pupils selected for academic potential (reasoning, maths and English), extracurricular interests and current school reference. No interview. Apart from junior school girls, top students from feeder schools including Rydes Hill, Rowan, St Hilary's Godalming and Halstead. Some 25 to 30 per cent from state schools. Sixth form entrance requirements include eight GCSEs, A*-C, with at least five at grade A or above, with an A grade recommended for the subjects to be studied (Tormead students usually far exceed these requirements). Girls entering sixth form from other schools are interviewed.

T

Exit: The vast majority of the junior girls sit the entrance exam for the senior school and 90 per cent go on there. Those who don't make the grade (although very few fail) are handled sensitively and are advised on 'a senior school better suited to their educational needs'.

About half stay on to sixth form. Four to Oxbridge in 2016, including Clare College's first ever female organ scholar; Birmingham, Bristol, Bath, Exeter, Durham and East Anglia all popular, with students opting for eg medicine, politics, chemical engineering, mathematics, psychology and history.

Money matters: Parents remark on the 'good value' represented by the school. At 11+, academic, music, sport and art scholarships, worth 10 per cent of tuition fees. For sixth form, academic, music, and art scholarships, plus internal sport scholarships are available. Full bursaries available at 11+ and 16+ on a case-by-case basis.

Remarks: A nurturing, buzzy school with a tradition of high academic standards that is not content to rest on its laurels. New facilities bringing it in line with its aspirations. Opportunities for pupils to find their niche, whether in art, sport, drama or music, while still encouraging experimentation and maintaining an all-round approach.

Tring Park School for the Performing Arts

Tring Park, Tring, Hertfordshire HP23 5LX

Pupils: 326; 64 boys, 145 girls full boarders • Ages: 8–19 (optional 3rd year in sixth form for dancers) • Sixth form: 143: 38 boys, 105 girls

Fees: Day £14,070 – £22,410; Boarding £23,715 – £33,540 pa

Tel: 01442 824255
Email: info@tringpark.com
Website: www.tringpark.com

Principal: Since 2002, Mr Stefan Anderson MA BMus ARCM ARCT. Fifties, single, no children. A highly personable man whose Boris Karloff-like photo on the school's website in no way reflects his immense charm and humour. A classically trained musician, he grew up in Canada and attended Carleton University, Ottawa; then moved to the UK and studied at the Royal College of Music and Emmanuel College, Cambridge, where he was an organ scholar. He spent 12 years at Wellington as assistant director of music, then seven years as director of music at King's Canterbury, before taking up the principal's post at Tring in 2002. Very much involved in education nationally: an executive director of the Boarding Schools Association, and a trustee of the National Schools Symphony Orchestra. Universally liked and admired by parents and pupils. 'I think he's wonderful. He's absolutely spot on with the kids,' said one mother. 'They all respect him, but they can have a laugh with him,' said another. 'Kind and courteous and very professional,' pronounced a third. 'Makes time for you, easy to deal with, very helpful and very fair,' added a fourth. 'He's brilliant, a character,' said a father, 'There's a great fun side to him.' The feeling is clearly mutual. 'I love it here!' Mr Anderson affirmed. 'The students can be high-maintenance, but it's never dull.'

Academic matters: Tring's results are proof that for the right children, the chance to do what they love actually enhances their academic performance. Only half the school day is given over to academic lessons, and the students here are selected solely on their performing abilities (if they pass the audition, applicants sit academic tests for diagnostic purposes), yet results just keep getting better. In 2016, 34 per cent of GCSE passes were A*/A. You could be forgiven for wondering if these results were made up of non-academic subjects such as drama and dance, but no: they cover the full spread including sciences and languages. In 2016, A level results were 32 per cent A*/A and 56 per cent A*/B, and 77 per cent got D or D* in BTec performing arts. Solid spread of academic subjects offered includes English lit, French, German, RS, history, geography, IT, and all the sciences. 'We push the academic side hard,' confirmed the head, who was brought in to improve Tring's profile in that area. Active and successful learning support department caters for wide variety of SEN, and roughly a quarter of students have either one-to-one or small group support. Parents report themselves very happy with the provision. One mother whose child has dyscalculia reported, 'She really struggles with maths, but she's had excellent support.' A boy with dyslexia told us, 'I've never had so much help as I've had here.' 'The support for dyslexia is brilliant,' said a father.

Those of us who remember the days when stage school was more often than not a byword for poor education can only marvel. But then Tring isn't a stage school in the old-fashioned sense, as the pupils were eager to point out, but a heady mix of high-level vocational and academic education, where the two strands rub together to produce very bright sparks. The former head boy has gone off to Manchester to read medicine, and one Tring alumna, a physicist, has recently started her doctorate. As the director of studies, herself a Cantabrigian, put it: 'It's very exciting working with students who are engaged and passionate with their lives. There's a joie de vivre here that spills into academic lessons.' That said, it's important to remember that this is a vocational school, one of only eight such in the UK funded by the DfE as centres of excellence for exceptionally talented young dancers and musicians. Tring's remit is to produce highly-trained performers who've received a rounded education; not lawyers and doctors who like hoofing.

Games, options, the arts: Believe it or not, Tring had actually played a football fixture shortly before we visited. They lost 11-0. 'But,' assured the head, 'we played with great passion.' Students do get together for an informal kickabout, or walk down the High Street to the local swimming pool, but there are no organised games on Tring's timetable, because there isn't time for them. Instead, half of every weekday is given over to vocational training, and, say parents and students alike, it's amazing. 'Equal to the very best available in this country,' said one parent. 'Inspirational!' said another. 'Second to none, absolutely fabulous,' said a third. 'My son's physical fitness has improved dramatically,' said a fourth. And everyone else said something similar.

Children in the prep (years 4-6) receive training in acting, singing and dancing. Thereafter, students specialise in either dance or theatre arts. Dance training covers ballet, contemporary, tap and jazz; drama training does pretty much the same, but less intensively and also covers voice, improvisation, and other aspects of theatre technique. And of course there's musical theatre and singing too. Tring isn't a specialist music school – aspiring concert pianists would feel frustrated at having to break off and jeté every time they'd sat down to practice – but the music department is strong, with several excellent choirs and all students given the chance to learn instruments and play in ensembles.

Packed programme of shows, plays, musicals and other performances throughout the year, all of them done to an astonishingly high standard. Sometimes students have a chance to do external work – ballet dancers regularly join English National Ballet for productions of The Nutcracker, for instance – but not that often. The school doesn't encourage students to be absent, and children wanting a school that will act as their agent and find them regular professional work should look elsewhere.

Boarding: With limited space and funds, the boarding provision was only rated 'satisfactory' by Ofsted in 2011, and we have to say we thought it pretty basic; we saw seven girls to a room, for instance. On the other hand, the 9-12 year old girls in question didn't seem bothered. 'It's fun! Like we're one big family! And if we're having a row, the houseparents sort it out and then we're all best friends again!' Pupils are encouraged to do what they think will make their quarters nice: thus the girls' accommodation was a profusion of heart-shaped pink fluffiness, whilst the boys' was as fresh and tidy as you'd expect rooms shared by multiple boys to be. New boarding accommodation planned to start in 2018. Feedback about the food was very mixed, with a number of parents expressing anxiety about how much and how healthily their children were eating, and several stories of boarders needing to pop into town to fortify themselves at McDonald's (a behaviour not confined to Tring students, of course). We ourselves were given a pleasant and nutritionally-balanced meal in the canteen, so it's impossible to comment on this further.

Background and atmosphere: Today's Tring grew out of the Cone Ripman School, founded in 1939 and itself the result of a merger between two previous dance schools. Originally located in London, the outbreak of war forced a move to Tring where the school shared premises with the Rothschild Bank at Tring Park Mansion House (strange bedfellows they must have been). In 1941, the school was able to move back to London but kept its Tring premises as a second school where boarders could be accommodated, and in 1947 both places were re-named the Arts Educational School, to reflect Grace Cone's and Olive Ripman's commitment to a proper academic education for their stage-struck charges. Gradually the two schools diverged, with London becoming more focused on post-18 training, while Tring continued to develop as a vocational boarding school. Eventually they became completely independent and in 2009 the Tring school changed its name to Tring Park School for the Performing Arts, in order to avoid confusion with its former partner. Originally for girls only, one boy was admitted in 1993, 'and that opened the floodgates'.

Still housed in the gorgeously flamboyant mansion in which it took refuge over 70 years ago, Tring Park School literally sings with activity and joy. Half the stunning wood-panelled entrance hall is glazed off as a dance studio, and we arrived amidst cries of 'Five, six, seven, eight, and right! Two, three, four, and left!', while Guys and Dolls mingled jauntily with a more demure strain from the ballet class next door. Everywhere we looked, we saw children enjoying themselves and eager to tell us so. 'Life here is amazing!' 'You get here and everyone has something to give!' 'Everyone's really welcoming!' 'It's so creative!' 'It just makes you want to dance more, being here. You get to see everyone's talent!' 'You have more time here for what you love, you're more connected!' twittered a group of frankly adorable young things. Parents agree. 'If you have a non-academic child, as we have, the enthusiasm and the passion motivates them to do better at everything. Our son loves it, he absolutely thrives on it,' said one mother. Another commented, 'The children are lovely, all so dedicated, and it really is like a family,' adding, 'When my husband and I are walking round the school, we wish we were there!' 'Every child comes out with poise and confidence from that place, they all know how to present themselves.'

The mansion's Grade II listed status has hampered some necessary modernisation – it took years to get planning permission for Wifi to be installed – but the school boasts an impressive array of newly-built dance studios. It has also received funding for an even bigger and better theatre to supplement the existing 176-seat Markova Theatre, while the new art centre will move from the site of Baron Rothschild's zebra cage to a new home next to the theatre. The surrounding tree-studded gardens provide a tranquil and soothing backdrop to all the artistic fervour.

Feathers do get ruffled occasionally. 'Inevitably at a school like this, there is competition, and I think there should be,' said one level-headed student. But everyone we spoke to insisted that the school also fostered care and affection amongst its students.

'We've always been taught not to compare ourselves to others, but to where we were last term,' said one sixth-former. 'If their best friend gets the part, the others still give her a hug,' said one mother. Another said, 'There is no real jealousy or one-upmanship over talent, and good performances are widely praised and discussed between pupils.'

Parents were less starry-eyed about school-parent communication, and everyone we spoke to agreed that it needed improving. 'Communications are not all they should be,' was a very typical criticism; 'they could be more regular and more informative.' Another said bluntly, 'We pay a hell of a lot of money for our child to go to Tring, and if I send an email I expect an answer.' The head acknowledged these criticisms with candour. 'I would absolutely agree. We need to upgrade our facilities so that we can have a parent portal. We email things weekly, but we don't have a newsletter as such. We have plans – our aim is to get a new iSAMs system (school information software). Staff are extremely busy here, but that doesn't excuse it, and I take it on board.' A new appointment, head of careers, was made recently to address concerns that families weren't getting enough information and help with students' UCAS applications.

We also heard disquiet from parents whose children hadn't been allowed to take the course of their choice at 14+ or 16+ after having already spent two or more years at the school. Specifics weren't forthcoming, but we gathered that this particularly applied to those with aspirations to a career in dance. 'This can be a more difficult adjustment than the school acknowledges, and it's you the parent who has to deal with your child's disappointment,' wrote one worried mother. But as other parents observed, a career in the performing arts is tough, and the head was adamant that the school always put the child's best interests first. 'I would dispute very strongly that we block anyone, but we try to get the child onto the course where we feel they'll succeed. If someone has unrealistic expectations, we speak to the child and to the parents. But 95 per cent of the time, parental, child and school expectations match up.' The great majority of parents we spoke to agreed. As one mother wrote, 'Tring provides a very supportive network for students who are struggling or who change their minds about whether vocational training is for them.' Another said simply, 'The support given by Tring's staff is exceptional. Our son is very happy there, and flourishing beyond our imagination.'

Pastoral care, well-being and discipline: To a person, parents praised Tring's pastoral care, with the boarding staff particularly singled out. 'The housemother was wonderful, and my son settled in really quickly,' 'A houseparent in a million' 'The houseparents are so switched on,' ''The houseparents comfort you if you're homesick!' 'They're amazing! They do so much for us!' were typical comments. The medical unit was also very highly rated: 'Informs you immediately if there are any problems,' 'The medical staff were exceptional,' 'Both pastoral and medical care have always been exemplary.'

T

Behaviour at Tring is exuberant but respectful. There are the usual sanctions for infringements, but the students want to be here and are generally keen not to mess up. Many parents commented on the children's excellent work ethic, and one boy added, 'My time management has become fantastic since starting here. You really do become reliable, hard working, responsible. You have to work hard.'

Pupils and parents: From a very broad range of backgrounds, and from all over the UK. Some from overseas (around 10 per cent of boarders), and EAL help is there for those who need it. Many of them new to boarding, or to independent schools, or to the world of performing arts, but all of them united by a common ardour. Inevitably, there are more girls than boys, with the current ratio being more than 2:1. Do the boys mind? 'No, because I'm friends with all the boys in my year,' said one young lad, 'and my confidence with girls has increased!'

Entrance: Children can join the school from age 8 to 16, but the commonest entry points are at ages 11-13, 14 and 16. Applications are increasing, particularly at 16+, and overall the school receives seven applications for every place. One-day audition process at which children show what they can do in dance, drama and singing. They aren't expected to excel in all three of these – although many do – but the school is looking for great talent and potential in the candidate's chosen specialism, 'and they have to show a real desire to learn,' says head. If they're successful in gaining a place but need funding to take it up, they're called to a second audition.

Exit: The majority of students continue on into the performing arts in one way or another. A few dance stars progress straight to major companies such as English National Ballet and Scottish Ballet; others might join the school's own dance company, Encore, for a rigorous third year of touring and performing, or take up places at dance schools such as The Place. Drama schools are also a popular destination: Laine Theatre Arts, Bristol Old Vic, etc. 'And we regularly turn out some good classical musicians,' adds head, although invariably these are singers – one recent alumna went on to train at The Royal Academy of Music and has already appeared with Garsington Opera and Opera North. Some go straight into professional work (Downton Abbey has mopped up several Tring alumni). And a number decide to go to university instead: one sixth former we spoke to was waiting to hear back from Trinity Hall, Cambridge, where she'd applied to read history. One medic in 2016 and one off to Boston Conservatory.

Much praise from parents and pupils alike for the way Tring supports and guides students' career aspirations. 'I'd love to get a job in a ballet company,' said one young male dancer, 'but my body doesn't work that way, I'm not flat-turned-out. But the teachers work with you to find other ways you can do things, and they're brilliant.' A parent whose son was now at college told us, 'He knows he can still call on Tring for help and advice, a relationship he really values.'

Money matters: Stonkingly high fees, as you'd expect with all this specialist tuition, but around one third of students are on some kind of support. Dancers who join the school at age 11, 12 or 13 can apply for funding from the government's means-tested Music and Dance Scheme. Dance students joining at 16+ may be eligible for DaDA scholarships (Dance and Drama Awards, another source of government funding). And Tring has its own scholarship fund for musical theatre and drama pupils, to which families can apply. Many Tring students come from families on modest or low incomes. Up to 100 per cent assistance available for those who need it.

Remarks: An extremely impressive vocational school that gives its students an excellent and well-balanced education. Children for whom the performing arts are central to their existence will feel they've come home the moment they walk through the door. As one mother whose daughter had been there eight years said, 'We cannot fault it. She's had a wonderful time, and the training has been amazing. Her work ethic is fantastic, she's very well-prepared for auditions, she's made friends for life, and she's grown into a wonderful young lady.'

Tudor Hall School

Wykham Park, Banbury, Oxfordshire OX16 9UR

Pupils: 332; 256 full boarders • Ages: 11–18 • Sixth form: 89

Fees: Day £20,745; Boarding £32,610 pa

Tel: 01295 263434
Email: admissions@tudorhallschool.com
Website: www.tudorhallschool.com

Headmistress: Since 2004, Miss Wendy Griffiths, BSc PGCE (50s). Educated at Queen Elizabeth Grammar School, Carmarthen, read zoology at University of Wales – still a trace of her Welsh accent. Previously head of sixth form at Tormead School, then director of studies at St Catherine's, Bramley.

Before our meeting we'd already been entertained by the sight of Miss Griffiths dancing and lip synching to Chic's We are Family in a film made by the girls of Todd (year 7 house). There aren't many heads we can call to mind who would even consider doing this, let alone be able to pull it off with such groovy aplomb. The video was playing on a wall-mounted screen, somewhat at odds with the restrained décor of the entrance hall. It's also on the school website, along with others – they like making films at Tudor Hall.

As a student she had plans to become a doctor, but while teaching in a Portsmouth comprehensive Miss Griffiths had an epiphany. After seeing how excited her class became during an 'ambitious' practical lesson she succumbed to pedagogy and has never looked back.

With her sleek bob and leather skirt, Miss G is poised and highly professional (albeit with a twinkle). She was described to us as someone who 'never slows down', which may account for the fact that in addition to the responsibilities of headship she is also just coming to the end of a stint as chair of the Boarding Schools Association in its 50th anniversary year. What about boarding schools then, we asked, are they still necessary? 'Almost more than ever', was the not unexpected reply. A boarding school is able to inculcate so much more than narrow academics: 'Instead of sitting at home glued to social media, at boarding school children have to be be social, they learn how to get on with everyone'.

Miss Griffiths still interviews prospective pupils and teaches a GCSE biology class – that's four lessons a week, very unusual for a senior school head. She lives on site with her husband, who teaches history at Sibford School; they have one daughter. Spare time, should there be such a thing, is for dog walking – plenty of Cotswolds on the doorstep for that.

To conclude, here's a little list of the the words parents used to describe Miss Griffiths: 'Outstanding', 'astonishing', 'highly professional', 'diplomatic', 'inspiring' and (we heard this one repeatedly), 'a great role model'. 'She just gets it', said one.

Academic matters: Gradual upward trajectory of academic results is testament to small classes (average 15), plenty of individual attention and by all accounts, dedicated and inspirational teaching. In 2016, 64 per cent A*/A at GCSE and 79 per cent A*-B at A level (39 per cent A*/A). Top performers at A level are geography, economics and maths. That maths is one of the most popular A levels speaks volumes for the teaching – head told us with regret how girls continue to arrive from prep schools saying they 'can't do' it.

Innovative work to inspire girls to stay engaged not just with maths but also science subjects. Super new labs for exploding jelly babies as well as more serious experiments. We saw girls in smart red lab coats investigating their own cheek cells under the microscope. Lively programme of extracurricular science clubs, visits to science fairs and National Space Centre etc.

We shared a delicious lunch with girls who had very different and exciting plans for their future – lots of gap years followed by courses from criminology to drama. No sense that sixth formers are all expected to board the non-stop university express – one told us how much support she'd had for her decision to go straight into interior design rather than take a degree in the subject.

Visiting speakers widen horizons as does head's initiative, 'Tudor in three continents', which includes travel scholarships for girls to participate in projects in India, Bolivia and South Africa; has recently become 'Tudor in four continents'. School has added a project that doesn't involve epic amounts of air travel: mentoring children at the Bolton Lads and Girls (sic) Club. Meeting less fortunate children in their own country, rather than thousands of miles away, has been a very profound experience.

Parents told us staff keep an eagle eye on each girl's progress and are quick to intervene if she appears to be lagging. 'Teachers work so hard to get the right results; if there's a problem they really drill down to find the root cause'. Girls love the fact that teachers are so accessible: 'there's always a subject teacher who can help if you're stuck on homework or revision'. What parents love is the individual attention given to their daughters' academic progress; all those we spoke to said they were confident no child would be allowed to struggle or fall behind.

SEN or EAL support provided individually or in classes but head says this is not the place for a girl with serious needs; 'we want all pupils to be able to participate fully in the curriculum'. Dynamic learning support team uses variety of approaches including latest educational technology such as iPad apps.

Games, options, the arts: School has put considerable efforts into improving sports provision and parents say that it's much better. Facilities are all present and correct including glass roofed outdoor swimming pool (not used in the winter) and plenty of pitches. Girls told us that a 'bigger gym' and a 'pavilion on the top pitch' would be great. Larger schools' A teams are likely to have the advantage so notable and sustained recent successes at county level in hockey and cross-country are all the more creditable. Individual talents in tennis (lovely courts in former walled garden), skiing and riding are well supported and a wider range of non-competitive options such as swim fit and zumba are offered in the sixth form. Girls also work with Carrdus School (Oxfordshire prep owned by Tudor Hall) and local primary schools to provide pupils with coaching and taster sessions in eg lacrosse.

Drama is offered at GCSE and A level but TH girls love to perform, whether or not they are pursing it as a subject option. Great results in LAMDA speech and drama exams too. Regular participation in Shakespeare Schools' Festival, plenty of theatre trips and a choice of stages – new (2015) studio theatre has eye-catching neon sign. Dance is accorded greater status here than at other schools and can be taken as a GCSE. Reaction, the audition-only school dance group, has been going for over 20 years; the house dance title is as keenly fought as house singing and drama competitions. Music, too, offers girls of all abilities the chance to perform – whether at school concerts, carol singing at care homes or carrying off trophies at Banbury Young Musician of the Year competitions.

The quality of the art, both in the studios and (perhaps a little infrequently) displayed throughout the school, fair took our breath away. Quite the best we can remember seeing anywhere.

Likewise textiles and photography. Style and subject matter went from traditional to unexpectedly edgy and challenging. The textile and art rooms stay open into the evening and at weekends and girls love the freedom this gives them to work on their projects outside lessons. Textiles currently housed in Portakabin but purpose built studios are in the offing. Leavers regularly go on to art foundation and fashion design courses.

Extracurricular options encompass just about everything from Model United Nations to the very popular dissection club. It seems not only can a Tudor Hall girl address a crowd and whip up a soufflé (if she's done the Leith's course), she can also eviscerate a frog. Parents approve of the way girls are kept very busy lower down the school, gradually developing independent study skills as they approach the relative freedom of the sixth form.

Boarding: The full Monty – two exeats per term and no flexi or weekly. Saturday school with lessons until 1pm and games in the afternoon, trips, activities and down time thereafter. Boarding is arranged horizontally – ie by year group – meaning that everything (activities, bed times etc) can be tailored to the age group. Works especially well at exam times – much easier if everyone around you is revising.

Year 7 boarders and day girls are based in Todd (named after the school's founders), a charming house with a large peaceful garden on the edge of the school grounds. It's as uninstitutional as possible with a large family kitchen, colourful soft furnishings and lots of toys and games. And, when we visited, a body on the sitting room floor. 'Just step over it, we're doing first aid,' the housemistress told us. Todd girls love putting on plays and concerts for their captive audience, they also enjoy 'special breakfasts', baking and Sunday excursions (day girls can go too). Todd girls have lower sixth buddies, described to us as a 'big sister support system'.

Dorms vary from two to six cabin beds; bathrooms are clean but on the functional side. Apparently they're 'due for a refurb'. Personal technology at this end of the school limited to mobile phones for 10 minutes a day. Skype etc always available, 'we never stop a child speaking to their parents'. Glad to hear it. Housemistress has set up a Facebook page for Todd parents who get daily photos and updates on their girls' activities.

Other houses (known as The 11s, The 111s and so on) are spacious and well equipped. Girls need no encouragement to personalise their space; walls were papered with photos, letters, bunting and many, many rosettes – plenty of keen horsewomen here.

Each boarding house has its own character and traditions so there's a real sense of progression through the school. Sixth form accommodation is designed as a halfway house to prepare girls for living independently. They can cook, are responsible for their own laundry and organise trips and activities. One such is the Christmas shopping trip to Paris (plus Disneyland Paris); no shortage of teachers signing up to chaperone that one, we imagine.

T

Background and atmosphere: One of the oldest girls' boarding schools in England, Tudor Hall was founded in 1850 by Rev T W Todd and his wife. In 1908 the school moved from London to rural Kent and on the outbreak of the Second World War it decamped to Burnt Norton, a small Cotswold manor house, to escape the air raids. Pupils, teachers and parents stayed here, even during the holidays, and old girls remember those times with great affection. It was a visit to the gardens at Burnt Norton that inspired T S Eliot to write his eponymous poem, a meditation on time, memory and original sin. Perhaps he would have penned something a little jollier than 'Garlic and sapphires in the mud clot the bedded axle-tree' if he'd visited a few years later when the Tudor Hall girls were in residence.

Surrounding area predominantly rural – grazing cows more common than passing traffic – but access to Oxford, London, Stratford etc pretty easy. Nearest town is Banbury. A great summer treat for the older girls is, we were told, to walk to the nearby farm shop, buy a picnic and eat it in a field. Wouldn't suit a committed urbanite, but that's not really the demographic which is, we suspect, one that is accustomed to town and country living and has the right shoes for both.

First time visitors may be surprised to find no busy reception desk; the entrance hall, with its bergere furniture, beautiful flowers and polished wood, is rather reminiscent of an exclusive hotel – but the welcome is warm and personal. Usual mix of buildings – not everywhere is country house gracious – but all well tended. School magazine and publicity material are similar – high production values but nothing boasty or brash. Come to think of it, that probably sums up the Tudor Hall pupil.

Pastoral care, well-being and discipline: Tudor Hall has long had a reputation for the highest standards of pastoral care, but don't confuse caring with soft. Yes, it's a nurturing environment, as all the best small schools are, but within that environment girls are encouraged and tested; challenged to overreach their own boundaries and try new things.

All the parents we spoke to felt that their daughters were in the safest of hands and cited many examples of occasions when tutors or other members of staff had gone above and beyond to help or advise them. Day and boarding parents get a weekly update from tutors about what's been going on and home school communication in general receives nothing but praise.

A couple of people we spoke to thought the downside of year group boarding was that it contributed to a somewhat stratified hierarchical atmosphere, but we didn't feel this was the case. Vertical house system, not to mention the mix of different clubs and sporting activities, must go a long way to defuse this.

Day girls are very well integrated and can join their boarding friends for trips and weekend activities, but it's a long day and, with Saturday school, a long week. Even year 7 day pupils don't finish until 6.45pm or later, although they will have had an hour or so's break, a snack and done their homework.

Regular socials with chaps from Radley, Eton and Harrow. The young gentlemen from Harrow are current favourites, but apparently this changes from year to year.

What do you gain from boarding, we asked a group of sixth formers? They all cited strong and lasting friendships; others valued the 'accessibility' of teaching staff and the fact that there's always someone around to help with academic work. 'It helps you become responsible and independent – and it stops you taking home for granted.' We like that last one but doubt it survives the summer holidays.

Pupils and parents: Most recent ISI report described Tudor Hall pupils as 'overwhelmingly positive in outlook' which sounds rather alarming – a posse of Pollyannas, perhaps. It would be so easy to fall back on the old stereotype of Tudor Hall girls as darling daughters of the home counties, what with Leith's, polo, doing the ski season, etc – but that wouldn't be fair or accurate.

The girls we met were friendly, thoughtful, comfortable in their own skins and definitely not the identikit result of an educational production line. There's no arrogance or sense of entitlement and definitely no hair flicking. Girls know they are fortunate and are very aware that the world beyond Banbury is considerably less shiny; it certainly won't be any the worse for having Tudor Hall alumnae in it.

Pride in one's school is not usually compatible with the teenage psyche, but Tudor Hall girls aren't too cool for that. Lots of daughters of old girls – always a good sign. Other old Tudorians include Katherine Hooker, tailor to Duchess of

Cambridge; Cleo Barbour, shoe designer; Julia Peyton-Jones, director of Serpentine Gallery.

Entrance: Candidates for 11+ and 13+ invited for 'taster day' (or day and night for prospective 11+ boarders) and assessment days with tests in maths, English and verbal reasoning. The tests are to 'ensure girls are compatible with academic pace' of school. Girls applying for entry at 13+ offered conditional places dependent on outcome of CE. All candidates are interviewed by the head who told us she is looking for 'character.' She believes that girls who are 'sparky about something' succeed because the school can channel their enthusiasm into other areas.

Exit: Art foundation seems to be most popular post A level choice and Oxford Brookes attracts quite a few. Bristol, Birmingham, Edinburgh, Exeter, Leeds, Newcastle, Nottingham are current Russell Group favourites; also one to Parsons fashion, art and design school in New York and one to the Academy of Contemporary Music. Occasional one or two to Oxbridge (one in 2016, and four medics).

Money matters: Fees at the slightly less eye watering end of the boarding range; day fees look like good value considering time spent in school. Academic, music, art, drama and sport scholarships (up to £1,000 pa) available at 11+, 13+ and 16+. Also textiles and dance at 16+. Means-tested bursaries to support new and current parents in financial need.

Remarks: Leave your preconceptions at the door and prepare to be bowled over. Whether your daughter is headed for fashion design or Oxbridge, under Miss Griffiths' dynamic stewardship Tudor Hall deserves a place on everyone's short list.

Tunbridge Wells Girls' Grammar School

Southfield Road, Tunbridge Wells, Kent TN4 9UJ

Pupils: 1,020 • Ages: 11–18 • Sixth form: 293

Tel: 01892 520902
Email: admin@twggs.kent.sch.uk
Website: www.twggs.kent.sch.uk

Headteacher: Since 1999 Linda Wybar, 50s. Educated at Blyth Grammar School and the University of Hull, where she read English and took her PGCE. She also has an MA in education management from the Open University, taken when her twin sons were toddlers. Linda's earliest ambition was to clean and tidy her parents' wool shop, but she soon decided she would prefer to be a headmistress and never looked back. She came south for her first teaching post and has taught in Kent schools ever since. Her first appointment, at a co-ed school, was a tough one where she 'learnt a lot about behaviour management and how to motivate young people'. Has worked in both girls' and boys' grammar schools: taught English for four years and then became head of department at Norton Knatchbull Boys' Grammar, where initially she was the only female member of staff, followed by deputy headship at Highsted Girls' Grammar, before moving to TWGGS as head teacher.

She still teaches English to a GCSE class. She says, 'The school prides itself on its blend of academic challenge and the wider life outside the classroom – expectations are consistently high but girls should still be able to pursue their passions where they can'. The school appears deceptively relaxed – 'there is lots of fun and laughter and we don't want girls to feel pressurised' – and she is proud of the exceptional pastoral care and guidance: 'a strong sense of community pervades the school; it is our greatest strength'. The girls say she is 'approachable and dynamic – she is very energetic and turns up to all the after-school stuff'. 'She is very passionate about the school and her assemblies are relevant, upbeat and encouraging, and she is in tune with the girls and well respected'. 'She is also quite strict and we can't get away with much', added a pupil. 'She is always available', said a parent, 'and you will always get an answer within 24 hours – you can feel the pride and pleasure she gets from the school'. She says she has been approached to lead independent schools and academies but feels there is still so much that is fresh and interesting to do at TWGGS, as the job is ever changing and nothing is taken for granted. She is highly skilled at obtaining funding, and next in her sights are a new science/technology block and a sports hall to replace the small, old fashioned gym.

Married with two grown up sons, she has a cottage in Cornwall where she and her husband retreat whenever they can. She loves good wine and food and the theatre and is a regular visitor to Stratford.

Academic matters: An unashamedly aspirational school with the results to go with it; girls are not pushed but expectations are high. In 2016, 80 per cent A*/A at GCSE with particularly good results in geography, maths, biology and English; 52 per cent A*/A at A level, with best results in economics and geography. Twenty-one subjects offered at A level including psychology, sociology, politics, economics, drama and music, with biology, maths and psychology being the most popular. Scholarship and academic rigour are two of the school's main priorities, but girls do not feel under pressure and younger girls are given a lot of help with time management skills. Setting in maths from year 8 and in science from year 10. Girls study three separate sciences from year 9 and most continue these to GCSE, but dual award is an option for some. Everyone learns French and German from year 7 and takes up Spanish in year 8, carrying on one or two languages to GCSE. All have to take a GCSE course in RS and most take the exam – 'it makes the girls think – especially the philosophy and ethics element,' says the head.

Close co-operation with Skinners' boys' grammar across the road eg PE and computing A level is taken at Skinners' and Skinners' boys come to TWGGS for Spanish and psychology, and there is also collaboration with subjects if there is a timetable clash.

Gifted and Talented girls are differentiated in the classroom and some bilingual girls are allowed to take their own language GCSE early – but are not taught by the school.

Girls stay in the same form for the first two years and then, after a shake-up in year 9 when they can request to be with their friends, they stay together until sixth form.

Good age range of teachers, some of whom have been at the school over 25 years but also take on a few NQTs each year – most staff stay a reasonable length of time and are generally keen to embrace change. Emphasis on constantly improving quality of teaching with regular staff appraisals. The small number of girls with dyslexia and dyspraxia are well supported within a mainstream setting; there are no special lessons or teachers. Support given to visually impaired and school can deal with mobility issues, but some of the older parts of the school can be quite difficult to navigate. A handful with EAL requirements feel well supported.

Well-equipped careers department with an independent careers adviser and careers education integrated into PSHCE lessons. All expected to do two weeks' work experience after GCSE – most find it themselves but school has good contacts if needed. Well stocked and well used library overseen by a helpful and enthusiastic librarian, who also runs reading groups for all ages in partnership with other local schools.

Games, options, the arts: Sporty school with lunchtime and after-school clubs as well as timetabled PE lessons. Sixth form encouraged to do some form of exercise but have to organise themselves, although staff are involved with teams and competitions. Floodlit netball and tennis courts recently refurbished and school has its own Astroturf, which means most matches are held on site. Fine record of achievement in county and regional tournaments: recent U19 netball county and regional winners; U19 regional hockey finalists; regional finalists in gymnastics and cricket and won gold in the U19 regional floor and vault competition. Supportive of girls who belong to sports clubs outside school and gives some leeway with homework if they are in after-school matches.

Drama a particular strength, and the school has its own performing arts centre with professional lighting and retractable seating, with numerous events throughout the year. Biennial whole school production and annual year 8 Shakespeare festival, year 9 drama festival and sixth form production. Drama and music departments work alongside each other on whole school productions. Girls also able to take part in workshops with professional actors and theatre companies and often team up with Skinners' for drama productions. Prefects run drama clubs for the younger girls. Drama also part of the curriculum in the lower years, albeit one lesson every other week. Girls can get involved in all aspects of production from costumes and lighting to script writing and scenery design. Drama offered at GCSE and A level.

The school's specialisms are English and music, and although it no longer gets extra funding, music is part of its DNA – 'there is music everywhere,' said our guide. About 400 girls have music lessons and take part in extracurricular musical events. Recently expanded music block with individual practice rooms and an ICT music room where pupils can compose their own music. Large array of orchestras, bands, choirs and ensembles and there are usually TWGGS girls in the National Youth Orchestra or Choir. The school gets involved with national music competitions, were recent national chamber music champions and take part in the National Festival of Music for Youth. Work hard on links with the community which enables girls to perform alongside other musicians like The Royal Opera House schools projects and orchestras in Tunbridge Wells. They also perform in local primary schools and in old people's homes. The staff choir sings regularly at school events. Usually a couple of girls a year go on to read music at university.

Good take up for art, although 'the equipment is not too elaborate,' say the girls; there are very few computers but they have their own kiln, and textiles particularly popular. All learn food technology for the first three years, along with graphics, textiles and resistant materials. Art displayed around the school and rotated regularly.

Huge range of clubs, many run by the girls, including the popular feminist society. Two of the most well-attended clubs are debating and CCF. Girls can join the debating society from year 7 and TWGGS is one of the strongest state schools on the debating circuit, taking part in many national competitions and often hosting the local rounds. TWGGS is the only girls' state school with its own CCF. 'My daughter loves the CCF and gets so much out of it in terms of leadership skills and working in a team', said a mother. 'It's another fun thing to do', said a pupil. 'You get to learn first aid and orienteering and it's a good way to get to know girls in other year groups'. A handful each year takes gold D of E and about 25 gain silver.

Masses of outings and trips – to museums and art galleries, history trips to Russia and Hampton Court, geography trips to Iceland and Devon and language trips to France, Germany and Spain. School runs an exchange programme with a school in India and has a regular expedition to Ghana – girls go to stay with a family in India for three weeks and Indian girls come back to stay with girls in UK and come to school. Places on the biennial trip to Ghana are keenly contested and girls have to take an assembly on their return. The school raises about £40,000-£50,000 per year for the Ghana Education Project and has built a girls' school there.

Background and atmosphere: The school was established in 1905 as an all-girls selective grammar. It is off a quiet residential street on the edge of Tunbridge Wells and backs onto open countryside. The original Edwardian buildings are solid and functional and visitors are greeted by cabinets full of silverware. Teaching blocks have been added over the years as well as a performing arts centre and music block and an attractive courtyard with flowering trees and benches where girls can socialise or revise. The school has its own Astroturf, tennis, netball courts and athletics field on site and a small gym and a large hall for assemblies – can't quite fit in the whole school. New sixth form block with a computer room and common room for each year group – sixth formers can also bring in their own laptops.

Strong links with the community and about half of the sixth form girls do some sort of voluntary community work: some teach a foreign language to primary children through music and others help with reading at local schools. Large numbers involved with fundraising for local, national and international causes – over £10,000 raised for charity each year; a different charity is chosen by the charity prefects each term. Younger girls wear tartan skirts and jumpers and there are strict rules about not rolling up their skirts, which staff enforce. Quite a relaxed approach to clothes for sixth form and they can wear whatever they like apart from crop tops, ripped jeans or sportswear.

Pastoral care, well-being and discipline: 'A highly successful and happy school,' say the inspectors, and the staff are proud of the high level of pastoral care. There is a robust anti-bullying policy with any problems being dealt with immediately; community and caring are regular features in assemblies and the school is 'big on respect'. Unusually for this type of school, there is no house system, but the strong pastoral care means no one gets left out – girls are encouraged to look after each other, with sixth form offering help and support to younger girls and a prefect responsible for each form. There is a year 7 buddy system for new arrivals in which girls are paired with a pupil from the year above for the first year, and all year 7s take part in a bonding day at Carroty Wood activity centre at the beginning of the autumn term.

Close liaison between form teachers and tutors, who monitor academic progress and general well-being and who are able to offer support for friendship problems in the lower years. There is an external counsellor, in school pastoral support with a walk-in office, and a school nurse, and mental health issues are discussed regularly. Good links with outside agencies if needed. Transgressions are few and 'a firm conversation usually does the trick'. The head has never had to exclude a girl permanently, but sometimes a girl might be sent home for a couple of days for a serious misdemeanour, 'often something daft and they usually turn out ok,' says the head. 'Discipline fundamentally self-imposed and based on consideration for others'.

About 70 per cent of girls eat in in light airy canteen – the food is good with plenty of choice. Sixth formers tend to bring in packed lunches and eat in their own kitchen, or use local facilities.

Pupils and parents: Parents generally supportive and proud of their daughters – they want them to excel in and out of the classroom. Families reflect the mixed social and economic background of the area within two or three miles of the school, but are mostly white middle class. 'Girls sparky but caring with a real ability to enjoy themselves inside and outside the classroom – they are determined and ready to work hard for their goals but also kind and supportive to each other and the staff'. 'There is no typical TWGGS girl', said a mother; 'the girls can become who they want to be and no one is moulded'. There is a strong sense of community helped by the very tight catchment area which means girls often know each other outside school. The head girl and her team of prefects play a significant part in the running of the school, including heading up some extracurricular activities as well as a role in pastoral care and support for the younger pupils. Girls go on to a wide range of careers – a significant number into medicine, business and accounting but also design and the arts, plus some into teaching. Old girls include Jo Brand, weather presenter Nazaneen Ghaffar and tennis champion Virginia Wade.

All parents are automatically members of the PTA, which organises social and fundraising events like an annual quiz night, the biennial ball and a whole school sponsored walk, and also runs the second hand uniform shop. They contributed £50,000 towards the new performing arts centre. Good communications between school and parents and 'you feel you are with your daughter all the way through, and you can get as involved as you want'.

Entrance: Entry into year 7 is via the Kent PESE Test, which is sat in the September before entry with tests in English, maths and verbal and non-verbal reasoning. There are seldom spaces in other year groups; applications direct to the school. Over 80 per cent come from state primary schools and the rest from local independent prep schools like Rosehill, Derwent Lodge and The Mead in Tunbridge Wells. The catchment area is tight and is currently about a two to three mile radius, with preference given to those living in specific parishes, but this can change from year to year. There are also 14 governors' places for those in the wider catchment area who do very well in the 11+. Sixth form entrance depends on point score from the best six GCSE subjects (including a minimum 6 in English and maths) and an A/7 grade at GCSE in any subject to be taken at A level (or in the case of a new subject, a related subject eg psychology would require an A grade/7 in science or English). Twenty or so join the sixth form but it depends on spaces and courses; girls settle in quickly and are made to feel welcome.

Exit: Most go on to a wide range of universities to study a huge variety of subjects including applied sports science and graphic design at Edinburgh, medicine at Birmingham, medical sciences at Exeter, civil engineering at Sheffield, physics at St Andrews, art and design at the University of Creative Arts, nursing at Nottingham and paramedic science at UEA. 5-10 to Oxbridge most years – seven in 2016. Girls occasionally go to university in Europe but none have yet gone to the USA.

A small number leave after GCSEs, some to local FE colleges or vocational courses where they can work at a different pace and a few each year move to independent or other local schools for sixth form.

Money matters: Most parents contribute about £40 per year into the TWGGS Fund which is for extracurricular activities such as tournament fees and transport to matches as well as visiting group music teachers, score sheets for concerts and prizes for speech days. It also helps towards the cost of drama productions, pays for pupils to take part in debating competitions and pays into the Southfield Fund to help those who are struggling pay for school trips and other activities.

Remarks: A consistently high performing school with a very tight catchment area which is always oversubscribed. It turns out confident, well rounded girls who are willing to take part and who have a strong sense of the wider community. 'All the promises have been fulfilled and my daughter is a different girl since she arrived at TWGGS – it has exceeded our expectations', said a mother.

Twyford School

High Street, Twyford, Winchester, Hampshire SO21 1NW

Pupils: 482; 15 weekly, 111 flexi boarders • Ages: 3-13 (boarding from 9) • C of E

Fees: Day £9,066 – £18,570; Weekly Boarding £23,370 pa

Tel: 01962 712269
Email: registrar@twyfordschool.com
Website: www.twyfordschool.com

Headmaster: Since 2010, Dr Steve Bailey BEd PhD FRSA; educated at Kent College, Canterbury, Southampton University and St Paul's College of Education (50s). Born and raised bilingually in Hong Kong before teaching history (all levels) at Winchester College for 30 years; housemaster for the last 12. A Fellow of the Royal Society for the Arts, research fellow of the International Olympic Committee, author of six books and with an international reputation as a historian of sport and the Olympic Games, it's no surprise that he has shaken things up a bit at Twyford.

Dr Bailey began by curtailing lessons to 45 minutes and encouraged teachers to deliver lessons beyond narrow CE requirements. Regularly observes teaching and makes no secret of his ambition for more creativity in the classroom; is keen to avoid 'death by worksheet.' Banished formal exams in the first two years of prep school and introduced extension lessons, known as Apprenticeships, in the timetable. 'Children are capable of far more than we sometimes offer.' Intellectual and erudite, is also a keen sportsman. Played hockey at county and regional levels and enjoys tennis, water polo and surfing. Wife Paula MSc (health psychology) has taught ICT as well as tutoring children with specific learning difficulties. They have three children, all in full-time education.

Entrance: Main entry points are nursery and year 3, although places are occasionally available in other years. Nursery places allocated according to date of registration; siblings have priority on waiting lists at other times. Short half-day assessment in November for those joining prep school the following academic year, which school says is 'not a rigorous hurdle.' Most pupils live within 30 mile radius, some weekly boarders further afield.

Exit: Nearly one third of boys leave for Winchester College, a steady few with music and academic awards. Other boys and girls scatter far and wide, but most popular destinations are Bradfield, Bryanston, Canford, Charterhouse, Cheltenham Ladies', Downe House, Eton, Godolphin, King Edward VI, Marlborough, St Swithun's, and Sherborne boys' and girls' schools. Tally of scholarships is on the up under Dr Bailey's stewardship; boys and girls gain a more diverse range of awards including academic, music, sport, all-rounder, art and DT scholarships and exhibitions.

Remarks: Main school building, a beautiful Queen Anne house, is set in over six acres of playing fields and surrounded by the South Downs. Moved to its present location in 1809 from premises in nearby Twyford and can probably trace its origins back to the mid-17th century. (A Latin grammar book has turned up bearing the inscription 'Twyford School, 1775'.) Boarders still live in original house, which has a pretty Victorian chapel, oak-panelled library, atmospheric old school hall and large modernised refectory. Teaching takes place in a collection of modern buildings dotted around quadrangles.

Lots of hard work going on for CE when we visited; most pupils aim to sit level 3 in subjects across the board (some level 2 if appropriate). 'Dr Bailey has increased the aims and aspirations of the children.' Maths set from year 4 and all subjects by year 6. French from reception, Latin from year 5 and study skills as a separate subject from year 7, otherwise all subjects taught as usual. 'Learning qualities programme' encourages children to think more independently and take responsibility for their own learning (praised in latest ISI school inspection). Classrooms are modern, bright and spacious; science labs are immaculate (including snakes!). Class sizes average 16-18. Children are divided up into three sets in the last two years, depending on their 'next school'. Boys aiming for Winchester and all other scholarship candidates join 'W set' in year 7, the rest are divided into two common entrance sets. ICT provision is well planned, with fixed terminals for younger ones and laptops for year 5. Year 6 up have tablets to enable independent research in geography, history and science lessons. Five SEN specialists help with (mild) learning difficulties and around 70 one-to-one sessions (including pre-prep) were timetabled when we visited. These are free, but school doesn't take children who need more than one session a week.

Traditional prep school sports for boys and girls, with matches on Wednesday and Saturday afternoons. First and second teams have an excellent sporting record in fixtures against other schools. School tells us it 'has addressed girls' sport' by drawing up C and D teams and organising more fixtures, and everyone gets on a team the majority of times. Pupils also compete in swimming, water polo, athletics, tennis, lacrosse and girls' tag rugby. School is a 'centre of excellence' for girls' cricket in Hampshire. Large gym and indoor 25m swimming pool sit side-by-side, with 25m traversing wall outside. Has several all-weather courts for tennis and netball, plus Astroturf for hockey and football. 'Sports day is fabulous.' Netball teams have had success at regional and national IAPS tournaments (with the U12 team winning the nationals in 2015) and individual footballers at national schools' level. Other pupils perform at county level in cricket, cross-country running, hockey, rugby and swimming. 'Court Cricket', invented at Twyford and played here for at least a century, is still in robust health at break times.

Outstanding art and DT departments, probably the best we've seen for quality of work. Small, permanent gallery at the side of two storey art block displays pupils' work throughout the year; standard of painting and ceramics is excellent. Artist in residence paints school scenes on site so children can observe brushwork – no surprise that number of art scholars is on the rise. DT is also very good with some really imaginative work (high level of design) on show, eg insect 'hotel'.

Music block sits in unusual amphitheatre setting overlooking tennis courts. Bright, airy performance space upstairs with several practice rooms on lower floor; more pianos are dotted around elsewhere in the school. More than 80 per cent of children learn at least one instrument, including the less usual, eg harp, drums and bagpipes. Lessons are fixed for older children and rotate for younger ones. School is a centre for ABRSM and Trinity College music exams and many pupils pass these at higher grades. Three school choirs, including a show choir, school orchestra and various ensembles give occasional concerts. Drama is improving, with a weekly lesson for all taught by specialist teachers and more performance space in Mulberry Pavilion, but 'dramatic aspirations could be higher ... we need a whole-school musical once a year.' Dance (ballet, modern and tap) is on offer as a lunch time club. Regular Shakespeare workshop for year 8 takes place after CE.

Apprenticeships (Saturday activities) are compulsory for all children from year 4. Activities become increasingly academic further up the school, and include ancient Greek, Arabic, critical thinking, debating, fencing, Mandarin, music theory, philosophy, photography and horse riding. Everyone chooses a different apprenticeship each term, and 'children often get their first choice.' Staff run weekday clubs after school, eg art, cookery, judo, water polo and yoga. Outdoor education programme, eg navigation, orienteering, shelter building and survival techniques, 'encourages children to solve practical and physical problems.' One residential course away for each year group every year; in school there is a treehouse complex with outdoor classroom and advanced adventure playground.

No longer offers full boarding, but can arrange for long-distance boarders to stay with local guardians on Saturday and Sunday nights (on average, there are 15 weekly boarders every term). Otherwise, most children board a few nights per week (68 stay one night a week, 38 for two nights and just three for three nights) from year 6 in preparation for going away to senior school and around 20 from Monday to Friday. Dorms for younger children; cosy two-man (or girl) cubicles for year 8s allow more privacy and the chance to room with a friend. We noted clean, well-appointed bathrooms, a comfortable common room and plenty of storage space for belongings. Boarders have limited use of mobile phones (matron keeps phones at all other times). Parents full of praise for boarding houseparent, also head of sport.

Excellent meals are served cafeteria-style and atmosphere is informal; children can sit where they like (we didn't notice staff on each table). Perhaps (enviably) this isn't needed, as school works hard to instill a broad set of values in its pupils. Regular services in chapel throughout the term are reinforced by anti-bullying PSHE lessons and constant vigilance by boarding and teaching staff (often around in the evenings running clubs or supervising prep). Everyone belongs to one of four houses and is assigned a house tutor from year 6. End-of-term Team Feast for house with the highest house point scores; individual high scorers are 'sent up good' on Fridays for lemon sherbet from the head (a Twyford tradition). Still has a friendly atmosphere, although parents say times are now more formal. Nevertheless they add, 'It still feels like you're part of a big family and [that] requires family involvement.'

Pre-prep is going from strength to strength with over 126 on the register when we visited. 'The nursery is outstanding.' Two classes in reception and year 1 grow to three in year 2, which is located in the newly built Forest Lodge which opened in 2014. Nestling in the trees, Forest Lodge provides three spacious, bright and airy classrooms for year 2 – windows at child height is a nice touch. Children grouped for phonics and spelling ability; reading is taught both individually and in groups. French and music learned from an early age. Homework is limited to spelling, reading and topic work, eg Knights and Castles. 'It's a really full-on day.' Has small SEN room and ICT suite. Lots of outdoor play; children spend an entire afternoon outside every three weeks and have access to small woodland area. All attend chapel services and use the pool and library. Puts on annual show for 'grandparents' week', where little ones can show off their music, ballet and ESB exam preparation. Clubs include gardening, hand bells, ukulele and recorder ensemble. Most go on to join prep school in year 3, causing prep school numbers to rise. Universal feeling from parents is that school is at capacity; would like to see new pupil numbers capped.

A relatively wide mix of families, but it's safe to assume that most are comfortably off. Two 100 per cent bursaries (means tested) for new children joining as weekly boarders in year 7; sibling discounts are limited to five per cent for third and subsequent children. Boys and girls are polite, confident and increasingly aspire to top schools. Old Twyfordians include Alexander Pope, Douglas Hurd, Hubert Parry, Mark Tully, Thomas Hughes and, more recently, The Apprentice winner Tom Pellereau. Very active Twyford Society keeps ex-pupils in touch.

Although well into the process of changing from 'a slightly scruffy, not very ambitious place' to one with a much greater focus on academic success, Twyford is still a friendly school where parents enjoy being part of the 'family'. Will continue to send a good number of boys to Winchester College, but is clearly aiming just as high for girls and boys going on to other schools.

Upton Court Grammar School

Lascelles Road, Slough, Berkshire SL3 7PR

Pupils: 1,250 • Ages: 11–18 • Sixth form: 300

Tel: 01753 522892
Email: office@uptoncourtgrammar.org.uk
Website: www.uptoncourtgrammar.org.uk

Principal: Since 2010, Mrs Mercedes Hernandez Estrada BA MA (40s). Previously deputy head teacher at Tonbridge Grammar School for Girls, Kent and, before that, assistant headteacher at Regent's Park School in Southampton, preceded by three year spell leading curriculum design for schools 'from Plymouth to Kent', says website. Husband is a drama teacher, busman's trips to each other's school productions something of a feature of married life.

Petite and engaging, she's very much the clever, industrious little girl grown up (and fetchingly doing the full Downton Abbey in a long dress for World Book Day on morning of visit). She inspires praise for her poise, glamour (has a wonderful complexion, too) as well as achievements which are both formidable and, in the case of fundraising, essential, with school built for 500 and now housing more than double the number.

Not desperately high profile, at least to parents. 'I don't really get to see her,' said one father. Not that they appeared to mind, given faith in the school – 'The best!' said one – coupled with the knowledge that pupils approach her freely, once they get to know her. 'Because she's so polite and proper, she can be quite daunting but she genuinely does care about the students,' said one.

When it comes to the importance of education, she doesn't mince her words. It is 'the key to breaking social barriers. With it, you're powerful. Without it, you could be lucky, but I don't trust luck.' No wonder, given her own experiences. Raised in industrial northern Spain, she was blessed with parents (steelworker and housewife) who saw education as 'the way you prepared your children to have a better future than you had yourself.' Encouraged by teachers, she was the first in her family to go to university, studying languages at Oviedo (speaks at least six, ancient and modern).

A thirst to communicate led her to travel but, in the event, no further than the UK, where she met 'someone' during a year's Spanish teaching at Bath University and never left.

Her affinity is, she says, with 'people who have high expectations of themselves,' something she relishes both here and at earlier posts at non-selective state schools, locations, including Haringay and Swindon, to some extent influenced by partner's career moves. 'It's great to work with people who want their children to do well and children who want to push themselves,' she says.

Starts each day by walking her two dogs in local park (their toys adorn a chair in her office) and bringing them into school where they're collected later by dogsitter. Provides valuable breathing space where she often does her best thinking.

Just as well as there's plenty to mull over, in particularly the best way of helping education set her pupils free regardless of financial or family circumstances, as it did for her. 'A selective school is for a lot of people the step into a life of possibilities and if I can make that happen, I will.'

Academic matters: Despite super selectivity, feel is 'more laid back' than other local grammars, reckoned one mother, who counted it a benefit. Pupils agree. 'The teachers will say pick the subjects you enjoy, not the subjects you're being told to do, or the job that will offer you the most money,' said sixth former. Similarly, while voracious appetite for learning is encouraged – some, who complete the European Computer Driving Licence in a term go on to take GCSE computing, for example – school doesn't go in for the M4 special executive exams lane, everyone sitting everything together.

Punches aren't, however, pulled. While 'sixth form is an exciting time, full of opportunities,' begins presentation, 'attendance is vital...A levels are much more difficult than GCSEs and students must make good use of their time, inside and outside of (sic) lessons.' That'll larn you... so how much excitement was that, exactly? Actually, given subject range, quite a bit. IB, though previously a big feature in wobbly A level years, is now, it appears, being sidelined as A levels, fortified with added Gove-inspired marking rigour, take centre stage. Recent additions to the subject roster include media studies and photography, which 'you won't find at other grammars,' thinks head.

GCSE offering up as well – Chinese trialled initially as a club then, as numbers climbed, promoted to full curriculum status in 2011. Japanese, however, didn't take off in the same way, lacking superpower appeal and thus felt by students to be less useful, reckons head. Progressive range of subjects isn't necessarily matched by enlightened attitudes to post-16 choices. 'Humanities are meant to be seen as more girly subjects just because boys are meant to be more mechanical,' said ...a girl. And while maths remains popular with all (and consistently the biggest A level subject), as elsewhere, physics is one for the boys. Sigh. Having said that, chemistry in last three years has overtaken biology as top science (psychology, previously attracting well over double the class sizes of physics, has retired for an early bath and recently only just ahead).

Results, as you'd expect, are commendable, though they do reflect school's determination not to make pyrotechnic stats its be all and end all, tending politely to let the other three local grammars nudge ahead. In 2016, 51 per cent of A level entries were graded A*/B. At GCSE, 57 per cent graded A*/A.

Language take-up and results have slipped a bit, with more D and E grades feeding through into lower take up at A level. But here, as in every other decent grammar school, you can end up picking holes in what is ultimately a high quality fabric. Parents give thumbs up to most subjects although one queried A level physics, where numbers have dropped by over a third in the past two years.

Quality staff are the key – and with an average class size of 24 and one to 16 teacher to staff ratio, they'd need to be. There was admiration for RS teacher who asked husband, a serving officer in Afghanistan, to field questions about the morality of war. 'A lot of teachers just wouldn't do that,' said pupil. Mind you, with crème de la crème teaching school status, you'd hope for such out of the box approaches. If lesson with whizzy English teacher, coaxing bottom GCSE set into life, top responses rewarded by decorous whoops, even 'phone a friend' system to encourage the unsure to seek help, was anything to go by, there's plenty about. Sixth form lessons were also rated very highly. 'Sometimes we're doing notes, but discussions can be quite open ended,' says pupil, with others praising science lessons' high practical to theory ratio in nine well-equipped labs.

Support, too, is comprehensive and well organised. Back up extends from clubs to surgeries, revision sessions (notionally voluntary but attendance strongly recommended and absences logged) and after-hours homework club. Everything is run either by subject teachers or, increasingly, by older pupils. Initial one-to-one sessions for year 11s, run by sixth formers, so successful that sixth form prefects (every year group has its own) hope to extend so that pupils through the school can book themselves an Oxbridge style one-to-one tutorial with fifth or sixth formers.

Decent resources although library, on borrowed time, can't, like its stock, be renewed. It's moving to fine new learning resource centre, leaving current premises, a nice old room with curved ceiling (not unlike cut and cover London Underground station). We'd have liked to see a few more initiatives to encourage less enthusiastic readers to buck the trend and pick up a book – though librarian, who bemoans decline in reading above year 8, does her best. Book champions event recruits pupils to defend a chosen title against all comers (and hopes to do more) while staff undismayed by majority of pupils in home clothes ('We're muggles,') had enthusiastically embraced World Book Day. We particularly enjoyed sight of food technology department dressed as fetching St Trinian's girls complete with a Miss Naughty flask, in the midst of their soberly-clad pupils.

It's not just gifted and talented who have a cracking programme – extension work embraces development of critical thinking and analysis (well-organised website is rich in detail) but those with learning needs, too. Unusual for an ultra-selective school, opts for full immersion rather than lip service, stressing importance of dignity and privacy, with warm, experienced team on hand to deliver the goods. Autism and dyslexia crop up with reasonable frequency. As with wheelchair users ('we rearrange as many lessons as possible so they're on the ground floor'), team copes with equanimity and a fuss-free and inclusive approach, from OT to physiotherapy.

Games, options, the arts: Although it's rather low profile on school's website, sporting talent is considerable. As well as individual successes (badminton and rowing at county/national level) – a small number also take sport/PE at GCSE and A level – there is also a decent run of good team results: girls' rugby fast becoming a star turn. Recent innovations include sixth form sports day featuring all the retro favourites, egg and spoon and sack race amongst them – brought back as centenary celebrations special and so popular it has become an annual fixture.

U

With plenty of non-team-based activities, timetabled and run as clubs, early morning kickboxing amongst them, recent converts praise choice and encouragement. 'My primary teachers made me hate sports at primary: here I love it,' said one pupil. It could all be part of a cunning plan to confound opposition as pupils delight in deceptive appearances. 'They think that because we haven't got an Astroturf, we'll be underdogs, and then we play,' said burgeoning rugby star with considerable satisfaction.

Current facilities may not impress but they're full of promise. Once huge field gets the makeover it's crying out for – and if proposed development deal goes through, this will happen – Astroturf and a sports hall are likely to give opponents considerable pause for thought.

Creativity, as witnessed by steady GCSE take up for fine art (small numbers continue post-16), is busting out all over on the approach to large art room, via staircase transformed by lovingly painted time line. Once inside there's – hurrah – a pile of satisfyingly authentic mess to one side and a huge cabinet of curiosities filled with pupil-made and ever so slightly wonky wooden boxes, each about to be filled with special objects. Quality continued in DT room, where fab new lasercutter, won with well-targeted bid for funds (hit rate increasingly impressive) was in midst of casting aluminium with hugely impressive results though 'terrible smell,' said teacher.

Drama splendidly high profile, with lively lessons (year 8s working in threes to create own walking, talking living dolls, two as puppet masters, third as puppet) setting the pace and productions a coming together of whole school talent, written by drama teacher and featuring enticing titles ('A stereotypical musical set in a high school' was recent effort) with productions and involvement by many, on and off stage.

Just 75 pupils have individual music lessons in school although many more 'almost certainly' learn outside. Day to day musical presence tends to be via individual involvement, with talented soloists showcased regularly in assemblies. Tone is set by list of enrichment activities, featuring enticing-looking extras for science, maths and English, and 'choir, band' for music. As to orchestra? 'I don't know,' says senior teacher. No more questions, m'lud. However, with its own nice suite and double handful of regular takers at GCSE music (though rarely beyond), there's plenty of potential.

As to extracurricular, there's much on offer, from Children's University, for years 7 and 8 pupils, with credit for different activities leading to awards, to D of E. Much appreciated, as were outings generally – rare enough currently to have Christmas present feel to them (field trips were considered a huge treat) and just about the only thing pupils, very happy with school, would add to wish lists

Background and atmosphere: You can see Windsor Castle from the road, we were told – and what better metaphor for aiming high? Aspirations apart, it's been all change, several times over. Founded as a co-ed selective school in 1912, it split into separate boys' and girls' grammars in 1936, reforming as co-ed only in early 1980s on the current site, wheel coming full circle in 1993 when it regained its original name. Alumni, known since 1915 as Old Paludians (marsh, or slough in Latin) have had no such identity issues. Only downright loser is original school building, whose remains lie beneath Thames Valley University tower block.

Immediate surroundings cope without too much sense of strain, well managed given numbers packed into site that was intended to cater for many fewer. Getting better all the time, however, thanks to the fruits of head's fundraising efforts which are increasingly visible: gorgeous new English block (marred temporarily by mud carried in from rained-on rugby players and distributed generously round pale wood floors).

More coming very soon, in the form of 12 new classrooms, vast café area and gym, which could see the removal of asphalt-heavy areas round the back and Portakabins. In the meantime, there's plenty of corridor candy to brighten things up, well curated by art department (relative emptiness of art rooms explained by volume of works on display) mostly terrific, with the very minor exception of slightly out-of-date staff pics (a few had left) and the odd, unlaminated notice with curled up edges.

While surroundings might be ultra modern, what won't change is the delightful formality of staff titles. Male staff, conventionally enough, are 'sir'; females, endearingly, are 'ma'am' (to rhyme with 'harm'), which replaced 'miss', formerly in use, which was reviewed and found to be lacking gravitas.

Applies to everyone: visitors and delightful admin staff as well as teachers, allowing many a personal Judi Dench/Skyfall moment and so ingrained that it's preserved in staff conversations, even when the pupils aren't around. 'It did strike me as different when I was called ma'am during my interview,' said head's PA.

Further proof of status accorded to backroom team is high profile website presence. School chef (pictured looking as if caught mid-soufflé crisis) is highly rated. With new canteen planned (much talked about, too – current one 'does its job,' say pupils, but that's about it) food is clearly a big thing and rightly so – we particularly liked the way that pupils are able to order giant celebration pizzas for friends' birthdays. Staff, too, are big on food, home baking a speciality – 'relieves the tension,' said one – end results regularly making it to the staff room as giveaways or charity fundraisers.

Pastoral care, well-being and discipline: Pupil support is commendably huge part of school's behind the scenes work and vital too, say warm team (separate director of student welfare as well as SENCo and three higher level TAs) who increasingly provide a drop-in shoulder to cry on service not just for children but 'sometimes staff, too'. Vital, as well, given that pupils, who may have only IQs in common, come from backgrounds that range from well to do to anything but, needing support that 'goes way beyond what we would class as the normal routine,' including, for example, pupils who are the main carers for family members with debilitating physical or mental health issues. Add in year in year out transition work (they run parenting sessions to ease fears, often linked to long distance commutes to school) and unsurprisingly, team reckon that they're busier than ever before.

No soft touch when it comes to boundaries, which are impressively clear cut, almost literally so in the case of the food line (two bins on either side of path) which mark start of food free zone. No nonsense approach extends to instant fine of litter pick if you're caught dropping rubbish; in-class bans on mobile use – a phone in the hand during a lesson means instant confiscation for minimum of a week (some older pupils voluntarily turn them in to form tutors for the day to reduce temptation). Uniform (worn by all, sixth form changing blazer colour but little else) is strictly enforced, breaches noted in homework book and, if repeated, on school record).

Goodness of all sorts is rewarded with house points leading to annual presentation of trophies, dominated by The Beast. So big it looks as if it could eat tiddler cups for breakfast, it's awarded for academic success, a (perhaps) not so subliminal message about what really matters in life.

May sound punitive, but isn't. Pupils, who worked on revised behaviour policy with staff, were in no doubt about sanctions which were, they felt, simple to understand and, because consistently applied, rancour-free. They praise the way they're given a say. 'The teachers know we'll be adults so they treat us like it,' said one.

Pupils and parents: Widening diversity of backgrounds, with over 40 per cent Indian, followed by Sri Lankan Tamil and Pakistani and white English (accounting for under seven per cent of intake) is a source of pleasure to former pupils: 'exciting and stimulating when you go into the school,' said one. It's the geography that defeats many parents, wide radius (home counties and London fringes) making socialising a near impossibility.

Pupils, on the other hand, are an incredibly cohesive group, who think before they speak. Quiet confidence when they do, underpinned with a rich vein of understated humour, is well worth the wait.

Entrance: Much made, on website, of school's popularity – over 10 applicants per place (145 in year 7) though less scary than it sounds and places are actually offered to one in four applicants. As so often, essential to keep eye on ball, without blinking: first documents relating to entry are online almost 18 months before Sept of entry.

Whole competitive process, drawn out during the wait for results, is predictably 'a nightmare,' says mother, who didn't tutor, 'but I think most do.' Families apply not just from surrounding boroughs, but, says admissions guru, as far away as Scotland and the EU. At least the tests, administered by Slough Consortium, take some of the pressure off pupils, who take just one batch of tests for four schools.

If unsuccessful at 11 plus, school remains off limits until sixth form entry when everyone, including school's own year 11 pupils, apply for places. Occasional places do occasionally crop up, however, and uniquely in the area, school hates to see a good candidate go to waste and may consider going over numbers (it's currently 60 above capacity) if there's a danger of genuine talent being missed.

Exit: A very few pupils leave after GCSEs, some to follow specialised courses, others because they want more freedom than school is prepared to offer (strict uniform policy sees sixth form wearing close to identical version of years 7 to 11 maroon, but in navy blue). A few take up apprenticeships; a very few drop out of education altogether. A shame? Head is forthright about reasons – often down to money – but crisply dismisses any thought of hand wringing about this or other inevitable disappointments. 'Life is not fair, we cannot pretend that we'll all be rewarded with what we deserve. However, if you cannot get what you want then maybe you need to be told to want what you get.'

For the most part, however, hard-working students and ambitions are well-matched. One to Cambridge in 2016 (natural sciences); one medic. Most to solid bread-and-butter subjects from accounting to civil engineering to pharmacy. Brunel and other London universities feature highly, as do Surrey, Southampton, Loughborough and Aston. The range, however, reflects school's admirable philosophy which trumps all. 'We encourage children to go to prestige universities but it's whatever is best for them,' said senior teacher.

Money matters: Government bursary fund to help 16-19 year olds who would find it hard to carry on education without financial assistance clearly flagged up on website.

Remarks: 'We try to allow students to develop themselves the way they want to be developed,' says senior teacher. Corridor with 'GCSE mocks star achievers' at one end and 'learn to knit' poster at the other just about sums it up.

Vinehall School

Mountfield, Robertsbridge, East Sussex TN32 5JL

Pupils: 260; 30 full/weekly, 30-40 flexi boarders. • Ages: 2-13 (boarders from 7)

Fees: Day £9,135 – £17,037; Boarding £20,034 – £22,218 pa

Tel: 01580 880413
Email: admissions@vinehallschool.com
Website: www.vinehallschool.com

Headmaster: Since 2011, Mr Richard Follett (40s). Married to Jo, who is head of juniors. The pair met as undergraduates at Liverpool University, and have two daughters – one in the prep, the other has moved on to secondary school. Educated at Latymer Upper School and grew up on the river in Hammersmith, West London, where he developed an interest in rowing which took him to international levels, until he was stalled by back injuries. He now coaches and selects for the Great Britain junior team.

Previous post was further along the Thames at Pangbourne College, where he was head of the junior school, housemaster of the junior boarding house and director of rowing. His career has also meandered through another waterside post, 10 years at Bedford Modern School, where he taught geography and headed up rowing; and through a comprehensive in inner-city Walsall, where his duties included tracking down and removing a boy who was dealing drugs to pupils.

While he's a self-confessed snob about coffee (you can be sure it's filter) his career path has taken him through all walks of life and delivered a man who parents describe as 'down to earth', 'very normal' and 'the perfect balance of tradition and innovation'. There's no cosying up to particular families or pupils – parents point out that the current head boy joined in year 7 from the state sector, and was appointed purely on merit.

Nowadays Follett's sports are golf, and cycling – because he can do that before his family gets up, and because it provides him with thinking time. 'I've planned some of my best lessons cycling to Rye,' he says. And he's a keen photographer – the walls of the school are lined with his action shots from home matches and school performances.

Entrance: There's an element of selection because all students are expected to take common entrance or the Cranbrook Grammar exam. Prospective pupils attend a taster day, and not all will be accepted. Those seeking places in year 3 upwards do a maths, English and verbal reasoning test. There are a small number of pupils with dyslexia and dyspraxia, but none with autism. This is more to do with geography than the school's attitude – the specialist Frewen College which caters for these conditions is just five miles away.

Exit: Most popular destinations in the independent sector are Eastbourne College, Tonbridge, Sevenoaks, Mayfield, Benenden, Battle Abbey and Winchester, but pupils go on to about 16 senior schools. Around 15 per cent go to Cranbrook Grammar at 13 each year, but it's rare for a child to leave at 11 for the other Kent grammars.

Remarks: If a pig could talk, should you eat it? Does a dog know it's a dog? These are lessons that children here wrestle with. Philosophy is big on the curriculum at Vinehall as a way of broadening education. 'Common entrance is quite prescriptive, it's rigorous and there's a great volume of knowledge required, but I'm concerned that we teach children to jump through hoops. But do they think for themselves?' says Follett. With concerns about this he started a lunchtime philosophy club, which has now extended to lessons in critical thinking in years 7 and 8, and Puzzle it Out sessions for the pre-prep. It's highly popular with parents and 'sold the school to me,' according to one. Others mention 'a lot of self-directed learning, which really lights the fire'.

Follett is also working hard on turning around the school's previous reputation as academically elitist – one mother admits that local talk almost put her off viewing the school. 'If they are a potential scholar they will get a scholarship, but we want every child to be happy,' says Follett. 'Not every child is going to get a scholarship, it's the minority, not the norm. Some schools put huge pressure on the children, they are driven by fear of not getting into the next school. We want to be academically excellent, but not for children to feel a failure if they find certain aspects difficult.'

It's clear he's no ogre; children walking past invariably talk to him, including a pre-prep child who announced fiercely, 'I've got a sore tummy'. As we toured classrooms, children clamoured to show him their work: 'Look at my Jungle Book story,' one beseeched him proudly.

The pre-prep comprises a nursery (from age 2) and kindergarten (from age 3) all housed under the same roof as reception to year 2 to enable easy transition. It's a modern, bright building with its own hall and library and a woodland play area.

One parent with children in both parts of the school feels that the pre-prep is more traditional. 'The two environments are very different, pre-prep is very formal and structured, and I'd like to see more freedom,' she said. But the school says that the last year has seen a continuation of new innovations in pre-prep teaching, including the use of iPads, a Mandarin club, and higher-order thinking skills sessions.

The prep is situated in a Victorian mansion built by banker Tilden Smith as his family home – the head's study has glorious views over 47 acres of school grounds and miles beyond. Corridors and staircases are lined with shields, each one representing a past pupil and his or her achievements.

There's a separate Millennium building – with subject classrooms arranged around a hub with a library at its centre; also a computer suite, science block, music building, and art, design and technology centre. Subject specific classrooms are used from year 5. Years 7 and 8 have a scholarship form and two mixed ability common entrance forms, with setting for maths.

Reporting back to parents is thorough. There's an Industry Card each half-term, which reports on how hard a child is working only, with full reports at the end of term. A system called Classroom Monitor breaks subjects into component parts so that parents and teachers can be better informed about specifics to work on – in maths it might say, for example, that a child is good at co-ordinates, but finds algebra difficult.

One-third of the pupils receive some form of learning support, which can range from work on posture using Swiss balls, because it can help concentration, to one-to-one support in lessons.

Mr Follett has appointed new heads of maths, science, music and art. 'The calibre of staff in the prep is outstanding,' said a parent. And all the parents praise the prompt attention to any worries. 'I had an issue this morning, they emailed back half an hour later, and it was done and dusted in an hour,' said one.

Everyone studies drama, and productions are staged in a theatre which could grace a small town – it has all the professional equipment and a 250 seat auditorium.

Sports facilities include an indoor swimming pool and a nine hole golf course. Follett has brought a sportsman's zeal to the school, and it's now 'very sporty', say parents. The school now goes on rugby tours, and teams take part in the National Schools Indoor Rowing League. Girls' provision has been revitalised. Follett says: 'Girls' sport now has a culture of competitiveness. I'm all for good sportsmanship, but I want them to win. Before they lost many of the matches, now they win more and show a determination which I'm told wasn't there before.'

No more Saturday morning school for year 7 and 8s – a previous bugbear for some children and parents. Instead, there is an optional enrichment programme for years 3 to 8 – including sports, crafts, and subjects such as astronomy, media and philosophy.

School day now shortened – lessons finish at 4.30pm with optional activity programme including supervised prep (whoopee! say parents) until the school buses leave at 5.25pm.

Boarding is popular, with around 60 boarders on any given night – half of whom will be regular boarders, and half taking up flexi-boarding. The school attracts a number of international boarders (around 25 per cent): currently seven Europeans, three Russians and one South Korean pupil. Full boarding is available from year 3, but junior boarders (years 3 to 6) have the option to board for four nights a week, while year 7 and 8 can opt for full or weekly boarding. There's also temporary boarding for occasional nights. 'I like it that they don't push boarding too much and you aren't deemed second class if you're not a boarder,' one mother commented.

Minibuses bring local children in from all points of the compass including Hastings, Eastbourne, Lamberhurst, Mayfield, Heathfield and Cranbrook. Some parents work in the City but there are also families who find it more of a financial struggle, and they say there is no snobbery. Those who have transferred from the state sector say it's been seamless and they've felt welcome.

Walden School

Mount Pleasant Road, Saffron Walden, Essex CB11 3EB

Pupils: 321; 53 boarders • Ages: 3-18 (boarding from year 5) • Sixth form: 47

Fees: Day £8,625 – £16,725; Boarding £20,460 – £27,285 pa

Tel: 01799 525351
Email: admissions@waldenschool.co.uk
Website: www.waldenschool.co.uk

Head: Since 2013, Anna Chaudhri MA Cantab, PGCE, 50s. Scholar of Robinson College, Cambridge, she attained BA first class Oriental Tripos and an MA. Research Fellow of Clare Hall, Cambridge, specialising in Caucasian literature, before taking her PGCE. Began her teaching career as a German teacher and examiner for Cambridge Arts and Sciences, then taught German at St Paul's Girls' School, before moving to Chelmsford County High School for eight years as head of German and careers. Deputy head at Walden School from 2009 before being appointed head. Her husband is emeritus reader in physics, Cambridge University, and they enjoy music, walking and travel. She is a published author of several research articles on Ossetic literature and editor of two books on related subjects.

Says that Walden School's strength lies in its size – 'Many schools in this area are tending to expand and form consortia, and provision at sixth form is often in large colleges, offering a multitude of courses but to very large classes. Walden School is a small but strong community, where all efforts are directed towards getting the best out of each pupil'. She is described by parents as 'fair, calm and very approachable' and is known – and celebrated – for her high expectations of the children in terms of behaviour and learning. 'She also has a freshness, which is unexpected,' says one parent. 'She says things like, "we'll just have to think flexibly about this one, but I'm sure it's possible".'

Head of prep school: Since September 2015, Sally Meyrick BA (Warwick), previously deputy head.

Academic matters: Nursery replete with staff given the number of children and infant classes that have a teacher and assistant, whatever the class size. Emphasis is on structured play in nursery but in years 1 and 2, learning becomes more formal in literacy, numeracy and science and children join in with prep school activities and assemblies. In the junior department, English classes start with 10 minutes of reading every day and languages are enthusiastically encouraged – Eco Club conducted entirely in the German language. Science labs are sensibly laid out with benches at the back and desks at the front to deter fiddlers. Wildly popular, food tech starts in year 5 and takes in health and nutrition as well as cooking.

'We offer a standard range of academic subjects, which allow successful progression to higher education and employment,' says senior school head. 'Our education is, however, inclusive and supportive, so that our pupils leave us as well-rounded young adults with a good moral compass, ready to make a positive contribution to society.' For a school whose policy is to select as wide a range of pupils as will fit into its relatively small yearly cohort and will benefit from its curriculum, Walden does well. There is a rejection of the tyranny of league tables and no policy of withdrawing borderline candidates in order to improve statistics. Small class sizes ensure that teachers get to know each pupil very well, and can tailor their teaching accordingly.

Value-added is above average (more than a whole grade across the board for many students) and maintained year on year, though achievement fluctuates according to who is in the year group. There's a good choice of GCSE subjects and no Ebacc obligation – 'our pupils are individuals and we want them to achieve the best they can without shoe-horning them,' explains head. In 2016, 24 per cent of GCSE grades A*/A. Cosy sixth form (most tutor groups only six) attracts those who can't face 'factory farm' sixth form colleges nearby. Groups vary in size for A levels (sometimes as few as six, though 18 in the biology class when we visited) and several new subjects recently added, though the weightier subjects such as further maths and science remain as popular as art and photography. In 2016, 54 per cent A*-B and 22 per cent A*/A grades.

Member of the National Association for Gifted Children – caters for the more able as well as special needs. Three specialists in a separate study centre with six assistants for class-based work. Dyslexics predominate but mild Asperger's, impaired hearing and occasionally a statemented pupil can be accommodated. School bumf suggests now a cap on the number with needs in each year group and the head won't admit anyone she feels the school can't support well. Established ESOL department.

Games, options, the arts: Walden School regularly slays the local giants on the sports field. Cricket, rugby, hockey, trampolining... 'There's a real percentage opportunity,' says head. 'In a small school with a lot going on, children get more of a chance to try everything.' At least half of pupils represent their school at some sport or other. Sports hall with sparklingly refurbished swimming pool in which each year group has a term of lessons. Two or three gappies help out. Spacious campus has acres of playing fields, hard tennis courts and a 25-metre swimming pool. D of Eers travel further afield.

Music is taught at least once a week all through the school and is a popular choice at GCSE and A level. Around 70 per cent learn an instrument but practice sessions aren't timetabled. The many instrumentalists make use of a large rehearsal space and there's a concert every term involving a rotation of the school orchestra, choirs and ensembles. Annual house music competition is a lively affair by all accounts.

Drama studio was full of seniors rehearsing Daisy Pulls It Off with gusto when we visited, on stage as well as behind the scenes. Annual plays for years 3 and 4, 5 and 6 too and the keenest thesps join drama club.

Workmanlike art studios with some impressive pieces – notably a display of teachers' faces interpreted bravely by their students; a couple every year get into art college. Artist in residence. DT room has a laser cutter as well as the usual CAD/CAM equipment.

Extracurricular programme has been re-energised of late and was praised by recent ISI inspectors for its breadth – from fashion and textiles club to industry days. A recent bank holiday weekend prompted a boarders' trip to Paris. Many trips out and visitors in to liven up learning, and residential trips build through the juniors – year 4s to Flatford, year 5s to Norfolk and year 6s to Wales for a week, with more elaborate journeys in the senior school – geographers to Iceland, for example. Clubs and activities go on at lunchtimes and after school. 'They get to do lots of things that we did as children and still fit in the academic work,' says a parent, gleefully citing Easter bonnets, maypole dancing, yoga days, forest school and a long list of trips.

Boarding: Truly flexible boarding with full boarders catered for as well as those who pitch up for the odd night, and around 60 pupils taking up the option. Some nine per cent are international students from around the globe – Asia, US, Eastern and Western Europe (a 35 year tie with German schools) – and are fully integrated into the English boarding school way of life. Separate boys' and girls' boarding houses (up to four in a room) in the main building. Location is a plus – 80 minutes from Heathrow, 30 from Stansted – along with the attention to pastoral care and no Saturday school, so plenty of trips out at the weekends.

Background and atmosphere: One of only seven Quaker schools in the country. Founded in 1702, this well-travelled school began life as Friends' School and was attached to a workhouse in Clerkenwell. Lifted off to Croydon and, when typhoid threatened, settled on the present site donated by two benefactors. Wide barren drive curves up to an imposing Victorian edifice supplemented by several additions of various vintages. Sixth formers congregate in a civilized double height space and appreciate the annual Ikea budget – helps build a sense of shared responsibility. Paths around the campus have been upgraded and grass tennis courts nurtured. Land on the school's perimeter was recently sold off for housing development but this hardly impinges on the school's feeling of space, with open areas right in the middle and dotted with picnic benches.

The youngest pupils benefited the most from the sale of land, the proceeds of which built their own domain in the shadow of the senior school. New spaces are cheery and purpose designed with the small in mind, each nursery and infant classroom opening onto an outdoor space and heaps of room inside. All well kitted out with interactive whiteboards and educational paraphernalia of all kinds and of course all have access to the facilities (sports hall, pool etc) and grounds shared with senior school as well as forest school at the far reaches.

Generally, the atmosphere of an unpretentious grammar combined with a small county school with tight community ties. With its well-worn, old-fashioned feel, a place where individuality is cherished, catered for and celebrated. 'My child said joining the school felt like "getting into a warm bath" after his previous, enormous rather impersonal school,' said a parent. Certainly an impressive modern application of the traditional Quaker values, which are still present, though some sense among wider school community that the inclusive and charitable Quaker ethos might be being somewhat diluted under new regime. Year 7s visit Bourneville, where they learn more about the Quakers (as well as visiting Cadbury World). Parents admit to being slightly irked by the modesty of the place – 'they don't like to trumpet their successes as is not Quakerly, but I guess that the product is more important than the PR,' said one.

The Quaker commitment to 'stewardship' is also driving a refurbishment of the tattier parts of the school's buildings. Now the paths have been spruced up and hedges lowered to create a more open and spacious feel outdoors, there are plans to tackle the heating system and windows and to increase the school's use of renewable energies and its general sustainability. There's also a move towards new technology – the ICT room is a veritable orchard of Apples and a new VLE is up and running.

Pastoral care, well-being and discipline: 'Quakers have been educating the individual since 1702 – it's only now that everyone else is catching up!' points out head. Indeed this is where the Quaker ethos comes up trumps. Pupils truly feel that their school values them and they in turn value it, and each other. Certainly the fact that the emotional and personal well-being of the children is paramount is palpable. Support and encouragement abounds. There's also a welcome sense of stillness in an increasingly frenetic world – school meetings and weekly assemblies begin with a moment of quiet reflection (which the head admits she misses at out-of-school engagements) and it's easy to see why this is a school that suits school-phobics or those bullied elsewhere. A mentoring scheme for year 11s – who select a teacher who'll be there for them if things get a bit much – is a safety net much appreciated by some in particular. No uniform for sixth form nor, in line with Quaker principles, any prefects – a quartet of senior scholars represent their peers.

Like the senior school, prep school a very supportive environment, where children are known and feel valued. Parents bask in the warm glow of the culture of kindness that pervades – 'The support shown by staff to pupils, and older pupils to younger pupils, results in a very happy learning environment and illustrates Walden School culture very well,' said one.

Three senior houses – Merell, Tuke, Lister – and three in the prep – named for famous Quakers Cadbury, Fry and Penn – but lots of competitions and an easy way for all ages to mix. 'Year 7s can talk to year 11s here,' confirmed our guide. Relatively short day with a 4pm finish (3.30pm in the prep), after an 8.30am start. Lunch is a choice of the hot meal of the day, pasta or sandwiches, all cooked and prepared on site, and at break-time pupils pay for their own sausages rolls and paninis, or can choose from a variety of fresh fruit.

Banned substances aren't 'condoned'. Where illegal drugs are concerned, cases are considered individually, but expulsion or suspension plus future random testing are likely outcomes.

Pupils and parents: 'I am not a Quaker but I love the idea of Silent Assembly and the emphasis on looking for the good/God in everyone, which runs counter to some of 21st century popular culture,' said a parent. Indeed Walden School pupils are candidly chatty youngsters who do recognise strengths in themselves (and others) and don't see areas of difficulty as weakness. Only a sprinkle of teachers and pupils from a Quaker background, though the governing body is still essentially Quaker. Day pupils come from a 30 mile radius – Cambridge is 20 minutes away – and boarders from London and the Eastern counties as well as abroad. Parents mainly professional and entrepreneurial.

Old scholars include BBC Blue Planet producer Martha Holmes, rock star Tom Robinson, Lord Newton of Braintree, educator extraordinaire Naomi Sargant and quite a few of the Rowntree clan. Alumni organisation now numbers more than 3,000 and they're kept in touch with a termly newsletter and invitations to school events.

Entrance: Prep school entry points are into the nursery at 3, and then 4 and 7 after a series of taster days to make sure they'll settle. Places offered on the basis of observation and individual assessment.

Thirty come in at year 7 (60 per cent from the prep, the rest from Dame Bradbury's, Howe Green House, Heath Mount, St John's, St Faith's et al, as well as local village primaries), swelled by another 10 in year 9 (from St Faith's, St John's and overseas). Entry is by interview and – not desperately difficult – assessment (evidence of intellectual potential to achieve C or above at GCSE). A third of pupils stay on to A level and any new sixth formers are generally from overseas.

Exit: After year 6, majority cross the playground to the senior school. A few leak out to local state and Cambridge independents. Post-16 exodus (45 per cent in 2016) to sixth form colleges beginning to slow as A level curriculum broadens. About a quarter tend to take a gap year and the rest make it to their chosen universities, including e.g. KCL and ICL, Reading, Exeter, Bristol, Bath, Sheffield, Loughborough, Warwick and Central St Martins.

Money matters: Nobody who could benefit from a Walden School education should be discouraged from applying on the grounds of finance, says head. Fifteen per cent of pupils receive means-tested bursaries, and scholarships are dished out to those arriving in years 7 and 9 for academic excellence, art, drama, music and sport. Sixth form scholarships are at head's discretion (maximum £2000) for those who contribute substantially to school life. Quaker bursaries for Quaker families.

Remarks: Calm, caring place for individuals who benefit from bespoke push, stretch and support.

Walhampton School

Walhampton, Lymington, Hampshire SO41 5ZG

Pupils: 360; 30 full, 30 flexi boarders • Ages: 2-13 (boarders from 7) • C of E

Fees: Day £8,550 – £16,650; Boarding + £6,063 pa

Tel: 01590 613300
Email: registrar@walhampton.com
Website: www.walhampton.com

Headmaster: Since 2012, Mr Titus Mills (Eton, University of East Anglia and Oxford). Has taught across the spectrum, latterly as head of The Paragon, an independent school in Bath, and prior to that as head of St George's International Junior school in Rome and deputy head of St Mark's C of E school in Lambeth. Named Titus after the family donkey. The kids from St Mark's sang 'Oh Happy Day' at his wedding to Jemima, who is involved in many aspects of school life, from meeting parents to arts and crafts. They have three young sons at the school.

Head is charming, his ease of manner no doubt stemming from his Eton roots; he is also warm, penetrating, and very enthusiastic. Mr Mills relishes a challenge: he has turned around schools in the past, and has a remit to do something similar for Walhampton. Not that it was failing, but he is there to make it fly – 'he's brimming with positivity,' said a parent.

Since taking up his post, head has swept through the school like a brisk wind, removing all dusty elements and making significant changes to staff, uniform, even the school emblem (the sticking out tongue has been lopped off the stag). There was 'lots of debris,' commented a parent. Another enthusiastic parent said that the head works 'at the speed of light' and will respond to an email request within half an hour with an action plan. Happy constituents indeed.

Entrance: Non selective. Tests for placing purposes.

Exit: To more than 20 senior schools. Canford and Bryanston most popular, followed by Sherborne, Marlborough and Radley.

Remarks: Walhampton is exceptionally lovely, with glorious buildings and grounds. But there's something more than that: a feeling that your favourite childhood fiction might come to life in this place. The prospectus dust jacket (no, we've never seen a dust jacket on one before either) is just like the map in the front of Swallows and Amazons – there's Portmere pond for sailing, Sandwalk pond for fishing; even a Curly Wurly mountain. For Enid Blyton lovers there's the Faraway tree and a Wishing Seat. Beehives sit in a wildflower meadow and there are stables, camps and bluebell woods.

Thoughtfully arranged library – books reserved for years 7 and 8 on one side, so the librarian can see if a crafty year 3 nips across to pick a book that is not age appropriate, although 'We don't really do [books full of teenage] angst here.' Library sessions each week, but library evidently used at all times: a jigsaw is always on the go – a child stressed out by a lesson calms down after five minutes with a jigsaw, the librarian told us.

This place's stately past is not completely diluted by its school present. Standing on the terrace during break, watching the children at play, it is extraordinary to think this is a school and not a home. The family feel is underscored by the fact that many teachers live on site with their families.

Children are a lively, happy bunch and properly young: they all play at break time, including the enormous 13 year old boys, who looked as though they should already be at a senior school, but raced around, twisting each other on a tree swing. There are the usual number of screens here, but children are equally likely to enthuse about an outside activity – riding, flags or the tremendously popular 'escape from Colditz': children have to escape from an area of the grounds, in the dark, and get up to the headmaster's study and ring the bell. Staff, equipped with miner's lamps as headgear, try to spot and stop them. 'Wet, windy and wild,' says the school mag, The Mercury. This is a school where they are not afraid to get dirty; or take risks.

Manners well to the fore: children leapt to their feet as we went around and held open doors, one small child moved out of our way, saying decidedly 'good evening,' (just after lunch). With much fanfare, Mr Mills introduced new comprehensible school rules and a merits/sanctions so kids understand what they've done right and wrong. Beach huts in house colours collect stag tokens, handed out for behaviour, effort and achievement – very popular with kids who love posting their tokens. Each half term the school, pupils and teachers alike, aims to develop a particular learning characteristic – perseverance at the time of our visit: clearly taken very much to heart by the children, and the determined cross-country runner who came in last, but persevered to the end.

Children feel that their views are listened to: school council got the water fountains it requested and also managed to secure something more yummy than banana chips at break. Food much improved since regime chance – it was certainly delicious on the day of our visit.

Head's main focus has been on increasing academic standards, and for the first time in the school's history two boys were awarded academic scholarships to Winchester recently. Subjects are traditional (Latin is compulsory), but learning comes alive here: the Battle of Trafalgar takes place on one of the ponds, and ditches are currently doubling as trenches for WW2 enactments. History, understandably, is a tremendously popular subject. The head is keen to take learning outside as much as possible and as a result this was one of the most deserted schools we have ever toured. 'Mud is part of the curriculum,' said one member of staff. Class sizes range from 15-20.

In the pre-prep the little ones have wet weather red dungarees, coats and wellies and recently enjoyed operations in a mud kitchen with wok and watering can. Ella and Daisy, the pre-prep hens, potter around happily. There's a new outside area, Owl corner, with bushes to hide in, a wooden stag to climb on, and a rope to pull yourself up a steep slope.

Learning support provided across the spectrum. Although most fit mild to moderate categories, there are a few children here with severe dyslexia. Whether or not children with severe learning difficulties are accepted depends partly on assessment and the balance of children in that year. Support charged as an extra, but 'not expensive,' said a parent. LSU provides 'exceptional support,' said parent of a child with dyslexia. 'No stigma,' and kids likely to help each other with difficulties.

Mixed age tutor groups for years 6 to 8. Pupils have some say in which tutor group they wish to be in and good relationships develop across the age groups, with pupils often helping each other out with academic or other difficulties.

Pupils know who to go to with problems and bullying is dealt with promptly. Parents feel that pastoral care here is very strong. 'The time and energy which goes into each child is remarkable,' said one. Most parents attend chapel on Friday nights – 'a lovely way to round off the week.' Kids say what they want to pray for – there's usually a rabbit or a finger shut in a car door (although the school is 'not deeply religious,' the mum added).

Head of sports sees those who claim they don't enjoy sport as a challenge and does his best to find an activity that a child will take to, archery or golf for instance. Great to see the girls learning rugby. Good sports hall and Astroturf, and funding for two new netball courts. Six Oppies (sailing boats to the rest of us) recently purchased. Riding is extremely popular and many boys ride although they tend to prefer games – anyone for buzkashi? (a Mongolian game played with the stuffed hide of a goat). Even if it's not your turn to ride, you can always go down to the stable and fling your arms around a pony.

Well-equipped music rooms and over half of pupils learn an instrument. Pop bands – The Stags and The Does – as well as a selection of choirs and orchestra. Joseph was in its final rehearsals, and sounded good – a hefty show for a prep school.

There are around 30 full boarders, with numbers increasing to 60 during the week with lots of flexi-boarding arrangements, the latter very popular with busy parents. For those who suddenly find themselves stuck in a late meeting, emergency boarding is a bargain at £35 a night. The Walhampton express runs weekly from London down to the school, one of the house parents travelling backwards and forwards to escort weekly boarders. Accommodation has been renovated and redecoration has been sensitive, younger girls having pink and frills, the older girls a more restrained version. Things are kept very neat – posters are carefully framed – no bluetac and tatty edges. Nice little kitchens with cereals for any time (Dorset muesli included, naturally), and tempting hampers of healthy snacks. All kids come into school on Saturday for activities and boarders have special trips out on Sundays.

Parents are well heeled, lots of professionals and business people. Apparently it used to be a school where grandparents paid the fees but this is no longer the case. Most pupils are from the surrounding area, including the Isle of Wight, but some also from London and overseas. Academic scholarships awarded to internal or external applicants from year 2 upward; sports scholarships of up to half fees from year 3 upwards aimed at those talented in a range of sporting disciplines who would not otherwise be able to afford to come to Walhampton.

W

Walthamstow Hall

Hollybush Lane, Sevenoaks, Kent TN13 3UL

Pupils: 628 • Ages: 3–18 • Sixth form: 104 • C of E

Fees: £11,040 – £18,810 pa

Tel: 01732 451334
Email: registrar@walthamstowhall.kent.sch.uk
Website: www.walthamstow-hall.co.uk

Headmistress: Since 2002, Mrs Jill Milner MA, PGCE (early 50s), educated at Maidstone Grammar School for Girls and St Anne's College, Oxford where she read English and took her PGCE. She took her finals at 20 and went straight into teaching, starting her career at St Helen's, Northwood where she taught English and drama. After a career break when her children were young she joined Headington School where she taught English and drama and was head of sixth form; moved on to Tonbridge Girls' Grammar as head of English and sixth form and acting deputy head in charge of curriculum development and timetabling. A passionate believer in girls' education and the 'transformational and life changing potential of education'. She is an ISI inspector, serves on the GSA Membership Committee and is a governor at Holmewood House and The Schools at Somerhill.

Married to Rupert, a retired teacher and businessman, whom she met at Oxford; they have two adult children and a daughter at the school. Her twin passions are reading and walking. Calm and relaxed but with a needle sharp intelligence. Easy and comfortable relationship with the girls who see her as approachable, and her door is genuinely always open. Says she 'feels truly privileged to have this job', and is passionate about the school and justifiably proud of the girls. Knows girls well and considers the finalising of the UCAS reference as one of the highlights of the job. Sees the school as her life's work and says that she could not imagine another school she would care more about.

Retiring in January 2018.

Head of junior school: Since September 2013, Mrs Diane Wood BSc. Educated at Manchester High School for Girls and the University of Durham, where she stayed on to complete PGCE in primary education after studying psychology. Also has Certificate in Education from Oxford Brookes University.

After teaching in maintained schools in Hampshire and Buckinghamshire, Mrs Wood moved to the independent sector, spending more than a decade in two Girls' Day School Trust schools – Sheffield High School for Girls and then Sydenham High School in London where she was a senior teacher.

Academic matters: Two parallel classes from reception upwards. Children are taught as individuals which means different abilities can be accommodated within one class with individual education programmes for the gifted and talented and anyone with SEN. They are set for maths from year 4. About 20-25 girls need some level of SEN support, mainly for mild dyslexia and dyspraxia and extra help with maths – two part-time teachers. Recent academic scholarships to the senior school, Sevenoaks and Kent College. Well equipped science labs with specialist science teacher. Emphasis on developing independent thinking and study skills and girls encouraged to think and find things out for themselves. Doing your best considered as important as being the best. Lots of cheerful art work about the place and three lessons a week with a specialist teacher from year 3.

At GCSE in 2016, 70 per cent of entries graded A*/A. Eighty-three per cent A*-B (60 per cent A*/A) at A level in 2016. Girls are helped to develop 'smart' study habits so they can take part in all aspects of school life – music, sport, drama, art etc and have an astonishing capacity for juggling time and taking things on. Curriculum and timetable very much set up for the girls and there is much discussion about teaching in the classroom and how to do it better. Girls take 17 subjects in first year including Latin, French and design technology. Creative textiles and a second foreign language added in second year. Most do RE GCSE early at end of year 10 with the majority achieving an A*. IGCSE in about 80 per cent of subjects and Pre-U in economics, philosophy and theology, English and maths. Particularly strong history department received Good Schools Guide Award for history teaching in the sixth form. Around 15 per cent of girls also take the GPR (Global Perspectives and Research project) Pre-U each year. Sciences taught separately from the beginning – top flight science teaching in modern labs part-funded by a grant from the Wolfson Foundation. Class sizes about 16 and not above 20 and much smaller in sixth form. Plenty of debate, discussion and interaction from early on – work in a team with teachers and lots of hands-on practical stuff. A 'stimulating, safe and challenging environment with high expectations for all,' according to one parent.

Most staff have been appointed within the last 10 years and there is a good range of ages and an increasing number of male teachers. A few staff flats on site for new young teachers. Three part-time teachers offer SEN support where required, mainly for mild dyslexics and dyspraxics. Extra help in maths and English offered in small groups to year 7.

In most cases girls can do the combination of subjects they want and 'twilight' GCSEs offered as extra subjects after school from 4.30-6pm for subjects that won't fit into the curriculum. Lots of help with UCAS forms from tutors and head of sixth form and sixth formers are taught in small seminar-type groups similar to university. Extra clinics to help children with homework and make sure everyone is doing as well as they can. All year 7 have to do cooking as part of PSHE and it is offered as an optional subject in upper sixth. Well-stocked and well-used library with panoramic views.

Games, options, the arts: 'Girls get involved in everything,' said one happy parent. Regular junior plays mean that all get a chance to perform – there are also gymnastics displays and class-led assemblies. Forty or so lunchtime and after school junior clubs include the usual music, art, dance and drama; chess is also particularly popular. Cookery club in the purpose-built mini-kitchen always oversubscribed.

Inter-house music and drama festivals and inter-house sport – all girls take part. All girls in years 7 to 9 do music, drama and art and about half take Trinity Guildhall drama classes. Lots of plays every year and most girls involved in drama in some way, either on stage, backstage or with the music and lighting. Plenty of space for performances in The Ship Theatre and main hall as well as the new drama studio – drama is offered as an A level. According to one mother, 'Everyone is given a chance to get involved in a smaller and less pressured environment than many other local schools.'

Lots of cheerful art work about the junior school and three lessons a week with a specialist teacher from year 3. Own kiln for pottery and carpentry also offered.Thriving senior art department, wonderful art and textiles rooms – both fine art and textiles can be taken at GCSE and A level and 3D design now offered. Music can be studied up to A level and is a big part of school life under inspirational new director of music. School has recently bought a harp.

Plenty of sport in the junior school including pop-lacrosse, a gentler version of the game played in the senior school, also netball, tennis, rounders and athletics. Swimming particularly strong and a number of girls take part in national and county championships. Sport popular in seniors too (new sports centre), many sixth formers continue with team games and there are a number of county netball, lacrosse and hockey players; the curling team are Kent champions. Girls usually find something they enjoy – gymnastics, fencing and judo are options for those who do not like team games and school has won the Judo National Congress two years running. Pilates, aquarobics and the fitness gym popular with the older girls. PE is offered as an A level.

Background and atmosphere: Affectionately and universally known as Wally Hall, it is one of the oldest girls' schools in the country. Founded in 1838 in Walthamstow as a school and home for the daughters of missionaries, it moved to its present Arts and Crafts building in Sevenoaks in 1882 – it was 'built on prayer with money raised from church collections', became the girls' grammar school under the direct grant system and is now a fully independent selective girls' school. The Junior school moved to its own building a couple of miles away in 1992 which allowed for the creation of a separate sixth form centre – the Emmeline Blackburn House, known as EBH. Girls have a self-contained unit for most of their lessons and private study as well as two common rooms, a kitchen and an ICT room. Much building and refurbishment, mainly from fee income, in the last 10 years, most recently Ship Theatre refurbished and new senior school sports centre opened in 2015; new sixth form centre under construction. The new entrance atrium (opened in 2012) has provided a modern, light and airy space and has linked the school together. Many parents attracted by the fact that this is a small school although, as one observed, 'Girls do well here and get involved in everything, but a very ambitious girl might need a bigger environment'.

Junior school down a quiet road on the edge of Sevenoaks in a large, light and comfortable Edwardian house with many additions – all sympathetically done. Fresh paint and everything in good condition with vases of flowers dotted about and an atmosphere of ordered calm and purpose. Lots of silverware displayed in the hall with cups for everything. Moved here from a house in the grounds of the senior school in 1992 and the short distance between the two means that the junior school has a separate identity but with all the benefits of a 'big sister' up the road. It uses some of the senior school facilities like the Ship Theatre and indoor pool but remains very much a self-contained unit with a different uniform and good facilities of its own including a large multi-purpose hall which doubles as a dining room – work about to start on a new dining room. Lots of outdoor space including the Dell with playhouses and bushes for making dens, plus use of an adjoining sports field.

Pastoral care, well-being and discipline: Leadership roles taken seriously and each junior school girl is given some responsibility – head girl, monitors, house captains, games captains or playing with the youngest children at break time. Year 6 girls run the library overseen by a librarian. Senior girls meet regularly with head to discuss their responsibilities and carry out self appraisals. Four junior school houses, all named after female authors, with plenty of friendly competition in music, sport, swimming etc; each house chooses a charity to support.

Senior school organised into three pastoral teams: sixth form, middle school (years 9-11) and lower school (years 7-8). There are six houses and this system means different year groups get to know each other. Competition between houses can get quite fierce (in the nicest possible way) eg sports competitions, inter-house performing arts festival, and each house chooses a charity to fundraise for. Members of the sixth form run the house events and organise rehearsals, costumes etc and all are expected to be leaders of some sort. Pastoral heads and form tutors provide guidance and mentor personal and academic well-being – girls review their own progress and set themselves targets and there is plenty of praise and recognition. There is good careers guidance and lots of time and care taken with UCAS forms and the school organises a programme of talks about university and beyond and also helps with work experience placements. Firm policies on bullying. Girls' views sought on whole school matters including food (which is extremely good) through school council and pupil/staff relations seem to be pretty good – they even invite their teachers to the leavers' ball. No Saturday school but girls often come in for matches, rehearsals, activities and Duke of Edinburgh. Assemblies three times a week, more than just a prayer and a hymn, and everyone expected to participate in religious education and regular collective worship (parents of other faiths may withdraw their children from these).

Pupils and parents: Broad mix of parents including high flying City types, local business people, medics, members of the clergy and youth workers. Mainly local English girls. About 50 per cent of mothers work. When the school was set up it was serious about equipping girls to follow in their parents' footsteps and become missionaries; they needed to be adventurous, resourceful and brave and much of this spirit lives on in the present school. The school's emblem is a ship sailing on the high seas, and at the end of their time at Wally Hall the girls take part in a special 'setting sail service' when they hand over their prefects badges to the year below. Girls tend to keep in touch and many old girls send their daughters here. 'Girls expect to do well and are not afraid to put themselves forward'; they tend to be grounded with a strong sense of purpose and of community and want to make a difference. Almost all girls in sixth form take part in voluntary service – nothing compulsory – many help with reading in local primary schools, working in charity shops and riding for the disabled and help out at the local old people's home (which was founded and is run by old girls). Girls not frightened to succeed in front of each other. The school works closely with parents and there is an active group that organises social events and raise funds for bursaries and 'frills'. Some indomitable campaigners amongst the old girls, who are often leaders in their field. Alumni include Beverley Hunt, Professor of Thrombosis and Haemostasis at King's College, London and founder of the charity Life Blood, also playwright and triathlete; Janine Gibson, editor-in-chief of Buzzfeed; actress Victoria Boreham; Rowan Pelling, newspaper columnist and broadcaster.

Entrance: Junior school non-selective. Most children join in the nursery and entrance is via an informal chat with the parents and a one hour taster session for the children to make sure they are ready to start school. Older girls attend a taster day when their English, maths and social skills are assessed.

Senior school entrance at 11+, 13+ and 16+. Not super selective. Interview with headmistress and written papers in maths and English in the autumn term before entry. Girls who do particularly well are then invited to sit for a scholarship in January. Entry into sixth form via interview, school report and a minimum of seven GCSES at A*-C with A*-Bs in the subjects they wish to study. About 40 per cent come up from the junior school but have to pass the same test as everyone else. Otherwise from a range of state primaries and local prep schools, eg The Granville, Derwent Lodge, Hilden Grange. About 10 girls join sixth form each year from other local girls' independent schools and grammars, often because of the wide combination of subjects available. Occasional joiners into year 10 if things have not worked out at another school.

W

Exit: About 50-80 per cent move on from the junior to the senior school each year but have to take the same entrance tests in maths and English as external applicants. Lots of discussion with parents about the next step and plenty of warning if it is thought their daughter won't pass into the senior school. Others to a variety of state and independent schools including Sevenoaks, Tonbridge and Kent College and eight or so per year to the grammars – girls are well prepared for all entrance exams including the Kent Test.

About 20 per cent leave after GCSE, some to co-ed boarding schools and some to the state sector. Around 10 per cent take a gap year, most straight to university to study subjects including medicine, maths, modern foreign languages and various sciences. Durham, Exeter, Leeds, St. Andrew's and Warwick popular. One to Oxbridge in 2016 (engineering); three medics and one vet.

Money matters: About 16 per cent of girls on some sort of bursary. Various financial awards from the Founder's Bursary which can cover nearly 100 per cent of fees plus scholarships in drama, music, art, and sport worth up to 50 per cent of fees. Help also available for current parents in financial straits. Sibling discount offered.

Remarks: Thriving girls' day school in leafy Sevenoaks. Produces quietly confident young women with a 'can do' attitude and an adventurous spirit. The strong academic results are a 'happy by-product' of all this.

Watford Grammar School for Boys

Rickmansworth Road, Watford, Hertfordshire WD18 7JF

Pupils: 1,389 • Ages: 11–18 • Sixth form: 434

Tel: 01923 208900
Email: BrownC@watfordboys.org
Website: www.watfordboys.org

Headteacher: Since 2015, Ian Cooksey, previously head of Dr Challoner's High School for Girls. Educated at Queen Mary's Grammar School in Walsall and Magdalen College Oxford, where he read biological sciences. Has spent his career in the state sector, first at stellar grammar Tiffin School, Kingston upon Thames, where he rose from biology teacher to assistant head. Moved as vice principal to Tomlinscote School, Frimley, before being charged with taking King's International School, Camberley, out of special measures, which he successfully achieved. Came full circle back to a state grammar when he joined DCHS as head.

A keen mountaineer, he is married with two small children.

Academic matters: An unashamedly academic curriculum. Everyone tries three languages, and takes at least one to GCSE. Latin and classical civilisation are important departments. Separate sciences at IGCSE and many continue to A level. In 2016, 78 per cent of A level entries were graded A*-B and 50 per cent A*/A; at GCSE it was 57 per cent A*/A. 'Outstanding' maths department; huge numbers take it at A level and most get A grades.

The only 'studies' on offer are religious and sports – the latter popular at A level as well as GCSE. The intake is undoubtedly skewed in favour of the top of the ability range, but since nearly everyone gets at least five good GCSEs, those who are less academic are evidently lifted by the same rising tide. 'There is plenty of mixed-ability teaching at KS3, so low-ability pupils are not ghettoized. They have their aspirations raised and it can be very liberating.' The school works with other providers where necessary – one boy learns basic skills at WBGS and construction elsewhere. 'You don't succeed with a broad range of students unless you are prepared to be flexible. We're very proud of the fact that boys with autism, dyslexia or dyspraxia succeed very well here. But they must want to work and to have their aspirations raised. With boys for whom this is not the appropriate school, we give them all the support and use our best influence to find the best place for them.'

Games, options, the arts: 'This is not an exam factory. It's about music and drama, sport and debating too.' Sports high profile here, particularly rugby, cricket and hockey. 'We're the best state school in the country for hockey. They can pick it up at 11 and take it to international level.' Football is not on the curriculum – although, said our guide, 'it can be difficult to get from one end of the playground to the other because of footballs flying about.' More individual sports like cross-country, athletics and sailing also popular, and the school houses a table tennis academy.

Nineteen places a year are awarded for musical aptitude and there are lots of music groups and ensembles, including a joint orchestra with the girls' school. The stunning music centre has a 200 seat concert hall as well as many practice rooms, a recording studio and a music technology suite. Very few take art GCSE or A level, 'though it's interesting how many keep doing art even though they're not working for an exam.' Food, a new addition, 'has taken off hugely', and there is a sixth form survival cookery club.

Plenty of clubs – from chess to debating – and trips away: sports tours, World Challenge, language exchanges, field trips, creative writing courses. Lots of work with charities eg Mencap.

Background and atmosphere: Has its origins in the Watford Free School, founded in 1704 by Mrs Elizabeth Fuller, which split into separate boys' and girls' schools in 1884; these were renamed the boys' and girls' grammar schools in 1903. Has the feel of a '50s grammar school – and, indeed, The History Boys was filmed here and at the girls' grammar. Polished wood, cream panelling, stone stairs, honours boards, oil paintings of previous heads. The long neo-Georgian main block and adjacent Master's House are grade 2 listed buildings. The add-ons of various architectural pedigrees culminate in the award-winning Clarendon Muse music building on the front lawn, splendidly clad in blue/green glass, which is also used by the Watford Music Centre.

Pastoral care, well-being and discipline: Has a critical mass of pupils who want to work hard. 'It becomes a virtuous circle – our boys tend to want to succeed, so exceptions become isolated.' Boys say: 'They're strict when they need to be strict, but they try to make it as fun as possible.' One who had moved from an independent school was happy to find it freer and more relaxed than his previous school. There are around 10-15 short-term exclusions a year, but few of these become permanent. 'This is a very ordered environment. They take responsibility for themselves, and we can trust them to do so.'

Pupils and parents: Wide social and cultural mix; about a quarter have English as a second language. Those with specialist places come from up to five miles away, though the third or so who get in on distance usually live within about a kilometre. OBs include actor and comedian Terry Scott; publisher and chairman of West Ham United David Sullivan; England rugby international Josh Lewsey; poet Michael Rosen.

Entrance: Don't bother to apply for one of the 190 places (increasing to 196 in 2017 and 226 in 2018) unless you live in the right WD or HA postcode. Forty-five academic and 19 music places, 60 per cent allocated to those who live in the nearest Watford postcodes ('Watford Area') and 40 per cent to those in the 'Rest of Admission Area'. Then 19 places to those who live nearest and haven't got a specialist place, then priority to siblings, including those with a sister at Watford Girls. After siblings, the remainder of the places are allocated by distance – usually less than a kilometre. NB Academic and aptitude tests now take place in September – sign up in May/June. A few students join the sixth form, with a minimum of six B grades at GCSE.

Exit: A few – up to a quarter – leave after GCSE, some because they didn't get the six grade Bs needed for sixth form study. 'It's rare for people to leave on bad terms. We tell everyone it's a seven year programme; the assumption is that everyone goes through to the sixth and everyone goes to university.' Medicine, economics and business all popular courses, a large proportion at Russell group universities. Twelve to Oxbridge in 2016.

Remarks: Very popular, high-performing, partially-selective school with a grammar school ethos. Boys work and play hard with results to match.

Watford Grammar School for Girls

Lady's Close, Watford, Hertfordshire WD18 0AE

Pupils: 1,200 • Ages: 11–18 • Sixth form: 400

Tel: 01923 223403
Email: admin@watfordgirls.herts.sch.uk
Website: www.watfordgrammarschoolforgirls.org.uk

Headmistress: Since September 2016, Clare Wagner, previously deputy head at South Hampstead High School. History degree from Bristol, PGCE in secondary history from the Open University, MSc in learning and teaching from Oxford and NPQH from the Institute of Education. Completed her initial teacher training at Upton Court Grammar School; then worked in a range of state and private schools, including North London Collegiate School where, as well as teaching history and politics, she was also head of middle school. Her own academic interests lie in 17th century England and 18th century France. She succeeded Dame Helen Hyde, who left her job after 29 years of headship to help refugees coming into Watford.

Academic matters: School unapologetic about its fast pace and openly urges prospective parents to 'choose carefully', although parents told us there is 'definitely give and take' once girls are in situ. When pressed about SEN, defers immediately to the ethos of treating the most rather than least able as having extra needs: 'we drive girls hard and never accept the minimum.' Girls across multiple year groups uniformly (and with pride) use the word 'challenging' when asked to describe their school. Whilst bright pupils clearly thrive in this environment, the least able may be less well suited. However, there is a learning enrichment department to support for girls with learning difficulties – 'we do the best we can for them, and they're happy'. Links with the local FE college enable the least academic to choose vocational courses to suit them.

School is one of only five in the country which trains in de Bono thinking skills – taught to all year 7 pupils and incoming staff. The approach, which teaches pupils to look at a problem from all angles, certainly seems to pay off. In 2016, 61 per cent of GCSEs were A*/A, with 51 per cent of A level grades hitting A or A* and 80 per cent A*-B in 2016 – impressive given school's broad church intake. No rigid setting system – girls are loosely set in maths in year 7 and in languages for GCSE. High fliers take triple science GCSEs, often leading to A level.

Staff and pupils say that maths is huge strength of school ('we have the largest A level further maths cohort in the area') with RS, Latin and art also getting a firm thumbs up. Sciences and maths are most popular A level subjects, followed closely by history: 'they all want to be doctors'. Two languages (girls can choose from French, German, Spanish and Latin from year 8) taken up to – and at least one at – GCSE. Strugglers in year 8 assigned a sixth form 'buddy' to tutor them in subjects they find tricky – with relationships often lasting way beyond a year or two. Unusually, EPQ now on curriculum so sixth form girls are trained in the necessary skills and assigned a specific tutor to guide their project. When it comes to university applications, girls say they are advised well and 'constantly reminded' to get involved in extracurricular activities to boost their CV.

Games, options, the arts: Girls can't decide whether music or sport is top dog – but there's plenty of both and all to a high standard. It's a very urban school, so playing fields are simply adequate, but there's an indoor pool, hard tennis and netball courts, impressive fitness suite and dance studio, and a fishes and loaves style feeling that the powers that be are skilled in making very limited budgets go an awfully long way. A and B teams are fielded for frequent matches in all the major sports, competing against fellow state but also private schools – 'and we often win'. A few grumbles from parents that if you're not picked for the A team from the outset, that's it – no chance, hence no real motivation to improve. Loads of opportunities for sports enthusiasts from year 10 upwards to help coach their younger peers in anything from swimming to football – one year 10 girl took it upon herself to start a club for year 7 girls who hadn't made it into the netball team – typical of the get up and go ethos that oozes from every corner of the school. Sport 'a bit half hearted' at the top of the school according to some parents, who did not feel that yoga was an appropriate use of the compulsory sixth form PE lesson.

School admits that musicians often 'have to work in awful conditions' but, having heard the senior orchestra in full swing, we don't think it's holding them back and parents concur, describing school music as 'first class'. There are choirs, orchestras and ensembles galore, music in assembly every day and over 350 girls taking peripatetic music lessons. Drama less prominent, incorporated into English rather than on curriculum, but still plenty of productions to involve budding thespians, some in conjunction with the boys' grammar school. Plans have been approved to give arts facilities a major facelift with a brand new centre. This should be completed by September 2017.

All girls have to participate in at least three extracurricular activities, mainly taking place at lunchtimes, one of which must be musical and one sporting. Clubs range from Spanish cinema and astronomy to 'groovy gamers', yoga or flamenco – definitely something to suit all tastes.

Background and atmosphere: Founded in 1704 by Mrs Elizabeth Fuller, the school originally taught girls to read, knit and sew as well as recite the Church of England catechism. It's come a long way since then and has none of that girly feel, but despite its multicultural cohort and thoroughly urban vibe, retains strong sense of a traditional grammar school (undoubtedly why it was chosen as the set for the History Boys). Panelled walls, parquet flooring and Victorian sash windows create a scholarly atmosphere and walls are laden with examples of work and information. There's an undercurrent of energy running through the school and an industrious and vibrant atmosphere.

Modern additions are the Food Factory ('we wanted to create a Caffè Nero style environment') – a casual dining room where girls can get hot food or healthy wraps and sandwiches – and the Hyde House maths block, completed in record time by the previous head side-stepping an earlier government's lumbering Building Schools for the Future programme by raising her own funds and organising the design and build. The library is well stocked and functional, ditto the food tech lab. Computers are everywhere, with girls allowed to use these for private study at their leisure, and there's a gleaming fleet of state of the art iMacs for music tech. The sixth form block isn't the most attractive we've seen but is certainly spacious, well kitted out with a small kitchen area, and usually mobbed with girls. Year 7s are gently eased into the school, spending their first year based in Lady's Close – an absolutely delightful modernised villa with its own beautifully landscaped walled garden – a sanctuary from the hustle and bustle of the main school.

The pièce de résistance is a fabulous futuristic glass dome (2015), an inspirational multi-use research facility (with a bird's eye view of the Elton John stand at Watford Football Club) which aims to extend the learning opportunities of A level science students. Funded by the Wolfson Foundation, it 'aims to nurture and inspire female scientists with high esteem, practical confidence and exceptional subject knowledge.'

Pastoral care, well-being and discipline: 'No major problems' – 'the worst we get is a stampede to the canteen on chip day.' School is, however, strict on uniform and behaviour: 'what other schools would deem nothing, we get cross about.'

It's seen as 'cool' to work hard and effort is rewarded as much as attainment at the annual prize-giving. Pupils set their own personal targets each term, with staff setting them clear academic expectations. Plenty of opportunities for responsibility at top of school. Head girl and four deputies elected by senior team and there are prefects for all subjects, music and sport, giving lots of girls the chance to shine.

Pupils and parents: Diversity at its best. Girls from all races, faiths and socio demographic backgrounds are here in one seemingly happy melting pot. We were struck by how supportive they were of one another and without exception they look you in the eye and speak with great pride of their school and all it offers. With the arrival of two new Jewish secondary schools in the area, cohort is increasingly Muslim, although parents say that 'for the most part' differences in race and religion don't hinder friendships. Families largely hard working, dual income and it can be 'a struggle' to get them along to social events, but the fabulous Christmas Fair raises around £15,000 annually. Political correctness can reportedly get the better of school on occasion, with one parent given a dressing down for asking on open day what percentage of girls were Jewish – and reports of class secret Santas being banned in favour of secret 'Friend'.

Entrance: Only those living in the very closest WD or HA postcodes need apply. Of the 180 year 7 places up for grabs, 45 academic and 18 music places are offered to outstanding candidates, 60 per cent of which are allocated for those in the nearest Watford postcodes and 40 per cent to those in the 'rest of the admissions area'. Eighteen places are then offered to those who live nearest but don't have a specialist place. Siblings are prioritised, including those with a brother at the nearby Watford Boys' Grammar. After siblings, remainder of places offered by distance from school to home. Sign up in May of year 5 for the aptitude and academic tests which take place in the September of year 6.

Around 100 new joiners into sixth form with at least six good GCSE grades, including As or Bs in chosen A level subjects needed for entry.

Exit: Some 90 per cent to university with a respectable crop to Oxbridge each year (seven in 2016, plus nine medics) and many to Russell Group. Apprenticeships also encouraged where appropriate. Expert UCAS advisor based in sixth form centre on hand to guide girls in the right direction, and pupils we spoke to offered very positive feedback regarding help with applications and personal statements. A 'Face the Future' programme in year 12 sees girls go through dummy application process for work experience, jobs and university, offering invaluable experience in interview technique – 'we really learned how to sell ourselves,' said one of our guides.

Remarks: WGGS manages to take rough diamonds of all backgrounds and abilities and polish them to a high shine. 'Phenomenal staffing' brings out the best in the girls and with the school's ability to deliver a truly rounded experience, you can be confident that you could send your daughter here, stand back and watch her achieve.

Wellesley House

114 Ramsgate Road, Broadstairs, Kent CT10 2DG

Pupils: 116: 74 boys/42 girls; 45 full, 52 weekly, 2 flexi boarders • Ages: 7-13 • C of E

Fees: Day: £11,640 – £18,957 pa; Boarding: £25,062 pa

Tel: 01843 862991
Email: hmsec@wellesleyhouse.net
Website: www.wellesleyhouse.org

Headmaster: Since 2006, Mr Simon O'Malley MA PGCE (late 40s). Educated at the Oratory School, Reading and at Aberdeen University. Previously a housemaster and later deputy head at Beaudesert Park in Gloucestershire. Ambitious and enthusiastic; has generated an energy and buzz about the school and is justifiably proud of all that it is achieving. Much liked and respected by parents. A keen sportsman, he still plays cricket and teaches English. Met his wife, Katy, while they were both teaching at the Banda School in Nairobi. Says managing parental expectations is an integral part of his job. Encourages parents and children alike to aim high but to be realistic, and on the whole the parents are a pretty happy bunch. He sees the school as 'kind, thoughtful and unique with traditional values but not old fashioned'. He does not rest on his laurels and is constantly striving to 'do things better'.

Katy used to teach art, and following the sudden departure of the art teacher not long before common entrance, brought her skills out of mothballs and got back into the art room. Five children won art scholarships under her watch (the current art teacher is also doing well, with three more scholarships in 2014 and one in 2015). Katy keeps a close eye on pastoral and domestic matters too. They two children, both at university.

Moving on in July 2017 to head Thomas's Battersea. His successor will be Gavin Franklin, currently a housemaster at Wellington College. Sport degree from Durham; represented British Universities at cricket and went on to play for Staffordshire and Warwickshire. Spent five years at the Oval, as performance manager in charge of elite player development, becoming a level 4 cricket coach, before moving to Wellington as assistant director of sport and English teacher. His wife Claire is also a Durham graduate and a teacher with an interest in sport; they have two young sons.

Entrance: Children can join at any time from 7 upwards – many from local day schools join at this age, with major intakes in years 5 and 6 particularly for boarders. Very occasionally children join for the last year but it can be difficult getting up to speed for common entrance. Girls' places always oversubscribed. Non-selective but entry via interview and reports and examples of work from the child's current school. Would only test if there were concerns about learning support or that a child might not thrive.

Surprisingly large catchment area with many coming from west Kent and East Sussex. About 15-20 from London with an accompanied minibus to Battersea at half term and exeats – headmaster keeps in close touch with London pre-prep heads. Scholarships and bursaries available. Discounts for army families.

Exit: To a huge range of senior schools all over the country with King's Canterbury the most popular, others to Harrow, Charterhouse, Eastbourne, Benenden, Downe House, St Edward's Oxford, Sutton Valence, Cranbrook and Epsom College. Great trouble is taken to pick the right school for each child and the headmaster tries to visit at least two public schools a term. Over a third have won scholarships in recent years (14 in 2016 including drama, academic, art, sport and all rounder). Children hardly ever leave at 11+ and the school does not offer coaching for the Kent Test.

Remarks: Wellesley was founded in 1869 in Ramsgate and moved to its current purpose-built site in 1898, a light and airy red-brick building which has been added to over the years and which is surrounded by flower beds and playing fields. It merged with St Peter's Court in 1969 and went co-ed in 1977. It does not have the rolling acres of some prep schools but everything is immaculate and every inch of the grounds is used – there is plenty of room for den-making, a pond, vegetable plots and even some igloos when it snows. The playing fields are divided by an elegant avenue of trees which has been colonised by a group of noisy, bright green parrots. Lots of refurbishment recently and the squash courts, shooting range and the sunny indoor heated swimming pool and barbecue area are all looking like new. The walls of the new games room were decorated by the children. The headmaster and his wife like to come back during the summer holidays to take a fresh look at the school and see what needs to be done. Sunny, comfortable, well-used library with lots of space to sit and read and where children can curl up with a book. Each year group has its own common room – recently redecorated thanks to the fundraising efforts of the Friends of Wellesley. Photographs of children past and present line the corridors and there are four rolling news boards around the school showing BBC headlines, birthday announcements, notices and photos of recent events.

Avert your eyes as you drive through the cabbage patches and retail parks of Thanet – it is worth it. Many parents drive miles to send their children here, passing other good prep schools en route. It is a school which embraces the whole family and where friends are made for life: 'My daughter's best friends are still the ones she made at Wellesley,' says one mother. Parents, too, make great friends here – many a mother has been known to weep copiously during the leavers' chapel service. Old Welleslians often end up sharing flats together and there are usually a couple of Wellesley weddings announced in the school magazine. It is a busy, happy school where there is great emphasis on fairness and giving everyone a chance.

Academic success is highly valued but good manners, tolerance and consideration for others are equally important. At the annual prize giving each summer, there are not only prizes for academic and sporting achievements but also the headmaster's prize which can be for anything from attitude and effort to just being a thoroughly nice person.

Younger boys live in Boddington House which is joined on to the main school and where they do most of their lessons and are cared for by a housemaster and a team of matrons, which gives them a very gentle introduction to boarding. They move over to the main school aged 10 where they are equally well cared for in large, light, airy and extremely tidy dormitories.

The girls live at the Orchard, set in its own grounds and surrounded by apple trees on the far side of the playing fields. The Orchard is run by Mr Nichol, who teaches geography and is in charge of the Thanet weather station, and his very elegant and bubbly Spanish wife, Elena, and it is very much a home from home. The Nichols have been in charge here for over 20 years and give the girls an exceptional start in life. There is only space for 43 girls so it feels like a large happy family and is always oversubscribed. Bright, light dorms, all named after Kentish apples, with an abundance of pink and teddy bears on all the beds. One mother who was reluctant to let her daughter board said, 'I cannot deprive my daughter of the Orchard experience, it's truly unique'.

The school motto is 'Open up a world of possibilities' and this is exactly what Wellesley does. There is great emphasis on the individual and 'children get noticed in a smaller school and get opportunities they would not get elsewhere', says the headmaster. Everyone has 'a chance to shine' and with so many activities on offer virtually everyone finds something they are good at. Everything from photography and art, board games and chess, boys' hockey and girls' football, judo, fencing, riding at the local riding school, archery, cooking, needlework for boys and girls, ICT where children can create their own computer programmes and even scuba diving, with the 'shrimp' course taking place in the school swimming pool – the list goes on. Golf is popular – there is a putting green in the grounds and the lucky few are allowed to play at Royal St George's nearby – this can lead to a certain amount of envy amongst the parents. The school is always open to new ideas and the girls have recently set up their own cricket club. Rifle shooting is a popular activity culminating in the annual parents v children shooting match – not just fathers and sons but mothers and daughters as well.

The average class size of 12 means that the school can support children at both ends of the learning spectrum. Children streamed from year 5 and setted in maths and languages – French (taught by a native speaker) and Latin are taught as part of the curriculum and Spanish can be taught by private arrangement. Very bright children can be stretched and academic scholars are either taught in a separate, accelerated class for the last two years or within the top stream – depends on the number of scholars from year to year.

A good team of teachers, with a healthy balance of age and experience. The children are 'pushed and stretched with full support, and the school has pushed our son to be the best that he can be,' says one happy mother. New computers, and two lessons of touch-typing a week as well programming and website design. High praise from the inspectors who judged that 'The curriculum is excellent, well balanced, stimulating and structured', lessons are 'challenging and interesting' and 'effective anti-bullying procedures include development of awareness of cyber-bullying through PSHE and ICT lessons'.

W

The school is quick to spot problems and about 20 per cent have some sort of learning support. The department is run by 'the wonderful Mrs Wallace' and there are specialist English, maths and language teachers – some children taught within the class and some withdrawn but lessons rotated so they do not fall behind in any subject; close liaison between learning support and class teachers. Will go the extra mile for children with bigger difficulties. An occupational therapist has designed a programme for dyspraxics. A small number of children work with laptops. In class EAL support available for those who need it.

The school has recently been awarded International School status by the British Council which means that all lessons must have an international dimension to encourage children to have a more global outlook – it recently took part in a European day of languages and is already twinned with a school in India.

'The school achieves things it shouldn't for its size,' says the headmaster and it certainly punches above its weight on the sports fields. He puts this down partly to the close bonds that develop in a small boarding community and partly to the support and encouragement from staff. They are frequent winners of the JET cricket and rounders national competitions, much to the envy and astonishment of much larger and apparently sportier schools, and are always represented at the annual national athletics championships in Birmingham. One girl has recently been selected for the England athletics squad and a boy for England cricket training. There is a long tradition of cricketing excellence and alumni include England captains Mann and Cowdrey as well as the Loudon brothers and Sam Northeast, plus three day eventers and Olympic medal winners William Fox-Pitt and Georgina Harland.

Music is part of the curriculum throughout the school with all year 3 learning the recorder and all year 4 the violin, and about 70 per cent continue with at least one instrument; they will find a teacher for any instrument – one child is currently learning the harp. There are instrumental groups and an orchestra and the choir sings in local churches and at weddings; a recent highlight was a trip to Venice to sing in St Mark's on Palm Sunday. Two school plays a year as well as smaller form productions at Christmas mean everyone has a chance to get up on stage. There are also poetry and musical recitals and children are prepared for the LAMDA exams.

Vibrant colourful artwork displayed all over the school with 'six of the best' selected to hang in the head's study. Masses of outings and trips; most year groups visit France and year 7 has an outdoor pursuits trip to the Lake District for an 'educational adventure'. Various charity fundraising events throughout the year from cake sales to sponsored swims and fancy dress days – when children can put their sewing skills to good use. Burns Night is celebrated each year with haggis and reeling and there is a programme of lectures from parents and visiting speakers.

Lots of traditional boarding school parents as well as local professional families and about 20 per cent foreign nationals – from Russia, China, Nigeria and Hong Kong, and also popular with Spanish who often come for a year. Arrangements can be made for children of other faiths, but most are happy to attend chapel twice a week and the full choral service on Sundays. Children not overly sophisticated and do not grow up too quickly but they are still self-assured and confident and are very comfortable talking to adults. The head and his wife invite the top year to dinner parties in their house where the children can dress up and hone their conversational skills. Usually about 60 children in at weekends with plenty going on and outings planned – ice skating, clay pigeon shooting, bowling or just going to play on the beach. The top year is allowed 'down town' into Broadstairs on Sundays where they can spend their pocket money – a much looked forward to privilege, and many opt to stay in for the weekends just for this.

The Friends of Wellesley House organises social events and fundraising activities including lunches for new parents, quiz nights, the bonfire night and other parties including the recent Wellesley Fest.

A small and extraordinarily caring prep school with traditional values which produces self-assured and considerate children who go on to schools all over the country.

Wellington College

Linked with Eagle House School

Duke's Ride, Crowthorne, Berkshire RG45 7PU

Pupils: 1,045; 835 full boarders • Ages: 13-18 • Sixth form: 465 • C of E

Fees: Day £27,120- £31,155; Boarding £37,110 pa

Tel: 01344 444013
Email: admissions@wellingtoncollege.org.uk
Website: www.wellingtoncollege.org.uk

Master: Since 2015, Julian Thomas BSc MBA FRSA (apparently 50ish, though looks about 27). Read computer science at King's College, London – not a common headmagisterial start. After launching into banking, light dawned and he took a Cambridge PGCE, winning a half-blue in Rugby League. Taught maths at St Dunstan's College and Forest School, co-authoring several text books. Thence, as director of studies, to Portsmouth Grammar and on to Hampton School as second master for four years during which he took an MBA in Educational Leadership (International). Prior to Wellington, was head of Caterham School for eight years doing great things. Engagingly, he tweets as @Welly_Master.

Instantly likeable. Relaxed, open, friendly and clearly capable, Mr Thomas relishes everything about the college and his centrality to it. Taking over a school so publicly identified with a predecessor isn't easy. However, he was clearly in sympathy with the Seldon ethos and values and, to a considerable extent, maintains them, though his emphasis is less on generally desirable lists of values and aptitudes than on each individual pupil. Remarkably, while we spoke to numerous staff, parents and pupils who evidently deeply revered his predecessor, no-one regretted the move into the Post-Seldon-Era – a tremendous tribute to Julian Thomas and his sensitive and sensible handling of the transition. In fact, as some parents, suggested, 'Everybody was feeling a tad exhausted – it's a wee bit calmer now.' Pupils feel known and engaged with. 'He'll just stop us and say, "What do you think of this?" about some idea or other. He really wants to know what we think.' And, 'He knows stuff about you. He'll just ask, "How did it go?" It's amazing.'

'Exciting,' was the word Mr Thomas used most often to us. And we heard it often from parents and pupils too. An astute appointment. Wellington will grow greater and richer in his care.

Academic matters: A place in which learning matters. We loved what one parent told us: 'It's cool to do well there – it's embarrassing if you don't.' College offers both A levels and the IB in the sixth form – 45 per cent currently opting for the IB. The IB Middle Years programme was dropped due to lack of uptake – a disappointing but hardly surprising decision. A level results are impressive overall. Maths and economics by far the most popular options – 2016 results saw 55 per cent of candidates achieving A*/A in the former and 85 per cent gaining A*/As in the latter. Ninety per cent of history candidates achieved A*/As – remarkable. Likewise, the seven Latin candidates all got A*/As. Minority subjects, eg some languages and art history, also outstanding though a less starry showing in eg English, business and photography. Overall, 70 per cent A*/A grades. IB diploma results similarly impressive though a bit more of a mixed bag, perhaps. The average score of IB diploma candidates in 2016 was 39 – outdone by no other UK co-ed boarding school. 'Our teachers seem to like teaching the IB more than A levels,' one sixth former thought.

Mainstream range of GCSE subjects offered and results in maths and all three sciences are excellent. Of the options, history, geography and Latin are especially popular – Latin with spectacular results; Spanish and Greek also sparkle. Good choice of languages but German no more buoyant here than anywhere else, sadly. Overall, 85 per cent A*/A grades in 2016.

But Julian Thomas no longer publishes examination results for national league tables. This is a part of the college's shift from raw results to a focus on value added. 'A school like Wellington has a duty to do what's right in education,' he says. 'The things that really matter can't be measured by league tables.' We agree. We approve. This approach is supported by eg Harkness Tables – large oval seminar-style tables to facilitate the sharing rather than the imparting of knowledge. And, as independent learners, the pupils do much of the preparation for lessons. Every kind of modern IT device and programme abounds but most designed, again, to allow for the sharing of learning. Mobiles allowed for eg messages re assignments and catch-up sessions and Microsoft Surface is embedded so that class participants can all contribute to the same piece of work at once.

Two-weekly cycle of lessons – each one hour long. Regular monitoring, reports and 'interims'. Staff:pupil ratio of just over 1:6 which is remarkably low, although actual class sizes are not smaller than average. Some parental grumbles about the high turnover of staff: 'They do go. They like to have Wellington on their cv and then they get promoted.' But many long-serving staff, very few of whom have lost the light in the eyes.

Everyone is assessed on entry for baseline skills. Remarkably high number of mild or other deficits picked up at this stage – sometimes coming as a surprise to parents. Good support for the 10 per cent of pupils on the SEN register. Emphasis here as throughout on independent learning. Help delivered individually or in groups. Some forego a second modern language for individual support and maybe take one or two fewer GCSEs. One-off subject help sessions abound.

Games, options, the arts: 'If I stayed here for twice as many years, I still wouldn't get round to trying everything,' is a cry we heard over and over. 'You have to sign up for everything you like the sound of in College Carnival (Freshers' Week to you and me) try it all out, then make a longlist, then a shortlist and then try and do what you really want to. But it's still difficult.. and there is class work too..'

Sports, clubs and enrichment activities galore and any teacher or pupil with an enthusiasm is encouraged to start a club of their own. So – a Tea Drinking Club when we visited where the members. er, drink tea. And a Ukelele Orchestra was in full swing. And our Concert Band is the biggest in the country.' 'Service' is central to the ethos providing numerous initiatives to work here and abroad with the less privileged or less physically/cognitively able. They walk the talk.

Rugby rules – this is a quintessential rugby school. However, girls' sports are now firmly on the agenda and the new arena, due mid 2017, will up both the provision and the profile of girls' sports to more of a parity. Though rugby will still rule! The third form can take dance as a curriculum option. We saw a class of excellent textile work but, sadly, not a boy in sight. WTV is an institution and produces professional quality broadcasting. New performing arts centre – a vast building site when we visited – will transform the provision in 2017. The auditorium will seat 1,300 and will be complemented by TV editing suite, recording studios, concert rooms etc. Drama and music pretty spectacular anyway – with high performance values in all media. Visits by professional companies of the highest order too, especially for the occasional Welly Arts Fests. Art in many media, DT and general creativity busting out all over. Trips, exhibition, visitors – it's all just too much!

Boarding: Seventeen boarding houses – 'inhouses' close to the main building, and 'outhouses' nestling in the grounds, some with their own dining rooms – each with its own character, provision, facilities, traditions, lore and argot and each seemingly inspiring loyalty and affection: even when, in the case of one, 'it's been on the upgrade list for the last five years'. Houses bar one are single sex. We were impressed by some small, high-ceilinged, rooms in which the clever use of stairs and a little mezzanine transformed the space into study bedrooms. High standard of bathrooms, showers etc. Lots of honours boards – new and old. Feeling that the character of a house much depends on the character of the sixth form boarders in a given year – some being more inviting and less exclusive than others.

Saturdays are full school days with lessons in the mornings and sports in the afternoons but most go home after that until Sunday evening. Around 150-200 boarders in school most weekends – obviously mostly those with families abroad – and a full programme of activities is on offer if you want it. Wisely, overseas boarders are distributed between the houses so everyone meets everyone. Four weekends annually everyone is required to stay in school. Occasional grouses about the disparity between the houses in terms of upkeep, facilities – and sofas. It's clearly happening, but too slowly for some. More water dispensers around the site would be popular and also the introduction of bikes on which to get around – even if only for the older students.

Careful and thorough induction and acclimatisation activities to help newbies settle in – and to support their jittery parents. Masterclasses give parents a chance to take on eg social media, teenage eating and coaching. Countless events offer parents opportunities to feel part of the wider Wellington community – embraced enthusiastically by many but, of course, not all.

Background and atmosphere: By top English public school standards Wellington, which opened in 1859, is an upstart newbie. It was built as a monument to the first Duke of Wellington (the vanquisher of Bonaparte) by a grateful nation and Queen Victoria laid the foundation stone. But it stands proudly with our most illustrious schools and, when you visit – and even more when you become part of the school – you cannot ignore the pride, the history, the tradition and the splendour of the place. Third form history is largely based on the college's own past and the extensive archives are a rich resource.

Four hundred acres – around half of which are playing fields, lakes (five of them), forest and gardens – embrace the college's main building – a surprising (given the essential Englishness of the place) exercise in low-rise, Rococo-chateau-redbrick designed by John Shaw Jnr (Prince Albert's choice). A very attractive frontage and the interior still boasts some attractive features. Chapel designed by G Gilbert Scott. Rarely for a school chapel of this size and capacity, this one has a warmth and genuine consolatory ambiance. 'It's one of the things you never forget,' a wise alumnus told us. 'Maybe because Wellington is so modern and progressive, we love the chapel because you can think over the college history and what it was like here before.' Numerous later buildings – mostly in red brick – are in sympathy – even the newest glassy additions – and we saw nothing here which was unpleasing to the eye. The Mandarin Centre – complete with gold Chinese dragons, lake, bridge and traditional gateway – comes as a bit of a surprise. Quads – especially the Combermere with terrific central huge bronze of The Iron Duke's horse, Copenhagen – are simply stunning and the upkeep of everywhere is impressive. The V & A is the hip modern café and meeting place – we felt quite at home. Excellent signage too, though a speed bump more or two might be an idea to discourage some over-eager visiting parents.

The forest and lakes abut the centre. The darkness of the close-growing trees add a welcome touch of the less-formal and structured and people do take themselves for walks there, especially when – as they will – closer relationships develop in the sixth form or when a breathing space and solitude are needed. But the school life provides little time for such things – even in the sixth, there is only 45 minutes of free time, between 9.00-9.45pm.

The atmosphere is orderly, friendly, purposeful and relaxed. The light in the eyes when you stop to talk to anyone – and everyone – is immediate. An air of engagement, quiet busyness and enthusiasm pervades the place plus a sense of privilege but not entitlement, and a focus on learning of all kinds. Parents seem universally thrilled: 'They generate a culture where it's all about having a go – nothing is impossible – there's such a buzz about the place.' 'It wouldn't suit everyone – you need a lot of energy and independence,' Interestingly, the word 'whacky' crops up a lot – meant warmly and kindly.

Wellington is now at the heart of a major global and national educational business. It has a portfolio of schools, several in China, and two academies here. This informs aspects of life on the home front – partnerships and exchanges and there is a Dukebox – an online sharing platform for the entire family of schools.

Pastoral care, well-being and discipline: Famous for it – well-being, mindfulness, restorative justice, coaching, leadership, counselling etc – they explore and practise it all. 'Our children – who are all so different – are equally happy,' said one parent. 'I'd give it 10 out of 10 on the pastoral side,' said another. Carefully structured pastoral care system – every teacher is also a tutor and attached to a boarding house. But self-discipline is the norm. A school with rewards and punishments but punishments are rare and exclusions far rarer. Repeated bullying will see you out but isolated episodes seen as an opportunity for learning. Virtually all staff have training in coaching and this, alongside the school's Basic Courtesies, Core Values, Eight Aptitudes, and Mr Thomas's Five 'I's – 'Inspired, Intellectual, Independent, Individual, Inclusive' – underpin the tangible moral purpose of the place. 'The Stiff Upper Lip is long gone,' we were told. Nonetheless, some of the most forbidding uniform rules we have encountered (especially for girls) – seemingly at odds with the school's ethos in other ways, but this is not something the master has got round to looking at yet. 'But I like them to look smart.' It's a Christian foundation but now pretty ecumenical, though with a 'gently Anglican' bent, we were told. Health centre operates 24/7. Vast dining hall (former school hall?) with excellent menus on a four-weekly cycle. We snaffled a memorable flapjack.

Pupils and parents: Majority of UK pupils come from west London and the home counties. School's weekly boarding policy adds to its attraction in the south east. Around 13 per cent come from state and non-prep schools; around 12 per cent from overseas – from 41 countries at time of our visit. Around a third of pupils based overseas are British expats. Interestingly, of the 715 UK-based boarders, over 100 are from non-British or dual citizenship homes at time of our visit. A genuinely inclusive and cosmopolitan constituency and a feature that is fostered by its schools overseas. Very few overseas boarders need EAL support – but those that do get individual help for which the college does not charge. Parents feel welcome here – 'I've never felt I shouldn't be on site. They are brilliant at involving us.'

Entrance: Around 190 pupils enter year 9 – some 110 boys, 80 girls. Around 900 apply. All candidates sit the ISEB common pre-test in the autumn term of year 6. References from present schools also sought. Long-listed candidates visit the college in January/February for an assessment day – a mix of collaborative problem-solving activities plus interview. Offers made in March – at least 65 per cent expected across all subjects at CE.

Around 25 boys and 20 girls join after GCSEs. Sixteen-plus candidates submit recent school reports and a personal statement about a year before entry. Applicants outnumber places 10 to one. Long-listed candidates attend an assessment day in November of year 11 and sit three papers in the subjects they mean to study in the sixth form, plus a maths skills test and an interview plus group discussion. References too, of course. Offers made on December 1 – A*s and As expected in all subjects – A*s in subjects to be pursued in the sixth. Internal pupils also expected to produce 6+ As but there is always 'leeway if they are good citizens'. Attention paid at all levels to characteristics such as independence, inclusivity, grit plus the college's Virtues

Exit: Penny numbers leave after GCSEs. Quite extraordinary recent record of Oxbridge places – 28 in 2016; exemplary by any standards. High numbers also to, especially, Bristol, Durham, Edinburgh and Exeter but Mr Thomas plans to expand the breadth of destinations and wants to provide 'tip-top advice on all options' – including the modern, high calibre, degree apprenticeships path. Also a good number to the US and Canada – Wellington has led the way in sending its leavers to good universities across the pond. Runs the best conferences on this as on many other subjects. Tremendous list of notable alumni includes: Christopher Ewart-Biggs, British Ambassador assassinated by the IRA, current politicos Crispin Blunt, Michael Spicer and Edward Garnier; Harold Nicolson, numerous sports jocks including James Hunt and Max and Thom Evans; arts and entertainment types eg Robert Morley, Nikolai Tolstoy, Rory Bremner, Sebastian Faulks, Christopher Lee, Will Young and Elize du Toit; the Beeb's Peter Snow and Robin Oakley; practically the entire British military including 15 holders of the Victoria Cross and hosts of other worthies in many fields.

Money matters: The international schools help to fund the school's burgeoning bursary fund – scholarships no longer carry any financial benefit. Funds now routed into bursaries. However, without meriting a scholarship no-one is eligible for a bursary. Bursaries means-tested as elsewhere and worth anything from 10 to 95 per cent of school fees. Some £1.7m and rising annually available. Prince Albert Bursary Fund offers life-changing bursaries up to full fees to entrants who would otherwise have no chance of such an education. Ten holders at time of our visit. Also the Jimmy Higham sports' bursary and the Sir Anthony Seldon arts bursary. Well worth checking out. Foundation supports the children of deceased military officers up to full fees.

Remarks: Hard to imagine it done better. A site and campus to dream about. A school with mind, heart, guts and a constant fizz.

Westbourne House School

Shopwyke, Chichester, West Sussex PO20 2BH

Pupils: 40; 59 boarders • Ages: 3-13 (boarders from year 3) • C of E

Fees: Day £9,960 – £17,160; Boarding £20,940 pa

Tel: 01243 782739
Email: office@westbournehouse.org
Website: www.westbournehouse.org

Headmaster: Since 2011, Mr Martin Barker BEd Exeter (40s), four years as deputy before – previously at Papplewick in Ascot. Married to Helen – she also teaches, masterminds special projects for the scholarship forms and organises charitable initiatives and donations. They met at university where she concentrated on primary, he on science and PE. Daughter and a son both at Westbourne and a place near the Everglades for what little non-Westbourne time they have. He's tall and approachable (kids agree), passionate about good teaching having been burnt by the opposite at a grammar school (in the 80s...). His initial brief was on the academic side (brought a database for recording marks to the school) and an impressive scholarship rate backs up the governors' appointment. So far he's also applied this talent for rationalising systems to the school day, delegation within the teaching staff and boarding options – the result is a more formal structure but parents say a more relaxed atmosphere, 'fewer meetings, the ones that happen count'. Reassuringly, he is most proud of the pastoral improvement – 'reduction in unkindness with the shorter break in the afternoon' – and that the kids are 'rounded and grounded – and so in demand for senior schools'. Still teaches year 8 chemistry and coaches rugby and cricket.

Entrance: Very local school – biggest commute 40 minutes away, 50 per cent of families London migrants. Also local farmers, entrepreneurs (some semi-retired), medics (St Richards Chichester nearby) and Rolls Royce. Diverse lot – double incomes, single parents and the wealthy. Reputation locally for pushy parents. Best entry point at reception/year 1 – 75 per cent – unfiltered for nursery and pre-prep, ability assessment for entry to year 3. SEN would have to be seriously limiting to be turned away – support both in class or with a small group extracted. Composition of intake dictated by composition of new families – waiting lists for years 2, 3 and 5 – very hard to keep spaces open later in school if siblings arrive en masse eg from London. Fifty per cent scholarships available for music and some for academic excellence. Means-tested bursaries available for current families, five per cent off for siblings. Continuation scholarships with links to Radley and Cranleigh – entry point year 7 at present, could be changed to year 5 to ensure they have the best chance in senior schools.

Exit: Boarders, from year 3 (though this is rare) must board a minimum of two nights in years 3 to 6, building up to minimum three nights in year 7 and full week (five nights) in year 8 – vital preparation for the 60 per cent who go on to boarding schools. Top three destinations are Brighton, Canford and Wellington. Portsmouth Grammar is the only popular day school but the train journey puts some parents off. Aims for half a dozen each year to eg Seaford, Lancing, Eton, Benenden, Hurstpierpoint, Cranleigh, Radley, Marlborough, Downe House, St Mary's Ascot, Bryanston, Sherborne. Scholarship hit rate an arrestingly high

35 per cent of all leavers. Eminent outgoers include R4's Marcus Brigstocke (funny) and the late Nick Clarke (news); Monarch of the Glen, Alastair McKenzie; England women's cricketer Holly Colvin

Remarks: Founded as a family school and the atmosphere remains – the original owners, now in their 80s, still live on site (just beyond some wire lions as you enter the beautiful grounds) and continue to be part of school life. Early Victorian main house, sandwiched between beach and the Downs, pupils here stay kids for longer than those in more urban schools and staff make sure they are ready for entry to secondary schools by the time they leave. Complete refurbishment of pre-prep in 2015 following roof fire.

School ethos grew out of scouting – the fleur-de-lys logo is sprinkled about and patrol leaders are voted in (panther, tiger, otter and owl) each term. In the summer the mothers of troop leaders (heads of school) present the prizes – this family involvement is characteristic, whether it is houseparents with children at the school, the parental barometer on teaching standards, support on the games pitches or siblings in different years. A parent could pick up at three different times each day – from nursery, pre-prep and prep – the hanging around can be frustrating but also means relationships are built and social events are surprisingly well-attended.

Children love it here – their favourite parts are the communal ones – form rooms, chapel, the millennium hall, picnics after Saturday morning lessons, BBQ night in the summer – the astounding attraction of a sausage in a bun! They respond to the humanity of teachers and understand the thinking behind structures in the school eg how cleaning works in dining room; that playing in bases (dens) in the boundaries (woods) is organised by rota now – to avoid any tussles or rivalries between age groups. Boarding is popular (one of houses was doubled in size recently). Six boarding houses in total, presided over by houseparents, caring matrons and fun gappers. Most boarders go home at weekends, often after Saturday matches.

ICT is omnipresent to free up staff and pupil time for learning and playing – ideally, as in the world outside. Four trolleys of Apple Macs, Wifi – no issues with gaming, kids say they save that for home if they are into it. Older boarders can use iPods before bed. Smartboards in every classroom – yet, as ever, only some teachers use them to the pupils' best advantage. Landlines on wall for calling home – no need or time for mobile phones or Angry Birds apparently. Newspapers as well as screens in the library (due to be revamped).

Breadth in the curriculum, backed up by good facilities. New food tech and science labs, French vocab on doors in main school, ceramics studio a popular retreat (sometimes there's hot chocolate and often CDs playing), stunning art, sparky technology projects, drama opportunities both on, back and above stage, a lake for kayaking (sailing soon), indoor pool and Astroturf. The purpose-built music school fosters a full range – harpists to advert theme tune composers, 80 per cent of children learn an instrument. Peripatetic music teachers mean a catch up period is vital for missed academic lessons.

The risk with such a range of well-supported subjects (and the results to match them) is choice and activity overload, no space left for aimless mucking around (the risk assessed alternative to climbing trees?). Shorter lessons, no time between them, a longer break in the morning, scholarship sets – the long prep at the end of the day is a crowd-pleaser since no homework – the disadvantage is that parents don't see books when they come home. The proof is in the pudding, though – really happy families.

W

Winchester College

College Street, Winchester, Hampshire SO23 9NA

Pupils: 690; all board • Ages: 13–18 • Sixth form: 280 • C of E

Fees: Boarding £36,678 pa

Tel: 01962 621247
Email: admissions@wincoll.ac.uk
Website: www.winchestercollege.org

Headman: Since September 2016, Dr Timothy Hands, previously master of Magdalen College School. A state school pupil turned down by Cambridge ('I was told by the careers adviser at my grammar school that I wouldn't get to university at all'), he studied violin at the Guildhall before reading English at King's College, London, then went on to St Catherine's, Oxford, followed by Oriel, where he ended up as a lecturer. He became housemaster at King's Canterbury, then second master at Whitgift School, then head of Portsmouth Grammar. He comes from a long line of teachers, including both parents and an ancestor who was schoolmaster on HMS Victory. Likes sport and music – was co-leader of the London Schools Symphony Orchestra and conductor of the Oxford University chamber choir, Schola Cantorum. The author of several books about Victorian literature and teaches English A level.

Married to Jane, a solicitor who read classics at Oxford; two sons.

Academic matters: Winchester offers Cambridge Pre-U examinations as a replacement for A levels in all subjects. The school takes a dim view of the latter, especially in modern languages which have been 'vandalised' ('you can now take an A level in French without reading a book!'). The Cambridge Pre-U has no coursework and opens up sixth form study as a serious two-year programme, studying three subjects in depth, with examinations at the end – a format now copied by revised A levels. Some mathematicians take four (or even five) Pre-U exams, sitting maths at the end of the lower sixth and further maths the following year.

Results always outstanding (50 per cent D1-2 – A* equivalent, and 75 per cent D1-3 – A*-A equivalent, in 2016), and the school continues to offer the shortest list of exam subjects of any reputable sixth form in England. Forget film studies and froth – here you will not find examined drama, classical civilisation, politics, business studies, PE or psychology. Chemistry and physics the most popular Pre-U subjects, followed robustly by history and English lit. Philosophy and theology on a roll at the minute. No great cornucopia of GCSE choices either: all boys sit IGCSEs in three sciences, maths, English, Latin, and any modern language so long as it's French, plus usually three other subjects which can include more languages. In 2016, 94 per cent A*/A grades at I/GCSE.

'Div' is the unique and highly-prized complementary programme at the heart of the Winchester ethos. It aims to instill a knowledge and understanding of British, European and world history and culture and, as such, is a true, liberal education. 'The boys and dons love it. It's the one bit of this over-structured world in which they can pursue their own intellectual interests.' It's a holistic approach that we expect to find in Montessori education and schools on the alternative end of the spectrum. 'It means the staff have to be of the highest calibre so that they can lead this cross-subject, cross-cultural tutorial,' a parent explained. Average age of teachers has come down significantly in recent years, and is now a youthful 38.

IT not cutting any edges, reflecting an institutional reserve about the digital world. Little, if any, work done on computers in a boy's first year (or two) here. Offers learning support for around 100 boys, mainly for mild dyslexia, dyspraxia and information processing. One boy registered blind, one deaf.

Games, options, the arts: The sport is 'brilliantly flexible', a parent told us. Enthusiasts can play as much as they want. 'My son went from the 4th team at his prep school to the A team here', chuckled one mum. 'There's a great spirit in the school sport', another told us, 'very unpressurised.' 'If you are determined to do no games, it's possible' (refreshing, and probably unique, to hear this said in a British public school). But some sort of physical exercise ('ekker') is compulsory. Main sports are soccer, Winchester College football (read the rules) and cricket (huge here – the cricket coach also runs the Hampshire U16s) but these are supplemented by everything from aikido to water polo. Fabulous playing fields and sports facilities of all kinds. Recent national competition wins in rackets, fives, fencing and cross-country running.

Music very important, very strong and very classical. James Blunt, Genesis and Mumford and Sons may have attended public schools but they would not have been Wykehamists. Two-thirds of boys learn a musical instrument; many learn two or three, taught by a long list of specialist teachers. Pipe organ very strong here (one Winchester boy we know was making a tidy sum playing weddings while still in sixth form). Music school includes 50(!) practice rooms, a music tech classroom, recording studio and editing suite. Vast range of musical ensembles and performance opportunities – weekly Tuesday concert and many more throughout the year – many open to the public.

Art and drama lively and of quality, though they do not quite enjoy the accolade of music. CCF compulsory in year 10, after which it can be replaced with community service.

Boarding: All boys board. First year boys are generally in rooms of four. By IGCSEs they're in doubles. All sixth formers have single rooms, except the scholars. A boy's life here begins and ends with his house. Houses, while still more autonomous than at any other school in the UK, have been brought some distance into dreary conformity in this era of Health and Safety, school inspections and the like. There is now a lot more consistency of discipline, food (all meals are eaten in house) and day to day routine and less competition between houses (and housemasters). Current crop of housemasters praised by the parents we spoke to. Accommodation and food improving but still seen as of secondary importance, both to the school and to (British) parents.

Saturdays consist of lessons until lunch, then sport, then reading, then prep. Most boys go out after chapel on Sundays – younger boys to lunch at home, older ones into town. The school's inflexible attitude towards Sunday boarding is a source of contention for a few boys who have to pass up outside sports fixtures.

Background and atmosphere: Founded in the 14th century by William of Wykeham, Bishop of Winchester, Chancellor to Richard II, and the sage behind the school's motto: Manners makyth man. Began in 1387 with a Warden, 10 fellows, two schoolmasters three chaplains, 70 scholars and 16 quiristers – the Winchester version of choristers. The bishop also founded New College, Oxford, with which the college maintains strong links. The quiristers are now educated down the road at the Pilgrims' School but continue to board at Winchester College and sing in chapel. So this is a quiet land of flinty walls, leafy quads, a venerable chapel, many other buildings of ancient date and visible history (the school was used as Cosette's Paris convent in the film version of Les Mis). Later foundations, eg Eton College, seem like modern upstarts by comparison. Not that the college hasn't kept building and acquiring. There are 10 boarding houses in adjacent streets, and buildings for all major disciplines. The college is now building a new museum in a converted stable to display its trove of treasures – paintings, porcelain, silver, scientific instruments, books etc.

The atmosphere is donnish – the masters are called dons here and the college has a language of its own (called Notions) for almost every aspect of daily life. The lack of girls, together with the school's academically elitist ethos, gives the boys the gift of unselfconsciousness rarely seen elsewhere. The school considered admitting girls under previous head – 'I started off thinking we'd do it', he remembered. In the end, they decided against: 'Girls dominate academically, especially in the lower years. To introduce that here would change the intellectual ethos of the school. What we do is distinctive – we do not have a wide ability range. It is the high quality of the boys' ability at the "bottom" that is key here.'

Surprisingly, the school has no formal relationship with Winchester Cathedral – who needs it when you've got such a superb school chapel (built 1392)? The cathedral is used for school choir concerts. 'It casts an ecclesiastical aura.' Has a 5+ year relationship with Midhurst Rother College (academy) and some pupils from the academy come to Winchester for a Saturday morning programme of classes.

Pastoral care, well-being and discipline: School rules cover 10 tightly spaced typed pages and make a terrifically good read. You will find a complex list of warnings about alcohol (depending whether wine, beer or spirits and where purchased) and learn that the possession of firearms or explosives is forbidden (with the exception of 'shotguns brought into school with parent permission'). Boys are also reminded not to wear 'T-shirts bearing slogans which are anagrammatical' (what harm is an anagram, we ask?). No hats. And before you ask, no earrings.

Mobiles allowed so long as they are 'inaudible and invisible'. School takes a hard line on drugs, but they remain a recurring nuisance. Unusually, for a school of this vintage, there is no sixth form bar. Housemasters run most aspects of a boy's life – pastoral and academic – but serious matters end up with the head.

Pupils and parents: Some 87 per cent of boys come from the UK. All pupils speak English as it if were their first language; around 20 pupils are bilingual. Quite a lot of Hong Kong Chinese families – who tend to coalesce at the academic hothouses of this land. 'Russians haven't found us yet,' commented one of the admissions staff (more likely, they shun it because it's single sex). Boys come from a large assortment of preps mostly in the southern half of the UK, with Pilgrims' School, Horris Hill, Twyford, The Dragon, Summer Fields and Sussex House leading the field. The school does not break its back to court parents – neither current nor prospective: there is one rather sober open day each year.

Parents we spoke to were keen to emphasise that though boys must be clever and academic to be happy here, they need not be geeks: 'There's a view that Winchester boys are anaemic swots. There are some very studious individuals here – yes, but there are also normal, clever but lazy boys who like their sport and are not averse to sunshine.' Not the place for hovering parents – signing on here takes a leap of faith and the school is set in its ways ('clear about what it wants and expects,' says the school). List of well-known old boys is long, but curiously unexciting. Lots of politicians, academics, cricketers, journalists, pillars of The Establishment.. and Tim Brooke-Taylor.

Entrance: You'll need to be on your toes. The school asks parents to register their sons after they've turned 8 but 'well before the end of year 5'. No need for early registration for those attempting scholarships – winning an award carries with it the automatic right to a place. Admissions for 'Commoners' are via the housemasters who see 25 to 30 sets of parents when the boys are 10-11, interview and test them (a short verbal and numerical reasoning test), get reports from existing schools and offer places to around half. A deposit is then requested and the place is firm, barring (rare) failure of the college's entrance exam which is taken two years later in May of the year of entry in all usual CE subjects (with Greek and German as additional options, but not Spanish). It helps to have an idea of which houses you are interested in – parents may arrange meetings with up to three housemasters. 'If parents are still unsettled after seeing three houses, this may not be the school for them', said the admissions department with customary directness.

Scholars and exhibitioners selected by exams in English, maths, science and a multiple choice 'general reasoning' test. Candidates must also choose three optional papers from among: Latin, French, Classical Greek/German/Spanish, history, geography, maths II or general paper II. Scholars live in 'College' – a separate house pulsating with hyperactive brain cells. The life of a scholar here is not for all, and we know of families turning down an academic scholarship (especially now that they bring no automatic fee remission). A half dozen boys come fresh into the sixth form via exam and a minimum of six GCSE A*/A grades (ie mainly A*s but the odd A won't rule you out).

Exit: In 2016, 26 to Oxbridge, and five medics. The rest to a predictable spread of the best redbricks. Increasing numbers (around 20 lately) to a distinguished list of top North American universities. Six As required at IGCSE to proceed to sixth form and, thought this is a low hurdle for most boys here, the college is said to be 'ruthless' (school says 'firm') about enforcing this rule. A handful of unfortunate boys receive 'the letter' each year.

Money matters: Since 2011, all scholarships – given for academic and musical ability; no sports, art or drama frippery here (though candidates with those talents may bring along a portfolio of their work) – bring zero fee remittance. However means-tested bursaries can be awarded up to 100 per cent of the fee where necessary. Music scholars, of which there are 10 (usually grade 8 by age 13), receive free tuition on up to two instruments and singing; music exhibitioners (closer to grade 6) get free tuition on one instrument. NB Charges an inexplicable £500 'entrance fee' (in addition to a registration fee and deposit).

Remarks: A very special place for intellectually curious boys and their teachers. Unique.

Windlesham House School

276

Washington, Pulborough, West Sussex RH20 4AY

Pupils: 351; 195 full boarders • Ages: 4–13 • C of E

Fees: Boarding £20,010 – £28,770; Day £15,990 – £24,990 pa

Tel: 01903 874700
Email: whsadmissions@windlesham.com
Website: www.windlesham.com

Headmaster: Since 2007, Mr Richard Foster, Head at Pembroke House School in Kenya, then at St Anselm's in Derbyshire for 14 years. Thoughtful, warm, much liked by parents and pupils. Incredibly busy wife Rachel is in charge of everything pastoral – parents give Rachel a ring and she races around the school to find the relevant child and tend to it. Three grown up children. Both Fosters refer slightly wistfully to Kenya as home and enthuse pupils with love for the region. Windlesham is the most child centred school Mr Foster has ever taught at – though he is careful to point out (perhaps with the more conservative parents in mind) that 'children [here are] liberated – not liberal.' In his 50s and will stay at Windlesham until retirement. Still teaches, and randomly covers all classes over the course of the year.

Entrance: Non selective. Academic assessment from year 1 upwards for setting purposes plus night's stay from year 3 upwards. Houses have different personalities, and tester night helps school decide in which house the potential pupils would flourish. Waiting list for many years. No scholarships, but means-tested bursaries available.

Exit: Pupils move on to over 30 different schools, including Eton, Marlborough, Lancing, Hurst, Brighton College, Bedales and Oundle.

Remarks: Gorgeous grounds, movingly beautiful even on the miserable day of our visit, with the elegant Queen Anne house standing at the end of a long drive past a mixture of woods, playing fields and golf course. Game rambling around (they don't shoot it here – just clay pigeons). Beautiful entrance hall with roaring fire adds to the impression of arriving at a country house hotel; one specialising in modern art – it's everywhere, and extremely good.

Feels happy and free – described by one parent as a 'tree climbing education centre.' There is a distinct feel of Famous Five here. The amazing grounds are fully used by the children; one parent described how the matrons have to drag them in to bed during the summer months, and how kids are out playing golf and cricket before breakfast – 'kids have the freedom to be children' (children with a nine hole golf course).

Parents and children all comment on the strong community at Windlesham -'it's an incredibly kind place', which aims to be a family home away from home. No uniform promotes the homey feel, although the strict dress code prevents a grungy look. There's no label competition here – 'they ruin clothes at school, so don't send them in anything good,' said one parent wryly. Birthday parties for boarders in the Fosters' flat – cake, treat food and all. Huge amount of energy devoted to pastoral care. Many staff live on site: one parent said 'they never clock off'. Another: 'teachers go over and beyond what they need to do; nothing is too much effort.' One parent described the 'brilliant support' from the learning centre and houseparents after a family death – they have a 'genuine love of children [here].'

High level of responsibility and support shown between children. Peer listeners appointed from the top class, peer mediators in each year- described lavishly by one of our guides as 'unpaid spies', but a peer mediator calmly countered with an example of a love/hate triangle successfully resolved by her and her counterpart. Any help from adults? 'No, of course not – confidentiality,' she said in a shocked tones. For prep age children, they are astonishingly responsible and outward-looking. This is one of the school's aims, with the head's mantra firmly in mind – be kind, be kind, be kind. Any bullying nipped it in the bud early. 'There's not a great deal of it,' said a parent, whose daughter experienced bullying which was dealt very efficiently.

No prefect or monitor system. All pupils in the top year sign up for responsibilities, and at the end of the year it is announced who will have been head girl and boy on the basis of performance.

Huge emphasis on good manners here: children pay good heed to the head's warning – 'get your greeting in before I do.' Good evidence of this on our tour: all pupils held open doors, flattened themselves against walls as we passed and leapt up in classrooms. Children are very aware of rules set down in the code of conduct, and there's open discussion of rules in school council (top year). 'Fatigues if you're really bad' – jobs such as cleaning the dining room.

Pupils can board from the age of 8 and there are 230 full boarders, 18 per cent from overseas. 'Boarding provision is exceptionally good,' said a mum, whose kids started as day pupils, and all ended up boarding at their request. Pupils agree – 'it's a sleepover that doesn't stop.' Homely girls' dorms, with posters, cushions, bears; spartan boys' fare, with coloured duvets the most cosy touch (despite the school's best efforts). 'It's the girls who need One Direction posters,' said one of our guides loftily. Girls also get bedside tables and lights – boys don't because of their tendency to play cricket in the dorms. At the end of the term, children give in a list of people they like, and are guaranteed to find at least one in their dorm the next term. Twelve is the biggest boys' dorm, six the smallest, nine-three for the girls. A little unfortunate that the girls' dorms are named after colours – 'azure,' 'saffron' etc – to suit their delicate natures? – whereas boys' dorms are sturdily named after senior schools -'Wellington' et al. Unfortunate indeed, but no other whiff of sex discrimination here.

There are two boarding houses, each of which has a male and female houseparent, a permanent matron, and a battalion of evening matrons who come in from the surrounding community to assist at bedtime, and make sure kids are clean with clothes sorted for tomorrow. Nightly showers, although boarders can relax in a birthday bath. Bathroom facilities extremely clean, but not all that new. Each year has a comfy room, reduced to cheerful bedlam for the boys, ordered comfort for the girls. No mobile phones or own computers, but phones all over the place for speaking to parents, Skype phones in the comfy rooms for those with parents abroad, and dormitory phones for good night calls to parents (time restricted to give everyone a chance).

Parents say school is just not the same for day pupils, who don't have the same access to activities or teachers as boarders. Kids love the autonomy of deciding what to do every evening: tag rugby, fencing, art, just hanging out with friends – and can always get help if there's problem with prep. Boarding is particularly useful as work steps up in preparation for common entrance, parents say – early bird lessons start at 7.15am, and work ends at 6.30pm, so it's a long day for commuters.

No pocket money. On school trips pupils are given a set amount to spend, which goes on the school bill as an extra. Boarders get tuck at weekend – not enough to rot their teeth (a chocolate bar, a can and packet of crisps). Can earn various treats, which are usually of an edible nature. Kids talk a lot about grub, one way or another. One pupil earnestly reported that someone actually stopped boarding for lack of crisps (although it should be pointed out that the food here is plenteous and good). Academically, parents and pupils are happy with most subjects, exceptionally so in some areas though French is 'not that popular,' say the kids and parents agree, citing a reliance on work sheets. School says it has taken on new teachers since our visit.

Another parent suggested maths is also a key subject that could be taught better, although the children we spoke to gave maths teachers a glowing report – 'if you listen carefully they're really funny – very sarcastic.' One teacher apparently tells stories of his life in mathematical fantasy (difficult to imagine how this might go...). Those fiddling with their calculator may find it deposited on the outside of the window sill, so that if someone opens the window it would smash – 'really cool,' says a pupil. The head says they are about to appoint an additional maths specialist – an acknowledgement this is an area with which some children struggle.

Head says English and science are exceptionally strong. Pupils agree about science -'one of the finest lessons.' The kids enjoy the interactive classes – 'we always do an experiment, and if you work hard, you can fit in two or three. We are doing chemical reactions, so I'm seeing things explode,' said one of our guides with relish. One science room just updated, others to be done soon.

Set for core common entrance subjects from year 5. French and Spanish to all, Latin from year 6 (can be dropped by those with learning difficulties to concentrate on more core subjects). Provision for Greek, Mandarin, Italian, Russian, Norwegian and Dutch. Basically if a child arrives speaking a language, they will be encouraged to keep it up, whatever it is. Equally if a child has a burning desire to learn a particular language, school will attempt to accommodate the urge.

Forms usually no more than 18, occasionally up to 20. Starts spotting potential scholars in year 6, and a formal academic scholars' group is established in year 7. Two academic scholarship groups at the moment containing 40 children. Some strong feelings about the scholars' group (where offspring have been both included and excluded from the elite), with the suggestion that scholars are more profiled and get more support than others – and have more chances to go on the fabulous biannual charity trips. 'Opportunities should be more evenly spread,' said a parent (although the forthcoming trip to Nairobi is open to anyone in year 8).

Year 8s do have some preparation for independent learning, but one parent thought kids are hand held a bit too long, and could do with a little more independence in personal care, and organising prep.

Rigorous reporting for parents: progress report monthly with attainment and effort, both child and parents get a copy, and a full report at the end of each term. Annual parents' evening (termly for juniors). 'Amazing level of communication,' say parents: written letters from kids every week, emails and phone calls. 'School responds promptly to any query, over and above what you would expect.' Another parent commented how welcome she felt at weekends – you can attend Saturday chapel, watch a play rehearsal or recital. '[You] never feel excluded as a parent – always welcomed.' Parental portal has live stream of events, also available for catch up, ideal for parents who aren't local. New sports complex and swimming pool under construction.

Three computer rooms, one reserved specially for junior use. Dell laptops and iPads to book out, also available to assist those with mild learning difficulties (about 15 per cent of children here). Learning development unit with head and team of assistants. Bright, well-stocked library, open from before breakfast until bedtime, news with a Tory bent – Telegraph and Times, with the honourable exception of the i.

Feels quite hunting, shooting, fishing, but manages not to feel exclusive. Sports are the usual public school fare. Parents are delighted that sports kit left hanging around at school is returned washed and pristine. Some criticism of sports facilities by parents, who feel that the swimming pool and equipment is rather tired – pupils too are keen for a new pool, and complain the Astroturf is rather worn. Changing rooms on the scruffy side. One parent felt that sports could be improved, and those in teams in the lower echelons should be playing more matches.

Most boarders are around at weekends (though it's possible to go home four weekends a term). Everyone's around on Saturdays: morning school, matches in the afternoon. Plenty of activities available – Capture the Flag is extremely popular at the moment; but also debates, mountain biking, gardening in the walled garden, shows and games – pupils can keep extremely busy if they want to (though some kids just want to live in the woods, and that's ok too.) Chess club is thriving, though the outdoor chess set is largely unused – 'but we do use a couple of the pieces for goalposts.' All love cooking club – you have to run fast if you want to sign up.

All have drama lessons, three productions each year, everyone who auditions is included in some way. Own theatre – the Malden Family Theatre – with visiting productions every term. Some rumblings from parents who are a bit tired of seeing the super-duper children starring again. Music compulsory all the way, but popular even with those who are not musical because of the inspirational director. Over 80 per cent play an instrument. Vast array of music groups of all complexions, from Miremba to rock choir.

Early years housed separately at Little Windlesham (reception – year 2). Relaxed setting, emphasis on flow and play. Tapestry method of contacting parents, who receive a video stream of their children in class directly to their email at work, which parents love. Described by a parent as being 'part of [the] big school – but very gentle, with a lot of time [spent] in their special oasis.'

The head says Windlesham would suit most types of kids, providing they join in and have a go at things. One parent suggested it would not suit a child who needs to be totally organised by others; nor is it a place for shrinking violets; although conversations with shy pupils suggested they could find their feet and flourish here. One parent emphasised that those who want their children to be day pupils should avoid Windlesham – all kids here will want to board eventually.

Parents from the foreign office, business, Forces, professions, and lots of expats. Some 20 different nationalities in the school, around 12 per cent non British. Assesses language skills on entry, but will give special assistance to learn English as a foreign language. Some 50 per cent of kids local, 50 per cent from abroad or other parts of the country. Parents like the mix of children from different countries, and to a degree, backgrounds – a few means-tested bursaries and no judgement, say parents; although four wheel drive likely to be parent vehicle of choice.

Several parents of leavers said their children are homesick for Windlesham: the move from this caring environment to senior school can be quite tough; but as a parent said, no one would want Windlesham to be less fabulous.

Woldingham School

Marden Park, Woldingham, Surrey CR3 7YA

Pupils: 550; 150 full, 150 weekly boarders • Ages: 11–18 • Sixth form: 175 • RC

Fees: Day £19,596 – £21,357; Boarding £31,332 – £34,113 pa

Tel: 01883 349431
Email: registrar@woldinghamschool.co.uk
Website: www.woldinghamschool.co.uk

Headmistress: Since September 2016, Alexandra Hutchinson, previously deputy head. Began her teaching career at Clifton College in Bristol, where she met her husband Chris, who is the head teacher of Royal Russell School in Croydon. Her other roles before coming to Woldingham have included spells as head of sixth form at both Wimbledon High School and Central Newcastle High School.

She plays hockey for a local team and also enjoys choral society singing.

Academic matters: Long-standing reputation for creative excellence now matched by burgeoning academics. Wannabe Carey Mulligans (school's best known old girl) might be applying in greater numbers but artistic temperament without solid academic performance these days no longer enough to secure a place. 'We're not St Paul's but we expect every girl to be capable of achieving 10 or 11 good GCSEs.'

Pupils' ability is above national average and progress made is one of sources of school pride – pupils move up about a grade based on entry level performance, helped by small(ish) classes, average 15 or so to sixth form, nine or 10 thereafter, together with bigger, earlier focus on setting (in maths and science) and banding (humanities) and lots of inspiration along the way, from thought bubbles surrounding topical articles (diligently completed by teachers and a couple of pupils, including head girl) to large type motivational quotes in English corridor: 'Only positive attitudes allowed beyond this point.'

While 100 or so speak English as a second or additional language, only half need support. Similarly, while all are screened for learning difficulties on entry, needs mainly mild to moderate, though school goes the distance with support, staffing recently ramped up to offer everything from in-class support to separate one-to-one and small group sessions. Though inspection report quibbled, pupils are in no doubt as to value. 'Wanted a school that didn't make me stupid,' says one. 'Here they knew I had difficulties but still felt I could be in the top set.'

Combination of setting in maths and sciences and banding (same group for humanities) allows strengths – and difficulties – to be recognised – though not currently offered in languages, potentially disadvantaging those starting ab initio in year 9. Overall, however, 'not about who's smarter than who but who learns differently,' said year 10 pupil.

With specific learning difficulties by far the biggest need, main form of help given is with organisation – watches, jewellery and memory sticks top lost property lists – and study skills, clearly a school-wide preoccupation, with emergency furniture stuffed into every spare nook and cranny, ensuring no one struck with urgent revision needs is ever more than a few feet from a desk.

More made of most able in recent years, now offered assorted intellect-stretching activities ranging from summer schools at prestigious US unis to encouragement to enter essay writing and maths competitions, plus law, philosophy or creative writing clubs and societies. Also encouraged to take EPQ, where jury currently out. Though results impressive, horribly time-consuming and thus may be destined for early bath.

None of that early exams for the brightest nonsense, however. 'What's the point?' thought director of studies (appropriately aka Mr Clever, according to Mr Men picture 'from wife' in study). Able mathematicians instead enticed with chance to do stand-alone additional maths qualification. (Replaces further maths, an off-putting IGCSE, which attracted few takers).

Suits actions to words with improved results both at GCSE and A level, gap closing between the two, with 55 per cent of A levels graded A*/A in 2016 and 81 per cent A*-B. At GCSE, 74 per cent A*/A grades.

Few trouble spots dim otherwise healthy glow, though mixed intake does mean that success in toughest subjects may always be uphill struggle for tiny minority of weakest pupils.

Subjects have been overhauled – nothing radical (will always be A levels rather than IB, for example), just gently progressive (pupils we spoke to felt food tech and business studies would be icing on curriculum cake). Cat's cradle complexities of GCSE option choices usually managed with aplomb (timetable room, floor piled high with discarded paper, presumably bears witness to the effort required to pull it off).Everyone now takes European Computer Driving Licence in first two years, budding techies now able to essay HGV version in form of GCSE computing as alternative to ICT.

Art outstanding, work including transformation series with delicately drawn human heart gradually metamorphosing into tree, one of a long row of eye-catching GCSE exam entries forming orderly queue like so many talent show entrants.

At A level, little to complain about, choice impressive and growing (slowly) with PE and media studies recently added and lavish sugar coatings courtesy of delicious-sounding subject-related excursions (sixth form physicists' chance to air surf in a wind tunnel surely top of wish lists).

Translates into broad base of interests reflected in roughly equal numbers taking arts and sciences at A level, maths and economics the single biggest subjects but followed by theatre studies, English about as popular as chemistry. Creative types particularly well catered for with three-way choice of art (textiles and history on top of fine) as well as music and musical technology. Even get bonus of own staff shirt code, smartly suited for conventional subjects, art and music signalled by occasional shift into denim.

Teaching generally excellent, staff putting in as much of own time as necessary to ensure pupils really understand a topic and help the unconfident to blossom. 'Started off as middle of the road and really came out of myself,' enthused sixth former destined for high ranking university. 'Turn shyness into quiet confidence,' said a parent of year 9 pupil who is now 'relished for who she is – this isn't just a conveyor belt for A and B grades.'

Traditional lesson formats rule though plenty of interaction – year 9 pupils deftly stretched during demanding poetry analysis by encouraging English teacher. Pupils enthusiastic. 'I love everything,' said several, science hands-on fun making it a list topper. 'We've set fire to a lot of things,' exulted year 8. Perhaps just as well not all eight labs have yet been refurbished.

Only handicap the considerable to-ing and fro-ing between lessons, noted by inspectors with some mild accompanying tut-tutting. Given that distance between buildings – it's a fair old trot from science, say, to humanities – remains a fact of life, school does its best with longer 55 minute lessons and five minute travel allowance time. Hard to see how gorgeousness of commute can be anything but a bonus.

Games, options, the arts: Pupils 'need to be robust just to take advantage of all the opportunities,' thinks teacher. Must be, too, what with 300 tough nuts studying drama or instruments (to diploma level), 200 having tennis coaching, remainder able to select from 80 activities so tempting that droves of day girls stay on to take advantage of extended day that runs to 6.30pm; Saturday activities, compulsory for years 8 to 10 (and a popular voluntary extra in year 7) provide another bite of the cherry.

Currently having a bit of a moment are fencing and riding, cookery course, run by Leith-trained school staff, another favourite together with debating – whither EU membership typically (and topically) meaty subject tackled by sixth formers and no doubt packing in the crowds.

Range of entertaining external speakers are additionally wheeled in to galvanise the troops, 'Vampires' the (blood-soaked) cherry on cake for year 7s in National Science and Engineering Week speech. Trips, equally abundant, range from art in St Ives and science in Peru, to music, excitingly 'TBA'...

Acres of space well used inside and out. Parent-pleasing eye candy provided by flight of stone steps rising up to outside swimming pool through series of lush grass terraces. More prosaic, though well used, is floodlit, sand, all-weather pitch and umpteen others for tennis/netball.

Sports rather less monochrome than recent match reports, netball accounting for seven out of the 10, would suggest, hockey faring well, appeal boosted no end by fab weekend tours to major European cities (Lisbon and Rome love the game, apparently).

School works hard to avoid sports and arts activities clashes by rotating priorities so all-rounders aren't torn between the two. While the championship fixated might not thrive, there's enough local success to keep competitive instincts honed, as well as sprinkling of individual county and national success (hockey, netball, British diving team), while enthusiasm and attitude are first class, pluckiness unswerving in the face of disappointment – 'close to coming second,' was typically upbeat report. Feistiness also an essential attribute (one girl was taking A levels as timetabled, despite breaking arm just before first exam).

Though same names tend to crop up in first teams, 'less good do get matches,' reckoned year 8 pupil, and commitment will do the trick every time. 'As long as they turn up for the training sessions then they get a go,' confirmed a mother, though further up the school it's a slightly different story, have-a-go mentality giving way to realities of tougher competition, so that keen but hopeless may be sidelined, says school. 'People say it's not sporty – but it's sporty enough,' felt mother.

Arts 'amazing,' thought parents, and similarly busy with much impressive showcasing for top talent, from what pupil review describes as 'raucous' production of Midsummer Night's Dream to local music festivals and energetic house music competition. Focus the knock-out Millennium Arts Centre packed with pupil-friendly extras including concealed high level walkways allowing safe access to lighting rig. Would-be Dorothys can even skip there along yellow brick road linking with main building. More beige, we reckoned, but what's a pantone shade or two between friends?

Boarding: Accommodation for boarders never less than clean and bright with smart, purpose-built storage in companiable shared rooms (maximum five, mostly two to four) with single rooms from year 10, en-suites the perk for upper sixth. Friendly feel that makes boarding feel 'more like home than home', said one pupil.

While thoughtful range of activities and outings filling the Saturday afternoon gaps for full boarders when others head home, top of pops is procession of supermarket delivery vans 'to sixth form houses,' stresses school (Ben & Jerry's soothing the exam nerves no official school meal can reach, apparently). Highlight, pizza Tuesdays, when 'it's BOGOF night,' explained senior pupil.

Background and atmosphere: Ticks all the right boxes. Promotional literature, some daintily served in tiny beribboned boxes, is so appetising that you're hard pressed to know whether to read it or serve it with after dinner coffee. Posh and Catholic? 'Yes,' says OG, without even a millisecond's pause for thought. But that was then. Much more inclusive now, says school, practical results including new-look, entirely washable uniform (smart blazer and tartan skirt all hers, deputy head responsible for sports kit featuring natty pink stripe on trackies.)

School is set ('nestled', says school) – downy image somewhat countered by reality of weighty-looking main building in best Victorian red-brick – in 700 acres, home to cattle, ponies, occasional Muntjac deer and assorted topiary, and extending to local station, drive alone a mile and a half and with enough land to spare for every pupil to have own smallholding (none of this 'you in your small corner and I in mine' nonsense here).

Moved here in 1940s, 100 or so years after foundation of Convent of the Sacred Heart in South West London, stopped being nun-run in 1980s when first lay head appointed, though still part of the Sacred Heart School worldwide movement. Buildings vary in appeal, original stable block augmented with inoffensive modern additions including agreeable chapel with striking stained glass windows (original is now the art room).

Appearances frequently deceptive. Archetypal 1970s block of apparently little promise big on enchantment within, from extensively revamped classrooms – most neutrally nice, pockmarked notice boards last hurrah of long vanished posters – to highlight of delightful dining room, done up to the nines and even into double figures. Food (once 'awful', said pupil) improved out of all recognition and now as nice as the décor, everything freshly cooked or chopped – none fresher than pedal-powered smoothie maker – sittings abolished as room for all (though sixth formers don't queue up). Thumb print log in ensures anyone missing a meal swiftly picked up – pupils' weight and height regularly checked, too. 'Phenomenal,' said a pupil.

With breakfast served in separate dining room (has own below stairs, slightly weatherbeaten entrance below imposing main reception) and regular deliveries of cereal and bread to boarding houses, supplies are plentiful and good, we're assured, even if common room cupboards seemed rather bare by mid-afternoon.

Spotless everywhere but not clinical, occasional sprawl of bags, one hanging off handle of table football game in year 9 common room, circular seating in one of boarding houses another favoured dumping spot.

Common rooms vary, some with stronger institutional whiff than others, lower sixth version particularly nice, with big windows and convivial seating with sofas positively crying out for company.

Pastoral care, well-being and discipline: Spontaneous hug and outpouring of exam worries by sixth former to teacher during tour of school said everything you need to know about quality of relationships between staff and pupils. That said, pays to mind not just your Ps – preparation, punctuality, presentation, politeness, personal responsibility (the five classroom-based expectations) – but your Rs as well. Respect for others, ourselves and the environment plus 'responsibility for our actions' all feature in the behaviour code, on top of faith, hope and social justice (we paraphrase).

Transgressions lead to (and almost always end with) detentions, escalated to withdrawal of privileges, assistance with domestic tasks and – rarely – suspension, removal or expulsion.

Peer-selected prefects, known as ribbons (after sashes they wear) help maintain status quo. With low key burgeoning jollity in revision session instantly quelled by look from supervising teacher, probably not too much of an uphill struggle.

Pupils and parents: Good spread of bus routes packs 'em in from Croydon hinterlands to Sevenoaks, while delicate balancing act with international pupils (make up around a third of boarders) from countries including Hong Kong, China, West Africa, Spain and Mexico (around a quarter of total) ensures no monocultures dominate. Blend creates 'lovely' atmosphere, thought former pupil, a current parent praising (rare) lack of fuss over appearance. 'Even sixth formers will have hair pulled back in a knot because there's nobody to impress.'

Somewhat changed from the days when, with parental permission, older pupils had leave to smoke, midnight feasts also tacitly accepted. Still unchanged, however, is the end product – pleasant, principled girls who, in keeping with best of Catholic educational principles, aren't just doing it for themselves but giving back to the world as well. Unwanted tuck goes to local food bank, these days (what would Bessie Bunter say?).

W

OGs often span the generations – one in, all in. 'Grandmother, great aunts, aunts and endless cousins attended. Bond that was formed so long is very strong and special,' said OG. Though heirloom education suffered bit of blip in recent years, school now doing far more to woo alumni, courtesy of assorted publications – kudos to 'The Wold' for pun-free environment: 'Wold news' or 'Wold-wide community' all successfully avoided – and events. Judging by numbers of pupils who mention family links, seems to be working.

Entrance: Most enter at year 7 (60 places – school's own exam, looking for Sats level 5, with the occasional 4), further 20 join in year 9 and sixth form, occasionally also in years 8 and 10. Reaches out to those in need. One pupil, disoriented after previous school closed and initially reluctant and last minute newcomer in year 10, now wouldn't be anywhere else.

Popular sleepover event for year 5s also helps school sweep for those with behaviour or social communication issues (may be better served elsewhere) though, if able to cope with the pace, 'we won't rule out the rather unusual'.

Approximately two candidates to each place. We like their requirement for well-rounded pupils with 'a genuine interest in education in the broadest sense of the word' (no laser focus on exam results alone, thanks very much).

Six formers will need minimum four Bs, two C grades at GCSE (though in practice will need to set sights rather higher, with As in desired A level choices). Current school reports also count.

Exit: Not everyone will make it to sixth form, hazard signs appearing early, year 10 exams now held in March so stragglers can be helped and alternatives researched in case results don't come good in year 11.

Post-GCSE brain drain to Charterhouse, once the big temptation ('was only the ones whose parents refused to let them go who stayed,' says OG), now halted. Many of top performers now staying on, though will 'inevitably' lose a few to rival attractions of the IB (Sevenoaks) and boys (almost everywhere).

Leads to broad spread of degrees at (mainly) quality destinations – as likely to head for anthropology at Manchester as economics at Durham. Two medics and vet in 2016, with five to Oxbridge and Hong Kong and US unis (Ivy League and others) also exerting growing appeal. Bulked up careers department stresses gamut of future options, policemen and soldiers attending annual careers fair as a satisfying counter influence to lure of cookery school and fashion journalism.

Typical year group can produce teachers – 'two of naughtiest friends ended up in schools,' said one OG – designers and a 'something in the city' or so. 'An all-rounder type of place,' reckoned former pupil.

Money matters: Not prodigiously endowed, reliant on bank loans and donations (we liked website urging former pupils, euphemistically, to connect or reconnect with the development office). New award to support OG's daughter at the school and £500 post-school scholarships, though less than eager beavers unlikely to be successful, what with requirement to 'consider their contribution to Woldingham during their time at the school' before applying.

Remarks: Delightful school with pupils to match, benefiting from first class leadership and a realistic day school option for anyone within striking distance of Clapham Junction. While not a place for academic no-hopers, ideal for above average (and often well beyond) who prefer teaching adorned with dollops of TLC.

Woodcote House School

Snows Ride, Windlesham, Surrey GU20 6PF

Pupils: 105; 35 full, 36 flexi boarders • Ages: 7-13 • C of E

Fees: Day £16,800; Boarding £22,500 pa

Tel: 01276 472115
Email: info@woodcotehouseschool.co.uk
Website: www.woodcotehouseschool.co.uk

Headmaster: Since September 2016, David Paterson, brother of proprietor and ex-head Nick, and previously deputy head. Born and educated at Woodcote he returned in 1992 with his young family after a career in the City. Joined as head of mathematics and became deputy head to his brother Nick Paterson in 2000. Woodcote is a real family affair with Nick Paterson still teaching English and Spanish, and Nick's son Oliver Paterson teaching maths and Spanish.

Entrance: Places offered following internal assessment test in VR and NVR and interview with the headmaster. No linked schools or significant feeders. ('Wish there was a pre-prep,' said one mother). All quite laid back. Non-selective, but will want to meet you and your son to ensure school and boy will suit each other. Some boys will have been on a list since birth, others rock up mid-term somewhere along the line. Most families are from London and home counties. In essence, the school is looking for boys who will put something into the school. Will take the odd hard luck story, a boy who has been bullied elsewhere or got lost in a larger set up. Head has a 'conversation' with prospective pupils and their parents, and will suggest a chat with the SENCo if it seems appropriate – nothing more formal than that. 'We are not going to say, in effect, "you are not clever enough for our school", but you have to be robust enough to cope. We want boys who don't mind getting their knees dirty. I wouldn't say we don't want sissies or prissies, but we want boys who want to be boys.'

There is a scholarship morning each March prior to September entry for boys joining the school as day pupils or boarders between years 3 -7. The owning Paterson family put up the equivalent of two sets of boarding fees (introduced to mark school's 150th anniversary) and divide as they deem fit – five boys could get 20 per cent of the available cash, or two boys get the lot, or sometimes nobody gets anything – school does not give them away for the sake of it. Must spot a spark or talent, academic, musical or sporting.

Exit: At 13 to all the top-notch public schools, from Ampleforth to Winchester, with clutches of academic, music and all round scholarships won. Lots to Sherborne of late, plus of course Eton, Harrow, Wellington. Parents given lots of guidance on future schools – evidently a strength of this place. WH parents are not always chasing Eton and down the list schools. It's all about what is best for the child, and plenty of other factors are considered. 'So the list of schools WH boys go on to does not always reflect the actual academic achievement,' said one parent. And any leaver will not have heard the last of Woodcote. Legend has it that popular long-serving master Colin Holman – a modern day Mr Chips – has been known to drop a note to many of the boy's new senior school housemasters when he remembers a nugget of useful information about them, to the effect of 'If he's like this, try this'.

Remarks: Superb example of that dying breed – the thriving family-owned school. Idiosyncratic – you will either 'get' this school or you won't. Sceptics ask where the owls are kept, but its parents and boys are so glowing in their praise it's unreal. Feels like a proper country prep, although it's just 40 minutes from London. Combines top notch teaching with tons of outside activities so that the boys are both mentally and physically challenged every day. But also makes time for them to do their own thing, so they are happy and flourish. Nice balance of nurture and push.

Unapologetically focused on doing its own thing – even the unusual brown and yellow school uniform seems a manifestation of a school confident in its own skin. Several parents mentioned how their sons had blossomed at this school, developing their personalities and interests. 'We aim to turn out a young man with good manners who is well-rounded, honest, trustworthy and friendly.'

You will see at a glance that this school isn't splashing your cash on fancy facilities, though new theatre recently completed – the place is delightfully worn at the edges. It really does look as if 100 boys have the run of the place. There's a relaxed feel, plenty of rough and tumble, all part of its charm. Not precious, but quite a cocooned existence. Known to sort out an odd bod or two.

Set in its own 30 acres, including some attractive woods, the main building is Regency and hits you with a real sense of tradition and history – ask about 18th century highwayman, Captain Snow, when you visit. But school has been in its present incarnation since 1931 when it was bought by the Paterson family. Old boys would definitely recognise the place – and that's the idea. 'The Paterson family is very strong and not swayed by fashion. They know what they want to provide and are very good at doing it,' explained one parent. Healthy sprinkling of old boys have their sons here.

Pictures of former pupils line the walls, and many of them were clearly recalled by Paterson matriarch Angela (Nick's mother) when we bumped into her during our visit. And the main thoroughfare, Red Lane, is a literally well-trodden path of black and red tiling, pitted and undulated from the patter of boys' feet over the years. Then the dining hall, where whole school, pupils, staff, visitors, all eat together, is decorated by the honours board and pictures of school founders. As they sit chatting together boys are clearly in a stable, traditional environment and confident about talking to adults.

Lessons are relaxed, but industrious. None of the staff 'just teach', they all wear a number of other hats so the boys see their teachers all the time, as much outside the classroom as inside it. Hence no forced formality about the classroom setting, but all is most respectful – staff exude an air of relaxed authority. Still boys scramble to their feet when visitors enter the classroom and to walk through the grounds with a staff member is to be met with a cacophony of 'Morning sir, morning sir'. Very small class sizes, average 10, never more than 14 and just four in the scholarship class we visited – having fun with the Kubla Khan. Fairly holistic approach to teaching as staff tie in topics across subject areas, so that talk of battlefields in history will link to their locations in geography. Staff more like synchronised swimmers, rather than everyone ploughing up and down their own subject lane. Parents full of praise for an enthusiastic staff always pushing for excellence.

Long day (8.20am to 6.10pm) for day boys, furthest of whom travel around 20 miles to school. First thing every morning is prep – sensible move as boys are nice and fresh and aren't able to get help from parents. Not a whiff of an interactive whiteboard around the place and school is currently rather conflicted about the role of ICT – never a huge deal here, where teachers largely prefer projectors and coloured pens. 'Many schools will find their fancy ICT suites defunct as everyone clutches hand-held devices like iPads now.' (Not that school has those either.)

'ICT is certainly a subject in transition and we need to decide what stance we will take'.

Nothing state-of-the-art about other facilities either, though the boys we met described them as 'good' – 'we've got everything', said one. It's a bit scruffy and ramshackle in places, but not because nobody cares, rather it's just rather battered in places as a result of hundreds of boys kicking around the place – it's clearly a home from home for them.

Woodcote is able to accommodate some special needs and has a dedicated SENCo to handle boys on the autistic spectrum, dyslexia and EAL. About 20 boys (but a fifth of the school, remember) have some type of learning support, for which their parents pay extra. Languages taught are French and Spanish – a significant Spanish entourage among the pupils and Nick Paterson is a fluent Spanish speaker. A few boys from Thailand and Russia and some 15 per cent of Forces families, who particularly appreciate that the place is properly focused on boarding (38 full and 22 flexi boarders), so that weekends are busy and boys are far more than simply 'minded'. School keen to get the UK/overseas balance right. Very good relationships between the boys themselves and then between themselves and their teachers. The overseas boys tend to spend exeats with their more local friends, leading to an informal exchange programme.

Years 3 and 4 are housed in a separate Juniors building to facilitate a slow integration into main school life. Lots of praise for junior head Mrs Woodall; 'She is so very kind to my sons,' said one mother. Similarly, year 8s are given a taste of teenage life when they spend a term during their final year living in Dominies House – within the grounds, but away from the main school and set up to give year 8s some preparation for their life to come at public school – not least a taste of going to and from school each day.

Parents struggle to put their finger on a stand-out subject – 'It's all fantastic', said one mother. 'Whatever the talent, they will bring it out' – but music and art mentioned several times. A Woodcote boy beat 13,000 entries to come second in The Sunday Telegraph/Saatchi Gallery prize. And if your son plays an instrument, however badly, he will perform – this place is big on performance opportunities. 'My heart was in my mouth as I saw my son approach the piano, knowing that he'd only been learning for a couple of weeks,' recalled one parent. Not much timetabled drama, but usually a production per term. Staff write the plays – they seem to enjoy it, though it's probably also a necessity to find parts for so many small boys.

The philosophy here is that it is good to be a big fish in this small pool. One mother with several boys at the school felt strongly that each of her sons had found an inner confidence at Woodcote. 'I don't mean they are cocky, in fact they are more polite now, but simply that they've all formed quite distinct personalities and developed a love of study that definitely wasn't there before'.

While things are rather cosy inside, outside the school the boys are spoiled for space, with 35 acres of grounds to run about in, and are encouraged to try out a huge range of outdoor activities. Boys are even kicking about on Rip Stiks during break. From the usual cricket, football and rugby, to the more unusual CCF, bushcraft and even clay pigeon shooting (for older boys) there is masses on offer. School takes its sport seriously and reckons to punch above its weight when taking on other (almost always larger) schools – has only lost 20 per cent of its fixtures over the last five years.

W

Keen on outdoor education, school considering a 'very small' smallholding, and an outdoor pizza oven is also on wish list. Shame more use not made of on-site swimming pool – but boys seem too busy with other things to be very bothered about this.

And fears that a non-sporty boy might flounder in this place are apparently unfounded as more indoor types can make the teas and help the parents park their cars on match days. 'In fact my incredibly non-sporty son even got a few games with the B team – all the rubbish players do,' said one mother. Other activities for the less physically inclined include archery and golf and plenty of indoor pursuits, even a turf club.

School has a refreshing 'let children be children' attitude and is happy for them to cook outdoors sitting around a campfire – not in a cavalier way, but just acknowledging that they will enjoy a few safe risks. Think Just William updated for 21st century. So not surprising to hear that these happy, busy boys sleep like logs. And of course with 75 per cent of pupils boarding, they sleep at school in clean and cheerful accommodation – small dorms with sea blue walls, punchy primary-coloured duvet covers. Largely settled for the night by 8pm (9pm for older ones), older boys three to a room, more as you go down the year groups, but even larger dorms divided into little 'pods' to give a homelier feel. All tidy. A fairly basic common room full of bean bags for when they want to collapse.

Sky Sports available along with controlled access to TV, phones, play stations and associated electrical detritus of modern life, but school would far rather they were outside or generally more gainfully employed – and they usually are. Lovely old-fashioned insistence that, Skype and emails notwithstanding, boys will write a proper letter home once a week. Weekends (starting after Saturday morning school) typically include sports matches against other schools, an outing and a service in the school's own chapel (a charming building – apparently an early flat-pack of the type originally destined to be shipped out to missionaries in the 1800s).

Parents are welcome to attend matches and chapel and lots do. In fact we were surprised to see quite a number of parents at a predominantly boarding school – even though several of them were actually parents of day boys dropping books in or sorting out for their sons to stay on for some or other evening activity. There's a full programme of popular Friday night entertainments including visiting speakers – recently a sports commentator and a seven peaks climber. Many day boys do ask to board in the end, so that there are more day boys in the lower school and only one or two by year 8. 'My son doesn't even always want to come home for exeats, he is so happy at school,' said a parent. School offers a graduated approach to boarding, three nights as well as seven, but this is aimed to be an introduction to boarding rather than a babysitting service, although it would be flexible about the odd night here and there.

Staff all casually dressed when we visited – no airs and graces here. You won't get a fresh paint-type royal tour, but will see the place warts and all – the showers, the worst dorm (the last awaiting refurbishment) and maybe even the popular Warhammer dungeon.

Very accessible and welcoming of parents – none of this waving them off at Waterloo in September and not seeing them till Christmas. Parents swing by if they are in the area and teachers happy to respond to 'Can I have a quick word' during a match afternoon in favour of any formally structured pastoral system. 'Pastoral care is fabulous', said one parent. 'You drop the boys off without a worry'.

Not flash or fancy; old fashioned in the best sense of the world; 'Traditional with a modern twist?' offered one mother. Warm and inclusive, quite a gem. A school with a heart and soul where boys will definitely be boys.

Worth School

Paddockhurst Road, Turners Hill, Crawley, West Sussex RH10 4SD

Pupils: 575: two-thirds boys; 229 boys, 73 girls full boarders; few flexi. • Ages: 11-18 (boarding from 11 for boys and 13 for girls) • Sixth form: 232 • RC

Fees: Day £14,970 – £22,050; Boarding £18,990 – £31,140 pa

Tel: 01342 710200
Email: information@worth.org.uk
Website: www.worthschool.org.uk

Head Master: Since 2015, Mr Stuart McPherson, previously a housemaster at Eton College and teacher of English. He took his bachelors degree at the University of Western Australia before completing an MA in literature and religion at Newcastle. He has also taught at Sydney Grammar School. He is married to Johneen, who is the director of studies at St Mary's Ascot, and they have four children.

Academic matters: All about 'academic worth' says the relevant section on school's website and you really can't blame them for indulging in the occasional pun. School has fair share of bright buttons. However, not all are 'are desperate high flyers,' thinks parent. More are having to gain altitude though, what with school upping the ante with six GCSE B grades or better required to make the cut for sixth form. Essential 'to stand realistic prospect of university success,' reckons school. 'Definitely becoming more academic,' agreed one mother, with slight regret.

Offers fully formed dual systems post-16, taught in class sizes averaging around nine (18 in the school as a whole). IB, currently taken by around a third of sixth form, pulls in some locals each year, drawn by rarity value and has strong European appeal (though formerly strong contingent from Germany has waned following changes to education system there). IB results averaged 35 points in 2016, ahead of world average. Popularity may increase further now IB subject choices are a closer match with A level options (psychology is the latest to be added). In 2016, 36 per cent A*/A at A level and 65 per cent A*-B. A levels continue to be exam of choice for the majority and a non-negotiable for some international students with specialisation already in their sights (maths and science for Chinese pupils, for example).

Sciences have been experiencing distinct off season, biology in particular, psychology broadly similar, with physics and chemistry probably not the best version of themselves, either. It's accounted for by status as third choice subject for many pupils, says the school, which stresses this is no longer the case and is also at pains to point out decent sprinkling of top grades. Also speaks of a 'renaissance' with sciences the choice of a third of current year 12 cohort. However, plenty of strong subjects including history, art and religious studies, languages in general starting to pack in the boys 'like you wouldn't believe,' comments staff member.

School doesn't shirk from shock of the new, or newish, with economics flourishing (felt to be good route to a crisis-defying well paid job) and government and politics A level on the way in. Unusually no DT, though with design element absorbed into art and successfully so, helping to spawn at least one budding architect in the process, doesn't need to be, thinks head. Ditto engineering which 'we incorporate into science and mathematics.' Lines on the sand are media and film studies. No snob factor involved. 'Just wouldn't be popular.'

GCSE results also very respectable with over 50 per cent A*/A in 2016. Pedagogues span the age range, some so unnervingly youthful you want whatever they have sprinkled on their bedtime cocoa, others long haul troupers, including one who has featured 'in every school photograph for the last 40 years, even the faded ones,' said pupil.

Have fair share of idiosyncrasies, presentation-focused English teacher responsible for high density notice-board achieving concours standard symmetry (writing quite literally on the wall), language specialist much admired for proselytising Spanish by highlighting party culture rather than demographics (yawn) as well as ways with vocab, word for 'potion' indelibly printed on IB student's memory following mime involving coffee granules and juice.

Overall, broadish palette of ability shades well catered for from the Oxbridge gang (about three or so a year) to the minority who don't have higher education in their sights, in line with one of the plentifully quoted St Benedict's dictums that the strong should have 'something to strive for,' the weak 'not be overburdened.'

Something school is definitely up for when it comes to support. International contingent are well served by EAL department which concentrates on weighting lessons towards nuance decoding – vital in science and maths exams where word games are all part of the fun (or perhaps not, judging by levels of concentration in EAL science class, ears almost audibly straining to grasp finer points of examiners' habits). Learning support department doesn't venture much beyond 'dyses' in mild form, Asperger's ditto, as 'we don't have learning assistants in the classroom,' (screening for all in year 9). Individual or small group support by withdrawal (often replacing language). What it does do, it does well, though: parents speak of children 'transformed' by support.

Day to day helping hands plentifully outstretched, felt pupils, sixth form learning prefects who run sessions in range of subjects, including Latin are popular with younger gang as can have edge over teachers who 'don't have the experience of teaching themselves,' thought one. More formally, anyone falling seriously behind will be supported through GCSEs with involvement of house tutors, learning support and addition of extra lessons in the hope, rarely unfulfilled, that galvanising effect will be sufficient to propel them into the sixth form. On rare occasions it doesn't, school will suggest search for suitable plan B school post-16.

Usually does the trick, think parents. 'Takes all comers, gets the best out of most children and they achieve their potential,' reckons one.

Games, options, the arts: Idleness, said St Benedict, is hostile to the soul, a message taken to heart here, particularly when it comes to sport. Website oozes Catholic take on muscular Christianity (a six pack, at least) featuring video that cuts away to reveal rugby team pitting strength against giant grass roller (and winning, naturally: it'll be a jumbo from nearby Gatwick Airport next). Deceptive, however, as you don't have to be terrifically sporty to enjoy it here, say pupils. Though football is finally acquiring the kudos supporters feel it deserves, rugby (which also musters six senior teams) continues to loom large on the sporting calendar.

School, thought one parent, is 'astute' at picking its opponents, middle rather than top rung, success consistent – with several unbeaten teams – if not always earth shattering, a few 'mixed' and 'disappointings' sprinkled through the end of school reviews (particularly good at quarter finals...). However, 'we're still really bad,' agreed group of pupils, cheerfully. On the plus side, there's no in or out crowd, change from days when rugby heroes were school idols (and life wasn't altogether plain sailing for less hearty). 'Completely gone, now,' says school. Pupils and parents agree. 'Friends can share emotional similarities even if interests are completely different,' thought articulate sixth former. Low stress environment allows sport and arts lovers to have their fill, others preferring not to do either with tolerance for all.

Attitudes haven't softened at the expense of choice. Plenty for die hard fanatics to get up to in the way of must-have team sports that tick all the participation boxes. While it's non-negotiable sport for all two afternoons each week and for Saturday fixtures 'not always popular with day pupils and weekly boarders,' most esprit de corps stuff is largely optional beyond year 9, 'though they like us to be in teams,' thought girl. Aerobics, fencing, golf and riding mop up those seeking a personal challenge, the perhaps slightly euphemistically entitled multi-sports catering for those who may not be. 'There's a lot of sport on offer but if you don't want to do it I don't think you have to,' thought parent.

Some sporty girls feel slightly short-changed as they're in a minority and therefore not stretched enough, thought a mum. Something school 'could do little about ... but will be rectified in the natural course of events as more girls come up through the school,' and benefit from 'excellent teaching.'

Gourmet facilities include assorted courts (smart Astroturf firmly padlocked, presumably against ovine marauders) as well as eight hole golf course. Nearby sports centre offers athletics tracks and 50m pool (would be even better if school had its own, thought a parent). Access to pitches the other side of busy 'B' road is via new bridge, following tragic death of a pupil there in 2011.

Two sports halls, smaller very slightly dingy; larger, approached through front door so heavy that even spectators could end up with a decent six pack, kitted out with decent fitness suite. Somewhat off-message vending machine in foyer, stacked to the gunnels with confectionary and drinks and thoughtfully putting back the empty calories that exercise has taken out, is being restocked with healthier options. (A second, in sixth form house, will retain sugar as principal ingredient).

If sports don't trigger necessary inspiration, terrific array elsewhere (billed as – wait for it – 'Worth extra' – groan) should do the trick. Drama includes three plays for different age groups in the summer term with lots of Shakespeare (added treat is array of beautiful costumes, many borrowed from the National Theatre). Music also strong, helped by super recording studio and Mac-rich room to hone technical and composition skills as well as sensibly soundproofed rock room for band rehearsals. Forty per cent of pupils have individual instrumental or singing lessons, orchestra (quite audibly not an earsore) particularly praiseworthy for size and boy participation. Abbey Choir, which sings weekly mass (website features a nice bit of plainsong) ditto.

Midweek afternoon given over to colossal range of activities which range from chess, very successful with substantial input from keen father, to community service: 'pupils are taken to charity shops....' (to serve, not for sale) as well as 'invasion games' (you have been warned).

Some, such as choir and jazz club, are vetted with auditions; most are entrée libre, many designed for IB compatibility. D of E-worthy, too, driving lessons apparently counting as a credit-earning skill – who knew? – and school, as a licensed centre, able to run and approve awards, popular trips (South America a favourite haunt) adding an edge of glamour.

Sparky individual achievements, too: sixth form are 'influential role models', says prospectus. Not half, with posts including public relations prefects (surely a first) whose duties include scouting for pupils able to take visitors on guided tours. Further down the school, one year 9 pupil has self-published own fiction, originally prep that outgrew the exercise book/took on a life of its own.

Creativity a-plenty elsewhere, too, with two wonderfully big art rooms, generosity of seniors' space influencing scale of artwork – few miniatures here. 'Means you aren't compressed,' says pupil. By way of demonstration, there's vast, decorated tree trunk, donated to the school and apparently taking root in art room. Pupil creations, some selected for display at the Saatchi Gallery, include orchid-like shapes strung along wires, while floor level delights include a sculpture with the precarious delicacy of a scaled up Jenga game and meticulous, technically brilliant paper and wood confections with concertina folds at crazy angles, like Escher on hallucinogens. Like pupils' poetry, seem to plumb otherwise hidden emotional depths.

Boarding: Boarders (vast majority full, 230 boys to just over 70 girls) have well designed bedrooms, tidy but not unspeakably so – boys' gloriously free of après-trainer whiff – fours and fives to a room, dropping to two in year 13; star of the show the solo accommodation for year 13 boys in smart, self-contained Gervase House, the only one to blend day and boarding pupils, and amply conveying undergraduate feel (more upmarket than many a uni) complete with tiny but perfect en-suites.

St Mary's, sole girls' boarding house, is a delight with well thought out bedrooms, duvets adding flashes of pink to light wood sea, and a common room you actually want to spend time in, best feature 'the pit' – lowered hearth area used for house mass and picnic style meals but, alas, never warmed by roaring fire, vetoed by health and safety.

Parents hope houseparent, just leaving, will have successor equally rich in humour and discretion, from curtains ('you'd be surprised how many don't close them') to conversations (office, just off quiet room 'isn't very quiet' so hears 'everything – and amazing what you pick up.')

Thoughtful touches include washing machines for 'emergencies, delicates and underwear,' says school. Girls only, however, as no boys so far have expressed urge to do own washing.

Background and atmosphere: De haut en bas, literally so, with two main groups of buildings taking up 25 of the site's 500 acres and separated by hill steep enough for twice daily ascents to form basis of daily fitness routine.

At the foot, approached by grand entrance (ornate electric gates, gryphon-topped portico, though you have to nip round the corner for commanding views over Downs) there's the stately pile originally built for Cowdray family and acquired by Benedictines, school's founding order, in the 1930s to mop up pupil overspill from Downside, becoming a separate school in the 1960s.

Teaching, meanwhile, goes on at the summit, school's very own mini Parnassus, with standalone main teaching block (a solid 1980s construction shortly to be extended) housing maths, humanities and languages together with serious looking learning resources centre (solid shelves and workaday displays suggest books as study essentials first, imagination firers second).

It's next to tranche of buildings, home to performing arts, science and the Pitstop, a small café-style eaterie (main low-ceilinged refectory – slightly apologised for; 'it is what it is,' says member of staff; much improved by paint job, mint green replacing previous appetite suppressing mustard yellow – is down the hill). They're clustered in loose extended courtyard arrangement, centrepiece a clock tower so wantonly Disneyesque you half expect it to sprout features and break into song.

Dotted through the site are the school houses, all nine of them, which come at you from every direction. Seen as hugely important centres of r&r for day as well as boarding pupils, they enable everyone to let off steam, enhancing sense of camaraderie as 'you spend a lot of time with your houses even if you're not boarding,' says pupil.

Communal rooms (too many to count – we did try) are swankiest for oldest, who also have study rooms, mainly shared if day, some solo if boarding, while younger day pupils stash stuff in lockers, tops cunningly (and frustratingly) sloped to prevent leaning towers of casually dumped textbooks.

While they take the same newspapers (in assorted shades of blue: Grauniad fans may pine) houses vary enormously in style, ranging from Rutherford House's touch of the Brideshead s (parquet and imposing marble fireplaces no whit disturbed by table football machine and mini bank of computers) to St Bedes's, the newest house, so far away from the main drag that only rooftop is visible on location map, which comes complete with soft furnishings co-ordinated in browns and greens (nicer than it sounds) and eco focus, much lauded though little understood. 'Didn't realise we even collected rainwater,' said pupil.

Pastoral care, well-being and discipline: Insulating tranquillity radiates both from surroundings and what one mother described as 'gentle, smiley' monks, though not a place to come for those with real issues with Catholicism or deep-rooted opposition to introspection.

Spiritual side is 'the heart of the school,' says one of many delightful pupils, impact felt most strongly in tolerance for others with soul-searching high up the agenda and a feature of student magazine which, like a thought for the day compilation, is jam-packed with worthy thoughts about happiness and love and, pick of the bunch, what nuns do all day (pray, apparently).

School temperament is accordingly mild. Even traditional post-exams photograph eschews standard shrieking, certicate-grasping, mid-air riot in favour of a nice, quiet group of girls and boys standing in semi-formal pose, looking slightly embarrassed at being singled out for glory.

Reflects notion of competition as being 'based on the idea of sharing excellence'. Though a possible handicap if opponents' idea of competition is to slaughter the opposition (school team recently lost debating competition because it was 'too politically correct,' says magazine report) seems to damp down house on house aggression despite ferocious-looking face paint applied, warrior fashion, before girls' matches. House music competition is the only event capable of triggering anything approaching blood lust 'because we organise it and it involves everyone,' felt pupil.

Pupils and staff spoke highly of events that blend spiritual with social rather than adversorial dimension in keeping with admirable Benedictine tradition of hospitality. 'Food is a very good reason to mix,' says housemistress. Civilised, too, with wine allowed for sixth formers on Feast of St Benedict 'but only with food,' and over 18s allowed to nip down to the local pub with permission (though hadn't been a single request when this reviewer arrived at the start of the summer term – unusual, thought member of staff). Many house parties, too, (not in the format most parents know and dread, we're assured) as well as 'young ladies' lunches' (young gents' versions, too) where pupils from same house or year group foregather in delightful panelled room to swap news and views in civilised surroundings.

Results in easy going, clique-free contact between year groups, think pupils. 'So refreshing compared with my previous school where the year 11s wouldn't talk to the year 10s. Here, everyone does,' says one recent arrival, who also praised unofficial problem sharing – girls' friendship issues the unsurprisingly regular hot topic.

Tutor groups, house linked except in sixth form, meet regularly; chaplains, one per house, are also useful listening ears. Pupils also felt that lectio devina – Benedictine tradition of reading sacred texts aloud and discussing themes raised – can be effective route in to problem sharing, akin to grown up circle time. 'You can raise worries – it's a personal thing,' felt one.

School recently reported that behaviour had hit an all-time high, and pupils we talked to felt there was little in the way of badness beyond missed homework deadlines, with normal sanctions consisting of warnings and a series of ever-lengthening detentions or, in the case of 'rude or inappropriate' use of phones (a worry as 'can access everything' unlike computers where school Wifi blocks undesirable sites, including Facebook) minimum 24-hour confiscation.

Not much obvious kicking over the traces in pupils we saw, who seemed born to walk rather than run (though sloping terrain is admittedly a fabulous natural deterrent), although some current models of decorum were, we were assured by pupils, former wild cards who have been 'subdued' as they come up through the school, ending up 'unrecognisably well-behaved.' Schools stays on top of things, confirmed parent. 'I don't get the impression that children drift off the radar. They're not allowed to misbehave or become lost sheep.'

Pupils and parents: Fair few Worthians wanting to spread educational joy to second generation, substantial overseas contingent, some from hyper-Catholic parts of the world. One Brit parent, while accepting school's need to get bums on seats, felt that 'you need to make sure that that percentage doesn't get out of hand.' Riches represented amongst parents, rags less so, though neither end of the spectrum dominates. 'You'll see the odd Rolls Royce as well as the odd beaten-up car,' thought one mother.

Lots of parent socialising, from informal curry nights to large scale events including masked ball fab summer fair complete with fairground rides, jazz band and a profusion of strawberries. 'A very jolly scene,' thought one.

If all goes according to plan, pupils will emerge from the Worth experience 'wise [and] intellectually astute,' (according to prospectus, size defiantly non-standard and so glossy you could skate on it). They are, as well (so much so that it was a relief to hear off-duty younger girls described as 'very screamy' by sixth former). One parent, with ultra-serious child, felt distinctly frivolous in comparison.

Pupils take great pride in individuality and proclaim absence of a particular school type, backed by staff who thinks school should 'allow people to grow into themselves – a pupil's inner talent could mean that you haven't mastered any one thing but are good at lots. We're 600 weird and wonderful individuals and we've got to learn to get on with each other.'

We admired fighting talk, though couldn't help but notice girls' near identical hairdos, most tumbling manes of mermaid-length tresses, varying in colour, finish as high gloss as prospectus.

Star former pupils include actor Robert Bathurst and publisher Sir David Bell, though sports dominated, from Tim Hutchings (athletics) to Tom Symonds (racing) and rugby (Nick Walshe). All admirable stuff. However, as old girls start to make their mark on the world aided by slickly run alumni society (which includes a 'Worthians in Property' group), we'd hope for more variety and quirkiness in years to come.

Entrance: Oversubscribed, says school, which advises registration two years in advance. Around 120 places a year, 40 in year 7, 60 in year 9 and 20 in year 12, occasionally in other years. Feeder schools many and various, majority independent, fair few Catholic (though not all) and also include local state primaries and secondaries, though with school bus network puts Tunbridge Wells, Haywards Heath and Horsham within reach.

Just shy of 20 per cent from overseas (Gatwick a 10 minute taxi ride away), some non-native English speakers, support offered though must be sufficiently fluency to cope with normal lessons.

Currently pushing convincing case for 11 plus entry by citing early leadership opportunities on offer to the brightest and best in years 7 and 8 when academic effort plus helpfulness and embodiment of Benedictine ethos can land a handful a place on school council or as prefects. Fine for boys, who can board from year 7 (with three nights a week flexi option), though it's day places only until year 9 for girls (might account for very low representation in current year 7 – just six out of 25-strong year group).

Exit: Up to a fifth leave after GCSE. Around three or so to Oxbridge most years (three, indeed, in 2016), wide range elsewhere recently. Lots to Russell Group and, in 2016, one to the Royal Ballet School, another to the University of the Arts and several off overseas. Economics, maths, business and management all popular, interesting combinations (history and theology, maths and philosophy) also a big feature.

Sixth formers praised careers advice, helpful email updates arriving at least twice a week, approach informative but low pressure. Many (more than average, it seemed) were postponing university applications with official blessing, gap years viewed as logical make your mind up time.

Money matters: Fees about on a par with nearest competitors. Good scholarships (music, academic and all-rounder) offering up to 40 per cent of fees (music also includes free instrumental tuition). Means-tested bursaries are also available though total fees remission generally capped at 50 per cent. Local, bright Catholic children can also apply for St Benedict's Scholarships – fully funded day places, one in year 7, two in year 12.

Remarks: 'At some schools, it's all about how clever or hearty and sporty you are – not here,' thought one parent. Another, with experience of several other leading Catholic schools, had no doubts. 'It's the pick of the bunch.' Encourages reflection, not out to dazzle, producing thoughtful pupils, distinctly themselves and quite definitely Worth it.

Wychwood School

74 Banbury Road, Oxford, Oxfordshire OX2 6JR

Pupils: 112; 41 full/weekly boarders • Ages: 11–18 • Sixth form: 25

Fees: Day £14,700; Boarding £22,200 – £23,400 pa

Tel: 01865 557976
Email: admissions@wychwoodschool.org
Website: www.wychwoodschool.org

Headmistress: Since 2012, Mrs Andrea Johnson BSc (50s). Comes from a family of teachers and doctors and intended 'never to do either'. She read chemistry at Durham, did a PGCE 'because it might be useful' and unexpectedly fell in love with teaching. Formerly assistant head at Tudor Hall where she worked for 20 years, she is the first head of Wychwood not to be an old girl. Teaches chemistry to year 7 and 11. Married to a retired scientist, two adult children, at least one intends to continue the family tradition and is training to be a teacher.

Mrs Johnson is energetic, genuine and very friendly – her presence is reassuring, rather like a wise owl, and one feels she could cope with anything (parents tell us that she does). Just as well really, since that's what you need to be able to do when you run a small school. And as far as Mrs J is concerned, when it comes to education, small really is beautiful. She sees Wychwood as a place that can be responsive to the needs of the individual, to educate girls who 'want to think and achieve but would sink in the hurly burly of a bigger school.' The school gets its fair share of 'burn out' refugees from some of Oxfordshire's super-heated girls' independents, but is equally a positive choice for many families from the word go. 'We enable any child who comes here to get the best possible exam results.'

Parents we spoke to were extremely supportive of Mrs J and tell us that they welcome her sensitive moves towards modernisation and determination to raise the school's profile.

Academic matters: With only 110 pupils in total, results would benefit from micro, rather than macro analysis, but they're respectable: in 2016, 48 per cent A*/A at GCSE – 69 per cent of pupils getting A*-B in all subjects – and 64 per cent A*-B, 40 per cent A*/A at A level. Small class sizes mean teaching staff can give every girl individual attention and customise their approach. We watched year 8s getting to grips with evaluating historical sources and you could almost touch the intense concentration in the room. In fact quiet and studious pretty much sums up the atmosphere of Wychwood. A display of beautifully produced project work showed Jane Eyre's end of term report, as well as prospectuses and other material from Lowood (somewhere that definitely wouldn't make it into the Good Schools Guide).

In a smart and well-equipped lab we came across the head teaching year 7 chemistry and yet more rapt attention and eager answers. The biology lab was festooned with a long, pink papier maché tube, 'That's a life-size model of the large intestine,' we were told. Length, not girth, we hope.

One thing we kept hearing about Wychwood was that 'teachers have time for you' and that 'they encourage us to follow our own interests'. The school will ('within reason') run a course for just one student; for instance, GCSE astronomy was taught for the benefit of a single star-gazing girl. In the sixth form, some A level classes might just be two or three strong – more like the tutorial teaching that goes on at the university down the road. Individual tuition in particular subjects can also be arranged and in some cases girls may repeat a year.

Girls take maximum of nine-and-a-half GCSEs and different strengths and interests are accommodated: double or triple science; both Englishes or just English language; psychology; art, textiles and, unusually, photography. Most do French and Spanish, German offered privately, as are GCSEs in, for example, Chinese, Japanese, Persian, for native speakers. Exchange trips to Spain and France in alternate years. All do short courses in RS and ECDL in ICT. At A level most popular subjects are maths, the sciences, photography and history of art.

Games, options, the arts: Textiles, art and photography each enjoy their own light and modern studios in a converted stable block decorated with impressive examples of students' work. As one pupil commented, 'for our size we have so many resources.' It was in the textile studio that we had a sneak preview of the new uniform 'unshortenable' skirt, designed by the textiles teacher. If it's successful she should patent it and make her fortune, but since it doesn't feature something that padlocks it to below the knee we fear that girls will always find a way. New uniform design has not been received joyfully, but is it ever? In fact, as far as we could see, Wychwood pupils seemed rather modest in their skirt minimising aspirations, compared to other schools we've visited.

Few mutters that Mrs Johnson isn't as supportive of the arts as former heads have been. School says that girls may opt for more than one GCSE out of art, textiles and photography but since they only take nine-and-a-half in total they often only choose one. At A level girls can do all three if they so choose.

There's a school orchestra and choir, a chamber choir and music lessons are offered in any instrument – harp seems to be a favourite. House plays, written, designed and directed by the girls, are performed competitively; LAMDA exams popular. D of E up to gold offered and Model UN.

If your daughter is sports mad and keen to play for the winning side then, with heavy heart, we suggest you look elsewhere. On the plus side, as a parent pointed out, 'you always get picked for the team.' Not that Wychwood is a complete stranger to victory: our guide was still buzzing from a recent and unexpected rounders success. As the head says, 'Girls learn to lose with grace, but when they win ...' On-site facilities include tennis, basketball and badminton courts, and fitness suite (in a rather gloomy basement room). Nearby off-site are an athletics field, Astro, and more tennis courts. Main opponents are Oxford High and St Helen's; years 7 and 8 play against The Dragon. School does all it can to support girls competing at high levels (county and national) in particular sports by adapting individual timetables etc. Rather surprisingly we discovered that there is a Wychwood equestrian team. No sign of horses trotting down the Banbury Road, rather girls with their own steeds compete on behalf of the school. Recent 'uproar' when timetabled sport was reduced to an hour a week during GCSEs. Schools say that this was to accommodate girls doing 12 GCSEs at the time. Timetabled sport will increase once option choices are rationalised. Quite right too.

Until the 1960s swimming took place in the nearby River Cherwell. Girls used to cycle down to a muddy pool called (for reasons lost in history) the Rhea, where non-swimmers were initiated by being dragged through the water on the end of a pole. Punting was also on the curriculum. There are delightfully nostalgic accounts of the Rhea and its rather whiffy mud in the school's centenary history book. Today's Wychwood swimmers use the Kidlington pool, undoubtedly safer but much less to reminisce about in future years.

Boarding: About a third of pupils board, a fairly even split between full and weekly or flexi. Parents book flexi boarding (usually 1-3 nights per week) at the start of term but school can, and does, accommodate pupils at short notice. Day girls can stay after evening activities such as trips to London or the theatre – bunk beds (only for occasional boarders) add to the sleepover excitement. We were told that news of major road works caused a spike in boarding applications – even fairly local parents appreciate the benefits when gridlock threatens Oxford's already notorious traffic.

When we describe the boarding as 'homely' it's a compliment as well as a reality check. Years 7-9 have large first floor rooms – sash windows and high ceilings – with three to four beds in each. School says mixing the age group helps foster sisterly ethos; colourful curtains and duvets, bedside clutter and lots of family photos and posters add to the family feel. There's wardrobe and under bed storage but no desks – homework takes place elsewhere under supervision.

Sixth formers have characterful single study bedrooms, mostly up in the eaves. Rooms have names such as North Pole, Elysium and Valhalla – harking back to earlier and less centrally heated times. What would their former occupants think about today's duvets and power showers?

During the week there's a table plan for supper – another way of making sure everyone knows each other – but things are more relaxed at weekends. Girls can make themselves snacks – they just go down to the kitchen and ask for supplies. Activities include film nights, Oxford-based bowling, ice skating and trips to Port Meadow along with regular forays to Camden and Bicester Village for shopping. Boarders also take part in community activities – most recently litter picking for Oxclean (voluntary but apparently rather popular). There's a big trip once a year to somewhere like Thorpe Park that's funded by old girls – day pupils can go too but they have to pay.

Background and atmosphere: The school was founded by a Miss Lee and Miss Batty in 1897 and has always been on Oxford's busy Banbury Road. Miss Lee, the younger of the two, was a pioneer, obtaining a first-class degree in English at St Hugh's and going on to lecture and become vice-principal. She funded the school from her earnings and continued to lecture in both Oxford and London. The school was named after Oxfordshire's Wychwood forest in 1918, having formerly been known unofficially as the Battery or Battery Lees, and a uniform of forest green was adopted. One of the early teachers, the redoubtable Miss Rendall, went on to found another Oxford school, Rye St Antony.

Today's Wychwood is still domestic in scale, the original brass plaque on the door (featured heavily in promotional literature) modestly announcing its presence in an area where a Latin primer, carefully launched, is bound to hit a venerable educational establishment. There's nothing flash here, no plate glass or modern architecture, but everything is well loved and cared for. Head of boarding is from the hotel industry – what a good idea – and facilities have been upgraded accordingly, although The Randolph it isn't. This was Mrs Johnson's first undertaking on arrival, strongly backed by the 'brilliant' governors, the chair of whom is a former pupil.

Pastoral care, well-being and discipline: Mrs Johnson says, 'a child can't learn if she is unhappy.' Parents say that pastoral care is outstanding: girls who need it are given time and space but this doesn't mean that the school can't be tough when called for. In a small community one person's actions can significantly affect all and Mrs Johnson will ask a girl to leave if she feels that the school can't accommodate her needs. As one parent put it, 'Yes, your daughter is an individual but she is also part of a respectful community.' Some grumbles that pupils arriving at odd times eg half way through a term can make things a little disjointed.

Famously democratic, girls are genuinely involved in decision making – much to the horror of the Daily Mail in the 1960s (plus ça change ...). The founders' original forward-thinking structure of councillors and 'citizens' with voting rights, responsibilities and privileges still operates today (albeit with a few modern tweaks). As Mrs Johnson says, 'We're so small that everybody can be involved.'

Lower ground canteen is as nice as a lower ground canteen can be. Girls mostly complimentary about the food – favourites are the breakfasts and Friday fish and chips. There are, and have been since the school's foundation, buns at break time. Cook deserves honourable mention for skilfully adapting meals so that girls with eg dairy or gluten intolerance can eat the same as everyone else.

Some might discount a school such as Wychwood because of its small size, but consider the benefits: it's responsive, girls notice there's a play or event on down the road (this being Oxford it's more than likely) and arrangements can be made to go double quick. Parents are very involved, professionals including medics from the John Radcliffe come in to talk to pupils – this happens in other schools but it's more likely to be a lecture than a conversation. Parents told us that Wychwood was uncliquey and that foreign students integrated very well. One commented that it was very good preparation for work because you 'had to get along with everyone'.

All schools say that they nurture every child as an individual, but common sense tells us that this is easier to achieve in a school of 120 rather than an academic super tanker of 800 or more.

Pupils and parents: Used to be known as the 'Dons' school' but draws from a wider pool these days. Majority of local parents are Oxford professionals – lawyers, doctors etc. Girls we met were thoughtful, independent-minded – lacking the swagger of nearby sisters perhaps – and fiercely loyal to their school and its ways. Lots of summer-born girls, fair few refugees from schools that were too big and girls going through upheaval eg parents' divorce. And then there are girls who visited on an open day and 'fell in love' with Wychwood.

Former pupils include Margaret Casson, architect, designer and photographer; Joan Aiken, writer; Vicky Jewson, film maker; Rebecca Stockland, opera singer; Matilda Leyser, actress and aerialist; Izzie Lawrence, comedian; Honor Fell, microbiologist.

Entrance: Girls join at age 11 from local primaries/preps and there's another influx from preps at age 13. Prospective year 7s spend a day at the school and are tested in maths and English. External candidates for sixth form need minimum of six GCSEs at grades A*-C and A*/A in A level subjects. Places may be available in other years, subject to interview and assessment.

Exit: Around 30-45 per cent leaves after GCSEs. This isn't a school that unthinkingly crams sixth formers onto the non-stop university express, although most girls do go on to further study. Art and design at Oxford Brookes and elsewhere popular; other courses range from chemical engineering at Surrey to midwifery at Birmingham City to food and nutrition in Hong Kong Girls have also gone on to be Norland nannies, Montessori educators, farriers and business entrepreneurs.

Money matters: Day fees on a par with local equivalents – OK, you're not getting the sports facilities but you are getting something pretty close to a customised education. Boarding comparatively good value. Academic, music and creative arts scholarships of approximately £1,200 pa available, as are means-tested bursaries.

Remarks: Charming pint-sized power house. Much-needed alternative to the academic overdrive of some other Oxford girls' independents (if it didn't exist someone would certainly have to invent it). A positive choice for many relieved families, one of whom described it as 'a jewel, we wouldn't want our daughter to be anywhere else.'

Wycombe Abbey

281

Abbey Way, High Wycombe, Buckinghamshire HP11 1PE

Pupils: 601; 558 full boarders • Ages: 11–18 • Sixth form: 170 • C of E

Fees: Day £27,564; Boarding £36,750 pa

Tel: 01494 520381
Email: registrar@wycombeabbey.com
Website: www.wycombeabbey.com

Headmistress: Since 2013, Mrs Rhiannon Wilkinson MA MEd (50s). Previously principal at Harrogate Ladies' College, one of many curves in perfectly rounded career that includes five years at Haileybury as director of studies and two at Cheadle Hume School where was director of pastoral system. Married with children – husband, Donald is a retired headmaster.

Choice of profession early and unwavering, thanks to family clan of fulfilled teachers (has happy memories of washing out paint pots in mother's classroom). Started in large comprehensives in Devon and south Manchester, then (sensibly ignoring relative's confident predictions of 'career suicide') spent 11 years in Hong Kong and Brunei schools where managing international and affluent families honed parent-whispering skills. Only career downside – has lived in school accommodation since age of 27. 'Probably makes me a sad person.' (Not on evidence so far.)

Far more to the post than simply ensuring all that excellence in terms of popularity and superb results carries on ad infinitum, from righting genuine wrongs – 'would always be first to admit if we make a mistake' – to curbing 'me, me, me' excesses, nicely. 'You can't run any school for an individual,' she says.

Key is transparent admissions process, ensuring name and glittering prizes don't blind families to school values. 'Want parents to choose us because truly know us, not based on the name.' Spends every Tuesday with prospective parents – 45 minutes apiece – to get message across.

Staff love her and she's getting there with parents. 'A true educationalist who is clearly passionate about the school – maybe too passionate,' commented one. 'I don't think you can be too passionate because if you weren't you would lose your enthusiasm when you face some challenging times,' counters Mrs W.

Weekend 'meet the head' lunch programme under way to increase exposure, linked to match fixtures for maximum efficiency. Has also put in the time with pupils, from individual meetings in top years to throwing jolly party at house in grounds for all 65 first years. 'By end of first half term, knew everyone by name,' says parent.

Expert knowledge extends to on-site wildlife, from nesting red kites to badgers, deer and – her favourite – Stumpy the Canada goose, named for deformed wings, tenderly cared for by school with occasional Jammy Dodger as a treat.

Girls like what they've seen of her: has achieved finely judged balance that hovers somewhere between friendliness and formality, thought parent. 'She's super, so there for them, doesn't go round being all huggy or anything – they're scared of her in a nice way and the staff are also very behind her,' said mother.

Unlike predecessor, doesn't teach – yet – and is eyeing up the timetable (shame to waste that Oxford history degree). May have work cut out with building programme – two new boarding houses on site of disused swimming pool. Also starting, in a quiet way, to build public profile – was quoted in The Times talking about the ability of boarding to rescue children from otherwise pressurised existence. Looking at results with jaundiced eye this might seem a tad kettle and pot-like but no, she insists, school does amazingly well with all-embracing support rather than 'trot on Smudgy' crack of the whip. Pupils might feel cocooned; they won't feel driven.

Academic matters: Easy to see results as inevitable consequence of admissions process – bright in, gleaming out. Results impeccable – 85 per cent of A levels and 97 per cent of GCSEs graded A*-A in 2016. 'Results are amazing,' said parent. 'Feels as if no barriers to what the girls could achieve.'

However, not quite the effort-free equation it might appear. Smaller numbers applying to come here means school has to spread admissions net just that bit wider than equivalent boys' school – and it's how they manage the talent that's their forte. Whisper it softly, but sexism is still rife in education, thought parent. Boys get the very best, but for 'the girl it doesn't matter quite as much, so a school like [this] has not got such a huge pool of clever children to draw from.'

There's also the darling daughter factor, thinks Mrs Wilkinson, where doting parents can't quite bear to part from their girls. 'They are very precious, daddy's little princess, the friends of mothers and hard to let go.'

Everyone here is bright – with compulsory Latin and attempt at classical Greek for all, wouldn't cope here if they weren't, though don't overdose on GCSEs, with 10 or 11 the goal for most, one girl insistent on 13 talked down to more manageable 12. 'Great achievement is bringing up girls who are competent but don't shine and getting them to get the really top grades,' said parent.

Not a place where learning support is rushed off feet: though 54 (around 10 per cent) are identified as having special needs, for most this translates into academic support – aka learning enhancement – to plug previous curriculum gaps, particularly for overseas pupils. Just five have help with SpLD, a further five working with EAL specialist – and every pupil in the school needs to enjoy the challenge. 'My daughter's somewhere in the middle [which means] she has a lot to strive for and works harder,' thought mother.

Key is micro monitoring. No slightly below par result is given the benefit of the doubt, no progress chart left unplotted, communication between staff of the instant message variety. Parents, pupils and staff know exactly where every girl is in every subject (pre-GCSE tracking grades include three for A* – high, secure and low – alone). If anticipated trajectory shows any signs of premature wilting, the SWAT team is ready and waiting. 'The ones that would struggle, they just spend more time with them. Literally, the teacher's all over them,' said mother. 'Nobody's going to fail their grades by accident,' agreed another. Timetable underpins the message – Saturday kicks off with breakfast at 8.00am with lessons until 11.50am (detention, scheduled for 8.20am, isn't compulsory, we were pleased to hear).

Tests, predictably, are frequent but well managed and not done 'in a kind of heartrendingly tedious way,' thought parent. Inevitably, some girls find relentlessness of approach harder to bear than others, but transmogrified into gratitude when desired grades came in. 'There are times when you think "wish you would stop hounding me and accept standard" but it's worth it in the end,' said sixth former.

Parental comments acted on. Issue with one teacher relating to lesson pace 'sorted out instantly and school kept us informed on an almost daily basis [until] problem solved,' said parent. One teacher, total convert to boarding, felt it enabled tiny changes where girl 'not quite herself' to be picked up and sorted before could escalate. 'It's that swift response to a change in demeanour – remarkable, rewarding and very satisfying.'

Staff fabness is the norm, best teachers trending at top of charisma settings and 'adored' by pupils for effortless ability to take scenic route through the curriculum and 'teach round the subject, which I think is really important,' said mother. (Latest inspection report gushes agreement.)

Among many favourite subjects history teaching gets rave reviews, sharing joint honours with maths. 'School encourages you to do the subjects you love,' says pupil. 'Very foolish to take on two years in sixth form to study subjects you're not committed to,' agrees teacher.

Fairly brisk staff turnover inevitable consequence of recruiting top talent – no weights are going to hold back rise to greater things for long. Recent departure of fab director of studies to become head elsewhere par for the course. 'If you're recruiting at the top level, it's going to happen,' said parent, one of many who perceive this as price worth paying for quality teaching, while long stay figures (average age 46 with 76 staff members here for 10 years plus) do send reassuring message of stability. Only niggle is that some departures could occasionally be better timed, thought one. More quality staff accommodation – school lags behind others in this respect – would also help, feel staff and parents.

While care and attention that goes into creating the finished pupil hugely appreciated by parents, we heard more than once that aspects of culture had been a tad joy-free. 'There's a sense that growing up is a serious business,' said parent. 'We don't laugh at ourselves, we don't question ourselves that much. We know what we do, we're good at it, deal with it.'

Similarly, when rules are broken 'there's no knowing smiles, no "I've got to give you this penalty, please don't do it again but we're still friends",' said parent. 'It's "we really expect girls of your age to behave much better than this and it's not funny at all".' Occasionally po-faced? Possibly, thought staff. 'I think staff felt they needed permission to let hair down,' says head.

Staff confirm that fun, once the three letter word that dare not say its name, is now out and proud – mostly. Immediate muting of clearly very jolly (and refreshingly noisy) Latin lesson heard when this reviewer hove into view suggests not all teachers have got the message that head is, as one put it, 'in favour of jollity.'

Girls, though, stress noses are removed from grindstones on regular basis. Everyone works hard but there's 'lots of laughing and joking in the kitchen,' stressed sixth former. 'Not so serious that you shouldn't be scared to come here. We know how to have fun.'

Games, options, the arts: As with other high-achieving schools, everything you'd expect in the way of stunning stuff to play, perform or create is on show on a nearby pitch, platform or podium. Bashful won't get you places though, thought parent. 'If you're not going to do grab the opportunities, probably wouldn't suit.'

Caters for all sorts in innumerable venues, sweet-toothed first years to Cadbury's World, skiers to Whistler, budding sixth form medics to West Herts Hospital and female highflyers past and present regularly celebrated with events and talks – subsequent pupil write-ups, even by youngest, are little gems of well-observed journalism.

The 550 plus weekly instrumental lessons are also somehow fitted in, handful most years reaching diploma standard, substantial numbers hitting grades 7 and 8. Drama, equally ambitious, includes day of Shakespeare miniatures – Titus Andronicus (and others) each done and dusted in just 30 minutes.

Games widely enjoyed and lots of them, team sports 'formidable' with even tiniest slivers of talent encouraged to flourish. Teams don't straddle the alphabet – size means lacrosse, for example, only reaches C after the first year when 'have more teams so as not to make the girls feel left out.' Sure footed pretty much across the board, football, netball, tennis and squash teams among those whizzing up to quarter final stage and above in national tournaments, sailors recently taking part in world championships.

Not so sporty thrive, happy to trade games for other interests, school good at helping find inner something ('funasize' weekend activity option sounds fun, bootcamp possibly less so). Music, drama, or art, 'they'll find a way of making that come to you,' said parent.

Marvel of timetabling helps to avoid overloads – one third year had opted for piano, violin, ballet, riding and extra lacrosse. 'Very tailored. I don't know how they do it,' said parent. Sheer willpower and not letting sun set on unfinished work was pupil tip though can lead to lateish finish (10pm rare but not unheard of).

Only small bone of contention was desire to embrace the new rather than stick to tried, tested and trophy-ed – one parent thought rowing, recently introduced, could be made more of. Another, however, had nothing but praise for polo, also new to the school and thus far a galloping success.

Boarding: It's all or nothing full boarding (unless you're one of the very few day pupils). School operates non-negotiable 'closed' weekends (following hols, half terms and exeats). No choice over houses either – decision is made by school and that's that, though with posh lighting, carpet and paint upgrade programme under way, will be few complaints wherever you end up – fabbed-up bits of Daws Hill, for example, well worth a visit.

Oldest and youngest pupils have own houses. First years get chickens for extra homeliness, upper sixth ditch poultry for first taste of independence – wear own clothes, too (sensibly point out that as universities don't insist on work wear, why should they?). Can be heady experience – school occasionally has to coax those briefly high on prospect of unlimited toast making and TV watching back into more humdrum aspects of school life.

In between (years 2 to lower sixth) girls join one of nine mixed-age houses (two more under construction), each with around 45 pupils. Older girls are enlisted as mother and granny substitutes, brilliant at 'been there, done that' advice, many issues resolved without recourse to adult intervention. Also compels older girls to keep conversation within age-appropriate limits, pointed out parent. It's rounded off with formality of timetabled slots with housemistresses and elected house prefect system (one housemistress uses two vote system, one for loyalty candidate, the other 'for one they'd really like to win – they're never wrong').

Add packed programme of evening and weekend activities, from shopping trips to ice skating and even, according to website, 'vegging out' (inverted commas – theirs – probably say it all) and parental approval pretty much universal.

Background and atmosphere: Entrance via one of High Wycombe's statement roundabouts makes countrified setting a particular pleasure. 'Abbey' is a misnomer (it's a nun-free zone, name for status purposes only) but from ecclesiastic trimmings in main building – an 18th century former mansion – to performing arts centre overlooking lake, with incredible number of performance areas (one handily combining grand piano and chaise longue for artistic swooning to music), school is very easy on the eye.

Founded 1896, school was 'new experiment' by pioneering Miss – later Dame – Frances Dove. One of Girton College's test batch of girl students and school's first headmistress, was every ounce a character, on-line portrait notable for fabulous, gravity-defying hair probably held up by principles alone.

Her aim – girls' education every bit as good as boys' through pursuit of excellence, development of talents, godliness and an understanding of the needs of others – remains top of the checklist. School's view is that even if her reaction to chicken nugget-making or 'baking with Mr Whiteley' sessions might be harder to call, Dame Frances would feel right at home with current ethos and achievements.

All happens on suitably inspirational site, originally belonging to Carringtons (current Lord Carrington is school enthusiast and regular visitor), enlarged by 1929 purchase of next door estate, Daws Hill, big enough to house a school all on its own, used for weddings and a good five minutes from main school by car (staff often drive, girls in its three boarding houses take compulsory scenic route). Has just got back World War II underground bunker, annexed after school was requisitioned as HQ for US Eighth Air Force – history department no doubt licking lips at potential for truly authentic lessons.

Little sign of world-weary London – and on and on – vibe here. Instead, children remain children – against the odds. Delightful 'Fairies' event (you'll have to ask for details – we're sworn to secrecy) where magical beings turn every house into (tinsel) town one night in Christmas term, appears proof against teen cynicism.

Was it really healthy to put so much distance between pupils and real life, wondered one older girl, worried for health of contemporaries' souls. Definitely, think parents, who appear simply relieved that school's imposition of rules, including bans on make up and travelling unaccompanied on public transport until reach 16, keeps them off the hook. 'Might be a bit ridiculous but means girls feel safe and can be scruffy and dirty when it's appropriate,' said parent.

They also love their jargon. Prefects, unofficially, are 'mons' (once monitors); booters the temporary lockers where pre-lunch gubbins is stowed. (And, oh, the relief of seeing a bit of learning sprawl, with books, calculators and even the odd sock in contrast to pristine conditions elsewhere.)

There's Big School (actually the school hall – smell, instantly recognisable, of 'dust, old wood and overworked brains,' thought staff member) overlooked by bust of Frances Dove, grim as death, a martinet in marble, exiled from classrooms where was scaring the teachers (a joke, they said – though we wonder..)

Add Gym Courtyard (gym went years ago), four boarding Out Houses, inside the school grounds but 'you have to go out to them' – well, of course – and Long Corridor – the through route that thinks it's a communal room – and no wonder that even long-serving staff freely own up to being occasionally surprised by unfamiliar nooks and crannies.

Pastoral care, well-being and discipline: Housemistress as personality cult may be dead but continue to exert considerable beneficial influence, experts in even-handedness and clued-upness, matron and tutor completing house triumvirate. 'You get this impression, if something's happened in the morning, housemistress will know about it by lunchtime,' said parent.

Not always a breeze. Some girls won't get on with others in their house – and sophisticated urbanites vs the rest can make for occasional trouble. Staff antennae don't miss much, however, and one parent was pragmatic. Daughter has 'realised that she's just going to have to get on with it,' she said.

Pupils and parents: With school seen as nearest you'll get to girls' Eton equivalent in terms of ethos, location and facilities (impressive list of joint social events adds to sibling feel), it's often purchased as part of matching pair. Old girls are solidly brilliant type you'd expect (reality TV slebs aren't their thing, so far) and include Rt Hon Lady Justice Butler-Sloss, Baroness Howe, plus star journalist India Knight and actress Rachel Stirling.

You won't find idle rich featuring in the parental mix: hard-working, high-flying, well connected and dual income professionals dominate – as indeed they must to stump up hefty fees, though still find time to attend matches.

Some reservations about amounts of money sloshing about. 'Do worry that when many of her friends have their own Addison Lee account daughter might have a warped view of what is "normal",' said one mother. School asks for birthday celebrations to be limited to pizza or noodle bar excursions to avoid escalation of party politics.

'Don't want them to be in a privileged little bubble,' agrees head, while pointing out that anyone who can afford the fees unlikely to be on breadline. Fast growing bursary programme will help those who can't – new boarding houses will lead to gradual increase in numbers to 600. 'Thirty extra girls over seven years won't dilute product,' says head.

Girls may cover the gamut of characters, outer appearance occasionally au naturel as regards make up but sharing hefty degree of inner self-confidence (it's the quality most commented on by parents elsewhere) and appetite for success. 'Good with strong, silent type,' said one parent. Won't be squashed and there's 'healthy situation where girls help each other [but] if you're not the type that is striving to do well, you'll soon be left behind.'

Entrance: Potential pupils will 'like their notebooks and fluorescent pens – busy little bees who love finding out the way things fit together,' says head – which might help when it comes to working way through complex entrance procedures and deadlines. Register 18 months to two years in advance for 11+ and 13+ entry and at least 15 months ahead for sixth form hopefuls – minimum nine A and A* GCSEs required. Pre-tests for all candidates.

Feeders include high profile preps in London and South East: Maltman's Green, Bute House, Francis Holland, Pembridge Hall, Glendower, Ken Prep and Garden House in year 7 (65 places – around 180 applicants). Godstowe and The Dragon at 13 (more competitive with 100 applicants for 25 places), separate exams for UK prep and overseas/senior school candidates). Around 25 per cent international pupils, Hong Kong, Malaysia and Nigeria most strongly represented. Thirty day places awarded to top performing locals.

Exit: Head's lightbulb moment was to stop post-16 exodus by giving fifth formers Through the Keyhole invite to previously, and pointlessly, top secret delights of upper sixth boarding house. While Westminster remains most desirable of alternative destinations (for some, lessons with b**s just too much of a lure) vast majority now stay on. With 25 Oxbridge places in 2016 and nine medics as well as Browns, Columbia, John Hopkins, MIT and the Rhode Island School of Design, why risk chances elsewhere, argues head?

Money matters: At five per cent off the fees, scholarships more gloss than dosh (hopefuls also need to invest six pounds in past papers); exhibitions worth £600 a year. Help for those in need via expanding bursary fund, donor generosity permitting.

Remarks: A classy, focused school, true to high-minded educational objectives of pioneering founder. Knows what it's about and makes year in, year out results look easy. Appreciative parents accept school for what it is and don't expect much in the way of radical change – except, that is, at Christmas, when the Fairies come to call. 'Encourages girls to dream big and shows them what is possible,' said one. 'We'd do it again in a heartbeat.'

Yateley Manor

51 Reading Road, Yateley, Hampshire GU46 7UQ

Pupils: 400 • Ages: 3–13 • C of E

Fees: £10,485 – £14,385 pa

Tel: 01252 405500
Email: registrar@yateleymanor.com
Website: www.yateleymanor.com

Headmaster: Since 2015, Robert Upton BSc PGCE MA (Ed) NPQH, previously director of studies at Bede's Prep in Eastbourne. Studied at Loughborough and Brighton universities and started teaching in Hastings; has led two Sussex state primary schools. He and his wife Olivia have two children.

Entrance: Taster days and informal assessments, though these are mainly to determine children's needs. Scholarships for academic all-rounders, creative and performing arts, music, sport and chess up to 50 per cent of fees and means tested bursaries up to 100 per cent. Sibling discounts. Numbers steadying after a small drop, but economics dictates a much greater proportion of late applications. Mostly local children from banking and service industry families; middle-class, not mega rich, with an ethnic mix reflecting the local population.

Exit: To up to 40 schools, mostly fairly local: Royal Grammar School Guildford, Lord Wandsworth College, Farnborough Hill, The Abbey, Guildford High, Wellington College, Queen Anne's Caversham etc; also Bradfield, Tormead, Sir William Perkins's and others, with a good smattering of scholarships. Girls have tended to move schools at 11, so numbers have been 60/40 boys to girls, but in current year groups far more girls are deciding to stay to 13 because (as a pupil put it) 'They enjoy being special in the last two years'. Senior schools report ex-Yateley pupils as confident and well prepared.

Remarks: Still well oiled and ambitious, but with a newish state of the art philosophy of education accepted staff and parents alike. Parents appreciate the updated curriculum; they say change, since the initial impact, has proceeded at a steady pace. The footprint of the school has recently doubled in size and a new creative and performing arts centre opened in September 2015. Rambling Edwardian/Victorian domestic building provides a pleasant, spacious if inconvenient centre to the school, with lots of later additions. Well-equipped classrooms in attractive '70s and '90s buildings. Satellite buildings, pitches, gardens (tended by pupils), plenty of grassy play space and a well used (vital) car park.

Children, confident and creative, speak of enjoying the drama, the masses of curriculum related projects and sport. Extracurricular is big with spectacularly competitive chess to the fore and a seemingly endless list of challenging activities, though parents comment that the school wisely only does what it can do well, not attempting to compete with local professional classes in dance, sports etc. Strong sports with loads of success for teams and individuals (catalogued at length in the school mag) and pupils going on to do well at national level in cricket, running, swimming and biathlon.

Tinies in the nursery have impressive centre at back of site with a lovely outdoor area featuring a pirate ship, track for colourful ride-in cars and lots of things to play in and push. Inside amazing construction toys and learning games, but this is nonetheless a cunningly planned learning environment where everything is carefully monitored and tailored to each child's need. Older children can come here to help at break times (and get a bit of TLC themselves). Social problems picked up by tutor system. Nurse (full time) is friendly and popular.

Crammed curriculum includes French and music taught by specialists from reception onwards. Latin from year 4, chess for all from year 1, Italian in years 7 and 8. The Prep Schools Baccalaureate incorporates core subjects, English, maths, science and French which are assessed through common entrance. It also includes a record of achievement in all other subjects such as humanities, classics, sport, art, DT and drama. Importantly key life skills: communication, thinking and learning, self-reviewing and improving are all tracked with respect to independence, collaboration and leadership. The school has its own woodland learning area.

The house system provides pastoral care, together with opportunities for responsibility for senior pupils. Tutor groups of six or seven pupils for supervising progress and encouraging self-awareness and independent thinking.

A number of children come and go by coach, with coaches leaving at 5.30pm after school. Parents and pupils can have school breakfast (lots do) and pay by voucher. Snacks are provided mid morning and for children staying to clubs in the afternoon. Masses of trips, both fieldwork and fun, and a full holiday activities course during the summer – so lots of help for working parents.

A happy, busy school with confident, outgoing pupils, underpinned by some impressive organisation.

Yehudi Menuhin School

283

Stoke d'Abernon, Cobham, Surrey KT11 3QQ

Pupils: 80; 71 boarders • Ages: 8–19 • Sixth form: 24

Fees: Day £40,986; Boarding £42,069 pa for those not on music and dance scheme

Tel: 01932 864739
Email: reception@yehudimenuhinschool.co.uk
Website: www.yehudimenuhinschool.co.uk

Headmaster: Since 2010, Dr Richard Hillier MA PhD (50s). Began his school career as a chorister at The King's (The Cathedral) School in Peterborough. Read classics at St John's Cambridge, and after a spell of teaching in St Andrew's and Durham, became head of classics and housemaster at Repton. Took up the post of head at the Oratory Prep School in Oxfordshire in 2006 and moved to the YMS four years later. Still sings as a freelance baritone when time allows. A true scholar who continues to be involved in academic research, he recently gave a paper in a Late Roman Seminar at Corpus Christi, Oxford: Arator: a sixth-century life reconsidered. Shares his office with fellow scholar Jimmy, a parson russell terrier. Married to Elaine, the school's exams and alumni officer, with two grown-up sons.

Retiring in December 2017. Successor will be Mrs Kate Clanchy, currently senior master at Westminster School. Degree in modern and medieval languages from Cambridge, masters from the Institute of Education and an MBA. Initially head of marketing for a French water company; French teacher at Dulwich College, head of modern langs at JAGS, deputy head at St Paul's Girls before joining Westminster in 2013. She's also a governor of Oak Lodge School for pupils with hearing difficulties.

Malcolm Singer is retiring from his post as director of music in August 2017.

Academic matters: 'It's not the best, but it's OK,' was how one student described the academic provision. Results are certainly OK. In 2016, 75 per cent A*/As at GCSE. A levels were 64 per cent at A*/A and 86 per cent at A*-B. This information isn't readily available on the website, giving the impression that the school doesn't think it of much interest; no one is here for the academics, after all. That said, the ability profile here is above the national average, and students want to do well on all fronts.

Most students take seven GCSEs from a narrow range of subjects: music of course, then maths, English, single or double science, history and German, the school's main language because conservatoires in Germany and Austria are popular leavers' destinations here. Other languages are also taught when the need is there, and Russian, Japanese, Turkish, Mandarin have all been offered. (French used to be very big at the school, but no longer, which we thought a shame.) At A level everyone takes music, and then chooses one or two further options from English, history, biology, chemistry, maths, further maths and German. No physics, because the low demand makes it hard to justify employing someone to teach it. 'That's a tricky one for us,' admitted the head, 'and I'd love to be able to offer it.' Art taught throughout the school and some lovely work on show, but not usually taken as an examined subject. 'I wish there were more options,' was a concern voiced by one student and echoed by others. But the school's academic music programme, a longstanding jewel in the YMS crown, was highly praised by everyone. 'It's incredible!' 'Amazing!' 'Inspiring!' 'Harder than at Juilliard!' were typical comments.

Impossible to build year groups as such, because of very small numbers. Instead, learning is organised in four groups based on key stages. D group is made up of pupils in years 3-6, C group of those in years 7-9, B group years 10-11, and A group years 12-14. Classes are very small, and all students get a high degree of individual attention. No SEN teacher, but the school's few dyslexic pupils receive ongoing support from the regular staff and teaching assistants; one-to-one tutorials where necessary. Strong EAL support, with students who need it given regular lessons with dedicated EAL teacher. 'I couldn't speak English very well when I came,' one student told us, 'and the school has really helped me.'

Games, options, the arts: Music is, of course, the school's raison d'etre, and at least half of each day is devoted to it. Everyone has a daily practice target to meet, and it's perfectly usual for the older students to do four or more hours a day. Younger students do less and their practice sessions are supervised. Pupils receive two one-hour lessons per week on their principal instrument, and half an hour on their second study, and everyone learns composition. There are also courses in classical improvisation, choral singing, aural training and general music studies. The result is a landscape of really stellar music-making in which the students live and grow. The orchestra is stunning, and chamber music is wonderful. Huge programme of concerts, including twice-weekly ones at the school given in the beautiful Yehudi Menuhin Hall, all blond wood and gleaming Steinways, and dozens across the UK and abroad. The three pupils we saw in concert had excellent posture, were compellingly confident on the platform, and gave virtuoso performances of great beauty and taste.

Sports and physical training are provided for in a delightfully esoteric way. Pupils have two hours of timetabled sport per week, chosen from a range of swimming (in the school's own indoor pool), football, PE, badminton, tennis, cross-country running and dance. Yoga is optional but encouraged, and an Alexander technique teacher is always available for those who want or need to see her. Annual football fixture with the Purcell School for Young Musicians in Hertfordshire. The latter usually win, it has to be said, perhaps because they number brass players and percussionists among them who tend to come up beefier.

Art is much-loved and drama has always flourished at the school: shows are staged in the Square Room, and a recent production of The Tempest was set quirkily in a boarding school. Plenty of trips to concerts, theatres, art galleries, museums, etc. The Duke of Edinburgh scheme has been running here since 2010.

Boarding: Boarding has been intrinsic to the school's ethos since its inception. 'We run a boarding day and a boarding week,' confirmed the head. There are a tiny number of 'day boarders', but they're in school from 8am until 6.30pm and are regarded as boarding pupils who sleep at home. The youngest students are weekly boarders and can go home at 4pm on Fridays. The rest stay on for Saturday morning school, after which they can go home if they choose, although many of them come from too far away for this to be possible.

Two boarding houses, both maintained to a high standard. The girls, and the youngest boys, live in Music House in quarters that we thought well-appointed and attractive. Students are grouped in 'pods' of broadly similar ages; same-age room mates can't be guaranteed because numbers are so small. Younger pupils share two or three to a room, older ones may get an ensuite to themselves: a new storey has just been added to provide this kind of accommodation. Pianos everywhere – Debussy's L'Isle Joyeuse drifted out dreamily from under the door of one room as we passed – and practice sessions are timetabled throughout the day. Until they're aged 11, pupils can practise until 8pm; thereafter they can go on until 9pm. We'd heard reports of students practising themselves into a decline, but the house staff and students we spoke to denied this. 'We patrol the corridors and we do stop students over-practising,' said the housemistress, 'but they learn commonsense.' 'It's very busy here during the day, and we want to sleep,' agreed a soignée young violinist.

The boys live in Harris House, which has a brand spanking new extension providing seven ensuite rooms and a kitchen for student use. Like Music House, it was clean, orderly, cosy and dotted with pianos. We liked the wall of clocks showing the current time in different countries around the world – 'We have pupils from every time-zone and it was a way of making them feel at home,' explained the housemaster.

As a rule, boarders have to be at least 9, but the school conceded that this wasn't rigid, and they have taken children as young as 8; we heard from one mother for whom this hadn't worked, possibly because children of that age are the exception here rather than the rule.

Students enthused about the improvement in the food over the past two years. We thought it pretty good too: a healthy and appetizing range from which even the fussiest eater could find something. Servery and eating area has been handsomely refurbished, and ranks as probably the most civilised school dining hall we've ever sat down in.

Background and atmosphere: Founded in 1963 by Yehudi Menuhin to give musically gifted children the chance to develop their potential to the full through a sympathetic curriculum, enhanced practice opportunities and superlative teaching in an immersive environment. Initially only for pianists, violinists and cellists, the portfolio has since been expanded to include double bass players and guitarists. The YMS approach has had its detractors and historically the school has known darker times, but some truly world-class musicians have come out of the place, although, the head insisted, 'it's not the purpose of this school to produce lots of little Yehudi Menuhins'. Tiger mums please take note.

Beautiful Victorian mansion setting in Surrey village suggests peace and harmony. Once inside, the feel is a curious mix of very relaxed and rigidly controlling. There's no uniform, the dress code is informal, and with the exception of the head, staff and pupils are on first name terms. But as a seasoned schools' reviewer, it was clear to us as we went round that this school doesn't like criticism, or what it perceives as criticism, and that it keeps a tighter grip on the way its pupils make music than the other specialist music schools. On joining the YMS students can't choose to continue on programmes at Saturday junior conservatoires, for instance, whereas at Purcell, Chetham's and Wells this isn't a problem. (Indeed, the school's Saturday morning programme would make this impossible.) The only exception to this is made for the double-bass players, whose teacher also teaches at RCM junior department and takes her YMS students there each week for the additional orchestral experience. And despite a packed calendar of performance opportunities, the system by which pupils are chosen for the most sought-after of these is a closed one (at other music schools it's often done by audition), and several pupils told us that they felt consistently excluded. 'They choose the students who are a safe bet,' said one, a remark which had everyone nodding vigorously, and others said, surprisingly, that in the time they'd been at the school they'd had hardly any chance to perform chamber music. 'We have to give pupils the opportunities that are right for them,' was the head's response. 'If you have a high-profile concert, you have to put the people in who will pull it off. It's not always easy to be fair on paper.'

However, students were adamant that the atmosphere between them all was supportive, and not destructively competitive. 'There's actually not much competition; I've never felt it here,' was a comment that everyone agreed with, and their relish for the musical experience here was unstinting. 'It's the best you can get for the age we're at'; 'It really prepares you for music college'; 'They are such good teachers!'; 'My violin teacher is like a mother to me'; 'For practice, it's so much easier to be here, everything is so close' – etc.

No parents' association. School's reason for this is that parents come from too huge a radius for such a thing to work. Ex-parents told us that they had felt kept at arms' length, with one even telling us that they never felt welcome. But the only current parents to contact us wrote, 'Headteacher and indeed other teachers are approachable and welcoming even though they must be under pressure also.'

Pastoral care, well-being and discipline: Yehudi Menuhin believed in the importance of a homely, family atmosphere in his school, and as we walked about, we saw children playing contentedly in the school's leafy grounds, cheering on their friends in the lunchtime concert, and generally appearing happy and at ease. Students attested to the kindness of the staff. 'The school's been really patient with me,' said one, philosophically. 'When I first came, I wasn't a well-behaved child. Anywhere else would have asked me to leave.' In this small, artistically-driven community, the kind of misbehaviour most schools have to deal with is rare. Pupils have worked hard for their place here and want to keep it.

Staff to student ratio is low, and there are regular weekly meetings about pastoral issues. 'If someone's falling through the gaps, it's picked up,' affirmed housemaster. However, all the staff we spoke to put much emphasis on pupils 'self-managing': 'There's a lot of autonomy here'; 'They just get on with it'; 'They're surprisingly mature'; and we did wonder if this sometimes meant pupils were left to flounder. The head emphatically denied this – 'I have never taught in a school which discusses, and, yes, cares for pupils at this level'. The students themselves offered slightly ambiguous observations, such as 'We do a lot of our stuff on our own in this kind of school'; 'The older ones usually take care of the younger ones'; 'The boarding staff are doing the best job they can.' However, inspection reports have consistently rated the school's pastoral care as excellent, and the only parents to respond to our appeal for feedback wrote, 'Pastoral care is very important to us since we live far away but have been happy with the attention so far in that area.' Despite several attempts on our part, we could not find any other parents of current students who wanted to talk to us, although we were contacted by parents whose experience of the school had been negative and who had taken their children away.

Pupils and parents: With 80 pupils on the roll, the school is the biggest it's ever been, and there are no plans to expand further. Just over half are from the UK (although this figure includes a few international families who have relocated so that their child can attend the school), the rest from overseas. Very broad range of backgrounds and nationalities makes for a truly cosmopollitan school community: students currently hail from the UK, Ireland, France, Germany, Switzerland, Spain, Poland, Bulgaria, Bosnia-Herzegovina, Serbia, Turkey, Morocco, Tunisia, China, Taiwan, South Korea, Singapore, Japan, Thailand, Brazil and Mexico. The common ground they all share is music: students have chosen to come here for the outstanding teaching, the support with practice, and 'being surrounded by musicians of this calibre,' as a student put it. It's a musical hothouse and has its fair share of eccentrics, but it's impossible not to be won over by the results. The young people we met were all really lovely: articulate, thoughtful, intelligent, personable, good-mannered and good fun.

Alumni include Nigel Kennedy, Tasmin Little, Nicola Benedetti, Kathryn Stott, Melvyn Tan and Colin Carr.

Entrance: Aspiring young musicians from all over the world apply from age 8 – there is no set entry point. The process is long and thorough: preliminary audition, then main audition, and if applicants get through both those hurdles, a three-day residential assessment during which they take part in all aspects of school life including instrumental lessons, academic lessons and boarding. Children have to be robust. A recent candidate played incredibly but wasn't ready socially, and no place was offered. Applicants' academic ability is not used to determine entry.

Unusually, students who join the school in the sixth form have to commit to doing three years. Year 14 is spent continuing with their instrumental tuition plus academic music and possibly another AS. This could be seen as another example of the school's determination to control its end product, but the year 14 students we met were positive about the experience, and felt it to be of benefit to their musical development.

A child must join before their 17th birthday, but otherwise a student's age isn't taken into account and the year groups aren't even. School won't admit into year 11, but happy for students to repeat a year and go into year 10. Students can join at any point in the year if there's space.

Exit: The overwhelming majority to music conservatoires around the world: at this rarified level, they choose the teacher with whom they want to study and apply to the institution where that teacher is based. 2016 destinations included Royal College of Music, Guildhall School of Music and Drama, New England Conservatory in Boston and Musikhochschules in Germany. Rarely, to university: one to Cambridge in 2016 to read music; previous students have gone to Oxford to read English and to Imperial to read biochemistry. Occasionally a student wishing to pursue broader academic options will leave at 16.

Money matters: Inevitably one of the most expensive boarding schools in the country, given all the top-calibre specialist tuition, but hardly anyone pays full fees. Families who have been continually resident in the UK for at least two years receive means-tested funding from the government's Music and Dance Scheme: the YMS is one of only eight schools in the UK to be so supported. For those ineligible for the scheme, the school has its own bursary fund: it has a good endowment, and fundraising is ongoing. Where they can, they match what the Music and Dance Scheme would pay.

Remarks: This is as unusual a school experience as it's possible to get, and one that parents need to choose with their eyes wide open. Don't send your highly academic teen here and then complain that they can't do triple science. Don't put your 8-year-old here if you want them to have lots of friends the same age. Try not to send your child here in the secret hope that they'll be the next Fritz Kreisler. But if the music offered here is what your child wants with all their being, and you believe that they couldn't be as happy anywhere else as they could be here, go for it.

London

M25
M1
M4
BARNET
HARINGEY
CAMDEN
HAMPSTEAD
HARROW
BRENT
HILLINGDON
EALING
KENSINGTON
HOUNSLOW
RICHMOND UPON THAMES
MERTON
KINGSTON UPON THAMES
SUTTON
A
B
HAMPSTEAD
CHALK FARM

ENFIELD
M11
WALTHAM FOREST
REDBRIDGE
M25
HAVERING
HACKNEY
ISLINGTON
NEWHAM
CITY
TOWER HAMLETS
SOUTHWARK
GREENWICH
LAMBETH
LEWISHAM
BROMLEY
CROYDON
M20

B
PADDINGTON
KENSINGTON
KNIGHTSBRIDGE
BELGRAVIA
CHELSEA

Junior Schools
Senior Schools
Junior & Senior Schools

LONDON

The Academy School

3 Pilgrims Place, Rosslyn Hill, London NW3 1NG

Pupils: 89 • Ages: 6-13

Fees: £18,375 pa

Tel: 020 7435 6621
Email: office@academyhampstead.com
Website: www.academyschoolhampstead.com

Principals: Mr Garth Evans (50s) and Ms Chloe Sandars (40s) are joint principals of this small Hampstead school, which they founded in 1997. Chloe studied at the Royal Academy of Music, followed by postgraduate work at Trinity College of Music, then played in a trio while teaching music part-time. Garth, whose great-grandfather accompanied Captain Scott to the Antarctic, was educated at Falkner House, Westminster School and Queen Mary College, London, where he read English. He started tutoring privately at the age of 16 ('to fund my beer money') and went on to work at Trevor-Roberts, where he met Chloe. As private tutors, Garth and Chloe developed quite a following and parents encouraged them to start their own school. 'They liked the way we taught,' says Garth. 'Their children were inspired and given confidence.' The pair are an excellent foil to each other, she calm and organised, he a passionate and reassuring instructor. Chloe has two teenage daughters, both of whom attended the Academy, Garth a teenage son and daughter. Garth's wife Bea (who teaches geography and acts as the school nurse) and Chloe's husband Andrew (ex-City, who runs the finances and also teaches history and maths) are very much part of the four-person leadership team.

Entrance: Though they have occasionally taken a younger sibling, this is essentially a school which begins at 6, once children have learnt to read. 'We start with specialist subject teaching from the word go,' says Chloe. Pupils join at every stage thereafter, including mid year, if a place is available and the school feels it can meet the child's (and the parents') needs. Maximum of 90 pupils, however, and the school tends to be fullest in the summer. Pupils are assessed rather than tested, taking part in a class to see how they fit in. 'We're happy to work with the very strong and the very weak,' says Chloe. 'The questions we ask are: "Do we think we can do a good job?" "Do we like the family?"' Occasional year 7 places for boys after the 11-plus exodus of girls.

Exit: To a wide range of schools but most get their first choice. St Paul's, North London Collegiate, City of London, Westminster, UCS, Highgate, Mill Hill, South Hampstead, Francis Holland, Channing, North Bridge House, with several scholarships. 'Sometimes we have to work with parents to adjust their expectations, particularly if they've set their heart on a specific school from an early age, but most parents trust our judgement,' says Garth. Others are just grateful for the help given in pointing them in the right direction. 'My daughter is not at all academic,' said one mother, 'but they did everything to find a school that worked for her and she is now immensely happy.'

Remarks: The Academy is by no means a traditional school and its approach is perhaps defined by the backgrounds of its heads, who spent their early careers mopping up the fall-out from a traditional education elsewhere. The basis of their philosophy is that all learning stems from a happy child. 'It really is true,' says Chloe. 'If children are happy, everything follows from that.' Year groups here are soft-edged ('We're very flexible about birth dates') and so are classes. 'The whole school is planned round the individual and how best to work with their ability. If there's a problem we solve it.' Class sizes of about 14, but pupils are moved up a set in the middle of a term or taken out of a class to be given additional support. A significant part of the process is instilling the essentials. Teaching, particularly in the core subjects, is rock solid and maths and English are thoroughly engrained. Though most pupils can read fluently on arrival, they continue to read aloud two or three times a week. Older children read for 15 minutes at the end of every lunch hour and all have a reading list and a carefully monitored reading record. Maths is unusually strong. 'Children like being good at maths,' says Garth, who believes that any subject, no matter how complex, can be taught well if communication is clear. As proof, on the day the Guide visited, his class of 11-year-olds had clearly grasped logarithms, a topic normally reserved for sixth formers. The effect lingers into secondary school. 'My daughter has stayed in the top maths set at a competitive school,' said one parent, 'I feel that's down to the teaching at The Academy.'

The Academy started out with just seven children in the premises of a Unitarian Chapel in Hampstead village. 'I looked at every church in the area,' said Chloe. 'Then one snowy evening I knocked on the door here and the vicar said, "Step this way".' The lower years are now housed in two dainty white Georgian cottages, with room sizes that reflect the era, older pupils are taught in the chapel. Facilities are relatively restricted with only a small library and science taught on the move, but pupils are engaged and enthusiastic. 'They give us quite a lot of freedom,' said one, 'but work us very hard.'

The school day starts bright and early with the first lesson at 8am. 'We always felt the best part of the day was lost if you started with assembly at 8.30,' says Chloe. There are no 'class' teachers (though the youngest do have one specifically devoted to their needs). The school believes that 'every child is special', but this is not a place that specialises in those with serious learning difficulties. It copes well, however, with those on the margins and a special needs expert visits weekly. Whatever the child's ability, most parents agree every ounce of potential is fully exploited.

Games are certainly not the raison d'être here and if you had a madly sporty child, whose primary motivation was to be captain of this or that, The Academy would not be an obvious choice. PE is taught on site by a sports teacher and swimming at the nearby Royal Free Leisure Centre, but there's little in the way of team sports. This is more a place where the question is who would like to be in the team – if the answer's yes, you're in. There is, however, a recently established netball squad and matches have been played against other schools in cricket and football, as well as handball, badminton and netball. Music and art are more of a priority. Double art every week, with woodwork on offer and a separate pottery room with its own kiln. Music, too, is taken seriously. 'We do a lot of singing, since it's very inclusive,' says Chloe and the school has a violin teacher and a 19-piece orchestra. 'It's a pretty odd orchestra, with one person on brass and 11 violins, but it's fun and they learn what it's like playing together. Occasionally, an exceptional player will raise the bar for everyone.' The annual school musical, which involves the entire school, is the highlight of the summer term. School food is packed lunch.

Pastoral care is what this school is all about. 'Children are nurtured and encouraged and set very simple objectives,' says Garth. 'We then build it up little by little and make them believe in themselves.' The Academy is inspiration for all, but particularly so for those who've lost their way or lost confidence elsewhere. 'We're good at turning them round,' says Garth, and parents couldn't agree more. 'It's a bit of a cliché,'

A

said one who'd sent two children from two different schools, 'but they do care passionately about the children. In the case of both my children, they were completely transformed both academically and emotionally.' The school has its own visiting counsellor, who teaches PSHE and is available for any pupil who wants to talk. 'They feel it's OK to cross a line with me,' she says. Boundaries here, however, are firm, just further back than might be the case elsewhere. 'We deal furiously with unkindness or making capital at someone else's expense,' says Garth. There is no expulsion. 'We never send them away, we just remove them from society from 8am-3.30pm unless they behave.' The school has a uniform – a navy sweat top with the school's logo – but it's not strictly imposed. 'We don't really mind as long as they're neat,' says Chloe.

Families are mainly Hampstead locals and the relationship with parents is fundamental. Garth gives out his mobile number and parents can ring whenever they feel the need, a privilege he say they don't abuse. The parents themselves are immensely grateful. 'This is the school we all wish we could have gone to,' said one.

ACS Hillingdon International School

Hillingdon Court, 108 Vine Lane, Hillingdon UB10 0BE

Pupils: 540 • Ages: 4–18 • Sixth form: 110

Fees: £10,280 – £23,110 pa

Tel: 01895 259771
Email: hillingdonadmissions@acs-schools.com
Website: www.acs-schools.com

Interim head of school: Diane Hren is holding the reins for the 2016/17 school year. She has previously been deputy head of ACS Cobham and helped to set up ACS Doha, becoming head of school there in 2012. She moved back to the UK in 2014, becoming head of programmes (education) for ACS International Schools.

Academic matters: Take a deep breath before you try to penetrate ACS's patchwork quilt curricula. Start with American-style pre-K – grade 4 with international add-ons including some IPC (International Primary Curriculum) units, language and cultural studies to grade 2, then Spanish plus PTSA (Parent Teacher Student Association) led multicultural weeks (grades 3-5); IB Middle Years Programme with Spanish or French, followed by the last two years of high school with the IB diploma, a fair range of AP courses (11 on offer), high school honours (which is really just 'regular' level, meaning not IB or AP), or a combination thereof. The early childhood programme is a nice blend of learning-through-play and structure, supplemented by specialist teachers for music, art and PE, and cultural classes. Language and cultural studies expose the youngest ones to languages represented in the school community. A different language and culture is featured each month, and children learn basic phrases, explore traditions and sample food.

So it combines American school roots with academic programmes, legacies of previous ACS International Schools leadership and the experiences of the sister campuses – sewn together, with some added layers of internationalism appliquéd on top to embellish the whole work of art. IB average in 2016 was 32 points.

Parents like the fact that the primary principal is very much around in the classrooms, engaged with the kids and monitoring progress. One of the few complaints is that some feel that homework is somewhat inconsistent, with more in the lower school than in the middle school. (School says it has a 'coherent homework policy published in its handbooks'.)

Two full-time counsellors in the high school at Hillingdon alongside an IB co-ordinator. School provides counselling on course selection and university and career planning – beginning in 9th grade. Students who are less likely to be successful with the full IB are given some early guidance, leaving it up to the student and family to decide whether to go for full diploma or certificates. About 60 per cent of students go the IB diploma route. Lots of monitoring and MAP (Measures of Academic Progress – a data-led approach originated in the US) tests to track progress.

The NLE (Native Language Enrichment programme – an ACS schools feature) provides mother tongue instruction. With a minimum of three students of similar ages and levels, languages are supported by classes funded by the school (if fewer than three, the school helps find a tutor but classes are paid by parents), scheduled after school for one hour each week. The idea is to maintain reading, writing and oral proficiency; typically on offer are up to 10 languages including Spanish, French, Dutch, German, Arabic and Japanese taught by native speakers. Parents appreciate this but say they'd like to see more, and it can be difficult to enthuse children about taking the mother tongue when their chums are doing 'fun' after-school activities, so they may revert to Saturday schools. At IB level, the provision ramps up to mother tongue language A courses (Japanese and Dutch currently offered). EAL specialists support pupils in regular classes; beginner non-English speakers are accepted up to grade 7 but after that some proficiency in English is required.

Games, options, the arts: After-school and lunch time clubs for all ages include crafts, Model United Nations, D of E, International Schools Theatre Association, National Honour Society, scouts and sports; there are even middle school magic and Lego robotics clubs. A popular Saturday sports programme for grades K-8 features basketball, tennis, football and baseball. There's been a proposal from the kids for a sleepover in the mansion to see if there's any truth to the rumour that Hillingdon Court is haunted. All suggestions obviously considered!

Quite aside from one parent's comment that sports may not be this school's strong suit, ACS Hillingdon has the highest uptake of the three UK ACS schools: 70 per cent of the students do extracurricular sports. Staff say it's not so much about winning and victory as it is about getting involved, having fun and being well-rounded. But despite all that fun and well-roundedness, the riot of banners and plaques prominently displayed in the gym are testimony to plenty of winning over the years. Recent notable achievements in boys' rugby, basketball and tennis, and girls' basketball and softball. Kids participate in the usual international school sports fixtures, travelling to other countries for tournaments. Sports fields are out in Iver Heath, about a 12-minute bus ride away; an impressive double gymnasium and tennis courts are on site.

Student art work is exhibited everywhere including revolving exhibitions in the head's office (a proud primary student was in the office taking a photo of this to send to his grandmother), and the centrally-located Bridge Gallery. Most music activities (including lots of music tech and a recording studio) are based in Harmony House. Primary music takes place in the main mansion, in a stunning room with high ceilings, sculpted crown mouldings, cornices, coving and massive windows overlooking the gardens – surely one of the most elegant international primary school music rooms on the planet. Many kids (grades 4-12) take private music lessons during the school day, and various musical ensembles are available for middle and high school students. Hillingdon's Got Talent is hugely popular for the whole school community. In fact, parents described the overall arts programme as 'phenomenal'.

When compared to other local international schools, community service at ACS Hillingdon seems a bit more focused on fundraising for good causes rather than hands-on action. That said, IB students do projects at an orphanage in Bulgaria (running for several years now), help in a local nursing home, and also do volunteer activities within the school.

Background and atmosphere: Located in a residential pocket of Hillingdon, a west London suburb on the former estate of Lord Hillingdon, the original Victorian mansion was used during the war as a nursing home. Modern buildings added onto the lovingly maintained 19th century house are a bit at odds with the beautiful proportions of the house, but do accommodate the school's many classes and activities.

Entrance through the manned security gates leads to a morning room conservatory, the reception area, a splendid ground floor entry room used for various meetings and events, the admissions office in a beautiful wood-panelled study, and the music room and high school library – several of which overlook the manicured gardens. The aim has been to give the kids access to these beautiful reception rooms, and not to restrict them to the modern parts where most of their classes now take place. The fact that the head's office is not in the auspicious rooms of the original house, but more centrally located at the heart of the school, says something about the school's values.

Lots of nice bright classrooms, generous space for art rooms, numerous science labs, music rooms. Two areas for drama (the auditorium and a smaller mirrored dance or drama rehearsal studio); two libraries, one each for primary and middle/high school, both located in the mansion.

Each section of the school is in a more or less self-contained area, which parents like. Pre-K and K have their own self-contained pavilion (a calm oasis on the day of our visit) with a small library and colourful outdoor play area behind the main house overlooking the gardens. Beyond the gardens are some outdoor sports grounds and tennis courts, and somewhere out there two vegetable gardens tended by students.

Though the school has won awards for its healthy catering, kids say the lunch room food is 'okay'; but parents love the touch fingerprint payment system as well as the school's flexibility, so kids can buy there or bring their own lunch without the need to handle money.

Hillingdon is one of four ACS International Schools (three in UK, one new one in Qatar), governed by a board of independent, non-executive directors (who typically have international and UK experience across a range of areas including education, finance and law). According to the school's website, the board 'supports the development and the day-to-day operations of the schools'. We interpret this to mean that they support the ACS leadership team that meets regularly and consists of the managing director, the heads of finance, marketing, HR, head of school and the three other ACS heads.

Pastoral care, well-being and discipline: Positive feedback from everyone, including parents, about the strong sense of community. The counsellors are reportedly excellent at helping students integrate into the school and families to cope with the transition to a new country and school, particularly at the primary school level, in addition to supporting the usual issues such as relationships, self-esteem and behaviour. They've also developed with teachers a cyber-safety programme for kids and parents, starting with the youngest children. No mention of serious behaviour issues; good home-school communication; teachers are responsive to emails.

Pupils and parents: About 40 nationalities: 34 per cent US, 14 per cent British, and, among many others, a recent increase in families from the Middle East. Parents are made up of a good many corporate expats (particularly finance and pharmaceuticals, many based at Stockley Park), US embassy and other diplomats, and private entrepreneurs. This international diversity is part of the school's attraction, according to many parents we spoke to. Some of the British students are repatriating from abroad and prefer to stay in the international school environment with its more relaxed and varied teaching approach. As is true in other London international schools, pupil turnover is lower than one might expect: about 17-20 per cent. Families (including staff kids) are staying longer.

A super-active PTSA organises events for parents to socialise and get acclimated with London, and also works with the school to make sure all new families are contacted. Buses are available and cover a wide net: from Maidenhead and High Wycombe to the west, Watford and Amersham to the north, central London to the east, and Heathrow and Windsor to the south. It's a combination of door-to-door or pick up point, and a very good late and late, late bus service is appreciated by families whose children get involved in after-school activities. (Pre K and K students are not allowed to take the late buses.) Forty per cent of the school's kids are bussed from central London. Parents love the availability of this service, but suggest prospective parents consider realistically the likely travel time.

Entrance: Non-selective; will admit students they feel they can serve and who will benefit from the programme. Admission based on previous school records and testing scores; family statements and references from previous school are preferred, though the admissions director understands that for last-minute summer transfers these are sometimes difficult to obtain. Additional assessment or writing samples may be requested. Academic English required for non-native speakers to enter grades 8-12, assessed through a test that can be sent abroad to the current school to administer. Decisions to admit students (grades 5-12) with diagnosed special educational needs are made in consultation with the specialists. It is sometimes possible – and recommended – that prospective students spend a day in the school.

Exit: Students generally leave because of family moves. Very few leave to attend other local schools: most juniors continue on to ACS Hillingdon's middle school and then the high school.

About 40 per cent of students go to North American universities (eg Boston College, Brigham Young, NYU, Notre Dame, San Diego State, Emory, American in the US, McGill, Uni of British Columbia in Canada); about 40 per cent go to UK (UCL, Royal Holloway, LSE, Warwick, Bath, Lancaster, Edinburgh, King's). A handful go to countries such as Japan (eg Waseda, Keio), Australia, Germany and Denmark (eg Technical University). Most of the UK applicants are IB students, though some AP candidates as well.

Money matters: ACS Hillingdon is privately owned by a for-profit corporation, fee-supported with no endowment. The school relies on income from fees, with surpluses reinvested in the schools to maintain high standards; it is evident that there has been continued investment in the school facilities.

Limited need-based financial aid is available from the ACS Foundation. Two full academic sixth form scholarships for talented pupils coming from state schools. No big development and advancement programmes; the PTSA does fundraising activities to support school programmes and events.

Remarks: This is a happy, internationally diverse school that is ticking along nicely. Some holistic soul-searching about this American international educational institution may well lead to interesting developments in the years to come.

A

Alexandra Park School

Bidwell Gardens, London N11 2AZ

Pupils: 1,485 • Ages: 11–18 • Sixth form: 385

Tel: 020 8826 4880
Email: office@apsch.org.uk
Website: www.apsch.org.uk

Headteacher: Since 2008, Mr Michael McKenzie MSC PGCE (late 40s) – educated at a comprehensive in Birmingham, he read chemistry at Nottingham, followed by his teacher training at the Institute of Education. Head of year at William Ellis School in Camden which he cites as one of his 'most enjoyable times in education', then head of sixth form at LaSWAP and a brief stint at Parliament Hill School. Subsequently, deputy and associate head at Beal High School in Redbridge. Familiar and comfortable with Alexandra Park School's ethos before he applied, as the founding head had been his teaching mentor.

His reputation had preceded him and phrases such as 'the consummate PR man', 'fantastic salesman', 'smooth' were not an exaggeration. This head could sell sand to the Sahara – and it doesn't take Einstein to suss out how this once mediocre comprehensive has now become top of the league of schools in Haringey. The head says: 'If I am called a salesman, it's only because my commitment to the product – in this case education – is unequivocal.'

We finally meet (after trying to pin this head down for a while) and are greeted as if we were royalty – beaming smile, firm handshake and the exuberance of somebody who clearly delights in their job. Friendly and chatty – one could almost forget the purpose of our visit and drift into a non-relevant conversation. But be not fooled – this head is very much on the ball, and relishes the school's many achievements and outstanding students. He constantly finds his students 'very entertaining', and delights in meeting different kids every year. 'I have a student now. who is possibly one of the brightest I have ever come across. I am so excited to see how it pans out for that person..I am constantly motivated by bright pupils and those who want to challenge.'

He is a state school head through and through and says he could never be beguiled by the private sector. 'London has a very interesting education system. One of the strengths of this school is the mix. We still have pupils from as far afield as Tottenham from when school's catchment used to exceed five miles.' However, he is realistic that this diversity has changed over time, as the school's popularity has reduced the catchment to 0.7 miles – which by virtue of its location (pricey Muswell Hill), will invariably make it more socially homogeneous. 'I can't control that element, but it will be a long time before that happens. There is still a good mix at APS, which keeps the school a little bit sane.'

Described by parents as being 'very much on the ball'; we imagine this head doesn't allow himself much downtime. Married, no children.

Academic matters: The proud recipient of a World Class Schools award, which means that APS belongs to a pretty exclusive club of only 19 schools nationwide. The award is given to schools who 'equip students with knowledge, skills and confidence to thrive in a challenging international environment where those who succeed take risks and continually pursue improvement.' APS's motto is 'success for all' and the school pulls off the very tricky achievement of being a successful London comprehensive welcoming the full range of abilities and social spectrum. 'Unlike other schools round here, it doesn't pick and choose. It's very inclusive,' said one parent.

The intake may be all-encompassing but the academic values remain traditional. 'We don't play any games with the curriculum,' says the head, and the school is notably strong on core subjects. 2016 results at GCSE: 81 per cent got 5+ A*-C including English and maths, with 38 per cent of grades A*/A. Most pupils take 10, including all three sciences. Spanish, French and Mandarin standard languages with Turkish also an exam option for GCSE and A level. Classics also a popular option with more than 120 pupils studying this at GCSE and A level.

Has specialist status as a science and maths school and an international school. More than 200 students last year had the opportunity of studying in partner schools in France, Spain, South Africa and China. Mandarin on the curriculum here and is more than token – students can spend time on an immersion course in Beijing, with 57 studying the language pre-GCSE, a dozen or so in the sixth form.

Some setting from year 7, depending on the department head – so maths and science are setted, English is not. When students first arrive, they are split into 'Alex' and 'Park' – one lot doing Spanish, the other French. This has been the subject of much heated debate as students are no longer offered the choice. One disgruntled parent told us: 'My family live in Spain, so I was very keen for my daughter to learn Spanish, but she was put into French and there is no room for movement.' Arts and media studies – unsurprisingly in this heartland of the media classes – are notably good so, to counterbalance the trend, has opted for a specialism in science and maths, with a dramatic upswing in results. Good vocational curriculum, with BTecs in sport, business, art, salon services and catering, some taught at the College of North East London. 'It means children who might have been less engaged have something positive and interesting to do, and those taking academic exams have the space to focus,' said one parent.

Strong gifted and talented programme – pupils take early exams in maths, statistics, astronomy and classics. Astronomy has become so popular that the subject caused much controversy last year as the school didn't anticipate how many students would want to do the course, and spaces were limited. One parent told us: 'When we heard that astronomy was being offered as a GCSE, we jumped at the chance – we're middle class after all, of course we'd want our kids to do an extra GCSE!' However, there were many disappointed students who didn't get onto the course at first, 'but credit to the school, they listened to parents and extended the provision', putting an additional astronomy class to cater for all 60 students.

Also notable SEN support under dynamic head of special needs, with additional support in year 7 for those who've not yet achieved the requisite level in maths and English. This school seems to succeed where other large comprehensives fail, in that the large bulk of students who fall in the middle are as well monitored as those at the extreme ends. One parent told us: 'My daughter was very middling in her primary school and didn't have much confidence in her abilities. However, she has really thrived at APS, and whenever I go to parent evenings, one would think my daughter was top in everything.' Another parent told us: 'My son was really floundering before he came here, but he has really blossomed. The teachers get him.'

A National Teaching School, indicating the importance the school places on appointing the best practitioners and ensuring they receive the latest training. The teachers have been particularly praised as being a young and enthusiastic cohort with infectious enthusiasm – although, as with all schools, 'you do get the odd one who makes you think, why are they still here – are they unsackable?' Such is their dedication to the job, that the school is open on Saturdays and Sundays for several weeks before exams, for students who feel they need an extra bit of support: 'This is all off the back of the teachers, and not because I ask them', Mr McKenzie assures us.

Popular sixth form – in 2016, a creditable 43 per cent A*/A grades and 70 per cent A*-B grades at A level; 32 subjects on offer – strongest include English, French, physics and 'a really happening' history department.

Games, options, the arts: Busy, busy, busy. Specialist music and drama with a media suite and dance on offer. The school has a vibrant and very well-resourced music department with large numbers of students choosing to study music at key stage 4 and 5 and also a range of vocational courses including music technology. Extensive extracurricular programme including three choirs, orchestra and jazz band and the department organises an annual concert tour to Europe. More than 250 students take music lessons; 25 peripatetic teachers. Every student is expected to study music and drama each week. Large scale productions of Oliver! and Grease have included around 60 pupils running the entire event, from on stage to backstage to front of house. The school also has an annual Shakespeare performance.

Art also popular, 'one of the reasons my daughter chose this school.' Lucky pupils can draw inspiration in the stunningly bright art studio overlooking the golf course, which the head says he's been trying to claim for years as his office, 'but the art team won't let me.' (We were particularly struck by a fantastic portrait of Barak Obama drawn by a GCSE student). Energetic visual arts with A levels in photography, art and product design, plus a creative and media diploma for those wishing to work on large-scale projects. Also a wonderful facility for textiles and those wishing to do fashion design.

Though relatively limited on-site space for sport, games spill over into adjoining Dunsford Park and plenty of variety to suit all tastes. Basketball, football (West Ham's wonder youngster, Reece Oxford, is a recent ex-student), netball, rugby and cricket are main sports, but judo, aerobics, trampolining, tennis, badminton, wrestling and rugby also part of the offering. Online student newspaper. Eclectic range of after-school clubs includes astronomy, knitting, fashion, pursuit cycling and cheerleading.

Trips a big feature, with more than 120 throughout the year including student exchanges to China (for those studying Mandarin), geography in Iceland, French in the south of France, art in Madrid, politics in Washington and design in New York. Good careers advice with visits to universities and higher educational conferences.

Background and atmosphere: Local parents lobbied the local authority to create a new school in the area and APS was eventually founded in 1999 on the site of a former FE college. A relatively constricted site, which feels more spacious due to the surrounding greenery of Muswell Hill golf course and Durnsford Park. The original mix of pleasant brick buildings, some from the 1950s, some from the 1980s, have been joined by a sleek modern extension (winner of a 2006 Civic Trust Award) and the sixth form centre.

Spatially, it is one of the decision makers for parents choosing (or not) to send their child to the school: 'I would say the lack of space at APS is the only downer at this school. At lunch time there isn't really anywhere for the younger students to hang out, so they gather in groups around the old car park.' However, this is shortly to change as the school is in the process of acquiring some of the land from the neighbouring golf course (which by the time this goes to print should be in the bag). Mr McKenzie says: 'Now pupils won't just wistfully look out onto all that beautiful green belt – they can actually benefit from it.'

Parents unanimous on the remarkably welcoming atmosphere: 'Everyone from the lady on the gate who checks uniform to the school receptionist makes you feel at home'. Even the police officer seeing kids onto after-school buses does it with a smile. Parents also enthuse about the school's multi-culturalism and inclusiveness ('They really try to be for everybody') and genuine concern ('It's far more nurturing than some of the other local comprehensives'). But concern is not cosseting. Mr McKenzie is also a very visible presence and is on the gate most days: 'He is very chatty to us parents – sometimes a bit too chatty and I worry that my daughter and her friends will think I'm terribly un-cool hanging out with the head.'

Pastoral care, well-being and discipline: Traditional values apply. 'Kids need firm boundaries and it's important for the school to set them,' says the head. 'We expect them to be at school, on time, in uniform, ready to work.' Smart red and black kit is strictly enforced. 'There used to be a gang who wore their uniform in a special way and that's now all ended,' said one parent approvingly. Mr McKenzie also tries to clamp down on big clusters of students hanging around outside the local café at lunchtime, occupying the pavements. Not the school's best PR (although we have to say there are very few other places for them to go).

Behaviour in general is 'excellent' and school aims to keep it that way by instilling a sense of responsibility. 'We're training pupils to choose to do the right thing.' Misdemeanors are promptly and firmly dealt with – 'When my son got into a fight, there was absolutely no messing. They threw the rulebook at him'. Whilst Mr McKenzie considers himself to be fair, he is not one to pussyfoot around; 'This is definitely not a non-excluding school. If a child is making it difficult for other children to learn and we have exhausted all other options – we will exclude.'

'Other options' could include a trip to The Bridge, a prospect so mortifying that the mere mention is enough to make even the tardiest of students get their act together. One parent told us: 'My son is a bright child and generally well behaved, but has the potential to be swayed by peers. He was sent to The Bridge fairly early on, to deliver a message to a teacher. A stroke of genius'. According to that parent, the experience was enough to ensure that her son was 'never late or naughty in class again'. After further questions, it pans out that The Bridge is a fully staffed, self-contained base providing a wide range of interventions to those 'who present challenges in class.' One parent said: 'I imagine that children with a nervous disposition would probably be terrified.'

Drugs not a notable issue. 'It's bizarre,' says the head; 'at a previous school we had an incident every week. Here perhaps they're more savvy, more mature and are listening to our advice.' Weapons, too, had been conspicuously absent until just one recent incident in school – but the offender was promptly excluded.

Year 7 has its own 'transition manager', and one parent we spoke to, whose child had joined from neighbouring Rhodes Avenue, told us that 'there were a few opportunities during the summer term for new students to spend a day at APS and be taken around to orientate themselves.' Pupils remain in the same tutor groups for five years with a director of studies for each year. They're also supported by learning mentors and counsellors. About 56 pupils with statements of special needs/ EHC plans have mainly cognitive rather than behavioural difficulties and the school copes well with autism, Asperger's and Down's. One parent told us: 'I shopped around many schools before I chose APS for my son because of his very particular needs. I have to say, they have been amazing for him. If he was upset they would know about it. And nobody laughs at you here for being different.' The pupils we met were a lovely blend of savvy, street smart and witty ('the only thing that's missing at the school is a statue of me') – whilst polite and thoughtful. They shared one common notion – that they were all really happy to be there and felt listened to and looked after.

A

Communication between parents and school clearly a strong point – 'All my emails, however trivial, get answered promptly'. And various methods of positive re-enforcement are used: 'We often get phone calls home or postcards telling us how well our daughter is doing.' They also have a commendation system of silver, bronze and gold: 'Their rewards system is brilliant. It makes the pupils want to do well. '

Pupils and parents: Wide social spread, from the comfortable middle-class suburbs near the gates to some of the most deprived kids in the country – 'a high proportion on the cusp of social needs'. Middle classes tend to dominate the PTA, which runs endless jumble sales and bazaars and is strongly involved in the day-to-day running of the school, but the kids themselves mix well. Very supportive parents – 'Parents helped set it up and want to make it work'.

Entrance: Around 1600 applications for 232 places. Usual priority to looked-after children, those with statements of special needs and siblings, then distance from the gates, which is now less than a mile (0.7 this year). The largest percentage (approx 20 per cent) from adjoining high-achieving primary Rhodes Avenue, as well as from Bounds Green, Our Lady of Muswell, Bowes, Coldfall, Coleridge, Hollickwood and Muswell Hill and another 30 or so local primaries.

Majority of existing pupils continue into sixth form of 340, with 70 or so joining from other local schools. External applicants for A levels should have at least five GCSEs A*-C, with Bs in A level subject choice. (The head has been known to invite pre-A level students to his office, to lay out the pros of staying on at APS, if he gets a whiff that they may abandon ship for another local sixth form.)

Exit: Some 20 per cent leave after GCSEs. Around 60 per cent to Russell Group universities, including regular places at Oxbridge and some medics. 'What is heartening is in the last three years these Oxbridge students have read a range of courses including English literature, law, history, maths, modern languages, music and natural sciences.' Other popular destinations include LSE, UCL, Manchester, Bristol, Bath, Nottingham, Warwick, Central St Martins, Queen's Belfast and Trinity Laban.

Money matters: Training school and academy trust status bring in extra funding.

Remarks: A notably welcoming place for children (and adults) from across the borough. Not an academic pressure cooker but a school with high standards for all.

Alleyn's School

Townley Road, London SE22 8SU

Pupils: 1,245 • Ages: 4–18 • Sixth form: 302 • C of E

Fees: £15,651 – £18,126 pa

Tel: 020 8557 1500
Email: registrar@alleyns.org.uk
Website: www.alleyns.org.uk

Headmaster: Since 2010, Dr Gary Savage MA PhD Cantab (40s). Previously undermaster at Westminster School, joining after 10 years' teaching at Eton, where his roles included head of history, community service coordinator and housemaster of the scholars' house. A historian of 18th century France, has a passion for watching sport (Ipswich Town supporter – he grew up in Suffolk and was state school educated) and for the arts. Has taught himself German, and he and his wife Natalie (a television and film producer) have a pied à terre in Berlin. Would like to encourage in his pupils his own appetite for learning.

'Imaginative....very charming...a good hand on the tiller,' say parents. Certainly a suspicion that he is more elitist in outlook than his predecessors, and parents fear that the school's liberal, creative ethos may be lost. Not so, he insists: 'I want our pupils to do very well in public exams – but emphatically not by turning Alleyn's into a hothouse. I want to expand horizons intellectually and socially without diluting or compromising the Alleyn's ethos. I want to work with not against the grain'.

Head of junior school: Since September 2015, Mr Simon Severino, previously head of St Andrew's Prep School, Eastbourne. He read geography at Oxford, started teaching at Culford Prep in Suffolk and then went to Dulwich Prep London as head of geography and deputy head. He joined St Andrew's in 2010. He is married with two young children.

Academic matters: English and maths taught in small groups from day one in junior school. Formal setting for maths from year 4 – 'For those in the B sets it's mostly about increasing their confidence and self-esteem'. Maths mentors come over from the senior school to help. Specialist teachers for French, music, art and PE from the beginning, and for every subject from year 4.

Support includes speech and language therapist, a literacy expert and learning support assistants – 'We've had children here with quite serious learning differences and we've done a great job with them. That's one of the things we're most proud of'. Pupils say: 'I like their attitude towards learning. The teachers help you to get better in a very calm way. The classes are very friendly.' Signs round the school during our visit proclaimed that it was anti-bullying week.

Used to be the junior partner of the Dulwich triumvirate of schools in academic terms. No longer: the increasing popularity of coeducation and a more selective entry has helped its rise up the league tables. 2016 saw 90 per cent A*-B and 70 per cent A*/A grades at A level; 92 per cent A*/A at GCSE. Maths much the most popular A level subject, as one would expect, but otherwise a good and broad spread of arts and sciences.

The head is 'passionate about non-examined academic enrichment'. He has instituted the Governor's research project prize, which is awarded for a piece of sixth form research – prize-winning subjects have ranged from an anthropological study on ape/human divergence to one on the mating habits of arachnids. He is encouraging a wider range of visiting speakers (the Guide listened to a fascinating talk by a Médecins Sans Frontières nurse; A C Grayling and the Archbishop of Canterbury have been other recent visitors), and has appointed a KS3 co-ordinator focussing on thinking skills – 'I want to celebrate the life of the mind without compromising our buzz, busyness and happiness'.

Everyone is screened during year 7 to help identify any learning difficulties. At the end of the year, staff get together to decide who is likely to need extra support or an ed psych assessment. Full-time learning support co-ordinator can give individual term-long learning skills courses to those who are struggling. 'They're very quick at picking up when things are not going right,' said a parent. 'We get detailed reports, and I really feel they're on the case.'

Part of the Southwark Schools Learning Partnership, which involves staff and students from 11 state and private schools sharing experiences and working together to improve teaching and learning. Now developing links with the state Sydenham and Forest Hill sixth form.

Games, options, the arts: Has always been viewed as the most liberal and arty of the local independent schools – and, of course, attracts many families from the creative professions. 'Fabulous' theatre (named after a post-war English master who set up the National Youth Theatre) hosts lower, middle and upper school plays as well as many sixth form and visiting productions each year. Full time stage manager, and students help with lighting and sound. 'The standard is amazing,' said a parent. 'They've really brought out my son's talents' – though inevitably it can be hard for lesser mortals to get parts in shows. 'But in the sixth form there's much more scope and they can put on their own performances,' said a student.

Large numbers play instruments – flourishing orchestras, choirs and ensembles taking part in masterclasses and performing at 'astonishingly high standards'. Very impressive art, with many taking it to A level and a very high proportion of A* grades. Not a school that is sniffy about media studies, which has its own well-equipped studio with the latest high-tech editing equipment. Food tech is a GCSE option and there's a popular cookery club.

Enviable sports facilities include floodlit netball court in the centre of the quad and floodlit Astroturf, alongside sports hall, swimming pool, acres of playing fields. Sport for all but excellence too: whether the 1st XI footballers who recently reached the final of the Independent Schools Football Association cup, the girl who plays hockey for England, the extraordinary water polo teams (boys and girls have reached the national finals in every age group and the U14 girls were national champions for several years running), the fives enthusiasts or the cycling club which meets at the Herne Hill Velodrome. 'There's so much on offer that everyone finds something they want to do,' said a pupil.

Volunteering is important – 'They take it very seriously' – and houses raise funds for their own chosen charities. CCF very popular – opportunities to try gliding, go camping, do adventure training, learn radio communication – as is D of E, with large numbers at all levels. Huge numbers of overseas trips: eg football tour to Germany, geography society expedition to Iceland, religious studies trip to India.

Excellent junior school art in newly converted studio, set up to resemble a fish tank during our visit with strings of fish hanging down the windows. Pottery popular: 'Edward de Waal did a workshop recently and showed us how to make our own kiln and fire our own pottery'. Colourful artistic displays all round the school, and the Dulwich Picture Gallery is a regular destination.

Everyone learns a stringed instrument in years 2-4 and a brass or woodwind instrument in year 5, and many keep it up. Clubs include jazz band, choirs and L'Orchestre de la Grand Salle. Plenty of other music and drama – school tends to attract creative families so lots of talent/parental encouragement. The day of our visit was hip-hop day and year 6, in tee shirts they had designed themselves, were busy learning dance moves. Africa and India days also combine art, music and dance, and Alleyn's Junior Has Talent competition is a highlight of the year.

Sport particularly strong in juniors, with the enviable senior school facilities including rolling green acres just next door. Large numbers of sports clubs include ballet and taekwondo; A, B and often C teams play against other schools in sports ranging from girls' football to biathlon. Pupils we met were very enthusiastic: 'I do seven clubs a week, nearly all sport'; 'There's something that suits everyone'.

Background and atmosphere: A direct descendent of the foundation Alleyn's College of God's Gift, set up in 1619 by Edward Alleyn, wealthy actor and proprietor of taverns, brothels and bear-baiting pits. Part of the foundation funded Dulwich College; in 1882, the upper and lower schools split, with the lower becoming Alleyn's Boys' School. It became a public school in 1919 and a direct grant grammar school from 1958, until that status was abolished in 1975. At that point it became independent and went co-ed. Other schools within the foundation include JAGS and several state schools.

Pleasant setting in between chic Dulwich village and trendy East Dulwich. Unpretentious red-brick facade of four-storey main building masks the main site, with its landscaped quads and acres of playing fields. A continuous development programme has, most recently, resulted in the dramatic Edward Alleyn building with its theatre, lecture room, sixth form area and Costa coffee bar, plus refurbed RV Jones science building with rooftop observatory. Large sports hall, music school and excellent library.

Junior school a very busy, buzzy place tucked away in a quiet corner of the senior school site. Light, bright classrooms include a conservatory and a playground that doubles as an outdoor classroom. Magnificent IT suite; iPads integrated into lessons – 'We have embraced new technology'; giant iPad in art room. Science garden has wildlife pond, herb, flower and vegetable plots and ex-battery chickens.

Parents attracted by its reputation for a liberal, stimulating environment, with its history as a direct grant grammar school and perhaps less pretension than some more traditional public schools – 'We weren't interested in putting our children through a system that gave them an over-inflated view of their position in society,' said one parent. Generous bursaries help the social mix.

Pastoral care, well-being and discipline: A very happy place, say parents, with good pastoral care and good communications – 'Any questions get answered immediately'. The head concurs: 'When things go wrong we deal with it carefully, kindly and robustly. We have a strong pastoral set-up with many layers, and we all work together to ensure that any children with problems are helped. Everything else is secondary to this.'

Lower school – years 7 and 8 – has its own building, providing a sheltered introduction to the senior school and, say parents, particularly good individual pastoral care. Year 9 upwards join houses, which give a family feel and opportunities for those who don't make school teams/plays to compete in inter-house events, eg music, drama and sport.

Head reckons only a handful of bullying incidents a year – 'It is a remarkable testament to the ethos of the place' – and parents agree. 'We've never come across any bullying. It probably helps being co-ed, but it is a very well-balanced place'.

Very few exclusions – 'I've had to do a couple of suspensions – for low level disruptions and disengagement – but we can generally get them back on side. Sometimes children give you no room for manoeuvre and you have to say it's not working. But we tackle these things educationally and pastorally from the beginning, and generally the children buy into this'.

Congenial atmosphere. School aims to 'encourage respectfulness between adults and children. We're after more than good manners: we want our children to have the confidence to communicate with adults'. 'All the people here are very friendly,' say pupils. 'Even if you're not best friends with someone, you just get on with them.'

Pupils and parents: More bohemian than the other Dulwich independents – 'It's always attracted pupils of journalists, rock stars and theatre people,' commented a parent. The least multi-ethnic of the three schools, probably because high-achieving ethnic minority families tend to go for single-sex education. 'I'd love to see us reflect more broadly the south east London community,' says the head, 'and I hope that a wider range of families will feel confident applying to us. I don't want us to be

A

a bubble community.' Pupils tend to be 'charming, articulate, incredibly polite,' said a parent. Has produced an unusual number of well-known actors, musicians and writers.

Ex-pupils include actors Jude Law, Nancy Carroll, Jessie Ware, Simon Ward and Julian Glover and director Felix Barrett; musicians Florence Welch, Felix White, Gabriel Prokofiev and Ed Simons; scientists Prof John Isaacs, Prof RV Jones and surgeon Prof Lord Kakkar; plus Air Marshall Sir Christopher Harper, writers CS Forester and VS Pritchett and former Sun editor, Kelvin MacKenzie.

Entrance: Tends to be very local at junior level – 'We try to be centred in the community'. At 4+, 20 places and some 200 applicants. No sibling policy – 'We could fill the place with siblings, and we like to encourage some diversity'. Intakes also at 7+ and 9+ – 'If they don't get in the first time, we encourage them to see it as a postponement and to try again later'. Assessment 'looks for children who can participate in a very busy and structured timetable'. 'We try to take in children who have a lot to contribute.

Main senior entry at 11, with 125 places and around 500 applicants. Reasoning, English and maths papers. Automatic entry for junior school pupils, but the occasional one who has been struggling may have a probationary year: 'We try very hard to make it work. We will see it through if we possibly can'. Generally a third of year 7 comes from the junior school, a third from local preps and a third from state primaries. 'We like to take as broad a range as possible, but they must be bright enough to flourish, to enjoy the pace and buzz of life here. We're looking for those who will have a fabulous time.' Around 15 places at 13, with English, maths and reasoning assessments. At both levels, two-fold interview process, in small groups and individually. Up to 20 places at 16 (but often fewer) – exams in three prospective A level subjects plus a critical thinking test.

Increasing popularity means that local families can no longer be confident of a place for all their children. Parents who went to Alleyn's themselves sometimes irked to find the academic bar has risen above their reach, with places going to those from all points east, west, south and even north of the river.

Exit: All junior school pupils have right of entry to senior school (one or two move elsewhere, often with scholarships) though everyone takes the 11+ exam and year 7 could be a probationary year for a child who is struggling to keep up. 'We value the real contribution of the child. A boy with dyslexia might have trouble with English but be brilliant at maths and go on to play for the school football team. We'd rather have a hard worker than someone who is bright but lazy.' The transfer exam 'is about celebrating hard work and achievement, not just about winning scholarships. Everyone gets a leaving certificate which includes details of what they have done for the life of the school.'

Few leave after GCSEs. Nearly all year 13 leavers to university, including Oxbridge (21 offers in 2016) and medical schools. Popular destinations are Bristol, Edinburgh, Leeds and Durham. Several to art foundation courses, one or two to drama school or music college, a few to American colleges, otherwise mostly to top UK universities to do a huge mix of subjects ranging from natural sciences to social anthropology.

Money matters: Enviably well-endowed with funds from the Dulwich Estate and from the Worshipful Company of Saddlers, which pay for a generous staffing ratio and the ability to carry out a rolling programme of improvements. Some 30 pupils on 100 per cent bursaries and many more on 50 per cent upwards – school is fundraising to increase that number. Scholarships (maximum £3000 a year) for music, art and sporting as well as academic excellence.

Remarks: Traditionally a liberal and creative school, beloved of south London media families, which is increasing its academic clout. Parents like the fact the children are 'well-balanced kids with lots to do'. One commented: 'We really feel we landed on our feet – it's a superb school.'

Allfarthing Primary School

St Ann's Crescent, London SW18 2LR

Pupils: 400 • Ages: 3–11

Tel: 020 8874 1301
Email: info@allfarthing.wandsworth.sch.uk
Website: www.allfarthing.wandsworth.sch.uk/

Headteacher: Since January 2017, Tom Holmes, previously deputy head at St Mary's in Richmond. Has also worked at Honeywell and at a primary school in Surrey. He is keen on sport eg touch rugby, cricket and cycling, and lives in Twickenham with his wife Kathryn.

Entrance: At 3+ into the nursery or 4+ into reception. Priority goes to siblings and then those living closest to the school. Attending the nursery does not guarantee a place in the infant department. For occasional places in older age groups contact the school to check availability and put your name on their waiting list.

Exit: Popular state choices are Graveney, St Cecilia, Burntwood, Ricards Lodge, ARK Academy and Bolingbroke Academy; odd one to Kingston or Surrey grammar schools. Around 30 per cent to independents, Emanuel, Ibstock Place, Wimbledon High School, Trinity and Whitgift.

Remarks: Situated on rather a busy corner, the tall 1920s building offers large, bright classrooms; eyes are immediately drawn to displays of children's work and art designed to capture imagination and interest. Standards are high and parents note a recent increase in monitoring and assessing progress across the age groups to ensure underachievement is picked up and addressed swiftly. Reception and nursery classes have indoor and outdoor classrooms, ample resources laid out thoughtfully. Early years classes follow the Read Write phonics programme offering a good grounding in literacy skills. Overall, school's results in English are impressive; lots of drama and speaking and listening activities are incorporated into the curriculum. Maths results not quite as high but catching up. Large inner-city mix; around 24 languages spoken in the school; everyone learns Spanish from year 3. Parents report good traditional teaching with interesting history and geography projects alongside whizzy IT; all classes can access iPads, MacBooks and trolleys of laptops. Graded outstanding, the school does very well in national assessments and has an above-average added value score. Curriculum is further extended with masterclasses provided by special partnerships with Graveney for ICT, Burntwood for sciences and Southfields for PE. School feels SEN help should be delivered as required through small group or individual teaching, in addition to speech and occupational therapists visiting the school.

Two multi-purpose halls provide space for PE, assemblies and lunches cooked on site in the recently refurbished kitchens. On site sports include lacrosse, football, hockey and cricket; older pupils are bussed to Battersea Park School for swimming lessons.

Sports days are held at Wimbledon Park where year 5 has a week of water sports, courtesy of the Friends Group. PTA fundraising has resulted in a new school playground, including outdoor classroom and nature zone, with growing beds for the children to learn about growing food, composting and studying mini-beasts. There is also new climbing equipment and table tennis tables.

Music features highly on the daily curriculum; super purpose-built accommodation with a dedicated music teacher. Opportunity for all from year 4 to learn an instrument, with many achieving grade 6 before moving to secondary school. Each child chooses a string or wind instrument for group lessons in year 3 and there is a budding choir that performs in the community. Parents say choir has really developed over the past year and are particularly impressed at the large number of boys who have joined in. Encouraging setting for musical families, currently something of a rarity for a state primary.

Remarkably good Friends of Allfarthing Group is an asset, raising money for all sorts of activities and equipment through traditional and creative ways. Friends contribute throughout the school, baking biscuits for meetings and fêtes and writing an introductory guide book for newcomers. Parent volunteers and staff recently collaborated to run a very successful lettuce planting project for the UNICEF Day for Change. Monthly book club lottery raises funds for the library and other book purchases. All tastes taken into consideration for after-school clubs, with parents and pupils suggesting some of the choices available.

Pupils are encouraged to voice their opinions through the school council and class reps, on school rules, sensible behaviour and other issues that benefit everyone's participation and enjoyment. A few rumbles from parents over staff changes and prospects of building works; most remain positive and feel the changes will be for the best. Overall a popular school, working hard to continually improve and develop provision, along with a number of little extras, or not so little, as the case may be.

The American School in London

1 Waverley Place, London NW8 0NP

Pupils: 1,350 • Ages: 4–18 • Sixth form: 240

Fees: £24,150 – £28,650 pa

Tel: 020 7449 1220
Email: admissions@asl.org
Website: www.asl.org

Head of School: Since 2007, Coreen R Hester (degrees in English literature and education, Stanford University), previously head of Hamlin School in San Francisco. Was ASL's high school principal from 1995-1997, when her children were both pupils there. Early in her career, Mrs Hester taught English at University Liggott in Michigan; she then spent 10 years at the Branson School as teacher, dean, college counsellor, assistant head and interim head of school. Was also previously director of the Western Region Educational Services.

This energetic Californian inherited a well-oiled machine in a newly-renovated campus. She has aimed to strengthen the already high-qualified teaching staff, looked at the role of support staff and reviewed the curriculum so that what is taught to 5 year olds makes sense when they are 15. Highly visible, 'larger than life', with 'lots of presence', she gets lots of praise from parents who describe her as 'so smart and insightful', and 'couldn't be more approachable'. 'She's a great communicator'. 'The impact she has had on the school is huge. She has really upped the game for the teachers. We think the world of her!'

Retiring in July 2017. Her successor will be Robin Appleby, most recently director the University of Chicago Laboratory Schools. BA in English from Dartmouth College, and an MA in English literature from the State University of New York at Buffalo. Began her career teaching writing and literature at the State University of New York at Buffalo, followed by teaching and administration positions at the Nichols School in Buffalo, New York, and Hathaway Brown School in Shaker Heights, Ohio. She then became high school principal at the American School of The Hague before joining the Global Education Management System (GEMS) organization in Dubai, first as deputy superintendent and then superintendent/CEO of the Dubai American Academy (DAA). Alongside her role at DAA, Robin served in her last two years as principal and brand director for the GEMS American curriculum schools. Robin is married to John Leavey, who is English and Dutch.

Academic matters: ASL's reputation is tops and an expectation of excellence must be pumped in through the air ducts; parents say that ASL aligns itself with the top US independent and public schools. Classes are no larger than 20 (15 is the average in high school) and children are encouraged to take risks and view mistakes as natural learning. To quote a high schooler, 'Being smart is admired here. It's not about showing off, it's about showing what you can do.'

The lower school's project-approach aims to develop attitudes and habits that set up these youngsters for life-long learning, with critical thinking skills and solid foundations. During our stroll through the lower school we saw a full range of teaching contexts – children working one-to-one with teachers and assistants, working in pairs, small groups working collaboratively on projects, whole class groups seated in a big circle on the floor playing a language game, or engaged in teacher-led instruction using an interactive whiteboard. Spanish is introduced from the start, and lower school classes occasionally spend the day at the school's learning centre in Canons Park for outdoor and environmental studies.

The middle school programme is designed to develop independence and organisation. While some parents initially worry that middle school begins at grade 5, a tad younger than the norm in many US and international schools, the structure is well designed so that grades 5 and 6 share one floor, and grades 7 and 8 another, facilitating the transition from primary to secondary education. 'Think of it as lower middle and upper middle school,' parents say. 'It works.'

High school is preparation for higher education with plenty of options in several subject areas, including over 20 AP subjects, making ASL one of the most prolific AP schools outside the US. In 2016, 89 per cent of AP exams taken by ASL students were scored at a grade 3 or higher (out of a possible 5). The school benefits from the work of a K-12 teaching and learning director who has overseen a review of the entire curriculum.

Older students say that this is a school where you need to be motivated and work hard. It's more of an unspoken expectation throughout, but all confirm there is good support in place and teachers willing to put in the extra hours to help. However, it comes a bit easier if you are proactive about seeking that help out. One parent said, 'If a child is highly sensitive, it is not always the kindest and gentlest place to be. But if they can access the education, it is a great experience'. All the departments are strong, improvements to language provision previously noted, although we have spoken to some dual-language families and kids who say they no longer consider themselves to be truly bilingual, having not maintained the other language.

ASL keeps up with US pedagogy, forging strong relations with leading US educationalists, such as Project Zero at Harvard, and not only sends teachers there to learn as part of the school's generous professional development programme but also hosts ASL learning institutes so other educators in the UK and abroad benefit. Technology is integrated into the classroom beginning in kindergarten. High school students bring their own laptops or can use the many on site.

ASL can handle students with mild learning problems; specialists provide individual support; spaces are limited and there's an additional fee for the programme. One parent we spoke to wanted to dispel the myth that ASL does not deal well with learning problems. Her child's problem, overlooked by previous schools, was diagnosed right away and the SEN team has been 'fabulous'. The English as an Additional Language (EAL) programme helps non-English speakers up to grade 4 come up to speed for better integration in the mainstream. Intermediate and advanced English speakers are integrated up to grade 10. After that, total fluency is required to handle the rigorous academics.

Average tenure is nine years which is good for international schools. Not only do 75 per cent of the teachers have higher degrees, so do many of the teaching assistants.

Games, options, the arts: Academics are important but so are the arts, sports and other activities, with a growing emphasis on community service. Framed paintings, drawings and photos by former students line the walls, forming part of the school's permanent collection and setting the bar for the arts. Everyone learns an instrument in the band or orchestra and sings in the choir through middle school. These enthusiastic musicians then take up seats in the bands and orchestras at the high school level. Opportunities available to travel in Europe with the choir and orchestras, or with the drama programme. Photo labs and art studios busy throughout the day. The new auditorium looks like a not-so-mini version of the Barbican, and it's always in use either for concerts and plays or hosting speakers.

Sports are part of the DNA at ASL but, unlike some stateside schools, sports at ASL complement the academics rather than competing with them. At least 85 per cent of high school students play on at least one school team. There are two gyms, a new swimming pool and 21 acres of playing fields a tube ride away (students are bussed there, though distance means that this is restricted to after-school activities) and a display case filled with trophies leaves no doubt about the school's athletic standing in the international school world.

Special interest clubs too many to mention – all the usual ones and lots of unusual ones, in school and off campus. The PCA funds up to £1,000 for a well-thought-out one-time project put forward by faculty, students or staff. The head also has a fund to support new projects: for example, the school's robotics programme began this way.

High school students accompanied by faculty members participate in annual spring Alternatives programme, choosing between recreational, academic or cultural activities done over four days. Community service with new emphasis on local interaction has 270 kids volunteering in charities and projects based within a few miles' radius. They're also building bridges with the nearby comprehensive school thanks to a student-led joint-school Lego robotics club initiative. The kids themselves form lots of service-related clubs that do their own independent fundraising for good causes they want to support. Students encouraged to assume leadership roles, challenge themselves and take advantage of London. Field trips, not just in London but all over Europe and Africa, organised to broaden perspectives.

Background and atmosphere: Founded in 1951 as an alternative to the British schools for London's burgeoning American diplomatic, military and corporate community, this London city school uses every inch of its space. Compact brick buildings set on a city block encase the 1,350 student body, which is at capacity. Security fencing surrounds the perimeters and smart security men keep a watchful eye on all comings and goings (no entry without a school pass or photo id). Outdoor spaces adapted to different age groups.

ASL has a strong and proactive board of trustees in the style of US independent schools. The lower school has a pod centre for each grade level; classrooms radiate from a central information space housing computers, reading corners and other teaching resources. The middle school students move around between classes more, and the high school is what you would expect: animated kids rushing around halls, definitely happy to be there. Pupil work is everywhere, for example an impressive student-designed notice board about the US elections conveyed both the US-essence of the school and the calibre of creativity and critical thinking these kids possess.

Middle and high school classes run for 80 minutes with an hour for lunch. Students bring their lunch or buy it in the cafeteria, which is very good, though many in grades 9-12 opt for the off-campus privilege. We hear some grumbles about pressure on lunch facilities; one parent said she was not particularly happy with the early timing of her lower school daughter's lunch sitting. Lower school students eat a packed lunch (from home or purchased from ASL) in their classroom.

Pastoral care, well-being and discipline: It seems that students at ASL work hard and play hard. The kids are motivated to try hard to do their best, to try lots of new activities or get better at the ones they excel at. While allowing for individual initiative and responsibility, the organisation and structure is in place to ensure plenty of support so that no one drifts off course.

Parents report few serious disciplinary problems, saying the school plays it 'close to the vest', and that if there are, they're dealt with quietly and confidentially. School rules not onerous but expectation is that they will be followed and the school will take transgressions seriously. When news circulated about a recent (and rare) cheating incident, the head responded swiftly and firmly. Parents say, however, that teachers and principals are not always consistent in doling out the consequences and sanctions which result from misbehaviour.

The school recommends that families abide by US drinking rules – no alcohol for under 21s – but this is difficult to enforce. If word gets back to the high school dean about a party, he phones the host's parents just to make sure they are aware. At times this makes him more popular with parents than the kids. No dress code, but jeans seem to be the uniform of choice. If you do see the odd shirt and tie, it means a team is off to an away game.

Students arrive at this urban school with different levels of 'street wisdom' and 'stranger danger' awareness. Parents appreciate the way ASL takes pains to speak frankly to parents and kids about the potential problems and equip students with the right skills to protect themselves. A noteworthy issue is that middle schoolers are sometimes targets for muggings in the streets of affluent St John's Wood. Perpetrators are usually other kids looking for the portable technology now standard kit for many students. Nobody ever gets hurt, but it happens a few times a year. Door-to-door bus service available in the morning and after school and also at the end of the after-school programme, covering central, north and west London.

ASL high schoolers do not have an advisory or home room teacher, a concern for some parents; instead, a dean of year looks after the year group, working in partnership with principals and subject teachers. In grade 11 deans hand over to the university counsellors, each of whom has a light case load so they can give plenty of attention to each of their charges. Daily bulletins and notices are sent by email to all.

Pupils and parents: The school may be in London but the tone is definitely American – let's call it 'global American'. Eighty per cent of the 1,350 students hold US passports, and half of those are multi-passport holders from dual-national families. There are 50 nationalities in the school and the group of great kids who turned up during break to meet the GSG visitor didn't contain a single American. As a rule, ASL students are bright, curious and confident, and willing to express their views about anything you ask them. But, as one middle school pupil observed, 'international passports do not make a place international; the school is pretty American'. The popular award-winning student newspaper The Standard debates this question from time to time. Non-Americans at this school are largely attracted by the academic, social and college counselling preparation for entry into US universities. Lots of 'third culture kids' (professional parents raising children in a country not their own), and expats from the finance world, though the transiency is diminishing as more families stay longer. As one parent said, 'If you are an American coming from another international school, it feels American, but if you are from the suburbs of Chicago or Westchester County, it feels international'.

The school has revised its mission statement to incorporate the 'global perspective', and 'bursting the bubble' is one of Hester's goals for the school, which she describes as 'somewhere in the mid-Atlantic'. After 9/11 the school heightened its security and understandably drew inward but now, Hester explains, 'it's time to bring ASL into London, and London into ASL', with more intentional planning for programming, including emphasis on community service activities.

There is a perception on the part of some parents that it's economic diversity that is lacking, with concerns that 'too many kids are fretting about the right trainers or Prada handbags, and the presence of a few kids so wealthy that their security guards come to school with them, which is a bit weird.' This is something the school hopes will change through its diversity statement – and a target to grow the financial aid pot.

It is worth noting that lots of ASL families are there for the second time. Families sometimes choose London as a posting in part because of ASL; it is regarded by many as one of the key attractions of moving here.

Entrance: Admission is based on school records, teacher recommendations and standardised test results (ERB/SSATs). Turnover is diminishing, with waiting lists at all grades, which means there may not be space for all family members. Unlike other international schools, ASL will only accept applications a year before admission; the first round of offers is made on 1 February. After that, it's rolling admissions.

Huge praise for the school's support for new arrivals – both parents and kids – including seminars, social events and newsletters. 'It's tremendous how much they reach out to pull you in, because they know you are lost.'

Exit: Most students leaving before graduation do so because of family transfers. For those planning to finish the course, university preparation work begins in grade 11 for students and parents. ASL's US Advanced Placements (APs) are welcomed by British universities, and although more ASL students are getting offers from top UK universities, most still opt for the USA. Graduates go on to Ivy Leagues, as well as the major state universities in the US (Harvard, Yale, Princeton, Stanford, University of Pennsylvania), the major players in Canada (McGill, Toronto) and British Russell Group unis (Cambridge, Bristol, Queen Mary London). A recent graduate entered University of Virginia as a prestigious Jefferson Scholar with full university funding.

Money matters: Tuition covers textbooks, laboratory fees and all required activities except for the music tour for band, orchestra and choir members. There are occasional additional expenses – usually travel – associated with some middle and high school classes. Tuition does not include expenses for trips related to extracurricular activities such as athletics, Model UN or service learning. Needs-based financial aid is available for tuition and also for school-related trips and activities.

Parents say there is a definite expectation that everyone (including staff) will participate in the school's fundraising initiatives; this presents a challenging adjustment for some, particularly families who are less familiar with a US independent school tradition. Besides annual funds, there is a major auction every other year ('Think Sotheby's,' one parent said.) Another parent said that the level of importance attributed to the expectation of significant donations is a lingering legacy of previous heads, and the days when a family's status at school was, albeit subtly, linked to the size of a financial benefaction, are long gone.

Remarks: In her opening letter to the parents the head spoke about 'striving for the best in American education'. Well, this school isn't far from that. The resources and facilities are excellent, attitudes are positive and results are good. Bright, curious, motivated kids do well here and those who are in the middle of the road end up surprising their parents.

Annemount School

18 Holne Chase, London N2 0QN

Pupils: 100 • Ages: 2.75–7

Fees: £8,850 – £16,125 pa

Tel: 020 8455 2132
Email: headteacher@annemount.co.uk
Website: www.annemount.co.uk

Head Teacher: Since 1993, Ms Geraldine Maidment (50s), previously head of Hilltop Nursery in Hampstead. First teaching experience was as an English teaching assistant in Vienna, during her University College London year abroad, whilst studying German and history of art. Worked at Sotheby's before teaching at Basset House School. A widely travelled linguist (she speaks five languages), she has visited and attended schools in many different countries. During a two-year sabbatical in Colorado, she did a masters in child and family studies at Denver University and joined a school board concerned with social and emotional issues of school age children. Has also been on UK local government committees related to early years and works as an educational consultant for pupils who need schooling advice at any stage.

Has two grown up daughters and five step-grandchildren, who have all attended Annemount. Parents say: 'She's very on the ball and intelligent.' 'She's not going to be your best friend,' commented one (another 'begged to differ'), 'but she's incredible with the children'; 'She's very strict, but in a good way'; 'She's very good at explaining what is going on and how we can help.'

Entrance: Main intakes into the nursery (2.75+ years), kindergarten (3+ years) and reception (4+ years). Both parents are expected to come on the school tour: 'I tell them you're making the biggest decision of your life for your most precious possession. You both need to be involved'. More or less first come first served into the nursery classes, with preference for siblings. Assessments for kindergarten upwards: 'They must be able to fit in socially and behaviour-wise, and they must be able to cope. Our classes are very busy, and the children need energy and stamina'. Discourages applications from families who live further than about four miles away – 'Children shouldn't spend hours a day sitting in a car'.

Exit: Some move at 4 or 5, but most at 7, to local independent schools, eg Habs' Boys and Girls, Belmont, Highgate, Channing, South Hampstead High, St Margaret's, UCS, North London Collegiate, City of London Girls, St Mary's and Lyndhurst. A few to local state primaries, eg Garden Suburb or Brookland.

Remarks: One of a quiet street of large, brick-built early 20th century houses in the midst of leafy and wealthy Hampstead Garden Suburb. The school, with small but bright and colourful classrooms, was built by grateful parents for the previous ex-governess owner, who was head until she died in 1993 at the age of 93. Large garden, divided into a nursery playground with Wendy house and grassy area and a playground for the older children with a climbing frame, sand table, sports equipment, planting areas and gazebo. Woodland garden created to celebrate the school's 80th year.

Inevitably, its ultimate raison d'être is to prepare the children for 7+ exams, but this does not overshadow school life – 'People feel we really understand children, their stages of development and their needs'. The early years concentrate on personal and emotional development: learning to listen, developing good social awareness and independent thinking skills – 'We encourage them to be well organised, plan ahead, problem solve'.

A broad curriculum with lots of practical emphasis. Cookery is used to learn maths, debating helps with language, chess with strategy and problem-solving, sports with coordination. Reception had just finished making its own playdough when we visited, another class had taken photos of the other houses in the road and made models of them, and in another were newly-hatched chicks. In year 2 children choose a project they present to the class – which can be on anything from Nelson Mandela to Arsenal. 'By the time they have heard about all the different projects, they know a lot about a lot of things.'

Children are assessed for developmental delays from an early stage and outside help may be recommended for anything from a lack of pencil control to poor social skills. 'We have a good bank of respected practitioners, and interventions work particularly well when they are very young. We recommend them to protect children's self-esteem and help them reach their potential.' Probably not ideal for a very boisterous child, or for one who cannot cope with change. 'We have had fantastic success with one or two Asperger's children, but this is not generally the place for them. We offer places if we feel we can fully meet the child's needs. It is most important that children's school experiences shouldn't be stressful.' Recognised by NACE for its provision for more able children.

Teachers a mix of youth and old hands – 'Some have worked with me for over 20 years, and we're like a family. We're more pedagogues than teachers'. Praise from parents: 'The children really love my daughter's teacher and want to please her', and from the ISI, which talks of the 'high standard of teaching skills across the school'.

Children have plenty of opportunities for, and find great delight in, taking responsibility as head boy, head girl or a member of the school council, which has regular lunches with the head, who also invites birthday children to tea. Many performance opportunities too, in concerts, plays and poetry recitals – 'We like to celebrate the arts'.

Strong emphasis on all matters green: composting, reusing, exercise, healthy eating, sustainable travel. Lunch boxes must contain 'real food': nothing processed or ready-wrapped. We saw children tucking in to salmon risotto, sushi, tortillas and pasta salad. 'Seemed annoying at first,' said a parent, 'but my daughter is talking about why certain foods are good for you and why some are not, and how she feels when she eats something too sugary.'

Unusually wide range of extracurricular activities for a pre-prep. Around a third of the children learn the violin at school – 'It gives them zillions of study skills, such as concentration and perseverance, and those who keep it up tend to do exceptionally well academically'. As the pupils move through the school, they are offered dance and drama, gym and swimming, French and computing as well as chess and recorder; also a very active and popular co-ed football team. 'When the children leave they have a whole breadth of experiences that stand them in very good stead later on.'

The head brought back with her from the States a belief in strong links with parents and the local community. Parents report lots of emphasis on getting together as families for meals and outdoor activities. The school runs parent education sessions, social events and plenty of whole school initiatives such as sponsored walks. Parents and grandparents come in to lead assemblies, help with topics, accompany school trips to anywhere from Hampstead Heath to the British Museum, talk about their jobs or hobbies. The PTA organises charity events, picnics and parties, and arranges school workshops, visits by theatre groups and farm animals as well as the annual garden fête.

'It's a very warm and friendly place,' said a parent. 'My daughter has thrived here and our experience has been brilliant. They do a nice mix of activities and she's really excited about learning.'

Archbishop Tenison's School

55 Kennington Oval, London SE11 5SR

Pupils: 525 • Ages: 11–19 • C of E

Tel: 020 7735 3771
Email: school@ats.lambeth.sch.uk
Website: www.tenisons.com

Executive Headmistress: Since 2006, Mrs Elizabeth Sims, BEd MA, who is also executive head of federated St Mark's Primary School. Initial degree in religious studies and English from Institute of Education, followed by MA in education management and administration. Previously deputy head at St Saviour's and St Olave's School. Passionate about young people's development and learning; has been involved in youth work since the age of 16. A member of the Tate Britain Advisory Council. Committed Christian. Loves reading.

Academic matters: At GCSE in 2016, 58 per cent scored five or more A*-C grades including English and maths. Pupils generally take nine or 10 GCSEs, though some take as many as 13. BTec results strong. School is particularly proud of its excellent maths teaching. RS is a compulsory subject for all years from the off.

The sixth form is a strength of the school and is improving rapidly year on year, with around 40 per cent of A level grades at A*-B. Small numbers of girls in sixth form, though this looks set to grow as word spreads of the opportunities on offer. Girls typically come from schools that are less scholarly in order to pursue more academic A level options here. School works hard at arranging visits to universities and setting up diverse opportunities for work experience placements. Extended sixth form centre with study room and kitchen seen as a great success by pupils. Large proportion of sixth formers have own laptops, subsidised by school. A sixth form psychology class we sat in on was impressive – students fully engaged, lively, full of questions, keen to participate and enjoying their learning.

Class sizes quite small, averaging 26 or 27 but can be as few as six per class in the sixth form. Learning support department assesses each pupil in the school and sets up extra support if needed. Those with SEN are withdrawn for individual or small group support or are provided for in-class with learning support assistant or classroom assistant. Lower sets are offered additional literacy support while more able are offered Latin, philosophy and thinking skills. Enrichment programme targets gifted and talented pupils and school claims to be always on the look out for opportunities to extend learning for the most capable. For those with behavioural issues, workshops are arranged on anger management and social skills.

Games, options, the arts: Sport is taken seriously and school does its best to organise a rich diet of sport for all pupils. Football and basketball perennially popular and a number of alumni play football professionally. Lots of teams and matches regularly arranged. Sport is played at nearby Kennington Park or a train-ride away at Motspur playing fields, where pupils play rugby, tennis and athletics most days. Swimming takes place in Brixton. Pupils in the past have been offered American football training with teams from the NFL.

Currently 25 students learn a musical instrument, including guitar, drum kit, saxophone and clarinet. Once a pupil has reached grade 2, the lessons are free. A very strong brass ensemble. Two choirs – gospel and traditional. School choir performs at homes for elderly and hospitals throughout the borough, as well as occasionally at Southwark Cathedral. There is an open invitation for boys to join the Pegasus Opera Singing Academy and currently about 10 boys are training to sing with this group. Samba band, piano club and rock school also on offer.

Around 20 boys take drama at GCSE and numerous theatre trips are on offer. Two school productions each year, 'though more likely to be a fun production than Chekhov,' says school. Strong art department housed in well-resourced sky-lit art studios at the top of the school. Outstanding artwork on display and frequent visits to art galleries encouraged.

Wide variety of clubs on offer, including philosophy, ICT, basketball and the very popular Debate Mate, which teaches debating to inner-city schools in areas of high child poverty. Easter holiday revision classes and Saturday school provision are funded by pupil premium payments for those who would benefit from extra structured support. Trips abroad arranged to Spain and France as well as a character-building trip to Herefordshire to foster teamwork. Boys who can't afford trips are helped financially by the school or by livery companies.

Pupils are encouraged to look beyond the school walls and some boys recently gave a presentation to TfL on safe and sustainable transport. Significant numbers of speakers visit the school each year, including authors, actors and CEO of Surrey Country Cricket Club. School goes out of its way to inspire the pupils to achieve through positive role models. Rapper Tinie Tempah made a lively addition to a recent school assembly when he presented a pupil with an award for his work against youth violence.

Background and atmosphere: School is very proud of its ancient origins. Founded in 1685 by Archbishop of Canterbury Thomas Tenison, who wanted to provide the first free education for boys in London. Its first home was in St Martin-in-the-Fields and the annual Founder's Day service still takes place in the church there. School moved to present site opposite the Oval cricket ground in 1928 and has an enviable view of the pitch on match days. Was a grammar school and this is still reflected in its ethos and outlook. The site remains a tight squeeze, particularly at break times, but no plans to look for another location.

Christian worship is an integral part of the school and religious assemblies are held twice a week. School has its own chaplain. At the heart of Tenison's are the values of 'justice, mercy and humility', which are combined with the school's core values of 'compassion, hard work, accountability, respect and trust'. School doesn't just pay lip service to these principles but takes them seriously and expects pupils to do the same.

Stable and contented staff – about 20 per cent have been here for more than 10 years. School states that 'when teachers do leave it is nearly always for positive reasons.' Roughly 50:50 male to female ratio. The teachers we met were enthusiastic, welcoming and dedicated to the school.

School is going fully co-ed, and first intake of year 7 girls arrived in 2015. 'We feel the time is right to offer our unique mix of Christian values, tradition and academic rigour to all young people, regardless of gender,' says the school.

Pastoral care, well-being and discipline: School prides itself on its pastoral care and there is a supportive, family feel to the school. Every pupil has a tutor keeping an eye out for them. On the morning we visited, one pupil was being looked after in a teacher's office while he let off steam before an incident escalated. The pupils know the staff are there for them at all times. Operates a zero tolerance policy on drugs, weapons and replica weapons but permanent exclusions are rare.

High standards expected regarding uniform; no baseball caps or trainers. Short hairstyles preferred on boys. Different coloured blazers for different age groups (younger pupils in blue and older ones in black); house ties worn throughout. Sixth formers wear business uniform and the ones we saw generally looked immaculate, with only the odd rebel not toeing the line.

One boy, quite new to the school, rated Tenison's highly. 'It's good,' he told us. 'The teachers are nice and I enjoy the lessons. They show us respect. It's quite cramped but not too bad. It's much better than my old school, though I go home for lunch as I don't like the food.'

Pupils and parents: Majority of pupils come from local area, mostly Southwark and Lambeth. Fifty per cent black African; 15 per cent black Caribbean; a growing Latin American contingent; small numbers of Asians; roughly 10 per cent white. Excellent attendance record. Pupils are generally proud to be at Tenison's and deputy head commented that 'we have to remind some of them to go home at a certain stage in the evening. They don't want to leave. They trust us and feel safe here.' Large proportion has English as a second language though it's unusual not to be fluent on arrival at school. Those requiring EAL support are growing each year.

School says that the 'overwhelming majority of parents and carers are supportive'. Recent PTA pampering evening arranged for mothers and carers was a great success and saw the great hall converted into a beauty salon. Regular newsletters sent out and parents are encouraged to read pupils' homework diaries. Parents are expected to work with the school in their child's education and development and to support the school in what it is trying to do.

Entrance: Seventy per cent of places offered to those of Christian faith; 30 per cent open places. Not as over-subscribed as previously due to free schools and academies opening nearby, but still not short of applicants.

Exit: Vast majority of pupils go on to higher education (many being the first generation in their family to go to university); only a few head for the world of training or work. Recent leavers to study eg law at Coventry, chemical engineering at Loughborough, art at Camberwell and pharmacy at King's College. One or two apply to Oxbridge most years. Huge spread of subjects studied at university, from computing to German and psychology.

Pupils are well supported with university applications including the writing of personal statements through charitable organisation which supports young people from disadvantaged backgrounds to attain a university place or another chosen aspiration. As school deputy remarked: 'If they don't get an offer from a university, it won't be because of a poorly written personal statement.' A handful of students opt for art college (Camberwell, Chelsea or Central Saint Martin's) each year; others prefer to study fashion. Some to drama school – most recently to the competitive BRIT School in Croydon.

School has built up strong external links including with livery companies – The Worshipful Company of Cutlers provides bursaries for those studying medicine at university and The Worshipful Company of Dyers awards a university bursary to pupils who attend City University. Surrey County Cricket provides funding for students who study PE at university and often lends its facilities. Strong links also with St John's College, Cambridge and pupils also have opportunities to become involved in mentoring schemes with LSE.

Remarks: A small school which is going from strength to strength. Archbishop Tenison's remains a safe haven in this underprivileged part of south London and has increasingly high expectations of its pupils, taking every opportunity to celebrate individual and group success. The teachers believe in the pupils and students are rising to the challenge.

Arnold House School

1 Loudoun Road, London NW8 0LH

Pupils: 260 • Ages: 5–13

Fees: £17,634 pa

Tel: 020 7266 4840
Email: registrar@arnoldhouse.co.uk
Website: www.arnoldhouse.co.uk

Headmaster: Since 2006, Vivien Thomas (50s). A user-friendly, down-to-earth chap with an easy warmth and an unscholarly taste in garish ties (red flowers and giant yellow fish on the day we visited). Makes a point of being accessible on school gate duty at least twice a week and is generally popular with parents. 'Relaxed, confident, intelligent, and understands how parents feel about their children,' said one. Educated at University College School, Hampstead, followed by St Luke's College, Exeter, where he studied PE and history. Had a trial for QPR aged 17 and dreamt of becoming a professional sportsman but, after failing to make the grade (at football, tennis and rugby), he turned his talents to education. Taught PE and maths at UCS, followed by a spell at an international school in Venezuela. He returned to London to become deputy head at Arnold House, then head of Keble Prep, Winchmore Hill. Married to Rowena, he is a man of varied interests, who 'struggles with golf', enjoys travelling and takes guitar lessons with 'a madman in Dollis Hill who used to play with Ginger Baker of Cream'.

Entrance: Application form (plus the usual £100 fee) due before child's second birthday, followed by an open evening held in April/May approximately two and a half years before the intended entry date. Interested parents (roughly 170 families for 38 places) are then invited to meet the head for a 20 minute chat. As always, it is the parents who are being assessed as much as the child. Don't say, 'I need you to get my son into Westminster'. Do say, 'I'd like my child to be happy and enjoy an all-round education'. Prospective pupils then invited for an informal one-to-one assessment and places offered 15 months before entry date. 'I hate the idea that it'll be down to the little boy, that he might be "not good enough",' says the head. 'What I want to know is, will he be a nice little boy to teach? When you open a book, is he able to be engaged? Or is he climbing the walls, unruly and impolite? I don't want it to be a skills-based test, and I find it astonishing that there are tutoring agencies for 3 and 4 year olds.'

Main entry point is into year 1, with occasional ad-hoc places in other years. Younger siblings and sons of old boys looked on favourably. Partial and full means-tested bursaries are available in years 5, 6 and 7.

Exit: Strongly 13-plus focused school. A wide intake means a broad exit, but high fliers get into all the top schools, often with scholarships to boot. Two-thirds go on to London day schools, with the remainder heading off to boarding school. Strong links with Westminster, St Paul's, City of London Boys, Highgate, UCS and Mill Hill. Boarders go to Eton, Harrow, Rugby, Marlborough, Winchester and Bradfield, amongst others. Over-ambitious parents are discouraged from entering their son for exams all over the place. 'After many years of headship I know the system inside out. I am very honest with parents. What may look like an opportunity to them is in reality a rejection letter on the mat. Granny's all keyed up, everyone is rooting for him, but I know it's just not going to happen. I'll say, "Your son is moving along quite happily, do you really want him to get that knock back?"'

Roughly 25 out of 30 boys get their first choice school; the remaining five or six take a bit longer. 'When boys are on the waiting list it's my job to turn that into an offer. We have excellent relations with schools, and that's when the prep school head really earns his corn.'

The school offers excellent results with less of the stressful, hothouse hysteria that so often accompanies the 13-plus experience. 'I offer places to parents who understand the Arnold House ethos,' says the head. 'They should want their son to join knitting club, cooking club, play music and sport, and not be getting anxious if he doesn't get three hours homework a night. We are here for bigger things than getting into a top academic senior school.'

Remarks: While some sniff that it is old fashioned, for others the traditional values of Arnold House are its strongest selling point. 'It's just like the perfect country prep school, but in London,' sighed one happy parent.

In the stressful, results-oriented atmosphere of the London prep school system, Arnold House is an artfully constructed oasis where boys can still be boys. Pupils are even encouraged to have snowball fights and inter-house conker competitions (safely supervised, of course). Admission is non-selective and the school frowns on hothousing, yet year after year leavers gain entry to the holy trinity of Eton, St Paul's and Westminster.

'These boys don't need to be pushed,' claims the head (rather airily). 'It's a question of 'nudging' and bringing a boy nicely, like a fine wine, to the point where he is ready.'

Arnold House was founded in 1905 with nine pupils by a Miss Hanson, who was keen to prove boys could be prepared for public school entrance by a woman. She was successful, and the school has now expanded to fill three adjoining houses in a quiet St John's Wood side street. The buildings lack any particular architectural pizzazz, but inside it feels spacious and well laid out, and is probably one of the cleanest schools we've visited. Even the boys' loos were sparkling, and instead of the usual dank, unloved urinals we found modern boutique-style plumbing with glossy lime green and red cubicles.

Entrance is into year 1, with 38 places split into two classes, though classes are smaller at the top of the school due to natural shrinkage. They are mixed up every couple of years to ensure academic parity and 'social refreshment'. Setting begins in year 3 for maths and English, with subjects taught by specialists from year 5. French from year 1, Latin from year 5, and ancient Greek is an option in year 7. No separate scholarship class, but boys with scholarship potential are identified at the end of year 7 and invited to join specialist lessons.

Lots of examples of creative, value-added education. The Compass Course in years 5 and 6 aims to foster independent thinking, public speaking and IT skills. Pupils work collaboratively to design an EU leaflet, make an animated film, write a play and create a charity PowerPoint presentation. Instead of the bog-standard year 8 battlefields trip, pupils spend time researching Arnold House old boys killed in WW1 before visiting France and finding their graves in the war cemeteries to pay their respects. An inspired way to bring history off the page. There is an embarrassment of before-school, after-school and break-time activities ranging from an 8am Quiz Club to Mad Scientist Club, Bug Club, darts, French Fun and Games plus all the usual sport, music and art activities.

Like many London schools has a shortage of outside space. There is an adequate playground, but boys must travel to the school's seven acre sports ground in Canons Park (35 minutes away) for games. The younger boys travel by coach, years 7 and 8 by public transport. ('You'd expect, with the fees we pay, that the boys wouldn't have to get there by tube', muttered one disgruntled parent.) Here there are classrooms, a theatre, tennis courts and pitches for football, cricket, hockey and rugby. Older boys play team games twice a week, younger boys once a week, and there are additional PE and sports sessions at local leisure centres. A busy fixtures list for A, right down to G teams, means that even the most athletically-challenged pupil has an opportunity to represent the school.

The music department is outstanding and has many scholarships under its belt. Some 85 per cent of pupils learn at least one instrument and many learn two. Twenty different ensembles on offer, from flute group to jazz and African drums, with lots of opportunity to perform in concerts. Years 7 and 8 can use the whizzy i-music suite for production, recording and podcasting.

Art is taught to a high standard and doesn't get quietly sidelined as exams loom for older pupils. No need to feign enthusiasm when pupils arrive home clutching yet another art project. We saw wonderful Cubist self-portraits from year 3 and some very accomplished papier-mâché shells that any parent would be proud to put on display.

SEN support is excellent and, with a year of free one-to-one sessions before charges kick in, is more generous than at many comparable schools. One permanent SEN qualified staff member is supported by three visiting specialists for dyspraxia, speech and language and occupational therapy. Pupils who need extra help are identified in years 1 and 2 and either given classroom support by the six teaching assistants, or allotted one-to-one sessions as necessary. Dyslexia screening for every pupil in year 4 as a 'final trawl' to identify those with SEN needs, which can often mean brighter pupils in which dyslexic tendencies are masked.

So what type of child does Arnold House suit? 'My son has been blissfully happy, but there is a certain rough and tumble that goes with a boys' school, and I think if they are very fragile they might find it easier at a co-ed. They don't have to be uber-sporty though, there's drama, singing, art, something for everybody.'

'We take the boys as they are,' says the head. 'We have boys with IQs below 100 all the way up to 140. Once we take a boy on we're looking to be together as a team for eight years.' He admitted that, occasionally, if a boy looks like he is struggling by year 4 or 5, he will have a meeting with parents to decide 'whether or not this is looking like a good plan'.

Behaviour at the school is generally accepted to be good. 'We expect the boys to rise to a certain level of behaviour. I don't know if you can teach kindness, but you can certainly teach consideration,' says the head. There's the usual system of sanctions and rewards with Good Citizenship badges for 'being a good egg' and Industry badges for trying hard. Senior boys get ties for art, music, games and responsibility. 'I'm always pleased to hear how strict the school is,' said one parent. 'My son is well-behaved, but I occasionally hear of other boys being told off, and they are properly told off.'

Bullying is rare but, as in all schools, it happens. Usually nipped in the bud early by class teachers, but suspension has been used when necessary. 'In 7 years I've had only four situations where I've had to step in,' says the head. 'There isn't a parent I've met who thinks their son could actually be the bully, so it always has to be thoroughly investigated.' The head is very hot on cyber bullying. 'If a boy is being talked about in a derogatory way on Facebook on Sunday night, then it's going to cause problems at school on Monday morning. Even if it happens outside school, I will deal with it.' Only one parent we spoke to was unhappy, feeling that a situation had been dealt with 'too late'.

Parents are a mix of multinational successful professionals, with 50 per cent close enough to walk to school (should they ever choose to leave the 4x4 behind) and others coming from further afield (Notting Hill, Islington, Highgate). Reputed to be a friendly, sociable parent body, though the higher-than-average fees mean there's a lot of wealth sloshing around. 'There are a few amazingly flash cars, but also plenty of beat-up cars like ours. It's an easy, mixed group and I've seen no snobbishness whatsoever.' This is not the place for wags, trophy wives or school gate show-offs. 'It's definitely not a "women who lunch" school,' said one mother. 'All the mothers have, or have had, interesting careers. At my son's nursery I was the only working mum and had nothing in common with anyone, so I find the professional ethos here a relief.'

School lunches would definitely win a triple gold star from Jamie Oliver. A very jolly cook was making roast beef, Yorkshire pud, parsnips and broccoli on the day we visited, and the gravy was even made with a dash of wine.

The Arts Educational School (London)

Cone Ripman House, 14 Bath Road, London W4 1LY

Pupils: 232 (182 girls, 50 boys) • Ages: 11–18 • Sixth form: 116

Fees: £14,500 – £15,860 pa

Tel: 020 8987 6600
Email: pupils@artsed.co.uk
Website: www.artsed.co.uk

Headmaster: Since 2012, Mr Adrian Blake (40s) BEd MAPgDip NPQH. Trained as an actor and worked professionally before finding he liked education and retraining. Started his career as lecturer in performing arts at North East Surrey College of Technology, followed by a spell as director of thinking and learning and advanced skills teacher at Greenshaw High School. Moved to Lambeth Academy to become assistant principal, then came to ArtsEd in 2009, initially as director of teaching and learning. This background may help explain his consummate ease with modern education and its jargon – unusual in a performing arts school head. A fast-talking enthusiast, who seems genuinely to know the names of every single ArtsEd pupil past and present. Still teaches 15 periods a week (extracurricular martial arts included), and greatly liked by parents and pupils alike. 'He is truly inspirational, and the children really respect him'; 'Very present in the lives of the students, and my son especially enjoys his lessons'; 'A very dynamic character whom the pupils love and want to impress,' parents told us. Married to a deputy head at a nearby state school.

Academic matters: Several of the pupils we spoke to said that they'd come to ArtsEd because they weren't excelling academically – 'I really just like acting, I'm just not into this academic stuff,' was a comment echoed by most. If so, they appear to have found the right school to help them find their academic feet. 'I'm enormously passionate about learning, and when you put creativity into leaning, everything is richer,' asserts head, and the figures support the claim. In 2016, 33 per cent A*/A and 62 per cent A*-B at GCSE, with 60 per cent of A level passes at A*-B and 23 per cent A*/A. Creditable results for an academically non-selective school.

Maximum class size of 24, and students are taught a core of subjects that covers all the basics, including French and the humanities. At GCSE students take double science; it's rare for anyone to take triple science, although not unknown. One mother attested to the subject's overall popularity: 'My son loves the lunchtime science club, which is really igniting his passion for the subject.' Homework is, according to everyone, kept to reasonable levels, and the children are given at least two days to complete any assignment – an important piece of commonsense in a school where pupils have so many other claims on their time. 'Although there isn't as much homework as at other private schools, I'm confident that the teachers are gauging the pupils' needs well, and I feel my child is in safe hands,' wrote one parent. Others were equally positive about the academic provision overall. 'The staff are very inspiring. Since being at ArtsEd my daughter has become very keen to succeed in her academic studies – I've never seen her so determined to do well,' commented a grateful mother.

In the sixth form students choose A levels, or a mixture of BTec and A levels, and at this stage the options are almost entirely arts-based: dance, drama, art, music, film studies, etc. English, history, and French are there for the more academically minded, plus maths, which is, according to head, very popular. No science A levels offered: the sixth form is built according to demand. Sixth formers we spoke to praised the teaching and the high level of individual attention given. 'The teachers are one of the reasons I love it here – they give you so much time,' was a typical comment.

Full-time SENCo offers support to the 25 per cent of students with dyslexia and other SEN, and this provision was particularly highly praised by parents. A mother, whose son moved to ArtsEd for the sixth form after receiving inadequate support elsewhere, wrote, 'With the help of the excellent SENCo team, my son has thrived and achieved really good academic results in all his subjects. He is more confident in his academic ability now and feels understood and supported with his dyslexia.' New dedicated sixth form SENCo as well.

Games, options, the arts: Students in years 7 to 11 choose to specialize in either dance or drama (see Entrance), but everyone receives classes in both disciplines. The vocational and academic teaching is interspersed throughout the day, and the amount of time students are required to spend in school increases as they move up: younger students stay until 5.30pm doing vocational work two or three days a week, in the sixth form it's every day. This is no hardship to the students or their families – it's what they all joined for. Lively and busy programme of shows and presentations including two major productions a year, all of them resourced and rehearsed to an extremely high standard. 'It's such a professional environment,' a sixth former told us, 'and the work ethic you're taught to have is fantastic.' 'You come in each day and there's such a buzz that you just want to stay!' said another.

Extremely good facilities, some of them shared with 'the degrees', as the ArtsEd undergraduate students are known here. The amazing Andrew Lloyd Webber Foundation Theatre that hosts the school's major dance shows and concerts is at the heart of the school, along with several smaller studio performance spaces. The school can boast many successes in national initiatives such as the National Theatre's Connections and the Independent Schools Association Drama Festival. Students are encouraged to get involved with all aspects of production, and film is also increasingly popular, with regular access to the purpose-built film and TV studio.

Music is taught at all levels and lots of instrumental lessons available. One recent leaver went on to the Royal College of Music to study the oboe. When we visited, the school resonated to the rhythms of an African drumming class, complete with enthusiastic whoops and wails.

'Sporty kids wouldn't like it here,' was the unanimous opinion of the students we spoke to. The school has no outside facilities of its own but the students go off site for sports each week, and there are regular kickabouts at lunchtime. But no one is here for the sport, of course, and with so much dancing going on, the children keep super-fit. Visual arts are also strong and creative, as the variety of work on the walls confirms.

ArtsEd isn't a stage school or an agency, the emphasis is firmly on academic success and vocational training, and it does not go out and seek professional performing work for its pupils. That said, professional directors and producers regularly come to the school looking for the right child for a particular role, and the head will always consider what he calls 'enhancing opportunities'. An ArtsEd year 8 pupil is currently appearing in Harry Potter and the Cursed Child and we met a young lad who'd enjoyed six months in Bugsy Malone. The industry likes ArtsEd youngsters, it seems. 'I know a high-level producer who won't consider stage school children any more, because they're prepared in a certain way – but he comes here!' remarked the head, with pardonable pride.

Background and atmosphere: ArtsEd grew out of the Cone Ripman School, founded in 1939 and itself the result of a merger between two previous dance schools. Originally located just off Oxford Street in Stratford Place, the outbreak of war forced a move to Tring in Hertfordshire where the school shared premises with the Rothschild Bank at Tring Park Mansion House. In 1941, the school was able to move back to Stratford Place, but kept its Tring premises as a second, boarding school. In 1947 both places were renamed The ArtsEducational School, to reflect Grace Cone's and Olive Ripman's commitment to a proper academic education for their young performers. Gradually the two schools diverged, and are now good friends but completely independent of one another (in 2009, to avoid confusion with its former partner, Tring changed its name to Tring Park School for the Performing Arts). ArtsEd moved to its present premises in a leafy part of Chiswick in 1989, renaming the building Cone Ripman House in honour of its founders. Cone Ripman House does nothing much for the eye on the outside, it has to be said, but has been extensively modernised and refurbished within and looks airy and streamlined.

The original Cone Ripman School was for girls only, and even today ArtsEd is still girl-heavy. This is almost always the case with performing arts schools, but seemed particularly so here. Of the 116 pupils in years 7-11, only 25 are boys; in the sixth form 35 out of 116 students are boys. A sixth-former admitted that she 'wished there were more boys', but the boys themselves were philosophical about it. 'It's a bit of a problem, but you make friends across the years,' observed a year 10 lad, equably.

Parents and students alike described this as a happy school. 'Everyone knows everyone, and everyone's so kind to each other'; 'It's a really nice atmosphere, it allows you to progress.' Parents concur: 'Our daughter has been at ArtsEd for two years and they have been the happiest school years of her life. ArtsEd is like a big family,' wrote one. Everyone praised the 'positive competitiveness' the school fosters, and insisted that no matter who got which part, 'we're in it together, we work as a team.' Chances to shine abound. 'If you audition for a part and you don't get it, you know there'll always be another opportunity,' a level-headed teenager told us. 'We offer developmental opportunities throughout the year,' confirmed the head, 'and parents will see their children do any number of things.' 'Watching your children in demonstrations of work is amazing; you can see them and their cohort growing in confidence,' agreed a parent. The young people we met were quiet, polite, respectful and proud of their school.

Awarded the Independent Schools Association Excellence Award in 2015, in recognition of 'excellent academic standards, alongside specialist performing arts provision and record numbers of pupils achieving places at universities and conservatoires'.

Pastoral care, well-being and discipline: Students work hard to win their place here, and still harder once they arrive, so behaviour problems are rare. Occasionally there are the friendship group issues that you'll find at any school. However, everyone here knows the importance of getting on with each other, and staff work actively to promote harmony and healthiness, both physical and emotional. 'In my old school there was a lot of bullying, but everyone here gets along, and the teachers always talk to us if there's an incident,' said a year 7 girl. Parents agreed: 'Staff are kind and approachable and my child has great respect for them.' The head was adamant that there were no eating disorders in the school, and the canteen certainly seemed well-used and well-liked, selling a commendable variety of healthy and appetising dishes. A few sixth formers live too far away from the school to travel there daily from home, and instead lodge in nearby digs (this isn't allowed for younger students). The school isn't affiliated to any boarding provider, but helps students find host families, and has set up an 'away from home' group that meets every fortnight.

All students are assigned a staff mentor in year 10, and in year 11 the head personally meets all year 11 students to talk about future plans. The school prides itself on developing 'emotional resilience and bounce-back-ability' in its pupils. 'We really grow the understanding, and we enable them to do their best at auditions,' said the head. Parents valued this aspect of the school very highly. 'The school emphasises professionalism in preparing them for a demanding and sometimes brutal industry,' was one comment. 'ArtsEd students leave school very well prepared for the big wide world,' was another. 'You make connections here,' a sixth former reflected, 'and you're well-connected when you leave.'

Pupils and parents: Inevitably, many of the children come from families of film-makers, actors, writers and dancers, but not exclusively so, and the students we spoke to were adamant that 'you don't have to have a showbiz background to do well here'. Not much ethnic diversity when we looked round, perhaps reflecting perhaps the differing aspirations of London's various communities. Most of the children we spoke to were local, but the school recruits from a wide radius – one year 7 student travels up from Brighton each day, and we met a sixth former who'd relocated from Ireland.

ArtsEd alumni include, to name just a handful, Julie Andrews, Darcey Bussell, Martin Clunes, Nigel Havers, Bonnie Langford, Tuppence Middleton. Finn Jones – the list is impressively long.

Entrance: Twenty-four places at Y7, but school won't take full number if there aren't 24 good enough to take. Places do come up in other years: always worth checking. Entrance is by audition: students can try out for either the dance or drama pathway – or they can try for both, in which case the school will offer a place on the one they feel is best suited to the student. Written assessment in maths and English is simply to gauge academic progress: the school is academically non-selective. A number of additional places available at year 12. Similar entrance procedure, albeit more detailed and tougher: audition, workshops, interview.

School looks for 'potential... that real passion', but not for would-be stars. As head observed, 'I don't do divas. Everyone's talented here. Staff are talented. We're all here because we're passionate about the arts, about education, about training.'

Exit: Typically with this kind of school, a few leave after GCSEs, having decided to pursue other life choices, in particular to study science at A level, since it isn't offered in the sixth form here. ArtsEd students have successfully applied at this stage to schools such as Latymer Upper and Tiffin. At 18, around 80 per cent to an impressive array of prestigious conservatoires: RADA, LAMDA, Royal Central School of Speech and Drama, English National Ballet School, London School of Contemporary Dance, Trinity Laban, etc. A number move upstairs to the highly regarded ArtsEducational degree schools in Acting and Musical Theatre. Some pursue a career in film at places such as Bournemouth & Poole or the National Film & TV School. Others go abroad to institutions such as the Julliard or the New York Film Academy. A few go into the industry immediately: a recently sixth form leaver went straight into playing the lead role in The Curious Incident of the Dog in the Night Time. A small number to university, mostly to read arts subjects.

Money matters: ArtsEd fees are remarkably reasonable given the high level of specialist tuition the students receive, and lower than those charged at many other independent schools in this part of London. For those who need help, the school offers means-tested bursaries of up to a third of the fees for students in years 7 to 11. In addition, eight full-fees scholarships are available in the sixth form. The school does not receive any government or local authority funding.

Remarks: A dynamic, purposeful, well-oiled institution where creative youngsters learn to work hard and achieve highly. 'With the school's expert guidance and support the transformation in my child has been remarkable,' said one mother, and another reported her daughter as saying, 'Mum, I don't think there's another school in the world that is as good and as fun as ArtsEd.'

Ashbourne Independent School

17 Old Court Place, London W8 4PL

Pupils: 270 • Ages: 16–19; plus small GCSE stream • Sixth form: 210

Fees: £23,250 – £24,750 pa

Tel: 020 7937 3858
Email: admin@ashbournecollege.co.uk
Website: www.ashbournecollege.co.uk

Principal: Since 1981, Michael (Mike) Kirby BApSc MSC (60s), who founded the college. Mr Kirby read aerospace engineering in Toronto (he retains a soft Canadian burr) and Birkbeck where he did a masters in statistics. Very tall, laconic and seemingly inscrutable, but a warmth and a smile escape him

A

occasionally and the man is momentarily revealed. After 32 years, unsurprisingly, he and his school mirror each other. Focused and clear-sighted, he has made a place where little distracts from work but where the work ethic is underpinned by the sense of support felt by the students. His involvement with the students is integral to the day-to-day running but the touch is light. 'I know a lot of them personally – they can be a bit wide-eyed and innocent but they're just nice kids and they're great fun.' He still teaches maths revision classes – as ever, we applaud – and, unlike many in his position, sees the students very much in their own home context. 'We positively encourage parents to get involved.'

Prominent member of CIFE (the Conference for Independent Further Education) and the British Council Education Counselling Service, he is the owner and proprietor of Ashbourne. This and the length of his tenure make him unique. He is keen that Ashbourne be recognised as a 'bona fide part of the independent school system', hence his resolve not to be the first resort for resit students – though they do come in penny numbers. He launched and continues to steer a pretty effective school.

Academic matters: Most students come for the two-year A level course, although one year and 18 month A level programmes also on offer – these popular with, mostly, overseas students. In 2016 A level results were 51 per cent A*/A, 76 per cent A*-B. Separate classes for those AS students who want to improve their grades – a growing trend. However, AS students who significantly 'underperform' – having been warned that they are in danger of doing so – are shown the door. No embarrassment at this – 'We filter,' says Mr Kirby. 'That's how we get the results'.

Small middle school offers two year (years 10 and 11) and one year (year 11) GCSE programmes but up to date exam results not readily available, so do ask searching questions.

At A level, 37 subjects on offer and all taught in small classes – seven is average, 10 is max and even ones and twos for some subjects. Maths much the most popular subject and with the most impressive results – tend to be mostly A*-B. Similarly with further maths. The sciences also taken by many – again with, generally, a decent crop of results. We witnessed one Eng lit class – all girls. Languages holding up well and business here, as everywhere, gaining a more mixed bunch of results. Unsurprisingly, no Latin, no Greek. All language teachers are native speakers. Lunchtime critical theory seminar much-praised and very popular: 'It's way beyond the A level syllabus so you learn about Marx and Freud and feminism and then apply the theories to film and literature. I learned so much from doing it that way,' an A2 student enthused. All lessons are two hours long. Teachers much praised for their enthusiasm and care. Many are long-serving.

Few SEN students with anything other than mild dyslexia/dycalculia/ADHD and neither building any good for those with mobility difficulties. No SENCo though SEN overseen by affable head of middle school. Mr Kirby says: 'The school is happy to accept those with SEN but makes no special provision beyond arrangements for exams.' A few here have extra exam time, a laptop in exams or a scribe.

Games, options, the arts: Some variance between the college, which claims to offer 'a very wide extracurricular programme', and the students, some of whom seem to know little about it – mostly, apparently, the Brits who don't live locally. However, much enthusiasm from those who do partake and especially from those who have gone on overseas subject-related trips with the college. We are told that the college has now appointed an officer who is specifically responsible for student activities and for ensuring that everyone knows about them.

Art is legendary here and the art room – where we were glad to see some mess – was full of concentrating artists and makers of textiles when we visited. Lots of colour and art seemingly derived from diverse influences. College runs a choir but no orchestra/ensembles. Lots of societies – held in lunchtime and after college; good college newspaper written by students. No sport to speak of and some join gyms etc (there's one next door) but, as everyone agreed, it's the price you pay. Very popular Christmas Revue in which virtually all take part – local fringe theatres are hired for these and other performance events.

Background and atmosphere: Principally in two buildings, separated by Ken High Street. 'Old Building' (in Old Court Place) is tucked down a side road – helpfully guarded by two policemen holding rifles (actually outside the Israeli Consulate) – and so discreet, it's very easily missed. Most sixth form classes take place here. 'Young Street Building' in – you couldn't make it up – Young Street opposite houses the middle school and the rest of the sixth form classes including a huge art room – by far the biggest of the school's rooms. Internally, both buildings are pristine – white walls relieved by stylish and undistracting prints and some larger artwork made on site. Plain carpet, bare wood stairs. Sofas only in one common room and the two staff rooms which are as severely workful as the rest of the establishment. There's nowhere to doss, nowhere to hide. You come here, you work. If you want to mess about, you go out. And they do. Ken High Street, the park, cafés and shops – it's all on the doorstep and, if the inside of the school is cramped, up close London is huge, spacious and full of things to do. Students would welcome kitchen space – somewhere to warm up lunch brought from home (daily eating out is expensive) – but every inch counts here and the common rooms are small. Lockers only for GCSE, art and photography students.

School has recently bought the upper floor of a period building at 47 Kensington Court, which provides, alongside extra classrooms, a new dedicated drama space with elegant top-lighting.

Can accommodate up to 250 students. Teaching rooms are definitely small. Interactive whiteboards in use everywhere and Mac PCs everywhere too. The library is all Macs and the shelves have text books and uni guides. Good music room – again, all tech, as far as we could see though there is, apparently, a piano and a guitar. Good film/media room and photography studio has dark room. A pervasive air of relaxed purposefulness. And a fantastic location.

Pastoral care, well-being and discipline: The parents we spoke to paid tribute to the excellence of home-school communications and this is true equally of local or UK-based families and the overseas ones. Few such colleges offer the community feel and nurturing to be found here – strengthened by everyone being on first name terms and easy exchanges of emails between parents and staff. Staff room doors are glazed and usually open – little sense of 'them and us'. Everyone has a personal tutor – the same throughout their time – 20 tutees to a tutor. This is not the place if all you want is processing to achieve results. The staff gain much praise for being on top of their game educationally but also for 'really caring' and being very approachable. Drug use would lead to immediate expulsion but this sanction very rarely used. Probably not your first shot if you've been ejected elsewhere.

Pupils and parents: Students come from state and independent schools in the UK, as well as from private schools abroad. Around half the students from around 40 different countries – the rest from the UK. Fewer Chinese than hitherto – more now from Vietnam and Malaysia but college recruits from Russia, Botswana, Ukraine and Kazakhstan and elsewhere. All students have to speak good English and must speak English during the school day – even when with compatriots. About 40 per cent of the students have dedicated English-language classes (no extra cost) – up to six per week – however, best not to choose Ashbourne if you need substantial EAL reinforcement. Of the UK students, around third to a half from the state sector. No boarding though college has halls shared with other educational bodies close by and in Hampstead. Some international students' families find their own more local accommodation. Slightly more girls than boys overall and girls vastly outnumber boys in the humanities. Students here don't look like rebels, dropouts or rejects but wholesome and focused – much as at any academic, independent school's sixth form. All relish the social mix and the internationalism. Students on bursaries complement the loaded with no discernible difference. 'It's a bit cliquey,' we were told, 'especially if you're not into smoking and drinking,' but that's what they do at this age – it's part of being a teenager and drugs seem not to feature here, unlike elsewhere. The principal notes that Ashbourne appeals particularly to 'pupils from good local girls' independents who want something different at A level'.

Entrance: January and September intakes makes for flexibility and a great help to those who need time to re-group after, perhaps, mind-numbing GCSE results. Entry via interview – telephone or face-to-face with either principal or director of studies plus a subject-related entrance test. Auditions for drama/music applicants and portfolio for those who wish to pursue fine art – in which the college has a distinguished tradition. Also, most recent school report/grades/predictions and a personal statement. Bs expected for entry to A level courses – though some flexibility. International students must have minimum 5.5 IELTS or equivalent.

Exit: To a diverse list of colleges and universities – London universities figure prominently, along with eg Edinburgh University. Four to Oxbridge in 2016. Courses taken mostly point to solid professions and vocations. Many ultimately into law and finance but this is no mere spawning ground for the suited professions. Creatives include artist and photographer Marion Sosa, fashion designer Chau Nguyen, actors Calum Witney and Vicky Pasion, and the writer Dane Weatherman (founder of the literary periodical Black and Blue).

Money matters: Some bursarial help for students of exceptional ability, especially in drama, art and music, which offer a very few full scholarships. Candidates assessed on the basis of academic and (where relevant) performance or artistic ability. Also a rigorous, wide-ranging interview.

Remarks: Solid, reliable and effective place to study. Not for socialites, smack-heads or slackers.

Ashmole Academy

Cecil Road, London N14 5RJ

Pupils: 1,490 • Ages: 11–18 • Sixth form: 365

Tel: 020 8361 2703
Email: office@ashmoleacademy.org
Website: www.ashmoleacademy.org

Head Teacher: Since 1997, Mr Derrick Brown MA MBA DipEd – degree subjects psychology and business. Formerly a scientist, but changed career when he realised it wasn't all about 'filling pretty liquids into tubes. It was actually quite isolating and I'm a people person.' He was advised at the time to become either a teacher or a prison governor. He opted for the former. Prior to headship at Ashmole, he was vice principal at Leigh City Technology College in Dartford and then senior deputy at Cranford School – both schools much the same size and diversity of Ashmole and in comparable outer London suburbs.

Recently turned 60, but 'nowhere near retiring.. I wouldn't know what to do with myself'. Quietly spoken, serious and tirelessly focused on getting things done, an outstandingly successful head. His drive and determination stem from his own 'not great' secondary school education which prompted him to challenge the state school system – in this case to turn a bog standard local comp into one with all the academic benefits of a private school education, without the fees. As he says: 'Why should only a privileged few have these opportunities? I want to make it available to all kids.'

Mr Brown vowed when he started at Ashmole to make an immediate impact on results: 'It was a fairly averagely performing school with not very high aspirations.' He took a hard look at the areas that were lacking and the following year results were already up by 10 per cent. 'I created partnerships with parents, worked on the discipline and talent scouted good teachers.' His 'football manager's mentality' of never being satisfied, and always finding something to improve on, has awarded Ashmole the title of 'super state school' according to the Evening Standard.

One gets the feeling that this head has little time or inclination for hobbies. With two grown up children of his own, any extracurricular activities he may pursue are of the more 'unusual' kind – which currently, he says, is revamping an old wreck he bought (we're presuming he means property). Although there's no resting on laurels for this head, he has already consolidated Ashmole's reputation as a provider of comprehensive education at its best.

Academic matters: This school hasn't been awarded the title of 'super state' for no reason. As the head says: 'Every subject excels here, no subject is weak.' Ofsted outstanding – it has managed to sustain many years of exceptionally high results. Strong value added. Entirely non-selective, so the results are impressive. Way ahead of the other non-selective schools in the area. 'There are no tricks here – all the students come from the local community.' Anyone can do well here, we were told – boys, girls, the less motivated, 'everyone exceeds their personal best.' Classes are setted in main subjects – 'mixed ability doesn't work except in certain areas', says the head.

In 2016, 85 per cent achieved five or more A*-C grades at GCSE, including English and maths, 36 per cent A*/A grades. A levels 26 per cent A*/A and 60 per cent A*-B grades. French is popular and there's a very strong exchange link with the twinned town of Le Raincy, a suburb just outside Paris. Spanish and German are also offered at GCSE and A level, but less popular.

Students are closely monitored and undergo assessments after every half term. The head says: 'If we see underperformance, we can intervene and work with the child individually to make them improve.' However, one parent we spoke to disagreed. 'Ashmole is a great school if you are the academic, studious type. However if, like my daughter, you don't fit the mould, you're going to have more of a struggle there.' Teachers are also closely monitored and parents feel that there is quite a high turnover, although the school says it is similar to most London schools. But if this is the case, it is not an unhealthy state of affairs anyway, according to the head. He says: 'A stable school with no turnover can be a recipe for complacency and disaster.'

A third of the school has English as an additional language – support in place to make sure they progress, either through extra help or (mostly) in-class intervention. Around a seventh have some kind of SEN – about one or two per cent with statements/EHC plans. Learning support is located within its own area, providing adequate space that caters for all needs. The weakest 30 or so students drop languages after year 8, taking BTec business instead, although this varies every year. These students have extra help with the basics.

Able, gifted and talented pupils – those who have all round ability across the core subjects of English, maths and science (around one in four students at Ashmole) – have their own programme designed for them. This bespoke Ashmolean programme involves a variety of activities which 'encourage aspiration,' whether this be by visiting higher education institutes or learning through Firefly, the school's virtual learning environment. However, one unhappy parent called it an 'exclusive' club and a very 'rigid' system; 'most students who are on the programme come on it straight from primary school and there seems to be little movement.' She also said that much is made of the G&T students and the privileges offered to them, which makes the other students feel less worthy. Another parent disagreed, saying that her child has been 'on and off the programme many times according to her grades.'

Games, options, the arts: The opportunities are plentiful and the facilities wonderful. Huge floodlit Astroturf court, playing field, sports hall and separate studio for dance, aerobics and net sports, but no pool. Outdoor table tennis on offer, which proves to be a very popular lunchtime activity. Outstandingly successful in both boys' and girls' football; the boys' football team recently won the Barnet Cup and the girls' team reached the semi-final of the Middlesex Cup. Rugby also a biggie and the year 8 rugby team won the Barnet Saracens tournament recently. One parent told us: 'Even if your child is not the academic type, the sports on offer can give them the opportunity to shine.'

Much acclaimed music department. Amy Winehouse was a former student (although head, who was here at the same time, says: 'Amy left us quite early on to join the BRIT school'). Having a music specialism, they are able to employ the very latest technology. Music scholarships on offer to help those with talent develop their skills, and an increasing number of pupils take individual music lessons. A full range of extracurricular music programmes also on offer, including an orchestra, jazz band, chamber string group, junior string group, brass band, senior wind ensemble, Latin rock band, two choirs and show band for the annual school musical.

Drama popular – big, well-equipped studio and major musical production each year. Standards are high – recent 'fantastic' production of Hairspray. Impressive art studios and some astounding individual pieces of art. The school has its own radio station and two recording studios. Plenty of lunchtime and after-school clubs, including film club, debating societies, mad for books club, philosophy, homework clubs and numerous language clubs. Enrichment groups offer a choice of cultural, entrepreneurial and environmental activities. 'The options here are great,' a sixth former told us. 'We're bombarded with courses and clubs which enrich us as people.' He was not wrong.

Background and atmosphere: This is a different school, quite literally, from the Ashmole of yesteryear. It had survived in pretty dire conditions for years but, on his arrival in 1997, the head organised the sale of six acres of school land and began a visionary building programme with the proceeds. The design of the new buildings was the result of collaboration between the school, a very proactive parent committee and the architect. Rehoming happened in 2004 at a cost of £14m. The result is a bright and spacious, well-mapped-out building, 'which is easy to navigate,' one parent told us. All subjects grouped into their own sections and everything immaculately labelled. No chance of getting lost here. The only confusing things are the different coloured named staircases, like the 'orange staircase,' which in fact is blue. The head told us: 'When we designed the building we wanted to colour group it into sections so, for example, people could meet at the orange staircase, but this wasn't DDA compliant for partially sighted people, so everything has to be kept white and blue.' Lifts are also available for students with disabilities.

Large, wide corridors with beautiful wall displays, seriously impressive artwork and a convivial atmosphere. As we progressed from section to section we witnessed quiet classrooms (with the odd exception), with an atmosphere that encourages work and discourages messing around. 'We have a policy at this school that lessons should be silent, unless they require a discussion. It helps to keep the class focused.' We also noticed a lot of reading going on – by individuals in the canteen and elsewhere. The head told us that he insists every student carries a book of their choice around with them. 'There is no such thing as doing nothing,' he said. 'One can always read.'

Set in 28 acres of land in quiet, residential Southgate, the outside of the school is none too shabby either, especially for a London comprehensive. Plenty of outdoor space. Remarkably free of litter and immaculately kept lawns, outdoor classroom and environmental area, fully equipped with wooden table and benches. So much excess land that Ashmole primary school opened on the premises in September 2016. 'There is such a lack of primary schools in the area, it makes sense,' says the head. We say: Start booking your kids in now.

The new sixth form block, kitted out with its own Starbucks, was opened in 2014. This was many years in the waiting, needed £1.3 million (raised through fundraising events and tightening of the old school purse strings), two contractors and various other obstacles. One student told us: 'It's so exciting, I'm just upset I'll only have one year to enjoy it.'

Pastoral care, well-being and discipline: Big on discipline. 'Not for the free spirit,' one mother told us. Strict adherence to their uniform code expected – no exceptions or students will be asked to go home and change. Lo and behold: if pupils are caught outside the school premises with a shirt hanging out, they will be seriously reprimanded, sometimes even face a detention. Mobiles, too, are strictly forbidden, except for the sixth form – confiscated immediately if found and, to add to the humiliation, parents have to go in to school and pick them up. While this has been a bone of contention with many of the parents, who like to get hold of their kids after school hours, others feel it is a good thing. 'If nothing else because there have been some phone thefts in the area, but muggers know not to bother with Ashmole kids as they never have phones on them,' one parent told us.

Zero tolerance of drugs, weapons and violence – on or off the premises. Much has been done to combat bullying, which has clearly been a problem at Ashmole in former years (as in many comprehensives of this size). CCTV cameras operate along main corridors 'to monitor any deviant behaviour that may occur' and when the new building was designed head specifically requested wide, open spaces free of 'little cul-de-sacs,' where vulnerable students could be cornered. As Orwellian as this may sound, bullying is now virtually non-existent and parents are very grateful.

Disruptive or abusive pupils are sent to the individual learning room, where they are under supervision, have no contact with their friends and hate it. Two or three days there usually does the trick, but head will exclude for serious offences – roughly five permanent exclusions a year. 'We just can't let a disruptive child continue,' he says. 'They are given community service and various other deterrents, but if they are hell bent on being disruptive, they're out.' The result of this is a school in which pupils feel secure and comfortable and everyone knows the score.

Each key stage has its own learning mentors and key stage managers whom pupils know they can go to if they feel the need. Parents aren't so convinced. One parent we spoke to said: 'It's not always made clear who we should be speaking to, or emailing. I have left messages on several occasions and no one has responded. I think the communication between parents and year heads could be improved.' However, for the most part, parents and students we spoke to seemed extremely happy with the school. One sixth former told us: 'I've loved every minute of this school. The sixth form is like a big family, even for external students.'

A large amount of interaction between the year groups, encouraged by the cultural and charitable activities. Pupils feel they have friends in all years. Charity work plays a vital part in the general ethos of the school and every year students and staff raise thousands of pounds for a variety of good causes. Overall, the school has a general sense of self-discipline and a fostering of civilised behaviour.

Pupils and parents: Vast ethnic mix, as you'd expect from the Southgate area, though more Cypriots – Greek and Turkish – than anything else. Main religion is Christianity of all sorts, the second is Islam. Mostly working parents, but a supportive and hard working PTA makes big contribution to the school's development. Pupils are cheery, ambitious, focused and involved. Notable former students include: Amy Winehouse, former S Club 7 member Rachel Stevens, musician Stephen Sidwell, goalie Mark Bunn, Oscar winning producer Mark King, The Feeling lead vocalist Daniel Sells and Channel 5 tsar Sham Sandhu.

Entrance: More than 1,100 apply for the 232 places – of which siblings will take around 80. You'll get in if you have a sibling there, are a looked-after child or live very close – otherwise no chance. 'I wish I had bought on Cecil Road years ago. Houses must be worth a fortune now', one parent sighed. Up to 20 music aptitude places; these pupils, along with others who show talent, are placed on the music scholarship programme.

Exit: Around 30 per cent leave after GCSEs, mostly for vocational courses elsewhere. The rest need to get Bs in the subjects they wish to study for A levels to stay on in the sixth form. Around a third to a half of sixth formers to top universities; generally a few to Oxbridge (none in 2016, but six medics); others to places like Durham, Warwick, London universities, Nottingham, Leeds. Science, law and humanities are all popular.

Remarks: Slick, sensible and effective. Check out the housing market.

Bancroft's School

611–627 High Road, Woodford Green, Essex IG8 0RF

Pupils: 1,121 • Ages: 7–18 • Sixth form: 239 • C of E

Fees: £13,290 – £16,323 pa

Tel: 020 8505 4821
Email: stephanie.wallis@bancrofts.org
Website: www.bancrofts.org

Head: Since September 2016, Simon Marshall MA PGCE (Cantab) MA MPhil (Oxon), previously head of the English College in Prague. Highly educated: classics degree (choral exhibitioner) and PGCE from Cambridge, later studying English at Oxford and taking an MPhil there in 18th century studies. He has been head of English at King's College Wimbledon and deputy head of UCS. A keen mountaineer and runner, he enjoys gardening, music and theatre. Married to Eleanor.

Head of prep: Since 2012, Mr Joe Layburn MA, previously acting head. MA in German literature from University College London, followed by a 15-year career as investigative journalist and TV reporter, primarily for Channel 4. Retrained as a teacher and joined Bancroft's Prep in 2004. Author of a trilogy of children's books. Married with three sons; two of them were educated at Bancroft's from prep onwards and one at a special needs school. Keen on running, cycling and West Ham United.

Academic matters: Classrooms busy, not over-orderly and relaxed in the prep – we wanted to look at the displays, all of which seemed interesting and not as predictable as they so often are. We liked the alternatives to 'said' and loved the paper collages showing variations on the Arcimboldo fruity face and the glittery, sparkly, firework ones. We also approved some of the interesting work in progress, especially the lesson on moulds – 'We had to throw them away as they were beginning to smell,' was a rueful observation. Year 6 has critical thinking lessons – 'to expand our minds, to think out of the box, to widen our imagination,' we were told, earnestly. We were impressed by the sensible 'traffic light' system whereby pupils assess their grasp of what they have learnt and where they need help. All entrants assessed for SpLD at 7 and SENCo-led help laid on where needed – mostly mild dyslexia.

Notable results across the board (in 2016, 89 per cent A*/A grades at GCSE) but maths is a star performer by any standards. English more of a spread, despite reports of some brilliantly inspirational teaching. Modern langs getting a boost – all year 7s learn German and Spanish; Russian is an option from year 9; Mandarin recently introduced. Greek and Latin have healthy numbers. Remarkable science results – especially in chemistry. History and geography also impressive. Few takers for art, music and DT – surprising, given the facilities – but a school which takes its academics seriously. No trendy subjects, though drama has seduced its way into the timetable and options list and programming introduced for year 8s. A particular, enlightened feature is that subjects can be chosen not, as elsewhere, from 'blocks' but from the whole curriculum. If they can manage it at Bancroft's, why not everywhere?

A level results similarly impressive – 90 per cent A*-B, 67 per cent A*/A in 2016. Maths and chemistry popular and successful. Demand for maths and sciences has led to creation of new maths room and science lab. Economics and geography good and, at this level, English also impresses. Greek and Latin survive, though the numbers taking modern langs are, we would suggest, a cause for concern, though may reflect the immense diversity of backgrounds here.

A place where serious learning happens and in which learning is taken seriously. The library, revamped with a stylish mezzanine floor beautifully integrated into the whole, is a proper scholarly resource – not something you see everywhere these days, when for 'library' you can so often read 'IT suite'. Pupils appreciate the library and its staff – 'they are fantastic – they get in anything you need'. Sixth form has a dedicated library and quiet study area plus university-type lecture theatre – used for societies, debates and visiting speakers. IT everywhere – lots of rooms with new PCs, including a tiptop language lab, which should give the languages a deserved boost.

Learning support department screens all at 11+ (the prep also screens at 7+). School has its first SENCo and all new staff get some training in SpLD. All on the LS register (mostly mild dyslexics) have an IEP and get some kind of individual support – the younger ones come out of different lessons each term and older ones get one-to-one. A TA in class helps those who are happy to be helped in that way. Lower sixth get help to 'develop individual learning skills'. 'They are wonderfully flexible over special needs,' said a parent.

Games, options, the arts: Exuberant sports, music and drama and lots of inspiring extracurricular stuff in the prep. Outgoing, relaxed and confident children from a vast range of local backgrounds, as you'd expect.

Sports are 'big' and well-resourced. Large playing fields on site plus vast sports hall with 25m pool. Five minutes away is school's own West Grove with pitches, courts, tracks etc. Achievement to match – triumphs in netball, rugby and cricket as well as tours in these and hockey to, eg, New Zealand, Australia, South Africa and Sri Lanka. Heartfelt pupil and parental complaints that sport is too elitist – 'if you're not in a squad, they don't give a monkey's' – seen by school as a priority and B and C teams have been developed, along with soccer. 'We are encouraging more staff to help so we can run more teams. It's something we need to work on.'

CCF is huge, very popular and enthusiastically pursued by those who surprise themselves by how much they get out of it, girls as well as boys – 'It's taught me how to get on with people I'd never mix with normally'; 'It's good that the sixth form help with it – you can have a bit of a laugh with them': not common in what is still, more or less, a London school. Thriving D of E and Sea Scout group with cubs and scouts.

Equally, steadily increased provision for arts across the school. Music and drama enthusiastic and popular – annual concert in Drapers' Hall the big annual event, with bands, solo performances and musical mix the main features. Vast range of instruments studied – music maybe more pop and jazz than classical, though we are told around eight classical concerts each year. Drama had a fillip with conversion of old gym to good, large studio and subject now on the curriculum at all levels. Not all musicals here, either – The Caucasian Chalk Circle and Macbeth among recent productions; year 9 and 10 performers taught to fence for their production of The Three Musketeers. Productions at Edinburgh Fringe Festival.

Art, electronics and DT departments produce lively work – we liked the clever clocks, mobiles and the remote control cars and, within the remit of the task, pupils are given their head to be creative with the actual design. Art, exceptionally well-displayed throughout school, originates in one of two brand new studios with kilns and exhibition space – light, spacious and full of quiet artists. Nice ceramics. Art could and should be bigger here – perhaps textiles and photography (on the way), as more than a club?

Tons of trips and tours – though some parental gripes about not enough places on trips for eager applicants. Extracurricular stuff is good, though some cries for more from the inexhaustible.

Background and atmosphere: Founded in 1737 by the Drapers' Company on behalf of Francis Bancroft as a school for poor boys; moved to Woodford from Mile End in 1889 into the present large and imposing red-brick Victorian gothic revival building – clearly designed to impress, with serious scholarly credentials by architect, Sir Arthur Blomfield, also responsible for Selwyn College, Cambridge, The RCM, much of Charterhouse, The Bank of England, Wellington, Eton Lower Chapel etc etc, as well as an astounding number of parish churches. This is one of his more benign and attractive buildings, with towers, crenellations and oriel windows, a splendid central quad and admirably generous corridors which, though originally intended for 200 boys, still feel spacious for today's quadrupled numbers.

A truly impressive school with twisty, brick staircases and leaded lights which grab eager 10 year olds immediately – 'I chose it because it was like Hogwarts': a unique selling point in Essex, to be sure. Large Great Hall – typical of date and type. Excellent Courtyard Building with colonnaded atrium and sitting area, dining room (all eat together; good food, though popular vegetarian option can run out too fast for true veggie latecomers, we're told), servery and sixth form common room and café: large and well-used. Some typically dismal 1960s add-ons but much better later additions (such as enormous multi-purpose sports hall) and adjoining buildings, eg vast head's house now used for admin and offices too, with head's garden open to everyone for quiet time and 'well-respected'. Very recent physics labs and modern language rooms and DT suite.

Integral chapel one of the best bits (complete with much-loved chaplain who is 'lovely, a wonderful person for a chat, a laugh and advice – he takes salsa club'), into which everyone comes once weekly for an ecumenical service. Brass plaques to former heads and a vast stained glass east window set the tone for the services, which are inclusive in all ways, given the mix of pupils. Chapel also used for arts events – words and music etc, a classy extracurricular feature here.

The prep school is in two conjoined, inviting-looking, modern red-brick buildings at the lower right hand side of the main school playing fields – two-storeyed and with big windows. From the main school they appear small and modest; the main school, viewed from the prep, looks imposing and a little awe-inspiring, but the prep children spend time in the main school, so that 'It's a bit scary as it's so big and the students are so big, but we had a meeting with the head so we know much more about it now and I'm not really scared any more'. Quite! And senior pupils trot over to visit their junior siblings in break too. However, the prep is its own world and, as you descend the slope to its entrance, between the playing field and the tennis court, a gentleness and palpable sense of fun envelops you.

The prep has splendid new rooms which have greatly enhanced its overall space and provision. New science, drama, music and DT rooms, a good-sized hall with flexible seating – lots of IT and new laptops. Around 23 children in a class, but the rooms are big and airy enough not to feel crowded – we did not feel the need to open windows, as one so often does. The library, recently refurbished, is well-stocked and a good mix of fact and fiction. Outside space good and super all-weather surface for littlies with monster chess set and apparatus – not surprisingly, 'Everyone loves coming out here'.

Parental tributes to general efficiency of school and its communications. Sense of order, purposeful activity and common sense all-pervasive.

Pastoral care, well-being and discipline: When asked what was good about the school, all the parents and pupils we spoke to – lots – said, as with one voice, 'the pastoral care' – we can't recall such unanimity on any other school feature anywhere. Tributes to the teaching staff, overall friendliness, care and attention given to individuals pour from everyone and are a delight to hear: 'My teacher is amazing – he's given me extra lessons every week. He's ordered in around 30 extra books just to help me. They'll help with anyone – not just the Oxbridge candidates'; 'The teacher gave my daughter as much time as she needed when she was struggling'; 'The staff commitment is excellent; pastoral care couldn't be better'; 'My children love it – they look forward to every day.'

Pupils and parents: From as far away as Potter's Bar, Winchmore Hill and Cheshunt, though most from between 10 and 20 minutes' drive away. Transport from local tube station to encourage pupils to look out of town towards green space for schooling. Vast ethnic and social intake – 'very well-handled by school,' say parents: around 30-35 per cent South Asian, 10-15 per cent Jewish, 40 per cent white. Most parents first-time buyers who 'work very hard to pay fees'.

OB notables include Dennis Quilley, Sir Frederick Warner, Sir Neil McFarlane, Hari Kunzru, Adam Foulds, Yolanda Browne, Andrew Saul, Anita Anand, Lord Pannick QC, Samantha Spiro and Mike Lynch.

Entrance: At 7+ – over-subscribed by about three to one. Testing in English – reading and writing – and maths for year 3 entry takes place on beanbags. Children seen (and offered doughnuts) in small groups with head and deputy – it's 'as informal and low key as possible'. Around 70-75 places offered – Bancroft's will be first choice for most applicants.

At 11, 50 come up from the prep. Around 500 apply for 70 additional places. Tests in maths and English plus interviews. In practice around a third of those whose first choice is Bancroft's will get in. Umpteen feeders, though several from St Aubyn's, Loyola and Woodford Green Prep. Around a half from state primaries.

Candidates for the sixth form sit the school's own entrance exam in two proposed A level subjects, need six As at GCSE plus the usual references. Around 20 places at this level – very few (around 10 per cent) leave.

Exit: Vast majority of prep school pupils – around 90 per cent – to senior school; a few to local grammars, including Woodford County High, Ilford County High and The Latymer. Others to join siblings or take up a scholarship elsewhere.

Around 10 per cent leave after GCSEs. Ten to Oxbridge in 2016 and 12 to study medicine. Other popular choices include Exeter, Imperial College, Bath, Durham and King's College London.

Money matters: Fifteen Drapers' scholarships offered annually at 11+ worth a quarter to a half of fees. No means-testing – based solely on performance at entrance exams. Also music scholarships worth half or quarter fees plus free tuition in one instrument. Several Francis Bancroft scholarship awards – means-tested but with a generous financial threshold, worth up to full fees, based on a sliding scale dependent on family income. Bancroft's Foundation set up in 2012 to mark 275th anniversary has already raised significant amounts to increase means-tested provision – enough to fund six Foundation scholars.

Remarks: A splendid school, catering for bright children and those who will seize opportunities. Deservedly over-subscribed. Brings glory to Essex well beyond its immediate catchment.

Beatrix Potter Primary School

Magdalen Road, London SW18 3ER

Pupils: 412 • Ages: 3–11

Tel: 020 8874 1482
Email: Info@beatrixpotter.wandsworth.sch.uk
Website: www.beatrixpotterschool.com

Headteacher: Since 1988, Stephen Neale MA Dip Ed Tech Dip Ed (late 50s). Growing older and wiser, he remains a popular hands-on head, described by parents as a real character, somewhat unconventional and very easy to get on with. Brave enough to make his own decisions and not a person to get tangled up in bureaucracy. Married to a Polish opera singer, with one grown-up son. His enthusiasm for travelling, links with other schools and exploring different cultures all over the globe influences many of the school's activities. Beatrix Potter has gained the British Council's Full International School's Award twice. A steam train enthusiast, Mr Neale also enjoys sailing and travelling.

Entrance: Admission to the school via the standard Wandsworth primary school admissions criteria. Looked after children and special needs pupils first, then those living closest to the school. Admission is usually oversubscribed, but if you are not lucky enough to get a place in reception, it's always worth calling the school for occasional places in the older age groups.

Exit: Pupils move onto a big mix of senior schools. Around 60 per cent to state sector: Burntwood, St Cecilia's, Southfields, Wilson's and Wallington Grammar. Forty per cent to independents, including Emanuel, Dulwich College, JAGS and Wimbledon High School.

Remarks: Good solid curriculum continues to be at the heart of this delightful primary school; all pupils are well grounded in literacy, numeracy and IT. Imaginative range of projects covering history, geography, sciences and international links are embedded into classroom work and the arts. Fab new technology suite and equipment, where pupils can contact children all over the world via Skype and Facetime. These links often turn into fantastic foreign adventures for pupils, and have led to the school being asked to host a European Link Project. The caretaker's house has been redeveloped so the school can offer accommodation to pupils and their teachers visiting from abroad.

It's not a pushy school, but everyone gets to where they want to go. School produces parents' booklets packed with information on how to support your child at home and get involved in their education. The ethos is all about being a happy, balanced person who is able to move on to senior school well equipped to cope in new settings. Head runs advice sessions for parents to assist them in selecting the right senior schools. Children with SEN are well cared for by full-time SENCo and her assistant, who run a variety of small groups for children with different additional needs. School is eager to work with parents and other therapists to help children achieve to the best of their ability. Since the refurbishments, the building is now fully accessible for children with physical disabilities. Kids City runs on-site breakfast and after-school clubs.

Mr Neale and architects have worked hard over the last few years to redesign much of the school, and there are now two classes right through. Outdoor spaces have been improved with courtyard areas, picnic tables and three outdoor courts and there's a large new sports hall. Sports coaches are brought in from local clubs for lacrosse, cricket, tennis, tag rugby and football. Parents say the arts are developing well, particularly now the school has separate spaces for art, dance and drama. Another bonus of the expansion is the new kitchen: the school can offer freshly cooked lunches every day. Initially the expansion process caused quite a few wobbles and rumbles from some parents. However, everyone is now in agreement that the school is able to offer more to its pupils while still maintaining its long-term reputation for being a warm, friendly community school. PTA and school governors are all very active and fundraise substantial amounts of money for both the school and various charities. Past and present pupils have many fond memories of the school. Some can't stay away, returning to do their teaching practice or even joining the teaching staff permanently.

B

B

Belleville Primary School

Webbs Road, London SW11 6PR

Pupils: 875 • Ages: 3–11

Tel: 020 7228 6727
Email: enquiries@bellevilleschool.org
Website: www.belleville-school.org.uk

Headteacher: Since 2001, Mr John Grove (50s) BEd MA, previously head at West Hill Primary School in Wandsworth. Two children, both at university; partner also works in education. A man consumed by his job, who found Belleville failing in 2001 and has worked uncompromisingly to make it the most sought-after primary school in the area. In his rare moments off, admits to being a season ticket holder at Chelsea FC. A visionary, who still gets unexpected hugs from the youngest of his charges as he roams the corridors.

Entrance: At 4+, 120 places, in four forms of 30, with an extra 'bulge' class in reception in 2016/17. Heavily over-subscribed. Usual local authority admissions criteria: special requirements, siblings and those living closest to the school (no more than around 270 metres away for a first offer). Popular on-site nursery takes 52 children each year, but nursery place does not guarantee entry to reception in main school.

Exit: Since Bolingbroke Academy opened up the road in 2012, approximately half to this non-selective school, which local residents campaigned for. Others to a range of local state and private schools, including Alleyn's, Dulwich, Whitgift, Putney High and Emmanuel (10 scholarships in 2016). A few sit successfully for Graveney School, Tooting, which has a grammar stream. A steady trickle to the Lycée Kensington and the German School Richmond, reflecting the number of European families in the locality.

Remarks: Glossy new site at Meteor Street houses a reception and a year 1 class, and will become a one-form entry campus for the school's full age-range, complementing the three-form entry at Webbs Road. Head admits intake will probably have to stop at 900, but clearly frustrated by lack of space in this cosmopolitan neighbourhood, where two-bed conversions go for £700k. 'My dream is to take one of these nearby private schools, turn it into a state school and expand,' he told us, his eyes gleaming behind their specs. 'Only one?' we asked. He smiled.

As well as a penchant for the state sequestration of private property, Mr Grove has a passion for doing things well. Housed in what was once a dark and gloomy Victorian maze, imaginative building work has turned Belleville into a really beautiful school, where old-time space and solidity meets modern light and technology. Walls have been knocked through, windows replaced, venetian blinds fitted in attractive colours, and everywhere painted to look bright and fresh. Intelligent, creative use of ICT is integrated into the fabric of the school and is awesomely good: iPads and tablets are mounted in every corridor, displaying slideshows of school events, offering information, etc. Classrooms have ICT projectors and interactive whiteboards, teachers use visualisers (for dinosaurs like this reviewer, that's a powerful digital camera that points downwards and projects onto the teacher's computer/projector screen, so that books, objects, etc can be magnified and displayed clearly to everyone in the room). We were gratified and impressed to see this head, at least, insisting that the children learn on both Macs and PCs, as well as on desktops, tablets, netbooks and smartphones, so that they can cope with whatever system a given environment has in place. But none of this has come at the price of old-fashioned excellence. Work on the walls showed both handwriting and content of a very high standard. Ofsted stated that 'pupils achieve exceptionally well', and everywhere we saw children working with a lively yet calm focus. 'The behaviour is excellent here,' asserts head, 'We have 800 children and I never have to raise my voice.' We believe him.

Specialist teachers are employed for art, music, PE, dance, French and computing, and the results are splendid. Wonderful artwork – inspired by, for instance, Van Gogh and Kandinsky – is everywhere, produced by the children from a modest-looking art room with love and skill. When we arrived, we were deafened by a terrific workshop on Sengalese drumming, which turned out to be a weekly event for all the classes. (One lad, so moved by the spirit that he couldn't sit still, suddenly left his djembe and did an impromptu breakdance, to fond applause). The children all learn French, and were keen to show us how much they knew.

SEN provision is strong and mostly integrated, with plenty of one-to-one support for individuals provided during regular lessons. 'We don't withdraw unless we have to,' confirms head. Parents report themselves satisfied: 'SEN support is really good'; 'The school's been brilliant both at pushing my abler child and supporting my younger one.'

Belleville was one of only five primary schools in London to be awarded the status of National Teaching School, and professional development is inescapably at the heart of everything it does. In each year group there are teachers whose core job is to improve pedagogy and teaching, and the children certainly seem to enjoy their lessons. 'The teachers are really nice'; 'The teachers are fair'; 'They really try and make the lessons fun and they do succeed'; 'The teachers are very good people,' were just a few of the comments we heard. Parents agree: 'We've been impressed with the enthusiasm of all the teachers'; 'The classroom assistants have been an invaluable resource'; 'The staff are brilliant and the academics are brilliant'; 'My children have always had fantastic teachers.' There was also praise for the many clubs on offer, both in and out of school, with parents particularly grateful for the breakfast and after-school clubs: 'They cover long hours, which is very helpful for working parents, and have a wide range of activities.'

The school prides itself on its diverse community, although its location in the heart of Yummy Mummy Central (as Clapham Common is locally known) inevitably accounts for the very high proportion of articulate, well-mannered, middle-class children that we met there, most of them Caucasian. We heard murmurs from a few parents of different ethnic backgrounds, who, while remaining extremely positive about the school, felt that it could do more to acknowledge their children's needs. Belleville's motto, proclaimed in huge posters everywhere, is 'Relentless Drive For Excellence and Equality', and it's possible that this relentless drive has occasionally knocked a few obstacles out of its path. We couldn't help noticing the almost universal youth of the teaching staff, with its few older members hived off to the school's smaller Meteor Street site, where, presumably, fewer people could be offended by their wrinkles and grey hairs. (And in fact they too will soon be mostly replaced by younglings, head assures me, but will be redistributed at Webb's Road, where they can hide amongst the 20-somethings in plain sight.) But by any measurable standards, Belleville is an outstanding school. 'My children are thriving at Belleville, and are valued,' was a typical parental comment. 'My child has done as well as she could do,' was another. 'I can't imagine her doing better at a private school'. Which is just as well, really; if Belleville gets any more successful, there won't be any left.

B

Belmont Mill Hill Preparatory School

Linked with Grimsdell, Mill Hill Pre-Prep School, Mill Hill School

   16

The Ridgeway, London NW7 4ED

Pupils: 494 • Ages: 7-13

Fees: £16,815 pa

Tel: 020 8906 7270
Email: office@belmontschool.com
Website: www.belmontschool.com

Head: Since 2015, Mr Leon Roberts MA PGCE. Taught for four years in the state sector, moved to Keble Prep as head of history for the next four years then became deputy head (academic) of Belmont in 2004 before being promoted to senior deputy head (pastoral) in 2010 and finally taking on the headmaster's role. Married with three young daughters, including twins, he enjoys cricket (playing and coaching, both boys and girls), walking and watching Nordic Noir drama.

Down-to-earth, hands on and with the same energetic style as the outgoing head, he approaches the job with the same consultative and open style – he's building on a school which is in great shape (which he's been involved in creating) and adding his own mark.

Entrance: Automatic entry from pre-prep (Grimsdell) to prep (except in some very rare cases). This accounts for two-thirds of the school's intake. For external candidates, there are two main points of entry into the school – 7+ (year 3) and 11+ (year 7). NB part of a group of independent co-ed/boys' schools that coordinate 11+ results, but forbid those who have accepted a place at one school from taking up a subsequent waiting list offer from another. Occasionally there are places available in other years – these are called 'chance vacancies'. Heavily oversubscribed from external candidates, so each expected to take reading, creative writing and maths tests together with a reference from their previous school

Exit: Some 95 per cent of Belmont students continue on to Mill Hill School, although all have to sit the CE exam (for setting purposes. It is not a qualifying exam for entry). 'Children for whom Mill Hill is not the right school will leave at the end of year 6; once in year 7, the children have a place at Mill Hill at 13+ conditional on continuing good work ethic and good behaviour.' One parent felt that the fact that Belmont goes up to 13 is a massive advantage. 'At 13 they are desperate to make the next jump and are confident to do it. They are not little 11 and 12 year olds floundering around.' Occasional transfers to boarding schools eg Harrow, Tonbridge and Stowe.

Remarks: Established in 1912 following the success of its senior school Mill Hill, Belmont Junior House opened its gates with one student – Harold Pearse Soundy. By the summer term 1913, it had 12 pupils. Originally a boarding prep for boys, it has been a day school since the 80s and co-ed since 1995.

Situated on the relatively quiet part of Mill Hill's Ridgeway, the school is in an enviable location – set back from the road and flanked by large houses, beautiful greenery and a stone's throw away from the small but popular Belmont Farm. Hard to believe that a 25 minute train ride will take you to the centre of London. Harder still after meandering through some 35 acres of parkland to the rear of the school – taking in the panoramic views of the Totteridge Valley. Undoubtedly the school's selling point, the grounds and its facilities are impressive for a London-based junior school.

For a sporty child, this must be nirvana. The grounds host seven rugby pitches, 10 football pitches (of various sizes to accommodate different age groups), three cricket pitches, five cricket nets, five rounders pitches, two Astro mini hockey pitches, six Astro tennis courts, six netball courts, a fully equipped gymnasium and a small dance hall. Finally, a 1,500 metre woodland cross-country course known as The Oti (in memory of a former student who died of sickle cell anaemia). Pupils also have the use of the new 25 metre indoor swimming pool at Mill Hill School for swimming lessons and clubs. As one parent told us, 'Forget this school if your child has absolutely no interest in sport; they'll be unhappy', commenting that it is the most disciplined department in the school.

Outdoor facilities also include a large wooden adventure playground, a variety of large established games including a giant chessboard, for children to use during break and lunchtime, and a gardening area where pupils tend seasonal plants and flowers. We spotted a little recycling area and then learned that Belmont has been awarded the much coveted Eco-Schools Green Flag Award.

After the spectacular exterior, the interior of the school comes somewhat as an anticlimax. The original 18th century house acts as the main entrance to the school and houses the function rooms, main reception area, staff rooms and the head's office. Whilst this has been tastefully refurbished (with the original beautiful winding staircase acting as the centrepiece), several of the classrooms on the upper level seemed on the cramped side and lacking in imagination. The science labs (in the Cloister Block) and the gymnasium particularly struck us as archaic and in need of a refurb.

That said, the Jubilee Hall, which accommodates most of the lower school classrooms, the dining/assembly hall and the head of lower school's office, is modern and airy. The school has a genial vibe, perhaps because it is not as formal as some of the other independent schools we have visited. Colourful and interesting displays of student work adorn the corridors, and the pupils we witnessed, whilst not particularly noisy, were 'spirited'.

Belmont pupils 'speak with confidence, whether in a classroom discussion, reading in an assembly or conversing with adults,' said their most recent ISI inspection. This was particularly evident on our tour when we met with school's council members – a bunch of 8+ year old boys and girls who were bright, articulate and bounced off each other like the future spokespeople they may one day become. They were confident, polite and hard pushed to find anything negative to say about the school. One bemoaned the fact that lunch should be better organised, whilst another commented incredulously that 'We've been to play other schools that don't even have their own cricket grounds' – which made him feel very lucky.

A Belmont child is a busy one. School opens at 7.30am for optional breakfast, and from there on in, a cascade of activities barely allows for an oxygen intake. Fifty clubs are on offer during lunchtime and after school, so if elastic or kicking a ball ain't your thing – why not try ancient Greek? Or perhaps origami, Dead Poets Society (we presume without Robin Williams), jazz band, Belle Plates or Bollywood dance, to name but a few. Popular after-school activities include chamber choir and horse riding. Fabulous trips (including a history trip to Venice) are offered from year 6 and above.

Clearly time is set aside for the curricular stuff, as results are well above national expectations. This, we are told, is achieved through 'excellent teaching' (ISI 2012), a broad curriculum that includes French from year 3 and Latin from year 6 and smallish class sizes. Teachers have annual performance reviews and their planning is monitored termly. No sluggards allowed here. A couple of parents we spoke to said that academia across the Foundation has definitely been stepped up a notch over the past few years. One parent told us: 'Belmont was always more of a nurturing school, but the goalposts seem to be constantly changing and you feel like you are kept on your toes the whole time.' In school's view, 'High academic performance is our number one target.'

Sats abolished in favour of continuous assessments from year 3. Most pupils are expected to continue through the Foundation, although places at Mill Hill are not unconditional. Any early problems, academically or behaviourally, are usually flagged up whilst the child is at Grimsdell school (the pre-prep), so there are 'rarely any surprises.' School says that because Belmont is part of a Foundation of three schools, it is important to look at the bigger picture. 'If we didn't feel a child could cope, we wouldn't allow them to progress to year 7.' These cases are few and far between, however.

The school has a small learning support department and is happy to accommodate children with mild cases of dyslexia and dyspraxia. Anything more severe, and 'we're not the school for them.' Small groups of gifted and talented children are arranged across the years, and most are prepared for the 11+ and 13+ scholarship awards.

Belmont is a Christian foundation based upon the principles of 'religious freedom'. Chapel services are obligatory, because if you start pulling pupils out, 'you lose the ability to say we can work together'. However, the school's pupils represent a wide range of faiths and cultures, so chapel services and assemblies are inter-denominational.

During our tour, we noticed the school undergoing building works – six new classrooms, two science labs and an impressive hall. Shortly after our visit, we discovered that Belmont, along with the other two schools in the Mill Hill foundation, was merging with the Mount School for girls (hmmm). The merger came as a great shock for parents who were informed by email, with no prior warning. School insisted that it was not planning a permanent expansion; pupil numbers have increased by some 55 or so, and boy:girl ratio is now more even. The Mount building now houses The Mount, Mill Hill International school.

Belmont Primary School

Belmont Road, London W4 5UL

Pupils: 470 • Ages: 3-11

Tel: 020 8994 7677
Email: office@belmont.hounslow.sch.uk
Website: www.belmontprimaryschool.org.uk

Head: Since 2010, Ms Verity Coates MA PGCE (40s). She has been in various roles at Belmont since 1996, including deputy head from 2005. She graduated with a degree in mathematics from Newnham College, Cambridge in 1987 and after a PGCE at York and a brief spell at a London primary school she worked abroad in Africa. On returning to England in the mid 90s, she started as a class teacher and SEN coordinator at Belmont and is fiercely loyal to the school.

Keen to press her commitment to state education, she appeared anxious about Belmont being perceived as the middle class answer to independent schooling. Tight-lipped when challenged on the question of Sats results and the high numbers of pupils who have private tutoring – she is determined that her staff also get some credit. Quite right too.

Entrance: Preference given to siblings. Next in the pecking order are those who live within the Primary Admissions Area – 'catchment' to you and me. In recent years, even living in the catchment has not guaranteed a place at the school. Children in public care and those with medical/social needs come high up in the pecking order. After that – don't even try. Parents are known to rent property within the area just to qualify, and then..? More hope from year 2, however, as a steady trickle leaves to go to prep school/move out of London. Places are snapped up, though, and school tends to be full all the way through to year 6.

Exit: About half to Chiswick School, although the numbers are decreasing with the advent of competition in the area. A clutch to West London Free School and Hammersmith Academy as well as the usual numbers to Twyford, Lady Margaret, Gunnersbury and the Green school. The rest (about 20 per cent) to local independents, including Godolphin & Latymer, Notting Hill and Ealing High, Latymer Upper, Hampton, Ibstock Place. The occasional one to St Paul's Juniors at 8 as well as at 11. Lots of outside coaching during years 5 and 6 to prepare for independent school entrance exams. Ms Coates asks for a financial contribution for the school reports required for entry into such schools.

Remarks: The reluctance of the head and her staff to welcome us to look round this super, oversubscribed, well-funded state primary (or indeed respond to our messages) bemused us – especially considering that Belmont is one of the most successful and popular state primaries in West London, with seven applications for each place.

Pupils bubbled with enthusiasm and love for their school as they showed us round. An abundance of facilities – from musical instruments, playground equipment, books and materials to the brand new stage for dramatic performances. Results are excellent, showing much higher than expected progress between key stages 1 and 2 and a quarter of pupils in their final year sitting the optional level 6 in reading and maths.

The school caters for an affluent corner of Chiswick and the catchment area is becoming ever tighter. Families from sumptuous houses in the Bedford Park area can no longer expect to get a place. Were it not for the council accommodation on the school's doorstep, you might not get the social mix one would expect in an inner London state primary school at all. Our first impression was that there was an unusually high proportion of white middle class kids; the head was keen to give precise statistics and told us that 52 per cent of Belmont's pupils are from minority ethnic groups (in this case Eastern Europe and a few affluent UK residents from say, Canada or Sweden). This ain't your typical London primary.

School is housed in a large, three-storey brick building that benefits from the high ceilings, large windows, well-proportioned rooms and wide corridors typical of Victorian buildings of its kind. A generous refurbishment programme has resulted in shiny polished floors and child-friendly primaries and pastels (plenty of aqua and primrose) painted on the walls – helping the building to fall firmly on the side of happy, modern school rather than gloomy Victorian institution.

Belmont is beautifully mapped out, with two classes at either end of each spacious floor, each one charmingly named after fruit – apples, pears, cherries. The main hall in the middle space between classrooms is used for play (reception and year 1 – lots of dressing up and imaginary play goes on here), assemblies (years 2 and 3 on the middle floor) and drama and gym (years 5 and 6 on the top floor). Yet more rooms house musical instruments galore (drum kits, pianos, flutes, various percussion), two well-stocked libraries, two ICT suites (the juniors have the luxury of one computer each, one between two for the infants) and dedicated SEN provision. Teaching up to the end of year 2 is mixed ability; setting in maths and English from year 3. Two sets – the higher being slightly the larger and having, therefore, up to 32 children to the lower set's 28-ish. The upper set has just one teacher, no classroom assistant being needed with these children because, of course, they are motivated and keen to learn. We couldn't see much problem with the lower sets either.

About 20 per cent of children identified as having special educational needs but a very small proportion of these have statements. School has coped in the past with more severe special needs, but children must be able to climb stairs.

About a quarter of pupils don't have English as a first language (about 43 different first languages other than English recorded) but no marked difference in the performance of these children – credit to the school. Dedicated part time EAL teacher as well as SEN coordinator with a team of teaching assistants give support in the class room. Sats results in all subjects are at least 10 per cent above local and national averages and are far higher by year 6. Those with EAL needs are seen individually or in small groups for as long as necessary, until they are up to the general standard. Teaching assistants support individuals, pairs or groups under the supervision of the SENCo. A reading recovery teacher sees individuals who, by year 1, are falling behind – with 'fantastic' results. When we visited, there had been a relatively high turnover of staff (head assures us that this is a result of career progression, maternity – no reflection on the school). Five male teachers – always a bonus. Years 3 to 6 have 40 minutes of French weekly. Everyone has two hours of physical activity weekly.

All classes have class music lessons and learn singing with a specialist teacher. In addition to class music, many learn individually – often more than one instrument. Recorder is offered to the whole of year 3 and there is a choir. Swanky staging facilitates an annual production from year 6. Other year groups, sometimes working together, also put on shows each year. Photographs on display suggest a high level of dramatic productions, much supported by parents, many of whom are 'in the arts'.

Good sports provision. A school sports partnership linked to Chiswick School and an outsourced sports programme (football, netball and athletics) in addition to members of staff teaching sport. On Friday afternoons here there is 'enrichment time', when for 30 minutes children can choose from a wide variety of activities, from Glee Club to comic making. Strong after-school club provision. These include, as well as the sport and music, Big Bang Science and Doughlightful – a clay modelling activity.

The Belmont Home School Association – PTA to you and me – raises between £20,000 and £30,000 each year. This has helped make the playground ever more luxuriant, with designated spaces for quiet reflection, a wilderness garden, covered areas for performances with costume boxes, lots of bike sheds, a super climbing wall painted by parents and plenty of gardening boxes replete with flowers, herbs and plants.

The early years spill out beautifully into carefully designed outdoor play areas, secure from the rest of the large playground. The nursery is particularly roomy and attractive – 52 places with sessions of a maximum of 39 children, an à la carte choice of mornings or afternoons or a combination of whole days and half time sessions. Three large rooms, own toilet facilities and a large kitchen area ('mummy sometimes comes in to help us cook', said an excited 3 year old) as well as access to the hall and library. Few chic little independent nurseries provide as much as this. Everyone eats in the school canteen and the number of pupils having cooked lunches delivered by the borough increases all the time. The rest bring their own.

Ofsted hasn't done a full report since 2007, when school was judged 'outstanding' (confirmed by an interim assessment in 2011). Head is greatly aided by a posse of 'liberal middle class' parents only too eager to help in all areas of school life, including arranging fundraising events to enable disadvantaged pupils who might not otherwise be able to afford to take part in trips etc. She is aided, too, by an excellent governing body, as well as by a good relationship with her local authority. A very small number of exclusions in previous years, but none for some time. A proper and well-understood system of sanctions. Also an established homework system with extension work on the school website for those who want to push their offspring further.

Many parents commented that they were sometimes frustrated by the blank wall that meets their follow-up questions on their child's progress and results. 'Teachers can be cagey', remarked one parent, 'which makes me nervous. I might be surprised'. If you can cope with this and a certain complacency ('we don't need publicity', remarked the head at one point), then this is a no-brainer – an excellent state school with most of the advantages of an independent school but without the fees.

Blackheath High Junior School

Linked with Blackheath High School

Wemyss Road, London SE3 0TF

Pupils: 319 • Ages: 3–11

Fees: £9,456 – £12,150 pa

Tel: 020 8852 1537
Email: info@blj.gdst.net
Website: www.blackheathhighschool.gdst.net

Head of Juniors: Since, 2012, Mrs Sarah Skevington (early 50s), LLB Sheffield PGCE, formerly head of the school's early years dept. She practised as a solicitor specialising in family law then retrained as a teacher. She has taught throughout the EYFS and key stages 1 and 2 at local state primaries including Brindishe Lee – 'outstanding' in every category – and Invicta, which she found both challenging and inspirational.

She went to school in Greenwich, at St Ursula's and has raised her family here. Her three grown-up children attended a co-ed school, but since teaching at a GDST school she really appreciates 'what single sex can do for girls', and as a working mother has 'sympathy for working parents'. In her spare time she likes walking in Greenwich Park and lots of trips to the cinema and theatre.

Mrs Skevington is calm, quietly spoken and welcoming. Her office is the home of Florence the labradoodle, who on the day of our visit had flopped silently beneath her desk, offering a tantalising glimpse of a grey furry foot. Children delight in walking Florence. A parent commented: 'Mrs Skevington is wonderful. She has grown into the role since taking it over and we are very happy with the direction the school is taking under her leadership. She is very good with the girls who really like her.' Another, 'She is professional, personable, level-headed, I could go on...'

She pays tribute to her incredibly hard-working staff, saying this is very much a Blackheath community school, 'it's culturally diverse and all the better for it'.

Entrance: By interview with parents and child. Whilst the child plays, the head is looking for parents who 'understand our offer', in other words are not super-pushy or those who might baulk at no formal homework in reception. Parents who will be happy here are looking for somewhere for their child to grow as an individual.

Exit: Most (some 80 per cent) move up to the senior school. If the head considers that it isn't the best place, will discuss with parents at an early point. Some off to boarding or Kent grammar schools.

Remarks: The junior school building is the original first GDST building. Inside is a beautiful Victorian school hall, brought up to date with the insertion of coloured panels into the large lantern skylight. On the sunny day of our visit the hall was full of bright colours, while children below practised their circus skills. A grand, double stone staircase sweeps down from the entrance to the classrooms on the ground floor, also featured in a wonderful portrait of the very first pupils and staff of the school. The walls feature quotes from inspiring women of our times: Maya Angelou, Anita Roddick and Deborah Meaden.

Classrooms are large, bright and airy, with one teacher and one teaching assistant in every class of 16 in nursery and around 48 girls in every other year group. Classes vary between excited exuberance at year 1 to quietly attentive year 5s. The library, recently rescued from an ill-judged make-over, has had its wonderful parquet flooring revealed, with new freewheeling bookcases in spring colours. Some girls are library prefects and make book recommendations. Playground in full swing at lunchtime was quite a sight, with girls busily making the most of all the different levels: there is climbing equipment, space to run around on hard surfaces, a sandpit in a separate area for the nursery, a maths hut, sensible sun canopy provided by the PTA, and even a small forest school, which the head admits is more concept than actual woodland. The girls' stripy summer dresses are just right for running around on a hot day.

Asked for an example of good teaching, the head cites lessons where year 5s designed an app, then linked up (virtually) with the nursery children, who tried out the app, giving instant feedback. 'Simple stuff done well,' says the head. She observed the head of English teaching girls about persuasive writing styles, saying the girls were hanging onto her every word, and later tried out their new skills writing to ask her to do away with homework.

A parent agreed her daughter is taught 'without feeling she is under pressure. Subjects are taught in an engaging, fun way which increases her enthusiasm to learn and do well.' Another liked the fact that 'the teachers use innovative ways to get concepts across – for example using a "money week" to make the concept of money and savings so much more exciting, and asking parents who work in the financial services sector to come into class'. The French teacher is the best of both worlds, a native French speaker, trained as a teacher in England. Currently there are iPads in group sets, but the school is working towards one for every pupil.

The junior school has 72 girls on the SEND register with needs such as mild speech and language difficulties, dyslexia, dyspraxia and other mild learning difficulties. Needs are catered for within the classroom through differentiation and TA support as well as small group and one-to-one withdrawal. The head says that dyslexia is on the rise. One parent who was appreciative of the school's support nonetheless found the part-time SENCo to be 'extremely stretched'.

Sport is set to have a change of pace with the appointment of another specialist PE teacher. To date, not the sportiest. Head and parents wish the school playing field was closer – it is a bus-ride away. To allow girls as long as possible on the field they have recently introduced a club prior to PE, so that parents drop girls off at the field. Dance is offered as part of the curriculum. Swimming is at the local pool.

Music flourishes under the 'talented and energetic' head of music: there are 150 music lessons currently timetabled each week for instrumental or vocal lessons – from beginner to grade 6. From the youngest performers in year 1 through to year 6, every year group entertains parents at an annual tea-time concert, and the juniors recently joined the seniors for a beautiful performance of Noyes Fludde at the Royal Naval College. Year 2 girls can have a generous 10 lessons for free on a new stringed instrument to really test whether they like it. The chamber choir is award-winning – four times in a row at the Beckenham Festival.

Girls recently displayed clay busts made in DT at Ranger's House owned by English Heritage in the good company of European masterpieces. We enjoyed the display of a recent holiday project where girls chose any piece of art to recreate photographically at home, with staff joining in too: super renditions of The Girl with A Pearl Earring, Frida Kahlo self-portraits, and our favourite: Mrs Skevington, the school caretaker and Florence posed as Mr and Mrs Andrews by Gainsborough.

A Stone Age workshop stopped just short of making fire in the school hall with two twigs, and seemed to be delivered by an actual cave man. The school makes the most of London, with girls popping out to explore the Cutty Sark, the front row at Wimbledon and further afield. Boasts over 50 clubs and must be one of the few junior schools with own radio station. A GDST alumna, Rachel Joyce, author of The Unlikely Pilgrimage of Harold Fry, adjudicated the annual poetry competition. 'They really do a wonderful job of including all the girls in class plays, assemblies, nativity plays,' said a parent. The hall is large with retractable raked seating so that everyone and their iPad can get a good view.

The co-curricular and extracurricular programme not universally popular with more than one parent who wished for more focus on academics. One said, 'I am not convinced the school is capturing the academic potential of all the children', and another, 'may not be a bad thing to ramp up the academics a notch.' The head says children are learning a great deal through structured play and that they don't drop everything for Sats, but nonetheless girls gain a plethora of level 5s, including girls who are more than mildly dyslexic and some level 6s, with girls exiting at 11 'ready for anywhere'.

Transitions are managed thoughtfully. Year 5s feel much more grown-up with the provision of lockers in their classrooms, as they begin to move around to specialist teachers. Year 6 pupils are made to feel special with a prize-giving and lunch with their parents before they head off to senior schools.

We agree with a parent who said, 'The school is friendly and welcoming – it feels like a family.' And everyone, but everyone, agreed on fabulous pastoral care, with one saying: '[It] is exemplary – the main reason we chose the school above others. Not only do the staff look out for the girls, they are encouraged to look after each other, and the buddy group system works well to encourage that. My daughter is thrilled that she can call some of the big girls her friends'.

Parents say the happy pupils we saw at lunchtime cannot wait to get to school in the morning. They might be described as 'bright and sparky, polite and well mannered, kind and empathetic. It's not for kids who want to be pushed, graded or constantly winning.' And as for self-portraits, a parent obliged: 'A nice mixture from different backgrounds and cultures who all want their daughters to enjoy learning.' One parent with a talent for slogan writing summed it up: 'Childhood is not a race and at BHH they enjoy the journey.'

Blackheath High School

Linked with Blackheath High Junior School

27 Vanbrugh Park, London SE3 7AG

Pupils: 352 • Ages: 11–18 • Sixth form: 68

Fees: £15,282 pa

Tel: 020 8853 2929
Email: info@bla.gdst.net
Website: www.blackheathhighschool.gdst.net

Headteacher: Since 2014, Mrs Carol Chandler-Thompson BA (in history) and PGCE, both from Exeter (early 40s), formerly head of the Girls' School, North London Collegiate, Jeju, in the Republic of Korea. Prior to setting up NLCS in South Korea, she spent seven years as head of history and politics at NLCS. Before that, teacher of history and head of PSHE at Haberdashers' Aske's School for Girls, Elstree.

The move to Korea was not simply in search of a headship or an international move, but enabled her to continue to be part of NLCS with the remit of setting up a school from scratch with a focus on the importance of the quality of teaching. She was drawn to the GDST for its 'girls first' philosophy but also the sense of community where 'older girls don't feel too superior to talk to the younger ones'.

Youthful, open, highly articulate and full of energy for the transformations in hand, she lives in Woolwich with her partner, Emma, and although barely having time for sport these days (though something of a triathlete), she enjoys the downhill run home from Greenwich towards the river when possible, and being back in vibrant London after the monoculture of Korea. Having said that, she misses Asia and we met her just prior to a holiday in Sri Lanka.

It's never easy following a longstanding head – her predecessor, Mrs Laws, was head of Blackheath High for 14 years – but girls and parents alike have quickly taken to Mrs C-T. She is getting to know each girl gradually, teaching the year 9s history, joining in on a D of E challenge, and inviting them in twos and threes to have lunch with her. A parent said, 'She is approachable, energetic, personable and committed and will clearly blend her own ideas and purpose to good effect within the school as her influence evolves. She has very quickly secured a place of affection and respect amongst the girls and staff.' A pupil: 'She's refreshing; different in such a good way'.

The ISI's verdict on the sixth form, 'good and sometimes excellent', is a somewhat lukewarm tribute amongst a sea of 'excellents' for all other aspects of the school. As well as reinvigorating staff and teaching, working hard to push back the administrative tsunami to protect space for 'thinking about teaching', so that they can rekindle their own subject passion, the head will be bringing her experiences from NLCS's highly successful sixth form.

And whilst she's very happy for the school to be known for the strength of its pastoral care, she will be focused on moving that reputation to highlight academics. Having heard her talk about her involvement in this year's 11+ selection process, we've rarely heard of such care and attention given to spotting potential beyond mere performance on the day. Every applicant is interviewed and given a chance to shine even if not the most polished at 11.

Also on the agenda is raising the profile of sport. Never known as a sporty school – amusingly illustrated by girls in the playground sitting chatting either side of the nets on the table tennis tables – the head has appointed a new director of sport.

She will be aiming to ensure no ceilings are put on the girls. 'Girls are stretched and pushed here but they don't succeed through the failure of others; it's about challenging themselves'. Whatever girls want to do, whether it's apply to Oxbridge or become a professional singer, the school will absolutely support them. The word 'aspiration' crops up a lot, and parents say, 'She was very quick to pick up areas which needed improvement and is addressing them eg widening the girls' aspirations... She is very thoughtful and passionate to further advance the school.'

Academic matters: Fifty-eight per cent A*/A at GCSE and 30 per cent A*/A at A level in 2016; results don't dominate league tables or the GDST leader board, but the head says it's about value-added.

No surprises curriculum-wise. GCSE science starts in year 9. Excitingly, as befits the Greenwich location, a handful of the top physicists are invited to study astronomy GCSE, alongside similarly selected state school pupils. Most lessons taught in mixed ability groups apart from maths, set from year 7. Computing, not ICT, thankfully. School, and the whole GDST, is keen on STEM subjects and a recent look to the future event allowed girls to have their eyes opened by an engineer, a dentist and a computer programmer. Art and design flourishes and is as popular as the single sciences. Plenty of keen actors: drama is a likely choice.

Proud to be one of the first schools to offer Mandarin. All pupils take Latin from year 7 plus a choice of modern foreign languages from French, German, Spanish and Mandarin. Some leeway for girls with SpLDs. Carefully structured language trips and exchanges, gaining in adventurousness as girls go up the school, taking in Paris, Trier in Germany, Castellón in Spain. 'Exchange trips with a school in Germany from year 8 onwards fostered her interest in and ability with the language, as did the encouragement to do work experience in Germany in year 12,' said an approving parent.

Things get more varied at A level with the addition of economics/business, further maths, music technology, textiles, theatre studies, politics and psychology. Highest grades recently in art and design and English literature. Biology, chemistry, business and economics rather bring up the rear and none of the mathematicians reach the tip of the top.

A parent said, 'Every subject area has had at least one teacher who has been inspiring and is completely trusted by the girls'. Our guides went further, telling us how much they appreciated the excellent standard of teaching; they could only think of one instance when a maternity cover teacher had not been up to scratch, but they felt it was quickly dealt with, and convinced us they wouldn't hesitate to raise this with the head of year. Another parent said, 'As a result of the excellent and inspirational teaching, she has developed a passion for the subjects which she intends to study at university.'

Co-curricular flourishes: eco week saw year 6, from the junior school, and year 13 geographers working together to experience what life is like for slum dwellers. During the recent election, the politics society organised mock elections with some pretty impressive drop-in guests, including all of the local party candidates, and a trip to Parliament encountered Andrew Mitchell, giving the girls the inside scoop on 'plebgate'. The newly introduced Wollstonecraft Programme, far more vibrant and modern than it sounds, offers girls from years 7 to 11 a non-examined choice of courses including the creation of Girls' Hour for broadcast (think R4 Woman's Hour), creating and marketing apps, global perspectives, and introduction to film analysis.

B

The clunkily titled Matrix of Knowledge course in year 11, subtitled A History of Western Civilisation in 23 Lessons, prepares girls for entry into the sixth form and Russell Group applications – it develops critical thinking, research and debating skills and culminates in explorations of the riches of London such as The Wellcome Collection and Sir John Soane's Museum. Theory of Knowledge takes this further in the sixth form. And whilst the school isn't considering IB, other elements from this such as the extended project are in place. Originality is the order of the day: one girl even grew her own skirt. A parent added: 'The school offers an excellent series of TED lectures'. The librarian said she's just had her book budget increased and girls say the selection is well-chosen and they can also request anything they want.

Plenty of praise for the school's career preparation. Girls are encouraged to start thinking of their aptitudes and possible options for their future from around year 9. There are trips to inspire. Girls in years 9 and 10 were given a behind the scenes tour of Microsoft by interns, who had each fought off 60 others – let's hope they are being paid. Sixth formers make use of online help from Unifrog. A parent told us: 'My daughter received excellent advice, encouragement and support from the careers teacher regarding a work placement in year 11, and an opportunity in year 12 to shadow an undergraduate at a Russell Group university.' Another, 'The quality of the guidance and the fact that it is offered early ensures that the girls can build a very strong application, when the time comes, for places in further education.'

The head speaks warmly of the SENCo, currently studying for a masters, who initiated the 'pupil passport', where each girl records what works for them and their particular learning style in the classroom. The senior school has 56 students with a form of SEN, including dyslexia, dyscalculia and dyspraxia, and currently one child with a statement/EHC plan. Girls receive in-class and out-of-class support, which incorporates differentiation or small group or one-to-one support, depending on need. The head has also appointed a separate EAL co-ordinator.

Games, options, the arts: Despite its location close to the edge of Blackheath and more or less alongside Greenwich Park, the school's five acre sports field with a pavilion and an all-weather pitch is a short bus-ride away. PE is compulsory for all and anyone can play on a team; in fact girls are horrified to hear of friends who never get to play for their schools. Winter sports are netball, hockey and cross-country. Summer sports are rounders, athletics and tennis. Girls benefit from the wider GDST network for competitions as well as local tournaments. Our guides felt whatever your sporting interest, it would be made available. They try fencing, trampolining, gymnastics, table tennis, football and dance. The annual Iron House race sees 40 athletes from across the school, including staff, showing their stamina in Greenwich Park, including the gruelling near-vertical climb to the top. It's a breeding ground for competitive runners.

Girls with a love of the wider outdoors enjoy D of E – everyone does bronze, with just a hard-core few making it to gold. Also on offer is an international three week World Challenge – previous trips have been to Namibia, this year to Peru. The cost is steep but girls raise the money themselves, rather than digging into the bank of mum and dad. There are also taster sessions in canoeing, sailing and horse-riding, and girls get a chance to go on PGL adventures to challenge any fear of heights and brave the English weather.

The school makes the very most of its situation in Greenwich, recently putting on a stunning production, Noyes Fludde, at the Old Royal Naval College, featuring singing, dance and musicians from across the school together with a professional tenor. The new head of music, a former professional drummer, has shaken things up. There are over 200 music lessons a week and extracurricular is chock full of music: orchestra, chamber choirs, samba band, rock band, ukulele orchestra, glee club and a number of percussion ensembles aptly named Beat It!, Percussionistas and Mini-mallets. There are biannual international music tours, and many pupils study at junior conservatoires. Everyone arriving in year 7 can take part in a taster scheme where they have the opportunity to learn an instrument free of charge.

There are clubs timetabled for each year group from Viking and Anglo-Saxon club in year 7 to Iron Woman, self-defence, debating club, crochet collective – who meet in the outdoor classroom – and an F1 club. Any sixth former can start a society.

The Theatre is a purpose-built performance space on campus, but pupils also put on plays at Greenwich Theatre. A parent enthused, 'The drama was outstanding...always thoroughly engaging and bursting with energy and enthusiasm.' A competitive audition recently resulted in the world premiere of creepy Coraline, complete with button eyes: an ambitious adaptation scripted by the drama teacher. Plenty of rehearsal spaces and professional equipment

High quality art is displayed around the school. We were lucky enough to see the GCSE and A level examination pieces, including dresses one might covet, much in demand for the end of school ball. The art teacher welcomes all into the studio, even if just to do their homework in inspiring surroundings.

Background and atmosphere: The first purpose-built GDST school, opened in 1880, it maintains the tradition of a thorough academic education for girls for highly competitive fees. The school is situated on one of Blackheath's fine Georgian streets, although now very busy with traffic. A tall, red-brick building with stone dressings, with the somewhat odd addition of a 1960s church, currently used as a dance studio. Some of the fine archival history of the GDST is here, but hidden away.

Development plans are in progress; first phase (including new sixth form centre) opened in 2016, with everything due to be complete by 2018. The old building will be refurbished, whilst an entire wing is replaced, and an impressive, glassy entrance hall is added, with the library and resource centre heading below ground. Old will meet new, with one of the school's original stained glass windows dramatically incorporated into the new building.

Parents enthuse about the school's warm atmosphere, saying: 'By the time my daughter reached the GCSE years, the teachers knew her as an individual rather than as a number'; 'very positive atmosphere, friendly, supportive, collaborative'; 'everyone is enthusiastic about learning and has an open mind to new ideas incorporating very well the different cultural backgrounds the girls are coming from.'

Old girls include talents in all areas, particularly the media, perhaps most notably: Mary Quant, Baroness Jay of Paddington, Labour politician, Helen Lederer, comedian, and Katie Stewart, cookery writer.

Pastoral care, well-being and discipline: The head has split the roles of deputy into academic deputy and pastoral deputy, and there is a new part-time school counsellor. Pupils who volunteer are given training in peer mentoring by Childline. Mentors are assigned a year group and available at lunchtime, before and after school. One we spoke to clearly enjoyed it.

Parents praise the emotional support given to the girls: 'The teachers frequently remind the girls of the importance of finding time for rest and relaxation in their busy schedule to safeguard their well-being in what will be a very challenging world.' The head, too, is keen to help ensure girls develop healthy mental habits.

The head girl team takes the pressure off one individual and shares around the privilege. They clearly feel listened to and that this is their school. They've initiated eating with the lower school girls once a week, like kindly big sisters.

Good links with the local community including an outreach programme. Pupils from a local primary recently visited for a Shakespeare workshop, where year 10 girls entertained with Horrible Histories style dramas. The transition to year 7 is thoughtfully handled – new girls take part in a summer school, more for fun than anything else, with cake-making and a picnic in Greenwich park, making sure no-one gets lost on day one.

Pupils and parents: Pupils come from a diverse range of backgrounds. Nearly one third are bilingual.

Who is this school for? Parents say: 'For children who are keen to try new things and get involved – the more you put in, the more you get out' or 'girls who do not fit into a stereotype but have their own thoughts and opinions'. The sixth formers we met seemed confident, sincere, happy and very mature: a delight. Without boys to impress, there were none of the false eyelashes or make-up we've seen at co-eds recently. Girls between lessons were exuberant, loud, even.

A mother with two daughters at the school enthused: 'My children are ready for anything; they have been prepared step by step from juniors onwards to become increasingly independent. They are totally trustworthy and sensible. They can cope with minor emergencies and they look after one another. They support one another emotionally and practically.'

One parent without a typical home situation told us how supportive pupils had been of her daughters and others told us delightedly of making new friends themelves. The PTA is active and seem a relatively down to earth lot, organising car boot sales with bacon butties.

Parents feel in touch with the school. They receive grade cards or full reports twice a term with detailed information about a girl's progress, as well as strategies and suggestions for improvement. School days are long, cue a sigh of relief from working parents: pupils can arrive at 7.30am and stay until 6pm. There are also minibus routes ferrying girls from all across Greenwich, Rotherhithe and Lewisham.

Entrance: There are 60 places at the 11+ stage and most recently there were around 190 applications. No guaranteed place for junior school pupils, but all year 6 girls take the entrance exam in maths, English and non-verbal reasoning. Senior staff interviews all candidates. Best performing girls attend an academic scholarship interview with the head. For casual places beyond year 7 applicants sit papers in English and maths. Given the proximity to Canary Wharf, families do move about. Will need a good reference from current school and finally, if all goes well, an interview for both pupil and parents with the head. Any SEN students with an ed psych report are granted extra time.

Girls come from a variety of primary schools, most commonly Blackheath Nursery and Prep, The Gatehouse, The Pointer, Halstow, All Saints C of E, John Ball and Brooklands. Pupils generally come from Blackheath, Greenwich, Charlton, Lee, Lewisham, Brockley, Eltham, Canary Wharf, Hackney and Rotherhithe. A few from as far away as Dartford and Chislehurst in Kent and Leyton, East London.

Into the sixth form, there are 60 places available, currently undersubscribed. The girls we met described lots of their peers being attracted elsewhere simply to try something new – and by 'boys'. The school's redevelopment and new sixth form building is adding 100 new places. You'll need a good range of GCSE results with A*/As in the subjects that you wish to study, plus an excellent school reference.

Exit: Subjects from anthropology at Bristol and Aberdeen to zoology at Leeds. Between a third and a half leave post-GCSE. Around half of sixth formers to Russell Group destinations eg Warwick. None to Oxbridge in 2016. Few linguists. It's a very arty list of leavers, heading off for art foundations, even a famous shoe design course, but balanced with plenty of scientists, medics, a medical geneticist and dentist. These girls have found their passions and are not afraid to specialise.

Money matters: Scholarships and bursaries for girls entering years 7 and year 12 only. Scholarships based on entrance test results to a maximum value of 50 per cent of fees. In addition, scholarships are awarded for art, music and sport at 11+. A bursary takes into account means, plus academic merit. The maximum value of the bursary can be the full fees. There are a variety of sixth form scholarships including four provided by HSBC.

Remarks: The girls may not be super sporty, but they certainly seem super happy, comfortable in their own skin and a great recommendation for the school. One to watch under the dynamic newish head with academic ambition and transformative building works soon to be unveiled.

Bousfield Primary School

South Bolton Gardens, Old Brompton Road, London SW5 0DJ

Pupils: 430 • Ages: 3–11

Tel: 020 7373 6544
Email: info@bousfield.rbkc.sch.uk
Website: www.bousfieldprimaryschool.co.uk

Headteacher: Since 2014, Helen Swain BEd MA, deputy head for last eight years. Has been in teaching for 26 years and joined Bousfield as a year 6 teacher some 20 years ago.

Entrance: Due to cuts in funding there are now 60 part-time places in the nursery on offer, rather than the previous 30 full-time places. Two parallel classes from reception to year 6, each with 30 pupils. Applications for the nursery are done through the school; applications to the main school are done via Royal Borough of Kensington and Chelsea.

No automatic transfer from the nursery to the main school – parents must reapply. Children who are in care or have an SEN statement are considered first, followed by siblings and then proximity to school (currently approximately 0.5 of a mile and shrinking). Distance measured as the crow flies. Places do become available further up the school, due to high mobility rates of pupils, so worth persevering. Hugely over-subscribed. As one current parent puts it: 'If you get offered a place here, you'd be mad to turn it down.'

Exit: Most popular secondary schools are Holland Park, Chelsea Academy and Lady Margaret's. Over a third go on to independent senior schools, including Latymer, City of London, The Harrodian, Putney High and Francis Holland. No special preparation given for those doing 11+ exams. School knows a large amount of tutoring probably goes on, but says pupils get plenty of exam practice anyway. Much parental advice and support given when it comes to choosing next school.

Remarks: Strikingly international, with 41 different first languages currently spoken at home. Sixty per cent have English as an additional language. After English, the most prominent

B

languages are French and Arabic. School sees this cosmopolitan element as a real strength and the high level of harmony being something to celebrate. A significant number arrive with very limited English. It is 'sink or swim, but usually swim.' Much language teaching on offer, including Italian classes laid on by the Italian Consulate and French to all KS2 pupils. Bilingual pupils tend to outperform monolingual ones. Much coming and going due to large expat intake. Lots of French families have departed recently due to job losses in the City. Only about half the class in year 6 have been there from reception.

Superb academic results, particularly given the huge EAL contingent, though school always looking to 'up the ante.' English, maths and science Sats results well above national average. There are plans afoot to introduce some setting for maths and reading in year 6, though lack of space means separating children into groups is a challenge. Pupils' progress is tracked carefully.

When we visited, children were beautifully behaved and all engaged. A sense of calm pervaded the school. Manners and presentation clearly high on the agenda. No uniform. Packed lunch or school lunch. Fruit given to the younger years, funded by government school fruit and vegetable scheme.

One full-time teacher and one teaching assistant in each class, as well as extra support staff for pupils with statements and EAL pupils in the early stages of learning English. A great team of dedicated staff, who 'put the hours in.' Many loyal, long-serving teachers (20 members of staff have been there more than 10 years), as well as newer ones. A strong team – 'no prima donnas.'

Bright, vivid displays throughout the school. Some classrooms smallish; every iota of space used. School is a 1950s listed building which makes expansion and development problematic.

Arts are very strong in the school, though not at the expense of academics. Lots of music, dance and drama going on. School believes performance helps to build children's self-esteem. Pupils are offered a rich curriculum, full of workshops, plays and concerts. More than 90 learn a musical instrument. Guitar and strings ensembles, two choirs but no orchestra. Parents attend practice workshops so they know what a good music practice at home should involve.

Plenty of sport – gym and games as well as after-school clubs offering tennis, football, cricket and even cheerleading. Swimming for years 3 and 4. Pupils take part in borough events (including athletics) in the summer term.

Quantity of homework has been reduced – parents were completing too much of the pupils' project work ('you can always spot the hand of a parent,' we were told) and copious amounts were being downloaded unthinkingly from the internet. Homework now more focused on the basics, with reading, spelling and maths given from early on.

Some children with SEN statements/EHC plans. More on the SEN register, receiving support of some kind. No specially trained teachers but school feels they have strategies and experience to help those in need. Has experience of pupils with Asperger's syndrome, autism, ADHD, emotional/behavioural difficulties and moderate/severe learning difficulties, as well as dyslexia, dyspraxia and hearing and visual impairment. School is not a centre of excellence for all of these – very occasionally pupils move to special schools, either when Bousfield can no longer adequately support them or when they move to secondary school. Staff say Bousfield is 'an inclusive school' that does its best to accommodate those with difficulties.

Strong parental involvement, with school questionnaires showing overwhelming parental support and high levels of satisfaction. Numerous opportunities for parents to attend curriculum workshops and 'book looks' (when they visit to look at children's books). Parents welcomed in at the beginning of the day.

Some wrap-around care available, albeit not all on-site. Breakfast club on offer and pupils can be escorted to a neighbouring school (with more provision) at the end of the day if required.

Bousfield has close connections with artist Quentin Blake, who attends prize-givings and pops in regularly. All leavers receive a prize at the final assembly and Blake says his spirits are raised as each leaver is celebrated. 'After the ceremony, I go away feeling that at this point in their lives perhaps they really have all won,' he adds.

A great sense of purpose permeates this thriving school, with pupils bright-eyed and focused, offered a lively, dynamic and interesting education. As one satisfied parent lamented: 'I just wish it could go on into secondary school.'

The BRIT School

60 The Crescent, Croydon, Surrey CR0 2HN

Pupils: 1,190 • Ages: 14–19 • Sixth form: 800

Tel: 020 8665 5242
Email: admin@brit.croydon.sch.uk
Website: www.brit.croydon.sch.uk

Principal: Since 2012, Mr Stuart Worden BA MA GTP (40s). Previously school's director of theatre, though involvement stretches back, one way or another, almost to its foundation in 1991. Before that, was all over the place (literally, not metaphorically – he's highly organised) as, like so many of school's staff, has combined education, education, education with production, production, production. Though past isn't yet mythologised, may yet happen, given that when whistles through key moments of his career, 'the years change each time,' says affable minder.

First act of our (possibly world exclusive) version opens in Chichester, where the 'first and only' theatrical type in his family (brother, also in education, got there by more conventional means), he was taken on regular trips to the theatre – 'virtually at the end of my road' by 'lovely' mother. Was hooked, particularly by the language, leading to writing/producer roles with everyone from the National Theatre to the Royal Exchange Manchester, Playwrights' Co-operative and Working Title Films.

Teaching cropped up early on, too, with FE/HE posts on the film writing MA course at Sheffield University in 1990 as well as a spell as drama teacher at Lansdowne College in Kensington, reprised during two years at the Chichester College of Technology in 1991-1993.

May not look like conventional head (he's creative industries smart, down to intelligent glasses) but is meticulous when it comes to rock solid efficiency of school administration. His ethos is creativity within a framework, from the details (photographic ID for visitors, lessons that run to time or he'll want to know why) to the big things – buildings, new and refurbished, that are no architectural folly but really work.

Wants students to leave not just with creative potential on the way to being realised but equipped with hard-headed entrepreneurial nous to back it up (there's praise in literature for a student's massive on-line following).

His long term involvement in community arts – helped create Steam Industry, a theatre for all initiative – has also led to blossoming of school's outreach programme which is increasingly varied and demanding, though also, he stresses, 'purposeful and long term.' Virtuous circle, too, as those seeking to make career in the area can opt for community arts practice BTec qualification – developed by school and so far unique in the UK.

Pupils work with hospice patients, asylum seekers and rape victims and also act as talented big brothers and sisters to pupils in new, much-needed primary that Mr Worden helped get off the ground – projects naturally including a home-grown musical. BRIT Kids, for local 8-15 year olds, includes community classes and free performances at local Ashcroft Theatre, themed day for tinies, too.

He attracts huge praise from staff. 'He's professional, a good leader, very polite, expects high standards and is very positive,' thought one, speaking for everyone else.

Pupils, too, like his friendly, hands-on approach. 'When I needed help with recording for radio, he was like, "give me a minute and I'll do it",' said one. As a result, takes a while for everyone to work out who he is, particularly those whose previous experiences with authority figures were of a bruising nature. 'He doesn't give out a principal vibe,' said year 11 pupil who had only recently clocked who he was.

Older pupils, though, had no problems with identification. 'Love the way he comes round, sits with us and chats,' said sixth former. 'Not like any principal I've met,' reckoned another. 'He makes an effort to talk.'

Perk of job is 'daily' feedback about pupil success (during GSG visit, it was smash hit involvement in London Fashion Week). As to qualities required by prospective students, he's 'not sure' where talent features in the equation or passion, either, come to that. Instead, stresses importance of being 'nice and kind. Creativity and the arts need you to be open and then you should be willing to share your skill with others. I think that's a special quality.'

Is regularly asked whether school might extend to cover wider age range or sprout satellite versions in the regions. Likely to remain a one-off, he thinks, an 'extraordinary' place that does far more than equip pupils for careers. 'Parallel with that is the sense that the school goes to so many people and uses the arts to enrich their lives.'

Academic matters: Wouldn't be hard to see school as a giant performing arts centre with added classrooms. Not that 'straight' academic teachers would thank you for the description, or principal, come to that. ('Not a Fame Academy' a recurring leitmotif in literature). Staff are either traditional types who 'come here because they think it's the right school to teach at and want to be part of what we're doing here' or creative industry professionals who want to teach 'in a place that specialises in what I'm skilled at,' thought principal. No passengers: choreographers, film makers, playwrights, composers all welcomed but need to commit to training: on the job GTP programme is particularly popular.

Academic staples are bunched together, with sociology, humanities, science and musical theatre in East Wing (actually the main building of Old Grammar school – pay attention at the back). While inevitable focus on performance can make it seem as if you're never more than two minutes from a rehearsal, rooms are well-soundproofed to avoid stardust leakage into classes.

Staff work hard to harness pupils' energy, GCSE groups enjoying animated discussions on causes of youth crime in lively sociology lessons, maths teacher moving us along from fidgety class, distracted by visitor. 'This is a creative enterprise,' says young, happy-looking teacher. Once here, it's a hard place to leave. Teachers, like pupils, praised 'inspirational' atmosphere – latest arrivals include new head of costumes, fresh from Eastenders – and warmth that 'sucks you in'. Though no coloured hair (something of a pupil speciality, though 'they get over it after the first year'), they span the gamut from blouse and skirt to finest beard, bomber jacket 'n' red trainers combo.

Star quality tends to reside in BTec results. Full-on approach makes results extra impressive. In years 10 and 11, pupils take BTec level 2 diplomas (counting as four GCSEs) as well as following well-equipped and solidly taught GCSE classes in core subjects – some streamed, if ability range demands it, subjects broadly EBacc-themed. Given intake at year 10 – nerve-wracking standing start for any teacher – results are spectacularly good when it comes to performance-related topics such as dance and drama, and pretty respectable in the must-do areas, too. In 2016 at GCSE or equivalent, 58 per cent gained five A*-C grades including English and maths (28 per cent A*/A).

Inevitably, still greater pressure for sixth form, with BTec diploma (choice of broadcast and digital communication, community arts practice, dance, interactive media, music, musical theatre, technical theatre, theatre and visual arts and design) the starting point with rich rewards (41 per cent D*s in 2016). Everyone also takes additional AS or A level(s) (15 subject choices) or additional BTec qualification. Results largely respectable – 44 per cent A*/B (12 per cent A*/A) in 2016.

Welcome flexibility allows teachers to devote whole days to some post-16 BTec modules. 'Means you really get to learn,' thought one, approvingly. Course options can lead to slight difficulties: not everyone, for example, is drawn to the sewing that's currently a must-do part of the visual arts and design and technical theatre arts courses – though discussions are currently under way on possibility of evolving a stitching-light option.

For those needing extra help – there's screening for all during May induction day – terrific SEN is a huge strength, generously accommodated, including cosy, cushioned area and Smartboard-equipped classroom – 'keeps sense of routine' – where struggling pupils (SpLD biggest need, also some ASD and ADHD) get parallel lessons at slower speed, multisensory approaches added 'until it works'. Most staff 'very supportive and recognise that approach builds self-esteem'. Doubters (and there are a small number) are won over by success stories, including pupil who went from U to A* in English GCSE.

Whatever the choice, it's a full-on commitment, eminently do-able for the already organised, efficiency step-change required for those who aren't, and a tough old regime for all which can come as shock to anyone expecting straight drudge for drama swap.

'Same as any old school but one where there's less time for academic subjects,' thought slightly jaded year 11 boy. Even with sensible timetable structuring separating academic and performing arts days, extra workload means 'you need to push yourself and get ready to learn.'

Games, options, the arts: Stuffed with opportunities for performance and just about everything that goes with it, arts naturally the main drain on space, from eight music rooms, all sound-proofed (plus innumerable additional rooms for individual lessons – drums, vocal, keyboard, bass all popular) to two theatres – one, Obi (as in benefactor Sir Maurice Oberstein rather than Kenobi) complete with two storey barn doors to make scenery shifts from adjoining scenic workshop easy peasy.

Textiles/costume design space in main building a pleasure to experience, too, recently remade with retractable door splitting teaching space, allowing GCSE students to spark off older pupils.

Hands-on stuff rules, however. Literally so in case of portable appliance test, pupils shinning impressively up ladders to check the lights. 'Need to understand what's dangerous,' said teacher (and a useful all-purpose teenage rule, too).

With students billed by specialism, (dancer x and musician y) in school literature and so much going on, can sometimes be hard to know where lessons end and the extracurricular begins.

Even college awards nights become performances, most recent complete with Great Gatsby staging and X Factor style audience votes (which would brighten up more conventional speech days elsewhere no end).

Driving everything is all-round enthusiasm, fuelled by wide range of sixth form specialisms and staff contacts – brilliant, of course – with some interactive media students, for example, getting chance to work with Aardman studios.

Sixth former taking BTec in technical theatre had had a ball working on Tim Burton-inspired costumes for Hamlyn, put on in local theatre and one of 40 productions through the year ranging from Artaud and Brook to Brecht, Caryl Churchill and much in the way of full-blown Shakespeare, many others with words and scores written by the staff and/or pupils.

Traditional educational add ons far from absent, however. Duke of Edinburgh runs conventional course (though Jack Petchey awards – imaginatively awarded for academic rather than community service excellence in years 10 and 11 – do not). Sport isn't neglected either. School has own Olympian to its name, and while council has hung on to school's (small) sports field, necessitating relocation of sports day (and other fixtures) to nearby Norwood Lakes, the keen have school gym – somewhat battered but serviceable – for basketball (popular girls' team, which meets on Mondays, 'vicious', thought year 13 boys, admiringly).

Background and atmosphere: Patriotic acronym is down to British Record Industry Trust – great and good still feature on governors' list – whose funding and influence led to school's foundation in 1991 (after Mrs Thatcher, fearing creation of home for resting thesps, had been won round – or so the legend goes).

They're hugely proud of what they've created, says principal, and with good reason. Despite growth of vocational training colleges covering the 14-19 age range, school remains a one-off, the only free (prospectus uses capitals to emphasis) performing arts and technology school in the country, state funded but outside LA control.

Set within easy walk from Selhurst Station – not likely to become new Hoxton any time soon – school, though not an obvious looker from the outside, is full of thought, care and taste when it comes to the interiors. Inevitable tired corners mainly in vintage old school building (site originally housed Selhurst Grammar), one of three of varying styles and vintage. Newest, light and bright, is very plush indeed though smart rooms and corridors largely rule throughout the site, with plenty of tarting up (paint 'n' porthole doors even in otherwise non-refurbished areas, for example).

Feel is urban grit, rather than Surrey Downs (even feels like a long way to leafy South Croydon) with undeniable pressure on space. No pupil common rooms, for example (one year 11 girl had asked teacher to keep an eye on possessions during the day – gladly done, too) – immaculate carpeting in many corridors provides comfortable sitting space for the needy (speckly stone finish remains in original school building) with one student sitting by banked lockers busily sorting out vast pile of music.

Little in the way of school jargon, bar slightly confusing names. (Blue Block, though lovely, isn't blue). Main (and alias-free) building, built new for school's opening, has been substantially refreshed. Features include internal windows opening out on to corridors (principal's office too, at his request, providing a window on to the world), walls liberally decorated with high quality art (everything from Aboriginal-motifs to Banksy lookalike and delicate Japanese figures disporting themselves against parchment backdrop).

Academic year, too, is unusual with five eight-week terms, interspersed with fortnight breaks. Officially 'best supports delivery of the curriculum and ensures students return refreshed', though according to one teacher, production demands mean 'you'll often find students coming in over the holidays'.

With the exception of occasional overt whackiness – bins spray painted in wild array of colours following theatre teacher's guerrilla decoration initiative over the summer holidays – what dominates is sense of all-through professionalism.

And while absence of uniform, bells (and whistles, at least off stage) may not tend towards the norm, expectations certainly do, with teachers unlikely to indulge in too much time-drift as 'students will tell you when break is,' reckoned one.

Pastoral care, well-being and discipline: It's a busy old day; lights up 7am, not dimmed until 12 hours later. Though 'no-one will be here all that time,' says principal, some will operate in unconventional hours – drama and dance students, for example, warming up in the early hours before auditions or classes, studios booked up way in advance so pupils can edit their films.

Outstanding attendance, particularly at sixth form level, testament to commitment but also in stark contrast, in some cases, to pupils' unhappy educational experiences elsewhere. Several talked about feeling 'like outsiders' in other schools. Here, blend of rigour and tolerance seems to suit everyone. 'I felt I'd found people like me,' reckoned one sixth former.

'We think it's a good place to be looked after,' says principal, who is particularly proud of large scale speed meet and greet induction where grizzled year 11 veterans help newly arrived year 10s to settle in.

Body image can (predictably) be an issue, countered by strong message highlighting the glory of the individual, school stressing its more unconventional successes such as Adele to ensure that identikit size nothings aren't touted as the only aspiration worth pursuing.

On-site counsellors, presence discreetly advertised to students via form tutors, provide additional back up, while healthy eating (just about the only niggle otherwise superlative inspection report could find) is now a major school focus, with year 10 science pupils reporting on savoury snack fat content to year 13 dancers, canteen staff challenging pupils 'in a friendly way' if appear to be opting for unhealthy/minimalistic lunch (those on free school meals compelled to have healthy meal, though 'it's not about being a dictator but guiding and supporting,' thought staff member).

Staff enforce gentle discipline – students in library, verging on slight chattiness in quiet zone, were instantly quelled by (silent) entrance of smiley but no-nonsense librarians. Creativity within a framework something of a necessity, especially with school jam-packed, recent BTec additions adding another 200 to sixth form so 'as much as can take without bursting,' says school.

May be a timetable but there's 'no "you will do this number of hours" – it's their school,' says principal. Adds up to atmosphere that engenders sense of independence combined with professionalism – a lesson for the future, as with sixth form pupils given permission to leave lesson to conduct library research, but with return time and teacher expectations clearly outlined.

Pupil voice is heard loud and clear, too, in everything from 'almost daily' cake sales to fundraising for forthcoming productions to active student council which recently voted to ban environment-unfriendly disposable cups at lunchtime, 'commit to bringing in refillable bottles'. No wonder giant painted portrait of the blessed Jamie on wall of bigger canteen dispenses saint-like smile like a South American folk hero by way of inspiration.

Pupils and parents: Education should be accomplished without removing innocence along the way, thinks the principal. 'Friends assume it's going to be like Fame, but it's really down to earth,' felt sixth former, though performers in particular exhibit healthy dose of chutzpah and aren't backwards in coming forwards, adding in a couple of pirouettes and a solo on the way in. We enjoyed early morning dancing huddles outside (professional-looking gurning, too, in one case) – and tales of close harmony rivalry in the canteen.

Though unified by drive – 'at an ordinary school she'd be the leader of the pack, here, she's in a class with 30 of them,' reckoned mother of aspiring dancer – school community otherwise diverse. Families range from chimney sweeps to the loaded, many drawn from immediate area, which is 'socially complicated,' says principal, characterised by side-by-side pockets of affluence and deprivation – eligibility for free school meals is above the national average, and school also runs 'BRIT loves Selhurst' campaign, offering free tickets to locals.

Entrance: Not for everyone. One talented singer-songwriter had opted instead for Guildford ACM. 'They advertise it as once you go there, 75 per cent of your future career is done, but I know it's hard work.' Some find the place for themselves – press coverage is pretty much non-stop. One girl, now in sixth form, paid first visit to keep friend company and ended up the one with the place.

A minority very local (15 per cent from Croydon), though vast majority (75 per cent) from South London, remaining 10 per cent, selected on raw talent, not postcode, can come from anywhere in UK. (School stresses desire to avoid impossibly long journeys, somewhat spoiling effect with X-Factor winner Leona Lewis, quoted as describing two-hour round trip as 'so worth it'.)

Oversubscribed all the way through, less so for those entering in year 10, massively for sixth form. For 14 year olds seeking place in year 10, process less daunting, though useful to muster clear ideas on what pupils would gain from coming here.

Technical courses based on portfolios followed by workshops the norm. Inevitably stressful for would-be performers. 'She got recalled, she cried, she stuffed up in her first audition and thought "that's it" – but got in,' said parent who felt school wasn't looking for fully formed talent (there are rumours of already successful child stars being turned away) but 'something in kids that they can bring out – they don't necessarily want someone who's completely polished and finished and looking for it as a way into the next big thing'. A fair comment, thought school. 'It's about unlocking potential rather than a finished product.'

Exit: In a handful of cases, some year 11 pupils may not make the sixth form, most after discovering that love for performing arts has worn off. 'Might get to age 16 and think, I don't want to be a dancer – I want to do something else with my life,' says principal. 'They might just change and that's a good thing.'

At least 70 per cent, usually more, do carry on into sixth form, and almost everyone, even those who leave post-16, go on to further and higher education elsewhere – most recent extreme example swapping bright lights for animal husbandry.

Principal stresses proof that employability issues amongst the young can be triumphantly overcome. According to school survey, 70 per cent of past pupils end up working in creative industries. A few are household names but this is definitely not yardstick of measurement. All, says principal firmly, are superstars even if not household names because 'are the best box office manager or record label executive.'

School's well-designed vocational courses, with an eye and a half on the future, help speed the process along. Community-related courses, for example, lead to a virtuous circle, helping local bodies and in the process raising future trained community facilitators – a growing area for well-regarded HE courses such as Royal Central School of Speech and Drama's applied theatre and education BA degree. Others end up at RADA, Rose Bruford, Drama Centre, East 15, Bristol Old Vic, Guildhall and LAMDA, or head off to university – Leeds, York, Sheffield and Birmingham among them.

Once through, you'll find their words, music, performance, directorial and backstage talents just about everywhere you look, from fashion shows to musicals, national theatre to community arts, in the UK and internationally.

Remarks: Vocational dazzler with some academic bright lights as well. An educational showstopper, and one you definitely won't want to walk out of half way through, which tempers sprinklings of stardust with lashings of nuts and bolts reality checks. That's what they say. We secretly think it's like collecting every school's coolest kids and putting them in one place. If we could set this review to music, we probably would.

Bromley High Junior School

Linked with Bromley High School

22

Blackbrook Lane, Bickley, Bromley, Kent BR1 2TW

Pupils: 314 • Ages: 4–11

Fees: £12,855 pa

Tel: 020 8781 7001
Email: admissions@bro.gdst.net
Website: www.bromleyhigh.gdst.net

Head of Junior School: Since 2012, Ms Claire Dickerson BA (Anglia Ruskin University). Since arriving at the school 14 years ago, she has seen the school from all angles: beginning as a year 4 class teacher before moving to reception and then taking on the headship in 2012, at a particularly exciting time as the school moved to its own version of a creative curriculum. We found her to be focused, warm, open and an accomplished wearer of heels. Parents tell us: 'She is very approachable and we feel that we can have access to her whenever we need it'; another said, 'Our daughter was thrilled on her first day when Ms Dickerson was able to remember all their names and she takes a personal interest in each and every child.' Her outside interests are skiing, swimming and theatre. She lives locally and has two grown up children in their 20s.

Entrance: There are two forms of 20 pupils at 4+ and an additional eight girls join at 7+. The 4+ assessments are in the January prior to entry and 7+ assessments are held in the November of year 2. Most recently there were 80 applications at 4+ and 20 for the year 3 places. Thereafter a waiting list for occasional vacancies.

Exit: Around 70 per cent move on to the senior school. Around a quarter leave at 11+ to attend local grammar schools. The school is very clear that it is not a prep school and girls will not be prepared for external testing, leaving them free to explore a broad curriculum throughout years 5 and 6.

Remarks: The new curriculum has freed the teaching from Sats: instead the focus is the creative and cross-curricular, which the head feels has inspired the staff and 'sparked' the girls. Reception girls might be sculpting a mermaid, but they are learning about building 3D shapes and developing their research skills by investigating appropriate sea companions. Parents seem highly delighted with the imaginative approach to learning; one told us: 'The teaching throughout has been

B

fantastic, varied, and full of different learning opportunities such as visitors and trips that have enhanced the curriculum'. One aim is to give each child the confidence to put forward their own ideas. Year 6 girls describe having 'talk partners' which change every three weeks, where they pair up to discuss topics, and that those who have finished their work will buddy up with a girl who might be stuck.

On polar fun day a real-life explorer shared tales of blubber and frostbite. Pupils dug up the grounds searching for archaeological artefacts on Roman day. We have seen plenty of Tudor houses built from cereal boxes and straw as part of the history curriculum, but never heard of them being set on fire to no doubt replicate the Great Fire. This seems to sum up the staff's ability to take things to the next level here.

The counterbalance to this is a careful teaching of the core subjects of reading, writing and maths. Maths is nearly always taught separately from the cross-curricular work. Handwriting is all joined up for most by the end of reception. A new system has been introduced for comprehensive academic tracking which, coupled with close home/school links, ensures that if a child does have a blip it can be talked about and supported. Homework escalates gradually, starting with some over the weekend in reception. There is a computing suite and years 5 and 6 each have an iPad which remains at school.

Literature is often at the heart of themes; World Book Day decorations adorn each classroom door, the library is well-stocked, houses are named after authors and the girls had recently enjoyed a visit from children's Laureate, Chris Riddell.

Girls like to come to the library at lunch times if they're in the middle of a particularly good book. Languages are taught to give girls a flavour of what they might go on to study: French throughout, then Spanish in year 3, German in year 4, Latin in year 5 and double French in year 6 culminating in a five day trip to France. Girls say they are ready for it, as they've 'been practising' with shorter trips such as the choir's weekend trip to Belgium where they visited a chocolate factory and also sang at the Menin Gate memorial at Ypres.

Girls benefit from being able to share all of the sports facilities of the senior school, such as the indoor pool, and are the current GDST gymnastics champions. Girls seem to try everything and are playing an increasing fixture list, including a few against boys' schools. A recent win against a local independent boys' school was particularly important says the head, not so much for the win, 'but knowing they can compete as equals'.

The music wing contains practice rooms and a high ceilinged performance space. Lots of individual musical tuition and girls learn the recorder in year 3. Wind and string ensembles and the chance to play with senior girls in the orchestra. The junior school is the reigning Bromley Festival schools' choir champion in its age group. A year 5 girl is currently playing Matilda in the West End. There are whole school drama productions twice a year. This summer it's the Mikado.

A tempting array of weekly clubs. Some sporting and musical, but also ballroom dancing, nature garden, chess club, circus skills, 'hot off the press' and our favourite: guinea-pig club.

The junior school building is tucked behind the senior school. Plain, brick-built, functional, some of the classes and the library have nice views across the tennis and netball courts to the woods of Jubilee Park. Plenty of playground space, mainly tarmac but the year groups are carefully divided: the reception children have a large weatherproof canopy and a pirate ship; there is a fake grass 'Teletubby' hill for the slightly older girls and plenty of space to run around for the Hawthorns, years 3 to 6. Making use of the grounds, the school has also adopted elements of the forest school outdoor learning.

The atmosphere is orderly but relaxed with children exuberant in PE and busy at playtime. Classrooms are large and utilitarian with meticulous displays. Girls were particularly neat in their uniforms of traditional summer dresses and grey wool blazers on the day of our visit. A parent: 'Every facet of the school seems to run like clockwork'. Confidence is most often mentioned by parents, with one telling us, 'Our youngest daughter is a completely different child since starting Bromley High. She has grown in confidence and has really thrived'.

Working parents may be delighted with the breakfast club, which runs from 7.30am. Additional fees for this and the after-school club. Had better hope that trains run on time, as late pick up fees are steep.

A large proportion of girls for whom English is an additional language, reflecting bilingual families. Just a few with a SEN. A part-time SENCo leads a team of eight teaching assistants who offer additional classroom support to any child needing a little more individual attention. One-on-one support is available where needed. Parents seem unanimous in the trust they place in the head and her staff and the 'nurturing' pastoral care to be found here.

Bromley High School

Linked with Bromley High Junior School

Blackbrook Lane, Bickley, Bromley, Kent BR1 2TW

Pupils: 560 • Ages: 11–18 • Sixth form: 110

Fees: £15,942 pa

Tel: 020 8781 7000
Email: admissions@bro.gdst.net
Website: www.bromleyhigh.gdst.net

Headmistress: Since 2014, Angela Drew BA PGCE MBA (50s). She studied English literature in Durham and then spent a year working with mentally disabled adults before entering teaching. She is an ISI inspector. Previously deputy head (academic) of Epsom College. She was head of English and drama at The Mary Erskine School in Edinburgh and has taught at George Watson's, Whitgift and Prior Park College. She teaches AS thinking skills from Y10. Friendly and open, she wears her headship lightly. A hope and ambition for the girls is that they will not just be prepared for the modern world but lead it.

After the departure of her relatively short-lived predecessor, Mrs Drew's initial year must have been spent on something of a caffeine high as she hosted 30 coffee mornings with groups of parents. 'She is passionate and proud of the girls, supportive and comes to so many events during school time and outside school hours. I believe she promotes the importance of an all-rounder with particular focus on the academics,' said a mother. Another: 'I think the headteacher has come into a well-established and successful school and she has made her mark. She has shaken up the PE department and this has improved. She has employed extremely good teachers and bought in different teaching methods'.

Married with a daughter reading English at UCL and a son studying history at Leeds, Mrs Drew enjoys reading and theatre and is a committed Evertonian. She lives nearby in rural Kent.

Academic matters: There has been a great curriculum shake-up in recent years, with most recent results not reflecting the wider choice of subjects available to GCSE students. As well as the expected core curriculum girls could choose dance, photography, classical civilisation, economics or additional maths. The sixth form offering adds in psychology, government and politics, business studies, plus a Pre-U in theology and philosophy. In 2016, 61 per cent A*/A at GCSE and 48 per cent A*/A at A level.

In the sixth form classes do not exceed 14 pupils, some tuition groups are just a handful, and girls seem unfettered to pursue their own interests. Indeed this seems to be a strength of the school. Subjects don't have to be chosen with any timetabling restrictions and our sixth form guides described being encouraged to find their passions, no matter how slowly these emerge, whilst teachers offer guidance with a weather eye to careers and UCAS applications. Mrs Drew: 'we're very focused on where they're going, but they are free as to how they get there'. Triple science, literature and maths are the core (and the mathematicians really shine). For two consecutive years, upper sixth girls have gained the Salter's Award for the second highest chemistry A2 mark in the UK.

The school isn't considering the IB but elements such as the extended project are not mandatory but on offer. Up to 16, few stray far from the more academic subjects: most take nine or 10, including several IGCSEs. Plenty of modern linguists, but curriculum changes have provoked a huge resurgence in classics – 39 girls are currently studying Latin in year 10. When we queried whether Mandarin is on the horizon, Mrs Drew says she is 'tempted'. DT, but no food technology: a swing too far from gender stereotyping? Having seen the girls' impressive rainforest cakes in the geography bake off, perhaps there is little left to teach.

More than 20 teaching staff have been with the school for over 10 years. The school's newly minted ISI report declares teaching to be 'exceptional'. Praise for the teaching from parents ranges from the extremely appreciative to slight wistfulness from a couple who have come up from the all-singing-and-dancing junior school. A typically balanced report: 'there are some teachers who clearly go above and beyond to be approachable and encouraging and these members of staff are well liked and respected by the girls.' The head has just appointed a new academic deputy, a former head of science at St Paul's Girls', who has encouraged independent learning and 'risky' lessons. Mrs Drew has also introduced external workshops led by graduates to cultivate good study habits for both pupils and parents.

Trips, masterclasses and competitions inspire free thinking beyond exercise books. Year 12s were recently boggled by a speech recognition lecture by a leading light at Google; sixth formers secured tickets to see Simon Russell-Beale perform their set text at the National Theatre; whilst GCSE artists took a study tour of Vermeer's Amsterdam; meanwhile year 11 biologists extracted the DNA from strawberries and the historians put Hitler on trial. Terry Waite was soon to take part in a cross-curricular 'brain day', discussing how he survived captivity.

The curriculum has switched from ICT to computer science, a new computer lab has been unveiled and GCSE and A level students joined 20,000 classrooms worldwide in two weeks of 'an hour of code'. Science labs are well-equipped and gradually being modernised. Meanwhile, girls have been proud winners of two Arkwright engineering scholarships. Serious contenders in the national Maths Challenges. Year 10s also recently won gold in the national Biology Challenge. A parent told us that the girls have so many public speaking opportunities it becomes 'second nature'. Those year 10s seem to be on fire, having also qualified for this year's Oxford finals of the international youth debating championship.

Maths is set immediately on entry; science is set in year 9 and English from year 10. As always, parental thoughts on the amount of homework down to the individual child's stamina: some think it's a lot, particularly in the exam years, whilst some 'could actually do with a bit more' lower down the school. Holiday homework 'keeps things ticking over'.

Only a tiny number of girls receiving one-to-one support for identified learning differences as support is provided in lessons. Most girls with SEN have dyslexia but a few have dyspraxia or are high functioning ASD. No additional fees for learning support. Those capable of working up to three years beyond their chronological age are offered extension opportunities within the curriculum and via clubs, competitions and collaborations across the GDST, maths masterclasses and a STEM day.

Everyone does work experience in year 11 after GCSEs. The head recently took a group of year 10s – anyone who wanted to come – to meet an old girl at Cambridge. Teachers are said to be 'plugged in' to additional opportunities such as CV boosting competitions to enter. The GDST alumni network of 65,000 is invaluable for arranging work experience. Café Scientifique is a drop-in lecture series where girls are exposed to parents and old girls with inspiring careers and life experiences. And those prepping for Oxbridge have the benefit of the whole network of schools to form a cohort.

Games, options, the arts: Sport is compulsory for all girls up until the end of lower sixth. Upping the ante – bringing the fixture list and ambition in line with the 25 acres and facilities – was one of the head's first priorities. She has recruited a new director of sport, previously head of netball at Alleyn's, and a male hockey coach. The U16A hockey team is currently Kent county champion Someone is keeping score as they tell us the hockey teams have played 123 fixtures in the last year celebrating over 300 goals. The Olympic size Astroturf is newly floodlit. Girls compete in netball, athletics, swimming, cross-country, rounders and are accomplished gymnasts. Increasing numbers getting to go on the bus, as the school fields A-D netball and rounders teams. Sixth formers are thrilled with the new gym, like a mini health club, for use with a buddy at lunch times or after school. Year 10s give zumba and aerobics a go. The school's indoor pool can also be used by girls' families one evening a week and Saturday mornings. Girls able to brave the British weather enjoy the bronze and silver Duke of Edinburgh challenges, compulsory in year 10, with a couple completing gold before reaching university.

More artists than musicians in terms of academic study, but a very musical school. Music theory is taught to years 7-9. We met a lone A level student, studying music tech. The majority of girls learn a musical instrument or have vocal tuition. Last year the senior school music tour was to Prague. One parent suggested there would be more take up of instrumental lessons if girls did not miss important lesson time. Some 24 peripatetic music staff teach to grade 8 on 16 different instruments and over 60 per cent played their way to a merit or distinction last year. There is regular success at Bromley and Beckenham Music Festival and girls have performed at Southwark Cathedral, the Royal Festival Hall and enjoyed tours to Spain and Normandy with choirs and ensembles.

Each year sees dance and drama productions with students performing, singing, playing in orchestra, and lighting, choreographing and undertaking backstage skills. One has a starring role in EastEnders.

High quality art is displayed around the school. We squinted through the door at the appealing art studio with mezzanine level as exams were in progress. Several pupils have exhibited at the Turner Contemporary Gallery. The DT facilities are extensive and enthusiastically used with the usual laser cutter but also a 3D printer.

Lunch time is deliberately long. Clubs range from the cosy such as 'knit and natter' and card games, the sporty – rugby, horse-riding or squad training – to the stimulating: robotics, DT divas and TED talks club. Musicians might try jazz, percussion or chamber strings. We were assured girls do not spend their

B

lunch hours cutting up cadavers but were intrigued to note the forensics club. Sixth formers are equally engaged running their own discussion group, most recently on the death penalty.

Background and atmosphere: The school opened in 1883, aiming to provide education for girls on a par with that of their brothers, and the first entrants described it as a bit like being in the army: there are photos of girls doing PE wearing ties. Originally in a Victorian building, the school relocated to its present site in 1981. The wooden honours boards line one of the modern corridors, their name in gold being something the girls still aspire to today.

The campus is spacious and green but with few mature trees to take the edge off the already plain buildings. The Parents' Association's most recent purchase has been sturdy wooden parasols to provide much-needed shade. Views come into their own from the upper floors – a science teacher jokingly referring to his lab as the penthouse. There is the large Crompton library – Richmal Crompton, the author of Just William, taught at the school – open until 5.30pm every day to facilitate homework. Sixth formers have their own large, light common room where they can eat their lunch, hang out on sofas and study in free periods. The dining hall is newly decorated in a zingy lime with lots of fruit and salad in evidence.

The grey and burgundy uniform here is particularly smart, with blazers on when not in lessons. The fashion seems to be for patent loafers with knee socks. Girls assured us that there isn't an 'it' bag culture. Sixth formers look smart and ready for anything in 'business attire', mostly jackets with skirts but they are free to express some individuality.

Girls burst out of lessons onto the wide carpeted corridors seeming relaxed. Asked to describe the school, a parent said, 'I feel there is pressure for the girls to succeed but above that I feel they push each girl individually to get the best out of them'; another, 'I feel the school is quite competitive – but very caring as most teachers know each girl individually and care for their welfare.' One of our guides said fondly of her time here since the age of 4: 'it's a really nice bubble'.

Pastoral care, well-being and discipline: Everyone we spoke to praised the school's pastoral care. 'I think the school provides excellent pastoral care. Teachers are involved and approachable and seem to work together,' said one. Parents universally expressed confidence in the school's ability to take care of any issues of bullying and felt that their daughters would be able to raise it. The school has one of the most thorough positive mental health policies we have seen, with a particular awareness of eating disorders, depression and self-harm as very live potential issues for students. There is a part-time student counsellor and 'big sister, little sister' pairs senior with younger girls.

Rules seem low key. Girls are allowed to wear 'discreet' make-up from year 9, earlier than many. Mobile phones to be kept in lockers away from lessons. From Mrs Drew's nonplussed response to our enquiry about any exclusions we gather that discipline is not something she has to worry about. Girls are engaging seriously with the current new wave of feminism and issues such as university rape culture. They have recently set up a LGBT club.

Pupils and parents: Although parents describe the school as 'mixed', it is not as culturally diverse as more central London schools with just over 10 per cent of girls speaking another language at home.

Mainly white British with a mix of other ethnicities including Chinese, German, Portuguese and Hindi. The majority of girls come from the local area of Orpington, Bromley, Beckenham and Dulwich via a direct train route, but a proportion of girls also travel in from rural Kent.

The commutes of working parents are well-supported with both a free breakfast club from 7.30am and a homework club after school until 5.30pm.

Entrance: Over 70 per cent of the junior school girls transfer to the senior school, the majority without an 11+ assessment, although some choose to sit the test. Places for outsiders are offered via testing in the January prior to entry in verbal and non-verbal reasoning and creative writing plus a short mathematics extension paper. We are told that competition is stiffening as pressure for places increases. Pupils with identified SEN are given 25 per cent more time.

Pupils join from a range of independent prep schools and state primaries including Breaside Prep, Blackheath Prep, Merton Court, St Christopher's, The Hall, Rosemead Prep, Oakfield Prep and St Olave's Prep. External applicants to the sixth form subject to GCSE entry requirements, school reference and interview.

Exit: Some 30 per cent leave at 16 to enter mainly co-ed sixth forms. Around half of A level leavers to Russell Group universities with Barts Medical School, Exeter, Bristol, Sheffield, Warwick, Loughborough and Nottingham amongst the favourite destinations in 2016.

Money matters: Bursaries and scholarships in penny numbers for girls entering at year 7 and the lower sixth only, including honorary scholarships and minor awards for artists' materials and music lessons. Academic scholarships based on entrance test results. Bursaries are available on entry to the senior school and offer up to full fees for the academically gifted who could not otherwise afford to attend. Parents should expect their finances to be scrutinised in detail on application and each year thereafter. Some sixth form scholarships for which candidates must prepare a written application.

Remarks: A selective school, offering a wonderful range of opportunities to widen horizons and develop new interests. Suits academically able girls with lots of drive.

Broomwood Hall

Linked with Northcote Lodge School

68–74 Nightingale Lane, London SW12 8NR

Pupils: 640 • Ages: 4–7 (boys), 4–13 (girls)

Fees: £14,790 – £18,185 pa

Tel: 020 8682 8830
Email: broomwood@northwoodschools.com
Website: www.broomwood.co.uk

Principal: Lady Katharine Colquhoun BEd (50s). Has a rather regal manner but her vision has seen this school mushroom from humble beginnings (handful of children in a local Methodist Church), to a thriving empire with over 600 pupils (as well as 200 boys at Northcote Lodge – the brother school down the road). 'She's remarkable,' one parent told us. 'Inflexible at times, and you have to toe the line with her, but she is seriously impressive.' Lady Colquhoun knows she has an able team behind her and believes the ability to delegate, which she learned as the eldest of five children, is her secret.

Lady Colquhoun has made the transition from headmistress to joint principal with her husband, Sir Malcolm. She still teaches literature to prep school girls, whilst he is in charge of administration and property. School has a board of directors which oversees both Broomwood Hall and Northcote Lodge and comprises the principals, heads, bursar, director of admissions and Patrick Colquhoun (Malcolm's son).

Headmistress since 2001, Mrs Carole Jenkinson BSc PGCE (50s). Varied career, including time as ski rep, with stints at International Tribune in Paris and British Council. Started her teaching career at Northcote Lodge. Universally respected and admired by parents; everyone we spoke to described her in glowing terms. She exudes calm wisdom. Very knowledgeable about senior schools of every hue and spends a significant proportion of her time visiting potential schools up and down the country. Teaches maths to year 7 and verbal reasoning to year 4, so has a good grasp of each girl's abilities and character before recommending suitable senior schools. Now head of all three Broomwood Hall schools: two lower schools in Garrads Road and Ramsden Road, and the upper school in Nightingale Lane.

Mrs Jenkinson is supported by Katie Paynter, who is responsible for the day to day matters at Garrads Road. Miss Paynter joined the school in 2015, bringing with her a wealth of experience in teaching and learning, most recently from Oakfield Prep and from the Shell International Schools.

Entrance: Lower schools hugely over-subscribed, non-selective and located in the heart of Nappy Valley. For reception class, parents must provisionally register their child in advance on the provisional list, and are invited to register formally and pay the £100 fee once they have attended an open day or individual tour. This is followed by a 'readiness assessment' around the child's third birthday, a year prior to entry.

School says it looks for a wide variety of characters rather than a type and aims to have a good spread of birth dates throughout the year, as well as a 50:50 mix of boys and girls. Forty reception places at Garrads Road and 80 at Ramsdon Road. Priority to siblings.

A strict one-mile radius rule applies which ensures all children can walk, cycle or scoot to school. Head encourages parents to apply to a number of schools in the area, to avoid disappointment. Not a huge international contingent – still predominantly well-to-do British families with some Europeans and Americans. Small number with English as an additional language are given support if needed.

Three forms per year in the prep, rising to four per year from year 7. Maximum 18 per class. Vast majority come up from lower schools. Those coming from elsewhere must register on the provisional list and provide a report from previous school. Parents have a tour and time with the headmistress, and prospective pupils spend a morning in the school where staff assess their academic ability in a classroom setting.

Girls come from as far afield as Fulham, Chelsea and Dulwich. A Fulham parent we spoke to felt that those who were not from the immediate area were made to feel like outsiders by parents – 'the Wandsworth brigade can be quite intimidating for non-locals as they stick together like glue.' The school itself bends over backwards to integrate the new recruits. Morning and evening minibus to Fulham and Chelsea. Places vacated by 11+ leavers are quickly snapped up by girls from a variety of local independent and state schools.

Exit: Most lower school girls to the upper school and the majority of boys transfer to Northcote Lodge. A few disappear at this stage to country preps (such as Cheam, Ludgrove, Farleigh and Cothill) and some opt for neighbouring day schools (Dulwich Prep, Dulwich College and King's Wimbledon among them).

About 20 per cent leave at 11, mostly to south London day schools (eg JAGS, Alleyn's, Streatham and Clapham High) or to boarding (Benenden, Downe House, Woldingham). More and more stay until 13 and then tend to head to co-ed boarding eg (Bradfield, Bryanston, Marlborough, King's Canterbury, Wellington and Epsom College). A few to single-sex boarding (Benenden, Cheltenham Ladies', Heathfield, Tudor Hall) and local day schools. High number of academic, sport, art and music scholarships gained each year reflect breadth and excellence of the education delivered here.

Remarks: The Garrads Road site is a substantial arts and crafts style Edwardian mansion, a stone's throw from Tooting Common. Large, pretty garden with lots to keep children occupied – hopscotch, vegetable patch, climbing frame, sandpit and outside classroom for reading on summer afternoons. Ramsden Road is on two sites – The Old Vicarage, a rambling, red-brick former parsonage, for the first two years and 50 Nightingale Lane, around the corner, for the next two years. Both feel homely, with tartan carpets throughout, a fabulous mural of former pupils going up the stairs and attractive displays at every turn. The upper school, also in Nightingale Lane, has a wonderful garden, including an amphitheatre where girls perform plays.

Schools have a relaxed, country feel; on the day we visited, pancake races were in full swing in the playground at Garrads Road and children and teachers were having a ball. One mother we spoke to felt Garrads Road was less academic than its Ramsden Road counterpart, but curriculum planning is done jointly and the same syllabus is followed. Good reports about the schools' support for children with dyslexia and nurturing approach given to any pupils who are slower off the mark. Teachers engaging and inspiring; these are lively places to work. The parents we spoke to felt the lower schools give a solid academic grounding as well as a joyful start to school life.

Reading is of paramount importance and the libraries are well-stocked and well-used. Classical music was being played in the background in one classroom on the day we visited, with calm, focused children enjoying their lesson. School rewards hard work in all areas: copious numbers of cups awarded to pupils (including for good manners and friendship). Head believes children have to learn that they will only win a cup when they have tried really hard and must learn to accept that they will not win every time.

Principal is keen that girls learn that hard work pays off and girls certainly keep their heads down in the upper school, although there is also great fun to be had along the way. Lots of lively young assistants, including Australian students and ex-pupils on gap years. School recommends tutoring for pupils who are having difficulties but is against tutoring just to get a girl into a certain school. Head believes it backfires once the tutoring stops and the child can't keep up at their next school. Setting in English and maths throughout school. Fantastic science labs. Some 60 upper school pupils receive some form of SEN support. School feels able to support mild dyslexia and dyspraxia but wouldn't be the right place for anyone with severe difficulties. Currently 30 children with English as an additional language. Good mix of long-serving and new staff, with some having chosen teaching as a second career. Biggest challenge is coping with teachers constantly going on maternity leave.

A very well-run, flourishing school that knows where it is heading. For those who want a modern education underpinned by traditional values, there is arguably nowhere better south of the river. Tea is served at the end of lessons, followed by compulsory supervised homework at school. Viewed as a godsend by busy parents, and children say they like being able to relax (save for rote learning) once they get home. Some parents, admittedly, would prefer homework to be done at home so they can keep a closer eye on their child's progress. Clubs, including flower arranging and glass painting, finish at 6pm.

Talented head of lower school music writes plays and composes scores for productions. Art and drama taken seriously. Substantial amount of sport on the weekly timetable. Full-size hard tennis court in the Garrads Road garden used for PE. Cricket, football and rugby pitches 10 minutes away on foot. One parent we spoke to felt this is 'possibly not the right school for a really sporty child,' though others disagreed and said there were plenty of matches going on. Wide range of after-school clubs, including karate.

The upper school is ahead of the pack when it comes to technology. Girls bring in their own iPads and older girls learn computer coding (which they love). Drama is a real strength, everyone is in two plays a year, one of which is biblical, 'so they know their Old and New Testament stories by the time they leave.' Flamboyant productions, including revues, well attended by parents. Bright art and DT studios, complete with impressive equipment. Art exhibitions include drawing, painting, carpentry, needlework and pottery. Eighty per cent play a musical instrument, with many girls reaching high grades. Four choirs, including a prestigious chamber choir for which there are auditions. Recent choir trip to the Vatican.

Good variety of sport on offer in the upper school, including netball, lacrosse, hockey, rounders, tennis and sailing. Some sport played on-site but girls regularly bussed elsewhere for more space. Some pupils currently performing at pre-county level. 'We've definitely become a sportier school,' says head. Lots of teams, so the less talented can play in matches too. Currently winning or drawing three-quarters of matches; school excels at cross-country and netball.

Principal believes old-fashioned values hold true and is keen on instilling good manners in her pupils. Children hold doors open for adults and look you in the eye when they talk to you. Pretty uniform and girls are required to have a comb in their backpacks at all times; ear piercing strongly discouraged. Pastoral care is a great strength of the school. A trained counsellor is at the upper school regularly to help girls with eg potential eating disorders, exam phobia or bereavement. Pupils select their own tutor and are encouraged to talk to them about both academic and non-academic issues and the system works well. Resident matron deals with cuts, bruises and tummy aches.

Delicious food – 'my daughter thought the food was great and she's quite a fussy eater,' said one parent. Younger girls sit together and are supervised by a teacher; older girls eat canteen-style. Girls are encouraged to make conversation and to hold their knives and forks correctly. Leith's has written a bespoke cookery course for Broomwood. All girls in year 7 have weekly cookery lessons in the sensational cookery department and during the summer term pupils put on their aprons and cook a three-course meal which they serve to their parents. Always a great success and highly anticipated.

Good communication between schools and home. Parents are encouraged to get involved in school life, from providing costumes for plays and painting scenery to nit checks. Lots of social events, including leavers' dinner – a swish black tie affair for parents, pupils and teachers. Massive amounts of fundraising for a school it has built from scratch in Ethiopia. Parents are very supportive of the enterprise, though one or two grumbles about not enough money being given to local charities. Drop off and pick up times involve huge numbers of mothers, either in gym kit or walking the family labrador, though schools note that more and more mothers work. Some joint upper school ventures with Northcote Lodge (debates, clubs and field trips) – but one mother we spoke to felt that in reality the girls and boys hardly mix and that this is a missed opportunity. Broomwood schoold are Christian; children say prayers at break time and the end of the day. There's also a weekly church service – 'but we don't bible-bash,' says head.

Schools turn out well-adjusted girls, fully prepared both academically and socially for the next stage. Broomwood celebrates success on all levels (cups are given for 'being a good egg' and for demonstrating originality) and parents emphasise what a great job it does in producing confident, happy and successful girls. As the school handbook firmly explains: 'We don't expect parents to become heavily involved in the minutiae of the learning process; we do expect you to leave your daughter's education to us and let us get on with it.' If you do that, your daughter will be in safe hands here.

Head acknowledges that parents are more demanding than a decade ago, but understands 'that the significant financial output for school fees means they inevitably want to know they are getting value for money.' Cheerful, well-behaved children abound here. Welcoming, gentle schools full of delightful children.

Bute House Preparatory School for Girls

Luxemburg Gardens, London W6 7EA

Pupils: 310 • Ages: 4–11

Fees: £14,625 pa

Tel: 020 7603 7381
Email: mail@butehouse.co.uk
Website: www.butehouse.co.uk

Head: Since 2012, Mrs Helen Lowe (50s), BA Oxford Brookes, LGSM Guildhall School of Music and Drama. Married to Phil, whom she met at drama school. They have two grown up children. Having 'got acting out of my system' she started her teaching career in big Essex comprehensives, where she taught drama. She is verging on the evangelical about the profoundly positive benefits a background in drama can have – 'everyone should go to drama school because it's all about people and understanding other people's point of view'. She then went on to teach at primary schools in Richmond and became the literacy consultant for the whole of the borough. Her experience in the independent sector includes being a drama teacher at St Paul's Girls' in the 1990s, curriculum coordinator at Lady Eleanor Holles junior department and head of juniors at King's House in Richmond, where she taught for three years. Bute House is her first 'stand alone' headship, ending the 20 year tenure of the formidable Sallie Salvidant.

Bright and bubbly, Mrs Lowe likes to make an impact. Never one to be seen without her pink lipstick, snazzy glasses and white blonde hair well coiffed. Her confident manner ('I'm very bossy,' she admits with a twinkle) could be overbearing were it not delivered with such warmth and humour. Parents remark on her enthusiasm and ability to make changes without a fuss. Good changes, that few had even noticed were needed – a whole school Christmas celebration at a local church for example. 'I am a great communicator,' she says. Parents agree. She holds open house individual appointment sessions where parents can discuss any of their concerns about the school. She not only puts her point across impressively but listens too. What's more, the parents listen to her, even when it might be news they don't enjoy hearing – that their daughter won't suit a school they have set their hearts on, for example.

She knows the girls properly, and by the time the 11+ process kicks in, she is well-equipped to write their reports for senior schools and advise the parents on the best school for each one, having taught all girls in their second half of year 5 and first half of year 6. 'I have the best interests of the child at heart,' she avers. This may not always coincide with pleasing the parents but it doesn't faze her. When it comes to decisions about boarding school, however, she is sensitive to the fact that this is a decision that affects the whole family, not just the girl. A refreshingly modern and human touch from a prep school that sends a fair few to the top girls' boarding schools.

Entrance: There are two entrance points: reception – a one form entry where 22 places are allotted by ballot (after taking into account siblings, which could mean that the number is easily halved), and year 3, when girls are selected after sitting the 7+ exam (in the January of year 2). About 400 girls are entered into the ballot, two years before entrance, which is then scrupulously and rigorously drawn – by the chair of governors, with the head, the bursar, the school secretary and a lawyer in attendance. No question of rigging, and absolutely no point in ensuring that little Emily can recite her 10 times table.

For year 3, about 200 register for 38 places. Assessments in English, maths and non-verbal reasoning are carried out in a relaxed way along with various activities which focus on team work and social interaction. The girls are carefully observed by a number of teachers and Mrs Lowe said, 'hand on heart', they weren't just looking for the most academically able and – don't choke on your skinny flat white – they have turned down girls despite their marks being among the highest. They are looking for girls who respond well to learning, with a positive and enthusiastic attitude. This is a school determined to maintain its mixed ability, academically non-competitive ethos (this and the ballot were the two non-negotiables in her interview, Mrs Lowe tells us).

No sibling preference at 7+ assessment, but school 'looks very carefully at sisters'. Occasional places thereafter are competed for by test, and the school has a waiting list for each year. Girls come from the local boroughs and as far as Barnes, Ealing, Kew, Putney, Wimbledon and north London. Vast diversity of backgrounds; the US and Asian contingent is fairly significant and a number are bilingual in combinations of French/Mandarin/Italian/German, to name but a few.

Exit: Over half each year go either to St Paul's or Godolphin & Latymer. Even if they don't go there, these are the two schools that most parents aspire to. The rest either board – Wycombe Abbey, Downe House, St Swithun's the current favourites – or go to other all girls' day schools eg Putney High, Lady Eleanor Holles, the Francis Hollands. Recently greater interest among parents in co-ed – Latymer Upper is becoming increasingly popular. Interestingly, around the same proportion of those who enter at 4+ as those who come at 7+ go on to the most academic schools. Bute girls trail scholarships: in 2016, the leavers were offered, between them, 16 scholarships (including several music awards).

Remarks: One can be forgiven for thinking that this is the prep school for St Paul's Girls' School; it used to be years ago, but hasn't been since the 1950s, and it's a dangerous mistake to make. Although Bute is lucky enough to share the St Paul's swimming pool and some games pitches, and is only a stone's throw away, it is an entirely separate and distinct institution. You may have won the jackpot to get your daughter in here in that she will have a fabulous education during her early years, but you haven't been granted a stepping stone into the hallowed halls of St Paul's Girls. There are no friendly ears to be bent. Iris will have as great a chance of getting in there from any of the good London preps as she does from Bute House.

An outstanding prep school, Bute House manages to combine solid substance with flair and panache. There is lots going on: the academics are excellent despite – or probably because of – its non-competitive ethos, but this is one of the most passionately competitive about sports of any of the girls' day schools we have seen. In the classroom, however, there is no setting, streaming or ranking, and marking is all done by comment: 'That's what contributes to the girls being so good and kind to each other – and makes it such an amazingly warm, happy and friendly place,' comments Mrs Lowe.

Learning support is known as 'learning enrichment' here – SEN and G&T girls occasionally removed from their lesson in order that their learning be 'enriched'. The head of the learning enrichment department is an SEN specialist, as are the other members of staff who both support those girls needing extra help and extend the more able girls. Teachers from the LED work in class alongside class teachers as well as sometimes taking groups of girls out of the classroom. The teaching is clearly, for the most part, inspired, and this is true of the learning enrichment programme too. Fifty-two girls are on the LE register, many needing only minimal support. This support is free. Those who don't speak English at home have one weekly support session. Some see the SENCo on a one-to-one basis and some in small groups. Ninety on the G&T register. School says that any difficulties are diagnosed early and dealt with as soon as possible.

We detected some sensitivity around the issue of special needs. The school says that it 'makes it clear in its parents' contract that girls with specific learning difficulties who need a great deal of additional support may be encouraged to look for another school that can meet their needs better'. A few parents, albeit under the old regime, felt that their daughters with learning difficulties were not getting sufficient attention compared with those who were 'gifted'. School is keen to point out that this is changing. A dynamic SEN teacher coupled with a change in priority and ethos from the top means that everyone here gets the attention they need. However, there does appear to be some tension between the non-competitive academic ethos and the fact that ultimately this is an academic school with parents who have academic aspirations. Mrs Lowe asserts that early identification of any issues should enable all the girls to achieve highly, and she is especially keen to ensure that every girl achieves to the best of her ability. She says she also looks carefully at the transition from year 2 to 3, since this can cause anxiety for parents who perceive that the new intake may well be more academically able, and the flood of new girls will result in their daughter becoming 'lost'. The strong non-competitive academic ethos comes as a shock to a lot of parents who are attracted to the idea of Bute House as a top prep school with a history of a relationship with St Paul's – often in competitive professions themselves, they find themselves feeling frustrated not knowing whether Molly is top of the class or not.

Any competitive instincts can find an outlet in the sports programme, however. Bute girls are known in the prep school world to be formidable netball players and there is a D team as well as an A so everyone should get a chance to play. Some mutterings among mothers that this is not the case – but we suspect that the kudos of playing in the A team is such that both daughter and parents aspire for that. Gymnastics is also very popular and of a high standard. Although gym squad, run by external coaches, is only for the most talented, school says that those not in the squad have plenty of opportunity to be involved in gymnastics. Excellent sports facilities, especially considering its inner urban site, with use of St Paul's pool next door, and swimming is strong – plenty of squads and galas so that everyone gets a chance. Mrs Lowe attributes the excellent team spirit among the girls to the lack of competition in the classroom.

Very young, innovative head of drama (complete with red glasses and severe fringe) injecting some exploratory imaginative work into the drama curriculum; the class we saw were all lying on the floor with their feet in their air waving their arms. Head of music also young and energetic – a benign 'Jack Black school of rock' type, he arranges lots of different groups, bands and orchestras ('smiley strings', 'string fever', 'jammy jazzers' to name a few). Girls have class music twice a week from reception through to year 6 and most learn at least one instrument, from the double bass through to the bassoon.

Rich curriculum – everyone does French from reception, Spanish from year 5 but no Latin at all. Specialist teaching from reception in drama, music, sport and art (and DT) as well as French. Specialist science teaching from year 4 and proper DT facilities – saws, work benches, as well as a well-equipped art room – first class and unusual in a London prep school. Huge superbly-equipped science lab and lots of outside space – netball courts as well as playgrounds, comfortable sitting areas and plenty of greenery. Every floor has stairwell storage for laptops, which are available for the girls to use when needed. Excellent library, well-stocked, well-organised (there are two librarians) and most importantly well-used. Lots of music rooms for lessons and practice. All the girls do one drama performance once a year. The show at the end of year 6 is a highlight, with a recent production being Annie.

The Bute building itself is a surprise – a somewhat futuristic 1950s neo-greenhouse farrago with add-ons in pine, pink render, louvred glass and warm-toned brickwork in a quiet Victorian terraced street just off fashionable Brook Green, five minutes from the Hammersmith jungle. It has a splendid atrium with the reception and offices and big screens with the news of the day, timetable changes etc; even the day's birthdays – rather nice. One eye catching and charming tradition is the corridor outside the hall, the walls of which are covered by little ceramic tiles, each one made by a Bute pupil as a record of their time at the school. The school, thereafter, in the head's words, 'is a bit of a Tardis' and one is not prepared by the hotch-potch exterior for the spaciousness – of each classroom, the immense hall and outside space as well as of the airiness and uncluttered feel of the whole.

The classrooms are a feast. Reception is big and there is plenty of space for everyone at the little tables and around the many activities. Everything is beautifully laid out – pencils in pots, a discovery table with 'new life in spring' exhibits – most remarkable – a canopied and cushioned book corner and lots of lovely dressing-up stuff including some pretty cool shoes. All the children use the garden, complete with lots of climbing things and a real – not a bouncy – castle and sandpit. Reception children have their own times when they also use large wheely toys. This is perhaps the most colourful school we know – everywhere are displays, pictures and models – all bursting with vitality, wit and fun. Many rooms, including the hall, are flexible, and divisible into two. All classrooms have smartboards and, oh joy! – all are air-conditioned. The girls eat in one half of the hall and drool over the food. 'It's just the best'..'it's cooked to perfection!' Free cucumber and carrot wedges are served at break and there are water-fountains inside and outside school.

If your daughter is lucky enough to get a place here she will have stimulating and exciting time, making good friends and building excellent foundations for her future. Your aspirations and ambitions need to be tempered, however; the school she ends up going to next will be right for her, but it may not necessarily be the one you had in mind when you set out on this odyssey.

The Camden School for Girls

26

Sandall Road, London NW5 2DB

Pupils: 1,003 • Ages: 11–19 • Sixth form: 435

Tel: 020 7485 3414
Email: csg@camdengirls.camden.sch.uk
Website: www.camdengirls.camden.sch.uk

Headteacher: Since 2010, Elizabeth Kitcatt BA MA (Institute of Education). Ms Kitcatt has been at the school for many years, joining from Parliament Hill School, where she was head of English. At Camden, under the previous regime, as well as teaching English, she was deputy head, responsible for 'teachers' professional development' and 'school improvement planning'. Looks a bit like Delia Smith and has the same reassuring, measured presence. Clearly strong on detail, but generally considered rather more cautious and less charismatic than her predecessor. 'She's a bit bland,' said one long-term parent. 'She's quite a lot stricter, but otherwise seems to have made little impact.' Determined to maintain the school's high standards and inclusive approach. Enjoys singing in her spare time.

Academic matters: Camden is one of the country's most successful comprehensives. Latest Ofsted rated it 'outstanding' in every respect (except attendance) and commented that 'it rightly deserves the outstanding reputation it has among parents and in the community'. In 2016, 77 per cent of pupils got 5+ A*-C grades at GCSE, including English and maths, and 45 per cent of grades were A*/A. But the sixth form is the jewel in the crown and A level results are stellar, with 75 per cent A*-B and 41 per cent A*/A grades. 'Top class curriculum,' says Ofsted, and that includes a hard-going compulsory core at GCSE of English, maths, science, philosophy and theology, physical education, French or Spanish and PSHE. Mixed-ability classes of about 28 pre-GCSE, 20 in the sixth form, and work carefully monitored with individual targets set at the beginning of each year. Homework, too, taken seriously, with detentions for slackers.

The sixth form decidedly less mixed-ability than the lower school, as only those who make the grades make the transfer. The curriculum here is traditional and academic with classics, history of art, ancient Greek (now to AS only due to government funding cuts), economics, psychology and philosophy supplementing the mainstream subjects. Extended Project Qualification (EPQ) also popular. Intellectual stretching taken even further for Oxbridge aspirants with after-school masterclasses covering everything from the Economic Downturn to The Wasteland. Much inspired instruction, particularly in the sixth form. 'It's like an old-fashioned grammar school,' said one parent. 'The teaching is really rigorous.' Lower down, there are those who struggle with more challenging pupils. ('Some teachers just can't control the class,' said one year 9 parent. 'There are subjects where my daughter has completely given up.') Though sciences are well taught with strong results, this is a noticeably arty school – possibly not the ideal place if medicine is your ultimate goal. Special needs well catered for, with sensitive individual support in class or by withdrawal in small groups. After-school homework club for dyslexia and spelling. Middle-class parents, too, tend to pick up the slack when students flag.

Games, options, the arts: 'Art and music are fantastic here,' said one mother with two daughters, one artistic, the other musical. Most parents (many in the media) agree. The school has specialist music status with dedicated music places at both 11 and 16, and this pool of talent forms the core of two orchestras (including a 70-piece symphony orchestra), various chamber music ensembles, three choirs, a wind band, a jazz group, a jazz choir and a recorder group. Both music and music technology offered at A level. Energetic and dedicated head of music. Art, too, is incredibly strong ('Art is really big in this school,' said one student fan) with powerful work on display throughout the halls and a glorious traditional art studio (formerly the gym), with a suitably bohemian skylight, as well as a pottery studio. Textiles equally vibrant. Art is the fourth most popular A level choice (after English, maths and history) with a good number of A*s. The keen also use the EPQ to extend their range (a short film made by a student was recently shown on the South Bank) and about 20 per cent of leavers go on to art-related degrees. Drama too – with the already professional among the sixth form – is strong, with an annual Broadway show and sixth formers mounting their own production; stage management is offered as an enrichment activity.

Sport, on the other hand, is probably not the school's forte. An on-site gym, outdoor netball court and attractive dance studio are supplemented by excellent facilities at Cantelowes Park, a few feet from the gates, but play-up, play-up and play the game is not really the ethos here. Plenty of clubs from art, technology and modern languages to specialist make-up and knitting, and sixth formers devote Wednesday afternoons to 'enrichment studies', ranging from creative writing to personal finance and tag rugby. All the more traditional ornaments, too, including a sixth form newspaper and a debating society. Though there's plenty going on, you do have to be self-motivated to make the most of it. 'My son was supposed to do football as an enrichment activity,' said one mother, 'but no one monitors it. He just has Wednesday afternoons off.' School trips (Austrian tour for musicians, ski trip) and work experience abroad organised annually.

Background and atmosphere: Camden, founded in 1871 by Frances Mary Buss, is an iconic school in the history of education. Buss – and her limerickly-linked counterpart, Dorothea Beale, who founded Cheltenham Ladies' College – were responsible for establishing three of the great landmarks in women's education. Buss founded North London Collegiate in 1850, and then, specifically for girls of more modest means, Camden, which opened in 1879 and until 1920 (when it established its own sixth form) regularly sent scholarship girls on to North London for sixth form. The school went comprehensive in 1977.

Relatively restricted site with a motley collection of buildings, from the high-ceilinged, large-windowed Victoriana through 60s concrete to red-brick modern. Good facilities with new science labs, a well-stocked library, modern computer rooms and classrooms and a building which houses design technology, English and music. Socially, the atmosphere is relaxed but purposeful. 'I was at quite a strict girls' independent school before I came to Camden in year 10,' said one sixth former, 'and I much prefer it here. You're treated like an adult.' Good food – pasta and garlic bread, curry – at reasonable cost.

Pastoral care, well-being and discipline: Deliberately few rules, but Ms Kitcatt is generally noted for having tightened up on the detail, clamping down on latecomers and absentees. Camden Compass spells out the behaviour code, but generally a strong sense of trust and girls are 'let out into the unknown' from year 9. That doesn't mean, however, their activities remain unobserved. 'The one time my daughter was absent without leave, you knew immediately,' said one parent. 'They really have the girls sussed,' said another, with a daughter who'd encountered considerable difficulties. 'I really feel they listened to my worries.'

Highly praised induction programme eases new pupils into the sixth from, where the approach is definitely 'young adult', with signing in rather than register and no requirement to be on site during study periods. 'We see it as transition between school sixth form and college,' says the head. Loose-rein it may be, but a strong team of tutors oversee 18 students each and offer advice on everything from study skills to gap years. Elected prefects organise the leavers' ball and help out younger girls. Parents in general think the outcome is all that could be desired. 'It's a terrific environment and produces really feisty girls, who are encouraged to think for themselves and question.'

Pupils and parents: 'Camden girls have a sense of their place within the world that is immediately recognisable,' said one former head girl, and who could dispute her standpoint? 'Girls are confident beyond belief,' said one parent with a more ambivalent view. Camden is a cool school, an obvious haven for the daughters of the north London, left-leaning media classes. Current and former parents include the sculptor Antony Gormley, Random House chief Gail Rebuck and Tate Modern director Sir Nicholas Serota, and old girls in the same style number Sarah Brown (wife of Gordon), Professor of Networking Julia Hobsbawm and actress Emma Thompson. The mainstream here is street-smart and sociable and frequently blessed by names like Hermione, Indiana and Genevieve. But while all participate in the uniform non-uniform of skinny jeans and stylish footwear, this is not a socially homogeneous institution. The school serves a catchment where the proportion of those eligible for free school meals is well above average, and it educates a plentiful sprinkling of refugees and asylum seekers, from Kosovo to Kurdistan. 'It's multi-dimensional and multi-ethnic,' said one mother. 'It's an urban experience, but excellent.' In the sixth form, there's a significant influx – boys and girls – from the independent sector.

Entrance: At 11, everyone sits an assessment test which places them in one of four bands – 28 admitted from each band. Preference within this to those with an SEN statement/EHC plan naming the school; then looked after children; then siblings; then those with exceptional medical or social need. Eight music places: three offered to those scoring highest in musical aptitude test; next 50 invited back for five minute instrumental performance audition to compete for other five places. Distance the tie-break for the remaining places – generally rather less than half a mile. Camden is definitely one of those London schools which people move house for (and sometimes only pretend to move house – a naughtiness the school clamps down on firmly). If that's your plan, living within a few feet of the gates is your only sensible course of action. In the sixth form, Camden goes co-ed, admitting a further 150-170 new pupils (from about 1,000 applicants), no more than half of whom can be boys. Once again siblings are given precedence (but only if the sibling is still at the school on the date the applicant starts). Other places are dependent on distance from the gates, academic references and GCSE grades, predicted and actual (documentary proof required for all three). Grade Bs essential in at least five subjects, including maths and English language. At this point, a further 15 music places on offer to those who play 'an orchestral instrument to a high standard.'

Exit: Quite a number leave at 16, either because they don't make the grade or because they prefer a sixth form college, apprenticeship or employment. Vast majority of leavers at 18 to further or higher education, including 15 to Oxbridge in 2016, and two medics. Sussex particularly popular, as are art foundation and music schools.

Money matters: Camden is a voluntary aided school and, as such, has to contribute 10 per cent to its buildings costs. Parents give generously and there is an annual fundraising appeal, with monthly donations from £10. Plenty of further fundraising activities, too, where celebrity watching is the order of the day.

Remarks: One of London's best and coolest schools. Suits the self-motivated, self-assured, creative individualist, particularly those who might find the atmosphere elsewhere pettifogging and unimaginative.

C

Cameron House School

4 The Vale, London SW3 6AH

Pupils: 119 • Ages: 4–11

Fees: £17,535 pa

Tel: 020 7352 4040
Email: info@cameronhouseschool.org
Website: www.cameronhouseschool.org

Headmaster: Since September 2016, Padraic Fahy, previously deputy head at Westminster Under School. Born in Galway, on the beautiful west coast of Ireland, he came to England after taking an English and German degree at the National University of Ireland, Maynooth. He joined the English department at the Hayesbrook School in Tonbridge and gained further experience as a subject leader at a secondary school in Clapham before joining the Hazelwood prep school in Otford, Kent, where he was head of English and head of house. He has also been deputy head (academic) at St Michael's Prep, and still lives in Kent. He enjoys reading, music, the company of friends and, when time allows, cooking and travelling.

Entrance: All children are assessed at 3, so no need to rush to get your baby onto a list; register up till a year before entry. A popular school – over 200 applicants for 20 places and school acknowledges how difficult it is to choose – 'It's heartbreaking to reject anyone.' Ultimately they look to create a class with a balance of the confident and the shy and some happily in between. They work closely with nurseries and rely on their reports (children come from a wide range including Pippa Poppins, Paint Pots, and Miss Daisy's). Putting school down as a genuine first choice always helps.

Exit: A few boys at 7+ or 8+ to, eg, boarding or Catholic schools (Ludgrove, St Philip's), but school actively discourages year 3 leavers so fewer and fewer now. School has fine tuned the 'stepping stones' options for boys who want to do 13+ common entrance and sends them for two years at 11 to, eg, Newton Prep, Fulham Prep, Sussex House, Wetherby or the Hampshire School Chelsea. Lots of advice given to parents from year 5 onwards.

At 11 girls and boys go to a broad range of schools each year – current favourites include St Paul's, Godolphin & Latymer, Westminster Under, Wycombe Abbey, Francis Holland, City of London and Alleyn's. They nearly always get their first choice school, we're told (due in large part to school's determination that parents choose the school that suits their child, whatever they themselves might prefer). 'And they interview beautifully because they're so confident.' One or two girls every year board at, eg, Wycombe Abbey or Downe House.

Remarks: A tiny (one class per year of about 20), cosy, pretty school, but don't be misled into thinking it's just chocolate boxy – Cameron House is a serious player in getting children into sought-after London schools. Wide range of ability, but what all children have in common is that they are confident and very, very smiley.

They are given a lot of preparation in the final year. In year 6, class sizes shrink so everyone gets more attention, compulsory homework club gives all children an extra hour at school and removes the pressure from the parents. 'We shoulder the worry, and the last thing we want is to see 10 year olds being counselled for stress.' A lot of staff channelled into year 6, when they do group work, prepare for scholarships, have mock interviews and confidence-building workshops. The formula clearly works – they get results, but no-one could describe this as a hothouse.

Approximately 15 children are helped with mild to moderate SEN – dyspraxia, dyscalculia, dysgraphia etc. The school takes a holistic approach. Learning support is timetabled and structured with clear IEPs drawn up – parents pay extra. Programme for the gifted and talented run within the class. In addition a select few are invited to join the Discovery Club and Explorers Club. Cautious approach to the gifted and talented programme. Children are identified towards the end of year 1 – 'We wouldn't want to have to say, "You weren't gifted after all!"'

A town house with not a great deal of space, but the soft plush tartan carpet throughout the stairwell, lavatories with pretty wallpaper, water filters, attractive blue furnishings and every teacher referred to by their first names – without even a Miss or Mister attached – give the school a homely, uninstitutional feel.

Children have fun here, whether it's enjoying music, drama or sport, watching caterpillars transmorph into butterflies or playing giant magnetic chess in the playground (a good excuse to see the lovely Lucie, to get the chess pieces). Even maths can be made to be an excuse to dress up and laugh – Bubbles the maths clown visited, the hall was filled with balloons and children came to school dressed as shapes. In Book Week everyone dresses up.

Nearly everyone plays an instrument or has singing lessons – the lessons happen in a little Wendy house type hut in the playground. Major dramatic productions – The Lion King, A Midsummer Night's Dream among them – take place in a closely guarded secret venue – 'Let's just say a theatre off Kensington High Street,' is as far as school will be drawn. 'We aim high' – list of impressive artistic accomplishments for such a small school includes getting to the final for young choir of the year at the Royal Festival Hall. They have an orchestra, string quartet and three choirs.

One of school's challenges has been to stop the boys leaving at 7+ or 8+ – signs of success. Although previous year 6 classes have had few boys, some none at all, when we visited there were an equal number of both sexes. 'Parents are starting to realise that they can get their boys into Westminster Under, St Paul's Juniors or Latymer at 11, and there are plenty of stepping stone options between 11 and 13.' Children are kept a lot more active here than at many similar schools. Games takes place three times a week – children can do cricket, football, hockey and netball as well as martial arts in the huge loft space at the Boudokwai centre. Lots of matches (most of which they lose, comments one parent) but the advantage of being a small school is everyone gets to have a go – it's not just the sporty types who do everything.

A lot of expat families, mainly from the US, Canada and Australia, reflecting the cosmopolitan area. We saw masses of glamorous long-haired mothers off to the gym after drop off. Lots of City types, but also more than the usual number of creatives – artists and actors, as well as doctors and art dealers. All parents are very involved and enjoy the open door policy of the school.

A charming school that will discover your child's strengths, nurture and support them.

Canbury School

Kingston Hill, Kingston, Surrey KT2 7LN

Pupils: 50 • Ages: 11-16

Fees: £16,110 pa

Tel: 020 8549 8622
Email: enquiries@canburyschool.co.uk
Website: www.canburyschool.co.uk

Headmistress: Since 2014, Ms Louise Clancy BEd. Spent 11 years as deputy head of Greenacre School for Girls, Surrey. Has taught at some challenging comprehensives. Teaches GCSE art and design. Described by one parent as 'down to earth. She just loves the children.' Another said, 'Her office is in the middle of the school and she hears and see exactly what is going on. The children like the fact that she is accessible and often pop into her office for a chat. She's easy to talk to but everyone respects her.' Married to a retired policeman. Two grown up daughters; one works in theatre and one in commerce. Now a doting grandmother. Enjoys baking and cooking, which she finds therapeutic, and is a dab hand at portrait painting. Loves travelling, with a soft spot for Cyprus.

Relishes being head here. 'I wanted to be a head of a small school where I could know each child's name. I just fell in love with Canbury,' she confesses. Ambitious for her school. Very keen to improve the teaching and learning on offer – wants it to go from good to outstanding on her watch. Parents feel she has turned the school around and believe she is determined to transform it further still.

Academic matters: A mainstream co-ed independent school that is able to support pupils of all academic abilities, especially those with SEN. 'We have a reputation for working with teenagers who have needs, but are not special needs teenagers. This makes us different,' explains head. Pupils generally take a maximum of nine GCSEs. Due to size of school, results vary greatly from year to year, depending upon cohort. In 2016, six per cent of grades were A*/A and 24 per cent A*-B, though has been rather higher. Science viewed as particularly strong (good showing of A*/C grades among year 10 GCSE science students in 2016), as are creative subjects.

'We are an independent school. We just do everything on a smaller scale.' School is good at targeting the differing needs of the individual pupils. Everything is done with the intention of making the curriculum as accessible to each pupil as possible. 'We personalise and adapt the curriculum, where we can. We teach to their strengths and we are continually reviewing the students' needs,' says head. Science lessons, for example, are practical-heavy as most pupils are kinaesthetic learners. School offers Spanish 'as it is more accessible for our learners than French.' For those who struggle with foreign languages, there is also the option of taking a BTec qualification in travel and tourism. 'We don't want their confidence to plummet so we offer an alternative where we can.'

One parent commented, 'The school is incredibly accommodating. They teach foundation and higher level GCSEs at the same time which must be a challenge'. Another parent said at times her son felt some lessons could be better, but overall most teaching was good. 'Spanish is excellent and maths clinic was a blessing. It meant my son could go over trickier topics again, often on an individual basis, which he found really helpful.' Maths is taught in mixed ability classes for first three years, then set thereafter.

Head explains, 'We do have a range of students with quite different needs. Some have no special needs at all but like being in a smaller school. They have looked at bigger schools and felt they were not for them'. Pupils have a variety of difficulties including slow processing, OCD, dyslexia, dyspraxia, autistic spectrum disorder and cerebral palsy. Others have health issues including transplant patients who need a gentler environment where they will not get knocked about in the corridors. Students with high anxiety and school refusers also come here for its nurturing atmosphere. School does not take on children with behavioural problems. 'Our pupils are happy and I won't take on new students who will disrupt our existing students. We do not accept children who are violent and nor do we take children with complex needs as we are too small. No intimate care offered. We only take pupils if we feel we can meet their needs,' states head matter-of-factly. She explains, 'We have able children who can't always get it down on paper. They just need extra support and they do well academically here.'

Many of the pupils arrive in a vulnerable state with shattered confidence, for a variety of reasons. Head describes how 'some arrive broken and we make them whole again. When they leave in year 11, they are fully functioning, productive members of society.' Pupils are very accepting of each other's needs.

Games, options, the arts: Plenty of sport offered, with five hours a week in key stage 3 and three hours in key stage 4. Weekly swimming lessons for first couple of years. Games afternoon comprises football, basketball, badminton, tennis, athletics, softball and cricket. Kayaking on the Thames and rock climbing also on offer for the more adventurous. Swimming galas, cross-country championships and sports days aplenty. Highly competitive house sport. School also regularly participates in borough events and some pupils perform at national level. Mixed teams, often made up of boys and girls from different year groups. Where possible, school uses Richmond Park for games lessons as well as its own playground, with a wonderfully bouncy surface.

Strong performing arts programme that mixes creativity with technology. Christmas entertainment is mostly student-led, where the teachers provide a skeleton of the production and pupils are expected to do everything else. Head convinced one of the many advantages of being a small school is that all pupils can take on a leading role. 'Everyone here gets the chance to be the star of the show!' she smiles.

Stunning artwork throughout school, including a huge mural of the headmistress. One girl proudly showed us her immaculate portfolio, bursting with striking images and thoughtful write-up. Photography very popular and school has own kiln. Students from nearby Kingston University come into Canbury to collaborate on projects with pupils.

Music taken seriously. Pupils were rehearsing enthusiastically for school concert on the day we visited and parents feel the 'singing is beautiful at Canbury'. Head comments, 'We have extraordinary pupils doing extraordinary things.'

Clubs to suit all tastes including doodling, Minecraft, karate, yoga and nail varnish art (which acts as an informal communication club). Homework club most days, which is popular with parents as homework can often be completed at school, resulting in less stress at home. Duke of Edinburgh award offered to silver level.

School makes the most of its location by arranging visits to the Science Museum, Kew Gardens and the Imperial War Museum. It bends over backwards to ensure all pupils get chance to go on annual overseas trip. 'No child is denied the experiences on offer.'

Background and atmosphere: Founded in 1982 by John Wyatt and housed in a large Edwardian villa on Kingston Hill, on the boundary of Richmond Park. His vision was that, as a small school, Canbury would be able to support the learning of all pupils. When founding headmaster retired in 1997, an educational charitable trust was set up, with a board of governors. Donald Campbell, speed record breaker, lived in this property and a house is named after him.

Maximum class size is 13. Currently more boys than girls but ratio fluctuates. One parent admitted that 'at times, the small size of the school has been frustrating for my son. He would have liked a larger group from which to make friends. It can be limiting.' Up to two adults per classroom. Speech and language and occupational therapists come in regularly, as does a counsellor.

Buildings a little frayed around edges but renovations imminent. Massive ground floor refurbishment planned to include new reception and school hall, flooring and lighting. Rooms are mostly multi-functional. Library currently some bookshelves in a corner of the hall but will soon inhabit a room of its own. Facilities include a fully kitted-out science lab, ICT room overflowing with Apple Macs and a stairlift. Pretty garden decorated with ceramic figures and flowers made by pupils. Study Support Suite, housed in the attic, is an oasis of calm where pupils are supported on a one-to-one basis and in small groups. No school kitchen due to lack of space so pupils bring in their own lunch.

Pupils seem unconcerned by lack of space. On the day we visited, pupils were happily playing at break time in the playground with balls flying in all directions. Much laughter and ready smiles in the corridor. Children seemed genuinely delighted to be here. On spotting the head, pupils bounded up to her and could not wait to share with her how they had found their GCSE exams that morning.

Pastoral care, well-being and discipline: A supportive and caring environment. One parent told us, 'My son had missed a lot of school and had had a terrible time before he came here. He has blossomed at Canbury. He has done everything he should do at school, and more. They certainly know how to get the best out of the kids.'

School is hot on discipline and 'British values are upheld'. Manners are important here. Uniform reintroduced by current head. Mobiles banned apart from at break times and lunch. A pupil once caught with a cigarette was sent home immediately. Another who had shaved his head was made to stay at home until his hair had grown back. No tolerance for inappropriate use of internet. 'If behaviour is good, they learn,' believes head. The pupils we met were polite and friendly and clearly felt at ease with their teachers. Hands-on head who is quick to tell pupils to smarten up if shirts are hanging out or ties are at half-mast. When pupils need to cool off, members of staff take them for a walk in Richmond Park to clear their heads. 'We don't mollycoddle them,' says head. 'We treat them like all the other teenagers in the country but when they fall, we catch them.'

School is keen to praise its pupils at every opportunity. They are given responsibility with a prefect team headed by head boy and head girl. Success is recognised through house points and badges on school blazers. Headmistress's letter is the ultimate reward. Achievements are celebrated in assembly and prize-giving.

Pupils and parents: Most come from within a 10 mile radius, in particular from Barnes, Putney, Wandsworth, Kingston and Hampton as well as Central London, but becoming increasingly local. A sprinkling from overseas. Head says parents are highly supportive and raise huge sums for the school. Current parents are teachers, barristers, solicitors, politicians as well as some media folk. Head believes they are 'the nicest people you will ever meet.'

Parents generally feel they are kept in the loop via weekly newsletter, though one mother complained that parents were not informed early enough about a teacher leaving. Talks regularly put on for parents, including how to cope with teenage anxiety.

Entrance: Non-selective. Pupils come here from a wide number of feeder schools including Parsons Green Prep, Hurlingham School, Finton House and the Lycée. Main point of entry is year 7, though pupils accepted mid-year if there is space. Applicants register during the year preceding entry and must supply their most recent school report, along with other relevant educational, medical, social and diagnostic information. This is followed by a visit to the school. If it is thought that the school can support the child, they are then invited for an assessment day, but others are declined before they even visit if head believes it is the wrong school for them.

Prospective pupils join in classes for the day where teachers set 'a number of tasks to establish the student's current level of ability in a variety of subjects'. Online diagnostic assessments also demonstrate the way pupils learn and their potential. Behaviour and interaction with other students is also important in deciding whether school can offer the pupil a place. Sometimes further assessment days are needed before a decision can be made.

Most special needs are identified prior to pupils arriving here but further assessments are carried out in year 7 and extra support is then put in place. Head is very frank with parents from the off and personally shows all families around. She wants parents to be aware of what school can and cannot provide. Numbers had been dropping in previous years but now school is becoming increasingly popular, so a year 7 admissions week in October has been introduced to assess larger numbers of applicants. 'The interest in us recently has been phenomenal,' says delighted head.

Exit: Roughly 80 per cent continue their education at sixth form, with others going on to apprenticeships, and a significant number progress to university. Pupils' destinations include Blossom House, Carshalton Boys', Coombe Sixth Form, Esher College, More House in Frensham, MPW, Richmond College, Waldegrave and St John's Leatherhead. One parent we spoke to felt the head has a good knowledge of suitable schools for her son and was supportive in helping find the right place for him. Head hopes Canbury can open its own sixth form, though this is still at planning stage. School tries hard to help pupils find relevant work experience and one pupil we spoke to was bubbling over with enthusiasm about her placement in a local primary school.

Money matters: Small number of bursaries up to a maximum of one-third reduction of fees available, to both current and prospective pupils.

Remarks: This school genuinely transforms lives. One parent commented, 'It has literally been a life saver for my son. They believed in him from the start. I can't speak highly enough of the school.' Another parent enthused, 'Canbury has allowed my son to be the man he should be.' Head says, 'We are the best kept secret in south west London but the message is getting out. We're being talked about. We really are a school like no other.' School motto sums up school perfectly: 'Unique. Happy. Inclusive.' A remarkable place.

The Cardinal Vaughan Memorial School

89 Addison Road, London W14 8BZ

Pupils: 990 • Ages: 11–18 • Sixth form: 390 (140 girls) • RC

Tel: 020 7603 8478
Email: mail@cvms.co.uk
Website: www.cvms.co.uk

Headmaster: Since 2011, Mr Paul Stubbings MA. Educated at Worcester Grammar school and Durham University, where he read classics. His conversation is littered with his experiences of 'damascene' moments – his love of Latin and Greek, his vocational calling to become a teacher. One wonders (though he didn't say it) whether it was a similar enlightened moment that drove him to fight for the headship and steer the school away from the dangerous rocks of conflict between the Westminster diocese and a section of the governing board. He certainly stepped into the breach when horns were locked over a tussle between whether the school should be a 'pan London Catholic school' or whether priority should be given to local residents of the borough. He was promoted from deputy head, pastoral – aka the enforcer, and feared by many in the role. He refers to himself in that incarnation as 'the chief chastiser – good at scaring kids, but not nastily'. One former parent described him at this time as a sergeant major, famous for issuing multiple detentions as snowballs flew on one of those rare fun-filled winter days. A smooth negotiator is certainly not the role one would immediately assume for him, but since he has taken the reins the school has been running without much jolting, and both parents and staff are delighted with his appointment. He is completely 'home grown', and has taught here in various roles since his teaching practice placement in 1988. He officially started as a classics teacher in 1989 and still teaches Latin to year 7.

Since morphing into the top man, he sees himself as more of an avuncular figure to the students and confesses that he misses the ongoing day-to-day bustle. However, he embraces having to articulate the direction of the school and describes his vision as the replication of qualities of Cardinal Vaughan himself – namely his energy and foresightedness, firmly rooted in a Catholic foundation. He regards the school as embodying the best of tradition and 'the old', whether is be the traditional hierarchy or the gowns the teachers still wear. 'The only times hierarchies don't work,' he says, 'is when they cease to be benevolent'. However, he acknowledges that change cannot be avoided: 'I have to row this school forward in order for it to stay the same'.

As we left his large modern study, he with a flourish of his gown, two boys were waiting outside whom he confided he was about to exclude. The lines here are straight and inflexible, and if you cross them you can be in no doubt of the consequences.

Academic matters: Consistently impressive results and school makes no bones about aiming for academic excellence in its comprehensive intake. Sunday Times continues to rate it as the highest attaining comprehensive school in the country. School has specialist status in mathematics and IT and computing is BIG here – computer science is now part of the curriculum – an innovation that puts paid to the any suspicion that the school might be stuck in the past. A level results 83 per cent A*-B grades, 54 per cent A*/A in 2016. Range of subjects offered not immense but includes economics, music tech, Latin, philosophy and sociology. It has to be said that the 'newer' subjects do not attract vast numbers. School also offers applied A level in business – Bs for most. Most popular – and successful – A level subjects are maths and Eng lit, both astonishingly good. GCSEs: again not a huge range of options – French and Spanish now the only modern langs, though Latin thrives and Greek is available at GCSE. Most popular subjects are engineering – a double qualification – French and ICT. Everyone takes RS. In 2016, 49 per cent A*/A grades overall and 87 per cent of pupils achieved five good GCSEs including English and maths. And remember, this is a comprehensive school.

This degree of success is not achieved by having independent school sized classes. In the lower school class sizes are 28-30, though music, DT, art and IT groups have 20 pupils. At KS4, class sizes vary but core subjects are taught in groups of 25-30. Most sixth form classes are under 20. Girls and boys seem to achieve similarly though there are some mutterings about AS candidates being 'encouraged' to drop subjects rather than continuing to A2 if it is felt they are unlikely to do well. Accolades abound – the Vaughan is in the top 20 of just about every league table, often near the top. It is regularly named 'top Catholic comp in the country' by those who have such plaudits to give away. Parents and pupils, for the most part, add to the encomia. No-one could eulogise the school's shiny new facilities – apart from all the IT stuff – or accommodation. The level of achievement here is down to the quality of the teaching and the staff and pupils' pride in the place. We heard of 'lovely teachers', the good monitoring of progress and much high praise, especially of the music dept. Bright pupils speak warmly of their 'inspiring' teachers – 'they are amazing – best in the business' – and they mean it.

All applicants are tested – to ensure that school takes across the ability range and to better enable banding once they arrive. School takes 'more than our fair share of statemented children' and it is a beacon of hope for those parents of children with significant difficulties, seeming, as it does, to offer real education in a compassionate community. Majority with SEN, though, are mild dyslexics and dyspraxics. Who goes where is decided, of course, by the LA but school is concerned about the sheer additional physical space taken by extra LSAs who accompany some of the children with more severe SEN. And this is understandable. Many rooms are small and rather poky and corridors are not spacious. Busy SENCo and others give in-class support but parents give mixed reports. One parent felt that her dyspraxic son's problems were picked up very late and that the support he was subsequently offered was barely adequate. Similar reports from others. School, however, tells us that such comments are 'vastly outweighed by parents delighted with our SEN arrangements'. School unashamed of its high octane essence. 'Here we have traditional, hothouse academic teaching. It can be a bit of a shock for those who come in from outside.' G&T pupils offered Greek – where else in the state system is this a growth area?

Games, options, the arts: Despite having to travel for 30 minutes on a bus (to Twickenham) for rugby and football, these sports are not only popular but also strong. Vaughan teams are not to be messed with and are widely respected by their competitors in West London. The first XI recently won the cup in the QPR league, the second XI, no slouches either, won the shield. Athletics and cricket in the summer. Fixtures on Saturday mornings, though if you get a detention you are in danger of being dropped from the team – no leeway there. There is also a gymnasium on site in the 1990s extension known as the Pellegrini building, painted in bright blues and turquoises; the well-known 'boys at games' fragrance welcomed us as we observed a volleyball game. Rock climbing, basketball, table tennis also on offer. Girls in the sixth form can play netball, and some do rock climbing.

Several parents referred to a divide in the school between the 'sporty' and the 'musical' side. Music is certainly as keenly practised, respected and given an equal, if not even greater status as sport, and we were very impressed both with the sumptuous musical facilities and the array of opportunities for performance. When we visited there was great excitement as the head of music rushed in to show Mr Stubbings an article in the Financial Times about a carol composed by one of their 15 year olds and performed on Radio 3. Large practice rooms and smart rooms for performance. There are several grand pianos for simple practice, you understand, and a plethora of choirs from the elite Schola Cantorum – replete with claret-coloured cassocks and leather-bound hymn sheets, providing music for the school's liturgies – to the sixth form choir and the school choir. As well as a full orchestra, chamber orchestra and various trios, there is the hugely busy Big Band that performs in concerts and events all over London.

Various venues are used for concerts including the Albert Hall, Cadogan Hall, St John Smith Square and Westminster Cathedral. The Schola goes on regular tours outside the UK, including Italy – all the grandest places in Rome – plus Spain, Greece, Holland, Germany, the USA and France. The Schola now has its own Songschool – just like in a regular cathedral choir school – in which the choir rehearses; a real boon. Those with a talent for singing also get the opportunity to sing in operas at the Royal Opera House as well as the ENO; recent productions have included La Bohème, Die Zauberflote and Carmen. More light hearted musical productions take place in the summer – Guys and Dolls, Sweeney Todd, The Pyjama Game, to name a few. Other than the annual musical there is little drama to speak of – never a strength here and not an academic subject. School's original main building began life as a theatre and we wondered why so little use is made of it in this way – the stage and gallery are intact, if a little dog-eared. Good art: we liked what we saw of the ceramics, sculpture, mobiles, printing et al – lively creative stuff – and equally good DT: wood, metal and plastic work. Three workshops and lots of benches means there is plenty of room to work and create. Engineering and graphics popular at GCSE – this is where lots of that work takes place. Plenty of imaginative and rewarding extracurricular trips and visits – especially for the musicians; parents glow.

Background and atmosphere: The Vaughan is located in posh Holland Park – wide, quiet streets lined by well-appointed Victorian villas and mansion blocks. Shepherd's Bush, on the other side of the monster roundabout round the corner, is a world away, whereas Kensington High Street – about 15 minutes walk the other way – seems a natural neighbour. Founded in 1914, the school is a memorial to the third Archbishop of Westminster, Herbert, Cardinal Vaughan. It began life as an independent school with 29 pupils but became a grammar school in 1944 and a comprehensive in 1977. Girls were first admitted to the sixth form in 1980 and their presence is firmly established. They are not just a token presence, either – the ratio is 60 boys to 40 girls, which is significantly higher than their cousin school in the neighbouring borough. No chance of going co-ed throughout – simply no room. The original building – Addison Hall, which Mr Stubbings affectionately refers to as Hogwarts – was a musical theatre, but its exterior – possibly what attracted its purchasers – is more reminiscent of a Rinascimento palazzo in pink stone. It now boasts an entrance with highly-wrought grillwork in which the school's motto, Amare et Servire, and crest are displayed. The Old Building, as it is known, houses years 11-13. The New Building was built in the 1960s and much added to since then. It has an attractive exterior with a pretty little garden and an impressive reception area, which abuts the main hall – full of pupils on supervised private study when we visited – no 'free' periods here. DT and IT are housed in the Pellegrini Building, named after a former head. Some roomy places inside but the overall impression is of a rather cramped school with little space – especially outside – and many rather bleak areas.

Situated in these leafy, pricey avenues, you'd expect an upmarket local school population. But it isn't so. School takes from all over, some travel from as far as the northern reaches of Barnet, Harrow and Hillingdon, others from the furthest reaches of Southwark, Merton and Kingston. The only common denominator is a commitment to the Roman Catholic faith. Previous head was wearily, but pugnaciously, defensive of the charge of being socially or academically elitist. He wrote, 'people ask why our pupils' performance goes so far beyond national averages. After all, our top results at A level and at GCSE, over the last five years, have improved six times more than national results. Is it because, as some would like to believe, we "cherry pick" pupils from privileged backgrounds? I don't think so.' Mr Stubbings, too, is often accused of running an elitist school, with only some eight per cent of pupils on free school meals (against 21 per cent in the local authority as a whole). His retort? Selection is random.

The life of the school is imbued with its Roman Catholic inspiration. Everywhere are photographs of pontiffs, cathedrals and the school's own choir singing in various glorious cathedrals. Year groups go on retreats at Tyburn Convent and at Farm Street and the school day and week are punctuated by regular mass, confession, Benedictus, Angelus and so on – all lessons begin and end with the Sign of the Cross and some teachers have prayers in each of their lessons – to a degree rare even in RC schools. But there is also a spirit of enquiry. Vaughan pupils address seriously 'the Dawkins delusion', 'the problem of free will' and 'the just war theory'. Philosophy pupils attend Heythrop College for talks on philosophy of religion, epistemology and ethics, and theology pupils explore the history of Israel. The ethos is embraced and warmly defended by pupils when appropriate. They are aware of the privilege of being here and of the secular – and other – pressures that might have it otherwise. While most parents express great satisfaction with the school in general, we heard a few murmurs from those who are less than ecstatic. 'It's fine as long as all goes well'.. 'they're not brilliant at dealing with problems'.. 'they're not great at getting back to you' – (school says, 'we pride ourselves on excellent communications with parents and prompt responses to their queries') – and 'it's best for the really bright'. School warmly disputes this too. And most are truly grateful for what they receive.

Pastoral care, well-being and discipline: Discipline couldn't be much tighter. The boundaries are clear and few transgress. Immediate expulsion for 'supply' of drugs – sharing them with a friend; fixed term exclusion for possession. 'We don't have a drug problem in this school because they know the score,' asserts Mr Stubbings. The senior sixth former who was our guide was so concerned with punctuality that he didn't allow us to admire the work in the art room. The atmosphere is orderly and you could hear a pin drop walking through the corridors during lesson time, despite the open doors into the class rooms. Occasional bullying is 'firmly and speedily dealt with'. The occasional idiot caught smoking in the streets – sixth form pupils are allowed out of school in breaks – is punished. 'If they're in my uniform it'll be exclusion,' says Mr Stubbings. We saw lots of Vaughan pupils out and about and they definitely do not frighten the horses. 'Old-fashioned good manners' expected and, in general, displayed. Catholic ethos underpins everything and is palpable. Sex ed taught 'by the RS dept for the moral side and the science dept for the biological details'. Four houses – Campion, Fisher, Mayne and More.

Pupils and parents: Pupils come from a wide area covering most of London, some from as far away as Hertfordshire and Surrey. Around half are from ethnic minority groups. Some 30 per cent speak English as an additional language. Here the offspring of a few of the well-heeled 'old' RC families from Kensington learn alongside those of their Filipino, Portuguese or Spanish live-in domestic staff and the children of Irish immigrants from Wembley, in a context hard to find elsewhere. Parents very appreciative of parents' evenings when teachers come to find them rather than the usual ghastly queuing for a two minute slot with a glazed-eyed teacher. Notable former pupils include actors Richard Greene – Robin Hood in earlier days – and Roger Delgado, footballers Bernard Joy of Arsenal and Fulham and the last amateur to represent the England national football team, Paul Parker, Kevin Gallen of QPR and Eddie Newton, novelist Helen Oyeyemi and comedian Dominic Holland. Also WWII flying aces Donald Garland VC and Paddy Finucane DSO and recent Olympic rowing gold medallists Martin Cross and Gary Herbert. Many seem, however, to have careers in the City.

Entrance: Pupils come from over 50 schools. Around 830 apply for the 120 places at 11+. At sixth form, around four apply for every place. Most of the sixth form entrants will be girls – lots from Sacred Heart – and the entrance requirements at that stage are primarily academic, although they do have to have been baptised and a priest has to attest to mass attendance – As and Bs in the subjects they will study in the sixth. School has long been (in)famous for the rigour of its admissions' criteria and stories abound of devoted little church-goers being rejected on account of imperfect catechism or knowledge of parables. 'Nonsense!' bellows school. Early baptism (within six months of birth), weekly attendance at mass, holy communion – all are taken for granted in applicants; no mention now of the 'family involvement' that was so contentious. Applicants split into three ability bands, 12 music places. School uses 'random allocator' for the 70 or so places that remain after priority places have been taken (Catholic children in care, siblings etc).

Exit: A regular mighty handful to Oxbridge (10 in 2016), all doing solid subjects at real colleges. Most of the rest to heavyweight universities to do heavyweight subjects – law at King's, maths at Imperial etc – and a sensible fistful to eg sports psychology at Bournemouth. A notable number to architecture and engineering. Some 10 per cent leave after GCSEs – most to join other schools, a few to employment, another few to other RC colleges.

Money matters: Voluntary aided. School asks for a voluntary contribution of £300 pa for the Governors' Fund and the vast majority stumps up – some more, some less, but no-one comes after you if you don't. A few instrumental bursaries for sixth form entrants who must have reached at least grade 6 on an orchestral instrument.

Remarks: Some see the Vaughan as a 'quasi grammar school' and its cousin in Fulham as a 'quasi public school'. Whatever label you attach to it, our view is that it is the kind of school many parents in London are crying out out for but few, very few, ever find. A unique opportunity if you are lucky enough to qualify, however it won't suit all boys. Be sure your son is someone who responds to rigorous discipline and doesn't flake (or rebel) under stern authority.

Central Foundation Boys' School

C

Cowper Street, City Road, London EC2A 4SH

Pupils: 906 • Ages: 11–18 • Sixth form: 192 (including 30 girls)

Tel: 020 7253 3741
Email: info@cfbs.islington.sch.uk
Website: www.centralfoundationboys.co.uk

Head: Since 2010, Mr Jamie Brownhill LLB (40s). Originally a lawyer, he worked as a construction litigator for city law firm Mayer Brown before deciding to retrain as a teacher at CFB in 2000. 'I wouldn't have gone to just any school,' he says. 'It was very much a sense of vocation and moral purpose that leads one from being a city lawyer to such a challenging environment.' And lucky for the school that he did make that choice – after just five years at the top, he'd completely turned it around and continues to work tirelessly to keep it on track.

Extremely visionary and not one for small talk, he is prone to sounding as if he's permanently giving a speech, making big, sweeping statements ('One needs to have a vision and follow it through'; 'There's a recognition that a head has an incredible impact' etc), which make him an impressive orator. 'Even in the corridors, he has important words of wisdom,' one pupil told us. Parents talk about being 'blown away' by him. One said, 'Our older sons were educated privately and we looked round 15 schools for our youngest, including private, selective and comprehensives – but this one stood out head and shoulders above the rest, largely because of Brownhill. He sets the tone, the culture and the expectations within the school and we love his inclusiveness, his energy, drive and commitment.' Praise indeed. Another commented, 'We love the fact that he's from the outside world – it gives him a much broader perspective than heads who have spent their entire careers within education.'

Rare is the day that pupils don't have some contact with him – he greets them every morning, runs weekly whole-school assemblies, teaches history to the lower years and he's usually out and about during changeover and break times. His office even overlooks the playground. Staff say he has a finger in every pie (which one admitted can be as frustrating as it is helpful), but ultimately they agree it's enabled him to make the school what it is, with the systems he's brought in for the likes of behaviour and targeting being described as 'nothing short of brilliant.'

Academic matters: GCSE performance has put this school in the top 10 per cent of schools nationally for added value, while the sixth form results mean the school is in the top 15 per cent of KS5 providers in the country – very impressive for an inner city comprehensive with 65 per cent pupil premium (in fact, it was nearer 80 per cent when the head joined). In 2016, 83 per cent got 5+ A*-C at GCSE, including English and maths; and 30 per cent of grades were A*/A, with the strongest results in maths, English, science and computing.

French or Spanish from year 7, with after-school provision available in the other. After-school classes also available for Mandarin, Arabic and ancient Greek (all of which can also be done at GCSE), though few continue languages to A level. Setting in English, maths, science, languages, geography and history from year 7, with a reassuring amount of movability. Homework in abundance – building up from an hour in year 7 to two hours in year 11 – and woe betide any student who doesn't hand it in on time.

In 2016, 62 per cent A*-B grades at A level and seven per cent A*/A. Subject choices are largely traditional – sciences, maths, economics and computing most popular – but the school is part of the Islington Sixth Form Consortium, meaning there's breadth to study the likes of photography, psychology, media studies and a whole wealth of languages at one of the other member schools.

Head believes the school's success is largely down to the fact that students are taught in classes with a maximum of 24. There's also a major push on the fundamentals in year 7 and 8, which ensures literacy, maths and learning habits (how you revise; how you organise homework etc) are up to scratch, ready for GCSE learning. Indeed, unlike many schools, where there's an overt focus on years 10 and 11, boys here are developed, with meticulous attention to detail, right from the off. 'It's all part of the culture of learning that is drilled into the boys from the day they start,' said one parent. 'It seems to me that the importance of learning is at the heart of every single piece of communication with the boys,' said another. Perhaps this explains why the boys we spoke to were not only enthused about their studies, but able to directly relate them to their futures. Even some year 7 boys were able to tell us exactly what they wanted to do with their lives and what they'd need to get there.

Lessons, which are all taught by subject specialists (most of whom have firsts or 2:1s in their degrees) are well-planned and, according to students, engaging. 'If you don't respond well to a teacher's learning style, they'll adapt it for you,' one told us, whilst several pointed out that teachers are always available by email or after school to go over anything you don't understand.

Teachers (over half of whom are female) say they are helped by the centralised system for dealing with behaviour (same-day detentions even for small transgressions), along with a painstaking focus on tracking and monitoring, which they say means they can get on with the job in hand. We noticed very few teaching assistants – they tend to be used on a temporary basis for getting a child's behaviour sorted. There's a mixed diet of practical, interactive lessons and heads-down learning. Food tech, for example, always involves cooking, whereas in the maths and languages lessons we witnessed, it was very much a case of chalk and talk.

SEN provision – which covers the usual dyslexia, ASD etc – is almost exclusively classroom based (and helped by those small class sizes, as well as setting) and offers exceptional outcomes for students, evidenced by the results. 'I couldn't have asked for better help throughout my son's education,' said one mother, whose son is dyslexic. 'He's had the "Why me?" moments when he's had to work much harder, but the school keeps him positive, as well as making sure he has attainable goals and extra support and time where he needs it. Dyslexia has certainly never made him feel he can't achieve as much as anyone else.'

Games, options, the arts: Football and basketball are the top sports, with boys doing CFB proud when it comes to competing against other schools. Cricket is on the up and there's also fencing, boxing, martial arts, table tennis and gym workouts. Whilst the school is good at playing to the boys' strengths (hence winning all those high level competitions), the head is adamant that sport here is for all. Pupils and parents concur. 'There's no stereotypical male bravado around sport at this school. In short, you don't get the jocks,' we were told. On-site facilities include an undercover Astroturf pitch, running track, a couple of gyms and two halls. Off-site, the boys do climbing, swimming and more. 'When a young person leaves here, they really know how to access the community's facilities,' says the head.

Music is integral to school life. Incredibly, every boy who wants to can borrow an instrument for the duration of his time at the school. We're not just talking recorders, but cellos, saxophones and clarinets. No wonder 150 students are heavily involved with the department. From 7.30am every day, there are rehearsals, whether for the three school choirs, orchestra, bands (including house band and concert band), string quartets, woodwind groups etc. The department's equipment is sophisticated and there's a 10-strong staff team, including two full-time music teachers. Expect to see a raised eyebrow if you use the word 'peripatetic' to describe the visiting teachers – this dedicated team say this is the only school in London they work in, where they are considered part of the school community, not just 'teachers who pop in' – the result of which is that they are more than willing to put extra time in for the three main performances per year. Parents describe these performances as 'amazing.' 'We nearly all had tears in our eyes at the last one,' one parent told us. Meanwhile, external opportunities range from singing in the Royal Albert Hall to providing the musical entertainment for local law firm functions. While many of the musical children are also academic, others aren't – and music gives them a great opportunity to excel.

A delightful, airy and bright art room is home to some serious artistic talent – much of it bold, brave and inspiring. Drama is also seen as important, with weekly lessons for years 7, 8 and 9 in the two-roomed, carpeted drama studio. There are three main performances per year, providing opportunities for both pupils in the lower and upper years. Debating also strong, they were national schools Debate Mate champions in 2013 and were third out 250 schools in the 2016 competition when we visited.

Day visits to all the usual museums and galleries that this school has on its doorstep, as well as French and Spanish trips (year 9, 10 and 11), an annual ski trip open to all and a rural activity trip for sixth formers. Extracurricular provision focuses on music and sport in the main, with other options ranging from cooking (particularly popular) to arts club and gaming to drama. The school takes full advantage of its location, with excellent links with the City.

Background and atmosphere: There could hardly be a more unlikely location for a school – smack in the middle of the City. Squeezed between, and overlooked by, law buildings and financial institutions, you walk in expecting it to be bursting at the seams. But this place is a Tardis, with a roomy outside courtyard (some of which is covered) and Astroturf pitch, along with ample classrooms of various sizes, break-out rooms, labs, halls, library, dining room, sixth form centre, art block, drama and more. The oldest parts date back 150 years and boast beautifully tiled walls and polished wood floors, albeit with a few areas that look in need of a lick of paint. 'The school even smells of tradition,' said one dad – and he's right.

The school originally opened in 1865 by Rev William Rogers (chaplain to Queen Victoria), who recognised the pressing need for more education in the City. Having initially used temporary buildings in Bath Street, the current purpose built school then opened in Cowper Street in 1869 and the Great Hall came four years later, by which time there were over 900 boys. Post-war, it became a grammar, then in 1975 the school returned to being a comprehensive, with various building works having taken place over the decades – the most significant of which is about to happen. 'The development project, which will cost between £30-£40 million, will involve a science block and a new reception, followed by a new art centre, then a four court sports hall – along with some more general landscaping and renovation,' explains the head, who points out that the works will be staggered to ensure minimal disruption.

During lesson times, the school is so quiet that you could be forgiven for thinking the place is empty. It's another story at break times, though, when boys inevitably let off steam – and with everyone changing lessons or having breaks simultaneously, it can be loud. 'It's essential, in my view, to avoid interruptions, so when we learn, we all learn and when we move, we all move,' says the head.

Pastoral care, well-being and discipline: Each year group is organised into eight form groups of 18 students and each of these forms has one tutor who stays with that form as it goes up through the school. Every student is allocated regular tutorials with this tutor. In addition, there are directors of learning (heads of year) who, once a term, do a detailed analysis of each student, looking at issues such as attendance (including at after-school clubs), punctuality, learning and behaviour. Then there's a house system, which generates all the usual leadership opportunities and cross-year friendships.

A high level of engagement with CAMHS means there are no waiting times for students who want to access mental health services within school and there are three student counsellors, focused on supporting students with any work-related issues. 'Students can access both, should they require it,' says the head.

No word gets used more by the head than 'community' and it's this ethos, say students and their parents, that ultimately makes the school such a supportive environment – a place that students want to be. Some older students told us bullying used to be a real issue, but that this head's zero tolerance has helped – measures such as teachers in playgrounds and even bus stops and underground stations, mean there are no longer any hiding places. 'There are instances of bullying,' one boy told us, 'but teachers are good at sorting it out quickly.'

The glass cabinet in the reception area sets the tone for discipline. Displaying beautifully hand-written notes from the headteachers in the 1800s, outlining intricately detailed rules around issues such as not throwing paper and not pulling other boys' hats off, this isn't just a light-hearted look back to harsher times. Indeed, the message remains crystal clear that boys must not misbehave, even slightly. Any that do find themselves receiving a short, sharp shock – notably an hour's detention after school that very afternoon. Talking in class, forgetting your PE kit, lacking focus, failing to hand in your homework – all these things will land you in deep water. No wonder Ofsted marked behaviour here as outstanding and we did not see a single boy failing to pay full attention in class. Teachers who come to visit can hardly believe their eyes. There are more serious misdemeanours, but only occasionally, and these usually relate to violence. 'There is the odd time when a boy flares up and hits out,' explains the head, although it's much less than it used to be, reflected by the drop from 190 exclusions per year before he joined to just 10 in the academic year we visited.

Boys are expected to dress immaculately both in and outside school. The messiest you'll see is an undone top button. 'I have a room with every piece of uniform in every size, so if a boy forgets something, they can borrow it,' says the head.

Unusually, sixth formers get a chance to do paid work in school, for example by working in the kitchen and doing lunchtime duties in the year 7 play area. 'It's not that they don't do voluntary work too. It's just that we don't want the students working every hour at Sainsbury's to earn money, which would get in the way of their work. It means everyone wins,' says the head.

There's a strong student voice here – the student council is taken particularly seriously and individual requests are often met too. 'One student in year 7 asked for there to be a skateboarding club and they set it up within a month,' one student told us.

Pupils and parents: There are 35 first languages spoken by students at this truly ethnically diverse school, it's English for 47 per cent of students, then Bengali (16 per cent). Nineteen per cent of students are white British, with other significant numbers being Bangladeshi, Somali, Turkish and Black Caribbean. Because of the banded entry system, some of these students come from neighbouring boroughs, as well as the whole of Islington. The students are a mixed bag socially too – both extremes of wealth and poverty, plus everything in between.

There's no PA, although parents are seen as key to enabling the boys' learning and there's almost 100 per cent attendance at the two annual parents' evenings and other talks and meetings. We found pupils to be articulate and enthusiastic, even in year 7, and there's already a huge sense of pride. Notable former pupils include Anthony Wedgwood Benn (before he became plain old Tony Benn), Kingsley Wood, Jacob Bronowski, Richard Seifert, Ronnie Scott, Martin Kemp, Trevor Nelson and Reggie Yates.

Entrance: More than 600 boys compete for the 150 places (180 from 2018). All applicants take CATs (Cognitive Ability Tests), with students split into four ability cohorts. Within each of these cohorts, the boys closest to the school get in. All sixth form entrants must have Bs in the subjects they want to study, including English and maths, as well as getting through a detailed interview. 'The way we see it, we have a short period of time to achieve a lot, so we need to know students have the right character and work ethic,' says the head. Attendance in sixth form is 98 per cent (compared to the average of 85-90 per cent for London) and the head intends to keep it that way. Usually, around 10 of the school's own applicants tend to get turned away, while around 25 new students come in (of whom 10-15 are female).

Exit: Around 60 per cent stay on to sixth form, those who don't have generally decided to study A levels elsewhere, including the private sector. Maths, engineering and computer science are among the most popular subjects chosen at university (although there is a huge breadth of subjects overall). Around 13 per cent to Russell Group universities; nine biomedics, one pharmacologist and one pharmacist.

Remarks: This extremely disciplined, well-ordered and highly academic, urban school runs a tight ship, giving boys who are prepared to toe the line a chance to leave with both excellent exam results and a genuine readiness for the modern world in terms of character, moral compass and work ethic. A hidden gem right in the heart of London, it is a school going from strength to strength and has the feel of a grammar, without the selection. 'It's a hugely well-kept secret, with many parents – including me – thinking, "Why don't all local boys apply?"' summed up one parent.

Channing School

31

Highgate, London N6 5HF

Pupils: 842 • Ages: 4–18 • Sixth form: 130

Fees: £16,050 – £17,580 pa

Tel: 020 8340 2328
Email: admissions@channing.co.uk
Website: www.channing.co.uk

Headmistress: Since 2005, Mrs Barbara Elliott, MA PGCE (50s). Mrs Elliott attended a girls' grammar school in Lancashire, then read French and Spanish at New Hall, Cambridge. Taught

C

in both the independent and state sectors before arriving at Channing a decade ago. Much liked by pupils and parents ('She brought new life into the school.') Gets to know pupils well at the outset by inviting year 7s in for a chat. With experience of all-boys, all-girls and mixed schools, she remains a firm advocate of girls-only education. 'I've seen girls in co-educational schools sitting silently for years. Girls here are not without an interesting social life, but here they have the freedom to be themselves and try new things.' Like her pupils, there's nothing of the wallflower about Mrs Elliott, whose fashionable red glasses and stripy tights signal her buoyant and breezy personality. Pomp and distance play no part in her regime (recently, for example, she happily sat crossed legged for morning assembly in a charity swop with a junior pupil), and she runs the school with a light touch. It's clear, however, she remains devoted to its future. 'I'm not about to leave,' she says firmly. 'Why would I go anywhere?' With four adult sons, all now successfully established, she's recently become a grandmother. Lives locally, and spare moments are spent walking (with her dog) on Hampstead Heath, 'making the most of London', and travelling further afield.

Head of junior school: Since 2008, Louise Lawrance B Prim Ed, 40s. Mrs Lawrance grew up in South Africa, where she trained as an English specialist. Then spent five years in the state sector in Burton on Trent before taking a 'gap' year ('I was in my late 20s and working every evening'), realising in the process that 'I was really meant to be in teaching'. Returned to the UK, where she spent seven years at Gems Hampshire School in Chelsea (now the Hampshire School), the last three as head of the pre-prep. A relaxed and sympathetic presence, she continues to teach the youngest, and you have no difficulty believing that her ambition – 'I spend my life trying to give girls the absolute best' – is fully realised. Married, with a young son.

Academic matters: A fundamental aspect of the junior school's approach is its personalised attitude to the academic; all are taught to a high standard, but not all are taught in the same way. ('One of my daughters needs – and gets – much more support than the other,' said a parent.) Bright and breezy teaching moves at a brisk, imaginative pace. (We watched girls create a 'storm' using a variety of sounds, for example, for a lesson on weather.) Specialists in ICT, modern languages. Art, DT, PE, drama and music throughout. Innovative new Spanish language programme engages all pupils in 'Spanish language and culture'. French also added in year 3.

IT firmly embedded from the off, with a dedicated IT room lined with Apple Macs, and iPads used as 'learning tools'. 'Somehow they see them as something completely different from the tablets at home,' says the head. 'Here they're used as dictionaries, for creativity and for research.'

Reasonably heavy homework load. ('My daughter couldn't manage more,' said the mother of a girl in year 5), but it's cool to work hard and parents, pupils and students all have high aspirations. 'The school manages a good balance between stretching them academically, while still nurturing them and treating them as individuals,' said one parent. 'I feel my daughter's pushed about the right amount,' said another.

Designated additional learning coordinator works with classroom teachers to put together appropriate learning plans. Children are sometimes withdrawn from lessons to work in a quieter space, but always follow the same work as their classmates. Gifted and talented also given additional stretch.

Channing is an academic school, but not one where academic achievement overrides all else. The intake here is slightly broader than at some of the local competition, and not every pupil will be cut out for straight A*s. ('Here, if a girl is outstanding at art, but not at maths, it's not the end of the world,' says the head. 'Some are exceptionally bright; others exceptional at something, but not everything.') Every girl, however, should get the best she's capable of, and often significantly more than might be expected. ('Some achieve more than you'd have ever have thought possible.') At GCSE, most garner a pleasing string of A*-As (83 per cent in 2016); at A levels, the dominant alphabet is again A*-A (69 per cent).

The sixth form is not huge – about 60 in each year – and nor is the subject range (19 on offer), but the core is serious stuff and the conventional arts/science divide is roughly in balance, with biology and economics attracting similar numbers to history and English (though few physicists). Maths tops the popularity stakes; biology and politics take away the highest grades. Good spread of languages, with Spanish, French, German and Latin all on offer at GCSE and A level, plus Greek as a twilight GCSE subject. Art history recently reintroduced to the post-GCSE mix.

The school prides itself on the quality of its teaching. ('We teach our teachers to teach,' says the head.) The Independent Schools inspectors found teaching 'excellent', and also waxed lyrical about the 'exceptional' quality of 'pupils' learning and achievement'. No doubt at all that value is added here – in every direction. Good take up, for example, of the research-directed Extended Project Qualification (EPQ). Technology, too, thoroughly embedded, with all girls issued with a school iPad 'to support research, investigation, creativity and communication'.

Special needs addressed by a qualified SENCo, called on to assist a range of difficulties, from the profoundly deaf to 30-or-so girls with mild visual impairment, dyslexia, or processing issues. 'We carry out appropriate assessment, but it's as much about helping teachers to adapt their teaching.'

Games, options, the arts: Art and music both unusually strong. Art ('absolutely amazing,' said one pupil) is housed in roof-top studios with stunning views across London. Strong emphasis on drawing as the basis of it all, but art rooms are lined with Macs and scented by oil paint. Plenty achieve external glory, with recent prize winners in 'Young Art' at the Royal College of Art and Haringey schools' film competition. Student work also displayed (and sold!) at a north London gallery. Music, always strong, has undoubtedly been enhanced by the completion of the new music school, which has added 10 practice rooms, a technology room and a sound-proofed percussion studio. Record numbers now take external exams, including the first set of musical theatre awards (with 23 distinctions). Plenty of opportunity to perform in-house – annual and lunchtime concerts, plus informal recitals – and in formats that range from string quartets and guitar ensembles to a jazz band and contemporary music group. Recent finalists, too, in Voice Festival UK.

Limited running around space on site, so probably not a first-choice for those who live for goals and glory. 'We have county level sportswomen, but they don't necessarily train here,' says the head. But if go-fight-win is not top of the agenda, keeping fit and healthy definitely is. PE compulsory throughout and the sleek and spacious new gym (nominated for an architectural award) and independent multi-gym make this a pleasure, with vastly improved opportunities for volleyball, badminton, cricket and dance.

Staggering range of school trips and activities, from history in Berlin and classics in Greece to a music tour to Madrid and regular theatre outings to the West End. Clubs follow prevailing interests and currently include feminist society, robotics, chemistry, classics, life drawing and creative writing.

Music undoubtedly a strength in the juniors too, with enthusiastic head of music working closely with her equally energetic colleague in the senior school. Regular music lessons, plus plenty of opportunities to perform in music assemblies, orchestra, brass and wind bands, string quartet and choir. Wide range of individual music lessons, with vast majority taking classes in anything from saxophone to harp. (The school currently has four harpists.) Does its best to ensure girls find an instrument that 'fits their character' and lets parents borrow rather than buy in the early stages. Three girls recently invited to join the National Children's Orchestra, and usually several music awards to senior school. Art, with its own designated room, also vibrant.

Large sports hall on site (recently vacated by senior school, which now has its own), plus well-used netball and tennis courts. Swimming takes place elsewhere, and the school has its own playing field a brisk walk away, used for sports days and rounders matches. Pupils have competed at regional and national level in tennis, swimming and cross-country.

Junior school head has significantly boosted the extracurricular offering introducing in- and after-school clubs ranging from judo and gymnastics to fencing, ballet and chess (with one Grand-Master-in-the-making competing in the U11 World Chess Champions). Busy schedule of visits (eg Neasden Temple, Sky Studios, engineering workshop) and residential trips for older pupils.

Background and atmosphere: School housed in four tall and graceful Georgian buildings on Highgate Hill overlooking one of London's most beautiful and under-visited parks. Backing these, head has done a serious job of rearrangement, making the most of a relatively small site with the addition of a new complex (containing the music school, the gym and a sixth form centre). 'If you're investing in your daughter's education you expect 21st century facilities,' she says. Now in the process of producing a £3m theatre. 'We've dug the foundations – all we need to do is raise the money.'

Established in 1885 by a Unitarian minister and two members of his congregation to educate the daughters of Unitarian ministers, the school's clientele has broadened, but it retains the founders' values of liberalism, democracy and religious tolerance. There's no prize-giving, for example, and the most valued award is a Conabor Badge, bestowed on 'girls of good character' (or, as one recipient phrased it, 'for being good'). 'Girls really aspire to be awarded a badge,' says the head. 'That's what most embodies the spirit of the school.'

Pupils are active and engaged, participating enthusiastically in both academic and extracurricular activities (15, for example, gained D of E gold last year, impressive numbers even for a much larger school).'I've never worked in a school where the focus on advancement and learning is so great,' says the head. 'They all have a common purpose. They're very ambitious and focussed.'

Set opposite its senior school, behind high walls and tall gates in Highgate's traffic-packed high street, the junior school's rather forbidding exterior belies the pleasures within. Located in what was once Fairseat, the fine Victorian mansion of the Waterlow family, the junior school moved into its current accommodation in 1926, retaining a generous slice of the original gardens (the remainder was donated to the community to become adjoining Waterlow Park). The expansive house (with far-reaching views) now contains large, light classrooms, a performing arts studio, music rooms, a practical room for science, and plenty of elbow room for all. The gardens, with their mature trees, also house an adventure playground. 'It gives them a freedom rarely found in London,' says the head. 'They can go into the bushes and make dens and still feel totally safe.'

Pastoral care, well-being and discipline: This is a calm and orderly place, but it has little to do with a system of tight rules and stern warnings. 'I'm not quite sure how the detention system works,' admits the head, who oversees 'a record of serious discipline' going back nine years which takes up just two pages.

Strong emphasis on student leadership, with two officers in every form – 'they hunt in packs' – including two head girls. Older girls also apply to become 'school officers' with designated areas of responsibility. 'A lot of girls aspire to the leadership team,' says the head. 'They have real influence.' As well as 'advising constructively', year 12s set up and run clubs and have recently sat on a panel interviewing a teacher for a job. 'I hadn't done this before,' says the head, 'but they were so clear in their thinking, so mature and perceptive.' The code of behaviour is also co-written by the girls. 'We live together in this community.'

Head's priorities are 'integrity, loyalty, scholarship and honour' – old fashioned virtues, adapted to a more complex modern setting. She acknowledges that the pressures on her students are greater than ever before – 'Not all girls sail through life without hitting stormy waters' – and the school works with parents all the way, helping minimise screen time and maximise mental and physical health. 'They believe in happy girls, rather than ones who are pushed,' said one mother.

Girls generally get on with minimal bullying and cliques. 'You know everyone here, you feel very comfortable and there is a real sense of joining together.' 'It's a very safe place,' said one parent. 'If your child is slightly quirky, you know they will still be fine.'

Junior school girls are well behaved – leaping to their feet to chorus 'Good Afternoon' – but building confidence is as critical as good manners here. 'My daughter used to be very shy,' said a parent, 'but performing in everything from music assemblies to poetry readings has made her much more self-assured.' The atmosphere is friendly and bustling, girls engaged and enthusiastic. 'My daughter loves the school,' said one mother. 'If we ever discuss moving, she says she doesn't want to leave. She has a wide variety of friends – the school's not cliquey at all.'

Pupils and parents: Essentially a local school, so no fleets of coaches to far-flung locations. Most pupils walk or come by public transport, from a broad sweep round the gates. 'Mainly north and west, though we do get a few from east London.' Parents are cosmopolitan (South African, European, North American, Asian), highly educated ('At careers fairs, if you shout, "Is there a doctor in the house?", there's a rush') and value education ('expectations are very high'). They're also 'tremendously supportive'. Pupils, quite often the daughters of old girls, are confident and motivated, thriving in this relatively small school.

Entrance: Main junior entry at 4+. About 200 assessed (ie observed performing a range of 'nursery tasks') for 48 places (two classes of 24) in January before entry, then whittled down in a second round. 'We're looking for bright girls, who are interested, engaged and willing to have a go,' says the head. The school's increasing popularity means they're now first choice for most applicants. A further handful of places at 7+ (but this entry point is ending in 2018), and a smattering of vacancies higher up. Most families, however, are here for the duration.

At 11, 300-400 sit the North London Independent Girls' Schools' Consortium exams for between 70-75 places, joining those coming up from the junior school to form four forms of 24. ('Junior school pupils don't have to sit 11 plus – it's a dream ticket,' says the head.) For sixth form entry, applicants are interviewed and expected to achieve nine or 10 A*s and As in GCSEs, with a minimum of A in the subjects they intend to study. 'I can sometimes bend the rules for existing students,' says the head, 'but we'd turn away someone from outside who didn't have the grades.'

Exit: The mode' is 'all-through', and the junior focus is to prepare girls well for the next stage, not for admissions elsewhere. ('We don't provide extra tutoring or practice papers'.) The

C

assumption is that all girls will proceed to the senior school without further entrance testing. ('Not having to do the 11+ is a real advantage,' said one mother. 'It enables you to have a longer term view of education, which is very appealing.') Last year a small handful left for other schools. Some to board, some to the state (including highly competitive selective schools, like Henrietta Barnett and St Michael's Catholic Grammar), one or two to other leading independents. Children who would really struggle at the senior school are also gently guided elsewhere. 'It isn't a question of having a bar that has to be met,' says the head. 'We want girls to thrive. Some children find the academic pace a challenge and flourish nonetheless, but if a girl's self-confidence starts to dip, we help the family find the best alternative.'

A few leave at 16 – to board, to co-ed, to local state schools. The rest depart two years later for serious subjects at predominantly Russell Group universities. Five to Oxbridge in 2016, then UCL, Nottingham, Leeds, Exeter, Bristol. About half go onto science-related degrees (with a good smattering of medics and vets). The head takes a personal interest in all applicants, interviewing each girl.

Money matters: Not a hugely rich school, but still does its bit, with five per cent of annual income devoted to 'supporting families, who hit hard times'. Academic scholarships at 11 worth 10 per cent off the fees, but music scholarships (grade 5 with merit minimum required) are particularly good, with up to 50 per cent discounts. In the sixth form, art, music and academic scholarships (of up to 50 per cent off tuition fees) on offer to existing ('We want to recognise their talent and not find them sloping off elsewhere') as well as external students. Bursaries also available at this point.

Remarks: A cosy, vibrant, local school in a very attractive setting, with high academic standards, up-to-date facilities and happy, motivated girls.

The Charter School

Red Post Hill, London SE24 9JH

Pupils: 1,202 • Ages: 11–18 • Sixth form: 315

Tel: 020 7346 6600
Email: info@charter.southwark.sch.uk
Website: www.charter.southwark.sch.uk

Head Teacher: Since 2013, Mr Christian Hicks (40s) grew up in West Norwood and was educated at nearby Dulwich College, then collected a BA in German studies and European literature at Bristol, an MA in English and American literature at Newcastle and an MA in effective learning at the Institute of Education.

Very likeable, open and seemingly far less ego-bound than some heads. Mr Hicks lives in Beckenham with his teacher wife and three young children – two boys and girl. Out of school he thrives on learning new things, recently taking up magic and completing the Yorkshire Three Peaks Challenge. What could be more useful in a demanding headship than a head for heights, stamina and the ability to pull rabbits out of a hat?

Despite his own alma mater, he is committed to the principle of comprehensive, inclusive education. Previously deputy head of Blackfen girls' school in Bexley and before that deputy head of the Royal Docks Community School in Newham. His move was not without ambition. The Charter School is never far from the dazzle of the spotlight, its every move noted and often written about in national newspapers by the influential parental and local body. The Charter School East Dulwich opened in September 2016.

Head jokes about his tough remit of improving on the already vastly improved academic standards. Has high expectations of his pupils, aims to challenge, inspire and be highly visible: he isn't too grand for break duty and is on the door with his headship team every morning and afternoon to greet, send off and confiscate any attempts to flaunt the uniform. He sees one of the most vital parts of his role as 'getting the right people on the bus' – the hiring and firing of an exceptional team of teachers.

Academic matters: Unfazed by the ending of modular assessment at GCSE, 75 per cent of pupils gained 5+ A*-C including English and maths in 2016. At A level, 67 per cent of grades were A*-B and 34 per cent A*/A.

Standard-ish curriculum at GCSE, including French, Spanish and Latin plus Mandarin for those with an aptitude for languages at year 7. The school has been teaching Mandarin with some success and finds it accessible for those with dyslexia. GCSE English results have soared, maths is solid, and sciences are strong. History and art and design are both popular and successful. Weak spots most recently media studies and RE.

Relatively few taking computer science, but the school is ahead of the curve in making the transition from ICT and is looking forward to pupils who have been coding at primary school joining in future years. A group of girls recently won a competition to design an app for a local business, whilst prizewinning games designers met the Duke of Cambridge at an enterprise event at BAFTA HQ.

A few less deskbound options such as catering, PE and performing arts and a handful of BTecs on offer – science, business, social care, engineering and ICT, with most success in business.

Head assured us that school will 'really push children who have been successful at primary school' – hence this school does well by the more able, with some 20 per cent of pupils generally achieving at least eight A*/As. Stand-out performances include lashings of A*s, but we noticed the school proudly trumpets the achievements of pupils gaining three Ds if this means that they have achieved well and are on track for their next step.

Best-performing subjects most recently at A level are: further maths and maths, biology, chemistry, fine art, English literature, history and a few -ologies. Languages seem a complete turn-off. Head says school is not alone in this. Aiming for an all-round academics, school will run subject even with a single pupil if necessary. Equal numbers of girls taking maths and a strong showing in sciences too.

Twenty-one teachers have more than 10 years' service – hard to believe as they appear extremely youthful. As one parent noted, 'teachers are mostly young and cool.' In fact one was so young and cool that we witnessed the receptionist assuming he was a pupil. Head and parents point out the calibre of staff attracted here by the unusually leafy milieu for an inner city salary. Head is very clear about his expectations of staff: 'don't come here if you're not prepared to work hard for successful outcomes for the students.'

A thrilled father of three girls told us that 'science teaching at The Charter is fabulous; several staff have Oxbridge PhDs and the teaching is inspiring.' Others said: 'Our children are inspired by their teachers and are really motivated to learn' and 'the staff clearly work really hard and are extremely conscientious.' Average class size at key stage 4 is 20, with 30 the maximum and some as small as five for 'nurture groups.' In the sixth form the average is 18.

With regards to homework and pressure one parent said: 'There is a good balance of homework throughout the term and a very balanced approach to exams,' whilst another warned that 'it's very intensive.' Parents kept thoroughly in the loop. The school is quick to bring them in to discuss a student who is not attaining their individual target for each subject. Coasting is not permitted.

The school dazzles in its business and enterprise specialism, creating aspiration in thinking ahead to future careers – opening students' eyes to the wider world and maximising their situation in London is a real strength. The school has links with PwC, King and Woods Malleson, O2, King's College Hospital, the Worshipful Company of International Bankers, Shell UK and more than 100 business mentors.

One parent tells us that assistance given to her son included 'mock interviews, workshops on CV writing, presentation skills and financial awareness workshops.' The CEO of the Science Council recently spoke to year 10s about STEM careers and a doctor from King's College Hospital runs an annual seminar on applying to medical school. Students also sampled uni life at Lille, London South Bank and Brighton and large groups are taken to both Oxford and Cambridge to inspire.

Someone here is in possession of an amazingly A-list little black book – a truly top-notch class of the great and good drop in to inspire regularly. Imagine the thrill of a Romeo and Juliet masterclass with none other than Joseph Fiennes; Jo Brand speaking to celebrate International Women's Day; Professor Sir Michael Rutter talking about his latest research to psychology students; not to mention professional Bollywood dancers teaching the Samba. Nor are they short of invites: the day prior to our visit 30 pupils met Boris Johnson at City Hall at a reception to honour the contribution of African and Caribbean soldiers in the First World War.

Head emphasises the value of the growing D of E programme in fostering key learning aptitudes such as resilience. Around 300 day and residential trips every year, from Bletchley Park to Belgium, Berlin and Beijing. London theatres are made good use of with trips to the National, Unicorn and Young Vic this year. One parent said: 'The school also works closely with many charities and my son was lucky enough to take a charity trip to Kenya this summer.' The school is aware of hardship issues and helps with small bursaries where it can.

Quite high numbers of SEN: around 20 per cent of students across the school cope with varying degrees of learning difficulties, so everything from specific learning difficulties such as dyslexia or dyspraxia to physical disabilities, autistic spectrum disorder or ADHD. Large learning support team of 23 staff, including specialist SEN teachers, higher level teaching assistants and learning support assistants, support students in mainstream classes but may also be able to offer small group withdrawals, extra literacy and maths intervention sessions, touch-typing, handwriting and reading clubs and input from a range of external agencies.

Games, options, the arts: Sports are compulsory – and the only time girls and boys are taught separately. Footballers enjoy links with professional clubs such as Millwall and Fulham FC. Cricket and rugby are on the up: the MCC coach cricket and the RFU rugby. The coaching team includes national class coaches in table tennis and aquathon. Students recently started play basketball competitively and are now enjoying BMX at Burgess Park.

Successes across the board, with pupils competing regionally and nationally, particularly the girls: the school boasts a national champion in rowing; under 13 girls' cricket team recently won the Lady Taverners' competition at the Oval; year 8 girls' rugby recently placed sixth in London; year 7 girls' netball team won the Southwark league. Over 500 pupils take part in after-school sports club every week.

The school appears rather boxed in by the neighbouring houses and plentiful sports ground of the neighbouring girls' school, but pupils use a playing field a five-minute walk away. Indoor sports hall is large and there is an on-site floodlit netball court, ball-court and Astroturf.

More than 200 learn a variety of 20 different musical instruments up to grade 8, with some lessons significantly subsidised and many trying an instrument for the first time. Two choirs and a jazz band, which may be led by teachers or pupils. Past students have gained places at the Royal Academy of Music. A favourite alumni is rising star Kwabs – The Guardian calls him 'the new Seal' and he has a recording contract with a major record label.

All pupils study drama once a week in years 7, 8 and 9, enjoying purpose-built drama studios and a flexible theatre space. A highlight of the dramatic year is the whole school theatre performance – most recently Guys and Dolls – featuring staff alongside pupils. A parent said of the art: 'I have been delighted with the art department. I feel the teachers really care about what they teach.' London galleries are frequented and facilities include a kiln, dark room, screen printing and Mac suite.

Lunchtime and after-school clubs include young historians, tennis, handball, track cycling, music theory, ukulele, African drumming and study skills. Pupils sign up on a first come first served basis. Most are free, with a small charge for tennis and swimming clubs.

Background and atmosphere: Smaller than most city comprehensives, The Charter squeezes into a plot a few strides from North Dulwich station and at the heart of Herne Hill. Built on the site of the defunct William Penn School, it opened in 2000 following a concerted campaign from parents in an area dominated by independent schools, but without a good state option.

Savvy parents realise that they have something of a find on their doorstep, but some nervousness persists locally around the legacy of the failed school, and the head is aware school has to work hard to ensure that no one child lets down the reputation of the whole amongst the local community. Ofsted has rated it outstanding twice since 2006.

Most of the buildings were remodelled rather than replaced. It is light and functional but now looking more than a little frayed at the edges, both inside and out. We wondered how a shy year 7 moving here from one of the cosy local primaries might make the transition. The head told us: 'This is a family school, a local school. When children move here they are often joining siblings or friends' – a third of every year group has school siblings. And everywhere in the mornings and afternoons one sees little gaggles of Charter pupils walking to and fro. Each year 180 new pupils join, but the school very often operates in year groups, with assemblies for each year. Lunchtime arrangements – a mix of indoor and outdoor seating under-cover – with year 7s heading to lunch 10 minutes earlier to avoid being overwhelmed.

Prior to lessons we noticed some boisterous boys in the corridor, but once lessons had commenced the atmosphere was exceptionally quiet and calm, with each lesson we viewed in both arts and sciences equally industrious.

Parents talk of happy children who are able to be who they want to be here. When the head was writing his mission statement, pupils asked him to add 'happiness' because that is how they feel.

Pastoral care, well-being and discipline: The relatively relaxed school uniform – polo-shirts and pullovers mostly, so no ties and without the blazers of the other nearby state seniors – is deceiving as to the school's culture of high expectations. Given the issues of the school in its previous incarnation, the school

C

set out to be something of an innovator in managing behaviour and is known for its no-nonsense attitude to discipline, which it balances with care. Behaviour officers, not in evidence on our visit, have a remit to swoop into any classroom to remove a student who has overstepped the mark. The head says that 'any pupil who is disrupting the learning of others will be in school until 5pm.'

More serious offences such as smoking will result in exclusion – gross misconducts are half what they were five years ago, although slightly up this year. The emphasis is on inclusion and working with pupils to find a way back to contributing positively. There is a whole raft of rewards including VIVO Miles – like air miles for good behaviour – extra school trips, presentations and a phone call to parents from the head or head of year.

Mobile phones are not allowed in school at all, except for sixth formers who must keep them out of sight. Any confiscated phones must be collected by a parent. No piercings other than one pair of ear studs; no hats, hoodies or outlandish hair colours.

Pupils should always have someone to talk to. There are strong relationships between staff and pupils, a tutor system, year 11 mentors for year 7s and a school counsellor. Even the staff get a buddy each.

Pupils and parents: A large part of the intake is from privileged Dulwich Village, Herne Hill and East Dulwich, but pupils encompass every kind of home life. More than 30 per cent of students are pupil premium students – the performance gap is significant but closing. On entrance, students demonstrate a wide range of ability but it is notable that by year 11, 56 per cent have risen to the two highest ability bands. A parent told us: 'This school is for children who want to learn, want to get somewhere in the world. It caters for all in that there is something for everyone.'

The school prides itself on its inclusivity and parents say it really 'celebrates diversity.' Forty-seven per cent of pupils describe themselves as white British, with black British African as the second largest group (11 per cent of pupils). Surprisingly few EAL students and whilst there are many bilingual pupils, 93 per cent have English as their first language.

Parents come from all walks of life. Very effective PTA has just bought a 16-seater minibus for inter-school sports matches.

Entrance: The hoo-ha over the school catchment area is in the past. Admissions criteria are looked after children, then siblings, then distance criteria using safest walking distance as a measure, which places the catchment currently at no more than 1,600 metres from the school. Parents in East Dulwich may want to get out their pedometers. No feeders as such but largest cohorts from Dulwich Hamlet Junior School, Dog Kennel Hill School, Heber and Goodrich local primaries.

The sixth form is more inclusive than many: pupils must have five A*-C grades including maths and English, with a minimum grade for subjects of study which varies.

Applications for places stand at seven to one. Crowded annual open days – often 2,000 attendees – are held in September for year 7 and November for the sixth form.

Exit: Nearly all to university, art or music college. Remainder to start gap year, apprenticeship or work. Recent destinations include Bristol, Durham, Birmingham, Edinburgh, Imperial College London and Leeds. One or two usually to Oxbridge (four in 2016).

Many pursuing other dreams have exited to equally prestigious destinations, such as RADA, major London art colleges and the Royal College of Music. Two pupils recently gained sought-after City apprenticeships with KPMG and investment company M&G, whilst the Queen recently presented one girl with a Southwark Council scholarship to pay all her university tuition fees.

Remarks: A truly local comprehensive and for those on the doorstep it may be the stepping stone to very good things. Well connected, with increasingly impressive academic results driven by a talented staff promising much for children who want to work hard and those who have previously found opportunities thin on the ground. For parents wondering whether there is life beyond school fees we recommend joining the open day throng.

Charterhouse Square School

40 Charterhouse Square, London EC1M 6EA

Pupils: 201 • Ages: 3–11

Fees: £15,105 pa

Tel: 020 7600 3805
Email: life@charterhousesquareschool.co.uk
Website: www.charterhousesquareschool.co.uk

Head: Since 2009, Caroline Lloyd (40s). BEd in geography from Exeter University (although her parents had wanted her to do a 'proper' degree). Her first job as an NQT was at Charterhouse Square School in 1994, straight after leaving university: 'I was young, determined and desperate to be a teacher.' Indeed Caroline (as she is known to staff and pupils), knew she wanted to teach from the age of 7 and 'used to line up my teddies, pretending they were in class.' However, she had a very specific idea of the kind of school where she wanted to teach and only five schools matched her criteria – Charterhouse Square being one of them.

During her 15 years at the school and prior to becoming head, Caroline experienced teaching in all year groups from nursery through to year 6. After leaving to start a family she returned six months later on a part-time basis as she 'missed teaching so much'. In 2008, the school was purchased by Cognita and the position of head was advertised. Caroline says: 'It was never my intention to become a head, but I was worried that someone new would come in and not see how special the school was' – so she applied for the post. After so many years at the school her application was seen as a natural progression by both parents and children. One parent told us: 'The school was good before with the previous head, but it's great now. The children have just blossomed under Caroline.' Another praised her for being such a consistently visible presence; 'She knows every pupil by name and is naturally great with children. The school just seems to run seamlessly.'

Tall, attractive and immaculately turned out she could have been separated at birth from the Middleton sisters and would look quite at home sipping Pimm's at a polo match. Her boundless enthusiasm for both her job and life in general is infectious but don't be fooled, this head is no pushover and knows that some people might go so far as to call her a control freak: 'I'm on the school door every morning and most afternoons. I feel that if communication is strong, we can get things sorted before they escalate out of control.'

One can't imagine too many things getting out of control at this genteel school, which has had no permanent exclusions in its 25 year history; the head concedes that her main challenge is 'managing over-aspiring parents.' She says: 'I've often had to remind parents that I'm actually on the side of the child, especially when they are being pushed too hard to get in to certain secondary schools.'

Entrance: Completely non-selective, entry is by lottery – unless you have a sibling who already attends. Twenty-six 3+ places offered each year and roughly 70 on the waiting list. No point planning the Caesarian or putting names down at birth, you can register up till the end of June the year before entry and a ballot is drawn on 1 July. Head says this comes as a shock for some parents: 'who have been used to pulling out a cheque book to buy their way in' and concedes that 'It can make me pretty unpopular.' Cheque book will, however, come in handy for £4,000 non-returnable deposit payable when accepting a place.

Exit: Most to high calibre selective London secondaries. Fierce competition for places at both (girls and boys) City of London schools and some pupils even pulled out early at age 7 or 10 by parents who think this will increase their chances of getting in. School says this is a shame and 'can be disruptive.' Other leavers to Channing, Francis Holland, Forest School, Portland Place and Queen's College, with a smattering travelling further north – eg Highgate and North Bridge House.

Remarks: Charterhouse Square School is located on the south side of historic Charterhouse Square in Smithfield, central London. The square was built on what was the site of a 14th century Carthusian monastery (an alms house and chapel remain) and also London's largest Black Death plague pit. The five-storey Victorian building occupied by the school, though smart enough, is easily missed among neighbouring offices and apartment blocks, but any lack of character, not to mention green space, is more than made up for by such a central location. This is a City school and parents know exactly what they're buying into when they make the decision to send their children here. One told us: 'I am able to drop my kids off on the way to work, which is one reason I chose this school. The other reason is that I noticed how happy and well-mannered the pupils were when they were out and about. I know some people think it looks more confined than other schools, but it works for us and my children are very happy here.'

Though it wouldn't suit those who like to plan ahead, most parents seem to welcome the diversity and 'range of abilities' that result from school's non-selective lottery-based entrance procedure. It's an unusual independent school in other ways: there's no uniform and it's first name terms for all teachers, including the head. One parent told us: 'I love this school for being individual with very individual ideas.' Another said: 'Coming from a convent school background I was initially horrified about the idea of first name terms, but I have to say it works very well and makes the teachers far more approachable to the children, without diluting any respect.'

Head has worked hard to ensure that hers isn't a one size fits all school: 'When I came on board, early years was very formal and a bit of a hothouse. Drama was only every other week and there were no school trips. I think it's about broadening the curriculum so that we can make sure that all pupils can excel at something.' Parents wholeheartedly agree. Teaching described as 'exceptional' and 'instilling a love of learning.' Years 4 and 5 are taught together so that they have the same teacher for two years before the all-important year 6. They work on a two-year curriculum, with the exception of homework, and English and maths textbooks. They are also ability grouped. One parent told us, 'I'm not really sure how it works – but the kids seem to understand it, so that's the main thing.'

Designated SENCo provides one-to-one support and booster groups for children with SEN, which accounts for a handful of the school's intake. The nature of the school building (five flights of stairs) may make it unsuitable for pupils with physical disabilities.

Pastoral care is paramount and school employs a number of highly effective strategies to help pupils feel safe. Older pupils can make use of classroom 'feelings boxes' to share concerns privately with teachers, and the 'buddy' system supports new pupils. Every parent we spoke to raved about this: 'It's a great system as it makes new children feel less intimidated and older children rise to the responsibility of looking after the younger ones.'

Our tour started in the early years foundation stage classes, nursery and reception. Nursery was having its annual 'animal dress up day' and we were greeted by tigers, bears and monkeys plus a couple of unidentifiable but colourful animals. Sweet little add-on area designed for role play was effectively outside, but covered by a canopy and surrounded by a high wall. This, we were told, was to prevent anything landing on the tracks of Barbican station, something that carries a huge fine (on an hourly rate!). Thankfully, this has not happened so far.

Small but well stocked library from where children are encouraged to take books home nightly, and a carpeted school hall with beautiful white piano and colourful wall display of ukuleles. Extracurricular activities such as judo and table tennis take place here and all children have the opportunity to learn a musical instrument. 'Informal' Spanish also offered in the early years. One parent said: 'I was amazed when we went on holiday to Spain last year, that my 5 year old daughter was able to communicate with a local in pidgin Spanish.'

Bright, neat, colourful classrooms were full of interested, happy and very polite children and the atmosphere of the school is extremely warm and friendly. Pupils who were leaving told us how they'll miss Charterhouse 'sooo much', especially the teachers. 'What I really like about the teachers is that they are all so friendly. Also, we are often asked to tick a box privately at the end of a lesson about whether we found the classes easy or difficult. If we are really struggling, we can sometimes get an extra private lesson.'

Despite the limitations of a tall and narrow building ('I often had to walk up five flights of stairs when I was pregnant,' the head told us), children don't seem to lack breathing space and fresh air. During the warmer months they spend their lunch break in the private Charterhouse Square gardens; when it's cold and wet they play in the school's 'jungle' downstairs. Organised sports take place nearby at Coram Fields or the Golden Lane Leisure Centre. Pupils do take part in inter-school sporting events, but no regular fixtures because of the issue of 'bussing children around.' One parent did say that this school is perhaps not the right option for the 'extremely sporty child', although another said that her two boys 'are extremely sporty and it meets their needs.' A highlight in the calendar is sports day: 'It's just such a joy, well handled and fun.'

No school meals prepared on site and no dining room because of limited space so until recently all pupils had to bring in a packed lunch. School has now organised for a company to bring in hot food in thermos containers, if the parents require. The head says: 'This system works very well and the advantage is that parents know what their children like and can order accordingly.' We are told the quality and choice is great, with meatballs, pasta, wraps, soups and stews on offer.

Lack of space may deter some, but Charterhouse Square is a wonderful option if you live and work in the City. This is a successful school and a happy environment in which pupils of varying abilities thrive and with comments such as: 'My child loves every day of her school life!' who could ask for more?

Chepstow House School

C

108a Lancaster Road, London W11 1QS

Pupils: 303 • Ages: 2-13

Fees: £18,720 pa

Tel: 020 7243 0243
Email: info@chepstowhouseschool.co.uk
Website: www.chepstowhouseschool.co.uk

Headteacher: Since 2010, Mrs Angela Barr BA Ed (40s). Has been head since school started. Previously head of the lower school at Pembridge Hall, another Alpha Plus school. Studied geography and education at Christchurch College, Kent University and then taught in a state school in Essex before taking off and travelling around Africa for a year, where she met her husband, Simon. 'I loved school and always wanted to be a teacher,' she says with passion.

Blonde, youthful, warm and attractive, head is a spirited, independent character who lives for the moment and is all about the 'doing now.' Asked where she sees herself in five years time she looks dismayed and then, grinning, says: 'on a beach with a gin and tonic.' She is very hands on and personally supports youngest pupils with their reading. 'I am a big believer in getting children reading,' she says. Also works hard to make sure her staff are teaching with all the different learning styles in mind – 'essential in a co-educational school.' Plenty of internal training – for assistants as well as for teachers. She says her biggest challenge is maintaining a sense of community among her 17 staff. When we visited a strong team spirit was evident. Head is very much a 'primus inter pares,' in the old style of monarchy.

Entrance: Non-selective, so it's a case of registration at or as soon as possible after birth (current cost £150 – non-refundable if you don't get a place). School allots five definite places a month, and tries to stagger them among children born at the beginning, middle and end of the month, so no advantage in booking your Caesarean for the first of September. Attempts are made to keep an even number of boys and girls and those who drop out are replaced like with like, as far as possible from the waiting list. That way they don't get a surfeit of, say, boys born in August. Priority given to siblings. Has recently opened a nursery class, additional reception class and year 3 and 4 classes and moved to new premises; is expanding gradually to year 6 and possibly year 8.

Exit: Pupils can now stay on until 13. Before this, large number of boys, as you would expect, to Wetherby, and girls to Pembridge Hall (via a test, but most have got a place). Bute House a popular choice for girls but not many jump through that hoop. A small number get to St Paul's Juniors and Westminster. Latymer Prep a popular choice as more and more parents opt for co-ed. The odd one to Thomas's, St Philip's or outside London.

Remarks: Born into the now well-established stable of Alpha Plus Group schools, the young colt that is Chepstow House barely wobbled on its hind legs before it was up and running. No doubt thanks in part to the huge demand there is for good schools in this leafy, sophisticated area of Notting Hill. However, the school has risen to meet that demand with style as well as results. Children look enchanting in their quaint red berets and jackets, girls in tartan pinafores, boys in red tank tops and grey shorts (some parents worry about their sons getting cold knees in the winter).

Classes named after birds – the further up the school, the bigger and more fierce the bird. Two classes of 20 in reception and year 1. Pupils start in Robins and Sparrows and then move into Woodpeckers and Kingfishers. For year 2, with exams looming in January, they divide into three groups of 12, with classes named after three types of owl – Barn, Snowy and Tawny.

With a teacher and teaching assistant in each class the children get lots of support and attention. French and music start from reception. Three sets for maths in year 2 and lots of differentiation in the lower years. Each child has the use of an iPad – technology skills are learned on the job rather than in a separate lesson devoted to IT. We saw 5-year-olds using their iPads in a geography lesson, as well as other imaginative methods of teaching, including reception children learning how to tell the time in the playground through movement and action. Good-sized playground is frequently used for learning, both academic and physical.

Any learning difficulties are identified quickly, says head. High standards are set for reading and writing and development and progress are tracked in-house with a reading test as well as SEN assessment. Guided reading from reception helps with comprehension. Head told us: 'If a child has not taken off in reception we know that they will need support in year 1 and someone will work with that child every day – either me, or one of my assistant heads.'

The sense of purpose is palpable. When we visited children were working on 'big write,' a weekly activity for years 1 and 2 where pupils learn to develop their vocabulary and style of writing.

Music is vibrant. The only male teacher here is the music teacher and he introduces pupils to a number of different genres – Portuguese singer/songwriter Caetano Veloso when we visited. A number of pupils have violin, guitar and piano lessons taught by peripatetic teachers. Colourful and expressive art adorns the walls. Evidence of physical activity everywhere; much-loved Little Foxes franchise gets them learning ball skills. Fencing and martial arts clubs in the morning. Swimming up the road at Porchester Baths, otherwise all sport happens on site. The children get fresh air and exercise come rain or shine. Delicious food cooked on site and there is a remarkably civilised atmosphere as the children enjoy their lunch.

Ofsted (who visited just two terms after the school launched) concluded it was good across the board. All credit to the way the head and her team hit the ground running. We suspect the esteemed government inspectors will be even more impressed when they return.

Parents from all over the globe – plenty of Americans, Australians and Canadians, a fair few from Scandinavia, Eastern Europe and Russia, as well as French and Italians. Attracts the less traditional English who prefer co-ed at this stage. Parents are in media, finance, law as well as in the arts. Head makes good use of the parents' experience. One parent arranged for someone from Sky News to give a talk in assembly while another hosted expeditions to private art galleries hosted by another parent. Plenty of trips, including the favourite Bushcraft as well as to churches and Science Museum.

Lots of smiling faces, both parents and children, when they arrive first thing. Head welcomes everyone and is proud of school's open door policy. 'We are not hiding anything,' she says. Nor does she have to. These children are very lucky indeed to have such a focused and privileged start to their education.

Parents are generally very supportive and enthusiastic. 'It's a tight ship – with high energy,' we were told. All good, but there was some regret from a few quarters that the pressure of the 7+ perhaps took the joy out of learning for the child who finds it hard to sit still and concentrate on reading and writing. All this has now changed, with the whole school move to considerably larger premises in Lancaster Road (bang opposite rivals Notting Hill Prep). This not only makes for a larger school at the bottom, with a new nursery class, but has also enabled expansion to the age of 13. There is no longer the pressure to enter and pass an exam at the age of 6 and there should be scope for much more drama and a structured sport department, two things the school has lacked so far.

Definitely one to watch if you live in or near this very oversubscribed area of London.

The Children's House School

King Henry's Walk, Islington, London N1 4PB

Pupils: 170 • Ages: 2–8

Fees: £13,050 – £13,815 pa

Tel: 020 7249 6273
Email: upper@childrenshouseschool.co.uk
Website: www.childrenshouseschool.co.uk

Head: Since 2016, Kate Orange CertEd (Wellington, New Zealand College of Education), previously deputy head.

Entrance: Register for nursery as soon as possible after birth and (crucially) register separately for nursery and pre-prep (deposits of £1500 and £2000 respectively). Places offered by date of registration and sibling priority. Most places in the pre-prep are filled from the nursery, but 'one or two' spaces available in reception, again based on date of registration. Considering expanding to year 6.

Exit: A few leave at the formal entry points to other schools at 4 and 5. 'Parents ask if we mind,' says the head, 'but our advice is always to do what's best for the child.' Twenty-eight start out in two reception classes, but numbers generally reduce to a manageable 20 by year 2. Vast majority of 4+ and 7+ leavers to North Bridge House or St Paul's Cathedral School; a few to eg City of London Girls' Prep.

Remarks: Founded as a nursery in someone's front room in 1973, when 'there was little in the way of early years provision and nothing in the way of policies and procedures', the nursery is now a fully-formed school, housed independently in a converted chapel in central Islington. Here children from 2 enjoy a rich and dynamic offering (including conversational French, dance and sport) taught by fully qualified teachers. 'It's a lovely, friendly place,' said one parent. 'They really care about each child.'

The pre-prep came into being when a former parent spotted a school to let in the local newspaper. 'Our nursery parents always felt it was a pity children had to move on at 4 and 5.' Now they can remain in the fold, housed in a petite and picturesque Victorian schoolhouse nestled in the shelter of its big brother church. 'It's idyllic, like Enid Blyton,' said one parent.

Mornings are devoted to the three Rs, with much of the work 'topic based'. 'We take an overarching theme and help children make links across the curriculum.' (Typical subject matter, for example, is Ourselves, in which children might explore the senses in science, study old toys in history, make a toy in design technology, and visit the Bethnal Green Museum of Childhood.) Often children work in groups. 'We like them to work collaboratively, one child supporting another.' A very creative school; arts and crafts is central to learning. Children might make shoebox interiors as a part of a home topic, create tetrahedron mobiles in maths, and paint and embroider textiles to study printmaking. Homework introduced gently in reception and year 1, with a more significant push towards 7+.

Specialist teachers extend the core. French and ICT, with a dedicated teacher and a full-class supply of laptops, throughout. Singing and rhythm taught by a music teacher, plus a weekly half-hour violin lesson from a professional violinist. 'We want the children to be at the end of passionate teaching.' Dance, too, taught by an external expert.

The school prides itself on being 'very inclusive' and a hard-working SENCo addresses both minor and significant difficulties. Good support, too, for those with English as an additional language, addressing the requirements of an increasing number of bilingual children.

Not the school for those looking for an early introduction to competitive team games, but a specialist teaches PE and ball skills (relay races, running, pitching) in one of the two large adjoining church halls. Well-equipped playground provides further scope for fresh air, exercise and, most importantly, play. 'We have a lot of play resources and use them to extend their learning with carefully planned activities.' Working the nearby community garden provides further time out of doors and educational avenues.

Plenty of 'enrichment'. 'The school is fantastic at making lovely things happen for the children,' said one parent. Two visits a term, a least one in the form of 'entertainment', plus numerous themed days (dressing-up day, book day, etc). All stay for after-school clubs (sewing, fencing, cookery, drama, football, arts and crafts and yoga).

School uniform minimal and practical (navy and white sweatshirt with logo). No hot food; children bring in lunch boxes, supplemented by a snack and fruit in the morning.

Traditional values of courtesy and consideration central to the ethos. 'Being kind is paramount,' said a mother. Monitors chosen weekly, with top-of-the school year 2 given increased responsibility. 'They're so helpful and dependable. If you ask them to do something, they'll get it done.'

One of the things parents like most about the The Children's House is its home-away-from-home atmosphere. In break, for example, children wander in and out of the school office. ('We're doing plaits,' confided one pair, 'can you help us?') 'There's no such thing as a closed door,' said one happy parent.

Founded by parents, The Children's House remains a parent-driven operation, with active participation from its Parent Committee. 'No one owns it. It's a collective.' All vote for the Council of Management, which administers the school. Unsurprisingly, families (Hackney and Islington media, City, lawyers and artisans) form a tight bond both with each other and the school, regularly arriving to read, organising the summer fair, quiz night, etc. 'We couldn't do it without the parents. They're amazing.' 'We're always made to feel welcome,' said one.

About 10 per cent of children are on means-tested bursary places, covering up to 100 per cent of fees.

C

Christ Church Primary School Chelsea

1 Robinson Street, London SW3 4AA

Pupils: 210 • Ages: 4–11 • C of E

Tel: 020 7352 5708
Email: info@chchchelsea.rbkc.sch.uk
Website: www.chchchelsea.rbkc.sch.uk

Head: Since 2009, Mrs Avis Hawkins, BSc NPQH (40s). Read psychology at Royal Holloway with a view to becoming an educational psychologist, but got the teaching bug while training at the Institute of Education. Started her career in a state primary in Lewisham, then opted for a school in special measures (now 'inadequate' rating) for the challenge; 'That made me the teacher I am'. Appointed deputy at Christ Church in 2000 and was the natural choice to step into the role when previous head retired.

Attractive, energetic and disarmingly open, she has both children and parents on her side; 'So personable and friendly,' said one. Another added, 'Not the kind of head who just sits in their office', though with the white and grey Danish-look furniture, complete with functional teaching table – no leather sofas here – she might be tempted. 'Open door' policy taken literally; pupils appeared in her study and opened up cupboards and drawers in her desk during our chat. Her wide smile only wanes when lamenting the tight budget. In response, she has recently created an enrichment assistant, who makes the most of useful local contacts, whom she invites to talk to hand-picked groups of children. Recent visitors include a fashion designer, artists from the nearby Saatchi Gallery, and volunteers from the Chelsea Physic Garden. 'I am taking experience-based learning and applying it to the curriculum', she explains. Married with three children, two at the school, her hobbies range from food to DJ-ing. There is no doubt she leads by example. DJ Hawkins is one to watch on the education scene.

Entrance: Vastly oversubscribed C of E voluntary aided school, with perennial waiting list. Priority given to siblings and families attending St Luke's or Christ Church, Chelsea; remaining places for other C of E families and locals. Takes from RBKC and Wandsworth, with a few from as far afield as Hammersmith and Lambeth. Single class intake at reception, with occasional places further up the school. One parent told how 'wealthy families used to take them out at 7', but it appears the wealthy have now got wise too, and none leave unless forced by relocation.

Exit: Increasing numbers, 30-50 per cent to independents, including Godolphin, Alleyn's, Dulwich, Westminster; lots bag bursaries and scholarships. Many to top London state schools: Lady Margaret, The Grey Coat Hospital and Chelsea Academy, plus newly established Fulham Boys School. One parent felt, given increasing numbers opting for independent secondary schools, more help could be given to parents with bursary and scholarship applications.

Remarks: Located in the hushed affluence of a terraced square, in an area of celebrated artists, writers and politicians, this charming Victorian school has an exterior that harks back to a bygone age, when Chelsea was no more than a collection of small parishes, and church, schoolroom and public house all clustered together on one corner. 'A village school in the heart of London' was how one parent described it and the charm lingers on, with lollipop cherry trees and a butcher's boy bike poised to deliver lunches to a nearby nursery. However, step inside and you have a Narnia experience: the interior has been redesigned to a spacious and functional plan, with chic grey walls, birch wood trimming and rows of navy pillars. Purpose-built in 2005, the main building on the north of Christchurch Street opens out to accommodate an internal playground for reception, with multi-coloured apparatus, as well as an open central stairwell and roomy classrooms for years 1-3. Behind doors we found a cookery room, art studio and ICT suite, as well as cosy beanbags in the reading room (emphatically 'not a library') and a multi-use hall with gym and dining tables. As one parent put it, 'Every nook and cranny has to be made useful'. Outside and across a wide pavement (or 'The Piazza') the older years occupy what was the infant school, opened in 1850 by the patron, Earl Cadogan, we are reminded on a stone plaque. Three classrooms housing the older years have a more studious feel, with individual desks facing whiteboards, but each has its own corner with plump cushions for bookworm breaks. Opposite stands Christ Church, a Victorian gothic parent building, visited on feast days and Fridays by the school, while at the fourth corner of this tiny crossroads is the playground, discreetly hidden behind a tall wall of ivy, masking the children's shouts from the genteel residents. The large play area has been landscaped to accommodate a sports pitch, gardening plots, a pergola and free play areas. 'I would like a bit more playtime,' sighed one child, and we were not surprised. Several parents commented how well maintained the buildings were, and one ventured, 'environment helps behaviour'. The charming neighbourhood is reminiscent of a scene from Mary Poppins; all it lacks is a dancing chimney sweep.

This is a school that claims to take a holistic approach to education, nonetheless, it manages to hit the spot academically. Class sizes are 30, with a 22:1 student to staff ratio, but with lots of small groups or half-class sessions at specialist subjects. The head assures us, 'if you're looking for a school at the top of the league tables, we're not the school for you', but it is hard not to be impressed by these children's achievements on paper. When we asked the children what the school could do better, they suggested more time in the library. Numeracy and literacy is managed by the leadership team as a through-school experience, not split into key stages. Verbal reasoning and non-verbal reasoning are taken in year 6, 'We pay lip service to the 11+ exams,' says the head. 'Aspiration is important'. The national curriculum is supplemented by half-termly 'curriculum weeks' when the whole school shares a topic. Recent themes include healthy living; fashion; local studies. We witnessed a Friday afternoon English class hard at metaphor and meter – no slouches here. Inclusion is a watchword too, with several SEN children supported within each year group. A range of difficulties, from dyslexia to ASD, are managed by a dedicated department and visiting OT, SLT, nutritionist and school nurse. The head welcomes the differences: 'it makes everyone aware of social behaviours'.

Not surprisingly, the staff profile is 'very static'; several boast 10+ years of loyal service, so the head continually makes waves with professional training programmes. The school forms an alliance with four other local primaries, mutually inspecting and monitoring each other and offering suggestions. The head also has a knack of finding restless retirees and enlisting them into some extracurricular activity: a retired headmaster takes gardening, as a curriculum topic, directing the wheelbarrows, tending the chickens and watering the kale beds. Another ex-teacher runs cricket sessions in morning break, and several volunteers have become student teachers, and later join the staff. As one mum put it: 'They are very good at growing their own'.

There's a daring zing to the curriculum, or, as the head puts it, 'I am trying to make the curriculum wide enough and rich enough so children can find their talents beyond the three Rs'. This is evident in music, where a specialist teacher with his own band inspires over 50 per cent of the school to take up an instrument. Youngsters can pick up a ukulele, trumpet or drums, as well as the more usual options, funded for a term by the school. Any child showing musical promise can go on to one-to-one lessons, at their own expense. As an Artsmark school, there's an artist in residence in each year group, who encourages messy creativity in an upstairs studio. Year 1 recently completed a metal-bashing project, while the corridor was arrayed with giant paper planets – another group's work. A recent leaver went on to star in the West End production of Matilda, a talent no doubt fostered in the ambitious Christmas and Easter shows; productions have included King Lear and Richard III (abridged!). A specialist sports teacher co-ordinates trips over the bridge for team games in Battersea Park or to the beautiful Royal Hospital pitches nearby. There's room for football and netball on the hard court in the playground, dance for boys and girls in the hall, and swimming from year 2 at nearby Chelsea Sports Centre. Lately, they introduced teams to borough tournaments, and the girls' netball team ran off with the cup. A mass of after-school clubs include Mandarin, chess, judo, and knitting as well as a kayaking experience up river to Putney. One parent had to pinch herself when faced with the list of clubs, for fear she had confused it with the exclusive school up the road.

Christian values appear modestly within the school, as a poster on the doorway or mosaics of Biblical scenes on the walls. There is daily assembly, led by the head, or a celebratory one each Friday, known by the visiting vicars as 'The Oscars'. Here the children applaud each other's achievements and two Students of the Week are named from each year. Other incentives to good behaviour include an afternoon's golden time, sparingly reduced for poor behaviour. Anything more serious involves meeting the behaviour specialist, but we had difficulty finding anyone who had ever witnessed this: one parent said, 'They are all incredibly well behaved and respectful', and 'the last thing they would do is exclude a pupil'. The youngest children have a designated 'shepherd' from year 6 to sit with them at lunch. The system looks after the lambs but also instils a sense of responsibility in the older pupils. One mum worried that responsibility was not always shared evenly between the children: 'They could mix up responsible roles, like reading in church'.

Unlike many London prep schools, the pick up was not dominated by hooting 4x4s; instead, parents chatted outside in groups. The school's community spirit was evident; 'phenomenal at bringing everyone together. Very welcoming', thrilled one mum. Many meet up crossing the bridges from Battersea. One dad stressed the 'connectivity between teaching staff and parents'. There are parent workshops in maths and English, with crèche, to coach parents in helping with homework. Day to day queries are dealt with by phone or teacher meeting. More than one mum reported how they got an overnight response from the head and an invitation to meet the next day. Children are a more mixed bunch than at some local schools, or as the head put it, 'a mix of privilege and none', though all looked equally smart when dressed in the navy and cherry uniforms and stripy ties. Perhaps on World Book Day when the children walk up the King's Road to Waterstones in their PJs, they appear more individual. Their eyes lit up in anticipation of the trip, and again when discussing the lunches. Parents and offspring raved about the improved catering. The kitchen is literally a home-grown affair, using eggs and produce from the school's garden, cooked up into healthy meals by two mums, who have a background in catering, with a sprinkling of advice from the community nutritionist. One of the cooks even delivers carry-outs by bike to a nearby nursery. The result is an education in healthy eating and sustainability. According to the kids, it tastes good too, especially the pizza and apple crumble.

We agreed with the mum who said: 'I knew it was good, but I was surprised how good it was'. A diminutive state primary school, which rivals the local independents in the brainy stuff but which displays ingenuity and imagination in its broad curriculum. The resourceful head syncs her band of dedicated staff and parents to strike up a winning tune and lively, inquisitive children take up the chorus. Well, Chelsea is famous for its smart set.

City and Islington College

283-309 Goswell Road, London EC1V 7LA

Pupils: 1,600 • Ages: 16-19

Tel: 020 7700 9333
Email: courseinfo@candi.ac.uk
Website: www.candi.ac.uk

Director: Since 2015, Peter Murray BA MA PCGE Oxon, late 50s, previously deputy director of sixth form. Read history at Kings College, London, before taking a masters in 19th century social history at Warwick. Drawn to teaching by an inspirational role model at school: 'If you've had a good experience, you think... I might enjoy that....and I did'. Cut his teeth in secondary schools in London and home counties, before moving to tertiary education in Richmond upon Thames College, arriving at Candi (as it is known) in 2000 to co-ordinate humanities, then as deputy for seven years. No stranger to the area, he grew up in Islington, supports the Gunners and saw his younger sister attend the college, operating under a previous name, in the 80s. 'She had a really different and a really good experience,' he muses. A keen runner and 5-a-side football player, and at 5 o'clock on a Friday evening, showed no signs of slowing down. Although his monochrome office has a touch of the impersonal about it, he expounds vividly on the college achievements, is conversant with the myriad different A level courses and glows with pride at his students' individual successes; 'a lot of our students come from a background where they don't have networking opportunities... where there is not a lot of academic success'. Describes the college as 'schooly, but it's not a school, it's not a university... like university, with safety nets'. Views his recent appointment to head as 'evolution rather than revolution', aiming to continue the progress of his predecessor in forging contacts with business and industry. 'There's a lot of advantage to be gained from networking and in London we are in a very good position to do that...building students' confidence and knowledge and an understanding of the world of work, building their aspiration'.

Academic matters: A sixth form college for A levels, sheltering under broader academic umbrella of City and Islington College and Westminster Kingsway College, has the advantage of offering a wide range of subjects (over 34 on offer when we visited), delivered by A level specialist teachers, in a tailor-made environment for 16-18s. Class sizes are kept to around 20 (22 max) in the popular subjects, supported by over 140 staff and technical assistants; smaller numbers attend the more unusual options, electronics, dance, graphic communication, Turkish. One parent was impressed by the flexibility in the timetable: 'They've been very open minded about changing course'. Mainstream subjects like physics have seen a surge in popularity, boosted by the college's two female physics teachers, while the college has extensive technical back-up for a range of practical

C

options including textiles, photography and media studies, whose students get to show final pieces at nearby Screen on the Green. In 2016, 37 per cent A*- B grades. The head describes the student experience as academically rigorous. Around 60 students take the Extended Project, which distinguishes independent learners and researchers. The staff are A level specialists, some with doctorates, some authors of school text books – and unanimously got the thumbs up from parents.

The head gives it straight from the shoulder about the Ofsted inspectors' tour. 'Overwhelmingly they were grade 1 lessons; I didn't have to hide anyone from them, there are no bad teachers here'. The management team he describes as 'fantastic' and 'sparky'; the parents' verdict: 'interconnects well as a team'. The head's mission to create links with industry and academia has a two-fold effect. Describing how aspiring medics get to sit alongside UCL students at the Royal Free Hospital, he commented, 'It is stimulating for the staff, and that comes back into the classroom'.

An inclusion co-ordinator supports a full range of special needs, from mild dyslexia to ASD, with one-to-one support in class or in separate smaller rooms, depending on the level of need. The user-friendly building, complete with lifts, accommodates physical disabilities too.

Games, options, the arts: Wednesday afternoons are for enrichment. Students who aren't lucky enough to be visiting the Supreme Court or meeting a Nobel Prize winning astrophysicist can enjoy more earthly activities, including football, basketball, netball, boxercise and gym, co-ordinated by a sports youth worker, off site. There's an in-house dance troupe and theatre shows, including an annual talent show and a Christmas production, which take place in the drama studio or at Islington's Almeida Theatre. Students from both music and music tech courses join with others in a combo band, though numbers don't allow for a choir or orchestra. The walls of the corridors display lively posters for a wide choice of clubs: history club, talking religion, talking politics, geo-justice, robot club, as well as political debates about local elections and the London mayor. Teachers make the most of the graphic design students in promoting courses: 'Why learn a language?' asked one eye-catching poster and 'Congratulations on completing your coursework' cheered another message. Trips out include London museums and Tate Modern; residentials for geographers to Derbyshire, while the RS class gets to visit a Buddhist retreat in Scotland.

Background and atmosphere: In an area that Dickens refers to as where 'London began in earnest', the college site at Angel stands at a confluence of the metropolis's business and residential life. To the south and east it touches the City with its commercial and banking quarters, to the north it embraces the mixed residential areas of Highbury, Finsbury and Holloway and the buzzing shops and bars of Upper Street. The college's sparkling glass, steel and chrome structure catches the eye, with its grey themed interior and a city garden. Past the turnstiles and uniformed security checks, the visitor is greeted by a large canteen/hall/chilling area on the ground floor, labelled 'a thriving hub' by one mum. Beyond this is the library, with its purple and grey colour scheme, and shelves of journals. Many of the rooms are convertible to smaller meeting rooms, with soft dividers and screens; an adjacent IT suite houses computers as far as the eye can see.

A tour up the glass stairwell, with Barbara Hepworth-style holes, takes us to the classrooms and workshops above. Textiles, photography, and visual arts studios look out over the many cranes and offices of the cityscape, while film studies are found further along the corridor they call Media Street. Disappointingly little to see of the students' artwork in the designer building, and one mum felt the art and design department could be more inspiring. However, a room full of recording equipment run by dedicated techies provides support for the many and successful media students (alumni include singer, Paloma Faith; actor, David Oyelowo OBE; TV presenter, Reggie Yates; and news reporter, Symeon Brown). Humanities and languages classrooms have a floor to themselves, with seven science labs below; fully equipped with the latest kit and a flock of white coats and goggles; 'It seems to be very well resourced,' commented one parent. A vibrant hub on the first floor, full of upholstered chairs and scarlet beanbags, houses the careers advice centre.

A lone horse chestnut tree on a patch of green breaks up the austere landscape of the grounds (this is EC1 real estate) while an all-weather court on the roof of the science building next door allows for floodlit matches. Students can take a break between classes at brutalist picnic tables or work up an urban sweat at a game of garden ping pong.

Pastoral care, well-being and discipline: Dress is teen-casual and it's first name terms for teachers; 'that doesn't stop them calling you Sir for two years,' laughs the head. The relationship relies on mutual respect; 'we are trying to turn them into young adults,' he says and students we spoke to were aware of the journey. 'It's preparing me for life after', said one. The young adults recognised the school's high expectations: three warnings for misconduct or poor work, followed by a 'cause for concern' notice. One parent reported that the tutor had been quick to notice when her daughter's new-found freedom had gone too far, and called a meeting; 'we all three of us got her back on track'. No bullying, except the occasional modern menace of cyber-bullying. A more serious misdemeanour involves discussion with the parents. Serious alcohol or drugs issues are rare and accountable to a disciplinary panel; 'there's less goes on here than in my own sixth form of 90,' owns the head. A mum praised the pastoral tutor system, for 'quite closely monitoring' a particularly shy daughter. The college is conscious that its population is at a fragile stage of adolescence, so employs a full time counsellor, alongside others including a mental health and well-being worker, 'As a society we are more enlightened,' explains the head. 'In the past people got on with it or sunk'.

Students with issues knew how to contact their tutor, and met with them every week in the normal way to discuss progress. They were in no doubt how to seek out help in applying for university from the full time careers officers; 'They are always telling us who to go to', said one. The higher education department offers advice on UCAS applications, explains personal statements, carries out interview practice using former members of staff and even helps plan gap years. They run a dazzling timetable of tutorials, eg applying for Oxbridge, medicine, teaching, nursing or apprenticeships, along with a range of informative talks ('STEM work experience for Girls' caught our eye) in addition to masterclasses in work-related skills such as online IT courses or young drivers' workshops. 'I talk to universities all the time,' says the head, which explains the respectable number of offers to competitive courses, though it was disappointing to find a capital-centric attitude in the students we met, who appear content to study close to home.

Pupils and parents: Starting afresh in a new sixth form, rather than staying at their secondary school, gives the students a real chance to reinvent themselves, and the ones we spoke to described a variety of reasons for choosing the college: 'it gives you more independence'; 'looking for somewhere you are doing things by yourself'; 'it's more diverse'; 'more subjects'; 'closest to home'. One parent commented about her daughter, 'She hadn't had a good experience, and had a lot of catching up to do with feeling good about learning...it's a place that gives inspiration to the students'. More girls than boys (60:40) and a typical urban cultural mix: 'The ethnic mix is a real mix; 30 per cent Asian; 30 per cent Afro-Caribbean; 30 per cent white,' says the head, plus a few international students who 'want to have a London experience'. With huge numbers of students, the variety of ambition was also evident: the high achievers gain scholarships with banking or legal companies, others apply for vocational courses, while some are content to munch cookies in the canteen. 'The scale allows the range,' explains the head.

Parents commented on the study body as 'a mixed bag of individuals...from far and wide' and 'it's very diverse'. They meet the teachers at the annual parent evenings, or at individual sessions with the tutor or course leader, if requested. Surprisingly for such a large cohort, the parents all felt involved, and emails and phone calls were answered promptly. The school sends out a termly newsletter, though no-one we spoke to had read it.

Entrance: Five Cs needed at GCSE to study three A levels, higher grades required to take four subjects, and the college sets its own entrance test for maths. Applicants are encouraged to visit the open day in November and apply before the end of January. Oversubscribed, more than four applicants per place, but interviews 2,500 before making offers. A nucleus of students from Islington and Hackney, and has a partnership with three local schools: Elizabeth Garrett Anderson, Holloway and Islington Arts and Media, which have priority, although current cohort attended 200 different secondary schools. A taster day at the start of July is followed by registration at beginning of autumn term and a last opportunity to finalise courses. A handful of international students, who board with local families.

Exit: The head is rightly proud of his statistics: 70-80 per cent to university, one fifth to the Russell Group, a few to Oxbridge (three in 2016). Popular courses are science, maths, business, economics, psychology, law, media. Several students praised the dynamic careers advice service, which supervises applications.

Money matters: Centrally funded by Education Funding Agency; international students self-fund. Dedicated college advisor supports applications for a host of bursaries, sponsorships and additional expenses, including travel. Parents pay towards school trips.

Remarks: City and Islington College offers students a new beginning with a wealth of courses and great facilities. The students are encouraged to take advantage of their position in the heart of London to forge connections with the world of work and academia. Throw in supportive staff, a savvy head and a blessed central location at Angel and no wonder they are off to a flying start.

City of London School

Queen Victoria Street, London EC4V 3AL

Pupils: 925 • Ages: 10–18 • Sixth form: 250

Fees: £15, 633 pa

Tel: 020 7489 0291
Email: admissions@clsb.org.uk
Website: www.clsb.org.uk

Head: Since 2014, Mrs Sarah Fletcher MA PGCE NPQH, an Oxford historian (early 50s). Previously head of Kingston Grammar School, where her regime was creative, modernising and human. Before that, a deputy head at Rugby and she has taught at, among others, Wycombe Abbey, St George's Montreux, Habs Girls' and Lawrence Sheriff Boys' Grammar in Rugby – a diverse and venturesome academic career. And an excellent preparation for one of the top jobs in the independent day school sector.

An inspired appointment. It put some noses – and a few other organs – out of joint. Her headship followed the long reign of an exceptionally popular predecessor. It raised eyebrows and, in some minds, the alarm; and her first term or two were not easy, involving, as they did, the sudden departure of two senior members of staff, which went down less than well with some older boys and their parents.

Mrs Fletcher – soft-spoken, pretty, candid, sensitive and determined – has the unreserved backing of her governors – The City of London Corporation. She has the vision, eloquence and, when needed, steel and an intelligent and enabling approach 'The best results come,' she told us, 'from trusting people and giving them the space to develop their own thinking.' Sound advice.

She is moving on in July 2017 to take on the new challenge of heading St Paul's Girls' School.

Academic matters: Offers A levels – but a move to Pre-U (NB Mrs Fletcher's brainchild some years back) is on the way, initially with biology, history and RS. Others may well follow. All in the sixth can opt to take the Extended Project Qualification in addition to three or four main subjects. Mrs Fletcher is keen to develop computing – already exceptionally well provided for – throughout the school and is on the look-out for a replacement for the ECDL – something with programming built in, a cry we hear everywhere. Links with IT companies being developed to further upgrade the offering. No weak subjects or depts – results at A level and GCSE uniformly impressive. Columns of A*s, As, a few Bs and very little in the lower order columns (92 per cent A*/A grades at I/GCSE and 73 per cent at A level in 2016).

Maths much the most popular A level but modern languages hold up and Latin and Greek battle on. Mandarin compulsory in first two years and, seemingly, catching on here rather more than elsewhere. Links being forged with schools and organisations in China. Economics and drama the only concessions to the more 'modern' subjects – no psychology, business or other 'studies'. Lots of academic prizes eg recent successes in Olympiads, the prestigious Erasmus Essay Prize and the international Juvenes Translatores prize. 'My son's teachers have all been wonderful – especially in maths and the arts,' a parent enthused. A second felt, 'My sons are always stretched to be the best they can be but never pushed. They don't let you become so obsessed with work so you can't do other things. The teachers plainly want the best for each boy.' Another was concerned: 'There seems to be a drive to climb the league tables. We don't want that. It's not why we chose the school.' But head assures us there is no shift in the school's aims in that respect. She teaches all year 9s (we do like that) and sees everyone with their UCAS form. Around 60 on the school's SEN register – mostly dyslexic or needing help with organisation. Not a prominent feature of the school's mix.

Good library – rather like a top notch public library in design and atmosphere but with 50,000 books, periodicals, CDs and PCs galore plus cases housing the more venerable volumes for show. Unique, in our experience, is the school bookshop – a real one. Super 'science lecture theatre' but memorable lectures seem to be on anything but science.

Games, options, the arts: Sports and arts praised unreservedly by parents despite the trek to the school's main sports centre at Eltham. 'They do fantastic things with them. The music tours are amazing.' More than half learn an instrument; many take LAMDA exams; much-praised joint productions with the Girls' School in eg choral concerts with a choir of 200+. Music tech facilities of a high order. Lively drama – productions at all age levels. Smallish, pretty basic, studio theatre but excellent main, flexible 150-seater theatre would do credit to an upmarket fringe venue. Weekly school publication The Citizen produced by students. Four high-ceilinged art studios – all do art and music to year 9 – and much varied and vigorous portraiture on display. We enjoyed the ceramics – especially the satisfying crunch of some material or other underfoot. DT on the bottom floor also lively and fun and more DT and to a higher level (as yet no GCSE) on the cards, to boys' delight.

Football is main winter game and the school is a powerful presence in inter-school tournaments. Basketball, cricket, water polo, swimming and athletics all strong. Current National Water Polo champs and champs in London basketball and football tournaments – no narrow academic focus here. On-site huge sports hall, weights room and pool. Sizeable Astros marked out as pitches. Rest happens 25 minutes' away at sports clubs around the metropolis. Some 200+ on D of E Award programmes; CCF surprisingly lively for a city school but offering mouth-watering, subsidised opportunities – 'I did a powerboat course and got my licence from it,' said one young man.

Excellent range of trips and tours with a focus on educational value and enrichment rather than the extravagance one sees elsewhere. Good use made of London and its riches – a three-weekly trip to somewhere in the capital made by all year 9s. Good range of clubs with a bent towards to the literary and the philosophical – we like The Diaspora Club, The Comedy Society and Modern Language Society, in particular. Many have their own sizeable domains – we passed The Railway Society room – 'thousands of pounds worth of kit in there,' we learned. Debating is popular and lively as is Model United Nations. Lots of outreach and charity work done out of conviction more than duty. Overall impression is of a varied, creative and quirky programme with plenty for everyone from sports stars to unashamed geeks.

Background and atmosphere: A school with a long, complex and obscure history. Its original benefactor, John Carpenter, and his executor intended his legacy to be for 'the finding and bringing up of four poor men's children with meat, drink, apparel, learning at the schools, in the universities, etc, until they be preferred, and then others in their places for ever'. The school as we know it today was finally established four centuries later, in 1837, first just off Cheapside, moving, in 1883, to Blackfriars and finally, in 1986, to a purpose-built, magnificently-sited, establishment between the Thames and St Paul's Cathedral. While it can no longer claim the nobly charitable purpose intended by Carpenter, it retains a liberal, progressive ethos, not least in its determinedly ecumenical attitude to religion and its generous bursary scheme, and, under its new head, much is being done in 'outreach' – eg working with The City of London Corporation's three academies, charitable ventures, multiple imaginative and beneficial links.

Wherever you are, great city buildings look in at you through many windows. And the river light is likewise inescapable. The building – which seemed over-warm and airless to us on a mild spring day – is wearing well. It's a little municipal – the signing, wide corridors and atria are reminiscent of an NHS hospital – but the whole is softened by relics from its previous home (we appreciated especially the row of Victorian leaded lights lining the dining room celebrating school luminaries), trophy cabinets, miles of red lockers – and the arts and crafts about the place. Displays stay up for rather too long, we gather, so that people stop looking. Extraordinary things like the fragment of a second century AD limestone Roman head of Mars found as part of an old riverside wall. Large 'concourse' used for events, adorned by plaques and statues to more school luminaries. Also, seemingly, hundreds of PCs everywhere. School houses are named for great figures in the school's history.

Pastoral care, well-being and discipline: Houses are 'important but not that important', we were told, ie sports, chess, intellectual competitions etc run on house lines but 'being in a different house never separates friends'. Sixth formers are grouped by shared subject teacher rather than houses. Every parent stressed how happy their son(s) were at the school. 'The boys in his class are so lovely – friendly, happy and always polite and nice to each other,' one told us, while a second said, 'it's a nurturing environment – they offer help, they set him up with a mentor and try to nip problems in the bud'. A third felt that the boys were 'very respectful of the teachers – it's a liberal ethos and it works'. And a fourth, 'The boys help each other in all kinds of ways'. Few discipline problems, though we heard one class giving a language assistant a bit of a rough time.

Pupils and parents: From all over London and the home counties. Mostly native English speakers, but a great diversity of home languages spoken including Chinese, Hindi, Russian and Tamil. Very few need EAL support. Brains the only common denominator – parents, who like the social mix in the school, are mostly professional, bright, urban and appreciative of broad and liberal educational values. 'They learn to respect everyone,' said one, 'and realise that not everyone can afford parties in limousines.' Formidable list of notable former pupils (known as Old Citizens) includes HH Asquith (PM 1908-16), Arthur Rackham, Ernest (Oh for the Wings of a Dove) Lough, Denis Norden, Julian Barnes, Daniel Radcliffe, Mike Brearley, Anthony Julius, Steven Isserlis, umpteen brainbox academics, legal eagles, cleverclogses of all sorts, among them three winners of the Nobel Prize.

Entrance: Highly selective. By competitive exam in English, maths and verbal reasoning in year 5 for 10+ (40-50 places for which around 160 apply), and year 6 for 11+ (60 places for which around 550 apply) and 13+ (40 places – ISEB pre-test at 10, followed by interviews and conditional offer based on CE – perhaps 350 apply) plus interview and report from current school. At 11+, two distinct competitions, with those after 100 per cent bursaries sifted by taking an online reasoning test in December. Around half of all entrants come from preps, the rest from state primaries. At 16, applicants are tested in their two top subjects – 20 available places for which 75 apply. The school courts the primary/prep sector early – admission in year 6 is unusual and they clearly steal a march on the rest.

Exit: Up to 15 leave after GCSEs, almost all to state sixth forms. All leavers go on to heavyweight subjects at good universities – around 15 per cent to Oxbridge annually (23 in 2016) and the rest to eg UCL, Bristol, Durham, Warwick, Edinburgh etc including six medics.

Money matters: Around 10 per cent of current pupils on 100 per cent fee remission via 'sponsored awards' available at 11+ and 16+ for bright candidates whose family finances would not stretch to fee-paying school without assistance. All applicants sifted via reasoning tests. Gross parental income to be below £45,000. Around 30 academic scholarships available at all entry points, worth up to 25 per cent of fees. Candidates invited to a 'demanding interview for which no preparation is helpful'. Sports scholarships – good footballers especially welcome. Music scholarships and choral bursaries – these for those who become choristers at The Temple Church and The Chapel Royal.

Remarks: 'A very down-to-earth school,' asserted a parent and we agree. An inspiring yet grounded school with solid values, providing vision, opportunities and a wonderfully civilised start in life for its lucky students. A jewel in London's crown.

City of London School for Girls – Prep

Linked with City of London School for Girls

39

St Giles' Terrace, Barbican, London EC2Y 8BB

Pupils: 90 • Ages: 7–11

Fees: £16,056 pa

Tel: 020 7847 5500
Email: admissions@clsg.org.uk
Website: www.clsg.org.uk

Headmistress: Since 2010, Miss Jane Rogers MPhil BA (London). Worked for 10 years in the state sector before moving to the Institute of Education as a science lecturer and educational researcher. Moved back into education when she took a post of senior teacher at the Lyceum School, after which she came to the prep, because 'I'm interested in academic excellence'. Educated at Chelmsford County High School for Girls, University College London (geography) and Institute of Education. Has two teenage children.

Entrance: Twenty-four hotly contested places at 7+, sitting nationally standardised tests in English, maths and verbal reasoning plus some spelling and writing tests of the prep's own authorship. Register your daughter early to be sure of her being seen: the school assesses a maximum of 150 girls, and is always oversubscribed. Of those 150, the top 50 are called back for a further day's appraisal, during which they're examined in English, maths, science and DT – this last because it allows the girls to be observed in practical activities and working as a team. The 24 places are then offered to those 'with academic ability and the potential to become independent, happy learners.' Girls are seen in the November of the year preceding entry; closing date for accepting or declining offers is mid-February.

Exit: Parents take note: entry to the senior school is not automatic. By Easter of year 5, reserved places (ie places that are guaranteed) are offered only to those girls 'who continue to develop'. Any child who joined the school later than year 3 doesn't get one at all, and must sit for a place along with the external candidates. Head insists that 'the vast majority go through' (90 per cent in 2016). Some parents' perceptions are different; see below. Destinations of those who do go elsewhere include St Paul's Girls', North London Collegiate, Francis Holland, Channing and Queen's College London. 'We've been hugely successful in placing girls at other schools,' says head. 'Schools like City Prep girls, and they don't get them that often.'

Remarks: Broad curriculum, with specialist teachers from the senior school coming in to teach music, art, DT, PE, Latin (years 5 and 6) and modern languages. The girls learn a different language each year: Spanish in year 3, French in year 4, German in year 5 and Mandarin in year 6. The idea is that the girls acquire an enthusiasm for languages which then helps them to choose the right ones when they go on to senior school, which is certainly commendable. It struck us as odd, however, that they only studied each language for a year before having to drop it and move onto the next one; a year 5 girl we spoke to admitted that she'd now forgotten the Spanish she'd learned in year 3.

As well as benefiting from the senior school teaching expertise, the excellent senior school facilities – swimming pool, sports hall, library, Astroturf, tennis courts – are also available, which doubtless explains why there's no difference in fees between the two (though prep fees do include lunch). Sports and gymnastics are strong, and music likewise, with the Y6s doing a Prep Opera every year. Impressive LAMDA results. There are also lots of residential trips which are perennially popular. Wide variety of clubs, and after-school care provides an opportunity for girls to do their homework as well as have fun. ('They have a register to make sure you don't wander off,' said one of our tour guides, earnestly.) Sixth formers from the senior school run clubs for the prep girls, which, says head, creates 'a big sister culture. They're great role models for the younger girls.'

Other than some worrying reports which we outline below, it took a long while for parental feedback to reach us about this school. Our first invitation was met with complete silence, and even a second appeal didn't yield very much. (This was in contrast to the parents of girls in the senior school, who were quick to tell us how happy they were.) Those who did eventually contact us agreed that the girls are worked hard but achieve highly. A couple remarked on the school's competitive nature: 'The girls are incredibly competitive, but also very supportive of each other, and have a strong sense of loyalty to their school,' said one. Another observed, 'If you're prepared to buy into the idea of City and have a daughter capable of swimming in its often competitive seas, it will be a worthwhile experience for her and for your family.' These parents emphasised that their daughters were enjoying their time at the prep, had made friends and embraced the opportunities on offer there.

However, some of these same parents expressed disquiet about the entry process to the senior school. 'The goalposts seem to have been moved,' said one couple, 'The message about not everyone getting reserved places is stronger now than it was when our daughter got in.' The same worried mother continued, 'Choosing to put a child through an entrance exam when they're 6 is not an easy decision; in our case we hoped to avoid the stress at 11+, which we now find we may not do. I suspect the feeling of rejection and the dent to self-confidence is higher if you don't get a reserved place from the prep and can't stay with your friends, than if you apply and fail as an external candidate.' Miss Rogers told us that an average of four girls leave City Prep's year 6 every year: two out of choice, and two who were 'advised to go elsewhere.' School figures show an average of three girls a year recently have not been given reserved places. This figure seems high to us, given both the stringent nature of the admissions process and the acknowledged high workload put upon the girls during their time here; and we did ask the head about this. 'Not all girls develop the same,' was her comment. 'Some go upwards and some go downwards,' adding, 'sometimes things happen in families to disturb girls.'

Parents and former parents are divided in their feelings about the school. On one side of the argument, accounts have been passed to us of recent City Prep girls whose confidence, and even health, had been so undermined by the school's approach that their parents voted with their feet and took them out. These parents write with angry eloquence about the school's 'complete lack of nurture and care' and claim that it 'values malleability and obedience over originality and sparky intellect.' They allege that there is poor support for special needs such as dyslexia, and that some of the teaching is substandard ('After we moved her, we discovered that she had been so poorly taught that she needed to relearn a year's worth of maths,' said one mother, and another mother reported an identical experience.)

The head insists that the school works closely with parents, and that the girls' happiness is paramount to her. 'We love quirky individuals. We've got lots and lots of those. Girls are allowed

C

to be themselves here.' And indeed, other parents told us that their daughters loved coming to school. One, whose child had excelled there academically, spoke of the school's 'really good pastoral side.' 'The prep is a nurturing and non-threatening environment,' said one mother whose child was now at CLSG senior, 'and I would have no hesitation in recommending it.'

C

Picking our way through such contradictory accounts was difficult. We can only conclude by suggesting that since entry to CLSG senior school isn't guaranteed, parents should think closely about whether City Prep is the right choice for their daughter or whether a prep school not linked to any senior school, but with a proven record of getting its leavers into the destination of their choice, might suit their family better.

City of London School for Girls

Linked with City of London School for Girls – Prep

St Giles' Terrace, London EC2Y 8BB

Pupils: 642 • Ages: 11–18 • Sixth form: 152

Fees: £16,056 pa

Tel: 020 7847 5500
Email: admissions@clsg.org.uk
Website: www.clsg.org.uk

Headmistress: Since 2014, Mrs Ena (pronounced Enna) Harrop BA MA MA MPhil PGCE (one of the longest list of degrees in The Guide!) (40s), a modern linguist, originally from Spain. Her previous incarnations include head of Spanish at Royal Russell and head of modern languages at Royal Grammar, Guildford. She joined City Girls as director of studies in 2010 and – unusually and remarkably – was appointed internally to the headship, clearly to the delight of the entire school. One of the most popular heads we have encountered.

You can, instantly, see why. She is the real deal. Formidably intelligent, chic, softly spoken, charming and beautifully articulate, her credo is the centrality of gender equality and the necessity of the modern world being gender-blind. And, as a head and the mother of three daughters, she lives the dream. Her (teacher) husband took her maternity leave when their last daughter was born. In the words of her pupils: 'She was – before she became head – a kind of figurehead.' 'The message of feminism she promotes in the school is so inspiring.' 'She is likeable, approachable.. collaborative, efficient.' One admitted, 'I was scared when she came on our school trip but she was so relaxed it wasn't daunting at all.' And another, 'When she became head we just thought it'd be great to have more of her.' And every parent we spoke to concurred.

'Independent learning' is a phrase you meet a lot here and, again, the head – with her list of degrees – walks the talk. 'I feel tempted,' she told us, 'to take at least two A levels at this school – economics and art.. and then there's..' A very modern head: a recent assembly was on 'All you need to know about pregnancy and childbirth' and she refers to 'the nappy barrier' to women's achievement. Behind her desk sits a text: 'Feel the fear but still do it.' With Mrs Harrop as role model, a City student will leave as well-equipped to take on and challenge the world – while remaining her essential self – as any young woman could.

Academic matters: Maths rules. As elsewhere with clever students, this has become the most popular – and successful – A level subject, and recent takers outnumbered those who take languages all put together. 'My girls are strategic,' explains Mrs Harrop, 'and they know that if they take a language they are less likely to get an A*/A than if they take maths.' The girls say: 'People really like maths – they see the use of it.' Other popular subjects – in an, admittedly, conservative range as befits the preferences here – are history, chemistry and English. Mandarin, after a very successful course to GCSE, now offered at Pre-U, and should markedly boost the number of language takers which, has, in any case, increased since Mrs Harrop took over. Overall, A level results included a remarkable 76 per cent at A*/A and 96 per cent at A*/B in 2016. GCSE results no less impressive with 96 per cent A*/As. However, although results are obviously a key factor in the school's success, the school itself puts the emphasis elsewhere – on, for example, independent learning and thinking.

Lots of computers and library has a bank of borrowable laptops. Librarian seen as 'wonderful', though library itself, possibly, not the most impressive feature – we were bemused by some strange cataloguing and location of books and it felt a bit tired. Although a third of the pupils speak a language other than English at home, almost none need EAL help. Around 12 per cent with a mild SEN of some kind, all supported as needed on an 'as and when' basis but no-one with major learning difficulties here. School not easy for those with mobility difficulties.

Games, options, the arts: Art is, according to all, wonderful. We saw some terrific painting and the results at A level and GCSE are phenomenal. Good hall for display of work and three studios, all richly and messily busy – the colour and variety of the top floor a refreshing relief. DT taken by all years 7-9 in good sized studio with 3D printer and laser cutter plus all else you'd expect. We enjoyed some lively work including inventive year 7 torches. Lots of music – individual, large and small groups, pursued with excellence and enthusiasm. Two good sized teaching rooms at top of the building plus numerous practice rooms. Drama in huge hall and Black Box Theatre at the top of the building. Well-designed literature for shows is evidence of classy production values all through. Draughty outdoor theatre a splendidly imaginative recent innovation – a bit like a Greek theatre, only colder.

Games, remarkably, mostly take place on site – planners found flat spaces, inside and out, for two tennis courts, a large Astro pitch, various other big enough spaces for a gym, 25 yard pool, table tennis, new dance studio (2015). Outside space overlooked by flats – the girls must get used to it. Non-selective approach to some teams gives all enthusiasts opportunities and it works. They do cross-country round the high level walkways. Many representatives in borough games and several notable individual successes on local and grander levels.

But perhaps the most exciting aspect of the extracurricular offering is London itself. 'There are all the galleries and museums – they are so easy to go to from here – you can get there in a double art lesson. It's one of the reasons I came here,' typifies the response. Young Enterprise, likewise, outside speakers, visits, lectures at UCL, the Royal Institution etc, trips and tours – all add to the stimulating mix and the avid seizing of a rich variety of opportunities here.

Background and atmosphere: One of the more surprising school locations in the UK. Navigating the Barbican complex is notoriously tricky, but if you negotiate the grey concrete and glass mini-village to its heart, you will find the school. You get there via brick-paved walkways and the school sits between the ancient church of St Giles, Cripplegate one way, with glass office blocks behind, while the other way are the Guildhall

Conservatory, the Barbican arts venue and the city flats with their valiant window boxes – and a large, flagged and lilied, ornamental pond between. Also surprising the eye and breaking up the harshness are the gallant trees and the improbable wodge of ancient London wall which squats defiantly opposite the school's main entrance. The school opened here in 1969 – the first, pretty much, of the reincarnations of venerable educational institutions needing new and purpose-built homes. A bold conception and it wears well. The inside is as stark and workful as Gradgrind could have wished, though lively displays and lots of big windows help relieve the Spartan architecture. Sixth form centre cleverly bolted on. You go in and out a lot as you negotiate the five storeys and we were glad we were not there on a cold wet day. Good-sized dining hall and jolly good menu – Wok Theatre, Italian/Indian Fusion and Big Bowl Salad looked tempting.

The original school began life in 1894. William Ward, who believed in giving girls a broad and liberal education with an emphasis on scholarship, left a third of his fortune – £20,000 – to the City of London Corporation for the foundation of a girls' school. Livery companies, banks and city firms continue to give financial support. The Corporation still administers this and numerous other schools and the board of governors is appointed by the Court of Common Council. The Corporation has an education strategy and its portfolio of schools gives rise to mutually beneficial links between City Girls' and state primaries eg for sixth form community service.

Famously diverse mix of pupils and staff as befits the school's situation in the heart of the city. 'Diversity' is a word you hear a lot here, in numerous contexts. Not least the effect of coalescing people from so huge an area. Likewise, we heard 'exciting' a lot. The girls say, 'It's always busy here – but in a good way, and being in the Barbican is so exciting!' Pupils are bright-faced, smiley, articulate and confident – with no trace of arrogance. They have a sense of their responsibilities to the wider world alongside their own personal ambitions.

Pastoral care, well-being and discipline: Light but 'tightly run' discipline. 'The teachers really care that the girls are happy,' a parent told us, 'and they deal quickly with problems.' 'No-one gets thrown out if they haven't had loads of warnings first,' girls told us. 'They bring in parents. It's mostly just poor behaviour over a long period but it hardly ever happens.' And most pay tribute to the excellence of pastoral care and their 'lovely' teachers.

Pupils and parents: They come from a vast circumference around the city – Chigwell to the north east, Harrow to the north, Shepherd's Bush and Fulham to the west – even as far away as Cambridge. 'It's helped me become a lot more independent and the school gives us "travel buddies" when we join so that we can get used to the journey with someone experienced.' Parents say: 'The mix of girls is wonderful. They're not a flashy lot and they not tarted-up either.'

Entrance: Numbers of applicants, as at other academically selective London schools, now hitting heights of absurdity and severely straining schools' resources, especially where, as here, physical space needed on assessment days is limited. School is no longer part of the North London Consortium so sets own exams in English and maths and what is graphically described as 'an interview with teeth'. Around 900 now applying for the 100 places at 11+ (or 850 for 75 places excl those applying from City's own on-site prep). Around 70 applicants for the 10-15 places at sixth form. Sixth form places conditional on school's own exams taken in potential A level subjects and on A*/As at GCSE in all subjects.

Exit: Around 15-25 leave post-GCSE to board or go co-ed or to sixth form colleges. Early warning – sometimes as early as year 9 – given to those who are unlikely to make it into the sixth form. Some parental criticism of the less than gentle manner in which this has taken place in the past but the Harrop regime is softening the approach, though the criterion for staying – ie no more than three Bs and all else at A*/A at GCSE – remains in force. Sixth form leavers are starry – nine to Oxbridge in 2016, with 10 medics and two to Ivy League colleges; the London University colleges also take a good number. Great range of serious courses – nearly a third STEM and number of linguists now rising. Notable former pupils include Claire Rayner, Hermione Lee, Alison Weir, Elizabeth Emanuel, Romola Garai, Winklemans – Claudia and Sophie – and Daisy Christodoulou. Also Anna Blundy and Dido Armstrong, who both did their sixth forms at Westminster. One wonders whether they still would now.

Money matters: Around 25 per cent on some kind of fee assistance. Bursaries from 25 per cent to 100 per cent. Unusually no academic scholarships, but music, drama and art scholarships of up to £1,500 a year at 11+ and 16+, and an 11+ sports scholarship.

Remarks: By any standards, a top school for girls, with an edge of excitement, modernity and realism. Makes the most of what it is, where it is. Said a parent: 'My daughter is incredibly happy there. She has blossomed. Her friends and the head are amazing. I've only ever heard good things.'

Coldfall Primary School

Coldfall Avenue, London N10 1HS

Pupils: 680 • Ages: 3–11

Tel: 020 8883 0608
Email: office@coldfall.haringey.sch.uk
Website: www.coldfall.haringey.sch.uk

Head Teacher: Since 1996, Evelyn Davies (50s). Ms Davies is one of life's 'superheads', a woman who has taken a 'bog-standard' primary and transformed it into a star act with an 'outstanding' Ofsted, three-form entry and very happy parents. Most find her open-minded and approachable. 'I had an idea', commented one, 'and she immediately said "let's have a chat about it."' Hard working and well-organised, she gets things done. 'She's not ticking boxes, she really gets involved in the nitty gritty'. An active opponent of testing, testing, testing, she's even been to parliament to protest, winning the admiration of her local MP ('if I were the minister for education I would grab Evelyn Davies and put her as a key adviser. That way our children would be well educated in every sense of the word').

Entrance: Places given out using the standard local authority formula: children in local authority care, followed by special educational needs, siblings and distance from the gates. Recent expansion means a bit of leeway for those living a few streets away.

Exit: A primary whose catchment fortunately straddles the borough's two highest flying comprehensives. The largest chunk of year 6 proceed to Fortismere, just next door. Sizeable (and growing) slice to Alexandra Park, down the road. Enviable success rate too, in grammar school entrance, then in dribbles to a wide range of local and distant establishments.

Remarks: This meticulously run school has everything going for it. Teaching here is enthusiastic and thorough, with staff constantly looking to improve performance. Academic standards are high and virtually every child reaches the government targets, many far exceeding them. Though the school has an 'unusually high' number of children with special needs, both those who struggle and those who excel are provided with plenty of booster classes. Not all parents, however, feel difficulties are necessarily dealt with sympathetically. 'Our son has considerable problems', said one, 'and we found the attitude very inflexible'. Behaviour is good and positive performance (particularly regular attendance) rewarded (classes compete enthusiastically for attendance teddies).

Facilities here can only be described as exceptional for a London primary. The original, large, low-lying Victorian schoolhouse, once a secondary school, has now been joined by a sleek, modern addition, providing extra classrooms and a new gym. Expansive grounds boast country-like playing fields, as well as two large and notably well-equipped playgrounds kitted out with basketball and netball nets, table-tennis tables and sheltered cabins. Pupils also benefit from the school's own allotments and nature trail, as well as access to nearby Coldfall Woods.

Sport played enthusiastically and successfully. Two hours of PE weekly overseen by a qualified sports coach and training approached with professional efficiency (gymnasts, for example, use flip cameras to study performance). Both boys and girls triumph in borough-wide competitions, boys winning recent golf and football championships, girls excelling in football and netball. Pupils also qualified for the London Youth Games.

Plenty of enrichment, in lessons and out, including chess (with championship-winning chess teams), French (taught by a native speaker), computer programming and cooking all part of the regular mix. Excellent range of clubs (including geology) and activities. Successful school choir has made appearances at the O2 and Barbican and one enthusiastic parent recently organised an entire week of dance with over 60 workshops and professionals imported from the West End. 'Things don't just happen here', said one mother. 'Everything is well planned and thought through'. Regular trips beyond the school gates include at least one visit to a museum, gallery and musical event for every pupil.

In the main (though not exclusively), parents are comfortably off Muswell Hill locals, so there's a good sprinkling of designer trainers in the playground, but this is low-key prosperity. Almost a third of pupils speak a language other than English at home. Both mothers and fathers (plenty of the latter at pick-up time) involved in making the school a success. 'All parents', said one enthusiast, 'are given an opportunity to contribute, not just non-working mums'. Many arrive at weekends to help with the gardening, and the thriving PTA organises summer and winter fairs, weekly coffee mornings, a Valentine disco, quiz night, fashion show and organic vegetable scheme. Sizeable sums are raised for playground, computer and PE equipment. 'There's a real feeling that everyone matters', said one mother. 'The kids are really blessed'.

Colfe's School

Horn Park Lane, London SE12 8AW

Pupils: 1,055 • Ages: 3–18 • Sixth form: 165 • C of E

Fees: £11,934 – £16,110 pa

Tel: 020 8852 2283
Email: admissions@colfes.com
Website: www.colfes.com

Headmaster: Since 2005, Richard Russell (50s), previously deputy warden of Forest School. Educated in Ireland and went on to read classics at Cambridge. He started his career as a Latin teacher; teaching initially attracted him as it would allow him to pursue his interest in archaeology and attend digs during the long summer holidays. Knows everybody and what they're up to, teaches Latin to year 7. He spent 15 years at Sevenoaks coordinating the IB programme; however, he has never thought it particularly suitable for Colfe's and is a great fan of A levels. A professional and pleasant person, say parents, easy to get on with and ambitious for his pupils. He lives in Blackheath with his wife, who works in the City. Nowadays holiday times see them heading for their house in Sicily, where they make their own olive oil.

Head of junior school: Since 2016, Catriona Macleod MSc. Worked at several London prep schools, becoming head of science and then deputy head at Streatham & Clapham junior school, head of juniors at Dunottar School, then head of junior school at Knightsbridge School. Has recently worked in a senior role at a free school in Hertfordshire.

Head of pre-prep: Since 2013 is Sarah Redman (50s) BEd. Mrs Redman was deputy head of the nursery and pre-prep school for some years before becoming head teacher. Parents comment on her warmth and friendliness, 'exactly the sort of person you can entrust your small child to'. Married to a fellow teacher, who is head of a local state primary, with three grown-up children, one of whom is an actress. She enjoys gardening, theatre, arts and crafts, the influence of which can be spotted around the pre-prep.

Academic matters: Well-planned academic curriculum in the junior school runs alongside inspirational sport and arts options. Six-year-olds upwards learn French and Spanish in alternating years. Mixed ability classes of around 18; each child is monitored regularly to check progress. Lively pupils perform well in both national and house competitions; particularly successful teams for maths and chess. 'A very caring school, where the teachers recognise every child as an individual.'

Exam results heading upwards most years – 62 per cent A*/A at GCSE in 2016, with particularly strong showing in maths and science and 44 per cent A*/A, 80 per cent A*-B at A level. Maths, English and the sciences are popular closely followed by economics and history. Most take nine or 10 GCSEs including a language, choice of German, French, Spanish or Latin. Whole school aim is to make classes active and stimulating; everything is in place for high flyers who might be heading for Oxbridge but also for those who might need to go more gently. Setting for maths, sciences and languages. History and maths departments are particularly strong performers; provision for accelerated learning groups for additional maths qualifications. Sixth formers can take Extended Project Qualification. Students with mild specific learning difficulties are supported by specialist staff. The library is a well-used resource, full-time librarian who also doubles up as head of careers, open until 6pm, during Easter holidays and to students on study leave. Outstanding advice and guidance on selecting courses and universities. The school recently ran a conference to introduce the option of going to university in the Netherlands.

Games, options, the arts: Arts and sports are strong all round, structured to suit all tastes and talents. 'Sport for all' policy means there is something for everyone, be it dance or being a member of one of the successful rugby teams. On-site facilities including a gym and 25m swimming pool, which hosts swimming galas, kayaking, water polo and lifesaving courses for year 10s. Additional large playing fields at Leathersellers' sports grounds a few minutes away by minibus on the Sidcup Road. Former Surrey and Kent opening batsman coaches cricket, and athletes often selected to represent Greenwich in the London School Championships. More or less everything on offer on the sporting front for juniors too, with lots of house competitions. Junior girls' netball team have been national prep school champions. CCF with its unique Army Air Corps unit popular, as is D of E, with many progressing to gold award.

Large art department includes printmaking equipment, a kiln for ceramics and a dark room. Parents comment on the energetic drama department; pupils encouraged to write and produce their own plays. LAMDA classes, stage management and technical theatre skills all on offer; impressive variety and number of productions. Up-to-date music rooms and individual soundproof practice studios; swing bands, orchestras, and choirs galore. Huge range of clubs and societies to join: particularly popular are maths, chess and debating along with many inter-house competitions, quizzes, drama, sports and concerts. Regular outings, theatre visits and trips abroad; sixth formers visit the Gambia annually to help build and maintain a school. Good participation in the arts, but relatively small numbers go on to take these subjects at A level, drama and media studies taking the lead over art, design and music.

Art is incorporated into much of the junior school curriculum and classrooms are bursting with interesting displays, models and sculptures. Specialist art teacher organises a big end of year exhibition. Musical education starts early with recorder in year 1 and ukulele in year 2. With around 80 per cent taking instrumental lessons, the school boasts choirs, orchestras, chamber groups, rock band and specialist brass programme. Creative drama, regular plays and lots of opportunities for performers in musical and dramatic assemblies. Dance workshops are popular and include everything and anything from flamenco to African dancing.

Background and atmosphere: Founded in 1652, to educate 'the poor boys of Blackheath' by the Rev Abraham Colfe of Lewisham. Later the school was left in the trust of the Leathersellers' Company, whose livery members make up a majority of today's governing body. Leathersellers have recently pledged an additional £1 million in bursaries. Was a state boys' grammar school for some years before opting to go independent in the 1970s rather than become a comprehensive school. Went fully co-ed in 1999. Strong links with six state schools, five local, one in the Gambia.

Corridors adorned with pupils' work and achievements; atmosphere is positive and busy with smartly dressed, friendly pupils and helpful staff. Bleak, utilitarian brick buildings softened by shrubs and trees; new Stewart building houses sixth form centre and Roebuck café.

Junior school in green and tranquil setting on the edge of the main school; new buildings are shooting up so the school can now accommodate three classes across the age groups.

Pastoral care, well-being and discipline: Pastoral care continues to be excellent and very much part of the school's ethos. Well-established house system in senior school; everyone attends regular house tutor meetings; years 8-11 are in vertical age groups, sixth formers and year 7s in separate groups. There are lots of opportunities for leadership and mentoring within the house system to help pupils develop maturity, gain confidence and a range of life skills. Frequent house activities and competitions ensure everybody is involved in the school community. School nurse and independent counsellor. Parents say home-school links are encouraged and the head of pastoral care is always available to speak with them. One commented that pastoral staff have done well in creating a supportive and caring atmosphere. Pupils seem thoughtful and considerate to others, older pupils particularly good at mentoring younger ones. 'A very caring school, where the teachers recognise every child as an individual.'

Pupils and parents: Mainly professional types from Blackheath, Lewisham, Lee and more recently other areas accessible via train links. Head is keen to recruit from as varied a pool as possible, so a lot of effort is made to encourage children from state primaries as well as independents to apply. Big old boys' and girls' society runs a number of activities and fundraising events. Everyone is invited to the annual service in memory of the founder Rev Colfe. A good all-rounder school producing an interesting range of pupils going into many different careers. Alumni list reflects the school's diverse range: Eric Ambler, author, Lord Vaizey, economist Kenneth Grayson, first professor of theology at Bristol University, to name but a few; also actors, musicians, politicians and sportspeople.

Entrance: Most join juniors at 3+ or 4+ via information observation morning. Year 3 no longer a main point of entry; assessment for occasional places further up the school. At 11+ interview, reference from current school and exams in maths and English. Sixth formers are offered places on the basis of an interview, reference and predicted GCSE grades.

Exit: At 11+ about 80-90 per cent move into the senior school; a few opt for local state grammars. Around 10-20 per cent leaves at 16+ for sixth form colleges. At 18+ to huge a range of different universities (majority Russell Group), including two to Oxbridge and six medics in 2016.

Money matters: At 11+ and 16+ scholarships and means-tested bursaries are available for drama, art, sports, music and academics. Around 20 to 30 per cent of pupils receive some form of fee subsidy.

Remarks: Pleasant, relaxed atmosphere. Provides a high standard of education without being overly competitive. Its focus on individual successes and promoting a balanced approach to life and learning is not to be underestimated in today's hectic world.

C

Collège Française Bilingue de Londres

87 Holmes Road, London NW5 3AX

Pupils: 695 • Ages: 5-15

Fees: £8,339 – £9,215 pa

Tel: 020 7993 7400
Email: info@cfbl.org.uk
Website: www.cfbl.org.uk/en

Headteacher: Since 2011, François-Xavier Gabet (50s). He has degrees from University of Lille – in teaching French and French as a second language. Has taught in French schools in France, Saudi Arabia, USA and Australia and was a French language adviser to the US state of Louisiana. Set up the first bilingual French/English school in Melbourne (while also teaching at Monash University).

He was the ideal founding head for this newish London school and arrived a year before it opened – to plan every facet. Despite his traditional website photo, when we met him he was fashionably turned out in jeans, turtleneck jumper and blazer – looking more like a high-tech dot-com CEO on London's Silicone Roundabout than what one might expect for the head of a prestigious French school.

Steeped in the high standards associated with French educational tradition, he is refreshingly internationally-minded and aims to help his multilingual students recognise the advantages of being part of a global network of schools. While well aware of the rigorous demands of the French system, he asks teachers to be flexible, creative and generous in their approach. He cares about the school's relations with the local Kentish Town community (he does not want CFBL to be a 'French bubble') and works closely with the board (whom he describes as 'capable, professionally-accomplished and yet humble') to find ways to improve this full-to-capacity school.

Fit, energetic and quite the coolest head this Good Schools Guide editor has met, he is married with a daughter at university in Belgium and a son in secondary school.

Head of primary: is David Gassian, and Cerian Maraviglia is the deputy head of primary.

Academic matters: The French primary model has two divisions – maternelle (reception and year 1) and primaire (years 2 to 6). At the junior section of the CFBL 50 per cent of children have French and English language instruction and 50 per cent follow the French national curriculum. Half the staff are UK qualified and half are French. The teachers are timetabled in such a way that when classes are being taught by French teachers, the English-speaking staff are freed up to support students whose English language skills need bolstering and to ensure that English literacy standards are of a high level.

There are two forms of 25 students each for the youngest classes, 30 per class from the age of 7+. Classes are of mixed ability but the combination of French and English teachers means that they are able to differentiate the curriculum. English and French as a foreign language taught up to four times per week. Other specialists include teachers of PE, music and ICT (interactive whiteboards in all classrooms), while the bilingual French librarian works closely with the teachers in developing the literacy scheme and creating class libraries.

The French secondary model has two divisions – collège (years 7 to 10) and lycée (years 11 to 13). CFBL offers the collège division, following on from the school's primary section. According to the new norms of the French educational system, all students in secondary school will be taught English for five hours a week and will begin a third language (German or Spanish) in year 11. They are also taught music, sport, IT and art in English.

Students (already working in French and English) have the option to join the International section of the DNB (Diplôme National du Brevet) where 45 per cent of the curriculum is delivered in English, preparing them nicely for the new international diploma (DNBI). They are taught history and geography two hours a week in English.

Parents have mixed views – some feel the bilingual programme gives their (French-speaking) children lots of good exposure and immersion in English while others say the level of English is not as challenging as they'd like and that it's essentially French with a few English classes. Bilingual school models are never straightforward, with different perceptions about what exactly it means. IT is taught weekly – some parents would like to see a bit more, but concede that with the extra time already devoted to languages, this would be challenging.

The pupils work long hours (approximately 30 hours per week) – the additional English language means more hours than usual – so parents should be clear on this before they enrol their children. This is in addition to the homework load. The French educational system is regarded as one of the best in the world and academic standards are not an issue here. It's deciding if you want to do this with the added challenge of a bilingual or trilingual programme.

No specialist SEN support but class teachers are able to provide some support and there is a part-time educational psychologist too. Parents pay for diagnostic testing. A speech therapist is available.

Games, options, the arts: Though extracurricular activities don't traditionally loom large on the French educational landscape, they do make a great effort at CFBL. More sports on tap here than is the norm for French schools – the football team practises locally and took part in an international tournament. Netball is popular with girls. The school is working on launching a choir and developing interest in instrumental music activities. Sixième students (first year secondary) go on a residential trip with outdoor pursuits activities aimed at integrating new students and team building.

CFBL has an exchange programme with schools in Uruguay, Valence and Berlin for students studying Spanish or German, and strong links with a school in Spain. Mandarin club recently introduced. The head hopes that these experiences will help students and parents value the importance of learning languages and about other cultures.

Background and atmosphere: The Collège Français Bilingue de Londres was born out of a previous French ambassador's call for increased capacity to meet the growing demand for French education in London. With funding from the French government and from French companies (we're guessing banks and perhaps Eurostar, whose London base is conveniently nearby), who formed a charity to acquire the school property, the school's mission is to offer a French curriculum in a bilingual context to 700 students. The school was at one time known as L'Île aux Enfants and located in a nearby building that now houses Le Petite École, a feeder primary school.

Housed in a Victorian school building in Kentish Town. The head is aware of the impact that the mass arrival of a French community in the heart of this traditionally working-class area of north London has had and is working to win over the hearts and minds of locals. Most families living in the area were attracted to the Victorian terraced properties and the 'gentrification' of the area is thought to be partly thanks to the school (as well, of course, as the long-standing local Camden School for Girls). Part of the neighbourhood charm offensive was the introduction of French language classes for the local community.

The school backs on to some picturesque residential streets, though it fronts onto a street that is less so, and a bit of planting and tidying of the outside pavements and garden patches would improve the first impression. Step inside, however, and it's another story. The refurbishment is brilliant, taking full advantage of the Victorian features, with high ceilings, large windows drawing in masses of light, brick and glazed tile walls and parquet wooden floors, while incorporating modern touches. The upper school library – with high ceilings and huge windows – is fully equipped with impressive French and English collections, loads of computers and armchairs. Cosy primary library in its own little building on the playground – most of the resources are French, although they are developing the English language collection.

A small portion of the central playground has been forfeited to create a bright and airy cafeteria. Lunches compulsory, with meat and fish served daily and vegetarian options available for those observing kosher or halal diets.

The school has recently acquired an outdoor space a five-minute walk away. This will feature a massive inflatable structure for sports and other activities and will be available to the local community too.

Part of the AEFE (Agency for Teaching of French Education Abroad), CFBL is one of an international network of schools directed by the French ministry of education. The school is managed by a 12-member board – six representing the companies that helped fund the acquisition of the building and six elected by the parents. Its goals are to provide continuity of education to the French expat community in London, but also to prepare students to go to the best French universities. In fact 80 per cent of students who graduate from the Lycée Charles de Gaulle head to British or US universities. The head feels that the internationally-minded, multi-lingual emphasis of the school serves to provide good preparation for these options later on.

Pastoral care, well-being and discipline: Parents are very pleased with the school, many jumping through hoops to secure places. A parent of a child with SEN described it as particularly caring and attentive to her child. Classes are smaller than most French schools – a maximum of 30 in a class, with a two or three form intake. Discipline is not a worry for parents – one parent speculated that the presence of more UK-trained teachers (there to deliver the bilingual programme) strengthens the pastoral care perspective of the teaching faculty (not always as high on the French teachers' radar). The school runs careers counselling through a jobs forum that parents help to organise. The school employs a full time nurse as well as a part time speech therapist and child psychologist.

Pupils and parents: The community is a blend of expat corporate types on international assignments and more permanent French families who have found themselves in London for other reasons, including entrepreneurs, local business owners and French nationals whose marriages have created bi-cultural families. Parents suggest that the socio-economic atmosphere at CFBL is less 'rarified' than one finds in the more salubrious environs of the Lycée Charles de Gaulle in South Ken. While some end up at CFBL by default (no room at the Lycée), others prefer this school. The size is another factor – even with its capacity of 700, it is much smaller than the Lycée. French families who find the Eurostar terminal at St Pancras convenient are increasingly moving into neighbourhoods that are handy for the train journey through the tunnel to France and for the school.

The community is about two-thirds French. Some parents feel the school is less international than they would like, while others who come from France find it very international by comparison. There is obviously an underlying French cultural and educational foundation, but it seems that with a school community consisting of many dual national families, they seek to honour all cultures and traditions. Parents are happy that the children integrate easily, although some say teachers don't make as much of this diversity as they might. A parents' association provides lots of volunteer opportunities for those who want to get involved.

Entrance: Due to the recent opening of new French schools in London, not as oversubscribed as previously. We hear that a maximum of 30 per cent of the places are allocated to children whose parents work for the consortium of French companies that helped to secure the school building. The list of partner companies is available for inspection if required.

Admissions priorities are: siblings (both primary and secondary), children from another official French school (local or abroad), including students following the CNED (the French distance-learning programme), then any miscellany of Francophones fortunate enough to get in. It seems there are some last minute surprises. The nearby La Petite École is a popular feeder, while others opt for local British independent schools while they wait for the coveted place at CFBL.

Exit: Some expat families move abroad and continue their education in the French system. Others, finding the fees an issue (though remarkably good value when compared to most London independent schools), enter local state schools. Students who are less confident about their French language skills may leave after quatrième to do GCSEs in the local British sector, although the English section at the Lycée Charles de Gaulle is an option for them. Most of the students head to the new Lycée International Winston Churchill in Wembley to enter their baccalauréat programme.

Money matters: The fees at CFBL are reasonable by London independent school standards (although CFBL fees are marginally higher than the Lycée Charles de Gaulle). As a charity, school engages in some fundraising activity – such as its annual gala event.

Remarks: An interesting school that embodies all of the academic rigour associated with the French tradition, but with a strong emphasis on languages and English. A sparkling little gem in the heart of Kentish Town, it is a bilingual environment with a truly international mindset.

Collingham

23 Collingham Gardens, London SW5 0HL

Pupils: 210 • Ages: 14–20 • Sixth form: 190

Fees: £7,200 – £20,700 pa

Tel: 020 7244 7414
Email: london@collingham.co.uk
Website: www.collingham.co.uk

Principal: Since 2012, Dr Sally Powell, BA PGCE MPhil DPhil (Oxon). Degree in English literature from Royal Holloway, London. Masters and doctorate in Victorian Literature. Teaches English literature A level for four hours a week and tends to

C

take the fast track group. Still passionate about teaching. 'It would be a deal breaker for me if I had to come out of the classroom,' she states. Enjoys gothic revival novels and is a huge Brontë fan. 'If I can teach Wuthering Heights then I normally do.' Has been here for 15 years, previously as vice principal and deputy principal. Over 20 other members of staff have also been here more than a decade. 'I'm the new girl!' she jokes. Loves theatre and art and often accompanies school trips to plays and exhibitions. One teenage daughter who is destined to come here for her A levels. 'She would come here now if I would let her!' she says. Warm, enthusiastic and welcoming.

Parents like the fact that head knows every pupil by name as well as their background. They describe her as 'easy to talk to,' 'kind' and 'wonderful – she champions the children.' Nobody we spoke to had anything but praise for her.

James Allder BA is the deputy and also teaches geography. Very knowledgeable about the school. They make a good team.

Academic matters: In 2016, 24 per cent of A level grades were A*/A and 52 per cent were A*/B; 33 per cent of I/GCSE grades were A*/A. A good mix of academic and vocational courses offered at A level with maths, business studies and economics currently popular. A staggering 25 subjects possible at GCSE, including Arabic, classical Greek and photography as well as the predictable mainstream subjects. Pupils generally take eight or nine GCSEs. Rare for pupils to come here to retake GCSEs – pupils tend to take them all here over the full two years, starting in year 10.

Pupils can either take A levels over two years or opt for the more intensive one-year course. For fluent French speakers, a dedicated A level class is laid on so they can complete the course at speed. No restrictions in terms of subject combinations, however unconventional. 'It is entirely bespoke.' Head feels that strongest departments currently are English, economics and chemistry but also singled out art as being extraordinary.

Revision A level and GCSE classes also offered at Easter (three weeks) and Christmas (three days), with intense practice of exam-style questions. Open to in-house pupils as well as those at other schools. Small groups guaranteed. Just the ticket if your offspring needs structured handholding in the exam run up. Head says it is a great way to recruit future pupils. Once they see what is on offer, many are keen to jump ship. Some 11+ and CE tuition also offered in the holidays and after school.

International students, though a tiny minority, have mandatory English classes for eight hours per week. All these students are prepared for IELTS test, a requirement for study at British universities. Where necessary, extra support is available either in groups or one-to-one. Many non-native speakers are timetabled to take classes in art, photography or PE in which they can work alongside fluent students and improve their language skills.

One of the college's main selling points is the small classes, with a maximum of nine pupils at GCSE and eight at A level. 'A luxurious way to learn and a luxurious way to teach,' says head. School bends over backwards to put on whatever class is requested, even if only one pupil is taking the subject, eg Japanese. Masses of individual attention. Mixed ability classes: some are highly academic, others distinctly less so.

About 20 per cent currently has some form of SEN – overwhelmingly mild dyslexia, dyspraxia or slow processing. College has taken high functioning autistic students in the past but you have to be pretty independent to thrive here, so not the place for someone at the severe end of the spectrum. SENDCo offers learning support on individual basis. Weekly study skills workshops put on for all pupils with topics ranging from how to organise one's files to how to take notes and how to memorise material. Pupils also offered one-to-one support from teachers, at an extra cost, either for a short boost on tricky topics or longer term help. For example, if you are dead keen to do economics but your maths is not quite up to scratch, you can have individual tuition with the economics teacher in school to get you up to speed. Parents welcome this in-house support rather than having to find an external tutor.

Many teachers here are academics, often with doctorates, and love the intellectual life. 'That is what makes our A level teaching so very strong.' College shares some teachers with Imperial, a stone's throw away. Deputy explains that 'the flexibility of our timetable means some teachers are part time and many of them do something else as well as teaching here. Both art teachers, for example, are professional artists. That gives a real depth and breadth to their knowledge. Lots of the maths department are musicians too.' One parent we spoke to commented that the majority of teachers are inspirational, though possibly not all.

Head is excited about the newly launched 'electus programme' which aims to stretch the most able. The bright sparks selected take additional classes, go on visits and write a dissertation over the summer holidays, similar to the EPQ. It is intended to be an opportunity to explore cross-curricular themes and provide something to talk about in their personal statement. Head is convinced there are more opportunities for able students here than at larger schools.

Games, options, the arts: Extracurricular provision limited. Pupils who are talented musicians or on the sports field tend to pursue these passions externally. 'By the time you are 16 or 17, you know what you are interested in. They are in London, so they can find a place where they can do whatever they want. We have students who are top end ballet dancers, tennis players, skiers or violinists and the school fits in around their lives and schedules. It is a different type of schooling,' explains head. One mother we spoke to felt many of the pupils here are not the sort who care much about making a sports team or school orchestra anyway. 'Collingham does not attract many of those types,' she said.

Two hours of sport per week for GCSE pupils, mostly football in Kensington Gardens, plus tennis and rounders. In the sixth form, students can choose between football and yoga. 'We play in a small inter-college football league but we are not particularly good,' confesses deputy. 'Definitely not a sporty school. Quite the opposite,' said one parent. Annual music concert is run by the students and includes varied performances from rap and computer generated music to drama and poetry recitals. 'We've seen it all. It's an open stage', and is apparently great fun. Everyone is encouraged to take part and money raised goes to charity.

High standard of art displayed on the walls around the school, despite the small size of the studio. Photography is popular and school has its own dark room. Pupils have had work exhibited at Royal College of Art competitions. Parents feel able artists thrive here. No drama performances at all. 'Not the school for you if you are looking to take part in musicals like Seven Brides for Seven Brothers or Oklahoma!' jokes head. LAMDA exams can be taken by those with a dramatic bent.

Plenty of trips and outings arranged including to Houses of Parliament, law courts and recording studios. Teachers are encouraged to get the pupils out and about as much as possible to support the curriculum, whether to attend lectures, visit exhibitions or see plays. Residential trips to Paris, Amsterdam and Florence as well as ski-ing in the Alps and walking trips to Snowdonia for the more energetic. A level pupils and GCSE pupils come together for these, which helps to foster a feeling of community which could otherwise be lacking. Activities week includes a charity walk, art and drama workshops and work experience. Everyone must get involved in some capacity, even if they are reluctant to travel too far afield.

Background and atmosphere: Founded in 1975 as Collingham Tutors. Based on two sites, half a mile apart, one for GCSE students and the other for A levels. GCSE pupils come over to use the two labs, the art studio and to study Spanish in particular. The building in Collingham Gardens was previously Gibbs' Prep School where Prince Edward was educated, and before that was a magnificent terraced home, with servants' quarters up at the top. Though the vast drawing room on the first floor has been transformed into a study room/exam hall, it has retained it grandeur. The whole building still feels like a home, with its thick carpets and ornate mirrors.

Pupils tend to get on well as a group. One parent we spoke to felt the distinct 'lack of nastiness and cliques' was refreshing. 'They are quite a sophisticated bunch, though.' A level pupils are free to come and go during the day, as long as they are back for their lessons. Supervised study periods between classes for first year of sixth form, so there is a little more structure and less to-ing and fro-ing than one might expect. GCSE students need to be in school all day other than lunchtime, when they can go off site, as there is no outdoor space. Most are thrilled to be able to enjoy the delights of the Gloucester Road in the middle of the day. Many lunch at cafés in the 'French quarter' in South Ken, though it has been known for pupils to head to McDonald's. 'They are generally far too cool to bring in a packed lunch!' laughed one mother.

School is good at celebrating achievement. A board of 'high fliers' is in pride of place in the entrance hall with their photos, grades and university places for all to see. Acts as a spur to the current students to try to get themselves onto the board in due course.

Pastoral care, well-being and discipline: Excellent. Lots of individual care offered. Everyone has a personal tutor who regularly meets with them on a one-to-one basis to discuss both performance and well-being. Half-termly target setting and termly parent meetings. Given the size of the school, anyone who is struggling is picked up at lightning speed.

Zero tolerance of drugs, alcohol or bullying. On the day we visited, there was a group of pupils standing across the street, cigarettes in hands. Though not ideal, head would rather that staff can see what is going on and who is out there than have them skulking down back streets. College will not accept any behaviour that will disrupt classes, though this is rare. 'There are very few opportunities for disruption, but young people are young people and they can make wrong choices from time to time..'concedes head. Pupils wear their own clothes and the dress code is 'informal but respectful.' Pupils are sent home for inappropriate attire. No hats or hoodies inside. 'There is a university-like feel to the place and most students rise to that challenge.' School occasionally needs to have a conversation with a pupil about garish hair but tends not to over-react if it is subtle. 'The worst thing for a student is for me to like it!' jokes the head. 'Essentially, it is an elegant building and we expect people to behave in an elegant fashion.'

Some pupils who come here have had a fractured school history, possibly because parents have moved around or because they have experienced bullying. Some have just fallen under the radar in bigger, more conventional schools and crave a fresh start. There is certainly a band of more fragile students. One mother commented, 'It is wonderful there is a school like Collingham to scoop up these children who have lost their way elsewhere. Once they get here, they can finally breathe again.' Another said the school had been wonderful with their child's depression and never judged her. 'Everything at the school was fitted in around her recovery.' In-house counsellor on hand to help with issues such as self-harming and depression.

Small, manned café in basement, open from early morning to evening serving main meals and snacks. You could eat all your meals down there. 'Sometimes I do!' quips deputy. All freshly cooked, made to order. Those with eating disorders can be monitored in a subtle way by the lovely cook. 'As a community, we are quick to pick up on what is going on'. Everyone seems to be looking out for everyone here.

Very rare to be expelled. 'If a child is getting the tone wrong then we are there to support them. We help them to develop those social skills.' Deputy explains, 'We will give them a second chance but not necessarily a third, fourth of fifth chance..'

Small classes help with low self-esteem. One mother commented that her two children have been transformed by coming here. 'Within six weeks they have become totally different children. I cannot praise the school enough for this.'

Pupils and parents: Over 95 per cent are UK students though the college is strikingly cosmopolitan with a diverse range of parental backgrounds. Ninety per cent of pupils speak English at home and five per cent speak French. Over half of pupils come from London and home counties day schools with another 20 per cent from British boarding schools. Steady flow of pupils from neighbouring Lycée, keen to have a more intimate school with a less didactic style of teaching. Others from eg Dulwich College, Eton, Westminster, St Paul's Girls' and Boys' and neighbouring Queen's Gate as well as boarding schools such as Bryanston and King's Canterbury.

Mostly affluent, dual-income professional families. Many from creative backgrounds, particularly the media. One mother commented that some pupils are very spoilt, though there are others from more modest backgrounds.

Good communication between the school and parents. 'Much more than you would find in other schools,' states head. Parents feel they are kept fully informed and that anxieties and concerns are acted upon. Head believes parents discuss matters freely with the school partly because 'there is no long gravel drive to navigate. We are much more open house. They come in off the pavement, straight into the hall and my office is just there.' Certainly not an intimidating school. Head says parents tend to be 'warm and lovely'.

Notable former pupils include actress Minnie Driver, author Paula Hawkins and assorted members of the Jagger clan.

Entrance: No open days. The vast majority comes through word of mouth. Prospective A level and GCSE pupils are interviewed individually by principal or director of studies, and must also provide a satisfactory school reference. Every student is considered on a case by case basis. 'We spend well over an hour interviewing a pupil with their family. We really try to get to know the family dynamics. We want to know how supportive they are going to be – that is important to us'. School would never take a pupil who had been expelled from their previous school for drugs because 'the parents who are sending their children to Collingham are sending them here in good faith that we are policing and monitoring, as best we can, our students' behaviour. We are not in the business of taking other people's problems'. Head admits it can be heart-breaking because they may have just made a silly mistake. 'They may be a delightful student from a delightful family but regrettably that is our policy'. She has a box of tissues at the ready in her office for inevitable tears which are shed when pupils are turned down or when parents and children talk about difficulties they have encountered at their previous schools.

Normally, 10 new students join year 10 and 20 join year 11. Entry is also possible throughout the academic year. Around 60 per cent of the GCSE pupils continue into the sixth form provided they have a minimum of five GCSEs at C grade or above. Those wishing to take maths or a science need a minimum of B grade in that subject at GCSE. Normally around 60 students enter the school for the first year of sixth form, with year 13 entry taking on an additional 10 A level pupils and 20 one-year pupils.

Exit: Those who leave post-GCSE tend to go to state sixth forms. Some return within weeks, as they realise it can be better to be a big fish in a small pond.

Most sixth formers head to university, many inevitably to London. Bristol, Leeds and Oxford Brookes also currently popular. Pupils select a range of courses including engineering, history and English. The more artistic tend to opt for art foundation courses at eg Central St Martins.

Some parents think it is 'Oxbridge or nothing' and Collingham feels it is key to manage parents' expectations. Oxbridge preparation includes extension classes and help with entrance exams. Mock interviews set up with experienced retired teachers so pupils have practice in being grilled by a stranger. One or two fallow years in terms of Oxbridge successes but some years there are three or four places. On average, one or two.

Money matters: Fees depend upon numbers of subjects being taken, length of course and whether full or part time. 'We try to keep fees as manageable as possible and we offer multi payments.' High performing students from state sector are sometimes awarded a means-tested bursary, to a maximum 30 per cent reduction in fees.

Remarks: Head explains, 'We are the last, or one of the last, domestic-orientated sixth form colleges in London. The others are very international. We have carved out a niche for ourselves that we are jealously guarding.' Parents and pupils rave about the friendly, supportive environment here and feel cherished in this intimate environment.

Coloma Convent Girls' School

Upper Shirley Road, Croydon, Surrey CR9 5AS

Pupils: 1,075 • Ages: 11–18 • Sixth form: 340 • RC

Tel: 020 8654 6228
Email: webadmin@coloma.croydon.sch.uk
Website: www.coloma.croydon.sch.uk

Headteacher: Since 1995, Mrs Maureen Martin. Won't be pinned down on precise career dates or age ('you can say "very experienced",' she says) while mention of the r(*tir*ment)-word strictly off limits.

A Coloma old girl, went on to take degree in economics (Bristol) and PGCE (London) with religious specialism (enhanced with her own extensive private studies) – perfect combination for cash-strapped faith school; counselling training (through church) a boon in honing skills in sensitive questioning.

When her husband's work with British Council – he is now head of physics here – took the couple overseas, Mrs Martin worked at schools in Uganda, Tanzania, India (where had first headship in a primary school), Mexico, and Malaysia, interspersed with short term teaching posts in the UK, also raising four children, now grown up. Was snapped up here and the rest is history (with slug of glorious future still to come).

Charismatic and with great presence, Mrs Martin is a high-vis head who leads, emphatically, from the front. If you didn't know who was in charge, stamp of authority on visitor notices that bear her name would soon put you right. Post is 'greatest privilege I could hope for,' she says – though delighted by award of OBE that staff and parents feel was long overdue.

She's universally rated as wonderful. Pupils are in awe ('in a good way,' thought mother) but Mrs Martin knows her girls and those we met in her office, after a spot of reassurance that weren't in trouble, were relaxed, chatty and articulate.

Tribute to strength as effective leader that everything runs smoothly when she's out helping struggling schools nearby – two in the Coloma Trust, plus ad hoc support for local primary, all going great guns.

Works incredibly hard to make it all happen and spare time inevitably limited. With interests ranging from sport to the United Nations, Catholic Church to humanism and the arts, reliant on reviews for cultural updates. Emphatically no complaints – it's her choice, she says.

Faith informs everything she does and the mind-boggling opportunities, academic and otherwise, offered here are all about making words in Lord's Prayer – 'your kingdom come ... on earth...' a reality. No wonder that even heads from well-heeled independents are known to marvel.

Academic matters: Consistently one of top comprehensives in the country for results and progress, achieved through blend of top teaching, forensic (and largely behind the scenes) analysis and, school's secret ingredient, exceptional choice for pupils. Everyone, high achiever or otherwise, can opt for subjects that they enjoy and thus will excel at. 'I've got way too many favourite lessons,' enthused year 10 pupil.

GCSEs for all in English language and literature plus maths, science, RS, a language and humanity. But it's the options list that's a thing of beauty – offered within the timetable where possible (art and design, business and communication and DT) and as twilight club if not (PE and Spanish) with music featuring on both lists to ensure enthusiasts don't miss out because of a subject clash.

With 86 per cent achieving five GCSEs including English and maths in 2016, 40 per cent at A*/A, immediate benefits obvious, breadth enabling vast majority to gain at least one A grade. 'Even weakest can be strong in some subjects,' says Mrs Martin. Pupils agree. 'Made me realise that I could push myself and my capabilities here,' said one.

At A level, with 67 per cent of grades at A*/B (32 per cent A*-A) in 2016, more of the same, with girls listing their dream subject combination (30 to choose from) and school (assuming large enough group to make finances and logistics work), making it happen – timetabling a marvel of ingenuity. Many complete four A levels and a handful do five, everyone taking PE, PSHE and religious studies on top. Firm emphasis on facilitating subjects with several nods to wider range of interests including health and social care and DT. No BTecs – money the major factor, though in ideal world, would offer both. No IB either – current system felt to offer breadth and to spare, grateful medics recently coming back to extol joys of leavening sciences with arts or a language.

Minimal setting and none in year 7 – avoids any sense of being programmed for failure. 'Spend the first year sussing out where they need to develop,' said parent. Class sizes sound big – maximum of 30 for first three years, 24 in years 10 and 11 and 14 in the sixth form (17.5 pupil to teacher ratio overall) but often far smaller, stresses school.

No resting on laurels. Even quiz former pupils on what could be improved – uni-standard referencing techniques, for example, recently added to sixth form curriculum. Strong staff team of just under 80 includes half a dozen or so former pupils influenced by strong desire to 'return the favour', as a parent put it, devotion to duty likely to be stand-out quality in application letters. Morale is high with happy blend of newcomers and long termers (23 have been here for decade or more), school a pioneer of in-service training and keen to welcome in new ideas.

Organisation is straightforward. Teachers teach, senior management manage, helped by data crunched anyway you want it, courtesy of resident expert. No decline too small to pinpoint or too difficult to reverse. Masses of lesson observations, positive reviews – what worked well, what could have worked even better – deliberate avoidance of corporate blame game and focus on collaboration emphasised by titles – team leaders rather than heads of department.

Girls, similarly, encouraged to put in the effort – long-ish school day can end at 5.00pm or later – but never to feel that 'school is continuously holding them to account,' says Mrs Martin. Take learning needs in their stride (just over 100 pupils with SEN, five statemented and 110 with EAL requirements), working with primary schools to ensure smooth transition and offering range of support that includes one-to-one and in-class help.

Results in calm, low-pressure atmosphere though 'plenty of organised noise,' says teacher. Trust in the school required – difficulties may not be raised until parents' evening, and one mother felt more feedback during the year would be useful. Overall, approach felt to be on the button. 'Some of daughter's friends at other schools are always stressing,' thought parent. 'Here, they prepare them gently.'

Games, options, the arts: 'Gives the children all the opportunities,' said parent. Every day jam-packed with total fulfillment for arty, active or both – helped by flourishing parents' association that's stumped up for new laser cutter for DT department (works wonders on wood) and refurbishment of two grand pianos (the two aren't connected). Community the focus for fundraising, 100-strong charity committee choosing different cause each year as well as supporting linked school in Uganda. Run special charities week featuring talent show and daily cake sales (carrot a dominant and healthy ingredient, stresses Mrs Martin) but not allowed to spill into vital learning time.

Pupils are expected to make the most of activities – Mrs Martin stresses impact on outcomes – and most stick to termly pledge to try something new, 70 sixth formers, for example, turning up for optional netball club. Those who don't tend to change their minds pronto – 'got a bit boring when everybody was leaving for a choir competition or a match and I was just sitting there,' said one.

Trips, likewise, ranging from French and German exchange trips to netball tours (South African in 2016) hone practical and socialising skills, while annual visit to Lourdes can be life-changing. And so what if it's budget rather than de luxe version? Twenty-five hour coach journey for year 9 Austrian ski trip was 'nearly the best part,' said pupil. Even year 7s pack in Disneyland excursion, teachers still smiling at midnight, despite coach's cargo of 'grumpy girls burned out with far too many sweets,' said parent.

While parents rate every area as 'exceptional', music is perhaps most exceptional of the lot, recently acquired specialist music status merely official acknowledgement of the fact. Think not just big but bumper-sized, with eight choral groups and 500-strong main choir (all year 7 pupils expected to sign up for practical demonstration of virtues of cooperation, regardless of singing ability). Also two orchestras, numerous bands including – amazingly – a six-strong harp ensemble and over 300 individual weekly music lessons (French horn, bassoon – even double bass to grade 8). While already run 40 events each year (schedule is described with heartfelt sincerity as 'hectic' – audition-only St Cecilia Singers' triumph in national choral competition one of many successes), 'to do' list constantly being extended, multi-school youth music festival latest to be added.

Just as busy and successful on other fronts. Out of school hours, high-energy clubs range from CCF (run with Royal Russell, local independent school) to D of E, though plenty of others – including chess and prayer clubs – of a more cerebral nature.

Sports also described as 'exceptional', say parents (no surprise there), from range (orienteering, kickboxing and handball all on the menu) to successes. Recent Croydon champions for cross country (year 8/8 and 10/11), indoor cricket (U15 and U13), table tennis (U13 and U16) often moving on to success at county, regional level and sometimes national level. Lacrosse particularly noteworthy. School one of few (possibly only one) in state sector to offer it, yet regularly trounces independents like Brighton College.

Teamed with generous facilities (two gyms, all weather floodlit sports pitches, field and track in extensive grounds). If three 50-minute sessions for first two years (two in year 9 and one in years 10-12) aren't enough, umpteen ways of filling any spare gaps, like early morning fitness sessions for those who don't get their kicks (penalty or otherwise) from team sports. 'Stuff happens at lunchtime, before school, after school and at the weekend, I don't know how teachers have a family life, to be honest,' said parent.

Background and atmosphere: Everything derives from living the motto, 'labore est vocare' which is known and understood by all, each lesson starting with a prayer. Parents approve. 'It's a good grounding to think of others and have a bit of reflection, whatever your spiritual beliefs are,' thought one.

Upholds values of educationalist The Very Reverend Canon Van Crombrugghe, who founded the Congregation of the Daughters of Mary and Joseph in native Belgium in 1817 in premises owned by Count of Santa Coloma. Convent opened 1869 in Croydon, school followed two months later (with just one pupil), moving to current home (with rather more) in 1965. Links with order still close, sister ('young in spirit and delightful in every way,' says Mrs Martin) running repository. Josephite brothers, meanwhile, went on to found St George's College in Weybridge, relationship as cordial as distance between the schools will allow. Initially independent, school joined maintained sector as grammar, becoming a comprehensive in the 1970s and merging with sister school, St Anne's, which survived flying bombs (commemorated by touching stained glass panel in chapel entrance) but couldn't withstand vicissitudes of shifting educational policy.

Site is neat, tidy (beautifully clipped shrubbery lines attractive paths), survival of original Victorian buildings (coach house particularly pretty) and inevitable Portakabin presence offset by tactical use of trees. Giant specimen is framed dead centre, to magnificent effect, by picture window in vast, airy performing arts hall, one of many improvements and new builds that keep coming, courtesy of non-stop grant applications and budget-finessing. Others include an all-weather pitch, sixth form centre, after-school users radiating industry under its curved roof, as well as 50th anniversary Jubilee Building, home of 'brilliant' art and boasting eccentric but charming turret.

Some economising elsewhere, low tech computers lovingly maintained rather than cutting edge, lunches paid for with real money and non-flushing loos or wobbly chair legs logged by pupils and staff on paper slips. With funding for just one technician and small but dedicated maintenance team, staff and pupils expected to treat this like home from home only better (slightly exasperated note in staff loos impresses need to keep the bowls clean...).

Girls as spick and span as the premises, non-negotiable school uniform policy including compulsory white socks or tights for juniors (helps make them more visible to motorists). No makeup or body spray or 'unnatural hair colourings and letters home stress importance of retaining modesty, even on home clothes day. Goes down well with parents. 'Not appropriate to be flashing your cleavage when you're 15 and going on public transport,' said one.

C

C

Pastoral care, well-being and discipline: Structure ensures continuity, with form tutors normally unchanged through to GCSEs. Each year 7 and 8 form group also gets two sixth form prefects to help with settling in process. School stresses importance of self-motivation and personal responsibility, parents expected to ensure daughters' punctuality, arrange dentist appointments outside school hours and to avoid term time absences (requests need to be made at least a month in advance).

Sanctions and rewards as clearly worked out as you'd expect, commendations awarded for effort and attainment and teachers encouraged to 'catch pupils being good in order to find opportunities for praise and rewards.' Misconducts awarded for everything from using mobile phones in lessons (they're also banned on school trips) to failure to sign homework diaries. Escalation of reports; exclusion for most serious offences – though a vanishing rarity, with a strong emphasis on forgiveness. 'We all make mistakes and need to move on,' says Mrs Martin.

Friendship issues usually resolved, though long-term bullies would be asked to leave if didn't change their ways (and with serious incidents kept on file for six years, strong incentive for them to do so). Clearly works – almost unheard of for pupils to be asked to leave. Little details all taken care of, down to staff escorts out of school and on to local buses – 'don't have to do it but helps keep the girls safe,' says Mrs Martin. 'Really lovely,' says parent, while bus drivers comment on courteous behaviour (witnessed first hand when they stopped this reviewer leaving vital bag behind).

And sensitive support extends also to parents who report that if family crisis strikes, will be contacted by dedicated pastoral head to see how they're coping and offer a sympathetic ear.

Pupils and parents: Bright, motivated pupils will do well – rebels or late sleepers may find it harder, though 'wrong sort of rebellion is tamed,' reckons member of staff. Important, stress parents, to be realistic about school's expectations. 'Have to be in at 8.10am and factor in your journey – if that's difficult for you then this is not the school for you,' said one.

Depth of religion, too, needs to be thought through. 'Can't lag it,' stresses mother. While sex education is offered according to government guidelines, you're left in no doubt as to school's stance, say parents (marriage first). Mrs Martin, a strong believer in lifelong impact of quality of relationships (met own closest friend on first day here) delights in happy integration of pupils who span range of backgrounds and circumstances and develop streetwise (but sensible) nonchalance, heading off to shops or homes in Bromley, Coulsdon and Crystal Palace on public transport. More affluent learn to appreciate good fortune along the way. Daughter 'realises what she has is pretty damn good,' said parent. Locals connected with the school – one in eight of women in Croydon, it estimates – feel the same way. 'I do as much as I can to support them,' said one former pupil.

Tend to live long and prosper – one recently made it to ripe old age of 107 and like pupils, have plenty of opportunities to be involved, from joining choir directed by retired head of music to helping organise events – harder if live further away but usually plenty of volunteers and warm welcome for all. 'Can turn up and go to anything on your own – not cliquey at all,' said parent.

Entrance: Five form entry – total of 150 in year 7. Applications from families from other faiths (number 7 on admissions criteria) or none (number 8) in theory welcome, but vanishingly unlikely to translate into offer of a place given 700 applications each year and 450 or so Catholic families ahead of you in the queue, though Mrs Martin never takes popularity for granted. 'We welcome everybody,' she says.

Early and whole-hearted commitment to Catholicism is required and attendance at mass, baptismal age and first communion will all need verification. Ever-shrinking home to school distance the tie breaker.

Around 30 per cent of sixth form from other schools, when faith criteria no longer apply. Minimum six GCSE passes with four B grades (Eng Lang and Lit count as one) required. Need to be on your toes as school barely advertises the fact – prefers those already in the know.

Exit: Lose around 40 post GCSE to co-ed sixth forms, mostly those taking vocational subjects and a few with longest journey time opting for an easier commute. Over 90 per cent of 2016 leavers either to university or art foundation courses, 40 per cent Russell Group. Five to medicine-related courses, one veterinary medicine, all sciences well represented though wide range also includes English, psychology and law.

Good Oxbridge record with some pupils most years (though none in 2016). Lead up to applications process predictably thorough with own, qualified careers advisor (a rarity), highly detailed website content and early planning – pupils in year 8 play interactive games that match interest with possible careers.

Money matters: Some funding for residential trips for parents on benefits.

Remarks: Awe-inspiring in every direction, bulging with extras despite limited funding. 'The school is like a clock tower: you need to make all the cogs work together,' said pupil. Swimming pool would do wonders for the mechanism. Caring hedge fund managers should apply direct to Mrs Martin.

Colville Primary School

Lonsdale Road, Portobello Road, London W11 2DF

Pupils: 392 • Ages: 3–11

Tel: 020 7229 6540
Email: info@colville.rbkc.sch.uk
Website: www.colville.rbkc.sch.uk

Head: Since 2011, Jagdeep Birdi BA QTS (40s). Studied history, English and education at Lancaster, then headed for the Big Smoke, where he has since taught across five different London boroughs. For the 11 years before he joined Colville, he was deputy head at Ronald Ross, Wimbledon, then at Sir John Lillie, Fulham.

Despite the school leaping from its place in the bottom 200 schools in the country to one of the top 200 since he joined, he's not one to wax lyrical about vision, strategy and grand plans. Not for him the stereotypical headteacher mini-speech packed with well-practised bullet points of what makes the school, and him, great. In fact, this modest, mild-mannered man even struggled to answer our questions about what it is that makes the school stand out, although you don't have to talk to him for long before his passion and dedication for both education and this school reveal themselves. It is this heartfelt, unaffected and laid-back attitude – in which aspiring for the best is seen as the most natural thing in the world – that staff say sums up his leadership style. This style, they told us, makes him approachable, collaborative and empowering and is ultimately responsible for him having made such a difference here, turning the school into one that attracts and retains excellent teaching staff and causes kids to treat the school's core values of respect, aspiration and perseverance as instinctive. It can be no coincidence that the amount of private donations have shot up under his headship – reaching over £100,000 in the last four years alone – which have led to huge improvements in three key areas: the physical environment of the school, the number of teaching staff (35) and the numer of extracurricular clubs (42).

Kids – of whom there are 400 (set to rise to 500 as the current 'bulge years' are officially replaced by double intake years) – feel they can chat informally to him too and do exactly that at lunchtimes, which he joins them daily to eat, while both children and parents are greeted by him at the gate every morning and afternoon. 'I know every parent and I know every child,' he says, again in a tone that suggests this is completely normal. 'His natural manner is to make us feel as if we're an important part of the school – that our views about the school matter as much as the teachers,' said one parent. Another told us, 'If you raise something with him as being in need of change, he will go ahead and make the change or give you a very good reason why he can't. I don't think you could find a more accommodating head.'

His first-floor office – a Big Brother set-up, with floor-to-ceiling glass overlooking the key stage one area of the school – seems an unlikely choice for such an unassuming leader. Until, that is, staff explain that actually, it means they can see when he's free to talk to and, perhaps more crucially, it places him firmly at the heart of the school rather than being hidden away in some corner office.

Entrance: After the customary priority for looked-after children and those with special needs, siblings are next on the list. Then it's down to distance, which currently stretches to 0.45 miles, although this is rapidly shrinking as news of the school's improvements spreads. Indeed, there are now over 200 applications for the 60 reception places. Even if families move to another part of London, they tend to stay, with some children coming from as far as Hackney and the far side of Barking. Cohort is truly ethnically diverse, with a whopping 46 languages spoken and no dominant group among them (even the most common language spoken apart from English only has 18 speakers). Refreshingly, the fact that 62 per cent of pupils come in speaking English as a second language is considered a bonus, not a drawback. 'These children know how to acquire a language – that's a good thing,' says the head, adding that diversity is seen to enrich the school. Seventy per cent of pupils at the older end of the school are on free school meals, whilst that figure drops to just 10 per cent at the bottom end, telling you all you need to know about the change in reputation of the school.

Exit: The largest share – half the pupils – go to the local comprehensive of Holland Park, whist around a quarter go to Kensington Aldridge Academy. The rest go to a wide range of comprehensives right across London, with a handful per year group now moving into the independent sector.

Remarks: 'Let's not beat around the bush – this school used to be appalling when my child, who is now in year 6, joined,' said one parent. 'Colville was the school that nobody really wanted for their child and the one that poor low-income families got lumbered with,' reported another from the same year group. But in the last five years, standards of attainment achieved by the school have shot up, with Colville having received two ministerial congratulations in the last two years alone – and the parents, particularly those of the older kids, can't believe their luck.

'Teaching was poor,' acknowledges the head. 'The school wasn't in a good place.' So what happened to all those substandard teaching staff? "A number of teachers chose to leave during my first few months,' smiles the head. 'Now we get top-notch teaching staff coming in and the teaching is rigorous, particularly in maths and English,' he says, adding that the school has specialist teachers for computing, games, art, music and French, all of whom teach from reception upwards. But it's not just the quality of the teaching staff – who we found to be successfully engaging children in every classroom we entered – that's noticeable here. It's the sheer number of them, with some classrooms we visited having four teaching staff for 24 children. Refreshingly, many are male and most of the teaching assistants are graduates. Even when these classes reach the 30 mark, it will be an impressive adult-to-child ratio and it clearly makes a difference. Indeed, we watched staff working their way round the classroom, making sure that every child understood exactly what was being taught and helping them with the nuances of their learning so that nobody is left behind.

The extra adult bods in classrooms also means there's more room for learning-through-doing. In fact, we didn't see one instance of chalk-and-talk during our visit, but instead clusters of desks in which small groups of children, helped by adults, worked together interactively to put the teacher's words into practice, often in fun and innovative ways. And before you wonder if all that makes for a chaotic and noisy learning environment, it doesn't. There is a noticeable sense of calm and purpose throughout this school.

Except, that is, at break time, which takes place in the reasonably sized tarmacked playground that takes up around half of the school's neat, rectangular plot that's tucked behind the fashionable Portobello Road and which is overlooked by high-rise flats and town houses. Playtime here does what it says on the tin, with raucous children running around loudly and happily and making full use of the new plush, large wooden climbing structures. There's also a school garden and separate edible garden (which, by the way, has links with Wholefoods in Notting Hill). Everyone seemed to be part of a group and we failed to spot one face that wasn't smiling. 'You don't get left out here because we have a playground buddy system,' one pupil told us. 'We once had an issue with another child upsetting ours, but the school put a stop to it immediately,' reported one parent, with others agreeing that any unkindness or friendship problems are generally nipped in the bud. A school survey, completed just prior to our visit, found that 99 per cent of children felt the school is a respectful environment, where are pupils are respected whatever their background.

Originally, the school opened in 1879 as Buckingham Terrace Primary, when six teachers – poor things – were charged with 550 pupils. During the WWII these pupils were evacuated and when they returned after the war in 1945, the school reopened as Colville Primary. The old laundry building (girls were taught laundry back in the day) has now been converted into a modern, welcoming space for reception, whilst another outdoor building, complete with glass roof both inside and out, is home to the nursery. The rest of the school is taught in the three-storey main building, where the (mainly) large classrooms boast high ceilings and such large windows that even with the blinds almost completely pulled down, the rooms ooze light. There are three school halls, one of which doubles up as the dining room – known as Le Bistro – where removable round tables are covered in red and white table cloths and even vases of flowers. 'We wanted to make it homely and the children love it,' a member of staff told us, although one pupil told us the one thing she'd change about the school is the food. That said, just 22 kids choose to bring in packed lunches.

The well-stocked library is a welcoming environment, complete with areas to spread out on cushions and read, whilst the art studio/come food tech room is huge and, again, boasting plenty of natural light. 'I never thought my son would like art, but he loves it now,' said one parent, who praised the specialist art teacher's links with local galleries, including the Saatchi

C

gallery. Music is also taken seriously, with the specialist teacher working in a large, well-equipped dedicated space. All children are given the opportunity to play instruments here, with a steady stream of six peripatetic teachers teaching in small groups and individually. There's a school choir (which has performed at the likes of the Royal Albert Hall) and orchestra. Other facilities of note include the break-out rooms for specialist support and the large ICT suite. Truth be told, much of the school could do with a lick of paint, and it's never going to look state-of-the-art due to the age of the building, but if you focus on the available space and how it's used, we think most people would be hard pushed not to be impressed, particularly for an inner city primary. And the £4.5 million refreshment looks set to make some exciting changes.

Sport is reported by parents and pupils alike to be fun and inclusive, with all the usual options, some of which are taught on site, whilst others, including swimming, involve a short walk to the local leisure centre. There are links with major local football clubs and Lord's cricket ground and dedicated coaches regularly visit to teach and enthuse the children. 'Sport is brilliant in comparison to other inner city schools,' one parent told us.

The school's motto, 'Inspiring success', is clearly not an empty phrase here, but something that they really aspire to for every child. Part of this involves setting – in phonics and reading from October half-term in reception, and in maths from year 2 – whilst another area of focus for the school is SEN. With seven statemented children when we visited, and plenty with extra needs ranging from those on the dys spectrum to those who may not have quiet areas to study at home, the school has made sure it is a learning environment where individual support is prioritised and provided both inside and outside the classroom. Without really planning to, the school has also gained something of a reputation for specialising in hearing loss, with three children in this situation attending at the time we visited. There's a big push on reading at home, with parents expected to regularly sign off reading records and there's a fair amount of homework, usually at weekends. 'Fridays aren't my favourite after school day,' admitted one parent. 'But I agree the homework is necessary as the children will be in for a shock when they reach secondary school otherwise.'

Behaviour is generally good, with pupils we met having a clear understanding of the school's behaviour code and, by and large, respecting it. A traffic light system in every class helps keep them on the straight and narrow too – nobody likes the shame of being moved onto red or, God forbid, purple (the extra colour that pupils tell us is saved for the likes of 'disrupting the class or being rude'). Youngsters who really overstep the mark find themselves in the head's office, although he says, 'the only time any child has had to be sent to me in the last six months was for setting off the fire alarm.' It also helps that good behaviour and work is rewarded with privilege points, which can be redeemed for toys out of the special cupboard when they reach increments of 10. 'Ten points will buy you a nice little toy, but if you save up 30 or 40, you can get something like a Bop-it,' one pupil told us, visibly excited by the prospect. Children who do particularly good work are invited to share it with key stage leaders and/or the head, as well as getting a special mention in class assemblies. The school says it's strict on uniform, but in reality, that just means that unlike in the past, when kids could wear any old red jumper, there's now a school version, along with the usual grey bottoms and black leather shoes.

Signs of life can be spotted early in the day here, with before- and after-school provision, as well as a breakfast café where parents can come with their children. In addition, the 42 before- and after-school clubs range from breakdancing to violin and ballet to gardening club. There are regular school day trips to the capital's museums, Kew Gardens and Holland Park (the latter for forest school), whilst year 4s upwards get to go on residential trips. Community links are a strength, with children involved with everything from Jamie Oliver's (for cooking sessions) to Salvation Army (where the choir performs to the elderly).

Parents are increasingly involved in school life. It wasn't always the case, pointed out one parent, who suggested the idea of having student reps to the head, which he promptly took up. 'The PA is increasingly active too,' she said, although some parents told us they'd like to see more events put on for parents to help bring the school community closer still, whilst another said a common complaint is that the school often only tells parents about school trips last minute – a shame as many like helping out on them, but don't generally get enough notice to get time off work. The summer and Christmas fairs are a very big deal here. 'One of our parents went to RADA and it meant last year's Santa's Grotto was better than Harrods,' says the head.

We found this school to be refreshing, unpretentious, aspirational and spirited. It is also testament to the fact that, with the right leadership, a poor performing school can become a school of choice within a short space of time – not just for parents, but children too. 'Every single day, my children look forward to going to school,' one parent told us. 'Everyone loves it here,' agreed one of the pupils we spoke to.

Connaught House School

47 Connaught Square, London W2 2HL

Pupils: 85 • Ages: 4–8 (boys), 4–11 (girls)

Fees: £15,000 – £16,500 pa

Tel: 020 7262 8830
Email: office@connaughthouseschool.co.uk
Website: www.connaughthouseschool.co.uk

Joint principals: Since 1991, Mrs Jacqueline Hampton (60s) and her husband, Mr Frederick Hampton MA RCA; both studied at art school. Mrs Hampton, aged 19, came here to lend a hand to her mother, Mrs Nancy Keane, who founded the school in 1952 with just six pupils, and never left. An intimate, cosy, family-run school, refreshing in this age of private equity backed independent schools. Mr and Mrs Hampton are very hands on and complement each other in their skills and strengths. She is form teacher for year 5 and he teaches English and art. Mrs Hampton describes herself as a 'big picture' person. She wants to see the children having fun while they learn and is determined to withstand the pressure, that faces all London schools, to turn into an exam sausage factory. However, she recognises that there has to be a balance and there needs to be some push to enable them to move on to good schools. The couple have two grown-up sons (both of whom were here).

One of their daughters-in-law, Mrs Victoria Hampton (30s), who runs the early years part of the school and has taught here for more than six years, is being groomed to take on the reins of headship. Not that she needs much training. She comes with a wealth of experience of young children, having started and run her own nursery in Oxfordshire, been deputy head of a nursery in Clapham, as well as having a host of qualifications for teaching young children – Montessori diploma, early years foundation degree, Hornsby diploma (dyslexia). She has two young boys of her own who will come here and loves being part of the fabric of the school. Gentle, pretty, with a mellifluous voice and perfect diction (which we suspect matches her handwriting), the children clearly love her as do the staff. She knows them all, is actively involved in observing and participating in lessons throughout the school and has already initiated and implemented changes and improvements. One of these was to bring the reception class (known at Junior One) up from the ground floor so that they can have plenty of space, free flowing between two large, high ceilinged rooms.

Although this is an independent, privately owned school, it has none of the trappings of a profit-motivated business. 'We are a school first that happens to have to run as a business,' say Mr and Mrs Hampton in unison. Phew – such schools do still exist. The Hamptons are wonderfully down to earth and direct. No kow-towing to demanding high net worth parents goes on here (and some parents do feel their concerns aren't listened to). The children are their focus. They know the children, enjoy the children, and put their interests above all else. They are proper educationalists, in the more traditional mould, and despite the competitive pressures common to all London day schools, are ensuring that music, art and drama are as central as the academics. They are firm believers in the theory that a happy child will be a successful child.

Entrance: At age 4 into reception (here called Junior One). Sixteen places for girls and boys. 'Very gentle assessments' take place when the child is 3 to ensure that they will get as much out of the school as possible. Children are assessed by two teachers and also have some one-to-one time. Absolutely no preparation is necessary. Priority is given to siblings and second and third generations. After that, proximity to school. 'The local community ethos is something we value very highly and would not like to lose,' says Victoria Hampton. Applications can also be made for entry into the upper end of the school. Academic and music bursaries are available to those applying at 7 or 8. Many come from local nurseries, including Great Beginnings and Paint Pots, and there is some liaison with nurseries after places have been offered.

Exit: All boys leave at 7 or 8 and tend to go to local prep schools such as Westminster Under School, Sussex House or Wetherby, the odd one going north to UCS junior school. The girls stay until 11 and generally opt for London day schools – Francis Holland, Clarence Gate, is currently the most popular, but many also to Godolphin & Latymer, City of London, More House, Latymer Upper, Queen's Gate and South Hampstead High. Those wishing to board generally choose Wycombe Abbey or St Mary's, Ascot. Despite leaving a very small school to go on to these much larger establishments, none of the pupils seems to be fazed – the confidence they acquire at CHS gives them the ability to cope in a broader environment.

Remarks: There is no danger of the slightly old-fashioned, wonderfully personal and child-centred ethos of this tiny school changing. The school has not expanded at all since it was first founded. It still occupies the same building, and is very small; you will know quite quickly if you love it or not, but if you don't, be careful not to write it off too soon. This is a rare little boutique in the increasingly branded, competitive world of London day schools and it offers a uniquely personal touch that many similar schools are in danger of losing. Despite its small size, good use is made of the environs. Hyde Park is only a short walk away, and children enjoy lots of outdoor activities there all the year round, including parachute games, obstacle races, rounders and football. Fencing, dance, and martial arts all take place at Little Venice Sports Centre. Tennis, football, hockey, basketball and the annual sports day happen at Paddington Recreation Ground. Swimming is at Queen Mother's Sports Centre in Victoria. There is sport every day of one kind or another. Although we heard some whispering from former parents of boys here – that the boys didn't get to run around enough and there were insufficient sporting opportunities – we could see no evidence of this. The Hamptons clearly understand boys well, with two sons and at least two small grandsons of their own.

Art and music are the main extracurricular strengths of the school. Plenty of music assemblies and lots of performances. Everyone takes part, and the large, high-ceilinged room in the middle of the building is a comfortable and intimate place to perform. We were treated to a mini concert, which included violin and recorder players as well as piano and singing – impromptu concerts of this kind are not unusual, we were told, and you can see how much confidence is imbued into these tiny performers as a result. The art room is a relatively dark, pokey room in the basement, but the quality of art that is produced defies the facilities. Perhaps to be expected, since both heads are trained artists. We saw small children beavering away at covering balloons in newspaper to create hot air balloons. We were shown wonderful wooden red buses and fire engines, built by the children, and split-pin dolls clothed in fabulous petite Victorian dresses and hats. Colourful displays adorn the walls – work obviously done by the children rather than touched up by the teachers (what a relief), and bright Chinese lanterns and colourful fish were bobbing from almost every ceiling.

Plenty of drama; each junior form does its own play once a year (these have included the Gruffalo's Christmas and Charlie Cook's Favourite Book), and years 4, 5 and 6 have performed Sleeping Beauty. Drama productions and concerts take place at the Carisbrooke Hall down the road or the Steiner Theatre close to Baker Street. Although this is very much a mixed community school with no particular religious bias, there is an annual carol concert in St John's Church, Hyde Park Crescent, which everyone is expected to attend. 'We would rather it were inclusive,' says Mrs Hampton.

Clubs are varied and numerous. The Hamptons make a huge effort to ensure that everyone from years 2-6 try everything. There is lots to try, from embroidery, pottery, board games and mini beasts to any kind of dance from country to zumba as well as chess and music. Full advantage is made of the school's cosmopolitan location – recent trips have included to the Globe Theatre, the Courtauld and the Tate Modern, the Celtic Harmony Camp, London Zoo and to the obvious museums – Science, Horniman and Transport.

You need not worry about little Freddie not getting enough attention either. There are only 16 pupils in a class – they try to keep an equal number of girls and boys in the early years. Junior One (reception) has two teachers and a qualified teaching assistant. Forms 1, 2 and 3 have both a form teacher and qualified teaching assistant in each class. All children use personal Fizz books (little laptops, as far as we could tell), there are MacBooks in every classroom and the Hamptons pride themselves on recruiting excellent teachers with 'diverse interests'. There is a competitive fives player on the staff at the moment. With such a small school, and class sizes, it is relatively easy to pick up any learning difficulties, we were told. They have a few cases of children with glue ear who may need speech and language therapy. Specialist therapists, for, eg, dyslexia are brought in at extra expense for parents but Victoria Hampton herself is a dyslexia therapist, and they prefer to keep as much support in school as possible. We were told that there is usually only one child in each year group who needs any kind of help at all. There are a high number of children with English as a second language, and although they need a reasonably good grasp of English at assessment, because of the high level of teacher support (and a recently introduced EAL club) they usually progress very quickly.

All in all, a very special little school which is loved by parents and pupils alike, where the children feel challenged every day and their parents are constantly amazed by what they know. 'The closest you can get to home schooling,' declares one. If that sounds appealing, take a little trip to Marble Arch now.

Coombe Girls' School

C

Clarence Avenue, New Malden, Surrey KT3 3TU

Pupils: 1,364 • Ages: 11 –18 • Sixth form: 300 (100 boys)

Tel: 020 8942 1242
Email: enquiries@cgs.rbksch.org
Website: www.coombegirlsschool.org

Headteacher: Since 2011, Mrs Deborah Walls (40s). As executive principal of Coombe Secondary Schools Academy Trust, also has oversight of Coombe Boys' and Knollmead, formerly a failing primary school but now undoubtedly destined for far greater things.

Her second time here – after teaching posts at Wallington High School for Girls and Langley Park, did stint in 1996 as head of languages, before being promoted to assistant head, moving back to Wallington as deputy head in 2003 and then closing in on Coombe again when was appointed in same role at boys' school. 'When you've worked [here] it becomes a part of you,' she says. 'It's more than just a job, it's part of your life.'

Discerning readers will also have clocked career focus on single sex schools which, yes, reflects Mrs Walls' strong belief that they're an educational essential. Means chance to find out who you are in safe environment, she believes. 'You can be yourself and let your individuality come out.'

Not that she wants anyone closed off from 'big world of opportunities,' as she puts it. Even before mixed sixth form, many co-curricular activities such as public speaking and ski trip are co-ed, while whole year groups of boys and girls have annual timetabled session themed according to age and interests – year 7s enjoy rocket making, year 8s self-awareness, while in years 9 and 10 there's more formal focus on options and higher education. It's diamond model light, the perfect scenario, thinks Mrs Walls. 'Gives the best of every world.'

Her family's talent for languages (grandmother, a teacher and languages expert, was a particular inspiration) meant career and specialism never in doubt, particularly when coupled with precocious ability to see flaws in the system (sussed, aged 11, the drawbacks of teaching languages in English). Enjoys travel, though helping own children achieve happiness and success are about as close as she comes to a hobby as, unsurprisingly, not much in the way of spare time pursuits.

Still manages to fit in some teaching but thoroughly enjoys organisational side of the role. Just as well as calls on time come thick and fast, from recent appointment as governor of King's College Wimbledon to beaming in advice to struggling schools, helped by colleagues. As Coombe is a national teaching school, also involved in growing new crops of teachers and bringing returners back into the fold. So many other requests to participate in kudos – and time – heavy research projects roll in that these days, writes risk analysis before making decision. No point spreading resources too thin, she says. 'We sit back and look at it from every angle first.'

While clearly a first class operator, also warm with great sense of humour but above all with burning desire to do her best for the girls, something that appears to permeate school consciousness. 'You may not hear much about her but know she has our interests at heart,' said one. They're also impressively confident in speaking their minds. When we asked year 9 pupil in her presence if she was enjoying producing complex-looking design for tote bag, we got a matter-of-fact 'no.' Sensitive to colleagues' needs, too. During tour, expertly bypassed trainee teacher in danger of losing the thread when confronted unexpectedly by head, assistant head and energetic note-taker.

Goals? With lots still to do, we're not sensing any appetite for a move elsewhere (though must be plenty who'd leap at the chance to recruit her). Parents value her strengths – 'Good combination of organisation, professionalism and approachability,' said one – and take her other commitments in their stride. While naturally delighted that appointment of new head at boys' school (former assistant head at Coombe Girls') now means Mrs Walls is here more often, parents have boundless confidence in school management's ability to cope when she's called away.

'Ideal person to lead the federation into its next stage of development,' was commendation from predecessor here. Professional and warm, she's supportive of other women attempting to get to the top and involved in local initiative for women leaders. We suspect that seeing her at work and clearly getting so much from demanding job is probably just as effective when comes to inspiring future generations of girls.

Academic matters: School 'honoured' that remains hugely oversubscribed – and not hard to see why parents would be bonkers to bust a gut securing place anywhere else if successful here. If daughter has tried out (unsuccessfully) for nearby grammars – and many have – don't worry, stress parents. The bright flourish here, some reckon more so than they would have done in the febrile atmosphere of ultra-selective alternatives where can take full marks just to get noticed.

Some of the seven school houses (all named after planets) are rather livelier than others, but come GCSE preparation time, everyone knuckles down to work, say parents – amply demonstrated by the results, with 88 per cent of pupils getting five good GCSE passes including maths and English in 2016, with 37 per cent of grades at A*/A.

Success founded on strong relationships between staff and pupils – confidence boosting a speciality. 'School has really built her up,' said parent of previously shy daughter. Staff feel well supported and, like parents and pupils, given regular slots where can raise difficulties and issues and know will be listened to. Asked if they ever go home, they laugh (but don't actually confirm that they do). Official school day, which runs 8.40am to 3.30pm with five 60-minute lessons, often extends into evening and weekend activities. School also unleavable in career terms, with 27 members of staff (average age 39) into their second decade or more. Newcomers or long-stayers, all exude palpable warmth down to smiley trio on duty to greet latecomers who run velvet glove rather than gauntlet, while row of clocks set to other time zones tells you how tardy you'd be in Buenos Aires.

Plenty of little touches – teacher (male) baking cake for GCSE geography pupils: 'Oh, Sir!' they shout, celebration breakfasts for good results, librarians who take no chances – up to year 8 'we read to girls and they read to us' – and offer full set of daily papers: The Times to tabloids. Above all it's a sense that girls are known and that teachers 'are rooting for them,' said mother.

Curriculum planned to nth degree – each subject served in parent handbook filleted into component parts with garnish of thoughtful enrichment activities, many of a useful nature (times tables tests for maths), others winningly desirable (geography trip to Paris for all year 7s). Some classes are set (maths in years 7 and 8 plus English in year 9), others in mixed ability groups (technology and languages), while science sometimes is and sometimes isn't, flexible approach dictated by range of each year group's ability and changing schemes of work.

Though there's extra stretch for gifted and talented, achievements in all their diversity are celebrated. Nitpickers might point to percentage of low achievers making expected progress in maths – currently it's just 32 per cent according to Dept for Education data. But given latest in series of letters from government, praising results, and stunningly high Progress 8 figures – numbers passing toughest GCSEs – any nits picked would be of microscopic dimensions.

For disadvantaged pupils (around a fifth) mostly a pretty positive picture, with half securing five or more GCSEs including maths and English. Low-ish numbers of pupils with SEN (currently 25, seven with statement or EHC plan), all supported in timetabled hours, with everything from teaching in lessons to room 41 – a dedicated haven for those struggling with sensory or emotional overload in or out of lessons. It's a rare pupil they can't cater for, SEN working closely with staff providing weekly briefing on needs and support. Similar system for EAL pupils including buddy system and catch up or slower paced lessons, though not needed by vast, linguistically competent majority.

Inevitably, families not above supplementing with tutors if pace of lessons leaves children behind. No criticism, says one, just normal for the area. 'A universal problem.' School feels shouldn't be necessary and points to numerous initiatives – tracking and lots of it, blips quickly picked up with extra catch up and revision sessions for anyone in danger of falling behind. 'Try to get the absolute best out of them,' thought parent and school reckoned to listen to parents and respond quickly, complaints limited particularly now anxiety over turnover of science teachers has slowed, department has no vacancies and (impressively) biologists, chemists and physicists are all teaching own subjects.

Post 16, there's a split screen approach, more academic subjects here, vocational at boys' school and 35 courses in total. Otherwise beamish Ofsted report had reined in lumens slightly – attendance and results were felt to be below par, some of brightest lured away by excellent fare on offer at outstanding local sixth form colleges.

School has responded by upping budget for careers and uni preparation and bringing in dashing new subjects including A level classics (follows success of Latin GCSE, taught out of hours with support from King's College School) plus government and politics and economics, each new addition somehow woven into the timetable by staff specialist (swears more fun than other hobbies – cryptic crosswords and fiendish Sudoku).

Smaller but significant perks such as sixth form snack exclusives (paninis, jacket potatoes and sausage rolls) and relaxed uniform code (we admired one girl's dazzling blue Doc Martens, just seen under sombre trousers and conventional shirt) have no doubt played part in improving results and pupil retention. Overall, 32 per cent of A levels graded A*/A and 52 per cent at A*/B in 2016 – up on previous year's results.

Games, options, the arts: In addition to all the curriculum must-haves, many wonderful-to-haves such as active Duke of Edinburgh. All this despite limited resources, felt to tail off only slightly in sixth form (dance would be popular addition to the menu, thought several pupils). Plenty lower down the school, though, with year 7s working on cross-curricular project, themed to 'my journey' which culminates in presentation to parents, as well as covering off everything from cultural diversity to healthy lifestyles, touch-typing and research skills.

It's all approached with dash and enthusiasm, visible also in enthusiastic art and DT, dresses cascading ruffles and crank handle wooden toys on display, walls brightened by everything from lavish, Rubens-style picture of woman's torso to accomplished year 9 self-portraits in chalks. Performing arts, felt by parents to have been a notch below par, now on the up again with revitalised productions, some at Rose Theatre in nearby Kingston, courtesy of new, dynamic head of music (peak beard, creative tie) and vibrant drama department.

Sports appropriately energetic, facilities – own grounds as well as impressively large sports hall – felt to give it the edge in comparison with many other more space-challenged secondaries nearby. Houses compete to speed run a mile round the grounds in aid of Sports Relief and teams frequently successful in outside events, year 7 football team achieving silver in borough event, trampolining a particular strength, one former pupil going on to become county coach.

Parents complimentary about achievements though wish lists would include extra coaching, funds permitting. 'It's not a level playing field,' said one with feeling, if not literal accuracy.

Background and atmosphere: Set in heart of New Malden, between lush Kingston Hill mansions and more workaday housing and on same compact site since foundation in 1955 as Coombe County Secondary School.

Original uniform, mustered for diamond anniversary celebrations, a smart affair, including woolly scarf and squashy felt hat. Though both have gone, other nostalgic touches remain, including original wooden bars in gym, space now repurposed as dance studio and occasional exam room.

Site is spotless, courtesy of maintenance team whose devotion extends to post-break litter-picking sessions. Plenty of greenery – year 7s have own grassy area and even the cut-down playing field, which could so easily be sea of mud, is a well-tended space, while small hedges, something of a planting favourite, brighten up odds and ends of space no end.

Niceness extends to other areas. Floral scent wafts from newer, far bigger sports hall. Particularly fragrant staff? 'Just what the cleaners use,' says teacher. And despite one parental comment that catering had suffered slight decline, range and quality looked impressive, all meals cooked from scratch by team in at 6.00am to add dainty finishing touches, no toasted sandwich minus its upmarket cardboard envelope or St Valentine's Day cake lacking an icing heart. And all served with sugar-free drinks and low prices (roast and a pud for £2).

Sixth form centre a building of two halves, one for quiet study (plenty of 'shushing' from supervising teacher if it isn't), common room on the other. Appears girl-heavy but boys magically appear at break time (just follow the sound of the football).

Rebuild of this and other less than gorgeous areas (flaking paint is pointed out by teacher with a certain relish) would be top of Mrs Walls' wish list. Pristine additions – geography recently re-homed while staff also have a posh room for best – show what can be achieved.

Pastoral care, well-being and discipline: New pupils eased in with visits to feeder primaries and summer school at end of year 6, including trips to London Zoo – website is big on reassurance, with relaxed pupils sharing tips. First day 'one of the best and scariest, felt was going to die but at the same time really excited.'

New or not, school makes no bones about expectations. With so much going on, likes pupils to get the full benefit of school life and stresses importance of punctuality, with sliding scale of detentions from 10 minutes with tutor after school for one offence to a one hour Friday session for five late arrivals – plus parent meeting. Request for term time absence unlikely to be considered, let alone granted, for anyone whose attendance drops below 98 per cent.

All other breaches (arriving in mufti, failing to stow outdoor coats in lockers, long, fake or varnished nails, using phones during school day) sanctions are strict and explicit, exclusion for 'defiance' the non-negotiable norm for persistent offenders followed by 'formal reintegration [where] your daughter's future will be discussed.' One to avoid, though, stresses school, it's only tiny minority who fail to obey the rules. Just as well, as there's now greater formality (compulsory blazers for all).

Plenty of support for families (we hope that 'talk to your teen' advice on website, containing conversation-igniting gems such as 'That looks interesting, what are you doing?' is as popular as it deserves to be). Parents accept need for rules with slight sigh

C

(decision to ban popular black leather, lace up trainer derivative caused a bit of angst), girls similarly philosophical, hitching up skirts again as soon as doorstep length inspection completed.

Teachers approachable and reassuring – 'Ones you click with are a comfort, especially at exam time,' said sixth former – and tough issues addressed head on, from mental health issues and grooming to bullying (including advice on how to cope if child is bully rather than victim...). School has at least one eye fixed firmly on friendship issues, pupils so effectively mixed and matched on arrival that pretty much guaranteed you'll leave with different mates from the ones you arrived with. Pragmatic approach of 'getting everyone to sit down and talk it over rather than screaming at each other,' said pupil, generally felt to be key to resolving majority of difficulties.

Pupils and parents: By far best known former pupil is children's Jacqueline Wilson, also Olympic athlete Anne Packer. Alumni association, only recently set up, promises to bring many more successful former pupils – plenty of creative and City types – back into the fold.

Regardless of background, packed with conscientious, hard-working sorts and notable for strong sense of community – tragic pupil death led to whole school rag week, everyone contributing, most popular event penalty shootout, sixth form boys doused with water if failed to save goals. 'What could be better?' said girl.

Entrance: From over 900 applicants, takes 210 in year 7, popularity inevitably resulting in a 'Honey, I shrunk the catchment area' issue (under two km in first round of offers), to school a source of mixed pride over popularity and sadness that so many who want to come here can't. Arrive from numerous primaries headed by Burlington Junior School, Christ Church C of E, Coombe Hill Junior School and King's Oak Primary.

Post 16, there's second chance at a place here, seven GCSEs with Bs or better in chosen A level subjects required. More places for girls – 210, compared with 100 boys – and priority for existing pupils, 40 per cent going to external candidates, who'll be vetted for academic potential and attitude to learning.

Exit: 'Aspire' programme offers Oxbridge taster events (with input from King's College School) and STEM-related courses, designed to ensure pupils get the rundown on full range of top careers and courses and don't settle for second best. In 2016, 24 per cent to Russell Group, two Oxbridge places and one medic. London unis – UCL, King's College and Queen Mary – regularly feature as most popular destinations, others to Bristol, Cardiff, Exeter, Leeds, Nottingham. Recent spread of subjects also includes law and modern languages.

Money matters: Asks for annual payment of £120 per family – voluntary, some families contributing more.

Remarks: Fabulous education, staff who can't tear themselves away and delighted parents. What's not to like? 'A pure comprehensive which is very rare and does what it does really well,' said mother. 'I wouldn't consider anywhere else because my daughter is so happy.'

Coombe Hill Infant and Junior Schools

Coombe Lane West, Kingston KT2 7DD

Pupils: 720 • Ages: 4–11

Tel: 020 8949 1743
Email: admin@chj.rbksch.org
Website: www.coombehillj.kingston.sch.uk/

Head of junior school: Since 2014, Mr Mark Clutterbuck, previously deputy principal at Chessington Community College.

Head of infant school: Since 2013, Mrs Janet Berry. SENCo and senior assistant head for three years prior to taking over the headship and a member of the senior leadership team. Has been at the school for 13 years, starting part time when her children were pupils and progressing through the ranks as they got older.

Entrance: Much sought after local school. The closer you live the better, although it may still prove difficult to get in. More than 550 first choice applications for 90 reception class places; over half go to siblings. Admission policy strictly adhered to – medical or social needs get priority. Occasional bulge years add an extra class. Some 99 per cent of junior school entrants automatically from the infant school. Others all local, round the corner.

Exit: Infants almost without fail to the junior school next door. One or two to local independent schools, of which there are plenty. Majority of juniors to local state schools, impressive number to the highly selective Kingston state grammars Tiffin Boys and Girls, more to Coombe Girls and Boys, others all over. With the improvement that has taken place in the current local state schools, very few pupils now move into the private system.

Remarks: Brilliant, buzzing, exciting state schools more than ever holding their own against the many local private sector schools. Very much an upmarket area; the pupils are a huge ethnic mix from a variety of backgrounds, with parents who help, encourage and enjoy the multinational involvement.

From the moment you walk into it, through the art gallery entrance, you realise that the infants is a lively school bursting with happy, interested children. A vast ethnic mix – about 60 per cent need some EAL support, mainly in class except in extreme cases. No attached nursery, so some children arrive speaking no English at all while others speak two or three different languages. The resulting mix is 'demanding but fascinating to work with.' All classes – five or more of up to 30 children in each age group – mixed ability. One full time teacher for each, plus a teacher's aide for at least half of the day and other extra staff who help wherever needed. All are highly trained and experienced, often current or ex-parents. 'The school has a really family feel,' we were told.

Fantastic semi open-plan layout, all on one floor, loads of natural light. Corridors of well-equipped classrooms, all with interactive whiteboards, computers and educational displays. Children's creations abound. Pupils enjoy themselves, eagerly joining in all activities. When we visited all of them were absorbed, participating and learning, and eager to show us what they were doing. Three excited year 2 pupils were delighted to take us round their school and point out their favourite places and activities. Fantastic IT suite, good lending library with videos, games, reading and maths schemes. Great art on display everywhere.

We were taken round the junior school by some senior pupils eager to show us everything that was going on. We didn't miss a nook or a cranny and were suitably impressed. Everywhere was clean, bright and full of happy, thoroughly involved children. Classrooms overflowing with interesting displays. Technology everywhere. Parents told us 'excellent teaching', 'fantastic, exuberant teachers', 'great facilities' and 'really like the way they make learning fun and incorporate different subjects in one lesson'. We were delighted to see a good number of male teachers, two of whom are heads of year. Classrooms a bit squashed but that didn't appear to matter; flexibility is the name of the game. All mixed ability but the brightest separated into four groups for maths and literacy. We were told, 'the teaching is something special, a real collaboration between teacher and pupil, teacher and teacher, and pupil and pupil, they all help each other'. 'No cramming, the education is broad and full, they are taught to debate and to question and to discover for themselves'.

Lots of music, singing and playing different instruments. Private lessons available for those who want to learn a particular instrument. Everyone learns the recorder in year 4. Our guides proudly showed us the range available for them to try. Great art on display in the atrium and, when we were there, models of Andersen shelters – 'very difficult to make!' For a state primary, the sport is exceptional. A brand new games area provides for cricket, netball, basketball, football, rugby and other sports, some of which they play competitively against other schools. Not enough, some parents think, but it is a privilege not there for all primary school children, so they are lucky. And they have their own heated swimming pool – two sessions a week for each class. Added to that PE and dance form an important part of the curriculum.

One of the special things about these schools is the massive amount of outdoor space. Plenty of room to run, climb and explore. Children certainly make the most of it – log cabin for special projects and areas for planting and learning. Imaginations soar. Infants also have the use of the heated swimming pool (in the junior school's section of the shared open land) in the summer term. Each class has weekly sessions, weather permitting.

Our guides led us proudly round their extensive grounds. Every class has an outdoor learning day once a year. As well as the usual play areas, there are wildlife areas, including a pond and a 'hotel' for insects, a vegetable garden – 'some we eat, some we sell' – and, really exciting, a pen for chickens whose eggs, of course, also get eaten.

Sympathetic SENCo who seems to really care for the children, making sure no needy child slips through the net. Several groups, run by learning support teachers, take pupils out of class where necessary, but never during a core subject. Non-stop records kept and a provision map for every child in the school. Those with behavioural problems get one-to-one support but they do try to make sure that they are given enough individual space. SENCo works closely with both the behavioural team and the class teachers, trying to tackle problems before they go too far. Says it's important to try and pre-empt difficult situations before they get out of hand. 'I really love my job'. Parents say, 'Children respected and nurtured. Bad behaviour not tolerated'. 'Quick to deal with problems'.

A large variety of after-school clubs which are extremely popular and introduce children to new skills and ideas. An hour a day, all taught by their regular teachers with a minimal charge to cover materials.

Mix of nationalities means cultural activities from all over. Most festivals are celebrated and any excuse for dressing up is grabbed. Knowledge of the world is part of the learning process – every child and every country is important. Music and art are an essential part of the school day. Parents rave about every aspect, haven't got a single criticism. Only worry, will they be able to maintain this high achievement level?

All in all, tip-top schools that have managed and absorbed the necessary expansion over the last few years and the broad ethnic diversity that is Greater London today.

The Coopers' Company and Coborn School

St Mary's Lane, Upminster, Essex RM14 3HS

Pupils: 1,400 • Ages: 11–18 • Sixth form: 450

Tel: 01708 250500
Email: info@cooperscoborn.org.uk
Website: www.cooperscoborn.org.uk

Headteacher: Since 2013, Dr David Parry PhD MA MBA NPQH. Previously deputy head of the school since 2005, including a stint as acting headteacher. Did his teacher training at the Royal Central School of Speech and Drama (where alumni include Rupert Everett and French and Saunders); his BA in English and education, along with his masters in leadership and management, at Open University; and his PhD and more recently MBA at the UCL Institute of Education. When we visited, he was studying for a GCSE in physics with year 11s. 'It's part of our growth mind-set culture – all staff take on board a challenge to show the students anything is possible,' he explains, providing other examples of staff learning to play the saxophone, to sing, to learn a new language or to walk the three peaks. Staff told us this aspirational culture was always implicit, but Dr Parry has made it explicit. Also known for bringing in clearer systems, along with zero tolerance around behaviour. 'Students' behaviour was always good; now it's even better,' one staff member told us.

Prior to this school, he was deputy head at Caterham High School. 'And before that, I suppose you could say I was professionally promiscuous,' he laughs, pointing out that he worked across both the independent sector (where he taught Alan Sugar's children) right through to challenging state schools in London.

One of the most hands-on heads we've come across, he greets pupils every morning at the gate ('The subtext is checking on uniform, but it is genuinely nice to welcome them every morning,' he smiles) and says goodbye to them every afternoon. He is available outside for every morning break time, has a genuine open-door policy, eats in the dining room every day, gets involved in extracurricular activities and school trips, helps with UCAS applications and teaches English. 'As a head teacher, I don't know how you cannot teach,' he says. 'All of us are shop floor operatives in this school, no matter what our role. We don't want to run a school where leaders are remote.'

Parents see him as 'old school, but always open to new ideas,' ('the perfect balance,' said one) and pupils say he's the kind of head that 'instantly demands respect', but is 'very approachable.' We found him a solid, authoritative type, but extremely friendly, open-minded and forward-thinking.

C

C

Academic matters: There's an assumption that students will do well here ('It's built into their DNA that they will want to succeed,' says head) and they do, with the school consistently achieving near top GCSE results nationally, and the proportion of pupils achieving the highest grades is significantly above the national average – 88 per cent of candidates gained five or more A*-C passes including English and maths in 2016, and 27 per cent of grades were A*/A. They are especially strong in English language, English lit, mathematics and art and design, but pupils also do exceptionally well in RS, DT, textiles technology and music. The most popular GCSE choices are history, German, geography and sport/PE, and fair numbers also choose Spanish and French.

At sixth form, pupils are offered a wide curriculum of traditional subjects but are also introduced to new courses – media studies, psychology and politics. Popular choices are the sciences, especially biology ('We buck the national trend when it comes to STEM subjects a A level,' says head), business studies, history, maths and psychology. In 2016, 57 per cent A*-B and nearly 27 per cent A*/A grades.

Spanish, French, German or Mandarin from year 7 (parents get to state a preference when they apply to the school), with a second language introduced in year 8, at which point Mandarin and German are also available. 'Modern languages are big strength of the school,' said one parent, reflecting the views of others. Pupils are setted for maths in year 7 and there's an element of setting in languages and sciences at GSCE. Homework considered an essential part of shaping pupils' academic experience, particularly in relation to independent learning and thinking skills.

Teachers renowned for going the extra mile both inside the classroom and out. 'No teacher gets an interview until they've taught a lesson which we find to be good or outstanding,' says the head, who adds that for every applicant teacher, he asks himself two questions: 'Would I want to be taught by them? Would I want my daughter to be taught by them?' If either answer is no, they don't get in, he says. A fair amount of emailing goes on after hours, for which both students and parents are very grateful.

Despite high results, the school is always working on improving grades and has introduced Go 4 Schools, an online tracking programme, enabling parents and teachers to login at any time to monitor how the student is doing, with both individual grades and overall grades, target grades and how they can improve, enabling all three parties to monitor progress and make any necessary interventions to keep grades on track. 'It really helps cement the three way partnership between students, parents and teachers,' says head and parents agree. 'We have a good idea of both where our children are relative to where they need to be,' said one parent. The bottom 15 students in the year are provided with extra measures, as are the 15 at the top. SEN has a strong team of six staff members, mainly providing classroom-based help for children with issues ranging from dyslexia to autism, although less than one per cent of these have been statemented. 'For major SEN issues, other schools in the borough are better equipped,' admits head.

Although the school is very academic, we found it to be the antithesis of an exam factory, offering a broad and liberal education, with a major emphasis on extracurricular activities that all students are expected to get involved in. 'If you're the kind of person that just wants to go to school from 9am-3pm then go home and forget about school, this probably isn't the place for you,' one student told us. Whilst PE accounts for the majority of the 142 clubs on offer, other subjects include music, drama, IT and all the academic subjects right through to beekeeping, chicken keeping and robot building. Many of the school teams enter national competitions – 94 of them the year we visited, reaching national finals in 33 of them and world finals in two. The debating team reached the finals at Oxford University.

Games, options, the arts: This is the number one co-ed state school for sport, if you take as the criteria the number of national level finals reached across all sports. International events are also regularly entered for, with the triathlon team having reached the world finals, coming second mixed team, the year we visited. Students took part in the opening ceremony of the 2012 Olympics and were also involved in the handover of the Olympic Flame for the Rio Olympics. Regular competitions against leading independent schools, especially in athletics, cross-country, badminton and swimming. Not surprisingly, the students we spoke to were deeply proud of the school's exceptional achievements and aptitude.

The rich curriculum ranges from circuit gym training to trampolining, cricket and netball to indoor rowing and PE remains compulsory throughout the school years, even at sixth form. Facilities, including a swimming pool, are impressive and sports trips are notable, including rugby tours to New Zealand and Australia, athletics training in Lanzarote and tennis training in Florida. 'The attention to detail in the coaching is second to none,' said one parent. 'Nobody is left out, with everyone given a chance to thrive,' said another.

Well-equipped art studios, with a studio offering individual cubicles for pupils who need a designated area in which to work. An 'open house' policy approach encourages independent work and, along with the clearly outstanding levels of work on display, creates a wonderful 'art school' atmosphere. Pupils consistently have work displayed in exhibitions around the country.

Drama standards are high, with two roomy practice areas, including a state-of-the-art renovated theatre, with retracted seating. Plenty of performances throughout the year, including one main annual performance – Singing in the Rain the year we visited.

Music also strong, with five school orchestras (including an all ability one), two choirs and regular ensembles and concerts. Expect brass band more than rock music 'as we like to keep things traditional,' says head. Around 180 students are taught instrumental lessons in school, with 54 music exams in school alone – with many more students learning and being tested outside school. Students take part in music festivals and competitions, as well as playing at significant events, such as the Lord Mayor's Banquet, and at a more local level within school, for example during assemblies. 'There's no shortage of volunteers and the inclusive and supportive ethos of the school means you never get students saying, "I don't think I'm good enough to play in front of my friends",' says head. Overseas trips, such as an eight-day Italy music tour to Lake Garda.

Huge range of extracurricular choice, with clubs before and after school and at lunch time, covering almost every conceivable area, from chess to fishing. Several clubs have been instigated and are run by pupils. 'The amount of opportunities is amazing – everyone tries something they never thought they would,' said one student. School trips are also big here, with around 40 domestic and 23 international ones every year. Besides the sport-based ones, there are language trips (year 8) and exchange trips (year 10) to support Spanish, German, Mandarin and French and other trips to explore interesting places such as Namibia and Botswana.

Background and atmosphere: A rich history dating back to 1536 when it was first established as a free school for boys. Its name came in 1552 when the Coopers' Company was asked to take over the running of the school. It was then located in Stepney, Tower Hamlets. In 1891, it joined foundations with the Coborn school for boys and girls and remained at sites at Mile End and Bow until it moved to Upminster in 1971. 'Our first students would have seen Shakespeare's plays,' points out the head, who sees their long history as central to the school's culture.

Now situated a good distance from the main road amid 25 acres of greenery, and home to a pond visited by ducks and geese, the school feels spacious, exceptionally neat and tidy and well cared for. And although some of the main school buildings from the 70s are looking tired, modernisation and development have seen new buildings regularly erected since the 80s, the latest being a sixth form block. Other smaller but notable modern developments include a solar panel roof, i-desks (with computers that pop up) and a state-of-the-art laser cutter. 'This school really listens to the students when it comes to the need for new facilities or equipment, so we never feel left behind,' said one student.

The school motto, 'Love as Brethren', appears quite literally in shining lights as you walk in the school and you won't find a student who doesn't believe it's central to school life here, with many using the hashtag

LasB when they sign off emails or post on social media. 'There's a real spirit of philanthropy and generosity of spirit here,' one student told us, and we too found the atmosphere to be happy and thoughtful, with students displaying a healthy level of boisterousness during break times, but heads down during class. Religion not in your face, but Christian values embedded into everyday life.

Pastoral care, well-being and discipline: Students describe the school as being a 'protective cloak' and 'like a family,' with the young people looking out for each other and staff on hand to help with any issues students may have. The school also buys into a student counselling service and clearly takes mental health issues seriously. 'Mental health is the single biggest issue facing today's young people,' says head. A house system, which consists of four houses, helps create vertical links, as well as the horizontal year groupings. Peer to peer mentoring, and around 150 sixth formers work with younger pupils.

Plenty of leadership opportunities, with a democratic process selecting school captains from year 12 pupils, who must apply for this prestigious position. The one boy and one girl selected hold office throughout their final year. School council plays a key role in the decision-making processes – including the appointment of senior staff. Pupils are given a sense of importance and are consulted on important developments. Reward system is fully utilised, including housepoints, certificates, postcards and phone calls home, letters from head and spotlight in assembly.

There isn't much room for making mistakes here, however, with zero tolerance to bad behaviour and very high expectations of conduct. These expectations, and the punishments for failing to adhere to them, are all outlined in both a contract that students have to sign before coming to the school, and a visually friendly charter. Staff are trained in them too, so that there is complete consistency, and parents are also expected to be on board. 'If students don't meet the standards, they can expect serious sanctions,' says the head. 'I'm quite happy to run Saturday detentions, for example, and I would exclude.' Indeed, he had permanently excluded a student the week before our visit for intimidating behaviour towards a staff member, although permanent exclusions are rare. Talking when teaching, or not focusing in class, are considered as bad as writing on school walls. 'I explain to students that there are two types of vandalism here – damaging something and damaging the education of others – and I tolerate neither,' says head, with other rules including no mobile phones (except in sixth form), eating only in allocated areas and very strict uniform rules, with not a silly haircut or rolled up skirt in sight. But whilst it might all sound draconian, we found unanimous agreement from parents and students that the rules and consequences are fair and ultimately prepare young people for the world of work. Bad behaviour here is simply 'uncool,' students told us, with one pointing out that the rules are so well embedded into school life that in reality, nobody really thinks of the school as that strict. 'There's a strong sense of students not wanting to let down the school or betray its past,' adds the head. Bullying rare because, according to students, 'mocking just isn't what we do here.'

Pupils and parents: Most students from aspirational families. Around 80 per cent white middle class, the rest of a mixture of ethnic minorities. Although it's a Christian school, there's an eclectic mix from all recognised world religions. Many parents are supportive of the school and help out at school events, with an active PA of about 30 members – good for a secondary state school. They arrange various fundraising events including a monthly sale of supermarket vouchers to parents and staff and they had just raised enough funds for a new minibus when we visited. We found pupils to be articulate, grounded, respectful and polite – traits for which they are known throughout the local community. They are very proud of their school, as well as extremely appreciative of having a place there. Everyone is welcoming – greeting visitors with smiles and hellos, saying thank you, holding doors open and even singing to themselves as they pass by.

Entrance: Unusually large number of feeder schools (around 100). Admissions rules and catchment area complicated due to the school's historic links to east London and wish to preserve the principles of the Coopers' Company and Coborn Educational Foundation.

Over 1,000 applications for just 180 places and a fair number go to appeal. Ten sport and nine music places, which hundreds apply for. All other applicants must be actively connected to one of the main world faiths. Some places for children of staff and former students; others by promixity; others to those who live in specific areas including Havering, Brentwood and Billericay.

Most stay on to the sixth form after GCSE. Around 50 places for students from outside but, again, massively popular with over 700 applications. Applicants need at least eight A*-C grades to be considered for a place, to be sympathetic to the school's Christian character and be willing to uphold its 'Love as Brethren' ethos by giving time to serve the school. Oversubscription criteria prioritise looked after children, highest predicted grades and then availability in specific sets. 'Our sixth form is equivalent to a grammar school, in terms of offering traditional subject choices and the fact that we take the cream of the crop,' says the head.

Exit: Around a third leaves after GCSE for one of three reasons: to study a vocational course at college, to study different subject choices at other local schools or (a few) to take up an apprenticeship. Almost none leave to go into low-paid work. Around three-quarters of sixth formers to university, which is high for the area, of which a third go to Russell Group universities; two to Oxbridge in 2016. Particularly popular are Warwick, Bristol, Durham, Birmingham, Bath, Exeter, Loughborough and Imperial.

School provides a range of opportunities to prepare for post school, including careers advice from year 9, conferences, workshops, competitions and special events at universities such as Nottingham and Cambridge. Many go on to study pure science subjects or vocational courses such as medicine, veterinary science and dentistry. Other popular subjects include psychology, economics, architecture, art history, journalism, politics and theatre design.

Money matters: The school allocates £10k to assist pupils that need help and also provides music and sports grants of up to

£500 through a bursary system from The Coopers' Company and Coborn Educational Foundation.

Remarks: World class in the true sense of the word, this school is a dynamic, exciting place to learn, preparing students for successful lives. Dazzling reputation in the local community and largely responsible for increased house prices in the Upminster area. 'If you're not one of these things – academic, sporty or musical – it's probably not the school for you,' pointed out one parent, whilst students say you need to be willing to put in more time than regular school hours and more commitment than the bare minimum. 'There's no room for just plodding along here,' explained one. But for those that fit the mould, it's outstanding.

Croydon High School

Old Farleigh Road, South Croydon, Surrey CR2 8YB

Pupils: 600 • Ages: 3–18 • Sixth form: 100

Fees: £11,751 – £15,516 pa

Tel: 020 8260 7500
Email: admissions@cry.gdst.net
Website: www.croydonhigh.gdst.net

Head: Since September 2016, Mrs Emma Pattison, previously deputy head (academic) at St John's School, Leatherhead. A linguist, she started her career at Caterham School, then moved to Guildford High, where she was head of modern foreign languages for the senior and junior schools. She is a keen piano player and singer.

Head of junior school: Since January 2015, Mrs Sophie Bradshaw BA (Ed) from Exeter, previously academic co-ordinator for years 3-4 at Ardingly Prep School.

Academic matters: Introductory courses in Spanish, German and French in the junior school to tempt young linguists. GCSE results creditable – 62 per cent A*/A grades in 2016. Good all-round education with a strong performance from the science, maths, English and modern foreign languages depts. French, German, Spanish and Latin offered; talented linguists can take up to three options at GCSE, putting linguists on a par with the scientists. Newly-decorated, bright, clean science and language labs, with recently updated resources. Parents report very solid teaching in maths; quite a few go on to take maths and further maths at A level. A tracking and monitoring system recently introduced to help move towards more individualised learning, the aim being to ensure everyone meets their potential. Year 9 girls encouraged to try out subjects and choose a balanced mixture of GCSEs before making A level choices – always guided towards their strengths.

Subject choices at A level now expanded; in 2016, 40 per cent A*/A grades, 74 per cent A*/B. Sixth formers link with Whitgift and benefit from a good range of sporting, artistic and practical enrichment activities. Accessible careers centre which maintains links with outside agencies; girls also encouraged to get involved in voluntary work, help run school clubs and undertake some supervisory roles with younger children.

ICT centre and library stay open until 5pm; library is run by a much-appreciated and knowledgeable librarian, who facilitates book groups and a number of other literary related activities. Pupils volunteer to assist in the library, designing information posters and leaflets. Girls say library comfortable to work in, with desks overlooking attractive grounds, a popular place to be – good stock of books, audios, periodicals and DVDs.

A few wobbles recently on the staff front but we hope now settled down in time for new head. Reasonable mix of long-serving and new, younger staff. Part-time SENCo organises some additional support provision which includes screening and study skills for all age groups.

Games, options, the arts: Something for everyone – energetic sporting calendar: hockey, netball, tennis, cross-country, rounders and gymnastics. School has won the netball national finals 14 times in the last three decades and is successful in many other national events. Large sports centre, which doubles as a private club, houses gym, sports hall, dance studios and pool, where the highly successful swimming teams train. Recreational sports include badminton, self-defence, table tennis, aerobics and salsa. D of E award scheme thrives, also regular field trips as well as adventure holidays, music tours and skiing. Year 7s go to an activity centre in Devon for a week of outdoor activities.

Traditionally strong music, say parents – instrumental tuition available on most instruments including tuba and harpsichord. Everyone has the opportunity to learn a string instrument in year 3 – quite a few budding cellists look set to impress. Wonderful choirs, orchestras and bands in-house and Fairfield Hall concerts are always a sell out, musicians are involved at local and national levels. Own annual chamber music composition competition judged by an external adjudicator. Music and drama departments work together to produce spectacular musicals each year. Surprisingly few choose to take music GCSE or A level, a shame for such an innovative group of musicians. Art teachers continue the open-door policy so pupils can use facilities – which include pottery studio and dark room – outside timetable classes. Imaginative art displays throughout the junior school corridors and classrooms.

Girls also get out and about and take part in national and local competitions; enthusiastic debating groups and year 7 recently made finals of a national spelling bee.

Background and atmosphere: Founded in 1874, the school moved in 1966 to its present purpose-built site, which accommodates the junior and senior schools. The buildings, which are rather utilitarian from the outside, provide excellent, well-proportioned rooms. Lots of refurbishment under way. Spacious landscaped grounds supply superb sporting and recreational space for both juniors and seniors. A few well-loved school pets enjoy the grounds too. Comfortable atmosphere pervades, possibly influenced by the many links encouraged between older and younger girls. All appears to be quiet and purposeful.

Pastoral care, well-being and discipline: School code of conduct is included in pupils' yearly planners; school rules are mostly common sense or based on health and safety requirements. Sixth formers train as peer listeners to befriend younger pupils. No outside counsellor, however referrals can be made through the school nurse. All girls are encouraged to look out for each other and respect each other as individuals. Teachers are available to pupils on a drop-in basis first thing in the morning.

Pupils and parents: Catchment area stretches from south London to rural Surrey, although the majority lives within a five-mile radius of the school. Pupils come from a range of backgrounds, mostly professional; proportionate racial mix with around a dozen different nationalities attending. Link with Shenzhen in China, so a small number of Chinese students are able to live locally to attend the sixth form. PTA runs fundraising events and sixth form fashion show often raises around £4000 for charity.

Alumnae: Jacqueline du Pré, Helen Chadwick, Elizabeth Laird, Jane Warr and Marilyn Cutts etc etc.

Entrance: From 3+ into the nursery, then by assessment from 4+ and subsequent year groups. At 11+ annual entrance test in November and informal interview with the head or deputy. All those offered places attend a special induction day during the summer term before entry. Automatic entry from junior school for academically able, who sit entrance exam only for scholarship purposes. At 16+, interview, report from the previous school and seven GCSEs, B grade for subjects to be studied at A level, A grade for mathematics, chemistry, physics and modern languages.

Exit: At 11+ around 80 juniors continue to the senior school; leavers tend to opt for local grammar schools or other independents. Around 30 per cent leave at 16+, mostly for co-ed schools or state sixth form centres and colleges. Nobody left at the end of year 12 in 2016. Great majority to university, a handful a year to Oxbridge (three in 2016); Nottingham, Durham and Manchester popular, otherwise anywhere from London to Edinburgh. Three to study medicine/biomedicine. Combined degrees becoming particularly popular, eg engineering or law with a modern language.

Money matters: Standard GDST scholarships and bursaries are available. Music, art, drama and sports scholarships for year 7 entrants. Jacqueline du Pré music scholarship and sixth form scholarships.

Remarks: Consistently good results across the board. Pupils appear highly-motivated and accomplished, but maybe too rigorous a place for a more sensitive soul.

Cumnor House School (Croydon)

Linked with Cumnor House School for Girls

168 Pampisford Road, South Croydon, Surrey CR2 6DA

Pupils: 400 (200 in co-ed nursery) • Ages: 2-13

Fees: £9,495 – £12,090 pa

Tel: 020 8660 3445
Email: registrar@cumnorhouse.com
Website: www.cumnorhouse.com

Headmaster: Since September 2016, Floyd Steadman, previously head of Clifton Lodge. A former Saracens and English rugby player, he used to be director of sport and head of the junior section of St Paul's Juniors (previously Colet Court). He became deputy head of Belmont Mill Hill, then head of Downsend, before moving to Clifton Lodge in 2013. He has also been national squad adviser for the RFU and director of the Sports Aid Foundation.

Entrance: Three form intake with 20 boys maximum in a class. Automatic entry from the school's Treetops Nursery, which parents told us they found a very attractive feature of the school. Otherwise, boys come in at 4+ for a taster day, which for most is nothing to worry about. Maths and English are checked to ascertain if the child will cope at Cumnor, but not formally assessed. Other entry points at 7+ and 11+. School aims to be as inclusive as possible, and all kinds of families pay the (very competitive) fees to send their boys here.

Exit: Given the school's non-academically-selective admissions process, Cumnor's exit record is truly remarkable. Students can be prepped for either 11+ or 13+ depending on parents' and boys' wishes, which, families affirm, the school is always careful to consult. Those who opt for 11+ are put in a dedicated class, and win places either at local grammars (Wilson's and Wallington's), or at independents such as Trinity and Whitgift, often with scholarships. Those who've chosen to stay until 13 also go on to a whole range of top-brass schools including Westminster, Eton, City of London and Tonbridge. Such is the school's success that refugees who come to Cumnor at 11 often pass at 13 with scholarships into schools which turned them down two years previously. 'We've been in the game long enough to know what the senior schools are looking for.' And year on year, the results prove them right.

Remarks: After years in the schools' reviewing business, we were nonetheless surprised by the fervour with which parents talked to us about Cumnor House. 'It's a lovely, brilliant school. I would recommend it to anyone and everyone!' cried one mother. 'The boys there are lovely young men, and the teachers are amazing, they always want to go the extra mile,' said another. 'It's been a really positive experience for our son,' said a third. 'We couldn't fault it.' 'No negatives, and nothing to regret. It's fantastic!' said a fourth. And this is just a sample.

Cumnor House is surely triumphant proof that single sex education from an early age can really work. If a How-I-Hope-My-Son-Will-Turn-Out contest existed, the boys we met here would all be candidates to win. Their manners are astonishingly good. Everywhere we were greeted with courteous smiles and handshakes; in one instance, even with a bow! Whilst they hurled themselves around the playgrounds at break-time, they were nonetheless well-behaved and considerate, both to each other and to us. 'You might want to walk quickly, 'cause it's raining,' urged one of our tour guides with anxious politeness.

Everywhere we saw evidence of lively and careful teaching, and the boys were vociferous about how much they enjoyed lessons. 'History is my favourite, because it's all about old things, and did you know that Henry VIII died because his bottom exploded on the toilet!' cried a year 2 lad enthusiastically. The older boys were more conservative in their praise, but no less warm. 'The teachers are very kind', 'They're inspirational!' 'Lessons are always fun', 'Because of my science teacher, I want to be a scientist,' we were told. Work on the walls was imaginative and of a consistently high standard. Strong SEN team supports boys in need of extra help; the school welcomes all learners, although the school acknowledged that boys with more than moderate learning difficulties would struggle at Cumnor, and we ourselves felt that this wouldn't be the right place for them.

Parents in search of flashy facilities might initially be nonplussed by Cumnor's honeycomb, let's-patch-on-another-annexe-here school campus. The main site used to be residential, and the impression is still of a large, rambling house full of staircases and inglenooks. Decor-wise, it would be fair to say that it lacks the feminine touch: somehow, despite the displays and children's books lining the walls, there isn't much colour in the place. Desks are endearingly old-fashioned, and occasionally downright scruffy. But honestly, who cares? The classrooms are all well-resourced, there's an excellent ICT suite, the boys radiate contentment and their achievements speak for themselves. And there's nothing scruffy about the sports facilities: the huge sports ground boasts £50k's worth of new cricket nets and a new clubhouse, the sports hall is adequate and the swimming pool block was warm, light and inviting, which may be why the reception teachers were all in the water with their young charges when we visited. Cumnor's swimming is very successful (the swim squad practises from 7am), and the school has won national as well as local competitions. Football, rugby, cricket and athletics are likewise strong, nurtured by a team of very dedicated PE teachers. Old boys include Mark Butcher, Alistair Brown, David Sales, Chris Robshaw and Elliot Daly.

For the non-sportsmen, however, there is plenty of other fare on offer. Music is flourishing, with over half the boys learning at least one musical instrument, and a pleasing variety of bands and ensembles to join. The school's choral singing is particularly impressive: previous fixtures include Salzburg Cathedral and the Barnardo's National Choir Competition (which they won). Drama is also lively, and the school puts on at least two productions a year. There are lots of clubs and societies, and the boys are encouraged to try new things. 'We don't want boys who are in at 8.30am and out at 3.30pm. We want them to take risks. We tell them, if you haven't auditioned for the school play, why not? If you aren't learning an instrument, why not?'

A few years ago Cumnor joined the Cognita schools group, thereby increasing its financial clout in a very competitive locality. The Lodge Schools on the other side of the Purley Way declined and fell during the financial crisis, whereupon Cognita bought up most of the site and asked Cumnor to open a girls' school (see our separate entry) and expand Treetops, their excellent nursery provision. Reception boys are also housed on this site in Woodcote Lane, and we wondered if that didn't provoke grumbles from parents dropping off more than one child. But no: the school runs a shuttle service between the two sites, and parents can choose to which one they deliver both sons and daughters, knowing that the school will safely ferry their children to where they need to be. (And this, frankly, is more than can be said for some of the parents; the thoroughfare outside the Pampisford Road site gets very exciting at drop-off time, as local residents will feelingly confirm.)

The Croydon area is multi-cultural, and one of Cumnor's greatest successes is the way that it takes a highly diverse group of boys – every colour and creed is represented on the school roll – and helps them all become polished and likeable English gentlemen, in the best possible sense of the phrase. It may not be the place for the kind of child who just isn't into school no matter how good it is; incurable mavericks would be exhausted by the ebullient enthusiasm and team spirit here. But make no mistake, this is boys' education at its best.

Cumnor House School for Girls

Linked with Cumnor House School (Croydon)

1 Woodcote Lane, Purley, Surrey CR8 3HB

Pupils: 175 • Ages: 2–11

Fees: £10,050 – £12,090 pa

Tel: 020 8660 3445
Email: admin.purley@cumnorhouse.com
Website: www.cumnorhouse.com

Head: Since January 2016, Mrs Dina Mallett BA Ed (Reading), previously deputy head at City of London School for Girls Prep School. She started her teaching career as a class teacher at Dulwich College Prep School (now Dulwich Prep London), becoming classical studies teacher, head of year and assistant director of studies.

Entrance: Two-form entry with up to 20 per class. Automatic admission for girls at Treetops, Cumnor's excellent and increasingly sought-after nursery. Otherwise, entry is 'mostly non-selective', and at 4+ consists of a taster day where the girls' literacy and numeracy is checked 'to see where they're at', but not formally assessed. 'Very rarely say no,' says school. But with a growing reputation in the neighbourhood, we suspect that will change. Register early to be sure of a place. Apparently there's means-tested assistance plus the odd scholarship available at 7+, but we couldn't find any mention of this on the website.

Exit: To an impressive range of local selective schools, often with scholarships. Recent destinations include Wallington, Nonsuch, JAGS, Caterham, Croydon High, Lady Eleanor Holles and City of London Freemen's.

Remarks: Opened in 2010 on the site previously occupied by Downside Lodge: when all the Lodge schools got into financial hock, the site was bought by Cognita Schools who turned it into Cumnor House Girls, to the delight of many local parents. Poor Commonweal Lodge School, now being busily converted into flats (it was the bit that Cognita didn't want), broods mournfully from afar over this happy and flourishing newish venture on the leafy Webb Estate, but c'est la vie. We don't think Cumnor House Girls will go the same way; the signs are too promising. 'We've a clear vision,' is school's explanation. 'Our aim is to offer girls choice at 11. That's what we're good at.' Are they academically aspirational? 'Without question. Girls cover the curriculum more quickly, so we're able to really push them on academically.'

There are girls here who joined the school when it was Downside Lodge co-ed, and as far as they're concerned, things just keep getting better. 'This is the best school anyone could ever choose', 'It's amazing here', 'I'd give the school five stars', we were told. Did they miss having boys around? 'Well, they were loud,' commented one girl cheerfully, 'so it's good that they're not here, really, and it's nice to have smaller classes.'

Whatever its secret, the standard of work here is high, all the more creditably given the school's non-selective intake. Literacy and numeracy are very strong, and the work on the walls bore testimony to imaginative and effective teaching. A girl who'd transferred to Cumnor from another independent school told us, 'I feel here they're pushing me a bit more.' But this clearly isn't at anyone's expense. The same girl added, 'There wasn't as much learning support at my old school, and Cumnor has a nicer atmosphere.' And indeed, we thought the learning support room was particularly welcoming. The SEN team is strong and vigilant, and difficulties are picked up early. The head meets with the SENCo every week, and 'dynamic support' is offered quickly to those who need it. We were impressed by the Games Club, a nurture group for girls with social difficulties, but also by the Quest Club for the gifted and talented students. We certainly saw some lovely examples of the latter.

Sport at Cumnor House Girls is 'MASSIVE!' and 'VERY,VERY important!' according to its young devotees. Rounders, netball, gymnastics, athletics and tennis are all on offer (but no football, which the girls said they would have liked; school please note), and all girls from reception upwards have weekly swimming lessons at Cumnor House Boys. 'They include everyone in the sports here and it's great fun,' insisted a self-confessed non-sporty type.

There was some gorgeous artwork on display, including a wonderful Olympic themed sculpture in the foyer; the art teacher, we were told, 'has many different ideas, she's amazing!' The school is also a firm believer in music and drama, with both integrated into the curriculum. Free instrumental lessons are offered to all girls in year 3, many choose to continue them afterwards, and the school fields two choirs and an orchestra. Wherever possible, they team up with the boys' school for drama productions; previous shows include Bugsy Malone and Aladdin. The hall struck us as rather old-fashioned, but the girls adored it, and told us, 'This is a very, very exciting stage!' Lots of clubs, including dance, chess, judo and sewing, and business club ('so we get confident in speaking') – though none of the debating, science and electronics clubs offered at the boys' school. Food technology is on the timetable (unlike at the boys' school, which seems to give rather more emphasis to the sciences in lessons too) and is very popular, and the school has a lovely garden which provides the vegetables for lessons – we were proudly shown shallots, parsley and runner beans. (On the subject of actual school lunches the girls were diplomatically loyal, which, after the stone-cold and unappetizing fare we'd been offered, we thought very praiseworthy of them.)

The girls themselves, smartly attired in a sensible and well-cut uniform, are the surest proof that this is a school doing well by its students. Lively, happy, enthusiastic, well-mannered and articulate, they were a pleasure to meet. Parents agree. 'It's a very child-orientated school; the girls are allowed to have fun,' said one. Other comments include: 'The teachers are very caring', 'My daughter loved it from the beginning', 'The academic provision is very good, and my daughter's become very confident', 'It's a lovely old-fashioned village-y atmosphere, and she's made some great friends', 'It's a fantastic school; I have no issues at all.' Our verdict: a blossoming school with much to offer; the clever choice for Croydon daughters.

DLD College London

199 Westminster Bridge Road, London SE1 7FX

Pupils: 500; 195 full boarders • Ages: 14–20 • Sixth form: 400

Fees: Day £7,850 – £19,990; Boarding £15,000 – £21,000 pa

Tel: 020 7935 8411
Email: dld@dld.org
Website: www.dldcollege.co.uk

Principal: Since 2013, Rachel Borland BEd MA. Originally principal of both DLD and Abbey College in London, until they integrated on a single, purpose-built site with student accommodation on Westminster Bridge Road in September 2015. Previously principal of Abbey College in Birmingham, as well as principal of the largest private boarding school in Nigeria. In addition, she's been assistant director of studies at the British Council in both Hong Kong and Jordan, and she also worked at Bath University.

A self-acclaimed workaholic, she is both amenable and easy-going – with no hint of the stereotypical authority of more traditional headteachers. Known among colleagues as being inspirational and collaborative. 'No decision is taken alone by me, although I'm inevitably the finisher,' she says. Typical day involves arriving at 6.30am, checking in with boarding staff, breakfasting with students, having quiet time in her office, then juggling the usual meetings and paperwork with meeting students and finally leaving early evening. 'I'm not a person who can sit still for very long,' she laughs. Travels a lot. The term we visited, she had gone to Nigeria, Dubai and St Petersburg, visiting schools and spreading the word about DLD. Students very much at ease chatting with her. 'We see her every day,' said one, although they add that they rarely have to bother her in her office due to the tight pastoral and academic support, which means other staff members are generally a first port-of-call.

Lives alone in Haywards Heath, Sussex. 'I love London, but I also love fields and space.' Her daughter is a houseparent at DLD and her son was educated through the Alpha Plus Group.

D

Academic matters: College offers a two-year GCSE programme, whilst a minority (usually those who are older or who have transferred from other schools where they started their GSCEs) do a one-year GCSE course. Most take seven subjects, from a list of 12 options including the basics, plus French, religious studies, art, graphics and drama. Russian, Chinese, Spanish, Italian, German and Arabic are available via individual tuition. Commendable results from a mixed ability intake. In 2016, 43 per cent A*-B and 67 per cent A*-C grades.

A level students get a choice of 33 subjects, including music technology, photography, film and media studies, sociology, psychology and languages, in more or less any combination. Art, economics, religious studies and philosophy are consistently popular, alongside English and maths. In 2016, 63 per cent A*-B grades and 38 per cent A*/A. BTecs also available in media production and business.

Some students are disaffected when they arrive, but it's rare for them to be anti-education after a few weeks. 'Because of the small class sizes – on average, 12 – they get lots of individual feedback and huge amounts of encouragement, and most start making progress very quickly,' says the principal, who also attributes their academic success to their focus on fitting the right course to the right student.

Parents can't praise the system enough. 'The small class sizes, and the extra attention that provides each child with, have been the absolute making of my daughter,' one parent told us. Another, who has had two children at DLD, said, 'DLD has a record of helping children who felt they weren't going to achieve anything in a regular school to really do well. There's something about the small class sizes, easy-going environment and quality of teaching that gives them a chance to break out of set patterns of underachieving and underperforming. It really shows, more than anywhere I've seen.'

The college can cope with a wide range of special needs, generally picking up several previously undiagnosed cases each year, including dyslexia, ADHD and autism. Thirty-four per cent SEN when we visited and those benefit from support with study and essay writing skills; individual help is also available at extra cost. 'Our SEN students get more or less the same level of results as the others, due to the amount of input from SEN department, which is run by a two-strong team. This extra help is critical,' says head. Accredited by CReSTeD, whose most recent report speaks of it as a unique school.

Very bright students also well catered for, with parents confirming that their children feel stretched and challenged in a positive way. Others point to the personalised approach of monitoring, feedback and target setting ensuring that students continue maximising their full potential at all times.

Indeed, educational expectations are high for all, with patchy work not accepted by staff. 'We believe in helping students believe they can move up to the next level,' says head. Many staff are from Oxbridge and some come from non-teaching backgrounds – the theatre, the City, the BBC. 'This means our tutors know exactly what employers really want from graduates and it also means they have great connections,' said one student. 'My music teacher, for instance, has invited in songwriters, a music lawyer and others to talk to us, as well as sending out our coursework from people in the industry to get feedback.'

Teachers only employed if they are accessible to students outside classes, with many not only being available on email, but on a live chat system. Students say they are treated as adults and for many of them, it's that mutual respect that gets them back on track with their education. The most recent ISI report states that students like being at the college and are very happy with the personal support that they receive.

Extended Project Qualification increasingly popular, with 12 students doing it when we visited, although head admits some drop off in first few weeks. 'It's a tough programme,' she says.

Games, options, the arts: A level art and photography are two of the most popular and successful subjects here, and the artwork we saw on display in the large and well-equipped art rooms was striking, with a notable creative energy among the students while they were working. 'I can honestly say every photography lesson is fun,' said one student. LAMDA examinations on offer and the DLD youth theatre puts on two performances a year.

All GCSE students play curricular sport at local centres on Wednesday afternoons, including football, basketball, tennis, netball, dance, rock-climbing and aerobics. Sports clubs and matches after school too, including cricket and yoga. On-site sporting facilities include a swimming pool and gym in the basement. 'But although sport is accessible and enjoyed by many students, DLD is probably not the best place for your child if they're really, really sporty,' one parent told us.

Music popular, with facilities including a recording studio and various practice areas, all of which are soundproofed. There's a vocal group, ukulele group, recording studio club and 59 students do private music lessons, including classical and jazz piano tuition, rock guitar, pop singing, singing and drum kit.

Extracurricular offering has improved in recent years, including Duke of Edinburgh Award, EPQ, debating and art clubs. Located in the heart of Westminster, it's no wonder the school takes full advantage of the galleries, museums and theatres practically on its doorstep, with overseas trips to the likes of Barcelona and Paris.

Boarding: The new site includes over 214 student beds (195 of which were being used when we visited) over 15 floors, with views over the Thames. More to be converted in the future. The areas are gender split, with younger ones on the lower floors. Strict curfews in the week from 9.30-10.30pm and, which are extended on Fridays and Saturdays until 10.30-11.30pm (depending on age). All full boarders, although some do visit home during weekends and half term and the school is very flexible when it comes to students wanting to visit friends and families. Boarders will often arrange their own activities for the weekend, but there are always free activities going on in the boarding house, including movie nights, quiz nights, zumba, birthday parties etc, along with visits to local museums, galleries and places like Harry Potter World.

Mostly single rooms, of different shapes and sizes, all ensuite. Some twin rooms share a bathroom. These rooms have a partition between beds that can be extended along the whole length of the room if required. 'It's the twin ones that are the most popular,' a staff member told us. Rooms are hi-spec, contemporary and minimalist, with a clear wow factor. 'I love my room,' one student told us. 'And because it's soundproofed, I can be as loud as I want and study in peace regardless of how loud anyone else is.' Weekly inspections mean they are kept reasonably tidy, although lots of unmade beds when we visited. Light, airy and spacious communal kitchen on each floor, complete with comfortable seating areas, fridge, freezer, microwave, kettle and toaster, but no hob or oven, with students expected to eat main meals in the refectory. 'It's a really sociable area,' one student told us.

Pastoral care for boarders includes a strong team of house parents, who are fully residential, run by a director of boarding and his assistant – who in turn is overseen by the vice president of principal welfare.

Background and atmosphere: Now one of 16 schools and five colleges owned by the Alpha Plus Group, founded in 1931 to provide tutoring for Oxbridge and Colonial Service entrance exams. After World War II it began to specialise in A and O level teaching. In 2004 it moved from Notting Hill to light, airy, refurbished premises in Marylebone; in August 2015 moved again, amalgamating with Abbey College in a new, purpose built site on Westminster Bridge Road.

On first sight, this shiny new building looks more like swanky corporate offices than any school, both outside and in, but a closer look reveals that education is very much at the heart of the design. A large open space – with huge projector screens on the wall, and which doubles up as a 350-seat performance area when required – forms the central atrium. Then the teaching and study areas – all arranged in colour co-ordinated zones so students can't get lost – sit around the edges. These facilities include six high-spec labs, a creative arts and media faculty, 40 tutorial rooms and an open plan library, study and ICT facilities.

Informal atmosphere, more akin to a college than a school, with staff and students on a first name basis and no uniform. But there's no room for slacking, with students engaged, inquisitive and busy both in the classes when we visited. 'Academically, it's tough, but people want to learn,' said one student. Helping students keep up is a vast array of break-out areas dotted around the different floors – some with individual booths for private study, whilst others have small or large tables for group study.

Active student council, which meets twice a month and organises plenty of charity events (breast cancer awareness day when we visited), as well as bringing about changes such the reintroduction of table football, although one parent told us she'd like to see 'more of a student voice overall.'

Fresh food available in the cashless refectory, which is reviewed by a food committee comprised of students and staff. Starbucks also on site. The day begins for students at 8.50am and finishes at 4.40pm, with enrichment extending that until around 6.30pm.

Pastoral care, well-being and discipline: Very strong pastoral system, which had recently been restructured when we visited, so that there are separate staff for pastoral and academic care. 'This is important because we do attract some needy students, including school phobics and SEN,' says head. 'There's no stigma if you need help,' said one student. 'Staff really care about you here,' said another. Parents we spoke to were very moved by what the school had achieved for their children pastorally. 'Staff are so kind and supportive that I'm welling up thinking about what they've done for my daughter,' one told us.

Electronic register is taken in every lesson and parents are texted or emailed if attendance becomes a problem. Each student has a weekly meeting with their personal tutor to talk about progress and future plans; three directors of studies and three directors of welfare work closely with the personal tutors. Expectations, rather than rules, are the norm here. 'My son kicked back about things like strict uniform and not being allowed to go out at lunchtime at his last school, and he's much happier here, where you're expected to turn up and do your work and be respectful, but without lots of petty rules and an authoritarian environment.'

Significant proportion of pupils smoke (nurse runs a stop smoking programme), but there's tough penalties for misusing drink and drugs – those under suspicion are sent for drugs tests, to general parental approval. Most students, even the most troubled ones, buckle down eventually, although head says occasionally things don't go to plan, with around two exclusions every academic year.

Sanctions include supervised study; also a system of verbal and written warnings based on employment law. Bullying is taken very seriously, although students told us the atmosphere is so relaxed and accepting that it's exceptionally rare. 'Nobody judges you here,' said one student.

Peer mentoring had around 60 students involved when we visited. 'It's improving my interpersonal skills,' said one student.

Pupils and parents: Students aged between 14-18 (with the odd exception up to 20), most of whom have come from private schools. Some have been ill; some have had mental health or other problems; some have found their previous school too rigid or too stressful. Others come from peripatetic diplomatic families. Some lack confidence and need to learn good working habits. Most thrive in the informal but structured atmosphere. Around 30 per cent from UK, with others mostly from Germany, Latvia, Ukraine, Malaysia, China, Burma, Vietnam, Italy, Kazakhstan and Russia. Little, if any, sense of community among parents, which one said is 'disappointing, but hardly surprising.'

Entrance: Everyone is interviewed and previous schools are asked for references and reports. Those going into the sixth form need a minimum of five grade Cs at GCSE; if they haven't passed maths or English they will need to retake these, alongside their A levels. No student who has been disruptive elsewhere is accepted without a discussion about the need for a change in behaviour. School is registered for 725 students, although only 500 when we visited. 'Our vision was always to open the new facility with 500 and build it up,' says head.

Exit: A few GCSE students move on elsewhere – perhaps to state sixth form colleges – but most go through to the sixth form. Those aiming at Oxbridge (two got places in 2016) are given an intensive course including lectures, seminars, mock interviews and individual tuition. Popular destinations include UCL, Goldsmith's, King's College, LSE, Imperial, Cass Business School and Bristol. Wide range of degree courses, with business studies, economics and specialist art areas being the most popular. Extra help also for potential vets, doctors and dentists, via a bespoke medical programme, with three or four a year going onto study these at university.

Money matters: Several scholarships available, worth 10-100 per cent of fees, on the basis on academic attainment, plus means-tested bursaries. 'I'm fortunate to have free rein to be sympathetic to the individual,' says head, who adds that she's keen to support the local community. Indeed, one local boy supported 100 per cent financially when we visited.

Remarks: This unique educational environment seems to capture all the best things about a college environment, combining them with the pastoral care and motivational structures that are more typical of school provision. All this takes place in small classes, with one-to-one help when required, in a state-of-the-art, purpose-built building in the heart of London, where students have the option to board on-site. The result is an informal atmosphere with an underlying structured regime where everyone is kept up to scratch. A fantastic place for the very bright, as well as re-motivating the disaffected, although not for young people who want a more traditional boarding school experience.

Drayton Manor High School

Drayton Bridge Road, London W7 1EU

Pupils: 1,560 • Ages: 11–19 • Sixth form: 360

Tel: 020 8357 1900
Email: adminoffice@draytonmanorhighschool.co.uk
Website: www.draytonmanorhighschool.co.uk

Head: Since 1994, Sir Pritpal Singh BSc MA FRSA, educated at Highgate School and London University, where he read chemistry (50s). Previously deputy head at Cranford Community School, prior to which he was head of chemistry, head of science and head of year in various other comprehensive schools, mainly in London. His own schooling (DMHS has academic links with Highgate) and, perhaps, his current school's early history as a grammar, underlie his approach, and grammar school virtues seem subtly to strengthen this non-selective comprehensive. Premier league football clubs could learn from Sir Pritpal's career. Put a good man in a moderately-achieving school and let him get on with it for long enough to find a vision, amass the means and expertise to realise it and then build on it. The high-flying Drayton Manor High of today is the result and Sir Pritpal – along with numerous other honours and awards – was knighted for services to education. Supported by many long-serving staff, notably the senior deputy head – here since 1983 – he is relaxed, candid, softly-spoken, smiley, winning in manner, and, though wholly on top of 'initiatives' and the latest government plans, is refreshingly free of edu-speak.

His tenure has not been without controversy. In 2008, he went head to head with Ealing Council over admissions. Accused of trying to select middle class children, the school was vindicated and the result is an admissions policy which allows children to come to Drayton Manor if it is the nearest school to their home. See below for explanation of what seems obvious. In 2011, the school was granted academy status. The attempt to seek parental opinion was only a partial success – very few replies. 'I like to think it was that they trusted us,' remarks Sir Pritpal, somewhat beadily and probably correctly. Those parents who do involve themselves are appreciative – 'he runs a tight ship... his staff are happy and, mostly, they stay... he is always there at parents' evenings and events'. This last is significant as some 'superheads' more or less disappear from the day-to-day life of their schools. Staff likewise pay tribute – 'he has added to the culture of the place and made it what it is today; it was hard work, especially on standards and behaviour. He took us back to the fundamentals and it has worked'. Drayton Manor struggled for decades but now, under professional management and sound educational principles, it is giving the local independents real competition.

Academic matters: Now outperforms other Ealing state schools and some of the local independents at A level – this reflecting, but only to some extent, the height of the academic bar to A level courses. Thirty A level subjects on offer plus extensive Wednesday afternoon enrichment programme which includes EPQ and citizenship courses worth half an A2.

Latin survives at GCSE with excellent results, though struggles at A level; German also battles on; best language results in French at GCSE and A level. Separate sciences at GCSE with exemplary results – much parental praise for staff, also in history and English. Starry A level results in government and politics, history, English, media and further maths. Overall, results impress – 54 per cent A*-B grades at A level, with 23 per cent A*/A, in 2016. A few non-A level sixth form courses available for those who don't make the grade at GCSE – site and facilities don't allow for more. At GCSE in 2016, 64 per cent of pupils got five plus A*-C including English and maths, with 24 per cent of grades A*/A.

Setting in maths from year 7, in science and languages later on. Enlightened approach re setting – 'We don't have an ideology – we look each year at what will work best' – and parents praise the flexibility of pupils moving up and down as appropriate. Library not huge for the size of school – good stock of popular fiction plus smallish, though interesting, stock of subject books. Parents say, 'I've got a lot of time for all the teachers – they require grammar school standards: our children have achieved even more highly than we had hoped, due to them'; 'They like lively discussion to promote learning.'

Around 20 per cent have some type of SEN: support is rigorous, systematic and professional under head of inclusion. Good links with primaries, baseline assessment on arrival, SENCo involvement with subject and class teachers and constant target setting and monitoring make for unusual progress. Thirty-four statemented children, 290 on school action or school action plus; eight with an ASD, 157 with MLD or SLD and 61 with behavioural or social difficulties. EAL support offered on a withdrawal or in-class basis, mentoring, masterclasses, tracking. Inclusion centre takes children on a last warning and is staffed by 'our best teachers', who offer individualised teaching to 'develop positive behaviour for learning' – a narrow curriculum, taught in small groups in 'a nurturing environment'. Those identified as gifted and talented are monitored by the intervention department, who check they are sufficiently stretched and challenged.

Games, options, the arts: Great range of sports, much success. Sporting ambition fostered in teams and individuals. Lots of showings in the higher levels of Middlesex tournaments and beyond – boys' 1st XI won the Middlesex Cup; both girls' and boys' football teams reached English Schools national finals recently. Netball and dance also outstanding. On site provision of numerous hard courts and field supplemented by nearby pitches – the best for a state school in Ealing, we are told. New all-weather surface in the offing. Lively drama, culminating in the key stage 3 expressive arts festival (art, music and drama) every summer including the inter-house drama festival, the Shakespeare Schools Festival and the school production attended by many of the feeder primaries as part of the transition programme. A good idea. Art is produced by an enthusiastic minority but we were not wowed by what we saw; most work, however, to be done on music where the talent has yet to be harnessed and developed. 'We're determined for it to be of the highest standard – we are working very hard behind the scenes,' says the head, acknowledging the problem. However, a flautist is part of the National Youth Orchestra and has performed nationwide. Food tech, DT and textiles all with specialist provision. New arts building – the Sir Montague Sharpe Building – opened in 2014. Lots of trips and visits – we are particularly pleased to see London theatres featuring prominently. Also, impressive range of speakers from the Big Outside.

Background and atmosphere: Began life as a grammar in 1930 and has the solid, handsome building you'd expect, though now supplemented by later blocks of varying quality around the central piazza – tastefully developed in recent years during multi-million pound developments, including large scale refurbishments to buildings and sports facilities and new science labs, with more in progress. Outstanding is the Frances Moore Building, named after much-loved deputy head. Impressively broad corridors. Venerable trees, well-tended shrubbery beds and a few hanging baskets greet the visitor, and the reception area is more friendly smiles than forbidding security measures. Pupils are well-turned out, the place is in good nick and we saw little litter. Classroom after classroom was engaged in orderly and seemingly quiet, collaborative work. Few eye-catching displays – though some good blow-ups of current pupils are an attractive feature – little to distract and a purposeful, no frills approach pervades the school. Lots of IT; trad school hall used for productions and gatherings. Good new-ish dining hall with new caterers and excellent and popular food – a particularly wide choice and reasonably priced. All foods prepared on-site using fresh ingredients and healthy options predominate – though we wondered about chocolate peanut butter cheesecake. Sixth formers have a common room for each year – spacious, well-used and appreciated. Pupils have a cleaning rota! Some sense that house system is underused and that pupils have little idea what those outside their immediate circle do. The head sees the truth in this and says, 'we're on to it.'

Pastoral care, well-being and discipline: 'We've had one smoking incident on site in the last 10 years,' says the head. One or two permanent exclusions or 'managed moves' annually for persistent disruptive behaviour. Very rare drugs incidents – 'they know that if they do that they jeopardise their own future'. Good structured pastoral care system, mentoring, buddying, quick pick-up on problems. We heard no reports of bullying not jumped on and dealt with. 'Care, courtesy, consideration and integrity come before anything else,' says the head. Staff call each other 'sir' and 'miss' as they pass in the corridors. Parents praise the inclusive atmosphere – 'everyone is included in awards, not just the high achievers but those who've made progress. The ethos encourages aspiration'. Also appreciation of the disciplined approach – 'they are hot on punctuality and attendance' – and the efficient staff-home communication. Uniform and sixth form dress code seemingly adhered to – though they don't look like automata either. Much in place to guide towards post-school life though some students felt it needed to start earlier and be more pro-active. Again, Sir Pritpal, wonderfully undefensive in the face of criticism, sees this as something he is happy to address – new careers coordinator now appointed.

Pupils and parents: From a very narrow chunk of Ealing these days as the school's popularity and reputation have grown. With a catchment area that takes in everything from the neat Edwardian terraces opposite, the detached grandeur of the Victorian houses a few hundred yards to the east and the council estates of west Ealing and Hanwell, the mix could not be richer. A vast range of backgrounds – 57 different home languages spoken and 34 per cent have English as second language. Lots of after-school classes, notably in ESOL and English, offered to parents alongside other support classes. Pervasive culture of aspiration melds and blends and whatever background you came with, you leave with a sense of your own potential. Notable former pupils include Lord Justice Sir Michael Fox, Martin Rowlands, artist/producer Steve McQueen, Jay Kay, Rick Wakeman and 'if I hadn't been a footballer I'd have been a virgin', Peter Crouch.

Entrance: Vastly over-subscribed. Lots of siblings. Usual local authority criteria apply but the successful court case means that children will gain a place at Drayton Manor if it is the nearest school to their home. In practice this means that if you live a mile from the school but it remains the nearest school to home, then you will have priority over children who live half a mile away but have other schools from which they can choose. Some 50 per cent come from five local primaries – Drayton Green, Hathaway, Hobbayne, Montpelier and North Ealing. Odd disparity in local population and in other local schools means that all years have more boys than girls. Entry to the sixth form depends on five good GCSEs including English and maths as well as other stipulated grades depending on your choice of A level – most subjects requiring Bs at GCSE. These requirements apply to existing students and to applicants from outside.

Exit: Around a third leave after GCSEs – to employment or vocational courses elsewhere. Virtually all sixth form leavers to university – several vets, medics, dentists and pharmacists; quite a few engineers; London unis, Manchester, Birmingham and Nottingham all popular. A partnership with Sir Pritpal's alma mater, Highgate School, sees shared expertise on careers workshops and Oxbridge preparation. Twelve medics and dentists in 2016.

Money matters: An annual £10 contribution is asked for.

Remarks: Get clear about the admissions policy and move house. This is about as good as it gets.

DUCKS Kindergarten and Infants School

Linked with Dulwich College: The Junior School, Dulwich College

87 College Road, London SE21 7HH

Pupils: 237 • Ages: 3m–7 • C of E

Fees: £7,995 – £14,115 pa

Tel: 020 8693 1538
Email: ducks@dulwich.org.uk
Website: www.dulwich.org.uk/ducks

Head: Since 2015, Nicky Black, previously deputy head. A Durham graduate, she joined DUCKS from Hornsby House, where she was director of studies, head of lower school and head of maths. She is particularly interested in creative teaching and active learning.

Entrance: Into the kindergarten, six places for babies aged 6-18 months; 18 places for toddlers and up to 40 places for 'ducklings' of between 2 and 3 years. The infants' school comprises nursery from 3+ to year 2. There are usually five to 10 places available at the nursery, then 10 to 15 reception places, with places occasionally emerging higher up the school.

No assessment for entry into the kindergarten, but children entering at 3, 4, 5 and 6+ will have an assessment to ensure their learning is up to date and at a stage where they can take advantage of everything the school has to offer. Priority throughout is given to the children of college staff and DUCKS siblings. We imagine the younger members of the college staff could keep the baby room next to filled. Given the small size, keen parents will want to register early.

Exit: Girls and some boys exit to a wide range of destinations, beginning locally with Alleyn's, JAPS, Sydenham High, Oakfield and Rosemead, spreading to Streatham & Clapham High School and St Dunstan's College.

The majority of boys (around two-thirds) move on to the junior school. There have been grumbles about the numbers being offered places in the past. The school says that realistically the college may not be the right school for every child.

Remarks: The teaching staff is mostly female, some mothers with relatively young children themselves, hand-picked by the head based on 'qualifications and enthusiasm'. Parents seem to feel this a place where children can be themselves free from pressure. One said, 'It has impressed me that the staff are willing to work individually with children at a pace suitable for that child in that subject.' Another told us, 'My daughter is not interested in academic subjects but the teachers have awakened an interest in learning in her.' One felt that the head enables children 'to develop at the speed that they require, unlike the hothousing that is encountered at some prep schools.' This means 7+ time won't be overly-pressured, which won't suit all.

Parents suggest that there is a good balance between the kind of learning through play where children are having so much fun they are oblivious to the learning and good, solid foundation skills teaching. 'Being taught how to count by jumping in puddles was a particular favourite of my sons,' said one mother. Another told us, 'My son rapidly caught up with his classmates in literacy skills, having moved to the UK from a country where phonics and literacy are started at a much older age.'

On our visit, the nursery children were busily and noisily involved in a variety of activities and play which only the trained eye would realise were carefully structured to deliver the early years curriculum – plenty of role play corners, freedom to go in and out, and excellent use made of glittery pasta. Their playground stretches up the grassy bank behind the school with forest school elements newly introduced at the top. Reception classrooms are large.

Head of the kindergarten says modestly that the school is not unique but doing what they do well. She cites her staff as following the children's interests in their teaching – she points out the artwork on the wall where a child has painted what he wanted rather than following the given theme, but it is still valued and appreciated. In the toddler room, currently decorated with a jungle theme, learning is very much child-initiated, with lots of sensory discovery.

No sightings of lunch, but pupils declared enthusiastically that the lunches are 'yummy' and 'tasty' – they are prepared on-site by DUCKS' own chef.

Achievements are celebrated in assembly, being invited to share a good piece of work with the head or with rewards including fruity tea. From year 1 the usual stickers, certificates, shields and trophies. Not a homework-free zone, but a parent said, 'just the right amount of homework and holiday work to keep the children ticking over.'

The school is committed to early identification of SEN – all pupils are carefully observed and assessed, if any SEN identified then work with the parents to establish the best support for the child. There are nine children with identified needs currently. The school recently admitted its first pupil communicating with British Sign Language – children, parents and staff have all received training with a BSL instructor.

Aims for PE set realistically for the age group, looking to develop spatial awareness, love of physical activity and play as well as social skills. Rather boy oriented, tag rugby, football and cricket on offer, and everyone learns to swim. A parent explained: 'The PE teacher is one of a kind, immensely talented and patient. The children have sports three times a week as well as extracurricular sports clubs if they choose. My son has at least five hours of organised sport a week.' Everyone learns to swim in the college pool.

Music is taught by specialists and all of year 2 learns the recorder. 'The music teacher pulls together amazing productions given the young age of the children.' Very able children are able to join groups at the junior school.

After-school activities every day of the week run until 4.30pm at a cost of around £4 per session offering an appealing mix of down-time or, for those with the energy, 3D modelling, swimming, ballet, football, netball and more. When there is always so much to fit into every day, lunchtime clubs can be useful: 'I love that my daughter has had the opportunity to start ballet with her friends at lunchtime', says a mother. So, clubs seem to offer redress the balance of the traditionally 'male' sport on offer for the girls.

DUCKS is so tucked away in Sydenham – one almost has to be in the know to venture in search of it when making the rounds of nurseries and pre-preps. If you are coming from Dulwich Village, Herne Hill or East Dulwich, it lies beyond a local curiosity, the Dulwich estate's antique toll-gate, which makes the road south of the college impassable to all but those willing to pay a pound a time to pass. Excitedly, we enquired as to whether DUCKS parents are given a toll-gate pass – not even staff are privileged with such a thing. Parents soon get the hang of the loop around.

A mere infant in terms of the almost 400 year old college, DUCKS recently celebrated its 20th anniversary. One might imagine that the school occupies only the large Victorian house fronting the road, but this is home only for the younger children: a good thing, as the rooms are slightly gloomy.

The majority of the classrooms are actually situated in a wooden-clad building looking over the playing fields and onwards to stunning views of the City and the glittering Shard. It looks very much like a cricket pavilion, echoing the actual pavilion used by the school until it burnt down in 1997 – the silver lining being the opportunity to create something which worked just for them.

The peace and quiet of the setting is a rare and unusual treat for any London family, and lends itself to numerous environmental themes, lots of muddy fun and gives rise to the names of the classes, all of wild birds. At the rear of the school are several soft surface playgrounds, segregated for various age groups, so plenty of space for letting off steam with no shortage of ride-on toys and a veranda ensuring children can play outside even on wet days.

The word used repeatedly by parents to describe the atmosphere here is nurturing. Parents told us, 'It is supportive of shy children but equally has the space and facilities for children who have boundless energy' and 'although not fiercely competitive, it does expect the children to stretch themselves.'

Whatever rumours of previous discord between staff and management have made their way to us, there have been key new appointments, teachers spoke of their happiness working here and much may now be set to change.

No concerns voiced with regards to pastoral care. One parent said, 'Outstanding pastoral care, and the school is good at communicating any concerns about our children with their parents'. 'They discuss bad behaviour in circle time in what appears to be a very meaningful way for the children.' Years 1 and 2 are all buddies to lower school pupils, whilst senior boys from the college visit as part of their community service.

Something about the building suggests a place more akin to a nursery than a school, but parents surprised us, saying it would suit 'a child responsive to structure who is keen to learn' and 'those who prefer a more free and easy approach to learning would probably find things difficult.'

The school is proud of its pupils' cultural and linguistic backgrounds, celebrating them throughout the year. Currently 17 children in the kindergarten are at least bi-lingual and 29 children in the Infants' school are bi- or tri-lingual. Far fewer, just a handful, have EAL needs.

The school praises the parents, who embrace themes and initiatives keenly, even recently attempting to pry themselves from their phones and tablets for a 'screenless week'. One mother with an eye for telling detail said: 'This is not a school where working mothers and stay-at-home mothers compete, or where a parent can achieve kudos by the quality of party bags at their child's party.' Phew.

One summed it up with satisfaction: 'Outstanding. I have wanted for nothing.'

Dulwich College: The Junior School

Linked with DUCKS Kindergarten and Infants School, Dulwich College

Dulwich Common, London SE21 7LD

Pupils: 222 • Ages: 7–11 • C of E

Fees: £18,915 pa

Tel: 020 8299 8432
Email: junioradmissions@dulwich.org.uk
Website: www.dulwich.org.uk

Head: Since 2013, Dr Toby Griffiths (40s). Educated at Whitgift School and the University of Edinburgh; completed a masters in educational psychology and a doctorate in educational psychology at Oxford. Previously a six year stint as deputy headmaster at Lanesborough School in Guildford, where he was involved in the management and marketing of the school in a parent-facing role: a good precursor to being head. He has also taught at Colet Court (now St Paul's Juniors), where boys are often on track to St Paul's, and eight years at The Dragon, where he was boarding housemaster and head of maths. Part of a teaching dynasty, his father taught at Whitgift for 38 years and his mother was a prep school head. He and his brother, also now a headmaster, were hockey blues together at Oxford. He considered teaching psychology, but from the moment he experienced the Dragon 'all bets were off' – he loves the junior school age group: 'their energy and enthusiasm, they seem so alive'.

Parents enthuse: 'He is approachable and responsive' and 'very much involved in every aspect of the college and knows the boys well'. Determined and no doubt extremely competitive: 'bring it on!' he said (with regards to a forthcoming school inspection).

The green spaces of Dulwich made moving to London easier. He lives nearby with his wife, Vicky, now working in the City. Their son is at the top of the junior school and daughter at nearby Sydenham High.

Entrance: Approximately 45 places available at age 7+, many taken by boys coming up from DUCKS, six to eight places in years 4 and 5. Register in the autumn preceding the desired year of entry. Tours most Friday mornings for prospective parents and autumn open days. Assessments during January in maths, English, verbal and non-verbal reasoning. Not looking for perfection, understanding of differing educational experience, but all round ability. Successful applicants invited for an interview and an activity morning; process now includes a taught element 'to see how boys react in a lesson situation and how well they learn something new'.

Dr Griffiths says the junior school has gone from being popular to very popular, with now over three applicants per place, and is increasingly seen as the 'start of the college'. Boys come from as far away as Greenwich, Orpington and Fulham, up to a 40 minute commute. The school lists an eclectic list of feeders at 7+ in addition to DUCKS: Herne Hill, Bertrum House, Broomwood Hall, The Villa Pre-Prep, River House Montessori and Babington House, seemingly not many of the nearby state primaries.

Exit: Almost all (at least 95 per cent) go on to the college. The head says that those who don't go on from the lower school are very rare, and only after extensive dialogue over several years regarding where they would thrive best, and then it is the parents' decision. We asked a parent if they felt their son was well-prepared for the next stage; they replied, 'absolutely. And if we didn't, we would feel comfortable raising any issues with the teachers and headmaster.'

Remarks: Once more sporty than academic, the balance has been redressed, and it is now much more of an all-round school. Dr Griffiths says, 'It had always been a through school, but at one time the boys from the junior school had taken their foot off the pedal whilst everyone else worked hard to get there [the college], so four to five years ago the bar was really raised to ensure primacy of the classroom'. It does mean that there is no need for exam pressure to dominate. Focus is on 'doing their best, not pass or fail'. Boys we spoke to were quite nervous about the forthcoming 11+ tests despite in reality the certainty of a place – all carefully designed to ensure they arrive in the college confident in exam technique and on a level playing field.

Big leap in scores of boys coming in this year. Teaching time has been increased by 40 minutes per day and all children now have two periods of French per week. No gripes about teaching reached our ears, quite the opposite: 'The boys seem fired up by what they learn. There has been a practical element to subjects which fires the imagination and creates interest.' Recent Academic Enrichment Symposium on the subject of movement saw 25 different speakers giving workshop on topics ranging from Masai dancing to Roman battles, kite flying to hovercraft.

Curriculum is delivered by form tutors with specialist staff initially for French, art, DT, music and games, with additional specialists in later years.

Parents pretty united on homework, saying, 'We don't feel it is intensive at all. Obviously there is homework, but we feel that it is suited to our sons' capabilities. There is extension homework for those boys who are more academic and help for those who perhaps find it takes longer to grasp certain things.' No holiday homework – other than when preparing for the 11+ exam. 'Doesn't feel too pressured re exams or testing'.

Improved rewards system – commendation certificates, bronze, silver and gold, are presented in assembly. Reports for parents show effort and attainment, which is appreciated by parents who conclude, 'it will likely do much to encourage the children.' 'Very little pressure on the lead up to exams. In general, we haven't known when the boys are due to have any sort of assessment. And while there is homework every day, it is rare that it will take more than 30 minutes'.

Surprisingly low levels of SEN. All children are screened for dyslexia on entry to year 3. Some may be referred for further testing and diagnosis. There are four full-time learning support teachers shared between the junior and senior schools. In the junior school, teachers work with individuals and small groups to provide extra support where needed, perhaps in terms of how their working memory affects spelling, organisation, numeracy, creative writing or comprehension. Less than two per cent receive EAL support, but many from multi-lingual families.

This is the time for experimentation. The headmaster tells us, 'We want boys to be and to try everything by the time they leave here – a rugby player, actor, musician, chess player, mathematician and writer'. Should not have to choose between a swimming gala and orchestra practice – the sporty head says he won't let fixtures take over.

'With 70 acres of fields there is no shortage of sport and it is all first class,' cried a delighted parent. All boys play rugby, football, hockey and cricket, everyone has the opportunity to play a competitive fixture, whether extra or intra school. Aim is for boys to represent the school in every sport – 'everyone gets to go on the coach and shake hands with the opposition', so far managed it for football. 'Our sons are not in the A or B teams for sports, but they always get to play matches and be involved in the sporting community'. Fitness should be a given with gymnastics, swimming, rackets and athletics in addition. Stars include a year 6 national breaststroke champion and several county representatives in cricket and chess. A highlight for many is the trip to the college's outdoor centre in the Brecon Beacons.

Everyone performs in the year 3 and 6 plays. The recent Bugsy Malone performed in the Edward Alleyn Theatre looked enormous fun.

Music department seen as first rate. All the boys in the junior school learn a stringed instrument in year 3 and a wind instrument in year 4, and perform in two major productions. Some 40 per cent then have individual lessons. 'Our younger son has decided to have extra violin and guitar lessons and we are not a musical family,' said a surprised parent. A year 5 pupil recently won the prestigious Bach piano competition, open to the whole college. There are opportunities to play in ensembles and orchestras and sing in the choir. Boys have performed at London venues including Southwark Cathedral, the Cadogan Hall and St John's Smith Square. Pupils benefit from the wider college co-curricular activities, recently taking part in Dulwich Creative by designing their own graffiti t-shirts.

These boys are readers – the library has 8,000 books and a full-time enthusiastically chatty librarian who insists that books are not just for book week, that she never tells everyone to 'shhh!' and that 'life's too short to finish a book you're not enjoying'. The Roald Dahl day is an annual fixture where everyone dresses up as their favourite character. Art projects line the walls, currently takes on Mark Rothko and work inspired by a trip to Tate Modern to study Henry Moore.

Just the swim squad and chamber group up and at it early. At lunchtime a couple of by invitation clubs such as madrigal and chapel choir, but also each year has choices such as karate, tennis, book club, chess, sewing and various music ensembles. After-school clubs have been extended (there are 95 in all) and now run until 5pm, with after-school care available until 6pm. Boys can do their prep in the homework club or try Russian, dance, cycling, magazine club or French aviation.

The location on the southerly edge of the college campus in a peaceful backwater just a stone's throw from the useful South Circular, and station makes drop-offs and collections pleasant. The building itself is modern and handily adjacent to the lower school, with a pitched roof, wide corridors upstairs and quite spacious classrooms. The library tucks under the roof, giving cosy reading nooks. Year 3s have their own playground.

We were impressed that year 6 boys were entrusted to lead us solo on our tour of the school, with only a little assistance from Dr Griffiths on time-keeping – not every school entrusts its pupils, of whatever age, to speak as they see fit with a visitor wielding a pen. It speaks volumes. Parents, too, speak of this level of trust between boys and teachers. One said of their son, 'He truly looks forward to being at school. He has had very supportive form teachers – strict, but fair, so there is an obvious level of trust.'

Boys seem to feel listened to and have seen their ideas put forward to the school council come to fruition, such as more play equipment for the playground.

A parent told us, 'This school excels in its pastoral care. We couldn't ask for better.' Others agree, 'They know the students very well and truly try to understand not just individual students, but the different dynamics amongst various groups of boys.' And in the case of a problem with peers raised with the school, 'The boys were supported, but given opportunities to address the issues themselves.' Teachers are seen as responsive – known to answer emails out of school hours.

Competitiveness abounds – house allegiances start here – but there is room for inclusiveness: all year 6 boys are prefects, rather than an elite group. And every year 6 child has a buddy in the lower years – our guides introduced them to us with grins as we went around: we might have thought they were siblings.

Parents say, 'The boys feel like they belong in the school and with each other.' And, 'The atmosphere is one of feeling included. It is not an exclusive school.' Parents themselves sound unpretentious and appealing, describing each other as 'friendly, relaxed, supportive of their children', 'from all walks of life', 'welcoming, fun, and interesting.'

As for the college as a whole, appearances can be deceptive and there is a rich social mix. Many say there is no type for whom the school particularly caters, 'it's tough to see what kind of child the school wouldn't be suitable for.' Several say: 'He can't wait to leave the house in the morning.'

A few academic scholarships at 10 per cent of the tuition fees, plus means-tested bursaries may be available for the very able whose families fulfil the financial criteria.

Dulwich College

Linked with DUCKS Kindergarten and Infants School, Dulwich College: The Junior School

58

Dulwich Common, London SE21 7LD

Pupils: 1,367; 130 full/weekly boarders • Ages: 11–18 • Sixth form: 470

Fees: Day £18,915; Boarding £37,017 – £39,480 pa

Tel: 020 8693 3601
Email: info@dulwich.org.uk
Website: www.dulwich.org.uk

Master: Since 2009, Dr Joseph (Joe) Spence BA PhD (mid-50s), a graduate in modern history and politics; the Irish histories and literature of his postgrad line his study walls. Previously headmaster of Oakham School and for 10 years until 2002 held the prestigious position of master in college at Eton, housemaster to the King's scholars, 'surrounded by the brightest'; it was here he found his vocation. His first decade at Dulwich College will coincide with the college's 400th anniversary, entwining their legacies.

Grammar school educated, he describes his career path as the 'story of accident', a happy one. The turning point was a friend's encouragement that one 'no longer has to be behind a desk as headmaster'. Immensely warm and charming, putting one at ease, the embodiment of the oft repeated 'Dulwich boys can talk to anyone'. He brings a sense of fun to those around him, appearing to wear his responsibilities lightly, preparing to ad lib a speech to a grand assembly as he says goodbye.

He is married to a lawyer, with two sons and daughter. He still finds time to write, recently penning a new libretto for a concert at King's College Cambridge, turning a poem written by PG Wodehouse's brother into a song. He wants these sustaining passions for the boys: 'My duty is to make sure that every Alleynian leaves with something intellectual... a passion which will be with him for the rest of his life'.

Parents, seeming to have adopted the Ofsted phraseology, unanimously declare him to be outstanding. They enthuse: 'a good orator, a great listener'; 'as fiercely passionate about the arts as academics'; 'a great presence and a motivational leader'; 'excellent, effective and innovative'.

His vision for the transformations in progress – physical and philosophical – start with 'get the classroom right, then everything else', but quickly go beyond with the desire to create a generation of original thinkers. You don't have to be a scientist or an artist here – 'learning that is free from the syllabus' allows boys to take risks in a dazzling (we've rarely seen such a weighty catalogue of riches) programme of challenges, national and international competitions, symposia, external prizes, performances and physical adventures.

Academic matters: It's well known that improving the academics was top of the agenda. The college is now in the top eight per cent for value added nationally and the master is confident that the best is still to come. In 2016, 85 per cent of I/GCSE grades were A*/A. Plenty of A*s in sciences, English literature, maths, French and Spanish. At A level/Pre-U, 61 per cent A*/A, and (again including Pre-U) 90 per cent A*-B. Maths is most popular by far, followed by physics, history, economics and chemistry. High percentage of A*/As in physics, plus history of art, English, further maths, history and art. A levels remain as the core upper school offer but individual heads of subject have the flexibility to offer Pre-U.

Academic teaching is described by parents as solid lower down the college but inspirational higher up. Thirty-five per cent of teachers in residence for over 10 years. The master says candidly that now only a handful are perhaps not on message, and he won't see boys stuck with them, which chimes with parents, who say, 'very good standard of teaching, noticeable improvement' and 'incompetence would not be tolerated'. They also describe staff as 'hugely committed'; 'they understand a boy's potential'; 'they set the bar high academically' and 'the daily report system is excellent'.

The master drives innovation. A key appointment is the director of science, formerly at lauded Brighton College. Turning things on their head, 'flip' lessons might give boys homework first, then the boys come in and discuss how they found it, or mini-whiteboards may enable a teacher to see at a glance whether boys have 'got it'. Boys were initially consulted on their view of assessments, and came back saying they actually felt there was grade inflation – pupil voice has been used in every key decision since. Staff share with each other a 'speciality dish' ie what is working for them in the classroom.

Curriculum is largely as one might expect; choosing options is quite complex. Languages have a particularly strong focus throughout. French, Spanish, Chinese and Latin are taught in the lower school, later on there is the addition of German, Italian and Greek. Appealing language trips: year 9s to Salamanca, year 11s to Florence. The boys describe them as holistic, taking in both language and culture, raising their passion for the subject up a notch. Exchanges take place too, but with boys considerately settled in host families in pairs.

The only setting is for maths. All pupils study separate sciences up to IGCSE and the college doesn't necessarily encourage the collection of an excessive number. Intellectual boys wishing to stretch themselves further between years 7 and 11 can enrol on the scholars' programme, described by one as 'the highlight of my week'.

Quirkier A level options include critical and contextual studies and ancient history. Liberal studies in the upper sixth in conjunction with the girls at JAGS allows boys to try something new: modern poetry, yoga, book-binding, Italian cinema and even ballroom dancing.

Also for sixth formers, the Dulwich Diploma, which looks to offer the depth of A level with the breadth of the IB: the three components comprise academic study, at least four AS levels and three A2s, an extended essay or research topic of their choice – recent examples Who Killed Sylvia Plath? and Is Medical Research the New Imperialism? – engagement beyond the classroom and preparation for life after Dulwich.

Whilst all of this adds up to a very full plate, parents say there are 'high expectations with excellent support through study skills sessions' and 'it's pretty intensive in terms of workload but not too high pressure'.

A team of four well-qualified learning support teachers are shared with the junior school, and provide support to individual boys with a diagnosed learning difficulty – 20 per cent. Eight per cent of middle and upper school boys receive EAL support.

Games, options, the arts: In year 7, whilst skills are built and some sports tried for the first time, rugby, football, hockey and cricket are all compulsory. By year 8 choices emerge, one being dropping rugby for fencing. Tennis currently squeezed for space with only three courts. No single sport is compulsory in the middle school but a plethora of teams make it tempting to get involved – skiing, rowing, fives, squash, cross-country and basketball, to name but a few. Years 10 and 11 may try golf, rock-climbing, self-defence, taekwondo and rugby 7s, whilst upper school choices aim to involve boys in sport however that may be, perhaps officiating or coaching as well as trying gentlemanly pursuits such as croquet, horse-riding and sailing. The school has responded to the national appetite for competitive cycling and boys are able to use the superb facilities at nearby Herne Hill velodrome.

Seventy acres of playing fields recently re-seeded, and rugby is the triumphant sport with 1st XV recently winning the NatWest Schools cup for the third consecutive year. Success, too, for the under 14s rowers, who are national champions, and the school supplies four members of the under 15 GB water-polo team. Boys we had lunch with laughingly said the only thing they didn't like was swimming as there was no point trying to keep up with the Olympic swimmers and water-polo players.

Dr Spence continues to ponder how one achieves balance amidst such rich opportunities: '50 boys will have played at Twickenham, that's a once in a lifetime experience', but are there 'boys who might have done better academically if they had not done so much?'

'Arts, music and co-curricular are outstanding'. We arrived just in time to be treated to a sensitive rendition of W H Auden's Stop All of The Clocks as part of that day's house poetry competition. The school has a rich theatrical tradition, a flexible theatre space, Chewetel Ejiofor and Rupert Penry-Jones are OAs, makes the very most of the London theatre scene, and each year produces three drama festivals and 24 performance pieces.

A parent said, 'What I really like is the drive to go beyond the curriculum and inspire'. This term's Dulwich Creative week was produced with all of the finesse and confidence of a national arts organisation gone guerrillan and saw art hijacks where every pupil – astonishingly even the babies in the kindergarten – produce a clay self-portrait, which then came together into one installation. A surreal note remains overlooking the cricket pitches, giant polyurethane mushrooms by international street artist Christian Nagel. A new 'found' space, The Store, chills to the bone, but provides an edgy, white-washed, informal rehearsal space which boys can call their own, which also houses art exhibits.

Art and DT facilities are light and bright, and where we found some of the most exuberant classes in full flow. We admired Grayson Perry-ish vases produced in ceramics classes, and groovy dog kennels in DT.

Numbers learning instruments peak in the lower school at 45 per cent of boys, falling naturally enough to 25 per cent by the upper school. Standard of musicianship varies from enthusiastic beginners to boys who are leaders of section in the National Youth Orchestra or principals at Glyndebourne and the ENO. The music department is in the process of upgrading: there is a shiny new Mac suite for music technology, a new acoustic percussion suite, and small and large practice areas. Another funky new facility is the electric 'shed', fully sound-insulated, a great place to let rip with the electric guitar.

World class performances from a formidable debating team, who recently trounced the competition at the Oxford and Cambridge Unions. Where next for the boy currently ranked number one in the world?

Long lunch hours ensure even the senior boys feel they have time for clubs and societies, which continue after school. For the lower school these might include fencing, card games, woodwork and Scouts. For the middle and upper school a sophisticated list offers Japanese culture, alternative thinking, finance, Norse and Germanic, ultimate frisbee and rocketry. Poultry society boasts its own hens; whether they are ever eaten is set to be a college myth. Our curiosity was piqued as to what goes on at the Gentlemen's Club (no-one seemed to know); presumably no cigars.

The careers office has a 2,000 strong network of former parents and corporate contacts: a recent event invited 40 such to the Dulwich Picture Gallery. Boys were instructed to read up on everyone's biographies then were sent off to network fiercely.

Boarding: There are 130 boarders, two-thirds in the sixth form, majority from China and Hong Kong but also Eastern Europe. The boarding houses are on the campus, modernised period houses decorated with OA sporting team photos: quite basic in our view, small-ish rooms with less than luxurious en suite bathrooms, but unlikely to worry most boys intent on studying and playing hard surrounded by friends. Common rooms with large screen for movie nights, table football and all-important toasters.

Background and atmosphere: Founded in 1619 by the wealthy actor and businessman, Edward Alleyn. He set up and endowed the Foundation, which distributes its surplus profits to a group of schools including Dulwich College, JAGS and Alleyn's. The college moved to its present site in the 1870s. The main buildings are stunning Italianate red brick designed by the son of the architect of the Houses of Parliament. Inside, the panelled Great Hall lined with the names of Oxford and Cambridge scholars – up until the wall space ran out in the 1960s – has featured in a Hollywood film or two, more often the site of Old Alleynian dinners, the master's library and the Wodehouse library (PG is an Old Alleynian), with a significant theatrical archive including a Shakespeare First Folio.

Sitting amidst vast manicured pitches, the college is a gracious and intriguing south London landmark. Closer up, the collection of modern buildings forming a large part of the teaching spaces, particularly in the lower school, are plain and nothing more than functional, quite possibly a bit depressing. The buildings housing the upper school feel fresher – Ed's place looks like a commercial café, and there is a huge common room, whilst a second one was sacrificed to create a popular 'work room' with banks of computers. Ironically for a school that appears so stunning to the passer-by, it's the fabric of the school which could currently disappoint parents if not boys.

However, we donned hard hat and work boots to inspect the then almost complete Laboratory, costing over £21m, which will put the college's science offer ever more firmly on the map.

The first phase opened in April 2015, the second in September 2016. Led by prestigious Grimshaw Architects – Cutty Sark, The Eden Project – It literally removes the divide between arts and sciences, including a 240 seat auditorium, as well as five IT suites and 18 glassy labs looking over the beautiful trees of Dulwich.

At its centre is displayed Shackleton's boat, a treasured college possession previously residing appropriately enough with a stuffed penguin in a chilly cloister. Conrad Shawcross RA, with a committed team of 10 boys, worked on an installation. Naturally it leads the way environmentally too. The finishing touch, which may transform the feel of the college as much as anything, is the bright idea of removing the central car park, replacing it with landscaped recreational and thinking spaces.

The Dulwich College partnership schools overseas thrive, the latest in Singapore, but the master is clear that Dulwich is his absolute focus: he has delegated all but top level sign-off. Similarly, although he has championed outreach and partnership with a London academy group, a pie-chart of time devoted would see this account for only 10 per cent.

Sartorial traditions define the college – 'colours' blazers are boldly striped affairs awarded in recognition of achievement. 'Buy a big size,' advises the school captain – they will be de rigueur come OA reunions. You need a spotters' guide to identify old school ties, there are so many for every society and event. The master sees the Christmas fair attracting 3,000 local residents as a way to prove that the school isn't 'stuck up'. He is aware that the uniform gives off mixed messages, but wants the boys to wear it with pride. Believes the school is and should be 'class, creed and colour-blind'.

School lunches seem due for a make-over, but boys won't starve. Students we spoke to in the lower school were amusing, boisterous; those higher up articulate, but not at all arrogant, and all with different interests. A regular visitor to the school said, 'The boys appear relaxed and happy, there's always plenty of banter and camaraderie in evidence'.

Pastoral care, well-being and discipline: A senior prefect told us he's a rarity, having been at the school all the way from year 1, but has relished meeting new boys – 'each intake year interests and friends shift' – and although the school is large, boys feel they know each other within their year. The transition points are handled thoughtfully, ensuring boys get to bond with each other, for instance on a Welsh adventure when joining the lower school.

Houses are named after great Englishmen, and wooden boards throughout the school see Drake, Spenser et al jostling for position – house competitions facilitate new friendships as well as much rivalry.

We were on the look-out for indifferent pastoral care, but found no evidence for it whatsoever, instead much praise. A parent – 'Boys know where they stand with the master, and whilst he's friendly and approachable, boys know he won't tolerate certain misdemeanours...hard line on bullying'. Another, 'He strikes the right note on being nurturing but also seeing that the boys get on with being independent'. 'A caring atmosphere which celebrates the individual,' said a parent of a child diagnosed with ASD. One noted realistically that 'pastoral care is good, but the biggest problem is to get the boys to overcome male pride and admit they need help.' Gross misconducts such as possession of drugs or bullying would result in consideration for exclusion, whether fixed term or permanent, rather than an automatic exclusion.

Pupils and parents: The college is academically selective and socially inclusive, with a very culturally and ethnically diverse population, augmented by the boarders. Lots of multi-lingual children who might speak Chinese, Russian, Spanish or French at home. Boys mentioned pupil-led assemblies: recent topics include homosexuality and discrimination. The school captain said: 'There is no Dulwich way. You don't have to conform.'

A parent: 'It takes boys who are sporty, academic, musical, artistic and a mixture of all those things. If your child is gifted in one area, they will soar here. If they are a good all-rounder they will be encouraged to be a great all-rounder.' And it may come as a surprise to find that parents describe each other typically as 'a good bunch of mixed, non-stuffy parents', 'un-snobbish and not cliquey.'

Alumni include Chiwetel Ejiofor, Bob Monkhouse, Raymond Chandler, P G Wodehouse, Nigel Farage, Lionel Barber, Sir Ernest Shackleton.

Entrance: Not the ultra-elite intake of a few London schools, but still a top 15 per cent ability profile. At 11+, half of the 75 boys arrive from Dulwich College Junior School and half from a variety of local primary and prep schools including Hornsby House, Blackheath Prep, Rosemead, Dolphin School, Oakfield, Honeywell, Belleville, Corpus Christi, Dulwich Hamlet, St John's and St Clements. Parents are asked to send a letter from a registered professional regarding SEN needs to ensure appropriate assistance with the entrance exam. At 13 + the main feeders are Dulwich Prep London, Northcote Lodge and Fulham Prep. Non-refundable registration fee of £100 for Brits and £200 for overseas candidates.

A good number come from the immediate vicinity of Dulwich, but Foundation coaches brings pupils from as far away as Notting Hill, Canary Wharf, Wimbledon and Chislehurst.

Exit: Recent leavers to over 47 universities including Bristol, Durham, Edinburgh, Exeter, Imperial, KCL, LSE, UCL, Warwick and York; 24 to Oxbridge in 2016. Increasing focus on global destinations, particularly Ivy League. Currently around a dozen each year exit to overseas universities – often the Chinese University of Hong Kong, a couple to Harvard, Dutch universities in the slip-stream but the list has also included MIT and UCLA.

Money matters: Currently 411 boys in receipt of financial assistance of various kinds – 145 have means-tested bursaries ranging in value from five to 100 per cent and 266 have scholarships, ranging in value from 10 per cent to one-third of tuition fees. 'Superb value for money,' said one parent of three privately educated children. 'Quite simply, Dulwich College far outstrips the rest in terms of communication, professionalism and results'.

Perhaps most exciting of all in terms of evolution is the college returning to its early 20th century past in launching a New Dulwich Experiment, championed by the master, which will see up to 50 per cent of pupils coming from families who cannot afford to pay full fees, opening up admissions to some of the brightest pupils from all backgrounds. In some ways it is a protective measure against becoming a school for the global super-rich, and the master freely admits it is 'enlightened self-interest', but partly funded by OAs keen to give something back, it sits very well in this already socially enlightened place.

Remarks: A school with a long tradition, with all of the prestige that comes with it, but now with a thrilling new dynamism which is raising the academic ante in every way, creating glittering new learning spaces and delivering a stunning co-curricular vision. Far more inclusive than one might imagine, the new bursary scheme needs to be trumpeted far and wide to ensure the school is on the radar of the brightest from all backgrounds.

Dulwich Hamlet Junior School

Dulwich Village, London SE21 7AL

Pupils: 390 • Ages: 7–11

Tel: 020 7525 9188
Email: office@dulwichhamletjuniorschool.org.uk
Website: www.dulwichhamlet.southwark.sch.uk

Head of School: Since 2016, Mrs Claire Purcell BEd (40s). Having gained her degree at what is now Southampton University and her first teaching post in a Hampshire school, Mrs Purcell headed to the Hamlet, rising from class teacher and senior manager with a music specialism, via deputy to the new post of head of school over the course of 20 years. Extremely modest, she is, however responsible, for the incredibly rich musical life of the school. One parent told us of her son punching the air when she was made head. We would have liked to spend more time with her but our visit coincided with year 6 Sats. She is devoted to music and family and we hear plays the recorder and sings wonderfully too. She has two young children.

Executive head since 2007 is Mrs Sonia Case BA PGCE (50s) who has no plans to retire. Since the school became part of a multi-academy trust, she has been executive headteacher of Dulwich Hamlet Junior School and The Belham Primary School, an exciting reinvention of a Victorian school in Peckham which she is building from the ground up. She has an office at the Hamlet, but currently splits her time, spending three days at the Belham, whilst this school continues to spin along like a well-trained top.

Mrs Case started life as an actress, including a role in the original series of Poldark, before moving into advertising and has worked in education for over 24 years. Prior to leading Dulwich Hamlet she taught at three state primaries in Bromley. Parents describe her to us as 'a driving force', 'dynamic', 'passionate' and she 'encourages readiness to learn by expectations of excellent behaviour'. We found her to be vibrant and full of fizz with a real passion for where the right style of teaching can make a difference to individual children. She has two daughters and two grandchildren.

Entrance: The main feeder school for Dulwich Hamlet is Dulwich Village Infants' School. No automatic entry from one school to the other. Unlike the infant school there is no faith stipulation governing admissions. The school is oversubscribed but not to the tune we had imagined from its local reputation, and there is always some movement on the waiting list after first offers are made. Stories of houses being rented nearby to get in persist, but are taken a hard line on by the local authority and are perhaps more focused on the infants' school than here.

Other admissions come from local prep schools such as Ducks, JAPS and Herne Hill and some other local state schools.

Exit: The majority of children fall into the catchment for the nearby Charter School and head straight there, whilst a percentage of both boys and girls move into the independent sector, to Dulwich College, Alleyn's, St Dunstan's or Sydenham Girls' School. Some children attend schools further afield such as the Grey Coat Hospital school and grammars in Bromley and Kent. According to parents, those preparing for selective entry elsewhere sometimes use tutors, more for exam technique than academics.

Remarks: The school consistently ranks near the top of league tables with regards to academic attainment. Ofsted, declaring it outstanding in every category, has long since moved on to other more variable territories. It does well by children across the board, but also by high attainers.

Teachers have two surprising qualities; they are young and quite often male. Mrs Case delights that they are enthusiastic and fresh from training, full of the kind of multimedia experience and latest thinking that invigorates what she describes as a 'glittering curriculum'. We concur that it is pretty sparkly and ambitious. A parent told us about a year 6 English lesson which involved tightrope walking. We visited shortly after Shakespeare week, where each year took a different aspect of A Midsummer Night's Dream and created a film to be viewed by the whole school and parents. Students study for LAMDA exams. STEM week answered questions such as 'can you eat a candle?' and 'how do you get the fizz in pop?' Prospective parents should brace themselves for a particularly high number of dressing up days – Roman, Celt, Greek, Indian and Shakespeare. Drama often comes into lessons with role-playing techniques used. There are currently striking papier-mâché sculptures of Ted Hughes' Iron Man around the school and we saw year 5 pupils creating blueprints of wild flowers inspired by Victorian women artists employed by Kew Gardens. Displays within classrooms are 'learning walls' whilst those in the public spaces, on lovely felt boards, exhibit the children's work.

A couple of parents said to us: the teachers have 'all been so different but have continually excited and stimulated my children'; they are 'approachable and accessible' and 'most are imaginative in their teaching and enthuse the children'. Setting of children is minimal as Mrs Case points out that removing the brightest would disadvantage those who would benefit from a higher level of discussion, but there is setting for maths from year 3 to enable more teaching resource where needed.

Parents describe sport as having improved dramatically since the school has had access to neighbouring sports fields. There are also courts adjacent to the school in use most days for either netball or tennis with specialist coaches. At least half of the students in each year group have represented the school, participating in football or netball tournaments, and many attend sport clubs before or after school. The cricket team – girls as well as boys – won the British Land cricket trophy, playing the final at Lord's. Years 4 and 5 are strong swimmers, both having won their Southwark schools swimming galas this year. A parent said of sport: 'the school balances a competitive spirit with inclusivity'. There is a minibus for away matches provided by the PTA. The cross-country team represents the school nationally.

The school excels in its musical provision. All children receive music lessons conducted by specialists, and then nearly three-quarters learn musical instruments up to grade 5 taught by peripatetic music tutors. Whatever the instrument, there's an ensemble for it – woodwind, brass, strings or guitars. Steel pans are very popular. The fusion ensemble developed an original composition, Londinium, which was presented with an award for innovation and performed at the Royal Albert Hall as part of the primary proms. There are two choirs, who have sung at The Scoop on the Southbank, the Young Voices Concert at the 02 and the Bromley Music Festival. Recorder playing is taken to a new level here, with an annual recorder festival featuring a workshop, performance from professionals and inter-school concert. We were lucky enough to hear the early music ensemble play at Dulwich Festival; the standard seemed so high they could provide the incidental music to Wolf Hall.

Parents are asked to make a voluntary contribution of less than £100 per annum to help fund the extracurricular, such as trips and specialist workshops.The school offers a wide variety of fun after-school clubs including cookery, knitting, magic, Lego robotics, yoga and clay, with some charges.

The school presents as a picture postcard Victorian school, with patterned brickwork and scalloped roof tiles, at the heart of picturesque Dulwich village, encircled by sunflowers in the summer, thrilling many a parent and passer-by with nostalgia. The school has had many incarnations, but the main building dates from 1897. On the sunny spring morning of our visit, the nearby village hall promoted a barn dance, whilst the petite row of shops sell ice-creams, children's shoes, beautifully curated art and school stationery: it's an idyllic slice of middle class Village London.

D

Through the gates it doesn't disappoint, in fact, the rear outlook looking across the Griffin Fields, unseen from the road, which the school leases for sports, is a hidden delight. Between the admin building and 'village building' housing the traditional high-windowed Victorian school hall is an Astroturf playground. There is free play, but also structured play at lunch time such as teacher-led football. We liked the Astroturf shady veranda of an attractive wooden classroom built with 'bulge' funding, for those wanting to escape the hurly-burly.

Space at the front of the school is newly transformed into a garden with raised vegetable patches, bug houses and composting and what will be a wild flower space for curriculum work. Lunches with an international menu can be eaten either in the refurbished dining hall or at circular picnic tables under a shady canopy in the playground. Above the dining hall are DT and food technology facilities which outclass those of several of the nearby prep schools. A couple of the celebrities familiar to everyone who lives locally were parents here and opened the transformed building. Year 5 participates annually in a project run by the Architectural Association. There is a large library and break-out space for year 5. And the whole school hall now boasts a sophisticated sound system paid for by the PTA. Given the school's focus on design and media, the ICT room uses Macs.

Pupils describe the school to us as 'fun and happy'. Despite the affluent catchment area, there is apparently more of a social mix than one might imagine. Certainly a wide range of languages is spoken within the school, from Urdu to Japanese or Hindi. A word which crops up several times from parents is 'inclusive'. The school has a full-time inclusion manager, and there is small room for one-to-one teaching. The school is also a Dyslexia Friendly School, though one parent mentioned being disappointed the school had not highlighted her child's dyslexia to her. Parents say that bullying is not unheard of but they trust the school to resolve such matters swiftly. They say: 'the general atmosphere seems to be caring' and 'they will go out of their way over the smallest issues to ensure every child is happy and included'.

The children of parents hopping onto the local trains and buses to commute are well provided for with a large dedicated classroom and qualified staff offering breakfast and after-school care. A parent described her peers to us as 'high powered with equally high expectations', which we are told is a fair portrait. Most seem grateful and appreciative, as one mother shared: 'I frequently find myself telling my kids I wish I could have gone to a school like theirs', whilst another concluded: 'quite simply a joyful experience'.

Dulwich Prep London

60

42 Alleyn Park, London SE21 8AT

Pupils: 850; 20 flexi-boarders • Ages: 3-13 (co-ed nursery) • C of E

Fees: Day £11,850 – £17,520; Boarding + £1,440 – £4,648 pa

Tel: 020 8670 3217
Email: registrar@dulwichpreplondon.org
Website: www.dulwichpreplondon.org

Headmaster: Since 2009, Michael Roulston MBE MEd (50s). Married with three children, educated in Ulster, he is warm and friendly, zipping about and offering to 'play mother' with the Darjeeling on our visit. First impressions aside, one senses his combination of vision, drive and no nonsense was forged during his first headship in the 1980s at The Model School – an informally religiously integrated school in Northern Ireland. His contribution to conflict resolution in the field of education was recognised by the BP Gulbenkian Citizenship Award in 1994.

After a stint in Japan as headmaster of The British School in Tokyo, earning him an MBE for services to education, he returned to the UK as head of Cranleigh Prep in Surrey. This is a man who clearly thrives on challenge and change, with his eye on the prizes – his and the boys'. We see him as a definite moderniser, sprucing up the old traditions, delivering a slickly presented school with a few fashionable nods – boules, allotments – without straying from his brief of happy parents and pupils at common entrance. Prior to our visit we had heard him described by parents as being 'rather like a successful CEO'. We found him to be business-like certainly, but not stiffly corporate. Yes, very 'on message', but sincere too.

He says of the school, 'It's fun, full of energy from the earliest years all the way though...every day you cannot but be inspired by what the boys do. They are valued, recognised and well-loved'.

Head of the pre-prep since 2011, Mrs Ruth Burtonshaw BSc Phd PGCE Dip dyslexia and learning, is an early years specialist.

Entrance: Admission is selective. Multiple points of entry but majority start in the nursery at 3+ (girls and boys), at 4+ (boys only) or at 7+ (boys only). Limited number of means-tested bursaries to new applicants in years 3 and 4, determined by academic assessment.

Exit: Don't think that entrance to DPL is a do-not-pass-go ticket straight to Dulwich College, but a large proportion of pupils do gain entrance – with others heading in a variety of directions, foremost Westminster, Alleyn's and Tonbridge. Recent leavers exited to 28 different schools. Conversation regarding choice of senior school starts as early as year 4, and headmaster claims that every boy achieves his first (guided) choice of destination. Good tally of academic, sport, art and all-rounder scholarships or exhibitions, with many scholarships offered to Dulwich College. Only two or three boys a year choose to leave at 11+.

Remarks: The main curriculum is fairly traditional. French from year 1 and everyone tries their hand at Latin. Spanish offered as alternative to French. We found the lack of fashionable forward-thinking options such as Chinese or Russian surprising when even the local state primaries are giving them a go. The head says Mandarin has been offered as a club in the past, but there was little interest.

Setting in maths from year 4, extended to all examined subjects by year 7. This really works, with parents confirming there is sufficient flexibility for boys to move within the year to find the right level for them, and to be encouraged by their ability in different subjects. In each of the classes we visited, young male teachers were particularly noticeable, in amongst the boys or sitting on desks, easily relating to the boys in lessons ranging from European history, via maths to music technology. Energy fairly resounds and parents of pupils at the lower school, particularly, describe it as 'buzzing'.

Almost 20 per cent of boys are identified with a learning difference, mainly mild to moderate dyslexia. The head says that the school will do its best by all, but any with significant difficulties may find themselves guided to a more specialist school such as Fairley House. Highly-trained specialists lead a good number of staff in the learning support department. We saw great learning integration in the older years with dyslexic boys using laptops alongside their peers; parents confirm that boys don't feel singled out in any way if they need extra help. Nonetheless, some comment with feeling on just how tough it can be and wish for a little more two-way communication with teachers.

Sport is well resourced, with fixtures both after school and on Saturdays. Seven full-time PE teachers, specialist coaching from year 4, more than 70 teams, and achievements at national level, particularly in rugby and swimming. Every boy has an opportunity to play. Parents say coaching is less good at the lower levels, and whilst clubs offer exciting opportunities from rock-climbing to kayaking, 'alternatives to the obvious sporting options are very limited in the younger years'.

Homework is as ever controversial. One mother comments that whilst the boys love the varied topic work, parents find it 'never-ending' at weekends.

Drama varies from year to year. There is a year 6 play and an upper school play each year. Year 7 classes have drama and each year 8 class is off timetable for two weeks to produce an original production. Art continues to year 8 with clearly inspiring teaching, new facilities and technologies. We were wowed by the boys' 3D acrylic sculpture after Jackson Pollock, and the excitement in the room as the boys made sophisticated digital animations.

Music is rich, appealing and widely pursued, with over 20 ensembles and choirs, concerts of every type at venues in and out of the school, such as the Royal Hospital, Chelsea and Southwark Cathedral. Ninety per cent of the boys from year 2 upwards study an instrument, many achieving grade 8 before they leave.

Clubs (only a few additional charges) and activities run at lunch-time for boys from years 1-4, but also 4-5 pm from year 5. Current options include Lego, Warhammer, movie-making, beekeeping, street dance, juggling, Greek, golf and gymnastics. Wide array of trips – no stone unturned on the London museum circuit; further afield during school holidays (often built into the fees) eg Pompeii and Normandy. All this plus a thought-provoking lecture series – featuring recently a holocaust survivor, notable writers, broadcasters and adventurers.

The school was founded as Dulwich College Prep School (DCPS) in 1885. Despite the confusion arising from its name, the school is completely independent from Dulwich College and is an educational trust with its own governing body. This has recently been clarified with the school now styled as Dulwich Prep London (DPL). Situated in a wide, quiet West Dulwich street a few minutes from the train station, the buildings, mostly fairly modern, crowd around the playground.

With just over 800 pupils the school is large, but we saw how the division of the school into four distinct sections, each with its own library and classrooms, really works – 'the boys are quite protected from feeling lost in a huge place, and they're fully prepared for moving on,' said a parent.

Parents from the nursery year to higher up the school all comment on the benefit of a single sex school where teachers are free to focus on knights, dinosaurs, bloody battles etc. If there's one thing this school seems to do brilliantly it's the ability to really 'get' boys and how they learn and put this into practice. There is wiggle time (dancing around between lessons), marble parties or even a pool table as a whole class reward – 'the motivation and excitement are huge'.

The school motto is 'one for all and all for one' and the houses are named after North American Indian tribes from Chippeway to Objiwas. The winning tribe raises their flag weekly up the pole in the playground and if this is all sounds incredibly macho, we hear the boys sometimes choose to sing ABBA as their victory song. Meanwhile others, who choose the calmer activities from book club to weaving and needlework, do so without fear of ridicule. Some parents transfer from a co-ed environment for exactly this reason.

While the head's emphasis on character and kindness rings true – right on cue we witnessed children relating the story of the Good Samaritan to their day – a couple of parents commented that it can take a good while to find your niche. 'If you're not good at sport, you're not popular in the playground.' This is a school which aims to develop 'resilience'. When asked which kinds of boys would be happiest here, parents suggest: 'the bright and the best', 'a self-starter, bright and athletic', 'you've got to be robust'.

No surprises that the majority of parents are highly affluent, most living within an expanding 10 mile radius of the school. However, we hear that there is a healthy mix from the scarily ambitious to the more laid back, so there is a good chance of finding like-minded souls.

School has one boarding house called (not so aptly in our opinion) Brightlands; this can accommodate 25 weekly or flexi-boarders from year 4. Rather a sombre looking house with a garden next to the pre-prep, it's been recently redecorated, and though the housemaster and his family are young and welcoming and boys rush around busily, we spied scary paint colours downstairs and 1950s style curtains in the dining hall. We wondered how this rated as a home from home compared to the boys' weekend surroundings. Definite fun, though, is one week a year when years 5, 6 and 7 stay from Sunday to Thursday; they experiment with life away from home and gain the Tomahawk Award for life skills such as button-sewing and bed-making.

The pre-prep early years department is a stunningly designed new-build – all wide open flowing spaces, blending indoor/outdoor, the classrooms give way to a huge covered sandpit for wet days. It has a delightfully green outlook surrounded only by playing fields, woodland and the grounds of Dulwich Picture Gallery. Nothing locally compares to the rural feel of this setting, a great comfort for any parent who didn't expect to raise their children in one of the world's biggest cities.

Girls are the minority but are carefully selected and more than hold their own. Parents of girls have little need for concern – except getting them in: applications are over-subscribed. Rainbow Club, staffed by regular teaching staff, offers care and activities pre and post school, from 8am to 4.45pm.

The head assists in girls' applications to local private and state schools. Almost all the boys move up to the prep.

D

Dunraven School

94–98 Leigham Court Road, London SW16 2QB

Pupils: 1,469 • Ages: 4–18 • Sixth form: 250

Tel: 020 8696 5600
Email: info@dunraven.org.uk
Website: www.dunraven.org.uk

Principal: Since 2003, David Boyle (40s), BA NPQH FRSA. Married with a young daughter. A north Londoner by birth, more than a decade at Dunraven has made him a thoroughly naturalised Streatham man, and proud of the success he's done so much to create. 'My main interest is work,' he explains (although he concedes a liking for literature and cinema) 'and after work, my family.' Under his energetic leadership, the school has achieved creditable results, and acquired a bewildering array of designations: High Performing Status, Beacon Status, Advanced Healthy School Status, Investors In People status – and on it goes. Along the way, it's become the most popular school in Lambeth with seven applicants for every place. Parents describe him as an excellent manager and highly effective communicator. The secret of his success? 'I love what I do,' he shrugs. 'And I like working with people who enjoy what they do.'

Head of secondary: is Jessica West; head of primary is Michaela Christian, previously at Fairlawn Primary School in Lewisham.

Academic matters: Results are a testament, says head, to the commitment of 'a fantastically creative and hardworking staff team.' At GCSE, 65 per cent of students achieved 5+ A*-C including English and maths in 2016 with 21 per cent of grades at A*/A.

Expectations are high. 'We start from the premise that the children will do well, and might do even better than we think.' Younger pupils are kept aware of how well the older ones are doing, and the benchmark is set higher each year. 'We're aiming for "astounding",' says head, with a modest smile, and indeed school was recently rated outstanding by Ofsted.

The curriculum in key stages 3 and 4 is broad and balanced, thanks to what's called the Dunraven Baccalaureate: English, maths, science, humanities, languages, and all the arts, because 'the kind of learning opportunity you get through the arts is invaluable.' Other subjects are also offered, notably DT, ICT and PE/dance. Visiting teacher from Westminster comes in every week to teach Latin, which is proving a popular option at GCSE and A level, but we thought the language provision could have been broader. French and Spanish are offered, with the G&T students given the chance to do both; but there used to be Mandarin. The impressive sixth form, housed in its own new purpose-built centre, is the most successful in Lambeth, and offers a wide range of academic and vocational courses – A Levels, BTecs, GCE applied and the AQA baccalaureate. In 2016, 32 per cent A*/A grades at A level (60 per cent A*-B). All Dunraven year 11s can apply to study there and most do, but places are sought after and are not guaranteed. Strong enrichment programme of activities, both on and off site, includes theatre and opera visits, excursions, exchanges, competitions, and residential trips abroad.

SEN provision is excellent and enlightened. The school has its own on-site speech therapist and parents were full of praise for the SENCo, who was described as 'fantastic', 'works like a Trojan', 'highly empathetic'. 'We felt that our child was properly supported throughout her time here,' was a typical remark. Hosts a specialist centre for children with speech, language and communication needs.

There were parental murmurs about their child being unable to study all his/her preferred subjects at GCSE due to timetabling issues (a problem not unique to Dunraven), but the majority of feedback was overwhelmingly positive. 'My child left with a love of all his subjects, based on great teaching,' was one comment. 'There is rigour in all that Dunraven does,' was another, and everyone we spoke to praised the 'constantly rising level of academic achievement.' The children agree: 'The teachers are good and you learn stuff,' said a cheerful year 7 boy, who'd been temporarily sent out for being cheeky. 'You make friends, you learn, every class is suited to you,' added a strikingly poised year 10 girl.

Games, options, the arts: You can do almost any sports here: in addition to football, rugby, cricket and basketball, there are opportunities for badminton, fencing, swimming, diving, the martial arts, boxercise, trampolining and ice-skating (using facilities at Crystal Palace). Engagement with games remains good throughout KS4. Drama, dance, art and photography are all popular, and the Soul Choir enlivens many a local church concert. Music is also strong, and the excellent Play It Live initiative, part-funded by the local authority, enables the children to work regularly with professional musicians.

Background and atmosphere: The school is approaching its 100th anniversary. Originally founded with a bequest from the Earl of Dunraven, it expanded onto its present site in 1950, moved into the Philippa Fawcett College in the 1970s, became grant-maintained in 1993 ('A very important decision for the school'), and became an academy in 2011. £20 million mixture of rebuild and refurb (under the last government's Building Schools for the Future initiative) now complete, including new sixth form centre. Some very inventive touches, including the use of recycled shipping containers for new buildings, which look incredibly smart and cost half of what was originally planned. Now has an attached primary school – the first reception children started in 2013 and moved into their permanent £5 million home in 2014. Primary school opened with reception class in September 2013 and will expand with a new class each year. School initially in temporary accommodation but moved into new buildings in summer 2014. The aim is provide a seamless progression from 4-18.

Smart blue and grey uniforms, own clothes for sixth form (with a requirement to be 'respectable'). Students work purposefully, and – during our visit, at least – an air of orderly quiet prevails. The pupils we met were polite and helpful. Even the malefactors hanging around outside the classroom who'd refused to go in, for reasons they were unable to articulate, knew what was expected of them. After chatting to us about how much they liked their school really – 'It's fun here...there are nice trips... a good after-school club, something to do every day' – they filed in equably to begin geography.

Pastoral care, well-being and discipline: Considering the size and diversity of this school community, we were impressed at how calm and purposeful the students were. The emphasis everywhere is on courtesy and consideration, and the pupils confirm this: 'The people are nice. The teachers are good and you learn stuff.' Parents praise the staff as 'incredibly supportive', and any bullying is dealt with swiftly and effectively with 'restorative justice' sessions and behaviour contracts. Very low turnover of staff tells its own successful story.

Pupils and parents: An inclusive, socially and ethnically mixed intake that reflects the diversity of the area.

Entrance: At primary level priority to looked after children, then siblings, then by distance. NB applicants must complete Dunraven's supplementary information form as well as applying through the LA. They will have an automatic right of entry to Dunraven Senior when they reach year 7. The head positively radiates excitement: 'This provision will eliminate the trauma of secondary transfer. Everyone will benefit. We'll be able to offer expertise and opportunities to enrich the primary experience, and their different pedagogical approach will increasingly influence us.' Heady times indeed.

Entrance tests put secondary applicants into one of five ability bands; the school, which is heavily oversubscribed, then takes 20 per cent from each band, allocating places in line with its (non-academically selective) admissions policy.

Exit: At 16, the majority (65 per cent) progress to Dunraven sixth form; a few move to local sixth form colleges, training etc. At 18, nearly all leavers go on to university, with an increasing number of top university successes every year, including Oxbridge (three in 2016), Bristol, Durham, Warwick, Edinburgh, York and Manchester. The rest take a gap year, or have a lead into work of some kind. Head says, 'The aim is to get to the end of Y13 with a choice.'

Money matters: EFA-funded academy since August 2011, and in receipt of many grants and awards in recognition of its academic success and work for the community.

Remarks: A dynamic, exciting, successful school community. Proof that you can have a comprehensive school that works for everybody.

Dwight School London

6 Friern Barnet Lane, London N11 3LX

Pupils: 345 • Ages: 2–19 • Sixth form: 70

Fees: £4,290 – £20,625 pa

Tel: 020 8920 0600
Email: admissions@dwightlondon.org
Website: www.dwightlondon.org

Executive principal: Since January 2016 Alison Cobbin BA Dip Ed MBA. Brought up in Australia and qualified as an English and history teacher at Macquarie University in Sydney. Moved to London in 1995 with her husband and three young daughters; worked at Dwight in various roles. Moved to a SE London independent school as pastoral deputy head before returning to Dwight as executive principal. Loves sport and was a competitive basketball and football player; now enjoys social netball, cycling and walking.

Upper school principal: Since April 2017, Andy Atkinson, previously director of the two International Schools of London.

Lower school principal : Since 2007, Mr Matt Parkin BEd DipEd. Has taught in the UK, USA and Indonesia. Teaching football and swimming as a teenager helped him find his vocation. Married; likes going running with his labrador dog ('though she is much faster than me').

Academic matters: Runs the IB programme at all levels. Year groups in lower school divided into two parallel classes with an absolute maximum of 20 in each. Lots of child-inspired batiks, pottery and art help create a vibrant atmosphere. IB learner profiles are displayed everywhere. IB primary years programme (IBPYP) well linked with the national curriculum, which keeps inspectorates happy and ensures children are well grounded with an international mind-set. All lessons in each half of term based around one aspect of the curriculum. Specialist teachers for music, art, PE, French and EAL. Homework important and can be done at after-school club.

In 2016, average IB point score 30 (out of possible 45). One or two students each year opt to take a Dwight High School Diploma, earning IB certificates rather than the full IB diploma. Average class size in upper school not normally more than 15. Good results for IB middle years programme exams with several top students getting more than 60 points out of 70.

Dwight has been designated an IB Open World School – one of only seven worldwide. This means that students from other institutions may register to take IB diploma courses at Dwight through the Pamoja Online courses, which may appeal to local sixth formers who want to combine IB courses with their A levels. By having Pamoja Online courses available to Dwight's students, the course options are much expanded, and it enables students to experience the kind of online learning that is increasingly common at university level.

French is introduced in primary, Spanish added as an option in year 7. Other languages considered on request at additional cost. Computers and interactive whiteboards available throughout the school, yet on the day of our visit we did not see students working on these devices in any of the classes we visited. RE is not an IB subject, though religious and other cultural traditions are addressed through other areas of the curriculum, and parents tell us that there are opportunities to celebrate these in different ways. Photos throughout the the school buildings depict many school trips, dramatic and music performances and community service activities, suggesting that a lot of learning is regularly extended out and about. After-school homework club for those who want extra help.

Parents receive a chatty weekly newsletter from the head, including updates on extracurricular activities available both to their children and themselves. Helpful and informative website.

Through the QUEST programme (at extra cost) the school can accommodate a range of learning needs, with the support of specialist teachers. The school has a sister school for more significant cases including statemented/EHC plan children.

EAL (also at extra cost) regarded as essential for children with two non-English speaking parents – two to five lessons a week, one to one or in a small group depending on needs. A mother tongue programme is available for Japanese pupils – the second largest group in the school (about 10 per cent) and some other languages (no extra charge is made if four or more students are in the same group and level). IB diploma students must be completely fluent in English. Language Heritage Day once a year sees everyone speaking their own language. Pupils of over 35 different nationalities, and full-time teachers of 15.

Parents say that what they like about Dwight is that it suits a great variety of children. 'I wanted a school where all of my children would be well served'.

Teachers are international and IB-experienced. They are always willing to help and respond quickly to any parent concerns. One parent told us her child said that Dwight teachers must go through a 'humour test' – you have to have warm sense of humour to teach at Dwight.

Games, options, the arts: Games obligatory once a week for each year group – the school has its own sports field 10 minutes away by minibus and uses other local sports facilities. They compete not only with local and national schools but also with international overseas schools. Parents say they like the variety of sports on offer – not only the traditional ones but a wider range: rugby, football, basketball, track and field, sailing,

D

ice skating... One Dwight student represented London in the National Schools Swimming competition.

Lots of after-school clubs. Strong music – about 15 per cent learn an individual instrument; there are rock, jazz and chamber groups. The choir has sung at London's 02 in Young Voices, and on the week of our visit, they were about to jet off to the US to perform with the Dwight New York choir at the Carnegie Hall. There is a music tech lab on a bright upper level that overlooks the music and art rooms below, and soundproofed rooms for individual tuition.

For the last period on Mondays, the pupils do mixed by year group community service projects. This helps to develop relationships across the ages, reinforcing the 'Dwight Family' concept.

Lots of outings to concerts, theatres and galleries as well as trips home and abroad. We saw photos from a science trip to Iceland, the Model United Nations Conference is popular, all year 6 students spend a week at an activity centre in Normandy (practising the French that they have been learning since they were 3) and some of them go on exchange to the Dwight School in New York. Older students have been doing community service helping to build in a Cambodian village. They raise funds, and roughly every three years students, parents and staff travel there to do volunteer work. The drama club was preparing to go to Cuba to study music and dance; while the year before the film club went to Hollywood. India is on the horizon.

Dwight London students are eligible to participate in the Dwight Global Leaders, a summer gathering of high school students from all over who come together at the Dwight Vancouver campus to develop leadership skills and learn about social entrepreneurship. This programme features big name motivational speakers from the world of sport, education and business (for example Monica Seles and Michael Bloomberg) and it receives high praise from the families of students who have participated.

Background and atmosphere: The school was originally founded in 1972 by Dr Stephen Spahn, chancellor of the Dwight School in New York. Previously known as Woodside Park and North London International School, the school recently changed its name in a rebranding exercise to Dwight London School, to heighten awareness of its association with the Dwight family of schools that now has campuses on Vancouver Island, Seoul and Shanghai. 'Dwight family' is a term used by staff and families alike. Dwight London has an advisory board of local parents and others who lend expertise and guidance and serve as a supportive sounding board for the principal in the strategic planning of the school.

The school is on four sites in two locations. Lower school is in Woodside Avenue. Kindergarten and reception based in their own little house, The Lodge, with its own garden for play. Half day and part-time options are available and there's a wraparound care programme from 7.30am to 6pm for the lower school.

Years 2 to 5 in the main building here have good sized, light classrooms with washing lines displaying student work. Each child has own drawer for storage. Computers everywhere. Media resource centres, a small library collection; great gym, which doubles up as the dining hall. Healthy food served from the kitchens next to it (where meals for the kindergarten are also prepared). Photos of all the year 6 student displayed in the passage with their personal blogs. Good music room and lovely art room. Year 6 has a separate and brand new eco-building with easy access to the specialist classrooms and playground; schools has green flag eco-schools status.

Playground not huge but much use made of local park for cross-country runs and scientific experiments plus compulsory swimming once a week at Trent Park. They also regularly use the school's own playing fields a short bus ride away.

The upper school is in the former Friern Barnet Boys' Grammar School and in nearby Jubilee Hall. The main building has recently been refurbished and is clean, bright and welcoming, making very good use of light throughout. The administrative offices and faculty room share the same corridors as the classrooms, which must strengthen the sense of community. Every wall is full of original and creative student art and photographs, and there are posters with quotes from Gandhi, Martin Luther King and Nelson Mandela, who we learned are the role models for the three upper school student houses.

The individualised approach we heard so much about from parents was evident during our visit. One Spanish class had just two students; in a lively drama lesson, students were planning the direction and staging for a Dwight student version of a Chaucer play; art students in a large art room with plenty of natural light were working on sketches and prints as part of a unit on 'celebrations'; and the design technology lab was a hive of activity with students measuring and vigorously sawing away as part of a woodworking project (hopefully all the fingers survived). A painted wall is a legacy of one student's project on graffiti as an art form. It was easy to see why the parents rave about the quality of the arts programmes.

The Jubilee Hall holds more classrooms, two science labs, the upper school library (closed for a few days when we visited, as the librarian was on a school trip) and a pleasant canteen open throughout the day (there are rave reviews for the new caterers), with a TV tuned into Sky News or the BBC. This looks out onto an outside playground where students engage in a bit of exercise during break or lunch, and a small world garden beyond with picnic tables and benches.

The school admits that conditions are a little crowded, and they are always on the lookout for new property in the area.

Pastoral care, well-being and discipline: The IB philosophy and emphasis on tolerance and global understanding are reinforced by the house system in the English tradition, with upper and lower school head boys and girls. Kids look tidy and seem happy, and although there is a uniform there are various options, so they can choose how casual or dressy they want to look. Parents love the small size of the school. 'It's a massive advantage. Everyone is known, everyone can shine and blossom.' It helps build self-confidence, and there's plenty of attention from teachers. As one veteran parent described it, 'The teachers really knew my son.'

Parents repeatedly assured us that they were not aware of any incidents of bullying, and the British ones in particular felt that the huge diversity of student backgrounds is a huge plus, with families inviting students home to share their family traditions during different holidays.

Pupils and parents: Dwight has a larger British student body than most other international schools in London, which seems to make it easier for international families to integrate into the local community. The impression from parents and from our visit is that there is relatively little sense of the 'expat bubble' in this international school. Long term families who joined the school in earlier incarnations (pre-IB) say they have been very pleased with the introduction of the full suite of IB programmes, and the interesting international experiences and friendships that Dwight's growing expat community brings. While they do see the turnover of families as a factor, many of these friendships endure and lead to exciting trips during the holidays to visit old friends who have moved on.

Parent Link works behind the scenes to support the school and organise the social events that are particularly helpful for new families. Parents can also volunteer in the school.

About half of families are local north Londoners. The rest are expats representing a mix of industries and embassies, though most live less than 30 minutes away. Parents appreciate the expansion of the area served by the door-to-door transport provided by the school. There is also a free shuttle service from the local tube stations and the free inter-school shuttle facilitating drop off. Most families have an international background, usually one English-speaking parent. Nationalities primarily British, then Japanese, and then a complete mix of many.

Entrance: Parents describe the school as 'selectively inclusive'. In all of our conversations (with parents and staff), no one emphasised 'academic results'. Though most enter in September, since the school serves expats, there are students entering throughout the year, from abroad and from local state schools. Interview and report from previous school only real requisites.

Exit: About 75 per cent of lower school pupils move on to the upper school; around half leave after GCSEs, moving abroad or to sixth form colleges. University counselling programme in year 12, but it seems parents often start earlier, commenting they'd like to see a bit more attention to this area. Sixth formers mainly to university, a lot London based but some overseas – eg recent admissions to Coventry, Goldsmiths, UCL, Durham, Exeter, Hertfordshire, Kent, Nottingham, University of Colorado and several Japanese universities.

Money matters: Tuition is marginally less than other international schools in London. Extras include school trips and activities such as Model United Nations and some after-school activities. Scholarships are available with testing in the early part of the calendar year.

Remarks: Dwight is a school where the education of the 'whole child' and the learning journey genuinely appear to be as important as exam results. As one parent said, 'When we visited other schools, it was a PR exercise where they told us about their tests, achievements, etc. At Dwight, they asked us about our children.' The school does all it can to provide each student with opportunities to pursue their individual interests, all within the IB context. 'It's a kind school.'

Eaton House Belgravia

Linked with Eaton House the Manor Girls' School, Eaton House the Manor Prep and Pre-Prep, Eaton House the Vale

3-5 Eaton Gate, Eaton Square, London SW1W 9BA

Pupils: 240 • Ages: 4-8

Fees: £15,390 pa

Tel: 020 7730 9343
Email: admin@eatonhouseschools.com
Website: www.eatonhouseschools.com

Headmistress: Since 2015, Annabel Abbott (30s), previously deputy head. History with primary education degree from the University of the West of England; spent nine months in Australia as a gap student teacher before joining Queen's Gate School. Moved to Eaton House in 2000, taught throughout the age range and was promoted to deputy head four years later.

Entrance: At 4+ non-selective – places are allocated on a first come first served basis with priority given to siblings, children of staff, ex-staff and old boys. Put your son's name down early – £50 for a confirmed place and £30 for a waiting list place. Deposit of a term's fees, two terms before the child starts, which is credited against your final term's fees.

Exit: At 7+ and 8+ mainly to London day schools – Sussex House, Eaton House the Manor, Westminster Under, Westminster Cathedral Choir School and Wetherby. A few head off to board at Summer Fields, Caldicott and the like.

Remarks: Traditional 3Rs curriculum with lots of added extras, particularly in the arts and science – the school boasts its own lab; boys enjoy potion and crystal making amongst their many experiments and discoveries. Pupils are divided into small classes, no streaming but informal sets for maths to ensure that everybody is meeting their potential and able to go at their own pace. As in the past, the school's aim is to give boys a good grounding and a full understanding in all maths and English topics, rather than rushing ahead.

No outdoor space so school days are very structured – boys are bussed to Hyde or Battersea Park every day to let off steam and play sports. Swimming takes place at the Queen Mother's sports centre. Good choice of after-school and optional weekend sports clubs encourage boys to choose and try out different activities. Chess lessons for years 2 and 3. An actor visits the school to help train the boys for junior debating club. Lots of spirited music and drama, which is reflected in the many assemblies, plays and themed days, which often see teachers dressing up too. Excellent choir for ones so young, performs at a local charity events and is thought to be adorable by parents and anyone lucky enough to catch one of their performances. Five small practice rooms in the basement for young instrumentalists – boys can learn piano, flute, violin, recorder and guitar.

Well-organised SEN supports children with specific learning differences; Move Fit group is run by physiotherapists for anyone who needs to improve coordination, and touch typing tuition for year 2 upwards.

Mainly local clientele with many parents working in the City as bankers and lawyers, although much more international than in the past. Staff and parents have high expectations for the boys as the majority move onto academically selective prep schools. Boys are set numerous challenges, both physical and intellectual, and well trained so they become familiar with class exams in preparation for the formal 7+ and 8+ entry examinations. Head and her staff are always on hand to advise parents about suitable choice of prep schools.

Bustling kitchen runs two lunch sittings a day; where possible the food is fresh and cooked on-site. Birthdays are special days, with boys bringing cakes or biscuits to share with friends and staff. Boys present as cheerful little chaps. School remains a popular and successful recipe for pre-preppers as ever.

Eaton House the Manor Girls' School

Linked with Eaton House Belgravia , Eaton House the Manor Prep and Pre-Prep, Eaton House the Vale

E

58 Clapham Common Northside, London SW4 9RU

Pupils: 200 • Ages: 4–11

Fees: £14,745 pa

Tel: 020 7924 6000
Email: admin@eatonhouseschools.com
Website: www.eatonhouseschools.com

Head: Since September 2016, Oliver Snowball, previously acting head of Kent College Prep. PGCE (London), MA in theatre studies (Goldsmiths) and BA in English (Nottingham). Started his teaching career teaching English and drama at Tunbridge Wells Girls' grammar, moving on to Kent College where he has also been housemaster and deputy head of the prep. He is married to Claire and they have two young children.

Entrance: At 4+ non-selective – put your name down early as a waiting list operates on a first come first served basis. Occasional places in older age groups, entrance exam and a visit to the school for an assessment day.

Exit: Francis Holland and Streatham & Clapham High most popular London next steps, with others to eg JAGS, Putney High, Godolphin & Latymer and Towmead. St Catherine's and Woldingham most popular boarding schools; others to Benenden, Downe House, Tudor Hall etc.

Remarks: New, stylish, bright, architect-designed building next to the boys' school. Three floors of classrooms with a huge basement activity hall/gym and ICT room; pupils share some of the boys' school facilities. The school opened in 2008 – one class of approximately 20 pupils in academic year group, so much smaller than the boys' school. Well-balanced academic curriculum; the girls are continuously assessed and 5 and 6-year-olds are screened to identify any specific learning difficulties. Part-time specialist SEN teacher and visiting occupational and speech therapists can be arranged when necessary.

Specialist subject teachers for the arts, French, science and sports. Forward thinking and gentle pastoral care, mentoring 'big sister' scheme to encourage older girls to look after younger and new pupils. Good selection of sports including all year round swimming lessons, dance classes for budding ballerinas. Lots of lively drama and music; tuition on any instrument is available and girls produce two dramatic productions every year. Wonderful art studios accommodated in the main building give the opportunity to work with a range of different media. Every term sees a selection of extracurricular clubs, along with an after-school homework club.

Staff have created a charming, traditional girls' school in a nurturing and relaxed atmosphere. Superb asset to the Eaton House group of schools.

Eaton House the Manor Prep and Pre-Prep

Linked with Eaton House Belgravia, Eaton House the Manor Girls' School, Eaton House the Vale

The Manor House, 58 Clapham Common Northside, London SW4 9RU

Pupils: 403 • Ages: 3–13

Fees: £14,244 – £17,424 pa

Tel: 020 7924 6000
Email: admin@eatonhouseschools.com
Website: www.eatonhouseschools.com

Head: Since September 2016, Mrs Sarah Seagrave (40s) BA Ed MA, previously head of the Eaton House the Manor Girls' School. BA in education and history from Durham and MA from the Institute of Education. She joined the Eaton House group of schools in 1993 as one of the founding teachers in the prep school. She taught history (her main passion) and Latin and was housemistress and year coordinator, taking on the headship of the pre-prep school in 2001. She became head of the girls' school in 2010 after an extended maternity leave,where she taught general studies to all age groups and enjoyed organising quizzes and history in action events. Cheery and practical, parents at the girls's school told us it really helps that she has young children herself and is able to relate to hopes and fears. She is married to Nick and they have two children, at the pre-prep and the girls' school.

Pre-prep head: Since 2013, Mr Huw May, previously head of Sydenham High Junior School. Has also headed Roedean Junior School and St Aubyns Pre-Prep. A professional singer for several years before taking up teaching, he is also an ISI inspector.

Nursery head: Since 2004, Mrs Roosha Sue (30s).

Entrance: Non-selective at 3+ and 4+ for the nursery (co-ed) and pre-prep – first come first served waiting list operates. At 8+ for the prep school internal candidates are continually assessed to ensure their suitability for the prep. External candidates sit an 8+ entry examination; academic, music, sport, art and design and all-rounder scholarships for 8-year-olds.

Exit: At 8+ small number of boys opt for country boarding schools. At 11+ a few move to London day schools – Dulwich College, City of London. Majority sit 13+ for a good mixture of traditional public schools – Harrow (most popular), Eton, Winchester, Radley and Marlborough – or day schools like Westminster, St Paul's, King's College School (Wimbledon) and Dulwich.

Remarks: The school opened in 1993 as a boys' pre-prep. Today The Manor hosts a co-ed nursery, boys' pre-prep and prep school and the most recent addition is a girls' school (see separate entry). All accommodated in an attractive Georgian manor house and its grounds in Clapham. Fortunately, the school sits on the edge of Clapham Common, which provides the ideal location for sports lessons as on-site outdoor space is limited.

The cheerful purpose-built nursery is the starting point and then on to the pre-prep. The same successful teaching methods are used as in its brother school across the Thames. Children are taught in small ability related groups within their classes. Pre-prep children also benefit from magic touches, which include structured creative writing classes and the all-important but often forgotten skill of handwriting.

Most boys go on to the prep school, where they are divided into two parallel classes per year group. Latin and French are introduced in the first year of the prep; most classes are taught by subject specialists and setting for English and maths.

School can support children with mild dyslexia/dyspraxia and ASD, an area that is being developed. Full-time SENCo makes referrals as necessary and runs a small team of teachers, most of whom have specialist training.

Bright airy classrooms, decorated with delightful art displays. Exciting range of art and design classes to suit all tastes and talents, wonderful top floor studio overlooking the London skyline. Music has been developing steadily – a good orchestra, string quartets, two choirs and frequent musical assemblies. Drama classes throughout the age groups, boys perform lively plays and sketches and a musical play each summer.

Parents are invited to help with stage designs for plays, hanging art displays and listening to children read. They are also active fundraisers for the school's charity of the year and annual fête. Supervised homework club, great choice of extracurricular activities and a holiday club. Overall a strong all-round school. Parents say the approach is fairly formal but, thankfully, less stuffy than it used to be.

Eaton House the Vale

Linked with Eaton House Belgravia, Eaton House the Manor Girls' School, Eaton House the Manor Prep and Pre-Prep

2 Elvaston Place, London SW7 5QH

Pupils: 90 • Ages: 3–8

Fees: £15,390 pa

Tel: 020 7584 9515
Email: admin@eatonhouseschools.com
Website: www.eatonhouseschools.com

Headmaster: Since 2008, Mr Robin Greenwood FTCL ARCM, BSc (40s) a scientist and musician. He was educated in South Africa, then London University, where he studied biological sciences. An accomplished pianist, he also studied music at Trinity College, London. Mr Greenwood taught at the Eaton House Schools before becoming headmaster of Wetherby Prep and then returned to the fold to become headmaster of The Vale. Parents say the school is like one big family and Mr Greenwood is always on hand to discuss their child's progress.

Entrance: At 3+ and 4+ non-selective entry on a first-come first-served basis. Children attending the nursery enter in the term leading up to the third birthday.

Exit: At 7+/8+ to eg Knightsbridge, Eaton House the Manor, Wetherby, Colet Court, St Philip's, Latymer Prep, Eaton Square.

Remarks: The Vale is a co-ed nursery and pre-prep school catering for boys and girls from 3-8. Traditional 3Rs curriculum with a focus on developing every child's abilities, both academic and non-academic. No streaming and class sizes are kept small to ensure lots of individual attention.

The school occupies a six-storey Georgian house just off Gloucester Road, complete with kitchens and a dining area. Facilities are excellent for a small school, although slightly tight. Well-stocked library, ICT room, multi-purpose hall and own science lab. No outdoor space – pupils go for short walk during morning break and midday playtimes are held in Kensington Gardens. Two afternoons a week children go to Battersea Park with the games master for PE lessons. Pupils are introduced to around 10 different sports, including tennis, cricket and athletics, with matches, competitions and summer sports days being popular events. Exciting whole class drama and music; with around a third of the children learning an instrument, everyone performs in the regular plays and musicals.

For those with SEN, a part-time adviser organises additional support as needed by pupils. The school welcomes visiting specialists including speech and occupational therapists to support pupils with individual needs. Home/school communication is considered paramount – reading and message books are exchanged every day and five simple rules for everyone to follow to encourage thoughtfulness and sensible behaviour.

The children also benefit from being taken out to visit a variety of London sites and museums. After-school clubs include French, cookery, chess, healthy kids and lifestyles. Mr Greenwood has an open door policy for parents which helps create the nurturing and friendly atmosphere and, most importantly, yummy lunches, say the young ones.

Eaton Square School

79 Eccleston Square, London SW1V 1PP

Pupils: 387 • Ages: 4–13 • C of E

Fees: £19,935 – £20,550 pa

Tel: 02079 319 469
Email: admissions@eatonsquareschool.com
Website: www.eatonsquareschool.com

Headmaster: Since 2010, Sebastian Hepher BEd (early 50s). Educated at Alleyn's and University of Greenwich. Began teaching career in state sector, at Hurstmere Boys' in Kent, followed by The London Nautical School. Joined Eaton House Pre-Prep in 1990, before being asked to lead Eaton House The Manor in 1993. Under his headship, the school grew from the initial embryonic phase to a thriving prep school. Married, with four children currently at four different schools, with the youngest here. Swims in his local lido every day of the year, come rain or shine. Avid reader of Russian literature. Warm and charismatic, with a good sense of humour. Every parent we spoke to described him in glowing terms. 'He is the reason people gravitate towards the school,' according to one mother. Teaches reasoning. Will also head the upper school that opens in September 2017.

Entrance: Main intake is at 4+ via assessment. The school runs several nurseries for children from 2.5 to 4 and these pupils are assessed by head of nurseries and head of pre-prep. They are given priority over other candidates and make up well over half the intake. 'It's not automatic but very rare not to accept a child from one of our nurseries,' explains head. Assessments, in November for external candidates, involve phonic and numerical activities, as well as colouring, cutting and talking to teachers. Between 100 and 150 external children compete for 30 places. Sibling policy, 'as we truly are a family school.'

Occasional vacancies further up the school are quickly filled from the school's waiting list, after the child has successfully completed a series of online tests and spent a day at the school in a classroom setting.

Exit: Most girls leave at 11 and boys at 13. Very few girls stay on for the 13+, usually those heading for co-ed boarding. Pupils progress onto a wide range of senior schools, both boarding and day. Rare to send more than a couple of children to any one school in any given year. Recent leavers to Eton, Harrow, Tonbridge, Charterhouse, City of London Boys, St Mary's Ascot, Beneden, Downe House, Roedean, Latymer Upper, Allyen's, Dulwich College, Godolphin & Laymer, Francis Holland x 2, City of London Girls, Queens College, Queensgate. Impressive number of sports, drama and music scholarships.

Head starts dialogue about senior schools in year 5, often encouraging parents look at boarding too even if previously dismissed out of hand by international clientele. Head acknowledges that 'London schools are not the place for the average boy' and that some need to cast their net further. Numbers of boys heading to boarding has increased noticeably and is 'beginning to bubble for the girls.'

Remarks: Situated in three large town houses in the heart of Belgravia. Separate buildings for senior prep, junior prep and pre-prep. One parent likened the children to mountain goats, as they make their way up and down the steep stairs.

Founded in 1981. Recently became part of the Minerva Education Group. Teething problems have left some parents feeling a little raw. One mother we spoke to said, 'The transition to the new ownership has been pretty bumpy, especially as it coincided with an escalation in fees'. Head feels some parental perception has been inaccurate and that school fees have not actually increased more than usual. Indeed, the second year of ownership has actually seen a reduction to the usual increase. On the positive side, Minerva has enabled the school recently to buy a building on Piccadilly overlooking Green Park for its new senior school, Eaton Square Upper School, which will open in September 2017 and eventually go up to 16.

Current head is credited with having pulled the school up by its bootstraps academically. It has grown both in size and standing on his watch. One parent commented, 'It used to just be a sweet, local school before Mr Hepher took over. He is much more ambitious and has taken it to another level'. Pupils now follow a more academically rigorous and broader curriculum. Excellent language provision. Spanish being introduced. Extra French classes for fluent speakers. Mandarin offered as a two year course from year 4, though pupils must commit to it for the duration and take a CE exam at the end. Latin for all from year 5.

Head abhors the culture of tutoring and believes 'we need to educate parents.' He has addressed the matter of intense competition for senior places with intelligence and worries that increasing number of schools using pre-tests works against late-developers. School prepares pupils well for senior school entry without being a hothouse.

Typically five reception classes and four year 1 classes. Class size fairly small, with a maximum of 16 up to year 5 and a maximum of 18 in final years. Currently only eight pupils in each year 8 class and 11 in year 7, giving plenty of scope for individual attention. Pupils are placed in sets for maths and English at start of year 2 but these are fluid, with 'plenty of room for manoeuvre'.

Parents feel pupils are well prepared for transition to senior school, partly because the curriculum is kept broad throughout. Once 11+ exams are over, girls 'latch onto boys' CE syllabus.' No time wasting allowed here, as can often happen elsewhere post 11+, much to the parents' delight.

From the start, all pupils are encouraged to be articulate and confident citizens. Head believes that good manners are essential. Each class has its own official greeter who comes to the front, shakes hands firmly and welcomes visitors on behalf of the rest of the class. A charming touch.

Thriving pre-prep department. Vibrant, colourful classrooms where emphasis is on practical work, consolidated by written work. 'It's hands on, creative learning here.' Impressive writing on display up the stairs. Everything is beautifully presented, from the work crafted by the children to displays produced by teachers. Charming library area where children can be found earnestly recommending books to each other.

As school is non-selective, there is a huge ability range. Full-time SENCo, supported by highly experienced learning enrichment team. Approximately 30 pupils currently having SEN support (mostly dyslexia, dyspraxia and dyscalculia), either one-to-one or small group sessions. Two children with statements. More able pupils extended through challenging extracurricular activities.

Pastoral care is well structured. Head worries about life being stressful for these children. 'We have a duty of care to shield children from excessive pressure which London and the system place on them. Parents who are anxious tend to pass that on to their children. I worry that we're causing a very anxious society. We want to make sure that children are happy when they are here.' Whole school comes together once a week for a reflective and celebratory reflective assembly at St Michael's Church, Chester Square.

Charity is an important part of school life. Huge amounts raised by parents and children. Head is aware of how privileged pupils are here and is hoping to get older pupils involved with visiting elderly residents who live on their own in the Square.

Teachers mostly in late 20s and early 30s; some 10 members of staff have been here a decade. One parent described them as being 'friendly, energetic and good at communicating with the parents. Just what you want'. 'We haven't had a bad teacher yet!' said another, whose children are currently in the middle of the school. Parents demonstrate their gratitude to the staff with a 'parent appreciation breakfast' once a year.

Sensational drama. Huge annual musical performed by year 5 and 6 children at Unicorn theatre in the West End. Professional theatre director hired for the occasion. Years 7 and 8 perform something more challenging such as a Greek play. Younger children perform on stage twice a year. Music also a central part of the school with over 100 pupils learning an instrument. Performances in abundance, from carol services to rock concerts. One parent felt that 'music is certainly more organised than it has been in the past.' Art taught to a high standard. Extra scholarship classes offered to the most artistic; the standard of portfolios is considered exceptional.

Despite its lack of outside space, school takes sport very seriously and coaching is excellent. Mainstream sports all offered as well as ballet, climbing, fencing and kayaking on the Thames. Pupils compete strongly in prep school ski-ing championships, recently bringing back a clutch of gold medals. Legendary swimming squad currently on a four year unbeaten streak. Unusually, pupils swim here from day one. Football also strong, with plenty of practice taking place in Battersea Park. All children make a team of some description. 'The problem is finding enough other schools who can field C and D teams,' laments head.

Extracurricular activity viewed as important. Sensational residential trips. Year 3 heads off to Sussex for a four day adventure. Years 4 and 5 go on a ski-ing and cultural trip to France where pupils practise speaking the language in context and also have daily French lessons. Snowball fights with the teachers apparently one of the highlights. One mother was delighted that the children were made to 'carry their own skis and make their own beds.' A novel experience for some, apparently. Pupils in year 6 go on a classical tour of Rome and Naples. Year 7 spend a week at a château in Normandy. At the end of year 8, pupils go on outdoor pursuits trip to Scotland to celebrate the end of common entrance. Head now setting his sights on a residential trip for year 2. Thirty-four clubs currently offered, at extra cost, including numerous sports, chess, storytelling and cookery.

Pupil composition is predominantly expat, with more than half the pupils from overseas. Americans, Australians, Italians, French, Spanish mostly, with a sprinkling from Germany, Russia and Asia. One mother observed that there had been 'a thick crust of oligarchs' children in the past, but not any more.' Significant proportion does not have English as their first language. School is committed to its international families and has an EAL system in place which supports every child who joins with no, basic or limited English. Currently 14 per cent of pupils require targeted EAL lessons, which are intended to 'help speed up the process of full inclusion in the classroom.' Many of the parents we spoke to felt that its international feel was an advantage. 'It is a British school in terms of manners, etiquette and uniform but feels international in terms of its welcoming and warm approach.' Rare for mothers to work. A sea of nannies at the school gate on the day we visited. Pupils mainly come from local area but radius extends as far as 'Kensington in the North, Fulham in the West, Battersea and Kennington in the South and Marylebone in the East.' School bus service in operation to and from west and south-west London for those who live further afield.

Parents are encouraged to become involved, from hearing children read to giving career talks. Strong sense of community here and very active PTA. 'When you go into the school, there is a smile on the staff's faces. It's not the sort of school where you drop your child at the door and never get to venture across the threshold,' explained one mother. Head feels parent body is caring and empathetic, 'partly because of the huge mix of nationalities. Parents who come here are quite open, as they have often changed city and country themselves. You need to be outward looking to do that and this feeds into their children. It creates a lovely atmosphere.' One-upmanship, so prevalent elsewhere in London, is refreshingly lacking here.

Heady mix of traditional British education with an international flavour. Children are happy here as they have the freedom to be themselves. Judging by stampede to get into the building at the start of the day, Eaton Square offers its pupils an joyful start in life.

Upper school opening in 2017 from age 11 upwards.

École Française Jacques Prévert

68

59 Brook Green, London W6 7BE

Pupils: 260 • Ages: 3–11

Fees: £5,600 – £6,233 pa

Tel: 020 7602 6871
Email: info@ecoleprevert.org.uk
Website: www.ecoleprevert.org.uk

Director: Since September 2016 Delphine Gentil. A former student of the École Normale Supérieure, she spent eight years as head of Brigueuil's school in Charente.

The école is under the auspices of the AEFE (French Agency for the French Education Abroad, run by the French Ministry of Foreign Affairs), which oversees a network of French curriculum schools around the world, and appoints the directors of all its schools. The northern European ones meet regularly, and they are are generally rotated every five years.

Entrance: Most children start in September, although as the community is an international one there is occasional movement during the school year. The cut-off date for birthdays is December, so those accustomed to September birthday deadlines may be surprised to find there are some younger peers in the class.

The admissions criteria are aligned with those of all AEFE schools. Priority is given to siblings, pupils coming from other AEFE schools abroad or in the UK (typically La Petite École Française in Notting Hill and L'École du Hérisson Hammersmith); academic ability isn't a factor. Siblings get preference. The school is normally over-subscribed with one or two forms in a year. Twenty-eight pupils admitted at age 4 and 16 new pupils at age 6. Parents recommend getting on the waiting list at the earliest possible opportunity and hanging on even if you don't get an offer for the first year, as vacancies can arise in later years. They also advise that if you aren't on the waiting list, and are not transferring in from a French school, 'you can forget it'.

Exit: Most pupils have gone to the London French Lycée Charles de Gaulle, where the director is able to track the pupils' progress, as the Lycée regularly sends progress reports back to Jacques Prevert. However, families also have the option of the College Français Bilingue de Londres in Kentish Town and the new Lycée Winston Churchill in Wembley. Some parents (Anglophones) opt to move their children into the English system at the end of the primary years. The school does not advise parents on specific schools, but the parents' association organises information sessions about the English system and the French Lycée organises a meeting in March about the French secondary system.

Remarks: French curriculum, with the addition of English classes taught by native speakers. Main language of instruction is French, in keeping with school's mission to promote bilingual education, which begins in kindergarten. As the children get older (8 upwards), some the subjects such as history, geography and eventually science are partially taught by English teachers working in parallel with their French colleagues.

Parents are pleased with the early childhood programme that integrates arts, crafts, singing and pre-reading skills such as learning letters. They move to the primary section at age 6, and are usually reading by the end of the first term. The school is exempt from following the EYFS.

Those in the primary section follow the prescribed French curriculum, which includes seven 'pillars': mastery of the French language, speaking a modern foreign language (English), acquiring basic knowledge in mathematics and science, developing a humanist culture, mastering common ICT, acquiring social and civic skills, and developing autonomy and initiative.

The first two-year cycle (roughly equivalent to British KS1) includes PE and sport, visual art, music and a modern foreign language (in this case, English, taught by native speakers). This is followed by a three-year 'consolidation cycle' (ages 8-11) roughly equivalent to English KS2. This is where the French imperative to teach grammar shines and the rigorous French history syllabus covers pre-history to the Middle Ages, the Enlightenment to the French Revolution, the 20th Century and the European Union. Geography is similarly Franco-centric.

Teachers are encouraged to integrate IT into the curriculum from 4-year-olds upwards. A cheerful library holds an impressive French collection; the English classroom holds the English language materials. There are no national exams for French primary school students; progress is internally assessed and there are detailed termly online reports.

Because pupils are not necessarily fluent English speakers, juggling the English language levels is a continuous challenge; English classes are streamed by ability groups from 7 years, and the school provides some support to help new arrivals in the English-medium classes. The curriculum includes English grammar and comprehension.

E

Though the school is crowded, it is orderly. Some special classes give teachers the opportunity to work with smaller groups. On our visit we saw lots of variety in teaching approaches and learning activity, including PE, music and artists at work, all the students looking engaged and happy. The Maternelle Grande children were making elaborate models of castles in anticipation of a visit to the Tower of London.

Typical of many French schools, there is no specialist SEN support, but teachers use their free lessons to provide one-to-one teaching to pupils who are lagging behind. More flexible than most UK schools, it is not unheard of for a particularly strong or bright child to move up a year, or a struggling pupil to stay down.

PE includes ice skating, rock climbing, acrosport and badminton. Music is taught by a specialist, art mostly by class teachers. Parents point out that while extracurricular activities are not a big feature of traditional French schools, here a super-involved parent body organises clubs for eg tennis, judo, karate, chess, arts and crafts and singing at nominal extra cost. Morning club from 8am.

Founded in 1974 as a smaller, more family-friendly French primary school alternative to the larger Lycée Charles de Gaulle in South Kensington, the school is in a large converted house. There is a small outdoor playground, and children sometimes have free time on spacious Brook Green.

Discipline is quite strict. Pupils have the same teacher for most subjects so they know each other well. Lunches (included in the school fees) are well balanced and freshly prepared. On Wednesdays, which are half days, those staying on for afternoon activities bring a packed lunch.

The community is an international one with many dual-national bilingual families: more than half are French or French/British, about 15 per cent are British and the remainder come from a variety of countries, with speakers of Spanish, German, Arabic, Chinese all represented. It's not unusual for students to speak three or four languages. However, parents tell us that the lingua franca is English.

Most families are local, but there is a school bus service organised by parents. Active parents' association, kept up to date by a snazzy online newsletter with video links. In this small community where everyone knows everyone else, parents feel obliged to play their part in committees, fund raising or generally helping out.

Subsidies from the French Government keep the fees down. French nationals are eligible to apply for scholarships.

For London families who want their children to have the advantage of developing or keeping up French language fluency in a small and friendly school environment, parents advise: 'Get on the waiting list'.

Eleanor Palmer Primary School

Lupton Street, London NW5 2JA

Pupils: 326 • Ages: 3–11

Tel: 020 7485 2155
Email: admin@eleanorpalmer.camden.sch.uk
Website: www.eleanorpalmer.camden.sch.uk

Head: Since 2003, Kate Frood MA,OBE (50s). Knew she wanted to be a teacher from the age of 8 and started her career doing just that at nearby Fleet Primary in 1983. Aside from a four-year stint as a maths consultant to Islington Council, has taught in Camden ever since. Trained when child-centred learning (as opposed to testing) was the focus, and this has remained fundamental to her approach. In order 'to keep her hand in and share ideas', continues to teach year 6 maths. 'She really knows what kids can do and – more importantly – what they can't,' said a mother. 'She makes sure every child is well-prepared for secondary.' Liked and respected by parents. 'She's a brilliant head, incredibly good behind the scenes and incredibly forward thinking,' said one. 'Problems are dealt with before they turn into problems.' Awarded the OBE for 'services to education' in 2014. One daughter who attended Camden School for Girls.

Entrance: Hugely oversubscribed, with about eight applicants per place for a single reception class of 30. Proximity is key and there's been much tut-tutting about families renting to squeeze through the gates. (Camden now scrutinises applicants carefully, particularly looking for those who own or let another address locally.) Full-time Camden-funded nursery of 26, but bagging a place here does not guarantee admission into reception (children have been rejected in the past).

Exit: Pupils here tend to go on to local community secondaries, generally the cluster round Dartmouth Park – William Ellis, Acland Burghley and Parliament Hill plus some to Camden School for Girls. A few, too, to selective state schools, and a further sprinkling to independents. By and large, however, this is a parent body committed to state schooling.

Remarks: Housed in a medley of low-built mid-20th-century buildings on a reasonably spacious, but very urban, site, the school has well-cared for and imaginatively used grounds, including an adventure playground and colourful entrance ornamented with art, fish, running water – and a prominent plaque declaring 'racism is unacceptable'.

Academically, the school falls firmly into the Outstanding category, with high standards in the core and a rich offering well beyond. Heavily committed to topic-based study, with themes such as World War 2 or Victorian childhood taught using imaginative links between history, geography, art and literacy. 'We see learning as an adventure,' says the head, an adventure explored through plenty out-of-school visits and and in-house contributions from story tellers, artists and experts.

The school has both a national reputation for maths teaching and a highly-praised literacy strategy. Children read daily for half an hour and end every afternoon with a class story. Great emphasis, too, placed on the best children's literature, with new titles added regularly and a handy booklet of recommendations. Year 5 studies and performs a Shakespeare play. French for all from year 3, taught by the classroom teacher. Homework (including daily reading and times tables) from the start, and ICT well embedded, with access to a myriad of laptops and iPads.

Eleanor Palmer is a 'teaching school' – one of just 350 in the country – teaching teachers how to teach. This, according to parents, can have both its upside and its down. 'It means,' said one mother, 'the staff are young and hugely energetic, willing to work after school and at weekends, but some are also pretty inexperienced.' Head, however, tends to restrict the rawest recruits to the younger years.

The ethos of the school has been shaped by the work of Carol Dweck – whose perspective is that effort and persistence are what really count. 'This teaches children to see mistakes and failures as positives and makes for a very energetic and inclusive culture,' says the head. So, no star charts, no ability sets; instead, each child is encouraged to achieve their personal best, with marking emphasising steps forward rather than what's gone wrong.

Special needs is led by the head, aided, in school, by support teachers and learning support assistants, and, out of it, by an educational psychologist and occupational therapist. Parents feel the SEN offering has improved in recent years. 'The head is very responsive and things like touch typing are now standard.'

Two hours of PE weekly, with a dedicated sports co-ordinator mentoring both those who struggle and those who excel, as well as arranging participation for all in out-of-school tournaments. Plenty of alternatives, too, to conventional team sports, with dance and skipping workshops, fencing and taekwondo sessions. The school is also 'very committed' to walking. Nearby Parliament Hill used for class activities and sports days.

Specialist music teacher visits twice weekly, overseeing a 'strings programme', which provides all pupils from the age of 8 with (free) group tuition by a specialist in violin or cello. Multiple opportunities to perform in concerts and musicals.

Head very much of the '50 things to do before' philosophy, and her objective is that all leavers should have completed a substantial tick list of activities, from growing their own vegetables to visiting a farm. Trips, trips, trips make the most of the wealth of galleries and museums a bus ride away, as well as of opportunities further afield (everyone gets four residential stays, ranging from camping in Epping Forest to a year 7 week at a Michael Morpurgo's Farm for City Children.)

As the leader of a 'multi-cultural community', the head has taken up the option to skip the daily act of Christian worship. Instead, the red-letter days of all the major religions are covered in assemblies and younger pupils are taught philosophy by trained philosophy teachers. The school is also a level 2 Unicef 'rights respecting' school, which entails listening to children's views and including them in such decisions as the fairness of team selection. Every class draws up a charter based on agreed rights, and then lists how adults and children will respect these. 'Once behaviour is seen in this way there is little need for rules,' says the head. Local councillors, politicians and lawyers, too, are invited in to teach pupils about their rights and responsibilities as citizens. Charity link to school in Sierra Leone.

Kentish Town is more affluent than formerly, particularly after a recent influx of French émigrés, and the popularity of the school means the sharp elbowed have gained ground in recent years, but you'll still find a good cross section of traditional locals and recent refugees alongside the organic set. About 20 per cent receive free school meals, a national average, but well below what might be expected for the location. As the head concedes, this can be a positive, as those from more affluent backgrounds provide 'a critical mass of high-achieving, motivated, liberal, middle class kids – so all my working class or refuge kids get caught up.' Parents, too, feel the balance works ('I think it still has that community-school feeling,' said one) and are full of praise for its warm and nurturing atmosphere. 'Our children have been extremely happy here – and very well educated.'

The Ellen Wilkinson School for Girls

Queen's Drive, London W3 0HW

Pupils: 1,400 • Ages: 11–18 • Sixth form: 400

Tel: 020 8752 1525
Email: office@ellenwilkinson.ealing.sch.uk
Website: www.ellenwilkinson.ealing.sch.uk

Headteacher: Since 2014, Ms Rachel Kruger, previously acting head. She joined the school in 2012 as deputy head. South African born, she is a maths and music graduate and a trained opera singer.

Academic matters: In 2016, nearly a third A* and A grades at GCSE. English, sciences, languages (including Arabic and Latin) all strong. A specialist maths and science college – a healthy proportion take maths, biology and chemistry A level (increasing numbers opting for physics with plenty of A grades). Arabic, further maths, psychology and philosophy are recent additions to the A level choices. In 2016, 41 per cent A*-B grades at A level. Several vocational options at level 2 and 3, including business studies, travel and tourism, health and social care and ICT. Runs maths and science taster sessions and masterclasses for feeder primary schools, with excited pupils trying out practical experiments in real science labs.

Some 50 per cent of students speak English as a second language – EAL support is excellent. 'Most speak English enough to be understood. The difficulties arise with subtleties of language – maths terminology, for example.' So both English and EAL lessons focus on the specifics of language, and learning foreign languages can help with sentence structure. Drama is particularly helpful for some girls who get little conversation practice outside school because their close female relatives do not speak English. Literacy catch-up programme in year 7 for those who need it, plus personalised online reading programme. Study support available instead of a second language in year 8, and optional support higher up supports learning throughout the curriculum. Good SEN help, in and out of the classroom. Extracurricular gifted and talented enrichment activities. Scores very well on value-added basis, and is probably the best-performing Ealing school that does not select on academic or religious grounds.

Games, options, the arts: PE facilities have been transformed by new sports and performing arts building. Plenty of outdoor space, with grass and all-weather hockey pitches and netball/tennis courts. Sport is popular and high on the agenda – 'Because we're an all-girls school it's cool to be sporty'. Successful basketball and netball teams, lots of clubs, eg dance, trampoline, badminton, ultimate frisbee, inter-form matches. 'We do competition here. We celebrate people taking part but we reward winners too. Students need to be resilient.'

Art studios ablaze with papier mâché, silk screen printing, life model drawings. The (smallish) canteen is decorated with exotic designs created during the year 7 arts and crafts day. Everyone does drama in years 7 and 8 and a fair number carry on to GCSE and A level. Plenty of performance opportunities: monthly concerts, Christmas musical extravaganza, school musicals, year 12 pantomime, orchestra, rock band, choirs and the wonderful Ukulele Ladies.

Gardening is a popular club – paths are lined with daffodils and crocuses, flowers bloom in brightly painted pots, herb gardens and vegetable gardens. Other clubs include Amnesty, debating, chess, film. Students go on geography field trips, D of E, language exchanges; they take part in mock bar trials, science, technology and maths challenges, debating competitions, classes with visiting artists, musicians and actors.

Background and atmosphere: Named for Mancunian Ellen Wilkinson, who was a Labour MP during the '20s, '30s and '40s, one of the leaders of the Jarrow March in 1936, and became the first female Minister for Education in 1945. The school sits amidst comfortable, leafy, mock-Tudor suburbia, though few pupils live in the immediate vicinity. Brick buildings, mostly one or two storeys high, flanked by grass and flower beds planted by the gardening club, with a tube line running behind a high wall round the edge of the playing fields. New sixth form centre and study rooms, library and resource area.

The only all-girls state school in Ealing. 'This makes them unselfconscious: they're happy to sit and make daisy chains in the summer, they're keen on science and sport, they're very appreciative of each other. They don't grow up quite so quickly.'

Pastoral care, well-being and discipline: Well-ordered. Girls are put in one of four divisions – similar to houses – and stay in these throughout their time at the school. 'It's like having a smaller school within a bigger school, with a family feel.' For some girls from difficult backgrounds, school is the most stable aspect of their lives, and discipline is based round 'catching them being good'. Learners of the Month are celebrated, awards for perseverance and commitment. Most are well-behaved girls, who give the school a good name. A member of the audience during a recent class trip to the National Theatre wrote to the school to praise the exemplary behaviour of its students.

Pupils and parents: Great ethnic mix, with around 20 per cent white, 20 per cent black, 20 per cent Asian and 20 per cent Arabic. The rest come from a variety of backgrounds, eg Polish, Chinese. Most of the well-heeled residents in the immediate vicinity patronise independent schools, though several Japanese girls from the local enclave have been choosing it recently in preference to their community's school. The catchment area tends to spread along the local tube lines and bus routes.

Entrance: Increasingly oversubscribed, with over 600 applicants for 216 places. Priority to siblings, looked-after children and those with specific medical or social needs. Then 10 per cent from linked Ealing primary schools. Other Ealing primaries get next preference, with the remaining places filled by those living nearest. In practice, this probably means less than two miles away.

About 40 girls from other schools join the sixth form each year, with a baseline of 5+ A*-C GCSE grades for A level courses, including Bs in their A level subjects. Those who don't make the grade can take level 2 courses.

Exit: The 30 per cent or so who leave after GCSEs tend to go to mixed sixth forms or colleges, or follow vocational courses elsewhere. A few high-fliers are lured by scholarships to local independent schools.

Sixth form leavers mostly go on to university, with a trickle to Oxbridge, but some potential students find it socially alien and the majority stays in London. Imperial is particularly popular; as are SOAS, Kings, Queen Mary, Royal Holloway and Brunel; recent others include Liverpool, Leeds, Lancaster, Sussex and Anglia Ruskin. Biomedical sciences, business and law figure highly, with English close behind.

Remarks: An increasingly successful and popular school. Huge social and ethnic mix, egalitarian traditions. Stable staff, nice girls, few discipline problems. For many pupils it is a haven and a springboard to academic success.

Eltham College

Grove Park Road, London SE9 4QF

Pupils: 1,080 • Ages: 7–18 • Sixth form: 210 (65 girls)

Fees: £14,340 – £16,245 pa

Tel: 020 8857 1455
Email: mail@eltham-college.org.uk
Website: www.elthamcollege.london

Headmaster: Since 2014, Mr Guy Sanderson MA (Oxon) PGCE (40s). Studied PPE and then modern history at Trinity College, Oxford. Having started out as a stockbroker in the City, he followed this with a stint at the UN High Commission for Refugees in Pakistan and Afghanistan before teaching at a series of academic independents – St Paul's, Whitgift, City of London Boys' School and Reigate Grammar, where he rose to head of sixth form and deputy head.

His office, newly decorated in tasteful grey with fresh flowers and framed photography of the boys in action, is a small sign of his modernising intent and ambition to make the school one of the country's best independent schools. However, it is important to him to be able to do this in his own time in his own way and not to be strait-jacketed by targets. The parents we hear from seem pleased the school is being given something of a shake-up. One confided: 'the new head is clearly very driven and personally career oriented. From my perspective this is no bad thing. If he does well it will mean that the school has done well.' Another: 'Excellent. Making his mark as a new head with refreshing improvements and upgrades. Sensible and approachable, academic yet realising sport and extracurricular activities make the school.' And: 'Determined to improve the school's academic standing, modern in his approach... he knows the pupils and is interested in them individually.' 'He is not, however, afraid to say no and stand steadfast by his principles.'

In tune with this dynamic image, Mr Sanderson tweets encouragement to the far-flung corners of Elthamians' daily activities. Boys will find his door open at lunch-times and he's delighted to find they drop in to suggest ideas for new clubs or initiatives. Year 7 boys are invited to his office on their birthday for a doughnut. In answer to our question as to whether there should be a head girl as well as head boy, he says that it is simply a case of the best person for the job and in the case of this year that means there is. With a wife who is a FTSE 100 head-hunter it's a topic of debate.

Mr Sanderson has relocated from rural Sussex with his wife and three children. A keen skier and open water swimmer, for the past two summers he's swam the Bosphorus. The family lives in a house overlooking the playing fields, together with the chickens, but not the pigs, from Sussex.

Head of junior school: Since 2010, Mr Edmund Cavendish (50s) MA (Oxon) PGCE. Studied modern history at Queen's College, Oxford. Deputy head at the senior school for five years. Prior to this, he was head of history and then head of sixth form during 16 years at Ipswich School, following four years at Merchiston Castle School in Edinburgh. This junior school setting was new for Mr Cavendish, but he relishes the enthusiasm of the younger boys and feels his experience of the senior school – he still teaches the Oxbridge historians – is helpful in enabling him to bring the two schools together, very much a focus since the arrival of Mr Sanderson, the new head of the senior school.

He dips in and out, ensuring he teaches something to each year so that he gets to know each boy. Another focus has been ensuring the stretching of the most able wherever their talents lie – this could be in the shape of elite coaching for the sporting or opening up the senior orchestras to junior musicians.

Parents say he is 'is a great champion of the traditions of the school' and 'I think the work he is doing on mental health is amazing and the implementations made mean a less stressful, more enjoyable schooling'. He lives close to the school, has been married for over 30 years and has two grown-up daughters, one working in Burma, the other for McKinsey, and two dogs that have as prominent billing in the framed photos in his office.

Academic matters: All of the usual curriculum subjects in the junior school. As well as French, Mandarin is taught from year 3, which boys describe enthusiastically as 'fun, but hard sometimes'. Boys are set for maths throughout and for English comprehension from year 5. ICT rather than computing at the moment. Terms alternate between DT and art. There is a focus on developing cross-curricular thinking skills via 'philosophy for children' whilst following a growth mind-set approach of challenging every boy to believe intelligence isn't fixed but can be developed. Plenty of fun workshops and curricular trips to the London museums and galleries on the school's doorstep as well as short residentials further up the school. No doted-on school pets – the science lab terrapins have been replaced by giant African snails.

A slightly mixed picture from the few parents we hear from regarding teaching. One satisfied parent: 'I have been nothing but happy with the teaching' and another: 'All subjects are taught to a very high standard'. Whilst for another: 'The junior school could do with the shake-up currently refreshing the senior school'. It seems this is very much on the cards. The boys we meet who strike us as fairly free and easy with their views are wholehearted in their praise: 'The teachers are very kind; when you are feeling stressed they help you' and 'They want you to get the best marks possible'.

The parents we spoke to welcomed the fact that testing here does not feel intensive throughout. Mr Cavendish elaborates that teachers 'don't over-hype' tests and that a new system of monitoring enables the school to build up a picture of how each child is developing. At the end of each half-term boys receive a grade card with a mark for effort and attainment. In years 3 and 4 boys tell us 'everyone is mad about collecting merits'. By years 5 and 6 it's no longer 'cool' to collect them but boys nonetheless make use of the teachers' comments. A parent reported: 'Homework seems OK: in year 6 it's around 20 minutes each day. There are revision packs during the holidays which aren't compulsory'.

In 2016, 81 per cent of grades were A*/A at GCSE and 60 per cent A*/A at A level (85 per cent A*/B), the latter an improvement on the previous year. Senior curriculum wise very trad but with a careful eye to future global employment prospects. More academic subjects have been added and the less academic such as sports studies removed. Timetabling isn't completed until each boy's preferences are accommodated.

Everyone does single sciences at IGCSE and the short-course RS. A Level additions are economics, psychology, government and politics, pure and further maths, unusually geology (a 30 year tradition) and newly introduced computing. Maths is the most popular A level and taken as an IGCSE. All those from the top sets taking maths early have consistently gained A* and mathematicians throughout the school regularly compete nationally. Years 8 and 9 have been finalists in UKMT for the past 3 years. There are very strong student numbers in economics: currently the second largest A level cohort. A glittering array of highlights from the science department. The physics department is recognised as a centre of excellence by the Institute of Physics with stellar grades; most recently a chemist was in receipt of the prestigious Roentgenium award; year 10s were also finalists in the Royal Society of Chemistry's challenge in Kent. The school regularly produces Arkwright scholars who go on to study engineering at the country's most desirable destinations. One Eltham geologist scored the highest geology A level mark in the country, losing a mere four marks.

French, German, Mandarin and Spanish are introduced gradually over the first three years with boys choosing a minimum of two. The head has appointed a new head of classics, introduced ancient Greek to compliment Latin and says all language appointments will be either Oxbridge graduates and/or native speakers. Italian is available and Russian off timetable. Whilst French holds its own with several studying French alongside their chosen degree subject at university, German is the second most popular language. Of nine recent Mandarin GCSE passes, only one was a native speaker. It will now be extended to A level.

Class sizes average 22 but with smaller teaching sets in all languages, maths, science and some creative subjects. A quarter of teaching staff have been at the school for over 10 years but the head says this is a changing picture. Keen to develop staff, he devolves leadership, empowering them to run with their own project ideas if it will benefit the school. One of our guides said of the teachers: 'They're all passionate about their subjects; lessons are very interactive'. The head tells us of a lesson he witnessed recently where the boys were studying glaciation using edible food stuffs. Parents are aware of teaching standards being consciously raised. A mother told us: 'In the sixth form the teachers help the students to get excellent A level results whilst keeping their subject alive and interesting.' For the most able, there is a new head of academic scholarship running a programme of debating, lectures from outside speakers and encouraging boys to prepare and deliver papers to their peers.

There is a full-time learning support teacher. All new pupils are screened on entry for possible difficulties. Around 10 per cent with identified SEN needs, the majority with dyslexia but a few with ADHD, ASD or communication issues. The school says that the majority of cases are quite 'mild' and most support is within lessons. A dyslexic pupil describes the school as: 'Nice atmosphere. Positive, helpful teachers'.

Despite the hard-working atmosphere and desire to up the academic ante parents do not feel there is too much pressure – the extracurricular provides relief from academic work, year round rather than annual testing is a relief, with not too much holiday homework and sufficient time left within the year for revision.

Games, options, the arts: No doubt that almost everyone is sporty but that seems to be mostly by dint of encouragement and breadth of opportunity. The core sports on offer in the junior school are rugby, football, hockey (on the up, reaching the regional under-11 finals) and cricket for two afternoons a week plus a brief gym or swim period. A mother sees the benefit of sports teaching by both male and female coaches. Boys are wowed by the coaches with national team experience. Competitive fixtures and galas, inter-house competitions plus clubs in which to try new things such as judo or basketball. Every effort is made to encourage boys of all abilities to don head-to-toe stripes and play for the school. This year every boy played rugby in at least one match fixture. There are plenty of individual successes too – one boy plays for Kent U11s cricket and three skiers were recently selected for the national training squad. The teaching of fencing must be good: we met one boy who tried fencing for the first time at a school open day and is now GB number two with highly ranked team mates to spar against. Boys also excel in chess competitions and LAMDA exams. One parent summed it up: 'The diversity of activities allows most children to find a niche that they can feel part of'. Far too many sporting triumphs to list here.

Rugby is the school's big thing: England U16 champions for two consecutive years, winner of the U15 Kent 7s this year and 13 county players. Hockey comes a close second with plenty of county players and this year's U16 winners of the Kent cup. And the summer months are no less high-achieving with the U15 cricketers also bringing home the Kent cup. Players of international standing are in good company, with a couple representing England in fencing, a GB skier and three England internationals and last year's U13 England chess champion. Games afternoons are compulsory, although PE lessons reduce to a single lesson by year 9. Coaches are often national players but the head stresses to them that they must have an interest in teaching not just the elite but 'the grass roots'.

Plenty of opportunities to try new things such as climbing or sailing. For those with a lighter interest there are clubs and societies for table tennis, basketball and pilates. With regards to having a go, the school aims for all boys to represent the school in an activity. Glad to see the girls as well as boys have a tug-of-war in the annual house competition.

Music is a significant part of the junior school curriculum and 85 per cent of pupils have weekly individual lessons, currently up to grade 5 – the high uptake inspired by a project which enables all boys in years 3 and 4 to receive five weeks of free instrumental tuition. There are several choirs and ensembles and an annual music concert. Plenty to aspire to: trebles enjoyed singing alongside the seniors recently at the Barbican with the LSO. Years 3 and 4 perform an annual play or musical, as do years 5 and 6. As on our last visit, however, we hear consistent rumbles about the focus on a talented few: 'the chosen ones reappear very often across activities'. The senior school is also proud of its musicians who achieve exceptionally well academically with the last few years, consistently delivering an Oxbridge place or two. Around 65 per cent of pupils learn an instrument. One parent told us: 'I was particularly touched to see my child play a string instrument in his first term as we are not a particularly musical family.' Choral singing is a high point. Ensembles, choirs and orchestras play across London's most stunning venues. Recently parents were treated to performances at Ronnie Scott's, the Barbican, St John's Smith Square, the Royal Albert Hall and beneath the hull of the Cutty Sark.

Boys' impressive artwork decorates the school. This is the first school we've visited with its own art gallery. The Gerald Moore Gallery, named after an Eltham alumni, also open to the public, houses school and external exhibitions – the curator shared the Arts Council funded Youth Uncovered exhibition where students had worked with a commissioned artist to explore what it means to be young in today's world. The exhibition assisted students to achieve offers from a top graphic design and fine art course, plus an offer to study architecture at Cambridge. Two Hayward tours have used the gallery space. All the art teachers and technicians are artists and pursue their own practices and an artist-in-residence has a studio within the department.

Drama is on the curriculum for all years 7 to 9 and is available at GCSE and A level. The drama department produces a major musical every year – most recent Les Misérables with student-led orchestra. Students also directed, acted, managed and teched a production of Richard III. Those jaunting to Edinburgh for The Fringe were rewarded with 5* reviews in the national press for their performance of Sweeney Todd. Plenty of distinctions in LAMDA exams and a place this year at the National Youth Theatre.

Clubs and societies often seem to be extending in tone but Dixieland band, 'magic: the gathering', slick sticks, run for fun, Fair Trade and Morris dancing caught our eye. Those looking forward to a far-flung expedition may need a head for heights with past destinations including Nepal and Borneo whilst students tackle D of E from bronze to gold.

Pupils are carefully prepared for university exits, including a new focus on US universities. A pathways programme ensures pupils are en route and prepared for possible careers, making use of the network of Eltham alumni for work experience placements.

Background and atmosphere: Originally founded as a boarding school for the sons of missionaries, boys attend chapel twice a week as part of a strong Christian tradition with caring for the community still an important part of the school's ethos. Since moving in 1912 to this elegant 18th century mansion, with a columned entrance, surrounded by 70 acres of green fields, it has grown in size, stopped taking boarders and girls have been part of the sixth form since the 1970s. Despite the increase in size, boys and parents refer approvingly to the school so often as 'small' that we check the pupil numbers. The atmosphere is peaceful but buzzy indoors and out; students engrossed in lessons or off to play sports with huge kitbags.

Apart from the elegance of Central Hall, now housing the humanities classrooms in style, with its beautiful wooden boards of Oxbridge scholars and charming sepia photographs of sports teams gone by, the school comprises a collection of blocks in various states of repair. The science block is so delightfully retro we expected to bump into the Enigma Machine at any moment. However, labs are being modernised one by one and an imaginatively conceived £14m development project will extend the sixth form centre out into the playing fields, mirroring the students' imminent transition to university – set to open in 2018, also providing new language classrooms, a new mathematics suite of classrooms and a well-being centre. The DT facilities comprise a series of large professional-looking workshops with a laser cutter, 3D printer and a CAD-cam suite. The library is large and well-resourced with books, journals or e-books which boys can borrow on their phones, with a separate sixth form area up a spiral staircase.

The chic grey paint of the senior school make-over is yet to reach the outpost of the master's office but classrooms are being transformed from top to bottom into brighter spaces with the boys' approval. The small library – 'we love David Walliams' – now boasts coloured beanbags popular for hanging out or doodling on wet days. There are separate outside spaces allocated at breaktimes to the younger and older boys. Art displays could be improved in our opinion, but boys are justly proud of a wonderful mosaic of London they helped to design and make to celebrate the school's centenary. It seems like a family home that can afford to get bashed about a bit without anyone worrying about the soft furnishings. The high decibels at break time only add to the atmosphere.

The school's most famous alumnus is Eric Liddell, the Olympic athlete who won gold in the 400m at the 1924 Paris Olympics, forever immortalised by Chariots of Fire, hence the Eric Liddell sports centre, which provides on-site indoor cricket nets, a 25 metre pool, dance studio and fitness suite. In addition £3.5m is earmarked to further develop the sports facilities including a new pavilion, second Astroturf and 4G rugby pitch. The sport almost always gets a mention from boys as a highlight of Eltham, but another boy sums it as having been 'supportive, caring and achieving'.

We asked to meet a few sixth form girls curious to hear about their experiences. Those joining from girls' schools spoke of wanting to find larger teaching groups for their A level subjects. Whilst all felt slightly nervous on arrival, they don't feel in a minority, as the numbers suggest. They spoke of finding the boys welcoming, the atmosphere competitive academically, offering them different points of view, but less 'cliquey' and more relaxed socially.

Pastoral care, well-being and discipline: A mother otherwise very happy with the junior school did tell us that she believed 'less confident children can sometimes be allowed to hide in the background'. There seems no doubt that it is a competitive place. At the same time, there is no need to conform: we hear that difference is accepted and quirkiness happily embraced – certainly borne out by the boys we met who seemed to listen to each other and respect individual talents. One thing that might unify boys here: we'd describe our tour guides as keen as mustard. Our overwhelming impression was of the boys' enthusiasm for their academic subjects. We raised an eyebrow at the idea of a Latin club at lunchtime, not a bit of it; two relived being caught out in a comprehension test by a tricky piece of grammar as if it was a narrowly missed sporting goal.

The school as a whole receives glowing praise for its pastoral care, the front line being form tutors. One mother told us of the care and consideration her son received during a difficult time at home. Co-curricular clubs run pre- and post-school, whilst a breakfast club allows parents to dash for the commute. Boys were keen to tell us about their efforts at charity fundraising and seemed modestly unaware of how they'd been chosen for leadership opportunities. Boys talk about 'we' much of the time and clearly feel proud of their school.

A careful and detailed anti-bullying policy and zero drug tolerance. Incidents are not unheard of but parents report that they were swiftly dealt with. Thought has been given to the potential misuse of mobile phones, which can be brought to school but kept out of lessons. Sixth formers are allowed out at lunch-times. A fairly strict, disciplined environment with quite a long list of sanctions available to teachers to keep efforts up to scratch academically.

The deputy head is the head of pastoral care in the senior school. Parents universally praise pastoral care here, one going as far as to describe it as 'exceptional'. This is certainly one of the best resourced pastoral care teams we have encountered: two qualified nurses, a doctor, counsellor and two chaplains. Boys wave to the nurse during our tour. When we quiz the head as to the school's consideration of the kind of mental health issues variously affecting girls and boys today he is engaged and has recently returned from a conference on the subject.

There is a newly appointed head of transition to ease in year 7s. Form tutors, the pastoral front line, are described as 'accessible and generally very quick to respond to any concerns' and will now stay with boys for their lower school and then middle school years. Communication between school and home is felt to be excellent.

We raised the news stories still to be found on a Google search of the school concerning the conduct of two teachers. The incidents were before the current head's time and concerned activities outside of the school but have resulted in a review of safeguarding and DBS checking procedures for staff.

Pupils and parents: The majority of students come from within a five mile radius, taking in Blackheath, Greenwich, the Isle of Dogs and Surrey Quays but also south to Bromley, Chislehurst and Sidcup, Orpington, Farnborough and West Wickham. Far fewer with different languages spoken at home than we see in central London schools. A tiny few international students. Working parents are catered for: pupils could be in school from 8am purchasing breakfast in King George's Hall, whilst the library is open for after-school study until 5.30pm, not to mention myriad activities taking pupils until the end of the day, often with no extra cost. Parents are described to us as including 'multi-millionaires' and the 'down to earth'.

What kind of child would Eltham suit? Parents mention 'all-rounders' and 'bright, motivated, independent children who will rise to a challenge'. The head says there is no Eltham boy; it will simply appeal to those who want to make the most of opportunities.

Entrance: Capped at 60 across three forms of 20 boys at 7+ entry and then rising to no more than 22 boys in a form for years 4-6. Candidates are assessed in maths and English, including an element of verbal reasoning and reading. Historically chances of getting in have been pretty good but applications are increasing. The same test subjects for entry at 8+, 9+ and 10+. Pupils mainly enter from local preps and pre-preps such as Babington House, Bickley Park, The Pointer School, Breaside and Colfe's. Open mornings in the autumn.

Academic standards are high and entrance to the senior school is by selection based on academic merit and on an assessment of the pupil's likely positive contribution to the school. Everyone needs a good reference, and computer adaptive verbal and non-verbal reasoning is now a feature of testing at every stage. The majority of pupils come through from the junior school and 40 to 50 external pupils join at 11+, with around five competing for every place. External candidates take entrance papers in English and maths. Those with SEN needs may be allocated additional time. New 11+ joiners hail mostly from local preps including: The Pointer School, Blackheath Prep, Breaside, Heath House and St Olave's but also Chislehurst CofE Primary. Only a few joining at 13+ but it is increasingly competitive entry point. Candidates sit papers in English, maths and a modern foreign language or Latin.

External candidates to the sixth form take an exam and if successful are interviewed. In recent years girls have arrived from the local GDST schools and St Ursula's Convent, amongst others. Candidates sit papers in two subjects of their choice. Offers made are subject to a minimum of six A*/A grades at GCSE including the four subjects of further study.

Exit: All but a dozen juniors head to the senior school, a quarter with scholarships. Those leaving do so mostly due to a change in family circumstance eg relocation, plus a few to the local grammar schools. The significant change is that boys from the junior school no longer sit an entrance test for the senior school. Other initiatives ease the year 7 transition and have built the all-through school feel: boys become familiar with the buildings, facilities and teachers.

Almost all boys stay on to the sixth form. The trend has been for departing pupils to head for Exeter, Nottingham, Oxbridge, Bristol, Warwick, Durham, Leeds, Southampton, Imperial and Loughborough, so one can be pretty confident of attaining Russell Group aspirations. In addition the school does particularly well by its medical students.

Money matters: A generous number of scholarships on offer at each entry point, which could be for academic ability or music, sport, art and drama (16+ only) – the financial reward varying from the token to the quite substantial. Everyone sitting the entrance test will be considered for academic scholarships, with further requirements for music, art and sports scholars. Fewer than 10 per cent of pupils are in receipt of means-tested bursaries, which could range from a helping hand to 100 per cent of fees.

Remarks: With an energetic head on the case and money being spent in bringing the facilities up to scratch, it could be a wonderful place to find a niche and increasingly achieve great things: heading in a more academic direction than of late but still extremely sporty.

Elthorne Park High School

Westlea Road, Hanwell, London W7 2AH

Pupils: 1,058 • Ages: 11–18 • Sixth form: 182

Tel: 020 8566 1166
Email: elthorne@ephs.ealing.sch.uk
Website: www.ephs.ealing.sch.uk

E

Headteacher: Since 2012, Mr Eliot Wong BSc PGCE Dip Ed NPQH (40s). Married with a school age daughter, Mr Wong is a West Londoner through and through. Educated at St Peter's Primary school in Hammersmith and then Burlington Danes, he graduated with a first class degree in mathematics at King's College London before following his vocation in teaching (maths). He still finds the time to teach further maths to a class of about five who choose to do it ('it's the most enjoyable thing I do') as well as running revision classes for GCSE. Sixteen years of his career have been spent in schools in Ealing. Previously deputy head at Brentside High School, and before that assistant head at Cheam High School. He has also worked at Cardinal Wiseman (head of maths) and in Woking.

Thoughtful, determined and with a razor sharp logical mind, Mr Wong has already achieved much improvement. Graphs depicting GCSE data are moving in a healthy northerly direction and the latest Ofsted inspection in March 2015 graded the school as Good (from a Requires Improvement in 2013) with the proviso that it only missed an Outstanding because there was only two years of available results data. Far from being disheartened by missing out on an Outstanding, Mr Wong sees this as an opportunity to innovate and change continually: 'once you achieve an Outstanding, there is a risk of complacency,' Mr Wong smiles. An advocate of Jim Collins' hedgehog principal, Wong believes if you focus on doing one thing really well everything else will fall into his place. In his view it's the teaching that you need to concentrate on. 'If you teach really well, behaviour improves and parents are happy.' He measures the quality of teaching in a number of different ways, including regularly observing lessons and checking exercise books.

A simple but effective change he has made is to the school's mission statement: from 'achieving in a learning community' to 'achieving excellence in a learning community.' He has introduced rigour, challenge and aspiration and observes that 'most staff have responded very positively'. A regular tweeter, he celebrates his students' achievements in the public sphere as well as making sure his school remains prominent not only on social media but also in the mind of the local authority, from which he has been effective in extracting funding (for the £14m expansion, for example, currently under way). He is proud of the liberal atmosphere that is immediately noticeable, but asserts that 'we are old fashioned in some senses – in that we work hard and show a positive and respectful attitude.' However, this is achieved not by 'imposing draconian measures' but through 'trust (and verification) and expectation'. That is the Elthorne way, he says, and applies as much to the staff as to the pupils.

Excellent teachers and motivated pupils are only two legs of the three-legged stool; another focus of his is parental involvement. He has introduced the 'text challenge', challenging parents to support their children with weekly texts about particular issues, in current affairs, for example. Mr Wong is deeply conscious of having to find ways to add value not only to aspirational families but also disadvantaged families. 'If you want to get the best out children you can't drag them, but you need to stimulate them with interesting, engaging lessons and the support of their parents.' This is the ACE formula – Achievement, Challenge, Excellence. It seems to be working.

Mr Wong is well respected by the pupils (they panic if they are on their phones when he appears in the playground), but parents speak of their frustration with his failure to respond to emails, and to complete references on time, and complain how difficult it is to get hold of him. An industrious, and thoughtful head, however (his office is decorated with hundreds of yellow post it notes), he is highly committed and canny.

Academic matters: Huge improvement in results since 2012. Nearly a third of all GCSEs awarded in 2016 were A or A*; at A level 26 per cent of grades were A*/A, 61 per cent A*-B (including BTecs, 50 per cent A*/A and 76 per cent A*-B). ALPS value added rates the sixth form as 'outstanding' for teaching and learning and results. Each year five or six pupils take further maths A level.

Elthorne Park is currently the top performing school in South Ealing and Hanwell (and has held this position for the third year running), and is in the top quintile of schools nationally in terms of GCSE attainment (including English, maths and two sciences). Out of 5220 non-selective, mixed schools in the country Elthorne recently ranked 91st in performance tables, putting the school in the top two per cent.

Ofsted identified particularly imaginative teaching in modern languages with high standards of marking. Over half the year takes at least one language and French, Spanish and German all get a good smattering of A and B grades, Polish too. A foreign exchange is organised for each language and about 50 pupils go on a language exchange each year. Elthorne's modern language results are in the top five per cent of the country. Mr Wong says he will support anyone who wants to learn Latin (and ancient Greek) but a visiting teacher will have to come in specially or the pupil will have to go elsewhere.

The quality of teaching is closely observed and monitored. 'Book looks' at least half termly to check that marking is up to standard and each teacher is observed three times a year. Each year to GCSE has six classes with about 26 pupils in each. Setting in maths from year 7, English and science also broadly set as well as modern languages. Excellent DT department, offering separate exams in food technology, textiles, resistant materials and graphic products. Music, drama and theatre studies are strong, as well as all three sciences, particularly chemistry. All departments run 'intervention sessions' to support pupils who are falling behind.

Some 75 per cent of students have been taking Ebacc subjects for some time but 'I will no way force every student to do subjects that aren't suited them,' avers Mr Wong. BTec courses in media, business and health and social care also available as well as level 1 courses in eg motor vehicle maintenance and salon services. The ASDAN Award Scheme provides a course in basic skills, life skills and general knowledge for those students who wish to limit the number of GCSE courses they study.

Innovative style of teaching includes 'flip learning'. Students in the sixth form (and some classes lower down the school), given an iPad and required to research a subject before a lesson. The lesson can then be conducted in a more discursive way – students therefore learn to think, as well as to carry out independent research.

Enrichment lessons form part of the curriculum for years 7 to 9 – an effort to broaden the academic experience so that pupils are not confined to Ebacc subjects. They might study, eg, Japanese or film. Gifted and talented pupils can used it as a springboard to enhance their skills.

One parent observed reluctantly that there remains a culture of low expectation at Elthorne, however, citing as an example the practice of basing target grades at GCSE on earlier

Sats results. Parents also commented on a lack of support with regard to A level choices and the university process. There is a lack of clear communication and flexibility about options, they say. This results in a few going elsewhere for sixth form when their inclination would have been to stay. School's response to this is that the senior leadership team now interviews every year 11 student and discusses the extracurricular guarantees made to every student, which range from travel abroad to gym membership and personalised help with Oxbridge applications. Communication when a child is not reaching targets, on the other hand, is very good, observed another parent. A subject teacher will send a text, and similarly if a child gets detention, the parents are sent a text.

The number of students with SEN is not high – less than 20 per cent – but a relatively high number of students (between two and three per cent) with Statements/EHC plans. 'They are attracted to us as we are a nurturing school, and they are well supported,' says Mr Wong. The SENCo has a team of 10. Children are supported in class as much as possible with teaching assistants attached to subjects. EAL tuition takes place outside the classroom. One parent observed how little support you get if you are a middle class kid with dyslexia – we have heard that before. Currently a £14m expansion project is under way, which already has the acronym ARP attached to it – the 'Additionally Resourced Provision for Special Needs'. This will be a hub of activity working to support chidlren with speech, language and communication problems and those with specific learning needs (SLCN – speech, language and communication needs). In addition, the new development will house facilities for all the students, including a new hall and drama studio, a life skills room and two extra ICT suites.

Games, options, the arts: 'Expressive arts are at the heart of our community,' says Mr Wong. We were impressed with just how much goes on in here – in creative arts, drama, music and sport. Elthorne teams have excelled in the borough in various sports including cross-country, netball, basketball, rugby, football and cricket. Girls' sports are especially strong. The current year 11 girls' netball team has been unbeaten for the past four years and the U13 girls' football team is national champion. There are regular competitions and matches – inter-form and inter-school as well as regional. An annual sports day, which includes track and field athletics as well as softball, takes place at Perivale sports ground.

For budding thespians there is the opportunity to perform extracts from Shakespeare plays at the annual Shakespeare Festival. In addition there is an annual major whole school production, often a musical (recently they performed Grease). Students get involved with all aspects of the production – costumes, choreography, music, set and props. Decent drama studio where lessons and rehearsals take place. Performances happen in the hall.

Gifted musicians are identified and giving lots of opportunity to compete and perform. Numerous concerts and recitals plus a classical music competition and annual rock concert. Plenty of ensembles – brass and guitar as well as a chamber and whole school orchestra. Macs in music rooms where students are taught music composition. The popular summer festival and barbecue brings together performances and displays – art and DT as well as drama and music.

Lots of trips and activities including annual ski trip and Spanish, French and German exchanges (with a twin school), as well as geography field trips and visits to eg Oxford University and the theatre. Plenty of extracurricular opportunities such as public speaking competitions, D of E, bushcraft and PGL trips, the STEM challenge (EPHS were recently regional winners) and UK maths challenge. A plethora of clubs take place after school, from debating to film and volunteering in the community.

Background and atmosphere: Elthorne may be in Hanwell but it stands out from other schools of its kind because it's situated on the edge of the seven and a half acres of green space that is Elthorne Park. Children can spill into this area during lunch break (supervised), and the football pitches and sports areas are a tremendous additional resource. The main buildings are positioned around a central courtyard – a mixture of low, single storey, temporary, and two storey buildings as well as the shiny modern sixth form centre. Eight modern, spacious and well -equipped science labs, a suite of specialist music rooms, a purpose built drama studio, four art studios with a dark room, graphics and kiln facilities. Specialist DT including food technology, textiles and resistant materials. Plenty of Macs available for use in graphics as well as in music. Large sports hall as well as separate school hall where lunch, assemblies and drama happens. Purpose built sixth form centre. A feeling of space – no cramped corridors and a comfortable well-resourced library.

Maroon uniform creates a somewhat dour impression and can be worn scruffily: 'they are not super strict about ties and tucking in shirts here,' said our guide with warm appreciation. This school is far from dour however, but vibrant and buzzy. While Mr Wong clearly has a firm grip, the school has a relaxed feel; children are not deferential but their behaviour seems to fall on the right side of the line.

Pastoral care, well-being and discipline: Mr Wong describes the school as a healthy mix of old-fashioned and more relaxed values. While there is a finely tuned system of 'levelled' detentions (ranging between a 15 minute personal detention with a teacher to a head teacher detention on a Monday night) as well as a three strikes policy and a system of internal isolations, the key element is trust. This can't be imposed, says Wong, through draconian measures, but through example and respect. He talks about 'the Elthorne Way,' an expectation of high achievement and excellence through a healthy symbiotic relationship between staff and pupils. Students appear relaxed, but that doesn't mean they aren't polite and well behaved. Mr Wong works hard and expects those around him to work hard, both staff and pupils. 'I believe in hard work and striving for excellence,' he says, 'I don't believe in excuses.' Trust is key – but trust with verification. We will trust them, he says, but we will check on them. The students have a voice – the student council have regular breakfasts and lunches with staff and there is an annual student survey. They, too, are listened to and treated with respect. When it comes to drugs and weapons, however, the line is clear and inflexible.

Parents warmly supportive – and appreciative – of the school's approach to incidents that happen outside school hours, often with the local community. They step in quickly and with tact and understanding. Behaviour – according to most parents – is 'on the whole good'.

Pupils and parents: Just under 50 per cent of families here are white British. The rest split fairly equally between black, Asian and Eastern European. Some support for EAL but most have learnt good English at primary school. Local Ealing families who, on the whole, are keen their children do well and will work hard with the school to achieve this. Relatively low number of pupils are on free school meals (25 per cent compared with a national average of 28 per cent). Stable student population.

Entrance: About 1,000 apply each year for 240 places in year 7. The four main feeder primaries are Fielding, Oaklands, Little Ealing and St Mark's – perception among parents is that Fielding dominates. As the primaries expand, so there is greater pressure on places. Proximity to the school the main criterion (after the usual criteria have been taken into account – children in public care, exceptional medical or social circumstances etc). Catchment has shrunk from a 1.5 mile radius to a one mile radius. Parents want their children to come here and consider it to be outstanding

– regardless of what Ofsted says. Siblings given priority. To get into the sixth form you need a minimum of 5 A*-Cs including English and maths with at least a B in chosen A level subjects.

Exit: Of the upper sixth approximately 88 per cent go on to university, in 2016, 43 per cent of these to Russell Group universities. Brighter pupils attracted elsewhere for sixth form, observed one parent. 'No NEETs for the past three years!', says head proudly. Some 93 per cent stay in education post-GCSEs, over 50 per cent stay at Elthorne to study advanced courses in the sixth form – over 70 per cent of these study A levels, but all sixth formers study advanced (level 3) courses. About 20 per cent each year go on to art school and one or two each year go to the BRIT school.

E

Money matters: A local authority funded, well resourced school – reserves we were told are greater than five per cent. Lower than borough average spent on supply staff, large proportion of budget spent on teachers and education support staff. Almost double spent on learning resources and ICT compared with local and national averages.

Remarks: Value added – an often overlooked measure – is strong here, Mid and high achievers will make significant progress, especially compared with their peers nationally. If you have a motivated child, keen to do well, this school won't hold him/her back but will inspire and work to meet that potential. A school with a genuine liberal arts and creative ethos. A precious gem in this age of emphasis on Ebacc subjects. Let's hope it will preserve its arty tradition as it consolidates the academics in the face of pressure from on high.

Emanuel School

Battersea Rise, London SW11 1HS

Pupils: 895 • Ages: 10–18 • Sixth form: 180

Fees: £17,572 pa

Tel: 020 8870 4171
Email: enquiries@emanuel.org.uk
Website: www.emanuel.org.uk

Headmaster: Since 2004, Mr Hanley-Browne (50s) MA (Oxon) in natural sciences and PGCE from Cambridge. Educated at St George's College, Weybridge. Previously taught biology at Sevenoaks for five years, assistant master at Charterhouse for nine and deputy head (pastoral) at Highgate for seven.

His vision has been to create a London school with a global outlook – there are links to schools in India, China, the US and Germany – and to be a top 50 school within the next four years: 'everyone comes from all over London for our creative arts, but we're not just that'. He recognises the weaknesses of A level but feels 'there is more good to A levels than bad, and also I don't wish to run the the IB alongside it.' Credited as being an astute businessman, he has transformed the fortunes of the school – it was struggling to recruit when he arrived – as its academic results have risen, so too its size has grown and it has become a first choice rather than back-up for other south London co-eds.

Lots of 'excellent's from parents asked for an opinion, appreciative of the transformations in progress and accomplished over his tenure. One told us: he 'has been absolutely first rate on the few occasions we have had dealings with him directly. A real asset to the school.' Another: 'approachable, forward-thinking, independent in the best sense – that is putting the rounded education and happiness of the children before league tables.' As we noted before, the word 'aloof' also crops up; a parent said: 'The children think of him as a bit of a distant figure; he could perhaps engage with them a bit more as individuals.' When we came across two boys at break-time and asking them for their views on the head unprompted, they were enthusiastic in their appreciation for everything he is doing for the school, but indignant he didn't seem to know who they each were. Mr Hanley-Browne's response was that he doubts he sees any less of his pupils than other heads of major schools and that he is inevitably spread rather thinly. Married to Rachael who works as head of leadership consulting in an executive recruitment firm, they live locally and love to travel as much as possible, most recently to St Petersburg and Moscow. Moving on in July 2017 to become CEO of the Alpha Plus group.

Academic matters: Both A level and GCSE grades have been steadily improving year on year. In 2016, 39 per cent of A level grades A*/A and 62 per cent A*/A at GCSE. Grades in chemistry and physics at GCSE are streets ahead of the rest. Strong results in maths but mathematicians sometimes outclassed by a huge cohort of historians who really shine at A level too. Politics and economics are also popular. Linguists in handfuls.

GCSE: all pupils study English, maths and one language from French, German, Latin and Spanish – French and Spanish are far more popular than German. Either double or single sciences; the decision on the final route is made during year 11. Pupils choose a further three subjects from a wide range: art, economics, classical civilisation, DT, drama/theatre studies, geography, history, RS, music and PE. Not complete freedom to choose. A Levels add in business, further maths, politics and psychology. The majority of pupils are now expected to take three A levels and the EPQ.

Twenty-nine teachers have been at the school for more than 10 years. The most recent ISI report offered a host of 'excellent's when referring to both the teaching and attitudes of the pupils to learning, noting the good rapport between staff and students, though almost every parent we asked about the teaching staff began carefully with 'on the whole'. One said: 'There are some exceptional, inspiring teachers across the school who can transform a child's understanding.' Another: 'Overall, I would say the teaching is very good with some excellent examples thrown in'. Some offer praise without reservation: 'My wife and I are astonished by how much she loves the academic lessons too; we can't remember that school was this much fun when we were teenagers.' Interestingly innovative, the head has been keen to try the Harkness method where teaching is done in a small group, with a maximum 16 of students sitting around an oval table with tablets for instant online access: it's felt to encourage participation and the exchange of ideas.

A little more than average numbers with a learning difference, but a well-qualified head of learning support with two assistant practioners, both with qualifications in the support of dyslexia. The school does not screen all on entry, only if making 'poor progress'. Those with an ed psych report will have a 'learner profile' created to advise class teachers of learning preferences, some small group withdrawal. A few extras on offer such as an early morning spelling club and homework club every day of the week. Pupils talk of the value of touch-typing lessons and a Cogmed course, designed to help with working memory. Some 12 pupils currently have EAL assistance.

As befits the happy and relaxed atmosphere of the school, children don't seem to feel too intensively pressured. A typical report: 'Children seem to be prepared for exams without being over stressed.'

All departments seem plugged into national competitions. Year 10 students entered and were shortlisted for the Cambridge triple helix science writing competition. A DT student was recently awarded a prestigious Arkwright Scholarship. Maths students are regularly successful in both the UKMT Maths Challenge and the Hans Woyda competitions. Science students compete in the annual Science Olympiad, over half taking home a medal. Two students have won prizes in the Peterhouse essay competitions in recent years, both of whom were later awarded places at Cambridge. This is also a well-connected school which has no problem attracting an impressive line-up of speakers, such as Samira Ahmed, Sir Bob Geldof, Professor David Starkey, Alastair Darling and Lord Coe. Rowan Williams came to talk to the literary society about the Christian symbolism in the Narnia series. Sir Tim Berners-Lee, possibly the most famous OE, is returning to the school in September.

A member of staff is responsible for Oxbridge applications and arranges university visits for all of year 10. Oxbridge candidates attend seminars held jointly across the Westminster schools group. Work experience begins in years 10 and 11. The sixth form makes use of OEs coming back to the school to give them advice on everything from surviving the first year at uni to spending a year in industry. There is an annual careers convention attended by more than 70 guests, working the parent body as much as former pupils.

Games, options, the arts: A parent told us: 'Emanuel does punch above its weight in sports for the size of the school. That is down to the encouragement the children get from the games staff.' Sport is a major feature of the school, with rugby followed by rowing the most popular. One parent said: 'If you don't like rugby you can have a problem'. Teams are kitted out in striking navy and gold stripes.

Facilities are extensive: apart from 12 acres of on-site games fields there is also access via a private gate to facilities on Wandsworth Common plus 14 further acres near Raynes Park. The sports hall includes a climbing wall. There is a large pool and a boathouse at Barnes for 75 boats. Rowing is historically the most successful sport at Emanuel with over 50 international and Olympic oarsmen in the record books. This year success for the girls: senior girls won gold at the National Schools Regatta whilst a junior girls coxed four won Wallingford Regatta and Bedford Regatta. And a recent year 13 boy represented GB and secured a silver medal at the world junior championships.

The school has also been awarded top 100 cricket schools status by The Cricketer Magazine. The 1st XI was unbeaten during 2015 in all of their competitive fixtures. Meanwhile at rugby the 1st XV have won six out of their 10 fixtures. Plenty of netball and hockey stars too: two girls were selected for London Youth Games hockey team and 10 selected for the event's netball team. Three girls have been selected at county level. Some would like to see more done outside of these core sports: there are naturally fewer matches and opportunities outside of the major sports.

Some 300 individual instrumental lessons a week, of all grades with many reaching grade 8. Recently, two pupils gained places to attend the junior Guildhall School for Music and junior Royal Academy of Music. It is common for students to gain choral scholarships to Oxbridge colleges as well as win places at music colleges. A good rehearsal and concert space.

Drama is a highlight with many OEs entering careers within the field of drama, film and television. Recently one boy starred in Dickensian. Most recently, the senior play was Brief Encounter; the junior play was The Lion, the Witch and the Wardrobe and the year 7s bonded over The Witches. A parent: 'I look forward to every concert or school production as it saves me a trip to the West End.' An enlarged theatre of around 100 seats was opened by Ralph Fiennes and Mike Leigh.

Passports at the ready – too many international trips, sports tours, departmental exchanges and adventures to mention covering what seems like the entire of Europe and further afield to India and the US. Over 40 clubs and societies: choir, computer club, drama club, technical drama club and Eton fives are all after school. Many others take place before school and at lunch time including one for Dr Who fans.

Background and atmosphere: A school with a history – founded in Westminster in 1594 by Lady Dacre. The school's magazine, Portcullis, has just reached its 300th edition. Unusually, it was co-educational from the start with just 10 boys and 10 girls. The boys then moved to Wandsworth in 1883 to the current building, originally a Crimean war orphanage. The school became a voluntary aided grammar school in 1944 until it resumed its independent status in the 1970s. In 1995 it became co-educational once more. The school is growing and will continue to do so up until about 960 pupils. There is a courtyard in the middle of the main building dedicated to three Queen Elizabeths. The first on the throne at the foundation; the second who planted the central tree, Queen Elizabeth, The Queen Mother; the third her daughter who made a royal visit in 1994.

A smart new bridge provides access from Spencer Park, showcasing the school at its best angle – called the Memorial Bridge in memory of the Clapham Rail crash in 1988. The railway line provides only a gentle rumble of trains going past. Despite this, the school has a fairly unique feel as a green oasis – the buildings' outlook onto the sports fields at the rear, particularly the outdoor café under the cricket nets, is very appealing on a sunny day. The library, at the heart of the old building, is remodelled to blend modernity with aspects of the school's heritage, including an archive area and 'family photo wall' of OEs. Large and well-stocked, with a spiral staircase and mezzanine, it lends out up to 500 books a week; teen fiction such as The Fault in Our Stars leads the way. This is a Christian school with Christian values and the chapel with stained glass windows remains on the first floor. Sixth formers have their own modern block with plenty of corners to hang out and a café akin to Starbucks.

The main building is impressive, but far more institutional and shabby inside than we expect – it even smells rather like a hospital. So, the news of development projects in progress – a £10m humanities building, which is almost complete and will include a film studio and a separate up-coming 'temple to maths' to include a maths café, grand foyer and lecture theatre – suggest the fabric of the school will start to match the head's ambition.

Parents report: 'Whenever you visit the school there is always a very happy atmosphere among the students and great camaraderie'; 'there has been an increase in the number of highly academic children at the school but I still feel that the school is not a pressure cooker'. Another: 'There is a definite atmosphere of letting everybody have a go at everything without judgement – it doesn't matter how good or bad you are'. 'It's fun and pretty cool,' added a student.

Pastoral care, well-being and discipline: A system of form tutors who see pupils every day combined with a house system and easy access to the head of year ensures that any problems that arise should be spotted and dealt with quickly. We hear they are quick to respond. Parents agree the school is supportive and caring. There are two chaplains, and a fully trained counsellor.

A detailed anti-bullying policy is in place, updated to include cyber-bullying, giving pupils, staff and parents clear guidelines as to what to do and a fairly long list of sanctions if pupils are not behaving with courtesy and co-operation. Every pupil carries a conduct card. Chocolate as a reward has been dropped for the sake of blood sugar levels. We hear one report of the school's rigorous discipline procedures seeming quite severe to newcomers. But there are also 'lots of parental talks to help support children.' Useful in a co-ed school, we're told by a parent: 'Their sex ed offering is similarly "full on", which I fully support'.

Pupils and parents: Coming from all over London and occasionally beyond as the school is within seven minutes' walk of the transport hub of Clapham Junction. Many parents work in the media or creative industries. The Fiennes family is connected with the school. The majority of pupils are white European in ethnicity, and reflecting the local area 26 pupils have French as their first language. Ten per cent are from overseas. Parents tell of us of making friends here, something that happens less at senior school. There is even a choir for mums and dads and socialising in the pub in Barnes whilst watching the rowing. They describe each other as 'committed and unpretentious'; 'friendly, mostly working parents'; 'down to earth and genuine.'

Entrance: Interested parties should note that registrations are capped so that all pupils registered have a one-to-one interview as well as the entrance exam. At 10+ capped at 180, at 11+ 600, at 13+ 150 and 16+ 120. One of the few London senior schools offering the opportunity to avoid all of the hoopla and stress of 11+ with a 10+ entry point, it is apparently still as competitive to enter, as at 10+ there are only 40 in a year group rising to 130 in year 7.

At 10+ and 11+ there are papers in English, maths and verbal reasoning. At 13+ English, maths, science and a language. At 16+ an English essay and three subjects of the applicant's choice (in subjects they intend to study for A level) and a reasoning test. Pupils with SEN will be considered for extra time if appropriate.

Some 70 per cent enter from state primaries at Y6 and Y7, higher than we often see, but it is a wide community. Students come in from over 200 feeder schools such as Belleville, Fulham Prep, Honeywell, Hornsby House, Hurlingham, Maple Walk, Orchard House, Our Lady of Victories, Thomas' Clapham and Wimbledon Park. Biannual open days plus several week morning tours per term.

Exit: In 2016, 15 per cent left after GCSEs, tiny numbers (one per cent) at end of year 12. Current popular university destinations are Exeter, Durham, Sussex and Essex plus Oxbridge (five places in 2016), with long tail of others heading off around the UK to pursue everything from PPE to product design.

Money matters: A generous number of scholarships and bursaries and unusually lunch is included in the standard fees. One in five have a scholarship. Fifteen children currently received 100 per cent assisted places, which the head hopes to roll out to 20.

Remarks: One to keep a decided eye on as it makes its upwards progress, and register early. Something of a boarding school atmosphere – open seven days a week in a day school format.

Falkner House

19 Brechin Place, London SW7 4QB

Pupils: 200 (10 boys in nursery) • Ages: 3–11

Fees: £8,910 – £17,610 pa

Tel: 020 7373 4501
Email: office@falknerhouse.co.uk
Website: www.falknerhouse.co.uk

Headteacher: Since 1999, Mrs Anita Griggs BA PGCE (60s). Educated at Queen's College, Harley Street, then studied history and economics at York University. Spent her early career at the Bank of England, before heading the economics department at St Paul's Girls' School.

Her mother, Flavia Nunes, was Falkner House's founding head and her father ran a successful boys' prep so she has the central London education system embedded in her DNA. Today she unites the best of British tradition with the decisively innovative. 'As soon as someone has a good idea, I would like it to happen,' she says. 'I'm an impatient person.'

Very much a hands-on head, she's at the gates every morning, constantly available to parents (her home number is on the school's website), pupils ('I don't teach, but I know the children from the back of their heads') and teachers. Forthright, purposeful and positive ('never think you can't do something'), she's also bracingly down to earth. 'While I want girls to be happy and successful at 11, I also want them to be happy and successful at 31 and 41.'

She has no immediate intention of passing the baton to one of her four adult daughters (two of whom work in the school). 'There are other things I could do with my life. I do it because I love it.' Parents definitely appreciate this. 'She's immensely charming,' said one, 'and really fights for the girls.' 'She's given my children the most wonderful education,' said another.

Married to a city lawyer, she lives across the road from the school and in her off-duty hours is an 'obsessive reader' and enthusiastic traveller.

Entrance: Register as soon as possible after birth. Some enter at nursery (including boys), but a nursery spot does not guarantee passage to the main school. In the January before entry, about 130 girls compete for 22 reception places in an assessment that looks for 'focus, working memory and enthusiasm,' as well as more elusive qualities such as 'grit' and good manners.

'A child cannot be prepared and we don't assess whether or not they can read,' says the head. Many will inevitably be disappointed, but parents are let down as gently as possible. 'No selection system is perfect. We don't get false positives, but we sometimes get false negatives.' Occasional places (an average of one a year) are again filled by assessment. 'I'd rather leave a space than have the wrong fit,' adds the head.

Exit: The 'next step' is considered thoughtfully, with parents invited in for a planning meeting in year 5. 'We take endless care to ensure girls not only get into the best schools but the schools that are best for them.' The majority, now as always, to London's academic girls' schools (Francis Holland SW1, Queen's Gate, St Paul's, Godolphin & Latymer, Putney High, City) but co-ed Latymer Upper is also attracting increasing attention. Reasonable numbers to board, with Wycombe Abbey, Cheltenham Ladies and St Mary's Ascot featuring strongly. Girls frequently leave garnered with scholarships, academic, music and sporting.

Remarks: Flavia Nunes set up Falkner House in 1954 with the intention of providing girls with the same standard of academic excellence enjoyed by their brothers – by no means a given in those days – and the school continues to provide a broad and challenging education taught by a dedicated, energetic and innovative staff. 'They're the real stars,' says the head.

Reading is central to the offering. All younger girls are expected to read nightly at home and a love of words and books is encouraged by regular attendance at two libraries, well-considered reading lists, a weekly library lesson from year 3 and freedom to bring in Kindles from year 4. Poetry is learned by heart and recited in class and competitions; recently launched own poetry anthology of verses 'every Falkner House child should know'. Girls become articulate and confident, both on the page and in conversation.

Beyond the three Rs, a rainbow of opportunity. French throughout (with a fortnightly French assembly), classics from year 3, Latin from year 5. Debating now part of the curriculum. The arts, too, taken seriously. Music strong and varied with plenty in the way of performance (wind band, string group, choir, chamber music ensemble). Art room buzzing and history of art taught from reception, with regular outings to museums and galleries. Dance and drama included in the core curriculum, year 4 produced a class film rather than a class play, and a popular after-school ballet club allows those who wish to take external exams.

Technology here is not just for display on the timetable, but blazing a trail – a hardworking teacher has reinvented the year 5 and 6 curriculum to be delivered on iPads. Recently Apple named Falkner House one of six groundbreaking schools worldwide for its innovative approach.

Homework and exams introduced early (the former in reception, the latter twice yearly from year 3). 'It's important for girls to learn to take both the test and the results in their stride; to learn their best is good enough,' says the head.

This is a selective school and few have serious special educational needs. Mild difficulties, however, are addressed successfully by experienced staff and high fliers given regular extension work.

Despite a handkerchief playground, sport played competitively to a high level. Coaches ferry girls to Battersea, Kensington Gardens, Latchmere Leisure Centre and Chelsea and from year 3 the school fields A, B, and often C squads in netball, athletics, swimming, rounders and cross-country. 'It's a culture of "play the game within the spirit of the game",' says the head. 'We do not kill to win.' Win they do, however, producing recent champions at the London Schools Swimming Association and the British Schools Team Fencing Championship. Numerous extracurricular activities include clubs, trips (abroad and to the head's house in West Sussex) and treats (on Founder's Day an English National Ballet soloist came in to teach choreography).

Fresh food cooked daily – and described as 'amazing' by our guides, with staff monitoring manners and a balanced diet. 'We've taken out all mention of healthy eating,' says the head. 'All children here eat healthy food, so why create more anxiety?'

The school is still located in the two spacious, multi-storeyed Victorian houses where it was founded and retains the echo of a post-war family home, with carpeted corridors and the head's office elegantly kitted out with antiques. Tradition, too, maintained with daily 'prayers' (Christian hymns and the Lord's Prayer) held in the delightful, parqueted assembly hall. All faiths welcome. Remembrance Day, carol service and the Queen's Jubilee accorded due dignity. 'The girls should understand the culture. That's not deprivation; it's enrichment.'

Other traditional strands include both a house and prefect system. Head girl, deputy and prefects appointed for half term stints, so most get a go, while other routes to glory include sports person or artist of the week, eco monitor and badge girl (responsible for helping the teacher).

Head's mission is to endow pupils with self confidence, independence of mind, kindness and good manners, and girls clearly enjoy the process. 'It's fun,' said one. Though the inevitable friendship groups form, all seem to get on. 'No-one is not friends,' said another. Top year girls are paired with those coming into reception, and this union of 'grandes' and 'petites' means new arrivals are never left stranded. 'We play with them and introduce our petite to our friends' petites.' Precocity definitely discouraged (no nail varnish, no jewellery and only 'sensible' shoes).

Parents kept at well-informed arms' length. 'I'd prefer them not to come in and hang up the children's coats – children come to school to learn independence,' says the head, who is also firmly anti-PTA. 'I'm very proud of that. I don't want some alpha mummy in charge. I'd prefer her to come in and give me her bright ideas.'

The home-school link, however, is strong, with parental involvement expected with homework and music practice. Parents regularly invited to attend events, from ballet recitals to Father's Day breakfasts. The school website, updated weekly, keeps all in the loop, while the flexible early birds and late birds system allows drop off and pick up from early morning till late afternoon. 'If you're stuck in traffic you can just telephone,' said one parent. 'It's fantastic for working mothers.'

Families mainly within walking distance, then spreading out to Hammersmith, Chiswick, Fulham and Battersea. Predominantly British, highly qualified, working in financial services, but also numerous global citizens. Unsurprisingly, some can be a tad competitive, something the head keeps firmly in check. 'If someone rings up to demand why their daughter's not in the netball team, you just have to say, "I'm sorry you're cross, but let's try and be reasonable. There are other people better at netball".'

Given the location, families tend to be affluent. The website includes requests for housekeepers and year 6 parents are politely asked to plan family holidays 'to avoid jet lag'. No formal bursaries or scholarships, but the school has always helped out existing pupils in financial difficulties.

Opening a boys' pre-prep for 4-8 year olds in Earls Court in 2017, plus a co-ed nursery.

F

Fern Hill Primary School

Richmond Road, Kingston, Surrey KT2 5PE

Pupils: 670 • Ages: 3–11

Tel: 020 8247 0300
Email: office@fernhill.rbksch.org
Website: www.fernhill.kingston.sch.uk

Headteacher: Since 2015, Adam Scott, previously deputy head, who has been at the school for over 15 years.

Entrance: Very popular, very oversubscribed, move very close. Usual local authority admissions criteria apply, which essentially means siblings and distance. Obviously catchment varies, but always tight – anecdotally an 800m radius most recently. Due to population bulge, Kingston has had a problem with reception place numbers and the school is expanding. Worth staying on the waiting list as there is a trickle of mobility in the area and odd spaces do come up.

Exit: Be aware that although packed with good primaries, North Kingston is short of secondary school places – though the new Kingston Academy should ease matters, and some leavers are moving on there. Many pupils progress to Grey Court in Ham, which is actually in the neighbouring borough of Richmond. Others feed elsewhere into the Kingston and Richmond secondary systems. Handfuls to the much sought after places at very nearby selective Tiffin Grammar schools (NB almost everyone in North Kingston uses private tutoring to try and get to these schools) Some plunge into the private pool (some always planned to), including Kingston Grammar (co-ed), Hampton (boys) and Surbiton High (girls).

Remarks: A top-notch school – regularly vies with neighbouring Latchmere for unofficial 'best in borough' award. Sets high standards, has high expectations and unsurprisingly attracts high numbers of the white middle classes who abound in this area. A real community school – just be aware that the community is North Kingston, swarming with young professionals hell-bent on achieving a first class state education for their brood. After the white middle classes, largest ethnic group is Asian. School says not all is leafy and lovely in Kingston and there is some social housing around, but this accounts for a minority of the cohort.

Ofsted rates Fern Hill as 'outstanding and providing an excellent all-round education', praising pupils' achievements both academically and in terms of their personal development.

Academic standards are good – generally around half the year group achieves at least level 5 in maths and science Sats. School acknowledges that many of its pupils enter the school with above average skills but, even so, these results are sparkling and seemingly achieved without too much pressure placed on the children – 'The parents are probably pushier than the school', commented one mother.

F

There's a distinct private school feel to the place – and not just because the children are beautifully turned out in smart uniform. Everything is orderly and fairly calm, but not sterile, children all appear engaged and on-task, overall a quite traditional feel to things. Children sit in groups around tables, but for year 6 move to rows to support the sense that year 6 is a special year and to ready them for their more formal secondary schools. Lots of praise for teaching staff – stable and nice mix of youth and experience, few men (but including deputy head with high parental approval rating). When staff do leave it is rarely to work at another local school. Teaching assistants everywhere (more assistants than teachers) some class-based, others working with individual children, more senior TAs leading activities such as PSHE, ICT etc.

School packs it all in via a tight timetable and has made real efforts to introduce more creative ways of learning, for example using drama to help pupils empathise with historical characters. Lots of cross-curriculum and project work helps to free up the day – eg non-fiction literacy as part of history, writing for a purpose. Teachers add breadth to the national curriculum diktats introducing supplementary topics of their choice. 'We are always looking at the curriculum and trying to find links'. 'Obviously some subjects need to be directly taught, but in other areas we can pull things together to make things less prosaic and more interesting for the children'. Homework manageable, about half an hour a week for years 3 and 4, rising to half an hour a day by year 6. School adamant that young children need a life and to have time to do other things outside school. 'Homework is not a central part of the school'. Tutoring for entrance to the Tiffin schools is huge in this area and school is reasonably relaxed about it but admits to some concern for any child who is hauled around to take lots of different entry exams.

Specialist French teacher; all pupils learn from nursery with every class having a short French lesson each week, with some language and vocabulary incorporated into the children's learning during the rest of the week. Several other teachers are confident French speakers and the long term aim is for all teachers to be able to teach French to their own classes. Also a specialist music teacher now comes in two days a week which, together with links to Kingston Music (and Arts) Service, has seen some improvements in this area – previously a little weak for this school. There is now a school choir and orchestra in which a few parents play too. Around 45 pupils learn an instrument and each year 3 has an opportunity to learn strings.

Gold award for art, kite mark for PE – school takes this side of the curriculum just as seriously as the academic work.

The school has a special needs/inclusion coordinator with a team of teaching assistants and a dedicated resource, the Rainbow room. Some 60 odd pupils are on the SEN register, six with statements. These children are taught with their class as much as possible, with one-to-one or small group sessions used to support this as necessary. EAL support is available but, although some 180 pupils have English as a second language, their English is usually good. Flexible ability grouping within each class, and there is plenty of room to take small groups out for focused teaching as necessary. School has had a good reputation for picking up any problems or learning difficulties early – some parental concern over whether staff will be able to maintain this focus as school expands.

School is very keen on good manners, politeness and respect. Overall pupil behaviour and attitude is great – for the most part these children are on-side and eager to learn. They abide by 'golden rules', the breaking of which results in the loss of 'golden minutes' from playtimes. (But other times they gain – we passed children returning from the playground after a five-minute, mid-lesson 'brain break'.) All the children understand the school's focus on the 6Rs – resourcefulness, resilience, reflection, responsibility, reasoning and respect – promoted around the place by Winnie the Pooh and his friends. 'We are generally very lucky that our children are well-behaved. But there are some little pickles that we need to manage, as well as looking out for the quiet ones so that they don't disappear'.

School environment enjoys all the advantages that come with having been purpose-built (co-incidentally in response to a shortfall in school places back in 1994) including wide doors and corridors and specialist toilet facilities for disabled children. Use of space is very good throughout. Classrooms are all a reasonable size, lots of outdoor activities for the tinies and separate playgrounds for nursery, infants and juniors (though again playground space at a premium as school size increases). Full-time social skills assistant on hand to encourage play and mediate where necessary. External facilities also include an environmental area and inner courtyard with amphitheatre feature.

New buildings include a sports hall, small hall and music room on the back of the school, together with alterations to the existing hall to make seven new classrooms, an art room, new special needs room and additional multi-purpose small group rooms. The field at the back of the school landscaped to include an all-weather surface, new football pitch and other playtime activities. Part of the school has become two-storey.

Great displays are all around; a lot goes on here and it is all written up, drawn, photographed, modelled, reviewed or rewarded in pen, pencil, paint, clay, crayon – you name it and it's probably up on a wall somewhere. It's not an especially tidy place, but nor is it sloppy – it's just a reflection of a busy school life.

Strong and competitive house system, busy school council with some powers and facilities all help promote positive peer groups. (Recent pupil decision was to swap the older girls' and boys' loos as it was felt that the boys would benefit from having an open window in their facilities. Pupil power in action.) Lots of after-school clubs, till 4.30pm. No other on site before or after-school care facilities, but the school does have a close association with the nearby YMCA Hawker Centre which provides breakfast and teatime clubs and will take and collect the children to and from school.

Parents feel involved, lots help and home/school communication is good. Colonised by the middle classes who are willing (and encouraged) to get fully involved in school life, the PTA is, as you would imagine, very active and well-supported. 'It's a very special place,' said a parent, 'and we all want to do our bit'. It's a secure, happy place with lots going on. Plenty of trips and visitors – everything from theatre groups to fire engines and animals. 'There's nothing boring,' said one dream pupil. 'We're always doing something fun'.

To our question, 'Any notable former pupils?' school answers positively, 'Not yet' – but you come away feeling that there certainly will be in 20 years' time. You would be delighted to have this state offering on your doorstep – which is indeed where it will need to be for your child to attend.

Fine Arts College Hampstead

   76

Centre Studios, 41-43 Englands Lane, London NW3 4YD

Pupils: 185 • Ages: 14–19 • Sixth form: 160

Fees: £19,500 pa

Tel: 020 7586 0312
Email: mail@hampsteadfinearts.com
Website: www.hampsteadfinearts.com

Principal: Candida Cave (50s) set up the college in 1978 with Nicholas Cochrane – who has recently retired as co-principal. They studied at the Ruskin School of Drawing and Fine Art, Oxford, started teaching at a tutorial college and found 'we were quite good at inspiring people'. The decision to set up a college of their own was something that just 'came about', but clearly had a market, and has grown steadily ever since. She remains a practising painter and playwright, while teaching art history. Parents and pupils are great fans of the warm and relaxed approach. 'Candida Cave is what all parents dream of in a teacher, but think they'll never meet,' said one. 'She's imaginative and nurturing, but not a pushover. My daughter just fell in love with her.'

Academic matters: A very broad, almost exclusively, arts-based curriculum (no science in the sixth form, though a few mathematicians). The visual arts remain, as one might expect, exceptionally popular. Photography is the number one subject choice (80 students this year) but also large numbers for fine art and art history, English literature, textiles, graphic design, film studies and media studies. The fine arts approach provides a strong traditional grounding (from classical busts and life models), which leaves many students with strong enough technical skills to bypass foundation courses. (The college also runs a two-term post A level portfolio course, to ensure preparation for art degrees and art college is tip-top). An extensive curriculum (29 subjects in all) of liberal arts, social sciences, modern languages (French, Spanish and Italian), and classical studies (Latin, Greek, ancient history and classical civilisation), can be taken in virtually any combination. Strong results overall at A level (21 per cent A*/A and 61 per cent A*/B in 2016), with English and fine art particularly stellar. Exceptionally high 'valued added' between GCSE and A level (fourth highest in the country) produced by caring teaching in small groups (classes never exceed nine).

'My daughter had failed spectacularly at two other fee-paying schools,' said one appreciative mother of a daughter now at a Russell Group university. 'She thought she was a dunce until they took her under their wing. They produced an incredible turn around and she went from Cs to As.'

Also offers GCSEs, with two year groups of about 20 in all. 'We find there's a real need in year 10,' says Candida Cave, 'particularly when schools start saying, you should drop this or that.' GCSE subjects include biology and some physics but probably not the place for nascent medics. In 2016, 30 per cent A*/A grades. Staff long-serving and enthusiastic (including three ex-students and Candida Cave's daughter), with a fair proportion who also have alternative lives as professional artists, film makers, etc. Teaching style relaxed but enthusiastic; student style, co-operative competition. 'It's very much teaching in discussion, they want to impress each other in a nice way,' says Candida Cave. Good information given to parents and pupils about progress, with fortnightly reports and two parents' evenings. Rated outstanding by Ofsted in latest report.

Games, options, the arts: Plenty of opportunity to display talent, with an annual art exhibition, music and drama recital, and short films shown at the local Everyman Cinema. (One girl was recently runner-up for the Young Film Critic Award at Bafta). Loads of outside speakers and cultural outings, with annual study trips to Florence, Paris and Venice. Not at all a hierarchical place, and students organise their own entertainment – 'a certain number tend to take the lead each year' – including charitable fundraising (for Breast Cancer awareness, the Red Cross, a local hospice) and other social events. Certainly not the ideal environment for the sporty (and few here care) but GCSE students have fencing lessons plus PE at a local sports centre and the college's long-standing football team plays against other sixth-form colleges. Popular table tennis, too, on site.

Background and atmosphere: Started in 1978 in the YMCA in Tottenham Court Road, teaching art and art history. 'We started because there wasn't anyone else specialising in the arts,' says Candida Cave. Moved to Belsize Park in 1982, started offering GCSEs in 1994, and then, in 2002, added a converted Victorian dairy, which now forms the hub of the school, providing rambling lateral space around a cobbled courtyard. A good mix of classrooms (some more spacious than others) and excellent studio space, for art, drama, photography (with its own darkroom for traditional-style printing) and media studies. The atmosphere is intentionally informal and teachers are called by their first names. 'The college was very much founded as a bridge between school and university. Many students come here because they're looking for something more flexible.' Students congregate in the common room, where free coffee is on offer, but no food supplied on site. Some bring sandwiches, the majority visit the multitude of local eateries. Dress code vaguely artistic and bohemian (the odd fur gilet and extreme make up, the majority in UGGs and tracksuits), but kept well within limits. 'If it offends, we tell them to dress properly. It's just common sense.'

Bought by Dukes Education in 2015.

Pastoral care, well-being and discipline: 'What we liked about the college', said one parent, 'is the industrious informality. They take the job seriously, but don't wear it too formally.' Pupils' work and well-being is immaculately monitored. Everyone has a personal tutor, whom they see for an hour and a half each week. The tutor goes through reports, helps with essay-writing and advises on university applications. All GCSE pupils sign in at 9am and again at 1.30pm. If pupils are not in class an email is sent to parents within half an hour. 'Pupils turn up because they want to,' said one parent. 'But, equally, they know that if they can't be bothered to turn up, the attitude will be, don't bother to come back.' Most have no problems with this. 'I've never been to a school before where all the other pupils want to learn,' said one boy. Students sign a contract of behaviour, so know exactly what is expected, and misbehaviour, social or academic, is followed by an oral warning, a written warning, and then a parental meeting. 'We've not excluded anyone for eight to nine years, and not even suspended anyone for a long time,' says Candida Cave. 'We're run here on mutual respect and they do seem to rise to that.' Most see the college as a place where they can be confident concerns will be dealt with quickly and in confidence. Definitely a haven for those for whom more boisterous or insensitive environments have just not worked. 'The college made my daughter believe in herself. I feel I owe them,' said one parent.

Pupils and parents: A mix of mostly local professional/artistic families, who tend to be profoundly relieved that their children have found such a civilised and creative niche. Some of those who come to do GCSEs have previously been educated abroad. Others have had enough of boarding school, or failed to fit into more conventional schools. Alumni include Orlando Bloom and Helena Bonham-Carter.

Entrance: All applicants are interviewed with their parents and the college makes offers based on two criteria: candidates 'really want to be here' and 'they intend to go on to higher education'. Minimum five GCSEs with C or above for A levels, but this liberal benchmark is generally well exceeded, not a few arriving garlanded with a multitude of A*s. Most from local independents and leading boarding schools, a few from the state sector and schools further afield.

F

Exit: Around 30 per cent leave after GCSEs. For the rest, a generous sprinkling into every permutation of arts and media – from film studies and fine art to fashion retailing and creative writing – but also to history, psychology and sociology. Sussex, Falmouth, Nottingham Trent and Leeds currently popular.

Money matters: One scholarship of 100 per cent (based on academic merit, a statement of why they deserve a scholarship, and an interview). Two of 25 per cent may be given for outstanding exam performance at GCSE ('We wanted to show we appreciated their intelligence.') A limited number of bursaries awarded to students who have previously been educated in the state system who would not otherwise be able to afford private education.

Remarks: A low-key, calm and friendly place, with strong teaching and results, particularly in the arts. Ideal for the 'arty, urban misfit' who has wilted in a more conventional environment.

Finton House School

171 Trinity Road, London SW17 7HL

Pupils: 320 • Ages: 4–11

Fees: £13,890 – £14,550 pa

Tel: 020 8682 0921
Email: admissions@fintonhouse.org.uk
Website: www.fintonhouse.org.uk

Head: Since September 2016, Ben Freeman BEd (design technology) PG Dip (educational leadership), previously head of Windermere Prep. Clearly a teacher at heart, he was born and brought up on the Wirral, educated at Rossall School and then the University of West of England, Bristol. A keen sportsman with something of the Bear Grylls about him, he enjoys outdoor activities including camping, walking and sailing and has previously competed in the London and New York marathons. Teaches DT and sport. He lives with his partner, Sarah, an outdoor instructor, and her three children,

Entrance: If you want the certainty of a place, get on the phone as soon as your child is born. Apart from siblings, who have priority, it is very much first come, first served. Two entrance lists – one opened in September, one in March, to give spring/summer born children a chance. Occasional vacancies higher up when the prospective pupil will be invited to spend a day at the school to see if he/she will fit. At least three places each year for special needs children, who will be assessed to verify that the school can meet their requirements; and the head will meet the parents. Places then offered to those whose needs can be met, on a first come, first served basis. Some state funding for statemented children. One means-tested place per year available via Sally Walker Bursary, funded by relations of the much loved ex-headmistress, as well as past and present parents.

Exit: Mostly after 11+, to a wide range of schools, mostly London day schools but a few to boarding. Current choices include Woldingham, Whitgift and JAGS followed by Trinity, Alleyn's and Wimbledon High. A handful, mainly boys, move on at 8. Several scholarships and exhibitions each year.

Remarks: Happy, informal, inclusive, buzzes with enthusiasm. A strong community-based school, very supportive and particularly good for those families with challenged children. Every parent we talked to was full of praise, several saying that their shy, unconfident children had blossomed beyond belief. A local school which, we were told, is reflected in the friendly feel of the playground at the beginning and the end of the day: 'It is full of relaxed, chatty parents, and we go on chatting even after the children have all gone into school.' Emphasis on inclusion, individuality and results without pressure make this a very special school.

The teaching staff are a great strength. Loyal and imaginative, some have been at the school since it started, in the mid-80s, and some have been away, had children and come back. Others are ex-pupils returning to relive happy memories. The rest just love the school. 'The ethos is wonderful.' 'I intend to teach here as long as I possibly can.' With half of the full-time staff over 40 and a third of them having been at the school for over 10 years, experience and continuity prevail. One parent talked about 'the same old projects, there's not enough change'. Sometimes the proven old is better than the new. Certainly these teachers seem to know and understand their pupils. From one parent of a special needs child: 'I can't describe how amazing they are; the care and support they give is unrivalled'. Another said, 'They quickly picked up on my child's shyness with adults; she is now much more confident'.

The teaching standard is high and the curriculum broad. We've been told that there's something special about the way Finton teachers operate, through relaxed, informal, but focused, learning. It does seem to work: we didn't see an unhappy child anywhere. Less homework than at most other schools yet all 11 year olds seem to get into their first choice of senior school. The children said: 'Everyone's kind and if you get something wrong, no-one laughs', 'Teachers are your friends', 'No matter who you are you are never treated differently'.

Four articulate, happy, enthusiastic year 6 pupils took us proudly round their school, across the playground to the reception block where three mixed classes experience 'fun learning'. 'We love reading stories to them'. There certainly seemed to be a lot going on. They pointed out the lift, 'which is only used sometimes', and embarked upon a straightforward and informed discussion about how some of their friends needed extra help. Then back across to the classrooms, in the main building. Two staircases, well decorated with projects and pictures, led to smallish classrooms, containing happy-looking children sitting round tables (in year 1) and at desks (in years 2-6). Interactive whiteboards, used imaginatively, everywhere. We saw everything: the well-stocked library which they are all taught to use properly in weekly lessons, the DT room full of fascinating projects, the lovely, light art room, the rather warm ICT room, the science room; it would appear they have all they need and creations abound. Eager children pointed out their favourites. Back on the ground floor, lunch is prepared in their on-site kitchen – suitable choices for all and staff on hand to make sure everyone eats a balanced meal. 'There's always something I like,' said one of our guides and the others nodded in agreement.

'This is our fantastic music block,' one of them announced as we crossed the playground again. A third of pupils in years 3-6 learn an instrument (brass, woodwind, piano). Lessons are timetabled on a rotational basis during the school day and there are special sessions for choirs and music groups. Individual practice is done at home. Most children take part in a number of concerts, in school and externally. Art and drama also hit a high note. Not long ago, nine pupils had their pictures selected for the Royal College of Art's Young Artist competition and their work was put on public display. Small plays are put on in the school hall, larger productions down the road in the nearby church hall, or at a local theatre. We were lucky enough to see a year 1 play, specially written with lots of songs. What fun they all had, and how well they performed. New specialist teaching rooms for music, DT and science in an innovative basement unit under the playground, plus new learning support building, enlarged classrooms and new playground.

Lots of sport, both compulsory and in after-school clubs. Matches played against all the local schools – appear to win pretty often, which says a lot for a small school. Currently the local swimming champions. A wide range of after-school clubs, sporting and creative, in which children are encouraged to take part. Wide choice which varies from term to term. 'We even have an early morning running club. The reward is hot chocolate back at school!'

Not an SEN school, but some places reserved for a wide range of educationally-challenged children: Finton House is committed to making sure that pupils of all abilities have their individual needs addressed. All children monitored from the start to see if extra help needed. Deputy head also head of special needs; her team includes a SENCo, a learning support co-ordinator, a speech and language therapist, an occupational therapist and seven learning support teachers. So there is plenty of help on hand for one-to-one support when necessary. Many opportunities for children to be taught individually or in small groups as 20 teaching assistants also on hand. 'The key is flexibility and the full classroom integration of all children.' Special one-to-one sessions charged extra but otherwise all is included.

Forest School

College Place, Snaresbrook, London E17 3PY

Pupils: 1,370 • Ages: 4–18 • Sixth form: 279 • C of E

Fees: £11,607 – £16,980 pa

Tel: 020 8520 1744
Email: info@forest.org.uk
Website: www.forest.org.uk

Warden: Since January 2017, Marcus Cliff Hodges, previously deputy warden and head of boys' school since 2005. Degrees in English literature and educational management from Cardiff University and London University respectively. Has also taught at Bedford School and Gstaad International School and been assistant head at Latymer Upper.

Head of prep school: Since 2012, Mr Andrew Noakes MA education, Open University (30s). Previously head of Northampton Junior School. Studied at Reed's, Surrey, then De Montfort, where he read European studies and French. He trained at St George's College; has also been director of studies at Bedford Modern Junior School. Described as 'calm and unflappable', he is married to a teacher and has two daughters.

Academic matters: In the pre-prep (4 to 7), children are taught in co-ed classes and follow the EYFS; in the prep they begin to experience single-sex teaching preparation for their later move to the boys' and girls' senior schools. Class sizes 16 in the pre-prep and 22 in the prep school. Teaching based on national curriculum with specialists brought in for art, PE, drama, foreign languages and, in particular, music. Expect to see lively but small groups of pupils actively involved in learning, lots of writing and artwork displays in and outside of the classrooms, and tiny, well-behaved pupils following behind their teacher in duckling-like fashion from one part of the school to another.

'Both of my daughters are scholars,' said one very pleased parent. Single-sex teaching in this co-educational environment 'creates a study environment that boys and girls feel comfortable with and which enables them to achieve their best', says school. Teachers are committed; about a third of them have been here more than 10 years and all of them are specialists in their subjects; also large number part-time eg music, drama and dance specialists. Most pupils are of above average ability. They do well across the board, notably in English, history, geography, maths and the sciences. From year 8, some setting occurs for maths, English, MFLs and science. There is a free choice from French, German and Spanish. Latin is taught to all pupils during the first two years, then it becomes a GCSE option along with ancient Greek.

In 2016, 68 per cent A*/A at GCSE and 52 per cent at A level. Extended projects, which allow GCSE and A level students to flex their academic muscles beyond the norm, are popular. With topics and titles such as 'A legal definition of torture' and 'Love and the Adversary' (a treatise on the representation of Satan in English literature), pupils demonstrate their capacity for critical thought.

Courses in both the boys' and girls' schools run broadly in line with the national curriculum. This leads some parents to make the same complaint heard of state schools, that lessons can have 'too much focus on teaching for success in the sometimes dull GCSE syllabus rather than to wider lateral thought.. but I think this is what happens everywhere'. Hence, by and large, parents also prize the school for its 'good academic expectations but not [being] too pushy'. As one parent echoed, 'I don't consider that [my daughters] are always adequately stretched, but the humanities and arts subjects appear to be particularly well taught', adding that they had turned down places at more academic schools in favour of Forest's 'more balanced experience'.

The number of academic challenges, competitions, tournaments and Olympiads these pupils enter is dizzying: maths challenges, chemistry masterminds, physics Olympiads, and even the informatics Olympiad – where pupils have competed in Thailand against the best young computer scientists in the world. Trips to eg the battlefields, Munich (history), Devon (geography), China, Russia, Japan and the USA.

Majority of pupils stay on at sixth form where courses include classical civilisation, government and politics (with visits to key places in London, Washington DC and New York, and supported by guest speakers such as Iain Duncan Smith, John Bercow, George Galloway and Nigel Farage), philosophy (a popular university choice) and economics. The A level economics department has links with the City of London, the Economics Association and Institute of Economic Affairs.

F

Extra support for those who need it; school publishes an excellent guide to independent study to help struggling pupils find their own answers or at the very least to formulate thoughtful and clear questions before asking for help.

Games, options, the arts: You will find them all here: aerobics, basketball, cricket, even fencing. Extensive playing fields, netball and tennis courts, various pitches, a sports centre housing two heated swimming pools, cricket nets and a fitness suite. At sixth form, PE covers sports psychology, history and exercise physiology. Pupils can try out other sports eg karate, cross-country and golf during activities afternoons and house matches. Several record achievements gained at county, regional and national level in netball, rounders, hockey, tennis, badminton and athletics.

F

A large (one of the largest in London) and busy music department with over 700 instrumental and vocal lessons a week. Every pupil has the opportunity to try out an instrument free of charge and pupils are encouraged to take the lead in musical activities, often leading to specialisms. With seven orchestras, 10 bands, 14 choirs and more than 40 specialist teachers, numerous opportunities to perform. School is extensively equipped with practice, recital and technology rooms. On the day of our visit one of the bands was preparing for a lunch time concert in the chapel, the norm at this school that presents more than 80 concerts and other performances a year both in and out of the school. Tours take place in the UK, Spain, Italy, Netherlands and France and the school regularly sends pupils to major conservatoires. Regular choral and organ scholarships to Oxford and Cambridge.

The prep school music department is led by a teacher prized for her ability to spot the 'differences between concert and worship' voices, as well as knowing how hard to push the youngest of performers to discover their best. Each May, the school organises Composition Week, where year 5 pupils are transformed into a team of songwriters, singers and composers to produce, for example, a signature melody inspired by the retelling of the legend of Arachne. The experience is 'demanding but rewarding' for the pupils, and this spirit is one of the prized characteristics of the school: even the youngest of pupils is stretched and pushed to learn.

Drama and art also taken seriously. The purpose-built Deaton Theatre seats 350 and has excellent lighting and sound equipment. Pupils act in large-scale productions and learn design or technical skills. As part of the house drama competition, they can select, cast and direct their own productions. A long tradition of excellence in drama with present and past pupils making successful careers in this area (the West End show Stomp was founded by former pupils) and pupils have been involved in many well-known television and theatre productions, including East Enders and The Bleak Old Shop of Stuff for the BBC, and a West End production of Oliver! Art and design studios are well-resourced and pupils allowed to develop their passion outside classroom learning hours.

Co-curricular opportunities in sport, music, drama, dance and visual arts. CCF linked to the Royal Green Jackets offers field days, annual camps and weekly training. The Duke of Edinburgh Award is popular. Other opportunities include student-led societies, video production, languages, musical theatre, and journalism. Pupils also take part in raising money for charity, in public speaking competitions, and community work such as visiting the elderly and riding for the disabled.

Prep school pupils make respectable contributions to a very lively school diary of events, such as the pre-prep nativity play, a dramatised festival service and an idiom recital day to mark the 400-year anniversary of the King James version of the Bible. They also have house competitions in eg acting, singing and rounders, and charity fundraising events. They compete in the UK chess championships and have hosted a prep-level junior science competition involving over 20 schools. They won a school prize in a wildlife foundation global art competition, with 10 year 4 and 5 pupils selected among entrants from around the world, including Hong Kong, Nigeria and Arabia. Cricket is popular but football is 'something special', and there are several teams and matches played in and outside the borough.

Background and atmosphere: Old and new exist side by side here. It is close to the bustling City of London and yet surrounded by the quietness of ancient forest. The St John the Baptist chapel, where pupils regularly congregate for services and other events, is at the heart of the school and reminiscent of a history that goes back to 1834 when it began with just 22 pupils. Although Anglican in tradition, the outlook is ecumenical to cater to the broad range of backgrounds, faiths and cultures. Pupils enjoy this and say, 'It is good to have the school come together and talk about different faiths.' Alongside the old are new buildings like the Sylvestrian Leisure Centre – built with the aid of a 'buy a brick' fundraiser organised by the parents' association, used by the public at weekends and as a quiet camp for Team GB during the 2012 London Olympics – and the Martin Centre for Innovation, with digital teaching and learning facilities for the whole school.

Tucked away from the main roads, and accessible by what resembles a narrow dirt track lane, the prep school stands as a closely hidden secret in its inner city surroundings. However, once we had cleared the highly secure, gated reception area to enter the school grounds, the bustle of life at the school immediately greeted us. We heard string and brass instruments sounding out from one of the many lunchtime concerts at the chapel, and saw brightly clad prep pupils at play or through their open classroom windows, merrily chanting foreign words in rote-like fashion. Pupils seem to be busy, happy and oblivious. They are taught in buildings alive with a heritage dating back to the school's foundation in 1834. Even with its Georgian buildings, this school has a distinctively bright, spacious and airy feel.

Pastoral care, well-being and discipline: Form and house groups, headed by a housemistress or master, provide a sense of belonging and stability. Because classes are small, community atmosphere is strong; 'pupils are well known individually by the staff,' say parents. Pastoral care gives each child 'the support they need to progress socially, morally and academically'. Housemasters and mistresses stay with a child through his or her time at the school and are there to advise on any aspect of school life. This continues at sixth form. Pupils are allocated a tutor who oversees academic progress, helps with university applications, and advises on careers.

There is heavy emphasis on the code of conduct in the school prospectus: 'all observed behaviour, which indicates a lack of mutual regard, will be fully investigated', 'the school stands firmly against any form of verbal or physical bullying or any behaviour which is intended to cause distress to pupils', and the 'warden may require the permanent exclusion of a pupil if.. it is in the interest of the pupil or of the school community'. Approach is good lines of communication. 'Children are encouraged to talk and are listened to' and to report incidents of bullying to an appropriate person, says school. 'Where bullying is detected, we acknowledge our responsibility to support both the bully and the victim'.

The chapel and chaplaincy are central to learning here. The chapel is where pupils begin and end each term with events such as breakfasts for parents followed by a welcome service. Last year all new pupils brought in a cardboard brick to build a 'prayer wall' showing their aspirations for the term. These included learning to read, wishing to play football for the school, becoming a monitor, making lots of friends and, simply, 'I want to make my teacher and parents proud.'

Parents say, 'Bullying – the school deals with this very well' and 'We hear mixed things about how long it takes the school to home in and deal with these issues; but no direct experience'. Most say their children learn 'in a secure, supportive and encouraging environment'. 'The children know they are lucky but they don't see themselves as special', says school. 'If children are not happy they won't learn; get that right and the grades will come.'

The best thing about being at the school, said a pupil, is the 'diversity. I like the mix, staff are kind, they encourage you to do the best you can do.'

Pupils and parents: A diverse ethnic mix. They come from the surrounding east and north London and Essex areas. Most are the children of professional parents and no-one speaks English as a second language. Past pupils include actor Ian Beale and cricketer Nasser Hussain.

Entrance: Main entries at 4 and 7 via play-based or literacy/numeracy assessments. Most from the prep move to the senior school at 11, joined by a large number from other state and private schools (English and maths tests). Variable numbers admitted at 13+ depending on spaces.

Exit: Prep pupils are automatically offered a place at either the boys' or girls' sections of Forest School and majority – over 90 per cent – take up the offer. Virtually all to university; 10 to Oxbridge in 2016, six to medical schools. Good mix of subjects across the range.

Money matters: Academic and music awards at 11+, academic, music and sports at 13, academic, art, music, drama and sports at 16. Means-tested bursaries only awarded as scholarship add-ons.

Remarks: A happy school with committed staff, and pupils who clearly display a strong sense of independence and enjoyment of school life. While remaining true to its traditional roots, this is a forward-thinking school, humane and open-minded, with both feet on the ground. Its clear grasp of the rich inter-relationship between the curricular, the co-curricular and the pastoral ensures children do well.

Fortismere School

South Wing, Tetherdown, London N10 1NE

Pupils: 1,700 • Ages: 11–19 • Sixth form: 450

Tel: 020 8365 4400
Email: office@fortismere.org.uk
Website: www.fortismere.haringey.sch.uk

Head Teacher: Since 2010, Mrs Helen Glass BA MA PGCE (40s), previously head since 2006 of Central Technology College in Gloucestershire. Studied English at Liverpool and Keele, PGCE at King's College London. Had a number of teaching and leadership roles in London and Gloucestershire before joining Central Technology College, which was then one of the roughest boys' schools in the country. She brought it back from the brink of closure and transformed its rating to 'good' (Ofsted talked of a 'remarkable journey').

She has imported to very middle class Fortismere some of the tactics that had wrought improvements in her previous setting, such as a hard line on punctuality, attendance and litter. She clearly has a steely determination and is evidently not a head to be trifled with, though on our tour a pupil did not hesitate to buttonhole her to check she had signed a form for him. 'Very hard working and ambitious,' say parents. Mother of two daughters.

Academic matters: A large proportion of bright, motivated pupils and also a greater than average number of pupils with SEN, with a relatively small mid range. In 2016, 51 per cent A*/A grades at A level, with 72 per cent A*/B. Similarly strong at GCSE: 45 per cent A*/A grades, and 86 per cent of pupils got 5+ A*-C grades, including English and maths.

The previous head had introduced setting for every subject from year 7; this has been loosened, but school still sets early for maths and science, whilst English is taught in mixed ability classes. 'I trust my faculty heads on that, but they must show that it works.' Relatively low class size of 24. Everyone learns French or Spanish in year 7 and promising linguists are offered Mandarin in year 8. They are encouraged to take two languages to GCSE; around 80 per cent of pupils take at least one. The top 60 per cent are encouraged to take triple science GCSE.

Teaching standards mostly very high with the odd exception, say parents. 'They expect of lot of the students – I think they push them very hard. They encourage and extend them, particularly with the personal projects in the sixth form.' Reporting system to parents 'has improved. They tell you what your child's target is, what level they're performing at now and whether that's okay. I've mostly found teachers very responsive when I've emailed them.'

The sixth form admissions criteria are 'closer to a grammar school', with at least five B grades at GCSE required for A level, and As for certain subjects eg maths. The small number of vocational options, with five C grades at GCSE as a boundary, include music technology, ICT, business, media and sports science. School also teaches classical heritage and global perspectives Pre-U courses.

Maths a very popular A level, alongside history (teaching dubbed 'exceptional' by parents) and English. Respectable numbers pursuing biology and chemistry, and – as one might expect in this liberal, intellectual area – philosophy, psychology, government and politics and sociology, though linguists disappointingly few.

'Amazing' preparation for Oxford, said a parent. 'It was all very low key, but there are several young Oxbridge graduates teaching at the school, and they ran workshops, put on seminars, did mock interviews, and put pupils in touch with other students who'd been through the process recently. It was all there, but it was up to the kids to push themselves that much further.'

With its large, segmented site and high pupil numbers, possibly not the most suitable school for children with learning difficulties, but many choose it nonetheless, 'and we do a very good job with them'. Those with statements/EHC plans – and there are a relatively large proportion of these, mostly with autistic spectrum and behavioural issues – have their own teaching assistant. However, 'we try to keep away from TAs velcroed to children', and they are included in class work as far as possible, with small group sessions to help them develop independent learning skills. Linc team helps those experiencing learning difficulties – temporary or permanent. The secondary department of the Blanche Nevile School for deaf and hearing-impaired children occupies an impressive building on the site. Some of its pupils join in the mainstream school activities.

Games, options, the arts: Fabulous newish music block, with recording studios, composing and practice rooms, plus multi-use performance spaces, mirrors the importance of the subject here (though few take it to A level). Symphony orchestra, big band and several choirs; community choirs and orchestras include parents as well as children; hosts Saturday music school. 'We play a key role in the local community.' Head doesn't envisage the abolition of music aptitude places having any effect on the quality of music-making in the school. 'We have always had a lot of hugely musical students – it comes with the parent body.'

Impressive displays of art and fabulous photography coursework around the school on our visit, plus bright papier mâché aliens and rats created by younger year groups. Photography a popular A level and one can see why. Drama also 'massive'. 'We're a very artsy school. It's our natural default setting.' 'Fantastic' production of Little Shop of Horrors included the actual plant from the West End show; sixth formers regularly take productions to the Edinburgh fringe, and help with GCSE drama performances.

Sports stars used to hone their talents largely outside school, but sport has been bolstered by increased amounts of time in the upper years plus the introduction of Colleges, or houses, which run weekly inter-college competitions and encourage non A team players to get involved. However, parents report that it is possible for the less athletically inclined to avoid breaking into a sweat, and it is fair to say that reports of sports team triumphs do not feature largely in school newsletters. Sports hall, tennis/netball/basketball courts, acres of playing fields and 'very popular' table tennis tables. The head would dearly like the renovation of the 'stagnant' disused swimming pool to be her legacy, but financial constraints seem likely to stymie this ambition.

Large range of trips includes 'brilliant and very well organised' week in Beijing for Mandarin speakers, exchange visits to France, Spain, Senegal and India ('though you do have to queue up at 7am with your cheque to get a place on the popular ones,' commented a parent), D of E, outdoor pursuits in the Brecon Beacons, ski trips, field trips and cultural visits. A steady stream of authors, scientists, politicians etc comes to give talks; librarian organises team of pupils to shadow Carnegie medal deliberations, reading and reviewing shortlisted books; teams enter debating competitions.

Background and atmosphere: Large site amidst leafy Muswell Hill Edwardiana has been the setting for a series of schools of all sorts, including private, state grammar and comprehensive. Fortismere was formed in 1983 by the amalgamation of Creighton and Alexandra Park Schools (another Alexandra Park School has since opened nearby). Site includes a hotch-potch of buildings from its various incarnations. North and South Wings linked by a quarter-mile pathway round the playing fields that can resemble a storm in the North Sea in inclement weather. Accommodation beginning to show its age, but bright and cheerful. Head has encouraged a multitude of notice boards – with college news, photos of trips, information on clubs.

Very much a community comprehensive with a relaxed atmosphere (subject to 'behaviour for learning' sanctions), and pupils strolling around in jeans and tee shirts. 'Proudly non-uniform', though with a veto on revealing too much skin or underwear. 'It's part of the ethos for children to be able to express themselves,' said a parent.

Pastoral care, well-being and discipline: Good transition system, with year 6s spending three days at the school in the summer term getting to know the site and teachers. Operates vertical tutor system, with 18 pupils of different ages from the same college in each group replacing old form tutor system. All staff – including admin staff – are tutors, 'which enables us to have small groups, and also increases student respect for non-teaching staff'. Mixed reviews from parents and pupils, some enthusiastic whilst others feel that the system needs time to bed in and become a tradition, and that they would prefer to spend the time with their peers.

Student leadership team, which includes head boy and girl and their deputies, has a meeting with the head each Monday. 'It has already had a real impact. They really challenge us about why we do things, and it makes me think about structures.'

Head's introduction of zero tolerance for lateness and absenteeism has shocked some families and delighted others, with one parent terming it 'draconian.' 'The behaviour here was good, but I thought it could be better,' says the head. 'If you are disrupting the learning of others, that is not negotiable. Parents complain, but when I tell them their child is stopping other people learning, they find that hard to justify.' She refuses permission for holidays in term time: 'We get a lot of poorly relatives in far flung places towards the end of the Christmas and summer terms.' In response to pupils' requests for carrots as well as sticks, Positive Points system gives house points for helpfulness, participation, tidiness etc and is widely reported in the newsletters.

Pupils mostly very happy and have good relationships with staff, but some parents feel that the pastoral system is variable. Some teachers 'do resolve your issues,' said a parent, citing the 'novel and interesting solutions' to stress suggested by her daughter's college head. However, 'I had a very unsympathetic reaction from the school to a family death. I found their policies very inflexible.' 'They didn't seem to be sensitive to the needs of my younger daughter,' said another parent, whose children had joined from a different education system. 'I really didn't feel she got the support she needed, and I felt that no-one had an overview of the situation. I also had no response to a very carefully worded email about a pastoral issue that had upset her.'

Permanent exclusions rare, and usually for persistent defiance or repeated breaking of behaviour policies. Will swap recalcitrant pupils with other local schools. 'We're good at managed moves – they can be very effective.' Will also use outside providers such as local boxing and football academies for those who clearly need a different approach. 'We prefer to try something different before moving to permanent exclusion.' A parent commented: 'There are some wild and woolly kids, but they don't tend to disrupt classes.'

Works in collaboration with the mental health charity, Place2Be, to provide therapeutic counselling for students as needed.

Pupils and parents: Largely affluent, liberal, middle class families – artists and musicians, writers and actors – plus quite a few looked-after children. 'It is a very political school. I have to remember that parents don't just read the Guardian – quite likely they write for it too,' says the head. These are mostly cool kids, relaxed and confident, proud to be at Haringey's most popular comprehensive. 'My daughters' friends are lovely,' said a parent. 'They meet up to study and all help each other.' Ex-pupils include singers Michael Kiwanuka and Jess Glynne.

Entrance: Takes 270 pupils into year 7. Those with an SEN statement/EHC plan naming the school – and there are many of these – will automatically get a place. Then priority to children in care, those with particular medical, social or emotional needs, and siblings, with the remainder by distance, usually less than half a mile.

Takes 110 or so outside students into the sixth form, from state and independent schools. Requires 5+ A*-C GCSEs for vocational A levels and 5+ A*-Bs for academic A levels, with higher grades for certain subjects eg maths, from internal and external students. Those who don't get at least three D grades at AS are liable to be directed elsewhere.

Exit: Small numbers (around 30 per cent) move on after GCSEs, generally for more vocational courses. Nearly all sixth form leavers to university: Sussex, Leeds, Manchester and Bristol the flavour of the moment; 12 Oxbridge and medical school places in 2016. English, philosophy, psychology, maths, law, geography all popular.

Money matters: Very active parents' association, the FSA, which underwrote the refurbishment of the sixth form centre.

Remarks: A popular and high-achieving comprehensive that successfully includes those with difficulties as well as extending the most able. Head's vision is for it to have 'an active mind, a finger on the pulse and a big heart.'

Fox Primary School

Kensington Place, London W8 7PP

Pupils: 330 • Ages: 4–11

Tel: 020 7727 7637
Email: info@fox.rbkc.sch.uk
Website: www.fox.rbkc.sch.uk

Executive Head: Since 2006, Mr Paul Cotter BA PGCE (40s), who is executive head of the federation of Fox Primary and Ashburnham Community school, Chelsea. Previously deputy head at Avondale Park Primary, North Kensington. As successful head of Fox, became acting head of Ashburnham, and oversaw the transformation of the smaller school at World's End. Sees the formal union of the two schools, both with multi-cultural populations but from different social spheres, as a positive; 'Fox has benefited from the whole experience. We've had to reflect upon our own practices'. Described as 'approachable' by the parents, and visible at the school door every day. Not content to sit back on laurels and watch the RBKC high-steppers bid for a place by renting a house on the doorstep, he is currently implementing the local authority's new entry system, with more equitable lottery-style admissions; not to mention managing a huge building project on the side.

Head of school since 2013, Ms Emma Madden BA (Cantab) MA (IoE); mid 30s. Like Paul Cotter, joined Fox from Avondale Park Primary in 2007, swiftly rose through the ranks of assistant, deputy, then associate head. Married with two children, husband works as an environmental campaigner. To call Ms Madden purposeful is an understatement. Barely through the door, we were treated to a lightning lecture on the school's educational approach, whilst she fielded calls for advice from staff. Parents are rightly respectful of her leadership qualities. A young dynamo in the school, she takes great pride in the school's training record, and quickly dismissed our suggestion she might have time for extra-mural leisure pursuits. She is at the door every afternoon, keen, committed and capable; but don't expect a relaxing chat over coffee.

Entrance: Oversubscribed with one and a half class entry (45 places) but plans to take two full reception classes in the new building. LA managed, prioritising looked after children, SEN and siblings. Current catchment area extends from Westbourne Grove in the north to Cromwell Road in the south, includes more billionaires' basements than you can shake a stick at, and a small local authority housing estate. Unsurprisingly, given the international demographic, some occasional places, but loyalty is encouraged; 'We only want people to come if they intend to stay,' says the head of school, with a nod at the 'state till 8' brigade.

Exit: Roughly half of all leavers go to Holland Park School, where results have soared, a few to Chelsea Academy. Others (with helping hand from a tutor) successful at top London day schools, including St Paul's Juniors, City of London Boys and Girls, Latymer Upper, Godolphin & Latymer. Parents say Mr Cotter makes no judgement about where the child goes, as long as it's the best fit.

Remarks: Perfection comes in small packages, and the teaching at Fox Primary is no exception. The small classes (two of 24 per year) and the impressive KS2 Sats results (the majority exceed level 5) have consistently put the school high in the league tables. The head pointed out they have been the highest performing school in the country for two years running. The key to its success is spotting and training good staff, of which they are justifiably proud, 'It has huge respect for teaching as a profession,' a parent remarked. The Mayor of London must agree, to have awarded the school the Gold School award. Emma Madden is unashamedly serious about the school's role as a training centre, providing professional development for two London boroughs as well as courses for newly qualified teachers and TAs. She even runs literacy and numeracy training sessions for parents. In addition the school is a maths hub for central and west London, sharing methods among teachers as far as Shanghai.

We were surprised to hear that, though energetic and youthful-looking, some staff had more than 10 years experience, and a few up to 20. The best of the newly qualifieds in training at the school are persuaded to join. 'There's a lot of support for young teachers', said a parent. 'I guess you want that fresh voice, but you want it to be quality'. The school has children with statements supported by the two special needs teachers, one a science specialist, but overall number of SEN children is lower than average. EAL proportions are high. One parent remarked how quickly the class teacher had noticed and dealt with her daughter's reading and maths difficulties. Support came in the form of small group work and individual attention; 'she's flying now,' commented the delighted mum. Currently not suitable for physical disabilities, but the new building will be wheelchair friendly.

The 1930s municipal school building sunk between chic terraces and mansion flats off Kensington Place is no great shakes. Classrooms are high ceilinged, utilitarian design, with steel framed windows, some brightened up by pots of geraniums. The younger years enjoy the ground floor rooms, where round tables in primary colours, a carpeted reading corner and bunting brighten the space. They make the most of their direct access to the rear playground, where netball posts share the tarmac with raised vegetable beds sprouting sunflowers and courgettes. Mounting a brick-built staircase to the half tiled upper corridors we met a class of older children, in quiet discussion at a large group table. Another group was colouring the Brazilian flag in a geography lesson, strains of gentle music in the background. We heard from one articulate boy that a parent had visited earlier to teach them some Portuguese in addition to the Spanish, taken in class. On the top floor a music activity had children, grouped in front of the white board, following acoustic patterns by clapping out rhythms. A display of the SS Windrush emblazoned the white walls of the oldest children's room in celebration of black history month, as had a visit from Lenny Henry. The children we met were unpretentious yet confident, happily engrossed in their work. PE in the hall, involved youngsters shooting hoops in sensible royal blue T shirts and track suits. No uniform otherwise, though Hackett rugby shirts were all the rage.

Parents, though devoted to the teaching methods, were unanimous in wishing for a larger site. 'It's a small patch of land that the school is squashed into', said one. 'To keep up with the level of teaching, the building needs to catch up,' said another. Sure enough, the front playground contained a gaping excavation on the occasion of our visit, promising a new extension for classrooms, a hall and teaching suite, to accommodate the extra 100+ children.

Fox values displayed around the school: collaboration, loving learning, independence, creativity mean there is a healthy balance of academic and creative subjects. All children learn recorder in year 3, with individual instrument lessons offered further up the school. A school orchestra practises before lessons. Shows are big at Fox, with end of year productions carrying an ethical message (Charlie doesn't just find sweets in his chocolate factory but Fox's moral values too). Previous productions have included Matilda, Grease and Mary Poppins, with class teachers scripting a part for every child. Parents are happy to watch three Mary Poppinses singing in chorus. 'They are really nice events,' said a parent, 'with a lot of real warmth towards the child who stands there'. Other children join the inter-schools debating team. A makeshift studio in a classroom at the top of the school allows the specialist art technician space to do her thing. We saw satisfying slab pots and displays of accomplished paper cutting. Some talented children's work had been exhibited at Leighton House Museum and The Tabernacle, Portobello Road.

An experienced PE teacher, 'adored by the children' ensures every child in year 6 represents the school in an activity: football; tag-rugby; hockey and netball run alongside judo and athletics in local leagues. Table tennis is a big success, with an all-weather table in the playground, and involves ex-Fox students in national tournaments. With many working parents, clubs after school in subjects such as martial arts, chess or 'thrifty accessories' are popular, one parent told us; 'The day people sign up, parents are queuing into the street'. There is a breakfast club for early bird children, and if they are still motoring after school, play care runs till 6pm, with tea too.

Founded in 1842 by a doughty female philanthropist, Caroline Fox (curiously under-celebrated at the school, we thought), when modish Notting Hill was no more than muddy fields. Originally a charity school for the local labouring classes, Fox Primary moved to its present site behind the antique shops of Kensington Church Street in 1935. Since then, the utilitarian architecture has withstood a sea change of bohemian chic in the neighbourhood, retaining a sturdy presence at the end of a quiet cul de sac. Within the high walls surrounding the school, some of the noble intentions of the founder re-emerge in a save the planet philosophy. A children's eco committee rakes out compost, feeds the wormery and monitors rubbish, and has achieved the Green Flag award. Solar panels operate on the roof, while a water butt supplies the gardening teacher with rainwater to cultivate some tasty extras for lunch. The chickens have now given way to beekeeping and two hives produce Fox honey, which is sold for school funds. These city children are not just playing farms, they grow their own lunch and even supply produce for a local restaurant.

This is a foodies school. Lunches are cooked on site, with meat delivered by Lidgates butchers on three days; the rest of the time it's a meat-free menu. Some choose to bring packed lunches. 'Food's excellent,' said a parent. Favourite dishes included chicken and rice and yogurt fruit compote. Fox publishes its own cookbook, with toothsome photographs by one of the parents. Not a turkey twizzler in sight, instead delicacies such as pigeon breast in fennel, top secret pancakes and a recipe from the high table: Mr Cotter's vegetable loaf. A Food Explorers week is an opportunity for children to try unfamiliar tastes. One mum welcomed the experience: 'I feel that if the other children are eating it, she will'. Trips out have included the Holland Park edible garden, London Wetland Centre, as well as the walkable South Kensington museums site. Older children have been to Whitstable on a geography field trip and paddle-boarding at the British Sailing HQ.

'We celebrate success a lot,' remarks Emma Madden, both among the four houses (named after species of Fox: arctic, desert, silver, red) and at afternoon assembly, timetabled at 3pm, to keep the mornings free for the most concentrated tasks. Children are motivated in class by the chance of becoming 'Star/Speaker/Reader of the week' or by competitions, eg 'Who can invent the healthiest snack?' with a trip to a local café as a reward. Homework is regular but not excessive, numeracy once a week, reading and spelling daily. Discipline is not an issue with such an oversubscribed school. 'Behaviour is very, very good', remarks Emma Madden; 'children need to have clear expectations'. Parents' concerns are managed by face-to-face meetings with teachers in the playground each morning, or by email. 'They are learning to control that,' said a parent, conscious that high-achieving parents are experts at monopolising a teacher's attention. The school's Twitter account, no doubt managed by one of the school's two network managers, is full of up-to-date bulletins of the children's day. Despite this, one mum felt notice of school decisions did not always get through. 'I know the information is there, but it's just letting the parents know...it's been a full time job keeping up with it all'. Parents' evenings twice a year bring opportunities to chat to the class teacher, as does the annual International evening, a festival of the multi-national flavour of the school.

The parents are a committed lot; 'Fox is fortunate as it is in an affluent area,' said one mum (very low numbers on free school meals). Despite the area being known for its cosmopolitan beau monde, the school's parents include a few past pupils as well as professionals from business, legal and arts spheres. Fundraising by the parents, via the usual coffee mornings and cake sales, has succeeded in equipping the IT class with a set of iPads. The PTA has charitable status and organises summer and winter fairs with the aim of creating benefits for children from all backgrounds – Caroline Fox would be proud.

For the fortunate who break through the over-subscribed entry lists, can breach the formidable railings outside and are not bewildered by the airport-style security checks inside, it is a rare find: a quality education with a broad curriculum, led by a staff with vision and commitment. As one mum said, 'It's a brilliant school and we are very, very lucky'.

Francis Holland School, Regent's Park

Clarence Gate, Ivor Place, London NW1 6XR

Pupils: 492 • Ages: 11–18 • Sixth form: 120 • C of E

Fees: £18,390 pa

Tel: 020 7723 0176
Email: admin@fhs-nw1.org.uk
Website: www.fhs-nw1.org.uk

Head: Since January 2016, Charles Fillingham MA, previously deputy head at City of London School, and this school's first male head. Married with a son and a daughter. French degree from the University of Wales, PGCE in French and German from Bristol

University and an MA with distinction in education management from King's College, London. His teaching career covers independent and state sectors, single sex and co-ed schools and he is also an independent schools' inspector as well a member of ACSL (secondary heads' association) governing council.

Academic matters: Small classes – especially at A level – are an almost USP here. No class is bigger than 25 and, in the sixth, 14 max – many are far smaller. For a relatively small sixth form offers a creditable range of subjects including economics, history of art and psychology. Most popular subjects tend to be art, biology, English, history and maths; the best results in RS, politics, geography, history of art and art. Economics less strong. Theatre studies offered at A level though not at GCSE. Outstanding results in many subjects – 56 per cent A*/A in 2016. Extended project (worth half an A level) can be taken in addition to A levels and challenges the most able.

GCSEs and, increasingly, IGCSEs (87 per cent A*/A in 2016) also include a good number of options – most popular are history, art and geography. Wisely, allows girls to take either three separate sciences or double science – we approve. Has introduced computer science.

SEN support is generally by withdrawal or out-of-lesson individual support. Most of those who receive help are mildly dyslexic/dyspraxic but additional support also for those perceived as G and T. Three-strong 'learning enhancement' team. 'We give girls extra support the entire time – it's simply part of what we offer,' says school, and parents concur: 'The girls can refer themselves for support and there's excellent liaison between the subject staff and the team'.

But the academic input here is far more than just good teaching. Weekly lectures by outside speakers open to all from year 9 up. Lots of trips hither and yon and good use made of privileged location and the proximity of the odd museum, Houses of Parliament, Bank of England or three.

Games, options, the arts: Minutes from Regent's Park, where most sports take place. Onsite is a tiny Astro playground – good for netball shooting practice but no more – but a good sized gym, fitness suite and, surprisingly, basement swimming pool, opened 1996 by, somewhat improbably, old girl Joan Collins – swimming one of the more competitive sports. Completely renovated to celebrate centenary of school's move to Ivor Place, in 2015, and with adjustable floor can accommodate diving and water polo as well as swimming. Sport compulsory for all, but lots of choice by the time you're in the sixth and zumba is a recent, popular addition – along with yoga and the use of the fitness suite.

Art is exceptional here – lots of it lines the corridors and we felt inclined to snaffle some of the best pieces to hang at home: really attractive, skilful, imaginative work. Top floor now houses the two studios, plus kiln, dark room, and printing press; views over the grey slate, Georgian rooftops and grey, steel satellite dishes must inspire artistic freedom, as it clearly burns bright.

Music also housed up here, though you'd not imagine the few small rooms result in the level of skill and performance managed by the girls here. Seventy per cent learn at least one instrument. Orchestras, choirs – large and chamber – and other ensembles thrive and surprise. Annual concert with the boys of Harrow School is a highlight. Music and drama combine to produce major annual show, plus drama competition – these draw in most, one way or another, though more drama – especially in the upper years – would be appreciated by many. Young Enterprise and Duke of Edinburgh Award scheme both thrive, along with more than 70 clubs and activities.

Background and atmosphere: Founded by Canon Francis Holland in 1878 at the instigation of his wife, Mary Sibylla, an interesting woman, mother of six, who pushed for the education of 'girls from the middle and upper classes' and later converted to Roman Catholicism. Moved from Baker Street to Ivor Place in 1915. The second school with Canon Holland's name was founded shortly afterwards just off Sloane Square; the two schools are run by the same foundation. Sibylla's letters were published by her children and make for touching reading.

Minutes from Baker Street and Regent's Park, the main building is a classic 1900s red-brick school – smallish classrooms, corridors, lots of floors and a wonderful hexagonal hall with three galleries and lots of polished wood. But the Tardis cliché really applies here. From the unassuming outside, you can't imagine how the school could accommodate more than a few dozen girls, but inside it goes on and on and has some surprisingly spacious areas. The library is also a decent size and has acquired a new area for computers in addition to the trad bookshelves and table space. Sofas and armchairs – we approve of that too. The stock is good, but some updating might inspire more to use books along with Google.

The hall – used for all major events – is not an ideal performance space but has extendable staging and clearly works. The acquisition of the adjacent Gloucester Arms pub and its consequent reopening as the Gloucester Wing was a major advance – school is on the lookout for a further property to enable further expansion, not in numbers but in facilities. Now possesses two good art studios, seminar rooms and a splendid, well-used lecture theatre. The old saloon bar is a useful space for drama work, charity activities and talks. School is an admirable mix of traditional and up to the minute – computer system recently renewed and everyone now wired in and up, as you'd expect.

Right at the top is the sixth form area and it's super – lots of space, though it can get crowded at breaks – with a roof top garden, a workroom, silent study area and common room with cooking area, sofas and lockers. Staff allowed in to pop marked work etc into sensible pigeon holes. School is accessible – lift enables wheelchair-users to get almost everywhere, though some corridors and steps make odd corners impossible.

The food is 'the best in London' – certainly the salads were lusciously inviting, as were the plates of fruit – pomegranates, passion fruit and melon slices: drool! Kitchen staff clearly popular with sixth formers – 'They are so kind – they bring us up hot chocolate and muffins,' we were told, and that really is kind, as four flights of stairs are involved.

Pastoral care, well-being and discipline: Universal praise for the pastoral care – 'the school could not be more supportive'; 'The staff are incredibly sensitive and caring. They are firm when it's needed, but you are always supported,' parents told us again and again. 'The staff are inspiring – they are more than just academic: they look after the whole child,' is another theme. Heads of year have overall responsibility and a counsellor visits weekly. Home and social difficulties – as anywhere – but few discipline problems.

Back-up for practical as well as emotional needs: 'The UCAS support here is amazingly impressive,' an Oxbridge hopeful told us. 'The school has been so on top of everything – you get at least three teachers helping, loads of sessions; our head of sixth is amazing and she makes us feel completely secure in how we approach our applications.'

'We want them to be confident and self-possessed but not trumpet about it. We are absolutely about nurture. We are kind and academic. Kind is central.'

Pupils and parents: Interesting mix. Professional families from all over – hence the higher than usual incidence of relocating ins and outs that results in places appearing at odd stages: academics, medics, thesps and financiers, as you'd expect. The very rich – 'There are a few "princesses" in the sixth form,' muttered one or two parents – along with those who struggle to find the fees.

F

Notable old girls include Theresa Villiers, Joan and Jackie Collins, Tamara and Petra Ecclestone, Emilia Fox and Holly Branson.

Entrance: From over 170 preps and primaries. Majority from Pembridge House, Bute House, Sarum Hall, St Mary's, Hampstead, St Christopher's, Hampstead, St Christina's. Applications via the North London Consortium – exams in English and maths plus interviews. Oversubscribed of course, but as for many parents whose daughters also apply to the other powerhouses in the area the school, for all its virtues, is not always the first choice, a good chance of a place at 11+ if your daughter is able and would fit in. Location in central London means that relocating families come and go more than elsewhere and places often occur in other years – it is always worth a call.

At 16+ very few are taken – school has a sizeable sixth form and is not straining nerves to cram in more. Perhaps two to three places awarded to, perhaps, 20-30 applicants. A*/Bs needed at GCSE.

Exit: Around 10 leave after GCSE and head for mixed sixth forms, notably Highgate – some come back. School will not throw you out if you have problems or your GCSEs disappoint – 'We take them in at 11: we'll stick with them till 18'; also several families whose daughters have found refuge here from unhappiness elsewhere. No identikit FH leaver – fledglings go everywhere including New York University, Durham, Warwick and Imperial College. Six to Oxbridge in 2016.

Money matters: A few bursaries and scholarships and worth enquiring, but, like most girls' day schools, not munificently endowed.

Remarks: Your clever daughter will be well taught and will do as well here as anywhere. Your shy and gentle soul will be loved and encouraged. Definitely no hothouse but a school that warms and nurtures. A gem in the heart of the metropolis.

Francis Holland School, Sloane Square

39 Graham Terrace, London SW1W 8JF

Pupils: 501 • Ages: 4–18 • Sixth form: 70 • C of E

Fees: £16,950 – £19,170 pa

Tel: 020 7730 2971
Email: registrar@fhs-sw1.org.uk
Website: www.fhs-sw1.org.uk

Headmistress: Since 2012, Mrs Lucy Elphinstone MA PGCE MEd FRSA (50s). Educated at Barnstaple Grammar School, Devon, and Newnham College, Cambridge (English). Very varied career, including stints in publishing, bookselling, catering, property and ghost-writing. Wide teaching experience from 3 to 18 years, and countless leadership roles including head of a pre-school, head of English at King's Taunton, director of studies in two prep schools, director of drama and resident tutor at Fettes College. Came here from Downe House where she was head of sixth form, senior leader and Oxbridge co-ordinator. Four highly successful adult children. Living in London for the first time since her 20s and loving the culture. Hobbies include ski-ing, watercolour painting, Scottish reeling and Victorian children's literature.

Keen to build up girls' resilience to help them deal with the challenges ahead, including multiple changes of career. Wants pupils to be confident risk-takers. In her assembly on the day we visited, she encouraged girls to take on board Christopher Robin's advice to Winnie the Pooh: 'You are braver than you believe, stronger than you seem, and smarter than you think.' One parent described her as 'ambitious for the school and highly visionary'. Another claimed, 'She's shaken the school up. It was good before but she has lifted our spirits.' Girls consider her to be 'a great role model.' Dynamic, vivacious and engaging.

Head of junior school: Since 2015, Caroline Spencer-Kruger, previously deputy head.

Academic matters: 'Low pressure in the early years,' says school. Reception children have naps after lunch in first term when sleepy. From year 4 it hots up, with summer exams in maths, English and science from then on. No setting but plenty of differentiation. The consensus among parents we spoke to was 'You need to be academically robust to cope here. There are so many projects and tests, and parents are expected to be able to support their offspring massively. It feels almost relentless at times.' More academic than senior school: 'The girls here are clever and motivated,' said one parent. 'Strong foundations are laid but the girls work hard for it,' according to another. The standard of work on display was astonishingly high. The girls themselves feel that they are well prepared for the 11+, but 'we don't feel too much pressure.' Year 6 pupils kept working to proper timetables once 11+ exams are over; no coasting here. Teaching is superb and staff considered by the parents to be high quality. Teachers come over from senior school to teach PE, science, French (from 8) and some art. Well motivated staff. 'We're a strong team'.

In 2016, 40 per cent A*/A at A level; 71 per cent A*-B. Maths and English currently popular, with ever-increasing numbers taking science and economics. Compulsory Extended Project Qualification in sixth form, introduced by head to develop girls' research skills and to prepare them for the next stage. Photography, art and design and computing recently introduced at A level. Eighty-seven per cent A*/A at GCSE. Spanish, chemistry and history results impressive. Setting in English, science and maths by year 9.

Excellent reports about provision now on offer to pupils with special needs: 'no longer just lip service,' said one parent. All pupils screened for dyslexia on arrival. A handful of pupils have EAL requirements and are seen on a one-to-one basis by specialist staff. Extra support continues to sixth form.

Some teaching described as 'fantastic', but one parent we spoke to felt there were 'still some members of staff who need weeding out. They aren't inspiring the girls and aren't getting the results.' Approximately a third of staff has been there at least 10 years. Recent appointments, particularly of younger members of staff, seen as very positive. Staff feel 'empowered' by newish head.

Academic success is recognised with flamboyant prize-giving at nearby Cadogan Hall, with performances by talented dancers and musicians. The girls were hugely excited to see staff wearing their graduation gowns and 'felt proud' to be part of Francis Holland. A great success, recently introduced by head, who is clearly keen to celebrate success in all fields.

Two parallel classes throughout senior school. Classes start at 16 on average and rarely go above 20 in lower years, diminishing to six to eight in sixth form. Would split sixth form classes if they exceeded 10 pupils. From year 11, all girls have an academic mentor, so everyone is fully supported and no one is left floundering. Girls genuinely feel that staff are keeping a close eye on them and that they are guided through university entrance 'incredibly well'.

Games, options, the arts: Sport now taken very seriously, at all levels, and is compulsory for all. Head believes, 'Sport is important as it teaches you that you can't always win, but you can pick yourself up and carry on'. Recently appointed head of sport who everyone is raving about. Well-equipped gym and netball/tennis court on site. Outdoor sports in Battersea Park, including tennis, hockey, athletics and rounders. Top years can try pilates, yoga, squash and boxercise as well as more traditional team sports. Most parents are delighted that fixtures are now arranged on Saturday mornings and the school wins the majority of matches.

Lots of music and drama in the junior school, including impressive end of year 6 musical. Girls take the initiative by providing the costumes, designing the posters and rehearsing on their own at break times. Great emphasis placed on creativity throughout the school. Junior choir from year 3 and a very select chamber choir for the most talented singers. Significant numbers learn Instruments from year 1 onwards. 'Girls need time to be bored. They should not have every moment of their lives timetabled.' Wants them to discover what interests them for themselves. Plenty of clubs on offer including chess, speech and drama, pottery, art and French.

Music is flourishing in the senior school too. Nearly 60 per cent learn an instrument. Choirs, orchestras, chamber groups and jazz groups galore. Two choir tours to Europe each year. Head wants creative and enterprising pupils and girls recently set up own theatre company. Highly successful theatrical collaborations with boys from nearby Cardinal Vaughan School, with minimal adult input. Parents consider drama to be a real strength. Speech and drama very popular with many reaching top grades in exams. Ballet taken seriously in junior school: compulsory in the first years, fabulous ballet studio. Highly anticipated Princess Margaret ballet competition every summer term – her daughter is an old girl – culminating in a final attended by governors and prestigious figures from the ballet world. Many take ballet exams, and talented pupils have auditioned to attend the Royal Ballet School Associate Programme.

Impressive selection of clubs including debating and philosophy, as well as animal club for younger girls. School has a renowned menagerie of animals, from gerbils and snakes to chinchillas, and younger girls get to take home animals for the weekend. Girls encouraged to become proficient in public speaking: debating club from year 6, and mock elections and English Speaking Union events arranged. Broad horizons and an informed awareness of current affairs expected. Plenty of time for fun, with highly-anticipated trips to Cornwall in year 6 and Canterbury in year 5.

Background and atmosphere: Set up by the Rev Francis Holland, Canon of Canterbury, in 1881 as a C of E foundation but all faiths welcome. Sister school to Francis Holland Regent's Park: the schools share a governing body, staff training days and have the same ethos. Same site as junior school, in a Tardis-like building behind Sloane Square. Head aware that being in the same place from 4-18 years has its disadvantages and is keeping her eye out for property nearby. Beautiful interior decorating: stunning new entrance hall lifts morale on arrival and upper sixth common room seriously plush.

School described as 'vibrant', and it was certainly buzzing on the day we visited. A real energy about the place. Francis Holland girls have a wonderfully stimulating start to life here, with devoted care and attention from outstanding teachers. No wonder there's a queue to come here.

Pastoral care, well-being and discipline: Junior girls have beautiful manners and stand up with military discipline when adults enter the room. Highly articulate and fluent. Very keen to show their projects to us when we visited and tell us what they had learnt. Highly engaged in lessons, from early years upwards. Pretty tartan uniform. One girl in top year thought it would be worth staying at the school just so she could get to wear the new kit. A very caring school in which older girls are expected to, and do, look after the younger ones. Year 6 pupils write and illustrate books for year 1 pupils. Lots of raising money for charity. All year 6 girls are prefects, though badges confiscated for poor behaviour.

Described by parents as being 'nurturing'. Lower sixth and year 8 girls are paired with year 7 girls in 'Big Sister' programme, to make sure they settle on arrival at the school. Head concerned that 'high performing parents have high expectations of their children.' Aware that girls can feel pressurised to perform and a well-being programme, including mindfulness, has been set up to help girls to cope, when it all becomes too much. Head is a trained counsellor and pastoral care is high on the agenda.

Strong ethos of service fostered, whether fundraising for school in Uganda or organising tea parties for elderly in Battersea. Girls are expected to give something back.

Head would expel a girl for drug taking; those caught smoking pay money to a cancer charity, phone their parents from head's office and do community service within the school grounds. Won't tolerate unkindness or rudeness and girls we met were fantastically polite. Sixth formers allowed out for lunch but 'school food is delicious so we prefer to stay at school for lunch and just go out for a coffee,' said one.

Pupils and parents: Happy, confident and charming girls who seem ready to take on the world. Well-heeled and polished with ready smiles. Couldn't wait to tell us how lucky they felt to be here. High octane, international families: mainly French, Spanish, Italian, Russian and American. 'A bewildering number of languages spoken in the playground at pick up time,' according to one mother.Most live within a three mile radius of school. Communication with parents now greatly improved with weekly e-newsletters and reports. 'We are delighted that we finally know what is going on,' said one.

Notable former pupils include Vanessa Mae, Sienna Miller, Cara Delevingne and Rose Tremain.

Entrance: Assessments at 3. Some 150 girls tested in January for 24 places. School assesses 'girls' potential and readiness to learn.' School was horrified when a parent asked about tutoring for their 3 year old and advises, 'Parents need to read to their children, take them to the park and talk to them. That's the best preparation for these tests.' Places occasionally available further up the school and prospective pupils are then assessed in the classroom setting. Barely a spare seat in the house.

At 11+, exams in English and maths, as well as half a day spent at school consisting of interview and taster lesson. Part of the North London Consortium Group One. Some 500 girls sit for 50 places. Bar raised each year. At 13+, exams in English, maths, science and French. For sixth form, by entrance or scholarship exams in proposed A level subjects.

Exit: Fairly evenly split at 11: one third to the senior school, one third to other London day schools and another third boarding. One parent remarked that she thought it would be 'a hard jump to go from Francis Holland Junior School to a large co-ed. Girls are protected here and can be quite gentle. I'm not sure they are always ready for the hurly burly of senior school.' Popular day destinations are St Paul's, Godolphin & Latymer, Latymer Upper, JAGS, North London Collegiate and City of London Girls. Current boarding favourites are Wycombe Abbey, Downe House and Cheltenham Ladies'.

A trickle leave after GCSE. Most sixth formers to university. Occasionally one or two Oxbridge places. As one girl put it, 'I have applied to Oxford, but it's just one of my choices. It's not made into a big deal here. My other choices are great too.' Art foundation courses also popular. Medicine, economics, history and psychology are favoured courses; Durham, Bristol and Exeter regular destinations. Increasing numbers to US universities, especially for liberal arts degrees, and not only those with a direct American link; others to Spain, France and Canada. Head of careers is a very successful recent appointment; she asks girls at beginning of sixth form, 'What is your dream?', and then helps them to chase it. Higher education fair organised by school. Girls well supported once they leave, throughout university and beyond if needed. Relations with alumnae now actively fostered.

F

Money matters: At 11, four academic scholarships, as well as music, art and drama scholarships. Bursaries at 11+, 14+ and four in sixth form. Daughters of clergy offered remission on a third of fees.

Remarks: This school is undergoing a transformation and the excitement is palpable. Expectations are high and challenges are being set, but the girls and staff know they have a strong leader and are following her willingly. 'An excellent appointment,' said one parent. 'We feel seriously lucky to have our girls here on Mrs Elphinstone's watch,' said another. Though small, this school is now punching above its weight. An exciting and exhilarating place to be.

Fulham Prep School

200 Greyhound Road, London W14 9SD

Pupils: 651 • Ages: 4–13

Fees: £15,708 – £17,445 pa

Tel: 020 7386 2444
Email: prepadmin@fulhamprep.co.uk
Website: www.fulhamprep.co.uk

Headteacher: Since September 2016 Neil Brooks, previously acting CEO of the Cothill Educational Trust and running the Old Malthouse educational study centre in Dorset. PE and geography degree from Warwick; was an officer in the British Army for eight years, serving with an airborne unit in Northern Ireland and Bosnia. For the past 16 years he has worked for the Cothill Educational Trust, successively as a form teacher, housemaster and headmaster of Cothill House. He is married with two teenage sons.

Mrs Jane Emmett, who took charge after the short-lived tenure (less than a year) of Richie Howells, founded the school in 1996 along with other members of her family (it is a family company with some external shareholders).

Head of pre-prep: is Ms Di Steven BEd, educated at Glasgow University with PGCE from Dundee and an NPQH. She has been with the school for a decade, has one son in the pre-prep, a second son in a nearby nursery. Clearly in touch with the concerns of the modern parent, juggling work pressure with teaching her son to ride a bicycle. She is thorough and thoughtful with a pleasant manner and high standards. Her IT expertise ensures that the pre-prep is very well equipped.

Entrance: Pre-prep is non-selective in reception, with 90 places offered on a first come first served basis. Priority and a discount given to siblings. Entry after reception involves spending a morning at the school. Automatic transfer to the prep. The prep holds examinations and interviews at 7+ 8+ and 11+.

Exit: Majority of pre-prep pupils move on to the prep. Has a reputation for getting each prep school child into the right next school. Results are impressive with regular scholarships and places at a variety of boarding and day schools. Keen to encourage more girls to stay until 13 but this very much depends on the choice of destination as many girls' schools want them at 11+. Varying numbers to Benenden, Bradfield, Charterhouse, Downe House, Dulwich, Emanuel, Eton, Francis Holland, Godolphin & Latymer, Hampton, Harrow, Kew House, King's College School Wimbledon, Latymer Upper, Putney High, St Mary's Ascot, St Mary's Calne, Westminster, Wimbledon High.

Opening a senior school for 13-18 year olds, with a new year 9 in the current site in 2017, moving to a new site in south Fulham in 2018.

Remarks: The school is on two sites: there are transport arrangements between prep (on Greyhound Road) and pre-prep (on Fulham High Street) to assist busy parents, and January exam candidates are given the opportunity to visit in November for a treasure hunt so that they feel more at home when they come in for the dreaded tests.

The curriculum is not straitjacketed, and parents appreciate its variety and breadth. Although one class is given an accelerated pace (selected according to pupils' school destinations) this would 'not be fair on the others who do not need it'. That said, there is an expectation that every child will be able to keep up with a dynamic academic programme. All are being prepared for competitive entrance examinations, and although some allowance is made for pupils from abroad, there is limited EAL support in school. Experienced and extremely caring SENCo supports those with mild learning difficulties. Parents confirm that if serious difficulties were to develop, a school move would be suggested. Pre-prep has its own SENCo, a 'godsend,' remarks Ms Steven, and we noted some very good examples of provision for different abilities.

Until year 4 pupils are classroom based, then they move round specialist facilities. Latin from year 5 and philosophy for years 4 to 6. Greek available in years 7 and 8. 'The teachers make lessons interesting, often involving games in them', pupils remarked to us. They also appreciate the way staff 'offer advice and support'. We saw a number of young, enthusiastic staff, with more males in evidence than is often the case. The school is keen to stress the role models provided by the female head of science (who is also a great skier), and the male head of art. Class sizes between 14 and 20.

A listed Victorian school building accommodates the pre-prep reception classes, library, activity room and ICT suite. Adjoining is a modern three-storey block for years 1 and 2 as well as the spacious gym/hall, dark music room and light art studio. Large, well-equipped play areas including fabulous Astroturf and garden with shallow pond. We saw plenty of imaginative play equipment that can be re-arranged with different themes.

Do not expect soft furnishings, carpets and tasteful flower arrangements, or a palatial office for the head. The prep school was originally a Victorian board school and the building still shows this, although it is light with high ceilings, classrooms leading off the wide corridors on several floors, and an impressive meeting room with raked seating. Welcoming library with enthusiastic librarian. Classrooms contain attractive displays and are well equipped with the usual interactive boards. Some access to laptops, but though good use is made of the intranet to support learning (a recent development), we felt that the ICT in the prep is not cutting edge (schools says, 'we have been very proactive in implementing a great deal of computer science, coding and digital literacy within our current programme.')

More boys than girls in the school, especially noticeable in years 7 and 8 when many of the girls have left for London day schools. Those girls that do remain can be assured of being given responsibility and participating in many sports. Pupils look happy and move about purposefully; they are polite and responsive but not precocious, though it takes a certain robustness to flourish here. Parents like the fact that 'there are all walks of life' and the school is not 'glitzy'.

Heaps for all to do here. 'There are lots of opportunities for children to try new activities, with loads of clubs from jewellery to street dancing,' commented a parent. 'There's also plenty of music, from award winning chamber choir to African drumming, orchestra and jazz group.' Music is a strength of the school with four choirs including school choir apprentices and chamber choir, a boys' choir, plus a parents' choir which sings at the carol service. All classes have two music lessons with three-quarters of the pupils taking individual instrumental or singing lessons in spacious accommodation. Pre-prep pupils learn the recorder and percussion.

The school has its own Astroturf, netball court and cricket nets, and there is one afternoon a week at Barn Elms. In years 3 and 4 every child is given the chance to play in a team. The second half of Friday afternoon is for sport, as are some Saturdays (though both of these may be avoided). The deputy head is especially pleased with the up-and-coming rugby players, and cricket is very popular. Girls play netball. The pre-prep makes frequent use of Hurlingham Park for games, swimming takes place at Fulham Pools and there's summer tennis coaching for years 1 and 2 in Bishops' Park.

Pupils show tremendous loyalty to the four houses. The house names fit the locality: Bishops, Crabtree, Hurlingham and Peterborough. Older pupils take their responsibilities seriously and look out for younger pupils. Even in the pre-prep pupils start to take responsibilities eg as house captains. All the houses raise funds for charities, and the school supports, for example, a local state primary for severely disabled children. Discipline system understood by all and parents believe any bullying is quickly acted upon. Pupils we spoke to were clear that the head sees anyone who seriously misbehaves, and cited swearing as a major offence. Matters are dealt with promptly. Strong communication between home and school, including an open door policy and regular daily contact, means potential problems are nipped in the bud.

Sibling discount; some bursaries for families in difficulties. Scholarships available for years 7 and 8.

Very much a local school, as evidenced by the numbers of bikes and scooters parked inside the gates. The pupils are polite and express themselves confidently; one parent commented that some parents choose Fulham Prep because they have been impressed by the behaviour of the children outside school and asked where they were educated. A 'really vibrant, caring school where pupils are nurtured and understood' is the parental consensus. No wonder it has grown so fast.

Garden House School

84

Turks Row, London SW3 4TW

Pupils: 479 • Ages: 3-11

Fees: £13,500 – £21,600 pa

Tel: 020 7730 1652
Email: info@gardenhouseschool.co.uk
Website: www.gardenhouseschool.co.uk

Principal: Since 1973, Mrs Jill Oddy BA. She also runs three pre-prep schools in New York. As a long-serving member of the administrative department – who appreciated the school's move in recent years to Turks Row just behind Sloane Square – proudly remarks: 'She has tremendous vision.'

Head of girls' school: Since 2014, Mrs Charlotte Crofton BA (modern history, Newcastle) and PGCE (London), who has been a year 5 teacher here for eight years. She works alongside the head of the girls' lower school – Mrs Julia Adlard, who was previously head of kindergarten.

Head of boys' school: Since 2006, Mr Christian Warland, with BA from Exeter, (40s), left his work in the City as a lawyer and seems here to stay. He has found the change very satisfying: 'We spent considerable time analysing what went wrong in the City whereas here we are constantly forward-looking and this is very positive.' An old Garden House boy himself (and son of the principal), his three sons have been, or are being, educated at Garden House.

All three heads value taking time to get to know the children, from shaking hands with them and making eye contact first thing in the morning to teaching. Head of boys teaches ICT to year 2 and current affairs to the rest.

Entrance: As part of the school's desire to involve parents from the start, the family is seen as a unit. Usually girls are interviewed by head of lower school in January for the following September and boys by headmaster in October/November. Regular tours are organised for prospective parents, Tuesdays for the boys' school and Wednesdays for the girls', and there is no entrance examination, thankfully, so it really is important to secure a place on the lengthy waiting list with £120 as soon as possible. The school states that GH children live in Kensington, Chelsea, Fulham, Battersea and Westminster and that English is spoken at home by at least one parent, so very much a day school serving its local, smart area. Once a place is offered, a registration fee of £2,000 is payable. There is a 10 per cent discount for all siblings. Around 50 boys and 45 girls join reception. Entrants at 8+ (by exam and interview) are nearly all boys, to replace the 30 – 40 who leave at this stage; scholarships and generous bursaries available at this stage. There is a small amount of coming and going as families relocate so it is definitely worth checking.

Exit: Boys leave at 8+ (30-40) and 11+ (12-15) for top London day schools, including St Paul's Juniors, Sussex House, Westminster Under, Northcote Lodge, Wetherby Prep; one or two to boarding prep schools such as Summer Fields, Ludgrove and Cothill House. Nearly all girls leave at 11; just under half go on to boarding schools including St Mary's Ascot, Downe House, Wycombe Abbey, with a consistent number to Francis Holland SW1, Queen's Gate, Godolphin & Latymer, St Paul's Girls' etc.

Some go on with academic, art or sporting scholarships and awards.

Remarks: The exterior of the school, originally a British army barracks, is well maintained, but what awaits inside is quite magical. We were struck by the attention to detail and aesthetics; the entrance hall is beautifully arranged with rocking-horse, pupils' models and high quality art works by professionals, including an appealing watercolour of the school by a parent, Martin Millard, whose wife helps in the library. Classical music plays and flower arrangements and lighting produce a calming, civilising effect after the noise and bustle outside. Every corridor and every room shows a care for the surroundings, whether it be the recital room, art room, well-equipped ICT suite or classrooms with vibrant displays, and this contributes to the attention paid to individual pupils. As a current parent remarked: 'This is above all a nurturing school, where boys and girls receive a wonderful education. It is so nurturing both for parents and children.'

Heads are proud of broad curriculum and use of cross-curriculum planning. Every class has a teacher and classroom assistant, with specialist teachers for music, drama, games, French, IT, ballet, Latin, fencing, art from year 2 upwards and RE in the upper school. Boys and girls are taught separately after kindergarten but come together for playtime and musical and drama performances, as well as some trips. Average class size is 15 for girls and 14 for boys, with mixed ability teaching for all and some streaming only in mathematics. There is a learning zone on the website and plenty of interactive boards and laptops for research. There is a well-qualified learning support team with a range of expertise, including speech therapy, so pupils can be assessed in-house; some classroom assistants are trained in dyslexia. Alongside the learning support, there is also a gifted and talented coordinator, and year 6 get help with creative writing and mathematics ready for 11+ exams. The boys and girls share the same broad curriculum, but many boys sit 8+ exams, so there is a different emphasis at this stage even for those staying till 11. Practice papers and internal assessments throughout the year help pupils to cope with different styles of questioning. Plenty of advice and guidance available to parents but tutoring is discouraged as unnecessary pressure.

The attractively-equipped kindergarten accommodates tiny tots in a separate building attached to Holy Trinity Church. There are morning sessions for 24 children and afternoon sessions for 12, and they share a play area with the C of E primary school over the road.

The behaviour policy, using traffic lights, is well thought out. A parent commented on how seriously the children take it and said that the red light is very rarely used – 'it is brilliant, a clear not emotional system.' The head was also reassuringly definite that she would have no hesitation in using the red light and contacting a parent if the need arose: if, for example, a child were bullied.

All three heads are keen for school to be fun and stimulating, as the enormous array of activities and events demonstrate. During our visit boys were producing leaves in IT and art enthusiastically for FebFest, and the older girls spoke of the delights of preparing music and performing at Cadogan Hall in the spring term to a packed audience. The FebFest programme, involving the whole school from year 2 upwards, is linked to a fictional character travelling the world and hearing music from many cultures and heritages. The school is handy for galleries, exhibitions, museums and concerts. Music is popular with pupils as the teacher makes 'music enjoyable using actions' and 'is not too serious but friendly.' We heard the boys singing with gusto, and the percussion teacher clearly had year 1 boys enthralled. Every year the chamber choir goes on tour to Normandy and sings in the chapel of Emmanuel College, Cambridge. The musical calendar is packed. Four productions a year at the Royal Court and the Christmas concert is held in the Holy Trinity Church. Numerous events and competitions include Varsity Challenge, House Shout and Garden House has Talent.

Sport is taken seriously with football, rugby, cricket, rounders, hockey, lacrosse, tennis, netball at nearby Burton Court and Ranelagh Gardens as well as swimming at the Queen Mother's Pool. As a parent remarked, 'It all happens seamlessly despite the school not having its own extensive grounds, as so much is in easy walking distance.' Pupils were keen to explain how inclusive the school is, with team places and encouragement even for the less talented.

Active and supportive PTA with a predominantly Anglo-American parent body. The pupils feel they are respected by the teachers; as one parent remarked, 'There is always a seasoned staff member who has expertise and experience alongside another with energy, who comes across as positive and not world-weary. The school is amazing'.

Fridays are half days, though older children can do supervised homework until 2.30pm. Popular with parents who feel younger children are ready for the shorter day by Friday, and with those who want to leave early for the country.

Not a cheap school, although the Harrods uniform is also available secondhand and there is a complimentary bus service at 4.00pm to Fulham.

Sparky teachers, male and female, give a sense of energy in a school community in which care, respect and kindness for all is very much the ethos.

Glebe Primary School

Sussex Road, Ickenham, Uxbridge UB10 8PH

Pupils: 593 • Ages: 3–11

Tel: 01895 671951
Email: office@glebeprimary.org
Website: www.glebe.hillingdon.sch.uk

Headteacher: Since 2006, Mr Nick Alford BA PGCE NPQH (40s). Previously taught in Weston-super-Mare, then at schools in London for 10 years before moving to Glebe Primary.

Married to a teacher (who is deputy head at an independent school). 'We talk a lot about education and compare notes,' he says. Young son attends nearby state primary school. 'I did think about him coming here,' he told us, 'but if he ever got picked to be in a school play or for the school football team then parents would always think it was because he was the head's son.'

A cheerful, down-to-earth chap who admits to being a long-suffering supporter of Plymouth Argyle. His other passions are cricket and music (The Smiths and The Beatles).

Parents praise him for being very approachable. 'He's always in the playground in the morning and knows every child's name,' one mother told us. 'It means he can spot potential difficulties before they become a problem.'

Entrance: For nursery places apply direct to the nursery and for the school apply through the local authority. Usual criteria apply.

Exit: One or two go to the independent sector and a few to local grammars, but the majority head to Vyners School in Ickenham (about half) or Douay Martyrs.

Remarks: Set in the deepest London suburbs (Ickenham tube is near the end of the Piccadilly and Metropolitan lines) and built in the 1970s, the school caters for a mixed intake. Ten per cent of pupils come from military families stationed at the local RAF base and often only stay for a short time. Most pupils are drawn from the local area but the catchment area has shrunk in recent years as the school has grown more popular. 'When I first started as head I used to see some local children walking away from Glebe to a primary school further away which had a better reputation,' said the head. 'But now I'm proud to say that those children are now coming back to Glebe and even transferring from the other school.'

Sats results are above the national average but the most recent Ofsted report found that 'more able pupils have not always done as well as expected.' However the head told us that this point has been addressed 'through setting and focus groups for more able children over the last few years' and as a result, level 5 Sats results have risen to well above the national average. There is a joint project for gifted and talented pupils with a neighbouring school and Glebe recently won the Hillingdon Maths Challenge. School also has links with nearby Brunel University – for science and PE lessons.

The school's go-getting motto is 'We can and we will!' and first impressions reminded us more of a private school than a state primary. Photos on the wall of the head boy, head girl and house captains show the ambitious nature of the place and the head told us that he was keen 'to replicate some of the best aspects of independent schools, such as widening opportunities in sports, music and introducing a house system and prefects.'

Much of the games teaching is delivered by a specialist sports coach. Sports include football, netball, cross-country, athletics, cricket and tag rugby (supported by an enthusiastic year 6 teacher). The school takes part in inter-school competitions and recently won the Uxbridge football competition.

All children get the chance to study a musical instrument. This starts in year 2 with recorders and free tuition on the keyboard from year 4. Parents can pay for tuition in violin, cello, clarinet or flute if they want their children to take music exams. Two guitar clubs after school and when we visited we saw a group of year 4 children strumming away confidently. School choir performs regularly in different concerts, including one at the 02 Arena. 'The music provision is wonderful,' said an appreciative parent. Former pupils include TV presenter Sue Cook and London 2012 athlete Julia Bleasdale.

The school is a regional centre for those with impaired hearing. The SRP – specialist resourced provision for hearing-impaired children – has two teaching areas and a speech therapy room. Each classroom has a Soundfield system, amplifying the sound of the teacher's voice. There are places for nine hearing impaired children and the school employs two specialist teachers of the deaf. All the children are on the roll of their mainstream class and school aims for them to be taught in class alongside their hearing peers, with support if necessary.

School has recently moved into a new two-storey building, to great parental relief, and can at last serve hot lunches.

Parents are very supportive and reckon the school has a strong nurturing ethos. 'It feels like a little village school and it has a very caring environment,' said one. 'All the children are aware of each other and support each other.' Another told us: 'I wouldn't hesitate to recommend it to anyone. I feel that I struck gold when I found Glebe.'

Glendower Prep School

87 Queen's Gate, London SW7 5JX

Pupils: 238 • Ages: 4-11

Fees: £17,490 pa

Tel: 020 7370 1927
Email: office@glendower.kensington.sch.uk
Website: www.glendowerprep.org

Headmistress: Since 2012, Mrs Sarah Knollys (rhymes with tolls) BA PGCE (40s), educated at Wycombe Abbey and St Paul's Girls', Exeter (a degree in French and Italian) and Roehampton Universities. Started teaching career as SEN assistant at Finton House School, London; rose from form teacher to maths co-ordinator, SCITT mentor, key stage 2 manager, senior management team and school governor at Allfarthing School, London, a busy state school in Wandsworth (1993-2000); founding head, Maple Walk School, London (2005-2012). Married to Christopher; they have two teenage sons.

Bright and bubbly, Mrs Knollys exudes warmth and is highly accessible. She is the kind of person who rolls up her sleeves and gets on with it, whether it be teaching netball, transforming school lunches or wearing her slippersocks round the school on Red Nose day and dressing up in something crazy on Fun Friday. She is a woman who gets things done – as can be seen from her previous job at Maple Walk, the pioneer New Model school which started 'out of a trunk' as she puts it, with two pupils, and increased exponentially to 150 pupils by the time she left.

This is her first experience of a single sex school. 'I thought I'd miss the boys,' she remarks, 'but I don't miss the scraps in the playground – and our girls are very feisty.' She loves the girls, she says, because of their enthusiasm for everything, their lack of shame about excelling in science and maths and the more stable class dynamic – which can often be distorted by a predominance of one gender, she explains. She makes herself available to the parents, emails are responded to promptly, and she is there every morning to greet families. She is particularly on top of the 11 plus process, which starts with private meetings with her as early as year 4.

She is a good listener and we were told by one girl that 'she took on board our suggestions so we have much better lunches now, we no longer have to serve the younger children their lunch, and the loos and sinks are much nicer.' Her visible presence around the school includes teaching year 6 Latin, supporting maths in year 5 and English comprehension in year 4. That way she can properly understand each child and write detailed reports for the senior schools as well as giving fully informed advice to parents. She has one-to-one meetings with everyone from the kitchen staff through to the teaching staff and the parents. No one gets special treatment but everyone gets proper attention. This is a woman who throws herself into every aspect of the job and has been seen wiping her tears away during a music assembly. 'These are my girls,' she says unapologetically.

Entrance: Selective at 4 years. Far too many applicants for the 36 places. The girls are assessed on an informal basis – essentially to see if they interact well and can do the basics competently. Any parent who thinks coaching at this age is a good idea – forget it now. Sensible sibling policy means that often there are a fewer than 36 places open to newcomers. The tinies are assessed for 40 minutes in small groups. Older children applying for an occasional place will be assessed for longer – a morning or perhaps a full day, careful note being taken on whether they can cope and how they interact with their peers. No particular feeder nurseries. Occasional places occur but school unlikely to fill them after year 5 – the cohesion of the year being seen as paramount. It's worth a call, though. Some bursaries available for needy local girls or those already in the school who fall on hard times. Unsuccessful applicants for 4+ entry and later applicants to the school will be placed on a waiting list for consideration should an occasional place arise.

Exit: Recently, quite a number to top boarding schools – among them Benenden, Downe House, St Mary's Calne, Wycombe Abbey. A wide range of offers from London day schools – including the odd co-ed one – but girls tend to go to St Paul's, Godolphin & Latymer, Francis Holland SW1, St James's and even as far afield as South Hampstead, North London Collegiate and Putney High. Always a handful of scholarships each year – art and music as well as academic.

Remarks: Think purple. Think elegant. Think Glendower. Natty purple berets, charming purple checked and striped uniform, purple website, purple chairs and folders in the class rooms, purple benches and tables in the playground as well as the purple scooters that the girls arrive on. Plush carpets and sweeping staircase in a building that feels much more like a comfortable home than a school. The 1830s white building – Thomas Cundy III? – on Queen's Gate occupies a large corner plot facing Stanhope Gardens. Part of the adjacent building integrated with the school through a major development and refurbishment programme. The resulting six storey building is remarkably spacious. An airy, panelled and white-painted entrance hall, complete with wonderful large Quentin Blake originals, greets the visitor and is also used, with the doors opened to the adjacent library, as an assembly space. Library attractive and well-stocked. Excellent displays of work everywhere, lots of up-to-the-minute equipment in all rooms, which are remarkably orderly with inviting and interesting-looking work and resources.

From the moment you enter Mrs Knollys' study with its oak panelled walls, large Victorian partners' desks and oil portraits on the walls, you know this is a school with history. Founded by two spinsters in 1895, one of whose eyes (Edith Lloyd's) follow you around the room from above the fireplace, Glendower is a charitable trust, and has always been run as a not-for-profit organisation. A nostalgic relief as spanking new profit-making companies pop up throughout the city, establishing expensive schools to meet demand.

Girls get lots of attention here. One teacher/assistant to 11 girls, class sizes of between 16 and 18. Not a school for those with serious SENs but school will pick up and support those with mild difficulties and make individual learning plans for those who need them. Between five and 10 per cent of girls are on the SEN register, more are being monitored. No stigma, just lots of support. There's a handwriting club during lunch break, some who have been diagnosed dyscalculic get support from outside – Emerson House for example; a learning support assistant will go into the classroom to give support with organisational/processing skills etc. No extra charge for this. Some five per cent come needing a little extra help with English and EFL is given in small groups or one-to-one as needed. Parents a real mix, US, Chinese, European – lots of bilingual, trilingual, English as a fourth language – but they are here for the duration – not much to-ing and fro-ing. Specialist teaching right from the start – French, music, drama and PE, and by year 4 almost all teaching is specialist. The academic programme includes DT and ICT, and Mrs Knollys is no Luddite – plans afoot to introduce tablets in the classrooms. Science is well-equipped and busy. The girls enthused about identifying cells under a microscope using iodine.

The post 11 plus programme is excellent and includes touch typing, Latin and lots of public speaking – balloon debating competitions against other schools is a popular one. Poetry competitions all through the school, poems recited by heart, girls vote for the winners and finals judged by eg famous actresses and poets. Lots of music – and the twice weekly music assemblies can feature anything from Bollywood dancing to a harp recital. Most girls play at least one instrument and many take musical theatre exams. 'Music is as natural as breathing here,' glows Mrs Knollys. 'No-one is concerned about performing and there are no divas.' This school is no slouch when it comes to sport either, despite having no grounds to speak of. They are fiendish at netball and compete at national level as well as against other local schools and among themselves in inter-house matches. We saw several girls snatch some precious moments during break to practise their shooting skills. Theatrical productions and swimming take place at Imperial College, athletics in Chiswick. The girls also play tennis and rounders. Lunch: 'we are no longer vegetarian!' – another change introduced by the attentive Mrs Knollys. Fish on Fridays. Only vegetarian options on Mondays but the rest of the week meat galore. Food cooked fresh on the premises and they eat in their own dining room – no packed lunches here – hurrah!

Godolphin & Latymer

Iffley Road, London W6 0PG

Pupils: 780 • Ages: 11–18 • Sixth form: 215

Fees: £20,148 pa

Tel: 020 8741 1936
Email: registrar@godolphinandlatymer.com
Website: www.godolphinandlatymer.com

Head Mistress: Since 2009, Mrs Ruth Mercer BA (50s). A grammar school girl from Preston, she read history at Bedford College, trained as a teacher at Oxford, and began her teaching career at a state school in Liverpool. Arrived at Godolphin & Latymer as deputy head in 1998, took up a headship at Northwood College where she stayed for seven years, then back to Godolphin, this time in the top job. Married to the deputy head of an Ealing comprehensive, with a grown up son and daughter.

Brisk, forthright, no nonsense, but wholly committed to the girls in her care and to single sex education generally. 'The best schools are those that can focus on the needs of the children they have, and boys and girls have different needs as they go through adolescence.' Gets to know all the new year 7s by rotating teaching history for half a term to each class. Parents praise her as grounded and hands on. 'She cheers the girls on at sports fixtures and helps set up the tables at parents' evenings'; 'The girls respond to her with respect and affection'; 'One of the best headmistresses I have ever met'; 'Very approachable, practical, common sense, progressive, genuine, deals with problems quickly and efficiently'.

Retiring in July 2017. Her successor will be Dr Frances Ramsay MA PGCE DPhil (Oxon) (40s), currently principal of Queen's College London. Educated at co-educational boarding schools, the Dragon, then Oakham, she read history at Oxford and her doctorate is in medieval history. Prior to becoming principal here at Queen's College, she was director of studies at Westminster School and master of the Queen's Scholars for 17 years. Parents at Queen's spoke of her 'vision' and her presence – 'she is always there', said one, 'and available,' said another. Married to Christopher, who is a professor of archaeological science at Oxford and has two teenage children. She is a keen horsewoman and rides on most weekends, enjoys alpine skiing and likes to visit historical sites.

Academic matters: Extremely impressive. In 2016, 94 per cent A*/A at GCSE, 77 per cent A*/A at A level, and a stellar points average of 40 for the IB, with one student achieving the maximum possible of 45. Even more impressively, this is achieved without (too much) pressure. All the parents we contacted were adamant that the school successfully balanced high academic standard with a rounded and friendly environment. 'Our daughter achieved straight A*s at GCSE whilst playing netball for the school, performing in school productions, and having a great time with her friends,' wrote one father. The school doesn't have a prize-giving because, they say, it isn't part of the G&L culture to single girls out for academic achievement: 'It's celebrated and praised, but we want the girls to take responsibility for their own successes.' The girls agree. 'We're worked hard here, but in a good way,' reported one. A parent confirmed, 'There is a competitive atmosphere in the school, and the expectations of the girls themselves are very high, but I think much of this is driven by the girls themselves, and I have not seen any undue pressure from the staff.' 'The amount of homework set is very manageable and appears to be less than other comparable schools,' added one mother.

Humanities continue popular, with a high take-up of subjects like English, history and philosophy. Interesting language curriculum: compulsory Mandarin in year 7, plus Latin, plus optional French, German or Spanish. The following year girls can drop the Mandarin, but only if they take up another language. From year 10 they can study Russian, Italian and Greek. Maths and science are strong and at least a third of the sixth form chooses to continue with them. 'The beauty of a girls' school is that the girls want to do everything,' says head, who is adamant that she would never consider bringing boys in at this stage.

Around 30 per cent of sixth formers opt to do the IB, which is now in its 10th year here, and Mrs Mercer admits to being a fan: 'I think it's a great programme, a philosophy of education rather than individual syllabuses tacked together.'

School says that it's 'very happy to receive applications from students with individual learning needs' – the term SEN isn't used here – and there are two members of staff employed to support them. That said, we have to add that not a single current parent of the many we contacted mentioned any such issues, suggesting that few girls here need this kind of help; and given the school's very selective intake, this many not be the place for pupils with more than mild difficulties. Parents of a recent leaver, however, were extremely positive that their daughter – who went on to one of the top universities – had received 'marvellous' support for her dyslexia from G&L staff, and were the more grateful that no charge for this help had ever been made.

All girls here treated as gifted and talented, and the emphasis is firmly on stretching and challenging everyone as far as they can go. It evidently works. As one parent wrote, 'The staff are dedicated to ensuring everyone achieves their potential and willingly give up their time to offer in-school clinics, extra lessons and other help when needed.' Another wrote, 'The amazing results speak for themselves.'

Games, options, the arts: Sport at Godolphin used to have a bit of an exclusivity tag, with parents complaining that their daughters got sidelined if they weren't good enough for the A team. Not any more: the school has worked hard to extend the provision, and the word that both parents and pupils now use to describe it is 'inclusive'. In fact, every parent who contacted us praised the sporting provision and described the sports teachers as 'incredibly dedicated.' Hockey, netball, basketball, tennis, rounders, cricket, gymnastics and athletics are all flourishing, and the number of teams has dramatically increased to around 12 per year group. The school already boasts a full size Astroturf hockey pitch, three netball courts and 12 tennis courts, but there's more to come. A new £6m sports centre offers badminton courts, volleyball, trampolining, a climbing wall, fitness room and a dance studio. Lots of extracurricular options on offer too, such as rowing, pilates, squash, fencing, karate, kickboxing and yoga, plus dance options including zumba, hip-hop and street. No pool in the new centre – to include one would have put completion back by another five years – but the girls we spoke said they were fine with it. 'If I want to swim, I go swimming!' was the prevailing view, and there's certainly enough else to do.

Music and drama have always been strong at Godolphin, and continue to be so, although oddly enough none of the parents we spoke to said much about them, choosing to concentrate on the sport instead. The Rudland Music School, with its contemporary glass frontage, is home to state-of-the-art facilities. Lots of choirs, bands and ensembles for girls to join, and opportunities to learn all the usual range of instruments. Several drama productions a year, some of them student-led, and everyone has a chance to get involved. These are staged in the Bishop Centre (named after a former headmistress), formerly St John's Church and now a marvellous multi-purpose performance space, with flexible staging and seating expertly deployed by the school's own dedicated theatre technicians. Speech and drama exams are a popular extracurricular choice.

Art, housed in a pleasingly scruffy corridor with paint-splattered walls, is clearly flourishing, with some wonderful work on display, and lots of girls choosing to take the subject for GCSE and A level. Loads of clubs on offer, covering everything serious and non-serious – we thought the Inaccurate Classical Film Society looked great fun – and the school arranges a remarkable 150 trips a year to every conceivable destination. Plenty of opportunities for community work, and all year 11s get involved with Model United Nations. School is non-denominational, but has a strong Christian society.

Background and atmosphere: Built as a boarding school for boys in 1861 and called simply the Godolphin School, it became an independent day school for girls in 1905, hooked up with the Latymer Foundation and was re-named Godolphin & Latymer. A few decades of state-aided existence followed, until it was threatened with going comprehensive in 1977, and, rather than lose its academically selective ethos, it reverted to being fully independent again.

The walk from bustling Hammersmith is short, but the streets become abruptly quieter and leafier, and stepping into the school grounds is like entering a time-warp: red-brick Victorian tranquility was our first impression, quickly succeeded by admiration at the school's ultra-modern thumbing-in system. These contrasts abound throughout the site and create much of Godolphin's undeniable charm. The school hall – far too small for whole school assemblies these days – is delightfully old-fashioned, and adorned with traditional honours boards celebrating scholastic achievement; the library is a miracle of modern planning in a limited space, offering different rooms for silent, quiet or collaborative study. Sixth form common room and study areas on the top floor are light, airy, well-equipped, and obviously used by the girls with relish and affection. Facilities everywhere have been tastefully incorporated alongside the original buildings, and the effect is an enticing blend of monastic calm and youthful buzz. A lovely garden, complete with pond, is used by the girls for quiet reading.

An average of 23 pupils per class, slightly high for an independent school, but no sense of pupils being packed in. Everyone praised the friendly, supportive and lively atmosphere. Dolphins, as they're known here, are an eager and zesty bunch, joining in and seizing the opportunities here with both hands. One mother summed it up: 'A lively group of competitive girls, all with different talents, but sharing a great enthusiasm for life.'

Pastoral care, well-being and discipline: Previously not rated that highly by parents, but as with the sports, the school has worked hard to raise its game in this area. There are two tutors per form group and the emphasis is on celebrating every kind of achievement. The result? 'Fair to outstanding, depending on the staff involved,' was one parent's verdict, but they all said how happy their daughters were and how much they loved their school. 'My daughter feels empowered and respected by the school. She feels the school belongs to her, not that she is a minion that belongs to it'; 'Pastoral care is diagnostic, not just a knee jerk reaction,' were typical comments. Communication with parents, once a source of complaints, is now almost universally rated as excellent.

Behaviour is relaxed, 'but there's no mucking about,' according to the students. No uniform for sixth formers, who are able to wear jeans provided they look 'appropriate'. For the rest of the school the uniform is modern, smart and smartly worn.

The variety and quality of the food came in for particular praise, with all parents and students seeing this as a vital part of caring properly for busy girls, and we can confirm that the smoked salmon and cream cheese bagels were wonderful.

Pupils and parents: As you would expect in this part of London, parents are hardworking, professional, mostly affluent, and ambitious for their daughters. Considerable cultural diversity, with numbers of students speaking more than one language, but inevitably less social mix than there used to be before the abolition of assisted places. Girls are confident, articulate, cheerful, and full of self-belief without being arrogant.

Entrance: Competitive, and becoming more so each year. At 11+, 820 applicants for 110 places, but school aims to keep the admissions process as fair as possible. School is part of the North London Consortium so uses their English and maths papers for the entrance tests, and every applicant is given two interviews. School looks for 'curiosity and a willingness to think for yourself: girls who are going to enjoy the learning experience here.' Emphasis also placed on primary school report. No guarantee of sibling places – girls have to be able to cope with the pace of lessons here – but, says head, 'I will always look very carefully at siblings, and for occasional places siblings are given priority.' About 25 per cent of girls come from the state sector.

At 16+ around 12-15 places available, all of them keenly competed for.

Exit: A small number – around 10 per cent – leave after GCSE to board, or to co-ed sixth forms at schools such as Westminster. At 18, almost everyone to university: 17 to Oxbridge in 2016, 12 to the USA/Canada, and pretty much all the rest to Russell Group institutions, including Imperial College.

Money matters: Music scholarships available at 11+ and 16+, art scholarships at 16+ only, worth anything up to 50 per cent of the fees. Around 10 per cent of girls on means-tested bursaries. Owing to its history as a state grammar, the school has no endowment, and the bursary fund exists solely through fundraising.

Remarks: To have your daughter offered a place here is a real gift. As one parent expressed it, 'I am a huge fan of Godolphin & Latymer. I have two daughters there, both very different girls, and both have really thrived.'

Grafton Primary School

Eburne Road, Holloway, London N7 6AR

Pupils: 532 • Ages: 3–11

Tel: 020 7272 3284
Email: graftonschool@grafton.islington.sch.uk
Website: www.graftonschool.co.uk

Head: Since 1993, Mrs Nitsa Sergides OBE (awarded in 2012 for services to education), 60s. Qualified as a teacher in 1973, followed by 19 years of teaching at another local school. Became deputy head of Grafton Primary in 1991, and head two years later.

Cypriot born Nitsa (as everyone calls her) is the embodiment of Mediterranean warmth. Her pupils adore her, 'lovely to all of us, talks to us like family.' Her teachers are loyal (incredibly low turnover of staff) and parents marvel at her dedication: 'She's quite amazing, her enthusiasm never wanes and she genuinely wants the best for everybody.' 'She is truly exceptional. Apart from her incredibly nurturing side, she has a gift of being able to get hold of every resource going for the school.'

Nitsa came to the UK at the age of 13 with teaching firmly on her radar; 'I think I was 7 when I realised that's what I wanted to be.' Now in her third decade at Grafton School, she still wants to make a difference. 'I believe that children must be given every chance to succeed regardless of background or ethnicity. We try to create opportunities some pupils may not otherwise have.' This could be a yearly trip to the coast (which for some pupils is their first experience of the sea), or the chance to learn a musical instrument.

One of Nitsa's proudest achievements is that she hasn't had to exclude a child for 11 years, 'I always believe more in preventative measures rather than reactive measures.' She also believes that, given the correct guidance, inner-city schools can be as good as any: 'My three children are all products of Islington comprehensives. My son is now a neurosurgeon and both my daughters are barristers.' Married for 40 years to an engineer, 'my bouncing board', she loves visiting art galleries and museums and spending time with her grandchildren. Such is her infectious enthusiasm that we left her office grinning.

Entrance: Standard local authority criteria of siblings, proximity to school and children in care etc. Competition for places is fierce – most recently 354 applicants for 60 places. As word spreads about this school there is concern about wealthier parents buying property in now trendy Holloway to get their kids a place, with predictable consequences for Grafton's rich diversity.

Exit: Mixed bag on offer for secondary schools in the Islington area. Most go on to Acland Burghley (if they live close enough), Highbury Fields, Highbury Grove, Mount Carmel school for girls, St Mary Magdalene and others including Islington Arts school, Central Foundation Boys' School, Camden School for Girls, Highgate Wood, Parliament Hill and William Ellis. A few try for grammars like Latymer or Dame Alice Owen and independents such as City of London.

Remarks: A tricky one to find, Grafton Primary sits adjacent to the Holloway Road, off Seven Sisters Road, accessible by car via a tiny slip road. Most pupils walk to school thereby avoiding the perils of Holloway's one-way system.

We were expecting great things and we weren't disappointed. Rated outstanding by Ofsted for the past 10 years and awarded the title of Beacon School, Grafton defies its demographics. A staggering 55-60 per cent of its pupils would qualify for free school meals (although in Islington, these are fully funded for all pupils), 25 per cent of children have SEN, 12 per cent with statements. Grafton is genuinely inclusive – big on equal opps for pupils with disabilities and a vast ethnic mix. One pupil told us, 'I have friends from so many different cultures and we are like a big family.' We heard the word 'family' used frequently and there is definitely a sense of unity and loyalty as well as pride in this school.

Grafton has recently become a teaching school, meaning that it now trains teachers and support staff from other primaries. It is also one of only a few pioneering schools to have been chosen to introduce the CAME maths programme (Cognitive Acceleration through Mathematics Education), which promises to have a significant impact on both pupil and teacher development. Maths is already a very strong subject at Grafton. Up to 20 per cent of year 6 achieve a level 6 in maths Sats.

On entering one is immediately struck by the spectacularly colourful lobby. Rarely have we seen so much artwork, sculpture, ceiling displays (including a wonderful tree of life installation which ran the length of the lobby and through the school's office). Grafton has partnerships with art professionals, a specialist art and design teacher and an artist in residence, believing that time given to creative subjects helps children achieve in other areas.

The interior of the school is charming, if a little cramped (could be because every inch of space is covered with student displays). The Victorian building is DDA compliant and has a lift for wheelchair users. A £3.5m refurb means all classrooms are now up to spec and there's a new sports hall and reception play area. Library is still a work in progress but promises to be a great space.

Outside is an oasis of calm – amazing, considering proximity to the very urban and not very pretty Seven Sisters Road. Grounds are fairly large for an inner-city school and in addition to the playground there is a quiet formal garden with benches for students to have lunch and read (undergoing a refurb during our visit) and a wildlife garden. This mini eco system with pond and bug hotel feels a million miles from the city. 'Many parents volunteer their time in the garden and elsewhere', we are told. At the end of the wildlife garden is a glass building that we thought was a greenhouse; it's actually the art room, a quirky space crammed with creative materials.

In the assembly hall we were treated to a music assembly in Swahili, just one of the 34 languages spoken here. On site translators assist parents from the three main non-English speaking groups – Somalian, Turkish and Bangladeshi, and the school told us, 'We do what we can to make parents from all sectors of society feel included.'

The pupils we met were a highly articulate bunch – happy, confident and engaging. They loved their school and the opportunities it offers. One told us, 'Julia Donaldson has visited the school and some Paralympians came to talk to us, which was amazing and inspiring.' Another said he loved the cricket and football 'and we've won many tournaments.' A few negative comments about the lunches (free of charge for all pupils) and we thought that some of the food did look pretty unappetising. It seems almost churlish to mention this when for some pupils it may be the only cooked meal they get in a day.

Parents and pupils generally seemed extremely happy with their school. One parent did mention that she would like more sporting activities within the school day as opposed to just afternoon clubs, although she added that the Grafton school day is such a busy one, she's not sure where they would fit it in. Another told us, 'The school is amazing at being proactive, especially with day trips. If they're not hopping on the bus to St Paul's Cathedral, visiting the zoo or going to art galleries and museums, they're doing a walking tour around London. That's the benefit of being so inner city with free bus travel.' The quality of teaching came in for particular praise. One mother told us, 'My older children go to private schools and I know that the teaching my youngest is getting here is better than they received at her age.' She also said that there is a very high ratio of staff to pupils – 1:6 in the first two years – again, as good, as if not better than at some independent schools.

Graveney School

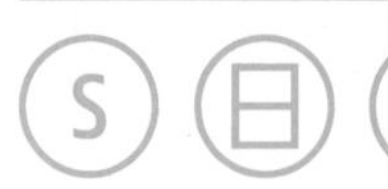

89

Welham Road, London SW17 9BU

Pupils: 1,947 • Ages: 11–18 • Sixth form: 679

Tel: 020 8682 7000
Email: info@graveney.wandsworth.sch.uk
Website: www.graveney.org

Principal: Since 1989, Mr Graham Stapleton MA (60s). Read history at Cambridge and started teaching at the school 40 years ago when it was Battersea Grammar School. Married with two grown-up children, his hobbies include reading (20th century American novels) and listening to soul and jazz. He has the air of a history professor about him. No immediate plans to retire as he wants to stay and oversee the new Tooting Primary School and the building of a new sixth form block. 'Fantastic and inspiring', declared one parent. 'He really cares about each and every student'.

Academic matters: School is regarded as one of the top 200 state schools in the country. In 2016, 58 per cent A*/B grades at A level, with 33 per cent A*/A. Thirty-five subjects available at A level – English literature the most popular and film studies recently added to the list. In 2016, 84 per cent of pupils obtained five or more A*-C grades including maths and English at GCSE, with 48 per cent A*/A grades. Focus is on the academic subjects. Some 85 per cent of students take triple sciences. RE is a compulsory GCSE. All students study a foreign language – French, Spanish or German (with Latin and Mandarin available as twilight subjects – before or after school).

Pupils are divided into ability bands as soon as they enter the school in year 7. They are banded largely by English scores and then set for maths from year 8 onwards. Extension programme for those nominated by teachers (includes PE, music and art as well as English, maths and science). Some concern from potential parents about what school is like for those who don't get into the top band (extension group), but anecdotes from current parents say that the next band (upper) is also very high achieving. 'Whichever band your child is in, the teachers will push them to achieve their best', said one mother. 'They seem to have a knack of finding out what motivates your child and then encouraging them'. There is movement between the bands so no need to panic if your child is not in the extension group. However, some parents complain about the high number of students in the extension classes – up to 33 in some cases.

Large number of students with special needs (55 with statements/EHC plans) – 'because we have such a good reputation', explains the principal. SENCo and various learning mentors look after these students.

Games, options, the arts: Everyone is encouraged to take part in team sport and play for their form or house. Sports include rugby, football, volleyball, netball, cricket, tennis, athletics and basketball. One parent complained that there is only one timetabled session of games per week but principal stresses that all students are encouraged to take part in one extracurricular sports club after school. Even PE classes are streamed, so students get chance to play with others of similar ability.

School puts a special emphasis on music. All children eligible for free school meals get free music tuition. Around 350 learn an instrument at school (taught by peripatetic teaching staff) and more learn outside school. Each year around five students are members of the London Schools Symphony Orchestra and some students go on to study music at university or music college. School orchestra has 40 students, and choir has 70. All encouraged to take part in a musical event or production. When we visited, rehearsals were in full swing for annual sixth form production – Annie Get your Gun (with 200 students taking part).

Background and atmosphere: School is spread out over two campuses so despite its size (around 2,000 students) it doesn't feel overcrowded. Formerly a teacher training college, the original Georgian building (now rather scruffy) houses the art department. Other buildings have been added on over the years. School was due for refurbishment before government budget cuts so now looks rather tired. However, new RIBA award winning sixth form block.

When we visited at break time, students were orderly and well behaved. Pupils all stood up when principal entered class – emphasis on good old-fashioned manners. No lockers, so pupils have to carry everything round with them, complained one parent.

School meals fantastic – delicious food and good selection, though some grumbles about the lengths of the queues. New lavatories for boys and girls (replacing the 'rather ghastly' previous ones) were built during 2014.

Pastoral care, well-being and discipline: Teachers really do seem to care about each and every student. When we visited we came across the head of art berating an A level student for not completing his coursework. Afterwards she confided, 'he'll get an A* but he needs to understand that he has to put in the work.' This attention to detail is followed through at all levels. We also met a year 11 student being mentored by the principal to ensure that he gains the all-important five A*-C grades at GCSE. 'Are you making sure your homework is handed in on time?' he enquired. 'Mostly', mumbled the student.

Pastoral care is very good and students with difficulties are mentored by students higher up the school who have been through the same experiences.

Pupils and parents: Parents include middle class arty types and a good cross-section of the local community. Pupils in the extension group (those selected by ability) travel from further afield whereas others live locally and walk to school. Pupils are proud to belong to the school. 'Now I'm at Graveney I believe I can do anything', a year 9 student told us proudly.

Alumni include Naga Munchetty, BBC newsreader, and Amol Rajan, editor of The Independent.

Entrance: For year 7 entry all applicants take the Wandsworth year 6 test. This selects 25 per cent of places by ability (63 pupils out of 2,000 who sit the exam), with 75 per cent selected on proximity to school. Sibling policy now applies to all pupils, including ability places (although it does not guarantee a place in the extension group: pupils still have to take the test to see which class they go into).

Students need five GCSE A*-Cs (including maths and English) to stay on into the sixth form. Most do and are joined by an extra 150 (over 1,000 apply for these open places). Sixth form popular with pupils from the private sector, especially from single-sex schools. 'I think they want a more culturally diverse environment', says the head, 'and of course at that age they want to meet the opposite sex'.

Exit: Up to 20 per cent leave after GCSEs, perhaps because they haven't achieved the crucial 5+ A*-C grades. Those with poor AS level results are also advised to find alternative courses. Around half to Russell Group universities (including 13 to Oxbridge) in 2016. Some to music, art or drama colleges.

Remarks: Pupils who manage to get in are assured of a top class education in a socially mixed environment. Local parents often turn down places at schools like Alleyn's and Dulwich if their children manage to get places here.

The Grey Coat Hospital

Greycoat Place, London SW1P 2DY

Pupils: 1,055 • Ages: 11–18 • Sixth form: 270 (30 boys) • C of E

Tel: 020 7969 1998
Email: info@gch.org.uk
Website: www.gch.org.uk

Headteacher: Since 2011, Ms Siân Maddrell BA (40s). Educated at Surbiton High, followed by a degree in French at Durham. After gaining her PGCE at Oxford, she began her teaching career at Grey Coat in 1992, soon becoming head of modern languages and one of the first advanced skills teachers in the country. Left Grey Coat in 2000 and later became the first vice principal of Pimlico Academy. Friendly, thoughtful, efficient and clearly devoted to her school. Takes great pride in her pupils and their achievements. Not above picking up stray litter in the playground.

'We want to enable girls to take charge of their learning, make decisions based on Christian values, live in the world as independent women and meet the challenges of the 21st century,' she told us. 'We just try to focus on our pupils. It's a very ambitious school and the students will tell you that the expectations and aspirations are really high for everybody. It's about empowering the pupils to do their best. We want girls to be confident enough to be able to seize every opportunity.'

Enjoys sport, theatre and travel – 'I'm very interested in other countries and cultures.' Married with two sons, so 'most of my free time is spent with my family.'

Academic matters: School is regularly rated outstanding by Ofsted. Recently received congratulatory letter from local MP and schools minister praising pupils and staff for position in the performance tables and saying 'it is clear that your school has equipped its pupils to be successful hereafter, both in terms of their readiness for further study and in terms of their readiness to enter the world of work in due course.'

In 2016, 82 per cent of students gained five or more A*-C GCSEs including English and maths, and 46 per cent of grades were A*/A. Girls take between nine and 13 GCSEs. At A level, an upturn with 64 per cent A*/B and 37 per cent A*/A grades. Grey Coat has recently been in the top 100 non-selective schools in the country in terms of GCSE results and progress. Good range of subjects on offer to GCSE, including Latin, business studies and computing. Pre-U offered in Latin, Greek and art history, all of which are taught at neighbouring Westminster School. 'The pupils love their lessons at Westminster,' the head told us. A level subjects include film studies and sociology as well as more traditional fare. Biology, English, history, maths, psychology and religious studies currently very popular. EPQ is becoming increasingly fashionable.

Grey Coat is a specialist language college and has an outward looking, global focus. 'We encourage an international outlook as well as strong grades,' says the head. 'It is important for our students to gain an understanding of other countries and cultures and to have an open and inclusive approach, as well as to develop their linguistic skills.' All students study Spanish and a second modern language (French or German). Most continue with two foreign languages to GCSE. Opportunities to study Mandarin, Japanese and ancient Greek out of school hours. Japanese exchange offered to girls in year 10; other exchange trips to France and Germany, as well as opportunities for work experience in Germany.

International May Fair for younger pupils is an annual highlight. Students are encouraged to represent a country – through fashion, food, dance, ecology and culture. The competition is judged by staff and the prize, awarded to the most impressive tutor group, is a trip to Paris. School is excellent at offering incentives to pupils; girls are encouraged to be competitive. Pupils regularly win local and national science and maths competitions.

Grey Coat prides itself on being an inclusive school. SEN pupils make good progress academically and are fully involved in school life. All year 7 girls are screened for learning difficulties on entry to school. Small support groups for literacy, numeracy and social skills run at lunchtime for younger girls. Five per cent have a statement of special educational needs. Gifted and talented extension programmes in place for more able.

Average class size is 26, with a maximum of 30. No setting in year 7. Year 8 pupils setted for English, maths, science and languages.

Games, options, the arts: Good level of participation in wide variety of sport. 'We are the Westminster sports champions in practically everything and we provide a rich variety of sports,' says the head. Opportunities for fencing, squash, ice-skating and athletics as well as team sports. Currently Westminster netball champions. 'We've struggled a bit with athletics as we have to bus the pupils over to Battersea Park,' admits bursar. Massive sports hall at Regency Street site. Annual gym and dance display.

Creative subjects taken seriously. Excellent facilities in art and design; these remain very popular subjects and the quality of art displays is very high. 'The standard of art work is mind-blowing,' according to one parent. Music and drama both strong. Instrumental and singing lessons are subsidised by school's foundation. Good range of choirs, bands, string and jazz groups and orchestra. Several concerts every year. Successful gospel choir recently reached semi-finals of BBC's School Choir of the Year competition.

Roughly 15 pupils a year achieve D of E gold award. Good spread of clubs, including maths challenge, debating, football, trampolining and creative writing. External inspirational speakers come in regularly to motivate and encourage the girls. Workshops led by outsiders a regular feature of the education offered here. School takes part in BBC News School Report, enabling pupils to make their own news reports for a live audience. Students develop their journalistic skills and have a ball.

Lots of time for fun here too. Talent show at the end of the Easter term is eagerly anticipated while staff pantomime is apparently 'the best day' of the school year. 'It's absolutely hilarious watching the teachers,' said one pupil. Post-GCSE celebration for year 11s includes a fashion show of their textiles work.

Background and atmosphere: Originally founded for boys – by eight merchants of Westminster on St Andrew's day in 1698. In 1706, Queen Anne granted the Grey Coat Hospital Foundation a royal charter and her portrait hangs in pride of place in the Great Hall. Original wooden boards detailing the names and donations of 18th century benefactors line the stairs. In 1874 Grey Coat Hospital became a girls' school, under church management. Whole school was evacuated during the war and its buildings suffered significant bomb damage.

A C of E school – head says 'Christian values play a key part in what we aim to do here.' Church services held each term either in Westminster Abbey or St Margaret's, including a service on Ash Wednesday and a July celebration to which new pupils (and their parents) are invited. 'It's a lovely event – beautifully done,' said a parent. Confirmation services take place at Westminster Abbey and school has its own chaplain.

School occupies two fabulous buildings in the heart of Westminster. Huge quantity of traffic and people encircling it on the streets outside. Strikingly beautiful building in Greycoat Place, freshly painted and well polished. Statuettes of Grey Coat boy and girl adorn the front façade of the school. Wonderful entrance hall, glistening with trophies and artwork. School celebrates the achievements of the girls at every opportunity. In 1998 the school celebrated its 300th anniversary by opening a new upper school building on Regency Street, having sold another site on Sloane Square.

Original building at Greycoat Place is used by the younger pupils (years 7 to 9) but lots of coming and going of pupils from one site to another. Fantastic new arts block, includes swish drama studios where recent productions have included Shakespearean plays and The Madness of George III. 'Drama is one of those things that is taken very seriously at Grey Coat and the performances are very professional,' we were told. Facilities hired out to National Youth Theatre in holidays.

Welcoming staff. Healthy female/male ratio and mix of long-servers and newly qualified teachers. 'A positive balance,' says the head. Turnover of staff can be high, with up to 20 per cent a year leaving, but 'there's no clear pattern.'

Symbiotic relationship with Westminster School. Grey Coats go there for lectures, some lessons and Oxbridge preparation, while graduate trainee teachers from Westminster come here to gain experience of teaching in a state school. 'It's wonderful for our students that they have these opportunities,' says the head.

Pastoral care, well-being and discipline: Pastoral care is a major strength of the school. 'Each girl is part of a tutor group family and a year group family, so each feels looked after here,' says the head. Strict code of conduct, but relatively few behavioural issues here. Older girls are given plenty of responsibility, with 40 prefects in final year. Girls can become ambassadors for their year group, having successfully explained at interview why they should be chosen. 'There is a strong sense of community here,' says the head. 'We have counsellors, student counsellors, and older students working with younger pupils. It's about creating a sense that we're all in this together.' It certainly seems to be working well. A learning mentor is on hand to help girls organise themselves if needed, as well as a drop-in school nurse.

Girls start off in smaller, lower school – helps them cope better with the progression to upper school. 'It's rare to hear of anyone being miserable here,' a parent told us. 'The school keeps a close eye on its pupils and intervenes quickly if things are going awry.'

Food thought to be 'very good, with lots of choice' according to one pupil. Vast quantities of pizzas being eaten at break on the day we visited. Oyster card system in place so girls don't need to carry money and the canteen is open from breakfast onwards. School is confident that 'we'd know if a girl wasn't eating.'

Head is justifiably proud of the excellent attendance record of 98 per cent throughout the year – rating it the third highest in the UK. 'All our pupils came in when the recent tube strike was on,' says the head. Pupils with 100 per cent attendance and punctuality for a year get a trip to the theatre.

G

Pupils and parents: 'A real mix,' the head told us. Twenty-eight per cent of pupils eligible for pupil premium. Two-thirds from minority ethnic groups. A quarter whose first language is not English – more than 50 languages spoken at home, including Yoruba, Swahili, Spanish, French and Dutch.

Big inner-city blend of families, including daughters of politicians and education professionals. School recently hit the headlines with the news that prominent politicians are sending their daughters here. Old Greys include TV presenter Sarah Greene and Tamsin Dunwoody MP. Recent leaver is Ebony-Jewel Rainford-Brent, the first female black cricketer to play for the England team (she presented awards at last prize-giving). Many old girls remain loyal to the school and return to the annual school celebration service in Westminster Abbey each year.

Entrance: Huge catchment area from the dioceses of London and Southwark. Pupils travel from as far away as Essex and Kent and are rarely local. Total of 151 places offered in year 7. Fifteen language places (following an aptitude test which 450 sit); 88 C of E places; 28 other church places; 20 open places.

Priority given to looked-after children, then siblings, church attendance for church places and a distance tie-breaker. The comprehensive intake is placed into bands following an assessment test – 25 per cent places to band 1, 50 per cent places to band 2 and 25 per cent to band 3. Offers sent out in March.

Open events for year 6 pupils in September and early October each year. Sixth form open events in November. Relatively little movement of pupils. 'We are a very stable population,' says the bursar. Once pupils are here, they tend to stay put, even if it means travelling long distances. In-year admissions are dealt with by the local authority. Some 30-40 boys in sixth form, all 'charming,' according to one member of staff.

Exit: Around a third leave after GCSEs, usually for schools closer to home or offering subjects not available here. Their places are taken by a fresh intake – the head says 'it's a fresh start for all.' Around 90 per cent go on to higher education. School encourages pupils to aim for top universities and some 40 per cent go to Russell Group universities as well as art college. Popular destinations include Oxbridge (four places in 2016), Exeter, St Andrews, Leeds, Durham, Nottingham, Bristol and Manchester. Popular subjects include medicine, sciences, maths, English, religious studies and classics.

Money matters: Parents' Guild raises money each year for both the school and charity. Recently paid for a beautiful stained glass window by Michael Coles. Parents are asked to contribute a small amount of money on a monthly or annual basis.

Remarks: A sensational mix of high academic standards strongly supported by caring and devoted staff. No wonder they are prepared to travel for hours each day to be part of this buzzing school. The girls we met were charming, articulate, interesting and purposeful. Their pride in the school was striking. Not only are they ambitious and successful but they're also happy. On the day we visited, groups of girls were sitting cross-legged on the tarmac playground at break time, chatting and laughing as though they didn't have a care in the world.

Grimsdell, Mill Hill Pre-Prep School

Linked with Belmont Mill Hill Prep School, Mill Hill School

Winterstoke House, Wills Grove, London NW7 1QR

Pupils: 187 • Ages: 3-7

Fees: £6,366 – £13,836 pa

Tel: 020 8959 6884
Email: office@grimsdell.org.uk
Website: www.grimsdell.org.uk

Head: Since 2014, Mrs Kate Simon (40s). A current Grimsdell parent, Mrs Simon is no stranger to headship. Between 2002 and 2008 she was head of the junior school of the Royal School, Hampstead (now incorporated into North Bridge Senior) and from 2008 was head of Girls' Upper School at Garden House School in Chelsea.

Entrance: Heavily oversubscribed, due in part to it being non-selective at age 3 or 4. 'I don't feel comfortable with failing children at that age', says the head. Most pupils come from within a five mile radius and there is a 'multi-cultural mix.'

Exit: The majority of pupils continue on to Belmont school. However, if the school feels that a child won't cope there, discussions about alternatives take place from year 1. 'We have to be realistic', the school says.

Remarks: Unfortunate name for a very pretty school. On a beautiful autumnal day, Grimsdell was the antithesis of 'grim'. Situated on Mill Hill's Ridgeway, but accessed via a small and very lovely private road, the school occupies the rather grand Winterstoke House. Originally a vicarage for the vicar of St Paul's and sold to Mill Hill School in October 1923, Winterstoke House was purchased to become a school boarding house to host some 42 boys.

The school became Grimsdell in 1995 – a newcomer compared to the other two schools in the Foundation. The reason for its formation was largely due to a Mrs Grimsdell, widow of an Old Millhillian, who bequeathed a large part of her late husband's estate to Mill Hill School. Following a request from the school governors, Mrs Grimsdell agreed that the benefaction be applied to create a 'much required' pre-preparatory school, and Grimsdell opened its gates. The school is situated adjacent to Mill Hill School but has its own grounds – not quite on the scale of the other two schools, but more than adequate for a pre-prep school.

This is a cute, cosy school. Nothing grand and pretentious, despite the impression given by its exterior. We were seated in a colourful and bright reception area with a large aquarium to gaze at while we waited to meet the head. Familiar sounds of over-excited kids emanated from one or two of the classrooms (and we were particularly struck by one over-zealous music teacher doing something very strange with her arms!)

All classrooms were light, airy and well equipped – particularly the Sunshine Room, which even in its name suggests something warm and nurturing. This is where pupils who need it go for extra one-to-one learning support. Specialist on-site teachers in music, PE and French are on hand and 4 to 7-year-olds have weekly keyboard lessons with a music specialist. The swimming pool at Mill Hill School is a great addition to the PE curriculum. Pupils use the theatre at Mill Hill School for concerts and performances. Cursive handwriting is taught from the start and we were quite amazed with the standard of year 1 handwriting displayed on classroom walls.

As with Belmont and Mill Hill School, Grimsdell's selling point is undoubtedly its idyllic surroundings. Pupils not only have access to 120 acres of beautiful parkland at Mill Hill school with its sports pitches, swimming pool and woodland, but they have their own great adventure playground and science garden to enjoy. A firm believer in the great outdoors, Grimsdell has its own forest school. Each session has a theme and activities can range from mini-beast hunting to fire building and cooking outdoors. With a school that states boldly in its prospectus 'there is no such thing as bad weather, just bad clothing', you had better be sure your little darlings have a healthy interest in outdoor pursuits. Forget this school otherwise – indeed discount the other two schools in the Foundation while you are at it.

Parents appreciate the expertise of the large Foundation, and the lack of pressure to take exams for future schools. One parent told us, 'Grimsdell is a secure and nurturing stepping-stone, which is illustrated by my own excited and eager children.'

Gumley House School FCJ

92

St John's Road, Isleworth TW7 6XF

Pupils: 1,125 • Ages: 11–18 • Sixth form: 200 (including 9 boys) • RC

Tel: 020 8568 8692
Email: general@gumley.hounslow.sch.uk
Website: www.gumley.hounslow.sch.uk

Headteacher: Since September 2016, Caroline Braggs, previously deputy head for 13 years. Read theology at Heythrop College, London University and then PGCE at the Institute of Education and MA at St Mary's College, University of Surrey. Extensive experience at three other Catholic schools before joining Gumley. A Ugandan Asian, arrived in Britain as a refugee with her family at the age of 6. Hobbies include theatre, travel and reading; school community reportedly delighted with the appointment.

Academic matters: For a non-selective state school, very good results. Compares extremely favourably with local and national averages. In 2016, 51 per cent A*-B and 22 per cent A*-A grades at A level. At GCSE, 81 per cent achieved 5+ A*-C grades including English and maths (59 per cent A*-A grades). Designated as a high performing specialist school and has a languages specialism. First school in the borough to teach Mandarin (taught all the way through from year 7 to 13).

Very committed to special needs and disability provision. Three fully qualified teachers and 14 learning support assistants. SEN catered for include physical difficulties and learning difficulties including ASD, dyslexia and and speech and language needs. To make sure they miss nobody, school's policy is to screen for literacy at the start of year 7 and organise support as appropriate throughout years 7-11 eg literacy tuition, in-class support, reading clubs or monitoring. Wheelchair access throughout the school seen as part of ethos. Sixth formers involved in helping younger pupils.

Important links with world of work. School's director of global learning and communication organises critical skill and competency development through programmes such as Young Reporter and science and enterprise projects with Imperial College, where girls compete with other schools. 'We want to prepare our students fully for the commercial and globalised world,' she explains. The school's motto is Vive Ut Vivas (live that you may have life) and the school extols this to the full with partnerships with schools in Africa, India, China and Singapore.

Games, options, the arts: Netball, hockey and athletics very strong – school regularly wins all local tournaments and pupils compete at county level. Eight tennis courts, all-weather surface hockey/football pitch set in spacious 10 acres. Dance and fitness studio (very popular) and two drama studios. Thriving orchestra (has performed at European venues) and plethora of private instrument lessons on offer. Annual art exhibitions, drama productions, poetry festivals – some of which are open to community groups and partners.

All extracurricular clubs (including science, debating, languages, geography, drama, art and sport) are free. The only extras parents have to pay for are LAMDA classes and private music lessons – 'but we do have money available for those on free school meals,' says the school.

Background and atmosphere: Founded in 1841 as a school and convent by the Faithful Companions of Jesus. The Queen Anne house, surrounded by lovely grounds, creates a peaceful oasis in west London. Superbly equipped library in former chapel (just the place for inspired contemplation) and sensational octagonal assembly hall for whole school events, plus school chapel for quiet sanctuary as well as worship. 'The school even has its own cemetery, which is unique,' said one parent.

Pastoral care, well-being and discipline: School prides itself on discipline. Truancy is very rare and school/home links are strong. Distinctive uniform – 'the colour brown is so unflattering, though,' complained one mother, although the school commented: 'The uniform can be brightened up by the striped blazer.'

Strong emphasis on religious, spiritual and moral formation of pupils. Very supportive staff. Two part-time counsellors (who make up one full-time post) and two pastoral managers support the heads of year. 'We have a zero policy on bullying but if it occurs we have very clear procedures and it's dealt with justly.' Special IT system to detect internet bullying. Peer mentors are trained to help younger students and look after the year 7 students particularly well.

School offers great support for students coping with exams. One mother told us that when her year 10 daughter was finding the workload difficult her head of year organised relaxation classes for any girls who were feeling stressed. 'It's not just about results,' she said. 'They really make sure that the whole person is happy.'

Pupils and parents: The catchment area covers a wide area of west London (from Hillingdon to Twickenham) so a broad mix of intake and 63 feeder schools. Majority of girls from Hounslow and Ealing, with others coming from Richmond,

Hammersmith and Fulham, Hillingdon and even Southwark. Sixty-four languages spoken – main one is Polish. Parents/ Carers are asked to make voluntary contributions for the school development fund.

'Our vision is of a Gumley family'; many former pupils send their daughters to the school. Parents concurred. 'Even though there are over 1,000 girls at the school, it doesn't feel that big and you feel that your child is looked after,' one parent told us. 'I can't recommend it highly enough,' said another.

Entrance: Non-selective academically at the age of 11 – but girls and their parents must be practising Roman Catholics (baptism certificate and written proof required from parish priest) and must attend mass every Sunday. Other entrance criterion is distance from school. School is heavily oversubscribed but places sometimes come up for non-Catholics so it's worth getting on the waiting list. Open policy with no faith requirement for year 12 (including boys – there is currently 40 in the sixth form including consortium students but students need to have five A* -Cs at GCSE and Bs in the subjects they wish to study at A level (for maths they need A*/A).

Exit: One to Cambridge in 2016; others to a range including many top universities to study eg medicine, engineering, biochemistry, Chinese, economics, architecture and languages.

Some students go for gap years or apprenticeships.

Money matters: Schools asks for voluntary contributions.

Remarks: A very caring school in lovely surroundings that achieves good results. Well worth a visit.

Haberdashers' Aske's Hatcham College

93

Pepys Road, London SE14 5SF

Pupils: 2,191 • Ages: 3–18 • Sixth form: 297

Tel: 020 7652 9510
Email: hreception@haaf.org.uk
Website: www.haaf.org.uk

Principal: Since 2008, Mr Declan Jones LLB PGCE NPQH (50s). A man totally in love with, and at ease with, his chosen sphere – 'this is an exceptionally exciting time to be in education,' he says. Grew up in Ireland, read law at Birmingham, then travelled the world for three years teaching English as a foreign language. Settled into a PGCE on his return and taught at various London comprehensives before coming to Hatcham in 1999 as curriculum manager. Became deputy head in due course, and was instrumental in expanding 'The Hatcham Brand' across Lewisham. Became acting head, then head in 2008, leading the school to its first outstanding Ofsted. Married with two teenage daughters.

A music lover, who is, in his words, 'very privileged to be principal here.' Extremely proud of the way the school has invested in children's musical ability. Particularly enthusiastic about the school's choirs: 'it pulls people together, because you're participating in a sound you can't make on your own.' A particular interest in 'growing your own' led to Hatcham becoming an all-through school in 2008 by taking on the then failing Monson Primary and turning it into an outstanding school in three years.

It's impossible not to be enthused by his passion for the school and his pride in its achievements. A number of parents, however, commented that he was rather remote from their day-to-day experience of the school, and that they saw more of the vice principal.

Head of primary phase: Since September 2015, Emily Gyimah, previously deputy head at Hatcham Temple Grove. Degree in primary education from Brunel; spent two years as a KS1/KS2 class teacher at Monson primary school and then taught for five years as a KS1 and literacy leader at Hatcham Temple Grove. She was then promoted to Haberdashers' Aske's Federation phonics consultant, a position she held for three successful years before returning to HTG in 2014 as deputy head.

Academic matters: On of the primary phase's unique selling points (the other is its music) is its German immersion programme, which pupils begin in year 1. According to the school, the children are taught for half a day, every day, in German, and staff with ability to speak German are actively recruited. It's had a big impact on the children's academic performance. 'Our phonics results went through the roof, because German is very phonic in the way it's spoken' with 'skilled and fluent German speakers coming up through the school ranks.' This is all excellent stuff, and we were thrilled to have 'Heads, shoulders, knees and toes' sung to us in German by a flaxen-haired child of 6 who could have stepped straight out of Hamlyn. Every primary parent we spoke to, however, told us a different story. 'My son's been doing it for two years now, and he can only tell me the nouns. He doesn't have any better grasp of German than if he'd been taught it in the usual way,' said one parent. Another said: 'It was sold to us as an German immersion programme, that they'd be taught in German every afternoon, but in reality, it's turned out to be a couple of afternoons a week and it's teaching things like colours and days of the week. It isn't immersion.' Even the most enthusiastic of school supporters said: 'I don't really know if they teach the German – just once in a while, maybe.' Quite a mismatch. School please note.

In 2016, 70 per cent of students got 5+ A*-C grades at GCSE, including maths and English, and 27 per cent of grades were A*/A. Very good results, the best in four years, at GCSE, though a decline at A level: 43 per cent A*-B, 19 per cent A*/A.

Parents are generally satisfied, with most reporting that academic standards are good. 'Homework is prolific,' said one parent, adding, 'but it's mostly well thought through, well explained and supports classwork.' One parent was unhappy, reporting that their very bright child was 'constantly bored during lessons' and that 'the curriculum, especially in science and maths, is very basic, and the teachers, with a few exceptions, are not willing to take pupils beyond it.' The school contests this: 'We have the experience to help G&T children to get on,' and the leavers' destinations are certainly good. Principal adds: 'We run The Brilliant Club for our academically able students. You join in year 9, and you're assigned a PhD student [from Goldsmith's over the road] and given a task to do.'

Wide range of languages – year 7s get to choose two from German, French, Spanish, Mandarin and Latin, and higher up the school there are opportunities to learn classical Greek. Sixth form courses are 'strongly academic' – no BTecs offered, only A levels; the IB was explored but rejected as not inclusive enough for HAHC students.

Our impression was that the academic performance is very creditable given the non-academically selective intake, and that the school is both enriched and held up to critical scrutiny by a highly articulate parent body who expect the best and give no quarter when they don't get it.

Games, options, the arts: The school has its own sports centre in Nunhead, and students can do cricket, basketball, volleyball, football, netball and rugby (when we visited, the rugby team were about to head off to play another Haberdashers' school in Monmouth). Sport plays an active part in the junior school curriculum, with basketball, athletics, swimming and football on offer and funding awarded for Saturday and after-school provision. School adroitly links this with academic achievement – 'you have to be in the reading group to be in Saturday football.' The Little Leaders Group offers leadership exercises for children who don't get out much at home. Plenty of trips: river walks, London Eye, museums, visits to the theatre, all helped by an active parent body. Good programme of drama, and children are encouraged to do public speaking in assemblies etc.

The primary phase music was uniformly praised. Class music begins in reception, everyone learns recorder in year 3, and in year 4 those who are progressing well – generally around half of the class – are invited to learn violin, cello or clarinet. 'It's the discipline and the dexterity; and it's much easier in year 4 than when you're an older child.' The lessons are free and all children are allowed to carry on in year 5 if they want to, which at least a third of the year group always do. Those who don't want to continue can still be involved with the junior choir, and the Haberdashers' Livery Company and Temple Grove Trust can award bursaries to parents whose children want to learn other musical instruments outside school. Lots of concerts and the choir busks in Lewisham Shopping Centre to raise money for the 999 Club.

The music in the senior school is astonishing. No other word for it. We see many schools which claim to have marvellous music, but they really do have it here. We sat, open-mouthed, through student performances of Soave il Vento from Cosi Fan Tutte (sung in Italian), Mozart's Divertimento No 1 scored for two clarinets and a bassoon, Bartok's Mikrokosmos on the piano – all of it delivered with exquisite taste, sensitivity, musicality and technique. Then, just as we were preparing to move on, the choir started a ravishing rendition of Lotti's Crucifixus and we sat back down again. 'It's like being at a professional concert,' said the vice principal, with pardonable pride.

Unusually for a state school, classical music takes centre stage here, but it's for the many, not the few. Virtually all the children learn at least one instrument, and the lessons are free. The school abounds with orchestras, chamber music, and choirs of every kind, and there are jazz bands too. Parents were uniformly delighted with this aspect of the school. We heard comments like 'all the music groups are fantastic,' 'there are concerts all the year round, musicals and even a school opera,' 'the music staff teach with ambition, enthusiasm and humour, and my children love it' and 'HAHC is a vibrant place where you are encouraged to fulfil your artistic potential.' We heard a murmur that rock music doesn't get quite the same encouragement, and the school admitted that this might be so. But what is on offer is so amazing, that it's hard to grumble. HAHC choirs provide the music for City Hall's annual Remembrance service as well as carols for Southwark Cathedral. The Haberdashers Company regularly asks school to provide chamber ensembles for events. As the vice principal put it: 'A very good part of this school is that the students gain the cultural capital to function beyond it.'

On a different note, the CCF also flourishes at HAHC, attracting some 160 students, and with a Corps of Drums that is, according to a visiting instructor, 'better than Eton's.'

HAHC is proud of all aspects of its enrichment programme. The school is 'thronged' with students after lessons finish, says vice principal – but parental feedback we received about it was mixed (music excepted). A common complaint was that it was hard to get information about the various clubs and activities and that a number of initiatives, such as Artsmark and D of E, had unravelled due to poor organisation or lack of assessors. 'All a bit half-hearted,' was how one parent described the netball, and another said that her children felt that 'a huge opportunity is being missed in terms of sport.. things just don't get organised.' These concerns were at odds with the school's excellent facilities and range of provision offered. Principal robustly defended the school's record on Artsmark ('I've handed out the certificates in assembly') as well as on sport, and college says that D of E is now thriving, with a coordinator in place and a plaque awarded by the Duke of Edinburgh recognising the its committment. The students we spoke to seemed happy.

Everyone agrees that debating is strong. Sixth formers have started a tutoring cooperative, coaching students from lower down the school and getting paid for it too. In general, HAHC students seem to gain confidence and skills from what is an unusually broad and intellectually stimulating extracurricular programme.

Background and atmosphere: One of the Haberdashers' 'family' of schools, both state and independent, and one of three schools in the Haberdashers' Aske's Federation, the others being Knight's Academy in Bromley and Crayford Academy in Bexley.

The primary phase was originally Monson Primary School, which was failing. HAHC took it on in 2008 and turned it around in three years. It is now rated outstanding. The school was being extensively refurbished when in 2010 a builder managed to cause a fire that gutted the place. The primary children and staff camped on various floors before moving into the new building in 2015.

Hatcham itself is divided between three sites. Jerningham Road, built in 1889 as a girls' school, now houses years 7 to 9 and is a very pleasing old Victorian red-brick, although some parents were critical of the state of the classrooms and toilets. We weren't shown these areas and can't comment (school says new toilets were installed in the summer of 2016). The older students study at the Pepys Road site, a rather gruelling 15-minute walk up Telegraph Hill. Minibuses shuttle pupils and staff between the various school buildings, all of which appeared well kept, blending tradition (stained glass, honours boards) with bang-up-to-date innovation and décor; in the parts we were shown, at any rate. School is co-educational, but in years 7 to 11 teaching is in single-sex groups wherever possible.

School-home communication much criticised by parents and we ourselves found this a difficult school to make contact with. (New direct lines for each school may help: until recently, all calls to any of the Federation schools had to be routed through the Haberdashers' Aske's Federation office, a system which parents loathed.) School counters that it has a policy that all emails must be replied to within 48 hours, that its communication is 'pretty good and pretty effective' and that all parents receive a handbook at the start of each year. But, acknowledges principal, 'these days there's a need for real-time information.'

Pastoral care, well-being and discipline: Behaviour at HAHC reflects the school's large and diverse intake, but is perfectly fine, and all pupils we spoke to reported feeling safe here. The uniform is smart and smartly worn.

Many people commented on the school's 'good and healthy' atmosphere. 'The children respect the staff and the staff are interested in the children themselves, what their interests are and what makes them tick,' said one mother. Another wrote: 'The atmosphere is friendly and good pastoral care is provided.' The young people we met were courteous, assured and proud of their school. 'It's very welcoming here, I've made a large group of friends,' said one. 'The music department is great at involving everyone'; 'there's a really nice community feel here and the older and younger students talk to each other' were typical comments. Parents report that SEN provision is much improved and HAHC is the borough's school of choice for wheelchair-bound students.

As we walked about the primary phase, this impressed us as a lively, happy and well-behaved community of children. There were a couple of dissenting voices, including one who claimed that if it hadn't been for the automatic entry to HAHC's hugely-oversubscribed secondary phase she would have moved her child to a different school. The majority of parents, however, told us they were very happy with both the academic standards and the pastoral care. 'My daughter loves it – she wants to go even when she's sick,' said one mother, and others agreed. Comments included: 'The teachers are always helpful'; 'well done to all the teachers keeping standards up during all the moving about'; 'the encouragement and welcome my daughter receives has made her time at the school a pleasure,' and, from a mother without much English, 'I think it's a good school, really, really good.'

Pupils and parents: Reflecting the area, this is a very diverse community both socially and culturally, with about 50 per cent of pupils coming from ethnic minorities. As one member of staff dryly observed, at the end of the school day equal numbers turn either right into the Telegraph Hill conservation area, where a five-bedroom house might go for £1.3m, or left towards New Cross and some of the worst social deprivation in London. A number of professional musicians send their children here for the music provision. The school appears genuinely to integrate all its various members successfully. Ofsted recently wrote: 'The promotion of racial harmony within the college's richly diverse community is exemplary.'

Entrance: Two form entry to primary school. Sixty places in reception, with four more available further up the school. Usual state school admissions criteria apply: looked after children, medical needs, siblings, proximity. Oversubscribed. About 25 children come up from the school's own nursery, but parents should be aware that a place at the nursery does not guarantee a place in reception.

Senior school massively over-subscribed, with at least 10 applications for every place. Some 64 pupils from primary phase year 6 have automatic entry. Ten per cent of places allocated on musical aptitude – these pupils are selected by aural test. Otherwise, standard local authority criteria apply: looked-after children, siblings, proximity etc. No longer uses banding. 'Admissions is a hot potato for this school,' admitted the vice principal. Appeals by parents are in excess of 100 each year, but be warned – the school's decisions are almost always upheld, 'because we're exceptionally compliant with the rules.'

About 60 to 100 sixth form places available to external students – no admissions tests, but a minimum of six A*-C grades required at GCSE, the same as for internal students.

Exit: Almost all primary pupils transfer to HAHC secondary phase, to which they have automatic right of entry. After year 11 about half progress to the school's sixth form, the rest to a variety of post-16 provision. Some don't get the grades necessary to move up to year 12 at HAHC and go to other local schools and colleges; a tiny number opt for Dartford Grammar and the IB. Careers officer follows the progress of all leavers, and the school is proud of having had no NEETS (young people not in education, employment or training) for five years.

Up to 10 per cent of AS students don't achieve the minimum grade Cs required to move up to year 13. At 18, about 70 per cent to university, including some 30 per cent to Russell Group. In 2016, two students to Oxbridge and three medics. Of the remainder, nearly a quarter take a gap year, often applying to university through HAHC once they've got their A levels.

Money matters: State-funded academy. Parents not asked to pay voluntary contributions, and vice principal looked astonished when we asked if they were. Unusual and generous provision of scholarships to the 10 per cent selected on musical aptitude – the school will partially fund them to train at the Saturday junior departments of the main London music colleges, the Royal Academy of Music, Royal College of Music, Guildhall and Trinity. In addition, instrumental lessons offered at HAHC are free to all students, regardless of ability or level.

Remarks: A large and flourishing comprehensive that's lifted above the crowd by its results and amazing music and attracts many aspirational families into the area. Plan early if you want your child to go.

The Hall School

23 Crossfield Road, London NW3 4NU

Pupils: 460 • Ages: 4-13 • C of E

Fees: £15,786 – £17,949 pa

Tel: 020 7722 1700
Email: office@hallschool.co.uk
Website: www.hallschool.co.uk

Headmaster: Since 2013, Christopher Godwin, previously head of Bedford Prep. Read geography at Loughborough, then masters in Middle Eastern studies at Durham. Joined Bedford in 1993 as second master and director of studies before taking over the headship four years later. With no experience of London schools, his post came as a surprise to some parents, although he quickly won hearts and minds with his keenness to maintain the ethos and values of the school, along with his gentle and unassuming nature and fresh pair of eyes. 'There's a track record of people taking this job who are greying and in their early 50s,' he laughs, 'but I hope I've brought a new energy to the school.' Parents and pupils concur, praising his emphasis on 'positive psychology rather than rules, rules and more rules,' as one parent put it. 'There's a strong pastoral element to his thinking,' said another.

Sees the next phase as making the school even more responsive to 'the world we now live in', with a growing focus on preparing boys for what their next schools require and embedding ever more IT into an already technology-heavy curriculum. Known for being open and available to parents and a great team builder among staff. Often seen out and about in school and is not precious about his office, whose conference table is often used by boys themselves. Teaches current affairs to year 5s upwards, geography to year 8s and frequently reads stories in junior school. Heavily involved in the assessment of boys. Keen and active sportsman, particularly rugby – now as coach rather than player.

Entrance: This is the top north London boys' prep school for those looking towards the country's top academic secondary schools, so competition for entrance is hotter than hot, with applications restricted to those registering before their first birthday – and even so, the school is three times over-subscribed. At 3, parents are invited in to discuss whether a child will apply to enter at 4 or 5 (32 places at 4, 22 at 5). 'This can be down to issues such as birth date, speed of development, grasp of English if they come from a bilingual family and, of course, the parents have a say too,' says head, although he stresses that it all comes down to the individual boy, rather than any set guidelines. All applicants are tested in the same year – 4+ entrants in January for September, 5+ entrants in late April/May for the following September – for which parents have been known to tutor their offspring at as young as 3 (although the school says it frowns upon this).

Boys are assessed in groups of six. 'We are looking for a hunch about their potential, measurement of underlying intellect that they'll develop in the long-term, as well as how interactive, sociable and curious they are and their ability to concentrate for appropriate lengths of time,' says head. 'It's very detailed, with lots of personal attention, so that we get boys who are right for the school and who we can take right through the school.' Inevitably, there wind up being strugglers and – as the head puts it – 'those who feel adrift from their year group', and these boys have been known to be guided elsewhere, although school insists this is rare and it's clear that increasing effort is made to help every boy keep up. Favours siblings, but no guarantees and many haven't got places in recent years. Occasional places arise higher up the school, with a formal registration process for the waiting list. 'They do a good job of picking the right boys,' said one parent. 'Those that don't get in shouldn't get in and those that do are generally a good fit.'

Exit: Around half to Westminster and St Paul's, with largish contingents to Eton and Harrow. Others to eg UCS, City of London, Highgate, Merchant Taylors' and Mill Hill. Sizeable minority to other mostly single sex boarding schools, though co-ed boarding schools becoming more popular (and increasingly encouraged by the school), including King's School Canterbury, Sevenoaks and Arundel. Exceptional guidance in secondary school choices. 'We encourage parents of boys in year 4 upwards to start looking widely. We don't leave it with a year to go,' says head. The match is made by a meticulously planned programme of assessments, which include annual verbal and non-verbal reasoning and day-to-day performance, and which are all tracked on a graph for each boy. Scholarship form in year 8 for those completing the demanding exams of Eton and Westminster, but not all scholarships derive from this form.

Remarks: Prep schools don't come more ambitious than this. Catering to the needs of boys who are intellectually curious, academic and highly motivated, this is a school that stretches them in every direction, the result of which is a cohort of fiercely intelligent and extremely articulate boys. Yet there's nothing precocious about them and we found the school environment to be surprisingly relaxed.

Two classes of 16 in reception, reshuffled to three of 18 in year 1. By year 8, four classes of 12 to 14, with a scholarship form and three fast common entrance forms. Staff are a broad age range, including at the senior end, and have notable experience and oodles of enthusiasm. 'They're strict, but you can have a real joke with them too,' said one boy, and we certainly found humour abundant in the classrooms and corridors, with a refreshing ease of communication between pupils and staff. 'The lessons are unbelievably interactive. You never just sit and listen,' said another pupil.

Specialist French, science, music, sport and ICT more or less from the word go. Latin added in year 5, Greek in year 7 for scholarship candidates. Setting in core subjects from year 5 and Latin from year 6. 'But even if you're in set 3, you're still really smart, so there's never a feeling of being bottom of anything,' said one pupil. Three sciences, taught in a more combined way than in the past. ICT provision has long been outstanding, with digital learning embedded into just about every subject and clearly apparent when we visited, with plenty of tablets being used across the board. Advanced coding and programming is praised, as is the collaborative work using shared computer files. Head still not resting on his laurels, though, with £250,000 spent on further ICT, including a new virtual learning environment. Homework starts gently, then builds up and peaks at two preps of 45 minutes for years 7 and 8. No Sats but exams taken very seriously, with all subjects examined twice yearly in the upper forms. 'The teaching is so good that you actually don't need to revise for exams,' said one boy, 'although most of us do anyway.' Does well in national competitions, such as the Townsend Warner History Prize and national Maths Challenges.

The school itself is divided up, with junior school (reception to year 3), middle (years 4 and 5) and senior school (years 6-8) on separate sites all within a short walk of this upmarket residential area. Junior school is made up of two well-ordered Victorian buildings, with the head living in a flat above. Middle school is a 1970s building that was probably cutting-edge at the time, but could do with a rethink in terms of use of good space now. Senior school is the original red-brick school building, with lots of quirky design features, including split level classrooms, which make for a cosy learning environment.

Classrooms generally on the small side, especially in the middle school, but well-ordered, and many are innovatively designed (especially the history room, with its very own upstairs library and historically decorated walls) and welcoming. Even the DT room, where boys were making splurge guns ready for their production of Bugsy Malone when we visited, is carpeted. Lovely, bright art room, with separate pottery room that boasts two kilns. Wathen Hall, which is the main hall, feels a bit past its use-by date and would benefit from something more airy and with better use of space. Well-stocked, two-story, library with library sessions once a week. Stand-out common room, known as the Pit, with a focal snooker table and split level, contemporary and airy environment.

Like most north London preps, outside space is limited, although the junior school has a colourful and imaginative playground, whilst the older boys use one all-weather pitch, which school admits 'can get crowded' at playtimes. Sport, however, is prioritised, with £2m recently invested in the sports field at East Finchley, which the boys are transported to by coach two afternoons a week, and where they play football, rugby, hockey, cricket and tennis. Gymnastics and fencing in Wathen Hall. Every boy gets a chance to represent the school at some point in a team game (nine football teams) and the school is currently looking to extend its fixture list outside London. Some parents concerned that sport generally favours the best boys, however. 'All boys get to play, but if you're good, you get much better training,' said one. 'If the boys aren't sporty, they're not really bothered with them,' said another. County and national representatives at chess, fencing, skiing and tennis. Annual skiing trips to France and biannual cricket tour of Sri Lanka. 'We competed against teams that got 1,000 runs in 10 games in the last tour. The quality of cricket was amazing,' said one boy.

Over 80 per cent of boys play an instrument, with an army of peripatetic teachers made available, on top of which there are two specialist music lessons a week for all. 'It's not unusual to find boys playing three instruments,' said one boy. Plenty of encouragement to join the large orchestra, string quartets, jazz group and choir, all of which regularly win music awards. 'You get to sing in some amazing places if you're in the choir,' said one boy, listing Southwark Cathedral, St Albans Cathedral and Eton Chapel. 'There are some great music trips too,' said another, citing a year 7 trip to South Africa. The annual bands night is popular and boys rave about the new recording studio. Drama taken seriously, with boys of all ages encouraged to perform in plays, concerts, public speaking and most notably debating. When we visited, an actor in residence (an MA student from the nearby Royal Central School of Speech and Drama) was about to begin his year-long post.

This isn't the kind of school where every boy knows each other (not helped by the lack of single campus) but school does what it can to encourage peer support, with older boys helping out in the junior school and becoming ambassadors for subjects, such as geography. From year 5 upwards, the four houses have so-called 'bungalows', which comprise cross-year groups of eight boys who meet regularly and are led by a year 8 boy to discuss topics such as new ideas for activities or views on the rewards system for good work. In addition, there's a lively school council, that makes a lot of recommendations around meals ('I really don't like the food,' admitted one pupil) and equipment for the playground, as well as decisions about various charity fundraising. Boys say the atmosphere is highly supportive. 'Everyone is really friendly here,' said one.

School accommodates all the usual SENs free of charge, including dyslexia and Asperger's, and is open minded about discussing pretty much any difference, provided the underlying intellect is there. 'My son is dyslexic and the school just took it in their stride, which had a hugely positive effect on his confidence,' said one parent. Learning support department, which is run by a full-time staff member (BEd and certificate in dyslexia), involved in identifying issues, as well as monitoring and supporting them either in the short or long term, bringing in outside expertise where necessary. Only one statemented child when we visited. Huge range of clubs, including cookery, Mandarin, model making, computer maths games etc.

Lots of links with the local community, with teachers offering services at other local schools, whilst boys join forces with other schools to do everything from enrichment maths to drumming workshops. Boys are also encouraged to help out at the community centre 100 yards away. More religious than many nominally Christian schools, but it's a culture that's easily accessible by boys of other faiths or indeed of none, with some assemblies more spiritual or modern or even focusing on current affairs, although expect daily hymns and grace before meals.

The jury remains out on how nurturing the school is. A strong reputation persists that it has a competitive atmosphere, with a focus on academics at the cost of emotional support. But the school itself, along with the parents and pupils we spoke to, made convincing arguments that problems are nipped in the bud, with good pastoral care from teachers, two matrons and the part-time school counsellor, who has links with the Tavistock Clinic. In consultation with parents, the school undertakes a pastoral review every three years, with clear recommendations made. 'Despite its reputation, I've found it to be an incredibly child-centred school, with a caring and supportive environment,' insisted one parent. 'I think people see academic success and believe it must be down to a harsh environment, but actually the environment is genuinely caring and warm,' said another.

School doesn't promote rules as such, but there are clear expectations (many of which are dotted on posters around the school), and sanctions to back them up, most commonly detentions. But boys say punishment can be inconsistent. 'You can wind up with a worse punishment for running to pass a boy a book in the corridor than being really rude,' said one. 'And sometimes you turn up for detention, but the teacher has forgotten all about it.' Parents told us there's far less bullying under the current head, who has made the message loud and clear to both pupils and parents that it won't be tolerated.

Parents mostly high-flyers – bankers, media types, lawyers etc – many of whom have extremely high aspirations for their boys, which can mean the head has his work cut out. Mainly local, but some travel from Notting Hill, Holland Park and Islington. Very active PA and parents socialise regularly, although some years are rather cliquey, with very strong personalities, according to the parents we spoke to.

This is a school that offers boys with high academic potential a dazzling start in life. Most leave not only with great academic results, but excellent general knowledge, huge intellectual curiosity and an appreciation of all things cultural. Myths abound that these are boffins that are hothoused, but in fact we found they are boys with a great sense of fun and who are highly motivated, genuinely enjoying being stretched. For the right boy, this school is hard to fault, but boys who wind up struggling could feel left out in the drive to achieve. As one parent put it, 'The school does all it can to help such boys, but if you don't have a particularly bright son, the bottom line is he's better off somewhere else.'

Hall School Wimbledon, Junior School

Linked with Hall School Wimbledon, Senior School

Stroud Crescent, London SW15 3EQ

Pupils: 205 • Ages: 4–11

Fees: £12,501 – £14,427 pa

Tel: 020 8788 2370
Email: enquiries@hsw.co.uk
Website: https://hsw.co.uk

Headmaster: Since 1990, Mr Timothy J Hobbs MA (50s), educated at Eastbourne College and St Andrews, where he read medieval and modern history. He founded the school in 1990 (see senior school entry) and as numbers grew and the school developed a senior and junior section, his brother Jonathan joined as principal of the junior school in 1999.

TJH remains head, oversees operations and devotes massive amounts of energy to preserving the original spirit of the place. Entirely child-focused and delighted to leave the detail and day-to-day running of the school to Jonathan. He's based on the senior school site, but visits almost every day and takes assembly once a week. 'Children are very at ease with him,' said one mother. 'Of course there's respect and formality, but they like him and aren't afraid of him.'

Jonathan M Hobbs MA (education management from OU) was also educated at Eastbourne College and then at the British School of Osteopathy. He is married with children; his wife also works at the school. Ably assisted by deputy Susan Harding, who is more parent-facing – his brief is largely finance and management.

Entrance: First come, first served for the 44 reception places, with priority for siblings. Holds assessments and interviews for occasional places in years 1 to 6 and requests report from previous school. Parents from wide socio-economic spread, a chunk – about 20 per cent – from overseas.

Exit: About two-thirds to HSW Senior School – entry is automatic, but the children sit the same exam as the external senior school candidates to give an idea of where they are. Others to a range of mostly London schools, eg Kingston Grammar, Surbiton High, Reed's, King's College Wimbledon, Ibstock Place, Emanuel.

Remarks: Like the senior school, a very free-thinking place, all about celebrating the individual. The current site is a former state school – it's been improved and landscaped, TJH himself doing lots of planting. An American garden was added after 9/11 and serves as a place of reflection and commemoration. Also incorporates a library in a colourful caravan. School backs on to Wimbledon Common and staff take full advantage of this with plenty of expeditions.

Mixed ability classes, each about 15-20 strong, within which children may be set different work, so treated according to their ability without feeling singled out for special treatment. 'We don't like to take the weaker pupils out and teach them separately because it's hugely important that they gain from hearing what their brighter friends say,' explains Mrs Harding. Huge focus on reading in the early years – they have to 'get it' and school won't rest until they do. Unique senior school homework and monitoring system called Flints begins from year 3 – it's based on a theory of 'little and often' testing to reinforce what's been taught in school. Most of the schemes of work, methods and innovations of the senior school begin here. Hence it follows components of the common entrance and national curriculum, with its own HSW-stamp on it all.

About 30 children need EAL or special needs support. School is happy to take on children with mild learning difficulties, visual impairment, dyslexia and dyspraxia. It had an autism unit some years ago, but no longer, and today it shies away from anything beyond mild needs.

Parents mention again and again the confidence their children gain at the school and again, like the senior school, a huge focus on encouraging the children to think for themselves. 'We want to rein back from too much guidance, noise and teachers' voices,' says TJH. 'Thinking needs time. We want to challenge their minds.' Plenty of opportunities for the children to have a go at everything – and the academic are valued as much as the artistic or the sporty. Overall the message is: do as well as you can, whatever your strength.

Very strong sport here. Like the senior school, the day begins with 30 minutes of circuit training – even in the drizzle – followed by tons of sporting activities, changing each week, rather than each term, the idea being everyone will do something they enjoy – if gym is not your thing, what about rugby? Hockey is currently flavour of the month and the school is sponsoring Wimbledon hockey club. Children apparently get used to all the running about. No swimming, though – no pool nearby, so travelling and changing times involved make it hardly worthwhile. If your child is not into sport would it be a living nightmare? We asked one of our year 6 tour guides what would happen if you didn't enjoy all the outdoor activity. 'Tough luck,' he replied grimly. School has recently bought some nearby playing fields and a farm/field centre in Wales.

Major music and drama productions each term, plus children prepared for external LAMDA exams. From year 4 children can join school choir and orchestra and get lots of performance opportunities. School provides a solid foundation in art – lots of inspiration surrounds the children in the classrooms and corridors – and they complete varied craft and design projects, everything from basic architectural concepts to costume and set design, bookbinding and mosaics.

Their ICT experience will not be so wide – as in the senior school, it will not be studied for its own sake. The children are taught the joys and frustrations of using books as a resource – 'They need to know that a sparkling new book may yield them very little of use, whereas a tattered old thing may be packed with good stuff,' says TJH. No interactive whiteboards in classrooms nor so much as a whiff of an ICT suite.

Longish day – from 8.50am to 3pm for youngest, and from 8.30am to 4pm for years 3 to 6: a lot to pack in. Outside lesson time the children play beautifully, with all ages mixing together. Particular praise for 'fantastic' field trips – 'I know I'm verging on hyperbole, but they are nothing short of magical,' said one mother: educational, but also full of great experiences and treats of the kind normally only available to a scout or guide these days, as not many parents are prepared to sit in the garden while their children fry bacon over a campfire or abseil down the walls.

Pupils' birthdays are celebrated on a major scale, with the child in question entertaining their parents and a few chosen friends at their class table for lunch. Then he/she stands on their chair while everyone sings Happy Birthday before they cut and share their Hobbs-baked cake. Even the most retiring soul basks in the spotlight for a few minutes. 'It's a wonderful ritual and the children love it so much,' said one parent. 'Those with summer birthdays spend inordinate amounts of time planning for the school celebration once they get back in September.' And as well as the cake, every child gets a present from school's own Father Christmas – again to show that they are valued as individuals.

Lunchtimes are said to be 'special' – lunch is served in a family way; from years 3 to 6 the children say grace and are encouraged to develop good table manners. 'I think children take the lunchtime ritual for granted while they are here, but after they have left they say it's one of the main things they miss,' said one mother.

The place is boy heavy (60/40, like the seniors), but mothers of girls don't seem to find this a problem – 'Teaches them an early and necessary lesson in how to hold their own in the world,' says one mother. Behaviour is good – no real need for punishments: 'The children quickly get to understand what is expected of them and rise to it,' says the school. Parents are generally delighted that all their children learn good manners, strong morals and simple courtesies almost by osmosis here. Writing thank you letters, standing back for others, saying 'Good morning' as you pass somebody in the corridor – all de rigueur.

Real mix of parents from all walks – bankers, lawyers, media-types, fewer working mothers than at senior school. A bit more sociable, too, with organised coffee mornings for everybody to get to know each other. Parents also help on trips and come into school to share any expertise they may have – recently a Japanese parent delighted with a demonstration of origami. 'I like the fact that the school offers all the best bits of a traditional education, while rejecting the silly stuff that goes on elsewhere,' said one mother. HSW school life won't be for everyone, but definitely worth a look.

H

Hall School Wimbledon, Senior School

Linked with Hall School Wimbledon, Junior School

17 The Downs, London SW20 8HF

Pupils: 250 • Ages: 11–16

Fees: £16,539 pa

Tel: 020 8879 9200
Email: enquiries@hsw.co.uk
Website: https://hsw.co.uk/

Headmaster: Since 1990, Mr Timothy J Hobbs MA (50s), educated at Eastbourne College and St Andrews, where he read medieval and modern history. Abandoned accountancy training in favour of a teaching post at Hill House International Junior School, which he left six years later, encouraged by parents, to set up his own school – the original Hall School Wimbledon Junior School. (In 1999 his brother Jonathan joined as principal of the junior school.)

Unmarried – except to the school, which TJH (as he likes to be known) hates us saying, but no better way to describe his passion and dedication to the place. An avuncular figure with quite old-fashioned (in the nicest possible way) sensibilities. He's a stickler for good manners, a strong advocate of books over computers and likes the children to be outdoors in the fresh air as often as possible. Alongside such Blyton-esque objectives, he espouses a rigorous and thorough approach to teaching, tested weekly in his personally devised homework system.

Works tirelessly at the sharp end and consequently gets to know every child very well. Does some teaching but, more pertinently, personally leads the many school expeditions – basically count him out for the summer term: he's 'on tour'. Traditionally has baked every pupil a cake for their birthday – 'a great way to focus on that child for half an hour and think about their needs in the coming year,' he says. But less keen on thinking about their parents – he's not interested really: he's all about the children. 'I've never met him,' said one mother who has been at the school a couple of years. 'He's very nice,' thought another, rather vaguely. 'But you'll never see him glad-handing at the gates.' TJH happily defends his position, 'I can't know and run the school properly if I'm seeing parents all the time: I have some excellent staff who do that. I am keen that parents speak to the right person to deal with their questions/ concerns. If that person is me, then I will meet with them.'

H

Opinionated on occasion, one gets the impression that it is his way or the highway – you either buy into his ethos of the school or go elsewhere. Admits he dislikes detail and dealing with the minutiae of running a school – 'He does tend to wander off,' agrees the school secretary – but he's absolutely your man for some blue-sky thinking, pushing the envelope, outside the box type of approach. Cutting something of a maverick figure, he and his school have a local reputation as being quirky; although actually he and the whole set up are much more traditional than reputation would have it. Outside school, he is interested in culture, particularly art, which he collects and hangs at the school.

Academic matters: For a largely non-selective, mixed-ability school, does well. The ethos is that learning should be a pleasure, not a chore, and that exams are not the be all and end all – as the prospectus says, 'Thought is the most important activity taking place at our school'. So no teaching to the test, other than, obviously, complying with the requirements of the GCSE syllabuses. A nod to the 'spirit and content' of the national curriculum, all combined in school's own Work Programmes.

Pre-GCSE the core curriculum includes English, maths, French, German, science, history, geography, religious studies (including a chunk of philosophy), art, DT, music and drama. At GCSE the timetable will be written around that year's cohort. No ICT GCSE (see below).

Children are encouraged to believe that all subjects are equal – poetry as valuable as science – with no more praise given to a mathematician than to a pianist than to an athlete. 'It sounds ridiculously clichéd, but we do faithfully honour the individual,' says TJH. Forget the league tables and think about the value-added. 'Some of our children will leave with a full set of A*s, while for others a collection of B and C grades will be a personal triumph and just as worthy of celebration.'

IGCSE is preferred in science – largely because they are, in school's view, 'more child-friendly – we are an international school after all'. Certainly the language used is simpler, making them more boy-friendly perhaps. In 2016, 30 per cent of GCSE grades were A*/A.

Homework is relevant, contained and limited to 45 minutes a night, all designed to reinforce what has been taught in the classroom. It's a system of the school's own devising called Flints. Based on a 'little and often' philosophy, the pupils get bite-sized exercises in four or five different subjects every night and are then tested at school on Friday morning in what is called a 'Flint Wall'. Some parental feeling that CE children pushed a little harder than the rest – which would be unsurprising. Hard to over-emphasise the importance of Flints, which are an enormous part of the school – 'My child is quite obsessed with them,' says one mother. Certainly parents can see exactly what is going on (particularly valued by those overseas). 'It gives trust and comfort that their children are being prepared at the highest level,' says TJH.

One area where children may not be so highly skilled is in ICT – TJH is not a fan but, bowing to the modern world, such technology is tolerated and available, with laptops permitted where it helps a dyslexic child. Desktop computers are available in a dedicated ET (Enabling Technology)suites and laptops are used on Geography and English field trips and for use when lessons are taught outside the school e.g. at its Oberon playing fields and pavilion for GCSE PE. TJH prefers that children are trained to use books as a resource. But it is worth noting that the Flint system is a highly sophisticated computer-based one, so although anti-ICT for its own sake, the school isn't exactly advocating chalk and slate – it's more of a philosophical position. DT is also not strong – really only facilities for woodwork and the subject falls off the curriculum after year 8.

The school says it has average numbers of special needs children for a private school. Lots of dyslexia, so surprising to hear from one parent that her child's dyslexia was neither picked up nor sympathetically handled – don't assume school has it covered. TJH says, 'HSW is diligent about not labelling children, hence possible explanation for this comment. Every child is assessed annually.' Head of Enhanced Learning (praised by a parent) who tries to meet most needs within the classroom – inclusivity is everything here. But it's not the place for anything other than mild needs.

Nearby Kingston upon Thames and New Malden have large Korean and Japanese communities and a third Hobbs brother has links in the Far East – reflected in school numbers. Mixed gender staff with several long-standing members steeped in Hobbsism.

System of deputies and senior tutors aims to devolve power down from the head. For the future, a sixth form is on the cards – parents would welcome it and school is similarly keen to get stuck into A levels.

Games, options, the arts: Lazybones and other such slackers need not apply. Get your children used to the great outdoors – they will be thoroughly aired here with lots of sport and all sorts of clubs. Every day begins with a wake-up call of 30 minutes' circuit training from 8.30am and loads of sport is timetabled throughout the week – some each day, bad weather rarely stops play. Rugby, hockey and netball feature large – no swimming facilities, though; two playgrounds on site and extensive playing fields and sports facilities nearby. More chances for girls to play in the teams as fewer of them in the school. Fantastic place for netball – borough champion, netball tour to New Zealand and football in Malta extremely popular. Boys' rugby tour to NZ recently added. TJH admits to feeling 'rather galled that Epsom, Cranleigh and Millfield get credit for having international players who are actually former HSW pupils who got their first touch of a ball with us'. The Levels, new play/sports facility at the junior school, used for PE programme and training ground for strong climbing tradition – lower circuit level provides two parallel obstacle courses and upper climbing level includes a traversing wall.

Drama in its many different forms runs through the timetable for all years. Every child has a role to play in his or her year group's annual performances and learns that production, lighting, costume and make-up are just as important as starring roles and comic cameos. Also dance laid on for girls. Well-equipped music studios and peripatetic teachers offer vocal, guitar, piano, woodwind, percussion, music theory and music technology lessons, plus an orchestra, choir and various ensembles. A long day school day helps the children fit it all in.

Hard to overstate the importance of field trips at this school – usually in the summer term and always led by TJH. They are educational – picking up on the history and geography of whatever location, eg Northern France and D-Day landings – but also provide an opportunity to talk through PSHE-type issues, undertake physical challenges and bond as a group.

Background and atmosphere: All very civilised. Original Victorian building has nice features including a 'country house-style' library filled with giant bean bags, although as one parent pointed out, the bean bags are more in evidence than the books. And no librarian – all a bit strange for a school that claims to value books so much. Not a glamorous place; some of the newer parts (from the 1980s and 90s) were a bit dismal when we visited, though the school tells us they have been recently redecorated. All floors are carpeted and windows curtained to minimise ambient noises. Walls are decorated with original artwork, including TJH's own collection. Not much of the children's work around the place – although we did visit early in a new term. Classrooms are of different sizes, but space is well used and no feeling of crush and cramp. Unusually for a secondary school, years 7, 8 and 9 stay put and the teachers come to them; from year 10 the more traditional set-up of children moving around.

The place is less boy-heavy – school says 60/40 (though it looked more like 70/30 when we walked around); it varies throughout the school, some years more boy-dominated than others. Although school says it desires equal numbers and a new campaign recently launched to increase numbers of girls to 50:50 by 2020, lots of very good girls' schools in the area make for strong competition. TJH says he is very mindful – and keen to change the fact – that some girls might not come to the school because of male feel to the environment. But no nasty role-modelling – children will see TJH gardening, cleaning and even hanging curtains.

An active place – outdoor pursuits-style uniforms say it all. Nice to see children (admittedly year 7s) actually playing at break time rather than skulking around trying to looking cool. Balls allowed – or rather encouraged – and we can't believe this place would have any truck with conker-bans and the like. 'They really celebrate childhood here,' said a parent. 'When it snows they are told to get sledging.' Similarly, where many schools would have a ban on running, here running outside is good.

Forty-five minute break mid-morning and a similarly decent break in the afternoon – on both occasions your child will be encouraged to get fresh air. Freshly cooked food for lunch. As well as a birthday cake large enough to share with their class and take a piece home, every child is given a Christmas present by TJH – 'They are simple acts of kindness to show each child that they matter to us'.

TJH conscious that some wariness exists over family owned schools and is keen to stress that the place is not a 'Tim Hobbs' production – 'There's a proper structure here, with Jonathan (TJH's brother and head of junior school) and I each supported by a very able deputy and a system of senior tutors'. We feel it would be some deputy that made much headway against a Hobbs brother – though TJH disagrees.

Pastoral care, well-being and discipline: TJH extremely strict on all interaction at the school, proud of the fact it is 'a very safe place', and of course its small size makes it reasonably easy to monitor. 'I've found that the school watches the children very closely, particularly as they get older,' said one mother. Few rules, mainly common sense. The fact that TJH displays his own art collection around the place speaks volumes – obviously no vandalism. 'We spend a lot of money on making the school nice and comfortable; they wouldn't write on their parents' walls and we don't expect it here either,' he says.

Little call for punishments as children quickly understand what's expected of them – 'We try not to create pointless barriers and rules'. But action will be taken if necessary – a child was expelled a few years ago for bullying, which the school 'loathes' and is the ultimate no-no here, widely defined to include even ignoring somebody: this place is very inclusive. Parents all mentioned how their children grew in confidence at the school. If somebody does do wrong, staff are 'shocked and upset' rather than angry. No detentions – school would not want to send a message that break-time activities were not important and could be dispensed with at will. Ever evolving, at one stage considered providing make-up lessons for the girls – in reality, probably no better way to put girls off the whole idea.

Pupils and parents: Sixty per cent from the rather prosperous local area – which is roughly mid-way between Raynes Park and rather grander Wimbledon. Others from Kingston, New Malden, Dulwich and Clapham, with a couple from Kensington, Knightsbridge, Barnes and the like, so a fairly up-market clientele, including the odd famous name. Children of all shapes, sizes, nationalities and abilities – parents similarly mixed bunch. No PTA or sports days (by design) so not the easiest place to get to know other parents, particularly if you haven't been at the junior school – though the school doesn't accept this comment.

Entrance: By assessment at 11+ – applicants spend a day at the school: interview with deputy, English and maths assessment and they take part in drama, music and games activities. 'We're watching for behaviour too – it's quite an elaborate process,' says TJH. Prides itself on seeing the good in all. Consequently this can involve two or three meetings with parents – all handled by long-serving deputy. 'While there is no such thing as a HSW child, we are looking for a good match.' Regular 11+ open mornings (four Tuesdays each term).

Exit: Some 10 per cent leave after common entrance. Pupils go all over the place – locally to King's Wimbledon, Lady Eleanor Holles and Westminster, alongside further afield Winchester, Cranleigh and Millfield and St John's Leatherhead. All out at 16, eg to Epsom College, but not to one particular school/sixth form.

Remarks: A happy school, brave enough to take on children that other London schools might well turn down. Children who are a bit eccentric will be comfortable and accepted here. A humane place that concentrates on all-round development (not just academia – so not for league table obsessed parents) and turns out confident, personable, polite and physically fit teenagers.

Hampden Gurney CofE Primary School

13 Nutford Place, London W1H 5HA

Pupils: 240 • Ages: 3–11 • C of E

Tel: 020 7641 4195
Email: admin@hampdengurney.co.uk
Website: www.hampdengurneyschool.org.uk

Headteacher: Since 1997, Mrs Evelyn Chua (40s). A firm and fashionably-dressed visionary, originates from Malaysia and is a pianist and former music teacher, and has worked immensely hard to transform this inner-city C of E primary to a school with beacon status, recently ranked third in the country.

H

A formidable figure, the children certainly respect her, the punishment of last resort for the naughty, but those who've experienced her teaching also find her an inspiration. No British embarrassment about supporting the gifted and talented, but equally determined that every child in this exceptional school will come out a winner.

Entrance: School is affiliated to the High Anglican Church of the Annunciation in Bryanston Street near Marble Arch, and gives priority to church-going applicants, so if sung mass and ample evidence of the Virgin are not part of your belief system, not the school for you. Don't relax your church attendance either once your eldest has secured a place – sibling priority only as a tie-break. Heavily oversubscribed. No automatic transfer from nursery to reception.

Exit: Results to make many a prep school head weep. Plenty of academic, music and art scholarships, as well as bursaries. 'We don't give specific preparation, but we just teach them very well,' says the head, and clearly 'very well' is very well indeed. Recent awards have taken pupils to Latymer Upper, City of London Boys and Girls, Notting Hill and Ealing, St Benedict's, Westminster Under, St Paul's Girls, Cardinal Vaughan and St Paul's Juniors, with others to eg Highgate, Queen's College, St Marylebone, Holland Park and Chelsea Academy.

H

Remarks: Long-serving head is clearly able to stretch and enthuse young minds and the busy, well-organised classrooms and dedicated staff (four male teachers) are testament to her management skills. Clearly no area of the curriculum here where good is good enough. Half the pupils come in speaking little English; the rest are prosperous middle class, many from international backgrounds, but nearly all those moving on to secondary school attain top marks in maths, English and science. Specialist teaching in PE, art, DT and music, with a rotation system of teachers two afternoons a week.

Particularly noted for its gifted and talented programme – this is definitely a school where it is cool to be clever. Mrs Chua has high standards and many students reach or exceed them – 'In year 6, some of the children are doing GCSE maths,' said one mother. But also strong (individual and group) out-of-class support for every child who needs it.

A fairly hefty homework diary, particularly for a state primary: 30-45 minutes a night in years 3-5, one hour in year 6, with English, maths and science set nightly and other subjects once a week. Optional holiday homework as well. Well-equipped ICT suite with digital cameras and laptops. Interactive screens in every classroom. ICT taught creatively with an annual ICT week, where even the youngest gets a chance to demonstrate their Spielberg potential.

Despite its restricted playground space, the school performs sporting miracles with daily sport clubs and specialists provided by the local authority to teach PE, netball, cricket, tennis, tag rugby. Young footballers play for Westminster and regular football competitions with other local schools. Swimming at nearby Seymour Leisure Centre.

Neat and practical red and grey uniform. Strong house system with houses named after eminent Brits and points for everything. Ample extracurricular activity, ranging from sewing and gardening to writing and publishing the school newspaper. Strong emphasis, too, on charitable fundraising. Residential trips to the countryside.

Heavy emphasis on attendance and punctuality (head firmly warns prospective parents against sinful thoughts of mid-term breaks). Escalating punishment system (warning, missing play time, time out, Mrs Chua) but minimum behavioural problems. Indeed classrooms are a model of well-ordered enthusiasm.

Founded in 1863 by Reverend Hampden Gurney, Rector of St Mary's Bryanston Square, the school's ethos is still strongly High Anglican, with compulsory attendance at weekly sung Eucharist and RE teaching firmly rooted in the Church of England.

Mrs Chua has collected many awards, everything from the National Association for Able Children Award to Service Excellence Award. Not unnaturally, most parents are immensely positive: 'You couldn't find a better education in the state system,' said one mother, who'd taken her children out of the private sector. And the articulate, confident and happy pupils are the school's best advertisement. One boy, asked about what he liked about the school, replied, 'Everything.'

The Hampshire School, Chelsea

15 Manresa Road, London SW3 6NB

Pupils: 314 • Ages: 3-13

Fees: £15,525 – £17,100 pa

Tel: 020 7352 7077
Email: info@thehampshireschoolchelsea.co.uk
Website: www.thehampshireschoolchelsea.co.uk/

Headmaster: Since 2014, Donal Brennan BEd (50s). Soft-spoken, bearded, kindly. A Kerry man, one of seven, who went to a tiny village school with two teachers and no electricity or running water: 'It was a fantastic place – education was everything there.' Always wanted to be a teacher. Read education, theology and art at Trinity College Dublin, then trained at the Froebel College as a primary school teacher. Taught at Hill House International for 25 years, where he ended up as under master, but wanted to head up his own school and was attracted by The Hampshire School's small class sizes and caring ethos. Not afraid to give parents his mobile number, and greets all the children personally every day – 'We celebrate the achievement of getting to school, and how you welcome children is hugely important.' Popular with parents: 'Approachable and genuinely caring,' was a typical comment.

Still teaches – his study doubles as a year 6 tutorial room – and a passionate believer in learning by doing: 'Climb the tree; afterwards you can write about it.' A music lover, for whom singing is an essential part of life; also still does the occasional Irish dance in his spare time. Firmly committed to the school's inclusive intake: 'Mixed ability is a reflection of real life. I don't believe it's healthy at a young age to be in a community that's already selective.'

Married to Rosie, a former science teacher, with two young sons.

Entrance: Entry points at age 3 into the nursery, age 5 into year 1 and age 8 into year 4 – informal interview and assessment, designed to put children and their families at ease. Small entry point into year 7, 'but we're quite selective at that age, because of needing to guide them to the right schools.' Occasional places in other year groups do sometimes come up – always worth enquiring.

Exit: To a wide range of destinations, mostly London day schools. Girls move on to places such as Francis Holland, More House, Queen's Gate, Emanuel, Latymer Upper, with occasional St Paul's Girls' and CLSG successes. Most leave at 11, but no pressure to do so, and some opt to stay on until 13 because they like it here. (The school has forged sporting links to other schools with 'small clusters of girls' at this age, which we thought eminently sensible.) Boys leave mostly at 13, to the likes of Latymer Upper, City of London, Emanuel, Dulwich, sometimes St Paul's and Westminster. Head is proud of the school's track record: 'No child here leaves without the school that's right for them.'

Remarks: Founded in Surrey as a dance school in 1928 by June Hampshire, mother of actress Susan. On moving to London in the 1930s the school became mainstream and for many years was seen as a very traditional prep. Since becoming part of the GEMS group in 2007, however, it has modernised considerably and now has a reputation for delivering sound up-to-date academics in an atmosphere of kindness and friendliness. Years 1 to 8 are accommodated in the main premises on Manresa Road, a wonderfully spacious grade II listed building; it used to be the Chelsea library and still has the same air of calm tranquility.

Sheltering beneath the architectural grandeur is some pretty impressive modern technology: a splendid science laboratory, one of the best we've seen in a central London prep; height-adjustable interactive whiteboards; individual computer desks in the classrooms; and an excellent ICT suite where we saw children hard at work designing a restaurant. None of this has come at the expense of tradition, however, and bookworms would adore the fabulous school library: cavernous, marble-columned, galleried, and home to thousands of books. We thought it looked a tad underused, but the forthcoming appointment of a librarian is set to change that, whereat this will surely become one of the great strengths of the school's provision.

The school hall was in the news recently when a piece of the ceiling fell down, but school is anxious to point out that it was a very small piece; all has now been repaired, and it remains a great space for PE, concerts, plays, assemblies and dance – the Chelsea Ballet School visits every week. Lovely spacious classrooms, and a well-sized and equipped garden for the children to let off steam. Team games such as rugby are played off-site in Battersea Park, and the children go swimming at Chelsea and Fulham swimming baths. Lifts throughout the building mean that children with physical disabilities can be accommodated.

Broad extracurricular provision includes judo, table tennis, fencing, archery, football, rugby, cooking, chess, cards, computing, debating, art, drumming, ukulele – 'We're constantly seeking to add to our clubs,' affirmed head, adding that they hope to lay on activities at weekends in future. Music provision is good and there are plans to get it better. Children can learn piano, cello, violin, etc, and take part in choir, and there are regular concerts plus the annual Summer Arts Festival. No orchestra yet, and drama is currently confined to class rather than whole school productions, although the imminent arrival of a second drama teacher will bring more opportunities in this area. Lots of trips, including annual week-long jolly for the older children to places at home and abroad. Parent body is dedicated and 'very proactive, very influential in supporting the family feeling of the school,' according to staff. Recent events organised by the PA include a Fathers' Day breakfast and a United Nations day where parents drew on their own variety of backgrounds to run stalls showcasing food from countries around the world.

We liked the pupil work that we saw on display, particularly the French, and this struck us as a school where children are free to flourish at their own pace. Teacher pupil ratio is 1:9, ensuring all students get the attention they need, and there's particularly strong SEN provision, both for those with diagnosed difficulties such as dyslexia and those assessed as gifted and talented. Full time SENCo is called head of enrichment, and is integral to the school. Speech and language therapist comes to the school to help on site. EFL is well catered for in-house: much demand for this, since this is a school with an international intake, reflecting the locality. Both parents and children very contented with their choice: 'The school gives an excellent balance between holding the kids accountable for high academic standards and a well rounded extracurricular activity programme,' was one parent's verdict, and a pupil told us, 'I like everything I do here!'

Early years are housed a few streets away in Wetherby Place, in premises which felt rather small when contrasted with the main school. However, there's been a lot of refurbishment, and it's clearly becoming known as a smart choice for local parents: there is a waiting list for reception places, and the school recently opened a third class to accommodate the increasing numbers. Teaching rooms are bright and airy, and classes are small: 13 max for nursery, 14 max for reception. We saw child-friendly, child-centred learning and positive reinforcement everywhere, and the standard of work on the walls was high. The little ones go over to the main school for lessons such as art and PE and to use the library and play areas, thus ensuring that they remain part of the wider school, and a shuttle bus means that parents can drop their children off to either site.

In both locations, we were impressed by the peaceful, happy atmosphere. The bottle green and grey uniform is smartly worn, and children move about with a sense of calm purpose. Kindness really does seem to be the way here, and everyone we spoke to agreed. 'The teachers never, ever shout,' was one comment, 'they're really sensitive to the needs of the children.' As a charming and articulate young leaver put it, 'I've loved this school. I would have stayed here until I was 18 if I could.' 'My daughter's been made really welcome here, and we couldn't be happier,' confirmed a father.

Perhaps not the go-to choice for those seeking non-stop high-octane buzz from dawn till dusk, but a successful and busy school for all that, offering a supportive and relaxed environment in which children can be themselves and achieve their potential without having to compromise their nicer nature.

Hampstead School

99

Westbere Road, London NW2 3RT

Pupils: 1,245 • Ages: 11–19 • Sixth form: 230

Tel: 020 7794 8133
Email: enquiries@hampsteadschool.org.uk
Website: www.hampsteadschool.org.uk

Headteacher: Since 2006, Mr Jacques Szemalikowski MA BSc PGCE NPQH CPhys MInstP (50s). This head needs no Red Bull! Positively explodes with energy, a dynamo. Five minutes in his company and you are left exhausted. With four young children of his own, this guy is driven. He is here to make a difference, and in his tenure as headmaster of Hampstead School, he has.

A graduate in astrophysics, and a teacher for 25 years before his first headship at The Warwick School, Redhill, Mr Szemalikowski is somewhat old school in his principles and discipline. A misbehaving student can find themselves holed away for the day in the exclusion zone, 'our naughty step' – a small building situated at the back of the playing fields. He makes no apologies for his rigorous approach to education, both for his students and staff members alike. His mantra is 'Every child can achieve, every child will achieve, whatever it takes' – and he does what he can to ensure this is not just hot air. He organises trips to Oxford so that his students can be aspirational: 'I want them to know this can be for them too. I want them to be the movers and shakers of the modern world.'

His staff are not allowed to rest on their laurels either. He doesn't do 'good' – he wants outstanding from his staff and they are expected to attend weekly regular after-school workshops in order to achieve this (the latest Ofsted report commented that there 'wasn't yet enough outstanding teaching.') A recent high turnover of staff, he says, was testimony to their 'tremendous training' which secured them promotional posts in other schools. Like him, don't like him, 'I'm not here to be popular, I'm here to get the job done.'

Hit the headlines recently for reporting the student author of a blog critical of the school to the police and to the universities where he hoped to study.

H

Academic matters: 2016 saw 57 per cent of pupils achieve 5+ A*-C grades at GCSE including English and maths. Consider that nearly half the pupils are bilingual (63 different nationalities), five per cent are statemented and nearly 40 per cent are on free school meals. Twenty-two per cent of grades were A*/A.

A level results 37 per cent A*/B and 15 per cent A*/A. In the top 20 UK state schools for continuing into science A levels after GCSE. Big emphasis on science, and there is the option of triple rather than double science for students who attain at least a level 6 at the end of key stage 3. Maths, too, is strong and the school is very involved in maths challenges with students achieving above national average numbers of gold, silver and bronze certificates. The school also offers free Saturday school maths masterclasses for gifted mathematicians from years 5 and 6 of local primary schools.

English and media are popular subjects, and students also have the option of learning Arabic and Italian (as well as French and Spanish). Bilingual homework support is offered. Pupils have six BTecs to choose from including catering and hospitality, and a wide variety of A levels including three new ones in philosophy, creative writing and culture and communication. No subject is offered at GCSE level which can't be carried through to A level. 'We don't stream, we set, so there is movement', the head points out. Maths, English and science setted from year 7. Every faculty in the school has a remunerated teacher responsible for gifted and talented children. There is a clear focus on standards and students are tracked from the moment they arrive. They have individual charts and are monitored six times a year. As soon as a student starts to slip, staff want to know why. An appreciative parent commented that the school is 'quick to congratulate children if they've done well – very good at praising.' Strong curriculum support and SEN help, notably those who arrive with little English, and catch up is rapid: 'Assessors couldn't tell the difference between SEN students and non-SEN students', we were told.

Archaic-looking but well-equipped classrooms, most notably the music department, where a large cash injection has meant up-to-date technology. Through their status as a technology college they have been able to implement a £0.5 million upgrade to the library, creating an independent learning centre combining traditional library resources with new technologies. (That said, the library is actually quite scant on books itself.) Masses of extracurricular activity perhaps also reflects the academic ethos of the school: the school's debating society has had spectacular success in Model United Nations – with ongoing victories both as a delegation and individuals. Involved in Jack Petchey Speak Out Challenge and has a Youth Parliament.

Games, options, the arts: Fizzes with activity – plenty to do. Music is popular and heavy investment in this department has meant that each of the school's 1,300 students is offered the opportunity to learn a musical instrument. Pupils can choose to join a wide variety of musical activities, including senior or junior orchestra, guitar orchestra, jazz band, junior choir and many more.

Enthusiastic drama – great on-site replica fringe theatre, partnerships with the Hampstead Theatre Club, Royal Court and Tricycle all help to inspire; a few students had extras parts in the Dustin Hoffman movie Quartet.

Strong sport, particularly football, basketball and table tennis. The football team recently won the Bliss Inner London Cup, becoming the first Camden school to win the trophy; the girls' basketball team won the Under 15 Championships recently. A team of students and staff also recently completed the 56-mile London to Brighton bike ride. Limited playing fields, but somewhat redeemed by its other on-site facilities including a basketball/netball court, a dance studio, a fitness suite, a multi-use Astroturf and an on-site pool (that could do with some love).

The plethora of extracurricular activities includes gardening (they have an allotment which grows produce for the catering department), poetry, rugby, dance and aikido clubs, plus several music ensembles. For the more dedicated student, those who lack quiet space at home and those who need extra help, there are after-school homework sessions.

Background and atmosphere: Hampstead Schmampstead – this school is no more in Hampstead than Arsenal (FC) is in Arsenal. Situated in between colourful but definitely not posh Cricklewood, Kilburn and semi-posh West Hampstead, you can see the flag before you see the school. Red and emblazoned with the school logo, the flag waves proudly high above this impressive large red-brick building. The main building, formerly the old Haberdashers' Boys' school, was built in 1908, and indeed on first appearance promises great things.

One is immediately struck by the amount of banners displayed on the building's facade: 'Best ever GCSE results', 'Read more, earn more, learn more', 'Leaders of tomorrow' and so on. Mr Szemalikowski, who has been on three trips to the USA (Chicago, Boston and DC), says it's very much an American thing to do: 'It reinforces key aspirations at all times.' Tear your eyes away, walk up the ramped approach, through a plate glass entrance into a fairly modern foyer and see more slogans – this time on a wall-mounted flat screen TV, and from the wisdom of Galileo: 'Measure what is measurable,' the theme of the week.

Currently in process of major redevelopment which will, over the next school year, see a a sports centre with four courts and an activity studio, a three storey building with a new dining hall, drama studio, music facilities, science laboratories and a large assembly hall, and two all-weather pitches, in place of the 60s building.

A well-equipped ICT and catering block (with industrial spec kitchens). Good sixth form centre with huge common room overlooking the central atrium. Lucky sixth formers can feast their eyes on yet more banners – this time displayed on the walls around the central atrium – (did we mention Big Brother?) Wheelchair access throughout – the school is completely DDA compliant. There is a disability resource which can cater for up to seven students with complex needs. These students are fully integrated into mainstream lessons.

This is a big, sprawling campus, and easy to lose your bearings, especially for new pupils coming from little primaries. Lest you forget where you are, fear not, everything is logoed – from school water bottles to the dustbins, another of the head's ideas of constant reinforcement of group identity. Pupils are a mixed and diverse bunch, but all seem to share a common loyalty towards the school and enjoy being there. One 13-year-old pupil told us: 'I love the responsibility they give us. I was on a panel to help elect the last deputy head of the school.' Badges are awarded to students who meet standards and display good behaviour – bronze through to platinum. Get platinum, you can have lunch with the head! Students' pride in their school is evident in the total lack of graffiti, vandalism and litter.

Commendable efforts to involve the outside world and lots of whole school charity work. An appreciation of the diversity of the school is prevalent – Black History Month, Gay/Transgender Month, a recent trip to Auschwitz, to name but a few. The school culture involves loads of celebration and rewards for achievement and improvement.

Pastoral care, well-being and discipline: If punctuality and attendance ain't your bag, this ain't your school. Mr Szemalikowski and the entire senior management team are at the gates to greet pupils from 8.40am, after which sluggards have to report individually. (Early risers' club offered from 7.30am onwards for an extra cost of 50p). Attendance has improved dramatically since Mr Szemalikowski came on board. He is completely intolerant of any absence during term time (other than illness) and allows pupils two days a year for religious holidays. 'Every day counts' is one of the school's many slogans.

He is the head that reintroduced uniform to the school, and according to an ex-student, it has made a huge change – 'now everyone is on a level playing field.' Different ties denote whether or not a student has been trained in peer mentoring, and any student feeling vulnerable can approach those who have. Automatic exclusion for fighting, drugs, alcohol or carrying a weapon (as was recently the case with a student found to be carrying a knife). The head walks around daily to keep in touch, and lo and behold, if a student is wandering aimlessly in the grounds, they are stopped and questioned – and only when Mr Szemalikowski is entirely satisfied with their response are they sent on their way. Good level of security – brings to bear the stark reality that you are in an inner-city school.

However, despite Mr Szemalikowski's robust attitude to discipline, one parent said, 'it doesn't go far enough'. She felt that students are given too many chances, although she did acknowledge that the exclusion zone is a good deterrent – 'my daughter was in there once, and has said she won't be going there again.' (It is a small outhouse building, which can hold up to six students at any one time, with no contact with their peers for the whole day). Classes seemed to be well behaved for the most part – with the exception of the odd class joker – and a good level of concentration in what they were doing. PE, however, was on the very raucous side.

Non-teaching heads of year are one of Mr Szemalikowski's brainchilds. The idea is that the heads of year are there solely for the pupils' welfare needs and not to be distracted with marking homework. It works brilliantly, one parent enthused. 'It means that if I have any concerns about my child I know I can contact the head of year, and they are always available to speak to, no matter what time of day.' Year common rooms are 'exclusive to Hampstead School' – the idea being that year groups can eat together at lunchtimes and the heads of year have their offices in there and are always available at lunchtime too.

Buddying, mentoring and restorative justice schemes all bolster pupils' sense of security, and bullying is rigorously kept in check. 'The House', situated a stone's throw from the Exclusion Zone, is a cuboid block on the perimeter where you go if you are troubled – or troubling – and is well staffed with welfare workers, counsellors and other supportive types.

Pupils and parents: From moneyed West Hampstead, to recent refugees in temporary housing, the demographic is diverse – all the more admirable when one considers how far the school has come. One pupil told us: 'I love the fact that one of my best friends is black, the other wears a hijab'. A real feature of the school, we were told, is that no ethnic groups predominate. Nineteen per cent is white British – the largest group.

Former pupils include Sadie Frost, Rachel Yankey, ex-MP Julia Drown, Alec Bogdanovic, Jake Lensen, Tobias Hill, Zadie Smith.

Entrance: From up to 71 primary schools (no named feeders; totally non-selective), and covering three boroughs – Camden, Brent and Barnet (admissions managed by Camden) – the school is now oversubscribed in every year. One parent, a born and bred Cricklewood local, remarked how the school used to have a 'terrible reputation', and no right-thinking parent, given the choice, would have sent their kids there – but she said, 'that's changed since Mr Szemalikowski came on board'. Oversubscribed sixth form both from internal and external candidates. Twenty year 12 places are available to external applicants that meet the entry requirements – which vary according to the level of course they want to pursue.

Exit: About 70 per cent stay for the sixth form, the remainder go to other colleges and sixth forms. Some 70 per cent of sixth formers move on to an impressive range of higher education – from chemistry at King's College, law at Bristol and maths at Leeds to a paid apprenticeship in aerospace engineering with Airbus, at University of Surrey (which was big news because the student beat a large number of applicants for the prestigious placement). One former student has become an international DJ and producer as a result of studying A level music at the school.

Remarks: The head's energy and vision has worked wonders on this school. A melting pot of culture and diversity, and a whole host of activities to keep even the most apathetic child interested. However, this school ain't for the faint hearted – large and imposing, and big on discipline and punctuality. In the process of much-needed redevelopment – at last.

Hampton Court House (Junior School)

Linked with Hampton Court House (Senior School)

The Green, Hampton Court Road, East Molesey, Surrey KT8 9BS

Pupils: 235 • Ages: 3–11

Fees: £12,735 – £15,615 pa

Tel: 020 8943 0889
Email: sarah@hamptoncourthouse.co.uk
Website: www.hamptoncourthouse.co.uk

Headmaster: Since 2001, Guy Holloway MA (Cantab), NPQH, known as 'Guy' to all, who is also head of the senior school.

Entrance: Into the nursery at 3, or year 1 at 5+, following an informal interview with child and parents. During visit child will be observed by the teaching staff for both academic and social behaviour, and will meet with the head of lower and early years. If applicable, a confidential report from the child's current school will be requested. Head wishes to ensure that parents are committed to the school's ethos and approach to learning. At 10, children are tested in English and maths. More selective in

H

recent years, but potential is still considered carefully. With approximately 35 languages represented at the school, the majority of students have at least one British parent. School runs buses from Chelsea, Kingston and Richmond and pupils come from central and west London and surrounding parts of Surrey.

Exit: Despite being an all-through school, pupils are all prepared for 11 + and 13+ examinations and scholarships. Most stay on, but some move to a very wide variety of destinations eg boarding to Bryanston, Kingston Grammar, Eton, Westminster and Tiffins. Not surprisingly there are also families returning abroad as work commitments dictate. Increasingly parents are choosing to keep their children at HCH senior school.

Remarks: Very special indeed is the opportunity for all children from early years to year 4 to receive a bilingual education in English and French with fluent French speakers, so all can become at least competent and develop good accents. From age 6, pupils can also follow the French curriculum for the Centre National d'Enseignment à Distance, which we saw in practice as a year 5 group successfully completed assigned writing tasks to time. Grammar is taken seriously, along with teaching accurate use of punctuation, as seen in pupils' books. All learn Latin from year 5 and Spanish is lively and enthusiastic. Language options include Mandarin. HCH is one of the leading prep schools for this in the UK. French is taught through other subjects (such as mathematics and humanities) and we saw year 1 pupils completing maths addition work happily asking questions in French and slipping back into English with ease. It all seemed perfectly natural and there was support from classmates as well as teachers.

Many nationalities are represented amongst staff and pupils and the curriculum reflects this, so children learn to appreciate and respect other cultures. We saw a year 5 English class tackling creative writing and were impressed by the articulate, confident responses to our questioning, whilst attentive year 6 pupils were appreciating Beowulf. Parents value the imaginative cross-curricular opportunities teachers take to make topics more meaningful eg Queen Victoria in history alongside Great Expectations in English. We saw year 2s, basing their designs on South American wildlife, making imaginative moulds in art, which would later be used to produce Fair Trade chocolates

As well as a concentration on the 3Rs, art, drama and music are seen as central to education here – hooray! Talented musicians are given every opportunity to perform and share in music-making, and more than 50 children have music lessons in school. IT is well provided for with a designated room full of Macs with big screens. All sports are taken by qualified sports teachers and everyone up to year 4 has weekly swimming sessions at Imber Court Pool, a short ride away. In addition, after-school tennis lessons are on offer with tennis specialists. Early years children have their own garden, and all can freely enjoy the wonderful space for outdoor play. There are trees to climb, grounds to explore including a sizeable pond, and the stunning house itself in beautiful countryside. One parent remarked, 'HCH is not an imposing, austere place: instead, very warm and welcoming. My child has had an amazing childhood at HCH. They read books and then play outside enacting them, letting their imaginations run freely'.

A French parent we spoke to was very impressed with communication and the fact that teachers are approachable, know pupils by name and show interest in the families attending. 'The school is small enough to defuse situations so difficulties can be resolved at an early stage.' School is flexible about keeping children down a year or bumping them up one in consultation with parents. This can work exceptionally well, especially in a case of mild bullying, exceptional aptitude or slowness, but it can pose a problem if the child is destined elsewhere.

SEN provision is considered 'outstanding' as far as Ofsted is concerned (praise for the IEPs), with a few requiring direct support for dyslexic traits and social and communication skills. There is specialist one-to-one EAL support.

The food is amazing. The chef also oversees all food at a Fulham free school and is a key player in the government's School Food Plan programme. We saw healthy, appetising food choices with plenty of seasonal options.

Freedom to run about in home clothes and be encouraged to gain a love of learning without the usual constraints can, in many cases, lead to happy, self-disciplined, motivated children. Nevertheless, some parents flee after a while and are not assured that the ethos works in practice or that all claims are realised. This is not the right school for those conservative parents who prefer a more conventional, pedagogical approach and obvious rigid hierarchical structures.

Hampton Court House (Senior School)

Linked with Hampton Court House (Junior School)

101

The Green, Hampton Court Road, East Molesey, Surrey KT8 9BS

Pupils: 106 • Ages: 11–18 • Sixth form: 20

Fees: £16,800 – £18,180 pa

Tel: 020 8614 0857
Email: admissions@hchnet.co.uk
Website: www.hamptoncourthouse.co.uk

Headmaster: Since 2001, Guy Holloway MA (Cantab), NPQH, known as 'Guy' to all. With his own Russian/German background, he is passionate about the importance of languages, both ancient and modern. He studied at King's College School, Wimbledon, before reading English at Peterhouse, Cambridge. He spent many years in Paris, first at the international PR firm, Burson-Marsteller, and then at the École Active Bilingue, where he was head of English in the section Britannique. For several years he was a volunteer with Save the Children UK, working with disadvantaged children. He is now patron of the children's charity Their Future Today, which supports abandoned and institutionalised children in Sri Lanka.

Part of the 1993 founding team which opened the Harrodian School, where he was director of studies, he is a co-founder of HCH. A committed educationalist, he lectures at the Institute of Education's London Centre for Leadership in Learning. He believes in giving pupils a global perspective so they have an appreciation of cultures and informed tolerance, partly borne out by the international flavour of his staff appointments, including a Spanish head of pastoral care and a German head of mathematics. He runs a weekly seminar – a comprehensive history of music course for all children in years 1 to 8 – and teaches cultural studies to years 10 and 11. He believes staff have a responsibility as role models, sharing the love of their subjects with their pupils. He acts on his beliefs, eg, he encourages all in the acquisition of vocabulary and shared his personal discovery, lustrum, in assembly on the day we visited.

Guy sees his future as 'married to HCH'. He champions creativity and is justifiably proud of the school's culture, which 'enables pupils to fulfil their passions' and nurtures individuals so that they develop quality relationships as a life skill. He is approachable and totally committed to the school's ethos: 'We believe in questioning our beliefs' and 'The primacy of the idea over the person'.

Alongside his fascination for psychology and learning, Guy has a diverse range of cultural and linguistic interests alongside languages, including foreign travel, literature, chess and concert-going, and he is an active member of the Rose Theatre Players. He enjoys directing films as well as plays (over 30) at HCH and recalled many ambitious productions to us with pride.

Academic matters: The study and celebration of languages and the arts are integral to HCH, which is a UNESCO associate school and the only school in the UK to be granted 'Institut Francais' status by the French government for its commitment to French language and culture. In a liberal, civilised, relaxed, atmosphere where staff are addressed by first names, individuals are encouraged to pursue their passions to the full, whilst learning how to appreciate art, music and drama. The staffing reflects this, with native speakers and professional performers as role models; so important. Undoubtedly languages are a strength at HCH with 54 per cent A* grades in French and 50 per cent in Spanish at GCSE in 2016. Everyone takes at least one language to GCSE, with nearly a quarter studying French/Spanish in the first year of the sixth form.

In 2016, 43 per cent of all GCSEs at A*/A. In 2015 HCH was given the Good School Guide award for best performance in English independent schools by boys in both psychology and Spanish. This is not a result-driven academic school; instead, the head describes it as a 'shared intellectual environment'. Pupils are prepared for 13+ as well as GCSEs and now A levels (first results summer 2017). As one long-standing parent put it, 'Don't expect one of the local hothouses without uniform. You won't find the mechanistic, predictable, step by step approach for all at HCH, but instead a joy in the educational experience where pupils gain a rounded introduction to life, and where it's not just about passing exams'. Unavoidably, not all parents are convinced, and some question the fact that, despite degrees, teaching staff do not necessarily have teaching qualifications, whilst others praise their 'inspirational enthusiasm' and the attention and support given to each individual.Ofsted has judged that 'the mostly good or outstanding lessons enable pupils to make rapid progress' and recognised HCH as 'good and increasingly outstanding'.

The school is a lead school in the Network of Excellence in Computer Science, with an emphasis on programming. 'If a child needs to be extended and takes a subject a step further, this is acknowledged and encouraged'. Pupils do need to be motivated and exert self-disciplin,e as this will not be imposed from above.

In 2015 HCH opened its gates to a newly-established sixth form led by experienced, traditionalist headmaster Tristram Jones-Parry MA (Oxon), previously head of Westminster and Emanuel, and teacher of mathematics. Guy explained that the decision was made initially to offer 'heavy duty A levels as well as psychology'. We caught the end of a physics lesson with a small, predominantly male group of the first cohort of sixth formers in one of three new specialist science laboratories. The sixth form has been in the spotlight with its novel late start. Lessons run from 1.30pm to 7.00pm and the school is linked with Oxford University research, promoting a later start for under 20s which aims to maximise the benefit of improved sleeping patterns. Sixth formers can stay on to enjoy a diverse range of speakers, as part of the Form Seven adult education programme involving topics such as Napoleon and the Battle of Borodino, women and enlightenment science, and 18th century French art history. We wait to see the results.

School is very accepting and inclusive of SENs. SEN department comprises a SENCo, who comes into school twice a week, plus three others: one maths specialist, one specialising in early intervention, and the other very experienced in dyslexia and dyspraxia. They work in small groups or one-to-one, as best suits the child. Seventeen per cent of pupils are on the SEN register – mostly mild to moderate dyslexia or dyscalculia, but school will support ADHD and dyspraxia. One parent commented how proud she had been of the way her daughter and friends had been deliberately protective and inclusive of a pupil with ADHD, and another commented on the positive staff approach showed, allowing the pupil to let off steam by running up and down the corridors when necessary.

Games, options, the arts: The arts and music are superb, with imaginative use made of music composition linked with filming and animations, and pupils winning prizes for artwork and photographs. Small classes mean staff all really know the pupils. Talents are recognised and promoted and the school is sufficiently small to be flexible, a great plus if your child carries out arduous sports or music practice or has to attend rehearsals outside school. Many do, including a current ballet pupil dancing at the Royal Opera House; others attend West End show rehearsals and music performances, and there is a genuine respect for the work ethic involved. As Guy comments, 'Our current national gymnasts complete hours of training a week, and that requires real commitment and dedication'. In the lunch break we heard a young Cambridge choral scholar master successfully putting the choir through its paces, practising a Rutter anthem in the Great Hall. More than 60 students have one-to-one music lessons in school.

There is a varied sports curriculum, with fixtures against local schools in football, netball, cricket and athletics with coaching in rugby VIIs and hockey too. Sixth formers can use a gym across the road if they wish. Each year group has one full sports afternoon a week and there are daily lunchtime clubs as well as after-school clubs in judo, archery, table tennis, football and athletics. The school grounds are extensive and include a netball and tennis court, football pitch and a smaller 5-a-side football pitch. Pupils enjoy running in Bushy Park and Hampton Court Green. One parent did suggest: 'There are lots of clubs but it would be good if they had some physical activity every day of the week, building exercise into their daily lives', although acknowledging that 'healthy eating is considered and the food is amazing'.

Background and atmosphere: Completed in 1757 by the Earl of Halifax, Hampton Court House was intended as an extravagant gift for his mistress Anna-Maria Donaldson and was designed by architect and astronomer Thomas Wright. He was responsible for special period features including a heart-shaped pond and enchanting shell-lined grotto with its painted blue ceiling with gilded wooden stars, and an octagonal ice-house now used for drumming practice. Set within nine acres, the beautiful Georgian mansion has a stunning entrance hall with columns, gallery, ceiling, fireplace, conservatory, winter garden with palms and dining room, all tastefully decorated and looking out at the vista of Bushy Park. After Mrs Donaldson's death the house passed through a succession of tenants and was sold to Marmaduke Blake Sampson in 1871. He was city correspondent to The Times and Argentine consul in London, and was responsible for adding the picture gallery. Much later it passed to the tea-planting Twinings, until in the 1980s, quite extraordinarily, it was a Save the Children home for refugee Vietnamese children.

Following considerable restoration and refurbishment of the house, the school started its life with a pre-prep and prep in 2001, expanding upwards until it opened its sixth form in 2015. The irregularity of the classrooms, along with the abundance of comfortable sofas and country house items of furniture, may seem quirky to those parents used to pristine, purpose-built establishments. Nevertheless, much thought has been given to light, and the ambiance is spacious; pupils are not as crammed in as they might be in some central London schools.

This school has a palpable atmosphere and culture of kindness. As one parent explained, 'HCH is a microcosm of society based on respect and developing useful, responsible citizens ready to take their place in the world.' Parents rightly value the warm welcome and friendships made at HCH with fellow pupils and staff. We noticed the relaxed way in which ages and genders mixed happily and naturally at lunch, moving about with ease, whilst parents are delighted at the way pupils support one another, enjoying activities such as camping, chess, or performing in concerts and plays.

Pastoral care, well-being and discipline: At HCH the belief in developing quality relationships is key, whilst reflecting and learning from one's mistakes in a community based on mutual respect. Guy explains, 'I may hold a door open for a pupil but expect a pupil to hold a door open for me'. First names are used throughout, but despite the non-uniform, each pupil has an almanack in which there is a clear code of conduct and dress. When we visited we were impressed by the pupils' smart appearance. Undoubtedly some individuals would not thrive in such a liberal, non-hierarchical setting, and Guy admits that it is important to match the individual to the right school and that some have left because of this. Parents often visit several times for reassurance, but tend to agree that 'The teachers know all the pupils, and because of the small nature of the school, they are often able to intervene and defuse situations'.

School actively promotes mindfulness, and nutritional advice and time management skills are included in a comprehensive well-being programme. In the past the head has expelled a boy over drugs, and is very aware of safety and security. He regularly chats with the gatekeeper, who can spot if a child is looking miserable or has a concern.

Pupils and parents: Pupils come from a 30 mile radius, with many from Kingston, Surbiton or Hampton, and there is a school minibus which collects from Chelsea, Richmond and Kingston. Not surprisingly, there is a number of international families including some French, who want their children to maintain levels of French 'whilst immersing themselves in English and English culture'. HCH attracts the unconventional, the liberal, the arty. As one parent summarised, 'we appreciate an all-through school where time is found to explore ideas and there is a conventional output but not process'.

Although a relatively new school with no sixth form leavers as yet, many ex-pupils have moved on successfully to universities including Oxbridge. Non academic achievers include environmental campaigner and filmmaker, Ayrton Cable, winner of Diana Award and nominated for the International Children's Peace Prize for his work in Malawi; two international ice skaters; many young actors and actresses eg Rupert Sadler, Harriet Turnbull, Nell Tiger Free and Isabella Blake Thomas; not forgetting a heavy metal singer, Austin Dickinson.

Entrance: Main entry points at 11+ and 13+. Interview for candidate and parents plus maths and English tests. Parents are welcome to visit more than once as it is essential pupil and family believe in school's distinctive ethos and approach to education. New sixth form applicants need at least six B grades with As in subjects to be studied at A level.

Exit: Will prepare for 13+ exams and, unsurprisingly, incredibly diverse range of destinations, including lycées abroad, state schools, Eton, Wellington, Westminster, Bryanston, Kingston Grammar, Wimbledon High, Surbiton High, with some scholarships, although in recent years more are staying on. There is some turnover of children because families move abroad, but those remaining develop a widening circle of friends. First cohort will go on to higher education in 2017.

Money matters: Up to three scholarships – academic, music, arts – each year, worth 10 per cent of fees maximum. All 11+ candidates are automatically entered.

Remarks: Ideal setting for individuals who can be trusted to be responsible and will thrive on civilised, relaxed values and learn from enthusiastic, approachable teachers who share their passions for their subjects. Several parents acknowledged, 'We visited three times before making up our minds because the school offers something different'. In recent years the school has become more selective, but the head, quite rightly, remains interested in individuals and what they have to offer. As one parent remarked, 'This is a place where it is ok to be different and ask questions, and not be considered a nuisance'.

Hampton Pre-Prep and Prep School

Linked with Hampton School

102

Gloucester Road, Hampton TW12 2UQ

Pupils: 223 • Ages: 3-7 (girls), 3-11 (boys)

Fees: £10,890 – £12,600 pa

Tel: 020 8979 1844
Email: admissions@hamptonprep.org.uk
Website: www.hamptonprep.org.uk

Head: Since 2015, Mr Tim Smith, BA, MBA (40s). Previously deputy head academic, The Hall School Hampstead, for five years, originally joining in 1994 as games and French teacher, becoming head of learning support and then head of middle school. Also deputy chair of governors in Camden state primary.

Full of the joys of spring. Actually, make that all seasons. 'I love coming into this wonderful place every day,' he exults on the website.

A linguist, he's arty (a regular at the Barbican; partner is head of exhibitions at the Royal Academy) but has only ever wanted to teach. 'Always wanted to play schools,' he says of childhood in New Zealand. Years of wrestling with nervy North Londoners haven't dimmed enthusiasm for career he describes as 'exciting, rewarding, engaging, motivating, joyful and hilarious.'

A shrewd operator, choice of SW London school with less toxic parental vibe – at least for now – compared with north of the river is deliberate. Ditto prep finishing at 11 rather than traditional 13, as many senior schools up year 7 intake at the expense of common entrance places. Keen to avoid ivory tower complacency, an occupational hazard for preps, he thinks (state schools often do it better) and keep the innovations coming to improve quality of teaching – 'the light at the heart of school'.

His emphatic approach has come as a bit of a shock to parents though (largely) in a good way. 'Quirky,' was a description we heard more than once. 'Eloquent,' ditto. Felt to have made real effort to get to know pupils. 'Had the measure of our son quite quickly,' said mother. Excitement of the job? Like other heads, says no two days are the same (we're dying to find the first school where they are). Unlike them, explains how. Easy to forget you're dealing with children, he says, who 'do lots of extraordinary and enlightening and motivating things no matter how hard you try or how much you want them to ... go in a certain direction.'

Doesn't pull his punches, particularly when it comes to nervy parents who tell him they only 'want the best' for their child. Do they imagine teachers 'munching on breakfast of baby seals and endangered penguins [and thinking] "I can't wait to come into school and be mean to children?"' he wonders.

Short shrift also given to their fears that strengthened links with Hampton mean school door, as one expressed it, 'no longer open for all boys'. Stresses that nothing is set in stone, academic standards largely going to be determined by intake and any change will be gradual – with no wholesale notices to quit. 'Won't be gathering children up by their ankles, and flinging them into park because they're not clever enough.' A relief all round, then.

Entrance: In crowded part of the world where limitless parental aspiration meets finite school places, school's willingness to go extra mile a real help for parents – one family wrestling with decision given mobile number to call during hols for extra reassurance.

Main intake at age 3 into co-ed nursery (20-22 places) and into boys only prep in year 3, when between 14-17 places on offer depending on how many boys leave at end of year 2 (some lured away by well-regarded state primaries). Screen for learning needs in kindergarten, then it's assessments for reception, and years 1 and 2, plus reports. Entry to prep currently automatic-ish for existing pre-prep pupils. Others have tests plus interview with head and report from previous school.

Exit: Girls at end of year 2 to local all-through schools such as Surbiton, LEH, preps (Newland House, Twickenham Prep) and state sector. In year 6, healthy numbers to Halliford, St James Boys' in Ashford and Kingston Grammar, while others such as Reed's make guest appearances. Hampton School, however, biggest destination of the lot with 19 places in 2016. Assured places scheme available from year 2 to year 5 based on combination of assessments, teacher reports, exam results and in-depth discussions by admissions committee unsurprisingly a huge parental incentive. Other boys welcome to sit 11+ on equal footing with external candidates.

Remarks: Relationship with big brother Hampton School wasn't exactly a secret even before change of name (from Denmead) in early 2016. Part of Hampton School Trust since 1999, founded in 1924 by one of English masters in own dining room after own son's left-handedness made him an educational pariah.

Pre-prep, just a hop, skip and jump away across pretty public park, is where it all starts. 'The jewel in the crown,' thought one parent. Housed in original school buildings with grassed front garden and miniature lych gate entrance, home-like feel and nurturing ethos makes it a popular standalone option for daughters as well as sons.

Long-serving pre-prep head, Mrs Murphy, gets star ratings from all for ability to get the best from pupils, effortlessly wrapping up fun and learning together with cross-curricular approach felt to be particularly successful (pirates covered by coordinates in maths, on board rules in English and top marauding destinations in geography). Lots of experienced teachers who make connections but ensure pupils 'make the vital links for themselves.'

New name means new uniform featuring friendly Hampton golden lion, but big news is complete prep rebuild, replacing shabby (without the chic) Portakabin collection, to all round relief. Attractive two-storey building houses eight airy classrooms, brace of IT suites, art and music rooms and efficient-looking library, all under nature and neighbour friendly living roof, angled to blend in with residential surroundings.

Plenty of greenery courtesy of allotment with raised beds and that horticultural essential, a potting shed, part of revamped outside space that also includes playing fields (shaping up nicely on day of visit) and all-weather area. Back gate on to Carlisle Park provides extra overspill games space, senior school's 27 acres and theatre also coming in handy for large-scale events.

Other changes are less root and branch than nip and tuck and made only where demonstrably better than what's gone before (we liked the lesson bell, lifted from French educational system and featuring mellifluous four-note leitmotif).

'What we do is based on substantiated, evidence-based, peer reviewed, professional practice,' says Mr Smith. 'We're not pulling mad ideas out of a hat.' (Harvard University, no less, called in to help with review of pastoral care). Far more emphasis on tracking – no doubting where your child is and what they're capable of achieving, while assessments are regular without being excessive and can't be prepared for (and don't get Mr Smith started on tutors – 'A racket'). Formal exams limited to maths and English, with verbal reasoning added to English and NVR to maths from year 4.

Team of 20 academic staff in the prep (equal numbers of men and women), 12 in the pre-prep (all female) and just under 30 non-teaching staff, including three gap year students.

Two sets for maths and English from year 4, three in years 5 and 6. Will often double up on teachers to support and challenge (school's headline staff to pupil ratio of 1:18 doesn't reflect this) while three-strong learning support team (same again for pre-prep) help small numbers (around seven) with ADD, ADHD and mild SpLD. Their highlight is the 'ladder of success' – top rung winners who successfully complete daily tasks acknowledged in assembly with 'huge, noisy fuss...' and edible prize. Individual support for EAL pupils (around 35 across whole school) in pre-prep and in class in prep.

Curriculum 'shouldn't be a mile wide but only inch deep,' says Mr Smith, who also comes up with own three Rs – 'richness, relevance and rigour'. Thus subject list doesn't bulge with the outré or unusual – French is only language taught, for example – but concentrates on core range done well, and given more time. Mr Smith is also bumping up recruitment of subject specialists – like parents, feels currently too many generalists, particularly in top years.

With staff training and appraisals also being revamped, teachers 'go the extra mile,' says parent, encouraged to go exploring if lesson takes a different tack. Universal praise for English, boys learning to 'critique their own work and improve it,' says approving parent. Love of books reinforced all the way through –school will set reading as only holiday homework, for example.

Maths felt to be improving, on-line resources used increasingly to advantage. Results in all-through confidence – year 3 boys eager to explain division by four ('divide by two and by two again'), others in year 6 yomping through hinterlands of mean and mode. 'Teachers aren't going to blow you out of the window if you get it wrong,' reported one. 'Make teaching fun.'

Exam pressure – which pupils agreed could be tough – similarly well handled, focus on preparation without panic. Boys able to rattle off practical techniques that help. 'Make the point, use a quote and explain,' said one.

Ad hoc prizes (including sweets and – from one teacher – even more popular tennis balls) are popular incentives, though discipline felt by parents to be excellent – 'Only takes a look for boys to be quiet.' Masses of reinforcement, from weekly award of courtesy cup in prep to flowers, cloth and special pud for best behaved pre-prep lunchtime table. Easily understood golden rules for younger pupils, though slightly tortuous house point system for year 4 upwards (fine detail runs to several pages) is being revamped. 'Too complex,' agrees head.

Trips range from creative writing workshops to suitably bloodthirsty Saxons vs. Viking experience – firmly linked to curriculum, while clubs span debating to cooking, changing by season. Otherwise, sport's the big thing, with three sessions a week and easily the highlight for majority of pupils. Biggest stars can, thought one parent, get the sleb treatment (the eternal problem) though another praised numbers of teams (A to D for rugby and football) and regular swapsies so Bs get at least second dibs on training and attention. Means that while truly uninterested might struggle, anyone who's keen but with a modicum of talent is felt on the whole to have a good time. Results justify the effort with frequent successes, school handicapped only by size (some larger Richmond-based opponents can choose from bigger pool of talent).

Swimming has been major casualty of timetable rejigging, axed in the prep (though still offered for years 1 and 2). Not everyone's happy about this – 'focus is on football and rugby to the detriment of any other sport,' said parent, but Mr Smith isn't budging. 'We're not going to use valuable curriculum time to teach them to splash around in some grubby pool when parents can do that themselves on a Saturday.'

Art, however, has had a reprieve. Initially pared back and rotated in 10-week blocks with drama and DT, will regain weekly slot on the timetable from autumn 2016 after fears that talented weren't getting enough time to hone work to scholarship standard.

With around 60 prep and pre-prep pupils learning instruments (beginners to grade 5), a choir, orchestra and wind band and several scholarships in recent years, performing arts are good, think parents, though anticipate better things to come. 'Don't have enough children, scratching, blowing, tweeting and trumpeting,' agrees Mr Smith. Added space for more of everything – instruments, informal as well as class-based concerts plus whole school annual production all on the way, activity across the octave and decibel range should increase.

Parents very sociable, newcomers quickly brought into the fold. While the many working parents can inevitably end up missing out on coffee mornings, 'Always someone who'll scoop up your child.' Helped by before and after-school care – 7.45am start (8.00am in the pre-prep), 5.30pm finish – more activities after school would make life even easier, felt one parent.

Mr Smith stresses (and will probably have to keep on stressing) that ethos of school won't change 'simply because ... we apply tenets of the admissions policy ever more carefully as time goes by.' Some current parents have yet to be convinced. Prospective parents eye up snazzy rebuild and growing numbers gaining places at Hampton and make up their own minds.

Hampton School

Linked with Hampton Pre-Prep and Prep School

Hanworth Road, Hampton TW12 3HD

Pupils: 1,200 • Ages: 11–18 • Sixth form: 380

Fees: £18,375 pa

Tel: 020 8979 5526
Email: admissions@hamptonschool.org.uk
Website: www.hamptonschool.org.uk

Headmaster: Since 2013, Mr Kevin Knibbs MA (early 40s). Joined Hampton as deputy head in 2007. Previously history master, head of lower school and senior master at Bolton School Boys' Division. Educated at King Edward VI Grammar School, Chelmsford and read modern history at Oxford (gaining two football blues in the process). A career schoolmaster who still teaches history to youngest boys. 'I happen to run a big business, but that's not why I chose teaching in the first place,' he tells us. Not one to hog the limelight. At his happiest when talking about the boys, of whom he is fiercely proud.

Very visible head who can often to be spotted at weekends on the touchline and towpath, supporting Hampton boys and chatting to parents. Friendly, approachable and generous spirited. 'I am lucky to lead a school that is on this trajectory and I want to keep it going. It's a privilege to be in this job. I love it. I hope that comes through.' It does.

His wife is one of the chemistry teachers. He has a weakness for off-piste ski-ing in Colorado.

Academic matters: Results going from strength to strength with record grades. At GCSE, 91 per cent A*/A in 2016. Boys performed outstandingly well in the free-standing maths qualification with over 90 per cent scoring top grade. Hamptonians also impress regularly in national competitions, including as winners of the UK Maths Trust challenge for two years running, and in winning essay and poetry prizes. In lower years, all boys study chemistry, biology and physics as separate subjects, computer programming and coding, at least one language out of French, German, Spanish, Russian or Mandarin, and Latin, which is compulsory in years 7 and 8. Setting in maths and modern languages from third year.

At A level, 66 per cent A*/A grades in 2016. Currently physics, chemistry, history, philosophy, German and Mandarin (short course) offered at Pre-U. At A level, maths remains perennially popular with regularly 30 per cent taking further maths. As one teacher explained, 'maths is like a magnet for these boys.' High uptake of chemistry, physics and economics too. In sixth form, all boys follow an enrichment programme which includes six week courses on topics including university life and finance, mindfulness and current affairs. School offers its own extended project qualification, with recent essays focusing on quantum gravity and the feasibility of time travel.

School is no slouch on the computer front, with eight different ICT suites and a new coding room. Boys bring in their own iPads and use them in every subject. School council currently hotly debating whether to replace text books with ebooks.

Around 185 pupils have some kind of SEN. Support offered tends to be small group intervention (currently around 40 such groups) with lunchtime drop in sessions popular, especially as exams start to loom. 'Some of our highest achieving boys are on our learning support register and that's how it should be,' states head. Forty pupils are classified as EAL, though none require additional support.

Over a third of staff has been at school for more than a decade. Each year roughly 10 per cent leaves, so constant flow of fresh blood, including some sparky graduates who are grabbed straight out of university and are trained on the job. Head acknowledges that 'we are a springboard school and people want our staff. Any of my senior team could run their own school but I am clinging on to them.' Approximately 40 per cent of teachers are female. 'That's changed a lot. When the boys leave here they know exactly who is in charge,' smiles the head. Pupils feel their teachers are friendly. One of the younger boys explained, 'Homework got the better of me at the beginning. But if you email a teacher to say you are struggling with the work, they are more than happy to go through it the next day. You just need to give them the heads up.' All the lessons we observed were lively and led by dynamic teachers, many of whom have grammar school backgrounds themselves and like the down-to-earth ethos of the school.

Games, options, the arts: School is well-known for its excellent sports provision, with at least 17 different sports offered. Over 27 acres of playing fields so all facilities (bar the Millennium boathouse) are on site and head has been known to joke that he would move the Thames if he could so that it could flow closer to the school. State-of-the-art, all-weather 3G sports ground very well used, including at break time when swarms of boys congregate there and kick balls about with great gusto. 'It's good for morale and improves concentration in the classroom,' states head. One boy told us that 'my mum loves the 3G grass as I never come home muddy!' Another told us that he fell in love with Hampton the moment he saw the huge number of pitches stretching into the distance. Sports practice mostly takes place at lunchtime to enable those travelling home by coach to participate. Football and rugby in the winter; athletics, cricket and tennis in the summer; rowing throughout the year. Minor sports include fencing, sailing and windsurfing. Boys can choose which sports they want to play and the school excels at most. As always, Hampton is competing at the highest levels in national schools' competitions and churning out some exceptional sportsmen, especially in football, rugby, rowing, athletics and cricket. Deserves its reputation for being one of the top football, rugby and rowing schools in the country. No hockey offered which one parent found 'disappointing, as many boys would be keen to play it.' School stresses importance of participation for all, and multiple teams are fielded in all age groups. One mother we spoke to was not so sure, saying that 'in reality, there may be some who struggle to make a team.' Starry old boys include Olympic gold medallists Greg and Jonny Searle as well as Surrey and England all-rounder Zafar Ansari.

Head insists that school is not just for those who can perform brilliantly on the games pitches. 'There are many quiet, effective learners who find their own niche. We want to make sure that all boys get opportunities'. Boys agree that 'there is no hierarchy of worth. Being in the first XV is not seen as being any better than being in the Voices of Lions.' School has worked hard to encourage this view and head is adamant that that academic, musical and dramatic successes are now celebrated just as much as sporting triumphs.

With over 50 clubs on offer, including model aviators, debating, and photography, there does seem to be something for every taste. Over 200 boys take part in D of E scheme each year. Adventure Society, open to all years, offers a heady mix of kayaking, power-boating, orienteering and sea-cliff climbing. For the more sedentary, chess is thriving: five teams regularly represent the school. One pupil is currently national chess champion. Beekeeping society is the latest club on the list.

Performing arts have taken off in the last decade and serious resources have been funnelled towards both drama and music. The Hammond theatre seats 380 and boasts a hydraulic orchestral pit, hi-tech lighting and sound systems and, one pupil told us, watching plays here 'feels like being at the West End.' Numerous plays performed every year, from junior plays to large-scale musicals such as Chicago and Les Misérables. Lower school play is normally a performance of an original work by a visiting community playwright. Well-equipped art/DT department, and some stunning artwork lines the corridors, though surprisingly few take these subjects at A level. School produces a steady stream of Arkwright engineering scholars.

Around 400 boys have music lessons, many on more than one instrument. Significant numbers attain grade 8. Two current pupils with diplomas. Plenty of performances from rock, jazz, keyboard to strings and boys have 23 music ensembles to choose from. Celebrated male voice choir, Voices of Lions, enjoys a high profile and performs at Edinburgh Fringe. The lively rendition of Drunken Sailor in school assembly was apparently 'legendary'. Nine Hampton musicians have received organ scholarships from Oxbridge in recent years.

Background and atmosphere: The school was set up over 450 years ago thanks to a bequest of property and land by local brewer and businessman, Robert Hammond. Formerly a grammar school (went independent in 1975). Situated in suburban West London, on a greenfield site. Not the most beautiful of schools, though the warmth and friendliness of both staff and pupils makes up for the lack of architectural splendour.

School is outward looking and has developed links in the local community and abroad. Boys help in local primary schools and put on a Christmas party for elderly locals. School provides a Latin class for GCSE pupils from local state schools. Also has an association with a safe haven in Malawi. Hampton is proud of being a 'beacon school' for Holocaust education and raises awareness of more recent genocides. Certainly not a school that just looks after its own.

Close ties with neighbouring girls' school The Lady Eleanor Holles School. Since the appointment of the new head there, there is 'an enhanced desire to work collaboratively, especially at sixth form level'. Schools already share much, including drama productions, language exchanges and Oxbridge interview preparation. School firmly believes it gives the boys the best of both worlds, and it is hard to disagree.

Pastoral care, well-being and discipline: School takes great care to integrate boys who arrive at 13 with the well-established 11+ cohort. Pupils are supported by a pastoral team, including their form tutor and head of year, as well as sixth form mentors, though one parent we spoke to said 'the lack of a house system and small tutor groups may mean that some boys may slip through the net, no matter what the school tells you.' Some reports of bullying in the early years, though parents felt this was generally stamped out quickly. Head runs a weekly pre-school drop-in for boys to approach him on any matter they wish and he meets with head boy and his deputies once a fortnight and jokes that 'they tell me how to run the school'. This head has his ear to the ground.

Head has helped establish Hampton as a national leader in mindfulness. 'We're one of the early pioneers of it,' he says proudly. Believes it is a useful tool for helping these boys deal with 'the ups and downs of teenage life in this high achieving setting.' Mindfulness, life issues and well-being/resilience taught for nine weeks as part of the curriculum in fourth year, followed by a top-up session before GCSE study leave begins. Numerous teachers, including the head, have also done the course. One pupil we spoke to admitted that 'it can be a struggle to balance everything as there is so much going on here, but mindfulness helps.' Boys can frequently be seen practising mindfulness techniques before exams and performances. Head believes that it is no coincidence that since it has become a mainstream part of the school, 'the academic results have improved and the school has become a kinder, gentler and calmer place'. Head adds, with a smile, 'If it's good enough for Jonny Wilkinson ...'

Pupils and parents: Diverse mix of boys. Many parents have state school backgrounds and choose it for its unpretentiousness. Increasing numbers of European parents whose sons are bi/trilingual. Languages spoken at home include Gujarati, Urdu and Korean. Many boys walk or cycle to school and older boys can drive, as long as they park at a distance. Extensive coach network (run jointly with LEH) attracts families from all over west and south west London and Surrey. Coach journeys with girls apparently awash with 'witty banter.'

Parents are very involved with the school, often helping with careers advice and fundraising. Head admits the parents can be demanding, but 'we're better off than some schools in that respect. We seem to attract families which do not tip over the fine line between aspirational and obsessional.'

Entrance: Highly selective. A 40 per cent increase in registration since 2011. Now more than six applicants per place. No sibling policy. Pupils generally enter the school at 11, 13 or 16. The 11+ route is normally for 125 boys; current batch from 75 different feeder schools (54 per cent of them joined from state primary schools, the remainder from preps which finish at end of year 6). At 13+ a further 65 boys enter the school, from about 25 different independent prep schools. Around 10-12 boys join in sixth form though few places up for grabs at this stage. At 11+, entry is via school's own entrance exam (maths, English and reasoning) plus interview and reference. For 13+ entry, boys must sit the pre-test at 11 and offers are made conditional on a satisfactory performance in CE or in the scholarship exam. Entrance at sixth form is via personal statement, head teacher's report, written and online assessment and interview. Boys must also get a good clutch of GCSEs, with a minimum six A*/A grades including English and maths. The staggered entry at 11 and 13 works well and one teacher made it clear that 'we're standing firm with the 13+.'

Head devotes hours to speaking to prospective parents and says he tries 'to be clear about our ethos to parents. The families we choose need to be on board. It has to be the right fit for their son.' Warns parents not to 'force the pace' but to aim to put their son in an environment where he will be happy. Looking for boys who are academically able, inquisitive and hard-working, but they also need heaps of stamina to keep up here. A willingness to join in and try new things is crucial. 'Along with appointing staff, it is the most important thing I do,' says head. He manages to make the selection process as personal as possible and sends out good luck cards to all 1,200 applicants before entrance exams. A characteristically thoughtful gesture.

H

Exit: School is keen to point out that 'we do not cull anyone post-GCSEs' and there is no minimum number of GCSEs that internal boys must gain in order to be allowed to stay into the sixth form. 'We do talk to parents and pupils openly, however, if a boy is struggling. They might choose to put in place a contingency plan.' Those boys who leave at 16 tend to do so because school does not offer the subjects they wish to study, such as photography.

About 25 to 30 boys head for Oxbridge each year (22 in 2016) in a wide range of subjects. Head explains, 'We don't get obsessed about it. It is certainly not a case of Oxbridge or die. Some boys actually turn down Oxbridge places if there is a better course for them personally elsewhere'. Vast majority tends to head for Russell Group universities. Occasionally, boys venture to the Continent while others choose medical schools, drama schools or conservatoires. Favoured universities at the moment include Warwick, Durham and Nottingham. Boys opt for a wide range of degrees from astrophysics to zoology. A handful disappears off to Ivy League colleges in the US, often on sporting scholarships. Twenty or so take gap years. As head of careers explains, 'We try to set out the options for the boys and support whichever path they want to take.' Boys regularly return for career advice long after they leave.

Money matters: Fifty-six boys are on full bursaries and another 127 are on substantial bursaries. Plans afoot to provide more such places and this is a matter close to the head's heart. 'In terms of the school's future, to maintain our grounded feel, and with fees going up, we need to make sure that more bursaries are available. We do not have a big endowment so have to do it through fundraising.' Academic, all-rounder, art, choral and music scholarships carry a remission of up to 25 per cent of fees. 'If there are financial issues, we do try to help,' says head.

Remarks: Hampton is riding high. Though head is conscious that 'we can sometimes hide our light under a bushel here,' they would be justified in shouting their achievements from the rooftops. There is currently a real energy about the school and boys appeared to be genuinely happy.

One of the aims of the school is for Hamptonians to strive 'for personal success while supporting those around them.' If the boys who showed us around are anything to go by, they are accomplishing their goal admirably. Hampton is producing young men of integrity. No wonder the head is so proud of them.

The Harrodian School

Lonsdale Road, London SW13 9QN

Pupils: 983 • Ages: 4–18 • Sixth form: 166

Fees: £13,800 – £21,105 pa

Tel: 020 8748 6117
Email: admin@harrodian.com
Website: www.harrodian.com

Headmaster: Since 1999, Mr James Hooke BSc PGCE (geographer). Educated at nearby Hampton Grammar, followed by Leeds university, began his career in the City but swiftly changed to teaching abroad at St John's School, Buenos Aires. Appointed deputy head at The Harrodian in 1994, he worked alongside, and impressed, the legendary Peter Thomson, becoming head five years later. Youthful in appearance, he continues to find seeing young people progress and develop under his watch extremely satisfying and is sad to see them go. This is a head who regularly takes lunch duties, checking queue hoppers, and happily chats with pupils over meals. He moves about the school with calm, purposeful authority, and is, above all, accessible and approachable.

As one parent observed, 'Although there have been changes as the school has grown in size, the ethos remains the same at the heart of it, and that emanates from the head.' What is impressive is that in a school of nearly 1,000 pupils, the head really knows them and takes pleasure in acknowledging their interests and achievements. Parents agree: 'Mr Hooke knows them all as personalities. He stands outside, on the pavement, or on the side of the pitch. The pupils feel connected and valued. He often praises them for things they do outside school and manages to be at everything'. Committed to the ongoing success of the school, he moves effortlessly from leading pre-prep assemblies, to a sixth form planning meeting, to selecting future pupils ('increasingly difficult as demand has grown,' he comments), to evening engagements such as a prefects' dinner in the City. For relaxation, this energetic man can be found on the ski slopes with the school trip or playing golf alongside pupils and parents. When we visited, he was about to participate in a weekend Surrey cycling event.

Mr Hooke has put in place a dynamic, experienced team of senior staff and looks after them, inspiring loyalty. Among them is the calm, capable, head of pre-prep, Ms Lucy Horan, who has been in place since 2004. Her previous experience was in the state sector – Our Lady of Victories in Putney and deputy head at the Oratory in Chelsea. Mrs Jenny O'Neill became head of lower prep in 2015, herself mother of three Harrodians, so 'I really know the school and Harrodian-style first-hand,' she informed us. She is determined to create 'an even stronger sense of team and community in the prep school'.

The sixth form is thriving under the stewardship of business-like David Behan, ex-City banker and Oxford geographer, who was appointed as head of economics, and who collaborates with senior colleagues to ensure university application guidance and careers advice is given and changes carefully engineered as new-style A levels work their way through.

Academic matters: 'This is a school which caters for individuals and allows all children to be themselves,' was the observation of more than one parent. A broad curriculum caters for different tastes. 'All take single sciences at GCSE', explained the head, 'to ensure they keep their options open'. Streaming in English, maths and languages. Bilingual pupils are expected to study two different languages and all benefit from being taught by wholly native speakers, as we observed. Latin and religious studies survive. No design technology but graphic design, photography, media and three-dimensional design offered. Unnecessary pressure is avoided but there is guidance so that, for example, pupils are made aware of the need to apply themselves in GCSEs since the AS has disappeared and these grades help to secure future university places. Pupils spoke of the Aspirational Universities Club which they had found helpful.

The standards continue to rise as the entrants are more selected. An impressive 83 per cent A* B at A level (52 per cent A*/A) in 2016 and 63 per cent A*/A at GCSE. Nevertheless, Mr Behan stresses, 'there is room for the individual for whom three Cs could be a real achievement'. The school is not setting out to be all about examination results, but nowadays there are plenty of high achievements to celebrate.

The number of pupils with SEN (notably dyslexia, dyspraxia and dyscalculia) is small, with one or two per form, and their needs are catered for both within class and with individual support from the experienced learning support department run by highly praised SENCo. The dedicated staff work alongside one another with individuals in a light, spacious, attractive, well-resourced room at the top of the building which, in days gone by, was the headmaster's geography classroom. Typically, a parent praised the provision and how her daughter wanted to go to sessions and had noticed the difference since she had received targeted support. In addition specialist one-to-one EAL tuition is provided for the few that need it.

ICT is well provided for with interactive whiteboards and dedicated spacious rooms although we did not see younger pupils with iPads or sets of laptops, and the staff commented that the emphasis remains on teacher/pupil oral interaction.

Games, options, the arts: The school employs highly-qualified sports coaches and the latest recording equipment to improve players' techniques and even offers PE A level. Smart dance studio accommodates dance, fencing and gym. Amazingly, for its location, there are 25 acres of playing fields, as well as two all-weather pitches, netball, basketball and tennis courts. On and off-site activities for sixth formers include gym and weight training, swimming, spinning, aerobics, body pump and pilates, as well as rowing. Sport is compulsory across the entire age range, with three or four lessons per week out of 30 for sport/PE. The emphasis is on participating, enjoyment and representing the school, with the Harrodian regularly hosting tournaments, swimming galas and athletic meets. For talented players there are opportunities, for example when we visited the U18 rugby had been almost unbeaten in a highly successful season, with U16 footballers reaching last year's ISFA final. The Ski Academy offers bespoke training in the UK and France for the squad which competes in the English School Ski Championships. The annual golf tournament is also very popular and pupils appreciate the wide choices, and sixth formers enjoy a sports afternoon each Wednesday. Attractive heated pool in colonnaded courtyard is open from April to October. The vast array of fixture lists is impressive, catering for a range of abilities, although a few parents we spoke to did not find the amount of sport lived up to their expectations. But one parent explained her son was 'offered a place at Winchester and declined as he wished to remain at the Harrodian and play for the A football team'.

'Music is superb,' was a parental consensus, with compulsory lessons up to year 9 and thereafter music and music technology available at GCSE and A level. More than half the pupils receive individual tuition across a full range of instruments and singing from beginner to grade 8. We came across one prep boy on his way to ukulele and a girl awaiting her grade 4 singing exam during our visit, outside the school's auditorium with its raked seating. All are involved in annual carol concerts at St Paul's Church, Hammersmith. Pupils really enjoy the annual Battle of the Bands, an X factor style competition for year 4 upwards. Harrodian rockers compete to participate in the Isle of Wight festival. A sixth former spoke enthusiastically of a choir trip to Athens, whilst younger pupils chatted to us animatedly about many other choir opportunities including cadets (boys), stilettos (girls), training choir, senior choice, chamber choir and the Sixteen. 'All are encouraged to perform in assemblies and so grow in confidence and anyone can audition for parts in productions,' parents informed us.

Artists are very well catered for and we watched seniors skilfully painting in oils and acrylics in one of the many attractive art rooms and admired fine displays. As one might expect in a school promoting creativity, diverse courses are on offer, leading to university places to read history of art and art and design. In response to a design and photography challenge, pupils were invited to create a First World War inspired design, and this will stay in one of the senior courtyard buildings until the end of the centenary in November 2018. Display cabinets in an entrance hall bulged with highly imaginative shoes created for a house art competition. Drama also flourishes and is very popular. Pupils perform at the Edinburgh Fringe and we met one talented individual who had completed her extended project qualification on set design. The school encourages public speaking and debating, which helps pupils to grow in confidence and puts the young at ease when conversing with visitors like us.

Background and atmosphere: In 1993 pioneering Sir Alford and Lady Houstoun-Boswall bought the then country club for Harrods employees with its 25 acres and sporting facilities, to realise their vision for a co-educational preparatory school where children could thrive in a civilised environment without unnecessary pressure. The school has grown from the original 65 pupils and 12 staff to nearly 1,000 pupils and an established sixth form.

The cream, well-proportioned building is beautifully pristine with its sweeping lawn and manicured neat lines. We saw discreet scaffolding camouflaging the latest sixth form building to provide further facilities. The gardens are immaculately maintained with shrubs carefully pruned, courtyards, olive and magnolias tastefully placed. One could almost imagine oneself in the country, looking out at the 25 acres of playing fields with pitches galore and, across the road, separated by stylish railings, the magnificent view of the river Thames. The exterior is matched by the interior with its sweeping staircases, vast entrance hall and spacious, well-lit rooms.

Pupils and parents with considerable experience of the school over the years comment on 'the warm, friendly atmosphere which marks this school out'. There is an outstanding sense of a vibrant community and this comes from the top. Both exterior and interior promote civilised values, and all seems magically removed from the traffic, noise and hurly burly of Hammersmith Broadway. No wonder some pupils do not see any need to move to board in the country. The institutional aspects of school have been skilfully replaced by synchronised clocks, so no bells, but carpeting and great attention to decoration.

The pre-prep is self-contained with its own bright, airy accommodation and a paved courtyard. The conservatory provides space for listening to readers and small group work and opens onto Astroturf where all the year round play takes place. The very attractive French-style garden, complete with water feature, provides a tranquil setting. The prep school is cleverly arranged so that, although senior pupils work in rooms alongside, the younger pupils are not intimidated. In fact the natural mixing of age groups is a pleasure to behold. Prefects organise year 4s to obtain sponsors for a charity Easter egg hunt, and science week took place throughout the school, from a workshop in the hall to Cancer Research teachers in the senior laboratories setting challenges. The coffee shop is another splendid touch, welcoming parents and visitors in the mornings and providing a convivial space for sixth formers, as well as the many comfortable three piece suites we spotted about the place. Lunches are served in a spacious dining room. Some parents and a few pupils we spoke to criticised the quality of the food. 'Too much pasta,' voiced several. The sausage and mash was very popular when we visited. The libraries are an additional bonus, lined with books and with librarians to hand. We were pleased to note the acquisition of familiar reading desks with lamps straight from the old British Library Reading Room, where seniors were studiously in silence. Again the community spirit prevails with annual events such as dads' reading morning for year 4 to year 7 and the annual year 4 Night in the Library event.

H

Pastoral care, well-being and discipline: Pupils of all ages we spoke to commented on 'the kind teachers' and 'the welcoming atmosphere'. Bullying they did not see as a problem because 'everyone is so kind to one another'. 'It's amazing – everywhere you go there is someone to talk to,' said one year 8 boy. Much has been put in place to promote this caring community and the mentoring scheme is an excellent example. Senior school students are selected and trained to provide one-to-one mentoring of younger pupils who they meet with regularly. They also run inductions for newcomers. There is a student leadership programme which gives year 11 and sixth formers the opportunity to develop and apply for roles as subject sports or community leaders.

The school has introduced mindfulness and life coaching for staff and students. A school counsellor is available for drop in sessions for year 7 upwards on a self-referral system whilst younger pupils require consent from a parent. There are timetabled citizenship lessons for year 9 and circle time for younger pupils. A student council meets regularly.

There is a healthy balance of gender and age among staff, who also reflect the school as a community and the desire of many to return. We encountered one Harrodian who had returned as a gap student and another ex-family member appointed to the staff. A young teacher's mother had worked at The Harrodian and Mr Hooke's own children attended the school.

The house system, rather than the usual house swimming galas and sports events, sees a flourishing array of staff and pupils zealously throwing themselves into planning and meetings. The pupils appreciate the house bake off, pumpkin carving competition, drama, music and house quizzes. Parents like the fact that 'Kids organise assemblies and ensure all children perform in front of one another'.

Pupils were very clear about the range of punishments leading to detentions and their fairness. There is no uniform except in the pre-prep but there is a clear dress code carefully explained in the parent handbook, and implemented. Parents commented: 'Some might say The Harrodian is an easier, relaxed school where anything goes, but it is no laissez faire country club. Far from it, there is zero tolerance for drugs or bullying. The school acts on bullying swiftly and effectively when it does occur.' A few parents suggested there could be more effort and consistency over pupils' awareness of others and politeness when moving around the school. However, parents feel they can see a member of staff promptly if they have a concern, and even approach the head informally, which they would not attempt at a more traditional school. The chair of PTA said that 'the school has no out of bounds areas, which means pupils can be happy, and feel free to express themselves rather than intimidated'

Pupils and parents: Notable former pupils include actors Will Poulter, Robert Pattinson, George MacKay and Tom Sturridge and musician Will Heard. Parents increasingly include entrepreneurs, those involved in advertising and public relations alongside professional families and international businesspeople. There is a real sense of continuity, with the chair of the PTA having been there since the school's foundation. Parents value the fact all of their children can spend their whole schooldays here.

Entrance: The catchment area includes Barnes, Mortlake, Putney, Sheen and Richmond, as one might expect, as well as stretching towards Ealing, Holland Park and Chelsea, with a few older pupils travelling from as far as Wandsworth or Battersea by train. Main admission points are at 4+,8+,11+,13+ and 16+, with the occasional places at other times. Non-selective reception places by informal assessment and date of registration. Siblings are given priority but not guaranteed a place. Admission to the prep and above involves exam and interview. There are a few places at 8+ for children from the Merlin School in Putney.

At 11+ there is a diverse range of applicants for some 25-28 places (exam and interview). At 13+, common entrance or school's own assessment plus interview.

Sixth form entry requires six or more B grades at GCSE and at least Cs in English and mathematics, plus A*/As in the subjects chosen for A level. Standards less stringent for internal applicants as external applicants sit examinations in mathematics and English, plus interviews in the subjects they wish to study at A level (six or seven external places) and reference from current school. As head remarks, '16+ applicants include those who have had enough of boarding, along with girls, in particular, who wish to escape from single sex London day schools'. Increasing numbers staying on after GCSE with new sixth form facilities.

Exit: A decreasing few at CE to trad boarding schools (Eton, Harrow, Charterhouse, Marlborough, Wellington etc) and the odd one or two to single sex London day schools (St Paul's Girls', King's College School etc). Majority stay on for GCSEs now with a few (five per cent in 2016) elsewhere e.g. to boarding or tutorial colleges. University destinations varied, ditto subjects, though economics and business currently very popular. In 2016, 65 out of 86 leavers to UK unis (Bristol, Bath and Leeds all popular – no Oxbridge this year), eight off abroad to study in Canada, US and Switzerland.

Money matters: Fees are in line with other schools in the locality. You will not, however, find much financial help as there are no entrance scholarships and limited bursaries are reserved for the unexpected emergency or crisis. Limited academic awards for internal candidates at 13+ and 16+.

Remarks: Head emphasises that 'The Harrodian is not an international school with high turnover of pupils: rather, the pupils reflect London's exciting and vibrant international community'. In this civilised setting, a very diverse, cosmopolitan community happily thrives. One parent of four commented, 'The school believes that if a child enjoys where they are, they are more willing to learn', and that has proven to be the case for her family. 'The school understands that every child is good at one thing and if you harness that, then there is a positive outlook'. Current parents believe it 'would not be the right choice for pushy parents or those who shy from informality and creativity'.

Harrow School

5 High Street, Harrow on the Hill HA1 3HP

Pupils: 820 (all full boarders) • Ages: 13–18 • Sixth form: 360

Fees: £37,350 pa

Tel: 020 8872 8007
Email: admissions@harrowschool.org.uk
Website: www.harrowschool.org.uk

Head Master: Since 2011, Mr Jim Hawkins MA (40s). Educated at King Edward VI Camp Hill School for Boys in Birmingham and read maths at Brasenose College, Oxford (he was a year above David Cameron and knew the PM slightly). Did PGCE at Oxford before first teaching job at Radley – perfect combination of teaching maths and coaching rugby and rowing. Head of maths at Forest School in Walthamstow, then deputy head at Chigwell School. Prior to Harrow he was head of Norwich School for nine years – 'a fantastic school in a beautiful city.' Norwich went co-ed during during his headship but there are 'no plans' whatsoever to follow suit at Harrow. 'We are very happy as we are,' he says firmly.

Proud of the fact that Harrow enables boys to enjoy being boys. With a plethora of activities from dawn till dusk, he reckons the school suits 'the kind of boy who wants to take the opportunities we offer and throw himself into things.' He says education at Harrow goes 'way beyond the exam syllabus' and that there's 'no better place for the really bright boy with a strong attitude towards life and learning, the sort of boy who is going to contribute and soak everything up.' School sends loads of boys to Oxbridge but head is equally proud of those who 'work jolly hard to get their As and Bs. They are some of our great successes.' When we asked who the school wouldn't suit he was unequivocal. 'It wouldn't suit someone who wanted a sixth form college sort of experience. Harrow is a highly organised, very busy school and it's very clear what the demands are.'

Dynamic, focused and urbane, with dashing good looks. Still keeps his hand in at the chalkface by teaching 'a bit of maths' to the youngest boys at the start of the academic year. 'It's really nice to have 40 minutes when you are focusing on something entirely educational,' he says. 'The key thing as a head is to find ways of interacting with the boys. Without that you lose touch with reality.' He makes a point of having lunch with boys and in the 'beaks' dining room' when he can. Very sporty – he rowed for Oxford's lightweight crew and was captain of Brasenose rowing. Ran the 10-mile Long Ducker, school's annual charity race from Hyde Park to Harrow, in 90 minutes, though laughingly admits that the director of studies did a faster time.

Loves his job, although he admits 'the highs are very high and the lows are quite challenging'. Says there are three main educational areas he wants to develop. First is the 'super curriculum' to encourage academic scholarship above and beyond the timetabled curriculum, research, independent thinking and university-style learning. Second is to look at preparing boys even better for university – he's already appointed a five-strong universities team with specific knowledge of Oxbridge, medicine and the US universities – and third is to concentrate on 'leadership and service'. School is already very active in local community (links with primary schools, tea parties for elderly, projects with Mothers Against Gangs charity etc) but head would like to do more. 'We want the boys to understand that leadership and service go hand in hand,' he says.

Wife Zoe is an artist and they have a young daughter. They live right in the heart of the school (along with their cocker spaniel) and regularly invite boys for breakfast – 'bacon butties and croissants.' Enjoys music, sport, reading and the theatre.

Academic matters: Teachers, parents and the boys themselves describe Harrow as an 'academic' school. Harrow's results don't appear in league tables – head says he's fed up with the 'one-dimensional snapshot' they deliver – but results are impressive. At A level in 2016, 65 per cent A*/A grades, 89 per cent A*/B and 85 per cent A*/A at IGCSE. IGCSEs taken in English, French, German, Spanish, history, geography, maths, as well as biology, chemistry and physics. Drama and PE introduced at GCSE recently. Thirty-one subjects on offer at A level – all the usual, plus business studies, government and politics, history of art, music technology, photography and theatre studies, with a range of languages. Maths is the most popular subject at A level, with nearly two-thirds taking it. Half the boys do four subjects at A level rather than the usual three (one boy recently did nine). Sixth form electives are a recent innovation for sixth form pupils – a chance for boys to experience university-style teaching in specialist areas and have increased from five to eight periods a fortnight, with boys taking three one-term courses – the last relating to their chosen university course. Cerebral subjects on offer include programming, the history of western art, the greats of European philosophy, psychoanalysis and its impact on European culture, conflict and creativity in creation, post-genocide Rwanda and financial mathematics. Now offers EPQ.

Dazzling array of languages on offer – French, German, Spanish, Italian, Russian, Turkish, Polish, Japanese, Arabic and Chinese. All three sciences are compulsory at IGCSE. School has its own observatory with three telescopes and astronomy offered as a GCSE. Timetabled reading periods and new seminar programme for years 10 and 11. At GCSE classes range between 14 and 20 pupils while at A level the average is eight and none are greater than 12. School caters for mild dyspraxia and dyslexia. One-to-one help given off-timetable, at no additional cost. Dedicated band of teachers (or 'beaks' as they are known at Harrow) includes many writers of scholarly books. Women make up 19 per cent of staff.

Games, options, the arts: There's no doubt about it, Harrow is a very sporty school, with hordes of teams regularly trouncing their opponents. Sport played five afternoons a week, 32 sports on offer and director of sport encourages even the less enthusiastic to 'have a go' at something. Main sports are rugby, soccer, cricket and Harrow football. The latter is played with a pork-pie shaped ball which absorbs the wet and can be propelled by any part of the body. Even though it's played in the depths of winter and is a very muddy affair the boys love it and only wish more schools played it (Harrow is the only one). When we visited pupils were counting the days till their Harrow football match against an OH team. Last year lots of their fathers had played and there was even one grandfather in the side – 'but we were very careful with him.'

Vast expanse of playing fields, sports centre with indoor climbing wall, weights room, 25m pool and sports hall, courts for tennis, rackets and squash, nine-hole golf course and Olympic-sized running track. School boasts national champions in rackets, fencing, fives and judo, two boys playing rugby for England and number of cricketers playing at national and county level. The mother of a gifted sportsman was full of admiration for the way the school nurtured her son's sporting talent whilst keeping him focused on his academic studies and helping him achieve stellar grades. 'The school sees each boy as an individual and were very supportive and flexible,' she told us.

Head of music admits that when he arrived there was a perception among rival directors of music that Harrow was 'an old-fashioned school where little value was placed on music and the arts.' To his delight he found the reverse was true and there's a 'wealth of musical talent.' Half the boys learn musical instruments and 50 per cent of these achieve grade 8 or better by the time they leave. Practice sessions timetabled for younger boys. Loads of orchestras, choirs and strong tradition of singing. More than 100 concerts a year, with recent performances at the Royal Albert Hall and Royal Festival Hall. Steady stream of boys to top universities and conservatoires to read music too.

Excellent Ryan Theatre seats 400 and is used for school and professional productions but annual Shakespeare productions take place in the beautiful arts and crafts Speech Room. A huge, wood-panelled half-moon, it boasts authentic Globe-style staging and seats the entire school. Wonderful art and, befittingly for a school where photography pioneer William Fox Talbot was a pupil, photography. DT, sculpture, art and photography now in a new state-of-the-art facility that also includes a new digital design suite. There's no lounging around with nothing to do at weekends either – scores of extracurricular activities to choose from, everything from the Alexander Society for boys interested in military history to the Turf Club for horse racing fans.

H

Boarding: All pupils board at Harrow. We visited two very different houses – Druries, which dates back to the 1790s and is a maze of charming nooks and crannies, and the ultra-modern Lyon's, or the Holiday Inn, as a few wags have nicknamed it. 'It's the best piece of real estate around here,' joked one boy, hugely appreciative of its light, airy, five-star rooms. 'There's room for us to move around and not cause too much havoc.'

Each house has common rooms, games rooms (kitted out with plasma TV, pool and table tennis tables), garden and 'yarder,' an area where boys can run off steam and kick a ball about. Two boys sharing is the norm in the first year but by year 11 (or even earlier) they get their own room, complete with desk, shelving, computer and, occasionally, en-suite shower. All pupils' names etched on wooden house boards, with head of house's name picked out in gold. Boys can make toast and heat up soup in their houses – 'and the more ambitious make Pot Noodles,' said one boy. We trust he was joking. Meals are eaten centrally and food gets a firm thumbs-up – from us too, if the lunch we had with sixth formers was anything to go by. Boys are allowed to go out for a meal with their parents on Sundays but there's no weekly or flexi-boarding. Two weekend exeats in the autumn and spring terms and one in the summer.

Background and atmosphere: Harrow is one of only four all-boys, full-boarding schools left in the UK (along with Eton, Winchester and Radley). Boys have been educated here since the 13th century, but the school was founded in 1572 under a royal charter granted to local farmer John Lyon by Elizabeth I (Lyon's, the newest boarding house, is named after him). The aim was for the school to provide free education for 30 local scholars, a number later increased to 40 by the governors. School sits in picturesque Harrow on the Hill, surrounded by 400 acres and with panoramic views across London – of it, yet remote from it, as we said last time. On a clear day you can see Canary Wharf from the head's study and it's just 25 minutes by tube to Green Park. Visitors to the undulating school site take note – flat shoes are a must.

School is steeped in tradition and history. The 17th century Old Schools contain the beautiful Fourth Form room, with names carved into every inch of panelling, from Byron to Robert Peel. It's also where Professor Flitwick's charm classes were shot in the first Harry Potter film (lots of tourists gazing admiringly when we visited). The stunning Vaughan Library, designed by architect Gilbert Scott (he also created London's St Pancras Station) has chess sets on tables and stays open late during exam periods. War Memorial Building commemorates the 633 OHs who died in the First World War. You can't help but be profoundly moved by the Alex Fitch Room, an Elizabethan wood panelled room with stained glass windows and a Cromwellian table, given by a grieving mother in honour of her 19-year-old son after he died in the First World War. She asked that it should be used for the purpose of boys meeting their mothers and that a light should always be left on over her son's portrait. Plaques and memorials commemorating quirky events are everywhere. Charles I rested here while preparing to surrender and little inclines have memorable names like Obadiah Slope, wittily named after Trollope's unctuous Barchester Towers character.

Harrow Songs are legendary. No Harrovian, either past or present, fails to mention the strength of feeling they engender and the lump in the throat they provoke. Songs have been an important part of the school since 1864, when the head of music wrote the first song, and they are considered to be 'a unifying force.' In November each year the whole school assembles in Speech Room in honour of its most famous alumni, Sir Winston Churchill, for the Churchill Songs. Like rival Eton, school has its own jargon. 'Skew' is a punishment, 'tosh' is a shower, 'tolley up' is permission to work late and so on.

Pastoral care, well-being and discipline: Pastoral care is meticulous, with highly structured system of resident housemasters, assistant housemasters and matrons. Harrow's 12 houses are integral to the school and boys are fiercely loyal to their own house. Some houses are regarded as stricter than others and parents we spoke to said it's important 'to pick and choose carefully.' One of the houses – West Acre – was recently the subject of an ITN documentary series, following the life of the school for a whole year. Housemasters in post for 12 years and as well as doing most of the admissions assessments each gives their house its character and reputation. They also work round the clock – 'at the beginning of every term I say to my wife "see you at the end of term",' one housemaster told us with a grin.

Harrow takes a pragmatic approach to technology and social media but the boys are so busy there isn't much time to sit around and play computer games. Pupils understand that bullying is 'completely unacceptable' and head says that it has plummeted, 'not down to zero, but pretty close.' School does a bullying survey every winter and housemasters, year group tutors, matrons, two school chaplains, health education tutors and school psychologist pick up on most things. Discipline is clear and firm but the place feels pretty relaxed, with boys knowing exactly where they stand. 'You are given freedom but if you abuse the freedom you would be punished,' one boy told us. Zero tolerance on drugs and use or supply in term-time or holidays means expulsion. Anyone found with spirits suspended and warned while smoking is handled through 'escalating sequence of sanctions imposed by housemasters.'

Smart uniform of dark blue jackets (bluers), grey flannels (greyers), white shirts and ties, plus, of course, Harrow's infamous boaters. Boys wear them or carry them and either love them or loathe them. They're allowed to write their names and draw pictures on the inner rim and spray them with varnish to protect them. Members of Philathletic Club (school's top sportsmen) get to wear bow ties. Sunday wear is black tailcoat and the whole kit and caboodle.

Pupils and parents: Pupils come from all over and school is proud of its 'broad and varied intake.' We said last time that it's the sort of place where a Yorkshire farmer's son will be sharing a room with the offspring of a City banker – and it still holds true. Between 10 and 15 per cent are progeny of OHs, while 20 per cent are from overseas (some expat, others from vast range of countries – 40 at last count). Twenty-five with EAL requirements. Most boys are C of E but there's a 'significant' RC community. Small numbers of all other main faiths or none.

The boys we met were engaging, appreciative of the fine education they get and very proud of their school. 'It doesn't give you a sense of entitlement, just a great responsibility to give something back,' one boy told us, while a sixth former who'd joined from a state school at 16 said that he'd been 'pushed and challenged' and that there was 'a lot more opportunity for debate' than at his previous school.

Parents reckon the school suits all-rounders who work hard and like sport. 'It's very disciplined and the boys are busy all the time so they have to be organised,' one mother said. 'There isn't any time to get up to any mischief and the boys are really tired by the end of term. There's a real camaraderie about the place and the boys make life-long friends. I can't fault it.' Another reckoned that even though it's 'strict,' any boy would thrive at Harrow, as long as they can cope with being in a large school where they won't necessarily be 'king pin.'

Long and distinguished list of former pupils – seven former prime ministers (including Sir Robert Peel, Lord Palmerston, Stanley Baldwin and Sir Winston Churchill), 19th century philanthropist Lord Shaftesbury ('a towering figure – we refer to him a lot,' says the head), Jawaharlal Nehru, King Hussein of Jordon, Lord Cardigan (who led the Charge of the Light Brigade), General Sir Peter de la Billière, plus countless other men of military renown (20 holders of the Victoria Cross and one George Cross holder). The arts and sciences are equally well represented, with a dazzling list of luminaries including Lord Byron, Richard Brinsley Sheridan, Anthony Trollope, Terence Rattigan, John Galsworthy, Cecil Beaton, Edward and William Fox, Richard Curtis, Benedict Cumberbatch and James Blunt, plus Crispin Odey (one of the UK's most successful hedge fund managers), Julian Metcalfe (founder of Pret à Manger), cricketer Nick Compton and Tim Bentinck (better known as David Archer).

Entrance: Very competitive. Around 600 apply for the 160 places on offer at 13. Prospective pupils supply school reference and sit pre-test in year 6; most are expected to be invited for assessment at the start of year 7, through tests and interviews. Offers are made – subject to CE or scholarship exams 18 months later. Sixty-five per cent expected at CE. 'Some weight' given to sons of OHs and boys' siblings – 'but brothers don't automatically get in,' said a parent. Boys arrive from more than 100 regular feeder schools. All-boys' boarding preps like Caldicott and Cothill top the pack but others from a myriad of co-ed and day schools.

Total of 24 new pupils a year into the 340-strong sixth form. Candidates need at least seven or eight A*/As at GCSE but many will have straight A*s. Candidates write a CV, plus letter to the head explaining why they want to come to Harrow, and take tests in their proposed A level subjects. The best attend a day of interviews and assessments.

Exit: Very few (four per cent) left after GCSEs in 2016, none at the end of year 12. Ninety-nine per cent to university – 25 to Oxbridge in 2016 and most of the rest to Russell Group, five to study medicine. Top destinations Exeter, Bristol, Edinburgh and UCL. Significant number opting for Ivy League universities in the US, recently including two to Harvard plus other top international institutions.

Money matters: School has given franchises to Harrow Beijing, Harrow Bangkok and Harrow Hong Kong, with a fourth likely to follow in the next few years. These are all successful enterprises carefully monitored by Harrow and also fund generous bursary schemes at home.

Wide range of scholarships and bursaries at 13 or 16. School offers means-tested bursaries of up to 100 per cent of fees to pupils who win a scholarship of any sort. Up to 30 scholarships a year for academic excellence, music, art or talent in a particular area (normally worth five per cent of fees). There are also Peter Beckwith scholarships for gifted and talented boys whose parents can't afford to send them to Harrow. Two awarded each year to boys aged between 10 and 13 – these can cover fees at a private school from the age of 11 and Harrow fees from 13.

Remarks: Parents looking for a top notch, blue chip, full boarding, all boys' school will be hard-pressed to beat Harrow. This is a school on top of its game.

Hawkesdown House

27 Edge Street, London W8 7PN

Pupils: 145 • Ages: 3–8

Fees: £15,270 – £17,565 pa

Tel: 020 7727 9090
Email: admin@hawkesdown.co.uk
Website: www.hawkesdown.co.uk

H

Head: Since April 2017, Jenny Mackay, previously deputy head of the junior school of Lady Eleanor Holles. Education degree from Oxford; has taught at Dulwich College, Eaton Square, Jumeirah English Speaking School in Dubai and Clapham and Streatham High in roles including head of English and head of year.

Entrance: There are two main entry points. The first is the nursery (20 places) and the second is reception, which is made up of two classes of 20. There are no open days; instead head gives individual tours with prospective parents lasting about half an hour with a follow-up chat in her office. This is key to see if the aims and ethos of parents are aligned with the school. The boys are asked for an introductory session in the year before they are due. This is purely to see if the boy would be happy in the school and whether it would be the best place for him. A variety of activities for a 20 minute session in the nursery adjacent to the courtyard, with opportunities for outside play. Those hoping to join in year 1 upwards spend an hour in the relevant class and are assessed in literacy and numeracy before being offered a place. The pupils come from a wide spread of local nurseries. There are no bursaries, scholarships or sibling discounts on offer.

Exit: Most to established London prep schools including: St Paul's Juniors, Westminster Under, Sussex House, Wetherby Prep, St Philip's, Latymer Prep. Others choose to board at a range including Caldicott, The Dragon, Summer Fields and Papplewick.

Remarks: The school was founded in 2000 by Mr and Mrs Loveridge and is part of a family group. This includes Devonshire House School and Lyndhurst House, both also in London. It is named after Hawkesdown Hill, in Devon, familiar to the Loveridge family, and where an ancient, gigantic, defence earthwork fortress was built. A colourful painting of Hawkesdown is on view in the entrance hall, a reminder of the qualities the school promotes – tradition, charm, community endeavour – and a source of inspiration.

The school provides a traditional curriculum with emphasis on the basics with literacy and numeracy sessions most mornings. 'This is necessary as the demands of the next selective preps are still very traditional, including English written composition and comprehension at a sophisticated level.' Topics and daily routine are deliberately timetabled to cater for boys' interests and enjoyment. We saw evidence of solar system models, astronauts, aeroplanes, castles, and, in year 1, an imaginative life cycle display with very neat handwriting and illustrations, under the friendly eye of one of the few male teachers. Undoubtedly, once the wireless network is installed and running, the boys will also be able to enjoy more ICT opportunities across the curriculum than existed at the time of a recent inspection – development of ICT a current focus.

One mother commented that having initially intended sending her son to a co-educational school, she now believes he would have suffered seated next to a girl with beautiful penmanship as boys have a definite rhythm of learning. 'They are,' as another parent acknowledged, 'wriggly'. That is catered for and understood completely by the staff at HH. French is taught from reception. No dedicated science laboratory, art or design technology rooms. The boys are prepared for serious entrance exams and given plenty of practice. 'The boys are not pushed too much and they have a good balance of work and play.' In year 1, for example, judo is added to the timetable with chess in year 2 and fencing by year 3. Violin, piano and singing lessons are available from year 1, as well as Mandarin, with plenty of after-school clubs.

Parents tell us that pupils with SEN are well catered for because 'the school is small and there is plenty of support'. We saw happy boys with hearing aids and the sparky, young SEN coordinator supports form teachers, ensuring that individual plans are monitored carefully and reviewed. Setting in maths and English is realistic and understood: 'Kids quickly know where they stand'. A speech and language therapist comes in weekly and boys are offered High 5s sessions before beginning lessons as well as booster groups. TAs work with boys who need extra help. This is not the school for someone with disruptive behavioural problems or physical difficulties because of the school's layout, but emerging problems are dealt with in a caring way.

Young teachers and teaching assistants, some from abroad, are lively and enthusiastic and support the boys with different languages, an important feature as this school caters for international families, and there has been a recent focus on EAL. Nobody has been on the staff for more than 10 years, but this is hardly surprising as it is a relatively new school.

One drawback, commented on by some parents, is the lack of space for a playgound. During indoor lunch break in their classrooms, the top year boys we saw looked extremely happy in K'nex heaven, constructing imaginative vehicles and missiles with great enthusiasm. Nevertheless, 'by the time the boys are in their final year they are big and notice the lack of space,' remarked one parent. They make use of Holland Park for PE in good weather, with football once a week, team games and formal matches arranged, and run around in Kensington Gardens enjoying plenty of controlled rough and tumble. Still, some boys, especially the older sporty ones, might find this frustrating. Judo is extremely popular, as are football, cricket and PE (no swimming). All boys play in fixtures against other schools at some point.

The house system with its homage to royalty, Plantagenet, Windsor and Tudor, has been revitalised to excellent effect. Parents are encouraged to be involved and are welcomed, once a fortnight, to attend Friday assemblies in the packed main hall. Boys are awarded pen licences, house points and many awards for tying of shoe laces and ties, good manners at lunch time and community spirit among others. The skills encouraged are spot on for this age and there's always a loud cheer for the winning house. The boys are taught to be courteous and polite and they respect the staff who know them so well. The positions of house captain, vice captain and prefects merit special house ties, rather than the normal school tartan ties (which do look a little odd against the blue and white check shirts). The navy blue and red uniform including blazers and caps is popular, and several parents commented, 'the boys look so cute'.

An important duty for the house prefects is to ring the large bell outside the dining hall for lunch, serve food and clear up. One parent remarked just how great it was that the boys sat in houses for lunch. 'The younger ones look up to the older boys. My son told me he had learnt all about Lord of the Rings from another boy at lunch.' This social mixing may account for the ease with which the boys spoke during our visit. One recent newcomer was highly appreciative of the way he had been made to feel welcome and, a sensitive soul, had clearly benefited from another boy's support. Lunch is extremely popular, even more so since the arrival of a new chef who has a great following. Special themed meals, such as for Wimbledon (with strawberries and cream) and Independence Day, are a real hit with even the fussiest boys.

A thorough mix of English and international families with a number of bilingual pupils. Most parents live within walking distance of the school and many work in the financial sector. HH is reassuring to the many new to the English examination system; right from the start, it provides advice, support and the necessary preparation to give parents and pupils a very happy start in a caring, environment without undue pressure.

Haydon School

Wiltshire Lane, Eastcote, Pinner HA5 2LX

Pupils: 2,010 • Ages: 11–18 • Sixth form: 500

Tel: 020 8429 0005
Email: info@haydonschool.org.uk
Website: www.haydonschool.com

Headteacher: Since 2006, Robert Jones (40s). Read economics at LSE and taught in Hong Kong for four years before returning to the UK. Moved to Haydon in 1999 and quickly moved up the ranks to become assistant head, then head. Married to drama teacher. Two sons – one grown up, one at primary school. Originally from Manchester, he's a huge Man United fan and looks rather like an ex-professional footballer himself. Still plays football and coaches Ascot United under 7s (his son plays for the team) and keeps fit by running a number of half marathons each year.

Academic matters: Specialist language and applied learning college offering more than 30 GCSE and BTec options. 'We want to offer as broad a curriculum as possible,' explains the head. Language provision is excellent, with students starting off with French and Italian or Spanish and German; older pupils can take on further languages such as Mandarin. 'Around 100 opted for Mandarin this year,' says the head proudly. In 2016 72 per cent of students achieved at least five A*-C grades including maths and English at GCSE (25 per cent A*/A grades); at A level 45 per cent A*/B, 21 per cent A*/A. Parents praise the quality of teaching and particularly the revision lessons offered around exam time.

Students need six GCSEs at A*-C (including maths and English) to study four A levels. Those who do not have a minimum of a C in English or maths are able to retake these and can study three A levels. One SENCo and a team of learning support assistants support around 20 or so statemented pupils. There is also a special centre where students can be taught in small groups.

Parents like the fact that class sizes are around 25, but some would prefer more streaming. 'At present in year 7 there is streaming just for maths,' said one parent. 'I would like to see this extended to other key subjects such as English and science as is the practice in other local schools'.

Games, options, the arts: School has scored successes in a host of sports – at both local and county level. Particular strengths are rugby, rounders and indoor athletics and there is even an ultimate frisbee team in the sixth form. New sports hall.

Haydon has benefited from new facilities in recent years, including £5 million art and design building and £2 million music and performing arts centre (three music rooms, drama studio and music mixing room. plus one-to-one teaching rooms). School has two orchestras, jazz band, samba band and wide variety of other music groups. Four big concerts a year as well as annual musical or play. Thriving art department achieves excellent exam results. Students can study art, textiles and photography at A level. Lots of school trips too – to France, Germany, Italy, Peru and Swaziland.

Background and atmosphere: School is situated on the edge of the Northwood Hills in Pinner, with spacious playing fields. Rather nondescript 1950s buildings – originally two grammar schools that merged in 1977. Lots of building work going on when we visited. Food in the sixth form café is so good that the staff choose to eat there. Food in the canteen for the rest of the school received less favourable reports but new caterers have been appointed. Some of the toilets need a little TLC but these are in the process of being refurbished. 'The boys' changing rooms are a real state,' one student told us, but we weren't shown these on our tour. We were very taken with the pool table and primary colours in the rather groovy sixth form common room though.

Pastoral care, well-being and discipline: A new positive reward system has recently been introduced. 'The reward system is a great motivator,' one parent told us. 'My child strives to get good news notes, commendations and other rewards.' Meanwhile a year 8 student said: 'I really look forward to the awards assembly. It's a way of showing how hard we are working.' One of the top awards means pupils get a special lunch with the head (mums sadly aren't eligible to compete for this award).

Students excluded for threatening behaviour or repeated disruption in lessons (four permanent exclusions last year). Parents are happy with school's approach to behaviour. 'I have always found that a high level of discipline is maintained from the minute the children arrive at the school,' said one. When we visited, students seemed well behaved and friendly.

Pupils and parents: 'Haydon has a really good reputation round here,' a student told us, 'and all my friends at other schools wish they were here.' The school offers both pupils and parents a chance to voice their opinions – parent voice group meets four times per year.

Entrance: Most students live locally (within a mile or so of the school). Admissions criteria are: children in public care, then siblings, then children living nearest to the school, then employees' children. An additional 60 students join in the sixth form.

Exit: A third or so of pupils leave after GCSEs – for college, other schools, apprenticeships or employment – and 10-15 per cent after year 12. Around three-quarters of sixth formers to university, and about a third of these to top universities eg Southampton and Nottingham. One to Oxbridge and one medic in 2016.

Remarks: A friendly comprehensive that really does cater for all, with strong vocational courses as well as the more traditional A levels – all taught to a high standard. 'I would have no hesitation recommending Haydon,' said one parent. 'I feel my children are lucky to attend the school.'

Heathside Preparatory School

16 New End, London NW3 1JA

Pupils: 400 • Ages: 2–13

Fees: £15,000 pa

Tel: 020 7794 5857
Email: info@heathsideprep.co.uk
Website: www.heathsideprep.co.uk

Headmistress: Since the school's foundation in 1993, Ms Melissa Remus Elliot MA PG Dip (40s), who is also joint owner. She grew up all over the US, following her father's work, and attended Duke University and The American University, Washington. She worked as a Washington intern and on several Broadway shows before moving to the UK and becoming a teacher. During three years' teaching she formulated an idea of her ideal school and set up Heathside with her business partner and co-head (now retired), Jill White, becoming the youngest head teacher in the country in her 20s. She also got an MA in counselling aspects of education at The Tavistock Clinic.

Married with four children, all at or graduated from Heathside, 'which gives me a good insight into what actually goes on in the classrooms'. Over-flowing praise from parents: 'a very open-minded and dynamic person, relentlessly striving to find ways to make the school better'; 'open and honest in a very refreshing way'; 'both pragmatic and inspirational'; 'extraordinary ability to retain a thorough portrait of each child'; 'unbelievably energetic and gung-ho'.

Entrance: Takes 2 and 3-year-olds into the nursery class. Most places go to siblings and those who sign up very early, though it's worth trying for an afternoon place if you have been less well organised. More join to form three reception classes of 15 each. Children visit for a day to ensure they and the school are a good match. 'If there is any question mark we may ask them to come in for several days. We try to be careful to make sure that the school suits the child. We don't take children with behavioural difficulties or serious special needs, and if we have any concerns about academic ability, we would speak in detail with the parents and teachers about whether we could create a special programme to support the child.'

Exit: Most move on at 11, the vast majority to the local independents: Highgate, UCS, North Bridge House and Belmont; also Haberdashers, South Hampstead, Francis Holland and Channing. Some to City Boys' or Girls', some very bright children to Westminster, St Paul's or North London Collegiate, and some who prefer a less intense environment to Aldenham. A few to local state schools, eg Camden School for Girls and St Marylebone. Generally a good haul of scholarships. Parents comment on 'Melissa's dogged commitment to find places for all her pupils. She reads children exceptionally well'.

The school has now added years 7 and 8. The first year 7 class (fully co-ed) has pupils who have already gained places at Westminster, St Paul's and City of London in year 9. Now dubs years 5-8 'Heathside High' and offers flexi boarding.

Remarks: Started in 1993 on the site – and with much of the equipment and quite a few of the staff and pupils – of a former prep school that had come to a rocky end. Occupies six buildings in the middle of Hampstead and has permission to

H

use the upper floors of a local pub during the day. Aims to let every child follow their strengths and interests, with plenty of extracurricular activities and fun, practical lessons.

The lower school is housed in a converted and extended church hall, which includes a music practice room, a hall used for gym, yoga, music and drama as well as assemblies, a nursery room with comfortable sofas, and art and science rooms. 'Science teaching brilliant – really hands-on and fun,' said a parent. 'And my daughter is very excited to be allowed to chop wood and use a glue gun in DT.' 'Can't imagine my kids being more stimulated or jolly,' said another.

Since the school is non-selective it includes a fair ability range, but teaching groups are small and the lower school has plenty of teaching assistants. 'Learning is really celebrated,' said a parent. Several ability groups for maths from year 1 upwards. 'Children have different ways of learning, and we group them accordingly. Some need lots of reinforcement, but we never assume that a child is no good at maths. We work in a way that helps them to understand, and once the building blocks are firm, they can fly.' When we visited, a group of children who found times tables challenging were learning them through pictures and stories, whilst another group (of year 4 pupils) were working on secondary level problems.

Several literacy groups – 'they are all good readers, but some have difficulty with writing'. These get intensive tuition in years 3 and 4, ready for the lead-up to year 6 exams. 'Because we don't have to prepare them for 7+ exams, it doesn't matter if they take longer to come through.'

French is taught throughout the school, with plenty of songs and games, by a teacher who talks entirely in French from the start. 'They think she only speaks French, and they learn amazingly quickly.' Latin is a 'massive hit,' said a parent; also a Mandarin club.

Inevitably the pressure rises as the 11+ approaches, but parents praise the imaginative approach. 'They're pushed in their ability to write essays and do comprehensions, but it's not a brutal régime,' said one. 'In a typical Heathside move, an ex-parent who is a literature professor comes in twice a week and encourages them to read and enjoy sophisticated texts. They're worked incredibly hard, but it's very exciting.' Has now added year 7 and 8 classes.

The full-time identified needs coordinator is renowned for helping with dyslexia and dyspraxia. One-to-one help costs extra, but most learn in compatible groups. The school would not suit an autistic child – 'We're too busy and active' – and would hesitate to take one with other behavioural difficulties – 'We have to think about the rest of the class.' However, a girl who came into year 4 with limited experience of maths 'blossomed, and got into all the secondary schools she tried'.

Small groups work at their own pace in various nooks and crannies. 'You may find your child having a lesson in what looks like a broom cupboard – but they are learning,' said a parent. Prose and poetry competitions, with everyone writing poems and learning a piece to recite, and plenty of drama from Macbeth to Pirates of Penzance. 'We do really challenging stuff, but in a fun way.'

The full-time music director is 'amazingly inspirational' – everyone learns the ocarina and recorder and many play the piano and other instruments too. Several instrumental groups and choirs, and termly formal and informal concerts 'spur them on'.

Chess is a big deal here – teams go off for weekend tournaments, and Heathside has been the English Primary Schools Chess Association National Small Schools champion for eight years. 'It's a big social scene,' said a parent, 'and they're very good at encouraging girls to play.' A 'huge variety' of other clubs including gym, art and science. Parents talk of 'amazing trips', including ice skating at the Tower of London and 'going to France for the day to meet pen-pals'.

The school's only outside space is a small playground with climbing frame alongside the lower school. However, nearly everyone from year 1 upwards goes to Hampstead Heath for an hour at lunchtime most days – the younger ones go three times a week – to climb trees, run around, build dens, play in the snow. The children also play sport every day, at UCS and Swiss Cottage; on Friday morning they have a swimming and multi-sports programme – ranging from rock climbing to judo – at Swiss Cottage leisure centre. Specialist coaches include an ex-international Sri Lankan cricketer and an ex-professional footballer, and the football, swimming and cricket teams are rarely beaten. Many teams are co-ed – 'Our best footballer is a girl' – and girls' sport was boosted by the arrival of a coach specialising in rounders, field hockey and netball. Sports day includes 'proper races' at Parliament Hill Fields running track.

Parents praise the family atmosphere, with friendships across the year groups. 'There's a real relationship between teachers and children,' said a parent. 'They are strict about talking and noise, because they have to be in a building that size, but then you see a child hurtling downstairs with no shoes on to do some photocopying for their teacher. It's an adventurous, common-sense and human approach.' Another parent commented that she is delighted with the 'close and intimate, nurturing atmosphere which generates a real appetite to learn. It's very warm, very flexible'. We have however had reports of a lack of response to parents whose child was experiencing difficulties. Organic lunches served daily.

Huge mix of families including some wealthy, famous parents and quite a few international families. But it tends to attract those who are not happy with the more traditional private sector ethos; quite a few have moved their children (often reluctantly) from state primaries. Parents tend to become closely involved: one dad runs a gifted maths club, another comes in to talk about astronomy, many parents help with festivals such as Chinese New Year and Halloween, others help run the library or become class reps. 'We're an interesting mix,' said a mother. 'Most people are very friendly and very engaged with the school.' 'We absolutely love it here,' said a father, 'and so does every other parent we've met.'

The Henrietta Barnett School

Central Square, London NW11 7BN

Pupils: 766 • Ages: 11–18 • Sixth form: 272

Tel: 020 8458 8999
Email: admissions@hbschool.org.uk
Website: www.hbschool.org.uk

Headteacher: Since 2014, Mrs Del Cooke BSc MBA NPQH (50s), previously head of Sir William Perkins's School in Surrey. Maths graduate with MBA in educational management, her broad experience covers the comprehensive system, sixth form college, adult education and boarding at Cranleigh, where she was head of maths, housemistress and finally deputy head. Although relatively new, she is increasingly seen as the embodiment of HBS – smart, quick-witted, friendly and empathetic. 'The girls want to hang out with her. She is like them,' summed up one parent. We found her instantly likeable, not remotely intimidating and surprisingly low-key. Made no dramatic changes so far ('It's such a fantastic school, you'd have to be pretty pompous to come in and turn it upside down,' she says), but is known as a visible head, particularly interested in getting the girls' views on various aspects of the school, and is clearly keen to focus more heavily on celebrating individual achievements. No bad thing, point out some parents, who say the girls can be 'far too modest, and need reminding how amazing they are'. Has a passion for music, playing a number of instruments, including self-taught bassoon. Married with three sons.

Academic matters: Consistently top or very near the top of both the GCSE and A level league tables. In 2016, 95 per cent A and A* at GCSE, 83 per cent A*/A at A level. Most do 11 GCSEs, four or five AS, three or four A2s. Results strong across all subjects at GCSE, with a bias towards maths and sciences at A level, which around three-quarters of pupils choose, although history and English also have a healthy representation. Languages prioritised, with French and German for all in year 7, Latin and Spanish for all in years 8 and 9. Plus an option of ancient Greek. Setting only for maths at KS4.

Myths about this school being an academic hothouse, where girls are worked like dogs, are prolific, and even the head was initially put off the job because she thought it would be so pressurised. 'I was resistant, assuming the girls would be working in a ridiculously intensive environment. But it's the girls who drive the pace of learning and if anything, the staff sometimes have to tell the girls to slow down!' says the head. Pupils and parents agree, with one saying her daughter had just been advised to 'take some time out of her revision schedule to do something more relaxing.' Girls are encouraged to be independent, albeit well-supported, learners from day one, with many setting up their own societies and visiting universities for extra lectures. During our visit, we saw one noticeboard with pages from HB Scientist, the sixth-form produced (and very professional looking) science magazine that is sold throughout the school, whilst plenty of posters around the school advertised forthcoming speakers that pupils have organised – Zadie Smith when we visited.

Competitive learning is frowned upon, making way for a supportive atmosphere and strong sense of co-operation, which everyone agrees is a huge aid to the girls excelling academically. Teachers could hardly be considered more dedicated, although many parents say more of them are needed. 'Every one of the teachers would be a good candidate for a head of department in a private school, earning 50-100 per cent more money, but they choose to stay here because of the quality of the school and the commitment of the girls, which makes them very, very special,' said one parent. Girls love the fact that many of the teachers have had (non-teaching) careers in their subjects, also praising the informal relationships they have with them and level of responsibility the girls are given. Homework is given if and when teachers feel it's required, rather than hours every evening for the sake of it.

Games, options, the arts: Historically sports not brilliant, although improved facilities – large multi-purpose Astroturf court for netball, hockey, football and volleyball – have helped, with the school increasingly winning at both a local and borough level and holding its own against some top private schools. Facilities also include four tennis courts, two average sized gyms, a state-of-the-art fitness suite with a good range of exercise equipment and a variety of pitches available on the nearby Hampstead Heath extension. 'Sport is very much on the up,' insists the head and there's a long list of exercise alternatives, including rock climbing, zumba, fencing, tang soo do, yoga, fitness, indoor rowing, cricket, badminton and dance. Rugby and athletics are also increasingly popular. No swimming due to lack of facilities, which disappoints some.

Thriving music department, with a symphony orchestra that everyone agrees is a joy to listen to, especially at concerts in the nearby ambient St Jude's Church. There are other orchestras and plenty of choirs, along with all manner of bands, including swing and rock. All pupils study music in key stage 3 and many go on to GCSE. Plenty of private tuition in a wide range of instruments, including double bass, bassoon and French horn, and there is an organ scholarship. Great excitement about the music wing built in 2011. 'Previously, we were taught music in our classroom or temporary huts, so it's a major thing,' said one pupil, who showed us the well-stocked rehearsal room and studio, with several soundproofed practice rooms. The same wing is home to drama, another lively department with strong facilities, with recent performances including Hamlet (year 9s), a play about Henrietta Barnett (year 7s) and a school-wide Our Country's Good.

Mirroring this wing, on the other side of the main building, is the DT and art block. Downstairs, the spacious DT room is home to all kinds of interesting inventions, including a Batman-style wooden chair and scooter that changes colour when exposed to sunlight. Meanwhile, the upstairs art room is a fantastic space, with some seriously talented work on display across all media. The wrap-around balconies on both wings are both aesthetically pleasing and provide an outside space for students to work during the summer months.

Lots of extracurricular opportunities, including Mandarin, Robotics (year 8 team recently got through to world championships in USA), creative writing, philosophy society, LAMDA, and many pupil-led activities. For instance, sixth formers currently teach Japanese to younger ones, as well as running a current affairs club, with speakers (invited by pupils themselves) including Melissa Benn and Lucy Holmes.

School trips, through each subject department, take every year group out once a year, with recent examples including Iceland (geography) and Greece (classics). 'It was easily the best holiday I've ever been on, just unbelievably interesting and fun,' said one pupil who went on the latter. French and German exchanges and Spanish trip to Seville. When we visited, 65 students were getting ready to head to the Rhineland for a music tour. Lots of day trips, particularly to theatres, museums and art galleries. Enrichment week, held in the summer, provides an entire week of outings. Own field study centre in Dorset, which every pupil visits for one week during her early years at the school.

Background and atmosphere: Founded in 1911 by formidable social reformer Dame Henrietta Barnett, the school is housed in architecturally stunning Lutyens designed buildings in upmarket Hampstead Garden Suburb. Not unlike the kind of buildings you'd find at Harvard of Stanford, it's also a beautifully landscaped campus. Facilities top-notch, particularly the colour-coded science labs and new swanky new wings for art, DT, music and drama, plus newly refurbished and extended library. Floors are polished parquet, classrooms are light and airy and corridors are tastefully decorated with everything from a recent photography competition to huge science-inspired pictures. Dining hall, where food is praised, and all-day café for year 10 upwards. Parts of the interiors could do with a lick of paint. But overall facilities feel spacious, with excitable students loving their environment, including after school, when something is going on pretty much every evening.

Pastoral care, well-being and discipline: 'No bells, no detention, no rules – it's so relaxed that if you came to school in your pyjamas no one would bat an eyelid,' wrote Tatler in its 2015 review, words that are now a source of great pride (not to mention humour) in the school 'simply because they are so true,' explained one pupil. Even a mention of the word 'discipline' will get you a blank look among pupils ('Why would you play up?' one said, genuinely bemused), whilst any occasional quirkiness that's perhaps inevitable among such an academic bunch is accepted as normal and certainly never teased. 'A few weeks ago, a whole class came out of art with painted-on moustaches and top hats from drama – it was so HBS,' laughed one girl. But this is no St Trinian's. Far from it, the girls' behaviour is impeccable and they always do their best, as well as being delightful and friendly. 'If a girl did step out of line, the teacher would just have a chat, adult-to-adult,' says the head, who believes it's the fact that the girls are treated like adults – with all the respect and trust that goes with that – that accounts for the lack of need for rules.

Bullying a non-issue, whilst a part-time counsellor is on hand to deal with any problems. Currently a big push on reducing the stigma of mental health issues, with several noticeboards pointing to relevant resources. Strong student council, which is particularly strong in recruitment and currently focusing on raising funds for the new library, plus lunch council.

Pupils and parents: Girls are extremely bright and eager to learn, as well as both interesting and interested. Clear team spirit, where girls in different years bond naturally as well as through schemes like the student-led 'vertical families.' 'Of course, you get friendship groups, but absolutely no cliques,' said one pupil. 'It's a real community where everyone knows you and supports you,' said another. The school has always had a wide catchment area, based as it was on the vision of providing education to bright girls regardless of their means, although since the arrival of league tables, some pupils come in too far for the head's liking. ('I do question whether it's a good thing for some to travel really long distances.') Those in London mostly walk, cycle or get the bus or tube (Golders Green). There's also a parent-organised bus service to cater for those who can't easily get there by public transport.

Great ethnic mix – about a fifth Indian and a fifth white British, the rest from a variety of backgrounds. 'The school is the multicultural, meritocratic face of Britain,' said one parent, proudly. PTA provides refreshments at events, along with the odd quiz night, but not as active as some, particularly for socialising. 'It's inevitable, with families coming from such a wide area and diverse backgrounds,' said one parent, which probably also explains why after-school social life is not as vibrant as elsewhere.

Entrance: It doesn't get more selective than this, with 2400+ applying for 100 places. Some families move house once they have a place; others travel for long distances. Verbal and numerical reasoning tests in September, then the top 300 are invited back for English and maths tests in October. Pupils come from 50-60 primaries. Priority to looked after children and up to 20 on pupil premium who have been ranked in the top 300.

For sixth form, approximately 600 apply for a further 45-55 places, with six A grades at GCSE minimum requirement, including As in intended A level subjects. Girls already in the school are also expected to achieve this requirement, although in reality most far exceed it.

Exit: Around seven per cent leave after GCSE, mostly to sixth form colleges. Twenty-nine to Oxbridge in 2016. Lots of medics and dentists (23 medics and seven dentists in 2016) and a good cross-section of all other subject areas. Team of sixth form tutors provide UCAS advice, including raising expectations of what can be achieved. Alumni include Sarah Solemani (actress and television script writer), Ros Altmann (pensions minister) and Debbie Wiseman (composer).

Money matters: Regular fundraising via PTA, pupil-led initiatives and a parental support scheme to which many parents regularly donate.

Remarks: One of the top academic state schools in the country, yet also one of the most liberal and nurturing; it's hard to exaggerate the emotional buy-in from pupils. 'The school becomes part of your DNA in a profound way,' said one. 'I don't know what happens when you get inside those four walls, but it is genuinely unique and stays with you for life.' Producing friendly, fun and delightful girls who come out with academic results that quite literally make the world their oyster, it's no wonder that top universities and employers love it too. 'My only sadness is that I can't see how it will ever be this good again,' said one pupil. A gentle and inspiring education for extremely bright girls, in a fabulous setting.

Hereward House School

14 Strathray Gardens, London NW3 4NY

Pupils: 168 • Ages: 4-13

Fees: £15,615 – £16,065 pa

Tel: 020 7794 4820
Email: office@herewardhouse.co.uk
Website: www.herewardhouse.co.uk

Headmaster: Since 2015, Pascal Evans, previously director of studies, and before that head of French, at Westminster Under School. Studied law, and practised as a pupil barrister before following his passion and becoming a teacher. Started his career at Colet Court (now St Paul's Juniors). A keen runner, he is married to Akiyo; their children are trilingual; he often teaches basic Japanese to classes after exams.

Entrance: Register by the time your son is a year old at the latest. Head sees all parents and boys, in groups of two families, when boys are 3. 'We make a significant commitment to finding the right boy.' Siblings guaranteed a place, the rest chosen on 'suitability' rather than ability. 'We could test to find the most academic, but we're not going down that route. What we're really looking for is a good chap to have in the place, a player rather than spectator.' Offers – conditional on staying till the age of 13 – are made one year before entry at 4+. Occasional places thereafter due to relocation, but those on the waiting list get first dibs. Occasional places at end of year 6.

Exit: The school won't prepare for entrance tests at 7 or 8. 'Our record at 13 is so strong, there's no need to exit early.' Highgate perhaps losing favour, with a fairly even split between between City, UCS, Mill Hill, Westminster, St Paul's and others eg Eton, Winchester, Haileybury, with regular scholarships. 'Our scholarship record is broadly comparable per head to the best schools in the area.'

Careful guidance given in the run up to CE. 'Parents here will typically ask: "What is the right school for my son?" rather than saying "which school can you get him into?" They really do want the best fit.'

Remarks: The school was founded in 1951 in its current red-brick Hampstead house. In essence it's still a family business, though now governed by a trust made up of members of the Sampson family, the owners.

Though not a school in which selection is made on academic grounds, almost every boy here is above average, with 'the top third as bright as anywhere'. Generally no setting until year 8 (occasionally from year 7), when the class is divided into a scholarship group and a CE group, with maths and French taught entirely separately and other subjects in small groups. Specialist teaching, in part from year 4, entirely from year 5. French from the start, Latin from year 5, Greek from year 8 (potentially from year 7), Mandarin now introduced to year 4. Teachers know boys well and respond quickly to their needs. ('Teachers are often outside during pick-up time,' said one parent, 'and will seek you out to talk about your child.') Learning support also fine-tuned, with two specialists to help the struggling ('in the majority of cases, boys come out the other end without a problem,' says the school.) A former barrister provides the stretch needed for the most demanding scholarship papers. Parents feel the school works well for all abilities. 'Our older son is very academic and remains challenged with lots of extra work,' said one, 'while our younger son is smart, but playful, and the school uses a very different approach to stimulate him.' Homework at manageable levels. 'It should be do-able in an hour if working at a steady pace.'

Sport is 'central to the school life'. Two afternoons of games a week, one on Hampstead Heath, the other in Brondesbury. Cricket and soccer particularly strong and every boy gets to play, with a first, second and third team. 'This is simply too small a school for a boy to be sitting on the sidelines handing out oranges. They love to represent the school.' Punches above its weight – the Colts remained unbeaten for nearly two years – but can struggle against the largest schools. Cross-country also taken seriously, with weekly lessons in the spring term. Fencing, tennis and hockey on offer as clubs, plus timetabled swimming at Swiss Cottage baths just down the road. Smallish playground with an intricate system of who uses what bit when – seems to work like a well-rehearsed ballet.

Almost every boy plays an instrument, half play two or more (the orchestra has nearly 60 members). Form concerts every term. Art, too, highly valued. Boys' work now hangs around the school ('we wanted to take art out of the art room') and a cricket-themed display now ornaments head's study. Pottery and DT also popular (though a cleverly crafted crossbow did have to be confiscated). Drama taught until the final two years, when academic works takes precedence. Major drama production every other year, with every boy involved.

Loads of clubs, including photography, fencing, tennis, typing, art, music theory, chess, Spanish and science. 'If boys want something else we make it happen.' Handy prep club, too, nightly from 4pm to 5pm (with flexibility to stay till 6pm). Popular annual ski trip, accompanied by head and parents, where card playing is often a focus of evening activity. 'We believe in cards. We don't see why they shouldn't learn to play whist and basic bridge.' First school disco held recently, so boys can 'learn how to treat a lady.'

Bright, high-ceilinged classrooms, originally the living quarters of an affluent turn-of-the-century family, complemented by relatively flimsy science and music space, which are top of the school's agenda for a make-over.

This small school revels in its size. It wants a family atmosphere and does its utmost to make this happen. 'Academic performance is based on the foundation that the school is happy.' All boys are known by name and all are given a position of 'meaningful' responsibility at the top of the school, with eight prefects, four house captains, and further captains for music, drama and games. 'Every boy must have his moment in the sun.' Parents definitely approve: 'Senior boys thrive on the responsibility and have the confidence to display a fair amount of individuality in how they fill their role.' Two senior boys, for example, are at the door each morning to greet each boy by name. There are merit prizes, with bronze, silver and gold awards, form prizes for effort and contribution to the community and school colours for non-academic achievements.

Elected school council has considerable sway. 'They wanted more pasta and sweet and sour chicken and that was delivered.'

Rules kept to a minimum. Beyond the basics, the main principle is that boys should treat one another well and make the most of what's on offer. 'Hopefully boys have a sense they are part of the system, not ruled by it. We're looking for good chaps, gentlemen with a general sense of decency.' Parents remark on how considerate boys are to each other – even out of school. Disciplinary problems only of the extremely minor variety like tipping chairs and talking in line. Staff eat lunch with boys every day to engage boys in friendly conversation. 'It's a great time to find out how things are going.' The head also meets with prefects weekly to discuss concerns they may have about younger boys. 'Everyone knows everyone else; older boys look out for younger ones; the more confident encourage the less so.'

Parents are typical north London professionals, with a cosmopolitan range of nationalities, generally reasonably local. Newly founded PTA, very much part of the school's drive for a sense of community. 'Everyone is very welcoming to newcomers,' says one recent arrival. 'My two boys, who joined higher up the school, have had plenty of invitations.'

Herne Hill School

111

The Old Vicarage, 127 Herne Hill, London SE24 9LY

Pupils: 288 • Ages: 2-7

Fees: £5,550 – £13,775 pa

Tel: 020 7274 6336
Email: enquiries@hernehillschool.co.uk
Website: www.hernehillschool.co.uk

Headteacher: Since September 2016, Ngaire Telford (pronounce Nyree), previously deputy head. All four of her children have been through the school, and she has worked here since 2007, first as EYFS co-ordinator. She is a New Zealander who qualified and taught there for two years before coming to teach in London in 1993. She has taught in both the state and independent sectors with experience across the whole primary age range.

Entrance: Three points of entry: into the kindergarten at 2+, into pre-reception at 3+ or into reception at 4+. Each entry point has its own registration deadline and assessment month, with some sibling priority given. Early registration is key, as this is the dominant factor in the allocation of places, hence there are elements of a mixed ability intake here.

There are approximately 40 kindergarten places. These children are then joined in the kindergarten by others, mostly from local Dulwich and Herne Hill nurseries, to make a total of 70. The array of parked scooters testifies to the proximity of the families who come here, but there are children from more distant parts of South London: Peckham Rye, Brixton, Clapham, and Crystal Palace.

Exit: All children exit at 7+, a few to the sought-after maintained Dulwich Hamlet school, the majority to the six independent schools in the area that top most parents' wish lists. Three-quarters of girls exit to James Allen's Prep School, Rosemead, Alleyn's or Sydenham High. Dulwich College heads the list for boys, followed closely by Alleyn's, then DPL and a few to Sydenham, Rosemead and others.

Remarks: The school began as a private nursery in 1976 and became an independent day school 10 years later. The meticulously planned spaces, including solar tiles on the roof, are carefully chosen by the school's director since 2005, Dominik Magyar, a Swiss businessman with an eye for detail and high standards. Surprisingly hands-on – during our visit, he phoned to consult on choice of chocolates for staff thank-yous.

There are three classes in each year from kindergarten to year 2. The parents we spoke to describe their children as 'always happy to go' and 'always loved it.'

Children certainly appeared very happy in every classroom, enthusiastically involved with their activities: making a potion of 'yukky' words, completing jigsaws of the organs of the human body, sequencing numbers to 20 by ordering themselves into a line, or working intently on laptops under the watchful eye of a specialist technician. Carefully differentiated learning was in evidence, allowing children to tackle the same topic within a single lesson at their own pace.

English teaching is definitely a strength – the co-ordinator we met on our visit was extremely impressive in her passion and attention to detail: one parent noted of her child that 'he learned to read at lightning speed'. The school is also very good at 'teaching' parents, with curriculum evenings every term and English hand-outs from Herne Hill known to be begged and borrowed by parents at other local independents.

There are some quirks – reading books are given, not chosen, until year 2; no pens for hand-writing by year 2 (only for display work) – but we noted the careful thinking behind every decision. Maths, previously a weak spot, has been strengthened with a new curriculum, training and some setting of years 1 and 2. School points out that children score well in their Sats, with 76 per cent recently achieving level 3. Homework consists of just reading and spellings until year 2, when there is a maximum of 20 minutes to get children into the swing of it for middle school. French lessons are with a native French speaker, and there are the usual cross-curricular science, French and book weeks. Comforting for the less competitive, the school considers what parents may be able to whizz up of an evening, in terms of costumes, and reflecting their sensitive pastoral care, provides something for any child whose busy parent has forgotten.

We've heard that pupils work very hard here and we don't doubt it, but in the reception classes there is still space for play with role-play corners. Every classroom bursts with cheerful artwork of a high standard and plenty of glitter.

A distinctive feature of the school is the high staffing ratios – up to four in a class of 20 pupils in the kindergarten, although plenty of young faces, as some of these are newly qualified or gap students. Some 25 per cent of the 50 staff has been there 10 years, and there are currently four male teachers. The school ensures that teachers across the year groups don't spend time on playground duty or hymn practice, but rather spend an afternoon each week lesson planning, pooling ideas. Parents are largely very happy with staff – 'they're totally committed' – but mention some highs and lows around teaching experience.

Currently less than 10 per cent of pupils receive learning support, mostly for mild learning differences. Many children with EAL but none needing extra support, as they are bilingual. Learning support teaching has been boosted with full-time staffing, and is sensitively handled – all children may have some lessons with these specialist teachers, so that it becomes the norm.

Music and drama top the list of parental satisfactions. As one said, 'amazing concerts, like a professional choir at year 1 and year 2'. Years 1 and 2 learn the recorder and specialists visit for individual music tuition, which parents are invited to listen in on if they wish. Space on-site is limited for PE – though enhanced by new hall – but the high quality of the coaching is a real plus – the school uses a well-qualified outside team coach and makes use of the various local playing fields, whilst swimming is a mini-bus ride away at Crystal Palace. New enlarged all-weather sports surface in the playground with nature trail at the rear.

Tucked just behind an imposing church, a short (steep) walk from the useful Herne Hill station, the school is housed partly in the well-maintained, large vicarage, together with a new building comprising the kindergarten to year 1 classes. This building really works, with some automatic doors and large, light classrooms with ensuite loos. New kindergarten classroom means children from 2 years old can now stay all day, new hall provides space for drama, PE and assemblies, and new kitchen provides hot lunches.

The nearby residential streets are lined with cars, making parking almost impossible, so that many parents switch to arriving on foot. Once through the doors, the open space behind both buildings is an unexpected delight, providing a large, soft-surface playground, and areas for den-making and gardening beneath the trees of a small copse.

Complete on-site wrap-around care, from 8am to 6pm and provided by Herne Hill staff, keeps things simple for working parents. It could stack up financially for full-time working parents: we calculate £1,000 per term per child for 8am to 6pm, but only a handful use it so consistently. There are many club activities after school too: gardening, drama, Lego, yoga, ballet, hip-hop, football, ball sports, art and a popular cycling club teaming up with the nearby Herne Hill velodrome.

What kind of child will thrive here? A parent comments: 'I think the school is great for developing confident, outgoing children, but suitable for all types of children – outgoing kids, quieter kids, studious kids and triers'.

Parents are perhaps a little younger than average, mostly busy professionals, but not too busy to be involved in the PTA, as the head says, 'just as much or as a little as they want'. One says of her experience: 'Parents are very friendly and supportive. We have made some great friends through Herne Hill.'

The fact that children arriving at 4+ have only a short time here before parents must think again about the choice of middle schools and more assessments is an undeniable downside of Herne Hill School. However, in our view, the quality of care, the pleasant environment and the high standards of early years teaching, particularly in English, make Herne Hill a definite contender for first choice of school up to 7 years.

One parent confided regarding her daughter's time here, 'A great start to her schooling, which I wouldn't change (even with hindsight of the year 2 assessment process). The children seem mostly unaffected – the pressure is on the parents.'

Highgate Junior School

Linked with Highgate School

3 Bishopswood Road, London N6 4PL

Pupils: 340 • Ages: 3–11

Fees: £16,965 – £17,970 pa

Tel: 020 8340 9193
Email: jsoffice@highgateschool.org.uk
Website: www.highgateschool.org.uk

Principal of Junior School: Since 2002, Mr Mark James (50s), BA theology Nottingham University, followed by a PGCE in English from the London Institute and an MA from King's College London. Grew up in Somerset where he worked for a term at Wellington School: 'I had far too much fun running around with the kids and decided then that this was what I wanted to do.' He started his career in the state sector – Tiffin Grammar in Kingston – followed by a decade at Dulwich College, prior to becoming deputy head at King's Wimbledon School junior school: 'It was there I made the transition from senior school to juniors, after my wife suggested I give it a try. I loved it.' This is the head who had the task of transforming Highgate boys' 7-13 prep into a modern mixed junior 7-11 junior school: 'When the school took the decision to go co-ed with the ambition to be academic and selective – it created a unique place in the market.'

Friendly, down to earth, all round nice guy – who certainly doesn't come across as being filled with a sense of his own importance, yet as principal of Highgate Junior School and head of admissions for the whole school, Mr James is THE guy to know for desperate parents vying for a place at the school. But he stands resolute and assures us that places at the school can only be obtained through a child's own merits and the Highgate assessment procedure: 'Parents can inevitably be disappointed if their child is not offered a place, especially if they already have a child in the school, but as I often say it has to be right for each child and the offer has to be justified based on the evidence we have'.

Popular with parents and pupils alike 'firm but fair', 'approachable', open to ideas', 'knows all the pupils and parents' 'involved in everything.' He is an enthusiastic can-do character, with a boyish charm and sense of humour (as was evident from the large jellybean jar crammed to the brim in his office). Married to a teacher – they have two daughters both who have both gone through Highgate School. One parent told us: 'It helps that he's had kids who have gone all the way through the school, so he knows the score.'

Of his role at Highgate School, Mr James says: 'I feel very lucky that I like what I do – what's not to like?' We couldn't help feeling the same as we stepped out of his office into the splendour that is the newly built junior school.

Head of pre-prep: Since 2012, Mrs Diane Hecht DCE (50s). Previously deputy head of St Columba's Junior School in Kilmacolm, she came south as two of her grown-up children had settled in London and feels that she has found a wonderfully similar school in Highgate. 'The girls here wear exactly the same tartan skirts as at St Columba's – it was meant to be!' Warm, efficient and enthusiastic.

Entrance: Hugely oversubscribed – 350 try for the 36 places at 3+. Sane and lovely pre-prep head admits that assessing 2 year olds has to be on the arbitrary side, so do not be amazed if your astounding tot just doesn't astound on assessment day. Teachers observe them at play in groups, look for capacity to listen and follow instructions, general sociability – so don't make them learn their letters the night before.

At 7+ your child will be up against around 300 others battling it out for 50/60 places. Assessments at this stage comprise of a reading test and an English and maths paper. Approx two-thirds of candidates will be invited back for a 'fun and interactive lesson' and a practical lesson which could be anything from art to music or science observed and, based on the outcome of that, will be invited for an interview: 'We are looking for an active and engaged child – a spark that sets them apart.' Other things count (where you live, parental statement etc), but not massively, it has to be said. No sibling policy, but 'every sibling is guaranteed an interview.' As far as school connections or being an old boy, no preferential treatment we are told: 'oh no, that doesn't exist anymore.' Definitely have a plan B.

Exit: Nearly all go from the pre-prep to the juniors and nearly all go from there to the senior school. 'If your child has got into the school you're going to try your utmost to make sure they stay.' Plenty of warning given to those unlikely to thrive in the higher stages. Pupils generally only leave for financial reasons.

Remarks: There are schools (and we've been to many many private schools) – and then there's the newly built, £25million Highgate Junior School, so brand spanking new at the time of our visit, the imported fossilised stone was still setting. Tucked into Bishopswood Road – one of the many prestigious roads that line the route from Highgate to Hampstead – this two year undertaking (financed by the judicious sale of former boarding houses) was a project of deep consideration. The powers that be were very aware that whilst it was important for the school to have some sort of artistic mark to it, they didn't want the space to look like a museum, 'but one which would have appeal and comfort to our younger pupils.'

On entering the building one is immediately drawn to a breathtaking feature wall in the reception area, which was the work of a specially commissioned artist. Portland fossilised stone provided the backdrop with a design which gently curves its way to the upper level. Reptiles and amphibians of various kinds are sculpted into the walls and at various points throughout the school, to encourage children to explore and discover different surfaces and textures as part of their learning exploration. We were also told that this was based on the Fibonacci principle of combining maths with biological settings. (At this point we nodded sagely, had no idea what was being said and felt very inadequate.)

Light, space and fluidity are the core elements of the design. Entering the bright circular atrium, you can observe the goings on all around on both levels. This feeling of transparency was very much key to the design 'so that visitors can see great things going on..rather than relying on pretty corridors of prepared displays.' The school offers bright and spacious classrooms, science laboratories, specialist rooms for art, DT, ICT, drama and music. Our favourite bit was the 360 retractable seat hall for assemblies and concerts etc. All classrooms, on the upper level or lower level, open onto a wonderful outdoor space. Balconies at the top – enclosed garden areas on the lower level with reading pods. The outdoor space also includes a small amphitheatre, a literary garden and a wonderful adventure playground, all surrounded by the extensive Highgate playing fields. Simply idyllic.

However, as we know from experience, a beautiful building doth not a good school make, so this school had much to live up to. We were shown around by two lively and phenomenally bright pupils, one of whom will no doubt be the brains behind something quite wonderful in years to come. The only pupil we have met to date who was trying to explain the ergonomics of desk sizes in the class in relation to the seating. But he did this without any pretentiousness, or awareness of how quirky this might appear. As one parent told us, 'most Highgate kids, are just regular kids, without an air of snootiness, or look at us – we're the rich kids. That's what makes it so special.' We had to agree: all the pupils we met were like any other – happy, spirited, at times noisy, curious and just very astute.

Hardly surprising when you consider what they have to do in order to get in at 7+ (if they don't come in via the pre-prep route). Once in, pupils can expect a challenging but fun time, 'the best' we are told. The day starts at 8.25am prompt and then it's full throttle into the learning day with the added injection of a smorgasbord of languages on offer. Unlike most other primary schools with 'only' French on the syllabus, Highgate Juniors can expect everything from French and German to Japanese, Gujarati and Russian, with the aim of instilling a love of languages, since they have no need to pass an entrance exam.

Teaching staff, who were praised by one parent as being 'beyond anything', struck us as being a particularly young and attractive bunch. A low turnover of staff and continuity throughout the school no doubt contributes to the school's success. Teachers are fairly heavily vetted and there is an open door policy for all classrooms, for regular observation: 'Each term we have roughly 30 observations, which are graded, and if they are not where we would hope they would be, we would need to do something to bring up their levels.' Fairly tough, some might say, but there are reputations to uphold.

Class sizes don't exceed 22, and are set from year 5 in maths. The school can cope with mild SEN, but because of its selective nature, numbers are quite small. Dedicated SENCo and part-time learning support person. School doesn't believe in much one-to-one; they adopt a more inclusive approach 'so that pupils don't miss out.'

Homework, we were told by both pupils and parents, was slightly on the heavy side. One parent told us: 'The workload can be a bit much at times, but my daughter doesn't struggle as she's used to it from pre-prep. I imagine if you come in at the 7+ stage, it might be more difficult.'

Academia aside, there is so much going on. 'Everyone has their chance to shine in the sun', says the head and sport is a biggie here. It would be difficult for it not to be with the phenomenal facilities on offer, both outdoors and at the Mallinson Sports Centre. Everyone gets the chance to play, we are told, and both juniors and seniors are known to do well in competitive sports.

Drama and music thrive. Many children take individual instrumental lessons and in addition to these, there is a school orchestra, and numerous ensembles. Drama is taught as a separate subject throughout the school, and there are termly drama productions within and across year groups. Active drama club.

Lots of extracurricular going on too. It's amazing that these young kids can cram it all in, but somehow they do. Robotics club, maths club, newspaper club, debating, Minecraft, Lego, creative literacy, chess and mosaic making are just a handful of what's on offer – not to mention the multitude of sports clubs (including water polo). Lunch time lectures are offered mainly by parents whose kids attend the school (and there is a veritable feast of who's who).

A very sociable school with 'a big heart', one parent told us. Tons of charitable events organised by the school's enthusiastic PTA. Indeed last year we were told they raised a staggering 50k for various charities, via the usual summer and Christmas fairs and school productions plus the less usual sales of teddy bear sales, friendship bracelets, umbrellas and pupil-designed cookbooks. Parents are in the main a prosperous bunch, but a couple of the parents we spoke to were not particularly high earners: they just decided to make their child's education a complete priority.

Pre-prep separately, delightfully (and permanently) housed. Starts at nursery – 18 morning or afternoon tots in lively spacious space both inside and out with smiley, lively teachers. Whole school theme of colour and light when we visited and lots of attractive work on show. Glorious herd of Elmer elephants made from plastic milk cartons and coloured paper. Lovely singing – the most in-tune bunch of rising 5s we've heard. An orderly, relaxed and friendly school. We saw much warm interaction between staff and small people and just wanted to stay and watch.

Highgate School

Linked with Highgate Junior School

North Road, London N6 4AY

Pupils: 1,140 • Ages: 11–18 • Sixth form: 298

Fees: £19,590 pa

Tel: 020 8347 3564
Email: admissions@highgateschool.org.uk
Website: www.highgateschool.org.uk

Head Master: Since 2006, Mr Adam Pettitt MA (40s). Oxford modern and medieval linguist. Taught French and German at Eton, Oundle and Abingdon and was second master at Norwich School, under Jim Hawkins, now head of Harrow – a formidable team. Has French wife and school-age children and is quite the most interesting, eloquent and thought-provoking head this veteran GSG reviewer has met in many a long school visit. Propelled by a sharply focused and incisively articulated moral and educational philosophy, Mr Pettitt is spare, brilliant and energetic. He must be an exacting – though supportive – man to work for. His pupils can only benefit from his firm commitment to outreach to schools and to those without their advantages, to placing an understanding of language at the heart of modern languages, and to educational values rather than exams and results. The results will follow where this approach leads. Parents are unstinting in their praise. The most inspiring head we've met in years.

Academic matters: Head has a refreshing disrespect for the bodies deserving of it: 'You choose the exam board on the basis that it will have the least distorting effect on the way you want to teach' – bingo! IGCSEs now in English x 2, sciences, langs and history and many subjects now opt for the Pre-U as an alternative to A levels. This can only enhance the nature and quality of learning. English and langs the first to head this way. Mr Pettitt the 'de facto head of MFL' at the time of our visit so langs getting the oxygen they needed and number of takers is sure to rise. Mandarin now through to sixth form; computer science a GCSE option. Maths much the most popular A level and, with further maths, has impressive results. Also strong are English, art, Latin, all sciences and RS. Tiny numbers take theatre studies, Greek, classics, music – school does not offer music tech nor other popular 'modern' subjects eg textiles, psychology and loses a few post-GCSE on that account. Number of subject options (24) felt by some to be a little limited, given the size of the sixth form, and some sixth formers would like more drama and art. However, good innovations include the 'knowledge curriculum' and 'critical method' courses. In 2016, 88 per cent A*/A at GCSE and nearly 64 per cent at A level/Pre-U. Lively, student-led conferences. Mr Pettitt takes all criticism on the chin and, given that over 70 per cent of the staff are his appointees, this – as everything else – is fast developing.

Head's inclusive approach is just that: 'The quality of the way you learn is critical and every child's experience is equally important. Every day is important – I am most interested in the way each one of us teaches and learns.' IBAC – Independence through Buzz, Aspiration and Collaboration – the new acronym around the place. So this is not the school that was, nor the one people think they know. The fabric – see below – is radically changing and the character equally so. This is encapsulated in the sane and sensitively individualised approach to SEN. The Victorian main building is not good for those with mobility problems though school says 'we will try to make it work by moving our routines and schedules as far as we can.' Director of learning support covers all three schools and is a renowned expert in autism. The support for all conditions and syndromes as they emerge is individual, tailored, supportive and 'concerned with management rather than labelling.' The very few with EAL needs are usually the very bright.

Games, options, the arts: Blessed with playing fields and space beyond the dreams of other London schools. If the educational philosophy and general zip in the place doesn't inspire you, the sporting facilities will. Girls' sport, some feel – school disputes – still catching up with boys'; football and netball still pre-eminent but plenty more on offer and played hard. Sports hall, pool, weights, Astroturfs, squash courts – it's all here. No country school could offer more.

Interior activities also privileged and currently being transformed by an enormous rolling building project that will add considerably to teaching space but also, it is hoped, to an eventual sixth form and arts campus. Drama and music thrive – many productions, concerts of all kinds and tours – art a little undemonstrative at the time of our visit but some lively colourful work around. Mills Centre provides studio and gallery space. Cultural life better displayed in the admirable school publications – professional-looking periodicals on history, politics, science, theatre and thought written and produced by pupils. Terrific range of clubs (they include 'vinyl and philosophy,' beekeeping, LGBT soc and feminist society), trips, exchanges and tours – extracurricular is praised by many but not fully taken advantage of by all. 'I used to feel that some pupils' cultural references were limited to Arsenal: great though that club is, I want them to see and know so much more,' comments the head, happy to stress to parents that while these opportunities are on offer it is up to pupils to take them up.

Lots of charitable and outreach activities for both staff and pupils – several staff now working at local state schools as part of community partnership work. This very much part of the Pettitt ethos – outreach is not a box ticking necessity here but an essential part of what it is to grow into a valuing and valuable person.

Background and atmosphere: A school with an up and down history. Founded as the Free Grammar School of Sir Roger Cholmeley, Knight at Highgate, in 1565 – former pupils still known as Old Cholmeleians. Became Highgate School in the late 19th century – and no longer free. The chapel, undergoing terrific refurb at time of our visit, 'complete brick by brick restoration, new roof, stained glass windows repaired and cleaned, apse painting restored etc; lighting and heating to render God's work less chilly and gloomy,' in Mr Pettitt's inimitable phrases – and main buildings are 19th century. Some impressive bits – old gothic central hall with Norman arches, leaded lights, wrought iron balcony and cantilevered ceiling and splendid new Sir Martin Gilbert library in old assembly hall. A real library which, unlike so many schools' learning resource centres, actually has books in it, alongside all its rows of PCs, and an atmosphere to encourage concentration and study.

By the 1960s, the school buildings (some considerably less felicitous), including boarding houses, were spread over the heart of Highgate Village – the premier north London suburb whose denizens refer to it as 'the village' and who are, understandably, rather smug about living there. Charter Building adds new subject rooms in a five-storey glass cube. All very high tech – interactive whiteboards and PCs everywhere. The whole site is now a mix of the new, light, glass-bound, airy and stylish, and the old, rather shabby, small passages and dark areas along which school operates a clever one-way system – but all likely to look a great deal smarter and more coherent in the next few years. Much tramping up and down the hill between the main buildings and the Mills Centre, playing fields etc, and each day sees orderly crocodiles with professional chaperones trailing along.

School suffered during the 70s and 80s and took time to recover its reputation. Girls joined the sixth form in 2004 and year 7 in 2006, and the whole school is now fully co-educational and fully rehabilitated. A Christian foundation and an inclusive one, with multi-faith assemblies and speakers from different religions on a weekly basis. House system – 12 houses – but no fanatical exclusive loyalty to these, rather a friendly rivalry in competitions etc and designed to encourage the mixing of year groups. 'It's a family school,' a parent told us. 'Not everyone is terrifically academic, though they really make the scholars work. They are very encouraging to everyone.'

Pastoral care, well-being and discipline: We saw only absorbed and concentrating classes with lively teaching. Discipline, as pupils gratefully pointed out, is not dependent on the whims of individual staff but 'whole school,' ie you know what is coming to you at every level should you transgress. Very little transgressing these days and we have seldom seen so few uniform infringements – everyone is smart.

Small classes 'very well-monitored,' say parents. 'It's extremely well-run,' we were told. 'We are kept fully informed and have lots of email contact with staff,' another told us. 'The teaching staff are so enthusiastic and they really care about my children,' another enthused. Occasional loutishness clearly frowned on by majority of pupils, who are a civilised lot. 'We have sent all our children there – they're so different academically and in their characters – but all have been happy.'

Pupils and parents: From a wide area of north and more central London, though most live near, if not within walking distance. 'Not ruthlessly elitist,' as one parent put it but lots of City lawyers, accountants etc with clear idea of what they want from the school. Pupils are friendly, happy and articulate. Most seem proud to be at the school and keen not to jeopardise their futures. Notable OCs include Rt Hons Charles Clarke and Anthony Crosland, Michael Mansfield QC, Johnny Borrell of Razorlight, Ringo Starr's son Zak Starkey of Oasis and The Who, Orlando Weeks of The Maccabees and DJ Yoda, Phil Tufnell, Sir Clive Sinclair, Alex Comfort, Nigel Williams, Sir John Tavener, Barry Norman, Gerard Manley Hopkins and Sir John Betjeman. Doubtless, old girl Cholmeleians shortly to make their marks.

Entrance: Wildly oversubscribed at every stage – on a scale we see most commonly with the grammars. Six hundred apply at 11+ for the 90 places available when the junior school pupils have been accommodated. NB part of a group of independent co-ed/boys' schools that coordinate 11+ results, but forbid those who have accepted a place at one school from taking up a subsequent waiting list offer from another. At 13+, only 6-8 places available; tests and interviews in autumn term of year 7. At 16+, 120 for 30. At 11, around 60 per cent from state primaries and 40 per cent – mainly girls – from local preps. The tiny 13+ entry mostly boys entering from the obvious preps – Arnold House, Devonshire House, The Hall, Keble etc.

Exit: Around a dozen, mostly boys, leave post GCSE to, mostly, Camden School for Girls, which has boys in the sixth. Around 90 per cent gain places at their first choice university – Bristol, UCL, Durham, Edinburgh and Leeds among most favoured; some now head to top US universities. Good numbers to Oxbridge each year. Economics, English and languages are popular subject choices.

Money matters: Scholarships – music and academic – at all usual entry points and now purely honorary. 'Much kudos, but not just to the particularly brainy but to those who exemplify scholarship (persistence, creativity, setting own agenda, leading learning in the classroom, originality),' stresses head. Bursaries up to the value of 100 per cent fees available each year and most go to those who get all or most of that amount. School makes extensive efforts via primary school visits etc to reach those who need to know.

Remarks: A new school in all but site and name – co-ed, modern, delivering a first rate education to the lively minds and limbs lucky enough to get in.

Hill House International School

H

17 Hans Place, London SW1X 0EP

Pupils: 930 • Ages: 4–13

Fees: £11,200 – £15,300 pa

Tel: 020 7584 1331
Email: info@hillhouseschool.co.uk
Website: www.hillhouseschool.co.uk

Principal: Since 2002, Richard Townend (early 70s) – organist, scholar, and son of the founder. The present head is calm, shrewd, gently impassioned by the vision of the school which he runs – and a wonderful foil for an egotistical and anxious world. The running of Hill House, while ultimately in his hands, is shared with his family. His beliefs are refreshing simple: 'bring children up with plenty of love and affection, and an example which allows them to understand the boundaries by which we must all live'. To that, and an inspiring academic education, add lots of fresh air, games, skiing and mountaineering, swimming and music. The morning of our visit, he was taking a vast choir practice of over 90 children, preparatory to a school assembly held at St Columba's Church. That isn't how most heads operate today – more's the pity.

After some stinging criticisms from Ofsted in 2014, the school found itself forced to address a range of health and safety issues, and to oversee some structural shifts designed to safeguard academic progress. It is a mark of the head's quality that he believes much good resulted from the whole episode. It was also very telling that the Ofsted debacle was chiefly notable for provoking an outpouring of parental, pupil and old pupil love and faith.

Entrance: Prospective parents have to go on a tour of the place – there's no booking: you just show up at one of the advertised times (these happen four days a week). 'Hardly sounds very onerous,' says the head, 'but just occasionally you'll get someone who tries to avoid it. No tour, no place. Simple as that.' If you like the place, then you fill in an application form. There is a waiting list, but – given the fast-changing plans of young parents and the fact that many go abroad – vacancies often crop up. The school tries to sidestep entrance tests, especially for the youngest children. Mrs Townend, wife of the headmaster, is in charge of admissions. She and her team make it their job to be friendly and accessible.

Exit: Most pupils go on to London day schools – destination of 2016 leavers shows how wide the school's outreach is: girls' destinations included Frances Holland, Godolphin & Latymer, St Paul's. Boys went to KCS, St Paul's, Dulwich, Westminster, inter alia. Boarding destinations included Charterhouse, Eton, Roedean, Wycombe Abbey. Two music scholarships to Eton and one to Uppingham.

Remarks: The youngest, aged 4 and 5, go to Small School to learn their rudiments – physical development, communication and language and social development. With lots of free play as well as structured lessons, the aim is to build up confidence and competence. They move from Flood Street to Pont Street when they are 5 or 6, and start to focus on English, handwriting, maths and reading, supplemented by supporting subjects as well as lots of music, drama and games. Then it's on to Cadogan Gardens and gradually learning to adapt to specialist subject teachers as well as the all-important form teacher. Aged 10 and 11, the girls and boys have separate classes, as they set about preparation for senior schools. Most girls leave at 11, while the great majority of boys stay to 13.

'The genius of Hill House,' said a parent, who is also an old pupil, 'is that they apply intelligence and thought to getting a child happy. Being happy means feeling reassured, not indulged. When they are surrounded by teachers who focus upon them with a fond and shrewd eye, they feel reassured. They can start to learn.'

There are three special needs teachers to support those with particular needs. The ethos of the school is to attend carefully to anything which may stand between a child and their ability to meet their potential, but also to guard against anxiety. 'Early intervention and calm management seems to level most things out very satisfactorily,' the head observes.

Staff reflect the school's commitment to diversity and cosmopolitanism – a spread of ages and backgrounds, but with a healthy quota of bright and fit young ones heralding from all over the word, as well as those from within London and the M25. This is a family school and, as presently constituted, nobody who isn't a Townend would appear able to climb to the very top of the tree. While this might work to demotivate a lesser teacher, the staff here palpably relish the wonderfully idiosyncratic extended family to which they, and everyone connected to the school, belong. The proof of that can be seen in the extraordinarily high rates of staff retention. The head's deep knowledge of his staff, and fond regard for them, is an eloquent advertisement for the school.

'Almost too much sport,' one parent said, 'except that it seems to embrace all pupils, and so the effect is everyone of them feels involved and wanted'. All pupils play sport at least once every day. Given that the school buildings are housed in the heart of Knightsbridge and Chelsea, this poses some logistical demands, but the sight of boys and girls in rust-coloured breeches is well-known to residents of SW3 and typically presages a visit to or from various indoor and outdoor grounds (Duke of York's, Battersea, Queen's Club – the list goes on for ever). Longer journeys are also made possible by a fleet of six minibuses, operated (as with everything else here) by in-house drivers. As well as all the usual rugby and netball, football, hockey and so forth, there are limitless opportunities for individual sports and a full complement of inter-school fixtures. A particular emphasis is placed on swimming – to which the late Colonel Townend, the school's founder, attached a passionate importance.

There is more art, music and drama than one can imagine. The head is a fine organist and, back in 1972, a fine two manual organ with mechanical action containing 456 pipes was especially commissioned for the school and installed in the music room in Hans Place. There is also a stock of over 300 orchestral instruments, which are loaned to boys and girls for the duration of their time at Hill House, and everyone gets a slice of the action. 'I've just watched my son play at Peter Jones,' said one parent, 'and my daughter at St Columba's Church. They're not prodigies, but they're thrilled to be involved. And so am I.' Among many other offerings, there is an annual Christmas musical as well as a regular dance and drama club. The school has three art galleries and children's work is displayed everywhere – all of it is framed. In a typical Hill House touch, the frames are bought at the local Habitat and knocked together expertly by the school's works department. The impression is terrific.

Hill House famously has an overseas annexe in Switzerland. Since 1960 this has been located at Glion, a mountain village over 700 metres above sea level looking out over Lake Geneva. The children are given an experience of a boarding school environment in the setting of a mountain village: there are geography CE project courses – and, of course, skiing.

The founder, Colonel Townend, opened the school in 1951 and was still in post in his 90s. His somewhat autocratic manner, the Knightsbridge address and the fact that the young Prince Charles arrived as a 7 year old newbie in 1956, have led many to assume that this is a school for toffs. That is quite unfair. Its vision has always been both forward-looking and international. It was among the very first of the so-called prep schools to welcome girls, its fees are a good deal lower than many local competitors, and its pupil constituency much broader socially than its elite addresses suggest. True, the place is superbly equipped, but it is also quite crowded, teeming with life. The children and staff are both industrious and relaxed. Both genders and all ethnic groups are fully represented at every level

There are a series of handsome London houses – Hans Place is the site of the original school and this is where the headmaster and school offices are located, but there are other houses in Flood Street, Pont Street and Cadogan Gardens. Two idiosyncrasies seen in each are revealing: a discreet investment by the school in the latest chemical technology to ensure the loos are odour-free (an issue in some schools) and the fact that all the catering is done in-house by support staff who have mainly worked here for years and years. No agencies, no fuss and consistently terrific reports of school lunches. The day of our visit we passed chefs chopping mounds of fresh carrots alongside mountains of fresh fruit. That isn't typical fare in school kitchens, more's the pity.

The school has a huge local reputation – arguably one of the few fixed points in that restless rootless world of Knightsbridge. It embraces the local community in the fullest sense, inviting local societies and residents' associations to concerts and plays and festivals, loaning its facilities at knock-down rates (or, where appropriate, free) and also doing a mass of fundraising for local children's charities.

The ethos of the school revolves around being tolerant, well-exercised, stimulated and kind, and contexts for nurturing each of these are embedded within every aspect of the school curriculum. There is a well worked-out chain of communication embracing form tutors, year and section heads, senior tutors and housemasters, all ultimately reporting to the pastoral deputy head (the only very senior figure in the school who is not a Townend) and finally the headmaster himself. 'What matters,' says the head, 'is that every child knows there is someone to whom they can confidently turn.' Anecdotal evidence suggests this is overwhelmingly true. 'The key to it all,' said a parent, 'is an atmosphere of great friendliness and patience, accompanied by an underlying structure and sensitive discipline.'

The school draws in families from south, west and east London – lots of children commute by bus and tube – as well as those who walk to school from various smart Knightsbridge or Chelsea Squares. We detected none of those snobbish hierarchies which, in some schools, can make relationships toxic. Parents are welcomed as part of the school community from the first minute, and many are first-generation users of independent schools. All form tutors – the first port of call between parents and school – set aside 30 minutes before and after school when parents can go and see them. There are reports at the end of every term (a particularly full one every summer) and an annual parents' evening to discuss children's progress with individual subject teachers.

The uniform is conspicuous but no more costly than others, but a big effort is made to keep extras to a minimum. Individual music lessons and Friday clubs are charged as (inevitably) are the trips to Switzerland. Some bursary help is available 'in exceptional circumstances' – the school works especially hard to try to look after families which have encountered bereavement.

Hill House challenges many of the complacent assumptions of our age. The fact that it's in Knightsbridge and that the uniform is so conspicuous could mislead one easily into inferring the opposite of the truth. The reality is a superbly effective and brilliantly resourced school – one which operates in a glorious time-warp in its preference for doing everything within the family and among the extended family: no school in the country can enjoy such deep loyalty from its support staff, which says a lot. Children of any race or social background will be gathered up here and utterly integrated.

Just like any family business, there are inherent vulnerabilities – and we suspect it may have been that which nettled the inspectors. But the commitment of the Townends to the constituency they serve is massive and wholehearted, and the palpable love and loyalty of all its constituencies (including old pupils), let alone their various successes, says everything.

Holland Park School

Airlie Gardens, Campden Hill Road, London W8 7AF

Pupils: 1,400 • Ages: 11–18 • Sixth form: 150

Tel: 020 7908 1000
Email: admissions@hollandparkschool.co.uk
Website: www.hollandparkschool.co.uk

Head: Since 2001, Mr Colin Hall BA PGCE (mid 50s). Born and brought up in Durham, he was educated at Durham Wearside grammar school. He graduated with a history degree from Sheffield and went on to to do a PCGE at Cambridge. His career has been meteoric. Each employer recognised his hunger and determination, as well as fierce loyalty (a number of references are reproduced in the staff planner for the benefit of his aspiring teachers). He arrived here from Longford Community School in Hounslow, his first headship; prior to that he had senior positions at Cheney School in Oxford and King Edward VI Morpeth in Northumberland. He still manages to find the time to teach English, which is the subject he has chosen to teach since his first job at Thurston Community School (now College) in Suffolk (his greatest joy, he says, is reading, and he read Sons and Lovers when he was 10). There is a more than a touch of Napoleon about him. A dynamo of man, we have rarely met someone who combines a seemingly unlimited supply of tenacity, fastidious attention to detail, boundless energy, aspiration for both pupils and staff alike and a total and passionate commitment to his vocation.

We were invited (unusually) to attend a staff meeting in the morning. Teachers here are (mostly) younger than 35 and Mr Hall invests as much nurturing and guidance in them as he does the pupils. Marking is assiduously scrutinised, lessons observed, goals and targets set. A canny head, he is also excellent at working the money and the room. The great and the good make up the body known as 'the friends of Holland Park'. Prizes such as the 'pupil premium award' are swept up, Alan Bennett attends whole school events, HRH the Duchess of Kent (known here as Katharine Kent) has her own set of keys to the building.

Deeply aspirational; 'no child is outside of our grasp,' he insists, 'no child is without ambition'. It does not surprise us at all that Michael Gove, the former education secretary, asked to come and 'observe Colin Hall' (although Mr Hall, with a disarming humility, says it did surprise him). Nor does it surprise us that when you Google him, Colin Hall appears among an elite band of 'super heads'. What is more surprising is that despite his Napoleonic appearance, parents describe him as having a big heart, a sensitive and empathetic approach. He also has a reliance on and affection for his trusted loyal advisers, the senior leadership team, but most notably his right hand man, David Chappell, associate head ('everyone is some sort of head,' remarked one parent. There are five deputy heads and five assistant head teachers as well as an associate head).

Academic matters: This is, unquestionably, a good fit for a bright, motivated pupil who has a particular flair for the humanities and English. A rigorous banding is applied across all subjects from the start. Band 1 pupils are considered by staff at pupils to be the crème de la crème. These are the ones taken on day trips to universities, for example and are the participants at the glamorous Perfect Tense event in the summer term when star pupils, selected by staff for 'outstanding achievement', are celebrated at a black tie awards ceremony in Holland Park – attended by the 'friends' of the school as well as by parents and staff. One pupil we spoke to remarked that 'even those in the top of Band 2 rarely get to go to Perfect Tense.' While this isn't necessarily true, school admits to the disparity in numbers – approximately 65 per cent of band 1 pupils compared with five per cent of band 4 pupils are likely to be celebrated at Perfect Tense. Pupils (and parents) are keen to move up a band if they can swing it.

All this contributes to personal drive and aspiration and the results speak for themselves. In 2016, 80 per cent of pupils got 5+ A*-C at GCSE including English and maths and 70 per cent of GCSE grades were A*/B. A huge improvement on 12 years ago when the pass rate for GCSEs was 45 per cent. At A level in 2016, 77 per cent A*/B, 53 per cent A*/A. Not a wide range of A levels offered, but all 'proper subjects'. English and biology currently most popular at A levels. Fewer than 10 take Spanish and/or French. A tiny few do design or music.

Teachers here are thoroughly committed. They have to be or they wouldn't last. Parents talk of a high turnover of staff, particularly in the maths department, but Mr Hall holds on fast when he strikes gold, with a talented teacher. Lots of opportunity for career development and promotion. English, humanities and art are all strong here and the staff, in those subjects, long serving. Class rooms could be mistaken for museums – ordered, uncluttered, tastefully decorated and minimal. Mr Hall's attention to detail spares no corner. Lesson plans are scrutinised, progress reports monitored and the delivery of lessons constantly observed and remarked upon. We were given copies of the lesson plans of every lesson we saw, as well as examples of marking. All extremely thorough and impressive. The lower bands have the advantage of the some of the best teaching. No one is allowed to coast here. Parents particularly enthusiastic about geography, history and English teaching. 'They lit a spark in my son,' remarked one parent, 'with a combination of inspirational teaching and incentivising notes of encouragement from the head'. However, another parent deplored a 'boot camp approach' – evidenced by an inflexibility and greater concern for the results and statistics than what might be best for the individual.

A measure of staff commitment is the practice of opening the school on Saturday mornings as well as for one week during the holidays – for what are called 'interventions'. About 200 children will come in on a Saturday to benefit from extra support and teaching. There may well be sports fixtures and practices on Saturdays too. As many as 600 students have lessons over the the Easter holidays. Teachers aren't paid extra for this. Their professionalism demands it of them. Parents are impressed by the thoroughness with which progress is tracked. 'If my son gets a lower result than expected, the teacher will ring me to discuss why this might have happened.'

Many pupils take GCSEs early (a practice that is unlikely to be able to continue under the present regime). By year 10 some have already taken four or five subjects including French, Latin, English literature, history and RS. A few parents regret this suggesting, that their children weren't allowed enough time to enjoy the subject and study in depth, cramming in a short time instead. Others feel disappointed that their child might have been able to achieve an A* in a subject if they had taken it at the normal time. Pupils we spoke to bemoaned 'the exam culture', the constant pressure and the stress this can cause.

Not the school for a child with special educational needs, whether mild or severe, and by Mr Hall's own admission 'you have to be very sure you can meet them.' The school does have lifts, so can accommodate physical disabilities, and perhaps even a case of mild autism. There are a number of students here with 'emotional and behavioural difficulties', we were told. Full time SENco but one parent remarked on the high turnover of people in this role. In class support provided wherever possible; occasionally a student may be withdrawn from class to be given extra support.

Games, options, the arts: Excellent sporting facilities – lots of outside space, Astro and tarmac for netball, tennis, football and cricket on the doorstep, as well as a spanking, shiny, well-equipped gym with basketball courts etc in the basement, not to mention the 25m competition swimming pool. One of our year 11 guides enthused about netball. Girls in the team are keen and committed and will turn up for practice at 6.30am on a freezing winter's morning. There are house matches every term and a house sports week. As well as rugby, football, cricket and netball, plenty of minor sports also offered, including lacrosse, badminton, table tennis, athletics and rowing, and there are netball and football tours as well as a ski trip.

However, parents agree that the uptake and quality of boys' sport is patchy. Football is popular and the school competes impressively against the local competition which includes Cardinal Vaughan, Burlington Danes, Chelsea Academy and Latymer Upper. Matches and practice sessions are timetabled on Saturdays. Rugby and cricket, on the other hand, have some way to go. Although two hours a week is allocated, most do little above and beyond this; 'My son is getting overweight and has no way of letting off steam,' complained one parent. Perhaps the work pressure is such that students are afraid of committing too much time to doing anything outside the classroom? Either that or, as one parent put it, 'the boys aren't being enticed to do more sport'. However, the school will support pupils' enterprising initiatives – setting up an American football club, for example. A cricket tour to Ampleforth College in Yorkshire caused a great flurry of excitement, but 'the standard is low and enthusiasm quick to wane,' observed one parent.

The major drama production of the year is performed not by pupils, but by staff. The leadership team puts on an annual Shakespeare play each Lent term, well attended by the whole school community; it is clearly a strong bonding experience. Photographs of performances adorn the walls, and particularly amusing characters (who can't act for bacon, confesses one of the leadership team wryly) are discussed for months afterwards. With the exception of an annual 'drama evening' in March where a wide range of age groups perform a selection of pieces – perhaps from the A level or GCSE syllabus – it would seem that there is little drama for the students, apart from what takes place in the classroom during a drama lesson, or when studying a play during English. Apart from the school hall, used primarily for assembly, there is nowhere to put on productions on site, and no mention of any attempt to borrow or lease any local theatres.

A small but impressive choir is growing in quality and stature, and is led by one of the talented deputy heads. We were impressed when we saw a number of double basses and guitars in a music practice room, owned by the school but available for pupils' use. Some pupils receive financial support from the school to play their chosen instrument. Lots of prizes for music. There is clearly very positive encouragement coming from the top (and it helps that Katharine Kent is a strong supporter of the arts, especially music). An orchestra gets cobbled together from pupils who play an instrument 'outside school', but there is little continuity. When we asked one pupil why there are not more musical groups, she replied tartly, 'probably because they can't make us do an exam in it.' School is part of the tri-borough music service (which includes Westminster, Kensington and Hammersmith); however, one parent talked of the music as taking place 'in fits and starts'. Peripatetic music teachers are not accommodated as there is huge resistance to any pupil missing an academic lesson to fit in an instrumental lesson.

One of the assistant head teachers runs the dance department, which is burgeoning. Two dance studios in the school, and several teachers; dance is a popular mainstream subject as well as after school activity. We saw boys and girls, gawky and graceful, making shapes and loving it. When asked about drama productions, most parents we spoke to talked of dance performances.

The art department is exceptional – and pupils heavily rewarded with prizes and praise for creativity. Mr Chappell, the exceptional associate head, is currently steering a very talented group of students from year 10 through to the sixth form through A level art in the bohemian environment of Thorpe Lodge. A run-down and enchanting building, once inhabited by the governor of the Bank of England and with its own magical gardens, Thorpe Lodge is situated within the school gates and a stone's throw from the main building. Here, the art students are given free rein to express themselves, and so they do. Huge self-portraits in oil, spectacular installations and a plethora of other work was currently in progress when we visited. DT is well equipped with several laser printers as well as 3 D printer. With the art scholarship students and a passionate teaching team, the school well deserves its reputation as an excellent choice for those with a creative bent.

Background and atmosphere: What you see now when you enter the shimmering glass building, replete with tasteful furniture, aesthetically pleasing fixtures and fittings, not to mention the delicate fragrance of Jo Malone candles, bears almost no resemblance to the 60s monolith that was Holland Park Comprehensive several years ago. Mr Hall and his leadership team (referred to by one parent, wryly, as the 'men in black': though there are two women on the team, the preponderence of young white men – who when we visited were wearing black gowns – give some weight to the analogy) have wrought a remarkable change. It neither looks, nor, more importantly, smells like a school. Fresh flowers, designer furniture (Ercol tables and chairs even in the classrooms as well as the front hall and communal areas), no mess, no clutter, and above all no damage. Everything is immaculate. The staff room is tastefully adorned with simple two seater pale blue sofas and blue Smeg fridges, banks of daffodils decorated the assembly hall on our visit, thoughtfully framed posters, paintings, poems and catechisms adorn the freshly painted walls.

The building itself is all glass and (sun) shine. Every one of the 1,335 pupils is housed here. With the exception of A level art in Thorpe Lodge, all lessons and activities take place in this one building. Everything is open plan, from the library to the unisex WCs. It's not possible either to smoke in the lavatories, or curl up in a discreet corner with a book – the building is easy to police and its corridors regularly patrolled. There is nowhere to hide. We were standing on the 'bridge' during break and it was like observing an installation – a river of smartly dressed, well-behaved young men and women moving seamlessly and smoothly up and down stairs and along the wide spacious passageways.

Pastoral care, well-being and discipline: Hall and his henchman is a phrase that slips easily off the tongue – even if it is said with some irony. There is little scope for miscreants. The leadership team members are ever present and enforce good behaviour – from attire to skullduggery. The open design of the building ensures that no misdemeanour goes unnoticed. If you're sent out of the classroom for poor behaviour – it's like being sent into a goldfish bowl. Uniform, attendance and behaviour all strictly observed. How else would the delicate Ercol chairs and tables that adorn all the classrooms contain not one scratch or speck of flicked ink or graffiti? These young adults are taught to take care of their surroundings, of themselves and of others.

In conversation, Mr Hall defies this appearance of zero tolerance. 'The development of individual relationships is so much more important than casting things in black and white,' he insists. He proudly states that no-one has been permanently excluded for five years, while accepting that sometimes the last resort is the only option. Parents are involved as soon as their child is excluded from lessons. Punishments include doing serious work over a period of two to three days – no break or lunch with friends. Restorative justice is a firmly held belief here – and constructive discipline.

Students are rigorously monitored. If they are disorganised, late or disruptive, are they getting enough support from home? Tutor system is key in pastoral care structure. If there is a lack of motivation in the class room, are individual teachers doing enough to support and guide – are work books being marked quickly enough, for example?

Pupils and parents: The school has had a glamorous history since its founding in 1958. It was the school of choice for the liberal left in the 60s (Tony Benn and Roy Jenkins both chose to move their sons from Westminster and Winchester respectively to Holland Park), and with Angelica Huston among the alumni, the school had a decidedly cool reputation. Colin Hall has restored much of this glamour during his 15 (plus) years. Although one parent referred to a 'champagne socialist' element among the parent body, it's no longer the choice of just the trendy left. A number of high profile members of right wing political parties are attracted to the school's rigour and aspirational ethos, but the creative, media element is still strong.

Located in one of the most fashionable and expensive corners of London, its demographic is very different from many schools of its kind across the capital. But only because standards are high. Parents who once might have saved and scrimped to go private are celebrating the fact that their children can be educated to such a high standard, funded by their taxes alone. You will still find here the odd Etonian or Wykehamist who has chosen to return to London in the sixth form. The catchment is narrow (currently a half mile radius) but it's not impossible to get a place if you live further afield if you can get in on the art scholarship ticket. Pupils here are smart, focused and polite. Ofsted rated behaviour outstanding and we agree. They know how much devotion comes from the top down into their education and they respond to it.

Entrance: The catchment area is getting smaller by the year. Now you have to live within about half a mile of the school to have a chance of getting in. About 1,600 applicants for 240 places. Can be as many as 50 appeals, with only a tiny few successful ones. Banding tests take place in the autumn of year 6. Siblings get priority; 24 places (10 per cent) are reserved for the specialist

H

'art aptitude test', with distance no object – 'you could live in Glasgow and get a place'. Normally about 380 apply for these 24 places. Applicants aren't interviewed, nor do they need to provide a portfolio, just two drawings under exam conditions. There's an art aptitude waiting list as well as a main waiting list – possible to sit on both. Large numbers from local primaries but particularly Fox up the road. Growing numbers from the independent junior schools.

Entrance into the sixth form is tough. 'This is a very academic sixth form' we were told – the high standard of the sixth form regarded as a role model to fuel the aspirations of students lower down the school. At least seven GCSEs graded A* to B including English and maths. Minimum of As in the subjects you want to study. Priority will be given to pupils from Holland Park, otherwise proximity to school will be the decider between two equally competing candidates.

Exit: After GCSE very few NEETs – almost all who leave join colleges, apprenticeships or other sixth forms. One or two to the independent sector but mostly to Holland Park sixth form (about 50) or to other state sixth forms (about 56) After A levels, 87 per cent to university. Around two-thirds to Russell Group Universities, including a few to Oxbridge. Quite a high number choose to take a gap year. Most popular are the London University colleges – particularly UCL and King's. Students choose to read a variety of courses from veterinary medicine, medicine, engineering and law, to English, classics, architecture and theology. A few go off to art college.

Money matters: Now an academy, but retaining its very close links with the Royal Borough of Kensington and Chelsea, it remains the area's flagship comprehensive school. Always well funded by the Royal Borough, this is now matched by funding from the Education Funding Agency. It has all the appearance of an exceptionally well-funded school, so we suspect Mr Hall is very clever at tapping any available and potential resources.

Remarks: Ofsted rates the school outstanding under every category – indeed 'beyond outstanding' in several, and the inspectors are superlative in their praise for the school. It would take a harsh critic to disagree. This is a sparkling environment and your child will emerge polished and bright if s/he is academically ambitious, prepared to toe the line and thrives under pressure. Comprehensive it may be, but it won't suit every child.

Holy Cross Preparatory School

George Road, Kingston, Surrey KT2 7NU

Pupils: 290 • Ages: 4–11 • RC

Fees: £12,570 pa

Tel: 020 8942 0729
Email: admissions@holycrossprep.com
Website: www.holycrossprepschool.co.uk

Headteacher: Since 2011 Sarah Hair BEd (40s). Joined the school in 2004; 'knows the school inside out,' say parents. She has spent time as a class teacher, maths and English coordinator at a previous school then director of learning at Holy Cross. Passionate about education and IT; she was one of the first teachers in the 80s to have a computer in her classroom. Teaches year 5 computing: amongst her many interests in new technologies is how IT can be used to support education today and in the future.

Married with three teenagers, one son and two daughters, she comes from a family of educationalists, a tradition she is keen to continue. Parents say she has a lively approach to school life and learning and they all appreciate her bright and cheerful personality.

Entrance: Non-selective at 4+; priority to siblings and Roman Catholics, although the school welcomes all faiths. Prospective pupils attend an introductory morning. At 7+ children are invited to visit for the day where they are assessed for their suitability for the school. Admissions staff are friendly and helpful, occasional places do arise and a waiting list is kept for interested families.

Exit: Girls move onto a wide variety of secondary schools eg Lady Eleanor Holles, Wimbledon High, Surbiton High, Kingston Grammar or top girls boarding schools eg St Mary's, Ascot, Benenden, Wycombe Abbey and Woldingham. A few to local state grammars and Holy Cross Senior.

Remarks: Whilst Holy Cross is not overly selective it achieves excellent results for all pupils. Well planned and thoughtful curriculum ensures high standards, so giving pupils the chance to cherry pick when it comes to choosing a secondary school. Reasoning is part of the core curriculum from year 3. Maximum class size is 22 and all classes have fully trained, high-level assistant teachers. Fantastic grounding in maths, English and IT, say parents. Specially structured English scheme used across the age groups, with a big emphasis on developing good essay writing techniques mixed with lots of speaking and listening tasks. This starts early, with even the youngest members developing the confidence to be able to stand up and address their classmates on a number of topics and share any special skills they may have.

There are four separate small teaching rooms for pupils needing individual support from the SENCo, and EAL is available as required. Drama and IT are linked to other subjects, helping to keep learning relevant and to encourage creativity. Well-resourced art and design rooms where pupils can engage with all types of media, much of which is elegantly displayed around the school. Impressive collections of pottery; the girls also benefit from having DT days, enabling them to plan, design and complete their projects as a whole. Science room full of active little girls in their goggles, with interesting experiments taking place and a specially designed area for baking and cookery clubs.

The old coach house is now the IT suite where pupils build websites and learn programming skills. The school has designed its own app for communicating with parents, and parents can contact teachers at any time.

Music is a serious subject with a full-time teacher coordinating and 13 visiting teachers. Early years classes learn recorder, then in year 3 everyone learns a brass instrument. Pupils are taught to read and compose their own music, and many go on to do exceptionally well, joining national youth orchestras and choirs.

The huge outdoor spaces offer lots of different play areas and all sports take place on site. Ample courts, three rounders pitches and own athletics track. Sports facilities are also used by other schools, for community activities and charity events. Pupils are keen participants in Surrey schools sports tournaments. Younger children have their own outdoor classroom and garden where they grow vegetables, harvest them and then learn how to turn them into soup.

Lovely Victorian buildings nestle comfortably next to modern additions; the new multi-function halls are cleverly built into the hillside so as not to lose any of the gardens. Unique setting for a school bordering London: eight glorious acres of well-tended grounds with views out to Epsom Downs, situated in a historical estate that once belonged to the crown and is now part of the pricey Coombe Estate. The house was once occupied by John Galsworthy, author of the Forsyte Saga; in 1971 the sisters of Holy Cross purchased the buildings for a school. Still retains many original features including beautiful stained-glass windows and a wood panelled library.

Warmth and the quality of relationships remain at the heart of the school and the well-established pastoral care system. Sister Ursula, the last remaining nun, has had a long influence on the school, teaching pottery and running the Welcome Room where parents and children come to drink her tasty cocoa and chat. New school council has recently evolved to give the girls a voice in the day-to-day running of the school and discuss the all-important issues of new play equipment and lunch menus. Girls are elected as officers, with each class providing two representatives; all very democratic. School council chooses charities to support, the girls run a number of enterprising fundraising events themselves, and they have an ongoing link with Build Africa. Parents are unanimous about the positive effects of the school's pastoral ethos. One parent told of the kindness shown to her daughter when she first arrived, making the transition to a new school so comfortable. Wednesdays are homework free to ensure that girls have time to visit friends and pursue outside interests.

A school that shines for its holistic, inclusive and caring approach mixed with academic rigour. Continues to be a fine example of 21st century education, and provides a wonderful start in life.

The Holy Cross School

117

25 Sandal Road, New Malden, Surrey KT3 5AR

Pupils: 941 • Ages: 11–18 • Sixth form: 200 (federated with Richard Challoner) • RC

Tel: 020 8395 4225
Email: hxs@holycross.kingston.sch.uk
Website: www.holycross.kingston.sch.uk

Headteacher: Since 2001, Tom Gibson BSc Dip Ed MEd NPQH (40s). Could be government poster star for rejuvenating benefits of headship – radiates fulfillment and energy, though also a possible fringe benefit of lifelong interest in sport. While original career plans as pro after studying PE at Loughborough came to nought (dawning realisation that wasn't going to happen, he says, hit him 'later than my friends'), teaching career, fortunately for pupils in his care, proved thoroughly acceptable alternative. Pretty much inescapable, given that computer has invariably said 'yes' to the idea. 'Whenever I do psychometric tests, always come out as a teacher or social worker,' he says, though without any discernable regrets.

Has viewed education from every angle, as a parent (four children through university, wife an early years specialist), teacher (in variety of co-ed special residential as well as single sex mainstream schools) and an inspector (of 30 or so schools when was seconded to Ofsted eight years into headship). Message he took home (and presumably back to school again) from assorted experiences was that even in struggling schools there's 'always something that's fantastic.' Here, fantastic is the norm, thanks in part to determination to ensure that staff creativity is unfettered by micro management. If teachers are professionals, he says, shouldn't require 'somebody on top of you telling you how to do your job.' Staff are definitely accountable – but must be allowed autonomy to do the job.

As a result, he's reassuring but often background presence to parents, strong, visible and approachable senior management team – 'the people you go to,' felt one mother – mopping up most day-to-day issues. Very definitely hands-on when required, however. When GSG visited, had just come off phone to LEA to arrange help for vulnerable pupil. He also (somehow) packs in a spot of teaching, including RS, as well as supporting some year 11 girls on reduced timetable.

Regularly sits in on other lessons, marvelling at other teachers' talents and happy to be outshone. 'Am I the best teacher? No, because that's not what I'm doing every day, and we've got some fantastic people here.'

Takes governmental caprice in his stride. 'Here long enough to adhere to political landscape without being blown off course.' Funding is one current concern (dominates meetings with other heads), recruitment another, though train and promote your own policy does wonders for retention rates (last big outside appointment was over five years ago).

'Teaching's a lovely job but we all need to feel we're progressing,' he says. 'The challenge is to ensure you can reward teachers financially and keep their interest up.' Seems to work, with many teachers there till retirement, though some younger staff are lured away by out of London quality of life – and lower property prices.

Praises his 'bright, skilled, sophisticated' admin team of action-packed enablers. Wish list is their command (collaboratively speaking), funding nosed out, ways and means found to overcome officialdom (recently built sports hall's pitched roof, for example, makes it multipurpose and thus LEA-compliant).

Job, though not entirely stress free – 'Of course there are times you worry' – remains endlessly fulfilling. 'Privileged that people trust their daughters to us,' he says – and goal is to repay trust by finding ways for every girl to succeed.

Academic matters: Won't disappoint, offering high-achieving home from home that should satisfy even those robbed of grammar school place – and all on their doorstep.

Results just what you'd hope for. Progress made between years 7-11 puts school in top five per cent nationally, GCSE results consistently good, congratulatory letters from top politicians par for the course. In 2016, 85 per cent achieved five A*-C grades including English and maths with 39 per cent at A*/A.

At A level in 2016, 25 per cent A*-A grades, 54 per cent A*-B. Impressive 33 subjects in total (34 counting 'other') offered post-16, including creative writing, human biology and media. Plenty of BTecs, too (from health to performing arts in year 11 and early years, hospitality, IT and science in the sixth form).

But also proud to care, with an overt stress on welcome for girls from all shades of the ability spectrum, something that doesn't always seem to be the case in results-hungry establishments elsewhere. School shines when it comes to learning support. 'Brilliant,' thought parent with dyslexic daughter. 'Help has been amazing.' Safe haven, staffed by SEN team, is open before and after school as well as during the day, with easy chairs, games and jigsaws among measures designed to bring temporary relief to pupils sometimes overwhelmed by lives.

And though there's inevitable worry over performance of disadvantaged pupils (about 10 per cent of school numbers), support is extensive, ranging from financial (uniform to term time and holiday activities) to academic (extra teachers recruited to provide one-to-one support). Mr Gibson is 'just as excited to have child who struggled at primary as someone at top of the class,' and backs it up with quality resources. Lower sets are tiny and get some of brightest and best teachers, thought parents. 'Tend to do better in bottom set than in other schools,' thought one.

Formidable efforts go into working out who goes where, with CATs baseline testing in June for September's year 7 intake, classes ordered according to the results – parents sometimes slightly miffed in the process, but generally mollified by subsequent extensive reshuffling as lights start to emerge from bushels.

Most able take 11 GCSEs including triple science, substantial numbers achieving government's EBacc measurement. Impressive as with just four core subjects (RS, maths, English and science), high take up of options (including geography and history) is down to quality of teaching (even notoriously snide 'rate my teachers' website bursts with praise and stars).

Dynamic history team – 'phenomenal and inspiring' among the many five-star reviews. Head of department is 'brilliant – daughter loves it,' said parent (who, like others, found it hard to name anything she wasn't delighted with) – and mentors colleagues in need of turbo-charged pupil-whispering skills.

Maths also strong through the school and set from year 7, English following in year 8. Sciences well-resourced (as you'd hope – this is school's official specialist area), biology and chemistry particularly so with five teachers apiece. Now pushing boat out for physics with recruitment of additional teachers. From also-ran girls' science subject, sixth form take up now moving into double figures (12 in current year 12), despite rival lure of psychology, currently single biggest A level subject.

Just-opened future technology learning room features banks of i-gorgeousness as well as natural daytime lighting, sizzling green chairs as well as licence to doodle (flip up tables double as whiteboards) and join clubs in electronics – leading to extra GCSE – and robotics. And if message about brilliance of science and technology careers for girls isn't clear, shortly to arrive 3D printer, next gizmo on the wish list, should be able to spell it out in a choice of colours and materials.

Well-established sixth form partnership with Richard Challoner (also Catholic, high achieving but with boys and co-ed sixth form) adds greater range of subjects (popular) and extra travel time between the sites (less so). 'You've got to get to know boys some time,' thought one pupil – it's just the five-minute minibus journey that's off-putting. 'Effort...' groaned sixth former, who like the others, much preferred the Richard Challoner pupils to come to them, avoiding 15-minute walk under A3 if minibus is full.

Games, options, the arts: If he could, Mr Gibson would get girls to trade online introspection for more sport. Though smaller size means slightly fewer games specialists than at larger schools (have three rather than five elsewhere), determination and creativity fills in plenty of gaps, from pupil self-starters organising 7.30am fitness sessions to PE-hating group sensibly offered civilised alternative of a walk in nearby Richmond Park.

Provides ball girls for Wimbledon, PE at GCSE and A level, and pupils see themselves as a sporty bunch, egged on by enthusiastic staff and helped by attractive sports hall which avoids box-like appearance common to so many of its kind, though most games are played in Kingsmeadow, just a few minutes' drive away.

Apart a few more matches for the keen, parents praised expectations ('high') and teams ('strong'), particularly netball (regular fixtures against girls' schools in the area, including independents such as Surbiton High) and handball (recent Kingston and London champions), cricket and trampolining.

Trips many and varied (year 7 camping, year 9 battlefields, sports and language trips, including French exchange) to suit every subject and pocket – trip to Thailand no jaunt for the entitled, requiring pupils to fundraise before working with disadvantaged children there.

Performing arts similarly no Sunday stroll in the park (with or without George). We saw year 7s performing confidently against tension-creating (and intentional) background dissonance, good preparation for rigours of Sondheim's Into the Woods, next on the to-do list (whole school production every two years).

Held together by boundlessly energetic teacher – has to be as 'only one we've got,' said one girl – who organises range of events, from rock and pop festival to musical tour of Kingston town centre – and felt to be talent spotter par excellence. 'Helps you find your inner music,' said year 11 pupil and, having discovered it, channels it into choirs, bands and – for the very keen – music GCSE and musical theatre A level.

Art, taught in enticingly cluttered studio heaving with work, 3D flower springing out from painted background; rhinoceros depicted with surprising lightness of touch a thought-provoking treat for viewer. Popular at GCSE, taken by about third of year 11 pupils, with 10 or so carrying through to A level where can specialise in textiles, art and design and – increasingly popular – photography (a must-do, thought teacher, for anyone planning glittering career as celebrity vlogger).

Background and atmosphere: Smallest girls' senior school in the area, 'though may not feel like it compared with primaries,' says Mr Gibson, with 900 plus pupils rather than the several thousand elsewhere.

Fancifully minded might see school façade, original building protectively flanked by two more modern wings, as embodiment of nurturing qualities that have endured since foundation in 1931 by The Sisters of The Holy Cross. Contemporary black and white photograph shows original five pupils and a rocking horse posing together in eloquent depiction of family atmosphere. Love, respect and living life to full all qualities school espouses today – though without drowning in cosiness, stresses Mr Gibson.

Religious dimension ever present – a cross formed from coloured glass blocks in sixth form centre contrasts with older stained glass in entrance hall – and never apologetically. Catholicism remains defining part of school life, with RS taken at GCSE by all, and compulsory part of sixth form education. Annual retreats offered to pupils and extensive support for Catholic charities including day centre for the homeless in London and orphanage in Thailand.

Homely atmosphere assisted by compact site, tucked into residential road close to centre of New Malden. School does best with existing material, small courtyards squeezed in between buildings – one with long, curved, bright blue benches for break time conviviality – though some more spartan areas remain: dining hall's main decoration is rows of lockers lining the walls.

Upstairs, there's the promise of far better things to come. In addition to serving decent coffee and chocolate muffins (a not very well kept secret from rest of school), sixth form centre is riot of colourful brilliance, with neon sign and psychedelic, curvy sofa in eye-bending electric blue and purple.

Uniform, however, is big on homeliness. School's approach is that 'smart uniform means smart brains,' says approving mother. Only issue has been over sixth form blouses – plain only originally allowed, parents unhappy. Happy ending with rules now relaxed and (subtle) patterns allowed to all-round relief. 'A minefield,' says Mr Gibson, with feeling.

No changes planned elsewhere. Years 7 to 11 wear non-negotiable long, green kilt. Not loved, but pupils get used to them and though expensive, made from parent-pleasing quality fabric that lasts. Even better, they're impossible to roll up ('Hurrah,' thought several mothers), which could be factor in several other local schools' decisions to opt for something similar. Summer skirt an improvement for some, owing to paler pattern that makes them 'less visible,' thought one pupil. But though uniform is instantly recognisable, not a taunting hazard – pupils travel without fear on local buses.

Similar approval for school's strict beauty products policy. It's absent from younger faces (at least, those we saw) and limited to natural look among seniors ('no lipstick, eye liner or cat eyes,' said one). Sixth formers, in default business attire, free to apply ad libere though sense of restraint appeared to rule.

Pastoral care, well-being and discipline: School that doesn't stint on detail – new head girl's name already on honours board early in autumn term. 'Treat every individual in holistic way,' said parent. 'It's not just about the academic progress, you get sense that they really do care.'

Settling in process for new year 7s starts with visits to primary schools in summer term of final year and carries on into first term, starting two days earlier than rest of school with just sixth form for company and let out early for lunch in first fortnight. Initial swaddling, including 'non-stop' enquiries about how things are going from teachers who know girls' names 'instantly', can feel a bit excessive, think pupils – but parents are delighted. 'A bit old fashioned – you could feel you're mothered to death but it's a good fault to have,' said one.

Pupil complaints and comments passed up the chain via Student Leadership Team – 'Have a lot of responsibility' – and mood is protective, controlled and gently aspirational. Bullying not common, thought pupils. And if it happened 'school would deal with it,' said one with confidence. Awareness of consequences felt to be undoubtedly helpful in putting off anyone contemplating unkindness – with notable turn of speed when parents need to get in touch. 'You can pick up the phone and talk to the people you want to talk to straight away,' thought one mother.

'Some parents say you can't be caring and high achieving,' says Mr Gibson. 'I say you need to be caring to achieve.' Succeeds, even when faced with challenging behaviour, in keeping girls in school. Appointment of inclusion manager and area where distressed can be supported without affecting education of others helps keep exclusion levels 'minute'.

Mental health problems, many linked to plummeting self worth, a growing problem, not helped by 'enormous amounts of aspiration,' says Mr Gibson. 'Expectation that everything's going to be A* weighs down on people.' School does its bit and more, with mental health-themed assemblies, training for pupil ambassadors and emphasis on coping skills for all to deal with anxiety, as well as more informal support (one parent praised cups of tea and chats available on tap).

Still 'probably not enough,' thought head, whose one (mild) bugbear is tendency for school to be seen by outsiders as sum of nurturing qualities. May be 'sweet, caring and academic,' (Mr G recounts qualities with air of one who's heard them many times before) but there's no absence of challenge – or innovation to meet it.

Pupils and parents: Religion the unifying element in school population that spans cultures, ethnicity and lifestyles, with around a fifth speaking English as an additional language and seven per cent receiving free school meals. Area covered extends from Hampton Court round to Chessington, Worcester Park and into South West London fringes (Morden, Mitcham and Wandsworth) as well as Kingston and Richmond, affluence rubbing shoulders with deprivation. Supportive PSA brings everyone together, while girls' friendships span the range. 'Daughter made such a huge variety of friends, from Roehampton council estates to [luxury homes] in North Kingston.'

Entrance: Securing one of the heavily oversubscribed 150 year 7 places a doddle as long as you meet the criteria (Catholic trumps all, with priority, after looked after Catholic children, given to regular – ideally weekly – and priest-endorsed attendance at mass) and remember to fill out the right forms (supplementary information as well as standard common application).

One member of staff thought non-Catholics might stand slightly better chance applying for in-year place, but we'd suspect slightly forlorn hope in a school which attracts applicants from almost 50 different feeder schools.

Additional 15 sixth form places on offer for non-locals (but still Catholic). Not unknown for families to move nearer to boost chances of success.

'When you've found the right school, fight tooth and nail to get in,' says Mr Gibson, sensibly tempering this with need to check admissions criteria to work out whether tooth and nail sacrifice, however extensive, will be sufficient to do the trick.

School big on empathy – will call parents pronto if there's waiting list movement. 'When place came up, the admissions head phoned straight away, said parent. 'Said they knew how anxious we had been. They really care.'

Exit: In 2016, 39 per cent left after GCSEs. Year 13 leavers head off in every direction (in recent years everything from English at Essex to politics at Glasgow; two to Oxbridge and two medics in 2016). Small but steady reverse flow of old girls returning as staff members.

Remarks: School notable for happiness, sense of security and combination of talent boosting and strong moral purpose. 'Seven years ago, didn't want to come here. Seven years on, don't want to leave,' said current head girl. After just a few hours there, nor did we.

H

Holy Trinity & St Silas CofE Primary School

Hartland Road, London NW1 8DE

Pupils: 210 • Ages: 4–11 • C of E

Tel: 020 7267 0771
Email: admin@holytrinitynw1.camden.sch.uk
Website: www.camden.schooljotter.com/holytrinitynw1

Head: Since 2013, Lorraine Dolan (40s) BEd and masters in education, both from the University of North London. Her first job as an NQT in 1996 was at Holy Trinity and St Silas; 'My plan was never to stay at the same school for long but to have an open mind.' However, when Annie Williams took over as head of the school in 2001, Ms Dolan, who respected her greatly, found it difficult to move on. Fourteen years later Ms Dolan started to get 'itchy feet', and when Annie Williams took a sabbatical Ms Dolan became acting deputy head and from there decided to move into leadership. She subsequently left Holy Trinity to take up the post as deputy head at St Paul's Catholic school in Wood Green. Although she says her time there was a 'great experience', she couldn't achieve what she wanted as a deputy head. When Ms Williams died in 2012, Ms Dolan had begun looking at headship and when the post was advertised, she applied, believing that she had the skills, understanding and experience to drive the school forward.

Tall, with waist-long fair hair, Ms Dolan looks on first impression like someone who might be in the world of media rather than a primary school head teacher. Although softly spoken and friendly, this ex-convent school girl is definitely no pushover and hides a steely determination. It is a prerequisite for this job. Any weaker souls would not survive the legacy of the former head teacher, who changed the fortunes of a not particularly good school to an 'exceptional school' (in the words of Ofsted) and was a woman who had edited the word 'compromise' from her vocabulary. Ms Dolan says, 'Annie was a force to be reckoned with.' Ms Dolan offers a more 'open door policy' than her predecessor and welcomes parent inclusion in the school. One pupil told us, 'she's very approachable and a great role model.'

She has been described by a parent as being 'very old school, in a good way.' She is very intent on bringing traditional values back into the school and has particularly clamped down on the school uniform, which was a bit hit and miss prior to her headship. As she points out, 'You either have a uniform policy or you don't; you can't have a bit of a uniform.' Another parent told us that Ms Dolan 'doesn't rest on the laurels of Ms Williams and wants to make her own mark. She is around most of the time and is often chatting to parents in the playground.'

H

Ms Dolan has a 24 year old son, whom she had in her early 20s, and who, she says, 'has been the making of me in many ways.' The product of Irish Catholic parents, Ms Dolan went to a convent school, where she says she was 'often challenging the system'. Her son forced her to be responsible, and although she wasn't thinking of a career in education at that time, was accepted onto a Montessori teaching course, 'which was perfect as I could take my son with me and leave him at the nursery'. Little did she suspect then where that first rung up the ladder would eventually lead. She and her long term partner are both members of a cycling club, and she also enjoys running: 'Keeping fit is a great outlet for stress.'

Entrance: After the customary priority for looked-after children, the primary admissions criterion is church attendance, either at The Most Holy Trinity Church across the road or at St Silas the Martyr in Kentish Town. Approx 60 per cent come via this route; the remaining 40 per cent of admissions are catchment based. When Ms Williams became head, the school was very much bottom of the parental-choice agenda, but the intake has altered and now gets more professional parents – particularly in creative and media related fields. Not too many, school hopes – 'we have a good social mix and want to keep it that way'. At the moment, remains a class and ethnic melting pot, with the largest minority being Bangladeshi.

Exit: Mainly to the local comprehensives – Haverstock, William Ellis, Parliament Hill, St Marylebone and Camden School for Girls – but school has also developed a relationship with The Hall, one of north London's leading prep schools, and some year 6 boys go there with bursaries before proceeding to leading London independent day schools.

Remarks: Housed in a typical Victorian schoolhouse, a meander from tourist-packed Camden Lock; one has to enter two heavy-duty doors to reach the main reception – the first to the playground and the second to the main building: 'We qualified for extra security', the head told us (part of their recent funding programme). However, once inside with its pristine, soothing interior, you'd never guess where you were – fresh flowers, polished parquet and a big red school bell are all from another era.

Teaching at the school is strong; a number of parents have pointed this out and cited a couple of exceptional teachers, one of whom – Kirsty Mccreadie, the current deputy head – held the school together after the previous head's departure and is described by parents as 'simply the most exceptional, passionate teacher – the cornerstone of the school'. Ms Dolan herself has been very successful in turning the maths results around – something she has been working hard to address. When she first came on board, results had been dipping, but her close monitoring seems to have worked – more or less everyone gets at least level 4 Sats, with around two-thirds now reaching level 5+.

The teaching staff are generally well qualified, with two MAs, one law degree, three teachers who speak fluent French (so French is taught convincingly from reception to year 2), and a couple of graduate teaching assistants who, according to Ms Dolan, arrived with 'passion and drive'. The excellent teaching is partly the legacy of Ms Williams, who had said: 'I'm very snobbish about teachers – they have to have been to a good university and to have travelled. It gives them a cultural understanding', and partly due to the current head who adds: 'All the teachers are clear about my expectations. It's not OK for one child to slip through the net.'

Despite the fact that the majority of pupils arrive at Holy Trinity with well below average attainment, the school is at the pinnacle of the league tables, with results in English in the top one per cent nationally. Literacy is taught for two hours a day, primarily through poetry and prose. This again, we are told, is largely down to another inspirational teacher – Luke Williams, a specialist drama teacher who teaches English and drama from reception to year 6, through the works of Shakespeare. Every year the school puts on a whole-school Shakespeare play, including every pupil and member of staff, and has now helped found a borough-wide Shakespeare festival with five neighbouring primaries. Hardly surprising then that, according to Ofsted: 'Pupils' empathy with the works of Shakespeare is quite remarkable'.

All the arts are fundamental to the curriculum. Music is central to the school and one parent told us that music largely formed her decision to send her daughter there: 'The school just feels amazing when you walk in. There is the sound of laughter and always someone playing the piano or another instrument.' Pupils can choose to join the jazz band or one of two choirs, or learn an instrument from a long list of specialist music teachers. However, drop-ins on any of the music groups have been abolished in favour of auditioning for them, as the head firmly believes, 'if you make that sort of commitment, you need to stick to it.'

Art is equally important, and despite limited square footage, has its own department; pupils' work is hung boldly throughout the building. Painting even spills out into the large urban playground (underneath the rattling of the Camden overground train), where one inner-city wall has been reborn as a rural, summer scene (with a 3D vegetable plot to extend the experience). We were particularly struck by an astonishing ceiling display in the upper school hall of famous London landmarks – the London Eye, St Paul's Cathedral etc, all made from paper mâché. The idea for this came from a walk around London with year 6 pupils, who were learning about architecture (from a parent architect) inspired by the imminent development works to the school. One parent told us: 'We're so lucky at this school, there is such a pool of talented and creative parents who can come in and share their skills.' Trips are very much part of the education. Visits to the theatre, opera, ballet and museums are planned on a regular basis.

Though about 40 per cent of pupils are not Anglicans, the Christian message is strong, with a thoroughly involved parish priest (Father Graham), regular church attendance and class mass held half termly. Grace is said before lunch. Lunch itself is entirely healthy, and mealtimes, too, are considered a development opportunity. Music is played and, on Fridays, tablecloths laid. A firm emphasis on good manners. The 'golden rules' dictate: don't talk with your mouth full; learn to use your knife and fork correctly. Rules elsewhere are equally clear cut. Attentive good behaviour is the norm, but for those who stray, the first offence means displacement to another class; further disruption means an encounter with the head.

Although standards may be firmly upheld, one parent complained that the pastoral care system is not great and there isn't much of a structure in place. However, the head says that whilst historically issues were not dealt with, she 'has worked very hard to get parents to trust that when they raise a concern about their child, whether emotional or academic, it will be dealt with and monitored.' The children are supported by the class teachers. They have weekly circle time sessions and are encouraged to share their concerns as well as develop their understanding about relationships with their peers.

The school takes a proactive approach to its parents, and offers core subject curriculum evenings to support parents with home learning. Parents respond with energetic fundraising – the PTA raises on average £4,000-£5,000 a year which goes towards buying new computers. Ms Williams herself was no ingénue when it came to fundraising and won considerable support from charities – a legacy continued after her death, with the Annie Williams Education Trust, set up by her husband, which has already received many donations.

Plans are currently under way to expand the school building and make it more accessible, the school being one of 10 schools in Camden identified as in need of updating. This will include a three storey extension at the side to house a new office, reception area and staff room and will allow the hall downstairs to be opened up into a large performance space. Classrooms will be increased in size (as they are rather on the snug side) and a lift will be installed, as this old Victorian building is currently unsuitable for anyone with a disability.

'Superb' is Ofsted's summary of the Holy Trinity and St Silas experience, and pupils agree: 'We love it here, we don't want to leave,' said one year 6 pupil. And a parent added: 'I just love the mixed demographic and the fact that everyone talks to everyone. I once saw David Miliband [a former parent], in the playground chatting to a mother in flip flops and pyjama bottoms, about the best pirate parties for boys.'

Honeywell Infant and Junior Schools

Honeywell Road, London SW11 6EF

Pupils: 694 • Ages: 3-11

Tel: 020 7223 5185
Email: office@honeywell.wandsworth.sch.uk
Website: www.honeywellschools.org

Head of junior school : Since 2001, Mr Duncan Roberts BEd NPQH (50s). Previously deputy head. Inspiring and popular head who is well respected by teachers, parents and pupils. Good sense of humour. Keen sportsman who enjoys swimming, football and playing water polo and instils in the children 'the importance of both winning and losing with dignity'. One parent described him as 'a born leader, but also a team player,' while another told us that 'he gets on with everybody.' Has two young children.

Head of infant school: Since 2004, Ms Jane Neal BEd NPQH. Previously deputy head, she has been at the school for 23 years in total. Two children at secondary. Softly spoken and reflective. Proud of her school and devoted to those in her care – 'a very safe pair of hands,' one parent told us. 'She's seen it all over the years and not much ruffles her feathers,' said another. Passionate about early years learning and keen on reading, walking, cooking and children's theatre.

Entrance: At 3 to nursery, although there's no automatic transfer to infant school at 4. Nursery offers 50 part time places, plus 14 full time places (39 maximum in a class). From reception, three parallel classes, with 30 per class. Usually one assistant per class from reception. A handful leave at the end of nursery. All must reapply to get from nursery into reception. Criteria for offers to infant school – looked after children, siblings, those with exceptional medical or special need, proximity to the school (as the crow flies). Once through to the infant school, each child is allocated a place in the junior school, though it's still necessary to reapply via the borough. Places do become available further up the school, so it's worth persevering. Incredibly popular – no problem filling vacancies.

H

Exit: All infants to junior school. Transfer over to juniors is generally smooth, thanks to system of reading partners (pupils) and induction sessions (parents). As one parent put it: 'There's just enough mixing of the two schools for the move to the big school to seem like a natural progression.'

At 11, roughly half to the state sector, including Bolingbroke Academy, Graveney, Burntwood, Grey Coat, Tiffin and Lady Margaret's. Those going to independent schools head for Alleyn's, Dulwich, Whitgift, JAGS, Emanuel, Wimbledon High, Streatham and Clapham High.

Much support and guidance given to parents when selecting a secondary school. Head knows that a lot of tutoring goes on at top of school and concedes that the right tutor can help with fine-tuning. As one parent told us: 'It can get pretty competitive around here at the start of year 6, though I think it's more the parents getting stressed than the children. The school manages to keep the kids pretty grounded but it can be fairly tense at times.'

Remarks: Schools housed in an imposing Victorian buildings, a stone's throw from Wandsworth Common. Infants on the same site as the juniors, though each has its own head, both of whom specialise in their own age group. Schools share a governing body, staff room and some facilities. Infants get to see the highlights of junior school, but lead separate existence day to day. As the head says, 'we get the best of both worlds.'

Schools are situated in a prosperous, middle-class area and the intake mostly reflects this. Junior head observes that a good proportion are 'advantaged children.' Thirty pupils per class. Around 17 per cent have English as an additional language but bilingual children catch up quickly, with weekly sessions for those who need extra support.

A total of 40 SEN children offered group and individual support in infant school. A small number of children with statements. Nurturing environment, especially in the early years. Forensic attention to detail when assessing the needs of each child – the school isn't just paying lip-service to treating each child as an individual. Excellent results at each stage. Head is aware that the middle achievers deserve special consideration too, not just the high flyers and the ones who are struggling. Infant School is currently focusing on how to make maths more 'girl friendly.'

Excellent Sats results, with a number of pupils gaining level 6 (head isn't complacent, though). The progress of each child in the school is monitored very closely and immediate action is taken if anyone is seen to be treading water. The current focus is on improving the standard of reading comprehension. Low turnover of staff. One assistant for each year group from year 3.

French taught to all pupils. Well-resourced school and heavily involved in teacher training.

A total of 75 SEN children in the junior school and support is given both inside and outside the classroom – in groups and individually. Playground can be a noisy affair in this large school. Lego club has been set up for quieter souls who find the hustle and bustle of break-time too much, as well as a cordoned off quieter zone, but some parents still say 'it's a bit of a jungle out there.' School council's requests listened to and acted upon.

Loads of outside space and vast amounts of equipment for the pupils. The infant school head told us: 'The children can do all the things here that they can't do at home.' Pupils have their own playground as well as the shared playground garden, complete with tepees, toadstools, fairytale bridge and enchanted forest – inspiring, imaginative and the envy of other schools. All-weather surfacing means that it's now used come rain or shine. Staggered use, so each year group gets the chance to use it. Jolly infant ICT suite, separate from the junior one, complete with jazzy multi-coloured keyboards.

H

Sport is a major strength of the junior school and is taken very seriously from year 3. Inter-house competitions recently introduced so 'everyone can take part' and house points hard fought for. Welcomed by parents, as some felt that previously only the sportiest were given the chance to play. School takes part in every tournament going – often with great success. Huge number of trophies on display to prove it. Swimming from years 3 to 5. Not just predictable sports here – cross-country and orienteering offered and lacrosse played at the highest level. Before and after-school clubs are very popular. All tastes catered for – tennis, Mandarin, knitting and baking. Early morning running club on the nearby common for pupils, parents ('mostly mums') and teachers. No uniform (apart from PE kit), after consultation with entire school community.

Gold Artsmark awarded to junior school for high level of provision in the arts. Huge orchestra with 60 members, as well as string orchestra. Individual tuition on a variety of instruments (recorder, violin, flute, cello), with regular concerts and performances for parents. The head's attitude is 'now you've got your grade 1, let's all enjoy it.' Recorder compulsory for year 3. Two choirs, so something for everyone, including one dedicated to popular music (scores from West End musicals). School hires drama facilities for year 6 production involving all 90 children. Recent productions include Bugsy Malone and We will Rock You.

This is a school which makes the most of being in the capital – lots of trips, visiting speakers and workshops. Year 6 outdoor pursuits residential trip to the Isle of Wight is a high point in the final year and everyone is encouraged to go.

Supportive, vociferous PTFA. Whether they're hearing readers, producing a snappy school magazine, fundraising or coming in to talk about their experiences, they're a force to be reckoned with. Excellent wrap-around care on offer, including holidays. Communication between parents and staff has improved recently with the sharing of teachers' email addresses.

School has strong links with the community and actively supports local charities. The importance of being a good citizen and of giving back to society – 'either in time, effort or finances' – is instilled in the pupils. Good manners are high on the agenda and behaviour is very good. Head stresses that school wants Honeywell pupils to be decent citizens, as well as achieving academically. No uniform, after lengthy consultation with the school community, and some pupils could do with smartening up.

Very welcoming. Happy staff and happy children, who are having an exciting time. Bright classrooms, with huge windows and colourful displays at every turn. Learning is made fun at Honeywell. The school produces articulate, confident children who are capable of working independently from early on. One parent told us: 'Honeywell's strength is that there is a feeling of community about the school. Everybody is looking out for each other.' As ever, the school is hugely popular but isn't resting on its laurels. Children get off to a flying start here and parents are willing to move heaven and earth to get their offspring a place. School produces independent, confident children ready to cope with the next stage of their education. Old pupils are always coming back to visit. As one parent told us: 'My girls loved Honeywell. I genuinely believe that it gave them the best possible start.'

Hornsby House School

Hearnville Road, London SW12 8RS

Pupils: 420 • Ages: 4–11

Fees: £13,245 – £14,235 pa

Tel: 020 8673 7573
Email: school@hornsbyhouse.org.uk
Website: www.hornsbyhouse.org.uk

Headmaster: Since 2012, Edward Rees BA (40s). Previously deputy head at Dulwich College Junior School, also an ISI inspector for the past 10 years. He grew up in Hampshire and became a keen cricketer while attending Charterhouse, playing in the past for the MCC. Today he lives in south east London and is married with a son and a daughter who currently attend Hornsby House. Parents say he is a sociable and hands on head, always willing to talk, and quick to respond to issues or concerns they may have. The school was founded in 1988 by educational psychologist Bevé Hornsby, best known for her pioneering work in the field of dyslexia.

Entrance: At 4+ into reception. Non-selective, places are offered on a first-come first-served basis from a waiting list, in order of the age of the child at the date of registration. Priority is given to siblings. Thereafter occasional places; prospective pupils sit assessment tests in English, maths and reasoning. Not as many places as there used to be at 8 as the majority of boys and girls stay though to 11+. At 8+, the school offers a few means-tested bursaries. Always worth applying for as it is not overwhelmed with applications.

Exit: At 11+ pupils move mostly to London day schools; popular destinations include Dulwich College, Alleyn's, JAGS, Whitgift, Emanuel and Streatham & Clapham High. A few choose the weekly boarding schools such as Royal Russell and Woldingham, with one or two transferring to boarding prep schools to sit 13+ common entrance.

Remarks: Over the last decade, Hornsby House has earned itself a good local reputation for offering a lively all-round education to pupils of varying abilities. A wide and carefully planned curriculum runs through this inclusive school, enabling children to develop at their own pace. All subjects are taught to mixed ability classes, with setting in mathematics for older age groups. Modern foreign languages are taught via a range of exciting topics and projects, French for reception to year 4, then Spanish for years 5 and 6. Parents feel teachers provide plenty of back-up work when needed plus extension activities for the more able pupils. Full-time SENCo with part-time specialists can offer support to children with milder specific learning difficulties, either individually or through small group work. There is an additional charge for one-to-one specialist teaching. The buildings are wheelchair accessible and staff are always willing to work with speech and occupational therapists as necessary. The school prides itself on developing potential in sports and the arts as well as academics, alongside helping parents to choose the right secondary school for their child. Proof is in the pudding: around a third of pupils are offered awards for music, art, sport or academics each year.

Whole-hearted teaching team with bags of energy; good mix of male and female, predominantly youngish, although there are some long servers. High staff ratio: two deputies, subject specialists, and all year groups have assistant teachers; reception classes have two each. A number of gappers add bounce to the sports and arts staff team as well as working as playground and classroom assistants. Many of these popular jobs go to past pupils; the gap year mentor remembers most of them from when they were in reception themselves.

Fairly compact site, cleverly designed by architects: it boasts lovely, light modern classrooms which sit side by side with the original Edwardian buildings. Whiteboards have disappeared in favour of the latest interactive technologies, all looked after by full-time technicians. Computing is very much on the curriculum. Minecraft, a newish club, helps with coding skills; pupils also use visual programming software. Art, drama, music and science have their own specialist rooms and teachers. Abundant arts and crafts on offer; Hornsby has been rewarded for all its hard work in art, DT and drama with Artsmark Gold. Pupils commemorated the 25th anniversary of the school by designing and constructing a fabulous mosaic in conjunction with artist in residence Tamara Froud. Drama teacher supported by an assistant puts on a variety of productions throughout the year across the age groups so everyone gets a chance to perform. Much looked forward to annually are the major year 4 and 6 productions. Music provision has developed in leaps and bounds since our last visit: two open choirs, chamber choir by audition and a small orchestra. Music room packed with instruments, mouth organs to African drums; pupils also benefit from workshops run by visiting musicians. Everyone learns the recorder and ukulele in class and individual tuition is available on some 11 other instruments. Considering the facilities and staff enthusiasm, some parents feel the orchestra is not particularly well supported.

Despite a lack of on-site space, sport is one of the jewels in Hornsby's crown; pupils use all the local facilities and are taken on sports tours. Main sports football, hockey, rugby and netball; all have successful teams, some impressive winning streaks and are always striving to improve. Cricket for all in the summer, proving very popular with the girls: definitely a few old girls who say they wish it had been on the agenda in their day. Anyone with physical difficulties or injuries can join in at their own level with the help of one of the stalwart sport assistants. Large underground kitchens and dining hall, which doubles up as extra space for gymnastics and dance. Parents and children like the open kitchens and serving hatch; children can see food cooking and what they're eating. 'Absolutely yum,' said two little ones.

All is brought together by the school community's positive, can-do attitude, and the house system which sees children of all ages working together on different projects. There is also a good choice of lunchtime and after-school clubs. Year 3 upwards get the opportunity to go on residential trips around the UK and France. Most families live locally; many are part of the strong Parents' Association, with some going on to become school governors. Parents we spoke to all commented on the friendliness of the children and the pleasant character of the school. In the final year pupils work towards the leaver's qualification the Hornsby House Certificate. This involves achievements including taking on leadership roles, displaying resilience during the year 6 trip to a Scottish activity centre, taking part in a charity event and speaking confidently in public: an ideal finale to the junior school years.

Hotham Primary School

Charlwood Road, London SW15 1PN

Pupils: 406 • Ages: 3-11

Tel: 020 8788 6468
Email: info@hotham.wandsworth.sch.uk
Website: www.hothamprimaryschool.org.uk

H

Acting Headteacher: Sarah Martin is holding the fort.

Entrance: The nursery class admits 36 full and part time children each year. Reception class of 60, including bilingual class. Waiting list for places in most year groups, which is an indication that someone is doing something right, considering four state primary schools in very close proximity, one of which is virtually next door. Admissions policy is administered by Wandsworth local authority so out of head's hands.

Exit: To a range of 15 different secondary schools. Maybe two or three a year go into the private sector but the majority are state school bound. Ashcroft (formerly ADT) is popular, but some also to Shene School, Burntwood, St Cecilia's.

Remarks: At first glance this looks like a typical Victorian primary school. It even has the original boys' and girls' entrances. The classrooms have high, light, draughty windows and are accessed by corridors and stairwells decorated with those funereal tiles so beloved of that era. The whole place cries out for a lick of paint and some TLC. Outside, the obligatory grey, hard playground is surrounded by a high wall.

However, what lies within tells a very different story. Take a closer look at that playground, for example – well-tended, well-planted flower beds all around the edge, each one the responsibility of one year group. Look further still and you come across a hidden, secret garden containing bird boxes, trees and plants to represent the four seasons, wood piles to provide homes for dozens of creepy crawlies and a quite amazing human sundial which looks very like a mini Stonehenge. All this surrounds a small classroom usually inhabited by the man affectionately known as 'Mr Hotham'. Retired, he then returned part time to give extra help to those in need and seems to embody the spirit of the school.

The classes are large (26-30 on average) but all supported by TAs. Twenty per cent of the pupils need EAL help, with full support on offer. Special needs pupils include those on the autistic spectrum, some dyslexic, some have cerebral palsy, some with language delay, some have ADHD. All are supported within the classroom as the school can see 'no point in doing anything else'. It's a 'place where we all learn from one another' and the wish is to see pupils become 'independent learners, to use their initiative and solve problems by using their fantastic, inquisitive minds'.

A bilingual stream has been introduced into the reception class and is making its way up through the school. In the bilingual class, around 15 per cent of the week is spent speaking French, and this proportion increases by year group so that by the last year the children will spend about 50 per cent of their time using French. Four French speakers on the staff and years 5 and 6 go on school trips to France. There's a link with a school in Paris.

Music is very strong, with choirs performing in Wandsworth events. All year 4s learn the clarinet. Swimming is taken seriously in KS2 when all children are taught in four ability groups over a six month period. Teams in football, cricket, netball, cross-country, swimming. After-school clubs in gym, yoga, photography, art, French. Very active PTA – recently completely refurbished the library. Polite, happy children in smart red, white and blue uniforms. Excellent handwriting throughout (would put many a private school to shame). As one parent remarked, 'Despite the presence of two excellent faith schools in the vicinity, Hotham gives a brilliant start to its kids. Its multicultural mix seems to work well.' Has won the Green School of the Year Bike-It award and two of the staff were finalists in the annual Teaching Awards.

This is a solid primary school offering a solid education to its local community from the nursery ('the best in the borough', according to one parent) to the final year, where discussion groups in the class are animated and passionate. One book which should not be judged by its cover.

Hurlingham School

122 Putney Bridge Road, London SW15 2NQ

Pupils: 325 • Ages: 4–11

Fees: £14,955 – £15,585 pa

Tel: 020 8874 7186
Email: admissions@hurlinghamschool.co.uk
Website: www.hurlinghamschool.co.uk

Headmaster: Since 2010, Jonathan Brough BEd (Cantab) NPQH (40s). Mr Brough (rhymes with ruff) was head of English at two boys' preps, deputy head of Bute House and finally head of City of London Girls' Prep before taking over at Hurlingham. Married to Harry, a leading ICT lawyer; they live in north London. Amicable, upbeat personality, he knows all the children by name and places a huge emphasis on happiness being central to everything that goes on in the school. Very popular with parents, staff and pupils, he teaches Latin and extension classes and is a much-appreciated supply teacher for all age groups when the class teachers are away.

One of those heads who takes an interest in everything going on around the school, be it new seeds for the garden or scholarship papers. He's recently enhanced house competitions with a rewards system and excellence book, and parents get sent surprise postcards informing them of their child's special achievements. An avid reader and writer since childhood, he particularly enjoys writing stories for children. He arranges for a good number of authors to visit the school, run workshops and book-themed events. Growing up in Devon, the son of two teachers, he has been surrounded by educational and literary influences all his life. When he awards himself some free time, he enjoys travelling and cooking, especially baking, which he hopes one day might make an appearance on the extracurricular calendar.

Entrance: At 4+ non-selective on a first come, first served basis, with priority to siblings and those living closest to school. Places do come up in older age groups, so always worth telephoning the school for occasional places.

Exit: Feeds a number of senior schools. Popular choices are Alleyn's, Dulwich College, Emanuel, Epsom College, Godolphin & Latymer, Ibstock Place, Kingston Grammar, King's Wimbledon, Lady Eleanor Holles, Latymer Upper, More House, Putney High, Queen's College, Queen's Gate, St Paul's Girls', Whitgift, Wimbledon High.

Remarks: Proudly mixed ability and does extremely well by its pupils. Reception class children are divided into three classes by date of birth. As children move through the school they are split into ability-related sets – maths from year 1 and English from year 5. The school is structured to ensure that everyone achieves success at their own pace to the best of their ability. Core subjects maths, English and science are all very strong and taught by subject specialists. No formal exams until they start practising for the 11+ tests. French is introduced in reception and Latin in year 4. By the age of 11 all the children take and pass an OCR 16+ entry level Latin qualification, demonstrating their skills in translating, comprehension and Latin coursework. The school is very keen to emphasise how the early Latin programme helps develop English and spelling skills. Children can try out other languages, including Greek, in after-school clubs.

EAL is available as necessary. SEN is catered for case by case depending on individual needs. There is a qualified head of learning support and three assistant teachers for small group work, one-to-one sessions and advising staff on differentiation within class. Homework is a serious matter and everybody is expected to complete it; lots of help available for anyone who is not sure what to do, along with a free after-school homework club. During year 5 parents have a meeting with the head and class teachers to discuss suitable secondary school choices.

Music and drama well embedded into the curriculum; a good variety of different types of theatre and concerts. There's a full-time dedicated music teacher and good proportion of pupils learn instruments.The corridors are well decorated with the children's art and designs; specialist art teacher from year 4 and the school boasts its own kiln. Well-planned traditional sports options, all taught by specialist coaching staff. Good choice of clubs each term, ballet in the elegant mirrored studio and karate being extremely popular. Particularly impressive karate, one of the largest school programmes to run in the UK, with about a third of the school taking part. This year they broke their own records with 100 per cent success in karate exam gradings.

Pastoral care is sensitively run; older children can become playground and reading buddies. There are five straightforward golden rules to follow and everyone knows there are consequences if they fail to stay within the boundaries. House competitions and activities enable children to mix and get to know other age groups. Lunch times look incredibly civilised for a junior school: youngsters sit in house groups, about eight children to a table, and tuck into tasty meals cooked on the premises. Tea is also provided for those who stay at school until 5:30pm.

The school is on a cleverly-designed compact site with a reasonable sized playground and bronze award eco-garden on the first-floor terrace. Lots to occupy children at playtimes: table tennis, climbing wall, giant games of Connect Four and chess, and a nature garden with a water feature for those who just want to chill. Recently graded outstanding in all areas and awarded Excellence in Education status by the ISI. Continues to go from strength to strength; parents comment that it's such a reliable school, and whatever happens your child's welfare and education will be looked after. The energetic Mr Brough is one of the safest pairs of hands for miles.

Ibstock Place School

Clarence Lane, London SW15 5PY

Pupils: 966 • Ages: 4-18 • Sixth form: 140

Fees: £14,985 – £19,200 pa

Tel: 020 8876 9991
Email: registrar@ibstockplaceschool.co.uk
Website: www.ibstockplaceschool.co.uk

Headmistress: Since 2000, Mrs Anna Sylvester-Johnson BA PGCE – known to all as 'Mrs SJ' (50s). Previously head of The Arts Educational School in Turnham Green, prior to which she taught at The Lycée and before that she was head of English at The Green School for Girls in Isleworth. An interesting and eclectic mix. Chic, svelte and very much in control, she is a mix of smiley and steely. That she has made the school the success it is today is beyond doubt. The splendid new-build that has transformed the school and the elegance and taste with which no visitor could fail to be impressed will be a lasting monument to her drive and commitment.

Head of prep school: Since 2015, Marion MacDonald.

Academic matters: A good mix of free and structured play in pre-prep school and happy, relaxed tots. A great sense of having fun while learning everywhere – we wanted to eat the yummy sausage rolls they were cooking and we loved the wheelbarrows they fill with plants each term – grow own veg. Both pre-prep and prep have iPads. Originally Froebel-inspired learning principles, though later educational thinkers also influence the sound and sensible curriculum.

IGCSEs in all core subjects now. A distinctive feature – and one of which we approve – is the insistence that all take two languages at IGCSE. German, Spanish, Mandarin, Italian, Latin and Greek all on offer, which we applaud. French the most popular and the most successful and the vast majority take this plus Spanish. Eng lit results outstanding, as are the results for those who take individual sciences, though dual award candidates' results weaker and parents report problems in the science dept which, school tells us, are now resolved. Geog and hist are popular options with most results A*-B. Physics and history among the top achieving subjects. Overall, an impressive 79 per cent of I/GCSEs A*/A grades in 2016.

Ibstock's sixth form is a relatively late bird – it began in 2006 – and its size now reflects its growing reputation and success. Philosophy, psychology and economics offered alongside the more trad subjects at A level – biology, English, psychology and maths being the most popular. All sixth formers now take the extended project qualification. In 2016, 55 per cent A*/A grades and 84 per cent A*/B. Small sixth form means, mostly, small classes – a definite plus.

Parents praise school's flexibility in moving pupils between sets when appropriate. No specific learning support unit but school supports mild dyslexics, dyspraxics and Asperger's children. Learning support – at an extra charge – given to 69 pupils at time of our visit. This school is assuredly not a haven for those who would struggle elsewhere and anyone who applies with this is mind 'is under an illusion from the distant past when the school was hippy-dippy!' One-to-one EAL support given to a few. The site overall would be tricky for a wheelchair user but the corridors – especially in 'new school' – are wide and easily navigable.

Games, options, the arts: 'We believe in competition – children are inherently competitive,' says Mrs S-J and plenty of opportunity to compete – in sports, debates, drama, you name it – both in and out of school. Good cross-curricular initiatives, much public speaking and sensible trips to worthwhile places. Usual range of sports supplemented by good range of extracurricular opportunities. Notable individual successes in many competitions and sports – representatives in several national squads. Music, art and drama all thrive (new performing arts centre). 'The teachers put a lot of time into the arts side,' parents told us. There's a warm sense of encouragement to try things out – witness the lively art and DT we enjoyed.

Background and atmosphere: In a nook on the edge of Richmond Park, between plush Sheen and the louring Roehampton modernist blocks of the late 1950s, sits the quite lovely Ibstock Place House, built in 1913 by Frank Chesterton (cousin of the more famous GK) and home of the Duchess of Sutherland until 1920, during which time she was Mistress of the Robes to Queen Mary and indulged her considerable taste in decorating the house. Between 1925 and 45 it was owned by the Paget family who brought in many mod cons eg a telephone system and a swimming pool. After three years of being requisitioned by the Ministry of Supply for scientists engaged in top secret work in radar development, the house was, in 1945, bought by the Froebel Educational Institute as accommodation for its 'demonstration school' – to practise the principles of the pioneering educationalist, Friedrich Froebel, whose fearsome bust still supervises the school gardens.

Rapid growth led to the building of the kindergarten and prep school buildings and various other add-ons until the quite magnificent extension to the main building – 'new school' – in 2011. The main building gave the new one something to live up to. Generously proportioned, elegantly decorated, now embellished with grand mirrors, large vases of opulent flowers, rugs, sofas and general country house elegance – all this must exert a civilising influence on young minds and spirits. New school, housing classrooms, labs and staff workrooms, is similarly appointed – ceramic tiled, spacious, with civilised loos and ample locker room, energy-saving lights etc. Well thought-out, tasteful and inviting. A sense of pride pervades the place and rightly so. Three buildings situated in the gardens opposite the rear of the elegant main house accommodate the tinies. They start in Priestman House, a delightful nursery with lots to do, lots of attention and an open door through which they run to the activities outside in their own safe and enclosed space. Attractive child-sized building houses the 6-10s. We were impressed by the number of books everywhere – a relatively rare sight. Orderly classrooms with very stimulating displays – we like the artwork inspired by Kandinsky and van Gogh, the clever Roman mosaics and the 'wow word of the week' palm tree. Good light art studio, and DT workshops with lively work. Year 6 pupils have their own building – Roberts House – which also houses good drama studio with retractable seating and gives them a useful transition between junior and senior schools.

Good, two-floor library with up-to-date stock, big chairs and a view of the school's 'woods'. Woods, orchard, 'bike city', two all-weather surface pitches and little garden make up main site's 10 acres of attractive outside space. 'Over the road' reached by a bridge is school's new performing arts centre, sports hall, drama studio, art room and two large pitches. Not the easiest place to get to – school runs pro bono minibuses for senior pupils from Barnes Common station in the morning and after school from 4 to 6pm. Several public buses stop on

Roehampton Lane, a short walk through the university campus. The popularity of 'bike city' is testament to the number of senior school pupils who cycle to school. Otherwise, you'll need a school run partner or three.

Pastoral care, well-being and discipline: Universal praise for the pastoral care and parents largely reported 'very happy children'. House system is key to the school and all appreciate the vertical groups in houses which make for a family feel. No drink incidents in anyone's memory, likewise few other discipline problems and bullying 'instantly dealt with – our investigations are always very thorough'. Some parental grumbles about high staff turnover – to the seeming mystification of Mrs S-J and definitely not seen as a current problem. Immensely sensible 'no bag' policy. You take your bag to your locker, take out what you need and can't go back for the next two hours. Result – no-one bashes you with a rucksack in a corridor, no heaps of bags at entrances and everyone has to think ahead. Hooray! Very attractive and sensible uniform worn, by most, with style and decorum.

Pupils and parents: The vast majority from the Putney, Roehampton, Richmond, Sheen areas. However, school contained children from over 250 junior schools when we visited, the most coming from Sheen Mount, East Sheen Primary and The Roche – after the school's own prep, that is. Active PTA and parents praise home-school communication. Parents a mix of professional, artistic, City and everything else. Notable former pupils include Emily Blunt, Nigella Lawson, Frieda and Nicholas Hughes and, head girl in the then top year, at the age of 13, Iris Murdoch.

Entrance: First come, first served at Priestman House (kindergarten) with priority to siblings. Now massively oversubscribed so names down as early as poss. Occasional occasional places on account of relocating families. At 6+, entry to Macleod House (prep), by individual assessment. At 7+ and 8+ papers in English and maths. At 9+ and 10+ English, maths and reasoning. Everyone is interviewed.

Register asap for senior school. Everyone interviewed for 11+ and all sit papers in English, maths and reasoning. Hugely oversubscribed. Some 500 children try for 70 places at 11+. At 13+, a few places for which there are 40+ candidates. At 16+, around 30 apply. A minimum of 57 GCSE points required (A*=8, A=7) plus As in A level subjects.

Exit: Up to 90 per cent of prep school children go up to the senior school, having taken the entry exam in year 6. However, Mrs S-J tells us, 'There is some humpiness that not all prep school children go up to the senior school. The two languages can be a barrier (everyone has to take two at GCSE). But we give them lots and lots of warning and we do help to find an appropriate school for them.'

Around 15 per cent leave after GCSEs. Bristol a popular university destination, followed by Bath and Oxford Brookes. Several to universities in the USA and Europe; two to Oxbridge in 2016. Lots off to study languages, others to a range including Royal Veterinary College. Generally several to art foundation courses.

Money matters: Music award available at 11+. Music, drama and sports scholarships at 13+ (no longer at 11+). Academic, creative arts and sports scholarships at 16+. Bursaries means-tested here as everywhere.

Remarks: Attractive school offering all-through education in a London suburb. Improving academics. Turns out thoroughly nice young people.

Ilford County High School

124

Fremantle Road, Ilford, Essex IG6 2JB

Pupils: 936 • Ages: 11–18 • Sixth form: 339

Tel: 020 8551 6496
Email: enquiries@ichs.org.uk
Website: www.ichs.org.uk

Headteacher: Since 2015, Mrs Rebecca Drysdale BSc (40s), who joined the school in 2012 as deputy and then acting headteacher. It was whilst she was doing her degree in geography at Coventry Polytechnic (now Coventry University) that she first caught the teaching bug. 'I had spent a year doing the Marks & Spencer's management training course and immediately took to the personnel side of things. This, coupled with the fact that I loved working with young people, made me realise teaching would be a great career,' she explains. Did her PGCE at Reading, then worked her way up the ranks across two comprehensives and a secondary modern (Chalfont Community College, Bucks; Copleston High School, Ipswich; Charles Darwin School, Biggin Hill), followed by a 10-year stint as assistant headteacher at Edmonton County School.

'I can be scary when I need to be,' she says (and pupils concur), but so long as everyone toes the line, she has a jolly and genial demeanour, as well as being both earnest and refreshingly unassuming – the type you feel would roll her sleeves up and get stuck in whenever needed. Staff describe her as a 'true listener,' taking on board everyone's point of views, which means that when she does make changes, everyone tends to move forward together. Teaches a little, 'but not as much as I'd like,' although she regularly does lunch and break duty, and students we talked to were clearly impressed at how often she chats to them in the corridors.

Sees her role as 'helping what was already a very good school to evolve,' although her attitude should not be mistaken for a lack of vision. 'I want this school to be the best grammar in the area,' she told us. 'I'd like to see people buying houses to try and get their sons into this school. I want people to move to Redbridge to come here.' Among the big changes she's made are overhauling the pastoral care system and increasing the emphasis on individual support for each child.

Academic matters: In 2016, 56 per cent A*/A grades at GCSE, with strongest results shown in the sciences and mathematics. French in year 7 and in year 8 pupils take up either German or Spanish as well. Everyone takes one language at GCSE, though few take two or continue languages to A level. No setting before GCSE and only then in maths, science and English. Besides maths and sciences, other popular GCSE subjects include geography, history and English, and every child has to take at least one creative GCSE in the likes of PE (particularly popular), art, music and technology. 'We call it EBac Plus,' says the head, who believes it enhances UCAS forms no end.

At A level, popular subjects include the sciences, economics, mathematics, history and government and politics. Most stick to academic rather than creative subjects, although sixth form enrichment ensures all students continue learning the arts. In 2016, 71 per cent A*/B and 41 per cent A*/A grades. Subject-based reviews help to monitor each subject and data tracking to monitor pupil progress helps spot and tackle underperformance; not that there is much of that here, according to parents. Maximum class sizes, at 30 (and 26 in the sixth form), are at the higher end.

Teacher profile on the older side, reflecting the low staff turnover and long-term experience. All teach their degree subject and many are examiners. Where possible, teaching is practical. Expect plenty of pongs wandering through the science block, for example, where one class was dissecting fish and another had their Bunsen burners all going when we visited. Meanwhile, a history lesson on WWII involved a mock trial for Hitler. In fact, all classrooms we visited were lively, with bright, perceptive students clearly hungry for detail and knowledge. Disappointing to walk past two classrooms with teachers shouting at their class, but maybe that's the price you pay for encouraging such energetic debate. School works on a two-week timetable.

Two-thirds of pupils with EAL requirements plus 30 or so who need SEN support, the provision of which is widely praised by parents. When we visited, there were students with cerebral palsy, hearing difficulties (including one who was profoundly deaf and also has vison impairment), plus all the usual – dyslexia to autistic spectrum. Can and does cater for wheelchair users, although there are some struggles with the old building – this will be made easier when the new ones are up. 'If students are bright enough to study here, we'll find a way,' says head, who says individual support takes place both in and outside the classroom. 'My son has a physical disability and we were initially told by people in the area that this might not be the best school for him, but they've been amazing at meeting his needs, whilst still academically challenging him,' said one parent. 'I've been particularly pleased at how they've built up his confidence. SEN support here is very nurturing and they regularly suggest things I've never even thought of.'

The creative curriculum is big here, with students taken off timetable for six per cent of the time in year 7 and four per cent of the time in year 8. Mainly involves students working in small groups to build habits of mind that will stand them in good stead beyond school – leading a team, being a team player, debating, time management, structuring a piece of work etc. We saw it in action during our visit, with year 10s having created a morning of educational activities for year 7s on World Book Day. 'These students devised the plan, worked out the detail, came to me to pitch it, then carried it through,' says the head, who is loathe to call them 'soft skills' for fear of depreciating their value. Other examples include students pretending their plane has crashed on a desert island (they work out how they will survive), commemorating National Holocaust Day and committing to learning a new skill (usually off the list of activities from the Duke of Edinburgh award which, by the way, is an option from year 9 upwards). A particular favourite for students is the project that involves them researching an area of London, then taking a fellow student on a guided tour. The preparation is impressive, with students writing to the likes of Downing Street to request going through the magic gates. By the end, students have learned skills including independent research, preparing engaging speeches, navigating a map and using the tube.

Games, options, the arts: Cricket and football are by far the strongest sports here. 'Cricket is the most popular and we're good at it; football is also popular, but we're not always quite so good at it,' smiled one pupil. Swimming and rugby also well-liked, whilst other options include basketball, badminton, table tennis, rowing, sailing and rock climbing. Boys here have a competitive streak and sport provides a good outlet, but that's not to say it's all about the best people, with several boys reassuring us that sport is inclusive, including sports day, 'which is very much for everyone', and sports relief, 'in which each house completes a triathlon – meaning you can do just one bit of it if you want'. Duke of Edinburgh caters for those who prefer walking and expeditions to actual sports. 'The focus here is on fitness for life, not just elite players,' sums up the head.

On-site facilities include an artificial cricket strip, two football pitches and a 400m running track. The impressive sports hall (where we saw enthusiastic boys thrashing each other at table tennis) houses a heated swimming pool. There are also four badminton courts, a full size basketball court, with two small courts and provision for volleyball, five-a-side football, and tennis. Upstairs there is a fitness/weights room, an aerobics area and a viewing gallery (which doubles up as a drama studio) and a 'theory room for people taking GCSE or A level' – currently about 50 at GCSE and 10 at A level.

Drama is compulsory for year 7s as part of the English curriculum, but beyond that there's only student-led drama clubs – not great for aspiring thespians. Even whole school productions are rare, although you do get some smaller productions and boys enjoy the annual Speakout Challenge. Art is a different matter, with rich, bold and inspiring work on display – including drawings, paintings and sculpting. We also saw students working on some particularly impressive photography. 'Art is core to cross-curricular work here,' one pupil told us. DT also dynamic, with spirited pupils working hard.

Provision for music is also good. 'This is my absolute favourite department. There are so many chances to learn and perform and there's plenty of sophisticated equipment,' one pupil enthused as he walked us through it. All students study music in years 7, 8 and 9. Over 100 children also have extracurricular music lessons and some exceptional talent can be found here. Some lessons take place at the Redbridge Music School and specialist music teachers visit to teach. Pupils have plenty of opportunity to develop their talents on piano, violin, cello, double bass, saxophone, drum, voice and more through orchestra, jazz ensemble, choirs and various bands. There are concerts and performances in London and abroad. But few pupils take art or music A level.

Extracurricular provision is largely sports-based and there's plenty of subject intervention to enable students to further and deepen knowledge in specific topics. Beyond that, there's a rich variety of clubs, groups and ensembles covering everything from astronomy to chess and gaming to debating club.

Day visits to all the usual galleries and museums (particularly for art) and fieldwork visits to the likes of Dover Castle, Epping Forest and the battlefields. Relatively thin on the ground when it comes to residential trips, however, with the exception of exchange trips (mainly to Spain, Germany and France), and sports trips have included Spain, USA and Caribbean in the past. 'We prefer to do lots of little things that help embed learning, rather than saving it all up for one big trip,' explains the head, who points out that there's no shortage of international focus. Indeed, the school has strong partnerships with schools and colleges in Germany, Spain, Switzerland, Denmark and Iceland and has British Council International School status. 'A lot of our international work involves video conferencing,' explains the head, who claims this makes the global emphasis of the school both more accessible and frequent, with examples including peer assessment with a school in Indonesia and a shared wildlife project with a school in Ghana.

Opportunities to volunteer are frequent, including sixth formers going into local primary schools to teach maths and modern foreign languages to small groups. 'I couldn't wait to do this because I remember how much it meant to me when an Ilford County High boy came and taught me in primary school,' said one pupil. A faith ambassadors scheme involves boys giving talks on what faith means to them (or not – one did a talk on atheism) and there's fundraising projects for local and national charities too.

Background and atmosphere: Founded in 1901 as Park High Grade School, the school was originally co-ed and located in Balfour Road. In 1929, the boys' school split, then moved to its present location in Fremantle Road in 1935. Although smack in the middle of a built-up residential area, the school has a secluded feel. And whilst the building itself is traditional (think sweeping oak stairwells, large wooden boards with lists of past notables and trophy display cabinets), the fabric of the school is undergoing dramatic change, which will lead to a new science block with 10 new labs and six demonstration classrooms; a new sixth-form centre; DT suite and more computer areas. 'We're bringing the school into the 21st century, with a purpose-built, modern learning environment that reflects our emphasis on learning through doing, but whilst still retaining the beauty of the original buildings,' says the head.

The changes will be welcome. Existing classrooms were built with much smaller classes in mind, at an average size of 44 square metres. Meanwhile, the science labs, whilst beautiful and Harry Potter-esque, are dated and poky. The idea is that once the new building work is completed, these old learning areas may be opened up and brightened up, hopefully providing areas such as a new music studio.

As it is, the school layout resembles a figure of eight, with two storeys of classrooms organised around the two adjacent squares, with green areas in the middle that pupils can use at breaktimes. The layout makes it easy for new pupils to find their way around, although we wondered how students here cope with the jump from extremely overheated classrooms to really cold ones. At the front of the school is the hall where assemblies and concerts take place – a decent size with that familiar old-school, musty smell. A new learning resource centre and library is airy, bright and welcoming, and hosts regular live and video conference talks by visiting authors; other visiting speakers; and a reading ambassadors scheme where older boys support younger ones. 'I love it here – this is my favourite part of the school,' one pupil told us.

The atmosphere here is bustling, lively and purposeful. We'd like to have seen the school corridors livened up with more displays of student work, but where they do exist, they are imaginative and intelligent.

Pastoral care, well-being and discipline: 'You don't learn until you get stuck,' says the head and it's an ethos that pupils here really do seem to get, making for a supportive environment, which balances the healthy competition between the boys. Where possible, form tutors – who are generally responsible for pupil welfare and progress – stay with their class all the way up the school. Meanwhile, the vertical house system means all boys have a head of house looking out for them too. The system provides opportunity for the boys to develop stronger skills in leadership, mentorship and responsibility, plus opportunities to develop relationships across year groups, right to sixth form. A visiting counsellor is available; the school regularly accesses Redbridge services for young people; and there are all the usual talks on sex, drugs and rock 'n' roll through to forced marriages and knife crime. 'One charity came in to do a drama workshop on domestic violence and that was particularly powerful,' says the head.

Year 7s receive peer mentoring from trained older pupils in year 9, 10 and sixth form. 'They're a bit of a role model for the younger ones to look up to,' one pupil told us. For one pupil, who joined at sixth form, this was 'one of the things I liked when I came, people always willing to help'. He told us that bullying, or rather the lack of it, was another nice surprise for him, as at his previous school 'fights were a common occurrence. It was a radical change for me – since I've been here I haven't seen one'. The head certainly seems to have a healthy attitude towards bullying. Whilst not making any arrogant claims that deny its existence, she outlined a strict anti-bullying policy and clearly treats it robustly and quickly. 'My child was bullied, but when I contacted the teacher, he had it sorted out within two days and he took me through all the measures he'd taken,' said one parent.

Boys are generally well-behaved here – reports describe the behaviour as 'outstanding' – which is no doubt helped by the clear warning system and strict rules, for example on uniform. 'But boys will be boys and they are naughty sometimes,' acknowledges the head. Indeed, there was an incident the day we visited. No permanent exclusions, although there had been 14 temporary ones half way through the academic year when we visited, mostly for fighting, saying mean things and bringing in banned substances. 'You are dealing with children and they make mistakes. The most important thing is to make sure they learn from them,' says the head.

Pupils and parents: Pupils come from a wide mix of ethnic backgrounds, with Asian (Indian, Pakistani and Tamil) the dominant group, then white British, white Eastern European and black Caribbean. They all come from the borough of Redbridge and some surrounding areas. 'The local authority drew up the smallest circle they could to fully encompass Redbridge, which means you get a little bit of neighbouring boroughs in there too, most notably Waltham Forest and Essex,' explains the headteacher, who describes the school as one of the few grammars left that are true community schools. 'We want it to stay that way,' she says firmly.

Pupils range from bubbly, stumbling and oblivious year 7s making their way between lessons, to the year 11s who are articulate, mature, friendly and inquisitive. In fact, the older pupils who showed us round asked us almost as many questions as we asked them – both rare and refreshing.

There's no PA here, to the disappointment of some parents, but parents generally have good involvement in the school, with almost 100 per cent attendance at parents' evenings and relevant meetings – and parents say that communication is good. The school does have some anxiety about boys whose parents 'have unrealistic aspirations for them' – the 'You will be a doctor!' brigade. But staff try to ensure parents understand exactly what the career they have in mind for their son entails, and to hit home that there are other jobs out there. 'If a boy's real interest and passion is for humanities and not science, fine, as that it is where they will get real satisfaction and achievement.' Work is also done from early on to emphasise that it's about the education, not just the grades. 'The qualifications will get you to the doorway, but you need more than that to walk through it – character, resilience and so on,' says the head.

Notable former pupils include Raymond Baxter, TV personality (Tomorrow's World), Sir Trevor Brooking, footballer, and David Miller, Deputy Chief Inspector of Air Accidents. Lots of presentation evenings hosted by alumni, including some of these big names.

Entrance: More than 850 boys in the borough of Redbridge and nearby compete for the 180 places available each year by sitting the 11+ examination. The test, which has recently changed to CEM (aimed to unearth the brightest children, not the most tutored), is administered by the borough. School manages its own admissions to the sixth form, with places offered only to boys with A*-B in their chosen subjects, plus at least eight Bs across the best of their GSCE results. 'It sounds counter-intuitive, but the idea is to get breadth as well as depth,' explains the headteacher. All sixth form entrants also require grade C or over in English and maths. Parents of pupils who get into this school say their sense of relief is huge, which is unsurprising given that it is the only boys' grammar in the borough.

Exit: Almost all (some 80-90 per cent) stay on to sixth form. Medicine and engineering are the most popular subjects chosen at university, although others include economics, architecture, dentistry, law and physics. Majority choose to study in London at eg King's College and UCL, whilst others go to Russell Group universities across the UK. 'If they're brave enough to go outside London, they're brave enough to pick far and wide,' says the head. Five to Oxbridge in 2016 and 18 medics, plus several optometrists, pharmacists and biomedics.

Remarks: This is a school that delivers a very high standard of academic teaching and much more besides, producing young men who seem genuinely well prepared for the wider world. It's not for the faint-hearted, with firm rules and high expectations, but there's a strong support system to back it all up, with a caring head and exceptionally experienced teaching staff. We found boys well-adjusted, happy and hungry to learn.

International School of London

139 Gunnersbury Avenue, London W3 8LG

Pupils: 401 • Ages: 3–18 • Sixth form: 68

Fees: £18,600 – £25,450 pa

Tel: 020 8992 5823
Email: mail@ISLLondon.org
Website: www.ISLLondon.org

Heads: Sarah Pearson has been principal of the IB Diploma College since May 2016, whilst Andrew Mitchell is head of the Middle and Primary School. Sarah was previously head of sixth form and deputy head at Parkside Community College in Cambridge; she has also been curriculum coordinator and assistant head of maths at Hockerill Anglo European College, after a successful international career in Taipei, Brunei and Botswana. Her husband is also a teacher and they have two grown up 'third culture' sons at UK universities. Andrew Mitchell BSc (chemistry, Nottingham Trent University) PGCE (Warwick University) MA (Open University) has previously worked for the International Baccalaureate Organisation in The Hague coordinating the Africa, Europe and Middle East regions. He has worked as a science teacher and held management positions in Portugal, Finland, Switzerland, the Netherlands and, most recently, as lower school principal and PYP coordinator at the American School of Bilbao.

Academic matters: The school offers the IB primary, middle years and diploma continuum. Some high school students opt out of the full diploma, earning instead an ISL High School Diploma. There's a good selection of IB courses, with more online through Pamoja Education. IB diploma average in 2016 was 31.

The major draw for every single family we spoke to is the 'terrific' mother tongue programme. It may cost extra depending on numbers, but mother tongue classes are offered from primary through to high school with about 16 IB languages leading to the added advantage of a bilingual IB diploma. If a new child's language is not on the list, they will try to find a teacher. EAL support is also strong.

Primary students have specialist teachers for music and PE; art is taught by class teachers. From middle school, specialists teach art, drama, music and PE (through grade 10). Strong level of support in primary classes with plenty of assistants for classes that can number up to 20. Some primary parents prefer the slight 'delay' in reading for younger children when compared to the local English schools. For families coming from countries where formal schooling begins at the age of 6 or 7, ISL's gentle introductory literacy approach at age 5 is more comfortable. However, others comment that while they're very happy at ISL, the range of English fluency may have an effect on the academic pace and rigour compared with other independent schools.

Engaged and cheerful children everywhere we went. A parade of primary students with yummy sandwiches headed to the dining hall, leaving behind open exercise books in their classroom, with individually written recipes for 'my favourite healthy sandwich'; middle school students debating the value of democracy and the advantages of a student council that can organise fun activities, in preparation for an upcoming assembly; CDT students sawing away at wood; art students busily tidying up their room to head to the assembly...everyone looked settled and at ease.

Parents generally happy with communication with the school although some say response to emails can be inconsistent and that while issues raised in emails seem to be addressed by staff, parents aren't always kept informed of the follow up. Parents new to the IB curricula sometimes may struggle if they don't attend the parent education events provided by the school. With families coming from so many different national education systems, everyone has his own idea about the 'right way' to do things. Managing these expectations and helping children adapt is part of the ISL challenge, and for the most part, parents report they do a great job.

Games, options, the arts: There's a mix of after-school clubs, though some primary parents would like to see more, and juggling after-school pick up can be tricky if a younger sibling has nothing to do. Usual international school sports such as volleyball, football, basketball and tennis, and triathlon offered too, with international tournaments. Primary PE and sports take place on site in the hall, small playground, or neighbouring park. Secondary kids go to a nearby sports centres or the park. Weekly swimming for all up to grade 10 at Brentford Leisure Centre. One parent suggests ISL may not suit the 'uber-athlete'; 'it's fun and competitive to a point, but for serious athletes, families join local sports clubs.'

Private instrumental lessons scheduled during the school day, with ensembles practising after school. ISL takes advantage of London as a vast field trip opportunity; early in the year there's a week when nearly everyone from grade 4 vacates the school for three to five day trips. Some incorporate team-building to integrate newcomers; in the middle years they're language-related (Beijing just added). Only the youngest and the IB students (except those on a biology trip) stay behind. Primary parents tell us that the idea of sending their 9-year-olds off on a residential trip 'takes some getting used to'.

Many community service opportunities on offer by school and students also organise their own. One returned to her native India to volunteer in a school for the summer. ISL has work experience programme for all grade 9 students; the school helps organise, or parents and students find their own placement. Though they're a bit young to work, it can inspire their thinking about what IB courses they may select. For one student it also led to summer job opportunities and a gap year project after graduation.

Background and atmosphere: A secondary school founded in north London in 1972, ISL was one of the first authorised IB diploma schools in the country. The school merged in the late 80s with the International Community College, a primary school founded by the Makarem family, becoming a full 4-18 school and moving into a former Catholic school on the North Circular Road in west London. The school is still owned by the Makarems, who recently opened schools in Qatar and in Surrey (buying Shell's former Dutch school). The group is managed by Amin Makarem, the founder's son, who oversees the leadership team of the three schools. Parents say the ISL's quite independent of the other two; not much inter-school activity at student level apart from some sports competition with the Surrey school, but we hear more collaboration is planned.

The building would not win any architectural prizes, but it is undergoing a major refurbishment to modernise and make more it attractive. The primary is located in an annex rented from the next door church; the school reports that it has no plans to relinquish this space even when the refurbishment is completed. ISL is a rabbit warren of hallways and stairwells with every nook and cranny utilised – the staff room, practically in the rafters, is a hive of energetic teachers planning and conversing in umpteen languages – a very positive vibe. Possibly due to building works under way, the school can feel cramped and disorganised and it's not easy to see any rationale to the arrangement of classrooms, corridors and public spaces. School leadership team is considering how to reconfigure things once the refurbishment is complete.

There's a two-level art room and a photo lab, a great CDT classroom, functional science labs of a certain age, a useful multi-purpose hall, a library (which will be relocated after the refurb) and lots of multi-use classrooms of various sizes. Middle and high school students share classrooms and primary share some of the language and specialist classrooms; primary parents reassure us that it's a happy family atmosphere, and of course the teachers are always supervising youngsters as they move through the building. However, the likelihood is that if a family visits ISL for the first time after seeing other international schools in the area, the facilities and environment may not quite measure up. One parent said that when they first drove up to the school, 'we could have cried', but having got past that, it was their first choice school, and they are very happy there. Despite the tight spaces, the students are friendly, polite and seem to move through the building in a pretty organised fashion, and it bodes well for world peace if kids of 50+ nationalities can get along so well in these relatively cramped quarters. The strong message coming from parents is 'don't be put off by first impressions'. Door-to-door bus service is available but with growing London traffic problems school strongly recommends that families choose to live in neighbourhoods like Kew, Chiswick or Ealing.

The school is aware of its limitations, hence the renovation programme. The Diploma College is now on its own site further north up Gunnersbury Avenue.

Pastoral care, well-being and discipline: The strong sense of community provides a solid foundation for the behaviour and discipline in the school, which is of course guided by the IB Learner Profiles. The school handbook directs parents to home room tutors for everyday matters, or the divisional principals, with more serious or school-wide concerns then directed to the head. Some less IT-savvy parents seem to be having some teething problems with a new online communications system. But their main concern is the welfare of their children, and as one happy parent said, 'at ISL children are treated like royals.' No big discipline worries came to our attention.

Pupils and parents: Possibly the most international school in the city if not the country; ISL's students come from 55 countries – the largest single group representing only 13 per cent. It creates fertile conditions for developing open-mindedness and international understanding for students, as well as parents and faculty. With many dual-national families, some kids hold as many as three or four passports. Parents love this environment where 'if you speak several languages, you're not unusual'.

Parents are also drawn to ISL by its smaller size and the friendly and approachable staff, who they credit with helping children to settle in so easily and comfortably, knowing 'how to manage the adjustment for children coming from very different school systems'. Teachers are approachable and deal with new children individually (and also help parents with tips to manage the family transitions). At ISL, this is more than marketing hype.

We hear that families interact socially outside of school; ISL parents believe that having their children learn to understand peers from all backgrounds is a huge advantage. Parents of older students report that their children meet at weekends, and most are happy for them use public transport to arrange this; week nights are spent at home with their noses in the books.

Very active PTA; many families regard the school as the heart of the community. They plan outings and orientation activities for new parents. Parents arriving mid-year are welcomed with newcomers' events and even English language lessons. One parent told us of a group of families who regularly take weekend trips around the UK. Another said she sometimes feels there are more activities for parents than for the kids. PTA got praise from everyone we spoke to.

Most are expats on temporary assignment in the UK, many based at the nearby Brentford business park or growing hub of international companies in Hammersmith, or one of the many embassies. A number lives within easy distance of the school, which makes managing the social life a bit easier, and parents know one advantage in living away from the centre of London is that their money goes further – bigger houses, bigger gardens.

Entrance: Rolling admissions allow students to apply from all over the world, all year round, although there are waiting lists for some year groups. Apply before Easter to improve chances. Admission is determined by previous records, a teacher reference, student and family questionnaires. Interviews are always welcomed (required for IB diploma). No testing (English language is assessed after admission); students with special educational need to provide diagnostic assessments used to determine whether the school can properly serve the student. Non-English speakers with good academic reports are admitted up to grade 10. During interviews there's a lot of discussion about the mother tongue programme and the possible fees for this service.

Although the school does not comment on a sibling policy, parents say they make an effort to ensure all children in a family get a place. Admissions director gets high marks for his thoroughness, efficiency, responsiveness and care and he can tell you about every student in the school. Though on first impression he may appear somewhat diffident, with his many years' experience working with ISL families 'he knows his onions'.

Exit: About 70 per cent go to UK universities, although more now applying to American universities. Some return to their home countries and ISL has a long history of helping students find the right fit in a wide range of countries – an important consideration for families. Even students who earn the ISL High School Diploma gain entry into UK universities. Very occasionally, a student may leave ISL to pursue A levels. Variety of UK universities popular; overseas destinations include Tokyo Science University, Kyoto University, Keio McGill, Technical University of Budapest, University of Chicago, University of Texas, Bocconi Milan, and École Supérieure du Commerce. Parents are advised to ask the school specifically about recent successes.

Money matters: No scholarships as such as most pupils have corporate support, but school will keep a child in extreme circumstances if a family financial problem arises.

Remarks: A school with a solid academic track record that has clearly won over the hearts and minds of its many international families. Many organisations, not to mention a few world leaders, could learn a lot about fostering global understanding from this school.

James Allen's Preparatory School (JAPS)

Linked with James Allen's Girls' School (JAGS)

   126

East Dulwich Grove, London SE22 8TE

Pupils: 300 • Ages: 4–11

Fees: £14,955 pa

Tel: 020 8693 0374
Email: Japsadmissions@jags.org.uk
Website: www.jags.org.uk/prepschool/

Headteacher: Since 2007, Ms Finola Stack BA PGCE Mont Dip. Currently working towards an MA. Co-founded Finton House School in 1987, before moving on to Cameron House as head in 1994. ISI inspector. Highly articulate, Miss Stack goes to great lengths to express herself as unambiguously as possible. One parent we spoke to described her manner as being 'quite restrained, which can seem chilly, though she is probably just being careful.' Revered by the girls. Parents describe her as 'kind' and 'sensitive,' and appreciate her professionalism. Finds time to boost those girls with low self-esteem. The consensus among parents seems to be that she is 'fair, reasonable and at pains to do her best for the girls and for the school...but she won't be bullied by parents'. Not a head that hides herself away in her study. 'Very visible,' commented one parent. Leads running club on Thursdays and regularly sports a tracksuit at galas and inter-house matches. Teaches RE. Three grown up sons. Her main interests are 'family, theatre and exercise.'

Head of pre-prep: Mrs Liz Channon, previously deputy head of Sydenham High Junior School.

Entrance: Entry at 4+ and 7+ in December and January each year. Highly competitive at both stages. Over 100 apply for 36 places at 4+. Open morning in October and school tours offered on Wednesdays. Reception teachers carry out assessments for 4+ entry through varied pre-reading, writing and number activities. 'Nothing to worry about,' reported one parent. 'The girls think they are just playing.' Written report from nursery requested. 'We're looking for academic potential. We're not looking for a specific type of girl. We offer places to a wide cross-section of girls with different dispositions and from a wide cultural base too.' School does not recommend tutoring as it creates a false impression of child's ability. 'We're not looking for the facts they know. We're interested in their thinking process. It is spottable.'

Maths, English and reasoning papers sat by prospective 7+ candidates. If girls meet the academic criteria, they are invited back for a reading test and interview with head. Report from current school requested. No sibling policy at any stage. Ms Stack comments, 'I do feel bad that sometimes sisters aren't accepted but we are entirely transparent in this. If we start muddying the waters, people will become confused about what we're doing.' All occasional places filled in double quick time.

Exit: Up to 90 per cent moves on to senior school (JAGS), often with academic, music and sport scholarships. Automatic entry to JAGS provided that girls are up to scratch in maths and English in years 5 and 6. If not suited to the highly academic environment of the senior school they are encouraged to look elsewhere. Head takes great care with those who are moving on: 'If a girl has received good support at home and at school but is still not making the progress we anticipated and it looks as though she will struggle at the senior school, then I'll work with the family to find the right school for her. It's a sensitive process'. All JAPS girls heading for JAGS must sit the entry exam on same day and in same circumstances as external candidates so they have access to scholarships and bursaries. 'This in line with us being transparent. It also helps the senior school to see the nature of the cohort they are getting,' explains head. Has introduced taster days in languages, sports, science, drama and DT for year 5s from other local schools who are considering the senior school.

Remarks: Prep-prep runs from 4-7 and is housed in a converted Edwardian mansion in Dulwich Village. Two parallel classes per year, with 18 per class, rising to 24 in middle school. 'A wonderful start on the educational journey,' remarked one parent. 'I can't criticise the school,' said another. 'It's a lovely, gentle, happy place,' said a third. Beautiful garden with immaculate lawn, pear trees, lavender and a summer house. Heaven on earth for children. Plenty of time is spent outside just being little girls, pottering about, playing and riding up and down the path on wheeled toys. Sensory garden includes a house for a hedgehog and instructions written by the girls on the gate to 'Look out for thorns!' 'A 4 year old is a 4 year old, however bright. Emotionally they are still very young.' No one is forced to grown up too fast here. How refreshing.

Praise and encouragement readily given. Girls are rewarded with gold leaves which they place on the gold leaf tree. On the day we visited, the tree was weighed down with leaves. One leaf celebrated a girl's ability to concentrate well, another was awarded for impressive show and tell presentations.

Even from early days, girls are given responsibilities and are listened to. They are taught to analyse problems and find solutions for themselves. Pupils from key stage 1 onwards have a school council. Girls recently suggested a 'Fun Friday' when they can let their hair down. Everywhere we looked at the pre-prep, the girls were busy but not frantic. One father summed the atmosphere up as being 'comfortably dynamic.' A winning combination.

No worksheet-driven teaching here. Girls are competitive and lively and there was a distinct buzz in the air on the day we visited. For bright, sparky girls, it's hard to imagine a more exciting environment. Possibly a little harder for those who are less academically whizzy. French teaching singled out by parents as being exceptional – French, PE and music lessons taught totally in French as part of the immersion programme. Accents apparently spot-on by the time they leave. Plenty of differentiation but not rigid setting anywhere.

Teaching considered very strong throughout. We hear reports of some outstanding teachers and certainly witnessed a couple on the day we visited, including a dedicated science teacher busy preparing equipment for the imminent solar eclipse. By year 5, all lessons are taught by specialist teachers.

This school is constantly looking to ways to improve what it delivers. Recently introduced reading sessions after lunch break to encourage girls to read more avidly. Makes the most of its links with the senior school. Older girls come over to help with projects and to give extra mathematical support to the very gifted as well to run language clubs.

Currently 17 on SEND register, mostly for dyslexia, dyscalculia and dyspraxia – no global learning difficulties here. SENCo and her team provide academic and pastoral support, free of charge. Pastoral care taken seriously with a successful buddy system in place to reinforce this. Librarians also provide a sympathetic ear for pupils who want to share worries with a non-teacher. The girls feel well nurtured here. Plentiful opportunities for enrichment offered.

Huge amount of extracurricular activities on offer as school 'wants to work out what engages a girl.' Clubs currently include sessions on climbing wall, portraiture, gardening and coding. Mostly free of charge. Shares sport facilities with JAGS, including swimming pool, pitches, courts and athletics track. Plenty of matches against other schools. Good variety of sport offered including football, hockey and rounders. Everyone makes a team and sport here is inclusive, C and D teams fielded when possible. JAPS hosts a netball festival in the autumn which is specifically designed for schools that cannot get matches organised for lower performing teams.

Head of music considered exceptional. Parents are transfixed by his enthusiastic conducting at carol concerts. Utterly dedicated – he attends everything from pre-prep children timidly playing Three Blind Mice to the year 6 play where he performs the incidental music. Huge variety of instrumental lessons and three-quarters play something right up to grade 7. Girls encouraged to perform as often as possible. Numerous choirs, ensembles, string and wind groups as well as orchestras. Music set to feature even more prominently with a community music centre planned. Parents report on the high standard of drama. Year 4 and year 6 put on annual productions, the latter performed in the senior school's theatre.

Impressive design technology and art department. On the day we visited, one class was trying to work out how thermoplastic is like chocolate. Girls were enthusiastic, engaged and enjoying themselves. Art studio jam-packed with animal masks, lino prints and still life drawings. Beautiful displays adorn the walls at both pre-prep and prep.

School makes good use of its London location. On the day we visited, the youngest children were preparing for a trip to the local fire station. The excitement, though contained, was palpable as these bright-eyed and articulate girls discussed the visit. Further afield, year 2 heads for Lille for a day, year 4 to Swanage, year 5 to Cornwall on an outdoor pursuits adventure and year 6 to Paris. When classes are mixed up at the start of year 5, three days of bonding on a bushcraft course occur. Pretty primitive – no running water and the girls have to cook their own food. 'Some of our girls would never normally do something like that!' comments head.

Multi-ethnic families from all over central and south London send their girls here. Coaches dart back and forth to Alleyn's, Dulwich College and JAGS daily. Every class has bilingual children and EAL support given to those who need it. Extra French conversation classes for bilingual girls. 'Lots of smart mummies with multiple children dashing about on the school run. Some fairly glamorous types with shiny black 4x4s and sunglasses, as well as a smattering of tiger mothers,' commented one parent, though school feels this is an 'unrepresentative appraisal.' Increasing number of families where both parents work. After-school care on offer is activity-based rather than glorified babysitting.

Parents remark on the sense of community here and participate in the life of school. 'It's important that the girls see we're a community, with teachers and parents all working together,' says head. Many come in to give presentations in assembly such as at Chinese New Year and Passover. Parents fundraise for projects, such as for a pond in the sensory garden. Head feels majority of parents is supportive and positive about the school but alert to the fact that 'some parents have strong views.'

Though some locals claim this is an elitist school that produces sharp-elbowed girls, school feels this is not the case. Head believes that 'above all, it's important all children here should be challenged, engaged and learn to give back. Given the advantages they have had, they need to ask themselves what they can then do to benefit others'. This ethos runs throughout the school.

JAPS deserves its outstanding reputation. With its enviable facilities, energetic teaching and dedicated leadership, it's unrivalled in this part of town. These charming, articulate and happy girls seem ready to take on the world by the time they leave.

J

James Allen's Girls' School (JAGS)

Linked with James Allen's Preparatory School (JAPS)

144 East Dulwich Grove, London SE22 8TE

Pupils: 775 • Ages: 11–18 • Sixth form: 200 • C of E

Fees: £16,515 pa

Tel: 020 8693 1181
Email: henrietta.kiezun@jags.org.uk
Website: www.jags.org.uk

Headmistress: Since 2015, Mrs Sally Anne Huang MA MSc PGCE. Previously head of Kent College, Pembury. Educated at Bolton School for Girls and Lady Margaret Hall, Oxford where she read classics and English. PGCE from King's College, London. Taught English and classics at Sevenoaks, where she was also housemistress. Sixth form housemistress at Roedean before becoming deputy head, a post she held for four years.

Head thinks that 'what JAGS does best is prepare young women for the modern world. That's the most important thing we do. We encourage intellectual curiosity, a sense of responsibility and purpose. We want the girls to lead purposeful lives.'

Girls adore her and are charmed by her easy manner and approachability. They see her as a very positive role model. Her open door policy means pupils regularly pop into her bright red study at break time, often just to stroke her three dogs and say hello. Teaches one lesson a week of classics to top year at the prep school, so knows many of the girls when they arrive. Also teaches philosophy to year 7 and civilisation to year 10. Knows impressive numbers of pupils by name.

Popular with parents too, who appreciate her warmth and energy. 'She has refocused the school,' said one. 'Mrs Huang is already very popular. It was a difficult job stepping into the gargantuan shoes of the previous head but she has injected modernity into the school,' said another. 'A breath of much needed fresh air!' commented another.

Lives next door so regularly nips over at weekends to catch up on work. Husband Alexis is Chinese but grew up in south east London. 'Multi-cultural, ethnic diversity is very close to my heart and so was a definite attraction of coming to JAGS,' explains head. Two teenage sons. Interested in children's literature, and is particularly keen on Marcus Sedgwick's novels. Loves theatre of all kinds, especially immersive theatre and heads to nearby Globe as often as possible. In the holidays, she is at her happiest walking her beloved dogs in Wales, where she has her home. Though brought up outside Manchester, she 'wants to be Welsh' and is an avid Welsh rugby supporter.

Academic matters: Strong results at A level, with 84 per cent A*/A and 96 per cent A*/B in 2016. Maths, biology, chemistry, history and English literature particularly popular. At GCSE, 73 per cent of all entries were A* and 95 per cent awarded A*/A. Girls normally take 10 or 11 GCSEs.

English department is particularly strong. JAGS was top of national league tables in Pre-U last year thanks to English literature results. No mean feat. Other Pre-U subjects offered are history of art and history. School is otherwise sticking to A levels rather than opting for IB. Head explains that 'a lot of the girls at JAGS are specialists so they might be better served with A levels and Pre U courses.' Modern foreign languages also well taught, with French, Spanish, Italian, Russian, Japanese and German offered. Two of these must be studied until end of year 9. Bilingual girls can take a foreign language GCSE early but otherwise pupils take all subjects at end of year 11.

Inspirational staff. Quality of teaching described as 'fantastic,' 'incredible' and 'superb' by parents. Some NQTs taken on most years but more than half the teachers have been here over a decade. Head explains that 'recruiting here is great, due to the reputation of the school.' Not uncommon for middle managers at other schools to jump ship to JAGS as regular teachers 'just to get into the system.' Males are well represented, making up around 40 per cent of the teaching body. Head observes lessons on a regular basis so knows her staff well and has been hugely impressed by the standard of teaching here. She acknowledges that recent upheavals in education have been a pressure on the teachers and she is also frustrated by the 'maverick' marking of A levels.

When academic problems do arise, parents feel they are dealt with quickly and efficiently. Setting in maths and French from year 8, though sets are fairly fluid with plenty of moving up and down as required. Surprisingly few take the EPQ but head hopes to encourage more girls to take it up in future years.

Historically class sizes have been large – reaching as many as 28 in the earlier years. Now, having moved to a five form entry, the maximum class size is 25.

Small numbers with special needs. School can support girls with relatively mild dyslexia, dyspraxia, ADHD, limited sight and hearing. Laptops and extra time in exams sorted for those entitled to it. Two SENCos in the school, one who focuses up to year 9 and the other from year 10 onwards. 'We don't have girls who need a lot of one-to-one attention here,' explains head. Girls have to be able to keep up with the snappy pace so would not suit a pupil with profound difficulties, though adjustments are certainly made to support SEN pupils where possible.

Games, options, the arts: Music is high profile and taken very seriously. All the parents we spoke to raved about the exceptional quality of music. Gustav Holst was a music master here for 16 years and school's main hall is named after him. Orchestras, ensembles, choirs and bands galore. Huge new music centre is now being built, including classrooms, IT suites and performance areas. Large numbers learn an instrument and play to high levels. Girls regularly win places in national youth choir and national youth orchestra.

Masses of sport going on. Netball and athletics considered to be especially strong but minor sports including ice-skating, golf, table tennis, skiing, yoga and kick boxing also popular. School boasts its own pool which is well used, even on the cold December morning we visited. Twenty-two acres of grounds, with pitches stretching far into the distance. Enviable amount of space for matches and practice, particularly when compared to sister schools in more central locations. One mother we spoke to complained that the sports department tends to focus on the most able, 'often to the detriment of those who do not excel as much.' School, however, feels that girls who are less able on the sporting front can at least play for their house, so everyone does compete at some level. Another parent felt that the school should try to concentrate on personal fitness more for those who were unlikely to make teams and that the state-of-the-art gym seemed underused. Extraordinary climbing wall to challenge all levels. Dulwich College lets JAGS girls share its boathouse, so increasing numbers taking up rowing.

Hugh amounts of collaboration with Dulwich drama department too. Middle school and senior school productions include a healthy mix of frothy musicals and more heavyweight plays, ranging from Grease and Thoroughly Modern Millie to Tristan and Isolde. Plays are considered to be slick and high quality and the set we saw would have put the West End to shame. School encourages girls to get up on the stage as much as possible, including public speaking in assemblies, but for those less keen on the limelight there are plentiful opportunities behind the scenes too. Saturday school of performing arts means extraordinary facilities can be enjoyed by the public.

The three art rooms as well as printing room reflect the popularity of this art throughout the school. All girls are encouraged to take one creative subject at GCSE, with roughly half opting for art. Displays of art and DT work around the school, including radios and board games, reflect the high standards. TeenTech Consumer Innovation Award recently won by two girls for a cycling jacket with lights on the shoulders to indicate the direction you are heading in was rewarded with a ceremony at Buckingham Palace.

Plenty of trips abroad: history department heads to China, RE girls to Israel, others do voluntary work in Romania, and the netball team has played in Barcelona. The cap on costs of trips has been lifted under the new head, with bursary girls being supported by funding from the school. Ski trips have been reintroduced. Head's belief is that not all trips need to have academic clout, that there is an awful lot to be gained socially and culturally from travelling abroad on school trips.

Background and atmosphere: Founded in 1741, by James Allen, master of Dulwich College, making it the oldest girls' independent school in London. His portrait hangs in pride of place in the hallway. Part of a foundation (including Alleyn's and Dulwich College) set up by Elizabethan actor Edward Alleyn. Increasing collaboration with close neighbour Dulwich, from music productions to cookery classes. 'Mrs Huang is encouraging more integration with the boys, which is very popular, as you can imagine,' laughed one mother. Part of the Southwark Schools Learning partnership which includes maintained and independent schools in the vicinity. Neighbouring schools share experiences and develop innovative practice.

Ethnic and socio-economic diversity is a fundamental element of the school's ethos. One mother commented, 'In the past it has felt more like a grammar school than a fancy private school. The new head seems to be smartening the place up but keeping the diverse student population, which is an important part of the school.' Girls accept and enjoy the variety of backgrounds here. 'We never judge each other on background or clothes. Not at all. We are very inclusive,' explained one of the pupils.

Christian foundation though the school wears that lightly as there are many girls here of different faiths and none. Charitable work is viewed as important. 'Girls are encouraged to have a social conscience,' according to one father. The Saturday literacy scheme is a typical example: year 10 and 11 year old girls help children from local primary schools with their reading at the weekend. Some girls love the experience so much that they volunteer two years running. One member of staff is just dedicated to community work, including at a local old people's home. JAGS also puts on Latin classes at Charter School next door. 'This sense of giving back makes us different from many other similar independent girls' schools' states head.

Outward looking school that is keen to be recognised on the national stage: Arkwright scholarships awarded annually to budding engineers, girls also excel at the junior and senior maths challenges as well as literary competitions. Inspiring range of outside speakers.

Pastoral care, well-being and discipline: A nurturing school. Current head has done a lot to improve pastoral care and girls have an array of people to turn to when they hit bumps in the road: form tutors, heads of year, assistant heads, as well as senior girls. Also informal 'family groups' within the school. The house system means girls in different year groups work together to fundraise, as well as with sport, music and drama productions. The girls feel there is always someone there for them.

Three school counsellors, including one from the local church and also a CAMHS counsellor specialising in mental health. Head assumed there would be many girls with mental health issues given the high achieving nature of the school and the high standards girls expect of themselves, but has been struck by how few there are with difficulties. She explains, 'We are managing it but it is definitely there. Teenagers are under increasing pressure.' Girls are good at looking out for each other here and assemblies on self-esteem and a 'happy being me' programme aim to address problems head on.

Bullying is rare and girls are taught the importance of being kind from early on. The way the girls interact with each other is crucial and the school will come down like a ton of bricks on anyone who misuses social media. Bringing the school into disrepute at weekends is also not tolerated. A girl would be asked to leave 'if she was having a negative impact on other girls', though current head has not had to expel anyone yet.

Pupils and parents: Over 50 languages spoken at home. Though some pupils are from affluent backgrounds, there is a sizeable proportion of the squeezed middle that is working very hard to pay the fees. Parents are doctors, lawyers, teachers, journalists, hairdressers, bus drivers and students, as well as many media folk. Most families are dual income.

Pupils come from far and wide, though majority from south east London. Handful from north of river and Kent. Coach service shared with Alleyn's and Dulwich means travel from long distances is manageable. One pupil we spoke to travels for three hours a day in total and she is not alone. Some pupils walk to school, others cycle or use public transport.

Good relationships between parents and teachers reported. Parents rave about the improved communication and love the fact that they can now email staff directly. Head has been delighted by how 'rational, liberal and educated' the parents are at JAGS and feels under less pressure from parents here than at any of her previous schools. 'I didn't expect that. Parents here have a great sense of proportion.'

Strong and active PTA that fundraises huge sums for school bursaries, as well as organising social events.

Entrance: Main points of entry are 11+ and 16+. At 11, around 500 apply for 120 places. Pre-selection assessment mornings in the autumn term, where girls are observed in a one-to-one context as well as group situations. The day consists of puzzle-solving activities, taster lessons taught by head and online tests in verbal, non-verbal and numerical reasoning. 'We know after this assessment day that there are some girls who will not thrive at JAGS. Largely, we take note of who participates, who talks first and who is engaged. We also take note of girls who are very quiet. This would not be against them but is useful for sorting out forms if they do come here.' Candidates are informed before Christmas whether they are to be allowed to take the entrance exams in January but vast majority is called back. Written tests in maths and English. Offers are made in mid-February and those who hold offers attend a Fun Day in early March. No sibling preference. Nearly 90 per cent of JAPS girls come straight up to senior school. They have automatic entry.

For occasional places in other years, candidates sit tests in mathematics, English and reasoning (non-verbal, verbal and numerical); 13+ and 14+ candidates sit an additional modern foreign language paper of 30 minutes (if they have a second language).

Places in the sixth form are dependent upon entrance exams based upon subjects to be studied at A Level, GCSE results, school reference and interviews with head and head of sixth form.

Exit: Around 15 leave after GCSEs, often heading for co-eds such as Westminster and KCS Wimbledon. A few new girls come in at this stage to replace the leavers and head intends to recruit more. Though she understands that girls who have been here from the age of 4 are keen for a change, she knows from experience that a co-ed school is not always in a girl's best interests. Every year some girls return within the first weeks of the autumn term, having missed the supportive environment of JAGS. 'We are happy to take them back, though we might not be able to accommodate their subject choices at this stage,' states head.

Most A level leavers head for university though some choose one-year courses at the Royal Academy of Music. Others make a beeline for art foundation courses, particularly Kingston, Camberwell and Central St Martins. Popular university destinations include Durham, London, Edinburgh, Leeds and Bristol. Increasing numbers to Oxford and Cambridge recently – 16 in 2016. One parent commented that, in the past, girls have not always ended up at the top universities but new head is changing that. She is focusing on giving pupils the confidence to apply for elite universities. Girls choose a wide variety of courses from biomedical engineering to history of art, but medicine is a particular strength, with three Oxbridge medics and eight off elsewhere, plus three vets, in 2016.

Huge careers lecture programme. School has a head of careers, head of further education, as well as Oxbridge co-ordinator. Help given with interview practice and with preparing for aptitude tests. Sixth form tutors help with the writing of personal statements, though head thinks girls tend to spend inordinate amounts of time on these.

Money matters: Art, music and sport scholarships available. At 11+ academic scholarships are worth up to £4,000 pa. Over 120 girls currently on some form of bursary, with over 50 on totally free places. A few 16+ scholarships of £1,000 awarded on the basis of GCSE results but girls keep it pretty quiet as bragging is frowned upon.

Remarks: One father commented, 'JAGS is everything you would want from a school. Girls are genuinely happy. They are given the chance to be what they can be.' Another said, 'The head is taking the school onwards and upwards. It was great before but Mrs Huang is changing things for the better.' JAGS produces articulate, ambitious, confident yet modest girls. Impressive on every front.

JCoSS

Castlewood Road, New Barnet, Hertfordshire EN4 9GE

Pupils: 1,260 • Ages: 11–18 • Sixth form: 325 • Jewish

Tel: 020 8344 2220
Email: admin@jcoss.barnet.sch.uk
Website: www.jcoss.org

Head: Since 2012, Patrick Moriarty MA Oxon MA (Ed) NPQH (early 50s.) Grew up in north London and attended Haberdashers' Aske's Boys School, before reading philosophy and theology at Oxford, then training as a teacher at King's College, London. Taught (RE and English) at Latymer in Edmonton, Bishop Stopford's School, Enfield, and Haberderdashers' Aske's School for Girls. Arrived at JCoSS in 2010 as deputy head. 'The opportunity of a new school was very exciting and I liked the fact that it was a faith school.' Despite his unlikely background ('I told them I wasn't Jewish and I was contemplating studying for the priesthood'), he started nine months before the school opened, helping 'finesse' the curriculum.

Breathtakingly energetic, genial and thoughtful, he has undoubtedly delivered on the promise of balancing an outstanding curriculum and outstanding pastoral care. Ofsted, pupils and parents agree on his manifold virtues. 'Exceptional,' say the school inspectors. 'The best head,' said a sixth former. 'He's done an amazing job,' agreed a parent. He's also recently received recognition at the Jewish Schools Award for his 'outstanding and inspirational leadership'. Married to a musician, his out-of-school hours involve heavy-duty family responsibilities (with two stepchildren, a 7-year-old and a toddler), but still manages to find moments to play the piano and organ.

Academic matters: High expectations of what would be achieved, and JCoSS's second set of GCSE results certainly didn't disappoint, with 40 per cent A*/A grades, immediately catapulting the school into the top 10 per cent nationally. At A level, 38 per cent of grades were A*-A (as good or better than many independents), and two-thirds A*-B.

Largely academic curriculum with most students taking 11 or 12 GCSEs (adjusted at the discretion of the staff). 'They could take fewer, but that would mean fewer options.' Modern Hebrew compulsory in years 7-8 (alongside French). In year 9, students can opt out of Hebrew and consider Spanish or Latin. Twenty-eight subjects on offer at A level, including psychology, sociology and further maths. Good take up of religious studies (20 out of 150 this year), which achieves notably strong results, as do psychology, English and sociology. Six vocational BTecs, too, in the sixth form (in health and social care, creative media, sport, IT and business). About 70 per cent of students do purely A levels, about 10 per cent purely vocational courses, others mix and match. 'Our aim is to break down the boundaries and get all our students successfully into university.' Energetic teachers, happy to go the extra mile, and teacher-pupil relations clearly strong. 'I feel my teachers are talented and charismatic,' said one student.

One of the distinguishing characteristics of JCoSS is the Jewish education. Students take six lessons a fortnight of Jewish education, five concentrating on Judaism, one on other faiths. 'The kids ask for it, and we feel part of being Jewish is loving your neighbour and understanding your neighbour's religion.' (At GCSE, the second faith studied is Islam.) Jewish education continues for all into the sixth form.

Provision for SEN commended by Ofsted as 'outstanding'. The school, after consultation with the local authority, decided to create a specialist autism unit, the PSRP, with seven places a year devoted to those on the autism spectrum who can access the national curriculum (regardless of faith). The aim is to integrate these students as far as possible into the mainstream. Some spend all their time with the rest; others about half. 'It's highly personalised,' says the head. 'It's a brilliant model because it allows the maximum flexibility and enables all students to recognise and celebrate difference.' One designated SEN teacher per year group in the PSRP, plus two or three learning support assistants, all with specialist training. Others with special needs (dyslexia, dyspraxia, etc) – about three or four a year – are also well catered for, with three SEN teachers and around 30 learning support assistants, given one-to-one tuition where necessary. 'Able and ambitious' programme enriches the core offering for those who excel in any area.

Games, options, the arts: Sport still relatively in its infancy and limited grounds mean it's unlikely to be a big priority in the immediate future. 'We need a wider range of sport,' said one student. Some all-weather pitches and a spacious well-equipped gym, plus a multi-gym. Some 150 external recent matches in netball, football and basketball, with pleasing results. Badminton a particular strength (recent Barnet champions). Rugby offering improving with enthusiastic encouragement from the sixth form. Elite sports programmes (with Saracens rugby coaching, Brentford and Southend football trials). Broad range of after-school sports clubs include sports leadership, table tennis, trampolining and modern Israeli dance.

Large art department with enthusiastic participants. Keen musicians enjoy chamber choir, jazz band, orchestra, guitar surgery. Good range of community involvement and social action: Duke of Edinburgh, Amnesty International, primary school volunteering, Israel club.

Background and atmosphere: Traditionally, London has not had enough school places for Jewish families, and JCoSS was established to be a 'pluralist' Jewish secondary, where all who 'self-identified as Jewish' would be welcome. 'Religiously, we were doing something different,' says the head. 'Here, whether you're Orthodox, Masorti, Reform or Secular, we believe that's a valid expression of tradition.'

Pupils feel the approach works well. 'At other Jewish schools, you might get the feeling that one person's opinion is not as good as another's, but that's not true here,' said one sixth former. 'There are Jews from lots of different backgrounds, but I've never seen an example of bullying on the basis of people's beliefs,' said another. 'We might disagree about Israel's stance for example, but we would debate it.' 'Religion is not pushed,' said a parent. 'It's discussed philosophically.'

The school is inclusive and ecumenical, with a strong stress on inter-faith activities, including visits to temples and cathedrals. Though 99 per cent of pupils are Jewish, last summer, for example, a Ramadan tent was erected in the grounds, where Christians, Jews and Muslims formed a circle of faith.

A long time in the making, the school finally opened on a leafy site in east Barnet in September 2010, with 150 pupils and 15 teachers. In 2012, a sixth form was introduced. Until recently this has been relatively small – with just 35 students per year – but numbers are now up to capacity as the junior years filter through.

Spacious (£48m) modern building, with wide corridors, large, light classrooms and excellent facilities. Calm and order reign throughout. Kosher food for all, with cool café for use of sixth formers, staff and visitors. Tight security on the gates.

Students generally mature and focussed ('During my son's GCSE year everyone really settled down,' said a mother. 'I was amazed how motivated they all were.') The head boy and girl actively involved in bringing about change – getting everyone to donate blood, inviting in speakers from universities, etc. Also generous with praise for fellow students ('He's amazing at art', 'She did a wonderful job,' are constant refrains.)

Pupils clearly enjoy the school. 'There's never been a day when my son has not been happy to go,' said one mother. 'When I asked him if he wanted to consider somewhere else for sixth form, he said, "Absolutely not".'

Pastoral care, well-being and discipline: The development of each student as a 'Mensch' – a person of integrity and honour – is the backbone of the school, and moral worth very much emphasised and rewarded (one prize, for example, for kindness, is voted on by students, another awarded for 20 hours volunteering).

Growing house system, with head boy and girl, plus deputies. 'Students put themselves forward, and are interviewed; it's a proper process,' says the head. Discipline is relaxed but clearly defined ('Chilled,' said one parent, 'but not laissez faire.'). 'It's generally a very inclusive and friendly place, good natured and human,' says the head, who has overseen a few fixed-term exclusions, but only one permanent exclusion.

Pupils and parents: From the highly observant to the not observant at all, with a reasonable sprinkling of mixed marriages. A good chunk live fairly locally, but pupils come from as far afield as St Albans and Essex, Harrow and Hackney. Many arrive by school coach, where firm bonds are formed. Parents are predominantly university-educated Jewish middle class, but a reasonable number are aided by the pupil premium and free school meals. All tend, however, to be focussed on similar goals. 'The great majority of our students intend to go to university and get professional jobs in the future, and think and act in that way,' says the head.

Entrance: Around 630 apply for 180 places, with about 400 putting JCoSS as their first or second choice. The school is mixed ability, but priority goes to Jewish children (proved by attendance at synagogue or involvement with Jewish education plus volunteering in the Jewish community). The admissions system is changing, reducing the priority given to feeder schools. 'We wanted to ensure there is room for children whatever primary school they have come from.' Order of acceptance is now: siblings; 18 places on distance; then, by lottery. The school does not expand the sixth form, merely fills the gaps. Minimum six Bs at GCSE for those considering A levels; five Cs for the vocational route. Jewish applicants are again given priority.

Exit: About 20 per cent leave after GCSEs. Some because they don't make the required grades, others to sixth form colleges or independent schools. At 18, virtually all to university, about half to Russell Group universities (Nottingham, Leeds, Manchester particularly popular), with one to Oxbridge and two medics in 2016.

Money matters: Parents are asked for a voluntary contribution to help underwrite unfunded Jewish education.

Remarks: A school with a clear vision, which, in six busy years, has grown from a hopeful acorn to an oak of excellence. An inclusive place producing excellent results and happy, involved pupils.

J

JFS

The Mall, Kenton, Harrow HA3 9TE

Pupils: 2,070 • Ages: 11–18 • Sixth form: 570 • Jewish

Tel: 020 8206 3100
Email: admin@jfs.brent.sch.uk
Website: www.jfs.brent.sch.uk

Headteacher: Since September 2016, Simon Appleman, previously deputy head.

Debby Lipkin, a schools improvement specialist who was acting as consultant at the school, is executive head for the 2016/17 school year.

Academic matters: Consistently in the top one per cent nationally of non-selective schools, JFS continues to achieve pretty stunning results. In 2016, 81 per cent of A levels at A*-B. At GCSE, 50 per cent of grades were at A*/A, although interestingly the percentage of students achieving five passes at A*-C including maths and English was 83, suggesting perhaps that the school's intake is top-heavy at the high-achieving end.

Teaching here universally praised. 'The school is incredible academically'; 'The teaching is amazing'; 'I feel I'm being really stretched, especially in maths'; 'The teachers praise you so much, they really notice your achievements,' said students, while parents added, 'The teachers for the most part are either good or wonderful'; 'Most of my son's teachers have been spectacular'; 'They really push pupils to achieve their potential'; 'The academic standards are excellent.' Strong uptake of the EPQ, and an ongoing and wholehearted commitment to A levels; only one BTec offered and there are no plans to introduce the IB.

Year 7 pupils set for English maths, Jewish studies, Hebrew and PE, but in mixed ability groups for other subjects. Excellent support for both high and low ability students, and a large and well-equipped SEN department supporting the latter. 'The support to my child has been fantastic – staff have bent over backwards to help him,' an appreciative parent told us. Ofsted commented in its most recent report that more need to be done to support those towards the bottom of the middle, some of whom don't make such rapid progress as their peers. Parents, however, told us that the school catered well for difference. 'My children are different in every way and the school's been brilliant with both of them.' 'The school has found a way to reward each of my children for what they do well.'

School is very well-equipped, with interactive boards in every classroom, and no fewer than 14 science labs. Indeed, science was praised as a particular strength of the school. 'The resources here are really good. The teachers are some of the best in the school, and they always get outstanding results,' said one young physicist, proudly. Annual science festival, and the department creates plenty of science leadership opportunities. One-year GCSE astronomy course available to sixth formers as an optional extra, and Science Support Club for years 7 to 11. We dropped in on the year 7 Math-A-Thon, a highly impressive but good-humoured event where you could have heard a pin drop as the competitors stepped up to the platform and got to work in an atmosphere of palpable excitement.

French offered to all year 7s and Spanish to all year 8s, along with Ivrit (modern Hebrew). However, modern languages came in for something of a battering from both pupils and parents – 'They aren't great, but this is no secret,' wrote one mother gloomily, and pupils we asked tended to concur, dismissing Ivrit in particular as 'the subject everyone intends to drop in year 10'. Whilst admitting that they'd had some trying staff shortages in recent times, school insists: 'We're fully staffed, and we've got some really cracking teachers in that department.' And at least one student agreed: 'I think the languages teachers have really helped me.'

History and politics are extremely popular here, and classical civilisation is a recent and successful innovation – 'a really good course,' according to students. Jewish studies widely regarded as excellent, and won universal praise for its intellectual breadth and inclusivity. 'It's been taught in a way that's allowed my son to challenge the material, rather than trying to indoctrinate him,' said one parent, and another confirmed, 'My children have felt comfortable to question the teachers, who have always responded well.'

Games, options, the arts: Impressive array of trophies on display reflects the opportunities and facilities for sport on offer: netball, football, badminton, basketball, trampolining, fitness, athletics, rounders – etc. When we visited, the school had just won the Middlesex Regional Cup for Football in year 12, and everyone we spoke to clearly enjoyed this part of the school's provision. Magnificent climbing wall very popular and much-used.

Superb artwork everywhere we looked, including some really huge canvasses – 'They're not short of ambition,' commented the head of art. Drama also flourishes on a big scale, staging musicals like Little Shop of Horrors, Guys and Dolls and Fiddler on the Roof alongside Shakespearean offerings such as Twelfth

Night and Much Ado About Nothing. Music is high-quality, lively and wide-ranging – 'The music department is really friendly.' 'They adopt you as one of their children if you go to rehearsals,' according to pupils. Students can learn 'any and every instrument', and there are regular concerts as well as an annual music festival and the ever-popular staff recital.

Sixth form newspaper held in high regard, and student journalism is strong throughout the school. 'Someone who likes to write and have their voice heard can always do so here,' said an aspiring reporter. 'Loads' of student-run societies, including the sixth form medical society, which lays on talks by prestigious visiting speakers – professors Jane Dacre and Alan McGregor recently headed the bill.

Lots of excursions, and many parents praised the year 9 trip to Israel – 'Incredible' and 'the highlight of my child's year.' High take-up of gap years in Israel arranged by the school.

Background and atmosphere: Founded in 1732, moved to Bell Lane in London's east end in 1832, where at one time it had 4,000 children on its roil and was the biggest school in Europe. The site was bombed during the war, and in 1958 relocated to Camden. Expanding numbers, plus the need to upgrade school facilities, led to the move in 2002 to its present purpose-built home in Kenton. The new school building was designed to be light and airy, to have learning at its heart, and to have the synagogue placed where it would be the first thing visitors would see. The latter is certainly the jewel in the school's crown, with beautiful stained glass windows and a library and study area in the gallery. It's in constant use, both for services and 'Lunch and Learn' sessions. Elsewhere the building is curvy and lightsome, with wide corridors and a progressive feel, although here and there carpets and paintwork were showing their age. Sixth form area is particularly inviting, with spacious and attractive study areas.

The school is divided into four houses named after leading lights in the Anglo-Jewish community (Angel, Brodetsky, Weizmann and Zangwill), and is orthodox in the sense that its denominational authority is the Chief Rabbi. However, it admits children from a wide variety of Jewish backgrounds, both practising and secular, including around 10 per cent from overseas. 'The school prepares you to mix with any background,' said a very likeable sixth former, 'it's great for getting you out of the Jewish bubble, and it's a great place to be secular as well as observant.' All faiths are represented on the staff, 60 per cent of whom are not Jewish.

We liked the liveliness and warmth of this school community. 'JFS is really good, really welcoming, and I settled in quickly,' said one student. 'You can have so many friends in all the different year groups, because there are so many activities,' said another. To us, as we moved round the school, the students seemed cordial, purposeful, orderly and well-turned-out, wearing their blue uniform with care (mostly); carrying themselves with confidence, and, we thought, joie de vivre.

Pastoral care, well-being and discipline: In 2014 parental complaints about some students' behaviour led to an unannounced visit by Ofsted and the lowering of JFS's status from Outstanding to Requires Improvement. Something of a shock, one imagines, but the school rallied, and following a monitoring visit from Ofsted six months later, was judged to be 'taking effective action to tackle the areas requiring improvement' and acting 'professionally and resolutely'. Measures have included restructuring the senior leadership team, new appointments on the governing body, improved information gathering about attendance, introducing a clearer sanctions policy, and working with an independent school improvement adviser contracted by the school's local authority.

Has it worked? Well, the school is, if anything, more oversubscribed than it was before, and responses from parents and children were overwhelmingly favourable. 'We have always been struck by the excellent behaviour we've witnessed in the JFS students we met,' wrote one mother. 'In my opinion, the recent downgrading only demonstrated what a ridiculous body Ofsted is,' said another.

'Everyone feels safe here,' was a typical student comment, and school says, 'We have a strong message to the students: bullying is not tolerated,' adding that recent surveys of parents indicated that 90 per cent of parents felt that bullying was dealt with effectively. That said, JFS is a big school, and a few people expressed concern to us that behaviours such as blanking and name-calling sometimes slipped under the radar. As one mother put it, 'The school deals with bullying very well once they're made aware that there's a problem.'

Pastoral care was very highly rated. 'There's so much support,' said a grateful year 7 child who admitted having taken a while to find her feet, and students throughout the school concurred. 'Any issues have been taken up when I raised them,' said one. 'The mentoring system is second to none', said another. Parents added, 'The staff are always easy to contact – I've only had trouble once in the past nine years getting a teacher to get back to me,' 'One of my children had some anxiety over exams and self-esteem issues. The school has been exceptional and extremely supportive over this.'

Everyone agreed that, despite the school's size, their child had felt noticed and encouraged. 'When choosing schools, we didn't want JFS because we felt it was too big,' wrote one parent, 'however, from the first day we could not have been more impressed. The transfer process from primary to secondary school was flawless, and both our children made friends quickly.'

Pupils and parents: A broad social mix of families, with about eight per cent on free school meals. Students are confident, articulate, 'sometimes audacious.'

Entrance: Heavily over-subscribed, with around 800 applications for 300 places at year 7. Check school's website for ladder of admissions criteria. Following the famous court of appeal ruling in 2009, students no longer have to have a Jewish mother, but families need to complete a certificate of religious practice. Around 35 external applicants are accepted to join the sixth form each year, on the basis of GCSE results and religious practice.

Exit: Around 10 per cent leave after GCSE to try something else. Of those who stay almost all go on to higher education, either directly or after a gap year. Some 70 per cent to Russell group universities in 2016, with 15 to Oxbridge, five to medical school and some to the USA. Usually a few each year to music conservatoires or drama schools. Gap year option arranged by the school to study in Israel is always popular, with some even doing a second gap year.

Remarks: Still the school of choice for Jewish families wanting the best education – both Jewish and otherwise – for their children. As one parent wrote, 'When my son received his place at JFS, my husband and I felt we'd won the golden ticket, and our feelings haven't changed.' As another put it, 'I can't imagine sending my children anywhere else.'

John Betts Primary School

Paddenswick Road, London W6 0UA

Pupils: 240 • Ages: 4–11

Tel: 020 8748 2465
Email: admin@johnbetts.lbhf.sch.uk
Website: www.johnbetts.lbhf.sch.uk

Headteacher: Since 2015, Jessica Mair BA QTS NPQH (late 30s). After a degree in drama and education at Roehampton University, earned her teaching colours at London primaries from World's End to the East End, before spending two years in Argentina, as deputy head of St Andrew's Scots School, which she describes as 'their equivalent of Eton...it was a very good experience, to be immersed in a different culture and way of thinking'. More recently, deputy head at Queens' Manor Primary, where, as head of inclusion, she was responsible for its special needs unit. She describes herself as 'a change agent', which gave her the courage to take up the reins at John Betts after a popular predecessor's 26 year tenure.

Visibly competent and professional in manner, she reveals the secret of her success: 'If you find out what a child is good at and make sure they are happy and settled, they will fly and make progress', a philosophy she acknowledges that has been handed down from her own headteacher at Queenswood. She and her 'very strong leadership team' have introduced careful changes in the traditional workings of the school, swapping individual desks for work tables, updating the curriculum to reflect a contemporary urban population and starting up an orchestra. Parents appreciated the changes: 'she's modernised us a bit... new staff, new ways to attract the children'. 'Very impressive, very together,' said one mum; also impressively quick up and down the many school staircases. 'I think it's important that children run to school', she laughs, leading by example.

Entrance: Vastly oversubscribed. Places are allocated by London Borough of Hammersmith and Fulham criteria: priority to looked after children, SEN needs, siblings, then according to catchment area, which in some years is no further than one tenth of a mile. Occasional places are snapped up, when families move abroad or out of town.

Exit: Fewer children leave at KS2 than in the old days, as shrewd parents have become more appreciative of the 'bargain' of a John Betts education. At 11, half go to independent schools: Latymer Upper, St Paul's (girls and boys), Godolphin and Latymer, Frances Holland, Harrodian; half to state secondaries: West London Free School, Hammersmith Academy, Holland Park, Twyford C of E High School. Occasional child to an independent boarding school.

Remarks: Eight classes of 30 (one per school year with a 'bulge' year for a double class intake), with a teaching assistant to support each class teacher, as well as learning support staff, for SEN children. The national curriculum is taught in a topic-based approach over two years, so both years 3 and 4 may be studying the same topic, but with differentiated work, to challenge them at the appropriate time. 'Our children are very good at asking significant questions,' comments the head. There is a 'London school turnover' of staff, including a new deputy and leadership team, who work alongside others, some of nearly 40 years standing.

The curriculum includes French from year 2, Italian from year 3 and students from nearby independent schools visit in the lunch-hour with an introduction to Latin. A feast of extracurricular clubs compliment the children's day: chess, coding (IT, to you and me); as well as yoga, netball, and skittleball. Years 3 and 4 swim at nearby Latymer Upper School and a football team, coached by parents, plays in a local league. One mum described how her son left school with the sports prize, and credited his confidence to the school's ethos: 'I feel he can deal with anything'. There is a tuneful school choir and, since the recent introduction of individual instrument lessons, a nascent orchestra. Performances for the parents have included Wind in the Willows, Fantastic Mr Fox and scenes from Harry Potter. Drama club, we heard, is 'incredibly well attended'.

John Betts, a Victorian physician and philanthropist, established the school in 1859 under a trust and it continues to operate as one of only two voluntary aided non-denominational schools in London. The founder's desk fills the head's office and his portrait on the wall oversees that his original vision continues, as a non-denominational school with Christian values. 'The values that are handed down at John Betts are still her,' a former parent told us. 'My son has been taught to be kind, and tolerant and independent'. Sitting on the north east edge of Ravenscourt Park, the building is sometimes mistaken for a church, with its stately gabled frontage and marble portico. The local area embraces both community housing and smart stucco villas of Ravenscourt Park, so there is a vibrant cross-section of locals, 'a good reflection of London,' commented the welcoming receptionist. A short bus ride down the road are the business hubs of Hammersmith and Shepherds Bush, but inside the school's sleek new lobby, you are greeted by an oasis of calm and orderliness. We were slightly bewildered by the labyrinthine layout of the school, the three buildings of contrasting age and style interconnecting with stairwells and walkways.

Downstairs the younger children enjoy a low level suite of modern rooms, and an ICT studio, with smoky picture windows, which open directly into the playground. A glass canopy shelters the children walking to and from the adjacent 1980s extension, which houses a year 5 class. As we peek in, groups of six children round work tables are chatting constructively about maths. The individual tip-lid desks are stacked outside waiting to be auctioned at the Christmas fête. 'They made it very static,' explains the head. 'Tables allow the children to have experience of moving round the room'. An old school hand-bell marks the boundary with the original Victorian school house with its raftered ceilings and gothic windows, where we find a multipurpose room for music, art and breakfast club as well as an interconnecting classroom for the two bulge classes. The lively displays of work hung from washing lines include rock cycles and ancient Greece, as well as a useful board of speech bubbles, encouraging the children to pipe up confidently with their own ideas: 'I noticed that...' and 'I disagree because...'. The head explains, 'We encourage chat'.

Behind the school, the playground has been given a make-over, thanks to the generous PTA, with an all-sports pitch, climbing equipment, a huge Four-in-a-Row and painted chess boards. Summer sports day is held in the open spaces of Ravenscourt Park.

There is just one hall at present, which converts to the dining room, with congenial round tables. Lunch is cooked on site, by a private catering company, and staff eat with children. Hot lunch is compulsory, to ensure the kitchen is viable, but judging by the aroma of the day's special, Moroccan chicken with apricots, with homemade bread and carrot cake as sides (vegetarian option too), there would be no difficulty persuading children to eat here. Whole school assemblies use the hall every Friday, and British Values (as recommended by DfE's Spiritual, Moral, Social and Cultural development programme) are promoted, in the form of kindness, tolerance, resilience etc. 'We're not just responsible for preparing them for the next step, but preparing them for the rest of their lives', explains the head.

Good behaviour is encouraged with gold awards at assembly, and house points for the three houses, Eagle, Falcon, Hawk (the school council's ice-cream sundae names for houses were vetoed!). Mindfulness and yoga encourage well-being among the students, and if these are too soporific, there's always Wakey Shakey in the playground. There were no reports of bullying – the school council explores both 'bullying' and 'victim' behaviour patterns, and the police visit to teach 'bystander awareness'. One mum reported, 'My daughter takes part in a little nurture group that is all about exploring emotions in a private space for children to talk'.

Teaching tailored to the individual is conspicuous round the school. One mum explained, 'They craft the lessons to engage everybody'. We visited a year 2 maths class, where the majority of the children were involved in a carpet time activity with the class teacher. Nearby a child with special needs was enjoying independent calculations at the computer, while a cluster of faster learners gathered around a table for extension work with the TA. The sense of industry and enthusiasm was contagious and we were pleased to see 'hands up' was still in favour here. 'They work really hard to differentiate and that takes a lot of work behind the scenes,' explained one parent. NHS therapists and SEN support workers visit the children with additional needs. 'Learning support might be for a more able child', explained the head. Despite this, one parent confided, 'tutoring does happen at the school'.

The staff got the popular vote from the children – 'my son just falls in love with each class teacher,' said one mum – and the 'family feel' of the school is upheld by having several ex-parents as employees; others run school clubs. Head takes advantage of the wealth of experience in the cosmopolitan community; we spoke to one mum whose sporting background was used to advise on specialist PE provision. 'I would not have put a hockey stick in a 5 year old's hands,' she said, but applauded the responsible way the specialist PE trainer had supervised the class, 'then the class teacher gets skilled up from watching,' she explained.

We heard about the 'very dynamic PTA' whose reps 'do a good job of keeping everyone up to date'. In addition, the head writes a newsletter each week, and there's a policy that all enquiries receive a response in 24 hours. Parents were aware they could have a quick chat to the class teacher after school, or make an appointment for a longer discussion. The head encourages face-to-face or telephone calls and has a firm view on emails: 'written word can be easily misinterpreted, clear communication is key'. Parents all stressed the 'very close community' feel of the school, and meet frequently at the many events, Christmas and Easter concerts, international day and the summer show, for which the whole school makes costumes, paints sets and sings (year 6s get the speaking parts). Parents help on school trips, popularly to the Kensington museums, Imperial War Museum and even The Royal Opera House, and years 3 and 6 get to go on residentials. 'It's a compliment to the school,' commented one mum, 'that I felt I wanted to put myself up for election for parent/governor....the PTA had quite a few candidates'.

Children looked smart in navy, white and grey uniforms with touches of green and yellow on their stripy ties. The school uniform list on the website speaks volumes: suitable shoes, hair ribbons and no zip up tracksuits. However, the website did come in for criticism from parents: 'desperately needs doing,' said one, who commented that the children on the school council would have a hand in designing a new one. 'The school council is not just a name, they are given autonomy,' she reported. A head girl and head boy are elected, along with prefects, giving the older children an opportunity to write a job application and undertake an interview, the head explained. 'It gives them exposure to talking to adults and public speaking experience'.

Possibly the best bargain in education west of Notting Hill; local authority funded. Extras for school trips made up by parents; PTA funds those who can't pay: 'We don't want any children to be priced out of the school,' said one parent.

Dr John Betts must look on with pride from his gilt-edged portrait in the old study to see how the school's original principles of curiosity and compassion are flourishing. Traditional and modern practices enrich the teaching, add to this mix a dynamic head, a lively modern curriculum and energetic parents, and – local fee-paying institutions beware – this school is a rattling success.

The John Lyon School

Middle Road, Harrow HA2 0HN

Pupils: 600 • Ages: 11–18 • Sixth form: 149

Fees: £16,632 – £17,268 pa

Tel: 020 8515 9400
Email: enquiries@johnlyon.org
Website: www.johnlyon.org

J

Head: Since 2009, Miss Katherine Haynes, BA MEd NPQH (40s). Attended Oxford High School for Girls ('No doubt, that's the reason I'm driven in the way I am'), before reading maths at Warwick, followed by an MEd. Then taught in the Midlands, becoming head of maths at Edgbaston High School, followed by Warwick School, where she first started out as a school inspector and took the professional training scheme for headship. Her appointment at John Lyon made her the first woman ever to head an HMC boys' day school, but she had no hesitation in taking up the challenge. 'I felt I could provide a different perspective and saw what was possible. I wanted to make it more academic and put it on the map.' Has acted decisively on this brief, expanding the academic and extracurricular offering and polishing the pastoral care. Parents undoubtedly appreciate her approach. 'She's vibrant and dynamic, with no airs and graces, no nonsense,' said one fan. In term time she 'lives and breathes' the school, and all praise her involvement with pupils ('She really has time for the boys') and their families ('We were so impressed she invited parents of new boys to dinner at her house'). Continues to work as a school inspector, and, in her limited free time, enjoys gardening and travelling.

Academic matters: Small class sizes (20-23 in years 7-9, 18-24 at GCSE, 10-16 at A level) mean that pupils are well-known by staff. ('A good relationship with teachers helps with their work,' says the head.) Currently reducing GCSE numbers from 10 to nine, 'to give more scope to go beyond the curriculum'. IGCSEs in maths, English and all sciences ('The exams are harder, but they make the transition to A levels smoother'). Carousel of languages, with Mandarin taster in year 8 (including a successful exchange programme with Harrow's sister school in the Far East), Latin from year 8, classical Greek from year 10. Post-GCSE, the school remains happy with A levels, adding classical civilisation, psychology, government and politics, music technology, computer science and, soon DT, to the subject range. Also major emphasis on the EPQ, with an impressive 100 per cent achieving A*-A for the third time in 2016. Results overall very solid (61 per

A*-A at GCSE; 44 per A*-A at A level), a reflection of the effort to instill self-discipline, hard work and high expectations. Parents believe the school gets the balance just right. 'The grades are good, but you're not made to feel awful if you're not at the top of the league tables.'

About seven per cent of pupils receive some sort of learning support (typically for dyslexia), which is provided by two specialist teachers in the learning support department. Those with English as their second language – the school does its best to accommodate families relocating mid year – also aided by a qualified EAL teacher. Gifted-and-talented programme, too, for those in need of 'enrichment'.

Games, options, the arts: Though the school overlooks some of the playing fields of Harrow, its own expansive 25-green acres are a five-minute minibus-ride away. These have recently been updated with a state-of-the art MUGA (Multi-Use Games Areas) pitch, providing excellent floodlit facilities for hockey and tennis alongside football and cricket (and archery!). Pupils also have access to Harrow's nine-hole golf course, squash and tennis courts (clearly made good use of, since one boy recently gained a tennis scholarship to the US). On site, there's a gym, 25m pool and fitness suite, with sporting options including basketball, judo, and badminton.

J

Drama a popular choice at GCSE and A level, with aspiring thespians busily practising their lines outside the two well-used drama studios on our visit. Boys also mount productions at Harrow School's Ryan Theatre and have the opportunity to work with professional companies, including the Donmar Warehouse, the Lyric Hammersmith and the Royal Shakespeare Company. Music – praised by parents as 'phenomenal' – benefits from a purpose-built recording studio.

A 'rounded' education given a firm emphasis, with a timetabled programme of 'skills-based' activities including everything from cooking to changing a tyre. Out-of-lessons options also extensive, with a particularly high take up of Duke of Edinburgh (an impressive 30 pupils successfully completed gold this year). CCF also on offer, as part of the Harrow School cadet force. Plenty of trips (football to Iceland, cricket to South Africa, joint ski trip with Harrow, Wellington and Dulwich) and societies, from computing to chess. 'It's a very broad-ranging education,' commented one contented father.

Background and atmosphere: John Lyon School – established in 1876 to 'educate local boys' – forms part (along with Harrow School) of the John Lyon's Foundation, and sits a street away from Churchill's alma mater in leafy Harrow on the Hill. The two schools have a happy, but not smothering, relationship, with heads of departments meeting for lunch, boys enjoying use of each other's more covetable facilities.

One of the head's greatest achievements has been a 10-year plan to modernise the outdated buildings. First on the list was the introduction of a dining hall. 'I wanted somewhere the whole school could sit and chat.' Moving the library to a new location has provided an attractive central space, where staff and students can socialise over a hot or cold meal (though the food itself is perhaps not a highlight – 'It's OK,' said one boy politely). Other, much-appreciated, improvements include a sixth form centre, occupying the entire Victorian school house, which provides both learning and leisure space for older boys. Next on the agenda is a flagship STEAM (the sciences plus art) building where DT, computer science and maths will unite with art.

A rebrand is also in the pipeline, which, it is hoped, will put the school more prominently in the spotlight. 'People describe us as one of the best kept secrets in London,' says the head, who clearly now intends the secret to leak out. 'We want to bring across the vision of what we represent: heritage and innovation, creativity and resilience.' Other widely acknowledged USPs include 'the family atmosphere,' the 'friendliness' and the attractively small scale. 'It's not too big,' said one father. 'Everyone knows my son's name, from the registrar to the guy who sits on the front desk.' Some feel the rebrand is long overdue. 'The school doesn't beat its own drum enough; it's sometimes seen as an also ran, which it definitely shouldn't be.'

Pastoral care, well-being and discipline: Great praise for the care and attention boys receive, with parents united in the view that the school does its utmost to develop every inch of potential. 'My son is a bright child, but not A*, nor is he massively sporty, but John Lyon is a lovely, nurturing, comfy school, which gets the absolute best out of him.' Confidence building in the public arena very much part of the package. 'My son has really flourished here and is turning into a nice young man who is able to talk to anyone.'

Boys generally motivated and ambitious with little evidence of teenage rebellion. 'We promote a code of conduct rather than having endless rules, so it's usually possible to pull back before declaring "time's up",' says the head. Even so, if that code is broken, lines are firmly drawn.

Girl-free zone compensated for by good links with neighbouring schools, so debating with North London Collegiate and Northwood College, drama with Royal Masonic.

Pupils and parents: Primarily local, very cosmopolitan, with over 50 per cent from Asian families, whose children will often be the first in the family to go to university. 'They're aspirational and hardworking and want to do the best for their children,' says the head. Boys are positive, focussed and keen.

Alumni include Michael Bogdanov, theatre director, Timothy West, actor, Stephen Pollard, journalist and Alastair Fraser, cricketer.

Entrance: At 11, 75 per cent come from local primaries (about 300 apply for 100 places, with increasing numbers making John Lyon their first choice); at 13 (when three or four forms expand to five), all from local preps, with main feeders Durston House, St Martin's, Orley Farm. The school is academically selective, but here the term 'potential' is not just rhetoric. All applicants are interviewed by senior staff (at 13, all by the head), with the intention of snuffling out 'those happy to be busy, active and willing to push themselves'. Small intake into the sixth form, plus occasional mid-year admissions.

Exit: A dozen or so leave post-GCSE for local sixth form colleges. Of the remainder, 70-80 per cent to their first choice of university, with significant numbers to leading London colleges (LSE and King's), then Russell Group (50 per cent) countrywide. University advice up-to-date and thoughtfully tailored to individual needs (including STEP classes for mathematicians). 'We're ambitious for boys and see what's possible,' says the dynamic head of university applications. High proportion to professional degrees in science (medicine, dentistry, etc), law, economics, architecture and finance.

Money matters: Good value. The John Lyon's Charity continues to help with means-tested bursaries.

Remarks: A small, thriving school, with historic links to Harrow School, which provides a well-rounded, well-grounded education in a welcoming atmosphere.

Keble Prep School

Wades Hill, London N21 1BG

Pupils: 220 • Ages: 4–13

Fees: £11,280 – £14,280 pa

Tel: 020 8360 3359
Email: office@kebleprep.co.uk
Website: www.kebleprep.co.uk

Headmaster: Since 2006, Mr Jed McCarthy (50s). Studied maths and management at Queen Elizabeth College, London, PGCE at the Institute of Education, then worked in state schools in Brent. Left the profession to spend five years in industry, but realised he 'really missed teaching' and returned to Orley Farm, where he remained for 16 years (as head of maths, director of studies and deputy head). A quietly-spoken enthusiast, Mr McCarthy has worked determinedly to build up the esprit de corps of pupils and parents and undoubtedly succeeded. Parents are lavish in their praise. 'He's always waiting at the gate and has a genuine interest in each boy,' said one mother. 'He's a very caring, very nurturing gentleman,' said another. Parents are also grateful for his availability and effectiveness. 'He's always ready to hear you out about any little gripe and he really gets things done.' Two grown-up sons.

Retiring in July 2017. His succcessor will be Mark Mitchell, currently head of Terra Nova School in Cheshire. He started his career as a science teacher at Ardingly, moving to King's House School and then Feltonfleet before joining Terra Nova in 2008 as head of science and then deputy head. Mark's wife Elanor is a teacher at the school, and they have two young children.

Entrance: Register a couple of years before entry at 4 but pressure on places is not intense. The school is non-selective. Some new entrants from the state sector at 11.

Exit: A small exodus at 11 to high-achieving local grammar schools and comprehensives but head hopes to attract parents who understand the benefits of a school that runs to 13. 'I believe in 13 plus,' he says. At that age, Mill Hill and St Albans are historically the two most popular choices, but horizons are expanding – 'we are sending boys to Highgate, City, UCS, Westminster, St Edmund's Ware and St Columba's'. Wherever pupils go, the school does its utmost to ensure the best match between boy and school – 'we know the boys very well and recommend on personality'.

Remarks: A small school, which hovers at around 200 boys in all, so class size is reflectively intimate, ranging from 12-15 in two parallel forms. In the early years the school follows the national curriculum, with add-ons such as French, which starts in year 3. The pace is accelerated and curriculum expanded as boys get older – 'we adapt it to the boys, easing into common entrance after 11,' says the head. Specialist teaching in music and PE in first two years, then further specialisation in art, ICT and French; by year 5, all subjects taught by specialists.

Enthusiastic teaching and boy-friendly approach. 'We try to make it very hands on,' said one teacher. 'We make models and castles.' Parents praise staff highly. 'My son is motivated, interested and enthused. It's a great credit to the teachers,' said a mother. 'The teachers are incredibly encouraging,' said another. In the past, the school has been criticised for not necessarily stretching the brightest, but the head has spent time, effort and money rebalancing that equation – 'and we're not finished yet'. A director of studies now has a clear brief and the brightest are given differentiated teaching in class and one-to-one support out of it. Boys are setted in English and maths from year 5, with informal setting in science, French and humanities.

The philosophy, however, is very much 'each child is an individual' and the struggling are equally well guided, with the full range of SEN support. The school deals comfortably with dyslexia and dyspraxia, mild autism and Asperger's. 'What I'm trying to do is not be the most academic school,' says the head, 'but to get all boys to expect more of themselves, set themselves higher standards and achieve them.' And parents confirm this is what happens – 'They really understand my son's strengths and weakness and really nourish him. I'm certain they meet all the boys' needs, even those at opposite ends of the spectrum'.

This is a small site and facilities are relatively restricted, though there is a French room and small science lab. Rebuild has brought more classroom space, a new science lab and an art room, allowing for relocation of the library, which had doubled as a music room. Limited space, too, for sports (though an attractive small gym), but games, played twice a week, are taken seriously. Rugby (reintroduced by the head), football, cricket and tennis are the main menu and a school minibus transports players to local and distant pitches. Rugby has put the school back on the prep school circuit. 'We mainly play other small local schools,' says the head. 'We lose more than we win, but we do play – and have tea afterwards.' Parents feel that even the sportiest get sufficient exercise and opportunity. 'A new PE teacher has invited a Tottenham scout to come to the school'. Numerous lunch-time and after-school clubs include puzzle club, movie club, common entrance drop-in club.

Has been going for 80 years, a lone prep school in an affluent suburban area of north London. Its aim now, as always, is to serve the local community, a community of small family businesses rather than City professionals. Many parents are first-time buyers. 'Our parents often want what they didn't have for themselves,' says the head. Many have Mediterranean roots (Turkish, Spanish, Greek, Italian, Cypriot) and a firm belief in family, and the school reflects those values with a strong family atmosphere.

Very much a traditional prep, it retains distinctive black and yellow blazers, formal good manners and neatly knotted ties. Boys still wear shorts in the warmer months and long hair is definitely frowned upon. Pastoral care is equally old school. 'We're looking for grounded, rounded individuals,' says the head. 'We cope well with all manner of children.' The aim is supportive rather than hothouse. 'We don't want to put pressure on ridiculously young. We want them to achieve, but not by testing to the eyeballs'. The mood is friendly and safe: 'If you're stuck on something,' said one boy, 'there's always a teacher to help you,' and the atmosphere is orderly and quiet, with bright noticeboards and well-run classrooms.

A 'big brother, little brother' scheme matches older pupils with younger ones – evident and unaffected warmth stretching across the age divide. On our visit, a boy at the top of the school, clearly revered by a recent arrival, praised his small friend for being able to tie his tie. Discipline is firm but certainly not draconian. 'Can you do it better?' is the gentle reproach. Pupils thrive on it. 'If I'm honest,' said one undoubtedly honest young man in his final year, 'I love the school and I'm going to miss it when I leave'. Parents are equally positive. 'We chose it because it's very friendly and has a great identity that boys can relate to. I wish I could find a school for my daughter that is as good as this one'. 'We love the school. It's a home from home,' said another. 'My son looks forward to going to school every day.' Keble is not a wealthy or notably well endowed place, but is undoubtedly a happy and safe haven, where all boys are treated with respect and respond in kind. A very secure place to start your school days.

Kensington Prep School

596 Fulham Road, London SW6 5PA

Pupils: 296 • Ages: 4–11

Fees: £15,897 pa

Tel: 020 7731 9300
Email: enquiries@kenprep.gdst.net
Website: www.kensingtonprep.gdst.net

Head: Since 2003, Mrs Prudence Lynch MA PGCE, a caring visionary, who seeks to equip her pupils fully for life's future challenges. After studying psychology at St Andrews, she obtained her PGCE at Goldsmiths. She has much experience in London preparatory schools, including working in the all-male environment of St Paul's Juniors.There she established the SEN department and taught maths, study skills and 'thinking' before moving on to heading the juniors at Notting Hill & Ealing, a sister GDST school. Small in stature and, trendily, rather than conventionally attired, she loves teaching philosophy, something she introduced into the curriculum in her first year. She scurries energetically around the school and, during our visit, we noticed how well she knows individual girls, thoughtfully picking up on any pastoral concerns. Parents like the fact that 'she listens, is not saccharine but respected by the girls and visible around the school.' They appreciate how forward-thinking the school is under her leadership and are 'blown away at how the children learn, not just academic subjects but how they learn to be emotionally aware'.

Mrs Lynch's ongoing zest to keep on testing boundaries, take risks and work collaboratively with her 'amazing staff' goes hand in hand with her clear regard for values, traditions and the importance of providing girls with opportunities to develop skills of resilience, reflectiveness, resourcefulness, reasoning and a sense of responsibility. Parents commented to us that as early as 5, 'The girls know what it means to be a resilient learner and to persevere.' The pupils we spoke to find her to be 'creative; her assemblies entertain us so we learn something new every day'. Her playful approach belies just how serious she is to take the school with her 'on a learning journey', maximising the stunning new learning facilities, alongside the development of coaching for staff as well as pupils. 'My passion is bringing staff on. No one can do it all and my team are experts in what they do. I value freedom of ideas and see my role as an enabler.' She confesses to being somewhat scatty; others supply the administrative skills. Staff retention is high, with many returners, and we saw several males heading English, maths, music departments as well as an assistant head.

A proud grandmother of three, outside school Mrs Lynch sings, reads, walks her dog, is a beginner learner of Arabic and a keen bird spotter. A trip to Uganda with a missionary friend has led to her paying towards supporting children there, and she greatly appreciates the large sums raised for charities by the girls with parental support. Mrs Lynch is immensely proud of KP's academic excellence and high achievements, but firmly believes that 'these are only possible with strong values, so girls feel safe and secure to become risk takers. Unless the culture is right girls, in particular, can't flourish'. Her office looks out on the bright, spacious playground with two adjacent courts and she commented on how, when she arrived, she introduced the climbing apparatus and equipment which allow the girls to place them 'outside their comfort zone', symbolic of the learning style favoured here.

Entrance: Girls come from 40 local nurseries and most live locally, many within walking distance. There are over 200 applicants for 44 places at 4+. Register any time up to September prior to entry the following September, with assessments in January. Girls are seen in groups of five or six and observed during play with every aspect graded. Mrs Lynch comments, 'I couldn't care if they can recite the three times table. I want to know if they understand the threeness of things in another context.' An understanding of English is important she advises: 'It's no good if they have no basic understanding of what is going on and what adults say to them'. At 7 + there are a very few places but it is always worth trying as occasional places do crop up. Siblings accepted provided they can cope, but this is not automatic.

Exit: Mrs Lynch is aware that most parents choose KP for its excellent results. She observes, 'Fewer are considering boarding schools and the majority want selective, academic girls' day schools.' Nevertheless in recent years girls have been awarded scholarships to Wycombe Abbey, St Mary's Ascot, Benenden and Downe House. Consistently offers are made to St Paul's Girls' School, Godolphin & Latymer, Putney High and Wimbledon High with a few to Latymer Upper. Twenty-seven scholarships in 2016: 14 academic, nine music, three art and one sport. Parents we spoke to who had experienced the ruthless competitive examination process commented on how they have complete confidence in the school system, and how well prepared the girls are so that they feel very secure. One recalled that the girls did knitting on a Friday afternoon to keep them calm. The process is carefully managed with plenty of meetings in years 5 and 6 alongside an Open Door for advice from the head, although her direct comments 'have ruffled feathers,' say some parents. As one parent remarked, 'The head is key in any school and she has a fantastic staff and very good relationships with other schools.'

Remarks: Founded in 1873 in Kensington, it was the first school to be established by the Girls' Day School Trust and today the only stand alone prep school in the group. In 1997 it moved to its present site, previously a secondary Marist convent in just over an acre of grounds. Mrs Lynch clearly values belonging to the GDST, which provides expertise and financial support alongside independence. The trust cares about the ongoing professional development of its leaders and staff. September 2016 saw the completion of a £2.7million building project appropriately titled Creative Spaces for Growing Minds. We saw the multimedia recording studio, and the eco greenhouse which complements the outside garden and pond. We were delighted to see the girls thoroughly enjoying their spacious classrooms with breakout areas and retractable doors, as well as the improved specialist drama, art, science and IT suites and two new lifts making the school thoroughly accessible throughout.

We witnessed a year 2 geography project work on the hi tech Explore floor. A carousel of 10 minute activities meant groups of six learnt about the United Kingdom in a stimulating, exciting way. Some learnt to use directions accurately and programmed small robots, others learnt to recognise London landmarks, whilst others learnt the difference between physical and human features. The girls we spoke to 'love the freedom to do what you like in learning. The teachers make maths and science fun.' Perhaps that explains why they do so well, winning the GDST Maths Competition in 2015 and in 2016, and four year 6 girls qualified for the UK MT Maths Challenge designed for years 7 and 8.

The dining room looks inviting with its bright colour scheme, modern lighting and freshly cooked food on the premises, which we sampled and enjoyed. There are a few classrooms with traditional desks but all have plenty of light and space. Accomplished artwork decorates walls, many of which are crammed with questions and ongoing thinking by pupils, not often seen on a school tour. Self-directed, independent and collaborative ways to learn abound, and in such an academic environment, girls need to be robust and willing to participate if they are to thrive.

With two courts on site as well as nearby Fulham pools and King's House Sports Grounds for sports day, girls are given plenty of opportunities to play in fixtures. In truth the games department is eclipsed by the starry music department. Girls perform at Cadogan Hall and there are three choirs, four orchestras, chamber ensembles and a main orchestra with over 100 players. A biannual overseas music tour takes place to Europe, for example to Holland and Venice, with a planned visit to Budapest. An artist in residence works alongside the art teacher as well as providing clubs. There is no pottery but we saw accomplished models. There is an extensive club programme which includes football and trips galore.

The early years section is superbly resourced inside and outside with free flow. The girls we saw were fully engaged in a breadth of activities without realising they were being assessed by experienced staff. One parent shared how 'the girls hear about fairies or the Big Bad Wolf visiting, and in year 2 a fairy lives in the classroom and girls can write to her if they have a concern and receive a reply.' Parents love their fact their daughters are happy and have fun at school. A director of individualised learning and assistant learning support coordinator ensure pupils are given extra support at different levels where necessary. This may be small group support by a teaching assistant or teacher within or outside the classroom. A school counsellor is in school three days a week. The online communication system supports homework with iPads and a learning platform showing how mathematics has been taught in the lesson.

Parents we spoke to remarked, 'The school has a lovely community feeling and right from the start girls know how important it is to be kind and good.' This is a caring, not a cosy school where girls need to be willing to be challenged. In 2015 inspectors awarded the school the highest possible grades across the board. They rated the quality of pupils' learning and achievements exceptional. This is not a school for the fainthearted, staff or pupils, but it is one where all share the excitement and creativity of learning. KP is the ideal school for a high flyer. The pace is fast and the girls are happy, have fun and are zippy.

Kew College

24-26 Cumberland Road, Kew, Richmond, Surrey TW9 3HQ

Pupils: 160 • Ages: 3-11

Fees: £11,025 pa

Tel: 020 8940 2039
Email: enquiries@kewcollege.com
Website: www.kewcollege.com/

Headmistress: Since 2013, Mrs Marianne Austin (60s). Read geography at Durham and then spent two years at Sheffield doing an MA in town planning before becoming a chartered accountant, working at the (then) Coopers and Lybrand. Initially fired to teach when her daughter began nursery here, she arrived at Kew College in 2002 and has never looked back. ('I love the school and believe completely in what we're trying to do'). Has taught in years 2, 4 and 6, became deputy head in 2010 and three years later took over the reins. Mrs Austin exudes calmness and warmth, and a determination to support and empower all constituencies including her staff, whose professionalism and commitment evidently help to inspire her own. 'We obviously want the children to feel secure and happy' she says, 'not least because we want to foster a culture which allows them to take risks. And that's a life skill for which the need will never go away.' Loves travel and skiing and spending time with her husband and daughter and with her family in Ireland.

Entrance: Children can start in the nursery aged 3 – there are two classes, one in the morning and one in the afternoon. Get their names down as early as possible – any time from birth. There's no examination or interview, though prospective parents are required, as a condition of entry, to attend an open morning to get a feel for the place. Priority is given to siblings, and to the sons and daughters of ex-pupils. Mrs Austin says this does not occasion resentment 'because it's transparent'. Clear belief that, so long as parents are invested, this is a school in which almost any child can thrive. 'My daughter came from the state sector,' said one parent. 'There are no airs and graces here, but terrific values.'

Exit: Everyone leaves at 11, many to the big hitters in West London – Hampton, Lady Eleanor Holles, Putney High, Emanuel, Kingston, Godolphin & Latymer, KCS Wimbledon, Notting Hill and Ealing High. Some boys go on to prep schools (St Paul's Juniors and Westminster Under). Boarding very seldom on the radar.

Remarks: Warm-hearted and effervescent learning environment. Staff are guided by the national curriculum, but teaching and learning go way beyond. In the nursery and kindergarten years, a clear emphasis on social skills and physical literacy, but of also being gently led into reading, writing and elementary maths. By the time children move into the infant house in years 1 and 2, ICT and science have become more fully integrated, and the children are becoming exposed to more specialist subject teaching. French (emphasis on lots of lovely sounds) actually begins in nursery, and 'understanding the world' introduces younger children to what will later become science.

Reading is huge here. Right from the start reading at home is encouraged. From year I, a 10 minute spell of nightly homework is also expected and, by gentle incremental steps, this is increased as children get older. A very industrious feel to the place, but none of the anxiety of a hothouse. 'They help children to extend their ambition in every way,' said one parent, 'but without getting het up.' Particular praise for thorough marking – 'lots of red and green ink, full of attainable target-setting and constructive comments,' said parent. Learning support is sensitively managed, with a SENCo and assistant 'The specific needs of children change,' says the head. 'Sometimes it's just a bit of anxiety'. Other issues, such as dyslexia, need longer-term support. But all children, however much or little help they receive, are fully integrated into the life of the school. Occasionally there are those with more significant needs, and every attempt is made to support them.

The school is housed in two big Victorian houses – classic west London stuff. 'We've been lucky,' says head. 'The original buildings were gifted to us by our founder' – something which has allowed the fees to remain at a relatively modest level compared to some. Now a third big building has been bought just alongside, soon to become home to many of the older boys and girls and to the art department. A further consequence will be the rehousing of the library – 'right at the heart of the school, as it should be', says Mrs Austin.

Although the present site is on the edge of being cramped – packed lunches on site are essential – there's no sense of crowding. Timetables have been carefully worked to minimise bodies having to jostle, and classrooms comfortably accommodate classes of never more than 20 children. There's no sense of claustrophobia – rather of light, of bustling creativity and of calm good relationships. At the back, just across the school playground is the Octagon – a purpose built block dating from about 2000 which houses younger pupils.

Masses of sport – football, rugby, netball and athletics especially, and plenty of swimming – with plenty of fixtures with other schools. 'It's lovely to win,' says the head, 'which, fortunately, they often do. Sometimes, of course, they don't – and that's education.' There aren't any rolling acres here, so there's a coach ride for everyone on a Tuesday and Thursday afternoon to sports grounds only five minutes away.

The school also hums with music (the Young Voices choir was practising when we arrived – a very joyful sound). A wind band, a strings group, a young voices choir, jazz band, and lots of beat and drumming, and masses of music technology. There's a special art day every couple of years with visits from the specialists at the V&A. Clubs, in and after school, have that same determined outreach – not only those with a digital and IT base, of course, but masses of dance and even one for Lego.

Pastoral care is taken very seriously. Every Monday, the head meets with staff and their first item of business is identifying pupils who present concerns. The school has identified a range of structures best calculated to serve the children's interests – a house system, of course (excellent for games) but also heads of year who liaise closely with form teachers to ensure a full and up-to-date flow of information and insight. Lots of outings, of course, and older children might take longer school trips – year 5 were at Hooke Court in Dorset during our visit. The school is evidently proud of its traditions as well as of its routines – Founder' Day each spring is a major jamboree, and allows pupils to come together with teachers and other friends of the school.

The policy of teachers of other years visiting all parts of the school frequently helps accustom young children to faces which might otherwise be unfamiliar. Before moving to a new class, there are 'transition' days to help acclimatise, and that extends to opportunities for parents to hear the reflections of parents with older children who've already made the journey. It's easy to spot the confidence which flows between the different constituencies here. The recessional at the end of each day eloquently combines pupil safety with a gentle exercise in toujours la politesse.

The wholeheartedness of the children (very apparent) is suggestive – they seem to have imbibed a confidence and optimism from other pupils and teachers and also, no doubt about it, from their families. This is a school in which the parents' investment – emotional, social and financial – reflects a deep commitment to education in the fullest sense. Parents are big fundraisers for the school (the school minibus and a massive investment in the library are recent examples). Mrs Austin is emphatic that the exchange of confidence and goodwill adds immeasurably to the potential of the school. 'Children all feel part of the bigger picture,' said one parent. 'I don't know quite how they do it, but it's exceptional. They think beyond themselves, and it spills over into everything.'

K

Kew Green Preparatory School

Layton House, Ferry Lane, Richmond TW9 3AF

Pupils: 275 • Ages: 4–11

Fees: £16,215 pa

Tel: 020 8948 5999
Email: secretary@kgps.co.uk
Website: www.kgps.co.uk

Head: Since 2004, Mr Jem Peck BSc (geography) PGCE (science) (both from Kingston University). Taught at St John's, Kingston for nine years, then moved out of education altogether for six years into the corporate world, where he focused on event production, marketing, PR and team-building. Gaining this wider perspective has been 'incredibly helpful' to his current role, he says, 'particularly for recruitment and driving the creative feel of the school.'

A very visible presence throughout the school, he teaches English and reasoning to year 6 and is often in and out of the classrooms. Enthusiastic yet calm, he gets down to the kids' level when talking to them. 'Unlike many heads in the private sector, he praises the children directly rather than turning his back on them to tell the parent,' one parent added. He has a door that's always open (except for the very occasional sensitive meeting) to his office – which, by the way, is both the most stylish and child-friendly we've ever seen for a head teacher, complete with sink-in sofa and swivel armchairs, matching navy furniture, open fire and more toys than many home playrooms have. 'Children know they can pop in whenever they want and they very often do, whether it's to have a jam on my guitar, discuss ideas to improve the school or just instead of going outside to play,' he says. During our visit, even kids that had recently left the school popped their heads in with big smiles. Does it interrupt his day? 'That is my day!' he laughs. 'Paperwork can be left.'

Parents, whom he greets every morning, tell us they also feel welcome to pop in any time. 'There's no need to email first – if you have a concern, you can talk to him, or indeed any of the other staff, that very day,' says one, although another told us, 'You can find yourself being pushed in a direction you don't necessarily want to go when you talk to him. For instance, he's good at persuading you that things you think are important are actually not.'

When not in school, you'll usually find him at sister schools Ravenscourt Park (primary) and Kew House (senior). He lives in Surbiton, has a teenage son and is a keen musician.

Entrance: Entrance is non-selective, with applications accepted on a first-come-first-served basis. This means you'll need to get in quick, particularly as this heavily oversubscribed school (which has some 90-160 applications for every 40 places in reception) accepts registrations from birth. Eighteen months before children are due to start, the school gives the parents a call to check they're happy to continue their journey. An informal taster day helps the children settle in and every year group has two classes of 20, with an equal gender split where possible. Occasional places (mainly when pupils leave because their families relocate) become available higher up the school, for which the school asks to see a report from the current school.

Exit: Significant numbers of year 6s leave with scholarships (nine in 2016) including academic, all-round, art, sport and music. Feeds a large number of London schools, notably Westminster, LEH, Hampton, Latymer, Notting Hill and Ealing, Kew House, Kingston Grammar, Surbiton High, St Paul's, St Paul's Juniors, Godolphin & Latymer.

Remarks: The story goes that Maria and Ted Gardener, owners of Ravenscourt Park Prep School (which was becoming increasingly oversubscribed) were walking along the Thames towpath in Kew, when they spotted a tall Georgian style building that they immediately fell in love with. 'Mrs Gardener was so keen to see more of it that she got on his shoulders to look over the wall,' says the head. A year later, in 2004, the school opened there.

Overlooking the River Thames at the back and Kew Green at the front, the location of this school is made all the more impressive by its neighbours – Kew Gardens – where pupils often drop by with teachers as part of their learning. By no means the largest of facilities, you won't get the likes of science labs or food tech areas here, but pupils get full use of these and other amenities at Kew House, the school's sister senior school. And although classrooms aren't huge, they are perfectly adequate for the small class sizes and all boast huge windows and high ceilings, keeping them light and airy.

In the basement is the staff room and the school hall, which doubles up as the dining room (and where the very popular food is made from scratch on site); the ground floor is home to the headteacher's office and admin rooms, as well as some classrooms; and the upper two floors house more classrooms (all well-resourced) and private study rooms, including for music lessons. All are spotless, welcoming and colourful, with masses of original artwork (not just paintings, but sculptures and textiles) adorning the walls and shelves, whilst the atmosphere is noticeably buzzy, both during and between classes. 'I don't expect military precision silence at any other time than assembly,' says the head. 'In fact, I'm pleased if the children are having lively discussions when they come down the stairs because it's bound to impact on their learning, whilst classes themselves tend to be very interactive.'

The single-storey building at the front of the school – again homely and packed with artwork – is the early years centre, whilst three innovative wooden, glass-fronted pods are used for music lessons and small group work for SEN. The playground at the back consists of a double tennis court and a smaller lower level, but fun-packed, outside play area.

The ethos, which aims to be the same as its two sister schools, is all about increasing self-esteem, encouraging children to be confident to ask questions and make mistakes without feeling intimidated – all with the overall aim of enabling them to flourish, not just as learners, but people. Parents are overwhelmingly supportive of this. 'This is a school that's all about celebrating attitude and effort, not just what is actually achieved,' raved one. 'Each class does an assembly once a term that parents attend, and it's wonderful watching the children get increasingly confident at speaking and performing. Even the quiet ones come completely out of their shell,' said another. Particularly striking is the friendliness of the school, with every teacher knowing every child's name, and the have-a-go culture, with children clearly keen to participate and try out new things. 'Life is so full of stopping children doing things and saying no, but we want to say yes, give it a try, see how you get on,' explains the head.

Parents we spoke to feel the pace at which the children learn academic subjects is spot on, picking up in year 5. 'If you're the kind of parent that wants to hand over a wad of cash to a school to turn your child into a genius, then this isn't for you,' one parent told us. 'I live near a school where you hear the teachers drilling times tables into them as they line up for lunch, and Kew Green is the polar opposite, giving kids a chance to be children rather than being forced into academic pressures, tests and exams from day one. The lovely thing is they still reach their full potential.'

Most of the parents we spoke to also felt that a refreshing aspect of the school is that the raison d'être is not getting bums on seats in the premiership senior schools, despite the fact that they do get many kids in there. 'The school gets that not every child is destined to wind up at the likes of St Paul's, whilst still managing to pave the way for the ones who are bright enough to get in without any need for extra tutoring,' summed up one parent. 'We want to recognise the strengths of every child here, and understand that not everyone is great at the likes of maths and English,' says the head, although one parent we spoke to says they felt pushed to apply for schools they felt were too academic for their child.

Lessons are based on the national curriculum, but with added enrichment, mainly in the form of workshops (bringing in small mammals and reptiles for younger ones and songwriters from the music industry for the older ones are two typical examples) and trips (to museums, galleries and of course Kew) that aim to bring learning to life. Poetry competitions through to maths challenges are another popular way of embedding learning beyond the national curriculum. There is setting from year 3 in maths and English, although head says 'it's a flexible feast,' and there are subject specialist teachers for art, music, PE and French.

French is taught from reception upwards, with Spanish, German and Italian part of the 50 extracurricular clubs on offer per week. Other clubs include sports such as judo, modelling, cooking, digital photography, computer programming, touch typing, writing, film club, children's newspaper, just to name a few. Whilst many of these finish at 4.30pm, the school is open from as long as 8am-6pm for an extra fee (includes tea). Parents and pupils say the level of homework is reasonable and flexible. 'If there's a birthday or a theatre trip, then it's fine to miss it,' says the head.

Teachers are well thought of. 'They don't just know some stuff, they seem to know everything,' one pupil enthused. 'If you ask them a question, their answer is 10 times as good as what you wanted it to be,' said another. Lessons, say pupils, are fun and never dull. One parent told us how his son arrived from a nursery where he'd been written off as a 'naughty boy.' 'The head of lower school at Kew Green, whom I can't praise enough, asked if I'd had his hearing tested and sure enough, he had glue ear. Two sets of grommets later, he was a different child and I can't thank them enough.'

There's extra (mainly classroom or small group based) provision for those requiring learning support (14 SEN when we visited, two of whom were statemented), particularly dyslexia, dyspraxia and autistic spectrum, via the progress centre, which is run by the school SENCo and three other staff members involved on a part-time basis. Specialist help, including speech and language therapy and OT, is brought in. 'If I could change anything, it would be making this a bigger department, with help put in place quicker, but what's amazing about this school and SEN is that issues are never brushed under the carpet or stigmatised, which has been my experience at other schools,' says one parent.

Creativity is central, with the school boasting an Artsmark gold award. There are weekly drama classes for all year groups and class performances to parents once a term, along with opportunities for larger performances at various touchpoints throughout the school. Film-making is also valued, especially in year 6 where, after the 11+ exams, pupils make a film in French, which is then shown at a larger school event with a French theme. 'It's a real highlight of the year,' said one parent.

Meanwhile, the range of art opportunities on offer in the weekly lessons is more akin to a secondary school, including fine art, pottery, ceramics, textiles, screen painting, Photoshop and more – with more than enough facilities to support it. Pupils' work has been exhibited at the likes of the National Gallery, Hampton Court Palace and Saatchi Gallery – testament to the artistic talent here.

Around two-thirds (190 when we visited) of pupils learn a musical instrument during the school day. 'You name an instrument and we'll teach it if a pupil wants to learn,' says the head, whilst parents told us they seem to find the right instrument for the right child. In addition, there are two choirs (upper and lower schools), a chamber choir (for which pupils audition), an orchestra and ensembles for guitar, strings and brass. There are plenty of music assemblies, which are just as likely to involve children who have only just started learning an instrument as more experienced ones, as well as opportunities to perform more publically. When we visited, year 4s were practising a song they'd written (lyrics and music) ready to perform later that week with a full orchestra.

Sport is valued here, although only tennis and netball takes place on the school grounds, whilst rugby, football, cricket, hockey, rounders and athletics are played on the green opposite. Other local facilities, such as Pools on the Park, Brentford Dryside Gymnasiusm, Westminster Sports Ground and Old Deer Park, enable students to participate in gymnastics, dance, swimming, cross-country, fitness lessons, athletics and traditional team-sports, for which there are specialist coaches. Years 3-6 take part in competitive fixtures with other local schools and the school hosts netball, football and rugby festivals.

K

Pastoral care is strong, helped by the high staff-to-pupil ratio and small class sizes, plus the fact that children are regularly reminded who they can talk to about any concerns. There are also class talks on issues such as positivity and anti-bullying and the students themselves have created a set of 'guiding principles,' including being respectful of others and listening to others. By and large, the children seem to live by them. In fact, the head says discipline isn't a word you'll hear much as behaviour is excellent. 'A simple nod usually does the trick if anybody oversteps the mark,' he explains. The last half-hour of lesson time on a Friday is dedicated to 'reflection time,' which allows teachers to reflect on individual or group successes and resolve any conflicts or concerns so that children don't have to carry them over the weekend. There are leadership opportunities for all year 6s, who are automatically made prefects and who regularly read with the younger years. 'The strength of the relationships across the school is very strong,' said one parent.

Residential trips include Norfolk for year 3s (team building and climbing); Devon for year 4s (orienteering and physical skills); camping in Snowdonia for year 5s (climbing, team building, camping and abseiling); and France for a ski trip for year 6s, along with a week of challenging water sports back in Devon. Other recent examples include netball trip to Brussels, choir tours to Paris, Venice and Tuscany and an annual year 5 visit to the Christmas markets in Lille.

The majority of children live within a three mile radius – mainly Kew, Chiswick, Richmond, Barnes and Hammersmith – most of whom walk, cycle, scoot or use public transport or one of the two school buses (use of cars discouraged, although in reality there is the inevitable jam of 4x4s at drop-off and pick-up). The pupil body is reflective of the area with the majority of pupils being of white British origin, with a quarter coming from European or ethnic backgrounds. Families are a broad mix of professions including media types, lawyers, bankers and quite a few celebs. Parents are encouraged to get involved in school life, often giving presentations on careers and interests, and there's a lively PA, called The Friends, which organises both social and fundraising events.

'My parents moved here for the school,' one pupil told us and it's easy to see why. This is a happy, friendly and nurturing school where the children are self-assured without being conceited, and where all abilities learn together, each flourishing in their own individual way. Probably not for go-getting parents that want their offspring to get top grades in everything, no matter what, or for parents who want their children to learn in a highly competitive or traditional environment. Not that it lacks academic rigour, with some impressive pupil destinations proving that the school caters for the very bright. A school for introverts and extroverts alike, we found the atmosphere to be caring, spirited and creative. 'It's the parents who have to drag the kids out of school at the end of the day here because they just have such a lovely time,' summed up one parent.

King Alfred School

Manor Wood, 149 North End Road, London NW11 7HY

Pupils: 652 • Ages: 4–18 • Sixth form: 106

Fees: £14,862 – £17,916 pa

Tel: 020 8457 5200
Email: admissions@kingalfred.org.uk
Website: www.kingalfred.org.uk

Head: Since 2015, Robert Lobatto, previously head of Barnhill Community High in Hayes. He has an Oxford history degree and has taught in several inner London comprehensives, including Highbury Fields School in Islington. He decided to leave the state sector because of its increasingly narrow focus on academic performance, he told the Ham and High newspaper.

Head of junior school: Mr David Weale BSc PGCE.

Academic matters: A school where exams are famously not the only priority. Pupils sit no formal exams until year 10, although each subject has its own testing process to ensure students are ready for GCSEs. That said, prides itself on being able to teach to the highest standards – 'if a child can get four or five A*s, we'll get them there'. Pleasing results at GCSE (most pupils take nine), with 53 per cent A*/A grades in 2016; disappointing 34 per cent A*/A and 66 per cent A*/B at A level. Exams may not be the main focus, but 'personalised learning' definitely is, and parents feel happy that every child is treated as an individual. 'We have no idea who the clever children are,' said one. 'All are special – they're not compared to one another.'

Not a vast range of subject choice at GCSE (curriculum languages French, Spanish and Latin); good variety at A level, with 24 options, and every attempt is made to accommodate any combination. The classroom approach, as with the whole-school approach, is relaxed. 'Teachers are not that strict,' said one senior school pupil. 'It can sometimes take quite a long time for lessons to begin, but you're still motivated to work.' Homework and marking, however, can be a bit too relaxed for some. 'The school believes that children should be children,' said one mother. 'I like the fact that it doesn't force them to do two hours a night, but sometimes I think they could push a little more.'

Sixth form particularly strong in the expressive arts (photography amongst the best in the country) and arts subjects (English, history); scientists generally find themselves in a minority. A few vocational options post-GCSE (business studies and music technology).

Additional support is available for students with mild specific learning difficulties – individually, in groups or in class. Students are monitored throughout their time at the school. Teachers build up a picture of pupils' learning profiles and identify those who might require specific intervention.

Games, options, the arts: Known for its creativity and the strength of its visual arts teaching; all lower school classrooms have ovens for baking and the school has its own forge. Thriving drama, with theatre, 'black box' studio and masterclasses often given by parents who are themselves leading lights in the profession; offers a performing arts BTec alongside theatre studies A level. There are two well-stocked libraries, one for seniors, one for juniors. Music is popular, with orchestras, band and ensembles of all kinds.

Sport played enthusiastically, but 'go, fight, win' is not what this school is about. 'We don't have a 1st XI in each year – often we just have a mixed-ability team.' The spirit, however, is strong, and an eager crowd turns out to support the home team. As well as the usual ball sports, sails three (school-built) boats on Welsh Harp, the Thames and Norfolk Broads. Games aside, for a London school it is an outdoorsy place. The large central playing field is at the heart of the campus and even on the rainiest day is filled with fresh air enthusiasts. Considerable emphasis on self-sufficiency. Den-building very much part of the experience and whole-year camping trips take place from year 4.

Extracurricular, too, is core. In the senior school, years 7-11 required to make their choice from a wide range of activities, from pottery to golf; sixth form options include screenwriting for films, emotional intelligence and Mandarin. Strong commitment to volunteering throughout, with pupils helping out at the local special school and raising significant sums for international causes (including building a school after the tsunami in Sri Lanka). Good careers advice (which kicks off in year 7) helps with GCSE and A level options and UCAS applications pre- and post-A level. As one might expect, green is high on the agenda – one of the first schools to introduce solar panels and recycling bins. Delicious, exclusively healthy lunches with plenty of fresh salads, yogurt and water.

Background and atmosphere: Founded by parents in Hampstead in 1898, original aim was to provide an education based on what was best for the child and encourage learning for its own sake. Part of the progressive movement, sees its kindred schools as Bedales in Hampshire and St Christopher in Letchworth. Moved to its current site, a leafy patch of north London opposite Golders Hill Park, in 1921, and has recently expanded, with a school building for the infants across the road from the main site at Ivy Wood, once the home of Anna Pavlova. Attractive, if compact, grounds, with a mixture of periods and styles (new fitness studio, music and drama block, lovely arts and crafts dining hall) grouped around a central village-like common. Star attractions include a wooded amphitheatre, an arbour (Squirrel Hall), formed from the sheltering branches of two ancient chestnuts, and a diminutive farm, complete with chickens, ducks and bees.

The original ethos – liberal, progressive, egalitarian, child-centred – remains core to the school's values today. Parents and pupils agree that the needs of each child are foremost. 'They try to act very holistically. They look at the individual and find out what makes them shine'. In many respects, too, operates as a large extended family, without the rigid age divide found elsewhere. 'It's a really friendly school,' said one year 9. 'Older kids look out for younger ones and you'll see sixth formers play with year 7s.' Most children seem to enjoy their time here. 'They skip into school every day,' said one long-time parent. 'Even after the holidays, they can't wait to get back.'

New Fives Court lower school building includes auditorium, cutting-edge art technology room with kiln and multi-purpose room for food science, rural studies and general science. ICT suite, learning support area and lower school library upstairs.

Pastoral care, well-being and discipline: Has always believed in minimal rules and flat hierarchy. Teachers are called by their first name and pupils are expected to be self-disciplined, co-operative and self-motivated. The mutual respect between teachers and pupils seen as one of the key strengths of the school. 'We trust them to be sensible'. The expectation, too, is that wrongdoing is likely to be an accident. 'We enable children to learn from their mistakes. There are no quick sanctions. It has to be worked through. Equally there are few reoffenders'. Those who cross the line between liberty and licence – 'being irresponsible in the science labs' or 'putting others in danger' – are given a 'blue form' and sent to the head. Children can be devastated. 'I've seen 16-year-old boys cry,' said a member of staff. Offences too serious to talk through – inappropriate behaviour towards their peers, bullying – can result in suspension. Expulsion for drugs on the premises, but can't remember the last incident, and the school has a 'huge' drugs education programme. 'The kids are pretty mature about sex and drugs,' said one parent. No uniform or dress code, but pupils tend not to push the boundaries, preferring standard-issue jeans and jumpers.

Four counsellors. 'We know what's out there and make it our business to be proactive'. Help, too, from other pupils – peer mentoring, school 'Cits', pupils' council. The end result is a happy bunch of kids. 'I've seen other parents go through miserable teens,' said one mother with two teenage children at the school. 'King Alfred teaches them a lot of confidence.' Non-denom – pupils of every faith and none.

Pupils and parents: An arts and media favourite, parents often choose it for its informality and creativity. 'They come from both ends of the spectrum. There are those who are so liberal they think we're conservative and those who are conservative with a small "c".' Popular, too, with former pupils. New converts are often those who disliked their own, more traditional school days: 'I'd have killed to go to a school like this,' said one. 'They make it such fun.' Pupils, mainly from the wealthier suburbs of north London (Hampstead, Golders Green, Highgate, Muswell Hill), are confident and articulate and expect to be given equal weight as adults. Quite a large international contingent – Americans, South Africans, Israelis, Swedish, Germans, Spanish, Italians.

Entrance: For entry into reception at 4+, names are put down from birth. Date of registration in relation to the child's date of birth (over 200 apply for 40 places in reception) decides visit order. 'We go down the list'. Prospective students come for a two-hour visit and are observed by teachers to assess children's readiness for the next stage of their education and 'whether the child is able to fully participate in and take advantage of the education offered by KAS'. Parents meet with the head and senior staff at the same time.

Entry for occasional places is also by waiting list order and the visits are half, full or two days, depending on age.

Over 100 apply for a handful of places at 11. 'A lot of thought goes into the mix of classes'. Not highly selective at A level – four GCSEs minimum for those already in the school; at least five at grade B or above for 10 to 15 or so newcomers, with A*-B in chosen subjects. All candidates, however, interviewed to ensure they'll fit into the school culture.

Exit: Majority of juniors (some 85 per cent) pass seamlessly on to the senior school. Around a quarter or so leave post-GCSE. 'Some children have been here since they were 4 and it's quite a long time to spend at one school.' About 98 per cent to further education, a good chunk (8-12 each year) to art foundation, then to the full spectrum of universities. One to the Royal College of Music and one to RADA in 2016; others to study eg history and Spanish at Leeds and biochemistry at Kent.

Money matters: Though not particularly well endowed, attempts to keep fees as stable as possible while keeping facilities up to date. No scholarships, a small number (about four) of means-tested bursaries in year 7 and sixth form.

Remarks: A kind, liberal, creative school that suits the self-starter, the sophisticated and the artistic (pupils and parents). Will get the best out of most children, but possibly not ideal for those who require competition in the classroom or on the games field. Good, too, for the square peg and those who might find a more traditional environment oppressive. Not a school for parents obsessed with league-table position or those looking for children who jump to attention when an adult enters the room.

King's College School (Wimbledon)

Southside, London SW19 4TT

Pupils: 1,395 • Ages: 7-18 • Sixth form: 396 (99 girls)

Fees: £16,590 – £20,400 pa

Tel: 020 8255 5300
Email: admissions@kcs.org.uk
Website: www.kcs.org.uk

Headmaster: Since 2008, Mr Andrew Halls MA (50s), previously head of Magdalen College School, Oxford, prior to which he was deputy at Trinity in Croydon and head of English at Bristol Grammar School. An impeccable trajectory. All preceded by a Cambridge double first in English, which is always encouraging. When you meet him you can see how well it fits him. Spare and fine-featured, quietly-spoken, assiduous and gently donnish without any of the waspishness that can accompany the brilliance – he is 'the compleat headmaster'. He is driven by the soundest of educational values. Hence his preparedness to modernise and innovate, even if the owners of tender toes squeal a bit, and hence his willingness to fight on behalf of pupils if he thinks any injustice has been done to them in public exams. A man of high principle and warm enthusiasms, especially for the partnership programmes undertaken by his school, real partnerships with local, national and international communities. You sense that the initiatives all schools need to take to maintain their charitable status are undertaken here from genuine conviction and principle, not just expediency.

Married to a fellow teacher, Mr Halls has two daughters. He is deeply proud of the school he inherited and to which he is devoted, and he pays tribute especially to his 'generous' staff and the generosity of spirit he finds in the school as a whole. He was a precociously young head when appointed to his first headship, to which he brought energy, vision and courage. Now, he is a wise and experienced leader – one who, seemingly, leads discreetly rather than with PR as his priority. The only parental criticism we heard of him was that they didn't know him or see him much. But one suspects he is discreetly everywhere. No questioning his quiet, dedicated authority and the clear assuredness of his vision. An exemplary head.

Head of junior school: Since 2006, Dr Gerard Silverlock (50s), affable, articulate and clever; despite having spent most of his career as a senior historian in senior schools (Millfield et al), a natural prep school head. Did his PhD on European disarmament 1918-25. Previously head of Aberdour in Banstead. Has four children of his own and is clearly held in much affection by his charges, who follow him about, demanding he sign their commended work, and seem determined that they – and not we, on our visit – are what matters. With which we entirely agree. Parents say he's 'approachable and easy to get on with'.

Academic matters: We liked the junior forum board which asked 'have you got ideas for improving life at KCJS?' and felt this was typical of a school which encourages its denizens to think, express themselves and enjoy school. And the achievements here are notable, among them winning for the three years prior to our visit the prestigious Townsend-Warner History Prize.

King's – or KCS as it is as often known – used to offer only the International Baccalaureate, but reintroduced A levels in 2013, citing the A* grade as a way of recognising exceptional performance. Mr Halls takes a balanced view and, though convinced of the IB's worth and breadth, is no blinkered zealot. Consistently excellent IB results: in 2016 pupils averaged 41 points out of 45 and 17 candidates gained 45 points. At A level, 76 per cent A*/A.

League tables of results can be read any number of ways, but the Daily Telegraph – when gauging success in A level, IB and pre-U results all together placed King's as the third highest ranking sixth form in the UK. The IB has been seen as a great draw for those who enter at 16 but as a mixed blessing by others. One long-serving parent – who was full of praise for the school – said: 'I sent my boys there despite the IB rather than because of it.' Another told us: 'We think it's fantastic and most can manage it, but it isn't for everyone'. However if you take it on, you can be assured that you will be taught it here as well as it can be taught, it will flex to support your weaker areas and challenge your strengths as they should be challenged. 'The IB is so much work – I don't dare tell my friends at my old school – but I do even more extracurricular stuff because we are all so busy all the time. I didn't know I could do so much,' enthused one girl. Nearly all sixth form courses now linear.

At GCSE – most now take IGCSEs – 96 per cent of grades were A*/A in 2016. A number take 10 or more, often adding a new language in year 11 – Russian or Italian. Most also take additional maths GCSE. No weak areas. Penny numbers of B grades in most subjects and virtually no Cs in anything. At all levels, the range of options is impressive. At IGCSE, pupils have choice of six mainstream languages; individuals also catered for – around 80 have English as an EAL. We enjoyed the notices on language room doors – eg 'Chiudere la porta!' Parents and pupils full of praise – 'The teaching is fantastic and the classes are very small. My sons have an excellent bantering, relationship with their teachers – it gets even better as they go up the school'. Excellent academic library with displays changed weekly plus private study reading room. New lower school of years 7 and 8 gives the opportunity for teaching outside the constraints of CE.

Around 10 per cent have some kind of SEN, though none with statements – mild dyslexics/dyspraxics by no means in the majority in this cohort: motor skills difficulties, emotional and communication problems and the more severe dyses all taken on and supported individually in class or via withdrawal, as needed.

Games, options, the arts: Powerful and impressive on all fronts and the advent of sixth form girls has given them an extra edge. A bit of a sporting breeding ground – in team and individual achievement they figure prominently in many activities, most notably perhaps in tennis, rowing, rugby, athletics and football. New sports pavilion; on-site sports hall, pool, courts (recently refurbished) and pitches and additional 'fantastic' facilities in West Barnes Lane. Opportunities for travel include D of E, endless sports camps, languages trips and exchanges, history, geography and classics visits – nothing obviously OTT and unnecessarily spoiling for the over-privileged. Excellent list of outside speakers/visitors brings the great outside and its challenges into school, eg Prof Sir Lawrence Freedman (think war studies and the Chilcot Commission), Mike Atherton, Simon Russell Beale, Carol Ann Duffy and Andrew (Churchill) Roberts all popping in.

Music, art and drama really exceptional. We found the art unusually expressive and free – especially rare in what is predominantly a boys' school – and felt quite exhilarated by the wit and life in what we saw in many media. We quite liked the fact that it was a bit messy too. Drama is legendary. The school takes shows to Edinburgh and sells out. Beautifully staged shows in the main theatre and little ones in the drama studio. Music likewise – housed, as so often, in less than shiny accommodation, but new music school rising apace; producing outstanding performances and performers in many genres. Chamber orchestra tour to Spain, concerts in St John's Smith Square and St James Piccadilly, The Cadogan Hall and St Paul's Cathedral. Debating and many other activities offer far more than your average teenager could do in twice the number of school years he has.

Much made of the school's partnerships with local state primaries and seniors. Sixth formers teach Latin at one and football at another. Clearly, much satisfaction derived from a special relationship with the primary school they support in Obera, Kenya, and we were moved by a modest description of just what that means in practice – both ways. This, plus the 1st XI cricket team's raising of over £50,000 for the Nelson Mandela Children's Fund, as a part of their South African touring activities, and the outreach programme, Junior Aspirations, involving teaching support for able boys and girls from state primaries, makes for a healthy interaction with the real world outside, which can only be good.

Background and atmosphere: Founded in 1829 as a junior branch of King's College, London – hence various ties still extant, eg the shared school and college colours. The move to Wimbledon was made to accommodate more boys – just over 200 – and 1911 saw the school being granted its independence. Junior school opened in 1912 and since then the school has grown and flourished abundantly. Its history – we visited in its anniversary year – is proudly, though not in-yer-facedly, celebrated in displays around the school, and most interesting it is too. Controversially, the sixth form has admitted girls since 2010 – not controversially inside the school (it seems an unqualified good thing) but clearly, the hard-working local and less local girls' schools are less than thrilled. The boys are converts. 'We were very excited at the idea of the girls coming – it was a bit awkward at first but everyone has come together now'.

The school faces a quiet corner of Wimbledon Common; the main building is solid, Victorian red-brick. We often describe a school's setting as 'leafy' – this is about as leafy as a top London senior school can get. Its neighbours are the imposing detached houses of the very prosperous and the more modest 18th century terraces and pub which still evoke a villagey feel. Behind the main building, the extent of the school surprises. Many later buildings – mostly functional rather than architecturally glorious, but the site overall is a pleasure to encounter. Vast, classic Great Hall with organ, WWII commemorative tablet, gothic window and splendid beamed ceiling – all as Hogwarts as you could wish. One-storey wooden music practice block – 'It arrived on a lorry and they just planted it there – quite surprising!' Most subjects in their own blocks or corridors. Good displays in most areas – we liked the maxims, eg 'Forgetfulness is the parent of poverty', which stimulate thinking, though we were told that some displays hang about rather too long. Wind turbine and solar panels contribute some power. Courtyards, much attractive brick paving, sculpture – notably that which marks the school's adoption of the IB with all its internationalism (Japanese stone lantern, African stone and wood pieces, Chinese lions etc) – and clever and well-tended planting make for a relaxed and pleasant place.

Physically attached to the main school, though also with a building or two of its own, the junior school shares facilities with the senior school and is integral to it. The two main buildings – one for the youngest boys, Rushmere, and Priory for the older boys – are in themselves worthy of note. Rushmere, formerly the home of sculptor, David Wynne, is a beautiful Georgian house with lovely decorative features and makes a surprisingly appropriate school for small boys. The younger boys are taught, 14 to a class, in the former bedrooms en haut and the older ones, 22 to a class, in the drawing and dining rooms en bas. Thence to Priory in classes of 18-24. All rooms are well-lit, well-aired and have good displays. The school also maintains two local pre-preps – The Squirrels and the Rowans – though entrance to the KCJS is not automatic from these.

Pastoral care, well-being and discipline: House system valued and relished by most. Also tutor groups, in which a pupil remains for his entire school life. System makes for a sense of security and consistency and ensures that you are known – valuable when it comes to UCAS forms. Parents praise the supportive atmosphere. 'It's been very good for my boys, who are all very different,' we were told. Although 'the success of the system depends entirely on the tutor – we've been very lucky, but it's not been so for everyone'. Some parents of boys who enter at 13 feel more could have been done to integrate their sons and help them make friends, but this has now been addressed by the appointment of a 'brilliant' head of middle school, a long-serving head of house who has 'transformed' their integration. Much parental praise for general school organisation, home-school communications and school's skill in picking up problems. 'They're usually onto it before you are,' we were told. 'If you get there early – at 7am – the car park is full of staff cars. They put in a huge amount of extra effort.'

School officers chosen via application, election and interview – the positions are coveted and hugely prized. Counselling service and chaplain to pick up birds with broken wings, but it seldom gets that far. Separate faith assemblies once a week. Smart plain suits and shirts for the sixth allow for some individual expression and no-one looks like a clone. Vast sixth form common room with TV, all-day coffee bar and a range of seating from the upright, austere I'm-here-to-work kind to the flop-on-a-sofa-just-leave-me-for-a-bit kind. Large dining room serves wide choice highly appetising food which almost all eat – staff and pupils ensemble.

The girls we spoke to were incredibly happy and none seemed to regret their move. 'We're much more modern – we feel more grown-up here,' was the consensus, but then of course, they didn't stay at their previous schools to experience the sixth form there, did they? They positively relish the house system – 'It was a joke in my old school' – and are wowed by the 'team spirit'. Perhaps a lesson for the girls' schools here, many of which cling to the idea that houses and team spirit are somehow olde worlde and passé (as indeed, they once were).

Pupils and parents: A real mix, as you'd expect: academic and professional parents alongside first generation immigrants with bright offspring on bursaries. Common denominator is brains and enthusiasm and they come from a very wide area. Good range of bus services means you don't have to grind through the traffic. Impressively eclectic list of former pupils

(OKs) includes Sabine Baring-Gould (wrote Onward Christian Soldiers), Dante Gabriel Rossetti, philologists Sweet and Skeat, Robert Graves, composer Robin Holloway, traitor William Joyce, the Beeb's Alvar Liddell, Roy Plomley and Mark Urban, actor Ben Barnes, musician Marcus Mumford and no fewer than five VCs.

Entrance: English, maths and reasoning tests for junior school and all 7+ and 8+ candidates are interviewed. Beyond that, those 'whose performance in the written papers suggests that they could benefit from the education which we offer' are seen. Entries at 7+, 8+, 9+ and 10+ – no longer at 11+, now the senior school takes 11 year olds. 'Our boys are bright. We are highly selective,' says Dr Silverlock, 'but we are not a hothouse.' With this level of aptitude, they would have no need to be. No automatic acceptance of brothers.

Now has senior school entry points at 11 and 13 (though junior school still goes up to 13). Registration deadline end of September of year 6 for 13+ and mid-November for 11+. Same tests in maths, English and reasoning in January for both, with best performers interviewed. Those offered 11+ places (around 40-44) do not take any further entrance exams; 13+ places (about 35) are subject to CE results or King's own scholarship exam. Most 13+ entrants – around 80 – come up from the junior school.

At 16+ they admit girls – 'very, very clever girls,' an admiring mother of boys told us – from a range of girls' schools, though predominantly Putney and Wimbledon HSs, usually attracted by the IB, or from Godolphin & Latymer, which does the IB but for a far smaller cohort. All 16+ applicants take tests in English, maths and a general paper and then have four interviews. The vast majority taken at this stage are girls, reflecting the greater number of applicants as well as their performance in the assessments. Roughly four applicants per place.

Exit: Most juniors to the senior school via The King's transfer exam in year 8 – around 90 boys go up. A few who would not thrive there are given plenty of warning and helped to find a nook elsewhere. Four in the last 13 years, which isn't much. 'When a boy is offered a place at any age, our expectation is that he will be here until he is 18'.

Very few leave post-GCSE, most stay on and head for the top universities – nine medics and 57 to Oxbridge in 2016. Rest to London University colleges or heavyweight provincials, eg Durham and Bristol, to do traditional subjects. Increasing numbers heading across the pond.

Money matters: Good range of scholarships and bursaries considering that, unlike the ancient foundations not so far away, this is not an endowed school. Increasingly, here as elsewhere, money being diverted into means-tested bursaries to attract the bright but broke. Well worth enquiring – up to 100 per cent fee remission possible in certain cases.

Remarks: It makes every kind of sense to get in early – the competition for places at 13+ and now 11+ being so tight. By any standards a top school offering an exceptional education under a notable head.

King's House School

68 King's Road, Richmond, Surrey TW10 6ES

Pupils: 450 • Ages: 3–13

Fees: £11,790 – £15,360 pa

Tel: 020 8940 1878
Email: schooloffice@kingshouseschool.org
Website: www.kingshouseschool.org

Headmaster: Since 2011, Mark Turner BA PGCE NPQH (40s). Studied French and Spanish at Bristol before training at Sandhurst with six years in the army. After leaving, taught at Merchant Taylors' before joining Durston House, Ealing where he was deputy head for nine years. Married with four children, two of whom are at the school. Feels he is lucky to head such a good, friendly, and mainly local school. Says it has a strong sense of community and provides a broad education. Parents like the fact that he teaches French to year 4, thereby getting to know the senior boys and say he's 'very approachable' and 'a classic boys' prep school headmaster'. Feel that he has made the school gentler. One of his aims is to unite the three sections of the school: at the moment they feel like separate entities. To that end, he spends more time in the junior section than his predecessor, which can't be a bad thing.

Entrance: From the term they turn 3, boys and girls at nursery level. Then reception, boys only, September after 4th birthday. No testing, places offered a year before entry in order of registration. Siblings take priority. A few more places at 7+ and 8+ subject to passing entrance test. Occasionally places occur at other times, each individually assessed. Mainly families from surrounding areas including Roehampton, Kingston and Barnes. Buses run from Chiswick and Putney.

Exit: A handful at 11+, trying to beat the rush, but the school does not give this much support. About two-thirds to boys' only London day schools at 13+ with St Paul's, King's College Wimbledon and Hampton all high on the list. Big range of boarding schools, with Bradfield, Charterhouse, Epsom, Eton, Winchester and Harrow amongst the current favourites. Several scholarships, both music and academic, most years.

Remarks: On three sites in leafy Richmond. Seems a happy, hard-working school. We were taken round by two delightful, polite and enthusiastic senior boys under the eagle eye of the school's marketing manager – we were certainly given the spiel.

Large nursery building on two floors. Huge, bright rooms with different areas for learning and play. Plenty of constructive fun to be had by eager under-4s, both boys and girls. Parents love it – one even said 'flawless'. Two outdoor playgrounds, one for physical play, one for creative/imaginative play. They think of everything these days. Send your children here and your sons get automatic entry to the junior school. Your daughters? They seem mainly to head off to the Old Vicarage.

The junior school – reception to year 3 – is just across the road from the senior. Two reception classrooms on the ground floor have their own outdoor play areas where all is still reasonably relaxed. It may only be the beginning of learning but they are definitely being prepared for the next stage; homework starts straight away. Writing practice first, then, when they are ready, reading. Only 10 minutes at a time but it's still homework for 4 year olds.

The rest of this rather rambling house contains two year 1 classes and three each for years 2 and 3. Average class size about 20. All have a classroom assistant as well as a fully trained teacher. It is at this point that the serious learning begins. More work, less play. Classrooms are not enormous but they are bright and buzzing. All the boys appeared happy and attentive. Space is at a premium, the library fills in a corridor and a piano lesson seemed to be going on in a passageway. The IT room contained a lot of slightly restless boys learning computer basics. But, no worry, there is plenty of room for burning energy outside in the big playground which, cleverly, has a partially covered area. Parents full of praise for Mr Gower, head of juniors, who they say is extremely approachable and quick to answer emails. He's usually there to welcome boys in the morning. Also, we were told, all children love Nurse Jo who cures all their woes.

In year 4 they move across to the senior school where they can take advantage of some bang up-to-do date facilities, of which our guides were rightly proud, and the real pressure goes on. Initially all classes are mixed ability and, apart from those subjects needing special equipment, are classroom based. In year 5 they begin to build up towards the common entrance syllabus and are setted in English and maths. Two science labs; DT and art rooms; two computer rooms including a suite of Macs for composing and design; a music room; a theatre where, our young guides boasted, amazing productions are put on; and a well-equipped music room. Parents say 'music used to be one of their weaknesses but is now one of their greatest strengths'. These are lucky boys.

There's plenty of outdoor playing space as well, for organised and free play, that area having been completely re-vamped recently. Parents say it's a 'shame there's not wider extracurricular'; 'there could be more broader based after school clubs'. We got the feeling that the emphasis is mainly on the curriculum, with the pressure to succeed being the be all and end all. A 21st century London problem? Or just a lack of understanding that there is more to life than passing exams? The head comments: 'We believe the breadth and balance of our curriculum is a strength and is far from being too focused on the academic. We also feel that while some schools reduce art, DT, drama and ICT to carousel lessons, we still give them regular lesson time up to year 8.'

We didn't see the 35 acre sports ground as it is a coach ride away in Chiswick, but we have seen a DVD and it looks pretty impressive. Senior boys go there twice a week and junior boys once. Rugby, football and cricket all played competitively – 25 rugby, 34 football and 20 cricket teams. Wow! And they have silverware to prove their prowess (including Prep Schools Rugby Nationals U13 winners). Tennis, swimming and athletics also figure. Astroturf area within the senior school grounds and a well-equipped gymnasium ensure plenty of PE.

Inevitably, in a non-selective school, there is a wide variation in ability but, parents tell us, lots of help in the junior school who are 'quick to pick up struggling children and help them so they don't get left behind'. Continual monitoring, boys needing specific help are given it free of charge – 'we give them the building blocks' – being taken out of class for an hour at a time. Free, individualised education programmes provided.

Strict code of behaviour both in and out of the classroom, weekly PHSE sessions and a pupil teacher ratio of approximately 12:1 ensure that the majority of problems are caught quickly. House and tutor systems also provide continuous monitoring. Parents say, 'communication lines excellent and emails responded to quickly'; 'quick to pick up on problems and good at keeping on top of them'.

Communication certainly seems to be a great strength; no parent could say they are not kept fully up to date. From the headmaster's termly letter to the weekly school newsletters, everything is covered. Information on matches, charities and school trips, contributions from teachers, prizes and praises – it's all there. An active and busy school.

Kingsdale Foundation School

Alleyn Park, Dulwich, London SE21 8SQ

Pupils: 1,560 • Ages: 11–18 • Sixth form: 200

Tel: 020 8670 7575
Email: info@kingsdale.southwark.sch.uk
Website: www.kingsdalefoundationschool.org.uk

Head: Mr Steve Morrison. Although he is keen for the school to showcase its achievers, he says: 'we are not just interested in the children at the top end'. The school believes it does well by pupils across the board. He says: 'We don't believe we've got it cracked, we believe we did not previously do enough because not every child achieved their potential'.

Academic matters: Results are on an upwards trajectory. In 2016, 40 per cent of GCSE grades were A*/A; 80 per cent of students got 5+ A*-C grades. The highest performing subjects were maths, physics, chemistry, biology, computer science, Latin, textiles, food technology and statistics. Still a long way to go at A level: average grade to date seems to be a C.

The school is proud of its high performers in whatever arena – the boy who entered the school with little hope, whose mother died during his studies but who turned down the opportunity to train as a professional footballer to enter the sixth form when he achieved nine A*s and three As at GCSE. He now heads to Columbia University with a soccer scholarship. Or, the highest performing child in the country – firstly, at GCSE she achieved 15 A*s and then achieved six As at AS level. There are several more on the same track right behind her. It speaks of individual talent, but also teachers who are able to nurture that talent with the right support and inspiration.

A broad and traditional set of GCSE options to rival many, includes triple science, Latin, economics and psychology. 'No vocational short-cuts', says the head. Pupils have the opportunity to study two languages, or one, from year 7: a choice of French, Spanish, German and Latin, with other languages as clubs, such as Mandarin. We watched a small French class of only 12 students taking place in the library. Students study a condensed key stage 3 in science, so that they can spend three years on their GCSE courses. Science labs are light, bright and modern with both benches for group work and lecture style seating. It's also a hi-tech environment. Every child has access to an iPad for home and school use, subsidised by the school, as well as PCs, Apple Macs and lap-tops.

Staff ratio is one to 10. The head says: 'pupils actually like the staff and staff actually like the pupils'. A parent said: 'a real strength of the school is the commitment of the teachers'. Our impression from talking to sixth formers is that for the motivated student the staff will be right behind them, as one girl said to us: 'all you have to do is ask'. Particularly in the approach to the summer examinations, the school is open seven days a week with evening revision classes, Saturday schools, Sunday schools and one-to-one sessions. As a pupil said: 'Kingsdale doesn't sleep and never leaves any pupil behind'. Ofsted in its latest inspection believed there is more to be done to challenge the most able pupils, with teachers required to provide more detailed feedback on pupils' work so that they can make progress.

Classes we observed were working quietly and diligently. When we enquired of a pupil about disruptive behaviour in the classroom she said: 'There was a lot to start with, but the teachers deal with it... it might make you laugh... but if you want to work you can'.

For nine successive years, it has been identified as a special school for inclusion. One mother said of her experience and that of her children: 'They've been treated like they have a voice. We've been listened to. It isn't a one size fits all school'. A mother of both a dyslexic and dyspraxia child talks of receiving everything she asked for. The focus is on in-class support provided by teaching assistants rather than withdrawal. There is monitoring of reading ages and provision of reading clubs, touch-typing classes, hand-writing groups, and GSCE support groups. Learning mentors provide additional support across year groups. There is also a school nurse for medical matters.

The sixth form is relatively new, opening in 2010 and now comprises 200 students. Courses include a baccalaureate programme comprising A levels, one AS level and an EPQ, plus extracurricular including D of E, or straight A levels. Also on offer: an access to medicine course. Ambitions are nurtured with trips to Yale and Harvard as well as the UK's most prestigious universities.

Games, options, the arts: The school has little outside space, but there are some courts and pitches behind the main building. To the rear is the new sports hall, seemingly made of golden plywood. It contains courts for basketball, netball, volleyball, badminton and more, plus a mezzanine for dance classes: ballet, modern, hip-hop and jazz. On the wall are posters of inspirational Olympians and female sporting role models. With a dynamic female sports director, there are teams and fixtures for every sport and some sporting stars among them: one boy was recently signed for Manchester United, another represented England at the Commonwealth Games 3000m and gained a bronze medal; one is member of the team GB gymnastics squad and one coach is a former Rugby U21 international player. There are 42 sports clubs on site and locally including: in-line skating, yoga, tennis, American football, go-karting, archery, fencing and trampolining, fencing, BMX bikes and cycling at the Herne Hill velodrome.

Music is truly outstanding and adds a real vibrancy to the school. The head of music, at the school long before the current regime, is renowned for her ability to inspire and her ambition for the children who may not have picked up an instrument before coming here. Every year the school hosts the Dulwich Festival Youth Concert and steals the show from the massed independent school ensembles – most recently with a group xylophone rendition of an especially composed medley of Bond theme tunes. Ensembles for every instrument imaginable running at lunch-times and after school, as well as steel pans, rock band, theory classes, jazz groups and chamber choir. The new music building is all curvy plywood and includes music practice rooms, teaching spaces and a recital hall with raked seating, plus a music tech suite. We heard a student's composition which sounded professional, akin to the latest pop release, and girls singing acoustically around a piano.

The art room displays accomplished textile GCSE projects, books rich with embroidered textiles and illustration. Within DT pupils study food and textiles technology and product design. A large, light DT lab with all of the usual workshop equipment, plus a laser cutter and CAD-CAM suite. The library seems rather gloomy, with dark blue carpet and a little low on books. The upper school library has computers that rise from desks.

There are lunch-time clinics for students who need additional help or are struggling with homework and plenty of academic clubs. The school works hard to offer opportunities for exciting trips that are accessible for all. There are annual language department trips to Europe and some more far flung: a sixth former told us of a music trip to Brazil, working with young children – 'I've never done anything more amazing in my life'. The 'trips of a lifetime' programme subsidises trips to destinations such as Japan, Namibia, Brazil, the USA and the French Alps.

Background and atmosphere: A local authority school which was cause for concern by the late 1990s, it was completely reimagined to the tune of £30m under a new management team and with the involvement of a design and innovation consultancy which placed the design of the new school at the heart of change, becoming a foundation school in the process. The design won multiple awards, including Building of the Year in 2005 from the Royal Fine Art Commission for its architects, and is now the most popular state senior school in Southwark and wears this badge with pride.

Situated south of Dulwich and Belair Parks, the school is located in a particularly leafy part of south east London. Its location on a residential street lined with multi-million pound homes, next door to Dulwich Prep London, makes for a calm outlook, surrounded by mature trees and safe-feeling journeys home via the buses on the South Circular or nearby West Dulwich overground station. There could be a bit of discomfort around a state school so surrounded by the plushest of independent education's finest – we get the feeling that there is only minimal sharing of facilities – but since the revamp and the climbing academic standards there is much to feel good about.

As you step through the sliding doors you find the most striking feature of the school: a huge, slightly humid central quadrangle, originally the school playground, now acres of green flooring enclosed with a glass roof – a central bed of tropical plants adding to the greenhouse effect. When it rains the noise on the roof is pleasantly loud. This futuristic central space is encircled by plywood banks of lockers on wheels designed to look like little houses, and most stunning of all a central 'egg' or pod, with fantastic acoustics and a steeply raked bank of seating for concerts and addresses. The usual dark school corridors have been cleverly done away with, instead wide, metal walkways encircle the quadrangle linking the classrooms on the first floor. Classrooms are light with brightly coloured walls. There is a freestanding lift linked to the walkways for wheelchair users. It's an exciting space. At lunchtime hot food is served here too, and there are tables outside. It's a versatile space that can be used for anything from art exhibitions to trampolining.

Pastoral care, well-being and discipline: A large school, significantly larger than the nearest local state co-ed senior school, but the school works to make it manageable, particularly for those joining the school at year 7, dividing into the upper and lower school and hosting induction days. There are buddies, junior and senior school prefects and a house system. Around a quarter of the student population is from disadvantaged backgrounds. Some 26 per cent of pupils speak English as an additional language. The uniforms, fairly smart black blazers and house ties, seem to be worn with a bit of a hastily assembled attitude, especially by the girls higher up the school – plenty of micro skirts with knee socks and half-mast ties. Ofsted was most complimentary about the behaviour of pupils in its most recent inspection, saying pupils 'show respect and courtesy to one another and to staff'. The pupils we talked to were polite and passionate about their school, appreciative of their teachers.

With discipline in mind, the school's very design is partly about transparency. Teachers can see what is going on everywhere, without anyone feeling monitored. However, a year 4 girl eager to leave no stone unturned on the tour of the school told us as we crossed the playground: 'There are fights. Not daily. You won't get into a fight if you're well behaved'. The head tells prospective parents there have been no exclusions for five years, but following a recent incident, where a pupil returned to the school after the end of the day resulting in a stabbing, the head suggested that the incident concerned an excluded pupil. Our enquiries amongst parents and pupils as to what has been changed with regards to safeguarding at the school in response to this incident have not yielded any firm information.

Most parents we encountered seemed excited by the school as a prospect. With such a large school there are inevitably diverse reports once pupils are there. One grandmother told us how quickly her shy grandson settled into the school and made friends – when he wasn't very happy with the school lunches he felt able to talk to the school about it: even better, they responded with changes. An easy-going mother was nonetheless disappointed to feel after two years that the teachers didn't really know who her daughter was at parents evening.

There was a certain freshness and honesty about the pupils at the open day we attended who told us: 'Kingsdale isn't perfect. Kingsdale admits its imperfections as a way to improve'; 'pupils are well-supported and grounded with room to make decisions for themselves'.

Pupils and parents: From all walks of life and backgrounds and from all across London. Many join in little bands from their local state primaries in East Dulwich, Herne Hill, Crystal Palace, Gypsy Hill and Forest Hill. But as there is unusually no distance criteria, students come from Clapham, Greenwich and beyond. We met a sixth former who had attended a local prep but after attending an open day and winning a music scholarship could think of no reason not to take up a place here instead. And the odd refugee from the uber-competitive selective schools that dominate the local scene. The head's invitation is for prospective parents to 'show up when you like: someone will show you around.

Entrance: Admissions via the local authority common application form – simply place the school as high up the list of preferences as possible for a chance of a place and await National Offers Day. Most recently applications stood at 11 to one. Pupils sit a banding test, in non-verbal reasoning, prior to the allocation of places, so that the school has an academically mixed intake. Numbers in each band will vary from year to year, so there is no way of assessing chances of a place. There is a complicated system of admissions criteria in terms of how places will be allocated – so complicated, the maths teachers are assigned to try an explain it to bewildered parents at open days – those winning a music, art or sports scholarship increase their chance but a place is not guaranteed.

A parent going through the admissions and scholarship process commented she wasn't sure she'd want the school in charge of evacuating the Titanic as everything was slightly chaotic. With so many applicants to places the school is possibly rather overwhelmed by the process, but gets there in the end.

Exit: Around 40 per cent of students achieve places at Russell Group/other top universities; two to Oxford in 2016 and one medic.

Money matters: Unusually for a state school, scholarships are available in maths, music, sport and art at year 7 entrance. The awards comprise additional tuition and coaching, such as £1000 worth of instrumental lessons for music and a scholar's programme – the musicians might attend workshops with professional musicians and the sports scholars take vocational qualifications in sports leadership. No need to be already at a high grade of accomplishment on your chosen instrument and sports scholarships are simply looking for 'potential' – candidates will be assessed for component activities and team work. Sixth form scholarships are also available in maths, performing and expressive arts.

Remarks: For those able to stretch to the local independents, there may be more peace of mind, particularly for the most able and ambitious elsewhere. For parents looking for a vibrant school with a growing academic capability and a uniquely inspiring daily environment, join the crowds heading this way.

Kingston Grammar School

London Road, Kingston, Surrey KT2 6PY

Pupils: 800 • Ages: 11–18 • Sixth form: 228

Fees: £18,430 pa

Tel: 020 8546 5875
Email: registrar@kgs.org.uk
Website: www.kgs.org.uk

K

Head Master: Since 2014, Mr Stephen Lehec, previously head of Aylesbury Grammar School. He joined Aylesbury as deputy head from Maidstone Grammar in 2006, becoming head in 2008. He has a history and English degree from Southampton and a PGCE from Oxford. Softly spoken (for a head) and personable, he works from an office so lush that it wouldn't look out of place in an interiors magazine or, at any rate, a Heal's ad. Not that he spends all his time there, with pupils telling us he's 'so much more hands-on than the last head.' Teaches year 7 history (and was trying to find time to start teaching sixth formers too when we visited) and meets regularly with pupils across all years. 'I never want to be the kind of head to say, "Remind me who you are,"' he explains, with pupils clearly impressed with how much of an interest he takes in them. 'He keeps us in the loop about everything that's going on,' added one. Meanwhile, staff praise his collaborative leadership style and his reshaping of the executive team that encourages more sharing and avoids anyone being able to say, 'That isn't my job.' Parents describe him as 'available', 'pragmatic' and 'open to suggestions'. 'There's no element of "Leave us to it, we know best",' one told us. 'He feels like a good set of hands,' said another. Refuses to overpush academia at the expense of developing the whole child; it's makes a nice change to meet a head who isn't obsessed with league tables – although, interestingly, the school gets the results anyway.

Lives locally with his wife and two daughters (one at the school; the other still too young to attend) and is a keen football, cricket and tennis player, having coached teams up to county level – although the school itself remains his biggest passion. 'If you asked my wife what's my biggest interest outside of work, she'd say "work",' he laughs.

Academic matters: Strong results across the board – in 2016, 61 per cent A*/A grades and 85 per cent A*/B at A level; 82 per cent A*/A grades at GCSE – although maths is the clear stand-out subject here, with pupils praising the brilliant teaching, and even those who say they aren't mathematical find it hard to resist. A whopping four maths choices alone at A level. 'We support people who want a bit of maths to supplement their qualifications right up to those wanting to study it at Cambridge,' says the head. For both GCSE and A level, other popular subjects include English lit, sciences (where there's a good gender split) and history, and the school also offers IGCSEs in maths, English, languages, and sciences. 'We're big on the facilitating subjects here,' explains the head, 'although lots of A level students also add on the likes of theatre studies, PE or politics.' Pre-U in economics and 70-80 per cent take up of EPQ – often with pupils revisiting areas they gave up for GCSE, such as Italian. Some pupils yearn for cookery, although they do get the opportunity to cook at home and bring in the fruits of their labour for assessment and tasting.

Language department – an uplifting environment, with bunting made from European flags hanging from the ceilings – currently musters 15 languages, with year 7 pupils choosing two options from French, German, Spanish and Italian, plus Latin. In addition, there are options to do taster courses in everything from Mandarin to Danish and Russian to Polish. By year 9, pupils can pick up other languages more formally, with all students studying at least one language for GCSE and many studying more. Greek taught in collaboration with Tiffin boys. 'Languages are fun here – it's all about interaction,' one pupil told us, with at least one lesson a week in the IT breakout area. 'You also get lots of one-to-ones with fluent native speakers.' IT very much embedded into learning here, with plenty of IT breakout areas across the subjects, many in full use when we visited. A little setting in maths and PE from year 7, 'but it's more tiering than setting,' says the head.

K

A new timetable system of longer, 50-minute lessons, has gone down well and the teaching staff are widely praised by pupils for providing interesting lessons and extra help when required, including extension classes and one-to-one tutoring. Not that the pupils are expected to give up oodles of their time. 'Far from it, teachers are really understanding that we have busy lives,' one told us. Indeed, despite the great results, this is clearly no academic hothouse. 'There's no sense of underachievement or failure if pupils don't get top marks,' said one parent. 'The ethos is more about encouraging and enthusing pupils,' said another, whilst a third told us, 'They seem to find individuals' talents that often the kids themselves didn't know they had.' Lots of professional development opportunities to help attract and retain the best teaching staff, and pupils report a mixture of strictness among staff. 'Some are really laid-back, whilst others will pick up on everything.'

Learning support department helps those on the dys strata, mostly mild, a few moderate. Learner profile compiled for all children seen by educational psychologist or specialist teacher – school a great believer in constant monitoring and tracking to ensure progress. Lots of laptop users and open to those with aural/visual impairment – 'so long as they can cope with the site.' One parent, with a child who unexpectedly became partially sighted, told us the school has been 'magnificent.' 'It was bolt from the blue for us and for them when she got this curious genetic condition, but they quickly assessed what they'd need to do to support her and to ensure she didn't stand out. They've been absolutely amazing.' Head wishes parents would be more honest about SEN at the time of applying to the school. 'Historically, a lot of prep schools and parents have hidden it, which is ridiculous as we could have been more helpful in supporting them if we'd have known,' he says.

Games, options, the arts: Sport, once seen as very separate to academia, is now seen to complement it and as such, there is more celebration of successes in assemblies and more house competitions and fixtures. Hockey, rowing and, most recently, cricket, are the three strongest sports here. The school has also boosted netball and football, once considered the poor relations. Good gender split (the school's best cricketers were female when we visited), with netball the only sport played only by one gender and even that is being redressed, with the school considering using handball as way of getting more boys into it. Other sports – of which there are 25 options by sixth form – range from spinning classes to sailing.

The rather unfortunately-named Cage (two onsite courts with soft surfaces) is actually well-loved by pupils, along with the school gym; although some sport takes place on the Fairfield – a field across the road from the main site, which is also used by Tiffin and maintained by the Royal Borough of Kingston – most sport takes place off-site at Ditton Field, a 22-acre facility a bus ride away that boasts six football pitches, three cricket, two hockey, eight tennis and netball courts and a separate boathouse on the Thames. A few grumbles from parents that there isn't more sport on site, although they quickly catch themselves sounding spoilt – this is London, after all. Pupils particularly love Ditton Field ('What's not to love? It's a fabulous open space right on the river, by Hampton Court,' said one), with pupils also enjoying the various other sporting venues used by the school, including St Mary's University and Hampton Court for Real (Royal) Tennis.

Plenty of sporting accolades, with 20 international level girls and boys at the school, and five currently playing at international level. Traditionally, the school comes in the top five schools nationally for hockey and amongst one of the best co-ed schools for rowing in the country – particularly good for a co-ed school, where they only have half the potential numbers of single sex schools. Around 80 per cent take up among pupils for Saturday and after-school sports.

Music a source of huge pride and joy, although it's seen by some, including the head, to have historically spread itself too thin, with too big a range of functions, so watch out for some more honed evening performances in the future. Three orchestras (beginners, junior and senior), four choirs (first year, juniors, seniors and chamber – which had recently sang at the Vatican when we visited), along with plenty of quartets and quintets from guitar to saxophone. Excellent facilities and around 250 private music lessons a week, many of which take place in the colourful contemporary pods, located in a school courtyard. 'Music tech is amazing,' added one student. 'You get to actually produce music from the word go.'

Drama outstanding, with an exceptional performing arts centre and professional staff from a theatre background, along with visiting actors (Samantha Bond's daughter Molly Hanson, a former KGS school captain herself, when we visited) helping with everything from LAMDA exams to drama school applications. Incredibly polished performances, including annual senior, middle school and junior plays, with at least 30 different parts – for example, Mike Bartlett's Earthquakes in London, for which they used proper airline seats on stage and filmed 500 minutes of scenes around London that were used for background. 'My son has really found his feet, thanks to the drama here – his confidence has grown immeasurably,' one parent told us.

Art and DT also excellent – masses of workshop/studio space, and we drooled over brilliantly conceived and executed works of art, both 3D and paintings, much of which you'd pay good money to hang on your walls. Professional quality furniture made by GCSE class, perspex clocks and clever ceramics make you want to get your hands gummy. The list of national awards, prizes and achievements fills several pages – not surprising, as this really is university standard, where no art forms are shied away from, including life drawing.

Co-curricular opportunities – which range from knitting to foreign language film club and from philosophy to debating club – fill a 40-page booklet, with many parents saying this is what gives Kingston the edge. Most pupils do at least one a day, with one telling us, 'I set up a new club myself – the economics society.' School usually open from 7am, with last staff leaving as late as 10pm. 'This school allows you to be the person you want to be and I think the clubs are a big part of that,' said one pupil, who said his passion for rowing has been supported throughout. 'Teachers' involvement in extracurricular activity is second-to-none,' points out the head. 'My biggest problem is telling them to hold back so they're not completely exhausted by the end of term.'

Masses of trips, with the school taking full advantage of all the theatres, galleries and cultural events the capital has to offer, along with national residential trips and international residentials to the likes of Iceland (geography), Rome (choir) and Gibraltar (netball) just in one half term, and many others such as South Africa (hockey), Sri Lanka (cricket), China (cultural exchange) Utah (skiing), New York (art and drama) every year or two. Plenty of languages exchanges every year. A hardship support fund seeks to assist those in need.

Background and atmosphere: Whatever you do, don't put the school's postcode in your satnav (which takes you to the back of the school, where there's no entrance) and even when you do find the front, be warned there's no parking on site (although, thankfully, there are good public transport links). But despite the metropolitan location that's a nightmare to get to, inside the school you quickly forget you're in the midst of Kingston's tarmac tangle, thanks to the relaxed, welcoming and buzzy environment. 'Honestly, you barely even notice the sounds of ambulances and traffic, if at all,' one pupil said.

The original building is an attractive, well-kept, old-fashioned looking grammar school (with a school hall of the ilk your parents would be familiar with), whilst newer, modern buildings provide plenty of bright, airy spaces to learn, with particularly impressive science labs. Good café for sixth form, with TV, stereo system, drinks and snacks (and always someone playing chess, apparently). Space isn't lavish here, by any means, though what they've got has been used wisely and it is less cramped than some of its central London peers. The next big project being planned is a multi-million three or four story building to include new changing rooms, space for engineering and art studios, bigger dining facilities (currently quite tight), additional library space and galleries with a real wow-factor – with the school hoping to build by around 2019-20.

Pupils – who wear white shirts and grey uniforms in years 7 to 11 (business dress in the sixth form) – look cheerful, both in lessons and during breaks, when they spill out into the various outside areas, including Fairfield during summertime. 'Yes, there's all the lovely "p" words – purposeful, peaceful and so on – but first and foremost this school is happy. Pupils like coming to school,' says the head, and pupils agree. Strong student voice, with recently reformed school forum changing the likes of the lunch queuing system through to mobile phone rules. Renewed catering means take-up among year 9s (when, traditionally, pupils have moved to packed lunches) is now 95 per cent and is still popular in the sixth form when students are allowed out of school for lunch if they wish. Good home/school IT links. Fabulous sixth-form development offices – a one-stop shop for exams officer, careers advice, head of sixth form and more.

Pastoral care, well-being and discipline: 'It's ridiculously caring here,' says the head – a bold claim by anyone's standards, but pupils and parents concur. Good system of heads of year, form tutors and heads of house – 'they get to know you really well' – along with a robust buddy, prefect, mentoring and house system that encourage friendship across the years, and plenty of positions of leadership among pupils, including older ones mentoring younger ones. 'I always say that, "If we don't catch you in the wash, we'll get you in the rinse," because it really is the case that if anything is bothering anyone, we have enough systems in place both to notice and to help,' says the head. Bullying and stress minimal. 'They're quick to pick up problems and keep parents in touch. It's in the culture of the place,' said one parent.

Discipline scarcely an issue here, with non-verbal and verbal warnings, misconduct marks, summons to head of year and occasional after-school detentions generally all that's needed – although head has excluded pupils for a day or two occasionally, for the likes of foul language and misuse of mobile phones. 'We need to show we won't tolerate these things on the rare occasions they do happen,' he says.

Pupils and parents: Mostly from a three mile radius (although increasingly from Clapham and central London), so at least they probably know how to navigate Kingston's surreal road system. That said, over 95 per cent of pupils come by bus, train, bike or walk. From over 150 primaries – some 60 per cent from state schools. Parents are a mixture of the predictably wealthy types and those who bend over backwards to afford it. School encourages plenty of parental involvement and there's a thriving parents' association. We found the pupils quietly ambitious and confident. 'You get the occasional princess type who has the best of everything, but you get that in all independent schools. In the main, the children here are grounded and pleasant,' said one parent.

Notable former pupils include Edward Gibbon (The Roman Empire one), RC Sherriff (of Journey's End fame) Michael Frayn, Jonathan Kenworthy, James Cracknell, Andy Sturgeon (imaginatively roped in to help with the reshaping of the school's landscape), 2012 Olympic gold medal rower Sophie Hosking and the founders of Not On The High Street, Sophie Cornish, and Hotel Chocolat's Peter Harris, as well as Ian Fortune, who was awarded the Distinguished Flying Cross (RAF version of the VC) for safely landing his Chinook with injured soldiers on board after being shot in the face through his helicopter windscreen in Afghanistan.

Entrance: The main entry points are 11+ and 16+ with some spaces available for 13+ entry. There's also an option to sit a 10+ deferred entry examination in year 5 to secure a place in year 7 (for which over 200 sit the test for around 20 places offered). More or less equal number of boys and girls. Interview seen as important – the school looks for potential, not just academic achievement, and it also helps weed out the overly tutored. Even at interview stage, the school is blind to whether the pupil goes to a state or private school. 'Unless, that is, they turn up in their straw boater, which some do,' says the head, smiling. Around 1,000 sit the 11+ test, with 360 interviewed, from which up to 250 places are offered for the 125 or so places they could fill. 'We're well aware people have more than one iron in the fire,' says the head, with lots of parents deliberating over issues such as, 'Do I go for Tiffin, which is free, or Kingston Grammar for its reputation?' School works closely with the feeder schools – especially at 13+, so as to not to encourage unrealistic applications. For external 16+, entry involves sitting exams in the A level subjects opted for, followed by interviews. Some 20-30 external offers are made every year.

At year 7, five forms of 20-25 pupils, dropping to an average of 16-18 in GCSE groups and to single figures for A level groups. 'I'm not convinced smaller class sizes necessarily affect outcomes, because good teaching should work in any size class, but it does mean we get to know the pupils better,' says head.

Exit: Around 80 per cent stayed on into sixth form in 2016, for which pupils need an A/B grade average in their GCSEs including A grades in their chosen or related subjects and A* in maths. Post A levels, 98 per cent go to university, 10-15 per cent after a gap year, with over 70 per cent going to Russell Group universities and an annual sprinkling to Oxbridge – 11 in 2016. 'We actually get quite a few pupils turning Oxbridge places down, for example to go to Royal Veterinary College or Imperial to study medicine,' says head (though no medics in 2016). Top destinations include Nottingham, Bristol, Birmingham,

Exeter, Manchester, London, Warwick, Durham, Southampton, Leeds – and a few to art and drama colleges. Biggest range of courses you could imagine, with maths, science, history and humanities among the most popular.

Money matters: Scholarships typically worth 10 to 50 per cent of fees available at all entry points and awarded on results of tests for academic scholarships and application and assessment for art, drama, sport and music. Bursaries worth up to 100 per cent of fees also at all entry points and means-tested – with the school aiming to fill 5-10 per cent of places a year this way. Worth a serious look if you are local, clever and strapped.

Remarks: There's no shortage of good schools in this area, all with their particular highlights, but this stands out for being relaxed and friendly, with an underlying buzz that seems to get pupils willingly and happily doing their best. 'There's a kind of intimacy about it that makes it the kind of school you wish you'd been to,' said one parent, whilst every single pupil and parent we spoke to, bar none, raved about the fact that the school really understands each child and what makes them tick. We found the extracurricular offering also stands out. Indeed, the ethos is all about developing the whole person, not just getting them through academic exams. A school that really lives up to its motto, 'Work Well and Be Happy', this is a place that sets young people up for a fantastic future.

K

Knightsbridge School

67 Pont Street, London SW1X 0BD

Pupils: 400 • Ages: 3–13

Fees: £18,201 – £19,380 pa

Tel: 020 7590 9000
Email: registrar@knightsbridgeschool.com
Website: www.knightsbridgeschool.com

Head: Principal and founder, since the school opened in 2006, Magoo Giles, (50ish) known universally and affectionately as Magoo. Married with two children, one in the school. Via Summer Fields, Eton, the Coldstream Guards and two years as personal equerry to the Queen, he spent six years as head of nearby Garden House Boys' School. If he wasn't a teacher from the off, he should have been – he exudes ebullience, dedication and high educational values. With the backing of 50 friends and family members, he got hold of the building on the corner of Lennox Gardens and Pont Street – formerly home of The Hellenic College – and began to create a dream come true. Magoo is energy, enthusiasm, loquacity and huge fun in pin stripes. He is not out to process children for any particular school but to ensure his school maintains the values, atmosphere and friendliness that make a sound learning environment for all. Parents praise his pastoral care for their children. His school was celebrating its tenth anniversary when we visited. Hard to believe it's not been a fixture for far longer.

Headteacher since September 2015, Shona Colaço MA PGCE MSB CBiol (50ish), previously head of science, director of studies and, finally, deputy head at Hampton Court House School; a biologist by training. Married and with two children, she has upped the profile of science in the school and has also developed leadership courses for her staff – which can, of course, lead to their leaving to lead elsewhere! 'I am as ambitious for my colleagues as for our pupils.' Parents approve: 'The school needed someone more academic'. If listening to Magoo is like being showered by freshly uncorked champagne, chatting with Shona is a reassuring glass of fine wine. She is calm, efficient, warm and experienced – and just as much fun as Magoo, only quieter. Their rooms adjoin, an open door between them, and you can't avoid thinking 'dream team' when you see – and hear – them working together. A wise and mature appointment for a fast-maturing school.

Entrance: Nursery is just for siblings and most entrants join at reception into which they take four classes with a maximum of 18 children in each. They close the lists at 200 applicants and Magoo sees all candidate parents and children – the child does activities with the head of early years while the grown-ups chat. Occasional places thereafter – younger candidates spend a day with their own age group and older ones sit tests and are interviewed. All is designed to ensure that children will fit in and involve themselves and that school and child will suit each other. Most from local nurseries eg Miss Daisy's, Tadpoles, Chelsea Pre-prep and Pippa Poppins.

Exit: Most girls leave at 11 either for local day schools eg Francis Holland SW1 (by far the largest number), Godolphin & Latymer, More House, Queen's Gate or Queen's College and a few for posh country boarding schools eg Downe House or Heathfield. Some boys also hop it at this stage to eg Dulwich College, Emanuel or Cothill. Both sexes take up places at Latymer Upper. The rest, mostly boys, at 13 to, again, Dulwich, King's College School and assorted day and boarding schools. Wise approach to children going to the best schools for them. This is not the school for you if you want your sprog spoon-fed for a school with a name you can brag about.

Remarks: On the corner of Pont Street and Lennox Gardens in a tall, six storey, once private, house complete with grand, limed oak staircase, back stairs, ballroom, erstwhile kitchens, spacious halls, interesting and large triangular corner rooms and lots of little rooms and passages. Few vestiges of the late lamented Hellenic College and its Grecian legacy can still be found about the place. An upmarket prep was the natural successor to its prior tenant and Knightsbridge School has quickly established itself as the natural school for its local constituency of sophisticated, moneyed and cosmopolitan residents. Despite its location, the road is extraordinarily quiet much of the day. The school encourages its families to walk to school, in the interests both of health and out of consideration for neighbours.

Quiet learning in every room. Every class has a teacher and an assistant. We have seldom seen such engaged children, at all levels. Bright, young (mostly female and blonde) staff – all smiles and energy. Curriculum trad and sensible, complemented by brand-new Macs and iPads and laptops with in-class charger units and all used with proper educational values rather than for their own sakes. We even spotted some books! Those on school's SEN register are supported in-class, in small groups and individually. Speech and language and occupational therapists come in as needed. Full time SENCo of whom warm reports. Tribute from one particularly grateful young dyslexic learner: 'Learning support changed everything for me. I don't go to ICT classes, I have one-to-one instead. I'd never have got to Harrow without her help.'

Much enthusiasm for many teachers eg 'he is brilliant!' Parents praise the care and attention given to their children. Rare and only gentle grouse from both parents and children is about a high turnover of staff – especially among the younger ones. To some extent this reflects the school's success in creating new leaders but, as one harder-nosed, parent observed, 'They all want Knightsbridge on their cv'. Also some wise and older staff, so youth and energy are balanced by experience and thoughtfulness. But the hope that a house tutor would stay with a child throughout its KS career seems unlikely to be fulfilled very often. Parental praise for academic support given to those who stay into year 8. Somewhat quieter praise for support given to those who take 11+ entrance tests. 'We need more help with English and maths and less other stuff when the exams are coming.' But this may express perennial parental anxiety more than anything else.

Art room on top floor with pitched ceilings and skylight. Art activities limited by space and resources but what we saw was imaginative and pleasing. Projects on eg 'fish' and 'looking out of the window'. No real DT though some textile work. 3D printer in Mac room. Though the (very well-cared-for) building has its airy spaces, on-site activity space is limited. 'We do miss having a playground.' One good gym in the basement is supplemented by the excellent and capacious facilities at St Columba's church opposite with its huge hall – used by the school for everything that needs real space. Otherwise, buses take children to local parks etc and no-one complains of a lack of exercise – despite the lack of space. Hot days make much of the place airless and stuffy, despite fans and windows.

Much of the ethos is encapsulated in and by the little KS book given to pupils. Its 96 pages include everything from The KS Code and Song (You're on the winning team all the way at KS/You get the most from every day); selective capital cities (no Brazil, Nigeria or Israel but Monaco?); rules of various games including poker; wives of Henry VIII; 12 famous women (one is Coco Chanel); famous speeches; 'thank you' in 24 languages; the periodic table; signs of the zodiac; instructions on how to tie a tie and some predictable hymns. It is quite wonderful, whisks us cheerily back to our grandparents' childhood and we will carry it everywhere.

Parents and children enthuse about the range and variety of activities and clubs on offer – impressive for a prep, especially a day prep. Lots of rewards (Supers) and some demerits (Subs) and a well-understood system for both. Trophies, cups and shields galore. House system which works vertically and horizontally and important for competition in sports, quizzes, arts etc. Effective tutor system clearly trusted by the pupils and especially in moments of anxiety or distress. Also Place2Be – recently won award – a counselling resource with its own room and handled with tact. Parental praise for the home-school communications which are frequent and close. Teachers in the junior school are Miss, Mrs or Mr plus First Name. On Magoo's door is, simply, Magoo. Food looked jolly good to us – especially scrumptious fruit bowls – but a few junior gourmets grumbled about lack of choice.

Most families live in Kensington, Chelsea, Belgravia. A few from such outbacks as Fulham and Battersea. Lots of Americans. But, at time of our visit, around 20 home languages spoken so an interestingly diverse constituency reflecting the neighbourhood. Smallish percentage of pupils need and get EAL help but the staff can muster several languages between them and induction of ESOL pupils is carefully handled. International families love the fact that so many are from overseas, 'so my children don't feel alien like they would in other preps – it's a real melting pot,' said one. Very lively and popular Parents' Association particularly valued by the recently arrived international families who make friends and quickly involve themselves. Five PA committees and a Knowledge Society which invites guest speakers for parental enlightenment, education and entertainment. Every parent we spoke to stressed how 'super-happy' their offspring were. Lots of involvement in local charities and eco initiatives – a palpable concern not to upset the neighbours – many of whom are current parents – clearly a priority.

KS Foundation – largely supported by parents – offers two 100 per cent bursaries annually for children in years 7-9. NB this is an important opportunity, especially for state primary leavers who want to go to senior schools which start at 13+. The commitment can extend to helping bursary-holders into senior schools which will offer continuing significant financial support. Otherwise, no fee assistance lower down the school unless in cases of dire, short-term need.

A lovable school with a warm and community feel that surprises in such a location. If you have no other reason, it's worth moving to Knightsbridge for.

La Sainte Union

Linked with LaSWAP Sixth Form Consortium

Highgate Road, London NW5 1RP

Pupils: 1,137 • Ages: 11–18 • Sixth form: 247 (48 boys); part of LaSWAP consortium • RC

Tel: 020 7428 4600
Email: admissions@lsu.camden.sch.uk
Website: www.lasainteunion.org.uk

Headteacher: Since 2008, Mrs Maureen Williams (40s). Educated at a convent school in Hampshire, read English and medieval literature at Exeter University before taking her PGCE at Digby Stuart College, Roehampton. Taught English at St Joseph's College, Croydon and La Retraite Roman Catholic Girls' School in Lambeth, before taking over from long-serving head Sister Teresa and becoming the school's first lay principal, charged with a mission to gently modernise while maintaining the traditions of La Sainte Union. A calm and competent presence; no doubt the school's illustrious tradition remains in safe hands. Married to a senior probation officer, she enjoys running, walking and good food in her spare time.

Retiring in July 2017.

Academic matters: One of Camden's top-performing comprehensive schools. In 2016, 75 per cent of pupils achieved 5+ A*-C grades at GCSE including English and maths, with 35 per cent A*/A grades – a significant achievement for a school with no academic selection, and not reached by any fudging of the exam system. Pupils here take a demanding curriculum, with nine and half subjects kept going until GCSE, including a compulsory modern language, ICT and RE. Has specialist status in science and maths and 25 girls a year take all three sciences. Everyone, however, benefits from the science enrichment programme, with a multitude of speakers from UCL and Imperial College (both of which offer work placements). 'Many of the girls come from backgrounds where there is limited experience of higher education,' says the head. 'The programme raises their aspirations.' Science results have improved significantly, though A level physicists are still a relative rarity. Setting in maths from year 7, broad banding in science, English and languages (French and Spanish) from year 8. The gifted and talented are led along at a brisk pace, taking some subjects early and adding to the basic diet with astronomy, geography, Italian and statistics. 'The school has some really clever girls,' said one mother, 'and they really nurture them.'

All abilities and interests, however, are well catered for, with young apprenticeships and diplomas increasingly popular. 'Not everyone has to be brilliant, but everyone has to achieve what they can,' commented a parent. 'They say, this is your goal, go for it – but not everyone's goal is the same.' About 70 per cent proceed to the sixth form, which forms part of the popular local consortium of four comprehensives, LaSWAP. A commendable

L

37 per cent A*/B grades at A level in 2016, though results post-16 are not quite as starry as at GCSE. 'We could raise the entry requirements,' says the head, 'and attract a higher ability cohort, but we know we can achieve these results without doing so.' Some 20 pupils have statements of special needs, including one with Down's; has wheelchair access by means of lifts. 'They try to help everyone,' commented one parent.

Games, options, the arts: Music is a particular strength ('super,' says Ofsted) and is based here for the entire consortium sixth form. The standard of singing is unusually high with a 'talented' voice coach in residence. Whole school enthusiasm manifested in a 130-strong gospel choir (a Tour Choice, which performed recently in Barcelona Cathedral), a year 11 jazz band and a strong chamber choir. About a third of pupils take individual instrumental or voice tuition.

Definitely not a 9am-4pm place – 50 clubs operating, before, during and after lessons, everything from rowing and trampolining to keep fit and cookery. For hard-pressed working parents, the homework club, with supervised study before and after school, is a real boon – as it often is for girls. Thriving art department. The spacious walled grounds include a decent range of pitches, made full use of for two hours' compulsory weekly sports, including rounders, netball, athletics, basketball, trampolining, football and aerobics. 'There's no sitting on the side here,' says the head.

Background and atmosphere: One of a number of schools founded by the Sisters of La Sainte Union de Sacre Coeur, a teaching order founded in the early 19th century. The Camden school has now been in the borough for the past 150 years. Housed in a gracious Victorian building (with later additions), maintains the stately and soothing presence of the former convent boarding school it once was. The classrooms in the main block are light and high-ceilinged, the floors polished to a mirror sheen, the gardens to the rear are elegantly laid out with a small orchard and an ample stock of summer roses (sensibly, girls are required to keep to the path and admire from a distance).

L

Though now very much a modern comprehensive, with a broad intake of practising Catholics from across the capital, still has the purposeful air of calm you might expect from its history. The last teaching sister departed in 2010, but the tradition of the founding order and those of the Catholic faith are well maintained. 'We see our mission as promoting the values of the gospel and spirituality, preparing children for a life centred on Christ, celebrating the sacrament and providing links with other parishes and the international LSU community,' says the head. Has its own pretty chapel and pupils attend mass on a weekly rota. Founder's Day is marked with mass – and ice cream.

Pupils wear the distinctive uniform of tartan kilts and white stockings with pride and recently voted to retain this particular tradition. Strong sense of community, both local and international, including its sister school in Tanzania. Vocal school council (with elections for president and vice president) has its say on bullying and school food as well as uniform.

Pastoral care, well-being and discipline: Despite its affluent north London location on the lower slopes of Highgate, intake is anything but indulged – 65 per cent of pupils from low income families, 10 per cent on free school meals. The student population reflects the Catholic population of London – a third speak English as an additional language; a sizeable percentage are first and second generation immigrants from Nigeria, Ghana, the Congo, Poland, South America and southern Europe. Parents are active in their own churches and in the school. 'There is a real sense of community,' said one. No linked parish but many families attend nearby St Joseph's, Highgate and St Dominic's in Kentish Town.

Pupils and parents: 'This is an inner-city comp,' insists the head, though anyone dropping in from outside might be excused for thinking the term doesn't match the orderly space within. Behaviour is generally exemplary but, for those who stray, bad marks and detentions, as well as fixed-term exclusions. Girls with difficulties are certainly not left to fend for themselves. 'Some girls are from families with real problems and they would rather be at school on weekends and holidays than at home,' said one mother. 'This is a safe place to be.' Offers both parental support and additional help with behaviour management and conflict resolution. Teaches about the temptations of drugs and alcohol but drugs are not a significant issue, at least on-site. Problems mainly concern friendship disputes that change social boundaries. Good induction day in year 7 brings pupils from disparate locations and homes together. 'My daughter has really blossomed here,' says one happy parent.

Entrance: Heavily oversubscribed year 7 admits 180 girls, mainly from Catholic primary schools. No selection on ability but must be practising Catholics with Certificate of Catholic Practice signed by their priest. Pupils arrive from seven boroughs (from Walthamstow to Barnet) as distance is measured by public transport rather than metres from the gates. Eighteen places offered on musical aptitude, with an aural test and a small audition. Entry to La SWAP sixth form requires mostly Bs for A level. All girls who enter between 11 and 16 base themselves at the school for the sixth form.

Exit: About a fifth to Russell Group universities, with UCL a favourite option. Popular subjects include English, history, business studies and art foundation. Medics get specialist coaching for BMAT tests. One or two to Oxbridge each year, and some medics.

Money matters: Despite the fact that two-thirds of parents here are on a joint family income of £30,000 or less, most manage the £100 a year voluntary contribution. 'Parents are very generous' and very active, constantly raising funds with second-hand uniform sales etc. 'This is not a rich school,' said one, 'but the school and parents make every effort to give the girls the opportunities that others might take as a given.'

Remarks: A calm and orderly universe, demanding (and getting) high standards of achievement from girls who might not always be expected to reach this high.

The Lady Eleanor Holles School

Hanworth Road, Hampton TW12 3HF

Pupils: 890 • Ages: 7–18 • Sixth form: 175

Fees: £15,693 – £18,945 pa

Tel: 020 8979 1601
Email: registrar@lehs.org.uk
Website: www.lehs.org.uk

Headmistress: Since 2014, Heather Hanbury, previously head of Wimbledon High. MA Edinburgh, MSc Cambridge in geography then land economy. Prior to teaching, she spent nine years working in various management consultancy roles in the City, then as a corporate fundraiser – 'real world' experience that both pupils and parents value. Moved into teaching because she was so frequently told she 'should' – 'but I initially resisted it because I don't like to do the expected,' she laughs. Eventually had a change of heart and took a PGCE with the express ambition of becoming a head. 'I always wanted to run things. I like making organisations efficient, effective and happy' – something that everyone agrees she's achieved, with bells on.

Began her teaching career at Blackheath High School in 1996, quickly rising through the ranks to head of sixth form, before moving on to Haberdashers' Aske's School for Girls, thence deputy head of Latymer Upper School. Teaches all year 7s for half a term each ('I get to know them, but more importantly, they get to know me – far better than helicoptering my way into sixth form teaching,' she insists). And although she does herself down when it comes to her teaching abilities ('I do the least damage,' she laughs), girls say she's actually very good. The only school where we've heard pupils describe their headteacher as 'very sweet,' they gush over her assemblies ('She recently did a fantastic one on friendship and talked all about the movie Mean Girls,' enthused one) and say she is 'involved,' 'interested' and 'approachable' – attending every event imaginable, even wearing sports kits to matches.

In school, she adorns glamorous suits (no staff member we met would have looked out of place at a wedding), hums with energy, has just the right amount of modesty (as is the LEH way), is quick to smile and laugh and is intent on injecting some fun into school life. Her office is among the nicest, largest and swankiest we've seen – in fact, if you replaced her desk with a bed, it could pass as a luxury boutique hotel room.

Lives with her husband in Hammersmith. Interests include bridge ('I'm not very good,' – there's that modesty again), cooking and theatre.

Head of junior school: Since September 2016, Mrs Paula Mortimer BEd (40s), previously head of St Christina's school in St John's Wood. A science specialist with a degree from Oxford, she has taught in preps and all-through schools, latterly as deputy and acting head of Channing Junior School. Also has experience as SEN coordinator. Still loves teaching. 'I have no plans whatsoever to stop spending time working with children in the classroom,' she says. A hands-on head, she is known for fostering honest, open relationships not only with staff, but with pupils and parents. Very committed to pastoral care. 'For me, a role as head is all about ensuring children are secure and happy first and foremost, as that's what makes them successful learners. They're two sides of the same coin.' Particularly keen to see children take risks in the classroom. 'That's how they learn.'

Academic matters: Great cross-curricular approach to much of the junior school teaching – something that the girls talk excitedly about, giving us example upon example. If they learn about the ancient Greeks, they make Greek vases. If they learn about circuits, they design and make a working toy car. Arts and crafts and DT throughout are unusual and clever – girls showed us examples of 3D mazes they'd made, along with personally designed carry-bags, clever photography, moving toys and home-made slippers. Even the plastic plates they use at lunch (where food has mixed views from pupils, but mainly good) are each designed by a girl in the school. Particularly great excitement about the animated films the girls make, using their own clay and cut-out models, in year 5.

The wow-factor science lab is designed for interactive learning, with five hexagonal shaped high tables with Bunsen burners and plug sockets in the middle with six stools round each, plus state-of-the-art flatscreen Apple TV on the wall. 'We recently hatched chicks in an incubator,' girls told us. The library, though inviting and well-stocked, is small and barely adequate for this number of girls – which staff acknowledge, although they point out that they haven't given up trying to work out a solution and they claim that the lack of brilliant library is somewhat compensated for by revolutionising the use of iPads in learning. Good traditional hall for productions, assemblies and younger girls' gym, and they use the fabulous senior school theatre. Decent ICT suite.

Back in the classroom, there's very little setting, although girls are sometimes taught in smaller, mixed-ability groups if it's felt it will aid their learning. French and extracurricular Mandarin are offered as languages, although the languages model is being reviewed. Specialist teaching in science, music, PE and computing from year 3, with everything else taught by the form teacher – then specialist teaching for everything from year 5.

Mild SEN catered for in the juniors – although note it's not called that here, with them favouring LDD (learning difficulties and disabilities). Help just as likely to be for a spelling group that need short-term strategies as for anyone with dyslexia or dyscalculia, which means no stigma. Short-term bursts of intervention is the name of the game here, with a major focus on arming the girls with tools and techniques to keep up with the fast academic pace.

Few teach academia better and it's done via thrilling, not drilling. 'What's the point in boring them into submission?' says the senior school head – although she admits it's not always easy, particularly around GCSE learning, 'which can be very routine especially for bright, lively minds.' 'I really admire the school's ability to go sideways in any subject, bringing in current affairs or going cross-curricular, for instance,' said one parent. Results outstanding – 96 per cent A*/A at GCSE in 2016. It helps that staff clearly delight in what they do and all teach their own degree subject. Pupils told us teachers are always available, with the staff room practically empty at lunchtimes, as teachers run clinics or answer pupil queries from their departments. Sixth formers increasingly help the younger ones ('It's easy for them to remember the bits people find tricky in years 8 and 9,' explains the head. 'And it's good for them too – there's nothing like teaching to help you learn yourself.') Traditional subjects taken at GCSE, with computer science being offered from 2017.

Committed to A levels, rather than the IB or Pre-U, with the academic offering upped via EPQ, plus an enrichment programme across every subject. 2016 saw 79 per cent A*-A grades (96 per cent A*/B). Good range of subjects, including classical civilization, psychology and economics, although maths and sciences remain the most popular. Sixth form feels quite a separate entity here – these older girls are revered and there are lots of sixth form only areas, including their smaller classrooms which cater for more tutorial style learning, in which there are no more than 12 girls in any one class.

Setting in maths during year 7, with groups reviewed annually. Languages include Latin, German and French from year 7, with the option of Spanish and ancient Greek added at GCSE (although French remains the most popular language at GCSE). The school has one of the biggest German A level cohorts in the country, and Spanish is growing. ICT embedded into learning, with increasing use of iPads in lessons. A culture of enquiry and exploration fostered throughout.

Meticulous record keeping for monitoring and targeting, although they don't make a big show of it to pupils or parents. We found girls have quite a competitive attitude to learning, although they are also quick to support and praise others' achievements, with lots of patting on backs and high fives. Some criticism from pupils around the timetable, which includes nine x 35-minute lessons. 'By the time you've settled into a lesson, that only leaves half-an-hour – and you've got four of those before break,' said one.

Few with more than mild learning difficulties here, for whom SEN support is embedded into classes, with some one-to-ones where required – and it must work as they get the same results as everyone else. Seriously good school to consider if you have mobility problems or are wheelchair-bound – flattish site, lifts and wide corridors, plus can-do approach – although we were surprised no girls in this situation when we visited.

Games, options, the arts: Legendary for sports and the facilities in this 23 acre plot are outstanding for a girls' day school, including three spectacular and very green lacrosse pitches (which many of the classrooms overlook – lovely, especially in summer); six outdoor courts; a massive modern sports hall; and rather elderly indoor swimming pool that had plans for a refurb when we visited. At the front of the school are grass tennis courts and croquet lawn ('embarrassing, really, but rather fun!' laughs the head). Some parents choose the school on the strength of the sports alone. Lacrosse, not surprisingly, is the main winter game and played to win – which they do. Rowing also a speciality – a welcome rarity in a girls' school, for which boathouse facilities are shared with neighbouring Hampton School, and they also collect lots of silverware. 'It's great because if you don't like running around after a ball, you can sit in a boat instead – although many do both,' says the head.

Other sports include gymnastics, netball, swimming, basketball, fencing, rounders, athletics, tennis and badminton. Don't like sport? Head told us there's plenty of girls in this situation and that's fine too, although one girl we spoke to felt sport can be a bit elitist. 'You start out with A-E teams in year 7, but now we've got an A team and half a B team – if you're not in those, you don't get anywhere near as much attention,' one of the older girls complained, although others disagreed with her, which led to an interesting debate. Sports tours to eg Barbados and America.

L

Superb junior sports too (great preparation for the legendary sporting culture of the senior school) and girls are lucky to use many of the older girls' facilities. In winter, the focus is on swimming, netball and gymnastics and in summer, on swimming, rounders, athletics and some tennis.

Artistic talent was being exhibited in the fabulous new art rooms and corridors in all its splendour when we visited – much of it so good that you'd hang them in your own home. Beautiful ceramics displayed in a glass cabinet. Lively textiles and photography.

Music exceptional – the Holles Singers reach the finals of the BBC Youth Choir annually. We lost count of how many other choirs there were – some for which girls audition, others open to all. Orchestras and ensembles galore, with bands ranging from rock and pop to jazz. 'Unbelievably, we even have a symphony orchestra!' smiles the head, wide-eyed. Sixty per cent of girls learn an instrument with a peripatetic teacher. Brass particularly popular, with many budding saxophonists. Plenty of space for all this in the shiny purpose-built arts block (where the arts studios are also based). Junior school girls have weekly music lessons in a good-sized dedicated room. Junior choir (for years 5 and 6 – you have to audition), chorus (open to anyone), orchestra and string group (which has performed in Hampton Court). 'My daughter adores her trombone classes – they really enthuse her,' said one parent.

Purpose-built theatre (again, in the same block) has the wow factor even when empty, but what a treat to hear a girl practising a solo song for the annual musical when we visited – she was amazing. Drama here is outstanding, with each year group performing something annually. The two big set pieces are joint musicals with Hampton School (years 11 up) and the summer musical (for years 7 and 8). 'They are something else – so professional,' said one girl. Drama is also big in the junior school and the girls love it, as we saw for ourselves during a practice session in the senior school theatre. Big singing and acting voices for girls so small – a treat to watch. The school takes part in everything from poetry recitals to debating competitions to Shakespeare festivals.

Extracurricular life here is thriving. Particularly lively debating society, model UN and lots of charity and community work, including going into local schools. D of E and CCF take-up good. Masses of day trips to museums, theatres etc, plus residential trips from year 7 upwards – language exchanges, ski trips and battlefields, among them. Other recent examples include Greece and Italy (classics), Berlin (history), Iceland (geography) and Geneva (with Global Challenge).

Background and atmosphere: The school was established in 1710 under the will of Lady Eleanor Holles, daughter of John Holles, 2nd Earl of Clare. This makes it one of the oldest girls' schools in the country. It began life in the Cripplegate Ward of the City of London, then moved to other premises in the City till 1878, thence to Mare Street in Hackney (that building now houses the London College of Fashion). The current school, purpose-built and designed in the shape of an E, opened in 1937. Such a long history is scarcely uncommon in many of our great public schools but rare in girls' schools. A palpable pride underpins the place. The staffroom has seen many distinguished names. They include Pauline Cox, former head of Tiffin Girls', Margaret Hustler, former head of Harrogate Ladies' College, Cynthia Hall, former head of Wycombe Abbey, and Frances King, former head of Roedean, who all taught here.

Very long, horizontal, featureless and functional, the two-storey main building doesn't delight the eye but then again, it doesn't offend it either. Inside, the corridors are wide, the rooms are light and everywhere is well-kept. Some areas are somewhat hospital-like, with lengthy corridors and polished wood floors. The pupils insist, though, that 'the thing that brings it alive is the girls.' Latest add-on – the arts, music and drama block – was finished in 2013 and provides the stand-out facilities mentioned earlier, as well as a jazzy new refectory. Big main library is well-stocked. Fabulous DT room, with much pride around the 3D printer ('I can't believe one exists, let alone being in our school!' said one girl). Lots of innovation in the cookery room – the girls were making their own versions of Bakewell tart when we visited. Excellent sixth form centre features small teaching rooms – ideal for a history seminar or session on poetic form. The sixth form library is notable – light and overlooking the pitches – as well as being well-stocked (including more mature books and careers and university materials), with neat tables for study and rows of PCs. Nice sixth-form café and common room too.

Focused and purposeful atmosphere. Girls are well turned out in grey uniforms and the sixth formers look fresh and neat in casual dress. A sense of order pervades throughout. It's cool to be clever and cool to be good at sport. And because they expect a lot from the girls from an early stage, there's a big push on them taking responsibility for themselves from the off. 'If you don't turn up for a practice, you don't stay on the team.' Strong links with Hampton School – just across the playing fields – not just in drama, music, rowing and coach trips as we've mentioned, but also in careers and university preparation and increasingly for the younger years too eg extracurricular clubs. 'It almost feels co-ed without having the distraction of boys in the actual classroom – what could be better?' delighted one parent.

The junior school building started life as an attractive old house, although build-ons over the years means that outside, it is now a rather dull looking three-storey block with a one-storey extension in unattractive brick and PVC windows. However, unlike preps elsewhere, it has fabulous outside space – real space. A super garden area with excellent climbing frames and other apparatus, courts and pitches, much of it, of course, shared with the senior school. Particularly valued by girls are the 'hedge homes' – little dens in the hedges abutting the brook separating the school from the grounds. The girls use pebbles for money and run these little domestic havens just as they would their brick and drainpipe equivalents.

Inside, everywhere is carpeted, which makes for quiet corridors and a civilised feel. Classrooms are airy and light, where teachers pack in the learning, although by no means all with chalk and talk – we saw plenty of interactive examples. A sense of purpose and attentiveness pervades, but it feels as if the girls are having real fun too – and their work is displayed in every corridor in witty, appealing and imaginative ways.

Academically, this school holds a reputation of being a hothouse, which clearly infuriates staff and parents alike. 'Come and see the school for yourself,' urges the junior school head, who believes the label 'hothouse' becomes lazy shorthand for selective schools that do well. 'They are just little girls who have a growth mindset.' The 'growth mindset' is a phrase you hear a lot here – with the school avoiding words like 'bright' and 'intelligent' like the plague. 'Those are fixed labels that are high risk because once you are told you're bright, you might not take risks in the classroom for fear of failing – and taking risks is how you learn.' Homework seems fair – 20 minutes a night up to year 5, then 40 minutes. 'The school understands that if you're a working parent, you might not have time to do hours of homework – I applaud that,' said one parent.

Teachers (who, disappointingly, when we visited, were all female) have lots of autonomy, teaching how they want to, not how they're prescribed to. They are, however, encouraged to constantly try new techniques (of their choosing) to keep things fresh. We found imaginative and lively examples throughout.

Pastoral care, well-being and discipline: Pastoral care strong, with deputy head of junior school at the helm. They take a proactive approach, with lots of staff meetings to discuss, 'Did you think what X did was out of character?' 'Did you think X has been a bit distracted lately?' etc. and they discuss it with girls if appropriate – and indeed parents, who they aren't afraid of calling to ask if everything is all right. Likewise, parents feel welcome to call the school. Girls praise the strong system of buddies, including coach buddy, house buddies and peer mentors, who help people out in the playground if they're sad. 'They even designed their own hats,' the girls told us, explaining that the buddy brings the woeful girl back over the little bridge into the junior school area to a special bench, where they can talk. 'It gives the peer mentor great skills of mediation,' one parent pointed out. Lots of leadership roles (science leaders, head girl, house captains etc) and there's a term of mindfulness teaching for year 5s. Plenty of opportunities for personal attention time – not just in the natural flow of the day, but via specific appointments, in which pupils are encouraged to share news about something amazing they did at the weekend as much as to discuss something that's worrying them.

Bullying minimal, due to zero tolerance attitude, anti-bullying assemblies, golden school rules, talks about making the right choices and – perhaps most innovatively – a contract that each girl signs every year. If they break the contract, the head shows them the document and their signature and they get a firm questioning session – girls consider this deeply shameful. 'Girls put a huge emphasis on best friends, so we do a lot of work around that, explaining that boys don't do this and they don't have to feel disloyal having more than one really good friend.'

Misbehaviour negligible, with little need for discipline – forgetting homework and calling someone a bad name is the worst of it, for which you get a 'sanction,' three of which in a half term mean you have to stay in during a breaktime. But it's very infrequent. 'You lose perspective of behavioural issues in a lovely school like this,' said previous head, recounting a story of someone who recently took the pebbles (remember the currency in the hedges) back to their desk in a plastic bag so they didn't have to share it. 'The result was huge gasp, shock and outrage – because that's as bad as it gets here.' Parents and pupils concur.

House system is a big deal here – there are even inter-house jigsaw competitions. 'It's about so much more than an annual sports day,' says the senior school head, and girls love the leadership responsibilities and opportunity to make new friends that come with it. Much praise for the pastoral care system – a clear structure and everyone knows who to go to. Teachers described as 'supportive mentors'. One parent told us her daughter needed to take significant time off and that the ongoing support from afar was 'incredible.' Good system of buddying, and a feeling that no transgressors would get away with it for long. No noteworthy sins of the drink/drugs/fags kind and minor bullying problems are dealt with swiftly. A culture of openness means that it's all right to tell someone if you're not happy. We were particularly impressed with the cyber mentor system, which involves sixth formers being trained to go into classes without teachers to discuss any online problems. 'The training means they know when a line is crossed and they report it to us to intervene,' says the head. In fact, e-safety overall is taken very seriously here, with a dedicated e-safety officer. School counsellor available three days a week. School wants to increase its offering around specific mental health issues. 'I think we're at the point we were with bullying 10 years ago – in that it's time to bring it out of the closet and admit it's ok to have issues and deal with them. It's about de-stigmatising,' says the head.

Despite the school's reputation of being highly pressurised and hothousing the pupils, it's the girls who seem to be the ones putting pressure on themselves, rather than it being imposed from above. 'It's just the culture of the school,' one girl told us. All are therefore grateful for the talks on how to cope, especially at exam time, and pupils told us they know where to go if they feel it gets too much. 'And we support each other too,' they say. One parent told us, 'I get especially fed up of hearing about the hothouse reputation as it's my experience that the school actually works very hard to take pressure off the girls, persuading them to rest in the holidays and to balance their work with fun stuff in term-time too.'

Low-level misbehaviour, such as forgetting homework, leads to a 'pink slip.' Three of those in a half-term and you get a strongly worded letter. But it's more carrot than stick here, with rewards of sweets if you don't get any pink slips and a class pizza lunch if your class does particularly well in something eg charity work.

Girls praise the mixing of year groups, which they say leads to friendships they might not otherwise have had – 'due to houses, extracurricular clubs and the buddy system' – but it didn't stop some girls complaining to us that there are cliques that can be hard to penetrate. Food much better than it used to be, girls told us. 'There's loads of choice too – you can grab a sandwich or have a full-on hot meal.'

Who wouldn't this school suit? Girls who aren't prepared to work hard, try new things (no matter if you're no good at it – it's the trying it in the first place that matters here) or who are set in a certain mindset, said the girls we met. 'You find yourself becoming someone completely different than when you started – it's really quite incredible,' said one girl.

Pupils and parents: Parents tend to be much like the pupils here – academically brilliant, with a go-getting attitude. Not all super-rich, with many parents holding down a couple of jobs to pay the fees, something that the school values as enriching the school community. 'There aren't as many very wealthy families as I thought there'd be when I joined,' says head. Lively PA, called The Friends, is open to both senior and junior school parents. Mainly white British, although younger years are more ethnically mixed, with the second biggest ethnic group being

Asian. From a wide area – Ealing, Windsor, Woking, Wimbledon and Chiswick, and all points in between. Public transport links aren't great, but an impressive coach map shows the multitude of routes they cater for (joint with Hampton boys' school) at the beginning and end of the school day (some later to cater for girls who do clubs) and which 50 per cent of the girls utilise. Juniors get a coach buddy to make the whole thing less daunting. The rest walk, cycle or dropped off. Lots of parents have boys at Hampton.

Word of advice if your daughter gets in: try to prepare her psychologically for the transition period. To get in at all, she'll have probably have been top dog in her pre-prep or primary school – here, she'll enter a melting pot, where everyone is academically superior. But whilst this can be difficult, girls find it humbling too – probably explaining why we found girls to be so pleasingly modest. No know-it-alls in sight. Overall, we found the girls to be conscientious and bubbly (the ones who showed us round didn't stop talking, such was their enthusiasm for seemingly every detail of the school) and very happy learners. 'My child loves going to school,' is a phrase we heard time and time again – and we saw for ourselves the reassuring skips down the corridors and beaming smiles in the classrooms. 'Anything you'd change about the school?' is one of our common questions to parents, to which we twice got the answer, 'Only that I didn't get to go there myself.'

Entrance: School's own entrance tests in English and maths at 7+, and top performers invited back for an activity session. About 48 places, split across two forms. Only two girls trying for every place, but don't be fooled – the older they get, the faster the ride, so best for tots who seem exceptionally bright and eager to learn. That said, they do take some borderline performers. 'Some show high potential, but have not had the fire in their belly if, for example, they've been at a pre-prep that just drills facts into them. We are looking for what girls are capable of, not what they've already achieved – along with a can-do attitude.'

Around a third of senior school entrants come up from junior department. Of the remaining two-thirds, there's a 33/66 mix of girls from state/private sector – around 40 different schools in total. Private ones include Newland House, Twickenham Prep, The Study, Bute House, Holy Cross Prep, Kew College. Four to five applicants for each place. Tests in maths, English, non-verbal and verbal reasoning and a problem solving paper. Expect the unexpected in the interview. 'We can tell a mile off if we are hearing not the girl themselves, but their parent or tutor. I'm absolutely allergic to that,' says the head, wincing. 'I don't even care if they do something silly in the interview – at least it shows they're being themselves.'

School sets its own exams for sixth form applicants, who need an A in subjects they want to study – and, in fact, As and A*s in pretty much everything. 'The odd B here and there is ok, but we want girls who can leap in with the rest and move fast,' says the head. Reports from current schools also count, along with an interview.

Exit: Some three-quarters of juniors move up to the senior department – low for an all-through school, but the school insists that in any one year, usually only three or four girls do not progress due to not being academically able. Thankfully, no exam separating those who get in vs those that don't – instead, girls are assessed on the basis of their classroom work and school exams and offered a guaranteed place in year 5. The few who don't make the cut get lots of support and extra help to prepare for tests to other schools and they may still sit the LEH entrance exam if they wish. Those who want to try for a scholarship also sit the entrance exams, along with the outside applicants. Those who do get a place, but decide to go elsewhere, opt for Tiffin Girls, St Paul's Girls or Nonsuch, with others going to Kingston Grammar, Sir Williams Perkins, St James' Girls and St Catherine's.

The school loses around 10 per cent of girls at sixth form – most to other high-level, but (crucially) co-ed, sixth forms. A few leave for financial reasons. Around 80 per cent to Russell Group universities. Destinations include Oxbridge (12 in 2016), Durham, Bristol, London, Exeter, Edinburgh, St Andrews and a few to Europe and USA (five in 2016). Mainly traditional degree subjects, with lots studying medicine (seven places in 2016) English, history, sciences. Notable old girls include Lynn Barber, Charlotte Attenborough, Carola Hicks, Annie Nightingale, Saskia Reeves, Jay Hunt and Gail (University Challenge) Trimble.

Money matters: Drive under way to increase the number and value of bursaries. Means-tested and reviewed annually. Academic scholarships worth up to 10 per cent of fees at 11+ and sixth form level. Music scholarships up to 10 per cent. At A level, academic, music, art, drama and sport scholarships available – each worth up to 10 per cent of fees. Music exhibitions worth up to 7.5 per cent – and that's at 11+ and A level.

Remarks: This is a school that bangs the drum very loudly about empowerment, constantly reminding girls they can do anything if they put their minds to it – and they excel in giving them the tools to achieve that. Not for the faint-hearted, the girls work hard – and we mean hard – but they play hard too. If your daughter has the potential to be a determined, committed learner with a can-do attitude, this could be her ticket to a highly successful future.

Lady Margaret School

Parsons Green, London SW6 4UN

Pupils: 775 • Ages: 11–18 • Sixth form: 185 • C of E

Tel: 020 7736 7138
Email: admin@ladymargaret.lbhf.sch.uk
Website: www.ladymargaret.lbhf.sch.uk

Headteacher: Since 2015, Ms Elisabeth Stevenson MA PGCE, previously deputy head at Grey Coat Hospital. Degree in mediaeval history plus later, part time, degree in early modern European history at Birkbeck. Taught history at Rickmansworth School before moving to Grey Coat in 2000 as head of history, then assistant, then deputy head. An excellent training ground for Lady Margaret with which it has much in common. Although only a year into her tenure when we visited, her leadership, innovations and smiley presence were palpable. Parents and girls seem enchanted by her – 'so involved and visible about the school'; 'she speaks so well'; 'look – her door is open, it always is – that speaks volumes' – and in fact, both doors into her room – to the atrium and to the garden – were wide open: she could hardly be more accessible. Entirely visible around the school, Ms Stevenson is completely invisible on the school website, even if you put her name in Search, which seems a shame.

A practising Anglican, she celebrates the 'Christian values' and the 'centrality of worship' to her school's ethos. 'It frames and shapes the day,' she told us. 'Every assembly begins with lighting a candle and ends with a prayer. And we say grace at the end of each school day.' But she will not rush to embrace the option of admitting 100 per cent of pupils on the basis of a shared faith: 'I think as a Church of England school we should serve everyone in our local community, not just the church community.' She has ideas and principles but is not dogmatic. 'I don't think education is something that happens to you. It's about engaging. Schooling should be characterised by kindness and engagement.' Girls concur: 'She runs a tight ship and is very organised but is so approachable!'

Academic matters: They are doing something right here. Despite a scrupulously banded intake, the results they produce defy any reasonable expectation. It must be all about aspiration and ambition. Psychology, Eng Lit, maths and history the most popular A level options in a range that includes history of art and IT. Thirty-four per cent of grades were A*/A and 66 per cent were A*/B in 2016. Fine art – see below – and history the most successful but few subjects saw many grades below C. Everyone takes core GCSEs which here include RS. Equal numbers for French and Spanish – no other languages timetabled. Around three-quarters take all three sciences. Almost 46 per cent of all subjects received A*/A grades in 2016 (84 per cent got 5+ A*-C grades including English and maths). RS, perhaps unsurprisingly, the stand-out success. We were interested in the approach here: 'Not all the RS teachers are from the Anglican tradition. They are very open to all religions and always willing to debate and discuss.' We toured the school and witnessed class after class of girls, head down or in earnest collaboration – evidence of the head's claims that 'girls don't have to be ashamed of working hard here.. they are ambitious and want to do well – even the naughty ones!'

Overwhelmingly positive approach. The school uses the WWW (What Went Well) remark and an EBI (Even Better If) comment on every piece of work. We think this a sound way of keeping teachers up to the mark quite as much as pupils. We enjoyed many features of work and evidence of thinking here eg the What Is Your Favourite Book display board and were intrigued by the choices: – lots of Roald Dahl (predictable), one Pride and Prejudice (estimable), one Ulysses (impressive, if implausible) and one 50 Shades of Grey (lamentable).

At the time of our visit, 10 girls had statements or EHC plans and a further 60 received some kind of SEN support. Level of support varies according to need eg differentiated work and resources, LSAs in lessons, withdrawal, small groups and in-class support where needed. SEN department runs homework club, reduced timetables and curriculum support sessions. Also external agencies provide eg additional therapies such as speech and language and drama. School would welcome anyone including those with mild ASD but the site prohibits entry to anyone with complex physical problems. Those who need EAL support also helped by the SEN dept and on a similar basis.

Games, options, the arts: Art is exceptional. It inhabits six separate studios and rooms including a designated oil painting room. We were delighted by some of the most interesting, careful and creative work in painting and drawing we've seen anywhere. Lively textiles, food tech lab and a sizeable DT workshop testify to the emphasis placed on head and hand collaboration here. Annual fashion show and competition display girls' own handmade work. Music likewise is celebrated here – both in theory (fabulous ICT suite for music) and in practice – lots of lessons, practice rooms, four choirs, ensembles and enthusiasm. Dramatic productions staged with verve and hard work and with impressive results. Until now, drama has not been a 'subject'. However, girls who chafe at the lack of timetabled drama will chafe – and leave for other schools in pursuit of it – no longer. Plan to introduce GCSE drama from September 2017 – Ms Stevenson very clear about its usefulness on the timetable in terms of character development, team work and expressiveness.

Energetic sports include rowing at Fulham Reach, games at Eel Brook, five minutes' walk away, or at Barn Elms, by public transport. Tennis in Bishop Park. Lacrosse, badminton, cricket – no shortage of sporting opportunities whatever your thing. And successes, both individual and in teams, across the board. 'Very well-run' D of E programme. 'Fantastic' dance opportunities – street to ballet on offer and parents rave about the choreography and production standards – 'they rehearse so hard!' A sense of trying everything and having a go.

Background and atmosphere: Parsons Green is a purlieu on the eastern edge of Fulham, in this hip part of London. A three-bed house will set you back around £1.5m. Facing the triangle of grass shaded by ancient plane and ash trees which is the actual Parsons Green, the school is housed in a row of attractive buildings from several eras. Parsons Green tube station is a convenient two minutes' walk away. The school has an interesting role in the history of women's education. Founded in 1841, Whitelands College was a teacher training college: 'to produce a superior class of parochial schoolmistresses'. Whitelands College School followed a year later. In 1917, when the school was threatened with closure, the remarkable second mistress, Enid Moberly Bell, rescued it and reopened it as Lady Margaret later that year. (She also moonlighted as the vice-chair of the Lyceum Club for female artists and writers.) Her life-partner, Anne Lupton, financed the purchase of the school's second building, Elm House and named the school after Margaret Beaufort, of whom Erasmus, no less, wrote on her tomb: 'Margaret, Countess of Richmond, mother of Henry VII, grandmother of Henry VIII, who donated funds for three monks of this abbey, a grammar school in Wimborne, a preacher in the whole of England, two lecturers in Scripture, one at Oxford, the other at Cambridge, where she also founded two colleges, one dedicated to Christ, and the other to St John, the Evangelist.' The school's transmogrifications since founding reflect the changing times and mores – from a grammar, to a voluntary aided and now an academy.

The Christian backbone of the school is proudly proclaimed by the 12 foot wooden cross with the Tudor rose ingrained on it which leans against the wall of the most modern of the buildings – a plate glass and marble statement – at one end of the extensive frontage. The two main buildings are handsome Georgian townhouses which retain some elegant features of their former selves and a mass of small rooms, passages and staircases. The school – when you are in it – is far larger than you'd guess from the outside, having accrued buildings, outside space and assorted additions. Most of it is well-maintained and treated with respect. We saw no litter. The girls, too, are well-turned out in their black with red stripe uniform. We witnessed the head turning down the odd collar and a girl or two pulling down a shorter than average skirt on her approach. 'She has smartened us up,' we were told. Sixth formers wear home clothes and treat this privilege with respect.

Excellent – and one of the best-stocked we've seen – library, a little cramped but full of girls actually working, something we do not often encounter. Good study areas elsewhere including one 'informal' and one silent one in the sixth form centre. Excellent Busby Auditorium – a real lecture theatre seating 140 – used for talks, rehearsals, presentations etc. Good and tidy displays about the place. One large tarmac playground. School food not seen as irresistible. About half bring lunch from home, most sixth formers go out to get it. But with pasta and salad bars, hot choices and fruit pots, it looked OK to us.

Pastoral care, well-being and discipline: Well understood pastoral care system. Problems first to form tutor, then head of year. School counsellor around two days a week for support. But girls attest to 'happier' atmosphere under new regime and a new emphasis on self-esteem. 'The head wants us to develop into confident young women.' When girls get into trouble – and in rare cases of exclusion – it is because of persistent behavioural lapses rather than anything else. Social media abuse a persistent hazard here as everywhere. 'We have a very strong community feeling but we do have girls who behave badly on occasions. We deal with it very quickly,' explained the head – this view supported by both parents and girls. Pastoral care described as 'amazing' by parents and school is assiduous in home-school comms. 'We have the numbers of absolutely anyone we might need,' said a parent. Parents also feel involved – 'they do listen to concerns'.

Pupils and parents: About as diverse as it gets. Some from local, affluent families who also apply for the local independents. Many from far less privileged homes. Great mix of backgrounds. Some 18 per cent speak a language other than English at home – a relatively small proportion given the school's location. Very active PTA – lots of drinks dos and other events. A few parents feel a bit pressured to involve themselves and cough up for school appeals but they stress these are, of course, voluntary and some keep away though everyone we spoke to praised the school's sense of community.

Entrance: Banding via non-verbal reasoning test which tests maths and a piece of independent creative writing. Sixty-seven foundation places reserved for girls who regularly attend C of E services. Fifty-three open places reserved for girls of any other, or no, religion. Applications divided into three ability bands making six categories. For each category, distance measurements are then applied. No priority for those with SEN unless statement or EHC plan submitted naming Lady Margaret. First priority to looked after, or previously looked after, girls, then (up to a third of places to) siblings. In effect, in the year we visited, this meant: 17 girls admitted from each of foundation bands 1 and 3, and 33 from foundation band 2. In the open bands, 13 were admitted from bands 1 and 3 and 27 from band 2. There was no point in living more than 0.3 of a mile away if you applied for an open place, but some foundation entrants lived up to five miles away. Church-going essential for the latter – at least twice a month for previous three years. Hundreds apply for the 40-50 sixth form places – applicants, like existing pupils, need six Bs at GCSE and between A*-B for individual A levels.

Exit: One of the most impressive leavers' lists we have seen from an academy. 2015 was a bumper harvest for Oxbridge with four entrants (though only one in 2016) and, while Oxbridge isn't the measure of all things, it suggests the school has an ambition for its alumnae lacking elsewhere. Otherwise, a good spread of universities from the newbies to the redbricks and, again, a diverse mix of courses chosen – from IT through midwifery to anthropology, including two medics in 2016. Rather extraordinarily, everyone seems to leave for either university or an art college. An interestingly diverse list of leavers over recent decades includes Diana Garnham, chief executive of the Science Council, Nigella and Horatia Lawson, Lady Zoe Barclay, actresses Kelly Hunter, Joanne Adams and Jessie Burton, film director Mahalia Belo, upcoming soprano Louise Alder, Martha Fiennes – oh, and Janet Street-Porter.

Money matters: Parental contribution asked for and willingly donated in most cases.

Remarks: Outstanding school for an ambitious, motivated, outward-looking girl. The anxious faces of the parents handing in their applications for next year's places said it all.

L

Langley Park School for Boys

South Eden Park Road, Beckenham, Kent BR3 3BP

Pupils: 1,690 • Ages: 11–18 • Sixth form: 625 (230 girls)

Tel: 020 8639 4700
Email: office@lpbs.org.uk
Website: www.lpbs.org.uk

Headteacher: Since 2013, Mr Steve Parsons (40s); has BA in history from King's College, MA in school effectiveness and improvement from the Institute of Education and the professional headship qualification, NPQH. He has lived nearby in Beckenham for many years with his wife Ruth, also a senior school headteacher, and could not quite believe the fortuitousness of the top job arising at Langley Park at just the moment he felt ready to take on a headship.

Having come straight from Dunraven School, the highly sought after south London co-educational state secondary in Streatham, where he spent seven years as deputy head, he would seem to be a very good fit. As Dunraven too underwent lengthy transition to new buildings, he is relieved to find himself in Langley Park's stunning new quarters post the spade-work. Prior to Dunraven he was assistant head at Crown Woods College.

The previous head was at the school for 15 years, and Mr Parsons is aware he has a lot to live up to, speaks highly of the past head's vision for the school and says it will be 'evolution, not revolution', confirmed by parents: 'the transition from the previous head seems to have been very smooth: we have not noticed any major changes'.

Parents told us: 'I find him inspiring and a great leader for the boys' and 'he seems a committed, positive and hardworking head'. We found him to be very approachable, focused, modest, extremely tall and not lacking in courage, not only in taking over from a much-loved predecessor but in resolutely describing himself as a fan of football – more armchair than playing these days – in a school where rugby is the sporting religion.

Academic matters: Thrillingly good results given the non-selective intake. In 2016, 80 per cent of boys achieved 5 A*-Cs at GCSE including English and maths, 30 per cent A*/A grades; a strong showing of A*/As in Spanish, music, statistics, physics, IT, computer studies and chemistry. English language GCSE is so good the school is in the top five per cent of results nationally. At A level 24 per cent A*/A, 57 per cent A*-B in 2016.

Everyone can find their level, with the seven entry forms at 11+ divided into eight ability-based learning groups at key stage 3, 10 at key stage 4 for English and maths. There is definitely no resting on laurels in sight: the head has ambitions for academic improvement, introducing the new year 7s recently to Dr Carol Dweck's Growth Mindset, inspiring them to believe they can do better and that everyone has the potential for success, a philosophy which will be taken up by the whole school. He's also aware of the need to future-proof students by teaching flexibility and adaptability to meet a barely imagined future job market.

Curriculum wise, at GCSE there is science at every level – so triple or general science and three art and design choices. Some creative options rarely on offer elsewhere at 16+, such as film studies, media studies, drama and dance, point the way to this being an amazingly artistic school. The idea behind the Langley Baccalaureate, promoted by the school instead of the EBacc, is that pupils are encouraged to retain an arts or creative subject when they're making their exam choices.

Pupils are also advised to study a modern foreign language, but it is not compulsory. German is twice as popular as Spanish and even more popular than French – more by tradition than design. The school has no plans to switch the emphasis at the moment. Special status in maths and computing with links to other schools to offer masterclasses. And the school is one of the few state schools offering engineering.

Apart from English and maths, the three sciences, particularly biology, are the most popular A level choices. There are also higher education oriented subjects on offer such as law, philosophy, psychology, economics, politics and further refined arts subjects – fine art and music technology.

On our visit the staff room was buzzing with a vibrant mix of grey haired and younger teachers including several former pupils. More than 20 per cent have been at the school over 10 years.

Parents see staff as hard-working and committed, enthusing: 'teaching staff are inspirational, very knowledgeable about their subjects and keen to stretch the students', 'the teaching is inclusive and of a high quality,' and 'assessment and feedback is thorough.' There is particular praise for English teaching, and the inspired geography teacher with packed classes who uses angel cake to explain coastal erosion – delicious! Pupils give rave reviews, mentioning teachers plugged into the wider world, bringing the latest research back into the classroom, and nothing being too much trouble.

Several parents we spoke to were in agreement regarding the relative lack of intense pressure and level of homework – very little or no homework during holidays – from lower school to sixth form. Whilst this could be good news for some, one, not alone, says: 'We live in such competitive times and I personally think my boys could be pushed harder'. The head disagrees, believing many feel the pressure on their sons is quite high.

Sixth formers are entrusted with independent study, nine free periods a week, and have several light and airy spaces, plus the café, around the school to work in, only lightly supervised by teachers based in semicircular goldfish bowl-like hubs. Pupils see the advantage of having their teachers close to hand – they always know where to find them when they need help. Students we saw were working diligently and told us, 'If you say to others "I need to work" they respect that'. The library with full-time librarian is open every day until 7pm.

The sixth formers we met impressed us with their drive and focus – they were determined on their university applications; one to Cambridge – and saw the school as doing everything to prepare them for their final exams: 'We work backwards from the final exam from week one'. Parents have confidence in the school's preparation for the next stage. Students speak of help with UCAS forms by a specialist, and joining with pupils from other south London schools in preparation for Oxbridge assessments.

With more than 30 learning support staff – visible in every class we visited assisting pupils – the needs of those with learning differences, particularly those with autism, are exceptionally well catered for here, attracting more than the average numbers to the school. The Sunil Centre, the base for learning support activities, is a discrete part of the school with its own courtyard garden and even magazine. Some 76 pupils are currently offered support and specialist input. Much is done in the classroom through differentiated learning, but the Sunil centre also provides quiet, smaller spaces and a separate exam room.

Four per cent of students have EAL requirements. The second most prevalent home language, after English, is French, followed by Lithuanian.

Games, options, the arts: A very sporty school – seven pupils currently play at national levels in sports from cycling to squash. Almost the only 'old school' features of the modern building are the traditional wooden boards in reception honouring sporting heroes.

A minimum of two hours sport a week is compulsory until the sixth form, and each Saturday one quarter of every year group represents the school in matches. 'We play the best of the best: all the independents', says the sports director of the fixture list. He commands an accomplished coaching staff, including former national league coaches, and 27 of the entire school staff are involved in extracurricular sport too.

No football; rugby takes centre stage in every way, not least the newly-seeded pitch in front of both the main school and sports building. On our visit it was still being cossetted behind fences, tantalising our guide who wondered if he'd ever get to play on it. The trophy cabinets bulge with local and national trophies for rugby, hockey, cricket and athletics. In the spirit of inclusivity, parents would like to see more matches for the lower ranked teams. New million pound hockey pitch. The under 16s were recently national champions, the first state school to make it to the top.

The school has held the Artsmark gold award for well over 10 years. The art department flourishes at an exceptionally high standard. Five students were recently chosen to have their work displayed in The Mall galleries at a Royal Society of British Artists exhibition, with two students being honoured as RBA scholars, a first for the school. The department holds an annual summer show where A level final work is hung for friends' and families' enjoyment in a local church. For those wishing to pursue the subject, a former pupil fresh from the cool of Shoreditch had recently returned to inspire budding graphic designers. The sixth form magazine was recently the winner of three national awards.

The 600 seat performance hall, also the home of the Bromley Symphony Orchestra, is rarely out of use. Dance is exhilaratingly popular here. Recent collaborations saw the PE department taking to the stage, whilst pupils provided an inspired interpretation of a WW1 love story as part of the school's commemorations. The riches of London's dance scene are mined, such as during a recent trip to see Matthew Bourne's Swan Lake at Sadler's Wells. A level dance is a new option. One parent: 'Our boys are not particularly interested in dance or drama; however, our eldest recently took part in a short dance performance during a show and loved it.'

A busy music department with dedicated practice rooms, large teaching spaces and a technology suite. Around 400 pupils learn an instrument, either during school or through private lessons mostly facilitated through a link with the Bromley Youth Music Trust. A dozen or so have reached the pinnacle of grade 8 and beyond, with some students performing in the National Youth Orchestra, the London Schools Symphony Orchestra and the London Jazz Festival. There are Christmas and summer Showcases, an annual music tour and gala concerts.

Several by invitation lunchtime and after-school music clubs such as wood and string quartets or, for something a bit different, cantabile, or Cuban band.

A society or club for most academic subjects each week plus a few extras such as Jaguar cars, GCSE dance, Christian union and scrum half clinic, which sounds as if it mends broken noses, but apparently is more about technique.

Enrichment really comes into its own in the sixth form, with everyone taking on a couple of new things as well as their A levels, which can be either a sport or arts subject. Most popular are rugby, football and table tennis, but almost a third of students are trying out Japanese, with others learning Dutch, counselling or taking part in the Duke of Edinburgh Award or a current affairs group, Think Tank. If performing arts is more their thing, students can experiment with dance, taiko drumming, creative composition or world music.

Background and atmosphere: The school has been through a number of metamorphoses in terms of buildings, names and indeed locations since its first incarnation in 1901: at one point a technical college, then a grammar school. Having settled on its current location in Eden Park, Beckenham, it eventually outgrew its buildings, leading to a huge development project to create the site we see today. Pupils moved in during 2012, whilst the old school was entirely demolished.

Appropriately enough, given the sporty nature of the school, on first sight the whole complex appears like a smart new sports centre with ample parking. The red-brick main building with curved roof and exterior walls appears hardly large enough to house over 1,600 pupils, but inside the design functions brilliantly, with large classrooms, mezzanine levels, spacious corridors hardly appearing to be corridors because of light from above and large break-out study areas for sixth formers. Everywhere are dazzling white walls and carefully hung student artwork.

Each of the lower years has its own small playground. During our visit, seagulls swooped down trying to snatch snacks from the boys – 'time to get the hawks out,' said a passing teacher, not joking apparently.

Pupils in the lower school wear maroon blazers, graduating to less eye-catching black ones. Then sixth form boys may wear a suit of their choice and girls have recently adopted a jacket of their own choosing – all look very smart.

Perhaps it was our exuberant guides, but as we walked the school we felt palpable excitement and energy amidst hard work. Everyone is agreed on the inclusive ethos of the school. One parent told us, 'The school is competitive but it seems to us that every aspect is valued at the same level. This is great as the boys always seem to be able to feel proud of some achievement: receiving a good grade, being in a team for rugby, being identified for great effort in art, having the opportunity to dance on a stage, working on a science project.'

Works collaboratively with new multi-academy trust formed by Langley Park Girls, Hawes Down junior school and Hawes Down infant school. Mr Parsons is a firm believer in the benefits of through schools, enabling a seamless curriculum, with benefits for teachers as well as pupils, enabling them to understand more closely the skills pupils arrive with. The Langley Park primary school opened in September 2016.

Pastoral care, well-being and discipline: School rules are traditional – no earrings for boys. Pupils need a cycling proficiency certificate to bring a bicycle to school. Respect, calm and litter picking mandatory. Mobile phones are allowed for sixth formers, but must be handed in lower down the school. The head says that exclusion figures are 'very, very low' and that 98 per cent of parents recently surveyed were very happy with the pastoral care and discipline at the school.

Form tutors are the linchpin of pastoral care. Several parents mentioned talking to staff on behalf of their child, but also reported problems being swiftly dealt with to their satisfaction.

There is deliberately no separate sixth form building, so that the younger years have role models around the school. The appointment of prefects by the head is like a mini job application – those putting themselves forward must each gather four or five recommendations from teachers.

Some thought might be given to the external sixth form candidates, who seem forever after to go by the unfortunate label of 'externals'. Our two tour guides both bore the label resolutely, but thought it unlikely their fellow externals, or indeed girls, would ever be school captain.

Pupils and parents: Parents as well as pupils are proud to belong to the school. We're told 'the term Langley Boy is one that is highly regarded and proudly stated.'

One parent explained: 'The school attracts gifted boys and later girls for the sixth form, who work in an educational environment that expects a lot of them. This high expectation draws parents that would normally be looking at independent schools.'

By far the majority of pupils are white British, with other white, black Caribbean and black African larger ethnic groups. The head describes his pupils as: 'confident, hard-working, proud of their school, articulate, supportive and active.'

Who will thrive here? Clearly the sporty, arty and academic, but parents add: a child who is 'well mannered, respectful, takes pride in their school's reputation, is a team player and competitive'; 'this school will allow your child to achieve their academic dreams and to bring out talents they never knew they had.' We'd only add the school seems to support and nurture ambitions and interests wherever they lie.

Communication with parents has been a weak spot and parents still shared a few niggles with us, but the head cites recent surveys of parental satisfaction.

Entrance: There are 210 places annually at 11+. With applications at just under three to one, chances of getting in could be far worse, but you will need to live within one mile of the school. Local estate agents say many move nearby simply for the school, creating something of a squeeze on prices. There are 45 local feeder primaries including: Balgowan, Clare House, Hawes Down, Highfield, Marian Vian, Oaklodge, Pickhurst Junior and Unicorn.

It's far harder to get into the sixth form: most recently 850 candidates fought tooth and nail for 150 places. Girls from Langley Park Girls School next door are subject to the same admission criteria as others.

Exit: Some 80 per cent stay on to the sixth form, with those leaving mostly going on to do vocational qualifications. The same proportion then head to university, very slightly more girls than boys.

Most popular recent destinations were Portsmouth, Brighton, Sussex and Bournemouth, with 25 per cent of those taking university places heading to Russell Group destinations such as Birmingham and Southampton. Three to Oxbridge in 2016.

Most popular subjects seem to be English, history, law, accountancy, engineering, physics and business with quite a few medically related (two medics in 2016), plus some budding pharmacists and psychologists. One lone actor, an aerospace engineer and a couple of architects.

Remarks: An exceptional example of comprehensive education with a sporting and artistic offer to match many an independent in smart new facilities. Easier to enter at 11+ (boys) than battle into the sixth form with increased competition from all around including girls.

Langley Park School for Girls

Hawksbrook Lane, Beckenham, Kent BR3 3BE

Pupils: 1,690 • Ages: 11–18 • Sixth form: 495 (64 boys)

Tel: 020 8663 4199
Email: info@lpgs.bromley.sch.uk
Website: www.lpgs.bromley.sch.uk

Headteacher: Since 2011, Dr Anne Hudson, MA BA PGCE PhD, (50s). Though local – lives in nearby Beckenham with husband Stuart, a retired teacher (no children) hence appeal of current job – this is her first professional move into suburbia. Was previously head of Central Foundation Girls' School in Tower Hamlets, her fifth inner-city comprehensive, the other four co-ed and all universally on the up, with one (Dunraven School in Lambeth, where she was deputy head) teetering on cusp of outstanding inspection score.

Precise (always a pleasure to encounter 'syllabi' in briefing notes), energetic (a keen cyclist who misses 'therapeutic' 24-mile round trip commute to last school) and articulate (diction so crisp you could serve it with dips at a cocktail party), she's notable for a jaw-dropping back story that's more Cry the Beloved Country than Être et Avoir.

Raised in Southern Africa, put aside early dreams of being a teacher when was sent to boarding school in 1970s segregated Zimbabwe – 'if we went to town, my best friend and I weren't allowed to sit at the same table' – and was confounded by 'boring history lessons' about Tudor and Stuart goings-on in distant England while civil war, raging on doorstep, was completely ignored. After dropping out of English and French degree at University of Cape Town, signed up for 'voluntary work' with Namibian resistance until deported to UK by South African-controlled government. You hope for tales of derring-do with bandolier over shoulder and grenade clenched between teeth but 'not heroic,' she insists, as 'they deported lots of bishops too.'

While working at Namibians' London HQ by day, took BA in economics by night followed by an MA in history and, teaching aspirations rekindled, a PGCE at Institute of Education (and has since been awarded a PhD in education by Leeds University). Started career as history teacher in Enfield with 'rusty' French on the side, criss-crossing London's eastern reaches to take up ever more senior posts. Spent seven years as assistant head at Deptford Green School in Lewisham, famed for transformation from near write-off to teacher's pet under headship of establishment darling Sir Keith Ajegbo, who also nudged Dr Hudson into studying for a doctorate ('an accident,' she says modestly) after she had accumulated a thesis's worth of raw data on whether citizenship can be a whole-school specialism. (Apparently it can.)

Teaches some PSHE and GCSE history lessons and is a highly visible and hands on presence – 'my sister saw her clearing rubbish round the garden,' said awed year 7 girl. Parents, who don't know her that well, equally don't see this as a problem. She gives out direct email address and is a reliable presence at school events – 'walks round saying "hello" at parents' evening,' said year 7 mother.

Desire for headship born not so much from personal ambition as clear-sighted grasp of its benefits – 'I could see that having power in the school could help you shape things.' Style is going down a storm with the pupils, who without exception cite reinstatement of own clothes day, banned for five years after bullying incident, as biggest achievement to date (Dr Hudson, you'd imagine, would hope for a legacy with a little more gravitas). Many (unprompted) praised her cheerful, high-profile presence round school. 'I've spoken to Dr Hudson at least three times,' marvelled year 11 girl. 'I didn't talk to the old head once.' 'She's far more relaxed,' confirmed a parent.

Academic matters: The reason parents send their daughters here. 'It was the academic side that appealed,' said one, who moved house specifically to secure a place. Plenty to shout about, too, with GCSE 5+ A*-C pass rate including English and maths 80 per cent in 2016 (head's declared goal is five good GCSE passes for all by 2020) and 36 per cent A*/A grades – particularly high percentages in single subject GCSE sciences and fast track languages, both reserved for most able. Students now take fewer GCSEs 'to reflect the increase in rigour' of the new GCSE specifications and allow more teaching time for each, with staff encouraged to include problem-solving and risk-taking into lessons.

Good news continues in sixth form. While new vocational courses are being added to roster that currently includes business, travel, health and social care with aim of broadening appeal (almost the only 'could do better' in otherwise glowing inspection report), the emphasis, says head emphatically, is unapologetically skewed 'towards the more able students'. Results – 48 per cent A*/B, 22 per cent A*/A grades in 2016.

Success doesn't, however, come at expense of the 200 or so pupils with special needs, many speech and language related (about 20 have statements). Good-sized and centre stage learning support unit, home to two key workers under direction of deputy head with SEN background, is widely appreciated as a whole school safety valve offering help for anyone under pressure.

Add enthusiastic teachers, including one working her socks off to spark discussion on ethics of designer babies amongst slightly somnolent GCSE biology class, and the technology head extolling the wonders of the computer programmed laser saw that cuts anything (Goldfinger would be envious, though less fussed by its ability to add detailed floral motifs) and it sounds like roses all the way.

Well, up to a point, Lord Copper. There's the odd wilting bloom. Success in some small but perfectly formed subjects (GCSE music, growing fast, consistently secures 100 per cent Bs or higher) is balanced by occasional whole-subject wobble (applied science a case in point). And despite GCSE success in languages, one of school specialisms (others are technology and sport) numbers die away post-16, with totals for German, French and Spanish scarcely into double figures (reflection, sadly, of national malaise). It's not for want of trying, what with Mandarin and Latin both available as popular lunchtime and after-school clubs, and the 150 EAL students, many bilingual, able to take community languages as additional GCSE. Currently, advanced linguists who take French GCSE early follow a slightly waffly culture-related programme with some cake-making but little academic bite in year 11. Head's plan to move them on to AS level work may help though, judging by less than encouraging results in other schools, it may not.

Then there's the little matter of boys' school next door which clocks near identical GCSE results to its neighbour – 'girls should do at least six per cent better,' says Dr Hudson – and is also seen as the place to go for sixth form sciences. Resulting mini brain drain especially in chemistry and physics is cause for concern but could soon be reversed with appointment of whizzy new head of science who comes with tried and tested Pied Piper-like A level recruitment skills. Shouldn't be rocket science – sixth formers who ignore hype and stay on for science are glad they did. 'Class sizes are very big in the boys' school – I knew the school and the teachers and the course seems to suit me,' said one.

Head wants everyone, including staff, to up their game, crunching primary school data so hard you can almost hear it squeak in effort to identify budding talent from arrival in year 7 and laying down the law with clear minimum academic goals for pupils (with hope, of course, that these will be routinely exceeded). 'Boys are often deluded about their own potential, whereas girls tend to underestimate themselves,' says head, crisply. If she has her way, however, certainly won't be the case for much longer.

Games, options, the arts: Sport highly rated. 'Amazing,' said one pupil. Lots to do and places to do it in – large if slightly sombre sports hall and gym inside and five tennis courts and an all-weather pitch in addition to five acres of green space outside. Old girls include Ellen Gandy, 2012 Olympic 100m butterfly finalist, and with current pupils making literal waves in diving and even water polo, and figuratively in squash, could be first of many.

Favours the competitive (lots of wins for netball and hockey squads in local championships) so 'you need to push yourself,' said parent. Theoretically, however, something for everyone and if the timetabled sport doesn't do it for you there's probably a club that will, from yoga to fencing. 'They really shine. You name it and they'll have it,' said pupil.

Robust though sport is, tends to be swamped by performing arts, which have pirouetted across website and ousted match results from shared online notice board, replacing them with close-ups of recent and seemingly non-stop round of acclaimed productions. Frequent high-quality, whole-school collaborations between dance, drama and music include large cast versions of Annie and Alice in Wonderland, which have gone down a storm, while with around 300 students learning instruments, there's a decent range of ensembles, too, including 50-strong jazz orchestra which recently toured China.

Mini BRIT academy feel never stronger than with dance: tap and street offered, but classical ballet a particular strength, masterminded (and frequently choreographed) by three dance teachers whose remit covers everything from hit versions of Twilight and Beauty and the Beast to GCSE, A level and, coming soon, BTec courses complete with glamorous overseas revision courses, all apparently done without drawing breath. Indeed, a new dance studio was recently opened by Deborah Bull of King's College London. Motto, unsurprisingly, is 'anyone can dance,' though, as sixth form boys as yet unconvinced, male performers are currently imported from next door.

In addition to 'look at me' events, lots of looking after others, with pupils from year 9 onwards lending a hand at local primaries while year 12s, who have Wednesday afternoons free thanks to miracle of timetable coordination, can opt to fill them with voluntary work, often as part of thriving D of E programme, open to all though you'll only get the go ahead if you're doing 'what your predicted grades say you should be,' said one. You can't keep staff away either: science teacher – a 'bundle of energy,' says head – awarded MBE for educational work in community.

Background and atmosphere: In its 90-year history (last 50 on current leafy site), school has had several Time Lord-like incarnations, beginning as a county girls' school, becoming a grammar in 1945, a comprehensive in the 1970s and achieving the full collector's set with academy status in 2011. Connections with the past haven't been sloughed off, however, with original society for old girls (known as Adremians) still going strong. There's also traditional, ultra-smart uniform much cooed over by outsiders, less so by current parents faced with dry-clean-only blue piped blazer and hard-to-press pleated tartan skirt. 'I get granny to iron it,' confessed one.

School design, mid-20th century standard issue, features two-storey main building with separate blocks for drama/sport, science (11 perfectly decent labs), sixth form and technology (newest and nicest of the lot with six well-equipped workshops), together roughly framing three sides of large and picnic table studded if slightly bleak courtyard (the main R&R outside area until student council secured leave to use 'head's own garden', a green and pleasant space round the corner). Effect is pleasant and unintimidating. New girls get maps and are quickly at home – in some schools you feel satellite tracking and emergency rations wouldn't come amiss.

Everyone now very nice about multi-million pound newly rebuilt boys' school (similar name, no relation). Wasn't always thus. Dr Hudson's predecessor fought plans all the way to Supreme Court and won what turned out to be pyrrhic victory as second application was nodded through shortly afterwards. Bridges now mended, cordial relationships re-established and girls offered use of new facilities, notably the hear-every-bat-squeak acoustically advanced auditorium – 'when boys aren't using it,' says head, without apparent irony. Big brother (though a benevolent one) rules.

Make do and mend philosophy only goes so far, however. An additional floor on top of sixth form building (including café and social facilities) has just opened, likewise a new dance studio. Head has planning permission for new music block.

Surprisingly little sense of overcrowding, and there's even a whole school assembly once a term or thereabouts – though 'if it were all boys, there would be accidents,' says head. (One pupil confessed to eating outside 'even when it's raining' just to get away from it all). Children seem to move in mysterious ways (possibly by converting themselves to compressed data format at busy times, more likely by learning to keep elbows in when using corridors). It's particularly noticeable at break, when what should be a scrum for the food and drink somehow isn't.

Mood is welcoming, helped by delightful, off-beat art displays (ceramic artichokes on sticks, anyone?) partial door 'n' floor refurbishment (light wood/portholes combo gives vaguely Nordic/nautical feel depending on preference), and homely areas including large, book-lined library, well used in and out of school hours, which hosts termly themed parties complete with cakes to keep reading top of mind when 'other things step in,' says librarian, diplomatically.

Pastoral care, well-being and discipline: Four houses; Lambda (yellow), Kappa (blue), Sigma (red), and Gamma (green) – fortunately no Brave New World Epsilon – as much an admin tool as a motivational one, used for imposing a little organisational clarity on eight-form entry. It's two forms to a house (block booking, no arguments) and little sense of feverish competition 'except on sports day,' say girls.

Friendship issues inevitably the biggest problem cited by parents, especially lower down the school. 'They look so grown up,' said worried mother who mentioned daughter's need to apply defensive make-up following pressure to fit in. If there is a problem, overwhelming pupil consensus is that there's always somebody to talk to – 'even the canteen people are friendly,' said one. Staff are often very popular, with tears on departure, though 'a few scare me, and I'm the parent,' said one mother. Relationships improve the further up the school you go. 'Students do have problems with teachers – no school's perfect but mostly they're great and there if you want them,' added another. Discipline, though firm, is considered: if there's out of character bad behaviour, staff will 'try to find out where you're coming from first,' said year 11 pupil, with exclusion very much a last resort and help provided, wherever possible, in situ.

Officially, form tutors are first point of contact, often staying with same group for several years. Parents praise ease of communication – teachers are listed in pupil planners and there are individual email addresses for all, up to and including head. 'If you expect other members of staff to give out their contact details you should be willing to do the same thing,' she says.

Highly effective school council, a model of its kind, 'lets teachers know what students are thinking, rather than what they assume they are,' said pupil, and gets things done – broken soap dispenser that had languished for weeks in one of toilets was 'fixed within days' after complaints. It's helped by involvement of sympathetic teacher who 'is on our side but is honest and will say if we're asking for outrageous things.' Youngest girls have as much of a voice as senior pupils and an equal chance of being chosen from full meeting to present ideas to head. 'You even hear what sixth form are doing,' said one.

Pupils and parents: Tight catchment area means many new pupils arrive with others they know. While behaviour is 'fairly standard for teenagers these days; you stop for 10 minutes to let them cross and nobody says thank you,' harrumphs slightly gloomy local, her experience seems exception rather than rule: on morning of our visit no sign of anything other than almost universal good manners. Lots of hands raised in salute to waiting cars as girls (boys, too – a symphony in blue and burgundy respectively) arrived in their hundreds.

In school, too, doors are routinely held open and there's general sense of courtesy towards others (helped, quite possibly, by numbers of teachers in corridors, though a benevolent rather than sentry-like presence).

Parents are necessarily local, many the hard-working exemplars praised by politicians of every hue. As a fair percentage commute to jobs in London, don't necessarily see much of each other, although with quite a few events (first class fireworks display, for example) 'opportunities to socialise are there if you want them,' said one.

Entrance: Large school, tiny catchment area (has shrunk to under a mile before now though normally hovers just over). Means that despite size of intake (240 places in year 7) it's routinely oversubscribed and there's always a waiting list. Pupils come from nine or so local primaries (Oak Lodge, Marian Vian, Highfield Junior, Pickhurst, Unicorn, Balgowan, Clare House, Hawes Down and St Marys Catholic Primary) though feeders in name only as attendance is no guarantee of place and distance (barring standard priority given to looked after children, siblings and now some staff children) is king. Estate agents testify to school's popularity. Parents vote with their square feet. 'We specifically moved to get a place,' says one (though other more dubious practices aren't unknown either).

Three-quarters stay into sixth form, again oversubscribed (minimum of 10 places available to external candidates, usually more in practice) and, like majority of local schools, co-educational, though boys so thin on the ground (around 20 a year) that spotting them not unlike real life version of 'Where's Wally?' A level places dependent on securing minimum of seven GCSE passes (about 50 turned away at application stage) with minimum B grades in four including chosen A level subjects, A*/As preferred for toughies like chemistry and teacher recommendations for languages. Anyone opting for performing arts will also need to pass audition.

Exit: A third or so who leave post-GCSE stay close, some moving to boys' school next door (with a few, who don't care for the size, moving back) while a very few opt for selective grammars like St Olave's and Newstead Wood or independent schools like Trinity School in neighbouring Croydon. A few head off to larger colleges to study work-related courses, though head keen to slow exodus of less academic – should have 'right to continue here even if not high flyers,' she feels.

No compromises when it comes to onwards academic journey. Almost all make it into higher education, nearly all first or second choice universities with Bristol, Leeds, Warwick, Southampton 'all popular,' says head of sixth form, and the most able encouraged to try for Oxbridge – normally a couple of places each year (two in 2016) and the same again for medicine. Law, business and administration, biological sciences and creative arts and design (including music and drama) head the list of subject choices, with social services, maths and English not far behind and a light dusting of languages and engineering.

Brand new careers academy 'will provide specific advice and guidance backed up with seminars, careers days, contact with employers and practice at interviews and skills'. School 'has been commended for its outstanding preparation of UCAS applications.'

Remarks: Short on square feet but, remarkably, feels as if has enough breathing space for everyone, helped by honest, intelligent leadership, enthusiastic staff and pupils who seem happy to be here and for the most part do well. A real breath of fresh air.

Lansdowne College

40–44 Bark Place, London W2 4AT

Pupils: 220 • Ages: 14–19 • Sixth form: 200

Fees: Day £19,050 – £20,950 pa; Boarding +£12,990–£19,950

Tel: 020 7616 4400
Email: info@lansdownecollege.com
Website: www.lansdownecollege.com

Principal: Since 2014, Mark Love BEd PGCLME (50s). Educated at Bristol Polytechnic and Sheffield Hallam University. Twenty-six years' experience of working in post-16 education sector, the majority with independent sector organisations. Taught A level economics, business and accounting and spent seven years as principal of Abbey College before becoming principal of CATS College London.

'I came into teaching to make a difference,' he says, and when you meet him, you're left in no doubt that this ethos has stuck with him – he celebrates example after example of young people's successes (often against the odds) in his conversations. 'Managing the college is not just business for him – he is genuinely caring, a really good man,' one parent said. 'He's really friendly, supportive and encouraging – you can knock on is door anytime,' said another. Teaches when needed – 'two terms of business studies last year' – but unashamedly spent his entire first year in his office, making dramatic changes. 'It was already a warm and welcoming college, but it lacked structures and a real sense of purpose,' he explains. Staff say he has injected 'excitement' and 'life' back into the place, while students describe him as 'really well liked' and 'a great guy.' We found him refreshingly honest – 'I never pretend we're perfect' – as well as down-to-earth, knowledgeable and very genial.

A former GCSE and A level examiner, he lists his main interests within education as team building and leadership, general management, curriculum development and pastoral care. His wife is an interior designer and they have two daughters. In his spare time he is interested in politics, rugby, football, film, reading, current affairs and travelling.

Academic matters: There is a small GCSE cohort of some 30 pupils, but this is essentially a sixth form college offering one year (first time and retake) and two year A level and an International Foundation Year (IFY) programme for non-UK students. Generally, around 15 per cent of A level students are retake students, with the remaining students completing their entire A level course here. Maths and the sciences are the most popular subjects (as well as the ones that get the strongest results), with significant numbers also opting for economics, business studies and art and design. Minority subjects include Latin, Russian and Japanese. In 2016, 77 per cent of the seven eligible students who took them passed five or more I/GCSEs at A*-C including English and maths. Twenty-three per cent of A levels were A*/A and 48 per cent A*/B (slightly down, compared with previous year). A traditional two-year I/GCSE programme is available from 2017 onwards teaching core I/GCSE subjects, plus a carousel of options that lead to students completing nine IGCSEs. Students joining the one year I/GCSE course complete.

Colleges like this stand or fall by the value they add whether on a student's expected grades as determined by ALIS or previously achieved AS or A level grades, and Lansdowne claims an average one to two grade increase at A level on its retake

L

courses. 'We're expert at getting people with Cs up to A/Bs, and at getting Cs for people who were predicted to fail.' Classes are small: seven is average – with one or two not unusual, especially for subjects such as Latin, although students we spoke to said, 'classes of 11 people are common.'

Although one year retakes remain part of the curriculum, the college is moving away from its 'crammer tutorial college' past to a college where, for two-year students, a range of clubs and societies, a student council, visits and excursions and so on are on offer (of which more later).

Abilities range from those who have failed first time round to those who need top results for competitive courses. 'But in a small class this range doesn't matter. Stronger students tend to pull up the weaker ones. If you put all the C grade students together they tend to stay at that grade. However, if we find we have a particularly weak group we may add on extra lessons.' Students have weekly exam practices in the hall where they will sit the real thing. 'If they do it once a week they don't panic when the time comes.' No exam study leave or June half term: 'We run our own revision programme. We teach right up to the last exam in the last subject.'

The college rarely accepts students with statements – 'we don't have the facilities or staff' – but they do have a SENCo, who oversees the 10 per cent of students who have a SEN, mostly dyslexia. Support for these students – whose learning needs are usually at the mild to moderate end – includes help both inside the classroom (specific teaching strategies and learning aids) and outside in one-to-one sessions, where necessary.

Very flexible timetabling means the college can offer any combination of its 29 A level and 19 I/GCSE subjects. It also enables sports stars or those with medical problems to fit in lessons round other commitments. 'Every single timetable is written for an individual. And they are organised for the convenience of the students, not the teachers.'

Around 60 per cent of the teaching staff, many of whom have higher degrees, have taught under the principal in his previous headships. 'I changed the staffing structure significantly when I joined, and I'm lucky to have what I call my "premier league," over half of whom followed me here. They're an amazing bunch,' he says. Students agree, describing them as 'approachable – including after hours' and 'going the extra mile.' 'Their teaching methods are inspirational,' said one, while another told us, 'They're never too busy to find time to help. But you do have to be proactive in asking for it – it's not a spoon-feeding type of learning here.' Ofsted, which has rated the college outstanding, commented on the teachers' 'excellent knowledge of their subjects,' while parents we spoke to raved about how teachers here really 'get teenagers – it's their specialism.' 'Students here have made a decision that school isn't right for them, and staff here seem to be spot on when it comes to giving young people more freedom, while at the same time providing scaffolding that keeps them in check,' summed up one parent.

Runs a medics' programme for those aiming at medicine, dentistry, pharmacy or veterinary degrees, and Easter revision courses, with plenty of individual careers advice and help with UCAS applications.

Games, options, the arts: Sport is not compulsory, except for GCSE students who have PE lessons at the Kensington Leisure Centre each Wednesday afternoon. The football team plays in a league, and the college intends to make more of its membership of the Independent Schools Association to play in more sporting fixtures. The basketball team is becoming more popular, but there's surprisingly little interest in other sports and exercise.

Plenty of creativity going on – photography and artwork adorning the corridor walls, a bright art studio, graphics room and 'fantastic' photography department with its own dark room. But each art related A level – photography, fine art, graphic communication – is restricted to an intake of 12 lower sixth students each year 'as there just aren't the facilities for more. Subject to planning permission, we're planning another art room on our flat roof at some stage, which would change that.'

Drama has been dropped as an A level due to low interest, and only about four students do the GCSE – but as an extracurricular option it's popular, with an annual talent show showcasing singing, theatre and stand-up in the large hall (complete with lighting rigs etc). Music practically non-existent – no A level or GCSE, with one or two students learning an instrument via a peripatetic teacher.

Every student has a double period to pursue the likes of debating club, chess, Spanish club etc. 'Extracurricular has always been good here, but it used to exist in a kind of scattergun way, making it inaccessible to many people, so we have integrated it into the school day.' There's an annual ski trip, a chance to do the Duke of Edinburgh Award, and a post-exam activities week that includes paintballing and a trip to Thorpe Park, visiting museums, galleries and other London sites or listening to outside speakers. They go ice skating, bowling and to the cinema together. There's a charity fund raising talent show, Christmas party and a summer ball, organised by the student council. However, it is fair to say that these students' main focus is on their studies and nobody would choose this college on the back of extracurricular options.

Boarding: Boarders – who make up around half the college intake – come from some 25 countries, including China, South East Asia, Baltic States, Iran, Nigeria and mainland Europe. All the under 18s reside at Princess Beatrice House (known as PBH), a 20-minute journey from the college, and a short walk from Earl's Court underground, while over 18s have their own facility called Pure Hammersmith, located two minutes' walk from Hammersmith station. Both are uber-modern, with light and airy rooms and communal areas – PBH includes a colourful common room with wall-to-wall windows, plus an attractive basement café, while Pure Hammersmith also has a state-of-the-art gym and cinema room. Both have laundry rooms. Principal describes the lodgings as 'like The Sheraton' and he's not far off – they are clean, well-kept, modern, well-equipped and welcoming.

PBH – where the vast majority of students live – is a historic building with accommodation that runs over four floors and comprises of a mixture of single dorms (the most popular) and shared (mostly two beds; a few three), all boasting oak floors and white walls, plus compact kitchens, including electric hob, combination microwave, fridge and storage (hob cut off for under 16s). Even the shower rooms are select, complete with upmarket fittings. Overhead storage means students have the chance to keep the actual living spaces tidy, although we noticed some were better at this than others. 'We do inspections three days a week, but you're always going to get some messier students than others,' smiled the houseparent that showed us around. 'The students here are made up of two distinct cohorts – under 16s, who are brought into college by their houseparents, and the under 18s, who make their own way,' she explained.

Curfews at PBH vary from around 9-9.30pm during the week, going up to 10.30pm at the weekends – and one of the nine houseparents is available at all times, including all through the night (they take the graveyard shift in terms). Breakfast and dinner are served in the trendy blue and white café on site, while a hot lunch is served from the college itself.

The boarders make full use of London, with plenty of organised excursions to museums, theatre, cinema, plus trips further afield to the likes of Chessington World of Adventures. If students travel without staff, they have to go in threes and there's a strict system for signing in and out. 'A lot of the international students come from urban locations overseas, so they're really comfortable travelling round the likes of Saigon or Rome – but this is London. I just have to explain to them that

I'd rather have them upset and cross with me than be unsafe,' says the principal.

The over-18s students at Pure Hammersmith get pretty much the same deal, but a little more independence – ideal for university preparation. 'You do get like with like, so the Chinese students stick together – or the Russian ones – which I think is a bit of a shame, but other than that I've got no complaints about the boarding here – people are friendly and we get to live in a fabulous location in gorgeous rooms,' one student told us. 'I have experience of other UK boarding schools and this is so different – we are so lucky,' said another.

Background and atmosphere: In a quiet residential street between Notting Hill and Queensway, the 60s building could be an anonymous block of flats. Inside is a maze of modern, airy and bright classrooms, science and language labs, art and photography rooms. Science laboratories, the dining area and many of the classrooms have had significant reinvestment. Noticeably, whilst there is a modern study centre with plenty of computers, magazines, reference material and past exam papers, there is no library – although nobody seems bothered. 'Who uses books for reference nowadays? We do all our research online,' said one student. No common room either, but students socialise in the canteen and on the small outdoor patio area. 'We also use Hyde Park a lot – it's only a two minute walk away,' a student told us. There's no denying the college is physically small, but they make good use of space and the honey-coloured oak, white walls, big windows and colourful artwork make for a contemporary and aesthetically appealing learning space. Students' biggest gripe around lack of space seems to be the smallish canteen, but even with this, they shrug it off. 'It's a small price to pay.'

Originally a primary school and community centre for the neighbouring synagogue, it became a college in the late '70s. Once individually owned, it is now part of Astrum Education, which also includes Duff Miller and Chelsea Independent Colleges, and is owned by private equity firm Sailing Capital. Happily, the firm is prepared to invest in the infrastructure, and building work has created more classroom space and freshened up the fabric.

Relaxed atmosphere – 'having no uniform breaks down a lot of barriers' – and definitely more akin to a university than a school. As such, not suitable for young people who thrive on firm boundaries or who are immature. School day from 9am to 5.20pm, and students like the fact that if they don't have lessons, they don't have to be in college. 'What attracted my son – and indeed me – to this college was a feeling. We just walked in and thought, "Yes!"' said one parent, who added that when her son started here, it 'was confirmed that we were absolutely right about this lovely place. He settled in within a couple of days and we haven't looked back.'

Pastoral care, well-being and discipline: Each student has a head of year and a personal tutor who keeps an eye on their well-being and progression. 'Because our groups are so small we can keep tabs on things and deal with any problems quickly,' says principal. Parents concur. 'This is such a smiley and caring college – students are in no doubt about its nurturing side,' said one.

But despite the laid-back feel, there is a stringent approach to punctuality and attendance, with a register taken at the beginning of each lesson. The college has a full time administrative officer who will phone or text any missing student, then their parents. 'Students are pretty good on both issues, which I put down to them enjoying the lessons and us having made a big effort in the interview to get them studying the right subjects,' says principal. College permanently excludes students who constantly ignoring warnings, although they've only had to do this once. 'Generally, there are no discipline issues here,' says principal. Exclusions also happen for a positive result to their random drug testing, 'although, thankfully we haven't had to during my time here'. No admission given to students expelled from other schools for reasons related to drug use. Bullying minimal, if existent. 'We haven't had any student ever tell us it's happened.' Students agree – 'It's really friendly here.'

Strong student council – we sat in on their meeting, which focused on an upcoming Halloween talent show, plus issues like whether they could get lockers.

Pupils and parents: A mix of backgrounds, including around 35 per cent international students from countries within Europe, Central Asia, South America, Africa and the Far East. 'My son says this diversity makes the lessons so much more interesting, especially in history and politics – it's been a real bonus,' said one parent – although there's no intention to go beyond 40 per cent international students, says the college. UK pupils come from a mixture of state schools and colleges for A level retakes, others are from across independent sector (day and boarding, London and elsewhere), and recent arrivals in London. 'They travel from all over London – and some from the home counties.'

Parents are invited to two parents' evenings a year – and know they are welcome to call up or email anytime in between. 'The communications are quite incredible here,' said one parent. 'Parents can talk to any staff member they want, to ask any stupid question – there's no "You can't talk to this or that person" or "Someone else can help with that".'

Entrance: The college is not selective, but does take into consideration previous results and coursework, as well as a student's target university degree and career thereafter. All applicants are given a tour and interviewed by the principal or vice principal. 'We use the interview to explore their background, then talk to them in depth about what they really want to do – and this tends to highlight what really makes them tick and what subjects will enthuse them. Often, the interview winds up being a kind of careers advice session, and it's well worth it,' says the principal. Around eight out of 10 interviewees are offered a place – 'the admissions process is so thorough that most only get to interview if we know they're serious.' September is the main intake, with a January intake for a five-term A level.

While around 25 per cent of A level students wouldn't be touched by other schools ('For us, talent and potential are more important than previous grades'), other students are academically gifted, going for top universities. 'Then there are the ones in the middle – including the ones who get seven or eight Bs or As, but where English language and/or maths is a D and their school won't allow them to stay on because of those Ds,' says the principal.

Exit: Of the GCSE students, around 80 per cent stay on for A levels. A level students nearly all to university – around half to top universities ranging from Durham to Sussex to UCL to King's College, with popular subjects including sciences, engineering and economics. In 2016, one to Oxbridge; four medics, one dentist and one vet. Several go onto art foundation courses, including the likes of Central St Martins.

Money matters: Several means-tested bursaries and academic scholarships up to 40 per cent of fees awarded each year, the latter via the spring term scholarship exam.

Remarks: Very good at concentrated and detailed preparation for passing exams, as well as being a fantastic place for young people who've had enough of school and want an environment with more freedom. The central London location is a big pull too, plus the staff who are determined to help youngsters reach their full potential.

LaSWAP Sixth Form Consortium

Linked with La Sainte Union, Parliament Hill School, William Ellis School

William Ellis School, Highgate Road, London NW5 1RN

Pupils: 1,000 • Ages: 16–19

Tel: 020 7692 4157
Email: laswap@williamellis.camden.sch.uk
Website: www.laswap.camden.sch.uk

Director: Since 2013, Georgina Atkinson, BA in business and French from Kingston University and L'École Superieure in Montpellier. Did her PGCE at London University, followed by a period of working in schools with sixth forms, teaching business. Subsequently, she worked for 10 years as head of faculty at Saffron Walden County High School in Essex, and then moved on to become assistant principal of Long Road Sixth Form College in Cambridge, where she stayed for the next three years. 'I'm passionate about education, particularly sixth form education and helping students find the right course to match their skills.' Georgina is also an Ofsted inspector.

Working across four schools is complicated; however, Georgina meets weekly with the four school sixth form directors and termly with the heads of the four schools that make up the LaSWAP consortium, to plan strategic overviews. The role of headteacher of LaSWAP rotates termly amongst the four school heads.

Ensuring consistency across four large comprehensive sixth forms is no mean feat, especially when the well-being of roughly 1,000 students is in question – a job made all the trickier by LaSWAP's free flowing arrangement, whereby students could have lessons in any one of the four schools that make up the consortium (La Sainte Union, William Ellis, Acland Burghley and Parliament Hill). To help manage this transient system, Georgina has recently introduced a consortium-wide web based system called e-Tutor, which is available to every tutor in the four schools, and a way of keeping tabs on each student and updating records: 'One of the major benefits of LaSWAP for students is the diversity of such a large place and the fact that students can commute between four different buildings – but because of this, they do need to be monitored.'

Each school already has its own director of sixth form, so Georgina rotates between each school. The LaSWAP office remains based in William Ellis School, but will move to the new LaSWAP building, under construction at time of writing, based at the front of William Ellis School and Parliament Hill School.

Academic matters: These four comprehensives, geographically within a few hundred metres of each other, created an amalgamated sixth form to provide the widest possible subject variety and range of qualifications. Lucky sixth formers here have a choice of a remarkable 41 A levels, as well as BTecs, NVQs, a choice of six vocational subjects, the new 'flagship' post-16 advanced maths studies, and post-16 GCSEs (for those who need to gain a grade C in maths or English) About 80 per cent of students follow a purely academic course, the rest take vocational courses, but those who want to can mix and match. Generally around 40 per cent A*-B at A level but cagey about 2016 results. The consortium's strengths lie in the visual arts (with consistently outstanding results) and arts subjects, like RE, film and media studies and English. Languages tend to perform well, but not many students take them up.

With such a wide and varied intake of sixth form students, we can't help wondering how the recent government move of abolishing most AS levels in favour of linear A levels will impact on future results. Georgina isn't overly concerned – in fact she welcomes the opportunity for students to learn subjects in a bit more depth: 'Students will learn how to learn more deeply and apply this. At the moment, many students acquire the knowledge for the exam, have the exam and then forget it.'

Some criticism for not always taking into account the wide range of ability in this relatively unselective sixth form, but not all would agree – 'In my classes, some people have 10 A*s and others mainly Cs, but I haven't found that a problem,' said one boy. A LaSWAP student, we were told, is one who wants to pursue 'more than just academic excellence, with its broad and innovative curriculum.' Teaching (with over 200 'highly experienced' sixth form teachers) is enthusiastic, knowledgeable and well prepared. 'Teachers are good, inspiring and they listen to you', one student told us, but another one grumbled that 'they enforce too much discipline here.'

All students are allocated a base school, depending on the subjects they choose or where they took GCSEs, but most study on a number of sites. Some subjects are taught on all the sites, the more rarefied – music technology, textiles and dance, for example – on only one. Each student is given target grades on entry based on GCSE results and is carefully tracked thereafter, with good exam preparation and help with study skills, as well as thrice yearly reports. 'The communication with home is excellent,' said one parent. 'If my son has done something well they email me. Equally, if he's not doing his homework, they'll let me know.' The academic side is clearly complex, but well organised. 'I wanted to change one of my subjects early on,' said a student. 'I went to see the head of year and it was sorted by the end of lunch hour.'

Games, options, the arts: The extracurricular here is a significant part of what LaSWAP has to offer, being as varied and extensive as the academic range. The activities, which largely take place on Wednesday and Thursday afternoons, provide 35 options, from ballet and debating to theatrical make-up, DJ-ing and maths masterclasses. Off-site sports include sailing and climbing. The programme is not compulsory, but everyone is encouraged to have a go, regardless of previous knowledge or expertise.

Sport is a biggie here and students with an interest in sports coaching and working with young people can enrol on the sports education and training programme which consists of level 1, 2 and 3 qualifications. If successful, students can progress until they achieve the advanced level 3 diploma in sports development, which leads on to university and/or employment. This takes place at the nearby Talacre Community Sports Centre.

Students also benefit from a wide enrichment programme of visiting speakers and volunteering opportunities that 'stimulate debate and interest in current affairs and the wider community.'

Background and atmosphere: The four schools (La Sainte Union, an all-girls' Catholic school, William Ellis, an all-boys' former grammar school, Acland Burghley, a co-ed comprehensive, and Parliament Hill, an all-girls' comprehensive) decided to unite their sixth form offering 35 years ago. Each school retains its distinctive ethos and students generally enjoy the change of pace. 'I really like the different atmosphere in each school,' said one. Students can enjoy the plush new common room that Acland Burghley has to offer – or the beautiful and serene gardens of La Sainte Union. However, the free-usage of all the various facilities that are not a student's base school has caused a bit of controversy with some students. One told us, 'I thought I'd be able to use the facilities of the other schools, but the reality is I would be asked to leave if I was in the common room of Acland Burghley after school, being a La Sainte Union pupil. It really is for lessons only.' The school says that this is because all students have to be monitored and safeguarded by their head of sixth form, which would be too difficult off site.

And surely even the most disgruntled of students can find somewhere to hang out during lunch times, as the location of these schools would be hard to match. Whilst Acland Burghley is a short walk from bustling Kentish Town with its plethora of restaurants, cafés and quirky shops, both William Ellis and Parliament Hill back onto Hampstead Heath.

Parliament Hill and William Ellis combine to form a joint co-ed sixth form, the other schools retain the pupils they take in at 11, and each has its own director of sixth form and heads of year.

One great plus of the model is the halfway house it offers between school and sixth-form college. 'My daughter originally wanted to leave and go to college,' said one mother, 'but once she'd started at LaSWAP, she found the teachers treated her with more respect and she was given much more responsibility for her assignments.' The advantage for students who opt for continuity is that they remain in familiar surroundings while meeting new people and conquering new horizons. 'In the earlier years, my daughter's friends were all local,' said one parent. 'In the sixth form, she suddenly had a whole new set of friends from all over London.' New students, however, don't feel excluded – 'I felt everybody was in the same position as I was,' said one. 'People had friends from their original school, but they didn't know anyone from the other schools.'

LaSWAP is careful about taking both existing students and recent arrivals to a more independent level of study, with a well-planned induction programme, including a thorough briefing on the outline of each course and relevant dates and department procedures. Students like the friendly, laid-back but organised approach and strong sense of community.

Pastoral care, well-being and discipline: All students register at their base school, where they take most of their lessons. Here they have a head of year and a tutor who monitors their work and well-being, with regular interviews to discuss problems and set appropriate targets. Also a confidential professional counselling service and regular PSHE, with outside speakers, group work and discussions. Georgina is also in the process of setting up a sixth form peer advising system around e-safety and well-being. 'Sadly, as we know, there is more self-harming these days, or at least more people are talking about it. We want to train willing sixth form students to signpost professional support services to their student peers around mental well-being and mindfulness.' Students are also offered the opportunity regularly to access the services of two dedicated higher education advisors.

When a student starts LaSWAP sixth form, they are given a detailed planner (which is a colourful diary-like book), which includes a mine of information. Everything from planning one's workload, to code of conduct and even evacuation points at the four schools. There is also a Who's Who list at each of the base sites including who is the child protection officer etc. (For this fantastic planner alone we thought it was worth enrolling at LaSWAP..)

Dress code is smart casual, and at enrolment the consortium will stress the importance of having at least five outfits which fit this description. However, Georgina says that they don't like to tell students exactly what to wear, but instead she suggests that 'perhaps they look at people who go to work – either from magazines or commuters – and get ideas from that, so as to prepare them for the eventual workplace.'

Pupils and parents: Students from a huge range of ethnic and social backgrounds apply from a vast swathe of north London. Despite the consortium's leafy surroundings on the eastern edge of Hampstead Heath, all four schools are inner-city comprehensives with a socio-economic intake reflective of the term. Generally, pupils are confident and mature and get on well.

Entrance: This year LaSWAP had just under 1,000 pupils who accepted a place. The number has slightly declined over the past few years because of other closer to home schools across London who have opened sixth forms. New entrants make up approximately 40 per cent of year 12. The entrance procedure is intricate, and careful attention must be paid to every step and date. First step is to register interest online. Then, armed with a ticket and a parent, prospective candidates attend the open evening in November. Applications must be submitted by post or by hand in early December – those who miss the deadline are put on the waiting list. All applicants who meet the deadline are offered a meeting at LaSWAP in February or March to discuss subject choice and given offers conditional on GCSE grades. Those with offers are invited to attend the one-day taster sessions held before the start of the summer holidays, when summer assignments are set. Post GCSE results, further enrolment appointments and places are confirmed. Now asks for at least five B grades at GCSE (rather than C grades, as previously) to study A levels. Pathways other than A levels ensure that individual needs are met.

Exit: Destinations are 'outstanding', and LaSWAP has a significantly above national average success rates to university in general, and Russell Group specifically – the most popular choices are Sussex and London universities, but across a wide range of degree courses: eg international relations, marketing, philosophy/politics, economics and business. Virtually all of their level 2 vocational learners go on to advanced further education, apprenticeships or employment – a third returning to LaSWAP for advanced applied courses. Four to Oxbridge in 2016.

Remarks: A good compromise between school and a sixth form college, with an extraordinary range of subjects on offer. Tends to suit the motivated and the self starter, but not ideal for those who will be distracted by studying on a number of sites or who require the disciplined parameters of a school sixth form to function at their peak.

Latchmere School

149

Latchmere Road, Kingston, Surrey KT2 5TT

Pupils: 918 • Ages: 3–11

Tel: 020 8546 7181
Email: office@latchmereschool.org
Website: www.latchmereschool.org

Headteacher: Since 2008, Mrs Julie Ritchie, CertEd BPhilEd MSI SIP (Special) (50s). Previously at St Matthew's C of E Primary School, where she was shortlisted for head of the year award. Qualifications (bucket-loads of them) include degree in multi-sensory impairment, a souvenir of decade-long post in the 1990s as deputy headteacher at Dysart, a Surbiton-based special school.

Grew up in Grimsby, drawn to teaching from an early age – something of a family thing as a brother is also a head, though neither of her two grown up children has so far been bitten by the bug. Inspects for Ofsted, a heart-gladdening experience, though never fails to feel thrill of returning 'home' afterwards. Though she doesn't teach – she's at her desk by at 6.30am as it is, notching up 12-hour days – she's available to parents first and last thing and regularly consulted by staff too. 'I've got a lot of experience and they know that,' she says.

Gets to know pupils well – no mean feat given numbers – and parents are duly impressed. 'She made a point of saying how well my child had acquitted herself in a school production. I was quite taken aback as she is someone who could very easily be missed', comments one.

Smiley and effortlessly calm, head rarely raises her voice. 'This is a no-shouting school', she says, and indeed it's as quiet as they come. Short, sharp blasts of the school bell that periodically lash the air are the only sound to puncture the serenity (not to everyone's taste but necessary to minimise euphemistically termed 'time drift').

Makes no bones about need for exceptional staff to deliver the goods, tough old selection process identifying those who, like able pupils, enjoy being stretched and 'have the potential to be outstanding'. With many taking on load-bearing roles, they need to be. School's best practice managers, one to a year group, carry the can for quality of teaching and learning, and 'could be heads in their own right'. Within the next post or so, they often are. Numbers likely to be augmented as fast track trainees, appointed under government Schools Direct scheme, start to make their mark.

Professional to her fingertips, caring too, head sees parents as the ultimate experts. 'We know what the child presents in school but it's at home where they pour their hearts out. If we feel they're not functioning, parents are the ones who know'. Her biggest buzz comes from seeing 'children achieve what you wanted for them'. 'Pupils love her and have unbounded respect,' confirms a parent. And so they should.

L

Entrance: Very oversubscribed, with 500 applying for 120 reception places and not a hope for anyone living more than a kilometre away. Solid core of 'aspirational' parents, some Forces families (there's a nearby army base). All year round wraparound care a boon to working parents. Looked after children have precedence, siblings (up to 50 a year) get second dibs. Only exception is eight-pupil Topaz unit where pupils may come from further away.

Virtual school tour will, hopes head, ensure that non-starters are gently discouraged online rather that getting taste of paradise during a face to face visit, only to have it whisked away again when logistics are explained.

Exit: Some to local independents eg Hampton, Surbiton High, with scholarships. A very few to Tiffin grammars (rarity down to ever increasing levels of competition, so over-subscribed that place hunting has become an extreme sport).

Majority to Grey Court School, Coombe Girls and Coombe Boys. Also the new Kingston Academy.

Remarks: Author Jacqueline Wilson's primary (and much changed for the better, she reckoned, when she revisited). Opened in 1936, just in time for Second World War (nearby aircraft factory was regular bombing target). Infant school added a year later – dividing wall in place until reunification in 2007.

Large site with playgrounds generously bestowed means most year groups have a space they can call their own in addition to larger shared areas for infants and juniors. Substantial on-site asphalt legacy is greened up with trees and bushes, plus veg garden in small courtyard, together with reception-only delightful green run between knee-high rows of plants (like nursery, have own secure play area). Tactical introduction of soft surfaces underneath sturdy and attractive play equipment for older children also helps, while nearby shared playing fields are used for some clubs, junior games and sports day, now back to traditional competition-driven format and considered all the better for it.

Inside, plenty of space with large classrooms for all. Spares too, as though school is geared up for expansion to four-class entry, will take time to permeate every year group. Two schools into one means inevitable layout quirks, corridor-heavy design putting well-stocked library on the through route. Potential dinginess offset by lots of colour, particularly in nursery and reception areas where primary colours rule and some toilets have gone green (paint rather than eco flush). Assumes more monochrome hues as you go up through the school, though brightened with lots of little extras including giant paintbrushes strung across art room ceiling and boards, inside and out, crammed with enigmatic clay masks.

Reigning delight is flashy new building housing year 6 classrooms upstairs, lunch/sports hall on ground floor. Also used for Monday morning whole school assemblies, smaller hall taking year groups two by two on other days, and notable for impressive red and blue light up buttons (disappointingly measure air quality rather than summoning International Rescue).

Though fab new buildings help, what really rocks parents' boats is success with non-standard issue pupils. 'Schools can all do the straightforward ones', reckoned one mother. 'What counts is how good they are with the off the peg kids'. Latchmere aims (learning, local community, laughter, loyalty, love and leadership) are oft recited, children 'accepted for who they are' and inclusion, very dear to head's heart, a big, well resourced, thing.

Despite leafy setting (Richmond Park within easy reach), pupil make up has a grittier, urban feel than you might expect, with challenges to match, including a few with difficult home lives and nearly one in five with English as a second language.

Staff, average age 40, around a third male (average pupil to teacher ratio of just over 21 to one) are expected to get on together, and get on they do. No coasting, either. Jaw-droppingly efficient systems still have enough give for teaching talent to flourish outside the box. One teaching assistant, a professional actor, has leave of absence to go on tour in term time, in return lending talents to sky's the limit school productions.

Mantra is constant improvement. 'Whatever we do, I ask staff how we can do it better next time', says head. 'And because they're bright, I only have to ask them once'. Accolades roll in, Artsmark award in head's sights adding to quiverful that already includes Sing Up and Sportsmark awards (both pure gold).

Most recent success is designation as Teaching School (an eat your heart out award bestowed only on the whizziest of establishments). Confers membership of six-strong alliance who pool ideas and resources, a boon when it comes, amongst other things, to pitching for extra funds.

Range of needs includes specific learning difficulties, speech and language and behavioural, emotional and social difficulties (BESD), while Topaz unit accommodates eight pupils with Asperger's, currently all KS2 but will extend to KS1, who join peers for some lessons, often with one-to-one support, but have separate base with own play area (small, nicely green, enclosed by no-nonsense fencing). Once identified (here, as elsewhere, some parents call in their own experts to speed up the diagnosis) support is unstinting, with nth degree differentiation in class taken as read. Pupil with memory and processing issues had checklist of stages to tick off on wipe clean board. 'Personalised it beautifully', thought mum.

Inspires 'very warm and fuzzy feelings' towards the school, said a parent, with size a plus point rather than drawback. Thirty-strong classes, bolstered with teaching assistant while nursery sessions (25 children in each) have two nursery nurses plus teacher. 'More people means more friends', felt a year 5 pupil, though in troubled times, 'there's a room you can go to if you're sad or lonely.' Felt, however, that some peer to peer disagreements are best resolved without teacher input. 'They can make it worse'.

Parents too, favour school over other highly regarded and smaller alternatives because of what one terms 'lack of prissiness'. Whereas artwork on display elsewhere was 'incredibly beautifully framed on the wall', only the best examples had made the final cut. Here, in contrast, it was 'messy, in a good way, with pictures from even the kids who couldn't draw'.

Resulting confidence is unmissable, pupils a winningly well mannered bunch, helped to become so by oft-stressed emphasis on social skills. Lunch for reception children is part of the curriculum, with big teacher input, emphasis on eye contact and handshaking, stressed through the school, ensuring the conversational niceties are a (nicely) observed feature of school life. 'Are you having a lovely day?' head was recently asked by pupil. Impressively, words 'self-control' were all it took to calm large group of pupils: here, it's viewed as innate rather than a skill to be learned and children live up to expectations.

Equally true of trips (year 5s just back from up to the neck mud in Ashdown Forest) and school clubs (including astrophysics and Techo DJ, both catering for the starry-eyed). School stresses that 'only exemplary behaviour will be tolerated' and sanctions are well understood. 'We have a consequences list. If we're too out of control, we get sent to the head', said a pupil.

Much more, however, in the way of encouragement, explanation and reflection, from popular blue room, shoe-free, carpet rich and decorated with skyscapes, to peer mediation and circle time. Very youngest join the debate, too, with 'brilliant' nursery head encouraging exploration of moral dilemmas, in one instance through medium of glove puppets.

Parents are also expected to do their bit – recent newsletter noting rise in pupil absences the week before half term. With current 'outstanding' status at risk if attendance plummets, nudge psychology designed to keep families onside seems to be working, thinks head.

Pupils tackle everything with gusto. Top perks include later lunch sittings and joy of second helpings for top two years (Portuguese chef's creative ways with assorted healthy options much admired, though occasional pizza and hot dogs days remain top favourites).

Responsibility also enjoyed from the off. Nursery children check themselves in online ('no need to be afraid of technology', reassures prospectus), while covetable posts for year 5 and 6 pupils include monitor who hands out free break-time snacks baked on the premises. Lessons are regarded with equal enthusiasm, consistency a big strength with two deputy heads stepping into the breach to cover staff absences. Teachers' approval counts. 'Oh, no, they'll be so disappointed in me', said reception pupil after mother threatened to expose mild cheekiness at drop off.

Relationships are excellent. 'I love all the teachers,' said year 5 girl. 'They're really kind and make lessons fun'. Even more so now, following introduction of creative curriculum, many months in the making and all the school's own work. Substantial ring-bound master plan so full of fizzing ideas that it probably glows in the dark.

Core subjects taught by class teachers, topped up by specialists for art, some sport, music and French (rapid progress made courtesy of native speaker means 'pupils are probably bored out of their minds when they get to secondary school', thought insider). Resulting variety is relished – diplomatically. 'Nice to have a change; not that you ever get bored with your teacher', said year 5 pupil.

Spritely lessons big on group or paired activity. 'Means you can share ideas or ask if you don't understand', said pupil. Recent highlights include 'Victorian' maths (everything in imperial measurements, dunce's cap for wrong answers); hands-on science, year 5s adding bicarbonate of soda to vinegar and inflating balloons ('we weren't meant to shake it but we did, anyway',) and drama-packed history lesson, with army trenches improvised from desks and teacher 'shouting' commands (though we're sure it wasn't very loudly).

Buzz, frequently mentioned, could well be down to synapses sparking merrily away in the background as staff respond to latest gauntlet thrown down by the head. School has many laurels but you'll never find anyone resting on them. Instead, there's a ceaseless quest for improvement, anywhere and everywhere.

Some setting (maths from year 2), high achievers treated to once a week sessions in small groups, one-to-one support scooping up small numbers at risk of Sats underperformance. Though results aren't the highest in the local borough, pupil progress puts them almost at the very top. 'They may not always get it right first time, but they don't give up and keep on trying,' said a mum. Latest innovations include recruitment of weaker readers to mentor younger pupils, some improving by more than a complete Sats level in the process. School has also introduced pupil challenges to up the excitement factor, reception recently wowing head with enormous sheets of paper covered with 'the biggest numbers they could think of'.

But though competitive instincts once more considered acceptable, children know when to rein them in. Unsuccessful year 6 candidate in election for one of four team captain posts was gracious in defeat. 'I am delighted and he has my full support', he said. Politicians take note.

Fundraising clout is substantial. A jolly crowd, forging friendships that often endure well beyond the school, parents are big on purposeful socialising, coffee mornings and cake-making featuring heavily in weekly school newsletters. Have their own choir, adding to pupils' very well regarded three, plus orchestra (healthy numbers boosted by local authority-subsidised taster lessons). Take school duties extremely seriously, finding the wherewithal to equip Apple suite not once, but twice as new technology succeeds the old. Also fund and manage school's own swimming pool which 'wouldn't exist without them', said insider, in constant use from April to October. Children adore it, two even asking for donations towards running costs instead of birthday presents (surely a first).

Not the school for anyone in search of 00 gauge miniature education. This is a scaled up version that works, thanks to a head who expects non-stop excellence, staff who buy in to the challenge and pupils who benefit from constant quest to do everything that bit better every time. 'It's such a lottery', said one mum. 'You buy the house and hope for the best. I just couldn't believe my luck'.

L

The Latymer School

Haselbury Road, London N9 9TN

Pupils: 1,369 • Ages: 11–18 • Sixth form: 439

Tel: 020 8807 4037
Email: office@latymer.co.uk
Website: www.latymer.co.uk

Headteacher: Since 2015, Maureen Cobbett (50s), previously head of All Saints' Catholic Voluntary Academy in Mansfield, Nottinghamshire.

Academic matters: Excellent GCSE results, making it the top performing school in Enfield borough and within the top six per cent in London, with 82 per cent A*/A grades in 2016. Pupils must choose a MFL from French or German in Y7 and they can then choose between French, German, Russian or Latin in Y8. ICT is not taught as a separate subject but incorporated across the whole curriculum.

Students study 10 GCSEs and the vast majority take the EBacc subjects with some opting for religious studies instead geography or history. It is important that academic success is supported by 'a life outside school' and students are encouraged to take part in the wide variety of activities on offer.

At sixth form the school offers 'nothing apart from an ashamedly academic programme', so no vocational subjects. The majority stay on at sixth form but another 50 join from other schools, so exam rates at 58 per cent A*/A and 87 per cent A*/B grades at A level in 2016 are commendable. Having a larger than normal sixth form means the school 'can teach a wide range of subjects, which smaller sixth forms struggle to offer'.

Parents agree that the school is 'very good academically' and it certainly makes plenty of effort to award academic achievement across all years. Year 13s are awarded prizes in specialist subjects too, such as mechanics, statistics and government and politics. Pupils who do not gain a subject prize have the opportunity to be awarded either a Latymer Lodge or school prize for gaining a high aggregate at A level. There are also open awards for special achievements in spoken English, creative work, instrumental performance, music composition and fieldwork. Prizes are awarded for service to the school in music, debating and service to the community, thus there is plenty of motivation to strive and to win here. 'They will take your child through the process and your child will pass the exams,' one parent stated confidently. Another said, 'I believe that both my children have been encouraged and guided to fulfil their academic potential. Classroom teaching is supported with a range of visits and activities to inspire as well as stretch.'

Where pupils have a special learning need, they will find help through the learning support department who also arrange mentoring for younger students from the sixth form. EAL students are supported well and achieve equally well at GCSE and A level.

Games, options, the arts: More than 17 different sporting activities offered (from athletics and badminton to volleyball and ultimate frisbee). Notable achievements include winners of Enfield Schools Hockey Champions and Enfield Football Cup, alongside a number of other firsts, seconds and thirds in regional finals for netball, tennis and cricket. In year 10, when pupils have the opportunity to specialise, and at sixth form, they can also take squash, golf, swimming, orienteering and dry-slope skiing in addition to the normal range of sports on offer. The school encourages active lifestyles and rewards pupils' enthusiasm for sport with a number of awards that recognise outstanding achievement both in and outside of school. These include hockey, football (for girls, not boys), netball, cross-country, rounders, tennis and cricket. All pupils have the opportunity to spend a week at Ysgol Latymer (the school's outdoor sports centre in Snowdonia National Park) for activities such as hill walking, orienteering, climbing, abseiling and canoeing.

Latymer had art specialism and so the subject has a strong presence outside the department, with work on display around the school and contributing to cross-curricular subjects (for example, year 9s painted the background scenery for senior drama productions of My Fair Lady and Hairspray). Experts visit to do talks and run special workshops in oil painting and sculpture, and the department runs visits to the London Institute, Tate Modern and Tate Britain as well as to Barcelona and Paris. As a result, examiners have commented on the good grasp pupils have of contemporary artists.

Drama is supported by trips out plus the big theatre productions that take place at the school each year: a main school production in November, a junior production in July, and the house drama competition every other year. The languages are supported by school journeys and exchanges through links with Russia, France and Germany; there have also been exchange visits with the Mwambisi school in Tanzania; other trips include geographers to Iceland, classicists to Italy, artists to New York, skiers to the French Alps, canoeists to the Ardêche, music to Austria, Belgium, Germany, the Czech Republic; sports to Holland and Italy. Other destinations have included Nepal, India and Malawi, and every other year there is a sports trip to Barbados.

A quarter of the pupils learn a musical instrument at standards ranging from beginners to beyond grade 8. As pupils advance through key stage 3 they focus on practical music-making wherever possible, covering projects on classical, jazz, pop and world music, with regular assessments every half term. There are five orchestras ranged from grade 3 to post grade 8, a concert band and several choirs. They perform at school concerts and many are invited elsewhere, such as the National Festival for Music.

Latymerians enjoy a rich range of extracurricular activities that shape life at the school; parents value its contribution to their personal and social development. House theatre and music productions; over 60 different clubs and teams run before, during and after school, and at weekends. Clubs cover art, gardening, chess and more. There is a Young Enterprise group, an economics society, a Christian union and clubs whose sole purpose is to raise funds for less fortunate children in developing nations while pupils learn more about their lives. We are told that the school's Amnesty International group is 'the largest and most active school group in the country'. The LAFTA (Latymer Awards in Film, Television and Advertising) is a fun and creative play on the Oscar-style awards ceremony.

Background and atmosphere: Tradition creates the atmosphere at Latymer. It was established in nearby Church Street in 1624 at the direction of Edward Latymer, a City merchant, who bequeathed certain property to trustees on condition that they were to clothe and educate 'eight poore boies of Edmonton'. His, and the 'generosity of the many others since', are remembered each year on the school's Foundation Day. Pupils are proud of this tradition and seem enthusiastic about the events that keep it alive. The school's motto – Qui Patitur Vincit (Who Endures Wins) – aptly sums up its spirit, and is the title of the annual talk. The school moved to its present location in 1910.

On the day of our visit it seemed very quiet, apart from the hum and beat of instrumental practice (including drums) in the music department and a flurry of students preparing for the school's major production in the Seward Theatre downstairs. Built on three acres of land and flanked by 12 acres of playing fields, which separate the school from the main A10 road, it looks deceptively small from the front. There are a number of outbuildings around the main one, added at various times over the school's life and capturing its spirit of progress: the great hall (1928), which seats over 1,000; the gymnasia and technical labs (1966); a performing arts centre (2000) and a sports/dining hall complex (2006). In 2010 the high-tech multi-purpose Seward Theatre (performance space, auditorium, media studio, art gallery and drama theatre) was opened. The school also has a number of rooms dedicated to specialist teaching, for example a suite of 12 science laboratories, six fully-equipped technology rooms, and specialist ICT rooms with wireless networks, an intranet and access to remote access learning. There is a large library, with separate learning resource and careers centres. Sixth formers have a large common room and quiet study area.

The school's traditional atmosphere is maintained by the old students' association (there is an old boys' football club and old students' badminton club). Ex-students are very much involved in school life, participating in school events, contributing to lessons, presenting school awards and setting up special funds. There is a rich sense of celebration of the past: each year a whole school assembly is organised for the 'grand Act of Remembrance' in honour of Latymerians who died in the two world wars. They sing the national anthem, read from the Bible, listen to a talk about war life and have a 'blessing suited to a multi-faith audience' pronounced by a local reverend. There is a book listing war casualties in the library, which pupils proudly pointed out.

Pastoral care, well-being and discipline: The 186 pupils in each year are organised into six form groups, and each form group belongs to one of the six house groups. They remain in these groups throughout their school lives, meeting daily for registration and form periods, including, in the lower years, PSHE lessons delivered by the form tutor. Each year group also has a head of learning (first port of contact for parents concerned about progress) who, along with the deputy head of learning, also acts as mentor.

House culture is strong. Each has a senior pupil to lead, democratically elected. Activities are organised by senior pupils and used to inject a sense of comradeship and teamwork across all year groups, and to make new year 7s feel fully inducted into life at Latymer. They do this via sports tournaments and various competitions such as cake-making, drama and music. Equally importantly, houses also operate non-competitively to organise community service activities and to help raise funds for charity (one house group raised over £80 in 20 minutes for Water Aid by taping water bottles to themselves). Together, this creates 'a strong sense of coherence and team working' among pupils at the school.

Pupils are expected to abide by the school rules and the home school agreement they signed with their parents on joining the school, but the school views 'self discipline resulting from wanting to learn' as a more important deterrent to poor behaviour. Although behavourial problems are rare and 'dealt with swiftly by the head of learning or form tutor', one parent did say that she felt the pastoral care side was not as strong as the focus on the academic side. However, other parents say pastoral care is excellent: 'Not only do my daughters experience excellent teaching, they also benefit from being at a school with a firm commitment to pastoral care. They feel safe, secure, confident and happy. While the academic side is challenging, it is not to the exclusion of everything else.' Another said she has 'always felt comfortable emailing teachers direct if I have a concern or question'.

Pupils and parents: Anyone and everyone who is 'very clever', though the school wisely lists acceptable postcodes in its admission criteria. Alumnae include Dame Eileen Atkins, actor, Simone Butler, bass player with Primal Scream, and Syed Kamall, Conservative MEP.

Entrance: Only those 'deemed capable of achieving higher grades of GCSE are considered' at this highly oversubscribed, selective school. Selection is by the NVR test as well as literacy and numeracy. A parent said 'it used to be harder to get into', but 1,900 typically apply for the 186 places, so many are still disappointed. Priority is given to looked-after children and those who live in designated postcode areas in the boroughs of Hackney, Islington, Waltham Forest, Haringey and Enfield. Offers also made to around 20 students who live in these areas and show 'exceptional musical talent and achievement' akin to grade 5. A further 20 places awarded to those on pupil premium.

At sixth form, 90 per cent stay on. An additional 50 places are allocated to pupils from other schools, bringing the size of the sixth form to 234. Sixth form is also oversubscribed with around 442 applications for these 50 places. Places are offered to students who achieve at least six GCSE grade As, including the subjects they wish to study at A level; they must also pass the Latymer test and live in one of the designated postcode areas.

Exit: Around 95 per cent go on to university or other forms of higher education in music and art. The school does not 'push Oxford or Cambridge though plenty apply, and plenty get offers' (15 places in 2016). UCL, Bristol and Nottingham also popular; courses include aerospace engineering, medicine, law, Chinese, Russian and Egyptology. Very few – one or two – leave to go straight into employment.

Money matters: The Latymer Foundation offers some financial assistance to pupils experiencing hardship.

Remarks: A peek back in time shows that some well-known former pupils like Baroness Claire Tyler (chair of CAFCASS and president of the National Children's Bureau), footballer Johnny Haynes and Sir Bruce Forsyth CBE all did well here. Pupils clearly still do. This is a zealously traditional school with pupils who show a healthy balance between hard work and play. There is some effort to keep with the times but the school's view is that 'If it ain't broke don't fix it'. Ofsted has a similar attitude and in its last report described the school as outstanding.

Latymer Prep School

Linked with Latymer Upper School

36 Upper Mall, London W6 9TA

Pupils: 168 • Ages: 7–11

Fees: £16,860 pa

Tel: 0845 638 5700
Email: registrar@latymerprep.org
Website: www.latymerprep.org

Head: Since 2001, Mr Stuart Dorrian BA, former long-serving head of English and of lower school in the senior school who was persuaded to take over the prep, with the chief aim of upping the academics (for which he ticked the box long ago). You'll be hard pushed to find anyone (pupils included) who doesn't instantly warm to his gentle, warm nature, his excellent listening skills and his clear enthusiasm for his domain. His office, a homely room overlooking the river setting, has an open door policy, in which pupils think nothing of popping in to tell him something they're worried about or to just pick up a sports ball. Meanwhile, his regular use of the term 'my school' is said with pride and passion, never conceit. He still teaches, some sixth form English and drama to his year 3. Parents describe him as being 'emotionally alert to children's needs', with 'a huge emphasis on pastoral care', but he is also regarded as a serious educationalist.

Retiring in July 2017. His successor will be Ms Andrea Rutterford, currently deputy head at Devonshire House prep in Hampstead. She has also headed year 3 and year 5 at Highgate Junior School.

Entrance: Highly selective, with around 220 competing at 7+ for the 38-40 places. They take an exam, with half invited back for some science-related activities and team-building exercises and observation. The gender split is nearly 50/50, with each year split into two classes of 20 (occasionally 21). Families are mainly local, within 30 minutes' travel time, although the reach of the school has expanded in recent years to stretch as far as Kensington and Notting Hill.

Exit: Almost all move into the senior school, although transfer is not automatic, with all pupils required to sit the entrance exam, but does not prepare for other senior schools.

Remarks: Rivercourt House, an attractive 1800s villa overlooking the Thames, is the main building. Full of light, with an elegant staircase and plenty of original features and creaky floorboards, it has the feel of a well-to-do, kindly, aunt's home and is an enviable environment for youngsters to learn in. Next door, Latymer House accommodates more classrooms, food tech, cookery, IT and art – all very well equipped, with plenty of space. Both utilise walls and corridors to the max to display children's work. Even a window had lovely artwork draped across when we visited.

Opposite the rather limited outside space is an odd 1930s building, whose outside spiral staircase leads to the Seahorse Drama Studio, with a truly professional feel. In addition, pupils also regularly parade down the underpass under the A4 to Latymer Upper to make use of facilities such as the dining hall, sports and music facilities and drama hall (with recent productions including My Fair Lady, Toad of Toad Hall and Peter Pan). Other links with the upper school include shared teacher training on inset days and teachers doing regular observations of year 7 teaching to get a feel for standards. All this, agree parents and pupils, makes the transfer into the upper school pretty seamless. 'They don't get scared because they're already familiar with it,' explained one parent.

Expect specialist teaching from day one, so whilst each class has its own form room, pupils go to subject-dedicated rooms to learn. Of particular note is the large, fantastically well-equipped art room at the top of the school, where pupils were busy painting clay pots they'd made, and a delightful, well-stocked library. Delicious baking aromas drifted out of the food tech room when we visited, whilst in the science lab, pupils could hardly have looked more animated.

The curriculum is future-orientated, with all pupils learning Mandarin and Spanish, and technology is genuinely embedded throughout all subjects, with regular use of iPads in class, including art. This is not at the expense of more traditional learning, however. 'We want them to read and write before they can swipe,' says the head.

Music is strong, with every child playing a musical instrument and half of them playing two, for which one-to-one tuition is timetabled into the curriculum. Big on brass, with lots of children learning the French horn or trombone, whilst the cello also remains popular. Two main choirs – enthusiast singers (no audition necessary) and the chamber choir – accommodate 90 children in total. Music tech also a focal point. 'I was certain my kids had no talent with music and I've been truly shocked what they've brought out in them,' said one parent.

The focus on sport that the upper school is noted for is seen as equally important here, with specialist sports coaches teaching both girls and boys rugby, football, netball, cricket, dance, rounders and – the particular strength of the school – swimming. New £14m new sports facility behind the 1930s building has revolutionised facilities. Sport is inclusive. 'Our aim is that every pupil leaves with one sport they like doing,' says the head. 'That might not sound very ambitious, but actually girls often fall away from sport because they're not given the opportunity to find something they love. Not here.'

Over 20 school clubs, including zumba, film studies, The Latymerian (school magazine), chess, bridge, drama, coding, Warhammer and karate. Most are free, although a few bought-in ones, such as zumba, do charge. No after-school care, but the prep room remains open until 4.30pm. Plenty of day trips to places including V&A and Kensington Gardens, whilst residential trips include Norfolk (year 5) and Italy (year 6).

This isn't a school that believes in lots of rules. 'There's just a general expectation of respect and being nice,' said one pupil. And with the exception of some year 6s who have passed their 11+ swanking around a bit, it's all pretty low-key, with a genuine feeling of innocence. About the worst behaviour you'll see, say teachers, is children running to the next class, when they should walk.

As for bullying, it's hard to imagine here. 'Of course children sometimes fall out, and there are situations in which children lack empathy or fail to see the implications of what they've done. But there's very little deliberate unkindness,' confirms the head. 'I think that's down to modelling by myself and my staff and the fact that, for the children, the absolute worst thing for them is feeling they've disappointed us. They can't bear it.'

'You learn through trying,' is an unofficial mantra of the school, with the staff encouraging intellectual risk-taking. 'We are constantly reminding the children that the point when you're not quite sure is the point when you learn,' explains the head. 'Getting to the top therefore isn't the be-all-and-end-all and we encourage them to see that and value the moment when they're not quite sure.'

There are pupils with SEN, including dyslexia and Asperger's, and they've also had students who are registered blind or deaf. 'We delight in being open,' says the head, explaining that anyone with any kind of learning challenge is encouraged to make full use of the upper school's learning support department (now known as the 'academic mentoring department' to remove stigma), which is run by three specialist and extremely well-liked women. 'They offer unbelievable support,' said one parent.

There's a lively PA, which does all the usual fundraising and organising of school fêtes and social events, along with each class having a 'rep' and 'dep,' who the head closely communicates with. 'If there's ever an issue or misunderstanding, the rep and dep won't encourage parents to write to me saying, "We all think this or that". It's much more a case of them coming to me informally and early to nip it in the bud.' Parents agree this works, and several praise the way they are encouraged to come into the school in the morning and afternoon, never hurried on as in some schools. They can also come in to help with reading.

We saw relaxed, engaged, happy and confident (but not precocious) children, who are clearly at home and keen to learn. 'You're encouraged to ask questions,' one pupil told us. 'In fact, if we are really interested in a particular area, that can drive the class in a new direction.' 'Teachers always tell us, it's our enthusiasm they want to build on,' explained another. For this reason, comment a couple of parents, it's probably not the best school for shrinking violets. 'I think a really quiet and withdrawn child might feel a bit lost here,' said one.

Unlike in the upper school, there is a house system, all named after birds. 'It gives a sense of healthy competition and gets them out of their year groups,' said one parent. There's also a school council, although it's not particularly active.

This is a charming prep that children genuinely adore. 'My child is often up at 7am fully dressed and asking when it's time to go,' said one parent, whilst another said, 'The children might not come out looking as neat as they went in, but you know they've had a really lovely time.' Despite the expectation on high academic achievement (which some parents say can be tiring), there's a big emphasis on a rounded education, and above all it's lots of fun, with warm relationships between staff and pupils. This throws some children who come from more formal pre-preps or primaries, with parents also sometimes starting off feeling slightly hesitant about how relaxed and open the atmosphere is. But they soon feel liberated and by half term in year 3, children seem to have fully subscribed to the ethos of the school. As one pupil summed up, 'this school is like one, big warm hug.'

Latymer Upper School

Linked with Latymer Prep School

237 King Street, London W6 9LR

Pupils: 1,180 • Ages: 11-19 • Sixth form: 360

Fees: £18,510 pa

Tel: 020 8629 2024
Email: head@latymer-upper.org
Website: www.latymer-upper.org

Head: Since 2012, Mr David Goodhew (MA Oxon), originally a local boy who has now moved 'back home', living 10 minutes down the road with his French wife, Céline, and their young son. Read classics at Oxford and previously deputy head of Durham School. Spends at least one hour every day walking round the school – visits lessons for a few minutes, which both pupils and parents say sums up his 'hands-on approach' and 'openness to ideas for change'. Not stereotypical headmasterly, parents and pupils describe him as 'very approachable.'

Academic matters: Grades have been steadily improving over recent years and although research from the University of Durham found pupils are achieving either in line with – or better than – their abilities, results remain a notch short of stunning. A levels in 2016 saw 76 per cent A*/A grades, with 95 per cent at A*-B. GCSEs were 87 per cent A*/A.

Key aspects of the innovative curriculum include the introduction of the UCAS-accredited World Perspectives, which has replaced the 11th GCSE in the middle school. Exploring global political issues, pupils love it and parents delight in their children 'watching more news' and 'talking about bigger issues at the dinner table.'

All year 7s learn Mandarin (carried on from the prep school, if they went) and all pupils expected to do a modern language at GCSE. IT has been ditched in favour or computing and coding and technology is genuinely embedded into all learning, with all pupils from year 10 upwards given an iPad. 'I do all my essays on it, plus I can do things like surveys,' said one pupil, while one upper sixth pupil has even designed a rowing app that is now used by the GB Rowing Team.

In 2010, the school decided to go linear with the A level syllabus, with all exams taken at the end of upper sixth – a format now common to most A levels. There are two benefits, claims the head – better results and six extra weeks back in the lower sixth, allowing teachers to go deeper into subjects.

Majority of teachers hugely admired, with several references to them going the extra mile and being 'very imaginative in their teaching methods'. 'Staff really care, not just academically but in a pastoral way,' summed up one parent. 'I could frankly hug all of them,' said another. 'The teachers try and inspire you – there's no fobbing off of pupils' questions, ever,' remarked a pupil.

Careers and university advice is outstanding, thanks to a knowledgeable and dedicated team, including a careers specialist and international university admissions specialist. The latter post was brought in due to the recent surge in applications to American universities – 12 off to USA in 2015 including three to Princeton, and six to Canada. 'Because of our rounded approach to education, it means our students are often drawn to the American university model of taking seriously areas like sport, music and drama, and the fact that you can delay specialisation,' explains the head.

Parents and pupils rave about the learning support department, which is now known as the 'academic mentoring department' (to remove stigma). Run by three specialist women who nobody seems to be able to praise more if they tried, pupils can visit for one-to-one sessions any time, whether they have severe dyslexia or just a piece of challenging homework, at no extra cost. The department's peer mentoring scheme is popular, whereby older pupils help younger ones, with benefits to both sides. 'If anything, the department could be bigger, though, as it's always full,' says one pupil, who adds that on results day, this is where you'll find students running to give staff a hug. School reckons on around 10 per cent needing some kind of support, with just two statemented.

Games, options, the arts: Famed throughout the western (London) world for rowing and football; these remain the school's strengths and are pursued with much enthusiasm and success. There's also notable accomplishment in swimming, netball and rugby, all of which are taught by professional coaches. Sport is also known for being inclusive, plenty of C, D and E teams, with enjoyment of sport valued as much as sporting prowess. One parent also points out how 'my son has been encouraged to try out sports he wouldn't normally opt for, which has been great for him.' Meanwhile, there are some strong examples of girls' sporting accomplishments, not least the fact that the senior girls' quad won Henley Royal Regatta (breaking three course records).

In the past a number of parents have complained that girls' sport has been taken less seriously than boys but the impressive £14m new sports centre (2016) – including swimming pool, sports hall and bouldering wall – should help to ameliorate this. Netball and cricket training takes place before school and at lunchtimes whatever the weather and there are greater opportunities for teaching more sports simultaneously, as well as enabling classes in fencing, climbing, yoga and pilates – no girls' football or rugby teams, though. Sports grounds at Wood Lane used by the England rugby team for training.

All pupils take DT, art, music and drama to the end of year 9 and then choose, although we wonder how they decide. Art is outstanding, with talented and impressively free and imaginative artwork in just about every media, displayed everywhere from the head's office to the four good-sized studios. Similarly, DT is fantastically equipped, with an emphasis on creativity. 'The people who maintain the school use this room, so it's built to industrial standard,' raved one excited pupil who passionately talked us through some of the machines. 'I once asked to build a stomp rocket powered table tennis ball dispenser for a project. I was allowed and it worked!' he added.

Performing arts also taken seriously, with a commendable theatre (plus other studios) and plenty of year group plays, plus an annual all-school one. Meanwhile, each week 800 individual instrumental lessons are taught by 40 visiting music teachers in air-conditioned, sound-proofed, purpose-built rooms. Group music lessons focus on getting children enthused with practical work, not simply focusing on theory. Singing takes place across several choirs through to grungy bands, and everything in between. Students even have their own record label, 32 Bit Recordings, with profits from releases going into the school bursary fund. 'The arts aren't considered an alternative to academia here,' said one pupil. 'There's room for people to excel in both.'

Astounding range of extracurriculars on offer, with over 100 clubs, as well as a good range of outside speaker. Trips, it seems, are organised to pretty much every corner of the earth, with the Horizon fund ensuring that no pupil is excluded for financial reasons. The annual 'activities week' causes much excitement, where students do anything from cycling coast-to-coast to building a shelter for teenage mums in Uganda. 'It all comes back to our rounded view of education,' says the head. 'Skills learned in leadership, resilience and teamwork matter every bit as much as academia.'

Background and atmosphere: Located on the banks of the Thames in West London, the grounds occupy a rectangular plot between King Street (where the main entrance is) and the busy A4 into London, under which runs a cunning underpass, through which children parade to the prep school, sports hall, pool and Latymer boat house.

But if you didn't know better, you could be forgiven for thinking the school is a church, since your eye is immediately drawn to the huge stained glass windows of the gothic, red-brick main hall, which is nestled behind a long, low gothic arched wall. Dating from 1890, the hall now has several smart newer buildings surrounding it, most recently the striking glass-fronted library and science block, while the old car park has been transformed into a charming 'piazza,' complete with giant outdoor chess set, which students describe as the hub of the school during nice weather and exam time.

Back in the main hall, expect portraits of old heads and war memorial tablets, along with brown glazed tiles on the walls and blue carpets on the floor, which very much set the mood throughout the old building, with its seemingly endless supply of nooks and crannies, hidden staircases and innovative linkages between buildings. 'Pupils can be here five years and still discover new areas,' said one pupil. Wooden lockers, which are dotted around the school, had just been replaced with metal ones when we visited ('so much nicer,' said a pupil), while the mezzanine areas of many classrooms give a nice warmth to many of the teaching areas.

In contrast, lots of light wood and huge windows feature in the newer buildings, the most exceptional of which is the science and library block. The ground-floor library is exemplary and one that many towns would be proud of – well-stocked, not just with books and DVDs but computers, with genuinely studious looking pupils. Meanwhile, the corridors of the three floors of science boast interactive periodical table, television with live newsflashes and even live lizards and fish (not together) behind glass, among other innovative features. 'We're just about to do a class on how much vitamin C exists in fruit drinks,' says one excitable teacher as we walk past one of the well-equipped labs. On top is a roof garden, weather station and observatory.

Other areas of note through the school include the huge dining room and the well-used sixth form common room, with plentiful and colourful booths and sofas. Outside, expect inevitable queuing and log jams at changeover times, as a result of 1,400 students in limited space, but nobody seems to really mind.

Originally a boys' school, girls started coming in sixth form in the late 1990s, after which it became fully co-ed in 2004. Now 50/50 across every year group, with the head genuinely astounded that anyone could think single sex is preferable. Certainly, nobody could argue that uptake for maths and science among girls isn't strong here. Active school council, which recently put together an initiative for more recycling bins and voted against bringing in a house system.

Pastoral care, well-being and discipline: There was a perception in the 1980s (and some argue, rather later) that the school was 'a bit rough,' admits the head. 'Not now. The behaviour is excellent.' Parents and pupils concur, putting it down to warm, mutually respectful rapport with staff, as well as pupils knowing exactly what's expected of them.

Head acknowledges that any school would be foolish to believe bullying is non-existent. What matters, he says, is what you do about it on the rare occasions it occurs. 'There's a big focus on encouraging pupils or parents to report it immediately, after which it's dealt with it quickly and sensibly,' concurred one parent. Despite the unfortunate headline from the Daily Mail in 2010, which read 'Sixth-formers at top private school expelled after being found with cocaine at "drunken" end of year prom,' the head says the zero tolerance to drink, smoking and drugs means it's not a problem now (and wasn't a big one then), which parents and pupils agree with.

Teachers genuinely interested in pupils' well-being, and although there's not huge interaction between the different year groups, pupils seem at ease with different ages.

Pupils and parents: Around 90 per cent from within a three-mile radius, who arrive by tube, bike or on foot. Diverse population for an independent school, which the school is clearly proud of. 'We attract a real mix from hedge fund managers, media types and academics living in leafy streets through to families on the White City estate, which is surely better than just those from a privileged bubble mixing with each other. What life lessons that does that teach you?' explains the head. Parents agree, describing the school as 'grounded'. 'Privileged, yes, but posh, no,' says another. Communication with parents – both via the school and the Parents' Guild – is considered good.

Incredible list of alumni, including Hugh Grant, Alan Rickman, Christopher Guard, Imogen Poots, Mel Smith, Gus Prew. Also Walter Legge and Raphael Wallfisch, and Pete Townsend's dad, who was expelled. Then there's Kulveer Ranger, Keith Vaz, George Walden, Joshua Rozenberg, Andrew Slaughter, Heston Blumenthal, Dr Hilary Jones and Lily Cole. 'If you're lucky, you get to meet one of them at a prize giving,' said one pupil. 'My sister actually got to shake hands with Alan Rickman.'

Entrance: Of the 160 places available at 11+, 40 come from the school's own on-site prep. Of the remaining 120, 50 per cent come from local state primaries, with the other half coming from other preps. Some 1,100 candidates altogether. But while the English, maths, reasoning and interview required to get in used to make the local area a tutor's dream, the head has dropped the reasoning in an effort to create a more level playing field. He's also dropped the 13+ entry as there was only ever a handful of places, which around 80 (inevitably privately educated) would apply for. 'That's just mean,' he says.

At 16+, over 200 candidates for 30 places. Although attracting a high calibre at this age, entry for sixth form doesn't set a ridiculously high bar, with the school expecting minimum eight or nine GCSEs including maths and English, with A or A* grades in the subjects they wish to study (or related subjects).

Exit: Careers and university advice considered second to none. Oxbridge (22 places in 2016), Durham, Edinburgh, Manchester increasing numbers to professional colleges for music, art and drama, including RADA.

Money matters: Founder Edward Latymer, a wealthy puritan, pledged funds on his deathbed in 1624 to educate and feed 'eight poore boies'. So when the previous head came into post in 2002 and there were just seven free places (even less than Latymer's pledge) he took action.

The school has since raised £11m specifically for the bursary programme, with 115 pupils now on means-tested bursaries (including 77 free places). That amounts to 12 per cent of pupils with some form of means-tested financial assistance. At 11+, academic scholarships (usually a one-off £1000) and music scholarships (one of 40 per cent, others up to 20 per cent). Sixth form drama (40 per cent), music, art and sports scholarships (nominal amounts).

Remarks: Oodles of pupil pride about pretty much every aspect of the school, with only minor niggles from pupils and parents. 'If you're not academic, you'll struggle. But it's not just about the academia as there's this constant focus on being well-rounded,' says one pupil. If you're after a school that encourages academic curiosity and a real passion for life, this is it.

L'École Bilingue Élémentaire

153

St David's Welsh Church, St Mary's Terrace, London W2 1SJ

Pupils: 120 • Ages: 3–11

Fees: £9,069 – £9,795 pa

Tel: 0207 224 8427
Email: admin@lecolebilingue.com
Website: www.lecolebilingue.com/html/pages/pagesuk/introuk.htm

Headteacher: Veronique Ferreira studied biochemistry at the University of Paris, and after obtaining her teaching licence in 1999 began her career as a primary school teacher in the suburbs of Paris, working with children with behavioural and academic difficulties. This gave her a lot of insights into the different learning styles of children, something that has shaped a lot of the teaching approach she has established at L'École Bilingue. Moving to London, she started in a French nursery school, but as parents continued to speak of their interest in a more bilingual programme, she pondered on how she might introduce a different sort of French primary school model in London. She focused on child development theories, looking at Canadian, UK (including EYFS) and French Breton bilingual educational models. Youthful yet wise beyond her years, her confidence is drawn from her solid foundation in pedagogical studies and the popularity of the school which was her brainchild. Her partner and the father of her daughter, Franck Laurans (head of administration), has provided the business knowledge needed to help her realise her vision for a school that is small, personalised and less rigid that the traditional French models where her students can 'find pleasure in learning'.

Entrance: L'École Bilingue is non-selective, but with only 15 places at the 3-year-old entry class, places are highly sought. Parents like the fact that, unlike other French schools, this is a transparent process. Priority is given to siblings (which can take up three-quarters of spaces), but after that it is first-come, first-served, so sign up early – from birth if you wish. (Nationality/passport are not a factor as in other French homologue schools). Vacancies for children older than 3 are subject to space; worth a call but most classes are wait-listed, so as soon as someone leaves (and with many expats, children do leave) there is someone to fill the spot. Note that if you miss out on the first round you need to proactively let them know you remain interested.

Exit: The head meets parents individually to discuss the options, and some non-native French speakers may at this point opt for 11+ exams (a very few leave at age 7 or 8) and a move away from the French system. Recent examples include Francis Holland, City of London Girls' School and Holland Park. As the school is part of the AEFE agency for French education abroad, year 6 pupils have automatic access to French secondary schools such as the two Lycées (South Kensington and Wembley) or the Collège Français Bilingue in Kentish Town, which follows the bilingual mode, and the vast majority go on to one of these. While moving from L'École to the ginormous French Lycée is a big change, the Lycée tries to place two L'École students in the same year form group, so that helps a bit. The school has noted that French students repatriating to Paris often seek out bilingual schools there to keep their English language strong.

Remarks: The curriculum is bilingual French and English, and although the French curriculum model is predominant, the head says that she has looked in depth at other curricula, including the national curriculum, the IB primary years and the international primary curriculum, and drawn on elements of all these. Some subjects are taught in French (French, maths, history), some in English (science, English, geography) and some are taught in both languages simultaneously (arts, ICT, drama, music). Children move between English and French medium classrooms so that they are immersed in the relevant language for that part of the day.

Though a small school, the limited space is used to good effect and is immaculately tidy. The compact library is brimming with French and English children's books, a cheerful space where we saw some one-to-one learning taking place; walls lined with colourful boards neatly display creative work by students of all ages; we noticed some tailors' mannequins with student-designed fashions – part of a broader project including all the London French homologue schools in celebration of the centenary of the Lycée Charles de Gaulle. Some special needs support (French and English) available; some children with statements/EHC plans in the school receive individual support either in-class or on a withdrawal basis. Teachers (19 in total, average age early 30s) are a mixture of French and English, all suitably trained and qualified. Staff turnover is higher amongst the French teachers than the English as they may be here as accompanying spouses or may move on to other French medium schools in London or abroad.

By all accounts, the pupils are busy and engaged in a wide range of activities. They are especially proud to have been invited – by recommendation of the French education inspector – to participate in the French Parlement des Enfants (a sort of 'junior parliament'). This event has influenced some of the themes and topics that have been studied by pupils in all the year groups. Other academic extras sometimes include a French mathematics competition for French schools in the north of Europe. French assessments are given in year 3 and year 6 to measure attainment against French standards; the school is inspected by Ofsted as well as the IEN French Inspector for the northern European region.

Year 3 goes to Brighton for two nights, year 5 spends three days in East Sussex and year 6 goes to Brittany for a week. The music programme is strong and some children do extra Suzuki violin and piano. Parents sang the praises (no pun intended) of the innovative music teacher who had recently done a 'bilingual Beatles' unit. As with other London French schools, many of the extracurricular activities are organised by the parents' association, and parents run some of the clubs, which include fencing, dance, art, choir and football. There are no competitive sports on offer; they use the local sports centre – where many students do taekwondo after school; from year 2 they swim at Imperial College pool. There are two major shows – the annual Christmas carol service and an end-of-year show.

We saw the former in final rehearsal – joyful voices,silver tinsel halos and red Santa hats.

Though the school is secular, the some of the ecclesiastical architectural features in the former Welsh church nestled in a quiet back street in Maida Vale have been put to effective use, making this a most unusual school building. An enclosed garden behind the school features a vegetable garden for pupils, an eco-pond (with resident creepy crawlies), and an area for messy hands-on learning with sand and water. There is an outdoor play area at the front of the school. A small multi-purpose hall is used for assemblies. Four-course lunches (optional) are prepared and served at school by cooks who know each child by name, chivvy those with picky palates to eat their vegetables and then report to parents on how many ate their carrots. Too much chatter is discouraged during lunches to encourage eating; an adult may read stories aloud instead.

There is a big emphasis on developing the 'soft skills' and the small size means that there is no anonymity in the school. Everyone contributes; everyone has a role to play. The appeal, parents say, is that at L'École they have found a near-perfect balance of strong (French) academic foundations in a very caring environment where everyone knows everyone. The intimacy of the school ensures that behaviour standards are high, and parents subtly suggest that the presence of several English teachers means that discipline is managed differently than in traditional French schools. Parents describe the children as 'kind' and very welcoming of new students. It's also highly inclusive. 'Birthday parties usually involve all of the siblings.'

Parents are big fans of this school, so much so that when they heard of the Good Schools Guide interest in meeting them, they organised a coffee morning (mostly mums, though one dad came) to share frankly their opinions about the school. The small size is an attraction – 'it's digestible for young children'. Another said, 'it's like comparing a mom and pop shop with B&Q'. One recent arrival accustomed to French schools voiced a concern that L'École may lack rigour; others from elsewhere in Europe and the US were delighted with the academic standards. Despite its small size, it appears that communication is patchy; some people seem to be in the know; others (particularly those new to the school) felt they were out of the loop. The school gate is definitely the place to find out what's happening. It seems that parents who are not fluent French speakers can find other parents willing to help and explain things.

Some 40 per cent of families are French (expat and local), 25 per cent are dual French/other nationals, 18 per cent are French/British, and some eight per cent represent other nationalities (including French-speaking north Africans, Canadians and others). Some international families also speak Arabic, Spanish, Italian, etc. Most families live nearby and walk to school, though some are drawn from as far as Fulham, Kentish Town, South Kensington and Hampstead. Because of the school's South Kensington origins, a bus that comes from the Brompton Road area serves families who joined the school in the early days.

The school is owned by founders Franck Laurans and Veronique Ferreira. Parents like the fact that this couple, who 'live above the shop', are firmly at the helm; they feel they provide continuity and sustainable leadership that secures the school's future – at least for the time being. Some subsidies come from the French government for French national students,

Described by one parent as small, friendly 'village' school that draws on the best of French academics and English pastoral education, this bite-size school in the centre of London is worth a visit by parents who want something a bit different.

L

London Academy of Excellence

Broadway House, 322 High Street, Stratford, London E15 1AJ

Pupils: 440 • Ages: 16–18

Tel: 020 3301 1480
Email: office@excellencelondon.ac.uk
Website: www.excellencelondon.ac.uk/

Headmaster: Since 2014, Mr John Weeks BA PGCE (late 30s). Previously deputy head at Brighton College. Married with two small boys, Mr Weeks is immediately engaging. He has a youthful energy and openness, as well as a boyish enthusiasm. Educated, as a boarder, at Cranbrook in Kent, he went on to read economics at Durham then qualified as a teacher of mathematics at Sheffield University. He arrived at Brighton College soon afterwards, first as a maths teacher (appointed by Anthony Seldon), then as housemaster as well as head of year and head of maths before becoming deputy to Richard Cairns. While passionate about social mobility and academic rigour, he says 'he never imagined he would be doing this but was lucky with the personalities he worked with'. Despite only having taught at one school prior to his appointment at the LAE, he says he was well prepared for the role after his six years on the senior management team at Brighton, as well as having two inspirational mentors in Anthony Seldon and Richard Cairns. Parents praise his commitment and approachability and comment on his passion for his students to aim high and reach their goals. He succeeded Robert Wilne, the founding head, who left two years after the school was set up in September 2012.

Academic matters: Only 'facilitating subjects' offered (what some might regard as 'proper subjects' or 'subjects favoured by the top universities.') These 13 include psychology, PRE (philosophy, religion and ethics), economics, further maths, French and Spanish. Maths and sciences are most popular at the moment. Very gradual increase in numbers taking modern languages. Students can also choose the Extended Project Qualification (EPQ). Additional languages offered outside the timetable include Mandarin, Russian, Italian, Bengali, Arabic, Urdu and Japanese. Opportunity to do an MPQ (mini project) in the first half of the first term, which is often developed into an EPQ. Exciting a thirst for learning and for academic endeavour is key here. The scholars' programme contributes to this incentive and prestige. Those who achieve high grades in exams may be awarded Governors' scholarships or Merit scholarships – the prize being financial support for resources as well as more trips to Oxford and Cambridge.

Maths and science setted according to ability – other subjects grouped but not according to ability (there isn't a wide range of ability in other subjects, says head). Results are good – but some mutter that, considering the selective intake, they should be higher. However the first two cohorts were not especially selective, counters school (minimum five grade Bs at GCSE) and they added a lot of value to relatively mixed ability groups. Value added scores impressive. In 2016, 49 per cent A*/A, 86 per cent A*-B at A level – a big improvement on the previous year; Mr Weeks' confidence was justified. English literature, geography and RE gained the highest percentage of A*/As.

For those students who need learning support (and there are around 40 on the schools' register with dyslexia, dyspraxia or ASD), the school says it takes a proactive approach to identifying any special needs. Not just those diagnosed with a particular

SEND will be given support. One of the assistant heads is the SENCo and learning coaches provide day-to-day support. Mr Weeks affirms that results for those with SEN match those without.

School day is long – the library opens at 7.45am, lessons start at 8.30am. At the end of the school day optional clinics take place where students can get further support. Teaching provision is effectively an 8am-6pm each day. Small tutorial-style groups and teachers who love their subjects make for lively, engaging lessons. Genuine participation and discussion rather than a more didactic approach. Parents wonder at the levels of support given to their children by the teachers: from Saturday classes and after-school clinics, to making themselves available by email until 11pm as well as during the holidays.

School regards itself as the 'academic pathway to top universities for students in Newham'. Three specialist 'pathways' are specified under the curriculum – law, medicine and Oxbridge – but there is bespoke preparation for a career in any field. Almost all progress to a Russell Group University, six to Oxbridge in 2016. High numbers (between 40 and 50) choose medicine. Head says part of the secret of their success is the high quality of teaching – teachers are largely specialists in their field (the biology teacher is a former doctor) – with excellent subject knowledge and a passion for their subject. They are able to conduct university-style lessons with lots of interaction – students here are taught to think, no doubt balm to admissions tutors' ears.

Games, options, the arts: Thursday afternoons are dedicated to clubs and societies. These range from the medical society to the Bollywood Dance society. There are 31 in total to choose from (but if a student decides there is a demand for a particular society, the school will facilitate the running of it). Currently python programming, the newspaper society (merged with the feminist society) and history of art are just a few that are student-led. Debating and Model United Nations are popular, as is chess. A number of competitions organised against other schools. One boy told us proudly of how he set up the LGBT society and raised over £400 from bake sales and non-uniform days. We observed students building a robot in the STEM society, and participating in a refreshingly polite and intelligent discussion about Brexit. Our politicians could learn a lot from these students' ability to respect the viewpoint of others and listen attentively.

A number of physical activities take place on Tuesday afternoons – with a huge choice of 21 different sports from girls' and boys' football, rowing, sailing and pilates to basketball, climbing, canoeing, boxercise, volleyball, yoga and zumba. Games take place at a number of different venues including the Olympic Park, Redbridge Sports Centre, University of East London and Lee Valley. Athletics in the summer can get very competitive in the run up to sports day when all six houses compete against each other. Students we spoke to became hugely animated about their house's performance in the javelin.

Drama and music a bit thinner on the ground. Apart from a guitar society there seemed to be little provision in the way of groups, orchestras or a variety of musical instruments. However music performances do take place during assemblies and there is a music room with a speaker system, microphone and guitars. Students get the chance to sing. There is a drama and improvisation society and a show takes place each term, which gives the students a chance to perform, whether it be a poetry recital, a band or dance performance. A play is produced in the summer after exams. Recently performed Macbeth directed by a teacher from Eton. The singers perform at a number of events, most notably at a reception at Lancaster House in front of the prime minister. One student we spoke to had high hopes of becoming an actor after completing his medicine degree. What provision we saw for drama was fairly sparse; however, since our visit school tells us that a student from the Central School of Speech and Drama now spends one day per week at the school, so that sixth formers will have regular access to drama.

Plenty of school trips. The students we met were buzzing from one recent trip to see Dr Faustus and another to listen to Naomi Campbell at the China Exchange. A thorough Outreach programme includes LAE students mentoring other students at local schools and voluntary work with local charities.

Parents thrilled with the opportunities their offspring have here. Opportunity is often their prime reason for choosing LAE, and is unparalleled here compared with other schools in the borough, they say.

Background and atmosphere: Founded in 2012, LAE was the brainchild of Richard Cairns, head of Brighton College, and Joan Deslandes, head of Kingsford Community School in Newham. They met on a bus in Beijing and found they shared a passion for the teaching of Mandarin (they both introduced compulsory teaching of Mandarin in their schools) as well as rigorous academic learning and a desire for social justice. Joan Deslandes needed somewhere to send her high fliers (Kingsford is an 11-16 school). Brighton College took two sixth formers each year from Kingsford, on full scholarships. These scholarships were funded by HSBC, which still continues to support the LAE today. However Joan Deslandes had another 40 high attainers at Kingsford, whose academic thirst still wasn't being met. With the inspirational energy of these two first class educators, the early seeds of the LAE were sown. Most agree that Richard Cairns was a driving force in gaining a groundswell of support from the independent sector, one of the innovative features of LAE.

The first sixth form only free school, it has the benefit of strong links with the independent sector. Six 'partner schools' – Brighton College, Eton College, UCS, Highgate, Forest School and Caterham – share resources, knowledge, experience and contacts. In addition strong links are being forged with Francis Holland and Putney High schools. The students are grouped into houses named after the partner schools. Some provide teaching support, and students from LAE are invited to seminars and talks at the partner school; others provide strategic advice, interview practice and contacts for university applications; others provide sporting facilities. Students in, say, Brighton house, will meet their 'sixth form buddies' at Brighton College, and will host a return visit from Brighton students.

School is housed in an unprepossessing 1980s former council office block on Stratford High Street. Functional and businesslike, but the edge is taken off by bright colours and idiosyncratic names (the large dining/study/common room area is called the agora – in Greek script), and walls throughout the building are adorned with wonderful large portraits of 'independent thinkers', from Coco Chanel and Elizabeth David to Srinivasa Ramanujan and Reverend William Buckland, saying profound things. All rooms are bright, light and airy, with tasteful wooden floors and pictures. Nothing here feels run down. All shiny, bright and fit for purpose. Many play chess in the agora during down time; 'we can't stop them playing chess,' remarked a teacher. Large comfy colourful sofas adorn parts of the space, with tasteful beechwood floors and tables and canteen for staff and students to eat together. School currently in negotiations with the Department for Education to see if they can expand into the next door building, but wouldn't want to get too big 'and become a sixth form college,' says Mr Weeks; the aim is 'to retain an independent school style of education.'

Pastoral care, well-being and discipline: Core values here are respect – and kindness; any breach of these and there's trouble. Students are driven academically so discipline tends to be good, says head. They concentrate on the everyday stuff – uniform, lanyards (zero tolerance on these not being worn), punctuality, not handing in homework. Lines of communication with parents fluid – they too will know when their child has been late or failed to hand in work on time. Mr Weeks did have to exclude four students recently for inappropriate cyber activity – every head's current nightmare. All four were found places at other sixth form colleges. He affirms that he is, and has to be, vigilant on cyber behaviour. This incident was picked up quickly, dealt with quickly and no shock waves ensued.

Students are grouped into six houses, with about 70 students in each house (from both year 12 and year 13). A head of house along with a team of five tutors in each house is in charge of these students' pastoral welfare. Each student's tutor is also responsible for their UCAS reference, PSHE and monitoring their academic progress. The tutor is the first port of call for parents. A tutor writes a report at the end of each term on the progress of the student, and parents also can meet the tutor and other teachers once a term.

We saw a mindfulness yoga session in full swing in the library. Plenty of opportunity to reflect and calm the mind, though in this instance it only seemed to be girls who were seizing this opportunity.

Pupils and parents: Unusually high proportion of first and second generation immigrant families – particularly Asian and black. Fiercely aspirational parents have a positive influence on the ambition of their children. Mr Weeks, painfully conscious of the very low representation of the white working class, has appointed a head of 'widening participation' to try to address this. Teachers remark on the curiosity of the students – they are kept on their toes, they say, by the students' complex questions. Students are dressed smartly but, apart from the boys' blue and gold ties, not uniformly.

L

The students we met, a mixture of year 12 and year 13, were the kind of people you would want to represent your country – model citizens. Thoughtful, articulate, mature, polite and with an ease and confidence that belied the backgrounds of many of them. Mr Weeks commented that their confidence comes on hugely as they progress through the school. One parent observed how much responsibility her son is given, which contributes to his mature behaviour. There is much competition for the prestigious roles of house captain (there are only six) and prefect, again fostering a positive and responsible attitude.

Majority of parents haven't been to university themselves and, while very supportive of the aspirations of their children and the school, some are brave enough to confess to feeling daunted as to how to fund tertiary education. Although, they say, school is very good at explaining the route to university and assisting with strategy and tactics, very little information or explanation is given to parents as to how to cope with the financing of it. 'I think they are scared of putting anyone off,' suggested one parent.

Entrance: Minimum of five As at GCSE with at least Bs in maths and English. School gets about 2,500 applicants and will interview about 1,500 for 230 places – according to their predicted grades. Fifty per cent of applicants are from students in Newham, other 50 per cent could come from anywhere. In future school is considering a measure for a certain proportion of students to be on free school meals – as a means of preserving a core aim of the school: to foster social mobility

Exit: Impressive – both in terms of the institution and the subject. Just under 60 per cent to Russell Group universities, a good number to STEM subjects (107 in 2016, including 44 girls), those who go to non-Russell Group universities mostly go to City, Greenwich, SOAS, Westminster or Bath. Most popular subjects are English and economics, closely followed by maths, biomedical sciences, history and politics and physics. Six to Oxbridge in 2016 and 10 medics – a higher percentage than many top independent schools. However re-entry into year 13 is dependent on sixth formers securing at least three C grades at AS level (or in externally moderated mock exams in the years to come)

About 15 each year take a gap year and come back during that year for advice and interview practice

Money matters: School is lucky enough to continue to have the benefit of the HSBC funding that was a legacy of the Brighton scholars' funding. This is not a luxury, says Mr Weeks, but vital in a climate of continuing government cuts, 'and we ask a lot of our teachers. The HSBC support,' he says, 'enables LAE to provide the complete education package which is experienced by the pupils of its independent school partners.'

The Hardship Fund, set up by the Worshipful Company of Innholders, provides financial support for trips and resources to those most in need, and the diligent few who are awarded scholarships also get financial help with resources and trips.

Remarks: London Academy of Excellence is – at the moment – is doing exactly what it set out to do. It provides a rigorous academic education to bright, aspirational students who are keen to seize the many opportunities that are on offer. Students here develop an easy confidence accompanied by a sense that they can do anything they set their sights on. An inspirational institution for anyone hard working and lucky enough to get a taste of it.

The London Oratory School

Seagrave Road, London SW6 1RX

Pupils: 1,340 • Ages: 7–18 • Sixth form: 360 • RC

Tel: 020 7385 0102
Email: registrar@los.ac
Website: www.london-oratory.org

Acting head: Pauline Devereux, previously deputy head (and author of The London Oratory School: A Celebration of 150 Years) is holding the reins whilst a new head is appointed. She is aided by Daniel Rooney.

Academic matters: Junior House boys are tested at the end of each term and reports are sent to parents, which detail their results, progress and targets. Otherwise, you get to meet your son's teachers only once a year. Some complain about poor communication lines between school and home, but say that on the whole they put up with this because they trust the school. 'You might not get to hear about a concert until two nights before,' remarked one parent. The school is totally integrated into the senior school – junior house boys even have lunch, as the senior boys do, in class rooms that become 'house rooms' at lunch time. However, there is little interaction with senior boys. Play times are organised so as not to coincide with the traffic of burly teenagers, and the whole of junior house has lunch at a different time from the senior boys.

Consistently impressive results at both GCSE and A level. School fiercely competitive with its notable rival – particularly regarding academic results. When considering A level scores school would like it be noted that they have a broader range of ability in their sixth form as their entry requirements are lower. What we like particularly is the range of subjects boys are choosing to take at both GCSE and at A level. Large numbers do maths and sciences – and a healthy helping of A*s in these subjects – but the humanities and languages are not neglected. History particularly popular, and double figures do art and DT each year. Heartening in an (almost entirely) boys' school to see this range, and we were particularly encouraged by a thriving German department. A level results in 2016 were 70 per cent A*-B and 24 per cent A*/A grades. At GCSE, 89 per cent of pupils got 5+ A*-C grades including maths and English; 53 per cent A*/A grades. School will endeavour to facilitate any language if there is a demand, however low the numbers – Russian, Arabic, Chinese, Portuguese and Polish all offered and a good solid classics department encourages a number of people to take Latin and Greek GCSE. A few go on to A level.

Good results can partly be attributed to good and committed teaching, but must largely stem from an excellent work ethic that is drilled in from the start. Homework is rigorously monitored and it's a detention for repeated failure to produce it. Setting from year 9 and a number of GCSEs are taken in year 10. Sixth formers have to work together in a large room during study periods. No lounging around on comfy sofas here. A member of staff is ever present to monitor behaviour and we were conscious of our noisy footfall when we peeked in.

The less academically able are offered a sixth form course in advanced business – a hybrid of two A levels and an AS, leading to qualifications in business and computing, a practical alternative to a sixth form college course for those who can't bear to leave. Plans afoot to introduce the Extended Project Qualification. Classes felt by some to be too big – can be as many as 30 at GCSE; sixth form numbers are higher than elsewhere too. However, with 10 or so a year gaining places at Oxbridge, the Sutton Trust continues to rank it among the highest performing state schools in the country. Standards here are high and pupils strive to maintain those standards.

SENs catered for – attracts standard numbers of the usual spread of needs. Currently school estimates there are approximately 40 with Statements/EHC plans – a range of those on the autistic spectrum as well as some with emotional issues, social and/or communication issues. School can accommodate pupils with cerebral palsy. By all accounts the SENCo is 'magnificent' and there is an army of teaching assistants as well as learning support staff. In-class help along with withdrawal where appropriate. Murmurings of discontent in certain quarters – particularly parents who have sons with no identifiable special need, but may simply be dreamy or disorganised. 'Faulty communication lines and support is not swiftly forthcoming' are the central complaints. Wheelchair-friendly and SENs seen, in general, as just part of life.

Games, options, the arts: Junior House boys are committed and robust. The day starts early with an hour's choir practice from 8am, if you are in the Schola. All boys play two instruments – one orchestral, normally supported by the piano. For potential applicants, who must be of at least average academic ability, musical promise is the only criterion which counts here, once you have demonstrated your Catholic credentials – all the boys have musical potential. Not all boys are in the Schola – some just follow an instrumental course. The Schola sings every Saturday evening in the Brompton Oratory. Junior house boys play every instrument you can name, under the care of innumerable peripatetic teachers of high quality, and use all the senior school facilities. They tour, record and give stunning concerts They work hard and play hard.

Not just music, sport too. Tag rugby is organised against other schools. They swim once a week in the school pool, and water polo is a popular after-school club. Plenty of other after-school clubs too – including Lego, programming and chess, but many boys are just too tired at the end of the school day. Art is vibrant and boys get to use the facilities of the senior school. They learn about eg Da Vinci in lessons then put their learning into practical effect in the art room. Not a lot of drama, but plenty of musical productions – again, use of the senior school facilities greatly enhances the experience. This is true, too, of science. Science is taught in the senior school labs, and they get the benefit of having specialist teachers from an early age – not just the form teacher.

This is a big rugby school and rowing is also 'massive', as our proud and enthusiastic sixth form guides told us – school has recently achieved entry into the Henley Regatta and won the National Rowing Champtionships. If your son is a keen football player he will struggle to find much here apart from the house soccer competition. Rugby fixtures against a huge number of schools including the top public schools, many on a Saturday. Six teams in the first form alone, and more than 20 in total, so plenty of opportunities for everyone to have a go. Boys are bussed to Barn Elms in Barnes for training – a round trip of not much less than an hour.

Water polo also popular, with fixtures against other schools; hockey, skating and basketball are other main activities at present – all weather 4G playing field installed 2016; also a good, well-used, on-site 17m pool and gym where you can see many rowers in training. World Challenge has more participants than any other school in the country – state and independent – and sends boys on exciting, self-financed trips of a lifetime. Also popular is D of E. CCF perhaps the biggest in any state school, both army and RAF – tours, camps and expeditions of all kinds. Lots of sixth involved in community work – helping at local schools and care homes, soup kitchens on Saturdays, the offices of a local charity etc.

A delightfully refreshing and modern attitude to educating boys: 'Arts are very important in a boys' school'; plans for a dance studio, which is in the pipeline. 'The boys will respond really well to dance classes.' That's right, says one parent, who remembers how much her son enjoyed knitting and crocheting while in the Junior House. Boys here will throw themselves into anything. The key thing is to make it fun.

Music is excellent, fuelled by those who come up from the Junior House, all of whom have exceptional aptitude. Some 600+ pupils learn at least one instrument. Bands, including the popular Seagrave Stompers, choirs and orchestras thrive and are well-housed in the arts centre. The chamber choir recently went on a tour to Prague, and recorded their first CD with music sung on the tour. The Schola Cantorum is a choir of professional standard and considerable significance in the world of RC – and secular – music: three visits to Rome in as many months, including representing the Vatican in Al Gore's Live Earth initiative. They record for films and TV, were one of the main choirs at the mass for the beatification of Cardinal Newman on the Papal visit to Britain and are regarded with deserved respect. They sing at the weekly vigil mass at the Brompton Oratory. A recent performance of St John Passion was by all accounts breathtaking – but this is the norm here. Concerts take place at St John's Smith Square as well as the school theatre, and there are plenty of other choirs – these boys (and girls) want to sing. A recent highlight was the girls' choir performance at the Vigil mass in Westminster Cathedral.

School's on-site arts centre is an impressive asset and includes stunning 300-seat galleried theatre in which full scale shows are mounted –a minimum of four performances each year, including one musical. When we visited, Sophocles' Antigone was in rehearsal – the sixth form play. Recent productions include Guys and Dolls, The Government Inspector and Henry V, as well as Joseph and his Technicolour Dreamcoat – performed by the junior boys. Good display spaces – a stimulating photo show by member of staff was good to see, along with a vast Paolozzi brutalist sculpture. Pupils go on to study art/art history and architecture at prestigious institutions. No photography or textiles on offer, though both are available in extracurricular clubs.

Lots of overseas trips in the holidays – foreign exchanges, cultural and historical visits. Rugby tours to far-flung places and singers and instrumental players performing far and wide.

Background and atmosphere: Founded in 1863 by the Oratorian Fathers, the school has recently celebrated its 150th anniversary. It moved to its present site and buildings – in the lee of Chelsea FC's massive stadium – in the 1970s and has worn surprisingly well. Splendid extension and refurbishment of main teaching area recently completed – nominated for architectural award. A bright glass central atrium with pods of different sizes round the edge – for smaller groups and lessons away from the main central area, which is the school library. This is where sixth formers come during their free periods. There is calm peacefulness, no doubt enhanced by the Seven Virtues of Man, which are encapsulated in images and text in panels that climb to the glass roof at the top. Around the outer edges the Beatitudes are depicted. On ground level in the centre is a stunning modern statue of Mary with an adolescent Jesus, complete with apron and the tools of his carpentry trade. A welcome change from the Madonna and child, and so fitting in a school where mothers and sons are working out this next phase in their relationship.

This stunning new development is a modern and dynamic contrast to the old-fashioned class rooms for years 7 and 8, complete with the old style wooden desks, storage inside and inkwell on top. Everyone eats by house in their 'house rooms' (aka classrooms outside feeding times) with six separate serveries. An unusual system, but it seems to work. Some rooms and corridors, notably in the sixth form areas, are scruffy and lacking in soul, but with plans for landscape gardening afoot for the sixth form garden, as well as the creation of a quiet room for reflection and contemplation, it is apparent that there is always attention on improvement and change. We liked the brick courtyard, Chapel Courtyard, with its lead flashing. No football in break and at lunch time here. Health and safety has stopped that. The infrastructure has undergone a profound makeover since we last visited and the boys and staff reinforce an air of engagement and pride, a sense of collaborative energy and achievement.

The chapel, opened in 1992 by Basil Hume and dedicated to St Philip Neri and St Edward the Confessor, is simple in design and has a warm and gentle feel. Services here are intimate and spiritual – only room for one of the houses each day and for the young boys in Junior House; part of the Schola sings, eg, Faure Requiem. Beautiful. Major ceremonies held in the famous, huge, Italianate Oratory Church in South Kensington. The Catholic ethos underlies all aspects of the school but not obtrusively or obsessively – it is simply a given and central also to the plans to develop the community involvement of the school. Long-standing commitment to local primary schools and charities – such as SURF and the SVP soup kitchen – with sixth formers carrying out voluntary work and the music department involved in outreach programmes.

The Junior House is not a separate school but a separate wing: the junior house, with four classrooms, a choir room and several practice rooms – as music is everything here – all recently refurbished. The junior house, rather appropriately, is situated in the heart of the music school. Old-fashioned classrooms, old-fashioned desks that lift up to contain a motley jumble of books and stationary. Music practice rooms adjoin and creakings of strings, blasting of brass form the background noise. Officially it is part of the senior school, but it is the part which takes junior-age boys (7-11). It operates rather like a choir school, or an old fashioned prep school – only without the boarding. It is one of very few state choir schools.

Pastoral care, well-being and discipline: The Junior House really is tiny, with only 80 boys in the entire school (20 in each of years 3-6) and can't really be regarded in a school in its own right. Parents talk of the shock arriving here after a state primary – 'This is not like a primary school. You entrust your children to the teachers here. You're not sure what goes on from the time you drop them at the gate,' said one parent. Ms McKay, who is junior house master – ie she runs the junior house on a day to day basis – is ex-RAF and feared by the parents, though loved by the boys. 'She obviously adores the boys,' said one parent, 'but I am a bit worried about approaching her.' Her attitude appears to be that the job of educating the boys is the school's, the less interference from parents the better.

Discipline in the main school is acknowledged to be tight – rules are strict and enforced strictly. Any mobile phones spotted on the premises will be confiscated and have to be collected by parents. Eight boys were expelled or left after two cannabis smoking incidents. 'You need a clear-cut policy, but you have to have a listening ear and heart.' The approach is 'compassionate', but zero tolerance for physical violence – automatic suspension for anyone who tries to sort a problem by 'raising a hand against someone else'.

House system – there are six houses with 200 pupils in each house – encourages friendships between the year groups and boys in the sixth can mentor those younger who need support over a subject or a problem. Parents mostly praise the staff for their pastoral care – especially the deputy heads – of whom one has been in the school for 20+ years since the start of her career and the other who is a past pupil of the school. However – as with the academics – a complaint we keep hearing is about communication channels and the prompt resolution of problems. There is a culture of deference among parents here, however, so it still takes some boldness to take a proactive step. The sixth form girls talk of close relationships across the two year groups – a benefit of having only 80 girls in total.

Previous head's shift in emphasis is taking time to seep through decades of rigorous and sometimes steely discipline. Aim is to see less 'reaction' and more proactivity, and that through charitable service programmes, and the self-reflection programme that goes with that, the young adults at the school will acquire a taste for 'goodness' and doing and being good. The sixth formers go on 'twilight retreats' at Heythrop College, where they attend talks and discuss issues of life over dinner. Part of this vision has been the establishment of the charitable foundation that is linked with the school, an achievement he is particularly proud of.

Pupils and parents: From a vast geographical area, most London boroughs, inner and outer – some leave home before dawn breaks to come here. Over 50 languages spoken at home; serious Roman Catholicism the only – but unifying – common denominator. A higher number of professional families than in most inner London comprehensives, and the school still has a traditional public school air about it. Parents are warming to drive to involve them in all ways – social, educational and practical. Parents' groups for sports, music and food, and more to follow.

A lot of boys in Junior House have brothers in the senior school, and 'being such a small school, the parents tend to bond quite closely and stick together,' said one parent. The pace is fast and it's 'hard core,' said another. 'While there is a sense of exclusivity – the bar is so high to get in and you feel so lucky – these are very normal boys, not precious and geeky'. A wonderful start in life for your musical, resilient, self-motivated, Catholic little boy.

Reports in the main school are now termly and home-school contact far more a normal thing, though complaints persist of parents not being kept in touch. Children appreciate the knock-ons of greater parental involvement and find it supportive and helpful. The boys themselves are relaxed, friendly, ambitious and hard-working. Classes are head down and concentrating. We heard no raised voices, saw few inattentive faces. Pupils have a sense of pride in themselves and in the school which one would wish to see replicated everywhere. The only boy who wouldn't like it here, we were told, was someone who didn't want to involve himself.

Sixth form girls are no mere modern import designed to boost results. They date back to a link with a girls' school in the 19th century and were incorporated into the sixth in the 1950s after a merger. Their numbers are small but, says head, 'they add so much to the school'. It was good to see girls and boys out and about in the lunch hour clearly in relaxed friendship and at ease – no cattle market or points system here. Popular among politicians – Tony Blair and Nick Clegg both sent their sons here. Notable former pupils include Simon Callow, rugby union star Michael Swift and Hayley Atwell. Oh – and David McFadden.

Entrance: Admits up to 20 boys at 7 into year 3, up to 10 of whom are choristers. All applicants tested for general academic ability and for music aptitude; potential choristers also tested for choral aptitude and suitability. Priority to practising Catholics who attend mass frequently, baptism before 6 months, siblings.

Entrance to main school simpler than hitherto, but heart-sinking for anyone other than an assiduously practising Roman Catholic family. In fact, don't bother to apply unless you are a pillar of your local church and known to your priest, who will have to vouch for your bona fides – both pupil's and family's; early baptism essential. After long-running legal battle no longer includes 'Catholic service' – eg church flower arranging – as part of points system. Admission process involves completing the school's Supplementary Information Form and a local authority Common Application Form. Nine hundred plus apply for the 160 places. Junior House boys transfer automatically and parents praise the seamless transition.

Sixth form also oversubscribed. Requirement is B grades in six GCSEs and at least a C in maths and English. This is the stated requirement, but parents we spoke to said the standard was in fact much higher. Beware the postman if your son looks like he won't make the standard expected at A level. A letter is likely to arrive during year 11 to warn that you need to find a place elsewhere. Forty places attract 200 applicants and, again, the RC credentials are what counts, plus 'expected performance at GCSE and suitability for an A level course which will be sought from each pupil's current school'. Girls join from Sacred Heart, Gumley, the Ursuline Convent and a few from Lady Margaret's. The current oversubscription criteria are based upon mass attendance, early baptism, siblings and attendance at the Oratory Primary School

Exit: All Junior House boys move up to the main school. Most stay on after GCSEs; almost 400 in sixth form. Regularly win Oxbridge places (10 in 2016), covering the range of disciplines. Over 100 to Russell Group, just over 30 elsewhere and two to study in US (MIT/Texas). Fairly equal spread of arts, sciences and practical subjects. Otherwise to good universities everywhere to read everything. Refreshingly few silly subjects pursued – these pupils have been properly taught and sensibly advised.

Remarks: Much that is excellent and not just the obvious – the music, the academics, but also the attention given to spiritual and emotional development. An ideal choice for a son (or sixth form daughter) who toes the line. Approach with caution if you have a scatty child who balks at authority.

Lycée Français Charles de Gaulle

35 Cromwell Road, London SW7 2DG

Pupils: 2,370 • Ages: 3–19 • Sixth form: 530

Fees: £5,385 – £11,271 pa

Tel: 020 7584 6322
Email: inscription@lyceefrancais.org.uk
Website: www.lyceefrancais.org.uk

Proviseur: Since 2012, Mr Olivier Rauch. Degrees in history and geography from University of Lyon as well as Agrégation (French civil servant educational leadership qualification). Previously head of lycée in Rabat and a lycée in Toulouse (which included a preparatory programme for the prestigious Grandes Écoles). Started career as a history and geography teacher. Married, with three grown up children who live abroad.

Urbane and distinguished, he is confident in his preparation, knowledge and previous experience of running large French lycées, yet a touch of humility makes for easy conversation. He's also head of the three satellite primary feeder schools.

Since the launch of a new school in Wembley in 2015, he and his leadership team have been working on the bigger problem of how to redistribute London's French school-age children into satellite French schools, and how to use the space this would free up at Charles de Gaulle – more student lounges, common areas and specialist classrooms. However, he knows families worry how the inevitable change in location for some might affect them.

Another goal is to assess the anomalies between the French baccalaureate and A levels that seem to impede his leavers' entry into some British university courses (medicine, for example).

Parents comment that discipline has improved since head's arrival – he thinks this may be a result of his close communication with students via the student council.

Academic matters: Lycée Charles de Gaulle is the premier French school in Britain and one of the largest in the world. The raison d'être is to provide French education leading to the French baccalaureate, regarded by many as one of the most robust school-leaving qualifications there is. With many dual national French-English families enrolled, the Lycée also offers GCSE and A levels.

The French model has the following divisions: maternelle (reception and year 1), primaire (years 2-6), college (years 7-10) and lycée (years 11-13). In primaire and college, the school offers the French curriculum in French. From the final year of college (year 10) students either move over to the British section to do GCSEs and IGCSEs followed by A levels or continue through to the French baccalaureate. Parent perspectives on the Lycée vary significantly depending on their own cultural expectations of what constitutes a school education, but most parents seem to feel that overall the kids are well taught, learning lots, enjoying the challenge and loving the school's international community.

Primary class teachers do everything (including art and PE) while specialists support IT and music. The quality of the art is down to the creativity of the teacher but we've heard of some great stuff with cross-curricular projects and older classes partnering with younger ones. Parents say there's 'frequent assessment and evaluation' so a struggling child is quickly identified. A primary parent with British school experience describes the French system as 'less flexible, but of high

L

standard.' Class sizes are about 28, with an assistant in each class. Classroom arrangements are fairly traditional, with desks in rows, though we saw some more varied arrangements.

College is another story. Some students entering college come from schools where the entire enrolment is less than the year group they are joining. Students move around for different lessons in what one parent described as an 'anonymous teacher environment.' Students have advisers whom they see for maybe 30 minutes per week and there's no expectation of pastoral care on the adviser's part. They monitor pupils' progress through frequent assessment and parents are kept informed. The problem is that it's public knowledge, so if you are bottom of the heap everyone knows, which can take its toll on the self-esteem of less confident adolescents. The survivors – and there are plenty who thrive on the mounting pressure – develop strong independent skills and learn to manage their time and work successfully, attributes French parents expect to see.

The French curriculum is followed in the French section for the oldest students (confusingly called the 'lycée'). In year 12 there are three French baccalaureate pathways: economics and social science, literature and science, where the subjects studied vary as do the number of hours devoted to each. The word is that there is pressure from both school and parents to go down the prestigious science route. Because so many students are fluent in English, many do a GSCE in English within the French bacc stream.

The international version of the French baccalaureate (which follows the French bacc curriculum but has more courses in English and leads to the same official French bacc exams) has recently been introduced, so it's too soon to evaluate. (Not to be confused with the IB diploma.) Students join this programme in year 10; transfer from this programme into the British section is only available in year 12 and depends on availability of space. No 'bacc-light' – this programme reputedly demands an even heavier time commitment than the regular bacc.

L

The British section offers the GCSE/A level pathway. Students must be fluent enough in English to manage. Discipline is also an issue – nobody with a rap sheet gets in. Occasionally this route is apparently recommended for students who may not succeed with the French bacc.

Year 10 pupils do a wide range of about 10 courses, including French of course, but also a third language (pupils are spoilt for choice – Italian, Spanish, German, Arabic, Russian, Greek and Latin on offer). French IGCSE exams are compulsory, which pleases parents, though there seem to be some questions about timing with kids sitting exams too early.

In year 11 students generally drop one or two subjects as they get into their AS level and A level subjects. Parents rave about the maths, chemistry and physics, but suggest that those interested in the arts tend to look elsewhere (French education is not noted for intellectual autonomy or commitment to creativity, which are fairly fundamental for art). French and PE are compulsory until year 13; since 2015, A level French is taken in year 13.

Deciding which route to choose – French bacc or British A levels – can be daunting. Those opting for the British tend to be dual nationals, non-French who joined the Lycée because their kids were in a French system and Anglophile French families setting down permanent roots in the UK.

The appeal of the French bacc is its strong global reputation, with its slavish commitment to developing intellectual rigour. But it's hard work, rigid, requires lots of memorisation and absorbing of new information. 'The French system crams knowledge into your brain – and we know the brain is a muscle that can be stretched,' said one French parent.

But some French students aiming for a UK university question the need to do the full-blown bacc when they can focus on more specialised A levels. Plus it's no secret that class sizes in the British section are smaller (about 12 compared to 28 to 30 for the French section) and the teaching style is more conducive to project work, class discussions and debates.

The French bacc classes, 'no wishy-washy child-centred approach,' are more traditional, 'cruelly elite' in a 'sink or swim' learning environment. 'Teachers instruct with minimal empathy. You listen and absorb the learning, which can be a challenge for students with strong personalities inclined to engage in debate and, God forbid, challenge the teacher.' Then there is the matter of 'loyalty to French heritage.' If they move to the British section some families lament the move away from the French educational tradition, even though it may be the right decision educationally. British section kids have more time for extracurricular activities. Places in the British section are competitive; with the Lycée full to capacity, expansion of this programme seems unlikely. But more French students are considering the advantages of the A level university pathway, so there are more applicants than spaces.

Ongoing discussion amongst parents about A level results. The small size of the A level cohort means there are limited courses offered and timetabling clashes can prevent kids from taking the courses they want, leading some frustrated families to change schools after GCSEs. It has also been suggested that some French parents whose children are in the British section have a hard time overcoming the 'pedagogical cultural divide' between the French and British systems; they simply don't understand the flexibility that British teachers have in delivering the curriculum.

The governance and management structure of the Lycée is naturally focused on the French curriculum. For a British deputy head, finding a way to sit within that institutional culture is undoubtedly a challenge. Although the policy of rotating the head makes sense for Lycées worldwide, it probably has an impact on attention to GCSEs, A levels etc in the British section. Each new head has to get up to speed with the whole (and for them, anomalous) British programme, along with all the other challenges of running such a large institution. It's a steep learning curve for even a top educationalist.

French bacc results are excellent, above the French national average. In 2016, 36 per cent of students got 'mention bien' and 42 per cent 'mention très bien' grades.

A levels are by comparison less impressive, though 58 per cent A*/A grades in 2016 (82 per cent A*/B). French A level results could be more impressive, given the context, although the school points out that students only have three hours a week for French and take the exam a year earlier than other schools. I/GCSE results show roughly 59 per cent A*/A grades in 2016 (British Section). Parents think this differential in results between the French bacc and A level has been taken on board by the head.

Although French nationality, language and heritage is the common denominator here, some kids are not completely fluent in French. It's full immersion, so if a child isn't capable of fully functioning in French by the age of 5, parents say they'll struggle when reading and writing begins. Others move their children out as they get older because parents lack sufficient French language to fully support them – unless they have a French-speaking nanny at home to sustain the French speaking day and supervise homework. English as a second language is taught from primary, with some setting for levels in consideration of the native speakers. In college, students are streamed for English. Other languages are available but no mother tongue instruction other than French and English.

For students with special needs, the educational psychologist and speech and language adviser recommends what sort of specialist might help manage the student's learning (dyslexia is not uncommon) but the school itself does not provide much support in-house. School has disabled access in all but one building but the logistics of the daily timetables and student movements mean that students with mobility challenges would struggle here.

Many teachers (average age early 40s) are civil servants, with professionalism and benefits for which French teachers are renowned. Forty-five per cent have been at the Lycée for more than 10 years.

Games, options, the arts: On Wednesdays, primary classes end early but extra activities like cooking, crafts, IT, sports and games are offered. Human Rights Club, Justice in the Heart and House of Students are student-led activities the British and French section students do together, but French section students have less time to devote to these.

Curriculum-related residential trips abroad include India, Berlin (history), Paris (Comédie Française), Greece (classics), Venice (Italian), New York (art), Moscow (Russian). Compulsory work experience programmes in years 10 or 11 are organised by parents.

A few hundred students do sports, many on Saturdays at the sports facility in Raynes Park, competing against London schools and schools abroad. There's a school sports day but parents warn: 'Don't expect to get a ribbon unless you place first, second, or third.' Music is popular, with ensembles, orchestra or choir to choose from.

Background and atmosphere: School was founded to serve London's French population, but also to further France's 'mission civilisatrice' – making French culture and education available to the Brits. During the Second World War it became the home of the Free French and the head sits in the office once occupied by General de Gaulle, so the school's name has meaning. British section was created 60 years ago to offer the French programme in English, but the differences in the French bacc and A levels meant that a marriage was not practical, so the British section sits within the organisation as a 'stand alone'. Over the years the Lycée has spread and now occupies a city block across from the Natural History Museum. If approaching the area during pick-up you'll think you've alighted at the wrong end of the Eurostar.

Part of the AEFE (Agency for Teaching of French Education Abroad), the Lycée is one of more than 100 overseas schools directed by the Ministry of Education and is governed by a committee including the French ambassador and other diplomats. Heads are rotated, with posts lasting up to five years. British section is managed by Kelvin Zane, dapper ex-deputy-head of a London comprehensive, whose fluid command of French has enabled him to adapt to this large French organisation. His UK experience is invaluable when it comes to matters such as child protection and Ofsted.

Facilities have been renovated to absorb increasing student numbers – a combination of inter-connected new build and Victoriana and using lots of cheerful colours. Buildings open out at the back to play area shared by all ages. Parents say 'it looks confusing, but the kids figure it out in a day or two.' Primary is in a building shared by upper classes on the top floor. There's a large hall for dramatic and musical performances, music and art rooms; PE is outside in the central yard, at local sports facilities or own grounds in Raynes Park. The yard has large canopies with seating areas to provide all-weather cover; no indoor play area.

A large library mushrooms over several floors, separated into college and lycée sections. Classrooms have desks in traditional rows. Computers in the libraries, study rooms and computer lab, but not much evidence of technology inside the classrooms.

Lunch is served in a bright, clean cafeteria. Youngest have their own lunch room; lunch is compulsory unless there are extraordinary dietary needs. Varied three course menu looks just short of Cordon Bleu by usual school standards. Considering that the chef turns out more than 2,500 meals a day, the food looked and smelled very appealing; fish always on offer for those with kosher or halal preferences.

School also boasts an impressive medical centre, staffed with sympathetic nurses and a full-time doctor. Parents are happy with home-school communication, and it's easy to have a quick chat with the primary teacher at dismissal. The formal communication cycle is 'front loaded' with year-group parent events at the beginning of the year; after that it's up to parents to seek out the teachers – but they'll be in touch if there's a problem.

Pastoral care, well-being and discipline: With such an enormous student body, parents' reports are mixed. Some parents insist the kids 'don't get lost, are well looked after,' while others say that once in college 'students are a number and their teachers hardly know them.' For students joining college, the school tries to put them in classes with three designated friends to ease the culture shock of coping with the sheer scale of the Lycée. This is less a concern for rising Lycée primary students already familiar with the environment.

Playground attendants are a prominent French feature – supervisors keeping an eye on everyone. College students may leave campus provided they have parents' permission (most don't); in the top years most go out for lunch. A nifty school diary is issued to track home-school communication; the back cover has every student's photo, identification and timetable so anyone trying to slip out can be identified and sent back to class.

The children are cheerful and polite; primary teachers remind them about the importance of greeting people respectfully. No lockers – backpacks are stored here and there. No reports of any significant behaviour issues; everyone knows what is expected. If students fall short, they may be given more homework or required to attend school on Saturday. School psychologist offers counselling for students. Secondary school year group leaders have offices in their own sections of the school, with a secretary to manage the 300 or so kids in each level.

Parents warn that drop off and pick up can be stressful. By staggering start and finish times the school manages the flow of traffic pretty well under the circumstances. But parents need to be prepared for the possibly overwhelming feeling of chaos and confusion at the start.

Pupils and parents: The French connection is the common denominator. Vast majority are French nationals with at least one French parent, some dual nationals (eg British/French), a few British. Other nationalities include Canadian, American, Italian, Spanish, Lebanese, Moroccan and Russian. Many parents are in London on short-term assignments – diplomatic, financial services, media, industry. The generously subsidised fees (not available in the British section) widen the socio-economic net, attracting families who may not normally aspire to private education. Parents prefer this more realistic reflection of society to the rarefied atmosphere of economic privilege that they associate with many London independent schools.

Students come from all over – some with long commutes on public transport – but they feel it's worth it. In some cases the main wage-earner commutes to France or travels internationally but the family has chosen to stay in London in order to keep the kids at the Lycée.

The APL (parents' association) organises after-school activities, raises funds, supports the athletics programme and serves as a sounding board for issues of community interest. Some non-French speakers say it's difficult to become involved. Eclectic list of 'vieux garçons et filles' includes Jacqueline Bisset, the late Natasha Richardson, Gyles Brandreth, Lady Olga Maitland, Roland Joffé.

Entrance: Registration process begins around April of the entry year, with decisions sent in early May. Highly over-subscribed, entry is described as 'a nightmare, haphazard and chaotic.' Families normally apply to other schools as well; some start off elsewhere to await an offer. There's a priority list of criteria: children of French diplomats, siblings (in primary only), children from another official French school (locally or abroad), including students following the CNED (the French distance learning programme), then any miscellany of Francophones fortunate enough to get in.

Siblings trump everything else in primary so families bank on getting one tiny first foot in the door, knowing the others are pretty much a shoe-in. One French national tells us she put her children on the waiting list from the earliest time allowed. Her eldest was unsuccessful but a few days after the term began the younger one was offered a place, posing a dilemma for managing two-school runs simultaneously. When she explained this to the school, they somehow magicked up a space for the second child.

Best tip for locals is to transfer from one of the official AEFE Ecole Homologuée nursery schools such as École le Hérisson, L'École des Petits (Fulham) or La Petite École. Feeders for primaire entry include the annexe schools – Wix (Clapham), South Kensington, Ealing and Fulham. Year 7 feeders include École Jacques Prévert, L'École Bilingue, L'École des Petits and L'École de Battersea. For year 10 (British section) and year 11 (French section) it's the Bilingual College in Kentish Town (CFBL). Beware, though – not all schools with emphasis on French language are official AEFE schools, so check the Lycée's website if you're banking on this as your golden ticket. Families do move on so vacancies arise mid-year, but school always refers to the waiting list. According to one successful mother, 'this is the only hope for a local family wanting their child to go to the Lycée' and requires strategic planning of Napoleonic proportions.

No admissions testing and once a child is in, parents have no worries about future entrance exams such as 11+ or CE.

Exit: The Lycée prides itself on its careers department, with advisers specialising in UK, US and French universities. Careers counselling begins in year 11; a major careers forum involves experts and university reps from three continents. Some parents feel more coordination is required to rationalise the Lycée exams and Oxbridge and Russell Group entrance criteria, and more focus needed on writing UCAS personal statements.

Roughly one quarter go to French universities, with 10 per cent of bacc graduates gaining entry into the Grandes Écoles. British destinations include Oxbridge, Manchester, Bristol, Essex, King's College London, Southampton and Surrey; American destinations include Rhodes Island School of Design, Virginia, McGill, Santa Clara and NYU. A few do gap years.

Money matters: A 50 per cent AEFE subsidy (except for those in the British section) makes for bargain tuition by London standards. Some welfare grants and bursaries – and APL has been known to rally when a family falls on hard times.

Remarks: This is a huge institution yet parents say children are happy, well taught and love the cultural diversity. The waiting lists are testimony to the school's overall success. With the French and Francophile population growing daily, it seems that the entente cordial is alive and well in this petit coin of London.

L

The Lyceum School

157

6 Paul Street, London EC2A 4JH

Pupils: 112 • Ages: 3–11

Fees: £15,060 pa

Tel: 020 7247 1588
Email: admin@lyceumschool.co.uk
Website: www.lyceumschool.co.uk

Headteacher: Mrs Vanessa Bingham, who took over as interim head following the abrupt departure of previous head Edwin Brown in July 2015, was appointed head in 2016. Mr Brown joined in 2014 when the founding heads sold the school to Minerva Education. Mrs Bingham is an experienced head, who has led schools in the UK and China, including managing the three schools in the Rego group. For the two years before joining The Lyceum she was interim head at several primary schools in England. Parents feel the right choice has been made this time. 'She's terrific..an amazing, galvanizing force..she's sympathetic to keeping the ethos of the school..it's in good hands.'

Entrance: Places at 3 (nursery) and 4 (reception) are offered on a first-come first-served basis with priority to siblings. A few places for 7 year olds and the odd vacancy later on (places awarded subject to assessment). Many families use public transport from Hackney or Islington but the demographics have altered in recent years, as more mothers are working or living close by in the City and several families live in the Barbican.

Exit: Majority stay until 11, with a few leaving earlier for schools like City Girls' Prep. The variety of senior school destinations has widened over the years to include City of London, Highgate, Channing, North Bridge House, Dulwich College, Queen's Gate, Forest School, South Hampstead, Frances Holland Clarence Gate and Portland Place. Also boarding schools such as Headington (Oxford) and Cheltenham Ladies'. Regular academic, art and music scholarships.

Remarks: A short walk from Liverpool Street and Moorgate, the building which houses the school was originally a distribution warehouse for the Radio Times. Apart from the nursery, the classrooms are semi-open plan and grouped together chronologically with a shared library and cloakroom in the centre. The bright strip lights in the hall are functional, whilst central pink chandeliers in the open plan classroom area are quirky and fun. We saw teachers working and sharing, encouraged to support one another, with plenty of resources. 'The relationship with the teachers is very important,' commented one parent of three, 'as the pupils see them as allies, friendly, someone to help them, rather than adversarial'. Another praised the fact that 'the children come out very comfortable with themselves, not brash', and another added, 'They develop interpersonal skills, are comfortable talking to adults' – as we experienced in our conversations with a group during our visit. There is a good balance of staff age with some long-serving teachers and energetic young ones. Some of the teaching assistants we met are old pupils, who loved the school so much they wanted to return. Each day begins gently with music playing as a signal for parents to depart. Specialists teach French (from reception), and music; afternoons are devoted to creativity and sports.

Year groups are paired for trips and non-academic lessons, or to make up the numbers for games. This results in the children knowing each other and looking after one another, taking responsibility without the need for houses or prefects. We saw small classes, 16 on average, each with a teaching assistant (including one chap), thoroughly enjoying their learning. In small classes friendships can become an issue, but parents remark: 'The school deals well with this and talks through any situation quickly and effectively. There is zero tolerance of bad behaviour.'

The school does not set out to cater for special needs and one parent with older children at the Lyceum told us she chose not to send her youngest child because she required more specialist support. Nevertheless, in recent years, the school has employed a SENCo and part-time speech and language therapist, which has helped as the needs of individual children have become apparent. Before parents accept a place, they are invited to meet the head to ensure they fully understand what the school is about before making a commitment.

Despite the urban location, the children all have plenty of physical activity and play on a daily basis. Nowhere for a dining room or on-site catering but while parents find the packed lunches a chore they accept that lack of space cannot be helped. Throughout the building there are massive silver pipes for filtering air. The school is sure they have 'less asthma as a result' but it is utilitarian – if post-modernist. There is a reasonably large, indoor courtyard, which works well for breaks and small sports, as well as a gallery/hall for drama, dance, music and gym, plays and assemblies. For half the year they use the local Broadgate Centre ice rink for skating and parents really appreciate the use of local facilities such as the vast Honourable Artillery Ground, Bunhill Fields and Golden Lane Sports Centre for tennis, swimming and netball. Clubs include judo, run by ex-Olympic athlete. One parent commented on the disadvantage that the children are taught the basic sports skills but do not have much experience of team fixtures and matches when they move on to secondary school. Another parent appreciated the fact that 'the children are learning to love the City and all there is on offer'. They come and go in their navy and white uniform, with smart caps for boys and felt hats/ boaters for girls. All the pupils we spoke to said they like the uniform and feel comfortable in it.

We saw a good mix of artwork in lively topic displays and a developmental whole school (nursery to year 6) set of colourful paintings of poinsettias in the hall. The school is keen to stress the many opportunities to perform, with regular plays, assemblies and concerts. The majority learn instruments and take examinations, and they reach a high standard of performance. We watched an impressive big band rehearsal and a chamber choir practice. As one boy proudly stated, 'It's great fun. For a small school, we can play loads of instruments'. Charlotte Barbour-Condini, an ex-pupil, was runner up in the BBC Young Musician of the Year playing the recorder.

Recently-introduced Mandarin clubs, plus an IT consultant, who has been working alongside the staff. The school is keen for children to be 'producers of content, not just consumers', and we saw children producing sophisticated animations, websites, mobile apps and even their own ebook. Much of this work is related to the Living History topics and annual year 5 and 6 residential trips to eg Edinburgh, Paris and Amsterdam. Parents praised these as being 'vivid and memorable', though one emphasised the need for careful budgeting, as they are in addition to the annual fees.

The emphasis is not on cramming and there are no end of year examinations, but parents feel that pupils are successfully prepared for secondary schools. One told us, 'The school doesn't come across as overly academic, however, it should promote its achievement in getting children into good quality schools.' Another said, 'I chose The Lyceum deliberately because I didn't want my child stressed out going to school'. All in all the consensus is that The Lyceum produces 'well rounded, happy children' and manages to strike a 'good balance between creativity and very good results.' No mean feat.

The Mall School

185 Hampton Road, Twickenham TW2 5NQ

Pupils: 320 • Ages: 4–13

Fees: £11,250 – £12,630 pa

Tel: 020 8977 2523
Email: admissions@themallschool.org.uk
Website: www.themallschool.org.uk

Headmaster: Since 2011, Mr David Price BSc (environmental science) MA (school and college management) PGCE (40s). Worked in a conservation unit for a few years before starting his career in a state primary school some 20 years ago. He has also been head of juniors and director of studies here. Previously he was head of English and deputy principal at Latymer Prep and before that taught at Melbourne Grammar School in Australia, where he lived with his family for three years.

Seems to be doing well in this, his first headship. Obviously knows the school inside out and so has been able to leap straight into action – no root and branch reformation, rather a gentle reorganisation in a few areas. Physically and procedurally, he's been tidying up the place and has improved the management structure, appointing a senior tutor for years 7/8 and a head of the 'middles'.

Tremendously affable, he has an open-door policy for staff and parents and consults widely before deciding anything, but he will always have the final word and is prepared to put his foot down where necessary. 'He's really personable, but don't cross him,' advised one parent. Parents generally seem to appreciate the fact that he's 'one of us' and 'a family man'. He lives locally with his Australian wife Lindy and two school-age children (a son at The Mall, and an older daughter), and 'he totally gets where we are coming from,' said a mother. 'He's got the same concerns as we do and I've got nothing but praise for him,' agreed another.

He's quite a stickler for the rules and likes things neat and organised – that includes the boys and their uniforms, and he's not above manning the school gates himself to check that all is shipshape. A precise person who believes that standards must be maintained in all areas and if you bother to have a policy you should follow it through. He's strict, but not feared – 'I would say the boys like him and have a lot of respect for him,' said one mother. 'He's easy to speak to,' confirmed our young tour guides. Not remote and office-bound, he still fits in some RS teaching, runs breakfast meetings with parent reps and attends all the concerts and sports matches. 'I think he's dynamic and wonderful,' said one fan. 'Nothing is too much trouble,' said another.

Out of school he enjoys walking, cycling and socialising, plus frequent trips to visit family in Australia.

Entrance: Non-selective at reception, it's first come, first served – register two years ahead. A DP innovation has been to invite boys joining in September to spend time at the school during the previous summer term. 'We obviously have a look at them and see reports from nursery, but it's not an entrance test,' he says. These infants join one of two mixed ability classes. Joiners thereafter will be assessed in English and maths, and anyone joining after year 4 will be additionally assessed in French and science. Almost self-selects because of its reputation as an academic school, although DP is keen to move away from possibly harsh connotations associated with that reputation. But even so, the bottom 25 per cent of pupils at The Mall end up in the top half of the national average. No dedicated feeder; The Mall takes from over 20 local pre-schools and nurseries including Jack and Jill, Sunflower, Windsor, Pavilion, Maria Grey and De Lacey. Scholarships available for outstanding candidates joining at 7+ or 8+.

Exit: No links to any one school, but does have a close relationship with neighbouring senior school, Hampton, whose head is on Mall board of governors. Typically two-thirds of leavers go to Hampton, King's College Wimbledon, St George's Weybridge, Westminster or Reed's. 'It varies according to parental mood and which senior school is flavour of the month.' Others to eg Charterhouse, Christ's Hospital, Eton, Harrow, Wellington and Winchester. Boys are expected to stay to 13+ so are not really prepared for 11+ exams, though a few do leave then, usually for a grammar school place.

Remarks: A well-established prep which knows exactly what it has to do and achieves more.

Things start gently, with reception and year 1 pupils based in a separate building, five minutes from the main school, on a fairly busy, semi-residential road; you can't drop off on site or outside, need to park up and walk. Parents like the fact that their little ones are physically separated from the older, bigger boys; 'I think it makes it easier for them as they start,' said a mother.

M

The infants' building is a converted Victorian vicarage, with two reception classes downstairs and two year 1 classes upstairs – maximum 22 in each class, generally around 18. Not masses of space for 80+ little boys, but neither are they jammed in. Bright classrooms enlivened with colourful displays. Lessons we saw were very settled and children seemed happy and focused. There is lots of topic-based work eg on space, where we saw some inventive designs for 'a planet unlike Earth'. Each class teacher has a full-time classroom assistant and there are specialist teachers for music and swimming – both strengths of this place, of which more later. Homework twice a week, spellings once a week and reading every night. Boys needing extra help with work will be peeled off for extra tuition with SENCo – no stigma, no extra cost at this level, but you will be charged higher up the school. Also a charge for help with EFL, but school says boys generally catch up quickly, typically within a term or so.

There's one large room, not grand enough to be called a hall, but where the whole infant school can gather for assemblies. Year 1s eat their packed lunches here too – no hot meals for infants – and reception pupils eat their lunch at their desk. Sounds messy, but school says it works.

Some nice touches outside – a bird box/camera and raised beds where the boys can plant – go some way to compensate for limited outdoor space including a sadly under-used grassy area ('little boys and grass don't mix,' said school).

Generally the atmosphere is relaxed, but not sloppy. All staff expect and receive respect – for example, the boys will be asked to re-enter a room if they have not entered it properly. 'I like the place and the pace here,' said one mother. 'It's perfect for little boys, with quite a lot of play-based learning in the early years as they improve their fine motor skills, then things hot up as they move through the school.'

From year 2 the boys move to the purpose-built main site, with 7+ entrants joining in year 3. Everyone automatically transfers to the senior section from year 4 (ages 8 to 13) to take up the common entrance curriculum. Years ago boys would be asked to leave if they did not make the grade – all that changed under the previous headmaster and Mr Price shares this same philosophy. 'I am here to get the less able boys through too and I like to see a wide range of abilities.' To this end school has a series of strategies to help and support the less able and is very keen on early intervention, 'the earlier the better'. Then in senior school there is a director of personalised learning, who develops individual plans. DP is also setting up a programme for non-academic scholarships and Mall pupils have already had some success in winning music, art and all-rounder places. Lots of mocks and target-setting, overseen by newly introduced 'academic tutors', aim to ensure early detection of anyone not working up to their capability. Currently 26 boys with SEN, mostly mild dyslexia and dyspraxia. 'From year 4 parents can pay for additional support if they choose', says school.

That said, academics is the focus here – no bones about it; that's why most parents choose The Mall in the first place. It's heads down every day as soon as the boys arrive, with assembly timetabled for just before lunch, so the work is done when the boys are at their freshest. Streaming and setting at the top of the school – in year 7 an accelerated class is introduced, from which come the scholarship boys, while the other class goes at 'ordinary pace'.

'It's a very good all-round school, but its USP is the learning environment – they have got it just right,' said a father. 'The all-round atmosphere is extremely conducive to learning,' agreed a mother. 'As we looked around it felt like we had come home. It's all brilliant from the get-go and I like the drive in this place. They let boys be boys, but also push them to do their absolute best.'

Parents seem to share an unerring confidence in this school and trust it to do right by their sons. There is an orderly, comfortable atmosphere and the boys are well-prepared for their CE. The ongoing tests and plenty of exam practice mean that the boys are so au fait with the whole procedure that it's no biggie when the important ones come around. 'They are totally familiar with what's expected and almost relaxed about it,' said a mother.

There is a fair amount of homework, including holiday homework – building up so that by year 7 there's about an hour a night, 1.5 hours by year 8. Teaching is strong across the board so it is invidious to pick stand-out subjects – 'Really it's all good,' chant parents – but suffice to say French ('extremely well-taught' by native speakers) history and music all mentioned time and again. All year 2 boys play recorder to get them ready and interested and 140+ boys go on to play instruments – we saw boys having great fun drumming and composing. There is also an 80-strong choir – 'It's one of the nice things about a single-sex school,' says one parent. 'Boys are simple creatures and follow what others are doing, so they don't see singing as "girly".' Plenty of chances to perform via regular productions – DP plans for the standard of school concerts to be even better. 'I think he just wants the boys to practise more,' said one mother. 'To make the shows a bit more polished'.

Facilities generally on a par with similar London day schools, with some outstanding features. There's a splendid theatre, a sublime swimming pool and a new sports hall. There are two full games afternoons each week and although school is lacking in lush grounds, it is but a short skip and a jump to the bosky expanses of nearby Bushy Park for football, rugby and cricket. There's not so much athletics or tennis and some parents feel sport is not taken as seriously as at some other schools in the area – with the exception of swimming, where the U10 team are IAPS national champions. But most agree that it does 'well enough' for their sons and praise 'smashing' sports staff. 'I wouldn't say it's for a very sporty child,' said one. 'It doesn't have the focus that it does in other schools, which irritates some of us'.

Not masses of extracurricular activities on offer, though there's all the usual art, DT, chess and of course a swimming club – it would be criminal not to make the most of their gorgeous pool. Offering of clubs has been beefed up to include computing, karate, judo and science. Some of the clubs are at lunchtime as it's already quite a long day (8.25am-4pm) but school has to balance this against the fact that many Mall parents are both working and would appreciate their sons being able to enjoy a longer school day.

Apparently there's no such thing as a typical Mallian: 'We prefer them to remain individuals,' says DP. But he will concede uniformity in that they are confident ('not arrogant,' he stresses), well-mannered and well-rounded young men. 'I think they are all quite different really,' agreed one mother. 'And I like the way they are encouraged to develop their own interests and skills'.

Staff have good relationships with the boys – good humour abounds, house points (plus or minus) moderate behaviour and are delivered with some theatrical flourish by school deputy. Head says there is something in The Mall's DNA that promotes good staff/pupil relationships here, bringing out the best in everyone. 'I'm continually impressed by the conversations we can have with them at a very early stage,' he says. Boys are encouraged and taught how to speak confidently in public and to vent their opinions through lots of debating activities. Pupil council and prefects' programme are all part of promoting leadership qualities in the boys. But they are equally encouraged to embrace sentimentality on occasion, such as the mothers' day breakfast (DP imported the idea from Australia) designed to tug at the heart strings: each boy paints a picture of his mother which he presents to her along with a red rose after reading her a poem – most mums cry.

There's a fairly cosmopolitan mix of families here with a wider diversity of cultural backgrounds than seen in other preps in this area of south west London – Asian, Chinese and European boys in the mix. 'I think it's fantastic that The Mall has such a varied population – it's not the rarefied exclusively white intake typical of schools around here,' said one mother. School minibuses run in the morning from Kew, Osterley and Kingston, other pupils from Hounslow, Isleworth, St Margaret's, Richmond, Twickenham, Teddington and Hampton.

Friendly bunch of parents – busy PTA does lots of fundraising but has recently changed its focus to include more social events to get people together. Class reps effective and take the role seriously.

Parents say they feel welcome in school and well informed. Lots of good advice about 'where next?' and DP has introduced a 'future schools information evening' to boost this area. The place is very upfront, it's easy to get to see staff and DP has introduced the Clarion call text communication system which parents have been crying out for. 'They've always been great if I've had a problem,' said a parent.'There's always a nice atmosphere and I feel very comfortable talking to them,' said another.

School runs a good and thriving thrift shop for uniform. Overall parents feel extras are relatively small, not many super-expensive ones, but neither is much available for free. Because The Mall is a small school there are not a lot of big expeditions and sometimes not enough takers to make an expensive jaunt viable. But that's not to say the boys don't get about; there's a year 3 residential trip to PGL Marchants Hill, older pupils to York and France, plus the occasional sports tour.

In all a happy, high-achieving academic school displaying a kinder attitude than of old – trying to be more inclusive. A settled, focused, organised place, which does exactly what it says on the tin.

Mander Portman Woodward (MPW)

90–92 Queen's Gate, London SW7 5AB

Pupils: 600 • Ages: 14–19 • Sixth form: 550

Fees: £25,953 – £28,122 pa

Tel: 020 7835 1355
Email: london@mpw.ac.uk
Website: www.mpw.ac.uk

Principal: Since September 2016, John Southworth, previously a vice principal. Engineering degree from Leicester and MSc in defence technology from the Cranfield Institute of Technology. Has been a major in the army, director of co-curriculum at The Perse, principal of Lansdowne College and vice principal of MPW since 2014. Parents at Lansdowne College commented that his army background showed through in his bluff manner: 'He's very much his own person. He said exactly what he thought, and it turned out to be right.'

Academic matters: Once primarily a 'crammer' helping students with short-term goals, such as exam retakes or Oxbridge entrance, today MPW is a thriving sixth form college, with over 70 per cent taking two-year A level courses. What marks it out is the range and flexibility of options on offer, with 44 subjects provided in any combination. A long day (9am-6pm) and 36 classrooms allow a timetable that suits almost all ('It doesn't always look pretty, but that's the price you pay for flexibility.'). The college also provides a stand-alone one-year A level programme, handy for aspiring medics moving from arts to science or those with weak results wanting to try their hand at something new. Results overall are strong (37 per cent A*-A, 68 A*-B in 2016), particularly in light of the wide-ranging intake, and a hefty dollop of star performers deliver top grades.

Without doubt, an exam-oriented place, with a persistent spotlight on the syllabus and exam technique honed by regular timed tests and ample supplies of homework, but students confirm it's far more than an exam factory. 'The teachers' knowledge is so broad, they make subjects more interesting because you're able to explore in more depth.' All pupils get plenty of close attention in classes never larger than nine – which means there's no place to hide. 'At my old school,' said one pupil. 'I used to sit at the back and not pay attention. You can't do that here.' Well-qualified staff, many of whom are public examiners or have published text books, receive extravagant praise ('brilliant', 'second-to none', 'amazing') not only for their expert subject knowledge but for their willingness to go above and beyond. ('Even when I was away from college in the middle of exams I would email them and they would reply within 15 minutes,' said one former pupil). Teaching style is egalitarian and conversational with technology firmly embedded in the delivery. 'Virtual learning is an efficient and engaging way of getting information across. There's now such a wealth of information available on line that students need to develop the skills to pare it down.'

About 50 a year take GCSEs (or IGCSEs) either as a two-year course for those joining in year 10, or as one year from year 11 (excellent for those recovering from ill health or recently arrived in the UK). Results good, with 32 per cent A*/A grades in 2016.

About a fifth of students here have some form of special educational need, and the school copes well with mild difficulties, with an SEN specialist, general learning and study skills and individual education plans. ('We're clear what we can do, and if we can't do something we will tell parents there are places much better equipped to help.') MPW continues to provide its traditional refuge for those taking resits, with a remarkably flexible range of options to allow for gap year plans. For overseas applicants looking to UK universities without the requisite qualifications, MPW has also recently introduced the University of London International Foundation Programme, developed and assessed by LSE.

Games, options, the arts: Art is a particular strength, with dedicated studios for ceramics, textiles, graphic design and photography. Music taught as an A level, but no school orchestras or groups, so 'not a big school for music.' Extracurricular, once very much an also ran, has become mainstream as MPW has developed its identity as a sixth form college. Today, you'll find the usual add-ons – student council, Duke of Edinburgh (bronze taken by all year 10s) and Bank of England Interest Rate Challenge. Sport has 'improved massively' (though, as one parent commented, 'It's still nothing like at school.'). Compulsory once a week for GCSE students, optional thereafter. Big menu of activities on Wednesday afternoons, with a fleet of coaches delivering to a host of venues. Well-qualified coaching staff in rugby, football and tennis, supplemented by experts in activities like golf. Rugby popular and successful, with matches against leading independents like Dulwich College and Epsom. Football, too, has an enthusiastic following. Those allergic to team sports can enjoy tennis, dance and yoga, and all students have free access to a local gym. Plenty going on outside the classroom: debating, poetry competition (this year's theme, Remember, advertised on whiteboards through the college), college magazine, widely attended lecture series. Students also make full use of local museums and theatres with regular trips. Diminutive basement canteen provides healthy-eating options, but local eateries a big draw.

Background and atmosphere: Founded in 1973 by three Cambridge graduates who hoped to apply the best bits of the Cambridge tutorial system to a school, providing more choice and less tradition. Now part of the MPW group, with branches in Cambridge and Birmingham, the London HQ is housed in a series of high-ceilinged, stucco-fronted Victorian buildings in South Kensington. Indoors, all very 21st century, with computers everywhere (including folding into desks). Excellent facilities, too, for the myriad of subjects on offer, including fully-equipped media suites, computing and film rooms, separate art studios for photography and ceramics, new drama studio, and five specially-designed science laboratories. Co-ed throughout (slightly more boys than girls), the atmosphere is grown up, academically disciplined, but socially relaxed. Pupils have a strong sense of community. 'We had an absolute blast, while getting the A level grades we needed to get on the courses we wanted,' said a recent leaver. The size undoubtedly helps. 'My year group feels like a family and I can approach anyone to talk to.'

Pastoral care, well-being and discipline: Pastoral care is central to the MPW approach. Each student is assigned a director of studies, who acts as the pivot of their personal and academic life (as well as the main point of contact for parents). 'It's very personalised learning. We feel if they're nurtured, they'll prosper.' Directors of studies gain a detailed overview of the student's strengths and weaknesses, help manage the workload and deal with other aspects of daily life. 'As well as reading 10 drafts of my personal statement,' said one overseas student, 'my director of studies advised me on practical matters like getting a GP and organising the paperwork needed for a school trip to Italy.'

A level students only required to be in college when they have lessons. GCSE pupils kept under close supervision between classes and given timetabled library sessions to complete homework. Parents are kept in the loop, with plenty of feedback, positive as well as negative. 'They shouldn't feel that every time they receive a call from the college it will be bad news.' Classrooms and libraries orderly and focused, corridors silent. 'The amount of time spent on behavioural management here is miniscule.' This serenity, however, is achieved by clearly defined boundaries. 'We're very consistent on enforcing the rules. You have to attend, have to behave and have to be on time.' Two or three generally expelled annually. 'The most common reason is a lack of work ethic, which is a corrosive influence on others.' Immediate expulsion for drugs, too, whether on the premises or off, and random drug testing. Fresher's week type activities help integrate newcomers. 'Over 50 per cent of the college is new in any one academic year, but these are well-rounded young people and make friends quickly.'

Pupils and parents: Significant number of refugees from leading independent schools, day and boarding, plus the usual international clientele (about 25 per cent). At A level, incomers are those looking for greater freedom and informality, or for A level combinations or subjects not offered at their current school. Pupils tend to be articulate, friendly and mature.

Entrance: More or less non-selective academically, but the average applicant will have good middling grades (three As, three Bs, a couple of Cs.) 'We have a strong top end, but we'll take someone with six Cs.' What they won't take is someone who doesn't fit the mould. All students are interviewed by the head or senior member of staff to establish whether they have a strong work ethic and understand that 'the price of freedom is behaving like an adult'. 'We're looking for the curious and motivated.' School references assiduously pursued. 'We want to be sure they're not involved in bullying or other misdemeanours.' International students given admissions tests and interviews. Majority of GCSE students stay on for A level, even if they arrive with other plans. 'Once they've seen it, they find they like the atmosphere.' Some join in the second year of A levels after a hiccup elsewhere.

Exit: In 2016, 37 per cent left after GCSEs and six per cent at the end of year 12. Normally 70 per cent or so to leading Russell Group universities (particularly in London – Imperial, UCL, and LSE all popular). Two to Oxbridge and eight medics in 2016. About 28 per cent annually to professional degrees (medicine, dentistry, veterinary medicine, science and law) and high numbers, too, to leading art colleges. Specialist preparation for Oxbridge, medics, lawyers, etc.

Money matters: Tutorial colleges will never be the cheapest A level or GCSE option, but most consider MPW good value for money. For the 'talented', there are a limited range of scholarships and bursaries and, for those planning 'worthwhile' travel in a gap years or holiday, there are also travel scholarships worth up to a £1,000.

Remarks: A positive, professional place, with strong teaching and outstanding pastoral care.

Maple Walk School

62a Crownhill Road, London NW10 4EB

Pupils: 200 • Ages: 4–11

Fees: £8,871 pa

Tel: 020 8963 3890
Email: admissions@newmodelschool.co.uk
Website: www.maplewalkschool.co.uk

Headmistress: Since 2012, Mrs Sarah Gillam, BEd from Homerton College, Cambridge. Originally Dorset born, but started her career at Lyndhurst House Prep school in Hampstead. She left education for a while to 'gain some experience in the professional world' but came back to education as she missed teaching and the children. Her 30 year career includes two middle school headships and one head of junior science. Prior to her role as head of Maple Walk, Ms Gillam worked for six years at the now defunct White House Prep school in Wokingham (although during her tenure, it was an outstanding prep school, she says). She was attracted to the post of head at Maple Walk 'because of its wonderful history and story' and because she felt it was a school with great potential.

Warm and likeable (she was very concerned that we should have nice biscuits with our coffee), slightly distracted but perhaps it was nerves, so keen was she to impress. However, the parents we spoke to praised her ambition for turning 'a small villagey school' into a 'proper prep school'. One parent told us: 'Ms Gillam takes very seriously the reality of living in London and has worked hard to make sure the pupils are well placed and prepared to take exams for secondary school. She has done this with a more rigorous curriculum.'

Ms Gillam herself says that she has been very keen to work on the process of transforming this school – already an amazing galleon – into a tighter ship with more rigorous applications and monitoring of crew. She has worked at strengthening the senior leadership team and now has an excellent range of advisors. Also an ISI team inspector, Ms Gillam says this can be a great resource for the school as she gets so many ideas from other schools as well as being able to confer with specialists 'who are at the top of their game.' She still teaches RE from year 3 upwards for one lesson a week.

Described as a very visible head who is always wandering around the school, is very approachable, open to ideas and someone who 'patently cares about her job.' She has an open door policy and as one parent said, 'is probably quite frustrated that more people don't walk through it more often.' Ms Gillam has three grown up daughters, one of whom is also training to be a teacher: 'If you have this as a vocation, it is something I would always encourage.' Any free time she has, she enjoys cooking, travelling and spending time with her family.

Entrance: The school aims to be a two form entry school, but this year it was one form due to lack of space. Some 200 applicants for 20 places per form. Siblings get preference, then in order of registration – waiting lists for several years ahead. The advice given is 'get them on the list as soon as possible.' For spaces higher up the school, the head meets the parents and the child has a trial day in the relevant class, 'to check that they will fit in socially and academically'.

Exit: To a wide variety of schools, including Aldenham, City of London, Emanuel, Queen's College, John Lyon, North Bridge House, Wetherby Prep and St James Senior Girls in the private sector, and St Marylebone, Hampstead School and Twyford Cof E School in the state sector. A fair percentage both from last year's cohort and historically have also been awarded art scholarships at Holland Park School.

Remarks: The New Model School Company (NMS) was set up by Civitas (but is now an independent entity) when research identified a gap in the market for a low-cost chain of not-for-profit independent primary schools. Maple Walk was the first NMS school, starting in a rented room in a sports centre off Ladbroke Grove in 2004 with one teacher, two pupils and school materials stored in a trunk. A year later the fledgling school of a dozen pupils moved to the upper floor of a church hall off Kensal Road. In September 2009 the school – by now with classes up to year 4 – moved to its own purpose-built premises in Harlesden, which have impeccable ecological credentials: a sedum roof, solar panels, a ground source heat pump, plus a no-car travel plan. It has added a form each year and now has a full complement of 200 children.

Although the school has had a reputation for being a no frills, low-fee-paying school and a decent alternative for the independent sector, parents we spoke to felt that it was now time to redress this reputation because, as one parent told us, 'it punches above its weight.' Another parent said: 'They do far more than you would expect from a school of this size and have really upped their game.' The general consensus seems to be that it delivers a great education and is a school which pushes each individual to strive. Indeed it made this year's Telegraph's top Ten Value Prep Schools: 'Excellent value for money', one parent said.

The education is traditional, with reading taught by phonics, French taught from reception, history taught chronologically and Latin taught in year 6. Maths is set from as early as year 1, but there is movement between sets. The school says: 'We recognise that within each class there are pupils of widely differing mathematical aptitudes and we aim to provide suitable learning opportunities for each of them.' The school follows the increasingly popular Singapore maths scheme, although this is 'often supplemented by other resources.' English is not set, but there is differentiation within the classroom for the more able and also for those who need more assistance. One parent told us: 'One of the perks of a school of this size is the small classes and that each class has a teacher and teaching assistant, so you know your child will get a lot of individual attention.'

The teaching was praised by parents and pupils alike: 'They have really nice teachers who know the children well.' 'Teachers are absolutely on it.' The head's after-school secondary transfer club introduces exam techniques to older children, and the year 6 class teacher 'is very experienced at secondary transfers'. 'They do their absolute best to make sure they are well prepared,' said a parent. Certainly parents are happy. 'They seem to be getting a very good grounding,' said one.

The school can cope with mild SEN – 'we don't assess children coming into reception, but we do ask parents to be honest and transparent and we may talk to their nursery if we have any concerns'. One-to-one literacy and numeracy assistance at extra cost; some children get speech and language support outside school.

Sport has very much been an area of focus for the school, with a 'competitive but inclusive policy.' Whilst onsite sport facilities are pretty basic, the school has the use of nearby Roundwood Park for tag rugby, hockey, football and netball etc. For the particularly keen, an early morning (7.30am) cross-country run is offered to both pupils and their parents. We were told of an inspirational PE teacher who encourages even the most uninterested of children to give competitive sports a try, even at the cost of sacrificing a win for the school. One parent said: 'My son is not great at cricket, but this teacher put together a team of all the least talented cricket players in the school to encourage them to have a go at a competitive game against another school. They loved it.'

An emphasis on children becoming confident public performers: the annual Craigmyle poetry competition (named for the charitable trust that paid for the new site and building works) involves everyone from reception upwards reciting a poem by heart, and there are public speaking competitions, music concerts and drama performances. 'The children are very confident,' said a parent. 'They have nice manners, they can talk to adults, they look you in the eye.'

This is a busy busy school. Lots going on to excite and motivate – indeed their most recent Independent Schools Inspectorate report praises the range of extracurricular activities. This includes photography, art portfolio club, Spanish, chess, dance, puzzle club, drama and football.

The curriculum is further enriched by a wide range of educational visits for all year groups, whether it's mud-larking on the Thames or visiting the Imperial War Museum. There is the year 5 residential trip, which has included a bushcraft trip where students are taught basic survival skills, and the annual year 6 week-long residential camp – which could be staying at a château in France or a PGL adventure course on the Isle of Wight. One pupil told us: 'I really like the variety of things on offer here. There's lots of great stuff to do, but it's also quite academic.'

The school copes well with its limited premises. 'Of course that would be the one thing I'd change about the school if I could, but without physically moving the school, there's not much you can do', said one parent. But the outdoor space still manages to squeeze in playgrounds for infants and for juniors – with a climbing frame, football/netball court with climbing wall (also funded by the PTA, Friends of Maple Walk). There are interesting looking outdoor 'pods' for music classes with peripatetic teachers. The gardening club grows vegetables in tiered beds and a butterfly/bee-friendly area is in concept. The children learn to swim at a local pool and try out a different sport each half term.

M

The active PTA has raised funds from auctions, casino nights and summer fairs to name but a few, for part-time specialist dance and sports teachers, and parents have donated computers, including a suite of Netbooks that travel round different classrooms. The school has a broadly Christian ethos, with some religious assemblies and nativity plays, but all faiths are welcome and Jewish and Muslim parents come in to talk about their religions.

Despite the low fees, it is still very much a white, middle class demographic – albeit mostly journalists, artists and musicians rather than bankers and lawyers. A much larger percentage of families now live locally (previously the majority from Queens Park and Willesden Green) and the fact that it is so predominantly white and middle class probably represents how the area has changed. But as the school says, 'it doesn't stop us hoping and trying to attract a more diverse demographic.'

Parents cite the 'village school' atmosphere as one of their main reasons for choosing Maple Walk. 'There's a nice, cosy, community feel,' said one. 'I liked the fact that it is small, pioneering and affordable,' said another. 'It's a really vibrant, eclectic community.' Parents emphasise how happy their children are – 'mine will look back and feel they've been part of something really special and exciting'.

Marymount International School

George Road, Kingston, Surrey KT2 7PE

Pupils: 250; 85 full, 14 weekly boarders • Ages: 11–18 • Sixth form: 95 • RC

Fees: Day £19,290 – £22,035; Boarding £33,020 – £37,360 pa

Tel: 020 8949 0571
Email: admissions@marymountlondon.com
Website: www.marymountlondon.com

Headmistress: Since 2010, Sarah Gallagher MA (40s). Educated at a convent school, she studied for her degrees at University College Galway. Previous teaching and leadership posts at boarding and day schools including Queen's Gate, Lord Wandsworth College, most recently St Leonards-Mayfield School, taught in Rome. Dips in to teach Latin at Marymount from time to time.

Attractive, stylish and poised, she is articulate and empathetic in her interactions with others, strategic in her approach. The girls say she is 'busy and important' but also approachable. 'Ms Gallagher is so intelligent that you just think to yourself you could not possibly have a conversation with her, but when you do she is lovely.' Can picture this head on Mastermind or in the finals of a schools' edition of 'Strictly'. Husband also a teacher, two daughters at university. 'I want to build on the strength already here, a tremendous appreciation for learning and its significance in the school and its application outside school. The girls are learning for life; building character and community is integral to this. It's an exciting place to work, parents and students are committed, the philosophy of the IB and RHSM [Religious of the Sacred Heart of Mary] and Marymount London are all compatible.'

In July 2016 she took over the headship of Marymount International School in Rome, leading both schools for a year before moving to Rome in July 2017. Her successor will be Meg Frazier, currently head of upper school at the Stone Ridge School of the Sacred Heart for girls, Washington DC (one of 147 Sacred Heart school in 30 countries). History degree from Dartmouth College, has over 25 years of teaching and admin experience in the Washington area in the Jesuit and Sacred Heart networks of US and international schools, plus worked with international boarders at Georgetown Prep in Maryland. Describes herself as an avid gardener and reader, a rusty golfer and a life-long sailor who enjoys cooking and travel. She and her husband have three children, one daughter studying in London and two sons both seniors in US colleges.

Academic matters: Marymount is a Catholic secondary girls school offering the IB Middle Years (MYP) and IB to an international community. The first (1979) girls' school in the UK to take up the IB in Britain, Marymount's grade 6-10 curriculum is built on solid institutional foundations. In 2016 pupils scored an average of 36, with 25 per cent earning 40+ points and 40 per cent awarded bilingual diplomas.

No resting on laurels; they've been reviewing the MYP to align it with IGCSE content, ensuring all topics are covered in the IBMYP context by end of grade 9. Head wants parents to be assured of MYP rigour: the priority is to be learning-driven, not taught to the test. Range of IB subjects and results is excellent. Lots of sciences, 'and we do lots of field trips', say the girls. The school is offering a relatively new IB course, environmental systems and societies, which satisfies either the IB science or IB humanities requirement. 'My sister likes geography and science so it's perfect for her.' Marymount's MYP covers the broad spectrum of disciplines, with the interesting addition of philosophy to introduce the girls to 'the language of philosophy' before they embark on theory of knowledge at diploma level, and now includes more coding, programming and robotics. As would be expected, religious education is also a key part of the programme.

School prides itself on the wide range of languages offered. Extra mother tongue support in German and French in grades 6-8 dependent on enrolment. Parents warn that languages are sometimes subject to demand and in a small school it's not always possible to satisfy all requests for second language. It seems that there are mixed messages here and prospective parents are advised to discuss this at the early stages to clarify. The school does its best to support girls in working out alternative options – as one pupil explained, 'a friend who speaks Thai is taking IB Thai mother tongue; she's self-taught with the help of a tutor'.

The school is wireless throughout; iPads now in grades 6-9 and will move up the grades as pupils progress; girls were excited to show off the first new Mac TVs, there are more to come. The library has undergone a complete refurbishment – it has 9,000 volumes and membership of London Library enhances the collection.

Classes never more than 16 and many, particularly at diploma level, only four to six, fewer still for languages. Some classrooms are designed with small seminar-style groups in mind.

The teaching faculty is an international bunch, average age 40s. Pupil-teacher ratio is six to one and staff seem to know most of the girls, affirming parent comments about supportive and nurturing environment with a caring individualised approach. Low turnover and enough long-termers to provide a cohesive core. Plenty of support staff and school nurse on site.

Mild/moderate learning difficulties and other issues managed collaboratively by the learning resource coordinator, teachers, parents and students themselves. Lots of individualised support throughout the school and the girls themselves were quick to talk about peer tutoring offered during free periods or after school.

The enrichment programme for able students has about 40 on the register. These students are invited to apply to programmes sponsored by Ivy Leagues (Stanford, Yale, Princeton, Johns Hopkins) and top tier UK universities. Additional provision includes extracurricular activities as well as resources which are made available to students for independent study and wider reading.

Games, options, the arts: Mix of competitive and non-competitive sporting activities available for all grades on and off site. If the school does not offer a particular sport they will help connect with local teams. Marymount is part of the International School Sports Association and they have produced an impressive record of results in soccer, badminton and tennis at championship tournaments hosted by member schools in different parts of Europe. One pupil training with the Chelsea Ladies' development squad and several play with the Richmond Volleyball Club. When girls were asked why they chose Marymount, one replied that she came for the sport and when you hear that one of their football trainers is with Chelsea, no prizes for guessing which team Marymount girls support.

Musicians have plenty of opportunities to play in ensembles and chamber groups. About 20 per cent take private instrumental or singing lessons; school boasts a 100 per cent pass rate in grade exams. Entry to the choir is by audition and choristers participate in school concerts and annual tours to European cities, performing in major churches and cathedrals. Teachers encourage girls to perform in local festivals and competitions.

Drama is inclusive and the entire community builds up to a major production each year; in true girls' school tradition male roles are played by the girls. Keen thespians can participate in ISTA (International School Theatre Association) festivals and when we visited girls were buzzing about their weekend ISTA trip to Stratford upon Avon. LAMDA examinations offered. Visual arts seem focused on painting and photography – the girls tell us that the art teacher is an inspiring photographer. Framed art by generations of pupils displayed throughout the school. New Fabrication Laboratory includes a range of 3D printers, laser cutters and other digitally driven tools.

Consensus is that the most fun of all is the 'international day', when everyone shares their culture and cuisine.'The Japanese do the best, and the [boarding] girls are already planning even though it's still months away'. Zumbathon – a fundraising activity involving the whole community beeping and bopping, swinging and swaying to music – was also highly popular and yielded no casualties.

As a Catholic IB school, community service involves everyone at Marymount. Middle schoolers do environmental projects that include cleaning along the bank of the Thames. Older girls volunteer in local activities including soup kitchens and schools and further afield join other RHSM students in projects working with children in places such as Zambia. All students take part in the spiritual life of the school and attend an annual retreat. Girls of all faiths come to Marymount and this provides opportunities for students to learn about other beliefs and traditions; care is taken to ensure that everyone feels comfortable at mass and prayer. We visited on a Hindu feast day and the girls said they had started the day with a Hindu prayer; Muslim girls wear their headscarves with confidence.

Boarding: Almost half the pupils board and there are four halls, each with its own duo of house parents. Boarding rooms (some bunk beds) and facilities are clean and pretty tidy. Boarding areas are kept locked during the school day unless a girl has a reason to be back in her room. Oldest boarders have the spacious shared bedrooms above and the remaining nuns living in a wing just off their hall. Sisters no longer teach but are very much part of the fabric of the school, occasionally eating or sharing cocoa and study evenings with the girls.

The school's proximity to Heathrow is an attraction for boarding parents; the girls say that the school's proximity to London is the attraction for them. The lure of London aside, boarders enjoy theatre and music trips as well as days out to the seaside (Brighton) and theme parks such as Longleat. There's plenty going on inside school too, including dance and music workshops and opportunities to explore and develop one's faith. Worth mentioning here that the school also takes weekly boarders from local (ie London) families and it is sometimes possible to arrange short-term boarding for day girls whose parents travel.

Clear procedures allow boarders off-campus freedoms to visit friends and family while ensuring their safety. One guardian who has long looked after boarders during half-term breaks told us that some older girls feel the school is too strict. She helps them, and their far-off parents who hear the grumbles, appreciate that the school is being cautious and not unreasonable. Two exclusions in the last three years of boarders who, after several warnings, broke the rules about leaving campus.

Background and atmosphere: Established in Kingston in 1955 by 10 nuns from the Religious of the Sacred Heart of Mary (RSHM), sent by the Eastern American Province. Mid-19th century French founder of RSHM aspired to provide charity for all classes through schools, homes and orphanages that worked interactively across socio-economic barriers. Schools opened in France, Ireland, Portugal, England, the US and later Latin America and the rest of the world. The first sisters who came to Kingston started a 'year abroad' programme for US university women, then a school offering the US secondary school curriculum. Early 70s saw the arrival of Sister Anne Marie Hill, a determined Irish mover-and-shaker, well known in international education circles and now executive director of the network of schools. She introduced the IB, making the school more relevant to its growing international student body and reflecting RSHM's original ethos. During the noughties Marymount had a series of heads as RSHM grappled with transition to lay leadership and during that time the board of governors was created.

In Ms Gallagher the sisters seem to have found the ideal head who brings continuity at the top, leading the school from strength to strength thanks to the partnership forged with the RSHM sisters and the board she describes as 'independent and experienced'. Enrolments are at an all-time high and it's all-systems-go for development plans aimed at enhancing programmes and facilities. School works closely with the other Marymount partners under Sister Anne Marie's guidance, meeting every six to eight weeks to discuss areas such as strategic planning and communication. Increasingly involvement with the international network of RSHM schools – 19 worldwide – is now bringing more opportunities to the pupils.

The school is based in an affluent part of Surrey occupying a large Edwardian house plus various more recent additions connected by walkways. Elegant grounds with lawns, manicured flowerbeds and sculpted hedges. 'The teddy bear topiary sold me', said one dad, 'How can you not love a school that has teddy bear topiary?' (We presume he had already consulted the GSG about minor details such as teaching and pastoral care.) Main house, with original wood panelling and stained glass, is head office and reception. The nuns are loved by the girls and parents appreciate their presence. Small school chapel is used by boarders and local community alike and plans to re-develop and open the ceiling to the rafters and heavens above are under way.

Modern blocks house multi-purpose classrooms, the library and university and careers counselling rooms. Another block has the gym (floor replaced recently), music rooms and auditorium for assemblies, all-school mass, drama. Yet another has more dorms, cafeteria (food is 'so-so', particularly at weekends), classrooms, infirmary, student lounges. A new quasi-Scandinavian wooden structure houses more small tutorial rooms just right for the many language classes and designed with IB language examination conditions in mind. Most of the buildings surround the garden and have big windows that bring the outdoors in and give a refreshing sense of space and light.

Pastoral care, well-being and discipline: Spiritual values underpin the ethos of Marymount, rooted in the mission of the RSHM, 'that all may have life'. These values are made explicit on the website: even the most casual browser will see them on every page, running alongside photos. School welcomes girls from all faiths but we think it might not be a comfortable environment for the girl who has none.

Plenty of support available at the school: academic, social, emotional and personal; more expertise called upon if necessary. The headmistress is well briefed and aware of anyone who may be feeling overwhelmed, unhappy, unsettled. Girls say she shows genuine interest.

Parents' Association hosts a welcome back family barbecue during the first weekend of the school year when boarding parents are there dropping off daughters so they are able to meet day families. One parent said the school went out of its way, allowing their daughter to board temporarily so she could start at the beginning of the year, before the family transfer to London took place. Another described how the teachers made an effort to encourage her daughter to join the orchestra for a big performance, even though her late arrival meant she had missed several rehearsals.

Pupils and parents: Marymount girls are internationally diverse, cheerful, articulate, academically motivated, quietly confident and as a bunch, quite enchanting. More aspirational than ambitious, they love their school and really enjoy having peers from all over the world. They look out for each other, especially new ones, and although one day girl says she wishes there were more ways to get closer to the boarders, everyone, including day parents, feels that the day girls and boarders are pretty integrated.

The girls are reflective about the realities of being in a single-sex environment. They feel they are able to focus more on learning, but they would like to find a 'partner' boys' school and the student council have made some moves in this direction. Trouble is that 'all the boys' (schools) seem to be taken', but they have not given up. Head is a big advocate of the girls' school advantage, having also worked in mixed schools. 'When adolescent girls become interested in boys, it can be frustrating to see how much they measure themselves against the approval of the boys in the group. Without that distraction they can develop as intellectually rigorous learners, they are their own people.'

The families that choose the school value the ethos of school, its Catholicism and internationalism, but are equally attracted to the IB. There are 40 nationalities in the school, British representing just over half. Other significant groups are German, Spanish, Japanese, Chinese, US, Australian, Korean and Italian. The numbers within these groups are balanced very carefully to facilitate integration. The school bus service extends into London to Sloane Square and more routes are under consideration.

Parents' Association organises events including outings for parents which are appreciated by newly-arrived expats.

Entrance: Local families are urged to attend one of the open days. Inbound expats on 'look-see' trips to London may book appointments. Girls' admissions based on availability and a review of school reports and teacher references. The headmistress interviews all girls prior to offering a place. English language fluency is required with exceptions made for younger students for whom English is a second language. Most classes have waiting lists so best to apply a year in advance though there is some turnover so you could be lucky.

Local feeder schools include Holy Cross, The Study, Fulham Prep, St Agatha's, The Grove, The Old Vicarage, The German School (Deutsche Schule London), Garden House, Unicorn School, Cameron House, Ursuline School. Day girls come from most SW London postcodes including Richmond, Wimbledon, Putney, Chelsea, South Kensington.

Exit: Small number leave to do A levels elsewhere. Most head to university and the chart we saw on the college counsellor's wall listing every 12th grader's destinations confirms that they are applying to many countries. Counsellor stays in close contact with parents, especially boarder parents, about each girl's plan and the process they must follow depending on the country of their destination. PSAT and SATs also offered.

One to Oxbridge in 2016; the rest go to eg Exeter, Edinburgh and Warwick. A good few to US as well as Japan, Munich, Netherlands, Libya and Egypt. Four to study medicine/biomedical science and engineering in 2016.

Money matters: School has no endowment so financial stability is maintained by tuition and fundraising initiatives. 'Being an international school and in the current economic climate, we need to be sure we are guarded and forward looking – we can't rest on our laurels.' The PA also fundraises for activities that support the school and pupils.

Scholarships (academic, art, music, drama, sport, community service) for grade 6 and 8 students. Some offered for grades 10, 11 and 12. Some financial aid available for means-tested students. About 20 per cent of the pupils benefit from this.

Remarks: Successfully serves a niche market of internationally-minded families seeking a girls' school with a Catholic ethos. In the words of one parent, 'We've been over-the-top-happy. The school provides excellent support and people from all over the world fit in and are welcome there.'

Merchant Taylors' Prep

Linked with Merchant Taylors' School

Moor Farm, Sandy Lodge Road, Rickmansworth, Hertfordshire WD3 1LW

Pupils: 300 • Ages: 3–13

Fees: £4,854 – £15,090pa

Tel: 01923 825 648
Email: office@mtpn.org.uk
Website: www.mtpn.org.uk/

Head of School: Since 2015, Dr Karen McNerney BSc PGCE MSc EdD; biochemistry degree from Newcastle and PGCE in primary teaching from Swansea. Also has a masters in educational leadship and doctorate in early years education. Taught in prep schools in north London and Hertfordshire before joining Northwood Prep (now Merchant Taylors' Prep) in 2001.

Principal: Since 1997, Dr Trevor Lee (50s). Educated at East Ham Grammar and Exeter University where he completed his BEd before cutting his teeth in the state system with a seven-year stint at Thomas Hardye School, Dorchester. Moved as housemaster to Dulwich College where he spent two of what he considers his most 'formative years', able to break free of government bureaucracy to 'actually teach and share one's passions.' Four years as deputy head at Durston House Prep in Ealing further sharpened his focus on academic excellence, and from here he became a member of Jesus College, Cambridge where, whilst simultaneously heading Hendon Prep, he completed his masters in education, with a special interest in pupil welfare. A doctorate from Hull followed in 2005.

Down to earth and engaging, a compelling educationalist refreshingly devoid of spin, with his feet firmly on the ground and a firm focus on the present and future success of his school. Sees his time to date at MTP as 'a rich and wonderful experience,' having taken it on at a time when it needed reform and renewal. Insistent that despite outstanding academic results, school is 'not a hothouse of academia,' although parents describe him as 'ambitious' for the boys, hot on 'making sure everyone's at the top of their game.' Happy to remind parents of the importance of roundedness: 'we have to respond to the requirements of our clientele but our own values cannot be stifled.' Describes school as 'a research-driven engine,' with success not being left to chance. No longer teaches, but holds assemblies for all year groups with, according to parents, the Wednesday assembly where he plays the guitar for the junior school children particularly popular.

A former member of the England rugby youth squad, lives in house on school grounds with wife Anne. Parents to two adult children, a son and daughter, both educated at Dean Close School in Cheltenham and now pursuing careers in management consultancy and veterinary surgery respectively.

Entrance: Selective. Vast majority join from hugely oversubscribed nursery located in former boarding house at neighbouring Merchant Taylors' School. Assessment at 3+ looks for 'teachability and sociability,' according to head. A few further places up for grabs at 4+. No further formal intakes, with ad hoc in-year applications dealt with on a case by case basis, but newcomers will need to be up to scratch. Siblings 'looked at favourably' but not guaranteed places. Class sizes capped at 20.

Exit: Major feeder to Merchant Taylors' School (MTS head Simon Everson sits on board of NP governors), with approximately 75 per cent of the cohort heading there each year at 13+, many with scholarships – an indeed has now merged with the senior school, as its name change shows. Good numbers also to Habs and John Lyon, plus some heading off in ones and twos to schools including Aldenham, Westminster, City of London School, St Albans, Mill Hill, Berkhamsted, Harrow and Charterhouse. A few each year (eight or so) peel off at 11+ to local selective grammars.

Parents speak very highly of support offered to boys around senior school applications and scholarships abound across the board, ranging from academic to music, sport and drama – and the school's first Queen's Scholarship to Westminster recently. One parent we spoke to said MTS was their 'back up school' – an indicator of the school's heady aspirations.

Remarks: Now changed its name from Northwood Prep to Merchant Taylors' Prep, as the merger has created a through school with the senior school where most of its pupils have always moved on.

Be careful not to miss the discreet entrance as you check out the bling real estate on the Moor Park Estate, amongst which the school nestles. A super spacious campus littered with grade II listed buildings lies behind the gates, steeped in history and providing boys with a village-like environment: 'I want the school to feel like a community,' says principal. Acres of fields provide sports pitches ('it was the acreage that really made it stand out for us against other local preps,' said one parent) and the overall impression is of a school that does nothing by halves.

No shabby corners at all, following a major renovation plan in 2008 which saw upgrades to changing rooms and music school, the building of a brand new theatre and relocation of the nursery. Spectacular new oak panelled dining room unveiled in 2014, representing the latest jewel in the school's gleaming crown. Classrooms housing quiet, studious students are spacious, bright and well organised throughout, with well-equipped outdoor play areas for all year groups. Parents report junior school to be 'warm and nurturing but very disciplined,' and say feedback from third parties regarding boys' manners is always top notch.

Despite the school's Christian ethos, at least 80 per cent of cohort from ethnic groups (mostly Indian) reflecting the local area, although principal states: 'we don't recognise cultural differences here.' 'Huge range' of social backgrounds, many from medical families, with principal only half joking that they could staff a hospital with the parents, plus many in the financial services sector, but also some from households massively stretching the budget to send their boys there. No plums in pupils' mouths. Boys come over as earnest and down to earth – a well-balanced and grounded bunch.

French from nursery ('a wonderful department,' says principal), with Latin from year 3 and Mandarin as an extracurricular option from year 4. Greek taught in years 7 and 8 'to a very high level,' according to principal – handy for those aspiring to starry destinations such as Eton or Westminster. Principal is passionate believer in setting not streaming and is absolutely against public ranking of boys ('very damaging'). Form groups mixed annually from reception to year 4, after which boys are placed in vertical tutor groups according to house. Setting begins subtly in year 1 for maths and English, becoming more formalised as boys continue up the school. Year 7 and 8 boys are split into three groups – a scholarship set and two others – although many from the 'lower' sets also win awards to their next schools. 'What's most important is getting a personal best from a personal baseline,' says principal and parents are clear that all boys are steered down the right path, whatever their academic level. Maths taught to the progressive Singapore Maths curriculum from reception onwards, 'with outstanding outcomes.'

Full-time SENCo implements personal development plans for the few boys that need them: 'although we're selective, we don't turn children with challenges away just because we feel they're going to shade the scores,' says principal. Parents find teachers open and approachable – 'they never hesitate to help,' said one.

Strong emphasis on broadening the spectrum to avoid one-dimensional academic output evident in areas such as drama, music and the arts: 'Many parents didn't understand the energy I put into building the new theatre,' says principal. 'It took a long time to persuade hearts and minds that soft skills are important.' But even the most academically ambitious parent couldn't fail to be won over at the sight of this jaw-dropping facility – easily the best we've seen in the area, complete with its very own ex-RSC director as head of drama. All boys in year 7 take a LAMDA speech and drama course (with a plethora of merits and distinctions to show at the end of it) to ensure top notch communication skills for those all-important school interviews. Ironically, given the theatrical facility, one of the school's most recent dramatic successes was year 8's performance of The Tempest, a roving performance around the grounds.

Music also high on agenda, with school's first guitar festival in 2013, as well as the introduction of a Young Musician of the Year competition. Some 40 per cent of the cohort studies an instrument peripatetically and all juniors learn the ukulele. The combined art and DT lab not the star attraction given the school's other standout facilities, and not a huge amount of artwork on display around the school, although a good standard of work is evident in school publications and parents describe the department as 'very creative.'

The word on the street is that school's sport is not so hot, but be prepared to be surprised. Rugby's not its strongest suit ('contact sports are not so popular,' admits principal) but the U13 hockey team is largely unbeaten and competitive cricket is also very strong. 'We want to put the best people in front of our children,' says principal. And so it appears: from the former England team hockey coach and specialist table tennis coach to the grand master chess coach (school has produced three England chess players since 2010), staff are exceptional. Occasional grumbles from parents that competitive sport is not as inclusive as it could be, often with only A and B teams representing the school, despite many keen, albeit less able, players.

Although always pushing for academic excellence, principal insists that pastoral care is a priority. Head of well-being appointed in 2011 to ensure balanced approach to academia – perhaps partly to counter high expectations at home – with curriculum devised accordingly. Boys keep gratitude diaries to keep their feet on the ground – 'it reminds us what we have got, rather than what we haven't.' said one, and 'it creates a "glass half full" culture,' says principal. Vertical tutor groups from years 5 to 8 enable older boys to support younger ones, and badges galore, commending everything from house merits to achievements in chess or science clubs, ensure everyone feels valued.

On-curriculum roundedness supported by broad range of extracurricular clubs, including the first investment club we've heard of in a prep school.

For working parents, school is open from 7.45am until 6pm. 'There's so much for the boys to do – really helpful for those of us who just don't have the bandwidth to drive them around,' said one parent. Homework considered by a few to be 'a bit on the heavy side,' especially for younger ones who are expected to read a whole book every evening. School 'expects a lot from parents' in terms of involvement, so perhaps not one for the woolly liberal 'just want them to be happy' variety, but the more typical 'ambitious' north London parent should be more than delighted with this very driven school.

M

Merchant Taylors' School

Linked with Merchant Taylors' Prep

Sandy Lodge, Northwood HA6 2HT

Pupils: 890 • Ages: 11–18 • Sixth form: 290 • C of E

Fees: £19,520 pa

Tel: 01923 845514
Email: admissions@mtsn.org.uk
Website: www.mtsn.org.uk

Head Master: Since 2013, Mr Simon Everson MA PGCE, born in Hertfordshire then educated at Solihull School and Cambridge (English) before completing a masters in philosophy at Nottingham. Has taught both in state maintained and independent schools as well as in Japan and was latterly head at Skinners' School in Tunbridge Wells, where he also took over a local failing school, guiding its transformation to academy status. Was adamant that very few schools would tempt him away but couldn't resist the lure back to Herts and MTS, where he took over 'a school with wonderful tradition, but one that's vibrant and relevant now.' Still 'loves the classroom' and 'borrows classes' when time allows. Moved immediately upon appointment to reintroduce significant financial benefits to scholars, with scholarships for the brightest and most able across the board now worth at least 10 per cent of fees: 'We are determined to seek out excellence and reward it.' Enjoys walking, bird watching, Scotland and is a recently qualified apiarist (beekeeper). An electric guitar sits tucked in the corner of his office – 'I wanted to put myself in the boys' shoes and remember how it feels to struggle to learn something new,' he says. Business-like and sincere. Married to Ginny, a psychotherapist.

Academic matters: A school populated by an intellectually curious and highly motivated cohort. Academic rigour – and ultimately success – is par for the course here but head is clear that they do not want to create a monoculture: 'We reject the philosophy of moulding children into specific types.' Boys inspired by staff who, in head's words, are 'fiercely intelligent –

no school is better than the quality of its staff', and are striking to visitors either for their youth, energy and enthusiasm or wit, wisdom and worldliness. Humour and empathy pervade the classrooms, evident as much in the way staff speak to the boys as the quirky touches around the buildings – we've never seen fairy lights or a Ferrari flag in a biology lab in any other school. Dead Poets Society springs to mind more than once on our tour.

Traditional curriculum, not known for any single specialism – boys as likely to read medicine at university as English – and, although one parent said that academically 'it's not for the faint hearted,' school adamant that it's 'not merely a conveyor belt to top results'. 'Exam results are a given,' says school; 'it's about what else they leave with.' Boys take IGCSEs in majority of subjects with consistently outstanding results: 87 per cent A*/A in 2016; with 66 per cent of A levels graded A*/A and 87 per cent A*-B. Flexible setting in maths from year 9 and science from year 10, with some 'banding' in English literature from that point too. 'We tend to separate out the boys who read; the ones who can handle Chaucer and Shakespeare with no problem'. Top half takes maths IGCSE in year 10, with one third also taking French a year early. It's French and Latin in the languages department in years 7 and 8 with the addition of German, Spanish or Greek in year 9, all available at A level. Around 60 per cent take the EPQ. Maths, economics and the sciences top choices at A level with around half the number opting for humanities and English but with no less stellar results. Small numbers for languages – although school still timetables minority subjects such as Greek even for lone students.

Excellent standard of art and DT, which has 'outstanding' teaching, according to parents – MTS has a produced higher number of Arkwright Scholars than any other school since the scheme began in the 1990s. This strength likely to snowball since the 2015 opening of school's cutting edge new DT building. Atmosphere surprisingly relaxed and no sign of the macho testosterone culture that's endemic in so many boys' schools. 'We achieve results by inspiring boys,' says head. Enrichment programme for most able scholars 'turns seamlessly' in Oxbridge preparation.

Learning support (mild dyslexia, dyscalculia some ASD) viewed in the same way as educating the most able children: 'they just need a slightly different educational experience to everyone else,' although school also quick to point out that even those with individual needs 'must be able to keep up with the pace here.' New SENCo 'with a wealth of experience' recently appointed to monitor and work with specific learning difficulties – but strictly no withdrawal from class. ESL students must be instantly able to access curriculum as are fully immersed from day one. Can accommodate pupils with mobility problems, including wheelchairs.

School really shows its mettle in university application process and careers advice, an area which head says has reached 'Rolls Royce quality.' Parents describe the UCAS application process as 'incredibly well organised', with each sixth former assigned to the head of department of their chosen subject who acts as advisor and referee. Personal references from tutors are the cherry on top of the holistic application process. Boys encouraged to begin thinking about future careers early with a 'World of Work' day in year 11, plus a joint careers conference with the girls of nearby St Helen's School. OMTs highly visible as mentors to current pupils, who are encouraged to use active database of over 600 old boys willing to offer work experience, and allowed time out of school to pursue such opportunities. A unique 'entrepreneur in residence' runs a start-up business from the DT building to give boys an insight into a world beyond the corporate giants who will doubtless be clamouring for their affections come milk round time.

Games, options, the arts: Sport seen as a hugely important part of the universal education at the heart of the MTS ethos, with sportsmanship and camaraderie as high on the agenda as winning. Part of the strong community feel comes from the whole school, including 80 per cent of the teaching staff, heading out to the (spectacular) sports fields together twice a week. Rugby, hockey and cricket are major sports and although there are varying degrees of success in the former (there was almost a hint of pride in the boy who self-effacingly told us he was in the 'least successful rugby A team on school record'), hockey and cricket are flying increasingly high with victories aplenty, and the fixture list growing annually to encompass more top schools. School boasts over 60 county and five national sportsmen and the U15 cricket team is county champion. This in no small part due to dedicated directors for each major sport (hockey coach is ex-England international), as well as regular visiting coaches; recently the Australian cricket team, who requested that their pre-Ashes tour training take place at MTS. Sport for all – every boy competes for the school as often as is feasible with as much celebration when the 'Super E' rugby team (unbeaten) brings home a victory as the more elite squads.

With over 20 minor sports from riding to kayaking, sailing and golf boys have no excuse not to find something they love. One of our guides was not overly keen on main team sports but was on the first team for fives. Two others were keener on playing electric guitar in their band – but that was seen as valuable too. One or two grumbles about lack of footie until sixth form, but that doesn't stop boys having a good kick around the quad at break times, and school provides goalposts for the purpose. World class facilities include all the usual suspects plus all weather hockey pitches ('better than the Olympic ones,' one keen player assured us), heated indoor pool, athletics track, lakes for sailing and kayaking, squash and fives courts, an assault course and fencing salle.

Endless opportunities to get stuck in outside of the classroom and sports field at lunch times and after school. Every sport imaginable, from sub aqua to cycling, has a society and there's chess, bridge or stamp club for those more inclined towards brain sports. Boys can flex their journalistic muscles by contributing to one of six school magazines or try their hand at societies ranging from the possibly unique dissection society to debating, most of these included in fees. Music and drama 'amazingly active,' says head, with ensembles and choirs galore, including Dixieland, Merchants of Groove and swing band in addition to a host of more traditional offerings. Two major theatrical productions take place each year in the Great Hall, in addition to smaller endeavours and a fiercely fought house drama competition. Parents rave about quality of productions, with recent extravaganzas including Grease. Active CCF (one of the largest in the UK) in conjunction with St Helen's, and D of E schemes offer super opportunities to follow outdoor pursuits and take part in trips to eg Morocco, Canada or Nepal. Huge sense of collective pride in relation to outstanding work with Phab, with funds raised throughout the year and an annual residential care week staffed by senior pupils, who consider it a great honour to be selected to take part.

Copious amount of trips. Rugby and hockey tours to South Africa and Australia and cricket to Barbados. Years 7 and 8 classics trip to Naples, geography to Iceland and history to Istanbul. Eleven language trips each year and six language exchange programmes across year groups.

Background and atmosphere: Founded in the City of London in 1561 by the Worshipful Company of Merchants, then the largest school in the country. Relocated in 1933 to its current location – a 250 acre site comprising a core of listed art deco buildings plus a host of sympathetically incorporated modern additions set before endless playing fields leading down to a lake that homes countless wildlife species. Visitors greeted by exquisite formal gardens and a handsome fascia. School lacks dreaming spires and turrets but gives an immediate sense of purposefulness and solid endeavour. Some areas (entrance hall, library, politics and economics centre, sixth form common room) more pristine than others but a sense of calm and mutual respect prevails.

'Civilised' a word that comes up again and again, along with a sense of a truly cohesive community spirit. Older boys mentor the younger, the whole school eats together (no exceptions, no packed lunches) and assembles together – 'invaluable', says head. 'We are a corporate body not a disparate group'. There's also a great sense of the traditional juxtaposed with gleaming new facilities – a feeling that a boy who has walked the corridors of MTS would not be remotely overwhelmed walking into an Oxford or Cambridge college for the first time.

Merged with ex-Northwood Prep, which has changed its name to Merchant Taylors' Prep.

Pastoral care, well-being and discipline: Discipline 'almost always low profile due to our hugely positive culture,' says school. Boys are not 'spiky' or 'entitled', transgressions rare and bullying almost non-existent ('I couldn't believe how much friendlier it was than my prep school', said one happy boy). Vertical tutor system praised almost unanimously by parents and boys with only a few grumbles relating to tutors moving on to pastures new mentally checking out in advance. For the most part, parents described them as 'almost part of the family', and many keep in contact with former tutees way beyond the A level years. Thriving house system facilitates yet more cross-fertilisation for friendships and opportunities for boys to shine in competitions, with pupils praising weekly house assemblies covering topics from 'the art of small talk' and 'how to tie a bow tie' to rocket building in teams. Plenty of chances for responsibility at the top of the school. Head boy voted in by 50 per cent student vote, supported by 10 elected monitors and a JCR of a further 30 boys. School run on Christian ethos, with services held in chapel and all faiths welcome, but there's also a Muslim prayer room and societies for all main faiths.

Pupils and parents: 'What makes a Merchant Taylors' boy?' we asked. 'Well, we don't really do posh,' came the smiling reply. Our opinion: smart, charming, self-effacing and diverse. Not a hooray Henry in sight or any trace of plums in mouths, but a group of boys wearing their school tie with humility and an awareness of privilege rather than entitlement. Fun to sit with (yes, even year 10s) in the dining room and totally at ease with adult company. Minds of staff and pupils alike on higher things than the tedious minutiae of shiny shoes and tidy haircuts obsessed over at so many schools. Head says school is 'always hanging on the coat tails of the pupils' enthusiasm', and keenly supports pupil-led initiatives, most recently a drone club, instigated by one young scientist. Perhaps because around a quarter of boys receive some level of financial assistance, social awareness is a key factor in their all-round pleasantness – 'It just wouldn't be the done thing to crow about wealth or status,' said one parent. 'Many families make huge sacrifices to send their sons here.' School concurs: 'Those from affluent backgrounds wear their wealth lightly'.

A school where three worlds don't so much collide as mesh. A hybrid London/country school with appeal to local, north and west London and Herts/Bucks families. The London crowd loves the spacious campus, laid back feel and multitude of sporting options on offer, especially in comparison to nearby competitors, and those from the shires enjoy the slightly edgier, more worldly feel than they find in schools closer to home. Reflective of local area, around 40 per cent British-Asian, a large Jewish contingent and all other main faiths represented. Wonderfully inclusive – 'there's zero tolerance of racism or homophobia,' boys told us – and although firm friendships are formed on the tube trains and coaches that transport boys in from eg Highgate, St John's Wood and Ealing, plus suburbs from St Albans and Harpenden to Beaconsfield and Gerrards Cross, all reported that new friends are constantly made through tutor groups, form groups which are mixed up each year, subject choices (from year 12 forms are grouped according to A level choices) and activities.

Unlike many secondaries, parents maintain close contact with school, attending events and committees in droves. Head reported around 200 attendees at one of his recent termly parent forums. In turn, school has unique relationship with many OMTs well beyond the A level years, with tutors speaking with deep fondness of past tutees' achievements. Actor and alumnus Riz Ahmed chose MT as the backdrop for one his first movies and Grammy Award winning OMT band Nero (the lead singer read philosophy at Oxford, incidentally) recently returned as the surprise act at leavers' ball. Other famous alumni include Nobel prize-winning medic Sir John Sulston, Lord Coggan (former Archbishop of Canterbury), Sir Alan Duncan and Boris Karloff, as well as a host of others from the worlds of politics, business, sport, the military and the arts.

Entrance: Selective with two main intakes at 11+ and 13+. At 11+ around 380 boys (roughly two-thirds from state primaries) apply for 60 places. At this point, applicants tested in maths, English and a general paper with those delivering the goods on paper invited back for a one-to-one interview ('not as intimidating as it sounds – they always leave with a smile on their face,' says school). Worth remembering that many will be applying for several schools, so not as competitive as it first appears. A further 100 places available at 13+ with fewer applicants (about two to one, though many places taken by boys from Merchant Taylors' Prep) for each place but larger hurdles to clear: boys are interviewed first in May/June of year 7 on strength of prep head's report with high fliers offered 'unconditional' places at that point in the expectation that the exam will present no problems. Those offered a 'conditional' place after interview will need to pass every paper in the CE-style exam in January. School clear that parents tutoring boys heavily for the exam 'are not doing them any favours – we're looking for intellectual curiosity, a passion for something, reasoning skills and ways in which boys can make a wider contribution to the school.' At 16+ exams in four A level subjects; offer confirmations depend on GCSE results.

Up to 40 or 50 feeders at 11+, with preps including Radlett Prep, Manor Lodge, Buckingham College, Reddiford and Gayhurst. At 13+ large numbers from Merchant Taylors' Prep, St John's, Durston House and St Martin's, plus a few each from The Beacon, Davenies, Orley Farm, York House and St Anthony's, amongst others.

Exit: Very little fall out after GCSE. Twenty-one to Oxbridge in 2016 with vast majority of remainder to top universities. London colleges feature highly (particularly Imperial, LSE and UCL) as do Birmingham, Bristol, Durham, Nottingham and Warwick. Very strong numbers to read medicine (three in 2016), economics and engineering but diversity across the board from sports science to English, humanities, law and the occasional one choosing film or drama school over university offers, or heading to university overseas.

Money matters: The old school tie doesn't come into the selection process and school prides itself on staying true to the ethos on which it was founded – to offer an excellent all-round education to boys from all walks of life and offer financial aid to those who would most benefit – these days, around 200 boys at any one time. Academic scholarships awarded to boys who perform particularly well in the entrance papers, with scholars benefiting from an enrichment programme. Up to five major academic scholarships at both 11+ and 13+ worth at least 10 per cent of fees. Also sport, art, drama, DT, music and all-rounder scholarships.

Remarks: A rare breed – a London school with a country feel, offering the best of both worlds to boys from the city and the shires. Sitting coolly around the top of the league tables, seemingly without trying too hard, a testament to teachers who inspire without applying undue pressure. Wonderful breadth of sporting opportunities for both the elite and the enthusiastic. Not the most obvious choice for macho rugby types, or for the parent hoping for their son to leave school with a public school swagger, but for those looking for an environment that actively encourages boys to 'lean in to difficult questions', get involved in enriching activities outside of the classroom, and that values the quirky and erudite, look no further.

Merlin School

4 Carlton Drive, London SW15 2BZ

Pupils: 220 • Ages: 4-8

Fees: £13,482 pa

Tel: 020 8788 2769
Email: secretary@merlinschool.net
Website: www.merlinschool.net

Headmistress: Since 2003, Mrs Kate Prest BA Music/Ed PGCE (40s). Studied at Oxford Brookes. Formerly head of pre-prep at The Harrodian, and before that, teacher and music specialist at Oratory Primary, Chelsea. Welcoming, lively and overflowing with enthusiasm, she treasures the school's unique, homely feel. 'We work very much as a team, which extends through staff, pupils, parents and even grandparents,' she told us.

Believes in the importance of communication and keeping children aware of the world they live in. Operates a complete open door policy, which parents told us works a treat. Prefers verbal communication. Always there to help and advise parents on the next stage. Lives locally and is married with three children, all of whom have attended the Merlin. Husband works in the City, so has no plans to move on. 'I'm not going anywhere,' she says. 'This is good. I love this school.'

Entrance: Non-selective. Parents attend an early afternoon talk and tour of the school. Places are then offered on receipt of registration – priority given to siblings, then it's first come first served. Advisable to view early. There are occasionally places higher up the school.

Exit: Some leave at 7 and the rest at 8. They go to schools all over and, apart from a high number to The Harrodian at 8 (no feeding but a link, whereby they are interviewed in November rather than examined in January), there is no particular pattern. Other destinations include Bute House, Putney High, King's College Junior School, St Paul's Juniors, Shrewsbury, Milbourne Lodge, Rokeby, Feltonfleet, Westminster Under, Broomwood House, Glendower Prep, Latymer Prep, King's House Richmond, Fulham Prep, occasional boarding schools.

Remarks: Located in a large, converted Edwardian house in a leafy Putney street, the school is homely, welcoming and cosy and initially appears quite old-fashioned in approach and look. We were shown round by three articulate, enthusiastic pupils – luckily they knew where they were going because we got completely confused. Good sized and light classrooms, well decorated with children's work. Very little evidence of IT influence. Several interactive whiteboards – head says, 'I want teachers in front of my children.' They have an ICT room, where all years have a lesson every week. Each classroom has a computer – used by the children in rotation. Separate science and art rooms. 'We dissect in year 3,' one enthusiastic pupil told us.

Class sizes are small (average 17). All classes are mixed ability. Some subjects are classroom-based, while others follow the teacher. Divisions according to ability in maths and English. Never a really competitive feel, apart from in an advanced maths class. Children seemed happy, relaxed and attentive – and eager to tell us what they were doing.

Drama and musical productions are an important part of the school year. Lots of music, vocal, instrumental and theoretical (not surprising with a music-trained head). Head still takes all the children for weekly classes. About a third learn violin or piano as an extra, with lessons rotated in school hours and practice done at home.

A spacious playground with Astroturf – plenty of room for outdoor play and sports practice. On the far side, purpose-built classrooms are occupied by year 2 classes. Well designed for indoor and outdoor use. Popular and experienced sports master ensures that everyone can try everything. Two training sessions a week in the playground (or inside if necessary), to build up co-ordination. Off-site practice once a week at a local sports venue. Fixtures against similar schools in football, hockey, cricket and rugby, but other sports on offer too. 'My bright, but not at all sporty, child gets to try everything and never feels that he's not excelling,' a parent told us. Chess is popular too – it's one of a host after-school clubs.

Dining hall in basement, and our young guides said the food, on the whole, is excellent. Sensibly, there isn't a great deal of choice. 'We have to try everything, but if we really, really don't like it, we are allowed to scrape it into a bowl,' they told us. All cooked in-house, with nutritionist's supervision. Catering staff have a list of all children with specific dietary requirements. School is very hot on manners too.

Warm, caring and fully-trained head of SEN, with two sympathetic assistants to make sure every contingency is covered. Good at identifying and dealing with problems. School says it is important to find each child's particular strengths. Early dyslexia screening for the youngest and full screening if suspected in older children is available. Continual staff meetings to discuss children and identify any possible problem areas. School runs own phonics, maths and spelling programmes and tries to give extra help in groups; if one-to-one is necessary, that is charged for. Always enough help in class, from gap year students and parent volunteers. An extra reading clinic in year 1. Occasional EAL pupils given extra support as necessary.

A happy, friendly school that builds children's confidence and prepares them well for the next step. One parent told us: 'My child has had an amazing experience. He has learned and grown and is ready to move on.' Another said: 'We have been really happy with the quality of education and care our son has received. They really find out what children are good at and make it happen.' Not for those who want acres of outside space, but a real home from home.

Miles Coverdale Primary School

Coverdale Road, Shepherds Bush, London W12 8JJ

Pupils: 250 • Ages: 3-11

Tel: 020 8743 5847
Email: admin@milescoverdale.lbhf.sch.uk
Website: www.milescoverdaleprimary.co.uk

Headteacher: Since 2008, Mrs Taranum Baig BEd with French, NPQH. Has studied at the Sorbonne. Previously acting head and deputy head of Dairy Meadow Primary, Ealing and acting deputy head at Stanhope Primary, Greenford. About to become an Ofsted inspector. Born in India and moved to London as a child. Conscientious and hard-working, though encourages staff not to stay too late at school, so they can get a healthy work/life balance. Gentle sense of humour. Likes travelling and heads abroad as often as possible. Enjoys tennis in her spare time. Married. No children. Head says her vision for the school is best summed up by a quotation of Martin Luther King, 'Intelligence plus character – that is the goal of true education.' Head adds, 'irrespective of background.'

Entrance: At 3 into the nursery. Admissions to the nursery are managed by the school office, but from reception to year 6 they are handled by LA, Hammersmith and Fulham. A place at nursery does not guarantee a place in reception. Heavily over-subscribed. Roughly 130 applicants apply for 25 places in nursery; 130 applicants for 30 places in reception. Intake drawn according to local authority's admissions procedure. One form entry.

M

Exit: Pupils go on to Fulham Cross, Phoenix High School and Hammersmith Academy. Some move to schools out of the borough. None to independent sector.

Remarks: School is named after Myles Coverdale, who in the 16th century produced the first complete printed translation of the bible into English. Today, the school accepts all faiths. About to celebrate its centenary. School has gone from strength to strength on current head's watch. She puts this down to high expectations of pupils and staff 'knowing the data' (school keeps a close eye on anyone falling behind), quality of teaching and an excellent team of governors. 'A combination of delivery and accountability,' explains head.

Housed in a vast red-brick, Victorian building in the busy heart of Shepherd's Bush. A mixed, multi-cultural area which is reflected in the ethnic diversity of the pupils. Sixteen ethnic groups currently. Largest contingent are West African, followed by white British/other. Sixty-six per cent do not have English as a first language. Languages spoken at home include Somali, Arabic and a variety of Eastern European tongues. Thirty-one per cent of pupils eligible for free school meals. Head acknowledges that a number of pupils come from unsettled backgrounds, so 'we can give them the stability they sometimes lack at home.' A very inclusive school.

Rated outstanding by Ofsted and placed in the top 100 schools nationally over last three years. Academically, each year group performs well above national average. Head confident that pupils can begin with low attainment levels but will have excellent results under their belts by the time they leave. 'We maximise potential.' Children fully engaged in their lessons and teachers full of energy on the day we visited. School works hard to narrow the gap between higher and lower attainers. Booster classes given to year 6 before Sats to make sure everyone performs well. A handful achieves a remarkable level 6 in maths and in grammar, spelling and punctuation before leaving. School has been awarded a gold club award by Boris Johnson for 'succeeding against the odds in improving pupils' aspirations and achievements.' Head is delighted that she has been made a National Leader of Education and the school has been designated a National Support School, in recognition of the continued school improvement work with other schools at local, national and international levels. A real feather in her cap.

Currently nearly 30 children with statements of special educational need. Early targeted support is the order of the day here, with maths and reading intervention groups for those falling behind. Specialist unit offers speech and language classes for children with language impairment (the only one of its kind in the borough). Pupils here are seen as being very much part of the mainstream school. These classes provide support for 20 pupils, between the ages of 3 and 7, in two classes of 10. Wide variety of difficulties catered for, from those who are unable to produce speech sounds to others who find it challenging to recall words. Most pupils then transfer to their local mainstream school at 7 or, if still in need of on-going help, stay at Miles Coverdale where they receive additional support. Full-time speech and language therapist. Children must have a statement before being accepted. A counsellor visits twice weekly to help with children with social and behavioural problems.

Strikingly attractive, bright and colourful school. Most classrooms are huge, often two rooms knocked into one. Food technology room where all pupils are given the opportunity to cook; large ICT suite; welcoming library, complete with dinosaur statue made by a member of staff. New library is wonderful: comfy sofas, bright murals of book characters and inventive furniture, all of which underline the emphasis on reading within the school. Even the most reluctant readers must be enchanted. Lots of small rooms dotted around the place for one-to-one support or small group sessions. Two playgrounds, one for each key stage, with plenty of equipment and a quiet area 'which doesn't get used very often!' Separate outside play area for reception pupils, complete with sandpits and water tables.

Staff consists of a mix of long servers of more than 20 years and more newly qualified. Low teacher turnover. Head keen on constant training of staff. 'We see ourselves as a learning community. We all need to keep learning. Every member of staff needs to keep developing to have an impact.' High pupil/teacher ratio, with two or more assistants per class of 30. High morale among the dedicated staff. One parent felt 'the teachers are close to the parents. They're welcoming and friendly. If you have an issue, they are happy to discuss it. They don't tell you to arrange a meeting and come back another time. They are very willing to talk to parents.' A teacher we spoke to happily gives up his free time to take pupils to events at weekends, such as chess tournaments.

Music is a strength of the school. Music co-ordinator encourages the children to join musical events going on out of school. 'I keep my eyes open for those with that something extra, then I push them on. I even go to the auditions with the parents'. Dynamic department which uses IT to great effect. Choirs put on performances for elderly in local nursing homes. Drama is also strong. Plays include an annual Black History performance as well as Christmas and year 6 productions. Poetry recitals, debates and presentations also encouraged. According to one mother, the performances are highly anticipated and 'parents always love the plays they put on.' Numerous outings and trips for all age groups including to Royal Opera House, Lyric Theatre as well as frequent workshops including with English National Ballet and maths magicians. Children are exposed to a variety of enriching experiences from Shakespeare to street dance. Head says, 'The reason for us arranging these activities is that the core of the children here doesn't have access to this sort of experience otherwise. I want them to be introduced to the multi-cultural aspects of British-ness, to British values.' Residential activity trip for year 6 leavers. A hugely busy extracurricular timetable on offer here.

The school participates in inter-school sport tournaments and events but a lack of silverware reflects the dearth of recent victories. Coaches come in from nearby QPR football club. Fencing and football popular and cricket also offered in the summer.

Extended school day available to help working parents with a breakfast club and a nearby after-school play centre, meaning children can do a 10 hour day. Pupils able to attend up to three clubs a week and all are free; current clubs include karate, basketball and dance. Homework club for pupils who need help. A popular five-week summer school is led by teachers and support staff and includes maths and literacy lessons as well as plenty of fun 'for those children who don't get away on holiday all summer.' Head very aware that many families struggle to cope and the school does all it can to give the pupils a chance to enjoy life as well as excel academically.

High parental satisfaction. Those we spoke to were very supportive of the school and felt there were plenty of chances to get involved. A number of the parents work here as support staff. One mother said she was happy to 'let the school get on with it' as she felt 'it takes good care of the boys and girls.' School reaches out to parents and adult classes are held within the school buildings during the day, including English, computer-literacy, sewing and bike-riding. Workshops also on offer which show parents how they can best support their children with maths. Coffee mornings held regularly at the school for parents. A feeling among the parents that they are very lucky to have found this high-achieving school. One mother we spoke to had experienced seven other schools before coming here and she believed that this one was head and shoulders above the rest.

Outward looking school which is very involved in local community. Teachers work with numerous outside agencies and school provides placements for work experience, teacher training and volunteering. Now has much higher profile within the community and is seen in a positive light by neighbours. Christmas and summer fêtes sponsored by local businesses. School takes fundraising seriously and raises a substantial amount for charity each year.

Head says, 'We are what we are. We're successful. The results speak for themselves'. Year 1's mission statement sums up the ethos of the school: to 'respect each other, sing out loud, smile often and work hard.' Head has certainly transformed this school from one which had 'a poor attitude and negative feel' to one that is firing on all cylinders. Seriously impressive on every level.

Mill Hill County High School

Worcester Crescent, London NW7 4LL

Pupils: 1,679 • Ages: 11–19 • Sixth form: 452

Tel: 0844 477 2424
Email: admin@mhchs.org.uk
Website: www.mhchs.org.uk

Headteacher: Since 2004, Geoffrey Thompson MA MBA (Ed) FCMI (50s). Formerly head of Duchess's Community High School in Alnwick, Northumberland. Educated at Campbell College, Belfast, then at St Catharine's College, Cambridge, where he read music. Started his teaching career at Langley Park School for Boys in Bromley, where he worked for 18 years, before moving to Norfolk as deputy head, then on to Northumberland. Though Mill Hill County has always been a school with high standards, his decade in charge has improved it significantly. 'Having a vision and a blueprint is not my way,' he says. 'You have a set of principles and good judgement, you make decisions with other people and the place grows organically.'

A dapper soul, whose own tie is always immaculately knotted, he has a dry sense of humour and a delightfully precise command of the English language. Married to a teacher (who also works in the school), he has two daughters and a son. Out of hours, he enjoys reading, particularly modern history, travelling and music.

Academic matters: One of the country's highest performing comprehensives. With 56 per cent A*-B grades, 22 per cent A*/A at A level in 2016, and 38 per cent A*/A at GCSE, this is a school which believes in an academic focus – 79 per cent of pupils gained five good GCSEs including English and maths. Apart from a handful of vocational qualifications in ICT and media, the curriculum is traditional, with a good range of modern languages (Spanish, French, German, Latin) and a quarter of pupils taking all three sciences at GCSE. In the sixth form – the largest in the borough – the 33 subjects on offer include sociology, psychology, economics and dance. Maths and science, however, are the most popular options (with 10 groups for maths).

Teaching strong throughout (with regular awards for science, geography and maths) and most subjects provide plenty of enrichment. In English, for example, there are Shakespeare and poetry workshops, in DT, direct links with industry. An undoubted strength of the school is the focused attention it offers for all. 'Every child is taught to their own individual abilities,' commented one parent. For those at the top of the spectrum, there are two members of staff to encourage A level students to aim for A*s and Russell Group universities, while those who struggle to make the A*-C benchmark at GCSE are offered a one-year course in which to resit. At this juncture, too, the school participates in a Barnet-wide scheme which sandwiches vocational college training with English, maths and employment skills. Largest number of SEN pupils in Barnet with a department reflective of their very varied needs (including provision for blind children). A raft of teaching assistants provides in-class aid and specialist staff oversee classes and support students beyond. 'It's quite an operation,' says the head.

M

Games, options, the arts: The school prides itself on its extracurricular offering, but there's little doubt that music is the jewel in the crown. 'There are few local schools that can hold a candle to us,' says the head with legitimate pride. He himself rehearses all year 7s to appear in the Christmas concert and from time to time plays the piano at assembly or a duet alongside a visiting professional. Standards throughout are exceptionally high. Recently, for the fourth year in a row, the orchestra is performing a joint concert with the Royal Philharmonic ('you have to be quite good for the RPO to come and play with you,' says the head). Meanwhile the school band will feature alongside that of the Royal Air Force at the Watford Colosseum. Regular lunchtime concerts, major concerts twice a term, large-scale musical in the Easter term, plus an annual European tour for concert and jazz bands. A full range of other sounds, including gospel, African drum and steel drum. Boys participate as enthusiastically as girls – 'unheard of,' says the head – and one talented former pupil performs regularly at Ronnie Scott's.

In sport too, the school has become a 'force to be reckoned with,' particularly in boys' football and girls' netball. Basketball and rugby also on offer and table tennis played enthusiastically by all. Excellent facilities for sport include a range of pitches, three playgrounds, gym, sports hall and in summer, six-lane track and three tennis courts. Art thriving, with a weekly art club and life drawing workshop run by the Royal Academy for A level pupils. Numerous guest speakers and in-demand trips (languages to Barcelona and Normandy, politics to the US, annual ski trip) to inspire and raise aspirations. Good range of clubs run early morning and after school (which can be difficult for those who live at a distance), plus D of E, World Challenge and CCF (shared with nearby independent Mill Hill School).

Background and atmosphere: Originally opened in 1931 as Orange Hill Boys' Grammar School, which then combined with matching girls' grammar in the 1970s. Merged again with Moat Mount School in 1984 to create Mill Hill County High School. The school, fringed by a good expanse of playing fields and forest, now sits on a hilly site with panoramic London views. There, however, the picturesque ends, with well-used buildings crammed together in an intricate hotchpotch to accommodate more students than ever. 'It is overcrowded,' said one parent. 'They're the victims of their own success.' Older parts of the fabric include some fairly basic Portakabins (which house dance and drama), but recent additions have provided modern labs, a sixth form centre, computer suites, seven new classrooms and an air-conditioned assembly hall.

The lack of elbow room doesn't seem to detract from the upbeat mood, with friendly and positive staff (on the day the Guide visited a member of the office team was ringing up a local primary school to ensure a forgotten jumper was returned to its owner) and parents praise the general sense of well-being. 'The school is very good at communicating,' said one. 'They keep us informed and I have the email addresses of all my child's teachers.' Another was grateful for the empathy shown at a difficult time. 'They were understanding and supportive when we had family problems.'

M

Not the easiest school to get to. No tube nearby, which contributes to the mood of semi-rural calm but can be difficult for those wanting to arrive early or stay late for clubs or games. Mill Hill became an academy in 2011, but still works closely with Barnet Council, particularly in its responsibilities for Oak Hill, a successful facility for 32 emotionally and behaviourally disturbed children, four and a half miles away.

Pastoral care, well-being and discipline: One of the first things parents tend to mention is the uniform policy. 'They're very strict on uniform,' said one. 'Everyone looks very smart.' The head sees uniform as a means of setting the expectation bar. 'We're very clear about what we say and insist that what we say is done. We aren't repressive, but you'd be unlikely to see anyone with their shirt tails not tucked in or their ties not tied.'

The head also spends one lesson a week making surprise visits to a range of classrooms. 'That way, you see what's happening. You chat to the children, look at their books. It's a co-operative relationship, but you could potentially see those same children in another context behaving badly.' The insistent focus on behaviour, attitude and good manners undoubtedly pays off. 'Most people who come across our students have positive things to say.'

Pupils and parents: About half the school's intake comes from the leafy and prosperous suburb of Mill Hill, with its high concentration of professionals and business families, but the intake is certainly not uniform. 'There are quite a lot of deprived children and the ethnic mix is huge,' says the head. It includes significant numbers of families who originate from the Indian sub-continent, Asia and Africa. Only a few, however, 'don't speak excellent English.'

Entrance: Mill Hill has entrance criteria guaranteed to drive north London parents into a neurotic frenzy, with 243 places at 11 sliced up into small print sub-sections. Lucky locals can benefit from one of the 90 guaranteed 'geography' places. But distance from the gates is frighteningly close (rather less than a mile). Siblings, too, are ensured a desk. After that children of members of the teaching staff (who have been working at the school for a minimum of two years). If there are 60 remaining places they are then awarded on aptitude and are split into: 24 for technology, 24 for music and 12 for dance. Technology is tested in two stages – a reasoning test in the summer term of year 5 whittles down about 1,500 to 240, the second round (in abstract reasoning and maths) held in September cherry-picks the rest ('it's harder than getting into Oxford,' jokes the head). Music equally competitive, with up to 400 auditioning, in two sections: listening and performance. 'You can, however, play a snappy piece on the classroom xylophone and come out higher than a carefully coached grade 4 violinist.' Dance candidates are selected by audition.

The large (and heavily over-subscribed) sixth form admits a further 40 to 60 pupils out of 600 applicants, with minimum entry requirements of six grade Bs at GCSE, including English and maths. Those wishing to study science and maths need As in their chosen subjects though, and most come garlanded with a string of A*s and As.

Exit: No one is ever asked to leave (except for disciplinary matters), but a fair few (25 per cent in 2016) move on after GCSE to local sixth form colleges, independent and grammar schools. In 2016, 85 per cent to uni, 45 per cent to 'most selective' including Russell Group (one of highest representations of any comprehensive in the UK, including one medic and two Oxbridge in 2016). Quite a number to drama and art-related degrees. A consistent trickle to the US.

Money matters: The transformation to academy status has released additional funds and these are now being used for building projects. Otherwise not rich, but not poor either.

Remarks: A cheerful, well-run school producing highly motivated, high achieving students. Exceptional music.

Mill Hill School

Linked with Belmont Mill Hill Preparatory School, Grimsdell, Mill Hill Pre-Preparatory School

The Ridgeway, London NW7 1QS

Pupils: 657; 100 boarders • Ages: 13–18 • Sixth form: 226

Fees: Day £19,641 pa; Boarding £26,502 – £31,326 pa

Tel: 020 8959 1176
Email: registrations@millhill.org.uk
Website: www.millhill.org.uk

Head: Since January 2016, Mrs Frances King MA PGCE MA MBA (50s), and about as experienced a head as you'll find anywhere. The first woman to head this school. Educated at Ashford School, Kent, read theology at Oxford, followed, later, by a degree in philosophy and religious ethics plus an MBA in international leadership (ie headship) in the independent sector. She taught

RS at Lady Eleanor Holles, Francis Holland (NW1), Guildford County and Tormead. Thence – as head – successively to Heathfield, Roedean and Beau Soleil in Switzerland. She's a bit of a one-woman Change Management Team, having overseen major adjustments in both her previous UK headships. This plus her recent headship in Switzerland must have made her the ideal choice, given Mill Hill's new international school, The Mount.

But she does it so well. And, despite arriving and making changes within weeks, she seems – to their great surprise, to have taken everyone – staff, parents, pupils – with her. She met all the pupils in groups of 10 and asked what could be improved. 'She won hearts and minds,' as one colleague put it. And sixth formers – not noted for embracing change – concur: 'My first reaction was, "oof! no!" – but then we realised what she had in mind and how good it was.' She is ambitious for her school, but it's not the leaping-up-the-league-tables type of ambition – 'We're not trying to be another Habs.' So she promotes eg leadership, teamwork, public speaking, inter-personal skills. 'Professional' in the best sense seems the aptest epithet. Clued-up on every educational innovation and tool, Mrs King is pre-eminently an independent-minded and creative thinker. 'The government is going backwards in so many ways. At Mill Hill, we are becoming ready for a world that is changing before our eyes. Twenty-first century employers will want personal skills because computers will be doing all the work.' Great appointment.

Founding head of The Mount, Mill Hill International School since September 2014 is Mrs Sarah Bellotti BEd (50s). Mrs Bellotti is steeped in international education, having spent 20 years teaching English in international schools in Rome and, latterly, nine years as the director of King's, Ely's International Study Centre. It has to be a dream job, this – a beautifully reimagined and refurbished school dedicated entirely to educating able children from overseas in English subjects via intensive language support to enable them to gain places at good English boarding schools – and down the road from and sharing the facilities of the main school. And she fits the bill. Intense and intensely committed to the task: 'I passionately believe in the international community – we celebrate internationalism here' – she exudes focused excitement and a determination to realise the considerable potential here. She spent her first year 'going across the world' spreading the word and recruiting pupils. At the time of our visit, there were 66, including, interestingly, 10 day pupils who find in the flexible curriculum etc something to suit their individual circumstances. Her new school is perfectly placed and equipped to make a real impact on this market.

Academic matters: Pretty trad curriculum though some interesting novelties eg an IGCSE in further pure maths and A levels in computer science and psychology, not found everywhere. Popular A levels are English, business studies and maths – maths being the stand-out success story in terms of results here. Results, otherwise, are a spread. Not vast numbers of A*s and a range from A-C across the board (in 2016, 41 per cent A*/A and 71 per cent A*-B grades). Popular GCSE options are geography, history, RS and French. Best results in all three sciences, art, Latin and statistics – popular and successful but replaced by further pure (see above) under exam reform. In 2016, 59 per cent A*/A grades overall.

Lots of changes under the new regime include an Innovation Hub – a room where techie things can be tried out. If the DT workshops and the work we saw there is anything to go by (eg stunning sliding work station) great things will emerge. Another King innovation is three-weekly progress reports – 'Before, if you were really good or really bad everyone knew but no-one really noticed the in-betweeners. Now you are monitored and have targets. It is more pressure but it's helpful.' And, of course, to counter the pressure, they now have 'mindfulness' and drop-in, stress-reducing activities like colouring. It had to happen. There are masses of catch-up classes, clinics and individual support. It's all there for the taking – though some sense among parents that the extent of what's on offer isn't always made clear – 'If we'd realised, we wouldn't have had a tutor. It was there in school for us all along.'

Good trad Piper Library – impressively full shelves though some stock needs updating and the bookshelves unaccountably not labelled. Good stock of periodicals. F/t UCAS teacher can be found in sixth form centre – 'She's brilliant'.

Interestingly, 20 per cent of the school's population is on the SEN register and we were told over and again how supportive the school is of eg dyslexics. Mrs King immediately enhanced the staffing and provision in general and the effects are obvious. 'Some of them are slow developers but they can be absolutely the children we want and do well by.' Support is given by individual and small-group lessons which are timetabled not to cut across pupils' other periods, following and reinforcing aspects of the main curriculum and teaching study and organisational skills. Learning support assistants intervene in mainstream academic lessons to support particular pupils or groups. School mainly caters for pupils with mild to moderate specific learning difficulties but also accommodates some statemented pupils eg those with impaired hearing.

The majority at The Mount comes for the one-year IGSCE course, though you can stay for anything from one term to two years. No IB. Small classes with a maximum of 12 pupils. It takes children from 13-17. All teachers have EAL qualifications/experience. Flexible courses depending on the level of English you arrive with. Pre-A level programme. We met several students on our visits – clearly a happy, stimulated and cohesive group who were enjoying a first class education.

Games, options, the arts: Long and pioneering tradition in the arts. We remember coming for an arts festival some 30 years ago and the vitality we met then has only grown.

M

Famously sporty and, while having fun, sports are taken seriously here – girls' sports, seemingly, as much as boys'. 'We have fields and fields and fields,' pupils enthused. Partnership with Middlesex University provides high level support for elite athletes. Good to see extension activities with sports scholars – with specialist staff to help them build and challenge themselves. Remarkable number of representatives in local and country teams across a range of sports – netball, cross-country, cricket, golf and – new to us – bouldering. Lots of teams in eg rugby and hockey so not restricted to the real jocks. School magazine reports – written with an honesty rare in such publications – attest to the earnest approach and a capacity for self-appraisal we seldom see. However, some feeling among the pupils that there was, notwithstanding, a lack of ambition and acceptance of below par performances when a bit more get-go might tilt the balance.

'You don't have to be sporty,' said one parent; 'there's so much else to get involved in.' Exceptional music dept and no lack of ambition in its vast repertoire and the 230 concerts and services annually for which it provides the ensembles, choirs, soloists etc. 'The standard varies from professional to er, well.. but they are so inclusive – everyone feels they can have a go.' House music and house drama on alternate years involve – intensely – just about everyone, as does the music competition. Patrick Troughton Theatre (capacity 150+), a rigged stage in The Large ie main hall, and a spacious drama studio with seating for a small audience. We were impressed by the range of art media: 'They encourage you to try everything,' a non-artsy sixth former enthused. We loved the variety in what we saw – no production line stuff. Impressive range of activities on offer. 'There is masses to do,' and lists and lists of clubs, outings and trips bear witness to that.

The Mount could accommodate three times the present number – it is spacious, superlatively kitted out; no expense has been spared. While some facilities are shared with the main school, there is little lacking here – own DT studio, plenty of outside space. The only shared teacher is one of the PE dept. Excellent range of weekend activities, again, shared with the main school.

Boarding: Boarders make up a fifth of the school population and most are full boarders, based overseas. They come from around 15 countries from China to Spain. However, only a third of them need EAL support, which is given individually and in groups when needed. Small number of UK-based weekly boarders. Boarding is set to grow here and not just for overseas pupils. The market for weekly boarding in the London of busy working parents is buoyant and Mill Hill is beautifully placed to supply it. Vertically-aged houses; all but one are mixed. Good bonding activities for newbies. Enticing and varied list of compulsory weekend activities includes outings eg theatre and music trips, catch-up and revision classes, sports, clubs and interest groups – lots of choice. Day pupils come in for much of it. Boarding isn't state of the art – no en-suites here yet – but most are in two-bedders of reasonable sizes and all year 13 boarders in singles. Good games rooms.

When we visited The Mount there were, among its 66 pupils, 24 home languages spoken. School will not take more than 25 per cent from any one country. Boarding takes place in the main school and The Mount's boarders are fully integrated.

Background and atmosphere: Founded by nonconformist merchants and ministers in 1807 in the then village of Mill Hill, safely located away from 'dangers both physical and moral, awaiting youth while passing through the streets of a large, crowded and corrupt city'. It's not just safe but high – ought to be called Mill Hill-on-the-Hill – and looks over the northern suburbs much as a more famous, boys only, school on a neighbouring hill does, only from a different angle. In many ways. A rare thing, a boarding school of this size – 120 acres – so close to the national hub and unique, now, in offering, as it does, coeducation from 3-18 with an in-built international school integral to its offering. In parkland with some glorious trees which still date from the planting of a former resident, the botanist Peter Collinson, the main building – colonnaded and with tall windows – makes a confident statement. Inside are some splendid rooms and many walls are lined with huge oil paintings of school worthies – again, this is a school which had, from its inception, no modest aims. Democracy rules here and even the grandest meeting room – The Crick – is open to bookings from pupils for meetings and discussions.

Countless additional buildings – many attractive, some functional – and dating from all eras. Walkways, staircases abound – 'You get used to stairs here'. We loved the rustic vernacular Winterstoke Library and were desperate to know what is housed in its little tower; we loved the McClure Music School (1912) redolent of an innocent age, and we loved the recent Favell Building (2007) – which houses humanities and the top floor of which is hung with huge flags from everywhere. An attractive chapel (1896) by Basil Champneys, architect of many notable scholastic buildings. The chapel – though obviously of Christian origins – is now very much an ecumenical hub, and actively celebrates all faiths and their key festivals. We visited over Harvest Festival but missed Rosh Hashanah, the week before, and heard about the preparations for Diwali on the week following. One of our guides explained about Ramadan and the difficulties of fasting. The chapel was decorated by self-portraits of the new year 9s who explain to the gathered classes why they depicted themselves as they had – an excellent way to start to get known and know others.

Away from the main corridor and atrium, some areas are pretty old-school Spartan and need painting or a general refurb. Others are mint and sparkling.

Strong and popular house system and here, unlike in many other schools, houses you belong to are actually physical houses – or, at least, parts of buildings. They are defined by a house colour scheme – you can't miss it in upper areas of the main building where the overhead light is retina-bendingly harsh. Parents praise the heads of houses: 'They deal with everything and they always phone you back'.

New sixth form centre will make staying on more attractive and the King revamp is upping the profile and quality of what Mill Hill sixth form has to offer in general.

Outstanding food – we can't remember seeing – or scenting – better. The home-made cookies made us want to curl up and stay for the day.

The Mount – formerly The Mount Girls' School – has been beautifully refurbished. It has lovely grounds, good-sized classrooms and a happy collaborative atmosphere. The pupils – from everywhere – mix well with each other and the boarders they share houses with in the main school.

Pastoral care, well-being and discipline: Universal praise for pastoral care – both when you need it and when you only need to know it's there eg on arrival in the sixth form. 'It was so welcoming!' 'It's not a school where people act up much,' we were told, 'and if you do hit trouble it doesn't define the rest of your time in the school. They try to help you and find out why.' Very rare chuck-outs, mainly for drugs and nothing recent. House structure is the bedrock of the overall care and support and much praise for house staff in general.

Pupils and parents: Boys vastly outnumber girls, especially in the sixth form. This is true in pretty much all co-eds but is markedly noticeable here, partly due to the number of local, first rate, girls' schools. However, again, Mrs King is working on redressing this and, in any case, girls, evidently don't feel outnumbered and no-one complains that provision for them is second-class. We did note an activity called 'programming for girls' and wondered.. Parents praise the inclusiveness – 'My three are all completely different and the school is brilliant for all of them'. Most day pupils live locally and are the, mostly, comfortably-off, ethnically mixed, professional families you'd expect in this prosperous part of north west London. Mrs King speaks, knowledgeably, of the local 'ambitious clientele'. Active Parents' Association – clearly very popular.

Most Mount students based abroad but it could also be an option for recently relocated families, for local or other UK pupils whose education has, for any reason, been interrupted eg by sports prowess, filming, illness etc because of the flexibility and the intensive courses it offers.

Entrance: At 13+, 80 come up each year from linked prep Belmont, which means 70 places available for outsiders. However, places now offered in years 6 and 7 at Belmont – the prep school is expanding, particularly in hopes of attracting girls. Entry to the senior school from Belmont is not competitive so well worth investigating. Exams in maths, English, science, French and Latin (if learned) plus interview and report. Places occasionally at 14+ tested similarly.

At 16+, 22+ places available and candidates need at least two As and three Bs (grades 7 and 6) at GCSE.

Exit: Uncompromising chucking out post-GCSEs of those who didn't make the grade stopped by Mrs King on arrival. At least two As and three Bs expected but there is flexibility – as there should be – for those who otherwise make a strong contribution to school life. We find this so heartening – not every school should be trying only to cater for the super-bright. Most of us aren't. Post-A level, one of the most impressively diverse list of leavers' destinations – in terms both of course and university – that we've seen. This suggests a real focus on developing the individual and not turning out an identikit product – we like this. One to Oxford in 2016 and two medics; also economists, linguists, thespians..

The list of notable Mill Hill alumni is equally multi-lateral: actors Jasper Britton, Patrick Troughton (Dr Who mk 2), Harry Melling (Dudley Dursley); Richard Dimbleby and Simon Jenkins; Francis Crick, Norman Hartnell, Bob Marshall-Andrews, Tanika Gupta and Dennis Thatcher.

Around 50 per cent from The Mount move to Mill Hill main school after, usually, a year. Some stay at The Mount for years 10 and 11. The rest to, mostly, other boarding schools better suited to their needs.

Money matters: More than 10 per cent of pupils receive some level of fee assistance and some few are on 100 per cent fee remission. Scholarships in academics, sports, arts all worth 10 per cent of fees – but bursaries available which can contribute, in a few cases, up to 100 per cent of the remainder. Three 100 per cent sixth form bursaries. Hardship fund may see you through short-term liquidity problems. 'Thorough' and regular means-testing, of course. Numerous smaller awards bring kudos and Mars Bar money. Some interesting one-offs eg The Grinton award – a senior school scholarship for a girl boarder who wants to study art and The Donald Hall award for someone who wants to take sixth form science.

Remarks: 'My school is a place where you can express yourself and do anything,' we were told. Spot on. Set to regain its pre-eminence in this part of the world, wider still and wider.

Montpelier Primary School

Montpelier Road, Ealing, London W5 2QT

Pupils: 683 • Ages: 4–11

Tel: 020 8997 5855
Email: admin@montpelier.ealing.sch.uk
Website: www.montpelierschool.net

Headteacher: Since 2003, Mr Am Rai (40s). BA in sociology, Birmingham Poly, MA in educational management and administration at University of London, Institute of Education. Married, two children. Very experienced head who had already worked in seven London state primaries prior to his arrival at Montpelier. He had been twice seconded to rescue failing schools. And you can see why. He is a man of very clear vision and sound, liberal educational principles. He is highly articulate, straightforward and frank in conversation. In two hours' conversation, we were wearied by no jargon, no pseudo-academic parroting, no political posturing – so refreshing. There is no disguising Mr Rai's confidence and his ambition – both personal and, more overtly, for his pupils. The results are there for all to see. Montpelier's most recent Ofsted – with only two days' notice – achieved a full house of grade 1s, and school is now a National Support School, helping others to improve. The results top the borough's and top most other boroughs too. The children are stimulated, creative, challenged, smiley and rewarded. A very good head.

Entrance: Oversubscribed at all levels but high turnover among local international community means that occasional places at all stages are not uncommon. All managed by Ealing LA and, if you have no special circumstances, you need to live up close and purposeful if you are to get in. And families increasingly swap their large homes in less well provided for bits of the borough for flats round the corner from this school.

Exit: Some leave for local preps at end of year 4. Of the remainder, around 30 per cent go to the local hotshot comprehensive – Drayton Manor HS. Around 15 per cent to Ellen Wilkinson HS – the local girls' comprehensive. The rest either to local RC or CE high schools or to the local independents – Notting Hill and Ealing, St Benedict's, St Augustine's. Increasingly, some to the Tiffins, to Bucks, Berks or Middlesex grammars, to St Paul's Boys' or Girls', Latymer Upper or John Lyon, and some parents even move house after their bright buttons gain places there or at eg Henrietta Barnett. No disaster schools in the area – another good reason for coming here.

Remarks: Sited on a corner of two quiet, tree-lined roads and adjoining a pretty park. The surrounding streets are similarly well-appointed, orderly and solidly middle class – this is suburban bliss, though the North Circular grinds along only a couple of hundred yards away. The nearest schools are all independent and, not surprisingly, they are the chosen destinations for a sizeable minority of Montpelier leavers.

Three connected school buildings, and only one – due for renovation – makes the heart sink. The latest is a clever extension housing reception and admin. Infants and reception on ground floor – makes sense. Four playgrounds with good play equipment though not over-provided with soft flooring. Reception classes have integral loos, so no tots trailing down corridors. No overheated classrooms here – though we visited on a dull January morning – and no class feels over full, despite 30 in each and staff. Windows have replaced doors wherever possible – school has a light and open feel. Reception in large classroom with a teacher, a nursery nurse, a student teacher and a teaching assistant. Corner with fresh fruit and drinks available all day for whoever feels inclined. Some 40 per cent bring food from home but the school lunch menu – outside caterers – looked varied and appetising.

Infants' classes full of quiet, concentrated activity – seven or eight things going on in each room – water, measuring, building, weighing, word work, writing etc. Every class has a whiteboard and IT used imaginatively round the school – connecting people and activities and joining things up. Learning legacy boards provide testimony to what has been learned during the term. Monitoring and appraisal embedded into everything – each child has her own targets for the core skills and a list of 'I Can' statements to keep parents abreast of what has been mastered and what still needs to be done. This complemented by the clever use of iPads by teachers who photograph work and load it onto a parents' portal so that latest work can be admired at home.

Lots of imaginative cross-curricular learning: displays everywhere are evidence of lively thinking and teaching. Year 2 work on portraits looked at what portraits can teach us rather than being merely an excuse to draw ourselves. Super project on Medusa – each child had made a Wanted poster with clever text – and another class displayed illustrations of The Lady of Shalott with sensitive use of quotes. Oxford Reading Tree used throughout with built-in encouragement for parental participation and each child has weekly guided reading session to build comprehension skills rather than just skimming speed. A good hall/gym, a nice little library – properly used for lending and reading – two IT suites, art room, and every class has an art week in which they can drop everything else and experience sustained and concentrated work on a project of their own.

Unusually strong music – 150+ learn an instrument in or after school – and school provides child care for siblings until 5.00pm to facilitate music activities. Everyone has an afternoon of sport weekly. Not much but better than many.

Remarkable amount of support given to those who need extra help with eg language, writing task or maths. We saw one-to-one sessions and numerous small groups in all available spaces. Also, for those with an SEN to whom – until recent changes in government SEN provision, at least – school has given exemplary support. And organised time made to equip those who arrive with no English with key words and skills. As socially diverse as any school in the capital. Around 55 per cent speak a language other than English at home – huge range of languages and cultures – among which highest proportions from the Middle East and Japan, then India and various bits of Europe. Families include a lot of 'corporate nomads' ie those with three or five year contracts who may be relocated anywhere on the globe. After-school language (French, Spanish, Arabic, Mandarin) and many other clubs.

The first thing that strikes you on an ordinary school day is how quiet it is and how class after class of 30 diverse children work absorbedly and happily together. In this large, highly organised school – and it is a large primary by any standards – children look relaxed and secure and, even amongst the smallest, there is a sense that school is about learning. Few behavioural problems – jumped on smartly when they occur. Head 'will exclude if a child is spoiling the lives of other children', but no-one excluded for bullying in eight years prior to our visit.

Parental talk of 'the warm community feeling', express gratitude that 'the children are looked after well and are happy,' and pay tribute to the truly multi-cultural ethos – 'all faiths and beliefs are celebrated'. Very active PTA and lots of community activities eg annual international food fair and remarkably effective fundraising summer fête.

Most staff – many are young – highly praised. Head is seen as dynamic and approachable by some and by others as remote and over-protective of his staff. No-one, however, wishes they had sent their children elsewhere, and none would dispute that he has made a stunning success of a school which, before, had been content to be good enough. 'We judge things by the happiness of our children,' asserts head wisely.

M

More House School (London)

169

22–24 Pont Street, London SW1X 0AA

Pupils: 212 • Ages: 11–18 • Sixth form: 32 • RC

Fees: £17,850 pa

Tel: 020 7235 2855
Email: office@morehousemail.org.uk
Website: www.morehouse.org.uk

Headmistress: Since 2014, Amanda Leach, previously deputy head here for eight years. BSc in sports science from Liverpool and PGCE from Exeter. Has taught at Cranbrook School, Kent, and Uffculme School in Devon. Spent a year teaching EFL in Rome. Joined More House in 1998 as a science teacher, and has also taught ICT and PE here. 'Why would I want to leave here? I love it so much,' she enthuses. Married with two daughters; husband is director of sport at Bedales. 'I love being outdoors with my family. My kids are into gymnastics. We are not allowed to sit still for very long at home!' Described by one parent as being 'approachable and down to earth, though we don't see much of her.' Another said, 'I love Mrs Leach. She is breathing new life into the place. She has lots of energy and is a total delight.' Enthusiastic, effervescent and warm. Can be seen cycling to school from Putney every morning and girls wave to her along the Kings Road as she races past. A breath of fresh air.

Academic matters: Wide range of academic ability. As one parent put it, 'There are less intellectually confident girls here who are nurtured, but there are also some very clever girls, whose parents have chosen the school because it is Catholic.' Core subjects taken in year 7 alongside Latin, history of art, dance, music and drama. All girls take two modern foreign languages and those that are bilingual can take that GCSE early. Maths, science and modern languages taught in ability sets. Religious studies compulsory for GCSE and many choose to continue with it at A level. Head favours the philosophy and ethics course as it 'encourages girls to question their spirituality.' Pupils take eight to 11 GCSEs. Thirty-six per cent A*/A in 2016 and nearly 60 per cent A*-B.

French currently popular at A level, though subjects wax and wane, depending upon the cohort. School happy to have only one or two pupils taking a subject at A level and class sizes seldom above four. Polish, Russian and Arabic all fell into this category recently, with no take up for physics or chemistry. Timetable built around what girls want to do and school tries to be flexible in terms of what it offers. Twenty-six different subjects currently taught at A level. In 2016, 66 per cent A*/B and 28 per cent A grades. Extended Project Qualification taken by lower sixth. No plans for Pre-U or IB due to school's size.

Head has tightened up on academic rigour, making some significant changes since her appointment. Templates now printed in exercise books to ensure that feedback from teachers is detailed and effective and that there is constant dialogue between staff and pupils. School is also getting better at monitoring girls, with assessment points five times a year to ensure those not making enough progress are quickly identified. Colour-coded boards in staff room help teachers to see when a pupil is falling behind in subjects other than their own and gives a more holistic view of each girl's overall progress. Staff appraisals take place more regularly and twilight sessions help ensure staff members are on board with changes being implemented.

Excellent provision for girls with specific learning difficulties. The department comprises a full-time SENCo, speech and language therapist and a part-time ESOL teacher. EAL girls have extra English support until it is up to scratch. School can support girls with dyslexia, dyscalculia and dyspraxia; currently one or two per year group have quite severe difficulties. Currently two girls with Asperger's. About 25-30 girls currently receiving one-to-one support, with others having help with maths and English in small booster groups. Some girls stop support lessons around year 9 and then come back to having support nearer to GCSEs. 'It is flexible. Girls can dip in and out, depending upon their need.' All subjects offer weekly intervention classes for year 11 and above, from October through to start of exams. One parent feels that 'girls have to flag up their need for support themselves, but once the school is aware of it, provision is made pretty quickly'.

Gifted and talented programme for the brightest pupils. 'The top end is identified within three or four weeks of being here. A learning mentor then sits down with them and asks them whether they are being challenged in each subject. We listen to them'. Extension work might include Italian classes for able linguists. School explains, 'It's not just a case of giving them an extra worksheet. It's more undercover than that, but we know who has a special talent or ability. We take notice, but they don't feel pressurized.' Scholars and gifted pupils are invited to join More's Household, which offers lunchtime talks, given by internal and external speakers. Girls here regularly enter and win external prizes, such as national poetry and storytelling competitions. One girl recently made the finals of The Big Bang UK Young Scientists Fair.

Games, options, the arts: Creative and performing arts at the heart of the school. Deserves its artistic reputation and currently boasts a textiles specialist, a painter and a mixed-media artist. Head believes that the art department is good at seeing where a girl's artistic talents lie and then giving her the opportunity to develop her interests whether in clay, textiles or fine art. Weekly, after-school life-drawing classes put on for sixth formers. Numerous visits arranged to London galleries.

Three-quarters of girls have individual music lessons. All year 7 girls play an instrument (brass, string or woodwind), bought through PTA fundraising. Strong choral tradition. All year 7 and 8 girls are in a choir. Optional thereafter. In the last choral concert, 130 girls sang alongside staff, parents and alumnae. Annual international music tour. On a recent choir tour of Rome, girls performed with papal choir in St Peter's in front of Pope and 75,000 spectators. All musical tastes and talents catered for, from chamber choirs to karaoke and geek club, which involves hand-bell ringing for the Christmas concert. 'The music is exceptional. All-inclusive. You don't have to be talented in order to be allowed to perform,' according to one parent.

Drama is another strength of the school. Sold-out drama productions of As You Like It and Grimm's Fairy Tales. Biannual play and musical which run on a carousel system. Musical is staged in a professional theatre. If a smaller production is put on one year then a junior production is also staged so that as many girls as possible can perform. 'Everyone is given a chance,' and certainly no shortage of opportunities for those who want to be in the spotlight.

'PE is being taken much more seriously than in the past,' according to one delighted parent, and sports department is well led. New PE kit has made a world of difference and hoodies without pockets mean that girls are more likely to catch the rounders ball. Practice takes place all over London, including the climbing wall at Imperial College, athletics in Battersea Park, swimming at St Mary's, Paddington and tennis in Cadogan Gardens. For the first three years, all girls participate in netball, rounders, hockey, athletics and dance as well as a healthy active lifestyle programme. Years 10-11 may also do circuit training, fitness classes, spinning and climbing and sixth form takes part in boot camp. Two girls recently selected to represent borough in London Youth Games netball team. Annual sportswomen's dinner in summer term celebrates athletic achievement. Teachers run the London marathon and raise significant amounts for charity in the process. 'The great thing about sport at More House is that everyone participates,' commented one parent. As head explains, 'We are competing against bigger schools. Sometimes we win, sometimes we lose, but all girls get the chance to play in a team.'

Plenty of early morning and lunch time clubs, such as a thriving debating club, as well as play-dough modelling and knitting for those who prefer something more sedate. 'We want the girls to keep their childhood as long as possible. We also offer flower pressing. We don't want girls to bypass that lovely age,' says head. Touch-typing compulsory for all in year 7. Confirmation preparation also offered. Most clubs are run by sixth formers and year 11 girls; some are run by professionals. Enviable overseas trips to Europe as well as ski-ing in America. Year 8 trip to France is a particular highlight, involving canoeing and camping overnight. Those that cannot afford the trips are subsidised, and alternative trips are also organised in London. 'Always lots going on here. That's why I am such a fan of the school,' said one satisfied parent.

Background and atmosphere: Founded in 1953 by canonesses of St Augustine at the request of a group of parents who wanted to send their daughters to a Catholic London day school. Since 1971, the school has been under lay management. Named after Sir Thomas More, the Tudor theologian.

In the heart of Knightsbridge, though not as glamorous as its location might suggest. Described by one parent as being 'essentially two houses in Pont Street with minimal outside space. Pretty scruffy and quite dark.' Much of the school (apart from the head's office and communal areas) was looking distinctly tired when we visited, but all has been transformed: classrooms ripped out, new furniture installed and redecorating throughout. One delighted mother told us, 'Mrs Leach has 'been busy tidying up the place, decorating where it was needed and making it more aesthetically pleasing.'

Head is determined that the school should 'not be a pressure cooker. We're not waiting for that top to blow off.' This is a very nurturing environment in which girls are constantly encouraged. One mother commented, 'At parents' evening, the teachers always highlight the girls' strengths and are keen to build on these, rather than just dwelling on what they can't do. It boosts the girls' confidence.' Very small classes which do not change from year 7 to GCSEs. 'That's my one gripe about the school. It would be good for everybody if the classes were mixed up regularly,' said one mother. Almost all classes have no more than 16 girls up till GCSE. Sixth form classes range from one pupil to 10 (but mostly much fewer). Family feel to school and all age groups mix well together, partly due to flourishing house system.

Pastoral care, well-being and discipline: Catholic heritage and ethos strong, with many crucifixes on display around the school. Currently 40 per cent Catholic, though there are girls of all faiths and none. School has its own chapel and the chaplain takes mass once a week. 'Catholicism is quite a big deal here,' said one parent. 'We get the balance right between Catholic and non-Catholic,' believes head. 'It's part of our foundation, to respect each other and to be kind. I'm not a Catholic, though I went to a convent school and then on to a missionary school, so faith is very much part of me.' Spiritual growth fostered here. Girls also raise decent sums for charity and this is seen an important part of their education.

Parents cite the pastoral care as being a main strength of the school, and those we spoke to felt that issues were dealt with efficiently and effectively. Head is keen that girls should develop a sense of perspective, and frequently reminds them that 'It's not failure you should worry about. It's how you pick yourselves up. I don't paint a perfect image of myself. We all have ups and downs. It's my duty to help the girls through their difficulties.' Head stands at the door each morning as the girls file past. She can usually spot when something is amiss with a pupil. Girls know they can, and do, knock on her door any time. Layers of support in place, including tutors, and all 'minis' (year 7s) have a 'big sister' in sixth form. Because it is such a small school, eating disorders and emotional difficulties are spotted quickly. Hard for pupils to hide under the radar here.

Excellent relationships between staff and pupils. Girls see their teachers as approachable. As one parent put it, 'The teachers know the girls so well, that's the beauty of a small school.' Occasional short-term suspensions for rudeness to a member of staff but head is not overly quick to punish girls. 'If a girl has messed up, she's going to get an earful from her parents. I tend to ask them what they'd do differently next time.' Saturday detentions recently introduced for persistent offenders.

Pupils and parents: Roughly 70 per cent British. International contingent from all over, including Spain, France, China, Russia, America and Middle East. 'A mixed bag. Some with lots of money, who are driven in and out by chauffeurs, and others who are struggling. Quite diverse, with a good percentage of different cultures,' according to one mother. Girls travel from all over London.

Parents mostly professional. 'I don't think I have the most demanding parents in London. That's a reflection of the girls who are here. These parents want the best for their daughters. They are not idealistic in terms of what their daughters are capable of. They are realistic and know we're going to do the best job we can for them', explains head. Parents feel the communication is good: 'We are kept fully informed, both with the good and bad. We are kept in the loop.'

Entrance: One open day only but private tours given by head throughout year. Part of North London Consortium with exams in English and maths. Prospective pupils spend a half day at More House in the autumn of year 6, which involves an interview with head and sample lessons. Interview is pivotal in many ways. Head always tells girls that they will be able to answer all the questions as they are about themselves, so no need to be nervous. Increasing numbers of applicants every year but lists are closed once 150 have registered. Normally 32 places available (two forms of 16) though some bulge years of 48 (three forms). Girls are either offered a definite place or put on the wait-list. Very few turned down completely and when they are it is 'because they are not More House material as they are off the scale at either end. I can't support the very lowest ability or very highest ability, given the cohort I've got. I don't want one girl on her own at the top. If a girl can't be challenged intellectually by peers here, she's better off elsewhere. It would be great for my results to take them on, but I won't do it,' explains head. Occasional vacancies further up the school are filled quickly. Three or four join in sixth form. Head says she is looking for potential as much as performance at each stage. 'I want to find the golden nugget that's hidden somewhere in a girl. I want to watch them blossom.'

M

Exit: About 60 per cent stay on for sixth form. 'The ones who leave are those who are too cool for school. I'd rather have the ones who want to be here,' explains head. Some depart for co-ed establishments or go to local sixth form colleges. Post A level, many go to art college. Others head to universities all over including UCL, Cardiff, Leeds and, recently, US colleges. One parent felt the school 'isn't striving to get everyone into university. That's not what they are about. They try to support the girl in finding out what is best for them.' Even if a girl is deemed to be Oxbridge material, there is no pressure on her to apply if it's not the right course for her. Usually one girl to Oxbridge every couple of years. School is now focusing on more careers advice for girls and is aware that it should tap into the expertise of its alumnae more.

Money matters: School offers a number of academic scholarships and exhibitions as well as creative and performing arts scholarships to year 7 and lower sixth. Entry bursaries for those starting the school in year 7, as well as special governors' bursaries offered in response to a particular set of circumstances, and come with provisions attached. Normally only awarded to girls who are already at the school and in examination years. Five per cent off school fees for eldest daughter when there are three or more sisters attending school at same time.

Remarks: If your daughter needs a large, competitive school with plenty of space, this is probably not the place for her. But, as one satisfied customer put it, 'If you're after an all girls Catholic school in central London, this is a great choice. It's not for everyone, but if your daughter wants a small, happy and supportive school, this couldn't be better. If I had my time over, I'd send my daughter here again like a shot'. Head is aware that many parents do not know about More House yet, but that 'word is getting out as we're getting better and better.' The way things are moving, this school is not going to remain a secret for much longer.

Mossbourne Community Academy

100 Downs Park Road, London E5 8JY

Pupils: 1,287 • Ages: 11–18 • Sixth form: 272

Tel: 020 8525 5200
Email: enquiries@mca.mossbourne.org
Website: www.mca.mossbourne.org/

Principal: Since 2012, Mr Peter Hughes BA (30s), who took over when founding principal Sir Michael Wilshaw left to lead Ofsted. 'They were big shoes to fill,' he admits, and although some parents say he's less inspirational and personable than his predecessor, he hasn't disappointed and is known for being both exacting and reflective. 'Yes, we've done well, but I always want to know how we can do better,' he says. An Australian, he came to Mossbourne as part of the Future Leaders programme, which identifies, supports and trains potential head teachers. He has taught at Pimlico and Highgate Wood, and was an advanced skills teacher. Gained his BA in education (secondary mathematics) from Charles Sturt University, Australia.

Big on marginal gains, many of the changes he's made are indeed peripheral, including introducing a lottery system to replace the pure distance criteria ('I wanted to stop parents trying to buy their way into the school by moving nearby') and offering an additional 10 per cent of year 9 places to those with the potential to become elite rowers. 'Originally we did this in year 12, but if we're going to complete against private schools, we need to train them at the same age they do,' he explains.

About as far from the stereotype of a headteacher as you can imagine, he is young and hip, with a shiny black office that wouldn't look out of place in a trendy media company. Not that he spends much time there. Mostly, he's out and about round the school itself ('I learned from my predecessor that you can't know a school from behind a desk') and he's also often off site altogether. Indeed, as CEO of the Mossbourne Federation, he now oversees not only the Mossbourne Community Academy, but the new Mossbourne Victoria Park Academy (secondary school), Mossbourne Parkside Academy (primary school) and the new Mossbourne Riverside Academy (also primary) in Queen Elizabeth Olympic Park.

Living in Canary Wharf, he is an early riser, often seen out running at 6am with the rowers.

Academic matters: Exceptional results: in 2016, 83 per cent of pupils got 5+ A*-C grades at GCSE including maths and English; 38 per cent A*/A grades. At A level, 71 per cent of grades A*/B and 42 per cent A*/A. Not only are these some of the best state school results in the capital, they are also all the more extraordinary when you consider that some of the pupils arrive in year 7 hardly able to read. That said, Hackney is experiencing a rise in the quality of students leaving its primary (and secondary, for that matter) schools, making Mossbourne a less steep learning curve for students than it once was.

School has remained in the top one per cent in the country for value added ever since it opened, a feat the head puts down to several factors. First, they've created an environment with a 'can do' attitude, where it's cool to learn. Second, there are exceptionally strong structures in place, with a strict uniform policy, ferocious discipline and meticulous monitoring with weekly target setting. The 'personalised learning agenda' is certainly not just government jargon at this school. Third, young and eager teaching staff provide top quality teaching, helped by great facilities. 'Three things are expected of the teaching staff here – giving high quality feedback; providing nurture and care; and being accountable for their results. The rest is up to them,' says the head. You'd have try hard not to do well here, he concludes – and it's true that, walking around, the culture is focused and calm. 'To step outside of that would actually be quite challenging.'

Although some teachers are better than others, they generally do whatever it takes to help kids grasp the subject and are nearly always prepared to go the extra mile, say parents. 'Whatever support you need, they'll give it,' said one.

The banded intake is set on entry in all the main curriculum subjects (English, maths, science, humanities, ICT and modern languages), with significantly smaller class sizes for lower sets and considerable movement between sets. Music, drama, dance, PE, art and design technology are not setted. Three modern languages on offer at GCSE – French, German, Spanish – as part of the core curriculum, and students also have the opportunity to take public exams in Turkish (large take-up), Latin (significant take-up), Bengali, Swedish, Italian. 'We meet the requirements of parents,' says the head, 'so if they speak a certain language at home, but want their son or daughter to learn it in a more formalised way here, we can accommodate that.'

Traditional academic sixth form, offering around 25 A level subjects, the most popular of which are maths (around two-thirds take this), English (around half choose this), history, psychology and the three sciences. Also on offer are Latin and classical civilisation, plus creative options such as music, art and drama.

Plenty of computers throughout, many built into the modern white desks – the result of which is that technology is very much embedded into learning. Homework is set in abundance, but head recently introduced a later 4.20pm finish for all, enabling students to spend the last period of the school day either doing homework, preparation for the next lesson or revision. 'It came about because we were asking ourselves if we could improve students' preparation for A levels,' he says, adding that some students lack a quiet space to work at home and that anything that stops homework becoming a battleground at home has to be a good thing. Crucially, though, students can use this period on some days to take up one of around 30 activities on offer – anything from bicycle maintenance to table tennis and from journalism to debating club – although only if they commit to doing their homework later on those days. 'The overall aim was to provide more structure around homework for year 7s, then slowly remove that structure as students move up the school, so that by the time they reach A level they are independent learners,' says head.

Saturday morning school not compulsory, but provides a safe place to do weekend activities such as the City explorers' club, revision lessons, Mandarin and other optional classes (including English for non-native speakers) and, of course, sports.

Outstanding autistic spectrum disorder provision via its own well-resourced teaching centre and well-qualified specialists. 'We take three children per year under this provision, which continues in sixth form and beyond, through the transition into college or work,' says the head. 'Everyone is fully integrated into mainstream school life here.' Parents are impressed. 'The help they've given my son around his dyslexia has changed his life. He went from struggling to write a paragraph in year 7 to writing reams of pages within months, and his growing confidence led to him moving up his sets too,' said one parent.

Games, options, the arts: Sports include football, netball, basketball, cricket and 'best in Hackney' for athletics. Rowing is big and continues growing, with links to the London Youth Rowing and London Regatta Centre, opposite City airport – originally a training centre for the Olympics and still a world-class training facility for the school's rowers. In 2015, a student got a full rowing scholarship to Washington State University to study architecture, whilst another student is first in her class at national level. Impressive sports facilities include a full size sports hall and rowing gym, while all grass sports take place on Hackney Downs. Next on the building agenda – expected around 2018 – is a performance pavilion, a dedicated space designed by Rogers Stirk Harbour + Partners, where students will be able to train on-site for rowing, as well as providing extra sensory provision for the school's autistic intake and enhancing the school's already notable music provision.

Music is a specialism here, with over 250 pupils having subsidised instrumental lessons. Junior and senior choirs and bands, along with an orchestra, all perform in regular concerts and performances. Meanwhile, the music scholars programme enables selected students to perform in public at the likes of the Jazz Café and Tower of London, and these students are also expected to share their learning back at school to help develop other students. 'My children had never done music before Mossbourne and I now have a leading guitar playing, violin playing child,' one parent told us.

Drama practice mainly takes place in the modern and well-equipped auditorium and lecture theatres, culminating in regular performances and an annual whole-school production, with recent examples including Charlie and the Chocolate Factory, Romeo and Juliet and Little Shop of Horrors.

Plenty of examples of skilled and creative artwork on show during our visit, showcasing strong artistic talent across fine art, clay, screen-printing and more. A dedicated A level art studio means students never have to compromise on space and time to work. 'I always think art is one of the unsung successes of Mossbourne,' one student told us.

Trips to Edinburgh, Belgium, the Isle of Wight, language trips to Spain and Germany; Spanish play, poetry competition, debating, links with London College of Fashion. Lots of careers advice. 'My son talks about his future a lot – way more than I ever did at that age. He has high aspirations,' one parent told us.

Background and atmosphere: Founded on the site of Hackney Downs School, once a successful local grammar school, whose alumnae include Sir Michael Caine and Harold Pinter. By the 1990s, however, it had become notorious as 'the worst in Britain' and was eventually demolished. Mossbourne was rebuilt on the same site, a tricky triangle bounded on two sides by railway lines. Founding principal Sir Michael Wilshaw worked alongside architects, Richard Rogers and Partners, to design a school (costing £32.5 million) which met his requirements. Now one of the largest wooden structures in England (known locally for looking like an IKEA, not least because it's huge and blue on the outside), it was created in a V shape, which holds in its arms a welcoming triangular social area, complete with tables and benches, basketball areas, table tennis tables etc.

Wilshaw believed that pupils need to be kept under constant observation, so the head's office and the classrooms all overlook the grounds. No corridors – hidey-holes for bullying – and no staffroom, since Wilshaw felt teachers need to be involved at break times and after school, when most trouble occurs. Inside (where the IKEA comparison still feels apt, such is the emphasis on modern, innovative and fresh interiors) the triple-height space is light and airy and learning takes place in 'learning areas,' which are split into themes of sport, history, music etc – including one specifically for year 7s, whose transition is a major area of focus. Glittering new sixth form centre.

In each glass-walled classroom – all of which have an open door policy – all students begin lessons by reciting the Mossbourne reflection: 'Throughout this lesson I aspire to maintain an inquiring mind, a calm disposition and an attentive ear, so that in this class and in all classes I can fulfil my true potential'. Sure enough, the students we saw did look attentive and interested.

Active school council and peer mentoring scheme for core subjects. Prefects in year 13. No house system. Pupils we spoke to were articulate, polite and delightful – oozing pride about their school. We were also wowed by the set-up here. It's bright, contemporary and spotless, with superb facilities and seemingly endless examples of attention to detail, including language booths and a huge amount of space for private study.

Pastoral care, well-being and discipline: Woe betide students who don't toe the line here, with staff giving out detentions for things like keeping a watch on during PE, untidy uniform and being more than 10 seconds late when the morning whistle goes at 8.40am. 'We work on the principle that if you sweat the small stuff, the big stuff takes care of itself,' says the head. 'Nothing ever escalates into anything more serious,' agreed one student. 'The most serious offence I've ever seen here is talking in class.'

Among parents, it tends to be the middle-class liberals who struggle, with some thinking teachers can be overzealous. There was also a feeling among some parents we spoke to that new teachers are particularly extreme. 'There's a joke that new teachers here don't smile until Christmas,' one told us. 'My son got a detention for writing his homework on the wrong page – I mean, come on,' said another. But most approve of the general ethos that if you set the controls, you ultimately give children freedom. 'The heavy-handedness has made my son very driven,' added one parent.

No physical contact between students is allowed ('If a boy has his arm around a girl, how do we know it's not making her uncomfortable, but she's too embarrassed to say, for example?' explains head) and no more than six people in a single group in the playground. Staff always on hand, with stairwells manned between lessons and students monitored after school.

Pre-GCSE pupils wear smart grey and red school blazers and neatly knotted ties, sixth formers graduate to business-like suits and skirts (at or below the knee). No piercings allowed, except for ears, hair must be kept to an acceptable norm. Mobiles banned and students not allowed to enter shops on their way home or loiter outside the gates in groups. Racism a non-issue, and the same can be said for truancy, with a 96 per cent attendance rate.

Pastoral care exceptional. Everything here is about students feeling safe and comfortable so they are ready to learn, with as much access as they need to school counsellors, who come in as and when they're required (the school works with a private company), plus plenty of senior teaching staff (including the deputy head) whose sole responsibility outside teaching is pastoral care. Few personal problems go unnoticed, whether self-harm or being picked on. At the first sign, parents are invited to come and speak to the staff, with two dedicated meeting rooms available. 'We very much believe parents are our partners and are fundamental to the success of the school,' says head. Bullying extremely rare and when discovered, it's dealt with swiftly and seriously. 'My daughter told me about a boy who came out in year 8 and there was no nastiness about it at all, with everyone being really accepting – that would have been unheard of in Hackney in the past,' one parent told us.

M

Pupils and parents: A large percentage of the intake comes from the adjacent Pembury estate, an urban sprawl which tends to hit the headlines for its shootings and drugs rather than its high educational aspirations. Two-thirds of pupils are from minority ethnic groups (many Turkish Kurds), two-fifths speak English as a second language, 50 per cent are on free school meals. But also a fair number of clued-up, middle-class parents – the kind who used to go private or bus their children out of the borough – who fight from a great distance to get their children the superb education the school offers.

Entrance: Some 1,500 apply for the 216 places, making it one of the country's most over-subscribed schools. The head is looking for a balanced intake: 'We want a comprehensive – we don't want a secondary modern'. Applicants sit cognitive ability tests to divide into four equal ability bands. Fifty per cent of places in each band are given to those who live within the inner zone (up to 1km from the gates); 30 per cent of places go to those in the middle zone (1-2km) and 20 per cent to those in the outer zone (2-3km). Priority is given to looked after children, those with a child protection plan, siblings, those with medical needs and children of staff. Further places by lottery, which head says prevents parents from buying their way into the school by moving into a property nearby, although some parents say the inevitable consequence of the gentrification of Hackney is that this feels less of a community school than in the past. Offers an additional 10 per cent of year 9 places to those with the potential to become elite rowers (zoning does not apply to this group).

The lower sixth form has 170 places. Applicants must meet the demanding criteria of seven A*-C GCSEs, including English and maths, with priority given to pupils already at the school – around 100 of whom generally secure places. All candidates, including those already at the school, must also meet the subject specific entrance criteria in their chosen A level subjects. Whilst successful external candidates used to come mostly from other Hackney comprehensives, they are increasingly applying from further afield, utilising the quick and easy train route from Liverpool Street.

Exit: Those who leave at GSCE leave mainly do so to do vocational qualifications or go straight into work. After sixth form, 90 per cent to universities, nearly half of those to Russell Group universities (a wide mix). Seven to Oxbridge in 2016. Broad array of subjects studied, including music, maths, physics, engineering, law, communications – and 4+ students every year go into medicine. Remaining 10 per cent mainly into apprenticeships, with around 4-10 students taking a gap year.

Money matters: Money not a problem at this well-resourced school – everything from the buildings to the technology is of the highest standard and whatever the head wants to get done he has the means to achieve.

Remarks: If ever there was a school proving that the right ethos, leadership and sufficient resources can provide not just a good education – but a great one – in the most deprived of areas, this is it. Everything about it is geared around the concept of passive supervision and students feeling safe, nurtured and ultimately ready to learn. This, together with the combination of high quality teaching, excellent facilities and strong discipline and pastoral care, means it's hardly any wonder that results are outstanding and that parents fight hard to get their kids in.

Muswell Hill Primary School

Muswell Hill, London N10 3ST

Pupils: 420 • Ages: 4–11

Tel: 020 8444 8488
Email: office@muswell-hill.haringey.sch.uk
Website: www.muswellhillprimary.co.uk

Head: Since 2014, James Wiltshire BA PGCE NPQH, 30s. Formerly acting head and director of standards at Canonbury School in Islington. Bearded, enthusiastic, dynamic – and very much liked by parents. 'He looks as though he should be in shorts,' said one, 'but his heart is in the right place.' On paper, can sometimes appear as though he's swallowed a policy document ('providing experiences that are stimulating and challenging', 'encouraging active participation in the learning process'), but clearly he's a man that gets things done. Since his arrival, he's revamped the website, revolutionised the management structure, and is now campaigning to rebuild the school. A busy, busy man.

Entrance: One of the most heavily over-subscribed primaries in the borough (586 applicants for 60 places last year). Having a sibling already at the school or living nearby are the two quickest ways through the gates, but 'near' means very, less than a quarter of mile if you want a realistic chance.

Exit: The school sits midway between two of north London's best comprehensives, so why consider anywhere else is the general parental view. Most leavers proceed to either Fortismere or Alexandra Park. A trickle, 'for those who live in funny roads', to independents, plus a few to various sought-after nearby grammar schools.

Remarks: Its last full Ofsted (2006) deemed this an outstanding primary, and there's little evidence this view should change. Results in year 6 remain rock solid. Teachers are a happy mix of experience and enthusiasm; most are in their 30s, with a healthy sprinkling of men. 'We're very happy with the teachers,' said one parent. 'They're very approachable and supportive.' The new management structure (giving responsibility for a number of year groups to three assistant heads) means classroom time is always in the hands of a qualified teacher (and parents have 'a point of contact' for concerns, gripes, etc).

Children eased gently into school life with parents allowed to stay in the early days. Good support for the basics, too, with an informative 'phonics workshop' for those unfamiliar with the jargon. French from year 3 (but 'only a little'). Good ICT, with plenty of coding. Science skills developed beyond the curriculum with final year pupils introduced to secondary school methods with classes at Fortismere. Philosophy, reasoning and 'reflection' from reception. Regular homework, with daily reading, weekly Maths and spelling, plus 'the odd project'. Comprehensive special needs strategy overseen by a SENCo, aided by learning support assistants in each class and out-of-school specialists when required.

The visual arts important here –'There's a lot of focus on art,' said one parent. As well as the standard fare, there's an arts week, art award, and involvement with a 'working' artist. School orchestra and choir (both provided in after-school clubs).

Sport 'huge'. Netball, rugby, dance, cricket, gymnastics, basketball, athletics and hockey all on offer, with external specialists honing skills to a high standard and plenty in the way of inter-school competition ('The trophy cabinet's not big enough for the trophies we've received,' says the head). But, if winning is the aim, the attitude remains inclusive. 'Football Friday' fields eight teams and eight groups of supporters (plus appropriate team shirts) and regs require three girls from each team to be on the pitch at all times. Good range of well-organised after-school clubs, from cheerleading and chess, to cooking and capoeira. (Paid for) before- and after-school clubs extend the school day for working parents.

Formed by the merger of an infant and junior school in 2000, the school now occupies an army camp of 60s low-rise buildings. Located on the site of what was once Muswell Hill Railway Station, there's lavish outside space, with an attractive, well-equipped playground for the youngest, good-sized courts and extensive running-around space (dotted with picnic tables) for their elders, plus a delightful wooded area and wildlife garden.

'Joy, Discovery and Diversity' are the defining themes of schooldays here, and parents agree that this is 'a really nurturing' place. Reasonably relaxed in a north London way, so no uniform. ('It's quite liberal, but I like that,' said one mum). Generally 'millennial' in approach, so clothes recycling point on site and pupils encouraged to walk to school. Broad cross-section of ethnicity and income, but the prevailing mood solidly middle class. ('It would be lovely to go for ice cream; let's find a date.') Fundraising, too, tends to reflect the area, with a concert of Vivaldi's Four Seasons a recent moneyspinner.

Generally a friendly, upbeat place, with parents bonding in the active PTA, which raises funds through a multitude of events, from quiz evenings and cake sales to fairs and fireworks night. Also active gardening and nature groups involved in 'site development'. 'It's a very nice community and I've made some very good friends.'

Produces articulate, confident children, who enjoy their time at school. 'My son looks forward to school every day.'

Newland House School

32- 34 Waldegrave Park, Twickenham TW1 4TQ

Pupils: 408 • Ages: 4–13

Fees: £10,875 – £12,165 pa

Tel: 020 8865 1305
Email: admissions@newlandhouse.net
Website: www.newlandhouse.net

Headmaster: Since 2010, Mr David Alexander BMus Dip NCOS (50s). Previously head of Norland Place School and Haddon Dene School. Warm, welcoming and with a good sense of humour. Very kind and doesn't have a bad word to say about anybody. Justifiably proud of his charges. 'Our 13-year-old boys are a delight, as are our 11-year-old girls. I'm very proud to know any of them. I like what the school has done for them.' Parents say, 'What you see is what you get. Pupils and parents respect him but he knows how to laugh too.' Believes one of his main jobs is to steer parents towards the right school for their child: he wants his pupils to be at the top of their game at their senior schools. The children adore him because he's such fun: he is currently keen for the school to buy a boat which can act as a floating classroom on the Thames. Holds a commercial flying licence and commands a reserve RAF squadron at weekends. Mr Alexander selects the head boy and head girl by deciding which pupils he would most like to have lunch with.

Entrance: Over-subscribed – best register your child as soon as possible after birth. Currently two main points of entry: 4+ and 7+. At 4+ entry is on a first-come, first-served basis, with siblings given priority. Sixty places available at this stage and a waiting list in operation. At 7+, which will be phased out after 2018 intake, pupils are tested in English and maths. Assessments for the 20 places take place in January for entry into the school the following September.

Academic and music bursaries available – up to 50 per cent of fees, negotiated on a yearly basis. Ten per cent discount for third sibling when all are in school together.

Exit: Predominantly private day schools, with Surbiton High, Lady Eleanor Holles, Hampton, King's College School and Kingston Grammar currently the most popular. A couple each year head for boarding schools such as Marlborough and Wellington. Girls leave at 11 and boys at 13. Girls can stay on to 13, but don't. 'It would be a leap of faith,' says head. Consistently high number of academic, sports, music and all-rounder scholarships. Head puts this down to outstanding teaching and the fact that the children are in a happy environment and so want to learn.

Remarks: Pre-prep is run by the approachable and calm Tracey Chong. All-female staff ('by coincidence') give it a homely air. A brand new pre-prep building has been built bang next door to the main school. Along with abolition of 7+ entry, this unites the two parts of the school and allows the school to offer additional places in reception. 'The teachers at the pre-prep are lovely and smiley and it rubs off on the children,' said one parent.

Classes at the prep are mixed ability, maximum 20 children. Lessons are lively and fast-paced with specialist teachers for PE, art, music and ICT from the start. Separate sciences taught from year 4. Children set for English, French and maths from year 5. Days are long, especially for those who start with the full cooked breakfast on offer at 7.30am.

N

Once the girls leave at the end of year 6, the boys are placed in two mixed ability classes and one small scholarship set; vacancies left by girls are not filled. Greek on offer to potential scholars. Parents love the fact that children get so much individual attention at the top of the school. 'A real strength,' said one. Children are well prepared for 11+, 13+ and scholarships. As the head puts it: 'We are a preparatory school. It's our job to prepare them for the exams for entry to their next schools.' Parents report that a massive amount of coaching goes on in the final years, of which the head is critical. 'It's not necessary. We are all fighting a coaching culture but people get sucked into it.' Head gives out CE results to boys as they sit around a camp fire on the year 8 trip to Wales. 'A lovely touch, and the boys never forget it. It's a gesture typical of the school,' said one parent.

Classrooms are spacious and light, with traditional wooden desks arranged in neat rows. Impressive ICT suite, tablets about to be introduced but head keen this shouldn't be a gimmick. The school enters a huge number of national and international competitions with frequent success. Recently won three World Maths Day trophies, out of a total of five awarded to UK schools. DT department is the envy of other schools and recently assembled a car for the Shell Eco-Marathon that achieved a mileage of 1,000 miles per gallon. Currently a group of senior boys is investigating the effect of tyre pressure on the environment and presentations have been made to MPs.

Plenty of choirs for each year group, new pop choir for year 7/8 boys is thriving. Several hundred individual instrumental and singing lessons take place every week. Lots of bands, ensembles and orchestras. Children have taken part in performances at the Kingston Music Festival and concerts at the Barbican with the London Symphony Orchestra.

Art clubs include weekend activities where parents can become involved. Local artists exhibit and sell their work in the reception area and include a couple of inexpensive pieces so that children can buy a picture if it catches their eye.

Sport is a real strength of the school. Boys play rugby, football and cricket; girls play netball, rounders and hockey. Swimming, cross-country and athletics also on offer and even more sport possible through numerous after-school clubs, including golf at neighbouring club. Main playing fields are five minutes away by minibus; two multi-purpose, all-weather courts and four cricket nets on site. Lots of tournaments and matches mean everyone gets the chance to compete.

Full-time head of SEN. Head believes 'a good learning support culture enhances what you do'. Provision for mild dyslexia, dyspraxia and dyscalculia, though not the place to send a child with severe difficulties.

Many long-serving staff. Head did away with 'teaching' and 'non-teaching' labels when he arrived. 'We're all teaching the children in different ways,' he says. One satisfied parent commented that staff were 'prepared to go the extra mile for the children.' Two gap year students help with sport and a French assistant teaches conversational French.

Parents are typically hard-working professionals. 'The school reflects the local community and lots of the children arrive at school on foot or by scooter,' says head of pre-prep. Active PTA raises substantial funds, half money raised goes to charity, the other half to the school – recently paid for a climbing wall. Activity-based wraparound club from 7.30am to 6pm.

A competitive, purposeful and demanding school which has retained old fashioned values (the pupils call the head 'Sir' and scramble to their feet when an adult enters the room). Pupils are challenged on all fronts and, as one parent put it, 'By the time the children reach year 5, they are under pressure to perform. It's not a soft school but, for the right child, there simply isn't anywhere better in the area.' One mother felt that 'it's not for the retiring child. I think they'd get trampled underfoot.' The head disagrees and feels the school caters for all personalities and abilities as there is so much on offer and so many chances to shine.

Newstead Wood School

Avebury Road, Orpington, Kent BR6 9SA

Pupils: 975 • Ages: 11–18 • Sixth form: 227

Tel: 01689 853626
Email: office@newsteadwood.bromley.sch.uk
Website: www.newsteadwood.bromley.sch.uk

Head: Since 2016, Nicholas Webb BA PGCE, previously deputy head. Degree in chemistry and geology; worked around the world for a variety of gas and oil companies before training as a teacher. Has taught chemistry and physics in a variety of schools.

Academic matters: Not so much an academic hothouse as the sort of place where if you don't work reasonably hard you're the odd one out. School places great emphasis on staff and pupils 'co-constructing' the learning experience and on staff leadership and development – they should be critical questioners and facilitate, rather than direct, learning. An active school parliament and there are both subject and house captains who feed into decision making and who support fellow learners. In addition to termly reports and annual parent teacher meetings, the pastoral team maintains home-school dialogue.

Building learning and thinking skills starts early; problem solving permeates the curriculum. The extended project in the sixth form is designed to promote independent study and breadth of learning. Exam results are consistently impressive, with popular subjects being biology, chemistry, maths, English lit, economics, history and psychology. In 2016, 80 per cent A*/A grades at GCSE. A level results no less creditable: 85 per cent A*-B grades and 56 per cent A*/A grades.

Strong enrichment programme – the usual timetable is effectively suspended for three weeks each year. KS4 students follow an elective option where they choose to study additional non-examined options, or devote time to volunteering or elite sport. Also a designated gifted and talented lead school – these pupils aren't noticeably singled out for special treatment but staff ensure lots to stimulate and push them. Dyspraxic and dyslexic pupils' coping strategies often uncovered during GCSEs. Individual education plans then agreed between pupils, parents and staff to overcome any difficulties with the support of pastoral and SEN team.

Games, options, the arts: 'Whatever they do, they do well,' said one parent and the evidence seems to support this. Good performances in hockey, netball and gymnastics and, though the school has no pool, it tops the results tables in national and county swimming events. Older girls help the youngsters.

The year 7 and 8 vocal ensemble was conceived and is run by sixth formers, one of several choirs and orchestras which perform regularly. Music is a real strength and taken seriously and at tempo here (better make sure you rehearse!); Vox CC, its senior choir, has performed at the Royal Albert Hall and in Prague. Drama is popular; 20+ student societies in anything from debating, politics, history, the environment, medicine to law, all run by year 12 pupils. Leadership and participation is very much what this school is all about and it's rare to find a sixth former who doesn't voluntarily take on extra responsibilities. For others, too, judging by the somewhat overwhelming stream of calendar reminders on the electronic board in reception, little excuse to be idle. Lots of after-school and lunchtime activities, as well as positions as sports ambassadors, Arkwright scholars to promote engineering in schools, language teaching in local primary schools, maths and debating competitions, Dragon's Den workshops and charity events – plenty going on.

Background and atmosphere: Set in a quiet residential area, has wonderful views across the playing fields towards the Downs, but the school buildings, though quite spacious, are unremarkable and jumbled – the 1950s, when it was established, not perhaps the best architectural era. Inside, the walls are brightened with artwork and benefit from the recent redecoration organised by the school's parent-run PET team. Various additions and upgrades; already has wonderful indoor tennis courts open to the public.

Pastoral care, well-being and discipline: Ongoing and slightly half-hearted battles regarding sixth form dress code but in the school's view it's churlish to make too big a fuss when most students behave and perform well. Students are generally not interested in acting beyond their years and the school encourages them to assess for themselves what's appropriate in different circumstances. More commonly issues arise through poor organisation or conflicting priorities, typical amongst bright, enthusiastic pupils.

As long as you are willing to work with the school, issues are normally swiftly resolved in liaison with staff and parents, the emphasis being very much on motivation rather than chastisement. Parents cite examples of a generally good response to concerns voiced, whether individual (friendship) or more general. The school is also alert to mixed expectations relating to academic and home life. In such cases, a counsellor and support teacher are available to provide guidance and support. A strong PSHE programme, which, eg, incorporates financial literacy, in which pupils can gain accreditation. Careers guidance is exceptional (a new Lifetime Achievement Award from Investors in Careers sits alongside their Gold Award). Abundant advice on university applications and longer term career planning. A well-stocked library provides a place to work outside of the classroom or a place for quiet contemplation.

Occasional incidents of bullying are addressed, with the girls themselves tending to side with the victim. Informal vertical contact is encouraged through extracurricular clubs and older pupils acting as mentors. The travel buddy scheme is a nice example, combining as it does environmental targets to reduce car use with accompanying year 7 pupils on public transport their first few weeks. Occasionally girls are to be seen eating and smoking outside the school grounds, but few complaints from local businesses and residents, who seem grateful to have such a well-thought of school in their midst – 'we'd all like our kids to go there'.

Pupils and parents: Said one parent, 'If they're really not up to and up for it, they won't enjoy it' – ie you need to be self-motivated rather than coached to get here. From a range of socio-economic and ethnic backgrounds. 'They stand out for being bright, self-confident and just getting on with it,' said one business regularly offering work experience to pupils from local schools. Both the Providing Excellence Together (PET) and the PA are active and effective, holding a variety of social and fundraising events over the year, as well as organising regular fairs through its careers sub-committee. Notable former pupils include Gemma Chan, Christine Hancock, Emma Johnson (clarinettist who came back to hold a masterclass at the school), Josie Long and Kim Medcalf.

Entrance: Most from local state primary schools. For year 7, entrance tests in verbal and non-verbal reasoning in September. Standards high, but the test experience 'more friendly' than for other local schools. Around 650-700 applications for 160 places. Preference to those who live within nine miles, then children of staff. When, very occasionally, places come available further up the school, those on the waiting list are invited to take an age-appropriate test and the highest scorers offered a place. Additional places are available for sixth form entry – including boys. A minimum of eight GCSE grades A*-B.

Exit: Those entering at 11 are expected to stay the course until 18 and only a few leave at 16, mostly to pursue specialist studies, eg performing arts or media studies. Nine to Oxbridge in 2016, one to US (Michigan), 75 Russell Group, 24 to medical and veterinary colleges. Southampton, London, Warwick, Exeter, Bristol, Nottingham, Durham, Manchester among popular destinations.

Money matters: Dedicated and enthusiastic PET and PA raise £30,000 to £50,000 annually, which funds the artists in residence each year and extra teaching resources. A covenant scheme and continuous fundraising events and activities to support the ongoing developments. Girls raise money for charities during house charity week.

Remarks: Capable and committed girls do really well here, most setting out on their future studies and careers well-qualified and equipped for the challenges ahead.

Newton Prep

149 Battersea Park Road, London SW8 4BX

Pupils: 662 • Ages: 3–13

Fees: £15,840 – £18,150 pa

Tel: 020 7720 4091
Email: registrar@newtonprep.co.uk
Website: www.newtonprepschool.co.uk

Headmistress: Since 2013, Mrs Alison Fleming BA MA (Ed) PGCE (40s), a grammar school girl and theology graduate. Previously head of Dulwich College Junior School for four years, prior to which she was deputy head at Highgate Junior School. A team inspector for the ISI and a governor of a local school. And, far more importantly, an ace head.

Forthright, articulate, warm and confident, Mrs Fleming inherited a large prep in good heart, good nick and with a massive new-build. She spent her first year listening, looking, learning and thinking. And now, subtly but decisively, change (all for the good, as far as we can judge) is on the way. This is summed up by Mrs Fleming's hope of relocating her own study away from the admin corridor to, ideally, somewhere at the core of her capacious school. Her aims are to maintain the school's 'academically ambitious' ethos while developing its parental involvement and community links (which included now defunct Kids' Company). In these aspirations, she appears to carry her own eclectic and inclusive school community with her. But there is far more of sound educational value afoot too.

Warm praise, especially from seasoned parents who have been part of the school under the last three regimes and who particularly value the increased headmagisterial presence around the school. 'She is always smiling and approachable,' we were told. 'She is independent-minded and has lots of ideas,' another enthused. A third said, 'She is fabulous. Really enthusiastic and has a really good combination of strength, warmth, leadership and vision.' We get the impression this is a pretty popular appointment.

Entrance: Oversubscribed at nursery stage when they have 48 places. Application process ensures an even balance of i) boys and girls and ii) of autumn, spring and summer birthdays. There's a waiting list and those who don't get in can reapply for reception. Sibling policy.

Informal assessment the autumn term before entry into reception. 'A gentle process'. Staff observe the children to see how they relate to adults, their peers and the world around them. 'Occasional places' happen occasionally. Year 1 or 2 candidates spend a day in class and take tests in reading, English and maths. Admission at year 3 and above by competitive testing. Any applicant for year 3 is considered for a scholarship (currently worth £250 per term) or a place backed up by a means-tested, top-up bursary. For a school only in its third decade, a surprising amount of financial help available. Most of those admitted at nursery or reception move smoothly up but this isn't guaranteed.

Exit: Leavers' lists are encouraging largely because there is clearly no stereotyped Newton product and they go to a wide spread of schools at both 11 and 13. Good range of scholarships – art, sports, dance and academic – won too. Year 6s to eg Alleyn's, JAGS, Emanuel, Dulwich College, City of London Girls, Sevenoaks, St Paul's Girls and the local GDSTs. Year 8s to similar plus impressive boarding schools (Wycombe Abbey, Wellington, Eton, Harrow, Bedales), Westminster and KCS. New role on the senior management team for a deputy head with responsibility for senior school transfer – a rare, if not unique position amongst prep schools. Watch the others scampering to follow suit!

Remarks: This part of London – behind the power station, which, along with a wide area round about was being comprehensively rebuilt and regenerated at time of our visit – is not generally appealing. To find an enormous, sought-after prep school housed, partly in an Edwardian block of debatable attractiveness and partly in impressive and extensive new build, is unexpected. However, one only has to enter the somewhat alarming steel wire cage that encloses the school to be transported into a very different and disarming world.

First impressions are formed by the children. They are happy, confident, relaxed, articulate, polite and eager to share their school with a visitor. They inhabit delightful spaces. Second impressions come from the place itself. From nursery, through lower school and up to the subject specific classrooms and studios of the top two years, each learning area is well-structured, full of colourful, stimulating and thoughtful displays and staffed by smiley, interesting teachers. We longed to linger – the language rooms ('souriez et entrez!') invite learning, the art rooms are full of creativity and a vast array of creative opportunities, the science labs and IT suites are sleek and the library is simply the best we've seen in a prep anywhere. Worth lingering especially here – exceptionally well-stocked, each child's reading is guided and encouraged and the children find that they have everything they need for research. A real understanding here that books can provide complementary riches, in so many ways, to the internet – which is equally well-used. Sofas, carpets, bean bags and cushions and hundreds of lovely books. Learning and inventiveness hums. We ventured into the RS room and were instantly involved in a fascinating discussion about the compatibility or complementarity of religion and science.

The old building, seamlessly now melded to the new, is old school standard eg green and brown tiles, sensible corridors, parquet. The new build is high, broad, confident with big spaces of the kind you'd expect from a sizeable and prosperous high school. The newest bits are breathtaking for a prep. A splendid auditorium and equally impressive, acoustically perfect, recital hall. Many senior schools would drool. Vast airy dining room with seriously inviting food, eaten by all. Scooter and bike park: 'they really encourage us to bike or walk to school – you get a special badge for it,' we were told. Sports hall, gym and other spaces for muscle stretching. Two art studios full of lovely stuff. We liked especially the monster sculptures – custom-built in some cases ('our librarian really wants a dragon to hang in the library'), the earth-colour tribal shields, the batik, the ceramics, the marionettes.

Outside space is equally enviable – there is so much of it. A huge all-weather pitch and various other good-sized safe-surface areas, well-equipped and colourful – for the different age groups. So sports thrive and, as parents crow, 'it's not exclusive – they have a C team and everyone has a chance'. Most delightful is the 'garden' – tucked away between car park and road but a rus in urbe idyll once you're in, with shady leafy nooks, fruit trees (one was a blackberry tree, we were solemnly informed) plots and beds, all well used by keen gardeners and for lessons of all sorts.

Around eight per cent have some sort of SEN – vast majority mild dyslexia, small numbers with eg ADHD or some speech and language delay in early years. Support is given either on an individual or small group basis by the director of learning development and teaching assistants in classrooms but head acknowledges that there is work to be done on the SEN side which will be welcome to parents current and future. Music too, now, under sparky new head of dept rising to match the stunning new facilities. We anticipate the Newton's impressive lists of art scholarships might well be matched by music similar in coming years.

Packed programme of events to celebrate 25th anniversary in 2016/17, starting with 'mass cake-cutting involving the very first Newton pupil (now a very respectable journalist...)', including whole school sponsored walk round Battersea Park and lots of volunteering by all ages, culminating in 'the first gala performance of our specially commissioned Silver Symphony at our end of year celebration at Cadogan Hall'.

About 20 to a class except for two nursery classes of 24. Pupils from all over south west and central London; locals walk or scoot to school. All speak good English though around 50 (nine per cent)are bilingual eg French, Spanish, Italian, Urdu, Arabic, Russian spoken at home. Small group EAL sessions for those who need them.

Best is the creative and collaborative ethos and the sense of community. Inclusiveness is key as parents testify – 'my children are totally different characters and it's been great for all of them' – and eccentricity is relished. (The history teacher gives WW1 bullet shells as rewards rather than house points.) There is little of the preciousness and snobbery one can occasionally encounter in other preps and the pupils feel part of something bigger than themselves. As they told us: 'Our teachers are so approachable. You can always ask for help'. 'You're not babied by the teachers.' 'There's no fear between the year groups. Year 3s often come and chat to us in year 8.'

A parent summed it up, 'We're going to be really sad to leave.'

Nonsuch High School for Girls

Ewell Road, Cheam, Sutton, Surrey SM3 8AB

Pupils: 1,313 • Ages: 11–18 • Sixth form: 370

Tel: 020 8394 1308
Email: office@nonsuch.sutton.sch.uk
Website: www.nonsuchschool.org

Headteacher: Since September 2016, Ms Amy Cavilla. Studied French and Spanish at Leeds; previously spent 12 years at Tiffin Girls, latterly as deputy head.

Jane Burton is the executive headteacher of the Nonsuch and Wallington Education Trust, which includes Nonsuch High and Wallington High.

Academic matters: Anything these girls do, they do not just well, but very well indeed. Exam results – 83 per cent A*/A grades at GCSE and 87 per cent A*-B (55 per cent A*/A) at A level in 2016 – put them towards the top end of grammar school performance and well into the rarified heights of super-boffin territory. A small number of children (just over one per cent) have learning difficulties, currently spanning physical disabilities and mild dyslexia.

There's some setting (maths from year 8, for example) but many subjects are tutor group based up to the start of GCSEs (girls take a minimum of 10.5). A generous handful will get 12 or 13 straight A*s, many going on to five AS and four A levels. Some complete GCSE maths in year 10.

A science and languages specialist, the school does both proud. Demanding GCSE triple science is taken by nearly all, taught in 11 well-equipped labs with adjacent prep rooms, and vast numbers carry on to A level, 85 doing chemistry alone. Girls study one language in year 7 and then choose two from French, German, Spanish or Latin and, from year 10, GCSE ancient Greek. There's even Mandarin, run as an after-school club for the linguistically adventurous. Lessons can be good fun – European Day of Languages was marked in year 7 by a Eurovision-style contest including 'Baby, hit me one more time' in German – and there are extensive study/work experience opportunities, currently European-based but no reason why, thanks to Skype and well-equipped language labs, girls shouldn't soon be at least chatting on-line to peers in China and elsewhere, believes the school. Arts are also on the up, with drama GCSE performances singled out for praise by exam board.

It's good to see a range of less traditional GCSEs on offer, photography among them (some stunning images in school magazine) and, unusually, astronomy. School has its very own dome, open to local societies, in a secure, passworded building, where budding Sir Patrick Moores troop for their own Sky at Night sessions. Not all the girls are alive to the magic of the constellations, though. 'It's just a telescope in a white dome,' said one, prosaically, when asked if a tour could be arranged.

Inevitably, pupils with a broad range of interests have to make tough decisions at A level, especially would-be scientists and medics. At A level critical thinking and the EPQ are offered. Judged solely by the results, the teaching clearly delivers the goods, and, for sixth formers especially, can be inspirational. 'You really see the passion in the teachers, you've got a different relationship... (The teachers) leave you to do the mundane stuff on your own, then use the lessons to explore the subject,' said one. Staff regularly go on to greater things elsewhere – one of deputy heads promoted to headship at Wallington High School, for example. However, the school is also committed to developing wider skills and is beginning to introduce a curriculum which develops independent learning, teamwork, communications skills and resilience. The culture of the school is shifting to encourage risk taking and to ensure students are prepared for the test of life rather than a life of tests.

Games, options, the arts: Monthly school newsletters invariably feature pupil sporting successes in school and out and there's huge enthusiasm for fiercely-contested inter-house competitions and even (a surprise) a burgeoning cheerleading team. Clubs abound; some, like judo, pilates and aerobics, run by outside firms and paid for, others, like lunchtime cycle club, exploring Nonsuch Park grounds, run by motivated staff (average age early 40s) and all done for love.

Facilities, including tennis/netball courts, playing fields, 400m grass track and floodlit artificial turf pitch, are good, while a deal with a private fitness firm has added a cavernous sports hall, small(ish) changing rooms and, in some parents' eyes, rather limited access (morning lesson time only) to a jewel of an indoor pool. Plans underway to build a new pavilion, all weather pitch, sports dome and running track.

Parents, though realistic about inevitable bias towards academics, feel sport becomes somewhat perfunctory higher up the school. 'If you have a very sporty child, you end up getting your fix elsewhere,' says one, though school fields respectable number of sports alumni.

Arts meanwhile are buzzing (possibly humming, too), with several children selected for national drama and music groups and so many learning instruments (650 and rising) in and out of school that you could staff a symphony orchestra several times over, with spares. With lots of highly regarded productions, recently My Fair Lady and Lawfully (sic) Blonde, house talent shows and a range of ensembles – some, like the flourishing Indian music group, are set up by the pupils – all nine practice rooms are usually busy at break time (forward booking, somewhat inevitably in these highly organised surroundings, is essential).

Add an excellent range of trips to Sorrento, Large Hadron Collider in Cerne, China and Costa Rica together with extensive community service options, and it's almost impossible not to acquire a CV bulging with career-enhancing goodies. Even year 7s compete to design and sell their own fundraising product, while sixth formers run a huge range of clubs and societies in school and at local primaries. CCF is optional (for year 9s upwards) and DofE (all levels) is run in conjuction with local authority.

Background and atmosphere: So quiet that the only thing a visitor hears is the clicking of the friendly PA's heels as she escorts you down grey corridors offset with lots of colourful photography and artwork to the staff loos (and waits outside to escort you back again).

The red-brick buildings, mainly three-storey and geometrically straightforward (though feeling anything but to the first-time visitor) date back to 1938, when the school, named for the next door palace built by Henry VIII, first opened. They're in generally good shape with lots of nice, bright rooms, many refurbished – art is especially appealing with vibrant-looking masks and wire sculptures. New sixth form block with library and study centre under construction.

From the plasma TVs giving regular updates on school events to smart card technology allowing girls timed access to buildings and fingerprint payment for meals, everything resonates with efficiency, though the motion-detecting lights, which can take a while to come on, give winter evening forays up dark staircases a certain adventurous quality. Even the loos have useful notices on the inside of the doors – 'I suppose it gives us something to read,' says a pupil.

The Nonsuch and Wallington Education Trust (NWET) was formed in 2015 and comprises Nonsuch High School for Girls and Wallington High School for Girls.

Pastoral care, well-being and discipline: Behaviour is generally excellent – lapses are so rare that there's a pause while girls struggle to remember what happens, the only recent incident of note being a brief online teacher-baiting episode in 2010, swiftly sorted with suspensions and detentions, and reinforced by new cyber mentors (girls, not robots) trained by CEOP, the on-line protection body, to keep everyone on the straight and narrow virtual road.

As for the rare underachiever – a relative term as they'd be a big success anywhere else – there's lots of help. Form tutors are the first point of contact for most issues and keep a watching brief on academic performance, working with the child and parents to resolve any underlying problems and organise a bit of extra support if required.

Most importantly, girls are extremely supportive of each other, often working and revising together informally, with younger pupils readily approaching older ones for assistance through the house system.

'There's the feeling that everyone wants to help,' says one girl, who agreed, as did others, that knowing their friends were looking out for them takes the edge off the anxiety that all accept as an inevitable, if occasional, fact of life. '"Serve God and be cheerful" is our school motto,' points out a sixth former, 'and that is our ethos.'

Pupils and parents: Parents 'very supportive', thinks school. Come across as a hard to impress bunch – 'ambitious, focused and driven families pushing to get their children in there,' said one mother – who expect the school to deliver against stiff competition from neighbouring girls' grammars, Tiffin Girls in next door Kingston in particular, and are quick to note any slippage in results. Does it matter? To this bunch, very much indeed. Having delivered their side of the bargain – producing bright, motivated daughters – it's up to the school to ensure they fly through exams and straight into Russell Group universities. Some have Oxbridge in their sights when their daughters first arrive. Not that they necessarily leave it up to the school, and novices assuming tutor traumas are behind them once their daughters start here are in for a shock. What one mother describes as a 'significant percentage' carry on having them tutored all the way through, not because they're struggling but to keep them at the top.

The girls, meanwhile, are a nice, modest bunch – braggadocio must be one of the least-used words in extensive vocabulary – and have a genuine and touching pride in each other's achievements. They're delightfully enthusiastic, too, writing reviews in the school newsletter that describe everything from competing in the local music festival and even 'a short geography trip in Cheam Village' as 'exciting,' 'great' and 'fantastic'.

And while they may be lacking in spontaneity, perhaps it's no bad thing, given their likely careers, madcap impetuosity being low on the list of desirable qualities for any budding brain surgeon or atom-splitting scientist.

Ex-pupil Joanna Rowsell won gold in the track cycling in the 2012 Olympics.

Entrance: Hugely over-subscribed (around 1,650 sit the exam) and highly competitive – numerous on-line/local press tutor ads say it all. Early deadlines, so essential to keep track. Selective Eligibility Registration Form, from school, must be in by mid August; first stage of tests in mid-September and second stage at beginning of October. Pass/fail results by end of October, but as more candidates pass than there are places, agony continues until March when offer letters sent out. Up to 10 places available on basis of score to children who have triggered pupil premium, 85 places awarded regardless of location (unless a tie for final place, when proximity is the deciding factor): remaining places go to top-scoring local candidates within catchment area, with 15 places ring-fenced for children who are residents of the London Borough of Sutton. No sibling priority. Waiting list for runners up runs to end of the academic year, then deleted unless parents advise otherwise; very occasional vacancies in other years determined by science, English and maths exams. Unsuccessful 11 plus or mid-term candidates will not be considered again until sixth form.

Limited intake in sixth form requires minimum GCSE average points score of 50, places offered on the basis of predicted grades.

Exit: Around 95 per cent to higher education; sends more girls off to read science subjects than almost any other school in the country. Twelve to Oxbridge in 2016, lots of medics (15 in 2016 plus 10 studying pharmacy) and many budding lawyers. Broad range elsewhere, from psychology, sociology and economics to editorial photography, management and art foundation. KCL and UCL currently most popular destinations.

Remarks: Does well by its seriously bright, highly motivated and caring girls. 'Unus pro omnibus, omnes pro uno' could be its alternative motto. While not necessarily a natural home for the seriously zany, its strengths in performing arts add a welcome swirl of colour to its more sober, science-based accomplishments. There's no getting away from it, however. Elsewhere, girls may just wanna have fun. Here, first and foremost, they wanna do well.

Norland Place School

162–166 Holland Park Avenue, London W11 4UH

Pupils: 240 • Ages: 4–8 (boys), 4–11 (girls)

Fees: £14,370 – £16,782 pa

Tel: 020 7603 9103
Email: office@norlandplace.com
Website: www.norlandplace.com

Headmaster: Since 2002, Patrick Mattar LRAM MA (early 50s). Degrees in music and education management and administration. Educated in Solihull. Came here in 1989, as head of music, straight from the Royal Academy of Music. This was followed by six years at Wetherby, first as director of music then deputy head. Returned here as headmaster in 2002. Married with two teenage sons and laughs that 'parenting does not get any easier!' Wife is director of lower school at Sussex House.

Music is his passion. Performs piano recitals at charity concerts, auctioned off by school. Parents rave about his talent. He admits that practising 'takes up a lot of time but I enjoy it.' Also admits to being a keen cyclist.

Softly spoken, with an infectious laugh. Parents find him approachable, compassionate and hard working. 'A superb head who has given great stability to the school,' enthused one mother. Another commented that 'the school is jolly lucky to have him'.

Entrance: Non-selective at 4 (48 places at this stage, half boys, half girls). Names down as soon as possible after birth; ideally the form will be dropped off at the school on the way home from the maternity ward. Places fill up sharpish. Each month, four definite places are allocated to two boys and two girls, on a first-come, first-served basis, so it helps it your child is born in the first half of the month. Other children placed on waiting list. Head jokes, 'Have your child in December or January when everyone else is too busy thinking about Christmas to register!' Siblings still have to register but get wait list priority and school has 'not yet failed to get a sibling in.' Head sees all parents (but none of the children) who have places in reception to explain the ethos of school. He considers it important that parents share his philosophy. Those with 'definite' places visit in the summer term just over a year before entry, those on the waiting list may be invited in the following autumn or spring term. Short, informal tests in English and maths for occasional places thereafter, as they materialise further up the school (though does not take in another class of girls at 8+ to replace the leaving boys). Head explains, 'We are non-selective but we are very much part of the London academic environment, so parents need to be aware that their child must be able keep up with the pace'. Nursery heads are seen as an invaluable source of advice about whether a child would suit the school and vice versa.

Exit: At 8, boys disperse to a range of schools including Wetherby, Sussex House, St Paul's Juniors, Westminster Under and Fulham Prep. A few head to country boarding preps, such as Caldicott. Girls' destinations, at 11, include Francis Holland (NW1 and SW1), Godolphin & Latymer, Notting Hill and Ealing with a sprinkling to boarding (eg Wycombe Abbey, Downe House). A couple of academic and music scholarships every year.

Head is aware that he is 'operating within a tighter academic belt' and that increased competition for London day places is a reality. School still gets similar numbers into same schools as it always has, 'though perhaps they need to work a little harder across the board to get there,' he smiles. Some parents complain about too much homework in the final years. Tutoring goes on here as elsewhere. Head finds it helpful when parents ask whether coaching is a good idea and encourages open dialogue, rather than secrecy, on this matter. He is conscious of the 11+ pressure but also notes that 'it's incredible how motivated, rather than battle weary, the children are by year 6. Many of the girls are switched on by the whole process and enjoy it.'

Head believes that 'if a child is struggling here, you have to be very careful about where you send them next. Sometimes boarding can accommodate a richer variety of pupils than London day schools.' Gives as much advice as parents want on the next stage but states 'it's always up to the parents at the end of the day.'

Remarks: Founded in 1876. Situated in the heart of noisy Holland Park Avenue in three large town houses, connected by steep stairs and narrow corridors. Bit of a rabbit warren. Not the most spacious of schools but good use is made of the two smallish playgrounds decorated with murals and climbing wall, so children have the chance to let off steam regularly. Staggered break times for practical reasons.

Mainly local families from Notting Hill, Holland Park and Shepherd's Bush. Most walk or come by scooter. Mainly professional families, many of whom are second and third generation Norlanders. Predominantly British, though with significant numbers of bilingual Europeans (Spanish, French and German). Fifty-five currently have EAL requirements, catered for through classroom differentiation and a year one EAL club. Alumnae include George Osborne, Rosalind Franklin and Arthur Bliss.

The school is structured around the fact that the boys scatter at 8 and the girls at 11. For the first three years, pupils are taught in two parallel (but age differentiated) co-ed classes. In year 3, the girls and boys are separated so boys can focus on 8+ exams while girls head down the 11+ route. Effectively, school becomes single sex from start of year 3, though spelling remains co-ed and some mixed classes are re-introduced once the boys' exams are over. Up to 24 per class, down to fewer than 20 in the one remaining class in the final years. 'We purposely allow numbers to fall off a bit in the last three years.' One parent we spoke to wished the school also offered 7+ preparation, but no imminent plans for this.

Parents favour the broad curriculum throughout. Lessons are exciting. Inspired science teaching with emphasis on experiments. Recently, year 4 girls have been busy imagining they were water particles. Specialist teachers for PE, art, music and French (which is introduced from the word go). Latin taught by head, post-exams in year 6. He also teaches reasoning to years 3-6 – 'A great way for me to get to know the children.'

Wide range of academic ability. 'As we're non-selective, we don't have a certain type of child. We love the variety we get.' Setting is fluid and discrete. School favours plenty of differentiation from the start (parents consider the most able to be well stretched and the weaker ones are effectively supported). From year 2, maths and English are divided by ability into separate classes and split lessons continue up to year 6. 'In effect, we are streaming pupils, though not for all lessons. What we are aiming for is very small group teaching.' It works well. Head says, 'I don't want rivalry amongst the children and we don't seem to get that.' Children do not fall by the wayside here, as they can do in larger establishments. Every child is kept on the radar.

All children are screened for dyslexia at the start of year 2, through a computerised test. Twelve currently have mild specific learning difficulties. School does its best to support those who are struggling but concedes the building lay-out is not ideal for those with physical disabilities. Visiting speech and language therapist. Some have one-to-one (at extra cost) or small group support. In lower years, pupils can attend early morning groups for consolidation sessions. Mr Mattar himself has undergone medical training to support a current pupil who requires extra physical help, reflecting the school's consistently caring approach.

No laptops or other devices brought in from home. Small ICT room where computer skills are taught in half classes. Other than researching, homework is not done on the computer. 'Parents support this – they are quite a traditional parent body.' Head is mindful of the fact that senior schools are old-fashioned in terms of entrance exam requirements (cursive handwriting, decent spelling, accurate punctuation and grammar). 'If that changes, we'll change what we do in school too,' he states categorically.

From year 2 upwards, the whole of Thursday afternoon is dedicated to games. Twice weekly PE lessons also taught in the playground or hall, with an emphasis on acquisition of skills. Football and cricket for boys; netball and rounders for girls; swimming for years 2 and 3; tennis, touch rugby and rock climbing. Years 3-6 participate in matches and tournaments with neighbouring schools. Though most children make a team at some point, head thinks it is important that children learn to cope with the harsh reality of team selection. 'It teaches them to persevere and prepares them for disappointment at senior school. We are encouraging, though, and get them to keep trying.' Some parents complain about insufficient sport, especially at the top end of the school, though most believe this has been partly addressed through the wide variety of clubs offered, including 'netball shoot off' and 'catch it' club. Number of clubs per child is restricted to avoid pupils becoming wiped out and to allow adequate downtime at home. Most clubs are run internally, others by external providers (chess, ballet and football).

N

Plentiful opportunities for pupils to play music together, from string and woodwind ensembles to recorder and guitar groups. Sixty-five per cent of pupils learn one or more instruments. Superb ABRSM results, from grades 1-6. Recently, over a quarter gained distinction. Large music room, chock-full of instruments including a set of drums, ready for samba playing on sports day. The whole of year 5 is currently trying to master the ukulele. Copious choirs. The chance of selection is high – 'that's the strength of a small school. Some are disappointed but that's life,' states head.

Art plays a strong part in the school. Large, airy art room. On the day we visited, there were stacks of clay on every surface and an assortment of mini creatures ready for the kiln. Children can try their hands at a rich variety of art, from weaving to screen-printing T-shirts. DT is combined with art in final years.

Abundant opportunities for pupils to take to the stage. Children here learn to conquer any fear of public speaking early on and giving each child confidence is an aim of the school. Younger years perform termly assemblies as well as a nativity play in the local church. A flamboyant musical in year 3 marks the boys' last year in style, as does the large scale performance put on by departing year 6 girls. Plenty of drama lessons and clubs to supplement the extravaganzas.

Parents feel that issues such as bullying are stamped out quickly and effectively. All pupils play together in the playground; 'very inclusive,' according to one parent. Everyone (including head, teachers and pupils), looks after everyone else. A very nurturing place. Without exception, the teachers we met were bubbly and enthusiastic. None has been here more than 10 years, though head believes he has a good number of 'seasoned ones' as well as a more youthful contingent.

Refreshingly, Norland is not afraid to celebrate individual achievements at weekly assemblies and termly prize-giving. Each Friday there is a 'sports person', 'musician' and 'art duck' of the week. Three head girls selected, one per term, in the final year. Ample opportunities for leadership.

Residential trips from year 3 onwards, becoming increasingly far flung as the pupils become more adventurous. All pupils go – no stragglers left behind, as can happen in other schools.

Parents are welcomed into the school and volunteers run library sessions. Head comments, 'The community of the school is a huge thing'. Lots of like-minded families who become close and go off on holiday together. Seemingly, a cohesive group of relatively unpushy parents. Emphasis on fundraising and children are expected to do their bit for charity, including getting their hands dirty. Head feels it is important for them to experience giving back, not just to be aware of it.

Very traditional school (from the berets and boaters to the emphasis on good manners and fair play) but combined with a forward-looking approach. On the day we visited, the school was awash with happy, sparky children who appeared to be thriving in this caring environment. According to one parent, 'the great thing about Norland is that it doesn't dim the flame of learning' through excessive exam focus. No wonder there is a stampede from the maternity ward.

North Bridge House Pre-Preparatory School

Linked with North Bridge House Preparatory School, North Bridge House Senior School

8 Netherhall Gardens, London NW3 5RR

Pupils: 410 • Ages: 2.75–7

Fees: £15,975 pa

Tel: 020 7267 6266
Email: preprep@northbridgehouse.com
Website: www.northbridgehouse.com/nursery

Head: Since 2016, Christine McLelland – who took over as interim head in 2015 following previous head Joanna Hockley's departure due to 'sad personal reasons' after a short tenure. She was previously deputy head of St Nicholas Prep in Kensington, and has taught all classes from reception to year 6 in London schools.

Entrance: Life begins at playgroup level and children are mostly siblings of current pupils. Then the nursery takes around 30 children out of the 120 applicants. Reception, the following year, takes the same number out of a similar number of applicants. Occasional places thereafter, but around 10 children out of 40-odd are taken into year 3.

Criteria are refreshing – first come siblings, then children of former pupils, then families who live closest and finally, those who fit the age bracket the school wants to fill. Makes a point of covering the entire chronological year in any class year group.

That doesn't mean no assessment. All applicants visit and parent and child are interviewed. So the emphasis is more on whether the child – and family – fit the school's ethos rather than on academic potential. The result is a spread of ability, ethnicity and just about everything other than location – most live within three miles of the school, many near enough to walk. Equal split of boys/girls. Runs a good coach service to obvious areas.

Exit: Virtually all move on from the junior school to the prep school in year 3, despite the different location. Those who leave at this stage mostly do so for single sex education.

Remarks: Arrangements can appear somewhat confusing to the uninitiated: the nursery and junior school are housed in two buildings moments from each other in Hampstead. The preparatory school lives off Regent's Park, whilst North Bridge House Senior School amalgamated with the Royal School in Hampstead in 2012 resulting in NBH Senior School moving to the Royal's central Hampstead site. Another NBH senior school, covering years 7-13, opened in Canonbury in 2014.

Life begins in the nursery building – a splendid Victorian house on Fitzjohn's Avenue, used as a nursery school for decades but only acquired by North Bridge in 1989. Classrooms are full of happily absorbed children. We saw year 1s engaged in water play and modelling while the parallel class had a friendly 'show and tell session'. Art was fun – we enjoyed Mondrian-inspired collages on the walls and appreciated the principle that 'everyone's work goes up – not just the best'. It's well-equipped – a music room doubles as an eating room, a good gym/hall for concerts and shows – and does not feel as crowded as some similar schools, though we found some of the rooms uncomfortably hot. Everyone learns French from reception and PE is four days a week. Outside space, again, compares well with comparable schools – some safe surfaces, a lovely wooden play train and caterpillar, with some covered nooks for secret conversations and conspiracies.

The Fitzjohn's site houses the playgroup, nursery and reception. The building on Netherhall Gardens is the main site for the junior school and has the year 1 and 2 classes. This is a quieter corner – a cul de sac overlooking the Finchley Road; the house is a five-storey red-brickery, interestingly sited between the British College of Osteopathic Medicine and the former home of Sidney and Beatrice Webb. It's a corner favoured by independent schools – South Hampstead Junior School is opposite and nearby, Southbank International (also owned by Cognita, the owners of North Bridge) is up the road, and others not more than a rubber's throw away. Efforts are made to stagger drop-offs and pick-ups. From the top of the main building splendid views – over to Harrow-on-the-Hill one way and to the North Downs the other.

As in the nursery building, every inch is covered in displayed work – much to intrigue and delight the eye. Classrooms are occupied by quiet and relaxed children, clearly engaged and interested. Music, French and PE are said to be the school's specialities – everyone learns music and a third or more learn piano, guitar or violin in school; choirs and bands. Outside space is less impressive, though. A marked out chess board and a climbing frame on the tarmac. Sports mostly at the Talacre Centre in Kentish Town. More could be done to make this a livelier area.

A full-time learning support teacher sees around 25 pupils regularly – up to three times a week – for varying types of support. Despite the manner of entry, nothing more than mild dyslexia/dyspraxia surfaces here. All children are monitored twice-yearly to check progress.

Junior and nursery school parents praise the friendliness and welcome they find here and feel what is offered at this level hardly differs from what the overtly academic neighbours do; however, the latest inspection report judged that the quality of education requires improvement.

North Bridge House Preparatory School

Linked with North Bridge House Pre-Preparatory School, North Bridge House Senior School

1 Gloucester Avenue, London NW1 7AB

Pupils: 490 • Ages: 7-13

Fees: £16,290 pa

Tel: 020 7267 6266
Email: prep.reception@northbridgehouse.com
Website: www.northbridgehouse.com/prep

Headteacher: Since 2005, Mr Brodie Bibby BA PGCE MEd (40s). Took his first degree in archaeology and ancient history at Exeter, followed by a PGCE at Roehampton, then taught in state and independent schools, including time at The Banda School, Kenya and as deputy head of Westminster Under School. Still teaches history, drama and games.

Energetic and efficient, he's a man who gets things done, but wants what's done to combine high achievement for all with happy kids protected as much as possible from the early pressure of the modern exam system. Parents rate him highly. 'He's really involved in all areas,' said one, 'and knows and welcomes every parent. You feel he's really proud of the school.' Has recently run the senior school during the previous head's maternity leave, but is now happily back on his own stomping ground, with more room to move around and year 3 now under his wing. His own son and daughter attended the school, always a recommendation.

Entrance: Most come up from pre-prep school. For year 3 entry from outside – around 20 places – assessment in January in English, maths and reasoning. Open mornings held throughout the year.

Exit: Plenty of guidance about appropriate secondary school starting in year 5. 'It's important to be honest with parents and make sure the school is the right fit,' says the head.

Most girls move on at 11 – most to Channing and many to North Bridge Senior in 2016, with a few to Queen's College, City, Francis Holland, South Hampstead and Highgate. Many boys to Mill Hill, with a few to City and UCS and singles to eg Westminster, St Paul's and Merchant Taylors'. Those who wish to continue to one of the North Bridge House senior schools in Hampstead or Canonbury are now more or less guaranteed a smooth passage, though occasionally someone may be asked to look elsewhere. Girls can now stay till 13, if they want to go on to North Bridge House Canonbury or elsewhere.

Remarks: North Bridge, one of the largest stand-alone prep schools in London, opened in 1939 in St John's Wood and is now part of the growing stable of schools run by the Cognita group. It is a school that has undoubtedly benefited from the recent relocation of its senior school to a new home. Now years 3 to 8 are grouped together on the same site, with considerably more elbow room.

Formerly a convent chapel, then a Japanese school, the site has gradually been updated to provide a spacious welcoming reception and good playground space. Still a bit of a rabbit warren (younger children are carefully guided round), but some impressive features, such as the lofty pillared and gilded assembly hall, two newly equipped science labs and music rooms.

Teaching – by friendly, well-qualified staff in classes of 20+ – is lively and fun, with the national curriculum followed in the early years, then stretched well beyond later on. 'My son is looked after really well,' said one mother. 'His teachers completely understand his strengths and weaknesses and seem to catch his imagination.' Pupils' progress is meticulously tracked on a database. Specialist subject teaching in ICT, French, music and games. French, taught by native speakers, from reception; Spanish added in years 3, 4 and 5; Latin and Greek from year 6. Plenty of 'professional development,' too, so teachers are kept on their toes. Classroom style is relaxed but orderly.

Children with special needs are given group work in class plus one-to-one attention outside if necessary. In years 3, 4 and 5, teachers are supported by assistants who help out with reading and group activities.

Girl-boy balance kept as even as possible in the younger years then in year 6 boys are hived off into a separate all-boys prep on the top floor to prepare for common entrance. The school prides itself on its support for those taking 11+ and 13+ entrance tests. 'The exams can be quite ruthless and it's important pupils feel good about themselves,' says the head.

Strong emphasis on art, music, drama and sport. The art room (home to art club and regular exhibitions) has now been freed up for use by all pupils. Music – with an orchestra, a number of choirs and plenty of informal concerts – is vibrant. Annual school play (recently The Pied Piper) attracts enthusiastic auditioning. Sport, played twice a week, offers a good choice for both boys and girls (kayaking, rock climbing, basketball, dance and table tennis in addition to the standard fare) and regular matches against other local schools. Two well-equipped playgrounds and afternoon break in the open spaces of Regent's Park, just across the road. The school is non-denominational, but pupils receive education in all major faiths.

Exciting range of out-of-class activities (at lunch and after-school) includes flamenco, yoga and cookery, as well as arts, sport and drama. Chess particularly popular, with a coach training potential grandmasters for national competition. Reorganisation has allowed space for a purpose-built library, with bean bags, newspapers and library lessons. Plenty of trips, including abroad (Rouen, Vienna). Energetic charitable involvement (recent fundraisers include a Readathon and cross-country run). Lunch, featuring traditional favourites like fish and chips and jelly with ice cream, is served in the assembly hall and eaten alongside the teachers.

Excellent communication with parents, with an informative handbook distributed at annual info evening and email access to teachers. 'They send you an email if they have any concerns and you can email them with anything that worries you.' Pastoral care, too, comes in for high praise. 'Problems are picked up immediately and dealt with sensibly and sensitively,' said one parent, whose daughter had experienced some low-level bullying.

Families live fairly locally (mainly Hampstead, Islington and Queen's Park), but are metropolitan and cosmopolitan (Russian, American, Chinese, Japanese, African), often in the arts and media. The approach certainly appeals to those who might find other local schools too formal. 'I like it because it's unpretentious,' said one father of three. 'It doesn't take itself too seriously.'

A successful school (which received 'outstanding' in every category in its last Ofsted report), but also a happy and friendly place which seems to find room for everyone to thrive. 'We get very good results, but we don't want to pressure someone into getting into a school. We let children be children,' says the head. A philosophy which clearly works. 'I really like coming to school in the morning,' said one girl in her final year.

N

North Bridge House Senior School

Linked with North Bridge House Pre-Preparatory School, North Bridge House Preparatory School

65 Rosslyn Hill, London NW3 5UD

Pupils: 330 • Ages: 11–16

Fees: £16,350 pa

Tel: 020 7267 6266
Email: seniorschool@northbridgehouse.com
Website: www.northbridgehouse.com/hampstead-senior-school

Head: Since 2013, Georgina Masefield BA MA PGCE (40s). Australian by birth, Mrs Masefield grew up in north London, where she attended Channing School. Then to UCL to do a BA in English literature and linguistics, followed by an MA in medieval literature. She also holds a PGCE and a masters of education from Buckingham University (where she has worked as a mentor and tutor). Started at North Bridge in 1998 as a supply teacher, moving quickly up the ranks from form teacher and head of art to head of English in the senior school. 'She's a fantastic teacher,' said one former pupil. 'Everyone she taught used to get A*.' In 2010, she left (temporarily) to become an adviser and then education officer for the school's owners, Cognita, helping to develop curriculum and standards across the group. ('I loved it, but in the end, I felt I wanted to shape and drive my own school.') Remains passionate about teaching. 'I still observe lessons, sitting where the children sit and doing the activities.' Glamorous and ebullient, she's also clearly effective, and the rate of change since she took over has been rapid and decisive. Married to an archaeologist, she has one son at university.

Academic matters: North Bridge Senior has never been (and has no desire to become) a hothouse, but there's definitely a sense that academic outcome has now been put higher up the agenda (with a considerable exodus of old staff and influx of new). In 2016, 90 per cent of pupils achieved 5+ A*-C grades at GCSE including maths and English, with 42 per cent of grades A*/A. Don't be surprised, however, if these statistics improve in the coming years. 'We're very keen to retain diversity,' says the head, 'but we also want pupils to leave with the best possible grades.' (Some parents feel the shift is entirely positive, 'She's really pushing the school in the right direction'; others are less convinced, 'I preferred it when it was a bit quirkier.')

Since taking over, Mrs Masefield has made a number of significant alterations, introducing specialist subject teaching in year 7 and increasing the academic content. All pupils take nine GCSEs, including English lang and lit, maths, double or triple science (about half do triple) a social science (history or geography) and a modern foreign language (those with dyslexia can be absolved). French from year 7, German and Spanish in year 8. Latin now compulsory in year 7 ('It's not only helpful for understanding English linguistics, but useful in terms of developing modern language skills,' says the head). A rich GCSE offering beyond the core includes textiles, photography, media studies, food technology, art, music, classical civilisation and (newly added) computer programming to complement the existing offering of IT.

North Bridge has always done well by those with mild learning difficulties, and about 10 per cent of pupils here need some sort of support (usually able dyslexics and dyspraxics). Lovely, large, bright dedicated room (with its own sofa), overseen by a full-time SENCo and a medley of part-timers (all with specialist dyslexia qualifications). 'There's no stigma attached to special needs here,' says the head of learning support. 'Children want to come.' Regular assessment for all and informal support with study skills, revision techniques and exam strategies available at break and after school on a drop-in basis. The school also has a lift, and can provide additional support for those with English as a second language.

Games, options, the arts: Always a creative place, particularly in the visual arts and drama, the new building has extended the range, with well-designed, dedicated space for textiles, ceramics and DT, as well as a new media suite (fully equipped with Macs), dark room and de-luxe food technology department.

Music teaching provided entirely in-house, with more music in the curriculum and a carousel of additional opportunities. Compulsory choir in year 7, musical theatre in year 8 and plenty of performance, including Battle of the Bands and clubs for close harmony singing, grade 5 theory and jazz.

For a small school, a very decent amount of sport, with a multitude of teams and access for everyone. Pupils already participate regularly in out-of-school competitions and sports trips and the new sports hall and newly landscaped grounds (with market garden and netball court) have undoubtedly improved on-site possibilities.

Perhaps the most popular innovation is the enrichment programme, a weekly 50-minute slot embedding in the timetable activities generally considered add-ons. 'If extracurricular activities just take place in clubs,' says the head, 'they tend to fall off the radar.' Now the whole school mingles in a choice of 26 varieties (changed termly), encompassing a broad and imaginative sweep, from archaeology and cheerobics to origami and animation.

Background and atmosphere: First established as a junior school in 1939, the senior school was set up in 1987. In 2004, the entire outfit (junior school, prep, and senior school) was bought by Cognita. The group runs 64 schools across three continents, but encourages each to retain its founding ethos. 'Here, it's to celebrate the individual in a caring way, to offer a wide breath of experience, to aim high and push pupils a little bit further so they exceed their potential,' says Mrs Masefield. North Bridge is Cognita's flagship and the association comes with undoubted benefits – centralised services and long-term planning – but some feel it's also accompanied by just a whiff of the corporate.

In 2012, the senior school separated physically from the prep school, moving out of the cramped site in Camden Town to take over the premises (and pupils) of the Royal School in Hampstead. The 60s building has now been entirely refurbished, combining all the positives of the era (acres of windows, light and spacious classrooms, outstanding views) with all mod cons. Comfortable, well-stocked library, with enthusiastic librarian who arranges tantalising displays of 'banned books' and interesting guest speakers. Delicious food (freshly baked bread, minted pea and quinoa soup, vegetarian option) provided by outside caterers. Free inter-school shuttle bus aids parents needing to pick up from the prep or pre-prep, plus a reasonably priced school coach taking in a broad sweep of north London.

Pastoral care, well-being and discipline: School prides itself on its family atmosphere and this, all agree, is one of its chief strengths. 'Kids really look out for one another,' said one happy parent. 'What I love about the school,' says another, 'is the way that everyone from the oldest to the youngest gets on. There's a real sense of camaraderie'. Others are upbeat about the individual, confidence-boosting attention. 'My son came home from a residential trip declaring, "Now, I'm not afraid of anything any more." He's really flourished at the school.'

Transition to secondary carefully managed, with the entire year contained on one floor and newcomers linked with year 11 'buddies'. Twice daily form periods make sure no pastoral (or disciplinary) issue is overlooked and head holds weekly open house ('Masefield Mondays') when pupils can come and 'tell me anything'.

An unpretentious and civilised place, where good behaviour and good manners are paramount. 'This is a nurturing school, but we have clear expectations and firm boundaries,' says the head. (The latter are now being made more explicit, with detention for uniform lapses, for example). Usual disciplinary ladder, starting out with discussion in form time. Good behaviour and achievement acknowledged by 'head's tea' and activities like ice skating and bowling.

New World of Work initiative, targeted at year 10, has upped the careers offering. Older pupils now do a week of work experience and gain a wider understanding of a range of professions (from local government officials to astronauts) through weekly speakers interviewed by the head or groups of students.

Three houses compete throughout the year (in maths, poetry and cake baking, amongst other activities), with winners rewarded with a trip. All of year 10 invited to apply for positions of leadership and responsibility. Prefects, house captains and head boy and girl appointed in year 11. Student voice throughout loud and clear. 'We want children to run things.'

Pupils and parents: Families generally local, many within walking distance, then trickling out to Highgate, Muswell Hill, Finchley. A few from further afield. Quite a cosmopolitan bunch, often less intensely exam focused than parents elsewhere in north London. 'They want a happy, stimulating, wide-ranging education for their children that won't turn them into nervous wrecks,' says the head. Pupils are often those who flourish in a more intimate, less pressured environment. 'When we looked at some of the bigger secondary school options, my son just hated the idea of them,' said one parent.

Entrance: Entrance is selective, but not unduly so. ('Pupils are admitted who are performing at or above the national average'). At 11+, considerable numbers from the state sector. Apply one year prior to entry, with a (flexible) closing date in December of year 6. A number of assessment days held in the spring, with applicants invited in in groups of about 20 for a two-hour assessment in English, maths and an informal interview with the head or deputy. 'It's quite relaxed. We want to find out how much they know and whether they'll fit in here and do well.' Those with 'scholarship potential' invited back to sit further papers or demonstrate skills in sport, music, art or drama. School does its best to balance the girl-boy mix, but still tilted 60:40 in favour of boys. Pupils at North Bridge House prep guaranteed entry at 11, but not at 13 (though they still get priority). Siblings, too, are favoured.

Exit: All leave after GCSEs, with plenty of advice and preparation (including interview practice) from year 10. Significant numbers to Camden School for Girls, Highgate, UCS, City, as well as to a range of sixth form and tutorial colleges (eg Woodhouse, DLD). Can now transfer to the North Bridge senior school in Canonbury.

Money matters: Range of scholarships, academic, creative (art, music, performing arts) and sport. Limited number of bursaries, but schools does its best to support existing parents.

Remarks: An inclusive, nurturing school, which gets the best out of many children who would struggle in a larger pond.

North Ealing Primary School

180

Pitshanger Lane, Ealing, London W5 1RP

Pupils: 721 • Ages: 3–11

Tel: 020 8997 2653
Email: admin@northealing.ealing.sch.uk
Website: www.northealingprimary.co.uk

Head: Since 2014, Sally Flowers, previously deputy head. She joined the school as assistant head in 2011.

Entrance: Wider catchment area now due to three form entry but pupils still need to live within a mile of the school to get a place.

Exit: Majority go to Brentside High, a few others to Drayton Manor, Ellen Wilkinson, Twyford and Cardinal Wiseman. A handful each year to grammar schools. One third go private – St Augustine's, Latymer, St Benedict's, Notting Hill and Ealing and John Lyon.

Remarks: Hidden away behind the main road, the sunflowers and flower tubs welcomed us in as we walked across the playground to the school entrance. The school is divided into three main areas. Reception and nursery classes are housed in a bright and airy modern building at the back of the site where outdoor classrooms are covered for use in all weathers, allowing free flow back and forth. 'The children are so lucky to have a new building and they love being able to explore inside and outside,' enthused one parent.

Years 1 and 2 are in equally bright classrooms and at the end of their corridor is a dedicated music room. There is also a hall where we observed new reception children doing a movement class. 'Bend knees!'

Children are also separated at play time: nursery, reception and year 1 all have their own separate playgrounds. Years 2, 3 and 4 have the back playground and years 5 and 6 are at the front. The school even has its own garden which backs on to Pitshanger park.

Years 5 and 6 are housed in the old part of the school (100 year old Victorian building). Classes here a bit cramped but bright wall displays, eg a display about the local Brentham estate in Victorian times, make them feel welcoming and warm.

Key stage 2 children are set for maths and we observed an able maths group being taught in the library, preparing for the Primary Maths Challenge. Around a third of year 6 students achieve level 6 in their maths Sats and results in reading and writing are among the best in the borough. 'We saw a great improvement in our reading levels after we introduced guided reading,' explained the deputy head.

Music and drama are particularly strong, with the school choir taking part in local music festivals. Children can learn the recorder in key stage 2 and there is also the opportunity to study the violin, cello or guitar. Each year the head directs the year 6 production; last year it was Bugsy Malone. 'The standard of the drama is really high, thanks to the head's passion for theatre,' explained one parent.

Sports are also very high profile, with a glass cabinet bulging with cups in the school reception. Netball, football and all the usual sports teams win prizes each year. There are numerous sports clubs before and after school most days.

Very active PTA organises regular quiz nights etc. 'As well as raising money, these events are a great way to meet other parents.'

Hot dinners are cooked on the premises – half the children have school dinners and half bring packed lunches. The school has a healthy eating policy – no sweets or chocolates are allowed in children's lunch boxes. 'We don't check the staff room, though,' quipped the deputy head. Senior staff are on duty at lunch time and there's a staggered system so that no one has to wait too long. There is also a tidy classroom competition each week where the school cleaners choose the tidiest class and their prize is to go first at lunch.

All the usual EAL, SEN and inclusion provision. Anti-bullying guidelines are adhered to and there is a buddy system where older pupils support younger pupils. Former pupils include Peter Crouch and Honor Blackman.

A very friendly and welcoming local school that achieves excellent results.

North London Collegiate Junior School

Linked with North London Collegiate School

181

Canons, Canons Drive, Edgware HA8 7RJ

Pupils: 316 • Ages: 4–11

Fees: £16,110 pa

Tel: 020 8952 1276
Email: office@nlcs.org.uk
Website: www.nlcs.org.uk

Head of Junior School: Since 2003, Mrs Jo Newman BEd (50s). An old girl of North London, Mrs Newman read geography and education at Homerton College, Cambridge. After leaving, she dabbled briefly with the idea of retail – 'I love people and I think I would have been equally happy in a number of jobs' – before starting her teaching career at Haberdashers' Aske's Boys' Prep. Deputy head of the NLCS First School, then moved briefly to Spain for her husband's work. On her return, spent three years as head of Channing Junior School. Warm, can-do sort of person, excellent at team building (her last three director of studies have moved on to headships elsewhere) and involving others. Cares passionately about education (part of a recent sabbatical was spent visiting schools in New York) and those in her charge. 'She knows every girl well,' said one mother, 'and really fights for their happiness.' Married to an accountant, with two adult daughters (both of whom attended the school), she spends off-duty moments cooking, visiting the theatre and walking.

Entrance: Some 250 try for 40 places at 4. A first edit establishes whether children have good basic 'pre-school' skills (such as holding a pencil and being able to use it) and takes numbers down to 90. A second evaluates 'learning, listening and following'. 'They look at pictures, play games, engage in conversation.' Reading and writing definitely not required. 'They will not be asked,' says the head firmly. Children assessed carefully in relation to those of the same age. ('There's rarely a month's difference in their assessment groups.') Much time spent, too, working with nurseries to encourage applications. An early refusal does not mean don't ask again. 'We try to get across to parents that, if a child is not ready at 4, please bring them back at 7.' At that point, a further 8-10 places, with about 127 applicants, again assessed in two rounds. 'We want to know what they can do, not what they can't; we'd rather they spelt "enormous" wrong than "big" right.' Also assessments for occasional places for those already registered.

Exit: Virtually all to the senior school. ('We're aiming to provide an all-through education and the expectation is that girls will move up to the senior school.') All sit the entrance test, however: 'Our research shows that it gives them confidence they're as good as those coming from outside.' For one or two this might not be the right route, and parents are advised well in advance. 'The art is to make the right decision for each girl.' Some girls leave to board, a trickle to leading state schools, such as Henrietta Barnett and Watford Grammar School for Girls, but no cramming for entrance tests. 'We prepare them for secondary education not for 11+,' says the head. 'Our aim is to instil a love of learning and a breadth of opportunity.'

Remarks: North London is, as it always has been, an unashamedly academic school, whose aim is 'to enable girls to recognise academic excellence and realise that it's attainable'. This is achieved through outstanding teaching and a holistic approach to learning, not by hot competition. Here the goal is always 'personal best' rather than 'beat your neighbour'.

National curriculum followed throughout, but work often goes well beyond and around it. (In years 2 and 3, for example, girls learn to play chess.) Classes throughout primarily taught by a form teacher, with specialist subject teaching introduced early on. Senior school staff ease final year girls into their prospective home, though the junior school also has its own subject specialists. A medley of foreign languages on offer (Spanish in year 3, German in year 4, Mandarin in year 5, French in year 6) as an introduction to the senior school range.

'Learning habits' (flexibility of mind, empathy, collaboration, resilience, reflectiveness, good judgement, self-assurance, curiosity, focus, risk-taking, persistence, initiative, originality) introduced early and made explicit. Year 6 guides on our trip were fully genned up on the terminology, pointing out their 6-year-old peers in full creative flow ('We're making pop-up sea creatures,' said one year 1. 'It's very creative and very fun,' glossed an older girl).

Homework from the off, with reading and spelling in reception and year 1. Older girls get about 40 minutes. 'It's not all work, work, work,' said one. 'You don't feel scared or embarrassed if you can't finish.'

Two school libraries, clearly much-loved habitats. Golden Book Oscars awarded for best author, etc, with teachers striding the literary red carpet dressed as Voldemort and other fictional stars. Prominently displayed list of 50 Books to Read Before You Leave Junior School ('I've read 47,' confided one year 6), with 'more mature' literature for the eldest.

Special needs carefully monitored. 'We look out for obvious signs in assessment,' says the head. 'We're very attuned to early identification.' Strong in-school support, led by a SENCo, for those with dyspraxia, etc. 'Every case has a conference.' The site itself works well for those facing physical challenges, and the school has, when required, incorporated additional aids, such as a hearing loop.

Extracurricular – 'the hidden curriculum' – very much the bedrock of a North London education, whatever your age or stage, and girls here are active and energetic participants, whether in the latest theatrical production or music competition. A multitude of after-school clubs (with late transport on offer) ranges from cookery to bridge, and many take a range of three or four activities each week.

Drama important, with an annual play for each year group and a major year 6 extravaganza. 'It feels like a professional play,' said one, 'with costumes and make up.' Over 90 per cent learn one or more musical instruments, with plenty of performance opportunities. (Two all-comers' choirs, plus an auditioned year 5/6/7 choir competing on the international stage.) Games three time a week, plus swimming lessons, plus after-school sports club, plus school teams. 'Squads are very exciting,' said one girl (and perform well against other schools).

Like its senior counterpart, the junior school was founded by the formidable Frances Mary Buss, one of the Victorian era's most dynamic crusaders for women's education. The school originated in Camden Town, but, in 1929, purchased Canons, the former home of the Duke of Chandos. The First School (reception to year 2) opened in 1993. Today, the junior school is housed in its own building, in two separate parts, one for the First School (with its own hall, library, adventure playground and playhouse); the other for years 3-6 (with a science lab, ICT suite and art studio). Girls also make use of the large, leafy grounds, senior school's excellent sports facilities (including pool) and dining hall.

Older girls poised, purposeful and articulate. An encounter with representatives of the junior school council demonstrated school democracy in action. Their aim: 'to improve the school'; their achievements: the introduction of an adventure playground, a bird feeder, a poetry competition (with a cup) and a raffle (with the prize of shadowing the head for a day). Sadly, a motion to supply sushi at lunch fell by the wayside.

Classroom teachers take responsibility for pastoral care, with a not-many-rules policy that stems from the founder. Discipline not really a significant issue. 'No one gets in trouble,' said one girl. 'If we do something wrong, we apologise.' Occasionally, there might be 'a warning' (for 'saying a rude word'), even more rarely parents are notified and the miscreant misses break.

More problematic issues dealt with sensitively, aided by a school counsellor and good communication with parents. 'We don't want little problems to become big problems,' says the head. She herself is very involved, with an 'open-door' policy. Parents kept well informed, with a regular curriculum newsletter, home-school diary ('Today x lost a tooth,' read one, the tooth itself carefully enclosed) and plenty of information evenings. 'Parents can be anxious, and we want to make them feel comfortable.' Parents themselves very proactive: 'All you have to do is mention an exhibition and they trot off to the museum.'

The school runs an extensive coach service importing girls from a large swathe of north and west London and Hertfordshire. Families – from all over the world – often have both parents working (so supervised breakfast and after-school care a godsend.)

A stimulating education, provided in an idyllic setting, producing articulate, confident, enthusiastic girls.

N

North London Collegiate School

Linked with North London Collegiate Junior School

Canons, Canons Drive, Edgware HA8 7RJ

Pupils: 1,027 • Ages: 11–18 • Sixth form: 240

Fees: £19,062 pa

Tel: 020 8952 0912
Email: office@nlcs.org.uk
Website: www.nlcs.org.uk

Headmistress: Since 1997, Bernice McCabe BA MBA FRSA (60s). Mrs McCabe grew up in Bristol, where she was educated at Clifton High School ('What I loved about my school was that it showed me the possibility I could do anything; it was very much modelled on North London') and Bristol University, where she studied English. Taught at a number of co-ed comprehensives in Bristol and London, including The Heathland School in Hounslow, before becoming head of high-flying girls' grammar Chelmsford County High. While here, she took an MBA because she found 'the broader aspects of education leadership' appealing. Her priority, however, now as always, is the quality of teaching. 'The children here are passionate about their subjects because the teachers are also passionate.' She herself continues to take all year 7 for English ('It gives you a fighting chance of knowing everyone') and invites a shifting kaleidoscope of girls weekly to cakes and conversation in her comfortable study. Younger girls are slightly in awe; sixth formers completely at their ease.

Went into teaching because she wanted 'to make a difference', and outside North London has been an energetic participant in the national and international education landscape. A member of the National Curriculum Review Advisory Committee since 2010, in 2013 she was appointed an expert adviser for the London Schools Excellence Fund. She also co-directs The Prince's Teaching Institute. Despite this demanding co-curricular schedule, she tries to limit her time on committees. 'The school is my number one priority; it's the most amazing, affirming place to be head of.'

Undoubtedly one of the UK's most glamorous heads, as noted for her fashionable dress sense as her shifting shades of nail varnish, Mrs McCabe may be softly spoken and stylish, but her priorities are clear sighted and she leads a school with the highest aspirations for both girls and staff. Down time (how does she find any?) is spent at the gym, the cinema, painting and gardening.

Standing down as headmistress in August 2017 to become director of international schools and educational strategy in NLCS Enterprises (NLCS Dubai opens in September 2017 to complement NLCS Jeju). She is spending more time working with NLCS Enterprises over the 2016/17 year, whilst the senior deputy head, as head of school, oversees the day to day running of the school.

N

Her successor from January 2018 will be Sarah Clarke MA (40s), currently head of The Queen's School, Chester. Read history and classics at Newnham College, Cambridge. Previously deputy head at Wellingborough School in Northamptonshire. Married to a history lecturer, with two teenage children. Avid supporter of Chelsea FC and loves to cycle, paint and write fiction.

Academic matters: North London provides an unashamedly ambitious, academic education, consistently sitting in the top five schools nationally in terms of its exams results. In the sixth form, it is one of the rare London schools to offer both the IB and a mixture of A levels and Pre-Us. Virtually all pupils do outstandingly well in all exams. (In 2016, 86 per cent of A levels were graded A* or A; average IB score, 41, with five getting 45 points. Similarly superhuman outcome at GCSE, with 98 per cent A* or A.) The head puts this down primarily to the quality of the teaching: 'We don't teach to the test, we work well beyond it.' Parents agree teaching is 'inspirational'. 'The staff remain stable but are never allowed to get stale.' Girls are expected to (and do) work very hard, with plenty of homework from the off. 'You work as hard as you need to or want to,' said one recent arrival. Research skills are carefully nurtured and girls learn how to address their workload in a disciplined and organised manner.

Post-GCSE, English, history, physics and maths are notably popular. ('No gender bias! Hurrah!' commented one parent.) Modern languages (six on offer including Mandarin, Russian and Italian) and classics are unusually strong, with Latin for all in years 7-9. Traditionally, many took five AS levels, with many keeping a balance of arts and science, but the new A level regime will reduce this to four, with any slack addressed by 'an independent research essay'. Parents praise the school's flexibility in meeting individual interests, particularly in the sixth form. 'There's no pick-one-from-column-A procedure,' said one father. 'They don't mind if only one girl opts for a subject. They're willing to give one-to-one teaching if necessary.' Girls are free to choose what really interests them. 'They'll only query something if they feel a girl is being pushed by her parents or considering a subject which would put her out of contention for certain degrees.' Equally, however, they won't micro-manage any downside once choices have been made. 'No one told us our daughter wasn't very good at history and much better at English, which she was doing as a fifth AS level. We had to fight for her to be allowed to change.'

About 40 pupils have some kind of learning support. All receive an 'individual education plan', with students seen by a SENCo without losing lesson time. Despite its extensive and complex site, the school is also happy to cope with physical disabilities – 'as long as the pupil can communicate and access the curriculum' – working with parents to ensure the right support is in place.

Games, options, the arts: You could never be bored here, though you might end up exhausted. Every possible interest is catered for, from philosophy to animal welfare. Last year, pupils had a choice of 40 clubs and societies, 30 overseas trips and 30 concerts and productions. Actors to the Edinburgh Fringe, musical groups to Tuscany, and eager proto-journalists produced enough journals and publications (50 this year) to stock a newsagent, on topics as diverse as economics to Ebola – not to forget the cutting edge Wintour, named after celebrated old girl Anna Wintour, editor of American Vogue. 'We feel it's the extracurricular involvement which helps produce the academic success,' says the head. 'There's something for everyone, something to capture the imagination.' Activities for senior girls take place after school, those for younger ones in the lunch hour. Finding time can still prove a problem. 'Sometimes it's hard to fit it all in,' said a year 8 girl. 'You have to decide.' No doubt, all part of the learning process.

Lacrosse is the dominant sport, though plenty of choice, too, for those not unduly captivated by fresh air and outdoor competition, with a fitness suite, trampolining and dance in a smart new dance 'space'. Well-used and buzzing art department, packed with enthusiasts and a range of high-quality work.

Extensive range of enrichment activities (Duke of Edinburgh, Model United Nations, debating, Young Enterprise) help develop public-speaking skills and an appreciation of the world elsewhere. The school has a strong international perspective and offers exchange programmes with schools in the USA, Australia and Germany. In 2011, North London opened an overseas campus in South Korea, NLCS Jeju, and students have the opportunity to visit the campus and do internships here. Charity also firmly emphasised, including raising money for and teaching at a school in Zambia and visiting a local school for severely disabled children.

Background and atmosphere: Founded in Camden Town in1850 by the formidable Frances Mary Buss, a highly effective crusader in the cause of education for women. (She also established Camden School for Girls, with whom North London continues to share a Founder's Day.) The school bought its current spacious, 30-acre semi-rural site in 1929 to use as a sports ground, and relocated here fully in 1940. The estate formerly belonged to the 1st Duke of Chandos and, during his time, Handel was composer in residence. The central core of the building is a country house of 1760, now joined by a multitude of varied later additions. Pupils appreciate their attractive surroundings. 'It's so beautiful,' said one. 'When I first came here, I was blown away by the grounds.'

The atmosphere is calm, orderly, and purposeful, and most find it an enjoyable place to be. A recent arrival from the junior school, when asked if she'd thought about alternatives, said, 'I stayed here, because I couldn't see a fault with the school.' Some parents, however, find it quite protective (a good thing or bad, depending on your perspective).

Though the school is academic and fast-paced, it's not pushy. There are no academic rankings or prizes below the sixth form, for example. That said, a girl who doesn't tick along at the same speed could be less content. 'The academic stuff is just baseline,' said one parent. 'They're expected to get involved in clubs, societies, music, sport and community service.' Some also feel that a girl who needs plenty of validation or isn't super confident may occasionally feel swamped. 'I do know people who have pulled their daughter out, though it's usually more about the parents wanting their girls to be top in everything, which is just not going to happen at NLCS.'

Long list of illustrious old girls includes: Judith Weir, Stella Gibbons, Susie Orbach, Marie Stopes, Stevie Smith, Myfanwy Piper, Dame Helen Gardner, Gillian Tett.

Pastoral care, well-being and discipline: Girls here are generally industrious and motivated and heavyweight disciplinary issues are rare. 'I can count on the fingers of one hand the number of girls I've had to see about a serious matter in my study,' says the head. Her general approach can be summarized as: 'give girls plenty of freedom, make them engaged and feel valued'; purpose and focus will then follow. It undoubtedly seems to work, and even the youngest here appear remarkably poised and mature.

This is very much an education preparing girls for life as well as exams. The head feels that single-sex education gives them the freedom and security to experiment and develop confidence. Career aspirations are set high and reinforced with photographs of high-flying former pupils ornamenting the corridor walls. 'Our old girls often work in environments of domineering boys from public schools and hold their own,' says the head. 'The school helps give them the courage to do that.' An active alumnae office furthers access to a valuable network. Student voice here is important and heard, with a school council and elected prefects – 'the Big 6' – who play a significant role.

Brown and blue uniform for younger girls, sixth formers can do their own things (big shawls this year's 'look'). Most appear stylish and smart, with few fashion extremes.

Pupils and parents: Mainly cosmopolitan, ambitious, middle-class professionals, many of whom run their own business or work in financial services. Girls come from every conceivable ethnic background (over 50 languages spoken at home), but an increasing number of Europeans (French, Dutch, Russian) and Americans, as well as the traditional high percentage of Asian and Jewish families. An extensive coach service, with long arms stretching out north, south, east and west, makes this a far from 'local' school. 'The girls reflect the demographic of London,' said one mother.

Entrance: At 11, 65 places for external applicants (joining 40 or so coming up from the junior school). Apply between June and November of the year before entry, with exams in English and maths in January of the year of entry. About 600 apply, with about 200 interviewed. 'We're looking for teachability and girls who will thrive and flourish with the pace of life here,' says the head. 'We want flair and interests, a decent vocabulary and logical ability.' Excellent at establishing whether these qualities exist. 'The interview process is very good,' said one parent. 'It's rare for someone to slip in who isn't suited.' About 20 extra places available at sixth form. Apply between July and November of the year before entry, with tests in four subjects. Occasional places awarded throughout to fill any vacancies, when those already registered will sit appropriate exams.

Exit: Once girls are in, the expectation is that 'we see them all the way through'. A handful move on after GCSE to co-ed or state schools (but a few find the grass greener elsewhere). No-one asked to leave on the basis of exam results. 'They do not cull,' said one mother. 'Even if a girl is struggling, they'll do everything they can to keep her if she is happy.' Almost all get into their first-choice university, with 36 to Oxbridge in 2016, nine medics and most to top universities in the US and elsewhere.

Money matters: North London has always prided itself on being affordable and accessible and offers plenty in the way of scholarships and bursaries. Academic scholarships (of up to 50 per cent of the fees) are awarded on the basis of performance in the entrance exams at 11 and 16. Music scholarships at 11 (girls must pass the entrance exam as well as the audition in which grade 5 is generally the expected minimum). Means-tested bursaries (reviewed annually) range from 10-100 per cent of fees and can be awarded in conjunction with scholarships. Bursary funding is partially underwritten by the South Korean franchise, and the school is looking for other projects to further extend these opportunities.

Remarks: An outstanding school for the girl who is quick and hard working and enjoys being busy and involved. Probably not the ideal place for those who might feel the pressure to be 'top' in an environment where everyone is.

North Primary School

Meadow Road, Southall UB1 2JE

Pupils: 420 • Ages: 4–11

Tel: 020 8571 7749
Email: admin@north.ealing.sch.uk
Website: www.northprimary.co.uk

Headteacher: Since 2015 Ms Nicola Forster BA NPQH PGDip (mid 40s). With a personal pedigree from the best Ealing schools, Ms Forster took a degree in geography and education at Roehampton, before beginning work in the first (of eight) London primary schools. She was promoted from acting head at Hathaway Primary to head at Ryefield Primary, Uxbridge, before joining North Primary, following its troubled spell making headlines over the solar eclipse. Inspired to teach by her mother's example, 'I learnt from an early age how you could influence children's lives through teaching,' she is at ease in her trainers and sportswear ('I'll put on a dress for the town hall!') despite having just run four times round the neighbouring sports fields with the children for Sports Relief.

Parents showed guarded respect; 'It's early days; we all look at results,' said one, who had had experience of four successive heads at the school, but they applauded her candour: 'her door is open, which parents do like'. Children approached her with ease in the corridor, addressing her formally as 'Mrs Forster' but responding familiarly, 'Yeah, cool!' Divorced with two teenage girls at the local secondary school, she is a keen runner. She has already introduced a new assessment system for the children and plans a shift of emphasis in the curriculum; 'We have very high attainment in literacy and numeracy; I'd like to increase the range'. In her first year, she has refurbished some of the buildings, including a stylish makeover in a Victorian classroom to create a colourful office for herself and her deputy, and is planning to install a multi-use games area to rival the local boys' independent school. She applauds her school's participation in the national evaluation scheme, Challenge Partners: 'it's really helpful to hear other people's points of view, to help us tighten our systems'. We forecast that, barring rare astronomical incidents, she is on course for a successful run

Entrance: London borough of Ealing admissions criteria. Many come via the outstanding children's centre next door, Grove House. Catchment area includes the residential area west of Hanwell and north of Uxbridge Road. Oversubscribed.

Exit: Most to local secondaries: Villiers, Dormers Wells and Greenford High school are popular choices. Some go to selective state schools: Tiffin, Upton Court.

Remarks: Astoundingly high Sats results have earned this school its reputation. The head attributes much of it to the expertise of the staff and good resourcing; the parents put it down to commitment of the families and community environment. Two form entry with 30 children to a class, supervised by one teacher and a teaching assistant. Despite 98 per cent EAL – 22 different tongues, mainly Indian languages, but some Somali and eastern European – the teaching is in English, and the school is proud of its EAL lead status. There is some EAL support for the 30 per cent who arrive without any English, and bilingual staff throughout the school and offices. The corridors sport a handful of translated signs, but if interpreters are needed, it tends to be informally, by word of mouth, between community groups. Lower than average numbers of SEN, nurtured in individual sessions or small groups in a corner of the hall. One mum was dissatisfied with the SEN support: 'My child has had one-to-one; it has sometimes been a bit tricky'.

The classes are named after flowers (Cornflower, Poppy etc) after the school's address in Meadow Road. No rural signs now; the school is in one of London's more economically deprived suburbs, with twice the national average on free school meals. Drawing from an area between Hanwell and Heathrow airport, and home to a large Asian community, Southall is famed for its productive and hard-working ethos. 'There are very high expectations from parents and teachers,' says the head. A dad acknowledged the pressure this puts on the staff: 'We've had an up and down period in the last few years...recently some teachers left', but he reassured us, 'teachers do get along with the pupils; the pupils are encouraged to achieve'. The head describes the staff as a real blend of ages and genders, some home grown, some from overseas.

A single storey brick and slate schoolroom, with ornamental weather vane, is what remains of North Primary's village school origins. Adjoining is a Victorian Arts and Crafts extension, in keeping with the scale of the residential street, while additional low-level classrooms from the 1970s spread out into the playground at the rear. 'The premises need a revamp,' said one parent, as the defunct climbing equipment in the rear vouched, but the high ceilings and echoey brick corridors, lined with pegs, lend an air of trusty tradition to the building. The reception and year 1 classes on the ground floor enjoy direct access to the playground, where there is an outdoor classroom, as well as a giant number square and Snakes and Ladders, painted onto the tarmac. Indoors the classes are peppered with scarlet tables and chairs, with carpet-time nooks. Upstairs year 2 was studying the Great Fire, with 3D help from a flame-ridden dolls' house in Pudding Lane. We saw some budding authors, composing alternative endings to traditional fairy tales.

The first floor hall houses a gym frame and ropes for PE and accommodates assemblies, including the popular singing assembly, as well as whole school gatherings once a week. Old and new buildings are connected by a modern dining hall, serving a halal menu twice a week, fish and chips with Eve's pudding on the day we visited. Beyond is a corridor resplendent with children's work (design your own Greek urn was our favourite), with a full library at one end. We peeked into a discrete sensory room, for SEN time, and an ICT room, hiding 30 computers inside tip-up desks. The upper floor classrooms are a delightful mix of modern and traditional: whiteboards displaying familiar columns of spellings and fractions, while high-ceilinged rooms are ventilated by the original telescopic winder poles. Lively year 6 classes were in session when we visited, discussing the construction of pyramids, while in a side room, a pair of young boffins were enjoying higher-level learning tasks, cracking a secret code.

Visitors are greeted at the door by a colourful montage of art on the walls, reflecting the diversity of the school, with a collage of religious symbols served up on paper plates, and an appliqué wallhanging of local landmarks, from the famous Southall water tower to shops selling Asian sweets. In the reception class exotic instruments lay ready to play at one of the many school celebrations: Eid, Easter, Diwali, Holi, Chinese new year; 'It's one big party,' laughed the head. Some take the form of shows for the parents, such as The Elves and the Shoemaker or the traditional nativity play, with contributions from their own Bollywood dance troupe. There's a diverse choice of sports, too, football, cricket, netball and golf, as well as an American football club after school. Sports day is held at the local Spikes Bridge Park. Plentiful after-schools clubs include the three Rs: reading, rugby and recorder, as well as a hip Digismart computer club; some charged extra, some free.

Mindfulness, from year 4, prevents the myriad amusements causing sensory overload. The deputy head keeps a model brain on his desk to teach the children the mechanics of destressing; 'It helps them deal with test situations,' says the head, and 'The stressed child would have a specific adult to link to'. Parents were satisfied there were no serious issues with bullying: 'In the main...it's a misunderstanding more than anything serious,' said one dad, and 'The kids are all respectful to the adults'. Communication with parents was felt to be good; 'there is a system', which includes face-to-face chats with the head or class teacher; 'Morning and night, someone is on the gate,' reassured the head. Emails to the office produce a quick response; 'School is good at getting back to you,' said one mum. The school has a Twitter account and a weekly newsletter, as well as a (disappointingly plain) website. There is a strong parent council – 'Which helps the standards...where some parents have issues, but don't know how to voice them,' said a governor – as well as a student council, which has been known to travel to the town hall for meetings with the mayor. Other school trips include the Kensington museums, the RAF museum and a residential to Surrey for the older ones, while the youngest children's outings include learning to make and post a mother's day card at the post office.

Dressed in their scarlet jumpers and white polo shirts, the children we saw were both relaxed and purposeful as they prepared for a trip to the local sports field. As one dad said, 'The kids feel safe and respected and enjoy going to school'. A strong PTA funds extras, such as new playground equipment, via quiz nights, a ladies' night and the lavish Mela, or summer fête, a cornucopia of sweets. The head was astonished at the generosity of the participants. One parent commented, 'It's a very good community environment, everyone is fairly local, the community helps with volunteering'. Another said, 'Parents are quite involved and do a lot to make sure their children do well... A lot of parents bounce ideas off each other; it's an Asian thing'. Some parents are former pupils. The head is quick to recognise the parental input: 'Children are very focused, families are very supportive; families are ambitious...the parents are like private school parents'.

A fusion of traditional and progressive values makes this school special, from code-breaking science lessons to

Bollywood spectaculars, from Gulab Jamun to fish and chips. The community support is palpable and the academic success skilfully orchestrated by the head and watchful governing body, who make the most of the rich diversity among the children, in language, culture and learning. North Primary is clearly a rising star in Ealing's firmament.

Northcote Lodge School

Linked with Broomwood Hall

26 Bolingbroke Grove, London SW11 6EL

Pupils: 230 • Ages: 8–13

Fees: £18,165 pa

Tel: 020 8682 8888
Email: northcote@northwoodschools.com
Website: www.northcotelodge.co.uk

Headmaster: Since 2015, Mark Smith, previously deputy head, and before that head of maths, at Caldicott School. Prior to Caldicott, he spent 20 years at Millfield, as housemaster and head of year 9. He is a keen sportsman, qualified to coach cricket, football and rugby and fond of the odd round of golf.

Entrance: At 8. At least two-thirds from Broomwood Hall, the sister school, round the corner. The others mostly local, although school minibuses bring in some from across the river. Parents and families attend an open day and meet the headmaster. If they all like each other, zap, they are on the waiting list. A year before entry it's assessment time. A couple of hours at the school include tests in English, maths, verbal reasoning and ball skills, an interview with the head and some carefully observed playtime, including a snack. If your son is offered a place, you have to cough up half a term's fees immediately. Fifty per cent will be refunded on first term's bill, rest will be kept until boy moves on. They feel this encourages only those really serious about the school.

Exit: Mainly to board at a wide range of public schools, including Marlborough, Wellington, Bradfield, Harrow and Charterhouse. Most of those continuing to day school have gone to Dulwich College. Recent scholarships include academic, music, sports and all-rounder. Inevitably some find the transition, from small protected school to large busy one, difficult at first, but school feels they are doing as much as possible to ease the path for them.

Remarks: A day school with the ethos of a boarding prep. 'A boarding school – but pupils don't bring pyjamas.' Boys arrive immediately after breakfast and go home late afternoon having already done their homework. Parents, a lot of whom have boarding school backgrounds themselves, like this as it takes off a lot of pressure. Lots of after-school clubs as well – quite a full-on day.

Small classes, never more than 16, and enthusiastic teachers, average age mid-30s, approximately 50:50 male and female, create a good learning environment. All mixed ability, but setting in maths and English starts in year 4 and increases through other subjects as pupils move up the school. Plenty of playground space for kicking balls around or net practice at break time. Boys appeared relaxed, open and polite, quite happy to talk about what they were doing. School thinks they should be 'confident but not cocky; polite and affable; ready for next stage at 13'. Feels appearance important too and clean shoes essential – much-used polish and brushes kept on bench in playground, just outside matron's room. Full-time matron, very jolly and welcoming – boys happy to take problems to her, a fully qualified nurse and a key figure on the pastoral care side.

The large, grade 2 listed Victorian building has been a school (first for blind children, then disadvantaged girls) for the last 100 years. Several new additions have helped bring it bang up to date and you have to get to know your way around – we walked up and down different staircases and in and out of the main building, but, we were assured it was all totally logical. Probably a good thing that the younger boys stay put in their classrooms and it's only the top three years that move about.

Good art and DT studios, busy busy, lots of different things going on. Up to date science laboratories – apparently imaginative teacher recently bought a shark from Billingsgate for boys to dissect: Jaws, how exciting! Well equipped IT room, used by the younger groups for computer studies and as lesson extensions by the older ones. Music timetabled for all and about half also play an individual instrument, at the moment trumpet is most popular. A variety of musical groups and an active chapel choir, which has toured in Europe. Well-equipped gym can also be transformed into fully functioning theatre for the complete dramatic experience. Drama lessons part of the curriculum, about a third take the LAMDA exam. Several productions a year, hopefully something for everyone. Public speaking also encouraged – could be reciting a poem, taking part in a debate or reading out a match report in assembly: 'We want them to be seen and heard'.

Sport is big and played every day. Karate part of the curriculum, compulsory for first two years – 'it's good for confidence, concentration and self-esteem'. Masses of black belts. Main outdoor sports football, rugby and cricket, either across the road on Wandsworth Common or at Trinity Fields, 10 minutes' walk away. Plays matches against other schools, sometimes at weekends, but, parents say, possibly not competitive enough. No dedicated, specialist sports teachers, which can mean boys not properly prepared. Lots more to try in after-school clubs, including cross-country, golf and shooting – definitely modelling itself on a country prep.

Regular residential trips for all, ranging from PGL in year 5 to outdoor pursuits in year 8 – good formative stuff. The usual French trips, rugby and cricket tours and, less common, yearly exchange with a South African school. Also plenty of excursions in and around London, making the most of what it has to offer. All trips and excursions compulsory and included in fees.

EAL not an issue as only accepts fluent English speakers. Caters for mild learning difficulties – one-to-one help available, but nothing too severe and definitely no disruption. Parents say teachers good at communicating and problems quickly identified and dealt with. School says as far as possible everything is in place to counteract any problems or if a boy is unhappy. All boys have prep diaries, containing school rules and all contact details – parents use these for important notes. A Christian school and, though other faiths are welcome, they must join in with daily assemblies and attend the weekly church service.

Northwood College for Girls

Maxwell Road, Northwood HA6 2YE

Pupils: 940 • Ages: 3–18 • Sixth form: 155

Fees: £10,353 – £16,221 pa

Tel: 01923 825446
Email: admissions@nwc.gdst.net
Website: www.northwoodcollege.co.uk

Head Mistress: Since 2009, Miss Jacqualyn Pain MA (theology and philosophy) MBA PGCE NPQH (youthful 50s). School has benefitted from the wealth of experience she brought with her, with two headships of other high flying academic establishments (Henrietta Barnet and St Albans High School), plus a stint prior to these as deputy head at Northwood, under her belt.

'Immensely proud' of Northwood College's recent merger with Heathfield – both of her staff's success in the seamless joining of two cultures ('a lesson on how to be in change') but also of the girls' willingness to accept and embrace their new peers. Also highly instrumental in school becoming part of prestigious GDST group, a move which, she says 'has not changed the culture of the school' but has provided 'a plethora of opportunities that a standalone school doesn't have'.

Understands her customer to perfection and has air of calm control that immediately makes you feel your money would be well spent at any establishment with her at the helm: 'every girl here achieves the best she's capable of. It's not just spin'. Value added stems from pastoral excellence, she says: 'we're not nice just for the sake of it – it's about academic outcomes.'

N

Elegant and understated, parents describe her as 'a great communicator' and say she takes no issue with dealing with problems raised, however small. Like all the best leaders, she's surrounded herself with a formidable senior management team who not only sing from one hymn sheet, but give a very genuine impression that they are as committed to the cause of excellence as she is.

Head of junior school: Since 2015, Mrs Zara Hubble (very youthful looking 40s), educated at Westonbirt School and City of London Girls, after which she took a Montessori nursery teaching course then a BEd specialising in KS2 at Southbank University. Cut teeth at St Hilda's in Bushey before joining Heathfield, where she taught year 6 and ultimately became head of year 7. Moved to Northwood as head as part of merger with Heathfield in 2014. Likeable, calm and poised, with two daughters at university. Keen skier and book lover.

Academic matters: Delightful Bluebelle House is home to early years girls – designed with a wonderful playground, outdoor explorer area (minibeast heaven), masses of IT and spacious, airy and inspiring classrooms where girls learn Spanish via action songs, yoga and ballet from age 3. Three reception classes of up to 20 girls also enjoy this space with life skills such as resilience already high on the educational agenda. Lessons we observed were engaging and interactive and girls highly articulate. Years 1 and 2 in Vincent House, with junior school housing years 3 to 6 – both immaculate, modern houses, with every available space proudly adorned with colourful art and meticulous handwritten work. Thinking skills – pioneered by the whole school from nursery through to year 13 – taken very seriously by all with pupils able to explain the purpose of De Bono thinking hats with enthusiasm and clarity. All girls screened for SEN in year 4 and supported in small groups either within or outside the classroom. Around 30 girls receive EAL help.

In the ferociously academic context of this corner of North London, school is by no means at the top of the pile when it comes to results – but neither does it either pretend or want to be. Value added is the name of the game and head is delighted to be in top four per cent nationally in relation to this, if not topping academic league tables. Broad-ish church intake, coupled with ethos encouraging every girl to outperform her potential, means that academic superstars can co-exist happily alongside their more pedestrian peers, with neither group feeling undue pressure. Head more interested in 'building a portfolio of skills relevant to each girl' than cracking the Oxbridge whip – 'girls need a raft of skills beyond the academic', she says. 'Soft skills can mean the difference between success and failure.' Listen up, neighbouring hothouses.

It's compulsory Spanish in years 7 to 9 in the languages department (not popular with everyone), with French or German as an option. Mandarin on offer from year 9. Classrooms we visited were formal in format – old school even – girls in rows facing the front and lecture style lessons. That said, lessons were interactive (think periodic table bingo) and when questioned in class, the girls we saw were incredibly articulate, confident and considered in their answers. Parents cite RS and English teaching as 'really impressive' and results bear this out, with the former producing 'ridiculously high' grades at GCSE and A level.

Girls take nine or 10 GCSEs from a traditional curriculum with compulsory language and three sciences, plus options including art, classical civilisation, drama, Latin and Greek, home economics, RE and textiles. IGCSEs now taken in some subjects, at the discretion of each departmental head. In 2016, 65 per cent of GCSEs scored A*/A. Similarly broad choice of A level options, although disappointingly low uptake of the more 'artsy' options – including English, history and languages – reflecting parent demographic aspiring to careers in the sciences for their daughters. 'Our families value STEM subjects,' says head. 'It can be a challenge to persuade them otherwise...but it's one we're happy to grapple with.' After sciences, psychology and RE most popular A level choices. Respectable A level results in 2016, with 65 per cent A*/B grades and 30 per cent A*/A.

Because large number of girls move through from junior school, any SEN usually identified years before arrival in senior school, with seamless transition a major benefit for girls requiring support. Most mild SENs managed in lessons, with only occasional withdrawals. School supportive of girls pursuing interests or sports to a high level outside of school and will adjust timetable to accommodate if possible. Bespoke programmes occasionally put in place, for example to help girls be more outgoing.

Independent thinking is school's raison d'etre – even, according to the girls we spoke to, above and beyond sport, music or drama. Girls formally taught Thinking Skills from nursery upwards with a full-time cognitive development director to ensure consistency of message and integration across all parts of the curriculum. Even the youngest in the school evangelise the benefits of eg looking at problem solving from different perspectives – 'teachers don't spoon feed us' and 'we're taught how to learn from our mistakes', we were informed. School is pioneering in its approach and is working towards Thinking Schools International status.

University application process universally praised by parents and girls. Dedicated full time careers and UCAS advisor delivers 'loads of one-to-one advice,' say parents, plus programme to provide every opportunity for girls to build CV. Teachers described by all as 'really supportive', offering extra classes in preparation for eg medical exams. Visiting advisors are frequent fixtures, eg mock university interviews with admissions staff from

Imperial College or staff at nearby Merchant Taylors' and endless internship opportunities both through school portal and GDST – one sixth former we lunched with was spending her summer interning at Nomura thanks to the latter, with another looking forward to her work experience in Beijing via the same route.

Games, options, the arts: Doesn't boast the most gleaming array of facilities we've ever seen and the field is tiny, but for what is essentially a London school, it's as well equipped as it needs to be. Stand out facility is the 25m pool – with everyone swimming all year round and weekly lessons for years 7 to 9. Sports hall has a new climbing wall (2015) used both in PE lessons and by clubs. Gym also attractive and well equipped, apparently well used at lunch times by older girls. PE and games compulsory to year 11. Tons of extracurricular sports on offer to suit all tastes – hockey, karate, basketball – you name it. Try as we might, we couldn't get the girls we met to extol the virtues of school's sporting prowess and, with just three compulsory games sessions per fortnight on offer, we wondered whether school was perhaps not the most obvious choice for super sporty types. Parents reassured us, however, that cohort includes a number of outstanding gymnasts, swimmers and even a British team triathlete – we stand corrected, but worth investigating further if your daughter is sports mad. The overall message for sport was: 'it's about right'.

Performing arts centre looks newer than it is and includes an excellent drama studio, recital hall with a sprung floor plus well kitted out music tech room and a plethora of instruments from steel drums up. Plenty of opportunities for budding thespians to throw themselves into productions, most recently Narnia for the lower school, and although there's no space for such performances to take place in a grand theatre, the assembly hall does the job. Parents describe music as 'absolutely fantastic' – for all tastes and levels – from a 50 strong orchestra that plays 'everything' from classical to pop, to jazz bands and chamber choir. There's hours of fun to be had leafing through the booklet detailing all the extracurricular activities on offer with something for everyone – from the active to the cerebral.

Despite junior school parents admitting that 'the academic is the most important thing,' school works hard to ensure balance with a dazzling array of extracurricular clubs which take place either at lunch time or after school. Something for everyone, with all major sports represented, ballet, martial arts, masses of opportunities for musicians to do their thing and everything else from outdoor explorers and gardening to newspaper club. 'Really extraordinary' major stage production each year – recently The Wizard of Oz – with the whole of year 6 participating and many behind the scenes roles up for grabs for lower year groups. Super catering, with lunches (included in fees) freshly prepared on site and all girls from reception up eating together in dining room. Hot suppers also available (charged as extra) up to 6.00pm and there's a breakfast club from 7.45am – great for working parents.

Background and atmosphere: Founded in 1878 in Endsleigh Gardens, Bloomsbury, with around 25 boarders and a handful of day girls. Headmistress Miss Buchan-Smith, concerned about the unsavoury influence of the Euston area on her girls, moved the school to its current site in Northwood in 1893. The current front building – red-brick late arts and crafts with leaded lights – was opened for 20 boarders and just two day girls. The Briary, next door, accommodated little boys, and although they are long gone, school pays tribute to those who went on to fight and fall in the two wars with an annual wreath laying at Ypres.

Joined Girls' Day School Trust (GDST) in November 2013 as a precursor to joining with Heathfield School (75 per cent of their girls made the move to Northwood), already a member of the Trust, the following September. Head reports that the governors thought 'long and hard' before taking up the rare offer of membership and all are delighted that belonging has not changed the culture of the school at all, 'merely provided a plethora of opportunities that a standalone school doesn't have'. Northwood girls now benefit from participation in GDST music and sport competitions, eligibility for travel scholarships, participation in conferences on eg Oxbridge application, as well as access to an alumni network numbering some 50,000 members, bringing a healthy pool of work experience and internships from which to fish. Staff also benefit from additional training and development opportunities, which bears obvious fruit in the classroom.

Beyond the main building and with notable exceptions (the quaint William Morris-esque, parquet floored reception area and quirky, characterful library) the site wouldn't win any beauty contests and space is at a premium, but the combination of disparate buildings somehow hang together nicely in their urban setting to create a cosy atmosphere – and all aspects are highly functional. The homely sixth form common room buzzes with chatter. Most striking to visitors is the calm – almost serene – atmosphere that pervades the school. Smiling faces are everywhere to be seen and parents and girls report nothing but kindly and supportive behaviour between girls. If leading from the front is the cause, then this pressure-free, friendly vibe is most certainly the effect of Miss Pain's presence at the helm.

Junior school in three purpose built buildings on same site and a handy hop, skip and jump from senior school – handy when girls reach year 6 and start to take a few lessons with their soon-to-be secondary teachers. We spoke to parents who had wanted their girls to have the option of moving to other secondaries at 11+ and won places at – in some cases – arguably more high flying schools. Invariably, none wanted to leave, thanks in no small part to the clever balance of nurture and academic rigour they enjoyed at Northwood.

Pastoral care, well-being and discipline: Not a negative word to be heard from junior school parents – 'they've really brought our daughter out of herself – we love the inclusive atmosphere', raved one and indeed girls are nurtured rather than pushed and, happily, few are denied the right to move into the senior school.

Minor transgressions only in the main and these, mainly tiny bumps in the road to adolescence, reportedly dealt with 'brilliantly and sensitively' according to parents who were full of praise for the pastoral side of Northwood life. Reports of girls experiencing 'the grass is always greener' effect and returning within weeks of departure, particularly for other sixth forms. 'There's just something about Northwood,' said one mother: 'everybody knows everyone'. 'Incredibly strong' house system plays into this, with fiercely fought competitions ('the life blood of the school', according to one pupil) in anything and everything, the highlight being the house music competition in which every girl participates. Bullying is a 'no go zone', say pupils. Older girls pick up concerns of their younger peers and head reports 'very few' eating disorders or instances of self harm – highly commendable in an academic girls' school – 'we don't value aggressiveness'. What about lost sheep? 'We grab hold of concerns early and work in partnership with parents', says head. Indeed, parents appreciate this approach and seize opportunities to attend school for talks on subjects such as social media and cyber bullying.

Pupils and parents: Majority from British Asian backgrounds although all cultures and religions represented (there's a multi-faith prayer room for free use by girls as and when) and a more sensible and earnest cohort you'd be hard pushed to find. No reports of cliques, with the majority of non-Asian parents relishing the opportunity for their daughters to 'stay younger a little bit longer' due to the positive influence of other cultures. Wide reaching coach routes transport girls from

Ealing, Edgware, Kenton, Gerrards Cross and Radlett. Proximity to Northwood station on the Metropolitan line gives easy access from both directions.

Entrance: Oversubscribed for entry at 3+ and 4+ with around three applicants for every place. Gently selective with nursery and reception places offered after observation in play. Head meets all parents: 'we're looking for children who are ready for school,' she says. Up to 10 new places at 7+, when applicants are assessed in maths, English and reasoning and by interview. Parents attracted to the junior school in the hope of selecting an all through school generally not disappointed as transition from junior school is a given (although junior school pupils do sit the same 11+ exam as outside applicants) unless it is felt a girl really wouldn't thrive in the senior school. Even parents of most able appreciate this ethos – 'the fact school doesn't have a policy of shedding pupils spoke volumes to us about its culture', said one.

Girls joining senior school from other prep or junior schools take the North London Consortium exam at 11+ plus an online CAT-style test and group interview, with around 30 places up for grabs and up to six applicants for every place. Another 20 join for A levels, with places conditional on GCSE results plus online test and interview. Occasional places in other year groups so worth a call if you're moving into the area.

Exit: Almost all juniors to senior school at 11+ with a small handful taking up state grammar places most years. Almost all stay on for A levels with vast majority moving on to Russell Group or new universities. Just two to Oxbridge in 2016; this explained by school's demographic with hard working, dual income families often not wanting daughters to move away for uni – hence many take places up at London colleges or others within commutable distance. Generally several medics.

Money matters: A few means-tested bursaries – up to full fees for particularly deserving cases. Scholarships for academics, art, music and sport.

N

Remarks: If neighbouring options are too academic, too large or too aggressive, Northwood is (in the words of Goldilocks) just right. Unfettered access to a world of opportunities in a supportive and purposeful culture await. In the words of one parent: 'girls come out happy, healthy and rounded'. What more could you want?

Notting Hill and Ealing High School

2 Cleveland Road, London W13 8AX

Pupils: 903 • Ages: 4–18 • Sixth form: 152

Fees: £13,425 – £17,262 pa

Tel: 020 8799 8400
Email: enquiries@nhehs.gdst.net
Website: www.nhehs.gdst.net

Head: Since January 2017, Matthew Shoults MA (Oxon) PGCE (Cantab) (40s). Spent two years in the civil service before teaching called: started off teaching classics at King's College School Wimbledon, then moved to North London Collegiate as head of classics in 2004, becoming deputy head and then senior deputy (combining academics with running the school on a day to day basis). His hobbies include amateur music making (violin and singing), hiking (Scottish Highlands and European Alps), cooking and crosswords.

Head of junior school: Since 2013, Mrs Silvana Silva, BEd (50s), who arrived at the school in 1989 as a classroom teacher and has stayed ever since ('I absolutely love working here'). Prior to her present elevation, she spent 11 years as deputy head, so has overseen a relatively seamless transition. A north Londoner by background, she attended St Michael's Catholic Grammar, before taking a degree in education at Roehampton University ('I always knew I wanted to be a teacher'). A positive, energetic and sympathetic force, much liked by parents and pupils, she's a great believer in the GDST (Girls' Day School Trust) ethos: 'I want girls to believe in themselves, be resilient, show integrity and have creativity embedded in whatever they do.' Married with one adult son.

Academic matters: The national curriculum is watched but certainly not slavishly followed in the junior school. 'We look at what state schools are doing,' says the head. 'Sometimes we find we're doing it anyway.' That said, this is the antithesis of a testing regime, and teaching is intended to make learning 'alive and fun'. 'If you don't enjoy school that's a real shame,' says the head.

Staff specialists for music, PE and science, supplemented by Mandarin and French experts seconded from the senior school. Language teaching is important and, while girls here have traditionally studied European languages, Mandarin has now been introduced in year 3 ('They're all very able and it really challenges them'), with a likely extension down to reception. Regular homework (once a week in year 2, four times weekly in year 5), includes 'open' homework topic, in which all participate, to encourage creativity. (The response to a recent exercise on Up and Down included a marble machine and a coke and Mentos explosion, wisely demonstrated in the playground).

The junior school is academically selective, so special needs tends to be on the mild side, but an in-house SENCo works with all classes to ensure additional requirements are met (including those of girls who need extra challenge or the 10 per cent with English as an additional language). More extensive support is available, but at an extra charge.

The Independent Schools inspectors have noted that at Notting Hill and Ealing, 'the quality of pupils' achievement and learning is exceptional', and this is certainly reflected in league-table topping results at both GCSE and A level (90 per cent A*/A at GCSE, 72 per cent A*-A at A level in 2016). Performance is high across the disciplines. 'One of the reasons we are so committed to girls' education is that no subject is seen as a "boys'" subject. We want girls to be able to choose freely, with no judgement.' Large proportion of A*s in economics A level with DT another winner, and good numbers proceed to degrees in science, engineering and medicine.

The school is keen that girls should retain breadth (post-GCSE, those specialising in arts, for example, will often retain one science), and is replacing the subjects relegated in AS level reform with the Extended Project Qualification (EPQ). Not, however, contemplating the still broader sweep of the International Baccalaureate. 'We feel it can jam up the time. We like the idea of girls having the freedom to pick up a book or be at a bit of a loose end to let their thoughts run free.'

Curriculum kept under constant, carefully-considered review, with modern languages recently given a comprehensive overhaul. 'It used to be a bit bitty, with a number of languages taught as a taster in the junior school. We decided we wanted one main language throughout, so girls could leave really fluent.' Mandarin Chinese was selected for its economic relevance, straightforward grammar, and tonal complexity (so difficult to acquire later in life). Now compulsory in years 7-9, there's an excellent take up for GCSE (where last year all 30 candidates gained an A*). Plenty, too, to make the language real, including a bi-annual trip to China. Latin compulsory in years 8/9, Greek an option from year 10, plus French, German and Spanish from year 7.

Teachers throughout are enthusiastic, well-informed and efficient. 'They always get straight back to me by email,' said one sixth former, while others stress administrative blips are dealt with immediately. ('When one of my daughter's teachers was ill during her exams, she was still made to feel really comfortable,' said a parent.)

Special needs addressed by in-house assessment (triggered by staff or parental concerns), and a dedicated room offers discreet space for drop-in support. More complex problems are directed to an external educational psychologist who the school knows well. A recently added lift allows those with physical disabilities to access the entire building.

Games, options, the arts: Though grounds are not expansive, sport here is important. A pool (where girls trained successfully for the national water-polo finals), an impressive All-England four-court sports hall (providing scope for table tennis, cricket, badminton and trampolining), and a range of well-enjoyed Astroturf pitches complete the on-site offering. Athletics and tennis take place nearby. The recent rebuild has also allowed the school to take exercise in a new direction, with the addition of a roof-top dance studio and fitness gym. 'We wanted girls to have choice, and for dance to be of the same high standard as netball.' Numerous teams compete at in-school, local and national level (including recent finalists in the Middlesex netball tournament, and defending champions of the Ealing cross-country). Sports courts, used for formal lessons and play, link the junior school with the senior. Hockey, football, netball all on offer to juniors, with A-D squads in netball and hockey.

Music, too, is high profile, with an inspirational director of music and enthusiastic take up at GCSE and A level. A multitude of private music lessons, and plenty of opportunities to play (symphony and chamber orchestra, plus regular concerts) and sing (senior choir, harmony choir, House Shout). Performance opportunities elsewhere, too, with choir tours in England and Europe. 'Fantastic' drama department in possession of a main and studio space, and a recent production of Lorca's Blood Wedding was well-received at the Edinburgh Festival. Art department staff includes professional artists, and nascent talent is encouraged by a weekly life-drawing evening class and art club. Good numbers do A level, a trickle proceed to art foundation and architecture courses.

Extensive range of extracurricular clubs, including some inventive student-driven additions, such as Ukulele ('I didn't expect anyone to turn up but there are now 23 members,' rejoiced its founder).

'Enrichment' in all directions at the junior school too, both on the timetable and beyond. Music unusually strong, with a dynamic head of music training up aspiring instrumentalists to join the 85-piece orchestra, and plenty of opportunity to perform in concerts, bands and choirs. Spacious art room and specialist 'art club' for those demonstrating unusual potential. Other clubs aplenty (before school, in the lunch hour and after hours) from science and chess to touch typing and gardening. Most of these high-energy girls participate in a cluster. Lively school council, with representatives from each class. School also divided into 'teams' to compete for an annual team cup. Loads of outings, from a hands-on pizza-making seminar at Pizza Express, to a 'bushcraft trip', where girls learn survival skills and witness history in 3D.

Background and atmosphere: The oldest school in The Girls' Day School Trust (GDST) portfolio, Notting Hill and Ealing was founded in Notting Hill in 1873 and moved to its leafy site in Ealing in 1930. Previous head waged a clear-sighted campaign to transform its jumble of tired buildings into a coherent, up-to-date whole. 'The school is on quite a small site and was joined together in random, annoying ways. It was very hard to find your way round.' Now, a dazzling reworking of the central core has retained the period façade, but added a glamorous glass-clad extension at the rear, providing plenty in the way of new facilities, including a spacious library and sleek assembly hall. 'It's one of the things I'm proudest of,' said the previous head. 'It's exactly how I imagined a modern learning environment.'

A new sixth form centre has also been added just down the road. Here lucky A level students get their own café, gym and relaxed work space with comfortable sofas. 'I love being here,' said one. 'It's such a nice environment.' No brother school, though some mutual events with Eton, Harrow and nearby St Benedict's.

Junior school located in its own well-kept period building (now refurbished with air-conditioning and new flooring), with a self-contained, green (Astroturf) and pleasant playground. Large, light library equipped with bean bags. Girls are keen readers, of fiction and non. ('Not everyone enjoys Harry Potter,' said one emphatically. 'I prefer books about mythical creatures, such as mermaids.')

Pastoral care, well-being and discipline: A school where pastoral care is given as high a priority as academic drive. 'There's enormous pressure on girls today, but there's also increasing awareness and understanding of adolescent mental health. We want girls to be successful and have opportunities, but also to look after themselves and see that the sky won't fall in if exams don't go as well as they'd hoped'. To bring the message across loud and clear, they talk to girls 'a lot' and rely on a highly experienced counselling team, but the school believes student well-being is everyone's responsibility. 'Every member of staff is part of the pastoral team. They know what to listen out for and how best to respond.' Girls clearly welcome this approach. 'I've nicknamed my teacher my "therapist",' said one sixth former. 'Whenever I have a melt-down, she offers amazing support.' Few (ie next-to-no) serious disciplinary issues and very light touch punishment. 'Detentions are quite rare,' said one pupil. 'We really respect the teachers, so don't want to misbehave.' Overall, this is a confidence-building place. 'When my daughter came here, she was very shy,' commented a parent. 'Now she's thriving.'

Pastoral care in the juniors, as in the senior school, is very much to the fore. At the start, four teachers are stationed in the the playground to help girls learn to take turns, make friends and share. Handy acronyms like TAG ('Tell them how you feel, ask them to stop, get an adult') embed coping mechanisms. 'We put it in place in first year, before they go to the bigger playground,' says the head. Once there, all girls have a partner, and older pupils patrol for difficulties. Girls are polite – one said 'Good morning' unprompted as we passed – self-possessed and articulate. Staff know girls well and parents have ready access at the end of each day, and by email and phone. 'They're always willing to listen,' said one.

Pupils and parents: Most parents here work, many in the professions (plenty of doctors, lawyers and media types employed at the nearby BBC). Girls' ultimate aspirations often lie down a similar path. ('Quite a number want to become dentists and doctors.') Girls are sensible, articulate, grounded and genuinely enthusiastic about single-sex education ('I prefer it without boys; it's far more relaxed,' said one) and about the school ('It was the best decision I ever made to come here,' said another.)

Entrance: At 4, 100 try for two reception classes of 20. At this stage, applicants are assessed just before their 4th birthday and observed in small groups carrying out 'nursery activities' (no formal reading or writing required). 'We watch them playing, interacting, talking to us,' says the head. 'We're looking for the potential to do well – finding it is based on experienced and intuition.' At 7+ – when 30-40 apply for eight places – testing is in maths, writing and verbal reasoning, plus an interview for those who pass this hurdle.

At 11, 90 places, with 45 going to those from the junior school, the rest from a multitude of primaries and preps. Hugely oversubscribed ('We don't give out numbers because we don't want to put parents off.') Post GCSE, 6-8 places. Offers at this stage are tailor-made, though predicted A*s and As are the norm. 'We won't take a girl unless we feel she'll enjoy working at the pace of our sixth form.'

Exit: A tiny leakage at 11 to senior schools elsewhere (St Paul's Girls', Godolphin & Latymer, Lady Eleanor Holles, Tiffin Girls'), but the assumption is that, once here, you're here for the duration, so no formal preparation is on offer.

A handful leave at GCSE to co-ed independents or state schools, but most remain happily till the end. Then, mainly to Russell Group universities (an encouraging 14 to Oxbridge in 2016, plus three medics). Girls very positive about the support given in the application process. 'We've been given incredible guidance,' said one mid-way through. 'They always tell us anything's possible and it's never too late to change your mind.'

Money matters: The Girls' Day School Trust is currently celebrating 140 years of providing high-quality academic education at a reasonable cost, and Notting Hill and Ealing undoubtedly lives up to the brief. Academic and music scholarships worth up to 10 per of the fees in year 7 (which can be supplemented by means-tested bursaries). Additional scholarships (art, music, sport, drama, all-rounders, as well as academic) worth 5-20 per cent of fees for those entering the sixth form.

Remarks: A forward-looking school providing a stimulating education, outstanding results and positive, confident girls.

N

Notting Hill Preparatory School

95 Lancaster Road, London W11 1QQ

Pupils: 325 • Ages: 4–13

Fees: £18,300 pa

Tel: 020 7221 0727
Email: admin@nottinghillprep.com
Website: www.nottinghillprep.com

Headmistress: Since 2003, Mrs Jane Cameron BEd (50s). Married with three grown-up children. She had run the Acorn Nursery in Lansdowne Crescent for 25 years, and parents there encouraged her to translate its ethos of teacher/parent partnership into a prep school. Approachable, dynamic, greatly respected by parents and pupils, 'terribly hands-on and involved,' said a parent. 'Problems get sorted out very quickly because she'll invite you straight in to see her.' Another said: 'She is the backbone of the school. She brings a committed energy and a genuine passion in the joy of learning. She is an inspiration to us all.'

Entrance: Has three reception classes; younger children are offered a gentler introduction with some shorter school days in the first two terms. Automatic places for siblings; the rest are allocated by ballot – separate ballots for boys and girls and for September to February birthdays and March to August birthdays. Ballot is drawn in May, 16 months before date of entry. Highest waiting list places allocated to those who signed up soonest after birth. Those successful in the ballot are asked to pay a £1,000 deposit. Places higher up by assessment. Some, mostly boys, join in year 7, and there are one or two bursaries a year available for children from state primaries. 'It was lovely to hear from a boy from one of the local high-rise estates [who had moved on to a top boarding school] that rowing was now his favourite sport.' Can cater for some specific learning difficulties and EAL.

Exit: About half the girls and a handful of boys leave at 11, with the rest staying on to 13. Leavers to day schools eg City of London x 2, Francis Holland, Godolphin & Latymer, Harrodian, Latymer Upper, Queen's College, South Hampstead High, St Paul's x 2, UCS, Westminster; or boarding schools eg Bedales, Brighton College, Bryanston, Charterhouse, Eton, Marlborough, Rugby, St Edward's, Wellington, Winchester.

Remarks: On the borders of achingly trendy Notting Hill (Hugh Grant expected to stroll idly by at any minute) and grittier Ladbroke Grove, with tubes on the Hammersmith and City line and cars on the elevated Westway forming the northern horizon, and Portobello market just down the road. The school opened in 2003 with 57 pupils in a 1900s school building (currently owned by Campden Charities) which still has the painted brick classroom walls and high windows of a classic Victorian school. Some Acorn parents found out that the property was available, gathered shareholders, and moved fast to secure the lease, and the fledgling school was set up within a whirlwind nine months. 'We got a band of great teachers together, some of whom still work here.'

There's a large hall with stage for assemblies, plays and concerts; art room adorned with clay models, papier mâché shields and a cardboard violin; small library with comfy sofa. A painted timeline starts in the entrance hall with dinosaurs and continues up the stairs and through the ages.

The upper school building across the road, purpose-built and opened in 2008, is shoehorned into an intricate space where a Belgo restaurant once stood. Wood-clad, with whitewashed walls, rooflights and curved ceilings, it includes a basement dining/assembly/dance and drama room as well as classrooms, science lab, music and computer rooms for years 4 to 8. It looks out one way onto Ladbroke Grove tube station and Chicken Village fast food restaurant, the other onto wooded slopes that border the tube line.

'I feel passionately that I'd like our children to be educated in the true sense of the word, but we also have to manage preparation for very narrow tests at the end of the road. We do aim to light the fire rather than just filling the bucket.' Children from reception upwards encouraged to express opinions, with plenty of small group discussions. Philosophy4Children and de Bono Thinking Hats systems used to encourage enquiring, reasoning approaches to learning. 'There is a real onus on independent thinking and this seems to give the children an enormous self-confidence and sense of self,' said a parent. Practical, fun teaching; year 2 was investigating friction and gravity using toy cars and ramps of books during our visit. Kung Fu Maths, a NHP invention, sees children awarded 'belts' in assembly for learning tables, knowing number bonds, solving problems of increasing complexity. 'The teaching staff at all levels are extraordinary,' said a parent. 'Their talent, enthusiasm and dedication are an inspiration to the pupils'.

As children move into year 4 and the upper school building, the pace of learning changes too. 'The early years are particularly gentle and nurturing,' said a parent. 'When they cross over the road they graduate to a much more serious work ethic. It's a very successful symbol.' Another commented: 'You see a real mix between academic rigour and the fostering of imagination.'

Non-selective system means particular needs do crop up. 'If a teacher raises concerns, the SENCo will observe the child in class and suggest strategies. For the first two years, we will give extra support and keep watching. If it becomes evident we can't meet the child's needs we'll discuss it with the parents.' The SENCo can give one-to-one help at extra cost; speech and language and OT experts available to visit.

Music is a particular strength. The school has twice performed pieces written by the 'amazing, hugely enthusiastic and charismatic' music master at the Schools Proms at the Albert Hall – most recently The Eagle, based on a Tennyson poem. Some two-thirds of pupils play an instrument and many join the choir, orchestra or ensemble groups. Plenty of opportunities to perform, in assemblies, concerts, poetry recitals, school plays – Hansel and Gretel was under rehearsal during our visit. Art imaginative and inspiring.

Sport was the only area picked out as a weaker link in last ISI report; Jane Cameron acknowledges the challenges a new-ish school (and particularly a co-ed one) faces in setting up a fixture list. Football (boys' and girls'), rugby, netball, cricket and rounders matches played with varying degrees of success; the swimming squad is apparently 'second to none'. Compact playground, so sport involves travelling: most matches, and many sports lessons, at the Linford Christie stadium; they also use the Westway Sports Centre and Kensington Leisure Centre.

Clubs range from Greek to chess to netball to lateral thinking; they make good use of London, with trips down the Thames, to a Hindu temple, to City Hall and the Olympic site; they go off to Normandy, skiing, on outdoor pursuits courses and field trips.

Much parental involvement, whether helping in the library, giving a talk on the nature of consciousness or on Leonardo da Vinci, giving a violin recital or running a crafts workshop. 'There is a constant stream of authors, musicians, journalists, actors and artists, not only dropping off and collecting their children, but generously volunteering their time and talent by speaking at assemblies and judging various competitions, such as poetry and public speaking,' commented a parent.

Great parental praise for the 'pervasive caring ethos' of the school. 'The NHP community is one in which the children show an enormous and unusual amount of empathy.' 'Every child feels valued, and different talents are truly celebrated. Children take great pride in the achievements of their peers, not only academically but in music, art and extracurricular areas.' 'Altruistic behaviour happens all the time. It is the way things work at NHP and what we treasure most.' 'We feel indebted to NHP for giving our children a love of learning, a sense of belonging and pride.'

Nower Hill High School

George V Avenue, Pinner HA5 5RP

Pupils: 1,880 • Ages: 11–18 • Sixth form: 373

Tel: 020 8863 0877
Email: admin@nowerhill.harrow.sch.uk
Website: www.nowerhill.harrow.sch.uk

Head: Since 2012, Mr Chris Livesey, BA from London in modern history. A Cheshire lad, who moved to London for his degree, continued his studies there (PGCE) and never went back: 'My first teaching job was at a comprehensive school in Wembley, and then I became deputy head at Nower High, where I stayed for the next 15 years before becoming head. I've basically had two long services in two schools.' Although he is loathe to admit that he must have been the natural choice to succeed the much respected former head teacher, we think few would've expected otherwise. One parent told us: 'Mr Livesey was always a well-respected deputy head and classics teacher and was always very visible.' Mr Livesey says that when he was offered the role of head teacher, he was 'extremely flattered to be entrusted with such a role at such a school' and wants to ensure that he gives the role his utmost level of commitment and hard work.

At 50+ years old, Mr Livesey manages to successfully combine a friendly and youthful demeanour with a straight up, very headmasterly, no-nonsense approach. One parent commented that 'children really like him, but when he walks in the room there is complete silence.' He loved his own schooling and as a result remains passionate about education. 'I went to an independent school in Cheshire – school was fantastic.' This head doesn't strike us as someone who will ever take his job for granted; quite the contrary – he enthuses about his loyal and committed staff, 'a very strong team of senior leaders, teachers and support staff', the lovely pupils and the general vibe of the place: 'You only have to look at the school's history to see that since it first opened its doors in 1929, the school has only ever had seven head teachers.' Heads, it seems, are at Nower Hill for the long haul.

He insists on a clean and tidy school, will not tolerate the dropping of litter and leads by example in picking it up wherever it is seen. One parent told us: 'Mr Livesey is forever picking up litter and he never asks anyone to do it for him.' And his presence has been noted by many: 'He is always on the school gates and walking around the school. He is transparent in a good way. He doesn't hide how he feels about where he wants the school to be.' Punctuality is very important to him, and he himself has something of a daily commute from Richmond where he lives with his wife (an assistant head teacher in Richmond) and their three children.

Academic matters: This Ofsted outstanding school is well known in the area for its academic standards. One local parent told us: 'Nower Hill has always had a good reputation, now it has an excellent one.' Part of its success could be down to its class sizes of 25 pupils, spread across 12 forms in a year group, part of it could be down to the dedicated teachers 'who always have their lines of communication open to parents' to the point where one parent told us: 'I feel a bit sorry for the teachers. They work so hard during the day and then call or email us back straight away if we have a query.' Ofsted said: 'The leadership of teaching and learning is exceptional.' And the head added that part of the school's success is that 'we pride ourselves on working hard for all learners.'

In 2016, 73 per cent of students achieved five or more A*-C grades at GCSE including English and maths; 38 per cent A*/A grades. At A level, 53 per cent of all grades were at A*-B, with 29 per cent at A or A*. 'For a not particularly competitive school, they still get the results,' one parent told us. Another said, 'The school does very well at stretching bright children, whilst at the same time providing a round education for everyone.'

The curriculum is wide and varied with 24 optional subjects offered at GCSE level (Mandarin offered as an extracurricular language), with more able students being offered the opportunity to learn ancient Greek and astronomy. An enthusiastic parent told us: 'The options in year 8 are fantastic. Students start their GCSE course in year 9 and they are given a chance to chop and change a bit for the first term and decide if it is the right course for them.'

Each student has been given their own tablet, which they can take home and use for homework. Quite extraordinary in a school of 1,900 pupils and clearly highlights the school's priorities in terms funding. One parent told us: 'It's things like this that make this school so progressive.' The head is quick to point out that this is an educational tool only and that students don't have access to Facebook or Twitter: 'Everything they need has been put on there for them.'

Parents have also welcomed an online app called 'Show my Homework' where students, parents and carers can access homework details and retrieve and submit work online. Students also have their own personal portfolio where they can store all their electronic documents, allowing access to them in or out of school. It is part of the school's Managed Learning Environment (MLE) for which Nower Hill won the award for secondary schools.

Excellent facilities for students with disabilities, including ramps, improved corridor lighting, lifts, handrails on steps, widened doorways for wheelchair access and yellow lines to assist visually impaired students. Roughly 13 per cent of the school intake is registered with an SEN. For those students, a well-supported inclusion staff team is on hand to offer extra support, including a SENCo, qualified SEN teachers, Inclusion manager, behaviour manager, mentor and counsellor. There is also extra support for maths and English

Games, options, the arts: The school has a very long tradition of strength in the arts subjects, which was evident as we walked round. Astoundingly good self-portraits from GCSE students were on display as well as an interesting montage of student-designed film posters. Several of Nower Hill's art students have had their work displayed in local art galleries, national exhibitions and at the Mall Galleries. Many continue their art studies post A level, at well-respected art colleges. Photography also strong.

Drama is popular and taken up in fair abundance. Big scale biannual musicals, which have included The Lion King and Oliver! Watford drama winners recently. The dance department offers a wide range of extracurricular dance activities including contemporary dance, tap, ballet, Bollywood, street dance and modern. There are many performance opportunities available both in and out of school; school productions, a dance showcase, summer extravaganza and a performance at the Royal Albert Hall.

Musical students have a choice of a dozen ensemble music groups and orchestras to take part in, including a soul band, and school hosts concerts several times a year. Some 400 pupils have peripatetic music classes, and groups include everything from steel pan ensemble to African drumming to a full 51 piece school orchestra. Well-equipped recording studios. One pupil told us: 'This school really caters well in all departments and has something for everyone.'

Sports play a big part in the school and there is a wide range of activities. The faculty prides itself on 'giving very generously of its time'. Sports include netball, basketball, handball, rugby, trampolining and indoor athletics. All clubs are fully inclusive. School athletes compete at borough, county and national level with 'considerable success.' Sporting facilities include a 3G Astroturf pitch, two tiered grass playing fields, six tennis courts, six netball courts a multi-purpose sports hall, fitness suite and gymnasium.

Aspiration is definitely a buzz word at Nower High, and an Aspire programme is run on Wednesday and Thursday lunchtimes for Y12 and Y13. This programme helps to develop 'interview, thinking and critical analysis skills, provides personal feedback and mentoring' to ensure students have the best possible chance at future employment. Training is also offered to become mentors for younger students and give older students the opportunity to run lower school science, sports and dance clubs as well as a variety of other leadership roles.

This school really puts a big 'C' in charity. It doesn't do things to tick boxes, or to excite an over-zealous PTA. Pupils seem to be charitable to the core. When we were there, a dedicated area of the school hall had been given over to black bags, full of clothes and toys for Syrian refugees: 'We like to instill charitable values in children of a young age.' School fundraising events have included a leavers' ball, pizza and quiz event and charity sports fixtures against staff. There is also the opportunity for sixth formers to work voluntarily in an orphanage in Romania as well as with elderly people in the local community. Events are planned throughout the year to raise money for their chosen charity – St Marcellin's Children's Village in Zimbabwe.

Background and atmosphere: Formerly Headstone Council School, this red-brick building on Pinner Road first opened its doors in 1929. The school's purpose was to educate 292 5 to 14 year olds with an average class size of 50. The school soon expanded to meet the ever-growing number of children resident in rapidly expanding North Harrow and Pinner. Its steady expansion has withstood many a hitch including the Second World War, when many of its male teachers were called up for military service and the playing field was dug up for trenches and air raid shelters.

Redevelopment work continued throughout the 60s and 70s (when the school became Nower Hill) – continuing throughout the 90s, which saw the start of a £2.75 million development programme, including a new 13 classroom block and the Gristwood Centre, housing music, dance and drama studios, a fitness suite and the sports hall. The school added a sixth form in 2006, which a few years later moved into its £4 million sixth form extension. The site was further enhanced in 2010 by the addition of a block of five science labs and a new English teaching block hosting 13 classrooms. This is one big site!

As a result, the site is a bit of a hotch-potch of buildings, none of them particularly pretty, but functional and purposeful and very much in keeping with large comprehensives. Plus, as every parents knows, schools are much more than bricks and mortar – and this school is so much more. The pupils who showed us around were extremely articulate, warm, kind and very proud of their school. Big mix culturally and harmonious atmosphere. Room after room was explained with equal enthusiasm (even the less aesthetically pleasing ones), and each montage on colourful walls was discussed in detail – especially those of past school trips. We were taken through a labyrinth of corridors and would've lost our bearings many a time if it weren't for our guides. There were a few nice touches we spotted on our tour, most notably the 'ancient' Greek columns outside the classics department (homage, possibly, to the head, who is partial to a bit of classics).

Other things worth mentioning include the spacious library, well-equipped with books and computers, and six different outlets for food and snacks, including a cold canteen for grab-and-go pastas and salads and a hot canteen. However, one parent did say that the downside of such a large school is the difficulty in accommodating everyone: 'My son finds school dinners all a bit stressful and too much of an effort to have something hot. There are just too many other kids and often nowhere to sit. I think they should stagger it more.' Sixth formers have now been offered the incentive of a £1 coffee and cookie in the common room, instead of traipsing to the local café and wasting valuable time.

Pastoral care, well-being and discipline: Discipline is 'bang on', one parent told us: 'For a school with this many children, you really don't hear of many incidents like bullying etc, and if there are, they are dealt with quickly and appropriately.' By all accounts Mr Livesey is a truly dedicated head, and he expects the same of his staff, where the well-being of his pupils are concerned. One parent told us: 'The teachers always walk out with the kids at the end of the day and often accompany them to the local shops. That way the shop keepers are always reassured that a grown up is with them.' Another said, 'You never ever see any Nower Hill pupils lighting up outside the school gates or nearby, like at other schools. The students here are very aware that they are representatives of the school and they wear their uniform proudly.'

Uniform is a very smart navy affair, with the odd splash of varying colours on the v-neck pullovers denoting the year group. All blazers have the school's crest with the motto 'service not self' emblazoned on it. Although strict on uniform, Mr Livesey does display a softer side, especially when questioned about the assortment of hair colour that passed us by (most noticeably green), on our tour of the school: 'I won't argue with a child about their hair. It's a very happy environment here and that's the main thing.'

In a school of this size, we wondered how feasible it is to oversee the well-being of all students and to prevent the more vulnerable ones from slipping through the cracks: 'We work very hard at keeping a large school, a small school', says the head. And indeed Nower Hill does seem to have a pretty robust infrastructure. There is a full-time attendance officer who works with parents around punctuality and is there to pick up on any possible issues. There are two co-ordinators for every year group and a well-staffed student support team. There are also two peer mentors for new students allocated to each class.

One parent told us: 'This school's motto should be above and beyond. They really do go the extra mile here. The lines of communication are always open if you need to speak to a teacher, and somebody always gets back to you pretty promptly.' Another told us how the school bent over backwards to help facilitate her daughter's studies after a long period absent due to ill health: 'Home tutoring was arranged for my daughter as soon as we needed it and the tutor was very impressed with the excellent support material provided to her from the school.'

Mr Livesey recently reintroduced a new house system to reflect the core values of the school. These six houses have been named after influential people who, together, inspire millions around the globe: Gandhi, King, Shabazz, Franklin, Bannister and Nightingale. The school sees the qualities of being well mannered, articulate, well behaved, hard working, smart and kind as part of the DNA, and reminders are displayed throughout the school. Ofsted said in the last report that: 'Student' behaviour is excellent..the school provides an orderly, welcoming environment entirely conducive to learning.'

The reintroduction of the house system has been welcomed by pupils. One told us, 'It's more fun and you become loyal to your house. It also promotes a healthy competition between the houses on things like sports days.'

As with any school, particularly of this size, disruptive pupils will always be an issue. However, Mr Livesey says that permanent exclusions are below the national average: 'We have very high expectations here. Any poor student behaviour is dealt with in a clear and consistent manner' through what the school calls its Ladder of Consequences. This includes an inclusion centre for students temporarily excluded from lessons, which is equipped with computers and other educational resources.

Pupils and parents: Pupils and parents pretty much reflect the general demographic of the local area of Pinner and North Harrow. Roughly 30 per cent white British, nearly half Asian and the rest a mixture of other ethnicities. Parents are largely professionals, pupils aspirational.

Entrance: Hugely over-subscribed. Approx 1,400 applications are submitted each year group for 300 places. Waiting list system is operated by the local authority. School catchment is roughly a mile, and you'll get in if you have a sibling or a looked after child. However, one unhappy parent told us: 'My only real gripe with the school is that the sibling policy stops at GCSE, so if you have a bigger age gap between your children, there is no guarantee at all that they will get in.'

Exit: Around 40 per cent leave after GCSEs, mostly to do vocational courses elsewhere. Over 95 per cent of Nower Hill sixth form students went on to university in 2016, with the rest choosing a gap year, an apprenticeship or employment. Quite a few medics and dentists each year; usually a couple to Oxbridge. Oxbridge admissions preparation with academic mentors who have themselves been to Oxford or Cambridge. Popular destinations also include elite art colleges and music conservatoires.

Remarks: If you live in the north Harrow area and are within catchment of this school, applying for it is a bit of a no-brainer.

Old Palace Preparatory

Linked with Old Palace of John Whitgift School

O

2, Melville Avenue, South Croydon, Surrey CR2 7YN

Pupils: 140 • Ages: 3 m–10 • C of E

Fees: £10,362 – £10,824 pa

Tel: 020 8686 7347
Email: schooloffice@oldpalace.croydon.sch.uk
Website: www.oldpalace.croydon.sch.uk

Head of Preparatory: Since 2015, Tim Horton, who has 23 years' experience of teaching in the independent sector. Previously at The Hall, Hampstead but has also held posts at Abbots Bromley School and Birkdale School, Sheffield. He graduated from Jesus College Cambridge. Married with four children. Interests include cricket, reading and cooking.

Head of nursery: Miss Jacqui Hines, NNEB (40s), two teenage girls, one a gold-medal gymnast. Formal title, day care manager. Feisty, fast-talking with supportive, calm deputy – 'I run around like a loon, she's yin to my yang' – and runs a tight-knit team of 35 full and part-timers. Started as second in command, promoted to current post three months in. Can't imagine doing anything else. 'Children are so lovely and innocent and speak their mind. Whatever you're pouring into them, you're shaping their lives.'

Entrance: First come, first served into often oversubscribed reception, with many girls moving up from separate and flourishing Old Palace co-ed nursery located on the far side of school playing fields, and which expanded three years ago to offer full child care from three months upwards. Individual age and development determines speed of progression through well-equipped baby, toddler, kinder, transition and finally pre-school rooms, with a gradual induction into school ways (school tracksuit is worn by the oldest, for example).

A fair few newcomers join the prep in other years and are quickly absorbed, with firm friendships quickly established, say pupils. Assessments, from reception onwards, are on the rigorous side, including tests in English, maths and reasoning as well as observation of their social interaction. Parents are also asked how they will support their daughter (some don't, hence early flagging up).

There's a fairly intense focus on exam preparation all through, intensifying in the run up to 11 plus (school runs workshops on the topic, open to pupils elsewhere). Aim is for year 5s to be working a year ahead with entrance exam success the acid test – school doesn't take Sats.

Nursery open 51 weeks of the year, highly in demand and with waiting lists to match (though most are eventually accommodated). For the baby room, early registration essential. 'We get women phoning us the day the baby's born.' No formal entrance tests though mobility is prerequisite for toddler room (most start aged 12 to 15 months); freedom from nappies or close for kinder room (around 2). Followed by transition room, while a fair few join in final pre-school year, the biggest group with 40 places and the only one with a minimum attendance requirement of three days a week (Tuesdays to Thursdays are the most popular). Elsewhere, it's down to parental needs (many work) and availability. Some children will do full 7.30am to 6pm days from the start, others attend just a few mornings or afternoons a week.

Exit: Around 65 per cent per cent progress to the senior school, often with scholarships. NB Year 6 is part of the senior school. Vast majority of leavers do so for 'nice' reasons, securing places at one of the highly desirable local grammars (Wallington High School and Newstead Woods head the list). A few others are helped to the realisation that senior school is not for them, 'though we would never ask anyone to leave,' says school. Perhaps not, though one parent was fairly devastated to be told bluntly by another member of staff during a meeting that her child was 'unlikely' to make the senior school (though this was followed by some fairly nifty backtracking).

For girls at the nursery, assumption (by parents and school) is that they'll go on into Old Palace reception. Though their passage there isn't automatic (there's an assessment), in practice 'all our girls get places,' says head of nursery. Boys tend to stay in independent sector, with Cumnor House and Elmhurst the most popular destinations, Park Hill Infants for those going on to state schools.

Remarks: Originally just across the road from the senior school, prep school was re-homed on Croham Hurst's leafy south Croydon site, just a short tram ride away.

Year 6s stayed behind in central Croydon as 'baby seniors', a move that brings structure into line with Trinity and Whitgift, the other two schools (both for boys) in the Whitgift Foundation's educational trio.

With a whole senior school to themselves, the 160 reception to year 5 pupils have oodles of space to play with and in, and all the trimmings, including vast spaces for DT and ICT. The separate nursery takes children from 3 months and is housed in its own building on the far side of the playing field.

Year 5s, as top dogs, acquire the trappings of seniority a year early. All can be prefects and have their own centre, located opposite reception classes 'so you see how our school goes round in circles,' says typically bright, eloquent and eager-to-please pupil. The most coveted perk, however, is sitting on benches rather than joining the hoi polloi on the floor for daily assembly, one of the many small formalities which, like grace said at the end of every meal, add a pleasantly traditional punctuation to the school day.

The range of architectural styles allows you to channel Malory Towers, complete with enticing attic rooms one moment, up to the minute modernity the next. Fresh-looking, white-walled dining hall with jolly pictures adding a splash of colour is particularly nice. Heart of the original building, facing on to the Croham Road, is Small Hall, an unromantic title for what's effectively a mini-mausoleum to Croham Hurst's founders – galleried, beamed and stuffed to the gunnels with ancient honour boards and a sketch of the second Croham head, Theodora E Clark, looking wistfully into the middle distance. Visitors of a gothic disposition could have a ball.

Plenty to gladden the heart – a library with splendid tables fringed with solid, comfortable chairs (each one donated by a former grateful pupil some 60 years ago) that should entice the most reluctant of readers (and there are a few). Palatial size creates a few technical difficulties. All roads tend to lead to back of the school, a sort of nesting place for the many fire escapes, while enthusiastic guides initially struggle to find any other pupils, making school's assertion that 'one of the few things you'll see is teachers at standing at the front and just spouting,' literally true, if not quite in the sense intended.

Parents have had their ups and downs with staff here and in senior school, not helped by uncertainty caused by some (expected) post-merger redundancies. Once found, however, lessons here don't disappoint, with a jolly English teacher surrounded by chatty, cheerful year 5s attempting a modern take on John Keats' Ode to Autumn. Technical glitch resulting in a temporary computer failure could have been the reason for all the smiles and interaction. Though you hope not, slight sense of apology when noise reached a smidge over conversational levels did suggest otherwise.

Would parents mind if teachers' voices remained the dominant sound? Debatable. There's good, solid curriculum, taught in classes of around 15, with pretty much everything for all, French from reception and a modern foreign languages 'experience' designed to fill a few cultural gaps on the way. Much is made of use of topics to link subjects with a unified theme, as well as learning for life (reasoning and evaluation as well as fact collection, carried on into seniors).

For most parents, preparatory is the key word, exam success its most obvious manifestation and a place either at the senior school or one of the local grammars the desired goal. Major focus, consequently, is on doing well. 'It is an academic school,' confirmed a mother. 'They've never tried to hide it.' Study the prospectus, with plentiful references to academic excellence and you can't say you haven't been warned.

Most coveted reward for success is a highly desirable celebration tea with head. It's within everyone's reach, school insists, based on the completion of 10 extension tasks designed to recognise 'all girls who rise to a challenge and are putting in lots of effort.' Not all parents are convinced. 'My daughter said "I'll never go to one of those tea parties, will I?"' said one.

Success-driven outlook could perhaps account for what some parents see as slight ambiguity towards learning needs. Though mild difficulties, headed by dyslexia, are officially something the school takes in its stride (even offering in-house consultancy), parents report mixed messages, in particular when it comes to all-important, high pressure exams. School seems to be trying harder to get it right.

Outside lessons, masses going on. Clubs are blossoming, from sewing to ballet, even including Japanese as a one-year wonder. Activities start young and increase fast – begins and ends with Indian Dance for reception but by year 1, there's a choice of seven. Popular lunchtime Christian Union club (Little Wigs) attracts a range of different faiths and delivers fun, unpreachy messages – on day of visit, pupils were busily decorating their faces with sticky spots as the prelude to a discussion about leprosy. Teacher in charge, enjoying it as much as pupils, was unfussed about missing lunch break. 'Who would miss the chance to do this?' she asked with evident sincerity.

Sport comes with different aspirations. Super facilities include use of senior school swimming pool and their own large playing field 'for best', say girls, featuring splendid coronation oak planted in 1953, and stretching away across to the nursery wing (their gym doubles as prep school dance studio). Miniature pavilion, aching to be used for classic mid-match teas, currently houses spare minibus seats.

Lots to do – girls were particularly keen on weekly lunchtime table-tennis session. Everyone plays in a netball or rounders team 'even if you're useless'. Big on inclusivity, low on wins. 'I like it but we always lose,' says one pupil resignedly. However, school says there are now more fixtures – and successes.

Reception pupils have a nicely kitted out separate play area as a gentle introduction to the rough and tumble of 'big' school, with a soft surface, sheltered spot for wet weather play and even a tiny adventure playground, grassed area with tree and three side-by-side Wendy houses, a mini estate in the making.

Music also flourishes, with a good range of free taster sessions in year 3 and many learning instruments, excellent facilities (a big, terraced room, piled high with xylophones and five practice rooms dotted round the place) and a decent range of groups, instrumental and vocal, headed by the audition-only Junior Polyphonic, which performs with seniors in Croydon Minster (high on parental frisson-factor).

As to the future? Mood in school is upbeat. One parent, also a teacher, praises 'careful engineering' that helped girls to feel part of a 'new and evolving thing'. Though most parents seem minded to agree, a few, particularly those whose offspring are still at subsonic speed compared with high flyers, or need a bit more support, view the Darwinian model with some reservations.

Nursery occupies former Croham Hurst Junior School, acquired in 2008 by the Whitgift Foundation, with former senior school on the other side of the playing field now housing Old Palace Prep. While 'we never used to feel part of the Old Palace structure', the nursery has now, under senior school headship of Mrs Jewell, been brought fully into the fold, getting the full corporate branding to the point where prospective parents, confused by location, occasionally get lost en route.

Though exterior gives the impression of rolling square feet upwards and outwards, it's a slight Tardis in reverse as top two floors are unoccupied and will remain so, if Miss Hines has her way. While success of nursery, which has grown from 26 to 104 in just three years, has Old Palace management gleefully rubbing hands at thoughts of future money-making potential, she is adamant that predominantly single floor layout and instant access to outdoors space is a non-negotiable.

Even the pre-school children, the only ones based on the first rather than ground floor, take turns to spend full days in recently built outdoor classroom so they can have free access to real if diddy tree for climbing (staff stand underneath just in case) and other outdoor highlights including fence strung with assortment of pots, pans and hooters, though high-decibel wind up fire bell – acquired at a car boot sale by bargain hunting deputy – has, unfortunately, gone missing. (Silence-loving local residents are chief suspects). Veg is enthusiastically grown, recently scooping three prizes in local produce show.

Head of nursery is particularly keen on directed play and staff are encouraged to watch out for and gently discourage aimless wandering: one pupil was enthusiastically helping to rake up leaves, the rest seemed happily occupied.

Lots to do inside, too (we loved the small staircase/ramp that permits endless up and down games – Escher minus the impossibility) and attention to detail is jaw-dropping. Every parent is presented with a daily record of child's achievements complete with photograph, while there are regular diplomatically phrased parenting tips covering everything from reading to cookery.

There's an equally thorough approach to everything from stopping pupils' work being over-prettified by staff ('if they draw a dog with three legs, that's what we'll display,') to discipline. With no refuge in naughty steps (or indeed, use of the word 'naughty' which is banned) anyone being unkind is talked to about their behaviour and the need for 'kind hands' repeated ad nauseam until the message gets through (time-consuming but effective, say staff).

No chocolate or crisps (and of course no nuts) rules firmly enforced with children bringing in fruit on birthdays, rather than cakes or sweets. School chef rustles up appetising breakfasts, lunches and dinners, all included in the fees, catering with aplomb for every dietary requirement, with meals served to older children in pocket-sized, delightful dining hall and to babies and toddlers in their own rooms.

Staffing is thoughtfully planned, with at least one experienced mum 'who has seen everything' in each of the bright, light and appealing rooms as instant source of wit and wisdom. Once in place, each room tends to keep the same staff group – children and parents appreciate continuity. Currently just one man on the team (hugely popular with all) though diversity is the name of the game elsewhere, with staff (like pupils) spanning vast range of backgrounds and cultures. Huge range of activities and events makes the most of this, from songs and counting in Italian to a recent visit by Rastamouse.

For pre-school group, ICT room, whiteboards, (optional) homework and uniform (trackies and sweatshirts) gently introduces some 'big school' elements. However, 'we're not a Montessori,' says head of nursery and parents expecting everyone to be reading by the time they leave are gently disabused of the notion: emphasis is on cultivating desire to learn so children are raring to go when they start in reception. Feedback suggests it works.

Old Palace of John Whitgift School

Linked with Old Palace Preparatory

Old Palace Road, Croydon, Surrey CR0 1AX

Pupils: 560 • Ages: 10–18 • Sixth form: 120

Fees: £12,771 – £14,070 pa

Tel: 020 8688 2027
Email: admissions@oldpalace.croydon.sch.uk
Website: www.oldpalace.croydon.sch.uk

Headmistress: Since 2011, Mrs Carol Jewell, MA PGCE DipEd NPQH CSBM (50s). Preceded by a brief spell as acting head and a longish one as deputy, a role she took on in 2005, having originally joined the school in 1997 as director of music. Before that, had assorted teaching roles in a 'tiny' London sixth form college, a Banbury comprehensive and then (after a spell in Wales) at top-rated St George's School back home in Edinburgh (she's Scottish born and bred) where she achieved first senior management role, before heading south again. Rambling cross-country route (even Virgin Trains would shun the franchise) was dictated by husband's burgeoning career, first in further education, then IT. 'I was always following on – it's one of those inevitable things,' she says, matter of factly.

Though a musician by training (at St Andrew's, where she studied with Cedric Thorpe Davie), a head by inclination and posture. Nobody with such an immaculately straight back could, you feel, be anything else. Melodious voice helps, and is also useful cover for wry wit that's probably kept largely under wraps in school hours.

Her office, formal but friendly, sets her off to a tee. Only drawback is its slightly thin, no doubt listed, walls that render conversations in adjoining office intermittently audible, though visitors distracted by outlook from study windows – delightful medieval garden with (in season) suitably onomatopoeic bees – may not notice. (General gorgeousness means ever-present danger of 'oohs' and 'ahs' overload).

Her appointment followed a turbulent time for the school, which in 2008 acquired nearby Croham Hurst, a failing and less academic secondary. Parents on both sides greeted the news with fury. 'Dangerously progressive' predecessor moved on somewhat rapidly.

Enter Mrs Jewell, radiating copious amounts of 'all's well' reassurance and felt to be a safe pair of hands. Expressive ones, too, says an old girl, who admired conducting technique. Mrs Jewell is now definitely the Sir Simon Rattle of the show, in overall charge of the whole kit and caboodle, prep and nursery too, with section leaders responsible for the day-to-day nitty gritty. School is now, think most, back to the road more travelled, bounded by the familiar trappings and traditions that were its pre-Dr Harris hallmark. 'Very committed to the school,' says one. 'She's bringing up the standards, getting it back to what it was. It had lost its way.'

Liked by many. 'Gorgeous,' was one verdict. Her emphasis on courtesy and manners is just the sort of thing parents want to hear. Naturally good, you feel, at rising above problems, though not remote, thanks to a strong dose of gentle self-deprecation. 'As a Scot, I probably have some very traditional and quaint ideas,' she says. Parents, confounded by her suggestion for rustic game at school fair ('it wasn't turnip throwing, but it was close,' said one), wouldn't disagree. Phrasing, too, can be a charming blast from the past. 'We don't need to have a fit of the vapours because we're expected to put out cups and saucers,' she says, explaining importance of hands-on role.

She's out and about a lot, running regular surgeries for parents, taking weekly assemblies at the prep school ('She's joyful,' was one pupil's verdict). Thanks to marvels of rigorous Scottish four-year degree, also teaches Latin to pupils in years 7 and 9.

Though parents understand her need to stick to the official script, some feel she can over-adhere to the party line, giving impression that their concerns aren't being registered. One mother felt she was treated as 'a child (rather than) an intelligent professional'.

'I've always thought of her as a softish music mistress and very quiet, but I think behind the façade is a robust personality,' says an insider. With some aftershocks from the merger still to be negotiated, it's probably just as well.

Academic matters: The long-drawn out nature of the merger, with juniors and some staff settling into Croham Hurst site in South Croydon (everyone was previously at Old Palace) perhaps accounts for varying shades of parental opinion that cover the pantone range. 'A Marmite school,' said one old girl of her time here, and little seems to have changed, with everything from effusion ('I wanted the best education my daughter could get and I've been really pleased,' said one) to praise with reservations. 'I have mixed views,' said another. Specific concerns include quality of maths teaching, felt to be variable, while loss of other talented specialists, notably art teacher, was also keenly felt. However, there's a sense that the worst is past. 'They've sorted the problems of transferring staff and children and it seems to have settled down now.'

Results bear this out, ranging from good to vintage: in 2016, A*/A grades in 57 per cent of GCSEs and 47 per cent of A levels, where 87 per cent were A*-B. Plenty of choice post-16, with a good range of two-year AS subjects (including dance, critical thinking, DT, philosophy and PE) plus normal A2 selection (nice to see both Latin and Greek offered).

Given aspirations of pupils and parents, you'd expect maths and sciences to lead the popularity pack, as indeed they do, with twice as many taking biology and chemistry as physics (and psychology). Predictably good showing for English literature (less rigorous English language not offered), French and RS, with history the aberration. Good range of languages offered, modern and otherwise, with GCSE French (taught in sets, as is maths) way ahead on numbers, as is Latin. Some pupils also take Gujarati (Chinese and modern Greek pop up in other years) while Russian is available as a sixth form option.

Parents who, like particularly discriminating sundials, tend only to record the top results are, in general, satisfied with how their 'good, good girls who want to please their parents,' as one put it, are doing. Mention of occasional 'over-exuberant' behaviour in recent inspection report causes head to bristle slightly – it's not a picture she recognises and tour of school elicits absolutely no signs of roaring, gorging or indeed anything untoward.

Not that we were encouraged to get too close. One drama teacher was notably unkeen on our presence. Elsewhere, we were ushered away from classroom doors if heads started to turn, for fear (presumably) of providing an alternative source of interest. Entertainment value (much appreciated in sea of tranquility) came in the form of really lively A level biology lesson led by an amiable teacher and involving a great deal of yeast. 'Smell this!' said animated student, thrusting a steaming, strongly scented beaker in our direction.

The overwhelming impression, based on brief glimpses of heads bent conscientiously over books, was of orderly, efficient learning in classes that average around 20 up to GCSE, dropping to far fewer at A level (three isn't uncommon) and where motivated, bright girls do their utmost to get their grades. Learning support, as with the juniors, is in place, with range of needs catered for, says head, including ADHD, though emphasis on pace and focus would indicate compatibility with mild difficulties only (and 'we're not equipped to take on children with serious SpLDs.'). With parents' experience in some cases at odds with official line, dyslexia in particular, it would be worth, if possible, asking to speak to parents who know the ropes.

In contrast, there's excellent joined up academic support. Stunning library, far more than a pretty face, features syllabus-linked book displays helping the focused to plan their own 'now read on' programmes: one conscientious modern language specialist was ploughing her way through Gabriel García Márquez's oeuvre to complement modern language studies. Key subjects also have timetabled clinics run by staff and older pupils, more informal help on tap, willingly given by tutors. 'You don't feel as if it's a hassle,' said pupil. 'They'll say "Come and find me".'

School is currently trying to up parental involvement, which doesn't come naturally to all. Website goes back to basics, highlighting (startlingly for some) importance of eye contact, praise and even turning up at child's concerts. Message reinforced in workshops. Head herself addresses parents on need to 'read aloud to your child every night, ideally into their early teens,' getting a fair few abashed looks in the process. 'I said "Come now, there's no need to look down and be apologetic",' she says.

A few idiosyncrasies to get used to, headed by two-weekly timetable – a breeze once acclimatised, apparently, allowing longer, more productive lessons – and separate though apart presence of year 6s. From the security of own 'little empire' as head puts it (two bright classrooms and pleasant courtyard garden), they make controlled forays into main school, while imaginative 'expanding horizons' curriculum knits humanities together, with Victorian life and times, for example, covered by church visit (RS) and river trip (geography). It all adds a dash of va va voom to what can, post 11+, be a fallow year.

As to the future? You could be picky and argue that an all girls' selective school should regularly trounce the equivalent boys' version. No chance thus far, with Whitgift the outlier, streets ahead especially at A levels. Trinity (co-ed at sixth form) does better too.

There is, though, potential to be stronger still, especially given head's uncompromising focus on quality over quantity. Though school isn't at capacity (it's down 20 in current year 7) she won't 'bring in girls to be miserable' to make up numbers. 'We allow a bit of scope but it's an academic setting.'

Games, options, the arts: Hockey sticks not really jolly, with parent mood neutral to apathetic. 'She doesn't like group sport,' said one father, while another confirmed that 'If your girl's sporty, you're not going to go to Old Palace.' Prospectus, by way of corroboration, doesn't go a bundle on action shots (girls raising hands in class is about as energetic as it gets) though fab new pool (devoid of pupils) does feature and is extremely popular, with plans to increase squad training for the best and lunchtime clubs for the rest soon. Recent introduction of football could also prove a popular move, bumping up the number of sports, dance and fitness-related extracurricular activities – which also includes Duke of Edinburgh – to a round half dozen.

Arts and DT include lively pieces, nicely displayed. Biggest buzz, however, comes from performance side, admirably embracing school's history and culture. Drama department plans to 'develop work that explores the theme of pilgrimage to Canterbury' (school was on the route). For the musically inclined, the take is topical rather than Chaucerian. While three smaller music rooms are used for teaching (with as much fabulous classic choral singing as you'd hope for, including monthly evensong in the Minster), biggest is dominated by thriving steel bands, one per year group, with many pupils playing in highly-regarded external ensembles like Croydon steel orchestra and heading off to Notting Hill Carnival.

Background and atmosphere: Some of the oldest buildings in use as a school within the M25. Site of Croydon Minster, dating back to the ninth century and long-time summer palace for assorted Archbishops of Canterbury, who abandoned it in the 18th century for a drier new build. Somehow escaped demolition, though endured a century's rough treatment as, amongst other things, a calico bleaching factory, before being given to the Sisters of the Church, who founded a school here in 1899. Visitors flock (by pre-arrangement) to gawp at early brick guardroom (now library), medieval great hall (one of south England's finest) and 15th century chapel.

The site, in current scholastic incarnation, works perhaps unexpectedly well, though with some of the more idiosyncratic uses of space, such as IT support housed in gallery pew off the chapel, an effort of will can be required to banish Hogwarts-related thoughts.

Though there's a bit of a sub fusc feel on the cathedral side (and little in the way of outside space) the school modernises where it can. However, those in search of light-flooded rooms are best served by the attractive Shah building across the road. Housing a large sports hall, attractive language and performing arts rooms together with super dining hall, where girls linger at the long, attractive dining tables complete with fresh flowers, it is also home to comfortable sixth form common room. 'They know how to live,' says teacher, surveying end of day overflowing bins.

With such an array of goodies to enjoy, it's unsurprisingly easy to forget the contemporary world outside, though total escape from Croydon's signature tower blocks is impossible – a prize-winning specimen rears up across the road.

Contemporary life does have its uses, however, what with the handy tram stop located a stone's throw away from the front door, though many parents prefer to drive. You sense slight disapproval from Mrs Jewell, who feels parents worry unnecessarily about the area. Even the 2011 riots, though not exactly the publicity you'd seek, left the school completely untouched. 'Parents are more edgy. The girls are fine,' she says.

However, while we're told that for hungry sixth formers the main city centre feature of note is the nearby McDonalds' lunch menu, location is an issue for a minority of families. 'Mrs Jewell won't have it but the middle of Croydon isn't what it used to be,' said a grandparent. 'If the girls are coming out of school late, you have to pick them up.'

For majority of parents, though, the charm of the school trumps the area. Variations of 'girls are so privileged to be here and they just don't appreciate it,' were heard more than once.

Pastoral care, well-being and discipline: These are, you feel, girls with high energy levels, carefully checked by fairly heavy staff presence in the corridors and on surging staircases: one pupil departs for the day trailing slipstream of bubbles aft, wand and detergent to the fore. Ban on mobile phones up to sixth form helps create calm atmosphere, thinks head, though wonders how long technological tide can be resisted. Outside, there's the wonderful Michael who mans the street crossing and is renowned for impeccably good humoured early morning banter and 100 per cent recall of every pupil, parent and sibling.

House system is the glue that creates the unifying bond between youngest and oldest pupils. Even year 6s elect officers, take an active part in meetings and 'may find themselves planning and speaking in assembly,' says head. Strong ceremonial aspect includes regular house assemblies in the delightful chapel as well as an end of term church service, with bannered-up procession down the aisle.

Pupils praise what one describes as a 'big support network with a form tutor and deputy form tutor'. Essential for girls expected to care for younger children where, says Mrs Jewell, 'life is not always easy,' and also the key to swift resolution of bullying ('friendship issues' as ever the biggest cause). 'My daughter had a problem with a friend but the class teacher called us and it was quickly sorted out,' said father.

Pupils and parents: Splendidly multi-cultural, spanning the gamut of faiths, cultures and backgrounds and seemingly an accurate reflection of the local area rather than gated ghetto for privileged Caucasians. Old girls (strong, loyal network – hugely active) approve. 'I go down for founders' day and it's lovely to see the church full of every colour and race under the sun, all wearing the Old Palace uniform. Very moving,' said one.

Families praise the sense of community while not necessarily playing much part in it. While there's equal involvement of both parents in their daughters' education (and fathers dominate at drop off and pick up), interest tails off when it comes to socialising with other parents, and the PTA survives, but sometimes only by a thread. 'It's something I can take or leave,' said one mother we spoke to. She wasn't alone. 'A very mixed crowd,' said another parent. 'Some are lovely individuals, trying to work very hard to pay the fees and keep their jobs so they genuinely can't get involved. With others, the idea of paying for an event is ridiculous because what are the fees for?'

Entrance: Like Whitgift boys' schools Trinity and Whitgift, has prep year within the senior school. Unlike them, also has prep school, making for slightly clunky structure with junior school ending in year 5, year 6 pupils moving across to senior school. Anyone arriving in year 6 from outside and passing assessment (English, maths, reasoning, social interaction and parental support) will gain automatic entry to year 7. Everyone else sits 11+ exams (similar content) though 90 per cent make it through. Those who need it will be allowed extra time (this wasn't, thought parents, the case until very recently).

Occasional places on offer up to year 10 – same subjects again but minus social interaction, plus satisfactory school report. School reports some readmissions when girls who secure grammar school place find it not to their liking. 'We don't crow,' says head. 'It takes courage to retrace your steps.'

Catchment area largely but not exclusively local, with increasing levels of interest from Wandsworth and Clapham fringes as London day school bunfight for places continues to superheat, and bus routes to all points on the compass.

At sixth form level, you're not left in any doubt as to what the school wants. 'Is Old Palace right for your daughter?' thunders large font heading, warning of the dangers of poor choices that could leave students to 'flounder' and feel 'unstretched, lost and overwhelmed.' The bottom line: don't leave home without a goodly number of B grades at GCSE as bottom line minimum and preferably better.

Exit: Almost everyone to well regarded universities including Imperial, Warwick and Durham. One to Oxbridge in 2016. Favourites are headed by science, chemistry and biomedics in particular. Law also popular, ditto psychology, otherwise broad range of subjects and destinations.

Money matters: Whitgift Foundation does what it says in the prospectus – some families suffer real hardship after losing jobs (and in case of one parent we spoke to, home as well) yet manage to keep daughters at the school, thanks to the near 100 per cent bursaries it can provide. Scholarships for academics, music and sport. One girl recently aided by a Bank of England scholarship to help her through university and beyond.

Remarks: It's a question of Annie, get your grades. Having had a period of thinking outside the box, this school seems to have hopped back in to give parents what they want – a decent, solid education in beautiful surroundings with few surprises. Message to outside world is just want you'd want to hear (unless sports success is the deal breaker). How well it matches up to the reality of life on the inside remains an evolving story.

Orley Farm School

191

South Hill Avenue, Harrow HA1 3NU

Pupils: 493 • Ages: 4–13

Fees: £13,284 – £15,324 pa

Tel: 020 8869 7600
Email: office@orleyfarm.harrow.sch.uk
Website: www.orleyfarm.harrow.sch.uk

Headmaster: Since 2013, Mr Tim Calvey (40s), formerly school's deputy head and art teacher, rocketed to headship following the sudden departure of his predecessor following an 'error of judgement' (worth googling, even just to learn what 'acrostic' means). Hailing from a teaching dynasty, grew up in Zimbabwe in the boarding house run by his father. Passionate about sport and art, got his teaching degree at Christ Church University before cutting his teeth at Northbourne Park School in Kent under an inspirational head 'who pushed all the boundaries,' then landing at Eagle House (Wellington College's prep) around the same time as Anthony Seldon took the helm at the senior school – spending a six year period there that 'shaped him.' In true Seldon style, impassioned by well-being and development – 'we have to find ways to release the pressure children are under.' A challenge indeed in this most competitive of postcodes.

Shades of Gareth Malone – sharp, quirky dress sense, warm charisma, palpable energy and a real human touch. Parents uniformly comment on how informal he is compared to other local prep heads. Happily donned Willy Wonka costume at behest of parent committee at recent Christmas Fair. Pupils describe him as 'effervescent' (well done that child's English teacher), 'enthusiastic' and 'funny' – the first head we have met known to wear Iron Man cufflinks. Rarely have we seen a head teacher so naturally connect with even his youngest charges, all of whom chat away to him merrily. If he ever fancies a change of direction, a career in broadcasting surely awaits. Feels 'huge duty of care' to bright children and warns destination obsessed parents that it's about the journey and that Orley Farm is 'not for them if they just want their child tutored – we don't want to be defined by either the name of the school or our grades.'

Lives on school grounds with wife Rachel, who teaches RS and science at the school, and his three children – all of whom have attended Orley Farm.

Entrance: Vast majority enter at 4+ from as many as 40 different nurseries with places oversubscribed by about three to one. Children are observed participating in a carousel of activities and head is clear: 'don't bother tutoring your 4 year old' – school is looking for 'sparky children' rather than those with perfect cursive script. Occasional places do crop up from time to time, mostly due to relocation, and around 20 places come up for year 7 when many girls, and a few boys, leave for 11+ schools. Short shrift given if potential parents are looking for prep merely as springboard to top schools. 'Have I put parents off with this attitude?' muses head. 'Probably.'

Exit: Huge breadth of destination schools with an impressive number to top academic schools (St Paul's, Westminster, Merchant Taylors' and Habs for boys and St Paul's, North London Collegiate, City of London and Godolphin & Latymer for girls), as well as Hampton, John Lyon, Aldenham, Northwood College and Notting Hill and Ealing Girls' School. A small handful each year to boarding schools.

Remarks: The only co-ed school in the area, Orley Farm occupies a Tardis-like plot fronted by a Victorian school building, tucked into a leafy residential area away from the less picturesque parts of Harrow proper. Having just finished an £11 million refurb programme, school boasts smart classrooms and facilities galore (barely a tatty corner in sight), plus not only the shiniest dining room for miles around but also a state of the art library (both 2015) designed to inspire the most reluctant of readers. Delightful grounds sprawl behind the main school building, providing space for all manner of activities – as well as the Orley Farm chickens (the box of freshly laid eggs we were given on departure, rather than the usual piles of self-promoting literature, could almost be a metaphor for how this school differs from others). Main playing fields amounting to some 40 acres are over the road, plus separate gym and sports hall, pool and Astroturf – how many London schools can claim such riches?

A holistic vibe in evidence at every turn. Recent introduction of the Creative Curriculum in pre-prep much welcomed by parents who feel it 'brings topics alive' for the school's youngest pupils, to the extent that they want to do more under their own steam when they get home. The Edge programme, which sees children participate in age-appropriate experiences from planning – then following unaccompanied – a route into central London on public transport to fixing a bicycle puncture or spending time with local elderly people, demonstrates that school is not just paying lip service to developing EQ as well as IQ. You can't help feeling that an Orley Farm education is about so much more than just powering towards the next school. There is, however, a questionmark over how unanimous parents are in supporting this approach – definite rumblings in evidence from those who would like school to fall into line with local academic hothouses and reports of parents demanding homework for their 5 and 6 year olds (then setting it themselves when not forthcoming). This is explicable by school's demographic, typified by its geography. Around 70 per cent of families are Asian, with the vast majority dual income professionals, 'incredibly committed to education,' according to head. Many Harrow School and some John Lyon staff in parent cohort. Pupils, thankfully, come over as carefree, likeable and down to earth – head 'can't stand arrogance.' Teachers reportedly 'go the extra mile' and pre-prep parents are delighted with recent appointments of young staff, whose ideas have been welcomed and implemented.

Curriculum broad, with majority of girls heading for 11+ and boys for 13+ exit. French and Latin in the languages department, with a taste of Greek at the top of the school. Gentle setting from summer term of year 2 and children are class taught for most subjects until year 5. Classes maxed at 21, often with smaller numbers in English and maths sets. Head says 'academic life is a given – we go a long way beyond what's expected.' Staff ratios are 'absurd,' he says, with a full time classroom assistant in every class up to year 4. Full-time SENCo plus some part-timers to assist those with additional needs. Around 30 children currently supported with anything ranging from organisational skills to mild dyslexia, with withdrawal avoided wherever possible. Open to taking children with greater needs, recently profound deafness, as long as they are able to successfully access curriculum.

DT and art in strong evidence, both with impressive studios. Head still teaches art – his lessons greeted with enthusiastic fist pumps from pupils. Drama on curriculum to year 8; school has a new studio (2015) plus dynamic new teacher who has breathed life into performances. Music, though, is the jewel in Orley Farm's crown, taught from the brand new music school, with choirs and ensembles galore ranging from the Fab Fives which sing 'funky' hits to the chamber choir who tackle three part harmonies with reported aplomb. Compulsory recorder for all in year 2 and over 90 per cent of all pupils learn a peripatetic instrument. Unsurprisingly, given facilities, sport high on agenda with 'strong' rugby and netball, a non-compulsory Saturday morning sports academy and A to E teams fielded whenever opposing schools are big enough to match their numbers. A few grumbles from parents that school could do more to develop those with less talent, but overall sports universally praised.

Four houses encourage 'healthy competition' amongst pupils and children are given positions of responsibility right from reception. We love the playground traffic light system used for solving disputes – no teachers involved, just worldly wise year 3 pupils to mediate spats. Each class has a form tutor as well as form teacher to monitor pastoral well-being. Psychodynamic counsellor on staff two days each week, with children able to self-refer for help with concerns related or totally unrelated to school (fears, phobias, stress). Extracurricular activities known as 'hobbies' not as broad or varied as at some schools but solid, with all the usual suspects. Wonderful, annual Expeditions Week which takes everyone from year 4 up all over the place from mountaineering in Wales to 'total emersion' in a French château. Best of all, it's included in the fees.

Going places under fabulous newish head. If you're looking for a school to drive your child hard towards academic superstardom and a ticket to a top academic secondary, Orley Farm probably isn't for you. If, however, you want them to skip joyously into school every day, have time to play when they come home – and quite possibly land one of those coveted top school places on the grounds of their roundedness, likeability and passion for learning, get your name on the list and cross fingers and toes (tutoring won't work).

Our Lady of Victories Primary School

1 Clarendon Drive, London SW15 1AW

Pupils: 204 • Ages: 4-11 • RC

Tel: 020 8788 7957
Email: info@ourladyofvictories.wandsworth.sch.uk
Website: www.ourladyofvictories.wandsworth.sch.uk

Headteacher: Since 2011, Mrs Deirdre McDonald BA PGCE NQPH (40s). After studying English at university, Mrs McDonald worked in publishing, then decided to train as a teacher. She has a long association with the school – she was a governor and taught year 6 for eight years before becoming deputy head and more recently head. Her own children are now at university but attended Our Lady of Victories. Forward thinking and inclusive – parents say she is a caring and committed head who's available to all families as and when they need her assistance. Her background in publishing and interest in literature and language has inspired and influenced many school activities. Definitely an artsy type, she enjoys cinema, theatre, reading and travel.

O

Entrance: Priority to Catholics in all categories; siblings only get preference if parents still regular worshippers. Ballot allocation decides places in inevitable event of oversubscription. Places sometimes come up in the older age groups (usually due to families moving away from London), so it's worth contacting the school for occasional vacancies.

Exit: At 11+, just over half of pupils move to popular Catholic secondary schools like Cardinal Vaughan, The London Oratory, Sacred Heart, Ursuline High School, Wimbledon College, Gumley House. The rest go to local independents (Emanuel, Ibstock Place, Latymer, Hampton) or to Catholic boarding schools (Worth, The Oratory School, Reading and the IBVM convents).

Remarks: A first-rate primary school tucked into the residential streets of Putney, in the parish of Our Lady of Pity and St Simon Stock. Originally run by the Sisters of the Poor Servants of the Mother of God, the school was handed over to the Diocese of Southwark in 1978. Housed in the former convent (there are several modern extensions), its compact site is well kept and decorated with an array of colourful artwork by the children.

School is exceptionally well accomplished in all areas. The majority of children achieve level 5 by year 6, with everyone's progress assessed each half term. A well-balanced curriculum is delivered throughout and children achieve particularly well in maths and English. French classes from year 1. The school has won silver and gold awards in junior maths challenges. Creative writing is strong and pupils do variety of science, history and geography projects each term. Older children practise verbal and non-verbal reasoning for the Wandsworth 11+ tests and are taught how to write timed essays.

The school has strong links with the parish – it celebrates a number of religious festivals and the local priest visits the school regularly. At holy communion, children process from school to church, a day rounded off with a visit to the ice cream van. The choir sings in the church and at local care centres. Music, led by a dedicated music teacher, is very strong. Lots of music lessons in school, concerts and the school's recorder group and choir attends annual Music for Youth festival. Pupils take part in the National Theatre's Primary Programme (workshops held in school and theatre visits), alongside trips to concerts and the ballet.

Impressive PE programme offers a range of sporting activities at Dover House Road playing fields and swimming at the nearby Putney Leisure Centre pool. Good range of clubs includes fencing, zumba and Latin. SENCo and visiting speech and occupational therapists supervise learning support. Head is keen to ensure awareness of SEN throughout the school. Regular in-house training days and some teachers attend training courses run by a school specialising in specific learning difficulties and differences.

Lots of fundraising for charity organised by the school and parents, with many of the events run by the children themselves.

Our Lady of Victories RC Primary School

Clareville Street, London SW7 5AQ

Pupils: 240 • Ages: 3–11 • RC

Tel: 020 7373 4491
Email: info@olov.rbkc.sch.uk
Website: www.olov.rbkc.sch.uk/

Headteacher: Since September 2016, Chris McPhilemy, previously acting head teacher (and before that deputy head) at St Mary's Catholic School in Wimbledon.

Entrance: Pupils come from the parishes of Our Lady of Victories, Our Lady of Mount Carmel and St Simon Stock. Priority goes to baptised, practising Catholics; all applications must be supported by letter from the parish priest. Siblings of families living within the parish boundaries get priority. Random allocation is used to offer places to other applicants. Children attending the nursery are not automatically guaranteed a place in the reception class, which is always oversubscribed. Contact the school for occasional places in older age groups.

Exit: To state schools and independents in many different directions. Co-eds St Thomas More, Holland Park, Emanuel, St Benedict's, Latymer Upper. Boys, London Oratory, Cardinal Vaughan, independents Westminster, St Paul's, Dulwich College and City of London Boys. Girls, Sacred Heart, Hammersmith, Gumley House, independents More House, Queensgate, Francis Holland, Godolphin & Latymer. A few to Catholic boarding schools eg St Mary's Ascot, Worth and Ampleforth.

Remarks: Very high standards across the curriculum continue to make this a successful and sought-after primary. All teaching is graded outstanding. Lots of attention to detail, personal successes, the pupils are encouraged to take pride in everything they do. Continuous assessment and monitoring ensure everybody reaches their potential, and those who need additional support are identified. Parents tell us enthusiastic staff always want to make sure the children really enjoy themselves and develop socially as well as academically. School aims to pick up SEN early; pupils are supported by differentiated teaching, specialist teachers and therapists in small groups or one-to-one. International clientele so lots of EAL tuition for those who need it.

Tall Victorian buildings with lots of stairs, however, good-sized classrooms, beautifully decorated; the school has gold Artsmark. Displays show that even the tiny children have beautiful handwriting. Nursery and reception classes have been redesigned so 3 to 5-year-olds are taught in a large, open plan space with its own playground. French starts at key stage 2, other languages via clubs, year 6 have French penfriends and make an annual trip to Cannes. Sadly, Latin has disappeared from the curriculum. After-school verbal reasoning club in the run-up to 11+ exams. Inner city location means outdoor spaces are tight, but they are well-maintained and decorated with mosaics made by the children. Younger horticulturalists grow many colourful flowers and shrubs through the gardening club which they organise themselves.

The school has a Sportsmark; multi-purpose hall is large enough for short tennis, gymnastics and ballet lessons. Outdoor sports take place at Battersea Park; professional coaches, including ex-Middlesex cricketer, teach good range of team games. Specialist teachers for both art and music, pupils can have individual instrumental tuition on a range of five different instruments, and often join the young musicians' performances at the Albert Hall. Enticing range of extracurricular activities, clubs, trips and special visitors; year 5s can complete their cycling proficiency certificates at school.

Parents say pastoral care is very good and inclusive, the weekly newsletter keeps everybody up-to-date with events and pupils are given a voice through the school council which meets regularly with the deputy head. Food is often on the agenda, as the school has Food for Life Award, everything is cooked on site and where possible locally sourced. Encouraged to be involved in the school community, parents run cookery classes, listen to readers and raise large amounts of money which go towards paying for improvements and equipment for the school as well as for outside charities. Catholic beliefs remain at the heart of the warm, family atmosphere of the school. First rate and first choice school for Catholic families in Kensington.

Palmers Green High School

104 Hoppers Road, London N21 3LJ

Pupils: 278 • Ages: 3–16

Fees: £10,380 – £14,760 pa

Tel: 020 8886 1135
Email: office@palmersgreen.enfield.sch.uk
Website: www.pghs.co.uk

Headmistress: Since January 2017, Mrs Wendy Kempster, previously deputy head for five years at Loughborough High. BSc from Reading; has also inter alia been head of maths and assistant head at Nottingham Girls' High. An ISI inspector and an advanced skills teacher, has been a governor at three different schools, and has been married for nearly 25 years to a senior leader in FE. They have three sons at university. She sings with the Bach Choir and enjoys running, cycling, swimming and playing tennis.

Academic matters: Single form entry lower school. Parents like the small classes and the fact that specialist teaching in art, DT, drama, PE and music is introduced to children from as early as year 1 and in some subjects from reception. While core subjects such as English, maths, science and humanities are taught by form tutors, from year 3 girls have specialist French tuition and year 5s have taster courses in a range of languages, including Latin. Year 6 girls receive specialist DT teaching. 'DT is really fun,' remarked one year 6 girl. 'We've been doing models of playground rides and we solder too.' Her classmate showed us some prototypes but admitted that the teacher helped her with the soldering part as 'I was a bit scared' – then again, she had only joined the school in year 5 and said, 'In my old school we didn't do any DT, they didn't trust us.' Parents comment on the 'teaching with substance'. Early introduction to subjects such as Latin and DT helps to develop the children's reasoning skills and their understanding of a wide variety of topics.

It is a very friendly school where teachers insist you come in and have a look around the classrooms and the children appear wholly interested in what they are learning and readily talk about their work. A year 4 science class shared with us what they were learning about the comparison of light and dark. Another class showed off their work on historical toys, including specimens they had brought in from home. Learning is supported by visits to places like the British Schools Museum, Hatfield House, Whipsnade Zoo and the year 5 residential trip to Flatford Mill where they develop their skills in navigation, using a compass, and trekking. The school magazine shows off impressive artwork and writing.

Consistently high GCSE results in the senior school though a disappointing drop to 61 per cent A*/A in 2016. Relationships between pupils and teachers are strong; class sizes are still small, between 10 and 16. 'That's why we chose this school,' said a parent. 'It was pretty tough to see how overstretched the teachers were at our previous state primary school.' With a teacher pupil ratio of 1:9, 'we get the attention we need', say pupils.

The school offers IGCSE French and Spanish and girls can choose either or both. A few girls study additional maths; firm favourites when choosing options are history, geography and ICT. Parents will be pleased to know, however, that the school is flexible towards subject choice catering to, for example, those who study a language outside school or who have taken a GCSE/ IGCSE early (frequently in a modern foreign language spoken at home), allowing them to continue to study the subject at school.

School believes in teaching 'children to work smart and play to strengths'. Moving more toward IGCSE because GCSE 'doesn't stretch the brightest of students'. Parents agree: 'No bones about the school being selective,' said a parent. 'I wanted my daughter to be in that environment.'

Majority of pupils do D of E bronze level and the UK Maths Challenge. There are visiting teachers, educational trips and residential stays to enhance learning – eg year 8 geography trip to Dorset to prepare pupils for their GCSE fieldwork, trips to Poland and Berlin for GCSE history and to the Isle of Wight where pupils study the impact of the festival. 'We've just returned from a trip to Spain,' said a pupil. 'Every morning we had Spanish lessons with a native speaker; even if we asked what a word meant they would explain it in Spanish.'

Pupils say the trips aid what they learn in the classroom: 'it's so amazing to go and see everything expanded... it is all very well learning from a text book...' They particularly look forward to the annual year 9 visit to the Guardian newspaper office as part of the English curriculum, where 'you get to see how everything is put into action, you choose the stories, you choose a name and print the papers'. They bring the papers back to school and stick the front pages up on the walls.

GCSE students are able to access AS level course material – this is mainly in modern foreign languages and for those who have already successfully attained an A* in year 9 and year 10. 'The main purpose is to enrich and extend language skills in preparation for taking A levels.' School says pupils often surprise others with their knowledge due to their early access to specialist teaching or advanced materials: one went for a sixth form interview 'and the interviewer said, "how did you know that? You shouldn't know that at your stage."' However, one parent said that highly able students could be better challenged: 'There have been several instances where the homework has been so basic that my daughter has become demotivated.'

Teachers generally described as friendly; head of history praised by pupils for making the subject one of the most popular. Head of maths also praised: 'In year 7 I didn't like maths and now I'm doing additional maths. They made me enjoy it and that's really good as it's so important. I know that's the case for lots of people in the class.'

No children at present who do not speak fluent English but EAL support can be provided. Around 20 to 25 girls are identified with SEN, mostly dyslexia, and a few pupils have autistic spectrum disorders (ASDs). They can have support in lessons and there is some help for the ASDs in social skills arranged by the individual needs coordinator, who can involve outside agencies if necessary. Extra classes before and after school and one-to-one tuition are also available at an extra charge.

The school helps prepare the girls for moving on to a sixth form elsewhere – 'We want to make sure they have lots of opportunities when they leave because of the opportunities they have had here. It doesn't matter if they are not strong academically as they will have other strengths which may help them to get a sixth form place somewhere.'

Games, options, the arts: Although the school no longer offers PE as a short course at GCSE, the opportunity and enthusiasm for sport across the years is evident. This is commendable given the shortage of sporting facilities at the school. Until 2012, the main hall was the only space available for assemblies, gymnastics, drama and exams. The Elizabeth Smith Hall now provides a multi-purpose space for all these activities and leaves the main hall free during exams.

Not much of a playground, just a small yard used by junior pupils, and there are no fields. Girls travel 10 minutes by coach to nearby Walker Grounds for outdoor games and to Southgate for swimming lessons. Year 10 and 11 travel to Southbury Leisure Centre for a range of sports. Still, nothing is lost and time is well managed so that, for example, pupils receive pre-lesson instruction in transit, 'with the added advantage that they don't stand freezing listening' on the fields. Parents certainly don't view this as a problem, since 'it's not that far and they are not in the bus for half an hour'. Another said: 'My daughter isn't particularly sporty but we go and support netball matches.'

Dance and gymnastics are taught on half term rotation, and netball is popular. They have won the Barnet Netball League for four years consecutively, 'playing bigger schools, who have 200-odd in each year group, where we have only 30 girls to choose from.' This is a small school where the girls 'know each other incredibly well', something parents attest to. Pupils from year 2 upwards compete successfully in the week long Enfield Primary Schools Gymnastics Festival and Enfield netball tournament; there is an inter-house netball tournament for years 5 and 6, and there is a school swimming gala.

Around half choose art and design at GCSE and the self-portraits mounted in the art corridor show there is plenty of talent here, as do pupils' willingness to talk thoughtfully about their work. Classrooms are well equipped with colour wheels for guidance and artefacts for inspiration, 'to help you make a decision about what you are trying to express through colours, shapes, textures, perspectives... which is helpful if you are not too familiar with art,' said one pupil. Another commented: 'We did 3D art and I found that is my niche'. She showed us the model of a figure drowning in money, explaining that it was to show 'how greed can take over... how too much money is never enough for some people. People always want just a little bit more.' The remedy? 'It depends on the sort of person you are,' she said.

Year 6s take the lead roles in the annual junior summer play (which includes pupils from year 3 upwards) – 'we put on a play, we sing and dance and dress up in nice costumes'. Titles are adapted and new characters are introduced to popular productions to ensure everyone has the opportunity to take part. One year they 'did the 12 dancing princesses and 10 of their cousins because there were 22 of us'. Around a third of the girls choose drama at GCSE. It is also popular as an extracurricular activity, as is dance: pupils have performed in the Nutcracker ballet at the Bloomsbury Theatre in Euston.

Not many take music at GCSE (15 per cent). At the time of our visit, there was only one girl studying music in year 11 and five in year 10. The music department offers timetabled lessons in different instruments: sax, trumpet, singing – but pupils say that if you want to learn an instrument not offered, the school will get a teacher in. Around 80 girls across the whole school take lessons inside school and many more take lessons outside school hours. Their music skills range from beginners to above grade 8. There is an open door culture in the music department where 'you can come during break if you want to practise your instrument'. There is a senior school orchestra and and two choirs, plus other instrumental groups.

Plenty on offer in terms of extracurricular clubs, though some (particularly working parents) say they would like to see more after-school provision. The school currently offers netball, choir, music, knitting, drama, debating, swimming and a Christian union, and tries to ensure everyone gets involved in something. As well as lunchtime and after-school activities, there's a gym club at 8am and weekend cross-country competitions, D of E expeditions and training. They also take part in eg inter-school debating competitions.

P

There is a 'very competitive' annual house choral competition. Pupils describe it as a 'bit like a musical but not'. The girls choose songs on some pretty powerful themes – 'about war, politics, women in power, the economy, green issues'. 'People sing, play instruments, costumes get dragged into that... but most important, you don't want your competitor to know what you're doing so it's very secretive, all covered up.' 'Green house won last year,' another butted in, 'yellow house won year before, and we won year before that. So far we're equal... but we're worried about what will happen this year [after we leave] so we will have to come back and see how they get on without us.' The audience for the house choral competition always includes some recent leavers.

Background and atmosphere: Founded in 1905 by a Christian Quaker called Alice Hum whose motto, By Love, Serve One Another, still guides the ethos here. The building was originally located in nearby Osborne Road and opened with 12 pupils. It had grown to 300 when it moved to its present location in Hoppers Road in 1918. The original and main building, Avondale Hall, is still the heart of the school. Classrooms and a dining room were added between the 1960s and 1990s. Over the next decade a new office block was built and more recently the new Elizabeth Smith Hall (with a couple of one bed flats above – which the school says will suit student teachers) and a medical room. The school could do with more space but as the site is on a residential street, neatly tucked between houses, expansion is difficult.

Despite its age, the school has a modern feel. The building is intimate and compact yet the rooms, hallway and stairwells are airy and bright. Most spaces, including the head's office, double up for other uses, and there are well thought out rotas for use of the hall and library resource centre to accommodate the needs of both the junior and senior pupils. The prep department shares the same building, and the linked pre-school (Alice Nursery) is about a mile and half away.

Whatever the school lacks in space it greatly makes up for in friendliness: if there were a prize for the most welcoming atmosphere this school would be in the running. Teachers invited us into lessons, and pupils showed impeccable manners. A science class in the middle of an experiment gladly redid the combustion exercise just for our visit – or so they claimed. Pupils are keen to talk about their work displayed on classroom walls, like the 'wonder posters' they created about different countries that took part in the Olympics.

Pastoral care, well-being and discipline: As a relatively small school contained in one building, it would be hard for any child's problem or unhappiness to go unnoticed – 'it is quite common for a member of staff to take a girl aside if she seems troubled in any way'. Very good staff-parent relations as all share the ethos of: work hard and your reward will be a good career.

Pupils told us that settling into the school was easy. 'If teachers can see you are struggling they introduce you to someone'. Pupils have two induction days before they start plus a three-day team building residential trip within the first few weeks of September, 'so we made friends straight away'.

Small group sizes here mean no-one gets lost. 'We have an open door policy so we can talk to any teacher and get help if we need to,' as 'you can feel closer to one particular teacher'. In such a small school teachers 'can spot if something is wrong', and pupils develop good relationships with their form tutors – two to a form – who sometimes stay with the groups as they move up.

The house system also helps them know and support each other well across the school: during the fire drill 'older girls must each grab a younger child and walk them to the meeting place'. Parents mentioned this 'nurturing environment' with girls 'across different year groups interacting and playing with each other' as one of the appealing characteristics of the school. Senior pupils mentor younger pupils and take up roles as head girls, house captains, form and other types of prefects. Prep prefects help out in the prep school, form prefects help year 7s to settle in and career and public relations prefects help out in their relevant areas. Sometimes they double up on roles to share duties. All junior pupils learn to be responsible by taking on roles like helping out in the prep school or library, or as head and deputy head girls. These roles – called 'duties' – alongside the range of extracurricular activities on offer, give pupils plenty to do and they both enjoy and thrive from the responsibility despite their busy schedules: 'I find it amazing that I'm a head girl,' said one pupil. 'I have prep duties two days a week; orchestra on Wednesdays, Thursdays is choir and on Friday we do library.'

This culture of active citizenship means that the girls are consulted on lots of important decisions. They formed a committee to help choose a new catering company for the school – the winner was not only chosen because of its great home made yogurt (which has gone on to become a favourite), but also because it creates menus linked to the curriculum. Pupils also formed a panel to choose a new uniform to mark the school's centenary – they hated the old green one, apparently. We walked into a geography lesson where the girls were being consulted on what colour book to use for a new GCSE unit. They went for green.

Behaviour is good and incidences of bullying are rare: 'I've never had a problem... you would know about it,' said a pupil. 'I've been here since reception and never heard of anything.' Another said, 'The worst is you have an argument with your friend but that happens anywhere.' PSHE includes lessons in study and life skills and careers guidance.

Encouragement to work hard includes a star chart, embraced by even the most senior pupils, with stars awarded for high results in the weekly French and Spanish vocab tests – 'if you get 10 out of 10 you get a star, it's a good way to ensure you learn the vocabulary'. Parents praise the commendation system because it means their daughters are 'given more to aim for'. Notices on classroom walls include injunctions to 'turn up on time', 'help friends', 'have a good attitude', 'show respect'.

Pupils and parents: Parents are mostly professionals and come from a mixture of cultures and backgrounds. There are no parent governors: 'it avoids problems if there are financial difficulties'. However, the parents' association organises events like theatre trips, quiz nights, the summer fair and other fundraising events and has raised money for benches for the grounds, an audio system for the hall and the school minibus. It also helps new families settle in, 'especially if you have moved to London from outside,' said a parent who moved from Cardiff.

Notable past pupils include Marion Tait CBE, prima ballerina and assistant director of the Birmingham Royal Ballet.

Entrance: Most pupils join the junior school from the linked Alice Nursery, situated about a mile and a half away. Entrance to the prep department at 4+ and the junior department at 7+ is by assessment of ability and potential by one of the primary school teachers. This involves a timed test for children in years 5 and 6 but is less formal for those in year 4 and below. Girls joining at 11 sit English, maths, science and reasoning tests, with those who show promise invited for interview. However, the vast majority come up from the lower school. The school welcomes 'pupils with special educational needs, providing that our individual needs department can offer them the support they require'.

Exit: Around 70 per cent move on from the junior to the senior schools, others to other independent or selective state schools in the area. Some parents would like 'a greater focus on preparing children for 11+ exams in the same way some other schools do'.

'We always say we have the largest sixth form in London. It just happens to be located in all our colleagues' schools.' Senior leavers move on to to a variety of schools, with roughly equal numbers to each of selective state schools, non-selective state schools and independent schools, including Henrietta Barnett, North London Collegiate, Dame Alice Owens, St Michael's, The Latymer, Woodhouse, Aldenham, Headington and Downe House.

Money matters: Academic scholarships, music awards and means-tested bursaries are available to cover up to 100 per cent of fees at 11+. There are also other internal awards related to progress within the school.

Remarks: A small, cosy and nurturing school that prepares girls well to move on to a wider world at 16.

Parliament Hill School

Linked with LaSWAP Sixth Form Consortium

Highgate Road, London NW5 1RL

Pupils: 1,116 • Ages: 11–19 • Sixth form: 224 (550 in joint sixth form with William Ellis, part of LaSWAP)

Tel: 020 7485 7077
Email: enquiries@parliamenthill.camden.sch.uk
Website: www.parliamenthill.camden.sch.uk

Headteacher: Since 2005, Ms Susan Higgins MA (Cantab) MA (Ed) (50s), previously head of Brentford School for Girls for five years. She studied English at New Hall (now Murray Edwards) College, Cambridge, after a peripatetic school career as her family moved around the country. The first Oxbridge student from her Bradford comprehensive, she was enthused by 'an inspirational English teacher' who was a Cambridge graduate: 'He made Shakespeare a really exciting experience and encouraged me to study English at degree level. He told me Cambridge would be a great place to study.' Although very much in the minority, with a lot of adaptation on her behalf, Ms Higgins nonetheless looked at Cambridge as a fantastic opportunity and draws on that experience to encourage her own students. One parent said: 'The girls love hearing about her experience of going to Cambridge as a working class girl...She's a great role model for them.' Ms Higgins likes to invite her ex-students who are at Oxbridge to have a cup of tea with current students at the school, in the hope they too may inspire.

Head of English at Walthamstow School for Girls for much of her career, taking time out to become deputy head at Skinners' Company's School for Girls in Hackney and spending time as a school-based PGCE tutor for the Institute of Education before returning to Walthamstow as deputy head. Still enthused about her profession, Ms Higgins says that teaching in her eyes remains 'a fantastic job to do' and an increasingly important one: 'Education is a rapidly changing landscape and it is impossible to get bored.' Definitely not one to rest on her laurels, even after 10 years at the helm of Parliament Hill School – she is also a National Leader in Education and mentors other teachers, which she says keeps her at the top of her game: 'Because of this added dimension of mentoring and advising people, I better know what I'm doing and be confident at it, otherwise I'd have little credibility.' (Ms Higgins also stepped in to help Acland Burghley School during a period of turmoil after their long-term head left.)

Well respected by parents and pupils alike (although we were told by one parent that 'she presents a formidable appearance'), this head is a strong and capable leader with a good back-up team. She has her finger on the pulse and is a very visible presence at the school. She calls her school 'a glass half full school' because it 'captures the optimism of the school' and she cares infinitely about her students, 'lights up when she hears that her students are doing well', we are told. Has two children of her own.

Retiring in July 2017.

Academic matters: A huge ability range here, with lots of bright girls and also plenty in need of extra support, whether educational or emotional. Accordingly, the school offers a range of options. Everyone studies for a core of GCSE subjects which includes maths, English, core science, RE, and short courses

P

in PE and citizenship. They can add on more GCSE subjects, or choose a vocational BTec from a range that includes business, art and design, ICT and health and social care, or go for a young apprenticeship. Most of the latter two options are taught elsewhere in Camden. Everyone is allocated to either French or Spanish classes for the first three years, and can start the other language in year 9; about a third take a modern language GCSE. Other popular options at KS4 include additional AS maths and triple science; ICT AS and photography GCSE are taught after school as twilight classes.

In 2016, 67 per cent of girls got 5+ A*-C grades including English and maths at GCSE; 33 per cent of grades were A*/A. English has been very strong, maths and science historically rather weaker. However, maths now taught in ability sets from the second term in year 7, and the curriculum has been redesigned substantially. Girls arrive at the school with, on average, much higher verbal than non-verbal aptitude scores – 'but as a technology college we focus on building up their confidence and aptitude in maths and science'. The science department has appointed some very highly qualified teachers over the last few years. Triple science courses very popular, with excellent results. 'They're very good at assessing strengths and weaknesses,' said a parent, 'and throwing lots of energy at weaknesses.'

Downgraded in 2013 from its 'outstanding' status to 'good' by Ofsted, under the new harsher regime, citing the gap in achievement between poorer students and the rest. The head is clearly still upset about this and says it was based on 'historical examinations results' and not teaching. Indeed, Inspectors were able to identify many successful features of teaching and learning. Homework and marking – aspects formerly raised by parents as sometimes inconsistent – were areas that Ofsted pointed out as having had 'key improvement'.

Although there has been little fallout since this report from either parents or pupils, Ms Higgins is determined to win back their outstanding status: 'We will continue as a school community to strive for better things...and to be regarded in the wider educational world as a leading school and professional centre of excellence.'

SEN provision has been 'transformed', with an assistant head leading the the way on SEN and inclusion. Few state schools feel that they have sufficient funds to provide all the help every child needs, but 'we feel we've made substantial progress'. The Extra Mile project targets under-achieving year 10 girls, who are mostly from white low-income families. The school is also a Potential Plus Partner School which aims to identify 'high learning potential students' by using a programme called Maurice B, which uses cognitive tests to help identify Oxbridge students.

Joint sixth form with next-door William Ellis School, with co-ed tutor groups. It is also part of LaSWAP, which includes La Sainte Union and Acland Burghley schools too, and has over 1,500 students. Each school teaches the core sixth form subjects, but students visit other schools in the group for more minority subjects eg film studies and further maths. The ability range encompasses those aspiring to read medicine at Cambridge and those working for an introductory BTec diploma in health and social care, with appropriate entry requirements. A scheme in conjunction with La Sainte Union targets very able scientists, who study together and take part in organised work experience and masterclasses. English is the most popular A level subject at Parliament Hill, with psychology second. In 2016, 20 per cent of grades were A*/A and 47 per cent A*-B.

Games, options, the arts: This is a very physical school and indeed the reason that many pupils choose it above others. Its stunning location almost begs one to be outdoors. Students have the opportunity to experience a wide variety of activities in physical education and the curriculum alone includes dance, swimming, gymnastics, tennis, rounders, cricket, athletics, fitness, invasion games and trampolining. A year 7 student can expect to participate in a minimum of two hours of PE every week as well as learn to swim at nearby Swiss Cottage baths. This doesn't include the extracurricular sporting activities: table tennis, badminton, dodgeball, football, cheerleading and various dance activities.

Dance is the real hot favourite at Parli Hill and one pupil told us that she chose the school because it was one of the few schools in the area that offers dance at GCSE level. Dance at the school comes in many varieties including PHS Dance Elite, contemporary dance and street dance, and there are many opportunities to compete for the coveted Camden Shield by entering any one of the numerous dance competitions, including Rock Challenge and Camden schools' dance festival. (Parliament Hill actually won the National Rock Challenge in 2014 and delighted students were asked to perform at Disneyland Paris.) School also hosts an annual Sweet Summer Dance Show.

Furthermore, year 10 students are offered the opportunity to work towards either a dance leaders level 1 award or a sports leaders level 1 award. Both are designed 'to teach leadership qualities and give students an opportunity to gain experience in leading sports sessions for their feeder primary schools.' Sports teams play successful matches against other Camden schools. School has two tennis/netball courts at the front of the school and a grassy area at the back where the football teams practise, plus a rather ageing hall for gym and badminton with a fitness suite. (New multi-purpose sports centre on the cards as part of the school's rebuild programme.)

Everyone takes DT GCSE, with a choice of four options. The single storey DT block was built to an environmentally-friendly design with a green roof, and forms the fourth side of a grassy courtyard, twisting up to meet the original Edwardian building. On another corner of the building is the performing arts block, clad in green glass, which provides music rooms and the dance and drama studios. The top floor corridors are lined with expressive, colourful and imaginative GCSE and A level photography and artwork, and textile designs hang in the stairwells. 'The art department really struck me', one pupil told us when she was looking at secondary schools. (Pretty good photography studio space too.)

Music popular here too and many girls have instrumental lessons and can choose from a variety of musical groups to join including orchestra, rock band, flute group, jazz, string and brass ensembles, or sing in the choir. Those on free school meals get free music lessons. One big annual musical a year (recently Fame) and one main play. Drama also popular and pupils have a large and fairly new drama studio in which to rehearse.

A breakfast club every morning at 8am and plenty more activities ranging from Italian and drama clubs to creative writing and documentary making. They visit museums, theatres and galleries, travel to China and go on physics trips to Switzerland. D of E very popular, as is debating – many students have competed passionately in the Urban Debating League and the Debate Mate Cup.

Background and atmosphere: Opened in 1906, has an idyllic site on the edge of Hampstead Heath. Plenty of grassy space, including a sculpture park and kick-around area. Buildings range from solid Edwardiana to the 21st century award-winning DT and performing arts blocks. Is at last in receipt of £25 million to rebuild the well-past-its-sell-by-date Heath Building. This long anticipated building programme should be completed by July 2018. Students, we are told, can still work in the existing building whist works are under way without being inconvenienced too much.

This large injection of cash, paid for by Camden Community Development Programme, will fund a new maths, English and science block, a multi-purpose sports centre and a dedicated sixth form building. Money will also go towards renovating the existing main Edwardian building (which was very tired in places when we did our tour, especially the loos, which could do with a major spruce up).

Harmonious atmosphere. Despite the huge range of pupils, both ethnically and socially, girls tend to get on well together, with few reports of bullying. Recently one of six in the country to win a Diamond quality mark for cultural diversity. 'Very much a community school', one parent told us – and very 'inclusive.' Bright and engaging students – one who travels from as far afield as Covent Garden because of the school's reputation: 'I started this school in year 8 as I wasn't very happy at my last school, and heard about Parliament Hill. I was particularly attracted by its location and outdoor space as well as the bright classrooms..I settled in pretty much immediately and everyone was so friendly.' And a parent added; 'The good thing about a school of this size is that almost everyone is going to find another like minded person to hang out with.'

Definitely a sense of personality at the school and of girls who know their minds: 'a lively atmosphere,' as one parent described. Posters reinforcing 'female power' are dotted around the school – most noticeably near the sports hall. Ms Higgins is very much a key player in reinforcing positive role models at the school. She says: 'Female empowerment is very much part of the ethos at Parliament Hill. Girls here have a real sense of themselves as individuals. These are girls who will make a difference to the lives of other people.'

Pastoral care, well-being and discipline: Many vulnerable pupils here, including refugees and those with learning difficulties, who get 'excellent' support, says Ofsted. Liaises with its feeder primary school to identify girls likely to be in need of extra help with making the transition to senior school: 'Our transition is acknowledged to be excellent and supportive – we work very closely with families.' School also works with outside agencies that provide therapy or counselling to those in need, with a designated key worker in school. It also runs many programmes to motivate disaffected pupils, stretch the aspirations of bright girls and ensure everyone gets a chance to broaden their horizons. One parent told us: 'The school works very hard at narrowing the gap between disadvantaged and non-disadvantaged pupils.'

Assertive classroom management keeps most lessons running without disruptions (although we did pass some slightly rowdier ones on our tour). Big on some areas of discipline like punctuality, attendance and school attire – no uniform, but the rule is 'no gaps, no straps, no shorts' and students will be ticked off if they don't adhere to this. 'It's a problem in the summer,' one student grumbled. Older girls are allowed to go out onto Hampstead Heath at lunchtimes, together with pupils from nearby schools, William Ellis and La Sainte Union, and locals have complained about litter problems. 'We're very concerned. The girls regard the Heath as very special to them, and we're doing work on social responsibility to educate them that it's for everyone in the community'.

Pastoral care is very good, report parents. 'I've always felt they know my daughter very well,' said one. 'They school has contacted me whenever they've had concerns, and they've dealt with any problems quickly and well.' Ofsted remarked how: 'Students speak of the school being an extended family where they feel safe and supported at all times.'

Pupils and parents: 'Amazingly diverse' student population speaks some 50 different languages at home, though few are at early stages of learning English. Over 200 refugees. Nearly half of the girls are on free school meals, but also good support from some local middle-class families. OGs include actress Katrin Cartlidge, BBC journalist Laura Trevelyan, Lola Young, Baroness Young of Hornsey and Emma Hayes, manager of Chelsea Ladies.

Entrance: Takes 180 girls into year 7, with admissions organised through the local authority. Priority for particular SEN, siblings, children in care and those with exceptional social needs. Then by distance – generally within a mile and a half. Those joining LaSWAP sixth form to do A levels must have at least eight GCSE passes including three C and two B grades; various vocational courses available for those with lower grades. Increasingly becoming the school of choice for parents living in the area and not (as was the case historically), second choice to Camden School for Girls.

Exit: Between two-thirds and three-quarters of pupils move on to joint sixth form with William Ellis school, part of LaSWAP sixth form consortium. Some join other sixth forms, eg Camden School for Girls or Woodhouse College, others go to colleges such as City and Islington or Westminster Kingsway to do vocational courses.

In 2016, three Oxbridge places (usually one or two a year) plus two studying medicine. Around a quarter to Russell Group universities, London universities, Sussex, Nottingham and Leeds popular for a range of subjects – eg biomedical science, pharmacy, physics, languages, history, English, architecture and psychology. Quite a few to art foundation courses.

Remarks: Popular girls' comprehensive in idyllic situation on the borders of Hampstead Heath, with a diverse but harmonious student population. Strong, popular head who is a driving force in building on strengths and tackling weaknesses. Aesthetically tired, but much needed cash injection will change that.

Parsons Green Prep School

1 Fulham Park Road, London SW6 4LJ

Pupils: 200 • Ages: 4–11

Fees: £15,585 – £16,830 pa

Tel: 020 7371 9009
Email: admissions@parsonsgreenprep.co.uk
Website: www.parsonsgreenprep.co.uk

Headteacher: Since 2014, Miss Helen Stavert BEd. Year 6 class teacher and numeracy co-ordinator at the school since 2011 and deputy head for two years prior to her appointment as head. Previously head of year 6 at The International School in Marbella and before that taught at a state school in Gloucestershire. Originally from the Cotswolds (did her degree at University of Gloucestershire in Cheltenham), she lives in Putney and unwinds on long walks with her dog and by practising yoga.

Now in her 30s, but easily passing for younger, she took over the headship following the departure of her predecessor after a year – liked by parents but she didn't feel she was the right fit. Some natural angst at the change amongst some parents, but those who have experienced Miss Stavert as a class teacher are spreading the word, saying to us, 'I believe she will thrive' and 'she is respected, committed to the school, approachable and caring about the children as individuals.' She continues to teach year 6 in the mornings.

Mrs Lucinda Waring (40s) is the founding principal (since 2001) and majority shareholder. Originally trained at St Nicholas' Montessori College in Knightsbridge, she founded her first nurseries at the age of 26. Naturally inspiring some envy amongst her high-flying parent body, she aims to remain firmly 'back office' but has stepped up recently to aid the transition of the new head. The school is very much her vision – to create a school where children could thrive without undue pressure; she is on top of every detail and the children know and greet her throughout the school. She is married with one child.

Entrance: Parents can register from birth (£150 registration fee). Once on the waiting list, entrance into reception via pre-entry checks, including a full academic report from current educational setting. Easy-going families preferred. Sibling policy: 10 per cent off for siblings.

The maximum number entering reception is 44, with almost twice this number on the current waiting list. Pupils enter from Fulham nurseries in the main. Occasional places in year 1 upwards (with references and assessment). A deposit of £2000 per family to secure the place.

Exit: Preparations for exit at 11 plus are thorough and commence from year 4. Perhaps there is little the school can do to alleviate the inevitable pressure parents and children feel, but one parent says, 'Children need to be confident enough to be able to think: yes, I can do it! That's what this school gives them'. Both the principal and head insist they will speak up in the face of ambitious parents to try and ensure that children will move on to schools where they will above all be happy. Recent destinations include St Paul's Girls' School, Godolphin & Latymer, City of London Boys', Dulwich College, King's College Wimbledon, Francis Holland, Putney High and Ibstock Place.

Remarks: The school has undergone a name change, becoming Parsons Green Prep (previously Eridge House). Despite the marketing-friendly name change, and ambitious air of the principal, there are no plans to expand the school: 200 pupils would be the absolute maximum.

The school was founded in 2001 in a formerly derelict Victorian villa in an enviable location and with that rare thing, some outside space behind a high garden wall, offering privacy and enough room to run around. The original building was restored and modern additions blended, offering new classrooms and the large assembly hall used for everything from staging productions to PE. The end result is a smart blend of light, modern-seeming classrooms large and small, wide enough corridors with spick and span displays and lots of stairs. Come August and with class sizes finalised, the staff may be busily swapping rooms so that each class is accommodated in the best possible space.

The playground is Astroturfed throughout, with just enough room for football, tennis and netball, and a good in and out space for the early years, with wooden play equipment and smaller quiet area with outdoor chess tables. Very physical older children may need more space, not that it will be easy to find in central London. The stockpile of micro-scooters racked on the playground walls points to pupils mostly living nearby.

The school sets out to provide a creative curriculum, but is well ahead of the curve at primary level in putting STEM subjects at the heart of the maths curriculum, following three years of careful training and planning.

Parents say: 'Reading in the early years is extremely well taught'. Maths and English are taught in small ability groups. One of the numeracy tools has been effectively adopted from Montessori methods. The Mac suite has been upgraded and there is improved wireless technology around the school. Years 5 and 6 have their own individual android tablets with keyboards.

We were impressed by the individual targets on each child's work in every lesson. Teaching aims to take pupils from their learning comfort zone, where they might be engaged but not excited, to their learning challenge zone where they are encouraged to take risks. The school is currently increasing its expertise in stretching the able, gifted and talented. We found children eager to talk to us in every classroom we visited, either explaining clearly what they were working on, or coming unprompted to share their work.

Parents praise cross-curricular topic work, saying 'subjects are really brought to life', such as the year 6 challenge to design a theme park, using mathematical knowledge to design the rides and calculate their profits, whilst utilising art and creative writing to design the posters. Humanities teaching seems fun, too: we observed Horrible Histories style hygiene tips for the Tudors, whilst philosophy for children inspires pupils to interrogate the world around them. Science day saw staff joined by a team from the science museum – children made gigantic bubbles, launched rockets and made goop.

French is taught weekly throughout the school with a specialist French programme, which continues after school, for those children who are already fluent French speakers. The occasional pupil exits to the Lycée.

Two assemblies per week. Christmas concert not a carol service. When we visited in October, they were looking forward to going crazy on Christmas decorations.

A third of the 36 staff has been at the school for more than 10 years. We have rarely heard so much praise for teaching assistants: in the main extremely youthful, so they have sufficient energy to keep up with their charges. 'Right people in the right places,' says principal and 'no staff who get stale'. Parents say: 'often young and enthusiastic about teaching'; 'lovely teachers allow children to be children'; 'willing to try a multitude of different ways to captivate children'. Teachers feel looked after by the school and are part of a very thorough programme of ongoing training. They describe themselves as 'creative, motivated and committed.'

Teachers are addressed (by everyone – parents, other staff) as Miss or Mr plus first name, so Miss Lucinda or Miss Helen, which we found a bit Beatrix Potter-ish, but the principal says, correctly, 'it's friendlier for the children'.

Most parents are content with 'sensible homework', none during school holidays until key stage 2, and there is a dedicated homework session at school. Children are deliberately not overloaded. Trips could be to the local community supermarket or fire station, but also make the most of London from Fulham football club on the doorstep to Pudding Lane. From year 3 residential trips begin with camping and a French day trip.

Seven per cent of pupils have EAL needs. The school seems to have fewer than average number of children with learning differences, but a SENCo in place to ensure their needs are met.

Parents universally describe children who love going to school and 'can't wait to get in at the gate'. We can report beaming smiles and diligent application in every class we visited, and parents agree, describing the school as 'a happy place to learn'; 'intimate, caring, quietly competitive' and 'children do not feel any pressure at all and yet are making good progress'.

Some gripes about sport persist: 'No way near enough sport,' said one parent and another added, 'Not enough boys in year 3 to field a football team'. However, sport is evolving: now offers tennis throughout the year with new tennis coaches, and a coach from Chelsea FC runs three after-school clubs each week. Year 2 upwards play football, tag rugby, cricket, netball, rounders and have weekly swimming lessons. The school has recently joined the Independent Schools Association, which means more sporting competitions. The usual summer sports day and swimming gala. The upper school makes use of Hurlingham Park. Keen sports players had better be early risers as squad practice takes place before school most days.

Children are taught guitar, piano, violin and now drum lessons – singing and guitar most popular. There's an orchestra and a choir.

'The summer performance is always excellent,' said a parent. Most recently A Midsummer Night's Dream and The Wind in the Willows. 'Would like more drama opportunities,' said another. A few entries for the LAMDA drama exams with several distinctions.

Chess is huge here, deliberately encouraged to develop logical thinking. Greatly improved clubs, say parents. Those now on offer pre- and post-school or at lunchtime encompass the fun and fashionable, including photography, fencing, orchestra, Mandarin, soccer, chess, baking, sewing, ukulele, running and study skills. Hot lunches and after-school clubs cost extra.

The school is very clear about the standards expected of the children, and parents see pastoral care as a real strength of the school: 'My child had been unhappy at a different school, but has thrived here'; 'I really like the atmosphere: it is very caring but with high standards of behaviour'; 'bullying isn't tolerated and the staff has been quick to act' and 'not much gets by the staff'. The new buddy benches in the playground have been a big hit, too.

Frequent mentions by parents of this school being well suited to a child who might be quite shy initially: 'a sensitive soul ' or 'young in year or late developers'. But parents with more than more child here, the majority, report it suiting all sorts of temperaments and abilities: 'outgoing children can shine'. A teacher believes it works well for 'bright children who are not afraid to take risks and who want to learn'.

Parents are without doubt a smart, city crowd: 'Friendly, international and professional with lots of dual-working parents,' said one. Many agree on a friendly welcome from other parents. Every other parent describes the school community as 'international' but the principal says this is more perception than actuality. Parent volunteers do everything and anything from weekend hospitality for the science lab chicks, to designing the logos for the houses, to being part of the eco committee growing and harvesting crops in the school garden.

Any parents with low-flying or tiger-ish tendencies, this may well not be the school for you. Those who are searching for somewhere to nurture and inspire happy, confident children – look no further.

Pembridge Hall School

18 Pembridge Square, London W2 4EH

Pupils: 410 • Ages: 4–11

Fees: £20,595 pa

Tel: 020 7229 0121
Email: contact@pembridgehall.co.uk
Website: www.pembridgehall.co.uk

Headmaster: Since 2012, Mr Henry Keighley-Elstub BA PGCE (40s), previously deputy head at Wetherby Prep. Educated at Eton and Leeds University, where he read classical civilization. He has taught history at Ludgrove, Cothill and Chesham Prep, where he was head of department and also senior master. As well as this being his first headship, it is also his first experience of an all girls' school, and one that finishes at 11 years rather than 13. 'I was worried about that at first,' he admits, 'but now I barely notice, and communicating with an 11-year-old girl is equivalent to talking to a 13-year-old boy.' Married to Sarah who works at IBM ('I have no idea what she does', he confides. 'Perhaps she's a spy.') They have a young daughter.

Mr Keighley-Elstub, slight of build, has an immediately warm, engaging and enthusiastic personality that makes even the stiffest person unfurl. His conversation is littered with verbs and adjectives like 'skip along' and 'groovy'. His upbeat, chipper approach is directed at everyone. As well as the girls, the parents and the teachers it embraces the peripatetic music staff, games staff and the odd visitor. Despite being an Old Etonian with an unusually complicated name both to spell and pronounce (think 'Keithly'), Mr Keighley-Elstub is remarkably down to earth. He attributes this to his Northern pedigree (his father was a Yorkshireman but practised as a GP in Wimbledon where Mr Keighley-Elstub grew up). His family used to turn up at Eton in a clapped out old VW, but 'that wasn't remotely embarrassing,' he avers. 'Eton's not smart at all. The greatest compliment anyone could pay me,' he continues, 'is to turn up to meet me in jeans.' If he weren't so refreshingly open you wouldn't guess it – he looks immaculate in his well-cut suit and playfully shrieks when he discovers the odd crisp on the floor in a classroom.

He loves music – his wife is a violinist and he has recently formed a staff choir. He is also an enthusiastic sportsman (running is his thing) and he is determined that the girls here start winning some matches for a change. He champions all departments – art, music, sport and drama – equally and works to get them all to enjoy working together rather than being at loggerheads, as happens so often. He is relishing the challenges of his first headship and is not unaware of the benefits of running a school that is part of the Alpha Plus group. He talks of the wealth of resources available to him, from legal to financial as well as the supportive but 'hands off' nature of the governing body. Although ambitious with lots of energy, he is clearly here to stay for some time – 'I couldn't leave while there is still so much to do,' he says. 'I want to transform a good school into an outstanding one'.

Entrance: Names down at birth – 'but realistically that means within two weeks of birth,' says head. He is keen to dispel the myth that you need to plan a Caesarean and father needs to put the form through the letter box as the baby arrives. It absolutely makes no difference at all on what day of the month your child is born. They divide the months into thirds and take an equal number from each third. Non-refundable registration fee (currently £150) does not guarantee you a tour of the school. Personal tours with the head offered as soon as you are off the waiting list and offered a place (something Mr Keighley-Elstub has recently introduced – prior to his arrival tours with a member of staff offered at deposit decision time – close to starting). The competitive market (for children more than the schools) and wealthy catchment of West London means that parents don't blink at paying these sort of sums without even being given the chance to see the school before making a decision. The alternative to long waiting lists is a selection process at 3, and that would mean 'we may miss the wild wacky ones that add colour to the place,' says Mr Keighley-Elstub. Nevertheless, close liaison with feeder nurseries (he mentioned The Acorn, Rolfe's, Strawberry Fields, Minors and Ladbroke Square) to make sure girls will manage.

Exit: Plenty of scholarships, academic, sporting as well as musical and artistic, each year (21 in 2016) and fine boards in the upper school hall to commemorate them.

Most popular day destinations in 2016 were Francis Holland SW1, Godolphin & Latymer and Latymer Upper. Most popular boarding destinations were Downe House, St Mary's Ascot and Wycombe Abbey.

P

Remarks: Situated in a particularly leafy, white stucco square in Notting Hill Gate, the lower school is in a tall building a minutes' walk from an identical building containing the upper school. In between is Wetherby pre-prep – the boys' equivalent – and also owned by the Alpha Plus group. In the basement of number 10 (the upper school) is Minors Nursery – another Alpha Plus establishment: no wonder such direct communication about the character and ability of the girls can be made.

Round the corner in St Petersburg Place is the splendid St Matthew's Church where whole school assemblies take place each week. We joined a river of red blazered and straw boatered girls as they walked immaculately to the church. An overwhelmingly white collection of girls for such a multicultural part of London; they are international – American, Russian, European as well – but only about 10 out of 400 girls receive EAL help. Mr Keighley-Elstub described the ethos as 'lightly Anglican' but a very English education, which seemed to be requirement of even the most foreign of families.

Girls here are well spoken, eager to please and confident. Lots of awards and prizes and opportunities to speak publicly and take responsibility to build that confidence. We were particularly impressed with an astonishing game designed by a 10-year-old girl out of a cardboard box, which intricately displayed the planets and included chance and question cards which she had devised herself. She then explained through a microphone how to play the game to an audience of about 450 people in the church, including parents as well as teachers and children.

Classrooms spacious, bright and airy with wonderful high ceilings and tall windows. Lovely wide corridors and staircases that seem to go up and up for ever. Lush red carpet (to match the uniform?) in the lower school, upper school mirrors the lower school but in blue. We saw some very impressive still life work in the very studio-like space at the top of the school, which had brilliant ceiling windows, creating an excellent space to be creative. Well-equipped science labs in the basement with a good old-fashioned full-sized skeleton in the corner. Super space in the basement for drama and productions with a wealth of colourful and imaginative costumes and hats. All years get a chance to perform: year 5s do a Shakespearean medley, year 6s do their annual play in the local Tabernacle Theatre. Both buildings have large halls which double as dining rooms at lunch time. Wide choice of healthy cooked lunches and imaginative fruit (watermelon and pineapple – not just your regular apples and bananas). How refreshing not to see children eating packed lunches at their desks.

P

Healthy number of male teachers and the arrival of Mr Keighley-Elstub has seen barely any staff turnover at all. He feels proud of having injected renewed energy and purpose into the place and acknowledges that when he arrived there was a lot of reassurance to be done. Parents were rattled and there was a lack of direction. Those we spoke to referred to a terrible lack of communication. Many considered moving their daughters but remarkably few did, explaining that the pastoral care remained excellent throughout and they didn't want to uproot a happy child. Emphasis is now on communication – particularly with parents; improvement and consolidation of the academics; and improvement of sport.

Girls are starting to win netball matches now – and we were proudly told of how they beat Glendower recently. Netball and hockey played in nearby Avondale Park and Holland Park, athletics at the Linford Christie stadium in Wood Lane and swimming at the Porchester Baths. Plenty of inter-house matches so that everyone can have a go. Tennis as a club rather than a school sport, and rounders possibly on its way out. 'I don't see the point of it,' says Mr Keighley Elstub. 'It's rather a poor man's cricket'. He is very open to the idea of introducing football and cricket for the girls but so far there doesn't seem to be the demand. Several outside spaces in both buildings for fresh air between lessons and 'unless there's the threat of a tornado out they go,' says head, who can't understand why the girls had been treated with such velvet gloves in the past, with the mere threat of rain resulting in their reading inside.

Three classes of 20 in each year. Setting only in maths from year 3. Serious preparation for the 11 plus starts in year 5 but the groundwork is now being laid much earlier. Mr Keighley-Elstub teaches years 5 and 6 so he can give well informed advice about schools. He is not afraid to tell a parent if they are being overly ambitious academically but will look at the whole child and advise which is the most appropriate school on that basis. Vast majority of parents here are in finance – though the odd one is glamorously famous, you wouldn't describe this as a trendy school. Mr Keighley-Elstub famously put a stop to the cashmere scarves as part of the school uniform and supplied by a parent: this isn't the image he wants to nurture.

Large, busy, and traditional with a dynamic head, Pembridge Hall can only get better and better and could be an excellent choice for your enthusiastic daughter.

Portland Place School

56-58 Portland Place, London W1B 1NJ

Pupils: 399 • Ages: 8-18 • Sixth form: 87

Fees: £19,995 pa

Tel: 020 7307 8700
Email: admin@portland-place.co.uk
Website: www.portland-place.co.uk

Head: Since April 2017, David Bradbury, previously deputy head of South Hampstead High. BSc in physics, MSc and PGCE, all from Keele, plus an MA in education from the Open University. Physics co-ordinator at Bangkok Patana School for a number of years; taught at Chase Terrace High and Newcastle-under-Lyme College; head of physics at Nicholas Chamberlaine School and assistant head at Alleyne's High School. Hobbies and interests include archery, cookery, cryptic crosswords, film, literature and music, as well as hill-walking and board games.

Academic matters: A broader band of ability than in most of the fiercely competitive London day schools – something the school takes pride in and, together with its small class sizes, sees as a 'unique selling point.' Only 12 in a class in years 4-6, an average of 15 in years 7 to 11 (we saw several smaller ones) and smaller still in the sixth form means that attention can be given to each child – you can be sure that there will be both stretching and confidence building. A godsend for the discerning parent who can see through the merry-go-round nature of 11+ and wants to ensure their child is educated rather than exam-processed. Hence the increasing demand for places lower down the school; there is now one class in each of years 4 and 5 as well as two in year 6. Piles on the value added – 'We're always near the top of the value added tables' is the boast.

No Latin or Greek at GCSE ('there isn't the demand from our parents,' we were told). Economics, computing, sport studies and media are offered, along with the traditional subjects. All pupils take at least one of French, Italian or Spanish, not much enthusiasm for taking up a second modern language. If your daughter speaks Italian at home, she is encouraged to do Spanish as her GCSE option. If you want your child to take a GCSE in, for example, Arabic, the school will facilitate it within the timetable, but the onus of paying and finding the teacher is on you.

At GCSE, 89 per cent achieved five or more A*-C including English and maths, 26 per cent of grades A*/A in 2016. The value added shows at A level, where the results are more impressive, most being in the B-D bracket, with a decent sprinkling of As (38 per cent A*/A grades and 66 per cent A*/B in 2016). We saw small tutor groups of as few as five – notably these were in science subjects. Clever ones, with offers from Oxbridge as well other Russell Group universities. Arts subjects tend to be busier (up to 15 in a group). Library manned by full-time librarian and a nice place to sit and read. Lots of fiction, used for competitions, book club and quiet study. As an academic resource it is risible (school prefers 'needs developing' and reminds us that the individual heads of departments keep library resources in their offices). Good IT suites and resources for the popular media and film options.

Setting in maths, science and English from year 7. Plenty of movement between sets, we were assured. Sizeable number of mild dyslexics but no additional support in lessons apart from general support from class teacher. Staunch policy of no withdrawals from classes (except once weekly for children who have EAL). School employs four specialist learning support teachers who will arrange to see children outside lesson time in groups of two or three to devise strategies to help them access the mainstream curriculum. No screening on admission. However SENCo oversees general provision and monitoring – 80 to 90 children perceived as having some kind of mild learning disability or difficulty and some have IEPs. Most with more than the mildest difficulties seek support outside school. Inside school, the attitude is healthy – 'I'm not treated as if dyslexia is a crime, unlike at my last school,' we were told. Two of the three buildings have lifts but school will be helpful if someone breaks a leg and move lessons to the ground floor.

Games, options, the arts: Well known for sporting prowess despite there being virtually no facilities on site. Pupils are bussed or walk everywhere – mostly to Regent's Park, with pitches and courts of all kinds, Seymour Place for swimming – and the results and achievements, given the conditions, are impressive. Years 7 to 9 have sport timetabled four times a week (one of the advantages of no canteen and shorter lunch breaks: time can be reallocated to sport). Football and netball tours of Barbados, swimming teams win competitions (Westminster champions five years in a row), masses of medals in cross-country and local honours in athletics and team sports. Pervasive pride in school sports, helped, no doubt, by classy Olympians on staff. However most really keen sportsmen and women do their serious sport outside school – girls' football a particular highpoint. Sport now compulsory to year 12 – one afternoon a week minimum of netball or football.

Music and drama similarly 'massive.' Music mostly means pop and jazz (we saw lots of ukulele enthusiasts). There are also a few violinists and woodwinders amongst the jazz pianists, guitarists, drummers and bassists who predominate, but eclectic range of music taken seriously. We were shown round by a budding actor in year 10 who enthused about the opportunities he has been given to develop his talent. Wholehearted, whole school productions annually – West Side Story, Singing in the Rain, The Producers and Annie are recent offerings; not on site as no suitable space but venues include the RADA studios in WC1. Upper school recently performed a resoundingly successful Richard III – which was then a sell-out at the Edinburgh Fringe. Lower school (up to year 9) recently performed Skellig as their annual production. Good-sized on-site drama studio can accommodate smaller productions (we were impressed with the assortment of costumes and props).

Art in the lower school is lively and inventive. We saw ink portraits in the style of Peter Howson, as well as Pop Art-style Creme Eggs. Fewer than 10 do art A level – facilities limited, though there is a textiles room and school excels in photography. DT similarly energetic – resistant materials, pewter casting, CAD and CAM, though all in rather small and poky rooms in basement. Lots of extracurricular stuff – when we visited a stress management workshop was being delivered to all GCSE students. Trips galore – we have seldom seen such a full programme. Much use made of London's galleries, museums and exhibitions, plus the nearby wider world and the opportunities it offers for field, sporting and other educational exercises, both here and abroad.

Background and atmosphere: This is a young school, founded only 20 or so years ago by the visionary head of science at St Paul's Girls', Richard Walker. His aim was to create a smaller independent co-ed senior school that wasn't super selective. Part of the Alpha Plus group, it forms one of their 18 UK schools and colleges, bringing the advantages of the economies of scale. Portland Place – the road – is a broad, straight thoroughfare in the heart of Regency London, two minutes from Oxford Circus to the south, two minutes to Regent's Park to the north. It is lined by august embassies (China, Kenya, Poland, Portugal) and the HQs of royal and learned institutions (architects, physicists, radiologists, anaesthetists). The main school building – Portland Place – identifies itself with a modest brass plate and is elegantly splendid. It is rare for us to compliment a school on its decor but a pleasure to do so here. Eye-catching blue carpet up and down the stairs (not just on the ground floor for show as elsewhere), magnificent ceilings, cornices, columns, capitals and fireplaces: nowhere more so than in the old ballroom, rescued from its carapace of false ceiling and fluorescent tubes and very much in use. All in tip-top nick. This building houses the lower years, the hall (used for gym and dance) and the top floors (formerly the servants' quarters) accommodate music and languages.

A second building in Great Portland Street, five minutes away, houses the upper years and has a breathtaking eyeball-to-eyeball view of the BT Tower, seemingly within grabbing distance. Harford House, also in Great Portland Street and with a facade resembling that of a corporate HQ, is home to art, drama and science. It's a logistical nightmare – five or seven storeys to be up and down all day, three buildings – and it all has to be timetabled, supervised and navigated. We suppose everyone to be very fit – a real bonus for children who need lots of movement and exercise if they are to perform well mentally.

No school kitchen. Pupils bring packed lunches or order in from local cafés (which deliver dozens of paninis etc in little brown carriers). Years 10 and 11 and the sixth hang out in the many cafés in or around Great Portland Street and just love the privilege of this kind of freedom.

Pastoral care, well-being and discipline: Definitely an informal feel to the place. Although pupils are not quite on first name terms with teachers, one can sense an equality in the relationships not seen in more traditional establishments. Good use of sixth form mentors for years 7 and 8 – really fosters inter-age group understanding and friendships, especially helpful in so small a school. Solidly structured pastoral care hierarchy picks up and deals with problems, but there's a pervasive sense of everyone looking out for everyone else. People seem to know each other's little brothers and sisters here. Parents praise the home-school communications and especially the termly parents' evenings. 'The teachers are mostly young and energetic,' enthused a parent, 'and you really get to know them.'

Pupils and parents: More boys than girls (about 60:40 in lower years) – simply because there are so many more girls' and co-ed schools in London. Mixed, as befits its location – trad, moneyed independent education veterans alongside newbies and newcomers from here, there and everywhere, blended with those who couldn't get into the 'academic' schools and for whom PP has been a jolly lucky find. From the whole urban sprawl – no longer just the north and west but around 30 per cent from east and south too. Mostly UK born and based but also from pretty much the rest of the globe, solar system and beyond, in a great undivided family. Brains? Yes, though common denominator more palpably pleasure, pride and enthusiasm for the place.

Entrance: There are 8+, 9+ and 10+ intakes (and 7+ from 2017) – partly to steal a march on the competition and partly to meet the needs of those who dread the 11+ circus and will do anything to avoid it (wise move). 'Informal tests' in English and maths with deputy/head of year. Year 7 has tests in English and maths and a chat with a teacher. For places at 12+, 13+ and 14+, same format plus additional test in science. School keen to dispel image that it's the go-to place for a child on the dys-strata. Child has to be able to cope and pupils who can't will be turned down. A few join at year 12, on flexible terms. They come, at 11, from a large number of schools – state and independent.

Exit: Wide range of post-A level destinations and courses, including sports and exercise science, mechanical engineering and forensic investigations at the newer universities. The odd one to study music and to art college, and one medic in 2016; London and Sussex universities popular. About 30 per cent leave after GCSE (mostly to non-fee paying sixth form colleges).

Money matters: No scholarships or bursaries offered at any point.

Remarks: Small, nurturing and refreshingly relaxed. A haven of creativity in the pushy academically competitive world of London day schools. A place for engaged, lively, normal kids – privileged, yes, but Sloanes, no. Becoming ever more popular as more and more people discover it. The challenge will be to maintain its ethos of 'broader academic intake' in the face of increasing demand.

Prendergast School

P

Adelaide Avenue, Brockley, London SE4 1LE

Pupils: 878 • Ages: 11–18 • Sixth form: 285

Tel: 020 8690 3710
Email: admin@prendergast-school.com
Website: www.prendergast-school.com

Head Teacher: Since September 2016, Paula Ledger, previously vice principal of Harris Girls' Academy East Dulwich. Masters in education management from King's College London. Has taught in several schools in the UK and abroad, overseeing PHSE, religious studies and humanities.

Academic matters: In 2016 at GCSE, 67 per cent of pupils gained at least five A*/C grades including English and maths. Over half were A*-B grades (28 per cent A*/A). Pupils join with only just above average profiles and achieve well, particularly in English, placing the school amongst the top 100 state comprehensive schools for progress at GCSE English, maths and three others. The school's specialisms may not mean too much on the ground, but music and languages continue to be a focus. Students study French and Spanish, with Japanese and Latin offered as clubs, whilst native speakers may add a qualification in their own language. Whilst there are certainly stars, with pupils from years 7 and 8 bringing home gold and silver medals in the recent UK junior maths challenge, maths GCSE is not so golden, but steadily improving. Strongest performing subjects most recently: all three sciences, textiles, product design, art, French and PE.

Ofsted says 'good and improving' at sixth form, but results are a key focus. In 2016 at A level, 39 per cent A*- B and 15 per cent A*/A. Mostly B grades and above in English, geography, textiles, art and sciences, with ICT currently weak. Figures show the sixth form is strong in terms of valued added – school points out that with pupils entering from over 40 local senior schools, there is a lot of 'training' to do. 'Maybe they've done really well to get their C'. School aims to give a wide choice of A level combinations, with an eye to what works for progression to university – nothing either too avant garde or soft an option. Theatre studies now replaces performing arts, indicating something of a statement of intent to raise the bar academically.

School trips which caught our eye include a visit to Greenwich ecology park to hold slugs and newts and a more appetising day trip to a French chocolate factory, whilst an amusing time was had at the Tintin museum in Brussels. Sixth form journeys alternate between Barcelona and Rome.

A third of teachers have been at the school for over 10 years. Several former Prendergast students and several staff have daughters at the school. Parents say: 'My daughter is really enthused by the teachers'; 'interesting projects in maths and languages (subjects that can often be dry to learn).' The average class sizes vary considerably between 12 and 30 with relatively minimal streaming. One parent noted, 'The lessons have led to many fascinating debates around feminism/young women today', and as if on cue, we observed a memorable history class where the teacher led the girls in a discussion of an original illustration depicting a hunger striking suffragette being force-fed.

Unusually, everyone in agreement that the level of homework and holiday project work is well managed, and not overwhelming: 'The school seems to understand that learning requires periods to rest and recuperate' and 'There is not a lot of pressure, instead girls seem self-motivated'.

Two per cent with statements/EHC plans and 10 per cent school action plus. The head of learning support is full-time and also teaches English. There is an intensive phonics course in year 7 for those with reading difficulties, otherwise some individual support and in class support in the main. 'We try to keep students in their classes wherever possible'. Praise for teaching staff from a parent of a dyslexic pupil: 'They seem to be able to balance the needs of individuals in the class and motivate across the board.'

The school bangs the drum in terms of the expectation that every pupil entering the school at year 7 will stay on to the sixth form and most do, with the addition of boys. There is a dedicated sixth form study centre. Every pupil has use of his or her own laptop for just a nominal cost. Sixth formers don't wear uniform, although almost all wear comfortable leggings or jeans and sweatshirts, a uniform of sorts. The school defends the lack of business suits, saying they have enough transitions to make at university.

Careers preparation starts at year 7 with a Dragon's Den style business enterprise day, with traditional work experience placements in years 10 and 12 and subject specific careers weeks. A new speed networking event for years 9 and 10 makes the most of the professional experience of the whole school community. Solid preparation for university applications including mock interviews with staff and industry experts and sensible advice on how to manage financially at university. For some, eyes are opened with summer schools and shadowing former pupils at Oxford and Cambridge, and 45 year 10 students each year attend a residential course at the University of East Anglia.

Possibly room for growth in leadership opportunities which currently include mentoring younger students, leading the school council, organising the year 13 summer ball, D of E and 'homework club'.

Games, options, the arts: Pupils may not be competing at national level in mainstream sports, but the school works hard to get them involved and active. Pupils in the lower years describe their peers as 'sporty', and 72 per cent take part in extracurricular sporting activities: pupils say 'it's a good way to make friends'. A shuttle bus takes girls to a sports field at nearby Bellingham.

Girls can continue their netball, hockey, athletics and rounders or try their hand at something new: the school is now embarking on touch rugby and girls can row at the London Regatta Centre. They've also invested in cycling and make use of Herne Hill velodrome. One surprised parent: 'I love the fact that my non-sporty daughter now loves football. No boys: she can get stuck in.' Girls are also clearly good with a pompom as the school team is ranked third in the British schools' cheerleading championships.

A new purpose-built music block, with practice rooms, a recording studio and teaching spaces open all hours for practising is a real strength of the school. Around 40 per cent study an instrument at some time during their school career, from beginners to grade 8. The school has an orchestra, chamber choir, its own recording label, Hill Sound and a biannual music tour. Musicians are carefully showcased at assemblies and prizegivings.

Strong art offer includes variants such as product design, textiles and photography. Thought-provoking work of a high standard is on display throughout the school, such as a dress made of the traces left behind by animals, dog-hair and glue in this instance – the student collected hairs from her Airedale until she had enough to make a dress – dedication indeed. Teaching has good links with appropriate courses such as Saturday clubs with University of the Arts. We suspect more could be made of drama with pupils, parents and school struggling to cite much except a large scale Shakespeare production.

After school and lunchtimes are busy with a wide range of clubs – cycling, walking, creative writing, gardening, debating, trampolining, medical society, chamber choir, orchestra and gospel choir, appreciated by pupils and parents: 'The staff show a lot of dedication and commitment to making the clubs such a success'. D of E at bronze, silver and gold is small but thriving. A homework club where kindly sixth formers offer assistance every day after school until 4.30pm seems particularly valued by the keen students we met.

Background and atmosphere: Turn the corner from a promising but still rather gritty south east London high street where betting shops and secondhand white goods crowd the pavements, and one seems to have fallen down a rabbit hole to somewhere altogether more delightful. Hilly Fields, saved from urban sprawl in the 19th century by high profile campaigners including Octavia Hill and William Morris, sweeps up steeply surrounded by fine examples of Victoriana, circled by an avenue at the foot of the hill – a leafy and highly desirable conservation area in the midst of urban Lewisham.

Originally founded in 1890 as West Kent Grammar School, Prendergast School now occupies two sites, a short, energising walk apart, at the top and bottom of the hill. The original Queen Anne style red-brick building perches atop the hill, reaching dizzying heights by the time one has climbed the numerous stairs to the maths floor and sixth form common room near the roof. The listed assembly hall is show-stopping. First discovered by this editor in a World of Interiors spread, it was decorated in the 1930s with pastoral murals loosely based on Aesop's fables by four RCA artists, including the only official female war artist of World War 2.

Both the original building and the remodelled building at the foot of the hill – all angles, glass, sharp graphite bricks and splashes of bright colour – make the very most of the situation. Baroness Beeban Kidron opened the newly completed arts, English and science blocks. The classrooms have something of a wipe-clean look and can seem a bit gloomy due to dark blue paint, but corridors are wide and windows cleverly oriented to capture views over the sedum roof to the tree-tops of Ladywell, Brockley and beyond to Kent.

In its long history the school has changed its name more than most. As Prendergast School. it is part of a growing federation of four local schools – Prendergast Vale, Prendergast Ladywell and the new Prendergast Primary – with some governance and funding provided by the Leathersellers' Federation.

The atmosphere seems to be that of a relatively small community school where many of the parents know each other well from their primaries. One told us: 'It's a very friendly environment', another 'feels part of a family'.

Parents say: 'The school is very inclusive. It never lifts the top students at the expense of the average or lower but tries to bring everyone up together'; 'The school feels encouraging and supportive, strict but fair'; 'The girls are allowed to perform, experiment and make mistakes in a safe, nurturing environment.'

Pastoral care, well-being and discipline: There are clear rules, everyone knows what is expected of them and parents say they are enforced. Pupils must have a note to leave their classrooms. No visible mobile phones, but nose-studs may be worn. One pupil tells us that teachers carry make-up and nail polish wipes and aren't afraid to dish them out. 'No time in school is wasted managing behaviour.' Pupils seem mostly keen and studious, borne out by higher than average attendance, although not without a few grumblers in a couple of the classes we visited. A mother told us: 'My daughter wanted to go to a school where she wouldn't feel out of place for being competitive and clever'; another agreed: 'There is a great work ethic which encourages the girls to try their best.'

Form tutors are the key liaison with parents and are considered sufficiently on the ball to pick up any concerns quickly and report back to parents. Bullying is not unheard of, but parents say the school is quick to step in: 'very caring and intervenes when needed.' One concerned parent noted: 'The school does not have a counsellor and there is not one within the federation'. A deliberate choice: the school points out that pupils will be advised to access counselling through their GPs if necessary, preferring to reserve her budget for education.

Pupils and parents: Students hail from ethnically diverse backgrounds with 68 per cent from a black or minority ethnic background – the largest groups being white British, African and Caribbean. Some 22 per cent speak a language other than English at home but there are no early English speakers here. A parent said: 'All children are individuals and the school allows for that. Diversity is celebrated.' Parents speak of the value of the social mix to their children's empathy and awareness. We were particularly impressed by the school's efforts to support the significant number of students who are young carers.

What kinds of pupils would thrive here? A parent: 'A child who enjoys working within clear structures and guidelines'. Girls we spoke to seemed a little bemused to find themselves at a single-sex school, the older ones rather looking forward to the co-ed sixth form. A parent chimed in: 'This school may not work for a girl who is desperate to grow up or wants the whole boy thing to happen soon. This school is about really close female bonding.'

A parent described her peers approvingly as 'laid back and not the type to hire tutors.' Friends of Prendergast School Association does much valued work, this year raising money for a journey to France, a dissection club and the purchase of iPads for use in geography.

Entrance: The School participates in Lewisham's co-ordinated admissions scheme. The majority of places in year 7 offered on the basis of home to school distance and the school no longer operates banding. There are only four forms of entry and 10 per cent of places are music places for which applicants can sit an aptitude test, and which trump distance criteria. The majority come from nearby primaries with Gordonbrock, a few streets away, the biggest feeder.

Entrance to sixth form – boys as well as girls – requires five GCSE passes at grades A*-C, with a B required in the subjects of advanced study. Sibling on the roll trumps distance at application stage. Progression to year 13 is dependent on attaining at least a D at AS level.

Exit: In 2016, just under half left after GCSEs and nine per cent after year 12. Every student who wants to go on to higher education attains a place. Some 30 per cent to the Russell Group including Exeter, King's College London, LSE, Warwick and York. None to Oxbridge in 2016, three studying law. Considerable breadth of courses a testament to interests nurtured and inspired. Recently, subjects have included international relations, chemical engineering, architecture, zoology, medieval languages, midwifery and American studies as well as places at leading art colleges including Central St Martins, Camberwell and Chelsea.

Money matters: Support given to some students in the sixth form – 50 bursaries given this year. Three Leathersellers' Federation bursaries awarded each year to students about to go to university, comprising £700 towards each year of study.

Remarks: Girls who arrive here often feel very lucky; we can see why. There is space to breathe in this leafy spot, where girls can be and find themselves.

Prospect House School

200

75 Putney Hill, London SW15 3NT

Pupils: 313 • Ages: 3–11

Fees: £16,410 – £17,100pa

Tel: 020 8780 0456
Email: info@prospecths.org.uk
Website: www.prospecths.org.uk

Headmistress: Since 2004, Mrs Dianne Barratt MEd. She has a breadth of experience, having taught in the UK and USA in schools ranging from large, challenging state primaries and specialist schools to selective independent preps, including Croydon High Junior School, where she was deputy, and JAPS, where she was acting deputy. Added to this is her first-hand experience of the London day schools with her own two (now grown-up) daughters. Parents we spoke to were impressed by her 'wide range of skill sets, dynamism and very down-to-earth approach'. A non-teaching head, Mrs Barratt ensures she is visible throughout the school, often out at early morning drop-off time, taking or attending assemblies, or on her many tours with prospective parents. All the pupils we spoke to appreciate the way she knows them all and is encouraging and approachable. A shrewd lady, nothing slips her attention and she is copied into all parental communications, intervening when necessary.

Parents remarked, 'Mrs Barratt chooses on the whole excellent high calibre staff and has expertly guided them in her mould'. She herself believes in 'Looking for excellence in delivery from the staff. Relationships are so important; the glue that holds the school together.' Her vision and ethos are consistently applied and shared with the staff, many of who have been with her since early in her tenure, and they respect her expert lead for the benefit of all. Parents greatly value the advice and expertise she shows regarding future schools, and her no-nonsense northern approach means they can be sure of realistic options. Not one for gimmicks and the latest educational trends, she only introduces changes after careful consideration to see their value for PHS. She likes to see pupils challenged and not worried about making mistakes: 'If a pupil always has everything 100 per cent right then I question the teacher and whether the task is too easy.'

She relaxes in lunch breaks with a crossword in the staffroom, values time with her family and loves travel. With her specialism in psychology and language and literacy teaching, she informed us of the enormous satisfaction she enjoys, providing care to pupils and a role model to younger staff in detecting and dealing with any emotional or behavioural problems at an early stage. She is proud that pupils are 'genuinely happy and enjoy coming to school. They like their teachers and their teachers care about them'.

Retiring in July 2017. Her successor will be Michael Hodge, currently deputy head (since 2004).

Entrance: Places are offered each year in order of registration, mainly at 3+ nursery with 30 places and reception (10 places). Year 3 usually has four places each year by registration and assessment. There are occasional places throughout other years as parents relocate. Most children come from local areas: Barnes, Southfields, Wimbledon, Putney and the odd few from Fulham. Almost all children speak a reasonable level of English and there is a variety of religions and nationalities. No sibling discounts, with only scarce bursaries awarded to bright pupils by the separate House Schools Trust.

Exit: Whilst a very few seek boarding schools, the majority move on to local day schools. Popular choices include King's College Wimbledon, St Paul's Girls' School, Godolphin and Latymer, Latymer, Hampton, Ibstock Place, Emanuel, Putney High, Kingston Grammar and Kew House. Consistently a large number of scholarships are awarded each year and the results are very impressive for a non-selective school. Parents we spoke to were in agreement and value the fact that 'Mrs Barratt has very firm views when advising on senior schools, considering every child regardless of ability from the view of where the child will do best and flourish'. They value her knowledge of their children and it is worth noting that 'she makes it clear that the school is not there to prepare pupils for 7+ examinations'.

Remarks: Prospect House School opened in 1991 and has two sister schools, Bassett House School in Kensington, and Orchard House School in Chiswick, which form the House Schools Group. Advantageous collaborations include sports events and access to IT support. The school expanded in 2013 with the acquisition of an attractive, refurbished building, five minutes away, providing a lower school for children 3 to 7. Upper and lower schools are set in attractive grounds with plenty of space for play and an all-weather sports pitch in the upper school sports area. A further development has been in house catering in both and the freshly cooked, healthy menus, with jelly a favourite pudding, are popular with staff and pupils. Mrs Barratt stresses that 'this is one school in two buildings rather than two separate upper and lower schools'. Pupils regularly enjoying visiting each other's building with younger pupils going to the library and older pupils reading to reception, helping to make gingerbread or sharing a puppet show.

Without pushing or focusing chiefly on the academic, parents are very complimentary about how Mrs B and her staff successfully ensure that 'each child is well-rounded, confident and performing to the best of their ability'. Pupils we spoke to agreed that 'Teachers are always helpful, kind and don't judge you and know us really well'. This is not the right school if you require loads of test results and school examinations, instead we saw how each individual is carefully tracked, personal development as well as academic, with extra support for strugglers and streaming for maths and English from year 3. French starts from nursery, Latin in years 5 and 6 with Mandarin after the 11+ examinations. A particular feature is the excellent use of ICT, which is embedded in the curriculum. PHS was the first independent school to be awarded an ICT Mark for Excellence by BECTA and has gone on to win best school in the UK for primary ICT. We watched a year 6 lesson in which pupils enthusiastically raced in teams to solve complex mathematical calculations on personal iPads in record time. Pupils in years 5 and 6 told us how they really like having iPads as 'they make learning fun and interesting'. Parents can login to the homework app so they can see all the homework set, and teachers often add messages to the tasks given to individuals.

An inclusive sports policy and plenty of opportunities to play in fixtures against local teams help to build pupils' confidence. This is not the school for a champion swimmer or tennis player but the purpose built hall for dance, drama and gymnastics, all weather sports pitch and local sports grounds are used for team sports including netball, rounders, football, hockey and cricket. One parent spoke of her son's enjoyment of his curriculum ballroom dancing as well as judo, one of a wide range of extracurricular clubs. Music is outstanding, a very high proportion of pupils learn instruments and are encouraged to learn two. We heard the accomplished part singing of the senior choir, and the long-serving director of music has high expectations which pupils seek to meet. We also saw younger pupils with their specialist teacher singing their hearts out in a teddy bear rock.

The school has a culture of nurturing and promoting children's confidence and happiness. Experienced staff acknowledge and support any difficulties and there is a qualified, experienced SENCo with a well-resourced team. The pupils are screened in years 1 and 3 for difficulties including working memory, and one new parent we spoke to was delighted at the way in which his dyslexic daughter had settled in and made progress. The SENCo refreshingly commented: 'Any child with learning needs deserves respect and the confidence to make mistakes and not be overlooked'. Detailed lesson plans ensure topics can be introduced prior to learning with strategies put in place. PHS has taken on a few casualties from other local schools successfully and there are good links with local speech and occupational therapists.

There is an active PHS Friends' Society and, in liaison with the head, plenty of social and fundraising events. As we were, parents are impressed by 'the politeness of the pupils and how they learn to be very good at talking to adults'. Parents are extremely happy with the excellent communication between home and school and mentioned only the acquisition of a school minibus to transport pupils back to school after matches as a suggested improvement.

A thriving school, successfully working with parents to produce happy, confident, grounded individuals, who enjoy learning and participating in an extremely well resourced, forward-thinking environment with its excellent senior management and communication.

Putney High School

35 Putney Hill, London SW15 6BH

Pupils: 976 • Ages: 4–18 • Sixth form: 160

Fees: £14,403 – £17,409 pa

Tel: 020 8788 4886
Email: putneyhigh@put.gdst.net
Website: www.putneyhigh.gdst.net

Headmistress: Since 2015, Mrs Suzie Longstaff, following a year as acting head after predecessor Dr Denise Lodge took a sabbatical to care for her sick husband. Before joining the teaching profession, Mrs Longstaff had a successful rowing career. Highlights including coxing the GB Women's VIII at the Atlanta Olympics in 1996.

Mrs Longstaff joined the school in 2009 as head of sixth form before being promoted to deputy head (academic). An economics graduate (Durham), she has a 'passion' for lifelong learning, something she has put into practice with acquisition of diploma (in computing) from the University of Oxford and MA (in education) from the University of Bath.

Junior school head: From September 2017 will be Pippa Daverson, currently director of innovation and learning at Kensington Prep. She began her teaching career at Rowdown Primary School, Croydon, before moving to Kingswood Prep in Bath, and has also been head of junior English at the Harrodian. Her other roles at Kensington Prep – where she spent 10 years – have been director of studies and head of English.

Academic matters: Relatively large class sizes in junior school (22 until year 3 when classes increase to 24), two classes in each year are taught in bright, spacious classrooms. Much of the old Victorian building was looking tired and in need of love and a lick of paint when we visited, but bright, confident girls wreathed in smiles and purple more than made up for the flaky state of the building. French is taught from reception, Spanish from year 5, philosophy and ethics from year 3. IPads encased in school colour – purple – used from year 4 onwards. 'A mixed blessing,' remarked one mother, although the girls clearly enjoyed presenting a project, having researched the material using the iPad as their main tool. There are also a number of laptops kept in storage outside the library for general use.

A learning support department is gradually starting to emerge; although school insists there has been one for the past three years, it appears to be still in a somewhat nascent state. Only one dedicated member of staff. She works from the Panda Room' (parent and daughter room) and sees about 17 girls on a one-to-one basis, with more girls supported around the school in their classes. Some of these have specific – mild – learning difficulties, some simply require a boost in confidence.

Very academic place – some seriously bright girls here, working very hard, but not too pressured. Excellent results – at GCSE in 2016, an impressive 86 per cent A*/A grades. Good performances in sciences, English and music. At A level 64 per cent A*/A grades (94 per cent A*-B). Fantastic to see in a girls' school that maths is the most popular choice at A level, by a long way. Parents say it is a happy school that holds its own against St Paul's and Godolphin & Latymer, though the feeling on the outside is that St Paul's is still a jump ahead.

P

In year 7, when girls are mainly taught in form groups, they average (a large) 28. School is quick to defend the numbers. 'One third of lessons in year 7 are taught in groups of 21/22 – maths, art and science. Furthermore, DT/ textiles is taught in half classes of 14. By year 9 only PHSE (life skills) is taught as a group of 28.' For sixth formers, the average class size is eight.

Good to see that girls are not over-burdened with lots of homework – theory is that they work hard enough during school day. No setting in year 7, but in year 8 they are set for maths. It's more a matter of pace than ability – all can still aim for A grades by the end. Studies all based around a considerably developed national curriculum which is pleasingly broad and flexible. Sciences all taught separately from year 8, when Latin also makes an appearance. Coding has been introduced and computing is now available at GCSE and A level. All girls have their own iPads. School happily retains minority subjects. Nice to see Mandarin on the list of modern foreign languages – now available as a GCSE and Pre-U subject. Writer in residence conducts workshops and classes promoting qualities such as independent thinking and learning.

No testing for SEN, but specialists on the staff, though the impression from the school is that it is not a huge specialist area, so not a first choice school for a girl with SEN problems. Extracurricular activities for the exceptionally gifted and talented.

Games, options, the arts: A great place for all-rounders as games and music are very well done here. 'Would be a shame to come here as a pure academic – you would miss out on so much,' sums up one parent. Storming sports results lately. School has produced GDST champions in netball, lacrosse and tennis. Playing fields are off-site (but close by) – the downside of London location. Rowing increasingly popular and successful, more than 100 Putney girls take to the river with a rowing club which runs seven days a week. The only girls' school with a boathouse on the Tideway.

Great music – choir tours are legendary and colossal, orchestras and ensembles abound and is introducing an orchestra in residence. 'I just cannot get over the music here,' said one mother to a chorus of agreement. A mixture of planning and fortune has seen the music department refurbished, with all the toys necessary for GCSE and A level composition. Lovely to see 16 girls a year take music GCSE – higher than the average elsewhere. New performing arts centre with professional sound and lighting facilities. Art also very good – average of 20 go on to A level, with eight or nine then to art school. Tons of extracurricular stuff on offer – over 200 clubs, from barbershop to zumba. Almost everyone does Duke of Edinburgh.

Apart from the academics, music and the outside speakers who come and talk to the girls are regarded by junior school parents as the main strengths of the school. A compulsory choir for years 5 and 6 – 'very good for the girls,' agreed the parents – as well as the more elite Small Choir. Lots of musical activities, groups, an orchestra – everyone grade 1 and above welcome. Not much creativity in the classroom, observed one parent – 'I now pay extra for my daughter to do an extracurricular creative club.' Increase in intellectually-challenging clubs eg coding, engineering, current affairs, debating, problem solving. Thirty per cent of extracurricular clubs are charged for.

Background and atmosphere: Set up in 1893 with 54 pupils in five scattered houses, coming together as one on its present site in 1918. Typically of London schools, the site is relatively small, but it really makes the most of what it has, with some beautiful gardens, and is something of an oasis off uninspiring Putney Hill. Just a few steps from this busy London road and you are in a far more rarefied atmosphere – parallels with Narnia and Mr Benn abound. And of course the upside to this urban location is fab transport links – short walk from tube and BR trains and streams of buses stop right outside.

Inside some super-smart facilities – spectacular library, swish new drama studio and language lab, but overall facilities won't blow you away with glitz and glamour. Doesn't matter, though, as everything underpinned with great teaching and wide-ranging opportunities.

Situated on the same site as the senior school, Putney High Junior is definitely part of the whole rather than a stand-alone school. Not only are the facilities shared – the design technology workshop as well as the performing arts centre, sports hall, outdoor courts and very attractive cafeteria – but girls in the junior school also get the benefit of specialist teachers and co-curricular clubs – particularly art and ceramics. Part of the broader Girls' Day School Trust, the school also benefits from the advantages of being part of a well-established and specialist group of schools. If you're looking for the 'wow factor' then look elsewhere. However if you want your daughter to have a solid start to her school career then this is a good bet. A safe but not sparkling choice for your bright, conformist daughter.

Pastoral care, well-being and discipline: Structure is key, but there is a nurturing ethos, and 'waspish behaviour among the girls is nipped in the bud,' observed one junior school mother. A noticeable softening in the atmosphere since our last visit. Staff and parents alike are much more smiley, open and approachable, we were told. Mrs Archibald, the very effective deputy head, frequently comes up in discussion with parents. She is head of pastoral care and music and the first port of call if there is a problem. There is a little post box, the 'Secret Safe', where girls can post any anxieties confidentially. This is checked on a regular basis and, by all accounts, those anxieties rapidly resolved. The buddy system, which involves year 6 girls pairing up with girls in reception as their Guardian Angels, contributes to the cosy atmosphere.

Parental praise for senior school pastoral care – knows the girls well and understands all the ages and stages they go through. Worthwhile life skills programme is used to discuss bullying, eating disorders et al. 'We pride ourselves on spotting problems early on,' says school. 'Obviously there are occasional issues, but we address them fast and in a supportive way.' Has introduced a mindfulness programme. Happy, well-motivated girls with things to do and places to go to are unlikely to spend much time in detention. The usual system of praise and punishment in place as and when necessary – house points, detentions, that sort of thing – but overall a happy ship. Good teacher/pupil relationships make formal sanction the exception rather than the rule. 'When a school is working well like this you can afford to be a bit relaxed,' is its view.

Tough rather than tender, no nonsense rather than nurturing – but the bright and robust will thrive. Can be rather rigid about rules and regulations – parents complain about a lack of a personal touch with standardised responses to their queries and of secretarial/admin staff at times not being as helpful as parents would wish.

Pupils and parents: A mixture of families – some from across the river, others from the other direction as far as Kingston and New Malden, but largely from the local environs in the junior school. A broad range of nationalities: a number of Asian families as well as the usual international mix of US, European and Scandinavian. Parents are hard-working professionals who want the best for their daughters and most step up at school events like the Autumn Fair, for example.

The hard-working middle classes abound and are really supportive of the school. Perhaps not surprisingly, as they are discussing their own daughter and her friends, most parents describe the girls as 'down to earth' and the place as 'not snobby or élitist'. Pupils are largely a full-on bunch, full of attitude and ideas – and might overwhelm those who don't shine in anything in particular, so not the obvious place for the shy or unconfident. School is proud of its girls and their 'can do' attitude – when confronted with a minor inconvenience, they just get on with it. Pupils are a reasonably smart, normal bunch with no wacky hairstyles, jewellery etc.

Parents very welcome to contribute – preferably via parents' association rather than helping within the school itself: 'They prefer to keep us out of the way a bit,' said one mother. The parents' association is thriving, seemingly a great place for a night out and one of the few we've come across that make special mention of welcoming single parents who might otherwise find some school events a little daunting. Newcomers will be swept up and supported. Generally the school is big on fundraising.

OGs bear witness to the wide range of talents encouraged at the school, eg newsreader Sophie Raworth, fashion designer Edina Ronay, gardening broadcaster Pippa Greenwood, author Sophie Kinsella, politicians Virginia Bottomley and Baroness Elizabeth Symons, journalist Melanie Phillips, sculptor Emily Young, Sandie Okoro, president of International Lawyers of Africa and entrepreneur Calypso Rose, a London young business person of the year.

Entrance: Selective at 4+ and 7+. No sibling policy. About 130 apply for 44 places in reception. The girls come in for an assessment that lasts over an hour. Each one is seen on a one-to-one basis and every member of staff is involved in assessing. Parents are present but not interviewed. They take girls who are born throughout the year, so a proper mix of autumn, spring and summer birthdays. At 7, the assessments last up to three hours. Girls sit papers in English, maths and non-verbal reasoning. Classes increase from 22 to 24 in Year 3, so a minimum of 4 places at 7+.

Selection at 11+, described by the school as 'by competitive examination (papers in English and maths, each one hour 15 minutes) and friendly interview'. If an average selective school is looking for the top 25 per cent, Putney is after the top 10. Don't struggle and coach to get your daughter here – school knows exactly the girls it wants and you either fit or you don't. 'They'll need to have been well-taught,' is the only hint we could glean for you. Competitive, lots of interest – 2,000+ at open day, 400 will sit entrance exam (and potentially nearly half of places will go to junior school brigade, less than a handful of whom won't qualify). Register by November the year before admission. Lots of locals, but as girls are older and travel independently, net cast slightly wider than for juniors.

At 16+, girls need at least three A*s and three As at GCSE, with A*/As in subjects they want to study at A level and at least Bs in maths and English. Used to have a reputation for weeding out at this stage, ie booting out those of their own who do not make the grades, but the head insists this is no more – a major relief for parents. Newcomers will need references and interview with the director of sixth form.

Exit: On average between 70-90 per cent of juniors continue into the senior school. A few choose boarding. St Swithun's recently popular 'but it largely depends on the family and their own connections with boarding'. A few prefer to go to co-ed schools – Latymer Upper is popular, and very occasionally some go to Ibstock. A fair few move to St Paul's, Godolphin & Latymer or Lady Eleanor Holles, or choose to move to a state school, eg Lady Margaret in Parsons Green.

School assesses each year and from year 4 they start to get a feel for who might not be up to the academic standard of the senior school. The process is carefully managed through year 5 and 'no one ends up without a good school'. Senior school taster days are organised for the year 5s, mixing with the year 7s. All girls moving onto the senior school have to sit the exam and interview, but there are 'lots of opportunities for scholarships – academic, music and sport'.

Majority move up to the sixth form, though around a quarter head off to co-ed or boarding elsewhere. At 18+ most to Russell Group, eg Bristol, Edinburgh, Exeter, UCL, King's College London; seven to Oxbridge in 2016. Subjects range from anthropology to medicine (four in 2016). US universities coordinator supports girls applying for American colleges (one to Stanford in 2016).

Money matters: Academic scholarships awarded on merit – all 11+ candidates automatically considered. Music and sport scholarships via assessment at 11+. At 16+, academic, music, art, drama, design and sport scholarships. Travel scholarships in modern languages and science for internal candidates only. Means-tested bursaries available.

Remarks: Super school best for very bright and diligent all-rounders who enjoy a busy life. An impressive and substantial offering.

Queen Elizabeth's Girls' School

High Street, Barnet, Hertfordshire EN5 5RR

Pupils: 1,129 • Ages: 11–18 • Sixth form: 150

Tel: 020 8449 2984
Email: office@qegschool.org.uk
Website: www.qegschool.org.uk

Headteacher: Since 2015, Mrs Violet Walker, previously deputy head at Northholt High. Psychology degree from UCL and masters in education from Brunel; she is an advanced skills maths teacher and a specialist leader in education.

Academic matters: 'A love of learning is our priority,' says the school, but the recent Ofsted report criticised the school for failing the students on pupil premium who are not making good progress. Contrary to this report however, the school's GCSE English results are considerably above the national average, as well as above average for girls. All the more impressive when one takes into account that nearly a quarter of the pupils comes from homes where English is not a first language.

The school generally produces commendable results. In 2016, 63 per cent A*-B and 32 per cent A*/A grades at GCSE. At A level, 23 per cent A*/A, 53 per cent A*-B grades. Biology, chemistry, maths, philosophy and ethics, sociology and psychology are all popular A level choices, alongside English and geography. Vocational courses in product design and business studies are also offered.

Strong focus on science as well as English, with everyone encouraged to include an expressive art and a technology subject amongst GCSE options; school is quick to point out that while the arts have always been strong, its main priority is to deliver a broad curriculum for everybody: 'We aim to deliver a high calibre of subjects across the board and not get labelled as one thing.'

Spanish taught in year 7 and more able pupils can study French from year 8. Languages set from year 8 but all other subjects taught in mixed ability groups. 'We tried setting for science, but the results didn't improve.' Maths has historically been one of the weaker subjects, 'but we've made lots of progress in key stage 3 and the school now has a high performing specialist school second specialism in mathematics and computing.' This has allowed increased investment and focus on maths, producing strong results at GCSE and A level. Homework club offered every day until 4.30pm with teachers in every subject on tap to help students.

Good SEN support, mostly within the classroom. Split level site unsuitable for children with physical disabilities: 'Because we're on a hill and because of the age of the building, we can't accommodate students with significant mobility issues.' Around 10 per cent of pupils have special educational needs, including specific learning difficulties, dyslexia and dyspraxia. The gifted and talented co-ordinator identifies very able girls, who are encouraged to take on extension research projects – 'but we don't want to be exclusive, others can join in too.' Good careers advice – has Investors in Careers status, recently renewed.

Games, options, the arts: Arts are big here. The QEGS bronze art award has been recently introduced to recognise achievement, focusing on personal progress. Annual arts festival is an opportunity for the school and its community to celebrate the events of the past year and includes drama, song, poetry and music.

Drama GCSE very popular, involving regular showcases for parents. Christmas production is written and directed by sixth formers and performed to the whole school. At Film Skool (an extracurricular activity) professional film makers and producers work with pupils who write, edit and direct their own films, culminating in a private screening in a West End cinema. SMAKS (Stretch your Media Arts Knowledge and Skills) is a programme of after-school workshops, designed to encourage students (as well as the wider community) to try new media skills, including theatre set design, cartoon caricature, and portrait photography. The school hosts two drama studios and media editing suites.

Music is also strong, though relatively few take it to GCSE or A level, where it is available through Barnet Music Centre. Senior and junior orchestras, a jazz band, and various ensembles depending on the strengths and numbers of the musicians. Links with the ENO.

Several (rather basic) art studios, with some eye-catching art dotted around, including a pop art display. Dance an increasingly popular subject, as is sport – including the less traditional, fencing, boxercise and roller-skating. Great indoor facilities include a mammoth sports hall, gymnasium and a pristine, Olympic size swimming pool; 'I only learned to swim once I started QE Girls', a 13-year-old student told us. Outdoor tennis courts. Girls have competed in county football and cross-country competitions. Girls doing PE GCSE often organise dance and games tournaments for local primary schools.

'There's so much going on, you're never bored to death', one pupil told us. And she wasn't wrong. On top of all the media stuff, other extracurricular activities include karate club, music clubs and debating societies, Portuguese, cheerleading, rock challenge, archery, football, swimming, Young Enterprise etc. Blossoming hacks join the journalism club and can take part in the BBC School Report. Trips abroad include skiing in the Alps, language trip, art/drama trips to New York and history trips to the battlefields of France and Belgium.

Background and atmosphere: First opened in 1888 as a grammar school; has been comprehensive since the 1970s. Hilly site on the edge of London's green belt, and set back from busy Barnet High Street. Buildings range from Victorian to 1960s. Rather tatty round the edges and could do with a major influx of cash for refurbishment – which doesn't look imminent: 'We're often at the back of the queue because our results have been good.' A parent commented that in her opinion, the only weakness of the school is that 'it is very old, with small, sometimes manky classrooms.'

On the plus side, the loos were revamped at a cost of £150,000 at the request of the school council some 15 years ago and have been refurbished regularly since (although many pupils still cited the toilets as a downside of the school). During our tour we noticed that new windows were being installed – something the school believes only happened because of the switch to academy status. 'Apart from that, and our sporting facilities which used to be shared, becoming an academy doesn't make much of a difference in real terms.'

After walking through a myriad of corridors which didn't seem to correlate to one another, over an internal bridge (which linked two buildings), we lost our bearings on several occasions. General impression is of bright, sparse spaces painted pale blue. Rather Victorian and wanting in imagination, we felt. None of this seemed to bother the pair of perpetually positive students who took us on our tour. So proud they were of their school, 'one big family', that it might as well have been Versailles.

Large, well-stocked library that was busy and buzzing (but what caught our eye was a student stuffing a sandwich in her mouth directly in front of a sign which read 'no eating in the library'). The canteen was pretty pukka too, with its mouthwatering and beautifully presented selection of hot food, generous salad bar and divine desserts. Thumbprint ID system.

The outside space is a pleasant surprise – beautiful grounds adorned with smart benches and a few small Japanese-style feature bridges. 'It's lovely in the summer for picnics', one pupil told us. Hard to believe we were only a stone's throw from Barnet High Street. Very much a community comprehensive, 'we have students whose grandmothers came to this school', with a relaxed atmosphere and confident, articulate girls, used to speaking up in public.

Pastoral care, well-being and discipline: Renowned for making new girls feel at home quickly – 'we want parents and girls to feel confident about their choice of secondary school.' The dedicated head of year 7 spends much time and effort visiting feeder primary schools in the summer term to meet students and staff. Sixth formers are also on tap to help out and plan team-building activities for the year 7s, which encourages each form to work together – 'a crucial part of the friend-making process during the first week of term.'

'One of the hallmarks of the school is that girls find the staff very approachable'. High expectations of good behaviour and discipline do not appear to be unrealistic. Only five permanent exclusions over the past 15 years or so and although 'regrettable', they were left with 'no other choice'. Clear policy on drugs and bullying, 'Obviously girls are exposed to drugs outside, but inside it is not an issue. Our PHSE programme is very good and we put a lot of effort into equipping girls to make informed decisions on all aspects of life.' The form tutor or head of year is the first port of call if a girl is troubled, but 'my daughter knows she can go to the head if she really needs to', one parent told us.

Students' progress is closely monitored with regular reports, academic reviews and parents' evenings. Great emphasis is placed on parents' inclusion – 'we are kept very well informed via texts, newsletters and emails.' However, the same parent added: 'Parents' evenings can be a bit shambolic. It often feels like speed dating without the fun. I feel it could be better organised.' 'Time for You' sessions have proved very popular; parents are invited to informal meetings every half term which cover topics from self-esteem and friendship to e-safety. Sessions also offered just for dads and daughters. 'My daughter did a Ready Steady Cook afternoon with her dad. She loved it and it was great bonding,' one parent told us.

Form time and assembly at 8.40am with lessons starting immediately afterwards. 'Students don't like to miss teaching time.' Various incentives and rewards schemes are offered to students who work hard and take an active part in school life

– anything from an inspired design for a sustainable home to a competition cooking food from around the world.

Pupils and parents: Pupils from across the board. One parent told us: 'You get pupils who come from massive houses in Hadley Wood, and those that come from the local council estate, nature of the beast – you just have to hope they respect each other.' However, higher than average percentage of girls on free school meals. Ethnically diverse – largest share is white British, 40 per cent, the remainder a variety of different ethnicities 'which reflect the population of Barnet as a whole.' Old girls: actress and singer Elaine Paige and actress Stephanie Beacham.

Entrance: Oversubscribed, but not heavily – roughly three applicants for every place. First in line are girls with statement of social or medical needs specifying the school, then siblings, then those living closest ('we moved into the area to get our daughter into the school') – which in practice tends to mean within two miles. Girls entering the sixth form (about 18 each year) need four grade Bs or above at GCSE, and many A level courses specify a B grade in the A level subject.

Exit: About a third leaves after GCSEs for selective sixth forms, co-ed sixth form colleges or FE colleges. Most sixth form leavers go on to higher education, courses including medicine, dentistry and law.

Money matters: Not a rich school – low down in the queue for government cash for refurbishment, but does its best with available funds. Loyal parent body works hard at raising money.

Remarks: A successful comprehensive with high expectations that produces self-assured girls used to discussion and debate.

Queen Elizabeth's School, Barnet

Queen's Road, Barnet, Hertfordshire EN5 4DQ

Pupils: 1,190 • Ages: 11–18 • Sixth form: 145

Tel: 020 8441 4646
Email: enquiries@qebarnet.co.uk
Website: www.qebarnet.co.uk

Headmaster: Since 2011, Neil Enright MA (Oxon) MBA NPQH FRSA (30s). Educated at St John's College, Oxford, and has worked here since 2002, rising to become head of department (humanities – a geographer), head of year, deputy head. MBA in 2010 from the University of London Institute of Education, which focused on aspects of leadership, management and systems of effective learning.

Gives a knuckle-crunching handshake and oozes authority, but is cordial, jovial and empathetic. Pupils admit they sit or stand up that bit straighter when he's around, 'but more because we want to impress him than assuming we'll be told off.' Tellingly, one of the first things he did was put a huge glass window between his (more company boardroom than headmasterly) office and the corridor, with pupils encouraged to drop in with any concerns. Although not a timetabled teacher ('the demands of my job don't allow it'), he takes geography lessons across all year groups when he can.

Converses easily with the boys, always eats in the dining hall at lunchtimes, attends every school event and has even been known to hang around at the bus stop after school to chat. Runs a very tight ship, with a well distributed leadership model. Areas of focus include driving innovation in the classroom and pastoral care.

Academic matters: Consistently top of the academic league tables, rivalling most schools, independent or state, in its exam results. Baseline assessment in year 7, then setting in all subjects (including sport), with half-termly tests thereafter. Testing very much part of the modus operandi. Many parents put off applying for fear of the stress (one parent told us she took her son out because 'the pressure was just too much'), but the school has heaps of motivational mechanisms in place, including personal tutors, who they see twice a day in groups, as well as having a one-to-one sessions every half term. Coaching and mentoring (including peer mentoring) also the norm. 'I arrived with good grades, but was a bit of a slacker, and the school soon sorted me out,' one pupil told us. Others talk about being 'carried along with the collective will to learn.' It also helps that hard grafting is admired, said another parent. 'In a lot of schools, you get teased for trying, but nobody's called a geek here. In fact, they somehow turn it around so that the boys look up to each other and respect others for trying hard in something, whether it's their subject or not.'

A*s the norm at GCSE (average 10 A*s). In 2016, 88 per cent A*/A grades. Languages popular, with all pupils taking French, German and Latin from year 7 and continuing one modern language (at least) at GCSE, with Mandarin, Spanish and ancient Greek offered as extras. First school to become 100 per cent EBac. A level choices are decided by tests in years 10 and 11 designed 'to tease out' aptitude. 'We don't rate GSCE results as a good enough indicator,' explains head. Seventy per cent of boys do four A levels, most get four A*/A grades (84 per cent of grades were A*/A in 2016); only a handful don't take maths, two-thirds some science, many do a mix. No fluffy options whatsoever.

Strong teaching, with good gender balance, in every department. 'They go well beyond the syllabus and really care about you enjoying the subject and doing well,' said one pupil, with boys particularly enthusiastic about geography and history. 'Every lesson aims to push these boys up to their ceiling, which is made easier when there's such a narrow ability range,' says head. Boys say healthy competition pervades the classroom as much as the sports field, but there's plenty of group work, with many classes we visited organised with desks in clusters rather than in neat rows. Class sizes around 30, dropping to 15 at A level. Lots of homework (one and a half hours in year 7, one hour per subject per night at A level). Technology embedded in lessons, but not much use of tablets.

Enrichment throughout, with boys regularly taken off curriculum, and extra-long lunch breaks allowing for the myriad of clubs that also run before and after school (favourites include public speaking, karate and sports). Some clubs pupil-led, including an impressive politics one, with recent guest speakers including Vince Cable and Alistair Campbell. An expectation to do the Extended Project Qualification, with subjects ranging from photography to ancient history. Big push on symposia with high-performing girls' schools, including Henrietta Barnett, St Albans High School and North London Collegiate. 'Whilst there are huge benefits to boys learning in an all-male environment, boys also need to be able to work with young women,' says head.

Special needs at this school tends to be on the gifted-and-talented end of the spectrum, although school can accommodate mild autism, Asperger's and dyslexia and every department runs subject-specific clinics to support the struggling and challenge the most able. 'Because difference tends to be celebrated at this school, and the learning is so tailored anyway, our son's special needs have really been a non-issue in terms of his education,' said one parent.

Games, options, the arts: Rugby by far the strongest sport, with all participating in year 7. Fixtures list includes all major independent schools in the region. England under-16 head coach coaches the rugby squad and the school fields up to D teams on a regular basis. Rugby 7s has also been running for 38 years, with school playing against 64 others, including Eton. Swimming, Eton fives, tennis, badminton, basketball, tennis, cross-country and fencing also popular. Plenty of county and national representation in bridge, chess and water polo. Eight-lane swimming pool, all-weather tennis courts, multi-gym and plenty of neatly trimmed green fields for team sports. But it's no big deal not to have sporting prowess in the obvious options, say students. 'I didn't like any of them, but have found I really do like tennis and swimming,' said one old boy.

Music department boasts three full-time music teachers, 17 peripatetic teachers and a music suite where boys can study A level music technology with all the latest recording equipment. Particularly strong orchestra and choir, both of which are open to all, plus chamber choir and ensembles, including Indian music, which boys run themselves.

Notable visual arts facilities, all open-plan, light and airy, with exceptional examples of mostly abstract work displayed throughout the school, including some choice pieces adoring the head's smart office. DT boasts all the latest equipment, with one pupil designing and making their own drone when we visited. Generally an academic attitude towards art, with many pupils interested in pursuing architecture.

Whole school drama performances take place in Shirley Hall, which has a decent sized stage and 400 drop-down seats (otherwise flat against wall when the hall is used for low-impact sports). New spacious food technology facility.

Name a country and there's probably been a trip there. Recent rugby tour to Sri Lanka, geography trips to Iceland, Switzerland and Sicily, music tours all over Europe, plus well-established language exchanges to Germany and France and set trips to battlefields, among others. Head keen that it's not always the same boys benefiting, either due to cost or ability.

Background and atmosphere: Plenty of visual reminders around the school that it was founded in 1573 by Robert, Earl of Leicester, with a charter from Elizabeth I. Rebuilt in 1932 by Hertfordshire County Council in a noble civic style with terrazzo flooring, parquet and panelling, all kept in spotless condition. Still well-endowed with land held in perpetuity and its own Foundation Trustees, QE went comprehensive in the '60s, reverted to grant-maintained status in 1989 and became a grammar school once more in 1994.

Q

Atmosphere is ordered, focused and positive and even at break times, there's no casual loitering. At lunchtime, for example, boys wolf down their lunch so they can fit in football or other activities before attending a lunchtime club. Meanwhile, in class, boys are absorbed and single-minded. You'll find no low-level disruption here.

Leadership responsibilities from year 11, when own suits are allowed. Ninety prefects voted for by staff and students, monitor lunch (fresh food produced daily), playgrounds and classrooms. School captain and house captains appointed from on high. Student voice heard through pupil conferences. Boys also involved in appointing new staff by attending a class, then giving feedback.

A 15-year estate strategy means there are always plans in place around buildings. Among the newest additions is a spacious new library, with 100 computer terminals and 5,000 books when we visited. 'When other school librarians tell me they struggle attracting pupils in their library, I'm amazed,' the librarian told us. 'Ours is so popular that we practically have to fend them off at lunchtimes.'

Café 1573 provides a Starbucks-like environment for sixth formers, whilst other years frequent the dining hall, a modern space also with its own branding and colour scheme. School even has its own (cashless) shop, selling everything from uniforms (much lower cost than in shops) to pens, with all profits ploughed back into the school.

'Pupil progression' (broader and less vocational than careers advice) embedded throughout, whilst loyal old boys come back to chat to sixth formers about university and subject choice. Some act as Oxbridge buddies for the next generation. Big programme of volunteering, with all sixth formers expected to do 40 hours over the school year (although most do much more), including working in libraries, charity shops, hospices, charity shops and even supporting the local MP's surgery.

Pastoral care, well-being and discipline: Pastoral care mainly from form teachers, and a real strength of the school's provision. Motivation comes from a plethora of rewards and praise, including house points, certificates, merit stickers (for younger boys), congratulatory emails and postcards sent home to parents, showcasing of achievements on the website and 'good notes' in the diary which must be signed off by parents (there are 'bad notes' too for offences such as persistent failure to meet deadlines, but these are far less frequent). Plenty of silverware prominently displayed to remind pupils of the school's achievements.

No real misbehaviour to speak of – pupils have good manners, wear their uniform well, and do their work when asked. Head puts it down to clear expectations, a strong sense of discipline that feels natural rather than forced, and rewards. 'Not the kind of school for boys who don't like taking orders or challenging the system,' said one parent. Indeed, there are fixed-term exclusions for persistent 'failure to carry out school protocols' or misbehaving in lessons and head says he would expel a boy on the spot for offences including violence aimed at staff, consciously creating racial disharmony or bringing drugs into school, although no boy has been expelled in his time. 'We make absolutely no exceptions and that message is very clear,' he says.

Pupils and parents: Contrary to popular opinion, this school is not full of middle-class families. Ofsted noted it's the national average in terms of deprivation, with quite a few boys in receipt of pupil premium. 'We take great pride in the fact that the school is a complete meritocracy,' says head. 'There is absolutely no other means of gaining admission than doing well in the test for maths and English.' Over 80 per cent of boys come from ethnic minorities, predominantly Asian. Around half speak English as a second language, although they're advanced bilingual learners and generally only need help with areas like idiom and inference, which the school happily provides. Many of the boys who make it to Oxbridge are the first generation in their family to go to university, and in recent years one was a refugee from Rwanda. Majority travel from London borough of Barnet, although there are boys from all over north west London and the surrounding home counties, who are served by good public transport links and a nine-strong coach system facilitated by the school. Pupils are quietly confident, grounded, polite and exude intelligence.

Parents are considered as key partners of the school, regularly communicated with via pupils' diaries, live reporting on the website and emails. 'I've never experienced a parents' association like it,' adds head of Friends of Queen Elizabeth, with parents doing everything from providing work experience and mock interviews to giving lectures, supporting concerts and fundraising. 'The annual Founders' Day Fete raises up to £25,000 and has parents taking the day off work the Friday before to help prepare,' says head, although a couple of parents told us it's 'unfortunately the same old faces that tend to help.'

Entrance: More than 2,300 boys apply for 180 places. Tests in September (register between May and mid-July), which although tough are made as comfortable as possible, with year 9s present to put applicants at ease, 'including playing hangman'. Boys told whether or not they have met the 'standard required' before they have to make their choice of schools, so they have nothing to lose by taking the test. NB Meeting the 'standard required' does not guarantee a place. Pupils come from around 90 primary schools, but the ability range is narrow, with most in the top 10 per cent nationally. Occasional vacancies between years 7 and 10, offered to those on the waiting list. No sixth form entry for external candidates. 'I see this as a seven-year education,' says head, who adds that he's seen too many schools that take external sixth formers essentially run as two separate schools. Automatic transfer to sixth form for nearly all students, although pupils have to be recommended for individual subjects.

Exit: Up to 15 per cent of boys leave after GCSE. Reasons include not making the grade; preferring a mixed sixth form; hankering after a more relaxed environment; looking for subjects the school doesn't teach, such as law and psychology; or winning scholarships to independent schools (although that's rare – most families pick this school over the private sector). Almost all who stay go on to top Russell Group universities, notably Nottingham, Imperial, UCL and Warwick. In 2016, 36 to Oxbridge, two to the US, 27 medics, one vet and one dentist. Typical subjects include economics, law, engineering and medicine. First-rate UCAS guidance provided to all boys.

Money matters: You wouldn't know it, walking around the school, but there's minimal state aid, with head saying he gets less money than many local comps. Gaps are filled with a voluntary £60 a month contribution from parents, funds from the Foundation and donations from parents, old boys and friends.

Remarks: A remarkable school that offers the top 10 per cent of learners from a diversity of backgrounds an exceptional and rounded education that even private schools struggle to compete with. Not for boys who may want to challenge the status quo, nor for the non-competitive. But for those who thrive in a highly ordered, hard grafting environment with an underlying sense of competition across all subjects, this is a great school that consistently turns out responsible young men with unbounded opportunities to succeed at university and their chosen careers beyond.

The Queen's CofE Primary School

Cumberland Road, Kew, Richmond, Surrey TW9 3HJ

Pupils: 405 • Ages: 4–11 • C of E

Tel: 020 8940 3580
Email: info@queens.richmond.sch.uk
Website: www.queens.richmond.sch.uk

Headteacher: Since 2011, Miss Katie Bentham (30s). Trained at Bishop Grosseteste College in Lincoln, part of the University of Hull. Began her career in London, at St Mary Magdalene C of E Primary in Westminster and Newbury Park Primary in Redbridge, where she also gained a masters in science education. Relocated to Scotland for her next job at Westfield Primary in Cumbernauld, then back to London and Marshgate Primary in Richmond, where she was the SENCo and part of senior management. Queen's is her first headship, and she was parachuted in after what appears to have been a bit of a hiccup with the previous incumbent. Our impression is of a pleasant and energetic lady who is working with steely determination towards that coveted Ofsted 'Outstanding'. The parents we spoke to hadn't met her in person, but, said one mother, 'The children feel they know her, and when they're at home they even refer to her as Katie!' (Head adamant that this doesn't happen in school.) 'Not afraid to make changes,' was one parent's verdict. 'Miss Bentham's great!' pupils confirmed to us, eagerly.

Entrance: Two-form entry, so 60 reception places each year. Usual admissions criteria: looked after children, medical needs, siblings. Thereafter, at least one parent must be a 'committed and regular worshipper' at one of the three Kew Anglican churches (St Anne's, St Philip & All Saints', St Luke's); after that, it's down to proximity. Rather convoluted – if in doubt, contact the school office. School is oversubscribed, but not dishearteningly so. Also worth applying further up, as much of the Kew community is professional and mobile, and occasional places do become available.

Exit: As you'd expect in this locality, a high number of private and grammar school places every year: Latymer Upper, Hampton, Lady Eleanor Holles, Tiffin, Kingston. Popular non-selective state school destinations include Christ's, Waldegrave, Sir Richard Reynolds and Richmond Park Academy. As with other state primaries, school doesn't prepare for 11 plus, and parents report that a fair degree of private tutoring goes on in the upper year groups. The children, however, were inclined to attribute their success to the school. 'It's really, really helped me get into the school I'm into,' said one engaging year 6 lad, who could have passed for Benedict Cumberbatch in his young days.

Remarks: Queen's, in a brand new building, is sited a stone's-throw from Kew Village, which inevitably accounts for some of the school's character. As far as we could tell, this was a London-accent-free zone, and all the pupils we met were chirpy, well-spoken, well-mannered and quite delightful. We suspect that there isn't huge social diversity, and we saw very little cultural diversity as we looked round the lunch-time crowds. (School says that it has above the national average number of pupils from ethnic minority groups.) But that said, the school works tirelessly to give the best school experience possible to its students, and clearly succeeds. Parents were incredibly warm in their praise, with the school's kind and friendly ethos mentioned again and again: 'A very positive culture of caring'; 'My two children love it there, they go happily every day'; 'The outstanding thing has been the care from all the staff'; 'The great strengths of the school are the atmosphere and the teachers, who are of a high quality and very dedicated'; 'A very friendly, inclusive environment'; 'Gentle and positive'; 'All the staff care about every child'. The children unanimously confirmed this. 'Is it friendly here?' we asked as we moved about the school, and group after group gave us an instant and emphatic 'YES!'

The Anglican faith is central to the school's ethos, and plays a greater part here than we've seen in any other C of E primary school. Fathers Nigel and Peter from St Anne's and St Luke's take assemblies every week, there's a Passion Play every year complete with crucifixion scene, and attendance at church services is regular and frequent: when we visited, for instance, the whole school had just returned from Ascension Day service. Even competitions can be devotional in nature, with the winning entries in the Easter Crosses competition making a colourful display on the school's website. But there was nothing dour about any of it, and the children impressed us with their cheerful and confident benevolence towards life, the universe and everything. There was also a happy awareness of other faiths, and visits to a synagogue and a mosque had been followed up with some lovely work.

The standard of writing and maths that we saw was very high, and Queen's academic record is sterling: recently, the Daily Telegraph placed it 10th in the country for its Sats results, and most children here achieve well above the national average, with a number of them successfully taking the level 6 tests (a pass at level 6 is expected of the average 14-year-old). Robust systems of monitoring are in place to make sure that children's performance is being tracked. One parent criticised the 'large and ill-defined projects' set for homework and felt that the school didn't do enough to push the children to do as well as they possibly could; whilst another, conversely, felt that the school put too much emphasis on getting the children to perform 'excessively' well in their Sats. The majority, however, said they were contented with the academic provision. 'Very good academic results achieved without extra pressure on the students', and 'an excellent academic environment' were typical comments. There are bang-up-to-date interactive whiteboards in every classroom, an attractive library and excellent, well-thumbed resources. SEN provision was 'not in the best place when I joined' according to the head, but both she and the SENCo have worked hard to bring it up to scratch, and we liked what we saw of the provision in this area.

Popular breakfast and after-school clubs are welcomed by working parents, and there's a lively programme of extracurricular activities, with music being a particular strength. Despite its small size, the school fields two orchestras and two choirs, and a wide variety of instrumental lessons are offered. 'The concerts are brilliant!' enthused one parent. 'Every time you go into school your hear children singing or playing music!' Views on the sports provision were a little cooler, with many parents and pupils (boys in particular) wishing there were more, but everyone agreed that it was getting better, and there was much praise for a recent cricket tournament. The head insists that the amount of sport at Queen's has 'dramatically increased' over the past year, and two swimming trophies in her office bore testimony to sport's being 'one of our vision priorities.'

Queen's is the only school in the country to change its name according to the gender of the reigning monarch – it was The King's School until 1953 – and is held in warm regard locally. A recent alumni evening was well attended and produced some misty-eyed comments in the visitors' book. But there's no question of things standing still.

School rebuilt under the Priority School Building Programme, new buildings open for business from September 2016, followed by further improvements to the grounds. These are clearly exciting times for a school that has much to be proud of.

Q

Queen's College Prep School

Linked with Queen's College London

61 Portland Place, London W1B 1QP

Pupils: 228 • Ages: 4–11 • C of E

Fees: £15,270 – £16,500 pa

Tel: 020 7291 0660
Email: info@qcps.org.uk
Website: www.qcps.org.uk/

Headmistress: Since September 2016, Emma Webb, previously deputy head of the primary section of the British International School in Riyadh. Degree from London University and PGCE from University of East Anglia; she has also taught at Davenies Prep.

Entrance: Most children join in the September after their 4th birthday. No formal assessment but entry to reception involves a parental interview with the headmistress. Two forms in every year, with an average of 16 in a class. Entry to all other year groups (if places become available) involves an assessment of the child's academic achievement and potential, an evaluation of social skills and school reports, plus a parental interview. Two open mornings, by appointment only, are held each term and parents who have registered are invited to attend.

Pupils are international, multi-cultural, multi-faith, with majority living locally and with English as their first language. 'We love a family.'

Exit: 'We prepare for choice,' says the school – and the results show a variety of destinations, with around 40 per cent choosing the senior school (all by competitive entrance examination, so the Queen's College Prep candidates on a level playing field with outsiders). Girls regularly win academic, art and music scholarships. London girls' day schools are popular choices, including both Francis Hollands, Channing, City of London Girls, South Hampstead High, Godolphin & Latymer, North London Collegiate and St Paul's Girls'. A few head for boarding at eg Cheltenham Ladies' College or Downe House.

Remarks: This small, traditional girls' day school is well situated, very close to Regent's Park. 'Surroundings really matter,' and the head's study with its soothing, grey and cream décor provides a calm setting for dealing with parents and daily concerns. School is housed in two tall Adam buildings – ornate ceilings and ground floor classrooms with columns and fireplaces. All attractively light and bright.

The imaginative use of space and excellent modern resources work well, from the ICT suite to the transformed first floor drawing room (with sprung floor for dance, drama and fencing). Basement has a well-lit music room, dining room and gym. It was good to see girls enjoying reading in the well-stocked library (with part-time librarian). Older pupils can bring Kindles in for leisure reading. Something of an Aladdin's cave when you climb up past the big, bright science room to art studio on the top floor. Large windows, with great views of nearby rooftops, fill the room with light. Good to see younger pupils creating colourful Elmer-inspired elephants – freely drawn rather than using templates. No kiln, but girls produce batiks in the senior school. Senior school theatre used for top year productions and All Souls Church at Langham Place for harvest and carol services.

School offers a broad curriculum. Each day begins and ends with form teachers – to help pupils organise themselves and their homework. Mornings are dedicated to English and maths and the timetable has been constructed to build in time for travel to various sports facilities nearby. Older pupils have longer days on Tuesdays, Wednesdays and Thursdays. Specialists from reception up for music, French, PE, ballet and musical theatre. Specialist art from year 1, Latin from year 5 and study skills in year 6.

Rather than girls going out of class for individual learning support lessons, the emphasis is placed on differentiation in small classes. Recently appointed male SENCo manages the department, reporting to the deputy head, and there is a clear policy with procedures in place to identify girls with SEN as early as possible. Outside specialists for speech therapy, occupational therapy and dyslexia – by arrangement with parents. School informs parents on entry that girls must be able to access the curriculum on offer: 'This is the right school as long as we can meet their needs.'

Parents are full of praise for the high standard of teaching and care taken to cater for individuals. The small class sizes help, along with the use of teaching assistants (unusually up to year 4). Underpinning it all, however, is an effective, carefully honed monitoring system for pupils' progress – implemented by the management team and used to share information at regular meetings. Parents told us: 'The girls are happy as they are treated as individuals and there is an excellent balance between academic and life experiences.'

Vibrant displays and imaginative artwork act as a stimulus for learning and celebrate the pupils' achievements. We loved the walk-in mermaid's cave for an 'under the sea' topic in year 1, complete with relevant books on display. 'The teachers really take trouble,' a parent said, adding that teachers dressed up as astronauts during a recent project about space.

The pupils we spoke to felt very well supported and encouraged by the reward system (includes head's commendations and house points). Setting in maths and, where appropriate, English from year 3. This works well. We saw enthusiastic teaching, with girls focused, challenged and thoroughly enjoying their learning.

School takes full advantage of cultural opportunities and there are two class trips every half term. A parent told us: 'For me this makes up for other areas as like other inner London prep schools, there are limitations to sports provision.' Having said that, the girls get a very wide and varied diet of sports, including tag rugby and football. They also use nearby Regent's Park and other sports venues across London (some form of physical activity timetabled each day for the older children). Younger pupils enjoy a lovely private garden across the way. Tennis is not in the curriculum. Enthusiastic PE staff run sessions at weekends and are willing to try out new ventures (trampolining when we visited). School wants the girls to work hard and play hard. Music and dance are very popular, with vast numbers seizing opportunities to learn instruments, sing and attend the dance academy that operates after school and in the holidays.

At morning break older girls socialise in the dining room, and at lunch times there are organised activities to enable them to relax, have fun and mix. We watched a lunchtime marimba ensemble rehearsal. Girls concentrated hard and produced delightful syncopated African rhythms alongside their enthusiastic teacher. The energetic dance teacher runs a variety of classes from ballet and jazz to street dancing and tap and the girls love it. The performing arts are a real strength of this school.

Confidence is a key word and is nurtured and developed throughout girls' time here. All the pupils we spoke to during our visit were polite, well mannered and happy. In lessons they readily explained what they were doing and were eager to throw themselves into activities, finding mathematics fun as they devised and budgeted for their own theme park or discussed performance poetry and how to communicate with an audience. They understand the importance of being kind, showing mutual respect to their teachers and each other. They are mindful of the code of conduct (present in every classroom and emphasised in assemblies).

Active parents' circle for fundraising and social events. Parents are encouraged to be involved, with two form representatives for each year. Communication with parents is excellent. Alongside the usual there's a general weekly newsletter. The school has also introduced specific year group newsletters with valuable curriculum information, key dates, details of pupils' achievements and splendid photographs.

Food is prepared in the senior school and parents complimentary about the weekly menu. The parent of a daughter with allergies felt very supported by the school. Smart uniform; only niggle expressed by parents was that they'd like winter hats to be reintroduced (girls love their summer boaters).

Parents told us that this is a school 'that raises the bar.' They praised 'the quality of education, staff retention, creativity and happy children' and said that above all it's a place 'that takes genuine pride in its charges and allows each individual to flourish.'

Queen's College London

Linked with Queen's College Prep School

43-49 Harley Street, London W1G 8BT

Pupils: 370 • Ages: 11-18 • Sixth form: 75 • C of E

Fees: £17,700 pa

Tel: 020 7291 7000
Email: admissions@qcl.org.uk
Website: www.qcl.org.uk

Principal: Since 2009, Dr Frances Ramsey MA PGCE DPhil (Oxon) (40s). Read history at Oxford and her doctorate is in medieval history. Prior to becoming principal here, she was director of studies at Westminster School and master of the Queen's Scholars for 17 years. She says the transition from Westminster to Queen's was seamless. A similar central London culture – intelligent teachers lead their own full lives out of school and many parents have sons at Westminster and their daughters here (as indeed does she). The education is broad and each child is treated as an individual and difficult to pigeonhole. Unusually for a head of a busy and high profile senior school, these two schools are the extent of her teaching experience. It is obviously more than enough. We couldn't find a parent to speak in anything but superlatives when describing her. 'Brilliant,' said one, 'outstanding,' said another, 'very very genuine,' observed a third.

We found it hard not to be bowled over too. As soon as you meet this highly intelligent and incisive woman you feel at your ease and charmed by her gentle but focused attention. Dr Ramsey is like a tiny bird, modest and seemingly fragile but beneath that delicate surface robust (but not steely) and capable of (almost) anything. Her husband is a professor of archaeological science at Merton College Oxford, where they met. Parents speak of her 'vision' and her presence – 'she is always there', said one, 'and available,' said another. Without any fuss and with a great deal of subtlety she has managed to turn round a prevailing sense of 'laissez faire' about learning. 'Yes, the bright ones would get to Oxbridge, but if you decided that learning was not for you, you could sit back and enjoy the ride without putting the effort in – and that's what's changed,' commented a parent. Now Dr Ramsey doesn't allow any girl to be overlooked. Everyone needs to focus at all times. As this has become more ingrained into the culture of the school there is less necessity to enforce it rigidly from the top. The intake is also becoming of a higher calibre academically as the word spreads. This has created some murmurs of dissatisfaction – a slight feeling among senior girls that the school is losing its creative flair and marshalling a more uniform collection. However, parents comment on the excellent appointments Dr Ramsey has made. She notices, too, when an existing member of staff could flourish in another department, and this is where she makes the difference. Bold and imaginative, she is unafraid to rock the boat, but she does it with gentleness and empathy.

Off to head Godolphin & Latymer in July 2017. Her successor will be Richard Tillett, currently senior deputy head at Harrogate Ladies' College. Degree in modern languages and history from Cambridge; taught history and politics at King Edward VI Grammar and was housemaster and history teacher at The Leys before joining Harrogate Ladies' in 2010 as head of sixth form. His wife, Dr Emma Longstaff, is a sociologist who now works in academic publishing, and they have a young daughter. Richard's primary academic interests are Russian history (he is a Russian speaker) and contemporary politics. Away from school life, he is an avid follower of football and cricket, and loves travel, good food and hill walking.

Academic matters: The trend is upwards and results get more impressive year on year. In 2016, 82 per cent A*-B grades at A level, with 57 per cent A*/A grades. GCSE results 77 per cent A*/A in 2016. The range of subjects is broad, but by far the most popular and successful subject – according to recent results – is English, closely followed by history. Philosophy and ethics is another popular department. Tiny take up of further maths and physics, though several doing biology and chemistry, and A*s uncommon in all these subjects. The number of girls doing a modern language at A level appears to be low too. This is despite the fact that there is a lot of language provision in the early years – in year 7 they do Mandarin, Spanish, French, Italian and German, and then can choose a second modern language in addition to French in year 8 and 9 before finalising GCSE choices. We swept through a corridor overhearing the songs and languages of different European countries that poured out of each classroom. Results in modern languages are good at GCSE – in French, Italian and Spanish. A shame that this doesn't seem to carry through – yet – to A level. This may change following the appointment of a new head of modern languages from North London Collegiate.

Classics department is lively, we were told, with lots of recital competitions, for example, organised by the London Classical Association, as well as plays, trips and activities. Top Latin set in year 9 is introduced to ancient Greek and a tiny few take GCSE. The take up of Latin is also low at A level; at GCSE approximately five each year take the subject, some achieving strong A* and A grades.

In some of the EBacc subjects (maths, English, history, geography, and French, but not sciences) the girls take the tougher IGCSE. Results in maths are excellent. No one has got below a B in recent years, with 19 As and eight A*s recently. Parents of girls in years 7 and 8 are excited to report their daughters discovering a love of science and enthusiasm for subjects they had never shown an interest in before. From 2018 girls will take the tougher IGCSE in sciences too.

Reports across the board about the excellent relationships between staff and pupils. Girls here are treated with respect and consideration by their teachers and we were told by a number of parents that the atmosphere was more similar to a university than a school – helped, no doubt, by the 'supervision style' class sizes in the sixth form. Our guides enthused about the teachers 'being there for them' and that they felt they could always trouble them – in or out of lessons – with a question or concern. Small class sizes (15-20) and sometimes tiny in the sixth form – contribute to the particular personal rapport that develops between teacher and student.

One SENCo only, employed four days a week. Emphasis given to literacy and numeracy in admissions process means candidates with 'spiky profiles' are unlikely to reach the standard. Although the SENCo can meet the needs of pupils with mild dyspraxia, dyslexia, dyscalculia etc, 'we are not a school that specialises in this,' asserts head. Girls needing extra support are rarely taken out of lessons but will have 'individual learning plans' which all their teachers will be familiar with so that support can be given all the time during every lesson. Laptops and extra time may form part of the plan. No EFL tuition but will give support for EAL if necessary.

Games, options, the arts: Sport here is surprisingly strong considering this is a central London all girls' day school – and a relatively small one, too. Lots of choice of sports – netball arguably the strongest, but girls can also play lacrosse, football and tag rugby in winter, rounders, cricket and tennis in the summer. Despite its urban centre – Oxford Street and John Lewis only a stone's throw away – Regent's Park is also just up the road in the other direction and the girls can walk there in 10 minutes. Plenty of fixtures against other schools – they normally field a first and second team – and games is timetabled heavily in the early years. Twice a week girls will have double games, once a week PE and once a week dance. A gym in the bowels of the school is well equipped and a great space for letting off steam and doing (almost) any kind of sport, dance, ballet or gymnastics and even spinning and zumba. The school's sports uniform – 'a hoody and leggings,' as one parent described it – is very popular with the girls, no doubt a positive influence on the relish for physical activity.

Enthusiasm for sport wanes somewhat in the senior years but they then graduate to yoga, pilates and zumba classes at the University of Westminster gym off Regent Street. Swimming takes place at the Marshall Street Leisure Centre. Work has been done to create a fuller programme with a wider choice of activities and to encourage the competitive spirit. The appointment of a dynamic head of PE is reaping dividends. 'We are working on two threads,' school told us, 'coaching for excellence and ensuring everyone has a go.'

Drama and music are flourishing, productions here are inclusive, exciting and impressive. A recent show, Belles of the Ball, was devised by the girls with the help of a visiting professional writer and was based on a women's football team formed during World War 1 to raise money for men at the front. In writing and producing the play the girls not only wowed an audience with their final performance but were able to extend and enhance their understanding of a particular period through a very personal and liberating female experience. We spent some time with the head of drama, a former actor, who impressed us with her spontaneity, passion and experience. Lots of lunchtime clubs connected with drama.

School has a full orchestra and a number of ensembles. We heard rave reviews of the singing and tales of girls who had shown no interest in music before starting here, now being entered into choral scholarships for university. Formal recitals and concerts held in the beautiful Waiting Room on the ground floor. Annual jazz concert and a healthy number of girls are starting to choose to take music A level.

The art on the walls and the sculptures on display take your breath away. The art room is creatively inspiring – a barn-like, large, long room with windows in the ceiling and sun beaming in from every corner. However, when we visited the atmosphere was distinctly chilly. The girls were focused but not relaxed. What should have been a buzzy, creative warmth was instead stiff and wary. Perhaps we caught it on a bad day, but we did hear a few reports from parents that suggested we weren't imagining it. Girls who take art have historically done well here; large numbers continue to apply for the handful of art scholarships at the 11 plus. This should be a strength of the school: whether it will continue to be so remains to be seen.

Plenty of opportunity to travel, whether on cultural exchanges with schools in Pennsylvania and France, for example, or on football and cricket trips to, eg, Sri Lanka.

Background and atmosphere: Founded in 1848 and given a royal charter in 1853, a pioneer in education for women, this was the first institution in Great Britain to give academic qualifications to girls. Still on its original site in four elegant, well-proportioned Georgian houses, internally it has often been altered through the years in order to provide the best modern education possible. There is a faint whiff of Victorian hospital about it, with some cold stone floors and forbidding doors; however, the William Morris wallpaper decorating the ground floor corridor, tastefully toning in with the pale green school uniform, together with the high ceilings, large windows and frescos, goes a long way to making the school feel tastefully familiar, and comfortable. The school, tucked between expensive doctors' private practices on Harley Street in the heart of central London, with the music blaring out of New Look and Top Shop only yards away in nearby Oxford Street, is deceptively large. The houses extend some distance to the rear and classrooms and corridors are large and airy. An exciting development extending up at the top of the building, 'the roof project', is currently underway, including new sixth form centre – which will give them an area they can both relax and work in.

The school is more intimate than many of its kind in London. Older girls frequently smile and greet much younger ones, a sign of refreshing vertical friendships. This is not a school paralysed by hierarchy. Our guides said the thing about their school they were most proud of was the 'community'. 'Everyone knows each other and everyone is involved,' they enthused. A wonderfully atmospheric, wood panelled library with grand fireplaces, dark green wallpaper and serious looking, distinguished people, staring down from paintings on the walls, is where the sixth form currently work. The Waiting Room is an elegant old-fashioned room with an arresting frieze on the ceiling, where once girls waited to be taken to their next lesson. Now PSHE talks are held here, small drama productions and concerts. One of the few criticisms we heard of Dr Ramsey was that she had decided to carpet this room: to make it more comfortable and warm was her view; it undermined the grace and history of the room, say her detractors. The 'goldfish bowl', a striking glass-walled computer centre in the heart of the school, is a startling modern contrast to most of the rest of the school, and just outside Daunt Books runs a book stall where parents can place credit and girls can buy books at will. Plenty of computers around the school and a number of classrooms have desks with drawers containing laptops.

Spacious dining room in the basement, colourful Perspex chairs cheering up the dank basement ambience. Large glass doors open out onto an attractive courtyard area, with surrounding benches, into which girls can spill during the warmer months. Lots of choice, sushi and salad as well as the usual pasta and potatoes. Sixth formers can go out at lunch and sample what Oxford Street has to offer.

Pastoral care, well-being and discipline: Year heads, known as year tutors, help to monitor each individual girl, and there are section heads to oversee, for example, years 7-9 and years 10 and 11. There do not appear to be any serious disciplinary issues. We were surprised to hear no mention of drugs at all among the parents. 'Girls here are respected and treated as adults.' 'They feel listened to, the atmosphere is more like a university than a school' commented a number.

Parents' perception is that there could be more collaboration with boys' schools in the area. School counters this, pointing out participation in the Model United Nations and debating in the London leagues which 'bring the girls into contact with boys', as well as musical events organised with Harrow school.

Pupils and parents: Traditionally regarded as a school that caters for the well brought up, upper middle class girl whose parents regard a good education as of the highest value. The latter persists, and while there remains a faint fragrance of aristocracy, the demographic, as in most central London schools, is highly cosmopolitan. A wide mix of nationalities, Middle Eastern, European and American as well as Scandinavian, Antipodean and Asian; but there is no EFL teaching so they have to speak good English. The culture of the school is very English, however, and the majority of the pupils 'tend to be British,' says head. Girls here are well mannered and polite. They will look you in the eye and can hold their ground. A number of parents said how pleased they were that their daughters had formed such good and healthy friendships. Their view is that the school selects grounded girls who are willing to take advantage of the opportunities on offer. There used to be limos parked outside on Harley Street delivering girls – not any more.

Two of the earliest students, Miss Buss and Miss Beale, went on to found the North London Collegiate School and Camden School for Girls, and St Hilda's College Oxford, respectively. Katherine Mansfield and Jacqueline du Pré also stand amongst the long list of distinguished old girls as well as, more recently, writers Daisy Goodwin and Imogen Lloyd Webber. A distinguished tradition and history in the making.

Entrance: Mainly at 11+ via the North London Consortium group 1 exam. Some 500 applicants for 60 places and the numbers seem to rise relentlessly each year. Unusually at Queen's everyone is interviewed, regardless of performance in the exam. Indeed interviews take place between October and December before the exam. 'We like to form a picture of the child without seeing her test results.' They are genuinely selective and are looking for someone who is going to enjoy getting involved and seize the opportunities available.

No automatic entrance from Queen's College Prep but a good percentage come from there. Otherwise over 40 different feeder schools, with about 15 per cent from local state primaries. Another (small) intake at 16+ subject to GCSE results and letters of recommendation from their previous schools. All prospective entrants at this level interviewed by the head of sixth form.

Exit: Some 30 per cent leave after GCSEs, mostly to board or move into the state system. Post A level leavers to top universities: one medic in 2016; others to eg Edinburgh, Leeds, Manchester, Nottingham, UCL, York, to study everything from art and design to science subjects.

Money matters: Several means-tested bursaries available at 11+ and 16+, funded by the Old Queen's bursary trust fund. Academic, music and art scholarships, for up to 25 per cent of fees, for both internal and external candidates. Would hope always to be able to find a way of keeping a pupil in need.

Remarks: An elegant school offering a broad education to bright, interesting girls. There is nothing generic about Queen's

College. A very individual place where each girl is genuinely treated as an individual Will suit your all-round daughter who will thrive in a structured, nurturing community that takes a personal interest in every child. Stimulating teaching with strength in both breadth and depth. An excellent preparation for life for a young woman in the 21st century.

Queen's Gate School

207

133 Queen's Gate, London SW7 5LE

Pupils: 691 • Ages: 4–18 • Sixth form: 84

Fees: £16,650 – £18,900 pa

Tel: 020 7589 3587
Email: registrar@queensgate.org.uk
Website: www.queensgate.org.uk

Principal: Since 2006, Mrs Rosalynd Kamaryc BA MSc PGCE (50s). Petite, chic and with a lovely soft Irish voice, Mrs Kamaryc immediately comes across as the warm, calm and practical person to whom you'd want to entrust your precious daughter. A mathematician who still teaches – in her case, the bottom GCSE set. 'I just love teaching,' she says, and 'counts it a privilege to walk the school' once a day.

Mrs Kamaryc has an impressive pedigree, this being her second headship. She began teaching in Scotland and spent 10 years as head of Wykeham House School, Fareham – via Forest School and Woodbridge School. Parents enthuse: 'She gives terrific support to the girls,' we were told. 'She's extremely capable, a very safe pair of hands with a very clear vision for the school.' 'Very approachable though can seem a little shy.' Her catwalk walk at a school fashion show wowed everyone. 'She commands respect but she can kick up her heels too. She's fun.'

Head of junior school: Since 2015, Mrs Sharie Neale. Educated in Northern Ireland and London University, where her main subjects were education and music. Has been a director of music at both senior and preparatory independent schools. Decided to pursue a career in teaching mathematics, retrained and arrived at QG some years ago, teaching in both senior and junior schools.

Interests include music – she is a church organist, sailing and watching rugby. Retiring in July 2017.

Academic matters: Up to 23 tots in the first two years – each in a good sized room with teacher and two teaching assistants. Happy, absorbed children are relaxed and busy in rooms that are stimulating without being frantic. Some older classes quite noisy with a buzz of activity but everywhere, even the art room, is orderly and purposeful. Quiet, sustained work for the oldest girls, who would change nothing about the school save its lack of outdoors, and really like their friends.

'It punches above its weight academically,' one parent told us and the results bear this out. French, English, maths, art and geography shine brightly. Tiny sets at A level – often ones and twos – a rare privilege and at half the cost of the top tutorial companies. They will run an A level course with one pupil and don't ditch the subject – or its teacher – if it has no takers in a given year. Art, French and maths have biggest numbers. If a subject has more than seven takers they split the group. Some depts seen as better than others. 'English and history are very strong; art is amazing,' we heard repeatedly and 'though the teachers are all lovely, their actual teaching isn't always great – a little dull and uncreative sometimes.' But A level results are remarkable these days, 47 per cent A*/A, 76 per cent A*/B in 2016.

Good range of GCSE subjects for so small a school. Ancient history and classical civilisation, Latin and Greek, computing recently introduced and lots of modern languages, including Mandarin, available – and not just for native speakers. Good results in English, geography, French, drama, art – but no weaklings here (75 per cent A*/A in 2016). 'We chose it,' said a parent, echoed by more, 'because it is not obsessed by exam results.' 'It's not a hoop-jumping school.'

School has 1.5 staff on learning support team – much praised. 'Incredible support for my daughter's mild dyslexia. Possibly not for much else,' thought a parent, and this is borne out by the head.

Games, options, the arts: Parents glow and when you make it to the loftily-situated art dept you understand why. The main studio entrance is festooned with trompe l'oeil blue velvet curtains and abutted by a display of white paper insects; inside is a huge range of work, all demonstrating boldness, creativity and imagination. 'We do some gruesome stuff,' chortled the dynamic and experimental head of art as we gaped at the 'urban zombies', the girl under a blanket of fresh minced steak and various startling depictions of blood and vomit. It was reassuring to turn to the multi-coloured shoes on every step of the staircase, the cardboard relief masks, the fun, wit, skill of it all. DT even more surprising; facilities include a laser cutter, 3D printer and vacuum former. Products we saw included acrylic pencil and iPad holders and electronic dice. We warmed to a girl (flatteringly, given our age) mistaking us for a potential parent, who insisted on telling us: 'If someone wanted to do product design, they really mustn't go anywhere else.' Art and DT results from here are outstanding.

'Our drama teacher is so dedicated and lovely.' We interrupted a rehearsal of Darkwood Manor – a bit of gothic horror written by the girls, gory in their white and cicatriced faces, blood and masks. No theatre, though a small semi-studio – 'we don't need a 100 seater theatre,' claimed a proud parent. Good music room with lovely Broadwood grand and reassuring number of real instruments plus modern keyboards with headphones. Many learn instruments and school music is lively and popular.

Sports regarded as much improved during Mrs Kamaryc's tenure, though almost all involves bussing hither and yon. 'We don't mind, it's not an issue,' parents feel, though some pupils we spoke to yearned for playing fields and pitches. It probably isn't ideal for your jumping bean, though on offer now are rowing, squash, fencing among others and girls love it all. 'We have 95 clubs,' we were told and a buzz of jolly fun activities and try-outs pervades the place. Some little sorrow that not everyone joins in with all this opportunity as fully they might.

Lots of music in the junior school – choirs and an orchestra. Very lively art; we encountered Dragolina, an immense dragon being constructed for the coming Chinese New Year – and were glad to see good old-fashioned crayon work. Tastes of French, Spanish, German, Italian and Latin as the girls progress through the school. Fun, but some parents query the purpose, 'they really don't know any French at all when they go into the senior school'. Teaching of eg science done by senior school staff. By bus to sports facilities all over the place – ensures plenty of indoor and outdoor sports. Lots of lovely after-school clubs three days of the week – 'So hard to choose, Mummy!'

Background and atmosphere: Queen's Gate is a smart, elegant road in anyone's book. You walk past this school and back again without knowing it's there, so discreet is its little brass nameplate. 'It's a fantastic location,' gush Kensington mummies, 'just like a house.' And so it is – three houses, in fact, knocked together and inside – apart from the fabulous cornices, ceiling roses etc, it's yer actual rabbit warren. 'Yes,' nods a wise mummy, 'but good teaching can take place in a tent.' We lost count of the number of floors and semi-floors above the basement (ICT, lab, lockers and gym and still somehow redolent of the butler's clipped footfalls and scurrying maids). Some upper floor corridors are so narrow that we fear future generations of Tubby Tillies may get stuck. Not that we saw any such here, of course.

Main entrance hall embellished with wall-mounted bell, a set of gongs, a digital clock, fire extinguisher, staff pigeon-holes, a vintage radiator, a vitrine bulging with silver trophies and a venerable wooden post box we couldn't open. All this somehow seemed to sum up the whole. Wonderful main hall confected from the two adjoining salons from the houses' glory days – newish wooden floor and matching brass chandeliers. No playground, just a couple of tiny roof gardens for the younger years. Otherwise, breaks are taken in classrooms – and these, on, admittedly, a dark January day, were some of the most overheated we have encountered. Pupils and staff were busily fanning themselves as the rude bell shattered the silence and doors opened. 'It does get very hot,' a youngster confided, 'and sometimes it gets very cold.' Black (for pupils and staff) and white (for pupils) dining rooms, wonderfully elegant and decidedly different. Food reckoned to be good – around half bring in their own. Some come for breakfasts which sounded more than worth sliding out of bed and down the road for.

Main library is a beautiful room with splendid polished oak tables and equally venerable stock in many cases (nothing wrong with that) and a lovely place to work. Sixth form has surprisingly spacious common rooms with sofas. Also a kitchen and a work room, but work decidedly not happening when we peeked in.

Junior school a few doors down from the senior school and an equally discreet entrance belies the warmth, fun and productive activity that goes on here. Rooms light and recently refurbished – and at a sensible temperature. Good sized hall – like the senior school, the old salon in grand architectural style. Good-sized library, well-used with a real, 'very hard-working' librarian shared with big sister school. Lots of multi-purpose spaces and facilities. Good IT suite.

No uniform, most dressed perfectly sensibly though this feature of the school clearly stresses a few. 'Some girls bring in ridiculous designer bags,' one mum kvetched, but no-one looked especially coutured to us – though perhaps we are not the best judges. Certainly a divisive issue for some – though not exactly on an 'in/out of the EU?' scale.

Pastoral care, well-being and discipline: Everyone praises the pastoral care. 'They are very good at sorting out individuals,' one father told us. 'My daughter is very happy there.' Another praised the good relations between the girls, fostered by the staff and the care taken to build inter-year relationships. A third described the amount of extra time and effort put in by the teaching staff. A fourth said: 'My daughter feels there is always a teacher to chat to if she has a problem' – and so on. Each term has a 'pastoral day' and a trip to France in year 7 is 'brilliant for bonding us'. Very little sense of serious disciplinary problems being on anyone's radar.

Junior school parents happy too. 'It's traditional, though the head is livening things up. It really suits my daughter.' Staff now mostly young and pretty international. We warmed to the sight of children spontaneously hugging their teachers (probably illegal!) A safe, cosy and well-structured start for your precious daughter. And once she's there, you could really forget about her education for the next 14 years and trust them to give her all she needs.

Pupils and parents: Head stresses: 'We're a very English school with an international community. Many of our parents came here from overseas as students – and stayed. We are a Christian foundation but we celebrate all faiths and cultures.' Evidence was the great excitement – and splendid dragon – we witnessed in preparation for the Chinese new year. Largest number of overseas nationals probably Italian, followed by French, Spanish, US, Aussies, Qataris and a few Russians. Much-loved by its old girls, many of whom are current parents; good supportive parents' group. Only, but repeated, gripe is that 'communications are not great' – a surprise to the school but something they are addressing.

Notable OGs include HRH the Duchess of Cornwall, various Redgraves, Sieffs, Guinnesses, Amanda de Souza, Jane Martineau, Nigella Lawson, Lucinda Lambton, Tracey Boyd, Aurelia Cecil, Trinny Woodall and Imogen Poots. Former head of MI5 Eliza Manningham Buller used to be on the staff.

Entrance: Around 100 applicants for each of the 23 places at reception. One 7+ competitive academic scholarship worth a third of the annual fees. Assessment morning with groups of 8-10 children given tasks and observed by the headmistress and other staff.

Around six applicants per place at 11+. Waiting list for all years, but occasional places occur so worth a phone call. A few in at year 12 but 'we are very selective' and A*/As at GCSE are a requirement. Head meets all prospective parents before anyone is tested on anything.

Exit: Around three-quarters of juniors to the senior school. Rest to a range of good London schools and a few to boarding. Almost all stay to A level. Of the 20 per cent or so who try pastures co-ed, boarding or state, some scuttle back tout de suite. Head says that she encourages them to 'be brave and look elsewhere' at this stage. You'd be brave – or rash – to move from so small and nurturing a community to a place where no-one knows a thing about you. Year 13 leavers go to a wonderfully eclectic bunch of good universities around the globe, with several off to the US. Oxbridge is not uncommon (one place in 2016), solid Russell group for most but around a quarter much further afield. Art, art history and classics more common than science, though one place to study dentistry in 2016.

Money matters: All 11+ entrants are automatic scholarship candidates and 25 per cent fee remission offered to high flyers. Art, drama, music and sports scholarships also available – apply on registering. Similar 25 per cent remission available to sixth applicants. Means-tested bursaries too, but no point in applying until a place is offered.

Remarks: A lovely school for lovely girls in a classy and sophisticated milieu. Tiny classes, delightful teachers, charming friends with a faint St Trinian's spicy edge. Not for you if you want gritty urban reality – except, perhaps, in the art room.

Radnor House School

Pope's Villa, Cross Deep, Twickenham TW1 4QG

Pupils: 347 • Ages: 7–18 (9–18 from 2018) • Sixth form: 86

Fees: £15,390 – £17,955 pa

Tel: 020 8891 6264
Email: info@radnorhouse.org
Website: www.radnorhouse.org

Head: Since 2016, Ms Rosie Gill (30s) – direct, warm, approachable, no side. 'She's terrific,' said parent, 'and personifies exactly what we like about the school: she has clear values, a lovely manner and a sense of the real world about

R

her.' Ms Gill was a GDST girl who attended South Hampstead before reading history at Nottingham. Her previous positions include running PSHE at The Hall, Hampstead and serving as deputy head (academic) at Sherborne Prep. She was also deputy at Radnor House before being appointed to the hot seat now that her predecessor has gone to run the 'new' Radnor House in Sevenoaks. Ms Gill seems very happy in her new role, and not remotely fazed by it: she is an excellent communicator with a crisp mind and a kindly, low-key way about her. She also has a notably lovely rapport with children, adjusting very naturally and adroitly according to their age and stage. Married with toddler son and a husband in business, she decompresses by cycling to and from home in Surbiton each day.

Academic matters: The school is taking its academic mission extremely seriously – but equally its commitment to the wider well-being of all its pupils and their families. Once you're in, they want you to stay and to work hard – and that, in practice, is what happens. The results tell a good story: 50 per cent of A level grades in 2016 were A*-B and 23 per cent at A*/A. At GCSE, 44 per cent of grades were A* and A, and at least as important was that the grades were earned from success across a broad spread of mainly traditional subjects, with many GCSE pupils taking two modern languages and Latin. The school doesn't want to be narrowly selective, but it emphatically wants pupils who may not believe themselves academically exceptional to achieve more highly than they (or their parents) might have believed possible.

'I can't praise the teaching too highly,' said parent. 'However clichéd it sounds, the teaching my children are receiving is directed towards them, and I really believe others feel the same.' Another added: 'We didn't want my son tutored within an inch of his life, and that's not necessary at Radnor. He's working hard, he's thoroughly stimulated. And the place feels personal.' The slight gender imbalance among pupils is ironing out nicely now, although boys still in the majority 60-40. This imbalance does not extend to the senior management team which currently has slightly more women than men.

The head is emphatic that the effervescence and ambition of the pupils owes much to the calibre of the teaching staff. A lot of care goes into both recruitment and retention and the turnover is modest – 'you need a bit of change,' says the head, 'but continuity is critical, especially if the quality is high'. There are strong suggestions everywhere that this is a happy ship into whose vision staff subscribe wholeheartedly. 'It's a career, not a job,' says Ms Gill. 'I always make that clear to applicants'. Despite the nationwide moans of a paucity of teachers in maths and sciences, she says she has always had a strong field from which to make a selection. All appointments are qualified teachers.

R

There are two SENCos – one, dealing with children up to year 8, works very much as a classroom support figure in order to ensure that those with special educational needs are being adequately supported. The other, working with older students, has a particular responsibility to ensure that such pupils are adequately prepared for public examinations, with consideration awarded in line with statutory allowances. The informal brief of both extends, of course, very much further – 'like any other teacher, they have to win hearts and minds,' says Ms Gill. There are a small number of children with special needs within the school, whose interests are strongly championed, says head, by all constituencies.

Games, options, the arts: This is a school which likes its pupils to be active – but, equally, aims to get them to buy into this by friendly example. Rugby, football and cricket dominate boys' sport, and netball, hockey and rounders the girls'. But the school doesn't welcome gender stereotyping. Over 100 boys and girls are now rowing, and mixed football and mixed hockey are not merely popular but being taken very seriously. It's also part of the school credo that everybody represents the school in at least one sport once a year, come what may – am ambition made possible because there are always two teams for each major sport within a year group. There are no games fields on site, but the University of St Mary's, Twickenham, with all those lush playing fields, is only five minutes away by minibus. So nobody is going short of green spaces.

At the time of our visit, the school was busily preparing for its forthcoming production of Oliver! – to be performed at the St Mary's University theatre. It has good drama and music rehearsal spaces in house, each of which is much used for the biannual house music and drama concerts. The latter is a focal point in every Radnor House pupil's life, since the democratising ethos embraces the arts vigorously and ensures these events are truly school-wide. There are some hints that the impact of the arts (and of after-school clubs) doesn't hit home everywhere: 'There's still some way to go,' said one parent, 'before the great majority of pupils are really buying into what's on offer'. The head is doughty: the annual exhibitions of pupils' GCSE artwork and musical compositions are, she says, among her very best moments – 'such a precious insight into the minds of individual children'.

Background and atmosphere: Radnor House is a very recent addition to the tough and competitive environment of senior independent schools. It was the brainchild of David Paton (a former head of sixth form at the Harrodian) who was head between 2011 when it opened and 2016. He retains the post of executive principal. In theory, it sounds a fraught arrangement; in practice, it seems to work excellently with Mr Paton spending a day a week here 'really to exchange news and share thinking,' head says. There is also a heavy-duty advisory panel of governors including the former heads of Alleyns and Hampton.

The school is housed in a handsome mid-19th century neo-Tudor fantasy, which was once the site of the home of the poet Alexander Pope – hence its name (Pope's Villa). There's a delicate and thoughtful balance which has been struck in its redevelopment: the reception areas (with a splendid glass atrium in reception) are of graceful proportions, and the back of the mansion overlooks the river. The combination of grass, water and sky reminds any visitor at a stroke that, whatever else, there is nothing humdrum here. There are lots of small staircases and moderate sized rooms, rather than great ballrooms, all piled high with IT, children's artwork and recent photographs of pupils in their various endeavours. The uniform is worn easily, comfortably – and the atmosphere is the opposite of starchy. Children (of all ages) meet adults' eyes and engage willingly and warmly, but there's no sense of their being ingratiating. A visit to the sixth form common room lunch break gave us a snapshot into something completely authentic and reassuring: low-buzz comfortable chat, interspersed by bits of work and people plugged into their phones. There is a sense of children who know they are enjoying many advantages in life, but who don't want to put on side. They are busy, capable and unpretentious – and draw much inspiration from their teachers who clearly are cut from the same cloth.

The head is rightly proud that 'our community engagement goes a lot further than fundraising'. All projects wherever possible focus on 'personal engagement in the cause of social transformation'. She cites the annual Make a Difference Day in which every member of the school, staff and pupils, takes a full working day out to make some kind of civic contribution.

Pastoral care, well-being and discipline: Pastoral care is based around form groups – of 20 pupils – with a form tutor, and year groups of 60 under a year head. These are the proactive pastoral figures, and two members of the senior leadership team are there 'to guide, enthuse and, where necessary, to be reactive'. The house system has also been relaunched recently, mainly for sport and social purposes, but with sixth form pupils acting as heads of houses in an effort to lend kudos and foment useful initiatives. The deputy head (pastoral) fronts most of the bigger pastoral issues, but there is an underlying commitment to transparency and accessibility which the head believes embraces all the staff. 'We see parents a great deal,' she says, 'because it's critical. We enjoy it, we value it, and we hope they do as well.' There have been no recent exclusions – the usual challenges of children aged 10-18, especially those associated with IT, are ones the school recognises, but it finds that a gentle guide on the tiller is usually all that is required.

Pupils and parents: Half termly 'assessment' reports give all parents a terse overview of recent progress and levels of effort. In addition to these there is a full written report for all years and an annual meeting between individual parents and teachers. Other meetings are arranged as and when the need arises.

Three school buses help draw in children from the school's impressively wide catchment – one goes to Chelsea, one to Ealing and the third to Wimbledon. Socially and ethnically, there is a real mix here and many parents are first-time consumers of independent schools. The pupils radiate enthusiasm rather than entitlement.

Entrance: The main point of entry for juniors is year 5 (or at least it will be from 2018, as the classes for years 3 and 4 are gradually phased out – a sign of the school's growing popularity). Children sit an English and a maths test and, if admitted, will be part of a cohort of 20 when they arrive. A further 40 places become available at the start of year 7, selection for which is decided via the 11 plus. There's also a sixth form intake: you need to put in an application in the autumn of year 11, and get ready to sit a range of interviews as well as taking the Yellis computer adaptive test. The underlying rationale is clear – its entry policy is sensible and humane. It becomes more obviously organised around academic testing the further up the school you go, but never to the exclusion of everything else. Siblings are prioritised, but only to the extent that they can fit in comfortably.

Exit: In 2016, the school sent out its first year 13 cohort into the world – half of whom (11 out of 22) achieved places at Russell Group universities and three-quarters obtained their first choice university. This is heady stuff for a school which opened its doors only five years ago. No Oxbridge yet – 'but that's only a matter of time,' says the head, 'and also only one of many ambitions we have for our wonderful pupils'. Some interest is being shown by pupils and parents in European and American universities, applications for which are being finessed by a dedicated member of staff. 'There is a trade-off, I suppose,' said one parent, 'between results and values. At Radnor House, I am confident they can achieve the first, and I'm certain they are achieving the second.'

Money matters: Lunch is charged separately, as are school trips, though a big effort is made to keep costs down. The fees aren't out of line with competitor schools, and the ethos of the school has the low-key quality which accompanies an underlying confidence. Some bursary help is available 'in exceptional circumstances' but this is part of the school's development has perhaps some way yet to go. Uniform is smart but not showy or expensive.

Remarks: Radnor House works hugely hard but has a sense of its underlying values and of the direction it wishes to follow – and these both mark it out as a credible and confident player in the independent school world. The atmosphere is calm as well as energetic, and the head and her colleagues communicate values which are humane and imaginative. It is now poised to become a school of first choice and thoroughly deserving of all the good fortune which comes its way.

Ravenscourt Park Preparatory School

209

16 Ravenscourt Avenue, London W6 0SL

Pupils: 411 • Ages: 4–11

Fees: £16,212 pa

Tel: 020 8846 9153
Email: secretary@rpps.co.uk
Website: www.rpps.co.uk

Head: Since 2015, Carl Howes, previously deputy head at Colet Court (now St Paul's Juniors). Natural sciences degree from Cambridge and PGCE from St Luke's, Exeter; has also been head of maths and second master at King's House School in Richmond. Married to Mel, a teacher at St Stephen's Primary School, Twickenham, and has two teenage children.

Entrance: Non-selective, the September after a child's 4th birthday. It is vital to register a child on his/her first birthday. Can't be registered before. After that it is a lottery. Siblings get priority, then names are drawn randomly and places allotted strictly to obtain an equal number of boys and girls.

Exit: Traditionally, to London day schools, but with changing local demographics, some parents now looking to send their children to top boarding schools. Therefore some boys are leaving early, although, as one parent said, 'this is not a light decision'. So, occasionally boys at end of year 5 to country prep schools or London day schools that go through to year 8 (Fulham Prep, King's House). Around a quarter of the rest to sister school Kew House, others to Godolphin & Latymer, Latymer Upper, Hampton, Francis Holland, Harrodian, St James, West London Free School, with 12 scholarships between them.

Remarks: Parents said before we visited: 'Not a hothouse', 'kind and nurturing', 'safe environment', and 'excellent communication'. We found no reason to argue with these comments. Teachers and children buzzed with enthusiasm, the atmosphere felt relaxed, although each time we walked into a classroom work stopped, the children leapt to their feet, chimed 'good morning' and stood there until we left. This apparently always happens and, we felt, emphasises the edge of formality at the school. However, everywhere we went we were made to feel more than welcome. Parents also feel 'there really is an open door policy'.

Founded in 1991 by Maria and Ted Gardener, former teachers, this school has grown and gone from strength to strength. Its most recent building, opened in September 2011, has enabled it to move from two-form entry to three, gradually adding 20 more children to each year. No problem filling the spaces. There is some feeling that it would, perhaps, have been better to have added two more years, thus solving the problem of boys leaving early. (They say this is not a problem.) Some parents feel perhaps too much emphasis on the business side, 'definitely an eye for profit above all'. For instance: 'Why do we have to pay extra for lunch, when it is compulsory and our children are not allowed to bring a packed version?'

Fantastic facilities. The new building has enabled the top three years to move into nine bright new classrooms, colour-coded per floor. 'We chose our own colours,' said our two of

R

our guides proudly. And, 'look we've even got a lift but we can't use it without permission!' Splendid new science lab with all the latest equipment; a light, bright art room displaying a friendship bench, 'to sit on when you feel lonely', being painted by the art club and, very exciting, including a kiln; a music room where children were reading notes displayed on an interactive white board – of course these abound; an ICT lab with a laptop per child, 'we're making our own websites'. Perhaps best of all, as far as our guides were concerned, was the new school hall/theatre: 'The choir sings from the balcony', 'we can learn to operate the light and sound'. All very impressive.

A tad more cosy, the rest of the school is housed in two buildings, with a separate good-sized dining block. All food cooked on site and children served at their tables by catering staff. Most meals are hot, always healthy and compulsory unless a child has a dietary problem. As we walked across the large, mainly tarmacked playground, our guides pointed out equipment for active play (including balls galore) and soft area for the younger ones to climb, slide and play safely. We were later informed that there is an imminently scheduled building project to update the whole playground. Our younger guides proudly showed their fully equipped classrooms, interactive whiteboards and all. Children's work, art and otherwise, on display all over. All pupils appeared happy and relaxed, quick to say hello and answer questions. Unmissable code of conduct pinned up all over. Our guides were quick to explain the provenance of the many badges they were wearing. As one parent said: 'Lots of smiley teachers, lots of smiley children, such a happy school!'

A reasonably varied curriculum, at least for the first five years. The importance of 11+ kicks in during the summer term in year 5 and children are given lots of homework for the holidays. From then on English and mathematics dominate until all entrance exams are over; afterwards lessons become theme based, more adventurous and relaxed; children take part in a whole range of different activities, home and away. Recently, year 6s wrote traditional stories which they then read to the reception classes. The change of pace must work well because the majority of pupils get into their first choice of secondary school, parents having been well advised by the head, of course. Rated excellent by ISI after recent inspection.

All pupils in years 1 and 3 screened for literacy and specific areas of difficulty. Parents informed of any problems and help given where necessary. Small group lessons focusing on literacy and motor skills, if needed, once or twice a week for half an hour. One-to-one help also provided occasionally, if absolutely necessary. 'No extra ever charged for special needs support'. Say they wouldn't normally decline a place to a child with pre-identified minor learning difficulties. A special needs room in each building. Teachers always available to talk to parents.

Extracurricular regarded as important and many different after-school clubs, sporty, arty, intellectual, musical. The range changes from term to term. Several orchestras and choirs, individual lessons offered on a wide variety of instruments. Recently a year 3 boy scored one of the highest marks in the country for his piano exam. A full programme of outings, cultural and academic, plus some residential trips for older children. All the usual charity fundraisers – luckily some parents take these very seriously and are happy to organise. They have already built one school in Burma and currently a major project is to raise sufficient funds to build another.

R

Reach Academy Feltham

53–55 High Street, Feltham, Middlesex TW13 4AB

Pupils: 642 • Ages: 4–19 • Sixth form: 75

Tel: 020 8893 1099
Email: admissions@reachacademy.org.uk
Website: www.reachacademyfeltham.com

Principal: Since 2012, Ed Vainker MA (30s). Following experiences as Teach First trainee in inner city schools and exposure to US Charter School movement, burning desire to set up school to right wrongs was born. His Eureka moment came in the US (he'd won an educational scholarship), when saw Waiting for Superman at cinema (got time wrong – was supposed to be Social Network but didn't want to waste babysitter) and stayed up all night, committing educational vision to paper. Serendipity was the clincher: a mutual friend introduced him to Rebecca Cramer, school's co-founder and secondary head (third co-founder, Jon McIntosh, remains a governor but doesn't have active teaching role).

The first in family to go to university (Bristol, geography) and a fellow Teach Firster, Rebecca shared Ed's sense of injustice over dismal prospects for bright but disadvantaged pupils who ended up with middling exam results, education and careers instead of the stellar opportunities they deserved.

The solution? A school where the partnership with parents wasn't just about education but everything from aspirations to parenting skills and diet. It needed to take the very young (makes Jesuits look like beginners) and stay small so teachers could get to know children, and their families, inside out. Families short on decent life chances were to be the prime beneficiaries. Feltham, only five miles from Hampton Court Palace but an awful lot grittier (government's latest deprivation index puts it in bottom third of areas for education) was the ideal location, particularly given authority's commitment to building new homes and schools for fast-growing population.

First pupils (reception and year 7) arrived in 2012 and a new primary and senior year has been added on each September since. With just the sixth form and years 5 and 6 to go, will have a full house by autumn 2018.

Rebecca and Ed are idealistic but clear-sighted, offering practical help where needed (including carpeting bare floors in one family's flat) but never letting poverty become an excuse for low achievement. They're hugely impressive. Rebecca is praised for pastoral and psychological expertise while Ed's the systems and strategy man with a brilliant little black book stuffed with useful contacts and a virtuoso approach to getting what he wants from normally intractable public bodies ('pre-schmoozing' was mentioned).

Both have understanding partners and young children – 'was planning to have a school dog but got a baby instead,' says Rebecca, whose just crawling son was a cheery addition to the morning meet and greet squad on day of visit.

Job could take over their lives but they work hard to ensure it doesn't and swear blind that a 5.30pm getaway is the norm, 'plus, of course, some email checking once the children are in bed,' says Rebecca. Personable and charming though with the essential steely edge where necessary, they also have the ability to make others feel at ease. One parent, distraught when child launched into a tantrum at a get-to-know-you session, was instantly put at her ease by Rebecca. 'She came over and spoke to me like a human being and made me feel so relaxed.' Staff think they're pretty fab, too. 'Rebecca stays so calm, I've never seen her phased or annoyed. She's always in control,' says one.

That said, children have a healthy respect for her. 'She's very much like "this is how it's going to be",' said one.

Now first stage one has been accomplished, it's on to phase two – a second school that will take pupils even earlier – pre-conception, if they get their way – and 'hopefully' bring together NCT (currently nearest branches are in well-heeled Chiswick and Teddington), local GPs, midwives and just about everybody who can ensure that parents get proper support from the very beginning. It's due for completion 2019 (fast by most standards but boringly slow motion for Ed, who got this school up and running in just 10 months).

Ed and Rebecca now envisage training up a brace of successors who share their ideals but are happy to take on a going concern rather than a blank page while they work on further expansion. 'Would they be younger?' we asked. 'We are young,' say Ed and Rebecca, indignantly.

Academic matters: Social justice is the driver, goal transformational education ensuring that every able child gets top results. They've demanded, to some initial consternation, as big a proportion of families from disadvantaged backgrounds as possible.

Though first GCSE results won't appear until summer 2017, school is already notching up the laurel wreaths, first all-through free school to garner an outstanding grade from inspectors and with good results (eg in year 1 phonics test) that put it way ahead of national averages. The acid test will come in 2021 when first year 11s home grown from reception sit GCSEs. The current year 4s are already working at same level as year 7 pupils – so it's looking good.

'We take an A at A level and work backwards,' says literature...'They expect great things for all of us,' agreed year 11 pupil. Only exceptions a couple of pupils who wouldn't cope with GCSEs, based here but taking vocational courses at other local colleges.

Crack team of teachers is key. Highly qualified and occasionally shoeless ('helps them feel grounded,' we were told), they're also known by their first names (means 'have power but don't feel bigger,' thought one pupil) and have no discernable 'off' button, replying to texts from early morning to late at night and over the hols).

'Seem to be there because they want to be there,' thought another. The few who don't self-select into new employment fairly quickly, but with 17 who've been here since the school first opened, most are clearly keepers.

Ark Schools group helps with training and all teachers, several former TAs among them, have a mentor and weekly observations. Though ethnically less diverse than pupils, it's not the whole story as a fair few also have first hand experience of achieving against the odds.

Curriculum is very much the school's own. Unsurprisingly, little quarter is given in lessons, from year 10s deep in semantic (and battle) fields as they analyse war poetry to year 2s dissecting Edgar Allen Poe's The Raven by way of a Hallowe'en treat.

There's role play to develop confidence for reception pupils and the involvement of senior school subject specialists (science, French) from year 3 onwards. Lesson length varies according to subject, little and often for languages but longer sessions (up to two hours for seniors) in literacy and numeracy, which dominate curriculum. Competence in both areas is a non-negotiable that's well understood by parents. 'If you want to go off and be a carpenter or something like that, there's no good learning that at school if your maths isn't brilliant,' said one.

Everyone is expected to take between eight and 10 GCSEs with art, music and MFL among the options – most bases covered though don't offer DT. Sixth formers will have choice of 18 A levels and two BTecs, plus electives (astronomy to photography – potential starter for extended essay project) and linked studies such as research techniques.

With pupils speaking 55 languages between them and English an additional language for 40 per cent, support network has to be robust – and it is, with before school catch up lessons and small group work for those needing a slightly slower pace.

Don't shirk from SEN and school is impressively dyslexia friendly (white backgrounds routinely replaced with pastel shades – far easier to read), while new resources are being added (sensory room is on the way). Stress, however, that while school is small, class sizes aren't – it's 30 or so up to end of year 11 – so wouldn't be the right environment for child in need of extensive small group or one-to-one support.

That said, parents confirm that the school won't give up on pupils with additional needs without a fight. Under a handful so far have moved on to more specialist environments and it's brilliant with those it can support. Rebecca's prizewinning account of school life for bright, autistic boy resulted in trip to education conference in Bulgaria where his speech on need for greater understanding of SEN, he told us, had audience in tears.

Games, options, the arts: Sense of togetherness permeates everything, from play featuring wisecracking teacher and pupil compere duo to school trips – six a year for primary pupils, with overnight stays from year 3, while all secondary pupils get a residential week in a university (Bath for year 7, York year 8 and Cambridge year 10) – 'a huge thing and a non-negotiable,' says Ed. Year 9s, meanwhile, work on Sports Leader UK and D of E qualifications (aim for silver in year 11). 'All part of making everyone part of the family,' said parent.

Smart thinking sees work experience happening in autumn half term to beat the post-GCSE rush. One year 11 boy encountered slebs on his – 'Dom Joly,' he breathed in star-struck tones, though not everyone's as happy. 'Rubbish,' said a girl, who had less fulfilling time with another firm.

Around 100 children learn a musical instrument in school (fair few enthusiastic beginners aiming for grade 4 in time for GCSEs) and even reception children, including the very shy, have acquired the confidence to perform in public within weeks of joining.

Art is also taking off, specialist teacher now installed, room uncommonly neat and restrained but filling up nicely with glittery stage sets ready to go for forthcoming production of Annie when we visited and some interesting individual work including year 9 pupils' rather beautiful Romero Britto-inspired designs.

Opening of second Reach Academy, on a bigger site, should mean more outside space all round. In the meantime, sporting successes are coming (senior girls' football, cross-country and shot putt) while colossus of a sports hall also goes some way to compensate, as does its rooftop Astroturf (with views of glorious sunsets views over Feltham) – though one parent felt it could be used a bit more often.

SEN support extends to after-school clubs – yoga 'very good for those with dyspraxia,' says head of sport. They're popular with parents, with football, table tennis and trampolining all generally oversubscribed

Learning outside the classroom is a big feature, like so much here, plugging social as well as educational gap. Down on the farm that's a gated hop skip and jump from the playground, Nigel the farmer supplies and vets the livestock: beady-eyed chickens, hoping for seconds of mealworms (top favourites) have plenty of star quality but are comprehensively outshone by the two pigs. Pupils can volunteer to be young farmers and learn responsibility by working here after school.

Meat and eggs are sold to the parents who can also sample other edibles (spices, rhubarb and tomatoes and even a batch of home-made chutney), and there's also a virtuous circle, with pigs (sensibly not named) fed spare break time fruit (unlimited for all) though government diktats consign most other leftovers to landfill.

Adjoining forest school may be more of a coppice but gets non-stop multi-purpose use – tents, mini-beast hotel, and balancing wire slung between two trees. And though compact (you can definitely see the wood for the trees), it's an oasis to many of the parents who help out here. 'Like a day out – felt that wasn't in Feltham at all,' said one.

Background and atmosphere: No bureaucracy-heavy place, this. It feels fleet of foot – even on the 'phone. 'We'd rather deal with you ourselves,' says friendly receptionist, who offers to sort out the visit direct with the principal (none of this transferring your call to umpteen other extensions, all with a voicemail on the end).

School's small is beautiful ethos makes it a rarity not just in its home borough of Hounslow but just about anywhere in Greater London. It achieved star status early on, seemingly the must-see educational destination of choice for range of ambitious politicians. Year 11s we spoke to had previously been quizzed by David Cameron (school was final official engagement before his post-Brexit resignation). Others who've dropped in include Lord Adonis, Boris Johnston and Michael Gove (though we bet we were the only ones to be offered school pud – complete with bowl – as a goody bag present).

Area, though not picturesque, is brilliantly connected for trains, automobiles (and of course many, many planes) though some parents prefer to collect, on foot if necessary, rather than letting even secondary-age children walk back on their own.

Inside, however, the school, designed from scratch by founders, is a well-thought out and attractive oasis of calm, from the separate primary and secondary meet and greet areas and playgrounds to the move to unisex toilets ('the boys' smelled and the girls spent hours looking in the mirror,' says Rebecca).

Life centres round five phases, each with its assistant head, made up of one or more year groups in own area consisting of classrooms off a multi-purpose central space (nursery, in own single long room, the only exception). Unless location is key (science, music and art) it's the teachers who move. 'None of this 100 kids rushing through the corridors to get to a lesson,' said parent.

Plenty, as you'd expect, on the wish list. New library needs more books; embryonic music tech room more tech. Donations come from a range of sources – Teach First, for example, was persuaded to part with some old sofas – ideal for the new sixth form centre which also boasts rooftop terrace and well-stocked fitness suite – but Ed and Rebecca are cautious about hitting the wellwishers' list too often. State education 'isn't really badly funded,' they reckon.

R

Pastoral care, well-being and discipline: There's a strong family feel here, starting at the gates (primary pupils enter to left, seniors to right), with handshake for all at start and end of the day 'without fail,' said parent. 'It feels lovely.' Inspirational quotes (JK Rowling, Ghandi, Martin Luther King) are juxtaposed with posters for Childline, and school is under no illusions as to some families' home life. For some, just getting children to school is an achievement, we were told by grounded family support worker. 'They deal with every angle of their upbringing,' said mother. 'Not just education but their social needs, too.' Practical support includes organising visits to the job centre, optician and food bank or – in one case – taking the children to feed the ducks at local pond to give parents a break.

Some pupils arrive so far behind their peers that may never achieve as much as they should, though progress can be dramatic – one primary school boy sitting quietly at the table to eat his lunch 'would have found it impossible when he first arrived,' we were told. Food really matters. For some children it's their first encounter not just with healthy diet but also with the social rituals of mealtimes. So there's food mindfulness in primary (distraction-free silence during first mouthfuls) to minimal choice menu, family service with older pupils serving younger ones, no packed lunches and home visits for serial non-eaters. Several new parents, initially nervous about fussy offspring, quickly reassured. One H2O refuser blossomed when was offered school's 'magic water for big boys.'

Elsewhere, children are guided towards the right decision by impressively low key but authoritative staff. 'Don't need to shout and scream, just clap their hands and everyone stops,' said parent. Incentives include payslips for good work and behaviour – exchangeable for golden time (primary) and activities (senior pupils). 'You get a lot of messages coming home telling you to congratulate your child when they've done really well,' said parent. Nothing flabby about two-step sanctions, however. First time senior school trangressors talk through reasons for poor behaviour while serial (or serious) offenders sit on their own in lessons and at break for a day, decision to readmit to polite society decided by class vote and communicated by buddy.

Parents, too, shoulder their share of responsibility. If a phone goes off in a lesson, will be called in to remove offending item and confirm they understand why. Similarly, late arrivals get automatic 30 minute detention, 'bad traffic' excuse a non-starter. 'Would need to have affected every car in the whole area,' says Rebecca, implacably. Tough love it may be, but after the initial shock, every parent we spoke to understood why it was necessary and appreciated the active encouragement to join in school life. All have open invitation to have lunch or, if worried about child's progress, sit in on lesson. 'Very open – there's nothing to hide,' said one.

Pupils and parents: One of several rumours we heard was of places awarded to wealthy parents identifiable by posh cars at drop off and pick up time. We diligently scoured the Tesco and Aldi car parks opposite at 8.00am and can report a pronounced absence of luxury marques.

Instead, there's a diverse community. Was 80 per cent ethnic minorities when first opened though there are now more pupils from lower income white families. Embryonic PTA, busily organising Christmas Fair when we visited, is doing best to create parent community – one mother, frozen out by the clique in previous, middle-class dominated primary, was full of praise.

Entrance: The school stresses – and stresses again – that its admissions procedure is completely transparent – if different to anyone else's. It doesn't stop suspicion creeping in, down to the long odds – over 1,000 families recently applied for the 120 reception and year 7 places (something that rivals even grammar school admissions) – that condemn majority to disappointment. Doesn't stop them trying (two parents turned up on day of visit to plead their case) – and second school can't come soon enough.

After looked after children come nursery pupils qualifying for early years pupil premium, followed by exceptional medical and social needs, siblings, others qualifying for pupil premium, staff children and those living within admissions area (chosen by electronic ballot). Transition process is painstaking, particularly when it comes to identifying those with learning needs. 'We'll go in and make sure it's identified early,' says Rebecca.

Main feeder schools are Victoria Junior School and Oak Hill Academy, geographical area covering Feltham, Southville, Bedfont, Hanworth and Hounslow (though early adopters include those from slightly further afield).

At the start, school was canvassing for pupils – and how. 'Rebecca came to our house and did an amazing presentation,' said one parent. Those who took a leap of faith and got in early thank their lucky stars. Neighbours who didn't and are on the waiting list (which does move, but at glacial speeds), wish they'd done the same. In the meantime, the rumour mill is whizzing round at speed while school does its best to highlight transparency.

It's currently having to repeat the process for sixth formers as applications are slightly thin on the ground for first intake – sheer newness means not yet a destination school for high achievers. We'd strongly recommend taking a look.

Exit: There's some relocation – including visa expiry. Will be some departures at end of year 11 (around a third, they reckon) as school sets the bar high for sixth form admissions – six Bs minimum, A grades required to study toughest subjects (eg maths, sciences, languages, history). Similar number of A*-C grades will see you on to a BTec.

For those moving on, options range from The Heathland School in Hounslow to Springwest Academy and St Paul's Catholic School in Sunbury). One parent felt school should do more to help with search. Don't hold your breath or expect much in way of handholding – school expects parents to do their homework and research alternatives. 'We don't spoonfeed,' says Rebecca.

Money matters: Sixth form bursaries for everyone on free school meals. As and when hardship bursaries also available – no pupil will miss a school trip because of lack of money.

Remarks: 'It seems too good to be true,' said parent. 'We kept saying "what's the catch?" There is no catch.'

Reay Primary School

211

Hackford Road, London SW9 0EN

Pupils: 250 • Ages: 3–11

Tel: 020 7735 2978
Email: admin@reay.lambeth.sch.uk
Website: www.reay.lambeth.sch.uk

Headteacher: Since 2014, Caroline Andrews BEd from Sheffield Hallam (early 40s). Taught at Chaucer Junior from 1996-2000, then at Wix Primary where she became ICT leader, followed by deputy then co-head. Established the first state French/English bilingual school along with French Lycée. Made head here in 2014. Hails from Nottingham. Husband works in TV. Has a young son at another school as she feels 'it wouldn't be fair for him to come here, with me as head.' Most of her spare time is spent socialising with family and friends. Travels to far-flung destinations as often as possible. Keen gardener and enjoys cooking, which she finds therapeutic. Parents are big fans. 'Down-to-earth,' according to one. 'She's brought a new lease of life to the school,' said another. Welcoming and friendly.

Entrance: At 3 to nursery and at 4 to reception. School, rather than Lambeth, is now responsible for own admissions, so children in nursery are more likely to gain a place in reception than was the case previously, 'though there is still no guarantee as we have 30 places in reception and 40 in nursery.' Priority given to those with a supported medical or social need; distance a child lives from school 'as the crow flies' also taken into consideration. Waiting list in operation for occasional places further up the school. 'When pupils leave, we can now move more quickly to fill the place,' says head. Oversubscribed: roughly six applicants per place.

Exit: Small minority goes down the fee-paying route, and those that do usually favour Alleyn's or Dulwich College. Popular state destinations include Graveney, Lambeth Academy and London Nautical. 'We invite secondary schools to come and talk to parents at the end of year 5, and then again before parents need to make the final decision in year 6,' explains head. After-school tutoring delivered by class teachers if requested, prior to 11+ exams. 'We do have a discussion with parents if we think the school they want is not right for their child, though. We don't want the children to be put under excessive pressure. They are well-supported and well-extended here anyway, so most would get places without tutoring in any case,' believes head.

Remarks: Three-quarters of pupils come from ethnic minority groups. Half speak English as an additional language. 'Though for very few is this a barrier to their learning. It's more of an asset,' states head. Nearly 50 per cent are eligible for pupil premium funding, much higher than national average. Most live less than 400 metres away. 'We have a hugely mixed intake. Some are from the high rise blocks opposite and others live in million pound properties,' comments head. Very high attendance rate.

Housed in a purpose-built, high ceilinged Victorian building in the heart of Lambeth. A surprisingly peaceful oasis in this very urban location. Great sense of space throughout. Huge double classrooms abound with plenty of room for breakout activities. Large hall for sport, assemblies and drama. Recently converted library with doors opening onto a courtyard where year 6 pupils can be found reclining on beanbags, devouring books on sunny afternoons. Separate playgrounds for different year groups, complete with a climbing wall and quiet area.

Thirty children per class. Head is confident that pupils' varying needs are identified quickly and that children do not fall through the net – 'that's the beauty of a one form entry school.' All classrooms have at least one additional adult on hand.

Learning is fun here and pupils were all full of beans on the day we visited. Much learning is done through project work, from nursery upwards. Shakespeare was being studied when we looked round and one pupil was writing painstakingly with a quill pen and ink. Homework involves reading, spelling and times tables until year 5. 'Then,' says head, 'we up the ante, with past papers and test preparation. We believe that the children are so busy at school, and are offered so many extracurricular activities that homework doesn't add much before that, especially in homes where English is not the first language.' French offered from nursery onwards, though soon to be replaced by Spanish. Close links with the Lycée in Clapham where Reay pupils have penpals.

Pastoral care is a definite strength. 'We take mental well-being very seriously,' says head. School places great emphasis on outdoor learning in its beautiful nature garden, which includes a parent-built greenhouse, a tree-house, a pond for frogs and a bug hotel. Bluebells and blossom were in abundance on the day we visited, making it appear totally magical. One area is set aside for digging and another for making mud pies. Each class grows fruit and vegetables, including strawberries, tomatoes and lettuce. 'The garden is an area where children can get dirty and appreciate nature. Some children otherwise do not get an opportunity to play outside in this way,' explains head. A full-time teacher takes individuals, small groups and whole classes for timetabled sessions outside. Head believes this area helps those who struggle to communicate, as some find it easier to open up when busy in the garden. Weekly mentoring sessions also put on by local charity to help pupils build their social and emotional skills through activities and sport. One parent we spoke to said, 'Everybody looks out for each other here. The bigger kids look out for the smaller kids. The children nurture each other as much as the teachers do!' One parent mentioned an incident of bullying but was full of praise for the speed with which the school stepped in.

School can support a range of special needs, particularly emotional, behavioural and social difficulties. Thirty-nine on special needs register and five currently have an Education, Health and Care plan. Most classrooms are on ground floor so easy accessibility for those with physical disabilities. Learning mentor offers one-to-one support for those who are need it, either socially or academically. She also supports families and makes home visits if required. Extra language assistance given to those who do not have English as their first language. Dyslexia screening available from year 2 onwards, as and when required rather than as a whole year group. Plenty of workshops for gifted and talented pupils and extra maths sessions laid on by local secondary schools. Art therapist and speech and language therapist regularly visit.

'We try to broaden their horizons through art, music and drama,' comments head. Vibrant displays throughout the school, including a huge African collage in pride of place in the hall. Pupils have the chance to experiment with a variety of materials from ceramics to batik and school boasts its own kiln. Gold Artsmark awarded in recognition of rich arts opportunities here. 'Children like the freedom of art and we want them to enjoy it. We value it as teachers,' explains head. Music is also an important part of life at Reay and school buys in additional music teaching. Full time music lead. Year 3 pupils learn recorder, year 4 the ukulele and year 5 has a class orchestra, with pupils playing instruments ranging from violins and double bass to saxophones. Some subsidised individual music lessons offered in top two years. Performances put on for parents, at variety of venues including the Albert Hall. No choir at the moment though head stresses 'we have a lot of singing so the whole school feels like a choir!' Annual nativity play led by year 2 and a pantomime by year 6.

School has an all-weather sports pitch where cricket, netball, football and hockey are played. We observed a lively game of football at break. All year groups swim from year 2 onwards. Running club takes place in a nearby park. Pupils compete in local tournaments and participate in cricket schemes at the Oval. Extra sport laid on before, during and after the school day including yoga in French and basketball in Spanish. 'We have lots of space both outdoors and in the studio for sport and dance. We are very lucky,' says head. One parent we spoke to, however, felt that 'sport is challenge. I wish they did more. I feel like my son could certainly do with more of a run out than he gets.'

Outside dance and drama groups use the rehearsal and arts space for free in return for putting on workshops for pupils. Good range of after-school clubs from cooking and coding to street dance, run by a mixture of outside providers and in-house staff. Reduced price for those on pupil premium funding. Gymnastics currently hugely popular.

Wraparound care offered before and after school, so pupils can be looked after for over 10 hours a day. Breakfast club from 7.30am, with toast and cereal galore. 'Lots of us on the staff are working parents so we appreciate the need for a longer day,' says head. Reay pupils can also enjoy holiday provision at a neighbouring school.

Pungent aroma of fish and chips emanating from the dining room on the day we visited. Children have a choice of salads as well as fresh fruit and vegetables. Some take in packed lunches, but most opt for school dinners. Herbs grown in the school garden are used in the stuffing at Christmas lunch. Head hopes more of their garden produce can make its way onto the children's plates. School has advanced healthy school status.

Trips aplenty to theatres, parks and sports venues. Residential trips for year 4 to Kent (along with pupils from other local schools) and year 6 spends four nights in France. Parents pay, but school subsidises trips and the PTA helps with funds for those who cannot quite stretch to it. Whole school ventures merrily, in a long line of coaches, to a Sussex beach every summer term. 'We take picnics and it's absolutely lovely, though exhausting. Parents come too,' enthuses head.

A family-orientated school. Specialist sessions organised for parents on topics including how to support their children with speech development. Many parents volunteer at the school, by listening to readers, helping with play rehearsals and escorting groups to swimming. Some give talks to older children about careers. 'Most parents are very supportive. We have an open door policy and encourage parents to come in and sort out problems promptly. It makes life a lot easier,' explains head. She also stands at the gate every morning and afternoon so parents can bend her ear about any issues then. Active PTA that puts on regular events, including summer and winter fairs and a school disco. Money raised recently spent on kitting out the new music room. Communication with parents has improved recently with reports of it having been fairly shambolic in the past.

A very friendly school, where kindness and good manners are considered important. 'We place an emphasis on the joy of childhood here. We want the children to work hard but also to enjoy their time at Reay,' says head. 'The children are proud of their school and we are very proud of them.' A happy, caring environment.

Redcliffe School

47 Redcliffe Gardens, London SW10 9JH

Pupils: 170 • Ages: 3–8 (boys), 3–11 (girls)

Fees: £15,630 pa

Tel: 020 7352 9247
Email: admissions@redcliffeschool.com
Website: www.redcliffeschool.com

Headmistress: Since 2006, Mrs Susan Bourne BSc (50s). Read chemistry at Manchester University. Previously deputy head of the Old Vicarage School in Richmond and taught chemistry in both the state and independent sector. 'I still love teaching and teach the year 6 science lessons.' The sort of sensible woman you could rely on in an emergency, her calm demeanour permeates the whole school.

Married to a management consultant ('he's my anchor') with three grown up daughters (Latymer Upper, Queen's Gate and Godolphin & Latymer), she took time out while based in Geneva and Paris with a young family so knows what it's like to be a parent both at home and in an international setting. 'She really understands,' said one mother. Now lives in Richmond but escapes most weekends down the M3 to cottage in the New Forest where she and her husband sail their boat ('but only in calm weather!')

Entrance: Entrance to the nursery is first come first served but it is advisable to put names down within 6 months of birth. Places are sometimes available at the last minute due to parents in this area applying to lots of different schools, so it's worth staying on the waiting list. Entrance to the main school is by assessment and an interview with the head. 'When we assess children for entry to the main school, we are looking for more than just academic ability,' said Mrs Bourne. 'We are looking for sociable children who are going to be happy here. For example, I choose children who are comfortable when separated from their carer.' Most children go through to the main school from the nursery. Two mixed forms from reception to year 3, then one form of girls in each year.

Exit: Boys go at 8+ to schools such as St Paul's Juniors, Northcote Lodge, Wetherby Prep, Westminster Cathedral Choir School and Sussex House. Girls leave at 11+ to a mixture of boarding and day schools with Benenden, Putney High, Queen's College, St Mary's Ascot, Godolphin & Latymer and City of London being popular recent choices. Regular music, academic and art scholarships.

Remarks: This well-established prep school is situated on two sites on Redcliffe Gardens – a busy thoroughfare taking traffic from north to south London. Although it has expanded over the last few years and now has 170 pupils from nursery age up to 11, it still feels small and intimate.

The upper school is housed in the original main building, which when you enter looks more like a rather scruffy family home than a school. The cosy atmosphere is continued in head's office, where visitors sit on a comfy but rather shabby sofa. However, when you enter the classrooms it's an entirely different matter. The recently refurbished hall in the basement (which is also used as a dining room) is splendid, and when we visited during morning assembly, a Mendelssohn concerto was being played through a brand new music system. (A different composer is studied each week.) Children filed in and sat with their eyes closed so that they could appreciate the music. When the director of studies asked them what they were going to do that day, one girl replied, 'have fun,' which summed up the attitude around the school. (The answer she was actually looking for was 'work hard!')

A new extension at the back of the school is light and airy, while the other classrooms upstairs, although a little cramped, have high ceilings and natural light. The top floors house the library and music room where piano, violin, flute, trumpet, guitar and voice are taught by peripatetic teachers. Music is one of the school's strengths, with some children gaining music scholarships to their next schools. The school orchestra plays at school events such as the carol service and prize-giving and there are concerts for parents and friends at least twice a year.

The pre-prep school, at St Luke's church a quarter of a mile down the road, comprises five bright and well-lit classrooms in the basement of the church (one for nursery and two classes each of reception and year 1). A large hall is used for indoor sports and lunch (which is trolleyed down from the upper school kitchen), and is also the venue for whole school assemblies on Thursdays and Fridays which parents are encouraged to attend. 'Sometimes it's standing room only as these have become such popular events,' explained the head proudly. Children use a specially designed play area outside, with climbing frames built on an artificial grass covering with toys and scooters available. 'We like to spend as much time outside as possible.'

The teacher to student ratio is high, with a maximum of 16 in each class. There are specialist teachers for music, sport, French and drama. Recent productions include Minibeast Madness by the pre-prep and A Midsummer Night's Dream by the prep school. Extra EAL lessons support children who require help (particularly when they first join the school) and a learning support teacher sees a number of children (around 10) twice a week on a one-to-one basis to help with specific learning difficulties such as mild dyslexia (but this costs extra). Most of the staff are women (three have been there for over 10 years), with two male teaching assistants and a male PE teacher, and this does give the school (especially since boys leave at 8) a rather female atmosphere. 'We would like to recruit more good male staff,' said the head.

Food is cooked on the prep school site and there are themed lunches for events such as Halloween and Bonfire Night. 'Children who have left the school write back to say how much they miss the food.' Parents are regularly invited in to have lunch with the staff and the children. 'We always feel very welcome at the school,' said one mother.

Children are bussed to nearby parks once a week for sports – football and netball in the autumn term, tag rugby in the spring and rounders, cricket and athletics in the summer. Weekly swimming lessons all year round at Fulham Pools. They compete against other schools and also have their own swimming galas and sports days. On Friday afternoons school finishes early and children can take part in a wide variety of sporting activities from yoga to judo. 'We used to finish early on Fridays to enable our families with country properties to leave London before the rush hour but more and more are staying on to take advantage of the sports clubs,' said the head.

Families are drawn from the local area – half the children have either one or two international parents. 'Most of the schools round here have a high number of international families,' said one American mother, 'but this school seems very British still.' Another mother commented: 'It's very down to earth for a prep school in this area and you don't need to worry if you turn up at the school gate in the morning with no make up on. No one will judge you.'

Former pupils include Emerald Fennell, Jemima Rooper and Daniel Radcliffe. 'He was rather a quiet boy,' said the deputy head. 'We ever expected him to become famous.' But Redcliffe is nothing like Hogwarts, and all in all this is a warm and cosy school with a nurturing environment. The atmosphere feels somewhat cloistered and it probably wouldn't suit a boisterous child who likes to run around a lot. But this could be just the place for gentler, less confident children to flourish.

Rhodes Avenue Primary School

Rhodes Avenue, London N22 7UT

Pupils: 622 • Ages: 3–11

Tel: 020 8888 2859
Email: admin@rhodes.haringey.sch.uk
Website: www.rhodes.haringey.sch.uk

Headteacher: Since 2015 Mr Adrian Hall BEd (30s). After gaining his degree in primary education from Leeds University, he worked as a reception teacher at Castleton Primary School, then moved up the ranks to his first headship at Churchfield Primary School in Enfield, a post he had for eight years. During this time – in which he worked in a wide range of schools, some in deprived areas – he earned himself an NLE (National Leader in Education) in recognition of his work in supporting not only pupils but also teachers and leaders.

Instantly likeable, he is warm and laid back – a high-fives-in-the-corridor kind of head who wants children to feel comfortable in his presence. 'He's the best head teacher in the world,' one child told us, with others describing him as 'kind,' 'funny' and 'really nice.' 'They hero worship him – and he's a brilliant teacher,' said one parent – indeed he teaches year 4s once a week. But make no mistake – he is also highly efficient and savvy about all things educational, and the policies he's brought in around discipline and punctuality have been unanimously welcomed. 'He improved an already brilliant school – that's no mean feat,' one parent told us.

Parents and pupils alike welcome the fact that he greets them at the school gates every morning. 'Within a week of arriving, he knew every child's name and he always chats to us. What's more, if you put forward an idea, he's on the case. He's an incredible man,' said one parent. Another told us, 'This isn't a school where you don't go to the head because he's the last port of call – he and the teachers are seen as interchangeable. Even if he's not having a good day, he'll find time for you.'

When Mr Hall is not at school, he calls himself a 'water baby at heart' and loves swimming and rafting. He also tries to spend as much time with his family as possible and explore London and the world: 'My son is fearless so we spend many a weekend at theme parks.'

Entrance: Admission by means of the local authority criteria – which means that, in order of priority, it's looked after children and SEN, then siblings and after that, living as near as possible. With four applications for every place, this generally means within a quarter of a mile. Local estate agents are big fans – the success of the school, and its neighbouring comprehensive, has had a significant impact on local property prices.

Exit: The school backs directly on to Alexandra Park, one of the borough's best secondaries, and over half of pupils proceed there. Others to Fortismere and Latymer, with the remainder attending a wide range of schools including JFS, the Compton School, Greek School of London, Channing and Dame Alice Owen's.

Remarks: Undoubtedly helped by the fact that most families live within feet of the gates, this is a school with a true community feel – a vibe that parents say it has managed to retain despite moving to three-form entry of 90. What strikes you as you enter the contemporary buildings (set amongst immaculately kept grounds) is the atmosphere of both fun and of purposefulness – a combination that many primary schools aim for and fail, often spectacularly. If ever there was an argument that schools benefit from great architects, this is it – the interiors meld the original 1930s building with the more recent extensions to create bright, light and modern learning spaces that are a joy to spend time in. The wide, carpeted corridors of the main split-level building are so much more than mere walkways, with private music lessons, art exhibitions etc going on throughout. The classrooms are big and airy, with huge windows – and the spongy-carpeted library is somewhere that several children told us was their 'favourite place.' The art studio is well stocked; ICT suite is up-to-date; and there are two school halls – one purely for PE, while the other is also used for assemblies, lunch and performances. Nursery (now full time) and reception are housed in a single story building that also boasts nice, bright classrooms.

Outside, there are separate soft-ground playgrounds for nursery and reception; years 1-3; and years 4-6 – each well-equipped for the age group in question (younger ones get masses of toys under a large shelter; middle school gets a great climbing frame; older ones get the likes of table football and even a bandstand). And the chickens – a relatively recent addition, which has a nod to the school site's origins as a farm, and which is extremely popular with the children. 'We are lucky,' one of them told us – neatly summing up the pupils' sense of good fortune. They wanted to show off every single nook and cranny to us, revealing what is a clearly a huge sense of ownership and pride in their place of learning.

Teaching staff – who are made up of a good mix of thoroughly experienced and young and enthusiastic teachers – are themselves fun. In every classroom we visited – and in the staffroom too – there was a feeling of merriment, creativity, learning through doing and of getting things done with a smile and a light touch. And it clearly works. The school has for some years consistently dominated the local authority league tables, with reading progress in the top 20 per cent of schools in the country, and writing and maths in the top five per cent. Ofsted can barely think of a word of criticism. Sats results are outstanding, with the majority reaching the highest levels. Though the pupils tend to be of above average ability on entry, everyone we spoke to agrees the school goes above and beyond.

Children are taught mainly by class teachers, with specialist teachers enhancing areas such as French, art and PE. Parents praise the themed approach to learning – with each year group studying a single topic every half term, with a cross-curricular approach thereon eg year 5's theme was Pole to Pole, when we visited – the history aspect speaks for itself, while in geography they learned about global warming and in English, they explored Shackleton's poems etc. 'You really get to see these themes come to life in the class assemblies,' said one parent – of which each year group or class does one a year.

Academic progress is charted minutely and parents kept well informed, with three parents' evenings and three reports a year. Strong support, too, for the struggling. 'My son has a special literacy person and she's fantastic,' said one parent. French taught from year 2 and 'parlez-vous' is supplemented with fun activities like a French breakfast, croissants included. Setting in years 5 and 6 for maths and English.

Homework is an ongoing debate among parents, with a 50/50 split between those who think there's enough and those who believe there should be more. As with the classroom teaching, there's an emphasis on making it enjoyable and it will often include a visit to somewhere in London, which the child then talks about in class. 'We try to merge home and school life as much as possible as home can be a real place of learning too,' says the head.

An 'inclusion leader' leads SEND, with a separate SEND lead in the early years centre – both cater for not only mild and moderate, but more severe, including pre-verbal and wheelchair using children. Their creative, child-focused support both in and outside the classroom has earned the school an Inclusion Quality Mark. 'My son has a specialist care team because of his needs and they were very impressed by how far the school was prepared to go to ensure he reached his full potential. It's just incredible,' a parent told us, while another said, 'Unlike other schools, they start with the child and adapt the school to them – rather than telling you how you have to fit in.'

Sport, music, art and drama are as high up the agenda as the three Rs and although, in the past, some parents felt that the obvious winners were celebrated to the detriment of the less brilliant, things are changing, with a push on inclusivity. 'We want every child to be able to compete, so we've introduced a squad system for football, for example, whereby 30 children get to compete, instead of the six children in the top team in the old system,' says the head. 'It's working – sport here is much more about participation than it used to be,' a parent told us. Not that the school intends to take a soft-touch approach to sport – indeed, it tends to sweep the board in local competitions, with shelf after shelf of silverware on display in reception. Minimum of two hours of PE a week, which includes netball, gymnastics, athletics and rugby at the core – as well as less obvious options including basketball, boating, golf and handball. Onsite facilities include the two sports halls and outside cage for netball and football, and they use public parkland just behind the school – visible from the head's office – for field sports. There are good links with the local tennis club, and year 4s upwards go swimming at a local public pool.

Drama regularly seeps into English lessons, and there are two extracurricular acting clubs, plus a whole-school Christmas production and class assemblies. Art is popular – with the specialist teacher teaching the likes of sculpting and printing, alongside more traditional art, the results of which are on display during the annual summer exhibition. 'We had to make a fish out of a trash can recently – I thought it would be rubbish, but it was amazing,' one child told us.

Music permeates the culture here, with many of the private music lessons by peripatetic teachers taking place in the corridors ('The real reason we do it is because we're short on private study areas – but the upside of this problem is that it's lovely to walk past the children learning anything from the cello to piano,' says the head). There's an orchestra, chamber choir, school choir and boy band – all of which publically perform – and children sing at the local tube station to raise money for charity at Christmas. Some year groups learn instruments as a whole, with past examples including cello, clarinet, recorder, drums and violin.

Extracurricular clubs include sports (ranging from cross-country to cricket), recorder, Spanish, French, street dance, coding, meditation, sewing, chess, pottery and drama. Lots of competitions entered and usually won, whether that's for the school's abundant and much-loved vegetable garden or for pupils' Christmas card designs. Breakfast club from 7.50am and after-school play centre on site 3.30-6pm, plus holiday clubs. Loads of trips and workshops, all related to the current topic, as well as two activity-based residentials – year 5 to Wales for a weekend and year 6 to Lincolnshire for a week.

This is a nurturing school, say parents, with a strong pastoral system, thanks to these key ingredients: class teaches that get to know the children well; deputy head is the lead in this area; school counsellor available one day a week; art therapy sessions available from the specialist art teacher; an open environment, in which children feel able to talk and communicate and feel they can see the head at any time; and a parent gym (in which parents can get support and guidance on issues like bedtime routines and healthy eating). Many parents, as well as the head, also believe that the no-uniform policy is relevant – 'It helps children feel comfortable and that they can really be themselves,' he says – and although not all parents support it, many come round. One parent said, 'At first I thought, "What will they wear each day?" and where will the sense of identity be around the school? But it's so nice walking in with all those bright colours and you can see it just sets them free. And believe me, there's no shortage of identity in this school. I'm all for it now.'

Plenty of praise is the recipe for good behaviour – with stickers going a particularly long way. 'By and large, the children's behaviour is immaculate,' says the head – with children saying hello, holding doors open and arriving in the classroom ready to learn. Children who don't follow the 'golden rules' are given 'refection' and if that doesn't work, parents are called in. 'And if children are racist, fight or bully, then we would go straight to the parents,' says the head. But bullying is rare and there are less than a handful of temporary exclusions, if any, each year – which the head puts down to their focus on inclusion and accepting difference.

Parents increasingly prosperous and professional, although around six per cent of pupils are on free school meals. The parents are a sociable bunch – and very supportive too. Indeed, the PTA is buzzing, with recent purchases from its hectic cycle of events (including fairs, raffles, sales, fireworks etc) including more computers for the computer suite and redevelopment of the key stage 1 playground. Those with interesting jobs – astronauts or newspaper editors – come in to share their expertise. Around half of the children are white British, while the remaining predominant ethic groups are other white backgrounds and Asian.

There's a big student voice here, with the student council having voted to bring in vegetable growing areas, among other things. In fact, the school is big on the outdoors generally, with all teachers trained in forest school. Mixed views on the food. 'It's horrible,' more than one child told us, while a parent said, 'It's a shame as food used to be one of their shining glories.' The head acknowledges 'it's mass cooked,' but adds that 'there are 12 different choices in the salad bar – all selected with the help of the school council.'

This is a friendly, upbeat local school where pupils have fun, get excited about learning and have lots of opportunities around responsibility – whether in school council, sports leaders and ambassadors, librarians, lunch teams, animal welfare etc. 'Pretty much every day, I thank my lucky stars that my kids go to this school. You can't ask for more than that.'

Richard Challoner School

Manor Drive North, New Malden, Surrey KT3 5PE

Pupils: 997 • Ages: 11–18 • Sixth form: 248 • RC

Tel: 020 8330 5947
Email: rcb@challoner.kingston.sch.uk
Website: www.richardchalloner.com

Head: Since 2015, Mr Sean Maher BA (40s). Previously deputy head, rising through the ranks after being offered first post here four weeks into teacher training in 2001. Leadership skills amply demonstrated during secondment to Catholic secondary in Kent, transforming it in just under 18 months from 'requires improvement' to 'good' by upping expectations, improving discipline and putting classroom walls back in. 'Anyone could have done it,' he says modestly. Award of Kent Headteacher of the Year 2015 suggests anyone probably couldn't.

A local boy, combined studies at Emanuel and St Mary's Twickenham (studying English and history) with helping out in family bakery in Raynes Park (nothing like removing freshly baked loaves at end of night shift for sense of fulfillment, he says).

Little ruffles his feathers bar increasing amount of time spent on plugging growing holes in funding – every minute not spent helping pupils is a minute wasted. Tidiness also a major preoccupation, all senior teachers issued with own litter pickers. As badges of office go, not glitzy (sadly, there's no short but moving presentation ceremony either) but important, sending unambiguous message about standards and expectations.

While convention matters – uniform code for sixth formers specifying 'conservative' haircuts unlikely to change – Mr Maher also promotes the 'right sort' of Jesuitical rebelliousness – standing up against the prevailing wisdom rather than 'pointless' defiance. 'Boys need to be able to articulate their views – and unfortunately in society there is so much they need to stand against at the moment,' he says.

Devout, kind and focused on the pupils, he's a popular choice. 'Has best interests of everyone at heart,' says mother. No surprise that would-be staff will be asked if they really love children. 'Can tell straight away if they're really very awkward with the question.'

Impressive without being intimidating – 'Serious' thought junior pupil – though older ones appreciate deadpan humour that's not far beneath the surface – and recently sang to whole school in assembly to demonstrate virtues of risk taking. 'He's down with the kids,' reckoned senior pupil – though Mr Maher isn't convinced.

Above all, a force to be reckoned with. His son, starting at the school soon, plans to 'come and have a cuddle if gets into trouble,' says Mr Maher. 'I said, "Son, if that's what you think, you've underestimated me".' We suspect that's unlikely to be the case for very long.

Academic matters: 'You won't see one child not engaged with their learning,' says head. Naturally we put this to the test during tour – and he's right. From year 7 French class on a virtual shopping trip – 'Un grand sac de Doritos Chilli 'eatwave s'il vous plaît' – to year 8 boys' thoughts on constructing a balanced argument in English – 'Always talk through problems, don't keep it in,' there's minimal fidgeting or disengagement.

Even class of year 10 maths pupils, all blazer-clad and diligently working through mind-expanding algebra in boiling hot classroom, and year 11 pupils who have gone straight from first GCSE (RS) to revision session (physics), are impressively focused if a tad goggle-eyed – there's no study leave here, just a collapsed timetable to keep everyone on task.

All contributes to cracking results. In 2016, 82 per cent of pupils achieved at least five A*-C GCSEs including maths and English, 33 per cent of exam grades at A*/A, with 25 per cent of A levels awarded A*/A and 56 per pent A*-B. Success down to inspired teaching delivered with dedication and plenty of innovation. Younger pupils now have own iPads (top years who have missed out as not here long enough to pay them off are philosophical about greater good) and even insets, last one involving staff treasure hunt, sound fun.

Teaching team is bursting with young talent, with plenty of senior teachers barely in 30s and now heads-in-waiting, some former pupils who were taught by 50 or so veterans who've been here for a decade or more. Old or novice, sense of pride in their work visible in corridor after corridor crammed with pristine displays – we particularly liked the Poetree, with poems nestled among painted branches and the swathes of playing cards in the maths corridor, each with probability problem.

Energy courses through the place – head is a strong believer in keeping boys busy and the pace is correspondingly brisk. Despite DT's demotion from core subject to option in line with government requirements, most boys still take 10 GCSEs, down from 11 (slimmed down to six for some SEN pupils). Reduction a possible relief given one former pupil's comment about ease of overdosing on arts or sport activities 'and then realising you've got an exam in a month...'

Most subjects are set from year 7 with two innovative transition classes in core subjects helping first years who hadn't hit Sats targets bridge gap between primary and senior school. 'Some present with big challenges,' says teacher, who's using colour-coded activities (red for independent learning, yellow for group work) to 'teach boys to learn.'

Everyone gets together for other subjects including DT (freeflow rooms, 3D printer and fab projects including programmable robotic cars). Well-resourced food technology, hospitality and catering a big hit with year 10 pupils, particularly top set types who find relaxation in creation of immaculate macaroons, sushi and crostini.

Range continues at sixth form level with 28 A levels and five Btecs, some high demand subjects (maths, history, geography and psychology currently top list of favourites) offered both here and at partnered girls' school, Holy Cross, others split between the two – timetable immensely complex to sort but currently working well, minibus plying between the two sites 'and easy to catch as long as you organise yourself,' said pupil. No plans for combined sixth form – with almost 500 pupils across two schools, semi-detached existence works better.

Generously proportioned and resourced learning resource centre, open on Saturday mornings and in holidays, provides a shelter for anyone having a rough time. Determined librarian's mission is to ensure that everyone reads – books must be carried at all times – while staff post current title on their classroom doors – maths teacher was deep in Candide; head tucking into The Jesuit Guide to Almost Everything, a recent gift from a colleague.

High expectations extend to SEN pupils – 76 pupils in much-admired ASD unit which takes LEA-referred pupils (all statemented or with EHC plan) plus 12 in years 7-11 with social, emotional and mental health needs who get imaginative support – life skills programme recently boosted with acquisition of aquarium and (very popular) pet guinea pig. Focus is on inclusion with help from 26 learning support assistants. 'The philosophy is very much "we want you in the classroom",' says Mr Maher.

Current SEN team praised by a parent for 'exemplary knowledge of needs' and commitment to pupils. 'Chilled out, calm and very good at working out what students' individual needs are,' thought dyslexic pupil – extends to letting sixth formers taking three rather than two years to complete courses. 'If you can't do it one way, you can do it another,' supportive teacher tells parents. Building on expertise with new MLD unit for 16-19 year olds.

First class communication helps hold the whole thing together. 'Every teacher knows what's going on,' said parent. There's plenty of support, from timetabled revision classes to informal chats over coffee, particularly relished by sixth formers. 'Get on so well, wasn't that teacher and pupil divide,' said recent leaver. And humour is always on tap. 'Aah, isn't he lovely,' says wording under pic of puppy outside science lab. 'He's a guide dog for the blind and if you don't wear safety spectacles, you might need one...'.

Games, options, the arts: Not the right place for staff in search of quiet life and 4pm finish, warns school. With many charity-linked events – rough sleep event in school grounds raised over £7,000 – extracurricular programme spilling over into weekends and evenings, trips (rugby tour of South Africa) and clubs including art, video and media as well as vibrant house system with 40 events – house music competitions demand original composition as well as normal solo and group acts, rewarding extra commitment with bonus points – not surprising that potential staff recruits are asked what can bring to the party.

Best to arrive at interview with at least one extra talent and be prepared to offer it freely (there's no extra pay). 'Do it because of the impact it has on the children,' says Mr Maher. Recent sports award event a case in point, with staff (and some partners) organizing sit down evening meal for 180 winners and their teachers, reflecting considerable achievements.

Head is delighted with considerable sporting achievements, particularly in football where teams regularly reach final eight or better at national and district level, though would love to see rugby doing even better especially given permanent underdog status against largesse of independent school resourcing.

Pupils, bar desire for a swimming pool – likely to remain on wish list for foreseeable future – had few complaints and instead were eloquent about the way that whatever their interest, school's encouragement had helped them discover it – and find themselves. 'If it hadn't been for here, wouldn't be playing at county level,' said sixth former.

Arts equally popular, teaching highly rated, dynamic music teacher leading erudite GCSE discussion on monophony, performing arts BTec recently added to the mix.

Impressive facilities include imaginatively revamped St Bede's building include airy first floor multi-purpose hall, while bright dance studio (head's ambition is to give it official standing on the curriculum) is good enough to be hired out to private firm who no doubt relish its up to the mark light wood finish and mirrored wall as much as the pupils.

There's big performance space (large theatre) and gem of a drama studio, once the gym – its transformation into flexible, well curated black-ceilinged space with roll on, roll off seating, a professional lighting rig and teeny but impressive sound and lighting box yet another brainchild of previous head, who also managed to carve out funding and space from a corridor for tiny recording studio which is, courtesy of acoustic tiles, very nearly soundproof. Together provide worthwhile settings for ambitious plays and musicals that range from Shakespeare to home grown, one production each year touring in Hungary. 'A massive inspiration,' said past pupil.

Sunny art room, rather empty on day of visit, contrasted with sombre but highly accomplished monochrome tableaux on display, screaming mouths skewered with 3-D spears. 'It's linked to fear and inability to express yourself,' said jolly teacher. Not a problem that afflicts many of the pupils here, judging by popular debating society propositions that range from pros and cons of immigration ('fiery' says diplomatic member of staff) to 'Is feminism still relevant?' (Yes).

Background and atmosphere: Catholicism at its best though you don't have to share Mr Maher's beliefs to get the most from it. Chapel is of modest dimensions, though removable partition ensures that the growing numbers attending weekly mass (chaplain is parish priest and a school governor) can be catered for though 'knows his boys – never takes more than 20 minutes,' says the head.

Tangible manifestations of faith are numerous but not relentless – our favourite was Eric Gill-like Madonna and child in entrance to new block – an alternative design for school's foundation, finally realised on 50th anniversary, marked by bussing whole school to Westminster Cathedral on double-deckers for a special ceremony.

Once undersubscribed and so rough that 'story was you had to nail salt and pepper pots to the table,' says staff member, school has changed markedly though perceptions, particularly among the smarter Wimbledon Village set, have been a bit slower to catch up.

Their loss. The immediate surroundings may not be SW19-friendly, but even the most aesthetically sniffy will enjoy beautiful greenery of the ancient Hogsmill River that runs beside playing fields, as well as astonishing transformation of school itself. With curved roofs, plenty of wood-cladding and even mellow(ish) brickwork school presents unified face to the world, avoiding normal piecemeal additions so often derived on a one thing after another basis. Even the little details like repainting all the external window frames grey make a huge difference.

Inside, many of the long corridors running length of main teaching blocks have been transformed with glass panels, smart blinds and bright white paint. Outside there's a 3G pitch (superior artificial surface that can take conventional football boots) and athletics track – pupils allowed on grass only in late summer, mingling – happily enough – on the tarmac for rest of year.

It's masterpiece of nifty financial footwork by previous head ('genius in finding and stretching money – turned school from 1950s dilapidation to one fit for 21st century,' says head). No wonder even backroom bean counters are jolly – a rare sight indeed.

Even yet-to-be-transformed areas with Crittall windows, grey-flecked lino and thick brown tiled windowsills, are so well-maintained that have a rather desirable vintage look, though once head's money-charming skills are fully realised (and there's no chance they won't be), will doubtless get the necessary upgrades.

Pupil areas have been given similar TLC, with sixth form combined social and study area and bistro a particularly desirable perk. Though occasionally used for special events, normally out of bounds for lower school pupils who can only yearn over passing trolleys packed with seniors only fizzy drinks (as can buy up the road, no point in not offering) as well as bacon, sausage and croissants for break (all cooked in-house). Chips (girls) and southern fried chicken 'n' cheese baguette (boys) the top 16+ faves though, judging by prodigious quantities of food enthusiastically put away by lower school pupils and numerous lunchtime choices (including pasta, paninis and a veggie option) nobody appears to be suffering.

Pastoral care, well-being and discipline: 'It's like a family business,' says Mr Maher who (though not by way of proof) reports boys in lessons occasionally addressing him as 'mum'. Literally so, as many teachers don't just come in singles but often in pairs and occasionally in sets. We ran out of the times we were introduced to one teacher and told that partner or a sibling (they even do a nice line in twins) also worked here.

Winner in what would be cracking Top Trumps game is the Maher clan. Mrs M senior works in the café (and unfortunately wasn't in on day of visit as we were dying to have critique of son's leadership style), Mrs M junior, his wife, is a chemistry teacher, brother taught geography here and son is a potential pupil.

As in best run families, school discipline is achieved effectively with minimum of fuss, down to 'passive supervision' – staff always there but presence is low-key, issues often resolved through informal chats with favourite teacher.

Head speeds departing pupils on their way at end of day (no doubt fitting in a final litter check) while other staff patrol local shops. Even former pupils don't escape (one 30-something pillar of community told off for poor parking, reported distinctly gleeful wife).

'Very calm here,' said recent leaver, who felt that while would always be some naughty boys ('Don't let them tell you there aren't' – they didn't) response would be speedy and compassionate. Having witnessed the barely discernible fall-out from just one incident – pupil briefly and calmly removed from classroom after melt-down – we can only agree. Response to inevitable unkindness is similarly 'fantastic,' said parent.

'If you focus on the small things, you very rarely get to the big things, so we focus on the small things unrelentingly, shirt tails, top buttons, sensible hair cuts,' says Mr Maher. Rules are strictly enforced with sensible concessions. 'I abhor locked rooms,' he says – and they aren't, well-stocked fitness suite (like dance suite rented out after hours) the only exception – a health and safety rather than trust issue.

There's authorised queue-jumping for autistic pupils otherwise overwhelmed by lunchtime noise, younger boys using the outside entrance, year 11s, swelled by privilege of age, allowed to arrive via the hall, biometrics guaranteeing speed service for all.

Deliberate litter dropping was, unsurprisingly, taken very seriously, punishment – donning high vis jacket and does a whole-school clear up – very definitely matching the crime.

Above all, success celebrated where and whenever it crops up. Basketball star blushingly praised for efforts is told by Mr M that 'will make a fuss in assembly,' while there's tea and cakes with the head for frequent 'above and beyond' award winners ('go to Waitrose the night before and clear the shelves,' he says) successes recorded on honours board (updatable paper rather than carved on wood). Senior teachers dispense the beverages, boys serve the food. 'A nice touch,' said parent. 'Do praise effort.'

Pupils and parents: Most illustrious former pupil is probably Spiderman actor Tom Holland. Others to into professions (law) or sport – including Britain's first wheelchair referee.

Family feel is pervasive, with 16 or so girls joining modestly co-ed sixth form (plus 30 or so who come over from Holy Cross) instantly slotting in, praised by head for sparkiness and openness to change. Can be harder for routine-loving boys joining in year 12, thought school insider – nobody's fault, just down to intensity of bonds formed in earlier years.

Entrance: With hefty oversubscription and around four applicants for each of 150 year 7 places, essential to be realistic. 'Effectively if you're not a practising Catholic and you're not in one of our feeder schools [Corpus Christi, Our Lady Immaculate, Sacred Heart, New Malden, St Agatha's, St Cecilia's, St Clement's and St Joseph's, Kingston], it's going to be very hard,' says Mr Maher.

Strength of faith matters (weekly church attendance is one of entrance criteria). Then it's down to home address (living in two local deaneries helps) and distance to school gates.

Post 16, minimum of 10 external candidates accepted including small numbers of girls, permanent members of the school's own sixth form. All faith criteria as before, most courses requiring B grade or better in related GCSE.

Exit: In 2016, 30 per cent left after GCSEs and a further six per cent at end of year 12. Around 70 per cent of year 13 leavers move on to higher education (83 in 2016) with around 16 per cent gaining places at Russell Group universities (24 in 2016) with Warwick, Nottingham, Portsmouth and Kent all popular. Often several to Oxbridge (though none in 2016). Just under a fifth carry on in further education and programmes, remainder opting for apprenticeships including Civil Service fast track and BBC broadcast engineering.

Remarks: Faith-inspired, purposeful leadership and energetic teaching deliver first rate education that's big on family feel and hot on detail. Inveterate litterbugs might struggle.

Robert Clack School

Gosfield Road, Dagenham, Essex RM8 1JU

Pupils: 2,070 • Ages: 11–18 • Sixth form: 491

Tel: 020 8270 4200
Email: office@robertclack.co.uk
Website: www.robertclack.co.uk

Headteacher: Since 1997, Sir Paul Grant MA (late 50s). Famously promoted from head of humanities at a time when the school was going to the dogs, he has since transformed it into such a success story that it still continues to attract the national media. The eldest of seven children from a working-class Liverpudlian family, he is laid-back and unpretentious – not the type to talk himself up, but with a clear sense of leadership bubbling away underneath. This combination, together with his unwavering belief that every single child can be excellent with the right schooling, has won him enormous and ongoing respect from pupils, parents and staff.

A keen football fan, who had once hoped to turn professional, he attended the Salesian Grammar School in Bootle, where a teacher inspired him to study history at Hull University. He completed a PGCE at Durham and an MA at London University, and taught in north Yorkshire, Australia and Newham before joining Robert Clack in 1990. At this point the school had such weak leadership that even the teachers who did try to keep order were fighting a losing battle. There was a serious gang culture, children smoked in the corridors and caused chaos in the community at lunchtime. Pupils rode bicycles inside and it was commonplace to set off fireworks indoors. In 1996, only 17 per cent of pupils gained five or more A–C grades at GCSE and the school was on the verge of special measures.

The humanities department, however, was going from strength to strength. Sir Paul was appointed headteacher with an emergency plan of action which included a tough, transparent code for bad behaviour and a new system of rewards. He suspended 300 troublemakers in his first week, even driving around to pick up truants, as well as talking to local shopkeepers, local councillors, council employees such as housing officers, and police. Most teachers welcomed the new regime, but some parents were livid. Sir Paul met every one and gradually won them round. 'People rolled about in the aisles when I said this could be an exemplary school – they're not laughing now,' he says.

Sir Paul was knighted for services to education a few weeks after the school received an Evening Standard award for excellence in challenging circumstances – and remains the only serving headteacher with a knighthood (and who is a deputy lieutenant). Larger than life in build and character and described by Ofsted as 'tireless', he is married with three daughters, two of whom attend the school's sixth form.

Doesn't believe in experimental leadership, preferring to lead by example and working with a clear system of praise and clear expectations around respect. Takes weekly assemblies and regularly visits classes, but laughed out loud when we asked if he had time to take any lessons.

Academic matters: Some 40 per cent of pupils have SEN and over 50 per cent have free school meals, but results have improved steadily from the 1996 nadir, give or take a couple of per cent here and there: in 2016, 66 per cent of pupils got five or more good GCSEs including maths and English and 27 per cent of GCSEs were A*/A grades. At A level, 60 per cent A*/B and 20 per cent A*/A grades. These results are way above the national standard for a school with such a big cohort (one of the biggest in the country and becoming even bigger, thanks to the recent introduction of the Premier League Elite Player Performance Programme for 20-30 boys in years 10 and 11 at West Ham Academy, adjacent to the upper site of the school).

Specialist school in science, maths, computing and modern languages – no mean feat in such a strongly working-class school. Everyone takes French and Spanish from years 7 to 9 and approximately 70 per cent take a GSCE in one of those. 'Our aim is to push that to 100 per cent,' says head, although French and Spanish A level take up is disappointing. Everyone takes double science, and 35 per cent take triple science, with others opting for the vocational applied science option – all with a healthy gender split. Other vocational options include health and social care, business studies, catering, beauty and ICT. Indeed, while many schools are cutting back their vocational provision due to their worry about league tables, this school ensures the vocational routes remain strong.

The ability range is massive, from those aiming at A*s to those who joined the school with a reading age of 5 or 6. Setting for every subject in years 7 to 9, then in core subjects of English, maths and science until GSCE options, where there is no setting at all. Lots of auditing of progress means significant numbers move right up through the sets, however. Parents and pupils feel homework levels are fair – enough to complement their studies, but not so much that it causes battles at home.

Learning support and mentor rooms where children can come to catch up on literacy and numeracy – perhaps because they've been off sick or they're upset because of family problems and can't cope amongst their peers. Meanwhile, SEN – which includes the whole gamut from mild dyslexia and ADHD to pupils with Asperger's, dwarfism, hearing and sight problems and cerebral palsy – all get plenty of classroom-based help if and when required, as do the gifted and talented. 'I've got cystic fibrosis and whenever I've had to miss school, the teachers help me catch up, without making me look singled out, and I get lots of passes to help me get the things I need whilst I'm in school,' one pupil told us. 'My son, who has Asperger's had to leave his last school after just three months because it didn't work for him, whereas here their laid-back, but tailored, assistance in

R

the classroom has enabled him to do really well,' said another. One parent of a student who had to take several weeks off due to Crohn's Disease said home tuition had been set up, plus the head of year visited them both in hospital and at home. 'It's a big school, with a lot of special needs, but nobody gets missed and the focus on kids each achieving their full potential regardless of any barriers is phenomenal,' she said.

The sixth form is part of the North East Consortium with three other local schools, offering more than 40 courses at different levels. Over 800 sixth formers in the consortium, including some 550 at Robert Clack, many of whom are the first in their families to stay in education post-16. No minimum entry requirements, as courses range from a certificate in motor vehicle servicing to further maths, though students who want to take A levels must have at least five grade Cs at GCSE. 'Despite the ever-increasing risk from Ofsted, we don't set the benchmark too high because we want to give these children a chance,' says head. Maths and sciences are the most popular A level courses, followed closely by English, history, economics and media studies. BTecs in business, IT and sport popular, as is beauty therapy, taught in an on-site beauty salon – 'we give everyone the opportunity to be successful here'.

Alongside a strict disciplinary procedure ('expectations of high standards are well-established and non-negotiable,' explains head), high quality teaching is seen as key to the school's success. 'Every child feels there is a pathway for them, with teaching that enables this pathway,' said one parent. The 'Robert Clack good lesson' template – which involves explaining to pupils the objective, interactive content and process of every lesson – is also much admired. 'The established and consistent approach means young teachers can come in and say, "I know for a fact this is what you're used to," and get on with teaching high quality lessons rather than trying to reinvent the wheel,' says head. Teachers – whose ethnicity almost exactly represents that of the pupils – are seen as inspirational and often going well beyond the call of duty. 'They show enormous respect for the students – it's not just expected the other way round and these kids really value that,' one parent told us.

However, whilst the school was, until recently, one of 12 outstanding secondary schools fêted by Ofsted for excelling against the odds, it is currently feeling bruised by being taken down a peg to 'good' in 2013. The only category that has, according to Ofsted, dropped in standards, is the teaching – with the overall assessment remaining one most schools would kill for – but the head nevertheless found the decision 'incomprehensible' and was appealing at the time of our visit.

Games, options, the arts: It's sport, according to the head, that is largely responsible for turning this school around. 'It was the quickest, most visible way to espouse excellence,' he explains. 'Sport develops things like pride, self-discipline, teamwork, confidence and empathy, all of which then feed through into other areas of school life. I really don't think we could have done what we have without sport.'

Today, it's considered no less important, with the school frequently borough champion at rugby, netball, football, athletics and cross-country. It has also been county champion at rugby and netball, a great achievement against the Essex selective schools, and recently won the first Essex title at cricket ('A dream of mine for a long time,' says head). A rugby academy attracts talented players to the sixth form. Pupils have competed nationally at sports ranging from netball to skiing and their team shirts are displayed proudly alongside photos and trophies. 'My son hated rugby when he arrived and now he adores it,' one parent told us.

A swanky leisure centre includes a sports hall and fitness suite, open to the local community outside school hours. There are also tennis and netball courts and a large playing field which includes a recent £5m all-weather, state-of-the-art surfaced pitch. Numerous sports clubs before, during and after school, as well as on Saturday mornings, range from hockey to dance to girls' boxing. Even Bangladeshi girls, a notoriously difficult group to enthuse about sport, excel in sport here.

Boys', girls' and mixed school choirs go from strength to strength, including entering national song competitions, hosting musical exhibitions and helping local primary schools with singing. Ex-pupil Sandy Shaw gets stuck in enthusing pupils when she can, including attending concerts where she has been known to throw out a tune or two herself. Impressive school orchestra, with one student a member of the London Symphony Orchestra, plus a jazz group. Instrumental lessons are free and there are regular whole school performances combining music and drama, as well as regular visits to the West End.

Plenty of artwork displayed around the school, with light, airy and spacious facilities for both this and DT, both of which have reasonable take-up at GCSE. 'Take away art and you might as well take away some of our students' ability to breathe,' says head, who cites research showing that art can act as window into the soul among some children.

School trips include a French exchange, sixth-form politics and history visits to Washington and New York and sports trips to Canada, Barbados, Germany and South Africa. Cultural visits to Italy and Spain; expedition visits to Egypt and Latin America. Residentials to Isle of Wight and day trips to France, among others. Head insistent that these trips are critical to children's development and the school (and students) raise funds to ensure nobody misses out.

Background and atmosphere: This is a mammoth, split-site school, named after local legend Bob Clack, who was mayor from 1940 to 1942. The lower school site, which houses years 7 and 8 and most of year 9 (as well as some sixth form classes), opened in 1935, the upper school buildings, half a mile away, in 1953. There's also the more recent West Ham site, adjacent to the upper school.

It is one of the most deprived areas in the country, with the tower blocks of the Becontree Estate – one of the largest in England – casting a shadow over the playground. Yet this is one of the most ordered, neatest schools we've come across – no litter in sight and, as one teacher put it, 'an oasis of calm in the midst of the chaos outside.' Despite the vast number of pupils, there are only a few 'pinch points' that lack space, the dining hall among them. The shabby prefabs put up 'temporarily' in the '40s have been replaced by newer (still-prefab, but higher quality) buildings which provided the lower school with 18 new classrooms, and there's a good science block and media block with facilities for drama, music and media studies, as well as the spotless beauty salon. No shortage of computers and whiteboards and lots of students' work displayed neatly throughout the corridors. No lockers, though, which bothers some parents. 'I worry for my son's back, having to carry everything around with him all the time – he's only little,' said one.

Pupils also impeccably neat in blazers and ties (not a rolled up skirt or shirt hanging out here), orderly in corridors (although several students moan about the one-way system) and attentive in lessons. Students we met wore plenty of badges, reflecting the school's emphasis on providing leadership responsibilities. Racism issues minimal, with students mixing in genuinely diverse groups outside classes. 'When the school changed, the head dealt with all issues of racism personally, and now the school's values of tolerance and respect for others are just normal,' one parent told us. School recently introduced its own hijab as part of the school uniform, after consulting for a year with all the Muslim female students in the school and their families. Active school council made up of 300 pupils (again more or less reflecting diversity of the school).

A breakfast and homework club – along with masses of extracurricular clubs in everything from cheerleading to astronomy and sports to debating – mean students often arrive as early as 7am and don't leave until gone 6pm. 'They don't just come home and hang around on the streets because they feel really supported to pursue their interests,' said one parent. 'The clubs have taken my kids to another level,' said another. Even the library – where the homework club takes place daily – is very popular. 'It's a safe, quiet and friendly place that you can get on with your homework,' said one student. Even outside the school, there's little trouble, with Robert Clack kids known locally for being respectful and well-behaved – a far cry from days of old.

Pastoral care, well-being and discipline: Every positive action gets a reward and every negative action is followed with a consequence – and every student knows it. Praise includes colours for sport, music and performing arts; lots of merit awards during assemblies; notes home to parents; words of praise from Sir Paul, among others. Meanwhile, the strict disciplinary procedure ('expectations of high standards are well-established and non-negotiable,' explains head) means detentions for low level offenses such as chewing gum, forgetting homework etc. Two such boys stood in one corridor when we visited, looking suitably sheepish. Pupil referral unit handles more serious transgressions, such as disrupting lessons, starting a fight or playing truant, with the ultimate sanction sending them home. It's all about nipping problems in the bud, along with consistent and clear boundaries, says head – and it works, with no permanent exclusions for over 10 years and pupils agreeing rules are generally fair.

Pastoral care – mainly from form teachers and school counsellor – admired by parents, who say children feel very safe here. Bullying a non-issue, which pupils put down to CCTV throughout the school and an ethos among students of looking after each other. 'I spilled my drink in the dining hall the other day and an older boy came rushing over asking if I was OK,' one pupil told us. 'My teenage son isn't the easiest to deal with and has had quite a lot of problems, but staff have put in so much time to steer him on the right path,' one parent told us. 'It's amazing how they've worked with him.'

Pupils and parents: Largely from the surrounding estates, though proximity to the school puts a premium on the prices of the few houses for sale in the area. Huge (and increasing) numbers of single parent families, as well as those with several generations of unemployment. This is an area with some severe poverty issues and one of the fastest changing demographics in the country. The school largely reflects this demographic, with around 45 per cent white working-class; 35 per cent Afro-Caribbean; 15 per cent Asian (mainly Bangladeshi); and the rest mixed race. Pupils are polite, resilient, articulate and hard-working. And although they are typically from under-achieving backgrounds, the school says most parents work in partnership with the school. School employs a parental adviser who visits families under stress and helps with housing, clothing and food allowances.

Entrance: Some 2,000 applications for the 300 places in year 7. Looked-after children get priority, as do those with special educational needs, then by distance from the upper school site – generally within just one kilometre. Large numbers from other schools join the sixth form.

Exit: About 60 per cent of pupils move up to the sixth form, up from around 20 per cent 10 years ago. Around half of those go on to university. Usually a couple to Oxbridge (three in 2016, and six to study medicine). A handful to UCL, Queen Mary's and Royal Holloway respectively, with other high profile Russell Group universities also featuring regularly among destinations. Some 70 per cent study maths and sciences, with the remaining 30 per cent covering virtually every subject going. The remaining half of sixth-formers go straight into work (many on apprenticeships), with significant numbers moving into the City. Plenty of careers advice and help with UCAS applications, and the school has high value partnerships with the likes of the Premier League, West Ham United, The Prince's Teaching Institute, Teach First and Business in the Community, all of which provide pupils with work experience or routes into careers, as well as promoting the work of the school. School is also sponsored by a number of firms and organisations, the most notable of which is the Royal Society of Chartered Surveyors, which supports many pupils through university.

School is working hard to build up alumni, with 2,000 ex-pupils so far involved in helping with interviews and work experience, as well as providing access to their networks.

Remarks: An exceptional comprehensive in one of the most deprived areas of the country. All roads here lead back to the ethos of the school, which is all about being inclusive, mutually respectful and aiming high. Excellent leadership by an unflagging head, who – against all odds – has transformed a failing school into one that is a source of huge pride for staff, parents and pupils and where every single young person is both encouraged and supported to reach their full potential.

The Roche School

11 Frogmore, London SW18 1HW

Pupils: 288 • Ages: 2.5–11

Fees: £12,330 – £13,320 pa

Tel: 020 8877 0823
Email: gcac@therocheschool.co.uk
Website: www.therocheschool.com

Principal: Since 1989, Dr James Roche BSc PhD (60s). Educated at St Paul's, read physics at Bristol and has a PhD in general relativity from Manchester. Taught for two years in a London state school then spent 19 years teaching A level physics and maths at London tutorial colleges, latterly as principal of Collingham College, Kensington, where his wife Carmen taught languages. She set up the Roche School and they are joint principals, but he insists that she is the 'principal principal, the éminence grise', and that he has been 'happily demoted'. Head teacher since 2010 is Vania Adams ('I have to obey not only my wife but her too'); she was busy rehearsing the very confident year 6 cast of the forthcoming West Side Story production when we visited.

Dr Roche reveals that he was 'very scared' of changing from GCSEs and A levels to primary teaching when he joined the school, 'but it was just the same. You just have to explain things so children can understand them.' He still runs scholarship classes in mathematics for years 5 and 6 plus any younger ones who are preparing for 7+ and 8+ exams. He has a weekly meeting with a boy in year 4 'who is interested in science – we talk about the photoelectric effect and e=mc squared and tectonic plates and all these amazing theories'. He also teaches some year 6 science. 'I'm just interested in the theory, because if I try an experiment it goes wrong...happily the other year 6 science teacher is very good at experiments.' He has the air of a loquacious, slightly eccentric uncle, and we can see why he is 'particularly well thought of' and 'marvellous with slightly off-beat children'.

If the school has a particular aim, it is to make learning fun. 'It's our business to encourage children who want to know things – to encourage their enthusiasms.'

Entrance: Most join one of the two nurseries, or the reception class. Non-selective, and first-come-first served at this level; those after a place higher up 'come in for a morning or a day. We hear them read, and talk about it, see what their writing is like, if they know anything about how numbers work. We're not looking for technical skills but for a basic understanding.' Some very bright children, but also happy to take children with learning difficulties 'as long as they can benefit from what we offer. If they don't have any enthusiasms, if they're not interested in stories, that's difficult.' Can cater for dyslexia, dyspraxia, Asperger's, Down's syndrome, speech and language difficulties, ASD, ADD and those with EFL needs as long as they have the ability to catch up with their year group.

Quite a through-put, particularly of international families, so worth trying for a place higher up. Some bursaries available, both to incomers and those already at the school.

Exit: A few leave at 7+ or 8+ ('we're happy to prepare children at any age'), but most at 11+ to eg King's Wimbledon, Whitgift, Ibstock Place, Kingston Grammar, Tiffin Girls and Boys, Putney High, More House, JAGs, Wimbledon High, Dulwich College and Latymer Upper. A few to boarding school eg Bedales.

Remarks: Carmen Roche set up Mrs Roche's Coaching Establishment in her West Kensington basement in 1983, largely to prepare children for 11+ and 13+ exams. In 1988, she bought the office block of a Wandsworth laundry in a quiet back street between the A3 and the suburban railway line, and, after some refurbishment, The Roche School moved in. Classrooms mostly compact. Building work has added a library (in concept stage when we visited), increased the size of the assembly hall and added some bright top floor rooms 'where you can see the weather approaching right across London.'

Teaching arrangements are 'adaptable to the needs of pupils across a wide range. Children learn at very different rates.' Three ability groups for maths and English from year 2 upwards. Specialist French, music, PE and art teachers.

Plenty of practice for 11+ exams. 'The biggest step we have to ask year 5s and 6s to make is to learn to read the question in detail and use the information they are given. They need to get the habit of precision, of engaging their intelligence.' With his tutoring background, Dr Roche finds preparing children for exams 'exhilarating'. 'Anything that's worth learning is going to be more or less difficult. If we can help children to be patient with themselves we do them a favour.'

High flyers encouraged to fly, whilst 'if you're in year 5 and you've forgotten something you learned in year 2, we're happy to explain it again. A child should feel no shame at not understanding something'. Not a competitive ethos: 'I hope that the slower ones feel just as pleased with their progress as the faster ones.' Great praise from parents of dyslexic children for the care taken in helping them progress. One-to-one tuition, for special needs or EAL, at extra cost.

When we visited, some of year 4 were learning about meditation and Buddhism – 'next week we're going to bring in candles and make a proper temple for a meditation class' – while others were off for games in Wandsworth Park. A year 1 class was having a practical lesson about perspective, whilst some reception children were painting clay pots they had made (school has a kiln). Year 2s were studying the ancient Greeks – 'such fantastic stories'.

Reasonable sized playground behind the school, which also contains the art room (art taken seriously; specialist art teacher) and some sheds about to be replaced by music practice rooms. All the usual sports played in Wandsworth Park, and many inter-school fixtures; after-school clubs (some at extra cost) include cricket, football, judo, netball, swimming, chess, drama and dance.

Lots of chances to act in plays, speak in public, play in the orchestra and in concerts. Children come out 'confident and caring', say parents, tend to 'interview really well', and 'are very proud of their school'. Cosy, nurturing atmosphere; children encouraged to look out for and care for each other.

Bullying 'does sometimes happen: we talk carefully to both sides'. Has never asked anyone to leave on academic grounds, 'though it could happen if a child was interrupting the education of other people, or really had no chance of understanding their work.'

Not a typical London prep. Parents talk of slightly disorganised admin, a great tolerance for eccentricities; a school that really does treat everyone as individuals. 'My two children – one dyslexic and one very academic – both loved it here.'

Rokeby School

George Road, Kingston, Surrey KT2 7PB

Pupils: 370 • Ages: 3–13

Fees: £12,894 – £16,056 pa

Tel: 020 8942 2247
Email: admissions@rokeby.org.uk
Website: www.rokebyschool.co.uk

Headmaster: Since 2007, Mr Jason Peck BEd. Joined school in 1996 as a year 4 and science teacher, becoming deputy head in 2004. Long term association – also has two sons at the school – 'means parents know what they're dealing with,' he thinks. 'He knows the school, how it needs to be run and the traditions,' agreed mother.

Despite influence of several inspirational teachers as he grew up (together with deeply scary cane-wielding head), was initially keen to train as a vet, only to realise during work experience that was thoroughly squeamish, not helped by cow-averse mentor. Absence of James Herriot moments led him instead to a spell travelling and running own business, arriving at Kingston University in mid-20s better versed in ways of world, he feels, than some younger out of the egg fellow students. Didn't necessarily agree with modish teaching theory but was able to rustle up sufficient veneer of enthusiasm to please tutors and perk was instant pupil rapport during classroom experience where proved himself to be an inspirational teacher.

First and only previous post was in tough middle school in Merton. Was surprised, 'perhaps naively so,' at depth of opposition when announced plans to turn to the dark side, aka independent education. Stunned by opportunities, educational and otherwise, and, bar briefly considering more senior science role elsewhere before management beckoned, hasn't looked back since.

Personable, interesting, open, has retained sense of humour despite very considerable challenges, and definitely needs it. After spending first year taking stock, has made several far-reaching changes, broadening curriculum so doesn't operate exclusively on work/sport axis with little in the middle. In addition to making much more of arts, has also encouraged specialist staff to teach all the way down to pre-prep (not right for all, he says; 'those used to teaching senior school pupils aren't always going to be able to cope with very young children').

School has long had first class reputation for securing year in, year out places at KCS and St Paul's, the competitive parents' most wanted establishments, and 'we have to make sure we hit them,' he says. Remains singularly successful even now with record competition, as demonstrated by school's waiting lists (knee deep in every year group).

You wouldn't guess it, however, from levels of parental sniping, which are considerable and take in everything from regular easing out of those deemed not to be making the grade to bullies being rewarded rather than punished, to staff disaffection and defection, and even parents being frightened to speak out in case results in repercussions.

In the far corner, however, are Mr Peck's enthusiasts, equally firm in their praise of his leadership, dismissive of any tales of Flashman-style antics in the ascendance and baffled by them, too. One, with several children at the school, was 'surprised' to hear about negative feedback. 'I love it. I think it does just what it says on tin and tries hard to make nice boys.' Unusual, in fact, to find parental opinion so polarised. Recent school inspectors, we're told, were equally bemused, encountering ferocious criticism in feedback forms, yet unable to substantiate any of points made during their visit.

Only areas that both sides agree on is that some of admin team can be fairly robust to deal with (not unusual, in our experience), and that when it comes to teaching science, Mr Peck is the best in the business (and, fortunately for lucky pupils, who also think he's pretty fab, it's something he still finds time to do, though not as much as he'd like).

Mr Peck accepts that 'as a head, some will like my style, some won't', but points to efforts to improve school communications – regular parent rep forums, often free and frank in style, cover gamut of issues, and complaints procedure is being reviewed. As to pupils being asked to leave, yes, 'if a boy is struggling, we will help him find a better school,' but tiny numbers involved – three in past seven years, isn't, to his mind, a big issue.

School insider wondered if turbulence might be linked to structure of board of governors which could appear to be something of a closed shop – not easy to put yourself forward for election. In the meantime, Mr Peck is keen to get all dissenters to identify themselves and talk to him. 'Much better if they're inside the tent,' he says. We tend to agree.

Entrance: Catchment tends towards Wimbledon and Putney rather than Kingston and up into Teddington/Richmond. Other parents almost incestuously local, with the neighbouring homes on what amounts to a mini-me St George's Hill, Weybridge estate (barrier-only entry to the private roads that surround it – school issues passes to non-residents). Some go further afield. But with the added convenience of next door Holy Cross, a similarly high-performing prep for the sisters, why would you bother?

At 4, start in reception, now non-selective: 'You'd end up testing at 2 – just not possible,' says head. A very few leave at end of year 2 to go either to King's College Junior or St Paul's Junior, paper queues forming to snap up spaces – recently had 80 applications for just four slots. Rest carry on through the school, regular assessments tracking progress based on initial maths and cognitive ability assessments in year 1.

Exit: Doing the business with KCS, St Paul's, Eton, Harrow, Epsom, Dulwich College and Hampton amongst desirable destinations. Head working overtime to ensure that out of many worthy candidates deserving of places, school gets its fair share (and ideally a few more as well). Ups and downs come with the territory (change in senior school admissions teams means entire getting to know you process has to start again from scratch) but evens out over the years. No doubt that it's getting tougher, leading to ever closer bonds with out-of-town schools from Epsom College to Charterhouse. Mr Peck admits to pressure to talk up candidates, but 'relationships with senior schools can only work on trust,' so isn't about to give in to it any time soon.

Remarks: What is it with schools and porthole windows? Nautical imagery? All at sea? 'Friendly underwater feel,' thinks delightful guide, a year 8 veteran of countless school tours ('I've done around 20') who shows us round and whose choicest oft-repeated phrases show every sign of being breathed on and rubbed with a shirtsleeve to bring back the shine.

Not till we reach newest building, recently opened by royalty, featuring said porthole windows, does world-weariness disappear. Can't blame him – place is gorgeous, a new home for lucky pre-preppers, all beautifully behaved; reception children, now liberated from shackles of prescriptive EYFS curriculum, quietly immersed in directed play (teachers and TAs also eat with them to create family atmosphere); year 1 pupils having a terrific time matching (and sampling) food with regions that produce them: potato farls from Ireland and, according to worksheet, fairy cakes from Kingston.

Older pupils get to use gorgeous new performing arts theatre with colossal screen, teachers bravely attempting live link with National Archive, chap dressed as slave intermittently beaming in, hoots and cheers from (otherwise immaculately behaved) year 8 boys marking the frequent occasions when computer said 'no'.

With exception of two science labs (neat collection of animal skulls – real – and Henri the skeleton – plastic), sports hall (clean and white, like the song says, with pitched, pine-lined roof that makes it airier than the norm) and assorted music rooms (tuneful violin solo wafting from windows – standard here is high), most classrooms run length of main building, newer addition running into sober, solid Victorian original. Gradual revamping is subtracting old-style slam lid desks (atmospheric but heavy to move owing to volume of stuff stashed by boys) and adding floor to ceiling wooden units – very swish – either side and over the top of whiteboards, not unlike show home bedroom makeover.

What won't change, however, are the classroom names, each brass plate proudly announcing name of historic figure or – more rarely – veteran member of staff. Renaming opportunities vanishingly rare, accorded only to chosen ones – normally Mr or Ms Chips types combining longevity with universal outpouring of love. Lessons delivered in commendably low-stress style by cheerful-looking teachers 'who just want you to feel OK,' thought pupil and are homily-light, preferring, he thought, to encourage older pupils to realisation of any gaps to be filled.

Class sizes reduced with recent division of year 5 upwards into three forms (was two until year 7), maths and English both set, smaller teaching groups the norm in music, head's goal to do something similar with other subjects including science. Lots of staff enthusiasm, including evangelical DT enthusiast honing latest batch of scholarship hopefuls, charismatic drama specialist encouraging boys to create living poster show as part of term-long project to save fictional circus from closure and art teacher presiding over series of excellent, if sinister, screaming faces (inspired by Messerschmitt – artist rather than German plane).

Few complaints from pupils. Latin 'a bit of a Marmite subject – though I love it.' Otherwise, science loved for 'experiments and interactive games in last five minutes of lesson' and, unusually, pupil praise for teachers' awareness of different learner types – auditory, visual and kinaesthetic.

Many highlights, reckoned parent. 'English and maths are good and the history is inspirational,' said one. Not everyone felt the same, some sensing staff disaffection. If so, were certainly hiding it well. One, with child in pre-prep, was thoroughly enjoying the experience. Another wished 'I'd known about school – wasn't on my radar. If it had been, would definitely have sent him here.' Website, apparently constructed for those already in the know, wouldn't currently help. Though it's not a place lacking confidence – 'the first 125 years' is the title of recent school history – its online parent comms currently needs, and is shortly about to get, an update.

In the flesh, however, plenty of non-airy-fairy robustness, not least when it comes to sanctions and rewards. The aim, says head, is 'to find one thing every boy can do well and help him do it even better.' There's leadership training for years 6 to 8 and masses of good work incentives, from house points to red books (not actually red... or a book) rarer than hens' teeth (once every three years, reckoned one pupil). Presentation by Mr Peck about as big as it gets, only disappointment the disappearance of sweets. Big on detentions, too, or at least the threat of them for range of transgressions. Pays to double check teacher's written homework instructions against what's written on the board and transcribe correct version into homework diary as 'can differ slightly,' thinks pupil.

Pastoral care 'excellent', thinks parent, with head quick to respond to queries, masses of notes all round school commending virtues of good manners (classes and individuals painstaking about standing for visitors) as well as clearly very committed and caring staff. Cheerful learning support teacher runs popular sessions, while library, despite top heavy fact over fiction title weighting, is clearly something of a sanctuary. There's little chatting space and year 8s plan to campaign for old pre-prep classroom to be converted into common room.

Pupils adamant that school won't tolerate bullying, which rarely goes beyond 'boys' banter', said one. On rare occasions it happens, it's a call to the parents and 'immediate' after school detention. Former transgressors might have conduct explained to them, be punished but then, later, be rehabilitated. Though some parents aren't keen, head felt second chances important. 'Who would want a child to feel that their life had already been written off?'

Plenty of opportunities for redemption, sport a major feature, though less dominant now than it used to be. Many more and different sports and far more emphasis on arts now than used to be the case. Teams go all the way down to F in lower years (less so further up the school, but 'everyone still gets games,' said pupil).

Could so easily be swamped by pressure and riven with nerves. And that's just the parents. Despite substantial gripes from some parents, results and atmosphere give it undeniable cachet as prep whose top leavers continue to have the entrée to some of south west London's most sought after senior schools. Currently, worth doing a spot of fact, and faction, checking before you sign up. Under which king, Bezonian, could well apply here.

Rosemead Preparatory School

218

70 Thurlow Park Road, London SE21 8HZ

Pupils: 350 • Ages: 3–11

Fees: £10,272 – £11,736 pa

Tel: 020 8670 5865
Email: admissions@rosemeadprepschool.org.uk
Website: www.rosemeadprepschool.org.uk

Headmaster: Since 2012, Arthur Bray, CertEd from Bristol University (50s). Highly experienced; prior to Rosemead, he was headmaster of GEMS Hampshire (now The Hampshire School, Chelsea) in central London, for 26 years. Previously, at Millfield Junior, he and his wife were both senior houseparents for 10 years. Also formerly chairman of the Independent Schools Association and director of the Independent Schools Council.

Father of two grown-up children whose childhood portraits line the walls of his study – a daughter who is now in a senior post at a London prep school and a son who is a director of a City firm. We found him to be easy to talk to and animated when sharing his knowledge of the nuances of how individual children learn. Perhaps the polished antiques suggest an 'old school' headmaster, but his door was deliberately open onto the corridor, where children milled about chattering between lessons.

There is clearly work ahead, with changes already begun with a view to both academic results and 'preparation for life', but avoiding babies and bathwater. The headmaster tells us he has been very aware of listening first and then implementing, 'evolution not revolution'. One parent commented: 'He is very committed to making Rosemead the best that it can be. He is energetic and determined.'

Retiring in July 2017. His successor will be Mr Philip Soutar BEd, current headmaster of St Wystan's School in Derbyshire, and previously deputy head at Ackworth Junior School.

Head of the pre-prep since 2005, Mary-Elizabeth Everitt BEd Goldsmiths College (40s). She started in the state sector, before teaching for 14 years at Dulwich Prep London. Friendly and quietly spoken, she is focused and clearly made of steely stuff.

Entrance: Describes itself as 'mixed ability'; the majority of children enter the prep via the pre-prep. Children may enter the nursery during the term of their 3rd birthday; at 4+ into reception or at 7+ into year 3. Whilst the nursery is almost fully subscribed, there are sometimes a few places available at the prep. Assessments begin the November prior to entry, with a 45-minute play session for the nursery or reception entry and language and maths exercises for years 1-6.

Means-tested bursary scheme with no limit on numbers. No scholarships. Maximum class size is 22 in the pre-prep and 20 in the prep. No strict sibling policy, but will be taken into account. Unless your family is of Von Trapp proportions, the discount for four or more siblings is unlikely to assist you.

Exit: Pupils exit at 11+, with the school aiming to leave choices 'wide open'. We sense determined parents, as children make three applications on average, for which they are prepared with one-on-one interviews as well as practice papers. Most recently, leavers to Dulwich, Alleyn's, JAGS, Whitgift, Trinity, Emanuel, Streatham & Clapham, Sydenham High, Bromley High, St Dunstan's and Royal Russell. Since Mr Bray's arrival, there has been a rise in both places offered and a higher ratio of awards, particularly academic, art and sport.

Remarks: A traditional curriculum ticks all boxes, but there is modernising afoot, which is going down well. The head cites updating the texts used in English, and in maths a new online tutor sets tasks at an appropriate level for each child, 30 minutes in class and 30 minutes at home each week, with parents able to dip in any time online to see how they are doing.

A carefully thought through decision to switch from the traditional French to the more globally relevant Spanish has been pretty universally accepted and lessons have been doubled to twice a week. Spanish commences in the pre-prep with singing, stories and movement. Next in line for overhaul will be history, geography and science, including an eagerly-awaited science lab. New ICT facilities have arrived including class sets of chromebooks and interactive screens. Humanities are supported by a wide array of trips, and highlights of the year are cross-curricular theme days and celebrations.

One of the first things the headmaster instigated is a new means of assessment, and reporting which looks at core skills such as concentration and organisation skills, as well as subject-specific scoring, all of which can be far more useful than a paragraph of commentary.

Staff mix – 18 per cent of staff in place for more than 10 years. Not a high turnover, but the headmaster has made appointments since arriving, ensuring there is now one male teacher per year group at the prep. Reports from some parents are not spotless – but others impress upon us the warm atmosphere between staff and pupils: one mentioned the 'strong emotions shown by all of the year 6 children as they leave the teachers they have grown fond of'.

With three classes per year in the prep, the class groupings sometimes change after year 3, once teachers have been able to assess how children work together. This can be a tad unpopular, as it isn't necessarily about friendship groups. However, classes are fixed by year 5. Setting for maths from year 3.

The anti-bullying policy has been carefully reviewed, with a buddy scheme throughout the school and year 6 visiting to read to the younger ones, and sharing special assemblies such as that for Chinese New Year.

Learning support, termed enrichment, has six staff, two of them full time, with one-to-one support for just under 10 per cent of the school. Very small number with EAL.

The fenced playground, high up above the street, is the venue for learning a variety of ball skills. Years 1 to 6 have a weekly PE lesson, a swimming lesson and a full games afternoon. There are two male PE teachers, and a female director of PE. With children taken to nearby Dulwich sports club and Rosendale playing fields for football, hockey, netball, rugby, tennis, cricket and athletics and making use of Crystal Palace's national training facilities for swimming from year 3, one parent commented, 'It's a small school with minimum on-site sports facilities, but they seem to offer a lot and children don't know or care that the sports grounds aren't owned by the school.' Rosemead regularly has children taking part at the ISA finals, both as individuals and in teams, and recently at competed at national level in football.

How high pressure is it? A parent who has had three children through the school reported: 'I think Rosemead gets the balance right – one of the reasons we chose it... the amount of homework is about right, more than your average state primary, but not as much as some of the more high pressure private schools in the area.'

Parents commented to us in no uncertain terms that art has been a real weak spot in the past, but we visited the large, new dedicated art studio and saw the specialist teacher in action – a highly talented former assistant from the pre-prep praised by staff and parents. The school now employs a local artist to take groups for sketching and painting, and pupils have been awarded 19 art scholarships to senior schools in the last three years.

R

The prep has more than its fair share of violinists, as all year 1 at the pre-prep learn violin in groups. Some 150 children have individual instrumental tuition, with several reaching grade 5 by year 6. There is a large school orchestra and two school choirs; ensemble clubs for cello, brass, strings and recorder; and an 'electric fusion band' which plays at the annual Dulwich Festival. A musical highlight is the major concert at the end of the spring term. One parent commented on the 'superb Christmas carol service in local church... very impressive'.

Clubs – morning, lunch-time and after-school – offer mainly sporty and musical options, with a good show of language clubs for Spanish, French and Russian. Increasingly, this is a school for working parents and the school is well set up to offer a full day from 8am to 6pm. Clubs start in year 1, most end at 4.30pm, and these can combine with after-school care for all, provided by a third-party, Kids City, with staff chaperoning children between sites and taking any parental emergencies in their stride.

This was a school in transition which, as anyone who has had the builders in knows, can be painful and disruptive but well worth the effort. When we visited the façade was covered in scaffolding, with smart new year 6 classrooms just revealed, together with a new library, bigger dining hall and ICT suites. Meanwhile, downstairs everything looked a bit shabby and utilitarian.

What will hold the school together as well as the headmaster are the parents – due to its strong sense of community as well as unique governing structure. Already established as an independent school for 70 years, in 1975 a group of parents took over the managing of the school and it became a limited company with an all-parent management team. It is now a non-profit making charitable trust. All but one of the governing body are parents of current pupils.

Notable and somewhat off-putting is the location on the edge of Dulwich – a bit of a no-man's land on the traffic-heavy South Circular road – however, we did note that once inside we could not hear the traffic and the location between two overground stations is convenient for commuting quickly into town. The prep looks rather like a tall, red-brick Victorian London school building, but was actually a rehearsal space for the Old Vic theatre, hence the school hall resembling a proper theatre complete with fixed stage.

Parents say, 'Children work hard, concentrate and give of their best.' And our visit backs this up. The atmosphere was calm and industrious, perhaps particularly due to year 6 exams looming. One parent described it as 'a down-to-earth, happy school that will offer an all-round education and ensure a good secondary transfer without putting children under huge pressure in the early years.'

Two-thirds of families live close by, often walking to school; the rest come from all over south London, some from as far as Bromley and Elephant and Castle. This is a school for active parents who want to get involved – fundraising isn't just for external charitable projects but for valuable extras around the school. Talking of active, a team of Rosemead mothers recently rowed the Channel.

The heads report being bowled over by the response to their appeals for help: turning a piece of wasteground into a sunny little allotment for the pre-prep over the weekend, or creating a rota of volunteer librarians for the new prep library. All of which builds a real sense of community. Parents are a mixed and reportedly friendly crowd – we certainly saw gaggles lingering post drop-off – but particularly evidenced by the Easter family ski trip, which is not just for pupils but unusually everyone: parents, siblings, grandparents, old boys and girls and their families too.

The pretty purple uniforms are a delight, but the stand-out feature of the pre-prep is the charming church building, sympathetically developed to create high ceilinged classrooms, with beautiful arches and bits of stained glass – a lovely space in which to work.

The pre-prep has assistants in every class and high staff ratios in the nursery. School commences in earnest at reception with some parents wishing for a greater emphasis on play: 'hardly any toys in the classroom, much like year 1'. Reception is very different in feel to the boisterous fun we saw in the nursery, but the head points out the gentle start with just 20 minutes of phonics a day compared with an hour in year 1.

It seems to be different things to different families – the pre-prep's church building brings back fond memories for some parents of what a first school should be like; more pragmatically, it could well be a port in a storm when faced with the ultra-competitive local options at 4+.

Royal Russell School

    219

Coombe Lane, Croydon, Surrey CR9 5BX

Pupils: 971; 126 boarders • Ages: 3-18 (boarding from 11) • Sixth form: 177

Fees: Day £17,190; Boarding £25,155 – £33,975 pa

Tel: 020 8657 4433
Email: admissions@royalrussell.co.uk
Website: www.royalrussell.co.uk

Headmaster: Since 2011, Mr Christopher Hutchinson BMet Sheffield, PGCE Cambridge FRSA (40s). He started his teaching career at Clifton College in Bristol, where he was head of physics and a housemaster. Thence to Wellington College as head of science and assistant director of studies, before taking over the headship of Newcastle School for Boys. Married to Alex, a fellow science teacher, he enjoys singing, squash, tennis and gardening. Committed to providing a stimulating classroom education alongside a robust co-curricular programme. He has been officer commanding the CCF and also master in charge of rowing.

Head of junior school: Since 2009, Mr James Thompson BA QTS (30s). Previously director of studies at Kingswood Prep, Bath, and then deputy head at Ardingly College Prep School. Married to Viv, head of a nursery school in Notting Hill Gate; prior to that she ran the marketing for the junior school. They have two young daughters who both attend the junior school. Mr Thompson initially trained as a PE teacher; his other specialist subjects are mathematics and geography. His passion for sports rubs off on the school – a keen skier, he has introduced an annual family skiing trip. He is also involved with a large charity, assisting them in running sporting events, and umpires for premier league hockey.

Academic matters: Small classes of around 18 in junior school, mixed ability, with setting for mathematics from year 3; staff aware of the need to include differentiation in all the lessons. Additional support is arranged as required in small groups or one-to-one lessons. ICT is used across the curriculum to enrich lessons; everyone is taught to touch type on specially designed colour-coded keyboards. Head keen to involve parents in their children's education – runs regular workshops to give parents a good understanding of subjects children are studying and encourages them to come in and work with reading groups. Once a term homework is suspended for a week for a creative home/school project, the idea being to get the children thinking and investigating different topics and ideas, then creating a piece of artwork. Children learn Spanish in years 3 and 4 and French in years 5 and 6, so they have a good grounding in two foreign languages ready for senior school.

Exam pass rates generally improving – 45 per cent A*/A grades at A level and 40 per cent A*/A at GCSE in 2016. Mathematics is one of the school's strengths with a number of pupils taking GCSE a year early and AS in year 11, carrying on to A level and further mathematics and the sixth form. A flexible approach is taken to setting; most classes are mixed ability and pupils move into sets for maths, English, science, and modern languages for GCSE. Good choice of GCSEs offered. Pupils can study dual award or three separate sciences, although only two languages – French and Spanish – available.

Recently upgraded ICT – everything is interactive with a parent/pupil portal which enables school computer system to be accessed from home. According to parents, good team of male and female teachers from the more mature to young sporty and artistic types. Healthy turnover sees new blood and new ideas coming in each year. Refreshingly unfazed by the league tables, staff are committed to ensuring every pupil reaches their potential. Whilst the school is academically rigorous, a focus on producing broad, well rounded young people.

ESOL tuition is included in the fees and is available for pupils whose first language is not English. Strong learning support department, a charge is made for one-to-one lessons. All departments run lunchtime and after-school clinics offering additional support to those who require it. Beautiful library and sixth form centre with small classes and individual attention. Added value is outstanding; sixth formers feed back very positively.

Games, options, the arts: Arts strong all round. Flourishing music department has earned an international reputation, orchestras and choirs travel far and wide to perform. Over 200 ABRSM exams taken by pupils each year – needless to say, pass rate is 100 per cent. Musical experiences are enhanced by workshops, excursions and working with professional musicians. Enviable suite of rooms, including a recording studio, lovely light practice rooms and a 200 seat concert venue. Exceptional music in junior school, 70 per cent of children learning an instrument, in addition to class music. Year 1s learn the recorder and the following year everybody learns keyboard and a string instrument. An orchestra, rock group, jazz and choirs all perform regularly at school and local events.

Lively drama department teaches all age groups, giving pupils the opportunity to try their hand at acting, directing and being light and sound technicians, whilst developing public speaking skills and learning to work cooperatively. Theatre history is also taught and pupils can become involved in helping to make costumes and set designing. Theatre groups visit the school to perform and run workshops, also after-school drama classes and trips to local and West End performances. Pupils benefitting from the recently opened superb performing arts centre. Martin Clunes and Naoko Mori are former pupils. Inspiring light airy art studios where students benefit from expert teaching and a great range of resources.

Just about everything is on offer from traditional sports to archery and windsurfing. Eager representatives at local, regional and national level sports teams and events, school and house matches – being physically active and enjoying sport considered part of pupil well-being. Lots of fun and successes. Teams are coached by outside specialists as well as in-house PE teachers. Extensive playing fields and courts of every shape and size, cross-country course through their own woodland, indoor swimming pool and sports complex, where £2m refurbishment was recently completed. All sporting facilities are well utilised and operate as a local sports centre for the public, parents and local clubs, adding to the community feel of the school. Community link with Coloma Convent for CCF. The range of clubs, societies and activities is almost unlimited. Large number of senior pupils participate in the Modern United Nations programme and the school hosts one of the biggest UK conferences.

Boarding: Boarding houses – one for girls and two for boys – have been refurbished and a full programme of activities runs at weekends especially Sunday afternoons, from spy games (start of year induction activity) to craft. Plenty of excursions, from Tower Bridge Experience to activity weekends – go-karting reckoned to be highlight of the year. Everyone encouraged to join in house competitions. Most boarders from overseas (Europe, Asia and the Far East), so strong multi-cultural dimension. Each boarding house has day pupils attached, too; they can arrive for breakfast and stay for supper.

Background and atmosphere: Hidden from the public eye beyond a long driveway lies a great school for the 21st century offering a remarkable number of opportunities for all tastes and talents. Once thought rather down in the doldrums, now offers stiff competition to other south London and Surrey schools. Open-minded and flexible in its general approach, the atmosphere is vibrant and purposeful, a very busy place. The senior management are thought to be caring and in touch with the requirements of today's parents and pupils. An optional extended school day.

Established in 1853 at New Cross for the sons and daughters of textile workers – one of the earliest co-ed schools. In 1924 purchased the Ballard's estate, an extensive, wooded, 110-acre site, which now houses both the junior and senior schools. Long history of royal patronage – the present queen has visited the school four times since the 1950s and the Earl of Wessex opened the performing arts centre. Lots of new buildings have popped up recently: a rolling rebuilding programme to upgrade and redevelop is under way and some rather unattractive 1960s buildings have been pulled down and replaced. Christian based, now multi-faith and boasts its own recently restored chapel – much of the original stonework carved by Eric Gill in the 1920s.

Junior school accommodated in its own buildings, on a lovely rural site opposite the senior school. Classrooms are bright and spacious, along with three well planned playground areas including an adventure playground set into the woodland. Brand new purpose built early learning centre and outdoor nursery classroom. Lovely child-friendly library – each class has allotted library periods and storytelling sessions. Classrooms are well resourced, the juniors have their own science lab and pupils enjoy the senior school facilities increasingly as they go through the age groups, including the performing arts centre, indoor pool and other extensive on site sports facilities (including new all-weather pitch).

Pastoral care, well-being and discipline: House system, nine houses, six exclusively for day pupils with sitting rooms for each year group to relax and socialise in during breaktimes and after school. Supervised homework sessions run each evening and day pupils can stay at school until 9pm (evening meals are included in the fees). Prefect system with head and deputy head boy and girl; each house has its own head of house and sports captains, so a large number of pupils are involved with aiding the day to day running and school functions.

Pastoral staff pride themselves on their knowledge of the needs of young people and understanding the whole child. Housemasters and mistresses together with the chaplain are always available to talk, pupils are treated as individuals and staff go out of their way to help sort out any problems. Small tutor groups also ensure parents and pupils are kept well informed about academic and personal development. School rules regularly reviewed, predominantly in place for everybody's security and safety. Quite strict uniform code and tip top behaviour expected at all times. Pupils tell us the food is delicious, plenty of choices and everybody eats together – the sizable dining hall provides the perfect place to enjoy the company of others.

Pupils and parents: From around 20-mile radius between Clapham Junction and the M25, Bromley, Dulwich, Wimbledon and Croydon. Fortuitously, the tramstop is opposite the entrance, making it an easy journey for many. Folk from all walks of life – many different types and characters, first-time buyers to children of old Russellians. Interesting mix of nationalities, the sixth form being particularly popular with foreign students. Very active PTA helps to organise the numerous social activities, car boot sales and fundraising for charity.

Entrance: At 3 and 4+, selective (informal teacher observational assessment) entry to the nursery and early years classes. At 7+ children are invited to spend a day at the school for an entry assessment to gauge their potential.

At 11+ exam (English, maths and computer-based verbal reasoning or cognitive abilities test), interview and reference from previous school. Small number of places are usually available at 13+ and 16+ for sixth form.

Exit: At 11+ most (82 per cent in 2016) continue through to the senior school. A few leave for local grammars – Wallington, Wilsons or Archbishop Tenison, Bromley. At 16+, around a quarter move on, a few to local colleges to study vocational courses. At 18+, all to university or art colleges, an increasing number of students choosing law, economics and veterinary sciences. One to Cambridge in 2016; Leeds, Manchester, Bath and UCL popular.

Money matters: All applicants for year 7 and year 9 are considered for academic scholarships via their performance in the entrance exam. Further scholarships are available for year 12 on the basis of GCSE results. Also junior, senior and sixth form art, music and drama scholarships. A limited number of means-tested bursaries. Five per cent discount for siblings.

Remarks: Confident and socially accomplished pupils, proud of their increasing successes across the curriculum. Solid reputation for producing cheerful young people, well-prepared for successful futures at university and in the workplace.

The Russell Primary School

Petersham Road, Richmond, Surrey TW10 7AH

Pupils: 296 • Ages: 3–11

Tel: 020 8940 1446
Email: info@russell.richmond.sch.uk
Website: www.russell.richmond.sch.uk

Headteacher: Since 2011, Samantha Leir, previously deputy at the school. Her first teaching job was at Russell in 1994. From there she went to work for the local authority as a lead literacy teacher. Returned to Russell as deputy in 2003. 'She's always been a huge part of the school,' said one parent.

Two sons who both attend schools in Surrey. Grew up in Wales, the only girl with four brothers, so rugby is a big part of her life. Supports the Ospreys (Swansea). Her sons and husband also play rugby. She enjoys reading, cooking and swimming.

Entrance: Currently one form entry. For nursery places apply direct to nursery and for school through local authority.

Exit: Most go on to Grey Court in Ham, a couple to local grammars (Tiffin Girls' and Tiffin School), a handful to independent or church schools (Christ's, The Green School, Gumley), or to Waldegrave School for Girls if they live in Twickenham.

Remarks: Set in four acres of grounds, feels more like a campus university than a primary school. While we were being shown round by the head we bumped into students with a teacher doing orienteering! 'We have more square footage of land per child than any other school in Richmond,' the head told us proudly.

A large single storey 1950s block houses the nursery. The building is rather tired looking, but colourful wall displays and mobiles brighten up the space. Nearby is the unit for children with severe learning difficulties. The school has specialist provision for up to five children at key stage 1 (aged 4 to 7) on the autistic spectrum. The unit is staffed by specialist teachers.

Originally two schools (Petersham and Orchard Junior) built in the 1950s, they joined together to form the Russell School in 1980. The original buildings are therefore a bit scruffy but the outdoor space more than makes up for them and a new school building is under construction. There is a nature area with ponds, an outdoor classroom, an allotment. They even have their own orchard and keep chickens. Hot school dinners are cooked fresh on the premises.

There are Gifted and Talented groups for maths and writing. A Battle of the Books competition is available for gifted readers in year 2 and year 4.

Music is important here. A specialist music teacher is at the school for half of the week. She is also responsible for the school choir and orchestra. Children can learn recorder, flute, guitar, violin and even the harp. There are trips to the Royal Festival Hall and each year the school takes part in the O2 Young Voices competition. 'My son was so proud to be representing the school at the 02 centre,' explained one parent.

Drama is also strong, and as well as a big Christmas production and a year 6 performance (last year it was based around the theme of Pompeii), there is a talent show for the whole school.

A recent appointment is the deputy head, who leads sport at the school. Lunchtime and after-school clubs include gymnastics, athletics, basketball, football, netball, judo and golf, as well as chess, Spanish and art. A private company (Fit for Sport) runs a breakfast club from 7.45am to 8.30am, and after-school care from 3.15pm to 6.00pm, both at extra cost.

Parents are drawn from across the social spectrum. Some children live in the huge mansions on Petersham Road while others are drawn from the council estate over towards Ham. The PTA organises social events and parents are encouraged to come into school for special assemblies. 'Since Mrs Leir took over we feel much more welcome at the school,' said one parent.

It feels like a village school and it's amazing to have such space on the outskirts of London. If you can turn a blind eye to the state of some of the buildings, then you'll feel very smug if you can manage to get a place for your child at Russell. Even more so when rebuild is completed.

Sacred Heart High School (Hammersmith)

212 Hammersmith Road, London W6 7DG

Pupils: 960 • Ages: 11–18 • Sixth form: 300 • RC

Tel: 020 8748 7600
Email: info@sacredh.lbhf.sch.uk
Website: www.sacredhearthighschoolhammersmith.org.uk

Headteacher: Since 2014, Mrs Marian Doyle MA NPQH (50s). Previously deputy head since 1997. Before that, she taught English and RE at Haggerston School, Hackney, Phoenix High School, Hammersmith and latterly Holland Park School, Notting Hill Gate. A world away from the previous head (a deeply traditional woman who reigned for 23 years with what girls describe as a combination of awe and fear), Doyle is softer around the edges and fresher in her outlook. Not only does she look more modern (she wore fabulous killer heels when we met her), but the school itself feels more alive, with walls now adorned with colourful canvases of the girls at work and many inspirational quotes. School systems (from admin through to bullying policies) have also had an overhaul, thanks to the head's key vision of the school being run seamlessly. A parent herself, she is big on boundaries and 'tough love', but is also approachable and smiley, and is regularly seen around the school, popping into lessons and talking to the girls at break times. 'She is very keen to make sure that we like it here,' said one girl.

Academic matters: Impressive results, by anyone's standards. In 2016, 85 per cent achieved five or more A*-C passes at GCSE including maths and English, 51 per cent A*/A grades. New sixth form opened in 2013. In 2016 A level results 61 per cent A*-B.

Maths the strongest subject, followed by English. RE, history and geography also stand out. In terms of languages, Spanish and French are on offer, and a group of around 15 girls are put forward for Latin GCSE, which they study at St Paul's. Science highly promoted, with 60 per cent doing science and maths post-16.

Each year group has five form groups, with setting across all subjects from year 7 into five or six groups, depending on the subject, with plenty of flexibility to move about as necessary. Class sizes vary, with many as large as 35.

Expectation under new headship for all pupils to do at least two after-school clubs (which they call enrichment), which has been accommodated by changes to the school day (which now comprises five 60 minute lessons and finishes at 3.05pm) and an expectation that staff stay longer to run these clubs on Tuesdays and Wednesdays. Outside facilitators brought in too. Subjects include all the usual suspects such as choir, sport, maths challenge, science clubs, drama etc as well as more unusual offerings including yoga and gardening.

One full-time staff member (qualified teacher, as well as a dyslexic specialist; has the national SENCo leadership award) is responsible for SEN, although no special unit. She puts in place three tiered levels of support – firstly, qualified teachers' support in mainstream, with the aim that specialist subject teachers can support in their areas of expertise; second (if necessary) additional support before and after school; finally (again if necessary) involvement of school counsellor or outside services, such as speech and language and occupational therapy. Difficulties catered for include dyslexia and other needs that are physical, such as hearing loss or severe long-term conditions, communication and language difficulties, ADD, ADHD. School also claims there are some serious mental health concerns. School reckoned there were 65 in total with SEN when we visited, five of whom are statemented/with EHC plan. Very rarely, if a child's needs cannot be fully met, the school works closely with parents and the local authority to find alternatives. Help for gifted and talented through a range of enrichment and additional opportunities.

'The help my daughter has received for her dyslexia has been second to none, including trying out a range of different techniques, and the communication with us has been excellent too,' said one parent. 'Her self-confidence has rocketed and she's doing really well in exams.'

School is designated as a national teaching school, leading the West London Teaching School Alliance, which means working closely with 28 other primary and secondary schools in west London to improve standards of teaching and share best practice on issues including initial teacher training, professional development, research and development, succession planning and mentoring. Head says it's her vision for the school to become known for its drive for excellence. 'I put the same level of effort into training and development for the staff as I do teaching the girls, because I believe the two are inextricably linked,' she says.

Although the teaching staff we saw were a pretty glum-looking lot (particularly unwelcoming when we went near their classrooms), girls are clearly impressed with their level of commitment. 'Lessons are really engaging,' said one. 'They make sure nobody gets missed,' added another. Indeed, girls are regularly reminded of a quote from one of the founders: 'For the sake of one child, I would have founded the society,' after which they're told, 'You are the one child.'

Games, options, the arts: For a small inner-city site, they certainly pack in the sports facilities, all of which are utilised to the max, with the girls doing at least two hours of PE per week and with the option of PE as both a GCSE and A level subject. In addition to the two tennis/netball courts (which double up as rounders pitches), there's a gym and activity studio for the likes of dance, pilates and yoga. The new £8m sports and science block – imminent when we visited – is home to a massive sports hall that can facilitate three teaching groups simultaneously. 'It's four times the size of our current gym,' enthused one girl. Also new is a running track and outdoor gym of the ilk you see in parks, all of which means the long-standing link with Hammersmith and Fulham Health and Fitness Centre will start to diminish. Rowing, softball, basketball and volleyball on offer, along with all the usual suspects, and after-school clubs include street dance, yoga, cheerleading, fencing, trampolining and football, among others. Plenty of inter-house sports competitions, the highlight of which is the annual sports day held at St Paul's fields (originally owned by Sacred Heart but sadly they sold it off years ago), and the school has increasing success in the borough in hockey, rounders, netball and athletics.

No shortage of peripatetic teachers for musical instruments including piano, flute, trombone, drums etc. There are junior and senior choirs, various ensembles, and the girls talk highly of the general music classes, as well as about the annual Battle of the Bands. 'Music is really good fun here,' one girl told us. We particularly like the random pianos in the corridors, all of which girls say get played regularly for practice, making for a lovely ambience when walking through the corridors.

Links to various theatres, including the Donmar, and the drama school LAMDA, give a flavour of how seriously drama is taken here, with annual all-school productions such as Hairspray and Annie. Art and DT studios are spacious, with state-of-the-art equipment and some extremely talented artwork produced by the girls. No cookery on offer when we visited, but this is being re-examined.

Background and atmosphere: The school, or 'convent of the Sacred Heart,' is built on a site steeped in Catholic history dating back to the early 17th century. During its 330 year history, four different orders of nuns have taught here. Today's Tudor-style, red-brick buildings were built in the late 19th century and there's no shortage of religious reminders inside, notably the huge, austere-looking religious murals all the way along the wide, spacious corridors of the cloisters, as well as the chapel, which doubles up as the main school hall. 'We have daily morning prayers,' said one girl, 'but apart from that, the presence of Catholicism in our everyday life is through the school's ethos and values.' 'The school provides a good moral compass, but there's no hard-line religion,' agreed a parent, who added that there's a sensible and modern approach to sex education too, within the context of the Catholic Church teaching.

In 1948 the convent school was reorganised as a secondary grammar school, continuing as a grammar school until 1976, when it received its first comprehensive intake. The school then took on academy status in 2012.

Most pupils use the entrance on Bute Gardens, whilst sixth form and visitors use the main entrance on Hammersmith Road, where you'll be greeted by a single receptionist behind an oak veneer desk and a couple of rows of cream leather chairs. The hum of traffic is loud, but it doesn't take many more steps into the school to feel as if you're in an oasis of calm – not at all what you'd expect from an inner-city comp. Even during class switch-over times, when the extra-wide corridors are packed with animated girls, it somehow manages to avoid the feeling of chaos that many other schools have (probably helped by the very strictly policed one-way walking system).

A steep stone staircase leads down to the converted basement, which forms the buzzy social space and café for sixth formers. The rest of the girls eat in the dining room which, head admits, 'could be more funky' and where the 'food is 'ok.' Those who have packed lunch eat at temporary tables that are laid out daily in the wide corridors.

Asked what they'd improve, girls told us they could do with more quiet study space, especially in sixth form. 'We are allowed to use the library,' said one, 'but it's not ideal.' Indeed, when we visited, the library was being used by an entire class and was by no means quiet, although in fairness it is two-story, with doors shutting out such sound on the top level. Well-stocked and imaginatively designed, the library is also very light and inviting. Classrooms are bog-standard, with stand-out facilities for drama and music. Great excitement about the new science block, which will transform this current provision beyond recognition.

Girls encouraged to be proactive, rather than spoon fed, with lots of emphasis on them doing things, rather than talking about things. When we visited, a group of girls had gone to Mexico to rebuild houses for those in poverty. A further group of six girls went to Lourdes with the Handicapped Children Pilgrimage Trust. Impressive amounts of charitable work overall, including £10,500 raised for a sister school in Kenya for disabled children via activities including sponging teachers, making teachers eat chilli, sponsored walks and rowing the distance of the Channel in the gym. School is also part of a worldwide network of schools in 45 countries which creates opportunities such as a head girls' meet up to discuss leadership ideas and pupil exchanges across different countries.

Plenty of school trips to universities, BBC, Houses of Parliament, businesses including JP Morgan and all the usual museums and art galleries. Residential trips largely music-related, including to places such as Austria and Paris, whilst whole school European ski trips take place each year.

Strong student voice, with elected student members having requested that the science garden become more appealing, as well as having offered responses to the school's Equality Plan.

Pastoral care, well-being and discipline: Although current head is considered 'less scary and strict' than her predecessor, she is equally dedicated to high standards, pointing out that your daughter will be in detention if she arrives even five seconds after the bell goes. 'The point is that in professional life, if you had a meeting at 10am, you wouldn't arrive just after 10am,' she explains. 'We also want a calm start to the day.' It clearly works – there are few detentions in reality, with the girls we talked to never having been late in their entire six years. Other zero-tolerance aspects of school life include school uniform (especially length of skirts) and good behaviour, although pastoral care is highly praised here, with all the parents we talked to calling it 'very nurturing and caring.' Pupils are frequently reminded they can talk to form teachers, non-teaching pastoral support managers, the chaplain or two full-time school counsellors. In addition, there are strong links with Child and Adolescent Mental Health Services (CAMHS) and the charity Mind. 'One of my daughters went off the rails and had some counselling, which promptly nipped it in the bud,' said one parent. Head is by no means resting on her laurels, though. 'Like most schools,' she says, 'we have seen an increase in mental health issues and are very aware we need to talk about it in a more real and open way.' Peer mentoring scheme between year 7s and year 11s encourages cross-year relationships and older girls to take a leadership role.

Pupils and parents: This is top of the state school list for many families, not only in west London, but as far as Islington (with Tony Blair's daughter being the obvious example). Although it's non-selective and fully comprehensive, the majority of families are middle-class and with English as a first language. That said, there is genuine poverty among some of the girls, with head reporting that this is increasingly the case. 'We have 14 per cent identified as having free school meals and many others with an income only just above the threshold where parents struggle to make ends meet,' she says.

Strong PA and links between parents generally. 'It's unusually sociable among parents for an inner-city comprehensive, with lots of mums' nights out, quiz nights and family-focused activities,' said one parent. Good communications between school and parents, although some parents think the annual parents' evening, which falls in the summer term, is far too late in the academic year.

Entrance: Parents keep an extremely beady eye on the admissions policy of this heavily oversubscribed school, and many are unswerving in their commitment to find some way for their daughter to become one of the approximately 198 pupils to enter year 7. But you'll need to start early, as all girls need to have been baptised before they were 6 months old (although we did to talk to one parent who did it slightly later due to illness in the family) and to have attended one of 11 feeder schools, all named on the website. If you meet all the criteria, you won't need to sweat so much about how close you are to the school. Be warned that siblings don't automatically gain entry and are sometimes turned away. Separate admissions procedures for girls with an SEN statement or the new Education, Health and Care plan. Parents praise the transition from primary school. Up to places for 40 external applicants to sixth form, for which you'll need eight A*-Cs, including subject-specific requirements.

Exit: Clear expectation to remain at the school to do A levels, with 80 out of 164 staying on in the first year of sixth form and 145 internal applicants for 2016 in the second year. Others commonly go onto Cardinal Vaughan or The London Oratory, with a handful going into the independent sector, including UCS, St Benedict's and Latymer Upper. One Oxbridge place amongst the first year 13 students – engineering at Oxford – with plenty of places at other top universities such as Bristol, Southampton, Leeds, Nottingham, York, Liverpool, Manchester to study eg English, history and medicine.

Remarks: An exceptional and relatively small inner-city state school that provides girls who are prepared to behave impeccably with a traditional education and sense of community that will set them up for life.

St Anthony's Preparatory School

222

90 Fitzjohn's Avenue, London NW3 6NP

Pupils: 310 • Ages: 4-13 • RC

Fees: £17,685 – £18,075 pa

Tel: 020 7431 1066
Email: headmaster@stanthonysprep.co.uk
Website: www.stanthonysprep.org.uk

Headmaster: Since 2010, Paul Keyte MA. Educated at Bloxham and Oriel College, Oxford, where he read philosophy and theology, graduating with a first. Fell into teaching during his postgraduate research (on Wittgenstein and Kierkegaard). 'I thought I'd teach for a couple of years before going back,' he says, but, instead, became hooked. Started out at Dulwich, where he taught philosophy and RE, before becoming head of liberal studies. Then to King's College Wimbledon, where he set up the philosophy and RE department and was under master (pastoral). 'You have to understand the shadow side, the theft and the bullying.' Then, senior master academic at Winchester and director of studies, deputy head at Highgate and at South Hampstead.

St Anthony's is his first prep school. ('I was attracted to the job because it was big enough to be interesting yet small enough for me to be a father.') An undoubted enthusiast, he remains passionate about teaching ('I feel anchored in the classroom'), and continues to teach RS to year 8 and 'learning enrichment' to all. Knows virtually all his pupils by name. A convert to Catholicism and married to a Catholic (who teaches at South Hampstead), he has one son (now at the school). Outside (and often imported) interests include singing, Schubert ('I learnt German to understand it better'), musicals and Leeds United (much to his pupils' amusement). Energetic, enthusiastic and intellectual, yet accessible, parents feel fortunate to have him. 'He's incredibly supportive and gracious,' said one parent. 'He's the reason we chose the school,' said another.

Entrance: Two form entry at reception. Tour, then register, as early as possible. Some assessment places reserved for Catholics, who also get priority on waiting lists. All boys are interviewed. 'I'm looking for teachability and sociability,' says Mr Keyte. 'They have to be able to cope with the pace and adapt to our style of teaching. We're not competitive, but we're famous for creating independent learners.' Boys from about 25 feeder nurseries, but Catholics have often attended nearby St Mary's or St Christina's in St John's Wood.

Exit: In large numbers to UCS, City and Mill Hill, then everywhere with chunks to Highgate, Haberdashers' and Merchant Taylors', a solid sprinkling to Westminster and St Paul's. Increasing numbers applying to top boarding schools (head has links with Winchester, Charterhouse et al). Plenty of scholarships, including for sport and music. No one is ever asked to leave. 'That's our duty, once they're here,' says the head. Occasionally, some may decide that the academic pace is not for them and are 'gently helped' to find somewhere else.

Remarks: The head's heavyweight presence sets the tone and is a good match with the school's highly qualified staff (many with Oxbridge degrees and interesting first careers).The school is split into two sites across the road from each other, each with its own spacious Victorian building. In the junior school (reception to year 3), you'll find a sweeping staircase, turn-of-the-century tiling, large light classrooms and a good-sized dining room (which doubles as an assembly and concert hall). Class size is kept to a maximum of 16-20. Specialist subject teaching in French and music from reception. Mandarin from year 1. 'We aim to send them from the junior school happy and well adjusted, able to cope with the demands of exams,' says the head. 'We're building the personality rather than drilling.' But skills are thoroughly inculcated. 'In the junior years,' said one mother of two, 'the teaching is very precise. They really get the handwriting and spelling under control, which reaps benefits as they get older.'

The move to the senior school in year 4 is accompanied by greater subject specialisation, more male teachers and recently renovated premises. Some setting in maths, flexible setting elsewhere. With increasing pre-testing in years 6/7, has introduced more specialist maths and English teaching. No scholarship set, but plenty of 'learning enrichment.' 'Exams require sophisticated skills and we introduce enrichment early on,' says the head. Philosophy, Latin, Greek, Arabic and now programming and robotics all on offer. The head also runs lunch-hour discussion groups which any boy can attend. Parents feel he has got a firm grip on the rapidly changing exam landscape. 'The school used to be not quite as rigorous,' said one mother, 'but now the head is really on top of it.'

Good support for SEN with two specialists, one with expertise in dyscalculia. Sophisticated early screening identifies those who may require additional support. Discreet withdrawal to two small bright dedicated classrooms for those who struggle as well as those who need stretch.

The arts, now as always, remain core to what this school is about. The head has tripled the number of music lessons and managed to acquire a baby grand as well as introduce a music studio. 'My head of music says, "No boy leaves here who couldn't do grade 5 theory",' he says happily. A fair number are gifted musicians, one carrying off a recent Eton music scholarship, another singing with the ENO. Outside school hours, boys are given plenty of encouragement with the school providing the weekend venue for Trinity Laban's by-audition-only classes. Other art forms not neglected, with a big annual Shakespeare production and two weeks of film-making post common entrance. A wide range of hobbies and clubs – logic and puzzle, general knowledge, chess, dance, touch typing – cover a range of enthusiasms (the lunch-time chess players packed out one classroom on our visit).

Not traditionally known as a 'sporty school', but the head is keen to give sport an increasingly important role. 'This is one area I'm working on developing. I'm passionate about what sport brings to children.' Traditional carousel of rugby, football, hockey, cricket, played twice weekly at Brondesbury, a 10-minute coach ride away. On site, the school has its own pool and two good-sized playgrounds. At St Anthony's, however, sport is as much about taking part as winning, with as many boys as possible participating. 'I'd rather the boys lost nobly and honourably than win for the sake of it. But there's nothing wrong with really nice sportsmen who get gold medals.'

As a family-owned prep school founded in the 19th century, St Anthony's was run in its own highly individual way, with a famously alternative 'vibe', creative and quirky, underpinned by a strong Catholic ethos. Parents felt concern when the school was taken over by the efficient operator Alpha Plus, but have found that a professional distance has been kept, while judicious investment has brought the infrastructure into tip-top shape.

The only all-boys Catholic prep school in north London (with an 'outstanding' Diocesan report), this remains very much a Catholic school (about 80 per cent of families are practising Catholics). 'Faith is part of the heartbeat of the school,' says the head. Prayers said morning and afternoon, as well as grace at lunch, and you'll find a crucifix in every classroom as well as the Catholic RE syllabus at common entrance. The head, however, feels the function of religion is not to exclude. 'We have a mission to provide for the Catholic community, but inclusivity is important.' And most feel included. 'Families with other beliefs get incredible respect,' said one Jewish parent.

Despite its slightly bohemian reputation, good manners and ethics remain key. Discipline here is done with the lightest of hands, but the boundaries are clearly in place. All teachers known by their first name and learning very much a cooperative enterprise. There's a golden toffee for those who've done something special (such as sing a song in the style of Johnny Cash), but those who break the code of conduct are entered into a 'green book' and parents are brought in to discuss anyone who's managed to rack up a third offence. Higher up the school, boys discuss what they've done wrong and what they've learned from it. 'I've only given one detention since I got here,' says the head. 'It never gets to that point. I try to give them a dignified exit.' Strong anti-bullying policies. 'The teachers are exceptionally kind and nurturing,' said one parent. 'They'll always do their best to help, whether it's finding a lost rugby kit or providing interview preparation for senior school tests.'

Parents usual north London lawyers, bankers and advertisers, but Catholic purpose means plenty of Italians, Germans and Spanish. Media parents often come with useful benefits. 'One allowed us to preview films, another offered tickets to the Wigmore Hall.' Boys are not necessarily the neatest, but are undoubtedly enthusiastic and individual. 'St Anthony's boys are never the same. There's no stamp.'

The St Anthony's School for Girls opened in Golders Green in September 2016.

St Augustine's Priory

Hillcrest Road, Ealing, London W5 2JL

Pupils: 461 • Ages: 3–18 • Sixth form: 90 • RC

Fees: £10,572 – £14,169 pa

Tel: 020 8997 2022
Email: office@sapriory.com
Website: www.sapriory.com

Head: Since 2012, Mrs Sarah Raffray BA (English and Latin, Manchester) MA (literature and modernity, Salford), 40s. With a career, seemingly, purpose-built for this post, Mrs Raffray is universally praised. She inherited a school with a venerable tradition but a recent, prolonged and very public upheaval accompanied by a mass exodus. It is a tribute to her energetic, frank and warm approach that the school is in such good heart and that it merits this, its first inclusion in The Guide. She knew what she was doing when she came here – 'I almost didn't apply but I had an "if not you, who?" moment and I absolutely believe in Catholic education, with a 21st century resonance. Unless you encourage people to sit still, go deeper and challenge things, everything becomes superficial.' School received an 'outstanding in all areas' Diocesan inspection in 2016.

From St Mary's, Shaftesbury, where she'd been deputy head, Mrs Raffray had previously taught at St Mary's, Cambridge (head of sixth form) and St Bede's, Manchester. All good Roman Catholic schools and providing solid experience for taking on St Augustine's – less well-known than her earlier schools but, under her aegis, this is set to change – and not just in the locality. Not least among her achievements is the unity and community she plainly fosters – her parents tell us: 'she has recruited many, really outstanding, teachers'; 'she is a figurehead with real presence'; 'a dedicated leader'; 'she walks the playground – it's good to see the boss of the shop at the door and she's not afraid to deal with difficult things..all her changes are good – she now needs to be even more ambitious'.

No fear of failing in that department. Lots of new initiatives and a wholesale upgrading of staff. Ten-year master-plan for capital development has commenced and will include a new hall, sports and drama facilities.

Head is relaxed, easy to talk to and very open. 'I can't bear the idea of a "safe" sixth form – we need to look after people but we need to be edgy too.. We're not afraid to say we got it wrong but we're learning all the time... ' One of the best appointments we have seen for years.

Academic matters: Small classes. A pervasive air of orderliness and atmosphere of quiet study. Pupils pay tribute to the outstanding teaching, especially of many newer appointees – 'they are real experts in their subjects,' enthuse parents. Range of subjects respectable but not huge – as you'd expect from a small school. IGCSEs now taken in all sciences, modern languages and English. Russian on offer, as well as Spanish and French. Ambition shown in the arrival of additional maths on the GCSE curriculum. Very good results in, especially, art, English and Latin GCSEs, biology and physics IGCSEs. In all, 66 per cent A*/A grades in 2016. A level results suffer from too many post-GCSE leavers but that is changing. A very encouraging 37 per cent A*/A grades in total in 2016, with the retention of academic high-flyers in the current sixth seeing changes here. Far fewer leavers than previously – the Raffray ambition taking effect – but more still needing to be done. Girls would like thinking skills or critical thinking lessons. But the sixth form, newly relaunched, is ripe for expansion – with its new centre, enrichment programme and extended school day – and we are confident that, given another year or two and the school's reputation growing as it must, they will be turning girls away.

Good learning support from f/t SENCo plus f/t learning support/literacy teacher and much p/t help from subject staff and a dyscalculia expert. Parents of dyslexics appreciative of the support their daughters receive – 'my daughter outperformed all expectations and will now get a great crop of A levels – we never dreamed it'd be possible'. EAL also supported. School flexible over GCSE subjects when SEN hinders achievement – 'They let my daughter stop French – which she was never going to get. So sensible!' And all parents we spoke to praised the value added to their daughters' academic aspirations by the culture of the school.

Secured links with the French Embassy and Sorbonne in London, thereby officially becoming bilingual hub. Offering bespoke French intensive learning to a hand-picked few.

Some sense that the extra-bright could be stretched more but this, too, is on the way with a new Oxbridge group – open to all aspirants – from year 10 up. Also, blow-up pics of successful former pupils around the place, pour encourager.. Despite improving academics, this school is not striving to be another league-table topper and quite right too.

Games, options, the arts: With sports fields like nothing we have seen elsewhere in London, St Augustine's is uniquely privileged. And they're not just extensive but quite beautiful. Good new Astro used for team sports and athletics. Unsurprisingly, PE is a GCSE and A level subject. Much praise for new head of sport and team – 'a new energy,' said a parent. Hockey, netball and lacrosse on offer plus fitness and taekwondo. Matches played with enthusiasm. D of E is popular and girls rave about their trips eg skiing in Switzerland and Bulgaria, geography trips to eg Iceland and to Morocco where they helped build a girls' boarding school.

We were impressed, again, by the enthusiasm displayed in the art and photographic studios – much experimentation, colour and free expression in textiles, paint and modelling. Pupil art well-displayed in every corridor. Lots of musical activities too – choirs and ensembles and all backed, now, by tip-top equipment – IT etc – and super large music room. Carol concert held in nearby Ealing Abbey. School badly needs an all-purpose hall (and will, eventually, get one) but drama and music thrive notwithstanding and the chapel lends its own peculiar magic to events. Much success in eg Young Enterprise, Youth Speaks, Youth Games, maths challenges and various writing competitions and a sense of striving for achievable goals.

Background and atmosphere: The school was founded in 1634 by Mother Lettice Mary Tredway CRL (1595 –1677) a canoness regular and abbess who, together with Miles Pinkney (Father Carré), founded a monastery for the English members of her Order in Paris. A pension for English ladies and a school were attached to the new monastery, of which Tredway was abbess till 1675, when illness compelled her to resign. The priory survived, along with the school attached to it, until the French Revolution, when the English canonesses were forced to flee. They returned home, where they were able to live out their life as a religious community. Eventually the community established itself as St Augustine's Priory in Ealing and the school has occupied its rather wonderful and surprising present site since 1915.

It's tucked into a corner off the North Circular as it rises to meet the A40, yards from the unlovely Hanger Lane Gyratory System – as the monster roundabout is grandiosely named. From the front, the school looks a hotch-potch of brick and pebbledash buildings of no particular distinction. However, surprises await. From the back of the building, the view over 13 acres of fields to the spread of the capital is astonishing. There are gardens, an apple orchard, a prayer garden, chicken runs, many mature and beautiful trees and the whole thing is, literally, an oasis. You don't hear the traffic, you just relax into this beautiful space. Many of the school rooms look over this – most notably, the exceptionally well-appointed sixth form common room and the art studio at the top of the building. The rear of the building also surprises – its monastic principles clear in the pastiche Norman windows, the row of windows on the floor above which would have been those of the nuns – now gone – and the simple cruciform architecture – more obvious when you walk the school itself.

'It feels like the countryside,' as a parent said. It also feels like a village community – lots of old girls and staff send their daughters here. Junior school occupies building at one end of the site – with its own meadow and nursery playground. Little demarcation between the junior and senior schools – seen as a plus by some while others feel there should be more of a 'step up' up at 11. Junior school itself is lovely – lively, imaginative activities with some pleasing mess (we hate sanitised nurseries) and happy, occupied children. Very orderly classrooms for older children and an air of productive purpose throughout.

We have seldom visited a school with so powerful a sense of commitment amongst its community. It's small – too small for a few – but the girls know each other and the strengthening of houses and inter-year activities are helping. Lovely features like the new outside theatre, the willow tunnels constructed by 'amazingly inventive groundsman' and a feeling that 'anyone who comes up with a good idea gets encouragement and, if need be, funding'. Lack of a proper school hall felt by everyone, but 10-year development plan now commencing should sort this as well as provide other much-needed facilities. All classrooms have names of saints or worthies – Thomas Aquinas houses science, St Cecilia music etc. Tuck shop and two refectories –

modern, bright and with 'excellent' food. Whole school now bristles with new PCs.

Much of the interior is nondescript, though all is in good order – clean and spruce. But the chapel – even to heathens like your reviewer – is a source of pleasure. With balcony, vaulted roof, splendid marble columns and altar, and white walls, this Douai-inspired centre of the school life induces reflection and calm. Monday assemblies and three-weekly mass for each year held here. Little Muslim prayer room, but that this is a Roman Catholic school is inescapable. Life-sized statues of saints, crucifixes, pictures and pious posters and messages are everywhere, yet under half the school population is RC and not all those are practising. However, RC values underpin the school's teaching and the girls we spoke to were comfortable with the ethos, and felt the ethos of community and equality will stay with them when they leave. No-one felt oppressed by it.

Pastoral care, well-being and discipline: Very few problems. Some legacy of past difficulties persists but, as with everything here, a sense that Mrs Raffray and her team are on top of it and there is little left to do. 'We have changed our bullying policy. There are clear sanctions.' Impressive newish deputy has pastoral role among others. Universal praise for pastoral care and equipping the girls for the wider world: 'The school allows them to stay as children in an environment which wants them to grow up too early,' a parent told us. 'There are lots of leadership programmes and a growing sense of boldness and confidence.' 'Our daughters are very happy.' Big Sister/Little Sister buddying between sixth form and year 7 newbies. Before and after-school care.

Pupils and parents: Roman Catholics (around 42 per cent of school's population) from Ealing and surrounds. Further 20 per cent are other Christians. Culturally and ethnically diverse, as you'd expect in this part of London – lots of Asians and mixed race families. Strong community holds all together. Middle class, professional families. Mostly from local primaries. School runs a minibus from Chiswick. No identikit pupil. Says head, 'The school has a tradition of accommodating girls who want to be different.' We met nothing but relaxed, articulate, smiley girls.

Entrance: Ealing is well-served by good local state primaries – many of them RC. Nursery and reception places available but waiting lists now in years 3 and 4. Few places in years 5 and 6. At 11+, 60+ apply for c12 places via exam and interview. Places available for year 12. However, all this is set to change. This school is now a player and, notwithstanding the good local state provision, the school's site and, now its academics and inclusive culture – along with the outstanding pastoral care and community feel – will drive custom. Get in quick.

S

Exit: Latterly a sizeable exit post-GCSE to state RC heavyweights, and local co-eds. That is set to change. All 18+s to higher education, mostly to good universities to read proper subjects eg PPE at LSE, plus one to the Royal Academy of Music. No Oxbridge in recent years but we met some impressive current candidates and would confidently predict success.

Money matters: Fees appreciably lower than those of local competitors. Worthwhile discounts for siblings. Academic/sports/music awards at 11+. Academic awards at 16+. All worth 10-20 per cent discount on fees. Bursaries for existing students in case of need.

Remarks: We came away with a bottle of their home-grown and pressed apple juice, and much more you couldn't bottle. This could be the school for which the cliché A Hidden Gem was invented, but we don't expect it to remain hidden for much longer under such inspirational leadership.

St Benedict's School

54 Eaton Rise, London W5 2ES

Pupils: 1,117 • Ages: 3–18 • Sixth form: 213 (60 girls) • RC

Fees: £12,120 – £15,300 pa

Tel: 020 8862 2254
Email: enquiries@stbenedicts.org.uk
Website: www.stbenedicts.org.uk

Headmaster: Since September 2016, Andrew Johnson, previously head of Stonyhurst. Educated at Bristol (French and Spanish) and Portsmouth (education management). Has also been deputy head at Birkdale and head of modern languages at Winchester, where he taught for 10 years. Started his teaching career at Douai in Berkshire. Married to Dawn, with two sons, both an university. Enjoys theatre, music and the great outdoors.

Head of junior school: Since 2005, Mr Rob Simmons BA, the second secular head. A historian, he spent time teaching in Dominica after graduating and, realising teaching was for him, returned to do a PGCE at Sussex. Has worked at St Benedict's for over 20 years, teaching mediaeval and modern history in the senior school and becoming a head of year before his appointment as junior school head.

Academic matters: Respectable results, especially bearing in mind the school is not highly selective academically. Nearly three-quarters A*/B grades at A level in 2016, 38 per cent A*/A. However, a starry place in league tables is not what they're about; school is keen to ensure each child fulfils their potential. Among those who got A*s, As and Bs there would have been a number who would have fallen by the wayside in a more pressured environment. EPQ gaining in popularity. A good range of GCSE subjects on offer with everyone taking RS. RS curriculum largely RC in content and other faiths learned about in PSHE. Excellent ICT facilities. The subject is well taught and IT skills used extensively in other areas including art and music. History, maths and chemistry most popular subjects at A level. In 2016, 45 per cent A*/A grades at GCSE. Modern languages reasonably popular and take place in language labs in the £6.2 million development.

Wheelchair access throughout the school (lifts and ramps) means they have been able to accommodate a number of children with severe physical disabilities. 'As long as we feel they would be happy we will take them.' Full time SENCo who occasionally withdraws pupils from lessons but prefers to provide in-class support as well as extra time pre- and post-school. Lots of support given to children with their organisational skills and the SEN room provides a useful base for children who need more help. Very positive noises from parents about the caring and supportive approach of the school to a whole range of special needs. At the other end of the spectrum, a gifted and talented coordinator runs a programme through the curriculum, but also does a lot outside.

Games, options, the arts: Rugby is huge here. It's the main winter sport for boys (they don't play football, nor do they row, and it's not the place for your son if he's mad about ballet) and school recently ranked the top rugby school in the country (currently slipped to fourth but we suspect not for long). Tours to Dubai, Japan and New Zealand. Girls as keen to perform well as the boys. Netball tours to Sri Lanka and Barbados. Full size Astroturf pitch.

Cricket, athletics, rounders and tennis in the summer. School uses 14 acres of playing fields in Perivale about a mile away and plays hard, winning more than losing. Games staff everywhere – proper professionals in their matching coaching kit.

On-site sports hall, sparkling multi-gym and fitness centre as well as fencing salle and dance studio. Fencing a major sports option with regular fixtures against other schools. Basketball, volleyball and yoga are also offered.

Less than world-class pupils appreciate the school's attitude to sports – 'everyone's given a chance,' said one in heartfelt tones, having experienced the 'if you're not in the first team you're nobody' syndrome elsewhere.

Music strong and there's a huge variety – a symphony orchestra, lots of singing – four choirs (strongly influenced by the Abbey choir), jazz band, big band, swing band, string ensembles and brass groups. (Almost) everyone gets involved at some stage and one parent remarked on how well talent is spotted and nurtured. Excellent facilities, three grand pianos and lots of uprights in tip top condition. An IT lab is dedicated to music, posters of Led Zeppelin and the Beatles decorate the walls, lots of computers equipped with piano keyboards.

Exciting art. Intensely imaginative, disciplined and creative sculptures are dotted around the school and spectacular oil paintings adorn the reception area. IT facilities dedicated to art in the attractive one-storey modern art/DT block. Before – and after – school study supervision in the library on offer, and over 80 clubs which include karate, history society, CCF, D of E, Saint Vincent de Paul charity fundraising, debating and current affairs. One boy keen to point out that if you want to do something new, school will make it happen.

Background and atmosphere: Founded in 1902 by the monks of Downside Abbey, St Benedict's is the only Benedictine day school in the country. Its sister schools are Worth, Downside and Ampleforth which, like St Benedict's, have all relatively recently started to take girls all the way through. (There have been girls in the sixth form here since the 1970s, from year 7 since 2008.) The Roman Catholic faith is evident in every aspect of the atmosphere and the environment of the school, its publications, its ethos, yet almost half the pupils in the senior school are not Catholic. Eighty-five-ish per cent are Christian including those from other denominations, and you will find Muslims, Sikhs, Hindus, and Jews. The only condition is that they must respect the Catholic faith and take part in the regular masses that take place throughout the school year.

The buildings are a mix of un-gloomy Victorian red-brick and various 20th century extensions, additions and blocks – some of which are wearing better than others. The Cloisters, a stunning development costing £6.2 million, is the first thing you come to as you enter the school and has the same contemporary feel as some of the underground stations on the Jubilee line. New sixth form centre and art and design building. Smooth concrete walls, aesthetic balconies, quadrangles and colonnades, an imaginative foil to the glorious abbey, which is situated across the playground and adjacent to the junior school. Whole school mass is said in the warm and totally unforbidding abbey, but smaller class mass is said in the intimate chapel in the modern Cloisters development – stunningly light and bright with a large window in the shape of a cross taking up most of the ceiling.

Junior school housed in very large, very attractive Victorian red-brick building across the playground from senior school (playground shared but times staggered so tinies not swamped by six foot rugger types). Playground also encloses new small area for tots. Building recently and carefully extended to provide lovely, light new hall and classrooms (and new extension to house nursery to year 4 currently arising apace). New rooms include excellent ICT suite with modern low tables and matching chairs and inviting, comfortable library overlooking the abbey and lawns. Interactive whiteboards in every classroom and well used. Leafy Ealing far more apparent here – super trees with space to grow and local family homes just across the way. Excellent displays everywhere – really interesting, too, on stone carving, perspective, shape and colour. A good orderly feel with happy, confident-looking pupils in a school recently commended in ISI report for excellent music and ADT. Pastoral care, too, clearly exceptional. A great start for your son or daughter and big school just across the playground. Nursery housed in super refurbished Victorian house just down the road. Last Ofsted inspection rated the early years foundation stage provision as outstanding.

Trust in the Benedictine ethos of respect for each other, and an unquestioned local reputation for quite exceptional pastoral care, have been battered by a storm of revelations. See the website for the report of an inquiry, commissioned by the school's trustees and conducted by Lord Carlile (who we rate as unquestionably independent). The school tells us that it has fully implemented his recommendations. It is now fully independent of the Abbey Trust; the governing body has a lay majority and a lay chair, whilst three members of the monastic community are governors and another three work at the school. It regularly reviews its safeguarding and child protection policies. The deputy head left in December 2015, following arrest on suspicion of possessing indecent images of children. No St Benedict's children were involved.

Against that background, parents and pupils pay tribute to the trouble taken over the smallest worry, and pupils feel supported and secure. Advent of girls throughout has also contributed to modernisation and a sense of opening up.

Pastoral care, well-being and discipline: Very strict – until the sixth form all children carry around a yellow card – reminiscent of the traditional satis cards (short for satisfecit – has he done enough?) in order that their behaviour – good and bad – can be constantly monitored. Parents are kept in the loop, they sign it each week and house points are affected. However, it's not inflexibly strict – school recognises that hcldren can get it wrong sometimes. Regular parent forums on, eg the dangers of ICT at home; school likes to keep the sixth form in at lunch time (though they can go out). 'There is so much to do here, plus there are a few too many muggings in Ealing.'

Pupils and parents: 'Pupils in state schools think we're posh but Latymer kids think we're common,' a sixth former told us. You don't get many posey trust fund kids here. Solidly middle class but a genuinely wide range of parents, a number of single mothers and families who have made huge sacrifices to get a good education for their children. A number of parents talked of how supportive the school was – not just of their child but of the family as a whole. One boy commented on how no-one is arrogant about money – the influence of the abbey means that everyone feels welcome. Mostly local. Some come from as far afield as Barnes or Holland Park. Just over 50 per cent are Catholic.

One girl we spoke to was keen to mention that girls are not treated as second class citizens, attributing it to the fact that there have been girls in the sixth form for over 30 years. There are good inter-year relationships. Mentoring schemes where the older ones help out with the juniors and whole school involvement in drama and music. Pupils here are extremely courteous and mature. Old Priorians (the official title for former St Benedict's pupils) include Julian Clary, Lord (Chris) Patten (who also sits as an advisor on the governing board), Peter Ackroyd, Declan Donnellan, Andy Serkis, Professor Denis MacShane MP and poet/songwriter Labi Siffre, as well as plenty of rugby players, including Hugo Ellis and Joe Simpson of Wasps.

Entrance: Non-selective at 3 or 4. Main senior school entry at 11 – though school will still take the occasional few at 13. Ninety-six places, 40 of which go to the children coming up from the junior school (almost all transfer automatically).

Entrance exams in maths, English and verbal reasoning. Most interviewed. Looking to discover what the child will give back to the school. NB part of a group of independent co-ed/boys' schools that coordinate 11+ results, but forbid those who have accepted a place at one school from taking up a subsequent waiting list offer from another. Sixth form requirements – a minimum of six GCSEs at B or above and Bs in A level subjects. A few join in the sixth form from local girls' schools.

It's no longer true that if you don't get in anywhere else you will get a place at St Benedict's. Although school is keen not to be too selective, as numbers rise priority will have to be given to Catholics and siblings.

Exit: Some 70 per cent of junior pupils move up the senior school; a few on occasion to Merchant Taylors', Latymer Upper, Notting Hill and Ealing, Cardinal Vaughan and London Oratory.

Virtually all sixth formers to good universities and to an impressive range of courses – no stereotypes here. Two Oxford places in 2016; others to eg Bristol, Nottingham, Durham, Exeter and Leeds for subjects ranging from aerospace engineering to theatre performance; four to art school. Some 20 per cent leave after GCSE to go to eg Latymer Upper, Catholic state schools or sixth form colleges.

Money matters: School has increased provision for scholarships and bursaries. About half a dozen on 100 per cent bursaries, lots of others get help. Academic scholarships at 11+ and at sixth form – up to 50 per cent fees and can be augmented by bursaries. 'Once a child is in if a parent falls on hard times we will do our best to help them.'

Remarks: We said, 'A wholly unpretentious, good, solid school with sound values that is never going to squash your child into a box. Exactly the school for your brightish but quietish child who would sink in a larger, or tougher, environment. An honest, hard-working place with a gentle and loving approach', and we still think that that is a fair description.

St Charles Catholic Sixth Form College

74 St Charles Square, London W10 6EY

Pupils: 1,200 • Ages: 16–19 • RC

Tel: 020 8968 7755
Email: admissions@stcharles.ac.uk
Website: www.stcharles.ac.uk

S

Principal: Since 2015, Mrs Elaine Taylor, previously vice principal. She joined the college in 2009 from St Francis Xavier College, where she had been assistant principal.

Academic matters: Whilst around three-quarters of the students follow traditional A level courses, St Charles also offers BTecs, certificates and diplomas, vocational courses and foundation skills in English and mathematics. The college also offers GCSE retakes for those wanting to improve their grades. More able students can take the Extended Project Qualification. Students are all taught to plan and develop their work alongside how best to manage their time. Being a rounded, thinking individual is part of the college's mission: everyone follows the compulsory general RE programme, which involves much critical discussion around the purpose and meaning of life through theology and philosophy. Students who are successful in completing the course gain the nationally recognised Certificate in Religious Investigation and Moral Reasoning. The school is well-known for added value, with 24 per cent A*/B and 55 per cent A*/C in 2016; this is no mean achievement for a mixed ability college. Spread across two floors, the library provides quiet areas for working and a good range of books, multimedia, newspapers and periodicals. Active and well-resourced learning support department provides assistance to students with a range of specific needs. The building is now fully wheelchair accessible. Intensive courses for students with English as an additional language are organised for small groups to ensure much personal attention.

Games, options, the arts: Impressive and modern sports facilities; sports block also incorporates new IT suites. Huge sports hall, four new indoor courts and fitness suite; students can also use the Birkbeck College sports ground for football and rugby. Basketball team has won the London Pioneers for three out of the last four years. Very strong art and design department puts on well-attended exhibitions, and a number of students go on to foundation courses at top London art schools. Drama and music are also popular and the school produces plays and musicals, with auditions open to all students. Film and media students are involved with projects run by the British Film Institute, enabling them to show and discuss their creative work with film and television professionals. Very enthusiastic and successful young enterprise team recently won Best Overall Company for North Central London. The college links up with other organisations to provide community outreach opportunities, be it helping older people gain ICT skills or mentoring other young people. Students can also become involved in the CitySafe initiative run by London Citizens, an organisation committed to improving young people's lives and skills and combating street violence.

Background and atmosphere: As you walk into the entrance hall, a peaceful and positive atmosphere is immediately apparent, the most inspiring design taken from Milan Cathedral. Everywhere is spotlessly clean, and well cared for corridors positively shine. The college is named after St Charles Borromeo, a 16th century Italian archbishop who believed strongly in the redeeming powers of education. Founded by Basil Hume in 1990, it continues to go from strength to strength. Quite overwhelming feedback from staff that St Charles is a breath of fresh air, organised, and with a positive attitude across all disciplines. The college is conveniently located in St Charles's Square, often referred to as The Little Vatican, due to the neighbouring Catholic primary and secondary schools, St Pius Church and a Carmelite monastery. Much about the college is designed around hope and inspiration, and a large amount of wall space is dedicated to portraits of students with accompanying testimonials and histories of their educational and career development. Interestingly, quite a few ex-students return to work at the college in both academic and non-academic posts.

Pastoral care, well-being and discipline: St Charles's continues to work very hard to ensure the best possible pastoral care and that every student feels part of the community. Everyone has a tutor group under one of the pastoral managers which looks after their progress and well-being. There is a referral system for students with academic and/or personal problems. An outside agency provides both male and female counsellors who visit the school on a weekly basis. The full-time chaplain looks after the small but beautiful chapel, where morning prayers are said daily and a mass takes place every Friday lunchtime. The chaplain is available to students on a drop-in basis. Whilst supporting students, he also organises voluntary work experience and charity work. Students are provided with a code of conduct, so everyone knows exactly what is expected of them in all aspects of college life and behaviour. Zero tolerance towards smoking, alcohol and drugs, all banned from the site.

Pupils and parents: Very diverse 21st-century London group of students, from all over the world, Portuguese, Filipino, Hispanic, Afro-Caribbean and Eastern European. About 80 per cent from ethnic minorities, many of whom are the first members of their family to have the opportunity to attend an A level college and go on to university.

Entrance: First priority goes to those with specific needs, then to students applying from four partner Catholic secondary schools, which makes up about 20 per cent of the intake. Other than that, fairly open access; students come from around 150 feeder schools. Everyone applying on time will be offered an interview to discuss their application and suitable course.

Exit: Approximately 75 per cent to university (358 in 2016), around 10 per cent of these to Russell Group, others to art colleges or FE colleges to follow vocational training courses or apprenticeships.

Money matters: College raises some funds by hiring out the excellent facilities including the large hall, indoor and outdoor sports areas and equipment, and spacious restaurant and catering area. The student bursary scheme provides grants for those in financial hardship while studying full time.

Remarks: Some remarkable achievements happen here. Great place for motivated and hard-working young people from all walks of life who want to move on, regardless of previous achievements or background.

St Christopher's School

226

32 Belsize Lane, London NW3 5AE

Pupils: 242 • Ages: 4–11

Fees: £13,770 pa

Tel: 020 7435 1521
Email: admissions@st-christophers.hampstead.sch.uk
Website: www.st-christophers.hampstead.sch.uk

Acting Head: Claire Bailey, deputy head, is holding the fort since the departure of short-lived previous head Carrie Symes.

Entrance: St Christopher's is one of London's highest-achieving academic prep schools, with results at 11 the envy of many of its neighbours. This, however, is a school which selects primarily on ability. Part of the selection procedure is standardised tests, so summer birthdays don't lose out. 'It is not an academic assessment. We observe how they play together and how they interact with other children.' The school operates a split entry and although all are assessed at the same time, girls with September to February birthdays will generally join in reception, whilst March to August birthdays join in year 1. Tests dates and results are co-ordinated with other leading selective north London prep schools. Early registration is essential (as near birth as possible) for those already resident in London. Entry lists are closed at about 300 to be assessed for 38 available places. The school, however, is always willing to be flexible for those who've just arrived. Siblings are given an automatic offer, unless it is considered 'they will not flourish'. Not flourishing, however, is fairly loosely interpreted. 'If you have two clever daughters and the third is not as bright, some parents think she'll upset the exit poll, but that's not the way we work.' Parents confirm that year groups cover a (relatively) wide spread of ability. Occasional vacancies after entry. One 100 per cent means-tested scholarship available per annum and other support available as necessary.

Exit: 'We're fortunate in London that there are so many great schools, and we are proud of the achievement of all our girls. There's no scholarship board here. We don't want to make some pupils feel instantly diminished.' That said, this is generally a school of bright sparks and ambitious parents and the majority proceed to the highest performing London day schools. City of London, North London Collegiate and South Hampstead top the list, with St Paul's Girls and Highgate close behind. Quite a number of scholarships amongst them. A handful to board and a few to Henrietta Barnett.

Remarks: St Christopher's was founded in 1883 by two local literary lesbians, but established in its current form in 1950 by the writer Rosemary Manning. It became a charitable trust in the 1970s. Housed in a large Victorian family house (with modern additions) in fashionable Belsize Park, this is a top-flight prep school for top-flight north London parents and the ethos and atmosphere are reflective of that. The education the pupils receive here is thoughtful and exciting. It concentrates on the fundamentals, but only after the fundamentals have been carefully considered. 'We have to ask the question "what are we educating children for?" It's a world we know nothing about, a world very different from our own.' The school has carefully analysed the impact of technology. 'The girls think technologically and it can be much more difficult to get them to listen to a story and concentrate.' The issue is addressed by concentrated focus on the task of reading and understanding and girls read aloud every day from reception to year 3 and regularly thereafter. 'If you can't read, you can't do maths.' No concessions are made when it comes to literature ('We don't use abridged texts') and Dickens and Lewis Carroll are digested in the original. An excellent library underlines the school's priorities.

Much of the timetable follows the national curriculum ('It would be foolish not to – there are some very interesting things – but we cut away the trivia. We don't reject it, we tweak it') and the approach is based on 'child-initiated learning' with pupils taught to question and take responsibility for what they learn. Work is then tailored to the needs of each pupil, with maths books, for example, customised to the age and stage. (Though those in need of learning support are in the minority – mainly younger siblings – parents consider this tailoring, too, to be strong.) Spanish ('one of the most widely spoken languages in the world') is taught throughout, Latin from year 5 and French as a club from year 3. Specialist subject teaching from year 4, with drama added to the curricular mix, joined by history of art in year 5. Flexibility of mind is encouraged by the inclusion of chess. ('It's a brilliant thinking exercise.')

Hard-working, well-qualified staff, particularly in the final two years. 'I cannot imagine better teachers than the maths and English teachers in years 5 and 6,' said one parent. 'They are really transformative.'

Despite the school's outstanding scholarship record, there is no scholarship class and no setting, except in maths in the final two years. Nor is this a school that crams for exams; preparation lasts just one term, when practice papers are given weekly. 'They're not missing core subjects from year 5, they still have time for all the extracurricular, they're not pressured and processed.'

The approach here is enriching and the school believes there is as much value in creativity as in the core subjects.

Music is generally considered strong and enthusiastic, with two music classes plus a singing class each week. What's learnt here is put into practice with a junior orchestra, a wind group, a string group, piano club, junior and senior choirs and a chamber choir. This is media-land, too, and there is also a thriving film club, where girls learn to make their own. Cultural outings are very much part of the offering, with regular visits to theatres and museums and a young writers' workshop.

Sport is perhaps less important than it might be elsewhere (some parents complain that unless you're in a team, this can be a rather neglected area). Netball court and gym on site and regular matches against other schools in netball and rounders. Short tennis is also taught in the summer term and senior girls play lacrosse. Swimming lessons only in year 3 at nearby Swiss Cottage baths, sports day held at Hampstead Cricket Club. Though the outdoor space here is not unduly extensive, it is used very effectively, with an outdoor classroom, an Alice Garden and a science-themed garden. 'Children today have a very boring existence, chauffeured here and there, and we wanted to create an environment where they were allowed to be imaginative.' Indeed, the thread that runs throughout St Christopher's is that a good education is stimulating, interesting and exciting. The extracurricular is therefore addressed as energetically, with everything from public speaking to self-defence and Indian dance and, while there may be a Florence Nightingale workshop, the message that banking is as worthwhile a career for girls as nursing is instilled with visits to the Bank of England and a mock Dragons' Den. All staff are required to run two clubs a year and the offering is extensive.

Four houses, Bronte, Nightingale, North and Pankhurst, provide the basis for inter-house competition. The school has a strong family feel, sheltered and relaxed. There are no school rules ('We just ask for respect in the classroom and for them to be polite to teachers.') Good behaviour is instilled by discussion. ('Why did you do that? How do you imagine that would look?') Occasionally parents feel that emotional difficulties are not picked up as quickly as they might be. ('If you mention a problem, they take it seriously, but it's not always spotted,' said one.) Assembly every Friday is non-denominational. School meals exclude pork, shellfish, ham and nuts in order to cater for all. The facilities here have been brought thoroughly up to date, too, with a smart extension providing additional classrooms and impressive IT. The uniform of green Aertex shirts and blue trousers is practical and durable.

Over a third of pupils live within walking distance and the rest travel from affluent nearby postcodes like St Johns Wood, Maida Vale, Islington and Highgate. Parents are often intellectual, professional, international and Jewish – and occasionally celebrities. 'They are interesting and incredibly well-informed. They are very involved and desperately keen to support their children's education.' ('Sometimes too keenly involved,' remarked one father. 'There are a lot of non-working mothers who once had high-powered careers and are now directing their energies on their children.') Occasionally expectations have to be gently adjusted.

A high-octane education producing confident, well-informed and articulate girls. 'The nice thing about St Christopher's is that it provides an excellent education without trying to breed a master race,' said one happy customer.

S

St David's School

23/25 Woodcote Valley Road, Purley, Surrey CR8 3AL

Pupils: 164 • Ages: 3–11 • C of E

Fees: £5,700 – £9,720 pa

Tel: 020 8660 0723
Email: office@stdavidsschool.co.uk
Website: www.stdavidsschool.co.uk

Head: Since 2011 Miss Cressida Mardell (40s) a classicist, BA PGCE. Before joining St David's in 2007 she was a senior teacher at St Christopher's School, Epsom. Parents appreciate her positive approach, hard work and sound judgement, alongside a jolly personality and a good sense of humour. She lives locally and enjoys holidaying in France and walking with her two lively Border collie rescue dogs.

Entrance: Most join the nursery at 3+ (18 places); another four places in reception. Non-selective at this stage; occasional places in year 1 upwards subject to 'satisfactory assessment'.

Exit: At 11+ most popular choices are the local grammar schools Sutton, Wilson's Wallington, Nonsuch and Tiffin's. Others to Royal Russell, Whitgift, Trinity, Old Palace, Greenacre and Woldingham.

Remarks: Mixed ability school, which skilfully blends academic excellence alongside a good range of musical, creative and sporting opportunities.

Founded in 1912 with just five pupils, by Welsh (hence school's name) sisters Margery and Mary Talfourd Jones. The school has thrived through the decades and today's multicultural clientèle is still proud of its founders' Welsh connections. Pupils join in the Eisteddfod Festival and fly the flag on St David's Day.

Dedicated class teachers run maths and English lessons mostly in the mornings and then teach specialist subjects in the afternoons. There is an ICT room and a room for arts, science and technology; pupils often split for these subjects so class sizes are around 10, optimising opportunities for individual attention and development. French is taught throughout the school and year 6 learn Latin. Specialist teacher visits three days a week to assist children with any special educational needs. Additional support is provided in small groups, one-to-one or in class at no extra charge. ESOL can be arranged.

Very busy music department has a gifted and talented choir, brass ensemble, string ensemble and rhythm group. Most pupils play at least one instrument; older pupils are introduced to filming and music composition with the occasional commission, most recently a jingle for Halfords. Some great achievements on the sporting front; St David's has its own large playing fields a few minutes' walk from the school building complete with tennis and netball courts. Gymnastics is particularly strong; the school has won the ISA competition on several occasions. Swimming is another area where pupils excel, with eight children being selected to train as divers at Crystal Palace for the Olympics programme. Parents felt clubs had been rather limited; this is now an expanding area, and the aim is now to offer a much wider choice of activities, after-school and at lunchtimes. Chess team have made it into Champion League finals for primary schools and the maths team recently came third in the Sutton Maths Challenge. After-school care (at extra cost) is provided by the Jancett Nursery Group until 6.30pm.

Refreshingly, St David's has retained its independence and remains a small charity with a non-selective intake, so far avoiding being swept up by one of the large education businesses. Very successful results at 11 into the local grammar and independent schools, especially considering the non-selective intake and inclusive approach. Terrific value for money.

St Dominic's Sixth Form College

Mount Park Avenue, Harrow on the Hill HA1 3HX

Pupils: 1,274 • Ages: 16-19 • RC

Tel: 020 8422 8084
Email: admissions@stdoms.ac.uk
Website: www.stdoms.ac.uk

Principal: Since 2013, Andrew Parkin (40s). Educated at St John's RC Comprehensive School and Queen Elizabeth Sixth Form College in Darlington. Studied music at Durham and Cambridge and started his professional career in London at The St Marylebone Girls' School. Went on to be deputy head at Sion Manning Girls' School in Kensington and then St Augustine's High School in Westminster. 'For 18 years, I worked in fairly tough comprehensives, which probably explains why the hottest topics for me are teaching, learning, attainment, consistency and attendance and punctuality,' he says. 'But I love the way that here, we get to combine these with informalities such as addressing each other on first name terms, as well as a greater emphasis on independent learning – the result of which is fantastic preparation for university.'

Not someone to hide away in his office, he greets students on the gate, observes lessons, teaches general RE (and occasionally some music) and regularly chats to students and staff. 'I'm not really a number cruncher – I don't believe that is what headships are about.' Clearly passionate about his role ('I absolutely love it! I feel I've got the most perfect job, with happy students that work their very hard, and no discipline issues'), he is also a keen member of several committees in the wider sector. Among the key changes he's brought to the college are a strong emphasis on teaching and learning, more peer observations, a hands-on leadership team and embedding IT into learning. Students don't have a bad word to say about him. 'He seems to know everybody's name,' said one. 'He's so approachable and easy going.' Parents similarly keen: 'He is absolutely fabulous – a supportive leader who's not afraid to get his hands dirty, rather than being just a figurehead.'

Both interested and interesting, he is keen amateur musician and is chairman of the BBC Symphony Chorus.

Academic matters: Some 29 subjects available in more-or-less any combination. Maths, history, the three sciences, economics and psychology are the most popular A level subjects – with strongest results in maths, chemistry, biology, history and economics (in terms of attainment) and history, classics, languages, music and art (in terms of value-added). In 2016, 66 per cent A*-B grades and 35 per cent A*/A grades at A level, with nearly all D*, D or M results at BTec.

Option to change subjects in the first week or two if you really loath geography or have just developed a passionate interest in Italian. Currently, students can take four subjects in year 12, dropping down to three in year 13, enabling them to keep options open. Offers level 3 BTec national and extended diplomas, ideally suited to those who don't like the sound of lots of final exams, which can be combined with one (extended course) or two (national course) A levels. 'BTecs are often undersold, but they afford our less academic students an opportunity to achieve highly and go onto the likes of York, Nottingham and London universities. The business studies one has validity and is taught well here,' claims the principal. In 2015, the college also brought in a core maths programme, which enables students to keep up with maths without taking the full A level.

Class sizes range from 2-25 and teaching is largely discussion-based. 'The teachers' subject knowledge is phenomenal – some have two degrees,' one told us. 'Teachers here are so inspirational and really passionate about what they teach,' said another, although be warned they are very hot on homework, being 'very strict on both completion and deadlines.' Professional development for teachers is a strength, with all having spent time in London schools. 'It's been great for them to see what life is like elsewhere – it's got them to reflect on their own practice and raise the bar,' explains the principal.

Good for those with physical disabilities – we met one wheelchair user, who couldn't praise the college highly enough. 'There's not one area I can't access,' she said. Students with hearing or visual impairments are equally impressed. Very few students with SEN, though. Support for them is 50 per cent classroom support, while the other half takes place in the Study Plus area, which other students access for anything from revision workshops to small project groups – all of which helps to prevent any stigma. 'Our son has Asperger's and the college has been brilliant – really going out of their way to help him on his terms and he got far better results than we thought he would,' one parent told us.

Offers the EPQ. 'They have a free choice of subject, but it makes sense to relate it to a subject they may do at university, and gives something to talk about at interview.' Large numbers of aspiring medics, so the college runs a programme of BMAT preparation and mock interviews. Excellent university and careers advice; has been awarded the Investors in Careers mark and has a designated HE and careers advisor. 'We're realistic and honest, and allow no poverty of aspiration.'

Effort and achievement grades given every six weeks. 'Our monitoring is much more frequent than they have time to do in schools. All our staff are focused on the sixth form – not on settling in year 7s or helping year 9s choose GCSE subjects, or indeed behavioural issues.'

Games, options, the arts: State-of-the-art sports hall includes a multigym and hall for badminton, table tennis and five-a-side football, with its use juggled between A level PE students and general recreation. Sport is not compulsory, but the hall 'has increased motivation and attendance. We've been pleasantly surprised that participation rates have been very high.' Indeed, the principal encourages all students to utilise the multigym, which is open from 7.30am-5.30pm. Outdoor space includes a five-a-side football/netball court and a football field set among beautiful woodland. There's at least one team for each of football, rugby, tennis, basketball, table tennis and netball – 'Football trials are particularly popular, with around 100 students applying for just 10 places,' one student told us. They do well in local leagues, and some competitions further afield, particularly for football and badminton. There's a cycling club and golf club, plus opportunities for cheerleading and street dance for those less competitively inclined.

Music is part of everyday life – we heard the practising for the annual bands' performances when we visited. Decent numbers (around 25) do A level, while seven peripatetic teachers cover individual teaching of instruments including piano, flute, strings, guitar and drums. Choir and orchestra both popular and good, with termly concerts providing opportunities to perform. Department comprises of teaching space, recording studio and rehearsal rooms, and there's a newly installed electric organ in the chapel, that is used by keyboard players. 'I've been known to pop in to play it for half-an-hour myself,' admits the principal.

Top floor art studios could be bigger and better, but they do the job and are reassuringly cluttered with colourful resources and some very talented work. Three teachers cover art, art history and DT, and the sophisticated artwork and fashion creations are exhibited in the chapel annually, with several students each year going on to art and design courses. Drama studio is ok, but any lack of cutting edge practice areas doesn't put off keen thespians, who put on an annual musical production, plus various productions throughout the year. Great excitement about the devised pieces being showcased annually in the so-called 'shack' – a covered outside space for which the college hires in tiered seating. 'With the sounds of nature and the London hum in the background, and the sheer talent of the students, it's all highly dramatic,' says the head, recalling that one performance required a pig's head having to be ordered from the butcher, then kept under health and safety conditions.

Volunteering and fundraising are important parts of the ethos. 'Charity efforts spring up out of nowhere.' Students do sponsored walks and sleep outs, work in soup kitchens, volunteer on a catholic farm, join a pilgrimage to Lourdes. 'There's a philosophy of respecting other people and helping the wider community.'

Long list of day trips and residentials. 'London is used to the max – theatres, museums, concerts, Houses of Parliament and so on.' Among the regular overseas trips are Great Wall of China (general trip, open to all), Washington DC (history and politics students) – and there's an annual exchange with a school in New Jersey. Other recent trips have included music trip to New York, art trip to Rome, general trip to Venice and classics trip to Athens. Extracurricular activities not obligatory, but widely taken up – including everything from flower arranging to sports. Guest speakers regularly invited in – including The Spectator's editor Fraser Nelson, Sir Bernard Hogan Howe, Mark Damazer and Phillip Coggan.

Background and atmosphere: Opened in 1978 in what had been St Dominic's Independent Grammar School for Girls, run by Dominican nuns. Sits on a hill above a leafy, gated estate of substantial houses with large gardens that could have strayed from the Chilterns, and amazing views across London – as far as the City and Canary Wharf on a clear day. By the entrance to the 28-acre site is the chapel, a peaceful and atmospheric building with lovely stained glass, 'the heart of the college'. Assemblies (each year group gets four a year, which are supplemented by the principal's Sunday night emails on a theme for the week, such as 'What is truth?') and introductory talks take place here, as well as morning masses, and Muslim students use a side room for prayer. Four large blocks make up the key teaching areas – Hume (humanities), Catherine (maths, English, languages), Aquinas (sciences) and Siena (sports hall and psychology).

The most recently developed facility is the remodelled library – among the nicest we've seen, in which the £1m investment paid for a bright, airy space, with multicoloured seats and two glass-dominated mezzanine areas, with masses of study space and computers. 'It's well staffed and equipped – we love it,' one student told us. Indeed, it's generally packed until closing time at 4.30pm.

No common room ('We don't need one – we're not a school,' says principal), with students gathering instead in the spacious canteen, library and the Shack, where an all-day coffee kiosk augments the canteen offerings.

Faith is a major part of the deal here, with the principal big on the Dominican tradition – with links with its sisters and brothers all around the country. Mass is held every week, tutor groups take it in turns to choose readings, everyone studies RE. 'We want our students to develop on an academic, personal and spiritual level. We want them to critically examine their faith, to mix with people from other faiths and hear why it is important to them. It makes a tremendous difference to what we can offer and how they develop in later life,' says principal.

About 60 per cent of the staff is Catholic, but all buy into the ethos. Prayers are said each morning and each tutor period. 'It is a moment for thinking outside oneself – a lovely sharing moment.' Very good relationships amongst staff and between staff and pupils and overall, there's a real buzz around campus – the atmosphere is relaxed, informal, yet hardworking.

Pastoral care, well-being and discipline: Any student problems tend to be ironed out by teachers or the college counsellor, the latter whose hourly slots over two days a week are always packed out. 'If I could afford it, I'd have her here five days,' say the principal. One parent whose family had suffered trauma were particularly impressed by the pastoral offering. 'They could not have done more for my son.' Mental health issues, particularly anxiety, on the up, reports the college – but that's no different to what any other head tells us. In the main, things tick over pretty smoothly here – and students were aghast when we asked them if there was any bullying. 'Unlike a lot of sixth form colleges, where you get cliques, this one has a really warm and friendly atmosphere,' said one. Strong student voice – changing everything from more loo rolls in the toilets and better air-con to helping organise events like the annual talent show and cultural day.

Electronic registration for every lesson means that everyone is accounted for: the pastoral team phones parent and student if the student is not in by 10am. If lateness becomes a regular occurrence, homework is late, a student shows lack of effort, or takes unauthorized absence, then they're put on warning. If they still don't pull their socks up, they are asked to attend supervised learning and teaching (detention basically – although they won't call it that). 'It's an opportunity for students who haven't worked hard enough that week to do so,' says the principal, although not many students wind up actually having to attend one. If there's still no improvement, parents are called in – again, it's very few students overall. Zero tolerance for drugs or violence, but no problems with either for many years – in fact, no temporary exclusions whatsoever in current principal's reign.

Pupils and parents: About 50 per cent Catholic, most of the rest Hindu or Muslim. Homogeneous in that all take their religious faith seriously, with the exception of one or two atheists (but no zealous ones, unsurprisingly). 'All students are serious about academic life – you need to be motivated and have a certain level of intelligence to get on here,' one student told us – indeed, the college offers virtually no vocational courses. And as there is a high level of competition for places, those who get in feel a great sense of gratitude. 'I feel really lucky to be here,' is something of a mantra.

White British is certainly not the majority here. 'Harrow is one of the most diverse boroughs in the area, and we are reflective of that,' says principal. Good mix in terms of class too – with many students the first in their families to aspire to university. Parents are nearly all highly supportive, with 97 per cent attendance at the annual parents' evening – doubtless helped by the fact that parents can drop in anytime between 9am-7.30pm and the principal stipulates that they do so. 'I insist every young person has someone to represent them because it's my experience that when young men and women get to 16, many parents take a back seat, and that's not what we want here.'

Entrance: About 30 per cent from its two partner schools, Salvatorian College and Sacred Heart Language College – the rest from over 100 other feeder schools, stretching as far as 1.5 hours travel away. 'I know someone who comes in from Kent,' one student told us, while one from Enfield told us it takes her 'an hour-and-10-minutes travelling one way – and that's on a good day.' 'Most of our students live in Harrow, but if you looked at a heat map of London, we'd have dots representing students' homes all over it, and I think that's great,' says the principal. 'At 16, people are old enough to make decisions and if they recognise excellence and are prepared to make an effort to get out of bed for it, then I'm all for it.'

Students from the main two feeder schools are guaranteed a place, providing they get at least five A*-C GCSE grades including English language. All other applicants must get at least seven A*-Cs and meet the individual subject requirements. These range from a C in English for religious studies to an A in maths for further maths. Priority to Catholics, then other practising Christians, then other faiths and no faith. Applicants must acknowledge their commitment to the religious values of the school in writing. Conditional offers are made in March and are based on academic references, including predicted grades. Any remaining places offered based on subjects with spaces and highest GCSE average score. Some spaces also become available after the first year. 'Many parents round here work abroad, so there's quite a lot of movement in the area,' explains the principal.

Exit: Around 90 per cent to higher education. London universities are very popular, as are Nottingham, Southampton and Warwick. Law and medical/biomedical subjects tend to top the tables. Fewer Oxbridge applicants than one might expect given the calibre of students (six places in 2016), largely because so many are prospective medics/dentists (22 in 2016).

Money matters: Free if you're under 19. Excellent and enlightened system of bursaries for students and staff to fund specific projects and trips.

Remarks: Greatly sought-after college in pleasant leafy location with high academic standards and a strong Catholic ethos of care for each other. 'A lovely place to work and study,' say staff and students.

St Dunstan's College

Stanstead Road, London SE6 4TY

Pupils: 900 • Ages: 3-18 • Sixth form: 148 • C of E

Fees: £9,411 – £15,978 pa

Tel: 020 8516 7200
Email: Info@sdmail.org.uk
Website: www.stdunstans.org.uk

Headmaster: Since 2014, Nicholas Hewlett BSc PGCE (30s): the youngest head we've yet to meet, but youth becomes him. He's still bouncing with excitement after two challenging years in post. After a brief spell in the City, he headed to King's College London to study geography, followed by a PGCE at the Institute of Education. Landing his first teaching job at Dulwich College, within three years he moved to Magdalen College School Oxford, as head of geography becoming housemaster, contingent commander of the CCF and director of the annual arts festival.

We were somewhat startled to hear a wish from a mother to hear him sing until we encountered his CV. Performing as a tenor soloist throughout his 20s he also sang at one time as a lay clerk for New College Oxford. In 2011, he was part of the team that helped to lead a flagship school on the island of Jeju, South Korea, under the banner of North London Collegiate School. He credits being a part of transition and the brilliant leadership and mentoring at these schools for his confidence to lead the reinvention here.

The aim is to create one college rather than two quite separate schools and invigorate academic ambition, which he likens to 'tightening the plumbing of this incredible, beautiful building' whilst retaining the inclusive, diverse ethos of the school – a cornerstone of which is the introduction of a revitalised extracurricular offer named the Forder Programme, inspired by a pioneering early head who took boys on adventures all over London. Mr Hewlett lives in Croydon where he grew up and his interests include travel, literature, cooking and antique maps such as the beautiful one adorning his office.

We hear nothing but boundless enthusiasm in return from parents: 'He is ambitious for the college and very driven to secure its success, which is laudable. He is not afraid of change and he has conviction'; 'He is approachable, friendly and clearly driven. He also has a wonderfully eloquent turn of phrase.' Our sixth form tour guide appreciates greater transparency, more student voice and one-to-one drop-ins.

Head of junior school: Since September 2015, Mr Paul Cozens BA (40s). He grew up in the south west, was educated at Millfield School and graduated from Exeter University with a BA in educational studies with music and French. Exceptionally non-corporate – even his suit looked relaxed on the day of our visit – Mr Cozens describes himself and the head of the senior school as a Venn diagram with a 50 per cent overlap of core values: Mr Cozens brings much to the party, including music and mindfulness. Previously deputy of St Paul's Cathedral School, his first posts were at South Hampstead High junior dept and the Beacon School before being appointed as director of studies at Newton Prep. He is an ISI inspector and now lives within five minutes' walk of the school. He describes his first year as 'invigorating' and 'quite a project'.

Parents enthuse: 'He is dynamic, interested, brave... he is open-minded and interested in new ideas'; 'he manages to uphold the college's traditions while keeping up with the current times'; 'just right for the age group – visible, involved, friendly and approachable towards the children yet also minded to get the very best from them he can.' Our guides were somewhat amazed: 'He's friendly: not what you think a headmaster will be like!'

Academic matters: Children and parents speak very appreciatively of the junior school teaching: an 11 year old pupil who had been at the school since the age of 3 reported: 'It is great to be able to work with fantastic teachers who are able to explain things in a way that you can understand.' A parent: 'I have always been impressed by how quickly each new teacher gains an understanding of our child'. Another: 'The teachers in the pre-prep were absolutely brilliant at devising lesson plans that engaged very young children, expanded their minds...and made learning absolutely fun.'

Despite these bright spots, Mr Cozens found plenty of scope for introducing structural essentials to the academics: namely, a new academic deputy, and heads of English and maths. A pastoral deputy head joined the team in September. A new focus on a more joined up subject leadership from nursery to sixth form will benefit the junior school curriculum. It will work the other way too: year 6 pupils moving on to the senior school will find Mr Cozens teaching some ICT in year 7. Maths is taught creatively and memorably: when children learnt about area they designed a shopping centre; to understand units of measure they created and drank 'mocktails'. As elsewhere, the school uses Mathletics software. Plenty for linguists to experiment with in preparation for senior school: Spanish is taught from nursery to year 1, French in years 2 and 3 and French, German and Spanish in years 4, 5 and 6. Latin is now offered by way of co-curricular 'classics'. Mandarin is taught as a club. A parent said: 'lots of opportunities for recognition' which aid enthusiasm for academic subjects. The maximum size of classes is 20.

There is testing, but it's more in the style of continuous assessments – children take it in their stride. Homework is deliberately light with little or nothing in the holidays. Parents talk of seeking out the school because of a relative lack of pressure. A parent with children of varying academic natures believes the school 'would suit a child who thrives in a less competitive academic environment.' Those who need stretching are thought of too: the most able in years 5 and 6 have English and maths lessons with year 7 from time to time. We hear some year 6 children did feel under pressure, however, come the run up to the 11+ entrance testing. The news that the school will become an 'all-through' school should prove welcome.

In 2016, 45 per cent of A level grades were A*/A (73 per cent A*-B), whilst 61 per cent were A*/A at GCSE. Mr Hewlett's been on nothing short of a mission, observing 200 lessons, mentoring and training staff with potential, doing significant pruning elsewhere, resulting in four pages of goodbyes in the latest magazine, appointing a deputy head academic with experience of both Westminster school and the state sector, and student have had to raise their game too. Pupils are now innovatively graded on 'learning characteristics' such as 'engagement' or 'organisation' instead of simply the hard to measure 'effort' as well attainment.

On the ground, a student told us of 'an influx of better teachers'. The head says that his team is now in place and it's a matter of embedding. Parents speak of a change of pace: 'We are very happy that our children are aiming higher than before. It certainly isn't too intense.' Another, 'I have been impressed by the energy and enthusiasm displayed by all the teaching staff'. Naturally, there is still work to do. One parent also praised the teaching but said: 'Class discipline is less good, with a high level of ambient noise irritating for the more engaged students.' Whilst a mother said: 'It may benefit from developing a more competitive atmosphere for the more able students.'

The head likes the principles of the IB but also the rigour of A levels, so has decided to drop the IB in favour of the college's own diploma. This will consist of A levels combined with 100 hours of co-curricular and a global perspectives pre-U short course taken in the first term of year 12.

Everything you'd expect at GCSE in terms of curriculum choices, including Latin, and the languages taught are French and Spanish, German is offered, but no Mandarin. PE for those not wanting to be completely confined to a desk. Beyond the compulsories, Spanish and history are the most popular currently. Barely a handful of Latin students. More artists than musicians. Mathematicians, single scientists and historians perform well. Things get a little more varied at A level with the addition of drama and theatre, economics, and business studies. Most popular sixth form subjects last year were: maths, physics, geography and art and design, with the most A* by far for the mathematicians. Plenty of artists, but no drama or music students at this higher level. Teachers are free to choose whichever exam board best suits their cohort. Class sizes are a maximum of 25 until GCSE, then 15 in the sixth form.

All of the parents we spoke to said that they don't feel their children are unduly pressured: 'The school has a policy of not setting homework during the holidays. A project is set for any children who would like to do something, but it is entirely voluntary'.

The school has always had above average numbers of SEN pupils. This continues: 95 students have learning support needs, 70 per cent of these with dyslexia. The learning support provisions are mostly catered for in the classroom. Additional supplementary sessions are available based on need. For those who simply struggle with a particular lesson there are clinics or after-school help in every subject.

Some 15 per cent of the senior college are registered with EAL needs. There is an EAL co-ordinator and students are supported in class and withdrawal. In years 10 and 11 some EAL students can study for the GCSE in English as a second language.

Plenty of trips, workshops, competitions, adventures and fun drop-ins. Actor Adrian Lester gave the drama students four weekly workshops; English students make the most of London theatres, recently feasting on The Curious Incident of the Dog in the Nightime, A View from the Bridge and Othello, and year 12 and 13 mathematicians returned with a slew of medals from the UK maths challenge.

Sixth formers have their own shadowy domain, soon to be overhauled, but which includes a large boarding school-style common room with sofas, snooker tables and hot food from the dining room. Changes to facilities include a new lecture theatre next year and sixth form study centre.

Games, options, the arts: It's all here in terms of sports facilities including a swimming pool, cardio gym and weights, with more currently being brought up to scratch at the Jubliee sports ground. Sports are compulsory. The core are rugby, football, hockey, netball, cricket and swimming. Some individual successes: a couple of boys play for their county cricket team. A parent: 'My son throws himself into all sporting activities...it has been an enormous boost to his confidence and self-esteem that his commitment and achievements have been recognized'. In contrast another said: 'The children have felt under-prepared for their matches.' Help is at hand, with a new director of sport who isn't just focused on the elite or fixture results, but wanting every child to 'reach their physical potential'.

Some 200 students learn an instrument, from grade 1 to diploma level. A sizeable uptake, but by no means the most musical school we've visited. A mother told us: 'The gifted musicians are few in number and there are few opportunities for chamber music or innovative use of the talent pool'. However, plenty to thrill the ears in a rich timetable of recitals and concerts – some in beautiful London churches. The musical head believes the musical life of the school is very good. The St Paul's Symphonia recently joined school musicians in a festival concert.

Seriously impressive art lines the corridors, particularly the self-portraits. Large, light and popular DT workshops, including a separate space for sixth formers to work on their projects. A 3D printer and laser cutter. Students feel drama has taken a step up and there are 'lots of opportunities' with the appointment of a new head of drama; there are now three or four productions a year. The lower school recently relished putting on Bugsy Malone complete with splurge guns. A cross-discipline 'gothic evening' included everything from gentle electrocution – the science dept – to one teacher reprising Kate Bush's version of Wuthering Heights. The drama studio looks very professional, all black, framed with lighting rigs, complete with sound desk. The inaugural St Dunstan's Arts Festival show-cases the school's music, drama, art and dance for the fee-paying public.

The Forder programme provides 100 activities a week, is compulsory and runs every lunch-time, but still with space for a lunch break. Pupils must try something creative, active and as a service. Sixth formers as part of the St Dunstan's diploma must lead, must do something new and must commit for a term. It gives students plenty to write about come university reference time. Sixth formers also gain leadership opportunities taking activities into the junior school.

Debaters find their voice in national and international competitions. We were shown rooms of shiny Apples and Dells – pupils will leave school with the versatility of understanding both. CCF offers army and navy experiences. D of E challenges run up to gold. A selection of fun-looking co-curricular – after-school, before or at lunch times: Mexican art and craft club, French culture club, Amnesty, Hans Woyda, draw and print drop-in, swing dance and fashion appreciation caught our eye – some additional charges for specialist sports classes such as judo.

We rarely mention food in our reviews. When we entered the incongruous, modern dining hall, which has a Pringle shaped roof and our guide claimed 'they are the best school lunches in London' we expected hyperbole. Behold – towers of jewelled couscous displayed in tagines, the freshest of baby-leaf salads, home-made soups in terracotta bowls, bread baked every morning to Paul Hollywood standard and eight varieties of seeds in copper buckets.

All of the usual core sports in the junior school, rugby, hockey, football, cricket, netball, rounders and tennis take place on the extensive fields to the rear of the school – great to see the girls doing everything, even rugby. There's a new head of sport who will be redressing the balance: more time on skills, less time on matches. Some individual stars with a couple of county players.

There is a functional music block, with delightful sounds emanating, offering teaching spaces, practice rooms for lots of individual instrument lessons and a Mac suite. Ensembles for everything, plus chapel choir, chamber music, big band and rock band. Music scholars perform at St John's Smith Square. As the children rise through the school dramatic opportunities grow in ambition. Pupils performed in a Shakespeare festival at Greenwich Theatre. One delighted parent said of her son: 'He went from preferring to be backstage when he first arrived to taking a central part in his year 6 school production.'

Given this inner city locale the residential trips with an outdoorsy focus are a particular high. Junior school children take part in the college's Forder programme of extracurricular activities three times a week. Clubs could be music ensembles, opportunities to try new things such as debating or animation but also simply down-time pursuits like knitting and yoga.

Background and atmosphere: The school foundation has its origins in the parish of St Dunstan's-in-the-East, established on St Dunstan's Hill in the City, the location of one of five schools ordained by the Archbishop of Canterbury and Bishop of London in 1446. By 1865 it was agreed to relocate the school to parish land elsewhere, where there could be playing fields and to be accessible by rail. The school was duly opened in its present location next to Catford Bridge in 1888. The school maintains its links with St Dunstan's-in-the-East, more commonly known as All Hallows by the Tower, and students take part in services and ceremonies such as the wonderfully curious 'beating the bounds'.

This relocation for more green space seems incongruous now as one approaches the school from the ever-congested stretch of the south circular between Forest Hill and Catford. The school shelters behind its red-brick gates next to DIY sheds, a railway station and inner city grot somewhat at odds with the pictures of children walking along a tree-lined grassy grove (the playing field presumably) on the website.

Inside the red 'Hogwarts' building is at once impressive and in places shabbily homely. High ceilinged, metro-tiled corridors, lots of staircases with wooden handrails – no sliding – and a galleried Great Hall with stained glass windows, organ pipes and a multi-media desk for productions. Classrooms for year groups tend to cluster together, giving students a home base and possibly adding to the 'small' school feel.

The already large and well-equipped library is about to be almost doubled in size, retaining the wooden panelling, but introducing two soundproof modern pods with a teaching capacity of six for tutorials, adding a flexible lecture theatre and incorporating learning support and enrichment. The librarian inducts all year 7s into the resources available for their studies, which include 6,000 ebooks. Interns from London universities will become subject mentors, helping with research skills or providing careers inspiration.

A whole new junior school building is in the pipeline, and architects have been appointed. In our opinion it can't come too soon. The external fabric of the existing junior school buildings combined with the heavy lorries rumbling alongside much of the outdoor space is unlikely to win over prospective parents, but with plenty of play equipment, a good art space, large ICT suite and bright, well-organised, clean classrooms inside pupils seem oblivious.

We observed a happy and relaxed atmosphere. One parent told us: 'our daughter describes the school as busy, lively, noisy and feels confident with many friends. Our son describes the school as friendly, very informative and very sporty and active with lots of good trips.' 'Down to earth, practical, energised and caring' seems to sum it up.

Junior school children also struck us as happy and relaxed. We witnessed reception boogying to 'Move It, Move It', year 2s in quiet concentration and those on the move holding doors open for each other politely. Parents say: 'It is a place where every parent feels comfortable leaving their child knowing that they will be looked after, they will be happy and they will prosper'; there is 'a huge emphasis on making them stand tall, but also stride out into the world with questions to ask 'and 'most importantly, the children are given lots of opportunities to be children, to do fun things and enjoy their lives at school.'

Pets lend a family atmosphere. We met Fluffy 'the slightly evil hamster' and children eagerly await Marley the rescue rabbit. Come lunch time they troop to the senior school dining hall for a lunch which bears no resemblance to 'school dinners'. Extraordinarily fresh.

Pastoral care, well-being and discipline: Junior school parents speak highly of pastoral care; as one said: 'My daughter is able to discuss problems or concerns very easily with her form teacher. My son is so at ease in the school environment he feels totally happy with any member of staff.' Form tutors are the front line. House captains have as part of their role being someone younger children can come to, whilst 'worry boxes' are a starting point to raising something with a teacher. Years 1 to 4 have reading buddies. On a year 4 DT day each child created a pop-up book for their buddy based on the younger child's interests. Children all belong to houses. The head is striving to give the children a sense of what this means: 'understanding the notion of being competitive, but realising that if you work hard and well together that will reap rewards'.

A senior school parent confided: 'the pastoral care for the children has always been and continues to be excellent', but the head wants no room for complacency and so has appointed a new deputy head pastoral. There are four houses named after the first headmasters. Uniform rules are fairly stringent and students look smart. No mobiles on during the day. No beards in the sixth form. And ties at the conventional length: hear, hear. Hoodies are specifically forbidden, perhaps in case of inner city associations.

Pupils and parents: Pupils come from the immediate but also extensive south east London neighbourhood stretching across Lewisham to Greenwich, from the west such as Dulwich and further south to Bromley and Croydon. Fleets of coaches but also independent train travel.

The school welcomes international students and the numbers of Chinese students in the sixth form are visible; we wondered at integration when a student was unsure where they lived during term. A new head of inclusion and enrichment might consider issues like this alongside the remit to create a school that 'teaches to individuality'. In the future, international students will not comprise more than 10 per cent of the student body.

The community is one of hard-working families, many of whom are first-time buyers: 'down to earth, friendly and approachable,' said one mother of her peers. Creative types will find themselves in good company too. Old Dunstonians are musicians, politicians, businesspeople, sportspeople and scientists. Professor Sir Martin Evans, Nobel Prize winner for genetics, the very Rev Dr John Hall, Dean of Westminster and Lord Grade of Yarmouth, former chairman of the BBC and ITV, are among them.

Entrance: For 3+ nursery places, informal assessment and interview with parents 12 months prior to entry. For 4+ entry to reception there are small group assessments held each November – tasks such as listening to a story or discussing shapes and colours. The school is dipping its toe with a new 7+ entrance which will include brief English and maths papers followed by observed drama and science activities. There are similar assessments for 'occasional places' in other year groups beyond year 3, arranged on an ad hoc basis.

Whilst once upon a time the school was struggling for numbers, that is no longer the case. Year 7 is full and applications are up by 40 per cent. We believe this still makes it a gentle option compared with many. The head would love to lead on something truly radical with regards to 11+ entrance testing; year 7 applicants are currently tested in English, maths, verbal reasoning and abstract reasoning. Successful candidates are invited to return for an interview with a teacher and to meet either head or deputy head. No need for any nerves regarding parental interviews: it's simply time for a frank chat about the particular quirks of St Dunstan's offer and vision for the future. Testing takes place in January the year prior to entry. Unusually, there is an 11+ preparation scheme in place (for a fee), preparing candidates from all schools for the exams across three Saturdays. Far more entering from the local state primaries than is often the case – pupils come from Lewisham and Dulwich primaries, but also Heath House Prep, Oakfield Prep, Rosemead Prep and the Pointer School.

A small group of 13 or so enter at 13+, after taking English, maths and verbal reasoning papers. Prospective sixth formers are also required to sit papers in English, maths and verbal reasoning. Same interview process and references but the offer is conditional to the GCSE grades achieved in August.

S

Exit: Whilst most junior school children move to the senior school, around 20 per cent historically head to local state and grammar schools. Most exit to university, with around 60 per cent to Russell Group (one to Oxbridge in 2106). An interestingly diverse list of subjects being taken up for further study as befits the curricular offer here, recent range included biomedical science, design engineering, architecture, film practice, chemical engineering and neuroscience.

Money matters: There are academic, music, drama, art and design and sporting scholarships available at 11+ and academic and musical scholarships at 16+. Pupils who perform well in the entrance tests may be invited for an academic scholarship interview.

Potential scholars for the co-curricular awards must jump through a variety of hoops from one minute monologues (drama) to a colour study in oil pastels (art). Bursaries are generous and could run up to 100 per cent of fees for the right candidates. Family incomes will need to be modest but by no means breadline to be considered.

Remarks: In the next few years those pupils and parents taking up places are betting on potential. As the head says: 'we're not the finished article'. This location has to be a bit of a stumbling block but we expect parents looking for an effective and inspiring coeducational experience in south London to find themselves sorely tempted.

St Elizabeth's Catholic Primary School

Queen's Road, Richmond, Surrey TW10 6HN

Pupils: 213 • Ages: 3–11 • RC

Tel: 020 8940 3015
Email: info@st-elizabeths.richmond.sch.uk
Website: www.st-elizabeths.richmond.sch.uk

Headteacher: Since 2014, Mrs Jane Hines BA (40s), after 10 years as deputy head and six as a class teacher here. Before that was based in Bristol, where had completed a classics degree before moving into teaching. Loved the subject but, coming from a family of dedicated, fulfilled teachers, no other career exerted the same pull. News of appointment greeted with delight by parents, who already knew her as voice of kindly calm authority and (correctly) anticipated more of the same. 'Very calm and quiet, a real listener – have never seen her anything other than totally serene,' said parent.

But it's not just about maintaining the status quo. Mrs Hines is as dynamic (supported by strong leadership team) as they come. 'Very receptive to ideas,' said approving parent (we suspect she gets to do a lot of listening). In a short space of time, has brought in specialist teachers (a rarity in any cash-strapped school), transformed the site and ensured everyone buys into the process.

Happy and united staff – revitalizing mix of long stayers and recent arrivals – are with her all the way, recruitment pinpoint sharp (though very high standards mean that a few don't make it past probationary period). 'Want this to be a place where staff can innovate and try things out,' says Mrs Hines. Remains 'the best job in the world,' she says. If she has one (small) regret, it's that she isn't currently doing more teaching. Though won't take on a full time commitment as 'Tend to be called away for meetings,' she does plan to teach one or two lessons a week. 'Important to have that connection with the children.'

Entrance: Despite priority for demonstrably committed Catholic families from four local parishes, there's hope if you're not. A bulge class, added every three years, (so 60 in 2016-2017 rather than 30) greatly improves changes of success for applicants from other religions (Eastern Orthodox followed by other branches of Christianity) or even none. 'We welcome applications from everybody,' stresses Mrs Hines.

Exit: Top Catholic senior schools for most. Vast majority (30 in 2016) to highly rated newcomer, Sir Richard Reynolds, others to Gunnersbury, Sacred Heart Convent, Cardinal Vaughan and The

London Oratory School. Some girls to Waldegrave and handful of pupils each year to independents such as Putney High and Hampton (use of tutors not unknown).

Remarks: Even in high-achieving Richmond, St Elizabeth's would be having a bad year if its leavers didn't exceed borough averages. In 2015, 100 per cent of year 6 pupils achieved at least level 4s in reading, writing and maths (average level was 5B). While not, of course, the only reason parents choose the school, knowledge that in addition to a loving, Catholic ethos in cosy, small-scale environment, child is going to end up with a first class education does wonders for peace of mind.

Cynics might wonder whether given the location – lush lower slopes of Richmond Hill – and motivated parents, school simply can't go wrong. But success is never a given. Even here, there's considerable variation in family backgrounds. Over half the pupils now speak at least one other language, some arriving with very limited English, initially lured into the language by talking about their interests.

Success for all comes about through focus on the individual. 'Don't rely on any one tool,' says Mrs Hines. Throughout, rewards are based on how hard you try, not how clever you are. 'Teachers don't just care about our marks – they care that we're happy,' says year 6 pupil. Staff in complete agreement. 'Tests do not lead our judgement,' stresses senior teacher.

Writers' wall, changed every half term, features stories that are a personal best for their authors, not just the same old top talents. 'It's the pupils we're proudest of,' says teacher. Similar spirit – rewarding effort rather than straight brain power – prevails elsewhere. When all the children who had represented the school in sport were asked to stand up in assembly, 'was almost everyone,' reports a parent. 'Not always the same sporty kids doing stuff.'

For older children there's a big push on community involvement as role models for reception pupils. Year 6 chaplains develop entire assemblies for them from scratch – prayers, story and activity, while play leaders teach them to take turns at break. 'Look after them as though their own brothers and sisters,' said mother. 'It's a lovely thing for them to appreciate everybody.' Fun, agreed year 6 pupil – 'though they can be a bit wriggly.'

It all helps towards gaining coveted Governor's Awards – mini D of E scheme with desirable badges awarded for service, skills and growing independence – vast list ranges from leading a school club to locating 20 countries of the world and cooking a healthy meal. Everyone – with support from school – gets bronze, extra keen go for silver and gold.

Less than secret ingredient in success is teaching staff, most women (the perennial issue of the missing men in primary school teaching) who are 'unbelievable,' said a parent. 'Exhausted at the end of term but they're still smiling.' Add dedication – 'All work well beyond their hours,' said mother – and with happy, united team working to high standards, most parents had a virtually blank wishlist. A few start with initial reservations about how the many teachers with own children here balance dual roles – but not for long. 'It adds to their commitment – and if someone goes out socially with teacher who is a friend, would always put their professional hat on,' said one parent.

Even staff job shares are a model of effective communications, full-time TAs – one per year group in reception to year 2 – who stay with the class all week providing valuable sense of continuity. 'Don't know how they coordinate it but they don't miss a thing,' says parent. Skill, love of teaching and ability to construct active, exciting lessons undoubtedly help, though the basics are never forgotten, evening sessions for parents – starting with maths – showing how building blocks are put in place between reception and year 6. Must be working as while literacy is popular – 'Can let your imagination go wild with stories,' said year 6 pupil – most children rated maths as top subject. 'Fun learning new things – teachers help you through hard questions but don't tell you the answer.' Whatever the subject, clearly enjoy themselves, from year 2 pupils' pictures themed to 'Sky in the pie,' to a bit of creative headscratching as year 3s produced self-portraits for their reports, instantly switching from productive conversation to joining in with teacher's song, marking end of the lesson.

While those needing a bit of extra support or stretch will have separate group sessions, school doesn't go in for setting – not good for confidence. Instead, success is down to differentiation – highly effective because all children are known inside out to every teacher – no unknown unknowns here. Learning needs taken in school's stride – won't turn anyone away and if can't support a pupil themselves (and with excellent training for TAs that includes support for dyslexia and speech and language development, there's plenty they can) will look outside, often involving Richmond's highly rated Achieving for Children team. On day of visit, upbeat play therapist had just finished a session in the school's bright, cheerful library, a comforting space to work through difficulties. 'Can let go of their feelings here.'

School food was only aspect of life that some parents felt could do with some (minor) tweaking. Constantly under review, says school, with pupils pre-ordering so last in the queue don't miss out on best sellers (pizza a favourite), everything cooked from fresh and a salad bar recently added. Staff vote with their cutlery sets (around half have school lunches) and Mrs Hines and deputy both (other commitments permitting) eat with the children every day, 'which shows how good it is,' they point out. On day of visit, absence of mess and cleared plates suggested was going down a treat with the pupils too.

With academics ticking over nicely, the most welcome development (mentioned by every parent we spoke to) has been loan of specialist teachers (music, sports and – coming soon – French) from St Richard Reynolds. Provides non-teaching time cover for other staff, a bit of smart planning that keeps costs down.

Parents are pinching themselves in disbelief over speed of change, with weekly class music lessons for all coupled with accomplished school productions – polished lunchtime rehearsal of Bugsy Malone under way when we visited, impressive dance movements accompanied by talented young saxophonist, reception diners, knives and forks poised between plate and mouth, a gratifyingly awestruck audience. With new instruments to try, samba drums a popular addition, and excitement of having some of work recorded, difference is tangible. 'I notice a big change in their enthusiasm,' says parent of previously less than keen child who now arrives home singing new songs.

Whizzy head of sport has revitalized what was previously slightly low key area, at school four days a week, in first thing and often on days off as well, and spending every waking hour dreaming up new and exciting things to do, report parents. Includes setting up swimming squad and running extra sessions to help prepare for matches. 'Lives and breathes sport and has a passion that's spreading through the school,' says Mrs Hines. Just needs suitably aspirational space – about to happen with Astroturf courts on junior playground – and school will be able to host fixtures at home rather than borrowing space from Christ's, neighbourly C of E secondary school just down the road.

All happens on a compact site where 'every spit of space is used,' says staff member. Cleverly done, corridors minimal, monoblocks of colour creating sense of calm so stimulation comes from the teaching rather than the paintwork (riots of colour very much last year's pedagogy...). It's especially notable in bright, pristine reception classrooms, slightly separate from rest of school, opening onto cheerful, well designed freeflow playground, natural wood fence and climbing frame a nod to Richmond Park which runs just the other side of the back fence.

Energy carries straight on into myriad activities before and after school – and at lunchtime, with even reception having a go (though wouldn't do more than one a week). 'Tons and tons,' said mother, including big band, breakfast club, cookery, art, lego club, and DT. Parents, too, are immersed in life of the school, commitment extending well beyond fairs and cake sales to arranging for external speakers to come in and give talks.

'School has a lovely feel to it,' said parent, 'and Mrs Hines has taken it on and beyond where it was before. Our children there are so lucky.'

St George's CofE Primary School

Corunna Road, Battersea, London SW8 4JS

Pupils: 231 • Ages: 3–11 • C of E

Tel: 020 7622 1870
Email: admin@st-georges.wandsworth.sch.uk
Website: www.st-georges.wandsworth.sch.uk

Headteacher: Since 2015, Sarah Collymore (mid 30s); BA in primary education from Northumbria University. Went straight into teaching at 21 at a school local to her in Newcastle, but then decided to come to London with a friend and never looked back: 'We visited at Easter to view some schools – St George's being one of them. I rocked up one day and 12 years later, I'm still here.' Hired initially as a teacher in early years, at the same time as her predecessor Janet Hilary (former head) – this irrepressible duo took the school from special measures and on the verge of closure to Ofsted outstanding.

A Geordie lass who oozes warmth and likeability – the kind-natured, sincere head that every school should have. Dedication for 'her' children is tangible, and she is clearly popular with both parents and pupils alike – a few of whom came up to her in the playground (whilst we were there) to congratulate her on her new post as head. If one great head was going to leave, she was the only other person for the job and the only one with enough experience to drive the school forward. And this is where she plans to stay; 'If you have the will and desire to serve a community that is where you stay. There is no question that my work is where what I do will make a difference.'

Mrs Collymore has been described as 'an outstanding teacher' in all the phases of primary education she has worked – from early years through to key stage 2, then to deputy head prior to becoming head. One parent told us: 'I feel very confident in Mrs Collymore's ability to lead the school.' Married with one step daughter (her husband runs an exclusion unit in a large secondary comprehensive), she laughed when asked what she does in her 'spare' time.

The passion and pure dogged determination that former head Janet Hilary put into the school cannot be overlooked. She clearly left an indelible mark on both the pupils and parents who we spoke to. One parent told us: 'I chose this school because I was aware of Mrs Hilary's work before becoming head of St George's, and I knew how she worked. Her skill was that she pulled parents and teachers together.' However, after 12 years in the post, Mrs Hilary felt it was time to move on and embrace other challenges. She was appointed executive principle for Floreat Wandsworth and Floreat Brentford, 'an opportunity I couldn't turn down.' But she does very much plan to stay in touch with St George's and maintain a close partnership with Mrs Collymore: 'We are the No.1 Ladies' Leadership Team after all!'

Entrance: After the customary priority for looked-after children, 50 per cent of the school places are offered for church attendance, mostly from the local St George's Church, although some have come from further afield. One parent told us she travels in from Brixton. 'I wanted my child to go to this school, so I drive him there every day.' The remaining half of the school's intake are siblings followed by distance, although alarmingly we were told that being on the same road doesn't guarantee a place: 'Because there are so many tall blocks, some of those residents won't get a place.' Cohort is predominantly eastern European/Russian, Caribbean, West African, South Asian, and an increasing proportion of South American pupils. A large majority comes from single parent families: 'Diversity is very healthy for us. It enriches us all.'

Exit: The largest share goes to the local comprehensive St Cecilia's CE, followed by St John Bosco RC, a new voluntary aided college. Other local comprehensives include Ark Putney Academy, Southfields Academy and Lambeth Academy. If you have a girl, Lady Margaret – 'virtually impossible to get in to' – as well as Grey Coat Hospital ('if it's good enough for the [ex-] prime minister..') – are the schools of choice. One parent did say that she worries about the lack of decent secondary school education in the area, 'but try not to worry about it yet.' However, the head remains positive about the regeneration of the area and the new demographic buying into these properties. She says: 'I believe that in two years we'll have a secondary school of choice on the patch.' Last year, for the first time in the school's history, one of their students was awarded a scholarship to Dulwich College, and has since become something of a legend in the school – a source of huge aspiration for the other pupils. The head told us: 'Nothing can come close to the feeling you get when a child from the Patmore Estate in South London tells you that they are going to Dulwich College and will study to become a heart surgeon.'

Remarks: Set amidst the Patmore and the Savona estates in Battersea, dwarfed by the numerous regeneration projects in the area (most notably Battersea Power Station and Nine Elms construction, which is right next door) and tucked away at the end of a residential street, this small one form primary school could be easily overlooked. Indeed we almost walked past it, which would've been a shame, as this wholly unpretentious school is quite a hidden gem.

Over the past four years, standards of attainment achieved by the school have been among the highest in the country, and its progress measures puts it in the top five per cent of schools. This year alone the school received two ministerial congratulations: for the phonics results (100 per cent) and for being one of the highest achieving schools in the country in terms of attainment and progress.

For any primary school this would be a major achievement, but for a school where the proportion of pupils eligible for free school meals is well above average, and nearly 60 per cent of the intake comes from homes where English is not a first language (32 languages spoken at the school), the sheer ambition cannot be underestimated.

The school's motto, 'The best we can be', is not a useless platitude, but something that they really aspire to for every child. As the head told us, 'We teach our children dignity and respect and teach them to come to school ready to learn'. No time is wasted in helping and encouraging children who speak other languages at home to begin to speak standard English; 'language is our bedrock because of where the different parents come from.' In reception, children are 'spellbound during phonic sessions by the teacher's funny hat, the silly songs they sing to keep them all on task and by the praise they are constantly given for their hard work. Phonics lessons are consequently a joy, and filled with giggling, gleeful responses.' Ofsted.

Teaching generally very impressive and children we saw were well behaved and enthralled in what they were being taught. Innovative use of teaching staff to create small focused teaching groups in years 5 and 6 has been highly successful, and means that no pupil is left behind, and all are able enjoy high levels of challenge in English and maths. Each class has one teacher and one designated teaching assistant, in order to free up one of them to give individual help to any struggling pupils. 'It's important to spend time with a pupil if they don't get it, before they become disengaged.' Fairly high turnover of staff because of promotion elsewhere. 'Being a one form entry, it is hard to promote staff at St George's, but as we're diligent with our funding, we never have a shortfall.'

Those with special educational needs progress exceptionally well because the assessment and understanding of their needs is finely tuned. Former head said: 'I find it difficult to believe that when I started here, apparently 72 per cent of pupils had special needs. Now there are 12 per cent. I believe too often children are labelled as special needs if they are under-achieving.'

Statistics and academia aside, the first thing that struck us on entering the school was how very serene it was. Nobody spoke in loud voices and staff almost glided to their various destinations – we could virtually hear a pin drop outside the classrooms we visited. Evidently, much thought has been given into making this school a calm, inviting and safe haven for pupils – the antithesis to many of their lives. The small, but stunningly immaculate and colourful garden which acts as a centrepiece for the school ('there are around 15 goldfinches in the gardens and we grow our own rhubarb and strawberries') offers pupils the opportunity to sit and read or reflect – and the dinner hall has been designed to overlook these gardens. This is all part of the 'Calm School Code' ethos, which everyone is expected to adhere to.

The second thing that struck (as we too glided from classroom to classroom on account of the very shiny floors), is how immaculate the classrooms were and how pupils demonstrated such pride in all aspects of their schooling, from their beautifully laminated workbooks (with some exceptional examples of joined up handwriting from the lower year groups), to their pristinely turned out selves in their smart navy uniforms with tied back or braided hair. As one parent said, 'The school is pretty strict on uniform, but that is because they don't want anyone to stick out.'

Very little wall space seems to be taken up by specific topic work but instead by an assortment of learning aids – phonics, maths, famous quotes, charts etc. One wall was virtually made up of aspirational charts. Pupils can belong to the 144 Club (children need to know all their times tables up to 12 and recall them quickly), the 20-20 Club for years 1, 2 and 3 etc etc. Perhaps the most prestigious of all of these is the Superstar award. It is the responsibility of each class team to encourage as many children as possible to become Superstars. All classrooms must have the 'HAPPY' chart (an acronym for homework, attitude, punctuality, participation, yourself)) on display and must demonstrate all aspects of 'HAPPY' to receive their badge. Teachers are responsible for talking to parents about how they can support with any of these areas. At the end of each term the children who have been awarded their Superstar badge receive a reward. Autumn term – Christmas movie at the local cinema. Spring term – party and disco. Summer term – trip to Chessington.

Aspiration seeps through the very foundations of this school, from the extremely well stocked and well looked after library, to weekly maths assemblies (where certificates are awarded to pupils who have completed maths challenges) – through to enrichment days at local independent schools such as Newton Prep, where years 4 and 5 get to use the facilities and are taught art, music, sport, science etc by specialist teachers. Some lucky pupils have enjoyed a trip to nearby Chelsea Football Club where strong links have been forged, whilst others sat in amongst the musicians of the Orchestra Vitae. One parent told us: 'Credit to the leadership team at this school for encouraging our children so much that they want to achieve, and then achieve more.'

Breakfast club on offer from 8.15am and after-school care offered until 6pm. A wide range of after-school clubs including dance, cooking, zumba, football, karate, tennis, choir and gardening. Participation in sporting competitions including athletics, cricket, golf, netball and basketball, and swimming lessons offered from year 4.

This is a proactive school in every conceivable way – no opportunity is left untapped. Instead of being bah humbug about the extensive building work in the area, the school has seized the opportunity to work with the architects, designers and builders on the Nine Elms Regeneration Project – and even managed to secure a substantial donation from its developers for a brand new all-weather sports pitch and art classroom.

If this wasn't enough, the school has set up a programme of motivational speakers for the older children and thus far the likes of Baroness Scotland, Sir William Atkinson and broadcaster Julie Etchingham have all come to speak at St George's. The head says: 'We want our pupils to have ambition and aspiration and this programme really helps them to think about careers and life choices.' Generous donations and sponsorship have also provided many rich opportunities for the pupils, including seaside trips (many pupils never having been to the seaside), theatre trips and funding for the new school uniform.

Unspoilt and wonderfully refreshing, the pupils we spoke to talked of becoming chartered accountants, vets, footballers and comedians. What came through were spirited, happy children with big personalities and a real sense of ambition. One particular pupil who was touchingly wise beyond his years, just seemingly so grateful for being at this school: 'I just wish there was a St George's secondary school for us to go to.'

St Helen's School

Eastbury Road, Northwood HA6 3AS

Pupils: 1,173 • Ages: 3–18 • Sixth form: 169

Fees: £11,421 – £15,978 pa

Tel: 01923 843210
Email: admissions@sthelens.london
Website: www.sthelens.london

S

Headmistress: Since 2011, Dr Mary Short BA PGCE PhD (50s) – did her PhD, in the politics of budget-setting in the 1920s, at Cambridge. Has taught undergraduates at Cambridge and pupils at independent schools including St Paul's Girls, City of London Boys and Haberdashers' Aske's Girls (deputy head). She has teaching in her blood and is married to a fellow teacher. Apart from history, likes walking, bread-making and travel. Aims to up the academic performance, partly by 'reviewing the admissions process to more accurately identify academic potential', but more by curriculum reviews, consistency of aims, better monitoring of performance, peer review of teachers, that sort of thing. Good relationship with her top-notch governors.

A smile of measured mischief, and a fascination with bringing the best out of each pupil. Her eyes light up when describing how the school is going about sorting out one of her more troublesome charges. 'Is quietly powerful', said a parent, 'I really, really like her, and so do the girls.'

Academic matters: 'Makes learning exciting, with no pressure', to quote a parent of her 4-year-old – gets crisper as they get older of course. Recent review and revamp of maths, English and languages: 'we plan the development of confident, fluent linguists from the age of 3'. Lots of ICT, good DT. A teacher and teaching assistant to each class in Little Saints plus a newly-qualified TA, some teaching assistants in junior school.

Not the top of the highly competitive North London academic tree, but no slouch. Lots of male teachers, lots of teachers who have had other professional lives before or even during teaching. Every pupil we talked to had at least one teacher they found truly inspiring. Pupils describe the atmosphere as 'competitive but collaborative': in maths, for instance, where randomly chosen pairs of girls help each other to tackle problems and be the best pair in the class.

In 2016, 55 per cent A*/A at A level, 87 per cent A*/A at GCSE. Good range of subjects in the sixth. The overwhelmingly popular subjects at this level are the sciences, maths, economics and history, with maths results particularly strong. Physics as ever with girls the slightly weaker relation, but school working hard to encourage and take-up is growing – the Heath Robinson Club is clearly popular and interest in engineering is strong. The cuttings that adorn the corridor walls in the science department are totally fascinating, and would repay an hour's dawdling. Sixth form curriculum enriched by EPQ (school hopes that eventually everyone will choose to take this) plus lecture series and university preparation courses.

Way ahead of the government on the EBacc: has been doing it for years, with a strong emphasis on having a second language. Tendency to do art and/or drama as the 'free' choices. Highly IT literate: great facilities and teachers who know how to use them. Students are able to: complement their A level programme with the St Helen's Portfolio, which comprises additional qualifications such as the European Computer Driving Licence; take up modules offered by the Open University; continue with languages they have studied to GCSE or acquire additional languages or study further mathematics; also recognises CCF, D of E, other clubs and societies

Thoroughly sympathetic to SEN, from the headmistress down. Everyone is screened at 7 and 11 for potential educational difficulties. 'We then discuss with parents how we can make it better.' Individual Needs Department created in 2013 with three staff providing support to pupils from age 7. School can and does support autistic spectrum difficulties, mild dyslexia and dyspraxia, mild speech difficulties and children with hearing impairments. Currently focusing on better provision for those who struggle with numbers – some children have extra help with maths. 'All take iGCSE maths – we have no intention of becoming a specialist centre for dyscalculics, but do want to become much more effective at picking up those who struggle with number work before they become paralysed by algebra!' Support, but not separate teaching, for those who have English as an additional language. Some 100+ children currently identified as Gifted and Talented and supported with 'differentiated work schemes and activities' and school is developing a programme for its academic scholars.

Games, options, the arts: The huge surprise for anyone visiting St Helen's and who, perhaps, has only seen it behind its sedate hedges and modest perimeter walls, is the unbelievable amount of space it has. Acres of playing fields, courts and pitches extend in all directions and you begin to realise that most of this end of Northwood is St Helen's. A vast new sports complex and superb, seemingly endless pool, in a stunning new building, in enthusiastic use. Lacrosse, netball, rugby, tennis, athletics, badminton and rounders all popular and many other games and activities available including pilates, aerobics, fencing, climbing and trampolining. Representation in lacrosse, swimming, cross-country, netball and badminton national teams and much success for school teams in all these sports plus athletics and rounders at impressive levels. Supports those who excel (and need time off for national teams) and has no beef with those who prefer music (but still have to do games). All do ballet, PE, music and speech and drama as part of the junior school curriculum.

Art, DT and drama housed in the June Leader building, named after school's outstanding, and aptly named, head of 20 years (1966-1986), the great builder of the school, both in physical terms and in terms of the quality of education and values promulgated here under her uniquely humane regime. First rate art, teachers are real artists and teaching combines strong basic skills such as life drawing with experimentation, breadth and understanding. DT bubbling and well taught if not as jazzily equipped as some (though there is CAD and a 3D printer). Dance and drama (some joint with Merchant Taylors') much enjoyed, especially in the context of the annual House Arts festival. It is good to see the arts so strong in a school whose spirit is essentially academic. The Centre is a new multi-purpose space for the performing arts and sport (converted from the existing gym).

Music is going from strength to strength with numerous orchestras, choirs and, bands. The jazz band has made a CD, the huge choir tours abroad annually, there are many and varied opportunities for performance in school and the wider community, including regular concerts at St John's, Smith Square, London.

Collaboration with Merchant Taylors' also in CCF. D of E and Young Enterprise also popular. Visits from profs, writers and theatre companies. Successes in debating, maths and physics Olympiads, technology competitions. Lots of trips – Madrid, Kobe, Ypres, Berlin, CERN, Kew, Rome, House of Commons, Paris, British Museum, galleries.

Underlying ethos of opportunity, progression and support. Hundreds of things for pupils to try and, when they latch on to one, the school will find ways of allowing it to be taken further – as far, indeed, as the girl can go.

Background and atmosphere: Founded at the end of the 19th century with a vision of education for the whole child, which it still holds dear. A spacious school, trim and imaginative grounds, relaxed, not at all authoritarian. Dark green uniform up to 16; conservative freedom in the sixth. Plenty of completed and planned development eg converting newly vacated junior school buildings into sixth form centre. Longworthe, one of the former boarding houses, is now used for before and after school care in which pupils with busy parents can spend a long day – breakfast and tea included and quiet places for prep and recreation. Nicely decorated rooms for sixth form relaxation and study (much studiousness observed).

Strong Indian, Tamil and Jewish (a strong JSoc and well-established links with the local synagogue) contingents, but absolutely no sign of segmentation or separation among the pupils, and parents report that it's like that with the ones they bring home too. Watch them swirl around you at break time and wish the world could be like that. Strong and growing relationship with Merchant Taylors', already noted, supplies all the male element the girls want, and no more.

Notable absence of the unhealthily thin. Eating is a social rite here – you stumble across snacking groups all the time. School encourages this with decent breaks, delicious cookies and time enough for lunch.

The junior school is an integral part of the whole. The nursery, Little St Helen's, and the junior school are all housed in buildings around this beautiful site and share many of the facilities of the senior school. Completely new junior school building. Much given to heartening mottoes: 'Enter with an Open Mind', 'Reach Higher than Your Dreams' – an improvement on the school's Latin one, which is an odd combination of conquering, crosses and daisies. Happy atmosphere, lovely bright uniform, civilised loos and teachers who say 'ladies, will you please take off your shoes now' to a crocodile of receptive 6-year-olds. It is natural for girls here to stay the course – now from 3 to 18 – and continue to feel that it's all in the family.

Pastoral care, well-being and discipline: Each individual teacher is expected to notice and to care how their charges are, and to react supportively and promptly to any sign of trouble. As a result, while teachers talk of all the usual friendship and family problems, the girls seem hardly aware of them, and prefects do not see dealing with social ills as a significant part of their remit. Relationships within houses, year groups and tutor groups all seem close, giving girls a variety of communities to turn to.

Staff/student relationships palpably cordial. 'A lot of our teachers are role models,' said one sixth former. 'They are so kind and helpful and it doesn't just stop in the classroom. They will keep helping you achieve what you want to achieve.' A younger pupil agreed, 'and', she added, 'you just have to be friendly here because everyone is. The teachers are so sweet – they really look after you – there's always someone to talk to and problems are sorted out really quickly.' 'Never a door closed, they always have time for you'. The same applies to the medical room, with its welcoming nurse, and the school counsellor (called a confidential listener).

Clear sanctions policy. System of warning and detention cards. MP3s/mobiles illegal in school time. No drugs incidents in living memory. The occasional foolish misdemeanour is dealt with individually but 'sanely. It's never public, it's not about humiliation – ever.' You're allowed to slip here.

Pupils and parents: Resilient, personable, happy, chatty girls who 'know who we are and why we are here', and whose attitude to problems is to 'tackle not buckle'. Alongside, that is, a deep-rooted conservatism: wary of the poetry shelves in the library and reluctant to take gap years (although the pupil we talked to whose ambition was to be an inventor was thought eccentric, she was still very much one of the girls). The head 'hopes to encourage greater risk-taking'.

Northwood is prosperous, with lots of large detached houses. Girls come from wide area – good coach service covers Beaconsfield, Elstree, Barnet, Amersham, Ealing, Hemel Hempstead and points between.

Old girls' network huge and devoted. St Helen's inspires great loyalty. Alumnae include Patricia Hodge, a great supporter, Vanessa Lawrence (director general Ordnance Survey), Lady Lowry, Luisa Baldini, Penny Marshall and Maria Djurkovic.

Entrance: School part of North London Consortium which shares tests at 11. First point of entry is at 3 or 4 by observation and interview. At 7 by tests in English and maths and interview. At 11, exams in English and maths; around 460 apply for approximately 100 places – not too terrifying as lots apply elsewhere but school is increasingly candidates' first choice. Junior school girls have to sit the exam too, and most make the transition. Around half of the senior school places are filled by junior school girls.

Interview and reference from current school as important as scores. 'Aim is to explore potential and to ensure that girls will be able to take full advantage of the curriculum and wider opportunities the school has to offer,' says the school. As ever true but never spelt out, parents should remember that they are on show too.

At sixth form, 'places are available for girls who the school considers will benefit from the educational programme offered and who will enjoy becoming members of the school community. We don't fix the number of places.' You need 7+ GCSEs at B+ including good grades in the subjects relevant to the A level choices.

Exit: Usually a smooth transition from LSH to the juniors and from juniors to seniors. Very few to local state grammars, boarding or competition: 'I asked my daughter if she would like to look at other schools; she looked at me as if I was bonkers.'

Around 15-20 per cent leave post-GCSE. All sixth formers to higher education. Handful to Oxbridge annually (five places in 2016, plus one to Yale), otherwise a wide spread of universities and courses (London, Sheffield, Leeds, Warwick, Birmingham are popular). About a third science-related: strong bias to medical, biological and engineering courses, with a high proportion of dentistry and medical offers (five in 2016). Careers advice considered by the girls to be top notch, and in general they have a much clearer idea than usual of what courses they would like and what careers they might pursue afterwards.

Money matters: Range of scholarships and means-tested bursaries. Bursaries awarded annually and are either awarded to girls whose parents could not otherwise meet fees or to girls whose families are experiencing temporary difficulties.

Remarks: Thoroughly impressive. Not in hock to the league tables, but plenty of ambition for its pupils, academically and otherwise.

St James Junior School

Linked with St James Senior Boys' School, St James Senior Girls' School

Earsby Street, London W14 8SH

Pupils: 249 • Ages: 4–11

Fees: £15,360 – £16,740 pa

Tel: 020 7348 1793
Email: admissions@stjamesjunior.org
Website: www.stjamesjuniors.co.uk

Headmistress: Since 2009, Mrs Catherine Thomlinson, BA in English and history from Roehampton (40s). A St James' disciple to her fingers' ends, having spent almost all of her teaching career here after being educated at sister school, St Vedast (brief spell in South Africa before coming back to the fold). Two children, a son and a daughter, both of whom attended St James from age 4 right through senior school. A thoroughly lovely lady who radiates kindness, humanity and good humour, and this despite having a shocking cold when we met. The study oft proclaims the head, we've found, and Mrs Thomlinson's was sparely but beautifully furnished, bright and calm. Amidst some exquisite pictures of quiet seas, a joyous tract reads, 'Let your light shine!' – and hers most assuredly does.

Despite her lifelong loyalty to the St James traditions, Mrs Thomlinson has not been afraid to modernise. She has pushed through substantial curriculum development, including DT, French and dance; and both boys and girls now do cookery, woodwork and sewing. Introduced interactive whiteboards for upper junior classrooms ('a fantastic tool'), and is looking to bring these in throughout the school. Major development of EYFS provision, following criticism in recent inspection report. Parents report improved communication. Continues to uphold strong emphasis on speech, drama and music, 'because they really touch the emotional intelligence'.

Entrance: 'We don't take children on an academic basis,' says head, and accordingly there's no entrance exam at age 4; instead, the school holds informal assessments that involve meeting both child and parents, plus a report from child's nursery where applicable. Children of alumni and siblings have priority, as do those whose parents registered them early for a place. School looks for 'a certain confidence, and for children and families who value what we value'. Places higher up the school occasionally become available, and children who apply aged 7+ take assessments in reading, writing and mathematics to establish whether they're able to manage within the standard of the established class.

Exit: Girls and boys now both stay on till year 6, with the majority (80-90 per cent) going on to St James Senior Girls or St James Senior Boys. The latter is out at Ashford (a very comprehensive coach service is provided by St James Schools). Children can be prepped for entrance to other senior schools at parents' request; 'we are happy to support all our pupils in whichever path they take'. Parents appreciate the automatic entry. Other destinations include Fulham Prep, Latymer Upper, Wetherby Prep, Hampton and St Paul's Juniors.

Remarks: A frieze of the goddess Athene gazes down benevolently from one of the foyer walls, and this may explain the air of gentle wisdom that really does pervade this unusual and admirable little school. It nestles quietly within residential streets, the outside resembling a monastery, with its high walls and expanse of sheer red brick, but the tableau through the security gate wasn't in the least forbidding. Children played cheerfully in a pretty, cloistered courtyard under the eye of a watchful but serene-looking teacher, and the whole was framed by light and airy corridors – a preponderance of new glass giving a modern, clean balance to the Victorian charm of the original building. The atmosphere, as far as we could judge, was one of kindness and peaceful activity. Parents all confirmed this: 'It's a very happy place.' 'It's an extremely happy school.' 'A warm and nurturing environment.' 'My child has loved being there from the very beginning.'

The school's ethos places an unusually high emphasis on generosity, mutual respect and 'being the best human beings we can be,' and achieves this through a number of distinctive practices. Every lesson begins and ends with a 'moment of stillness'. Such moments 'give you that sense of ease and reflection,' says head. These pauses, as they're known, are popular with parents and children: 'It gives you a chance to be still,' said a year 6 child, whose demeanour was courteous and mature beyond his years. Parents agree. 'One of the main benefits of St James is the peacefulness,' was one comment, and 'One of the reasons we send our children to the school is to learn early on to take a pause, allow the noise to stop,' was another.

All the children, even the little ones, learn Sanskrit, in accordance with the school's belief that the Eastern philosophies have much to teach us; and both children and parents insisted to us that this was one of the things they 'really loved' about the school. St James describes itself as 'multi-religious', and philosophy itself is a very important part of the curriculum. The school teaches a Socratic method of dialogue and questioning, and the children are taught to develop open-ended questions and to debate as a class ('No putting-down of others' opinions is allowed,' says head firmly). The school motto – 'Speak the truth, be generous and kind, be your best' – seems to mean more here than such saws do in other schools. St James's policy of teaching boys and girls separately, then bringing them together for social activities (break-times, lunch, productions, trips, etc) may also be a key factor in establishing such good relationships between the children. 'You can see the boys, but you don't always have to be with them,' said a grateful year 5 girl, with which one of the boys countered, 'The girls think they're best, and we just get on with being even better.' We suspect this is amiable posturing: a number of parents confirmed to us that their child's closest schoolfriends included those of the opposite gender.

Academic performance is strong, with the standard of written work exceptionally high, both in content and accuracy – all the more impressive, given that the school's intake is not academically selective. 'I'm a great advocate for academic rigour,' confirms the head, adding, 'but I'm just as passionate about children finding out what they love.' All classes have weekly sessions in the well-stocked library, run by a dedicated librarian, and there are regular visits by children's authors. ('My son very quickly developed a love of reading,' reported a satisfied parent.) SEN provision is good, with about 30 EAL children cared for within the classroom set-up. We applaud the emphasis on using Shakespeare as a teaching resource at all levels, more so than in any other school we've visited. We saw verses from The Winter's Tale charmingly illustrated by the reception children, and read some excellent commentaries on Polonius's advice to his son ('To thine own self be true') by the year 3 boys. 'We love Shakespeare,' the head acknowledged. 'We did A Midsummer Night's Dream and The Tempest last year. And Mozart's The Magic Flute. We have a great cultural reservoir to draw on – why not give them the best material?' Why not indeed.

And in fact the drama on offer is very impressive, with all the children involved in at least one performance every year. 'We like big productions!' beamed a member of staff, before hurrying off to oversee preparations for Fiddler On The Roof, for which the school hired the Britten Theatre at the Royal College of Music because 'we like to be ambitious'. Previous big productions include My Fair Lady, The Railway Children and The Sound of Music. For in-house performances, the school's hall has been recently refurbished and hosts frequent verse-speaking, plus dance for both girls and boys as well as drama productions. Music is strong, with 70 children taking instrumental lessons at school on 'pretty much anything they want', and regular concerts, often featuring the school's orchestra. The children sing every day in assembly – repertoire by Mozart, Purcell and Vivaldi is popular – and have music lessons every week. Artwork of an astonishingly high standard adorns the walls, produced in the attractive art room under the gaze of the stuffed menagerie up on the shelf: a goose, a grouse, a heron and a weasel.

All children have a period of games or sport every day, be it gym, dance, swimming or ball skills, and the upper juniors (years 3-6) go off-site once a week to Barn Elms to hone their skills at netball, rugby, cricket, athletics, cross-country and the like. There are lots of inter-school competitions, and the children told us proudly about recent triumphs over Wetherby and Fulham Prep. Swimming is held in nearby Fulham Pools, and ISA golds and silvers have been a feature of recent years. St James Junior is a member of Forest Schools UK, with two of its staff trained as Forest Leaders, and there are many trips to Minstead Study Centre in the New Forest. 'I've been seven times!' enthused one upper junior boy, 'and I enjoyed it SO MUCH!' A varied programme of outings closer to home has encompassed museums, art galleries, theatres, and the usual London fare. Excellent range of lunchtime and after-school clubs includes guitar, yoga, cookery, gymnastics, model-making, archery, fencing, lacrosse and the perennially popular Mad Science Club. The head actively encourages all her staff to take up hobbies themselves, and the staff music band, we're told, is going from strength to strength. Use of ICT across the school has increased, although actual ICT lessons are still for year 6 only. Children are 'encouraged to use ICT at home,' which may or may not be enough preparation for the increasingly ICT-based curriculum they'll face at senior school. But the junior school's stated priority is to develop clear cursive handwriting in its pupils, and from what we saw, they definitely succeed.

Food here is vegetarian, so that all the children can eat together, and is included in the fees. We were impressed by what we saw: a delicious-smelling vegetable curry, fresh bread being baked, home-made leek and potato soup, and lots of genuinely appetizing fresh fruit. The number of clean plates testified to its popularity with the young clientele, and one solemn little girl was particularly enthusiastic about it to us as she lowered her elbow into her coleslaw. No problem, though – the lower juniors (years R-2) wear smocks down to lunch, which we thought eminently sensible.

All aspects of the pastoral care were rated excellent in the latest inspection report, which commented on the 'family atmosphere of mutual respect,' adding that 'the pupils thrive in the positive, caring environment' and are 'very well cared for.' The pupils concur. 'It's fun here,' 'The teachers are very kind,' 'Everyone is really nice,' 'You don't feel you have to be afraid of anything,' 'You can be yourself,' 'You can be proud of yourself,' 'The teachers are proud of us and they trust us,' were some of the many tributes we heard. This is all the more inspiring, given that the School of Economic Science, which founded the St James schools, attracted some very different comments from its embittered pupils a few decades back.

But all that is history. St James Junior impressed us as such a kind and enlightened medium in which to culture young minds, that we occasionally had to remind ourselves that this was a school we'd stepped into and not a Botticelli painting. It was almost a relief to see one small boy aim a punch at another, to hear an indignant cry of 'I was first!' and to meet a teacher who was unmistakably knackered after her morning's work. But these tiny wrinkles only served to throw into greater focus the sweetness and calm of this remarkable community. Not a school for budding Piers Morgans, we suspect. But who cares?

St James Senior Girls' School

Linked with St James Senior Boys' School, St James Junior School

Earsby Street, London W14 8SH

Pupils: 320 • Ages: 11–18 • Sixth form: 65

Fees: £18,330 pa

Tel: 020 7348 1777
Email: admissions@sjsg.org.uk
Website: www.stjamesgirls.co.uk

Headmistress: Since 2014, Mrs Sarah Labram BA (40s), formerly deputy head (academic) here. A classicist with a degree from King's College London, she is totally imbued with the St James ethos: a former pupil and head girl, whose two daughters were both educated at the junior and senior schools. She joined St James in 1996 as a classics teacher and has risen through the ranks to become head of department and then deputy head.

A hands-on head with a winning combo of directness, warmth and enviable serenity, she is often out and about around the school and clearly knows her pupils well, chatting easily with them in the corridors. Has an open-door policy, with pupils popping in to say anything from, 'It's my birthday, would you like a piece of cake?' to 'Can I tell you about my sports achievement?' Refreshingly, pupils also have no qualms about poking their heads into her office to ask things like, 'Can you sign our permission slip to stay in at lunchtime to practice dance?' if nobody else is around. 'She's definitely not a head that you only see for bad or serious stuff,' one pupil explained, and although they welcome her lack of preciousness and her cordiality, they are quick to add that underneath it all, she commands respect. 'I was late for assembly the other day, and I won't be doing it again,' one pupil said. Parents feel they're in safe hands and praise her responsiveness, kindness and efforts to involve them eg to give talks (a dad had come into talk about climbing Everest when we visited), try out the school food, hear updates about the school and present their own views etc. That said, her introduction of the three new roles of head of lower, middle and upper school means any parental concerns are usually dealt with lower down the food chain.

Teaches Greek to year 9s. 'Teaching is what I love and classics is my passion – I'm not giving that up!' she laughs, adding that it ensures that she understands what's expected of other teachers. 'I soon see if something works or it doesn't,' she explains. 'And the inevitable informal chats in the classroom give me an insider's view of pupil needs too,' she adds. Lives in south east London and hobbies include theatre, classical music and walking.

Academic matters: Girls take the IGCSE in the three sciences, for greater rigour. At GCSE, 78 per cent A*/A grades in 2016. Stunning success in art, biology, classics and physics, and at least respectable everywhere else. At A level the 19 subject options include theatre studies, Spanish and history of art. In 2016, 83 per cent of A level entries were graded A*-B (51 per cent A*/A). Results creditable in most subjects – few grades below B – and art, economics, French, and physics particularly impressive. School also offers EPQ to give students the opportunity to get deeply involved in a subject that interests them, to pull together learning from other subjects and to develop extended research and writing skills – all good preparation for university.

As with the boys' school, philosophy and spirituality are a major part of school life. Yes, girls are expected to work hard (we saw heads down in every classroom we visited) but every lesson is underpinned by the kind of big questions and ideas that form the cornerstone of all western and eastern wisdom traditions – but without being tied to the dogma of one. The result? Girls are encouraged to get the magic, awe and wonder of each subject – the wow-factor in addition to good, solid teaching. Plus, we found the girls could link pretty much everything – be it Latin, English or those knotty teenage issues like body image and social media – to guiding philosophical principles. 'It's not just about philosophical and spiritual concepts, but how they might be important when, say, you're trying to understand the relevance of maths in your life or how integrity might be important if, perhaps, you fall out with your friends,' explains the head. There's also a big push on mindfulness, meditation and quiet time (five minutes at the start and end of every day). 'I love the way they create space for inner reflection and how the school is so confident and unapologetic that this is their offering,' said one parent. 'If you don't buy into meditation or mindfulness, it probably isn't the school for you,' said another.

Sanskrit is continued for those who join from the junior school (introductory course offered to those joining in year 7) and available as an option at GCSE and A level. At least one a year chooses to study it at university. 'It's great for grammar,' says the head, 'as well as for the philosophy and culture that surrounds it. Plus, it marks you out as interesting and it's well respected.' In addition to Sanskrit, French and Latin from year

7; and Spanish (for those who don't carry on Sanskrit) and classical Greek (for the most able linguists) from year 8. Setting in English and maths from year 7; Latin and French from year 8; and science from year 9. Homework taken seriously – an hour and 10 minutes for year 7s, building up to a couple of hours a night in year 10 and 11. All the usual monitoring and targeting, with girls all initially tested in year 7, from which they are ranked (although they're not told where they sit).

SEN mainly consists of mild to moderate dyslexia, dyspraxia, dysgraphia and dyscalculia, with some mild autism and ADHD. Support mainly classroom based, with some one-to-ones and small group work taking place outside the classroom. 'Dyslexic girls often find Latin particularly hard, so we'll do small group work on study skills instead for year 8s, for example,' says head. 'The scaffolding they've put around my daughter has been amazing – it feels like they really care about getting her the best outcome,' said one parent. Strong gifted and talented provision. ICT not embedded as much as in some schools, though there's a decent ICT suite.

Heavy on careers advice, with girls given opportunities for 'tastes of reality' all the way through – much of which is embedded into lessons – with advice at every stage, which become increasingly intensive from year 9 up.

Games, options, the arts: This is a compact inner city school, so anything involving running takes place at the Chiswick playing grounds or Barn Elms multi-sports facility, both a coach ride away. On site, they cram in netball, aerobics, gymnastics, health-related fitness and dance etc and off site lacrosse, netball, athletics, rounders and tennis are the main sports. Does well in regionals and nationals for lacrosse (two Wales and one Scotland under-19 for lacrosse when we visited), along with some successes in cross country and netball. 'There's a drive to improve variety,' says the head, pointing to the recent introduction of football, table tennis, karate, cross country running and gymnastics – although this is mostly after school, to the disappointment of some pupils we spoke to. 'I wish there were more sports and more space,' more than one told us, and it was disappointing to find that some had reached sixth form having not been enthused by any sport. 'Sport is the one downside here,' some parents agreed, with one elaborating: 'It would be nice to see more of the less naturally sporty girls helped to find one sport they can love for life and to appreciate the value of teamwork that comes with that.' They have their own adventure club – the St James Challengers – and D of E. No swimming.

Artwork here is exceptional – and is, not surprisingly, on display throughout the school, much of it professionally framed. Two good art rooms in which, largely, the traditional skills are taught by much-admired staff. Visiting instructors add to the core curriculum. No DT, although they do run workshops.

S

Singing is huge – every Wednesday and Thursday, the pupils get together to sing and we lost count of how many times the summer concert was mentioned. Orchestras, choirs, ensembles galore – for which practice is before school or at lunchtime – and 75 were taking individual music lessons from peripatetic teachers when we visited.

Drama popular and lively, with a new drama studio providing a great dedicated space that can be fully blackened out. School takes part in the Shakespeare Schools Festival. Years 7-9 and 10-13 alternate in doing a play or musical every year (the older ones teaming up with the boys' school – with other joint events including the summer concert, leadership days and dinner and dances for the sixth-formers.)

Small, but much used, cookery room, with year 7s taught not just how to cook, but a wider perspective of the role of food in societies and a way to use it as a form of sharing and nurturing relationships (eg they cook lunch for elderly folk from local old people's homes).

All the usual day trips you'd expect in the heart of London – theatre, ballet, museums, London Zoo, Bletchley Park etc – plus plenty of residentials, to the likes of Isle of Wight, Devon and further afield to the battlefields and Greece. Community service trips to places like Calcutta and South Africa, where the girls get involved in housing street children. Occasional overseas trips for choirs and sports teams etc.

Extracurricular clubs impressively varied – everything from politics club to computer science and Italian to arts – which take place before school, at lunchtimes and after school. Minerva Society particularly popular – after-school talks, including the likes of politician Natalie Bennett. 'I've been blown away not only by the quality of people these girls get – and it's they who organise the speakers – but by the quality of the questioning from the girls,' said one parent. 'They are more insightful, sharp and ethically on point than my colleagues that I attend talks with.'

Background and atmosphere: Founded, along with its sibling junior school and senior boys' school, in 1975 by the School of Economic Science (SES) (see our online review of the senior boys' school for background and history), at which time the school was based in Queen's Gate, later moving to Notting Hill Gate and then, in 2001, to its current location in a leafy residential West London street.

Located down a quiet road, within sight of Olympia, the main gate leads into an attractive courtyard, which forms the centre of the whole school, in which the junior and senior schools co-exist happily. Indeed, there's nothing remotely unusual about seeing young boys and girls making their way along the polished wooden-floored corridors here – which is really rather nice and makes for a smooth transition from juniors up to seniors.

It would be unfair to say this three-storey school is bursting at the seams, but there isn't a great deal of elbow room, with compact (but very light and airy) classrooms – which probably look smaller than they are due to the clunky, traditional wooden desks, all facing forward for chalk-and-talk type teaching during our visit, although we were assured there's plenty of interactive teaching too. School was building a new sixth form centre nearby when we visited, which will free up space for a (much needed) larger library (the plans are extremely impressive), another science lab (in addition to its existing three) and some expanded classrooms. Good-sized and well-equipped music room. Big and airy school hall, plus gym and a refectory, all sitting on top of one another. Overall, the buildings are well cared for – lots of white-painted corridors, blue carpets, good wall displays and useful noticeboards. Outside space is limited, though care has been taken to provide little trellised alcoves for quiet chat around the tarmac playground, complete with climbing wall, and there's also the courtyard.

The food is vegetarian and the tables are laid invitingly – hot home-cooked food plus fresh fruit, salad, bread and cheese. Girls love it or hate it (older ones are more enthused). We loved it.

Girls seem down-to-earth, happy and supportive of one another, many draping their arms around each other as they walk from classroom to classroom. 'I can't think of a girl here that you wouldn't describe as nice,' one pupil told us. Plenty of room for difference, with no feeling that there's a St James 'type' and plenty of room for growth if your daughter arrives as a shrinking violet. 'My daughter was terribly shy, but now speaks publicly, is head of house and organises outside speakers for the school. I'd never have thought it possible. She has blossomed as an individual, thanks to this school,' one parent told us. Girls aren't overly sophisticated, but not too sheltered either. Academically, hard-working, conscientious and reflective. The sixth form have privileges – no uniform, going out at lunchtimes etc.

Pastoral care, well-being and discipline: Highly praised, with the form teacher – who moves up the school with the class where possible – at the heart of pastoral care. And if you can't talk to your teacher (which all girls told us they could), then there are plenty of buddies and mentors. All the spiritual and philosophical emphasis mentioned earlier undoubtedly helps guard against the usual teenage problems. And although there's no school counsellor, there's a trained well-being coach. Bullying rare. 'Girls are sometimes unkind, but it's usually down to thoughtlessness and we deal with that quickly when we need to,' says the head. Pupils concur. Plenty of assemblies on everything from LGBT to mental health. House system taken seriously – with girls all wearing their house T shirts on Fridays and alternating in eating in the staff dining room.

Misbehaviour, when it happens, is low-level – chatting in lessons, failing to hand in homework on time, untidy uniform etc is about as bad as it gets, for which you get 'a slip'. Three slips in one half term lead to a detention and three of those leads to an extended detention, which basically means community service and reflection. 'At that point, you'd want to be looking at the root cause,' explains the head. We met several sixth formers who'd never had a single detention. Only one temporary exclusion, and no permanent ones, under current headship. No school council when we visited (suggestions box instead), but it was about to be implemented.

Who wouldn't fit in? Girls who don't appreciate quiet time. 'There's lots of wriggling and squiggling at first – that's normal, but then they get so used to it that it becomes completely normal, then by year 12 and 13 they are such advocates,' says the head. We found she was spot on. 'I'm so passionate about the value of meditation,' said one sixth former. Also not a school for the highly competitive. 'You don't measure yourself against other people here,' one pupil told us. A parent added, 'Whilst this is an airy and bright school, despite its metropolis location, young people who need to be very physical would find the St James offering challenging, I think.'

Pupils and parents: Mixed as befits its west London location. Around half white British; a fifth from Asian backgrounds (many of whom are attracted by the influence of the eastern philosophies); and the rest a huge mix including Chinese, black Caribbean and Eastern European. English as a second language a non-issue as even they speak English well. A tiny minority of the staff are members of SES, some are ex-pupils, but the vast majority of pupils are now from families who have no direct connection whatsoever. When we mentioned SES to the pupils we met, they shrugged their shoulders. 'We know it was relevant to the founding of the school, but it's just not part of our school life now,' said one. Some pupils travel significant distances, mainly from the west, with some taking at least an hour on public transport, though most pupils are more local. A growing contingent from the north west pocket of London eg Willesden and Hampstead. Parents range from the relatively wealthy to those who save every penny to send their daughter here. Lots of dual income families. Quite a few old girls' children come here. Lively PA, called The Friends, with all the usual quiz nights and stalls at sports day etc. One parent was disappointed by the lack of class reps. Former pupils include actors Emily Watson and Sasha Behar and novelist Laura Wilson.

Entrance: St James Junior girls move seamlessly through – NB now at year 7 rather than year 6. The rest come from preps and state primaries – around half from each. Main prep feeders are Pembridge Hall, Orchard House, Chiswick and Bedford Park, Glendower, Ravenscourt Park Prep, St Nicholas Prep, The Falcons School, Bute House, Garden House, Kew Green Prep, Thomas' Battersea and Thomas' Kensington. Some also from St Mary Abbots, Barnes, Belmont and Fox primary schools. Around 200 apply for around 25 places (the other 25 taken by juniors). School is part of the North London Consortium so tests in maths and English. School's own reasoning test day also includes activities in baking, art, drama, dance and science. Plus an interview with the child and their parents. There's the odd space available in most higher years. Entry criteria for sixth formers is at least five GCSEs A*-C, including at least an A in the subjects chosen.

Exit: Around a quarter leave after GCSEs – all for good, healthy reasons: some to co-eds, some to schools that offer alternative A levels or courses, often to colleges, occasionally to board or to nearer home. Some gap years. Around 70 per cent to Russell Group universities, with popular destinations including Bristol, Exeter, Durham, York, King's, UCL and SOAS – and increasingly, East Anglia. One to Oxford in 2016. Science or medicine related courses popular, the rest choose across a vast range – art through to zoology and everything in between. Many pursue careers in which they contribute to the community, notably teachers, medics, nurses and working for charities.

Money matters: The school operates a means-tested bursary scheme. All current and future parents may apply. Future parents need to be registered with the school. This is not a rich school so don't look for masses of help.

Remarks: This small school is 'like a family', according to the pupils we met, and we got that impression too. Girls are supportive of one another and this, coupled with the emphasis on spirituality and philosophy, makes it a school that provides so much more than the academic rigour, which is a given. They take the view that it's no good being a straight A* student academically, if morally you are a C student. No wonder the school turns out such generous-spirited, honourable, sharp young women who know not only how to reach their full potential, but who have grown up understanding how to use that potential to the advantage of wider society. A gem for ethically minded families.

St James's Catholic Primary School

260 Stanley Road, Twickenham TW2 5NP

Pupils: 732 • Ages: 3–11 • RC

Tel: 020 8898 4670
Email: info@st-james.richmond.sch.uk
Website: www.st-james.richmond.sch.uk

S

Headteacher: Since September 2016, Louise Yarnell, previously head of St Norbert's Catholic Primary School in Lincolnshire.

Entrance: At 3 to nursery (52 places) and 4 to the main school (90 places). St. James's is a Roman Catholic school serving the four parishes of St James (Twickenham), St Francis de Sales (Hampton Hill), St Margaret (East Twickenham) and St Theodore (Hampton). Priority given to those baptised within a year of birth who are devout, practising Catholics. Siblings given priority. Heavily over-subscribed, with more than two applicants for every place. Occasional places become available in higher years, though there isn't huge pupil mobility. 'We don't lose many pupils further up the school, only if the families relocate. We certainly don't lose them to private schools'.

A place in the nursery does not automatically lead to a place in reception – 'though it is very rare for this not to happen'.

Exit: Between 20 to 50 per cent to independent schools. Hampton Boys' is popular and 'girls go everywhere', including Tiffin Girls' School, Gumley House and Waldegrave. One mother commented that many parents have chosen historically to go down the independent school route due to the dearth of good state secondary schools nearby – 'especially with the Oratory having reduced its catchment area'. That looks set to change with the new St Richard Reynolds Catholic High School in Twickenham starting to be an extremely popular destination.

Remarks: School has high academic standards, coupled with a strong Catholic ethos. 'Faith is central to what we do here. It is made explicit to parents. If you are a Catholic teacher, part of teaching is a mission as well as a job'.

School is large, spacious and well-run. Housed in fairly new accommodation in a leafy cul-de-sac. Light classrooms with generous windows and colourful displays abound. Two huge halls, well used for sport, dance, plays and assemblies. Glorious outdoor space where children can let off steam. Climbing frames, trees and quieter areas for those in need of tranquillity. Plenty of greenery surrounding the school. Rolling playing fields at the back and local golf club on the other side give the school a distinctly country feel.

School is at full capacity, with three parallel classes of 30 children from reception up to year 6. Children very engaged and focused when we visited and some impressive manners in evidence. Very strong academically. Rigorous analysis of progress and attainment of each pupil at each stage. School aware of the importance of pupils becoming independent thinkers and thinking skills now embedded in the curriculum.

Small turnover of staff with a respectable number of long servers. Specialist teaching for art and some games. Masses of lesson observations going on – at all levels – to maintain high standards.

School believes that sport is a vital part of the curriculum and it is taken seriously here, with the school competing at a high level. Recent borough athletic champions and 12 children competed at the national swimming championships in Sheffield – 'a great achievement, as they're normally dominated by private schools'. Football, netball, rugby, cricket and tennis on offer. Reciprocal sharing of swimming pool and games pitches with The Mall, prep school next door.

Music is strong. A symphony orchestra, three choirs (chamber choir is by invitation only), two rock bands and about half of key stage 2 pupils have private music lessons. Musical events arranged with local schools and there are opportunities to perform at the Barbican in the London Symphony Orchestra's Discovery Series.

S

The art department definitely holds its own. School is excited that, as part of the Take One Picture scheme, pupils have been selected to exhibit their work at the National Gallery.

Number of children requiring learning support is quite small. Limited number with IEPs but one-to-one help is on offer for those in need. 'Our special needs children make exceptional progress and are very well provided for.' Full-time SENCo and part-time learning support staff. George Tancred Centre is based at the school and caters for 10 children with moderate autism. Regular opportunities for these pupils to be included in lessons at the main school but they can withdraw back to the centre when activities become too distracting. Their playground is separate from, but adjacent to, main school. The pupils with autism are 'very much part of our school.' Pupils from the main school can choose to visit and play with the children from the centre at break times.

No wrap-around care on offer but plenty of before and after-school clubs, so the school day can be extended to help working parents. A variety of tastes catered for at clubs – football, cricket, basketball, French, Spanish, Italian, Jamming Together and ballet. Basketball is currently very popular. Plenty of school trips on offer. Year 6 get a week in Norfolk and year 5 head for Dorset as part of the history curriculum. Day outings include visits to art galleries and RHS gardens at Wisley.

Children at St James's are expected to work hard. Lots of homework from reception onwards, culminating in a couple of hours a night by year 6. Parents are generally supportive of this. Some tutoring goes on in the top classes – school is relaxed, as long as it does not become excessive.

Significant number of bilingual children – mostly Spanish, French and Italian. Parents are welcomed into the school and appreciate the open-door policy in place. Staff know most of the families well and believe parental involvement in the school is invaluable, either on trips or within the classroom. 'We'd be mad not to include them.' Parents are a fairly affluent, middle class group, reflecting the local area. Minuscule percentage on free school meals. Very active PTFA raises £30,000 annually. Money recently spent on the early years garden and subsidising school trips.

School has an excellent reputation in the local neighbourhood and parents feel lucky to have secured their child a place. At the start of the day, hordes of children in jolly yellow and grey uniforms race along the pavements on scooters. Ongoing problems over road congestion outside, however, and local residents aren't always happy. As one parent put it, 'it's a big, busy primary school. In the morning, the traffic can be horrendous'. School encourages less driving to school and has even gone so far as to employ numberplate recognition surveillance for repeat parking offenders.

This is an outward-looking school that offers an excellent academic education in a nurturing Catholic environment. Ably led and with high expectations of pupils, staff and parents, it's impressive on many fronts.

St Margaret's School (London)

18 Kidderpore Gardens, London NW3 7SR

Pupils: 160 • Ages: 4–16 • C of E

Fees: £11,532 – £13,359 pa

Tel: 020 7435 2439
Email: enquiry@st-margarets.co.uk
Website: www.st-margarets.co.uk

Principal: Since 2008, Mr Mark Webster BSc (early 50s). Educated at Highgate School and University College London (where he read psychology), PGCE at Cambridge. Spent 15 years at the Royal School, Hampstead (first in primary, then IT, psychology and maths, before becoming deputy and acting head). Never planned to become a teacher – 'If you'd asked me early on what job I wanted to do, I'd have said teaching was 999th out of 1000'. A chance encounter changed his mind. 'I was working in publishing, when I met someone who said their job in teaching was fantastic. I'd never met anyone who felt that way about work.' Now equally enthusiastic about his chosen profession, Mr Webster continues to be hands on in his approach and still teaches mathematics.

We were initially struck by Mr Webster's bold shirt of candy coloured stripes, which belies his very calm manner. He is not extrovert by any means (as his shirt may imply), but is calm, thoughtful and extremely warm and friendly. He takes the time to consider our questions, and responds diplomatically and graciously. Parents unanimously agree that he is a 'brilliant head teacher and a real leader.' During our meeting there are a number of students who pop into the head's office for a variety of reasons ranging from charity fundraising questions to other Christmas related issues. Clearly students feel he is very approachable, and whilst he does operate an open door policy like some other heads – unlike other heads, students actually take him up on this.

He says one of the benefits of working in a small school is that 'I have the privilege of knowing every student.' He enjoys the proximity and seeing the children grow up: 'You feel you can make a significant difference.' Unlike, he says, a much larger school, where perhaps you don't have the hands-on input: 'I can sleep well at night as I know I've done my very best.' Fundamental to his approach is the view that education is about instilling a sense of curiosity – 'Qualifications are a passport to the next stage, but if you remain curious you will never be bored'.

He himself retains a passionate interest in art, history and reading. Also plays football for Highgate Old Boys. A tactful, sympathetic enthusiast, Webster is a good fit for this family-like school. Possibly slightly unusual to have a male head teacher in an all girls school, but that doesn't seem to bother the parents. 'He is wonderful, we are so very lucky.' Married to a teacher; they have two young sons.

Academic matters: St Margaret's recently topped the Sunday Times' Small Schools' league table. When you consider that in 2016, 65 per cent of GCSEs were graded A*/A, it's not surprising, especially as the school is relatively non-selective and the ability range always includes the very able and those with more modest aspirations. One parent told us: 'I was a bit worried as I do have a very academic daughter and I thought she might not reach her full potential, but the luxury of a school this size is that teachers can cater for each individual in a mixed ability class.'

GCSE options include Spanish, French, art ('which is amazing' one student told us), psychology, history, geography and drama alongside the compulsory subjects. All girls are required to take the science trilogy (taught in a compact, but efficient lab) and the vast majority go on to do at least one science A Level. A modern language is compulsory. (Japanese is soon to be introduced as an extra curricular language).

Setting introduced when necessary but, with limited space, teaching is usually differentiated rather than physically separated. Extremely low turnover of staff (the French teacher has been there for 25 years) – 'I've only had to write one reference in eight years', the head told us. This is largely because most departments are very small 'so teachers can actually make the role their own and achieve what they actually came into the profession to achieve.' This consistency can only be a good thing for the well-being and academic progress of the students.

School does cater for pupils with mild SEN, 'we don't have the depth of resources for learning support that a larger school would have,' says the head. Two SENCo support plus a couple of teachers trained in dyslexia and dyscalculia, but the main support comes from classroom teachers. All abilities equally well catered for – 'We aren't results-driven and we try to exhaust every avenue'.

Games, options, the arts: The head's view is that education is a 'can-do', 'must try' matter, and inspired by the celebrated art historian Sir Ernst Gombrich's attitude: 'You don't have to like it, but it's important to understand why other people do. We compel them to try lots of things. They may moan, but we make them give it a go'. Drama is taken seriously. Shakespeare is now a biggie here. 'Our drama teacher has a big pedigree in Shakespeare.' From year 7, pupils have a non-Shakespeare year where they are encouraged to devise their own pieces to perform. The head says: 'We want to encourage them to devise their own roles by exploring situations.' Other productions have included Matilda and Wind in the Willows. Music, too, is important with a variety of traditional and less traditional extra-lesson options – anyone who wants to can join the ukulele club: 'It's a very egalitarian and upbeat instrument.' A number of choirs, plus a junior school orchestra. At least half of girls have private instrument lessons at the school. Art immensely popular, with excellent results at GCSE: two studios, one reasonably spacious, the other definitely petite. Dance popular.

Outside space, too, is relatively restricted, with a largish garden transformed into an Astroturf playground. A local hall is used for gym and the school now has a sports area for netball, tennis and other sports two minutes' walk away. Minibus takes girls to Hampstead Heath for rounders or running, to Hendon Leisure Centre for aerobics, rock climbing and badminton and the Welsh Harp for rowing. Inter-house and inter-school matches from year 4 upwards. In David and Goliath mode, the school is unafraid to compete with much larger north London schools like Channing, despite the fact that 'We often lose'. One parent told us: 'For the super sporty, this school may not be your first choice'

Plenty of extracurricular going on: street dance, choir, theatre, cookery, cheerleading, philosophy, orchestra, chess, tennis and origami. Trips local and international, from walks on Hampstead Heath to Tuscany and Iceland.

An unusual incentive which the head introduced is '125' (a tribute to the school's 125 anniversary), which provides pupils with a list of activities to attempt before they leave the school: 'Since 2013, to complement the academic, performing and sporting curriculum we offer, the girls undertake activities throughout the year as part of the school's Skills Grid. The range includes the practical, the cultural and the altruistic: everything from touch typing, learning a magic trick or "doing something nice for someone who can do nothing in return".'

Background and atmosphere: Founded in 1884 and one of the oldest schools in Hampstead – it moved to its present site in a quiet, suburban Hampstead road in 1943. A large, elegant red-brick house accommodates 155+ girls and the head says, 'The house element has become a pivotal cornerstone of how I think about the school. Everything emanates from it being a house – the relationships, the attitudes etc. We've spent quite a lot of money on knocking down a lot of walls.' We believe he meant that both literally and metaphorically.

Fairly recent building work has completely altered the layout of the ground and lower ground floors to incorporate a new school hall. The idea was also to open up the ground floor as much as possible to give the house a much more open plan feel, thereby creating more light and space. Everything is transparent – even the head's office. The school has also added a pretty roof terrace to encourage reading and quiet study for the upper years.

On entering the building we were treated to the melodic voices of a few girls doing choir practice. We watched for a few minutes entranced. It all added to the warm and cosy atmosphere of the St Margaret's experience (it helped that it was nearly Christmas at the time of our visit). We were struck by how deceptively big the school seems on the inside. Yes, there are areas which are exceedingly tight and narrow, and would definitely not suit any physically impaired student, but the floors upwards seemed endless and the corridors often led into quaint hidden areas. Although classrooms were snug, they were adequate for the number of students in each class (no more than 20). None of the students we met or chatted to seemed particularly fazed about the spatial issue. As one parent said, 'they don't know any better, as some have been here since infants and go all the way through.'

We were charmed by the lovely reading area for the juniors and the loft-style library. It definitely felt as if we had entered a bygone era – not a conventional school by any means (think the Brontës). This, it seems, is what some parents most love about the school. One told us: 'Both the head and the school are very unusual in education and sadly part of a dying breed – not caught up in the madness of it all, but eminently sensible.'

The girls who showed us around were happy, polite and totally unpretentious. We were taken aback by one student who openly admitted she had had 'difficulties' in some areas, but unlike other schools she had been to, everyone at St Margaret's was 'friendly and caring.' (Again, another of the school's many charms is that it didn't select one of its obvious 'stars' to show us around the school and do the whole PR thing).

Senior and junior schools both occupy the same building and have the same head, with different uniforms but little separation between them. Uniforms are smart – red and white in the junior school, black and white in the senior. The uniform was changed a few years back for the seniors as they didn't like it. Girls are listened to here. There are two 'agony aunts' (senior students) available at all times for confidential chats and a school council. One pupil told us: 'We voted for a tuck shop at the school council and now we have one. We can choose what is sold.' The school has three houses and pupils of all ages work together to raise funds for charities of their own choice and compete at sports.

The small friendly and homely atmosphere 'allows the girls to achieve whatever they can – but in a safe, non-confrontational environment', said one parent.

Pastoral care, well-being and discipline: Discipline not a significant issue. Though head insists this is not the garden of Eden, disciplinary issues tend to be confined to infringements of uniform – 'We can live with earrings if there's no drink or drugs'. Bullying – 'We get a case every year' – is dealt with promptly. Detentions, it seems, are an alien notion: 'we haven't needed to give one since 2011.' One parent who is a teacher herself working in an inner city school told us: 'I have to laugh sometimes when my daughter comes home and says "OMG! One of the girls threw a pen in class".' Girls generally very well behaved and extremely supportive of one another – 'an extended family', one said.' Another told us: 'My daughter went through a very difficult time one year because of social media. I was alerted to this by her form tutor, who in turn had found out from three of her close friends, who were very concerned. She was closely monitored and supported throughout and got through it.'

Parents, too, tend to be very supportive; they are known to choose the school for its caring environment: 'You get ups and downs with some of the girls, but if you ever get a problem it's dealt with straight away,' said one. Most parents feel one of the school's greatest strengths is its pastoral side, allowing girls to fulfil their potential and know exactly who they are. One parent told us: 'This school allows every girl to flourish. It formed my daughter into the happy, caring girl she is today.' Another told us: 'What struck me about this school when I first looked around, and what still remains true five years later, is that the girls all seem to have that wonderful, quiet confidence. Not that brash sense of entitlement that some wealthy kids can have.'

The school has its own head of pastoral care but also relies on a school counsellor when needed and proactively encourages bondin' with a variety of trips. 'The girls mix across the years and are often close to girls in the year above and below,' said a parent.

Pupils and parents: Nice, well-behaved, confident girls from a cosmopolitan range of backgrounds reflecting the school's north London location – a large chunk of second generation French and Italians. A fair number come from within walking distance, then in an arc stretching from Wembley to Islington (school minibus on offer for those who require it). Very much a family school in every sense – 45 per cent of pupils are sisters or relatives of current or ex-pupils. 'A lot of people like the sense of support and nurturing.' The school rarely advertises and most newcomers hear about it by word of mouth and favourable newspaper coverage. The internet has slightly altered the traditional intake, as it is accessible worldwide. One parent told us: 'What I like most about the parents who send their girls to St Margaret's is that they defy the Daily Mail stereotype of bling parents.' Daphne du Maurier was a pupil.

Entrance: 'Loosely selective.' From reception to year 2 assessment involves girls coming in for the morning and working with the class teacher. A handful of places offered from year 3 upwards and potential candidates take a standard set of English and maths assessments. Guaranteed transition from within at 11. 'Once we've made the commitment, unless there are particular special needs we can't support, we stick to it.' External candidates take English, maths and verbal reasoning exams. They do operate a basic sibling policy: 'We're not über selective, but we have rejected siblings if we don't feel the school is right for them.'

Exit: About 75 per cent of junior school girls stay on to the senior school, though a small number move to more selective senior schools such as Henrietta Barnett or South Hampstead High School. There's no intention of opening a sixth form, despite parental requests: 'One of the things about being a small school is that you are aware of the things you can't offer, in terms of space and subjects, which is why we will never have a sixth form.' However by then most parents agree it is time to 'move on.'

Notably successful with applications at 16. Most popular choices at that point are local co-ed sixth forms like UCS, more selective schools like St Paul's, and similar atmosphere girls' schools like Channing. A reasonable number goes to the state sector – St Marylebone particularly popular, and a few to Woodhouse or the Ark Academy. Good guidance on offer at both 11 and 16 – 'It's really important to make an informed choice. Not every school will suit every girl and they are used to being supported here'. School also works with them on interview practice and personal statements. One parent told us: 'Prior to looking around a few schools, I was advised to by Mr Webster to look out for things which would never have otherwise occurred to me – like to not be swayed by all the high tech stuff.' St Margaret's girls generally get their first-choice sixth form.

Money matters: Not an expensive school by any means, though a number of girls receive bursaries to cover all or part of their school fees: 'A reasonable proportion on some sort of financial help.'

Remarks: A gentle, nurturing school with a strong and secure family atmosphere providing a stimulating, tailor-made education. 'A little gem,' to quote one parent, though possibly not the ideal venue for the child who needs plenty of space to run around or one who requires the challenge of a big stage.

St Mary Magdalene Academy

Liverpool Road, London N7 8PG

Pupils: 1,183 • Ages: 4-18 • Sixth form: 130 • C of E

Tel: 020 7697 0123
Email: firstcontact@smmacademy.org
Website: www.smmacademy.org

Headteacher: Since 2005, Paul Hollingum has been executive director of the trust that governs the three SMMA institutions, including the primary and secondary schools and the specialist school for 14-19 year old pupils diagnosed with autism. BA (economics) Wolverhampton Polytechnic; PGCE, Birmingham University, MA (Education) Institute of Education, University of London; previously taught economics, business studies and law in selective and independent schools, deputy head of Wilson's School, Surrey, head of Raine's Foundation School, London. This is his first experience of an IB school.

Fair hair and complexion, sparkling blue eyes, he appears approachable and steady; he speaks with humility about what has been achieved in a few short years at SMMA. Describes SMMA as a 'new breed of church school'; the international dimension of the IB and the notion of service to the whole community links nicely to the Christian ethos of service. Mr Hollingum's long-standing involvement with China through the British Council has had an impact on SMMA and he continues to work as an advisor to schools there. He manages this thanks to the strong leadership of head teacher Victoria Linsley, to whom he leaves the day-to-day running of the secondary school. A parent tells us he is often on the school gate greeting everyone; he's 'visible to all'.

Founding head teacher is Victoria Linsley BA (history) Nottingham, MSc (history) and PGCE from Oxford. A Lancastrian, she has worked in London comprehensive schools for 20 years, and as a consultant with failing and special measures schools. She has previous experience as a deputy head at Broomfield School. This slim, petite, youthful head teacher is an energetic dynamo who notices everything and does not miss a trick as she roams through the school giving stern looks to students who may be pushing the uniform boundaries, while generously doling out affirmative 'well-done's to beaming students in classrooms and corridors. A few approach, eager to share something with her. Proud of the school, its facilities, resources and especially students, she does not shy away from talking about areas for improvement. It seems the Hollingum-Linsley chemistry has created magic at SMMA.

Head of primary school: Since September 2016, Ruth Luzmore, previously deputy head of Clerkenwell Parochial CE School.

Academic matters: This is the only state school in Greater London to offer the International Baccalaureate Primary Years Programme (IBPYP), and families familiar with this programme, found in schools worldwide, will feel at home here. School speaks positively of the clarity and direction of the curriculum and how this covers and at times exceeds national curriculum requirements. Parents are complimentary about school's talent for recruiting good teachers, who themselves represent a variety of nationalities, though there have been the usual challenges of dealing with staff absence and turnover due to maternity leave, relocation, etc, sometimes causing a break in continuity for the children. Specialist teachers offer music, PE and languages; class teachers do the art. Good results at key stage 2 Sats, with children regularly achieving level 6.

In keeping with the IBPYP philosophy and the school's own global education priorities, pupils study French (years 1 and 2), Spanish (years 3 and 4), and Mandarin (years 5 and 6); Latin is an after-school option. Pupils take lots of trips around London to see museums or take part in workshops linked to their units of inquiry (sometimes at modest cost). Years 5 and 6 take residential trips into the countryside. A parent told us: 'I love the varied and engaging approach to learning, and there is consistency across the subjects that helps children explore things in a more holistic way.'

SMMA describes its specialties as humanities and global citizenship, and this involves eight key concepts: citizenship, social justice, sustainable development, diversity, values and perceptions, inter-dependence, conflict resolution and human rights. For the 11-16 year olds, this is essentially a non-selective inner-city comprehensive preparing locals for GCSEs using the national curriculum, but aligning it with common entrance assessment standards at the end of year 8 so they can track progress. A good range of GCSEs are on offer and the school sets the bar high. Parents say that the kids know they are expected to achieve; students appear to be serious and committed at school and parents confirm that there is an expectation that pupils will work hard and to the best of their ability – whatever that is.

At sixth form, which offers the IB and A levels, the profile changes; more students come for the final two years and there are admissions criteria – not all year 11s are offered sixth form places. Parents credit the school leaders with working hard to help local families understand the advantages of the IB. There is an expectation of high achievement that is underpinned by what parents and students describe as a strong programme of pastoral care and sense of community. Pupils know they will be supported. Class sizes are 30 for years 7-8; for GCSE classes they are limited to 25 (streamed for core subject areas), and at IB class sizes are limited to 15 but often much smaller. In 2016, 76 per cent got 5+ A*-C grades at GCSE including English and maths; 23 per cent of grades were A*/A. At A level, 59 per cent A*-B and 36 per cent A*/A grades; average IB point score: 34.

The school's emphasis on global citizenship is demonstrated in a variety of ways, perhaps most notably, according to the parents and students that we spoke to, through the language programme. Most take French, Spanish or German and many also do Mandarin: year 7 students who have scored well on the school's language aptitude tests are invited to study Mandarin and sometimes Latin through the Inspire Programme in addition to a modern European language. There are several overseas travel opportunities and a special emphasis on Mandarin and China. These global dimensions are also enhanced by partnerships with schools in places such as Finland, China, Senegal, and Jerusalem.

SMMA is one of the few UK Confucius Classroom Schools. Funding from the Chinese government promotes the study of Chinese culture and languages through teacher exchange; two teachers from China also help to plan visits to sister schools in China, and help with cultural studies and festivals within the school. 'Chinese New Year is really something here,' we hear. Mandarin is on offer at GCSE and IB level.

Another important partnership is with Deloitte, which supports the school and students in many ways as part of its corporate social responsibility programme. Deloitte staff work with students and provide expertise to help prepare them for life after secondary school.

The parents can't praise the teaching staff enough and the pupils agree. They are described as hard-working, committed, quick to respond to parents, and they motivate students to learn and to work to their full potential. Most are local, but some have international experience, a few from European countries. It seems that it is a satisfying place to work; the turnover is quite low. Two young Oxbridge grad tutors are based in the library to help students with essays, maths or any other academic challenges. Parents say the teachers are good role models for the youngsters and help instil a sense of pride. 'They work hard at setting a high standard; they go beyond the call of duty. They will give kids – even the bright kids – a bit of a kick up the backside and say, "We can do better than this".'

This is offered within the context of a C of E perspective, but it is an inclusive school with students of all faiths, and parents say the religious aspect is subtle and low-key. Good support for SEN.

Games, options, the arts: Lots of after-school sports (including competitive teams) and other activities on offer in the primary school – such as Japanese art, chess, book club and gardening. Some of these activities are run by senior school teachers and coaches and even sixth form students (earning D of E points), and make use of the senior school's impressive sports facilities – one of the advantages of being a through school. An annual school-wide Shakespeare project supported by the Young Shakespeare Company culminates in performances, both dance and drama, by the students. Dance is popular, pupils excel at table tennis and were national champions recently.

Although parents say there is a good range of activities on offer, one remarked that the school had not been particularly flexible about approving a student absence in order to take part in a special activity outside the school during term time. The school responds that they have authorised term time absences for children attending both sports activities and activities related to the arts, eg TV, film and stage work. Parents and pupils are excited by all the extracurricular opportunities on offer here.

The school has a roof eco garden with a pond, tall grasses for insects, chickens, an aviary and bird feeders with cameras installed by students for filming and observing the hungry visitors, all making the place a mini wildlife haven in the heart of urban Islington. On another part of the building are rooftop sports facilities. D of E from year 10 upwards counts toward the IB Creativity, Action and Service (CAS) section. Pupils recently worked on a community project creating drawings of the local area to inspire a colourful mural on permanent display at a local train station. An extended school day on Mondays and Tuesdays offers sports, Mandarin language and culture, arts, community involvement and cooking. Parents talk enthusiastically about this programme and the variety of opportunities it affords.

The school makes good use of its networks – sometimes through its partner schools around the globe, or through parents – to invite all sorts of guest teachers and performers to work with students. They also take advantage of 'virtual networks', having Skype conferences with students in other countries. Younger classes go on camping trips, sixth formers have an activities week in Cornwall; on alternate years there are trips to partner schools in China – parents and students rave about these; they have travelled to Berlin, to Mexico and also to Senegal, where they volunteered in a local school and learned about African music.

The school has impressive sports facilities considering its urban setting, including a sports hall. Netball, basketball and football teams are all in training; and perhaps because of the Chinese links, pupils have won national table tennis competitions.

Music is popular and all year 7 and 8s learn musical instruments – we walked in on a group listening to a just-finished recording of a pupil playing her own composition. World music features highly here, and rather than full scale orchestras, the school features numerous small instrumental ensembles.

Pupils were keen to talk about the school's twice-yearly drama productions, which can involve everyone interested. 'If you are in year 7, you may not get the lead, but there is a part for you.' All sixth formers encouraged to volunteer, not just IB students with their 150 hours of CAS.

One student told us about Chapel Club, led by the full-time chaplain, which she had enjoyed earlier in the day: they had read and discussed biblical proverbs, which she said 'was something refreshing in the middle of day.' The school definitely has a C of E ethos, but there is no pressure to conform.

Background and atmosphere: While there has been a Saint Mary Magdalene School here for 300 years, the development of a 21st century 3-19 academy offering the IB programmes was an initiative of the church in partnership with Islington council and opened in 2007. The facilities are truly dazzling. Modern, minimalist, pale-coloured wood, carpeted throughout with lots of light pouring through windows throughout the building. The design and layout ingeniously mask the school's vast size. There are two floors largely reserved for sixth form, and all the floors overlook a large open courtyard area where the canteen and dining area is based, a gathering space effectively at the heart of the school. On the ground floor is the theatre, along with the 'noisier' specialist teaching rooms. The school is immaculately tidy without feeling sanitised; beautiful displays throughout celebrate student classwork and art, and most of the classrooms have lots of internal windows so that pupils at work are easily observed from the walkways. 'Open and transparent' is the feel.

Ms Linsley believes in the importance of maintaining an orderly, organised environment for her pupils. Rising above the central communal area is the two-floor library (one level reserved for sixth form) with chapel (more of a quiet room) above – imagine it as a structure built on 'stilts' at the first floor level – so they are easily accessible by crossover walkways all from all floors. Classrooms are spacious and more than ample for the class sizes – nowhere did we see students crowded and cramped – and there are copious specialist teaching rooms: the art quad even has a built-in large kiln studio and an IB art studio, so that students can leave their partially-completed projects out without worrying about accidental disturbance by others. There are music rooms with practice spaces, recording facilities, etc, there are ICT suites; and there's a spacious classroom for the school's high achieving autistic and Asperger's pupils, who also intermingle with the other pupils.

The primary and secondary schools share the same site but are quite separate, so the primary students have their own space while benefiting from use of the secondary school facilities. Lots of windows throughout make for bright classrooms and many have access to outdoor areas – either to the garden or balconies. The library is welcoming and well-stocked.

Pastoral care, well-being and discipline: The IBPYP features a built-in 'character education' element through the IB learner profile, which is amplified by the school's Christian values (Commitment, Empathy, Forgiveness, Hope, Independence, Integrity, Thankfulness and Tolerance). Golden Values are highlighted throughout the year, and school fundraising events support causes such as the Nepal earthquake and other good causes.

Rather than traditional form tutors SMMA has teacher 'academy guardians' who manage multi-age groups of lower secondary student 'families'. They stay in the same groups as they rise through the years, and everyone likes this pastoral continuity. In sixth form they become part of a new 'family' of combined first and second year IB diploma and A level students, who meet with their guardian regularly. They also serve as mentors to younger groups of pupils, enabling them to learn from their older peers about what lies ahead in the sixth form. The family groups are named after continents, emphasising the school's global outlook. Guardians are the first port of call for any concern and it seems they are quick to return phone calls or emails. Communication is a strong suit, according to the parents.

Though we gather there are definitely some pupils who are more motivated to learn than others, behaviour, as such, is not an issue. The school is non-selective and has a highly diverse socio-economic student community, but there are expectations and consequences for absence; pupils who arrive more than seven minutes late to lessons may be refused entry by the teachers. This sets the standard. One parent told us, 'There is a very rigorous code of discipline; they don't kick them out, there's a sort of "3-step programme". Kids who don't want to fit in with the standards of behaviour tend to move on.'

It is also interesting to note in the 'tips from sixth formers' that pupils 'should not use up too many hours working in a part-time job', suggesting that this is a community where pupils need to earn their pocket money.

Younger pupils wear uniforms, and on the day we visited were immaculately turned out – impressive. Sixth form has a sensible dress code.

Pupils and parents: The students we met were a multicultural mix – both 'home bred' and recently arrived. They speak of the strong community feel; the continuity of the mixed-age 'family' groups is reassuring. One previously home-schooled student said she chose SMMA over an independent London IB school because she was so impressed by the 'great' teachers she met during the open day taster sessions. 'They are so supportive and really helped me adjust to the system here'. She said that she felt there was less pressure at SMMA than she sensed at some of the independent schools she visited. Another said that the sixth form is enhanced by the international perspectives gained by having classmates from all over the world. 'You get a glimpse into all sorts of cultures here. That is very motivating and makes you want to know more about those people and places.'

Entrance: The primary school has one-form entry with classes numbering 30 pupils, boys and girls evenly mixed. 'It's quite cosy', one parent told us. Because of admissions criteria, all the students are local Islington residents and represent a wide socio-economic mix; from children of affluent professionals to the children of immigrants and asylum-seekers in assisted housing. Looked after children and siblings are given priority, and as it is a C of E school, church attendance is also taken into consideration, with distance given lowest priority. Heavily oversubscribed.

Year 7: 180 pupils admitted on the basis of strict criteria. After looked after children and siblings, and those coming up from the primary department, 70 per cent open places (by proximity) and 30 per cent foundation places (children attending an Islington C of E primary school, with proximity as a tie-break); 18 places (no catchment criteria) based on language aptitude tests at both year 7 and year 9. For IB, a minimum of seven grade B GCSEs, including English and maths, with A grades to study science and/or maths at higher level; for A level, a minimum of five grade C GCSEs including English and maths, with B grades in A level subjects.

Exit: Most move up from the primary school to the secondary department. Around half per cent leave after GCSEs; even SMMA students applying to sixth form must go through an admissions process. University and career counselling is good, and this is one of the areas where the Deloitte partnership is helpful. 2016 destinations include LSE, Surrey, St Andrews, Exeter, UCL, King's, Durham, Leeds, Sheffield and University A&M Texas.

Money matters: Most parents happy to pay for school trips, though there is support for those who find this a challenge. ParentPay cards also serve as ID cards and enable parents to replenish student accounts for lunch money.

Remarks: Students say: 'There's something for everyone here. Even if you don't like a subject, you can learn to enjoy it. They don't give up on kids here and you develop a lot of independence.' The students we met were a memorably impressive bunch – perhaps a bit too smart, ethically-minded and work-focused to be uber-cool, but the sort any parent would be proud to own up to. Kudos to the C of E and Islington on this impressive success story.

The St Marylebone C of E School

64 Marylebone High Street, London W1U 5BA

Pupils: 1,072 • Ages: 11–18 • Sixth form: 317 (79 boys) • C of E

Tel: 020 7935 4704
Email: info@stmaryleboneschool.com
Website: www.stmaryleboneschool.com

Headteacher: Since 2014, Ms Kathryn Pugh MA (Cantab) PBCE NPQH (mid 30s). A Cambridge graduate with first class honours in English, she joined St Marylebone in 2005 as an English teacher and learning co-ordinator, and was promoted to assistant head in 2008, before succeeding the long-serving and legendary Elizabeth Phillips OBE. This is only the second school she has worked at. She arrived here after cutting her teeth (as she puts it) at Riddlesdown Collegiate, a large co-ed comprehensive in Surrey, where she taught English and drama. Straight after leaving Cambridge she spent four years working in business and media, and worked in theatre and communication for 18 months in Malawi, as well as working for The Teacher Support Network, an educational charity.

Tall and willowy, Miss Pugh looks more like a Chanel model than headmistress. She cycles to work each day and is described by her pupils as 'inspirational', 'accessible', and 'empathetic'. We were regaled with tales of her contorting herself into yogic positions during English lessons as well as her passionate encouragement of 'complete randomness in lessons'. Said to be a fruitarian, she is described as looking strikingly beautiful in her red cape, while standing in the midst of girls in green cartwheeling and cavorting. She 'mucks in – not afraid to get her hands dirty during the fairs'; and 'She's so dynamic,' enthused one parent, 'everyone wants to do their best for her, both her pupils and her staff...the school is lucky that it has so many years of someone so ambitious and committed.'

We spoke to her surrounded by her senior management team. This is a woman who clearly prefers to see herself as prima inter pares. Her predecessor was a great delegator, and responsibility continues to be very much shared. She wants to talk about the school and its achievements and defer to her colleagues. She is deeply uncomfortable when the questions focus on her. Appreciative of a strong and supportive team, Ms Pugh is doing sterling work channelling the goodwill of both her staff and a diverse parent body.

Academic matters: Results are excellent. At A level, 66 per cent A*-B with 50 per cent A*/A in 2016. School keen to point out that girls who take further maths and chemistry perform brilliantly. While English is the most popular subject, school does have 10 STEM ambassadors, and offers two sixth form maths/ICT scholarships to students likely to go on to study STEM subjects at university. Psychology, sociology and economics among the options – the first much the favourite, with a spread of results.

German now phased out in favour of Spanish. High take-up; French and Spanish students achieved excellent results with a high percentage of top grades – a great improvement since our last visit. Supervised study periods during year 12 help the less-disciplined with their homework. Relatively good teacher:pupil ratio, with setting from the start, and school invests in retaining good staff. Our student guides were keen to tell us how many of their teachers had doctorates and were specialists in their fields.

Offers a good choice of subject options – 'an amazing variety,' enthused one parent. A future skills award and child development have replaced health and social care; dance, Latin (now compulsory in years 7 and 8) and business studies canter alongside the front runners at GCSE and all are in the ribbons. Ninety-three per cent 5+ A*-C grades in 2016 including maths and English with some outstanding performances (43 per cent A*/A grades). RS results are knock-out and the curriculum is praised for its earnest inclusiveness. The Englishes are good, so are the single sciences. One full class takes triple science each year, though most take the double award. Maths more than respectable. School does, after all, have a maths and computing specialism as well as performing arts. All students study both French and Spanish in key stage 3 and over 75 per cent take at least one language at GCSE. Art and history strong and popular. School has policy of taking some subjects – ICT, RS – early to excellent effect.

Gifted and talented programme now called Aspiration and Challenge, with the idea of achieving excellence for everyone. High Achievers' programme for those with high academic ability; Scholarship programmes those talented at dance, music or drama. Two SENCos, a full-time SEN teacher, learning support assistants and specialist centres for students with learning difficulties. It is a centre of excellence for severe emotional and behavioural difficulties. Can provide for moderate physical difficulties too. EAL is an important area also (about half of the cohort speaks a language other than English at home) and this department plays a vibrant part in celebrating cultural diversity.

Games, options, the arts: This has a performing arts specialism – with 14 places awarded to those talented in dance, drama or music. It is perhaps not surprising, then, that sport has a lower profile. That is not to say that there are not opportunities available, and there are a surprising number of athletically ambitious girls. Our guide was a pentathlete, excelling at high jump, long jump, shot put, 800 metres and hurdles, participating in clubs both in and out of school. Cross-country is also popular. Grey Coat Hospital School is the big rival at netball; they also play Portland Place and Holland Park. Plenty of inter-house sports competitions too (five houses across the year groups – Hardwick, Dickens, Barrett, Nightingale and Wesley). Annual sports day at Willesden Green. Other sports on offer include football, trampolining, rugby and tennis as well as the D of E awards scheme. They have managed to fit an underground sports hall into this already over-filled space and have a seven metre climbing wall. Sport very much available even if not always enthusiastically taken up.

Dance, drama and music are outstanding and production values are high. 'The girls take huge pride in their performances,' we were told, 'even if not everyone can take part. It is inspirational.' The inspiration is further fuelled by the innovative and outstanding three storey building that incorporates the visual and performing arts space, with dance studio and gym in the basement. This makes a huge difference – not least to the amount of space it frees for other curricular activities. In all respects the arts reign here. You can make everything from jewellery to ceramics and print your own photos. Up-to-date laser cutters in the well-equipped DT workshops. Graphics also well regarded. Debating, dance and musical performance of all kinds thrive. Scholars' concert happens in the Wigmore Hall; some musicals, eg sixth form production of Chicago, performed at the Rudolf Steiner Theatre; whole school production of Grease in the old-fashioned, polished-wood-smelling school hall.

Some disagreement among parents as to whether there is an opportunity for everyone to get involved in these productions and performances. Grumblings in some quarters that only the best are given roles – and here, there are a lot of girls considered to be glittering. So your aspiring Milly who doesn't quite make the grade may well end up sitting on the sidelines for much of her school years. School quick to point out that over 150 pupils across the school took part in whole school production at Christmas. We, like Ofsted, were impressed with range of other co-curricular activities which don't necessarily require high-confidence performance skills: book clubs, green committee, Young Entrepreneurs, Fair Trade group etc. However, opportunities like GCSE photography work in the highly professional Metro Studios only available to the three or four girls whose applications to take the course are considered sufficiently impressive. This is the reality of a state-funded school, but it must be trying for the also-rans and would-bes.

Background and atmosphere: Tucked between Princess Grace Hospital and Marylebone High Street and close to the teeming runway that is the Marylebone Road, the school is a leafy, contained oasis of calm and purpose. St Marylebone Parish Church is a focus point and contributes to the peacefulness. This is where assemblies and concerts happen as well as religious services. A closely-knit jungle of buildings from red-brick Victorian, complete with heavily green gloss painted corridors, to modern glass and concrete are packed onto this one compact site. Further down the High Street on Blandford Street is the sixth form building, which is modern, purpose-built, and feels more like a tiny university campus than a school.

Five forms per year, and with only 750 in the main school with up to 330 in the sixth form, St Marylebone is a relatively small inner London comprehensive – and this shows. As intimate as it can be, spread over two sites, it is an unintimidating place, with plenty of smiles and polite greetings between staff and pupils as well as between the pupils themselves. No space for lockers, so girls have to learn to be adept at carting their lives around with them and being organised about what they need for each lesson. Lunch is eaten in form rooms, though year 10 examinees and upwards are mercifully allowed out to settle in the numerous cafés round about at lunchtime. Sixth formers have their own canteen in Blandford Street.

Pastoral care, well-being and discipline: Pastoral care is very strong, affirm several parents. As well as there being systems of support in place among the staff and pupils, there is a strong mentoring facility between the older and younger pupils. This is an intense time of life for any teenager, but one senses that in this school the experience can perhaps become more intense than elsewhere. School says that the intensity is 'offset by a very caring community feeling which identifies and helps deal with problems' – and denies that this is a school of 'precious princesses'. Maybe it is part of the performing arts culture.

Girls, on the whole, very supportive of each other, though there is a lot of competition and this has to be managed. Behaviour is good. Cases of bullying rare, we were told. A smell of smoke doesn't linger in lavatories here, and a zero tolerance approach means that your child may well end up with detention just from talking in class. The bar is high, girls feel lucky to be here and want to behave well. Parents commend the fluid communication lines whenever a problem arrives. Lots of positive feedback when a struggling girl starts to perform well, as well as the more obvious commending of high performance. Much appreciated are the proper, old-fashioned termly reports which don't just parrot at you what the class has done but actually talk about your own daughter. Good, realistic and collaborative target-setting also works.

Pupils and parents: Broad social mix, made up of the heady variety of backgrounds and cultures that you would expect in an inner London comprehensive. Much more middle class than many of its kind, however, because this is the golden apple if you are after an excellent education for your creative daughter who also likes to perform. A higher proportion than usual of parents are actors, barristers, artists and, yes, even bankers, than you would find at just any ordinary central London comprehensive, many of whom have been privately educated themselves.

The gritty detail is there are approximately 65 per cent from ethnic minority backgrounds and from 90 different countries. Over 50 per cent of pupils are bilingual. More than 60 languages spoken at home. Sixty per cent C of E members; the largest second religious group is Muslim. School clearly tries hard to integrate the social mix – has an annual World Culture Day among many other initiatives – and attracts fierce loyalty. Girls travel some distances to get here – from as far as Hackney in the East to Ealing and Shepherds Bush in the West, Kilburn, Kentish Town and Islington in the north as well as Wandsworth and Southwark in the south.

Entrance: As maddeningly oversubscribed as you would expect – something like 1,000 applicants for 150 places. Looked after children and those with statements have priority. Sixty per cent C of E places, 40 per cent 'open', with distance the only criterion. Fourteen places annually given to those with outstanding aptitude in an aspect of performing arts (music, choral, dance or drama). Applicants divided into four ability bands with equal numbers accepted from each band. Tie breaker of how near to the school you live. In the sixth, 330 places – priority to existing students, though they have to fulfil requirements (minimum of five A*-B GCSEs, with at least C grade in maths and English). Boys are taken into the sixth and, again, more apply than there are places for. Performing arts and maths/ICT scholarships for sixth formers. School receives five applications a week for occasional places.

Exit: One-quarter leaves after GCSE and goes to sixth form colleges, the independents, eg Latymer Upper, or other state schools, eg Camden, largely for a greater range of A level subjects or more vocational courses. Most stay, though entrance to the school's own sixth form is not a given, even for their own, and 20 per cent left after year 12 in 2016. Sixth form leavers to good universities and a range of courses; five to Oxford and Cambridge in 2016 and three medics. A few each year to read music. Students go on to study a decent mix of arts and science subjects, from bio-medicine at Edinburgh to Spanish and Hispanic studies at Bristol to criminology at Manchester. A few each year to read music, usually several to art foundation, dance foundation and drama school – immediately or after a gap year.

Money matters: National funding programmes largely cut so bidding for extra money from various sources takes up a lot of time. The result, however, is a school that is well-staffed and well-equipped, if not to lavish private school standards.

Remarks: If your daughter is outgoing, confident and creative this is an excellent choice. St Marylebone is an exceptional school. It has the benefits of the moral ethos of a Church of England school but is ethnically diverse and serves many different communities. With a bright young head at the helm, its future looks as rosy as its history.

St Mary's School, Hampstead

239

47 Fitzjohn's Avenue, London NW3 6PG

Pupils: 300 (12 boys) • Ages: 2.75–6 (boys), 2.75–11 (girls) • RC

Fees: £7,305 – £13,500 pa

Tel: 020 7435 1868
Email: enquiries@stmh.co.uk
Website: www.stmh.co.uk

Headmistress: Since September 2016, Harriet Connor-Earl BA (religious education) from Brighton, previously director of studies and boarding housemistress at Ardingly Prep. A committed Catholic, she is married to Tom and they have one son, Conan. Enjoys family skiing holidays, cooking and renovating her house in Brittany.

Entrance: No specific deadlines, Places go first to siblings, then to Catholics, then to non-Catholics. Parents generally tour the school nine months before entry, sign the acceptance form and pay a deposit. Nursery arrangements are particularly parent friendly. Children are admitted from 2 years and 9 months and can stay to lunch or all afternoon with minimum notice. Boys make up a third of nursery entrants. A few further places for girls often become available in year 3. Some bursaries available.

Exit: About 85 per cent to leading academic secondary schools – South Hampstead, Francis Holland, Channing, Queen's College plus City of London, North London Collegiate, Highgate, St Paul's Girls etc – quite a number with scholarships. Also to selective state schools (St Michael's Catholic Grammar, Henrietta Barnett). Secondary school advice is a strength, starting with individual parent meetings in year 5. 'Most trust us and listen to what we recommend', says the school. Boys leave by the age of 6, many to neighbouring Catholic prep St Anthony's.

Remarks: Founded in 1871, by the Congregation of Jesus, the school moved from Belsize Park in 1926 to its present building, a turn-of-the century mansion with polished mosaic floors and vast country-like gardens. Against this gracious period backdrop, facilities are thoroughly up to date, with a super, Mac-filled IT suite, large, new assembly hall and well-stocked library located in the panelled former billiards room. In 1992, when there were too few teaching nuns to manage the school, a charitable trust was formed to continue the good work under lay management.

A non-selective school, it still manages to pull off high-flying results at 11. Teaching (as described in the recent ISI report) is 'excellent' – sharp, lively and very pupil focused. 'The teacher worked out my daughter in three minutes', said one parent. Praise is appropriate and immediate. 'My daughter had been struggling to write a longer essay. On the day she did so, the head immediately called her in and gave her two merit points. It encouraged her so much'.

The brightest are stretched through a curriculum enriched with plenty of arts-related activities and sport. 'We wanted to make it more relevant and incorporate risk taking and thinking independently'. Interesting extra work for those who need stretch (lunch-time puzzle club, for example, is a big hit).

Fluid ability grouping throughout, then setting in maths and English in year 6 in the run up to 11 plus. Excellent support for strugglers, too, with three special needs teachers providing help in class and out of it (in lovely, bright teaching space). 'The learning support is fantastic', said one mother with a daughter finding maths a mountain. 'Very few independent schools are non-selective, but St Mary's does very well by all'. Another told us: 'You really feel they care about every single girl. If someone is not up to scratch, the response is "what can we do to help them shine?"' External specialists are invited in to keep absence to a minimum.

Strong sport, with a double court for netball and a well-equipped gym. All the usual team games (rounders, netball, hockey, football), plus swimming at Swiss Cottage baths (for years 3 to 6) and athletics in Regent's Park. Gymnastics particularly popular, with pupils competing at regional and national level. High achievement too, in music and excellent dance and drama (including an all-encompassing production in year 6). Heaps of clubs (Latin, Spanish, needlework, craft, lingua franca) and plenty of trips (year 5 to an adventure camp in Devon, year 6 on a five-day break in France to meet pen-pals and make croissants, little ones to a farm and the seaside).

Boys are well integrated and given appropriate scope in the Big Boys' Club, in which football is played and steam let off on imaginary motor bikes. 'It lets them be boys in this all-girls environment', said one mother.

Very much a Catholic school, with about 70 per cent Catholic parents. 'I think one of the most wonderful things about it is that the Catholic ethos permeates every aspect of the children's life', said one. Those who wish can be prepared for first holy communion by much-loved Father Chris on his twice-weekly visits to the school chapel. Pupils participate in mass and study Catholic Christianity. 'Many of our parents have had a Catholic education themselves and want that for their children' – but even those who haven't feel included. 'As a non-Catholic', said one parent, 'I was quite concerned at the outset, but Father Chris is so lovely and gives such interesting talks. They really teach the children how to be good and loving members of a community'.

Pupils are beaming and notably well-behaved (not a peep was heard when our guide was chatting to one teacher as children queued to leave the room). 'We really work hard at being positive. We want to catch children doing the right thing.' Plenty of rewards for those who are caught doing things 'the St Mary's Way'; those who slip up are gently reminded of 'expectations'. 'We want pupils to do their best.' Most pupils adore the school ('my daughter can't wait to get back after the holidays') and parents are equally appreciative. 'You're never made to feel unwelcome, you never feel you shouldn't be there', we were told.

Mostly professional families from Hampstead and the surrounding areas, with a wide range of backgrounds (from Europe, the US, Asia and the Far East). About half speak at least one other language at home (with good in-school support for newcomers on the foothills of English). Mums 'really involved' (with reading, bazaars, the library, uniform sale). Despite its Hampstead location, this is a fairly understated place and, unusually for a prep school, offers a number of full bursaries.

S

St Michael's CofE Primary School

240

North Road, London N6 4BG

Pupils: 465 • Ages: 3–11 • C of E

Tel: 020 8340 7441
Email: admin@stmichaelsn6.com
Website: www.stmichaelsn6.com

Head Teacher: Since 2013, Geraldine Gallagher (40s), BEd Liverpool University. Was NQT in a 'semi-rural' primary school with a mixed catchment, then went inner city to work in a primary school in Hackney, an experience she called 'very good although challenging at times.' She left after a year to teach at St John Evangelist School in Islington where she worked her way up to becoming deputy head. Sixteen years later she was ready to embrace the demands of becoming a head and saw the post advertised for St Michael's CofE: 'I grew up in Islington so had heard of the school and it had always had a pretty good reputation, so decided to go for it.'

Focused, 'I've wanted to be a teacher since I was 14', grounded, and knows the score. Ms Gallagher was only too aware that this was not an easy school to take on, with its prominent milieu of extremely hands-on parents (a positive in many ways but could arguably marginalise the power of a new head). She says: 'In the main the parents here are very supportive, but like most people if things go out of kilter, they will let you know.' However, judging by the feedback we've had, she need not worry. One parent told us that Ms Gallagher has already turned things around for the better in so many ways since starting: 'Parents now know where they stand with her and with the school as she has clear rules and guidelines.' Another said: 'She is a fantastic head. Before she came there was a lot of discontent and the school was in quite a bit of turmoil. The school was operating on the ethos of an old head and it became a situation of us and them between parents and teachers. Ms Gallagher has brought consistency to the school and moved it forward.'

With three of her own children at the school, this head undoubtedly has a vested interest in its success, both academically and pastorally. As one parent pointed out, 'The ethos here is very much that you get out what you put in.' Married for 14 years, any extracurricular time that Ms Gallagher has is spent with her family on days out and the odd swim or two.

Entrance: Heavily oversubscribed at nursery and reception. Around 100 apply for 52 nursery places. The 60 reception places are allocated on a points system, 14 points being the maximum. (Four points for church attendance at St Michael's Church, three for living in N6. Thereafter, local Christians, siblings, other faiths.) Christianity very much part of the ethos. Open days every term and, if a vacancy is available, parents are welcome to look round. Places do arise, particularly in the higher years when some pupils leave for the private sector.

Exit: On the border of three boroughs – Haringey, Islington and Camden – St Michael's sends its leavers to as many as 30 secondary schools. About half to independent schools (many with scholarships), particularly Highgate, with which the school has a close association, and City of London, but also Channing, UCS, Westminster, North London Collegiate, Haberdashers' Aske's and South Hampstead, plus top grammars Henrietta Barnett, Latymer, St Michael's Catholic Girls and Queen

Elizabeth's Boys. A considerable chunk each year to Fortismere School, the popular local comprehensive in Muswell Hill.

Remarks: One of north London's most sought-after primary schools, St Michael's has high academic standards and a high proportion of pupils who reach well beyond the government's expectations at 7 and 11. This partly reflects the intake (largely middle class Highgate), but is also due to strong teaching – recently boosted by an overhaul of the teaching structure. 'Much more academic,' one parent told us; another said, 'The school is now back on track and on its way to becoming very successful again.'

The shift in the teaching structure came about following a period of upheaval at the time when Ms Gallagher was appointed head over two years ago. She says, 'I don't believe in old style leadership and pointing the finger. I knew the school had been though a difficult time, but I believe in working together to achieve the best teaching model.' This included bringing in several new members of staff and making some of the existing ones non-teaching heads of phases, which freed them up to oversee the efficient running of the year groups. While some parents were initially resistant, others feel their children are really reaping the rewards. One told us: 'There is a huge difference in what my son gets for homework to what my older daughter got at that age. It was a bit haphazard before, now it's more structured – not hothousing, just wanting each child to reach their potential.'

This is a school that doesn't rest on its laurels – which it probably could do quite comfortably by virtue of its catchment. A dedicated teacher/parent partnership ensures that even the least engaged child will derive something because of the constantly stimulating and original methods of teaching. Pupils will still enthuse a year later about how 'a spaceship landed in their grounds', which they were allowed to explore – after which they were encouraged to write a story about the experience. This was courtesy of some very innovative parents, who together with the English leader spent hours creating the spaceship, and Troy, the 'legendary' school manager who ran into each classroom shouting that a spaceship had landed, amidst loud noises and flashing lights.

This year saw a camper van book bus parked in the grounds to encourage pupils to go in and read during break times (a cool spin on the old mobile library). Other stimulating learning tools include a charming open reading shed in the grounds funded by parents, a play pod with an assortment of recycled goods to encourage imaginative play and an allotment run by parent volunteers. We also loved the idea of a 'kindness wall', which we spotted in a couple of the classrooms, and which, we are told by one pupil, 'encourages us to write nice things about each other.' The pupils we chatted to were an astute bunch, happy and friendly. We even got treated to one spectacular card trick by a pupil who said he loved the school because the teachers 'let me do magic.' Another pupil told us that as a Muslim he liked how a Christian school 'embraces other cultures.'

Parents are an unusually energetic bunch – the school's Parents' Association (SMSA) is possibly the most committed we have come across. Last year alone they raised an astonishing £61,000, through events such as a bonfire night, battle of the bands, fun run and, the pièce de résistance, the annual parents' pantomime. This, we are told, can rival anything seen in the West End and is the highlight of the school calendar. One parent told us: 'What makes this school so special is the dedication of parents. Because we are a church school with no extra funding we can only get the extras we want if we raise the money ourselves. It does create a lovely community atmosphere, but forget it if you want a school where you can just drop your kids off and not get involved.' For a recent production of Dick Whittington, it was not unusual to see parents rehearsing or building sets until midnight, on top of the jobs they do during the day. Luckily for the school, parents include actors, musicians and set designers.

Excellent drama, with two or three plays annually, plus a nativity play and annual summer concert. A good range of sport – gymnastics, football, tag rugby, tennis, cricket, netball and basketball – taught in lesson time. Swimming, taught in years 5 and 6, is particularly strong.

Fantastic and varied extracurricular programme provides a wonderful resource for working parents. Breakfast clubs start as early as 7.45am and for the particularly energetic early bird fencing and gymnastics are offered. The quieter soul can indulge in a bit of Latin or creative writing, and an early morning maths club is also offered for 'invited pupils.' After-school activities include football, netball, dance, drama (led by the school's celebrated drama teacher, Bob Williams CBE), orchestra, French, chess and fortnightly film club (pupils have won several awards for film reviewing as part of the National Film Club).

Charity a big part of the school's ethos. On the day we visited parents were arriving with hampers to distribute to the local community and a bus-load of senior citizens arrived for their annual Christmas party. At this much anticipated event, year 6s dress up as waiters and waitresses to serve food and give out individually handmade cards and wrapped presents.

Good SEN department. Specific programmes designed for pupils who are classified as SEN or statemented (roughly 16 per cent), and access to regular sessions with art, occupational, and speech and language therapists. Each classroom has an adjoining intervention room for those who need extra help with maths, English etc.

The school is a couple of hundred yards down from pretty Highgate village – barely visible from the road, but as you approach the main gates the beauty of this building and its grounds can be appreciated. Founded in the mid-19th century as a school to train young locals to go into service, by 1852 it was on its current three-and-a-half acre site with the intention of not only providing an academic education, but also cultivating the spacious grounds as a farm. The green fields and listed Victorian buildings have since been joined by a block built in the 1970s, two large, well-equipped playgrounds and a large, new all-weather court. Both building and grounds are extensive and it is easy to lose one's bearings. The only gripe we heard from parents was about improving the concrete play area. One parent told us: 'I appreciate it is all about funding, and it's definitely better than it was previously, when it looked like a camp site, but there has been just talk for a long time.'

St Michael's Catholic Grammar School

Nether Street, London N12 7NJ

Pupils: 760 • Ages: 11–18 • Sixth form: 270 (50 boys) • RC

Tel: 020 8446 2256
Email: office@st-michaels.barnet.sch.uk
Website: www.st-michaels.barnet.sch.uk

Headmaster: Since 2012, Julian Ward BA PGCE MBA (60s). Born in Lancashire and educated at the Pilgrim School, Bedford, and Manchester University, where he read modern history and economics. Then went on to study for an MBA at Bradford, before deciding that 'business was not my cup of tea' and training to be a teacher at Christ's College, Liverpool. ('I enjoyed every minute.') Has spent his entire professional career in London, where he started out teaching economics in 'front-line' local authority schools (Bishop Challoner in Tower Hamlets, John Paul II in Wandsworth, Sir John Cass's Foundation and Redcoat in Stepney), before moving to St Michael's in 1988.

Became sole deputy head in 1995, and his close working relationship with his predecessor, Ursula Morrisey, means he sees his current role more as evolution than revolution. Throughout his time at the school, has been a driving force in setting the highest academic targets, helping move the school from a middle-of-the road grammar to one that consistently sits at the top of the league tables. Since becoming head, has put particular emphasis on improving the percentage of A*s at A level, developing the gifted and talented programme and improving the school-parent partnership. A measured presence with a firm vision of what the school is about. 'Girls like him,' said one mother.'They think he's strict, but fair.' 'Very dedicated,' said another. Married with three adult children, he continues to teach citizenship and RE.

Retiring in July 2017. His successor will be Michael Stimpson BSc MSc MA MA PGCE NPQH (40s), currently head of St Bernard's Catholic Grammar in Berkshire. Degree in natural science and teaching certificate from Durham; went straight into teaching physics and much later completed his masters in astrophysics part-time through Queen Mary, University of London. He also holds two masters degrees in educational management (one in Catholic school leadership). Has spent most of his time in selective and Catholic schools, including a spell as head of sixth form at St Michael's. Keen on the role of extracurricular education – and of the Duke of Edinburgh's Award in particular, for which he has given up many weekends in his current school. He is married with three children and enjoys literature; walks in the wild bits of Britain and listening to the music of Westminster Cathedral Choir. He is a fellow of the Royal Astronomical Society.

Academic matters: St Michael's has won numerous awards (including Sunday Times State Secondary School of the Year 2013) for providing an outstanding education and is now one of the country's leading secondary schools, always sitting within the top 20 grammar schools (often in the top 10) nationally at A level, usually in the top five at GCSE. 2016 saw 82 per cent A*-B grades at A level. At GCSE, 85 per cent A*/A. Teaching is undoubtedly a strength ('There are very clever teachers who provide very good teaching,' said one parent) and the school works hard to maximize both pupils' and parents' aspirations. 'We give a great deal of time to thinking about it,' says the head.

All the girls accepted here are bright, but St Michael's still offers significant added value, with a packed, fast-paced curriculum ('You need to enjoy academic work and want to find out about things,' says the head). Almost all take 11 GCSEs, including a large compulsory core, which includes English, maths, history and/or geography, RS, a science (about a third take all three) and a modern foreign language (large numbers take two). Language offering particularly vibrant, with French, German, Spanish, Latin and Italian all on the timetable, and Japanese and Mandarin offered outside it. Italian and Spanish particularly popular A levels (as well as psychology, RS and maths). Sixth form has its own building ('St Michael's is really two schools, with two distinct regimes,' says the head, 'a girls'-only school in years 7-11, and a co-ed sixth form college'). Only small numbers with special needs, but strugglers are provided with generous support. Homework is pushed hard. 'If you're ill you have to catch up on what you've missed,' said one mother.

Games, options, the arts: No playing fields and only a handful of courts, so team games not a forte (no hockey, for example), but a spacious new-ish sports hall (the largest school gym in Barnet) is used to the full to deliver high standard athletics, netball, volleyball, gymnastics, table tennis and badminton. Professional basketball and netball coaches bring out the best in nascent stars and the school is successful at local and regional level in a number of sports. The top performing school in the borough's inter-sports competitions for girls.

Academic music is excellent, with dedicated practice rooms and a recording suite, though the head is pushing for higher standards of extracurricular involvement. 'Lots of girls participate in choir and orchestra, but I would like us to have greater opportunities for high quality performance.' Large, well-equipped art and DT studio (offering material technology, food technology and graphics) with plenty of enthusiastic participants.

Good range of clubs (mainly in the lunch hour rather than after school as many pupils live far away) and trips (including skiing, modern languages and faith-centred activities, such as retreats and a visit to Lourdes).

Background and atmosphere: Founded by the Congregation of the Sisters of the Poor Child Jesus in 1908 as a prep school in the grounds of its convent. In 1958, a girls' grammar school was launched to share the site, and eventually the prep school was closed to allow the grammar school to expand.

Still quite a compact school housed in a motley collection of periods and styles. The Grange, which now accommodates the sixth form, was once a 19th century private house, and has the elegant proportions reflective of this history. The main school was built in the 1950s and comes with large windows and bright views. Modernisation is a constant theme (and drain on finances), but recent additions include an air-conditioned multi-media suite and sixth form study centre. Classrooms remain a mix of old and new, but all are equipped with interactive whiteboards. Attractive gardens, once the convent orchard, are graced by a monkey puzzle tree, large redwood and shrine to the Virgin Mary.

The school, which is voluntary aided, is conducted by its governing body as part of the Catholic church and the Catholic ethos remains fundamental. Prayers are said daily and every pupil attends a weekly religious assembly, as well as mass on Feast days. But this is contemporary Catholicism. 'They go to mass, but they don't expect them to be cleaning the vestry floors,' said one parent. Attractive chapel with superior stained glass windows by Patrick Reyntiens, a master craftsman whose work also features in Liverpool and Coventry cathedrals. Girls put their faith into practice with charity work, helping in the community and giving food to homeless. Generally, the atmosphere is kind, warm and supportive. 'Academically, they push them to their limits, but they do look after them,' said one parent.'There's a very nice feeling to the school.' 'No one gets lost,' said another.'It feels very safe.'

Pastoral care, well-being and discipline: The primary aim here is the formation of responsible and committed Catholic citizens. 'We try to create a relaxed and happy atmosphere,' says the head, 'but we expect high standards of behaviour, self-discipline and responsibility.' Those from bohemian families are advised to think carefully about their choice. Even those who aren't acknowledge that the regime is firm. 'There is very strong discipline, which can irritate the girls,' said a parent. 'They will stamp on anything – possibly too hard.'

The pre-GCSE years have a slightly old-fashioned air. 'There's no talk of drugs,' said one mother. 'They do go to parties, but there's no big modern teenage culture.' Girls leap to attention if Mr Ward is spotted in the corridor and pupil pressure as much as teacher pressure patrols the classroom. 'My daughter said to me in astonishment, "a new girl in the school keeps answering the teacher back. Nobody will be friends with her. We like our teachers. They're on our side; we're on theirs".'

In the pre-GCSE years, uniform strictly enforced, with purple skirts at the knee or close to it, no jewellery or make-up. In the sixth form, mufti is permitted and the dress code becomes 'decency'.

Pupils remain accountable for what happens outside the gates if in uniform. Few problems, however. 'Most people who come here are impressed by the behaviour and friendliness of the pupils.'

Pupils and parents: Cradle Catholics from all over London and the world, with increasing numbers of Eastern Europeans, particularly Poles. Not as skewed to the professional middle classes as some other grammar schools, with more new immigrants (33 per cent do not speak English as their first language at home).

Entrance: Not perhaps as tricky to get into academically as some of the other North London grammar schools (390 apply for 96 places), simply because of its single-sex faith criteria. That said, the Catholic hurdle is not for slackers. Applicants at 11 plus must provide proof of first holy communion and at least one parent must also be a Catholic with a written reference from their parish priest stating they attend mass on Sunday with the applicant. There is no catchment ('you can come from Sheffield if you want') but only girls who meet the religious criteria are allowed to sit the admissions tests (in verbal and non-verbal reasoning, English and maths). Sixth form applicants are not required to be Catholic (about 20 per cent come from other faiths) but 'must subscribe to the Catholic ethos'. At this stage, there are a further 60 places (open to boys and girls with at least six GCSE passes at A* to A, with at least an A in the subjects they wish to study and no lower than a B in English and maths). Boys in this relatively large sixth form remain in the minority, with about 30 a year. 'The boys have to be quite brave,' said one parent.

Exit: Roughly 15 per cent of girls leave post-GCSE, to nearby sixth form colleges, like Woodhouse, or larger co-ed selective schools. Most sixth formers go onto the older universities. Good handful each year to Oxbridge (nine places in 2016), guided by the school's own Oxbridge specialist, plus several medics/dentists. Others to a range from archaeology at Manchester to theoretical physics at Durham.

Money matters: St Michael's is a voluntary-aided school and parents are expected to contribute towards the cost of the buildings and facilities. 'The school would fall down otherwise,' says the head. An annual contribution of £275 a year is asked for and 90 per cent of parents contribute something. 'We don't go chasing the other 10 per cent.'

Remarks: A happy school, with firm discipline, high expectations and outstanding results.

St Olave's Grammar School

Goddington Lane, Orpington, Kent BR6 9SH

Pupils: 1,011 • Ages: 11–18 • Sixth form: 365 (145 girls) • C of E

Tel: 01689 820101
Email: office@saintolaves.net
Website: www.saintolaves.net

Headmaster: Since 2010 Mr Aydin Önaç (50s) BMus BSc ARCM FRSA. A grammar school boy himself, who grew up on a council estate in Derby. Trained at the Royal College of Music as a pianist and still devotes several hours each week to the piano, but found it impossible to make a living as a musician and took a maths degree at UCL instead. After a short spell in the City, he found his vocation as a maths teacher, got a job at Hemel Hempstead, and began a rapid rise to the top. St Olave's is his third headship, after Tewkesbury School in Gloucestershire and Fortismere in north London. Two grown up children from his first marriage, and two teenage step-children in his second; his wife also works in education.

Ambitious and energetic, Mr Önaç has also been something of a controversial figure during his career. After reputedly receiving a 'golden handshake' of £40k to take on Fortismere School, where he introduced 10 per cent selection for musical pupils, he left after only four years for St Olave's, where he has driven already-impressive results still higher and made Cambridge the school's most common university destination, with an average of 30 leavers a year gaining places there. 'The challenge for me was keeping the school at the top,' he told us, 'A lot of heads tend to duck that challenge, but I revel in it.' Parental enthusiasm for the school's performance is universal, but the feedback we received about the head suggested that parents feel kept at a distance by him. Comments included, 'Not enough interaction on a personal level,' and 'Not really a people person.' Mr Önaç's response to these observations was surprised and robust: 'I attend every single school function, and I try to be very visible. I have an open door policy, and I welcome people coming in to talk to me.'

Academic matters: By any measure, St Olave's results are top-notch. In 2016, 84 per cent of GCSE results were at A*/A, with maths particularly strong. At A level, 72 per cent of grades were at A*/A and 94 per cent were at A*-B. 'We have the very highest aspirations for all our students, and that translates into having the highest expectations. It's a given at St Olave's, as far as I'm concerned,' says head. Parents and boys alike describe the staff as 'dedicated', 'professional' and 'enthusiastic'. Students are encouraged to go well beyond the demands of the syllabus. 'There's a focus here on going further than the curriculum, on exploring and expanding your knowledge,' said a very personable sixth form girl. Boys from years 7-11 confirmed that the teachers were 'really good at spotting where you might need help.' 'St Olave's promotes independent learning, it has done from the beginning,' reported a satisfied parent. 'Our son can structure his own time without needing any input from us.' 'The academic rigour of lessons is great: our son is challenged, and he has the opportunity to share his ideas in a supportive atmosphere,' said another. 'High-achieving in a relaxed learning environment,' said a third. 'Our approach can be summed up in one word: scholarship,' affirmed the head.

Very broad curriculum, encompassing everything you'd expect, and a few things you wouldn't: we were particularly pleased to see the new food technology room, and to hear that cookery was a popular part of the lower school curriculum. Lots of emphasis on computing, and robotics has taken off in a big way. Latin is compulsory in year 7, and Greek, Japanese and Mandarin are all offered as extracurricular options, but a recent decision to axe (school prefers the phrase 'phase out') Spanish and drama from the curriculum has ruffled the waters somewhat. The head urged us not to dwell on the matter, but parents and pupils alike told us they were disappointed about it (or, in the words of one, 'annoyed and angry'). We put these concerns to the head, who responded that the school had had to cut its cloth because of forthcoming government cuts, 'and we just haven't the numbers to fill a GCSE set.' According to the website, both subjects were popular and successful, so this struck us as a little odd.

School has now moved to a three-year KS4, so that students will choose their GCSEs in year 8 and begin their courses in year 9. At sixth form level, the school remains wholly committed to A levels (as opposed to the IB or Cambridge Pre-U). 'We prefer the depth,' said the director of studies, 'and complemented by a vibrant extracurricular provision, they suit our students best.'

Games, options, the arts: There can't be many state schools where rugby and Eton fives are the main sports. Fives is hugely popular, with many boys playing it every day ('It's quick and easy, and you can play it in your uniform!'), and the school's rugby teams regularly win success at both local and national level. Cricket is also big here – the school toured recently to South Africa. Broad range of other sports, including tennis, hockey, football, swimming, basketball, squash, badminton and athletics. The arts are also strong. 'The music is fabulous here,' said the head fondly. 'The jazz band is terrific,' agreed one parent, remembering a recent concert in Croydon's Fairfield Halls. Lots of choral singing, with all tastes catered for – 'I sing in six choirs!' one boy told us, proudly – and the school supplies all the choristers for the Queen's Chapel of the Savoy (one of them recently won BBC Radio 2's Chorister of the Year). Children can learn almost any instrument here, including the organ in the school hall, and take their skills into the school's many orchestras and bands. We're pleased to report that drama is also strong. A few years ago, there was just one annual production, and that was for sixth formers; now there are plenty for everyone, several of them directed by the students themselves. Lots of wonderfully cerebral stuff going on in clubs: we saw a superb English version of a German children's classic, translated and published by the students themselves, plus erudite student-produced journals for the Law Society, the History Society, the Medics' Society, and more. Boys report being made to feel welcome in all the activities they tried. Ambitious and enticing programme of trips and excursions: in recent months, students have had the opportunity to visit Iceland, New York, Paris, Greece, South America, central Africa – the list goes on.

Background and atmosphere: Originally located in Tooley Street, Southwark, St Olave's received its royal charter in 1571: display cases in the corridors show treasures from its archive collection, and watercolours show the school at its various stages. It moved to its present spacious site, complete with beautiful modern chapel, in leafy Orpington in 1968, in quest of more space and its own playing fields – also, perhaps, to get away from the threat of being turned comprehensive. Long and proud history of being academically selective, with which the present head is completely in tune: 'I believe this country neglects its brightest youngsters at its peril. They are the wealth creators and the job creators of the future. I spent 22 years in the comprehensive sector and I remain dedicated to its aims, but I'm also completely committed to giving these students the education they deserve.'

And yet, with all that was going on, and every reason for the Olave's air to be full of buzz and liveliness, we can only comment on what we found, which was a curious guardedness whenever we hove into view, not least in a reluctance to let us talk to the students without a member of SMT present; although, on our pressing the matter, they did agree. All staff, from the head downwards, reacted with surprise and displeasure when we passed on parental criticisms (perhaps, like some other high-achieving and over-subscribed schools, they don't often hear them), and a couple of the older staff simply refused to talk to us, actually getting up and walking away when we tried to ask them questions. One parent, whose son is doing very well at St Olave's, described the school as 'incredibly defensive', to which the head's response was, 'We don't have anything to be defensive about!' Others, however, have described a very different experience. 'On the few occasions I have needed to contact staff by email, their response has been prompt and helpful,' wrote one mother. 'Our sons have been incredibly happy at the school and we cannot fault it,' wrote another.

S

Pastoral care, well-being and discipline: Mixed responses from parents, with some praising the school's 'very caring ethos', and others saying that bullying issues took too long to be resolved. Strong prefect system ensures older boys take responsibility for leading and mentoring the younger ones, and highly selective intake plays its part in developing the very strong work ethic apparent in lessons. 'It's almost unheard of for behaviour to be poor here,' says the head.

Pupils and parents: From all over the borough and beyond; nearly 50 per cent from ethnic minorities. Less diverse socially, with only two per cent of students on free school meals. Extremely supportive and active parents' association, which works tirelessly to raise funds for equipment, facilities and travel opportunities.

Entrance: Roughly 1,000 boys apply for 124 places, and an additional four places are offered to choral scholars who must pass the same stringent entrance tests.

New admissions policy for entry into year 7. First stage is logic, maths and English test in September. Those who pass invited to sit second stage English and maths test later in the autumn. First and second stage marks combined to give final score and the first 124 applicants in rank order offered places.

Around 500 boys and girls apply each year for the 110 sixth form places on offer to students from other schools. Grade point requirement for sixth form entry for internal as well as external candidates has been upped to 64 from best nine subjects, with A* counting as 8 points, A as 7 etc (nothing lower than B is counted). Those external candidates whose predicted grades meet these requirements will be asked to take written tests in their four chosen A level subjects.

Exit: At 16, the great majority to St Olave's sixth form, although between four and eight per cent of Y11 students don't get the grades needed and have to leave. A few also eased out at 17 (school prefers the phrase 'fail to meet the published criteria') if they haven't got the grades at AS 'or equivalent internal examinations' required (three Bs) to progress to Y13. At 18, everyone goes to university: majority to Russell Group destinations; 37 to Oxbridge and 26 medics in 2016.

Money matters: State-funded grammar school, supported by Bromley education authority and the Diocese of Rochester. Parents invited to pay around £500 pa in voluntary contributions to help pay for faciltiies, etc.

Remarks: For the bright, motivated boy who is prepared to knuckle down, St Olave's is an excellent fit. As one parent put it, 'Very good, very impressive, very supportive. And we haven't had to pay for it.'

St Paul's Cathedral School

2 New Change, London EC4M 9AD

Pupils: 247; 30 boarders (boy choristers) • Ages: 4-13

Fees: Day £13,200 – £14,211 pa; boarding choristers £8,218 pa tuition free

Tel: 020 7248 5156
Email: admissions@spcs.london.sch.uk
Website: www.spcslondon.com

Headmaster: Since September 2016, Simon Larter-Evans, previously head of boarding, housemaster and head of English and drama at the Yehudi Menuhin School. He studied ballet at the Rambert Academy, then spent four years as principal dancer, performing in the UK and abroad. After 15 years' working in commercial management, publishing and IT industries, he gained a first class degree as a mature student in English literature, drama, theatre and performance from the University of Surrey, and a PGCE from the Institute of Education. He has been a teacher of English and head of year 9 at St Edward's School, Oxford, and a teacher of English and drama at Pangbourne College. He is married to Dawn, a director at KPMG.

Entrance: Seventy on list for 20 available places at 4+ (though planning to expand to two form entry), so best to put children down early. Informal assessment in November before year of entry. More places at 7+ when boarding choristers (boys only) also start. January assessment and short test for day children (also taken by those in pre-prep); informal audition with director of music for choristers, followed by formal audition and same academic test as day children. More places for choristers at 8+ and occasionally 9+. Choristers' fees paid by Dean and Chapter of St Paul's Cathedral with parents paying boarding fee. This will carry on even if a boy's voice breaks early. If in need, bursaries available for day children also. School is keen to build up a fund and expand this.

Exit: At 11+ and 13+ to a mixture of London day schools and top boarding schools. Majority of girls at 11+ though school eager to keep girls and maintain balance. Choristers mostly to boarding schools at 13+. An impressive number of music and the occasional academic scholarships. Westminster appears high among day schools, with Alleyn's, City of London (girls and boys), Dulwich College, Highgate, Forest School and JAGS also featuring. King's Canterbury popular amongst a wide selection of good boarding schools. Recently, Eton, Stowe, Uppingham and Oundle have all offered academic and music scholarships. Famous ex-pupils include Alastair Cooke (England cricket captain) and Simon Russell Beale (actor).

Remarks: A small school, nestling in the precincts of St Paul's Cathedral, providing an excellent all round education in a traditional setting with a formal, spiritual context to everything it does. In amongst the hustle and bustle of the City of London, an oasis of orderliness and calm. Boy choristers have been around since 1123, originally linked to a grammar school which became St Paul's School, London, about 400 years later. Only tenuous links remain. In 1989, the Dean and Chapter decided to expand the tiny choristers-only school to include day boys as well. Girls arrived in 1998 and the school grew to the size it is today.

Two low concrete towers house the classrooms and are linked by the school hall, the gym, the library and various other communal activity areas. We seemed to wander up and down and across as enthusiastic pupils showed us their school but 'once you know the two towers it's easy,' they assured us. Three lovely bright classrooms for the pre-prep years, two each for years 3 and 4, then subject-based doubling up as home rooms from year 5 onwards. A building project to house new boarding accommodation plus extra lower years classrooms at planning stage.

Broad-based curriculum with all subjects well taught. Parents praise 'inspirational teachers' who are 'passionate about everything they do'. Average age 39 seems about right. Our guides also spoke enthusiastically about their teachers, singling out science and Latin/Greek as exceptional. Certainly pupils did look happy and absorbed in the excellent science lab; however, the French class we looked in on appeared chaotic. Mixed ability classes throughout with some discreet setting, particularly in years 7 and 8. Previously some complaints about lack of preparation for 11+ entrance exams, but school is driving this forward and has made important changes, revamping part of the curriculum and timetabling non-verbal reasoning, study skills etc into earlier years. Parents very happy about this. Creative writing, apparently, a great strength. Latin compulsory from year 5. Modern languages not the strongest point, though French taught from the beginning and Spanish available as an extra. Interactive whiteboards in classrooms and new IT suite. All special needs problems dealt with by head of learning support. Teachers flag up concerns and he is immediately involved. Any necessary help is provided, mostly free of charge. Additional staff available for one-to-one and in-class support when necessary. Parents kept fully in the picture and involved from the beginning.

Reasonable art. Studio also contains a printing press (given by the Stationers' Company) and a kiln for firing imaginative clay models. Location excellent for visiting Tate Modern as part of extended art lesson. Drama strongish and everyone gets a chance to take part in a production. As one of our guides said, 'If you're not particularly musical, you can still do drama and have fun'. LAMDA exam course available.

Inevitably the greatest strength is music, huge both instrumentally and vocally. Virtually every child in the school learns an instrument of his or her choice (no bagpipes!). Choristers learn two, piano being compulsory. Over 300 music lessons given each week, beginners all the way to grade 8. At least six different choirs plus 15 orchestras and ensembles from classic to rock band. Something for everyone, you might say. For musical, creative children it is a great place to be. Opportunities abound. Choristers are in the minority but it is their talent that is the backbone of the school. The day school exists because of them and they are getting a wider breadth of education because of the day school. Thus both sides are gaining a huge amount and it is important to maintain the balance. Choristers are acquiring an excellent academic education and day pupils are seeing, hearing and being involved in music of an exceptionally high standard. All of them are equally at home in the cathedral, which they treat as an extension of the school. Assemblies and occasional special services held and the majority get the chance to sing there. A parent told us, 'The Christmas service was something to behold.. about six or seven different choirs were fielded, including a combined one which seemed to involve most of the school'.

Choristers have a pretty heavy schedule with singing practice before school every morning, evensong on Tuesdays, Wednesdays, Fridays and Saturdays plus Saturday morning rehearsals and Sunday services – alongside a multitude of other occasions when they have to perform. They now have Monday evenings off as well as Thursdays. Seems only fair after an action-packed weekend. School stresses the importance of watching the development of their voices and becoming more aware of change – necessary with the earlier physical growth that now occurs. Thirteen-year-old trebles are rarer. Both the cathedral's director of music and organist are also committed to their personal development and nurture.

Separate boarding house with two resident qualified nurses; common room with snooker, table football etc. Many choristers live relatively close by and are allowed out with their families during free time in between services at weekends, including Sunday evenings (though they must be back in time for before-school Monday rehearsals). Those without nearby families are taken out by staff on duty at weekends.

A father said, 'Sport at the school is active, fun and inclusive'. Despite its inner city site, it is well catered for. Pupils are bused to Coram's Fields and Regent's Park for seasonal activities. Matches fielded against other schools in hockey, football, cricket, rounders, fencing and netball. Have been runners up in U12 London Schools' Cricket Association Cup, winners of the Girls' Football South London Tournament and pupils have been selected for the U10 National Fencing Squad and the U11 Surrey County Cricket squad. Also swim at local baths recreationally and competitively. Prep has rubber surfaced playground, marked up for ball games, where teachers also arrange impromptu games and sports practice. New, larger, grass and woodchip playground with climbing equipment for the pre-prep. Older children allowed to play quiet games here but not allowed to climb.

A variety of after-school clubs, mainly on Thursdays to enable choristers to join in, but on other days too. Range from cookery to dance to computing etc. Bound to be something for everyone. Also children may stay to do supervised prep at school, charged as an extra but useful for working parents. Plenty of outings and expeditions, academic, cultural and sporty, home and occasionally abroad. A lot to see within walking distance as well.

Parents stress the happy atmosphere – 'it has been the making of our little boy' – (of a chorister) and 'our unsettled, troublemaker has been transformed' – (of a day boy). 'Very good discipline, they don't tolerate bad behaviour'. General feeling that children are treated as individuals, academically stretched and made to work to their own levels; that the school is 'well managed and well ordered'. Much of this appears to lie in the vertical tutor system. Pupils are assigned to a tutor from day one and, in normal circumstances, remain with him/her until they leave the school. Thus tutor groups mixed in both ability and age and there is easy rapport between all children across the school. The older ones love helping the younger ones.

According to parents, excellent pastoral care, particularly for the boarders. 'They get well cared for, individual treatment and feel they are part of a family'. Several raved about the deputy head (pastoral) who, they say, really carried the school through recent difficult times. Definitely feel there's a good team in place now.

St Paul's Girls' School

Brook Green, London W6 7BS

Pupils: 744 • Ages: 11–18 • Sixth form: 222

Fees: £23,013 – £24,741 pa

Tel: 020 7603 2288
Email: admissions@spgs.org
Website: www.spgs.org

High Mistress: Since 2006, Ms Clarissa Farr MA, who previously spent 14 years at Queenswood, the last 10 as head. She has also taught English in Hong Kong, in a Bristol comprehensive and in a sixth form college in Farnborough.

As the established incumbent of one of the most exposed headships in the land, she exudes an elegant, intellectual confidence that could intimidate nervous potential parents and pupils. 'She seemed aloof initially,' said a mother, 'but she's much warmer when you get to meet her.' As a parent commented, 'You could easily get the wrong impression of her – she seems like a cut-glass ladies' college type – but my daughter really likes her.' 'Mine is really scared of her,' admitted another, 'but I noticed that the head girl and her team are all very relaxed with her, and they all clearly value each other's opinions.' Another added, 'She's always around, she knows them all by name. And my daughter says she'll sometimes give her particular look that makes you feel very important – as if you're the one person who matters.' By all accounts always present at school events, 'even the smaller drama club productions'.

Retiring in July 2017. ; her successor will be Sarah Fletcher, currently head of City of London School.

S

Academic matters: Pretty close to unbeatable. School can afford a lofty disdain for league tables as it is always at or near number one (57.7 per cent A*s and 93.8 per cent A*/A grades at A level in 2016; 92.9 per cent A*, 99.5 per cent A*/A at GCSE/iGCSE). The common claim to prioritise a broad education is undoubtedly justified here: many parents chose the school amidst a plethora of offers from other London powerhouses for this very reason. 'It really does feed a broader intellectual curiosity,' said one. Another commented: 'The teaching is second to none – exciting and stimulating. The teachers really get the children and make the most of them.'

Those few with special educational needs often have coping strategies in place before they arrive, but the school is well set up to help. 'They've been astonishingly good at responding to my daughter's needs, and put in plenty of support for her,' said a parent, 'so it hasn't been too much of an issue. But they have made it clear that she is expected to meet the standards of the school.'

There is a tight group of almost entirely academic subjects at GCSE and A level, which includes Italian, Chinese and Russian in the wide range of languages, though with relatively few takers at A level, and the recently added government and politics and theatre studies A level. Maths is by far the most popular A level subject, as one would expect, with a fairly even spread between the runners up biology, chemistry, English and history. Most A levels (19 out of 23) and the Pre-Us are linear, with all exams at the end of Year 13.

The school considered offering the IB but decided against it. 'We decided that A level and Pre-U are more flexible instruments – you have time to do things outside the curriculum that are not measured, and you can be a specialist or a generalist. It also gives more time for the bespoke Paulina unique co-curricular opportunities.' These include the Senior Scholarship project, which sees girls between Years 12 and 13 carrying out projects with titles ranging from 'Is There Beauty in Chaos?' to 'Visualising Polytopes in 4 Dimensions'; and the Friday lectures from luminaries such as Shami Chakrabarti from Liberty and documentary maker Michael Cockerell on his latest work, 'The Life of Boris Johnston'.

Games, options, the arts: With a legacy of Gustav Holst as first director of music and in-house composer, music has always been exceptional. Indeed, the recently renovated music department and singing hall – 'where Holst and Miss Gray [the then high mistress] listened to girls singing' – are an important nerve centre of the school. There are orchestras, music ensembles and choirs open to all, but the symphony orchestra and senior choirs are by audition only and perform at astonishingly high levels.

Art, too, is high profile. When we visited, the impressive coursework for the school-directed art GCSE course was on display in the hall. 'Art here is very special,' commented a student. The top floor art rooms include a terrace with a panorama of the London skyline where girls learn about architecture. There are spaces for digital art, animation, ceramics, sculpture and print-making as well as painting and drawing. DT is a GCSE option only as part the art and design course but an example of the talent was an impressive pupil-designed bus shelter that adorned the entrance drive when we visited.

Drama has perhaps been a poorer relation in the past. 'Music and art have always been great strengths,' says Ms Farr, 'but theatre studies is my second subject, and it struck me that drama had not developed to the same level, so we have evolved a separate drama department.' It is a successful GCSE and A level option (though a mother commented that she was unusual in encouraging her daughter to take two arts subjects at GCSE: 'Lots of parents only want their daughters to do academic subjects'.) The purpose-built Celia Johnson Theatre hosts several annual school plays, with smaller scale productions in the drama studio. Students devise and direct their own plays, including the year 12 Colet Play, which has been performed at the Edinburgh Fringe on several occasions. Girls also join in St Paul's Boys' School productions.

Lacrosse is the main sport, with 7.30am practices for team players ('they all love it, so it's fine', commented a less devoted pupil), international tours and players often making county and area squads. The school also competes successfully at sports including netball, basketball, rowing, cross county, fencing and swimming. However, there are opportunities for the less talented too, with teams down to D and E in the lower years. 'My younger daughter is in a team even though she's rubbish,' said a parent honestly.

One parent commented: 'It's very inclusive. There's choirs and orchestras anyone can be in, and the same for drama and sport.' Amidst so many very talented girls, however, some of the younger ones in particular can take time to gain confidence and find their niche. 'My daughter plays an instrument but hasn't been asked to take part in anything so far. She and her friends like singing, but they found the choir too highbrow. And they were very disheartened when none of them got through to the second round of auditions for the school musical.' Another parent said, 'There are huge opportunities, but it's up to them to make the most of it.'

Huge numbers of clubs, seminars and trips: writing courses, physics and maths competitions, conferences in Paris, museum visits in St Petersburg, dance shows and debating competitions. 'The girls get caught up in the energy of the place,' says Ms Farr, and a parent commented, 'My daughter always comes home having done amazing things.'

Background and atmosphere: Some 400 years after John Colet founded St Paul's School 'for the children [not girls, naturally] of all nations and countries', the Mercers' livery company, guardians of his estate, decided girls were also worthy of an education and set up St Paul's Girls' School. Its red-brick main house, designed by Gerald Horsley, with marble-floored corridors, and panelled and galleried great hall, has a gracious, traditional and peaceful feel. 'But if you go in at break time it's very buzzy,' said a parent. 'They're all running round the hall, there's music blaring out.' Lack of uniform gives an informal air, with most girls dressed in ubiquitous jeans or shorts and tee shirts.

Ms Farr recognises that the school has an undeserved reputation for being 'very formal, starchy, cold, highly competitive, ruthless and unforgiving'. But once families join, she says, 'they find it's much friendlier than expected, and more informal. We like to do things in a friendly, collegiate way.' Parents agree: 'It's a much more normal place than you'd think from its image. It's much nicer from the inside than from the outside.' 'They really care about the individual.'

Impressive admin: 'It's really well run, which means a lot to us,' said a mother. 'Induction week in particular is brilliantly organised. They told the girls what would happen, and it did. They're very accommodating and very professional.' Another said, 'Unlike at my son's school, I don't feel I have to stress about homework and deadlines. I leave it to them.'

Pressure to achieve tends to come from highly-ambitious girls and their families rather than from the school. However, some feel that the school could do more to mitigate anxieties. 'Success is taken so seriously that it sends out a message of pressure,' said a parent. 'Lots of girls really worry about how they are going to do in school exams. You can feel very unsuccessful if you aren't brilliant.' Some parents of younger girls feel the homework can be overwhelming. 'It tends to take much longer than intended because they're perfectionists,' said a year 7 parent. 'She and her friends take all evening doing homework.' 'I don't know how they cope if they miss anything, because lessons move at such a fast pace,' said another.

'We had the preconception that you had to be pretty, funny and clever to fit in here,' said a mother. 'But my retiring daughter has come home beaming from day one.' Another said that her daughter has found it tough: 'It took her a while to make friends. Coming from a state primary was particularly hard from a social point of view. But she's already gaining in confidence. They make the girls feel really proud of being there.'

Girls are encouraged to take the initiative. 'If you come up with an idea, the school will back you up and support you all the way,' said a sixth former, citing the in-house second-hand clothes shop, housed in a restored Victorian coal cellar that previously acted as a junk room, set up and run by students to raise money for local charities.

Pastoral care, well-being and discipline: 'I like to think it is a kinder school than it was,' says Ms Farr, who has increased the emphasis on the pastoral side. 'We have clear boundaries but lots of room for independent expression. We treat the girls like adults as soon as possible.' 'There's a marked lack of rules,' agreed a parent. 'There's a respect and a feeling of equality between teachers and girls.'

Some of these highly-ambitious girls do succumb to eating disorders or other expressions of teenage angst, but the school is very conscious of the problem and encourages a relaxed approach to eating. The food, said a pupil, is 'amazing. I feel as if I am eating in a restaurant every day. Food is important to Paulinas.'

Small tutor groups of 12 girls keep the same tutor for two years in the lower school and three in the middle school. The sixth form has a vertical system to enable those in different forms to share experiences. The sister scheme sees girls from the middle and upper schools help new girls settle in, and two year 13 girls are attached to each lower year group, available for mentoring and encouragement. 'The sixth form isn't hived off in its own area but is very much part of the school. The girls are role models and figures to look up to for the younger ones.' Two 'very approachable' school nurses, a school doctor and three councillors make up the non-teaching pastoral team.

Pupils and parents: Intellectual, ambitious, often multi-national families. 'I sometimes feel that my daughter's in a minority having two English parents. Lots of girls speak a second language fluently.' From a range of backgrounds – journalists and artists, academics and scientists, with a large proportion of bankers and lawyers ('You can spot those with bursaries,' said a parent wryly, 'because their dads aren't bankers.') Largest single cohort from Bute House, which regularly sends up to 20 or so girls here; the rest from a wide range of preps and primaries across London and beyond.

'There is a view that you must be super-confident to succeed here,' says Ms Farr, 'but girls vary here as much as anywhere. We do have a place for sensitive, quieter girls, and we enjoy the challenge of bringing them out. However, some parents still don't feel that their daughter is tough enough.' Parents agree that eccentricities are well tolerated. 'Of course the top dogs are the cool girls,' said one, 'but you can be a total geek and it's not a problem.'

Old Paulinas include (amongst many) Harriet Harman, Shirley Williams, Carol Thatcher, Stephanie Flanders, Rosalind Franklin, Rachel Weisz, Imogen Stubbs, Marghanita Lanski, Dodie Smith and Rachel Johnson.

Entrance: A computer-based test in November, aimed to be tutor proof and to identify 'girls with intellectual potential', deselects around 20 per cent of applicants. 'There's a vast industry preparing girls for St Paul's, and we don't want to miss bright sparks who haven't been tutored.' The rest take maths, English and comprehension exams in January, with those short-listed invited back for interviews. 'Our admissions process is a very careful, solemn business. We try to make it humane as well as thoughtful, and we discuss every candidate in detail.' The school optimistically asks parents to state if their daughter has been tutored, 'though we know they will answer what they think we want to hear'. They are trying to increase the proportion of successful state school applicants (currently around 15-25 per cent), and run a series of enrichment days for gifted and talented year 4 and 5 children from local state primaries. Parents are given information about bursaries and encouraged to attend an open evening. 'We don't positively discriminate, but we do try to see through disadvantage.' The school is clear that it is looking for a particular type of girl. 'Our girls devour intellectual material very quickly. Those who want to work at a slower pace will be happier elsewhere.'

Exit: No-one is asked to leave because of poor academic performance (though they might reconsider someone who showed a lack of interest in learning). 'We make an undertaking to see them through, and every year we take through one or two girls whose GCSE performance is less than starry.' Minimal numbers leave after GCSE (a few are tempted off to co-ed sixth forms, particularly Westminster).

Vast majority stays the course and moves on to do mostly solidly academic subjects at a very narrow range of top universities. Around half get Oxbridge places (51 in 2016); 11 medics; 13 off to Yale, Harvard and other Ivy League universities; virtually all the rest to Durham, Edinburgh, Bristol, London and Russell Group universities.

Money matters: Various music scholarships at 11+ which are currently the value of tuition in two instruments. The same music opportunities are available at 16+ along with art and drama scholarships, each worth £250 a year. The school aims to fund 20 per cent of girls through its means-tested bursary programme – 'we would like to feel that any girl from any setting could plot her way here' – and staff visit likely families at home to ensure they are not running a fleet of Ferraris from a multi-million pound mansion. Those on 100 per cent bursaries also receive a grant towards music or PE lessons, school trips, textbooks and travel.

Remarks: Unmatched environment for girls who thrive on hard work and have an appetite for intellectual experiences. 'What is on offer is exceptional. They have so many wonderful opportunities.'

St Paul's Juniors

Linked with St Paul's School

245

S

Lonsdale Road, London SW13 9JT

Pupils: 450 • Ages: 7-13 • C of E

Fees: £18,771 pa

Tel: 020 8748 3461
Email: spjschoolsec@stpaulsschool.org.uk
Website: www.stpaulsschool.org.uk

Headmistress: Since September 2016, Maxine Shaw (40s), previously head of Hazelwood School in Surrey. Environmental Science degree from Queen Mary, PGCE from Bishop Grosseteste, PGDEdMan from Brunel. Deputy head at Wootton Lower School and head of Pilgrims School, both in Bedfordshire, before joining Hazelwood. She is an ISI inspector, on national education committees and has an interest in the creative curriculum and personalised learning. She has three teenage children.

Entrance: Has 36 places at 7+ and a further 36 at 8+, in classes of 18 boys each. In the January of the proposed entry year, applicants sit the school's bespoke entrance tests in maths, English (combined comprehension, reading and spelling), verbal and non-verbal reasoning. Always sought-after, competition for places increasing sharply, with applicants from 'literally hundreds of schools'.

If 7+ and 8+ are no pushover, entry at 11+, which guarantees a place at St Paul's, starts to resemble the Krypton Factor. Around 400 applicants try for just 20 places. Up to 10 of these are reserved for candidates from state primaries, who apply in year 5 for deferred entry in Y7 (or the Fourth, as it's known here). In this way, explains head, state-educated boys are given a level playing-field: instead of competing against heavily-prepped boys from the top independents, they're only up against boys from other state schools. If they don't succeed, they're free to try again in their year 6 for the remaining places, along with all the independent school applicants (who can only apply at this time).

Because of the very large number of boys applying, the first filter is the ISEB online pre-test, sat in December of candidates' Y5 (deferred entry) or Y6. This consists mainly of reasoning, English and maths questions, and the top 100 scorers are invited to take the entrance tests (English and maths). Finally, the 30 best of these are called for interview. All of those 30 boys will be very bright, so what's the school looking for at this stage? 'A boy who's going to enjoy himself here,' says head, 'Someone intellectually curious who wants to learn, and with good talents – he's likely to have something going for him outside school.' Insists that 'we're not looking for a particular character type.' NB There's no filter test at 7+ and 8+; all such applicants come to the school to sit the entrance papers.

Exit: Boys are expected to transfer to St Paul's senior's at the end of year 8 (Upper Third), and parents sign a form confirming that it'll be their first choice of senior school, 'but in reality we can't hold them to that,' says head. Indeed, changed its name from Colet Court to St Paul's Juniors in September 2016 to emphasise the link. Typically, out of 90-odd leavers, a maximum of half a dozen might go elsewhere, almost always to boarding schools such as Eton and Winchester. For boys who join at 11+ the place at St Paul's seniors is unconditionally theirs – 'If it's a mistake, it's our mistake.' For those who joined at 7+ or 8+, the places are conditional, and very rarely – 'in fewer than one case per year group' – there'll be one for whom St Paul's isn't right ('if they're struggling academically on more than one front'). School insists that in such cases the school always works with the child to bring him up to scratch, and all parents confirmed the tirelessness of the teachers in this regard. When asked if any 'weeding out' took place, previous head didn't initially understand the phrase, and then looked shocked when he did. 'Our aim is completely to get 100 per cent of our boys to St Paul's. And that's what usually happens.'

Remarks: A huge and splendid map of London hangs on one of the main walls, dotted with pins that mark where each individual pupil travels from in the mornings. We commented on what a very wide geographical area it was, and the head agreed, but added, 'You have to be a bit careful of the map, though, because the boys like to pick out the pins and put them back in Heathrow Airport.'

In many ways, this enjoyable little quirk sums up the St Paul's Juniors ethos: learned, rooted in tradition, intellectually elitist, yet still a very boysie boys' school where boys have a great deal of fun. The school has had its detractors down the years, who have blamed it for being uncaring and inflexible, but hand on heart, we found no evidence of such things when we visited. Quite the contrary.

'An enormous amount of looking after went on in the first two years,' commented a mother whose son had been four years here, starting aged 7. 'He couldn't have been more gently brought into the school. The staff were amazing.' Another, who has had multiple sons go through the school, confirmed, 'We have not had the sense that it's the pressure-cooker that it's reputed to be. The teachers are friendly, accessible and attentive, and the pastoral care is very good.' 'It's a kind place,' stated a third. One of the Y8 boys we spoke to said that he would miss his teachers when he went up to St Paul's seniors, because 'they get to know you very well, and they're like friends.'

The fees are not quite so friendly, and ensure that the school is more culturally than socially diverse. Only 5-10 per cent of boys are on any kind of bursary assistance (although for those few the subsidy can be up to 100 per cent), but there are sibling discounts of a kind: if you have three or more sons at the school, you get a whopping five per cent off the bill. Yay! However, bursary provision now increasing: a new scheme 'offers more generous support to families with household income up to £120,000'[!].

Founded in 1881 by Samuel Bewsher to secure numbers for St Paul's, our impression was that the Juniors still finds itself pushed off the sofa now and then by its big brother, which seems consistently to grab the biggest share of the financial pie and the nicest spaces on the site. St Paul's is having a multi-million pound makeover, but it was impossible to find out if any of it was coming the Juniors' way. 'We're pretty confident that there'll be something.' Meanwhile, the buildings remain drab and ugly – on the outside, at least – and it's hard to find anything positive to say about them, except that 'they're not about to fall down'. The entrance hall is underwhelming, there's a nasty little garden courtyard, and the reference section of the library was recently bagged by St Paul's seniors for its expanded boarding provision. (These older brothers, eh?) Nonetheless, life here is simply buzzing and the Juniors has plenty of reasons to be proud, not least because its pupils love it here. Every parent who contacted us – and there were many – confirmed that their son was having a whale of a time. And the boys – animated, enthusiastic, well-mannered and full of fun – were proof of it.

St Paul's Juniors is about excellence, and absolutely all parents and boys praised the teaching here. 'Exciting, challenging, and very intellectually stimulating,' was how one parent described the atmosphere, and others agreed. 'The teachers have inspired him to work hard'; 'The academic pressure and demands are very high, but the atmosphere is cheerful and there's a sense of community'; 'The teaching is superb'; 'The teaching is excellent, and always keeps the boys interested'; 'The teachers are fantastic, and really great at making things seem easy' were typical comments. Standards and expectations are extremely high, and the work we saw bore this out. Writing in particular was accurate, lively, witty, informed and a pleasure to read. Maths is exceptionally strong, with the best of the young mathematicians regularly winning national challenges, but all boys are encouraged to achieve; again, many parents told us of how supportive the teachers had been ('they all love their maths teachers'). The learning support room looked a little bare to us, but the very experienced SENCo got a huge vote of confidence from everyone, boys and parents alike. There are no current pupils with dyscalculia – which is unsurprising, given the demands of the entrance tests – but there are pupils with dyslexia, dyspraxia and 'shades of autism and Aspergers', and the school disputed our suggestion that only mild cases would flourish here. 'We have to assess every case that comes to us, but if we thought a boy was suitable for St Paul's Juniors, we'd put our backs out to accommodate him.' Several parents praised the languages here, although there are actually very few on offer: the only modern language studied is French, at which many pupils excel, with Latin and Greek also taught. The boys we spoke to said they would like to learn Spanish: school please note.

Is there too much homework? Some said yes, others said no. Some parents lamented that homework dominated evenings and weekends and could take their child hours to complete. But all agreed that the homeworks were enjoyable. 'We think a lot about homework and we're pretty sure that we don't overload: we did a survey recently with comparable schools and found we weren't setting the most. We do sometimes say to them that there's no need to do so much, but our boys are very competitive as well as bright and conscientious and they often go beyond the tasks set.' It was also hinted that parents were not wholly without the competitive gene themselves, which might account for some of the more spectacular assignments handed in. The Good Schools Guide, of course, is written by parents for parents, so we couldn't possibly comment; but we were impressed by how very articulate and assertive this parent body was, particularly the mother who told us that her son hadn't been offered a place first time around 'because of oversubscription'.

There is a vast amount to do here outside of lessons, ranging from a quiet little club for Four In A Row to a full-scale production of Guys and Dolls, one of no fewer than eight drama productions mounted every year. Music is outstanding – boys can learn anything, even the organ in the school hall – and the school fields any number of orchestras, ensembles and choirs. 'I cannot say enough positive things about the music department,' cried one parent. 'It manages to foster and encourage the talents of both beginners and accomplished players. The breadth of offerings is staggering. The boys are tremendously lucky to have such a committed music department at their disposal.' On the wish list is a bit more light in the art room, but the quality of the artwork on the walls is astounding, so something's clearly going right.

Perhaps the most popular and successful extracurricular activities here, however, are the sports, which feature very prominently in what the school offers. The facilities, many of which are shared with St Paul's seniors, are superb, and the boys can do rugby, football, cricket, tennis, volleyball, fencing, athletics, aikido – the list goes on. All the boys we spoke to adored this part of their life here; which is as well, because they're expected to be highly committed in their chosen sports, and weekends are often dominated by training and fixtures. 'Demanding, but worthwhile,' was one mother's verdict. Another's praise was more ambivalent, and seemed to refer to more than just the sport: 'You have to be willing to live with a certain amount of stress if your son goes here. The whole family has to make sacrifices.' The school agreed unapologetically with this last statement. 'Parents do have to get behind the school.'

Undeniably, life at St Paul's Juniors is not a walk in the park but an eagerly-contested run. The boys who get here – and the school does seem to know how to choose them – clearly find it exhilarating. As one engaging young man put it to us, 'I love it immensely here. I can't think of any faults.' Parents are pretty much convinced too. We heard disquiets about a lack of parent-school communication ('compared to my other children's schools, it's dreadful'); that parents were too often shut out of the picture ('they're not interested in the parents now that they have the raw materials needed to manufacture the next generation of Paulines'); that boys sometimes formed into cliques based on sporting ability, leaving others alienated. But for each of these concerns there was a parent who told us the opposite, and even the most critical added, 'my son loves the school and everything he does there, so all my criticisms are pretty much irrelevant.' Interestingly, a phrase that came up again and again amongst parents was 'This is the right school for him.' The school knows a St Paul's Juniors pupil when it sees one, it appears.

So don't worry if your extremely bright son isn't offered a place here. There are many ways in which to be brilliant, and this one won't suit every clever boy. But for those for whom this is the right place, St Paul's Juniors is very, very impressive, balancing superb academic provision with genuine kindness and care. Top of its class.

St Paul's School is currently under investigation following recent allegations of historic child abuse, said to have taken place between the 1960s and 1980s. In separate incidents, two St Paul's Juniors (formerly Colet Court) teachers resigned in 2013 after being arrested for alleged impropriety.

St Paul's School

Linked with St Paul's Juniors

246

Lonsdale Road, London SW13 9JT

Pupils: 945; up to 35 boarders • Ages: 13–18 • Sixth form: 400

Fees: Day £23,481; Boarding £35,169 pa

Tel: 020 8748 9162
Email: admissions@stpaulsschool.org.uk
Website: www.stpaulsschool.org.uk

High Master: Since 2011, Professor Mark Bailey (50s). Career has included both academia and education: former head of The Grammar School at Leeds, he has also been a fellow at Cambridge and at All Souls, and professor of late medieval history at the University of East Anglia, with whom he continues to be involved. Found time to be a rugby international (1984 to 1990) and is now president of the Cambridge University Rugby Club. A thoroughly engaging, astute, relaxed and kindly man, the complete reverse of what one might expect of the high master of such a venerable institution as St Paul's. We meet many head teachers who are fonder of their school than of the pupils in it. Professor Bailey, extremely clever himself, still cherishes the achievements of others. A people-person through and through, who likes 'reading, walking and the wines of the Rhone Valley'. Talks with a refreshing lack of jargon. Married to an HR consultant, and with a teenage son and daughter.

Self-imposed mandate on coming to St Paul's was 'Not to meddle with what this school does outstandingly well; leadership of exceptional institutions is as much about stewardship as change.' That said, he is skilfully overseeing a vast programme of refurbishment that is transforming the 1960s site into a school for the 21st century, and steering both school and students towards greater meritocracy and social responsibility.

Academic matters: The St Paul's recipe for academic stardom remains the same: cream off the very brightest, recruit the very best, light the blue touch paper and stand clear. The resulting sparks illuminate the sky. As one boy put it, 'The real pleasure about being here is going off-piste academically.' Another said, 'The quality of the teaching is beyond compare. It really pushes you further.' Parents agree. 'The teachers are brilliant at their subjects'; 'They're highly skilled at imparting their knowledge'; 'The teaching is simply superb'. A recent inspection report summed it up: 'The effectiveness of questioning in lessons, both from pupils and teachers, is outstanding.'

Broad and challenging curriculum includes ancient history, engineering and technology, and an excellent range of languages, Italian, Russian and Greek among them. Exam success is seen as a by-product of the boys' broader intellectual development, but it ain't a bad by-product: 96 per cent A*/A at GCSE in 2016 and 85 per cent A*/A at A level (98 per cent A*/B grades). Amazing science building offers 18 laboratories, but such is the subject's popularity that, according to staff, 'space is still tight'. Beautiful library, silent and inviting, and facilities everywhere are excellent, although we were amused to see far fewer interactive whiteboards in the classrooms than we'd seen in a state primary school the week before. Interactivity here is still verbal and cerebral perhaps, rather than fibre-optical. Huzza! But we applauded the really intelligent decision to install air-conditioning in all teaching rooms, ensuring that minds stay alert in the muggiest of weather. (How many times have we seen pupils wilting in the heat of south-facing temporary classrooms?) Specialist support is given to those few students identified as having special needs, but this isn't the place for anything more than mild cases.

There are no plans to introduce the IB, which the high master describes as 'enforced breadth'. Various subjects eg modern languages and philosophy and theology now Pre-U. A levels now nearly all linear; boys take three or four (five if they take two maths) and can add EPQ.

You can feel the thinking going on here. Academically, a very special place.

Games, options, the arts: Superb facilities include six rugby pitches, six football pitches, five cricket pitches, swimming pool, courts for rackets, squash and fives, and its own boathouse stuffed with sophisticated rowing craft. The students wax lyrical about the sport on offer here – 'Sport for me has been the highlight here'; 'There is so much!'; 'It's a big part of my life at St Paul's'; 'Most of my friends have been the ones I play sport with' – and we saw dozens of boys throwing themselves about the playing fields in organised and impromptu games of just about everything.

Music and drama are both extremely strong; concerts are held in the world-class Wathen Hall, and new Samuel Pepys Theatre was recently opened. Art is taught in a magnificent suite of rooms, and the engineering and technology room is surely every young boy's dream. Clubs cater for every taste, although oddly enough we didn't see any, despite having arrived at lunchtime; even the four lads we finally came across in the 3D art room turned out to be revising their French ('I don't know why they're doing it here,' mused the art teacher). But the student-produced magazines we read were testament to the vibrancy of this community of thinkers: page after page of exceptionally mature, sparkily written articles on cinema, sport, current events, modern architecture; a real treasure trove of ideas.

Boarding: St Paul's is a day school – one of only two to be included in the Clarendon Commission's 'nine great public schools of England' – but it does have a very small community of boarders as well, a quarter of them from overseas, who seem to exist to justify the superb round-the-clock catering which all the boys, day and boarding alike, can access if they need to. Boarding facilities have been recently upgraded, and the boarding provision was praised in a recent ISI report. Study bedrooms, common room and TV room, music practice rooms and computer suite. At least two hours' prep a night followed by supervised activities eg music or sport keep boys busy during the week. Many boarders go home at weekends, often after Saturday morning sports matches.

Background and atmosphere: Founded in 1509 by Dean John Colet, and moved four times before arriving in 1968 at its present riverside home in leafy (and very wealthy) suburbia. A £77 million redevelopment has transformed much of the site. Visitors now are presented with an exceptionally elegant, blond, modern school campus; an architectural version of the Paulines we met, really, and with the same air of informality and purpose.

Having survived the Great Plague, the Fire of London, the Civil War and the 20th century, St Paul's can afford to relax and enjoy its own success. 'Academic rigour and loose ties' was how one parent described St Paul's today, and this was echoed by the high master: 'It has the feel of an über-grammar school. It's more like a university than any other school I've known.'

It's cool to be clever here, and so, inevitably, there is peer pressure to do well. This is mostly positive, say boys and parents, and drives everyone on, although one parent added, 'If you were at the bottom of the class, SPS would be a horrible place.' But high master denies this emphatically: 'More time than ever has been put into teaching underachieving boys and providing better support.' And another parent observed, 'The bottom of this particular pile still represents an extremely high level of achievement.' We saw boys working with good humoured focus for an eccentric and witty geographer who was padding around in Muppet-motif socks, interspersing teaching points with cheerful insults which the boys lapped up and batted back, in time-honoured boys' school way. (But there was a detailed scheme of work on the board that accorded with modern practice, demonstrating that old and new styles of education can be blended successfully.)

Indeed, SPS remains an extremely masculine community, where the testosterone coming out of the circuit-gym knocks you over at 20 paces; and perhaps this shows most in the school's being unaware of just how masculine it is. The sur master insisted that there was much 'mutuality' between the Boys' School and the Girls' School, but this was flatly contradicted by the Paulines we spoke to, and by one mother who felt that the school could do much more in this regard. We were ourselves surprised to find a large-scale female nude looking breastily down on us as we ascended the art department stairs, and more surprised to find another one as we went down a different way. There were no male nudes on display, and we couldn't help wondering why, out of all the subject matter that might have been on show, the school had chosen these particular canvasses. There are 'no plans whatsoever to admit girls at any stage of the school; no parents, boys or staff have ever suggested it' (high master). Which, if they want to go all Rubens-y about the stairwells, may be a good thing. But the Paulines we met were very personable young men, and the same mother who wanted more contact with SPGS also affirmed, 'Paulines are lovely, decent boys, really articulate, fun, clever and very nice.'

Pastoral care, well-being and discipline: Vertical tutoring system, ie mixing the ages of form groups so that younger and older boys are together. The concept is simple: boys will listen to their peers sooner than their parents, so utilise the more experienced boys for pastoral care and to lead extracurricular activities. It's been in place for over 10 years, and is clearly popular. As one parent commented, 'From the moment they arrive, the 13 year olds meet boys in every other year and get a sense of what they might do.' Tutors stay with the boys throughout their time at the school, and, says school, often become family friends – the advisability of which the school may be reviewing, in the light of recent events (see below). The nature of this hand-picked community means that bad behaviour is rare: 'There's an intuitive understanding of where the boundaries are,' says high master. 'I've never seen any evidence of bullying here,' was a typical student comment, and sur master concurs: 'We have very, very few boys that would do what could be called bullying more than once, and if they do, we apply school sanctions quickly.'

The school, along with St Paul's Juniors, is currently under investigation following allegations of child abuse between the 1960s and 80s.

Pupils and parents: One of the most expensive day schools in the UK, and compared with similar institutions, financial support for poorer families is small – see Money matters. The result is a community which is highly diverse religiously and culturally, but not socially. Parents mostly ambitious and successful professionals with sons to match, hard-working and free-thinking. Old boys list reads like a Who's Who of Influential Britons: a sample includes John Milton, Samuel Pepys, Field Marshal Montgomery, Isaiah Berlin, Oliver Sacks, George Osborne, Rory Kinnear – and Nicholas Parsons.

Entrance: State-educated parents who are starry-eyed for their children but don't know the entrance procedure should start reading it now. SPS takes about 180 13-year-old boys each year, but it's impossible to go there directly from a state school. The 13+ candidates apply either from St Paul's Juniors, whose 80-90 boys nearly all go on to the senior school, or from any other prep school – usually those in the London area. St Paul's Juniors has its own admission procedures at 7+, 8+ and 11+; see our separate entry, and don't leave it any later than September of your child's year 6 (be grateful: it used to be year 5). Prospective Paulines sit an online common entrance pre-test at their prep school, on the strength of which about 350 are invited for interview. The school then makes conditional offers: boys have to get at least 70 per cent at common entrance. The school is looking for 'intellectual curiosity and embracing of novelty'. About 20 more boys also join in the sixth form, which at SPS is called the Eighth.

Exit: In 2016, 54 Oxbridge places (includes one pupil who turned down his Oxbridge place to go to a US university), the rest to Bristol, Durham, Imperial, Edinburgh, UCL and other top universities. An increasing number (34 in 2016) obtained places for USA universities such as Harvard, Yale and Princeton. Most popular courses: economics, engineering, geography and medicine.

Money matters: Only five per cent of students receive any form of means-tested bursary assistance (although for those few the assistance can be up to 100 per cent of the fees) and scholarships are honorifics only – £60 pa and a silver fish in memory of John Colet. However, a more generous bursary scheme now on offer with support for families with an income of up to £120k(!) Some remission for families who send three or more children to the school.

Remarks: For very bright, confident, motivated boys who like to think for themselves, St Paul's provides a truly unrivalled education. A unique start in life.

St Peter's Eaton Square CofE Primary School

S

Lower Belgrave Street, London SW1W 0NL

Pupils: 340 • Ages: 3–11 • C of E

Tel: 020 7641 4230
Email: office@stpeaton.org.uk
Website: www.stpeaton.org.uk

Head: Since September 2016, Miles Ridley, previously assistant head (inclusion).

Entrance: Ten part-time nursery places. No automatic transfer to reception – must re-apply and meet criteria. Nearly all of the nursery places go to baptised children whose families worship regularly at St Peter's Church Eaton Square; preference after that to siblings, then to baptised children who attend other churches without their own church school. Families come from a wide area and a huge range of backgrounds – 'duchesses to dustmen'. Apply through the local authority, with supplementary school form, during autumn term a year before entry. Takes 50 children into reception, again according to criteria.

Exit: Girls to Grey Coat Hospital, St Marylebone, Lady Margaret's; boys to London Nautical, Pimlico Academy etc. Over half to independent schools: Westminster Under School, JAGS, City of London, St Paul's, Godolphin & Latymer, Emanuel, Streatham & Clapham High etc. Children not encouraged to move on to independents at 7 or 8: 'We won't go out of our way to support it. It is disruptive, and our children do very well getting the places they want at 11.' A parent commented: 'Why would you want to move earlier when they all do so well here?'

Remarks: Very popular and over-subscribed central London primary school, tucked away in a side street just round the corner from Victoria Station. Consistently excellent, lively teaching, with each child's progress closely tracked. The majority of pupils reach level 5 in year 6: a huge achievement. Languages strong: Latin from year 3 upwards. Dedicated IT suite with 30 computers. Inclusion manager has responsibility for EAL and G&T as well as those with SEN. Teaching assistants deployed to support children as needed. Parents also pitch in as eg volunteer readers. Good at spotting problems with vulnerable children and liaising with outside agencies where necessary. 'We always cater for a wide range of needs.' Two reception classes of 25; higher up, the children in each of years 1/2, 3/4 and 4/5 are divided by age into three classes over two year groups.

'We are blessed that we have really fabulous music.' No orchestra, but peripatetic teachers for recorder, violin, drums, guitar, piano and brass, as well as class music lessons, trips to concerts at the Barbican etc, singing at the Royal Albert Hall and at Friday's Sung Eucharist service. Very little space for sport on site – the hall is used for gym and PE and the small, soft-surface playground has a climbing wall along one side. However, they swim at the Queen Mother Sports Centre (notable successes in galas), play sports in Battersea Park and Hyde Park (year 1 were off for a multi-skills session when we visited) and borrow Westminster School's Vincent Square sports site. Professional sports coaches run twice-weekly sessions, and football, cricket and tennis teams play in inter-school matches. 'It's such a cramped site that we try to get them out as much as possible.'

Enrichment is a buzz word here and there are plenty of outings – 'It's a fabulous situation: everything is on our doorstep' – to eg the V&A, National Gallery, London Zoo. Year 6 visits Sayers Croft field centre in Surrey. Girls from Grey Coat Hospital do work experience at St Peter's, and pupils visit Westminster City School for their science week. Strong tradition of raising funds for charity.

St Peter's was first mentioned in an 1860s survey as an infants' school in Ecclestone Square. Moved to its present site, donated by the Marquess of Westminster, in 1872; became an infant and junior school in 1949. Building and site compact, but even the basement nursery classrooms are light, bright and cheerful; youngest classes have their own indoor/outdoor partly-covered play area. The upper floor classrooms, carved from the top half of a hall, have beautiful large, round windows. Airy feel but very cramped for space: every nook and cranny has at least three different uses. A major building project in 2012 remodelled the school to create sufficient classrooms to introduce two forms incrementally into each year group.

School follows Anglo-Catholic tradition and there are services at school and in Westminster Abbey as well as in the strongly-linked namesake church: clergy pop in and out and are available for counselling. The church interior, redesigned after an anti-Catholic arson attack 20 years ago, is a beautiful, simple, open space which 'lends itself to our nativity plays' and is also the setting for year 6 productions, concerts and speech days as well as services.

A tightly-run ship: children are neat and tidy, with tucked-in shirts and tied-back hair. They are orderly in class and move quietly around the building. The atmosphere is welcoming, friendly and purposeful. Parents appreciate the combination of excellent behaviour, kind ethos and inspiring teaching. 'It is a warm and safe place,' said one.

Active PTA which organises social events such as Burns Night and helps with eg Easter Fair. This is not a local school – families come from a wide area – but there is a strong community of parents, many of whom also meet at church events, and including those who attended the school themselves. Children who have moved on to secondary school come back to do work experience and spread their news. 'We know they do well wherever they go.'

St Philip's School

248

6 Wetherby Place, London SW7 4NE

Pupils: 109 • Ages: 7–13 • RC

Fees: £14,700 pa

Tel: 020 7373 3944
Email: info@stphilipschool.co.uk
Website: www.stphilipschool.co.uk

Headmaster: Since January 2016, Alexander Wulffen Thomas (30s), who was previously deputy head at Westminster Cathedral Choir School. He was educated at Stonyhurst College and Durham University, where he read Russian. He worked for a specialist risk consultancy before joining WCCS in 2010.

Entrance: Boys come from local pre-prep and primary schools and most live within three miles of the school. Entry is into year 3 (10 boys) and year 4 (10 boys). School over-subscribed at both points but so far the temptation to select purely on the basis of ability has been resisted. Priority is given to brothers of current pupils and to Roman Catholics. After that, references from schools and observations made during an activity afternoon form the basis of any decision to offer a place. The school is well aware that for some parents St Philip's may represent a fall-back option; understandably it prefers to offer places to boys and parents for whom it is a firm favourite. It's hardly a gamble; there are plenty of parents who simply like what they see so the school does not need to change its modus operandi.

Exit: At 13+ roughly half to London day schools and half to boarding schools, including St Paul's, Westminster, Dulwich, The London Oratory, St Benedict's, Harrow, Winchester, Ampleforth, The Oratory (Reading), Eton, Worth.

Remarks: A school with few pretensions and a big heart, St Philip's feels like a large, slightly unconventional family. It reflects the best of Roman Catholicism; the religious ethos that underpins the day-to-day life of the school produces genuine humanity and flexibility in the education of the young boys for whom it caters. The boys themselves are confident, polite and enthusiastic and willingly engage with any interested adult.

About 80 per cent of pupils have British passports but many have dual nationality, with numbers from Europe and South America. However, this does not mean that the pupil body is a transitory one and most stay from beginning to end.

School says that there is 'room for eccentrics here', and we saw evidence to support this, although 'quirky' might be a fairer description. Staff are a good mix – many are young, several have been there for years, even decades. Stable staffing has not led to stagnation; teaching we observed was dynamic, technology is used to good effect across the curriculum but without sacrificing the rigour of more traditional methods. The balance seems just about right. In a year 8 Latin lesson boys were highlighting words they had problems remembering, followed by a session based around a series of pictures to assist those who were visual learners. The image of a shouting clam (clamo – to call, shout) or a vampire sinking its teeth into its victim's jugular (neco – to kill, slay) certainly seemed to do the trick.

Music has a high profile; more than half learn at least one instrument. The young director of music is one of the country's top organists: he has played the organ for the Pope and is credited with the number of music scholarships and exhibitions won recently by St Philip's pupils to eg Ampleforth and Winchester.

Differentiation in the earlier years and streaming in year 8 enables effective teaching across the ability range and impressive results at 13. Learning support is offered both inside and outside the classroom for the relatively few boys with mild learning difficulties. School accepts that life is not always easy for some children, often through no fault of their own, and sensitive, expert counselling is also available for those perceived to be in need. Parental expectations are managed through trust and 'not being too dogmatic'. They are 'having to raise the bar', but some parents we spoke to expressed concern that the academic push does not come early enough for the pre-tests and opportunities are missed.

School housed in a red-brick Victorian building cleverly arranged to best accommodate pupils (and staff). Science and ICT are situated on the top floor, 'the only purpose-built part of the school'. Sport takes place off site at Barn Elms playing fields (which are currently being redeveloped in 'an exciting fashion') and at Fulham Pools. The parents' association is very active and, allegedly, organises 'the best match teas in London'.

The outdoor space into which boys spill enthusiastically at break and lunchtime is something of a gem: a garden rather than a playground. It is an oasis of green with fruit trees, climbing roses, shrubs, flowers, vegetables and herbs. The boys play games around and within the vegetation as well as in the slightly more open areas where table tennis tables and badminton nets are erected. There are quiet corners for the quieter boys and plenty of staff on duty or simply outside because it's a great place to be. School admits that 'by year 8 the boys are outgrowing the space', but, of course, that is exactly as it should be.

St Saviour's CofE Primary School

Shirland Road, Maida Vale, London W9 2JD

Pupils: 240 • Ages: 3–11 • C of E

Tel: 020 7641 6414
Email: office@stsavioursprimary.co.uk
Website: www.stsavioursprimary.co.uk/

Headteacher: Since 1994, Ms Lindsey Woodford, BA in education from London University. A warm, humorous, approachable woman with none of the lofty airs that waft around some heads. 'She's fun and she's ballsy, but she's strict. It's a winning combination.' Happy to muck in, she even joined a team of parents in a sponsored swim to raise £12k to Astroturf the playground. 'I don't know many other headteachers who'd don a wetsuit and swim 3.5km in the Thames. She's pretty game.' Her office, far from being a scary place, is crammed with 100-200 soft toys which have colonised every available surface. She is ably assisted by Ripley, her border terrier, who is adored by the children. Pupils who have done well (or are perhaps just feeling a bit glum) are occasionally awarded 'Ripley Time', which means being allowed to sit in her office for a supervised stroking session.

In her spare time Ms Woodford enjoys embroidery, crime novels, antiques and baking. We can vouch for her excellent homemade biscuits (gooey peanut butter flavour the day we visited). Very much hands on – small children approach her for a hug as we walk through the playground (and you can't fake that). Previously deputy head at St Michael's in Highgate, following stints at schools in Bucks, Brent, Haringey and Ealing, so oodles of experience. A local girl, she was born at nearby St Mary's Hospital and attended Parliament Hill School in North London. She is married to the contractor who created the nursery in 2000. The ultimate accolade comes from a grateful mother. 'I'm proud of how my daughters have turned out and I feel they have been formed by Ms Woodford as much as they have by me. I owe her a lot.'

Entrance: Heavily over-subscribed one form entry school. Over 90 applicants for nursery and 140 for 30 reception places. Nursery is mornings only, though afternoons are available for a fee. No catchment area; pupils come from as far afield as Camden, Kentish Town, Kensal Rise and Harlesden. After the customary preference given to looked-after children, admission boils down to enthusiastic worship at one of two affiliated churches, St Saviour's and St Mary on Paddington Green. This means 'at least three Sundays every month for at least a year before application'. Prospective parents might want to reconsider that sneaky lie-in every fourth Sunday, as admission is uncompromisingly awarded to the 'most frequent worshippers'. And don't even think of slacking off once you've got your foot in the door as progress from nursery to reception depends on continued regular worship – a rule that is enforced. 'We hate to lose children but it does happen,' admits the head.

Admission for siblings languishes way down at no 8 on the list of criteria, though occasional places in later years are well worth applying for as later places are awarded 'on need'.

Exit: Pupils progress to a wide variety of schools. Favourite state schools include Greycoats, St Marylebone and Twyford High School, plus Paddington Academy, Holland Park and St George's. The head is also very open to the independent sector

('We love a good badge') with pupils winning places at Highgate, St Paul's Girls', Latymer Upper, City of London, UCS, Merchant Taylors', Channing plus boarding schools like Christ's Hospital and Wycombe Abbey. It's enough to turn an expensive prep school head green with envy.

'For the last two years we've got a child into Colet Court [now St Paul's Juniors] at 11 plus. We're very proud of that.'

Secondary transfer meeting in September where both state and independent school admissions are explained and various bursaries and scholarship options discussed. 'It's never too early to come and talk to me.' Parents who are considering the independent sector are given advice from year 2 onwards, plus suggestions for specific tutors. Ms Woodford is brutally honest about a child's chances of success. 'I don't mind where children go on to as long as it's the right school for that child'.

Remarks: Nestling in a quiet side street amongst the tall wedding cake mansions of Maida Vale, this Ofsted outstanding state primary has won more awards than you can shake a stick at. But, despite the wealthy area, this is no middle class ghetto school.

'It's truly comprehensive,' said one parent. 'You've got people who live in million pound houses and families who live in local authority housing by the canal. Everybody just gets on with it and befriends each other.'

Broad international mix with 35 languages spoken (the largest groups being white British, followed by Eritrean and other African). A tranche of bankers, diplomats and media types alongside a large number of low income families just above the free meals threshold. Twenty-four children on free school meals (approx 10 per cent) when we visited, though the number waxes and wanes. Winner of Mayor's Gold Club Award for succeeding against the odds in improving pupils' achievements. 'It doesn't matter to us that we get a badge for it, what matters is our free school meal pupils do at least as well, if not better, than other pupils. We buck the trend,' says the head.

The socially and culturally diverse mix makes the school's outstanding results all the more impressive. Over 60 per cent of pupils regularly achieve level 5 in Sats, and they are top of the Westminster league table for pupils achieving level 6 (expected level for 14 year olds). 'They really encourage each child to discover something they can excel in, whether it's art, English, maths or anything else,' said one happy parent. 'It's not just about sitting exams, it's about becoming a well rounded, caring, bright little person who wants to learn.'

Our immediate first impressions were that St Saviour's is an exceptionally smiley school. We got eye contact and a friendly grin from pupils and adults alike as we waited in reception, and the smiles kept on coming throughout our tour. In an age when so many children look down and mumble when addressed by an adult, the confidence of these pupils shines out. Clearly, the social graces are given the same importance at this state primary as they are in the private sector.

Bog-standard Victorian school building, but preferable to the cramped conditions so often seen in converted premises used by some London independents. Here the classrooms are large and light-drenched with walls of vast windows. Trad architecture could feel forbidding in dark stairwells, but they've done their best to create a bright, cosy and well cared-for learning space. Walls covered in excellent artwork. Comfortable sofas, toys and a multi-sensory room in the early years section. Pupil loos are clean and colourful (no smells) and only one wet tissue apologetically stuck to the ceiling.

Separate junior and senior playgrounds. Outside space is limited, typical of most inner city primaries, but they've made the most of what could have been a rather dank concrete area. Good range of outdoor toys including space hoppers, a climbing wall and some rather grand-looking trees in pots. Small side garden growing potatoes, rhubarb and herbs and we even spotted the head's mum who had popped in to tend the plants. Truly a family-oriented school.

Setting starts in reception, with four groups per class. Some groups might have just two pupils, while others are much larger, depending on the needs of each individual year group. Teaching assistants work with higher ability as well as lower ability pupils. 'We focus on what each child needs.' Weekly Spanish lessons from reception onwards with a linguist Star of the Week award.

Regular pupil progress meetings to identify and keep track of underperforming pupils. Each child on the SEN register has a target sheet so progress can be tracked in lessons and support groups, and to ensure no child slips through the net. A qualified SEN specialist working part time is ably supported by battalions of TAs trained in many different types of strategies and interventions. Success of the school's support safety net self-evident in outstanding results for all pupils, regardless of background. 'I have a dyslexic daughter and they are very clever with their thinking,' said one mother. 'If you can't learn your times tables they'll come up with another way to teach them to you. They teach each individual child, rather than sticking to a formula.'

Provision in sports and the arts is a huge strength at St Saviour's. Thriving PTA holds monthly fundraisers to generate over £65k a year, most of which is used to fund three specialist teachers for art, music and sport. This means, in addition to the standard PE hour with class teachers, all pupils have a weekly session with a professional sports coach. There are also dance lessons with a West End choreographer, covering fun stuff like Bollywood, musicals and Strictly Come Dancing. Then there's swimming in year 4, cycle training in year 5 and the year 6 pupils do a course of horse riding lessons in Hyde Park. Opportunities to try tennis, golf, cricket and tag-rugby and to compete in teams against other schools.

Art is taken seriously here and is of a high standard. The PTA-funded artist in residence works with each year group on a project relating to subjects they are studying in class, for example year 3 pupils made a giant sarcophagus when they were studying the Egyptians. We saw excellent William Morris designs done by year 5 while studying the Victorians, screen prints of the Tudors by year 4, and some awesome studies of real fish done by gifted and talented pupils. Pupils identified as G&T in art are given additional opportunities to work on projects with visiting artists (such as designing the 3D climbing wall), plus there are regular drama and music workshops run by outside experts.

For working parents there's an (oversubscribed) wrap-around care scheme running up to 6pm and a two week summer holiday camp. All staff members (including the headteacher) are responsible for an extracurricular club running from 3.30-4.30pm. Pupils can choose from horticulture, ICT, arts and crafts, media, football, website, cooking, construction, choir and many other options. More innovatively, there's a coding club, and coding is also taught as part of the curriculum in years 3 and 4. 'Coding is a big buzz in education at the moment and we're right at the forefront of that,' says Ms Woodford.

What sets St Saviour's apart is the head's boundless enthusiasm and creativity. 'What we do here is we don't say no. We consider all ideas and are willing to try new things'. STEAMco was a concept some parents had seen at a festival. It's now an annual day when lessons are suspended and every corner of the school is given over to different creative activities such 3D printing, learning the ukulele, an apothecary's garden, dance, sculpture, making furniture out of newspaper, launching home-made rockets, cooking and much more. Pupils are free to browse at will – some try everything, others stick with one experience all day. Year 6 pupils built an electric goblin eco-car designed to spark an interest in engineering, which they subsequently raced at Goodwood. Then there's Maths Week. Every class pitches a business idea to Ms Woodford and she decides whether to 'lend' them £20. The class must turn a profit and pay her back, plus one per cent interest, by the end of the week. Business pitches mostly involve making and selling various sweets and cakes but pupils have fun and grasp the idea of profit, loss and interest.

Pastoral provision is outstanding. Each child selects two staff 'listening partners' that they can talk to about any fears or worries. Some staff members are chosen by 20 children, others just a handful, but even the catering staff and site manager have their listenees. Then there is a Buddy System in which each year 6 pupil is paired up with a reception 'buddy'. The buddies read and play together, go on trips and can be invited to tea by the respective parents. There is a daytime 'sleepover' where pupils bring a pillow, toy and sleeping bag and lie in the art room reading stories to each other.

Few behavioural problems. A general policy of positive behavioural reinforcement, high expectations and aspiration seems to work well. Much ado is made of the Star of The Week system, with postcards sent home, a mention in the newsletter and announcements at school. Four houses (named after planets) and team points awarded for a variety of endeavours. 'The school is strict and that's what I love about it. They will not tolerate any bullying and they don't like cliques either. Pupils are encouraged to be friends with everyone, so nobody is left out,' said a satisfied parent.

St Vincent de Paul RC Primary School

250

Morpeth Terrace, London SW1P 1EP

Pupils: 250 • Ages: 3–11 • RC

Tel: 020 7641 5990
Email: office@svpschool.co.uk
Website: www.svpschool-primary.org.uk

Head: Since 2015, Mr Nathaniel Scott-Cree, previously deputy head at St Vincent's Primary School in Marylebone.

Entrance: Always oversubscribed. Nursery children are not guaranteed entry into the main school at 4+. Priority given to practising Roman Catholics, with distance from the school used as a tiebreaker. First priority goes to looked after Catholic children, then baptised, practising siblings, then baptised Catholics. A waiting list is kept for occasional places.

Exit: Most pupils get their first choice secondary school. Popular choices include Sacred Heart, London Oratory, Cardinal Vaughan and St Thomas More as well as independents including Westminster Cathedral Choir School.

Remarks: School was founded in 1859 by the Sisters of Charity of St Vincent de Paul to enable them to work with the poor of Westminster. Moved to current premises in the shadows of Westminster Cathedral, conveniently next door to St Paul's bookshop, in 1974.

Pupils come from a wide variety of backgrounds. Around three-quarters speak English as an additional language. Fairly compact site – outdoor space has been redeveloped to create three separate play areas for nursery children, infants and juniors. Cleverly designed, with lots of greenery and modern play equipment. Pupils also use the playgrounds and local sports facilities for team sports and have a dedicated sports coach for all PE lessons. Inside, school is light, modern and well designed. Peaceful chapel is very much at the heart of this friendly and well-disciplined school.

While this is a Catholic school, pupils are taught to understand other faiths and cultures. Good behaviour, thinking of others and cooperation goes without saying. Pupils are monitored regularly to assess their progress and there are plenty of parents' evenings, giving everyone the opportunity to discuss their children. Written reports at the end of each year.

Alongside the national curriculum, the arts and sports, pupils benefit from being taught Spanish from the age of 7. Latin is introduced in year 4. Academic results are exceptional. Staff have high expectations and have created a good learning ethos. The SENCo coordinates additional needs and runs a Units of Sound online literacy development programme for dyslexics. There is also a school counsellor.

Multi-coloured and multimedia displays of artwork adorn classrooms and corridors. Large, multi-purpose hall where children practise for termly concerts and plays and musical performances. School is part of the Westminster Cathedral Choir School outreach programme and the choir performs at Westminster Cathedral as well as singing regularly at family masses. Well-stocked music room with an impressive selection of instruments – from glockenspiels to bongo drums. All have singing and music lessons, provided by a dedicated music teacher. Pupils talk excitedly about how they are encouraged to create their own music. Small charge is made for individual lessons on a wide range of instruments.

Sixth formers from neighbouring Westminster School work as volunteers, acting as classroom assistants and helping to run school clubs. ICT room doubles up as a cinema for film club.

Not a place for those who wish to sit on their laurels. Energetic PTA meets regularly to discuss the organisation of numerous fundraising events for the school. Each family is asked to make a small annual contribution towards the maintenance and building fund – for the benefit of the present community and to ensure continuation for future generations. Pupils are active fundraisers and run regular charity events. The school also works with Mission Together, a charity that encourages children to care about mission through prayer, learning and fundraising.

A lively and impressive school that produces caring and thoughtful individuals. Recently downgraded by Ofsted to 'requires improvement', largely due to lack of challenge at KS1. However, parents praise it to the rafters and pupils say they look forward to going to school.

Sarum Hall School

15 Eton Avenue, London NW3 3EL

Pupils: 180 • Ages: 3–11 • C of E

Fees: £13,905 pa

Tel: 020 7794 2261
Email: admissions@sarumhallschool.co.uk
Website: www.sarumhallschool.co.uk

Headmistress: Since 2008, Mrs Christine Smith BA Cert Ed RSH (SpLD) (50s). Previously at Lochinver Prep in Potter's Bar, where she is now governor. Originally taught home economics and textiles at Edmonton County School, which she left to bring up her two daughters. Subsequently returned to teach deaf children, later becoming director of studies at Lochinver and setting up their learning support unit. When her children left home, she wanted a new challenge and 'fell in love' with Sarum Hall the moment she visited. Believes she's known for being kind, fair, calm, trustworthy, experienced and well connected in the educational world and, on the whole, parents agree, adding that she's 'lovely', 'nice,' 'always smiling' and a 'great listener.' 'Whether it's staff, food or sports day, if you have something to suggest, she'll seriously consider it,' said one parent. Mostly office bound, although she does greet the girls, teaches SRE, and dines with them, daily, along with all the usual lesson observations, assemblies etc. Not a captain that socialises with her crew, we feel, although the head points out that she has an open door policy and provides a long list of ways she supports her staff including organising end of term meals out. Married to an actuary, with interests including tai chi, cooking, theatre and martial arts (she spent time in Beijing learning about swords).

Entrance: Main intake in September after 3rd birthday. Parents are advised to register their child as soon after birth as possible (non-refundable fee of £100), visit the school on a working day two years before said child is due to start and then confirm their continued interest in writing. Non-selective, although priority given to siblings and children and grandchildren of former pupils (of whom there are many). The rest of the 23-24 nursery places are based on the head's decision. 'I meet with all parents and am looking for those who understand that the arts, and indeed play, are as important as academic learning for children's development,' she says, although presumably that's all of them, unless they failed to research the school before applying. It's all a bit vague for our liking; we feel that fitting in probably plays a vital part.

Exit: Almost all to their first choice of school at 11: Channing, City Girls, Francis Holland, Godolphin & Latymer, Highgate, Immanuel, North London Collegiate, South Hampstead, St Helen's and St Paul's. Unusually for a north London prep, a fair number go on to board too, at the likes of Cheltenham, Queenswood and Wycombe Abbey. Recommendations as to the next school very much the head's own, for which she uses her 'first-hand knowledge of the girls, together with the teachers' recommendations, results, tracking data, and my knowledge of the families, which the teachers are not always privy to.'

Remarks: Nestling among the opulent period homes of this leafy north London street is a contemporary, RIBA-lauded, purpose-built building, with no less than three secured doors to get inside the learning environment ('Safeguarding means a lot to our girls' parents,' explains the head). Inside the building, which was completed in 1995 (although the school itself dates back to 1928), the combination of high design standards, light oak floors, high ceilings, masses of natural light and (recently) air conditioning makes for a welcoming, airy space in which to work, move about and play. White walls are tastefully decorated with displays of the girls' work from across the curriculum and there's no shortage of colour, ranging from the odd single fuchsia wall here and there to groups of pastel colour chairs. If anything, there's over-use of pink, but this very much sets the mood of the school, which parents repeatedly refer to as turning out 'very well-mannered young ladies.' These are girls that will hold the door for you even if you're still half way down the hall and who, from year 2, leap to their feet when the head enters and chorus 'Good morning, Mrs Smith.'

Not that there's any compromise on academic learning. The head's unwavering vision of the school focuses on being both academic (with an expectation that girls go onto further education and huge praise from parents about girls being superbly prepared for 11+), as well as having a strong emphasis on the arts.

New national curriculum forms the cornerstone of learning, but without the dreaded Sats and with embellishment of other subjects, including French from reception, Mandarin in years 4 and 5 and Spanish for one term in year 6. Specialist subject teaching in music, IT and French from nursery, science from year 3, English, maths and humanities in years 5 and 6. Some setting in maths. Big emphasis on cross-curricular teaching, with girls preparing for a performance of Frozen when we visited, having made the characters (art), in preparation to perform the play (drama) in French (languages). Great attention to tailored learning, with plenty of classroom assistance and additional work, for instance, for those sitting boarding school entrance exams.

Music, art and drama all thriving. Music facilities include a spacious ground-floor room, with no shortage of instruments, while the rooftop extension provides three practice rooms and the so-called Rainbow room, which is used for rehearsals, workshops, fencing, the well-being programme (relaxation, yoga etc) and a resting place for girls in nursery after lunch. Majority of girls study one or more instruments after year 2, with plenty of opportunity to perform in assemblies, recital evenings and frequent concerts. Junior and senior choirs, open to everyone. 'My daughter does 8 music-related things a week including choir, music theory, music lessons and two instruments,' lauds one parent.

Drama taught in the Rainbow room, school hall and upstairs in the new playhouse, with performances generally including double year groups, and including recent examples of A Midsummer Night's Dream and Olivia the Musical. Also sit the English Speaking Board exams (and LAMDA if requested) to build up communication skills. Fabulous high-ceilinged studio art room, with girls studying sculpture, textiles, woodwork and more. Facilities include a printing press and kiln. Plenty of outings to exhibitions, including the Royal Academy, with which the school has close links.

IT suite has 16 computers organised on round tables, with half the class using it at any one time. Chrome books and iPads also used in the classroom, although not to any great extent. Well-equipped science lab, with a teacher having introduced sustainability in a big way to the school. Sunlit, well-stocked library, with soft beige carpet and big wooden table in the middle, with 12 colourful chairs and plenty of visits from authors, such as Helen Peters and James Mayhew.

Nursery and reception areas nurturing, with a good mix of tables and chairs and dedicated play areas, including an (again pink) indoor wigwam and freeflow outdoor space on the balcony, with two stylish 'SH' embossed canopies to keep the sun off young skin. Plenty of mingling with older girls, thanks to buddying and monitor opportunities, along with a shared play time once every half-term.

Outdoor space had been recently refurbished when we visited and although by no means vast, it's exceptionally well-planned and welcoming, with a new two-storey playhouse in the middle of the play area to provide more surface area of play (and welcome shade on hot days). Girls are free to use the lower level during breaks, whilst the upper level is used for drama, small group workshops and exhibitions. Girls particularly love the five colourful beach-huts. 'With the middle three, each of the houses chooses what goes in them,' explained one girl. 'Our one has sporty things, and the other two are for crafts or being creative.' Surrounding this and the adjacent sports court are wormeries, raised beds and an environmental pond, allowing children grow vegetables and herbs and do gardening club, all of which have helped the school achieve Green Flag status. 'In terms of being green, they've achieved a lot, even by Camden standards,' said one parent.

Daily sport (netball, hockey, rounders, soccer, cricket and tennis) takes place on the court or in the assembly hall, which doubles as a gym for both dance and gymnastics, and triples as a theatre. Swimming once more part of the curriculum, at nearby Swiss Cottage Baths one afternoon a week for one term for year 4. Cross-country at Primrose Hill. Annual sports day becoming more competitive and challenging, after parents complained it was too gentle.

Pupil voice much improved in recent years, with eco team and school council having made changes to snacks, lunch menus, uniforms and are regularly involved in décor decisions.

Breakfast club from 7.30am, and homework club until 4.30pm, included at no extra cost. Over 40 after-school clubs (photography, chess and draughts, yoga, board games among them), also included in the fees, unless outside staff need to be brought in. Plenty of outings, particularly to London museums and galleries. Residential trips to Norfolk for year 5 and a château in France for year 6. Homework introduced gently in year 2, rising to around an hour a night in year 6.

The girls themselves 'aren't the most savvy and streetwise,' as one parent put it. 'But all the parents I know like it that way,' she added. 'It can make the transition to senior school a bigger deal, but having nice, polite girls is a good trade-off,' said another. Behavioural problems minimal and nipped in the bud, with strict use of policies and procedures. 'Positive rewards for good behaviour and our constant emphasis on Golden Rules help,' adds the head. 'These are different to school rules because they're about how we should behave, rather than what we mustn't do. We are gentle, kind and helpful. We listen and are honest and work hard. We look after property. We don't hurt anybody's feelings' etc. If a girl doesn't work hard, or indeed underperforms for any other reason, her case gets taken to the weekly curriculum meeting and a plan put in place, with full parental involvement.

Great food (all clean plates when we visited and we cleared our own too) prepared daily on site, with vegetarian option and great excitement about puddings such as Arctic roll and sponge and custard. Served in dining room, with pastel spotty tablecloths to brighten up the four rows of long tables with benches, where staff eat with girls after grace has been said.

Christian background, but head quick to point out that they support other faiths. 'We say the Lord's Prayer daily, go to church three times a year and the vicar comes in for some assemblies. But I recently invited a rabbi too.' Big on charitable fundraising, with each house choosing a children's charity each term, then arranging activities to raise money for it.

Parents and pupils reasonably multicultural, but mainly affluent, white, middle-class. Plenty of bankers, lawyers and barristers. Many girls have brothers at The Hall and Arnold House (and head tries to coordinate term dates). Bursary fund, which is means-tested. One girl on it when we visited, with another about to join. Many of the governors have a connection to the school and have been there for many years, with (unusually) no set system of election or removal.

Learning support unit has one dedicated member of staff (trained to RSA level 7) who comes in four days a week. Copes with mild dyslexia, dyspraxia (five children in total when we visited) and the 'gifted and talented' at no extra cost. Support is mainly in the large dedicated room, but some classroom assistance too. Two deaf children when we visited ('The school has been incredible with meeting her additional needs and going the extra mile,' said the parent of one) and one child with a visual impairment had just been offered a place. But whilst school is well laid out for wheelchair access, no child who uses one has ever attended. Won't take children with serious behavioural difficulties, although never had to turn anyone away or asked a child to leave. Outside help brought in for speech and language when required. School nurse recently brought in, who doubles up as school counsellor. 'Both my kids were flagged as needing extra help,' said one parent. 'The school kept me informed, we had meetings and they made innovative suggestions, all of which has meant the children are now on the right path. I can't fault it.'

This is a small, intimate, highly structured and extremely traditional girls' prep in a stunning modern setting that gets children of a broad range of ability to reach their full potential, without too much pressure. 'I've got three girls at the school – one very academic, one shy and musical and the other in between, and they all shine,' said one parent. 'The school has a knack of fostering natural talent,' said another. Its emphasis on the arts and play, alongside academic learning, means it's not for the tiger parent and and its preciousness, emphasis on authority and very high expectations around manners means it's probably not for the non-conformist child either. 'But if you toe the line, this is a lovely, fun school that you see girls skipping into.'

Servite RC Primary School

252 Fulham Road, London SW10 9NA

Pupils: 244 • Ages: 3–11 • RC

Tel: 020 7352 2588
Email: info@servite.rbkc.sch.uk
Website: www.serviteprimaryschool.co.uk

Executive Head Teacher: Since 2002, Mrs Kathleen Williams BEd NPQH (40s). Has spent all her teaching career in borough of Kensington and Chelsea. Previously deputy head of St Mary's Primary, Ladbroke Grove. Married with a young child, who (she hopes) will soon be a pupil here. 'I couldn't think of my son going anywhere else. I want him to have the grounded education which Servite provides,' she says. Loves theatre, opera and all things musical. Friendly, capable and calm; an experienced pair of hands. Servite works in partnership with less serene local schools, in order to help raise standards and strengthen leadership. Head is ably supported by associate head teacher, Claude Gauci, who takes over the reins when she is out nurturing other schools. They make a robust team. Head admits that teaching is a demanding profession, but 'we're lucky. It's a privilege to be part of this happy school.'

Entrance: At 3 to nursery but a separate application is required for entry into reception. If they don't meet the strict criteria, then nursery children don't make it through to reception. Oversubscribed: approximately 60-80 apply for 30 places in nursery and 170-200 vie for 30 places in reception. Ever-decreasing catchment area (currently about half a mile). Pupils come predominantly from World's End estate and Earls Court. Priority given to baptised, practising Catholics who worship next door at Our Lady of Dolours. Occasional places further up school, though pretty rare due to low pupil mobility. V few non-Catholics. School currently at full capacity with 30 pupils per class.

Exit: Not a feeder for one particular school. Vast majority go to local Catholic state schools, including Cardinal Vaughan, Sacred Heart, St Thomas More and London Oratory, as well as a handful each year to Chelsea Academy. One or two go down the independent path, usually to Queen's Gate on bursaries. No special preparation given for 11+ and school seems to have escaped fanatical tutoring which goes on elsewhere in final years. A breath of fresh air.

Remarks: This successful school is tucked away behind an unprepossessing façade on the Fulham Road, opposite Chelsea and Westminster Hospital. Surprisingly spacious once inside with large, light classrooms and three playgrounds for different year groups (the one for the smallest children particularly colourful and welcoming). Impressively large hall which transforms into a dining room, gym and theatre and boasts sophisticated lighting and sound equipment.

Head believes Servite offers a broad education, which encourages self-confidence and independence. Children are well prepared for life at secondary school by the time they leave. 'Servite gave my daughter the firm foundations on which to build,' said one grateful parent. Parents value the close association with the church which backs onto the playground. Pupils visit on holy days and every week one class celebrates mass there. Only three school rules – follow instructions; use kind and helpful words; keep hands, feet and objects to yourself. Pupils seemed to be adhering to these when we visited, though last rule appeared hardest to uphold.

Significant proportion of male teachers now. Staff consists of dedicated long-servers whose average age is 40. Appear devoted to the school and appreciate its family feel. 'They go the extra mile,' says head, 'and attend events at weekends such as school family mass with parents. No matter where the teachers live, they come to these events and the parents really appreciate it.' New teachers aren't taken on if they won't make a strong commitment to the school, beyond the classroom basics. Palpably strong relationships between teachers, parents and pupils. 'We have an open door policy,' says head, 'but within a structure. Not mayhem! Boundaries are set in a respectful way and issues are dealt with quickly.' One parent said, 'The school is professional but understanding'. Problems tend not to fester for too long.

Academic standard has been raised and school now boasts impressive results. Able children are extended through creative writing groups and extra maths support. Some bright sparks achieve level 6 in maths. Links fostered with Imperial College and Royal Institution to extend knowledge and develop understanding of science. Spanish, music, dance and art taught by specialist teachers. Homework every night from the beginning. Project work given to older children to encourage effective time management and independent learning. School has pupils with a range of special needs, including autism, cerebral palsy and moderate specific learning difficulties. Behaviour support, learning support and pupil referral units offer considerable help to those in need. Currently five children with statements.

School reflects the international, mixed community in which it finds itself. Head comments that many pupils come from 'poor, working families, where parents are often in domestic service.' Many families struggling but tend not to be on benefits. One in five pupils is entitled to free school meals. Roughly 60 per cent has English as a second language. Many pupils hail from Philippines, South America, East Africa and Western Europe. Main languages spoken at home are Spanish and Tagalog. Extra language support catered for through small targeted group work and some one-to-one support on offer. Parents happy with speedy progress made by those with limited English on arrival. 'Now you wouldn't know which ones were behind with English when they started,' commented one.

Fantastic, flexible wrap-around care on offer but school admits it's hard to sustain at a competitive price. Includes breakfast at start of day as well as tea, activities and opportunities to do homework at the end of the day. Children can be looked after from 8am-6pm. Parents aware they are lucky and are the envy of other schools nearby which don't have extended care on-site.

Impressive range of sport on offer and given as taster sessions. Netball, football, athletics and swimming taught either on site, in Battersea Park or Chelsea baths. Dance and gym compulsory. A wide assortment of clubs including taekwondo, yoga, zumba and street dance. Football, drama and cooking currently very popular. Parents pay for these. Good use made of the local community and has strong links with neighbouring Chelsea Football Club. School participates in 'Educate through Sport' initiative and an English reading programme offered by the club. Paul Canoville, first black player for Chelsea, regularly visits the school as part of its programme to promote positive attitudes towards racial diversity.

Excellent use made of its central London location. 'You name it, we've been there!' says associate head. From designing apparatus for Cirque du Soleil acrobats to jump over in the Albert Hall to PGL visits to Weymouth, the pupils have fun here. Parents pay for school trips, but school helps those who are genuinely struggling to meet the cost. School payment plan in operation and parents encouraged to save for trips on a weekly basis.

Impressive art, drama and music. Annual art show to which parents are invited. Fantastic, carved Viking longboats on display and amusing portraits done by pupils of the staff line the stairs. Christmas nativity put on by youngest children and year 5 performs The Passion at Easter. Two nights in July are devoted to a musical production, generally led by year 6 leavers, and about which parents rave. Years 1-6 learn a class instrument, including ocarina, violin and ukulele. Currently 75 taking one-to-one lessons in piano, violin or guitar.

Effective communication between school and parents via weekly newsletter. Parent council is parent-led and discusses initiatives such as school meals and uniform. Money raised by PTA tends to be spent on travel expenses for school trips, restocking library and equipment for playground.

School lives by its motto: 'Learning to love and loving to learn.' Family feel to the place. Children skip in each morning and enjoy their time here. On the day we visited, ambulance sirens blared incessantly on the road outside while the children danced around merrily in the playground, totally oblivious to the noise and fumes that engulfed them.

Above all, a welcoming school. No wonder head won't be considering anywhere else for her son.

Seven Kings High School

Ley Street, Ilford, Essex IG2 7BT

Pupils: 1,583 • Ages: 4–18 • Sixth form: 483

Tel: 020 8554 8935
Email: contact@sevenkings.school
Website: www.sevenkings.school/

Executive Head Teacher: Since 2008, Ms Tracy Smith BA PGCE (50s). Educated at St Martin's School, Brentwood. Read history and sociology at Warwick, PGCE at Goldsmith's College, London, then taught at Barking Abbey School for seven years. Moved to Seven Kings as head of sixth form in 1995, then deputy to former head Sir Alan Steer, and a key player in the team which transformed this east London school into one of the country's most successful comprehensives. Prior to taking over the headship, she led a project on Assessment for Learning carried out by King's College, Cambridge and the Institute of Education and continues to sit on many influential committees, including the Regional RSC Headteacher Board. Dynamic and go-getting, yet grounded and level-headed, she seems to embody everything that is great about this school and is passionate about getting the best for the kids here, as well as being utterly determined that no child gets left behind.

Setting up the Seven Kings Primary School, whose new buildings opened in September 2015, has meant she's been in her office more than usual ('I can tell you more about mixed metals than you'd care to know,' she laughs) but for the most part, staff and pupils agree she's a visible part of everyday school life, often seen around the corridors and classrooms, as well as eating with the students in the dining room daily. Not overtly authoritarian in her manner, she is nevertheless clearly respected and admired by pupils, parents and staff. Married with grown-up children, she is a keen West Ham supporter and spends down time watching football, going to the theatre, hill walking and travelling.

Jane Waters is head of secondary and Kate Beaumont is head of primary.

Academic matters: If achieving top grades is your priority for your kids, then you have very little to fret about at Seven Kings. Despite its 'very average' intake, Seven Kings seems to sail effortlessly to the top of the league tables. Eighty-five per cent of GCSE candidates in 2016 achieved 5+ A*-C grades including English and maths; 35 per cent of grades were A*/A. The hugely oversubscribed sixth form produced respectable results – 61 per cent A*/B grades and 29 per cent A*/A.

This is a school that starts with outcomes required, then finds the best means to achieving them. 'This is no exam factory, but we do know the syllabus and the exam requirements, and we also know the kind of teaching that works,' explains the head. Pupils concur that the teaching is both vibrant and innovative, with faces in classrooms looking hungry to learn when we visited. 'Teachers here bring subjects alive,' one pupil told us. 'There's constant encouragement to probe the teachers because they want everyone to grasp the subject really well,' said another, who added that even if you email a teacher at 8pm, you often get a reply. High expectations for teachers, who are expected to enthuse children at every opportunity (they must engage with at least six students when on 20 minute break duty, for instance). 'Someone once said to me, "You just do what it says on the tin when it comes to teaching," and it's one of the best complements we've had,' says the head.

Monitoring, tracking and a 'can-do' culture also contribute to academic success. 'You won't find a pupil we haven't spoken to in the past three weeks about their learning,' says the head, who adds that every student receives two formal one-to-one interviews about their academic progress per year, in addition to many more informal ones. Pupils praise the marking system that means they've given comments, rather than grades. 'Understanding what you've done well and what you can do to improve is more helpful than just a mark,' explained one. Also popular is the 'passport' that all kids in KS3 get. 'The children get visas to add in for good work, eventually being made a "scholar",' explains the head, who adds that she encourages a strong triangular relationship between students, teachers and parents to ensure that everyone is on board with learning outcomes in a well-communicated way.

English, maths and science by far the strongest subjects, with learning for science very practical (one of the labs is university-level), meaning that bangs and smells are part of the fabric of school life, with around 50 experiments going on a day. 'Students rave about science here,' says the head, who points out that the school is a recognised centre of excellence in this subject, with some staff sitting on the boards of top science organisations.

Three languages on offer – French, Spanish and Mandarin – with well over two-thirds of the students studying at least one language at GCSE. Setting only in maths 'because all the evidence shows that setting doesn't work and puts a ceiling on young people's achievement,' says the head of secondary school. 'Research on boys in second sets, for example, shows that they are much more likely to move to the third set than the first set.' Plenty of academic after-school clubs, as well as after-hours opportunities providing support with homework and coursework. Plus other clubs for sport, arts, dance, radio, Amnesty International, Model UN, chess, model airplanes, astronomy, film and more.

Eighty per cent stay onto sixth form, where students get to choose from 22 A levels, of which science and maths are the most popular. One pupil, who moved from another school into the sixth form, told us, 'Teachers here give you a step-by-step guide to research, writing essays and getting through exams, whereas at my previous school, you're just expected to get on with it yourself.'

Seven Kings has a national reputation as a centre of excellence for disabled children. There is a specially adapted entrance and well-equipped medical centre, plus the classrooms are accessible by wheelchair. 'We are unbelievably inclusive, which brings such a richness to the school,' says the head. In addition, there's a well-staffed highly-skilled SEN department (23 per cent SEN when we visited, with 54 with statements/EHC plans), providing exemplary provision. 'If we can get it right with vulnerable children, we can get it right with all of them,' believes the head, who says they cater for the usual range of special educational need.

Games, options, the arts: Two hours a week of PE, with very few complaints from pupils. Football, cricket, netball, rugby, long-distance running and athletics all core to the curriculum, with notable successes in cricket, football and long-distance running. Judo and fencing recently added to the growing list of sports. Facilities include an Astroturf pitch, front field, sports hall and gym, along with table tennis tables dotted throughout the outside areas.

Music highly valued, with spacious and well-equipped practice areas. Years 7 and 8 are on a scheme whereby the whole class learns a particular instrument together, with past examples including recorder, clarinet and trumpet. There's a school orchestra, jazz band, ensembles (including strings), as well as student led bands. Staff are employed to teach guitar and drums, as well as 35 lessons a week with peripatetic music teachers.

Plenty on offer for aspiring performers, including an extra period for drama in year 7 and 8 and all students in year 8 expected to take part in story telling to parents. 'We think it's is a great way of developing confidence and oral skills,' explains head. KS4s put on an annual community play, focusing on issues relevant to them, with examples including the riots and refugees. Meanwhile KS3s perform monologues, as well as group productions. West End theatre groups regularly invited into school to do workshops, with students also being invited on trips to theatre performances, and there are whole school performances annually too.

School day trips to museums and galleries, as well as residentials to the likes of Berlin (history), Barcelona (art and culture), Vesuvius (geography) and Japan (science).

Background and atmosphere: The school started life as girls' grammar in the 1930s, and some remaining original features give a feel of the inter-war years, with an expansive spread of low rise brick buildings and a Betjemanesque assembly hall ideal for listening to the clock ticking away the exam minutes. Modern additions include the lecture theatre, glass entrance hall and shiny new science labs. Stand-out facilities include the spacious and well-used library; the DT facilities with impressive window displays of students' work; the well-resourced sixth form private study areas; and the sixth form common room, a great space with youthful wall art. Lots of colourful displays of students' work throughout the school, including huge canvases of artistic portraits. Inside the tall-windowed classrooms, the focus is on learning.

This is a place where the school motto is more than some inaccessible Latin phrase that nobody can pronounce. '"Friendship, excellence, opportunity" are what we're all about on every level,' says the head, with pupils and parents agreeing wholeheartedly. Mutual respect is also more than a hollow phrase, with students allowed in their classroom at all times, including break ('it's their school, so their classroom,' says the head) and students overwhelming report that they feel valued by teachers. 'The head thanked the parents for giving them such great students at a recent event – and that pretty much sums up the attitude towards the kids here,' one parent told us.

You'll find no shortage of leadership opportunities and student voice, with a vast array of headship roles for students, as well as plenty of pupil involvement in everything from designing the new primary school and its uniform to observing and feeding back on lessons and providing ideas to improve learning. You'll even find students on the school gate to monitor lateness 'because there's nothing like having to explain to your peers why you're not on time,' says the head of secondary. Peer mentoring also popular. We found the older students confident and articulate, although the head says a lot of work goes into achieving that. 'Many come in quite passive and quiet, but our mantra is that a quiet student isn't a good learner,' says the deputy head. Innovative courses and workshops help, including a day of circus skills in year 7 (which takes pupils out of their comfort zone and reminds them that if you put your mind to it, you can often do things you never thought you could) and a teambuilding day in year 12. Staff get similar treatment. 'For example, we got new staff to do The Big Paint, which reminds them about how it feels doing something new – like the kids have to every day – and helps develop empathy,' explains the head of secondary.

Pastoral care, well-being and discipline: Seven Kings serves a neighbourhood that has social problems and deprivation typical of many parts of urban London. But despite its relatively stark surrounding streets – and the fact that many students come from difficult backgrounds – the school itself is an oasis of purposeful calm. Discipline is assumed, corridors are quiet, classes orderly. That's not to say there's no bad behaviour. 'We have 1,500 hormonal kids,' says the head. 'Of course we have discipline problems.' Most are nipped in the bud, though, thanks to clear expectations and sanctions (mostly detentions), with exclusions kept to a minimum (two in total by the current head). 'What helps the most is that we can get it right with each child because we know them on an individual basis,' says the head of secondary school. 'For example, this week, a boy was misbehaving and when we looked into the cause, it turned out he didn't feel he was achieving success in class. Once we dealt with that, the problem stopped,' she says. The point is, she continues, that children often don't have the skills to navigate their way through what is a very complex world to grow up in 'and we never forget that when we're dealing with these young people.'

S

No wonder pastoral care and well-being are high on the agenda of every member of staff at this school, with particular attention from form tutors, year leaders, staff mentors and the full-time student counsellor. The school also buys in counselling support from outside agency Here and Now as and when required, as well as offering yoga and meditation sessions and occasional 'drop down days,' when the timetable is collapsed to focus on issues such as how to revise and stress management. 'In year 10, my daughter suffered from clinical depression. Her grades dropped and she didn't want to be in school. But the school pulled out all the stops to help her and she's now thriving at LSE,' one parent told us.

Bullying happens, but is rare. 'I experienced it in year 7,' one student told us, 'but the teachers took it really seriously and managed to stop it.' Pupils value diversity here – ethnically and in terms of disability, among other things – which students say helps in promoting a culture that values difference. No-one from years 7-11 let off-site at breaks or lunchtimes. Lots of talks around drugs, drinking and smoking, sex, eating disorders and cyberbullying.

Pupils and parents: This is a neighbourhood comprehensive, with students mainly living within a one-mile radius (some years, it's just half a mile) and coming from around 40 feeder schools (although most come from just four of these). More than three-quarters come from Indian, Pakistani or Bangladeshi backgrounds and 19 per cent are on free school meals. In the main, parents are very involved in their children's education – something that is very much encouraged by the head, who organises curriculum evenings, a 'test the temperature' evening (parents' evening early in the term), as well as breakfasts with the senior leadership team. Parents even get the opportunity to be taught a lesson to see how it feels, followed by help from staff in how best to support their child's learning ('for example, we encourage parents to say, "Tell me something about your day" rather than just "How was your day?" which is a closed question,' explains the head of secondary school). 'By the Christmas holidays in year 7, parents really know what we're all about,' says the head. Parents aren't, however, a cake-baking, raffle-holding crowd and, to the disappointment of some parents we spoke to, there is no PTA. The kids themselves work hard and, and on the whole, behave well. 'They are bright and ambitious and absolutely gorgeous,' says the head.

Entrance: Over 2,000 local candidates apply for the 180 year 7 places, with a waiting list well into the hundreds. As it's completely non-selective, children in the looked after system/ those with a statement/EHC plan are prioritised (following the admissions code), followed by siblings, after which it's down to distance. Around 80 per cent go through to the sixth form, with around 2,000 applying for the remaining 140 places. Successful applicants need six Cs or above at GCSE, with B in their chosen A level subjects (A for science and maths).

The Seven Kings Primary School opened in 2015 with 120 reception children. The impressive looking new-build forms part of the new all-through school which will grow by 120 places a year (588 reception applications in 2016).

Exit: Out of 180 students, some 70 per cent go on to sixth form. The rest leave after GCSEs, mostly to do vocational qualifications, other courses, apprenticeships or go straight into jobs. Of those who leave after sixth form, 95 per cent go to university – about half of those to Russell Group, including York, Birmingham, Leeds, Nottingham, Bristol, Bath, Cardiff. LSE, Imperial and Kings. Around half choose science degrees, with six medical students in 2016, plus four to Oxbridge. The rest go to other good universities ('Some choose not to go to a Russell Group,' says the head) or destinations such as internships in the City. The remaining five per cent who don't go to university either take a gap year or go into apprenticeships (one had just gone into Louis Vuitton when we visited), art college or straight into the jobs including in the City.

No shortage of help with UCAS applications, and careers advice is embedded into the curriculum from year 7, with lots of work experience and enrichment. 'Opportunities that look good on your CV or university application aren't just encouraged – they are really promoted,' said one student

Remarks: This is a school with high aspirations, and the academic rigour can be tough because of the pursuit of excellence. But the results prove it's achievable, with a wide range of strategies ensuring that every student is pushed to reach their full potential. But there's fun to be had here too, with students clearly enjoying school life. Particularly notable is how respected they feel by the teaching staff, which clearly contributes to the good behavioural record. Parents who send their offspring here can be confident they will reach or exceed expectations, as well as coming out well-rounded and ready for university and/or a decent career. We found the headteacher particularly inspirational.

Sheen Mount Primary School

254

West Temple Sheen, London SW14 7RT

Pupils: 533 • Ages: 4–11

Tel: 020 8876 8394
Email: info@sheenmount.richmond.sch.uk
Website: www.sheenmount.richmond.sch.uk

Headteacher: Since 2009, Mr Ian Hutchings BSc PGCE NPQH (30s). Previously deputy head here (since 2005) and before that at St John's Kingston and East Sheen Primary.

Having inherited an already successful and thriving school (he received huge backing from parents and staff to get the headship) the challenge has been to maintain and improve it. Parents seem happy with his progress, with one describing him as 'a top man' and another as 'on the ball'. He's younger than some of his pupils' parents, but evidently a strong enough character to deal with a rather full-on cohort of mothers and fathers, locally famed for their hands-on involvement with the school. Operates an open-door policy and also usually around in the playground before and after school. He's 'fair, approachable and responsive,' say parents and any lack of experience is more than compensated for by his fresh approach and openness to new ideas.

He has a calm and considered demeanour, which seems to permeate the school. Focused and a little corporate on occasion – talks about 'free flow access to outside space' and 'delivery of ICT'. But behind the jargon one senses a caring man, very pleased to have this job and bursting with enthusiasm and ideas for primary education. Genuinely enjoys the company of the children – takes some cover lessons – and they like and respect him in return, although his dry sense of humour sometimes goes over their heads.

Married with a young daughter. Enjoys skiing in the holidays.

Entrance: Ridiculously small catchment area; you'll need to live very close to get a place at this oversubscribed school. Cut-off distance is normally between 300 and 500m and families moving to the area ask estate agents if houses are 'Sheen Mountable?'

In common with many schools Sheen Mount has added an extra reception class. With 90 in the year group, will mean larger than usual numbers of siblings taking priority in the next few years, accommodated in new building. School will slowly increase in size to around 600 by 2020. and says it's worth asking about occasional places higher up the school – but reality is hardly anyone leaves this place if they can avoid it.

Exit: Some 60 per cent hotfoot it to the independent sector, having used this place as a state 'prep'. Some 20 different schools feature on Sheen Mount's list of secondary destinations – literally one here, one there, from St Paul's Juniors to Wimbledon High, but always a contingent to Hampton Boys, Surbiton High (girls) and Ibstock (mixed). The other 40 per cent search for a state school to match their charmed primary experience at Sheen Mount – parents openly yearn for a senior section to this school. Hardly any opt for the nearest secondary school option, Richmond Park Academy, although head commends its 'amazing resources' and says he tries to encourage the good state options available. Most popular local state choices are Grey Court and Christ's, with Waldegrave Girls an option for those living that side of the borough. A few (again just one or two) to the Kingston grammars. School is alive to the requirement for information about independent schools and invites their representatives to its various 'future schools' information evenings.

Remarks: A super school, locally lauded as the best in the area, tucked away behind the stylish residential streets of up-market East Sheen. 'It's like having a very local private school on our doorstep,' said one mother. 'We do recognise how privileged we are.'

Underwhelming at first glance, hidden from view next door to a pub (but a gastro-pub of course and owned by a TV chef), the scale and scope of the school doesn't hit you until you get inside. The site is much larger than it first appears with buildings recently refurbished and seamlessly extended (including new reception block) so that there are no obvious 'new' and 'old' parts to the school. Classrooms are big, bright and airy, first floor ones with a relaxing view of treetops. Playgrounds and playing fields have also been revamped so there is an outdoor classroom, a science garden, an allotment, lots of climbing equipment and overall a huge amount of greenery for an urban school.

But nice though it is to have everything ship shape, it would count for nothing were it not for the top-notch learning environment here. School's strong teaching team is quite young, pleasingly includes some male teachers, and has developed its own curriculum. 'We are not constrained by the national curriculum requirements, but rather pick and choose what adds value; it's a really creative, cross-curricular offering,' says head. Seems to pay off big time – Ofsted rates the school outstanding, Sats results are sparkling and its value added score is particularly impressive when you consider that the unremittingly middle class intake here means that Sheen Mount pupils are no slouches from the off.

There's a purposeful, industrious atmosphere in the classrooms. Children are really involved with the lessons and uber keen to share what they are doing – there was an audible groan from children not selected to answer a question or show some of their work. The vocabulary and empathy of even the youngest children as they answer questions about a piece of writing is startlingly impressive. Cursive handwriting similarly strong. The children do their work in a learning journal which moves with them through the school. This fits in with the cross-curricular approach to teaching and makes it easier to check progression; for example if a child's target is to improve use of punctuation, progress can be seen across all subject areas. The only subject not in the journal is maths, which is handled separately, but with equal focus. Mantra is 'excellence in all things' and to this end head has introduced more rigorous target setting and progress monitoring, all aimed at getting a better handle on each individual child. 'I believe that our high academic standards are almost a by-product of our efforts to make sure every child achieves their full potential, wherever that may lie,' he says. Special needs support is led by a full-time inclusion manager supported by a part-time teacher and a high proportion of teaching assistants throughout the school. Happy to take children with Down's and autism and most physical disabilities, as only one part of the building is not accessible by lift. School statistics show relatively high numbers of pupils with English as an additional language, but head says figures are misleading. Many children are automatically badged as EAL when in fact they may be newly arrived from Scandinavia with English a fluent second language and present no more of a teaching challenge than any native of East Sheen.

French is taught from year 1; recent year 6 trip to France. There are weekly music lessons from a specialist teacher and a great dedicated music space, well-resourced with instruments. Head likes his technology and as well as an ICT suite children have use of netbooks and WiFi in their classrooms. Parents describe recent art and drama showcases as 'outstanding'. 'The children perform with huge confidence, and whether it's a big show or a class assembly, they all speak so clearly and every one of them is involved,' said one. Loads of artwork on display around the school.

Quite a wide offering of sports for a state primary school with plenty of support from parents; for example, a qualified coach/mother runs the thriving netball club. A few moans about school's unwillingness to promote excellence and competition – 'those seem dirty words in a state school' said one parent. 'It's all about just taking part'. As well as its own grounds, including a smart open air, heated, swimming pool, the school uses nearby Richmond Park. School also takes full advantage of all the outreach opportunities offered by local clubs, such as Harlequins rugby coaching. Plenty of trips and lots of extracurricular, although one mother felt her daughter was offered more opportunities than her son, who was not enticed by yoga, street dance and cheerleading clubs. Breakfast and after-school club provides care from 7.30am until 6pm, run by outside company, Fit for Sport. With no commitment required, parents who suddenly find themselves in need of help can book via website as late as the night before.

School describes its approach to behaviour management as 'positive'. There are five golden rules which are rarely broken. Every child starts with week with 20 minutes of golden time and will lose two minutes for every transgression, as well as a visit to head so that they can 'explain themselves'. But these children are polite and well-behaved for the most part and rarely take the walk of shame to his office. Parents very happy with pastoral care, describing it as 'excellent' and say home/school communication is good. 'I think parents will always be hungry for as much information as possible, but I think Sheen Mount does well enough', said one. Simple example of good school/pupil communications is the school toilets – children were consulted about the new colour scheme (girls voted green and boys purple if you were wondering), theory being they are more likely to value the space, and keep nice, something they've been involved in choosing. There's also a 'bubble box' in classrooms where children can post any concerns, which will be picked up by their class teacher.

Slight criticism of school dinners in our last review obviously stung. Head at pains to show off rebuilt school kitchen where all the food is prepared from fresh; not so much as a sauce or a pizza base bought in. We watched children tucking into a proper roast dinner, served on china plates rather than dreadful institutionalised plastic trays. Not masses of choice (though there was salad and fresh fruit) but actually nice that everyone was eating the same, sitting around in small groups rather than long benches. Children can bring in their own packed lunches and some do – but they are not segregated and can sit with friends who are eating school dinners. All very civilised.

About the only negative in the last Ofsted report was pupil attendance. Nothing to do with truanting here, but apparently caused by parents taking their children out for term time holidays. Some of the families have links overseas, or older siblings at private schools with longer holidays. These affluent types consider that the school's disapproval and only available sanction, the £50 (national figure) penalty, is a price worth paying for their convenience.

However that's not to say that parents are generally disdainful of this place – they all recognise it is a gem and are happy to give generously of their time and money to ensure the place is superbly resourced and has great facilities. Their support is a real USP of the school and goes above and beyond the norm. 'We are absolutely on board, there's no them and us,' said one. 'It's a bit full on,' ventured another. 'Because we all live locally and walk to school we all get to know each other and it's hard not to get drawn in.' Parents who prefer to keep their distance, beware.

Big wow to the PTA, which gets involved with major building projects and raises seriously impressive sums – typically £40,000 a year, but on occasion they have raised that through one big event alone. 'We raise so much money it is almost embarrassing,' said one mother. 'But there are also some purely fun events and I'm glad we now support outside charities as well'.

Definitely a cut above the (above) average state primary. Turns out confident, articulate pupils, who have enjoyed a really positive educational experience. Great sense of community. Fail to get involved at your peril.

Shrewsbury House School

107 Ditton Road, Surbiton, Surrey KT6 6RL

Pupils: 320 • Ages: 7-13 • C of E

Fees: £17,385 pa

Tel: 020 8399 3066
Email: office@shspost.co.uk
Website: www.shrewsburyhouse.net

Headmaster: Since 2010, Mr Kevin Doble BA (law and political sciences) PGCE (40s). Educated at St John's College, Johannesburg and has a postgrad degree in management. Previously second master and acting head at Edge Grove prep and before that head of English at Newlands School and Vinehall prep. This is his first experience of a day school, although he likens it to 'a boarding school with no beds' because of the breadth of opportunities on offer to Shrewsbury House boys. 'I know that the move I made to Surrey was a crackingly good one,' he says.

Parents appreciate his softly softly approach. He's contained, but passionate about his work. Eloquent, focused and evidently relishes the vivacity of the school day. He's made a few changes (parents say largely logistic and for the better) and his staff appointments and promotions are popular. 'He's great,' said one parent.

Seemingly not enough hours in the day for the head – and the pupils he calls 'these little guys.' He cuts a rangy figure as he makes his presence felt around the place, at the gates morning and night and out on the touchline as often as possible. When he can be lured inside, he directs operations from his homely 'oval office' (named from its bay window looking out over the playground) and packed with books, art, sports memorabilia, and a big green leather sofa for his many visitors. Keen to keep up a continual dialogue with staff, parents, pupils and other heads, he's quickly gained a reputation as very approachable. Still fits in some teaching – takes each year 5 class for a lesson a week in English. 'My son is riveted by his lessons,' said one mother. 'He was telling ghost stories off the cuff the other day and evidently had them spellbound.'

Parents seem supportive and pupils evidently feel comfortable around him too. One mother told us that she overheard a boy asking why he had to have his hair cut short for school – 'and the head took him seriously and gave him a proper response, not just a "because we say so" answer.' Meanwhile another parent commented: 'It's rather a cliché, but he really does seem to combine youthful enthusiasm with respect for this school's reputation and heritage.'

He loves sport and has had great success managing the Saxon Tigers U15 and U17 squads for England hockey and in coaching cricket. Chairman of IAPS committee for sports. Lists his recreations as (more) sport, drama, children's literature, opera, painting and drawing. Keen traveller, enjoys going out for meals and generally 'recharging' during weekends and holidays.

Entrance: At 7, there are up to 50 places available, with around four applications for each one. Currently receiving requests to register children at birth. Most come from pre-preps, including its own Shrewsbury Lodge (off-site, formerly Milbourne Lodge junior school, merged with Shrewsbury House in 2010), Weston Green, Wimbledon Common Prep, The Rowans, Park Hill, Linley House, Lion House School, The Merlin and Athelstan House. Around 25 per cent come from the state system. While 20 years ago this was a very local school, now 50 per cent of pupils are bussed in from over five miles away.

The head believes that too often a school's admissions criteria will be overtly focused on one thing – 'usually a unilateral adhesion to academic demands' – and he personally eschews the notion of early assessment as 'ridiculous at that age.' But he acknowledges that the school has to ensure its boys are up to the above average requirements of coping with an intensive day. So Shrewsbury House does it slightly differently, with two types of entry – conditional (non-competitive, formerly called guaranteed) and competitive. But be warned, the 35 or so conditional places are snapped up sharpish and your son will still be gently assessed to ensure he'll be able to cope at the school. These tests are held in the autumn before anticipated entry and are for families for whom the school is first choice and are therefore happy to cough up half a term's fees as a deposit. Once these places are filled, then the remaining dozen or so competitive places are up for grabs by the boys who achieve the highest scores in non-verbal and verbal assessments. Some bursaries available.

This place is all about 13+ and there is no support or preparation for boys looking to move at 11+. Look elsewhere if you have your eye on other senior school destinations – it's not the path for you.

Exit: At 13, boys progress to an impressive range of some 15 senior schools, including King's College School (Wimbledon), Hampton School, St Paul's, St John's, Epsom College, Wellington, Charterhouse, Tonbridge and The Royal Grammar School (Guildford) – 11 scholarships in 2016, including to KCS and St Paul's. A few go to Eton and Harrow. Parents describe the head as 'very knowledgeable' when he discusses future schools for their sons, first of all in year 5, and he prides himself on his personal relationships with all the leading senior school heads. 'I know all these men and understand exactly how their schools are ticking on,' he says. Has launched a scheme to send Shrewsbury House heads of department out to senior schools to improve their grasp of what's expected. Also talks of plans to track boys after they leave. 'I like his idea of making Shrewsbury House accountable,' said one mother. 'It's not just about getting them through CE and not caring past that – he seems to want to make sure the boys are equipped to thrive beyond this school.' Head particularly pleased to have enticed Anthony Seldon as a governor – 'it's not his usual thing at all.'

Remarks: This is a first class prep, where academic rigour is balanced by an equally strong offering in arts and sport. Although your son will need to be above average academically to cope here, with that proviso, the school says it takes a range of abilities. But be warned. As one mother advised: 'It's not intensely academic, but I wouldn't recommend it for a boy who just scrapes the test. It's quite full on.' Others agree it is not for the faint-hearted. 'You have to be quite committed to come here,' said a parent, 'and that includes parents as well as boys.' 'They are run ragged,' said another. 'But they come home happy.' Add to the academic and extensive extracurricular offering a packed sporting programme, rehearsals, performances, charity initiatives, competitions and trips and you'll get the picture – these are busy boys.

Located on a quiet road in an up-market residential area of Surbiton, the school is one of the UK's oldest preps and celebrated its 150th anniversary in 2015. It is based around a Victorian house, but with additional purpose-built classrooms and impressive facilities, all on a six-acre site, including a playing field and a further seven acres at Almshouse Lane, which includes all-weather pitches and pavilions.

Broad-based, eclectic curriculum is delivered by a talented teaching team, much praised by parents. 'They are inspiring,' one mother told us. Every teacher is a qualified subject specialist and sports coaches have all been outstanding in their fields – the promise here is that whatever his ability, every boy will be taught and/or coached by someone with real expertise. 'I can't praise the teachers enough', said a parent. 'They seem to be here morning, noon and night, and weekends, and even holiday time clubs are starting now. They go beyond just teaching them. I walk away from parent evenings thinking "wow, I wish I'd had teachers like that".'

It's a longish and busy school day, but the boys seem to rise to the challenge, arriving by 8.15am and staying until at least 4pm, and very often 5.15 or 6.15pm when involved in extracurricular clubs or sports matches. All the extracurricular you can shake a stick at – from cookery (very popular) to rifle-shooting – or they can just stay and do their prep. Homework is 30 minutes to one hour plus per night, right from the beginning. Quite concentrated in term time, but now none in the holidays. 'Work is pretty relentless and they have high expectations of the boys', a mother told us. 'The motto is "aim high" and they do.'

Although the head believes there is generally too much testing, measuring and scoring in education these days, Shrewsbury House boys are set and streamed, comprehensively tracked and given plenty of exam practice. 'But I prefer to concentrate on performance, rather than results,' he says. 'If you get top performance, the results will come'.

Any special needs provision is given in the classroom setting, with staff supported by the special educational needs co-ordinator and a learning support teacher. Less than 10 per cent of boys have a learning difficulty or disability. All pupils have English as their first language or are fully bilingual.

Average class size is around 16 (fewer as boys move up the school and into sets), with an eight-to-one pupil-teacher ratio overall. We saw some lively lessons, but always in a focused way, with all the boys on task. A French lesson, taught by a native speaker, with boys vying for an opportunity to speak, was typical. Similarly, lots of fun and experiments in science. There's a particularly rich English timetable – year 8s were getting on swimmingly with The Rime of the Ancient Mariner, having just finished some Dickens. Asked if they found Dickens 'hard', as per recent media coverage, they replied, 'no, because we had just done Othello and it was much easier than that.' Most classrooms are equipped with computer-integrated desks and the few without have Netbooks instead. Some great subject-specific classrooms, including a lively and bright maths room (50 boys won gold in the National Mathematics Challenge recently) and one of the best history rooms we've ever seen –

a modern museum feel to the place with the teacher's own collection of helmets and weapons secured to the wall. Boys allowed to handle sometimes, which evidently helps bring the whole subject to life for them – a Shrewsbury House team has won the national Townsend Warner History Competition twice in the last few years. Even the Latin room, not traditionally a 'must-see' destination, was decorated with the teacher's own artefacts.

Music and sport are real strengths of this place. The school has an outstanding local reputation for sport, and several parents mention it as a deciding factor in their choice of Shrewsbury House. Major sports played are football, rugby and cricket, but, unsurprisingly with current head, hockey is now writ large on the radar and other activities including fives and basketball have been introduced. School gives equal weight to the 'very good' and the 'not quite there yet' theory that many will get there in the end – as long as they are given the chance and not fobbed off with some French assistant keeping the fourth XI busy. It's not unknown for boys to move from G team to A team during their time at the school. 'If you have a sporty son the school will embrace and develop that and take it to the max,' said one mother. 'But equally, my other son was not sporty at all, yet still received top-notch coaching and was proud to represent the G and H teams.' This expert coaching, coupled with the huge pride the boys have in representing their school, undoubtedly gives them the edge and makes them formidable opponents – they have a 70 per cent win rate across the board.

Despite this renown and head's own predilection for the sporting life, he seems almost irritated by the 'sporty place' label. 'We actually spend more time on music, but that's not as well known because sport is such an outward-facing part of the curriculum and tends to attract more attention,' he told us.

Music is the other stand-out subject here. Around 85 per cent of the boys take instrumental or singing lessons and they get plenty of chances to perform – there are 25 different musical groups and regular concerts, with jazz and brass band especially popular. 'The standard is incredible,' said one parent. The boys put on six plays a year and everyone is expected to get involved at some point, even if only as the back of a horse or with a single line – it's all about getting them out of their comfort zone sometimes. LAMDA examinations another recent innovation.

Lovely to see the splendid library heaving at break times. Total of 6,000 books, lots of magazines and good attendances for author visits (lately Josh Lacey, Robert Muchamore, Ali Sparkes and Charlie Higson). Reading club for lower years. Boys also sitting drawing, following how-to-draw guides or just copying pictures of tanks out of reference books – so they are evidently not all out on the sports field.

Boys we saw were well-behaved – in fact an extremely courteous and friendly bunch. They won't get away with slacking, slouching or scruffiness as high standards prevail throughout, but overall the atmosphere is positive and they get plenty of praise where it's due. Healthy competition for 'plus points' – like house points except individual boys can win personal prizes, usually books, as well as credit for their house. Minus marks for minor misdemeanours, such as running in corridors or forgetting a book. Overall parents find school discipline is straightforward and consistent.

Some disquiet over variable school/home communications systems in the past – school says it has addressed this now and parents agree headway has been made. One big improvement is the instigation of a parent consultation evening, where the boys come with their parents to discuss their progress with teaching staff. This replaces a not very enticing invitation for parents to come in to discuss 'problems and difficulties'. Parents are also invited to head's biannual 'state of the nation'-type briefings and to a programme of lectures on subjects like happiness, self-esteem and revision technique. 'In the past the school gave you the feeling that they intended to get on with the job all by themselves and didn't welcome our input,' said one parent. 'But now it feels like more of a partnership.' Thriving parents' association does its bit too – organises lots of social dos alongside more heavyweight initiatives including £40,000+ project to refurbish the school's Irving room in celebration of its 150th anniversary.

A high achieving, all-round school, wonderfully purposeful and more inclusive than a first glance might suggest. Head seems to have parents and pupils on side.

Sir John Cass's Foundation Primary School

St James's Passage, 27 Duke's Place, London EC3A 5DE

Pupils: 291 • Ages: 3m–11 • C of E

Tel: 020 7283 1147
Email: office@sirjohncassprimary.org
Website: www.sirjohncassprimary.org

Headteacher: Since 2014, Mr Tim Wilson BA MA (Cantab) (mid-30s). Grew up in rural Nottinghamshire, where he attended the local comprehensive, before proceeding to Cambridge, taking his first degree in education at Homerton College, followed by a masters in children's literature and phonics at Churchill College. Arrived at Sir John Cass after teaching in Cambridgeshire primaries and three years as deputy head of Princess Frederica C of E Primary School in Brent. Sir John Cass was already on sparkling form, and Mr Wilson has seen it as his mission 'to see what's good and polish it.' Has introduced specialist subject teaching in French and art and started the process of refurbishing the more 'tired' space. A sympathetic and thoughtful figure, his aim is to ensure the school 'excels in music, art, sport, maths and English – and goes the extra mile.' In his spare time, he enjoys making the most of London, with regular visits to theatres and galleries.

Entrance: The only state school in the Square Mile, Sir John Cass has until recently been restricted to one class per year, but, in 2016, accommodated the primary-school 'bulge', with a one-off additional reception class. Historically, about 100 apply for the 30 places on offer, with priority given to those who worship regularly at St Botolph's, Aldgate. Desk space decided thereafter by a mixture of church attendance and distance from the gates. The school also runs The Cass Child and Family Centre, an attached children's centre with full provision from 3 months.

Exit: To a wide range of secondary schools, north, south, east and west, notably to City of London's sponsored academies in Hackney (where City-dwellers gain some preference), selective state schools, and leading faith schools across London. One or two annually to the independent sector. (The head has recently started working with City of London School for Girls to help prepare pupils for 11-plus testing, and supports children to apply for scholarship and bursary entry at City and other fee-paying schools).

Remarks: Sir John Cass traces its roots back to the school established by the alderman of that name in the churchyard of St Botolph's by Aldgate in 1710. The current gracious grade

S

II* listed building – described by Pevsner as 'neo-Baroque-neo-Hampton Court' – dates from 1908. It formerly housed a secondary school, with all the benefits that implies, including broad corridors, large classrooms and a generous assembly hall. Its listing also relates to its 'boardroom', a glorious panelled reconstruction of a merchant's home dating from 1669, with a plaster ceiling and 17th century hand-painted panels, where lucky members of the student council enjoy regular meetings. 'It's quite a big building,' said a parent, 'but it still has a very intimate, personal quality. It really feels like a family, not corporate in any way.' As well as recent and on-going refurbishment, there are plans for a £5m extension and modernisation, and local building works will ultimately give the school access to a leafy square.

Academically, Sir John Cass has long been recognized as one of the country's best primary schools. Despite the fact that many of its pupils come in with well below average attainment, virtually every child here reaches the expected government benchmark and an exceptionally high proportion soar well beyond it. Success for all is guaranteed through excellent, experienced teaching, and, often too, by high levels of staffing, which enables children to be taught in small groups when small groups are most needed. (Two teachers, for example, work with reception and year 6.) 'The teachers are incredible,' said one parent. 'They give lots of extra support for whatever kids require.'

Huge emphasis is put on reading from the outset. ('I'm less about children catching up than getting it right from the start,' says the head.') Each classroom has a designated quiet space for private study, and pupils get plenty of extra support, both from City volunteers, who come in to hear children read, and parents, who are encouraged to make nightly reading as customary as tooth brushing. Good, well-stocked library, with full-time library coordinator, and year 6s are furnished with take-home Kindles to embed the literary habit. Regular – but not crippling – amounts of homework. Years 4,5 and 6 use laptops in class, but this is not a place which believes that technology is always the answer. 'Four year olds need to interact with each other and the natural environment,' says the head, who has removed whiteboards from the nursery classroom.

A firm believer in the broadest possible education, the head has introduced a fully qualified native speaker to teach French. (The class we visited seemed encouragingly well beyond bonjour and merci.) Art, too, now has a refurbished studio and expert teaching three days a week, with several nascent Picassos reaching the finals of a recent Diocese of London art competition.

Music a celebrated strength, with a long-established Strings Programme giving all children in years 4-6 a weekly music class and a smaller group session to concentrate on technique. Performance developed further at Christmas and summer concerts, and star performers (who often achieve grades 4/5) invited to study at specialist music colleges and play at the Guildhall. Outstanding choir, under legendary choirmaster, has also made plenty of public appearances, (including on the Queen's Christmas speech). African drumming and dancing recently introduced in year 2. Performing arts group meets twice weekly to study drumming, dance, drama and vocal techniques, all taught by specialists. 'Performance makes pupils more confident and articulate,' says the head.

Sport goes well beyond the statutory minimum, with a recently recruited sports coach developing skills in rugby, hockey and multi-sport in the expansive school gym as well as swimming at several local pools. Unsurprisingly, Sir John Cass generally represents the City of London in inter-borough competitions for tag rugby, cross-country and swimming.

A significant proportion of children here receive the pupil premium and/or come from families whose native language is not English, and additional needs are taken seriously. The attached nursery is very much seen as the foothills of primary, with children encouraged to get muddy and explore materials. Special needs is led by the deputy head, aided by number of teaching assistants specialising in English as an additional language. A Tavistock-trained councilor also attends weekly.

Lavish menu of trips, both in London (Buckingham Palace, Natural History Museum, Regent's Park) and beyond, which 'help pin down history and geography'. Out-of-London jaunts include a week-long stay at the beautiful Cass Centre in Hampshire's Brecon Beacons, and a country-town mouse exchange to Caunton Dean Hole in Nottinghamshire, where urbanites can get up close to cows, fresh air and pond dipping. Lunch-hour and after-school clubs include chess and Lego, football and art, as well as inexpensive breakfast and after-school care.

Behaviour throughout is exemplary, with classrooms quiet, orderly and attentive (misdemeanours generally confined to coats not hung up properly on pegs). 'All the children get along,' says the head. 'There are no dominant groups, no cliques.' All seem to get along with him as well. One tiny child came up and gave him a big hug, another waved to him as we entered the classroom.

As a voluntary aided Christian foundation, the school has a strong, traditional Christian focus, with a bible corner in each classroom, Christian assemblies and regular church attendance. Whatever their views, parents welcome the faith structure. 'My family are not religious, but I really value the fact that my kids learn about religion with children of all backgrounds,' said one mother.

School lunch eaten by virtually all with appetising food cooked daily on site and crudités laid out (and consumed) on all tables. City Gardeners work with pupils on a well-tended roof garden, so children can eat what they grown, and a project with Leith's cookery school ensures everyone leaves with a repertoire of 12 dishes in their personal recipe book.

About 30 per cent of families are City residents, the rest are from adjoining boroughs. Though number on free school meals has diminished as more professional families move into the City, the school remains unusually diverse. The head has worked hard on developing the PTA, bringing everyone together. 'The school really represents London,' said one mother. 'It's very open-minded, very inclusive. For me, it's like a dream.'

Sir John Cass Redcoat School

Stepney Way, London E1 0RH

Pupils: 1,489 • Ages: 11–19 • Sixth form: 498 • C of E

Tel: 020 7790 6712
Email: info@sjcr.net
Website: www.sjcr.net

Headteacher: Since September 2016, Paul Woods, previously head of Bishop Stopford's C of E School in Enfield. He comes from Enniskillen in Northern Ireland and has over 20 years' experience working in London schools.

Academic matters: Consistently near the top of the value-added tables and has three times been ranked the most improved school in the country. Most pupils come in with lower than average achievement, but in 2016, 70 per cent got 5+ A*-C grades at GCSE including English and maths (23 per cent A*/A grades). They come from a huge range of primaries and many have

S

difficult home lives. 'Our first focus is on behaviour, on creating a climate for learning. Then we engage them with exciting teaching.'

Although downgraded by Ofsted to inadequate in 2014 (see Pastoral), the latest report, in November 2015, returned it to its former outstanding status, talking of 'high quality and energetic teaching'. New year 7s are tested and placed in sets for maths, English, science and RE. These are fluid and there's plenty of scope to move up as one's English improves or down should the maths start to prove tricky. There are vocational as well as academic courses at KS4, for example in science and IT. The school keeps a close eye on pupils' progress, targeting those who need extra help to ensure that everyone gets the grades they need to move on to the next stage. 'They have very high aspirations for my daughter,' said a parent. 'They push the children very hard to succeed.'

It is a specialist language college and everyone studies two languages for the first three years, from a choice of French, Spanish and Bengali, continuing at least one to GCSE. There is also a choice of 11 languages in twilight classes (for parents as well as pupils), and many pupils take a GCSE in their own native language before year 11. Many go on French or Spanish exchanges. The school has links with an instituto in rural Spain, and children who have rarely left the East End of London have found themselves travelling to school by horse and cart.

It also has a business and enterprise specialism and good links with Canary Wharf and City firms, with some offering work placements, scholarships to cover university fees and jobs after graduation to talented students. Sixth form business studies students can have mentoring from business partners, visits and seminars, lectures and summer internships. One pupil recently spent the summer in America, having won a coveted place on a student leadership programme.

The large sixth form, with some 600 pupils, has its own new centre, including a library, IT suite, common rooms and a popular café. It offers a variety of vocational courses alongside A levels and GCSE retakes. Many students come in from elsewhere to join those moving up, and quite a few have relatively low qualifications. Some start with intermediate level courses then move up to higher levels en route to university. Science and maths A levels are particularly popular and successful, alongside psychology, RE and sociology. In 2016, 46 per cent A*-B, 15 per cent A*/A.

About 10 per cent of pupils have some kind of special need. 'We have an elaborate academic support team. The governors have decided to invest heavily in this and it is a very worthwhile investment.' Gifted and talented pupils are also identified for extra support. Learning mentors and assistants work through teachers and directly with pupils, helping to track their progress and ensure they know what they need to do to improve. There are regular extension and catch-up classes. Staff recruitment is not a problem, with over 60 applicants for a recent RE vacancy. 'We have a high profile and we attract high quality applicants.'

Games, options, the arts: Sports facilities include a swimming pool (everyone learns to swim by the end of their first term) and a sports hall with space for basketball, badminton, football and cricket. Football and basketball teams play enthusiastic and successful matches against other schools. Table tennis, boxing and fencing are also on the agenda. A level sports science students coach younger pupils.

Actors perform at the Mile End Theatre and the steel band has played at the Albert Hall. Guitar club and a gospel choir, and many pupils have individual music lessons. Trips to operas and musicals. A school ski trip in the Easter holidays, D of E, ice skating, rock climbing and canoeing trips. Sixth formers organise societies, including Christian Union and Muslim Students' Society.

Background and atmosphere: Formed in 1964 by the governing body of Red Coat School (established in 1714 for boys born within Mile End Old Town) and the governors of the Sir John Cass Foundation (a charity set up in 1710 by Sir John Cass for poor children in the East End of London). The school is owned by the Foundation, one of London's oldest educational charities, and Founder's Day in St Botolph-without-Aldgate church is one of the highlights of the school year. Its present site, with its pleasant red-brick buildings, dates from 1965. It is right in the middle of the East End but in a deceptively rural-seeming setting with a city farm opposite, a park next door and the school church and its tranquil graveyard beyond.

The school has been refurbished to include up-to-date science labs and learning centres stocked with computers. These are open before and after school and on Saturday mornings, with learning mentors around to help. Many pupils have no computer at home, nor quiet space in which to do homework. The great hall with stage and balcony doubles as a lecture theatre and can accommodate the entire school for assemblies. 'These are important for setting the behaviour tone for the school.' Lower school pupils wear a traditional uniform including a blazer, which becomes more informal higher up the school. Honours boards line the reception area. Although this is a C of E school, the vast majority of pupils are Muslims and they have their own prayer room.

Pastoral care, well-being and discipline: An orderly atmosphere is central to the ethos of the school. 'Security and mutual respect are very high priority. First of all we make them feel secure and safe, then we start to cultivate respect for all. A feeder primary school may be less traditional than we are but we're confident that when they come here we'll get them into our ethos by the end of the first half term.' The atmosphere is indeed calm and orderly, with some exuberance in the corridors between lessons but quiet concentration in the classrooms. There are CCTV cameras throughout, which, say staff, discourage vandalism and add to students' sense of security. Staff check on the destinations of those wandering the corridors between lessons.

By all accounts very little racial tension and very few exclusions. 'We do very occasionally have some challenging behaviour but it does not threaten the learning environment. We try hard not to exclude if we can possibly avoid it.' Two qualified counsellors on the staff. 'It's a very happy school,' said a parent, 'but the kids are expected to knuckle down and achieve.'

The 2014 Ofsted visit resulted in a downgrade to inadequate, largely due the school's failure to monitor a sixth form Islamic society. In particular, it was criticised over a Facebook site set up by the society that contained links to hardline Islamist preachers – a move that could have made pupils vulnerable to radicalisation, it is claimed. The report also criticised separate entrances, playground and common rooms for boys and girls. Local educators accused Ofsted of over-reacting. In November 2015 Ofsted restored its outstanding status, commenting that the previous head had 'driven improvement relentlessly to bring about rapid change'.

Pupils and parents: About two-thirds of the pupils are Bangladeshi, the rest from a variety of ethnic minorities, including many Somali refugees. Parents mostly very supportive of the school and its high expectations for their children. They join in maths workshops and twilight language classes and become involved in the numerous community projects. Pupils form strong peer groups. 'There's a very strong ethos of care for one another,' said a parent.

Entrance: Some 1,200 applicants for 208 places. Everyone is placed in one of four ability bands, assessed by the standard Tower Hamlets primary school test, with equal numbers of places offered from each band. This is a C of E school, so it does allocate a minority of places to committed Christians. Thirty-six places go to worshippers in a recognised Christian church, with looked-after children, social and medical needs, living in one of the listed parishes and then siblings in order of priority. The other 144 places have a similar priority order, but 20 are offered to first-born children. Families in the area tend to be large and siblings would otherwise monopolise the intake. Distance from the school is the tie-break.

The sixth form is also highly over-subscribed, with over 1,000 applicants for 300 outside places. Most advanced level courses require five or more A*-C grades at GCSE including English and maths, with some higher stipulations eg an A in maths for maths or further maths A level. But those with lesser qualifications can take lower level courses, and the majority of pupils from year 11 go through to the sixth form.

Exit: Those who leave after GCSEs – about 10 per cent of year 11s – mostly go on to another sixth form or straight into a job. All year 13 leavers for the past three years – and some of these may have spent several years in the sixth form improving their qualifications – have gone straight to university. For social and cultural reasons, the vast majority choose London universities, but some venture further afield. Has had several successful Oxbridge candidates (none in 2016). 'I am confident that once they start coming back to tell our students about it we'll have more applicants.' Some students return to the school as teachers or learning mentors.

Remarks: A beacon of excellence in a deprived area of London, which takes in students with low levels of attainment and sends the majority off to university with commendable exam results. Committed staff insist on good behaviour, provide expert teaching and inspire high aspirations. 'It's gone from strength to strength,' said a parent. 'It's a great school.'

Sir William Burrough Primary School

Salmon Lane, London E14 7PQ

Pupils: 379 • Ages: 3–11

Tel: 020 7987 2147
Email: admin@sirwilliamburrough.towerhamlets.sch.uk
Website: www.sirwilliamburrough.net

Headteacher: Since 1995 Mrs Avril Newman (60s) BEd, first class honours from Goldmith's, who has spent her whole teaching career in Tower Hamlets. She is a national leader of education, a JP and has been honoured with a Freedom of the City award. A lover of theatre, books and travel, she is married with two grown-up children. Mrs Newman cited her greatest achievement as the integration of rigorous attention to academic standards with high emotional intelligence; qualities she noted 'don't always go together' but, in this case, are evidently modelled from the top. A warm, positive and articulate woman whose delicate stature belies a strong and dynamic force. She believes that every child should aspire to the highest possible standards in reading, writing and maths regardless of social or cultural background; the testimony of which lies in the reputation and success of the school and the low turnover of staff. One parent remarked: 'She is amazing, she really listens', and another described her as 'very accessible' and 'very good at dealing with a problem'.

She has an open door policy, literally (during our visit the lively community toddler group was in full swing just outside her office), and encourages parents to come in and talk face to face with her about any problem. Communication between the school and parents includes monthly 'Cup of Tea Mornings', described alternately by one parent as 'Avril meetings', providing a forum where parents make suggestions as to how things can be improved.

Back in 2011 Sir William Burrough was one of the first primaries to become a converter academy in Tower Hamlets which, at the time, was politically controversial. Now, she observes: 'We are waiting for the future to catch up with us.' Whilst there was mention, sensibly, of succession planning, Mrs Newman added that she has 'no plans to leave soon'. When the time does come for her to retire, she is confident that the strong deputy and leadership team will ensure there is a smooth transition and stability will be maintained.

Entrance: A highly over-subscribed school in a highly populated area means that the appetite for places is fierce: most recently 180 applications for the 45 places on offer in reception. Customary priority is given to looked-after children, siblings then proximity – and last year you needed to live very close indeed (within 260m). The recent changes to the welfare system have resulted in some local families moving away so places in the later years do crop up.

Exit: Mostly a spread of local secondary schools with the occasional child attending an out of borough independent or grammar.

Remarks: In a densely urban area with the entrance tucked up a dreary back street, there is something quite magical about stepping through the gate into the friendly and colourful atmosphere that immediately greets you. For a Victorian building spanning three floors, it is surprisingly light and airy with windows open and homely curtains billowing against a soft breeze. Children's artwork adorns all surfaces, proudly including some deft pencil drawings depicting, as one articulate boy observed, 'sociality in the city', as well as a net suspended from a classroom ceiling decorated with sumptuous rainforest paintings; a project complimented by a trip to Kew Gardens, one of many trips to take full advantage of the city's resources.

The classrooms are roomy and colourful, all with interactive whiteboards, and the library has a calm, attractive ambience. Unusually for a state primary, there is a dedicated and fully-equipped computer room backed up by widespread use of iPads. The recently refurbished reception classrooms are calm and comfortable with integrated toilets and a separate outdoor play space. The indoor gyms are a bit on the small side but there are two of them, and for physical activity they are more than made up for by the fine outdoor provision. A series of outdoor spaces surrounds the school building, including a dedicated 'dance space' where children can dance to music outdoors during lunchtime; two multi-sport pitches; a netted cricket area; and a vast array of play equipment including a trampoline. When we visited, during playtime all children were busy climbing, skipping, playing table football or foraging in the wooded area making 'camps'. An advantage of reigning for 20 years, Mrs Newman has overseen the planting and maturing of the lush trees that encircle the playground, adding an abundance of green to this urban oasis.

Sats-wise, over the last three years 95 per cent of pupils achieved level 4 or above in the three Rs, well above the national average, and most recently 29 per cent reached level 5 or above. A National Support School, SWB is amongst the 200 top performing primary schools and in the top eight per cent for the progress of all children, regardless of background, the hard data testimony to the school's academic approach. All children, apart from those with particular special needs, have learnt to read and write (in cursive!) by the end of reception, when they partake in a graduation ceremony complete with mortar boards and gowns. Once the basics are established, the Accelerated Reader and Accelerated Maths schemes kick in: online, personalised programmes which motivate through quizzes, prizes and international competitions. Families are able to win what amounts to a small library between them once they have read a million words: 'our way of ensuring children have books at home'. Other incentives include a maths Olympics, where children win rosettes for knowing their times tables, and a spelling bee.

All this takes place in the mornings, with the afternoons dedicated to the creative, experiential learning of the International Primary Curriculum (IPC). Sir William Burrough was one of the first primary schools in the country to introduce the IPC, which adopts a global perspective alongside a thematic, topic-based approach to learning. In a project on the Romans, children traced each other's bodies to create a life-size collage and went on to act out The Battle of Marathon. The children make their own movies and animations using iPads and, if the plot demands it, a green screen.

An energetic and effective use of partnerships brings in professional coaching in fencing, judo, rugby, hockey and handball alongside reading, number and chess partners from City firms. A newly established link with the Worshipful Company of Musicians complements the already lively musical culture in the school, including a 60-strong choir and a ukulele ensemble. They even have a choreographer-in-residence who ensures that every child in the school gets moving, appreciated particularly by one parent who felt that 'dance is fantastic' at the school. After-school clubs include film and animation, Spanish, sailing and debating. Years 3 to 5 build up their independence on residential trips offering challenge and outdoor adventure. Year 5s and 6s get to learn Latin. There is a breakfast club from 8.30am and a teatime club that runs until 4.30pm, facilities that were much appreciated by many of the working parents we met.

The school's 'You Can Do It' programme 'keeps levels of confidence and resilience high, and is deeply woven into relationships of respect, tolerance, kindness and courtesy'. We saw this in action as children held open doors, enquired about the welfare of others and remarked that 'we all comfort each other'. There is an emphasis on continual practice and one pupil commented that 'if you are unsure, there is always a teacher next to you'. A caring infrastructure is evident from the youngest to the oldest: there is a room dedicated to part-time and summer-born reception children and year 6s were helped to feel calm before their Sats through afternoon yoga sessions. There is also a system of peer support via year 6 school monitors, who look out for the younger children, and year 4s who help the reception classes learn to read.

S

All SEN support is offered in the classroom by teachers and TAs 'in the moment of learning' rather than in separate sessions or groups. This is a genuinely inclusive school with an expansive cultural mix. A small majority of pupils are from Bangladeshi heritage, others are of Somalian, Eastern European, Chinese and white British backgrounds. Some 75 per cent of pupils speak English as an additional language, though most are London-born and speak English when they arrive: the school's mastery of words proclaimed by repeatedly finishing as runners up in the English Speaking Union's Pan London Debating Tournament. Parents describe it as 'like a family', 'creative, friendly, inclusive' and one pupil commented 'they accept everybody who comes here'. When faced with the question of what the school might be able to do better, the pupils understandably struggled: 'I would change the sausages into hot dogs' and 'get a bigger trampoline' were about it.

Over her 20 years as headteacher, Avril Newman has been inspired by the words of John Tomsett: 'A truly great school grows like an oak tree over many years'. Under the talented and passionate guidance of its head, Sir William Burrough has matured well like the trees in the playground. A happy, inclusive and high-achieving urban primary.

Snaresbrook Preparatory School

75 Woodford Road, South Woodford, London E18 2EA

Pupils: 164 • Ages: 3–11

Fees: Day £8,202 – £10,968 pa

Tel: 020 8989 2394
Email: office@snaresbrookprep.org
Website: www.snaresbrookprep.org

Head: Since 2013, Mr Christopher Curl MA BEd TEFL, studied English and drama at Exeter. Taught in a mixture of prep and senior schools, including his own, King's Canterbury. Has been boarding housemaster, head of English and drama and in charge of co-curricular activities. Third headship – chose this school because of its size, family atmosphere and autonomy. Active and involved governors – including some of the original founding family – give him scope to shape the school. They also give lots of practical support, from HR to decorating. 'On some other boards you see some three times a year for large lunches and no one knows who they are,' says the head.

He aims to 'make learning more interesting' while 'trying not to fiddle with everything', especially since the school already has an outstanding report. Parents think he strikes a good balance, especially in the difficult role of following 'a much-loved, very long-standing incumbent'. One said, 'He is doing a great job of listening to parents and making positive changes.' Parents describe him as a 'very visible', 'open, approachable', and a 'supremely capable steward' who 'genuinely cares about the school'.

He is hands on, helping with drama and musical productions, at the gate before and after school, and teaching. Every Monday he starts with year 6 and works his way down to the nursery, teaching the older ones current affairs and conducting story time sessions with younger pupils. He likes to avoid being 'this remote head who sits in an office'.

Head also provides weekly lunch time cover for his secretary, so he 'gets to see the front of the organisation, what she is dealing with, what's happening, who comes in, what people are saying'. He thinks that 'if as a head you stop doing the kinds of things other members of staff are asked to do, you become out of touch'.

Entrance: Most come in at nursery and go though to year 6. There is a low-key family interview with the head; sibling priority. Places higher up subject to a family interview and in-class assessment. Pupils come from various nurseries in the local area, from Canary Wharf and Stratford out to Epping, Woodford Green, Romford and Loughton, and beyond.

Exit: Many go on, some with scholarships, to eg City of London, Forest, Chigwell, St Edmund's Ware and Bancroft's. Others go off to grammars such as Woodford County High and Ilford County High.

Remarks: Small size and family atmosphere mean pupils settle in quickly. 'You don't have to be scared to talk to a year 6 because everyone knows each other,' a pupil said. One parent said that during her son's first year at the school he has 'waved to and greeted any older pupil we met in the street. And the bigger kids have invariably waved back.'

The main school is set in a 1930s Victorian house and was managed by the same family for 50 years. Its small, quaint classrooms are close together and the corridors are dainty, but it is an intimate rather than cramped feel. The nursery and reception are housed in a separate, purpose-built building overlooking a small playground, with the hall and a multi-purpose library room on the other side of the playground. Beyond that is a covered sensory garden, designed and constructed by an architect governor. The children grow plants here, and experiment with different climates and seasons. There is a huge blackboard where they chalk to their heart's content and above it a huge, colourful mural painted by year 6s.

The governors, as mentioned, are very much involved in everyday school life, often to be seen popping in and out. They helped to extend the hall to create more storage space, they have helped decorate the staff room and to build the new canopied decking area outside the nursery so pupils can enjoy year round outdoor play free of leaves and rain. 'They are very sensitive to the needs of the staff and children,' said the head.

Single form entry, with class sizes of roughly 24 in the infants and 18 in the juniors, and plenty of classroom assistants. 'It is mixed ability here,' says the head. 'What is exciting is seeing children who didn't come in as high fliers leave having made massive progress.' Most extra support for those with learning difficulties is provided in class, with a part-time specialist available as required.

French from nursery, optional German and Spanish, year 6s learn Latin and also embark on self-directed projects. Lots of investment in IT. We saw year 5s listening to a live commentary on an Arsenal v Southampton match and learning how to extract key information from a database to write up their news reports.

The school adventure service challenge is 'like a mini Duke of Edinburgh... we do camping, rowing, bird watching, cooking and it's lots of fun,' say pupils. Years 4 and 5 were excited about the annual trip to France where they visit a chocolate factory in Boulogne (they like this better than the snail farm). Whilst in France they spend time with penfriends and complete a shopping task in French, although some confess they have found ways around this: 'Luckily the lady that was serving us knew English'. Year 5 has a history trip to York and year 6 an end of year trip to Shropshire.

Before and after-school clubs include the usual range of sports plus country and maypole dancing, scooter club, creative writing, art club and knitting. Popular sports are football and netball, and considering how small the school is, they do well: 'Once we played in a tournament and there were two Snaresbrook teams in the football play-off and they ended up playing each other,' a pupil said with pride. There are no fields here so pupils take a minibus to Redbridge Sports Centre and Ashton playing fields.

One parent commented: 'I feel the school works hard to optimise the use of space available.' At breaktimes a daily games timetable saves the tiny playground from being dominated by football (football still an option at lunchtime when playtimes are staggered) and the children can try out a different game each day. 'Our new games teacher came up with the idea,' said a pupil. It was inspired by Olympics sports such as handball, dodgeball and basketball. Most of the children take part and girls and boys play together. Other activities are on offer, too – they can read, do art, play table tennis. The head says: 'In my last school we had acres and acres of green grass and the children didn't use it as well. Here they are much more appreciative, and the lack of space can be an advantage rather than a disadvantage.'

When we visited, years 1 and 2 were in the hall preparing for a dress rehearsal of Rise and Shine. 'All have a part to play in the production,' said their teacher. The school tries to offer a taste of a wide range of drama and music, and each class gets a chance to perform. 'Lots of parents come to see the productions whether they have children in that year group or not.' Around 20 per cent of children learn to play the recorder, violin or flute.

House system gives everyone a chance to shine in different areas. 'Browns usually win on sports day, blues dominate swimming, yellows are good at choir singing and pancake races,' a pupil told us, 'so we each have our fair share of glory'. The many charitable and fundraising activities include readathons, movie nights to raise funds for Redbridge Night Shelter, sports events for the NSPCC and Great Ormond Street and harvest collections for the British Red Cross. Year 4 girls created a magazine, 'packed with quizzes, gossip and pictures. They made £61 by selling it to everyone'.

Pupils help inside school too. A year 6 pupil said of the nursery: 'We come in our free time and help the children and teachers with projects. It's also fun for us as this was our room when we were in the nursery.' It invokes a sense of service: 'This morning I was holding the door for a parent and I heard one of the year 4s say, "Dad, when I'm in year 6 I will be able to hold the door, I will say good morning to everyone".'

Support is good, say parents, with teachers always willing to discuss and address problems. Plenty of incentives and rewards for doing well, including Good Marks assemblies and commendation awards. The merit board includes an award to teachers for 'making a good start on the return after holidays'.

A new system of online live reports, with up-to-date comments from teachers that parents can access at any time, has replaced yearly written reports. The plan is to produce a detailed picture of how each child learns and how they are progressing.

Very active parents' association – '40 donations for the bake sale the other day', said a member – with an impressive participation rate considering that many, if not most, families have two working parents. Hotly-contested annual pancake race involves children, staff and parents. After examining video evidence following one race, the head sent out an urgent email saying parents had in fact lost and parents retorted: 'Mr Curl, wait till next year.'

South Hampstead High School

3 Maresfield Gardens, London NW3 5SS

Pupils: 913 • Ages: 4-18 • Sixth form: 164

Fees: £13,839 – £17,547 pa

Tel: 020 7435 2899
Email: admissions@shhs.gdst.net
Website: www.shhs.gdst.net

Headmistress: Since January 2017, Vicky Bingham, previously deputy head at Guildford High. Educated at the European School in Brussels; BA from Oxford in Latin and Greek literature, ancient and modern philosophy; PGCE in classics from

S

Cambridge. Started her career teaching classics at Guildford High; off to St Catherine's Bramley as head of classics, before returning to Guildford as deputy head in 2010. Signs are this place will carry on buzzing as before.

Head of junior school: Since 2013, Mrs Gabrielle Solti BA PGCE (40s), previously head of Notting Hill and Ealing Junior School for 10 years. A welcome home-coming – she commuted from Hampstead while working in Ealing and previously taught at Trevor-Roberts, after which she was deputy head of Primrose Hill Primary. A highly experienced and much-admired head whose tenure here began simultaneously with that of the prevous senior school head, Helen Pike (now heading Magdalen College School) – providing a significant injection of energy, inspiration and ability across both schools.

Mrs Solti is that ideal junior school head – highly professional but intensely and personally committed to her school, her charges and to educational values. She is articulate, voluble and manages to be warm and vehement all at once. Realistic about her 'market', in this most aspirational part of the capital, she says, 'We are competing against other very good schools. People in this part of town are prepared to drive their children to wherever they think is best.' Mrs Solti's pupils may be thought the best judge of where – and who – is best. 'She's not like normal teachers who may just say, "oh, get on with it",' one seasoned year 6 child explained. 'Mrs Solti has children herself so she knows what we're going through.' Whatever it is that they are going through, one would wish that all children had some of it.

Academic matters: Cross-curricular learning is embedded here in the junior school and our guides stared when we told them about the rigid subject boundaries we met elsewhere. 'Oh no, we used Excel, Word and Paint for our geography project research on families – there was a lot of maths, especially geometry, when we made graphs when we used the census data,' we learned. Unusually, the girls are very aware of the school's approach to learning: 'They try to get us to have an open mind,' one told us. 'So they set us homework like 'Black or White' or 'Seven' and we can explore it any way we like.' We loved the big display board on Animal Arguments, on which were posted many questions eg 'Do we underestimate animals?' and 'Should products be tested on animals?' and 'Is it right to breed different species in captivity?'

'Learnpads' and laptops are there for the borrowing. Very good library in each building. Lots of trips out of school to support subject learning eg the Kew Steam Museum and the Henry Moore Foundation, Vikings in York, French battlefields etc. No slacking but no-one seems to want to slack. 'We're pushed hard in reading,' one girl told us. 'The librarian tells us that we can read harder books so we try and we really like it!' Good identification of those with special needs – mostly the occasional dyslexic, dyspraxic or ASD child. 'We enable them to go on and have a very successful time here whenever possible,' says Mrs Solti.

S

Outstanding academics. And, with a few historic glitches, has been so since its venerable inception. Results at GCSE are hard to beat – 2016 GCSEs totalled 90 per cent at A*/A. A levels somewhat disappointing – 66 per cent A*/A in 2016 – though one feels that they will soar higher with greater stability. Tiny numbers get lower than a B in anything. Surprisingly few linguists – modern, especially. Overall, the results speak for themselves; school feels that 'people need to be absolutely confident about the results in all subjects'. But it is not a cramming operation. 'We can get the results and we can have fun doing it.' And there is vastly more on offer here than work. Bucketfuls of Science Olympiad and Maths Challenge medals at all levels. Masses of activities – intellectual, artistic, cultural – to stimulate the intellect, and all is characterised by a spirit of enquiry and exploration. Much is done to facilitate it by way of cross-curricular programmes, a constant questioning and a valuing of independent learning. A seriously hard-working school, but one which feels friendly, collaborative and focused.

EAL and SEN support given unstintingly where needed but the truth, of course, is that if your needs in these areas are more than minimal you are unlikely to be here in the first place. The new building is blissfully accessible. The new sports and multi-purpose games area also means that those with mobility difficulties no longer have to leave the building in order to exercise.

There is every reason to expect South Hampstead to regain its pre-eminence – academic and cultural – amongst the elite London girls' schools.

Games, options, the arts: Sports have never been South Hampstead's selling point but things are changing fast. Well-resourced sports facilities at the Cumberland site provide for more than 20 sports and the new sports hall is now revolutionising opportunities on site. More sports now on offer and more teams to join. Football, cricket and rugby on the timetable. Much individual success including several in national teams. Gym, dance, netball, hockey, tennis and athletics especially strong. Sensitivities of sixth form girls, so long and carefully catered for since the days of compulsory hockey in freezing mud, now, ironically, need attention again. We cackled when some told us, 'It's very nice that they put on all these things like zumba and yoga and rock climbing but actually what we really like is old-fashioned team games like netball!'

Art and DT block to the left of central atrium provides ample space for all kinds of artistic efforts including ceramics room and kiln. Art, drama and music – always strong here – now in golden age of creative energy – witness excellent displays of independent-minded work and fabulous musical performances. Year 9 pupil became GDST Musician of the Year recently. Writers' groups, experimental drama and exploring in every field of creative intellectual life. Girls pay tribute to the excellent extracurricular provision – especially the programme of outside speakers which would do credit to a university. Beautiful school publications, many worked on by girls, and one elegantly produced by Condé Nast. Over 50 clubs each week and lots of trips. Vast take up of the Duke of Edinburgh Scheme. It is hard to see how a day school manages to do so much.

Background and atmosphere: One of the most prestigious and venerable of the Girls' Day School Trust's schools. South Hampstead's senior school had been housed in a single imposing Victorian red-brick mansion for most of its 140-odd years. Various more modest buildings were added but all except the latest science block, the Waterlow building and the sumptuously decorative Oakwood were crushed beneath the bulldozers in 2013. And a magnificent phoenix rose steadily from the ashes over the following 18 months. The new build – opened in a gloriously celebratory evening in January 2015 by old girl Helena Bonham-Carter – is breathtaking, not least because of how much space has been found in what seemed a cramped site. From the immense sports hall deep in the core of the Hampstead hillock on which the whole stands to the sedum roof-garden overlooking much of north west London, all has been finished to a fine sustainability spec – Douglas fir louvres, solar shading, photovoltaic roof cells, energy efficient glazing and air cooling, motion-sensored lighting – not that any of this obtrudes when you wander the spacious teaching areas, wide corridors, subject rooms, library, recital room and studios to meet every modern scholastic need.

The older buildings are connected to the new one by bridge or corridor. All the new classrooms are good sizes, smaller ones for sixth form teaching. Plentiful loos on each floor.

And changing rooms have hairdryers! Plasma screens and whiteboards all over the place. Music and DT well-equipped. The building is perforce long and relatively narrow and some rooms, mostly the departmental offices, have no natural light or ventilation, but light and space prevail everywhere else. All is finished in subtle light blues and white. And devastated old girls seeking their physical alma mater might be consoled by knowing that bricks from the old building were cleaned and used where possible. A remarkable achievement.

Junior school sited in two handsome Victorian red-brick buildings surrounded by lots more of a similar kind in lovely, quiet, tree-lined, similar Hampstead streets. If your junior school has to be in London, what could be nicer? In number 12 you will find reception to year 4. Number 5 houses years 5 and 6. Outside, reception tots have a new safe surface with play equipment and, inside, we observed happily absorbed groups of children involved in all kinds of educational play. Year 4 were all researching 'rivers' in all manner of interesting and exploratory ways. Everywhere we met the quiet buzz of happy learning. Every face was thoughtful.

Pastoral care, well-being and discipline: Excellent relationships between girls and staff and girls and girls in the junior school. 'No-one is mean,' it was explained to us. 'We're all very independent but we do encourage each other.' Much praise from parents and girls for the new house system brought in by Mrs Solti. 'It has brought us all together,' we were, somewhat paradoxically, told. And other Solti innovations also appreciated. 'We are smarter and more sophisticated now,' a worldly-wise year 4 child confided and a year 6 friend concurred. 'The school felt a bit wobbly before but it feels more steady now.' Wobbliness certainly not felt by parent body – this school has been solid and stable for yonks. Much praise too for the school council and girls clearly feel their views are taken seriously. 'They got the new playground equipment because of what we said.' And girls acknowledge the fairness of the regime in other ways. 'The art displays change regularly and it's not always the best artists whose work goes up but people who try really hard.' Huge array of extracurricular opportunities – much goes on before and after the school day and is there for those who want it. PTA and parental involvement across the board. This junior school offers robust, stimulating and creative learning in a secure, warm and nurturing environment. It's ambitious without being pressurising, cosy without being lax. For your bright, energetic, creative daughter, a perfect start. We would wish them more space to be able offer this start in life to a lot more deserving girls.

'We have very few rules. Those we have are to keep you safe, secure and harmonious. If there are any others, we shouldn't have them.' Senior school acronym is TORCH: Toleration, Open-heartedness, Respect, Care and Helpfulness. 'We talk to them a lot about friendships. We are tough on bullying – especially cyber-bullying.' But incidents are few and all girls we spoke to – all ages – remarked on the friendliness and supportiveness of their peer groups. Much parental praise for the pastoral care: eg 'My daughter's form teacher was on the case even before I was'; 'The girls and staff are mutually friendly and respectful – there's no "them and us"'; 'The way the teachers know the girls is very impressive'; and 'My daughter's teachers are wonderful mentors'. Praise from the girls for school's approach to difficult matters. 'If there's a problem, they confront it, head on.' Some mild chafing over the emphasis on uniform and dress code and a sense that this is a 'tough' school ie one in which 'you learn social skills you wouldn't learn in a gentler environment – it doesn't have a small, cosy feel'. But a consensus that the girls here have fun and learn through fun. As one mother told us, 'The school has the idea that the girls have to be happy first'.

Pupils and parents: High proportion lives locally, even close enough to walk, though others live an hour or more away. From both state and independent sectors and from diverse backgrounds. Around 30 different home languages spoken. This is the premiere girls' school in leafy, classy, intellectual, arty and moneyed Hampstead with the clientele to suit. Parents have high expectations of the school and the school meets them with a high degree of pre- and post-school provision. Parents are heavily involved with the school at all levels and the head and staff need experience and confidence to work with such a demanding but rewarding clientele. Girls are committed, energetic, clever, articulate, creative, independent and delightful.

Entrance: Application forms available to download during a two week period in the September two years before entry into reception; school assesses all those who apply within this period. Some 250 apply for the 24 reception places (so, you have to see it as taking pot luck) and around 130 apply for 24 more places in year 3 (applications close in the November of the year before entry). Immense care is taken over the assessment at both stages and, clearly, the school would love to be able to take more of the able and sparky little girls who apply. Reception assessment is play-based. All are seen in the November prior to entry in age-based groups of 12-13 with four or five staff observing and interacting. Mrs Solti sees all applicants herself. A hundred of the 250 return in January when the school 'looks for a range of personality types' and aims at a balanced year group. No shying away from summer birthdays – 'we expect a little less of them' – which is good to know. Year 3 applicants tested in maths, English and non-verbal reasoning and interviewed. 'We take it seriously and take a lot of pride in it,' says Mrs Solti, while acknowledging that the process, of course, is a something of a lottery. She understands entirely the anguish and anxiety of parents. 'All we can do is be as understanding as we can.'

Fifty-five places at 11+ for which 450 apply via the North London Consortium. Two classes (about 40) come up from the junior school. A few in after GCSE if there are spaces in their subject classes. Entrance exam in two subjects plus general paper.

Exit: Virtually all juniors to the senior school. Some 15 per cent leave after GCSEs. A few to state sixth forms such as Camden School for Girls, and a few more to join their brothers at UCS up the road or to eg Westminster but, otherwise, about 85 per cent sensibly stay put. Sixth form leavers to everywhere good to do everything interesting. A good handful now to US universities and the rest to eg Oxbridge (nine in 2016) and other well-established universities/colleges. Impressive number of engineers and economists and several medics but a sad dearth of linguists, despite exemplary results. Notable old girls include Helena Bonham-Carter, Lynne Featherstone MP, Suzy Klein, Angela Lansbury, Joanna McGregor, Rabbi Julia Neuberger, the late Lynsey de Paul, Fay Weldon, Olivia Williams.

Money matters: Academic scholarships worth up to 50 per cent of fees awarded based on performance in entrance exam. Music scholarships also worth up to 50 per cent. Bursaries also awarded on academic merit and financial need.

Remarks: 'This will be the most interesting school in London,' said Ms Pike shortly after arriving. Strong staff will sustain the interest and more in the brief interregnum and we will watch with considerable interest to see what Mrs Bingham makes of this always stimulating and vital place.

Streatham & Clapham High School

261

42 Abbotswood Road, London SW16 1AW

Pupils: 645 • Ages: 3–18 • Sixth form: 80

Fees: £9,702 – £18,033 pa

Tel: 020 8677 8400
Email: enquiry@shc.gdst.net
Website: www.schs.gdst.net

Head Master: Since 2012, Dr Millan Sachania MA (Cantab) MPhil PhD (40s). Former comprehensive student who gained a double first and a doctorate in musicology at Cambridge and then stayed on as a music tutor for five years. After (shock, horror) reading an undergraduate's paper on Beethoven's Ninth Symphony, he decided to train as a schoolteacher and acquired a PGCE at Kingston University. Was impressed with GDST experience at Croydon High while following the course, and after stints as head of music at a girls' school in Windsor and deputy head at a co-ed HMC school in north London, was delighted to accept this post. 'Are you married?' we asked. 'Yes, to my piano'.

Parents praise his 'phenomenal attention to detail'. One told us he was 'not an obvious choice, but perfect', while another reckoned 'we are lucky to have him'. Other parental comments include, 'definitely an individual', 'quirky', 'incomparable' and 'probably just what we needed but not everyone's cup of tea'. The girls seem to love him – 'even though he uses words we've never heard before'. Has a 'rescued' Bechstein grand piano in his study, which they are definitely allowed to tinker on.

Dr Sachania is amazed by the energy of both the school and the girls, which he feels derives from their cultural diversity. Impressed with their intelligence and really wants them to broaden their horizons and achieve beyond their potential 'across the width of endeavour'. Says he has an holistic approach and doesn't believe that pupils should obsess about being competitive with each other. He wants each girl to find her own forte and achieve her own personal best.

Has already made a few changes – some popular, some less so – and there are more to come. Lessons have been shortened. Head says that 'shorter equals sharper and if necessary lessons can become double'. The sixth form, which is in a separate building, now has its own popular café area while a small lecture theatre is used for a variety of activities, from musical recitals to the once-a-week head master's lecture period.

S

Head of prep: Since January 2015, Thomas Mylne (40s), previously deputy head of the Gatehouse School in east London. BA from the University of Brighton and PGCE from the Institute of Education; he has also taught at an east London primary school and been deputy head (curriculum) at Wimbledon High Junior School. Interests include cinema, travel, music and cycling; he is married (his wife works in publishing) with two daughters.

Academic matters: Two classes throughout KS2, with potential for growth in KS1. Girls happy, relaxed and proud to show us their work and talk about what they were doing. Good learning support. All children assessed on arrival at junior school, targets set each term and parents involved early if problems arise. Head meets all teachers once a term to ascertain that children have reached the expected levels.

'The school has really pulled its socks up' – that's the view of one parent we talked to. It offers a broad curriculum covering all the core subjects, and a wide variety of co-curricular activities to ensure pupils can learn and discover in depth. Economics A level and English IGCSE (to replace GCSE) recently introduced. In 2016, 38 per cent A*/A at A level (68 per cent A*/B), and 70 per cent A*/A grades at GCSE.

Setting in maths, sciences, modern languages and, occasionally, English. Class sizes are maximum of 26, many groups in the sixth form in single figures. All staff friendly and enthusiastic – average age 42. About a quarter have been at the school for more than 10 years, giving stability and a sense of continuity to a school that is growing and changing. Plenty of men on the team – four out of five of the senior leadership team are male. All pupils are expected to take four additional subjects alongside the core at GCSE; a selection of 12 on offer to which they can add ancient Greek and astronomy if they wish. Parents say science and humanities are now particularly strong. Head sees each year 11 girl individually with her parents to discuss A level choices.

One of the first things the head did was to introduce Kinza, a compulsory enrichment programme offering a range of over 30 topics which the girls study one afternoon each week in the Michaelmas and Lent terms. Staff run courses in subjects they don't teach (including forensic science, beekeeping and Arabic) and mixed age groups work together. He says the course is 'emblematic of my educational philosophy'. His aim is to create 'civilised human beings equipped with a philosophy for living'.

Bubbly and enthusiastic head of learning support in school three-and-a-half days each week. School has inclusive policy, as long as girl passes entrance test. Statemented children have individual teaching assistants who produce strategies to help them deal with problems. Otherwise school provides help in small groups for 20 minutes once a fortnight from year 7 to year 9, and before school, after school or at lunchtime for years 10 and 11. One-to-one help has to be resourced externally.

Games, options, the arts: Surprising to find a girls' school in a leafy London suburb with its own sports grounds and an enormous, all singing, all dancing sports hall, plus a dance studio and fitness centre. Plenty of cups to indicate sporting success. Football, hockey, tennis, athletics and lots of indoor sports – something for everybody. National gymnastic champions recently and notable successes in acrobatics, fencing, tennis and netball. The only criticisms from parents are that the school 'needs to offer more for C teams to improve their skills' and 'the sports department needs better organisation and more staff'. Needless to say, this is being addressed. One mother told us: 'The school is truly inclusive – my non-sporty child loves sport'.

Music strong (as you would expect with a musically talented head master), with lessons compulsory up to GCSE. Several choirs, orchestras and ensembles. Roomful of keyboards specifically for compositions. Parents say art facilities are 'brilliant' and we were impressed too. Large art room, smaller one specifically for the sixth form and separate pottery room with its own kiln. Drama also right up to standard; new creative arts building under construction. When we visited the whole school was involved in A Midsummer Night's Dream, with non-performers making costumes and painting scenery.

D of E taken pretty seriously – girls go trekking in Morocco's Atlas Mountains and have reached base camp of Everest. Most participants reach at least silver level.

Background and atmosphere: School was founded as Brixton Hill High School for Girls in 1887 and was one of the earliest GDST member schools. It later became Streatham Hill High School, housed in the building now occupied by the junior school. Current building was originally Battersea Grammar School.

This merged with Rosa Bassett School to form a comprehensive in Tooting, allowing Streatham & Clapham High School to move to bigger premises in 1993. Large, light classrooms are a good legacy and the new buildings have created a spacious, well-equipped school, with facilities suitable for the 21st century, with more major building work under way (new sixth form floor just completed). The four-and-a-half acres of ground they stand in are miraculous in this busy area of London.

School dining hall has relaxed atmosphere and offers reasonable selection of food, which girls said was always pretty good. Plenty of staff around to make sure everyone eating properly. School lunches are compulsory up until year 11. Sixth form café is popular and older girls like having their own area to meet and chat.

Junior school's unattractive building (school reports major refurbishments, 'including the installation of a very attractive oriel window') belies exceptionally light, large classrooms and happy atmosphere inside. Building benefits from the fact that it was once a senior school in terms of the facilities and space it provides. Enormous sports hall, where girls can play hockey, and excellent outdoor area with adventure playground and enough space for rounders and tennis, guarantee plenty of fun, games and team training.

We were shown round by enthusiastic, confident girls who led us from the well-equipped nursery (with own outdoor play area) to busy reception classes and virtually every corner of the school. 'Do you want to see the loos?' they chirped. Huge library contains vast range of books and specific reading lists for each year. We also spotted shoes created out of recycled material and models of school areas (our guides proudly pointed out their own creations). Light art room with terrific views over London – 'whenever we do art, we know we're going to do something really messy', said our guides. 'It's such fun'. Science room was locked (health and safety) but they showed us well-equipped computer room and music room. Interactive white boards and computers in all classrooms.

Pupils' general feeling is that this is a happy, focused school. Parents say the support given to pupils is second to none. Although the school says the expectations are definitely there for girls to achieve and do their best, parents are adamant that it's 'not a hothouse'. Comments included 'there's no excessive pressure', 'they are allowed to be individuals and gain confidence', 'they mix across the year groups and get to know each other better that way'. One told us: 'At parents' evenings, they really do seem to know and understand our two very different daughters'. Another, with an exceptionally bright daughter, said that the way classes are divided, sometimes by ability, sometimes mixed, works a treat. 'My daughter is never bored', she said. 'The expectations of each girl are relevant to the goals she has been set'.

Pastoral care, well-being and discipline: Deputy head mistress is in overall charge of pastoral care and system is in force for identifying problems early. Parents say communication is exceptional – emails are answered immediately and problems dealt with sympathetically. A parent told us of 'some unpleasantness...handled and dealt with properly and quickly'. Another talked about 'problematic disorder' in a particular class, which was 'completely sorted out by the head of department within a week'.

House system ensures girls work together as teams, across year groups, competing to gain house points at all levels. Each form has a representative on the school council, alongside form captain, so ample chances to raise welfare problems. PHSCE programme deals with topics such as relationships, moral issues and citizenship in a sensitive and informed way.

Deputy head mistress says that school aims to deal with problems promptly. It acts positively in rare bullying-type incidents, normally resolving quickly and amicably. Sixth form mentor teams are invaluable – girls often prefer to talk to them rather than a member of staff. Year 9 form mentors help girls transferring from the junior school.

Junior school parents told us: 'Communications are very good. All the staff are positive and professional.' The only thing they felt could be improved was sport. There's always something.

Pupils and parents: Mainly from the surrounding areas of south London and from variety of backgrounds – moneyed professional classes and entrepreneurs to local shopkeepers. Typical GDST range of ethnic and racial diversity.

Around 85 per cent arrive from the junior school and others join from state and private schools. Parents of girls in state primaries said they like the smaller size classes, which gives all girls a chance to be involved. Ex-pupils include June Whitfield, Angela Carter, broadcasters Maryam and Nazanine Moshiri, soprano Elizabeth Llewellyn and V&A curator Susannah Brown.

Entrance: Applications for co-ed nursery can be made from birth to 2+. Children join at 3 and spend morning with nursery teacher in term prior to entry. School 'is looking for happy, inquisitive children'. Girls then move into reception (more places become available) in September following their 4th birthday. Informal one-to-one assessment with foundation stage co-ordinator. Further intake at 7+ when girls are assessed by head or deputy head and take tests in maths, English and verbal reasoning. Written report from previous school also needed at this stage.

Competitive – interview and exam at 11+ and 13+. Those coming up from the junior school at 11 have to pass a test in year 5 and also sit the 11+ exam. Prospective pupils are interviewed in groups at 11+ and individually at 13+. At 16+ minimum of six GCSEs required, with A*/A grades in subjects to be studied at A level, letter from previous head and interview with SCHS head master and sixth form head. Early registration for all levels suggested as waiting list is limited. Occasional places crop up at other stages, subject to relevant testing.

Exit: Around 90 per cent from the prep to the senior school. Not automatic – they all sit assessment test in year 5. Girls whom teachers feel will thrive are offered guaranteed places. Some leave at 16 for local comps, sixth form colleges or boarding but around 60 per cent – and rising – stay on. Around same proportion usually head for Russell Group universities. Dedicated coordinator supports Oxbridge hopefuls (two places in 2016).

Money matters: Typical GDST school fees, so more reasonable than elsewhere. Several non-means-tested academic scholarships available and number of means-tested, subject based scholarships/bursaries at 11+ and 16+. All curriculum-related non-residential trips included in fees.

Remarks: Streatham & Clapham High is on the up. Take one newish head master, add a good handful of enthusiasm, pep up the curriculum, add ambition and belief, introduce Kinza, tune a grand piano and – eureka – numbers rise. It would certainly appear that something is working. There is now a consistent waiting list for places and numbers staying on for A levels have rocketed from 36 per cent to over 60 per cent. As one parent told us, 'The new head master is having an amazing effect'.

The Study Preparatory School

Wilberforce House, Camp Road, London SW19 4UN

Pupils: 320 • Ages: 4-11

Fees: £12,525 pa

Tel: 020 8947 6969
Email: admissions@thestudyprep.co.uk
Website: www.thestudyprep.co.uk

Headmistress: Since 2011, Mrs Susan Pepper MA PGCE NPQH (50s). Educated at Godolphin & Latymer School, read history at Somerville College, Oxford. Previously head of history and deputy head at Francis Holland. An interesting move/appointment for someone with previous experience only in girls' secondary schools, but it is generally felt she has found her niche. 'She is focused and dynamic but a softee at heart'. Determined to develop and expand the school while maintaining its 'excellent ethos'. Has delighted parents by bringing in school lunches, with all food cooked on site. Has invested in ICT software and hardware and in-class staff training, and improved and streamlined communications. Parents say, 'very approachable, not at all forbidding', 'never hurries us in conversations', 'our children are in good hands', 'manages expectations well and gives good advice'. They feel that her knowledge of the senior school system has distinct advantages. She displays a commitment that should move the school from strength to strength. She will listen to others' points of view, but will always drive through what she sees as necessary change. Her mantra is 'do the best by every child'. One mother said, 'gives the girls lots of respect and makes it easy for them to talk to her'. Teaches RE to years 5 and 6; runs the debating club for the older girls and pony club for the younger ones. Definitely feels that the move was the right decision. We think she could be right. Married with one grown up son. Enjoys riding, keeping ex-battery hens, gardening, reading and cryptic crosswords in her spare time. When, we wonder, is that.

Entrance: Non-selective at 4+ by ballot and thereafter by assessment. Registration any time up to 18 months before entry. No point in rushing in at birth, it won't make any difference. Sibling priority. Mostly from local Wimbledon area but some from Kingston, Wandsworth and other surrounding areas. The usual cosmopolitan mix of nationalities and backgrounds found in London schools.

S

Exit: Mainly to local day schools, often with scholarships (record 25 in 2016), including academic, music, sport and drama. Wimbledon High is at the top, with, amongst others, Lady Eleanor Holles, St Paul's Girls, Putney High, Surbiton and Sutton High Schools and Kingston Grammar. A few to boarding schools such as St Mary's Ascot, Benenden and Wycombe Abbey. Mrs Pepper really does try to make sure that the schools girls try for are the most appropriate. At the beginning of year 5 there is a general talk for all parents, after which she schedules individual sessions to talk them through their daughters' futures. 'She never hurries us and is so reassuring'.

Remarks: A happy school full of lively, enthusiastic girls. Parents love it and have nothing but praise. Couldn't find anyone with a serious criticism, but working parents would love a homework club. All feel that their daughters are nurtured from day one and are not overly pressurised. 'Huge strength is all are treated as individuals and their differences celebrated'.

Over 120 years old. The Study was originally just that, one room, three pupils, one governess. It soon grew and moved to 4, Peek Crescent, purpose built in 1905, now Spencer House, accommodating the prep school girls. About 20 years ago another purpose-built school was bought and the pre-prep department moved to Wilberforce House, approximately 10 minutes walk away across Wimbledon Common. The result? One school, two buildings, great teaching and tip top facilities.

Two year 2 girls took us round Wilberforce House. Articulate and enthusiastic, they were keen to show us every nook and cranny. Remembering with joy. Colour coded classes for all levels. Reception now fully high tech: 'we never had computers like these!' But 'we've always had interactive whiteboards'. All classrooms light and bright and busy. In year 1, we walked in just as a butterfly was emerging from a chrysalis – very exciting. Elsewhere, a show and tell session held everyone rapt. Everything is done to provide a happy, relaxed learning environment. Plenty of art on display. Low level loos for the youngest and basins with bear shaped taps. Excellent library with ICT area. Fascinating DT projects. To help with transition, year 3 girls go to Spencer House for drama and art each week.

We were taken round Spencer House by two bright year 6 girls, eager to tell us what they liked best about their school. Seemed to be pretty well everything. Good-sized hall which doubles up as stage for plays and concerts and, on the day we visited, space for a charity fair. Very keen on their charity work: 'Year 6 choose the special ones for the summer term'. The whole school gathers there at least once a term and on special occasions as, for instance, harvest festival. One parent said, 'Spencer House seems a bit small', then went on to say 'facilities fabulous'.

Well-equipped library; excellent science room: 'we can use proper equipment'. High tech ICT room where all have a lesson once a week; as in the lower school, interactive whiteboards everywhere and computers abound. Art room under the eaves, with displays continuing on the walls along the corridor. Individual music rooms named after famous musicians, a wide range of instruments taught. Several choirs and a variety orchestras and groups. Raved about 'our amazing music teacher; really teaches in a fun way'. Music a great strength and leads to several scholarships to senior schools. Drama also huge. Props room known as Narnia; easy to see why. Our guides said, 'everyone does cooking' but we did not see where. A blip, we are assured: both sites have excellent kitchen facilities. (Certainly the 'snack lunch' we were given at the end of the tour was most impressive.) An exceptionally wide range of clubs before, after and during school. 'Latin club at 8am is great'. A parent said, 'something there for every girl, bright or not, will always find a way to shine'.

Teaching appears excellent. Relaxed for the younger children, form teachers covering most subjects; more specialists in the upper school. Those we met were friendly, welcoming and keen to inform. Girls like them all. Average age mid-40s, over a quarter having been there for more than 10 years. Sad lack of males, but head said good ones are hard to find. Average class size 22, never more than 24.

Weekly staff meeting for whole school when specific problems can be discussed. Up-to-date, well-informed learning support co-ordinator. Continuous assessment and plenty of help for those who need it, including the very able. One-to-one when necessary, charged as an extra. EAL lessons also provided, when needed, at extra cost. Comprehensive anti-bullying policy. Believe it is important to provide equal opportunity for all children and 'encourage them to think beyond the school gate'. Head feels they are particularly good at building up confidence. Apparently, teachers go out of their way to make sure that each child 'has a moment of glory'.

Good play areas outside both houses, with separate sections for the younger pupils. Sport and PE very important. They say it is all about 'enjoyment, opportunity, success and celebration'. Good variety, taught by specialist teachers. Competitive matches from year 3. National prize winners in netball, cross-country and athletics. Now have their own sports field. 'Head of sport has amazing drive and enthusiasm'.

Surbiton High Boys' Preparatory School

Linked with Surbiton High Girls' Preparatory School, Surbiton High School

3 Avenue Elmers, Surbiton, Surrey KT6 4SP

Pupils: 160 • Ages: 4–11

Fees: £10,086 – £15,924 pa

Tel: 020 8390 6640
Email: surbiton.prep@surbitonhigh.com
Website: www.surbitonhigh.com

Headteacher: Since 2015, Sally Ralph BEd (50s), educated at a Gloucestershire grammar where she was head girl, followed by University of Bath. Mrs Ralph moved to London in the 1990s, teaching at Feltonfleet and Rowan Prep before becoming head of St David's in Ashford. She has now taken up the headship of the boys' preparatory school after five years as acting head and deputy head of both the girls' and boys' junior schools. An appointment much approved of by parents, pupils and colleagues, who tell us she is a gifted mathematics teacher as well as a dynamic leader of young men. She remains active in the classroom, working with all age groups on a weekly basis and as the maths specialist. She has a passion for gymnastics and has had a liaison role between school and the British Gymnastics Association. A keen follower of many sports, who enjoys reading and trips to the theatre, she has two grown-up children, one of whom works in the finance department at Surbiton High.

Entrance: At 4+ informal assessment days are held in November each year for 44 reception places; also two-form entry into year 3 via maths and English tests. Occasional places in other age groups.

Exit: At 11+ regular academic, music, drama or sports scholarships (15 in 2016). Most go to local day schools Hampton, Kingston Grammar, Reeds, Royal Grammar Guildford and KCS Wimbledon. A few to Tiffin and other Surrey grammars, with the odd one to boarding school.

Remarks: A growing reputation for inspirational teaching. In the early years, pupils are taught mostly by their class teachers, with subject specialist teachers for modern foreign languages, sports and music throughout the school. Class sizes are between 18 and 22; each one has team teachers so boys can be taught in ability groups. Year 3 upwards sees the introduction of specialist teachers for all subjects.

Mathematics continues to strengthen across the age groups. The curriculum is developed and updated on a continuous basis, lots of themed projects run to link subjects together. 'Did you know you share 50 percent of your genes with bananas?' remarked one little lad, who was busy making a DNA model in the science and art room. English and drama are embedded across the curriculum; spending the day as a Tudor child provides the stimulus for all sorts of history, arts and literacy activities.

The school is noted for being particularly good at helping children develop listening and speaking skills. Enthusiastic speakers read and write their own poetry, others join the debating club or the school council. French from reception, later on Spanish and Mandarin are added, delivered by The Dragons of Europe; boys work towards CE level 1. Popular annual event is the French musical breakfast; parents enjoy the choir while year 6s don bow ties and act as waiters serving coffee and croissants. Classrooms and corridors are bursting with displays of both academic and artistic work, demonstrating that there is plenty of imaginative teaching going on.

All subject knowledge is broadened through the use of the latest technology. Year 3s upwards all have their own iPad while younger boys can access school iPads. Focus groups, Friday drop ins and maths clinics are available to all pupils wanting to catch up or extend their work. Learning support staff are on hand to assist with a variety of mild SpLDs, touch typing is delivered through a club, and EAL is arranged as required. There are lunchtime clubs, academic, creative and active to choose from, breakfast club opens at 7:30am and there's an after-school club, which working parents find very useful.

With the acquisition of additional premises adjacent to the main school, the boys' prep is in the first phase of a long-awaited expansion. The school now has space for two classes in each year group. Reception and years 1-3 are based at the newly acquired and refurbished Charles Burney House, while years 4 to 6 remain at the original site in Elmers Avenue. Both buildings are large Victorian houses with small but well-equipped playgrounds. Boys benefit from a fabulous 39 acres of sports grounds in nearby Hinchley Wood, which includes tennis/netball courts, all weather hockey pitch, rugby/football pitches and a pavilion. Adjacent to the sports ground in is a lovely wooded area which allows numerous opportunities for adventure and learning outside the classroom, from pond dipping and observing wildlife in their natural habitats to family camping weekends.

Sport is a great strength throughout the three Surbiton schools. The physical education programme covers skills and techniques required for basketball, hockey, gymnastics, athletics and tennis. The main school sports are football, rugby and cricket. An extensive fixture list ensures all boys get the opportunity to represent the school in competitive matches. PE display cupboard shelves teem with awards and trophies.

Music continues to be high profile; the school arranges visiting instrumentalists and tuition for any instrument is available. In year 3, everyone gets the opportunity to learn a stringed instrument, the following year a brass instrument. Lovely music room brimming with instruments; boys have an impressive choice of choirs and ensembles to join. All the boys get the opportunity each year to be in musical and dramatic productions and assemblies.

Parents feel older boys are well prepared for 11+ exams and looked after all round in a calm and sensible way. Each boy is allocated a mentor to help with practice interviews and any queries. Mrs Ralph guides parents through the process of choosing the right senior school for their son. Parents are unanimous in commenting on the success at 11+, due to how well the school manages everyone's expectations.

A child-orientated school full of learning opportunities, where cheerful and articulate boys are also allowed to have fun and encouraged to be kind and thoughtful, with opportunities to link up with the girls' prep.

Surbiton High Girls' Preparatory School

Linked with Surbiton High Boys' Preparatory School, Surbiton High School

95-97 Surbiton Road, Kingston, Surrey KT1 2HW

Pupils: 300 • Ages: 4-11

Fees: £10,086 – £15,924 pa

Tel: 020 8439 1309
Email: girlsprep@surbitonhigh.com
Website: www.surbitonhigh.com

Head: Since 2015, Clemmie Stewart BA English literature and education (30s). Educated at Bedales and Winchester University, she has taught in both the independent and state sectors. Her teaching career started at Farleigh Prep, followed by several years at Talavera Junior School in Aldershot. In 2014 she joined Surbiton High as director of teaching and learning and was appointed headteacher the following year, after proving herself to be an outstanding English teacher. A go ahead and enthusiastic personality; parents we spoke to feel she is an asset to the school and will continue to steer the girls in all the right directions. She is always smiling, say her charges, which makes us feel happy. Talented all-rounder herself, Miss Stewart was a music scholar at Bedales and a horsewoman with success in the show jumping world. A country girl at heart, she loves travelling and exploring during the holidays, during term time she enjoys running and walking her dogs. She is a fan of many sports including Formula 1 and football, and an avid reader, and has a particular interest in how children's education advances continually.

Entrance: At 4+ girls are invited to attend informal child-friendly assessment mornings. Grouped by seasonal birthdays, autumn, spring, summer, this ensures each child is assessed with others of similar age and developmental stage. Several members of staff observe prospective candidates doing simple tasks based on stories and nursery activities. From 7+ and for occasional places girls sit assessment tests in maths and English.

Exit: At 11+ nearly all girls progress through to the senior school; regular scholarships are awarded for music, drama, art, sports and academics. One or two go to local grammars or a boarding school. Occasional parent still moans about girls being not prepared for other schools, however majority of parents feel why go through the stress, when you have one of the best senior schools in the area at your fingertips? Occasionally a pupil can be advised in year 5 that they might fare better in a less selective school.

S

Remarks: Bubbling with activities, academic, sporting and creative, the school grows from strength to strength. Ms Stewart favours an innovative approach alongside traditional teaching, which she feels enables pupils to exceed their targets and make outstanding progress. Lovely bright interlinking reception classes with their own small play area. Early years provision was highly praised in recent ISI inspection; parents agree; pupils are given an excellent grounding in language, literacy and mathematics. Form teachers cover all subjects until year 2, subject specialists, including maths and English teachers, are introduced from year 3, adding breadth across the curriculum. Inspiring co-curricular links connect subjects effortlessly: a chocolate workshop leads to a fair trade geography project, African dancing and story writing. The possibilities are endless, exciting stuff and always something to look forward to, girls tell us.

In addition to stand-alone lessons, drama is embedded into class teaching through creative role-play, history in action days, and storytelling, helping to develop a range of communication skills. Imaginative art and DT displayed in classrooms and corridors, pupils are exposed to a variety of media. Older pupils can use senior school facilities and are taught by some of the senior art specialists. Three languages are offered, Spanish from reception, French is added in year 2 and Mandarin in years 4 and 5. Pupils are continuously monitored; targets are set to check progress and ensure no one slips under the radar.

School prides itself on encouraging children to become active learners with a big focus on language skills and decision making. IT strategy is always advancing with each pupil having an iPad, some lessons have gone digital, and girls are definitely tech savvy, say parents. Lots of praise from the parents for teaching staff, who are good mix of youth and experience and considered an inspirational bunch. Our guides were eloquent, proud of their school and keen to explain everything from their art and science projects to learning to skip when they were younger.

SEN, termed as learning enrichment, provides specific support to individuals with mild SpLDs, usually dyspraxia and dyslexia. Pupils are cared for on an individual basis, via one-to-one sessions or enrichment groups. Gifted and talented activities run to extend knowledge and, if appropriate, some girls are offered scholarship training. EAL is arranged as required; the school has quite a few families from Korea and South Asia.

Music continues to flourish; everyone learns to play a string and a brass instrument, with a good number of pupils having individual tuition on more than one instrument. Dedicated and well-resourced room for music theory and pupils get the chance to try their hand at composition. Host of choirs, ensembles and orchestras, with plenty of opportunities for solo performances; girls and boys often join forces on choir trips, musical and dramatic productions. Good selection of outings, residential trips and visitors are arranged for many interests. Around 70 clubs, world explorers, newspapers, jewellery making and dance to mention a few; there are also breakfast and after-school clubs.

Parent-teacher partnerships are well developed; majority of parents feel the school communicates with them effectively in traditional ways and more recently via social media. Pastoral care has a positive and family feel to it and school is always keen to develop social interaction; mixed age groups sit together for lunch, and reception class all have a year 6 buddy. Everyone is allocated to one of the four houses and encouraged to voice their opinions and ideas through the school council. Parents and pupils are active fundraisers for the school and charities; mufti day with an ice pop sale is a firm favourite for fundraising, girls tell us.

Sport has come on in leaps and bounds since our last visit; this part of the curriculum is given equal importance as academics. As with many inner-city schools, on site space is fairly tight. Known as LOC, 'learning outside the classroom' mostly takes place at their 39 acres of sports grounds and woodland close by in Hinchley Wood. A specially designed physical education programme teaches the skills needed for netball, hockey, rounders, tennis and gymnastics. In addition to this they also cover athletics, health-related fitness and team building. Netball team is extremely successful; girls start to compete in year 3 U8s, regularly reaching the finals of the national netball tournament. Boys' and girls' preps participate in mixed athletics and netball events; netball team recently came fifth in the London Youth Games, while the athletics squad came third in Kingston borough finals. Girls can also join the ski club, which uses the local dry ski slopes and competes regularly. Adjacent to the sports ground is a newly acquired woodland area, offering further opportunities for outdoor pursuits and eco-projects, planting vegetables, discovering wildlife and camping trips; the prospects are plentiful.

A single sex school with co-educational opportunities as the boys' and girls' preparatory schools often link together. A happy, vibrant school for inquisitive and active girls. Unstuffy atmosphere but traditional ethos that fit comfortably with modern teaching and an innovative outlook.

Surbiton High School

Linked with Surbiton High Boys' Preparatory School, Surbiton High Girls' Preparatory School

Surbiton Crescent, Kingston, Surrey KT1 2JT

Pupils: 1,000 • Ages: 11–18 • Sixth form: 235

Fees: £15,387 pa

Tel: 020 8439 1309
Email: surbiton.high@surbitonhigh.com
Website: www.surbitonhigh.com

Principal: Since 2008, Ms Ann Haydon BSc (40s); arrived with an excellent reputation from a sister United Learning school, Guildford High, where she was deputy for five years. Previously she taught geography at Putney High, moving to Sutton High as youngest ever head of department. She's proved a dynamic and committed leader, who is able to make positive changes, while keeping the staff on side. Sport and music have been her key development areas; both are now in the outstanding bracket. She has also introduced a variety of specialist learning coaches and mentors to help develop subject areas and new skills. Parents appreciate her and feel she has been incredibly good at taking the school forward, making major improvements to the girls' education across the board. Definitely a lady who gets things done, said one parent. Her inspirational and innovative leadership has been recognised: recently she was awarded a distinction in the Pearson Award for headteacher of the year in a secondary school in London and the south east, for excellence in education.

In addition to managing all school affairs, she is personable and takes a hands-on approach, teaching geography to year 7 and hosting regular form captains' lunches to ensure she gets to know her pupils. She likes pupils to be 'rounded and grounded', feeling that excellent results will naturally follow. She endeavours to encourage a 'can do' attitude and is proud of all that the girls achieve. She is also a member of the governing body of several other independent schools. Outside school she has many interests including travel, good food, fine wines, sport and the arts.

Academic matters: Results are climbing steadily with everyone aiming high. Fifty one per cent of A level grades A*-A in 2016, with 85 per cent at A*-B. At GCSE, almost 70 per cent of grades were A*-A. Maths results usually very good with large numbers taking further maths getting A*/A. Class sizes are large-ish at 24, sets for maths, languages and practical subjects are smaller. Teaching is vigorous and interesting, so pupils need to be on the ball. Year 7s kick off with learning the all-important, often forgotten skills of note taking and how to organise themselves and their bags; easier than it was, with modern technology. 'Teachers want us to become independent and active learners as soon as we can,' explain pupils. Classes we observed had a good multisensory element with pupils looking eager and engaged. Stringent monitoring of all pupils; no one is allowed to fall by the wayside. Weekly drop-in clinics, maths and English for all, other clinics are mainly for supporting GCSE and A level students. Everyone studies at least two languages: core languages are French, German and Spanish, but girls can also opt for Mandarin, Italian, Latin and Greek through to A level.

Technology is everywhere: an assistant principal for digital strategy arrived a couple of years ago, so progress in this area has been speedy. The latest technology is used to enhance lessons; everyone has an iPad, but don't worry, social media blocked, so no distractions during class time. Staff and pupils are trained to use personal organisers; iPads, digital archives and learning spaces are available to every department. Comfortable ICT suite set up in semicircular tiers so everyone can see the board easily; girls commented on the staff's sterling research work to find the best software for them.

Bustling library is an active resource centre, with reading clubs, creative writing workshops and external speakers to boost interests, alongside books, magazines and DVDs in different languages. English Department runs a literary society, which meets weekly for tea and topical discussions on books, film and theatre. To inspire and teach the girls all aspects of writing there is a writer in residence. He collaborates with teachers to run artistic projects, helps prepare students for national competitions and has launched a student laureate programme for creative writing.

SEND learning enrichment staff run study skills groups and support pupils with mild dyslexic and dyspraxic type difficulties. Touch-typing classes are taught by an outside provider. Korean mentor and translator and two part-time EAL teachers work with girls whose first language is not English and prepare them for IELTS or similar exams. Gifted and talented programme offers a good range of co-curricular activities and extension tasks, special classes and mentors for scholars and Oxbridge preparation. School is keen to emphasise these classes are about offering equality of challenge to the most able pupils.

Sixth formers are well prepared for university life with lectures and special visitors to encourage them to look widely at the choice of courses available to them. Again, the school takes an all-round approach to pupils' futures; a leadership coach provides guidance and training for interview technique, public speaking, commercial awareness, careers, and preparing personal statements and workplace application forms. Young Enterprise gives the sixth formers an opportunity to try establishing their own businesses, designing products to sell and distribute in competition with other schools. The entrepreneur in residence works with pupils to help develop key work and life skills for business. The head is aware that while technology is changing rapidly, the skills for successful living do not, and she takes seriously the responsibility to provide opportunities for pupils to develop their leadership and entrepreneurial skills.

Games, options, the arts: Now a paradise for sporty types; 'sport for all' is coupled with the pursuit of excellence: the aim is to provide the best for everyone whatever their ability. The school has 39 acres of grounds nearby in Hinchley Wood, an immense asset for a town school. 'Super 6 Sports' are netball, hockey, rowing, skiing, gymnastics and tennis, each with their own head and coaches. Fitness centre for aerobics, zumba, other sporting choices including golf, athletics, badminton and riding. Former BBC rowing club boathouse has recently been snapped up by United Learning, and an experienced team of coaches trains rowers from novices to national eventers.

Riding club takes place in Cobham at the Silvermere centre. More competent and competition riders, some of whom have qualified for national championships, can join the equestrian team. Surbiton High has the largest and most successful school ski club in the UK; young skiers use a local artificial slope with extra sessions at the Snowdome. Each sport has its own head, professional coaches and mentors to manage events and arrange exciting annual tours all over the world. It goes without saying, girls are hugely successful locally, regionally and internationally; currently seven pupils are trialling or competing for GB. Surbiton Advanced Sport, known as SAS, is a specially designed programme for elite sports performers to help them balance academic work with a high level of training and competition.

Art department was preparing for an exhibition at the time of our visit to show off the talents of creative pupils. Impressive displays of large oil canvases, textiles, DT, photography and ceramics in well-resourced open plan studio with its own printing presses, kiln, dark room, computer suite and art library. Everyone can get involved in drama; masses of productions to ensure everyone gets the chance to perform. If singing or acting is not your thing, you can try stage management, set design, props or costume making. Year 9s write and perform plays for the house drama week; girls also perform at the National Theatre and an annual Shakespeare Festival. Energetic and inspiring head of music has developed the department beyond recognition, according to customers. From jazz to chamber music there is a full range of orchestras, bands, choirs and ensembles to join for differing abilities. 'I can't believe the great choices my sister and her friends have,' lamented an old girl. Music and drama are now thought to be thriving departments, which often collaborate, resulting in some stunning performances both in school and at the local theatre. Despite this, take-up at A level of these subjects is quite low. Clubs and societies offer something for everyone; there are around 70 to choose from, as well as the popular D of E and outings at home and abroad.

Background and atmosphere: The school is part of the United Learning Group, an independent Christian educational charity which runs and sponsors several independent schools and academies. Surbiton High now owns an entire block of buildings; the two most recent acquisitions are a large Victorian building which houses the junior section of the boys' prep school and Mary Bennett House, a modern building that has been developed into nine new classrooms, and a large flexible learning and event space. In the centre of these buildings are multi-sport courts and a grassed area for recreation, fundraising events, a performance space, and home to the school chickens, cared for by the chicken club girls.

Despite it being quite a large school, everyone comments on the friendly atmosphere. Voluntary work in the local community continues to flourish, with the hospital visiting scheme and the Friendship Hour: elderly residents are visited or invited to school events, summer and Christmas parties.

Pastoral care, well-being and discipline: High praise for pastoral care. When talking to one prospective family visiting with their (generally) sweet 11 year old, school staff assured them that 'we'll still like her when she is 15!' 'And they do,' says that mother; 'the pastoral care is really very good.' Most parents report an immediate and effective response to any issues. Generally a well-behaved bunch – largely complying with the zero tolerance policy on drugs, drink and cigarettes. Smokers hauled before Ms Haydon even if they were caught out of school hours and uniform. School nurse on site, doctor available weekly. Good induction routines for year 7s, followed up with 'big sister' mentoring programme. Healthy culture of 'telling' about problems and school quick to support anyone in difficulty and any of their friends who may have been involved. Not a bitch-fest – girls say their classmates are supportive of them. Parents pleased that school somehow manages to keep cliques and queen bees under control.

Pupils and parents: Predominantly busy, hardworking UK families, many of whom travel into the city for business. The clientele generally reflects the local population. Over the last few years the school has been attracting girls from slightly further afield due to good transport links; mainline train station approximate 10 minutes' walk away. Local community also includes a growing number of international families, particularly from Southeast Asia and Korea, who are well represented at the school. Many parents are involved in the PTA raising funds for the school and charities. One mother, a relative newcomer, told us that what impressed her most was how welcome new parents felt when attending fundraising and social events. Alumni: Mollie King singer and songwriter, Chemmy Alcott, Olympic skier, Nicky Morgan MP.

Entrance: At 11+, most junior school girls move directly onto the senior school. New entrants take assessment tests in English, maths and, then for their interview write a personal statement and provide a report from their primary school. Not elitist, but parents say it has become more selective than it used to be, as its reputation grows. At 16+, approximately 10 places for external candidates to join the sixth form via an interview, GCSE results with As in the subjects to be studied at A level and report from current school.

Exit: Some move on after GCSEs to local state sixth form college or perhaps boarding school. At 18+ around eighty per cent go to top universities (Birmingham, Newcastle, Durham and Exeter all popular). In 2016, four to Oxbridge and two medics plus one to University of Michigan, USA.

Money matters: Perceived by parents to offer good value for money. Help with fees is available through means tested United Learning and Church Foundation assisted places and bursaries for the daughters of clergy. Competitive scholarships are offered for academics, music, art, drama and sports at 11+ and 16+.

Remarks: An ambitious arena for driven girls ready to embrace life and all its challenges. Never a dull moment, owing to the school's growing reputation for offering outstanding provision across the board at a reasonable price. Recent ISI Inspection confirmed this, awarding the school excellent in all categories and exceptional for pupil achievement.

Sussex House School

68 Cadogan Square, London SW1X 0EA

Pupils: 180 • Ages: 8–13 • C of E

Fees: £18,600 pa

Tel: 020 7584 1741
Email: registrar@sussexhouseschool.co.uk
Website: www.sussexhouseschool.co.uk

Headmaster: Since 1994, the engaging, cultured Mr Nicholas Kaye MA ACP, Cambridge English graduate followed by music research (60s). Whilst deputy head here, following a brief spell at Asra Hawariat School in Addis Ababa, of which he is a trustee and fundraiser, the opportunity arose to acquire the school from the Vernon Trust, which he seized with typical energy, creating an independent charitable trust. Sussex House has never looked back, going from strength to strength, achieving the recent accolade of Best Prep School award. Parents admire this 'erudite man' and the boys sum him up as 'diverse, really talented, passionate about music, poetry, architecture, and a playwright'. His study/Victorian parlour is crammed with book shelves containing leather-bound volumes and novels by past Old Cadogans, an ornamental pianoforte ('The best pianoforte is the concert Steinway in the ballroom,' remarks the head) along with a cornucopia of porcelain, potted plants, objets d'art, furniture, rugs and oriental carpets illuminated by wooden lamp stands with large lampshades.

As one might expect in this very traditional institution, there are school photographs, house shields and embroidered banners made for the Jubilee and carried in procession on special occasions such as the annual All Souls' Day Requiem at St Mary Magdalene, Little Venice, which we attended. Conducted by Mr Kaye, this was an uplifting service in which the Sussex House choristers sang exquisitely. Mr Kaye enthusiastically teaches 10 periods to the top years with a focus on creative writing and literature. All the parents we spoke to agreed 'he has an excellent rapport with the boys'. One parent remarked, 'The headmaster has a key role in setting the tone of the school. Even more amazing is the fact that he sees the best in every child and gets the best out of every child.' Another commented, 'He teaches the VIth English in his study and they appreciate their elevated status. The sessions are challenging, quite adult, like an Oxford tutorial'. He is very ably supported by his PA/registrar who firmly declares, when questioned on the future, 'We are certainly not ready to hang up our boots yet!' And fortunately they show no signs of it.

Entrance: At 8+ and only later if there happens to be a place available. Thirty-six pupils are selected on the basis of a rigorous, competitive entrance examination in English, maths, reasoning and interview. Strong English is a key requirement and there are no boys in the school with EAL requirements; however, it does cater for up to 23 boys on the SEN register who are given support without additional charge. Parents suggest, 'Not a school of mixed ability, although mild learning difficulties such as dyspraxia are dealt with'. Prospective parents are all given a personal tour by the registrar, meet the headmaster and are invited to a special evening led by members of the VIth form. The majority of boys live within a few miles of Cadogan Square. Regular feeders are Garden House, Eaton House, and other central London pre-preps. There are no sibling discounts on offer but bursaries and scholarships are available according to need and are up to the full remission of fees in cases of genuine need.

Exit: Majority to Eton and Winchester, some to Harrow, just under a third going to London day schools such as St Paul's and Westminster, with some major academic, art and music scholarships in recent years.

Remarks: Mr Kaye chose the aspirational school motto 'Lead me to the rock that is higher than I', and, as he explains, 'This implies a journey which, unlike climbing Everest, is never complete'. Unusually for a day school, there is an Anglican school chaplain who leads important services in the local church which acts as the school chapel.

This is a distinctive, remarkable school which is unashamedly academic. After being greeted by gowned school marshal, Sergeant Khim Sherchan, formerly of the Gurkhas, you are ushered into a grand Norman Shaw arts and crafts town house with William Morris wallpaper, stunning fresh flower arrangements, a realisation of Morris' tenet 'Have nothing in your house that you do not know to be useful or believe to be beautiful'. Parents who would prefer something more modern and spacious, where boys can let off steam at break times kicking a ball, should look elsewhere. Up the wide, ornate mahogany staircase is the ballroom, which provides a venue for daily assemblies, lessons around polished tables and tea time concerts. These concerts are an example of how every effort is made to encourage budding musicians at all levels. The music is stunning and every year concerts with a professional orchestra take place at the Cadogan Hall along with an annual musical at the Fortune Theatre. We heard a talented 9 year old play the violin with incredible skill and learnt he is also a valued member of the football team. One parent we spoke to remarked, 'The school is small enough so that each boy finds a niche.' Creativity abounds and is an intrinsic part of life at Sussex House along with its nurturing approach, and why many parents choose it over other top prep schools. As a parent commented, 'The wonderful drama is performed in the West End, giving unparalleled opportunities for this age'.

During our visit we saw some excellent architectural models in the making, in readiness for the annual exhibition with the theme of Iconic Chelsea. The clubs and art lessons include opportunities to do pottery and oil painting as well as making use of laptops for presentations about artists. The subject specialist staff are long-serving and popular with their pupils. All the boys we met commented on how the staff are prepared to give up their own time to help individuals.The boys themselves are a superb advertisement for the school: intelligent, polite, lively, responsive and articulate. 'They are confident without being arrogant,' commented a parent, adding candidly, 'That is not to say that they are not sometimes boisterous, and need careful handling in this confined space by their form teacher and/or the deputy head.' They are given Stars for rewards and Stripes for punishments. The sixth formers are prefects and wear gowns unless they fall from grace and are no longer allowed to wear a gown: a great incentive. They have opportunities to exercise at Battersea Park at least twice a week, and A, B, C and D teams regularly play fixtures against other schools. The school day includes regular walks to Nicholls Hall for gym, fencing and music. Fencing is excellent here and the school magazine The Cadogan records many sporting achievements and activities, as well as superb poetry. The classrooms for younger boys still house old-fashioned lacquered desks, which are confining, and it is important to be aware that break times are spent inside the school, which would not suit all boys.

Average size of classes 18, with 12 in the top year when a scholarship group is formed. The curriculum is carefully tailored to suit the needs of individuals who will sit various school examinations. Mr Kaye would love to have a six day week, 'but that is not possible', so much is packed in: orchestra practice and Greek before school, for example. As there is no dining room or kitchen, boys must bring packed lunches; 'not ideal,' state parents, but lunch time is a social occasion with the form teacher followed by numerous, popular clubs including architecture and discussion group. One ex-parent remarked on how 'well-rounded SH boys are', and that out of 250 boys at Eton in her son's year, three of the 12 chosen for the Eton debating competition were SH boys. The boys we chatted to would love to play rugby, but revel in football alongside options such as fencing, tennis, cricket, golf and swimming. They appreciate the spacious new science laboratory and find the art they do inspiring.

For those parents seeking a Summer Fields in central London, Sussex House fits the bill. Parents agree, 'It really does prepare boys for boarding at 13+ and gives them a wonderful, well-rounded platform'. It is not surprising that so many Old Cadogans hold the school with great affection. They include novelists Edward St Aubyn, Jason Goodwin and Richard

Mason, along with actors Daniel Radcliffe, Jasper Britton, and Christopher and Jay Villiers, composer Michael Csanyi Wills, and many more recorded in the annual, very impressive magazine.

Sutton Grammar School

267

Manor Lane, Sutton, Surrey SM1 4AS

Pupils: 900 • Ages: 11–18 • Sixth form: 270

Tel: 020 8642 3821
Email: sgs@suttonlea.org
Website: www.suttongrammar.sutton.sch.uk

Headmaster: Since 1990, Mr Gordon Ironside MA PGCE (50s). Read physics at Cambridge, then taught maths at Alleyn's and Sutton Grammar before becoming deputy head in 1987. Married to a fellow teacher, he has three grown-up children who all attended Sutton grammar schools. One son continues what has become a bit of a family tradition and teaches in another local grammar school. Head is involved in a lot of charity work; he is a governor of the local hospital school and adult education college. Affable, hard working and thoroughly dedicated to education all round. Parents say he is always on hand and has the confidence to allow his staff to run their own departments. They appreciate his experience and all the guidance he offers their sons. Head has many interests in the arts, sports and enjoys the occasional round of golf.

Academic matters: Highly selective and always in the top 10 per cent of the highest achieving schools. Needless to say, it delivers mostly excellent results: in 2016, 75 per cent of papers were graded A*/A at GCSE; 60 per cent A*/A at A level (88 per cent A*/B). The school specialism is science – all three sciences are very strong and many pupils opt for the science and maths route at GCSE and A level. Very inspiring large and light labs, greenhouse on the roof and boys breed trout and salmon to release into the River Wandle. Two physics teachers run electronics project clubs and boys have won UK Engineer of the Year and Intech science awards.

Top performing pupils also excel in maths and physics Olympiads. Sixth formers help to teach science in primary schools, while some local schools visit Sutton Grammar to experience working in a lab. Early work experience is arranged in hospitals for those considering careers in medicine. Head stresses that staff work hard to make sure the curriculum is balanced with arts and humanities. Parents say the fairly dynamic English department really stretches boys, as well as organising fun activities with plays and poetry. No classics, modern languages only. Boys can choose from French, Spanish and German. Rigorous computing skills are taught – AIDA qualifications in year 9, leading to GCSE and A level computing. Good mix of male and female staff, most of them long serving. One boy told us 'it's great that the teachers guide the whole way through school'.

SENCo oversees SEN provision throughout the school for a small number of pupils with statements, SpLDs, sensory impairments or high functioning ASD. Refreshingly honest approach from head, who says this is not school's area of expertise and stresses that pupils have to be able to cope and enjoy the fast moving and competitive environment.

S

Games, options, the arts: A fabulous 27-acre sports ground in Cheam, used by pupils, old boys and Surrey football clubs. PE staff make a tremendous effort to help boys find sporting pursuits they enjoy, from table tennis to county league cricket. Around 12 football teams and three rugby sides compete in fixtures list, along with a host of house sports competitions. The school also boasts its own largish heated open-air swimming pool. Standard D of E programme and well established CCF (run with Nonsuch Girls School). Parents say the sporting opportunities for all are a great credit to the school.

Some impressive art displays around the school, although only a small number choose to take GCSE and A level art. Many more opt for the design and technology path, either in graphics or electronics.

Chamber groups, orchestras and choirs engage in a range of musical pursuits, including A Cappella singing. Tuition on any instrument of a boy's choice can be arranged. Composer in residence runs an annual composition festival. Music and drama departments team up with Sutton High School (neighbouring girls' school) for concerts and plays, including a biannual musical production. Both schools and parents pull together to produce fabulous productions. Drama on the curriculum: a reasonable number of boys go on to take GCSE and A level theatre studies. LAMDA courses and exams on offer too. The old gym has been converted into a drama studio (for which a talented pupil has designed a lighting system).

During the summer term there is an annual activities week; trips include foreign travel, adventure sports camps and a year 9 visit to the First World War battlefields. Others attend first aid training courses and some older pupils try their hand at teaching in local primary schools.

Background and atmosphere: The school has always been single sex. It opened as Sutton County Grammar in 1899, charging fees of two pounds and 10 shillings per term. More or less everything you could want is on site, so it's all fairly compact. New buildings are constantly popping up (latest additions are a two-storey maths block, new sixth form centre and bigger dining room.

Playground areas are small. Boys from year 10 upwards are allowed to go off site during the lunch hour. Sandwich bar in the playground (known as the Snack Shack) helps to relieve the lunchtime crush. Stylish but small newly designed canteen serves hot meals. Everything runs like clockwork in this traditional focused grammar school. Boys are well-behaved, motivated and articulate.

Pastoral care, well-being and discipline: Traditional house system and year group tutors look after pupils' welfare. One parent told us she felt confident that problems were dealt with 'very swiftly.' Boys taught to respect others and take responsibility for all aspects of the school and themselves. Everyone is expected to follow a strict but fair code on behaviour, hair and uniform.

The school has a no-nonsense approach to discipline and stresses to pupils that silly behaviour wastes valuable time. Parents' information evenings and discussion groups run on a wide range of topics, often led by outside speakers. Parents are canvassed on subjects they'd like to know more about each term and pupils are welcome to attend too if they wish.

Pupils and parents: Parents are mostly professionals from all kinds of backgrounds – wealthy Surrey and south Londoners along with those from less affluent areas. Great mix of brains from all over the world, 30 to 40 per cent of the boys are from other cultures. PTA is an impressive group, raising around £60,000 each year for the benefit of pupils and for school developments.

School runs mock test days for around 2,000 children each year wanting to prepare for 11+ entry into selective grammar schools. When an application for a government grant to convert classrooms into a science lab was unsuccessful, PTA stepped in to help with the cost. The Suttonians have a very active old boys' network and a large number of them remain involved with the school. Famous alumni include Brian Paddick, Christopher Bigsby, David Bellamy and David Farrar.

Entrance: Places are highly sought after, with around 1,500 boys competing for 135 places at 11+. School sets its own exam, reasoning paper, English and maths. Currently no catchment area, so highest scorers win the places. At 16+, approximately five competitive entry places are available for newcomers to the sixth form.

Exit: Almost all to university, although the occasional pupil takes up a specialist apprenticeship in the workplace. Twelve to Oxbridge in 2016, 14 studying medicine in the UK and in Europe with good numbers also opting for veterinary sciences. Others to a range of top universities, with London colleges, Southampton, Exeter, Bristol and Warwick all popular.

Remarks: School offers fantastic opportunities for those who make the grade. A must for academically able and enthusiastic young men.

Sutton High School

55 Cheam Road, Sutton, Surrey SM1 2AX

Pupils: 663 • Ages: 3–18 • Sixth form: 75

Fees: £9,471 – £15,990 pa

Tel: 020 8642 0594
Email: admissions@sut.gdst.net
Website: www.suttonhigh.gdst.net

Headmistress: Since 2012, Mrs Katharine Crouch BSc NPQH. Biology degree from Leicester. Joined Sutton High School in 2003 and has held many roles including head of biology, head of pastoral and deputy head.

Head of junior school: Since 2015, Anne Musgrove. With a BA in education studies from the University of Warwick, she has over 20 years' experience of teaching in both the independent and maintained sectors including a number of years teaching in Australia. Formerly deputy head (academic) and acting head at Putney High Junior School, she joined Sutton High Junior School as deputy head in 2014 and was promoted to head of junior school. She continues to pursue her interest in art and art history by visiting galleries and museums in the UK and overseas.

Academic matters: Traditional junior school which aims to offer a broad and balanced curriculum to suit a range of tastes. Carefully structured early years stage focuses on instilling basic literacy and numeracy skills through structured play whilst also developing independence and confidence. Moving up the school, everything appears to be well planned, with lots of music, drama and sport alongside traditional subjects. Setting for maths from year 4 and English from year 5. Impressive foreign languages programme: French starts in the nursery, years 3 and 4 are introduced to Spanish and years 5 and 6 start German and Latin. Teaching staff includes a few old girls; all are unanimous about aiming to pass on and develop a love of learning and natural curiosity in their young charges. SENCo, and a part-time specialist teacher for small group work or one-to-one tuition, assist children with mild specific learning difficulties or differences. There is also an EAL coordinator.

Solid results across the board in academics and the arts; 55 per cent A*/A at GCSE and 44 per cent at A level in 2016 (73 per cent A*/B). Head is very aware that today's young people need a range of skills and accomplishments to succeed in the competitive 21st century world; provision throughout the school is being reviewed and updated. Teachers are currently trialling the best way to maximise each individual's potential; consequently, girls are set according to ability and their strongest learning style. School appreciates the importance of ICT skills, offering DiDA (Diploma in Digital Applications) and GCSE qualifications and an ICT club. Separate or dual award science. Maths fairly strong all round, although some parents feel that less confident mathematicians should be identified and assisted much earlier. Good, practical help is also available: everyone is taught about budgeting and money management. Very impressive results for Latin; French, Spanish, German and Latin are offered throughout the school, with Greek run as an after-school class. Decent number of trips both here and abroad. Lots of girl-power on the staff – female majority – who are all committed to ensuring there are no ceilings or barriers for any pupil. Small number of pupils with mild dyslexia are monitored and supported by the SENCo; provision for EAL.

Sixth formers undertake the Extended Project Qualification to help prepare them for university. Girls say it's quite a lot of extra work alongside A levels, but they generally consider it a good thing to do. Enrichment course enables sixth formers to look at a wider range of topics and skills from cookery to philosophy. Friday afternoons are set aside for community service and fundraising activities. Girls collaborate with Sutton Grammar boys for a number of activities, including the Challenge of Management conference, giving them the opportunity to gain an insight into the business world. Biannual careers fair invites representatives from many companies into the school to pitch career paths and ideas to the girls.

Games, options, the arts: Fab facilities and very active and successful sports department. Enormous gym and 25m indoor pool, which is open to pupils and their families at weekends and in the holidays. Gymnastics is popular and there is a beautiful new dance hall for budding ballerinas and dancing divas. Sporty girls compete in house and in local competitions, and do particularly well in county athletics and cross-country championships. Assortment of sports tours organised annually to all parts of the globe.

The arts fare well across the school, particularly music: dedicated music teachers, lots of practice rooms and music technology suite. Different choirs to choose from, traditional to gospel, depending on the girls' interests. Fine groups of young instrumentalists play in a range of ensembles; tuition can be arranged for any instrument, subsequently, dynamic and well-thought-of orchestras. All this considered, rather a low take-up of GCSE and A level music. In-house and joint music concerts and drama productions with Sutton Grammar. Largish hall for drama, department always welcomes volunteers who'd like to help with staging or learn to use lighting equipment. Girls also have the opportunity to take the LAMDA acting and speaking exams.

Light, airy art rooms and a separate sculpture hut for pottery, an area where girls are particularly successful. Artistic types are offered the full range of art and design courses through to A level, being able to choose from painting and pottery, textiles, and resistant materials. More inventing and designing for all age groups goes on through the Young Enterprise Scheme.

Some lovely creations, textiles, paintings and sculptures, are displayed around the school. Lunchtime and after-school clubs, for which an additional charge is made, offer further opportunities for sports and music. Most subject teachers run drop-in clinics to provide extra support for individuals and extension work.

Well-stocked library in the junior school has aptly been renamed the Discovery Zone. Colourful corridors lined with children's art, poetry and other achievements. Neat and amenable girls appear beautifully behaved, happy and involved in their work. Drama is incorporated into the English curriculum and taught by class teachers; girls are encouraged to take LAMDA grade exams, organised by visiting teachers. Dedicated music teacher works extremely hard and successfully, producing two big concerts each year, as well as regular musical assemblies. All pupils learn keyboard and recorder in class; individual tuition is available on any other instrument.

Background and atmosphere: Founded in 1884 with just a handful of pupils. Over the years, as pupil numbers have grown, neighbouring buildings have been purchased alongside a rolling building programme to keep pace with modern demands. Latest additions include the sixth form centre and sports complex.

In the midst of all the buildings, well-maintained gardens and sports areas create a cloistered look. Busy pupils move round the site in an orderly way. Girls have a good local reputation and the school is always interested in setting up community links, the most well known being their work and artistic pursuits with Sutton Boys Grammar. Old Girls' Association has a reunion at school every year.

Pastoral care, well-being and discipline: The headmistress is very keen to review and develop the pastoral care, so that she can build on the good foundations. All new entrants are allocated a buddy to chat to and to help them overcome any small problems. Professional counsellor visits weekly and there is also a school nurse. Head is clued up about the emotional needs and external pressures that affect young people. Form tutors and heads of year monitor academic progress, personal welfare and development. Student council helps compile the code of conduct in partnership with staff, giving everybody a chance to have their say.

Pupils and parents: Good mix, socially and ethnically; lots of local business families and City types. Others travel from the edges of south-west London and various parts of Surrey; school is conveniently located close to Sutton station so attracts a wide catchment. School minibus services from Wimbledon, Southfields, Epsom and Ashtead areas. The Parent-Staff Association works to arrange social events and to further sporting opportunities through the parent-run clubs Otter and Centipede. Staff and parents organise an annual multicultural evening. Interesting group of old girls include Dora Black (Lady Russell), Susan Howatch, novelist, and BBC correspondent Sue Littlemore.

Entrance: Girls can join the nursery from their third birthday onwards and move onto reception at 4+. Younger children attend an informal play session before being offered a place; from 6+ girls sit assessment tests. For entry into other years telephone the school to enquire about occasional places.

At 11+ examination in maths, English and online non-verbal reasoning tests plus an interview with a senior member of staff. At 16+ entrance test consisting of general papers, verbal reasoning and interview with the head of sixth form. At least eight GCSEs, grade A or above in subjects chosen for A level.

Exit: At 11+ around two-thirds of the junior girls move to the senior school. Remainder move to co-ed or local grammar schools. Girls who are not suited to the senior school will be advised in year 5 to give them plenty of time to look for an alternative.

At 16+ some move to co-ed or grammar school sixth forms (20 per cent left after GCSEs in 2016). At 18+ more or less everybody goes to a wide variety of mostly top universities or art colleges. Science, maths and dentistry courses for about half. Others to study history, languages and art, one gaining place on BBC Broadcast Engineering sponsored degree and apprenticeship. None to Oxbridge in 2016.

Money matters: Academic scholarships at 11+ and 16+ based on top performance in entrance or public exams. Other small scholarships awarded for art, music, drama and PE. Means-tested GDST bursaries are also available.

Remarks: Would suit those who want a single sex education in a calm environment. Parents and friends are looking forward to the head bringing all the school's strengths out into the light. A school to watch?

Sydenham High School

19 Westwood Hill, London SE26 6BL

Pupils: 600 • Ages: 4–18 • Sixth form: 70

Fees: £12,348 – £15,702 pa

Tel: 020 8557 7000
Email: info@syd.gdst.net
Website: www.sydenhamhighschool.gdst.net

Headteacher: Since April 2017, Katharine Woodcock, previously senior deputy head at Queen's College. French and Russian degree from Bristol and PGCE from St Mary's College Twickenham. Has also taught at Oakham, where she was became housemistress. She has two children.

Head of junior school: Since 2014, Ms Claire Boyd, previously head of lower school and on the senior leadership team of Ravenscourt Park Prep. She has a politics degree from Royal Holloway College and a PGCE from Roehampton.

Academic matters: French for all from 4, Latin is taught to the top two years. Masterclasses at senior school for years 5 and 6 (most recently in maths, science, history and Spanish); sixth formers run clubs and activities. Junior school currently caters for range of mild SEN: dyspraxia, dyslexia, dyscalculia, Asperger's, autism, ADD, ADHD and EBD, but all must be able to manage the curriculum. Some specialist support available.

Of course the school has an eye to results and, given its broad intake, achieves well. In 2016, 63 per cent A*/A at GCSE and 80 per cent A*-B, 45 per cent A*/A at A level. But it hasn't lost sight of the need to relieve the pressure and inject fun into, in particular, years 9-11.

Many activities designed to develop personal learning and thinking skills and break the routine. A parent attendee at the year 7 study skills workshop throws up her arms: 'Why oh why didn't schools teach me good habits so early on?' Year 12 has a busy schedule of outside speakers to help pupils make decisions about their future, plus a professional skills programme aiming to develop skills in eg networking, teamwork and problem solving. In younger years an annual off-timetable day encourages them to reflect on themselves as learners using anything from Dragon's Den workshops to mixed discussion groups.

Staff clearly recognise technology's potential to engage pupils. In its first year, the maths blog with lesson podcasts received over 37,000 hits in the run-up to GCSE, indicating the high standard of teaching in this area. Other web-based tools are available and staff welcome email contact, particularly during study leave and from parents with concerns. Pupils can take some GCSEs early to free up time for other interests and areas of study. Science is an area of strength – two year 10 and sixth form pupils recently won national awards and another sixth former a Nuffield bursary to study cancer treatments at King's College. Getting science GCSE out of the way in year 10 doesn't deter pupils from taking it up again in sixth form and beyond. Care is taken to highlight the relevance to different careers, leading to a high proportion taking science-based degree subjects. Their flying in the face of gender stereotyping is a source of great pride at the school.

As you move around the school, there's a real feeling that pupils and staff feed off each other's enthusiasm. The teacher looking on almost smugly, they positively fall over themselves to show off their geography presentations. The GDST network also provides a wider forum for experience and idea exchange, impressing many parents. 'Staff are endlessly inventive and flexible in meeting different pupils' needs.' It helps being relatively small. 'Many pupils leaving after GCSEs are surprised how much they miss being known to staff and the reassurance that familiarity provides,' said one parent and, as many others, identified it as a real asset which the school often doesn't do enough to promote. SEN pupils are well-catered for too. There is dyslexia screening and other testing in year 7 and the Learning Strategy Team provides by all accounts excellent tailored support with a clear focus on inclusivity. Says the head, 'We know girls don't want to feel different, and if printing exam papers on yellow paper helps some of them, then why not do it for all?'

Games, options, the arts: Stalwart and welcome efforts from newer staff to raise interest and standards in sports are reaping rewards. Regular netball and hockey clubs are well attended and successes against local schools are notching up. Rugby, football and cricket also have a keen following – they are not girly-girls. Trampolining is popular and, to encourage the less sporty, there is dance (very popular), fencing, golf and scuba diving. The latest addition is rowing; the team trains alongside Dulwich College and will be competing for the first time this year. Even so, most parents agree that this is not the best place for the more competitive, 'never happier than when on a games pitch' girl. The separation by a short bus ride of the main school site from the major eight-acre sporting facilities is probably a deterrent, but also the distraction of other strong departments, most notably music and drama. However, recent initiative, the SydElite programme, gives monitoring, mentoring and workshop support to talented athletes balancing high level sport with academic and social life.

Supervised and informal music and drama rehearsals are very much in evidence around the school, with girls so absorbed that they barely seem to register your passing. Even those not opting to take exams get involved and opportunities abound. In addition to two junior and two senior drama productions each year; a variety of choirs and orchestras, ranging from wind, guitar, string and jazz, perform regularly with an expanded schedule of diverse concerts in the school's new 90-seater recital hall, complete with music technology department. A number of girls have auditioned successfully to appear in West End shows and the school choir has performed at many prestigious venues, including the Royal Albert Hall. Standards are high, but above all girls seem to relish the freedom of being able to join up with friends and enjoy themselves. The slightly chaotic art room is overflowing with talent and more and more are going on to study art-related subjects at university. Usual range of extracurricular clubs, including D of E and some, such as ICT, maths and DT, designed to bolster academic progress. More unusual tastes – code-breaking, Japanese and fashion – are catered for too. Recent additions to enrichment activities include cookery for years 7 and 12 and first aid, photography and indoor rock climbing for year 12.

Background and atmosphere: The original Victorian buildings where the school opened in 1887 are across the road. In 1934 the school transferred to its current main building which is slightly set back and surrounded by a jumble of more recent additions, most prominently the music block and sports hall. While they provide welcome facilities they, and the sixth form block, rather detract from its overall elegance. Away from the busy road with buses struggling up the hill, you can imagine girls sunning themselves on the terrace overlooking the large Astroturf pitch bordered by mature trees. Inside, a relaxed, friendly and purposeful air with girls unselfconsciously running from one lesson to the next. 'So nice that they don't seem to feel the need to have the latest phone or bag.' Intimate feel in the sixth form block. 'Some felt uncomfortable being in a small independent girls' school but those of us left behind really appreciate it.'

Good facilities in junior school, new library and IT suite, classrooms brimming with lively displays. New playgrounds, additional classrooms and specialist science, art and ICT facilities were all recently added; more redevelopment in progress to improve appearances and movement between floors. Close links with senior school – head spends an afternoon a week in the junior school, takes assembly, which girls love and say is a very special time. Year 6 girls permitted to wear senior uniform.

Pastoral care, well-being and discipline: Parents praise staff for understanding girls' different character traits and identifying individual strengths, focusing on those in order to develop all-round confidence. Nice touches such as cards of congratulation posted home and the odd hug in the younger years. They also sense a 'spirit of sisterhood' and 'moral strength' amongst the girls, which prompts them to be mutually supportive and keep each other in line, generally without disciplinary measures from staff. The school prides itself on understanding girls; the needs of each year group are carefully considered and programmes developed to support them. A full-day of PSHCE each term often involves outside speakers and is designed to engage pupils fully. There is a clear underlying message. If they are to succeed, they must take the initiative and think for themselves.

S

Pupils and parents: Tends to attract creative parents – as well as some from established professions – of varied social, cultural and racial backgrounds who don't feel their girls would completely fit the mould elsewhere. They and staff tend to think of the girls as 'edgy, quirky and boundary-pushers' though they don't overtly appear so (little evidence of uniform rules being stretched). They want their uniqueness to be celebrated and for them to have the freedom to be themselves. For most it is a careful investment calculated to bring maximum return – many first time buyers. Old girls include actress Margaret Lockwood, Philippa Darbre (scientist), Sophie McKenzie (author), Sandy Powell (Oscar winning costume designer), Claire Bennett (fencing champion) and Winifred Gerin (writer) and Apprentice finalist businesswoman Bianca Miller.

Entrance: Informal entry assessment at 3+ – 'gives us an edge over some of our competitors who do formal assessment –

children skip out of here, find experience enjoyable, even fun.' 'Weed out the stroppy and difficult' so hope it doesn't fall on a day when your child's in a bad mood.

Of around 200 applicants for senior school; 40-50 girls join the 30-plus coming up from the junior school. Most are from local preps and state primaries, although also from Wandsworth, Bromley and, since the opening of the East London overground, from north of the river. Many have brothers at Dulwich College. The head and senior teaching staff interview all girls, inviting them to talk about something they are proud of. They also take an entrance exam in English and maths in which they are expected to attain equivalent to level 4 or 5 in national curriculum KS2. Occasionally places come up in other year groups and the school is keen to expand its sixth form (currently there's capacity for 35 students in each of Years 12 and 13). Overall there's been a drop in numbers in recent years, which the head attributes to the effects of the economic downturn and more boys' schools opening up to girls.

Exit: Around two-thirds to three-quarters of juniors to senior school. Rest to a range of schools, both state and private, including other GDST schools. Progression to senior school expected but not automatic. After GCSEs some feel they have outgrown the school. Cost-saving, convenience and co-education are also factors and about 50 per cent leave; some to go to local state schools or co-ed independents and some to board outside London. Of those who stay, occasional Oxbridge places (one in 2016) and others going to eg York, Warwick, King's College London, Manchester, Exeter.

Remarks: The school doesn't have an instant wow factor but there's a palpable, almost defiant, energy running through the place. It seems to say, 'I will be who I want to be'. Girls emerge independent thinkers and confident communicators. All credit to the school that they become so in a happy, mostly settled environment.

Sylvia Young Theatre School

1 Nutford Place, London W1H 5YZ

Pupils: 263 (25 boarders stay with host families) • Ages: 10–16

Fees: £13,500 – £13,800 pa

Tel: 020 7258 2330
Email: info@sylviayoungtheatreschool.co.uk
Website: www.syts.co.uk

Principal: Since 1981, Sylvia Young OBE (70s). The founding principal, she is something of a legend in London's theatreland and has been supplying junior talent to the West End stage for over 30 years. With some early training, she decided 'performance was not for me', but soon realised she had a knack for spotting and inspiring talent in others. She started on a small scale, working with local children at a youth club in east London, then launched a full-time school at the suggestion of one of the parents. The school is her passion and she now lives on the site with her husband. Two grown-up daughters have both entered the profession, one (Frances Ruffelle) as a Tony-winning actress and singer, the other (Alison) as a theatrical agent. Her granddaughter is the pop singer Eliza Doolittle. Sylvia Young is a sympathetic soul, whose persistence and drive has developed the school from a walk-on role to full stardom. 'It's the Oxbridge of theatre schools', said one parent. She was appointed OBE in 2005 for services to the arts.

Since 2005, Ms Frances Chave BSc PGCE (40s) has been the academic and pastoral head. Ms Chave read maths at Exeter University, followed by a PGCE at Southampton, then taught at two large comprehensives (Cranford Community College and Feltham Community College), before helping to set up a third, Overton Grange School in Sutton, where she was deputy head. 'When I decided to move on, I wanted something completely different', she says. Sylvia Young is about as different as it gets and Ms Chave has steadily improved the academic offering, particularly on the science side. A strong and sensible presence, she enjoys theatre, 'but only as a spectator', and in her spare time plays golf and other sports.

Academic matters: The school has long been known for the high standard of tuition in the performing arts, and has put increasing emphasis on the more academic side of the curriculum. 'We decided early on we didn't want our pupils to lose out by coming to a theatre school', says the founder. The school is unusual in that it hives off academic lessons into three hard-working days on Mondays, Tuesdays and Wednesdays, leaving Thursdays and Fridays free for professional studies. The subdivision is reasonably demanding. 'Both staff and students have to be very focused,' says Ms Chave. Unsurprisingly, the academic curriculum is more compact than you'd find in a mainstream school – so no PE (no need with all that dancing), geography or DT – and the emphasis is definitely on the arts. All pupils study English lang and lit, maths, science (core and additional), expressive arts and drama to GCSE, when other options include music, art, media studies, history and Spanish. English, drama and theatre studies are the most successful GCSEs, but the head has worked hard to bring up attainment in science and maths (both of which are set).

Results are respectable, and 2016 saw the percentage of pupils getting five or more GCSEs at A*-C including English and maths at 70, with the percentage of A*/A grades at 28. 'Most of our pupils do better than expected', says Ms Chave. 'If you're somewhere you really want to be, it does have a knock-on effect'. Parents agree: 'My daughter was at a mainstream academic school before. Here she's achieved because she wants to, not because she's being pushed'.

The school, which is non-selective academically, tests all pupils for learning difficulties on entry and copes well with moderate problems, from dyslexia to Asperger's. 'We have two children here on the autistic spectrum, one's a great dancer, the other a great actor'. Well-qualified SENCo oversees help in class and out, with teachers kept well in the loop. Inevitably, lessons here are interrupted by professional work, but no one is allowed to lag behind. 'We have very good systems in place to catch up,' says Ms Chave. 'Every week staff write out what has been covered in class and what has been set for homework and everyone gets a copy'. Students are expected to make up what they've missed in their own time. 'They're amazingly adaptable, they just fit straight back in'. When a professional engagement is protracted, staff liaise directly with on-set tutors.

Games, options, the arts: The performing arts are of course the raison d'être of this all-singing, all-dancing institution and Thursdays and Fridays are devoted to the training needs of aspiring stars. Many of the performing arts staff are themselves working professionals and don't spare their students from the profession's harder knocks. (At one lesson the Guide attended, the class was asked to vote on the best singer.) Students are set by ability across the age range in all the performing disciplines – so, for example, a talented year 7 may be in the same ballet class as a less nimble year 11. Everyone studies all aspects of drama, music and dance, with classes ranging from voice production to recording technique, and all take annual LAMDA exams in speech and drama. All pupils, too, are represented by the in-house

Sylvia Young Agency and put forward for professional work, ranging from West End musicals (the school regularly supplies cast members for Matilda and Billy Elliot) to advertising voice-overs and language tapes. 'You have to understand what a real performance is like', says Sylvia Young, 'and you have to learn that you may not get picked because you're not right for the part, no matter how talented you are. It's part of the training'. The school takes care, however, to ensure work doesn't interfere with academic priorities. 'My daughter has GCSEs coming up and they don't allow her to go off every five minutes', said one parent. 'School work comes first'.

Background and atmosphere: The school started out by running part-time classes in the 1970s, then opened full-time in Drury Lane in 1981. In 1983 it moved to Marylebone and in 2010 transferred into spacious premises in a converted Christian Science church just behind Marble Arch. The refurbished building provides excellent facilities for both the vocational and academic, with 10 purpose-built studios, two computer rooms, two science labs, two bright art rooms and a small library (mainly used for catching up with homework). Priorities, now as always, remain the family atmosphere and care of and attention to children, whether they're constantly in work or destined for a civilian career ('we do sometimes have to tell parents a child doesn't have what it takes for performance'). Regardless of the eventual outcome, all are equipped with valuable 'transferable skills' – confidence and the ability to communicate well and work with adults: 'The aim is to ensure they're secure in themselves', says Sylvia Young. Parents say pupils take on board the virtue of industry. 'They know the world they're contemplating is fiercely competitive', said one mother, 'and it's not going to be an easy ride. They learn a very strong work ethic'. Though clearly those who've gotta dance or act or sing (or all three) are ideally served here, the school works equally well for those who might want to enter the profession in more self-effacing roles. 'They teach you about every aspect from choreography to TV'. Twenty or so pupils board with London host families (generally present or past parents), often in groups of two or three. 'The woman my son boards with is marvellous', says one mother. 'She picks him up from the theatre at night, makes sure he does his homework, and arranges fun evenings of singing or games'.

Pastoral care, well-being and discipline: This is a school which is essentially about self-discipline, and disciplinary problems of the mainstream sort are rare. 'We don't have bullying', says Sylvia Young firmly, 'just children being silly sometimes'. The school monitors each child carefully, with an individual log kept on each. 'The children know they can come to us and we'll listen'. Parents feel confident their children are happy. 'My son feels so lucky. He is doing what he wants to do every day and there aren't many adults who can say that'.

The school has a strong disciplinary structure. 'We're very firm about the basics,' says Ms Young. Rules are clearly spelled out – no make-up, no micro skirts, no uploading of photographs onto the internet (a serious danger in a school where celebrity is a daily fact of life) – and consistently enforced. 'Other schools have these rules, but at Sylvia Young they really impose them', said one parent. 'It's quite old fashioned'. Two uniforms, one for academic work (white shirts, blazers, jumpers and ties), another for vocational days (tracksuits and unitards). Both are neatly worn.

Pupils and parents: Parents cover the full range. 'They're not pushy stage-school parents at all', says Ms Young. 'They're a very normal group, from all backgrounds'. Though certainly some are affluent, many really struggle to send their children here and travel considerable distances to do so. The children, of course, are as diverse as the parents, but significantly more talented than the average. They're all here because they really want to be. One parent told us: 'My son, who'd been at a local primary school, said when he first saw Sylvia Young, "Mum, it's amazing. I just fit in there".' Others who fitted in equally well include Billie Piper, Denise van Outen, former Spice Girl Emma Bunton, Jade Ewen from The Sugababes, Nathan Sykes of The Wanted and the late Amy Winehouse, whose father has set up a scholarship in her memory.

Entrance: The first entry point is year 6. 'Year 6 is a good time to come', says Sylvia Young, 'because either pupils can continue into year 7 or they have time to go elsewhere. A few decide it's not what they want'. Most enter at year 7, with the occasional place at other times. At all ages, the audition is the most important part of the process. The school offers a preliminary audition, with low-key workshops. Those with most potential are invited back to perform two drama pieces (one from Shakespeare and a modern work), a song and a dance. Candidates also sit academic tests in English and maths. 'But we're not a grammar school. We just need to feel happy they'll cope with the pace and be able to get done in three days what most do in five'. That said, the stronger an applicant is on the professional side, the more leeway is given academically. Motivation, too, is carefully examined. 'There's a lot of discussion about what the child wants and what the parents are looking for'. The school sees up to 500 applicants for 40 places at 11.

Exit: Pupils are assessed at the end of years 8 and 9, which provides an opportunity for families to reassess their child's career path. Currently all move on at 16 (though the school is developing plans for a sixth form). About half go on to specialist colleges, often with scholarships or bursaries to study dance, drama or musical theatre; the rest to traditional academic sixth forms to do A levels and then frequently to study drama at university. Destinations include The Arts Educational School, Hurtwood House and Elstree UTC, which offers technical training in the visual and creative arts. School has close links with central London tutorial colleges (Lansdowne, Duff Miller etc) and some pupils move on to these.

Money matters: Three official scholarships (one full and two half), and many more get some sort of help. Quite a number put their theatrical earnings towards the fees.

Remarks: A school which combines a sound academic background with outstanding vocational training and professional opportunity. Hard work, but hard work undertaken with purposeful pleasure.

Tetherdown Primary School

Grand Avenue, London N10 3BP

Pupils: 420 • Ages: 4–11

Tel: 020 8883 3412
Email: admin@tetherdownschool.org
Website: www.tetherdownschool.org

T

Headteacher: Since 2013, Tony Woodward BEd music (late 40s). Started off teaching on his home turf of Solihull, West Midlands, at a 'challenging' primary school where he became music and art co-ordinator. He came to London in 1997 to work as head of juniors at Rushy Meadow Primary School in Sutton, where he stayed for the next four years. Following this he became deputy head at nearby Robin Hood Junior School, and then moved on to become head teacher of another local school, Warren Mead Junior – prior to his headship at Tetherdown. His work in Surrey also saw him as a local leader in education, supporting leaders of struggling local schools and as an additional Ofsted inspector.

Primary schools are where this head has always wanted to be: 'It means I get to work with a whole range of ages from 4 to 11 year olds.' His parents were both road safety officers who went into schools to teach, so being around this as a young boy gave this head a taste of how teaching can really make a difference to children. Indeed, in the last two years since Mr Woodward took over the daunting mantle of one of north London's leading state primary schools, he has already set about trying to make a difference to the school by introducing a lot more sport into the curriculum. One parent told us: 'Before Mr Woodward became head, the school was solely about academia and there was not much time factored in for anything else. '

Mr Woodward has since appointed a PE co-ordinator and a PE coach, and has set up a wide variety of sports clubs, both curricular and extracurricular, including football, netball, hockey, gymnastics and swimming. The school even won Haringey Sporting School of The Year recently and has won several trophies for football, tag rugby and cross-country. He is himself a keen sporting man (which is perhaps why it is so important for him) – trampolining was his specialty, and he came second in the European Championships at the height of his competitive career.

One parent praised the new rigour which Mr Woodward has imposed in his short tenure at the school: 'There seems to be a lot more organisation around the admin side of the school and with regards to homework – which was getting a bit haphazard before he came on board.' Another said: 'Mr Woodward has a positive manner and a clear vision of how he wants things to be.'

This is a head whom we suspect quietly worms away behind the scenes rather than being a front of house guy. That's not to say his presence is not noted around the school (some say quite visible), but he doesn't come across as a massive PR man. He does the job he was employed to do, but don't expect a big sales pitch, or well rehearsed spiel. He likes to unwind by playing the piano and cooking.

Entrance: The school admits 60 pupils in reception, but there's still fierce competition to get in. In the past it was only siblings and those living feet from the gates who stood a chance, now at least an address in the same street might reasonably be expected to do the trick. (Needless to say property prices nearby have their own exotic micro-climate.) One family (we are told) is even in the process of building their own house virtually opposite the school to ensure entrance. Parents can view the school in the autumn term prior to entry, kids visit in the summer term before they start.

Exit: Lucky pupils whose parents bought wisely in the area are also pretty much guaranteed a smooth transition to one of the capital's best comprehensives. Smug parents, who've sorted it all by the age of 4, tend to assume their children will proceed to Fortismere, and the vast majority do go on here. The rest to North London grammar schools such as The Latymer or leading independents – including a fair chunk to Mill Hill School and Highgate and a few to Channing. ('This is Muswell Hill,' said one mother; 'parents tutor without hesitation.')

Remarks: Despite a recent Ofsted demotion from 'outstanding' to 'good', Tetherdown remains one of London's top performing primary schools. This is a school which regularly sits near the top of the local authority league tables and, even in an average year, over 50 per cent of pupils reach level 5 in English and maths. 'Teaching is consistently good, with some that is outstanding,' says Ofsted. Parents would agree, but there has been a high turnover of staff in recent years, which has been noticed and commented on by pupils. One told us: 'There were so many teachers and teaching assistants that came and went in year 4 – none of them seemed to last more than a few weeks, I'm not sure why'. However, the head is keen to point out that that was an exceptional year and not the norm (and the shortage was mainly down to maternity leave). 'There was a period of instability, but we are back on track and currently have a very stable staff team.'

One reason for its demotion by Ofsted was because 'a few high-attaining pupils are not always sufficiently challenged'. One parent told us: 'Tetherdown is a great local school if your child can just get on and do the work and doesn't need extra intervention in any way. However, if your child is particularly able or, conversely, has any special needs, it doesn't cater well for that.' However, another parent strongly disagreed: 'My child does require extra help and the school does have good SEN provisions – his needs were picked up on early on. But I would say that you do really do have to push for everything and communication is not as good as it could be.' Communication is something the school has been working on a great deal: 'We have an open door policy – parents are invited to feed in as well as receive feedback.'

With meticulous monitoring, more than a dollop of regular homework (one and half hours weekly up to year 3, then a whole lot more), and dedicated parents willing to supervise nightly reading from reception to year 6, you get some idea of how good results happen. The school follows the national curriculum but adds its own flourishes, with a good emphasis on making learning fun – whether this be tricky Tudor recipes, studying maths with the help of a visiting Maths Clown or sharpening up those multiplication tables in Beat the Parents at Mental Maths. 'The children have a lovely education,' said one parent. Pupils are rewarded by pyjama days and a system of rewards. Pupils are grouped, extended and supported according to ability. Recent requirement for the inclusion of modern language teaching is provided by French lessons from year 2, and the school is looking into the possibility of Mandarin.

Plenty of stretching and thinking in all directions, whether in an opera workshop or an after-school street dance club. Plenty of creative parents, too, who come in to share their expertise. All children learn to play the ocarina (Peruvian recorder) and individual instrumental tuition, subsidised by the local authority, is provided during the working day. Sport, which was previously the weakest link, is now more expansive and better equipped. In year 6, all children learn swimming and travel outside the school for specialist coaching. Breakfast club and plenty of lunchtime and after-school activities eg choir, drama, gymnastics and spy club. Regular school trips include an annual outing to the seaside for years 2 and 5, as well as visits to the British and Science Museums and trips to the local mosque.

Virtually all parents and pupils live within a few surrounding streets and the school has always offered an exceptionally tight-knit community. Expansion has marginally diluted the atmosphere, but has brought advantages. 'It used to be very much like a village school, where everyone knew each other and older pupils looked out for the younger ones,' said one mother with children at both ends of the spectrum. 'That was comforting, but sometimes your child didn't have a particularly wide choice of friends. Now there's plenty of scope.' Indeed, the school prides itself on having a 'wide mix of cultures, religions, backgrounds and languages.'

All classes are supported by exciting innovations in technology and children learn to communicate learning through a variety of platforms, including multi-media presentations, pupil-led video articles, iPad technology and even create their own apps.

The school has no uniform and rules are kept to a minimum. 'We have just three rules. Respect yourself, respect others and respect your environment. If you respect yourself you are going to work hard to become the best you can.' Parents admire the way these principles are implemented. Those demonstrating behavioural challenges are given the same support as those with academic problems – with intervention and targets. Children are encouraged to get involved: with the school council; with each other's welfare (by becoming play leaders and buddies); and with the broader community (for example, running a soup kitchen at harvest time). They are also lavished with praise. Regular 'Achievements Assemblies' recognise work, effort and attitude. Anti-bullying is promoted throughout the school (as was evident by a large wall montage entirely devoted to bullying), because bullying has been an issue in the past. 'We take bullying very seriously, like any school, but we make children very aware about bullying, we liaise closely with the parents and we always use circle time and assemblies to make children aware.'

Tetherdown is located in North London's prosperous, professional Muswell Hill and the parent body is a mirror of the locality, with plenty of engaged parents who devote the same attention to reading rotas and library duty as they give to successful careers. However, one parent said that the school could do more to maximise the use of parents: 'There are many parents like me who are at home now, and have a variety of skills and could help more, but the school is not as proactive as it could be at utilising us more.' School maintains that parents are welcome 'to volunteer their time to share their expertise, support admin tasks and promote the school's high expectations', although they have found that parents are most often taking the opportunity to return to work.

Very active Parent School Association (PSA), which raised £25,000 last year and used the money to underwrite school trips, build a new woodland play area in the junior playground and contribute towards reading books and general resources. The head is very supportive of the PSA, which has been welcomed by parents. He says: 'Finance for the school is always one of our biggest challenges. This school is one of the lowest funded schools in Haringey because it is perceived as being in a wealthy area. What money we have, we invest in staff.'

Parents at the school are highly ambitious for their kids and for the school, 'some wanting a private school education from a state school.' One disgruntled parent told us: 'This used to be the school of choice in the area, but now according to our local newspaper, is the one you go for if you can't get into Coldfall, Muswell Hill or Rhodes Avenue.' We remain confident that it will resume that status again.

Thames Christian College

Wye Street, London SW11 2HB

Pupils: 125 • Ages: 11–16

Fees: £14,160 pa

Tel: 020 7228 3933
Email: info@thameschristiancollege.org.uk
Website: www.thameschristiancollege.org.uk

Executive Head: Since 2006, Stephen Holsgrove (50s) PhD. Studied engineering and ICT; before setting up Thames Christian College he worked as a development director of a software engineering company. Married to Catherine; three daughters, who all attended the school, two are now pursuing their own careers, the youngest is studying performing arts. Catherine is the school registrar and runs all the administration. Head and governors are all committed to making a difference to future generation's education and lives. They hope that in the future Thames will be a model for further similar establishments.

Academic matters: A non-selective school doing extremely well by its pupils, who mostly outperform their predicted grades. In 2016, 91 per cent of pupils gained 5 A*-C grades including maths and English, with 48 per cent A*/A grades – a record year. The school commits to ensuring that, wherever possible, everyone achieves at least a C grade in English and maths. The ethos is to bring out the best in each individual and encourage pupils to find and develop their strengths. All pupils are monitored, small classes, setting for some subjects, as well as small group teaching for those who need it. Head of English is a bestselling author of English curriculum materials for 11 to 16-year-olds, so ideally placed to help everybody achieve the highest results. Good range of GCSE and IGCSE subjects to choose from; the options are tailored to each year group's preferences. Alongside maths, all study personal finance to prepare for running their own budgets, be it financing university or setting up a business. Everyone studies Spanish and there is an annual trip to Spain for a mixture of sightseeing and intensive Spanish lessons.

Lunchtime and after-school enrichment classes offer the opportunity to study in more depth. Ideal for those who need stretching. The school strives to broaden young minds with a variety of cross-curricular activities, eg medieval murder mysteries to solve, design a Tudor king's football kit, and film making. Thames is building its reputation for understanding how different types of pupils learn best. Whilst doing very well for its brightest pupils, it is also able to bring on pupils with specific learning differences: dyslexia, dyspraxia, mild Asperger's and those who have not fared well in much larger establishments. CreSTeD listed, the school has a dedicated team of learning support teachers. It prides itself on attracting well-qualified teachers, some of whom also work in their own industries, giving pupils an insight into the world of work and how certain skills and qualifications can translate into careers. Parents feel they are prepared to go the extra mile to assist pupils in their learning.

Games, options, the arts: Excellent art department nurtures much budding talent and achieves outstanding results. Art curriculum has recently been redesigned to give pupils the option of taking two art GCSEs, graphic communications and fine art. The graphics element includes a brief designed by a creative director of an advertising agency, who is a visiting lecturer at the school. Part of this course involves pupils having to pitch their ideas for client presentations. Design and technology curriculum introduces pupils to ceramics, woodwork, sculpture and textiles. PE teacher and various specialist coaches offer a range of different sporting activities and team games. The school uses local sports centre facilities and the various courts and pitches at Wandsworth common. Strong drama, led by a working actress; pupils study the LAMDA Bronze Certificate and other LAMDA qualifications. New keyboards and mixing desks are part of the update to the music department, there is a band and choir, and two professional singers amongst the staff. Tuition on any instrument can be arranged and many pupils choose to have individual instrumental lessons. The school has links with a primary school to give pupils the opportunity to work with children in the community. Community projects involve drama, music, art, sewing and a mentoring scheme. Friday afternoons are dedicated to clubs. Each term a selection of clubs and societies: eg inventions club, textiles, debating, current affairs and creative writing.

Background and atmosphere: Founded by executive head and his wife, Thames Christian College opened its doors in 2000 with 12 pupils; today it accommodates over 120. Having viewed secondary school choices in London for their own children, the Holsgroves decided there was room for something a little different, and decided to set up their own school. The underlying principles of the school involve individuals and values alongside top service delivery. Their aim, to provide suitable education in a safe environment, has paid off: the school generally expands year-on-year. The atmosphere is about hard work and caring for each other rather than flashy facilities.

Pastoral care, well-being and discipline: As a Christian foundation, the school's ethos centres on mutual respect, Christian values and understanding others' opinions. Pupils of all faiths and backgrounds who share these values are welcome. School rules are very clear and non-negotiable, expectations are high: behave sensibly, work to the best of your ability and be considerate to others at all times. Teachers need to be able to channel their energies into teaching rather than having to deal with discipline issues. 'We do have strict rules here,' say pupils, 'and things like bullying or any type of unkindness are not tolerated.'

Pupils and parents: Wide catchment area: families come from all over London and Surrey – the school is located a few minutes' walk from Clapham Junction. Pupils come from a variety of backgrounds; ethnic and social mix typical of the surrounding areas. Parents are encouraged to be involved and work collaboratively with the school, particularly with fundraising and religious festivals and celebrations. Thought to be a committed bunch, with shared values and hopes for their children's futures.

Entrance: 11+ test to assess potential and ability. Non-selective.

Exit: At 16+ most continue to A level or (occasionally) IB at maintained and independent schools in London and further afield. Destinations in 2016 included Alleyn's, Francis Holland, Parmiter's, Dartford Grammar School for Girls, City of London Freemen's School, Chislehurst & Sidcup Grammar School and Seaford College.

Money matters: A not-for-profit organisation; fees are inclusive, making them very competitive in comparison with other independent schools. Small number of means-tested bursaries available at the head's discretion. Up to five scholarships a year of up to 20 per cent for pupils joining year 7 for academic, art, music, performing arts and sport.

Remarks: Small is beautiful. A unique school set up to meet the needs of individuals. Able children are stretched, and for those who find school more of a challenge there is plenty of support.

Thomas Jones Primary School

T

St Mark's Road, London W11 1RQ

Pupils: 235 • Ages: 3–11

Tel: 020 7727 1423
Email: info@tj.rbkc.sch.uk
Website: www.thomasjonesschool.org

Head: Since 2001, Mr David Sellens OBE (for services to education), BA English, Goldsmiths (40s). Cut his teeth in teaching at New End Primary School in Hampstead, where he worked for five years as the youngest member of staff; 'I had a lot of energy, and the head at the time afforded me the luxury of opportunity.' His energy and enthusiasm swiftly saw him on the leadership team, at a time when the national curriculum was being implemented. However, feeling slightly constrained and wanting to do things his way, he started looking for a post where, he says, 'I could make a difference.' The role of deputy head came up at Ashburnham school and the young, enterprising Sellens, bursting with ideas, hotfooted it straight from artistic and aspirational Hampstead to a school south of the river in dire straits; 'I was suddenly thrust into an environment where results and aspirations were very low.' He and the new head, working closely together for sometimes up to 80 hour weeks, turned the school around over the next four years into Ofsted outstanding and awarded beacon status. Shortly afterwards, he was alerted to the fact that nearby Thomas Jones Primary School was on the verge of closure and, keen to become a head teacher, he applied for the post and promptly set about changing the fortunes of the school. Fourteen years on, he has exceeded the expectations of even the most optimistic.

In his second decade of tenure, Mr Sellens still appears like an enthusiastic and irrepressible newbie to the post. He is a hard man to pin down and his boundless energy sees him flit from one room to another, starting with the 8.45am meet and greet of all pupils and parents at the school gates; 'You'll like this,' he assures us; 'apologies if it gets a bit loud with the bell.' He describes his approach as radical rather than traditional. He teaches year 6 pupils English and says he doesn't pay 'too much attention' to the national curriculum. When asked if he sees himself as a bit of a maverick (after all, this is a head who walks into assembly eating a bowl of porridge and banana extolling the virtues of having a healthy breakfast, a head who ditches the traditional end of year musical, opting instead for Under Milk Wood), he says that although this comment has been levelled at him many times, he sees himself more as an individual who occasionally likes to 'buck the trend.'

Mr Sellens admits that he is 'incredibly fussy' about a lot of things. 'I'm fussy about [the state of] buildings, pupils' attire, their demeanour.' He also insists that pupils make eye contact with people and greet visitors with a handshake: 'He has meticulous attention to detail', one parent told us. This head is also big on homework – year 6 pupils can do up to two hours a night. Even with this 'bossy' approach, he says that he doesn't face much protest from pupils or parents, as there is a sense that 'it is being done for all the right reasons and the outcome is extremely strong.' One pupil said he was 'controlling – but in a good way.'

Brought up on the south coast, Mr Sellens says he was the typical story of an 'industrious' child from a humble background who won a place at grammar school and worked hard to better his situation. He always carried with him a strong sense of social justice which is what motivates him daily; 'I want to give every pupil the opportunity to shine, to look back and think they don't have regrets and it doesn't matter what they do, as long as they enjoy doing it.' When asked if he has any children of his own, he replies 'no', then pauses, has a think and says 'yes, 235 of them!'

Entrance: The catchment is so small for this one form primary school that you virtually have to live in the grounds to get in (we kid you not – one pupil who lives two doors away last year didn't qualify. Such was the outcry, she eventually managed to secure a place). The head says he is sometimes overwhelmed by the number of prospective parents, 'some with children who have yet to be born.' Distance from the school is now measured from the centre of the school outwards. (Mostly therefore to those in the nearby housing estate and their siblings).

Exit: Mainly to the local comprehensives – Holland Park or new Kensington Aldridge Academy; some try to gain bursaries or scholarships to independent schools. Last year, three children secured bursaries and scholarships to nearby Notting Hill Prep and further afield Christ's Hospital, West Sussex and King Edward's, Surrey.

Remarks: There are primary schools, and then there's Thomas Jones Primary school. Former secretary of state for education Michael Gove has waxed lyrical about this school on many occasions, claiming in one speech that it offers a better education than nearby £19,620 pa prep school which taught the heirs to the throne. He said: 'There are state primary schools every bit as ambitious, as supportive, as exciting, as the smartest of private prep schools – like for example, Thomas Jones Primary in West London.'

Named after Thomas Jones of North Carolina – a passionate crusader against the evils of slavery in the early part of the 19th century – this state primary in the borough of Kensington and Chelsea (a short walk from bustling Ladbroke Grove) is as true to its ideological namesake as it is to his inspirational work. By any stretch of the imagination it is a major achievement for a primary school serving a deprived inner city area to secure a rolling five year average of over 99 per cent of children achieving level 4 and above in maths and English – about three-quarters achieving grade 5+ and a few achieving level 6 in maths (often top in the borough for both subjects). What makes Thomas Jones's achievement even more remarkable is that barely any pupils who sit the tests come from an indigenous English-speaking background, with one in three speaking Arabic as their first language. Moreover, 30 per cent of last year's cohort were on the SEN register.

Nowhere is London's diversity of culture or chasm of social inequality better highlighted than at this school. One side of the school (Lancaster Road) is flanked by grand period properties where a three bedroom maisonette can set you back a mere £2m. The other side (St Mark's Road entrance) is a stone's throw away from a large, austere housing estate, 'not fit for purpose' we are told, which accounts for roughly 70 per cent of the school's intake. More than half of the pupils live in difficult circumstances and are entitled to free school meals; some of them, we are told, 'don't own a desk and do their homework on an upturned tray or in the local library.' One parent we spoke to told us that the strength of the school is its diversity, 'and that it caters for all.'

There is nothing ordinary about this school – certainly not if one compares it to other inner city state primaries. The interior is so immaculate and shiny we could see our own reflection in the wooden parquet flooring and the walls looked as if they had been freshly painted; 'we keep them white so it's easy to match and cover any dirt marks.' When asked how they manage to keep a primary school of 230 children so unbelievably pristine, Mr Sellens tells us that the pupils demonstrate real pride in the school and often ask to be on the 'cleaning rota.' For a bog standard (architecturally speaking) 1970s prefab, as this school is from the outside, the inside came as quite a revelation. Light and bright 'to create an illusion of space', the open plan and organic design is quite remarkable both in terms of its functionality and aesthetics.

The artwork which adorned the walls had been carefully selected and beautifully displayed, and we were particularly struck by some stunningly creative models of castles made from toilet rolls and other household objects, displayed outside the year 3 classroom. We also liked a large, colourful mosaic of Elmer the elephant with a large caption reading 'It's good to be different.'

And then there are the candles! This most certainly was a first for us and we wondered whether this was part school and part holistic retreat. Large (glass-encased) scented candles, wafting scents of vanilla or lavender, flickered on teachers' desks in all classrooms bar the ones with the youngest pupils. The result was a calm, almost hypnotic ambience, 'the antithesis of what some students get at home,' the head told us. We even heard classical music (from Schindler's List) emanate from the year 6 classroom as they were in deep discussion about their current literature book. As Ofsted remarked, 'Immersion in the plays of Shakespeare and high quality literature, such as Lord of the Flies, has instilled in pupils a love of literature and has enabled them to reflect with confidence.'

No doubt the school's recruitment policy has played some part in its outstanding achievement. Many teachers are recruited straight from university and stay for a few years before moving on, possibly to jobs outside London where they can more easily afford a home. 'Some of them are very talented, they are enthusiastic and idealistic..they want to teach in this type of environment – even if sometimes they don't stop for very long.' It is now a teaching school and can train its own. Sellens attributes the quality of what is afforded to pupils to his skilled and deft team and especially the deputy Lindsay Johnson, who exudes gravitas and energy. She has worked at the school for 20 years and is, in Sellens' words, 'the lynchpin of the school's success.'

We were taken on a tour of the school by six well-mannered, extremely articulate and very lovely pupils of varying ages, who each in turn solemnly shook our hands, looked us directly in the eye and said 'welcome to Thomas Jones primary school.' This editor couldn't have felt more revered if she were the Duchess of Cambridge. Pupils were as pristinely turned out as the school they inhabited. Hairclips and bobbles matched their uniform and we were hard pushed to find a strand of anything out of place. The head told us it is extremely important to him that all students look exactly the same and 'exquisite in their uniform, so there is no way of telling their background.' Those from deprived backgrounds can get help with the cost of the uniform.

Future plans for the school include a beehive, which the school says is its modest way of contributing to the eco-system and 'teaching the pupils to care for something.' This will add to the existing mini outdoor nature reserve set amongst pretty, manicured gardens and (slightly sparse) play areas. Indeed, dare we say it, our one criticism of the school would be the lack of outdoor facilities (although we appreciate this is an inner city school) or much time given over to sports, which seems to be a criticism echoed by a couple of parents we spoke to. One told us: 'There's not much in the way of drama or sports at this school which is probably indicative of most state schools nowadays. Sadly, when schools are monitored so closely, something has to give.' However, netball, football and athletics teams, training after school, sometimes with professional coaches, have enjoyed significant successes in borough leagues in recent years.

Ofsted – which regularly rates the school as outstanding – has praised it for high aspirations: 'Year 6 pupils don white coats for science lessons and eagerly respond to the school's expectation that they are preparing for university.' We also noticed that pupils called their smart navy blue school bags their 'briefcases' and year 6 pupils are expected to pick up a daily newspaper, because as one former student told us, 'pupils need to experience language they don't normally use.' It is not unusual, according to Mr Sellens, to hear the children talking about going to university or becoming barristers or doctors when they leave school.

Everything about this school is aspirational. You won't find a 'home corner' filled with dolls, cookers or microwaves in the gorgeous and colourful nursery. Instead there is a medical corner filled with realistic medical apparatus and costumes. Similarly, we loved the weekly interchangeable corner in reception which encouraged playing various professional roles such as doctor or teacher. It has a gold healthy schools award and year 4 children were recently treated to a trip to a Jamie Oliver restaurant and have been learning how to make sushi wraps using healthy ingredients – and fish fingers and baked beans are banned from the school menu because 'we want to afford them food they wouldn't get at home.'

Thomas's Battersea

Linked with Thomas's Clapham, Thomas's Fulham, Thomas's Kensington

28-40 Battersea High Street, London SW11 3JB

Pupils: 547 • Ages: 4-13 • C of E

Fees: £16,959 – £19,155 pa

Tel: 020 7978 0900
Email: battersea@thomas-s.co.uk
Website: www.thomas-s.co.uk

Headmaster: Mr Ben Thomas MA (40s). Educated Eton, Durham and ultimately at the Institute of Education. First teaching job, aged 26, head of Thomas's Kensington, a bit of baptism by fire. After four years took over headship of Battersea and parents now say 'outstanding' and 'really has his finger on the pulse'. Says that this definitely affected his style of headship and believes that it makes him less didactic. Vice principal of the group, Jill Kelham, based at Battersea, has, apparently, been a huge help to him. Has built up excellent teaching team, including well respected heads of year, and now believes his main function, as far as parents are concerned, is advising on senior schools at 13+. Visits several of these each term and feels he really does know the heads. Parents praise his 'excellent advice'. Says that the school should be about 'enjoyment for the lower school, learning for the middle school and achievement for the upper school,' and is a big believer in the most important school rule, 'be kind'. One of the four principals of the whole group of Thomas's London Day Schools, originally founded by his parents, David and Joanna Thomas in 1971, describes himself as the headmaster, 'doing the fun stuff', and his brother Tobyn as the administrator controlling finance, buildings etc. It is a huge business and would appear to be extremely profitable, though some parents feel that the fees are increasing a little too fast. 'Four to five per cent is a bit steep in the current financial climate.' Married to Katie, a full time mum, with three children all at the school and totally satisfied with his current existence. 'I love being head. It's great for family life'.

Leaving in July 2017 to chair the Thomas's board. His successor will be Mr Simon O'Malley MA PGCE (late 40s), currently head of Wellesley House. Educated at the Oratory School, Reading and at Aberdeen University. Previously a housemaster and later deputy head at Beaudesert Park in Gloucestershire. Ambitious and enthusiastic; has generated an energy and buzz about his current school. Much liked and respected by parents.

Entrance: Mainly at 4. Competitive and oversubscribed. Register as soon as possible, preferably at birth. Assessments in November prior to entry in September the following year. Three applicants for each place offered. Up to six boys and girls per hour's session. Looking for children who 'have a measure of confidence, are responsive, sociable, with a light in their eyes.' Sibling priority but not absolutely guaranteed. Occasional places further up the school when candidates are assessed while spending half a day with their peer group. Written report from previous school also necessary. More places at 11+ but majority of these tend to be taken by children from Thomas's, Kensington.

Exit: Very few leave at age 7 or 8 as no preparation for these exams although, inevitably, the odd trickle whose parents are scared they may not make it later. At 11+ to St Paul's, Godolphin & Latymer, GDST schools, Francis Holland SW1, Downe House, Wycombe Abbey, St Swithun's. At 13+ to Eton, St Paul's, King's College Wimbledon, Westminster, Winchester, Dulwich College, Alleyn's, Charterhouse, Bryanston, Marlborough and Wellington. Impressive range of destinations at both levels with some scholarships.

Remarks: A big, busy, slightly chaotic school for cosmopolitan parents who want their children to have the best English education money can buy. That is what they want and, to a large degree, that is what they get. Plenty of opportunities for pupils to excel but withdrawn types might find it all somewhat overwhelming.

Occupies an attractive, listed ex-grammar school building, with many modern additions and plenty of playground space. This last is easily transformed into a car park at the beginning and end of each day as public transport not particularly convenient. Has own fleet of buses which convey children from Kensington and ferry the whole school to sports venues etc. All the facilities for a broad curriculum. Great science labs – 'we do chemistry, physics and biology here,' said our youthful guides – computer suites and all the modern aids to a tip top education. New music centre, with 245 individual lessons taking place each week on instruments that range from piano to cornet; an orchestra, various bands and ensembles, choirs at all levels (recent concert had the school orchestra playing alongside the Southbank Sinfonia) and their own choral society where they are joined by parents from the other schools and members of the local community. Two great art studios and two pottery rooms with their own kiln. Imaginative creations displayed all over the school. We particularly liked the charcoal drawings lining one staircase alongside a written request to please not rub against them. And, of course, being a Thomas's school, the drama is outstanding with huge productions by each year group being put on over the year. 'Only drawback', said one parent, 'is that they are always musicals. Not much use if your child can't sing'. School assures us there's always something for everyone. Great Hall where they perform is pretty splendid.

Lots of sport, say it takes up about 20 per cent of the timetable from year 3 onwards. All the usuals with sculling added in the summer term at the top of the school. Matches inter-house, inter-Thomas's and against other schools. Great gym and school playground excellent place for organised and unorganised games. Also use facilities at Battersea Park, Barns Elms and the Wandle Centre. Youngest children, reception to year 2, have fantastic and imaginative rooftop playground on high.

Academically, teaching deemed pretty good, though lots of coaching still occurring in the last years. 'Just as insurance,' say the parents. We did feel that this was definitely more about anxious and ambitious parents than inadequately taught children. As in all the schools, some specialist teaching from the beginning. Mixed ability classes, with setting in maths and English only, until they reach the upper school when they are divided into those doing 11+ and those staying on and academia becomes the be all and end all, with all classrooms subject-based and a tutor system coming into operation. Not a wide choice of languages, although 11+ leavers have the option of German, Spanish or Italian after their exams. French from reception, Latin compulsory from year 5.

Enthusiastic, experienced head of learning support who also teaches maths in the lower and middle schools and study skills to years 7 and 8. Determined to catch children early so that they can let go of support by year 6 or 7. Works closely with class teachers, showing them how to help pupils. Mainly milder end of the spectrum but one-to-one teaching available for more serious problems and laptop training when absolutely necessary. Parents always involved and communication apparently good.

Probably most cosmopolitan of all the Thomas's schools, with a wide ranging mix of international parents and 19 different foreign languages spoken at home. About 25 per cent of children on the EAL register. A few of these need extra support which is well provided. School celebrates and appears to make the most of this range of different cultures.

Thomas's Clapham

Linked with Thomas's Battersea, Thomas's Fulham, Thomas's Kensington

Broomwood Road, London SW11 6JZ

Pupils: 635 • Ages: 4–13 • C of E

Fees: £15,846 – £17,916 pa

Tel: 020 7326 9300
Email: clapham@thomas-s.co.uk
Website: www.thomas-s.co.uk

Headmaster: Since 2012, Mr Philip Ward BEd (50s). One of the first heads appointed to the Thomas's group of London schools from outside of the Thomas family dynasty, in person Mr Ward is the very image of Hugh Bonneville as the Earl of Grantham. Perhaps it's his winning charm as head of the Clapham family, bonhomie, liberal sprinklings of the word 'chap', not to mention the labrador behind his desk. Any similarity ends there, however, as we found him to be a highly astute, strategically minded leader. Very persuasive; anyone wishing to challenge his point of view could need some determination not to be swept along with him.

Educated at Reigate Grammar School, he read history and PE at Exeter University, thence straight to Uppingham where he became director of PE and chair of the games committee, ascending through the ranks finally to headship of Feltonfleet prep in Surrey.

As he talks he often refers to 'we': part of a husband and wife teaching double-act. His wife Sue now teaches year 5 here. The move seems something of a surprise but they are enjoying being in London, able to nip into town for an evening. It also went down well with their two grown up children. Milly, the chocolate lab, comes to school every day and has been known to get lucky with the odd cupcake or two not meant for her. They like to get out to the Surrey Hills at the weekends for long walks if they can. During the week, there are a lot of late nights, and missed dog walks.

We were impressed by Mr Ward's delightful manner with the children as we went around the school. He knew the name of every child we met. Some parents were sagely reserving judgement, but others were bursting with 'excellent!' already. One parent told us, 'The children love him' – we could see why.

Having taught at a senior school, he knows what's in store for children later in terms of pressure, and for now wants them to have fun, a childhood.

Entrance: The school advises that successful applicants register their children before 18 months, but if we're correct in seeing Thomas's Clapham as very much in the ascendancy, together with much more of an eye on marketing, then 'register at birth' is still our advice. Pupils are selected at an informal assessment day at 3+, most recently seeing 180 children for 80-ish places. And with no 7+ entrance, this is pretty much it.

This is a neighbourhood school in the main: children arrive from more than 30 different local nurseries. Those at the Thomas's kindergartens in Battersea and Pimlico are guaranteed an assessment, but not a place. Strong sibling priority, but no guarantees. Sibling discounts for up to four children. They look for children who will 'have a go' and are genuinely keen as well as sociable and co-operative within a group.

Very occasionally places available higher up the school. Fifteen to 20 Thomas's Fulham pupils move over to Clapham at 11+, their transition now given much greater care and consideration.

New-style show rounds every few weeks, for groups of six or eight prospective parents to meet the head and see the school – more intimate than previous hall talks, very deliberately sending out a new, more personal and welcoming message from the off.

Exit: The word from parents and pupils is that they have 'absolute confidence' in the school enabling them to reach their guided first choice. Around 20 leave at the end of year 6, 65 at the end of year 8, with some 65 per cent off to board in some shape or form. To 28 different schools in 2016; London destinations include James Allen's Girls' School, Wimbledon High, Alleyn's, Dulwich College, Whitgift, Trinity, King's College and Emmanuel; further afield Wellington College, Tonbridge, Marlborough, and St Mary's Ascot are among favourites.

Remarks: The school opened in 1993, and is housed in a huge four-storey Victorian red-brick, typical of many London schools of the time, this one formerly a girls' grammar school in the centre of prime, residential Clapham. Inside, shining maroon tiled corridors, very London tube like, multiply the children's voices at every change of lessons – it's reassuringly loud and exuberant. Reception classes are housed in groovy-looking pods with an in and out space – fun, but quite compact, and perhaps a bit warm in summer – with so much vibrant work hanging from the ceilings, it's like being inside a mobile.

The dining room needs some reinvention, currently high windows and too small, so that pupils eat in shifts. The food seemed no better than 'school dinner-ish' to our eyes, and it was Friday, but plenty of fried food as well as more healthy options. Large rear playground for breaks and games, with roped-off picnic tables for those who don't want to run around.

Specialist teaching introduced gradually up the school. Year 6 splits between those going for 11+ and 13+, with former getting much special preparation with past papers. Latter get exam technique and revision strategies in year 8, with a creative post-exam programme of extension subjects. The staff is a stable one, with 15 teachers having been at the school for more than 10 years. In his bid to make the school less autocratic, head introduced a new senior leadership team. Small changes have included greatly reduced homework and a less intimidating approach to school exams. Curriculum being revamped to include thematic inquiry based learning.

Parental praise for the teaching: 'Our children have enjoyed a multitude of inspirational teachers who go the extra mile'. 'Very supportive and nurturing whilst at the same time instilling the need for self-discipline and effort.' 'Apart from the French department, which needs a serious overhaul, the standard of teaching is superb. They manage to engage the children with original and inspiring teaching whilst also ensuring that the essential rote-learning/repetition aspects are in place.'

New director of computing and much investment in hardware. French is taught from day one by a native French speaker, but there is work to do for the new head of modern languages, who is expected to 'revitalise the department': indeed, a new approach emphasises international awareness alongside language learning. Latin from year 5, Mandarin now taught in year 4, Spanish a possibility in future.

Around 10 per cent of children have SEN, mainly dyslexia. Emphasis on differentiated learning and in-class support, but some withdrawal for one-to-one lessons. Strong learning support team assists some 150 pupils with a spread of learning differences, including a more able group. Refreshing for a London prep to be so proud of its efforts in this regard.

Great art facilities in a modern, light and bright separate block and an experienced newish head of art (formerly from Feltonfleet) is sensitively designing projects for each year group. Exciting to see a whole row of potter's wheels, and we were wowed by the impressive group of sculptures children had made by wrapping themselves in foil, inspired by Kader Attia's Ghost installation. Cookery a new addition. A film-maker in residence, a former head of art, is no doubt ensuring every moment is captured for the sharpening marketing act, as well as helping children to record and present multi-media projects across the curriculum. New DT specialist.

Sports fixtures list expanded with the aim of enabling everyone to play for a team. New sports ground on the edge of Wimbledon Common with pavilion and changing rooms. For the high achievers some glamorous tours such as South Africa too. Girls play netball, hockey, rounders and athletics. One parent told us: 'The head of sport gets the most amazing results out of the children, training and praising in just the right measure, and always there with a cuddle if they hurt themselves. The kids would throw themselves under a bus for her. The girls hold their own very well against schools with a far bigger pool of pupils and better facilities and the trophy cabinet is weighed down with the evidence of that.'

Boys play football, rugby and cricket. In part to keep the boys beyond 11, the head has beefed things up. We saw two current and former professional rugby players coaching the boys at the cricket nets, using an iPad to compare each boy's batting with that of a famous player. Further thoughts are hockey for the boys and lacrosse for the girls. Weekly swimming off site for years 1 to 4. Ballet part of the curriculum from reception – cue a class of tinies performing to parents and their iPhones on our visit. Mostly girls latterly; the boys who continue are often talented.

Performing arts are an outstanding feature – highlights have included a performance at the Albert Hall in celebration of childhood. A parent commented: 'There seems to be something on every week! It is quite astounding that children are so confident and unfazed by the opportunities to perform, either in sport or on the stage.'

Some 350 children have individual music lessons, currently beginner level to grade 8. A wide range of groups and ensembles, and frequent recitals, soirées and concerts. Those with gifted voices may be invited to sing in the chapel choir, whilst 'new voices' and senior choir provide opportunities for all to perform.

More than 60 before and after-school clubs include fencing, debating, golf, computer coding, newspaper publishing, running and Airfix modelling (run by the head).

Special days for everything, with plenty of outside expertise brought in to deliver workshops. 'Make a difference day' caught our eyes, with children heading off in mini task forces to spend time in genuinely helpful projects across the community, such as making decorations for their local hospice, visiting a Christian Aid centre and sending cards to sick children. Pupils seem to get out and about, get stuck in and see things for themselves. 'Woodland Adventure' on Wimbledon Common is 'by far the most popular day of term'.

Strong focus on PSHE. A new 'Inspiring Living' course is a philosophy of the school as well as a taught subject. A key component is a new focus on mindfulness (including new landscaped Mindfulness Place), and Mr Ward is at the forefront of the curve. 'We're going to do mindfulness together... more thinking time, more time for reflection,' he says with enthusiasm. We applaud him, but wonder how he will stop his mind spinning with ideas and objectives during his allotted four minutes.

Head and team have set out to reinvent school's pastoral care systems. The head has been known to drop external meetings and return from conferences to pick up immediately on anything that arises. A parent confirmed: 'They take issues such as bullying seriously and take measures to address it instantly.' Parents describe the atmosphere as 'Very caring, and competitive in the right way, ie set out to win, but it doesn't matter if you don't, as long as you try your best'; 'Positive, determined yet caring and fun' and 'Nurturing'.

The head says, 'Every child wants a bit of metal on their shirt' and so there are now myriad opportunities to lead and take responsibility: as well as the usual heads of houses and games there are prefects for subjects or for eco and charities, even flag captains.

Parents are not first time buyers in the main: many boarding school educated, and an impressive bunch of achievers. One parent described them as 'Vocal! Very involved in all levels of school life.'

Thomas's Fulham

Linked with Thomas's Battersea, Thomas's Clapham, Thomas's Kensington

Hugon Road, London SW6 3ES

Pupils: 418 • Ages: 4–11

Fees: £12,645 – £18,372 pa

Tel: 020 7751 8200
Email: fulham@thomas-s.co.uk
Website: www.thomas-s.co.uk

Headmistress: Annette Dobson, 40s, opened the school in 2005. A slightly low key dresser with a laugh that reaches her eyes, one only has to look at her feet to see that snappy shoes and clear-headed dedication are not the sole preserve of Theresa May. Wanting to be a teacher from the get-go (maybe influenced by her mother's voice teaching in an adjacent classroom), she swam into the professional A stream by graduating from Homerton College, Cambridge. After a spell at North Bridge House, she crossed London to Thomas's Clapham, heading up the lower school, collecting a postgraduate degree and completing a study in phonics.

Thoroughly aware of the need to keep abreast of the numerous practical and technological changes in her world, she still keeps her feet firmly in the playground by maintaining a close, personal involvement with each child. On Monday mornings she stands by the door and shakes them all by the hand and, far more amazingly, remembers their names, a nice touch that illustrates the emphasis she puts on manners as well as her commitment to approaching her charges as individuals. Genuinely passionate about improving her school, she even spent her sabbatical visiting educational establishments around the world, although luckily she shows her human side by admitting to having eaten pretty well along the way.

Entrance: At 4, a non-academic assessment takes place in January for September entry. Eleven years of experience makes the head fairly certain about the kind of child that would or would not relish the opportunity of beginning their education here. She is tactful but clear that it is potential team players as well as bright individuals she is looking out for. There is a strong sibling policy (on average about half the slots go to siblings), which usually leaves a minimum of two children applying for each remaining place. Parents can feel very pressurised; one observer said that a 'parent was completely manic to get child in', but the process is fair with advance information for parents, and one child came out saying, 'I like this big school'. Places do become available further up the school, mainly due to the constant whirling merry-go-round that lands London parents anywhere from Manhattan to Moscow at the drop of a city chapeau. At this stage, children spend half a day at the school to make sure they will fit in and also need a letter from their previous school.

Exit: As you would expect from such a professional outfit, detailed practical information and knowledgeable help on the which, when and how of senior schools is handed out to help parents navigate this educational minefield. Boys seldom bail out early to go to alternative prep schools, mainly moving on to automatic places at Thomas's Clapham for the last two years before common entrance, some already having done the pre-assessment tests for senior schools, including Eton, King's College Wimbledon and Wellington. Some girls also go to Clapham for 13+ entry but a large proportion takes the 11+ and continues their education at a range of schools including Benenden, Downe House, Godolphin & Latymer, Putney High and St Paul's. Scholarships are won but the head confirms that there are not many available at this stage, and this is not an academic hothouse, a point echoed by one parent who felt that a very clever child might not get as far here as in a more competitive environment. Parents seem pleased with the advice given on senior schools and the head's statement that they 'aim to work in tandem with parents to find the best fit for a pupil' is backed up by the results.

Remarks: This youngest outpost of Thomas's private empire has settled in a handsome Victorian school building, gazing out over the top of a smart new asphalt athletics field, at the green park beyond. Nineteenth century it may be, but with sparkling two-tone brick, huge windows and a tidy colour-coded interior, this is definitely not a modern version of Dotheboys Hall and there is absolutely no air of laissez-aller neglect: in fact the energy and enthusiasm of the school is almost instantly apparent.

With walls covered in pictures from an exceptionally imaginative art department housed in a large beamed outbuilding and neat, well-conceived timetables for music and games on the stairs, the atmosphere is vibrant. Happy, eager children look you straight in the eye and teachers appear to be enjoying themselves as much as their pupils. Judging by the cheerful munching of buns at break and excellent reports from the head girl, the food served on primary coloured plates (matching the house colours) keeps the energy levels up through a satisfyingly full school day.

Particular praise is handed out by parents of reception teachers, one commenting that her child coming into the school with zero skills did 'really well in her first year' and others saying that almost all the class are pretty independent, at least at the laces tying end of the scale, by the end of the year. All the way up reading is heavily encouraged, with pupils taking home a daily diary including a book page that parents have to sign off. A library complete with cheerful librarian is nestled under the roof. Maths is taught imaginatively, not just as learning numbers but as a link to other subjects, and science appears to be popular, apparently due to explosion experiments, luckily under control in two purpose-built labs. French is introduced in reception and croissants and conversation feature in a biennial French day in Fulham and a week's trip to France for year 6. History and geography are both taught with the emphasis on connections to the outside world, and with classics added in years 5 and 6, round out the rest of the curriculum. Like most schools with an ecumenical viewpoint, RE is taught from a moral guideline and historical angle.

The arts – particularly music and drama – form a central part of life, over half the children learn an instrument and nearly three-quarters sing in a choir. Very popular plays are put on in the school's own theatre by all year groups, and after-school or lunch time clubs encourage would-be gymnasts, thespians, musicians and ballet dancers to go further and take external exams, such as LAMDA and the Royal Ballet School. All children, including those whose idea of art is to splash a lot of paint about (actively encouraged last year by a gigantic Jackson Pollock themed bonanza) are able to learn the fun that can be had out of being creative.

Despite the practical problems of operating on a small campus set in bricked over West London, the head (a fresh air fiend) runs the full mile to bring the outdoors into the pupil's daily routine. Little ones do PE and ballet, in the lower school they have general games and later on they can pick from a wide offering of conventional single sex sports. Some take place in the park opposite, which is regularly filled with small people jauntily dressed in the school's red and blue uniform complete with stripey socks. Otherwise they walk or are bussed to nearby facilities, a necessary evil for London schools and which makes the head look longingly at the space available to her peers in the country. Despite the logistical problems, there is enthusiasm all round about games, both competitive and recreational, and particular pleasure when a team beats other schools in the group. Sporty children can choose further exposure by joining popular extracurricular clubs for gym or judo, golf or tennis, while swimming, sailing and kayaking are available if they want to get wet. Classroom themes regularly incorporate outside expeditions, both in London and further afield, often with the help of the Exploration Society to give them a more adventurous time away from the tarmac.

Takes an early warning approach, starting in reception, to spotting any learning problems, which are jumped on quickly by full-time staff, backed up by specialist help from the outside. The head, who used to teach in this field, reckons that it is part of her job – 'we love off-piste children here, they are so often better at problem solving' – to help find the solution to each child's difficulties. Equally, she feels that tutors should only be employed to mend a particular gap in the wall rather than act as structural engineers, a policy which can be hard to get across in a city full of aspirational parents. Rules clearly exist but are wisely enough applied to make for few confrontations and the vice-head is on standby to have words with the inevitable, occasional small child trying it on. All the last year are encouraged to take a responsible role and show particular pride in overseeing the playground, although they sensibly admitted that they grabbed a teacher pretty quickly if anyone looked in need of first aid.

Twenty-first century technology connects parents, described as cosmopolitan, via a Twitter feed, and a newly updated portal allows them to follow their child's every move. Most of the content is popular (particularly the photographs), but one parent remarked that she preferred talking to the teacher rather than looking at her boy's exploits on an iPad. The head, however, convincingly counters this by saying that she will never allow face-to-face contact between teachers and parents to be lost. In another minor quibble a mother said that she was probably old fashioned but found receiving online reports irritating, as she likes to keep the real thing. An unsurprisingly lively PTA backs up the school and works its socks off to raise money for charity with the Bake Sale streaking home in the popularity stakes. Thomas's ethos to 'give not take' seems to have sunk in well as children often donate a book to the library to mark their birthdays and sometimes turn up with money for charity that they have raised off their own bat.

Promoting the Thomas's motto Be Kind quite so prominently might have backfired, but the evidence of the success of the strategy is everywhere. From the top ('fabulous, fantastic head') to the bottom (smiley children leaving the assessment clutching balloons), this is a school that really does succeed in doing what it says on the shiny tin.

Thomas's Kensington

Linked with Thomas's Battersea, Thomas's Clapham, Thomas's Fulham

277

17-19 Cottesmore Gardens, London W8 5PR

Pupils: 362 • Ages: 4-11 • C of E

Fees: £18,840 – £20,001 pa

Tel: 020 7361 6500
Email: kensington@thomas-s.co.uk
Website: www.thomas-s.co.uk

Headmistress: Since 2012, Miss Jo Ebner BEd MA PG Dip Couns Cert FT NPQH (late 40s), previously head of the Royal School, Hampstead (now absorbed by North Bridge House and owned by Cognita); 'I got the school to a place where it was worth buying,' she says. Educated at North London Collegiate (where both her mother and her daughters were at school too) and Homerton, Cambridge, she also trained at the Tavistock Clinic as a school counsellor and completed her MA at the Institute of Education, London. Tall and statuesque, Miss Ebner has long brown, lustrous hair, is highly emotionally intelligent, with a self-deprecating sense of humour. She has three children – now in or approaching their 20s – and shares her comfortable office with her adoring golden retriever, Maddie. Her first teaching job was at Primrose Hill primary school ('from the age of 7, I was determined to be a teacher,' she avers). She set up the first counselling service when she was at South Hampstead High School. She also taught at a primary school in Willesden and at the North West London Jewish Day school as well as a successful stint as deputy head of The Hall junior school in Hampstead. A deeply committed educationalist, she is heavily involved with the GSA (Girls' Schools Association), serves as a governor of several schools, including St Mary's Ascot, and has written several articles on parenting.

One of the first things Miss Ebner did here was to remove the position of lower school head. She is very much in charge of the whole school. While she operates an open door policy and parents praise her direct approach when dealing one to one, her reputation at the moment is that she can be distant, 'certainly not cuddly,' observed one, but 'very cheerful, involved and approachable,' said another. She teaches religious studies to year 2, and set up a mindfulness course for parents, staff and pupils – 'it is really helpful in the run up to exams,' she confides. She regards communication as being vital, 'the bottom line, as with any relationship, is that it's about trust.' A transparent approach will nip things in the bud so she makes herself available – parents can drop in to discuss any issues with her. However, she doesn't cosy up to them – avoiding the dinner party circuit so that she can remain objective about what is in the best interests of their children.

Passionate about investing in her staff and striving for the highest quality of teaching, whether through further professional development or promotion, she is regarded by parents as having made shrewd recruitments as well as keeping good teachers and teaching assistants who mature and develop under her leadership. Her teachers value her big picture approach to their futures and the encouragement she gives for them to seize opportunities. She set up a bespoke masters programme for all Thomas's staff, in conjunction with Roehampton University. At the time of our visit a few teachers doing this masters programme were enthusing about their research on, eg, the pros and cons of setting.

Entrance: Three classes of 20 (split 50:50 boys and girls), so in theory, 60 places at reception. However siblings take priority (though will only take siblings they think will thrive) so you should expect only about half that number of places. Over 100 tinies are interviewed the year before entrance. They are not looking for children who have been tutored and prepped but who are adaptable, willing to get stuck in and have plenty of initiative. The pace is fast here and your child is likely to have a number of different teachers during a typical day. Register at birth to be sure that you get on a list for assessment. Once the list reaches 180 it will close and your only chance will be a waiting list place, currently limited to 50 names. Occasional places rarely arise but there is a formal assessment at 7 and 8 plus where school will consider applications of up to 10 children for each of years 3 and 4. School only ever offers a couple of places at this stage.

Exit: There is an option to continue to Thomas's Battersea from 11 to 13 and about a third choose to do this, mostly boys and girls who are going down the boarding route – automatic transfer, subject to the head's recommendation. Some of these have been successful at the pre-test during year 6 and are armed with offers from top 13+ schools from King's Wimbledon and St Paul's to Eton and Winchester. Lots of help and preparation to ensure the transition is smooth, as despite being part of the Thomas's group, they are different schools with a different make up and transition isn't necessarily seamless. Battersea teachers come to the school to meet the children who are moving, and a number of events are organised to help with integration, from games in the park to cupcake decorating, as well as coffee mornings and drinks parties for the parents.

Otherwise a range of schools as one would expect as there is a broad range of ability here. Latymer Upper currently very popular, a few to the Harrodian, City of London and UCS. Girls tend to favour Godolphin & Latymer, some go to Francis Holland (mainly Sloane Square rather than Regent's Park), one or two to St Paul's, South Hampstead and Queensgate. Boarders tend to choose St Mary's Ascot, Downe House, Wycombe Abbey or Cheltenham Ladies College. A cluster of academic scholarships as well as the odd music and drama scholarship each year.

Miss Ebner makes it clear that the school does not prepare pupils for 7/8+. If you want your son to apply to Colet Court, Westminster Under etc, you're on your own – the school will not do any extra preparation. Boys do still occasionally leave at

7 or 8 to go to these schools – it's not impossible – but it is not something the school will actively encourage.

Remarks: A stimulating, creative but also nurturing school in a very fashionable corner of London, Thomas's Kensington has a cosmopolitan flavour to it without being flashy or ostentatious. Children here are privileged but not spoilt, and fizzing with energy that a highly dedicated team of teachers channels very successfully. Thomas's kids are exuberant, confident and very, very busy. Lots of drama perhaps contributes to their looking you in the eye and explaining things with an articulate awareness that belies their young age.

Situated on three sites in a leafy, salubrious triangle of elegant properties at the south west corner of Hyde Park, Thomas's Kensington was the first school in the Thomas's quadrumvirate (the others are Clapham, Battersea and Fulham). Founded by Joanna and David Thomas in the early '70s and the family members are still the proprietors. Their two sons, Ben and Tobyn, are heavily involved as joint principals. Joanna and David, who have a flat above the junior section of the school in Victoria Road, are still very present around the school. The involvement of such a charismatic family and their wholehearted dedication to the place gives it a distinctive, family feel. Joanna and David Thomas are highly respected among the parents who generously donate to the CAIRN trust, a charity they set up to educate children in Nepal.

All three buildings are elegant, spacious and well looked after. Reception children enter the junior section on Victoria Road thorough a little passageway and wooden gate into a secluded garden and play area. Lots of scooters and bikes parked inside the black wrought iron gates of the pale blue painted Georgian mansion. Most kids live close enough to walk and scoot so there is a refreshing lack of Chelsea tractors at drop off. Lots of fresh air for all; the little ones are split into small groups from each class at playtime and spill out into the little Astroturf courtyard between the reception classrooms. This is just one example of how the classes are mixed up here so that friendships can be refreshingly fluid betwixt classes. From year 1 they walk 10 minutes to Kensington Gardens for fresh air and exercise.

School is mixed ability – assessments for entry are not primarily focused on any kind of academic prowess. This, and the tendency to take siblings, makes for a broad range. Lots of focus on reading. Children are listened to four times a week and a 'mystery reader' regularly turns up at school. To one child's (and his father's) enormous delight one week the mystery reader was his grandfather reading via Skype from the USA. Any difficulties are picked up quickly by class teachers and any special educational need is coordinated by the SENCo and her team. Parents praise the school's responsiveness when support is required, and an occupational therapist as well as a speech and language therapist come regularly into school. A number of children go to the Kensington Dyslexia Teaching Centre (just around the corner). Controversially, school made the decision to teach mixed ability maths and English groups all through the school until year 5. The decision was made partly as a result of the masters research that one of the teachers is doing at Roehampton. The evidence apparently suggests that setting is not beneficial to either the less or the more able students. A number of parents of able mathematicians are not supportive, parents of children who are not at the top of the game are more open to the idea. School says the research is still ongoing. French is setted – some strong French speakers in the school. Spanish and German offered as after-school clubs (parents recently requested Italian, so this is to be introduced). Latin taster in year 4 and then taught as part of the curriculum in years 5 and 6.

The creative and performing arts and sport are all given a lot of emphasis here and the school positively hums with activity beyond the classroom. Thomas's children stand out as being sparky and articulate, and the extensive drama and dance provision must play some part in this. All children, girls and boys, do ballet during their lower school years. Chelsea Ballet comes to the school to teach pupils once a week. Each year group puts on a large-scale production in the theatre. We watched year 4's fabulous production of Aladdin – worthy of any professional production, complete with tiered seating and first class lighting as well as stunning costumes. Watched by parents, staff and pupils, but what was particularly noticeable was the warm support of fellow pupils, one year 6 boy spontaneously rising to his feet to make a congratulatory speech at the end of the show. Year 6 will perform Arabian Nights at Imperial College. Music also flourishes – everyone given a violin to learn in years 1 and 2. A number of groups and choirs to participate in, including a full orchestra and a chapel choir. Concerts are performed at the Cadogan Hall as well as on site. Lots of sporting fixtures – primarily against the other Thomas's schools, but others too, eg Fulham Prep. Main sports – netball, hockey and rounders for the girls, football and cricket for the boys, plus tennis for both in the summer term. Parents praise the inclusive approach – children are encouraged in music and athletics, for example, even though they might not be showing a particular talent.

Even more impressive than the wealth of opportunity within the school is how much energy is put into a community spirit and to giving something back. From the CAIRN charity – Joanna and David Thomas's baby – supporting children in schools in Nepal, to various outreach programmes in local state schools, children here are busy raising money or sharing resources and thereby instilling and being instilled with a sense of public responsibility, generosity and kindness. Independent:state school partnerships have been established eg providing and teaching Latin in local state schools, collaboration between orchestras and choirs, and whole school community days when children from each year group carry out various projects in the community from reading to local nurseries to art, drama and music productions. The TSF (Thomas's Schools Foundation) is focused on working with local state schools, to widen educational opportunity and to provide bursaries. Joanna and David, together with Ben and Tobyn, are all actively involved in leading the whole school community to support the Foundation.

A remarkably cohesive and vibrant school. Bubbly children that are nevertheless polite and well behaved; 'It can be noisy,' acknowleged one parent, 'but with laughter not screaming.' Privileged, yes, but spoilt, absolutely not. These children are developing a strong sense of social responsibility and couldn't be better prepared for the complex global environment they are growing up into.

The Tiffin Girls' School

Richmond Road, Kingston, Surrey KT2 5PL

Pupils: 996 • Ages: 11–18 • Sixth form: 306

Tel: 020 8546 0773
Email: contact@tiffingirls.org
Website: www.tiffingirls.org

Head Teacher: Since January 2016 Mr Ian Keary BA NPQH, previously head of school at Glyn School in Ewell. Before Glyn, was assistant head of the Tiffin School, the equally desirable

T

boys' grammar, for four years. Taught PE, worked in maths and IT department and was head of year 11. Sporty – PE, rugby, cricket, energetic skier. Despite being presented by pupils with model of Marvel character The Punisher, also has cracking sense of humour (say former colleagues).

Academic matters: Outstanding results, of course, but how could they not be? If you get in here, you will be super-bright, be stimulated by your peers and superlatively taught and you will get the level of results that is normal and expected here. In 2016, 91 per cent of GCSE grades at A*/A and at A level 96 per cent at A*-B and 76 per cent A*/A. Few GCSEs gain anything lower than B grades. Of the mainstream subjects, only the Englishes and sciences get a fair sprinkling of Bs – all the rest are largely A*/A.

Sciences are popular, languages less so. Latin survives and does well. Drama and art excel at GCSE. At A level, 20 subjects available plus EPQ and an enrichment programme – taken with Tiffin Boys. Maths has by far the most takers with the majority achieving A*/A. Also popular are biology and chemistry, English, psychology, economics and physics. French and Spanish the only languages. Latin jointly with the boys' school and tiny numbers take music; few but increasing takers for DT. Lots of Oxbridge graduates on the staff and we heard nothing but praise for the teaching.

The stringently applied entrance criteria mean that few with learning difficulties clear the hurdle. However, the school is very accessible and would be a good option for your bright daughter with mobility or other physical difficulties.

Games, options, the arts: Rowing an increasing strength – very rare and pretty special for a girls' state school and it's now on the KS3 carousel of sports – the J15 squad has won gold at the Kingston Small Boats Head. Cross-country and volleyball similarly impressive; handball and zumba available alongside traditional sports (over 350 sports fixtures in 2015/6). Most games played on site: full sized Astro, eight tennis/netball courts and two adjoining gyms. Year 10s upward can use local leisure facilities for eg swimming and fitness classes. Sixth form required to do one hour's sport a week – but many do more outside school. Involved in Wimbledon ball girls programme, and plenty of trips to national sporting venues. Flourishing Duke of Edinburgh. Lots of trips – sensible, subject-based and not too exotic for most wallets though the US ski trip option seen as prohibitively expensive by many.

Art – judging from the massed and massive canvases that grace the corridor walls – is quite exceptional: figurative and topographical paintings which you want on your walls – brilliant use of mixed media and collage. The same applies to the ceramics and textiles. We loved the highly glazed ceramic shoes along one walkway – and art, though taken at A level by far fewer than the talent would suggest, is a key strength here. Two A level students selected for the 2016 Royal Academy A Level Summer Exhibition from over 1400 entries nationally. Music seen as very good if somewhat exclusive – this despite school's strenuous efforts to involve everyone: witness the carousel in year 7 in which everyone has a chance to try out instruments with the encouragement to learn one; and every girl in year 7 sings in the year 7 concert, after which many join whole school choir, for which there is no audition. In this, as in some other respects, the school's reputation seems to be lagging behind the reality. Drama clearly a major school occupation and great gusto expended on productions. Good programme of outside speakers and visits to museums etc. A great sense of the girls themselves using initiative to up their overall experience.

Background and atmosphere: In 1638, Thomas Tiffin, a prosperous brewer, left £50 so that the town clerk could choose a boy 'from ten years of Age, or there abouts' and educate him so that he might gain an apprenticeship and 'git his living'. His brother John left a further £100. There were further benefactors – eg Elizabeth Brown who wanted 'the Children of the poor inhabitants of the Town of Kingston... to read the English Tongue and learn some Godly Catechisme...' and Edward Belitha who, in 1717, left money specifically, and to his eternal credit, for the education of 'twenty poor Persons' Daughters'. However, no actual school was founded until 250 years later, after decades of local wrangling, when two 'lower middle class' schools – one for each sex – were established in the 1870s and named after the Tiffin brothers.

Initially, the boys and girls shared a school building – girls upstairs; the fees were modest and scholarships were offered. The schools blossomed and, in 1899, the girls moved to splendid new accommodation in St James's Road where they remained until a second move in 1937. Further expansion led to a another move to a former boys' secondary modern school building between Kingston and Ham. All went well until 2003 when a ferocious fire demolished most of the teaching block and a lot of coursework. They talk of it still, down Kingston way. The final result of the fire was a terrific new building, at the centre of the present school, and which rescues the site from being sadly undistinguished to having a centre full of light and a sense of generous spaciousness.

The wide new corridors are hung with impressive canvases mentioned above and, in fact, the framing, glazing and hanging of the girls' art makes a major impression on any visitor. The hang is rejigged three or four times a year – we applaud. No classrooms seem crowded and we enjoyed the mix of layout – some are eyes forward to the teacher behind her desk, others are arranged in tables for four and a wandering teacher. Whiteboards are everywhere and used imaginatively. Large school hall but also good drama studio with clever retractable seating. Good facilities for music, music tech and applied arts. Recent re-site of the sixth form centre with common room and work rooms, putting it back at the heart of the school; library moving to new accommodation and classrooms converted to science labs. Security has been upgraded with keypad entry for students. Site is litter-free and functional and mostly in pretty fair nick, though some careful planting could humanise it considerably. Good food – really good – and on a cashless system.

Pastoral care, well-being and discipline: Some of the best-presented girls we've seen. When we visited all the girls we saw looked comfortable and tidy in mid-blue jumpers, knee-length grey skirts and, seemingly compulsory, long hair. Sixth formers just have to look respectable and they all do. Excellent system of two head girls and six deputies and a team of eight house officers who oversee the house system including all house events and house based fundraising. The head girls and deputies oversee wider community outreach, whole school charity fundraising, and school community events. The girls we met were adamant about not missing boys during their seven years. 'We see the Tiffin boys all the time,' we were told. All those we asked said they would send their daughters to a girls' only school.

Praise for the head of pastoral care. The usual problems of highly motivated, clever girls, though no more here than anywhere. Some sense among some parents that not all staff have pastoral care as a priority. School stresses how much is done discreetly and behind the scenes, with PSHE and citizenship programme for all year groups; and certainly we liked what we saw of girl-teacher relationships. Few transgressions of the drugs/drink/smokes kind.

We have never met a more articulate, intelligent and thoughtful bunch of girls. They credit the school for giving them the confidence to hold their own in any context: 'They make you take an active role.... Everyone has to take an assembly at least once a year... You get very used to doing PowerPoint presentations, debating and we have masses of practice at presenting ourselves.' A quite extraordinary sense of pride in the school pervades the place: 'We love singing the school song... I wish we saw more of our old girls... we could learn so much from them.'

Pupils and parents: Pupils are the very bright daughters of highly organised and ambitious parents – historically not local, and there is some resentment amongst those who do live locally that this, the pre-eminent academic state school, has not until recently served their community. A knock-on is that, although tight friendship groups are formed inside the school, the demographic and logistics mean that socialising outside the school and in leisure time is less easy and some pupils and parents are saddened by the fact that girls live too far away or social life is not valued at home. One mother told us that only one girl in her daughter's class lived within walking distance, and others told us that developing a social life did not rank high in the priorities of many of the parents. The school now prioritises applicants from local postcodes, which should in future build a more local school community. It also has clever ideas like getting year 10 parents to talk to the parents of girls in the year below and share experiences. Parents' evenings of all kinds – but there is a sense among some that once the big push to get a place at the school is over, too many parents sit back and don't involve themselves as they could.

Most parents voluble in their appreciation: 'They strive to bring out the best in the girls'... 'if ever we have a problem you can always talk to someone — they are good at getting back to you'.. 'they are hot on time-keeping... and academically amazing'. Some parental scepticism too: 'It suits the academic, the focused, the conscientious. It wouldn't suit the erratic, the eccentric, those who are academically one-sided.' School strenuously refutes this and it is true that the range of opportunities and activities is impressive and the list of leavers' destinations is as varied as you could hope to find. It may just be that some pupils choose to focus exclusively on academic work and not take advantage of other opportunities.

Notable former pupils include Ritz muralist Helen McKie, actresses Jill Gascoigne and Katherine Parkinson, Lynne (Eats Shoots and Leaves) Truss and Olympian sculler, Sarah Winckless.

Entrance: This is probably the paragraph you are reading first. Some 1,600 applicants for the 180 available year 7 places. Worth noting is the fact that the selection dates are constantly changing and parents are advised to keep up to date with the school's website (currently, register by early September, first stage of test in early October and second in mid November).

Stage one is a 'sifting' test of English and maths multiple choice questions. Places allocated on the basis of results of stage two test, including written maths, reading and writing papers. Sixty places offered to girls living in the inner area, or being eligible for pupil premium funding and living in the inner or designated areas. Other 120 places to those living in designed area. Inner area based on local electoral wards, designated area on local postcodes.

In reality, the tests are sat by some of the brightest girls in the south east. A healthy tutoring industry thrives in the local boroughs, greatly boosted by introduction of maths and literacy tests.

At least 20 external sixth form places, with applicants judged on year 10 grades and GCSE predictions.

Exit: In 2016, lost 22 per cent post GCSE ('mostly voluntarily, for a variety of reasons,' says school). Further two per cent depart at end of year 12. Thereafter Tiffin girls leave for good courses everywhere. In 2016, 29 to Oxbridge, normally 80 per cent to Russell Group. Medicine (25 places in 2016) and engineering, history and English predominate but really there's nothing they don't do – and do well.

Money matters: All families asked to contribute £30 per month to school funds.

Remarks: Don't apply if you live in an undesignated postcode or if your daughter is only average at school. If she is super-bright, loves to learn, to think and take part in everything, you could find no better school – anywhere.

Tiffin School

Queen Elizabeth Road, Kingston, Surrey KT2 6RL

Pupils: 1,193 • Ages: 11–18 • Sixth form: 398

Tel: 020 8546 4638
Email: admissions@tiffin.kingston.sch.uk
Website: www.tiffinschool.co.uk

Headteacher: Since 2015, Mr Michael Gascoigne BA, 40s. Knows the school inside out – joined as history teacher after completing PGCE (Institute of Education) and training in some tough schools (think recreational chair-throwing). Subsequently became head of history here (1999), head of sixth form (2004) and deputy head (2009) – each promotion fortuitously happening just when was debating looking elsewhere (no coincidence, we suspect).

First generation in family to go to university, bursary to independent school firing career ambitions, though initially directed at policing or law. All changed when he took a temporary teaching post and thoroughly enjoyed it.

Humane, as articulate as his pupils (and that's a big compliment), he's a thoroughly likeable man who understands how boys tick and values his staff (he ensured teachers' room got much needed refurb ahead of other deserving projects).

It's no cinch. Constant pressure on budgets (spends a lot of time fundraising), and dealing with problems out of his control are the main downsides – as (occasionally) are the hours he puts in. Arrives at 7am and leaves whenever ('wife would say it's not early enough,'). We'd suspect it's often close to 12 hour day, plus Saturday mornings.

All so far outweighed by the good parts, headed by relish for challenges ahead. 'No virtue in standing still,' he says – putting it into action with three million pound building programme and forging ahead with plans to ensure school becomes an ever more influential local presence through outreach and collaboration. 'A lovely guy, approachable, reassuring,' was one parent's verdict. Combines insider knowledge with at least one eye on future developments. 'No shoe-filler,' thought parent. 'Has his own ideas and agenda.'

Academic matters: Rich balance of subjects from year 7 based on fortnightly timetable. Slightly more English in first year, separate sciences from year 8 but, impressively, keep up art and music as well. Latin for all, also religion and philosophy and fortnightly session on 21st century life. Everyone takes separate sciences, one language and (unusually for non-religious school) religion and philosophy at GCSE plus three options ranging from humanities to Latin and Greek, PE, dance (a rarity anywhere, let alone in maintained sector) and DT.

In the sixth form, have retained AS courses as well as impressive breadth (choice of around 20 subjects – including those rarities, Latin and Greek), most pupils narrowing from four at AS to three A levels (maths, sciences and economics consistently popular) plus games session and non-examined enrichment course (with Tiffin Girls).

Class sizes (average of 30 to end of year 9 dropping to 24 in GCSE years and 16 in the sixth form) no barrier to exceptional results, with 81 per cent of GCSEs graded A*/A in 2016 as were 61 per cent of A levels (87 per cent at A*/B).

And not a question of taking the best, shoving on to academic conveyor belt and letting them off again at the other end (though with the prizes coming thick and fast, from Arkwright Scholarships to 99 boys gaining gold certificates in Junior Maths Olympiad or the Junior Kangaroo and year 13s winning the Student Investor Challenge – top out of 10,000 teams – they probably could). Progress 8, new government assessment tool, puts school in top five per cent for the value it adds between year 6 and year 11 – so complacency certainly isn't the order of the day.

Staff stability helps (20 on the books for at least 10 years – average age of teachers is 40 and 44 for all staff) – though recruitment as problematic here as anywhere else in London – property prices mean 'move out in droves'. Magic ingredient is school itself. 'There's an attachment that grows on you,' says Mr Gascoigne. Some churn is healthy – 'don't want all staff to be here for years and years,' but with most teachers leaving for senior posts elsewhere, controllable, so new staff can learn in an experienced department.

Subjects generally organised by corridor (and door colour – though with pea green for geography, dark green for physics and something between the two for biology, it pays to mug up on pantones). Doesn't take long to work out where you are, say pupils and in any case, there are plenty of clues, like the helmet ('Norman,' said tour guide, authoritatively) in history office and pickled lobster-like creature ('a crayfish – has flatter and wider tail') outside the science rooms, though guide voiced slight disapproval at location – 'out of place, should be biology when this is clearly chemistry.'

School catches boys in magic few years between arriving packed with enthusiasm and ideas and losing it to adolescent cynicism, says head. One boy arrived in sixth form with a fascination for fungi. 'Not the usual thing but we knew he'd love it here.' Helps to be proactive about trying new things, we were told by pupil, though come as you are and you'll be accepted. 'Here it's cool to care about knowledge,' agreed school insider. Certainly true of tour guides, thrilled to be here, erudite and delightfully tickled by oddities of school life – the mystery bricked up door 'to nowhere', the religion and philosophy office – 'strangely placed as the classroom is downstairs.'

Perhaps unsurprisingly, few pupils have statement of SEN – just 0.2 per cent, just a tenth of the national average. That said, school caters for range of learning needs – though at 31, numbers are still low – ranging from hearing and sight problems to specific learning needs and Asperger's. Support comes via TA plus part-time additional needs literacy specialist who helps boys with dyslexia or organisational issues.

To teachers with the right approach (and parents struggled to find any without), they're a dream audience. Homework is 'about right,' thought pupil – neither excessive nor inflicted with a heavy hand. Instead, teachers will guide rather than lead, mention for example that there's a test coming up and leave the boys to make the connection.

Ability to suck up facts may be profound (it certainly impressed us) but these boys don't tolerate dull teaching. 'It might sound naughty,' said one (it doesn't, honest), 'but if I'm sitting in physics being lectured on the forces acting on a ball falling from the sky, I'm likely to be less interested than if I'm looking at a cross section of a cell,' (they build their own from plaster of Paris and plasticine and they're awe-inspiring). Head agrees. 'It is not good enough to sit at the front and feed them facts. You need to know your subject, and to encourage them always to ask questions – that's how they learn.'

Games, options, the arts: Breathtaking. Just one issue of fortnightly head's newsletter (essential reading if you want a cross section of day-to-day life here) included the latest school trips (GCSE and A level art students to Venice, year 9 classics to Bath, year 7 to London Zoo), sporting success (cross-country) and performing arts, with 'particularly active' dancers doing their stuff at half time during the 2016 Four Nations rugby final at Olympic Park and working with the Royal Ballet and Ballet Rambert. Year 8s learn capoeira, a couldn't-be-better fusion of dance and martial arts. Pirouettes have never before packed such a punch.

Sign up for the choir and pupils could end up performing with world class orchestras – Mahler's third with the LSO, Stravinsky with the LPO and Tannha ser at the Royal Opera House in just the last few months, plus choir tours all over the place, as well as appearing on the Blankety Blank Christmas special hosted by David Walliams. They're not blasé, though can be tiring. 'Came back from Royal Opera House and fell asleep in my uniform,' said one veteran.

There's something to impress wherever your eye, or ear, falls, from art (surreal paper scissors and screwdrivers, mounted on clock mechanisms and ticking away the hours – message, if there is one, too deep for this reviewer), to rugby – 16 teams – almost a quarter of all pupils, who regularly give independent sides a drubbing – and rowing. Saunter through nearby Canbury Gardens of a Saturday and you'll often see boats waiting to be launched and some of the 100 boys involved warming up with a few laps by the bandstand – one of the few state schools to offer it at all, let alone on this scale.

Other sports – cricket (main summer sport), basketball, badminton, tennis, cross-country and athletics – are also available and to equally high standards.

Timetable helps, with music, drama and dance allocated six periods between them in year 7 – more if you add on games – and equal to science or maths. Means school 'can grab you early,' said parent, who'd seen son suddenly (and unexpectedly) blossom into a talented singer. 'Everyone's got something different to them,' said one.

Sometimes spark a new idea (one year 8 boy, initially reluctant to try dance, had already reached post GCSE level; another had done 15 nights on stage at the Royal Opera House). But it's not just the conventional who flourish. 'If you want to learn the sitar or electric guitar or bongo drums then teachers let them,' said parent. 'The point is that they realise that the pleasure out of music is performance.' Top singers may end up as choral scholars but first year string players, scratchily delivering first orchestral performance, will get equal levels of applause.

'We encourage participation way beyond the lessons – school is not just about simply collecting the certificates,' says the head – and pupils praise resulting diversity. Trips are vital part of the process – and not just educationally. 'Playing pool in the evening changes things, you see boys in a different light,' says the head. And while missing lessons does create practical issues, school's view is that benefits outweigh need to catch up later.

In a day that stretches well beyond either end of official hours (dance rehearsals starting at 6.30am were the earliest we discovered – though choir, drama and sport require similar commitment) boys' ability to manage all their interests and academic work on top can be a worry to parents. Some, naturally organised, learn self-management early. But even the borderline chaotic somehow get through. 'My chronically disorganised son coped because he really wanted to do it,' said parent.

Background and atmosphere: Three cheers for Thomas and John Tiffin, brothers and wealthy Kingston brewers who between them left £150 in the 1630s to invest in the education of deserving boys. Canny investment in land by executor did their memories proud, though it wasn't until the late 19th century that eponymous school was finally opened (original site now home to local primary). They moved to current location in 1929, acquiring 30 acres of playing fields in Thames Ditton in 1948 (now owned by the old boys to kybosh any thoughts by rapacious governments of cashing it in for housing). Became voluntary aided, converted to academy in 2010 and are currently keeping close eye on opportunities created by potential expansion of grammar schools.

We don't doubt that J and T Tiffin would be chuffed with what their legacy has achieved. Behind the public persona of the horribly packed and inevitably anonymous open days is a warm, friendly school that's hard to leave. Many don't – or not for long. In quick succession we met retired deputy head, now back as a governor and unofficial archivist (school can trace every old boy since 1880) and former pupil, now a PE teacher here. 'Feels like home,' he said. 'I've even used my house key to try to get into the sports hall.'

Warmth extends to the admin team who keep cool while staying on top of copious amounts of lost property, from Tupperware packed with spectacles to the many missing bags – 'boys pick up the nearest one if worried about being late.' Jumpers ditto.

Pupils notice and respond. Helpful, caring teachers are 'best thing about the school,' said one, who had successfully mounted campaign to get a school corn snake (sadly on study leave – or serpentine equivalent – on day of visit). 'Wasn't dismissed as a silly idea.' Head finally gave blessing – once proper care plan had been presented and agreed.

From head's formal garden with sundial and homely bird feeders (lovingly tended by gardening parent) to cricket pitch, and MUGA surface which ...'is a pitch,' says head (amid in the swirl of jargon about multi-surfaces, G4s and suchlike, all you really need to know), site is greener and bigger than partial views from the three streets (and modern flats) that frame it would suggest. (Art rooms, appropriately, provide best panoramic view).

Definitely has its architectural moments, from historic – attractive 18th century listed building housing classrooms, uniform shop and IT (marked by dainty china figurines) to last century (1990s art and DT block). There's also cutting edge modernity in attractive two storey circular learning resource centre, bookcases radiating out from central desk and complete with spiral staircase inside (sixth form only) and sedum roof (outside).

Its twin (or close) is on the way, replacing vintage Portakabin, current home to dining hall. 'Dilapidated,' says head, erring on side of understatement – though doesn't stand in way of quality meals, sweet and sour chicken and pasta with basilico sauce among the highlights. Once complete (Jan 2018), will be thing of beauty, providing kitchen and dining hall downstairs, five new classrooms and IT suite on first floor.

Outside, careful design with smaller footprint will add more playground space and greater streetside appeal with glassed windows even offering reflections of the 14th century Lovekyn Chapel, the oldest building in town (though they don't own it – rather to their relief given the costs of upkeep). Means more streetside appeal for this distinctly average patch of Kingston – so a public benefit.

Though money is invariably tight (and tighter here than many assume), careful juggling ensures it goes where most needed. Yes, a few tatty staircases could do with a paint job but the displays are bang up-to-date, performance spaces are many and varied and even the gothic-windowed, red-curtained old style school hall also has thoroughly modern lighting rig. While Macs reign supreme in IT, spick and span food technology room stays well up to temperature and DT, still offered to A level (one of the only local schools to do so) remains beautifully dovetailed, nobody's complaining.

Pastoral care, well-being and discipline: School can't take on all the weight of world's anxieties, says Mr Gascoigne. Pressure to succeed – 'not unique to selective schools,' he points out – that flows down from management to teachers and pupils isn't helpful but can be overemphasised – and certainly the pupils we saw seemed notably uncrushed and extremely cheerful.

He sees social media demanding instant response, impossible to switch off, as a greater contributor to anxiety. School works with mental health worker who's in school for a day and a half each week and includes drop in system. 'We can't solve every mental health problem but can do best to help,' he says.

Merits for good work, contributions to lessons, attitude and helpful acts (in that order) more sparingly awarded after year 7. Lead to certificates, presented in assembly. Best of the lot is head's certificate (platinum) though it doesn't come along often. Dark face of the coin, demerits, treated with caution by teachers.

While will always be the odd behavioural issue and very occasional exclusion (for normal offences), it doesn't happen often. Most other difficulties (occasional missing laptop key) are caused by overdoing the joie de vivre that's inevitable consequence of considerable freedom. IT rooms, with prefect supervision, open at break, for example. 'Boys are not yet the finished product – will make mistakes, do things they shouldn't do. We're ultimately training them for independence and maturity in the real world,' says Mr Gascoigne.

There's much talk here of levels of happiness. Competition kicks in early – brilliant for bonding. Houses have recently increased from six to eight with rise in pupil numbers – one year 8 pupil, who'd moved as a result, initially very torn, though now wearing new tie with great pride – though form competitions, starting early in year 7, are also hard-fought. 'We sung [sic] our hearts and souls out,' writes first year pupil in newsletter of inter-form singing competition held within weeks of joining the school.

Pupils and parents: You find generations of local families who have come here, as well as fair share of celebrities, more tending towards performing arts and sport than straight brainbox, Nobel-winning fame as you might possibly expect.

Big hitters (literally in some cases) include sportsmen Alex Stewart (cricket) and Rob Henderson (rugby) as well as artist John Bratby and Jonny Lee Miller, an ex-husband of Angelina Jolie (probably happier being noted for starring role in Elementary). School is mounting major drive to round up alumni (especially the successful City types) and encourage them to do their bit for support.

Many current families need no urging. Joining the PTA is a good way to get in the swim and there are also subject-specific spin off groups fundraising for rugby, rowing and – probably the busiest of the lot – music. Each has own little community – 'Have got a whole load of new friends,' said one mother.

Main ethnic groups are white British, Indian and Asian. Area isn't immune from deprivation and school argues good case for looking beyond official tally of disadvantaged pupils based on free school meals that government data puts at just 11 out of the 140 finishing KS4 in 2015). If assessed based on other measures – postcodes, social class and levels of education (significant number of parents didn't go to uni, for example), school's intake broader than it appears. Keen to broaden mix still further, in line with government thinking – possibly through changes to admissions policy. Definitely a case of watch this space.

Entrance: Entrance day could be a tourist attraction all on its own, Kingston streets packed with small boys and their parents queuing to get in. Same crowds turn up in Sutton and even Slough to try their luck at selective schools there, says head, so not as daunting as it looks.

Admissions now favour locals after considerable legal to-ing and fro-ing overturned previous cross-London (and further) free for all. Now there's a 14km priority area extending to Kingston, Wimbledon, Thames Ditton, Surbiton, Richmond, Hounslow. Better all round, says head, shorter journey times ensuring that more can enjoy the before and after school activities.

Also more places – now 180 year 7 places (was 120 just a few years ago) allocated in two-stage admissions process, each consisting of English and maths assessments, weighted so as not to disadvantage younger candidates. Some occasional places in other years – new candidates only – those sitting but unsuccessful at 11+ can only try again for sixth form, when need (as do existing pupils) minimum five A and three Bs at GCSE (or numerical equivalent) with A*/As in three of four desired A level subjects. Around a third of sixth form are new.

'Didn't think I'd get in,' said pupil remembering the agonising wait after merry round of entrance exams. One family was poised to accept independent school place, knowing that fees would be a struggle. 'Would have been the unluckiest boy in the school. Here, feel like the luckiest.'

Exit: Vast majority to Russell Group, regular large contingent to Oxbridge (22 in 2016, plus 18 medics).

Money matters: Asks for voluntary donation – if possible £520 a year per child, to some a chunky sum. Understood that won't be affordable for everyone – pay what you can. Over the years, it's funded goodies including new labs and cricket nets – and there's also (discreet) help with uniform costs and school trips for those in need.

Remarks: Engage, inspire, excel, is the motto. It's more like a check list than an exhortation. Delivers 'well rounded, well read, normal human beings,' said a parent. 'It's an independent education provided by the state and we are very fortunate.'

Tower House Preparatory School

188 Sheen Lane, London SW14 8LF

Pupils: 190 • Ages: 4–13

Fees: £11,859 – £13,452 pa

Tel: 020 8876 3323
Email: admissions@thsboys.org.uk
Website: www.thsboys.org.uk

Headmaster: Since 2009, Greg Evans BSc, MA, PGCE. Was director of studies at Sussex House for five years and at Kings House Richmond for nine years before that. Early 50s. Genuinely loves his job and lives for the school. 'I always put the boys first. I keep their interests front and centre when making any decisions,' he explains. Wife is Icelandic and they regularly escape to their place in Reykjavík. Teenage son and daughter. Self-confessed sports nut. Recently taken up spinning at the gym in an attempt to stay fit. Currently enjoying the challenge of learning the trumpet for first time. 'I am not an empire builder but I like to think I have improved the place.' Boys adore him; parents hold him in high esteem. An exceptionally dedicated head.

Entrance: Non-selective. First 18 to register are guaranteed a place. Siblings very rarely turned down – 'there would have to be something spectacularly wrong, as family is at the core of what we do.' Before entry into reception, boys spend a morning in school to see whether they would cope in this environment. From year 3 onwards, potential pupils sit assessments in English, maths and reading and have an informal interview. Places generally fill up three years in advance with bulging waiting lists, so sensible to put names down as soon as possible. Not unknown for parents to check out the school before their son is born. Vast majority registered by first birthday. Occasional places further up the school are snapped up quickly. 'We could probably almost double in size tomorrow but we wouldn't be the same school. People come to us for a reason. We are the only single-sex, single-form boys' prep school in south west London and we are not giving up that niche on my watch!' states head.

Exit: Each year roughly a third goes to St Paul's, KCS Wimbledon and Westminster; a third to board (Charterhouse, Wellington, Eton); a third to other London schools (Hampton, Emanuel). Head states, 'From a recent cohort of 20, I am very proud that boys went to 15 different schools. We make sure that the boys go to a school that is suitable for them. It's not a responsibility that I take lightly. I tell parents very plainly to their faces that if I think they are trying to send their son to a school where they are going to be unhappy, that this will effectively be a mental scar on them all the way into adulthood.' Parents feel head knows their sons inside out and that he offers well-informed advice about senior schools. Robust numbers of art, music, drama and sports scholarships. Vast majority stays through until 13; only a handful has left at 11 in the last eight years.

Remarks: School is located on a residential street in East Sheen, on the edge of Richmond Park. No rolling acres on site but school is creative with space it does have. The façade is not beautiful, though the new build for reception pupils is a great improvement on the Victorian privies that it has replaced. Head also admits it is not ideal being situated under the flight path. 'We have learnt to live with the frequent shadows being cast as a 747 goes past – we get on, it accentuates our hearing!'

Warm, happy, family feel to the school but it is nevertheless ambitious. One form entry with 18 in reception, roughly 20 per class thereafter. One mother commented that its small size was one of its selling points: 'Boys all know each other well and that gives them confidence.'

Junior and senior sections on same site, with plenty of interaction between the two. Older boys hear younger ones read and help them out at lunchtime. A healthy amount of hero worship goes on. Junior school considered to be gentle by parents, a place where little boys can be little boys. Every Friday morning reception boys head for the forest school where they build dens, climb trees and jump in muddy puddles. Some parents we spoke to felt that the transition from one part of the school to the other was hard: 'It's a big leap to go from such a nurturing junior school to a full-speed London prep at the end of year 3, but this has to happen at some stage.'

Has been single sex since it was founded in 1931 with just three boys. Head sees single-sex schools as a no brainer. 'Boys and girls develop differently. If boys are educated away from girls at this stage we can take away some of the pressures they feel to keep up with them. By the time they are 13, the gap is hardly there at all'.

Emphasis on impeccable manners: boys are expected to shake their teacher's hand and look them in the eye as they say goodbye at the end of each day and decent table manners are expected. Great sense of tradition here. Pupils all know the words to I Vow to Thee, My Country by the time they leave. Head wants them to look back on their prep school with a sense of pride. 'We send well rounded, polite but humble young men onto their next schools.'

House system is at the centre of the school. Boys are apparently more scared of getting a rocket from their head of house than the headmaster. 'They don't want to let the side down. We're a small school and it is very apparent if you stick your head above the parapet. We have a sense of collective responsibility here'. Community spirit is important. Pupils play music at local care homes, clear the river bank of weeds and regularly raise money for national and international charities.

No academic scholarship class 'as it would be divisive and that goes against everything that we stand for.' If a child is sitting a scholarship, then teachers put on supplementary lessons as necessary. Head insists, 'We are not a slave to pre-tests but we provide lunchtime workshops and extra practice for those boys who are taking them.' Though uncommon here, head believes that tutoring is a mistake: 'If your son needs to be tutored to the hilt in order to squeeze into a school then you're doing him a disservice and you are setting him up for a fall in the future'. Head aims to deliver a bespoke education, 'a Harley Street approach'.

Most able boys are well stretched, with setting in some subjects from year 3 onwards. According to one mother, the top set for Latin in year 8 certainly gallops along at a fair crack. One parent commented that 'if your son is clever, he will do very well at Tower House. The average boy finds it a little harder.' Another disagreed and felt that, given its non-selective intake, the school caters successfully for all abilities.

Reading is taken seriously and a reading wall records numbers of books read by each boy during the term. For the group of pupils who reads the most, a huge bag of sweets awaits. Library is enticing: jam-packed with adventure books and offset by jazzy mood lighting. School ring-fences weekly reading sessions in the library for each class. Boys feel like secret agents as they proffer their fingerprints to take books out. Impressive numbers of boys win prizes in national literary competitions and regularly get their work published in anthologies.

Currently 35 have some sort of mild special educational need, usually dyslexia. Small group booster sessions offered; 10 per cent receive individual support from full-time SENCo. Tends to be for English but help also given with study skills and advice on improving concentration. Rare for a boy to need support throughout his time here.

Very successful on sports front. The envy of every other prep school in London with its access to the Bank of England's beautifully manicured sports grounds, just a stone's throw away. Rugby, cricket, football, swimming, basketball, hockey, tennis and dance offered. Head comments that 'we are often described as punching above our weight but this suggests we are plucky losers, which we are not.' Excellent sports tuition from a host of specialist coaches. Head smiles, 'We've moved away from the enthusiastic history teacher coaching the first XI!' School is particularly strong at cricket, reflected in its eagerly-anticipated biennial sports tour to Barbados. All senior boys included, irrespective of sporting prowess. 'Everyone can go along – we have a media group that blogs, sends tweets back home and produces magazines. I force myself to go too,' jokes head. All boys from years 3 to 8 make a team of some sort; everyone represents the school at least once every term. One father stated that 'Tower House can hold its own with the great names in the prep school landscape.' Headmaster rows enthusiastically up the Thames every year with year 8 boys in the Great River Race.

'Art in every form is stretched and pushed here and it constantly amazes me. If you are creative you should come to us,' states head. Inspirational art teacher is supported by two talented artists in residence. Boys get the opportunity to experiment with a multitude of resources from ceramics and textiles to glass and film. Fantastic DT – boys keen to get out the saws, vices and hammers at every opportunity. Music is thriving too and 80 per cent learns an instrument. There is something for everyone on the music front including two choirs (all welcome), two rock bands, an orchestra, a swing band, a woodwind ensemble as well as string and jazz groups.

Drama deservedly gets the headlines and head beams when he talks about the drama here: 'I have the most gifted head of drama in the country. Boys will crawl over broken glass for him. He has ambitions for the boys which many other people wouldn't even consider. It is my job to ensure that his ambitions are taken seriously. We see how far we can push it'. To date, Tower House is the only school, prep or senior, that has produced a full length feature film which premiered in the West End. Head explains, 'We don't try to replicate that every year, though, as it would take over and we'd get a reputation for being a bunch of luvvies!' Head sees drama productions as being great team-building exercises as everyone can contribute, from the ultra-confident thespian who delivers impassioned speeches to the lower-key boys who would rather focus on props or lighting. If a boy wants a part in a play then one is created for him. The current record is 91 boys involved in one performance. Here, as elsewhere, school lives by its motto of 'an opportunity for every boy'. Starry ex-pupils include comedian Jack Whitehall, actor Robert Pattinson and documentary film-maker Louis Theroux.

Pastoral care is a priority. School has ring-fenced well-being and resilience sessions every half term. Boys are encouraged to de-stress regularly, whether through yoga classes, practising meditation or running before school in Richmond Park. 'We aim to give the boys the toolkit by which they can face the pressures of modern life'. Head has noticed outside pressures on the boys are increasing, not only academically but also on the co-curricular front, such as selection for sports teams and musical ensembles. 'Parents sometimes over-expect,' he laments. 'I'm in my 22nd year in a south west London prep school and think that I have seen most cases of parental pressure, and hope I know how to deal with them'.

Current clubs include debating, chess, touch-typing, sewing and maths games. One parent we spoke to felt that the clubs on offer could be more ambitious and less sport-centric.

School aims to make fees as all-inclusive as possible so parents do not have to keep reaching for the cheque book throughout the term. Unlike many schools, learning support lessons, clubs and residential trips are not seen as extras. Full and part funded means-tested bursaries available from year 3.

Mostly professional families. Both parents tend to work but also many mothers do not. Pupils and staff generally live close enough to walk or cycle to school, heading in from East Sheen, Putney and Barnes, so snow days are unheard of here. Parents rave about the excellent communication between school and home. Active and vocal PTA. Parents give talks to boys about their careers, in a variety of fields including medicine, law and journalism. Cosmopolitan mix, including significant numbers of Scandinavians and Spaniards at present. This cultural diversity is celebrated with themed lunches. Head has introduced a grandparents' day and thinks it is important to involve them in their grandchildren's education, particularly as so many of them foot the fees.

Healthy numbers of male staff who parents think provide a very positive role model. Recent staff revue, put on for parents, included priceless sketches from Only Fools and Horses and 'Allo 'Allo. Head cites this as being 'indicative of the confidence that staff have in themselves and their warm relationships with parents.'

A remarkably inclusive school that feels like a traditional boarding prep. One mother commented that 'it does what it says on the tin. It prepares them very well for senior school'. Another parent went further: 'The headmaster and his staff have one single objective – that of educating boys to the highest possible standard, whilst nurturing extracurricular talent, instilling courtesy and the highest moral values.' Undoubtedly, Tower House is thriving.

Trevor-Roberts School

281

55-57 Eton Avenue, London NW3 3ET

Pupils: 180 • Ages: 5-13 • C of E

Fees: £13,890 – 15,600 pa

Tel: 020 7586 1444
Email: trseniorweb@trevor-robertsschool.co.uk
Website: www.trevor-robertsschool.co.uk

Headmaster: Since 1999, Simon Trevor-Roberts BA (50s). Son of the founder, Trevor-Roberts studied at Westminster School before reading English at Aberystwyth. In 1983, he joined his father Christopher in the family firm, where he learnt his trade by example. (He has since been joined by his sister Amanda, who heads up the junior school). Mild mannered and reflective, he has a very clear sense of what the school is about: 'We try to get children to enjoy the process of learning.' Continues to teach maths to the 13 plus candidates, because he's found he, too, now has the knack of putting things across clearly. 'I shadowed my father for a long time and learnt how to do it by osmosis.' Parents find him immensely approachable and engaged. 'You always have complete access to the head and he knows all the kids incredibly well.' Married with two grown children, both of whom attended the school.

Entrance: Register as soon after birth as possible. About 80 sets of parents are contacted when their child is 1 and offered a tour. Those who wish to proceed confirm this in writing, and the school assesses the first 50 children on their list in the September prior to the calendar year in which they turn 5. 'We're not expecting any preparation, but we want to make sure it will be a happy transition,' says the registrar. 'We're looking for inquisitive children who want to learn. Getting that is more a dark art than a science.' The school generally tries to give priority to siblings, 'but only if it's the right school'. Often takes in one or two more in year 4, when the year group divides into two classes.

Exit: Girls mainly – though not exclusively – at 11, generally to Francis Holland, South Hampstead and other north London favourites. Most boys (and some girls) at 13, to a wide range of day and boarding schools, including regular placements at City of London, Eton, Harrow, Highgate, Latymer Upper, Merchant Taylors', UCS and Westminster. 'The head is very good at managing parental expectations,' said one former parent.

T

Remarks: This is a family-run school with a very distinctive ethos, deriving in large part from its origins. Founded by the current heads' father in the 1950s with just 14 boys, it was originally seen as a refuge for the 'unteachable'. 'My father had a reputation for taking those whom other schools had given up on and getting them through entrance exams to leading public schools,' says Simon Trevor-Roberts.

Today, the school can take its pick of north London's brightest, but continues to select a mixed-ability (now co-educational) intake and provide a tailor-made education for all. 'They want every child to work to his or her potential and really do treat every child as an individual,' said one parent.

Children start in year 1 in a class grouped according to the calendar year of their birth. In year 4, this is rearranged to allow everyone to be in place for secondary school entrance. One class of 16-18 in the early years, two classes in years 4 to 6, then a single form again for the final two years. 'We like to move children around so they're not in the same group for eight years,' says the head. 'It give us the flexibility to allow those who require it a bit more time and accelerate those who need it.' Parents confirm this is skilfully managed. 'They're constantly readjusting their approach for different levels of learning, but not in a way that disturbs the children.'

Specialist subject teaching from the word go, with a classroom teacher for the core subjects, but music, history, geography, science and art all taught in their own space. 'It keeps the week fresh.'

Plenty of imaginative teaching by intelligent (including many Oxbridge), though not always qualified, staff. French from year 1, Latin from year 5, some Greek in year 8, Mandarin taught as a club. Special needs addressed by weekly sessions with the learning support coordinator and outside specialists.

Everyone staying for the final two years sits common entrance. 'We take it very seriously,' says the head. 'Eleven plus is about flexible problem solving; by 13, it's more structure on the page.' Senior schools praise the 'structure on the page' received.

Very good at ensuring the basics are in place. 'Sometimes you have to be a bit tough,' says the head. 'We insist that children use a pen rather than touch type. If you have to write an essay under exam conditions, you have to be able to discipline your thoughts.' No truck with overly formalised exam training. 'Non-verbal reasoning is not a subject,' he says crisply.

Formal homework from year 3, starting out with 20 minutes in English or maths ('It shows them how to work by themselves and for themselves'), up to two hours a night for the top forms. 'They do work very hard, but the atmosphere still manages to be reasonably relaxed,' said one mother.

Good relationships with staff are fundamental ('The teacher is not someone they're trying to hoodwink,' says the head), as is the view that effort should be lauded over achievement. 'Children are perfectly aware there's competition elsewhere, they don't need it reinforced. We want them to be in competition with themselves.' Good work is rewarded with a 'digniora', with recipients queuing in the lunch hour to have their accolade verified and registered. Three merits win a token (designed to reflect the season) to be spent at independent local shops.

Breadth well beyond the exam curriculum is given enormous emphasis. Outstanding music – 'We love music' – with a dynamic head. Taught in the classroom from years 1 to 6, with the addition of numerous ensembles (brass, jazz, string, woodwind, chamber choir, rock band) and much external participation (at the Royal Festival Hall, St John's Smith Square, etc.) Twice weekly art lessons (one in year 7) in a bright art department at the top of school, with its own kiln. Extra art and DT on offer for enthusiasts on Wednesday afternoons.

Cultural values that have largely been submerged elsewhere – 'Everyone is encouraged to have a novel on the go' – with half an hour of silent reading daily after lunch. Poetry and drama matter and prove great confidence builders. 'My son almost died of nerves the first time he had to read out a poem,' said one mother, 'but now he loves drama and performing.' 'The plays are unbelievable,' said another.

Plenty of fresh air and exercise, with a good-sized, well-equipped playground, including popular table tennis, miniature railway and chicken coop ('the chickens are a great comfort to quieter, shyer children.'). Primrose Hill, a few hundred yards from the door, enables twice weekly games. Definitely not a school, however, where 'go-fight-win' is on the agenda. 'Children love sport, but I don't want a First Eleven ethos, with the captain of games strutting around,' says the head. 'We do play matches against other schools, but everyone has a go.'

The senior school building, a fine example of the arts and crafts, was the founder's own home and still offers delightful domestic interiors with William Morris wallpaper in the front hall and mid-century classic tables used instead of desks in the top forms. The juniors are housed in their own building with a separate dining room and science lab.

The atmosphere is civilised but structured ('It's a nice mix of the very strict and the nurturing and kind – teachers are always willing to talk things through.'). Pupils sit down to eat their biscuits at break before rushing off to the playground. Everyone has a hot lunch, served through an open hatch, 'so they can see where it is made.' Staff share the dining hall with pupils. 'Eating is socialising.' Food is freshly prepared on site using local produce.

Manners and uniform are both reasonably relaxed (no backs against the wall here). Light blue polo shirt for younger children, dark blue for older ones. Trousers and skirts, 'something reasonable'. 'Jeans are fine, jeans hanging off the hips are not.'

Often the school of choice for the liberal, media intelligentsia (including some famous names), the type of parent who genuinely believes in the well-rounded education, not the rush to the top of the league tables. (Competition here, though it undoubtedly exists, tends to be on the level of how many operas your child has seen rather than where the family went skiing.) Mainly local, some from Notting Hill, Queen's Park, Islington. The head feels 'there's no typical child, but I've heard people say our children are very kind.'

Trinity School

Shirley Park, Croydon, Surrey CR9 7AT

Pupils: 1,009 • Ages: 10–18 • Sixth form: 286 (70 girls)

Fees: £15,906 pa

Tel: 020 8656 9541
Email: admissions@trinity.croydon.sch.uk
Website: www.trinity-school.org

Headmaster: Since September 2016, Alasdair Kennedy, previously deputy master at Dulwich College. Educated at Fettes; degree in engineering and PGSE from Cambridge. Has taught physics at Rugby and Sevenoaks as well as Dulwich. Married with three boys and has a keen interest in all sport (a Cambridge rugby blue) and in music, playing the piano, double bass and guitar.

Academic matters: Results particularly good at GCSE with steady rise in top grades (89 per cent A*/A in 2016). At A level, 90 per cent A*-B and 60 per cent A*/A in 2016. Business studies, chemistry and economics down over previous years, though school 'expects the new head of department to swiftly turn this round...' Lots of stars, however, with biology, Eng lit, maths (far and away the single biggest subject) and further maths amongst the large-entry subjects regularly achieving 90 per cent at A*/B or above. School trawls in the prizes, too, awarded for everything from investment to science plus Maths Olympiad gold medals. Finalists in international safe-cracking competition (success determined by physics know-how, not gelignite).

The school is open-minded to range of teaching techniques, from whizzy interactive lessons to more conventional didactic ones. Plenty of both going on as far as we could see. Best, certainly as a spectator sport, are those that spill out into the corridors – we enjoyed watching group of boys whizz humming tops down long lengths of rope to demonstrate Doppler effect. 'Sums up boys' education, boys who are doing boys' things but with real enthusiasm – that's how lessons should be.'

Admirable get-ahead approach sees early start made in key subjects. Some of maths GCSE basics, for example, covered in year 8, reckoned a parent. Helped, too, by enthusiastic teachers managing largish groups (20 average class size, maximum 24) with aplomb, considerable stock rotation seeing oldies replaced with a fair few first jobbers (also cheaper, pointed out parental cynic). Includes some former City bods who have made their money – and enjoyed spending it, too; see staff car park for details. 'Proof that they are doing the job because they really want to,' thought a sixth former who had seen teaching standards rise during his time at the school, Another praised 'great young teachers' with inspirational lessons notable for minimum of note-taking drudgery.

When worst anyone can say of teaching is that it can be 'a tad bloodless,' there's not much to worry about. Some inevitable variance – a literature-averse child encountered English teacher who interrogated parents on son's interests so could 'get him reading' and hasn't stopped since. Another, less fortunate, '... arrived not liking reading and left feeling just the same,' said a mother, who felt a few more initiatives based in large, well-lit library – book clubs and the like – wouldn't come amiss. Individual subject libraries come in for particular praise from older pupils.

Universal appreciation by pupils and parents for staff attitude that blends amiability with professionalism. 'Friendly but with a distance, which I liked,' thought a mother. Tolerant of parent visits, too, in contrast with other schools where, said a parent, 'you feel that you're totally unwanted and you shouldn't go past the gate.' We even heard of a dedicated mother sitting at the back during maths lessons. Parents feel confident that on the very rare occasions that issues with teachers crop up they will be listened to and the problem quickly resolved. Pupil absences well handled, knowledge gaps quickly filled.

Homework, too, normally well managed. 'Not excessive and if there's occasional congestion, will get in touch,' thought a parent who, like others, rated home school communications highly. 'Teachers will always email back and apologise if they haven't done so immediately' – though felt that occasionally had to nudge the school a bit to get different departments to communicate with each other if, for example, sports or music looked in danger of overwhelming academic commitments.

Only unspoken issue is dreaded letters home, sent to around 20 boys underperforming in year 10 exams and unlikely to make the grade at GCSE. Rumours abound. Felt by one mother to be an anomaly in an otherwise compassionate environment. 'School takes them in, then they're thrown back,' thought a mother. School stresses that letters are invariably the last stage in a programme of interventions which work in almost every case, all but three from recent batch making it through to sixth form. 'Our intention is that everyone will stay on.' Points out, however, that for pupils struggling at the bottom in high-achieving school, it may be better to move to different school where confidence and performance are often transformed.

School understandably wary (and weary) of changes to A levels and GCSEs. Fine for school, but pupils only travel this way once, so important that 'not in the vanguard of untested novelty.' What matters above all is 'the quality of the people standing in front of children day in and day out.' On the basis of results, it's in plentiful supply.

Games, options, the arts: Super at sport, stunning at music and while not exactly hiding its light under a bushel – 'exceptional' is school's own verdict – you'd be hard pressed to find much to carp at, bar occasional organisational blips. 'Gave up asking which kit to pack years ago as never heard back,' sighs a parent.

Show enthusiasm here and you'll be encouraged to find your niche, with fair share of trophies making their way to display shelves by way of proof. Team sports are rugby, hockey, swimming, golf, cricket, tennis, with many a final reached but perhaps slightly fewer of the top prizes scooped than a few years back. School thinks that while those in search of year in, year out national trophy glory would probably still head for Dulwich or Whitgift, it depends 'how you measure sporting success.' If formal premiership existed, school would score a top 10 place.

Several parents described some under the surface frustration that needs excising. 'There's so much talent that could be converted into success,' said one, who thought more input from talented individuals – there are currently 40 regional and county players doing wonders in everything from triathlon to high and triple jump – might nudge teams to greater efforts.

Pupils clearly enjoy what's on offer – pressure of a low key nature, enjoyment pretty much guaranteed, inclusiveness stressed. Some of lower teams named after colours rather than letters, a disguise presumably aimed at avoiding discouragement. High tolerance for the less keen who are just 'happy to tick along.' Some pupils, according to parents, see relegation to alternative indoors activity as a positive perk, particularly on chilly afternoons.

School principally known, however, for its music, which is so good – drama almost equally so – that parents mention school in same breath as top specialist music colleges. Music is everywhere, strains of flute and keyboard piercing the air like shafts of sunlight, dedicated staff teaching 500 individual lessons a week and top quality instruments as standard (school first in London to boast all-Steinway line up, though arguably trumped by recent chance for top string players to play a real Stradivarius). Around 100 pupils a year are involved in professional productions, appearing everywhere from national radio and TV to Ronnie Scott's, Glyndebourne and Royal Opera House. Six on tour in US on day of visit.

Musicians and singers are 'picked up, nurtured, taken off and encouraged,' said a parent. With the exception of bit of below the bar-line muttering about recent departmental changes, nothing but praise. No wonder some of the most talented pupils even turn down grammar school places to take advantage of seemingly endless opportunities. Choice of 50 ensembles caters for super-talented and less so, with enthusiastic beginners getting as much of a kick out of performing as gifted peers. Even school mag describes arrival of girls as 'adding a different octave' (on a more prosaic note, their presence means boys smell better too, according to school nurse).

Stunning and sometimes unsettling art that, in the case of naked (female) mannequin, arms outstretched against cross, part Borg, part Passion, haunts the brain for hours afterwards. DT is a similar wealth of traditional skills delivered with novelty, with bells, whistles (and entrancing flashing lights). Extracurricular programme is rich, particularly in first three years, with 150 lunchtime clubs and much in the way of community work. 'My son's passions are covered 100 per cent,' said a mother. Another said 'everything' is on offer, from foreign trips (Spanish students to Salamanca, photographers to Florence) to domestic outings (sixth form psychologists to London Zoo to study spider and other phobias).

Icing on the cake would be for DT (popular GCSE and A level choice) to be joined on the timetable by cookery. Particularly galling, felt mother, as at least one of local state schools now has boys arriving home with gourmet dishes on regular basis. 'It just doesn't get on private boys' schools' radar, but who is going to cook for these boys when they grow up? The world has changed.' More cookery coming soon in Portakabins freed up by soon to be renovated pavilion (no exam though).

Background and atmosphere: Pupils and staff don't beat about the bush when describing school. Comments include 'ugly' and 'like a 1960s conference centre,' but as they point out, 'what matters is what goes on inside.' There's no getting away from it, though. Acres don't roll so much as jut, grey building block frontage effectively though bizarrely concealing considerable greenery at the back.

Even so, immediate vibe is welcoming and slightly quirky, from multitude of well-lit spaces (many accessorised with pianos), cheerful staff and clear affection for surroundings, to pleas to 'visit us' prominently displayed on website. School essence summed up by picture of animated science lesson, pupil on what looks like giant vacuum cleaner (actually a hovercraft) being chased by laughing teacher, other boys cheering them on from the side. Certainly looks like fun, though tolerant, grown up feel makes school far more than cheeky young whippersnapper to staid sister and brother schools (Whitgift and Old Palace respectively) that make up the Whitgift Foundation. Baffled by the relationship between them? 'You're not the only one,' says school.

Extent of what a parent describes as 'sibling rivalry' between the two (mainly) boys' schools can only be guessed at (heads are coy about this). Parental rumour mill has it that decision to have girls in sixth form here – popular with all, though fairly low vis for youngest pupils – went to the wire because of fears that popularity, already at a high, would impact on application numbers at other Whitgift schools. Alarm understandable given school's many natural advantages. May not have quite the same presence as more historic establishments but then nor is it on quite the same scale, with smaller roll and more personable feel that has even parents with children elsewhere sounding slightly wistful when they talk about it.

Pastoral care, well-being and discipline: Taken very seriously. Sixth formers trained as mentors. Issues, including bullying, appear rarely but are swiftly and effectively sorted when they do. 'When another kid picked on my son it was dealt with sensibly,' thought a mother.

Year 6 juniors, known universally as J-bugs on account of 'being a bit annoying' in addition to short stature and giant backpacks – 'you get used to it,' thought one, with slight weariness – go straight into the mix with minimal cossetting and equanimity, furnished with map and high expectations. 'Teachers expect you to be on time from the second week,' said one, who clearly didn't see it as a problem.

Plenty of rewards, ranging from post-duty free lunches for prefects (who can recommend other pupils for commendations but don't wield much in the way of sticks) to teachers' end of term treats, including whole class outing to Nando's (dream choice). Conventional sanctions through system of 'signings' in homework diaries. Three strikes and it's a Saturday detention (chief crime usually not handing in homework on time). Lots of nurture on site, including school nurse, sympathy on tap (first visit goes unremarked, second in a term flagged up with phone call home).

Pupils and parents: Parents approve of the mix. 'A real balance in the classes, ages and races,' thought one. State primaries (some local, many further afield) field just over half of the pupils and around 45 per cent come from preps. Good bus services – mainly within a 10-mile radius (Oxted, Wandsworth, Dulwich, Farnborough and the like).

One parent thought addition of girls in sixth form was great for boys but 'wouldn't send my own daughter.' School disagrees – the ebullient and confident may flourish here but so, equally, do 'the more reserved. In the same way, we have bright, strong, talented and shyer boys.' Girls themselves, including one who visited out of curiosity but signed up on strength of head's presentation, felt that a range of characters is catered for, though sufficient confidence to voice views in male-dominated classes was a character essential. Much pride that current girl physicists, though a minority, outshining the boys, who are 'a bit annoyed that we're better.'

T

Amongst the parents, little one-upmanship. Fewer feverishly competitive types than elsewhere and socialising so much fun that events attract complete outsiders. No pressure to attend events but the many who do tend to stay late. 'Have left car outside school overnight...' said one.

Entrance: In some cases, actually preferred over local grammars, particularly for super-talented musicians if fees can be found. Praise doesn't come much higher.

Biggest intake (70) is in year 7. Also takes around 42 boys in year 6 and a further 20 in year 9. All sit papers in English (comprehension and essay) plus maths and VR, shortlisted candidates attending interview. While desire to boost results has pushed up entry standards (papers broadly the same, pass mark higher), won't turn away those who need support as long as they can cope academically, range of difficulties happily accommodated. Another 30 are added in the sixth form.

Exit: Some to specialist music schools including Yehudi Menuhin, testimony to lure of music excellence here (generous scholarships too). Others, occasionally ('handful in eight years,' says school) for less happy reasons (London exposure to drink and drugs the inevitable issues) are eased out but with discreet generosity that usually guarantees a second chance elsewhere. 'They don't blank them out but leave it open to go to another place,' said a parent.

After A levels, vast majority head to university; six to Oxbridge in 2016 plus five medics. Other top destinations include Bristol, Southampton, York, Edinburgh and Manchester, plus Royal Veterinary College and normal London suspects (King's, Imperial, UCL) as well as US (Rutgers). Huge range of courses taken, music and sciences of all descriptions well represented, from bioveterinary sciences to mechanical engineering.

Money matters: Exceptionally good for support. Scholarships worth between 10 and 50 per cent of the fees awarded for academics performance, plus music, sport, drama, art and (less common) design technology. Supplemented by excellent range of bursaries from Whitgift Foundation, which ensure that the gifted but less affluent won't miss out on a place.

Remarks: Grey outside, bursting with colour within. 'The school of the moment,' said a parent. Top sporting talent may haver slightly but if academic strength, music and general joie de vivre are your bag, practically perfect in every way. Forget the slightly unpromising surroundings. When the atmosphere is so buzzy that one parent said she even looked forward to the school run, you know you're on to a winner.

Twickenham Preparatory School

Beveree, 43 High Street, Hampton TW12 2SA

Pupils: 281 • Ages: 4–13

Fees: £10,245 – £11,100 pa

Tel: 020 8979 6216
Email: office@twickenhamprep.co.uk
Website: www.twickenhamprep.co.uk

Headmaster: Since 2005, Mr David Malam BA Southampton (history), PGCE King Alfred's College, Winchester (40s). Has been at the school for over 15 years, having joined as a history teacher, then deputy head. Before that taught in junior and first schools in Southampton (unusually including a year in a reception class) and at Logos International School in Cyprus, teaching ages 7-16.

He's very popular with pupils, gets to know them all well and is warm and funny around them. 'They are very fond of him, but also really respect him', said a mother. 'He has natural authority and never needs to shout; has a great gift with children', said another. 'He's better with the children than with parents', said a third. 'Personally I agree it's all about the kids, but lots of parents seem to want indulging and he's not good at that side of things'. However, those that know him best say he is 'an excellent headmaster'.

He's a great sports fan, especially football and squash, and he has also played chess at a high level. Lives locally, married, with five children who are, or have been, at the school. 'He treats them just the same as anybody else, they're not his favourites', said our year 6 tour guides confidently.

Entrance: Non-selective at reception, and while perhaps not necessary to register at birth, think about it by a first birthday. Although it behaves and sounds like a church school, there is actually no religious requirement in the admission criteria; if you are happy with the ethos they are happy to have you. That's not to say school will say yes to everyone; you've got to fit in socially, behaviourally and academically. Largely a local intake. Other places are occasionally available and subject to assessments in English, maths and reasoning. Bus service runs from Richmond and Twickenham. Aims to maintain its 50:50 ratio of boys:girls.

Exit: Girls at 11+ to Lady Eleanor Holles, Surbiton High, Wimbledon High, Sir William Perkins, Kingston Grammar, St Catherine's. At 13+ boys to Hampton, Halliford, Reeds and St George's. A few to St Paul's and King's College Wimbledon. Usually a healthy number of scholarships.

Remarks: A popular co-ed prep which prides itself on its positive, family atmosphere and strong Christian ethos. Non-selective, so not packed with academic boffs, but it's no place for a slouch either – increasing numbers of scholars attest to the academic thrust here in recent times. Not as pressured a place as some Surrey schools, but still seriously ambitious for its children, who are indeed going on to win places at the county's top senior schools. Carefully guided by Mr Malam, Twickenham Prep children will not sit many entrance exams – no more than two or three. 'The eight or nine some do is ridiculous,' he says. 'It's unnecessary; we know our children very well and therefore know which school will suit them best'.

Specialist subject teaching from the off in French, ICT, music and PE. By year 4 all teaching is subject-specific, with pupils moving from room to room for their lessons. No streaming, but setting for maths from year 4. Latin for most girls from year 5 and for boys when they move onto the common entrance programme. French for all, with a little bit of Greek and an introduction to Spanish for those up to it. Nice small classes, typically of 18. Homework is reasonably low key; 'I don't see it as a means of destroying family life,' says Mr Malam. Starts gently with some reading and spelling up to year 2, then one to two homeworks a night, reaching 40 minutes a night by year 6. Thrice-weekly homework clubs similarly take the pressure off family time.

Pupils seem well-engaged with their lessons, and the school's atmosphere is calm and purposeful. ISI inspectors judge teaching here to be always good, and sometimes outstanding, with provision for children with learning difficulties or disabilities said to be 'excellent'. However, it is not the place for a more serious special need, and none of the LDD children currently on roll are statemented.

Music is something of a strength here – there's a large choir and 80 per cent of pupils are swept up for music lessons and get plenty of opportunities to play and perform. Sport is often a bugbear in a small-ish set up like this one – on-site practice space is limited and it's hard to beat some of the larger schools in the area. But on the plus side, the school does have use of Hampton Football Club's facilities, which are directly behind it, and has notched up some major tournament wins of late. Parents appreciate the fact that the school's approach is inclusive, with all the children getting an opportunity to play competitively if they want to, with C teams fielded if necessary. Swimming from years 1 to 5 off site. Year 7 and year 8 boys pick up squash and badminton too.

Nice extracurricular clubs, including music and movement, historic adventures and sewing for pre-prep, and touch-typing, table tennis and knitting for prep pupils. Wrap-around pre- and after-school care. Mr Malam, and therefore his school, is a big fan of the Mind Lab (thinking abilities and life skills) programme which is timetabled as a weekly lesson. Typically the children play strategy games and learn about lateral thinking. The idea is that this work makes pupils more adaptable and less easily fazed when encountering a new problem for the first time. Mr Malam seems to have converted parents, who praise the programme. 'At first I thought it was some sort of hideous team-building exercise beloved of large organisations, but in fact it does get the children thinking in a different way', said one. 'They think they are just playing games, but really they are learning. And with all the verbal and non-verbal reasoning involved in many entrance exams these days, it does seem to give them a great basis for working things out'.

More mind games come in the form of chess – another Malam passion – or 'obsession' as one mother wryly observed. The school has built up quite a reputation as IAPs champions, English Schools national finalists and borough champions. Grandmaster Daniel King works with the school, involving up to 50 of the children regularly, with up to 30 of them going on to play for school teams.

Parents view the school as very strong pastorally – again, ISI says its provision in this area is 'outstanding'. The school is a really nurturing place; welcoming and warm, a gentle and kind environment with no sharp edges. Watchwords for the pupils are 'calm, courteous, courageous and considerate'. 'And they don't just pay lip-service to those words, they really count for something here,' said a mother. Discipline not really an issue – teachers use positive reinforcement ('Praising a child who is doing well has quite an effect on a child who is not doing as well themselves', says Mr Malam). Losing or winning house points an equally effective device here.

And as you'd expect from a Christian school, bible-based religious education is taken seriously here and children say prayers together. There's no affiliation to any one church, but close links with nearby St Mary's which the children visit for Christmas and harvest services. Assemblies are Christian-based, with a bible story/theme and a moral message. School has its own hymn book, teaches the Lord's Prayer, hosts visits from local Christian community and other faiths.

T

But that's not to say that the families at this school are all regular worshippers or indeed even Christian – several we spoke to were in fact agnostic or atheist or practitioners of another religion entirely – but obviously these parents share a willingness for their children to be taught about Christian values. 'We don't believe in ignorance of other religions and so have people in to talk about other faiths and cultures too', says Mr Malam. 'Generally I find our parents want their children in a school where they at least understand the ethos, rather than put them into a more secular environment.'

Attracts professional and business-type families, mostly local from Teddington, Twickenham, Sunbury and St Margaret's. The name Twickenham Prep is actually something of a misnomer, as the school is actually in Hampton – it was originally on Twickenham Green and chose to retain its by then well-established name when it relocated in 1992. Set in unexpectedly peaceful and leafy location behind a busy road, the main school building, Beveree, was once owned by John Blow, King's Musician to Charles II, and is grade 2 listed. Overall not masses of space, despite major extensions, but school makes the most of what there is and has sectioned off some space for a well-used amphitheatre and an adventure playground. New nature trail gets pre-prep children exploring the outdoors.

And, lest it all sound too unruffled and worthy, the children also have great fun along the way. A recent fundraising auction of promises saw one boy's family successfully bid for him to take over as headmaster for a day. He took a lesson, spoke to staff, was included in an interview and allowed to introduce some of his own for-one-day-only initiatives. These included arranging for an ice-cream van to visit at the close of school and awarding headmaster's commendation certificates to genuine supporters of Fulham football club.

Increasingly strong academically, it's offering its happy and settled pupils a good all-round education, generally allowing them their pick of all the best local day schools. Holding its own in an area packed with competitive offerings. Not pressured or pushy, rather kind, inspiring and creative.

Twyford Church of England High School

Twyford Crescent, London W3 9PP

Pupils: 1,484 • Ages: 11–18 • Sixth form: 505 • C of E

Tel: 020 8752 0141
Email: admissions@twyford.ealing.sch.uk
Website: www.twyford.ealing.sch.uk

Executive Head Teacher: Since 2002, Dame Alice Hudson MA (Oxon) (40s), educated at Slough Girls' High and Leighton Park, then St Hilda's, Oxford, where she read English. Previously deputy head at Brentside HS, also in Ealing, and prior to that taught at Central Foundation Boys, Islington and Maria Fidelis, Euston. Joined Twyford in 2000, first as deputy, then acting head and appointed head in September 2002. Married to Michael Lyon. He works for the Bank of England ('more public servant than banker,' she says). He is Roman Catholic, she and their four children are Anglican. Her eldest daughter was given a place at Oxford to read modern languages having completed the sixth form here; daughter 2 also a linguist at Cambridge; her son also attends the school.

'The first five years were Herculean,' she says, 'cleaning out the stables'. (She comes from a family of classicists and her conversation is littered with references to the ancient world.) There was the thorny issue of a divided community: the haves and have-nots. The crude observer would put it in plain black and white terms – the churchgoing but poorer and underachieving black community as opposed to the playing-by-the-book, aspirational and privileged white community. Ms Hudson takes a more sophisticated approach. 'The cultural capitalisers and disenfranchised,' she elegantly puts it, 'overlaid with typical inner London underachievement issues connected to socio-economic disadvantage, race and gender'. Whichever description you prefer, Ms Hudson was determined to 'harness the diversity of the student/parent body'. 'Exclusions were high,' she continues, 'and I didn't want to exclude, but to sustain a positive culture.' She proudly announces that she has now achieved three of her original goals: fixed behaviour and attainment, fixed cohesion, fixed aspiration. An intelligent and sensitive woman, she explains she learnt from watching the children; 'you have to read your institution,' she says.

During her tenure she has introduced a public school style house system (there are seven houses named after cathedrals, including Truro, York and Canterbury), a process of electing head boy and girl, the new post of school chaplain (allowing her to employ high calibre teaching staff who are not necessarily practising Christians), Latin and geology. Ms Hudson is a team player and her team consists of all the staff, all the students and all the parents.

Refreshing to see the head of a challenging, big state comprehensive not just running a business but also a passionate educator, lover of youth, life and learning. Not always the case in this inspection and results driven age. Parents and pupils admire her quiet authority (you could hear a pin drop in the assembly she took when she stopped mid-flow to say, 'distressed to hear three people talking', looking directly at them across the packed school hall). This, combined with more than a superficial knowledge of all the pupils as well as their parents, her infectious enthusiasm, disarming modesty, and striking physical presence – 'Miss Hudson is everywhere,' said one admiring 15 year old – and her sensitive awareness of every nuance, all contribute to making her an outstanding head. Lucky school.

Twyford is now part of a Multi Academy Trust – Twyford Church of England Academies Trust, with a sister school in Greenford – William Perkin Church of England High School (a free school that opened in 2013). William Perkin was awarded an Outstanding Ofsted in 2015 and Twyford results remain as strong as ever.

Operations at both schools are 'directed strategically from the centre'. Ofsted, reporting in May 2012 (unsurprisingly, rating the school 'outstanding' in all categories), also picked up on this concern among parents. Dame Hudson is channelling an enormous amount of energy into the project but if there is anyone who has more passion to spare and who has the team building skills to pull off her vision, she is your woman. Again, unsurprisingly, Ofsted agreed.

Karen Barrie, associate head teacher since 2013, was previously deputy head at the school for nine years. She is a mathematician with a degree from Manchester.

Academic matters: Results just get better and better in this academically, non-selective school. In 2016, 73 per cent A*-B and 41 per cent A*/A grades at A level. Top ability students complete extended project – mostly with A*s. Choices include economics, music tech, photography (very successful), psychology, sociology. Biggest improvement is in sixth form – head's especial baby – 'it's a reliable place for your high-achieving child.. we chase them much more in the sixth form', but the less academic well supported too. In 2016 GCSE results saw 90 per cent of students achieve 5+ passes at C or above (including English and maths), with 34 per cent A*/A grades.

ICT (we saw loads of computers) a developing area with interactive whiteboards in every class room and a well-developed VLE. Head sees wisdom in steering the less academic to the practical and creative which 'can be studied alongside A level'. Visual arts are a considerable strength of the school with significant numbers of students going on to art colleges; 16 art foundation applicants in 2016.

Twelve per cent have SLD or SEN ('disproportionately high number of children with statements,' remarks Hudson, 'skewed towards the severe end'). About five per cent of these include those with autism (across the spectrum). All pupils are well supported, either by regular staff or from outside. 'They will be valued and survive here,' says head, 'and parents are also given support – we have very good home-school links.'

Since she arrived there has been a tremendous push on languages and it became a specialisation (along with music) several years ago. 'We identify potential linguists in year 7, accelerate them in French and, in year 8, give them a choice of German and Spanish.' The person responsible for the language programme 'is a zealot' she says. All children have to learn to speak the language, not just from text books, and there are numerous exchanges, to China as well as to the obvious European destinations. Latin is taught once a fortnight and pupils can also choose to do it after school. It's not just a hobby, but also a GCSE option. One girl we met who moved here from the Middle East achieved an A* in GCSE Arabic at the end of year 9. If there is a demand or a talent, the school will make it possible to follow that talent and achieve the potential. Setting in most subjects (including science, maths and languages, English and the humanities) from year 7. From year 9 boys and girls are separated in the top two sets in English. There are at least eight sets straddling seven forms plus a tiny nurture group for the extreme special needs. Parents remark on the fluidity of movement between sets, 'you don't just get labelled as D set.' RE very much a feature of everyday school life and supported in the sixth form by two conferences each year, often with outside speakers on moral or spiritual topics. Curriculum taught on an alternating two-week cycle, which some find confusing at first, but they get used to it.

We heard some mutterings about the SEN department not always picking up strugglers (without statements) as fast as it should nor providing the continuous support needed. We wonder whether the major advances at the upper end of the ability range are sufficiently matched by rigorous attention to those who are finding work hard. However, school points out that the SEN department screens all students at secondary transfer and some 25 per cent are offered extra literacy and numeracy help. Students with SEN support achieve much more highly here than elsewhere (some 80 per cent achieving 5+ A*-C GCSEs as against an average of 23 per cent). There is no doubt that the formidable Ms Hudson, with her passionate eye for detail, would not like to give less than her full attention to everything, but it's a question of priorities. Expectations are undoubtedly high. Referring to one boy, who happens to be of African/Caribbean descent, who recently achieved eight A*s in his mock GCSEs, Ms Hudson says, 'unless he achieves 10 A*s when he sits the exams, we will have failed him.' When it comes to academic achievement, Ms Hudson comments, 'The big issue is that although we are doing well as a comprehensive state school, an independent school would be expecting those results. We need to push beyond.'

Games, options, the arts: Remarkable playing fields (albeit rented, not owned), well-concealed along this urban high street site. Netball especially strong here, but you can choose to play hockey, tennis, football, cricket and basketball too. Inter-form competitions are a major event. Everyone stays to watch the big matches: another one of head's effective community-knitting devices. Dance and athletics popular. Rugby coached by pros from London Wasps. Consistent successes in many sporting areas and representation in borough and regional levels. Thriving art, and stunning music (some parents confessed they wished sport was given as much emphasis as music). The church influence from gospel to choral filters through at every level. A main orchestra plus smaller groups and ensembles present opportunities for lots of live performing. At every assembly there will be live music. When we visited we witnessed a potential Rumer, singing from the heart as she accompanied herself on the piano. Music and music tech facilities impressive and well-used (including the state-of-the-art audio-visual recording studio). Drama is popular and lively and as well as smaller studio performances throughout the year the main event is the massive whole school production that takes place in February. The King and I and Oliver! have recently been performed and one parent commented on the enthusiasm and commitment of her usually shy and reluctant daughter while acting as one of the boys in Oliver!

There is a good work placement programme, though we heard some talk of the aspiring white middle classes with lots of contacts in the world of media and law etc getting plum placements while the less advantaged among the black community ended up working in the charity shop in Shepherd's Bush. School keen to point out that there is support (large database with useful leads, past placements etc, plus an 'Aspirations' conference run annually which invites successful black professionals and entrepreneurs to speak about their work), but the students have to take initiative to tap into that support. The pushy ones are sorted by the end of Lent term, the more lackadaisical are scrabbling around for something a week before they have to start towards the end of the summer term. You can take a horse to water and all that. Pupils enthuse about the number and quality of trips and expeditions – everywhere from St Petersburg to the New Forest for every activity imaginable – photography to water skiing. Lots of charity work.

Background and atmosphere: School tucked behind rare bit of green along the Uxbridge Road. Main building, grade 2 listed The Elms, an elegant, early Georgian house, built 1735, well-preserved and sensibly painted in blues, houses the admin and offices side of things. A diverse mixture of less distinguished and pretty scruffy later blocks, A, B, then, unaccountably, D and M, house rest of school. Rather alarmingly nicknamed The Cage is the large central piece of tarmac surrounded by fencing where 650 pupils line up in alphabetical order each morning. A logistical challenge in a disciplined corporate environment, at Twyford C of E High School it's like sliding a knife through butter. Some attractive modern buildings have emerged organically, including a wonderfully peaceful chapel, a contemporary and refreshingly un-institutional cafeteria (more Café Nero than trad school cafeteria), state-of-the-art performance centre, creative media suite with radio station and refurbished music areas.

Black uniform with white shirts creates somewhat sombre impression but most pupils look tidy (head strides around, not averse to pointing out, amicably, 'shirt!' to any wearer of stray shirt tails) and overall impression is of a good-humoured, confident mix of the boisterous and the purposeful. No uniform for the sixth. Huge ethnic diversity – 52 per cent from non-white British backgrounds, of whom the largest number from Afro-Caribbean families; Asians make up next biggest group. Christian principles in practice evident in staff's approach to all aspects of this richly diverse community. While Anglicanism predominates, all churches and faiths are celebrated and explored here and everyone feels part of the school. Two minutes' daily silent reflection before lessons – 'everyone is quiet', said a sixth former. 'Faith has a big profile here', says head. 'We place a high premium on formal acts of worship.' Everyone attends a termly communion service and there is a weekly voluntary one. Assemblies are inclusive but have an unashamed Christian bias. 'The key to inter-faith issues,' believes head, 'is to be clear about what one's standpoint is.' She talks of the validity of each individual's own 'faith journey'. 'Spiritual matters are neither embarrassing nor taboo here' – a big claim but it feels legitimate. Pupils, though seldom deferential, respect teachers – there is a good working relationship between staff and pupils at all levels. 'They stretch you as far as you can go – but not beyond what you can do,' reflected one sixth former.

Pastoral care, well-being and discipline: Well-established system of form tutors first resort though pupils able to talk to whichever member of staff they choose. Heads of year back up the tutors and pupils have regular meetings to check on targets, progress, happiness. Chaplaincy team also available. Interaction between ages encouraged – actively by sixth form mentoring of younger pupils and system of form reps. School recently mixed up tutor groups in the sixth form to avoid tutors having particularly strong bonds with the 'home grown' students and less good ties with the newcomers. School council much appreciated – 'It has a lot of power over changes and we can meet the governors,' we were told. Few serious problems – most pupils feeling that offending in school time and on school property 'not worth it' and seemingly a bit immature, though usual crop of minor misdemeanours.

Pupils and parents: As above, huge ethnic mix, Christianity being the unifying principle though 30 places reserved each year for those from 'other world faiths', and Christianity itself taking in Russian/Serbian/Eastern Orthodox along with other denominations. Pupils come from wide geographic area – Brent, Hounslow, all over Ealing and further into town. Most, though, from Christ the Saviour Primary school, half a mile away, and nearly 50 other primaries. More girls than boys for 2016 intake, though this not generally perceptible. Princes and paupers here – all social strata represented and cheerfully interrelate.

Entrance: Now here's the rub. To get in you not only have to be practising a religious faith but have all the badges and medals to show it too. For year 7, 150 foundation (Christian) and 21 world faith (other religions) places, all based on family's attendance at church/place of worship for at least five years along with home's distance from school. Worth checking this out in detail before losing your heart to the place. No-one is fooled by rapid conversion when your child is in year 6 – though it is still – widely and unsuccessfully – tried. Nineteen music places. Sixth form, hitherto less stringent, now oversubscribed 11:1. They must be getting something right. For external places in the sixth form students must meet individual entry criteria for courses as set out in the sixth form prospectus (minimum usually a B with one or two exceptions) and must be in sympathy with aims and objectives of a C of E school.

Exit: Some 20-40 per cent leave after GCSEs. Vast and creditable range of courses and universities. Six to Oxbridge in 2016 plus eight medics and several off to art foundations. The increasing uptake of the extended project has resulted in glowing feedback of pupils' performance in interview and an increasing offer of scholarships.

Remarks: This is an outstanding school. Don't make the mistake of thinking it's anything other than a highly successful inner London comprehensive, however, with all the challenges that entails.

Unicorn School (Richmond)

238 Kew Road, Richmond, Surrey TW9 3JX

Pupils: 170 • Ages: 3–11

Fees: £6,495 – £11,910 pa

Tel: 020 8948 3926
Email: registrar@unicornschool.org.uk
Website: www.unicornschool.org.uk

Headmaster: Since 2013, Mr Kit Thompson, previously deputy head (academic) of Twyford School in Hampshire. Has needed to keep a tight hand on the tiller to maintain school's highly

U

individual, non-pressurised yet astonishingly successful course – where else do pupils routinely turn down places at top London secondaries like Godolphin & Latymer or Lady Eleanor Holles? – whilst resisting undue interference from articulate, heavily involved parents who, as school owners, enjoy having their say. It's a big ask.

Entrance: Single form all the way through and non-selective for those who arrive in the nursery aged 3 – 'you can't measure intelligence by the way a child holds a pencil' – though arrivals in other years are assessed in English and, in juniors, maths and reasoning, too.

As for special needs, around 17 have some form of support, none statemented. 'We get what we get', though school stresses that long term, it 'can't cater for severe learning difficulties'. Success here, however, is much praised by parents. 'At my daughter's previous school, she was having issues with her reading, so she was in my mind a special needs child. When we moved her here she had so much encouragement she just blossomed – it was the best thing we ever did,' said one.

Clientele very local – you only have to watch traffic grinding along nearby South Circular Road to see benefits – with few coming from further away than Chiswick or Barnes and 50 per cent or so within immediate Kew/Richmond vicinity. Most hear about school through word of mouth recommendation or personal experience – 'I am an old Unicorn and had always said that my experience was so good that if I were able to send my children there I would,' said one mother.

Though horribly over-subscribed with many children registered at birth – would be even earlier if parents had their way – school is keen to point out that despite reputation of being 'impossible' to get into, there's a regular trickle of occasional places, often freed up when parents with mega-important jobs relocate. (Means-tested bursaries are available, too, covering up to 100 per cent of the fees and awarded at the discretion of the governors.) New arrivals include occasional prep school refugees in search of a less traditional mind set.

Conversely, there's also (very small) reverse migration. School's ethos, low on formal tests, high on parent involvement, ranging from reception swimming (prepare to get wet – no passive poolside role here) to ferrying children to activities (there's even a mum's choir that regularly wins first place at local music festival), isn't for everyone. 'The school operates so closely as a community that I think they'd feel outside if they weren't part of it,' though some frantic working mothers send nannies or fathers as proxies and 'it's really not that arduous,' emphasised one mother.

Exit: Nothing unconventional about secondary school destinations. You name it, they get in, with a spread that includes Tiffin Boys, West London Free School and Grey Court plus independents including: St Paul's Girls, St Paul's Juniors, Hampton, LEH, Latymer Upper, Godolphin & Latymer, Francis Holland, Ibstock Place, Harrodian, Radnor House, St James Boys' and Surbiton High as well as occasional boarding places (Tudor Hall, Downe House, Bedales). Some scholarships most years.

Children usually sit exams for three or four secondaries, one aspirational, one probable, one backup and almost invariably end up with several offers, usually including first choice schools. Some, particularly if in search of elusive place at one of 10 times oversubscribed Surrey grammars may take rather more (invariably at parent's behest).

Preparation is covered with subtlety, starting in earnest only in year 6 when weekly tests, including post-swimming maths on Friday (not much enjoyed, judging by slightest of grimaces) are introduced. School's approach can require a parental leap of faith, especially for those more used to all-through exam-driven atmosphere of traditional preps. But though government tests were dropped some years back after it was decided that vertigo-inducing league table heights didn't compensate for stress levels generated, school's in-house assessments ensure staff are on the button when it comes to pupils' progress (results invariably put them streets ahead of national or indeed independent sector averages), with small group teaching by maths and English specialists to speed up pace for most able (gifted and talented by any other measure) and slow it down for those needing a little extra help.

Commendably, setting by stealth approach is so low key that, unlikely though it sounds, children who mentioned it seem genuinely unaware of its purpose. 'You start doing tests to see what suits you,' says one. They also speak warmly of teachers' reassuring presence when 11 plus nerves strike. 'I trusted them and they made every school sound great. You felt you could talk about anything,' says one.

Remarks: With its lovely double-fronted Victorian villa home opposite Kew Gardens, the school radiates solid values and has a price on its head to match – similar pads up the road go for multi-millions, so current management team must bless prescient school founders for acquiring freehold 40-odd years ago.

Colourful Jan Pienowski-style murals, conceived by the children and realised to interior designer standards by a group of talented parents, add colour to the light wood and pastel-shaded décor, as do the rainbow leitmotifs that permeate school like letters running through a stick of rock. Parents will need to cultivate familiarity with the spectrum as each class is named after a colour with the oldest (year 6 in old money) housed on top floor (the younger the class, the fewer the stairs) and known as ultra violets, a witty touch not so far extended to their form chairs which, though colour coded for other years, are an anti-climactic grey.

Uniquely (it's thought) school is run as a limited company with one share per family, governors fulfilling dual role as board directors and an annual general meeting with state-of-union presentation by the head. While parents occasionally exceed their brief – 'because it's a parent-owned school, they feel they have a say in everything,' said one – there's a real 'do as I do' top-down ethos which extends to pupils who can serve on school council from infants onwards, or, in the case of the oldest, read stories or play games with nursery children, greatly enjoyed even though they give up some of their break time in the process. 'We help calm them down,' said one.

All in all, it's a happy continuation of the ideals that prompted the school's foundation in 1970 by a group of parents and teachers disenchanted with the fun-free learning inflicted on children elsewhere and in search of education with a creative spark. Once routinely described as bohemian or alternative, that's not the case now, say staff and parents (with a mere hint of politely gritted teeth) and the school excels at providing a child-centred education that's the real deal – short on edu-babble and 'stand and deliver teaching,' long on intelligence, spontaneity and enjoyment.

Much praised by all are the Thursday afternoon clubs that replace lessons for juniors, with 20 options or so ranging from sailing in Slough to riding at Ham House – most covered by the fees with a contribution for the priciest. A similar number and range of after-school activities is also on offer. In other years, however, trips don't have to be big to be clever with a one-stop bus journey for reception, dressed as evacuees, proving a stand out success.

As you'd expect, high calibre teachers come as standard issue here, a notably bright bunch of buttons who are required, like parents, to '... enjoy [our] philosophy and be happy to blend with it. Choosing staff...is perhaps more tricky than in other schools. While they're looking for particular skills to fill a gap, we're looking for a match and fit to the ethos, too.' Most are skilled up to the eyeballs; one, home grown, is just finishing her degree, and Oxbridge 'though not the be all and end all,' is well represented as are sports, with several high level players helping to lead football, netball, hockey and rounders teams, amongst others, to success.

The care taken over recruitment pays off handsomely with high grade work the norm, ranging from art (credible Catherine of Aragon glove puppets with papier-mâché heads and fabric bodies made by year 5s) to science (8 and 9 year olds all red-fingered after creating their own bicarb of soda and vinegar volcanoes).

Bottom line is that teachers love to teach and give pupils access all areas passes in lessons, encouraging them to think for themselves. Three Men in a Boat and Chaucer are on the menu after the 11 plus is done and dusted (no post-exam torpor here) while popular philosophy lessons let children choose which big questions to discuss. (One boy's place at St Paul's Juniors was secured when he enthusiastically told interviewer he'd studied 'nothing'.)

And it's not just the top years that benefit, with reception children ditching Wheels on the Bus for Maybe it's Because I'm a Londoner, delivered with tasteful guitar backing and full complement of aspirants rather than Chas 'n' Dave pub-side bellow. 'We were learning about London and some of the children started asking about the war so we ended up having a glorious week,' explains teaching assistant.

Recently installed kitchen means welcome addition of hot meals, though children still also have option of bringing in a packed lunch, if preferred.

Aspirations may be vast, space less so. What space there is, however, is worked hard outside with a newly refurbished greenery-rich main playground divided into an Astroturf netball/football/running around area (fore), an action-packed, vibrant area filled with new and exciting equipment (midship) and quiet zone (aft). The latter sensible, given proximity to gardens of the no doubt vociferous well-to-do burghers of Kew. Rejigged interiors with corridor-free airy hall and previously poky first floor of coach house annexe re-synced into natty class music area with matching practice room next door (much used, with 130 timetabled instrumental lessons each week). Similarly upgraded is the reception and nursery classrooms downstairs, both bright and cheerful with their own secluded and plant-filled mini walled garden. Nature is a big thing – a consignment of eggs with pre-confirmed hatching date is bought in each spring from nearby ethically-sound farm. Chicks are returned, hens to have fulfilled life as layers, cockerels to face somewhat curtailed future – best to draw veil.

Parents are unfussed by size. 'It's typical for London,' says one, who also points to proximity of both 'the' Gardens opposite and the Old Deer Park (home of London Welsh RFC), both extensively used by school, latter for games.

Pupils, a loyal, friendly and articulate bunch (predictably in an area stuffed to the gunnels with highly educated professionals) have few complaints, either. While there's the occasional bout of out-of-teacher's-hearing bullying disguised as friendly teasing (mainly girls), it's dealt with quickly and effectively once reported and backed by a carrot-heavy rewards system, with prize-giving every term and a roll of honour featuring pupils and, pleasingly, teachers too, who nominate each other for doing the right thing.

Small, but with learning presented as a huge à la carte menu and not just the assessment-driven prix fixe, this is a special place. 'I can't believe that sitting multiple exams instils a love of learning. If we can teach children to enjoy learning, that's a gift for life.' No wonder school is loved by parents who even apologise for non-stop praise. 'I feel like I'm blowing the school's trumpet,' says one. Not bohemian – easy to rhapsodise, though.

University College School Pre-Prep

Linked with University College School Junior School, University College School

36 College Crescent, London NW3 5LF

Pupils: 128 • Ages: 3-7 (4-7 from 2017)

Fees: £14,682 pa

Tel: 020 7722 4433
Email: pre-prep@ucs.org.uk
Website: www.ucs.org.uk

Headmistress: Since 2015, Zoe Dunn BEd PhD NPHQ (late 30s), an Eng lit specialist with an impressive pedigree and all in this neck of the woods. After four years at The Hall, down the road, Dr Dunn went to The Royal School – up the hill, and now taken over by North Bridge House Senior – first as deputy head and latterly as head of its junior school. After a sabbatical term on a Winston Churchill Travelling Fellowship, she founded and then led a local faith free school – The Rimon Jewish Free Primary School – down the far side of the hill for four terms. A brief maternity leave over, she took up the post here. She sparkles and charms. Clearly super-bright, she is also simply super and you want to find her children to benefit from her enthusiasm and energy. Herself a mother of a toddler (when we visited), she lives locally and engages her charges in lots of local affairs eg charities and arts activities. Keen on outdoor learning and forest school – 'so good for team-building' – she has also revived the house system. Parents are happy: 'She's very strong. All her changes are positive.. She understands the parent body.. She couldn't be more supportive when there are problems..She's pretty powerful but she's so approachable she somehow takes people with her.' One of three good recent appointments for this family of schools.

Entrance: September 2016 saw the last intake of girls and the last nursery intake. Register (boys only for 4+ entry) up to a year before starting reception. Siblings get no preference – 'We have to maintain the academic standard of the school'. Occasional 5+ and 6+ places.

Exit: Though entry not automatic, most boys go on to the UCS Junior Branch, as the name-change to UCS Pre-Prep suggests. Some to eg St Paul's Juniors, Westminster Under. Girls to South Hampstead, City Girls, Channing. Both kinds to Belmont, The ASL, The Academy, Highgate, Heathside.

Remarks: Tucked away down College Crescent, you wouldn't know it was there, but the anonymous entrance conceals a surprisingly roomy little pre-prep and a bit of a gem. Now overlooked by the imposing brick and glass grandeur that is the newly reinvented and rebuilt South Hampstead High School, UCS Pre-Prep comes as a surprise. But, if you are keen on a 4-18 trajectory through one of London's best schools, this is where you can start. Class names all follow the bird theme (school was previously called the Phoenix) and are named Hummingbird, Barn Owl, Puffin etc. The nursery is a delight and full of good things – including its own little loo in an alcove. Lots to stimulate and lots to absorb, and all the littlies here were clearly absorbed in diverse ways.

Good use of a whole range of teaching and learning media throughout, including interactive whiteboards – often as 'input' at the start of a class to set in motion whatever learning activity is planned. Also iPads and netbooks, but Dr Dunn stresses the importance of traditional skills too. Learning support given in small groups or one-to-one for EAL (25 per cent of the children speak a language other than English at home, though only 10 per cent need support), SEND and as a booster for those showing gifted/talented tendencies.

Some 35 per cent of these tinies play an instrument (having lessons in school from 4 years old), and all children participate in the twice annual performances, such as Aladdin, which take place in the large theatre auditorium at UCS senior branch – very exciting for all. Specialist art teacher produces wonderfully imaginative work in these creative buds. And art room has a wall that can be endlessly painted and repainted – such a good idea. Selection of so few from so many clearly works. A non-teaching staff member told us: 'The little ones climb out of their buggies or cars and run for the books. They cry if they can't get at them fast enough.'

Outside space is very limited but enthusiastically used, with playhouse and tunnel slide over safe surface flooring. School also has allotments and use of nearby fields and a surprisingly large gym at the top of the building. Also makes use of facilities – sporting and others – at big brother schools.

Families live in the NWs, some Ns and the odd W postcode. Sixteen home languages spoken at the time of our visit and all cultures celebrated when appropriate. School is linked to one in the high Himalayas and a teacher goes out each year carrying artwork from UCS Pre-Prep and brings back similar from a very different place. Parents seem universally happy despite hiccups like The Great Hot Lunch Controversy – resolved democratically, we gather (children bring their own lunches). Unstinting praise for the teachers: 'we're so lucky. phenomenal..amazing..' Summed up by one parent: 'There was never a day when my children didn't want to go to school.'

University College School Junior School

Linked with University College School Pre-Prep, University College School

11 Holly Hill, London NW3 6QN

Pupils: 254 • Ages: 7–11

Fees: £17,370 pa

Tel: 020 7435 3068
Email: juniorbranch@ucs.org.uk
Website: www.ucs.org.uk

Headmaster of Junior: Since 2014, Mr Lewis Hayward MA Oxon MA ed management (OU) PCGE, a classicist (late 40s). An interesting former life – he began his teaching life in EFL in i) Nairobi and ii) Saudi. Thence to the relative quiet of Holmewood House and Highfield preps' classics depts until he left for Highgate School in 2009, where he became deputy principal. Efficient, professional and articulate, Mr Hayward is a modern head. He is voluble about the mega plans for refurb and new build which will bring up to date this charming school on its compact site, but he is also a man who greets every child by name and who knows not only the bricks and mortar but the concerns and qualities of his charges. 'Stretching without cramming' is his academic credo, and the parents we spoke to recognised this approach. 'He's slotted in very well,' said one parent who's known the place for years. 'He doesn't just say the right things but he works hard and is very approachable.' Another agreed, 'He wants to meet everyone's expectations.' A third told us, 'He had big boots to fill but all his changes seem good.' A sportsman, he runs nine miles daily as part of his commute from south London. He's in school by 6.30am to avoid the crowds and have quiet time. Energetic, focussed, clever – a good appointment for this special prep.

Entrance: Sixty boys are selected at 7+ from the 210-odd applicants. Two part assessment – i) a series of concentration and listening exercises and ii) a formal exam including comprehension, maths and NVR. Newbies join those who come up from the school's own pre-prep (from which entry is not automatic – they sit the same exam) or other local preps eg Hampstead Hill, Golders Hill, Mulberry House. NB Sibling policy dictates that 'Having a sibling (current or former pupil) at the school does not confer automatic admission into the school. Siblings must go through the same process as all other applicants at their chosen point of entry. Siblings will not be admitted if we believe that they are unlikely to cope and thrive within the academic UCS environment or if we think that their admission in preference to another candidate would be unfair.'

Exit: Virtually all to the UCS Senior School. Any who, by year 4, are not cutting it are supported with one-to-one, and those very few who clearly wouldn't thrive in the senior school are helped by the head to get in to gentler, more appropriate, schools elsewhere. Notable leavers include Sir Roger Bannister, Julian Lloyd Webber, Hugh Dennis, Ian Katz.

Remarks: In the heart of gorgeous Hampstead village, though you could live there for years and never know it was there. Purpose-built in 1928, the main house is functional rather than beautiful but still works well. Supplemented by a small science block and smaller arts block, the school covers pretty much all indoor needs on site and the sizeable rebuild and refurb – which clearly Mr Hayward is itching to start – will upgrade and modernise as needed.

Academic excellence is a given, and the children here are sponges who mop up everything intellectual, cultural, esoteric, thrown at them. Several long-serving and much loved staff give character, stability and stimulation. In 2016, a UCS junior team reached the final of the Prep Schools' Science Quiz and they regularly star in the Primary Schools' Maths Challenge. Average class size 21. A few need EAL help and are supported by SENCo as are those with mild learning difficulties – all closely monitored.

Parents enthuse, but mostly about the quite extraordinary range of extraccurricular activities on offer – we've not met anything quite like it at a cramped London prep before, and wonder how on earth they do it. Before-school activities include G&T clubs – open to all – in maths, English, coding, German, Mandarin etc. More at lunchtime and even more after school. 'More than I could have imagined,' beamed one mum, 'almost too many. My son wants to do all that's on offer but he simply can't.'

We watched several lessons and were struck by the diverse teaching methods employed by the much-praised staff. The French names for the parts of the body were being learned by groups of boys, sprawled on the floor, drawing jambes, poitrines, gorges etc. Boys in a drama class were wide-eyed and thoroughly engaged in an instant reaction game – no hanging back or bashfulness here. Self-discipline rather than rules, rule here – most classes were lively but controlled and we also saw several in which boys were silently reading, clearly lost in their own imaginary worlds.

Arts thrive – stunning theatre work on proper plays – The Dream and Private Peaceful most recently. Everyone in top three years gets involved. Serious music – an orchestra, two choirs – each 50+ strong, big band and numerous smaller instrumental ensembles – and everyone takes part in the big annual concert. Virtually everyone scrapes or blows something – 'We get 'em playing,' asserted impressive head of music. Very good art displays in corridors, though some few classrooms sporting boringly blank walls. Art block houses studio and DT room – classes split between the two. We loved the Japanese ceramic pots which boys had made and were decorating in authentic style as we watched. Laser cutter, 3D printer etc and we were impressed by the torches being designed via CAD and then made in the subterranean DT workshop. Best was the super cookery kitchen. Year 6 boys cook a three course meal for staff and parents and it all smelled gorgeous. Good-sized labs in science block, inhabited by enthusiastic boys plus a corn snake, tarantula, bearded dragon and some startling tropical fish. Good-sized library, well-used and sensible tracked reading scheme, punctuated by quizzes to monitor progress. Parents help with reading.

Although on site outside space is limited to little more than a rubberised playground (a small adventure trail is also planned), sports thrive. Outside table tennis and table football. School uses nearby fields (new pavilion on the way) plus sports facilities at the big brother school down the hill. Earlier complaints about few opportunities for those not in A or B teams seem to be being addressed now. Lots of trips – field studies to Norfolk; west country rugby tour; ski trip to Italy; football trip to Spain; art trip to Nice, Amsterdam or Barcelona and a year 4 field studies trip to Normandy.

Strong social network across this very diverse community. 'My son sees a lot of the other boys outside school.' Inside school, too, communication thrives – 'Every class has a council rep who can express grievances and they really do listen to them. The kids feel understood.' 'Older boys mentor the newbies so it's a bit like having an older brother in the school.' 'They just don't tolerate bad behaviour.' Parents stress the friendliness of the place: 'They were wonderfully supportive of me when we had difficulties and I was very emotional.' Consensus: 'It's a lovely, embracing and supportive school for boys from varying backgrounds, interests and personalities. My boys are all quite different but it was the right school for all of them.'

University College School

Linked with University College School Pre-Prep, University College School Junior School

Frognal, London NW3 6XH

Pupils: 886 • Ages: 11–18 • Sixth form: 310 (80 girls)

Fees: £18,792 pa

Tel: 020 7435 2215
Email: ssadmissions@ucs.org.uk
Website: www.ucs.org.uk

Headmaster: Since 2013, Mr Mark Beard BSc MEd (early 40s), a chemist. Mr Beard came from Brighton College where he'd been deputy head with a period as acting head between the redoubtable Seldon and the remarkable Cairns – a good place to cut headmagisterial teeth. He is credited with this school's greatly increased number of Oxbridge entrants. He began his career at King Edward's School, Birmingham, where he is remembered as 'a jolly good chap', thence to St Paul's School, as head of chemistry. Mr Beard is married with two young children and enjoys squash, reading and ancient history.

He is energetic, open, likeable, relaxed and clear-sighted. He follows a loved and warmly respected head, Ken Durham, and big shoes can be hard to fill. However, 'I came in to be myself,' he asserted when we met. 'I set out my stall openly and clearly from the start.' Mr Beard's appointment to this major school as a first headship is a considerable vote of confidence. He flustered some in the school community when, in his first term, he cracked down on aspects of this traditionally 'liberal' school – notably its somewhat relaxed attitude to uniform. 'I have been keen to explain..that liberal scholarship is not the same as liberal attitudes.. There is a school uniform and it is to be worn properly at formal occasions; you should be punctual to lessons, mind your manners and if you have homework, you do your homework.' Many parents applaud. 'Things needed tightening up,' one told us. 'I think he'll make it stricter, smarter and tidier – but within the ethos of the school,' thought another. 'It's early days,' said another, long-term, parent. 'He's less overtly charismatic than Ken – more cautious and considered. He will be a very good influence but it's a slow burn.' Sixth formers concur: 'He's growing on us. He'll do interesting things over time.'

Academic matters: Mr Beard's charges have not let him down. Recent results have been some of the best in the school's history with 71 per cent of A levels graded A*/A, nearly 93 per cent A*-B in 2016. At GCSE, 88 per cent A*/A grades. Impressive by any standards.

Far freer choice of GCSE and A level subjects than elsewhere including no blinkered – in our view – insistence on the holy trinity of sciences. Twenty plus A level options, with psychology just added. Much teaching material tailor-made by school's own staff – that's proper teaching. Universal praise for the English dept. 'It's phenomenal,' drooled a parent. Very good languages dept and exchange system. Mandarin is growing seriously now and a new short course in Italian is on its way to the sixth. School has switched to the Pre-U for languages, DT and English. We approve. But teaching praised across the board. A sense of academic work being serious but also offering infinite opportunities for thought, exploration and discovery.

Parental approval of Mr Beard's instant moving of A level mocks from March to January. Much appreciation of staff dedication. 'They're always there if you need help. There's a young bunch of teachers and many run extra classes for those who need them,' we were told. There are also support mechanisms such as regular tracking and reporting back to parents, to help boys who need pushing.

All are screened in general literacy, numeracy and reasoning on entry. Mild SEN seen as no problem here. Two full-time and one part-time learning support specialists. Individual support either by withdrawal or classes before and after school – also for those with mild EAL needs.

Games, options, the arts: The school has traditionally focused on inclusivity over winning – an excellent principle but one which can elicit grumbles. 'They don't put the money into it,' a parent told us. 'If your son is motivated and competitive and wants extra coaching etc I'd look elsewhere,' opined another. Boys concur. 'There are lots of talented boys here,' one said, 'but they don't get the opportunities.' However, this is clearly changing now. Regular Saturday fixtures for up to 18 teams including C and D teams and many extracurricular clubs/practices in eight key sports taking place before school, after school and lunchtimes. School enthusiastic about recent sporting triumphs, which include the 1st XI football team lifting the cherished London Schools Cup.

Under Beard, there is greater emphasis on performance. There is now an 'elite sportspersons' programme', additional soccer and cricket coaches, increased games options and other initiatives to allow pupils to reach their potential. Recent results in several sports including some individual triumphs suggest that, indeed, a fuse is burning here and may start crackling soon. Mr Beard wisely reminds us that the school motto is 'Paulatim sed Firmiter' ie Steadily but Surely. They have county/academy rugby players, hockey players and cricketers, England (ISFA) footballers, tennis players very high in the national rankings, international swimmers as well as individual rowers and fencers. Planning permission granted for a new pavilion on their 27 acres of playing fields in West Hampstead.

'The music and drama are simply brilliant,' a parent enthused. Music has long been exceptional here and we noted the number and quality of ensembles eg the symphony orchestra, chamber orchestra, several chamber groups, umpteen bands of all kinds including jazz and swing and excellent choirs. Well-provided for. Many pupils take LAMDA exams to high levels. Students write and direct their own plays and performance values are high. DT and art are outstanding. Evident creativity, freedom and experimental ethos and the dept has more the air of an art college than a school. Many media, some wonderfully bizarre and arresting work and all good stimulating stuff.

Far more interesting sounding clubs and extracurricular activities than we meet in most schools. Friday afternoons are given over to sixth form enrichment and staff follow their own enthusiasms in running classes such as Latin American film culture, wine tasting, life drawing, rock climbing, Literary London. Pupils set up clubs to pursue their own interests so we found a medical ethics society, a law and justice society, an eco-friendly club and beekeeping among many others. We wanted to sign up to them all.

Far from being a crammer in atmosphere, independence in all things is key. 'If your kids are self-starters, motivated and organised there is so much on offer, but they have to make the effort to get it. They don't come after you,' an appreciative parent explained. 'There is so much on offer even for the less academic child,' said another.

Exceptional outreach activities include collaboration at all levels with several state schools and pupil volunteering.

Background and atmosphere: The main buildings, dating back to 1907, are solid and imposing but rest comfortably on the southern slopes of the Hampstead hill. An unusual history. Founded by the University of London and various interested liberal intellectuals in 1830, it was designed to give an education to boys from dissenting (ie not conformist C of E) families and, initially, had no form of communal worship – unique at the time. Also no corporal punishment and no boarding. Its earliest incarnation was in Gower Street, hence the designation of Old Gower for an alumnus. So, from the off, it was regarded as 'liberal', and the tradition has been proudly maintained. What does it mean? 'It means, "no rules just for rules' sake",' ventured one parent, and that's at least part of it. Another parent quoted a prep school head: 'It's a school for mavericks.' While we like this observation, we feel it's a bit off the mark and UCS suggests that, while the great majority of pupils are far from being mavericks, the school is inclusive and can certainly accommodate them. Perhaps best summed up by a veteran parent: 'It's a wonderful, liberal, free-thinking school – you can look however you want to look, whether whacky or entirely traditional. They are accommodating and accepting and they celebrate difference.' It also still means no RE or religious assembly and a spirit of tolerance and inclusiveness.

A terrible fire in 1978 destroyed the huge Great Hall but the rebuilt version is almost overwhelming in its size and gravitas – wood panelling, stucco ceiling, huge organ and brass chandeliers. All eat in the handsome panelled refectory – all refectory tables and forms – with a strangely monastic feel. Droolly enthusiasm for the school food. 'No-one complains here,' we were told, and the menu was about the most varied, tempting and creative we can remember.

Later buildings include: the 2006 sports centre with excellent pool – also used by the local community; the sixth form centre with large and well-appointed common room, study areas – with and without PCs – and an excellent all-day café; the Lund theatre – a large and flexible space in which most productions happen and which is constantly in use; a 1993 block with well-designed and well-stocked library – with carpet; plus music dept etc. Site now feeling a touch full (head prefers 'compact') although space still for super vegetable garden and beehives, three Astro pitches/courts and little green nooks for sitting and relaxing. Some smartening up needed hither and yon – a little paint and patching will do wonders and a rolling refurbishment programme is under way. The emphasis here is not on every kind of here-today-obsolete-tomorrow IT gizmo but on rock solid teaching.

Girls arrived in the sixth form in 2008 to both trepidation and excitement from staff and boys. But it has worked, and not too much to the detriment of relationships between the school and its all-girl neighbours. 'The boys love the girls coming in the sixth form – it works very well,' one veteran parent assured us. 'They take very confident girls – the multi-tasking, vibrant, feisty ones – and they settle well.' The girls we spoke to bore this out, but they also paid tribute to the efforts made to integrate them before term and to help them quickly make friends once the year began.

Pastoral care, well-being and discipline: Houses are called 'demes' here and matter, but not too much. Praise for the Beard tightened-up regime. 'Some of the younger boys were getting lippy and needed reining in.' But equally, parents, pupils and OGs keen that the school's treasured 'liberalism' is maintained. 'It isn't a school for those who need a highly regulated, organised system,' explained a devotee. Another parent concurred, 'It's very friendly and informal. It's warm and family-like.' Much praise for the home-school communications. 'I have mobile numbers for all my son's teachers and they reply to emails almost before you've sent them.' Even warmer praise for the 'deme' wardens: 'They are phenomenally good on the pastoral side.' Mr Beard has a light touch but a firm view. 'We want them to be the problem solvers of the future, not the problem causers. That's partly what a liberal education should be about.' Few discipline problems. Leavers reflect thoughtfully on their schooling: 'You learn to manage your time. They cultivate you into someone who can deal with a high level of intensity in your work. They build it up so that you don't really feel how much more deeply you are thinking. You become very independent and self-reliant in this school.'

Pupils and parents: From all over north and central London. Pupils are as diverse as the capital itself. They are articulate, thoughtful, independent. Parents are achievers, ambitious, cultured, moneyed – for the most part – and involved. 'Increasing numbers of middle class parents have to work hard to find the fees,' acknowledges Mr Beard.

Entrance: About two-thirds of 11-year-olds come from the junior school in Holly Hill. They move up without needing to take an entrance exam. At 11+, 350+ boys, mostly from local primaries, try for 30 places. Exams in maths, English and reasoning in January. Around 40 per cent of applicants thereafter invited for interview. NB part of a group of independent co-ed/boys' schools that coordinate 11+ results, but forbid those who have accepted a place at one school from taking up a subsequent waiting list offer from another.

At 13+, 300 boys apply for some 30 places – mainly from local preps, eg Arnold House, Devonshire House, The Hall, Hereward House, North Bridge House, St Anthony's and Trevor-Roberts, but also Notting Hill and Westminster Cathedral Choir School. Pre-test in year 6 in maths, English and reasoning. About 150 return for an activity morning and interview in the October of year 7. Offers conditional on performance at CE.

At 16+, some 200 apply for around 40 places. Most entrants at this stage are girls, but no actual quota – entry on merit. Girls come from eg City of London, Francis Holland, North London Collegiate, Channing, South Hampstead. Some from Highgate School. Also from St Marylebone School, Hampstead School and William Ellis. Selection via November assessment and about 50 per cent of applicants interviewed. Assessment is an objective test of thinking, reasoning and problem-solving. All offers conditional on GCSEs.

Exit: Everyone goes off to a good university to read a proper subject. London University is a favourite; many also to Durham, Manchester, Leeds, Bristol, Nottingham. Impressive numbers annually to Oxbridge (14 in 2016, with 11 to the US and nine medics/vets). The vast range of subjects they pursue is testament to the individuality fostered here.

Notable Old Gowers include: Tristram Hunt, actors Hugh Dennis, David McCallum and Bertie Carvel, journalists Ian Katz, Jonathan Freedland and Paul Dacre, Thomas Adès, members of Bombay Bicycle Club, Will Self, Justin Stebbing, Chris Bonington, Roger Bannister, John Barrett.

Money matters: Around £1m a year disbursed to pupils who would not otherwise be able to afford UCS. At the time of our visit, 52 pupils were on 100 per cent bursaries – one of the most generous provisions in the UK. Most of this funded by the letting of school facilities to the community, charitable work and donations. No academic scholarships but music schols worth up to 25 per cent.

Remarks: A very good school and set to rise even higher under energetic and confident head.

Waldegrave School

289

Fifth Cross Road, Twickenham TW2 5LH

Pupils: 1,280 • Ages: 11–18 • Sixth form: 280 (80 boys)

Tel: 020 8894 3244
Email: info@waldegrave.org.uk
Website: www.waldegrave.richmond.sch.uk

Headteacher: Since 2006, Mrs Philippa Nunn, BSc from UCL in zoology, MA in educational management from Greenwich, PGCE and NPQH (50s). Appointed a National Leader of Education in 2011. Married with two daughters at local state schools. Was previously head of the Holt School in Berkshire, an all-girls 11-18 comprehensive. Started teaching science in 1987. Currently teaches ICT.

A calm, glamorous presence. Parents are all big fans. 'She's fantastic. She's a real person. Very approachable. As a mother of two girls she really understands.' Some staff have been teaching here for more than 25 years, which 'adds strength to the ethos of the school'. Introduced a house system to promote a greater sense of loyalty and belonging and to enhance student leadership opportunities.

A keen sports enthusiast, she plays hockey at Teddington, tennis and real tennis are passions. She's also training to become an Ofsted inspector.

Academic matters: Consistently achieves good results in English, maths and science GCSEs. French, history, art, drama, RE always good too. The success rate in A*-C grades is well above the regional and national average; 85 per cent got 5+ A*-C grades including maths and English in 2016, and 51 per cent of grades were A*/A. Top of the Sunday Times Parent Power list for 11 to 16 schools for four years; now has a co-ed sixth form – opened in 2014 – with 75 per cent A*-B, 40 per cent A*/A grades in first A levels.

Quality of teaching is excellent. 'They're all so dedicated. I can't fault them,' said one parent. Achievements are recognised at assemblies throughout the year and at Celebration Afternoons at the end of the year. High academic standards are expected and some parents say that there is pressure on the students to get good grades. 'My daughter had to do French GSCE when she didn't want to do it as the teachers knew she would get a good grade.' But provision is made within the curriculum for all abilities, and modest acts such as helpfulness to the school or to others are duly acknowledged and rewarded.

Lessons are given in broad ability tutor groups initially, but setting for maths, science and languages occurs early on in the first years. In subsequent years, setting in other subjects if appropriate. All are entered for 6-10 GCSEs; some do up to 13 after discussion with parents and staff. Short course subjects such as ICT and PE well subscribed with good results.

Appointed as one of the first 100 Teaching Schools, and is also a National College for School Leaders National Support School. Designated area in an independent learning centre for gifted and talented girls and those with other special needs. Provides 'enhanced specialist teaching provision' for six girls with speech and languages difficulties/autism. With an incredible cultural diversity (43 different languages), EAL support is strong, even offering a lunchtime club for all age groups. On the subject of lunchtime, a great deal is compressed into a very short 35 minute break: careers advice, ICT, rehearsals for choirs and bands, puzzle club, homework clubs. Similarly, lots of before and after-school activities. A breakfast club at 8.00am every morning with badminton on offer at the same time for the more energetic. After school up until 4.00pm – choice is much more varied with a high take-up rate.

Games, options, the arts: Good range of sports offered – rounders, tennis, volleyball, athletics, rugby (with the Harlequins). Classes in the fitness suite, cricket, rowing (linked in with Walbrook Rowing Club) and table-tennis. Hidden from view from the road is a huge outdoor green area with tennis courts and marked-out running track. New sixth form block features four court sports hall.

School regularly wins regional netball leagues and was recently the Middlesex hockey champion. Also borough winners at netball and rounders. Running club is popular with 40 girls doing a 5k run twice a week with four teachers before school. (The head attempts to join them once every half term.) Head positively oozes enthusiasm, listing her school's sporting achievements. Another of her aims is to improve participation in sport. Gymnastics is strong – both a multi and traditional gym on site. A dance studio was funded through the National Lottery.

Extra opportunities include bridge, drama (big production every alternate year and an annual joint production with Hampton Boys' School), study skills, chess, art, music theory, ICT, choirs, rock bands and full orchestra. Art and music are both strengths. Year 7s all learn the recorder and in year 8 they get the chance to play the ukulele! When we visited we were

W

blown away by the bird sculptures made in art lessons, inspired by their sister school in Madogo, Kenya.

After-school clubs include extra languages, eg Mandarin GCSE and there's even an astronomy club which parents can also attend. These cost extra but the pupil premium funds places for those who qualify.

Background and atmosphere: Original 1930s building has been added to over the years. Science labs are housed in newish block and brand new sixth form building opened in 2014, housing new sports hall and dining room. Outside play area transformed with money from the PTA with an outdoor theatre and landscaped surroundings. Food freshly cooked on site, and a biometric system for payment. Some girls take sandwiches. 'I don't want them having a slice of pizza and a muffin every day,' explained one parent. The girls themselves give this school a buzzy atmosphere. A former pupil remarked that 'all girls is a positive rather than a negative.'

Pastoral care, well-being and discipline: No real behavioural problems. First years are invited to spend a day in the school to find their way about and practise their journey to and fro – puts a stop to later excuses about buses being late. They also start the term a bit earlier before the older ones arrive. Prefects help out with the younger ones, organise charity events, welcome visitors and play an important leadership role in the school. Each tutor group elects a representative to attend the school council, which in turn represents the school at the Richmond School Student Council. All good training ground for debating and public speaking.

School is honest about bullying and admits that, like the poor, it is always with us. However, stringent efforts made to put an end to it. Girls, staff and parents exhorted to report any incident straight away and assured that something will be done.

Pupils and parents: Although the school has no religious affiliation, the majority of the pupils are Christian. More than 25 per cent are from an ethnic minority. All come from the surrounding borough of Richmond, which is known nationally for its high level of professional parents. A local parent declares it to be the sort of school where 'decent folk will be prepared to break all sorts of rules to get their daughters in.' New (co-ed) sixth form is making this school even more desirable.

Entrance: Fully comprehensive intake. It is the only all girls' state school in Richmond so is always oversubscribed. Much to the head's relief, all admissions are dealt with by the local authority. Despite clear and rigid guidelines about admissions policies there are always appeals. Priority to those with special needs and those in public care or who are deemed by the LA to have a particular need, to siblings, daughters of staff and those living in priority areas. Most girls will have attended local primary schools in the borough. Six places are available in total in the school for those with speech and language difficulties or those on the autistic spectrum – invariably very oversubscribed.

Forty out of the 280 places in the sixth form are for boys but majority of girls' places will be taken by Waldegrave students. Five A*-C GCSE grades needed for entry, with Bs in the subjects to be studied at A level.

Exit: In the past students have gone to Richmond Sixth Form College, Esher College, Strodes College or to sixth forms of independent schools. This has changed as the new (oversubscribed) co-ed sixth form enables around 50 per cent of girls to remain at the school to study for A levels. 'We hope to be sending students to Oxbridge and the Russell Group universities,' explains the head, and indeed five Oxbridge places in 2016.

Remarks: A really buzzy school. 'It felt more dynamic than the other schools we visited,' said one parent. This school has so much going on that you're a lucky girl if you manage to get a place here. Now with the new sixth form you're even luckier.

Wallington County Grammar School

Croydon Road, Wallington, Surrey SM6 7PH

Pupils: 1,026 • Ages: 11–18 • Sixth form: 349

Tel: 020 8647 2235
Email: enquiries@suttonmail.org
Website: www.wcgs.org.uk

Headmaster: Since 2013, Mr Jonathan Wilden (30s). Educated at St Joseph's College, Ipswich; studied geography at University of Wales (Lampeter), postgraduate degree from Bath, NPQH. Mr Wilden has taught in a number of south London boroughs and was formerly deputy head at Evelyn Grace Academy, Brixton. He joined Wallington as deputy headteacher in 2010.

Academic matters: You'd assume top grades in everything, all the time, and for the most part you'd be right, with results that make for the world's most boring game of Scrabble (depending on interest levels in vintage Swedish pop groups). In 2016, 72 per cent A*/A grades at GCSE. At A level, more of the same with nearly 84 per cent of grades at A*/B, 56 per cent at A*/A.

Being bottom in a class of over-achievers can be a lonely place but here, stigma is neatly sidestepped – or at least addressed with humour. 'I know when x and y first met, but still I am in the bottom set,' says prizewinning poem in newsletter. 'I don't think you have to excel. They give their form order so everyone knows who's bottom but from what I can tell, nobody is given stick, or jeered or sneered at,' confirmed one mother. All this despite the fact that the cleverest are 'ridiculously clever', say boys, citing a sixth former, nickname King Language, who taught himself ancient Greek to A level standard in three years.

While it would be awfully easy to ramp up the pressure – 'you can just push them, there's no limit to what you can get out of them,' says a teacher – the school knows where to exercise restraint. 'Extremely tedious' ICT GCSE was axed, leaving pupils free to concentrate on achieving 10 or 11 cracking GCSEs – eight core subjects, economics and business studies amongst the options – and up to four A levels, though 'they suggest only doing three so we get good grades,' confirmed sixth former.

Around 80 per cent opt to keep going with a non-related but much-loved subject post-16 – one boy, hoping to study economics at university, was sweetening the pill of straight sciences and maths with art – virtuoso timetable juggling ensuring that just about every sixth former, somewhat amazingly, is able to follow chosen subject blend.

There used to be occasional frustration over use of supply teachers to cover long-term staff absences but things have improved, think parents, and there's non-stop praise for staff, many seen as an inspirational force for good: '...the only reason my son wants to study classics at university,' said a parent. Another pupil, initially planning to be an architect, was ambushed by the fascination of psychology. 'It's the way it weaves its way through society.'

With everything from innovative blood points awarded in history and classics – the more the gore, the better the score (one boy even made a Medusa cake) – to year 9 English students filming themselves looking moody and disenfranchised in (sub) urban dystopia (a 'gritty portrayal of life' says one – or as close as you get in leafy Wallington) it's not hard to see why teachers and lessons are so highly rated.

Consistent overall quality makes the very occasional slippage round the edges that much more noticeable, with a few more C grades in A level biology and physics than you'd expect and a tiny number slipping into D and E hinterland. Home influence can be a factor, thinks head. 'Though we have the conversation each year about how the subjects should be what the pupil wants to do, there is parental pressure to do the sciences even if they're not their best or favourite subjects.'

School, though, is far from passive. Flair-filled initiatives include book clubs and mini-libraries dotted around classrooms to get non-readers hooked (a surprising number see the printed word as a duty not a pleasure), while learning support for the 20 or so pupils with dyspraxia, dyslexia, ADD and ASD/Asperger's ranges from buddies to lend a hand with organisation to morale-boosting training as cyber mentors. Even parents are paired with others whose children have similar needs.

Add an extensive range catch up clubs and sixth form mentors who help year 7s in lessons and offer a listening ear outside and rigorous plotting of academic trajectories, and it's hard to slip through the cracks. 'We know pupils better than ever before,' reckons head.

Games, options, the arts: Sport is 'central to school life' says prospectus (music merely 'flourishes'). Lots of team finals (rugby particularly) and individual success (water polo gold at London Youth Games). Hockey is in decline; football, recently introduced to the relief of many, on the up – though relegated to the public park down the road. Only rugby and cricket grace the well-kept sports field. While the talented are encourage to sign up, adulation for sporting legends is low key and there's plenty of kudos to spare if, as a fair few do, you direct your talents elsewhere.

Outside school, pupils regularly reach the finals of national maths, science and spelling challenges. Inside, the arts are well represented with traditional ensembles and a popular Battle of the Bands, though eclipsed by 'Singstaff' – a teacher talent show. (Previous head's version of 'Man after midnight' complete with 80s big tie lives on in legend, so we're told, though sadly not on Youtube). Drama bristles with high quality productions running the gamut from mainstream (including a well-reviewed Oliver!) to the quirky – sixth formers were 're-imagining' classics, 'the more eccentric the better,' said one, who planned a new take on the Odyssey. Art also has its idiosyncrasies, highlights including a jolly slimline Michelin man lookalike crafted from cling-film wrapped wire.

Lots of charitable activity with sixth form boys about to embark on moustache growth – 'few have the manliness,' says one – to raise awareness of testicular cancer, with Wednesday afternoons for years 11 upwards dedicated to enrichment activity (facial hair nurturing presumably being a 24/7 preoccupation) and science-based links with local primary schools a speciality, with would-be medics passing on resuscitation techniques and future scientists launching rockets on the playing field (arts types, meanwhile, prudently watched the fun from indoors).

Around 80 per cent of pupils, it's estimated, attend at least one of the 50 plus clubs that plug any gaps in the timetable, most with a strong academic raison d'être (physics geek club about as frivolous as it gets) though D of E is also on offer. There's even the Hutchins über-club, the society's society, that monitors the rest and 'aims to push the academic boundaries,' says a pupil, by ensuring other clubs are delivering suitably nourishing intellectual fare to their members.

Background and atmosphere: 'The deputy head told us to practise personal humility and professional will,' said sixth former. 'You never get too big for your boots but you're committed to doing well and going about it in a nice way.' Judging by polite clouds of year 7s trailing grinning deputy school captain to plead for coveted school pins, awarded for participation, it's a lesson learned early on.

Not that an indomitable spirit is anything new, surfacing during World War II when the school, then fee paying (it became a grammar in 1944) stayed open during the Blitz, despite two direct hits and substantial damage.

School's homely feel is 'such a cliché,' said pupil, rather crossly, but inescapable, while the presence of girls – first two joining in 2000 though one only lasted a fortnight, today making up a fifth of sixth form numbers – brings 'a different dimension,' says the school.

Slightly battered charm, with some areas just for best (like green and pleasant quad) and lots of period details add to the charm. But behind all those curvy art deco brass-topped bannisters, the sixth form art room nicknamed Middle Earth (it's sandwiched between two others rather than home to a bunch of hobbits) and an abundance of gothic gilt lettering, there's a definite appetite for change.

Recent additions include funky new sports hall, twinkling away on the far side of playing field with wow factors a-plenty (automatic doors, which have reset to manual, are the only feature not playing ball) which has allowed large scale musical classrooms elsewhere. Sixth form study area replaces the library, which has taken over the gym; new labs in science block extension.

Food technology classroom features chairs in a zinging green that almost matches the walls and banks of ovens. Popular with everyone (there's already a school recipe book). Has also wrought miraculous reduction in queuing times at popular fundraising lunchtime barbecues.

Only loser is the sixth form common room, now given over to classics, though pupils take this in good part – 'we've lost a common room but gained a subject,' said one. A small patio constructed, by way of compensation, for their exclusive benefit, is little used, pupils congregating instead by the front entrance, as if waiting for a school bus that never arrives, while girls use their loos as a walk-in wardrobe, with a mish-mash of coats, books and make-up stashed under the washbasins. 'Surprising,' said sixth form boy, with masterly understatement.

Pastoral care, well-being and discipline: Things are back on an even keel after a period of what school terms 'low level misbehaviour' when pupil respect towards staff dipped. 'Towards the end, you felt [a previous head] was off the ball,' confirmed a parent. 'I was surprised at the amount of latitude.'

No chance now, with a rigorously applied code of sanctions (with input from pupils) and (existing) practical measures including a separate, well-patrolled areas for each year group, (though sixth formers, rather hurt at implied lack of trust, would like more mixing of the age ranges).

Wonderfully waffle-free policies ('scorn cheating,' exhorts section on sporting aims in pleasingly Tom Brown tones) leave no doubts as to what will and won't be tolerated. Drugs won't, though offenders expressing suitable contrition may get a second chance thanks to an informal 'you take ours, we'll take yours' agreement with Sutton Boys and Wilson's. (No guarantees, however.)

Incentives to behave are thick on the ground, from the six houses which 'exert an emotional pull,' said a pupil (victors' flags in the hall provide at-a-glance summary of current success), to ties that bind, with a cornucopia of neckwear on offer for games, arts or brainpower-based accomplishments.

Family links have been strengthened, too, with work and well-being themed workshops for parents (who also get on-tap access to form tutors, front of house contacts for day to day issues), though attendance for those living or working some distance away can be tricky.

Proof that it's all working just fine is provided by parental endorsement and pupil approval of pastoral head – 'he's tops,' said one. Tiny numbers, usually three or four at most, stay after school for Friday detention. More serious Saturday version vanishingly rare, says school.

Pupils and parents: Crimewatch's Nick Ross and the late Chris Woodhead of Cognita are best known old boys (Douglas Allen, later civil service chief Lord Croham, was debut pupil in 1927). Others include Surrey cricketer David Gibson. List is currently all male – old girls are, presumably, still chipping away at the glass ceilings.

Pupils temper intelligence with humanity – a useful quality for tomorrow's top scientists, lawyers and medics. A trustworthy bunch, too – possessions can be left confidently in the open bag storage areas, widely used round the school instead of lockers, ditched after a pupil vote.

Sixty per cent come from ethnic minorities and approximately a quarter speak English as an additional language. 'Culturally very mixed, more so than a lot of schools, so that attracted me,' said a parent.

Entrance: Year 7 candidates sit the Sutton Grammar Schools Selective Eligibility Test (SET) in September. Several grammars then carry out additional tests but Wallington CG does not. Currently, after those with the school named on their EHC plan and looked after children, places given in rank order from the SET, with up to 10 places for boys on free school meals and 15 for those in specific local postcodes, then children of Opia Trust schools staff, then by distance. Final 13+ entrance exam in January 2017.

There are around 50 sixth form places for external students (including girls), based upon GCSE results.

Exit: A few leave after GCSEs (13 per cent in 2016) though for almost everyone else it's straight to university after A levels, with 70 per cent to Russell Group members and around eight or so off to study medicine, dentistry and veterinary science. Other popular subjects include maths (though numbers have declined over past few years), economics, history, engineering (all sorts), physics and biomedical science.

Dip in Oxbridge success rates seems to have been resolved and eight pupils achieved places in 2016. School has taken advice from big hitters in other top schools to ensure that only hopefuls with a realistic chance of success are put forward. Head also plans subject-specific clubs (medicine, law, architecture) run by sixth formers, with eminent old boys invited in to offer advice and set work.

Remarks: 'Wants the results but isn't pushy in the way another school might be,' said a parent. Cleverness, even brilliance, is there in force but never in your face and tempered with good manners and charm. No wonder pupils are attached to their school and 'boys cry more than the girls,' said a (male) sixth former when it's time to leave.

Wallington High School for Girls

Woodcote Road, Wallington, Surrey SM6 0PH

Pupils: 1,420 • Ages: 11–18 • Sixth form: 365

Tel: 020 8647 2380
Email: info@wallingtongirls.org.uk
Website: www.wallingtongirls.sutton.sch.uk

Headteacher: Since September 2016, Richard Booth.

Buck will stop with previous Wallington head, Jane Burton, who has been appointed to the permanent position of executive head of the Nonsuch and Wallington Education Trust (NWET), widely seen as merger of the two grammars. She has overall responsibility for both schools which share a team of trustees but retain own governing bodies. Girls will, however, see no changes on day to day basis, stress governors.

Academic matters: Expectations exactly as you'd expect and terrific results to match – 82 per cent of 2016 GCSE entries at A*/A, 84 per cent A*-B at A level and 56 per cent A*/A. School, however, reinforce message that it's 'not an exams factory' and there's no sense of undue pressure from girls we spoke to. Subject choices surprisingly wide-ranging with media studies and DT four different ways at A level as well as a few GCSE rarities including photography (like Latin, offered as a twilight course) as well as business and psychology (rated by school for honing research skills). Everyone must do separate sciences in decent, bright labs (juniors 'tend to have same teacher') and at least one language at GCSE (school specialism), and it's two for all from year 7 (choose from French, German and Spanish – school will do best to accommodate preferences though GCSE numbers roughly equal for all three).

Forms (each recruited en masse to one of seven houses) taught together in year 7 so can stick together – almost literally as 'so big that for the first few weeks you just tend to follow each other round,' said one. Minor criticism of maths is that with sets kicking in only at the end of year 7, can be a drag for most able first years, who have sometimes covered the ground already. One pupil, clearly at top end of ability range, felt it could be a bit 'boring if you knew the subject already.' 'At my daughter's primary school, they started doing some year 7 work, so it depends if the teacher realises,' thought parent.

Current school preoccupation is need to upweight thinking skills. Manifested at GCSE in fusion of philosophy and ethics with RS (short course taken by most) and in the sixth form with philosophy of religion and ethics as one of go-ahead A level options (school doesn't do the IB) as well as an extended essay project that encourages independent research. Though there are masses of subject specific events, typical month including trips to Royal Observatory, Maritime Museum and War Horse for physics, history and drama students respectively, spanning the year groups and adding interest for all, are real stars of the show.

Swapping round groups in years 7 and 8 sensible 'as it means you meet new people', thought pupils, who have nothing but praise for staff, echoed by parents who extolled staff emphasis on morale boosting rather than pressure – slow boil rather than pressure cooker. 'You pick it up when you have parent evenings. Even subjects you think your daughter's not very strong in, the teachers are very encouraging,' said one.

Day to day, however, plenty of evidence of varied teaching styles that put a premium on initiative. Most recent inspection report was critical of over use of chalk and talk – now pared back to a minimum and group work something of a feature – 'we get 20 minutes to collaborate,' said year 7 pupil – and choice offered wherever practical: menu of experiments adds interest to science.

Lunch swipe card also acts as library ticket – food for the soul and stomach in one magnetic stripe – and everyone is instructed to have live book and not be scared to use it when reading is called for, which it often is – though all the girls we spoke to were enthusiastic readers, school diligent about keeping the light burning. If book is missing 'you'll be in trouble,' said teacher, with ferocious smile – in practice, means 'you get moaned at,' said pupil.

Just about every core academic subject has own club, some involving older girls. Space also freed up wherever possible to assist with private study. Library open all hours (or a fair few of them) while sixth form have own small but nicely kitted out conference room which can be booked out for meetings and quiet work.

No doubt where interests lie, however, with massive 140 currently taking A level maths, and sciences fab, too – 100 each for biology and chemistry and respectable 80 for physics. School dismissive of any suggestions elsewhere that girls can't and won't do sciences as here they can and will – in their droves. Their popularity, influenced by what can be 'lots' of parental pressure, thought teacher, inevitably puts many other departments in the shade, though 'we're winning,' says English teacher, who has seen rising A level numbers for Eng lit as well as Eng lang and combined. It's helped, she thinks, by growing desire by would-be employers to see evidence of broader spread of interests. Slightly disappointed by attrition rate into year 13, though in part, she reckoned, down to misapprehension that A level is a breeze – GCSE with a few more complicated bits – when 'it isn't.'

One parent felt that, in common with other local grammars, 'you can tell from the mixture of girls that with some, their English may not be very strong,' which she thought might affect the popularity of the subject. That said, all-round enthusiasm is inescapable. What are school's biggest things? 'Everything here is a big thing,' said year 8 pupil with just a hint of reproof.

Games, options, the arts: Lots love sport, some don't and academic thrust can divert some who might otherwise be doing great things on the pitch, thought girls. While school scoops gold Artsmark award amongst others, sports equivalent is the conspicuous absentee on website roll of honour, with PE just about sole area not raved about by inspectors. Enjoyed by pupils, however. 'They have fun and that's part of it all,' thought mum. Its standing on the website, lumped together with art and design, drama and music, under 'expressive arts' with no accompanying blurb pretty much says it all, as does minimal timetable presence – two sports/PE lessons a week, dance and gym dominating in winter, great outdoors (including cricket, rounders and tennis) to the fore at other times.

Small and hardy bunch go on to take PE for A level (currently half a dozen) and winners, both team and individual, including two budding sixth form football stars, recently awarded vast sports scholarships by US universities. Add favourable feedback and rapidly improving facilities, and will to ensure higher profile – and results – seems to be there.

Vast field, all-weather pitches (no Astroturf as yet, though four new tennis and netball courts recently added to existing two) joined by magnificent sports hall, a yodeller's paradise, mirrored dance studio on top just as nice and no gizmo spared, including retractable goals, dividing net allowing two classes to have simultaneous lessons.

Building, shaped like flat-bottomed sausage roll with rounded corrugated metal top, so bizarre-looking that to start with 'everyone was against it,' says sixth former. Now assorted delights are clear, 'we love it'. 'Amazing,' agreed parent. Anything in danger of despoiling pristine floor, such as trampolining, is relegated to old gym, which also incorporates very compact fitness suite, housed in section of main building beyond school hall and now largely disused or converted section (antediluvian-looking changing rooms now used for storage).

Art and drama very strong, quality excellent, visible manifestation of school's desire to encourage pupils 'to be who you are.' All, from year 7 girls to sixth form, praised teachers' desire not to impose but to guide, with thorough briefing and lots of encouragement to personalise tasks en route to completion. Thus masses of faces in art room (less scary than amazing but rather terrifying giant masks in school hall) are hugely different in style and design. We also loved pictures of lamas bearing staff names and chosen to 'reflect personality'. One gorgeously cuddly example (creature, not teacher) with fetching crop of fleece was felt to be particularly accurate representation of staff member's 'wacky hair'.

Painstaking creativity also a feature of relatively recent tech block, 'best in the country,' thought pupil and, according to recent school survey, achieves some of highest pupil and parent happiness ratings around. Spreads the joy with lots of outreach to local primaries, separate building worth clocking for extraordinary through corridor, narrow but incredibly high, like passageway for emaciated, super tall giraffes. Teachers diligent in 'explaining techniques', most projects starting with short list of designs and questionnaires designed to canvass friends' views ('You can ignore them but you have to explain why.') Projects included one of the most sensible we've ever seen – year 7s making covers for school planners – practical, fun and gorgeous (owners had gone to town on personalisation – initials as well as frills and furbelows a real feature). Those who stay the course end up with fab A level creations including terrific lamp complete with fronds of LEDs and mood lighting. 'Took three months to make.'

Lovely music – particularly strong on vocals (recent finalist on TV The Voice is former school pupil) with five choirs – Glee and 60-strong gospel choir both audition only (latter mostly seniors; year 7 girls delighted that one of their number had just won place), junior and senior versions open to all. Joint orchestra with Wilson's School down the road a happy union of brass and percussion (mainly boys) with strings (mostly girls).

Enthusiastic teaching team feel GCSE numbers (currently around 17) could be higher. Though accept the necessity, slightly miffed that small number of A level students are currently having lessons at Wilson's and are fighting good fight to boost numbers so pupils can be brought back into the fold.

Background and atmosphere: Founded just over 125 years ago in 1888. About six minutes by bus from Wallington station, it's a fairly easy trek compared with boys' equivalents (detailed knowledge of public transport essential for first timers, emergency rations desirable) and presents unthreatening face to the world, brickwork, if not mellow, certainly not likely to frighten the horses (not that you'd see that many on these crowded streets).

Has embraced cultural diversity (and won an award for it, too) with gusto, recent events ranging from Japanese drumming to fab-sounding international evening where girls and families ate, drank and danced way round the world, each table in school hall themed to a different country.

Warren-like corridors are brightened wherever possible with rows of pictures, space at a premium with seven year 7 forms feeding through. Generous-sized lockers, dotted round the place, a well-used necessity. 'I could get winter coat, all books and full PE kit in mine,' reckoned pupil. New teaching block also on the way. In the meantime, subjects are ranged together wherever possible, occasionally dual use (modern languages lesson might take over English room, 'though never a problem as teachers always bring all the resources with them,' says pupil).

Food was 'pretty good' except for the cheese, seemingly added to rather more dishes than you'd like. 'Texture a bit of a problem,' thought pupil. However, does offer much enjoyed freedom for déjeuner sur l'herbe, on outside tables and even in classrooms ('though not hot food,' thought year 7 pupils, as 'that would be a health and safety issue.'

Has now formed a multi academy trust with Nonsuch High.

Pastoral care, well-being and discipline: School excels here with common sense approach with earlier start and finish (8.25am to 2.50pm) and prompt close on Friday afternoons, packed programme of after-school clubs (sports, including badminton, football and hockey the most popular) mainly Mondays to Thursdays only, ensuring that everyone (including hard-pressed teachers) can start weekends promptly and with clean conscience, felt school.

In addition to form tutor and head of year, those with problems have access to what one girl described as 'superb' counsellor, accessible at all hours and 'like a second mum', as well as caring staff who have manifest understanding of pressures that go with life in top-achieving school and go out of their way to deal with them. Sports staff on hand for one pupil who 'went to them when feeling low just to spend time there and kick a ball around.' A huge help, she reckoned. Younger girls seemed largely content with system and own company – they tend not to approach older girls, who don't seem to have troubleshooting role, and in any case could be 'hard to find,' thought one.

As to bullying – incidents rare: 'one a year, if that,' thought year 7 pupil, while older girls marvel at school's success in avoiding issues that friends and family elsewhere report as being routine. 'Younger sister has all sorts of problems at her school,' says sixth former. 'Here, even though it's such a big year group, there's not even one.' School also praised for approach to those at the bottom of the academic pecking order. Teachers' policy is, sensibly, to compare the potentially down-hearted with the rest of the country. 'Don't remind us of our grades. We might be at the bottom here but for a lot of schools, that would be right at the very top,' said sixth former. Others praised teachers' way of dealing with those struggling with the pace. 'Will go on to the next pupil but then come back to you and often see you in private to sort things out,' reckoned year 8 pupil.

Though rule bending won't be allowed (range of sanctions in place, from confiscation of offending items to letters of apology through to exclusion), little more, thought pupils, is usually needed than quiet chat. Behaviour policy states that 'staff are expected to use praise and appreciation many more times than they use sanctions.' Feedback suggests it's highly effective.

Pupils and parents: A super bunch – parents as well as pupils. No-nonsense, lacking affectation, warm and, reckoned would-be mum, 'not too up themselves.' Really appreciate school's many virtues – head girls who speak of seeking office 'because we want to give [something] back' coming across as genuine rather than CV glory chasers.

'I've seen a lot of friends and they're all very different. Some are laid back, some studious, some sporty. I think a mixture of girls seem to be able to fit in really well,' reckoned mum.

Arrogance definitely absent from this picture, good manners and charm still in evidence even under trying circumstances. On crowded open day when had been on duty for over four hours, enthusiastic escorts (guided by presumably exhausted staff, pleasant to the end) were tireless in efforts to ensure nobody missed a thing, even after end of official visiting time.

Entrance: Popularity not hard to fathom given numbers who came to hear the head's talk on open day. Not so much standing as queuing room only, despite promise that on-line version of talk would be posted the next day. Pill sweetened by red-robed gospel choir blasting the hordes with high quality, high energy numbers including (appropriately) 'Ain't no mountain high enough.'

Would that it were true. Even the best grappling irons in the business may not be enough to haul you up these particular slopes. Following early September deadline for applications, anything north of 1,300 hopefuls sit mid-month VR and maths papers. The 700 or so who pass will hear in sufficient time to include school on CAF (common application form), though with only 210 year 7 places to fill, majority will go away empty handed when formal offers are made in March.

School, however, keen to inject a little hope into the process, points out that with sizeable numbers also doing the grammar school rounds (Nonsuch, Tiffin Girls and Bromley bunch) means that 'you could argue it's more like 1,300 for a total of 400 [year 7] places'. Lots of locals, open day blazer brands representing seemingly every primary and prep in the area, extending out to Croydon and Tooting. Distant reaches of London and Surrey not much represented – doesn't appear to have huge geographic catchment (though if results go up much further, it probably will).

Cleverness, though essential, doesn't have to be extreme, is message (though in many cases you'd imagine it is). 'Overwhelmingly, come with at least a level 5 in Sats, and if likely to achieve this in year 6, would be of similar ability to pupils at the school'.

Tests are designed 'to be accessible to all, whether tutored or not,' with exam content 'based on ground covered to end of year 5.' However, if content, particularly when it comes to VR, hasn't been covered, brief trip to WH Smiths or similar for a bit of mugging up can provide useful familiarisation.

Exit: Lose around 10 per cent after GCSEs, almost nobody at end of year 12 (one per cent in 2016). Destinations ooze academic credibility though there's a decently mixed bag: one girl we talked to was part of a select group contemplating career in sport. Picky might hope for a few more to Oxbridge (five in 2016) but around a third make Russell Group. Twenty to medical school in 2016; art college popular. Around a fifth take a gap year.

Remarks: Thoroughly genuine. School speaks of warm, friendly and purposeful atmosphere. Yada, yada, we thought, another bland statement. Yet from the minute you meet teachers and staff, coping with crowds and doing with smiles what Jesus did with loaves and fishes, you have impression of a school that's genuinely living the mission statement. Though equally desirable, not all grammars are the same. We loved this one.

Walthamstow School for Girls

292

Church Hill, Walthamstow, London E17 9RZ

Pupils: 900 • Ages: 11–16

Tel: 020 8509 9446
Email: info@wsfg.waltham.sch.uk
Website: www.wsfg.waltham.sch.uk

W

Head: Since 2012, Ms Meryl Davies BA (50s), who we found to be easy-going, enthusiastic and energised. Prepared to go against the grain if it's in the best interests of the school – which staff, parents and students unanimously admire – it feels like there's really nothing this determined head couldn't handle.

Having studied French and linguistics at Sheffield University, she stayed on to do her PGCE. 'I loved my own schooling in North Wales, so teaching was a long-time ambition,' she says. Immediately attracted to some of the more radical teaching techniques of the 1980s and the more gritty comprehensives of inner London, she found the reality was quite an eye-opener as a young whippersnapper, but one she nonetheless embraced, with one of her earlier jobs working on a London barge with school refusers to get them back into mainstream schooling. 'Working at the raw edge of education is an experience I think all teachers should have – you get to really understand what makes young people tick,' she says.

After moving on to Graveney School, Tooting, she moved up the ranks to assistant head, then took up a deputy headship in Elliott School, Putney, one of the biggest London comps at the time (where she was seconded briefly to take on a headship of a school on special measures). She then moved to Cator Park School for Girls, Bromley, before coming to Walthamstow in 2012. Disappointingly, results (5+ A*-C GCSE including English and maths) dropped a whopping 14 per cent after just a few months of her joining, but it's widely acknowledged this was largely down to an earlier decision to get all year 11s to do a pilot course of double maths. With fine grading among the tactics she's since introduced, results are not only back on track, but the best the school has ever had. Seen by staff as an enabling, empowering leader, she regularly encourages others to front meetings. She teaches French to the lower school, runs a Monday surgery for parents and answers emails at weekends, seeing her job as 24/7.

'Teaching has been my vocation and London schools have been my life and passion,' she says. 'It sounds trite, but if you think about how many lives we have an impact on, I think working in education is an amazing opportunity and responsibility.' Lives in South London with her partner and has three grown-up children.

Academic matters: Excellent results across the board, with the school consistently among the top performing non-selective schools in the country. 'There are no specialist subjects at this school – we aim to do well in everything,' explains head, although the school has a specialist status in maths and computing, which has done no harm to results in these areas. In 2016, 78 per cent of students gained five or more GCSEs (including maths and English) at A*-C and 26 per cent were A*-A grades – some of the best results the school has ever had, which the head attributes to a combination of high expectations, inspirational teaching, regular monitoring and target setting and a broad approach to learning experiences.

No setting, except in maths from year 7. 'Historically, the school has never done it,' says head, 'and this works for us.' French or Spanish from year 7, with a taster in Urdu, and Latin also available at GCSE. At the end of year 8, students take part in the Languages Festival, a celebration of all languages spoken or studied in the school and the girls perform in a foreign language in front of their year. Latin offered as an additional language at GSCE.

Targeting and monitoring are huge, with personalisation of study plans meticulous in detail – one of the key reasons no student seems to get left behind. 'It's forensic,' smiles the head, who can talk at length at how girls are identified for different types and levels of help, depending on their individual needs and the way they learn. Peer mentoring is also a focus, with older pupils trained to work regularly with younger ones around student support.

A tour of the classrooms revealed engaged students contributing animatedly and with much smiling. Students we spoke to agree this is the norm, with plenty of references to 'engaging,' 'interactive' lessons that 'are never dull.' 'Teachers want to see that everyone is on board and thriving in their subject,' said one student. The head points to the growing focus on sharing good techniques around teaching and learning, which she hopes will improve consistency of teaching methods across the school (something they've been criticised for in the past). Low staff turnover, with one parent commenting, 'Lots of teachers have been here a very long time and it means they have strong attachments to the school.'

Phrases like 'That's not good enough' are not part of school life here, where the emphasis is on enabling and encouraging effort in much more positive ways. 'You won't hear it said to the students or staff,' says the head firmly. 'We pride ourselves on having a healthy atmosphere where we make people feel confident, not self-doubting.' The school motto, 'Neglect not the gift that is in thee,' resonates here, according to staff and students, who add that school is, in the main, fun.

Whilst the school doesn't claim to stand out in terms of SEN, around a quarter (nearly 24 per cent) require SEN support (almost double the national average for schools) and a similar figure (27 per cent) speak English as a second language. No wonder the language and learning department has a 16-strong team (some of whom are teaching staff), catering for the usual remit – everything from mild dyslexia to mobility problems (there's good wheelchair access here). Most support is classroom based and there's a plenty of focus on looking ahead so that gaps are prevented from widening where they needn't. 'I've been massively impressed by how much effort the department puts into my daughter's needs and how well they communicate with us about it,' one parent told us. 'The school is incredibly personalised and inclusive.'

Games, options, the arts: 'Sport is a large feature of this school,' states the head and there's certainly no shortage of options – cricket, basketball, tag rugby, football, rock climbing, netball, trampolining, dance, self-defence and more – which are mainly offered on site, either in the sports hall or so-called MUGA (multi-use games area), which consists of a large, hard-surfaced area of courts. Sadly, no school field, although there is some outside green space, including a landscaped woodland area, which is sometimes used for PE. Meanwhile, the local YMCA, which is in easy walking distance, is used for swimming and fitness classes. The school regularly competes against other schools, and there is some representation at regional level and occasionally national, with one former student having made the Olympic squad for volleyball, and another for athletics. School is also involved in the NEC Wheelchair Tennis Masters. 'Some other schools around here don't seem to value sport, but this one really gets that link between physical exercise and learning well in the classroom,' one parent told us.

Impressive art facilities, consisting of two main studios, which are spacious, bright and airy, with students' creations in everything from ceramics to textiles and graphics to portrait work exhibited throughout the school. A particularly attractive year 8 Grayson Perry vase project, displayed in glass cabinets in one major corridor, couldn't help but catch our eye. 'We all have a great sense of pride when our artwork is displayed – there's a feeling of "I did that and my school appreciates it",' one student said. Lots of cross-curricular projects, such as maths through art, plus plenty of visits to galleries and exhibitions. The school runs an annual exhibition of self-portraits by year 7s, which appears as part of the Walthamstow Arts Trail, attended by celebs and general public, and which raises money for their link school in Pakistan.

Drama very popular and seen as a key part of increasing the girls' confidence and ability to speak out, with lots of performances by individual year groups and whole-school performances every other year, such as The Wizard of Oz. Strong links with the Unicorn Theatre in London Bridge. School also involved with Shakespeare Schools Festival.

The biggest things to come out of the music department here (which has two music classrooms and a decent number of practice rooms) are the highly acclaimed steel pan bands, which regularly perform in public spaces, including the Royal Albert Hall. It's been a tradition at the school for decades, with a steel band ensemble in every year group, which rehearses every morning. There's a whole school orchestra, although it's not huge, plus school choir and various ensembles and bands, some of which are student led. Four peripatetic teachers come in to teach instrumental lessons. The annual Modern Languages Festival involves each class in year 8 learning a song in the language they study and performing with their class in front of the entire year group. Dance is also valued, and seen as key to team-building.

Food tech is innovative, with plenty of competitions and links with outside organisations – ranging from an annual project with foodbanks, in which students learn to make dishes with very limited resources, right through to trips to fine dining restaurants in top hotels.

Extensive enrichment, including trips (eg black history month trips), workshops (eg in STEM, and also for young lawyers and for young doctors), events (eg Girls Can Crafting and Coding Event), entry to competitions (eg WSFG Cycle Planning Awards, Jack Petchey Speak Out Challenge) and links with other schools (eg primary schools are invited to the school for science days). The girls even run their own bank, through a longstanding link with MyBnk.

Extracurricular clubs include multimedia, origami, languages, sport, gardening, engineering and debating. 'Whilst these clubs are not compulsory, they are actively encouraged,' says the head. We attended a meeting for the International Club, where a group of students were busy planning all kinds of exciting initiatives, particularly schools they have strong links with overseas – including the Goodwill Secondary School in Roseau and Dominica and Ambore Read Foundation School, Ambore, Pakistan. Plenty of fundraising for the school in Ambore (over £15k to date), while teachers have travelled there to officially open the school and deliver lessons. 'These international links are frequently the subject of school assemblies and we are currently exchanging messages with students in Dominica via our Google Community,' says the head. School also has live pen-pal links with schools in France and Spain and holds the British Council International School Award (for outstanding development of the international dimension in the curriculum).

Background and atmosphere: Main building – with the classic grade II, red-brick grammar school look – was built in 1911, although the school itself dates back to 1890, when it was opened as a private school in West Avenue, which later moved to nearby Church Hill House. In 1911, the school was taken over by Essex County Council and in 1913 moved to its present site on land originally part of the Vicars Glebe. The school has since been enlarged in 1918, 1928, 1962, 1974 and 2010 and the resulting combination of new and old builds works seamlessly, with no need to even leave one building to enter the next. After a period in the late 20th century as a grammar school, then as a senior high school for 14-18 year-olds, in 1986 the school once again became a school for girls aged 11-16.

In the old part of the school, expect oodles of original features, from the parquet flooring and wall tiles to traditional radiators, with the oak panelled school hall forming the centrepiece, whose walls bear the names and achievements of past students. At the other end of the spectrum is the 2010 building, which includes the new Norris Hall, providing an impressive theatre-style auditorium. Spacious classrooms and labs boast masses of natural light, and there are some attractive break-out areas, including one with brightly coloured orange and black sofas, known by the girls as the 'Easyjet Lounge.' A vast dining hall has mixed reviews of the food from students and the library is a good size. Everywhere – and we mean everywhere – is scrupulously clean and tidy.

Outside, the stand-out feature is the Greek Theatre, built in the 1920s and which has a circular arena with steps up to a stage on one side and pillared portico on the other. There's a reasonably sized green space surrounding the theatre, plus a rooftop area (to the 2010 building), accessible from ground level, with plenty of chairs and tables. Students also use the MUGA area at break times. Overall, there's a rural, village feel here, even though they're only five minutes from the Victoria line – with enthusiastic students clearly enjoying their environment and plenty of reassuring signs that they're genuinely having fun. The only rude interruption to all this is the hideous end-of-lesson 'bell' that sounds more like some kind of nuclear alert.

The school day runs from 8.45am – 3.30pm, although breakfast club students arrive from 7.30am and extracurricular activities run after school daily, with girls also given the opportunity to stay on to do work after school if, for example, they struggle with finding the space and quiet to do so at home.

Pastoral care, well-being and discipline: Pastoral care primarily comes from form tutors, with students describing teachers as 'approachable' and 'caring', and girls clearly feeling safe and nurtured. Peer support is also strong, with some formal mechanisms in place, although for the most part, it's natural, with students instinctively looking out for one another, especially lower down the school. A part-time counsellor is accessible via referral from teachers and learning mentors, and there's plenty of emphasis on exploring issues that others school shy away from – from female genital mutilation to forced marriages. The school is Stonewall approved and there's no shortage of multi-cultural events and projects to ensure everyone's background feels valued. Big on fundraising, especially for linked schools in other countries. Transition for year 7s is notable, with the school running a highly successful summer school to get a head-start on team-building, and the school has recently introduced a mindfulness course for year 11s.

Strong student council (which, like most, seems to focus on food and toilets) and plenty of leadership opportunities, including interviewing staff, which reflect the emphasis on trust being given to the girls. 'Teachers are strict when they need to be, but for the most part, there's a strong reliance on self-discipline here,' says the head. Indeed, although there are school rules, you're more likely to hear talk of rights and responsibilities, with girls very much feeling a sense of ownership in this school.

Bullying occasionally occurs as it does in any school, says the head, although there are plenty of anti-bullying policies and the fact that this is a 'telling' school means students are quick to speak out not just about themselves, but any friends in trouble. 'Our staff are trained to notice signs,' adds the head, 'and when it happens, we involve parents quickly.' No permanent exclusions as long as anyone can remember, with fixed term exclusions well below the national average, usually given out for very rare instances of aggressive behaviour.

Pupils and parents: Multi-ethnic population, with students from over 50 countries – a great source of pride for the school, which celebrates this rich diversity in everything from assemblies to individual projects. Majority of students from Pakistani origin, followed by white (not just British), then black Caribbean and black African, with the fourth largest group being Indian. 'Mind you, this changes all the time,' points out the head. Girls seem confident, articulate, aspirational and optimistic. 'I could take any of my daughter's friends and they'd have a very clear idea of where they want to be in two or three years' time,' said a parent of a year 10 student.

Parents equally, if not more, aspirational, expecting a lot from their girls, with almost 100 per cent attendance at parents' evenings, consultations about subject options etc. Parents are also regularly invited to take part in questionnaires and parent forums and they are consulted about policy. No PTA, however, which is a disappointment to some parents.

Former pupils include Baroness Scotland, Jacqui Harper (BBC news) and Jeanette Kwakye (Olympic sprinter).

Entrance: Heavily oversubscribed, with some 700 applying for 180 year 7 places. Non-selective, the school follows the borough's entrance criteria, which favours girls in the looked after system/those with a statement of SEN/EHC plan, followed by siblings, then it's down to distance. Those who get in mainly live less than a one mile radius. Occasional places further up the school when families move out of the area.

Exit: Vast majority of girls go on to sixth form college or local school sixth forms. 'They clammer to have our girls,' says head. The two main local colleges are Sir George Munoux Sixth Form College and Leyton Sixth Form college, whilst schools include Highams Park, Heathcote, City and Islington, Latymer, City of Westminster and Forest School. Most go on to study for A levels, with a heavy emphasis on sciences, whilst a few do BTecs. 'They are career savvy and know exactly what they want to study and why,' says head. Those after more specialist courses are prepared to travel, with some commuting up to a couple of hours every day.

Remarks: This is a relaxed and happy school, yet it's purposeful, vibrant and aspirational. The strong academic atmosphere, which is backed up by a great pastoral system, means there's no reason any girl should get left behind. We were particularly encouraged by the extent to which girls are encouraged to express themselves and to challenge stereotypes and indeed the status quo where appropriate. A true community school that believes passionately in the research that a single-sex environment empowers girls to realise their potential, this is a place that proves with the right teaching and school culture, anyone can thrive.

Westminster Abbey Choir School

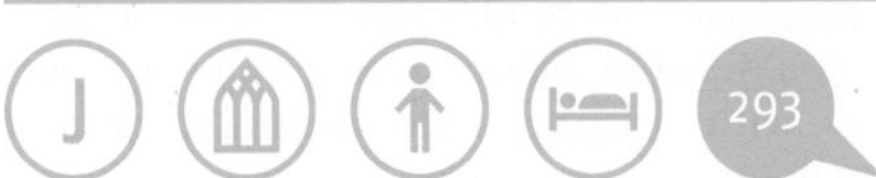

Dean's Yard, London SW1P 3NY

Pupils: 30 (all boarders) • Ages: 8–13 • C of E

Fees: Boarding: (after subsidy) £8,240 pa

Tel: 020 7222 6151
Email: headmaster@westminster-abbey.org
Website: www.westminster-abbey.org/choir-school

Headmaster: Since 2002, Mr Jonathan Milton BEd (50s), married, formerly head of The Abbey School in Tewkesbury. Bred, if not born, into the choir school tradition – he was a choral scholar at York. Music was his degree subject, though he now teaches geography. A gentle man, whose quiet, friendly manner betrays a profound love of his unique school, the tradition it enshrines and the community of boys and staff which gives it ever-fresh life. Clearly, an inspired appointment. Mr Milton is, at once, a traditionalist and a moderniser – exactly the right balance for the place. 'When I came, there were no carpets or curtains and it felt tense – that's now completely gone. It was dark too. We've tried to make it gentler.' He showed us the little IT room next to the dormitories: 'a marvellous way for boys to stay in touch – much simpler than writing a letter. And the staff communicate with parents every week electronically.' Gentler the school may well be but he has also tightened the academics, keeping step with the outside world in which senior school places are no longer assigned in little chats between heads of 'big' schools and trusted prep heads. Mr Milton's openness, thoughtfulness and warmth are mirrored in his boys. Those we talked to were similarly relaxed, candid and friendly. Head and boys share their view of life here, 'It's tough, you get very tired but.. it's fabulous.'

However, currently unwilling to meet the Guide and he feels that it 'seems not really to be appropriate for a school such as this and prospective parents can glean all the information they need from ISI reports etc'. Parents, of course, may disagree.

Entrance: No formal entrance test day or the like. Over the year, school will see around 25 boys for voice trials – usually in ones and twos – and usually in year 3. The master of the choristers will hear them and the head will chat to the boy and parents and, if the lad looks promising, he will be invited back to spend a day in the school. This will include a more formal voice trial, a chance to play his instruments and testing in maths and English. What is looked for is not grade 8 in six instruments but musical aptitude and the kind of attitude to music, community and learning that make for a happy and successful Westminster Abbey chorister. 'They have to enjoy being part of a close-knit team and they must have personality and character,' says Mr Milton. Academic brilliance is less important though, clearly, the boy must enjoy learning. Of the 25 they see, places may be offered to between four and six, on average, though one or two may be invited to come back some months later.

These days, more than half come from state primaries and can be caught up and supported where necessary. 'With year groups of six or seven, we can tailor-make classes,' says head. School fees are subsidised by the Abbey and no-one, however impecunious, should be put off applying if their boy is a natural chorister. Funds will be found. 'Some pay nothing at all,' says Mr Milton. Boys now come from further afield – Yorkshire and even overseas. Quite tough for an 8-year-old, you might think. 'And,' says Mr Milton, 'few of our parents would have chosen a boarding school – when they see it, they realise it's a way of life.' Yes. This represents the most amazing opportunity for the right child and a peerless preparation for life.

Exit: An astonishing list of leavers' destinations over the last three years. Many win music scholarships to prestigious schools and many win academic and/or art scholarships too. Recently, Eton, Winchester, Westminster, St Paul's, City of London, Tonbridge, King's Canterbury, Uppingham, Charterhouse, Oundle, Sherborne, Ampleforth, Bryanston, Wells Cathedral, Lancing, London Oratory.

Remarks: This is the only choir school in the country which is only a choir school – no day pupils, no girls, no non-choristers. Average class size six, maximum is nine. In a way, that says it all. The place hums with quiet activity – mental, physical and musical. It all happens in a tall, unobtrusive building in Dean's Yard – right under Big Ben, the Houses of Parliament and Westminster Abbey. Dean's Yard is a grassy square lined by augustly solid houses. Opposite is the modest arch which leads to Westminster School – no connection with the choir school except that the large pupils and the little choristers see each other passing all day, which makes the business of scholarship and growing up in this – the heart of the great centre of London – seem quite the normal thing.

Five floors accommodate all learning, admin and living space. All is freshly-painted and feels light, comfortable and well-cared for. There's a super ground floor 'music room' used for assemblies and the like – a splendid stained glass window commemorating Purcell and the other masters of the choristers, who between them make up a history of English choral music – Gibbons, Blow, Simon Preston et al. Classrooms are small with conventional desks and whiteboards and it all looks a bit dolls' house in scale – enhanced, when we visited (during exam week) by the very cuddly teddies (for good luck) sitting reassuringly on desks. More teddies in the dorms which – it is a boys' school – are, if not Spartan, certainly not prettified. Bunk beds with integral cupboards in airy rooms. Good shower rooms, good ICT provision and a very nice sitting room with sofas, piano, TV, books and games and feeling really snug.

Everyone does standard prep school curriculum but flexibility can be built into the system with such small classes and so small a school. Individual help is the norm. No boys with SENs, we are told, though the odd mild dyslexic may creep in. A boy with dyslexia would find chorister-life tough, says Mr Milton – what with having to read music and a foreign language at speed and so on. 'It wouldn't be fair.' Yes.

Sports take place via buses to Battersea Park, The Queen Mother sports centre in Victoria and water sports in Docklands – Mr Milton is a keen sailor. They kayak, rock climb and sail and Mr Milton sees this – and the opportunity to get away from the closed chorister world – as essential for good relations.

Evidence of boy-life and wit abounds. WACS Lyrical – the boys' own noticeboard – details competitions, initiatives, jokes and notices – full of fun and ideas. The art room, open in the evenings, similarly lively – we were terrified by the huge multi-tusked cardboard, paper and paint beast which 'would be tamed by listening to Palestrina'. Boys enjoy textile work, DT – they make fan-powered vehicles for racing – and knitting: 'very popular', we were told. Obviously, music is central to life. Singing practice in the song school happens each morning and each afternoon before evensong – except on Weds and alternate Mons. Instrumental practice is timetabled and very much a normal part of everyday life. Musical guests and ensembles visit, there is a composer in residence – a real privilege for such boys – and school takes full advantage of the concert halls and galleries roundabout. Likewise, the school goes into local primaries – boys take their instruments – to inspire others, 'just to give music a boost'.

What do the boys say – and their parents? 'You have to be very independent and organised,' a seasoned 12-year-old told us. 'You can't rely on your parents to pack your bag and find your pencil case – you have to do it all yourself. You have to manage your own revision and music practice.' (Sounds like a course in choristership might be handy all round.) 'It is very tiring – I'd like to have more of a rest after concerts.' On the other hand – 'singing all the special services we do is brilliant. We did a special service for the spies! [100 years of MI5]. They just looked normal. They don't wear T-shirts saying "I'm a spy".' And 'We're on TV, we go on tours and make CDs.' 'It can be exhausting,' said a parent, 'but they bounce back. It's unbelievably rewarding.' And they clearly enjoy the abbey community with whom they share Christmas and Easter meals and so on. A choristership here is a treasure. A huge commitment for boys and family while it lasts, but a gift for life.

Westminster Cathedral Choir School

Ambrosden Avenue, London SW1P 1QH

Pupils: 180; 29 full boarders (choristers) • Ages: 7–13 (4–13 from September 2017) • RC

Fees: Day £17,697; Choristers (boarding) £9,282 pa

Tel: 020 7798 9081
Email: office@choirschool.com
Website: www.choirschool.com

Headmaster: Since 2007, Mr Neil McLaughlan (40s). Married with a young son and daughter, and a man who radiates humour, decency and charm in equal measure. Read philosophy and politics at Durham and spent a few years with Andersen Consulting in London before embarking on a teaching career in 1997. After spells at Stonyhurst and Worth, he took up a post as head of English and director of development at Downside School, before joining WCCS as headmaster. He hopes to be there 'for the duration.' Parents hope so too. 'Lovely guy!' said one. 'So easy to approach!' said another. 'An extremely dedicated head and a great promoter of the school,' said a third. Typically modest, he hopes to do 'lots and lots of small things right.' We think he's doing lots of big things right too. Under his visionary yet kindly leadership, this has become an inspiring school that is going from strength to strength.

Entrance: Main entry points for day boys are at 7+, where 14-15 places are available, and 8+ (a further eight or so places – mostly for choristers). Applicants sit tests in English, maths and non-verbal reasoning in January of the year before entry. Occasional places in other year groups, notably at 11+. The school is always oversubscribed, and, once boys have met the required academic standard, will give preference where possible to practising Roman Catholics and to boys with a brother at the school.

Choristers, who must be Catholic and boarders, join at 8+. Would-be probationers have to pass informal and formal tests with the cathedral's master of music, as well as succeeding at the academic assessment; and if they manage all that, they spend two nights at the school to see whether chorister life will suit them. Only then will they be offered one of the six available places. As the school's popularity grows, so inevitably does the competition; there are now half a dozen serious candidates for each choristership, and for the first time in over a decade, the school has not had to go recruiting for them.

Up to full fees assistance for choristers; none for day pupils, whose families just have to fork out. As a result, there is more cultural than social diversity here. Boys come from a wide range of nationalities, among them France, Spain, Italy, Russia, Ghana and Korea, making this a truly international school. With some 80 per cent of the boys now from Catholic families, the school is less religiously diverse than it was, but remains open to day boys of all faiths provided their families are happy to support the school's Catholic ethos.

Opening a pre-prep for 4-7 year olds in September 2017. Entry by assessment. Most are expected to continue on to the prep school after English and maths tests.

Exit: The head has worked tirelessly to raise the school's profile, and WCCS's exit record is superb. Boys regularly leave for boarding schools like Eton, Harrow, Winchester, Radley, Downside, Charterhouse and King's Canterbury, and for a raft of top London schools, including Westminster, St Paul's, UCS, City of London, KCS Wimbledon, Latymer Upper, Dulwich College and the new Wetherby senior school, often with music scholarships. Others to Cardinal Vaughan and the London Oratory. 'The school is much more linked into the senior schools than it was a few years ago,' reported one satisfied parent. 'Oh yes, the head's always going on about schools,' confirmed one of the boys, equably.

Remarks: The school was endearingly shabby once, but not any more. A five-year programme of refurbishment has just finished, and everything is now bang up to date. Visitors are welcomed in the beautiful glass-fronted foyer, where handwritten Music for mass schedules from 1905 are hung beside huge photos of current pupils radiating health and cheeriness. Throughout the building, ceilings, floors and lighting are all new, and all the classrooms are gleaming and well-resourced, with interactive whiteboards in each one. Large and much-loved playground, covered with Astroturf, where boys play 'crazy games' on the climbing apparatus. 'That was a real selling point for me,' said one parent. 'The boys have a chance to be boys.' 'The way to the heart of little boys is good food and football at playtime, and WCCS excels in both,' confirmed another. We didn't try the football, but we can confirm that the food is splendid, a delicious combination of tasty and healthy.

Boarding facilities have also been upgraded. We can't comment on the refurbished boarders' common room, because a curmudgeonly old trumpet teacher therein told us we were interrupting his lesson and to get out, but we did manage to see the sleeping accommodation, which was cheerful, light and airy. The rigours of chorister life notwithstanding, feedback on the boarding experience from both parents and boys was uniformly positive. 'The key thing,' says head, 'is to have good, kind people around the boys, good accommodation and excellent food. An army marches on its stomach.'

Years ago, parents had disquiets about aspects of WCCS. Nowadays, they cannot find enough superlatives with which to express their delight. 'We have been thrilled by both the teaching and pastoral care provided by the school.' 'The staff generate a wonderfully positive energy.' 'It's an amazing school, the teachers are so kind!' 'You couldn't choose a better school, I recommend it to everyone.' 'A wonderful warmth and care is present everywhere.'

A father of a new chorister told us, 'My son absolutely loves it. He's thrilled to pieces. The first weekend they were eligible to go home, he didn't want to come.' (Poor mum!) And a mother of two day pupils wrote, 'Happiness is guaranteed at this school; it is such a nurturing, caring and stimulating environment. I can honestly say that the only problem I have ever had is to find a way to drag my boys out of the playground and back home at the end of the day.' What's behind this remarkable success? 'The one ingredient a Catholic school should have is joy,' said the head, simply and without any side, when we asked him,.

There is joy in the teaching here, that's for sure. A quiet revolution is taking place in the WCCS curriculum that made this reviewer go all excited and wobbly at the knees. Schemes of work have been painstakingly redesigned, with scholarship and a genuine love of learning at their heart. 'The idea is to present knowledge as a unified whole,' explained the head, 'so for instance, whilst they're studying Adam and Eve in RS, they'll be doing CS Lewis's The Magician's Nephew in English. Likewise, we use geometry and graph-plotting in maths to support map skills in geography, and they'll draw antique maps in art at the same time. If the boys are doing the human body in science, they'll look at what the Greeks and Romans discovered about it in history.' The boys we spoke to praised the lessons as 'really good fun,' adding, 'The work's challenging, but in a good way'.

Much emphasis on poetry, with poems studied every week, as well as learnt by heart and declaimed. 'We want them to know the great poets of the English language,' said the deputy head, and to further this, the school has produced its own wonderful anthologies, where the selection is 'unashamedly classic.' In addition to regular English lessons, boys receive two lessons a week on formal grammar and punctuation, and Latin is compulsory from the off – 'Latin is crucial for grammar, it's not an academic luxury,' insisted the deputy head. 'As an international school, the story of the world's great civilisations interests us. But children of this age also need connections, and they need the basics.' All those who have wrung their hands at the disjointed, shallow content of so many modern lessons, lift up your hearts and hope.

This is clearly a scholarly yet joyful environment, and the quality of student work we saw reflected that. We read, misty-eyed, a set of poems by the year 7s about Westminster Bridge (inspired by Wordsworth's sonnet) that were outstandingly creative and well-written; likewise, a history essay on Thomas Becket was not only mature and insightful, but skilful and lucid in its use of language. But mightn't this approach favour only the brightest? WCCS's SENCo emphatically denied it, asserting that boys at the school with SEN benefited from understanding how language works. We were impressed with the support the school gives to those with dyslexia and dyspraxia, as well as to ESL students, such as the two grave and courteous Russian boys we saw having extra English tutorials. And all the staff we met were purposeful, well-bred (curmudgeon excepted), cultivated, devoted to what they do and, according to parents, 'incredibly dedicated.'

As you'd expect, the standard of music here is outstanding. The choristers are completely immersed in music-making at the highest level (listen to the downloads on the website, and marvel), and the day boys, swimming in the same element, also achieve great things. We saw year 8 boys composing their entries for the school's Christmas carol competition, and heard much excellent instrumental playing as we went round the school. 'The music programme is amazing,' enthused one parent. 'My son's piano playing has come on by leaps and bounds in just a few weeks.' Many pupils achieve grades 7 or 8 in their chosen instrument(s) by the time they leave.

Football, rugby and cricket are the main sports here, played at local pitches, and swimming and PE are held at the nearby Queen Mother Sports Centre. Lots of extracurricular activities, including debating, philosophy, chess, scrabble, code-breaking, the Airfix model club, current affairs, and cross-country running. 'But where do you run?' we asked, glancing with some surprise at the surrounding streets. 'Oh!' said our tour guide, 'Green Park, Hyde Park, St James's..'

Lucky lads, you might think. And they are, of course. But what struck us most about this lovely little school was how considerate, well-mannered and sanguine about life its pupils seemed to be. They are achieving great things, while remaining likeable and happy boys. As one mother wrote, 'My son is neither Catholic nor musical, but has been recognised for other things he has to contribute to the school. They're grounded children with good values. It's a perfect place for my son to grow into a confident young man.' We agree with her. For boys fortunate enough to come here, this is as near perfect as it gets.

Westminster Under School

Linked with Westminster School

   295

Adrian House, 27 Vincent Square, London SW1P 2NN

Pupils: 288 • Ages: 7–13 • C of E

Fees: £17,718 pa

Tel: 020 7821 5788
Email: anne-marie.mccarthy@westminster.org.uk
Website: www.westminsterunder.org.uk

Master: Since September 2016, Mark O'Donnell, previously the head of St Martin's Ampleforth and also head of Alleyn's Junior School in south London. Educated at Stonyhurst and St Ignatius College, New South Wales, he has a masters in education from Harvard and a postgraduate diploma in education from Oxford. He is a Fellow of the Royal College of Arts, a Duke of Edinburgh assessor and an alpine ski leader. He is married with three sons.

Entrance: Academically selective (very) at 7, 8 and 11. Some successful applicants are merely 'well above the national average', about a third 'far above'. All candidates need to read fluently well beyond their chronological age and approach the unexpected logically and imaginatively. No obvious feeders, though all the usual central London pre-preps represented. At 11+, a reasonable chunk from state primaries, most of the rest from schools which end at year 6. (The school encourages entrants from 'those leaving at a natural point.') Twenty-two places at 7 (175 applying), a further 22 at 8 (175 applying), then 28 places at 11 (250 applying). At 11+, now uses computerised pre-tests in December before written exams for call-back candidates. About 40 invited at each stage for interview and further testing. 'We want to understand each child and decide if this is the right school for them.' What makes the fit? 'The school is about passion, enthusiasm, determination and a hunger for achievement. We're looking for boys who are independent, intellectual and individual. Everybody here loves learning.'

Exit: About 90 per cent go on to the senior school (including all those who come in at 11), with a good number of scholarships (nine in 2016), but the school is equally happy to prepare for entrance and scholarships elsewhere. About a dozen each year to Eton (often those with family connections), some with major scholarships (two King's Scholars in 2016). Generally a couple to Winchester, and sometimes a sprinkling to City, Dulwich, Alleyn's, etc.

Remarks: Academically top of the tree. Well-qualified staff (a number with PhDs) provides teaching that is mostly strong, lively and challenging. 'We're looking for boys who will think and problem solve. We want them to work things out, not be spoon-fed.' Most boys seem to relish the offering. 'I really like all my lessons,' said one. 'The teachers are very enthusiastic and if you have a problem they just want to help,' said another. However, the pressure to be high in the rankings comes as a shock to some.

Specialist teaching in all subjects from year 5. In English, boys are encouraged to 'develop their own voice'. Books are seminal, with even the smallest scouring the library shelves in their lunch hour. Reading lists updated termly and topped up with an in-house bookshop and regular swapshop. Weekly maths competitions hone skills both for lessons and the Intermediate and Senior Maths Challenge, where plenty achieve gold and beyond. Maths and science extension club. Programming from year 3. French throughout, taught by native speakers. Classical studies combined with Latin from year 5, stand-alone Latin from year 6, Greek in year 8. Annual Latin play competition. 'There's a real sense of intellectual endeavour,' said one parent.

Thorough monitoring, with internal exams November and June, plus mocks in the Lent term of year 8, as well as regular subject testing. Lots of rewards for achievement with cups and shields for virtually everything. 'They really ram home competition,' said one parent. Homework load significant at all levels. An hour a night in years 3-5, an hour and a half in years 7 and 8. Some parents have voiced the view that supportive homes are essential. The school says this shouldn't be necessary: 'We don't require parental support and you absolutely don't need a tutor. If you need a tutor, you shouldn't be at Westminster.' However, one parent commented that tutoring is 'rife'.

New arrivals at 11 – two forms of 12-14 boys – are given Saturday morning lessons from the moment they're accepted, then segregated for lessons (but not other activities) in year 7. 'We give them lots of attention, before dividing up the whole year group into scholarship and CE forms in year 8.' Those from state primaries can find the transition taxing. 'Catching up to common entrance in two years was difficult,' said one parent. 'There was an enormous amount of work and my son found it stressful.'

Few struggle in the conventional sense, but an experienced SENCo provides support with study skills, exam technique and organisation, arranging clinics where help from peer mentors is particularly productive. Plenty of 'enhancement', too, through debating, history of art etc.

Music of an exceptionally high standard (many boys with grade 8 and beyond and plenty of music scholarships to senior schools). Head of music (also musical director of National Youth Music Theatre) oversees over 500 lessons a week, an outstanding choir and biannual music trips.

Not everyone's idea of a sporty school, but the athletic ante has been raised recently with the addition of a number of well-qualified coaches. ('One boy attends the Chelsea football academy one day a week, but still manages his academic work.') For a central London prep, notably well-endowed with playing fields, and the expansive garden square opposite the front gates provides an ample supply of pitches and courts as well as an adventure playground. Games twice a week, with regular inter-house and inter-school tournaments in football, hockey, cricket, tennis and basketball. Recently-acquired sports hall just down the road (also able to accommodate mass gatherings of parents) offers further scope for indoor games, including judo, fencing, karate, wall climbing and nets.

Exciting theatrical tradition maintained by an 'inspirational' head of drama, with three productions annually (recent highlights include Lord of the Flies, School for Scandal) and a new performing arts centre. Art now housed in its own light and lovely double studio, with a self-contained art history library. Clubs every night (history, Mandarin, debating, etc). Chess (taught by a Grand Master) particularly popular, with 90 members and England players. Competitions galore, including hotly contested Scrabble tournament. (Some find the atmosphere slightly too competitive. 'They don't just have a Scrabble club or a chess club, they have a Scrabble competition or a chess competition.')

Plenty of external speakers and trips in London and further afield. (Recent adventures include classics to Sorrento, cricket to South Africa, geography to the Grand Canyon.) Philanthropy a core value. 'They learn to enjoy giving and love raising money for disadvantaged children.' (Parents and boys raised £45,000 last year, £18,000 in the popular Readathon.)

Founded in 1943 as a class of 17 boys located in the senior school, then decanted to Ecclestone Square, the school took up residence in its current spacious premises in Adrian House

– a red-brick Victorian former hospital – in 1981. The Under School continues to share both governors and outlook with the senior school, allowing the same careful planning over future development. A large new building, directly opposite the existing school, opened in 2013, providing a lofty dining hall and indulgent stretches of well-equipped teaching space.

Discipline not an issue. 'You don't have to shout at Westminster; we encourage good behaviour through positive behaviour management and high expectations.' Certainly, one boy unbidden held open a door, all answered questions readily and politely. Immaculate uniform, perhaps, not a priority. In PSHE, 'they learn about emotional intelligence and empathy for others. We talk about life. We want them to be able to talk with us about anything and it will be OK.'

At 7 and 8, parents primarily prime-central-London (often City) high achievers. At 11+, more diverse, with pupils coming from as far afield as Dagenham and Guildford. Plenty of bilingual, multicultural homes. Parents tend to be proud (and occasionally pushy). Boys are extremely articulate (one 8 year old, asked how he'd cope with a broken arm, responded, 'I would just have to become ambidextrous') and can undoubtedly be boffiny ('Thus, you can see,' explained one 11 year old).

No scholarships, but a few means-tested bursaries of up to 100 per cent at 11 (which take the recipient through the senior school). 'Our philosophy is that the children who can come here should not be prevented from doing so for financial reasons.'

An exciting, demanding education for the intellectual, industrious child.

Westminster School

Linked with Westminster Under School

17 Dean's Yard, London SW1P 3PB

Pupils: 742; 186 boarders (44 girls) • Ages: 13–18 • Sixth form: 381 (127 girls) • C of E

Fees: Day: £25,258 – £27,600 pa; Boarding: £36,462 pa

Tel: 020 7963 1003
Email: registrar@westminster.org.uk
Website: www.westminster.org.uk

Head Master: Since 2014, Patrick Derham MA (50s), previously head of Rugby School. At 12, he was sent to live and study on the naval training ship Arethusa, run by the children's charity Shaftesbury Homes to prepare young men for the navy. Two years later the ship was abruptly sold due to financial difficulties and, with a day's notice and little idea what a public school was, he arrived at Pangbourne College on a bursary. He eventually became head of school and read history at Cambridge (first class degree), and feels 'my life was transformed by education.'

Taught at Cheam School and then Radley, where he was head of history and a housemaster for '12 very happy years' before being advised by the warden there to go straight for a headship. Five years as head of Solihull were followed by 13 at Rugby, before landing the headship of 'the home of liberal education – the perfect culmination of my career.'

His background ('my mum still lives in a council house in Scotland') has clearly been a powerful motivating force in his commitment to widening access to a good education – as he points out, 'all the great schools were founded with that intention.' At Rugby, he set up the Arnold Foundation to provide bursaries for children who need the stability of a boarding education ('we didn't just cream off the brightest middle class kids'). He is a trustee of the SpringBoard Bursary Foundation, a national charity modelled on the same lines, and vice chair of IntoUniversity, which gives disadvantaged children academic support and mentoring to raise their aspirations.

'He did an amazing job here and will be brilliant at Westminster,' said a Rugby insider. Very down to earth, personable, fantastic speaker, say Westminster parents. 'You feel like you can trust him'... 'He really cares about getting to know everyone'... 'I like it that he already knows who I am and who my children are'... 'Very responsive to comments'... 'My daughter thinks he's great'.

Clearly no ivory tower head, he loves interaction with pupils and teaches A level history. Parents watching their sons compete in the recent National Schools Rowing Regatta were delighted to see Derham there cheering on the teams (they won the championship eights' title for the first time in the school's history).

Married to Alison, a teacher, with two grown up children. Westminster seems to be in very steady, to say nothing of inspiring, hands.

Academic matters: With these very bright pupils, 'you can teach for the love of the subject and focus on the exam when need be,' says the head. 'It's a breath of fresh air,' said a parent. 'Intellectual risk taking is encouraged. They're never not challenged.' 'It's incredibly inspiring,' said another. Many of the teachers are experts in their fields, encouraged to follow their interests. 'I cannot believe there is a more stimulating place to teach in the country,' said a teacher. 'It is so much more liberal than at my previous school,' said a sixth form student. 'It's not constrained by the syllabus – it's learning for the sake of learning. It really allows you to get a proper understanding outside the exam baselines.' Pupils tend to internalise that love of learning. 'They read and they question and they challenge,' says the head. 'In my first lesson one asked me, "Where is the evidence?" I'd never been asked that before.'

Everyone encouraged to include a practical subject, eg art, electronics, drama, music, at GCSE. Huge range of languages includes Dutch, Arabic and Portuguese. Several parents commented that inspirational teachers had sparked their sons' interest in subjects they had previously hated. 'He'd always been a bit of a maths boy but now he is flying at English and languages too. They've understood how to teach in a way that suits him and developed all these new interests.'

Top exam results are, nonetheless, part of the package, with 98 per cent A*/A at GCSE in 2016. At A level/Pre-U, the results were 90 per cent A*/A grades and 97 per cent A*/B. New thinking skills course – designed as a more challenging alternative to critical thinking A level – introduces sixth formers to the elements of informal logic, and helps prepare for university entrance skills tests such as the Oxbridge Thinking Skills Assessment.

High academic ability is obviously a prerequisite, but study skills coordinator works with all those who need support for eg mild dyslexia, dyspraxia or Asperger's, or just lack of organisation, helping them with the skills needed to cope with learning at different levels as they move up the school.

Links with local state schools Grey Coat Hospital and Harris Westminster Sixth Form – the latter sponsored by Westminster School – see sixth formers from these schools joining in German, Latin, art history and drama lessons with Westminster students. 'They've done a really good job at integrating us,' said a Westminster sixth former. 'I'm as good friends with students from outside as anyone else in the class.' Joint senior management meetings with Harris Westminster staff: 'We are going to learn from each other.'

Games, options, the arts: An almost overwhelming range of extracurricular opportunities. Societies often stem from the particular passions of both staff and students, ranging from feminist to secular to geography. English society may see Simon Russell Beale answering questions on playing King Lear at the National, whilst Piyush Goyal, national treasurer of the Indian Bharatiya Janata Party (BJP) party, tells the political society about Indian public affairs. 'I set up a society and had an ambassador from Panama come to talk,' said one student. 'Staff are really supportive when you want to set up new things.' Huge range of journalists and politicians, scientists and thinkers drop in to give talks; poet in residence inspires creativity. Trips everywhere: climbing in Cataluña, Beijing exchange, art history in Venice. Years 9-11 go off for a week's climbing, sailing, hill walking or camping at home or abroad.

'Phenomenal' music, with professional standard orchestral concerts at St John's Smith Square and the Barbican, carol service in Westminster Abbey, masterclasses, eminent musicians from Nicola Benedetti to Ian Bostridge giving evening concerts. One parent felt that 'unless you are excellent you won't get a look in,' whilst staff point out there are house concerts and ensembles for the less stratospherically talented. 'We like to think there is room for everyone.' Drama equally high performing – Guys and Dolls a recent sell-out but much cerebral fare too, plus house drama and GCSE/A level pieces – and again huge talent required to bag a role in the large scale school productions.

Art, too, 'wonderful', with much emphasis on traditional drawing and painting skills, life classes, film making facilities and a darkroom. Plus, of course, easy access to all of London's galleries and museums. 'My son had no artistic ambition when he arrived, but is now doing art A level. They have totally inspired him,' said one parent, whilst another commented: 'They let these academic boys be so creative – they feel free to explore.'

Sports – known as 'Station' – take place on Tuesday and Thursday afternoons, mostly on the enviably large playing fields in nearby St Vincent Square plus adjacent sports centre (in a previous life one of the Royal Horticultural Halls). In Westminster liberal fashion, no particular sport is compulsory, with a huge range of choices from sailing to judo to golf to girls' football. 'You wouldn't send a very sporty boy to Westminster,' thought a parent, who was grateful that her keen but not-particularly-athletic son had been in teams which he would have been unlikely to make at a more overtly sporty school. However, particularly successful at rowing (and was basking in the glow of recent success at National Schools' Regatta when we visited), fields nine football teams with 'at least respectable' results, and 'we do very well at niche sports such as rock climbing [third in the Independent Schools' Championships] and fencing [bronze medal in U15 Foil]'. Often dominates the London School Cross-Country Championships and the Westminster Secondary Schools Swimming Gala, with pupils representing Westminster in the London Youth Games, and is successful at fives and real tennis. 'You are encouraged to try lots of things and find something you are passionate about,' said a student.

Volunteering taking on increasing importance with newish head's passion for outreach, with nearly all Westminsters teaching music or setting up debating societies in local primary schools, working on Hampstead Heath or learning sign language to communicate with deaf children. 'People are really involved and really making a difference,' said a student. 'Staff have the time, passion and faith in us to let us get on with things.' Phab week – where year 12 Westminster students host young people with physical and/or mental challenges, taking part in creative activities and seeing London together – is a 'life changing experience'. 'With privilege comes enormous responsibility to give back,' says the head.

Boarding: The last Anglican monastery in London now houses Purcell's, a girls' boarding and boys' day house with attached chapel. Five other boarding houses, all in or near Little Dean's Yard and all of which include some day pupils. Many rooms surprisingly spacious; younger boys in College, scholars' house, in dorms of up to eight, whilst upper years have their own rooms and those in between may share with one other. 'Because these are all old buildings, the room arrangements can be random, and sometimes we have to improvise.' All boarders are cared for in relaxed fashion by housemaster (male or female), some with own family; resident tutor and matron also on site. Breakfast and supper in College Hall, the medieval dining room of Westminster Abbey, which day pupils may also join.

The only full boarders are sixth formers, and Saturday evenings tend to be quiet, though school is increasing organised weekend activities, particularly for the 10 per cent or so of overseas sixth form boarders.

Boarders have supervised prep sessions, and there are evening activities in the sports and music centres after prep, but those after a full-on boarding experience jammed full of organised activities may want to look elsewhere. 'He likes it for the independence and to be with his mates,' said a boarder parent, whilst another said, 'It feels like a convenient b&b. Much better than having to pick him up at late after a rehearsal or lecture.' However, a sixth form boarder commented on the 'serious sense of community you can only get from living with others. The people in your own house become quite special to you.'

Background and atmosphere: Whilst some other great public schools overshadow their environs, Westminster is an integral but discreet part of central London, largely located in the walled precincts of the former medieval monastery of Westminster Abbey. Its main buildings surround the square of Little Dean's Yard, known as Yard, where pupils spill out after lessons to chat or kick a football or practise basketball. The Abbey, next door and with its own private entrance, serves as the school chapel, used for twice weekly services plus carol and other concerts.

Westminster had become a school by 1179, with pupils taught by monks of the Abbey at Westminster. It survived Henry VIII's dissolution of the monasteries in 1540 and has been in continuous existence since the 14th century, with Elizabeth I celebrated as the school's official founder.

'It is an incredibly tolerant and civilised atmosphere,' said a parent. 'Unlike other schools, they don't try to mould pupils into a particular product. They are quite laissez-faire.' Parents of quirky students are relieved to find a school that is very kind and accepting of eccentricities. 'If he was at any other school he'd be toast,' said one. 'Some schools can be so unforgiving: Westminster is the complete opposite.' Another reported that it has 'catered brilliantly' for each of her very different children. 'It's so wonderful to see these kids spark off each other.'

Pastoral care, well-being and discipline: Tutors attached to each house oversee the academic side, whilst housemasters look after all else. One parent felt that both have too many charges to know her son well. 'I feel his well-being is my responsibility, not the school's. I don't think anyone there knows him well in the round.' Others, however, described the pastoral care as 'exceptional', and a student said, 'I have always found the school really responsive. Your housemaster is always there and will take care of everything from not feeling well to having too much work.'

Pupils expected to be proactive, motivated and organised, with very full timetables but no compulsion to take part in organised activities. 'But anything you want to try, there's some way of doing it,' said a student.

Pupils and parents: 'Lots of people said I wouldn't like Westminster,' reports the head. 'They told me the pupils were arrogant, staff unmanageable, parents difficult. None of this is true.' Westminster families undoubtedly tend to be wealthy, intellectual, metropolitan, cosmopolitan and no doubt demanding, but most parents are extremely supportive of the school. 'It is very hard to withstand this full on praise and delight.' 'I am a real believer.' 'Fantastic on every front.' And from an initial sceptic: 'I am increasingly fond of it.'

Girls entering the sixth form report a much easier ride than they might have expected. 'I had heard rumours about the boys being awful and arrogant – but they weren't,' said one. 'Some would show off in lessons to begin with, but they calmed down pretty quickly.' 'I suspect they look for a certain confidence,' said another. 'If you were insecure you might find it intimidating.' 'It was quite a shock to the system at first,' said a third, 'but we can hold our own.'

'Westminster imbues in you a sense that it is fine to talk to anyone on equal terms,' said an ex-student. 'You have a real feeling of being special.'

Parents – nearly all are Londoners, with even boarders mostly coming from within the M25 – offered a cornucopia of outings to Dulwich Picture Gallery, tours of Westminster Abbey and the Houses of Parliament, plus quiz nights, drinks parties, concerts in the Abbey, and the opportunity to attend expert lectures with their children. 'Parents very friendly and there's a good sense of community and involvement,' said one.

Old Westminsters span the centuries and the professions: the massive list ranges from Ben Jonson, John Dryden, Robert Hooke, Lord Lucan, Kim Philby, AA Milne, John Gielgud, Tony Benn, Corin Redgrave, Helena Bonham-Carter and Imogen Stubbs to Dido and Mika.

Entrance: Register by the end of year 5 for 13+ entry (boys at state primary and other schools that finish at 11 may apply to Westminster Under School). Computer pre-tests in English, maths and reasoning in year 6; high performers who also have a good report from current school called for interview, which includes short maths and English tests. Those with conditional places sit either the Challenge scholarship exam or CE (pass mark 70 per cent) in year 8.

For 16+ places, register between summer and October of the year before entry. Applicants – boys and girls – take exams in their four most likely A level subjects, and are interviewed.

Exit: Excellent and detailed preparation not only for Oxbridge but for American university entrance, with school trips to visit east coast universities. 'The school has been very supportive from an early age,' said a student, 'keeping us up to date with when to take subject tests and when to visit colleges.' Good preparation too for medicine, which is amongst the most popular degree subjects alongside liberal arts.

Up to half of sixth formers do, indeed, go to Oxbridge (58 in 2016, with 16 off to leading American universities and 12 medics), most of the rest to London universities, Edinburgh, Durham and Bristol.

Money matters: A number of means-tested bursaries of up to 100 per cent of fees available at 13+ and 16+; applicants must live in London. Bursaries also available at 11+; boys spend two years at the Under School before moving on automatically to the Great School. Eight Queen's Scholarships awarded at 13+; recipients must board, and the scholarship covers half the boarding fee. This can be topped up by a bursary in case of need. From 2017, four 16+ Queen's Scholarships for girls too. Five exhibitions at this level. Up to six music scholarships at 13+ worth 25 per cent of day or boarding fee, plus free instrumental tuition. No 16+ scholarships.

Remarks: One ex-student commented that Old Westminsters of her acquaintance have gone into a far wider range of careers than those from other schools. 'They seem to be following their passion. Westminster instils a belief that you can do whatever you want to do.'

Westminster Tutors

86 Old Brompton Road, London SW7 3LQ

Pupils: 40 • Ages: 14–99 • Sixth form: 40

Fees: £4,600 – £23,500 pa

Tel: 020 7584 1288
Email: info@westminstertutors.co.uk
Website: www.westminstertutors.co.uk

Head: Since 2007, Ms Virginia Maguire BA MLitt (40s). Was previously director of studies at David Game College, and lectured at a Thai university for five years, publishing articles on sociolinguistics and aspects of Thai culture. She read English at UCL and gained distinction in her MLitt in English Studies from Strathclyde University. Her own mother took her A levels at Westminster Tutors. As well as running the college, she acts as SENCo, teaches English and delivers the PSHE programme.

Academic matters: This is a tiny organisation with under 50 pupils, most of whom are taking or retaking A levels. The retakers – who may be there for a term or a year – are often high achievers who narrowly missed a place at a top university, and may be adding on another A level to improve their chances next time. Those who come for the full two year course tend to be attracted by the very individual attention. 'A lot of students who haven't coped well in a big school setting do well with us.' There is also a very small number – some five in all – taking or retaking GCSEs.

In spite of its size, the college offers a wide range of subjects, ranging from Greek to law to physics, by dint of having a large pool of freelance tutors it can call on, many of them Oxbridge graduates. These may be students working on PhDs, musicians, writers or experienced teachers moving towards retirement who want to keep their hand in. 'I will try to find someone to teach anything – I keep an eye out for what we are likely to need.' A large proportion of lessons are one-to-one, and each student has an individual timetable: drawing these up to suit teachers and students is a fiendishly complicated exercise.

Around a third of students have special needs of one sort or another, mostly dyslexia. The one-to-one system also copes admirably with, for example, the very bright girl with Asperger's who likes being immersed in two-hour-long lessons, and the boy with ADHD who works best in short bursts, including supervised homework sessions. 'It's like having one's own private tutor,' said the parent of a pupil who had floundered elsewhere, 'but in a friendly college setting.' 'My daughter's motivated at last,' said another. 'She's actually keen to go to school and to get on with her homework.' The school has links with an educational psychologist, and will adapt teaching according to her reports, but cannot cope with severe behavioural problems.

Exam results are highly creditable for such a mixed, totally non-selective intake. 2016 saw 59 per cent A*-B, 37 per cent A*/A at A level, 50 per cent A*/A at GCSE.

The college also offers private tuition for mature students who, for example, want to study medicine and need science A levels, helps with common entrance exams, and specialises in preparing outside students for Oxbridge, medical and law school applications. The head originally set up Uniprep as a separate company, but it is now merged with the college. She specialises in medicine and dentistry preparation plus LNAT, and her Oxbridge graduate tutors provide preparation for their respective degree courses. The college also runs half term and holiday revision courses. 'We work very well across the spectrum from special needs to very bright.'

Games, options, the arts: Art and photography are both A level options. Students visit the linked David Game College in Notting Hill to use its facilities, either joining an existing group there or forming their own. A 'wonderful art teacher' provides enrichment classes as well as taking history of art students for fortnightly gallery visits. The college is handy for the South Kensington museums and for theatre trips.

Sport is not a high priority, but the college does field a five-a-side football team, and weekly sports sessions are held at Chelsea Leisure Centre on the King's Road. One ping-pong table – being used as a desk when we visited. Because of lack of space and facilities, the college cannot offer drama, dance, PE or media studies courses.

Background and atmosphere: The college was founded in 1934 and is one of the oldest tutorial colleges in the country. It is now one of the David Game group of colleges, which includes some 25 institutions in the UK and overseas.

It is based in two adjoining townhouses near South Kensington tube, and most of the space is decidedly compact. Staff and students share a common room. 'We're really small so we all mix in together.' Library, IT room, physics room and biology practical room that decidedly resembles a small kitchen (chemistry students use the labs at David Game College in Notting Hill).

Pastoral care, well-being and discipline: All students have personal tutors – one of these 'is brilliant with wayward boys: we give him the younger ones who need to be constantly chivvied'. But the head is the personal tutor for the A2 students, supporting them through UCAS, as well as being the main point of contact for all parents. 'If parents have any concerns they always deal directly with me.'

Non-attendance at any lesson is swiftly followed by a phone call – first to the student then, if they don't reply, to a parent. But otherwise the atmosphere is informal: 'We're not oppressive about rules. It's easier to have a cooperative environment'. Students organise dinners or parties, with the head boy and girl in charge of younger pupils; only over-18s are allowed to drink alcohol. Bad behaviour unlikely to go further than a recent incident of older students placing bets for younger ones at a shop down the road. 'A warning is usually as bad as it gets. If I'm cross they know why.'

Pupils and parents: Eclectic mix of those with special needs and others who have not thrived in the rough-and-tumble of larger, more traditional establishments, combined with high achievers who come for the expert teaching.

Entrance: By interview with the head. 'We talk about what they are doing now, what they are hoping to do, their university goals. I look at their results so far and their school reports. But we're non-selective academically, and my main criteria are whether they are going to be happy, suit our way of teaching and fit into the college. We don't want to upset the harmonious atmosphere here.' She will not take students who have been expelled elsewhere for serious behavioural problems, drug or drinking offences, but will probably turn a blind eye to one-off misdemeanours, and rarely turns people down. 'But sometimes I can sense attitude problems, and I might not be so encouraging about them coming here.'

Exit: Over 90 per cent to higher education, including over half to Russell Group, ranging from nutrition at Nottingham to English at York and mathematical computation at UCL. Advice is always geared towards finding a course appropriate for the student, 'some students are not suited to university, but we always try to direct them to some sort of higher education. We try very hard to find a course that's right for them.' Recent destinations for such students include an apprenticeship and a BTEC in mechanical engineering.

Money matters: As one would imagine, the one-to-one staff:student ratio does not come cheap. However, fees are comparable with other tutorial colleges that have much larger classes. Up to four A level scholarship places. A few statemented pupils funded by LAs.

Remarks: Has developed a niche providing one-to-one teaching for gifted students with special needs, and also helps prepare potential medics and Oxbridge candidates. The rest come because they are attracted to the cosy, friendly, supportive atmosphere, 'and you can be sure they getting the best chance to achieve,' commented a parent.

Wetherby Preparatory School

Linked with Wetherby School

48 Bryanston Square, London W1H 2EA

Pupils: 325 • Ages: 8–13

Fees: £20,610 pa

Tel: 020 7535 3520
Email: admin@wetherbyprep.co.uk
Website: www.wetherbyprep.co.uk

Head: Since 2008, Nick Baker BA PGCE (early 40s). A grammar school boy, he hails from Bucks, was educated at Dr Challoner's and University College London, where he read geography, before qualifying as a teacher at Newcastle University. He has taught geography in a range of schools, including Holloway Boys comprehensive, head of year at Borehamwood, a former state middle school, and head of geography at Chesham Prep School (where he went as a boy, is now chair of governors, and where his two sons currently are). He has taught at Wetherby Prep since it first started in 2004, initially as a senior master before becoming deputy head, and his brief continues to expand as he has also headed the new Wetherby Senior School since it opened in September 2015.

Tall, broad-shouldered and youthful, with a reassuring laugh that echoes from his belly, Nick Baker is hugely popular, with parents, pupils and staff as well as colleagues in the wider prep school world. A keen supporter of Watford Football Club, he celebrates their victories at whole prize-giving events as well as in his blog and emails, and even the many Chelsea supporters among the families here share in his delight and enthusiasm. Open and affable, his weekly newsletters in Wetherbuzz frequently include anecdotes about his two boys and what his family is getting up to. Hot on values and manners, one of the many 'challenges' he initiated is the Politeness Challenge. 'Much the best news is hearing that Wetherby boys are good house guests,' he says. Parents like the fact that he is so present, both around the school and at the many social events organised for teachers and parents, the Headmaster's Ball, or 'pub nights with dads', for example, as well as the Come Dine with Me event where teachers cook and wait on the parents. The adjectives that we heard most often were 'very professional', 'excellent communicator' and 'very driven and opinionated', but what is most apparent and consistent is that they trust him.

Entrance: At 8 into year 4 (when 200 sit for 40 places). Boys from the pre-prep have automatic entry. Everyone else (including from other Alpha Plus schools like Chepstow House, but apart from siblings who also enter automatically) sits papers in English and maths during an assessment day at the school and also takes part in group activities.

Exit: An impressive number to top academic schools, especially considering the range of ability in each year. In 2016, nine to Eton (including a King's Scholar), and five each to St Paul's, Harrow and Charterhouse, with Marlborough and King's Wimbledon popular too. Others to eg Bradfield, Stowe, Wellington and Bryanston. Increasing numbers to the new Wetherby Senior School (15 in 2016).

Remarks: Wetherby Prep, and its brother, pre-prep Wetherby School, are currently riding high and widely regarded by parents across London as the jewel in the Alpha Plus crown. Slick as a well-oiled machine, Wetherby delivers precisely what its parents demand: high quality teaching, a broad and extensive choice of activities and sports and exceptional communication. Many of the parents are bankers and Wetherby is the prep school equivalent of a well-resourced City institution. Boys here are polite (everyone stands up when you enter a room – 'our parents like that,' says Mr Baker) but sparkling and not squashed. One occasion which captures the spirit of the school is the prize-giving assembly which takes place every Friday in the Church of Annunciation behind Marble Arch. Parents and children cram into every corner and, after singing a hymn, prizes are distributed. These can be anything from the history prize to the prize for the best joke – let alone for sporting achievements (like running the marathon). Mr Baker conducts the whole occasion with warmth and humour. He clearly knows every child well and there is a lot of boyish banter. A cauldron of competitiveness, when house points are read out there are huge whoops and cheers. These boys really care if their house is ahead – especially if it's about the amount of food waste they are managing to avoid. We also witnessed a charming joy in their peers' achievements. The best kind of competitive spirit. We were most impressed when boys not only moved aside to let us sit down but also folded and cleared our chairs for us amid the chaos of cricket bats, violins, hockey sticks and trumpets at the close of proceedings.

Situated behind Marble Arch in leafy Bryanston Square, the Georgian building is grand and spacious. The signature red painted front door welcomes you into a smart, light, high ceilinged entrance hall, complete with wood panelled, gold leaf scholarship boards and lists of head boys, prefects and house captains of the school. Boys pile past heaving musical instruments and sports equipment, looking smart but tousled in cricket gear, grey and red blazers and caps. A sweeping staircase takes traffic up the several flights, a small back staircase channels them down. All the classrooms are large, light and airy, well-equipped and organised. The basement not only houses a couple of very well-equipped science labs, a fitness suite with rowing and running machines, and the dining room, but also a pet snake which boys can stand and stare at to while away any spare minutes in their busy day. Every boy has his own red locker – no need to lug every book and file around with him the whole time. School laptops seem to be littered at strategic points around the school and are available for anyone to use. There are also 20 desktop PCs in the library, which doubles up as an ICT suite where the boys learn coding, touch-typing and animation.

From year 4, boys are setted in maths and English and have specialist subject teachers; most other subjects are setted in year 6, when they also start Latin. Three classes per year, with about 20 in each class. With automatic entry for siblings and boys from Wetherby School, alongside selective entry for others, the school is mixed ability but, Mr Baker observes, 'the academic demographic gets stronger year by year. The average CAT score used to be 112 and is now 120.' Full-time SENCo, assisted by one other person, gives support to children with mild learning difficulties, including dyslexia, dyspraxia and mild autism. Support provided ranges from touch-typing to reading groups as well as one-to-one session in maths and literacy outside the classroom. Approximately 16 in the school are getting support at any one time. Lots of prizes and rewards including a meeting with the head – the Headmaster's Good Show – to commend outstanding work. One young 9 year old told us proudly that he was 'very good friends with Mr Baker' as a result of his regular chats with him.

Sport is strong and getting better and better each year, both in terms of what is offered, the facilities and the teams' performances against other schools. The Park Club, in Acton, is now their home ground, and although some parents complain of traffic and the length of time it gets to bus them there, most were very enthusiastic about the excellent facilities, the space and the fact that they no longer need to box and cox in various places around central London. Boys play rugby and football in the winter, athletics, tennis and cricket in the summer. Their annual sports day is a major fixture in the calendar. There are plenty of other sports on offer too – hockey (including roller hockey), horse riding, fencing, rowing, rock climbing and badminton. One gets the impression that when Mr Baker goes to his Alpha Plus governors to ask that the tap be turned on (to make provision for another club, for example), it will be done. Lots of popular 'fathers and staff' fixtures too, in cricket and football.

Parents enthuse about the 'excellent' music. 'Despite the fact that my son is sporty, his favourite club is choir,' observed one father. Dynamic head of music has a modern and innovative approach. Plenty of public performances, impromptu as well as more formal. Breakfast concerts happen twice a term, there is a junior and senior school recital and a band as well as an orchestra and a chamber choir. Art is well organised and cross-curricular. We saw lots of lino cuttings and Mac books in the art room as well as impressive pieces of work around the school. In DT they were building clocks, and there is a dark room for photography, but the 'backbone of the department is printing,' we were told. Drama could be better, Mr Baker acknowledges; some parents, more brutally, described it as 'almost non-existent.' They use the Rudolf Steiner theatre up the road for productions, 'but it's so difficult to get good drama teachers/directors,' explains the head.

Parents here are slightly more diverse than those at the pre-prep. The numerous school buses run like clockwork and depart and arrive when they are meant to, enabling many parents to entrust their boys to the school transport, so they come from as far as Islington in the north east to Hammersmith in the west. Lots of well-heeled bankers and lawyers, and a smattering of celebrities – what would you expect in this part of London? – but a refreshing mixture of cultures and backgrounds. Nick Baker's openness and inclusivity – both in the weekly Wetherbuzz newsletters as well as in his public addresses – help to contribute to a real family and community feel. An outstanding school, polished and professional, and an excellent foundation for your all-rounder son.

Wetherby School

Linked with Wetherby Preparatory School

11 Pembridge Square, London W2 4ED

Pupils: 343 • Ages: 2-8

Fees: £20,595 pa

Tel: 020 7727 9581
Email: learn@wetherbyschool.co.uk
Website: www.wetherbyschool.co.uk

Head: Since 2009, Mr Mark Snell BA PGCE (mid 40s). Educated at Eastbourne College, University of Westminster (a degree in business studies) and Brighton University, where he gained his teaching qualification. His first job was at Eaton House the Manor. Utterly down to earth, direct, no nonsense and unpretentious (although one parent observed that his 'oikishness verges on the pretentious given his background'). With his buzz cut hair style and his gruff manner, Mr Snell is so robust and hearty he could pass for the manager of a medium sized football club. He is also deeply committed and completely devoted to the boys and their needs. 'I enjoy life and don't give a stuff what anyone thinks of me,' he says. Most parents love him ('he still makes time to for me to discuss my son even though he's no longer at the school') though a few dissenters bemoan his encouragement of the alpha in these already uber alpha boys.

Deputy for two years before taking over as head, he is completely au fait with the ethos of the place and is hugely respected by his fellow Alpha Plus heads. ('Nick Baker is a great bloke,' he says. Nick Baker – head of Wetherby Prep – thinks the same of Mark Snell, though he put it slightly differently.) Previously head of maths at King's College Wimbledon, and prior to that he taught at Westminster Under where, he says, he really cut his teeth and learnt a lot of what he knows now ('though I'm thick as two short planks,' he repeatedly assured us). Despite his 'street' manner, he was born into prep school aristocracy and teaching is very much in the blood. He was brought up in a south coast prep school with his three siblings. His father inherited and ran Mowden School near Brighton (now the prep school to Lancing College), and the wider family are involved with Ludgrove Prep School (in Berkshire). His wife also teaches ('though she is much cleverer than me'). They have a son and a daughter, both school age.

His subject is maths, and though he kept telling us how dim he is, he had us stumped on more than one occasion as so many of his explanations were put in arithmetic form and he relishes statistics. Teaches maths to years 3 and 2, and loves it, he says. An added advantage is that he really knows each individual and can give informed advice on where next. 'If parents choose not to listen, that's fine,' he says; 'that's their prerogative, but I know the schools, understand the assessment data, and I know the boys.' Very accessible – to the boys especially, but to parents too. Many spoke of their complete confidence in him, his judgment, and his recruitment of teachers ('you feel confident that he will never employ a duff,' enthused one parent). A loyal Seagulls fan, his faux wood panelled study (a present from parents, along with most of the colourful decorations) has several Brighton and Hove flags and memorabilia and is brimming with evidence of his personality and the affection families past and present have for him.

Entrance: Non-selective. Register the month your baby is born, and ideally the day he is born. If you try to register any later than when your baby is 3 months old, you're too late. School gets approximately 35 applications a month – or about 360 a year for 88 places (four classes in each year group). Staggered entry by the month to avoid a preponderance of December (say) babies. You only get to see round the school if you are going to be offered a definite place. If you are on the waiting list there is still hope, but not a lot. Parents feel they have a golden ticket if their son gets a place here and are unlikely to turn it down for anything other than 'act of God'. Lots of international families and a number of children speak more than one language at home, but not much EAL support needed, as most arrive here fluent in English. No longer as local as it once was, parents prepared to travel far for the first class education they feel their son will get here.

Exit: High numbers to the most academic prep schools. In recent years as many as 40 per cent to Westminster Under or St Paul's Juniors. Increasing numbers, currently 45 per cent, to Wetherby Prep, where entrance is automatic and the standards are rising, so why go through the stress of exams? The other 20 per cent elsewhere – eg locally to Sussex House or to board at Ludgrove, Summerfields, Caldicott or Cothill.

Remarks: The Wetherby brand is currently putting even Balenciaga in the shade. It is hard to find anyone, past, present or potential parent, who doesn't positively glow about the school. They single out the quality of the teaching – not only does Mr Snell recruit excellent teachers but he motivates them and makes them go the extra mile. Homework is 'innovative and thorough'. Communication with parents is 'exceptional', plus the 'school really understand boys and how to educate them.'

Lots of competitions and games inside the classroom as well as out. Learning here is fun, whether it's a project on the Romans or a fabulous end of year party, which incorporates an ice cream van and a bouncy castle. School is lucky enough to be able use the square opposite and the boys get lots of fresh air and exercise during breaks throughout the day. Reception and nursery children have their own outside playground, complete with springy tarmac and climbing wall, which is in constant use. On top of this they have several gym and swimming lessons (at Kensington Leisure Centre), as well as sport (in Hyde Park and Westway) in the afternoons. Lots of football and tag rugby in the winter, cricket in the summer. Plenty of fixtures against other schools, in swimming as well as field sports, and an annual sports day at the Wetherby sports grounds – at the Park Club in Acton. Dads' and boys' Saturday morning football is hugely popular, as are chess club, martial arts club, arts and crafts and drama. The choice of clubs is huge, from chess and cookery to Lego and French.

Plenty of music too – a choir in each of years 1, 2 and 3 as well as the wonderful Wetherby singers, created for those who couldn't make it into the choir but still love to sing. 'They make a terrible noise,' growled Mr Snell, 'but parents love it.' More than half the school learns an instrument – peripatetic teachers for guitar, violin and piano. There are instrumental concerts at the end of each term in St Matthew's church up the road as well as impromptu recitals in the hall. Drama part of the timetable as well as offered as a club. There is a performance at the end of each term, and the year 3s perform a major production (in recent years Peter Pan and The Jungle Book) at the Tabernacle Theatre.

Despite being non-selective the pace is fast here. Boys are expected to work hard right from the word go. We saw boys as young as 3 and 4 reading and writing (beautifully). Standards are high and everyone is aspirational – teachers, head and parents alike. Children who need support are usually identified early – good systems in place for spotting and diagnosing any difficulties. What is done about it next depends on the level of support required. At the more severe end – boys with moderate learning difficulties – many parents choose to take them to Emerson House in Shepherds Bush to get that support. Others are taken out in groups for extra support – it could be the top, middle or bottom group in maths or English; others may have one-to-one support lessons. School employs one full-time and one other teacher who has half her timetable, dedicated to learning support.

Maximum class size 22 [there are 22 boys in each class]. Boys get a lot of attention in the classroom. Ratio of pupils to teacher (or teaching assistant) is high – more than one teaching assistant in every class room as well a lot of floating teachers. Lots of differentiation – and boys taught according to academic capability not according to syllabus. 'We teach them when they're ready to learn'. Only in the final year, year 3, are they grouped according to ability, in maths, English and reasoning. Relatively high number of male teachers (14) unusual for this age group. 'We can attract a different kind of teacher – Alpha Plus pays very well, especially at this level, and we rarely lose anyone to another school,' says Snell. Although they couldn't fault the education in the classroom, some parents boldly suggested that more attention could be paid to the importance of moral values. The idea of being 'nice' to each other, so focused on in girls' schools, is missing here, they said. These are alpha boys with alpha parents and, parents observe, there is a limited public spiritedness where writing cheques replaces baking cakes.

School is currently expanding up to 360 pupils. The new building in Pembridge Villas, once the site of Chepstow House, is already being used for reception and Little Wetherby (the nursery). Also opening another pre-prep, Wetherby Kensington, in 2017. Despite an increase in the number of places, we doubt there will be less pressure on them. A busy, successful, well-run, well-resourced school, full of happy, spirited boys. For as long as this formula remains the same Wetherby is likely to remain the brand parents want.

Whitgift School

300

Haling Park, South Croydon, Surrey CR2 6YT

Pupils: 1,341; 108 full/weekly boarders • Ages: 10–18 • Sixth form: 338 • C of E

Fees: Day £18,618 pa; Boarding £29,704 – £35,522 pa

Tel: 020 8688 9222
Email: admissions@whitgift.co.uk
Website: www.whitgift.co.uk

Head: Since 1991, Christopher A Barnett BA MA DPhil (60s). Previously second master, Dauntsey's School and before that head of history at Bradfield. Married to Laura, psychotherapist and author, four grown up children, one daughter, three sons who all came here, all scaling assorted dizzying career heights from bloodstock agent to Twitter supremo.

First post was in higher education as economics lecturer at Brunel in the 70s, combined with political research for MP. Logical, given impressive string of qualifications to his name, Oxford and history-based for the initial bunch, including doctorate; extras from – amongst others – Downing, Cambridge where he's a fellow commoner (more important than a college lecturer; less than a bye-fellow, apparently) and French government (who wouldn't want luscious-sounding Chevalier dans L'Ordre des Palmes Académiques?).

Switched from higher to secondary education because of power of education to 'impact on the whole child'. Also, you suspect, to provide suitable canvas for his innovations. 'A minefield of ideas,' as colleague put it.

Supremely confident (quality shared by pupils). Rather than endure months of time-sapping debate on funding decent grand piano when first arrived here, simply went out and bought one. Can even stop rain and replace with sunshine – we saw; we believe. Performed similar trick when Patron Duke of York visited. Father shared knack, so 'everyone booked their holiday when he did.'

Unsurprisingly, shuns dead hand of risk-averse culture, leading decisively from the front and exuding vim and vigour, even more energised now, he says, in contrast to other heads who 'fade away' in final years.

'Building a country,' reckoned one parent. Thinks massive, from annual replacement of framed photographs of school achievements lining corridors to big-canvas projects, borrowing £8 million at commercial interest rates to fund sports facilities paid for by rising pupil numbers – now 1,400+ from 875 when arrived – and greater economies of scale.

Probably best known for love of natural world, from dog inclusion policy, horses ditto – school racing syndicate is about to be reinstated, equine visitors not unknown – to assorted wildlife, particularly exotic birds. 'A bit like Dr Doolittle,' thought mother. 'He feels that it gives boys a sense of calmness', reckoned another (boys say they quickly get used to peacocks' shrieks at exam time). Though pushmi-pullyu yet to make an appearance, other treats include wallabies, turacos and, our favourite, photogenic cranes waiting (unsuccessfully) by back door to be let in (backstage team 'specially trained' in deep-cleaning the mats).

With so much on the go, Dr Barnett delegates 'hugely. If I can engage every one of my 200 staff, then that's 200 times the power of me.' Unsurprising that for some parents he is a slightly distant figure 'pulled out for public occasions,' though agreed that deputy heads and heads of year are able day-to-day managers.

Supporters praised individual take on the role. 'I suppose you've got to have someone a little bit off centre, not toeing the academic line too much,' thought mother. 'A lovely man, very approachable – not completely aloof,' said another. One member of staff expressed fervent hope that, paraphrasing Ramsbottoms, she would have many sons to her name so could send them there.

Emphatically not a timeserver, Dr Barnett is a man who relishes ability to make things happen, sparking like a Catherine wheel (favourite description of his hero, Disraeli). Style may not please all – but then, nor did Disraeli's.

Has announced that he will be retiring in July 2017. His successor will be Christopher Ramsay, currently head of The King's School, Chester. MA from Cambridge in modern and medieval languages; PGCE from Durham. Has also headed King's College Taunton and been deputy head at Cranleigh and head of languages at Wellington College. Quick thinking, fast talking, intensely communicative. Three children in school from the juniors to the sixth form.

Academic matters: The full English but with continental option – A levels, IB (bilingual option for most advanced French speakers), BTecs and even the occasional Pre-U (occasional top ups for those requiring extra stretch). Extended essay qualifications and the like just about the only no-goes – IB covers the ground, feels head.

Results consistently good. In 2016, 63 per cent of A levels graded A*/A, 89 per cent A*/B. IB marks impressive at average 41. Maths leads subject popularity by a mile, sciences follow, English and humanities put in good showing. Rest – PE, computing and music among them – lag in single figures at the rear.

GCSEs (IGCSEs in English, maths, science, languages) similarly healthy with 81 per cent graded A*/A in 2016. Ten sat by most. Options chosen from relatively compact range bar terrific languages (three rather than two studied) with Japanese and Mandarin already on offer and Arabic and Sanskrit possible future additions. DT hugely popular (we were shown wide range

W

of delightful projects ranging from solar-powered beeswax storage unit to hockey stick unit).

One outsider wondered how staff can cover the range effectively, especially with same teachers for A levels and IB. Their idea, says head. Teachers, a level-headed bunch, averaging late 30s with a quarter into second decade, agree. Benefits of pupil choice outweigh double preparation time, said dedicated scientist, while some subjects with low A level numbers (such as DT) positively gagging to have a second go at IB now previously dreary syllabus is getting a makeover.

No shortage of teacher talent – former senior bods have gone on to headships everywhere from Magdalen College School to RGS Worcester. School has been academic non pareil in the area and 'the crème de la crème in every respect,' says local and could 'be in the top 10 [nationally] again,' says head, though not a fan of league table glory, however.

Classrooms have trad feel (admittedly hard to compete with new build excitement elsewhere), pupil numbers around 18 per class, 10 in sixth form. Behaviour immaculate – all rise for adults. Fun year 7 maths class working out probability by throwing dice, sixth form biologists fighting coursework deadline (easy listening music in background to counter tension).

Well on the way to building an education that ensures those focused on academic excellence get their fill, but will customise for those with exceptional sports, musical or other talents – fistful of scholars desirable but making A*s the priority for exceptionally gifted violinist headed for music college is pointless, thinks head.

Good reports for most subjects. More experienced teachers tend to be kept for best, thought a parent, focused on GCSE years and above, though any problems raised (including those with individual teachers) are quickly sorted at whatever stage. Increasing provision for the 10 per cent of pupils with SEN (largely dyslexia though also ADHD, ASD, three statemented), team about to increase to six, including two full time teachers. Currently around 30 EAL pupils from 20 different nationalities.

Homework sensibly organised and, though workload is ramped up from around year 8, staff stick to allocated days and good at helping absentees catch up on missed sessions while 'emails fly back all the time for boys who can't quite manage it.' Felt that would be useful to have drop in clinics and clubs in key subjects focusing more on lesson content exam technique – and we heard of parent being 'actively encouraged' to seek private tuition when child fell behind. Summer school opened for first time in 2015.

Head librarian in senior library (cosier separate version for juniors – some subjects also have their own areas) talked enthusiastically of ways and means to boost reading interest, from book clubs to brunch events. With many boys glued to laptops at break, blind to lure of enticingly packed shelves, looked like an heroic endeavour.

While the academically capable flourish, parents warn that while school 'does what it says on the tin,' pays to be on the ball, proactive parents getting in touch the second a report shows unexpected (downwards) grade movement. Former coasters are in for a shock. 'They do expect you to work to your optimum and you always need to be performing.'

Practical teacher input praised – one boy, struggling with twin demands of homework and role in musical, had rehearsal time halved so able to catch up. 'We can't speak highly enough [of the school],' said mother. 'Their expectations of the boys really surprised us, that everything was possible.'

Games, options, the arts: 'We allow pupils to follow their passion,' feels head. 'I'm only really interested on what we can do for the individual child.' Means pupils don't have to go to university to find out who they are, he reckons (though we worry about all that existential angst forced to find other outlets...). Finding niche can require strong-mindedness, however. One up-and-coming rugby star – Harlequins hopeful – had given it all up for love of singing.

For the natural joiner, undoubtedly paradise, and starts early with all new pupils getting free golf and instrumental lessons (though not simultaneously). Much of massive co-curricular programme included in the fees (100 or so options, from animal to Islamic club). 'So many activities that by the time you leave, you'll have other interests,' thought sixth former.

One mother felt that sporty, academic or artistic groups of boys tend to follow separate paths. Once, perhaps, said pupils, but no longer the case. 'Have friends with very different interests,' said one.

Sports facilities terrific, luring in outsiders from Surrey cricketers to Olympic hopefuls – approving quotes dot prospectus. Goodies include assorted pitches where seriously rugged hone skills to sports centre with squash courts, fencing salle and fitness suite, as well as swimming pool (different depths fit all, from armband armies to water polo teams). There's even a Transformers-style sports hall (now you see it, now it's a 1800-seat conference centre).

While talent levels mean pupils who would have made top teams elsewhere may not do so here, even C and D teams often win against other schools' As and Bs, while starry coaches including Colin Pates (Chelsea) and Steve Kember (Crystal Palace) are doing for football what is already the norm for rugby, hockey and the rest. Almost easier, in fact, to list sports that don't feature amongst over 100 national titles secured in past five years.

Performing arts also getting substantial injection of resources with International Music Competition for string players, inaugurated 2013, soloist opportunities and fees the prize, and attracting talent from Eastern Europe. Six full scholarship boarders now in residence with more to follow; all potential soloists, reckons head.

With sell-out musicals, some outstanding actors (one has already written and starred in own play) and 380 learning an instrument, some to diploma level, performing arts already in good shape, spaces indoors and out, from Founder's Garden to old swimming pool, all imaginatively used for everything from Shakespeare to sell-out musicals (West Side Story was in rehearsal when we visited), concerts ranging from beginner strings to Mahler at Royal Festival Hall.

If there's a corporate refrain, it's 'best anywhere'. Only parental niggle would be more access to facilities. Pool, for example, is 'amazing' but opportunities to use it outside the timetabled six weeks a year would be appreciated – tricky, admittedly, given extensive use by outside groups. Bottom line, though, is that 'if you're good at something, they've got all the facilities in the world,' thought mother.

Boarding: They've upped ante with boarding (new house catering for 100 13-18 year olds opened 2013). Bright and beautiful, partially powered by solar (though water 'too grey' to recycle, says new boarding housemaster – one of the many staff with rugby-fuelled handshake).

Features super common rooms, welcoming but airy, uncluttered feel, upmarketing furnishing (new Yamaha piano) and Subbuteo for juniors, snooker (and superior view over greenery) for seniors next door. Beds specially ordered for seven footers and, amazingly, every fragile-looking wall-mounted loo so far intact (must be made from same makers as indestructible cushions).

Highly successful, it's reckoned and, with 40 full boarders at weekends, no forlorn few testing the echoes. While activities generally good they sounded a little low-key when majority are off on voluntary exeats. Actively not trying to create traditions (can be where problems begin, is view of school, which numbers consecutive year groups 1, 3 and 5...).

Background and atmosphere: Ancient name, lovely and unusual site – cross between wildlife park and landscaped RHS outpost. Whipsley, perhaps? Don't expect acres of Tudor panelling, however. Though school was founded in 1600 and current site was owned by Henry VIII (and home to Lord Howard of Effingham, son a very early old boy), most is vintage 20th rather than 17th century (well worth seeing fascinating archive) and pleasant rather than grand in feel, despite commanding hilltop view over south Croydon.

Deep community roots, however, not only endure but extend each year, involvement ranging from extensive financial help for families of pupils in need to vast year-round outreach programme costing around £100,000 and involving 55 local schools, each spending a week at the school with dedicated classrooms and seconded staff with sessions covering sport, arts, science and languages.

Audition-entry weekend arts academy, for local children as well as school's pupils, runs wildly popular courses incorporating drama, dance and musical theatre.

Numbers standing up well to scrutiny and, as the biggest leading independent boys only in the area, as well as highly academically successful, so you'd hope. Theoretically a matching pair with Old Palace, the girls only school also in the Whitgift Foundation, though not an exclusive relationship – joint drama and music productions with Croydon High and St Andrew's C of E High School, too.

Trinity the big rival – 'You have to say 'T' word,' counsels pupil, though others would like more contact. Head says tricky logistically and for now, schools likely to keep dancing to individual tunes.

In unlikely event that new buildings don't deliver wow factor, outside loveliness certainly will, from Founder's Garden, created for 400th anniversary and graced with very own new rose, to Whitgift water gardens, tape cut by Sir David Attenborough, who was bowled over by visions of loveliness before him, rare emerald starling adding final touch of enchantment.

'We were blown away when we saw it,' said mother. Doesn't stop, either, planned science biodomes each featuring slice of life (flora and fauna) from round the world. Like the Eden Project, says head, only better (from educational perspective at least – though does win on location). Butterflies soon on order. Giant tortoise being debated.

Pastoral care, well-being and discipline: Big on nurturing from day one with older boys mentoring younger ones (a few blank looks from mentorees-in-waiting) on top of formal tutor system. Older pupils often turn to subject teachers for 'excellent' ad hoc support.

Fab induction trip to Lake Garda for year 6s (heavily subsidised) within first few weeks works wonders even for the very shy. Great care taken to create school within a school, 10+ and 11+ intake in own very pleasant building and, with the obvious exceptions such as art, music and games, form-based for lessons, and even a separate house system. Only question mark was over slightly bleak asphalt-covered junior playground, bins the only ornament. When quizzed, pupils and head unanimous in stressing year-round use for ball games (surrounding windows correspondingly battle-weary), rendering any embellishment undesirable.

Masses of boys can mean occasional testosterone overload, though any low level disruptive behaviour is effectively sorted out as pupils move up through the school. Fisticuffs rare but not unheard of, though parents tend to take this calmly. 'Typical of boys' schools,' said a mother. Ditto pupils. 'It happens. It's better just to deal with it,' said pupil.

Though corridor supervision appeared low key, boys reckoned teachers were never far away – even super sixth form common room has head of year's office in corner, though clearly gaze is benign, judging by relaxed crowd sprawled on easy chairs, one minus shoes. Hot on effective sanctions, too, reckoned a parent, with school services – times spent doing something useful, such as lunchtime litter clearance or cloakroom tidying, cordially loathed and thus highly effective deterrents.

Head plans mass pupil engagement programme – will see around 700 over next year in small groups for elevenses, lunch and tea. Though mainly for success stories, is also asking for teachers to refer boys who may need little extra pepping up to join them. May answer plea by one parent for more sugar to help medicine go down. 'I think I'd like it to be a little less pressurised and use more carrots rather than sticks.'

Pupils and parents: Many Croydon-based, or close; nearby grammars and Trinity the main alternative senior schools, with around 60 per cent of intake from state primaries (preps were in majority when head first joined school, but feels that links with community have boosted appeal to first time buyers). Increasingly attracts those from further afield – into deeper Surrey and even north London with boarding opening it up to the world (Taiwan the latest country expressing desire to forge links).

With old boys numbering TV illusionist Derren Brown, actor Martin Jarvis and Premier League star Victor Moses amongst ranks, average career hard to define, though being a reasonably tough personality to make a success of life here and later on probably helps. 'I think if you can't hold your own then you're going to sink,' felt mum.

For the right child, however, approach works wonders. 'If he'd gone to one of the state schools I don't think he'd be the confident young man he is now,' reckoned mother. 'He's much more able to walk into a room full of strangers and hold a conversation.'

Easy-going parents can come as a relief to newcomers. 'Thought they would be very highbrow and stuffy but not at all.' Terrific socialising, too. 'We have the best time...we went to a quiz night, there's a summer ball, it's everyone mucking in,' said one.

Entrance: Entrance exam early Jan, day at school. Majority sit 10+, 11+ or 13+ exams (maths, English, VR). Fewer at 12+ and 14+ (maths, English and science). Likelies invited back to interview. Sixth form candidates need seven GCSE passes with A*/As in A level subjects (similar for IB), though possible to enter to take BTec sport, in which case five A*/C passes will suffice. Interesting advent of dual sixth form streams, second for less academic but highly sporty. Head talks with winning enthusiasm for need to educate nation's footballers post-16...

Exit: Little fall-out – around 20 per cent leave after GCSEs; those with below par AS results often redo a year or retake modules. Occasionally pupils 'advised' to look elsewhere. 'Nobody is ever directly asked to leave,' said senior pupil. Vast majority who sail on reach splendid destinations. Offers from all the big beasts (Warwick, Southampton, Bristol, UCL, Edinburgh etc) and pupils clearly well thought of – one had received Oxford IB offer of 38, high but not stratospheric. Big range of subjects from geography to performing arts and professional sport. Seventeen to Oxbridge in 2016 – 'What you're paying for,' said parent. Nine places to read medicine.

Money matters: Scholarships are one of Whitgift's huge strengths; the number of bursaries and amount of financial help makes school a possibility for those from most deprived of backgrounds. Sensitively handled, too, with those in need of extra funding for school trips given subtle means of applying so need never miss out. Aim is for one in three boarders (mainly music but possibly sports as well) to be on full scholarships.

Remarks: 'Happy and high achieving,' thought a parent, with traditional virtues pushed but never, under sparky headship of Dr Barnett, a dull place to be, even though Zoological Society of London has declined request for elephant. Natural home for academically inclined, sportsmen and performers and ideal not just for wallabies and flamingos but also for confident joiners who may not yet have settled on their passion in life but relish process of discovery.

William Ellis School

Linked with LaSWAP Sixth Form Consortium

301

Highgate Road, London NW5 1RN

Pupils: 870 • Ages: 11–18 • Sixth form: 245; joint sixth form with Parliament Hill School, part of LaSWAP

Tel: 020 7267 9346
Email: info@williamellis.camden.sch.uk
Website: www.williamellis.camden.sch.uk

Head: Since 2011, Mr Sam White, chemistry graduate and previously deputy head of the London Oratory. Good news, say parents: 'He has an exceptionally good manner with boys and parents.' 'The boys like and respect him.' 'Whenever I go in I see him chatting with a boy, and he seems to be genuinely interested in them.' A pupil concurred. 'He has been really keen to get to know us all. He is a good influence on us.'

He was appointed after the school had suffered a budget deficit, got through two heads in quick succession and been slated by Ofsted. A year into his tenure, Ofsted returned and pronounced the school 'good', quoting a teacher's remark that 'The headteacher is leading and pulling everyone here along.'

He felt that he was taking on 'a challenge, but manageable... it was a school that desperately wanted to improve'. His first job was tackling behaviour – 'we needed to re-establish clear boundaries' – and his first two years saw a high rate of temporary exclusions, which has now dropped significantly. He has also continued the work on improving the quality of teaching and, despite some initial staff turnover, maintained teacher morale and encouraged staff to work collaboratively to produce good schemes of work.

Camden is one of the few areas of the country where no schools have converted to academies, and the local schools (which collaborate as a joint sixth form, LaSWAP) work closely together. 'I get lots of support from Sue next door [at Parliament Hill], Maureen across the road [at La Sainte Union]...'

Academic matters: Huge ability range, with year 7 reading ages ranging from 8 to 17. In 2016, 67 per cent of pupils got 5+ A*-C grades including English and maths, with 23 per cent A*/A grades. Parents report that English, once a weak point, has been turned round by the 'very impressive' newish HoD; the school now teaches the IGCSE English language.

The school has a language specialism, and everyone starts French in year 7, with around half studying it to GCSE. School has links with the nearby Collège Français Bilingue de Londres. Most take up either Spanish or German in year 8 (offered in alternate years), but this is no longer compulsory, and some spend extra time on English fluency instead. Latin and Mandarin are taught in clubs, and fundraising enabled a recent sixth form Mandarin and geography trip to China.

Around a quarter of boys take single sciences to GCSE. Those with a more vocational bent can take OCR science, and choose from various other courses with a large coursework element such as business studies, travel and tourism, and ICT. Some spend a day a week in years 10 and 11 at Westminster Kingsway College studying eg catering, construction or motor mechanics.

Fluid grouping rather than setting across the curriculum from year 8 (school hopes to group maths and science from year 7 in future) at the discretion of each faculty head. 'If a set of boys has a particular weakness in a subject we may put them together for a term, but there's plenty of movement.' Some parents would prefer more rigorous setting, but praise the willingness of staff to go the extra mile for boys at all levels. 'They will take time and a lot of patience with those who are bright but not pulling their finger out. I don't feel they are just settling for the easiest way of getting them through exams.'

Parents are mostly optimistic, though one complained about a lack of homework. 'We've found the teaching really good so far,' said another. 'My son is very happy here and seems to be doing well.' 'My son, who is very academic, is being well supported,' said another. 'I had severe reservations about some of the teaching during my son's early years here,' said a long-standing parent, 'but I don't now. I've never felt I had to get a tutor in.'

Teaching assistants are increasingly being trained to help with particular subjects, or with behavioural or language difficulties, rather than being velcroed to a particular child. The school uses some of its pupil premium funding (alongside sponsorship) on its City Year team of volunteers, who act as mentors, support teachers in class, run breakfast and homework clubs and supervise in the playground. The funding also helps with small group and one-to-one teaching, particularly in English, as well as counselling and interventions to improve attendance.

Joint sixth form with Parliament Hill School, which is part of the LaSWAP consortium that also includes La Sainte Union and Acland Burghley. This enables a wide range of courses including a choice of 41 A levels, as well as BTecs, NVQs, vocationally applied subjects and post 16 GCSEs (see LaSWAP entry for results info). Students stay in their base school (which for William Ellis boys will be their own school or Parliament Hill) for the majority of lessons, but may go elsewhere for minority subjects.

As well as working with Camden to provide one-to-one careers advice, school uses Future First, set up by old Elysians, to help it keep in touch with alumni and get them involved in giving careers advice, work experience and mentoring. It organises career sessions here and brings back old boys to talk about their work.

Games, options, the arts: A large trophy on the head's table when we visited is the house cup. Houses (named after local historic buildings: Lauderdale, Burgh, Willow, Keats and Fenton) have been reintroduced and are run by 'young, enthusiastic staff'. Pupils gain house points by competing at sports and taking part in talent shows, spelling bees, chess, model building, cake sales et al.

Year 7 and year 9 have a week camping at the school's field centre, The Mill, in Surrey. Boys also go on ski trips, language exchanges and field trips. 'The extracurricular activities have improved markedly over the past few years,' said a parent, citing her son's sessions at the Royal College of Music, playwriting with professionals, theatre and concert trips, Model UN.

Football and basketball are the most popular team sports, but rugby is up and coming – the RFU provides coaching and talented players are encouraged to join local clubs. The eight table tennis tables get enthusiastic use. Takes part in the annual Camden Shield boys' competition, which sees teams from six Camden secondary schools compete in football, table tennis, basketball, badminton, athletics and cricket. Pupils report that team sports peter out in the higher years: 'The teachers do try, but we tend to get a bit lazy in years 10 and 11.' The school has a newish sports hall, with facilities for PE and basketball and a multi-gym, and the playground doubles up as five-a-side football pitches. Sadly, the school cannot afford to hire the field next door, groomed for cricket when we visited, but it does play games on other parts of Parliament Hill Fields and uses the athletics track there. Clubs include cricket, running and trampoline.

Light top floor art rooms display impressive work; a sixth former was recently a finalist in the Camden Art Competition, and students have exhibited their work at the local Lauderdale House. Some parents find the music provision underwhelming, but there are choirs, ensembles and a range of concerts for all, from beginners to advanced musicians, often in conjunction with Parliament Hill School and La Sainte Union, which form a joint orchestra with WE. There are also workshops and masterclasses run by professional musicians. The head of music 'has been very supportive of my son writing and performing his own music,' said a parent, and a school group recently reached the finals of the Roundhouse Band Slam competition. School subsidises instrumental lessons for boys on free school meals.

Not a school that goes in for full-scale musicals, but has recently opened a new drama studio and there are many smaller drama performances, such as the recent drama club interpretations of the Ancient Mariner and Christmas Eve in the Trenches at the Winter Concert. Pupils work with outside organisations such as the Donmar Warehouse, and take part in the Shakespeare Schools Festival. 'They do it thoroughly and well,' said a parent.

Background and atmosphere: William Ellis was a public-spirited businessman who founded several schools in the mid-19th century, believing children should be taught 'useful' subjects such as science and to develop their reasoning faculties, rather than rote-learning religious tracts and ancient languages. William Ellis School, the only one of his schools that still exists, was founded in Gospel Oak in 1862 and recognised as a boy's secondary school in 1889. It moved to its present site, on the edge of Parliament Hill Fields, in 1937. Originally a grammar school, it turned comprehensive in 1978; the red-brick vine-clad buildings still have a grammar school feel. Work is starting on extensive new sixth form study area and classrooms.

'My son has had a very happy time here,' said a parent. 'He has a sense of belonging and pride in his school. It fosters a nice attitude and spirit in the boys – confident but not arrogant.'

Pastoral care, well-being and discipline: As mentioned, one of the head's first actions was to tighten up on discipline, with plenty of fixed term exclusions in his first couple of years. He also appointed a new and effective head of pastoral care. This has helped to cut down on the low level disruption that once marred many lessons, and has made boys feel safer inside and out. 'They are much stricter on uniform than they used to be, and you no longer have to hack your way through a posse of boys smoking round the gate,' said a parent. Year 7 has its own quad, with table tennis and picnic tables. The year 7 head has links with most of the feeder primary schools, and boys are invited to summer school before they start.

One parent commented: 'The pastoral care is very good. A few years ago I went through a difficult divorce and they were brilliant at supporting my son.' Another said, 'Whenever I've emailed to ask questions, I've had an immediate and pleased reply. They are extremely responsive to an interested/meddling parent.'

Increasing emphasis on carrots rather than sticks, with boys earning house praise points for good work and good attitudes, from persistence to creativity. 'Relationships can be much more relaxed once ground rules are established,' says the head. Deep Learning Days, part of the PHSE curriculum, see timetables dropped for a day in favour of discussions on relationships, including peer pressure and bullying, careers and the world of work, with plenty of outside speakers. 'We try to make it circular – get the boys to present back to their peers what they have learned. Recently 25 year 9 boys did a play for the rest of the school.' One parent commented on her despondency at a lack of creativity in the PHSE teaching, but another said, 'They are very good at raising the boys' social and political awareness. They don't shy away from issues that can be sensitive, such as homophobia and religion.'

Pupils and parents: Huge ethnic mix, with fewer than a third of pupils from white British background, and others ranging from Irish to Turkish to Somalian. Huge social mix too, from the large social housing estates of Gospel Oak to the multi-million pound houses of Dartmouth Park. 'There were cliques lower down the school, but in years 10 and 11 everyone hangs out together and we all get on,' said a pupil. 'The fact that the boys come from a huge range of backgrounds doesn't seem to matter one bit, which is a very impressive trick for a school to pull off,' said a parent. Old Elysians include Toby Young, Robert Elms, Sean French, Andrew Sachs and Len Deighton.

Entrance: Usual admissions criteria for 125 year 7 places (130 from 2017): looked after children, medical and social need, siblings, up to 12 musical aptitude places, then by distance (usually up to about two miles). Generally around 300 outside places for LaSWAP sixth form consortium, with an intricate admissions system and a range of entry requirements for different levels of courses.

Exit: In 2016, 45 per cent left after GCSEs. Most (70 per cent) to LaSWAP sixth form. Some go off to eg Camden School for Girls, Woodhouse College, St Marylebone, Fortismere or FE colleges. Around 20 per cent of LaSWAP leavers to Russell Group universities. Usually a couple a year to Oxbridge.

Money matters: Voluntary aided by the William Ellis and Birkbeck Schools Trust, but otherwise is as hard up as most other state schools.

Remarks: Small boys' comprehensive in idyllic situation on the borders of Hampstead Heath, now emerging rapidly from the doldrums under strong, popular and enthusiastic head. 'It can only get better and better,' said a satisfied parent.

Wilson's School

Mollison Drive, Wallington, Surrey SM6 9JW

Pupils: 1,125 • Ages: 11–18. • Sixth form: 300

Tel: 020 8773 2931
Email: office@wilsonsschool.sutton.sch.uk
Website: www.wilsonsschool.sutton.sch.uk

Head: Since 2014, Nathan Cole BA PGCE (30s), previously deputy head. Read history at Nottingham and was a postgrad at Cambridge. Began his teaching career at Saffron Walden County High and joined Wilson's in 2006, rising through the ranks to become deputy head in 2010. An expert on the history of Italian fascism, he is also a keen musician.

Academic matters: One of a handful of grammars in the area, all high achieving (comparing their results is like differentiating between shiny, perfect apples from M&S and Waitrose: look hard enough and you might find the very occasional blemish but it's scarcely worth the effort), and the natural home of the innately clever child who is 'looking at getting four A levels at A grade and going to a Russell Group university', said a mother.

It doesn't, however, always do quite so well by the merely bright, not through neglect but because 'only certain people can put up with being bottom of the pile', though that's a relative term. All achieve startlingly good results (so many finish with A*s in maths, taken in year 10 by most able, that it's practically de rigueur). Setting is fairly extensive, starting with maths in year 8, followed by sciences, English and all languages except Latin in year 9. Eleven GCSEs are the norm – eight core, including separate sciences, and AS level ICT among the options for the remaining three. In 2016, 89 per cent A*/A grades at GCSE.

GCSEs are followed by four AS and A levels plus either a formal extended project qualification (EPQ) or an internally assessed project. Modest menu of carefully chosen subjects – there's no psychology, for example (the demand isn't there, says school), though the numbers taking business studies are growing fast and economics is something of a star performer – bad financial news apparently does wonders for recruitment. Latin, though compulsory in year 7, doesn't have such an obvious current appeal higher up the school and is a 'Marmite' subject, said a pupil – though the keen are very keen and currently around 50 continue in year 9, when it becomes optional.

You're left in little doubt as to the big hitter subjects. Maths, daddy of them all, is taken by over two-thirds of pupils at A level with 90 per cent of entries securing A*-A grades (how many other schools have to ponder the potential problem of overcrowding?). It accounts, together with the sciences and economics, for almost twice as many entries as all the remaining A level subjects put together. Boys work hard 'because they know they'll get good grades, they know it's useful and they enjoy it', says a maths teacher – and that seems to hold true across the range of subjects. Overall, 95 per cent A*-B (75 per cent A*/A) at A level in 2016.

Like beady-eyed shoppers, pupils know how to choose a basket of carefully matched subject goodies and exactly what they're worth in enhancing career prospects. Teachers use this to their advantage. 'We tell them early on that if they want to work for companies like Siemens or Deutsche Bank, all the meetings are held in German', says one. Coincidentally, numbers taking German A level (in terminal decline elsewhere) have recently shot up from single figures to around 20.

Lots of help on offer, with academic review meetings with tutors to discuss progress, and valued catch-up clubs in just about every core subject, introduced originally for GCSE pupils but now, by popular demand, run from year 7. Support also for those with learning difficulties – some borderline Asperger's and dyslexia crop up now and then but you don't sense it's a big feature of school life. Generally, 'teachers know when to apply pressure and when to ease off – they're very good at reading the students', said one. Having said that, strength of character and robust self-confidence can be required if you're towards the bottom of the academic pack – occasional pupils suffering from sense of being 'at the bottom end of the academic scale,' as one mother puts it, leave early (school says this has not happened for some years), though it's felt that school is now far better at talent spotting and encouragement all the way through.

Atmosphere, however, is generally friendly and remarked on by visitors. One philosophy boffin 'said he'd been to plenty of schools where it didn't happen,' says a teacher and indeed it's unmissable. 'Teachers are very open,' said year 7 boy. The trust between teachers and pupils, slightly jokey but respectful on both sides, is evident and staff are missed when they go – one department head has recently been poached by private school for double the salary, it's said. Given emphasis in the prospectus on financial investment in top notch teachers, you have to hope that other even better funded institutions don't come to see staff list as akin to a particularly moreish educational tasting menu.

Games, options, the arts: Take a hobby or sport, preface with the words 'one of the top schools in...' and that's pretty much the gist. School boasts that 'boys are never bored' though to be honest, even if it laid on nothing, they'd undoubtedly find ways of deriving nourishment from the most barren of intellectual landscapes. As it is, activities ooze from every pore – 'So many, it's silly,' says sixth former – with the usual suspects, including tip-top CCF (now one of the largest in the country in conjunction with a local girls' school) and D of E to gold award; some, like ecology, Freethinkers and even Rubik's cube clubs, set up by boys themselves.

As a sports specialist, school excels here as elsewhere (though 'we'd choose this school every time even if they didn't own a tennis ball between them,' said a parent). 'Paradise for the sporting boy.' Certainly true if you're fiercely competitive. 'There's a sort of elitism and you do have to be pretty good to get into teams,' confirmed a mother (school says it now fields up to F teams on occasion). Lots of incentives, including medals for anyone taking three wickets out of five or scoring over 50 runs, and a range of sports tours, some more enticing than others, with list offering cricket in Barbados and badminton in Bulgaria. 'I know which I'd choose', said would-be parent. To prove the point, reception area is stuffed with glossy photographs of sports champions, including Olympic hopefuls. Badminton and judo are among notable high points for individual players, though school is no slouch at team sports either, specialising in football while nearby Wallington County Grammar went the rugby route. Both now do the duo, with further rugby provision planned, ensuring double the competitive fun.

The un-keen and non-sporty get by, however. 'Nobody hates anyone who's bad at football', said one pupil, while from year 9 the timetable is compassionately arranged to allow students to choose how to fill two compulsory sports periods a week. 'My son isn't sporty and that's ok', said mother, whose child has opted for martial arts over team games.

While it's easy to define school in terms of conventional subjects you'd see as shorthand for academic excellence, that's not to underestimate success elsewhere. DT, for example, is a popular AS option, not just because it's fun but because it's valued on 'serious' academic courses such as chemical engineering: 'admissions tutors say it's really useful because of all the planning and the way you have to take things apart and think them through', said successful student. Work on display routinely, as you'd expect, exceeds the brief (one particularly stunning electric guitar scored full marks at GCSE). School has also created a trio of hovercraft, as you do (though no plans as yet to bring back the much missed Folkestone/Bologne route).

Indeed, extension activity is way of life here. Students acquire European Computer Driving Licences – often a sixth form add on – in year 9, while ICT GCSE has been ditched as 'too boring' in favour of programming lessons. 'Celebrate your inner geek' cutting is pinned up on one of corridor walls.

Art, too, is excellent (staff blog, containing trenchant views on the Turner prize, amongst other topics, is well worth a read) and approached via snazzy light blue corridor and toning floor which serves as exhibition area. Unusually, life drawing classes are taken from GCSE up (and very good the results are, too).

Music, meanwhile, is one to watch, with new director of music lured away from Tiffin School. Professional choir director now in post, and choirs are embarking on a new touring schedule; three orchestras and selective choirs already going great guns, plus open-to-all school productions – excellent Les Mis had cast of 200. All year 7s get specialist free instrumental or vocal tuition and there are plans for a parents' choir; you can't help feeling that school's professional debut is but a baton's downbeat away.

Background and atmosphere: Many grammars give the impression of being a throwback to the 1950s. This one doesn't – 'deliberately', says school. Just as well, though it'd be perfectly justified in slipping into something a lot more traditional, what with the impeccable credentials: founded in the 17th century in Camberwell and, with the exception of a 38-year closure in the 19th century after a financial scandal, going strong ever since and celebrated its 400th anniversary in 2015. In 1975, lured by the space and local council's pro-grammar stance, it moved to its current premises, once part of Croydon Airport, and commemorated in nearby street names like Dakota Close and Hurricane Road.

While it's not a looker from the outside, with square brown buildings set uncompromisingly in a large, plain playing field, like so many upturned cardboard boxes, the interiors aren't half bad. Corridors might be on the pre-loved side ('it's because the buildings have been here since 1666 that they want to keep the old look,' said a pupil, with great presence of mind, if not architectural accuracy) but the classrooms, full of lovingly tended displays, more than make up for it. Science labs, too, slightly dishevelled from the outside, are a hive of well-resourced activity within.

No shortage of impressive large scale areas, either, including the traditional main hall – recently refurbished – which harks back to a glorious academic past (with still better to come, naturally) and a vast sports hall and gym (replacing expensive to maintain swimming pool and available for hire). But there are also more intimate and surprisingly luscious touches. The south canteen – as distinct from north canteen – (they don't go a bundle on fancy names; library has resolutely not morphed into a learning resource centre, for example) has cutting edge lighting, un-school-like black and orange walls and doubles as an attractive additional concert venue. Years 7-8 now have own brand new lower school with dining hall and classrooms.

Pupils whizz purposefully round the site, assisted by traffic calming measures including one-way staircases (suggested by student council). Like the school itself, they look initially unremarkable (crests and striped ties are the only distinctive features). All in all, a lesson in not judging by appearances.

Pastoral care, well-being and discipline: Motto is 'Non sibi sed omnibus' (not for oneself but for all) and quite right too, given the huge emphasis on belonging, with forms recruited wholesale into one of six not overly competitive houses, and 'nobody a guest or merely tolerated'. It's helped by approachable form tutors, first point of contact for pupils and parents, who stay with the same group for two to three years – 'easy to talk to when I had worries,' said a parent. Each form has two tutors throughout years 7-11, with pupils in years 9-11 registered and tutored in small groups of 15. First class settling-in arrangements. Year 7s take precedence in the lunch queue during their first term, though after Christmas it's every boy for himself (works well, say pupils, with 'delicious' meals on tap even for latecomers).

When problems crop up they're 'churned through until they're resolved, no matter how long it takes'. Anxiety can be a problem and school is doing its best to pinpoint early onset symptoms and treat them quickly. On-site counselling is available, together with a popular mentoring system which gives year 7s a sixth form buddy who reaches the worries that staff can't because they realise that 'we're going through hormones and can relate to us', explained one. Pupil support manager coordinates regular one-to-one meetings between teachers and pupils who may be liable to struggle to meet expectations.

School makes no bones about what constitutes unacceptable behaviour, though if there's bullying (it's rare, stressed one boy, who had suffered at his primary school), understanding of the bully as well as the victim is encouraged. 'They can't help it because they have issues, we do it in PSHE', said saintly year 7 pupil. One parent felt tolerance might occasionally err too much in the offender's favour, making recidivism a distinct possibility.

Detentions are widely used, or at least threatened (and immediate for unauthorised movement of instruments, thunders sign outside music room) though there's some wiggle room – it's three strikes and you're out when it comes to late homework, for example, and even the penalty is a starter detention lasting 10 minutes. With plenty of chances to step back from the brink, pupils considered the system a fair one.

W

Pupils and parents: Pupils are an unbounded delight. Hugely focused (one 11-year old was busily teaching himself to multi-task, 'so I can be as good as my older sister – I don't like sexism') and, boy, do they talk, with an almost evangelical desire to draw you into their world, apparently without drawing breath, though the kinder ones do pause occasionally to allow dull-witted adults to catch up. Some have their lives sorted aged 11 – most lean towards the professions (research science, accountancy and law all featured on careers shopping list). Not too dissimilar, in fact, from many of the parents.

School proud of its diversity – families encompass every major culture and religion and, currently, speak 40 languages between them. As to parental involvement, the opportunities are there, but 'not handed to you on a plate. You have to search them out', says parent, who recommended a spell as a parent governor as the best way of seeing inside the works.

Alumni include actor Michael Caine, fashion designer John Galliano, opera singer Mark Stone, mountaineer Paul Deegan and aviator Sir Alan Cobham.

Entrance: 'Boys here are clever but not geniuses. If they're doing very well at school, with high level 5 English and maths Sats tests in year 6, then they are clever enough to get in.' Ignore the horror headlines that tell of 10 applicants per place, school stresses, as it's simply the same children sitting each exam and the reality is more like four to one. No advantage in having a brother here.

Parents need to keep an eye on the calendar to avoid missing late August/early September deadline to register with the school for the entrance exams. There are two, English and maths, 'not Everest but Ben Nevis, with a brisk wind'. Nothing is officially harder than key stage 2 work, though the word on the street is that final maths question can be a twister designed to give the most able chance to show the innermost workings of their minds. The English paper is based on comprehension, 'something every child is doing in primary school', though parents can help by building child's vocabulary and knowledge of literary techniques.

School is grimly resigned to inevitability of widespread tutoring though strongly disapproves. Has ditched verbal reasoning paper because 'we know it can be coached for'. For the same reason, doesn't make past papers available. Parents also urge caution. 'I really don't think you want to tutor your child and get them there under false pretences because they won't be happy', says one.

Pass/fail results in early October tell you if child is still in the running, giving enough time to include the school (essential that it's your top preference – non-selective backup choice should come further down to avoid missing a place) on council-wide school application form, with 150 places offered following March to highest placed candidates. Where there's a tie break, Sutton children have preference with distance to school the final deciding factor. Some join in the sixth form. Again over-subscribed, with offers based on current school's report and places awarded to top GCSE performers.

Consulted on, but rejected, plans to go co-ed.

Exit: Very few leave post-GCSE. The rest – top subjects, top universities (85 per cent Russell Group) – all absolutely as you'd expect, and lots of it. In 2016, 15 medicine places plus two to US Ivy League. UCL, Southampton, Nottingham and Warwick among other popular destinations.

A pretty healthy number to Oxbridge (21 in 2016) although one sixth former thought grammars, placed awkwardly between better funded, Oxbridge fixated independents and more socially acceptable comprehensives may be faring less well. It's the case especially with screening essays for subjects like humanities, here a by the book DIY effort, elsewhere, he reckoned, toned and honed with expert out of school help. 'We don't have the immense preparation independent schools get or the bias comprehensives enjoy.'

Money matters: 'We are very grateful for the voluntary funding we receive from parents; they are very generous', says school.

'May the money keep coming,' adds a parent. 'We are in an area where it is needed.'

Remarks: Bright, clever and funny, and that's just the staff. Hard not to warm to a school where a pupil, asked what he likes best, says, 'everything's my favourite subject,' though wicked sense of humour ensures it remains a Pollyanna-free zone. A wonderful place if you're effortlessly clever, terrific for robust characters who need to work at it. Parents of bright but sensitive stragglers, however, may care to do a bit of soul-searching before calling in the tutors.

Wimbledon Chase Primary School

303

Merton Hall Road, London SW19 3QB

Pupils: 730 • Ages: 3–11

Tel: 020 8542 1413
Email: wcps@wimbledonchase.merton.sch.uk
Website: www.wimbledonchaseschool.co.uk

Head Teacher: Since 2001, Mrs Sue Tomes (60s) BEd NPQH. She arrived at the school as a French teacher over 30 years ago, ascending through the ranks as head of French, senior mistress and deputy head, and finally took the helm. Parents can't praise her enough for her almost lifelong dedication to the school and its pupils. Considered hard working and cheerful, one of those rare characters who makes time for everybody and everything, say parents. Popular with her pupils too; 'She is a lovely person,' one small pupil informed us.

Mrs Tomes maintains her links with France and is an avid supporter of teaching primary school children modern foreign languages across Merton. Part of her philosophy is that the children should be exposed to many different opportunities and experiences to help them discover their talents and develop as interesting and fulfilled youngsters. She and her staff aim to deliver the highest quality, meaningful, relevant and memorable education to all.

Retiring in July 2017.

Entrance: At 3+ to the nursery and 4+ into reception. Now expanded to three-form entry. Non-selective; applications must be made through Merton Council, usual admissions criteria. For occasional places in older age groups contact school or the council.

Exit: At 11+ majority to Ricards lodge, Rutlish, Raynes Park, Ursuline, Wimbledon College and St Cecilia's. Others to Sutton Grammar, Nonsuch, Wilson's, Wallington High, Tiffin, Wimbledon High, Kingston Grammar and Whitgift.

Remarks: Continues its long-held reputation for being one of Wimbledon's favourite choices for primary education. Very well thought of all round; academic expectations and achievements are high. Pupils are set by ability in maths from year 4. Stunning Starts, Marvellous Middles and Fabulous Finishes are how staff capture the children's imaginations and talents through the creative curriculum. Pupils are taught via many different media: lessons can include acting, music, dancing, art, design and technology. History and geography topics come alive through a variety of exciting activities. Everyone feels the positive impact and thrill of the creative curriculum; most notably these exciting projects have helped the children develop their writing skills. The arts make up an important part of the curriculum; full-time music teacher and specialist teachers for choir and orchestra also run brass groups, recorder club, drumming club and boomwackers percussion group. Teachers from Merton Music Foundation visit the school every day to give individual instrumental lessons. Musical evenings, assemblies, plays and concerts provide plenty of occasions for everybody to show off their performing skills.

Sizeable premises for a primary school, originally built as the girls' County Grammar in 1924. Playing fields, cricket pitch, tennis courts, a lovely wildlife area and gardens provide numerous outdoor and sporting opportunities. The children grow fruit, vegetables and flowers and are taught about which plants will attract particular birds and insects. Nursery and reception classes have their own specially-designed playgrounds attached to their classrooms, with new wing added to create space for expanded intake. Now space for 730 pupils. Stylishly-designed new building to accommodate classrooms, cookery room, specialist music rooms, an additional ICT suite, gymnasium and after-school care rooms. Some parents felt that the expansion and building would be disruptive for pupils, but now all appear to be in agreement that despite the odd hitch, the new space and facilities are an advantage for all.

Over 35 native languages are spoken by pupils; effective EAL programme; consequently nearly everyone does very well in Sats. Inclusion manager coordinates SEN, with two specialist teachers and a team of teaching assistants; also a visiting speech and language therapist and a play therapist. The school is fully wheelchair accessible and has a 16 place unit for children with speech, language and communication needs. Pupils attending the unit join with the main school in the afternoons for the creative curriculum, sports and music activities.

Exceptional range of clubs and activities. Friday film club run by a parent in conjunction with the British Film Institute has produced some successful young film critics. Far-reaching pastoral care; older pupils can train as peer mediators and playground buddies; any child feeling unhappy or needing to talk to an adult can post a note in the worry box. Parent support adviser is available to any parent who might wish to discuss their concerns. The Wrap Around Centre enables the school to offer a breakfast club, full-time nursery places and after-school care.

Parents are very much partners at Wimbledon Chase, assisting with hearing children read, clubs, general maintenance and the upkeep of the extensive grounds. Fundraising is also high on the strong PTA's agenda; dedicated parents' room, the nerve centre for meetings and a relaxing cuppa. Always keen to involve the wider community and improve their skills base: non-parent volunteers are welcome; a local volunteer has taken on responsibility for maintaining the wildlife garden.

An exceptional and innovative school and community with pupils, parents and staff all apparently delighted to play a part. Enthusiastic children bounce into school each morning eager to know what the day holds in store.

Wimbledon High School

Mansel Road, Wimbledon, London SW19 4AB

Pupils: 923 • Ages: 4–18 • Sixth form: 150

Fees: £13,470 – £17,328 pa

Tel: 020 8971 0900
Email: info@wim.gdst.net
Website: www.wimbledonhigh.gdst.net

Headmistress: Since 2014, Mrs Jane Lunnon BA (Bristol) (40s). A North London Collegiate School alumna, read English at university and, after an initial career in marketing, decided she'd prefer to teach. Immediately found a job at Wellington College where 12 years saw her progressing to head of English and assistant director of studies. Then to Priors Field as head of sixth form and, later, deputy head. Returned to Wellington in 2010 as senior deputy to Anthony Seldon, who, she says, taught her to 'be ambitious in your aims'. She played a key role in the leadership team, working to increase the profile of girls in the school. Thence to Wimbledon High. She and her husband, who is still at Wellington, have two teenage children and live on the college premises.

Wedded to girls only education, Jane Lunnon is determined that 'academic excellence is underpinned by outstanding pastoral care within an engaging curriculum and equally stimulating co-curriculum'. She believes in the need to develop the girls' confidence and self-belief, combatting what she refers to as the 'intensity of self-effacement in women'. Says it's a real privilege to run a school so full of magic and alchemy with very bright girls and outstanding results. Believes in model leadership and that the girls should have 'the capacity to be secure and go out into the world with confidence'. Enthusiastic and talks non-stop – apparently very popular with parents. Warmly supported by the GDST, Jane Lunnon has exciting plans for development. What has been done already during her short tenure is mind-boggling.

One of only the GSG's second set of identical twin heads: her sister, Jenny Brown, took over as head of St Albans High in September 2014.

Head of junior school: Since 2003, Kate Mitchell BEd MA (50s). Formerly deputy head at Alleyn's Junior School, Ashville College Junior School, Harrogate and Stamford Junior School, Lincolnshire. Knows every girl and every parent. Parents say: 'easy to talk to, professional, approachable and dedicated'. Girls love her. Teaches verbal reasoning in preparation for 11+ and hears infant readers. Non-controversial. Has been around for over 13 years, but no plans to move on. Do we hear parents breathing a sigh of relief?

Academic matters: A top junior school – a brilliant kick-off into the world of single-sex private education. Creative curriculum, ensures breadth and motivation, a desire to learn and discover. Based on literacy, tying in maths and linking in all other subjects in many different ways. Kate Mitchell says: 'Phenomenal! It really works.'

All children screened for SEN on entry and again in Y2. Approximately five per cent need extra help. Constant watch kept by the learning support coordinator who works with teachers to ensure all SEN pupils are accommodated in lesson plans – typically for barriers to learning such as dyslexia and dyspraxia. Progress tracked and peripatetic one-on-one help provided where needed. EAL not a problem despite the number of bilingual children in the school. Specialist coordinator/mentor for the gifted and talented.

Without doubt an academic school. Testing starts at entrance level in the seniors and progression from the junior school is not automatic. Classes are bigger than many – up to 28 – but decrease when setting starts in year 9, averaging 22 for GCSE classes and fewer for A levels.

Senior school curriculum is broad and demanding. The 'gentle' years, before GCSE, introduce them to the joy of learning. They are encouraged to explore and challenge. Excellent support for all the core subjects but there is some feeling that optional subjects are assessed less frequently which, given that the girls are encouraged to cover a wide range, seems, to some, unfair. But, then, it depends on your feelings about assessment.. Some parents feel that they would like to see their daughters' course work assessments more often – 'it would be good to be more involved'.

Many GCSE subjects on offer and the last few years have seen a considerable shift to IGCSEs. Outstanding results. In 2016, 93 per cent A*/A grades at GCSE and 67 per cent at A level (91 per cent A*/B). A double-edged sword this – some very bright girls are then tempted away by top schools with mixed sixth forms. However, there is also a steady stream coming in to the sixth from other schools, including some from the state system and rumour has it that some of the girls who leave WHS are not – as so often – completely happy with their moves.

Games, options, the arts: Not, historically, the sportiest of schools but that is changing. A fantastic swimming pool and large sports hall in the grounds, alongside great games facilities 10 minutes' walk away on the site of the old All England Lawn Tennis and Croquet Club. Parents say, 'it's a pity they don't swim regularly once a week'; nonetheless, they are rightly proud of their swimmers: national, county and regional prize winners; their hockey and netball teams who tour internationally every second year; their cricketers; and, recently, of their star rowers, one of whom came fourth in the National Junior Sculling Head. Skiing, taekwondo and fencing have also produced winners and there is an equestrian team waiting in the wings, an annual tennis tour to Portugal and a netball tour to Spain. So – a great range of sporting opportunities. Of course, they are also proud to ball-girl at the Wimbledon Tennis Championships every year. We met some of the Y7 sports enthusiasts and were impressed, not only with their achievements but also their confidence and ability to talk about them.

Very strong in music and drama. Fantastic music, vocal and instrumental, a particular feature of the whole school. Plenty of opportunity to start early. Specialise in different instruments each junior school year – percussion, recorder, keyboard, brass. Events, concerts, performances and regular musical shows. GDST Young Choir of the Year finalists in 2015; have sung at Queen Elizabeth Hall and the Royal Albert Hall. Musicals, concerts and plays put on in the ultra modern Rutherford Centre, which is much enjoyed by juniors and seniors alike. Some 80 per cent of senior school have individual music tuition and all of Y7 are members of the drama club. We were lucky enough to walk in on the senior chamber choir practising for a concert in St John's, Smith Square and, at the end of our visit, to hear some 'jamming' which included exceptional piano playing. Impressive. Several girls reach grade 8 in their choice of instrument and some work for diplomas, both classical and jazz. One Y13 girl was crowned GDST Musician of the Year in 2016.

Our guides proudly showed us the Rutherford Centre, a great facility for all the performing arts. Plays, musicals, plenty of dramatic opportunities for everyone – on and off stage. Sixth form drama students are now regulars at the Edinburgh Festival.

Clubs galore; the list is endless and imaginative: from art to biomedicine, debating to the Duke of Edinburgh (three golds in 2015), scribbling to engineering and many more. Also several trips and expeditions (including senior and junior World Challenges) organised each term, home and abroad. A busy, buzzy school where idling is not encouraged and plenty of time is given to co-curricular activities.

Background and atmosphere: This GDST school had its 135th birthday in 2015 and was top of the league table that year. A somewhat unexciting entrance to the building belies the buzz that you get as you walk round it. Stone staircases lead to bright corridors, windows onto the happy, busy atmosphere that emanates from both classrooms and laboratories. Girls look relaxed and involved. Rooms subject based. Teachers and parents, as well as students, can have coding lessons in the ultra-modern computer room. We gather a complete overhaul of the building is due complete with a lift.

Sixth form has its own house with relaxing and study areas, common room and café. The girls are allowed to wear their own clothes from the Easter of Y11 onwards, and 'have fun playing ridiculous games'. Relationships with teachers are easy and they are absolutely not spoon-fed. They say the lack of boys 'doesn't fuss us. In fact, it's probably less hassle'.

Our junior school guides – happy, vivacious year 6s – obviously loved their school and were quick to show us everything that was going on. A library on every floor – 'we're at the top and ours is the best!' (Well, it did contain a large display of cups.) All children, from the youngest to the oldest, looked thoroughly involved in what they were doing and were keen to explain their activities to us. They grow up as they (literally) go up the school building.

We saw the youngest, at ground level, sitting on the floor or clustered round tables, listening to stories, gathered in small discussion groups, immersed in what they were doing: learning to learn. Easy access for outside play.

Upstairs, larger classes for the older children – average 24. Two years to each floor. Still a generally relaxed feeling of informality, outdoor clothes falling from their pegs in the corridors. Jolly-looking classrooms with plenty on the walls. Every child looked interested in what they were doing. Specialist labs for the older pupils. High tech equipment used but not excessively. IPads recently introduced into Y3 but school says not totally wedded to them yet. Homework for years 4, 5 and 6 periodically done online.

Pastoral care, well-being and discipline: Happy, high-achieving pupils all seem relaxed and discipline problems are rare. Junior school parents say: 'Girls are supported but not mollycoddled'; 'develop confidence as they go through'; 'well prepared for move to senior school'. A zero tolerance policy on bullying, though, according to parents, not all problems are well handled. The school says 'any sniff of such behaviour and we act – this is why we have student peer counsellors and run resilience weeks and a range of seminars including one on "failing friendships".'

All are screened on joining the senior school, whether they are juniors coming up or new entrants. Any anomalies are picked up and monitored and parents immediately involved. The school is very aware that capable and high achieving children can often mask their need for support and that the crunch point is at the beginning of Y10. All problems, however mild, are taken extremely seriously and teachers are constantly on the look out for signs of eating disorders etc. 'Learning to learn' lessons are wisely given in year 7.

G&T children are offered weekly enrichment afternoons in years 11, 12 and 13. The school is active in the London Challenge that enables talented girls from neighbouring (but less privileged) schools to participate in particular projects.

House system encourages a good mixing of age groups and, parents believe, increases confidence and crosses all boundaries. Masses of fundraising, either for the school or for special concerns and charities. Parents say: 'helps them learn about money'. Girls clearly look after and care for each other.

Pupils and parents: Not yummy mummies, more parents keen to get the best education possible for their daughters. Often both working. No school transport, so either live within walking distance (about half), or on a good public transport route. Some 22 per cent speak a language other than English at home. All keen to give their children a good, well-grounded education. A school that encourages individuals, so anyone could fit in. The majority have a good sense of community; a thriving Parents' Association.

Notable former pupils include: K M Peyton (author of Flambards series), Professor Lynn Reid (first woman to achieve rank of professor of experimental pathology in UK), Professor Marilyn Butler (first female rector of Exeter College), Michelle Paver (author of Chronicles of Ancient Darkness), Margaret Rutherford (actress) and Eboni Beckford Chambers (played netball for England).

Entrance: Selective at 4+. Testing in November prior to entry. Specially designed, supposedly relaxing, activities in a nursery school environment. 'We're looking for potential, not what they already know.' If successful, a follow-up in January. More places available at 7+ when assessment covers English, maths and verbal reasoning, together with an interview that includes reading. Occasional places higher up. No sibling priority. Intake mainly from local Wimbledon and surrounds.

Selective at 11+: group assessment (interview) in autumn term a year before entry; then, in January, tests in verbal and non-verbal reasoning plus a short, creative problem-solving writing task. An interview with the head may follow. Offers made at beginning of February.

At 16+: a taster day in May alongside girls in own Y10. In November, tests in verbal reasoning alongside up to four 20-30 minute written papers in the subjects they want to study at A level. Those wishing to study art, music or drama interviewed by head of department. All candidates interviewed by head and director of sixth form and take part in a short group discussion on a current media issue.

Exit: Most junior girls move on to the senior school but take note, this is not guaranteed. Tests in year 4 identify those who may not make the grade and parents are pre-warned that their daughter 'could be better off in a senior school with a slightly slower pace'. This can also apply to less able siblings. All the rest offered senior places, some with academic or music scholarships.

Occasional moves to pastures new, often with a scholarship, recent destinations including St Paul's Girls' and Kingston Grammar. Some head for local grammars.

A few at leave at 16+. Of the remainder, together with those who join from other schools, a good handful to Oxbridge (eight per cent in 2016) or London and the rest mainly to other Russell Group universities. Nine medics in 2016, one to study in US. According to parents, the advice and guidance they are given about courses to follow and choice of university is second to none. Nearly all get to where they want to go.

Money matters: Academic and music scholarships on offer in Y7 – parents are disappointed that there are none for drama but there is a new sports scholarship. Many more offered at sixth form level in a wider range of subjects – academic, art, drama, music, sport. Perhaps this would be a good time to reward long stayers, who have been at the school all their lives, rather than mainly to tempt new entrants?

Remarks: Quite a school. It's extraordinary what has been packed into a relatively small space in the middle of a busy London suburb. First of all we were startled by a head who exudes enthusiasm and finds sitting silently impossible (though she does listen, too, and answers questions); secondly, we were taken round the school by some very chatty Y9ers whose fervour and ability to talk matched their head's. This school produces bright, open minded, self-motivated girls. Jane Lunnon has some major improvements in mind. An excellent school for girls who want to open their minds, co-operate and grab what is on offer.

Woodford County High School

High Road, Woodford Green, Essex IG8 9LA

Pupils: 906 • Ages: 11–18 • Sixth form: 312

Tel: 020 8504 0611
Email: head@woodford.redbridge.sch.uk
Website: www.woodford.redbridge.sch.uk

Headteacher: Since 2010, Ms Jo Pomeroy (40s), MA in English language and literature (St Andrews), BEd (Open), NPQH. Spent two years in a comprehensive in rural Scotland before going to work in France at a mixed grammar school for three years. It was at this high achieving international school that she became aware of 'what can be achieved', 'what is possible' and 'what bright students are capable of if they are given enough challenge,' she says. So the aim here 'is for students always to be working just beyond what they are comfortable with'. Back in the UK she spent another three years working in a comprehensive school with strong bias towards European languages and at that point 'got interested in management, in getting into position where you could make a bigger change'. Sure enough, at her next appointment at a girls' grammar in Surrey, where she spent 16 years, she eventually became deputy head. 'There is enormous satisfaction in seeing incrementally what can be achieved in one place,' she says. Academic life at Woodford is very much influenced by this passion for great leadership as well as head's English teaching background. 'What excites me the most is working from what you may be able to stimulate in your own life and career and then being able to share that with students so that they can enjoy challenges themselves.'

Academic matters: Best results in Redbridge. These are bright girls taught by committed teachers, a third of whom have been here for over 10 years. As a selective school (there are only some four students with SEN), it has maintained an outstanding record of achievement, with 78 per cent A*/A grades at GCSE in 2016. And these stats despite most students – in fact well over half of the school population – speaking English as a second language. 'The joy of being in a school like this is that it is self-propagating: when students come in and they see other students valuing learning and success, and working hard on collaborative projects, it really affects everything else they do.'

Impressive mentoring structure in place where older pupils mentor younger ones. There are literacy mentors who provide targeted additional support for year 7s where needed, and this 'sustained focus on academic literacy across the curriculum has been highly successful'. Head says, 'I have an interest in a great many subjects and I think the joy of English being my subject is that it takes you into everything, history, philosophy, art and music, and it is wonderful being able to investigate and enjoy literature and other languages as well.' These pupils have the opportunity to be mentored in other subjects as well, by sixth formers who relish the opportunity to 'give something back', though 'teachers still keep a close eye...'

In some classrooms desks are arranged to encourage interaction between students, not only with teachers. In the English department, year 7s are introduced to Shakespeare texts usually reserved for later years and invited to write an essay on what they have learnt. They also have lots of opportunity to visit theatres. Pupils take two languages from year 7 (French and either German or Latin). English, languages and science are all strong here and around 87 per cent of girls take triple science GCSE. Lots of information and support provided to both students and parents on choosing options. GCSE computing now offered and in KS3 an integrated DT, electronics and programming course.

In the sixth form, where roughly a quarter of students come from other schools, girls either take four A levels, three plus the EPQ or three plus AS maths over two years. Woodford maintains good A level results with 69 per cent A*/B grades, 42 per cent A*/A, in 2016, with students off to Oxford and Cambridge and on to medical careers. Academic mentoring and university preparation at sixth form, and guidance to final transition here is second to none, or in one parent's words, 'really very strong'.

Games, options, the arts: Head's commitment to leading a school that offers plenty of opportunity to be stretched is evident across the whole curriculum. Reasonable range of games on offer – badminton, athletics, netball, rounders, gymnastics and dance – and girls can pursue their interest in multi-cultural dance options such as Bhangra, African and street dance. Games either take place outside on the field and tennis courts or indoors in the newly built Lottery funded sports hall. Outdoor Greek theatre recently restored. The girls do well at games; they recently reached the UK badminton national finals, and they seem willing to try their best at everything, keen or not: 'Sport, I'm not good at, but it's a popular subject.'

Pupils speak highly of the sports leadership qualification offered in years 10 and 11: 'It gives you skills in being responsible, listening skills and classroom theory. We learn to create lesson plans.' Another said it 'opens us up to new areas; we realise there is more to our skill set and that motivates and opens us up to aim higher'. D of E also offered.

School does well at art and has had pupils featured in a Saatchi exhibition. Major drama event each term as well as an annual musical (most recently, Anything Goes!) plus a summer production run by teachers and a spring production organised by students. A beautiful patchwork tapestry displayed under glass in the technology department harks back to the days when the school offered textiles. These days the girls focus their design skills in technology, where they recently emerged winners of the National Technology Design Prize.

Instrumental and vocal lessons at all levels on offer, though most who learn do so out of school. Many are involved in one of a large number of ensembles and clubs: guitar, singing, Carnatic music. There is a large junior choir and band, a folk group, a brass project (all year 8 pupils learn a brass instrument), woodwind ensemble, and a staff choir too. Girls have also participated in Redbridge Choral Festival at the Royal Albert Hall.

Lots of trips to support lessons and extracurricular activities, including expeditions to eg Ghana, Morocco, Indonesia, China, Cambodia and most recently Nepal.

Sixth form enrichment programme includes dance, cookery, computing, BSL sign language, art, sports and an extended period of voluntary service. Older students preside over all manner of different extracurricular opportunities, such as talks, clubs and charity events, and there is a society for everything – even to discuss current affairs. 'We have house competitions,' head says, 'and sometimes there can be more drama off stage than on stage.' But because there is no adult intervention the girls learn to work together and develop great teamwork skills – 'a real success and selling point of the school.' All comes good in the end, as evidenced by the year 11-led assembly held on the morning of our visit. In their well-structured presentation the girls demonstrated what they had learnt about self, learning and approaching life, showing extraordinary wisdom and the ability to work together. Head says, 'They listen to each other very well, and coming up the school younger students see this and that sets their aspirations.'

Background and atmosphere: Main building dates from 1768 when it was built as the country manor home of the Highams; school opened here in 1919, and its venerable features lend an atmosphere of tradition – from the beautiful open air Greek theatre that stands in the grounds near to the tennis courts, to the hymnals still used in assemblies – 'I'm not a Christian but I enjoy it', a pupil remarked.

With its small classrooms, narrow stairwells and corridors, the school has an intimate feel. The lack of space noted at our last visit will be remedied by a new building due for completion in July 2017. There is a larger than average sixth form of 280 students. Still, the girls lack nothing in terms of modern resources, thanks to a very active PFTA.

Pastoral care, well-being and discipline: Pupils receive support from their form tutors and also have prefects to help school life run smoothly. 'Teachers are approachable, and there are some small classes so you get to know everyone.' When issues of bullying come up, 'once staff are aware of it the response is immediate and caring'.

Lots of careful thought has gone into ensuring peer support is strong. 'Our greatest glory is not in never failing but in rising up every time we fail,' says a poster on the PSHCE board in the corridor. The board provides information about the peer support service run by older pupils. 'So important,' said a pupil; 'petty things getting out of hand is rare.' Pupils say they 'can't imagine peer support not being there. It's natural.' Also, 'Form prefects develop close relationships so you stay in contact even after leaving, like on Facebook.' House groups are active and help mobilise the girls to get involved in drama performances and fundraising events for the chosen recipient of charity week. Events like the five-penny race are popular and encourage heated competition, raising as much £2000 in one hour.

Career support is good. There is a university success board to inspire the girls and year 11s have a review day including one-to-one meetings with teachers. Year 12s spend two hours per week in voluntary service, often working with children or the elderly or the disabled. 'It's a steep learning curve and you find yourself going back for several months.'

Pupils and parents: Multi-ethnic population: over 40 languages spoken here and there is a significant Tamil and Indian population. One parent said, 'My daughter benefits from being with children from many different ethnic backgrounds'. Parents support the PFTA as an opportunity to solve many of the school's cash problems (£25,000 raised for digital language lab, a minibus and external lighting).

Girls seem confident, resilient and creative. Former pupils here include Lucy Kirkwood, playwright (RSC, National Theatre), Sarah Winman, best-selling novelist (When God was a Rabbit) and Peggy Reynolds, Radio 4 broadcaster in the arts.

Entrance: Massively oversubscribed for year 7 places and has just expanded from four forms of entry to six. CEM entrance tests are used for the borough's only two grammar schools (the other being the brother school, Ilford County for Boys). It is one of just three all-girls schools in the area (the other two are independent and Catholic). Common catchment area with boys' grammar school. Head says the girls are tested on 'wit rather than what's been studied in the classroom'. Nearly all girls stay on to the sixth form, joined by 30 or so from other schools.

Exit: A few (around 10-15 per cent) leave post-GCSE but nearly all that stay go on to university. Subject choices are academic but varied: physics, law, medicine, languages (most likely French), mathematics, geography, English or economics. A few go on to study business or architecture. Some success in applications to top universities and competitive courses with two Oxbridge places in 2016, plus one to Harvard, 22 medics and five dentists. Other destinations include UCL, Queen Mary's, Kent, King's College London, Birmingham, Nottingham.

Remarks: With the great pastoral and peer support in place and strong academic atmosphere there is no reason why a pupil should not do well here. The message from pupils to any year 6s considering the school is: 'If you love academic study, close relationships with teachers, clubs and societies, and you want to get involved, this is the place for you.'

Woodhouse College

306

Woodhouse Road, London N12 9EY

Pupils: 1,336 • Ages: 16-19 • Sixth form: 1,336

Tel: 020 8445 1210
Email: enquiries@woodhouse.ac.uk
Website: www.woodhouse.ac.uk

Principal: Since 2013, John Rubinstein BSc (50s) – read maths at Sheffield University where he achieved a first class degree. It was during his PhD that he decided teaching was his vocation: 'Part of my duties as a postgrad was to teach undergraduates, which I really enjoyed, and I realised then that this was what I wanted to do.' His first teaching job was at a comprehensive in Manchester – prior to getting his first post in London. His third teaching job was at Woodhouse College in 1994 as a maths teacher. He stayed there for the next 10 years, only leaving when he was offered the post of deputy head at a school in Haringey. He came back to Woodhouse in 2008 as deputy head, and was promoted to principal five years later.

Originally from Yorkshire, this softly spoken head seems totally devoid of any of the salesman techniques often displayed by other heads – that's not to say he's not enthusiastic about the school or his pupils, he is clearly extremely proud of both, but no doubt he feels, as we do, that Woodhouse pretty much sells itself. Students and parents alike describe him as 'very approachable' and one student told us: 'Mr Rubinstein is always wandering around the learning zones and often spends ages with pupils helping them out. You can email him anytime and he always gets back to you.' Even after nearly 30 years in the teaching profession, maths is still his passion and he still teaches four maths lessons a week which equates to a full A level week: 'It keeps me in touch with students, with the experience of colleagues, but most of all because I love it.' He even taught his own daughter, who is an ex-Woodhouse student: 'I warned her that it might be slightly strange, but it worked out fine.'

His wife is also a teacher and they have three children – two of whom attended Woodhouse and are now at university. Mr Rubinstein has many other strings to his bow – formerly an Ofsted Inspector for 15 years: 'I gave up a year ago as the workload was getting too much and I was fed up of staying in hotel rooms'; he also enjoys running and has taken part in many half marathons and 10k runs. 'I have done the Crouch End 10k run for 13 years in a row and now train some of my students.' Recently nominated the school caretaker for a CBE for 20 years of service to the school: 'he is the glue that keeps this community together.'

Academic matters: Woodhouse is one of the country's leading sixth form colleges, always in the top five nationally, usually in the top three. This is essentially an academic place, whose main focus is on A levels. In 2016, 29 per cent of grades were A*/A and 64 per cent A*-B.

Undoubtedly a key part of the success is enthusiastic, experienced and focused teaching. One parent told us: 'I can't say enough about the teaching at Woodhouse and how they inspire students. My son had no real intellectual curiosity before going there. Now all he wants to do is discuss the Russian revolution.' Another said, 'The teachers really seem to know our children individually and their particular traits.' The consensus seems to be that 'they're excellent at monitoring and keep their finger on the pulse.' Mr Rubinstein says that close monitoring of students is vital as some students choose the wrong subjects, and they are under so much more pressure than they used to be. 'If a student is underachieving, there will be a case conference and a discussion of perhaps reducing the amount of subjects they take. They will also be offered extra supervised study.'

The principal welcomes the introduction of the new A level system. He says that although results will change, 'we won't just be teaching towards an end of year exam. Pupils will be able to explore their subjects more deeply.'

A wide range of options on offer, with 32 subjects in almost any combination. Maths is the most popular A level choice (with 45 per cent taking it) and results are notably strong. One of London's largest providers of A level science, with many going on to science-related degrees. Four languages, including Italian, and an abundance of 'ologies', from sociology to music technology and the extended project also available. The EPQ is taken by over 100 students each year and yields high grades. One parent said that 'the fantastic selection of A levels, including classical civilization, really excited my daughter when she was looking at sixth forms, and this is what swung it for her.' From next year Japanese and Latin will be offered at GCSE level as an extracurricular option.

Though the majority at Woodhouse tend to favour professional courses at university, social science and arts-based studies are strong, with thriving theatre studies, economics, English literature and geography. 'Independent learning' is high on the agenda. 'We want students to prepare for lessons, so they can understand and interpret the information, using the teacher and their fellow students as a resource,' says the principal. Motivated students respond well to this approach. 'Teachers assume if you're interested in your subjects, you will want to read around them,' said one. 'They don't force you to work, but they'll give you the resources and make themselves available to you,' said another.

Enormous amount of help is offered to pupils with their UCAS forms. A teacher is on hand every Tuesday after school to offer any extra help for university applications, and Mr Rubinstein is also very involved in the process and runs mock Oxbridge interviews.

All students have access to two learning mentors – one for humanities, the other science and maths. One full-time SENCo, plus one part-time specialist providing individual support for those with dyslexia and dyspraxia and a learning mentor to help with study skills. The buildings are 99 per cent adapted for those with physical disabilities.

Games, options, the arts: Woodhouse prides itself on providing 'a broad and civilising education' and all are expected to take part in at least two six-week courses of 'enrichment'. Most relish the opportunities to develop new skills in everything from observational drawing to street dance. Duke of Edinburgh and Amnesty International also on offer.

Some of the art we saw on our tour were simply outstanding – something we honestly weren't expecting: 'Traditionally the more academic subjects are most popular here, and although art and drama are taken by smaller numbers, they are very successful. Several of our graduates go on to art colleges.'

Dance is also a strong curricular subject here and the college has two lovely, bright, mirrored dance studios. Sports facilities, too, are good, with a new sports hall and new floodlit 3G football pitch. Official team sports include football (girls' and boys'), netball and basketball, but individualists can also enjoy cross-country, squash, trampolining and kick boxing. 'If there isn't a club that you'd like to do,' said one student, 'the sports department are happy to try and set something up.'

Music, which was previously a 'neglected' subject, now has its own dedicated separate building outside, with a well-equipped practice room and a music studio, which works in conjunction with other Barnet schools, and offers lessons from peripatetic teachers.

Woodhouse students like to get involved and there's an active college council. Plenty of outside speakers and activities including art trips, foreign exchanges, a ski trip and the opportunity to undertake voluntary work abroad. Debating has traditionally been strong at Woodhouse and the college takes part in the Model United Nations competition, which hosts around 40 different debates a year in various Institutions, including Woodhouse.

Background and atmosphere: Located in a pleasant leafy suburb, Woodhouse began its educational life as Woodhouse Grammar School in 1925, but became one of the capital's rare sixth form colleges in the 1980s. With some 700 new pupils a year, the college is significantly larger than a traditional school sixth form, but smaller than a FE college.

The original stately Victorian façade (deriving from its former incarnation as the home of ornamental plasterer Thomas Collins) has now been joined by a motley timeline of newer buildings, leaving it today with well-equipped facilities. The bright, open plan Learning Zone is one of the most recent innovations, offering space to work in solitary silence as well as in small groups, and supervised open-access IT. In 2014 the college managed to raise two million pounds for a two-story, purpose built mathematics facility. 'Quite a lot of students here can't work in silence at home and don't have the facility to do the "hard hours",' says the principal. 'We wanted to create learners who can work on their own.'

To a former Woodhouse student, the college internally would be barely recognisable. However, what still remains is the strong sense of individuality that Woodhouse was always renowned for – and is still clearly evident in the students we witnessed strolling around the grounds. All creeds, colours, dress codes, hair colour, piercings welcome (well, maybe piercings not 'welcome', but they're there). One student told us: 'I never feel we are judged on anything here. We know grades matter, but that's really it.' Another student told us: 'I've never been as happy as I am coming here. I used to loathe going to school, but now I'm worried about my time at Woodhouse going too quickly.'

The students we met all felt extremely independent and loved the free reign the college allows them. However, one student grumbled that she tends to go out for lunch in North Finchley High Road (a five minute walk), as the canteen is too small and can't often accommodate everyone – a sentiment echoed by a parent, who suggested that perhaps the lunch hour should be extended.

Values here are traditional. 'We believe in honesty, hard work, mutual respect and taking responsibility for your own learning.' The atmosphere is generally enthusiastic, as much for work as for play. 'Here it's cool to work, cool to be involved,' said one student. Another told us, 'There's a massive sense of community. There are always things happening.'

Pastoral care, well-being and discipline: Not every 16-year-old is ideally suited to the self-motivation required by an academic sixth form college, but here high expectations are supported by a well-thought-out tutorial system and plenty of individual guidance, 'My son sees a guy two or three times a week, whom he likes and respects,' said one mother. 'When he was having trouble at home, they really kept an eye on him.'

The principal is all too aware that students these days are under a lot more pressure than previously, 'and as a result are a lot more fragile and there is more self-harming.' For this reason, they invest time in what they offer pastorally, including a pastoral manager and a counselling service. One student told us: 'The pastoral care here is excellent. There's pretty much someone you can talk to 24/7, if you needed to.'

The college sees itself as a bridge between school and university, and new students are eased into this more adult world with an induction day in the summer before they start. The enrichment programme helps aid new friendships beyond the classroom. 'Everyone makes friends ridiculously fast because there are so many people in the same position,' said one boy. However, one parent did say that her child found the transition from school to college 'socially quite daunting if you don't know anyone, as pupils are always rushing off to their different classes or study period – it's unlike school where you get to know your peers over time.'

Boundaries are firm and there's zero tolerance on punctuality. 'It's an issue they have to grasp,' says the head. 'If they're not making the effort, why should other students suffer?' However, unlike most sixth forms, there is no morning registration, instead pupils go straight to their class and their ID registers them when they swipe it at the entrance turnstiles.

In lessons, students are attentive. 'If a teacher leaves the room, people get on with their work,' said one boy. We witnessed some of the most attentive and eager students we've come across, who were happy to talk with enthusiasm about what they were learning. 'Issues found elsewhere are not even on the radar here,' notes the principal gratefully, 'We have pupils from quite challenged backgrounds, but I have thrown out just one student. Parents agree that discipline is firm but reasonable. 'They run quite a tight ship, but it makes them responsible,' said one father. 'When my son's attendance was only 90 per cent, he had to see the senior tutor every week. As his attendance improved, he went less frequently.'

Pupils and parents: An eclectic mix – 'some nerdy kids, some cool kids, all sorts, colours and creeds.' The core is probably typical of the reasonably prosperous 'squeezed middle' of north London, but with a far higher ethnic intake than you'd assume from the location, and a far higher proportion of those who require some type of financial support.

Parents tend to be involved and supportive, students upbeat, mature, outgoing and energetic. 'They want to do well and they want to enjoy themselves,' says the principal. 'They're trying to get the balance right of working hard and having a good social life.' A parent agreed: 'My son is so happy. He really appreciates the fact that people are there because they want to learn, not because their parents are pushing them. Most students here are trying to better themselves and work really, really hard.' Past students include journalist Johann Hari, comedian Michael McIntyre and actress Naomie Harris.

Entrance: Priority is given to applicants from one local secondary school, Friern Barnet (although that accounts for roughly 20 places and they still need the same entry requirements). After that, it's predicted grades and/or interview. Competition is ferocious (about 4,500 apply for 700 places), particularly for in-demand subjects. 'We can afford to be choosy,' says the principal, 'but we're looking for a range.' All applicants with minimum predicted grade requirements (evaluated on a points system, with specific grades for individual subjects) are given a 20-30 minute interview (with optional parental accompaniment) in the February/March prior to entry. 'We're looking for maturity,' said one teacher. 'We want them to demonstrate that they are committed to A levels and really want to work, but we also want people who will get involved on a wider basis.' The interview is frequently of as much benefit to the student as to the college. 'We often spend it giving careers advice,' says the principal.

Travel time is also taken into consideration. Students come from as far afield as Highbury, but the school 'generally considers an hour and a quarter by bus the maximum desirable distance.' Applications available from the time of the open day in November until the closing deadline in January. All candidates require a confidential report from their current school and must be between 16 and 18 when starting at the college. The college operates a waiting list for the reshuffle that often takes place after results day in August.

Exit: Over 95 per cent to university – slightly over 50 per cent to Russell Group universities, with the most popular destinations being London universities, Warwick, Kent, Manchester and Sussex. Most popular subject choices are economics, law, engineering, business and psychology. Nine to Oxbridge and 16 medics in 2016, plus one student off to the US on a full scholarship, (the second student in two years to go to a US college). Good advice about careers and courses, including a full time careers co-ordinator.

Money matters: Parents are asked for £100 contribution for the two-year stint, enabling the college to keep up to date with books and underwrite the enrichment programme and facilities (those who can't afford it, don't pay). A £50 refundable deposit also required for text books. The college has attempted to replace some money lost through EMA cuts with bursaries.

Remarks: An upbeat environment, with strong teaching and results. A firm stepping stone between school and university.

Wren Academy

Hilton Avenue, London N12 9HB

Pupils: 1,200 • Ages: 4–18 • Sixth form: 220 • C of E

Tel: 020 8492 6000
Email: firstcontact@wrenacademy.org
Website: www.wrenacademy.org

Executive Principal: Since 2007, some 15 months before the academy opened, Mr Michael Whitworth (40s). Previously head of Kelmscott School in Walthamstow. Born and brought up in Northumberland, he graduated as a historian and has recently taught history and religious studies. After working in both private industry and the civil service, he entered teaching and has worked in schools in London, Hertfordshire and Essex. He was attracted by the 'unusual opportunity to create a brand new school from scratch', and built up the school's reputation very rapidly. 'I think the governors recognised my capacity to stick to a task and see it through.' Understated but extremely caring, say parents, very driven and with sights set very high. Married with two young children.

Principal of the secondary school: is Gavin Smith.

Academic matters: This is a comprehensive, but the nature of the students in this leafy area means it is primarily an academic one. The biggest initial challenge was achieving a truly comprehensive intake: the previous school on the site had a very poor reputation and Barnet has a variety of popular state schools, including three grammars. However, within a short space of time Ofsted stated that 'the teaching at Wren is stunning', and this is not something you read very often. 'As well as maximising achievement – because children need that currency to move on – we teach learning skills and aptitudes,' says the head. 'Children need the capacity to think for themselves. They are encouraged to seek out their own answers, to be flexible and take risks.' In 2016, 84 per cent of pupils achieved 5+ A*-C grades at GCSE including English and maths (42 per cent of grades A*/A). Second cohort of sixth formers achieved 22 per cent A*/A grades, 53 per cent A*-B in their A level exams.

Parents are enthusiastic. 'The teachers are very wisely chosen.' 'They're great at finding and encouraging talents.' 'They really encourage them to aim high.' Newsletters all include brainteasers for parents and pupils to solve, and articles on ways of building learning power.

English, maths and science are taught in single sex classes. 'This gives us opportunities to stretch children in gender-specific ways. For example, in English boys can look at their powers of reflectiveness and empathy, whilst in girls' maths classes we can encourage them to take risks and concentrate on answering quickly. It helps to broaden their skill sets, and they enjoy it.' Research suggests that girls taught in single sex groups are more likely to continue with maths and science, and a good percentage of girls is choosing single science GCSEs.

The school sets for English, maths, science and foreign languages from part of the way through year 7. 'We like to get data of our own rather than relying on Sats results.' Everyone studies a language (generally French, though some take Japanese or Spanish) and most are expected to take it to GCSE.

The specialism of design and the built environment enhances rather than dominates the curriculum, says the head. 'It influences our culture and our ways of thinking about tasks. We have a high emphasis on creativity, and each task has a creative phase, a planning phase and an evaluation phase. But we also have the opportunity to plan projects in architecture and civil engineering.'

Those who need extra help are identified at the beginning of year 7 and follow a six week key skills programme to help bring them up to speed. There are also after-school support groups that help with spelling and comprehension. Although some get one-to-one help from teaching assistants, 'the aim is for everyone to be unsupported in lessons eventually. We do what helps them to access the curriculum in the appropriate lesson.'

Games, options, the arts: The school week includes three extended days, with compulsory enrichment activities from 3-4pm. These range from samba band, Latin and knitting to debating. Staff and students learn together and either can win Excellent Learner of the Week awards.

Houses – named for Wren churches – give the main opportunities for sporting rivalry, but football, netball, basketball, badminton and athletics teams also take part in borough and regional competitions with increasing success. There's a sports hall, netball courts and a football pitch. Pupils can take sports GCSE or BTec, and enrichment options include rugby, trampolining and table tennis.

Art, design and technology very strong and creative – as one would expect in a school with a design specialism. Music is keen – there's an orchestra, samba band, gospel choir, Indian drumming club. Drama also finding its feet; eagerly awaited annual school musical – eg Bugsy Malone and Hairspray. Wren's Got Talent showcases singers, magicians and musicians.

Background and atmosphere: Named for Sir Christopher Wren, designer of St Paul's Cathedral, which reflects its C of E status and specialism in design and the built environment. Opened in 2008 on the site of a failed school next door to Woodhouse College. Partly refurbished but mostly newly built, it has an open plan feel, with roof lights and large north windows, grey carpets and aluminium cladding. Steps leading down from the entrance hall to the library, 'the heart of the school', are lined by ledges where children can sit and chat, under treble-height rooflights, giving an amphitheatre-like atmosphere. Corridor walls are decorated with graphics of the footprint of St Paul's Cathedral, and with murals quoting inspiring biblical texts eg 'Be willing and available to provide support and guidance to others'.

The school is sponsored by the London Diocesan Board for Schools and by Berkhamsted School, which provides some of the governors. The schools work together on areas such as curriculum development, Wren students go over to Berkhamsted for activities, including a year 7 residential retreat, and Berkhamsted sixth formers visited Wren to give their views on appointing a new head of sixth form. 'It's a partnership, and we hope that both schools will get an equal amount from it.'

Primary school on the same site adjacent to the existing school opened in September 2015; will eventually become a complete all-through school.

Pastoral care, well-being and discipline: 'The teachers don't tolerate any bad behaviour,' say parents. 'It is a lovely, safe environment for learning'; and indeed the school had a supremely ordered feel during our visit. Three different breaks and lunchtimes help. So does the design of the building: staff and pupils share uni-sex toilets, and there is no staff room, so everyone socialises in the restaurant. 'It's a philosophy that when staff and students share the same space there is passive supervision, and students feel secure. They're encouraged to sit in here and chat – it's part of the curriculum.' 'Focus days' concentrate on matters ranging from sexual health to university choices.

Much emphasis on good manners and courtesy. Common sanctions include litter duty and community service. There's a Reflection Room for 'those who would benefit from time on their own'. Pupils have a high degree of autonomy, with plenty of opportunities to get involved in the way the school is run, from becoming prefects to interviewing potential teachers to taking part in curriculum reviews. 'In return, they generally play their part. There's a high level of buy-in.'

The chaplain, who plays a counsellor-like role, is generally considered a good egg. The only parental criticism is that some feel the school doesn't take their views on board. 'When you start a new school you have to put in place structures that will work. We opened with a very clear idea of what we wanted. We've always listened and explained to parents, but we haven't always amended our ways as a result.'

Pupils and parents: A diverse range, about 25 per cent white British, and characteristic of this leafy outer-London suburb; mostly 'ambitious people who want to do well'. Pupils have taken GCSEs in 13 different home languages. Active PTA which organises quiz nights and festivals, organises second hand uniform sales to raise funds.

Entrance: Takes 180 into year 7, with 90 foundation (church) places and 90 community places. First priority for community places to looked after children, those with SEN statements or exceptional medical or social need. Points for having a sibling at the school and for attending a Barnet primary school, then by distance – generally within about half a mile. For foundation places, points for siblings and for regular church attendance, with distance as a tie-break. Has waiting lists for occasional places in other years. Internal and external sixth form applicants need at least five B grades at GCSE including maths, English, and the subjects they want to study at A level; prospective maths, further maths, science and French students need A grades in these subjects. At least 25 external sixth form places.

Becoming an 'all through' school: first cohort of children joined reception class in 2015. The primary will grow one year at a time until school has children from 4-18 (in 2022).

Exit: In 2016, 42 per cent left post-GCSE, seven per cent after year 12. Around 50 per cent of first year 13 leavers to top universities; two to Oxford in 2016.

Remarks: This young school has already established a reputation for high teaching standards, courteous students and excellent enrichment activities. Likely to go from strength to strength.

Midlands and East of England

Bedfordshire
Cambridgeshire
Derbyshire
Leicestershire
Lincolnshire
Norfolk
Northamptonshire
Nottinghamshire
Rutland
Staffordshire
Suffolk
Warwickshire
West Midlands

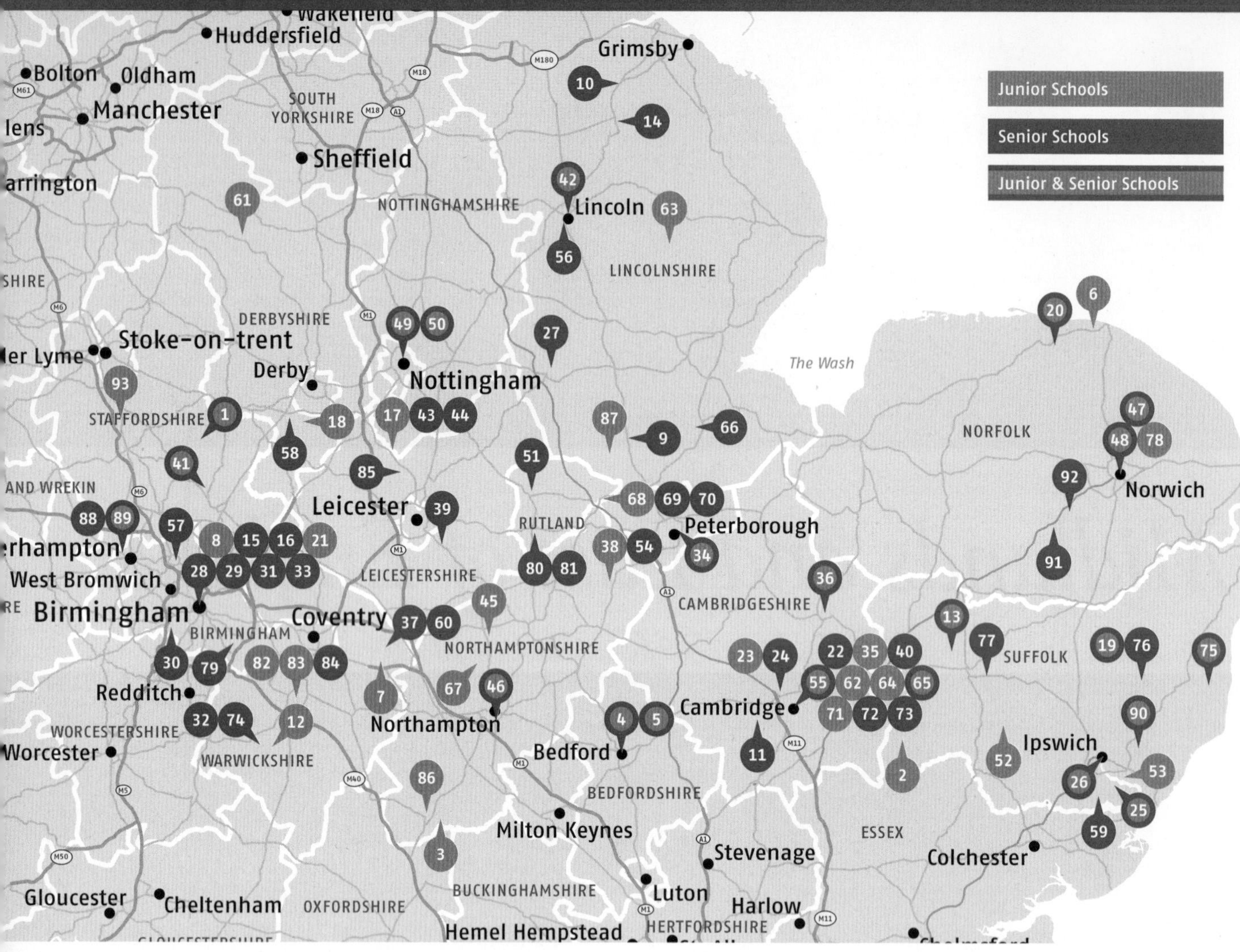

MIDLANDS AND EAST OF ENGLAND

A

Abbots Bromley School

High Street, Abbots Bromley, Nr Rugeley, Staffordshire WS15 3BW

Pupils: 270; 56 boarders (5 boys) • Ages: 3–18 (boarding from 8) • Sixth form: 67 • C of E

Fees: Day: £4,518 – £15,357; Boarding £17,040 – £28,305 pa

Tel: 01283 840232
Email: enquiries@abbotsbromleyschool.com
Website: www.abbotsbromleyschool.com

Executive head: Since April 2017, Maggie Shackleton, currently head of Sutton Coldfield Grammar School since 2010. She takes over from Victoria Musgrave, who was parachuted in to revitalise the school in 2013 after an ISI inspection criticised senior management.

Prep school head: Since 2015, Mrs Wendy Gordon, previously deputy head.

Academic matters: This not a results or league table driven school. Abbots Bromley, referred to affectionately as AB, will not kick a pupil out if her GCSE performance suggests that her A level results will damage the school's ranking. When we asked some girls if that happened at AB they looked amazed and replied with tough logic, 'Of course not, you'd be offered more help and guidance.' There is plenty of advice and help given at AB but one of the advantages of being a small school – there are about 30 in the sixth form – is that it is possible to tailor girls' needs and aspirations to suit them. The recent inspection noted and applauded that. Instead of shoehorning pupils into subject blocks, the school, where possible, builds the curriculum around pupils' choices. At best this approach is seen as inspirational and encouraging and not an opportunity for copping out.

Exam results are commendable for a school which is non-selective; 35 per cent A*/A at GCSE in 2016 and 46 per cent a A level. Girls and teachers seem immensely happy with the opportunities they have to pursue the sciences. In a mixed school these are frequently seen as 'boys' subjects' but here they are pursued enthusiastically. Small classes are greatly appreciated, too. There is a mass of information about subject choices in the excellent booklets that come with the prospectus.

Maths and English are setted for ability but sets are not rigidly static: movement up and down is in response to progress and confidence. Good dyslexia help is available as well as EFL tuition for those 10 per cent who need it. Those we talked to from abroad spoke with genuine fondness of the school, the way in which they had been welcomed and their involvement with dance and other activities. One mother told us of her dyslexic daughter who had struggled agonisingly at her previous school, but once at AB had 'taken off. There's such a wonderful mixture of love and expertise at the school. She's blossomed.' Sixth formers help younger girls with maths and other subjects as a genuine extension of that 'family feeling' as well as points towards their Duke of Edinburgh Award.

Everything at the prep school is achieved within a framework of carefully drawn up curricula and an intelligent timetable. For instance, conversational French is taught from the kindergarten, as is swimming. The school trumpets healthily the fact that the ratio of teacher/pupil is much more generous than government recommendations – but then parents are paying for it. Early years education is seen by those with whom we spoke to be particularly good value for money.

Games, options, the arts: Two unique features of AB are the Alkins School of Ballet and the Equestrian Centre, adding depth and variety to a school experience which is genuinely broad and challenging. Ballet may be fun but, be under no illusion, it requires dedication, with a mixture of sensitive response, physical control and courage. Outstanding results for performing arts and dance BTecs. Vocational dance, by audition, involves about eight hours a week; the alternative is dancing for fun, for a sense of release, for 'enrichment'. Both involve commitment. Several students have gone on to perform professionally via the Royal Academy of Dance and other prestigious schools. The excellent director of ballet, a former examiner with the Royal Ballet, and his wife, a former international ballerina, know that the career of a dancer can be cut short and does not last as long as many professions. For that reason they encourage students to do three A levels along with preparing for their BTec and beyond. 'We want them to have the widest possible choice.' Marvellous equipment – lots of barres and mirrors – but more importantly, fabulous teaching in spacious studios.

The superbly equipped equestrian centre is reached via a beautiful tree lined avenue and clearly has everything a budding rider needs to move on to Olympic honours. Indoor, floodlit outdoor, bring your own horse or hire one of the school's – you name it. Girls may learn to ride from 6 years old and there have been a number of startling successes both at horse shows and with BHS examinations, the top one of which counts for over 100 UCAS points as well as a teaching qualification.

These two activities are more than hobbies: they really do contribute to the well-rounded character of the school. AB is not an academic hothouse nor a school for trendy air heads aspiring to have their pictures in Country Life: it is a school which offers education at its broadest and most stimulating. It challenges and nurtures the brain as well as plugging into a lively, creative life of spiritual freedom and energy, artistic expression involving movement in response to music, what the school calls 'enrichment'. The Renaissance was right to combine horsemanship with learning.

Art is exciting and popular with examples of girls' work all over the place, helping to make the passageways of the original 19th century building less formal and intimidating. Plenty of drama, with plays being written and performed by the pupils themselves in house competitions. One wing of the school is dedicated to music, with over 20 individual practice rooms where girls who are now grandmothers practised scales in the morning after cold showers. Now there are computers for composing on after warm baths, as well as a keyboard studio. Music and singing are very popular, with most girls learning at least one instrument and a much travelled chapel choir – Italy, New York, Paris, San Francisco, Lichfield – and a Cantoria Choir that sings regularly on Radio 4.

Matches against bigger schools (and most are) are played with much zest and skill, with county players in many fields. Another school commented to us, 'Abbots Bromley girls always play with tremendous determination'. 'That's part of the ethos of making the most of our abilities and opportunities,' a pupil told us without a whiff of self-consciousness. Hockey, netball, football, cross-country, tennis, swimming, rounders and athletics are all on offer.

One of the great delights of the Abbots Bromley Prep School adventure is what it calls 'enrichment' (what might more prosaically be referred to as hobbies). There is 'enrichment' before lunch four days of the week, and these periods of serve to alter the tempo of the day and tap into a different part of the psyche. Some activities are charged for, such as riding, dancing (Abbots Bromley, as a whole, is brilliant at both these activities), tennis coaching, speech, music and drama lessons. Members of staff follow their own interests and – the best moments for teachers – share what fires them up. Thus there is craft club, ICT skills, art club, choir, ukulele ensemble (all those little Georgette Formbys!). There are also masses of sporting activities including netball, football, swimming, trampolining and athletics. And you can revisit old haunts by journeying to the sports hall and swimming pool bang next to where the prep school once was.

Boarding: Boarding is increasing in popularity. Younger girls share with three or four others, sixth formers have individual bedsits of a rather higher standard than they are likely to find at university. Girls we spoke to were most enthusiastic about boarding, 'but I can't get my mum to agree,' said one frustrated girl who is stepping up her nights of flexi-boarding. 'Perhaps then she won't notice I'm not at home.' Two free taster nights are included in every term's fees, which means that the great majority of the girls experience boarding from year 3.

Boys' boarding house opened in 2015 to accommodate male sixth formers and students from new AB International College, which 'provides a variety of courses for overseas students'.

Background and atmosphere: The village of Abbots Bromley has a population of fewer than 2000 and was recently cited in the Sunday Times as an outstandingly good place to live. Most of the pupils and teachers at the eponymous school would agree. There are so many listed buildings in the High Street that the village is preserved at its best: handsome, understated and welcoming. The school itself has two sides: in fanciful terms the mind and the spirit. The academic and intellectual side is what you encounter when you enter from the street and thread your way past the large 1960s building, through narrow alleyways separating the 19th century buildings of the original foundation to the visitors' car park and thence to reception and the head. If you drive towards the equine block, however, you come to the sports fields, the huge Astroturf and the stunning view of Cannock Chase. Here, too, is the grass running track where the school recently had to buy new loudspeakers to make announcements heard above the sound of the girls cheering on their housemates and friends.

Originally two schools (St Mary's and St Anne's), AB was the first girls' school in the Woodard Foundation and is one of the oldest girls' public schools in the country. Woodard was unwilling initially to found a girls' school: he couldn't see the point of girls' boarding schools. Various friends, sensing Woodard's blinkered vision, persuaded him to accept the idea and ultimately he allowed Abbots Bromley into the Woodard Foundation. Six years later, on the other side of the street, St Mary's was founded as a less expensive sister school. The Woodard Schools are religious foundations, but Victorian Anglicanism was very class conscious and St Mary's was for the daughters of less wealthy parents. Later ages were more squeamish about such distinctions and in 1921 the two schools on either side of the road became as one. Later they were linked by name as Abbots Bromley School for Girls.

On the St Mary's side of the road there is a splendid injunction to motorists from a bygone age: 'Please do not stand your Motors on This Side of the Road'; on the other side of the entrance is a fiercer notice: 'Private property: no trespassing.' This is the home to the swimming pool, sports hall and medical centre (and previously the prep school, which has now moved across the road to join its big sister). The mixture of senior and junior parts of the school contributes to that sense of affectionate unity that pervades the whole place.

The 19th century builders were generous with the size of their windows. Whatever the original motives for such huge windows – wide open at night, no doubt – they are a delightful addition to the facilities and contribute much to the rooms, which are airy and spacious. The lovely and inviting library is in the process of being made even more attractive, science labs have been improved, IT is efficient and attractively laid out and the boarding facilities are homely and inviting.

The school chapel is, in keeping with Woodard's principles, the most obvious and memorable building. It has height, majesty and atmosphere and will be even more impressive when the lighting is improved. It is clearly central to the atmosphere of the school and though there is no longer daily chapel for all, one or two girls we spoke to told us that they sometimes went to sit there and think. On Fridays the whole senior school attends eucharist and 'it's a wonderful place to sing in.'

The sixth form wing, with its delightful common room, cooking areas and comfortable bedsits, offers an induction into university. As part of the practical preparation for leaving home and school, sixth form girls do some cooking and are responsible for their own laundry.

The facilities of the prep school, back on the main school site, are excellent and the prep school children spoke excitedly – there was a lot of high octane energy around – about the satisfaction of navigating themselves around the building, the sense of being a part of the whole. One or two even volunteered the surprising view that the new set up is an improvement because if it's raining on Thursdays you can go to chapel without getting wet. Godliness and common sense: just what you would expect from a Woodard school.

Girls we spoke to, and how happy they were to talk, expressed huge happiness and delight in their school. 'If I have children,' said one sparky girl, 'I would definitely send them here.' Others nodded in agreement before she added, 'if I could afford it.'

Pastoral care, well-being and discipline: The old adage about family warmth and trust in each other is as true and apparent in AB as any school we have visited. It's partly the size. 'I know every girl in the school,' one happy inmate told us. 'That helps a lot.' Girls and staff greet each other with warmth and interest as they move about. We saw some inspirational teaching born of mutual respect and genuine interest. Classes were lively, active and worthwhile, and outside the classroom the willingness of staff to spend time with the girls and listen, advise or help is much appreciated.

There is much scope for interaction across the age range in the houses, whether it is in the dining room where houses eat together, playing and watching inter-house sport, performing together in plays and concerts, going on outings and trips. Clear anti-bullying policy and girls we spoke to said they felt happy and safe. As far as adults are concerned, girls can turn to their housemistress/ master, form tutor, sixth form mentor 'anyone whom they trust.' Some parents have moved to be nearer the school. That's always revealing.

Pupils and parents: There is a genuine elegance and style about the girls but they are not remotely pretentious or posh. Those we met were forthcoming without being arrogant and were innately courteous and good fun. Many spoke of the joy of being at AB because 'you don't have to pretend to be anything other than yourself'; they didn't feel they would be happier at a school that was co-ed throughout. They love the village and the village seems to love them; dads spoke approvingly of visits, 'do you know of any other school which is bang next door to a jolly good pub?' Mums spoke of the love and support given by the school and the fact that the girls are happily busy and involved. Those parents who were disenchanted by the previous regime are now coming back on board. The Commemoration Day, when the whole school walks down the centre of the High Street in costume and singing hymns, continues. 'We like the tradition: it's slightly mad but great fun.'

B

Entrance: Non-selective into the prep. Every child has talent. 'We accept boys and girls of all faiths and abilities.' Pupils may arrive at any stage, providing there is room. Obviously the start of term is the best time but the school is flexible about that. We met children who joined in the middle of a term and who spoke so happily about the way they had been welcomed in by everyone. Taster days are available.

Most of the girls at the prep school move on to the senior school, for which they are well prepared. Others come from abroad, locally and further afield. Entry is, by and large, non-selective: the school is looking for potential, for girls who will contribute and stretch their potential, for girls who will appreciate the variety of activities on offer.

Sixth form entrants – including boys – are assessed in English, maths and by interview.

Exit: Some 20 per cent leave after GCSEs. A mix of sixth form destinations from Oxbridge to art school to Royal Ballet to Case Western University, USA. Courses range from dentistry to accounting and finance; three medics in 2016. There is no cloning these girls.

Money matters: The school offers scholarships into year 7, year 9, year 10 and year 12 (academic, dance, riding, music, art, sport and children living in the village). Riding and ballet are extras: expect some £800 a term for ballet and stabling around £90 a week. Bursaries may be available. Don't be afraid to ask the bursar.

Remarks: It is surely right to see AB as a special school, a school with delightful idiosyncrasies and unique possibilities; a school which really does nurture individuality, offering unrivalled opportunities to pursue dance, the performing arts, music and riding as well as good academic teaching. In 2014 the school celebrated its 140th anniversary and it is now leaping into the next decade with 'courage braced and faith rekindled.' These are exciting times for an exciting school.

Barnardiston Hall Preparatory School

Barnardiston Hall, Nr Haverhill, Suffolk CB9 7TG

Pupils: 220; 24 full boarders • Ages: 6m–13 (boarding from 7)

Fees: Day £7,830 – £13,050; Boarding £18,045 – £19,575 pa

Tel: 01440 786316
Email: registrar@barnardiston-hall.co.uk
Website: www.barnardiston-hall.co.uk

Headmaster: Since 2012 Tim Dodgson BA (history – London) PGCE (40s). First joined the school as newly qualified teacher in 1992. Moved to Bedford Prep, returning married and with a young family to Barnardiston as head of history and pastoral care. After a brief sojourn as deputy head at Sedbergh, he returned again to Barnardiston as deputy, before stepping into the position of headmaster. His wife, Emma, also teaches at the school and both of their children attended before moving on to senior schools. The family live in the main school building. Has an easy-going manner, calm and a good listener – something of a foil for the principal's more extrovert style. Has no plans to move.

Principal and owner is Colonel Keith Boulter, Cambridge theology graduate and hockey blue (60s). Barnardiston is one of several schools and institutions run as a family business. Was headmaster from 1990, and despite passing the reins of day to day management to Mr Dodgson in 2012, he remains a force in the school, teaching mathematics, helping with games and choir work and followed everywhere by children, like the Pied Piper. Retains a certain bluff, military manner with great geniality and is greeted with wild enthusiasm and respect wherever he goes in the school. 'Who has camped in the garden with their teacher?' he asks. A forest of hands goes up. 'Who acted in the play? ' – hands up again (slightly different lot). 'Who wants more homework?' groans and shouts of 'Not me!' His early career in the Royal Army Educational Corps and, later, administering Gurkha schools, has helped shape the school's philosophy. Married, with a grown-up family, and lives in the grounds of Barnardiston. His daughter is head of the pre-prep department and his three grandchildren all attend the school.

Entrance: Non-selective. Pupils accepted at all stages through the school. A number come up from the nursery (6 months-3 years) to pre-prep. No formal exam but previous school reports are looked at and the children meet the head. Taster days are arranged for older children who attend classes, whilst particular needs are noted, and referrals/advice given to parents. The school has provision for educational support and few children are not accepted. Limited bursarial help for overseas pupils and siblings.

Exit: Most go on to a range of local independents at 13 – the Leys, the Perse, King's Ely, Felsted, Framlingham, Rugby, a sprinkling further afield (Gordonstoun recently). One or two leave at 11 for local state schools. Good guidance is given to parents. 'We suggest they visit three schools, two likely ones plus a wild card,' says the head. Pupils all get to where they want to go – a few scholarships each year.

Remarks: A country prep with a strong, slightly quirky character, very much the creation of its owner, Colonel Boulter. With a rural setting, agricultural rather than chocolate box picturesque, it has a splendid indifference to the customary marketing gloss. Boarders live in the main building, an Edwardian villa, alongside the headmaster and his family.

Subject teaching takes place in the converted stables which surround the courtyard, and the purpose built pre-prep department. A series of Portakabins are still in use, though no one appears bothered; in fact, the pupils see the strengths; as one pointed out in the 'temporary' science lab, 'We never have to worry about dropping liquids on the benches – they are so old!' The decorative theme throughout is inspired by the Colonel's travels including elephants and giraffes, displays from Tutankhamen's tomb, wooden carvings, ornamental ponds and, unexpectedly, two full suits of armour standing guard at the end of a passage.

Indoor sports and ballet take place in a marquee (heated), supposedly temporary but no plans to change this. School has a small theatre with raked seating and facilities for sound and lighting – 'We all learn to do it as well as act' – and productions are all-out efforts of the whole school rather than an elite group. Music, a particular interest of the Colonel, is well taught and popular; around 50 per cent learn an instrument.

No formal gardens or prefects' lawns here; the grounds resemble an adventure playground. Approached by a drive full of potholes ('We know the fees aren't wasted on tarmac,' said a parent, approvingly), skateboarding is allowed, as are tree climbing and den building, there is a miniature railway, a bouncy castle – all tastes catered for. Announcements are made over a PA system, known as the 'bing-bong', that operates all over the school; slightly disconcerting at first, rather like a tube station, but pupils like it and think it is sensible.

A lot of parents are commuters and chose the school 'because the pupils seem so happy and relaxed, very different from London schools,' said one. 'Mine have all made tons of friends and have a crack at anything going,' said another, though also warning that 'it's not a place for namby-pambys.' (We think that remark is directed more at parents than pupils.) Adventure and independence encouraged from the outset with form sleepovers. 'We camped with our teacher in the garden when I was 6!' said one pupil, and this spirit continues up the school. Orienteering very popular (Prep National Champions), camping expeditions, and all team sports played with gusto. Long-awaited Astroturf is now installed. Parents welcome the unfussy attitude but warn: 'If you like things Just So and organised months in advance then it might not suit'.

Classes are small, average 14, and setting begins early in the key subjects. Latin and French from early on, though Latin is dropped in the top three years by some. Those who might struggle in other schools find areas where they can shine. 'The staff are brilliant at building confidence,' say parents, who approve of the less stressful approach. Educational learning support is provided in the special needs department (known as The Bridge). Needs range from an extra boost to cases at the mild end of the autism spectrum, dyslexia and dyspraxia. There is also EFL and support for gifted children. A few children have statements and are LEA funded but the school won't take pupils they cannot help.

Boarding facilities are on the top two floors of the main building. Though approached by a slightly depressing staircase, the facilities themselves are comfortable and homelike. Boys and girls occupy separate floors. Bedrooms, mostly four bedded, are light, well-decorated and some have en suite bathrooms. Rather posh bathrooms in fact – think department store loos – good lighting, warm and clean. Friendly matrons, who remain on duty until the younger boarders, at least, are in bed and asleep. Boys, who form some two-thirds of the boarders, also have a common room on their boarding floor with an enormous screen for weekend viewing. The girls have one in their bedroom but, I was assured, there is no signal so can only be used for DVD watching. Mobiles, for all pupils, are looked after by the school during the day and boarders are allowed to use them for only limited periods. 'Can be hard for some, at first, especially those from abroad, but we want them to join in real life here,' said the headmaster. Weekend outings to local towns/ places of interest are arranged for those, largely from overseas, who stay in school. With notice, it is possible to remain through the half term holidays also. Occasional boarding is popular and encouraged towards the top end of the school, especially for those moving on to board at senior schools.

This is a tremendously jolly school where a sense of adventure is encouraged. Most pupils thrive and go on to do well at senior schools. 'We often hear of former pupils becoming prefects or house heads,' we were told. Perhaps not suitable for those with hearts set on scholarships to the top flight schools, but definitely worth looking at for those who appreciate a less stressful, unstuffy, purposeful atmosphere and a staff dedicated to the needs of its pupils.

Beachborough School

Westbury, Brackley, Northamptonshire NN13 5LB

Pupils: 340; 90 weekly boarders • Ages: 2.5 -13 (boarding from 7)

Fees: Day £10,236 – £16,074 pa; Boarding + £28 – £30 per night

Tel: 01280 700071
Email: office@beachborough.com
Website: www.beachborough.com

Headmaster: Since 2013, Mr Jeremy Banks BA MA (40s), previously deputy head for seven years. Prior to Beachborough, he taught at Dulwich Prep London, where he was director of studies and housemaster. His own mother was a headteacher, and having realised relatively young that he too had a way with children, he subsequently did a degree in education studies and geography at Warwick University and a masters in educational leadership (distinction) at Buckingham. A very visible presence throughout the school, he is smiley, energetic and enthusiastic.

Married to Sophie, who is head of Beachborough's junior department, The Boardman. Also a Warwick graduate (education studies and music) and considered a strong female role model in the school. They have three daughters, all at the school.

Entrance: Main entry (non-selective) in September, but can and will take from any time, with the school having grown by 100 pupils since the start of the recession. An informal 'taster' day, with teacher-led assessments, gives the school some idea of a child's strengths and weaknesses. Every year group has two or three classes with a maximum of 18 per class (three sets for English, French, maths and science from year 3 upwards). Some financial assistance is available for parents in difficulty via means-tested bursary provision.

Exit: Around half of year 8s leave with scholarships and all reach the pass rate for their chosen schools, the most popular of which are nearby Stowe and Bloxham, with others including Oxford High, Akeley Wood, Warwick, Oundle, Millfield and Headington. A few leave at 11 for schools like Royal Latin, nearby grammar.

Remarks: Set in an impressive rambling country mansion, once owned by MP Sir Samuel Scott, the school has a good range of modern blocks surrounding it, the newest of which is a huge sports hall that many senior schools would be proud of. Others include a very good sized school theatre, science block that usually has Bunsen burners in full swing, and a smart Boardroom Building, where children from nursery up to year 4 are based. There's also staff digs, where many of the 40-strong teaching staff live, including head, two deputies and the head of boarding. All the classrooms are light, airy and inviting. The school hasn't always been based here, however, having originally been founded in Folkestone in 1910, after which it moved to Ewell, Purley and then Stockbridge, finally settling three miles from Brackley in 1942.

The fact that the children use the same school entrance as visitors says it all – this school is all about inclusivity. So whilst the reception areas still have the typical 'smart hotel' look of many rural private schools, there's a refreshing emphasis on displaying children's artwork and there are practical touches like the fridge (albeit hidden behind tasteful built-in cupboards)

B

by the front door so pupils can collect anything they've made in cookery lessons on their way home.

Total of 30 acres of lush countryside for pupils to enjoy – and they really do. We happened to visit on a sunny April day and at break-time, children were running and jumping all over the front lawn, but on rainy days they simply don boiler suits and wellies. School has its own farm and sells its own sausages, and there are plenty of dedicated gardens dotted around, including the nursery sound garden and early years vegetable garden. Forest school means you'll often see pupils taking classes outside, and when we visited there was even a replica of a trench in one field. This formed part of the school's 'enrichment week', where the timetable is regularly collapsed so that teachers can focus all subjects on a single topic, in this case World War I.

'Enrichment week' and a few other examples aside, lessons up to year 6 are based on the national curriculum. In addition to core subjects of English, maths and science, all children learn history, geography, French (from age of 5), Latin, religious studies, art, DT, music, computing, drama, PE and games. Years 7 and 8 geared towards CE and scholarship exams. Subject specialists teach children from year 5 upwards. Average class sizes of 14 to 18.

In the past, Beachborough wasn't regarded as very academic. But whilst the previous head referred to it as a 'gentle' school, the current head now prefers the description of 'happy, ambitious and challenging' – a combination that pupils and parents agree pretty much sum up the changes he's brought in, ie encouraging a greater academic focus which stretches pupils, although never aggressively. So whilst year 1's computing lesson might focus on coding and older children can expect lectures from the likes of Professor Matt Jarvis from Oxford University on black holes, you'll also find display walls throughout the school celebrating the efforts of the less academically inclined.

Good provision for those requiring learning support (dyslexia, dyspraxia), via the learning support department. No charge is made for this – nor, incidentally, for tea and prep time after school; before- and after-school care; or most residential school trips, which include a year 2 trip to Amersham, whilst older year groups go to PGL, HMS Belfast, Spain, Paris and the Lake District. There's also a focus on gifted and talented via the school's able child programme. Self-assessment and peer-assessment are priorities and there's a big push for children (especially the gifted and talented) to be encouraged to allow themselves to take intellectual risks with a view to learning from them, rather than getting stuck in the notion that they must achieve the best marks first time.

Sport is central, with some pupils at regional or national level in sports such as trampolining and cricket. But this isn't a school where only top athletes are celebrated. Every child is involved in team games and team photos displayed around the school are not just of the A and B teams, but also the Cs, Ds and Es. Moreover, whatever their level of sports prowess, children get to compete against other schools, enjoying match teas and hearing their names read out in assembly. The school regularly puts out four or five sports teams to play against other schools. Girls play football and cricket too, which one parent says reflects 'how Beachborough isn't a boys' prep school with girls, but a proper, genuine co-ed school,' where incidentally there is pretty much a 50/50 gender split in every year. Swimming club every week at Stowe School's pool, four miles away, and the newest sport in the school is triathlon, in which 30 children take part every Saturday.

Music is big here, with around two-thirds playing an instrument ranging from piano to bassoon, and all year groups have weekly class music in a charming music department at the top of the school. Year 1s and 2s get to try out the violin, recorder and percussion keyboard for 20 weeks before deciding if they want individual lessons. Two choirs, chamber choir and junior choir, for all year 3 and 4 children. Music tours include places like Bruges.

Weekly drama and art classes for all year groups too. Year 8s perform a Shakespeare play every year, while years 7/8, 5/6 and 3/4 also perform annually, with recent examples including Treasure Island and Pirates of the Caribbean Curry Bean. Years 2 and under do a Christmas play. Art – which is overseen by not just a head of art but professional artist – is imaginatively displayed throughout the school, and other activities include Young Enterprise, golf, Mad Science, tennis, archery, craft clubs and dance.

USPs include no Saturday school and a flexible approach to boarding. This includes up to four nights a week, and nearly half the children aged 7+ stay over at least once a week. This is no sleepover, though, with organised activities for boarders, a clear boarding school culture and all the strict rules you might expect, such as bedtime for oldest pupils at 9.15pm and silent reading before lights out. Dorms, which are located on top floor of main school building and which have girls' rooms on one side and boys' on the other, are well kept, welcoming and cheerful, with stunning wall art (Narnia for girls; war planes for boys). Long-serving school matron is based here. As one pupil, said, 'Some of us have never boarded and you don't feel left out because of it.'

Food is popular, with one pudding known as 'bird seed' (Rice Krispies coated in custard) easily the best loved course. Children eat calmly at long wooden tables, with teachers sitting at each end, and grace is said before and after each meal.

The code of conduct is clear, including 'being friendly is easy and it can make the world of difference' and 'always do your best, whatever the challenge.' By and large, the children seem to live by them, with pupils (and indeed parents) saying the school feels like one big family. Bad behaviour taken seriously, with a naughty bench for the younger children (although it's not called that), but the focus is on prevention. Head says that whilst it's natural for children to fall out from time to time, they don't allow this to descend to bullying, which he puts down to an anti-bullying policy, great pastoral care, a focus on rewards for friendly behaviour and the fact that little problems don't grow due to positive interventions. Parents and pupils agree. Active school council, which had just voted in increased choice in school meals when we visited.

The pupil body is almost exclusively white and, besides the 10-15 per cent Americans, almost all English. But this is unsurprising, given that the majority of children are local, with some coming from Towcester, Bicester, Banbury and Milton Keynes. Parents mainly from farming industries, motor racing employees (Silverstone is round the corner) and hedge-fund managers. Lots of family events, with the Beachborough Association putting on things like murder mystery evenings, coffee stops, quiz nights and an annual camp-out on the front lawn, for which tents were starting to appear when we visited.

This is a happy, nurturing school, set in beautiful surroundings that are truly utilised, and run by a dynamic husband and wife team. We found the children to be confident, polite and animated and completely lacking in arrogance. 'I've done things I'd never have thought of – like archery,' said one pupil. 'I love the fact that we're always celebrating people. I've learned that everyone is good at something,' said another.

Parents talk about the 'special atmosphere' and 'emphasis on inclusivity', as well as the 'individual attention that each child gets.' 'This place is a hidden jewel,' says one parent. 'The children are encouraged in whatever direction they want to go and the staff have a way of getting the best out of them.'

Bedford Girls' School

Cardington Road, Bedford, Bedfordshire MK42 0BX

Pupils: 750 • Ages: 7–18 • Sixth form: 200

Fees: £9,036 – £12,699 pa

Tel: 01234 361900
Email: admissions@bedfordgirlsschool.co.uk
Website: www.bedfordgirlsschool.co.uk

Headmistress: Since 2010, Miss Jo MacKenzie BSc MSc (late 40s), previously deputy head of Ipswich High School GDST. She went to school in Australia (her family emigrated there when she was 5) and studied geography and economics at the University of Western Australia. Says teaching has always been a 'real vocation'. When she returned to the UK she did a PGCE at London University's Institute of Education and, later on, an education masters at Leicester University. Began her teaching career at Bromley High, then progressed to Blackheath High, Alleyn's and Ipswich High.

She was appointed head of Dame Alice Harpur School in Bedford in 2009 and a few months later jumped at the chance to take reins at the newly created Bedford Girls' School – formed when Dame Alice Harpur merged with sister school Bedford High. 'It's a fabulous opportunity to combine the best of both schools and decide everything from scratch,' she says. 'It feels like a new school, but with the history of both. The place has a real heart to it.' Under her leadership, the girls have had a say in everything from the school's new name, uniform and emblem (a stylish, swirly eagle) to the curriculum (including thinking skills and international studies in year 9) and the house system.

Head still teaches geography and in her first year acted as a year 7 form tutor too. 'It keeps you in touch with the girls,' she says. A passionate advocate of girls' schools, she points out that 'girls learn differently to boys and thrive in an all-girls' school. They stay on task, they are encouraged to take risks and they learn about leadership. They don't become anything token.' Head has the chicest office we've seen in a long time – all sleek and modern, with a glass desk and huge vase of white lilies. The vast curved office window looks out over the school entrance, so head doesn't miss a trick. Has long-term partner and lives in house on school site. Parents admire her clear vision for the school and say she's warm, approachable and an impressive role model for pupils. Almost as impressively, she runs marathons (her best time is 3 hours 37 minutes).

Head of junior school: Since September 2012, Mrs Carolyn Howe, previously deputy head and acting head of pre-prep at James Allen's Prep School in London.

Academic matters: Around 20 per cent do the IB – average point score a creditable 36 points in 2016. A level results not published separately. Most girls take 11 GCSE subjects – 65 per cent A*/A grades in 2016.

Staff are keen that school should offer lively, innovative teaching and we saw some inspiring lessons, including a philosophy class where year 9s stood in a circle to debate their views on the question 'Is it worth risking your own life for someone you don't know?' Sixth-formers like the fact that the school encourages independent learning while giving them a lot of support. 'The basic ethos here is that the school has high expectations, but in a positive way,' one girl said. 'They want us to do well.' Strong links with Bedford School (boys' school down the road and also part of the Harpur Trust), including joint drama, music, debates and CCF.

Year 7s choose two languages from French, German and Spanish, as well as Latin. Maximum class sizes of 24 in years 7 and 8, but this reduces as girls get older. Full-time SEN co-ordinator tests girls regularly – help for dyslexia and dyspraxia available either one-to-one or in small groups. Providing iPads for all.

Games, options, the arts: Keen to make a name for its sporting prowess. Excellent on-site facilities include a floodlit, all-weather pitch, 12 tennis courts, six netball courts, a gym, fitness suite and sports hall. Nearby new playing fields with club house, six lacrosse/rounders pitches and a community orchard opened in 2016. Indoor pool (decked out with jaunty bunting when we visited) and uses pool at former Bedford High site. Main sports are hockey, lacrosse, netball, cross-country, tennis, rounders and athletics, but rowing is growing rapidly in popularity – shares boathouse on the Great Ouse with other Harpur Trust schools. Up to the age of 16 all girls get at least five hours of sport per fortnight and many do loads more – 'We encourage everyone to be active,' the dynamic head of PE told us. Regularly fields four teams per year against other schools and sometimes six.

New music department is now housed in a former architects' practice bought by the school. When we visited, trumpet soloist Alison Balsom had just performed the school's official opening ceremony. Her message to pupils was to persevere, take risks and not give up if they get knockbacks – inspiring advice. Five choirs (four of them open to all), three orchestras, a dance band – something for everyone. Art, textiles and DT very popular – from drawing, painting, printing and sculpture to digital art and installations. Drama is part of the curriculum up until year 9 and can be taken for GCSE, A level and as part of the IB. When we visited GCSEs were about to begin and drama teacher had brought in a good luck cake for her year 11 students.

Own radio studio – year 10 girls broadcast their own 20-minute programmes (music, interviews, debate) every Wednesday morning. Girls encouraged to get involved in Young Enterprise, Model United Nations and D of E. Extended lunch break from 12.35 till 1.45pm so girls can take part in a wide variety of cross-curricular activities. Pupils in year 7 to 9 expected to do two every week, while year 10s and 11 take one. Activities on offer include everything from designing and building a green-powered electric car to knitting, as well as sport, music, languages, culture, book clubs and CCF.

Background and atmosphere: Both merged schools (Bedford High School for Girls and Dame Alice Harpur) founded in 1882, part of the Harpur Trust, a charity benefiting from the legacy of Sir William Harpur, a Bedford merchant who became Lord Mayor of London in 1566, and his wife, Dame Alice. In May every year Bedford Girls' School (owned, managed and supported by the Harpur Trust) celebrates the school's birthday and commemorates Sir William Harpur's generosity. Dame Alice Harpur School moved to present Bedford Girls' School site in 1938 – on the banks of the Great Ouse and a short walk from the town centre. The charity took the decision in 2009 to 'rationalise their provision of education in Bedford to one independent girls' school, one boys' school, one co-educational school and a pre-preparatory school', and so Bedford Girls' School was born.

One parent told us that Dame Alice Harpur (where his daughter was originally) had always been 'very good at making girls feel they can achieve and succeed,' and that the ethos is the same following the merger – 'It has helped my daughter to be organised, confident and happy,' he said. Junior school opened in 2010, senior school in 2011 and whole sixth form in 2012. Has launched house system – very popular with girls, six houses (Austen, Franklin, Parks, Nightingale, Hepburn and Chanel) named after inspirational women. House meetings every two weeks, lots of inter-house competitions and a cup presented at the end of the year.

The girls also helped to come up with the new school's values – which encourage them to be 'bold, imaginative and reflective'. Parents say the merger has been handled well, but admit that integrating two schools 'takes time'. They were rivals in the old days and some girls have stuck with their friendship groups. But new school ran a raft of integration activities in the early days of the merger and they seem to have worked pretty well. Sixth-formers we talked to showed a fierce loyalty to the new school and said they'd almost forgotten who was where before.

The junior school is in a large Victorian house opposite the senior school, with delightful gardens and brightly decorated classrooms. Individual iPads now issued to all and used throughout the curriculum. Enhanced curriculum inspired by philosophy of the IB. Strong links with the senior school, with sixth formers popping over the road to help juniors with their reading. Parents we spoke to were full of praise for the way the transition from the junior to the senior school is handled. Year 6 girls go to the senior school for science lessons and take part in a host of activities there. 'It felt like a very natural transition,' one mother told us. 'There were no nerves on my daughter's part by the time she got to year 7. She was raring to start.'

Sixth form girls get an assortment of privileges and responsibilities. They wear smart grey business suits and have their own sixth form garden, plus a café serving coffee, sandwiches and hot food. Open from 8am till 3pm and decked out with metal chairs and a black and white tiled floor, it looks like an upmarket brasserie. Sixth form also gets its own common room – the girls take it in turn to choose the music at break-time (JLS when we visited). Has had substantial revamp with silent study area, described as 'light, contemporary space' for work and rest, also added. Twelve sixth formers voted on to leadership group each year, including head girl, two deputies and house captains. The cohort we met were full of ideas to help incoming sixth formers, including a personal welcome letter, bonding days and a blog. School council consisting of form captains and reps meets once a term. Whole school assemblies held twice a week, as well as year group assemblies too.

Pastoral care, well-being and discipline: Each senior school form has a form tutor – girls keep the same form tutor in years 10 and 11 and all the way through the sixth form. Uniform of grey skirt, white blouse, damson jumper and blazer to age of 16, but the head has removed 'petty' rules. Shoes no longer have to be lace-ups, hair doesn't have to be tied back (apart from in science and practical subjects) and pupils are allowed to bring mobile phones into school (junior girls must hand them into their teacher). Behaviour isn't an issue here. Sanctions range from lunchtime detentions through to suspension and expulsion, but the latter haven't been required since the merger. 'The girls aren't goody-goodies, but they want to learn,' says the head. The pupils agree – 'Everyone is quite grown up here,' one told us.

Pupils and parents: Girls come from all over (from as far afield as Luton, Milton Keynes, Northampton, Cambridge, St Neots and St Albans) – by car, train and a network of school buses. Some parents make considerable sacrifices to send their daughters here. 'A few come from fancy backgrounds,' one mother told us, 'but everyone mixes in together.' Communication with parents is good – full report or parents' evening each term, and progress sheets sent home in the October half-term. Parents can ring daughters' heads of year any time – 'It's as little or as much contact as parents would like,' says head. PTA organises a plethora of events, including quizzes, parties and a fundraising ball for 300.

Old girls include the late fashion designer Jean Muir and former world champion badminton player Gail Emms.

Entrance: Not ultra-selective. Prospective junior school pupils attend an assessment day, where skills in writing, reading and maths are assessed (separate assessments for entry into years 3, 4, 5 and 6). They also take part in art, science and a circle group discussion in a second round.

Main senior school entry points are in year 7, year 9 and sixth form – via interview, assessment and report from previous school. Prospective pupils have informal January interview in small groups with the head – 'I'm looking for girls who enjoy learning, girls who have a joie de vivre,' she says – and return a couple of weeks later for exams in English, maths and verbal reasoning. Half of the year 7 intake comes from Bedford Girls' School's own junior school (parents we spoke to were full of praise for the way the transition from the junior to the senior school is handled). The others come from a vast range of state primaries and preps. Ten to 15 new girls join sixth form every year – they need five GCSEs at A*-B (and at least Bs in subjects they want to take for A level or IB).

Exit: Nearly all junior girls move up to the senior school. Loses a few pupils at 16 – some 20 per cent in 2016 – girls who want boarding or subjects not offered by the school. After A level/IB, 95 per cent go to university, including many Russell and 1994 Group. Popular subjects include medicine, biosciences, physics, English and history. Sixth formers told us they felt well supported by their tutors and the careers department in organising work experience, making university choices and the UCAS process.

Money matters: No scholarships (would rather reward excellence via prize-giving at speech day). A number of means-tested bursaries available for academically strong pupils whose parents would otherwise not be able to send them to the school.

Remarks: The merger has got off to an impressive start and the new Bedford Girls' School buzzes with energy, enthusiasm and innovation. A lot of good schools in and around Bedford, but this one looks set to hold its own.

Bedford School

De Parys Avenue, Bedford, Bedfordshire MK40 2TU

Pupils: 1,059; 230 full and weekly boarders • Ages: 7–18 • Sixth form: 258 • C of E

Fees: Day £11,682 – £18,027; Boarding £19,815 – £30,489 pa

Tel: 01234 362216
Email: admissions@bedfordschool.org.uk
Website: www.bedfordschool.org.uk

Head Master: Since 2014, Mr James Hodgson (40s), educated at Wellington College and Durham (classics) before being scooped up on the milk round by Ernst and Young and spending a couple of years as a trainee accountant. In his 20s a cricketer hovering around the fringes of the professional game – and uninspired by the world of finance – wrote to Cambridge on the off-chance of a late place on its PGCE course and turned up trumps, meaning he could pursue his long term ambition of running a boarding house as well as playing regular top class cricket, ultimately earning a blue.

Spent six years teaching in Sydney before joining Tonbridge School as boarding housemaster and director of admissions. Latterly senior deputy head of Magdalen College School, Oxford. Impressed on joining Bedford by the boys 'completely at ease' with the staff and each other – 'presenting awards in my first assembly, every single boy shook my hand, looked me in the eye, smiled and said thank you – quite something for a large group of teenagers,' he says. At peace with Bedford not quite hitting the dizzy academic heights of Magdalen but plans to up the ante a little 'for pastoral reasons – results are just a passport to the next level'. Passionate about boarding ('it develops the whole person') and ready to take on the challenge of keeping it thriving at Bedford. Parents feeling the effect of this already with the recent introduction of a full schedule of celebrations for leavers, including their own speech day followed by house events and a leavers' ball – 'a fitting end to a super education,' in the words of one.

Youthful, energetic and 'really personable,' according to parents – not just a safe pair of hands for parents to hand their sons to, but dynamic, likeable and inspiring. Accessible to pupils – has open door for a period each morning where pupils can come to discuss anything. Presence at matches and performances (with the occasional personal note of congratulations to performers afterwards) noted and appreciated by all. Married to Rachel, with four teenage children.

Head of prep school: Since 2013, Ian Silk (40s), previously deputy head of Bishops Stortford Junior School and former housemaster at Ardingly College. An English and drama specialist, brims with enthusiasm about all aspects of the school – most particularly the spectacular new theatre (2015) shared with the upper school and the town. Married to Sarah, with two sons both at the school – 'they are chalk and cheese,' he told us, 'but the school is brilliant for both of them.' Knows most boys by name – lots of heads do but this is a large prep – and has lunch with all new joiners in small groups.

Academic matters: Solid academics, especially given broad church intake and large proportion who joined at 7+. 2016 saw 60 per cent of GCSEs graded A*/A; 54 per cent A*/A at A level and 80 per cent A*-B, with an average IB score of 36 out of a possible 45 – testament to a focused and dynamic teaching staff ('second to none,' said one happy parent).

English and maths set from outset but rejigged along the way. Class sizes capped at 24, shrinking to a pleasing eight or nine for many A level subjects. All take 10 GCSEs, with around 30 per cent taking four full A levels in year 13 (mostly including further maths). Boys opt for either A levels or IB in sixth form. IB numbers 'a bit low' according to head with just over 15 per cent currently opting to take this route. School aims to boost numbers to around a third of the cohort.

Well thought out curriculum with separate sciences and all boys learning at least two languages. Maths and sciences extremely popular options at A level as well as good take up in geography ('a very good department,' says head) and economics. German, Spanish, French and Latin on offer in the languages department, with Mandarin available as a twilight option, but rather low take up of these at A level. PPE an interesting offer in year 10 and parents praised standard of 'inspirational' RS teaching.

Dedicated SENCo in prep school with two supporting specialists and strong emphasis on training whole staff to support individual needs (mild dyslexia and dyspraxia; a few with mild Asperger's). Around 20 boys receiving support. Close communication with upper school a great strength: 'we hand parents and children over individually so nothing falls between the gaps,' SENCo assured. Boys with SEN (mainly mild dyslexia or dyscalculia) given bespoke care in upper school with the department tailoring help according to each boy's individual needs. Strong ESOL team caters for overseas students, who are offered extra English language sessions in place of another language and about half of them take IGCSE ESL instead of English.

Head acknowledges lack of strong articulation of sixth form – super facilities abound at Bedford yet no dedicated centre for years 12 and 13. Parents identified career support as an area in need of improvement – 'so much more that they could do' – and recent appointment of dedicated UCAS and careers specialist hopes to raise school's game in this area. UCAS application process highly praised, with parents barely needing to get involved in the process: 'exactly as it should be', although head hopes to up future Oxbridge numbers.

Games, options, the arts: Prep has a fully inclusive approach to sport, putting out as many as 18 competitive teams for fixtures, so everyone gets a ride on the bus and a post-match tea at least once a term, whatever their ability. Sport is the lifeblood of Bedford and although the list of recent accolades is too long to list (in all sports from rugby and cricket to swimming and golf), senior school also maintains it's not just for the elite and says it offers all boys 'the same time on task' when it comes to training – the input and expertise from the directors of all major sports filtering down to even the lowliest of teams.

Are less gifted boys afforded the same kudos as the macho sporty crowd, we asked one sixth former? Apparently yes, since the introduction in recent years of colours for art, drama and academia in addition to sport – a welcome addition signified by a colourful array of scarves – and special striped blazers for those awarded cricket colours. Parents, too, concur that school 'absolutely allows boys to be all-rounders'. It's a rugby, hockey, cricket school – with strong rowing too (how many schools have their own boat house on a beautiful stretch of the river Ouse?) but plenty of other options to choose from: you name it and Bedford offers it, from archery or rifle shooting to pilates and fencing. National and international honours in all main sports plus golf and fencing, and boys have gone on to play for their universities and even their country in most sports played at Bedford, where the main challenge for staff is finding competitor schools strong enough to give them a good game.

Music of a 'fantastic calibre' according to parents, with a state of the art, super modern music centre – designed by award-winning architect Eric Parry and apparently positioned opposite the pavilion so that the director of music can keep one eye on the cricket scoreboard whilst conducting the school orchestra. Hugely popular (and, crucially, non-selective) junior choir, plus chapel choir for years 5 and up, as well as instrumental lessons on curriculum for years 3 and 4. Choirs, orchestras and bands a-plenty in the senior school, a brand new music technology suite, gleaming new fleet of iMacs (2014), a recording studio (Desert Island Disks with the head a recent highlight), rock room and inspirational recital hall – used for weekly performances by pupils and recitals from visiting professionals. Something for everyone and parents say even the most reluctant musician is inspired to join in. School's enthusiasm for making music illustrated by wild enthusiasm (parents and boys) for the annual house music, 'the best competition of the year,' by all accounts, which sounds like a cross between 20/20 cricket with boys, faces painted and fancy dressed, raucously chanting and cheering on their housemates, and young musician of the year ('as soon as the singing starts, everyone is silent,' explained our guide).

Possibly the most stunning theatre we've seen in any school opened in 2015, built on the site of a former Moravian Church, with original features sympathetically included to complement the modern architecture – all exposed brick and floor to ceiling glass. Shared with the town, and able to seat over 280, the theatre not only hosts school productions (recently Shakespeare's The Comedy of Errors by the prep and Henry V by the upper), often in conjunction with Bedford Girls' School, but also productions by visiting companies. A full-time technical director takes care of special effects and shows boys the ropes with lighting and scenery.

Super work of exceptional quality, themed to ignite passionate creativity amongst the all-male cohort by their inspiring male head of art (who doubles up as games teacher), festoons the interiors of the junior school. We loved the Viking shields crafted in DT and the fabulous gargoyle masks produced in year 8 art. Not a still life in sight. Outstanding work on show in the senior art and DT departments, with some mind-blowing projects on display in the year 13 workshop – no wonder so many move on to study engineering at university.

A non-stop merry-go-round of extracurricular activities keeps boys busy outside of the classroom. In the space of one lunch time we watched junior boys hunting for creepy crawlies in bug hotels, singing with gusto in the junior choir, planing chess boards in the DT suite, creating games in the ICT suite, building sets for the school play, having a good old fashioned kick about. Options in the upper school range from public speaking to a very popular CCF in all three branches, run in conjunction with Bedford Girls'. Trips and tours galore for all manner of interests from sports tours to choir trips, academic excursions and – occasionally – just for fun.

Boarding: Junior boarding in purpose-built Eagle House for up to 32 boys from year 3 and up, although most start after year 5 as either flexi, full or weekly boarders. A real home from home feel, thanks in no small part to super houseparent couple, as well as plenty of nicely furnished, comfy spaces with lots of personal touches for boys to hang out after school hours. Spacious dorms sleep between four and eight boys, who make them their own with pictures, posters and duvet covers from home. When prep's finished (supervised, in dedicated room for all bar the year 8s), there's a homely common room equipped with computers, a kitchen for snacking and a basement games room with table football and pool on offer. Where boys find the time to use these facilities, though, is anyone's guess, as there's also a full programme of after-school activities each day to take advantage of. Mobiles and other gadgets allowed but must be put on charge in the prep room overnight.

Around half the junior boarders are either Forces or overseas (from mainly Russia, China and Spain), so there are plenty around at weekends once Saturday school (compulsory for all from year 6) and Sunday chapel are out of the way, to enjoy outings ranging from go karting or high ropes to bowling or the cinema, often followed by a takeaway or one of the housemaster's legendary barbecues.

Six senior boarding houses – four on site and two just a short walk away – offer intimate and cosy homes from home for the 40 per cent of upper school boys who board here. Charming in that none are purpose built, the houses are adapted Victorian villas, each with its own character – all with a fraternity house feel. Described as 'an extension of the housemaster's home', the houses are bright and spacious, with reassuringly untidy dorms (we secretly approve – boys must feel at home to be quite so slovenly) and the kinds of communal spaces day boys would probably die for (Xboxes, pinball machines, pool tables, chess tables – you name it). In keeping with rest of the school, modern facilities are juxtaposed with traditional artefacts (shiny fleets of computers beneath panelled honours boards) and boys have the freedom to come and go during the course of the day. Masters describe the boys as 'like brothers', one commenting that 'there's nothing better than seeing a huge sixth former strolling to breakfast chatting to one of the year 9s'. Many boarders are former day boys fed up with the daily commute – parents love the fact that boys can 'grow with the school'.

Over 65 per cent of boarders are there full time so plenty of buzz at weekends, with regular trips and outings as well as free run of sports facilities and time for valuable R&R. Compulsory Saturday school for all.

Background and atmosphere: Don't be put off if you approach Bedford from the M1 via a somewhat grotty suburban high street, at the end of which you catch first glimpse of the school like an oasis in the architectural desert. School takes great pains to remind us of 'the other half' of Bedford which lies behind it – smart rows of Victorian villas (two boarding houses among them) leading down to a beautiful river bank. The school itself has the feel of a university campus about it – the buildings, a delightful mix of old and new, surround the manicured playing fields. The main building is all turrets, spires and a bell tower, with a magnificent hall as the central point and classrooms on four levels.

Impossible to choose a stand-out feature or department as each and every addition to the school has been made with care and deliberation to fuse function and form effectively. From the professional-looking cricket pavilion to the super modern glazed music school (who could fail to be inspired in here?), stunning library full of gleaming new books – but with the antique ones carefully displayed – and the cottage-like art building, set in its own sculpture garden, the whole campus gives the aura of a school offering roundedness in the purest sense of the word. The word chapel doesn't quite do justice to the glorious building where weekly services are held – the school accommodated amongst panelled walls inscribed with war memorials of fallen OBs.

Prep school 'nicely contained' in a corner of the vast Bedford School campus, one of its main benefits is that it enjoys unfettered access to the wealth of facilities of the upper school – as well as a fair few of its own. Classrooms ranging from the antiquated 'Inky' (incubator for fledgling Bedfordians) to more modern purpose-built additions sit around a central Astro play area where boys let off steam at break times. A boys' own paradise which simultaneously feels separate from and integral to the upper school and offers everything young boys could hope for, whatever their interests.

Sports facilities unsurprisingly top notch. Super weights room would give most private gyms a run for their money and there's a 25 metre swimming pool (reportedly 'rather chilly but nobody minds,' according to our guide). Recent refurb and renovation of tennis courts and cricket pavilion (2014) – opened by England captain and Old Bedfordian, Alastair Cook.

Pastoral care, well-being and discipline: 'Zero tolerance' anti-bullying policy in the prep school with clear protocol in place for inevitable – albeit rare – lapses. 'We show as much understanding to both sides as possible,' says housemaster. School counsellor available for boys to use for anything from home sickness to help with social skills.

Brotherly atmosphere in upper school helped twofold by small houses with a family feel and vertical tutor groups where boys can get to know others from all year groups, with the tutor being the first port of call in the event of a problem. Head describes school as 'a fantastic community,' with everyone pitching in to help with greater problems relating to mental health or general well-being should the need arise, and parents describe the way boys support each other through the inevitable occasional difficulty as 'magic to watch'. Teachers available to parents via email, with responses to queries and concerns flying back through the ether at great speed.

'Strong discipline makes a place happier', says head, and major transgressions are dealt with by the amusingly – and aptly – named vice master. Strict protocols followed in relation to serious misdemeanours with repeated conduct warnings leading to detentions. 'Absolutely no leniency' when it comes to dealing with drugs, either inside or out of school, says head. Timetable collapsed five times each year to focus on PSHCE with age appropriate focus on drugs, internet safety etc.

Pupils and parents: Parents say they have never met a Bedfordian they didn't like – their trademark being an ability to mix with all age groups with an easy, understated confidence. Many OBs in parent cohort, which is healthy mix of traditional types and first time buyers – lots of professionals commuting into London. Buses from Luton, Milton Keynes and Hitchin and easy access from Harpenden by train makes for a broad catchment, with the majority living within 40 miles of school and commuting for up to an hour. Just over 15 per cent overseas boys from 24 countries across Europe, Asia and Russia.

Entrance: Mainly at 7+, 8+ and 11+ into the prep. Not heavily oversubscribed but looking for the right fit, ability to keep up and fully participate in school life. 'At 7 some boys might not be there yet,' says head, 'but we encourage them to try again later.' Assessments in English, maths, NVR, creative writing, an in-school day – and that all-important report from current head. Large contingent from nearby pre-prep and fellow Harpur Trust member Pilgrims and around 30 per cent from local state schools.

One hundred and forty boys join year 9 with about 60 per cent of these moving up from the prep. Some 50 additional places for those coming from other preps (Aldwickbury, Beechwood Park, Kingshott, Lockers Park major feeders) and state schools. School sets own online entrance examination at 13+. A few extra places at 14+ then about 25 more into sixth form, when hopefuls will need six good GCSEs to go on to do A levels (at least Bs in the subjects to be studied; A grades in maths and sciences). Not ferociously competitive for day boys but boarding places are at more of a premium.

Overseas pupils often offered places conditional to taking ESL, billed as an extra.

Exit: Almost all transfer from the prep to the upper school with the odd exception departing for the state sector or, for international boarders, their mother country. No prep for CE or formal advice on other destination schools, but existing pupils sit the same test as external candidates for setting purposes. Parents report a seamless transition to upper school, with boys better prepared for workload than those joining from other preps.

About 10 per cent head to pastures new post-GCSE. Good range of destination universities for those that stay on, with a handful to Oxbridge most years (seven to Oxbridge in 2016) and around 75 per cent to Russell Group – Warwick, Sheffield, Imperial College and Durham feature heavily, with majority going on to study heavyweight academic subjects – lots of sciences and a few to medicine each year (one in 2016). Small numbers opt for creative options or languages.

Money matters: At a shade under the £30K mark for full boarding, relative value for a school of this calibre in comparison with the competition. Good clutch of scholarships and bursaries for entry into years 7, 9 and 12, with art recently added to the list and golf scholarships in conjunction with nearby Woburn Golf Club. Generous – up to 35 per cent of fees, non-means tested, up for grabs 'for boys with exceptional talent' – and buoyant reserves in the hardship fund. Just under 200 boys across the school currently hold awards, with around 10 per cent of these on 100 per cent.

Part of the Harpur Trust but financially independent and benefiting from an extremely active and benevolent OB network.

Remarks: A rare beast – an uncompromisingly single sex school offering flexible day and boarding options without losing its traditional public school appeal. Thriving and successful, with happy pupils and happy parents – a place where all boys can hit their personal best, whether it's on the sports field, in academia or in the arts. Understated confidence and purposefulness abounds. A school of established excellence ready to be taken to the next level by dynamic newish head. All in all, a really super option for those looking for top notch day or boarding – as long as your sights are firmly set on an all-through education at Bedford.

Beeston Hall School

West Runton, Cromer, Norfolk NR27 9NQ

Pupils: 113; 60 full, 14 weekly/flexi boarders • Ages: 4-13

Fees: Day £7,500 – £16,950; Boarding £18,750 – £23,000 pa

Tel: 01263 837324
Email: office@beestonhall.co.uk
Website: www.beestonhall.co.uk

Headmaster: Since September 2016, Fred de Falbe, previously head of St Richard's School in Herefordshire. Began his teaching career aged 18 in Honduras, before gaining a BA in theology at Manchester University and a PGCE from London. Joined the film business, later going back to teaching after a year in Australia. Since then he has worked in state secondary schools in London and Devon and been deputy head at Knightsbridge School. Married to Juliet, a keen rider who has built up a business in renewable energy; they have three children.

Entrance: Non-selective. Pupils mostly join in year 3, transferring from local state or pre-prep schools, but numbers increase steadily throughout the school with year 8 the largest year group. Discount for two siblings or more. Older pupils attend an informal assessment day. Can accommodate mild to moderate learning difficulties but all must be able to follow the curriculum. Not for those with behavioural problems. Has now opened a pre-prep for reception upwards.

A plethora of scholarships (up to 20 per cent of fees) offered for academic excellence, art, music, sport and general all-round ability for all ages, plus means-tested bursaries and in-house help for parents who fall on hard times. Sibling discounts if three or more children are at the school at the same time.

Exit: Nearly all stay to the end of year 8, the majority going on to out of county boarding schools – recently to Rugby, Ampleforth, Eton, Harrow, Oundle, Stowe, Tudor Hall and Uppingham; some to Gresham's and Norwich School. Careful guidance is given and pupils all get where they want to go and win a good clutch of awards in the process – the 20 leavers in 2016 gained 13 scholarships.

Remarks: Despite roughly equal numbers of day and boarding pupils, the school retains a strong boarding feel; the way the day is structured means many day pupils remain into the evening for activities and supper (no extra charge), and very often the pupils themselves want to change: 'My son began as a day pupil, saw the fun and wanted to board – it was his decision,' said one mother. A predominance of pupils are from

B

county boarding families, know what to expect and settle quickly: 'The atmosphere is so welcoming and friendly, lots to do'; 'Older pupils look after younger ones; it is not hierarchical at all.' They make friends for life: 'Friends last beyond senior school stage'; 'My daughter has done her gap year travel with [Beeston] friends.'

Lots stay in at weekends (35 is usual) and there are regular exeats, at least once each side of half term. The recent introduction of flexi boarding on designated nights is popular, though full boarding remains the choice of many, especially higher up the school; by year 8 virtually all are boarding full time. Parents chorus approval for the way pupils are prepared for senior schools: 'By the time my son left, he had developed the confidence to cope in a much bigger school'. Year 8s have their own house, with a kitchen for making toast, and a common room. This slight separation encourages a maturity of outlook and helps with the transition to senior schools.

The children create a good impression. Respectful but, at ease, good relations with staff ('none of that giving them The Look', as one mother put it), unforced good manners, standing up for visitors and holding doors open, for each other as well as adults. Traditional lunch (served at tables, with grace and passing the water jug) for the whole school, including staff, daily organised games and lots of off-duty playtime punctuate the day. No prep before year 6, 'developing a good reading habit matters most,' then 20 minutes a day, increasing in year 8 especially for scholarship hopefuls.

Idyllic setting, close to North Norfolk coast and nearby NT Felbrigg estate. Sweeping lawns and a Regency house are the centre of a mixture of newer builds, extensive sporting, music and art facilities. Everything spick and span with notices such as 'please walk ON the grass' and 'why not hold the door for someone?' Walls crammed with details of daily happenings, pupils' work, art, photographs and achievements. Dog-friendly site, some in class with their owners (staff) or spectating matches.

Small, mixed-ability classes until year 4, then setting for English, maths, science and languages. French starts in year 3, Latin from year 6 and Greek in years 7 and 8 for some. The year 8 scholarship form gives intensive preparation for those in the running for senior school awards, focussing on individual requirements rather than hothousing a group. Parents feel standards have improved, staff flag problems straight away via emails or the tutors, and setting is genuinely flexible. Regular effort grades, reports and consultations, but staff are always available for informal chats.

An educational support unit based in an attractive suite of rooms, with excellent interactive displays and hard to resist games, is run by a sparkling and vivacious teacher who makes attending a session fun and a privilege; 'we have drop-in sessions and parties and children really do see coming here as a treat'. Pupils agree, with roughly a quarter receiving help of some sort, usually in English and maths.

A well-designed and stocked library with wonderful squashy sofas to recline on is staffed throughout the day, including breaks and lunchtime. Pupils have timetabled library lessons for changing books and quiet reading. Art is taught in a barn-style studio with a mezzanine floor devoted to pupils creating a portfolio of scholarship work. Each has their own desk and work area and can come and go when they have spare time, leaving work in progress where it is, undisturbed. Music is one of the school's strengths with 90 per cent of pupils receiving instrument tuition in timetabled lessons. There are excellent facilities, rehearsal and practice rooms and a host of different choirs, bands and ensemble groups. Great encouragement, with all pupils joining the junior choir and auditions gradually introduced in the higher forms. Concerts, small and larger staged events, take place throughout the year and all pupils get a lot of performance experience.

All the usual team sports, and one of the benefits of being a relatively small school is that 'everyone gets regular match play,' said a parent. Games are played every afternoon. Pupils also sail on the nearby Broads (own fleet of Toppers) and can have shooting instruction (prep league champions). Plenty of choice for after-school and weekend activities: fencing, beach picnics, fashion shows, cookery club, trips to local attractions such as Bewilderwood, theme days and Beeston's got Talent, now a well-established contest. Charmingly, the highlight of the week for many pupils remains the visit of the ice-cream cart 'in the summer months.

A traditional, but not hidebound, country prep with vitality and warmth and a well-deserved reputation for nurturing its pupils, who are ' friendly and confident, willing to give things a try'. Given a solid grounding, Beestonians go on to do well and make the most of their senior schools.

Bilton Grange School

Rugby Road, Dunchurch, Rugby, Warwickshire CV22 6QU

Pupils: 293; 100+ boarders • Ages: 4-13 (boarding from year 4)

Fees: Day £9,510 – £18,345; Boarding £23,190 – £24,990 pa

Tel: 01788 810217
Email: admissions@biltongrange.co.uk
Website: www.biltongrange.co.uk

Headmaster: Since 2013, Mr Alex Osiatynski (30s), previously director of music of the Loughborough Endowed Schools foundation. Educated at Dulwich College and Oxford; PGCE at Roehampton. Has also taught music at Gresham's, The British School in the Netherlands, Smithdon High and Oakham. Married to Freya, with two young sons.

Entrance: Non-selective but placement test and interview for candidates – academic potential looked for (aim is to find something at which each child can excel). When spaces available children can enter at any time. Typically two form entry in pre-prep and three forms in older years, roughly 60:40 boys to girls.

Exit: Majority to senior boarding schools. Popular destinations include: Rugby (about 50 per cent), Uppingham, Repton, Oakham, Bloxham and Oundle, with typically some 10 scholarships a year, including Foundation ones to nearby Rugby School. Odd grumble that school is not well disposed to those who flee Bilton at 11; school's defence is that early leavers miss out on scholarships, responsibilities and the excitement of the final year, including cementing life-long friendships. Plus side is that occasional places appear for those from schools that finish at 11.

Remarks: Main school, decorated and extended by Pugin in the 1840s, consists of an elegant mansion complete with grand entrance bordered on two sides by high red-brick walls, stunning Pugin chapel used almost daily (all children, irrespective of faith, expected to attend) and superb, uninterrupted views across the Warwickshire countryside. Inside, the trappings of 21st century classrooms and teaching blend seamlessly with classic wood panelled halls (teeming at break-times with earnest youngsters playing chess and snooker), acres of windows, tiled floors and creaking floorboards.

Looks, feels and is a traditional 24/7 country prep, with good old-fashioned values, frequent assemblies and, in line with its boarding ethos, full Saturdays (from Y4). Pitches, playing fields, a nine-hole golf course, large sports hall and well-maintained swimming pool make this a haven for the sporty, yet even the most studious child would be hard-pressed to dismiss the Bilton outdoors. Intrepid explorers are free to investigate the 100 acres of grounds and woods, grow their own veg in the organic garden, participate in outdoor crafts or toast marshmallows on the fire pit – even an outdoor classroom complete with log benches and swings – all duly risk-assessed.

Sport and the open air are a major constituent of school life, but the arty are abundantly catered for. The director of music is boosting quality and quantity of music (most play at least one instrument but aim is to involve all) – choirs, concerts, bands and orchestras perform regularly; drama is consistently strong and popular, with the creative arts and DT abiding favourites. Activity weeks are emphatic highlights of the school year; our guides jabbered enthusiastically about the posse of daredevil activities – climbing, canoeing, 24-hour survival – and jolly japes: mud diving, arm jousting and mandatory dorm raids.

The work hard, play hard ethos is tangible, but pressure isn't. Even in the final year prep is completed in school, a conscious move by the school to keep a lid on what can be a difficult and demanding time. Small classes, some setting in prep and wide curriculum for all – even tinies are treated to drama, dance, ICT and French. All try Latin. No weak lessons. RE popular (do ask about WOW), maths divides, reading is ably supported by good teaching, knowledgeable librarian and well-stocked library. We were treated to two science lessons (loved the lively informative posters, the work of artistic scientists, adorning the modern labs), a lively whizz and bang session and a traditional chalk and talk, perhaps typifying the breadth of approaches and styles. Indeed, we were reliably informed, by our young tour guide, 'Teachers look at the type of learner you are such as audio [sic], visual etc and try to teach you in that way'.

No BG mould – former pupils include humorist Miles Kington, actor Alexander Hanson, composer Sir Arthur Bliss (organ on which he learned to play fully restored and in regular use) and film star Rupert Evans, but BG children are easily identified by their impeccable manners: they ask to be excused from the table, shake your hand, look you in the eye ('We practise that,' say staff), stand when an adult enters the room and speak with confidence, interest and knowledge but no tinge of arrogance. Universally good rapport between staff and pupils; school exudes warmth. It's a lovely, cosy environment to grow and be a child in and, 'regardless of ability, they get best out of them,' say parents.

Can cater for a range of needs, particularly the dys-strata and ADD, but nothing heavyweight – 'My child is dyslexic but I always felt they were delighted to have him, no sense they were doing us a favour'. Takes a genuinely broad church, celebrates diversity, welcomes and looks after all. 'Learning support staff are so fab, so lovely and so helpful,' said one delightful, delighted youngster, but odd parental mumble that knowledge of SEN across core teaching staff is patchy.

Parents praise pastoral care, 'Staff are good at setting boundaries and stamping on transgressions before they become serious'. Boarding houses are light, bright and comfortable. Communal areas offer TV, gaming, board games and jigsaws. Facilities and rooms (up to nine per dorm) clean and cosy but not clinical (encourages youngsters to decorate with posters and teddies). Atmosphere in boys a little formal, more relaxed in girls. Mixed reports in recent times about both quantity and quality of girls' boarding (do ask how many full, 11+ girl boarders), but new housemistress a unanimous hit. 'She has transformed things for the girls. I try to persuade my daughter to come home during the week but she never does'.

Eclectic parent body – new money, old and those with very little who work long and hard to pay the fees. Plenty happening socially and just as friendly, inclusive and welcoming to parents as they are to pupils – even a Saturday parental networking breakfast complete with bacon butties and croissants.

Aims to offer a truly rounded education where all are encouraged to try out new things, have a go, take part. Staff say, 'We let children explore the ox-bow, not just row down the river. We want them to take a risk, make mistakes, work out the rules.' Parents agree, 'BG children are enthused by life and learning.' One added, 'Thanks to Bilton, my daughter has had two extra years of childhood and a relatively untroubled path to adolescence – that's worth thousands to us.'

A breath of fresh air – a welcoming prep that builds confidence in the shy, empowers the gifted and is equally ideal for the imaginative, rumbustious child who can turn a tree into their castle. A tad boys' own (precious children would hate it), but those who are happy to join in, with a little rough-and-tumble along the way, should have the time of their lives.

The Blue Coat School

8

Somerset Road, Edgbaston, Birmingham B17 0HR

Pupils: 564 • Ages: 2–11 • C of E

Fees: £7,737 – £11,898 pa

Tel: 01214 106800
Email: headssec@thebluecoatschool.com
Website: www.thebluecoatschool.com

Headmaster: Since September 2016, Noel Neeson BEd NPQH (40s), previously head of St Peter's Lympstone. Educated at Notre Dame High in Glasgow before reading maths at his native city's university. A lifelong supporter of Celtic, he spent two years as a prep school teacher at St Aloysius College in Glasgow before moving south of the border to Crackley Hall, Kenilworth, where he became deputy head. Turned around a failing Catholic primary school in Leamington Spa before being appointed to St Peter's. Married to Juliet (whom he met on the staff at Crackley Hall); they have a young daughter and son.

Entrance: Usually at age 2 into pre-prep or 7 into prep when number of forms expands. Waiting list for the new-build nursery. Most children signed up at or near birth. Most move up through the school. Some places (dependent on natural wastage) at all levels especially at 7. Vast majority come from Edgbaston and Harborne but many from the greater Birmingham suburbs.

Exit: Very successful in delivering what parents want – entry to the highly selective King Edward Foundation schools where the majority go. Others to Solihull, Edgbaston High, Bromsgrove, St Georges. Some scholarships, academic and musical, every year to the flagship independent schools, King Edwards' and King Edward VI High School for Girls.

Remarks: The school was founded in 1722 by the Reverend William Higgs as a co-educational charity school (making it one of the earliest co-ed schools in the country). It moved to its present site in 1930, and it is hard not to fall in love with the buildings and grounds. The façade has an elegant simplicity, with surrounding lawns and playing fields that are the envy of

B

many city senior schools, and allow for the keenly anticipated annual family outdoor events such as bonfire night and the fête. The school has continued to invest in buildings and the latest additions are a new nursery, classroom block and library. Sports facilities are excellent and parents can take out membership of the sports centre which includes use of the swimming pool. The glorious college-style chapel is one of the many encouragements for the wonderful music.

The school has its eyes firmly fixed on providing inspirational teaching and learning. Since it closed its boarding houses, there has been a determination to maximise the excitement of the learning experience within the time the children are in the school. Well known for its innovative approach to modern languages, it has currently has settled on a programme of teaching French and Spanish from year 2 onwards. Parents complain that the enthusiastic teaching sparks endless nagging from their children to take them on foreign visits. Science is taught in a proper laboratory and is excellent preparation for secondary school with lots of practical work.

Friday afternoons offer a brilliant enrichment over and above the mainstream curriculum for the juniors with cross-curricular options such as philosophy. 'It is about breaking down the boundaries,' says school. The children love it. 'I don't want the weekend to come,' said one 10 year old aspiring philosopher. Art includes an ongoing outdoor sculpture project that is added to each year. As well as high quality traditional music making, there is music technology at an advanced level and African drumming. IT facilities are impressive with new suites of computers. 'Only problem is that the children's use of iPads at school puts us under pressure to buy one at home,' complained one parent. In year 3 the children move to a separate house, which offers a wonderful, homely environment as they move from pre-prep into prep, and they now have a brand new year 3 library. In years 5 and 6 there is serious attention given to preparation for secondary school. There are specialist subject teachers and the children start moving from classroom to classroom to get ready for the hurly burly of senior school life.

'Without a great deal of fuss being made of it, almost everyone gets extra lessons at some stage in their school life here,' said one parent. 'None of the children make anything of it – certainly no stigma attached.' Much of this is within the normal fees. As the children get older, key subjects are streamed and extra groups created as necessary. 'We meet the children at their point of need and move them on,' and the individual approach comes through strongly. 'We don't say every child excels here. How can you say that in a school with a wide ability mix? But what we do say, and deliver on, is that every child flourishes with us'. The approach to the ubiquitous 'gifted and talented' is refreshing. It is not 'Are you gifted and talented?' – but 'How are you gifted and talented?'

Pastoral work is at the core. The house system operates not just for competitions but to give opportunities for older children to look after younger ones, and the houses are single sex so at the end of lessons when most children go to their houses, boys can be boys and girls can be girls. It does mean an extra pair of shoes though – slippers for the house.

The range of activities is very impressive. The school says it aims to offer high quality options for every type of child, and all the children we spoke to were keenly involved in more than one. There are the usual major sports (the school regularly puts out A, B and C teams) and a number of minor ones – judo, for example. One parent said, 'The heart of the school is music, but there is a real drive to develop sport too.' The school has links with Aston Villa and local clubs and is forging new ones with Moseley Rugby Club and the University of Birmingham. There are more coaching sessions and specialist coaches now and the deputy head is a former head of sport – so other schools they meet for fixtures had better look out! The music is brilliant. Most of the children sing in a choir. This, the whole chapel experience and the polished school productions get the children used to presenting to audiences, and they did strike us as unusually confident, in an open, friendly way. The school welcomes a great many visiting speakers, who often run workshops in areas as diverse as Shakespeare and the Aztecs. There are lots of theatre and concerts visits.

Highly conscious of its charitable mission, there are scholarships and means-tested bursaries from 7 and the headmaster works hard at partnerships both in the state and independent sector. Blue Coat is part of the King Edward VI High School for Girls Teaching School Alliance, giving varied professional development opportunities for staff.

Chapel is central to the life of the school. 'Its messages permeate everything we do.' Parents can come along, and lots of children get their first experience of performance – singing, playing, public speaking – in the chapel environment, opportunities parents really value. The school reflects Birmingham's multi-cultural population and, while maintaining its Christian identity, focuses on the shared values between all the faith groups that are represented. 'The children simply don't see the faith and racial divisions', said one parent. 'The school fosters harmony'.

The Edgbaston establishment is pretty well represented in the parent body – lots of medics (the huge Queen Elizabeth Hospital is just round the corner), lawyers, accountants and businesspeople, but it is widened by those with means-tested bursaries. They are an ambitious lot, but come to understand that Blue Coat is much more than just a means of entry into the coveted senior schools.

Bourne Grammar School

South Road, Bourne, Lincolnshire PE10 9JE

Pupils: 1,323 • Ages: 11–18 • Sixth form: 301

Tel: 01778 422288
Email: admissions@bourne-grammar.lincs.sch.uk
Website: www.bourne-grammar.lincs.sch.uk

Head: Since 2005, Jonathan Maddox (late 40s). Educated through the direct grant system in Hertfordshire and read maths at Oxford. Always knew he was going to teach – 'for me it's about passing it on, not changing the world.' Worked in private sector until took the job at Bourne. 'It was the largest school that I had applied for and was the highest achieving academically.'

He has big plans for the school, which is expanding rapidly. By 2018 he plans to have eight forms at year 7, taking the numbers up to 1,500. Not all parents support this expansion – 'no longer a local school for the area,' say some. Always very oversubscribed, but in recent years the catchment area has grown. 'Every pupil who achieves the 220 pass mark will be offered a place, and has been recently', he told us. 'Funding is tight, but I run a tight operation and have some very able governors, so we have been able to find the money for expansion.'

Head knows every pupil by name, no mean feat. He teaches year 7 citizenship and year 11 maths. Liked by pupils, well respected and described by one parent as 'incredibly hard working,' although another said he is 'not a people person.'

Academic matters: Unashamedly an academic hothouse. In 2016, just over half A*/A at GCSE – only to be expected at such a selective school – and 41 per cent A*/A at A level. Most children take 10 GCSEs in a wide range of subjects. Computing at A level was dropped, now reintroduced. Systems and control (a modern version of DT, 21st century electronics and manufacturing) rising in popularity, ably supported by rows of computers and a new systems and control block opened by the Duke of Edinburgh. Spanish taught to all for GCSE. French and German also offered. Textiles, food tech and 'oily rag' DT recently dropped throughout the school. More 20 subjects to pick from at A level, including law. Sciences and maths most popular.

The lessons we observed showed hard working, well-mannered students. Parents talk about the fast pace of teaching, with those who can't keep up expected to catch up in their own time. Fine for the conscientious. This lot had their heads down and were getting on with it. Studious, busy and intense – so busy that time couldn't be taken from lessons to show us around. This lot are under pressure but many appear to thrive. Students are tested constantly. All know their targets, as do parents. If targets aren't attained, letters are sent home and privileges removed, particularly in the sixth form. 'Sub-standard work is not accepted and tests have to be resat if not up to par,' said one parent.

Learning support available for those who need it. Total of 91 students have SEN – in-lesson support arranged and one-to-one support available outside lessons.

Games, options, the arts: They're a competitive lot here when it comes to sport. Rugby, football, netball, cross-country running, cricket and athletics all have clubs and teams. 'The girls' PE teachers are excellent and incredibly dedicated,' said one parent, 'but the boys' teachers, even though excellent, I have to say I've been disappointed with, as the clubs and teams can be a bit hit and miss. I think this is because most of the male teachers have other roles within the school, so paperwork seems to take over at times.' Others disagree. The parent of a year 7 boy told us that 'sport is excellent,' while another said: 'Sport has greatly improved over the years.'

We didn't get the impression that it was sport for all, with teams for all abilities. But the keen are encouraged. Interestingly, individual stars get a mention in weekly bulletins, even those playing in teams.

Music and art well represented. About 10 per cent of students have extra music lessons timetabled on a rolling rota. Older students given preferential slots so as not to interfere with studies. Lots of bands, school orchestra and choirs at lunch times. Most clubs focus on sport and music, but Arabic for beginners and Christian Union also on offer. How well attended these are, we're not sure.

Artwork throughout the school (a dominant display in the entrance). Art A level fairly well supported, more so at GCSE. Now that textiles, food technology and DT have been dropped from the curriculum altogether it does raise the question about the more creative students moving elsewhere for sixth form. Drama has improved and 'the plays are very good – excellent in fact,' said a year 13 parent. Theatre studies and music studied up to A level, but few take music.

Lots of school trips, ranging from New York to local field expeditions.

Background and atmosphere: Founded in 1921, the school has been at its present site, on the edge of the small market town of Bourne in the Lincolnshire Fens, since the 1960s. Plenty of space but very utilitarian. Not a lot of soul in this place, but it isn't helped by the functional, block architecture. At lesson changeover corridors and staircases are crowded. A bit overwhelming for visitors and year 7s, but all very orderly. Disappointing to see rubbish lying about after breaks. Currently redeveloping and refurbing to make space for increased numbers.

School has always been mixed but boys wear black, girls green, and they look as if they are from two different schools. Nobody seems to know why, but it's tradition, so why change it? Sixth formers wear business suits.

Competition is rife here so it's not for the faint-hearted. Most pupils seem to cope well, though. The quieter, less able or diligent can fall by the wayside – we got the impression from a few parents that it was very much 'sink or swim.'

Sixth form block light and airy. A well-liked tutor on hand to offer advice and UCAS help. Upstairs area for quiet supervised study – some of it compulsory, particularly for those not making the grade. Concentrated, calm atmosphere, with an academic hum throughout. Sixth formers allowed into town at lunchtimes (unless privileges have been revoked) and have flexi-study afternoons at home.

Food available in the lunch hall and cafeteria area. Vending machines dotted about as well. 'I would like food to be served on plates rather than plastic trays,' one sixth former told us, 'but it's good and there's plenty of choice.' Pizza slices available daily, chips once a week. Pupils pay daily but parents can buy a squid card (top up card) which shows what their child is eating and spending and most do this. Some take a packed lunch. Outside seating available – good to see.

Pastoral care, well-being and discipline: We got the impression of a well-disciplined school and parents backed this up. Pupils well behaved in class and around the school. Most look smart, too. 'Bullying, if it happens, is stamped on quickly', said one parent. 'There were the odd tizzies in year 7 and 8, but these were sorted out very quickly and ever since my daughter has sailed through', said another. 'I like the fact that the child has the same tutor and form from year 7 to 11.'

Set structure of management team and teachers. 'They have a very odd system where you can only see four teachers on a parents' night as they are too busy,' a parent told us. 'This means that you only see the ones who teach subjects your child is struggling with and some you never meet at all – all rather negative.' Others disagree, saying that it's 'a good system.'

Some parents we spoke to said the school is 'excellent up to year 11' but thought it could perhaps ease up a bit in the sixth form and give the students more leeway. 'The teachers are excellent, though, and they really care,' said a year 13 parent, 'but I do feel that the school in general is too results driven and needs to be a bit more human at times.' Perhaps a bit more carrot and less stick.

Parents praise pastoral teachers. 'They know the children, understand them and speak to them like a parent would,' we were told. The odd gripe about pupils 'getting lost and sinking without trace', but teachers generally thought to be 'very proactive and inspiring.'

Pupils and parents: Pupils used to be from Bourne and the surrounding villages – quite a large area, given the rural nature of the county, and parents would move to improve the chances of their child getting a place. Pupils now coming from further afield because of the increased numbers. 'Sadly, it's no longer a local school and that spoils it,' more than one parent said.

Majority of parents are professionals and this trend is increasing as the catchment area widens and parents are prepared to let their children to travel rather than pay school fees. All parents aspirational for their children so mainly supportive and interested. The pupils we spoke to (they gave up their precious time at break) were pleasant, open and chatty.

Entrance: Pupils sit the 11+ in September for entry into year 7 the following year. The qualifying score is 220 and places are offered according to the school's 'oversubscription criteria.' Pupils tested for verbal and non-verbal reasoning. Higher up the school, youngsters take the 12+ or CAT test, subject to places being available. There aren't many, though. Sixth formers must achieve six GCSEs at grade B or above. English language must be grade C or above. Most pupils from local primary schools and the odd independent. They travel from Peterborough, Stamford, Market Deeping and further afield too.

Exit: Some 20-25 per cent leave after GCSEs, usually to other sixth forms or vocational courses at college. Most go to university (four to Oxbridge in 2016, including twins off to read medicine and law respectively). Subjects diverse. The odd one straight into employment or an apprenticeship, occasionally into the Forces. Increasing numbers taking gap years.

Remarks: Unashamedly academic and aiming higher – one of the top selective state schools in the county.

Caistor Grammar School

Church Street, Caistor, Lincolnshire LN7 6QJ

Pupils: 682 • Ages: 11-18 • Sixth form: 184

Tel: 01472 851250
Email: enquiries@caistorgrammar.com
Website: www.caistorgrammar.com

Headteacher: Since January 2017, Alistair Hopkins MA (English, Oxford), previously deputy head (academic) at Bablake School in Coventry. Worked as a journalist on The Yorkshire Post and The Western Daily Press before turning to teaching. Five years at Bradford Grammar School, then head of English at Woodhouse Grove school and at Wolverhampton Grammar before joining Bablake. Enjoys cycling and cinema.

Academic matters: In 2016, 38 per cent A*/A at A level. Options include classical civilisation, sport and PE, government and politics, RE (philosophy and ethics). Sciences, maths, Eng lit and history particularly popular and strong; DT and MFL good too, but small numbers, as with art, music, RS, PE and ICT (no performing arts/theatre studies); good uptake of class civ. Strong GCSE across the board – 54 per cent A*/A in 2016; 10/11 taken: must do a language, three sciences, RE; German, history and statistics the most popular options.

Outstanding for teaching and learning in last Ofsted, which is far from common. Staff 'have a passion for helping pupils to do the best they can', endorsed by pupils we met – they are 'outstanding', 'fabulous' (sixth former), 'they have their own personality', the history teachers are 'really brilliant' and make lessons very exciting. Two termly assessments for effort and achievement and the longest comments we have ever seen on yearly reports; parents are given lots of data so they can see how their child is doing in relation to the year and their own prior achievement. Girls do surpass boys in their results but not all the time and not by much, and boys here exceed boys nationally.

SENCo qualified to test for dyslexia (provides free individual support with spelling) – can accommodate anyone who passes entrance test, will deal with them on an individual basis, but nature of school site (lots of steps, some narrow corridors) would make it very hard for someone with a permanent physical disability. Doesn't screen all children for dyslexia but scrutinises test results in year 7 to identify any significant discrepancies and contacts all parents re any special needs at entry; in class support possible but kept minimal to suit children's feelings about it; G and T programme.

Games, options, the arts: Specialist sports college and hub school for regional schools' sports partnership, lead school in Lincs for national school games initiative; awarded Sportsmark seven times. Medium size sports hall, modern fitness suite, two extra indoor spaces for PE; two netball courts (year 9 girls county champs); extensive playing fields (two plus floodlit Astro) with pavilion half a mile away.

Plenty of timetabled sport for all: usual sports – lots of fixtures – plus orienteering, archery, martial arts, water sports; individual achievements at county, regional and national levels, eg swimming, riding, sailing; close links with local sports clubs and other organisations. Outdoor pursuits residentials, abundant trips – skiing, netball tour to Barbados, football to Holland, Germany for World Cup, sixth form to Senegal and China.

All key stage 4s do level 1 sports leadership award in lessons; various other leadership awards; year 12 students have hosted and led county conferences for secondary children. Astonishingly, four students chosen to carry 2012 Olympics torch (one donated hers to the school) and ex-head boy was one of the seven younger generation athletes who lit the cauldron in the opening ceremony (surely a record for any school). A girl's design for the Paralympic mascot one of 12 national winners.

Much improved music accommodation, including fully soundproofed drum practice room; music taught throughout key stage 3, exams at GCSE and A level if wanted. Orchestra, choir, several instrumental ensembles; timetable suspended for day of annual house music competition. Sixth formers do Trinity/Guildhall performing arts awards.

Although no theatre nor drama/dance studio, school play and house drama competition are high profile – most recent production, Les Misérables (performed in town hall), much acclaimed. Possibility of doing dance GCSE at another local school. Good results for GCSE art but low numbers at A level. Modern food tech room – cookery club, lessons for sixth formers, entries in Future Chef comp.

Lots of encouragement to get involved in the wealth of extracurricular activities – 'The teachers are very good at pinpointing your special talent and encouraging you to develop it'. Busy D of E; excellent school newspaper, with lively and entertaining articles and colour photos and illustrations – won Best Newspaper in the prestigious national Shine competition, with praise for the 'sensitive handling of the death of a teacher'; sports newsletter; masses of clubs, eg eco, Amnesty International, chess, pottery, Czech for beginners, global student forum, public speaking, Young Enterprise. Extensive range of trips – outdoor pursuits, London, Ukraine, Iceland; France, Germany and China exchanges; link with schools in Senegal and Morocco.

Many house activities run by students and leadership opportunities in performing arts, literacy, languages, maths. Awards evening is a wonderful celebration of the great range of achievements in and out of school – the ones you would expect plus solo gliding, volunteering at the Olympics, being the Young Mayor of North Lincs, working with young disabled athletes, even a trophy for moral courage.

Very good careers programme from year 7 – year 8s have a Real (jobs) Game day; all do work experience in year 10 and year 12s encouraged to find placements too; all year 11s interviewed by head about future plans. Annual events to develop employability skills – enterprise days, sixth form challenge of industry conference, newspaper days, plus visiting speakers. Year 13s praised help with university applications and interviews.

Background and atmosphere: Founded 1630 by Frances Rawlinson, Rector of South Kelsey. Grant maintained from 1991-2000 – when risk of closing in 1960, as numbers were very low, pupils marched 26 miles to Lincoln to save the school from a merger (consistently very oversubscribed now). In 2000 became a foundation school, then converter academy 2010. String of outstanding Ofsteds (grade 1s for everything in the last one) – the only school in Lincs to have been included in Ofsted's Hall of Fame on four occasions; 2002 became a beacon school (for academic excellence), twice received a School Achievement award. As a high performing specialist school became humanities college as well from 2008; gifted and talented lead school. Much bemedalled – Charter mark status twice; investor in people six times; healthy schools and international school awards.

Situated close to centre of Caistor, a small market town. Trad red-brick buildings a mix of 17th century and 1930s, '80s and '90s styles. Some of the labs are limitingly small – about to start work on a new building with better science facilities. Reasonable ICT resources; very new food tech room. On two sides of a close around the attractive, ancient parish church, which gives rather a homely feeling (despite the view of the burial ground). Original ironstone hall with oak panelling and ceiling dating from 1631 in daily use – an impressive environment for detentions. Smallish library with pedestrian decor has lots of engaging fiction but narrow range of magazines and newspapers. Some drab corridors, enlivened by many attractive photos of pupils' activities and art.

Modest sixth form centre in Casterby House, once a large private residence – we thought some of the common rooms looking the worse for wear could do with a makeover, but were assured that the students 'like them the way they are'. More dull décor in the cafeteria but good choice of food made on site from local ingredients (much more important in the scheme of things) and a highly regarded catering manager – students enthused about the Xmas dinners (upmarket veggie dish too). Small garden with very attractive paving to commemorate an assistant head and lab technician.

Ethos of 'strive' and 'excel', in the words of one of the younger pupils, with 'a great sense of fun' (parent); friendly, supportive, harmonious community with friendships across years, small enough for everyone to be known and treated as as an individual; 'There's a huge ethos of respect, for teachers and each other, that permeates throughout,' (parent); big focus on leadership from an early age, with opportunities to develop confidence in public speaking. Even has a very engaging school cat. Christian flavour – annual one day seminar for year 12s to engage with ethical and political issues. Active, highly-regarded school and sixth form councils; views of parents, staff and pupils canvassed via regular questionnaires.

Three houses – lots of competitions, often organised by sixth formers, including a pancake race. Uniform is black, grey and white – girls can wear 'formal black trousers' instead of a skirt; sixth wear office-type clothes. We were charmed by the sartorial diversity displayed, including a three piece suit with fobwatch and bow tie; winkle picker shoes and a stylish red and black floral number – evidence that individuality can be expressed.

Pastoral care, well-being and discipline: Usual structure of form tutors led by heads of different parts of school. Rules emphasise reason and consideration for others. Not heavy on sanctions – extra work, 'the occasional detention', but 'takes an extremely hard line' on drugs; 'When problems arise we try to involve parents at an early stage'. School sets great store by smartness – untucked shirts now a thing of the past, thanks to the head of the pastoral system, who has also tightened up on classroom behaviour – 'zero tolerance policy'. Pupils say (reassuringly): 'You know where you are'; 'People behave well from respect rather than harsh rules' (sixth former).

Counselling service plus drop in health clinic. Sixth form prefects and volunteers act as student counsellors, attached to lower forms – younger pupils trust and have a high regard for them. Very little bullying as open site, staff much present and head 'gets involved if there's any bullying'; any such issues are dealt with in an understanding way; 'There's always a teacher you like you can talk to'; code of cyber conduct being written by school council. Good induction for year 7s includes sleepover in gym (good for bonding with classmates and teachers) – new children settle easily, even if coming alone from their primary school. Rewards for good behaviour and work – £10 gift vouchers for winners of many merits.

Pupils and parents: Mostly white British, reflecting local population; over half from catchment area. LA school buses for years 7-11 (sixth have to pay a contribution), plus parent-organised transport for some out of catchment areas (can cost over £1,000 a year). Active Friends' Association – parents involved in activities and fundraising; the ones we spoke to very happy with the teachers, friendly atmosphere, well-organised parents' evenings and regular communications ('Parents feel valued and are seen as partners in their children's education'). Very thoughtful, articulate, appreciative and polite pupils.

Most notable old girl is Dawn French, 'But we're sure there'll be many more quite soon'.

Entrance: Organises own admissions procedure (close to that of other local grammar schools) – two VR tests taken in September (results available before deadline for LA preference form); takes top 25 per cent of ability range. Year group of around 94 – over-subscribed. Need to live within 6.5 miles of Caistor on or before September 1 of year of application – goes by highest score, then highest score for out of catchment area candidates.

Years 8 and 9: similar VR tests; year 10: VR test plus maths and English papers. Sixth: minimum five A*-B at GCSE, at least B for would be AS subjects plus C in English and maths – about 25 join from outside.

Exit: Some 15-20 per cent leave post year 11 for nearby sixth form/FE/agricultural colleges to do vocational/performing arts courses not on offer at Caistor or to join family businesses.

Almost all year 13s progress to often very good universities, with generally several to Oxbridge (two in 2016, and five medics); others to eg Newcastle, Sheffield, Durham, Nottingham, King's College London, Edinburgh, Exeter, Leeds, Warwick, York, as well as less high-powered ones, to do a tremendous breadth of courses – sciences, history, social sciences, law popular. Others to the Forces or jobs with training.

Remarks: A very strong contender if you are after sound academic values and achievement, with firm discipline allied to encouragement of talent and individuality, plus a good dollop of heart.

Comberton Village College

West Street, Comberton, Cambridge, Cambridgeshire CB23 7DU

Pupils: 1,675 • Ages: 11–18 • Sixth form: 354

Tel: 01223 262503
Email: thecollege@comberton.cambs.sch.uk
Website: www.combertonvc.org

Executive Principal: Since 2001, Stephen Munday CBE MA PGCE (late 40s), a Cambridge economics graduate who still teaches economics to the high flyers in the sixth form. Goodness knows how he manages the time as he's a bit of a superman. He's executive principal of Comberton Village College, and chief executive of the Comberton Academy Trust that also incorporates Cambourne Village College, a newly established school in Cambridgeshire, Melbourn Village College and The Voyager Academy in Peterborough. He manages his time well and spends three days a week on average at Comberton. 'I'm totally in awe of him,' said one mother. 'He expects a lot from his staff and pupils and is duly rewarded.' He went in to teaching straight from Cambridge: 'there is a proper purpose to it.' Well liked and greatly respected, he towers over the school, figuratively and literally. 'He attends virtually everything and speaks very well,' said another parent. A regular church-goer and a keen follower of sport, he was awarded a CBE for services to education in 2013; we can see why.

Head of school is Peter Law, and Lorna Conroy is head of sixth form.

Academic matters: High achieving for a non-selective school. An impressive 38 per cent A*/A grades at GCSE in 2016, and 73 per cent got 5+ A*-Cs including English and maths. At A level, 62 per cent of grades were A*-B and 31 per cent A*/A. 'They keep a close eye on them and let us know immediately if work isn't being handed in,' said one happy parent. All students study Spanish to GCSE, year 6s given a Spanish activity book before they join to give them a head start, and bright sparks (about five per cent of the year) are encouraged to take another language too. French and German also on offer, with Latin taught outside school hours. There were mutterings about extra language lessons after school which could be, whisper it, a disincentive.

'They know how to motivate year 11 boys,' said one parent, another added: 'Lots of after-school revision sessions; the teachers go the extra mile.' The bright are identified and encouraged, the less able equally helped along. 'What I like about the school is that they are flexible,' said another parent. 'If the pupil aims high and works hard, it's recognised and they are moved up a set; excellent.' Lots of vocational courses as well as academic. Lessons we observed involved plenty of interaction with teachers and pupils. Some seemed noisy, but controlled chaos was the order of the day. Odd to see one pupil in geography lolling with her legs across her friend, but if it works?

Impressive artwork and busy noticeboards; we admired all the pictures for the photography prize lined up outside the geography rooms. Given the International School Award for the fourth time. This global outlook links Comberton to schools in six countries, Europe and worldwide, offering chances for exchanges and visits. Room for 'disruptive and bad pupils' – happy to report was empty during our visit. The thriving sixth form, opened in 2011, bedding in well in new building with all mod cons.

A school open to all. SEND very well catered for with almost 20 per cent having some sort of extra support. A very inclusive, understanding environment for those with particular needs. A new block opened in 2015 as an Asperger's centre to cater for up to 40, many from outside the area, built to satisfy demand. Self-contained, well run and funded SEN department housed within main body of the school and run by well respected staff. This offers sanctuary and calm for those that need it, either temporarily or permanently. Individual programmes set up for many; most join mainstream lessons where appropriate.

Games, options, the arts: They're a sporty lot. Plenty of teams and after-school practice, possibly more notable for enjoyment than success. Rock climbing wall in the gym. All the usual sports as well as less common such as dodgeball and handball. Disappointing to hear that only the boys are put into sets for PE lessons; what about the sporty girls? Lots of sports facilities including the sports centre shared with the community including a heated open air pool. One of the gym areas could have done with a good hoover. MCC cricket hub for Cambridge. They're good at golf, too, and have chance to go off site for it, as well as rowing and leadership, where the older pupils coach primary school children. Sport viewed as 'inclusive and fun' by our ambassadors, who were looking forward to sports day. Endeavour awards as well as competitive prizes at this event. Sixth form includes various sports academies.

Dance, drama and performing arts well supported. Lots of after-school and lunch time clubs including orchestra, jazz, brass and Friday choir as well as dance in their impressive studio. Soundproof music rooms for practice. End of term performances held in the new performance hall where visiting musicians hold recitals. Rehearsing for Les Misérables when we visited, all year groups involved. Odyssey performed last year and then taken to the Edinburgh Festival, where it got five star reviews. Successful debating team and well supported D of E going from strength to strength and now offered up to gold award.

Background and atmosphere: Founded in 1959 as a village college with 240 pupils, it's grown rapidly to accommodate the growing villages around Cambridge. It's never lost the community college ethos, with the wider community sharing many facilities, but is now a vast sprawling site on the edge of the village, still with plenty of room around it. Became an academy in 2011 and opened the sixth form at the same time. Functional rather than attractive, the older parts look tired compared to the light, airy modern areas. It's a vast place and could seem intimidating to a newbie coming from a small village school. Successful induction days help overcome this, with year 10 and 11 mentoring newcomers. There's no house system, but year groups are tight, with each designated a 'social area' at lunch time. 'We would like to have more covered space,' said a mole, 'and have campaigned for it, with some success.' Table football and ping pong in the year 8 area, plenty of benches dotted about for al fresco dining. No complaints about the food, apart from lack of choice towards the end of the queue. Healthy eating encouraged and a new cashless system to try and speed things up as complaints made about lack of time. Forty minutes to feed so many does seem rather ambitious.

Uniform is a rather dull grey polo shirt and sweatshirt, with year 11 wearing black, all a bit utilitarian. A strong school council that is well represented. Good to see that year 11 still has an important role in seniority despite the new sixth form. No noses being pushed out of joint yet.

Pastoral care, well-being and discipline: Excellent, according to many, and well supported by parents. A large school that could be intimidating, but it doesn't appear to be a problem. They have strong anti-bullying policies that involve the pupils. 'There are a lot of us and sometimes there will be problems,' said one on-message ambassador. Perpetrator and victim are brought together on neutral ground for group discussions. They work hard to avoid punishment and problems are usually resolved without further action having to be taken. Pupils stay with the same form tutor from years 7-11. There are form reps, counsellors, mentors and teachers to turn to. 'They know their pupils well,' said one happy parent. 'We know who to turn to,' said one pupil. Pastoral care praised by many. 'It's a huge school but they are very supportive and notice if things are going wrong.' 'My daughter really struggled in year 7 and it got to the stage where she didn't want to go to school, she was so anxious, but once the school got involved she was transformed. Her head of year put her at ease and found her a mentor as well as a home support worker. I couldn't have asked for more and now she loves school.' 'They go that extra mile,' was heard more than once.

Pupils and parents: Bright, chatty, relaxed children who know they are lucky to be there. Majority of parents middle class, many Cambridge academics. But a strong mix including the less privileged, and all seem to slot together. Pupils and their parents appreciate the education they are getting.

Entrance: Surrounding villages south of Cambridge in the catchment take precedence after sibling rule. Lots of appeals due to population growth, and popularity of the school can make admission a nightmare. Numbers lower down the school being reduced as new school opened at Cambourne, within the same Trust, easing pressure of numbers. Entry into the sixth form requires minimum of five Bs including English and maths for those wanting to study A levels. They want serious sixth form students and all are interviewed.

Exit: Some two-thirds leave after year 11 to other local sixth form colleges to study A levels or take vocational courses. Newish sixth form becoming more popular each year. Pupils from other non sixth form schools also joining, some from as far afield as Bedford. The odd one straight into work, two-thirds to university. One Oxbridge in 2016, a third to Russell Group universities.

Remarks: A huge school that serves the community well, and encompasses it. We can see why it's so popular; pupils relish it and parents want them there. The new, well supported, successful sixth form is the cherry on the cake.

The Croft Preparatory School

Alveston Hill, Loxley Road, Stratford upon Avon, Warwickshire CV37 7RL

Pupils: 400 • Ages: 2–11

Fees: £7,308 – £11,514 pa

Tel: 01789 293795
Email: office@croftschool.co.uk
Website: www.croftschool.co.uk

Headmaster: Since 2012, Mr Marcus Cook, BSc PGCE (late 30s). Started his teaching career at the Robert Smyth School then took a break to become a professional rugby player in England and France. Resumed teaching as a PE teacher at Eastcote Lawn School, Warwick followed by Arden Lawn School, Arden before joining the Croft in 2002 as director of studies, head of boys' games and head of geography. Became deputy head in 2008. Still involved in the games department.

Married with two children who both attend the school. Wife, Gemma, is head of PSHE and a member of the girls' games department. A German short-haired pointer completes the family.

Head remarks, 'The Croft School is an incredibly special school affording its pupils an opportunity to embark on their learning journey with challenge, enthusiasm and interest, in a caring, supportive environment. We are keen to develop our pupils' EQ, emotional intelligence, to further enhance their abilities and to create an entirely rounded individual.'

Entrance: Inevitably, this being a day school which does not bus pupils in, most live nearby. Children are admitted from the age of 2 but may join at any time, space permitting. Moving up through the school is automatic, but applicants over 5 have a preliminary assessment during an induction day to see if they will need extra support.

Exit: Mostly to local day schools: Warwick School for boys, King's High for girls, the grammar schools in Stratford and Alcester, Bloxham, Bromsgrove, Princethorpe, King Edward VI School, The Kingsley School, and others. Occasionally pupils move to other prep schools to give them the experience of boarding before moving on to senior schools. A clutch of places to some seriously academic schools, such as Eton, Cheltenham Ladies' College, Cheltenham College, Oxford High School, and Magdalen College School.

Remarks: The Croft is unusual in being privately owned. The original school was founded in 1933 in Stratford, but the current proprietor and principal, Mrs Thornton, bought The Croft in 1981 with her late husband, moving the school to its current 30 acre site five years later. The original farmhouse and outbuildings, the barns, the stables, tractor sheds and milking parlour have been developed and adapted into a charming campus, surrounded by the timeless fields and spinneys of Warwickshire. The delightful Mrs Thornton has taught art at the school for years, and is responsible for the lively pictures and mottos high up on the walls, reminding everyone that this is Bard Country. 'All the world's a stage...' 'Fair thoughts and happy hours attend on you' and other uplifting messages adorn the buildings, along with beautiful mosaics and strategically placed works of art. Even on the misty grey November day of our visit, the overall effect was of brightness and colour. 'I am sure that children can learn better in beautiful surroundings,' she says, and that seems to be borne out by academic results as well as the obvious happiness of both staff and pupils.

Visitors to the school receive an instant impression of fun. Bright flags flutter and information about parking is translated into 'parking des visiteurs' or 'parking du château', the latter a reference to the wonderful motte and bailey castle erected outside the main house by Mr Thornton. 'Sens unique' reads another sign. Arriving a little early, we enjoyed the peace and distant views before becoming aware of a babbling, bubbling sound moving up to a cacophony of laughter, chatter, scraping of tiny wheels, shouting and even some singing. It was break, and the youngest inhabitants were making the most of it, pushing barrows of leaves, riding trikes and tractors, sliding through tunnels and having a whale of a time.

The senior part of the school is well laid out around what must have been the original farmyard. It all feels very homely, with children and staff scurrying around, smiling and laughing between lessons. Even the ground staff were beaming, and not because they didn't have to teach. 'It's a very happy place,' one told us out of earshot of any member of staff. (The views of ground staff are always worth hearing. They often know more about what a school is really like than teaching staff.) Early years section now restructured so that a child's 'learning journey can be personalised, rather than being structured in formal class groupings'.

Classrooms are bright, airy, very well-equipped and imaginatively inviting. We saw wonderfully inventive and detailed teaching going on. It became obvious that children are inspired to reach for the stars while standing firmly on the grounds of linguistic and scientific accuracy. 'We learn from detail,' one young child told us, proudly. No patronising in the lessons we witnessed and admired. If the questions were difficult they were phrased in a manner designed to suggest that the answers were within range after applying careful thought. The children were keen and alert and clearly enjoyed the sense of challenge. 'They really do learn how to learn,' one father who has had two children through the school told us; 'as a result their entrance into senior school is seamless.' Conversation with staff at senior schools confirmed that impression.

Housed in a tiny room is the head of learning support, positioned where she can provide privacy or move out to those needing attention. Staff are alert to special needs.

Music is a core subject throughout the school and the results are much appreciated in the locality. Choirs, orchestras, smaller groups, jazz concerts and dance; the annual carol service in Holy Trinity Church, Stratford and more. Over 80 per cent of pupils in prep learn instruments, and currently a range of 15 instruments is taught. As a result of some skilful architectural rearranging of an existing building, the school now has a superb space for performing arts which is also used for assemblies and religious services. Not only are the seats cleverly designed and laid out but lighting and sound equipment, thanks to the nearby RSC, is superb and brilliantly utilised. No wonder the children appear so fearlessly confident, though without a trace of arrogance or smugness.

Delicious, freshly-produced food in the pleasant dining room (periods of silence to 'ease the momentum of the day'); pigs wallowing in mud and dreams; sheep (but are they real?) watching the grass; a lake for making all sorts of discoveries, and an exciting forest school burgeoning into life; birds spotted and catalogued by the head groundsman; a model train set (in need of privatisation); an adventure play area; that castle. It is a Fern Hill of a school where it is shiningly obvious that the sensitive nurturing of children is what makes it dance.

One parent we pushed to say something critical about the school announced after much thought that at times it could seem a trifle precious. That was immediately brushed aside by another parent who said that it was the children who were precious to the school. We left them locked in semantics while the children fleeted themselves carelessly, close to the forest of Arden.

Culford School

Culford, Bury St Edmunds, Suffolk IP28 6TX

Pupils: 601; 200 boarders • Ages: 3–18 (boarding 7) • Sixth form: 138

Fees: Day £8,610 – £18,450; Boarding £21,585 – £28,484 pa

Tel: 01284 385308
Email: admissions@culford.co.uk
Website: www.culford.co.uk

Headmaster: Since 2004, Mr Julian Johnson-Munday (late 40s). Educated at Norwich School and Leicester University, where he read English. Previously housemaster at Cranleigh and deputy head of Mill Hill (during his tenure he studied for an MBA at Durham). Unpompous, affable manner but makes no bones about the clear direction of the school and the setting of targets for staff and pupils. Is intent on raising the school's profile and has overseen a busy programme of building. Seeks to maintain and support the school's boarding provision (currently nearly 50 per cent) and is not enamoured with flexi boarding options, as he believes this could compromise a vital spark of the school. His wife, Jo, is the school's marketing and foundation director and they have one son.

Head of prep school: Mr Michael Schofield BEd (mid 40s), taught history and games at a boys' grammar school for five years and head of 11-18 day house. Then at a co-ed school where he was sixth form master, head of politics and games teacher. Most recently, at Culford Senior School, ran a senior boys' boarding house and was senior housemaster (part of senior management team). Has always taken an active role in coaching all major games along with, most recently, being master in charge of school golf, plus supporting charity work such as the British Heart Foundation, for the past 11 years. Outside interests include dog walking, mountain biking, skiing and reading historical novels.

Academic matters: Strong performance at GCSE (45 per cent A*/A grades in 2016) and A level (29 per cent A*/A, 59 per cent A*/B) – impressive considering school is not ultra-selective. Head remains calm about occasional downward blips in results, saying with disarming frankness that 'year groups do vary in ability'. Average class size is 17 (seven in sixth form) with setting in the core subjects of mathematics, English, sciences and languages. All pupils study at least one modern language (French, German and Spanish on offer) with Latin available as a GCSE option too. In mathematics, high ability pupils take IGCSE in year 10 (all gain A*/A) and additional maths in year 11. Science is very strong and has superb facilities; roughly half do separate sciences at GCSE. Learning support has its own department and is well resourced.

Pupil support across the curriculum is arranged either on a withdrawal basis or outside the timetabled day. A popular programme of seminars and tutorials with high level speakers for the gifted and talented and potential Oxbridge punters.

The school day includes eight periods (four on Saturday), plus after-school activities. Day pupils don't leave until 5.30pm.

Games, options, the arts: Outstanding sports provision includes a 25 metre indoor pool, floodlit Astroturf, games pitches galore, fitness suite and squash courts. The indoor tennis school attracts students from all over with its elite training programme run by professional coaches. Similar regimes are now available for rugby, hockey and swimming. Many pupils train for and take part in athletics events at county and national level and the whole school does two 80 minute periods of sport each week.

New theatre and dance studio are well used, with two major productions each year (some taken to the Edinburgh fringe) and plenty of choirs, orchestras and ensembles. Large numbers take instrumental or singing lessons and a pupil recently won a choral scholarship to St John's College, Oxford. Art and design are strong subjects in the school with good results at GCSE and A level. Plans are afoot to improve the present facilities.

CCF and D of E popular; CATS – Culford Adventure, Training and Service – is designed for fourth years who don't want to do CCF, and includes first aid, life saving, fair trade and outdoor pursuits. Links with schools in Malawi and India; as well as raising funds, pupils visit to help with general maintenance.

Boarding: Just under 200 full senior boarders and 15 or so flexi, accommodated in five boarding houses, including one co-ed house for the prep school boarders (35 full and 20 weekly and flexi). Good range of evening activities; weekends may include eg a trip to the beach or to Norwich, quad biking, white water rafting, a movie or magic night.

Background and atmosphere: Sublime setting in 480 acres of landscaped parkland, complete with Grade I listed bridge and gardens designed by Humphrey Repton. The main building, originally owned variously by the Cadogan and Cornwallis families, is 18th century. The school moved to its present site in 1935 and has maintained the original fabric to a high standard and made full use of its assets. Lord Cadogan's morning room is the head's study – complete with distracting vistas of the park. The grand visitors' lavatory installed for a visit by Edward VII is still in situ, together with a photograph of the royal visitor. In the grounds, a series of newer and, for the most part, well-designed buildings house classrooms, science laboratories, sports and boarding facilities. High standards of maintenance throughout are helped by generous bequests from old pupils – a notable feature.

Unhurried, almost relaxed air about the school. Excellent staff/ pupil relationships, plenty of banter, easy but respectful. Headmaster greets pupils by name. Girls' uniform, featuring an ankle-length pleated skirt, could be a turn-off for some, though we were told by pupils that it is 'comfortable and cool in summer'. Parents describe the school as a 'hidden gem.'

Pastoral care, well-being and discipline: One of the school's great strengths, and the one most frequently mentioned by parents, is the care of pupils. Tutors and house staff deal with everyday matters but the headmaster keeps himself very well informed and can be the key figure at a moment of crisis. 'My son was confused about his future,' one father told us. 'The headmaster took him out for a walk with the dog and that seemed to sort everything out.' Emphasis is on consideration for others – kindness and politeness towards staff as well as to other pupils, and few discipline problems.

Pupils and parents: Majority of pupils are drawn from professional and business families from within a radius of 50 miles. They include a fair sprinkling looking for a different pace from that offered by some of the other local schools. About 20 per cent of boarders are Forces children and just over 10 per cent from overseas, including a cohort of 10 from Germany, who attend for a year. Families are tremendously loyal and many pupils are the children of Old Culfordians.

Entrance: Admission at 7+ and 11+: entrance papers in English, maths and non-verbal tests, plus satisfactory school reference and recent school report. Entry at other ages consists of similar papers at age-appropriate levels, again with satisfactory school reference and recent school report.

At 13, admission is by examination, school report and interview. Around three-quarters join year 9 straight from Culford Prep, with the remainder coming from local state and prep schools. The school report and interview are as important as the exam result – the head knows what he is looking for. Sixth form entrants need seven good GCSEs, with at least Bs in the subjects to be studied at A level.

Exit: Prep school pupils prepared for common entrance. Around 95 per cent proceed to senior school at 13. Around a quarter leave after GCSEs; just over 10 per cent to return overseas. Almost all go on to university, wide range of destinations including Russell Group institutions.

Money matters: A complex web of scholarships and exhibitions available at main entry points (normally worth between 10 and 20 per cent of the fees). Academic, music, art and sports awards are on offer, together with bursaries for the financially hard-pressed, including new foundation academic scholarship at 13+ and 16+ for candidates with Oxbridge potential. Reductions for Forces children and siblings. Overseas pupils charged at a slightly higher rate.

Remarks: A thriving, happy school with excellent foundations and confident leadership. It deserves to be better known than it is.

De Aston School

Willingham Road, Market Rasen, Lincolnshire LN8 3RF

Pupils: 927; 68 boarders • Ages: 11-18 • Sixth form: 167

Fees: £9,858 pa; Day free

Tel: 01673 843415
Email: enquiries@de-aston.lincs.sch.uk
Website: www.de-aston.lincs.sch.uk

D

Head: Since January 2017, Simon Porter, previously one of the deputy heads at the school.

Academic matters: Unwilling to disclose exam results, though generally some 60+ per cent of pupils achieve five or more passes at GCSE A*-C with English and maths, with A level A*-B grades in the high 30s. They are on top of the pupils, offering support for all. Gifted and talented spotted in year 7 and nurtured throughout their time at the school. Lunch time sessions offered to explore subjects in more detail, plus a broader church such as chess, discussion and quizzes. G&Ts also help with the younger years with learning support. The less able are monitored constantly and 'pulled along,' to quote one parent. Learning support very effective, with lots of extra tutoring available. We spotted quite a few one-on-one lessons on our tour of the school. 'My child is dyslexic and got tremendous support in the early years. Less so further up the school but, to be fair, he hasn't needed it as much. I know he is being constantly monitored though and they will step in if necessary.' EAL unit quite large, 59 students, effective and proactive. Many of these students are the boarders who pick up the language impressively quickly.

The main subjects are set early on. French for all up to GCSE, German on offer if enough takers. Lots of impressive artwork on show. DT room had a lovely smell of varnish and very well equipped. All parents were happy that the teachers knew their children well. The head is very proud of the school's value added record. Class sizes average 24, but can go up to 34. All pupils well behaved and attentive. A couple in isolation: obviously Monday morning not going well for some. But all was dealt with calmly and effectively. Some year 13s helping out with the year 7s; looks good on their UCAS forms. Many long-serving staff and many more are ex-pupils.

Sixth form block fairly new and well equipped. Large common room and lots of IT rooms being well used. Quite amusing to see that the 'unsupervised' room had a CCTV camera in it so the teacher in the 'supervised' room could keep an eye on them, including what was on their computers. Pleased to note that all was well. Lots of A level choices on offer, all the usual academic plus 'softer' subjects such as media studies and photography. English and history seem to be strong contenders. BTecs also available. Lots of careers advice, encouragingly, university not being the only option. School recently awarded Careers Mark accreditation.

Games, options, the arts: A sporty school with loads of pitches and facilities. No swimming pool but Astroturf and courts as well as a large dance studio and fitness suite. Massive sports hall. Plenty of silverware on show in reception area. Pleased to note that there is sport for all; the enthusiastic but less talented get chance to play in teams as well. Lots of lunch time practice sessions. Rugby dominant but girls' hockey and netball strong.

Enthusiastic director of sport offering vocational training for sixth formers to help younger years including junior schools. Competitive inter-house sports day every year.

Instruments taught within school but not a huge take up. Opportunity for pupils to show their talents in many shows and end of term performances. Plenty of rooms available for practice. No school orchestra and very few bands, but choir sessions for all.

Drama popular with whole school involved in annual production. More than one drama studio, all well used. D of E up to silver on offer and becoming more popular. Plenty of theatre visits and school trips including World Challenge.

Boarding: One of only 34 state boarding schools. Has always been a boarding school, originally to accommodate pupils from the far flung corners of rural Lincolnshire. Boarders are virtually all foreign students, but with the right to be educated in the UK. Most from Europe, particularly Spain, and a large contingent from Hong Kong. The occasional child with parents in the Forces. Many of the foreign students dip into the school for a couple of years to perfect their English.

Attractive large Victorian boarding house. Dated but spotlessly clean. Maximum of three to a room, most in pairs with the odd single room. Nice to see the rooms were slightly messy – teenagers allowed to be teenagers. Plenty of room available for more boarders, but 'we have as many as we want.' Virtually all are full boarders. Large communal areas, including a room with piano. The sixth formers are able to use their own common room in the school (accessed through a door from the boarding house). Plenty of trips. Friday night is cinema night. Saturdays spent in Lincoln or further afield at theme parks, shopping, sports venues or theatres. Well-liked housemaster incumbent since 1994. Plenty of outside space. Visitors welcome and friends allowed to stay. Tea and toast making facilities for all. Lots of prep sessions and a roll call at 10.30pm to ensure all sixth formers are back. Pretty relaxed about phones. An independent lot, but they know their parameters. 'We aren't allowed to go to parties,' our guide told us. 'It's annoying, as we'd like to go, but we accept it.' Very strong friendships forged within the house.

Background and atmosphere: Opened in 1863, it recently celebrated its 150th anniversary. Initially a boys' grammar school with boarding facilities for the farmers' and workers' sons who were too far away to travel daily. Still housed on the original site on the edge of Market Rasen, a pretty, small town well known for its racecourse. It has been extended extensively. A massive site with lots of land around it, including numerous sports pitches. A veritable rabbit warren. 'We get given maps in year 7 and it took me about two weeks to find my way around,' commented our guide. One of the tidiest, best-kept schools we have visited. Immaculate paintwork throughout; they must have a tremendous caretaker. A very nondescript black uniform, but all students are smart and polite. Lots of 'sirring' going on, surprisingly even from the staff member who accompanied us. Interesting to note that we were not allowed to tour the school with our guides unaccompanied by an adult – not that they had anything to hide, far from it, just school policy. We weren't sure whether to be insulted or reassured, but it's the school's safeguarding policy. Sixth form wear their own clothes but 'no jeans or bare shoulders.' Very much more relaxed relationship between sixth form and staff. It's a large school, particularly so for the county, but the bedding in period seems to stand them in great stead. 'When my daughter started she struggled at first, but was helped along her way and given huge encouragement.'

Pastoral care, well-being and discipline: Discipline is hot. They don't stand for any nonsense here. Pupils isolated if need be, often for the whole day. We were openly shown the list of detentions for that day. Most misdemeanours involved rudeness or insolence, the odd uniform malfunction. The school has very clear rules that the pupils are expected to follow. 'Most pupils accept that they are in the wrong, take the detention and see the error of their ways.' A very proactive intervention teacher who understands teenagers. 'We offer a safe secure spot where they can come and have a chat.' Sympathetic but firm, working closely with educational support department. Counsellors readily available if need be. 'Refreshingly, the school acknowledges bullying happens,' said one parent. 'The protagonists are brought together by the head of year and it's usually sorted out without parental involvement.' Pleased to hear that one child was moved into a different group with members of that form asked to help out and offer support. Sixth formers trained to spot bullying and how to handle it. Parents and pupils know who to turn to for advice. Active school council that meets every half term. School open to suggestions from members.

Pupils and parents: A true comprehensive. Parents can be local professionals or on the minimum wage. All are supportive and back the school wholeheartedly. Pupils can travel a long way, up to an hour, but mainly from the northern half of Lincolnshire. Some 80 per cent of them are bussed in. A long list of primaries, up to 30, sending pupils, many just the one child. Many children are third, fourth or fifth generation to attend. And then there's the boarding contingent.

Entrance: First are siblings, then local children from a wide area. The boarding is open to all who qualify ie British citizens, EU passport holders and those who have the right of UK residence. Most boarders are interviewed and references asked for before being offered a place. Entry to the sixth form requires 5+ GCSEs at A*-C or higher depending on subjects studied. The school is expanding, so very unusual to not get a place.

Exit: Around 50 per cent leave after GCSEs, most to vocational courses locally; one off to Harrow on a scholarship in 2016. Between 15 and 20 join the sixth form from other local schools. A large handful leave after year 12, mainly to apprenticeships. 'Employment prospects aren't good for young people in this area so if an opportunity comes up it is hard to turn down,' says school. The majority, up to 70 per cent, leave in year 13 and go on to university, many to local ones such as Lincoln. None to Oxbridge recently, but historically one or so each year. Interesting to note that almost 20 per cent go straight into employment or apprenticeships at this age. Gap years taken by very few.

Remarks: Quite an unusual place, with the boarding contingent adding a cosmopolitan flavour to a conservative community – good to see. A truly comprehensive establishment, open to all and serving the community well.

Edgbaston High School for Girls

Westbourne Road, Edgbaston, Birmingham B15 3TS

Pupils: 495 • Ages: 11–18 • Sixth form: 105

Fees: £11,982 pa

Tel: 01214 545831
Email: admissions@edgbastonhigh.co.uk
Website: www.edgbastonhigh.co.uk

Head: Since 2006, Dr Ruth Weeks BSc PhD. A Birmingham girl born and bred, she describes this part of her interesting and successful career as 'coming home', but with no disloyalty to her earlier jobs. A chemist by training – that's how she gained her PhD – she was about to begin academic research on muscles when the demands of her husband's career caused the family to move. In the course of her career she has been deputy head of Haberdashers' Monmouth School for Girls and head of Redland High in Bristol. So there's bags of experience here and a lot of intelligence.

A past GSG entry mentioned, with gentle irony we hope, the King Edward V1 consortium of schools as being the leaders in Birmingham education. Dr Weeks' response was vigorous, sharp and impressive. There was almost a suggestion of Elizabethan 'foul scorn'. 'We know what we are,' she said with asperity, 'and we know who we are.' The school is heavily oversubscribed but Dr Weeks and her SMT meet all the prospective pupils and their parents and visit them in their schools as well. The result is that right from the start of each girl's time at the school there is a warmth and understanding. The business of meeting so many parents and children – many times the number for whom there are spaces – is enormously time-consuming, but helps to spread a feeling of goodwill. It's also a shrewd move to keep in contact with local primary schools. Parents told us it was that personal touch that swung it for them and their daughters. Dr Weeks teaches chemistry to years 7 and 13, two significant years.

There is a whiff of the CEO amongst a number of modern heads; heads perhaps dominated by governors who see schools as businesses, and positions in league tables as proof of excellence. EHS does not feel like that, and a mention of the distressing frequency of schools getting rid of pupils who have failed to impress at GCSE and are therefore in danger of lowering A level league positions drew something approaching a snort from this elegant and intelligent head. 'Of course we don't,' she replied to our question. 'We have a job to do.' Actually, very few pupils fail to perform well at GCSE. Nonetheless, there is a caveat to all this. See Entrance.

It is said by some that before she arrived the school had become a trifle sleepy. Without being remotely bombastic or hectoring, Dr Weeks has injected new life into this distinguished school – the oldest independent school for girls in Birmingham. With wisdom and intelligence, concern for staff and pupils and an overall appreciation of the school's potential, together with a clear eye for what is needed and an infectious sense of humour, she has made the school more attractive to parents and increased the range and variety of what is now a broad and progressive curriculum as well as a stimulating extracurricular programme. It is a school for happiness, but not at the expense of academic endeavour and success. It might well be that the happiness that pervades is based on academic pride and pleasure.

Academic matters: There is much rivalry over academic prowess and education amongst the many fine schools in Birmingham. Many parents with whom we spoke cited a school's position in the league tables as the clearest indication of academic thrust. That depends. Some schools home in on a limited number of subjects, with their sights fixed exclusively on league tables. Probably because the ratio of staff to pupils is very generous, EHS is able to offer a very wide range of subjects – 27 at GCSE, including classical Greek and Latin, with 45 per cent A*/A grades in 2016. All that and a range of 30 subjects at A level (41 per cent A*/A and 75 per cent A*-B grades). It's a broad range, producing pupils with a wide cross-section of academic skills. Parents like the availability of choice, perceiving it as individual attention – smaller classes – and avoiding stereotypes. We witnessed some marvellous lessons with lively teachers who, rather than treat the pupils as if they were Strasbourg Geese, encouraged questioning and discussion and were rewarded by a lot of both. There is a palpable fizz in the classrooms. Fizz but no aggression.

Supporting this broad choice of examinable subjects is an extraordinary bank of extracurricular activities, always connected with matters academic. Thus the chess club is allied to mathematics; Lab Rats to science; Chinese calligraphy to art; knitting to textiles; creative writing club to English; Crest Awards to science; Mandarin for beginners etc. We gave up after counting after 30 options. No time is wasted: some sessions take place at lunch time, some after school.

Games, options, the arts: A recent building which has made a considerable difference is a wonderful performing arts centre called – for obvious reasons, when you see it – the Octagon. In itself it is a very attractive and versatile building and an ideal space for concerts, plays – senior and junior productions – assemblies, exams (aaargh), ballet and other activities. It was there that we were privileged to watch an unforgettable impromptu performance by the school's hula-hoop champion. A unique delight and rarely seen in schools of such calibre. There is masses of music and everyone seems to be involved in concerts of varying kinds. Art contributes much to the creative soul of the school. Three studios offer a variety of media including ceramics, printmaking and graphic design as well as traditional painting and drawing. Annual visits to Paris, Florence and Rome. As far as sport is concerned this school is pretty healthy: football, cricket, hockey, basketball, fencing, tennis, netball, rounders and cross-country are pursued with great enthusiasm. To have 14 acres of playing fields in this city school is very useful; to have a fitness suite is wonderful; to have a recently refurbished swimming pool – over 50 years old – is rare; and to have an all-weather pitch seems a real bonus. And it's nearly all happened since the school awoke under the perceptive wisdom of the Great Doctor.

Background and atmosphere: 'The aim of this institution is to afford to the girls of this important neighbourhood an education which shall be the best that this age can afford'. So said Miss Alice Cooper, the first head, in 1878. They are words that would be echoed nearly 150 years later. The founders were keen to make available a broad, liberal education and EHS has always been characterised by its non-denominational approach to teaching and learning, education rather than grade accumulation. A glance at the current list of governors confirms that the Quaker and Unitarian roots remain deeply embedded in the school. The atmosphere is friendly, warm and non-judgemental. Friday assemblies in the Octagon are spent silently listening to music; 'It's cool,' said one girl to us. Lots of charitable work. The reaction to our question about racial mix was a puzzled look. 'We're all happy,' was the answer. Silly question.

E

We had the doubtful privilege of reaching our destination via Five Ways roundabout. Thus it was already a pleasure and a relief to arrive at the handsome entrance. There we were greeted with warmth and courtesy in the car park by a groundsman. The warmth of our reception was constant, wherever we went. The atmosphere was palpable. Grounds staff, incidentally, are always very good indicators of what a school is really like.

An impressive array of new buildings has sprung up in the last few years. We visited the new, state-of-the-art sixth form area complete with comfortable chairs, books, improving magazines, tables to work at, facilities for making coffee and tea and a balcony terrace for dreaming. Why not? A marvellous room for discussing the great things of life and considerably superior to many universities. Five new specialist classrooms help accommodate all those subjects taught. The general study area has also been extended and significantly upgraded, to provide a wireless network, laptop computers and interactive white boards. All the gismos. We visited the wonderful new library, which is now almost double its original size, with research and fiction sections as well as a fully equipped ICT suite.

Sparky teaching. Lively brains. But who remembers that 'education is what you remember when you've forgotten everything you were taught at school'? Wherever we went we were greeted with friendliness and courtesy and a welcome current of humour.

Pastoral care, well-being and discipline: This is a very friendly, happy school where teachers and pupils seem to get on well with each other with mutual respect and affection. Form tutors and individual subject teachers have a recognisable role to play but there are more layers than that. The arrival of new pupils aged 11+ does seem to bring out the kindness of the older girls. Time and time again girls told us how easy it was to settle down on arrival, not only because there is a mentoring system in place where sixth formers 'shadow' the younger, but because of the overall atmosphere.

Pupils and parents: Pupils come from all over Birmingham and beyond. Parents are a loyal bunch who are keen to do what they can to support a school for which they feel gratitude and fondness. There is an active and enthusiastic parents' association which has its own website.

OGs include Molly Dineen, film-maker; Lydia Hislop, journalist; Professor Sally Davies, chief medical officer at the Department of Health; Robyn Jones OBE, businesswoman; Philippa Lett, top model, and Kate Williams, author and TV historian. Plus current pupil Malala Yousafzai, girls' education activist and Nobel Peace Prize winner.

Entrance: Many join from the prep at 11, others from local primaries. Maths and English exams plus interview. Entry into the sixth form requires a minimum of six GCSEs at grades A*-B (including English and maths), plus good grades in prospective A level subjects. Progression from year 11 at EHS into the sixth form and from the lower sixth to upper sixth is dependent in all cases upon sustained good progress and attitude.

Exit: Around 15 per cent leave after GCSEs. Huge variety of universities and subjects. Most years some Oxbridge places – two to Cambridge in 2016, plus one medic; Birmingham is the most popular destination. A few gap years. Good, careful advice and help reported by parents and past pupils. Certainly no suggestion of pupils being compelled against their wishes.

Money matters: There are moves afoot, as with so many schools in Birmingham, to raise money to make the school more accessible to parents who need financial help. There are bursaries and scholarships available. Interested parents should not be embarrassed to ask.

Remarks: 'Rigour with kindness' is one summary we were given. Both words are appropriate. It's a wonderful school for the warmth and affection which pervades, along with academic toughness. The breadth does not hide the toughness: it succeeds not through a shapeless smudge but through wonderful, rigorous teaching and the right choice of subjects. It is attention to detail that makes the system work; that, and a shameless love of learning.

Elmhurst Ballet School

249 Bristol Road, Edgbaston, Birmingham B5 7UH

Pupils: 188 (118 girls, 70 boys); 163 full boarders • Ages: 11-19 • Sixth form: 74

Fees: Day £18,378 – £19,047; Boarding £23,556 – £25,395 pa

Tel: 0121 472 6655
Email: enquiries@elmhurstdance.co.uk
Website: www.elmhurstdance.co.uk

Principal: Since 2010, Jessica Wheeler BA NPQH (30s). There can't be many people in the world, never mind the UK, who combine professional dance experience with top notch educational management expertise. But Elmhurst has found it. Laban trained, she then became resident with the Laban dance company. Moved into teaching as freelance and guest teacher. Tough London comprehensive that employed her to teach dance spotted the charisma, energy and determination and she was fast-tracked to assistant headship before moving with a team of super fixers to work magic in one of the worst schools in London.

Aspirations since arriving at Elmhurst are to make it the dance school of choice in the UK and beyond. Her vision is a holistic one – to ensure talented dancers are also healthy and wise – and this is being realised through detailed, methodical planning, management and monitoring. She is stunning in every sense, and warm with it.

Brilliantly supported by artistic director Robert Parker, the driving force behind the increasingly world-class dance side of the school. He had a meteoric career through the Royal Ballet School, into the company and to Birmingham Royal Ballet as principal dancer. He knows the industry inside out and inspires huge respect in the young dancers. Coming from a Billy Elliot background, he is driven and self disciplined but also hugely charming, brimming with enthusiasm and cares passionately about the experience Elmhurst gives its young dancers. And he has collected a commercial pilot's licence along the way.

Academic matters: Given that admission is entirely done on dance potential, results are good and the principal and new deputy are determined to continue the upward trajectory for GCSE and A level results. Ninety-five per cent of pupils gained five or more A*-C grades at GCSE including maths and English in 2016 (34 per cent A*/A). At A level, 14 per cent of grades at A*/A in 2016, 32 per cent at A*/B. Academic staff are up against students who say all they want to do is dance, but while they might be guided by their hearts, they are surrounded by adults who know you can't dance for ever, however talented you are.

Principal and her team have brought in changes to ensure any dip in academic performance is picked up and acted upon swiftly. She is building a curriculum that will play to the strengths of young dancers who are increasingly getting their five A*-Cs at GCSE. Baseline testing for children coming in to allow individual target setting and tracking of progress year on year. Most importantly, there is now transparency for students and parents about where things are heading.

School is rightly proud of its serious A level programme – dance, music, art, English and maths are on offer – and hopes to introduce geography and biology. Most dance schools give up on academic side at 16 but there is a philosophical commitment here to the value of an academic training, heavily underpinned by the practical consideration that a student who is seriously injured at 17 or has simply grown a bit too tall must have alternatives to a dance career.

Classes are around 20 – smaller once options are chosen. A real strength, parents tell us. Some streaming for EAL students and English exams are very careful chosen to meet the individual's best needs. Teachers all comment that the discipline and focus of the dance studio infuses academic lessons. The issue is sometimes getting the students to speak at all (they are so used to the silence of dance class). Teachers are very conscious that many of the students are kinaesthetic learners and match their teaching styles to maximise this.

Games, options, the arts: This a rigorous training for the most gifted and resilient. The artistic and dance side of the curriculum takes up about a third of the students' time up to 16. Then, as they head towards their three-year National Diploma in Professional Dance, it takes up two-thirds. Training is in classical ballet but there is also a strong emphasis on jazz, contemporary and other supporting dance styles. There is an assessing out process in year 9 and year 11, when students who have not developed as dancers as expected are asked to leave. Process is done as compassionately as possible and warning given in good time for families to find an alternative. About eight per cent of the cohort assessed out across these two key stages.

Recent major review of the programme drew on the views of the professional dance companies, ensuring students are prepared for the demands of the dance industry today. Increasing number and diversity of visiting artists, directors and choreographers, running workshops, masterclasses and lecturing to enrich the students' experience.

Partnership with Birmingham Royal Ballet (reason why Elmhurst moved to Edgbaston 10 years ago) is the icing on the cake for the artistic side of the school. It means getting top quality dance teachers is much easier than anywhere else outside London and students get the chance to perform regularly with the company. Even the youngest can audition for children's parts in productions like The Nutcracker. Also allows for easy professional exchanges.

Dancers simply don't do risky contact sports but Elmhurst is keen for them to try everything else and takes its responsibility for overall fitness very seriously. Attractive fitness suite has been created and staff and students are encouraged to use it. They also share sports facilities and coaches with a nearby mainstream school.

With no sports fields, there are no obvious spaces for younger children to run around but school's pretty, landscaped grounds give a sense of openness to the site.

Friday afternoons have been developed as an off-timetable fun time for learning new skills and offering enrichment and students love it. Sport, art and craft, academic clubs, drama, student-led choreography projects and yoga. Keen to showcase the students' talents outside dance, the school takes part in a host of national competitions – poetry and short story writing, for example, have seen recent successes.

Heart of the school is the excellent 250-seater theatre where the many performances take place, culminating in the outstanding end of year productions.

Boarding: Accommodation for the vast majority who board (just under nine per cent from overseas) is excellent, with many single and double rooms. When we visited the girls had set up their own beauty studio for pamper time with the help of a beauty-trained member of the house staff.

Sixth form accommodation has now moved into a purpose-built space nearer the main campus. This better links the sixth form experience and the rest of the school. Prior to this, one parent felt that when the children were younger they were in a very protected, small environment and then at 16 were suddenly launched into independent living. Students and parents commented on the recent increase in weekend activities, making the most of Birmingham, once Saturday classes have finished.

E

Background and atmosphere: The moment you walk into Elmhurst, you arrive in a huge dance studio, where there is invariably a class going on. From that point, you are in the ballet world. Students move around the corridors as though they are still on stage. They are graceful, hold themselves beautifully and even when they are chatting outside a maths classroom manage to group themselves as though in a corps de ballet. Most of the time they are either in dancewear or track suits in which they naturally look elegant and purposeful.

Staff comment on the maturity with which students relate to adults. Students we spoke to were articulate, able to express themselves confidently and had plenty to say. No bells and the atmosphere is calm and quiet. Something about the absolute dedication to a highly disciplined vocation infuses the whole place. Drive is there in academic as well as artistic classes. 'I have never been in classes with fewer discipline problems,' one teacher told us. 'The children succeed more than they would in other schools because all the time they are asking "how can I improve?" They do that in their ballet and they have that attitude to their GCSEs too.'

School's recently developed 'live, dance, learn' slogan captures the holistic approach to dance education. This is also underlined by 'the Elmhurst way', four statements posted all over the school to remind students and staff what it is all about – choose the right attitude, be there, make someone's day and have fun. We like the sentiments – they give an adventurous and humane dimension to the gruelling discipline of the ballet world.

Pastoral care, well-being and discipline: There has been a huge amount of heartbreak over the years about 'assessing out,' the process at the end of years 9 and 11 when students are told if they are good enough at dance to carry on. Elmhurst has done much soul searching as to how they can make this stressful time as bearable as possible for everyone concerned. They have introduced pre-assessment, which allows teachers to give early indication to both students and parents if things are not looking good. In some cases it can be turned around and every opportunity is given, but sometimes, no matter how much they work, it just can't. At least everyone knows sooner rather than later and the school support swings into action, looking for other alternatives (of which there actually are a lot). Pupils may not end up as Giselle at the Bolshoi but they could still have a career in the dance industry.

Overall, Elmhurst has moved way beyond the usual pastoral care. Students' health and well-being is at the core of everything and systems are in place that recognise the unique nature of vocational ballet training. Dedicated medical centre, with qualified nursing staff, on-site GP appointments, physiotherapy services, dance psychology, dance nutritionist, sports massage and chiropractor. New health and well-being centre aims to 'foster a closer working relationship between healthcare, artistic and boarding staff; thereby championing the ideology of a holistic approach to health and well-being whilst continuing to improve dancing ability and on an international level could help answer questions surrounding bone mineral density in professional dancers and improve dancers' quality of life.'

The school is ahead of the game – linking with university researchers to ensure pre-emptive strategies are in place to keep the students dancing at their peak. More in the pipeline – working with international researchers to develop motivational programmes based on the psychology of success. Probably because of the emphasis on well-being, there are virtually no cases of anorexia. Principal told us that during her time at the school there have only been two diagnoses (both of which had positive outcomes) and that this is proportionately far fewer than at her last school (a large comprehensive).

The school holds student inset days, much like those for staff. Outside agencies come in to run workshops and talks on subjects like e-safety, cancer, injury prevention and choreography. Staff make every effort to ensure that parents have the same information to complete the circle and ensure maximum input for the students.

'The children are simply in love with what they are doing,' one houseparent told us in an attempt to explain the enthusiasm and buzz about the boarding experience.

Pupils and parents: Most are encouraged to apply by their ballet teachers and all are there because they want to dance. There is a real warmth in relations between staff and students and between the students themselves. One boy told us: 'I have finally got friends who have the same interests as me.' Everyone we spoke to stressed the very special people here and the friendships made. 'I have become a different person,' said one girl. 'I am independent and confident now that I am doing what I love.' Parents commented on the way the school by its very nature encouraged independence. 'Our son is noticeably more mature and independent that his contemporaries at other independent boarding schools,' observed one father.

Not surprisingly, parents are quite intense. They are acutely aware of both the dangers and the strengths of opting for a specialist vocational education at 11. A number choose the school because they can see that it tries very hard to keep the academic doors open.

Parents are more obviously desperate for their children to succeed than those in other schools (although given the limited employment opportunities with the world top ballet companies, they know that not many can). This gives an edge to how they relate to the school and one or two thought some parents were reluctant sometimes to approach the school with criticisms. The last thing they want is for their child to be asked to leave. Those with children about to start auditioning for their first jobs were unsure if the school was doing enough to support them, although they recognised it did as much or more than other dance schools. A parent whose child had just had a minor injury wanted to see even more physiotherapy and counselling support. But even the most anxious parents agreed that their child couldn't be happier.

Former pupils (known as Old Elms) include actresses Helen Baxendale, Hayley Mills, Juliet Mills, Jenny Agutter and Joanna David, singer Sarah Brightman and ballet dancers Dame Merle Park, Diana Fox and Isabel McMeekan.

Entrance: Entrance is entirely on artistic merit. Auditions are held at various times in the year in the UK and overseas, although the overseas auditions are increasingly conducted via DVD submissions and then by Elmhurst staff travelling to host auditions overseas. Children will have had ballet lessons before they come and the school has links with some of the best local ballet teachers around the country. The school also runs its own associate classes for the under 11s in Birmingham, Sunderland, Manchester and Plymouth as outreach. Also visits some very challenged primary schools to talent spot. Students are reauditioned at the end of the third year (year 9) and fifth year (year 11) and places are either confirmed or not.

Exit: Around three-quarters leave after GCSEs, though 90 per cent of these leavers go on to further dance training. More than 80 per cent of sixth form graduates enter dance related employment within six months of graduating – increasingly to join internationally prestigious companies. A graduate placement scheme has been introduce to allow students who don't gain immediate employment to stay at the school to sustain audition-ready fitness. The odd student for whom the idea of a ballet career has palled by the time they are 19 head to university. When we visited one had just got an offer from York to read English.

Money matters: Given that the fees include all the specialist ballet tuition, they are reasonable. Many UK families are able to take advantage of two government funded, means-tested, bursary/scholarship schemes. Music and dance scheme (MDS) for those aged 11 to 16 and dance and drama awards (DaDa) for the sixth form. Awards are highly competitive but all credit to the government for ensuring highly talented children can get the specialist training they need, regardless of parental income.

Remarks: The only purpose-built ballet school in the country, this is the ballet school to watch. Elmhurst isn't afraid to look beyond the intense and sometimes claustrophobic ballet world. It challenges the conventional thinking that young dancers must be silent sponges soaking up the technical knowledge of their teachers. With the school's rising academic profile and development of pupil voice, the dancers coming out of Elmhurst are critical learners ready to take ownership of their own careers.

Elmhurst is not the Royal Ballet School and in that sense it has to fight really hard to prove itself. There are no laurels to rest on here. It reinvented itself when it moved to Birmingham and it has the drive and energy of a young institution hungry for success. The Royal Ballet School is still the first choice for the majority of families but Elmhurst is biting at its heels, offering something new and very special.

Fairfield Preparatory School

Linked with Loughborough Grammar School, Loughborough High School

Leicester Road, Loughborough, Leicestershire LE11 2AE

Pupils: 523 • Ages: 3–11

Fees: £9,396 – £9,678 pa

Tel: 01509 215172
Email: registrar@lesfairfield.org
Website: www.lesfairfield.org

Headmaster: Since 2013, Andrew Earnshaw, an effervescent mid 40s. Educated at Bacup and Rawtenstall Grammar School and Lancaster University. Has worked in both the state and independent sectors and also at The British School in Saudi Arabia. A deputy head at Beeston Rylands School before becoming headmaster of Nottingham High Junior School at the age of 34. Resembles an Anglicised version of Pep Guardiola and, like the Manchester City supremo, his organisation is at the top of the Premier League. A MAMIL (middle-aged man in lycra) who recently sizzled through a coast-to-coast ride, zooming through its 120 miles in eight hours. Humorous, perceptive, self-deprecating and with not a hint of the arrogance that some heads display, his popularity within the school with children, staff and parents is obvious. Like Guardiola he has invested his resources wisely: £8m has just been pumped into a stunning development of the pre-prep department, which has created a swirl of interlinked buildings: clear evidence of his vision and style.

Some heads can struggle on their second headship as they adapt to new scenarios. Not Mr Earnshaw. He wants to be known as 'a head who says yes, rather than ... I'll think about it'. Consequently, this is an original community where staff are given the freedom to develop ideas for themselves: witness the fantastic forest school, created in a former wasteland at the edge of the playing fields, where pre-prep children can become mini celebrities in their jungle, as they learn to build a fire, cook, create dens and play plenty of hide and seek. In a school of such size (there are more than 500 pupils on the roll) the head still appears to know every child by name, and to accompany him on a tour is a joy as both children and staff are genuinely pleased to see him. But he is not some kind of trendy who just want to be the kiddies' friend, for this school combines the wisdom of the past with the freshness of the future. For example, boys still wear caps and girls wear straw boaters in the summer. He wants his charges to look smart, so is often telling boys to tuck their shirts in. Everyone is stylish and polished .... and every child has use of an iPad to complement their learning. Academic standards are high. It is, as he says, 'cool to be clever'.

He must clearly survive on about three hours sleep a night – uniquely in our experience, he both writes a card and rings up each parent to give a report on how each of the 70-odd new pupils has fared in their first week. Perhaps his most engaging and inspiring idea is his Wheel of Fortune. This gives children who have won 100 behaviour points for good conduct by the end of the academic year the opportunity to spin the giant wheel in assembly and win, for example, time off homework or a tea party with the deputy head. The most popular segment is 8, for, if the wheel stops there, the spinner is given eight wet sponges with which to splatter the headmaster at break-time in the playground.

His wife teaches here too and his two sons attend the school.

Entrance: Non-selective at 3+ into the nursery; entry to the pre-prep at 4+ depends on a judgement of a child's readiness for learning. From year 3 onwards tests are more formal with boys and girls sitting papers in English, maths and NVR. No scholarships or bursaries are available, although there is provision to support families if there is a sudden change in circumstances.

Exit: Nearly every child – some 90 per cent – remains within The Loughborough Endowed Schools Foundation; girls progressing to Loughborough High School or Our Lady's Convent School, boys to Loughborough Grammar School. A high proportion of academic scholarships at the Loughborough Schools are also won by Fairfield pupils. Scholarships have also recently been won at Oakham, Repton and King Edward's School, Birmingham. For the tiny minority of children who won't be academically fitted to the demands of the senior schools, this will become obvious by year 5 when Mr Earnshaw will start conversations with parents to identify the most sensible options at the end of year 6.

Remarks: Touring with the head gives an accurate insight into the strength and naturalness of staff-pupil relations. The children were polite and bright. Everyone was genuinely pleased to see Mr Earnshaw and answer his questions and tell us about what they were studying. When we asked one class what life was like at Fairfield, they responded with 'fun', 'great' and 'marvellous'. When we found ourselves in the playground next to a jumpered goal post, to be hit by a shot of some power, the striker could not have been more apologetic and concerned that his volley might have hurt.

Pupils are expected by the end of their time to have a reading age at least two years in advance of their chronological one – a flair boosted by the spacious and well-stocked library and the fact that books can be read following a scheme that combines the best of the now with classics like Swallows and Amazons and ends with a quiz. French is introduced in the pre-prep and curriculum time is found for German, Spanish and now Italian in the more senior years. Some five per cent of pupils make use of the SEND provision, provided by a specialist team of teachers.

Competition is much encouraged. Boys and girls can enter for LAMDA examinations and we met a boy who had recently triumphed in a local Young Innovators' Challenge where he was tasked with designing a weight-bearing structure. And so he had knitted a bridge which withstood a 10kg weight. The clubs and activity programme takes place before school, at lunchtimes and after school. The variety is predictably vast, ranging from touch typing to first jazz, strategy games to dance. There are choirs and orchestras, netball, hockey and rugby clubs, a school council and even a harp ensemble. Music takes place in a splendid building which is used by both prep and senior school. Fortnightly concerts are programmed whilst the string instrumental project for every child in year 2 safeguards the future. Dramatic productions feature every year for each of the year groups, recent epics being Aladdin and Joseph and the reception's version of Whoops-a-Daisy Angel.

Sport is very strong. Boys follow a termly pattern of rugby, football, cricket and athletics; girls compete in netball, hockey, rounders and athletics. Facilities are outstanding – the grass would grace Lord's or Wimbledon – and somehow the sporting staff still find time to organise and run the Loughborough Town Sports, held at Loughborough University, for over 40 local state primary schools.

As the school is a part of the Loughborough Endowed Schools, there is a natural long-term vision for both parents and their children. Unlike many prep school-senior school relationships, Fairfield is independent within the Loughborough group and thus the head, in tandem with his governing body, is more able to make quicker decisions about the curriculum and development than would generally be the case in similar schools. And so, staff were closely involved in the planning of the new pre-prep building: one of the many highlights here being the custom-made carpet of inspiration. Schools often now have key words, like honesty, perseverance, loyalty and enthusiasm, plastered around the walls. These can very quickly these can blend into the background and go unnoticed. Not so those embellishing the fabric of the carpet here, which pupils can view each time they walk along it.

The soul of Fairfield is in great part created by the fact that this is very much a family-based school. Many mothers and father have been educated here. Some 40 per cent of staff have their children in the school, along with the Earnshaws' two sons. Recently the head welcomed a child of a fourth-generation family.

It is unsurprising therefore that the Fairfield PTA is so well involved in the life of the school, providing, for example, the funds for the creation of the forest school and being at the core of the community. It is a very sociable body, organising beer & curry nights, a Christmas fair, golf competitions and trips to the pantomime. Parental literature is exemplary – a model of its kind. The Kindergarten Parents' Information Guide, for instance, answers every 'frequently asked' question and all those that are not, as it details the expectations regarding uniform and personal appearance, the curriculum and school shop opening times. There is even a paragraph on what to do if head lice are spotted.

But it is the people who make it fizz. A new member of staff spoke of 'the great, supportive team' who had helped her through her first weeks, and at lunch, as we savoured our lamb orzos, we found ourselves sitting with a year 4 boy. We asked him what his teachers were like. 'Kind and funny,' he replied. 'How?" we questioned. He munched away. 'Well, like at assembly Mr. Earnshaw told us how he became bald. It was because he tore his hair out to give it to a rhino who needed to grow a longer horn' (for those who don't know these things, apparently rhino horns are made out of hair). He munched some more and then came out with his last line. 'Teachers can be bit sulky when you don't do your homework.'

F

There is an ease, a positivity and an endeavour about it all. Wrap-around care is provided by specialist staff. Breakfast club begins at 7.45am. There are parents' information evenings (recently focused on anti-bullying and e-safety), and the head teaches handwriting to year 3. The inspectorate of 2016 had it right when they described it as 'excellent in every aspect'. Fairfield will appeal to most types of child.

As it obviously does to the parents. A new parent, after three weeks in the school described both her and her boy's experience as 'fabulous'. According to another, 'children really enjoy it,' whilst a third remarked that 'the teachers are great,' citing the fact that if a child experiences personal problems then 'the pastoral care is excellent'.

With ultra-competitive fees, the drawbacks of a Fairfield education are hard to imagine – apart from the eclectic gastronomic fusion, which appears to mix Bakewell tart with chocolate krispie (surely a filling cruncher).

So, if you are lucky enough, as a prospective parent, to live in the wide catchment area – buses run from Leicester, Nottingham, Derby and Melton – do put Fairfield on your visit-list.

Foremarke Hall (Repton Preparatory School)

Linked with Repton School

Milton, Derby DE65 6EJ

Pupils: 470: 66 full, 50 weekly/flexi boarders (two thirds boys) • Ages: 3–13 (boarding from 7)

Fees: Day £8,805 – £18,921; Boarding £20,730 – £24,504 pa

Tel: 01283 707100
Email: registrar@foremarke.org.uk
Website: www.foremarke.org.uk

Headmaster: Since 2011, Richard Merriman, who easily matches his surname as he fizzes along into his late 50s and dresses in tasteful tweed, entirely in keeping with the kind of country school that Foremarke is. Educated in Loughborough, both at the grammar school and the university, he took a multi-faceted teaching degree in PE, sports science and geography. Like many a prep school headmaster, he trained as a secondary school specialist and spent the first phases of his career in senior schools in Kent and Dorset, before moving, at the end of the 80s, to a position as director of sport at Kimbolton. Throughout this time, he still developed other interests: securing, for instance, an MA from Leicester University in English local history – special subjects being churchyards and gravestones – whilst his flair for singing saw him as the front man of a band, Johnny Cool and The Iceboxes, who warmed things up in Kentish pubs and clubs with their early rock covers. Now his shoes have changed from blue suedes to brogues.

He then progressed to two headships, initially at Wolborough Hill in Devon, before moving to Birchfield School in Shropshire Now in his fifth year at Foremarke, he is clearly in his element, endowing his school with an assurance and an ambition that can only be sparked by his kind of varied experience.

His study is a room of some glory and very much reflects the man. Elizabethan and Georgian portraits of Foremarke's former families embellish the high walls – some other heads might have been myopic enough to have taken them down in favour of some 'marketing shots'. Copies of Wisden are lined up on one of the alcove bookshelves, revealing his life-long love of the sport and his times as a minor county cricketer. He still plays for the MCC.

Popular with his staff, for the work he does and the example he sets; they describe him as a 'kindly person who inspires confidence' and 'clearly wants the best.' When he arrived, so colleagues advised us, the school was rather departmentally driven – no doubt meritorious but fragmented in its operation. Now it is very much a single entity. Pre-prep staff, for example, from their base in a splendid new building, are included in everything. Training days are inclusive. Failure is acknowledged. All share in success.

A century ago, RM would have been the sort of character who men would have wanted alongside them in the trenches; for the inter-dependence of Foremarke's children, staff and parents is obvious. As we left his study, we noticed, somewhat tucked away, a silver-framed photograph of the head in filmic James Bond dinner dress; unshaken, pistol raised to the sky.

Entrance: This is essentially non-selective, although those who wish to enter from year 3 onwards will be given introductory papers to assess their abilities in English, maths and reasoning. The expectation and the reality is that children will progress to year 8, ultimately following either scholarship or common entrance systems of study. The learning enhancement department numbers four and works both in and out of the classroom, providing individualised and small-group guidance for those in need of assistance, especially in literacy and numeracy. There are up to 20 overseas students (all who have been assessed) and this international spread is encouragingly wide, students coming from Japan and Russia, Hong Kong, Spain and China. There is an EAL department to assist in their transition.

All admission matters are in the hands of the school's registrar, Ruth Merriman, a character full of Irish warmth and wit. The role of headmaster's spouse, especially in a boarding and day school, is a trappy one and, in certain institutions, Fawlteyesque squabbles for supremacy can ensue. This could not be further from the truth here, where headmaster and registrar are a conspicuously strong duo. Their daughter joined Foremarke in year 4 and is now at Repton, so empathy with parents is a given.

A range of scholarships and awards are available – for academic prowess at 7+ and for prowess and promise in music, sport and drama at 11+.

Exit: Being Repton's preparatory school, it is hardly a surprise that around two-thirds of year 8 students advance to the senior school. Other popular schools, from a wide selection, are Cheltenham Ladies' College, Harrow, Rugby and St Mary's Calne. Alumni include Georgie Twigg – a GB hockey gold medallist at Rio, the actor Tom Chambers, and England U21 footballer, Will Hughes.

Remarks: Shakespeare had it that 'all that glisters is not gold'. Foremarke's website is amongst the best we have seen; dazzling with high-quality photographs and text, a selection of enticing videos (one of which reminded us of an opening sequence to the Great British Bake-Off) and more menus than one would find in a chain of restaurants. Like many, it claims to be 'the leading prep school in the Midlands' (a phrase increasingly reminiscent of the 'best beer' Heineken advert) but does it live up to its promise?

Certainly, it makes a stunning start as, at the end of a long, well-tended, rhododendron-fringed drive, the Georgian hall comes into view, resembling part of a wing at Blenheim Palace. As we drew up, a gardener (hard to credit in early November) was cutting one of the perfect grass rectangles. Everything is immaculate. Sweeping steps herald the entrance to the front hall where sofas and log fires deepen the style. Home-made biscuits are served with coffee.

Throughout the school the facilities are impressive. Many join the pre-prep where play areas, consisting of a wooden adventure trail and a green area with tunnels and mounds that looks like something out of Tellytubby land, introduce the new building. The great majority of Foremarke's infrastructure is presented with similar polish.

The £6 million quad development, along with the adjacent Thomas Davies building, features rooms of a scope and flair that would in no way be out of place in a senior school, and, indeed, would be superior to many. Tremulous pupils, however, might not be too encouraged by the sign on the door of the history room which instructs entrants to 'abandon hope'.

The library will inspire, as will the theatre and the sports hall. The triple highlights, though, are the Charles Jennings music school (named after Handel's librettist) and the exceptional art studio and DT centre. We especially liked the pencil portraits in the former, while the latter is the pit-stop for four electric racing cars. These compete on circuits such as Goodwood and Rockingham, the school holding the course record at Aintree, on the track – adjacent to the Grand National fences – that used to host the British Grand Prix.

It is a truism that the most important factors in a school's success are the students and the staff, but the buildings and the beauty of the grounds at Foremarke all help to set the tone. Taste for the best of both the ancient and the modern is all-embracing.

This was also evident in our tour of the boarding houses. Full, weekly and flexible boarding options are available and around 40 students are in on weekends, cared for by the dozen members of staff who live on site. The girls' house, Nightingale, has a cottage-style feel to it and could have been decorated and furnished by a joint design team from Laura Ashley and Cath Kidston. There are two boys' boarding houses, Francis and Burdett, the first being distinctly more impressive than the second. Francis's rooms take their names from their original function: hence there is the Gun Room and the Wine Cellar, the Still Room and the Butler's Pantry. As in Nightingale, the rooms are spacious and elegant. Burdett, although perfectly acceptable, is of a lesser standard. It is to be refurbished by Easter 2017.

Consequently, the only carbuncle is the dining room, where space is cramped. So, staggered sittings have to operate; all of which impacts on ideal timetable patterns. Here, too, design plans for a major reconstruction, which will see facilities allowing the whole school to dine simultaneously, are well advanced. The food, however, is fantastic; as evidenced by our spectacular Thai curry. (Foremarke won the Tatler Award for the Best School Food in 2014, whilst The Week magazine awarded a similar accolade in 2016).

At lunch, we talked with some girls from year 3 whose 'best things about the school' were flapjacks on Wednesdays and 'golden time' – 'where we can do drawing'. On the same table was a year 8 boy, hopeful of a place next year at Eton, who was of the outlandish opinion that Foremarke was 'the most rounded school in England'. We challenged him to detail his knowledge of all schools from Durham to Cornwall. He smiled, and without a touch of Trump-like arrogance, cooly explained that he could not imagine a better school, 'for all that it has done for me'.

And it is clearly not just because it prepares the way for students to enter some of the best senior schools. The extracurricular holy trinity of sport, music and drama sparkles. Girls play hockey, netball and rounders, boys football, hockey and cricket. A multiplicity of teams exists for sportists at every level and the school celebrates the Foremarke Football League which runs alongside the pattern of school fixtures. This year Barcelona (still without Messi) were the winners. There is sailing on the lake, athletics, fencing (a year 6 girl has recently won The IAPS national épée title), swimming, triathlon and even an equestrian team.

Music fills many pages in the Foremarke yearbook – The Preptonian – detailing the calendar of concerts, both in and out of school, and the excellence of orchestras, ensembles and choirs. The chamber choir sings at Remembrance Sunday at the National Arboretum in front of 5,000 people. This year's senior dramatic production was Twelfth Night. There are class plays too, and visits from the Young Film Academy and the Young Shakespeare Theatre Company.

Given this whirligig of opportunity, parents gush about the Foremarke brand of education. One Russian mother, for example, who had met the head in Moscow, had scoured England for a school that would be flexible enough to allow her daughter to develop her high class ice-skating. According to her, 'everything is superb'. Another reported that her family's transfer from Yorkshire had gone well because of 'the excellent academic experience and also the experience of life that Foremarke gives'. A third said that... 'Staff cannot be faulted. They take them way beyond the curriculum.' When asked about the lead up to year 8 examinations, the view was that 'they are very good at managing the pressure and making the hard decisions regarding common entrance and scholarship selection.' Parents kept well-informed by the school's weekly newsletter (the Foremarke Flyer), text-alerts working smoothly if triggered by late cancellations. We were left with the words .... 'Children have such fun. They're tired and they love it.'

And so, does Foremarke, founded in 1945, live up to its marketing promises after its first 70+ years? If it is affordable – fees might be too much of a stretch for many – our visit confirmed that the shimmering straplines are justified. It is, perhaps, an indication of the school's standing that, in the county of Derby's recently produced edition of Monopoly, Foremarke has been awarded a green square: rather appropriately, given its heritage, Regent Street. As all Monopolists know, the third green property is Bond Street; where jewelled gold glitters. There is plenty more to be discovered at Foremarke.

Framlingham College

College Road, Framlingham, Woodbridge, Suffolk IP13 9EY

Pupils: 705; 240 boarders (most weekly/flexi) • Ages: 2–18 • Sixth form: 90 • C of E

Fees: Day £8,172 – £18,634; Boarding: Prep £35–£38 per night. Senior £23,920 – £28,981 pa

Tel: 01728 723789
Email: admissions@framcollege.co.uk
Website: www.framcollege.co.uk

Headmaster: Since 2009, Mr Paul Taylor BA. Read history and politics at Exeter University. Formerly lower master (deputy head) at King's School, Canterbury, and before that director of sport at Tonbridge School. Very friendly, charming without overdoing it and a good listener. Aims to 'produce a decent, rounded human being who looks you in the eye' and believes the school's good performance should be better known outside East Anglia. Wife, Amanda, is secretary of the Framlingham Society and they have four children – two at university and two at Framlingham.

Head of prep: Since January 2016, Matthew King. History degree from Nottingham; began his teaching career in Surrey before moving to Dorset, where he met his wife Emily while both were teaching at Dumpton School in Wimborne. Deputy head and then head of Pennthorpe School in Sussex, where he spent eight happy years before being appointed head here. He is a keen sportsman and writer who has taught subjects ranging from geography to drama and from cricket to ancient history.

Academic matters: Setting begins early for English and maths in the prep, and higher up for other subjects. French in pre-prep and Latin from year 7. Help for mild difficulties, notably dyslexia, but the curriculum is not geared for those who seriously struggle. Extension programmes are developed for 'exceptional students' (head prefers this to 'gifted and talented').

Performs well at both GCSE and A level, though not highly selective – strong commitment to pupils of varying ability. In 2016, 48 per cent of A levels were A*-B. At GCSE, 44 per cent A*/A grades in 2016. Some sixth formers take EPQ

SEN provision well established. Emphasis on supporting the pupils' needs – a register (updated termly) is kept to inform staff across the curriculum of any difficulties. Timetabled access to small group and individual tuition avoids pupil withdrawal from mainstream classes. All pupils must be capable of following the academic programmes at GCSE and A level. Provision for ESL also excellent – separate classes as well as individual tuition. Facilities well thought out, well designed and un-flashy. Exceptional library and design and technology building. Classes kept small, average size 12.

Games, options, the arts: Excellent provision for all sports. Artificial surfaces, new indoor pool and fitness centre (well used, especially by girls) – hosts many tournaments. Sport is important – all pupils take part competitively, whatever their level of ability. Music and drama popular too. Brand new theatre/performance studio and many pupils take drama options at GCSE and A level. Well attended regular public performances – pupils recently took The Importance of Being Earnest to the Edinburgh Fringe. Concerts held in local churches – Framlingham and Orford, as well as Ely Cathedral. Big takeup for D of E, with numbers reaching gold awards. Curriculum also supported by extraordinary plethora of clubs and activities.

Boarding: Prep school boarding is on the top two floors of the original building with spectacular views from every window, redecorated dormitories (mostly four to six beds) and common rooms – no twangy old sofas. Flexi-boarding very popular, and nearly every child from year 3 stays at least one night; 'The whole of year 7 and 8 seem to stay on Wednesday and Friday nights,' say pupils, partly no doubt, because there is Saturday morning school for these years.

Senior school boarding houses well planned and comfortable enough, though girls' quarters, unsurprisingly perhaps, are more home-like and with better decoration. Three houses for girls and four for boys. House competitions range from cross-country to crabbing. Pupils come and go with their own swipe card; most go home at weekends, unless from abroad.

Background and atmosphere: Founded in 1864 in memory of Prince Albert, Queen Victoria's husband (his statue takes pride of place at the front of the school). Senior school in imposing Victorian main building in stunning setting, perched on a hillside with a gorgeous view across the valley to 12th century Framlingham Castle. A variety of buildings added over time, none of them particularly distinguished, but well planned to make good use of beautiful and extensive grounds. Stupendous view of the castle from many perspectives (head has bagged dress circle view from his first floor study).

Prep school in idyllic setting down the Suffolk lanes. The original manor house has been rebuilt and remodelled as a memorial to former pupils killed both world wars. Remembrance is taken seriously and VC citations are proudly displayed in the panelled hall. This is a school for exploring and enjoying; massive oak staircases, terraces on which to play games or take off into the ravishing grounds. The country house atmosphere of the main building is complemented by a modern, multi-purpose hall used for concerts, assemblies and plays and well-designed buildings for DT and art, science and technology. Newish classroom block is reached via a covered passageway; spanking new dance and drama studio.

Nursery and pre-prep occupy their own purpose built accommodation and play areas, but are very much part of the same site. Notice boards with details of after-school clubs, sport and music cover the walls, including one headed Celebration, and pupils proudly point out their names and faces.

A tone of respectful informality throughout. Pupils well-mannered and noticeably calm, even at lesson changes and in the dining hall at lunchtime.

Pastoral care, well-being and discipline: Policy of incorporating day pupils into boarding houses is now well established and a great success. Many pupils do 'occasional' boarding. A parent told us: 'I can email the housemaster directly if my daughter wants to board at short notice – on the same day, on occasion.' Anti-bullying posters dotted around school and any incidents picked up on quickly. 'The housemaster got to the bottom of the matter on the same day,' said one parent, 'and the boys are still together in the same house.'

Keeping sixth formers in the house system creates opportunities for leadership. As a relief from house responsibilities, sixth formers have their own common room and social areas – plans afoot to create a technologically sophisticated sixth form centre. The school's 150th anniversary in 2014 was a launch pad for this and other initiatives. The head rightly lauds excellent pastoral track record but emphasises that 'the family is more important. Schools can over-claim for themselves'.

Pupils and parents: Pupils are mainly drawn from middle class East Anglian families. In some cases, several generations have attended the school. A strong body from abroad, notably Germany and the Far East. Head sees the school as poised to appeal as much to the Oundle and Uppingham market as to its Norfolk and Suffolk constituency. Excellent reputation locally and no problems recruiting.

Pupils well-mannered and friendly, very at-ease in their school, 'Not precocious, but not scared of adults either,' is how the head puts it.

Entrance: For entry to the nursery and pre-prep, pupils are invited to spend a day (or morning) for an informal assessment; same for year 3 upwards but their day includes an entrance test. Scholarships at 11+ for entrants to the senior school – academic, music and sport. At 13, pupils from prep accepted 'on the nod' – assuming they can cope with the academic rigour of the college. CE and interview for everyone else, though tests in core subjects (English, maths and non-verbal reasoning) can be arranged for pupils from schools that don't do CE. The interview is key and head also takes prospective pupils' school reports seriously.

Significant numbers enter after GCSE, with places offered conditionally on the basis of an interview, school report and a minimum achievement of seven A*-C passes at GCSE/IGCSE or equivalent. Overseas candidates also sit tests in English and maths.

Exit: Everyone in the prep is prepared for common entrance. All but a handful transfer to the senior school (results help decide setting in year 9). Almost all sixth formers go to university, with traditional universities well represented. Head is aware of need to identify and support Oxbridge potential early – one to Cambridge to read medicine in 2016, with others off to Ivy League, Exeter, Durham and Newcastle. The place of careers advice is stressed – he believes it should be seen as separate from the university application process. Parents rely on the school as an expert resource.

Money matters: A range of scholarships awarded for outstanding academic, musical, artistic and sporting excellence at 13+ and 16+. Further means-tested bursarial help is available as needed. Reductions for siblings and Forces families.

Remarks: A well run, unstressful school, with happy pupils and high levels of achievement in all areas.

Gresham's

Cromer Road, Holt, Norfolk NR25 6EA

Pupils: 811; 279 full boarders • Ages: 3–18 • Sixth form: 213 • C of E

Fees: Day £9,225 – 23,700; Boarding £24,150 – £32,970 pa

Tel: 01263 714500
Email: admissions@greshams.com
Website: www.greshams.com

Headmaster: Since 2014, Douglas Robb MA (Edinburgh) politics, MEd (Homerton, Cambridge), previously head of Oswestry School. A post-university spell of teaching in Zimbabwe and at Fettes College helped decide his career. Following a post teaching politics and economics at Loughborough grammar, he taught and was a housemaster at Oundle for 10 very happy years which 'totally persuaded me of the benefits of boarding.' Quite a commanding physical presence (a former rugby player), extremely quick-witted and entertaining, a live wire. 'He is confident enough to be able to listen to us and sometimes change his mind,' we were told by a pupil, and it is clear that he has 'picked up the vibe' of the school. He thinks 'it is dangerous to try and change a school; find one that's good and help make it the best. A school has a life of its own; I am a caretaker for a short time.' Believes the house system is central to the success of pupils learning and integrating well into school life. It can also help during the teenage years with 'opportunities for conversation and friendships, both amongst peers, but also with staff.' Has high expectations of his staff and spells out the commitment at interview; 'I pin them down, no woolly promises to help will do. This job is a vocation.' He is scornful of phrases such as 'work-life balance', believing that, in term time, successful teachers must be prepared to involve themselves far beyond the classroom itself, including meetings at odd times; 'Ten o'clock in the evening is not unheard of.' Is fortunate to be inheriting sound finances and is planning new boarding and music facilities and a sixth form centre. Is keen to continue raising academic standards – 'I never heard of a head wanting to lower them' – and to emphasise the central importance of boarding to the ethos of the school. Will accept pupils 'so long as they are prepared to work hard,' and their parents are realistic and in support.

Is married to Lucinda and they have three children (all at Gresham's). He is enjoying north Norfolk life, 'countryside, dogs, getting to know people.' Maintains keen interest in rugby, also golf, skiing and travel and 'proper holidays'

Head of prep: Since 2003, Mr James Quick (50s) BA in economic history, PGCE (Durham); began teaching at The Dragon School, then St Edward's, Oxford, where he was housemaster. Did teacher exchange at Geelong College, Australia before coming here. His wife, Kim, teaches English, history and Latin and their four daughters, all but one at university stage or beyond, were at Gresham's. Sparkling-eyed with a youthful appearance and manner, he is clearly at ease with both staff and pupils, but does not overdo the bonhomie in chance encounters. Has a modest manner and the attractive quality of being quick to praise colleagues. Says, 'Everyone can chip in ideas and rely on each other'. Continues to teach his subjects, history and classical studies, 'doing what everyone else does here'. Says there is no defined Gresham's 'product' as such, but believes hallmarks of pupils are 'the confidence to be themselves (we have room here for the odd squeaky wheel), kindness, a sense of humour, and being prepared to Have a Go.' Sees family in spare time and is a dedicated runner. He recently took part in the Round Norfolk Relay, volunteering for the Thetford – Diss leg at one o'clock in the morning. He is a happy head and in the right job.

Head of nursery and pre-prep: Since September 2016 is Sarah Hollingsworth (30s), previously director of pastoral care at Oswestry School. She has had various early years and KS1 roles and is a trained ISI inspector.

Academic matters: Without the restriction of teaching for the common entrance (abandoned recently), there can be greater flexibility in the curriculum in the prep school. Excellent languages: the younger years (2-5) learn a number of languages with the focus on fun and communication. French is taught from year 6 with Spanish and Latin options from year 7. Other languages (eg German, Mandarin) can usually be accommodated on request. Science taught in designated labs, sometimes using the more sophisticated facilities of the senior school. There is mixed ability teaching up until year 4, then setting in most subjects, though 'these are flexible and pupils move up and

G

down'. Pupils have their ability stretched by differentiated targets, rather than being 'pushed'.

Educational support well-resourced, with five specially trained staff (two full-time) who are also class teachers. Caters for mild difficulties such as dyslexia, Asperger's, and other emotional problems, for example, low self-esteem. About a quarter of pupils receive help, either in one-to-one tuition, small groups, or support in the classroom. Brilliant library, bursting with delectable titles, displays, opportunities to enter competitions and with an enthusiastic, full-time librarian, who does everything to encourage reading as an enjoyable habit. Open all day long (boarders can use it in the evening for project work), the atmosphere is quiet: 'we don't insist on a deathly silence, but purposeful reading does need peace and quiet'.

Class sizes between 12 and 20 in the senior school, and setting for most parts of the curriculum, mean pupils get focussed attention. Parents think the size of the school allows for pupils to develop at their own pace, though several also mentioned, not as a criticism, 'there is definitely more push; things are less easy-going than in the past.' Pupils generally take at least 10 GCSEs; 50 per cent at A*/A in 2016. For the sixth form, there is the choice of A levels or the IB with between a quarter and a third taking the IB. The requirement for one of the six subjects studied to be a language puts off a lot and, as an exam, it is perceived as 'stiffer' than A levels. The previous head's attempt to enforce the IB for all by 2016 met with strong parental resistance, and was abandoned as a policy in favour of the status quo: all may, none must. The present head is clear, 'IB is an excellent exam and we encourage it, but it is not, and never will be, for everyone.' Creditable results across the board at A level with 34 per cent A*/A, 63 per cent A*-B grades. Good IB results: average score of 35 points.

Around a fifth receive extra help with SEN, mostly dyslexia, dyscalculia, sensory impairments and poor self-esteem. The need for help appears greatest in year 9 and 10 and lessens as pupils progress through the school, perhaps finding their feet. The department is well staffed with full and part-time teachers, one devoted to teaching ESL, and help is offered individually and in small groups. Care is taken to ensure that individual difficulties are made known to subject staff. New entrants are screened to flag any problems early on and close relations nurtured with feed junior schools. Charged as an extra, but there is a termly cap on fees at £500.

Games, options, the arts: Outdoorsy lot who make the most of the facilities and seem to agree with the 'healthy mind, healthy body' outlook. All the usual team sports: rugby, hockey (for boys and girls), netball and cricket, with lots of match play for everyone and good coaching for those taking things seriously. In addition, pupils can choose shooting or kayaking in years 7 and 8. School also hosts training camps, some residential, in cricket, rugby and hockey, in the holidays. Swimming is compulsory in the lower forms and an extra activity higher up. Weights room, rowing machines, yoga and cross-country running all popular. 'I often go for an early run; it is one of the reasons I like boarding,' we were told by one girl, and it is obviously not a place for those who prefer stewing indoors. The few who seriously dislike team games are treated humanely and allowed to do shooting (this is Norfolk), sailing, fencing, cycling and swimming higher up the school. Pitches, Astroturf and courts for tennis and squash galore, and a rifle range (members of the club have been junior ladies champion four years running, and several pupils have been selected to represent Britain in the U19 rifle team). D of E popular at all levels, with around 30 reaching gold each year; CCF and the BASC course (British Association for Shooting and Conservation) are options.

The reputation of the school's drama department and facilities is renowned and the school has produced several professional actors, Olivia Colman (Broadchurch and Rev) most notable. With professional facilities (Auden theatre hosts touring companies as well as being used for several school productions each year – excellent sound and lighting systems, dressing rooms, proper auditorium, the lot), drama is a very popular extra activity: 'It was a reason to come here.' Parents loud in their praise: 'It is incredible what they can stage; lots of opportunities to develop a serious interest in stage management, lighting and sound as well as acting.' At least three major productions each year; it can be a real springboard for pupils who want to go on to study at drama school or university.

The performing arts, particularly music and drama, have status in the prep too, and are very well taught within the curriculum and as extra activities ('one of the reasons we chose the school'). Dance is on the curriculum in the lower forms and an extra activity later on. Drama is timetabled throughout the school; performances take place in the hall with larger productions in the Auden Theatre at the main school.

Music is equally valued – roughly half the school has timetabled instrumental tuition and there is a wide variety of choirs, ensembles, bands and orchestras. Despite a revamp for the Britten centenary in 2013, accommodation is under par and new facilities are a high priority on the head's building programme, which includes a new music school and sixth form centre planned for September 2017.

Well-designed building devoted to art, textiles, and DT – splendid displays of pupils' work, excellent facilities and all manner of projects undertaken. Opportunities to use oil paints from the start, life drawing classes regularly held and artists in residence inject their own talents and energy into this thriving department. Superb exhibition space, lots to feast the eyes on – a really dynamic place to develop a talent. Art and design have their own rather eye-catching building in the prep too, with spectacular displays of pupils' work (including designs on backs of chairs) and every inducement for creativity. 'We do textiles, mosaics, woodwork, mess generally'.

Boarding: Strong boarding feel, but day pupils are well integrated having their own bed and/or desk, in their house, and though flexi-boarding is not actively encouraged, 'We happily accommodate pupils overnight on occasions when they are here late for rehearsals, performances or other school events.' Pupils do swap around quite a bit; choosing to board in the sixth form is popular; others, sometimes for financial reasons become day. Houses are comfortable, well lit and decorated with thought given to making things home-like, for example decent-sized kitchens that are actually used for cooking and eating in, rather than miserable little kitchenettes with a toaster and electric kettle, standing room only. Houseparents and matrons are always about, pupils return to their houses at break and lunch; bedrooms mostly shared between two or four.

The academic/pastoral divide is blurred; house staff teach their own subject alongside their pastoral duties. Lots stay in at weekends and there are plenty of organised activities though not what the head calls 'enforced jollity.' Houses sit together at their own tables in the revamped dining hall. The food 'has improved, we get more salads' (this from a girl) but we thought it still a bit on the stodgy side – room for improvement. Some houses have fruit always available, but not all, a source of some grievance, we discovered. Straightforward uniform; jacket and trousers for boys ('suits' in the sixth form), calf-length tartan kilts and new, light blue tweed jackets (rather chic) gradually replacing the old blazers. Coats hardly worn and if needed (one thinks of bracing North Sea breezes), 'We wear what we like so long as it's not too outrageous.' How sensible. Home clothes once the timetabled day is over and at the weekends.

Background and atmosphere: Founded originally as a grammar school (1555), rejuvenated in 1890s by George Howson, a headmaster with 'advanced' views in education. He introduced the teaching of sciences, abandoned corporal punishment and encouraged pacifist thinking – practically unheard of then. Set in over 170 acres of woodlands and extensive playing fields, school buildings extend on both sides of the old Cromer road leading out of Holt (pupils cross via a bridge) and are a mixture of styles and quality ranging from magnificent Edwardian and art deco halls and libraries with grand staircases, stained glass etc, through to more run of the mill classrooms, the innovative art and design block and the famous Auden theatre. Pupils get plenty of fresh air doing the brisk walk between lessons in different parts of the site. There is a well looked after air about the place and a programme of refurbishment of various houses is under way together with further planned developments.

Prep on its own site, though only a brisk walk from the senior school, on the edge of Holt, North Norfolk's stylish market town. Mostly new buildings of one or two storeys, of varying design, set in the midst of extensive grounds, adventure play areas and piazzas; 'pupils have to play in sight of the gazebo'. Certain facilities such as sport, swimming pool and the theatre are used at the senior school, but in the main, it operates autonomously. Parents queue up to praise this relaxed and happy school where 'childhood still seems to last the right length of time'. One parent thought, 'My son came out of his shell here, he became a different boy'. A number of families have both Norfolk and London bases, but choose Gresham's for its 'less pressured atmosphere' over the more hothoused approach found elsewhere.

Pastoral care, well-being and discipline: Careful attention is paid to ensuring prep school pupils' well-being and happiness. As well as the usual offers of counselling well displayed, there is a 'worry box' to post in 'anything they want to discuss, however small it may seem'. Staff keep a weather eye, particularly in changing room areas, which are always supervised.

Nothing but praise from senior school parents too; 'My three boys all settled quickly and never felt out of things as day pupils,' was a remark we heard over again. The school focuses particularly on those not coming up from the prep school in year 9, and there is a 'buddy' system in place. 'Our son found it hard to begin with, but the school continued to support him; they were brilliant and he is really happy there now.' The small size of the school means staff and pupils all know each other and relationships are forged, which can help if there are difficulties at any stage. Good interaction between the different year groups and friendly, still respectful staff/pupil relations.

Apart from usual minor misdemeanours, a well behaved lot. There is a clear anti-bullying policy (lots of awareness notices on walls), counsellors and a school chaplain as well as matrons and house staff all keeping an eye out. Well understood rules on illegal drugs (zero tolerance), and alcohol: over 18s may drink ('enjoy a pint ' is the phrase used) either in the school's own bar or the Feathers in Holt; no PDA (public displays of affection), but few overstep the mark. The need for teenagers, sixth formers particularly, to handle stress is taken seriously with regular sessions on relaxation and quick intervention if a pupil is struggling. Sixth formers also choose their own tutors: 'they have to teach one of the subjects we are studying, it helps with university choices but of course liking comes into it too.'

Pupils and parents: Friendly pupils, unflustered and polite, with just the right amount of door-holding and rather less hair flicking and self-conscious teenage behaviour than usual. Un-flashy, country school, 'It's a Barbour and boots place.' Day pupils are drawn from a large area of north Norfolk, many travelling for an hour each way; boarders from all over the country but predominantly East Anglia. Mostly farming, professional and business families with a sprinkling of county boarding families, plus lots from London – many choose the school for the contrast with the fiercely competitive schools in the Capital. Some move to Norfolk for this reason, both parents commuting, or one remaining in Norfolk during the week so children can be day pupils. About 20 per cent from overseas, mostly Europe.

Arts, sport, science and technology are all well represented amongst former pupils, who include Benjamin Britten, WH Auden, Sir Christopher Cockerell (inventor of the hovercraft), Sir James Dyson (vacuum cleaner), Tom and Ben Youngs (international rugby players), Lord Reith (first director-general of BBC), Prof Alan Hodgkin and Olivia Colman.

Entrance: At all ages and stages from 3 (nursery and pre-prep), 7 and 11 in the prep school, although they will try to accommodate when possible at other times. Some year groups fill quickly, so first come first served. Accepts a fairly wide spectrum of ability, but admission is not a foregone conclusion. Informal assessment in the early forms, the same plus maths, English and verb. Pupils from the maintained sector often join for years 7 and 8 in preparation for the senior school.

Roughly 80 per cent of senior school have come up from the prep school, others from a mix of day and boarding preps, some from maintained sector. No common entrance; an assessment day is held for year 9 entrants in Lent term for following September. Tests in English and maths plus reports and references from current school. For sixth form, predicted grades (usually a minimum of A*/B in six subjects including those to be studied and minimum of C in English and maths) plus school report and interview.

Exit: Great majority, 80 per cent at least, go through the school to year 8 and move up to the seniors. All take the 'exit' exam, those not likely to make the grade are warned in good time. Those wishing to go elsewhere at 13, and there are a few most years, are prepared individually for the necessary entrance exams – Ampleforth, Charterhouse, Framlingham, Norwich School, Oundle, Rugby, Stowe, The Leys and Uppingham are popular choices.

A few to Oxbridge (one in 2016), sizeable numbers to London (Imperial, Kings and UCL) plus the other Russell Group universities. Wide range of subjects studied including a regular few to drama school and music colleges. Varying numbers (some 15 per cent) leave for pastures new after GCSE, usually in the maintained sector, plus the odd one for vocational work (gamekeeping a recent one). Head approves of pupils choosing vocational work and believes it reflects the diversity of the school.

Money matters: Thanks to a long association with the Worshipful Company of Fishmongers and its generous financial underpinning of the school's finances, a number of valuable scholarships and bursaries are on offer. Academic scholarships worth up to 50 per cent of fees offered for year 9 entry (can be topped up with a bursary, if financial need is demonstrated), drama, music, art and sport awards also offered, for up to 20 per cent. In the sixth form, scholarships are offered to those who do brilliantly at GCSE (if not already in receipt of an award) and help is forthcoming if families fall on hard times, at least to enable pupils to get through to the next public exam. Usual sibling discounts for three or more at one time.

Remarks: Well-established country boarding school with a deserved reputation for the encouragement of the arts, particularly music and drama. Its relatively small size and position make it a good choice for those looking for a broader educational experience within a school with a strong pastoral ethos. The twin paths of the IB and A levels will remain under the present head. Hard to think who would not thrive in this happy, well-run school.

G

Hallfield School

48 Church Road, Edgbaston, Birmingham B15 3SJ

Pupils: 565 • Ages: 3m–11 • C of E

Fees: £8,592 – £12,036 pa

Tel: 01214 541496
Email: office@hallfieldschool.co.uk
Website: www.hallfieldschool.co.uk

H

Headmaster: Since 2012, Roger Outwin-Flinders – a sparkling 50-something. Intuitive and incisive, he grew up in Lowestoft, the most easterly town in the nation, where he 'could see the sunshine first in the morning.' Educated at Lowestoft Grammar and St Paul's College in Cheltenham where he read geography and PE. Spent his early teaching career in north London, Sussex and Worcestershire before becoming, at the age of 33, one of the country's youngest headmasters when he took up position at Wycliffe College Junior School. Still sporty (ask him about his paragliding adventures in Mauritius and his plans for his first parachute jump), after eight years at Wycliffe – in which roll-numbers nearly doubled – he moved to Fairfield School in Loughborough, a part of The Loughborough Endowed Schools Foundation. There he had a similar impact, being a driving force behind the establishment of their music school which is a hub of excellence for both junior and senior departments. Given this background, governors would not have had to mull long over their 2012 appointment, for here is a man who epitomises all that a head should be. For, as each member of staff and pupil whom we met testified, he has revolutionised his school.

Formerly it was, perhaps, overly-concerned with the detail of its balance-sheets. Now it quite clearly has a more concentrated educative focus and, most crucially of all, a soul. Nowhere is this better illustrated than by the recent introduction of Hallfield's Children's Charter. Many schools have tried to navigate this route but it so often stops with a wall-display or a few trite sentences in the back of a prep diary. Not at Hallfield; for here every child is given a fold-out aide-memoire of business card size which centres the school's ethical heart. It explains the meaning of being good friends, good citizens and good learners. The card is with pupils at all times and is therefore a constant reminder of their school's expectations and ambitions.

Like all five-star heads, Mr Outwin-Flinders works around the clock, and then some more, but somehow still has the time for everybody and everything. In a school of such magnitude (numbers are the best part of 600) he has a mastery of names and represents a blend of traditionalism and modernity that parents clearly find highly appealing. For instance, one of his mantras is the word 'standards', which he applies both to appearance (children are conspicuously smart; shirts are in) and to language. He does not tolerate 'we was'.

But this is no tweedian figure from a past time-warp. In partnership with his equally admirable wife, Tania – Hallfield's communications officer – he has instigated a series of communication and literary initiatives that have helped to promote the school and move it into the premier division. Surfing through their lucid website will make that clear, but it doesn't end there as the range of supporting literature is of equal quality. Both an elegant termly magazine The Hallfield Focus – which incorporates a section for The Old Hallfieldian Society – and a weekly e-newsletter are produced. Borders are coloured by a Farrow & Ball type of lichen green, a subtle contrast to the rather deeper green of the uniform. This is a clever modern touch, complementing the shield, with its date of the school's foundation, 1879, still at the top.

Over the past year both the level of enquiries and open morning attendance figures are up, further underlining the fact that this is a school which excites. That Mr Outwin-Flinders is proud of it all is obvious. So should he be, but there is no tint of self-aggrandisement about him: his staff and children are given the credit for Hallfield's success. Like a would-be Olympic high-jump medallist, he talks about the need to keep 'raising the bar'. His major role, he states, is 'to open doors and let people go through them.'

Entrance: This is a selective school with a current boy-girl ratio of 55:45, girls and boys being assessed for their suitability to learn from 2+ onwards, whilst more formalised tests in English, maths and reasoning are set for those who wish to enter from year 3 and above. A small number of bursaries is available on a means-tested basis.

Exit: As Disraeli observed, statistics can lie; but these ones don't, for the fact that Hallfield pupils have won 126 scholarships to schools such as King Edward's Birmingham, Edgbaston High School for Girls, Priory School and Solihull over the last four years, and in 2016 achieved a 75 per cent pass rate for grammar school entry, constitutes the clearest evidence of the school's academic power.

Remarks: Unsurprisingly it all starts at the beginning and with the sense of a new belonging. The head writes welcome cards for each of the new arrivals during their first week. This, though, can hardly compare to the excitement sparked by the gift of a teddy bear (The Hallfield Bear) to all reception children.... And so, an unofficial competition starts as to where each bear can visit. We met one animated 4 year old who, having built some kind of rocket in the garden (assisted by his father), seemed convinced that his teddy had gone to the moon. The recent ISI report rates the school's EYFS provision as outstanding in all areas.

This surge of excellence continues as pupils make their transition to the more senior years. Given the 11+ aspirations of parents the academic pace is a strong one, but the pupils are comfortable with it and benefit hugely from recent reforms such as the half-hour of reading-time that takes place in the post-lunch period. SEND organisation and tuition – as recognised by this year's ISI inspection – is outstanding. The line between confidence and arrogance can be a thin one, especially for those academically blessed, but all those whom we met possessed the kind of humility and openness that would delight any parent. When they were asked to sum up their school in a single word the normal gushy ones such as 'fun' and 'amazing' featured. More revealing were the words 'changing' and 'trustworthy'. As in all high-ranking schools, Hallfield is unafraid of change; not because it clings to that odious phrase 'going forward', but because it knows the truth that only through change can things improve.

And reform is transparent. On an annual basis, a 'further information' brochure is published which sets out the 'aims for the year'. These, for 2106-17, include integrating the newly-established forest school more fully into the curriculum and providing a splendid entrance area for the pre-prep which will, no doubt, spruce up its current rather tired appearance. Use of tablet technology will be extended throughout the school.

If children have faith in the school's flair for change, then so do the teachers. Longer-serving staff talked with great warmth about the more concise and efficient systems of management and tuition techniques that have been put in place, whilst new staff stressed to us how friendly and supportive everyone had been. Thus, an atmosphere has been created where, they reported, their pupils 'don't want to go home'.

This is in great part due to the kaleidoscope of activity that the school provides. For a school so close to the centre of Birmingham, it is good to see that the playing fields are so extensive. This enables the school to run many teams in football, rugby and cricket for the boys (twice in the last three years the footballers have reached the national finals, played at St George's, England's headquarters) whilst the girls – known as The Vixens – form a similar number of teams for fixtures in hockey, netball and rounders. All children in the upper school take part in cross-country, gymnastics and swimming. Badminton is a special strength and nearly as many boys are in the dance club as girls. The school won the national championship in chess a few years ago.

Musically the pattern of quality is the same as specialist teachers lead choirs, orchestras and ensembles. Recently a senior girl won a place in the National Children's Choir and an Old Hallfieldian has just reached the last eight of X Factor as part of the girl-group Four of Diamonds. Drama, too, is spectacular; arguably the highlight is the Shakespeare Week for year 6 where the Young Shakespeare Company come in and take the children from base-camp to a performance-peak in five days: last year Hamlet, this year Romeo and Juliet. Designs for a new performing arts centre are well advanced.

Externally, links are strong – not only with other independent schools but also with local primaries. Hallfield runs holiday courses and masterclasses, and the head's recent appointment as a governor of St Catherine's School in Athens will open up a series of exchange opportunities.

As with any school, not everything in the garden is lovely: not least as a result of the current badger-invasion which has created an explosion of muddy pyramids outside the head's study window. The gym will shortly be fitted out with new flooring and acoustic panelling that will soften the noise. The car park will soon benefit from more investment, designed to produce a more ordered flow. And soon, we hope, it could be sensible to amend the distinctly bizarre system of form nomenclature, which sees every new member of staff working under an irrelevant initial from a former master or mistress. A recent appointment has just taken over the letter 'u'.

These, however, are tiny blemishes. On our visit parents lauded the school, stating that they were 'so delighted with the pastoral care' as 'everyone is treated as an individual'. Another said that her girls 'had thrived so much', whilst a mother in the pre-prep remembered that her son's 'tears at the start' had rapidly dried because 'all the staff are absolutely fantastic'.

All commented on the school's ultra-slick emails and texts – another stylish idea from Mrs Outwin-Flinders. Electronic communication actually seems to work here, and everyone benefits as parents are kept up to date with what has happened and are sent reminders regarding future events.

Consequently, a kind of golden triangle has been drawn: one that combines children, staff and parents in a triple quest for excellence. Of late, alumni relations have been developed and the fact that an Old Hallfieldian is, by custom, invited back to address the school at speech day gives a completeness and a vision to it all. Last summer the first girl at the school, who joined in 1995, was the guest of honour.

The Hallfield Pen has the words A World-Class Education on it. That, perhaps, is for some international panel to judge, but this school, for all that it does and for the new insights that are bound to spring from such a committed head and his team, is very much one to consider.

Hills Road Sixth Form College

Hills Road, Cambridge CB2 8PE

Pupils: 2,312 • Ages: 16–19

Tel: 01223 247251
Email: HR-Admissions@hillsroad.ac.uk
Website: www.hillsroad.ac.uk

Principal: Since 2008, Linda Sinclair (50s). Studied languages and linguistics at Essex before entering the banking world. Decided that wasn't for her so took her PGCE. Came to Hills Road in 1988 as a business studies and economics teacher and has never left. 'I only expected to be here three years but it just sort of evolved,' she says. Much admired by parents. 'She has great strength and gravitas, is very caring and very clear about Hills Road's values,' said one parent. 'A fantastic leader who is very good at sorting out the finances,' said another. An admiring father described her 'relentless drive for improvement and to keep going forward.' She struck us as a very competent, able woman, approachable, friendly and warm, but with a steely determination and clear vision of what she wants for her college – ideal qualities. She still teaches the EPQ so keeping her hand in.

Leaving in July 2017. Her successor will be Jo Trump, who has been deputy principal here since 2009. She has also been consortium manager for the S7 Consortium of Surrey Sixth Form Colleges and before that, assistant principal at Farnham Sixth Form College.

Academic matters: In 2016, 79 per cent A*-B at A level, 49 per cent A*-A, impressive but to be expected. It's the added value score that is interesting, meaning that many students did better than predicted from their GCSE grades; excellent. Vast number of subjects offered – 36; all the usuals with a few oddities such as archaeology, and 'soft' subjects like film and media studies and photography. Something for everyone. Maths by far the most popular subject, sciences highly regarded too. Lots of artwork and posters throughout the college. Nice to see outside the maths and chemistry rooms pictures of previous year groups with all their university destinations and courses shown – inspirational stuff. 'There's definitely academic pressure,' said one parent, 'but a lot of that pressure comes from the students themselves. They have high expectations, as does the college.' 'Lots of work but lots of support,' said another parent.

Specialist study skills team supports students with special educational needs and highly regarded. 'A very proactive team who helped my son enormously,' said one parent. 'My dyslexic son was supported all the way through his two years by the team; they got psychologists' reports and helped him hugely with his organisational skills.' Another parent, who has a child on the autistic spectrum, said 'We chose Hills Road because the specialist study skills team so impressed on the open day, and they delivered, which was excellent.' Team not just for SENs; lots of help for the slightly disorganised and stressed as well.

Games, options, the arts: This place is not just an exam factory. Every student takes on an enrichment activity in lower sixth, many carry them on to the upper. Lots of competitive sports on offer, with successful teams and, being in Cambridge, good rowing opportunities. Lots of choirs, orchestras and bands well supported; 'I got to meet so many different people that I would never otherwise have come across by being in the jazz

H

orchestra,' one student told us. Drama and dance with lots of performances, many directed by the students. One parents told us about the student-made production about Hills Road for prospective students. 'It was excellent quality. That is what Hills Road is about: opportunities to do anything if you put your mind to it.'

Lots of trips on offer. Duke of Edinburgh award, Hills Road radio show and the Phoenix (in-house) newspaper other choices.

Background and atmosphere: Based at the old boys' school grammar site, Hills Road opened in 1974 as a sixth form college when Cambridgeshire reorganised its education policy. Situated very close to the centre of Cambridge, it is surrounded by university colleges and often taps into the university for well-known guest speakers, who are invited by the students.

Attractive older building with modern blocks joined on, aesthetically pleasing; new maths, performing arts and PE building. All based around a quad. This place really is like a university; no trace of school here. The only difference is that all students still live at home, so get their washing done. 'The transition to uni is so easy as, effectively, they really are there anyway,' said one parent. 'They study in the same way as university students, so it doesn't faze them when they actually become bona fide ones.'

The place is vast, and many worry that they will struggle when they first start, but very few do. Lots of comings and goings, as they must only attend timetabled lessons; great for the independent spirit, possibly not so great for social cohesion. But many spend most of their days there as lots of study areas too. Open to all, the geeks, nerds, boffs and bookish are easily absorbed; they are with kindred spirits here. Masses of computers dotted around the place, all being used diligently. Plenty of social space as well, including the Hub, with lots of squashy sofas, humming quietly. This lot know where they're going and are determined to get there; focused springs to mind. Probably not a place for those lacking self-motivation, discipline and diligence.

The student council is a powerful force within the college, independently funded by its own bursary. It organises regular social activities and implements social policies to reflect the views of the students. We visited just before the elections, and the seats appeared to be hotly contested.

Pastoral care, well-being and discipline: Pastoral care appears to be excellent. 'Even though the place is so vast, they seem to know the individual,' said one parent. There's a specialist guidance team, with lots of monitoring and tracking, so no-one slips through the net. Personal tutor groups of about 20 mean the tutor gets to know the student well. Lots of counseling available if need be; 'no-one is invisible'. 'They know what makes this age group tick,' said parent. They should; they've got 2,000 of them on site and a very specific demographic to aim at; but they seem to do it well. Lots of advice from the careers department, excellent to see specific folders containing notes from previous Oxbridge interviews.

'Both my children loved being there,' said a parent, 'and made some very firm friends.' Another parent, 'My son wanted to go to Hills Road as it's the best. He initially felt a bit intimidated when he realised how bright some of the other students were, but he quickly found he could match them and it spurred him on.'

Pupils and parents: Most students are from the feeder schools in Cambridgeshire, with another 10 per cent coming from out of area. Some 15 per cent of the total intake comes from the private sector. All parents have high aspirations and expectations for their children, as do the students themselves. As expected, most parents are professionals, many academics – this is Cambridge, after all. All parents we spoke to were very supportive, and happy with their child's experience here.

Entrance: B grades over above at GCSE are the basis, but don't be fooled; the college is so oversubscribed they can pick the brighter students, and they do. All in-area candidates who put the college as their first choice are interviewed, quite a task considering the numbers involved. Offers are primarily based on GCSE profile rather than students' personal qualities, but during the interview it's made clear about expectations and work ethic. Out-of-area ones less likely to be interviewed.

Exit: Virtually all go on to university, with large numbers doing medicine, sciences and veterinary studies. Some 50+ a year to Oxbridge (67 in 2016, plus 28 medics). Nearly 60 per cent to Russell group. A large number, up to 40 per cent, taking gap years, actively encouraged by the college.

Money matters: The college has 'outstanding' financial status and has also been very successful in recent years in bidding for a number of QIA grants to support innovative projects and share good practice.

Remarks: Not just an exam factory, which could be the initial perception; their enrichment studies incorporate the wider curriculum and turn out well-rounded, bright, independent learners. Not suitable for all, but those with the right mindset flourish, and the parents know it. Classed as outstanding by Ofsted during their last two visits and voted Sixth Form College of the Year recently by the Sunday Times; enough said.

Histon and Impington Infant School

New School Road, Histon, Cambridge, Cambridgeshire CB24 9LL

Pupils: 287 • Ages: 4-7

Tel: 01223 568826
Email: office@histonimpington-inf.cambs.sch.uk
Website: www.hiischool.net

Head Teacher: Since 2015, Jonathan Newman.

Entrance: For mainstream schooling – within catchment. For the assessment unit – LA referral. Not necessarily from within the accepted catchment area – parents can and do express a preference.

Exit: Most to Histon and Impington Junior School.

Remarks: Histon and Impington are popular, vibrant villages (not far from central Cambridge) which benefit from the through nature of schooling – Impington Village College is close by. Opened in 1912, the infant school is in a quiet residential cul-de-sac (opposite is its feeder early years centre – an attractive, modern development). Austere exterior gives little indication of the welcoming, child-friendly interior. Modernisation has provided an ample hall, new classrooms and surprisingly spacious library with its own suite of computers. All classrooms have direct access to a playground – cheered up with several purpose-built structures including a jolly, two dimensional, palm tree. Large playing field for picnics and games is across the road.

The school is one of two in the Cambridge area with an in-house assessment unit. This specialised unit (a standard sized classroom within the school) is run by a long serving SEN teacher and the deputy head. The unit (in place since the mid 80s) is seen as a 'half way house' – programmes are devised with a view to getting pupils back into mainstream education wherever possible. Up to 10 attend at any one time and most pupils' needs come within the autistic spectrum, with social skills and language development high on the agenda – a visiting speech and language therapist comes in two mornings a week. Integration is clearly important and absolutely no stigma attached to needs – 'Infants don't see differences like adults – they're very accepting. It shows all the children how different needs can be accommodated and teaches them to be tolerant'. Every child from the unit – always referred to simply as class 4 – joins the rest of the school for assembly, break and playtime and they're assigned to a mainstream class which is visited regularly (frequency of sessions depends on the individual).

Those in mainstream classes who have special educational needs (approx 24 per cent overall) are supported through timetabled withdrawal and/or designated classroom assistants. The sensible and sympathetic part-time SENCo is based in a cosy room in the centre of the school. She also spends one afternoon a week in the assessment unit and liaises closely with the early years centre – all very helpful with the cross-fertilisation of ideas and possible referrals to the unit.

School is lucky enough to have a designated room for timetabled music lessons and individual violin tuition is available (provided by the county). Those in year 2 get to play recorders and a singing club, which includes children from the assessment unit, meets at lunchtime. Also on offer, for a nominal charge, are lessons in French (years 1 and 2).

The catchment area doesn't include much social housing but the school feels a healthy mix of children. A strong community spirit and plenty of parental help within the school. An active school association raises money for 'icing on the cake' and runs several clubs, including one to encourage kids to love and value books – each week children can buy a stamp, which is saved until the end of term, when a book sale: a great idea.

A popular school where the assessment unit is recognised to be a big plus for pupils and teachers alike. A civilised and effective arrangement which respects the needs of all within the community.

Impington Village College

New Road, Impington, Cambridge, Cambridgeshire CB24 9LX

Pupils: 1,335 • Ages: 11–19 • Sixth form: 266

Tel: 01223 200400
Email: office@impington.cambs.sch.uk
Website: www.impington.cambs.sch.uk

Principal: Since January 2016, Mr Ryan Kelsall, previously vice principal.

The former principal, Robert Campbell, is now executive principal, with a view to growing the academy trust.

Academic matters: A school with a split personality. Up to year 11 a good village college that attracts all sorts and abilities. In 2016, 39 per cent A*-A grades at GCSE, 81 per cent got 5+ A*- Cs including maths and English. Outstanding results place it amongst the top performing non-selective schools in the country and they are improving each year. Most pupils take 10 GCSEs and do one language, though they can study two from year 7. Spanish, French and German all on offer with Japanese and Latin available as enrichment, and star linguists actively encouraged. Sets for maths, sciences and languages. Performing arts, music and dance all very popular. Courses also offered in catering, product design and computer science. The able are encouraged and the less able given a helping hand. The occasional parental muttering about middle-of-the-roaders being overlooked, but this is becoming more of a rarity. They cater for a broad church up to age 16. Maximum class size up to 32.

Our guides were keen to show us the science block including the plants and pond. They were very excited about the ducklings that had hatched and were hoping to show us some. Sadly, the next batch were still in incubation. Lots of artwork on display and busy noticeboards. We were even shown the isolation room for the not so obedient; happy to report it was empty. Children well behaved and cheerful. The college has not permanently excluded a student for over 8 years.

And then we turn to the sixth form, housed in the old school gym, but you'd never know it. Unusually for a state school the sixth form, which is international, has offered the IB for 20 years. In 2016 the average point score was 32. A levels also studied, but by fewer pupils; no maths offered, just English, biology, humanities and the arts. A level results variable. In 2016, 12 per cent A*/A and 44 per cent A*-B grades. 2016 BTec courses offered: business, media, sports and performing arts. Also a football scholarship programme with Histon Town Football Club. Some 45 per cent of students are international, hosted by local families. The majority are from Italy, Poland and Germany, with many from other parts of Europe and from further afield. All mix well, and the ones we spoke to were very impressive, adorned with nose rings and piercings and quite charming. Some 40 per cent of sixth form do not have English as their first language, but lots of support offered and they come on in leaps and bounds. 'The international students really raise the game in the sixth form,' said one parent, 'and the locals follow accordingly, excellent.' 'The IB is ideal for the all rounder,' said another parent, 'and instills the discipline to study.' Noisy and messy common room – they don't keep Impington tidy here – but a happy, friendly bunch. Rest of the sixth from block scattered with superior artwork from past and present students. Lots of computers available, all in use.

A school open to all. Up to a quarter have special needs including some in wheelchairs. The spacious Pavilion provides sanctuary for those that need it, with some individual lessons taught there as well. All attend mainstream lessons where appropriate. Lots of in-class support offered too. 'My son, who is on the autistic spectrum, receives 25 hours a week of support. He is never singled out but discreetly helped. They are very sensitive about striking a balance. Their door is always open to me as well; I couldn't ask for more.' 'They think outside the box,' said another parent.

Others comment: 'The school is very supportive, lots of extra help if needed.' 'There was lots of homework in year 7 but it seems to have dwindled off in the last few years, but they are doing well, so who am I to argue?'

All parents positive about communication with teachers, some a bit more critical about getting through on the phone: 'It's very difficult to get the phone answered sometimes.' We have to agree with this. Email contact constant, with homework timetable posted online. All information available for those who look.

I

Games, options, the arts: Lots of sports pitches and good facilities including an indoor pool and sports complex shared with the community. We were informed that the rugby and football teams were doing well. Lots of sport available including oddities such as dodgeball. Plenty of teams including trampolining, and much after-school practice. Impington widely renowned for its drama, art and music. The performance school, a cross denomination of all the arts combined, actively supported by pupils throughout the school; Cabaret recently staged to rave reviews. Orchestras, choirs and rehearsals for numerous shows abound, and provide an opportunity for different age groups to mix. Dance studio well used by both sexes. Plenty of instruments studied to high grades and lots of practice rooms.

Duke of Edinburgh popular; many do bronze award. Plenty of school trips and a well produced school magazine. Active social media.

Background and atmosphere: On the edge of Cambridge, IVC celebrated its 75th anniversary in 2014. Having opened just before war broke out in September 1939, it is housed in a grade 1 Bauhaus designed building. Slightly austere and intimidating, but very much of its time. Inside, it comes into its own. Lots of curving corridors and light airy parts with plenty of open spaces. The original building has sympathetic additions.

I

Its ethos is very much of a community college. Open to all, with adult lessons held on site and a room for the community to use during the day. Nice to see a school sitting in the middle of the village for all to use. Interestingly, no prefects appointed – true egalitarians here. Aim is 'to create independent and internationally-minded students from the day they arrive' – whether local or from overseas.

A happy, busy place; the students seem very proud of their school. Pity they don't believe in keeping it tidy. Disappointing to see lots of rubbish lying about, particularly after breaks. Students know their rights and fight for them. Uniform battles have prevailed, to the extent that one young man turned up in a skirt to protest that girls could wear them in summer but the boys could not wear shorts – we believe that he won his point. All students wear sweatshirts, year 11s in a different colour. They don't look particularly smart, but functional. Sixth formers wear their own clothes. Interesting to see some quirky characters: lots of different hair colours and lengths, and that's just the boys. Multiple piercings on some of the sixth formers. 'We aren't draconian here,' says the head. 'We have no ruling on hair. We don't make it an issue so it rather defeats the purpose; they quickly get bored with pink hair if there's no reaction.'

'The school is very inclusive and the pupils are very tolerant,' said a parent. 'They accept diversity and all are welcome, which is a fabulous ethos to have.' Another parent said, 'Despite its size they know everyone. I really appreciated that the teachers had pictures of all the new year 7s so got to know them quickly.'

In response to previous complaints about lack of space to eat lunch (the dining hall is not big enough to accommodate everyone), the prom (reception hall) is now open to students at break and lunch with new tables. 'We are constantly asking for better facilities; they eventually listened to us about the toilets and did something about that,' said another guide.

Pastoral care, well-being and discipline: Pastoral care excellent. All parents very positive, particularly those with children using the Pavilion. 'I know if there are any problems someone will be in touch immediately,' was said by more than one parent. Teachers seem to know their pupils well, and there is lots of mutual respect. A new vertical house system is being introduced, so there will in future be lots of interaction between year groups – something lacking at the moment. It's meeting resistance from some, pupils and parents, but they're ploughing ahead with it.

Discipline has been improved in the last few years. Fewer complaints about 'disruption in the class and quieter ones being overlooked.' A strict disciplinary procedure in force and all comply, resulting in no expulsions for over eight years. 'My children are happy in the school and despite its size took to it really well,' was a frequent comment from parents. 'A happy place that involves the whole community,' said one.

Pupils and parents: Most pupils from feeder schools to the north of Cambridge, some from Cambridge itself. An eclectic mix of backgrounds. Parents range from academics and medics to the seriously underprivileged. All pupils seem to mix well and are tolerant of each others' foibles. Most parents have very high expectations, as do their children. The pupils we met were bright, chatty, confident individuals. Easy to talk to and proud of their school and all it stood for. Every parent we spoke to was very positive.

Entrance: At age of 11 from local primary schools. Appeals often succeed, hence the large class sizes. Those with special needs usually gain a place. Any student moving into the catchment area is offered a place to study here.

Entry to the sixth form requires 5+ GCSEs at C grade or above including English and maths for A levels, B grades or higher for the IB.

Exit: Some 60 per cent leave after GCSEs, the vast majority to other local sixth forms to study A levels or vocational subjects. A handful into employment or apprenticeships, the odd NEET. The remaining 40 per cent stay to study the IB or A levels and are joined by local students and the international contingent. As expected, these leavers are spread far and wide. The majority to university, many to European and American ones. A few straight to employment, over 10 per cent take gap years. Generally one a year to Oxbridge – to study physics, in 2016. Subjects very varied but performing arts and drama seem popular choices

Remarks: A true village community college. It attracts some bright sparks but is very inclusive of the less able and the different. Good to see them all in it together. The international sixth form makes it a true ground breaker in the state system. A well run place that has true community spirit.

Ipswich High School

Woolverstone, Ipswich, Suffolk IP9 1AZ

Pupils: 505 • Ages: 3–18 • Sixth form: 55

Fees: £7,839 – £13,374 pa

Tel: 01473 780201
Email: admissions@ihs.gdst.net
Website: www.ipswichhighschool.co.uk

Head: Since 2013, Ms Oona Carlin BSc, studied biochemistry at Imperial college, London. Previously deputy head at Putney High (GDST) and before that head of chemistry at the Royal Masonic School. Early 40s, elegant, but not over-polished, and approachable. Having a wide experience of different schools, including two years at the English school in Bogota, Columbia, she is convinced about the benefits of a girls' school, 'Leadership opportunities and a free unfettered choice of subjects,' plus of course all the benefits of belonging to the Girls' Day School Trust for networking purposes in the long term. Going down well with parents, 'Mustard – getting to know the place from top to bottom'; 'Has the right tone and approach and seems to have clear ideas of the school's direction.' Is unflustered by numbers leaving for pastures new after GCSE. 'It is a choice some make but we have so much to offer in the sixth form and those key months preparing for university entrance.' Wants to help girls find their strengths and play to them. A keen hockey player herself (plays for a local Ipswich side – sometimes against her own pupils) she has been known to cover a games lesson for an absent colleague; quite unusual. Has a down-to-earth attitude, 'Someone who will get things done'. Being with family and dog-walking are her main relaxations.

Junior school head: Since 2009, Mrs Eileen Fisher BEd. Previously deputy principal (juniors and early years) at St Margaret's School, Edinburgh. Married, with a teenage family and two dogs. Down-to-earth and fun. Has an infectious enthusiasm, whether speaking about the new library, her recent training to deliver the forest school programme or a liking for the colour pink (very evident). Chair of GDST junior heads and appreciates the support this network gives. 'We can share ideas and concerns – what works and what doesn't, without worrying about giving the game away,' she says. Teaches her own subject, English, and also maths.

Academic matters: There is an integrated curriculum in the junior school, though maths is taught separately with sets from year 4. Regular SEN review days; staff use a 'traffic light' system to identify difficulties as quickly as possible. Science, art and cookery taught in specialist classrooms in the senior school for year 6 to help the impending transfer.

High levels of achievement continue in the senior school. In 2016, nearly 70 per cent of GCSEs awarded at A*/A and at A level 39 per cent. Mathematics and the sciences are all strong. Although the school is very aware of the pressure for top grades, it encourages a broader view of education, and subjects on offer include photography, astronomy, food science and Mandarin. All pupils study at least one foreign language at GCSE and Latin also has plenty of take-up. Setting for maths begins in year 7, though approach is flexible. 'Quite often a change of teacher is the key to understanding.' We agree. Half-termly effort grades and regular reports help to keep a focus and parents in the picture. All pupils are screened for learning difficulties on entry and any problems are picked up early and help offered, either one-to-one or in small groups. As a selective school, difficulties are generally mild dyslexia or problems with processing information. Sixth formers have study/tutor rooms at the top of Wolverstone hall, the main building, with spectacular views. 'We are so lucky to be at the top; the climb is a bit aerobic, but worth it.' Small teaching groups and plenty of guidance in the necessary study skills. There is a hard-working, but relaxed air, 'most of us get on with work without anyone saying anything.'

Games, options, the arts: All team sports played competitively and well, notably hockey. The recent Project Leapfrog, a GDST investigation into PE provision in all its schools, recommended that the school engage more outside coaches. This has been adopted; despite a bedrock of talent there was a need to develop skills and match technique. 'Things had got into a bit of a rut,' was a comment we heard from several. The head's personal interest is very welcome. Sports hall and swimming pool (also available to the public out of school hours) and plans are under way to include a dance studio and a fitness suite. School aware that not all girls enjoy team games and encourages plenty of alternatives, including yoga and pilates, riding (school has an equestrian team), sailing and fencing. Recognises that enjoying games or exercise generally may be a matter of confidence. The girls all appreciate the spectacular grounds and the space for fun at breaks as well as for games.

Music and drama both strong. About half the school has individual instrumental/singing lessons and regular concerts are held at nearby Snape Maltings (Aldeburgh) as well as at school. There is a Young Musician of the Year contest alongside choirs, orchestra and ensembles. Diverse repertoire explored in orchestras and ensembles – something for everyone. Performs a musical and a play each year. The Hayworth theatre with flexible staging and raked seating holds 300. 'We did Bugsy Malone, my sister was Fat Sam!' said one girl, jumping with excitement at the memory. The theatre is well used for drama lessons and clubs as well as performances. Junior school multi-purpose, parquet floored hall, with stage used for regular performances in Friday assemblies, musicals, plays and a recent Strictly Come Dancing contest, has proved wildly popular. 'I did it with my sister, we did the Charleston and 20s stuff,' an enthusiastic pupil told us. Separate art, textiles and DT building. In year 7, 'We make clocks, egg holders, coat hangers and a soap dish,' the idea being to understand the materials involved and learn some necessary techniques. Food science is 'having a moment,' on the timetable for years 7-9 and available as an option thereafter. Several well-designed, home-like kitchens (sixth form has its own) within a separate building. Taking a creative subject at GCSE is, surprisingly, not compulsory.

Activities on offer after school for juniors as well as seniors include riding, cookery and knitting as well as the various music groups.

Background and atmosphere: One of the earliest Trust schools, founded in 1878 and transferred to its present site at Wolverstone Hall 20 years ago. Approaching the school along a tree-lined avenue surrounded by sheep is to feel a lift in spirits. 'It makes me feel pleased turning into the drive every morning', said one pupil, and the girls are all aware of their luck in enjoying such surroundings. Set in 84 acres of landscaped lawns, terraces and views towards the River Orwell, the hall itself, with pediments, urns and panelled drawing rooms, might easily double as the set for a period drama (or indeed, as a wedding venue – which it is). This is the hub of the school. Lunch is eaten in the orangery with seating on the terrace for sunny days and the Grab and Go bistro nearby for girls to get a quick snack, or lunch if they are short of time. The sixth form occupies the top floor (several flights, no lift and a reminder on the walls that in the past, servants, usually girls, carried buckets of coal and water up the very same stairs) with its own study areas, common room and well-equipped kitchen. A large separate teaching block, the sports hall, swimming pool and theatre are close by. Various outbuildings have been converted for art, DT and food science. The walk between the various buildings gives the chance for a breather and helps to foster contented pupils. Everything spick and span and well ordered.

Junior school is a bright, purpose-built, two-storey building sharing the spectacular grounds of the senior school. Recent sprucing up includes clapboarding the exterior – 'not sure I like it,' said a pupil. A bit reminiscent of Center Parcs, maybe. A well-stocked, redesigned library at the centre of the school, has flexible seating (look out for the Sellotape chair) and play areas. Pre-prep and nursery have their own defined area of the building and separate playground. Decent sized and light classrooms, lots of work displayed and traditional desks – 'we are allowed to decorate the inside of the lids!'

Very stylish grey blazers with a grosgrain trim and grey skirts (cerise jackets in the juniors) give way to own clothes in the sixth form.

Pastoral care, well-being and discipline: Frequently cited as a strength by parents. 'Nothing is too insignificant for them to bother with'; 'some slight bullying was dealt with well – a lot went on quietly behind the scenes'. The policy of changing the form groupings at years 7, 8 and 9 is designed to help foster good social relations and help counter any tendency for cliques to form. 'Intense friendships can prevent girls mixing well. We usually have a few requests to stay with established friends, but most accept the benefits of a regular shake-up'. There is a seating plan for each lesson, also changed regularly, to reduce the anxiety of constantly wondering, 'Who shall I sit with?' It also helps teachers get to know pupils quickly. The houses, named after eminent women, are largely used for social, sporting and charity events. Year 7 pupils are all befriended by senior girls. Good-tempered though respectful relations are the norm between staff and girls. Few, if any, serious problems with behaviour.

Pupils and parents: Almost 70 per cent travel to school on designated coaches from the many pick-up points in a wide catchment, mostly Suffolk and north Essex. The journey is seen as part of school social life. Mostly professional/business and some farming families; many parents commute to London on certain days. The girls are friendly and charming, easy to converse with but not overconfident. Good mixers.

Entrance: Informal assessment for those joining in reception (nursery is non-selective), informal tests in maths and English managed during a visit to the school thereafter. All pupils assessed for SEN. At 11, the majority come up from the junior department with another 30 from local state/independent schools. Entrance tests in English, maths and verbal reasoning, plus a report from current school. Juniors transferring also take the tests. For sixth form, at least five GCSEs at grade B, A for maths.

Exit: Nearly all juniors move up to the senior school. Around half the year group leave at the end of year 11 – some take advantage of the grammar schools operating just over the county border, others to sixth form colleges or local co-ed independents. A few choose boarding further afield. Post-A level the great majority leave for top flight universities: six to Cambridge in 2016 (Anglo-Saxon, Norse and Celtic perennial favourite); Birmingham, York, Royal Holloway and Nottingham Trent also popular. Good range of subjects studied with a clutch heading for drama, performing arts and theatre courses (one in the US) as well as two medics, four engineers and three apprentices in 2016.

Money matters: As one of the GDST schools, the fees represent excellent value. Academic, art, music, drama and sports scholarships are offered at 11 and 16 for up to 30 per cent of fees. Means-tested bursaries are also awarded for demonstrable need and academic merit, up to the value of full fees. Fee remission of up to 50 per cent for staff children – as in all Trust schools.

Remarks: A thriving academic environment for girls who relish drama, music and sport in a glorious country setting. A day school with a boarding feel.

I

Ipswich School

Henley Road, Ipswich, Suffolk IP1 3SG

Pupils: 1,093; 45 full/weekly boarders (two-thirds boys) • Ages: 3-18 • Sixth form: 235 • C of E

Fees: Day £13,137- £14,403; Boarding £21,462 – £26,643 pa

Tel: 01473 408300
Email: admissions@ipswich.suffolk.sch.uk
Website: www.ipswich.suffolk.sch.uk

Headmaster: Since 2010, Mr Nicholas Weaver BA (30s). Read engineering at Jesus College, Cambridge. Previously deputy head (academic) at Portsmouth Grammar, and before that taught physics at the Leys School, Cambridge, the Royal Grammar School, Guilford, and Radley College. Tall, elegant, with an approachable, unruffled manner. He is keen to develop what he calls the 'growth mind-set' – a strategy for developing the potential of all pupils, with a particular eye on those identified as academically able. The Academic Excellence Programme is designed for this 'elite' group, although open to all comers. Changes to senior management structure have resulted in a more streamlined, collegiate approach; all posts are now advertised externally. He is married and has three children, all at Ipswich Prep.

Prep school head: Since 2009, Mrs Amanda Childs BA MA, Dip Ed (late 30s). Previously deputy head of Alleyn's Junior School, following a teaching career at various independent schools and an international school in Bangkok. Dedicated and determined to introduce the school to changed teaching practices, for example in teaching reading. Extremely au fait with all current educational fashions but steers her own course. Believes in clear boundaries and instilling in pupils respect for each other's differences. Married to Martin, a journalist, and they have two daughters, both in the prep school.

Academic matters: Prep school class sizes fluid, and range from 18 in reception to 24 in years 5/6. Form teaching in most subjects, with setting in maths and English from year 5, and specialist teaching for certain subjects in years 5 and 6. All pupils are screened on entry for specific learning difficulties and emotional/behavioural problems are quickly picked up on. The School Action Plus programme is designed to support struggling pupils with the aim of them being able to cope, eventually, in the senior school.

Pupils are encouraged, even pushed, to work hard. Whilst not an academic forcing house, there is no place for coasting in the senior school. The brightest of the bright will be fast tracked – lessons before school for some and there is a programme of enrichment, including lectures and seminars, geared specifically at these pupils – 'We are hoping the head doesn't over-do all the elitism and Oxbridge stuff,' commented a parent. Homework is now called PSC, which stands for Preparation, Stretch and Consolidation – 'No one remembers,' said several. Though selective, the school has quite a wide ability range, but despite the head saying, 'we recognise the hard-won B grade', there are not many of these in evidence. In 2016, 65 per cent A*/A grades at GCSE. A level results saw 51 per cent A*/A grades. The head has made clear his priority to raise all teaching in the school to exceptional standard and school expects pupils to have the solid achievement of an A grade at

GCSE for subjects studied at A level. Sixth form is no place for slacking, with compulsory enrichment programme alongside A levels. No demand here for IB, as curriculum seems to be diverse enough.

All year 7 entrants are tested for SEN, but as this is a selective school, the needs identified will often be to do with organisation, mild dyslexia, or for ESL, for which support is offered outside the timetabled day. Head has introduced drop in clinics at lunchtime so any pupil can seek help informally.

Games, options, the arts: A recent shift in emphasis in referring to the 'co-curricular' rather than the 'extracurricular', with a designated assistant head in overall charge (formerly head of sixth form). First division player in all the team sports – frequently area and national finalists, most recently in hockey. Sport is for all, and the school often fields teams from A-D. Other sports on offer, and played highly competitively, include karate, sailing and equestrianism. Also entered a winning pair in the national finals of Eton fives. School recently bought nearby sports centre, complete with sports hall, fitness gym and floodlit Astroturf hockey pitch.

Music is taken seriously, with a third of pupils taking individual instrumental lessons and a variety of orchestras, choirs and ensemble groups which perform throughout the year. The chapel choir, besides a regular slot singing evensong at St Paul's Cathedral, tours both at home and abroad. The Annual Ipswich School Festival of Music brings internationally-renowned musicians to perform at the school in masterclasses and workshops. Britten Faculty of Music is based in a state-of-the-art purpose-built music school, opened in 2015, with a concert hall and recording studio still to come. School hopes this new facility to become one of the region's main musical hubs, attracting performers from Suffolk and beyond.

Drama GCSE is offered as an enrichment sixth form option (no theatre studies A level) and several productions are staged throughout the year. The sixth form recently performed Seussical-the-Musical, based on the works of Dr Seuss. Thursday afternoon activities include CCF and Duke of Edinburgh plus a long list of clubs and societies including photography, journalism and robotics. If the club isn't already there, it can be started.

Prep school walls covered with art/science work – some of it spectacular – and there is an interesting menu of music, drama and other activities, both within the school day, and at after-school clubs. All year 3 pupils learn a stringed instrument as part of the curriculum; new music school.

Boarding: The boarding house is a short walk away, occupying its own grounds – which include the school Astroturf – in a suburban road. Common room and boarders' kitchen; breakfast, dinner and weekend meals eaten in the boarding house. No Saturday school but EFL lessons available on Saturday mornings.

Background and atmosphere: The school has occupied its present site since 1852, but it has a medieval foundation (Cardinal Wolsey is an illustrious old boy) and the school's history is well-recorded and treasured. In addition to the original, rather gloomy Victorian structure, there are some fine and functional 20th century buildings which adjoin each other by a series of passages, steps and covered ways. Later additions include the sports facilities and sixth form building, which overlook the playing fields – a focus for relaxation as well as sport. There is a school chapel and a library of exceptional quality and design with windows by John Piper depicting the seasons. Everything is well cared for and maintained. Odd fusty corners in the older part of the school offset by displays of pupils' work, posters and subject information. Pupils by and large polite rather than courtly but clearly intent on their pursuits. Straightforward uniform policy, with sixth formers allowed the latitude of wearing their own clothes. Conformity seems natural here though 'slight oddballs have been successfully integrated'; especially if they are clever.

The prep school has occupied its own purpose-built premises next to the nursery and pre-prep since 2006. An eye-catching building which, though striking and affording fine views of the town, has limited play areas and no grass whatsoever. Pupils are taken over to the main school playing field to let off steam in the lunch break, and have timetabled access to the sports facilities. At the end of the school day, the playground transforms into a car park for collecting parents.

Pastoral care, well-being and discipline: The prep school is quick to respond to problems as they arise with contact via email and the head available before school each morning. Pupils charming, though we felt that the ones we met (year 3) were inhibited by the presence of the registrar, acting as chaperone.

Usual house and year group tutorial system in senior school with a separate identity for years 7 and 8, each form keeping the same tutor. The school chaplain, a full-time member of the teaching staff, plays a key part in the pastoral set up. The matron has her room strategically placed near the hard play area, a reassuring presence at break and lunchtimes. There is a strong expectation that pupils are well-organised and can cope with the pressure, though all know where to turn if in difficulties. Despite the city location, little flouting of rules, and a system of merits and detentions seems to keep the odd backslider on track. Occasional serious offenders dealt with firmly.

Pupils and parents: Mix of farming, professional and business families from the rural reaches of East Anglia together with those from Ipswich itself or other towns, mostly in Essex. Quite a lot of parents are London commuters. Extensive network of bus routes bring many pupils to school, and of the 40 or so boarders, over half come from overseas, mostly Europe and the Far East. Boys continue to outnumber girls by about 2:1 in years 7 to 11; the influx of girls to the sixth form – often from the nearby GDST school – gives a better balance, though girls remain in a minority. Pupils appear to be well able to cope with the rigours of the school; perhaps not ideal for those lacking in confidence or who thrive on pushing the boundaries.

In addition to Cardinal Wolsey, notable old boys include the author and illustrator Edward Ardizzone, physicist Sir Charles Frank and the writer Rider Haggard (King Solomon's Mines).

Entrance: Admission to the nursery is by registration. For reception and years 1-6 entrance assessment includes reasoning, English and maths. Children are also observed at play. Main points of entry are at reception, year 3 and year 5. Pupils come from a variety of schools and a wide catchment area, 'though half have a Colchester postcode'.

The majority join the senior school at 11 (year 7) with many coming up from the prep. All take the same entrance exam (results are used to organise setting in year 7). A report from the pupil's present school and a chat with the head are also required. At 13 (year 9), another 30 or so are also admitted via common entrance or school's own exam. Pupils do need to have above average ability to pass and to flourish. Entry to the sixth form requires six GCSEs with at least Bs, preferably As in chosen A level subjects.

For overseas admissions school will now consider UKiset applications (online testing system) rather than paper-based tests.

Exit: For most juniors, an easy transition to the senior school. A few leave for maintained schools (there are flourishing grammars in Essex). Any thought unlikely to cope in the seniors will have been given fair notice. Around 20-30 per cent leave after GCSEs. Majority of sixth formers leave for university with a leaning towards the Russell Group, particularly Exeter, Birmingham, Nottingham and London universities. Five to Oxbridge in 2016, and the head is keen to push up numbers; one vet and two off abroad.

Money matters: Queen's (academic) Scholarships equivalent to 50 per cent offered at 11 and 13, based on pupil's performance in the entrance examination plus interview. Means-tested bursaries can cover the full fees if necessary. Scholarships are also available in music, art and sport at 11 and an all-rounder at 13. A full range are offered at sixth form, together with a number of means-tested bursaries.

Remarks: A well run, urban school, with many opportunities for bright, motivated pupils to excel.

Kesteven and Grantham Girls' School

Sandon Road, Grantham, Lincolnshire NG31 9AU

Pupils: 1,201 • Ages: 11–18 • Sixth form: 313

Tel: 01476 563017
Email: mailto@kggs.org
Website: www.kestevengrantham.lincs.sch.uk

Head: Since 2015, David Scott (50s), previously deputy head. A maths graduate, he has taught at the school for 25 years and his own daughter was a student here.

Academic matters: In 2016, 58 per cent A*/A grades at GCSE; 35 per cent A*/A at A level. Most girls take 10 GCSEs in a wide range of subjects, with the vast majority taking at least one language. French, German and Spanish are the options. High quality framed artwork displayed throughout the school, including a charming mural done by a group of previous year 13s. Newly opened art and drama block and large DT room full of equipment. New sixth form block, still being furnished when we visited. Very bright and cheerful with lots of computers and space, comfy sofas and quiet areas too. Maths, sciences and geography well supported with, typically 40 per cent taking maths A level and half doing biology and chemistry.

The lessons we observed showed focused, happy, relaxed, alert girls. We were greeted with broad smiles from everyone, staff and girls, whatever age and subject. Lovely to see. Amusing to see year 8 girls litter-picking in the newly planted gardens. We were assured it was for a geography project. Killing two birds with one stone, very enterprising. Would have liked to see more windows open as most classrooms were very stuffy. Claims that the new blocks had air conditioning, but no sign of it working yet.

'Lots of homework but they seem to keep on top of it,' said a year 13 parent. 'The girls seem very relaxed even though they are under pressure to achieve,' said another parent. 'I was worried that my daughter was struggling in one subject and needed extra private tuition so went to the school about it. They very quickly came back to me, persuaded me it wasn't necessary and they could offer extra help. It was the right decision, she got the help she needed and did well'.

Learning support available for those who need it. There are 49 on SEN register and 271 registered as 'gifted and talented'.

Games, options, the arts: Despite the school being an unashamedly academic hothouse, the girls are encouraged to broaden their horizons. Lots of sport available. All the usual for a girls' school and then a bit more. Rugby team very successful and thriving. The girls have chosen to play lacrosse and volleyball this year (via the school council). Equestrian team fifth at Hickstead last year; water polo well supported – the U16 team is rated second in the country. 'Sport is well represented lower down the school but dwindles as you get higher up,' said a year 13 parent. Long list of achievements and successes in the lower years, though.

Music and art well represented. More than 200 learning musical instruments. Lovely to hear piano practice as we toured. School has been successful in the annual Grantham Music Festival. Lots of music clubs and orchestras. Newly opened art and drama block. Rehearsals going on and props being made for end of term productions.

Plenty of clubs run by sixth form girls for younger ones, including science, history, drama and various sports. There's a year 7-12 gardening club and a coffee and culture club for the A level girls. Lots of school trips including exchanges to France, Germany and Spain and the opportunity to go to Japan in years 10/11. World Challenge expeditions to Vietnam and Cambodia.

Background and atmosphere: Founded in 1910 and still on the same site overlooking the town of Grantham. Attractive Edwardian main building, evocative space with Chesterfield sofas and high ceilings, with boards of head girls' names mounted around the old hall. One name stands out: Margaret Roberts, who came back in 1980 as prime minister Margaret Thatcher to open the new Roberts Hall. Lots of new-build tastefully added, most recently in 2014. Gardens still present, thankfully, newly planted (funded by the PTA) after building work. Resident ducks still in situ. School feels spacious, lots of room in corridors and elsewhere (apart from a crammed car park). Good to see lots of tables and benches outside. Immaculately kept; thank you, year 8 geographers.

The girls wear a plain uniform disliked by some parents. We got comments such as 'uniform standards have slipped recently,' and 'my only grumble about the school is the uniform. It's really scruffy and too similar to other schools. They need to wear it with more pride'. One mother even said, 'I'm fed up with seeing indecently short skirts'. Can't say we noticed. We understand that if the skirt is rolled up to be too short – girls will be girls – the owner is told to wear trousers, which are also part of the uniform. Didn't see many wearing them, though. Sixth formers wear their own clothes.

School lunches are a hot topic with a reputation for excellence. 'Nothing like normal school lunches,' was a comment we heard a lot. Two years ago there was a major overhaul, at the request of the girls. Food is now sourced locally and cooked on the premises. It was costly to set up but the head was keen to make it work. Lots of choice, well-supported and looked delicious.

Powerful school council. The girls are listened to, mostly get what they ask for and are given choices. 'A school for the girls'. Rather than one head girl and deputies there are three of equal stature. The head feels that the role is too demanding for one girl who is also working hard towards her final grades (hear, hear). The girls work as a team and have their own office. 'We need three of us to look after the head,' said one with a smile.

The school is competitive but the girls seem to want everyone else to do well too. Lots of support for each other and from staff. Mutual respect all round. Nice to see bunches of flowers in the hall to welcome visitors. Each form takes their turn. When we were there, the year 7s had left bunches for the incoming year 6s on their taster day.

A very strong house system with lots of competitions, ranging from usual sports and choirs to baking, sweet making, story telling and pantos. 'The house competitions are very competitive, but nicely so,' said a parent. 'What is so good about them is that there is something for all, not just the sporty, and all the girls are very involved with them. And it is fun'. Ambitions among the younger girls to be house captains in year 13.

Pastoral care, well-being and discipline: 'Pastoral care is superb', 'the head of pastoral care is an absolute diamond' and 'I've never had to worry about them' are some of the comments from parents. Says it all, really. Every parent we spoke to had glowing praise for the systems in place. 'Any problem my daughters have had, and there have been very few, have been dealt with very quickly'. The girls are moved around in year 9 to mix them up. 'The form changes in year 9 are handled really well. Initially my daughter was devastated and I wondered if it would work. But it did. The school knows what they are doing,' a year 12 parent told us. Another parent said, 'My daughters have been very, very happy there and I'm very sad that my youngest is now leaving'. Discipline not mentioned by any parent; obviously not an issue.

'I can't fault the place,' said one parent. 'The girls are confident and ambitious, far more so than I was at their age'. 'They work hard and play hard and are rewarded appropriately,' said another parent. 'The school turns out confident, independent girls who don't take any nonsense'.

Parents, pupils and teachers spoke about the family atmosphere in the school. The girls referred to the 'KG family' and the 'KG army'. The school twitter account is keenly followed by a lot of old girls and firm friendships appear to be made.

Pupils and parents: Pupils are from Grantham and the surrounding villages. Some come from as far as Melton Mowbray and Nottingham. There are 76 feeder schools, mainly within a 20 mile radius. Quite a large area because of its rural character. Bright girls from quite a broad spectrum. But, as expected, most parents are professional with ambitions for their daughters. All we spoke to were extremely supportive of the school and very happy with it.

The girls we met were delightful. Every age group sat down together with us. All were chatty, keen to engage with us and each other, very open and happy. Supportive of each other and proud of their school. The KG Army reigns.

Old girls include Margaret Thatcher, Professor Val Gibson (professor in high energy physics and fellow at Trinity College, Cambridge) and Clare Tomlinson (Sky sports presenter)

Entrance: Entry into year 7 after sitting the 11+ in September. This test is standardised across Lincolnshire to select the top 25 per cent. About 300 take it, 200 achieve the target grade and 174 are admitted. Allocation is based on distance from the school and the sibling rule. The school is oversubscribed, but not heavily so. Sixth formers have to achieve six GCSEs at grade B or above, preferably with As in the subjects they wish to study at A level.

Exit: About 10-20 per cent leave after GCSEs, mainly to study more vocational or creative courses at the local college. A handful into employment. Each year 25 or so from other schools join the sixth form. Most go to university; usually several Oxbridge places. Many to other top universities; maths and geography popular subjects, but very diverse range. Gap years popular recently.

Remarks: A well-rounded school, not just an academic machine; these girls are happy and receiving a broad education. 'Nice things happen to nice people,' says school, and the girls are nice. Hard to see where the competition is locally, and why pay when you've got this on your doorstep?

King Edward VI Aston School

Frederick Road, Aston, Birmingham, West Midlands B6 6DJ

Pupils: 825 • Ages: 11–18 • Sixth form: 260

Tel: 0121 327 1130
Email: enquiry@keaston.bham.sch.uk
Website: www.keaston.bham.sch.uk

Head: Since 2004, Colin Parker (50s). He has a history degree from Liverpool and higher degrees from Leicester and Warwick. He spent three years working in the insurance industry before starting teaching in a large comprehensive and then moved to the selective sector. We were very impressed to see him in the play area at lunch time and the boys tell us that he is out there every day 'noticing things'. They regard him as approachable, down to earth, informed and caring about everybody, positive and with an incredibly clear vision for the school and for the boys that we see he has communicated very powerfully. Parents tell us he is out in the playground at the end of school too, and they also find him friendly and easy to talk to – 'he is a brilliant role model for younger teachers', one parent told us.

Colin describes Aston as having always been understated, and he himself is an attractive mixture of unassuming and dynamic. He avoids the ego-driven style of headship and puts the boys at the centre of everything. He treads a thoughtful path between his own, and historically the school's, firm Christian principles and the multi-faith world that is today's Birmingham. His sense of purpose is engagingly mixed with his sense of humour.

Colin is the most senior head in the King Edward's Foundation, an ancient and illustrious Birmingham institution. His experience and wisdom are keenly sought regionally and nationally. He is chair of governors of a primary school and governor at Aston University Engineering Academy. He is an accredited professional partner for newly appointed heads and on the Department for Education's Professional Conduct Panel. Married to Jo, a head of maths; they have three children.

Academic matters: Aston is academically selective and the strong results reflect that. At A level in 2016, 41 per cent of grades were at A*-A, 72 per cent A*-B. At GCSE A*-A grades were 61 per cent. That puts the results well above the national average at A level and at GCSE the progress made by students in their best eight subjects was in the top seven per cent nationally. The science and mathematics results are exceptionally good and huge numbers opt for these subjects at A level. Reflecting patterns in other all boys schools, English and modern languages are not appealing to the same extent, though we were excited by the English department's initiative to explore the male identity and consider texts that examine what it means to be a modern man. A modern language at GCSE has not been compulsory in the past but is going to be from September 2016. There is the broad, though not exceptional, range of the subjects you would expect to find at an academic school. All the subjects to get you onto a prestigious course at a selector university are there.

There are 120 boys in each year group in classes of 30. For optional subjects after year 9, group sizes are usually around 20-

K

25. Unusually for an all boys school, a majority of the teachers are female and they reflect more fairly than many Birmingham schools the cultural make-up of the city. The deputy head and head of learning support are both female.

Over 10 per cent of the intake comes in with identified learning support needs, usually dyslexia or autistic spectrum. Support depends on the level of need and ranges from a teaching assistant with a boy most of the day to occasional meetings to help with organisation. This is all funded by the school. The school says it picks up quickly on any problems that haven't been identified at primary school and the appropriate support is there. For a highly selective school, we were impressed. The boys themselves spoke warmly of the willingness of teachers to give extra help at lunchtimes and the success of the student mentor programme. One boy who had joined the school at sixth form from a non-selective school told us how quickly the school had picked up on his lack of a strong work ethic and he is coasting no longer! There are strong induction programmes in place, not just for year 7s but also for those moving into the sixth form. One parent described induction as 'fantastic'. Parents also applauded the student mentoring scheme. 'I've been telling my son to do his homework as soon as he gets it, for years. But it is only since his sixth form mentor has said it that he has started to listen!'

Students spoke warmly of the support in place for university admissions both in terms of general UCAS advice but also help for those preparing for university entrance exams of one sort or another, including Oxbridge. Parents say that the information is very full but directed at the boys, not them. We think that is probably right at the sixth form stage. There is a comprehensive programme of careers advice from year 7 with outside advisors brought in at various stages.

There is at least a double lesson a week timetabled for enrichment activities, which are wide ranging and include volunteer work. In major exam years, there are sessions on stress management, yoga, mindfulness, aromatherapy. Some of these are supported financially by the parents' association.

Games, options, the arts: The school has been a lead in local sports partnerships for a number of years. For an inner city state school, facilities are excellent. Rugby is the big passion but plenty of boys relish their hockey, cricket and football. There are overseas rugby tours. By year 10, there are options for boys who don't like the conventional team sports. The boys assured us that the sports department is as interested in those who are not natural sportsmen as those who are. All the boys study fitness and health issues relating to sport.

There is a range of extracurricular activities including Amnesty International and all three Duke of Edinburgh Award levels. Houses compete in sporting and academic events – such as the house chess competition.

Music is high status. 'Sensationa,l' as described by one parent. The Big Band regularly tours in Europe. There are bands and ensemble groups for all levels. The Head is determined that boys whose families do not have the background to support an interest in music at home will have that opportunity at the school. Indeed he believes that extracurricular activities are essential for providing the cultural capital that many homes cannot offer and he directs school money into ensuring the chances are there. Parents told us their sons find the opportunities inspirational.

House drama competitions are keenly contested, and a highlight of the drama year is the annual musical theatre production with the nearby King Edward V1 Handsworth girls' school.

Background and atmosphere: The architect of the 1883 school was JA Chatwin, who worked with Pugin and Barry on the Houses of Parliament, and the confidence and optimism of that founding period continues to pervade from the Chatwin bricks today. The school is squeezed into a site in the middle of one of the poorer areas of Birmingham that has always housed waves of immigrants. Today it is largely Asian working class, and the downside of having been on the same site since 1883 is a lack of space and a rather tatty immediate environment. There has been building going on since 1883, some of it very sensitively done, but there is a sense of a lot of people in a very small area. The school is hoping to expand onto some nearby wasteland, but the negotiations are taking a long time.

The boys are very conscious that they inhabit the oldest of the King Edward Foundation buildings and they are hugely proud of their history. There are old school photos adorning various walls as a reminder of the shared past, and a large memorial plaque with the many names of boys who died in the two World Wars. Each year November is a time for remembering the lives of individuals who died in the wars, and the boys relish the stirring stories. There are honours boards in the library, portraits of past headmasters, a rousing school song and carefully cherished archives. The boys are encouraged to understand that they are part of something bigger than themselves today and they all can add to the school's rich history.

The juxtaposition of that sense of the past that you find in many long-established independent schools and the ethnic make-up of the school today is thought-provoking, to say the least. Often described as the 'most Brummie' of the King Edward's schools, Aston has always reflected the changing nature of the local community in ways the other schools haven't. The school is majority Asian but there is a mixture of white, Afro-Caribbean, Chinese, Eastern European. It is less established middle class than the vast majority of UK grammar schools and its achievements are all the more remarkable because of that. The school has set out to attract families on free school meals, widening its social intake, and it is very successful in doing this.

Virtually everyone is involved in extracurricular activities, in travel, in music lessons, so by the time the boys leave, the school has ensured that they have had many of the experiences that are part of the fabric of traditional British middle class life. There is a huge sense of motivation and focus about the school.

We were told by various groups about The Aston Man. This ideal was conjured up by a past senior teacher and is embedded in the consciousness of all the boys. The Aston Man is well rounded, sticks to his own moral values, is unique and stands out from the crowd. One boy, in Kipling-like terms, described The Aston Man as 'a young gentleman, gracious in defeat and respectful in victory'. His choice of language was used without a hint of irony, was spoken with considerable pride and was greeted with serious nods from the other surrounding boys.

Pastoral care, well-being and discipline: What is particularly striking about Aston is the way it has moved on from traditional stereotype of boys' schools. Perhaps it is the large number of women teachers, perhaps it is the fluidity that the school has always needed to deal with the ever-changing Birmingham ethnic population.

To start with, we never heard anyone talk about 'boys', it is always 'students' or 'the young people'. The students spoke easily about emotional problems and explained the various formal and informal ways in which the school supported them through the difficult times they all experienced at some stage. Parents confirm that the school encourages the boys to talk to someone if they are not happy or don't feel safe. There is a school counsellor, a system of anonymous emailing to the safeguarding officer, a series of little podcasts that deal with teenage problems that the boys can access from anywhere without anyone being able to identify them, and student mentoring for personal problems, particular strong through the house system with older boys supporting younger ones. One parent told us her son had used it because he was unsure of himself and lacking in confidence. No big problem, but the student mentor had been a great support. The boys say the teachers are outstandingly kind and they feel known and cared about as individuals. Teachers spoke about the staff briefings where any personal difficulties a boy might be experiencing are shared immediately and action agreed all together. Parents spoke warmly of the speed with which the school reacts to any parental concerns. Staff can all be contacted via email and replies are prompt. All this is against a backdrop of a very thorough and thoughtful personal education programme.

The approach to discipline issues is absolutely clear. Behaviour that is against the values of the school is not tolerated and there is the usual range of sanctions. The school is not afraid to use fixed term exclusions for the more serious offenses such as stealing, or speaking very unacceptably on the internet or in person. However, everyone told us that it is a very forgiving school and the approach to punishment is essentially redemptive, and seen by boys and teachers as a way of improving the individuals involved. Once the punishment is done, there really is a fresh start. Staff spoke of one of last year's vice school captains who had been excluded earlier on in his school career but developed over time to allow him to win one of the school's coveted student leadership positions. The head's view, which he shares with despairing parents, is that mistakes are far better made in school than outside. The school's main aim is to ensure that the boy is back on the path to becoming a good citizen, and parents see this. It is telling that there have been no appeals against fixed term exclusions.

Pupils and parents: Over half the sixth form comes from families where neither parent has a university education, but there are also a fair number of professional families, and those with a business background. Families largely come from north of the city centre – but it is not a school that draws exclusively from the leafy suburbs of Sutton Coldfield or Solihull. Possibly the large proportion of Asian families skews the career aspirations towards the medical professions and engineering. Families are very motivated to support the school. There is a strong Parents' Association and parents feel that the school actively encourages parents to be involved. The Parents' Association raises serious money each year by organising parking for Aston Villa matches.

The boys are a delight. Serious and earnest, deeply loyal to the school, they are aware of the privilege of being at a King Edward's school. They appear to genuinely care for each other. They like being in a single sex environment and tell us they make lots of friends with girls at KE Handsworth through joint activities and on the Green Buses which bring lots of them to school. Teachers say the boys don't have to define themselves against girls and are more open talking about emotions than boys are in mixed groups.

Entrance: Although Aston doesn't demand the top marks in the Birmingham 11+ exams, don't be lulled into thinking it is anything other than highly competitive to win a place there. The numbers sitting the 11+ are eye watering and the relevant age group is expanding all the time in the Birmingham area. The criteria and technicalities of the entrance exam are clearly explained on the King Edward's Foundation website. A new criterion has just been introduced giving preference to pupil premium children. About 40 places are offered at 16+.

Exit: In 2016, seven per cent left after GCSEs and 13 per cent at end of year 12. Of year 13 leavers, virtually all make a university application, mostly to Russell Group universities and other high tariff institutions such as Aston, Loughborough, Bath. Other popular university destinations include Birmingham, Warwick, Nottingham and the London universities. The most popular university courses are engineering, medicine (five places in 2016), dentistry, economics, pharmacy and history. Up to eight go to Oxbridge each year (two in 2016).

Remarks: Aston is a remarkable school by any standards and boys who get offered a place must be regarded as amongst the most fortunate in the West Midlands. It is a revelation, both in how education for boys can work to encourage gender intelligence and equality and also in how ethnic diversity can be tackled within the context of a traditional grammar school. Birmingham wrestles with the challenges of a multicultural city where a minority of the population does not want to integrate with aspects of British culture. Aston does not make heavy weather of this but goes steadily on its way promoting the values that have served the school and its boys superbly for many generations.

King Edward VI Camp Hill School for Girls

Vicarage Road, Kings Heath, Birmingham, West Midlands B14 7QJ

Pupils: 1,021 • Ages: 11–18 • Sixth form: 330

Tel: 01214 442150
Email: head@kechg.org.uk
Website: www.kechg.org.uk

Head: Since 2012 and after nine years as deputy head, Mrs Linda Johnson. Previously spells at Yardley and Sutton Coldfield, 'but this is the place for me. I love it here.' Says she was surprised to be advised to apply for the headship, and even more surprised to be awarded it. The crown sits lightly. Parents and pupils alike speak of her approachability and friendliness, though 'she's no pushover,' said a father admiringly. On the website Mrs Johnson writes with a refreshing lack of jargon, 'the students who leave us should be feisty, caring, confident young women.' 'She's a superb role model,' a mother told us. 'Feisty, yes, and with a wonderful sense of humour, but she doesn't take her eye off the ball and is both dedicated and fun.' That word 'fun' cropped up frequently during our tour which was, in itself, a lot of fun. 'We're fond of irony, here.' If you have the opportunity, ask about the Princess Award and its faintly politically incorrect prize of a bar of chocolate. Pomposity is as rare here as weeds on the centre court at Wimbledon. Popular with staff and pupils, Mrs Johnson enjoys teaching history and 'seeing the girls in another light.'

Mrs Johnson has sat at a round table in Downing Street with luminaries of the educational world. That she and her school won their approval need not worry anyone. This school is an academy, 'which means we don't have to do the boring parts, but it does mean we can do more arts and drama in the lower school, and it's a great help financially when it comes to improving our facilities.' This became increasingly evident as our visit progressed.

Mrs Johnson is no slave to the more bullying aspects of the modern educational system where grades rule and targets preside. But she made the point in her gentle, intelligent way that there was a need to be aware of targets, but not to be driven by them. And for individuals, it is helpful to know where they are. Targets are useful in a personal way, but not to be used as whips and goads. There are many teachers in the state system who would be relieved to hear that.

Academic matters: In view of the entrance system, exclusively and entirely via exams, it is not surprising that the academic standards of the school are very high. After all, it would be disgraceful if they were not. For those who are hooked on exam results there is plenty of evidence to show the percentage of A grades, B grades, etc (in 2016, 57 per cent A*/A at A level and 85 per cent A*/B, 84 per cent at GCSE), and looking at the published lists offers at least one interesting set of results. The most popular A level subjects are biology, chemistry and mathematics. What is initially surprising is that those three subjects also have mixed results. The reason for this was explained to us by the head mistress. Many of the parents wish their daughters to apply for medically related courses. The school often recommends that some girls do an alternative subject, recognising from experience that they may well not be up to passing the top grades in their subjects at A level. Parents, ambitious for their daughters, insist. The result is that a few fail to achieve their chosen course and therefore need to pursue another subject at university. Many schools these days try to forbid the pupils from doing subjects for which they will not achieve high grades. They're worried about their position within the league tables. This school does not need to worry, nor does it need to dominate the academic link between students and school. The pupils learn to contend with perceived failure, which is a useful lesson. Having dealt with that, it is worth emphasising even here that the grades are extremely good and achieved through intelligent pupils and some brilliant teaching.

K

Games, options, the arts: There are plenty of good facilities for those who enjoy games. Tennis courts, swimming pool, rounders, hockey pitches, etc. The girls play with enjoyment and success. Nobody who is keen on sporting activities need feel frustrated by the lack of opportunities. As far as out of school activities are concerned there is a rich and varied diet. Russian, Chinese, debating, lectures, orchestras, choirs, sports, mathematics club, art club, spelling bee, engineering society etc are all available and pursued with enthusiasm. What is clearly outstanding is the music. In a purpose-built music block, many instruments are played and the singing is outstandingly good, with concerts all over the place, and last year the chamber choir and strings group went to Slovenia. Lovely music echoing out as we walked through the school, inspirational teachers and happy, inspired pupils.

The drama is excellent. We witnessed part of a rehearsal going on where there was clear evidence of involvement and enjoyment. There is a Christmas pantomime every year where the script is written by a member of staff. It has long been the wish of the head mistress to play the part of the fairy godmother, but she has never progressed beyond the wicked witch. It remains an ambition which is annually thwarted by the member of staff who writes the play. More serious dramatic performances take place. It is in fact one of the wonderful features of the school that packed into an extraordinarily busy day and in pursuit of good enough grades to move onto worthwhile universities they still have time for many extracurricular activities. That is a credit to their energy and the dedication of the superb staff. Adjoining the school and sharing the extremely attractive campus is the boys' school. Music and drama are two obvious ways in which the boys and the girls can integrate and enjoy the shared resolution of performing convincingly and appropriately.

Background and atmosphere: The school is one of the five voluntary aided, selective, 11-18 grammar schools which belong to the foundation of the schools of King Edward VI in Birmingham. There are links with the 1552 foundation. The history of the school on the website is fascinating to read, not only because of the different heads but because it offers a history of education for girls from its foundation in 1883. The school moved to its current site after the second world war and is on land owned initially by the Cartland family – not, apparently, Barbara Cartland. As you walk around the delightful buildings you occasionally spot a stained glass window in memory of some excellent head mistress or event. There is nothing incongruous about these. They serve to remind everyone of the successful past from which the current school springs.

Later additions include new STEM building – adds two laboratories and three new classrooms while an existing lab has had top to toe refurbishment after pupils won 'design a lab' competition. Currently fundraising with Camp Hill Boys to extend the sixth form building.The atmosphere is lively, friendly and purposeful. Pupils greet one with an openness and friendliness that is delightful and clearly the relationship between staff and pupils is very happy. We witnessed some astonishingly lively and inspirational teaching and as one of the pupils we met said, 'There is always such a buzz and excited atmosphere. The teachers are brilliant and such fun.'

Pastoral care, well-being and discipline: The pupils are bright, the staff rejoice in this; the staff give generously of their time, knowledge and enthusiasms and the pupils exult in that. There are inevitably cases when people fall beneath the general feeling of happiness, and there exists a system of support and advice, both from senior girls and members of staff. Different age groups breed different problems. Tutorials are held on a regular basis and individuals supported where necessary. 'It all works very well,' said a young girl to us.

Pupils and parents: It would be hard to say which is the ethnic minority in this wonderful school of mixed cultures and backgrounds. What is apparent from the moment you enter the school is the friendships and shared pleasures that different groups seem effortlessly to enjoy. In the religious studies lessons, for instance, we were told of the energetic and noisy debates that can dominate lessons when religions are being discussed. It all seems healthy and conducive to friendship and understanding. Many of the parents move house in order to be able to send their children to the school. The children can come from anywhere providing, of course, they pass the exams. Parents appreciate the trouble that is taken with their daughters and those whom we spoke to were universally happy with what was going on in the school.

Entrance: There are 150 year 7 places. Entry is by examination in non-verbal reasoning, verbal reasoning and maths. The answers are sent off to Durham University, which marks them and sends back the scores. The school now prioritises up to 20 per cent of children on pupil premium who have achieved the qualifying score, so the charity founded in 1552 is returning to its original purpose of helping less privileged children. There has been much activity undertaken with local Birmingham primary schools, and the latest admission criteria reflect this aim. The intention is to open up the opportunities to a wider range of pupils, though there is no intention to lower the standards required.

Exit: Vast majority – about 85 per cent – stay on to the sixth form with a few more leaving after year 12 (3 per cent in 2016). The most popular careers centre around medically related fields (19 places in 2016). When the girls are in the sixth form they get excellent advice about career possibilities and requirements building on the advice which they were given when they chose their A levels. Most pupils go on to good universities where they perform well; six to Oxbridge in 2016.

Remarks: This is an extraordinarily good school. It demonstrates how it is possible to set high standards and to achieve them not through perfecting the technique of sitting exams, but as a result of talented teachers sharing their interests with intelligent pupils. It is absolutely not an exam hothouse. It is a school of great happiness and joy celebrating intelligence and love of learning. Nothing stuffy, nothing pretentious, just love of excellence.

King Edward VI Five Ways School

   30

Scotland Lane, Bartley Green, Birmingham B32 4BT

Pupils: 1,212: 837 boys, 377 girls • Ages: 11–18 • Sixth form: 411

Tel: 01214 753535
Email: headspa@kefw.org
Website: www.kefw.org

Head: Since 2012, Mrs Yvonne Wilkinson BA PGCE NPQH. Read Geography at Northumbria University. She was the first ever female deputy and acting head at King Edward V Five Ways during an interregnum before joining Holy Trinity School Worcester as head. Then on as head to Gateways School in Leeds, a girls only senior school where she was responsible for introducing boys (up to age 11) before being invited back to Five Ways to become the first female head.

Mrs Wilkinson is, in more ways than one, the Real Thing, and is leading the school to new heights and breadth. While it's impossible to believe her career is the result of ruthless greasy pole climbing or excessive restlessness, it seems that King Edward VI Five Ways was always her Holy Grail. If there was any restlessness, it is over now. No plans to move on and if there were, we are told, many staff and pupils would barricade her in.

Friendly and forthcoming towards pupils and staff (though on her own admission she cannot know everyone), those who do know her speak warmly of her friendliness, encouragement and lively sense of humour. She is articulate, thoughtful, witty and gutsy, when necessary – Yorkshire, but not the dour, monosyllabic kind. Listens generously; addresses the whole school regularly in assemblies and 'has interesting things to say,' one worldly senior pupil told us.

What she values most, she says, is the sense of warmth and friendliness that pervades the school. Greetings and smiles are genuinely exchanged. Ground staff, always a useful indicator of what schools are like, volunteered that to us and we felt it from the moment we walked in. Mrs Wilkinson is deeply committed to widening the access of pupils coming to the school. To this end all the King Edward schools are involved in visiting primary schools and establishing links. Even more effective is that primary school children visit Five Ways and attend classes prepared and run by sixth formers. We met a group preparing for a music class using rhythm and tone. The involvement, the thought, the care and the skill they showed in working out the best ways of making the lessons interesting and fun was wonderful to observe. 'We want to encourage children from all backgrounds – all faiths and none. We have a vast catchment area. The only criteria for coming here is success with exams. Once they're here we want them to feel they can achieve anything worthwhile.'

Mrs Wilkinson is married to Robin, an award winning narrow boat designer and engineer. They have two children, both at university and both working towards careers in medicine.

Academic matters: The school pointed out to us that they were 'voted top school nationally at GCSE 2014 in Department of Education performance tables.' The head is on record as saying that she's not really particularly keen on league tables but feels honour bound to shout with joy when the results are really good. Inevitably she does a lot of shouting, though time and time again we were assured by pupils and staff that 'this is not an exam factory.' We saw some wonderfully clear and challenging teaching and witnessed bright, motivated pupils who responded with genuine involvement.

'The curriculum is student led,' the head told us. 'We start with a blank page and see where the demand lies.' Some 28 subjects on offer at A level – all the regulars plus more niche choices such as philosophy, product design, geology and classical civilisation. Most popular were maths, chemistry and biology; the least popular Spanish, religious studies and Latin. At A level in 2016, 48 per cent of all entries were graded A*-A (80 per cent A*/B). GCSE results also impressive with 40 per cent A*/A.

Without diminishing the importance of the early stages of the school, where good academic habits are inculcated, impressive GCSEs are earned, friendships made and confidence nurtured, it is the sixth form which seems to be the jewel in the crown. The Five Ways School sixth form prospectus is a work of art. It's an advertiser's triumph, a shamelessly alluring document celebrating the impressive facilities, the wonderful opportunities, the well-trodden path leading towards good universities, lucrative jobs and heaven knows what. To be fair, there is a good story to tell: lots of subjects to choose from and a wonderful sixth form centre in which to draw breath, drink coffee, discuss the Great Things of life, use the IT suite, the resources room, the study areas. Plenty of help given to pupils going into the sixth form from below or entering from outside, always a nerve-wracking experience. The tutors and career guidance counsellors clearly do much to help and we were constantly told how helpful everyone had been. 'The induction is wonderful,' a parent told us.

Many do the Extended Project Qualification (EPQ), regarded as excellent preparation for university in that it gives pupils the experience of researching and writing up to 5,000 words on a topic of their choice. Another worthwhile activity is the ACE (Alternative Curriculum Education) programme. At Five Ways it is compulsory, 'delivered during curriculum time with students opting for one activity per term during the lower sixth year and in the autumn term of the upper sixth.' Lest all this sounds as if the sixth form is separate and aloof from the rest of the school, there is an excellent mentoring and leadership system that creates strong bonds between junior and senior, contributing much to the overall atmosphere.

Games, options, the arts: The number of extracurricular activities on offer, one of which must be taken up, supports the feeling that there is life beyond exams. The majority of these take place during the lunch hour and include fencing, D of E, chess, debating and no fewer than seven drama productions a year. And for those pupils who can't get enough of their academic subjects there are maths and biology workshops.

Excellent sporting facilities. A cricket pitch which could host county games and with a wide fixture list; a swimming pool with sound and lighting for aquarobics. (Please, no synchronised swimming.) Good rugby pitches, new artificial grass pitch, sports hall, tennis/netball courts and a climbing wall.

Recent additions include new changing rooms and sports pavilion. Virtually everything you can think of. Sport is where house rivalry becomes most obvious and involved, there's inter house rugby, football, netball, hockey, cricket and the notorious tug o' war. More of that later.

On the arts side there are drama and dance studios and music technology. We didn't see a great deal of art or music during our visit, although the facilities are in place, and we were told that about a tenth learn an instrument. Choir, orchestra, ensemble, samba and swing band practices must make for very harmonious lunch times.

Recent rugby tour to Canada and other sports tours to Italy, Barbados and Ireland. Lots of trips abroad. Eight last year, including Africa, India, China, New Zealand and Chicago. Five Ways; five continents.

Background and atmosphere: Originally sited on the Hagley Road at Five Ways, the school moved from its congested location in 1958 to current attractive 30-acre site in Bartley Green, seven miles to the south west of the city centre, bordering Bartley Reservoir and looking out to Frankley Beeches – even boasts own observatory. In 2003, KEFW became the only co-ed state grammar school in the West Midlands.

The grounds are immaculate – bravo, that delightful gardener – and the whole campus feels pleasantly contained and smartly arranged. Arriving at reception, and we did it more than once, is a delightful experience, not only because of the welcome given from behind the counter but also the smiling, friendly pupils.

Among the entertaining literature given to parents of potential pupils or clapped out Good School Guide scribblers is a pamphlet entitled Five Ways in Figures. Rather fun, it's almost a spoof on the mania for statistics, but it tells you very succinctly a lot about the school: £40,596 was raised for charity in 2013 and fees are £0! There are 1,300 library books, a 100 per cent exam pass rate and KEFW is working with 24 local primary schools. It claims to be one of the top five co-ed state grammar schools nationally. A veritable feast of stats.

Pastoral care, well-being and discipline: 'Firm and fair' was the response we received when we asked about discipline. That would seem a reasonable summary, judging by the behaviour of the pupils we saw, both collectively and individually. In groups they were friendly and helpful when accosted; on their own they were forthcoming and easy. Many told us how safe and happy the school felt. Parents seemed pleased with the arrangements and the trouble the school goes to help the unsettled, the anxious and the nervous.

Head believes in trusting people, hence BYOD (bring your own device), a policy that is believed by many, though not all, to boost self-esteem. This vastly reduces time spent policing individual use of phones, tablets and laptops and, as Mrs Wilkinson says, wasting valuable hours and energy poking around suspiciously looking for what isn't there, instead of rejoicing in what is there.

One boy told us at some length how he felt responsible for the school in the sense that if he behaved badly – he wasn't specific – he would be weakening the structure of the school's society. 'The school is part of me as much as I am part of the school.' He had clearly given the matter a great deal of thought. He wasn't alone in that.

Pupils and parents: There are 60 different ethnic backgrounds in the school and pupils with 30 different home languages (so says Five Ways in Figures). About two-thirds boys. Parents we spoke to expressed pride and pleasure in having their children at the school. They come from a wide variety of backgrounds but feel that the melange works very well. So do the pupils with whom we chatted. Distances deter not: pupils come from all over Birmingham and 40 per cent beyond: Worcestershire and the Black Country.

Entrance: Very competitive. For entry at age 11, 1,800 pupils chase 180 places. Priority for up to 20 per cent of places is given to those on pupil premium and looked after children, as long as they achieve a 'qualifying score', otherwise anonymous pupils accepted by strict order of scores. No interviews, no concessions for siblings or proximity to the school. All applicants are required to complete an application form for King Edward VI Grammar Schools and the preference form supplied by their resident LA. Each of the Edward VI schools counts as a separate choice. One boy told us of the examination, 'I went in with a name and came out as a number.... But here I am.'

Sixth form applicants (including those from within the school) must apply formally. Minimum requirement is GCSE A*/A in subjects to be studied at A level plus at least B grades in English and maths. The school is hunting for new pupils and is shameless in its intentions. 'We welcome applications from students currently studying in other schools....We typically offer about 50 places to external applicants.' This does not necessarily endear KEFW to other schools but Birmingham is fortunate to have some pretty strong rival establishments.

Exit: About 10 (eight per cent in 2016) leave after GCSEs, mostly as a result of GCSE grades. Almost all sixth form leavers go on to traditional universities. Ten to Oxbridge in 2016 – numbers might have been higher but for a 'fear of failure' among more modest pupils. Birmingham, Leeds, Nottingham and Sheffield all popular destinations. Eleven to study medicine in 2016; 536 offers from Russell Group unis.

Remarks: KEFW is a crackingly good school of its genre and in terms of naked exam scores out-punches many high profile independents. The pupils we met were universally articulate, natural and forthcoming. We returned the day after our visit to watch the inter-house tug of war. Here were the young academics, apparently taking the whole thing as seriously as experiments in the chemistry labs. To the untutored eye, both looked equally dangerous. But house rivalry, though fierce, was nothing to the tug of war – and war it was – between senior boys and teachers. Could that seriously academic member of staff, whom we had witnessed the day before disseminating knowledge so interestingly and with such clarity, be the same man who was lying on his back, purple in the face and muttering eternal curses because his side had lost? Yes, this is an academic school, but that's by no means all. There's plenty of fun to be had too.

King Edward VI High School for Girls

Edgbaston Park Road, Birmingham B15 2UB

Pupils: 572 • Ages: 11–18 • Sixth form: 155

Fees: £12,042 pa

Tel: 01214 721834
Email: admissions@kehsmail.co.uk
Website: www.kehs.org.uk

Principal: Since 2013, Mrs Ann Clark. Educated at Bradford Girls' Grammar School, where she won a scholarship to Girton College, Cambridge. Read modern languages, specifically German, French and Spanish. Now teaches German A level, and French to half of the new girls. 'It's good to see how they're settling down socially and academically.' They, for their part, enjoy being taught by her. 'She's very approachable and clear headed,' seems the most common verdict. Attributes, incidentally, acknowledged by parents who like her a lot. She has more than 25 years' experience of teaching in state schools and university, and before becoming principal was deputy head of Heanor Gate Science College in Derbyshire.

One problem Mrs Clark had to face on appointment, not that it seemed to worry her, was the heroic and legendary qualities rightly attributed to her predecessor and the inevitable comparisons. Initially there were some curmudgeonly comments and eyeball rolling, but that was in anticipation. Now, even that educational organ, the Tatler, praises Mrs Clark. And so do we. Mrs Clark does not belong to the duchess style of head: she doesn't sweep along corridors scattering staff and pupils. There is a gentle elegance and grace about her, a quick and ready sense of humour combined with strong inner strength. Very experienced and wholly lacking in pomposity. Mrs Clark has two children of her own. She understands the ethos of the school and is building on it. Confesses to loving it all. Parents we spoke to were full of admiration

Academic matters: This school makes no arrangement for separating groups of 'gifted and talented'. Clearly there is no need, since the girls who have jumped the considerable academic and intellectual hurdles in order to arrive are, by definition, gifted and talented. One inspirational teacher – we didn't meet any who were not obviously passionate and fired up about teaching and, noticeably, not just their own subject – told us there were no cohorts, no clipped wings, no shaping and conscious moulding into a 'type'. What is required and encouraged is intellectual curiosity: 'creative living and critical thinking' – to reach for the stars with feet on the ground. Literally and metaphorically. There is the desire to investigate and discover through intelligent experiment, and the never-ending search for truth confirmed recently by the school's animated involvement with the most recent eclipse. As for that search for truth, look around. 'Trouthe schal delyvere' ('Truth will conquer').Those words of Chaucer appear above an entrance to the school, intended as the foundation stone laid in 1938. The great man would have been pleased, as was a recent inspector who wrote of the search for truth in the school: 'The school has established a practice of probing enquiry and clear investigation in lessons, rather than delivery and acceptance. This has been welcomed by the pupils, who consequently participate eagerly and successfully.' This we can confirm and very refreshing it is.

It seems almost vile to talk about grades and exam results against such a background of learning and scholarship. This school is not driven by Ofsted's occasional bullying and blackmailing techniques, the manic drive for grades and league table success. 'We take it all in our stride,' one girl told us without a trace of arrogance or smugness. Time after time KEHS Birmingham is up near the top of league tables and not merely because of the bright, hard-working pupils, the dedicated teachers and the excellent facilities though, of course, all that is important. It's the ethos, the atmosphere, the energetic quest for knowledge and discovery. Anyone judging this school by its exam results alone would be the sort of person who might see potential in Michael Angelo's pieta in Bruges as a useful door stop. Nevertheless, quite rightly, the school does publish its academic successes, but more as an offering than a drum roll. This is well summed up by a sentence on the school's website: 'The ethos of the school is one whereby we want all girls to develop a love of learning and respect for the life of the intellect that will continue throughout their lives as well as achieving highly in public examinations.' Beautifully put and with the right emphasis. But for those now salivating at the prospect of feasting on delicious statistics, here are some: in 2016, of the 20 different subjects taken at A level, 74 per cent of grades were A*/A and 91 per cent A*/B. At GCSE in the same year 92 per cent of grades were A*/A. More important than any of this is the breadth: the academic syllabus stretches beyond the question of grades. About 30 percent of A level candidates do mixed arts and science subjects. The most popular subjects are maths, chemistry and biology followed by history and English. Good results; happy candidates.

As mentioned, the academic facilities are excellent. There are seemingly hundreds of science labs. Probably fewer than that, but all impressively kitted out. Wonderful library where books are taken out and read and the librarian recommends, introduces and discusses with the girls what they have read. Sounds obvious, but it isn't universal practice. Yes, this school is wonderfully equipped, but there's more to it than that. One area everyone can rejoice in is the blogs section on the school website. Pupils and staff blog tirelessly on a huge variety of subjects. Staff keep a gently tactful eye on pupils' blogs, mostly out of interest as censorship 'rarely required.' In some ways the blogs act as a sort of drip feed for mind and spirit: uplifting blogs on how to keep happy; challenging blogs on matters of the intellect. Fascinating stuff from the academic staff; exciting topics from younger bloggers. A serious distraction for anyone with deadlines to meet. Everyone should read these blogs but you can't hurry. One girl described the blogs as the beating heart of KEHS. Some heart!

Games, options, the arts: A previous visitor remarked, 'this is one of the few schools where enrichment is genuinely as important as the academic'. In fact there seem to be no barriers between enrichment and academic. They feed on each other and the energy generated by both creates a powerful, tangible warmth. The cookery classes, for instance, are stimulating and rewarding, and not just in obvious ways. This is an option for third year pupils and they combine the joys of creating delicious food with scientific considerations involving different herbs and spices, temperatures and mixtures. When we visited, discussions were ranging from developing countries to healthy living, from farming to supermarkets. So many topics drawn from one activity. And that is what happens here.

Art is extraordinarily good right the way through the school in the bright, open studios from where KEHS has recently made a Big Hoot in Birmingham. Read all about it. Superb ceramics. Amazing drama, where we saw some wonderfully innovative work involving movement and dance, creativity and imagination, all run by a teacher whose energy and passion would have made a Catherine wheel seem like a jacket potato. The City of Birmingham has one of the finest concert halls in Europe; KEHS has one of the finest concert halls of any school we have visited: the Ruddock Performing Arts Centre, shared with the boys of King Edward's School next door. Bags of music, with a tremendous variety of concerts, from smaller intimate lunch times to large, sweepingly impressive symphony concerts. Parents spoke of them with much enthusiasm, even if they didn't have a child of their own playing. Music studio recently upgraded, also have Mac music suite running Sibelius.

Sport is prolific with excellent results. Swimming, football, hockey, netball, badminton, fencing, tennis, indoor rowing, snorkelling, gymnastics, on and on goes the list. You name it, it's available and KEHS girls, as one pupil told us, are up for anything. Tours abroad, including a memorable and all-conquering trip to the Caribbean, are a joyous part of the overall experience. Not just the matches. In this school of impressive academic prowess it's good to observe the standard and, indeed, the significance of extracurricular activities.

Wonderfully bright and enthusiastic sports staff. These are not the weight-lifting, whistle-blasting, muscle-bound bone-heads of yesteryear. They are intelligent, thoughtful and genuinely involved in all round well-being. They are the ministers of well-being; something deeper and more significant even than sporting triumph. Moments of activity and physical involvement are balanced with moments of silence, of stillness, 'de-stressing': the effect spreads right through the school. The result is that everything – intellectual and academic activities, music and art, friendships and sporting rivalries – all seem to blend into one harmonious whole, blossoming in the amazing amount of extracurricular activities on offer and the pervading happiness.

Nor is the school exclusively self-involved. Far from it. The sums of money raised for local and international charities, the different workshops run for local primary schools, the visits and the hostings all confirm the responsible and generous position of the school reaching out to its surrounding community.

Background and atmosphere: 'What a lot of schools were founded during the brief reign of Edward V1,' someone said to us the other day. It isn't quite like that – only King Edward's School for boys was founded by Edward VI – but there are eight schools of King Edward VI in Birmingham, six state and two – including this one – independent. All are part of the same foundation and all bursarial work is carried out jointly. The high school was founded in 1883; it followed King Edward's School to its present site next door, in fact adjoining, in 1940. Thus, as is often said, both schools have the best of both worlds. The campus is delightful: pleasing red-brick (but not the aggressive shade), with a dignified sense of space, without any egocentric pomposity. The result is an atmosphere of happy, busy activity: intent but not too intense. Just as the girls felt they could take things in their stride, so the staff seemed happy to stride along with them. One mum told us of the excellent individual help girls could expect from their teachers, at almost any time. Most schools boast of the happy family atmosphere of their establishments. We heard no-one extolling happiness here. No need to: it just is. No one talks of breathing, either.

Pastoral care, well-being and discipline: 'It's all built on trust', we were told. As a result there is no obvious hierarchy amongst the girls, no prefectorial system, no head girl. But there is an unobtrusive structure of which everyone is aware. It's based on an awareness of those around you, a shared endeavour and common sense. Girls who had recently arrived spoke appreciatively of the warmth of the welcome they had received and the friendliness of the older girls. Sixth form tutor groups are composed of a mixture of upper and lower sixth. This not only dilutes any stultifying sense of hierarchy, but makes it much easier for new sixth form girls to settle in. The sixth form council meets regularly with the director of sixth form to discuss any suggestions and ideas. When a new sixth form centre was being considered, there was much discussion about where it should go. In the end it was decided to adapt rooms within the main building so as to avoid any feeling of separateness or aloofness. Jolly nice it is, too. The cake looked delicious.

Pupils and parents: Wherever we went we were met with open friendliness, a willingness to chat and ready smiles. There were plenty of moments of quick and enjoyable repartee. They were amusing about the business of sharing buses and transport with the boys at King Edward's. Both groups come from a wide catchment area: Lichfield, Bromsgrove, Wolverhampton, Solihull etc. A healthy and delightfully friendly ethnic mixture ('we love arguing in religious studies'). Parents, mostly from professional backgrounds, feel involved and 'part of the community.'

Entrance: Everything you need to know about entering the school is clearly laid out on the school's excellent website – note changed timings of entrance exam, now in October of previous year rather than January. The examinations are particular to KEHS. At 11+ three papers (two English, one maths) – no reasoning. Emphasis is on creativity and potential rather than what the candidate has been taught. Applicants might be faced with some creative writing or a poem to elucidate, but whatever is required, the school goes to great lengths to ensure they have selected the right girls. That is when the majority enter the school, but there are occasional places the following year and post-GCSE into the sixth form. Winning a place into the sixth form is, as with everything here, more than just a question of grades. There are exams in the relevant subjects, 'tough but fair' interviews and consideration of the previous school's report.

Exit: Very few leave after GCSEs (about 10 per cent in 2016). An alarming amount of schools these days offload pupils who have not done very well at GCSEs and so probably won't help their A level league tables. KEHS does not do that and remains faithful to its commitment. The school's integrity is justly rewarded: very, very few drop below a C grade and most go on to a good spread of universities (Exeter, Durham, London (Imperial, KCL), Manchester and Bristol currently popular), generous helpings of Oxbridge and medicine (nine and 16 respectively in 2016), and thence to impressive jobs. The variety of university subjects chosen is impressive and a tribute to the school's help and advice. It is never a sausage machine.

Money matters: Under the heading of Bursaries and Assisted Places on the school's website there is a sentence of Boswellian longevity. There then follows a crisper sentence which will encourage many. 'Currently almost a quarter of girls in the school receive some form of bursary support thanks to funding provided principally by the Foundation but also by alumnae through donations and bequests.' There are energetic and determined efforts to make the school increasingly accessible financially to a wider range of parents. This is proving successful.

Remarks: This is certainly a top academic school but it's more than that. It's a community where intellectual lessons are imbibed for life along with emotional and creative experiences; where disappointments are often confronted with courage and triumphs with modest pleasure. And lest this all sounds a bit earnest, it is worth emphasising that we were constantly made aware by lively, cheerful pupils – and staff – that for the most part life at KEHS, Birmingham is a lot of fun.

King Edward VI School (Stratford-upon-Avon)

32

Church Street, Stratford-upon-Avon, Warwickshire CV37 6HB

Pupils: 699 • Ages: 11–18 • Sixth form: 300 (84 girls)

Tel: 01789 293351
Email: office@kes.net
Website: www.kes.net

Headmaster: Since 2010, Mr Bennet Carr BA FRGS (40s). Undergraduate studies in geography at Queen Mary's College, London, then PGCE at Institute of Education, followed by The Bishop's Stortford High School (head of geography and sixth form, assistant head). Influential deputy headmaster of St Olave's Grammar School, London, for eight years.

Enjoys the independence that has come with academy status and likes being at a small school where he can get to know pupils and be 'at every production, every concert and every match.' Fanatical about small details making a big difference (shirts tucked in, skirting boards retouched every Friday evening). Parents say he has hugely improved communication. Married with two daughters.

Academic matters: GCSE and A level results are very strong. In 2016, 75 per cent of GCSEs were A*/A. At A level, 62 per cent A*/A and 86 per cent A*/B. English and French departments have chosen to follow the Pre-U rather than A levels, as they believe it better suits the needs of their students (no immediate plans to extend this to other subjects). A growing range of A levels – the 'usual suspects' plus PE and Greek. Psychology recently added to the A level offering, and uptake has been enthusiastic.

KS4 is spread over three years. This allows additional classroom time for curriculum enrichment and, alongside slightly extended lesson times of 45 minutes, gives more time for teachers to extend and enrich learning in the increased time available. All boys take English, English language, maths, triple award science, a language (French, German, Spanish or Latin) and RS as compulsory GCSEs, with three options (which include Greek and ancient history). Two DT options at GCSE (electronics and resistant materials). Mandarin has replaced French as the compulsory foreign language in years 7 and 8 and is taught along with Latin.

At A level, as with many boys' grammar schools, sciences, maths and further maths are popular. Economics, geography and history also well represented. A good few take German and one or two take French and Spanish. Regular reports and half-termly grades, together with target challenge grades, including marks for punctuality, attitude in class, homework etc. As a state school, classes are not 'independent sized' – 28 in years 7 and 8. From year 9, when options are chosen, numbers tend to drop to around 20. At A level, groups are much smaller and the head says: 'I will run an A level course for one student if it's the right subject for them.' Students say expectations are high and teachers are 'always there' if they need help.

Brightly lit and well-stocked library (temporarily housed). Very good ICT facilities and Moodle for homework/research etc. SEN provision not huge but the school does have boys with mild dyslexia, dyspraxia, and Asperger's. Students performing below their personal challenge grades are supported in a variety of ways, including mentoring by senior staff and older students. SEN students are identified, monitored and supported and SENCo works with the school nurse, parents and outside agencies as appropriate.

Games, options, the arts: Sport is important – and well supported. Rugby is still strong and the new director of sport is a former professional player. Rowing, fencing, cricket, athletics and hockey are also offered to a high level. A fantastic sports hall (also used for assemblies, concerts, school productions etc), with a proper fencing piste. Very large and lovely playing fields a mile up the road to which the boys walk. Although the school is naturally keen to excel, all are encouraged to join in. Boys can choose whether to be in 'participation' or 'performance' groups. A-D squads in rugby, so room for more than just the successful handful. Rugby and cricket tours, both in the UK and overseas.

As you'd expect, drama features strongly. There is a lovely drama studio and lots of productions within the school, using, among other venues, the Guildhall where Shakespeare himself would first have seen and participated in stage plays. Very strong link with the RSC and the school is able to access its expertise, costumes, and even its stage on occasion. As well as the 'usual' drama activities, the school has also run Edward's Boys for the last 10 years (a company exclusively producing 'boys' plays' from the early modern period – the only one in the world to do so). Run by the deputy head (pastoral), it has a growing reputation. In a one-off break from their boys' plays repertoire, they performed Henry V at the RSC Swan in 2013. Not many schools can pull off a trick like that.

Lots of music. Previous head's policy of offering a free term of instrumental tuition to every year 7 boy has been maintained as 'sheer genius' by current head, because of the enthusiasm and talent it unleashes. School runs more than 20 choirs, orchestras and chamber ensembles and offers lessons in all mainstream orchestral instruments. About a quarter of the boys take music GCSE, a handful at A level.

Some lovely artwork, and a good, well-lit studio, though facilities are not outstanding. Separate, small building for A level students, where each has his own space to spread out. Some impressive A level work on display. Not a huge subject for the school (about 20 per cent do it at GCSE). Much of the design enthusiasm seems to be channelled into DT, offered in resistant materials and electronics, where the boys get very thoroughly stuck in. Around 40 per cent take DT at GCSE, and there are large, well-equipped, buzzing workshops.

D of E is popular. Most boys take bronze and many go on to higher awards. Lots of other clubs, including debating, bellringing, astronomy and Greek.

Background and atmosphere: Known (inevitably) as 'Shakespeare's School,' this is a place where the history is not so much sensed as inhabited. Classes are still taught in the half-timbered 'big school' where Shakespeare himself would have studied – a fabulous room with an extraordinary beamed and cantilevered ceiling and ancient desks pitted with centuries worth of schoolboy initials, all still in situ. This sits directly over the Guildhall, where Shakespeare's father presided as the high bailiff (mayor) of the town. Until very recently this was used as the school library but is now being renovated for less intensive uses, such as small concerts and drama productions. Just next door is a gorgeous chapel with 15th century wall paintings, where weekly assemblies are held.

New reception area has made the entrance to the school much more welcoming for parents and visitors. Boys are expected to form part of the welcome team. Beyond the Tudor glories, much of the school consists of fairly unremarkable 20th century blocks, but these are well maintained (the head won't tolerate anything less) and serve their functions well. New sixth form space – sixth form is now co-ed – with its own café, which bucks the generally utilitarian trend. Labs are modern and properly kitted out. Halls, studios and ICT suites are impressive.

Sitting in the heart of Stratford, just a couple of minutes walk from the RSC and the river, the school is very much in the heart of the town and significant effort has been made recently to increase positive contact between the students and the local community. As well as involvement with the RSC there is an expectation of service to the town, through the talking newspaper, local hospice and a school for children with special needs. The students know that their conduct and appearance will be noted for good or ill, and seem very keen to make a positive impression.

The head lives within the school campus and says he rarely leaves the gates between Sunday night and Friday so there is a sense of constant input. The general atmosphere is one of students who are proud of their surroundings – thoughtful, engaged, purposeful and confident (but far from cocky).

Pastoral care, well-being and discipline: Pastoral care is at the heart of the school. Second deputy head focuses exclusively on pastoral issues and there is also a school counsellor who visits weekly. Careful induction of the year 7 boys with a buddy system and from year 8 vertical tutor groups are operated within four houses, enabling support and good relationships between different year groups. Pupils mentor one another and raft of 20 elected prefects and five senior prefects must explain at interview why they think they are fit for the job of head boy.

Students say there is 'practically no bullying' and that they would intervene immediately if they saw anything going on. 'The most important things we're learning are to work as a group and be part of a wider community,' we were told. No significant issues with alcohol, drugs or smoking.

Tight control of uniform (the headmaster is regularly spotted at bus stops checking that the boys' top buttons are done up), and boys stand when visitors enter a room. That said, the atmosphere is friendly. Boys say staff are very helpful and always available if they need support. Parents told us that the boys' happiness comes first and that the head makes it his business to 'be everywhere' and ensure that everyone feels valued.

Pupils and parents: With a catchment area that takes in Coventry, Solihull and part of Banbury, as well as some fairly leafy Cotswold villages, there is a wide mix of background and outlook. Some farmers' sons, many from professional and academic families. The boys are courteous, confident, thoughtful and articulate. Currently four per cent EAL pupils. Parents are engaged and astute, very supportive of the school and heavily involved in fundraising for sports, performing arts, and school facilities. They clearly feel confident that their sons' potential is being nurtured and prized here. Old boys (apart from Shakespeare) include Reginald 'Rex' Warneford VC, poet Richard Spender, actor Tim Pigott-Smith, musician Neil Codling (Suede) and the biblical scholar Arthur Peake.

K

Entrance: Year 7 entrance tests are administered by the local authority (for this and the other four Warwickshire grammars). Distance from home/siblings not taken into account. Currently about three applicants per place, although this has been rising. Girls admitted to the sixth form since September 2013 (currently 84 in the school), with around three applicants per place. For sixth form, at least eight strong GCSEs required (4A, 2B, 2C) with As expected in their chosen AS subjects.

Exit: Very few leave post-GCSE. Most stay on to take three or four A levels (some take five). After A levels pupils leave to do everything from classics at Oxford to apprenticeships at Jaguar Land Rover. A strong selection of universities, both in the UK and abroad, including ten to Oxbridge in 2016. Plenty of engineers and economists; otherwise a range from astrophysics to brewing and distilling to Chinese.

Money matters: Three voluntary groups run by parents raise substantial amounts (used to assist boys who may not, for example, be able to afford sports tours or the right kit for D of E). The students say there is no sense that you can't ask for help, 'even if it's just a day trip that costs £30,' and that they all fundraise together to reduce the costs of major trips and exercises.

Voluntary contribution to school fund of £365 (a pound a day) per family each year – used to subsidise extracurricular life. Plentiful leaving scholarships awarded to A level stars (these contribute to their first university term). Additional leaving scholarships available for specific subjects, such as veterinary science and medicine, plus numerous other awards.

Remarks: A flourishing school that is developing an impressive offering under imaginative leadership and achieving results that will turn many independent schools green with envy. A brilliant place for bright boys to flourish, with great emphasis placed on provision for all – from sporty to geeky. Ensuring the boys' happiness is regarded as an essential precursor to academic accomplishment.

King Edward's School, Birmingham

Edgbaston Park Road, Birmingham B15 2UA

Pupils: 856 • Ages: 11–18 • Sixth form: 213 • C of E

Fees: £12,375 pa

Tel: 01214 721672
Email: admissions@kes.org.uk
Website: www.kes.org.uk

Chief Master: Since September 2016, Dr Mark Fenton MA MSc PGCE PhD (40s), previously head of Dr Challoner's Grammar in Buckinghamshire. Educated at Brentwood School, Essex, followed by Peterhouse, Cambridge (history), graduating with a first. PGCE at the Institute of Education, followed by PhD (on how parents choose schools). An impressive career, hitherto exclusively in the state sector, starting at a mixed comprehensive in Chelmsford, then King Edward V1 Grammar, where he taught history and politics whilst rising to assistant head. Moved as deputy head to Sir Joseph Williamson's Mathematical School in Rochester before landing at Challoner's. Taught A level politics until 2014, when he took on an executive headship one day a week of a free school in Ealing. Is one of about 100 heads appointed a national leader of education by the National College for Teaching and Leadership.

Academic matters: Switch from A levels to IB (in 2010) was a risky move for the school and it's still earlyish days to gauge the long-term impact on admission numbers. Judging by the social media debate some parents clearly have doubts, but school is unswerving in defence of the IB: 'It offers a breadth of knowledge and intellectual challenge for students' – and certainly endorsed by impressive rounds results. In 2016, pupils averaged 39 points, with five boys achieving the maximum 45 points.

In 2016, 87 per cent of GCSE grades were A*/A (A*s 61 per cent) – a fantastic result. Academic achievement is a clear priority. That said, an emphasis on fun and practical learning is still in evidence – maths Olympiads, robotics competitions and field trips aplenty (including recent visits to Pompeii and Guyana and rugby tours to Malaysia and China).

Games, options, the arts: Drama is legendary, with the senior annual productions – often hard-hitting musicals with casts of thousands – being the must-see event of the year. Much of the performing arts outside lessons is joint with the girls' school (King Edward V1 High School for Girls), so there is a large pool of both student and staff talent to draw on, but even so, it knocks spots off anywhere else in the region and possibly nationally. There are lots of other productions through the year too, so masses of boys and girls get involved. 'Of course, we audition, so not everyone can tread the boards,' says the director of drama, who works across both schools, 'but if they are really keen, we find them plenty to do backstage'. The end result is that far more boys go off into theatre-related courses than you might expect in such a conventionally academic school.

There is music everywhere. From the swing bands to the choral society to the symphony orchestra ('up to National Youth Orchestra standards,' said one parent), boys are surrounded by opportunities to hear or participate in high quality music. The only down side of all the fabulous music and drama is that boys report going to university can be a bit of a let down. 'Not as good as school,' is a comment often heard from old boys who have taken the dedication and talent as the norm throughout their KES days.

The unswerving professionalism of the whole thing is enhanced by the new Ruddock Performing Arts Centre, which is shared with the girls' school. Named after its benefactor (old boy, successful financier and chairman of the Victoria and Albert Museum, Sir Paul Ruddock), it includes a stunning concert hall – 'acoustics are as good as Birmingham's Symphony Hall,' says the justifiably proud head of music – a drama studio kitted out with the latest technology, and a dance studio with views over the university botanical gardens and girls' playing fields, saying loud and clear, 'We take the arts seriously'.

Main school sports are rugby, hockey, cricket and athletics, but there are more than 20 sports to choose from in total, including water polo, where the school enjoys national success. Thanks to the glorious 50 acre site, the school has six rugby pitches, five cricket pitches, an outdoor athletics track and a £2m hockey Astro pitch with pavilion. The elite squads are national standard and the school is in the middle of a major redevelopment programme with new sports hall, gym and additional indoor recreational space all on the way.

The list of extracurricular activities is long and deliciously idiosyncratic. There is a Living History Society (again gaining from being joint with the girls' school) that is the only historical re-enactment school group in the country. They hold their public gripped at many a historic building event. Then there is a Graphic Universe Society, Agora, the joint philosophical society, the Parliamentary Society and so it goes on, all led by wildly enthusiastic members of staff and senior boys.

Background and atmosphere: Founded in 1552 by King Edward VI, and now the flagship of the King Edward Foundation group of nine Birmingham schools, including King Edward VI Camp Hill, an excellent grammar and the school's main academic local rival. The school moved to a famous Charles Barry building in 1836, but this was demolished and the school has occupied its current 50 acre site since 1936. It sits next door to the King Edward VI High School for Girls, sharing some facilities as well as a healthy social life (while waiting in reception, we watched a procession of nervous boys drop Valentines cards in a special box, to be collected later by one of the girls).

The original red-brick buildings – interiors slightly scruffy with chipped paintwork and scuffed floors ('our corridors have got the shiniest floors,' says school) – sit at the heart of a growing network of shiny new-builds, including the £5m modern languages, science and sixth form centre. Honours boards align the walls, there's constant activity in the corridors and a feeling of fun and friendship prevails. Formalities are conspicuous by their absence and on our tour, a caretaker tidied a patch of lawn, ready for the scattering of a local benefactor's ashes: 'Miss Davis – she went to the girls' school but believed in what we are doing here in terms of assisted places – and so left us £2 million.' Outstandingly successful fundraising programme, raising £15 million in the last six years, an incredible feat for a day school during a recession.

Pastoral care, well-being and discipline: In their first few weeks, new boys – or 'Shells' – receive lessons covering areas such as bullying, safety on the journey to school, how to manage homework and even how to find their way around school. Ongoing PSE programme covers sex and drugs education. School believes drugs are less of a problem than 10 years ago and stress is now a more worrying factor affecting boys. Some of the teachers are trained in counselling and the school has an Open Door Youth Counsellor who comes to school once a week. Parents describe the pastoral care as 'exemplary' and 'outstanding'. Head of pastoral care is singled out by one parent for 'his dedication and commitment to make KES a happy and healthy environment'.

Pupils and parents: Many of the boys are from Birmingham and surrounding areas but some come from as far as Walsall and Derby. Some 60 per cent of boys are from ethnic minorities. No boaters or wing collars here – so not for parents (or pupils) who enjoy a bit of pomp and formality. The boys we saw hurtling through the corridors were a bit scruffy, and there was plenty of noise but the enthusiasm and ambition was infectious.

Parents' comments are resoundingly positive, although some respondents to a recent school-commissioned survey flagged the need for 'more frequent and informative feedback on their son's progress'.

But when it comes to the bigger picture, parents seem reassured. As one mother of a current year 10 boy commented, 'As a parent, you are made to feel that your son counts and is important – not just another number, lost in a large school.'

Old boys include two Nobel prize winners, the painter Edward Burne-Jones, politicians Enoch Powell and David Willetts and writers from JRR Tolkien to Lee Child and Jonathan Coe (who both recently spoke at the school).

Entrance: Highly competitive – 700 candidates for 125 places at 11+. Entrance tests in English, maths, verbal reasoning. Application deadline was earlier in 2016 – end of September, exam early October. Five or so places available at 13+, and another six to 10 places for sixth form entry, dependent on interviews, GCSE predictions and headteacher's report. Academic and music scholarships available (50 per cent funded) as well as means-tested assisted places – now 35 a year. About 30 per cent of pupils are given financial support through these schemes and 10 per cent have free places.

Despite healthy competition from other Foundation schools in the area, demand is high and parents warn about the tough entrance exam. 'I don't think it would suit a boy whose academic ability is below the range – possibly getting to the school by cramming and coaching,' commented one parent of a son on an assisted place. 'KES is excellent if your child is clever and hard-working but not so if they start to struggle to keep up', said another parent. 'It can be a bit sink or swim'.

Exit: Most – around 90 per cent in 2016 – stay on to the sixth form and almost nobody leaves at end of year 12. Twenty-five Oxbridge places in 2016. Other universities include nearby Birmingham (a two minute stroll across the road), Durham, Warwick, Bath and London unis. Twenty-six medics in 2016; economics and engineering also popular. A few parents voiced concerns about how well the IB would serve their children when applying for UK universities where A levels are still the norm, but so far, such concerns are clearly unnecessary.

Money matters: The school is admirably committed to continuing to increase the number of assisted places available. More than half of latest applicants applied for one. The King Edward Foundation chips in £1.2m towards these and successful fundraising has contributed another £5m+. The Assisted Places 100 Campaign aimed to raise £10m to fund 100 places and the school reached that target in June 2016.

Remarks: The exuberance and drive of the place hit you the moment you walk in the door. What it lacks in shine and ceremony is more than made up for in energy and ambition. Switching over entirely to IB with no transition period was a bold move, but so far, the signs are good. No hushed corridors or austere masters here. It's less about the polish and more about the passion. Diverse, caring and fun but underpinned by an intellectual rigour and clear pursuit of excellence.

The King's (The Cathedral) School

 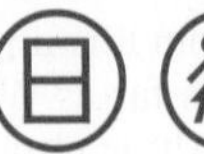  34

Park Road, Peterborough, Cambridgeshire PE1 2UE

Pupils: 1,198 • Ages: 8 – 18 • Sixth form: 354 • C of E

Tel: 01733 751541
Email: headteacher@kings.peterborough.sch.uk
Website: www.kings.peterborough.sch.uk

Head: Since 2014, Darren Ayling (40s). An English graduate who was heading for an academic career before realising that he preferred the tuition work he was doing to fund his PhD. On job training within the independent sector followed. Deputy head at Ipswich School before joining King's for his first headship and first job in the state sector. 'I have always wanted to work at a cathedral school so jumped at the chance to come here.' Attends evensong on his way home every week. 'He's still settling in,' is what many parents are saying, 'but we expect him to make changes.' 'He has a hard act to follow,' came up more than once, the previous incumbent having been in situ for 20 years. 'He is always at the school gates at the end of the day and is very friendly,' said one mother. 'I liked the way he introduced himself to me and my son on an open day and shook his hand. He engages well with the children,' said another parent with three children at the school.

He has plans but is easing himself in gently. 'I have taken over the school when it's in a very strong position so need to maintain that. We are one of the best comprehensives in the country and I want us to be the best of all state schools. I would like to see the school more outward looking and receiving the national recognition it deserves.' He will be teaching the EPQ to sixth formers when he introduces it in 2016.

Academic matters: A creditable 46 per cent A*/A at GCSE in 2016. Thirty-one per cent of A level grades A*/A, 57 per cent A*-B. Most pupils take 12 GCSEs, about to fall to 11 as ICT has been removed from the core to allow for computing. Latin now available at GCSE. All pupils take French or German at GCSE, many take both. Many take music up to GCSE – it is a cathedral school.

Pupils are setted for English, maths, languages and the sciences. Fabulous upgraded science blocks with all mod cons. The walls are wired up so energy usage can be checked. Monitors everywhere, all very high tech. A very proud teacher explained it all, but way beyond us. They all seem to understand it though, thankfully. Take note of the orrery in the gardens (a model of the solar system) – the physics teams' pride and joy. 'It's used to play football on too,' whispered an off-message mole. They even have a weather station, the first one at a school in Peterborough. Lots of talk of visitors from Singapore, China and the US to view it all.

'Loads of homework,' said one parent, 'but they just get on with it.' 'We know immediately if they are not doing their homework,' said another. Lots of talk of close contact with staff and immediate responses. 'My daughter felt she was being overlooked in some lessons and that her teachers didn't notice her. I spoke to the head of year about it and everything was dealt with very well, and solved almost immediately with them involving my daughter and how she could improve too.' Fun French lessons for the lower school. Hard at work in maths and English, very warm, stuffy classrooms, a bit of fresh air wouldn't go amiss. Impressive artwork on display, in reception area as well as around the school. Newly refurbished art room, bright and airy. Good to see DT and textiles work prominently displayed. 'There's good recognition at this school,' said another parent. 'They are quick to acknowledge achievement and make sure we know as well.' Nice sixth form block with vast common room and outside seating. Recently wired up for Wifi, television on the wall; 'We are allowed to watch it at break and love watching Wimbledon,' said one mole. A large, ornate library that covers two floors. 'One visitor asked us why we don't knock it down and build a swimming pool,' said one of our horrified guides.

Low numbers needing SEN support, but those that do are well catered for. 'I had doubts about sending my son, who is statemented, and have been really surprised about how well he is doing and how well supported he is,' said one happy parent. 'He is easily coping with the academic pressure and they have adapted to meet his needs.' Excellent.

Games, options, the arts: Plenty of sport played but mutterings from parents about 'cancelled games.' Lots of after-school practice and enthusiastic participation. 'My girls are desperate to play sports but there don't seem to be that many teams,' said one parent, but then adding, 'they take their kit every day and are always doing something, be it badminton, hockey, netball or in the gym; they love it.' All the usual sports including rugby, football, hockey and netball along with cricket, rounders, volleyball and trampolining. The playing fields are about a mile away, with the athletics track even further, so a quick trek across town at least once a week for lessons. Not to worry, it keeps them fit, gives them a bit of independence and teaches time management. 'We need to work out how long it will take us and if we can grab a snack before we go,' said one informer. Large, newly revamped gym with newish fitness suite overlooking it. House competitions hotly contested with enthusiastic captains encouraging participation. Sports day relished. 'Everyone gets points for competing,'

As to be expected from a cathedral school, music is important here. Choristers from the school, eight or nine from every year up to year 8, sing daily at the cathedral, and it's a big commitment. Evensong and early services including two on Sundays, plus all the Christian ceremonies. 'The choristers are like a family,' said one mother. 'The ethos of the choir and the discipline involved is a great leveller.' Choristers sing up to year 8 (at the behest of the cathedral, girls no longer continue as choristers throughout the school). 'I don't think the choristers receive enough acknowledgement from their peers,' says the head, 'something I wish to rectify, as their commitment is enormous.' Choirs, orchestras and bands abound, 17 extracurricular ones in total, with practices throughout the week. Many performances at the cathedral as well as at school. Almost 30 per cent of pupils have peripatetic instrumental and singing lessons. Large numbers reach grade 8. Mention must go to the organist who had just been offered an Oxbridge scholarship.

Drama productions enthusiastically talked about and supported. A new drama teacher spoken of with awe. Animal Farm as a musical a recent production. As You Like It, set in a circus, taken to Germany. Some productions run by sixth form for lower school. Other plays for the whole school to partake in. A newly refurbished hall with a new balcony section.

D of E well supported and lots of school trips, subject ones, including a geography trip to the Himalayas, as well as the usual ski trips and Auschwitz.

Background and atmosphere: One of only four state cathedral schools in the country. Founded in 1541 by Henry VIII with 12 students, it was originally housed in Peterborough Cathedral. Moved to its present location in the 1800s. An attractive building on a leafy street in a salubrious part of central Peterborough. Surrounded by houses, it is very discreetly sited and is hardly noticeable. The site is now full so no room for expansion, hence the sports fields being so distant. Henry VIII still dominates the school, with a large portrait looking down on them in the dining room. Prefects wear flowing gowns so stand out from the masses. 'We wear full length ones on cathedral days, shorter ones for the rest of the time,' said one of our guides.

Every pupil has a swipe card that they use to access locked doors and buy lunch. Not to be lost, as access then denied. Amusing to see the year 8s locked out of the sports hall after they'd been on a run; not one of them had remembered their card. Our superior guides in their flowing robes talked to them about 'forward planning.' Nice to see these temples of wisdom fix the exuberant year 8s with a steely glare when they tried to barge through the door before us.

Healthy eating a priority here. 'Fish Friday is chip day,' said with a big grin. Food well liked, even though it does seem to be regularly on the agenda for the school council. Represented by two from each year, this august body gets results.

The pupils look smart in their burgundy blazers and striped blouses or ties. Some of the smartest we've seen, with echoes to its illustrious past. The school has gone from private, to grammar to comprehensive, introducing girls as recently as the 1970s. But don't be fooled, this is no ordinary bog standard comprehensive. It feels, and is run, like an independent, with its ancient history and links to the cathedral.

Pastoral care, well-being and discipline: The Christian ethos runs through this school from top to bottom. 'This is a faith school and a cathedral school, inclusive and tolerant with a mission to live life according to our faith,' says the head. 'They pray for family members in assembly and are excellent if anything goes wrong,' said one parent. Another said, 'They visited when a family member was in hospital,' and from another, 'They kept an eye on my daughter when my marriage broke up and were excellent.' Lots of mentoring of younger pupils by older ones. A very happy atmosphere, a genuinely caring place. 'My child loves it here,' was said more than once. 'Pastorally excellent,' said another happy parent. 'My son struggled as there were problems at home. They mentored him and turned his life around.' 'They see the children as individuals,' was another comment.

'I chose King's because of the discipline and structure and their excellent values,' was said by more than one parent. Discipline is hot, they don't stand for any nonsense and parents back this to the hilt. The pupils know where they stand and know the consequences.

Pupils and parents: Happy, relaxed children and equally happy parents. All are ambitious. Fair to say that the majority of parents would be classed as middle class professionals. Very few less privileged and a low percentage of other ethnic backgrounds, very unusual in Peterborough. 'We have a very supportive parent body,' says the head. 'All parents are ambitious for their children and fully back the school in all it does, which is excellent. Disciplinary matters are backed to the hilt by them.'

Entrance: Fifteen pupils into the tiny junior department in year 3, up to nine of which will be choristers. They all gain automatic entry to the senior school in year 7. Seventy-four year 7 applicants, and non-choristers in year 3, admitted on religious grounds. Children of worshipping members of the Church of England, or Methodists, confirmation of five years' worship required. Children of staff and then siblings next in line, then other faiths, then by distance. Twelve year 7 places offered on academic ability, three music scholarships. 'We have children from other faiths at the school as these parents also appreciate our ethos,' said the head. Many more applicants than places, particularly for the academic ones. Pupils come from a wide area, as far afield as Huntingdon, Leicestershire and Oakham, adding to the private school feel of the place.

Entry into the sixth form requires a minimum of seven GCSE passes with Bs in the subjects studied. But don't be fooled: this is the minimum required, but as it's so oversubscribed, accepted grades will be much higher. Sixth formers come from equally far afield, many from the private sector. No religious criteria at this stage.

Exit: In 2016, almost a quarter left after GCSEs, mainly to follow vocational courses, plus further four per cent at end of year 12. An extra 50 join the sixth form. Virtually all go to university, most to their first choice – many Russell Group. Two to Oxbridge in 2016, eight to study medicine. The occasional one to an apprenticeship, becoming more popular. Quite low numbers taking gap years.

Remarks: A happy, nurturing school that is by far the best in Peterborough, and the parents know it and work hard to gain admission. Amazing how many families turn to religion at times like this, but who can blame them?

King's College School (Cambridge)

West Road, Cambridge, Cambridgeshire CB3 9DN

Pupils: 412; 34 boarders • Ages: 4–13 (boarding from age 8) • C of E

Fees: Day £11,505 – £14,625; Weekly Boarding (boys) £22,770; Choristers £7,650 pa

Tel: 01223 365814
Email: office@kcs.cambs.sch.uk
Website: www.kcs.cambs.sch.uk

Headmaster: Since 1998, Nicholas Robinson (50s). Studied English at Anglia Ruskin; PGCE in maths at Goldsmiths. Always knew he wanted to teach after spending a gap year at a Suffolk prep school and getting the bug. Five years at Eltham College where he set up an orchestra; headhunted by Worth School in Sussex as a housemaster at 29. Came to King's as head. A bachelor, immaculately turned out with a quiet wit. Sings with the chapel choir twice a year when large choruses needed. Has been known to conduct orchestras. A keen skier.

Well liked by parents. 'I have a great deal of time for him; he's very friendly and approachable.' 'He is why we chose King's,' was another comment. Another parent not quite so sure. 'He is doing a great job but I would like to see him more engaged with the parents and children. I was disappointed he didn't speak to us about where my son should go next, but, to be fair, his deputy offered great advice.' He has increased numbers at the school from 290 to 425. Lots of building work and refurbishment. They're running out of space but have plans to squeeze in a much-needed sports centre in 2016. 'He's a good thing for the school.'

Entrance: Some children registered at birth, or before. All 4 year olds spend over an hour with the pre-prep department, so 'we can get the feel of the child.' Be warned, they're looking for bright bunnies. Siblings, past pupils and fellows of King's given priority. Parents also have a chat with the head. Entry at 7 after assessment. Chorister scholarships for up to five boys in year 4. Open to any boy in the world if he passes the audition, and many try. All choristers (boys only) offered scholarships of up to two-thirds of fees or more, plus free piano lessons. Means-tested bursaries of up to 100 per cent at age 7, available for all. Children come from a wide commutable area, many from Suffolk and Hertfordshire, some boarders further afield. Many parents ex-Oxbridge, academics, medics, City people. Generally a good cross-section. All very ambitious and the driving force behind their offspring.

K

Exit: The occasional one at 11, but very unusual. No 'evictions'; they work hard, with the help of learning support, to keep them going, and then guide parents to make a 'sensible choice' for the next step. Only one has been 'moved on' in the last 18 years before age 11. Virtually all leave at 13. Over half to local independent schools in Cambridge, particularly The Perse and Leys. Eton, Uppingham, King's Ely and Oundle all popular too. Every chorister offered a music scholarship. About a third of all leavers get scholarships, many music, some academic.

Remarks: Founded in the 15th century to educate the choristers, now housed on one site off a leafy road a brisk walk from King's College. The choristers are an iconic sight walking through the streets in a croc in their Etons and top hats heading for chapel. Primarily a day school with 34 boarders, all boys, 24 of whom are choristers, the rest – some of whom flexi board – in the upper years. The choristers are an important part of the school, famous throughout the world, but are treated like any other pupils within lessons. But their life is different. Compulsory boarders from the age of 8 when they become full choristers, they attend six services a week at the chapel during the university term time, practice for an hour and half before school (in a purpose built acoustic room) and again in the evenings. Weekends during the university term means three more services. They travel the world touring and, of course, there is that carol service every Christmas Eve and the service on Christmas Day. The head plays Father Christmas every year. It's a big commitment with many sacrifices made by the families, but very rewarding, and the boys thrive on it. Every care is taken to make sure they don't suffer academically or personally. 'My son, a chorister, has struggled at times with his work, but the support from the staff is excellent.' They still get to play in the teams but practice is out; there just isn't time. If a boy's voice breaks before he leaves he is still included and part of the set up.

These children are bright and teaching is excellent, with some well-loved, gregarious characters amongst the staff. The special needs department, one of the first to be set up in the country, is very proactive. 'The school contacted me very quickly when my daughter started to struggle with her maths. She was offered extra help immediately, which was excellent.' Lots of support available if needed. All parents commented on how well the staff knew their children. 'We like the school for its "ballsy" attitude,' was said by one parent, with many commenting on the relaxed, but focused atmosphere. Lots of new computers available. Plenty of artwork about, modern science labs and a very well equipped DT room. A large, stuffed library attended by a librarian who appears to be a school stalwart. Knows every child, loved by all. Every parent was happy with their child's progress and had confidence in the school. Pace increases further up the school with a scholarship class in year 8. 'They are realising my child's potential,' came up more than once.

Lots of after-school clubs, chess highly recommended, but music dominates. A fabulous music department, and that's excluding the angelic-looking choristers. Virtually every child plays an instrument, many two or more. Lots and lots of chamber groups, choirs, orchestras and quartets. If you can think of it, they've got it. A new organ in situ, played by many, and lots of acoustic rooms for practice, including the church-like room for the choristers.

Music aside, sport is playing an increasingly big part in school life. Many more top-notch staff employed, with more teams available and better results. A new sports centre in the offing. 'Team selection can be a political minefield,' said one parent. 'I don't envy the staff but they handle it well.' The playing fields are at the front of the school, giving the impression of lots of open space – a bit of an illusion: every spare inch of the site is utilised.

A friendly, happy school, pastorally excellent. Bullying usually nipped in the bud very quickly. One father mentioned that an incident had been allowed to escalate before being 'handled excellently.' A mother praised the handling of manipulative children by the male form teacher. 'He was sensitive, calm and firm.' 'The school's policy of keeping parents at arm's length and bringing the children together is the right one,' said one wise mother. A school counsellor available for all and the children are happy to consult. Older pupils mentor younger ones with a buddy system.

The boarding house is also on site. Functional, but immaculate with modern facilities. Bright, airy dorms, duvet covers brought from home, sheets changed by the boys. Housemaster (a woman) praised and loved by all. An open door policy for the parents and homesickness dealt with kindly. Misdemeanours dealt with quickly. 'Punishment comprises chores, just like I would at home.' Tuck boxes brought out once a week with matron providing more on Saturday evenings. Dog walks on Sunday morning. Very much a family atmosphere, with parents included, as they often pop in mid week and, if local, walk the choristers back from chapel.

Bright purple blazers and sweatshirts make the children stand out. 'My son hates his sweatshirt so gets through a blazer a year.' Girls' summer dresses not popular with parents or pupils. Do note the purple carpet throughout the modernised buildings. Sartorial whimsy, perhaps?

All parents seem happy that the school is on one site and many spoke of the 'family atmosphere.' Every parent we spoke to was delighted with the school and would strongly recommend it. We can see why; you can't help but feel the relaxed ambience. The children are bright and friendly, completely stress free and at ease with their teachers. But don't let that fool you. There is a rarefied atmosphere of intense learning – and you may get to hear some excellent singing as well.

The King's School, Ely

Barton Road, Ely, Cambridgeshire CB7 4DB

Pupils: 853 (including King's Ely International); 169 boarders (inc KEI) • Ages: 7–18 • Sixth form: 171 • C of E

Fees: Day £9,330 – £19,869; Boarding £21,012 – £28,764 pa. KEI Day £20,673 – £27,627; Boarding £28,434 – £36,519 pa

Tel: 01353 660700
Email: enquiries@kingsely.org
Website: www.kingsely.org

Principal: Mrs Sue Freestone GRSM Med LRAM ARCM (60s), who joined the school as head in 2004, and became principal in 2013. She is again in charge of the senior school, after the brief tenure of Alex McGrath as head. Trained at the Royal Academy of Music and Bristol University. Was formely head of Sibford School, and before that conductor and director of music at Colston Girls. Very energetic, approachable and unstuffy, with strongly held convictions and an expectation of high standards for herself, the staff and pupils.

Head of the junior school: Since 2008, Mr Richard Whymark BA (Ed) (40s). Previously head of Stonar Junior and before that head of boarding and deputy head of Salisbury Cathedral School. Has an engaging manner and a natural flair for communication – with pupils and parents alike. 'He is usually around at drop-off time', commented one parent.

Firmly believes a good head needs 'a strong voice and a reflective personality – no room for big egos'. Has an easy rapport with students and is clearly a respected presence – on hand to sort out spats. Art, travel and gardening are all interests but, clearly something of a romantic, his passion is for restoring Morris Minors. Has two children at King's and wife Joanna also teaches at the school.

Academic matters: Parents praise the emphasis on effort and progress in the junior school; certificates and prizes are awarded for these as much as for attainment. Both ends of ability spectrum well served, with support and extension classes available. 'Confidence is encouraged, but not cockiness', commented a mother. Tutor groups are reshuffled each year, to break up cliques and expand friendship groups. A buddy scheme operates throughout the junior school and problems are quickly dealt with. The top year groups use some of the senior school's facilities and are taught by specialist staff as a way of managing the transition from junior to senior. Setting in maths and English from year 3. Languages introduced early, with taster lessons in Japanese, Mandarin and Arabic. French, and Latin from year 7.

Though increasingly selective at 11 and 13, the bar is not quite so high as for certain of the Cambridge schools close by. Considering the reasonably wide ability range, the school is achieving very respectable and frequently glowing results. Pupils are setted for most of the core subjects; close attention is paid to individual progress, and though not an overly pushy school, 'drifting along with little effort will be spotted', a mother remarked. Twenty-four subjects offered at GCSE (52 per cent A*/A in 2016) including single sciences, Latin and Greek. Religious and moral philosophy is compulsory. Twenty-seven subjects offered at A level with economics, mathematics and psychology all popular, and 43 per cent A*/A grades overall in 2016. Those with specific educational needs, such as dyslexia, are well accommodated. There is individual support available, together with a drop-in clinic, and a close eye is kept on subjects chosen at GCSE, with a flexible approach to certain subject choices allowed.

King's Ely Junior International offers 11-12 year olds intensive English language tuition alongside a wider range of subjects in preparation for 13+ senior school entry. King's Ely International prepares 14-16 year olds with sufficiently good English to take IGCSEs and be able to enter UK independent schools, including this one. The classrooms and boarding accommodation are separate, but the head is encouraging greater fraternisation with the main school: 'It can only benefit all pupils'.

Games, options, the arts: A strength of the school is what happens outside the mainstream academic timetable. Tremendous range of opportunities, from rowing at 6:30am to singing in cathedral services. Music predominates, with more than 50 per cent learning an instrument, and ensembles, choirs and orchestras galore. Junior school includes the 22 boy choristers, who alongside daily rehearsals, services and instrumental practice have a demanding schedule of recordings, concerts and broadcasts. The girls' cathedral choir recruits from the senior school. This is the first scheme of its kind in England, and is the inspiration of the present head, herself a professional musician. It will be interesting to see if the idea is taken up by other co-educational schools connected with cathedrals. The choir sings regular cathedral services, as well as touring and performing elsewhere. The musical training given to these girls will prepare them for advanced study and choral scholarships at university. A new initiative is sixth form male choral scholarships.

Sport remains central and important, though perhaps 'not the be all and end all as at some schools,' said a parent. Besides regular hockey, rugby and so forth, there is an emphasis on the more recondite sports, especially rowing, which is taken very seriously. The school has its own boathouse, pupils keen enough to be up with the lark and even some Olympic potential.

The Ely Scheme (outdoor pursuits programme) runs compulsorily in year 9 and 10, and many continue. It includes kayaking, rock climbing and navigation, and pupils are encouraged to join either the climbing or kayaking club. The culmination is a major expedition, which could be traversing the Cuillin Ridge or the Picos de Europa, or climbing in the Alps or the Himalayas. Teaches self-reliance, responsibility and leadership skills. Many join D of E too.

The teaching facilities for art and design are impressive – as is the teaching. Eye-catching displays of recent work are quite outstanding and several pupils, thus encouraged, go on to study at prestige institutions, notably in fashion and design.

Boarding: Boarding houses are clean and comfortable, rather than deluxe. Boy choristers live in the Choir House during term time, Christmas and Easter holidays, with the housemaster and his family. When not practising or performing they are encouraged to play outside and the housemaster takes them on excursions during stayovers. Girl choristers have their own boarding house, complete with grand piano in the common room. They have weekend chorister duties about once a month, and stayovers – periods of intensive rehearsals and services – at the beginning or end of terms and half terms. The Old Palace (former residence of the Bishops of Ely) is now a sixth form centre, with boarding space for 26 girls.

Background and atmosphere: Occupies a sublime position adjacent to the cathedral, partly within the close itself, but largely in a sprawl of buildings (some medieval, others purpose-built) nearby. Glimpses of the cathedral, the Ship of the Fens, tantalise from many windows, notably from the head's office, in the Old Palace; hard for conversation to compete with the Romanesque masterpiece behind. The cathedral's presence is both seen and felt, but the school also has a close relationship with the town through a variety of initiatives with other schools and local organisations. Frequent road-crossing is managed by pupils safely and with aplomb – it is just part of school life. Other buildings include The Monks' Barn, which houses the dining room (think National Trust restaurant – food, if anything, even better), jolly atmosphere, staff eating with pupils. The library has been re-ordered, also within the ancient fabric, but retains a monastic feel.

The junior school ccupies a site on the edge of the main school campus. Slightly bleak approach around the back of the senior school but the buildings themselves are well planned and designed. Attention is paid to the grouping of different classes, so years 3 and 4 (and so on up the school) are accommodated together, with their own suite of classrooms and play area. Youngest pupils cluster round a courtyard with a Tarzan trail for play time; years 7 and 8 slightly apart in their own building.

Pupils and parents feel they are listened to, and heard. The school council, a forum to discuss new ideas, is taken notice of by the powers-that-be.

Pastoral care, well-being and discipline: The Christian foundation of the school has a strong influence on the community. Rules are few, though strictly enforced, particularly for those boarding, but there is an atmosphere of trust. The head is very aware of the pressures on pupils and feels 'peer perception' can be 'the hardest nut to crack'. Emphasis on enjoyment as well as achieving.

Pupils and parents: Largely professional, business and farming families, drawn from surrounding Eastern counties; Kings Lynn and Cambridge both send cohorts (quick, easy train services). School believes 'it is in no-one's interest for pupils to travel more than half an hour each way'. Overseas contingent (about 12 per cent) including those in the King's International Study Centre. Past pupils include Alan Yentob, the tenor James Bowman and Olympian Goldie Sayers.

Entrance: Assessment for entrance at 7 consists of diagnostic tests and informal interview. Entry to King's Ely Acremont for ages 2 to 7 (pre-prep, though this term is not used by the school) is by informal assessment and most progress up to the junior department. Screening for dyslexia and dyspraxia at entrance. Moderate difficulties can be accommodated but all pupils must be able to benefit from the full curriculum, with minimal extra support. Those applying as choristers (boys only) must also pass the necessary voice trials.

Own exam at 11 to senior school and at 13+ to senior school, through a common entrance style exam (or common entrance itself). About 75 per cent of senior school entrants have come up from the junior school and the remainder from a mixture of local-ish schools, Framlingham Prep, South Lee and the Cambridge prep schools. Numbers well up and competition for places is increasing. Entry for the sixth form – minimum of six grade A*-C passes at GCSE with at least Bs in chosen A level subjects.

Exit: Virtually all make the transition from junior to senior school at 13. The exam also decides setting for year 9. The occasional pupil not suited to the senior school is identified early and support given in finding another school in good time, but leaving is generally due to relocation. Up to 50 per cent of students leave after GCSEs, often for Hills Road or other sixth form colleges. Post A level, the majority leave for Russell Group universities to study a wide range of subjects, with a number going to colleges of art and design and performing arts courses; three to Oxbridge in 2016 and one to Princeton.

Money matters: Boy choristers in the junior school get a 50 per cent fee remission, with 33 per cent scholarships in the senior school for those who remain in the school choir, and for senior girl choristers. The new male sixth form choral scholarships offer a 50 per cent fee reduction. Other reductions for clergy and Forces families and top-up bursaries for those in financial need.

Remarks: The school has an atmosphere of purposeful learning, and provides plenty of opportunities for all types to shine. A strong, happy school where the Christian ethos is taken seriously.

L

Lawrence Sheriff School

Clifton Road, Rugby, Warwickshire CV21 3AG

Pupils: 895 • Ages: 11–18 • Sixth form: 301

Tel: 01788 542074
Email: lss@lawrencesheriffschool.com
Website: www.lawrencesheriffschool.com

Headmaster: Dr Peter Kent (50s), joined in 1997 as deputy head and has been head since 1999. Originally from Liverpool, studied English Lit at Sheffield and then to Leicester to complete an MBA in educational leadership and a PhD in school culture. Title of thesis: 'Can you shape a school's culture?' Conclusion: 'Yes, but only in partnership with the students and parents.'

Previously head of English at Liverpool College, found himself comfortably ensconced in the independent system but wanted to work at a state grammar. Upon discovering Lawrence Sheriff (LSS), he was 'blown away', finding it 'very unusual, very distinctive.' As head, he sees his role as 'keeper of the culture', but clearly not happy to rest as a mere custodian, he declares himself driven by a 'power to innovate'. Gwen Temple is a strong second-in-command; there is a certain missionary zeal about their enthusiasm for the school, made clear as we chat over pizza and sandwiches in the sunny meeting room. But their appetite for success (unlike our appetite for the pizza) is clearly a healthy one.

Empowering underprivileged pupils is a priority for Dr Kent. He wants LSS to be the 'community grammar' for Rugby, and governors have drawn up their oversubscription criteria to allow priority admission status for those in receipt of the pupil premium.

Married with three children, two sons attended LSS. Although far from home and in kicking distance of the school that invented the odd-shaped ball, he remains a resolute Liverpool FC supporter.

Academic matters: In 2016, 62 per cent of GCSE grades were A*/A. At A level, 35 per cent A*-A grades, 67 per cent A*/B, a fairly impressive result for a less-selective sixth form.

Lawrence Sheriff was designated a special school for maths and computing in 2008 and became a National Teaching School in 2012. Having rejected academy status back in 2011, the school converted to an academy in 2014.

A three-year key stage 4 enables students to take their exams early and allows greater flexibility for pupils and staff – all part of a wider ethos to provide a 'personalised' curriculum, tailored to the needs of the student. Central to this is the popular enrichment programme – not a dodgy science experiment, but a selection of additional half hour lessons scattered across the normal school timetable, where teachers get to teach something that they are passionate about. When we visited, choices ranged from astronomy to Sudoku, German film to knitting (yes, in a boys' school). Most students take an enrichment class for a term but some will stick with it for a whole year.

Games, options, the arts: The school playing field is a good mile away from the actual school, but worth the walk, with five rugby pitches and an Astroturf field. Plenty of inter-school matches in eg rugby, hockey, football, cricket. Thanks to Sport England funding, the school is also a centre of excellence for table tennis. Several sports tours have been arranged in recent years, including trips to Barbados, South Africa, Uruguay and Chile. Most of the traditions that do exist at this largely informal school revolve around sport, and house rivalries run strong (houses Caldecott, Simpson, Tait, and Wheeler are named after former heads and benefactors).

It feels like a school with more sporty than arty tendencies, but on our visit we witnessed a gusto rehearsal of The Tempest in the impressive old Victorian mock-Tudor main hall, affectionately dubbed Big School and used for the majority of larger performances and concerts. Students from the nearby Rugby High girls' school collaborate on drama productions at sixth form. Orchestra, choir and jazz band.

Background and atmosphere: The origins of the school date back to 1567 when local benefactor Lawrence Sheriff left money for a school to serve local children. It moved to its present site in the 18th century, and became a grammar school in 1906. The school is now the selective boys' grammar for Rugby and the surrounding area, with the building owned and maintained by the governors, and running costs funded by the local authority. The school still receives an annual proportion of its funds from Rugby School as a legacy of the original bequest.

The site is an eclectic, rough and tumble mix of buildings-through-the-ages with many recent add-ons to cope with the expanding school population (the number of boys is now at around 900, up 50 per cent since 1990). Over £4m has been spent by the governors in recent years on new laboratories, workshops, studio space and a spacious sixth form centre with a huge common room, study area and separate canteen with part of the original Victorian section recently refurbed.

While it may not boast the gloss and grandeur of nearby Rugby School, the boys' pride in their school is clearly undimmed. Students must follow strict uniform rules: 'a smart uniform makes a smart person', said one year 10, pointing out that staff often refer to the boys as 'gentlemen'. 'So it's important that we feel like one', he explained.

A town centre location at the edge of a busy main road is accompanied by a rigorous security presence of ID checks and entry systems, introduced in 2010 following an Ofsted inspection. Space does feel at a premium and green areas a bit lacking, but there is a bustle and banter in the corridors and playgrounds that all testify to a 'happy' place.

Pastoral care, well-being and discipline: 'Happiness' is an integral part of the school culture that Dr Kent and his colleagues have worked hard to promote. 'If students are happy, then learning is enjoyable,' explains Kent, who has introduced some pretty innovative measures in pursuit of such happiness. The school has a vertical tutor system where each house has eight tutor groups made up of students drawn from years 7-13. Tutors stay with students throughout their seven years in the school, thus ensuring continuity of pastoral support. It was controversial when introduced, but seems to work. Boys speak of 'strong bonds' and 'mutual respect' between year groups.

One of the stated aims of the vertical system is to reduce instances of bullying. While the school is emphatic that bullying is not an issue, one parent that GSG heard from did allege examples of physical violence among boys. An Ofsted inspection in 2013 was specifically tasked with examining such allegations but did not find any evidence of bullying and concluded that the school's safeguarding and bullying policies were 'very strong' and that the students 'were responsible and independent and had positive attitudes towards each other'. The students themselves also set up a committee to look at reports of bullying but disbanded it after six months when no evidence of any incidents could be found.

The school remains proud of its disciplinary record (no child has been permanently excluded in 30 years) and insists that academic achievement does not take precedence over student welfare. 'The results are brilliant but I'm more proud of the culture and the values we have created', says Kent. One parent we spoke to did refer to an 'exam factory' tendency at the school, but others pointed out that as a selective grammar, it is inevitably best suited to high academic achievers, who thrive in this environment.

A particular challenge for the school is the number of boys with disorders such as ADHD and Asperger's, more prevalent among those with exceptional talents in maths and computing – a specialism at the school. A group has been set up to help support students who find social situations difficult and the boys we met talked about some of the 'more socially introverted' students and how they benefit in particular from the vertical tutoring system.

Pupils and parents: Lawrence Sheriff boasts the oldest PTA in Britain – and has an entry in The Guinness Book of Records to prove it. But the committee is far from antiquated. With discos and curry nights a-plenty, the aim is clearly to put the 'fun' into fundraising. Parents are kept in the loop with a weekly newsletter and every year surveyed for feedback. Complaints about the absence of a cloakroom and lockers are a popular gripe, as is the walk to the sports field. One father of a year 9 boy took umbrage at 'mildly threatening' letters received regarding his son's absenteeism, blaming it on the importance placed by school league tables on attendance. But overall, parents had high praise for the school, with a number remarking on how they felt their input and involvement was 'valued'.

The boys who took us on our tour were, indeed, 'gentlemen'. Other than a few moans about long dinner queues and reluctant attendance at school choir practice, these were a group of boys proud of their school, brimming with self-belief but without a trace of arrogance.

Student population is majority white British, with around 20 per cent ethnic minority.

Entrance: Selective entry based on 11+. Year 7: 120 places with three boys competing for every place; some preference to those on pupil premium. Half of the places are secured for local children, with the rest from about a 10 mile radius, including Coventry and Birmingham (although one child did recently apply from Gateshead). Nearly half of the sixth form students join from other schools; entry requirements include GCSE points roughly equating to eight B grades, including at least B in English and C in maths; A level subjects require a B or higher at GCSE.

Exit: Around 95 per cent go on to university – mainly Russell Group, with five to Oxbridge in 2016, plus four medics and one dentist; other popular destinations Loughborough, Coventry, Nottingham, Nottingham Trent, Birmingham and Bath. Despite the high university uptake, one boy insisted that there is no pressure from the school in this direction. 'If you don't want to go to uni but want to be an apprentice somewhere, that's fine – that's encouraged.' There is a tangible sense of equipping the boys for the 'real world'. Careers lessons start in year 8 with many boys drafting their first CV by the age of 13.

Money matters: No fees to pay, but the head is still very conscious of money as a potential barrier to entry and there are additional funds to help families with costs of uniform and school trips. As already mentioned, the school has also succeeded in changing the admission policy to favour those on the pupil premium.

Remarks: While poorer in pocket than its more famous public school cousin, Lawrence Sherriff can boast a wealth of ambition, drive and talent. Traditional in appearance and high-achieving on paper, it is a school striving – and succeeding – to be much more than a league-table topper.

L

Laxton Junior School

Linked with Oundle School

East Road, Oundle, Northamptonshire PE8 4BX

Pupils: 263 • Ages: 4-11 • C of E

Fees: £10,185–£11,175 pa

Tel: 01832 277275
Email: lat@laxtonjunior.org.uk
Website: www.laxtonjunior.org.uk

Headmaster: Since 2008, Mark Potter (40s). Studied geography and history at Liverpool's John Moore's. Initially wanted to be an accountant but after work experience changed his mind. Worked at St Mark's in Ipswich before heading overseas with Shell International Schools to Nigeria and China. A young family prompted his return to the UK as deputy at Laxton. Within six weeks offered the post of head at the age of 32. A senior member of the Oundle team, he is still finds time to teach maths to year 6. His boyish enthusiasm is infectious. Well liked by parents and pupils. Most parents call him by his first name and he knows most parents and all of the children by name. 'He's very open and proactive,' was one parent's view. 'Wonderful,' was another's. 'He knows what he's doing.' Very much a family affair: his two children are pupils and his wife works with the early years. 'I didn't appoint her; that would be too much,' he said.

Entrance: Entry into reception is non selective but the children have three visits to the school prior to starting so staff get to know them. Entry after that depends on previous school records. Assessment for the older pupils. Reasoning paper and maths and English tests for key stage 1, Saturday exam for older ones. 'There is no pass or fail as such, but it allows me to discuss the child's prior learning with the parents. We do not have a one size fits all approach here as all children are different.' Some are kindly advised the school is not for them, but not many. Means-tested bursaries available and a scholarship offering 10 per cent off fees for two years to a year 5 pupil. Spaces are available, but not many. Children come from a 25 mile radius of Oundle. 'Any further than that and we discourage them as it makes the day too long,' says the head. Broad mix of parents, some able to pay fees without noticing, others working hard to do so. A friendly bunch, very welcoming to all.

Exit: The main cohort, averaging around 75 per cent, to Oundle School as day pupils. But it's not a dead cert. Every child has to sit the entrance exam. Lots of advice and support given. Those not suited kindly steered towards a different route. The remaining 25 per cent to other local independents, mainly Stamford Endoweds and Oakham plus Kimbolton. The odd one to a boarding prep. Unusual for a child to leave the private sector. The occasional one leaves prior to year 6 to join local independents that have automatic transfer to the senior school.

L

Remarks: Founded in 1973, Laxton Junior is part of the Oundle School network. Originally housed in one of their buildings, it moved to its present site in the picturesque town of Oundle in 2002 and doubled in size. The current well-designed modern building that flows well is light and airy with all mod cons. Great to see proper old fashioned style lift top desks in use, albeit modern ones. Lots of computers, a whole IT department, in fact. Our guides showed us the new 3D printer with great pride. Plenty of space inside and out and, despite being a modern building, not at all bland. Lots of posters and displays throughout, a lovely sunny book corner and well-used library.

The children are bright and cheerful, as are the staff. We were greeted with friendly smiles by all on our tour. Our guides were very entertaining and enthusiastic and more than happy to chat. 'I think it important that our children have good inter-personal skills and know how to greet an adult by looking them in the eye and giving a firm handshake,' says the head. And they did.

Teaching appears to be excellent, with extra support offered, free of charge, if needed. 'The school is totally proactive and offered extra help without any prompting. It's done quietly and effectively in free time so no lessons are missed. We are constantly updated about progress and couldn't ask for more,' said one happy mother. All parents commented on how well staff knew their children and motivated them. 'A fabulous all round education,' came up more than once. The lessons we observed showed happy, involved children. Fabulous reception area with lots of dressing up gear. 'Golden time' is free time for the infants on Friday afternoon, if they have earned it. Lots of good equipment including a touch table for number sorting. Our guide was very keen to help with this, as were we. But it wasn't needed: the young reception boy had it all under control and was more than keen to show us his prowess, which was excellent. Pity; we were dying to have a go.

Music is strong here. Fabulous large music room stuffed full of instruments. All year 2s learn either the violin or cello and most carry on with it. There are 240 individual music lessons taught each week. Many children learn more than one instrument. Lots of ensembles, orchestras, groups and choirs. Amusing to see all the instruments piled up outside the music room.

Plenty of cups on display for sport. All the usual, as expected, including a girls' rugby team. 'I would like to see the head at more of the away matches, but he is very busy man.' One parent wanted to see more sport in year 2 rather than so much emphasis on music, but conceded that in the following years more time was allocated. The whole school swims once a week in Oundle's impressive pool. Lots of team photos on display and they are delightful, not the usual formal poses but full of fun and not what you might expect. Plenty of outside space, including a lovely woodland garden with pond and bridges where time is spent searching for minibeasts. We were not successful in our search, unfortunately, but had lots of fun looking.

Plenty of after-school clubs including debating, gardening, chess and all the usual sports and drama. Also a very popular street dancing group. One parent who wanted to see some different clubs, 'perhaps a politics one,' was the only dissenting voice. Most said there was too much choice and restrictions had to be made. Lots of school trips, residential and day.

A friendly, happy, relaxed school. Pastorally excellent. The older children spend a lot of time with the younger ones, including walking them across the road at lunch time to the dining halls shared with Oundle School. The head has onsite dining facilities on his wishlist, but the children seem to enjoy the walk in the middle of the day. Every parent very positive about the pastoral set up. 'The school cares, so much so that when my son first started and wasn't settled they allowed me to attend at playtime to observe that all was well. And it was.' Another parent commented, 'it's a lovely community.' Active school council with representatives from all years who have just introduced a 'friendship bench' in the playground. 'It's where you can go if you are feeling sad, lonely or cross. It's like a buddy bench. Sit there and someone will come and join you to make sure all is well,' one of our guides told us. 'We chose the school because of the pastoral care,' was a frequent comment.

The children look smart in their uniforms, white tartan pinafores or skirts for the girls and smart blazers for all. 'I would like them to wear caps,' was one mother's comment. A smallish school, but the size is what attracts many parents. 'It's family friendly and the children are lucky to be in such an environment. They promote independence and confidence as well as a good all round education.' As one mother succinctly put it, 'If there was anything bad about the school my children would be out of there.' Quite.

Leicester Grammar School Trust

London Road, Leicester, Leicestershire LE8 9FL

Pupils: 860 • Ages: 10–19 • Sixth form: 239 • C of E

Fees: £12,342 pa

Tel: 01162 591900
Email: admissions@leicestergrammar.org.uk
Website: www.leicestergrammar.org.uk

Head: Since 2001, Christopher King (50s). Read geography at Durham, returning to do a masters 18 years later. Started work at Wessex Water Authority as a planner. Very ambitious, realised would not get far in water so turned to teaching. Rose through the ranks via Rendcomb College and Kimbolton and was head at Leicester within 12 years. Chair of the HMC in 2015, unusual post for head of a relatively new school. A dedicated and popular head, he can be found on the touchline at most fixtures and is always present at parents' evenings and concerts. Teaches year 7s on rotation and knows all the children by name. 'I wouldn't want the school to be any bigger as I know every child and write reports for each one. That could change if numbers increased and it would spoil the school.' An all round sportsman, rugby and cricket feature highly on his CV, but musical too. Recently climbed Mt Kilimanjaro with his three adult sons.

'Friendly and approachable with a very high presence around the school,' is one parent's description. Another mentioned he was 'slightly crumpled but very welcoming.' Can't say we agree; very well turned out the day we were there. Most parents hadn't had many dealings with him but all spoke highly of him and had great respect for him. A parent who had closer contact described him as 'going the extra mile to make sure my children were happy and settled.'

An ambitious man with big ambitions for his school. When appointed, LGS was located in the city centre. 'We had outgrown the premises and had no sports facilities, so a decision had to be made. Did I make the school more exclusive academically or do something more radical? In 2002 I proposed to the board that we move the whole school to an out of town site. It took four years to find the site, get permission and raise funds, but we started building on a 75 acre site in February 2007 and moved in for the beginning of term in September 2008. It costs us £33 million and was officially opened by the Queen and Prince Phillip.' And he's not standing still. Another £4 million expansion under way to provide more labs, better sixth form facilities and a larger headmaster's office. 'I wanted to create a school that is not only the best academically but thrives in sports, music and drama as well.' Until recently, the fastest growing independent school in the country.

Academic matters: This lot are high achievers. In 2016, 78 per cent A*/A at GCSE and 60 per cent A*/A at A level, 85 per cent A*-B. Most pupils take 10 or more GCSEs. Chemistry is compulsory – most do all three sciences – as is one language. French, German, Spanish, Latin or Greek are the choices. DT well supported. Caterham provides a kit car to build each year. Last year's was driven round the grounds by the head. Twenty-four subjects offered in sixth form, mainly traditional academic ones, no 'soft' ones. From 2016, students will study four A Levels and will not take AS exams. Maths, further maths and the sciences are what this school is about. 'The children are stretched but not to breaking point,' said one parent. Another parent wasn't quite so happy: 'I would like to see the foot slightly less on the accelerator. They are driven very hard.' Another parent said, 'The school doesn't seem to be very flexible when it comes to changing sets, up rather than down.' 'Teaching is good, excellent in many subjects and support is there. But I do worry slightly that the child in the middle, neither flying or struggling, might get overlooked,' commented one parent. Many staff are old pupils.

The lessons we observed showed bright, engaged pupils, very keen to join in. Year 7 maths obviously inspired by their teacher, lots of arm raising and enthusiasm. Year 8 DT getting on with it, with very chatty, welcoming year 12s working hard on their own next door. Happy year 8s and teacher having fun cooking. Year 10s analysing Wilfred Owen poetry and keen to share the experience. The prep class sang to us in French. Sixth form classes varied from one-on-one in German to three studying philosophy. More in economics and labs. We liked the greenhouse just outside one of the labs, used for seedlings and cuttings during biology experiments. All focused. For such an academic hothouse there's a very relaxed, happy feel to the place.

Learning support available. One child with a statement of educational need. Thirty-two with cognitive/literacy need, seven with physical needs and nine pupils with EAL, all fully supported. 'My child is dyslexic and was given extra English lessons rather than studying for a second language', said one parent. 'It was very well managed with no fuss and he achieved an A and A* in his GCSEs, which shocked and delighted us.'

Games, options, the arts: Sport becoming more of a focus and gaining momentum. Ex-internationals now on the staff and superb facilities on offer. Boys and girls playing at county level in hockey and cricket; netball, athletics, badminton, squash and golf too. Internationals in fencing, volleyball, orienteering, sailing and swimming. Others playing rugby for the county or for a local premiership academy. Overseas team tours in most sports. More than one team represented in most sports. 'The sports facilities are fantastic but I don't think they make the most of them, there only seems to be emphasis put on one rugby team per year, so it's a pity for the less able but equally keen players,' said one mother. The girls showing us around didn't agree, stating that 'there were lots of teams and practices.' Every parent commented on the 'fantastic facilities' that include numerous pitches, grass and Astroturf, lovely airy swimming pool, huge gym and a dance studio with mirrored walls. Oh, the joys of being in new premises.

Music and art very strong, particularly in the lower years. 'I specifically chose the school because of their strong music department,' said one mother. 'And if you play an instrument it's compulsory to be in some sort of band or group, which I think is excellent. It means that for a LGS pupil it is the norm. My daughter has made many friends, and in different age groups, as they are put in bands according to their ability.' 'Delighted to see boys in the choirs,' said another mother. Interesting that the music department is below the maths one. 'We get to hear lots of practising and notice improvement during the week', one sixth former told us. There are 28 bands, orchestras, choirs and groups that meet to rehearse weekly. Lots of opportunities to perform with monthly, termly and annual events. Also a music tour.

House singing and karaoke hotly contested, as is house drama. Yearly drama productions, rehearsals ongoing for school play The Exam. Last year it was Sweet Charity.

Lots of artwork on display, particularly in the art wing and it's good. Many of the teachers successfully sell their own work, other work by local artists brought in and displayed. A pity interest drops off in the sixth form, but those that carry on get very small tutor groups.

Background and atmosphere: Founded in 1981 and originally located on the old grammar school site in the city centre. It opened with 94 pupils, but no sixth form. Ten years later it had 500 and a sixth form. There is also a junior school that opened in the early 90s on a separate site. Now both are together on the 75 acres at Great Glen. Long driveway conceals the school from the road. Large signs and flying flags announces its presence. All buildings are new, but can't be described as architecturally appealing, in our view. Functional rather than aesthetic. It feels like a mixture of a hospital and an airport, when you drive in. A one way system with parents seemingly dropping off on the move; no one stops. Very efficient but slightly soulless. But what can you expect from such modern premises? The first thing you see when you walk through the sliding front doors is the large library. It's an academic school and they are drawing your attention to it. Inside is light and airy, lovely wide corridors so no overcrowding. Laid out simply and effectively. Still feels a bit like an airport though, but not unpleasant.

All very high tech. Fingerprint recognition is used for entry to the library and for lunch. 'Once my son saw that he was desperate to come.'

Pastoral care, well-being and discipline: Discipline not mentioned by any parent, which was interesting. Behaviour obviously not an issue. 'It's a kind school,' said one parent. 'The staff keep a close eye on the pupils and seem to know if something is wrong.' Another parent told us, 'I chose the school because they accept that not every child is sporty. They don't force them, but allow them to find their own niche. They are very much about including rather than excluding, and are very accepting of the quirky.' Another parent was more blunt: 'The geek or nerd will probably be safer there than anywhere else. They are very accepting of the oddball and eccentric and just seem to absorb them.'

All parents we spoke to were happy with the school.'Child focused' and 'children not frightened of the teachers'. 'Easy to get in touch with the school and emails answered promptly'. Lots of comments about problems being 'nipped in the bud' and 'dealt with quickly'. One parent did think the school had 'been caught on the back foot when it came to internet bullying, but quickly got itself up to speed and were keen to learn where they needed to step in'.

Student support run by the sixth formers, ably assisted by the school nurse. This is a counselling course that over 40 of the sixth formers take, with a class a week for eight weeks. They then use these skills for mentoring the younger years. The nurse also offers pastoral support. 'I was stressing about my AS levels last year and she was lovely and really calmed me down and helped me plan my time properly,' one of our guides told us.

Some parents felt rather isolated from the school, physically rather than emotionally. The vast site with its one way system and well planned traffic control doesn't encourage stopping for a chat. 'Because the school is away from the town centre it's not as social, for children or parents. They all seem to come home straight from school rather than socialise. A good thing in many ways, but not always', said one mother. There is a coffee shop on site that sixth formers can walk across to during the day, only to be used by staff, visitors and sixth formers during school hours. Apparently built at the request of the year 11s who were very miffed to be moving out of the town centre – where were they going to go on a 'date?' We suspect some parents are delighted with the move.

Pupils and parents: Pupils come from a wide area, but mainly from the city and environs. Pupils reflect the demography of Leicestershire, with 25 per cent of from Asian backgrounds. This percentage is slowly increasing. Parents forward-thinking, not bothered by tradition and mainly from professional backgrounds. Many connected to the hospitals and university in the city. 'We have parents with high aspirations for themselves and their children,' said the head. 'The mix works. We adhere to the principals of Christianity but faith, race and gender aren't important. Everyone mixes well and parents are happy with the moral stance of the school.' The children we met were all very welcoming, friendly and engaging, more than happy to chat. 'Well rounded individuals, confident but not arrogant, such a good reflection on the school,' said a parent. 'I chose the school because it is forward looking, modern and multi-cultural, which reflects our society.'

Every parent we spoke to would happily recommend the school. 'I have three children at the school who are all very different. But all are happy and fit in well, which says a lot. If they're happy, I'm happy.'

Harry Ellis, England Rugby International and British Lion is an old boy now returned as a teacher.

Entrance: Entry at year 7 based on an entrance exam covering maths, English and verbal reasoning. Some candidates interviewed. Over half come from Leicester Grammar Junior School. There is no automatic transfer; all sit the entrance exam. Another 20 or so come from the prep class that is a year 6 group taught within the senior school. These children come from local primaries and gain automatic entry to the senior school as they have already sat an entrance exam. The remaining children mainly come from surrounding state primaries.

Entry to the sixth form requires minimum two As at GCSE in chosen A level subjects and at least four B grades. All external candidates are interviewed. Some 20 or so join the sixth form each year, mainly from state comprehensives. Very occasionally one will come from nearby boarding schools.

Exit: Very few leave after GCSEs, and this is decreasing. If they leave it's to the local sixth form college.

Vast majority of pupils head to a Russell Group university, majority to first choice. Three Oxbridge places in 2016. Almost 20 per cent each year study medicine or medical courses; engineering and physics also popular. Gap years becoming more common.

Money matters: Discount offered for more than one child, five per cent for two, 7.5 per cent for three and 10 per cent for four. Means-tested bursaries available as well as academic, sporting, music and art scholarships.

Remarks: The new kid on the block is making its mark. Has more of a feel of a state city grammar than a private school. But forward-thinking parents who aren't interested in tradition, status and history are flocking to it. LGS offers very competitive fees, produces excellent results and the facilities are tremendous. Your child can complete all of their schooling here, as long as they make the grade. We think the competition will be sitting up and taking notice, and so they should be.

The Leys School

Linked with St Faith's

Trumpington Road, Cambridge, Cambridgeshire CB2 7AD

Pupils: 562; 250 full, 120 home boarders • Ages: 11–18 • Sixth form: 200

Fees: Day £14,985 – £20,760; Boarding £22,605 – £31,035 pa

Tel: 01223 508904
Email: admissions@theleys.net
Website: www.theleys.net

Headmaster: Since 2014, Martin Priestley. Oxford PPE graduate. Claims to be an accidental teacher. Originally wanted to be a diplomat and applied to join MI6: 'I fancied being James Bond.' Whilst waiting for vetting to join the fast stream civil service, taught, and caught the bug. 'The civil service was not for me, too much use of the in and out tray.' Previously taught at Uppingham and was head of Warminster before joining The Leys. Attracted to the school because of its size, 'it's a big small school.' Knows every child. 'I was worried when the last head left as he was so good,' said one parent, 'but Mr Priestley has been very impressive, I like his style, he is very open.' 'He communicates with parents every week via the schools comm; we are very much kept in the loop.' Another parent said, 'He has changed a lot, modernised the school and is making good use of social media.' 'He is at every function and moves around the pitches talking to everyone during matches.' A German speaker who doesn't have a long commute, through the door from the hallway of his impressive looking headmaster's residence. We were privileged to meet Twiglet, his blind dog, obviously a regular in his office.

Academic matters: In 2016, nearly 67 per cent A*-A in GCSE, 41 per cent at A level. Impressive results that seem to be achieved without a pressure cooker environment. Lots of clinics available for those needing extra support, most voluntarily seeking it. Parents kept well informed about academic progress. 'The children are taught to work hard and do their best; what more can you ask for?' French, German, Greek, Latin, Chinese and Spanish all offered at GCSE, many doing two languages. Pupils set in maths for all year groups and sciences from year 10. One parent would like to see more choice of subjects at A level. Most are covered but no politics or photography.

Excellent facilities, computers everywhere with iPads for each pupil. Very impressive art on display including pottery; lots of art rooms with fabulous smell of paint and oils. Sixth formers working on mezzanine floor. Fully equipped DT room including a whole computer suite. Beautiful large library, children encouraged to take books out, free reading periods up to year 9. Lessons we observed showed friendly staff and chatty children. A very relaxed atmosphere but don't be fooled, they were working hard. Noticeably less formal between teacher and student further up the school. Enjoyed listening to the discussions in A level theology; couldn't resist joining in – this lot were very harsh on drivers. Seemingly very young teacher who had the group eating out of his hand, but maybe we are getting old. School on Saturday, all day, for years 9-13, lessons as well as sport. They make good use of Cambridge; lots of chances to go to lectures and listen to eminent speakers.

Learning support lessons for some 50 pupils year 7-11, twice a week in small groups, sixth form weekly one-to-one lessons for 21. Around 16 other pupils monitored throughout the term to make sure their needs don't change. Good support offered and parents are pleased. 'My daughter was disengaged when it came to studying until the school spotted her dyslexia. They offered tremendous support, and still do. She is now completely focused.'

Some 15 per cent of pupils are from overseas, 35 different countries. Around 40 students have EAL requirements. These pupils have three English lessons a week and extra privately funded lessons available if required. Integration activities for all. Monitored throughout their time at the school to make sure language skills not holding them back academically. Many long serving staff, some living on site.

Games, options, the arts: This is a sporty school, renowned for it, with excellent facilities including all-weather pitches. Lots of teams for all year groups. Accepting of pupils who have outside sporting commitments and willing to offer extra support academically if needed. Interesting to see they have a girl in the cricket team; she's there on merit, excellent. Good to see that pupils play within their own age group whatever their abilities. 'It is good for them socially to be with their peers,' said one wise mother.

The school is very keen to emphasise that it is 'not just about sport.' And parents backed this up. 'Their plays are excellent, much better than some I've seen in Cambridge,' from one parent. Lots of drama clubs and productions throughout the year. An inspirational, enthusiastic drama teacher who pulls everyone along with her.

Music excellent, housed in its own school with a very proactive director. Eighteen music rooms including a recording studio and recital hall with excellent acoustics. Professional musicians perform at lunch times. Lots of music lessons, 200 a week. Many talented musicians including ex-choristers from the local prep schools. Loads of bands, choirs, orchestras and groups. Boarders often practise or jam in the evenings.

D of E compulsory in year 9 and 10. CCF from year 10; interesting that they don't have a RAF contingent, yet, but they do have a rifle range.

Many school trips to all over the world. Trekking in the Himalayas this summer, three weeks in Southern Africa for biology last year. Numerous sports tours and subject trips.

Boarding: Pupils are split between 11 houses, including three day houses, and assemble there for registration and notices. The day houses have the same facilities as the boarding ones but without beds. School offers two sorts of boarding, full or home. Home boarding pupils stay at school until after prep and go home about 9pm. They are allocated a space within the house and are in all aspects boarders, except they don't spend the night. A popular option with many parents and pupils. Some 70 per cent board, with 50 per cent of pupils being full boarders and 20 per cent home boarders. Very much a family atmosphere, pupils on first name terms with staff and obviously very tight with each other. Sixth formers share light out duties and often pop in to chat to younger age group to make sure all is well.

Lots of house competitions for snooker etc. Year groups 9-13 housed together; sixth form have their own common room but often join younger age groups. One specific house for sixth form, mainly for new joiners. Lots of facilities including piano that is well used. Younger years share rooms, up to six in year 9, sixth form have their own rooms. Tea and toast-making facilities available, oven available for sixth form. Nice to see some of the dorms were messy. Clean, modern bathrooms, plenty of them. Matron described as a 'superstar' by our guide. Parents agree. 'It really is home from home and they do all they can to make sure everyone is happy,' said one parent. 'They are in a lovely environment and the housemistress really is a surrogate mum.' 'The younger girls have a "big sister" in the house that they choose and she will look out for them and help them settle in.' Prep supervised up to year 11; each pupil has their own desk in prep rooms. Phones and iPads taken away at night from younger years.

Lots of activities offered at weekends and evenings; they are kept busy. Sixth formers make the most of 'Cambridge boarding' and often head into town for dinner at the weekends, choosing to spend time in the city enjoying what it has to offer. Curfew of 10.30pm adhered to. Sixth formers also have a club with licensed bar. Pretty flexible approach to parties. If parents and host parents agree they are allowed to stay away overnight at weekends.

Background and atmosphere: Founded in 1875, The Leys is the only independent co-educational boarding and day school in Cambridge. Went co-ed in 1981. Situated on a 50 acre site a stone's throw from the centre of Cambridge. The buildings surround open playing fields so all feels very spacious. Lots of building undertaken over the years but fits in well with the original red-brick slightly gothic original ones that are beautiful inside and out. Founded by the Methodists, the school still has a strong sense of religious community with chapel services for all, whatever their denomination, happy to join in. Parent like the ethos. Note the original Wesley chapel, one of the earliest built, as a memorial to pupils killed in WW1,a perfect example of the arts and crafts movement. The school was evacuated to Scotland during WW2 with premises being requisitioned for a military hospital. Lots of talk of ghosts in the basement, but we didn't see any.

The big small school is an apt description. Large enough to be well supported and funded by generous benefactors, so offering excellent facilities and teaching, small enough to be intimate, with individuals recognised for who they are.

Pupils and staff lunch together, staff on a mezzanine floor, but many joining pupils. Delicious food we can vouch for. There was a quiet buzz within the dining hall: calm and orderly but relaxed.

Pastoral care, well-being and discipline: 'We are hostile to bullying,' says the head. Problems usually picked up quickly within the house, often resolved by pupils themselves. The house system is very effective with tutors and houseparents, as well as matron, getting to know the pupils well. They spend a lot of time together and quickly pick up if there are problems. Plenty of counselling services on offer if needed. 'There is a very strong community at The Leys,' said one parent. 'I was surprised and delighted at how well the teachers look after the pupils.' Another parent said, 'Pastoral care is the school's biggest plus point. My child is so happy there and as they are happy they work hard.' 'My child has a voice and is listened to. Problems are dealt with sensitively and well.' It's not just academia here. 'They encourage the pupil to be the best they can be, and not just at studying.' Pupils are listened to. A new initiative is just being introduced by the pupils themselves offering a point of contact for those with race/gender/sexuality issues – very on trend.

Introduction to the school treated seriously. All year 9s invited to spend 24 hours at the school before they start in September, day pupils as well, a very effective method that our guide still spoke about. Lots of bonding sessions to create a community.

Discipline wasn't mentioned by any parent as it doesn't seem to be an issue. The head has had to exclude one pupil for drugs. 'We don't have a zero tolerance policy, but it's close to zero. I know teenagers dabble, but warnings are usually heeded. I'm a great believer in second chances, but not third.'

L

Pupils and parents: Parents are very much 'Cambridge,' academics, entrepreneurs and medics and many more doing the London commute, hence the popularity of home boarding. Popular with Fen farmers as well. Many pupils second and third generation to attend the school. Most live within an hour, boarders as well, apart from the overseas contingent.

Pupils mostly well-rounded and self aware, friendly, welcoming and chatty. They can see there is more to life that just qualifications. A 60:40 mix of boys and girls. No obvious divide between boarders and day pupils.

Entrance: Every child is interviewed prior to the test. Year 7 intake of around 30, mainly from state primaries. The main cohort, about 70, joins year 9, mainly from local Cambridge prep schools. St Faith's is part of the foundation and a feeder school. Competitive entrance exam. Their own English and maths plus standardised verbal and spatial reasoning tests. Oversubscribed so they can take their pick.

Sixth form entry five Bs for current pupils. Same for new arrivals but As and A*s preferred. Between 25 and 30 join, mainly to board from day independents, the occasional state school pupil.

Exit: Some 25-30 leave after year 11, mainly to the excellent local state sixth form colleges. Very unusual to lose a pupil to another independent school. The occasional one doesn't meet GCSE hurdle, but again unusual. As expected most to university, RAU and Harper Adams represented by the farming contingent, others to eg Newcastle, Readong, Exeter, Durham, Edinburgh and London. One to Oxford in 2016. Around 20 per cent take gap years.

Previous pupils have included tennis player Jamie Murray, a couple of rugby union stars, journalist Martin Bell, the current King of Bahrain and a previous King of Tonga – an eclectic mix.

Money matters: The usual scholarships and bursaries. One full scholarship a year from the Wesley Foundation including all trips. The mindset behind this was so that no other pupil would know they were on a scholarship.

Remarks: A lovely place to study. You feel as though you are in the countryside but are minutes from the centre of the city of Cambridge so you get the best of both worlds. 'I don't begrudge a penny we have spent,' from one happy parent. Known locally as 'the friendly school,' we can see why, it is.

Lichfield Cathedral School

The Palace, The Close, Lichfield, Staffordshire WS13 7LH

Pupils: 423 • Ages: 3–18 • Sixth form: 38 • C of E

Fees: £8,070 – £14,370 pa

Tel: 01543 306170
Email: thepalace@lichfieldcathedralschool.com
Website: www.lichfieldcathedralschool.com

Head Teacher: Since 2015, Sue Hannam. She already knew the school well, having arrived as deputy in 2009 and doing two stints as acting head before she finally took over. Sue studied at Innsbruck University and the College of Law and, following a degree in English language and literature at Birmingham, she taught in state schools and also qualified and worked as a solicitor, so LCS has gained a wealth of educational and wider experience. She probably needs this experience, being the fourth head at LCS in five years.

Sue used to lecture in law at Reed College whilst in legal practice, and that legal ability to get quickly to the heart of a problem and sort it out has come in useful, with parents saying that over the last year there has been a sense of everything under firm control, and the school has rediscovered its sense of direction. 'She is a doer', said one parent. 'A fantastic asset', said another. She is dynamic, determined, thoughtful and much loved by staff and pupils. 'Sue is fantastic. She cares massively about the school and that cascades right down. She has the support of the whole staff', said one staff member.

Academic matters: LCS is non-selective and its intake around the national average of ability. Results at GCSE and A level are good considering that, above national averages as well as showing excellent value added. At A level, 56 per cent of grades were A*-B in 2016. At GCSE 40 per cent of grades were A*/A. Class sizes throughout the school are small – 16 to 20. There are learning support staff and teaching assistants in the junior school and learning support staff in the senior school who, parents tell us, pick up concerns quickly and set up six week intervention plans that are regularly reviewed. Sometimes intervention is shorter than that with the emphasis being on responding to individual needs as flexibly as possible. There is a robust tracking system in place all the way through the school and the head, with her new deputy who has a background in state school leadership, has moved quickly to get lesson observations and more staff training in place. The two of them have introduced line management for middle leaders and department reviews, all contributing to the rapid pace of progress in the school.

The school structure allows for careful transition at the various stages. The nursery up to year 4 classes are housed at

Longdon, a glorious rural setting, about four and a half miles away from the Cathedral Close on the edge of Lichfield. Then years 5 and 6 move up to the main site, but in their own hub. They start to share a few of the senior school facilities – the year 6s were very excited about using the science labs – and have some specialist academic staff, but they have their own space and there is a very strong, secure, nurturing feel about it. When they move to the senior School in year 7, the transition is very easy for them both socially and academically, with enough that is new for it to feel exciting.

The Longdon site has lovely outdoor play areas and allows for a forest school. There are tracksuit days twice a week so there is no restriction on getting muddy. There are kitchens in the classroom for the younger ones and some of the curriculum is taught through cooking. There are regular cross-curricular, cross-school enrichment projects going on, some of which engage with the local business community, something the school is seeking to develop further. There is an etiquette week coming up, sponsored by a local cutlery maker who will provide each child at Longdon with a cutlery set while the school will talk about the gracious art of entertainment, culminating in a pupil-organised tea party.

For a small school, academic options are wide. Pupils can study French, German, Spanish and Latin. Option blocks are based on the pupils' free choice, and if the timetable can't manage a particular subject or combination, the school has run twilight sessions. The expressive and performing arts are very strong throughout the school up to A level.

Games, options, the arts: Music is a huge part of school life. For a small, non-academically selective school, the standard is unusually high. The choristers have a demanding timetable and wonderful musical opportunity. There is no longer boarding so choristers (boys only) now have to live within travelling distance of the cathedral for the early start. There is also a girls' cathedral choir which sings one evensong a week and combines with the boys on feast days. The school emphasises that it nurtures all musical ability, not just those who sing in the cathedral choir. There are 18 weekly rehearsing groups with various aspirational ensembles that allow pupils to move on in time to the senior ensembles. A large number of individual instrumental lessons happen.

The school is very keen to take its music to other schools and is part of a Music Share initiative which aims to improve singing provision in local schools and beyond. The music diary is full and varied, with a lot of performance opportunities, both within the school and cathedral and also out in the community, which the school sees as part of its wider mission. Just before our visit, the senior school had put on Offenbach's La Belle Hélène. The director of music is forging ever-closer links with the cathedral music team, which has oversight of life of the choristers, but he sees the school as a centre for musical excellence for far more than just the cathedral choirs, and believes that music should be something enjoyed and experienced by all.

Performing arts generally are very strong. There are drama clubs and performances going on all through the year and all through the school, in the school halls as well as other local venues. Particularly at the junior end, there is a big emphasis on getting everyone involved. Pupils can take English Speaking Board exams. Lots do and achieve highly.

The year 10 boys told us: 'We are not being big-headed but we are all quite good at sport. There are lots of competitive people in our year'. The school is very conscious that small schools on restricted sites have to work hard to make sport high profile and LCS is trying its best, and pupils told us sport is now really on the up. There are some sports facilities on site, a fundraising campaign is currently underway to build a new multi-use games area in the grounds, and great use is made of all the excellent local facilities – eg Lichfield Hockey and Cricket Clubs. The sports department tries to put out as many teams as possible with the aim of getting every pupil playing in a school team a few times a term. That, of course, is highly laudable, and combining that approach with ensuring the gifted games players get involved with outside clubs is a way of beefing up what is on offer. They also encourage non-team sports – trampolining, orienteering, golf. At the juniors' Longdon site, male sports coaches have been employed to run lunchtime sports activities.

There are plenty of other activities on offer, some of which link with the enrichment whole school programme.

Background and atmosphere: Any school in the shadow of a cathedral has a very special feel about it. The children have Monday assemblies in the cathedral and use it for other special occasions. The Palace that houses offices, dining facilities and other functional rooms was the 17th century Bishop's Palace, a beautiful, classically-influenced stone building. 'We are its custodians', says the head.

There have been boy choristers educated here since the early 14th century. The prep school in the Close started in 1942, moving to its current location in 1953, and there has been expansion ever since. Girls were admitted in 1974. The secondary school began to develop in 2004 and the sixth form opened in 2010. The school acquired another junior school at Longdon Green, moved year 4s and below out there, creating the additional space on the Close site for the expansion. Behind the Close frontage are more purpose-built classrooms, recreational and sports spaces. The sixth form centre is in one of the old Close houses and the sixth formers said it was an oasis of calm during the A level period.

But the school does not just enjoy the cathedral atmosphere as a decorative add-on. The pupils are aware that they belong to something special and that the wonderful location brings with it responsibility. The year 10s (not a year group usually renowned for social conscience) talked to us about being in the public eye as they walk along the Close between buildings and coming to and from school. 'We have a responsibility towards all the tourists. We are part of the life of the Cathedral Close and tourists need to see how much we respect that', they told us.

For the head, it is the cathedral and all that means that differentiates the school. Part must be the music, of course, but she understands this in a much wider sense. There is a strong charity arm where the whole school regularly comes together to raise money and awareness of the needs of the wider society, but in fairness, a lot of independent schools see that as part of their mission. What the head has done that is unique is to set up an accredited ethical leadership programme that runs right from EYFS through to the sixth form. It gives validity to and recognition of a whole range of activities and behaviours throughout the school, building up layers of ethical understanding as a child gets older through practical day-to-day choices. It is a tangible way of saying to the pupils: we are about a lot more than exam results. We have the highest expectation of you to live in an ethical way in all you do and to understand what we expect of you as an adult in the outside world. 'This is what the world needs', says the head. It is excellent to see a cathedral school stepping up like this. It is a powerful justification for such schools, and the community is incredibly lucky to have found a head with this vision. It also has the potential to be a meaningful outreach for the cathedral with each generation of pupils. The cathedral can be seen as another support system for the pupils and then, as they leave the school, for them, their families and friends as young adults. The ethical values cascade out.

Parents and pupils talk about the family feel of the school. Both sites are small enough for everyone to know everyone else. The pupils are very protective of each other. There are strong, positive relationships between pupils and staff and communication between staff and parents is highly praised. 'We all have the teachers' emails,' parents told us. 'If we raise a concern, the school is onto it straight away and gets back to us really quickly'.

Pastoral care, well-being and discipline: Parents say the standard of behaviour is high and any suggestion of deviation from this is stamped on immediately. They also like the fact that the school does encourage pupils to resolve minor difficulties themselves, so they grow up feeling empowered and confident without always having to run to an adult. The school has high expectations in terms of use of language and the pupils rise to it. The worst things we heard about were 'girls being difficult – I certainly wouldn't call it bullying' or the occasional bad manners. Pupils say the teachers are 'quite strict' but that there is much mutual respect.

Because of the fact it is small and the way it is structured, there are many roles of responsibility for pupils and the aim is that all children have a leadership role. Because the year 4s are the top year group at Longdon, they take lots of responsibility that in a more usually structured school they wouldn't have until year 6. The children love it and really rise to the challenges. It is this stress on leadership that makes the new accredited ethical leadership course such a strong path for the school to cut.

There is a sense that excellent pastoral care must be at the heart of a school that defines one of its strengths as working with each child as an individual. Parents note that every member of staff, not just a form tutor, takes pastoral care as their responsibility, and there appears to be constant contact between teachers and parents when concerns are raised on either side. We thought this might get a bit much, but no one at the school did. It is seen as part of the family atmosphere that is warmly embraced.

L

Pupils and parents: Pupils come from a wide area and now the school no longer offers boarding, some choristers are likely to have long journeys. There are a number of school minibuses that bring pupils in from areas not on a main rail or bus route. The train is a good option for older children, 10 minutes walk from the school and on a main line through Birmingham.

The Longdon pupils are engaging, bright and adore their school. A recent ISI inspector described the seniors as 'confident with lots of humility' and we would endorse that. Parents compared LCS pupils favourably with the aura of 'arrogance' they perceive in pupils going to the well-known selective West Midlands schools. The school is encouraging pupils to understand multiple intelligences, and they don't end up thinking that because they have an A*, they are the best. They understand they all have gifts to offer to a wider society.

Families live in Lichfield and around, with quite a number from the Sutton Coldfield area. This hidden gem of a school could be drawing from the populations around Stafford, Wolverhampton and Burton. Our impression is that there are a high number of families that are first time independent school users, who are attracted to the school because it does not conform to their prejudices about the fee-paying sector.

Entrance: The school is non-selective, except for the choristers, who are auditioned by the cathedral and school directors of music. Currently expanding, now is a good time to get children in.

Pre-school children are informally observed during a series of visits to the school. Beyond this, entrance is dependent on assessment, interview and reports from the present school. The assessments are to ensure the school can support the pupil in a way that will ensure all of them flourish. Entry into the sixth form depends on GCSE results.

Exit: A few leave at 11 and some choristers at 13, with a few moving at 16 to colleges that offer a wider range of qualifications. But increasing numbers are staying on for the sixth form. Given the wide academic range in the sixth form, pupils go on to more diverse post-18 options than at many independent schools. Some go to good universities, and there are usually one or two off to read music, but the school is very clear that its role is to find out what is right for the individual and support that rather than feeling that everyone has to go off to university. Apprenticeships and other forms of training on the job are encouraged. One boy is going into fashion design this year. It is all about finding the inner passion and facilitating that.

Money matters: Fees are roughly what you would expect for a small school out of London. There are a number of scholarships, music of course, but also sport, art, drama and academic, plus a small number of means-tested bursaries. Learning support is not charged as an extra. Wrap-around care at both sites is at extra cost.

Remarks: The north of Birmingham destination for a musical child, particular one with singing talent.

The west midlands is a competitive area for secondary schools in particular, with very strong academic independent schools and free state grammar schools. LCS is a strong contender for families who don't want a highly charged academic powerhouse and exam factory but something with a very distinctive ethos.

Lincoln Minster School

The Prior Building, Upper Lindum Street, Lincoln LN2 5RW

Pupils: 518; 66 boarders • Ages: 2–18 (boarding from year 3) • Sixth form: 92

Fees: Day £9,006 – £13,158; Boarding £20,490 – £31,050 pa

Tel: 01522 551300
Email: senior@lincolnminsterschool.co.uk
Website: www.lincolnminsterschool.co.uk

Principal: Since 2015, Mark Wallace, previously principal deputy head at Kingston Grammar. Studied maths with computer science at Queen's Belfast; began his teaching career at Cambridge House Boys' Grammar before joining Caterham School, where he spent 14 years. Has played hockey at national level; coaches this and cricket as well as playing golf, enjoying TT racing and gardening. Three children.

Head of prep: Since 2012, Mrs Fiona Thomas BEd NPQH, early 50s, with a warm Welsh lilt and a clearly discernible understanding of children and all things educational. Now in her third headship, most recently she was head of King's College Junior School, Alicante. Married with two daughters, she lives close by in school accommodation and oversees both the pre-prep and prep departments, which are about quarter of a mile apart. You are guaranteed a cordial welcome here from Mrs Thomas and her enthusiastic team.

Academic matters: Spanish taught from nursery, French from year 3 with specialist staff. Thematic teaching also brings in the opportunity for tasters in Arabic (studies of Ancient Egypt), Mandarin, Portuguese (the World Cup) and even a few words in Welsh (a nod to the head..) – no fear approach to languages and much enthusiasm abounds here. Each new termly theme starts with a WOW day – year 3 about to study ancient Egypt were archaeologists for the day and managed to find and dig up Egyptian artefacts in the school grounds – imagine that..

IT features big time, staff and equipment are up to speed and the combination of using modern technology to deliver traditional teaching works well. Classes are busy and purposeful, with children proud and happy (eager, even) to share their work and ideas. Most class sizes somewhere between 14 and 18, two-form entry, room for a few more here and there but plenty of individual attention and support as necessary. Non-selective means a broad spectrum of ability; no extra charge for in-class support, small additional charge for a higher level of support if required. Much use is made of senior school space and expertise, allowing rock-solid specialist teaching of all subjects from year 4 upwards – 'really sets them up well for senior school,' according to parents. Older prep children use the recital hall for orchestra and the sports hall for games, and the proximity of Bishop Grosseteste College just around the corner brings student teachers into the talent pot also. Links with senior school build in the last two years of prep with activities such as a forensic science day opening up young minds to a world beyond.

Spacious, airy classrooms and eight impressive labs in the senior school new build, some with far-reaching views across the Trent plain. All very well-equipped with state-of-the-art IT equipment creating an environment that's clearly serious about teaching and learning. There is a real pride about the place with plenty of quality work on display and a general sense of order and rigour, all wrapped up with warmth and bonhomie. Wide corridors with carpets and plenty of natural light create an almost corporate feel – more businesslike and less school-like than the norm. Parents recognise the importance of the huge value added by this mixed ability school – seems it is down to strong pupil/teacher relationships and lots of individual support and attention as and when required. In 2016, 31 per cent A*/A grades at GCSE, and 51 per cent A*-B and 26 per cent A*/A grades at A level. The three sciences are taught in rotation at key stage 3, then separately and fully beyond that, leading to plenty of As and A*s in triple sciences.

French and Spanish taught, other languages occasionally on demand as extracurricular options. Basic range of subjects on offer at GCSE with most studying 8 or 10 subjects. Wider range of subjects at A level, all the usual trad subjects plus a few less common ones such as graphics, psychology, sociology and travel and tourism.

Average class size 17, max 24. Pupils say teachers have 'an infectious passion for their subject'; typical is the Earl Grey Society – other teas (and biscuits) are available – an extracurricular activity run by the English dept offering university seminar-type sessions to discuss a shared love of literature and broaden both reading and horizons. There is a clear work ethic; teachers look busy and focused, as do pupils, but no sense of hothousing. A chilled-out common room for sixth form sits alongside a silent study area, with a teacher on duty and plenty of uni prospectuses and careers advice around to guide and inspire.

Easy access to the local university brings additional academic range and scope; use of their library for sixth form extended projects, masterclasses and an introduction to engineering are all there to be experienced and enjoyed. Mild and moderate learning difficulties catered for; around 80 identified as SEN, a handful have statements, rest mainly dyslexia, dyspraxia, occasionally ASD. No extra charge for specialist support.

Games, options, the arts: This is the Minster school and therefore the cathedral link is not insignificant, and is regarded by parents (and staff) as a 'very special feature of the school'. Boy and girl choristers (20 or each) have a busy schedule and a weekly assembly is held in the Chapter House (to which parents are invited) and prize-giving is an inspirational annual event taking place in the cathedral itself. Plenty of high quality music throughout; name an instrument and they play it, parents misty-eyed and proud at concerts and recitals. They say you don't have to be musical to come here but it 'still touches you'. Standards are incredibly high, with a number of orchestras, bands and groups making for a busy concert programme and occasional radio and TV appearances. Cathedral choristers enjoy a busy life and can be day or boarding; choral scholarships available, normally 50 per cent off full fees (boarding and tuition). Choir rehearsals take place on four weekday mornings and weekends are carefully balanced with 'a busy one followed by a lighter one' to allow for a life outside school. Chamber choir performed on Howard Goodall's chart-topping album Inspired.

GCSE express music course for year 9 pupils allows them to complete the full course two years early. Cookery is an adventurous experience here: teacher is ex-military so only for the brave. Butcher a chicken? 'Why not? After all, it's cheaper than buying chicken portions so great prep for uni,' say grinning pupils. Wealth of extracurricular choices in addition to the music options; all the usual plus rarer alternatives such as rowing and remote-control car club. 'Flamboyant' head of art so plenty of wow factor in that department, stunning work on display. Drama is thriving and all year groups are encouraged to take part; it's 'taken seriously here,' say staff, and taught to A level.

Trad sports – hockey, rugby, cricket and rounders being the main team games on offer in the prep; numerous talented runners enjoy cross-country challenges and sailing is enormously popular, culminating in an annual regatta. Swimming taught up to year 2 off-site and a shared Astroturf at the pre-prep is a valuable resource. Parents run a Saturday morning swim club at a local pool and help out with fixtures throughout the year. Sports field is a short walk away from the senior school in Lincoln's conservation area and the newish sports hall and new Astroturf have fuelled the school's already high standard of team and individual performance. Rugby and hockey are king, but football, netball, basketball and tennis also popular. Plenty of recent success in rugby 7s as county plate winners in three age groups and county champions in U15 girls' cricket. Also has riding teams who compete regularly at events across the country and, just to prove this really isn't an unsophisticated backwater at all, polo now on offer and growing in popularity, with parents too, who particularly enjoy the après polo activities. Sailing offered as an extracurricular activity; a high level of involvement in the Duke of Edinburgh Award scheme and a very full outdoor and adventurous programme; Young Enterprise regional finalists.

Small-ish city but school has big ideas and knows that there is a big world out there, so no sense of isolation. Rugby tours to Italy, geography trips to Iceland and Switzerland, annual ski trips and more besides extend opportunities to explore and learn about the world beyond – but these are grounded young people; fundraising to cover their own costs is not unusual here and is to be admired. Project India is a venture close to their hearts, working to provide essential aid in Southern India. Sixth formers visit for up to three weeks at a time to create buildings for the deaf, community cafés, clearing land for fruit farms and teaching English, with the occasional cricket match thrown in just for fun.

Boarding: As part of United Learning (formerly UCST), it now houses boarders – most seniors, just four junior pupils – on four sites, three on school campus. Latest, The Mount, for years 3-8, including choristers, opened May 2015. Bucking the trend with boarding on the increase, a few Forces children remain; boarders are a 50/50 home-grown and overseas mix; full, weekly or flexi boarding all available. Plenty of investment in boarding; it's holding its own in a dwindling local market and recent investment is paying off as boarding houses are revamped and refurbed on a rolling programme; big expenditure on girls' boarding over last few years. Serious funding in this area indicates a real commitment to boarding into the future. Weekends for boarders involve cinema, theatre, 10-pin bowling trips, barbecues on sunny evenings and the annual summer camp is a real highlight; midweek there are plenty of opportunities to join a smorgasbord of school activities, go swimming, learn karate or join the Guides or Scouts.

Background and atmosphere: Formed in 1996 through a merger of the Cathedral School for Boys, St Joseph's School for Girls and Stonefield House School. In 2011, St Mary's Preparatory School merged to form the new preparatory school. It is now well-established and developing a clear identity locally. It's good to see it settling after what parents describe as a 'few uneasy years' post-merger, though to be fair, all admit the children were fine and any merger wobbles were amongst parents. Onwards and upwards, lots of positivity from parents now – 'choosing LMS was a no-brainer' – and the prep moved to a new site in 2014, allowing more space for both prep and pre-prep – the latter now able to spread out a little more on the original site. Both are a mere stone's throw from the ancient cobbled streets of the Minster area, tucked away in quiet residential roads. A handful of boarders, residing in a junior boarding house nearby, sharing a range of evening and weekend activities with younger senior school boarders.

Very newly moved in at the time of our visit, and with the paint barely dry, the prep school is bright, light and airy with large well-equipped classrooms, a science lab, hall cum dining room, art room, IT room and library. Predominantly housed in a large red-brick Victorian house, flowing straight through via a newly constructed extension to link to the adjoining stable block; pupils can really spread out here and good use is made of all the space available. Outside there is a tarmac playground and small adjoining field, well-fenced and surrounded by trees. Car-parking is limited on school days (the playground is opened up for evening functions), the one-way flow system allows for quick drop-off and pick-up and the staggered start and finish times help with this.

Christian-based but attracts all faiths and none. Religious services (including communion) held at the Minster, but not an issue, nobody pulls out. Five school houses, named after cathedral cities, attract fierce loyalty and healthy competition between pupils of all ages. A mix of building styles and eras, some rented from the Dean and Chapter; hugely attractive and spacious new buildings sit cheek by jowl with the old; a converted Victorian school building is wonderful for drama with its bell tower, leaded windows and brick arches and sits alongside a stunning contemporary £10m music school, recital hall and sports hall. It is hard to tell which are school buildings and which are not: they all seem to intermingle across this concentrated historic quarter of the city, which includes the Minster and, interestingly, a school-owned pub. The profits from the pub provide useful additional funds for scholarships; anxious parents need not worry, it's not a place for pupils, but thirsty locals can enjoy a drink here, safe in the knowledge that they are supporting a good cause.

Unsurprisingly in this somewhat ancient and crowded setting, car parking is extremely limited. Apart from special occasions and evening events, when the playground can be used, it's street parking for all. Sixth-formers bemoan the lack of parking (and the army of zealous local traffic wardens), wise parents manage it by avoiding the journey altogether and sensibly taking advantage of the school transport: 12 buses carry pupils on from all directions, as far afield as Nottingham.

Pupils (unprompted) tell us that 'the food here is very good' – huge spacious dining room, part of which becomes a café at break time, all very civilised. Themed lunches are popular, especially Italian day.

Pastoral care, well-being and discipline: Parents are a hugely supportive bunch, lavish in their praise of staff. A 'warm and welcoming start' for confident and shy alike in pre-prep, say parents, 'family-orientated with great care and support' and 'a hunger to learn through fun lessons'. Good manners are important, as is respect; 'Bullying, incorrect uniform and chewing gum are big no-nos,' say pupils. All seems quite low key but take it as read that anything more serious than that is prohibited and brings severe reprimands. Tutors are always on hand to help pupils and answer parents' concerns. A pupil mentoring system works well and means that prefects, too, are approachable, even by the younger members of the school.

'Business wear' is the order of the day for sixth form and they are an unusually smart lot. Below sixth form it's a uniform with an attractive and distinctive striped blazer (a view not necessarily shared by pupils) for both boys and girls. Good to see so many sixth formers in school during our summer term visit – it's unusual during what is normally regarded as a term of study leave by most schools. It's a healthy sign when pupils are offered taught revision classes and extra individual tuition right through and up to exams, and wisely they grab it with both hands – they simply want to be here.

Pupils and parents: Large number of first time buyers with a mix of professionals and businesspeople – farmers, hospital and university staff, Siemens employees – most working locally, plus a fair-sized commuter set heading to London and other cities beyond the county borders.

Parents tell us that they like the fact that this is a 'through school', ie 3-18, and are also fans of the school's commitment to 'old-fashioned principles of respect, discipline, manners, consideration of others and kindness – right from the earliest stages'. Parentmail system keeps them up-to-date with info and news.

Thoroughly charming yet sensibly grounded pupils, hard working and ambitious, unafraid to look you in the eye and chat easily. Notable former pupils include: Jack Harvey (motor racing), Lizzie Simmonds (Olympic swimmer), Alice Ross (pastry chef at Michel Roux's Le Gavroche), Sophie Allport (renowned ceramic designer and businesswoman), John Scarborough (education officer, Cameron Mackintosh).

Entrance: Prep school entrants mostly either into nursery or reception classes, though large intakes recently at year 3. Space allowing, pupils accepted at any age/stage; informally assessed though not especially selective.

Formal assessment day for senior school places at 11.The majority of pupils come from the prep school; other popular sources include St Hugh's Prep, Woodhall Spa and Highfield's Prep, Newark, plus a myriad of other prep and junior schools. External applicants attend a personal assessment day in January, the intention being to indicate and understand the breadth of ability or potential, although entrance is not based purely on ability.

Exit: Nearly all prep school children move up to the senior school. A few depart to state sector after nursery and some also to local grammar schools at 11, but most stay. Over 80 per cent go through to sixth form. Wide variety of university destinations: in 2016, 30 per cent to Russell Group, with one to the Royal College of Music. Award-winning virtual careers library, which can be accessed from computers outside the school, is a tremendous resource for leavers.

Money matters: Well-endowed under the auspices of United Learning. Scholarships for academic, art, music and sport. Means-tested United Learning assisted places.

Remarks: Forget preconceptions of Lincolnshire being a flat and remote county: you can commute to London from here without too much difficulty, indeed many do; and the school occupies a magnificent setting high on a hill overlooking the rooftops of the historic quarter of the city with views of the Minster from (almost) every window. A happy and successful product of a four-way merger, no doubt tricky at the time but thriving now that the dust has well and truly settled, and the place ticks like a well-oiled machine.

Loughborough Grammar School

Linked with Fairfield Preparatory School, Loughborough High School

43

Burton Walks, Loughborough, Leicestershire LE11 2DU

Pupils: 950; 70 full boarders • Ages: 10–18 • Sixth form: 264

Fees: Day £11,775; Boarding £25,929 pa

Tel: 01509 233233
Email: admissions@lesgrammar.org
Website: www.lesgrammar.org

Headmaster: Since April 2016, Duncan Byrne, previously second master at Cheltenham College. Studied modern and medieval languages at Cambridge, where he was a choral scholar; has been head of modern languages at Colfe's and Whitgift and assistant head at Habs' Boys.

Academic matters: As with much we encountered at Loughborough, the academic programme is carefully thought out. For the first three years the emphasis seems to be on learning for pleasure – or the pleasure of learning. Breadth rather than an exclusive drive towards good grades is the aim; a genuine wish to stimulate a sense of enquiry and wonder as well as accumulating knowledge. Clubs and societies outside the classroom seek to support that – see the list of clubs and activities below. 'We aim to eliminate any barriers surrounding the classroom,' one member of staff told us. All boys take nine GCSEs in addition to a further programme of religion and philosophy, PHSE and outside activities. Some Latin and less Greek is taken at GCSE and Latin is on offer at A level.

The excellent website and prospectus give generous information about the academic side of the school. Those who thrive on statistics can positively gorge themselves, revelling in small percentage differences between the popularity of subjects from year to year and the percentage of A and B grades. They will see that, in general, the sciences, maths, politics and economics seem the most popular, but they will also note that 28 A level subjects are on offer. Breadth of choice is encouraged and where difficulties matching a pupil's choice of subjects, the school will seek to accommodate. For those who still insist on reading league tables, Loughborough scores well. In 2016, 60 per cent A*/A grades at GCSE and 42 per cent at A level. Facilities in support of their enlightened approach are excellent, with a delightful and much-used library – not quite as big as it looks in the pictures – a superb language laboratory and a state-of-the-art new science complex; new maths building under construction.

Games, options, the arts: Plenty of sport and healthily enjoyed, 'though you don't have to be good at sports to make friends,' a youngish boy told us. Rugby probably the most popular game but has also had some notable successes at football, both locally and at international level, cricket, cross-country, basketball and tennis. In addition to pitches close to the school buildings, about 40 acres of specially-levelled games pitches, a cross-country course and a grass athletics track near Quorn, about four miles away. Pupils are driven there and back. The scene from the superb pavilion is most impressive.

Extracurricular activities include a thriving CCF section, the popular D of E award scheme, debating, chess and bridge, the last three obviously helping to break down any barriers that might surround the classroom. Bridge, in particular, popular and successful, with players moving on to national and international honours. We were assured 300 chess players – amongst other things, a thinking school.

An excellent drama studio, of which the school is justifiably proud, leads on to 'stunning productions' in conjunction with the girls' High School. The new music school, run by a wildly enthusiastic head of music, has seen more and more people learn instruments (year 6 pupils all do). Singing is increasingly popular and the choirs and orchestras go out and about nationwide and overseas.

Boarding: Two separate boarding houses run by housemasters with their own families, both in the heart of the school. School House, for senior pupils, has room for over 30, of whom about 65 per cent are from at least five different countries. The rest tend to be Forces children. Housed in a delightfully quirky, mid-19th century listed building, it was the headmaster's house, as witness the mosaic floor in the hallway and the welcoming Latin message over what was originally the front door – ask the housemaster to translate, if you can't: he is primed. No longer a green baize door – he and his wife (a teacher) live cheek by jowl with their extended family. The boys' accommodation is approached via an amusing rabbit warren of stairs and passageways and comprises shared bedsits before seniors gravitate to rooms of their own. Pleasant recreational facilities as well as kitchen and laundry. A resident house tutor. The genuine family feel is further enhanced by the cleaning ladies, some of whom see their posts as hereditary, obviously care about the boys and know them well – another example of that community feeling.

Denton House for juniors (10–13 years) takes up to 18 boarders and is decorated cheerfully and imaginatively in a building which was once a private house and still retains that feeling. In addition to full boarding, flexi and weekly boarding are welcomed when space is available. Lots of weekend activities on offer. Occasionally boys choose to do a stint of boarding in order to help them feel even more at home in the school. Pupils from abroad receive support and encouragement from the housemaster's wife, a trained EAL teacher. Cautious noises about increasing the amount of boarding and both buildings are in line for refurbishment.

Background and atmosphere: Founded in 1495, moved up to its present site in 1850 and now part of Loughborough Endowed Schools, sharing the delightfully spacious and leafy campus with Loughborough High School for girls and Fairfield School, the co-educational prep. Though independent of each other, the three schools share the same governing body and a number of facilities.

For those parents who cannot decide between co-ed or single sex, Loughborough could be the answer. The main quad with its Tennysonian Tower and cherry trees is a delightful fusion of old and new buildings blending in sensitively across the centuries. In fact, the whole campus feels more like a university, an impression confirmed by the school's approach to the pupils, who are treated as burgeoning adults. Sixth formers, currently having their designated centre upgraded, may have lunch in the school refectory or in town and the house system is designed to be 'healthily competitive and fun' (that word again).

Boys come from a wide variety of ethnic backgrounds, but diversity seems genuinely celebrated and seen as an opportunity to enlarge mutual understanding. Boys look you in the eyes and smile. They seem very much at ease with each other and the staff – that includes non-teaching staff as well. The departure of the head groundsman after nearly 40 years of loyal service was marked by a ceremony at the top of the tower while below the entire school gathered to cheer him – a real community.

Pastoral care, well-being and discipline: 'I think the best thing about this school is that they trust you,' a leaver told us. Another said, 'I'll be a bit sad to leave but I'm ready now. I think they've prepared me well.' He then added wryly, 'Well, I hope they have.' Small tutor groups, not selected on purely academic grounds, help form friendships and understanding not only between pupils but also with staff who seem, in general, much appreciated – 'They always seem to have time to help, even the weird ones'. A good anti-bullying policy in place, but all the boys we spoke to said that it really wasn't an issue and that they felt supported and understood. One or two offered the theory that going home in the evenings helped diffuse any tensions. All sixth form boys are made prefects, giving them a sense of responsibility and belonging; senior prefects are elected by the boys concerned – a system which seems to work well and is another example of the important part trust plays in the running of the school.

L

Pupils and parents: Not a school for toffs; one which absorbs about 25 per cent of boys from ethnic minority backgrounds and a wide cross-section of parents. The ones we spoke to felt involved and part of the community. Buses come in daily from a radius of about 20 miles as well as the local area. Boys return home at 4pm unless they are staying on for extra-mural activities. Approx 35 boys from Hong Kong and mainland China as well as other parts of the world. An impressive variety of famous old boys testifies to the feeling that Loughborough does not do pigeon-holing eg Shiv Thakor, cricketer, Amit Guptor, film director, Felix Buxton, dancer, and Ben Hammersley, journalist.

Entrance: By own examination at 10, 11 and 13 or CE at 13. Selective more on the grounds of suitability than academic ability. It does not set out to be a specialist school for learning difficulties but all boys are screened for dyslexia on entry and help is available from learning support. About 50 per cent of pupils come from Fairfield, Loughborough's prep school, and the rest from primaries and other preps. Caters for pupils who transfer at age 10 by having a year 6 class which is integrated into the senior school to prepare them socially and academically for continuing into year 7.

Sixth form entry is based on GCSE results. Conditional offers made after interview with the headmaster, report from present school and predicted GCSE grades. Overseas pupils are required to sit examinations in those subjects they wish to study at A level.

Exit: About 10 to 15 per cent leave after GCSE, usually in pursuit of courses not available at Loughborough. Virtually all sixth formers go on to university: eight to Oxbridge in 2016 (one medic) and five other medics. London unis, Durham, Exeter, Birmingham, Bath and Newcastle popular. No outstanding subjects, but a greater proportion reading for science-based degrees than the humanities.

Money matters: A number of scholarships at different levels are available – don't be afraid to ask. A 25 per cent boarding fee remission for Forces children.

Remarks: A civilised school at ease with itself but constantly looking to improve. Ask to see a copy of the regular newsletter from governors to parents and guardians, a document which aims to keep the whole community aware of the thinking behind decisions and aspirations – not many schools do that. A happy school where boys are encouraged to pursue worthwhile individual goals, while having fun. Highly regarded locally and by connoisseurs further afield. A special community preparing boys sensitively and intelligently for university and beyond.

Loughborough High School

Linked with Fairfield Preparatory School, Loughborough Grammar School

Burton Walks, Loughborough, Leicestershire LE11 2DU

Pupils: 568 • Ages: 11–18 • Sixth form: 154

Fees: £11,472 pa

Tel: 01509 212348
Email: admin@leshigh.org
Website: www.leshigh.org

Headmistress: Since 2011, Mrs Gwen Byrom BSc MA PGCE (40s). Lots of varied experiences and qualifications gathered during her ascent to the headship of Loughborough High. She read biochemistry at Manchester University, followed by a masters degree with the Open University. Later she added psychology to the quiver of subjects she is qualified to teach. Has taught in a grammar school in Kent, then head of junior science at Solihull followed in fairly quick succession by Bedstone College, Roedean and, most recently, Cheltenham Ladies' College as vice-principal (pastoral). If you trawl the internet, you will find very complimentary words from some ex-pupils about Mrs Byrom. She says that Loughborough High is the best place she has ever taught at with the best staff she has ever worked with. 'This is the place for me. This is what I've been dreaming of.'

Teaches philosophy to year 7 to get a feel for the girls as they come into the school. 'I love the interaction and I want them to have the confidence to express doubts about what I say and to argue with me, the head. We discuss a wide range of issues and I think that helps them to know me better. It certainly helps me get a feel for the pulse of the school. I hope these lessons are perceived as enrichment. They certainly are for me.'

Girls we spoke to said how approachable she is, what a good listener. One group described her as 'mumsie', a term which clearly surprised, if not baffled her. We've heard headteachers called worse things. Keen on single sex education, which is just as well all things considered. As a scientist she is aware that girls in single sex schools are more likely to pursue the sciences than in a mixed school where sciences are perceived by boys as their prerogative. Overall she seems to have gone down well with parents, who speak appreciatively of her thoughtful, gentle approach. Some query whether she is fierce enough, whether she is as determined about league tables as she 'should be'. Others say 'she is a motivator, not a battle-axe, and there are more important things than league tables.' There's a compromise lurking there.

When we asked about plans for the future she became tremendously excited about iPads for everyone. Faced with an ageing Luddite who shamelessly prefers books, she visibly turned up the heat, arguing with something that WB Yeats might have called 'passionate intensity.' It was a magnificent and sincere performance. As one worldly father said, 'Oh, she's got bottle'.

Married to a physics teacher. Five children.

Academic matters: Loughborough High doesn't feel like an academic oven nor an intellectual boiler: it does feel like a skilfully-used slow cooker where the right temperature serves to permeate the ingredients with interesting tastes and infusions. GCSE and A level results are clearly published for interested parties to see and analyse and in today's climate, where schools are increasingly run as businesses and driven by targets, it is right that staff and pupils should celebrate good results (76 per cent A*/A grades at GCSE and 57 per cent A*/A, 79 per cent A*/B at A level in 2016, in case you are interested). But that sort of success doesn't seem to be what this school is really about; that's not what seems to unite teachers and pupils in mutual respect, interest and concern. There's plenty of talk in schools about 'happy family atmosphere.' Loughborough High certainly has bags of that, but what is more interesting is the palpable feeling that genuinely shared academic interests and concerns hint at another level of happiness and satisfaction. Neither seems at the expense of the other. That's what comes over as the heart of the school. And that doesn't happen by chance. It involves hard work and attention to detail; it requires genuine love of learning and enquiry from teachers and pupils alike.

Potential parents can look at the website and see the results, the choices available and the variety of opportunities beyond the classroom, but that's not what impressed us most. We witnessed a fabulous teacher who described herself as being 'as nutty as a fruitcake' enthuse and encourage a group of sixth formers who were trying to decide what topics they wished to work on for their EPQ during the summer holidays. Music Therapy, The French Revolution and Literature, a fiendishly difficult sounding science investigation: 27 girls were volunteering to pursue their chosen topic over the summer holidays. They were liaising with teachers to act as personal tutors over the holidays. The decibel count was high and happy. These were not necessarily what Australians call Pointy Heads: they were girls of spirit and zest, girls who might, as one teacher put it, jump in puddles.

We heard girls talking about the wonderful help given in choosing universities and the right course; we heard teachers saying what fun it was to teach such lively and interested girls, 'though they can drive you mad'; we heard girls talking about the extra help teachers were prepared to give. 'Everyone realizes how lucky we are to have so much support,' said a girl. It was a feeling echoed over and over again. In the splendid library we met a girl reading Plato's Symposium for pleasure and keen to discuss it and another bursting to talk about Churchill and the Gold Standard; we saw some thrillingly exciting textile work, inspired by a teacher who would have been totally camouflaged in a herbaceous border. And to extend that theme, the breadth and number of GCSE subjects on offer – 23 in all – ranging across a very wide spectrum suggests the thoughtful planning of a skilful plants person who wants people to wander and pick whatever delights.

There was the faintest whiff of cordite and revolution amongst those artists who wanted to do more art and design but felt they were being prevented by the preponderance of maths and science. As might be expected, the facilities are excellent; the teaching superb.

Games, options, the arts: The recently refurbished Astroturf, a huge area, is shared with the boys – though not simultaneously. Hockey, netball, cross-country, tennis, athletics, rounders, soccer and cricket. Plenty of county players and more, though the delightful girls who showed us round said that they found the games too serious and just wanted to take exercise. So they went to the gym. No shame in that. Music is phenomenal. Housed in a superb modern building it isn't actually, but it feels as if it is, the centre of the whole Loughborough complex. Inside there is a wonderful sense of activity and involvement orchestrated by the seemingly tireless music teachers. 'Music is what makes my daughter so happy at Loughborough,' a father told us. 'None of our family is musical but my daughter has taken to singing and loves it. It's been the making of her.' In fact there are 15 choirs, including a senior choir of a 120. Overall it is a thrilling place. Other extracurricular activities include the Duke of Edinburgh Award, in which over 70 girls are involved; debating, chess, bridge – the latter particularly popular. The girls we spoke to were thrilled that they are now allowed to join the CCF section. It is a sombre thought that one of the first women officers to be killed in Iraq was a former pupil.

Background and atmosphere: Founded in 1850 and one of the oldest girls' grammar schools in the country, it is now part of the Loughborough schools empire that includes the boys' grammar and Fairfield Prep, run by a central governing body. But, important this and fiercely protected, each of the three schools on the very handsome campus is autonomous. Boys and girls do some lessons together – politics and psychology, for instance – and they share the music school, but overall they have separate identities with their own teaching blocks and accommodation. For those parents who cannot decide between single sex and co-education this might seem the perfect arrangement. As for the atmosphere, it is purposeful and friendly. Girls seem very much at home in the sensitively run set up and 'we are given the opportunities to air our views.' There is a wonderful variety of meals in the excellent dining room with cheerful, friendly kitchen staff contributing to the overall sense of well-being.

Pastoral care, well-being and discipline: Over and over again we heard comments about how friendly and helpful the staff are; how they are helpful not only with academic matters but with social and personal confusions. 'There's always someone to turn to,' seemed a subliminal refrain. There are anti-bullying guidelines in place but girls looked astonished at any suggestion they might need invoking. There is a genuinely warm and mutually shared feeling of interest and respect between staff and pupils.

Pupils and parents: Pupils come in from a 40 mile radius covering Leicestershire, Derbyshire and Nottinghamshire, and we have heard stories of families moving to be nearer the school. Parents we spoke to felt involved, consulted and considered. 'You can be sure of straight and honest feedback from staff at parents' evenings,' one father told us, 'none of that politically correct foggy stuff. What's more, the teachers really know the girls.' That certainly sounds refreshing.

Entrance: About 40 per cent of entries come from Fairfield, the Loughborough prep, the rest from local state and private junior schools. Intakes for year 7 are assessed in English, maths and verbal reasoning; the next three years the same plus a foreign language paper. Entry into the sixth form is via GCSEs, reports and interviews. Typically A or A* grades are required for those subjects to be taken at A level plus at least five B grades which must include maths, English and science. No wonder they get good A level results.

Exit: Up to 15 per cent leave after GCSEs for a variety of reasons: boarding, sixth form college or a subject which is not on offer at Loughborough. Girls told us that very few left because they were fed up. One to Oxbridge in 2016 and six medics, and lots go to Russell Group universities. Much success with university places in a variety of subjects: sciences are popular, plus philosophy, politics, modern languages, classics, music and architecture.

Money matters: There are a number of scholarships and bursaries available. Don't be afraid to ask.

Remarks: The best of both worlds with superb, inspirational teaching and alert, interested girls. Not a hothouse dedicated to clawing up league tables, expelling anyone who doesn't contribute to that, but rather a genuinely academic school where learning is prized and pursued with a measure of joy and satisfaction. A very happy school. A very good school.

Maidwell Hall

Maidwell, Northampton NN6 9JG

Pupils: 123; 110 full/flexi boarders (two thirds boys) • Ages: 7-13

Fees: Boarding £19,026 – £25,350; Day £16,500 pa

Tel: 01604 686234
Email: headmaster@maidwellhall.co.uk
Website: www.maidwellhall.co.uk

M

Headmaster: Since 2001, Mr Robert Lankester MA PGCE (50s). Educated at Elstree School, Charterhouse and Selwyn College, Cambridge, where he read history. Worked as city stockbroker for seven years before deciding he wanted to teach – 'the best decision I ever made.' After PGCE at Durham, he spent 13 years at Uppingham, 10 as a housemaster. Enthusiastic and focused, with firm, no-nonsense approach. School has thrived under his leadership and introduction of girls in 2010 – 'a very exciting development,' he says – has gone smoothly. Head says girl numbers won't go above 50 at the very most. He's adamant that Maidwell will remain a small, full boarding school but transitional boarding for two or three nights has recently been introduced as an option for local day children. Loves teaching and still manages to fit six periods of geography for CE pupils into his busy week. 'He is an exceptional headmaster,' one parent told us. 'He believes in bringing the best out of every child.' Married, with two grown-up children. Carey, his charming Montessori-trained wife, is very involved in school life. She is in charge of the girls (housemistress will be appointed once the new girls' house opens), head of swimming, teaches drama and does a host of boarding duties (boys and girls). Family lives in leafy wing of the main school.

Entrance: 'We have a very broad intake,' says the head. 'Our target is to get the pupils into their first choice of school at 13 and we've succeeded in that for the last 13 years.' Boys and girls arrive from pre-preps and state primaries and visit a year prior to entry for informal assessment – maths, reading, spelling, non-verbal reasoning and relaxed 10 minute chat with head. Smattering of scholarships and bursaries available – though 'there isn't a bottomless pit of gold.' Head keen to dispel the notion that pupils have to be extrovert, outdoorsy types. 'Any child would thrive here and it's unusual for me to say no,' he says, while his wife comments that the pupils are 'nurtured and looked out for.' All have a 24-hour boarding trial the summer before they start, 'just to get them (and their mothers) used to the idea.' Most pupils live up to two hours away and are from rural areas (Lincs, Notts, Rutland, Leics, Cambs, East Anglia etc) but a few come from London area. Handful (under 10 per cent) from abroad, including Spain, Japan, China, Thailand and Russia. Some children of Old Maidwellians. Old boys include Earl Spencer and former poet laureate Sir Andrew Motion.

Exit: Boys progress to a wide variety of senior schools, including Uppingham (most popular), Eton, Radley and Stowe. School reckons girls are likely to choose co-ed schools like Stowe and Oundle, or single-sex Queen Margaret's, York and Tudor Hall. Two or three scholarships a year.

Remarks: Eleven miles north of Northampton, in a pretty country village. School was founded in 1913 and moved to present 44-acre site in 1933. Main building is an imposing 17th century turreted mansion overlooking its own lake (pupils must pass swimming test before they are allowed anywhere near it). Spacious grounds mean children can build camps, climb trees (the favourite tree is called Radar) and play hide and seek and British Bulldog in their spare time. We visited on Shrove Tuesday and arrived in the middle of the annual (and hotly-contested) house pancake race. Lots of debate about how high the pancakes must be tossed, with welly-clad director of studies joking 'there may have to be a stewards' inquiry.'

Classes are small. Maximum 15, but more likely to be around 12. Two streams in each year group (maths setted separately) and lessons taught by subject specialists. Traditional curriculum (including French and Latin, and Greek for senior pupils). Extra one-to-one SEN provision (from three-strong SEN team) at extra cost for those with mild dyslexia and dyspraxia. Despite gloomy headlines about reluctant readers, most pupils read avidly. They all have 20-minute reading period every day after lunch, either in dorms or outside on sunny days. Current favourite authors, the children informed us, include Michelle Paver, Conn Iggulden and (still) JK Rowling. All do ICT and touch-typing. School assembly each morning, with prayers read by a pupil and thought for the day from a member of staff, plus a service at the church in the school grounds on Sunday mornings (lots of parents attend too). Relatively young teaching staff – 19 full-time, two part-time. Head and his wife, director of boarding, two matrons and three gap students live on site.

Sports-wise, the school punches above its weight. Head is particularly proud that Maidwell recently won the national under-13 cross-country championship – quite a feat when they're up against far larger schools. Pupils play sport six days a week – boys do rugby, hockey, football and cricket, while girls do hockey, netball and rounders. Sports hall with cricket nets, climbing wall and squash court. Rowing on the lake in the summer and weekly swimming for all in school's own indoor pool. Loads of activities during break-times, evenings and at weekends, including crafts, carpentry, textiles, school magazine, gardening, clay shooting and outdoor pursuits trips. When we asked two boys whether they ever got bored, they looked puzzled. 'Of course not,' they told us. Music, drama and art good. Two-thirds of pupils learn musical instruments and music practice is timetabled. Two major concerts a year and choir sings an anthem in the church every Sunday. Art is very popular – everything from surrealism to gargoyles – and on the drama front, there are lots of plays, musicals and public speaking events.

All meals are cooked in-house. Lunch is a formal affair, in a light, airy dining room with long, narrow tables. Grace is said at the start and finish and a member of staff sits at each end to serve food, encourage good table manners and chat to boys and girls. Tradition of one boiled sweet after lunch still firmly in place (plastic tub solemnly passed from pupil to pupil) and £1 of tuck on Sundays. When we visited, a group of jolly 12-year-olds tucked into a lunch of beef pie and pancakes (stylishly served with slices of lemon) and chatted enthusiastically about the school. Food gets the thumbs-up from pupils. As head says: 'We're aiming for the good bits of Jamie Oliver but we still have fish and chips on Fridays.' Breakfast and supper are more informal. House system in place, with head boy/girl, prefects and four house captains. House competitions range from rugby and cross-country to water polo and conkers, with points scored for the annual house cup. 'It's taken very seriously,' the head boy told us.

Boarding is at the very heart of the school. Lots of parental access (church, matches etc) but boarders must stay at school at weekends. Leave-out weekends (from lunch on Friday till Monday evening) every second or third weekend. Pupils can be weekly boarders during their first year but most opt for full boarding from the start. Boy boarders are housed on first floor while girls get the self-contained top floor of the school. Boys' dorms (up to six per room) are wholesome and shipshape while girls' dorms (three to six per room) are decorated with jolly bunting, Keep Calm and Carry On posters and lots of Cath Kidston (there are plans for them to move to a purpose-built house of their own in due course). Older girls' bathroom looks straight out of an interiors magazine – chic circular basins, tongue and groove and laminate flooring.

Pupils are courteous, well-behaved and good company. When benefactor Oliver Wyatt was once asked about the ideal Maidwell pupil, he described him/her as the sort of child who 'was invited to someone's house and invited back again.' His view still holds true, with Maidwell putting an emphasis on being kind, well-mannered and tidy. Boys look smart in navy cords, striped or check shirts, ties and tweed jackets while girls wear corduroy culottes, blouses and smart jackets. Perhaps unusually in this day and age (but very popular with parents), mobile phones, PSPs and iPods are banned (although final year pupils can listen to iPods in their dorms). Boys and girls are allowed to watch key sports matches and a film on Saturday nights, while older pupils see the nightly TV news, but no TV apart from that. Boyfriend/girlfriend relationships actively discouraged. 'We are resistant to the idea of girls and boys "going out",' says the head. 'We talk it through with the pupils and I am very clear that we are not having it.' All pupils write a weekly letter home – 'we emphasise how much it means to parents,' he says.

Discipline isn't an issue here. 'It's because we're a small school and everybody looks out for each other,' say staff. 'You don't get division or ganging up because it's so close-knit.' Parents agree. 'We love the fact that because it's slightly smaller it has a real family atmosphere,' one mother told us. 'It gives children the opportunity to shine. Everyone gets to play in a team and everyone is in the school play.' Meanwhile a father commented: 'I'm delighted with all aspects of the school. The teaching staff are great and the boarding care is just superb.' Head is adamant that it isn't a 'snobby' place either. 'Privilege has no place in this school,' he says. 'Everyone is equal here.'

Maidwell Hall remains a traditional, full-boarding prep school that has stuck to its full boarding guns and held its own in a declining market. Small enough for everyone to know each other but big enough to offer a first-rate, all-round education, it encourages pupils to work hard, get lots of fresh air and have fun along the way.

Northampton High School

Newport Pagnell Road, Hardingstone, Northampton NN4 6UU

Pupils: 699 • Ages: 3–18 • Sixth form: 130

Fees: £9,981 – £13,356 pa

Tel: 01604 765765
Email: nhsadmin@nhs.gdst.net
Website: www.northamptonhigh.gdst.net

Headmistress: Since 2015, Dr Helen Stringer, previously vice-principal (curriculum) at the Stephen Perse Foundation. Educated at Danum Grammar School in Doncaster, Yorkshire; history degree from Bristol; completed her masters and doctorate, specialising in mid-16th century England, at Sussex; teacher training at the Institute of Education in London. Over 20 years of teaching experience includes Channing, JAGS and Leicester Grammar.

Head of junior school: Since 2012, Mr Ross Urquhart BSc (40s). Previously head of Broughton Manor Prep School and deputy head of Milton Keynes Prep School. A PE and geography graduate from Brunel University, he has a passion for sport (tennis and skiing) and has taught all junior school subjects. Married to Nicola; they have two daughters, both at the school.

Academic matters: Glowing recent ISI report judged the school's EYFS provision to be 'outstanding' in every category, highlighting the fact that girls here are 'happy and greatly enjoy the setting'. Own junior school SENCo, who works with each class once a week as well as offering one-to-one learning support before school and during lunch breaks. Mild learning disabilities catered for plus enrichment opportunities for gifted and talented. Like other GDST junior schools, it combines first-rate delivery of the curriculum with a nurturing environment where girls feel safe and secure. Most year groups have two classes, three in year 6. Class sizes range from 16-24. French from year 1 and ICT lessons once a week for all. Teachers (16 full-time) have good working relationship with their counterparts in senior school, meeting regularly to discuss curriculum.

School says girls 'mean business' and recent results prove the point. Most recent ISI report said 'the quality of the pupils' learning, attitudes and basic skills is excellent' and noted girls' focus, concentration and progress. These comments are borne out by 2016 A level results – 77 per cent A*/B, 53 per cent A*/A. Sixty-four per cent of GCSEs A*/A. Most take at least nine GCSEs. Dual award science available or three separate sciences. At A level girls can choose from 28 subjects – all the traditional ones, plus classical civilisation, critical thinking (AS), economics, food, nutrition and health, government and politics, PE and psychology. Four girls recently piloted AQA's Extended Project Qualification and more will follow suit in coming years. In addition, Latin taught from year 7 and German and Spanish from year 8.

Staff very keen on preparing pupils not just for university, but also for workplace beyond – from skills days for all to work experience placements for sixth formers. A year 12 keen on studying veterinary science, for example, spends part of Friday afternoons working for a local vet, while in recent years several have won paid internships at HSBC.

Believes in being as inclusive as possible – full-time SENCo gives one-to-one support and in groups, as well as to gifted and talented.

Two-thirds of teachers are women, a third men. Clear policy on homework – year 7s, for instance, get nearly seven hours' worth a week. Laptops given to all from year 11 up – cost incorporated in fees and school gets them back when girls leave. Classroom teaching supplemented by specialist speakers, theatre visits, lectures and trips abroad (including annual expedition to Normandy each year for year 8s).

Games, options, the arts: Prides itself on its sporting achievements. 'We have élite teams but believe in fitness and enjoyment for all.' Girls do netball, hockey, swimming, squash, tennis, badminton, rounders, cross-country, athletics etc. Sports hall, dance studio, fitness suite, Astroturf, netball and tennis courts, plus three hockey pitches and 25m five-lane swimming pool.

The music department is located at the heart of the school and boasts everything from an orchestra, choir and jazz band to a strings group that played at the Royal Albert Hall a few years ago. More than 160 girls have individual music lessons in school. Drama is very popular too, and girls take it at both GCSE and A level. Annual school production (from Charlie and the Chocolate Factory to Hamlet) performed in main hall, which seats 650.

Art really has the wow factor. Department gets outstanding results and many go on to do art, architecture, graphic design and fashion later on. Head of art believes in encouraging pupils to expand their ideas and creativity and her approach pays dividends. When we visited, just ahead of the school's annual arts festival, the walls were a feast for the eyes – from a dress made entirely of bottle-tops by a GCSE student to etchings, screen prints, oils and collages.

Other activities include community service, Young Enterprise and D of E, as well as voluntary lunchtime clubs like printmaking, ceramics, public speaking, book group and eco-team. Resourceful group of year 10 and 11s produces their own online school magazine, complete with 'what's hot, what's not,' fiction, poetry, recipes and even an agony aunt.

Music, drama, art and sport galore in the junior school, plus activities like sponsored spellathon, cyber fashion show, talent show, hobbies convention and trips to pony club, music festivals, museums and art galleries.

Background and atmosphere: Founded in 1878 by committee of local church people. Moved from historic Rennie Mackintosh building in centre of Northampton to purpose-built, two-storey building on the outskirts of town in 1992. Envious visiting heads frequently comment on 'intelligent' and 'very civilised' design. Set in 24 acres so plenty of space to run off steam. Main building is designed in a figure of eight, with two pretty courtyards in the middle. Corridors decked out in school's trademark blue with a few bright pink IKEA sofas dotted around to provide light relief. While some schools appear noisy and hectic, this one is refreshingly calm and orderly. All girls encouraged to use well-equipped library, which boasts 12,500 books. Full-time librarian on hand to help them develop their research skills – no relying on Wikipedia here.

Junior school is housed in same building as its older sibling. Modern building means all classrooms are airy and spacious, with oodles of storage space for books, coats and PE kit. Classrooms at lower end of school open on to their own enclosed areas. When we visited, one had been temporarily transformed into a mini racing track, complete with scooters, toy cars and cardboard petrol pumps. All classrooms equipped with overhead projectors and most with interactive whiteboards too. Own hall for assemblies, dance, ballet and gym and library. Around £3,000 spent on new library books each year – Michael Morpurgo, Dick King-Smith and Anne Fine are girls' current favourite authors. Pupils get the chance to air their views at school council meetings. Previous head was astonished when girls vetoed his plans for a school disco and said they'd like a barn dance instead.

Pastoral care, well-being and discipline: Excellent pastoral care in junior school. PSHCE lessons given over to issues girls may face, such as eating disorders or friendship problems. Teachers give girls opportunity to play old-fashioned (and very wholesome) playground games like Grandmother's Footsteps, What's the Time, Mr Wolf? and Stuck in the Mud, with aim of getting everyone involved.

Senior girls say it's a friendly and welcoming place, with approachable teachers who 'really care'. Very good at settling new girls in, with induction days the term before they start and imaginative new Big Sister, Little Sister initiative, where sixth-formers keep an eye on new year 7s. School council, with reps from each year group, and new house system in place. Girls belong to one of four houses – Hestia, Selene, Artemis or Demeter. Lots of house competitions, from drama and singing to sports and film-making. Head girl is voted in by girls and teaching staff, along with leadership team consisting of deputy head girl and two more deputies for social services and charity.

Rules on drugs, alcohol, smoking and bullying all clearly stated, but girls and staff say these aren't issues here. One sixth former told us: 'It's just not what we do.' Another joked: 'No one would even dare.' If concerns about work or behaviour do arise, letters sent home to parents. Saturday detentions imposed if eight work or behaviour reports in one term are sent out, but no one can remember it ever happening.

Stylish new uniform recently introduced for 11 to 16 year olds – blazers, crisp navy and white blouses, navy skirts. Sixth-formers wear own clothes but must look smart – no strappy tops, short skirts, hoodies, jeans or trainers. Oldest girls have their own common room, café and study room. School lunches are wholesome and served up in three light, airy canteens. Lots of choice – hot meals, salads, vegetarian options, dessert, fruit and yogurt. Recent school dinner competition asked girls to design their own meal, and as a result obliging catering staff served up couscous, tacos and even square-shaped chips. Some girls bring packed lunches from home. Very working-parent friendly, offering early supervision and breakfast from 8am, supervised prep sessions till 5pm and after-school club till 6pm.

Pupils and parents: Parents give school a firm thumbs-up. Two-thirds of girls are from families where both parents work, and with this in mind recently introduced breakfast club – for parents as well as girls. It opens at 7.45am and has proved hugely popular, particularly with the dads. School reckons typical Northampton High girl is 'outgoing, articulate, hard-working and caring', while head girl says approvingly, 'You are allowed to be yourself here'. Pupils from a mix of rural and urban backgrounds. Many live in Northampton and surrounding villages, but some travel in (by school minibus) from as far afield as Brackley, Daventry, Wellingborough, Milton Keynes and Bedford. Parents, a mix of professional types, county set and self-employed, very supportive of school. 'It has a real buzz about it,' one mother told us, while another said: 'The school seems to embrace everything and everybody. When we go to a concert or play the pupils do everything, whether they're conducting the orchestra or doing the lights. I really feel the girls are being prepared for the outside world.' Eclectic list of old girls includes former MI5 boss Baroness Eliza Manningham-Buller, novelist Anne Fine and Olympic swimmer Caitlin McClatchey.

Entrance: Pupils admitted to nursery (open for 46 weeks of the year) on a first come, first served basis. After that main entry points to junior school are reception, year 3, year 5 and (increasingly) year 6. Prospective pupils visit for a half day, doing assessments in English and maths, before hearing whether they've got a place. Not completely full at the moment – 'possibly due to our selective entry, not that it's particularly high,' says school. Senior school main entry points are at 11, 13 and 16. Girls sit school's own entrance exam (English, maths and verbal reasoning) in January prior to entry. Half arrive from the junior school, while rest come from wide range of local primaries. A dozen or so enter the school at 13, mostly from preps like Spratton Hall, Winchester House and Beachborough. Up to 10 new girls join sixth form each year. All need minimum of five GCSEs at A*-C, including English and maths, but school likes to see at least Bs in proposed A level subjects.

Exit: Virtually all juniors progress to senior school. 'Robust tracking system' and any concerns get flagged up early on, but school says, 'We very rarely find ourselves in that situation'. About a third leave after GCSEs, mainly heading to co-ed schools like Northampton School for Boys. Virtually all sixth form leavers to higher education. Good spread of degree subjects, including aerospace engineering at Nottingham, hispanic studies at Warwick, textile design at Leeds and bloodstock and performance hosre management at the Royal Agricultural University. One to Oxbridge in 2016 and three medics.

Money matters: Several scholarships on offer at 11, 13 and sixth-form level – academic, arts and sports. A number of means-tested bursaries available too.

Remarks: A happy and high-achieving school that nurtures and educates girls throughout those all-important teenage years. School prospectus says, 'Kindness, courtesy, service and fun go hand in hand with striving for academic success,' and pupils certainly bear this out. With its increasingly sparkling achievements, a school on the up.

Norwich High School for Girls

Eaton Grove, 95 Newmarket Road, Norwich NR2 2HU

Pupils: 823 • Ages: 3–18 • Sixth form: 132

Fees: £10,290 – 13,542 pa

Tel: 01603 453265
Email: admissions@nor.gdst.net
Website: www.norwichhigh.gdst.net

Head: Since 2015, Mrs Kirsty von Malaisé, previously deputy head at Putney High. Educated at the Purcell School of Music and was a scholar at the Guildhall School of Music and Drama, before reading English at Christ's College, Cambridge. She was head of English at two London state schools before moving into the independent sector. A former Young Musician of the Year finalist, Kirsty's interests include music and mountain walking. She is married and has one pre-school son.

Head of juniors: Since September 2016, Nick Tiley-Nunn, previously deputy head at The Old School Henstead. BA in primary education from Canterbury Christ Church; has also taught at Woodbridge School and been assistant head at Radnor House. He is a regional lead for primary maths and author of 'How to teach primary maths – anyone can feed sweets to sharks'.

Academic matters: Lessons are stimulating and fun in the junior school. 'They've got to be worth getting out of bed for,' says the school, and much thought goes into structuring the curriculum. Lots of different 'Days' eg Victorian Day, Business Day, Tudor Day – suggestive of the cross-curricular approach that so enlivens the senior school. Try-outs in four different languages and lots of trips.

'They encourage a work ethic,' a senior school parent told us. Small classes – few are taught in groups of more than 20, 12 in the sixth form. Results impress across the board and initiatives support enriched learning – not just hoop jumping. Newish head of co-curricular developing lots of different courses as 'a break from the purely academic'. At A level, Eng Lit, maths, chemistry and biology top the faves – maths being notably successful. Fewer language takers hitherto – though results are good – but this now on the rise. Art, history and geography also shine. At GCSE, history and geography the most popular options but results in art, classical civilisation, languages and music are startlingly good. Englishes and maths show more of a spread but all get A*-C with a high proportion at the upper end. Mandarin and computing now offered at GCSE too. In 2016, 64 per cent A*/A grades at GCSE and 45 per cent at A level.

Emphasis – especially in sixth form – on independent learning – hence many areas for quiet study. Lots of short term individual support for those struggling with individual subjects. 'If you're stuck you can go to a teacher – you're never made to feel embarrassed. They encourage you to come.' And sixth form helpers for younger girls struggling with a subject – good both ways, we feel. Everyone screened in year 9; much praise for special needs teacher. At the time of our visit, 21 pupils in the senior school and 38 in the juniors were receiving some form of extra support in their learning – timetabled additional help – mostly one-to-one, support within the classroom and a variety of other specialist interventions by internal or external staff – depending on need.

Good library with 'our lovely librarian'... 'the best of the changes'. 'Drop Everything And Read' scheme = 15 minutes of 'out' time, a new idea. Gorgeous fiction library and good programme of visiting authors.

Games, options, the arts: Excellent sports provision and we were inspired – coming as we did in summertime – by the six grass courts spread around the gardens – what a treat! Plus the new all-weather hockey pitch a short walk away. Universal approval of the new games afternoon which makes for more time on pitches and courts and better squad development. Improved performance as a result and general praise for new head of sport and the introduction of teams for those not destined for sporting stardom. Sports hall and 25m pool.

Really lively junior school art eg Van Gogh-inspired yellows and blues and scenes from Narnia in evocative charcoal and impressive Greek vase pictures. 'If you do a good one it gets framed and stays for years and years till you come back as a teacher and see it again!' The arts thrive throughout the school and design, in particular, is celebrated here. Lively art and textiles – an innovation much appreciated – girls enthuse about their teachers and we loved the wittily designed, cleverly made bags and shorts. 'The fashion show is one of the really good changes,' the girls told us. Good drama, now with fab new drama studio and well-equipped tech gallery overlooking the hall. Dance an innovation, again much enjoyed. Much success in arts and sports – everything done with huge energy and drive.

Despite neglected accommodation – major refurbishment underway at time of our visit – music is a glory with acclaimed head of dept: 'Fantastic, amazing music teacher who really pushes our talents'... 'she gets everyone involved'... 'she's taught me that it doesn't matter if you're not specially talented – she got me playing the glockenspiel and ocarina and now I'm taking grade 3 piano!' And much more of the same. Around a third learn an instrument in school and more outside. The Chamber Choir recently won Barnardos' Choir of the Year at the Royal Festival Hall (resulting in concerts at the Royal Albert Hall, St John's Smith Square, Barbican etc and other 'professional' engagements). Annual music tours – an astounding 79 girls went to Tuscany recently. Previously sung in St Marks, Venice; Salzburg Cathedral; St Thomas', Leipzig; St Nicolas, Prague. Regular concerts and service in the Norwich Anglican Cathedral and occasional appearances at the RC one too. Not just classical – popular and musicals done with pizazz.

Woods, fields, jungle gym and main school facilities provide outdoor life for juniors. Year 5 girls recently won the regional paper's Young Poet of the Year Award.

Background and atmosphere: The first senior school opened outside London by The (then) Girls' Public Day School Company, now the Girls' Day School Trust (GDST). So, a notable and venerable institution with nearly 140 years of excellence to celebrate. Housed, principally, in a delicious 1820 residence on the generously proportioned, tree-lined Newmarket Road – one of the main roads connecting the city with the country. The school has been sensitively extended over the decades and there is much, internally, to delight the eye – splendid cornices, ceilings, plaster friezes, galleried atrium and sumptuous stained glass. Preserves former conservatory as part of the staff room and The Gadesden Room – elegant with splendid cornice and ceiling rose plus super long table for small scale events. No harm done to young minds to be educated surrounded by such architectural felicities. Attractive garden with lofty trees and grateful bird life contribute to sense of overall harmony here. Forest school for the younger pupils – laid out on logs under trees used as classroom area and also chat space – very relaxing.

Modernisation has brought high tech facilities in the hall, drama studio, lang labs etc and in 'the portal' – efficient school/home intranet used by all to access assignments and staff email. Much of school now trim and polished though here and there a dab of Polyfilla and a splosh or two of emulsion needed.

N

Junior school in beautiful 19th century Stafford House over the way from senior dept, newly decorated and revamped when we visited. Tots in Polliwiggle Nursery – that being the Norfolk word for tadpole, don't you know? Good, colourful clutter here and there – not one of those sanitised juniors; atmosphere is relaxed, orderly and purposeful. Lovely library with beanbags invites curling up and wallowing.

Very stable staff – almost half have been at the school for 10 or more years and the numerous new appointments seen as adding strength and breadth to the provision. Most staff seen as very efficient, though we picked up that a few could be better at home/school communication.

Pastoral care, well-being and discipline: Junior school parents very appreciative: 'I was sure about sending her from the day we went to look round when she was 4. She just got stuck in and loved it and there's always such a good atmosphere.' Others concur: 'It's a happy, productive, busy place'.

Year 7s into The Churchman Centre – a gentle transition from wherever they've come from into senior school with adored head of year – 'any time you want to talk to her, she's always there'. Sixth form centre in old Lanchester House plus excellent new extension with study areas, small teaching rooms, huge careers room – 'we get lots of help with uni choice' – lecture theatre and super-cool café. Good food – special praise for Nick the Chef who will do special diets if needed without fuss. Girls in six 'companies' – houses to you and me. Also longer break times – 'so we're not late for classes any more' – and more comfortable uniform. New emphasis on communication and sharing responsibility. No prefects – all sixth form girls have responsibilities – taken seriously by most. Parents are warm in their approbation – 'The teachers are good at seeing the girls' point of view.' Minimal discipline problems sorted out by pastoral staff – if it gets that far.

Pupils and parents: Among the most articulate, courteous, thoughtful and quietly assured girls we have met anywhere. Families from Norfolk and North Suffolk – not much competition in the area if you want a top quality academic girls' school. Buses run from Dereham and North Norfolk and more are planned. Mostly, local professional, business, academic, medical and farming families with a tiny number for whom English is their second language. Celebrated old girls include athletes Anna Bentley (fencing), Emma Pooley (cycling); authors Rafaella Barker, Pat Barr, Jane Hissey, Stella Tillyard and Anne Weale; sopranos Jane Manning and Elizabeth Watts; composer Diana Burrell, up-and-coming theatre director Genevieve Raghu, dress designer Ann Tyrell, scientist Jennifer Moyle and a nurse called Edith Cavell.

Entrance: Nursery from 3 and not oversubscribed – the locals being, seemingly, a little slow to seize their opportunities. Assessment via a play day when they look for manual dexterity, interaction, responsiveness etc. Reception has 20 and a further 20 by year 3. Again, currently not too much pressure on places but, as the place starts to zoom, this is unlikely to stay the case.

Over 20 local schools regularly send pupils to NHS senior school. Not, currently, wildly oversubscribed at any level other than at 16+. But when reputation catches up with reality here, what with the newly energised staff and the effect on both results and general satisfaction, that is unlikely to remain the case. Get in while you can. At sixth form, the word is already out. Far fewer now leave after GCSE and, of course, lots want to come – from local state schools and even the odd local independent. Not hard to see why.

Exit: Most juniors move, gratefully, to the senior school.

Fewer – some 30 per cent – now leave after GCSE, for the local boys' school, recently turned co-ed, or anywhere else. Post A level, most to sensible courses at good universities – two to Oxbridge in 2016; others to a mix of the soundly academic eg history at York or chemistry at Birmingham to the soundly vocational eg aerospace engineering at Leicester or retail management at Surrey. Altogether, a sense that people go where they should.

Money matters: The GDST isn't a rich organisation but under its current management much energy is going into upping the bursary provision. Academic and music scholarships at 11+. Academic, music, drama, sport and art scholarships at 16+. Bursaries at 11+, 13+ and 16+ on a means-tested basis. Over 50 students in receipt of bursary assistance in the senior school at time of our visit

Remarks: Best summed up by pupils: 'I've been here since reception and the school has just got better and better.' 'You're allowed to develop in your own way – there's no limit to what you can do.' And parents: 'I wish I could put my sons in dresses and send them there.' Now, there's a thought...

Norwich School

70 The Close, Norwich NR1 4DD

Pupils: 1,091 • Ages: 7–18 • Sixth form: 327

Fees: £13,725 – £15,060 pa

Tel: 01603 728449
Email: admissions@norwich-school.org.uk
Website: www.norwich-school.org.uk

Head Master: Since 2011, Mr Steffan Griffiths MA (Oxon) classics, BA (Open University) English literature (40s). Educated at Whitgift School, where his father was headmaster, and had a spell at Timbertop School in Australia as a 'Rentapom', before Oxford. Taught classics and games at Tonbridge School, then Eton (also deputy housemaster) before returning to Oxford for appointment as usher (deputy head) of Magdalen College School. Has made a confident impression at Norwich, where his relaxed, low-key style has been welcomed all round. 'He seems right for the school now,' commented pupils, though a mother we spoke to said, 'I am not sure I would recognise him in the street.'

Acknowledges and defends the rapid expansion of the school in recent years to admit girls throughout; proportion now nearing 60:40, and nearly even in the sixth form. No dramatic changes planned, and says he is 'very impressed by what I find here.' Has chosen to teach his own subjects (Latin and Greek) at GCSE and A level. He is married to Harriet, who teaches at another school, and they have three children, two at the lower school.

Master of the lower school: Since 2007 is Mr John Ingham BA (history), previously head of Rossall School Juniors. Cheerful and down to earth in style – an enthusiastic advocate of the school's recent inclusion of girls (his daughter was an early pioneer). Very accessible, teaches (mostly history and maths), not hidden away. Easy, relaxed relationships with the pupils. He is married to Mandy, who works in the school's games department, and they have one daughter, now in the senior school.

Academic matters: Closely-knit staff in the lower school, including plenty of men, teach pupils in smallish classes (under 20) with emphasis on encouraging a love of learning. Pupils need to be above average in ability and confident readers to benefit from all the school offers.

The senior school bar is set high by a committed and enthusiastic staff of over 100. Parents and pupils acknowledge the outstanding quality of the teachers – many are leading lights in their own disciplines and write the textbooks. A father spoke of 'highly intelligent, motivated teaching – the pupils are lucky'. 'My favourites are fun, as well as making us work,' said one boy, and a sixth former praised' the way we are made to think – it blows your mind at times!' Academic pressure is there, 'but it's more self-imposed; we are under pressure from ourselves', said a girl. 'It's hugely competitive, but most of us like that'. The head is frank – 'those who struggle to keep up just wouldn't be happy here' – and parents agree that 'scraping in and not thriving is worse than not getting in, in the first place.'

Examination results excellent; A*/A grades par for the course at GCSE (72 per cent A*/A in 2016). Options with a high take-up include Spanish, photography and 2D design. Latin, perhaps surprisingly, is not popular and Greek even less so. A levels again mainly sciences, maths and history, though music and philosophy are both popular. The art and design department has national recognition. Sixty-two per cent A*/A grades in 2016. School provides plenty of help with university applications – 'we received emails about courses our son might be interested in nearly every week', one mother told us, preparation begins early. Some resentment about the dominance of Oxbridge in all this – masterclasses and interview advice for suitable pupils can irritate. 'It really bugs me – one teacher kept saying, "you'll need this for your Oxbridge entrance", when only two in the group were doing it.'

The school provides plenty of support for study skills and revision. Though there is limited SEN provision, a new post has been created to provide specialist learning support. They will organise extra time in exams for dyslexics and help is available after school (either from school staff or outside specialists) but pupils must be able to follow the whole curriculum.

Games, options, the arts: The message is 'get involved'; enormous variety of clubs, sports, musical activities and drama productions. Pupils are 'very diverse, nerdy, sporty and cool types', said one mother.

Sport is compulsory throughout. The greatest importance is attached to the competitive team sports – rugby, cricket, hockey, netball – and the best are creamed off into the coveted A and B teams in each year. 'The boys can be cocky if they are in the teams,' said one girl, and the star status of the first XV is evident, though the girls' success in hockey and netball is giving the boys a run for their money. Playing fields a bus ride away. Those who don't catch the selector's eye do Potted Sports, having a go each term at different activities – mostly rowing, fencing, and non-team games.

Music is taken seriously and at least 70 per cent of pupils are involved in some kind of instrumental group, band or choral society. The school educates the cathedral choristers but also has its own chapel choir, which leads school worship and performs at concerts. Over half the school learn an instrument and there are regular music competitions including House Shout, in which everyone takes part. 'Music is cool,' said everyone we spoke to. Each year the school stages a major musical production – eg Guys and Dolls and most recently Les Misérables, involving at least 50 pupils. New plenary space for theatre and conferencing. The school runs a popular sea scout troop (own boathouse on the river), which is one of the largest in the country.

Background and atmosphere: The cathedral close setting gives school bags of style and the blessing (or curse) of a number of medieval buildings to occupy, mainly clustered to the north of the cathedral. 'The site has to be negotiated,' says the head, and though the city location has great benefits, the drawbacks are lack of space and privacy. 'We have to remember we are on view all the time,' said a pupil; another commented, 'There is nowhere to spread out and play football at breaks'. 'The cathedral is in all we do and is a huge strength,' says the head, conjuring up visions of pupils strolling through cloisters or popping in to say prayers, but in reality it is, understandably, out of bounds after the daily assembly each morning and used on an ad hoc basis for special events, services and concerts. As a tenant of the dean and chapter and occupying many listed buildings, the school is limited (some would say mercifully) in what alterations they can make. Elsewhere in the Close they have converted a 60s office block into science labs. Pupils wander calmly around; 'promenade' time is built into the timetable, no rushing or bells. School is stuck, it seems, with the unlovely canteen built circa 1970, but pupils don't seem bothered – the bag racks area next door appears to be the hub of the school, with pupils clustered there continually.

Lower school is on its own site a short walk from the senior school between the edge of the Cathedral Close and nearby river Wensum. Built in the 1970s and designed around a central hall and library with classes mostly at ground floor level, with views of the adjacent playing field.

'It's a happy school, non-fussy, non-pernickety – no waving fingers for the wrong sports kit', said a mother, though uniform is worn throughout – bright blue blazers exchanged for black suits in the sixth form. Badges – house, prefect and sporting – are worn by many. Pupils look cheerful and friendly, though we did not see much in the way of door holding. Their confidence is promoted and achievement applauded in all areas. 'It can be rather, "look at me",' said a mother, and a father summed up, 'Success really matters and the going is hard if you're not a high flier at something'.

Pastoral care, well-being and discipline: For a school where expectations of pupils (and parents) are high, getting the pastoral bit right is the key. Pupils stay with the same tutor up the school and houses a important for sport, music and drama. Staff are quick to respond to parental worries (via email or phone); there is a counsellor that pupils (or parents) can see confidentially (many do), and a much-liked chaplain – also a member of the staff. Prefects are a select group with privileges and are chosen via what sounds like a terrifying process of written application, weeding out by housemaster, interview, final choice. Pupils agree with the sense behind most rules, though a mother said, 'The bright boys who want to buck the system...get detention after detention, report cards, things can escalate.' Not a school for the non-conformist.

Lower school pupils are cheerful and confident, engagingly honest – 'My only gripe is the weird food', said one boy, 'so I eat a lot of pasta'. Another boy said, 'I love singing, maths, and history; I just like being at school'. Pupils here have a very full and active day and need resilience to flourish.

Pupils and parents: The great majority from within 20 miles and from professional, business or academic backgrounds; very few ethnic minorities (a reflection of East Anglia). Parents are aware of, and in the main regret, the school's aura of privilege. 'It is not a good social mix. My father and grandfather came to this school from a council estate in the 1930s when it was direct grant. It is much more bourgeois today'. There is wide support for means-tested bursaries and one father suggested, 'Put the fees up and offer far more bursaries to widen the social catchment'. 'We do what we can, and wish it could be more', acknowledges the head.

Entrance: Entrance exam (English, maths, NVR) plus interview at 7+. About 40 places available, generally oversubscribed. Pupils filter in higher up, mainly from other local prep schools, and the year group rises almost to 60 by year 6. Cathedral choristers (boys only) must get a school place before auditioning for the choir. 'The Master of Music is looking for boys with strong musical potential, usually expressed in a clear voice, a quick ear and a lively intelligence.'

Main senior school entry points 11+ and 13+. Of the 90 places available at 11, half go to pupils from the lower school (unsuitables warned and weeded out in good time) and the rest take an entrance exam – maths, English NVR, plus a morning of assessment and a private interview with a staff member. Another 30 places available at 13 (exam again or CE, plus interview) and a further 30 at sixth form stage (minimum six Bs at GCSE plus interview). 'We are looking for a base line of academic ability; this is a pastoral imperative', says the head. Competition varies year by year, but roughly two-thirds of applicants successful.

Exit: Vast majority of lower school pupils have a smooth transition to the senior school. Hardly any leave after GCSEs. Top drawer universities in the main, with a good bunch to Oxbridge (14 places in 2016, and nine medics). Heavyweight subjects, mathematics, sciences, engineering and law all popular. Around 15 per cent take a gap year.

Money matters: Fifty per cent off for cathedral choristers (boys only) and staff children. Variety of scholarships for academic, music, art, and sporting prowess, usually 10 per cent, though a few 100 per cent awards for sixth formers joining from the state sector. Limited means-tested bursaries.

Remarks: The grammar school style makes it an excellent choice for the bright, motivated boy or girl who will benefit from all the school offers. Not a school for natural non-conformers or those who need to challenge authority.

Nottingham Girls' High School

49

9 Arboretum Street, Nottingham NG1 4JB

Pupils: 830 • Ages: 4–18 • Sixth form: 143

Fees: £9,729 – £12,681 pa

Tel: 01159 417663
Email: enquiries@not.gdst.net
Website: www.nottinghamgirlshigh.gdst.net

Head: Since April 2016, Julie Keller (30s). Heads of single sex schools seem to fall into two categories – those who stress their school's excellence with the single sex nature just being one of its characteristics and those who stress the excellence of the focused nature of the single sex education offer. Julie Keller is firmly in the latter camp. Not only is she passionate about single sex education but she has everyone in the school behind her vision. For Julie, only girls' schools have the expertise to ensure the best education for the next generation of female leaders. And with her as a role model, Nottingham Girls' High students should break every glass ceiling going.

Julie is a dynamo – fast talking, confident, absolutely on top of her game; she was deputy head at the school before taking on first the executive headship of the junior school and then the senior headship. She knows the Midlands well, having a degree from Leicester in economic and social history, and before she came to the Girls' High, had worked in a demanding mixed comprehensive in Nottinghamshire. She has a background in pastoral leadership but has also been head of history. Staff tell us she is inspiring, approachable and good fun to work with and they respect her honesty and integrity. They say that since she became head she is really looking at every aspect of the school to hone development plans and up the game.

Girls love her open door policy. She has a study right off a central corridor and has encouraged girls to put their heads round the door and share news. 'She knows all about us all', say the girls in awed tones. On our brief walk with her to the dining hall, she must have exchanged a few relevant words with every single girl she passed. Her priorities are to stretch and challenge the top end, to ensure teaching and learning is absolute top quality and make extracurricular and enrichment activities work better – all of which are moving rapidly in the right direction with the whole school clear about the aims and behind them.

Head of junior school: Since September 2016 Laura Fowler(BA Education), who arrived at the school with a wealth of headship experience. She had been acting head at a state primary school in Essex and head of juniors for six years at Leicester High. She is absolutely on board with the aspirational vision of the whole school and has incredibly quickly got to know all the girls. Being new has allowed her to run meet-the-parents sessions where she is sharing her aim of strengthening relationships and wanting parents to fully engage with the school. Laura, who comes across as both wise and approachable, believes in getting in the classroom whenever she can and is doing some teaching in all year groups. Her staff and the girls love her open door policy.

Academic matters: Academically, there is a buzz about the junior school. There is much technology in evidence and the girls are confident users. As in the senior school, girls in years 5 and 6 have their own iPads and the girls in years 3 and 4 share class sets. The head and the staff tell us that there is constant reflection on excellent practice and that they are very conscious of modelling the behaviour they want the girls to develop. 'We show the girls that it is OK to cross things out – work doesn't have to be beautifully tidy to be exciting and interesting'. What an excellent approach to find in a girls' school. There is no obsessing about exams and assessments. Year 6 girls go away for a residential trip the week before the Sats. Teaching assistants work with class teachers where intervention is needed to ensure progress. This can take the form of pre-teaching a topic, so girls go into lessons already confident. As in the senior school, staff benefit considerably from the broad GDST links with access to cutting edge teaching and learning research and professional training.

The intake is selective and results are very strong. At GCSE A* grades in 2016 were 44 per cent and A*/A grades 73 per cent. A Level results for 2016 are getting back up after a slight blip in 2015, with 14 per cent at A* and 51 per cent at A*/A. Being part of the Girls' Day Schools Trust means the results are not only intensively dissected internally but also by the Trust as a whole, and the school consistently comes in the top few for value added calculations. Maths is outstanding but so are the humanities.

The head of educational support leads on learning difficulties, and parents whose daughters have had experience of this speak highly about it. Girls would not normally come out of lessons for this unless the decision has been taken leading up to GCSEs that they should take less than the standard 10 subjects. Programmes are individually tailored and there is no additional cost for this. Class sizes are up to 24 in the senior school and around 12 in the sixth form and it is expected that there will be sensitive differentiation within a lesson. Recent introduction of mentoring sessions, exam technique classes, subject coaches and peer mentors is resulting in a stronger support network for everyone.

Girls are identified for possible Oxbridge entrance in year 9 and well prepared from then on. Every girl is issued with an iPad and these are enthusiastically embraced by staff, girls and parents. Whether it is emails – 'We can just send a quick email to our teacher to explain why we are going to be late for a lesson' – or uploading text books and homework, or constant reference for research in lessons, these tablets are now seen as essential to maximising efficient progress for every girl. Girls email individual teachers with small queries about work and staff send much appreciated short emails to parents when someone has had a good day.

Games, options, the arts: The head has put excellence in sport, music and drama as a top priority. Sport in particular has not had the strongest reputation locally in the past. The head wants not just superb school performances but increasingly to see the girls succeed at national level. One of the first things she has done is to ensure that girls can continue with both sport and the performing arts so there are not the timetable clashes that can cause such frustration. Activities are now timetabled before school from 8.15am as well as at lunch times and after school. Girls can miss registration times for activities – 'You don't get excellence without giving it time', says the head. You need facilities too, with a spanking new 350 seater performing arts theatre completed in November 2016. Money has gone into sports as well with an upgraded Astroturf and new sports hall boasting a splendid climbing wall which even the reception class uses. 'We are building risk-taking and resilience all the way through,' the head of outdoor education told us. There are grass pitches offsite used for lacrosse and other games. Outdoor education has a major through-school emphasis. From fire-pit Fridays, where groups of girls take it in turns to cook lunch outside, playing instruments, singing and just enjoying being together, to climbing Kilimanjaro or the new climbing wall which sixth formers are encouraged to use in their non-teaching time, to joining the exploration society, where they build shelters and make fires, girls have every opportunity to develop confidence in their ability to relate to the physical world.

Music in the junior school is massive and virtually every girl plays an instrument. The concerts are wonderful, we were told by staff and parents, and there are lots of them, including tea concerts where every girl who is learning an instrument can play, regardless of level. It is this inclusiveness that parents love about the drama too. 'It is not all about over- rehearsing the stars,' one parent told us. 'There is the energy and naturalness you get when everyone is involved'. Outdoor spaces have been imaginatively used to create areas for each age group and a sense of woodland environs which is quite remarkable. There is an outdoor wooden amphitheatre and an outdoor learning area with low ropes and tyre swings which is regularly shared with local primary schools. As in the senior school, there is Firepit Friday when groups of girls spend their lunchtime in the outdoor education area, building a fire, cooking on it and doing camp fire things. Much anticipated by all. There is a feel of adventure about the place – when we arrived, the reception class were in harnesses up and down the climbing wall.

There is similar encouragement to engage with the wider society. Lots of charity work going on and the school won the lord lieutenant's award for voluntary service. They make videos to support local charitable causes, work on the national citizen service scheme as well as produce endless cakes for fundraising sales.

Background and atmosphere: Occupying several houses, in an increasingly gentrified Nottingham suburb, the school has capitalised on what is a relatively limited space to Tardis-like effect. The old sits next to the new creating a smart, imaginative yet unpretentious feel. Evidence of massive upgrading and modernising is everywhere – a new DT resistant materials suite, food lab, graphics studio, textiles and refurbished labs. The sixth formers have their own labs, art studio, library study area and sixth form building with common rooms and tutor spaces. Technology is everywhere with LED screens in useful public places announcing the myriad of events taking place. The dining room is light and modern with impressive food. Most city day schools are not offering chilli infused extra virgin olive oil to go with fresh salads. There was particularly delicious syrupy flap jacks too the day we visited.

The old and new buildings that make up the junior school sit remarkable well together. One moment you are walking on a stunning Minton floor and then through to the Rainbow Room, a wonderful vibrant space that links two buildings. There is a lovely new library and ICT suite and a good size multipurpose hall. Both staff and girls believe they belong to something very special. The head wants there to be a strong bond between every single girl, her family and the school. The school is working on lots of ways to show the parents they are part of something great. They are encouraged to come and watch a special lesson, to engage with the school on every level, attend IT seminars on safety and workshops on phonics and modern maths methods. Twitter is used very effectively and much appreciated by busy working parents. When girls are away on trips, staff send twitter photos to give the parents a glimpse into what is going on. New parents are phoned a few days into the start of term to check all is well.

The head of the senior school, Julie Keller, spent the year before she took over as head running the junior school as well as doing her senior deputy head job. It has meant there is real synergy at every level between the junior and senior schools. Julie says, 'I saw such a lot of excellent practice in the junior school that I have been able to share across the senior school'. Laura Fowler thinks it is wonderful having a senior head who loves the junior school through and through and really knows how it works. The girls value knowing the senior school head who still spends time there every week and the year 7s who got to know Julie so well last year are quite proprietorial about her now they have moved into the seniors.

The girls and staff all know they are in a modern, forward looking and confident 21st century school where there is an expectation that they will become tomorrow's leaders. The atmosphere is very aspirational and very individual. 'You can be the best you want to be here', say the girls. No gender stereotyping or any other sort of channelling of girls. Without labelling it as such, the school is giving the girls experiences of how to network, an area that research suggests lets women down at senior level. Here the girls learn about it through the buddying systems, mentoring, even drama competitions which the sixth form write and then work with the younger ones. Everything is about expanding who they know all the time. The Girls' Day School Trust is part of the networking. Girls say they get to know girls in other trust schools at trust sports rallies for example, and then continue to build the friendships online. The trust alumni events allow sixth formers to start forging those all-important professional connections.

N

Relations between girls and staff are conspicuously warm and relaxed, as indeed are the relationships between staff. 'We all get on and it's good fun', said staff members. The leadership team is relatively young, all at the top of their game and brilliant role models for young women. Well-being of the girls is high on the agenda but so is staff well-being. There is a sense of the spirit of good learning rather than the law – no-one sets homework if there is not a real point to it. 'We say to parents if the girls say they haven't got any homework tonight, then talk to them and go out and do other things.' We were pleased to hear that there is a determined attempt to fight the perfectionism that often dogs very bright girls. No-one has work sent back because it is messy. Girls feel listened to by the staff and therefore take ownership of school structures.

The girls have picked up that they are in a very special place and relish the girls' only environment. 'It is very calm here', one earnest 8 year old told us, and 'so we can try risky things whenever we want to.' The idea that girls can achieve at whatever they want is embedded early. The head says the girls have high expectations of themselves and learn quickly and deeply. 'It means we can do so much with them, take them out of school lots, go off timetable to explore practical skills and everyone still makes exceptional progress'.

Pastoral care, well-being and discipline: There are lots of transition projects and joint activities with the senior school – for example, a year 6 and 7 hockey tour to Holland. The year 9s help with the junior sports day. A big sister, little sister buddy scheme operates between sixth formers and year 6s. The junior girls come across as happy and courteous and very excited by all the school offers. They couldn't tell us fast enough all the clubs they attended and the residential trips that were coming up during the year. Lessons, they say, are fun, and if they have difficulties teachers are really helpful. They are not nervous about talking to teachers if they are miserable either, although they clearly are also encouraged to believe everyone has a responsibility for everyone else's happiness. Teachers, we discover, are quite amazing and know that you are unhappy even when you haven't said so. The girls relish the many leadership opportunities they have as they go through the school and liked having their say at the school council. Best of all – you get to choose your own food at lunchtime.

Pastoral care is highly rated by all, in part because of the palpably strong relationship between girls and staff. There is a group of pastoral specialists who have lots of experience of year 7 and the sixth form. In years 8, 9, 10 and 11 the girls stay with the same tutor who gets to know their strengths and foibles in considerable detail. They can't swop out of a form just because they have fallen out with their best friends. 'We want to show the girls that you can rebuild relationships and sort out difficulties,' the head tells us. The school nurse is top quality and fully involved in the pastoral side as well as health. Families who had suffered emotional challenges couldn't speak highly enough of the whole staff's support.

The girls had considerable difficulty of thinking of any disciplinary breaches. The best they could come up with was being 'on report' for late homework. The head, however, says she is firm and will exclude for bullying and e-safety issues. But this is not a school where there is any sense that bad behaviour gets in the way of purposeful activity.

Pupils and parents: Articulate, lively, confident girls who know they are going places. Parents cover a fair cross section, both in ethnic and socio/economic terms. Many families with both parents working. Bursary support widens the range of families that come. Quite a number of families where mothers and grandmothers are old girls. Parents are buying into the school's aspirations and they support wherever they can. New formal parent groups are being trialled with parent reps. Excellent communications is high on the agenda and all the technology, which goes alongside traditional methods, is helping tremendously, though it is the strong motivation to make it all work on a personal level that tells.

Entrance: Girls spend half a day in the junior school being informally assessed. 'We want to see if they are going to be happy here', the head says. There are half termly sessions for 2/3 year olds – 'Tots have Fun' – where the school gets a chance to observe younger girls over time.

Unusually, there is no entrance exam for the girls in the junior school to enter year 7. Other girls sit papers in English, maths and verbal reasoning and there is an informal interview plus references from current school. The emphasis is on looking for potential.

At sixth form level, girls are invited to spend a day at the school, sample preferred A Level classes and have an informal interview. References are requested from the current school and conditional offers are made from December onwards. Generally the school is looking for an average of grade Bs across eight GCSE subjects, including English and maths, with grade A in some subjects to be taken at A level.

Exit: Most juniors to senior school. There is no formal assessment for junior school girls to join the senior school, but if the rigorous internal monitoring and assessment process suggestions someone may struggle with the pace of the senior school, this is discussed with parents in year 5.

Although more girls than the school was comfortable with left after year 11 in the first year the boys' school took girls into the sixth form, this tide seems to have been halted and the vast majority are now staying through to university. They go to a range of strong universities, a few each year to Oxbridge (two in 2016) but the school is 'not obsessed with it'. Medicine and engineering very popular (six medics in 2016) and other than that, a wide span of the disciplines. On the rare occasion something goes wrong on A level result day, parents say the school is spectacularly good at working with the family

Money matters: As with other GDST schools, fees represent very good value for money. It is clearly not a school dripping money and endowments but on the other hand there is a style that money can't buy. About six per cent of income goes on means-tested bursaries.

Remarks: Many girls' schools would wilt under the news that the long established and renowned boys' school just along the street was starting to take girls into all year groups. But the Girls' High seems to relish the challenge. It has allowed them to celebrate their expertise in girls' education and there is no doubt everyone in the school sees their school as the one that is forward-thinking, energetic and innovative. There was more of an exodus than they would have liked in the first year but it has not taken the hit some thought it would and the novelty seems to have worn off. This is a first rate, 21 century offer with academic rigour but informal in feel, without establishment stuffiness. The new strapline is 'Be Extraordinary' and everyone believes they can.

Nottingham High School

Waverley Mount, Nottingham NG7 4ED

Pupils: 1,009 (113 girls) • Ages: 4–18 • Sixth form: 250 (67 girls)

Fees: £9,465 – £13,824 pa

Tel: 01158 452232
Email: enquiries@nottinghamhigh.co.uk
Website: www.nottinghamhigh.co.uk

Headmaster: Since 2007, Mr Kevin Fear BA PGCE (40s), educated at Douai and Southampton University. Taught at The King's School, Chester, from 1986, joined Nottingham High, 2000, as senior teacher, 2004 deputy head with academic and marketing responsibilities. Married to Denise; two children: girl at the Girls' High and boy at the junior school.

Approachable, open, modest, has overseen considerable building development and improved staff conditions since his appointment. Very focused on communication with parents via surveys, also his blog (worth a read) and is one of only a few HMC heads on Twitter. Keen to maintain the school's high standards in all areas and continue to produce well-rounded boys who enjoy school life, don't feel pressured to achieve and would perform well at interviews. Interested in IT and sport, especially football.

Head of juniors: Since 2013, Mrs Clare Bruce MA (40s). Educated at Hutchesons' Grammar School in Glasgow, read English at St Andrews and did PGCE at Loughborough. Spent two years in business. First teaching post at Grace Dieu Manor School in Leicestershire, then moved to Derby Grammar School. Head of Derby Grammar Junior School for four years. Has two children and enjoys reading and keeping fit in her spare time.

Academic matters: Very special infant school, for 4 to 7-year-olds. Brain gym twice a day; lots of physical and creative activity; individual and group support for learning needs. Uses specialist staff from junior school for ICT, swimming, music, Spanish, French, chess (part of the curriculum) plus main school sports, music and drama facilities.

Very good key stage 2 results across the board; sets, in a fluid way, for English (some very well-written letters on display) and maths. Strong ICT – especially in conjunction with maths (pupils participate in an online global competition), blogs created for topics. All classrooms have electronic whiteboards much used by teachers. Spanish and French from year 3 – pupils give sessions to the infants; also thinking skills. Attractive learning support room – full time co-ordinator: mostly in-class support with some outside (no charge); can handle dys-range.

Very strong and consistent all round, with maths, all three sciences, economics (all very popular), history, politics and government and English lit particularly successful at A level. Other choices include music technology, philosophy, psychology, Spanish. Sixty-two per cent A*/A grades at A level in 2016. All do AS general studies and some do the Extended Project Qualification and AQA Bacc; small numbers for languages, DT and art; will run subjects for only two students (if staffing allows). GCSE 2016: 71 per cent A*/A – most get 10, high numbers with all A*/A; two languages common.

Also does very well in all three science and maths Olympiads, sometimes attaining international level. National successes at chess (very popular, international level too), DT and finance competitions; pupils attend chemistry and physics camps/competitions at universities and achieve well in regional Latin and Greek reading competitions. Teachers enthusiastic and dedicated and have friendly, good-humoured relationships with the pupils.

The large library is managed by enthusiastic professional librarian with a generous budget – lots of current fiction, DVDs, full range of broadsheets, including French and Spanish newspapers, and magazines; reading widely popular and encouraged, eg through a cleverly designed inter-form competition for year 7s based around certificates, chocolates and publicly posted charts (this is a school that understands how to motivate boys). Twelve good-sized science rooms, including five very modern, half lecture hall style, half lab; well-equipped language classrooms; masses of tip top computers and electronic whiteboards everywhere.

Learning support department, headed by a full-time qualified coordinator, covers mild learning difficulties and disabilities (the dys-range), ADHD, Asperger's, and would try to accommodate physical problems – provided the required academic promise is present. She advises subject staff and provides (free) individual or small group support outside the class, eg with spelling – a year 8 boy spoke very appreciatively of his dramatic improvement in this since joining the school. The gifted and talented are identified and receive plenty of extension opportunities inside and outside the classroom.

Games, options, the arts: Very good playing fields a short bus ride away; on site a large, well-equipped modern sports hall with a fitness suite and climbing wall, full-size indoor hockey pitch, cricket machines, indoor swimming pool with canoes.

Outstanding achievements nationally and internationally in orienteering (very popular), rugby, squash, swimming, but not dominated by sport – other spheres well regarded too; plenty of opportunities to be in school teams. Also successful at bridge, badminton, chess (lots involved); hockey, archery, tennis, cross-country, golf, athletics and cricket (Barbados tour) on offer too.

Very strong and diverse music – orchestras, ensembles, bands, choirs, a recording studio; success in national competitions; tours to Barcelona, Venice and New York; pupils in national and Nottingham orchestras and choirs; very attractive recital hall with drum kit, small organ and Steinway, used for concerts and master classes with professional musicians. Joint musical events with Nottingham Girls', eg Carmina Burana, Pirates of Penzance, Guys and Dolls and a chamber music festival. Curriculum drama coming soon but no purpose-built theatre nor studio – conventional Founder Hall used for performances, eg Latin comedies – impressive choice.

Good art – varied media: painting (regular life drawing class), print making (three presses – two old, one modern), ceramics, sculpture (we saw some very inventive masks, created with a visiting sculptor), pottery; talks from visiting artists; local trips plus weekend residential in York or Leeds and visits to London, Edinburgh, Liverpool for sixth. A very large, well-equipped DT room with two ICT suites.

Parents value the 'wealth of experiences' on offer: several lunch time clubs, which pupils help run – reading, arts, politics, debating, philosophy, community action; CCF with all three services, D of E, scouts; house choral verse speaking competition (organised by sixth formers – a challenging task); external general knowledge and spelling competitions; various house charities; year group councils. Masses of trips – World Challenge to Siberia, New York/Washington, Hadrian's Wall, Rome, Sorrento. Unusually, year 11 and 13s are trained in how to deliver language lessons to reception and year 4 classes.

Junior school uses senior school sports facilities, eg indoor swimming pool – very good range of sports. Lots of success in national chess competitions at all ages (all play regularly in year 3). Dance, eg street variety, popular, now part of PE curriculum. Good music opportunities – free music tuition for all year 3s; well-equipped music room. All year groups do a drama production; interesting artwork in various media – Artsmark awarded.

Wide choice of lunchtime clubs including games, magic, practical science, fencing, jazz; eco and school councils; lots of competitions – house and external: general knowledge, poetry reciting, public speaking. Several trips ranging as far as London, Poland, Austria (skiing) and all year groups have residentials: a farm, outdoor pursuits centre, York.

N

Background and atmosphere: Founded 1513 by Dame Agnes Mellers in memory of her husband – originally situated in the Lace Market; moved 1868 to present site. Attractive mock gothic façade with two quads; later expanded by opening up the cellars to create a third floor, plus externally featureless 1970/80s additions. A lot of dreary carpeting and a few corridor walls in need of brightening, though often improved by displays of pupils' art work, big colour photos of pupils engaged in various activities and educational posters. Maintains contact with its early 20th century past, eg the large portrait of the spectacularly heroic Rev Hardy VC, accompanied by a case of his medals. The White House, a freshly decorated separate building formed from two Regency villas, is aptly used for sixth form politics and economics classes and also contains a small kitchen for the cookery club.

The most remarkable modern addition is the recent atrium-style sixth form centre on two levels – the Brasserie is a space for snacks and relaxation; the colourful, circular Pod contains one large-screen television, two Playstations, a music centre and pool table; at the top is a large light area for private study, chilling (we saw two boys playing shove ha'penny and were pleased that at least some low tech games survive) and discussion work. On the ground floor is the spacious dining hall used by the rest of the school – good choice of hot, cold, snacks and veggie.

Established in 1905, the current junior school building was purpose-built in the 1970s in the grounds of the senior school; large classrooms and attractive well-stocked library. Infant school opened 2008 in a very attractive mock Regency building across the road from the main junior school. Cheerful décor, large hall and music room, lovely art room with rafters and cookery section on top floor, ICT room with infant-friendly, coloured keyboards and versatile screens. Large, colourful classrooms all with very good displays, interactive whiteboards and access to outside.

Parents (and Mr Fear) say it is a happy place where pupils of all kinds are accepted. The younger boys we spoke to had found it easy to settle in and thought people friendly and the teachers helpful.

Now accepts girls into any year group.

Pastoral care, well-being and discipline: The main focus is the vertical tutor groups of 24 where pupils remain throughout their time at the school, staffed by two teachers – parents praised this. It encourages the helping of younger ones by older ones that is a feature of the school, eg prefects work with younger pupils in form groups; sixth formers help with lunch time maths workshops. Thoughtful transition arrangements for the new year 7s, including no homework for the first month. Parents say any issues are dealt with well and quickly, although one felt pupils could receive some more praise – 'a bit more carrot than stick' (school points out the head and deputy see pupils with distinctions regularly).

A sensible, comprehensive anti-bullying policy – the pupils we spoke to didn't see bullying as a problem – and a strict drugs policy: out for supplying and almost always for possession/using. Pupils apply to become prefects; house and school captains are chosen with input from pupils and staff.

Pupils and parents: About 40 per cent from the junior school, the rest from various independent and local state primaries. Most from the city and its suburbs plus others from as far afield as Chesterfield, Grantham, West Hallam, Matlock, Lichfield. Predominantly white British with a substantial Asian contingent and several parents who make sacrifices to send their children to the school – down to earth teenagers who are neither arrogant nor snobbish, take academic achievement as a given and are very interested in the other activities too. Plenty of communication with parents – two detailed colour newsletters (Connect) a year and fortnightly electronic newsletters.

Old boys cover a wide political spectrum including Ken Clarke (Conservative), Ed Balls and Geoff Hoon (Labour), Ed Davey (Lib Dem); also DH Lawrence, Geoffrey Trease (author); Gordon Richardson (ex governor of the Bank of England), Jesse Boot (founder of Boots the Chemist's), Jonathan Charles (BBC news presenter); Andrew Turner (international athlete), Henry Nwume (Olympic bobsleigh team).

Entrance: Individual assessment through games activities used to assess potential for learning for reception children, and national curriculum based numeracy and literacy assessment for years 1 and 2, plus classroom based practical activities observation (for both). For entry to junior school, exam in English and maths based on national curriculum and reasoning, plus observation during an afternoon's activities, to assess social skills, and informal interview – looking for above average academic potential and some spark. A few places available at other ages.

For year 7, exams in English, maths and reasoning plus interview for all non junior school candidates – looking for above average ability with some extra spark. About 70 places available for outside candidates: about 100 interviewed after exams have been marked. Can take up to 120 but won't lower standards to maintain numbers. A few places available for years 8-10 by academic and general interviews. Sixth form entry (mostly girls): interview plus Bs at GCSE in AS/related subjects and C or better in others.

All years now open to girls (most in lower classes of both infant/junior and senior schools, plus sixth form).

Exit: Automatic progression from the infant school to junior school in most cases. Virtually all progress to senior school from junior school unless relocating.

Almost all to a broad range of universities – majority to Russell Group and other top universities, for a wide variety of courses (medicine, vet science and dentistry popular – 15 in 2016); a respectable number to Oxbridge (seven in 2016) and the best London universities, mostly for maths, sciences and business management/economics.

Only a few leave after GCSE for sixth form colleges, often to do courses not on offer at the school or for financial reasons.

Money matters: Part scholarships not related to parental incomes; means-tested bursaries from year 7 (up to full fees) awarded on basis of entrance exams and interviews; music scholarships (auditions in June); bursary support for foreign trips. Bursary fund developed as part of the 500th anniversary celebrations.

Sixth form: Ogden Trust science scholarships up to full fees; school bursaries up to full fees.

Remarks: A very strong all-round school, achieving academic and extracurricular excellence while keen to avoid being a hothouse. As one parent put it, 'They know boys – they work them hard, feed them well and give them lots of exercise.' And they are beginning to get to know girls.

Oakham School

Chapel Close, Market Place, Oakham, Rutland LE15 6DT

Pupils: 1,058; 544 full/flexi boarders • Ages: 10–18 • Sixth form: 410 • C of E

Fees: Day £16,650 – £19,350; Boarding £20,250 – £31,575 pa

Tel: 01572 758758
Email: admissions@oakham.rutland.sch.uk
Website: www.oakham.rutland.sch.uk

Headmaster: Since 2009, Mr Nigel Lashbrook (50s). Educated in one of the last grammar cohorts at King's Heath Boys' Technical School in Birmingham. Only pupil in his year to get into Oxford (Hertford College – chemistry plus lots of rugby), first in his family to go to university. Part of his final year at Oxford involved running some undergraduate classes; 'Have you thought about teaching?' he was asked (in a good way) so DPhil plans were changed to teacher training. 'I just loved it', he says.

His first post was Manchester Grammar School where he taught chemistry and coached cricket and rugby. After eight years he went from this academic day school to an academic boarding school, Tonbridge. At Tonbridge he was head of science and chemistry, a housemaster ('I finished being a housemaster just before the advent of email', he says with a smile), plus a term as acting head – good preparation for his next move, the headship of King's Bruton in Somerset.

Seven years into his Oakham headship and Mr Lashbrook seems to be a man in his element. Parents describe him as 'very friendly', 'affable' and 'approachable' and so he is, although that relaxed bonhomie belies the super-efficiency with which his school is run. We thought Oakham had a particularly collegiate air – Mr L is obviously extremely good at picking the right staff and delegating to their strengths. He's also forward thinking and alert to shifts in what Oakham parents want from their boarding school. At the time of our visit a new boarding package was being launched to replace the three nights a week 'day boarding'. There is now a five-night option (costing 95 per cent of the full boarding fee). Apparently it's something that families who live further away have been asking for.

He identifies parental attitudes as the biggest change he has seen during his career. While he feels that parents wanting to be more involved is a cause for celebration, 'the pressure of unrealistic expectations can be a great cause of anxiety for children. We work hard to get parents to see the bigger picture.' At Oakham, as elsewhere, the emphasis is on enabling children to become independent learners, to see 'fail' as 'first attempt in learning'. 'We want to unravel the cotton wool,' says the head.

Mr Lashbrook still manages to do 'a tiny bit of teaching' and as part of his commitment to lifelong learning plans to take diving lessons; 'the pupils like to see staff doing new things.' To this end Oakham supports staff who wish to undertake study for masters or PhDs (in education related subjects, of course).

He lives on site during term time but has a family house nearby from where he 'commutes' in the summer and Easter holidays (when Oakham's commercial directors 'sweat the assets', running high profile sports academies and other events). His wife is an economics and geography teacher – 'they make a great team', said a parent – and two of their three now adult children were educated at Oakham. Down time is for golf, cricket and the theatre. Is there anything he wishes he'd been able to do? 'Play the saxophone'.

Academic matters: In 2016, 43 per cent of A level grades were A*/A (74 per cent A*/B) with 62 per cent A*/A at GCSE (IGCSEs in core subjects). Double award science only (IGCSE), French, Spanish and German are the language options. Around a third of sixth formers take the IB and results are impressive: 2016 average of 37, over a quarter of takers gained 40 points or more and one pupil achieved the maximum 45 points. Geography seems to be the most popular choice of A level, followed by maths, biology and economics. We were a little surprised not to see more A*s at A level, especially given the very respectable number of leavers off to medical school and Oxbridge – proof of above and beyond teaching at all levels. 'Look at the bigger picture,' says a voice in our ear (it's the headmaster ...). We always do, and so do parents who choose Oakham for their children: 'We like the way they celebrate hard work as well as good grades,' said one.

We heard a great deal from Mr Lashbrook and his staff about the Oakham approach to teaching and learning. Words such as 'holistic' and 'enrichment' aren't just eduspeak here; lessons we observed were hands-on, pupils were working at their own pace and one felt that teachers saw them as individuals rather than a class. In the DT department (school has Design Mark) we came across a group getting to grips with ancient history in the form of early video games, telephones, cassette recorders and a BBC Micro. 'So what is a mix tape?' we heard one ask. Sigh.

The learning support department was settling in to new top floor premises when we visited – lots of technology but quiet, calm spaces too. Staff had chosen some wonderful pictures, all by 'our' pupils, we were told proudly. 'Mild' SEN – mainly dyslexia but also dyscalculia and dyspraxia – catered for via small group teaching, individual lessons or in-class support. Lots of study, organisation and revision support, all described by parents as 'brilliant'. What's even more brilliant is that there is no charge for this service.

Senior academic mentor (formerly the formidable sounding 'master of scholars') is responsible for intellectual stretching of those with academic awards and Oxbridge candidates. We couldn't help feeling that this role (especially under its previous title) seemed a little un-Oakhamian. Not at all, we were told; the scholars' society is 'elitist but not exclusive', members aren't necessarily academic scholars: some have been talent-spotted by housemasters. After all, there are established pathways to extend and develop sporting, musical and artistic talents. Chosen pupils attend a seminar programme designed to play to particular specialisms and nurture 'genuine intellectual curiosity'. Whole school enrichment week in the autumn term is also designed to challenge and surprise all pupils. Most recent theme was the enticing sounding, 'rules and rebellion'.

The Smallbone library (named after a former head), is impressive, the foyer doubles as an exhibition space and was full of pupils' art work; it's also used for parent meetings. Upstairs though it is absolutely silent. Certainly no talking, no whispering and no headphones. 'Up here pupils can hear themselves think', the librarian told us (very, very quietly).

Games, options, the arts: A word to the wise: don't trot out the cliché 'sport for all' if you're visiting Oakham – unless you want to run five times round a rugby pitch and do 100 press ups as punishment. Director of sport actually shuddered at such a last century idea. The distinction is a bit lost on us because that seems to be what happens, even if the emphasis these days is on health and fitness as much as competition. Huge choice of over 30 sports, from sailing on nearby Rutland Water (Oakham's sailing coach devised and hosted the inaugural Water Quidditch World Cup) to polo (water and four-legged variety), and all take part, whether by competing or supporting. Outstanding facilities including 40 acres of grass pitches, two floodlit all-weather pitches, multi-purpose sports hall, squash and fives courts. The cricket square hosts county matches as well as school fixtures.

Over 100 pupils played in national finals in lots of different sports and the school will create 'pathways to foster individual talents, whatever they are.' Oakham's recent sporting honours are evenly spread between boys' and girls' teams with the girls' 1st X1 football team carrying off the Independent Schools Football Association trophy and the U15 rugby team reaching the NatWest Vase final. The 1st XI boys' hockey team came runners up in the U18 Hockey Schools Cup Final.

Drama and music are big news with countless opportunities to perform at all levels. The aim is to maximise participation as well as foster individual talents – at whole school plays, hymn practice or small in-house showcases to build the confidence of first timers. Over 300 pupils sing in school choirs and the chamber choir recently reached the finals of Songs of Praise School Choir of the Year. We were lucky enough to join an audience of townspeople and pupils at one of the weekly lunchtime concerts in All Saints Church. Young and old sat rapt in the pews, listening to virtuoso trumpet and oboe soloists give spellbinding performances. When asked, 'Why Oakham?' a prospective parent sitting nearby simply said, 'It's the music.'

Impressive numbers of A*/As for art and DT at GCSE; specialist teachers in all disciplines including sculpture and textiles, visiting artists run workshops. The courtyard of four art studios was formerly the town prison and the new exhibition space was a workhouse – Oakham can truthfully say that its art takes no prisoners.. Wonderful sculpture studio where pupils can create in clay and mixed media on a large scale and even learn stone carving. Not huge numbers taking these subjects at Pre-U/A level but the results are excellent. Pupils regularly go on to top art schools and to study architecture.

New 'Exploring Learning camp' for younger Oakhamians is a swashbuckling, Treasure Island-themed, problem-solving adventure in the countryside.

Boarding: Over half the pupils board and what with lessons on Saturday morning plus matches and other activities in the afternoon, day pupils probably feel as though they do as well. Parents of younger day pupils acknowledge this but say that the children like the chance to finish homework before they leave and enjoy time out in the common rooms. Quite a few local day pupils turn up for the Sunday goings on too. Food is praised by all – parents and children alike. All food is prepared in house and everyone eats together in the Barraclough. There doesn't seem to be any falling away of deliciousness as the day goes on – we heard no complaints about dreary boarders' suppers here. The homemade bread and soups, carvery nights and Sunday brunch came in for special praise.

One 'leave-out weekend' each half term. 'Transitional' boarding (two to five nights a week) is offered to lower school pupils (10-13 year olds) but the day boarding option of up to three nights a week for upper school pupils has been retired. 'It didn't meet the needs of families who live more than an hour's drive away,' we were told. Instead parents can opt for an up to five night a week package that comes in at 95 per cent of the full boarding fee.

Boys' and girls' middle school (age 13-17) boarding houses are on either side of a large playing field known as 'Donkey' (Doncaster Close). All upper sixth (known at Oakham as 'seventh form') pupils are based in two houses in Chapel Close, next to the market place. There are four lower school houses (two boarding) away from the main campus where younger children can enjoy their own space. Rooms that we saw were fairly standard issue – cabin beds with desks underneath, two or three to a room in the lower years, individual study bedrooms on the ground floor for the lower sixth. All the doors we looked behind in the boys' house featured, as ever, empty noticeboards, massive shoes and Lynx. Common areas are large and well maintained with the usual exhausted soft furnishings, big wooden bowls of apples ('we keep trying,' smiled the housemaster, indulgently resigned to choosing fruit on the basis of what makes the minimum mess if used as a missile), pool and table tennis tables. Year group integration fostered by lots of competitions and activities.

Youngest boarders do prep in the house library supervised by a member of staff or prefect until they're ready to work independently. Sensible rules about screens of all kinds, Wifi turned off at 10pm; youngest must hand in everything before bed. The term's programme of matches, activities, exam dates, UCAS deadlines and the like is up in an A3 frame near the entrance and makes exhausting reading. 'We like to do a lot,' said the housemaster, adding, 'This isn't babysitting, we put our heart and soul into boarding at Oakham.'

Background and atmosphere: Drive into the charming eponymous town (there's a butcher, baker and by the looks of things no shortage of artisan candle makers), past the Whipper-In hotel (Oakham is home to the Cottesmore, one of England's oldest hunts) and in the corner of the cobbled market place you will see 'Oakham School' announced in fine wrought iron. Oakham and its near neighbour Uppingham were both set up as free grammar schools by Archdeacon Robert Johnston in 1584 to teach Latin, Greek and Hebrew to the sons of their respective towns. The two schools' fortunes and size waxed and waned over the next 300 years – as late as the end of the 19th century the original one room school house was still Oakham's only teaching premises.

The main site is a horseshoe of teaching and boarding accommodation and if there is a lack of fine or grand architecture then it is more than amply compensated for by the bright green fingers of a first-rate grounds team. If there were Good Schools Guide awards for best-kept school grounds then Oakham would certainly be on the podium. School is very proud of the courtyard garden with its grass-free lawn designed by near-neighbour Bunny Guinness. It's overlooked by the biology labs and no doubt the 30 varieties of native plants that make up the lawn provide a useful study in biodiversity.

Fair bit of Monopoly-style buying up of town sites – latest is a former pub which is about to be reborn as a performing arts centre; the town's old police station is set to become school's pastoral hub (we don't know who will occupy the cells). Town and gown weave seamlessly in and out – one of the first lessons new pupils receive is about road safety, although we imagine that motorists are held up by pupils crossing, more often than the reverse. Our sixth form guides observed the school's road safety rules to the letter, despite absence of any traffic, we're pleased to report.

Sensible uniform of black crested blazers, white shirts, ties (boys only) and below the knee black and white kilts for the girls. All seems to be worn as intended: smartly and un-customised. Seventh formers sport the dreaded business dress – although apparently it's not dreaded at Oakham. 'We really look forward to wearing it,' our sixth form guide told us.

Pastoral care, well-being and discipline: Pastoral care was singled out for its high quality and 'generous scope' in most recent inspection report and we couldn't find anyone who disagreed. The parents we spoke to commented how observant teachers were – quick to spot and then get to the bottom of changes in mood or attitude. Like most things at Oakham the pastoral system is commendably well-organised and implemented with genuine interest and concern, not a whiff of weary lip-service to a box ticking set of 'guidelines'. The head of pastoral care told us how important it was that she and her fellow tutors teach: 'it keeps things real', she observed. Tutor groups are small and pupils keep the same tutor throughout their time in each section of the school. Boarding house matrons are all trained in youth mental health care and are 'eyes and ears' and girls often pass on concerns they may have about boys (who can find it harder to talk). Add to this a 'house family' and buddy system and every child should know plenty of adults or fellow pupils to whom they can turn if necessary. All pupils do a body and mind course that stresses the interdependence of mental and physical well-being. Respect, for oneself and others, plus very clear boundaries, govern relationships between pupils.

Pupils and parents: 'You get all walks of life here,' a parent told us. According to Mr Lashbrook the Oakham demographic is solid middle class, 'definitely not socially elite'. Pupils we met officially were clean cut and refreshingly uncynical (they always are) but those we saw from a distance didn't appear to have revolutionary tendencies either. Oakham probably isn't the place for determined bohemians or incipient Bolsheviks, but we've no doubt that the school would welcome them with a smile and find them plenty to do. Around 15 per cent from abroad – mostly Europe. Former pupils include Stuart Broad, Tom Fell, Josh Cobb (cricket); Alex Goode, Tom Croft, Matt Smith, Lewis Moody (Rugby); Crista Cullen (Olympic bronze, hockey, 2012); Matthew Macfadyen, Greg Hicks, Richard Hope, Lydia Rose Bewley (actors); Miles Jupp (actor/presenter); Thomas Hescott, Katie Mitchell OBE (directors); Phoebe Gormley, Sarah Curran (fashion/business).

Entrance: At age 10 and 11 from over 30 different preps and primary schools – exams in maths English and verbal reasoning. At 13+ CE mark of 55 or over or, for entrants who don't take CE, school's own papers in English, maths, French and science. For lower school pupils (age 10-12) progress to middle school is automatic. Around 50 new pupils enter the sixth form each year; they need a minimum of seven Bs at GCSE including the subjects they wish to study, plus satisfactory personal and academic references from previous school. All candidates are interviewed.

Exit: Some 15 per cent leaves after GCSEs. Around 70 per cent to Russell Group universities, good numbers to medical schools, others abroad to Canada, Europe and USA. School employs a Yale Fellow who oversees preparation of candidates for US universities. Ten to Oxbridge and ten medics in 2016. Oakham has been awarded the Career Mark for its excellence in careers guidance and several parents commented on how good the higher education, apprenticeship and careers support was.

Money matters: Comparatively good value, especially the boarding. Even more so if you consider that SEN support is free of charge and parents of day pupils are not charged for evening meals if their children have to stay late at school for activities. Wide variety of scholarships at 11+, 13+ and sixth form. Means-tested bursaries also offered, applications considered on individual basis. Ten per cent discount for Forces families.

Remarks: 'The Oakham of today started when we went fully co-ed in 1971,' the head told us and it's true that though the school is proud of its origins, four centuries of history are not its defining feature. This is a clear-eyed, energetic, forward-thinking school, aptly summed up by its motto, 'Et quasi cursors vitai lampada tradunt' ('And, like runners, they pass on the torch of life').

Old Buckenham Hall School

Brettenham Park, Ipswich, Suffolk IP7 7PH

Pupils: 208 (138 boys, 70 girls); 48 full, 47 weekly/flexi boarders • Ages: 3–13 (boarders from age 7) • C of E

Fees: Day £8,913 – £18,078; Boarding £16,677 – £23,553 pa

Tel: 01449 740252
Email: admissions@obh.co.uk
Website: www.obh.co.uk

Headmaster: Since 2015, Tom O'Sullivan, previously deputy head and head of science at Mowden Hall School. Law degree from Durham; worked in retail and pharmaceutical industry before seeing the light and getting a PGCE from Cambridge. Keen sportsman; has also taught at Beaudesert School in Gloucs.

O

Entrance: Pupils enter at nursery, reception and all years up to 7 and 8. No linked feeders, though the majority of pupils come from within a two hour drive. Non-competitive entry through interview and formal assessment plus reports from previous school. Pupils can enter the school on a daily basis and, if they wish, become a boarder at a later stage. A small, but constant, group of pupils come from abroad.

Exit: The school believes that the process of selecting the right choice of school at 13+ can't begin too early and certainly by years 5/6. Popular destinations are those schools fairly close, eg Uppingham, Oakham, Oundle, Stowe and Framlingham, but a clutch to Eton, Harrow, Wycombe Abbey, Cheltenham College, Winchester. Encourages parents to cast a wide net at senior school stage rather than staying within the safe and familiar choices. A significant number of pupils receive awards and scholarships.

Remarks: Alert, friendly and naturally courteous children – standing up for adults, holding doors etc. Classes are small (fewer than 16 generally) and with setting in the higher forms in preparation for exams/scholarships. The tone throughout is purposeful and light-hearted – one example is the use of Spanish and French in labelling, eg 'le bureau du Directeur'.

Music and drama enjoy excellent facilities and highly motivated staff ensure that children make the most of what's available. The full ability range is catered for and SEN is undergoing a full review. The school feels that the withdrawal of pupils with specific difficulties 'does not, in itself, necessarily address their needs – a highly competent teacher plus in-class support may often be the answer'.

One of the school's great strengths is its framework of pastoral support for each pupil. Arrangements for tutor groups and boarding houses constantly appraised and changes are sometimes necessary as staff come and go. The school is looking particularly at the needs of the older pupils. Well-organised and attractive boarding houses, careful thought having been given to the facilities and decoration. The slightly dismal air that can prevail in dormitories and common rooms has been completely avoided – no sagging sofas and ancient cast-off furniture. In years 7 and 8 pupils can decide whether to be a dorm leader or sleep in their year group bedrooms. Boarding is so popular that many board full time despite living close by – 'My friend boards even though she lives less than a mile away!'

Full boarding is run on an 11 day model described by the school as 'unique' – essentially it means that pupils spend every other weekend in school. Weekend activities are certainly appealing: clay pigeon shooting, night orienteering, trips to the Suffolk ski centre and local point to point. If that's not exciting enough, there's even the chance to go shopping in Bury St Edmunds.

Old Buckenham Hall is set to expand from its traditional county boarding base, keen to reach parents who might not naturally consider a prep or boarding option for their child. Positions itself as a largely non-selective family school, the majority boarding in the higher years. The pre-prep school runs on a day basis with boarding (weekly and full) becoming available in year 3. School aware that the decision to board needs careful thought and transitional boarding of two or three nights a week is available together with taster weeks.

The school has been quick to respond to the need for flexibility and operates a variety of collection times for pupils both in the prep and pre-prep. The majority of pupils come from within a radius of 40 miles, but quite a number come from further afield and the school operates a taxi service to the airport for those who need to travel abroad.

O

Orwell Park School

Nacton, Ipswich, Suffolk IP10 0ER

Pupils: 293; two-thirds board • Ages: 2–13 (boarders from 7)

Fees: Day £7,110– £17,790; Boarding £20,580 – £22,860 pa

Tel: 01473 659225
Email: headmaster@orwellpark.co.uk
Website: www.orwellpark.co.uk

Headmaster: Since 2011, Mr Adrian Brown. Arrived at Orwell Park from Ipswich School, a former professional Essex cricketer and Cambridge Blue. Affable and down-to-earth, much like the pupils in his charge, he lives in the headmaster's house at Orwell Park with his wife Nicole; three children at university.

Entrance: Entry points at 2+ and 4+ (by taster morning in class and a home visit), 7+ and 11+ (tests in maths, English and reasoning, plus a report from the previous school and interview).

Exit: Post-CE, Orwell Park's pupils spread across the UK to top-drawer boarding schools – Eton, Harrow, Winchester, Gordonstoun, Ampleforth, Rugby, Oundle, Uppingham and the like – and local day schools, with no more than four or five per cohort heading in the same direction. Some 15-20 scholarships every year, covering the full range of subjects.

Remarks: One of the most jaw-droppingly gorgeous schools we've ever seen – and it's a prep. Visitors are defied to supress a sharp intake of breath as an idyllic Suffolk leafy lane gives way to impressive wrought iron gates and a sweeping drive heralding a handsome Georgian mansion with late-Victorian additions. Built by a local philanthropist as a venue for royal house parties, it's complete with its own observatory and clock tower, but has been a school since 1937. A combination of effortless elegance (chandeliers and oak panelling in the dining room, ornate tiles and floor-to-ceiling windows in the orangery assembly hall) and down-to-earth, workaday practicality (music practice rooms in the basement) is an appropriate reflection of its clientele – 'the children here are quietly confident,' says head. Indeed the pupils, aged 2+ to 13, who have a 'number one' uniform for best and sweatshirts for every day, are very at home in such grand surroundings. Undoubtedly this is helped by the fact that head knows them all by name (a tour of the school has him checking on this week's second team rugby score with one of its stars, and congratulating a self-effacing young man on the outdoor skills shown on a recent camping expedition).

Every day at Orwell Park begins with a tutor period or an assembly. The timetable also includes a quiet reading slot and there's a serious emphasis on academic attainment, with streaming throughout the juniors. Latin is taught from year 6 – 'they love it' reports head – and includes translation from English to Latin, virtually unheard of even in senior schools these days. Ancient Greek is taught to year 8 scholars, but French is the main MFL, with Spanish and German options at year 6.

Learning support is for all – welcoming drop-in centre is open all day until late evening with an impressive mind-mapping approach ordering thoughts for any task or project. A SENCo oversees a team of five or six who support dyslexia, dyspraxia, dyscalculia, mild Asperger's and ADHD, but only those who are able to manage in the mainstream. Children are assessed on entry and advised on whether or not the curriculum will suit. After that, any difficulties are dealt with as and when with particular help for spelling, handwriting, reading, maths. Real focus on study skills in the run-up to CE with one-to-one and small group sessions as well as dual teaching in class. Outside agencies are co-opted as necessary – OTs, SALT and physios. Each junior class has a qualified teacher plus assistant and there are six gap helpers, mainly young Aussies.

This is a Mac school and they're everywhere – in the music room for composition, throughout the classrooms and in two dedicated ICT rooms, not to mention the iPads currently being trialled by the heads of department with a view to introducing mobile learning in the near future.

A performance culture – you name it, there's a competition for it (verse, singing, public speaking), usually house clashes or routing the local independent school league opponents on the 110 acres of stunning playing fields, which reach from the French doors of the most impressive salons right down to the shores of the Orwell. Growing bodies are encouraged to run free (though no further than the ha-ha for safety reasons). Junior girls love to make dens and shops in the trunks of the thickets and there's a genuine army-built assault course in the woods. Courts for tennis, squash and netball as well as an Astro, cricket nets, nine-hole golf course, sizeable indoor gym and the most inviting outdoor pool, set in a walled garden complete with barbecue area and reached by means of a wisteria walk. Idyllic.

Art has an inviting airy space and work is of an impressive standard. Prospective senior school scholars have their own area and may work on their portfolios independently. DT is generously equipped and a popular class. Heaps of extracurricular clubs, including clay pigeon shooting, and a stargazing club run by local astronomers in the school's own observatory.

Impressive £1m pre-prep building opened in 2013, making space for 80 under-4s with a large hall and teaching rooms as well as outdoor learning areas under the curve of an undulating contemporary roof.

Leadership is key here with the recent introduction of the OPS challenge – a mini D of E with long hikes and camp-outs – and outdoor pursuits holidays to Normandy for year 6s and the Ardèche post-CE. Positions of authority bring with them real obligations – head boys and girls are relied on to help run the school and there are dorm captains, house captains and prefects. 'Everyone has the chance to prove themselves if they want to,' says head, 'just by putting their names down.' The Alston lecture series inspires nascent vocations by inviting parents to come in and speak about their careers.

Increase in boarding numbers recently, locals as well as international students, and options are flexi (min two nights), weekly and full. Dorms are spacious with spectacular views and populated by pupils of the same year group plus a year 8 dorm monitor to keep them in order. Evening and weekend activities range from sailing to crochet to trips to the zoo.

Oundle School

Linked with Laxton Junior School

Great Hall, New Street, Peterborough, Northamptonshire PE8 4GH

Pupils: 1,103; 852 full boarders • Ages: 11-19 • Sixth form: 404 • C of E

Fees: Day £16,785 – £22,065; Boarding £26,175- £34,440 pa

Tel: 01832 277125
Email: admissions@oundleschool.org.uk
Website: www.oundleschool.org.uk

Head: Since 2015, Mrs Sarah Kerr-Dineen, previously warden of Forest School. Read English at Cambridge followed by postgraduate study at Oxford and NPQH. Taught at Open University, Kelly College (now Mount Kelly), Oxford High School (where she was an acting subject head) and St Edward's Oxford (for 13 years – she was boarding housemistress and responsible for the pastoral care of 80 girls, then director of studies). She is married with four adult children and her interests include reading, walking, theatre and music.

Academic matters: Possibly the most academically selective of all the co-ed full-boarding schools. Results are good – 89 per cent A/A* at I/GCSE and 61 per cent A*/A at A level/Pre-U in 2016. Many end up with a mix of qualifications, depending on the subjects taken: Pre-U (linear, no modules), a more rigorous alternative to A level, is the only option in 10 subjects: chemistry, English lit, history, history of art, philosophy, German, Italian, Spanish, Chinese and physics. No weak spots but Latin and chemistry perceived to be especially strong. Staff teach beyond the curriculum, investigate, explore and extend. All sixth-formers follow a non-examined general studies course which includes weekly lectures, discussions, debate and more.

It's not only cool to work but to do so with pace and purpose. Staff say pupils are a delight: 'Teaching is a serious business but students help make it fun, they have a good sense of humour, you can let your guard down a bit.' Not all are angels all of the time: 'My child had a problem concentrating and was allowed to change groups to get away from another child who was messing around'. We dropped in on a couple of lessons to find pupils engaged and on task, aided by some inspirational teaching. Parents happy with school but not gushingly so; they choose Oundle because their baseline is excellence and, for almost all, Oundle delivers. Very few parental moans: ad-hoc report times irritate some; girls, top students and strugglers (ie borderline B/C grade at A level) do well but feel some middling boys could do better; parent portal on wish list, but appreciative of extensive use of email.

School will support and encourage those with mild SEN, mainly specific learning difficulties but Asperger's and other SEN considered, so long as child is good university fodder. Parents say approach is matter of fact, no pandering: 'This is what we have, this is what we will do.' Help given with study skills plus whatever is identified in ed psych report. Minimal one-to-one help available but support for all (SEN or not) from individual departments. Pacey, demanding curriculum means EAL students need excellent English prior to arrival.

Good and ever improving facilities; latest jewel is the SciTec block with 16 well-designed labs. Whizzy new Adamson Centre languages block has state-of-the-art everything including an 'international suite' which 'provides a perfect venue for language conferences, films, lectures from visiting speakers and competitions'. The super 20,000 volume library stays open late and offers a book-ordering service. Flagship, innovative DT (BBC B computer started life here) – a veritable hive of activity and inspiration when we visited – continues to thrive. Industrious atmosphere, wonderful, woody workshops with casting, lasers, wind tunnels, micro-electronics and CAD all adding to the scintillating sensory experience. Mr Bean's car may have vamoosed but others remain, in various glorious states of build and disrepair.

Games, options, the arts: All major sports pursued including rugby, football, hockey, netball, squash, fives, water polo, rowing, athletics, aerobics, cross-country, golf. Recently became a Marylebone Cricket Club Foundation Hub, working to improve coaching for local state school children. Good facilities include a multi-sports complex with sports shop, pool, an outdoor synthetic athletics track, rifle range etc. Generally hold their own, win some, lose some, with a few key successes along the way including notable individual honours and national team selection – not bad considering sports schols only recently introduced. Parents say, 'Not all coaches are equally capable and enthusiastic; lower teams very much at mercy of master in charge but genuine sport for all – if they can put a team out, they will'.

For the stage-struck the charming Stahl Theatre, enjoyed by school and locals alike, provides a professional venue for touring companies as well as for esteemed pupil productions. Busy music department has recently formed a partnership with the Royal College of Music, a huge nod to the very high standard of musicianship. Two-thirds learn an instrument though far fewer perform. Music and drama lean towards the exclusive, pupils and parents grumble that those whose trumpet blowing is enthusiastic rather than virtuoso, or who hide their dramatic light under a bushel, are unlikely to be placed centre-stage or even on-stage, making it difficult for late developers to get a look in.

Art popular and prolific. We saw superb sculptures and castings, plus exquisite fine art. Yarrow Gallery regularly hosts visiting exhibitions as well as pupils' own masterpieces.

Millennium marked by pupil-design inspired, vibrantly coloured stained-glass windows made for the school chapel, a lively foil to John Piper's sedately beautiful east windows.

Field trips, exchanges, tours and expeditions galore to the near, the exotic and the remote. Extraordinarily varied list of activities known as 'voluntaries' are, paradoxically, compulsory for younger students; courses range from knitting, beekeeping and bridge through to junior economics, dance and DT. Virtually all do D of E. CCF compulsory in the fourth form, remains a popular choice thereafter. Optional fifth and sixth form community action programme recognised as a class-leader, not just holding hands with the elderly or cleaning out chicken sheds but tough stuff too, including street sleeping to help understand the harsher side of life and instil a 'give-back' culture. A busy school with little let-up, though all get chance to let their hair down via active social programme now enhanced by transformation of old fives courts into social centres.

Boarding: The 13 self-contained, well-maintained boarding houses have unique personalities; according to Oundelian, the school's own rather chic publication, Sanderson is 'intimidating', Laundimer 'friendly'. In reality school mixes pupils to ensure no cliques, or types ('the Scottish house' notwithstanding) – apply early if you yearn for a particular house. Compulsory chapel on Sunday plus two other weekly slots.

Background and atmosphere: Situated in the delightful market town of Oundle, with its gentle, honey-toned Cotswold stone, the school was founded in 1556 as the local grammar. In 1876 the school split into Laxton, for the sons of tradesmen and local farmers, and Oundle, for the sons of gentlemen. Full co-education came in the early 1990s and Laxton was brought back into the fold as a day house in 2000. Today it's hard to distinguish the extensive school campus and its 1,100 pupils from the eponymous town. Size matters; fortunately house loyalty endures.

Pastoral care, well-being and discipline: No time for prolonged hand-holding – pupils heed the emphasis on self-reliance – but HMs and personal tutors help and support. 'Most youngsters get something wrong at some point. We keep our ear to the ground and lines of communication open. We watch them try and sometimes fail, try again. We pick them up, dust them down, help them move on.' Parents say some HMs are excellent, stress there are no weak ones, but caution that HMs vary in outlook, attitude, expectations and communications. All dine in-house which means a careful eye can be kept on eating issues, friendships et al. Odd comment from parents of girls that house system is more geared up for boys, citing fewer events with parents, and more fall-outs between girls (no more than anywhere else, we suspect); certainly the girls we met were friendly, articulate and clearly had a sense of community. Parents of boys praise the range of house activities, camaraderie, and parental involvement; 'We appreciate the even-handedness of staff in dealing with issues'. Parents who live afar are especially approving of helpful, prompt and detailed home-school comms and of school's honesty about 'incidents'.

All incidences of bullying taken seriously, work done with victims and perpetrators. On the very rare occasion when things don't work out, students may be sent home to rethink, or supported in their quest to find something that suits better. 'Sometimes a fresh start elsewhere is all that is needed. All will make fantastic adults, we simply have to help them through the stupidity of adolescence.' Pupils at ease with each other and with staff, though some older students confess to feeling a little stifled by rules and ready for the freedom of life after school. Rules are fair and the school, perceived to be 'very, very strict', upholds the policy re drugs and sex – instant out. Those aged 18 allowed controlled access to pub and alcohol (understandably strict – a former student once tried unsuccessfully to sue school after a drunken fall several years earlier left her permanently disabled). Hot on electronic footprint, work hard to ensure youngsters understand cyber dangers.

Pupils and parents: From all over UK, including strong Scottish contingent, currently over 120 prep schools represented. Close family ties, some 12 percent are offspring of OOs. Twelve per cent from continental Europe or the Pacific Rim. Parents range from the professional to farming folk – open minded, ambitious. Not an obvious choice for first-time buyers but those who opt in are justifiably proud of their acquisition. School says London parents are the trickiest; 'They want the Oundle experience but on weekly boarding terms' – little chance of that, we suspect. Social credentials abound but social club this isn't, some parents keen to be more involved and for greater social interaction and parental events but a tricky feat for what is a genuine boarding school with a global community. Exeats a rarity; officially one per annum but flexibility when essential.

Pupils are bright, friendly, articulate and courteous. Uniform adhered to, girls look glam in their swishing culottes, boys business-like in dark suit and tie. OOs include Arthur Marshall, Cecil Lewis (aviator), Peter Scott (ornithologist), A Alvarez, Anthony Holden (royal biographer), Richard Dawkins, Professor Sir Alan Budd, Charles Crichton (film director), Bruce Dickinson (lead singer of Iron Maiden – allegedly expelled following a rock-star style prank).

Entrance: Rigorous at 11+, 13+ and 16+. Waiting list (up to two years) with sibling preference (a third have a brother or sister in the school). Feeder schools are well primed and start preparation early. The registrar makes it his business to ensure only those who will succeed are entered. Minimum CE requirement of 55 per cent in English, maths, French and sciences but in reality those accepted typically average 70 per cent (scholars do even better). Officially no pre-testing but runs practice CE day in November, 'to avoid disappointment'; those not following CE are assessed early via assortment of tests. Sixth form entry requires minimum three As and three Bs in GCSEs but competition for handful of places at 16+ means successful external applicants typically have fistfuls of A and A* grades. As with many popular, larger schools, when visiting you are unlikely to meet with the head (unless specifically requested); potential Oundelians are left in the very capable hands of trusty registrar.

Exit: Nearly all move on to the sixth form and thence to university. Mainly traditional courses at traditional universities – with Newcastle, Bristol, Exeter, Durham and Manchester favoured destinations. Forty per cent take arts degrees with the rest split between social sciences and sciences; history, economics and engineering the most popular subjects. Plenty of extra help for those wishing to apply to Oxbridge – 30 successful candidates in 2016, and four medics, though school says it is sometimes surprised by who is accepted and saddened that some outstanding students are turned away. Increasing numbers head across the pond thanks, in part, to well-versed influence of US staff.

Money matters: Range of scholarships awarded at 11+, 13+ and 16+, most limited to 10 per cent of fees. Bursaries as high as 100 per cent available in cases of proven need; apply at least two years prior to entry for help, expect to fill in extensive forms designed to unearth every last sou. No automatic sibling or forces discounts but Old Oundelian bursaries for the sons and daughters of OOs.

Remarks: A very busy school, ideal for the resilient, confident, energetic, academic child, who thrives in a large, pacey setting, rejoices in a heavy, focussed workload and delights in an abundance of extracurricular activities. Average all-rounders should head elsewhere, stragglers will struggle, strugglers will likely be lost in the milieu. For those who can, Oundle does. Anyone considering a full-boarding education for their motivated, able offspring should shortlist Oundle.

The Perse School

55

Hills Road, Cambridge, Cambridgeshire CB2 8QF

Pupils: 1,556 • Ages: 3–18 • Sixth form: 350

Fees: £12,516 – £16,032 pa

Tel: 01223 403800
Email: admissions@perse.co.uk
Website: www.perse.co.uk

Head: Since 2008, Mr Edward Elliott (40s), who has been at the school since 1997. Educated at The Royal Grammar School, Worcester, then St Anne's College, Oxford, where he got a first in geography. Tried commerce (a graduate trainee at De La Rue) but quickly moved to teaching at the Whitgift School in Surrey. Married to Sue, a paediatrician, with two young daughters and a son. Certainly a finger very firmly on the pulse at The Perse as well as in the wider education community, though 'not swayed by current trends in education to make knee-jerk reactions,' surmised a parent.

Head of prep: Since 2014, James Piper BA PGCE (30s). Previously deputy head of Bilton Grange. Educated at S Anselm's and Repton. Read classics at Durham, PGCE from Pembroke College, Cambridge, and is completing a masters in educational leadership at the University of Buckingham. Started teaching career at Aysgarth, then spent 11 years at the Dragon School (was head of classics and housemaster of year 6 boys' full boarding house). Married, with three children. Outside interests include cricket and golf.

Head of pre-prep: Mrs Sarah Waddington, BSc MA PGCE.

Academic matters: Parents cannot speak too highly of the Perse Pelican Pre-Prep. Deserves its reputation as one of the hardest schools to get into for the best possible reasons. The Perse's trademark academic thoroughness starts here, even if the youngest pupils don't realise it. Children in the nursery (usually around 32) are encouraged to love learning and to ask questions, supported by happy, friendly staff.

School defines 'The Perse DNA' which is present in all stages. Of course the prep school is academic, with intellectual, fast-paced, sparkling learning, but there's also an emphasis on extracurricular activities – not just 'a school for bright nerds and geeks'. Sport, music, drama, outdoor pursuits... there's even rocketry at the prep to prepare pupils for the award-winning rocketry society at the Upper. New whizzy science department under construction, with current one destined to become a computing lab.

Brainpower is not thin on the ground in Cambridge and the Perse aims, and achieves, high academically to meet its market. Even given the genes, results are impressive across the board – 93 per cent A*-B and 81 per cent A*/A at A level in 2016. Pre-U and International A level are offered alongside A levels. Three-quarters IGCSE and the other quarter GCSE, with 94 per cent of grades A*/A in 2016. Heads of department have the freedom to choose the exam they feel offers the most rigour and currency. Results are of course stellar in maths and science, yet history, geography and languages are also among the popular sixth form options – a hint to the breadth of education on offer here. The Perse has developed its own course in engineering technology and makes innovative use of IT. 'Global studies' in year 7 offers a taster of a range of languages – Mandarin, Japanese, Arabic, Portuguese and Italian. All labs recently refitted to highest standard and computer science now lauded as 'the fourth science'. More than 60 students each year involved in the Higher Project Qualification (HPQ) – 'intellectually liberating' says head – and the sixth form equivalent, the EPQ, is also popular.

SEN provision is excellent, although head prefers the term 'learning maximisation'. All pupils are screened on entry, with the result that 120 pupils are supported, including those perhaps running at 80 per cent capacity who would not be spotted elsewhere. On-site SEN teacher plus liaison with educational psychologists, who all feed through to director of teaching in a concerted effort to work around the barriers. 'The school's reputation for only concentrating on high flyers is not borne out by the extra sessions, reviews and learning aids that have been provided for my child,' said a parent.

A few parental rumblings about the school's commitment to nurturing young teachers, some of whom don't come up to scratch straight away. The school points to its significant new teacher induction and continuous professional development programme, with mentoring from more experienced staff.

Games, options, the arts: Surprisingly for a day school, manages to keep two or three sessions a week for games and other extracurricular activities right through the school – 'almost too many to choose from,' say pupils. This is, in the main, a very popular policy and pupils relish the opportunities to develop sporting, musical or dramatic skills, and various adventurous options on offer – notably CCF (RAF only, unusually, and a popular choice for many girls). There's also the Perse Exploration Society, which runs trips in the UK for younger pupils, as far afield as Vietnam and the Himalayas for the eldest. A new option is the Wilderness Group offering further outdoor pursuits activities. Excellent sports hall block includes squash court, weights room and a large and well-appointed fitness suite; school employs a fitness coach who provides guidance and fitness programmes for students and staff. Much effort has gone in to providing a wide choice of sports and fitness opportunities for girls, who show their appreciation by their enthusiasm.

Art is rich and colourful, evidence of inspirational teaching, and includes ceramics and printing. Local artists exhibit in The Pelican Gallery within the teaching space. Impressive lecture theatre doubles as drama studio seating 180 – productions have really grown in recent years. New (very neat) music building – an extension to existing block – provides plenty of teaching/practice rooms, as well as space for larger ensembles and rehearsal hall to accommodate full-scale symphony orchestra with chorus. This doubles as a concert hall and is made available to the local community. About two-fifths learn at least one instrument and musical activities of all types flourish – baroque string ensembles, jazz, brass, wind and chamber groups, choirs and music technology. The school's musical excellence now seen by parents as a principal reason to apply and attracting correspondingly good budding musicians. New performing arts centre rising apace on the upper school site. Most prep school pupils take part in three or four activities after school or at lunchtime very week.

Background and atmosphere: The school's history – nearly 400 years of it – is chequered and includes embezzlement in the 18th century, an assault on the head in the 19th and an incendiary bomb hitting it in 1941. Since 1960 it has occupied award-winning, purpose-built accommodation on a 28-acre site. Buildings are low, few higher than two storeys as is customary in this part of the world, but although not imposing; they are inviting and well integrated into the site. Hall doubles up as dining room, necessitating daily quick setting out and packing away of tables. Meals taken by staff and pupils together perhaps explaining the unusually orderly atmosphere. Two Astroturf pitches, very attractive, tree-lined playing fields, real feeling of space. A new outdoor pursuits centre and an additional full-size all weather pitch recently completed, with new sports pitches on 21 acres of land at Little Abington. New performing arts centre is scheduled for completion during 2017/18. Good careers room and resources in sixth form centre, which also has a well-used common room area, expanded to provide a separate work area.

Prep pupils have their own campus five minutes from the upper school and their own all-weather pitch (also used by upper school students).

Pastoral care, well-being and discipline: Pastoral care is taken seriously, with nurses on-site at both prep and upper schools, and there's a school counsellor and a pastoral safety net made up of tutors and heads of year. Interestingly, the house system was dusted off a few years ago to fill a gap in pupils' enthusiasm for extracurricular activities. Reintroduced as eight houses for pupils in years 7 to 11, leadership opportunities are appreciated by those lower down the school.

International links are being forged 'to prepare students for a world where employment will be global,' explains head. Exchanges to Spain, France and Germany as well as Sewickley, near Pittsburgh. Member of SAGE – Strategic Alliance of Global Educators – consortium of 10 schools from around the world (UK, US, Australia, Singapore, Hong Kong, China...) who share best practice and work together on a range of projects. Also involved in Christel House charitable foundation to establish first class schools in the most deprived areas of the world – Perse staff have been seconded to Bangalore and Cape Town.

Parents appreciate the school's meticulous planning and communication, making life easier particularly for those juggling several offspring – all information is provided well in advance and with great attention to detail. Emails from pupils and parents are responded to swiftly, 'even on a Sunday night,' marvels a parent.

Although common sense prevails in all corners of the school and its operation, there is room here too for eccentrics, who only add to the increasing richness of Perse life.

Pupils and parents: A school for the 'intellectually curious' says head, although fees prohibit mass takeover by bright children of poorly-paid Cambridge academics. Head is committed to ensuring that the school is a cosmopolitan meritocracy – a million pounds is spent on means-tested financial support for pupils aged 7 and over throughout the prep and upper, with more than 120 receiving fees assistance. There is indeed a real mix of backgrounds – rare in independent schools – which the school is certain contributes to the development of all pupils' emotional intelligence, preparing them well for life in the real world.

School ceased taking boarders in 1993, two years before girls arrived in the sixth form; it became fully coeducational in 2012, though still two-thirds boys. Most girls blossom here, with opportunities and resources few girls' schools can offer. Pupils are relaxed, unpretentious and natural – many come for the science but find they relish the sporting and artistic possibilities they discover. Majority live close by, though some from as far as Ely, Saffron Walden, Newmarket, Royston and elsewhere. Annually, a very few from abroad, under special guardianship scheme, seen as bringing new and refreshing dimension to school life. Distinguished list of Old Boys includes Sir Peter Hall, Rev Dr John Polkinghorne, David Tang, Dave Gilmour, Pete Atkin, Sir Mark Potter.

Entrance: By assessment: 'observed play' for nursery (32 places) and reception (about eight places); entry into prep for external applicants (another 30 places) by the school's own entrance tests in English and maths and verbal reasoning, as well as an interview and report from the previous school.

Competition for places at The Perse Upper is not as fierce as the rumour would have it and pales into insignificance next to London's bunfight. At 11, roughly two and a half applicants for each place – 60 come up from the Perse Prep and another 50 from local juniors and preps. Sixty more are added at 13 (largely from King's College, St John's College, St Faith's). Entry is by tests in English and maths and verbal reasoning, as well as interview and report from the previous school. Also a short humanities video and questions exercise.

Entry to sixth form is by interview and a subject test for scholarships, with all offers conditional on GCSE performance – usually above 70 points required, with A*/A in A level subjects. Most joiners come from local girls' independent schools (Stephen Perse, St Mary's) and the maintained sector.

Exit: Most – about 95 per cent – move from the prep to Perse Upper. Others to eg The Leys, Stephen Perse Foundation, King's Ely. Around 20 leave The Perse after GCSE, choosing Hills Road Sixth Form College in the main, but vast majority go on to The Perse's sixth form. Medicine hugely popular (40 offers) and many depart for top medical schools. Thirty-nine to Oxbridge in 2016, one to Harvard, rest to wide spread of other universities – three quarters Russell Group. Bristol, UCL, Durham, Exeter popular. Engineering, medical and natural sciences preferred subjects, but history also recurring.

Money matters: Scholarships are mostly five per cent, occasionally 10 per cent. Determined to maintain its direct grant tradition and increase the amount of means-tested financial support available to bursary applicants. Recently spent over £1m on fees assistance for families who could not otherwise afford a Perse education. All sixth form applicants are now considered for an academic scholarship based on their performance in the entrance tests; they can then apply for a maximum of two other scholarships (art, drama, general, music and sport).

Remarks: A co-ed academic school and a 'cosmopolitan meritocracy' which prepares students well for the real world, not just intellectually but also emotionally.

The Priory Academy LSST

Cross O'Cliff Hill, Lincoln, Lincolnshire LN5 8PW

Pupils: 1,871; 50 boarders • Ages: 11–18 • Sixth form: 519

Fees: Day free; Boarding £11,200 pa

Tel: 01522 889977
Email: general.enquiries@prioryacademies.co.uk
Website: www.priorylsst.co.uk

Head: Since September 2016 Jane Hopkinson (40s). Studied maths and chemistry at UEA in Norwich. Planned to be an accountant but work experience put her off. PGCE in maths found her returning to her roots to teach in girls' grammar school in Grantham. Joined the academy eight years ago, rising to deputy head here before headship at another school, returning here as head. Not very well known by parents yet but not expected to be in a school this size. 'I deal with the head of year. The head oversees the school rather than the pupils,' was one parent's take on it. 'She has a strong management team in place,' from another. All happy with plenty of online communication from new head. Still finding her feet but settling in quickly, particularly as already familiar with the school and the Trust. Quietly spoken, effective and efficient, she strikes us as a lady who will 'get on with the job.' Has plans 'to keep driving forward and to develop the staff.'

Academic matters: In 2016, 89 per cent achieved 5+ GCSEs A*-C including English and maths, with 33 per cent A*-A grades. Sixty per cent of grades were A*-B at A level, 31 per cent A*?A. Excellent results for a non-selective school but it has to be noted that 10 per cent of each year are admitted after an aptitude test. 'It's made very clear from day one that the children are here to learn,' said one parent. 'Guidelines are laid out before they start and are expected to be adhered to regarding homework and study,' said another. Gifted and talented spotted early on and nurtured, but not to the detriment of the less able. Children assessed every six weeks after each module and parents kept well informed. 'My children go to school every morning knowing what it expected of them, which is excellent,' said one parent, who went on to say 'the school is very much education based, they are there to learn, not taught how to behave, that's up to us.'

Science popular throughout the school with a modern planetarium within the new science block inspiring budding scientists and capturing imaginations. Excellent facilities, including modern labs and separate ones just for the sixth form. Plethora of computers throughout the school including impressive IT area. DT room home to a robotic lab including a 3D computer. You name it, this school has it when it comes to facilities. French, German and Spanish offered. All year 7s study Latin for 13 weeks – excellent; also available up to GCSE. Many take two languages, all have to take one, French or German, for GCSE. Gifted and talented take triple science and many do two languages as well. Streaming from year 8 in sciences, maths and English.

The lessons we observed showed smart, engaged pupils with enthusiastic teachers. All pupils leapt to their feet when we entered the room, except for the sixth form, of course. Pupils welcoming and chatty, lots of 'missing' and 'sirring'. Year 8 physics chatty and enthusiastically working on circuits. Sixth form still life art class concentrating hard and producing great work. Framed artwork throughout the school. Every GCSE and A level art student donate one piece from their portfolio to the school. Impressive gallery in large reception area. Library home to 15,000 books.

Maximum class sizes of 34, years 7-11, 26 in sixth form, but usually much smaller. About 10 per cent of each year has EAL requirements, higher for the boarders. Support available through learning support department and sixth form mentors. Every SEN student has a student profile explaining their needs and best way to support them in the classroom and at home. Parental involvement encouraged. EHC plan students have designated learning support assistant working with them. All parents spoke highly of the LS department. And all parents said their child 'was reaching their potential.'

Large sixth form, over 550 pupils, housed in separate modern block, not far from the boarding house. All wear smart business suits and look the part. Most sixth form teaching done in this block. Large – no, massive – common room full of Chesterfield sofas and a TV broadcasting the news. Canteen for exclusive use, breakfast, lunch and snacks available. Amusing to see many students playing cards. Not quite a den of iniquity but possibly future poker players being hothoused here, not that we saw any gambling per se. Lots of computers and supervised free periods for year 12s in particular.

Games, options, the arts: Every facility you can think of when it comes to sports. Indoor 60m running track, outdoor all weather track, climbing wall, trampolines, massive sports hall that splits into three, gym, swimming pool, dance studios all housed in new sports centre. Pitches galore. You name it, they've got it. Sports choices rotated frequently so everyone can try everything. PE compulsory up to year 11. Lots of after-school sports practices and clubs. Teams for all abilities. They even have their own spinning room alongside the fitness suite. As to be expected from the facilities, lots of silverware in the cabinet and certain individuals high achieving outside school as well.

Music and drama both popular. Nearly 90 students have in-house lessons. Impressive music school, including recording studio. Loads of bands, orchestras and choirs, performing frequently. Lots of plays and productions, including whole school shows. Fabulous debating chamber used for cross year group debates et al.

D of E to gold and, unusually for a state school, active CCF with on site rifle range. Both well supported. Plenty of school trips, far and wide. One parent commented that not everyone got to do D of E because of large numbers and often 'names pulled out of a hat' when it came to school trips. 'It's frustrating: if a child is keen to do D of E they should be able to do it, likewise with the social school trips. But I understand that it's difficult because of the size of the school. I suppose it's a lesson that you can't get everything you want,' was their philosophical take on it.

Boarding: Boarding introduced for sixth form in 2012 and classed as outstanding in recent Ofsted report. Housed in a modern purpose built building, Robert de Cheney House. Over 50 pupils, virtually all from overseas, some expats, board. Some 50 per cent join the sixth form for a year only, a handful for a couple of terms, the remainder for the two years. Large drive now being made to attract more boarders, particularly Forces children, many of whom already attend the school. New head of boarding highly regarded by parents and pupils alike. Parents appreciate the boarding blog to keep up with goings on and talk of quick response to emails. All students have their own locked rooms with en suite facilities – do they realise how lucky they are? Girls on one floor, boys on the other, with common room and dining facilities on the ground floor. Very much like uni accommodation, and they are allowed a lot of independence. But all have to be on site to do 2.5 hours compulsory prep daily, either supervised in the dining room or in their own rooms, all of which have desks.

There is a 10pm roll call every night but apart from that they can come and go as they like. Allowed out until midnight at the weekend and head of boarding more than happy for them to stay with friends as long as parental permission given. They have a kitchen to bake cakes and cook in at weekends. Bake Off competition hotly contested, apparently. They change their own bedding and have chores to do such as emptying the dishwasher and light cleaning in communal areas. Plenty of trips at weekends, many don't take this up as Lincoln is a short walk away, but again flexible approach to this. Compulsory team-building trip at the beginning of autumn term enjoyed by all. Head of boarding gently prises young men from computers if need be. Very flexible: one pupil has a weekend job, others attend evening clubs off site. Keen runners ran the Lincoln half marathon. School facilities, such as fitness suite, available for out of hours use. No restrictions on phones or social media within boarding house. A sensible rule as many have parents in different time zones. Despite numerous nationalities and languages a cohesive atmosphere prevails and freedoms not abused.

Background and atmosphere: Founded in 1992 on the site of an old girls' grammar school, this school has grown dramatically. Now the largest school in Lincoln, if not the county. Housed on a massive site on one of the main roads into Lincoln, the school is deceptive. From the main road you only see the old, attractive, red-brick school house. But once within the grounds you realise how vast the site is; it's like entering a Tardis. Pupils and staff walk miles during the day. 'We definitely manage our 10,000 steps,' said one guide. Walkways covered so no drowned rats during lesson changeovers. 'I would like to see the leaks repaired more quickly,' said another guide.

Some very savvy financial planning and foresight saw the school benefit from government introduction of academies in 2006. Funding applied for, and got, for massive development including the planetarium, new sports centre, debating hall and sixth form, including boarding house. The whole school immaculate and well cared for. No sign of litter or detritus. Good to see one of our guides pick up the only sweet paper in sight. Older parts of the school slightly more shabby than the modern. The school site feels very much like a campus. Plenty of open space including lots of water features, ponds, gardens and statues. Sad to see plaques in the memorial garden. Each year has its own garden for break times. They even have a chapel with underfloor heating, very popular at certain times of the year. A nice touch in the chapel – please note the labyrinth outside – is the 'blue book.' Each student signs it on their first day and 'signs out' on their last. Our guides were proud to show us their names and spoke with great pride about how it makes them feel they belong.

Pastoral care, well-being and discipline: Discipline is hot. 'Guidelines, rules and regulations are set out before they start and are expected to be adhered to,' said one parent, 'and they are.' All parents mentioned this and were full of praise about it. Another parent told us, 'the whole class had to write a letter of apology to a teacher because of bad behaviour, even those not involved, and I fully support that.' Uniform deviancy also picked up on immediately. They don't stand for any nonsense and the pupils know and respect that. Pupils look smart in their ties, blazers and regulation trousers or skirts.

There is no denying the school is large. Each year group is the size of a small school. But there don't seem to be any problems with new starters feeling lost or out of place. Induction days and bonding sessions are successful. Every year 7 goes on a team building trip to their facility in France during their first term. Lessons take place within the form so friendships quickly formed. Heads of years and tutors appear to know their pupils well. Forms stay with the same teacher for many years.

Pastoral care complimented by all parents. Peer listening scheme with years 11-13 offering advice to younger years. They can talk live on the computer to these mentors about any problems encountered. Counselling services on offer if needed. The atmosphere within the school is informal and relaxed despite, or because of, the strict discipline. Pupils know what is expected of them and act accordingly, with miscreants sorts out firmly, quickly and efficiently. There is an effective school council with its own budget. Latest purchase was mirrors for the girls' toilets. They also asked for, and got, more choice in the canteen.

Pupils and parents: Parents are ambitious with high expectations and very supportive. Pupils come from a wide area, many from small rural primaries. Parents very impressed with facilities, as are pupils, and the school's reputation, so concerted effort made to get their child a place at the school. Children from all walks of life. Many Forces children from the nearby air bases. Pupils friendly, welcoming, happy and focused.

Entrance: The school is oversubscribed despite offering 240 places in year 7. The area covered is wide with 50+ feeder schools, each being allocated at least two spaces. Pupils come from as far afield as Grantham to the south and Gainsborough to the north. Non-selective except for 10 per cent chosen by aptitute test in technology.

Entrance to sixth form 'open to all' but subject-specific for certain grades. Boarders interviewed by Skype. New sixth formers are mainly boarders.

Exit: Very few leave after GCSEs, between one and two per cent, usually for vocational courses at local colleges. The vast majority go on the university, 91 per cent getting their first or second choice. Eight Oxbridge places in 2016. Apprenticeships becoming more popular and being embraced by the school. Very few take gap years and the odd one straight into employment.

Remarks: A school offering tremendous facilities and education. Very much the feel of an independent school with fantastic facilities and very enthusiastic teaching staff, as mentioned by all parents. Its reputation precedes it, and we can see why. As one parent said, 'please thank The Priory for its contribution to my son's education.' Quite.

Queen Mary's Grammar School

Sutton Road, Walsall, West Midlands WS1 2PG

Pupils: 940 • Ages: 11–18 • Sixth form: 346 (91 girls)

Tel: 01922 720696
Email: postbox@qmgs.walsall.sch.uk
Website: www.qmgs.walsall.sch.uk

Headmaster: A modern linguist, self-confessed Francophile married to a French woman and spending his holidays on a melon farm in France, Tim Swain is lean, intense but with a real sparkle in his eyes. He is an Old Marian, has spent his whole career at QMGS and is now a QMGS parent with his two sons having gone through the school and his daughter just started in the first year sixth. So he has been ideally placed to ensure the rigorous academic traditions of the school are maintained while being determined that the school shall get better and better under his watch. 'He is that unusual combination of visionary and practical', says one of his younger colleagues. He is overseeing a gradual ongoing expansion of the school, that has resulted so far in, among other things, an extended school hall and an impressive sixth form centre, funded in part by his very successful capital projects bids and partly through his inspiring fundraising campaign with Old Marians and parents.

Teachers and pupils speak of his 'common touch'. His school walks are peppered with questions such as 'How is your day so far?' to young and old alike. His eagerly anticipated school assemblies are interactive – pupils are expected to respond to questions he might throw out at any stage – but he is also renowned for sharing his own experiences and challenges with pupils, something they much appreciate and remember. With a school population that is majority non-white, Tim Swain is very aware that he has to make an increasingly conscious effort to get to know and understand the diverse communities from which his pupils now come. He is keen to engage with parents and is pleased with the response to the parent seminars that the school runs on topics that are every parent's nightmare such as drugs and e-safety. Parents confirm his success in this area, describing him as 'inspiring', 'open-minded', 'progressive' and 'fair'.

During 2016-17, will become CEO of The Mercian Trust. Successor is Richard Langton MA, currently deputy head at the school.

Academic matters: As expected in a selective school, academic results are very good. In 2016, 78 per cent of GCSE grades were at A* and A. At A level, 71 per cent of results were A* to B and 41 per cent A*/A. Sciences and maths are strong in terms of both results and numbers taking A level, and DT is also high profile, with its visits out of school to show how design works in business and public spaces. Modern languages are encouraged and the school has Confucius Classroom status as a centre of excellence for Chinese teaching. Class sizes are about 25 and it is hoped as the school expands to keep a good ratio. There are regular catch-up classes timetabled and pupils say that the teachers are very supportive. Academic rigour stretches beyond the classroom to an emphasis on individual research wherever possible. Strong careers education programme – including much advice and opportunities for success in STEM areas, but also an emphasis on developing the soft skills needed for success in the work place. Annual Futures Events when Old Marians, specialists in a variety of fields, meet with pupils and final year pupils share their application experience with first year sixth. Learning support on offer for those with specific difficulties. Teachers are strongly encouraged to keep abreast of pedagogical developments; there is a teachers' learning group, coaching groups, research projects and open door days when any teacher can go and observe another's lesson. Parents describe teaching as 'enthusiastic and supportive'.

Games, options, the arts: Range of sports with much rugby and hockey success. Lots of cricket going on. Modern sports hall (sports block refurbished), fitness suite and indoor pool. Girls play netball and girls' sport seems to be building up a bit. The idyllically situated outdoor centre on the coastal edge of Snowdonia is near enough to make an easy weekend journey in school minibuses. It is much used for CCF and bonding visits as well as for history, geography, biology field trips and modern language immersion courses. 'The children are learning as much out on the hillsides as in a classroom – it reflects our holistic approach to education and commitment to character education,' one member of staff told us. Boys do the cooking and cleaning and there is no TV – all features parents heartily commend!. Two additional properties recently added. Visits to, for example, France, Spain, the States and China are regular features, usually with a subject rationale such as a recent Red Sea diving biology trip, and these, along with the school's European work experience programme, allow the school to give substance to its international dimension. The school encourages pupils to get involved in external competitions and participation is celebrated in assemblies even if they don't always result in success. Sixth formers in particular are encouraged to engage in community work beyond the usual fundraising – all participate in a service option. There is a link with a studio school where sixth formers, who all undertake a service option, mentor younger students, as well as a well-established mentoring system for younger QMGS pupils.

All year 7s learn a musical instrument and individual talented musicians are given plenty of exposure, helped by addition of new music suite with own recording studio. There are regular concerts and plays and a new drama society.

Background and atmosphere: The school has built its ethos on 'four pillars' – academic purpose, international outlook, enterprising spirit and generous approach. These spell out the seriousness of the school's intention to ensure boys can develop their full humanity and be confident expressing emotion and sensitivity as well as resilience in the face of challenges. Staff who have come from other all boys schools comment on how collaborative and supportive the boys are of each other, as well as showing the confidence and a willingness to embrace leadership opportunities that you might expect to find in a boys' school. They like taking on difficult topics and staff say that while there is boyish banter which girls coming into the sixth form can find a bit trying at first, overall there is a degree of maturity and sensitivity over gender and race issues. The atmosphere is earnest without being dull and pupils tell us it is cool to work hard.

Pastoral care, well-being and discipline: There is an instantly impressive atmosphere of courtesy, both towards visitors, as one might expect, but also between the boys themselves, which is more unusual. Staff say the school is small enough for a personal approach, both in terms of getting to know the boys and their concerns, but also when it comes to any discipline issues. The approach is strict but supportive, benign not draconian – though everyone was clear that when it came to drugs there was a zero tolerance policy. The school believes in educating wrong-doers, not just meting out uniform punishments. Pupils are shown how to fix what they have done wrong where possible and there is an emphasis on talking problems through. Parents tell us that when required the school confronts challenges full on, making difficult decisions to maintain the standards, ethos and reputation of the school and then communicate appropriately with parents, listening and responding in a timely manner, to maintain their support.

Everyone seems happy with the pastoral care. Pupils extol the virtues of the heads of year, and the sixth form girls have a dedicated member of staff to whom they can go with any pastoral concerns. At a recent parent survey of year 8 pupils, 100 per cent of parents said their sons were happy at school and felt safe.

Pupils and parents: The school has been active in recruiting from under-represented sections of the community and it now rightly prides itself on having a socially much more mixed cohort than most grammar schools. Pupils come from all economic bands in the community and are fairly evenly distributed, so it is not open to the usual anti-grammar school lobby of being entirely populated by pushy middle-class families. It is about 70 per cent non-white and there is a palpable sense of drive coming from families who see the school as a pathway to a different world. There aren't many 14 year old boys who will look you in the eye and say, 'It's an honour to be here,' but that is what we heard from one after another. Relations with teachers are good – in part because of the stability in the staff, so that many relationships are built up over the whole seven years, and in part because all the extracurricular involvement allows each side to get to know each other in fresh contexts. Parental expectations run high and along establishment lines – the school tries to wean both parents and pupils away from always considering careers only in medicine. We got a sense that this is a centre of real social mobility, with both the philosophical commitment and the energy to show pupils how a strong education can liberate and push the bounds of community expectations. QMGS pupils are snapping at the heels of the old Establishment – and social change starts here.

Entrance: The numbers applying are going up at both 11+ and 16+. There are about 1,200 applicants for the current 120 11+ places. The admissions exam is a joint arrangement with other local grammar schools (to avoid children sitting too many exams) and includes verbal and non-verbal reasoning, literacy and mathematics.

At 16+ about 80 join year 12 each year from outside. Entry requirements are minimum of seven A*to Bs at GCSE with at least a grade A in subjects to be studied at A level

Exit: A few leave at 16+ (seven per cent in 2016), usually for more vocational programmes, but far more join the school at this level. Further five per cent left at end of year 12. Around 70 per cent to Russell Group, including Oxbridge (four places in 2016), with a large swathe taking STEM subjects. Fourteen budding medics and dentists in 2016.

Money matters: It is free! There are regular voluntary oversees visits, the costs of which must put them out of the reach of some families, but these are often planned well in advance and pupils are coached in how to raise their own funds.

Remarks: One parent said to us, 'Why Queen Mary's GS? Well, why not? As Walsall residents we are fortunate to have an example of excellent education in our borough, and if your son can achieve the entry criteria it offers a great opportunity to get the best education on offer.'

Even by post-industrial West Midlands standards, Walsall is not attractive, but Queen Mary's Grammar School is a cultural oasis and powerhouse for social change in this urban sprawl. Its extensive grounds give a sense of space, and the 60s buildings are being renovated and extended. But there is a sense that the buildings are still a constraint and more flexible space such as that in the new sixth form centre is needed. It is a school with a mission to transform lives, and there is a brisk sense of purpose about every aspect, from the morning whole school assembly where the excellent headmaster's address whipped us through 'character education', before we were on to sixth formers encouraging participation in various activities and competitions that had or were taking place (good presentation skills training here), to the general focused moving around the school. Unusually, in our experience, our visit was organised entirely by members of the school council, who also run governors' visits and visits from anyone else who wants to get to know the school. The school is consciously working on the social polish so the pupils can meet their independent counterparts on an even playing field. This is a school that is raising community aspirations and deserves its growing excellent reputation.

Repton School

Linked with Foremarke Hall (Repton Preparatory School)

R

Repton, Derby DE65 6FH

Pupils: 648; 443 full boarders • Ages: 13–18 • Sixth form: 287 • C of E

Fees: Day £25,242; Boarding £34,026 pa

Tel: 01283 559222
Email: registrar@repton.org.uk
Website: www.repton.org.uk

Head: Since April 2016, Alastair Land, previously deputy head at Harrow School. First class honours in natural sciences from Cambridge; taught biology at Eton, where he also ran the CCF. Moved to Winchester as master in college and senior housemaster before joining Harrow in 2012. As well as involvement in CCF, he has directed house plays, organised and competed in endurance challenges and chaired an adventurous training committee. His wife, Madeleine, is a maths teacher; they have a young son and a newborn.

Academic matters: In the past Repton produced sound but unexceptional exam grades, but these have been well and truly been put in the shade by recent results. In 2016, 53 per cent A*/A, 82 per cent A*-B grades at A level. GCSEs strong too – 59 per cent A*/A grades. Lots of maths and French GCSEs taken a year early. Most subjects setted according to ability. Traditional teaching methods, with all pupils allocated an academic tutor to monitor progress. Year groups of 110 to 120 in years 9, 10 and 11 (or B block, A block and O block, as they're known here) and up to 150 in both lower sixth and upper sixth. Class sizes are 15 on average.

Wide choice of subjects on offer, including business studies, PE, drama and politics. Everyone does French, and keen linguists can take Spanish or German from year 9 too. Youngest also take either Latin or classical civilisation. Pupils very much encouraged to read for pleasure. Well-known names and Old Reptonains are invited to lecture pupils and give careers advice. Guests have included BBC foreign correspondent David Loyn, Holocaust survivor Freddie Knoller and diplomat and environmentalist Sir Crispin Tickell. Spectacular multi-million pound Science Priory is complete with animal centre, observatory, ecological research centre and 3D lecture theatre. Teachers' reports on academic work (effort and achievement) emailed to parents every four or five weeks, plus usual end-of-term reports too.

Learning support available in small groups or one-to-one and individual education plans for each pupil to monitor progress. Relevant information and strategies passed to subject teachers to ensure support continues in class and pupils agree that teachers go the extra mile to help them. Teachers we met seemed to have boundless energy and enthusiasm. Prep from 7 to 9pm on weekday nights (all day pupils stay till 9pm too). Youngest supervised, the rest work independently in their houses.

Games, options, the arts: Sport goes from strength to strength. Boys' main sports are football, hockey, cricket and tennis, girls main sports are hockey, netball, tennis. At the time of our visit the boys had recently won the national U18 hockey championships (they have now won it twice more) and the girls have clinched the national U18 title a record breaking nine times between 2005 and 2016. Overall, the hockey teams have won an impressive 30 national titles since 1995. Five old girls are in the current England and GB ladies' hockey squad and two were part of the team that won gold in the Rio Olympics. Football is pretty impressive too; school has strong links with local academies and several pupils are connected to professional football clubs. Cricket, tennis, and netball report similar triumphs. A clutch of county and test cricketers are regularly produced. The school regularly fields three teams per year group, sometimes five. Impressive sports facilities, including sports complex, large indoor pool, water-based and sand-based Astros, 16 outdoor tennis courts, two indoor tennis courts, squash and fives courts. CCF is compulsory for youngest pupils and then can opt to continue or choose D of E or community service.

Unusually for a school, there are three art galleries in the village, exhibiting the work of pupils as well as resident and visiting artists. Artwork is on display everywhere throughout school – a huge abstract painted by former pupil Matthew Drage hangs in pride of place in the headmaster's hall and particularly caught our eye. Money made from hiring out school artwork to local businesses goes into pot to fund foreign trips for art students – very entrepreneurial.

Music is huge, with around 250 individual instrument lessons a week. Stunning refurbished music school in former san, with 200-seat recital hall, recording studio, 16 practice rooms. Vast array of orchestras, choirs, jazz bands, string quartets etc, annual musician of the year prize and RockIt competition for budding young rock bands. Series of subscription concerts held throughout year for school and community attracts musicians of international renown. Everyone does term of drama in year 9 and some go on to take it at GCSE and A level. Plethora of productions now take place in the newly renovated auditorium, throughout school year, including house plays, lower school production and charity cabaret.

Boarding: School prides itself on being a 'seven-days-a-week boarding school' – each pupil is allowed three Saturday nights of their own choice a term at home ('privilege weekends'). This helps to ensure that the school 'doesn't empty at weekends,' says a member of staff. Weekend activities on offer, or SLOPs as they are known (Sunday leisure options) include cycling in the Peak District, paintballing, trips to Clothes Show Live etc.

The house system is integral to the school. Each house (four girls' and six boys') has resident houseparent and prides itself on having 'family atmosphere'. All pupils eat breakfast, lunch and supper in their houses. Food is cooked in-house and every pupil we talked to claimed the food in their house was the best. We were invited to lunch in a girls' house and it was one of the most delicious school lunches we've had in a long time – chicken pasta, homemade focaccia and excellent chocolate brownies. Vegetarian and gluten-free options always available too. Lunch is the most formal meal of the day, often attended by guests from within school and outside, and students are encouraged to chat and be sociable. Mealtimes also give houseparents the chance to keep an eye on whether pupils are eating enough. Youngest pupils tend to be in dorms of four, sixth formers have their own study bedrooms with wash basins. Houses also have quiet rooms for working, kitchens to make toast and pasta and mixed-age common rooms, where pupils from other houses can visit at specified times.

Background and atmosphere: On the banks of the River Trent (the head's study is in a free-standing medieval tower overlooking the river), the school is absorbed into the village of Repton rather than dominating it. Pupils are kept fit as they hurry between boarding houses up leafy lanes and classrooms, sports centre, games pitches etc. With a busy B road running through the village, Repton is by no means a sleepy idyll, but the school lends the place a certain vitality. The central part of the school is based around a 12th century Augustan priory. School founded under the will of Sir John Port, who died in 1557.

Good blend of ancient and modern architecture. Two-floor library in old priory building is breathtaking. National Literacy Trust has published report saying a third of today's students don't use their school library, but this isn't the case here. When we visited a happy group of year 9s were reading (everything from Bill Bryson to Conan Doyle) in comfy leather armchairs. Library criticised by inspectors in past but latest inspection said situation had been 'amply addressed,' with first-ever full-time librarian brought in and million-pound make-over.

Once boys only but fully co-ed since 1991 – boy/girl ratio roughly 54/46. School is big enough to create a 'buzz' and maintain standards of real quality but is small enough for everyone to know each other. Pupils and parents say it's a very friendly place and the latest ISI report specifically commented on the school's 'sense of community'.

Pastoral care, well-being and discipline: House system underpins everything at Repton. As one housemistress says: 'We are here 24/7 and I see each one of my girls every day.' Plenty of people for pupils to talk to if they need a sympathetic ear – including house prefects, matrons, houseparents, house tutors, school counsellor and chaplain. Head boy and girl plus heads of houses and raft of prefects. New pupils given a mentor, someone who has been at school for at least a year, to guide them through the early weeks. Mobile phones allowed but only at certain times of day and youngest must hand them in to prefects at night. All pupils attend chapel twice a week.

Clear school rules, with written tasks for minor breaches and detentions for more serious lapses. Meanwhile policies on drugs, drink and smoking are unambiguous. Zero tolerance on drugs – as deputy head for pastoral side of school says, 'Repton isn't a second-chance school'. Drinking and smoking both yellow-card offences. Sixth formers socialise in the JCR on Saturday nights. Any misconduct of behaviour incurs loss of privileges (or 'lopping', as it's known in Reptonese).

Uniform is compulsory and looks very smart. Dark suits for sixth formers, while boys wear blazers and ties and girls are clad in grey skirts, blazers and a V neck jumper of their own choice in a 'quiet' tone – pale pink, mauve and grey seem to be favourites. No nail varnish and minimum make-up.

Pupils and parents: A very down-to-earth, straightforward lot – polite, ultra-proud of their school and appreciative of the opportunities it gives them. Pupils come from all over – north, south and everywhere in between. Around 10 per cent from overseas. Past pupils of school include writers Christopher Isherwood and Roald Dahl and Top Gear supremo Jeremy Clarkson and gold Olympic medallists Georgie Twigg and Shona McCallin.

Entrance: Students arrive at Repton from a large number of schools. Roughly half from Repton's own prep up the road, Foremarke Hall, other half from prep schools like S Anselm's, Terra Nova, Terrington Hall, Malsis, Orwell Park and Swanbourne House. Not overly selective – director of admissions says the school doesn't state common entrance pass mark required, but in previous years it has been 50 per cent. About 30 new teenagers into sixth form each year – they need minimum of five Bs at GCSE, but preferably As in chosen A level subjects. School takes pupils with special educational needs who can cope with the curriculum – every case considered on individual merit.

Exit: Nearly all go through to sixth form. Over 60 per cent of sixth formers to top universities; seven to Oxbridge in 2016. Others to eg Durham, Edinburgh, St Andrews, UCL, Warwick and York and top American universities including Harvard. Each year a number of pupils are awarded athlete scholarships to American universities for tennis, football and hockey.

Money matters: Range of scholarships on offer – academic, music, art, DT, drama, ICT, sport and all-rounder. Also Foremarke scholarships, given to children who want to transfer to Foremarke Hall for years 7 and 8 and then on to Repton.

Remarks: Repton is definitely on a roll. A happy school that offers an all-round education in the wilds of Derbyshire. It gives students time to be themselves, whilst opening their minds and nurturing their interests and enthusiasms. As the head girl told us: 'I'll be very sad to leave here. It's a special place.'

The Royal Hospital School

Holbrook, Ipswich, Suffolk IP9 2RX

Pupils: 750; 450 full/weekly boarders • Ages: 11–18 • Sixth form: 243 • C of E

Fees: Day £14,535 – £15,900; Boarding £19,998 – £29,995 pa

Tel: 01473 326200
Email: admissions@royalhospitalschool.org
Website: www.royalhospitalschool.org

Headmaster: Since January 2016, Simon Lockyer, previously second master at Portsmouth Grammar. Has also been housemaster and head of department at Wellington College. The son of a naval officer, Simon was educated at Blundell's School, Devon, on a military bursary after which he went on to gain a BSc in microbiology at Newcastle, a PGCE at Cambridge and a masters at Buckingham. His first teaching appointment was at Bishop's Stortford High School in Hertfordshire. He is married to Abigail, who grew up in Suffolk, and they have three young children.

Academic matters: Sits comfortably between the highly selective Ipswich schools and the maintained grammar schools over the county border. The introduction of day pupils and their increasing numbers mean that academic achievement is rising across the curriculum. In 2016, 38 per cent of GCSE grades were A*/A. Pupils have noticed the increased rigour of the timetable, bemoaning that 'he stopped games on two afternoons and we have to do science and languages instead'; not strictly the case, though games have been moved to an after-school slot one afternoon a week to make way for lessons. A modern language is compulsory up to GCSE. All year 7s now have taster lessons in German, Spanish and Latin before selecting one, in addition to French.

Over 25 subjects offered at A level; maths and the sciences very popular. Sixth form purely academic; in addition to A levels, students follow the sixth form enrichment programme, which provides an opportunity to teach useful skills and gain extra qualifications; popular topics include ancient Greek, law, sports leadership training and a handy-sounding course, the seven habits of highly effective people. In 2016, 21 per cent A*/A grades, 49 per cent A*-B.

School has creditable results considering wide ability range, which includes some 80 overseas pupils for whom English is a second language (also responsible for stunning results in Chinese and Russian). Overseas centre can help them gain a good grasp of English. Over 100 have identified specific educational needs, but the majority of these are mild, and require only class-based support. More serious problems with literacy and numeracy, often a result of Forces families having a disrupted education, are given extra help from the start. Timetabled support can take the place of learning a second language. Mobile learning programme is seeing pupils issued with tablet computers.

Games, options, the arts: Development of indoor sports facilities including largest climbing wall in the region, new strength and conditioning and fitness suites, martial arts studio and refurbished sports hall. Also launch of Graham Napier Cricket Academy.

A big part of the school's attraction is the exceptional range of sports and activities. Games on three afternoons; all the seasonal team sports, and though not an elite sporting school, the variety is a big plus: rock climbing, squash, shooting and kickboxing a glimpse of the 70 plus activities. 'We never have nothing to do,' said one pupil, and it is definitely not for lazybones. Gigantic sports hall (or gymnasium), a separate enormous, indoor pool in another vast building and, if you've any energy left, 96 acres of playing fields.

But sailing remains key activity, with undreamed of opportunities for learning the craft and progressing in a sport that is often ruled out for many on grounds of cost. All year 7s receive a full week's instruction: 'We want to find ability among those who are not "dynastic" sailors,' says the RYA (Royal Yachting Association) instructor. Over 100 take to sailing seriously, on the water three or four times a week in one of a fleet including 60 dinghies – from beginners' boats to Olympic classe – four Cornish shrimpers and four powerboats – all replaced every three years. The beauty of the school is the location, overlooking the river Stour and near the Alton reservoir – no trek in a minibus, and 'nothing but the extremes of cold stop us sailing'. Many gain RYA qualifications, enter sailing competitions and have a recreation for life; Sailing Scholars get individual tuition from RYA advanced instructors. School teams compete successfully and there are sailing trips to the Med and further afield every year.

Mouth-watering new music school opened by John Rutter, who is patron of the school's annual concert programme, performed by home-grown and professional performers. Recitals hall with spectacular acoustics complete with two grand pianos, 10 others in practice rooms, all brand new and all Bechsteins and Faziolis (Rolls Royce in pianos). Composition suites bursting with equipment. Some 50 per cent learn an instrument; a plethora of orchestras, bands, choirs and ensembles to join. Pupils in the marching band that accompanies Divisions, the regular pupil parades, receive free music tuition.

Art, photography, graphics and product design all housed in separate building with large permanent display area with gallery for pupils' work. A separate print room (formerly manual training centre) harks back to earlier times, and there is serious encouragement for all craft and design skills, with many pupils working on projects outside class time.

Every spare moment filled with activities. Four sections of CCF: royal marines, navy, army, air force compulsory in years 9 and 10, but many continue: 'It encourages leadership and responsibility,' we heard from pupils as well as parents. D of E popular at all stages up to gold. Car maintenance, medieval society, Scottish dancing – choices for all tastes.

Boarding: Boarding houses are comfortable, with well-planned central areas for table tennis, pool and computers, huge kitchens for making snacks (all pupils have tuck lockers) and bedrooms, single or shared, are en suite. TV room stuffed with leather sofas said to be the least used space (though it was the housemaster saying so). The infirmary is a 26 bedded medical centre with a full time nurse; there's a school doctor and dentist (NHS), and a counsellor who can be seen confidentially.

Background and atmosphere: Long, proud association with Royal Navy and seafarers gives a distinctive feel to this large co-educational boarding and day school, and many material benefits. The Royal Hospital School was founded in the early 18th century at Greenwich to educate boys for service in the navy. Moved to its present site in the 1930s, when school received a bequest from the estate at Holbrook together with a generous endowment. The old school building is now the National Maritime Museum. The current buildings and layout, on a grand scale, are inspired by the original work by Christopher Wren at Greenwich. The pillared entrance, a massive hall with columns, marble floors and oil paintings, is awe-inspiring and regarded by pupils with affection and pride. The grounds, with wide promenades and parade ground, have the well-kept air of a military establishment, but pupils revel in the space, the vista of the river Stour and the tangible connection to naval history.

Became co-educational in 1991. The phased withdrawal of naval funding, begun in 2005, came with a parting present of £18 million for building projects and a general sprucing up. Day pupils were introduced to broaden the intake and make up the financial shortfall, but school retains the naval connection. Pupils all use navy speak, such as Stations, Mess, and Civvies, and regular parades or Divisions are a regular part of school life. Saturday morning hymn singing in school chapel is a feature and not seen as an imposition. 'It's fun, who doesn't enjoy singing?' say pupils. 'They sometimes grumble, but generally enjoy the parades,' we were told by a parent. 'It is one of those bonding experiences looked back on with affection'.

Pastoral care, well-being and discipline: Friendly house system counteracts the (possibly) daunting size and scale of the school, and we heard nothing but praise. 'Excellent support in the house, matron was key in helping my child over a bout of homesickness'; 'Matron does a lot more than simply dole out medicine'; 'Staff seem extraordinarily available.' Cries of approval (pupils as well as parents) for disciplined atmosphere and several parents spoke of lives being transformed by all that's on offer. 'Motivation is more likely in school work if they are interested and busy out of the classroom.' Food neither praised or criticised; we saw hearty fare, perhaps not enough in the salad line. Day pupils are increasing in number and fit in to the house system, with many remaining well into the evening to take advantage of everything going on.

Older pupils allowed out at weekends, but taxi fare and trek to Ipswich dowse enthusiasm, especially as school operates The Nelson Arm (supervised bar) discos and other events. By the end, a few chafe at restrictions but most think the way things work is fair, and they all know what the position is on banned substances (expulsion) and relationships (courting allowed but strictly outside lesson time). For many there is never a dull moment – 'I can't imagine having more fun at university' – but quieter types fit in just as well.

Pupils and parents: At present the majority of pupils are boarders, of which 15 per cent are foreign nationals, mostly Chinese and German, with a sprinkling of other Europeans. Day pupils largely drawn from Suffolk/north Essex. About a third have a naval background (grandfathers count) and it is unsnobbish. Day pupil numbers likely to increase as naval boarding subsidy is withdrawn. Parents speak highly of school's social mix: 'He rubs shoulders with pupils from all backgrounds and this experience will be useful all his life'; 'There is no arrogance or sense of entitlement.' Great sense of ease and camaraderie between staff and pupils but courtesy insisted on. Pupils appear confident, open and friendly.

Entrance: The majority enter at 11 via entrance tests in maths, English and verbal reasoning. At 13 plus another 30-40, respectable common entrance performance needed, and there is another influx in the sixth form. A reference from the current school is essential and all prospective pupils have an interview with the head.

Exit: Around 20 per cent leave after GCSEs, mostly to sixth form colleges, the majority after A level for higher education. A wide choice of subjects and institutions chosen; not an Oxbridge factory – though three places in 2016, plus four medics – but heavyweight universities well represented. Significant numbers take a gap year, often for travel and following courses abroad.

Money matters: Complex range of awards and bursaries. School offers a limited number of academic, sporting, drama, music, art and sailing scholarships each year. The value of the award is at the discretion of the headmaster and can be topped up with a bursary. Bursaries of up to 100 per cent of fees, depending on parental means, and siblings get a 15 per cent discount. Forces families claiming the continuity of education allowance (CEA) are also eligible for discounted fees. Greenwich hospital bursaries for the children of seafarers also available, depending on family income.

Remarks: Long association with Royal Navy brings privilege and a sense of service. Would suit the socially outgoing, give-it-a-go types, especially sailors. Excellent full boarding provision.

Rugby School

Rugby, Warwickshire CV22 5EH

Pupils: 807; 650 boarders • Ages: 11–18; 13–18 from 2018 (boarding from 13) • Sixth form: 360 • C of E

Fees: Day £21,378; Boarding £34,071 pa

Tel: 01788 556216
Email: enquiries@rugbyschool.co.uk
Website: www.rugbyschool.co.uk

Headmaster: Since 2014, Peter Green MA PGCE (early 50s), previously head of Ardingly. Educated at St Joseph's College, Dumfries, then University of Edinburgh, where he read geography. Although he comes from a family of lawyers and judges he always wanted to be a teacher. Studied for Cert Ed in religious studies and PGCE at St Andrew's Foundation for Catholic Teacher Education (now part of the University of Glasgow). First job was at an inner-city comprehensive in the Gorbals. He taught at St Olave's Grammar in Orpington and then Strathallan before moving to Uppingham, where he was head of geography, a housemaster and introduced all-rounder scholarships. Spent five years as lay second master of Ampleforth, followed by seven years as head of Ardingly College, where numbers rose from 720 to 950 under his watch.

A vastly experienced and engaging head (wearing fetching bright pink socks when we visited), he talks fast, sensibly and enthusiastically and is full of good tales and ideas. He says 'the whole person is the whole point of education at Rugby', and while this isn't a unique declaration for a head he believes Rugby is 'uniquely placed to make the claim.' Doesn't teach these days – 'I'd sack myself,' he jokes – but spends as much time as he can talking to pupils and staff and observing lessons. On the day we met he arrived hotfoot from discussing Lake District geomorphology with the youngest pupils in the school.

He's enjoying his job at Rugby – 'we have fantastic children here and it's a wonderful environment to work in,' he says. He finds the school's history a huge inspiration but emphasises that while Rugby is 'traditional,' it isn't 'traditionalist.' Delights in the fact that he's sitting in Dr Thomas Arnold's study – with a portrait of the great man, Arnold's own (surprisingly small) desk, a hidden key rack above the fireplace and the spiral staircase in the corner that pupils used if they wanted to talk to him privately.

The head says that Rugby is 'phenomenally strong' but is always looking for ways to improve – whether it's blended learning, flipped classrooms, character development, teaching tolerance and respect or engaging pupils in STEAM (science, technology, engineering, arts and maths) subjects. He's particularly proud of the fact that there isn't a Rugby type. 'The duckbilled platypus and the behemoth can be equally at home at Rugby School,' he says. Like his predecessor (Westminster head Patrick Derham), he wants Rugby to remain as inclusive as possible. The Arnold Foundation offers 100 per cent funded boarding places to pupils whose parents are unable to afford the fees and since 2003 well over 100 youngsters have benefited from the scheme.

Wife Brenda is an English and learning support teacher at Rugby. They have two children, a son who has just finished university and a daughter who has just started. In his spare time he enjoys reading, opera and the opportunity 'to pray and be silent.'

Academic matters: Rugby has a tradition of innovation – it was, for instance, the first school in the country to teach science as part of the school curriculum in the 1850s – and this continues apace. The school offers the IGCSE in most subjects and A levels in 29 subjects (plus the Pre-U in physics, chemistry, biology and art and design). Around 50 students a year take the Extended Project Qualification (EPQ), which was developed at Rugby via a pilot qualification called Perspectives in Science and involves an extended piece of research on a topic they choose themselves.

In 2016 nearly 60 per cent A*/A grades at A level/Pre-U. Fifty-one per cent A* and 81 per cent A*/A at GCSE. 'The head is definitely on an academic mission,' a parent told us. French, German and Spanish offered at GCSE and A level, with exchange trips to Montpellier, Vienna, Madrid. Wonderful new language block, with 11 classrooms, two language labs and computers and software in every language. Sixth formers can study an ab initio language, such as Russian or Japanese. Pupils also write, edit and code their own online magazine, Page Polyglotte.

Most do three separate sciences at GCSE. The sciences are housed in an imaginatively refurbished Victorian building, with lecture theatre, seminar rooms and labs. Learning development department offers support for those who need it (for EAL as well as specific learning difficulties), either one-to-one or in small groups. Enrichment programme for all pupils, with additional weekly sessions for academic scholars (140 currently). All pupils have their own laptops, supplied by school and charged to parents.

Teachers are skilled and experienced. Many pursue their own academic research and the school is producing its own document on approaches to teaching and learning at Rugby. School runs parallel sets (including two top sets) in English, maths and the sciences.

Games, options, the arts: Rugby has overseen a huge investment in sports facilities in recent years. It has the only listed gym in the world and, of course, the famous School Close, where William Webb Ellis first ran with the ball in 1823 and invented the game of rugby football. Members of the 1st XV are very proud to play on it, along with leading players and teams who visit from all over the world. More than 200 TV crews pitched up to film at Rugby ahead of the 2015 World Cup and the school featured in the opening ceremony (Prince Harry and Jonny Wilkinson had cameo roles in a video shot at the school). Immaculately maintained playing fields, with 13 rugby pitches and five cricket squares. Locals use school's three Astroturfs, tennis courts and 25-metre indoor pool.

Sports centre, with squash courts, polo pitches and fitness centre. Boys play rugby, hockey, soccer, cricket, tennis and athletics while girls' main sports are hockey, netball, tennis, rounders and athletics. Other sports include badminton, fives, rackets, basketball, fencing, gymnastics, tai chi, pilates, dance, aerobics, riding, polo, clay pigeon shooting, sailing and triathlon. One girl is the current under-19 British champion in wakeboarding. Huge number of sports tours – recent expeditions include hockey and netball to Australia and Singapore, rugby to Japan and Canada and cricket to Sri Lanka and Dubai.

Music department has more than 40 practice rooms, a recording studio and small concert hall. Music is magical, with masses of orchestras, choirs, ensembles and rock bands. Total of 600 music lessons a week. An impressive variety of drama productions at school's fully equipped theatre. Pupils stage a major school play and musical every year, plus a house drama season and annual arts festival. Art, design and photography flourishing and a third of sixth formers study related subjects at art school or university. Lewis Gallery, a light, airy space cleverly converted from old squash courts, runs programme of exhibitions by pupils and outside artists.

Boarding: Sixteen houses in total – eight for boys, seven for girls, plus Marshall House, a co-ed house for year 7 and 8 boys and girls (all day pupils), which will close in 2018 and is no longer accepting applications. Each boarding house has up to 60 pupils and the furthest is no more is than a 10-minute walk from the heart of the school. We visited soon after the school's annual pushcart race, hotly contested by all. The victorious house had a jaunty skull and crossbones flag fluttering from a top window.

Pupils eat breakfast, lunch and supper in their own houses – 'it encourages a real sense of community,' a parent told us. Food gets the thumbs up and there's plenty of it, including snacks in morning and afternoon breaks and in the evening. In a recent move, all but the sixth formers hand in their phones, tablets and laptops before bed each night. The new rule has brought a few grumbles from pupils, 'but nothing but parental support,' said a housemaster.

Houses are very wholesome. The boys' houses used to be less ritzy but are in the process of being upgraded. A house we visited boasted a cinema room, neat as a pin laundry, tuck shop (the 'stodge' in Rugby-speak) and individual studies for all. Each year group has their own common room and dorms vary from singles for sixth-formers to dorms of four to six for younger pupils. 'Your house is your home,' one boy declared.

Housemasters and housemistresses all live in (many with their own families) and see pupils as they come and go during the day. Youngest have to be back in houses by 9.30pm (lights out half an hour later), while sixth-formers return by 10.15pm (they don't have to be in their rooms till 11pm, though). Tutors are house-based and see their tutees formally at least twice a week, as well as when they're on duty.

Background and atmosphere: Founded as a grammar school in 1567 by Lawrence Sheriff, purveyor of spices to Elizabeth I. Moved to its present site in the centre of Rugby 200 years later. Home of the famous Dr Arnold and immortalised in Tom Brown's Schooldays. With its red-brick, Victorian schoolhouses the site feels rather like north Oxford. Pupils like being based in a town, close to shops and cafés. One told us: 'You get a sense of the real world. We aren't in a bubble.'

Glorious Victorian library, the Temple Reading Room, provides a quiet, inspiring place to work. Pupils attend chapel three mornings a week and on Sundays. Chapel – Thomas Arnold is buried beneath chancel steps – is majestic and awe-inspiring, with walls adorned with tablets in memory of famous Rugbeian writers like Lewis Carroll and Rupert Brooke. School chaplain describes the chapel as 'the base' of the school and pupils say it's a place where the whole school sings its heart out.

School went fully co-ed in 1993 and boy/girl ratio is now 55/45. All wear smart uniform for lessons. Girls sport distinctive ankle-length grey skirts, now redesigned so they can run in them. Girls say they really like their skirts – they suit everyone and you can wear woolly tights and leggings underneath to keep warm in winter, they told us. The only gripe from boys is that their tweed jackets get 'a bit smelly' in the rain. Prefects – or levée as they are known – wear different ties and gold buttons on dark blazers. Four buttons for heads of school (boy and girl), three for heads of house and two for school prefects – a simple and subtle way to work out exactly who's who.

The sixth form has impressive new Collingwood Centre, housed in a former Catholic secondary school on the edge of the site. Careers, economics, philosophy, business studies, art history, PE and politics departments are based there (politics classroom is set up as a mock House of Commons, even down to the green leather seats) and centre is used for studying, socialising and school events. There's also the Saturday evening Crescent Club, where sixth formers are allowed a maximum of two drinks (wine or beer) with food.

Pastoral care, well-being and discipline: School has put an enormous amount of time and effort into its pastoral care. It is also one of 10 schools across the UK chosen to work with the PSHE Association on the development of a new character curriculum, which aims to develop skills and attributes like motivation and resilience.

Each pupil is given a copy of the school's Guidelines for Life, which covers everything from its anti-bullying policy to relationships and where and when boys and girls can be in their free time. Policies on smoking, alcohol and drugs all clearly laid out. Expulsions are few and far between – two in the last five years. Public displays of affection (PDAs) between pupils banned – 'couples must behave in a way which would be appropriate if a member of staff were in the room,' says the school.

A host of opportunities for pupils to make sure their views are heard. 'Councils are huge here,' declared the head boy. He's right – there's a social council, music council, academic council, sports council and changes council. School is good at picking up on problems before they escalate. 'There are lots of people looking out for them,' a teacher told us. Cleaners spot things and chefs notice if a pupil hasn't eaten much at lunch.

Pupils and parents: Pupils come from all over, many from London, Oxford or locations within two hours' driving distance. Around 10 per cent international students. Parents are very supportive of the school. Many are sons and daughters of Rugby alumni and one described pupils as 'unpretentious, natural, spontaneous, courteous, tolerant and unstuffy.' Illustrious former pupils include Rupert Brooke (a girls' house is named after him), Lewis Carroll, Robert Hardy, Tom King, Salman Rushdie, AN Wilson and Anthony Horowitz. Not forgetting, of course, Harry Flashman and Tom Brown.

Entrance: No more 11+ admissions. Local children can sit exams in year 6 for deferred entry in year 9. Others sit aptitude pre-test and interview in year 7. CE pass mark is 55 per cent but average is higher. Boys and girls come from more than 300 feeder schools across the country, including The Dragon, Bilton Grange, Packwood Haugh and S Anselm's.

Around 40 new pupils (mostly girls, but some boys) join in the sixth form. UK candidates need at least three As and three Bs at GCSE. They sit sixth form entrance exams and have a house interview. Potential scholars are invited back at a later date for scholarship interviews. Keen competition for sixth form places.

Exit: Virtually all to university – around 94 per cent head to Russell Group universities most years. Bath, Bristol, Durham, Edinburgh, Leeds, Manchester, Newcastle and UCL are popular choices. On average, 10 to 15 Oxbridge places a year; 12 in 2016, with four others off to US/Canada, plus three medics and a vet. Gap years 'less fashionable' than previously and interest in US universities is growing.

Money matters: Complex range of bursaries and awards. School offers academic, music, drama, art, DT, computing and sport scholarships – it led the way in 2003 by limiting scholarships to 10 per cent of the school fees, although this can be augmented to 100 per cent if family need can be shown through a means test. Bursaries of up to 100 per cent of the fees, depending on parental means.

Remarks: This famous public school takes huge pride in its history and traditions – and quite right too – but it is genuinely innovative and forward thinking, especially when it comes to academic matters. Boarding houses have a real sense of community, pupils are welcoming and unpretentious and facilities are second to none.

S. Anselm's School

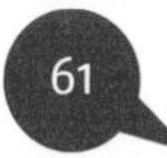

S. Anselm's Preparatory School, Bakewell, Derbyshire DE45 1DP

Pupils: 230; 31 full, 4 weekly, 30 flexi boarders • Ages: 3–13 (boarders from year 3)

Fees: Day £9,600 – £18,150; Boarding £22,500 pa

Tel: 01629 812734
Email: headmaster@anselms.co.uk
Website: www.sanselms.co.uk

Headmaster: Since 2012, Mr Peter Phillips. Head of Cundall Manor in Yorkshire for 13 years; built up school from around 80 to some 400 pupils. Started as a surveyor before seeing the light and becoming an English teacher. Head of English at Yardley Court and Dulwich College then director of studies at Cargilfield in Edinburgh.

A tall man, by any standards, he does not belong to the pinstriped, lapel-tugging, bullfrog school of heads. He is a thinker, a man of intelligence and vision, of great kindness, strong-minded and determined, and not easily swayed. Above all, he is dedicated to the welfare of the pupils. He does not like being pushed about by autocracy, but will listen for hours to children's worries and concerns. Some parents have complained that he is something of a recluse, that he doesn't come out to see them. The pupils we met – and they were marvellously forthcoming and natural – said how much they like him because he takes such a keen interest in them, makes a fuss of them when they are sent by their teachers to show him a good piece of work, and so obviously cares about them.

Though he denies being a Luddite, he knows nothing of computers and announced early on in his time at S Anselm's that he did not do emails but was always willing to talk. All emails go through his wife, Sarah, who has a delightfully zany sense of humour and helps look after the girls in the evening. He teaches 18 lessons a week and referees some matches. Pupils enjoy his lessons and he enjoys the contact.

He has encouraged some of the older staff to leave, causing some disquiet among a few parents and indignation from those staff. The overall feeling amongst the parents we talked to was a sadness that even teachers have to move on, but an acceptance of the inevitability. This has not been a St Bartholomew's Day Massacre of the not-so-innocent over-50s: he has displayed considerable wisdom in retaining some of the finest teachers on merit, reputation and – importantly – a willingness to accept his enlarged expectations. One experienced teacher said that due to the new demands of helping at weekends she now knew the pupils better.

Perhaps most exciting has been the arrival of a cohort of young, lively, talented and dedicated staff. Many of them followed Mr Phillips, along with children and families, from Cundal Manor. Their arrival caused much excitement among the parents and children, and they are a most delightful and engaging group. Parents queued up to tell us of the new buzz in the school, the energy and drive, the sense of purpose and fun, the fresh air. Even we could feel it. When we wandered out during break and saw the running, the chasing, the laughter, the sense of timeless delight, it felt as if we had taken a detour with Thomas Traherne: 'Boys and girls tumbling in the street, and playing, were moving jewels. I knew not that they were born or should die; but all things abided eternally as they were in their proper places.'

Mr Phillips has given up the rather grand and slightly intimidating study of his predecessors, and now inhabits a smaller but delightful room overlooking the beautiful gardens. As the visitor glances around he sees a rugby ball in the (unlit) fireplace, a set of bagpipes on a table, a model steam train made by one of the science masters (an inspirational teacher whose lesson we had observed earlier), and a pile of papers. No badges or hints of office, no pomposity or sense of importance. The same is true of the website. Search as you may, you will not find one of those proprietorial messages from a head looking like a stockbroker or as if they were fresh from a stylish garden party, urging you with false modesty and marketing acumen to come and visit. With a dash of daring, S Anselm's has done away with all mentions of the head and doesn't have a prospectus. 'The school belongs to, and exists for, the children.' You'll only find the head's name on the copy of the recent inspection report, and pretty good it was. He doesn't do swank nor is he interested in suits and tailors. He greeted us in bright, pinky-red trousers and sweater.

Entrance: Mostly into the nursery and pre-prep, which is superbly run with first class teaching, according to happy parents. The overall head of the pre-prep is 'wonderful' and children in the prep look back with fondness and an early whiff of nostalgia. But anyone may apply at any stage if there is room. One parent told us with huge appreciation of how her son, joining as a boarder a little later than the main group when the family moved up from London, had been welcomed with kindness and consideration by boys and housemaster, and had settled in very quickly.

Exit: The school has an excellent reputation for scholarships, achieved through excellent free-range teaching rather than force-feeding. Parents talk of the way teachers assess their pupils realistically and sensitively. A few parents, of course, have unrealistic demands and expectations, but the head is good at nudging them towards greater reality, even though that doesn't always endear him. Public school heads said they appreciate the lively, inquisitive approach of Anselmians, their willingness to get stuck in and their articulate courtesy and friendliness. Varying numbers to Eton, Harrow, Shrewsbury, Oundle, Fettes, Uppingham, Winchester, Downe House, Repton and Malvern.

School has expanded to secondary level: S Anselm's College (day only) opened with year 9 in September 2015 on the same site.

Remarks: The school has been through a turbulent period over the last five years. Numbers dropped, and morale amongst many parents and staff dipped, and they told us that a few years ago they were very worried. With the arrival of fresh blood and new energies, numbers and morale are looking up, with a doubling of intake into reception and increased numbers in the main school.

Mr Phillips has restructured the timetable in the junior prep. English and maths is the staple diet in the morning, 'when the children are at their most alert', with other subjects in the afternoon. We listened to an exciting and challenging science lesson. When asked to describe their teacher, pupils said, 'distinctive, epic, fun, super, funny and heroic.' They were still yelling out adjectives as we left the room. Art teacher wearing spectacularly bright trousers; 'I love getting messy in art,' said one enthusiastic painter with rainbow coloured hands and face. Excellent artwork everywhere, not just in the large-windowed studio. We saw groups of young Romans planning a three course dinner which included stuffed doormice. They were off to Chester soon to explore all things Roman there. 'Don't mess with this man,' said our guides as we entered the classroom of a gentle-looking man. 'He teaches karate.' A woman was teaching the value of a sensible diet in a brilliant lesson incorporating geography, chemistry, history, common sense and health.

Another of the head's ideas is for the whole school to share a topic and approach it from all angles. When we visited it was lighthouses, so there were pictures of lighthouses everywhere, calculations of light travelling, weather maps etc. Teachers described the excitement of approaching a topic right across the school from the youngest to the oldest, the way that seems to unite the pupils in a common aim, enabling them to share and exchange knowledge. A visit to a Northumberland lighthouse involved camping: the buzz, the fun and the almost unnoticed accumulation of knowledge.

Saturday mornings are voluntary up to year 6, but the take-up is enthusiastic. There is the excitement of starting to learn Spanish, and Latin and Greek are, in the words of one distinguished exponent, 'full on'.

Terrific facilities include a well-designed music block where we watched children rehearsing for an arts evening. About 90 per cent of them learn an instrument. The wonderful sports hall is, perhaps, even slightly improved following the recent fire during the winter holidays. The library is being extended and improved, a proud 10 year old librarian told us. Now there are plans for a real farm with real animals and the real hard work that goes with it, and a domestic science building.

Boarding facilities are excellent and improving all the time. In fact, under the new 'amazing and seriously mad' master in charge of boarding, according to parents and children, it is becoming ever more popular. Weekends are action packed and hugely enjoyed. 'He doesn't want to come home,' one parent told us, and talking of home, not long ago a group went up to Sheffield to help with the Archer Project. On that occasion it took the form of sleeping on cardboard on the streets in the rain with some young homeless people and some hardy members of staff. A thought-provoking experience. 'Boarding is just the greatest fun!' children said to us over and over again.

These feelings of excitement, pleasure and happiness seem to permeate right through the school – including the gardeners and maintenance staff and the charming and friendly cooks. (We had the most delicious lunch of roast pork and all the trimmings.) All of them are, of course, vitally important contributors to the overall happiness and smooth running of the school.

No doubt the excellent food contributes to the success of S Anselm's sport, which is taken seriously and played with zest and skill. County players abound in all areas, and there is huge excitement, though not at the expense of academic work. Or so they say.

S Anselm's celebrated its 125th anniversary with an elegantly produced book, with a forward signed by The Duchess of Devonshire. In it the writer comments on the founder's choice of motto : 'Esse Quam Videri......to be and not to seem to be'. It's a wonderful motto extolling the virtues of honesty and, to use that overworked word, transparency. Several people have suggested to us that Mr Phillips fits the message behind that motto. He may not be universally popular – people who need to make changes rarely are – but he is now presiding over a deeply happy school with parents falling over themselves to tell us how pleased they are with the current set up. Such bubbling enthusiasm is rare.

St Faith's

Linked with The Leys School

Trumpington Road, Cambridge, Cambridgeshire CB2 8AG

Pupils: 535 • Ages: 4–13

Fees: £11,865 – £14,955 pa

Tel: 01223 352073
Email: admissions@stfaiths.co.uk
Website: www.stfaiths.co.uk

Headmaster: Since 2011, Mr Nigel Helliwell BEd MA (London), previously head of Brentwood Prep for six years. Began his career teaching maths and PE at Ilkley Grammar School in Yorkshire, then moved to preps in East Anglia and south London. A qualified independent schools' inspector (sets a lot of store by 'lockers and loos' – St Faith's are exemplary) and an accomplished sportsman, having played rugby and cricket at county level. Married to Jane, who used to be a senior manager in a housing association and now enjoys helping the pupils with their reading and cheering from the touchline. They have one son and an Irish jack russell. Head eats with the children daily and personally hand-delivers birthday cards (there was one in his pocket on our tour). Has made a quiet impact – though, as he says, the challenge was only to lift the school further into the stratosphere. However, the 'subtle improvements' have not gone unappreciated by parents who have noted that his communication with them is now more frequent and that there's a useful parents' handbook, improved website and a hard copy calendar as well as electronic to keep all in the loop. Higher standards of appearance and manners – 'so important in the world of work today,' he says – have also gone down well, as has his wise advice on potential next schools, born out of diligent personal research. 'Mr Helliwell has suggested senior schools for my son that were not even on my radar, yet they have proved to be spot on,' said one mother.

Head is complemented by a hands-on bursar who is keen to keep the campus shipshape and parents particularly praise his marshalling of the new 'drop-off zone', arranged in collaboration with school's neighbours in the interest of good relations and less stressful mornings.

Entrance: Strong demand for places so names on the waiting list as soon as possible advised. Entry to pre-prep is offered by the head after a parental visit and a meeting with the child at their nursery. For all other years there are assessments in English and maths. Sibling policy gives priority on the waiting list.

Exit: About half to The Leys – otherwise to eg the Perse schools, Uppingham, King's Ely, St Mary's, Oakham, Felsted. Past pupils include Maynard Keynes, Christopher Cockerell (inventor of the Hovercraft), Sir John Tusa and England rugby player Alex Goode.

Remarks: Head's aspiration is to develop St Faith's national profile to be similar to that of Oxford's Dragon School and – minus the boarding – it's a dead cert, thanks to a child-centred educational philosophy that turns out sparky individuals with high all-round expectations and the skills to meet them.

The caps are gone but the 'distinctive' red, black and white striped blazers remain – rather Marmite. St Faith's opened in 1884 as a boys' school (girls joined in 1995). It shares the same Methodist foundation as The Leys and lives in a mixture of buildings on the opposite side of Trumpington Road, from the comfortable traditional to the buzzy contemporary. On the deceptively spacious site, behind a quirky ironwork fence designed by a local artisan, pre-preppers are accommodated in superb new edifices whose child-friendly architecture won a national design award. Inside, curvy walls, brightly coloured floors and cartoon doors make it a fun learning environment for the children – and staff, we imagine. Certainly a lively phonics lesson was in progress when we visited – year 1s having a blast with an enthusiastic male teacher – 40 per cent of the teaching staff are men and there's a healthy range of ages. 'The teachers show immense enthusiasm for the individual child,' said a parent. 'They constantly strive to find out who your child is and what makes them tick.'

All three 'Foundation' (reception) classrooms open onto an outdoor decked area and tinies have their own adventure playground, secluded from the older pupils' more traditional but no less well-equipped domain, which stretches across the site. Three classes of 14 children in pre-prep, with average of 16 children per class all through the school and a teaching assistant in every one; around 40 per cent girls. Classes are arranged in houses and there is a 'strong family feel,' say parents. Whole school assembly weekly, but every child has four assemblies in various permutations. All fit in the hall, which is complete with drop-down projector screens and professional stage lighting and sound for the many productions.

Pyramid educational philosophy here – school does well for all but can really extend those at the top, encouraging them to achieve at a national level. One of the head's major changes so far has been to extend lesson times from 30 to 50 minutes with a five-minute changeover – allows pupils to engage more deeply with their work. Reporting to parents has also been tightened – now grades for attainment as well as effort every half term for 7+. Parents' evenings are formal in the first term of the year and followed by 'tutor surgeries' in the other two. Academic achievement is generally well above the national average, although a minority of children, including learners with difficulties and/or disabilities (LDD) and any with special educational needs (SEN), are aided by the friendly learning support unit.

Very inclusive ethos – 'responsibility is given to all, not just the select few,' says head. All top year pupils are prefects and there is a ladder of leadership skills from a young age. So much so that this year all four heads of school at The Leys, Perse and Stephen Perse Foundation are Old Fidelians. Regularly two dozen scholarships a year to good senior schools – half academic and the rest a mixture of art, drama, music and sport – reflecting the high level of attainment across the board.

Languages are a way of life – doors, windows, books and even the head's office are labelled in Espagnol and the school is recognised by the Spanish embassy as being in the top 10 in the country for teaching of the language. Year 4 drama production is all in Spanish – 'the language is totally integrated,' says head. Latin from age 9, French from 11, Greek for high-flyers in year 8 and Cambridge University students teach ancient Greek. Trip to Pompeii is popular. School really on the button with computer science – out with the ICT and in with a new head of digital learning, who brings programming to children aged 9 plus, with general keyboard and communications skills for those younger. Everyone from year 3 up has an hour of engineering each week.

'It's easy to judge the quality of sport by the scoreline,' says head. 'Music, art and drama are less easy to rate but we have a lot of success.' Professional artist works full-time alongside the teacher, advising, inspiring and also working on his own commissions. Pupil artwork on display could be mistaken for GCSE. All over the age of 7 are treated to DT in the best-equipped workshops we've ever seen in a prep – vast doors allow huge pieces of professional machinery to be wheeled in and out. Results are impressive and scholarships are won. School hosts the IAPS national DT conference. Eco-garden at the front of the school, designed by pupils in a fellow's memory, is a well-considered place for quiet contemplation. Director of music is ex-King's College and although all levels of talent are appreciated, the most gifted do well and include members of the National Youth Orchestra and regional choirs. Superb music rooms double as a performance space and there are banks of Apple Macs equipped with music tech software, used by everyone over the age of 4.

Indeed, sport is a real strength, with seemingly invincible teams and individuals in most disciplines, but all have a chance to represent the school in teams A-D. Good acreage of playing fields a minute's walk across the road, including the usual pitches and two Astros, used by all over the age of 9 twice a week, plus clubs. 'Main sporting competition is now national,' says head. New £3m – from school's own funds – sports hall hosts regional and national competitions.

All aged over 7 are welcome in the library any time and it stays open after school for prep and reading. School day finishes at 3.40pm but optional (and mostly free) activities until 5pm. All-roundedness is encouraged and a surprising amount can be shoehorned into the school day – 'our sports mad boys have also been able to learn to play musical instruments to a high level, with minimal conflict,' reported a parent; 'my children are never bored,' said another. Family breakfast from 7.15am is a very popular option – a chance for parents to catch up with the kids, eat a hearty full English and avoid the worst of the city traffic. Lunch is three hot options as well as sandwiches, a salad bar and choice of puddings and fruit – all you can eat.

St Hugh's School (Woodhall Spa)

Cromwell Avenue, Woodhall Spa, Lincolnshire LN10 6TQ

Pupils: 181; 10 full, 60 weekly/flexi boarders • Ages: 2–13 • C of E

Fees: Day £8,535 – £14,349; Boarding £19,527 pa

Tel: 01526 352169
Email: office@st-hughs.lincs.sch.uk
Website: www.st-hughs.lincs.sch.uk

Headmaster: Since 2013, Chris Ward BEd, late 30s; first headship, previously deputy head of Worksop College Prep. He spent several years as director of music at St John's-on-the-Hill School in Monmouthshire, though now does some science teaching. Approachable, visible and welcoming to pupils and parents. A keen and competitive rugby player, spends Wednesday and Saturday afternoons refereeing matches or supporting from the pavilion, mingling with parents over a cup of tea.

Believes that St Hugh's is unique in Lincolnshire, as a stand alone co-educational prep school, providing all round care and catering for everyone. Is proud that 'when St Hugh's pupils leave they are able to stand on their own'. Parents feel that he has given the school 'a new lease of life' which they hope will continue.

Recognising the shift in the demands of modern parents for flexible boarding, he is transforming boarding under newly appointed houseparents and UK gappies to a more cosy, warm and family experience. Keen to build and strengthen the nursery provision to provide sustained growth in pupil numbers over the years and enhance the structure and shape of the school day.

Married to Angharad, who has traditional prep head's spouse's role, with three children, all pupils at the school.

Entrance: Majority of the children rise through the ranks of the school's nursery and pre-prep with some recruitment in year 3 and 4. Prospective pupils spend a day at the school for assessment. A web of school minibus routes brings children from a wide area.

Exit: Seventy-five per cent go on to independent senior schools in Lincolnshire and the A1 corridor, Uppingham, Oundle, Oakham, Repton, Stamford. Further afield Sedbergh and Barnard Castle. The remaining 25 per cent get places at local grammar schools, usually at 11 (some go at 13).

Remarks: Located in the attractive, former Victorian spa resort of Woodhall Spa, in the midst of what was RAF heartland, St Hugh's is situated in a leafy avenue of traditional, Edwardian villas. Founded by the Forbes family in 1925 as a boys' boarding school, loyalty to the school has been strong and successive generations of often farming families continue to be educated here. A charitable trust since 1962 and co-educational since 1981.

Whilst first impressions are of a modest establishment, once through the door the extent of the buildings and facilities become immediately apparent and the newly-acquired playing field now allows the grounds to be described as extensive for a school of this size. New Astroturf; this addition to the functional yet well-maintained sport shall and swimming pool provides a sporting facility gold, particularly for the hockey players. An adventure playground and nature pond – increasing use of the natural environment, staff undertaking forest school training, part of a green school kitemark. Boarding facilities in the upper echelons of the main school house, well away from classrooms.

Nursery and pre-prep classrooms flow through a building across the playground from the older children. Bright, well-resourced and full of colourful displays, features common across the school. Corridors adorned with interesting displays and children's work provide a sense of pride and commitment from staff. Good specialist facilities for science, music, art and DT with whiteboards in each classroom, a dedicated ICT suite and wireless connectivity throughout the school.

St Hugh's pupils have been successful in achieving scholarships, particularly in sports, music and arts, and it is the head's plan to strengthen further the number of academic and all-rounder awards. In the early years foundation stage the new department head has developed numeracy work, and investigational skills in mathematics is a focus of teaching and learning. Specialist French starts in nursery, increasing across subjects so that by year 5 all teaching is by specialists, with German and Latin being introduced and setting for mathematics and science. Classes are grouped according to ability from year 5 with an average of 14 in a class. Whilst teaching broadly follows the national curriculum, there is a weekly session for senior pupils to enhance independent learning. Ten per cent SEN, mainly dyslexia and dyspraxia though several children with statements/EHC plans. Personalised learning plans, good coordinated strategies between SENCo and teachers, with one-on-one support where required.

Everyone is given the opportunity to contribute to the school, either on the games field, musically or in drama, but it's sport that rules the roost. Focus on traditional team sports and swimming, and everyone encouraged to play in a team. Good fixture list mainly against local independents but outlying location involves lengthy travelling times. It really is 'sport for all' – no one is left out. Hosts an annual netball tournament using boarding accommodation for teams from far afield.

Music flourishes with three-quarters of pupils from year 3 playing an instrument up to grade 8. Plenty of performance opportunity with termly concerts and musicals, and public recitals for the two choirs; two orchestras with seniors scaling symphonic heights; string and wind ensembles. Joint production with drama each year – recently the Wizard of Oz and Bugsy Malone – though plays, sketches and nativities, as well as assembly presentations, give lots of scope for budding luvvies. Elocution competitions too.

Expressive arts thrive in well-equipped, dedicated rooms with specialist art, pottery and design technology workshops and weekly scholarship classes. Textiles and cookery are included throughout the curriculum.

St Hugh's pupils get out and about on numerous curriculum enriching visits and outings. Years 5 and 7 have residential French trips and year 8 a week's outdoor pursuits experience. Biennial hockey and rugby tours to Dublin and South Africa.

Positive reinforcement is key to rewards and sanctions with gold points accumulating for the benefit of the pupil and their house. Not just academic achievement: effort, good behaviour and citizenship are all equally recognised. We were wowed by the Wow board where individual exceptional achievements are displayed. When needed, clearly defined sanctions escalating through report cards to detentions. Parents feel very well informed about their children's progress through teacher emails and regular reports.

Pupils and staff are polite, friendly and welcoming; evidence of real rapport between teachers and pupils, anecdotal comments tinged with humour and respect; no doubt that every child is known well here. Citizenship prized – and awards presented at weekly assemblies. St Hugh's Award for actions above and beyond – recently presented to one of the house captains who went home for a night to bake a cake to cheer up a young house member who had sustained a complicated broken femur on the rugby pitch. Strong house structure (named for three previous heads) with sporting, general knowledge and arts competitions and fundraising activities. Peer mentors in years 7 and 8; worry boxes discretely placed for confidential concerns.

Attuned to changing needs (and a declining number of Forces' children), the metamorphosis of boarding has seen a rise in the number of children deciding for themselves to board weekly or occasionally. A programme of investment has provided houseparent accommodation and upgraded bathrooms, and will create common rooms available to all and improve storage space, much needed as the bedrooms accommodating up to nine children are not large – though not always full. Friday nights are the most popular – great fun, and for the price of a babysitter, no early morning rising for parents to make Saturday school. There is a small number of full-time boarders, who are well looked after at weekends and kept busy. Everyone (children, teachers and parents) agrees that the food is 'fantastic', with plenty of choice. The place is absolutely spotless throughout the boarding and school sides.

Parents tell us that they 'love the wonderful family atmosphere' and that the children 'mix throughout the year groups and are very supportive and encouraging of each other'. One parent told us, 'I have seen older year groups, unprompted, clapping and encouraging the little ones as they walk through the dining hall to go to perform in a play, which gave them such a boost'.

St Hugh's turns out well-rounded children who are polite and self-confident. Happy children – and parents.

St John's College School

75 Grange Road, Cambridge, Cambridgeshire CB3 9AB

Pupils: 453; 25 full, 3 flexi boarders • Ages: 4–13 (boarders from 8) • C of E

Fees: Day £11,391 – £14,313; Boarding £22,602; Choristers £7,533 pa

Tel: 01223 353532
Email: admissions@sjcs.co.uk
Website: www.sjcs.co.uk

Headmaster: Since September 2016, Mr Neil Chippington MA (Cantab) FRCO (40s), previously head of St Paul's Cathedral School. Music scholar at Cranleigh, organ scholar at Cambridge, Fellow of the Royal College of Organists; music is certainly in his blood. Came to St Paul's from Winchester College, where he was a housemaster for eight years, and having himself been a quirister (chorister) at Winchester Cathedral. He is a keen cyclist and runner who regularly takes part in half marathons and triathlons, usually for charity, and recently completed a 280 mile three day cycle to raise money for Leukaemia Research. In addition, he has a strong interest in travelling and has over the years led school trips to a wide range of countries including Jordan, Iran and Turkey. He is married to Leisle, who is also a teacher, and they have two sons.

Entrance: Oversubscribed but not overly so. For entry at 4 the children are 'assessed' – using sequencing and other methods which, even at such a young age, show their potential – as are the parents. 'We want parents to have a feel for the place and we see what they want for their child. If we agree, we can work together.' Don't be complacent; children here are bright. At 7, assessments in English and maths and child is observed during half a day at the school. 'It's all about the child fitting in and coping.' Chorister bursaries for up to five scholars, all boys, at 8, of at least two-thirds of the fees. Means-tested bursaries for those who would particularly benefit. At 11+, potential music scholars welcomed as boarders, with scholarships available. Siblings take priority and then boy:girl ratio to keep the numbers even. Children come from a wide commutable area around Cambridge, or further afield for boarders. The majority of parents are academics, medics from Addenbrooke's or employed on the Silicon Fen,with a Newmarket contingent as well. Many work in the City. All parents very ambitious for their offspring, but nicely so and welcoming to newcomers.

Exit: The odd leaver at 11 but very unusual, usually heading to the state sector. No 'evictions', but occasionally, after much discussion and agreement, the occasional one will be moved on to 'somewhere they will be happier at.' Virtually all leave at 13. Lots of help with future schooling. 'They guide us away from making the wrong choice.' Over half of the year get scholarships/awards, academic as well as music. At least 50 per cent go to local private Cambridge schools, the rest off to board: many to Perse Upper; St Mary's, The Leys, Uppingham, King's Ely, Eton, Oundle, Rugby and Stephen Perse Foundation all popular.

Remarks: The school is owned by St John's College and was originally set up in the 17th century to educate the choristers. Now housed on a leafy road in Cambridge opposite the college's playing fields, which they share, in three adjacent houses, recently redeveloped to include new outdoor woodland area on what was once the staff car park. On entering the main building the first thing you see are the choristers' gowns hanging in the hallway. They are very proud of the choristers, rightly so. They travel the world and are very talented. But once in the school they are just normal pupils. There are no 'stars' in this school so no cabinets full of trophies on display. They have them, but discreetly hidden in the dining room. The life of the chorister is slightly different to other pupils as they start practice at 7.30am, running through to the start of school at 9am, and again after school for a couple of hours. It's a massive commitment but handled well. The school ensures they don't suffer academically or personally.

A very tactile school. 'If a child needs a hug it gets one.' Many parents spoke of their children 'being allowed to be children and not to grow up too quickly.' 'They are imaginative and modern about learning,' said one parent. 'We are told very firmly to leave the education of our child to them and not to stress about exams. It works, the children are pushed, achieve highly but don't feel under pressure.' No exams until the penultimate year. Children taught to have enquiring minds and embrace learning. Mindfulness is taught to all, even the little ones, and stands them in good stead for future years. Hugely supported by parents. 'All of the teachers are of a similar mindset and embrace the concept and love the children. They wouldn't be here if that wasn't the case.'

Lots of after-school clubs, but not until year 3. Enrichment programme each Thursday afternoon for 9-13 year olds explores cross-curricular work across arts and sciences, plus My Mind programme, which includes tai chi for year 4. As expected, loads of music, not just for the choristers. The majority of the children learn an instrument, many two or more. Bands, choirs, quartets galore. All the usual sports teams, well supported. Drama very popular. Very impressive artwork framed and displayed throughout the school. A large, airy, newly refurbished art room where the older children can pop in and set to. 'All children can draw by the time they leave St John's,' the very enthusiastic art teacher told us. Timetables are flexible. Extra tuition offered, some at no extra cost, very quickly if needed. Individual needs department proactive. They are on top of the children academically and extra time allocated towards subjects for those aiming for certain scholarships.

A small contingent – including all choristers – boards. 'It means we can manage their time well rather than it being wasted travelling.' Larger numbers boarding higher up the school, many weekly, some flexi. Clean, bright, mixed boarding house. Lots of comfy sofas, snooker and table football. A large kitchen with huge table. 'Our parents can come and see us and have a cup of tea with us after services,' said one chorister. Very much an open door policy for parents. Strict rules within the house. No child can enter another dorm. No mobile phones in the boarding house and, very contentiously for our chatty guides, no tuck. 'They decided the choristers were getting too much sugar so cut tuck to twice a week and have now cut it out completely,' was the outraged comment. 'So when we go home we beg our parents for sweets.' There used to be accompanied visits to town with the older ones going in threes, 'as long as one of us was wearing a watch,' but these have now been stopped. 'They said all we did was buy sweets, but we only had £2 so what can they expect?' from our opinionated guide, 'and how do they expect us to manage money if they won't let us out to spend it?' All said with very good humour and a big smile. We feel our guides have a bright future ahead of them. Homesickness handled well. One pupil allowed to bring her rabbit last term. Lots of contact with parents, though not before bed, in private phone booths. 'Please note the phone number for Childline is listed on our contact lists pinned to the door.' This guide will go far. Dormitories clean and tidy. Bunk beds, six to a room max. Boarders change their own bed linen. Duvet covers brought from home. Houseparents loved by all, children and parents. 'I couldn't ask for more from them and the receptionist is magnificent.'

Uniform stands out with bright red blazers. 'The uniform is too expensive,' said one rather disgruntled parent, 'particularly the blazers.' The girls wear a rather dowdy summer dress, far too dull for the bright, exuberant characters donning them. 'Pastorally excellent,' was said by every parent. 'There are issues, usually girls and their friendships, but the school handles them sensitively and effectively.' The year 8s mentor the incoming year 5s.

Nearly every parent we spoke to felt 'we are very lucky to have our children at St John's.' We can see why. Certain schools have 'that feel', and this one does. It's a joyous place that's buzzing. Lessons are alive, the children are working hard, utterly engaged. And they are happy, exuberant, confident little people, from the youngest up. Children being children, nurtured through some tough, turbulent times, meeting adolescence with equilibrium and well set for future schooling. Long may it continue.

St Mary's School, Cambridge

Bateman Street, Cambridge, Cambridgeshire CB2 1LY

Pupils: 624; 82 full/flexi boarders • Ages: 4–18 • Sixth form: 94 • RC

Fees: Day £9,120 – £14,877; Boarding £27,210 – £31,608 pa

Tel: 01223 353253
Email: admissions@stmaryscambridge.co.uk
Website: www.stmaryscambridge.co.uk

Headmistress: Since 2007, Charlotte Avery (40s). English degree Oxford, PGCE Cambridge. Taught in various schools, deputy head at Highgate where she oversaw the transition to co-ed. St Mary's is her first headship. One of triplets, all with Oxbridge degrees. A formidable intellect who is determined to get her point across. Dedicated to girls' education. Brisk and efficient but also kind and caring. Obviously stands no nonsense. Well liked and respected by parents. 'She can talk the hind leg off a donkey, but in the nicest way,' said one parent. 'She's brilliant, a whirlwind with great enthusiasm who carries everyone along with her.' Many parents spoke of her great vision and the 'huge changes she has made.' Others spoke of how she has promoted internally. 'A very nice person, tough and a great leader.' Very high profile and attends all school events. President elect of national Girls' Schools Association for 2017. Interesting to note that she is an Anglican but head of a Catholic school.

Head of junior school: Since 2016 is Matthew O'Reilly. Read German and politics at Newcastle. Travelled the world teaching adults English for large businesses and interpreting. Returned to the UK to do his PGCE and started teaching in senior schools. Disliked this, so turned to juniors instead. St Mary's was his first job and he has worked his way up to head. Very well liked by all parents and settling into the role well. 'He is a young man with a quiet, calm, manner and great enthusiasm. I was delighted he was appointed head.'

Academic matters: In 2016, 68 per cent A*-As at GCSE, 50 per cent at A level. Impressive results from girls instilled with great self-belief and a strong work ethic. 'The girls work really hard but have great fun too,' said one parent. Lots of support for

S

all, whatever their abilities. Parents kept well informed about academic progress and spoke about 'prompt responses' from teachers. Science and maths very strong with lots of science clubs. Fabulous new science hub, incredibly well equipped. Year 10s were working hard at an experiment and good to see large sixth form groups doing sciences. Spanish, French, German, Latin, Greek and Mandarin all offered at GCSE. Many girls do two languages, though small groups for A level languages.

Inspirational quotes throughout the school from renowned women. Good to see a noticeboard about exam week and preparing for them. 'Don't panic' was one piece of advice. 'A very proactive school,' was one parent's comment. Another parent said, 'How I wish I'd had teachers like that.' Lots of computer suites and iPads filtering through to all pupils. Certain social media sights blocked – good. Food tech offered at A level. A younger age group was cooking when we were visiting – some delicious smells wafted our way.

The junior school is now a short walk away in Chaucer Road, in a lovely old house with lots of outside space. Girls taught here as per state system. One teacher for all subjects, but with specialist input throughout. Again lots of inspirational quotes, particularly from the founder, on the walls. 'They get a very good start here,' was said more than once. French for all and Mandarin taught to all but a few who have extra tuition when needed. All girls actively encouraged: 'You can do it,' is what a lot of parents said their daughters were being told.

Average class sizes of 20, smaller in the sixth form. Many teachers long serving. Learning support lessons for those that need it, about 100 SEN on the register, all with milder needs. 'My daughter needs extra support and time and the school couldn't have been more supportive helping her plan her work and revision as well as extra lessons.' Some 48 students have EAL classes, all in the senior school. Many more from overseas who no longer need this support.

Games, options, the arts: Quietly sporty and successful, cabinets full of silverware are testament to this. County cross-country runners, hockey players and netballers. Pitches situated a 10 minute minibus journey away. 'Sport for all and there are no sporting prima donnas,' said one parent. All talk about plenty of teams and 'masses of sports clubs.' Touch rugby on offer. Sixth formers have the chance to row. A jointly refurbished city rowing club's boathouse will mean that rowing will be available to all senior girls shortly. Gymnastics popular. Sports rotated throughout the year so always something for everyone.

Drama very popular with lots of productions, clubs and workshops. Parents very enthusiastic about performances. Drama GCSE one of the most successful subjects; most gained A*. LAMDA popular and encouraged for overseas students.

Art is big at St Mary's and it has a very strong reputation for it. Impressive art on display throughout the school. The art school is situated next door to the main building. Sixth form art scholars' photos displayed in the reception area. Each sixth form student has their own space; we admired the quality of the work, ambitious and eye-catching.

Music highly thought of here. Orchestras, choirs, bands, ensembles galore, in both junior and senior schools. Our visit coincided with mass rehearsals at the junior school. Every room was full of performers practising. Music as a career actively encouraged.

Numerous sports tours and subject trips. D of E for all, up to gold award.

Boarding: The boarding community is international. Some 20 countries represented, with those from south east Asia being the largest cohort. Currently 87 girls board, 42 of whom are in the sixth form. Only three boarders, none of them in the sixth form, are UK based. The majority are full boarders, though flexi boarding is offered. 11-16s currently housed on the top floor of the school with upper sixth girls based across the road in tall, narrow Edwardian interlinked houses. From 2017 all boarders will be housed in a newly purchased residence a short walk from the school on Brooklands Avenue. Current facilities are bright and airy and newly redecorated.

Girls are encouraged to personalise their space. Some rooms slightly messy, many cluttered, but homely – good to see. Younger girls in rooms of four, older groups in pairs. All upper sixth formers have own room. Pleasant communal areas, tea and toast making facilities for all. Girls taught to do their own laundry. One father couldn't understand why boarders were allowed so much freedom – 'why do they need to go into town to buy sweets?' – but we suspect the boarders disagree with him. They are kept occupied with church on Sundays, optional, and plenty of trips to Alton Towers and the like. Parents keep in close contact and are happy their daughters are 'safe and supervised.'

The year 13s' facilities are more like a house share. A small common room and kitchen where they are allowed to cook at weekends. A bit of a rabbit warren with its narrow staircases and corridors, but comfortable, clean and tidy. There's an alarm on the door to police any miscreants – not that we felt there were any.

Disappointing to hear from sixth form day girls that the new boarders don't mix socially with them. Lots of effort made to include them in sixth form socials but not many takers and very few attend the Leavers' Ball. Doesn't appear to be the case lower down the school: parents spoke of daughters going to stay with friends who are day girls.

Background and atmosphere: Now the only girls' school left in Cambridge. Founded by Mary Ward, an innovator of education for girls, St Mary's opened in 1898. Based on a strong Catholic ethos that is reflected throughout the school. All religions, and none, are welcomed and embraced, with the spiritual welfare of the girls being of paramount importance. There is a resident chaplain, a small chapel where services are regularly held, parents welcome to attend as well, and whole school services regularly. A strongly Christian school that believes that 'every girl is of equal value and has something to offer.' This belief permeates throughout junior and senior schools.

Outwardly the school is not particularly attractive. Squeezed into the centre of Cambridge along a large part of Bateman Street, the 70s façade is quite low key. But once inside the school it's another matter. Modern additions have been incorporated well, including new science hub opened by Dame Mary Archer in September 2016, and it's interesting to tour the school going from ancient to modern: it adds character and works well.

The original building, once a residential house, is beautiful. Now home to the admin and head's office with boarding upstairs. The magnificent staircase and large bay windows looking out onto large gardens reflect back to another era. The gardens are well used – the grass could have done with a cut when we were there – with plenty of benches, an outside gym and table tennis table.

Sixth form housed in a separate building that used to be the junior school, across the road. Smaller classrooms for teaching, a dance studio, gym and showers; please note the hairdryers and straighteners. A beautiful building that has recently been refurbished. Comfy-looking common room, kitchen (we spotted the toast and Nutella), and outside space for dining. Interesting to see a sign up in the kitchen to say only English should be spoken. Impressive library with sixth form girls quietly working. Silent study rooms and less quiet ones, but all working hard in them. Good use made of Cambridge and all it has to offer.

The junior school reflects the senior school, with large gardens and an attractive, airy building. Pretty sensory garden and vegetable plots for each year. Both schools are very much 'girls' schools.' The empowerment of women, strong women, is a theme throughout. The girls seem to absorb this. Unaffected and naturally pretty. Very little make up worn and no strutting divas to behold – thank goodness.

Pastoral care, well-being and discipline: All parents praised the pastoral care. Very few bullying claims. Happiness and joy with strong moral values is their mantra and the girls take this on board. But girls will be girls, and the school knows it. Spats and sniping dealt with calmly and efficiently, usually with very little parental intervention. Parents spoke of a happy school with 'no queen bees or cliques.' A junior school mother said, 'some parents get too involved, collaring teachers at every opportunity. They are too protective to the detriment of others.' But that's junior schools for you. Most parents trust the school and know their daughters are 'safe and happy.' School knows how to deal with girls and their problems. A counsellor and female lay chaplain available if needed, and staff appear to know the girls well.

Instilling self-esteem and confidence is very much an ethos of the school and many parents spoke about it along with the Mary Ward philosophy that they have great belief in. 'My daughter was very shy when she started but they have brought her out of herself and her confidence now is amazing.'

Pupils and parents: Parents are very much 'Cambridge,' academics/medics/professionals. Many are old girls. All spoke about the values of the school and how important that was to them. About a third are Catholic. All very pro single sex education, even the mother who said, 'I was very anti single sex education initially, but St Mary's suited my daughter best and she's thrived.' Girls from a 30 mile radius around Cambridge with about 25 per cent from overseas.

The girls were interesting. Charming and unaffected in both schools. It was quite revealing to see the sixth formers, slightly scruffy, but not in a bad way, and minimal make up. As one mother said, 'they don't care what they look like as there's no-one to impress.' Amen to that.

Entrance: Entrance tests for all, even the reception children, who have a chat with a member of staff, count, write and sort shapes, 'to see if they will fit in.' Don't be fooled: they are looking for bright sparks. Skype interviews for those overseas. Most girls are interviewed. The senior school is oversubscribed and the junior school full from year 5. Automatic entry from the junior to senior school, with only one girl in the last five years weeded out in year 5. Quite a large intake at year 9 when girls arrive from the local prep and state schools, and from abroad to board.

Exit: Around 40-50 per cent leave each year after GCSEs, mostly to the excellent state sixth form colleges in Cambridge. The odd one to a co-ed independent, but quite unusual. Sometimes a girl is advised not to return for sixth form, but it's very unusual, and as far as we could tell entry to sixth form was automatic for current pupils as long as they have a clutch of good GCSEs.

One to Oxbridge in 2016 and one medic; London a very popular destination, reflecting the international profile of the girls. Sciences, medicine, vets and engineering very popular. The head is embracing apprenticeships and encouraging girls to explore this option.

Money matters: Scholarships up to the value of 20 per cent of the fees awarded and bursaries of up to 50 per cent available. Two Ogden Trust mathematics and physics scholarships open to lower sixth candidates from the state sector, means-tested and can be worth up to 95 per cent of day school fees.

Remarks: A girls' school offering a tremendous education to young women. Being instilled with the belief of the empowerment of women from such a young age, these girls will go far. There'll be no glass ceilings for this lot.

Spalding High School

Stonegate, Spalding, Lincolnshire PE11 2PJ

Pupils: 980 • Ages: 11–18 • Sixth form: 249 (32 boys)

Tel: 01775 722110
Email: enquiries@spaldinghigh.lincs.sch.uk
Website: www.spaldinghigh.lincs.sch.uk

Head: Since 2014, Michele Anderson (40s). BEd in home economics from University of the South Bank in London, but has always taught geography. Her first headship. A Londoner who previously taught at selective and non-selective schools in south London and Kent, new to Lincolnshire. 'I was looking for a headship but was very particular about the school I wanted. As soon as I walked through the door here I knew as "the feel" was just right,' she says. Finding her feet with plans for 'fine tuning and funding.' Parents are positive about the new incumbent. 'She's fantastic; she knows exactly what she wants and where she wants to take the school,' said one enthusiastic mother. 'I like her and she has integrated herself well, getting to know everyone,' said another. Getting her face known locally and forging links with other schools in the area. Still teaching geography to the year 8s and 9s, 'I love teaching and the worst thing about being a head is that I can't do more of it.' Well aware of teenage angst. 'In the upper academic ability groups stress and anxiety levels are much the same, whatever the gender. We laugh a lot and eat cake here, and it helps. I have never been to a school with so much cake.' Husband is a househusband, a great eye opener for the girls. 'I couldn't do it without him.' Daughter recently started here.

Academic matters: As expected for a selective grammar, results are good. In 2016, 45 per cent A*/A at GCSE (97 per cent gained at least five A*/C grades) and 27 per cent A*/A at A level (61 per cent A*-B). 'We get lots of homework,' said one of our guides, 'but they teach us how to manage our time and motivate ourselves. We are pushed to work at the best of our ability.' 'They are pushed academically,' said one parent, 'but are well supported.' All parents report feedback from staff is very good. 'If there is a problem we are made aware of it.' Spanish, French, German and Latin – good to see at a state school – on offer at KS3 to GCSE with French or German (alternate years) and Spanish A level – lowish take up at A level, but growing. Most take the triple science GCSE, sciences popular at A level. Sociology, sciences and psychology top A level subjects. The lessons we observed showed diligent girls working hard; this lot have got their heads down and are getting on with it.

Class sizes are large, up to 30. The occasional boy in A level science groups – they get good results, hence their presence. Gifted and talented are spotted from year 7 onwards, meaning extra work and more challenges. Art very popular with a thriving department that achieved gold Artsmark in 2015. Great to see the art rooms decorated by the girls from the gifted and talented group; they are given a free rein with the paints and their creativity. IT lessons for all, year 8s building their own websites. A relief to poke our head in the computer rooms and experience a blast of cold air from the air conditioning.

Some of the other classrooms were stifling and stuffy – outside temperatures much the same though, to be fair.

Tech block very well equipped with lots of girls' work on display. They have a lathe, laser and 3D printers, quite unusual for a girls' school – no sexism here, hurrah. Textile room impressive. More cake being made in the food tech rooms. Sixth form has its own IT rooms, plenty of computers available. Tea and coffee making facilities in the roomy common room along with a microwave. A new tea urn is a recent purchase.

Number of pupils with EAL is 36 and rising, so more provision being made. Quite high for a rural area, but many Eastern Europeans settling and now educating their children locally.

Very few pupils on SEND list but provision made, usually within the classroom. Individual or small group support available from specialist teachers if needed.

Games, options, the arts: The cabinets are stuffed full of silverware at this school. Quite a few girls playing sport to county standard, or higher. They have a budding golfer and a competitive riding team. All non-school sporting achievements are acknowledged and accommodated. 'My daughter is sometimes away playing at a tournament and the school staff are very understanding. They give her full academic support.' Lots of teams throughout the school, including chances for the less able, but enthusiastic, to play. Interesting to see that they play lacrosse, unusual for a state school. Also successful football and cricket teams. Plenty of pitches, including Astroturf. No swimming pool but impressive gym and fitness suite that is well used.

Plenty of girls learning musical instruments, tapering off in the upper years. Singing lessons very popular. Lots of clubs, sport and drama, as well as orchestras. Drama is a popular GCSE and A level subject. Whole school involved in productions of eg Oliver! The lower sixth runs clubs for younger girls including drama, pop choirs and orchestras. Winter and spring concerts held each year involving all year groups. Each subject has a club as well. All clubs are run at lunch times as after-school not successful because of the large area girls travel from. D of E offered at bronze and gold level and the school has recently become a licenced centre.

Background and atmosphere: Based at its present site for 50 years; the 60s architecture is not particularly inspiring. Go inside and it's another story altogether. The head's description of 'the feel of the place' is apparent straight away. We were greeted with smiles from the girls running a cake stall in reception for charity – yet more cake. The main building has lots of bright airy spaces. Large windows letting in lots of light. Some very narrow staircases and corridors but no sense of overcrowding. All very disciplined at lesson changeovers.

A school in the heart of the Fenland town of Spalding that has a strong sense of community, and is very much involved with it. A large school, that must seem vast to some of the girls coming from tiny village schools in the outlying rural areas. They're aware of this, and every girl is visited at her junior school prior to starting in year 7 – an admirable undertaking, as there are 70 of them. Successful induction days help, and a summer school is now attended by virtually all newcomers. Friendly year 8 mentors on hand as well.

Plenty of outside spaces for al fresco dining dotted around the school. Just as well, as according to one mother: 'There just isn't enough room in the dining room for the girls to sit down and eat together, something that I think is important.' Food given high praise by our guides. Delightful to walk outside and pick up the scent of roses from the flower beds.

Uniform in the process of being changed from short skirts to longer pleated ones. 'I would like to see the girls in blazers,' said one mother, 'but the pleated longer skirts are definitely an improvement.' Sixth formers wear their own clothes, but need to be smart.

A strong school council that appears to have influence. 'We campaigned for an extra study period and got it,' said a guide.

Pastoral care, well-being and discipline: All parents we spoke to praised the discipline. 'The girls know where they stand and what is expected of them,' was said more than once. 'They have a very strong mobile phone policy, that is adhered to strictly, excellent.' Pastoral staff are also teachers, a policy the head is very keen on. 'It means the pastoral staff know the girls well as they are with them in the classroom.' It appears effective. One parent told us, 'They quickly picked up an issue with my daughter and were in touch immediately.' Pastoral issues appear to be dealt with quickly and effectively. 'They know my daughter and the other girls well,' was said more than once.

The girls stay in the same form up to year 11 and are encouraged to socialise within that group. So much so that in year 7 they are not allowed to gather in other form rooms. 'It stops one room being completely overcrowded and makes us tighter with our own form,' said a mole. Sixth formers are encouraged to be mentors and have the Jackson Room, where younger girls are encouraged to go to discuss any worries. Training is given to the volunteers who seem to be able to alleviate most tensions. Good to see that the school is aware of mental health issues and 'girls' problems' in general.

Pupils and parents: The brightest girls in the area, from all backgrounds. Unusually for a grammar school, the vast majority of girls are not from privileged homes, reflecting the area itself. A small, but growing contingent from Eastern European and Asian backgrounds. Friendly, happy girls with high aspirations, matching their parents. Many girls are second or third generation in their family to be pupils.

Entrance: Lincolnshire 11+ selection test sat by all pupils. All those who attain the grade are usually accommodated, even though the school is slightly oversubscribed. Pupils come from a large area covering South Holland, out to Wisbech and Peterborough in Cambridgeshire, with over 70 feeder schools. Entry to the sixth form, which is growing, requires six GCSEs grades A*-C including English and maths. Grade B or above in the subjects to be studied for A level. A growing number of transferees join every year, from the grammar school and other local schools in the town.

Exit: Up to 70 per cent stay on to the sixth form, with those that leave mostly following vocational courses.

A few to the local boys' grammar. The vast majority of sixth formers go to university, about 25 per cent to Russell Groups. Occasional Oxbridge. The odd apprenticeship or Forces. Very few gap years taken.

Remarks: A friendly, successful school that many aspire to, and parents relish. Often chosen over local private education on offer, and we can see why. The policy of eating lots of cake is obviously working.

Spratton Hall

Smith Street, Spratton, Northampton NN6 8HP

Pupils: 386 • Ages: 4-13

Fees: £9,600 – 14,175 pa

Tel: 01604 847292
Email: office@sprattonhall.com
Website: www.sprattonhall.com

Head Master: Since 2014, Simon Clarke BA (40s), who had been deputy (and pupil) at the school before taking over as head. Educated at Trent College and University of Surrey, he brought a wealth of experience when he returned to Spratton from excellent schools such as Gresham's and Millfield, where he was head of English and drama. A good deputy never upstages his head, so people may worry that a deputy taking over will not command centre stage effectively, but Simon's valuable experience as six years as deputy is much appreciated by everyone. He knows the children, parents and staff and hit the ground running. He understands the essential USPs of Spratton and is determined to build on them. He hasn't frightened the horses by imposing some grand new plan on everyone, but with considerable charm and diplomacy is moving the school forward to ensure its premier position in the region.

The already excellent pastoral care is enhanced by a magnificent kindness tree where children and staff add leaves to recognise acts of goodness and understanding. The already stunning academic rigour is enhanced by his emphasis on independent learning. Already at the forefront nationally in the use of IT, he runs very regular staff training to introduce everyone to get more advanced IT in the field of teaching and learning. He has a very strong senior leadership team round him. Parents love the fact that he meets and greets everyone as they come into school and when parents collect at the end of the day. 'It stops any small niggles building up,' he says. He has three children at the school and his wife is immersed in classroom life. He exudes a warmth and sharp intelligence (perhaps it is those piercing blue eyes) that gives confidence to the school community.

Entrance: Get your name down now! This is one of those schools that fills up from the maternity ward. Most children join in reception. There are occasional places higher up the school, as families leave the area. Children registered for reception visit the school on five occasions during the summer term before they start in September. They are observed and assessed by staff. If teachers have major concerns they are discussed at length with parents. Any year 1s and 2s will come in for a day and again be informally observed followed by an in-depth meeting with the family. Anyone wanting to join after that will take tests in reading, writing, spelling, maths and non-verbal reasoning.

Exit: The head talks to parents at the start of year 5 about future options and expects to meet with each family individually that year. Most go onto the big Midlands public schools, Rugby, Oakham, Oundle, Uppingham. There are an impressive number of scholarships – academic but also sports, drama, music and DT. The head built up relations with these schools when he was deputy and is well positioned to advise parents on where is right for their child.

Remarks: Yes, it is a brilliant all round school, to which parents testify and children confirm by not being able to agree on what is best about Spratton, but it is also a school that is a big hitter nationally in a number of areas, perhaps most notably IT. This is deeply embedded. The school uses the tablets which all the older children have not just for word processing and research but for changing the very nature of teaching and learning. Children film their own science experiments to review at home. Teachers film their introduction to new topics and post on the school intranet. The staff training programme and rate of innovation is impressive.

Learning support is exceptional in its flexibility, rigour and inclusivity. There is no extra charge for it. If your child has been away from school for a week or two, or is just unwell and needs some intense work to catch up on, say, maths, the learning support kicks in. If a child has mild learning difficulties or dyslexia, there may be one-to-one sessions, or work in small groups when the team can see that is more helpful. Parents comment on the significant progress made by the children and how the fact you need some extra help from time to time is regarded as the norm for making the best progress you can, rather than something about which children and parents feel a bit embarrassed. Small class sizes (about 16 in a class) help, of course, as do the teaching assistants who are an integral part of the personalised learning agenda,and are as well informed as teachers about the learning needs of every child. Parents spoke admiringly of the quality of the teachers. The head of pre-prep, herself a totally committed and enthusiastic leader, says her first criterion for appointing teachers is that they must be inspirational, and we saw some of that.

Closely connected, and central to the success of the whole story, is the pastoral care. This is where the school's holistic view of the child is really lived out on a day by day basis. There are daily senior management team (SMT) meetings, to go through not only the smooth running of the day (of which more later) but the progress of individual children. 'We nip any problems in the bud', members of the SMT reiterated to us. Intervention is swift, effective and, parents tell us, discreet. The pastoral care and support staff have the reputation for sticking with a child who might be a bit quirky and not conform to everyone's idea of the perfect pupil. On the very few discipline problems that get beyond the forgetting-the-correct-equipment level, the school has a reputation for being firm but caring. In the prep department, classes are mixed up every year so the children get to know the whole year group well.

The house system is seen by staff as being key to the positive sense of community. As well as the usual competitions, children get house marks for pleasing behaviours and can lose marks for the reverse. These house totals are read out in assembly every week and when we visited, there was a palpable hush of anticipation and sitting forward on seats as the results were announced. The houses are also responsible for raising money and awareness of specific charities that the children choose. The house system allows for a number of significant positions of responsibility at the senior end of the school. The school is keen that year 8s do experience leadership, and even those who are not getting the coveted top positions have opportunities to take on other responsible roles.

Rarely do we come across a school where the parents are in complete awe of its efficiency. Usually there is the odd grumble that the school doesn't keep us informed about a minor change, but at Spratton, it is the parents who are worried about not quite coming up to scratch and letting everyone down by forgetting some date that has clearly been flagged up by the school. 'Highly professional' and 'superbly organised' are words parents come up with first when asked about the unique qualities of Spratton. 'Run like a commercial business,' said one, 'fiercely efficient'. It is an incredibly well-oiled machine as far as communications are concerned and very much appreciated.

S

On a more informal level, parents can have breakfast at school with their children when they drop them off, a boon for the busy family.

Everything else is in place, as one would expect. It is a broad curriculum, including French from year 1 and Latin from year 6. Cookery has recently been added to the design and technology curriculum and regularly comes top of the popularity stakes. One of the many male teachers delivers some of this, presenting a very encouraging role model for the boys. There is no doubt that in years 7 and 8, there is an emphasis on common entrance. Most parents want this, but one or two told us that others found it all 'a bit intense'. The pressure clearly builds up, but most felt it was carefully managed so as not to overwhelm. There is setting quite early and tests with revision are introduced soon to ensure everyone is exam ready in time. Even the 4 year olds have spellings to learn once a week.

There is a lot on offer on the extracurricular front. Sport is strong and the school does well competitively particularly considering it is not huge. Cross-country is popular and successful. The aim is that every child will play in a team and it is certainly not just the A teams that get regular fixtures. Each team has its own coach. Arts are a strength. Most of the children take individual instrumental lessons, which feed into the high quality of the school music making. There is a drama production in the school theatre each year for every year group as well as drama club productions. Artwork hangs all over the school – the aim is that every child should have at least two pieces on display at any one time. A recent term's theme of Alice in Wonderland produced some brilliant work in a range of media.

The original building exudes Georgian elegance and calm. Much of the teaching takes place in purpose built classrooms as the school has developed the site since it took over in 1951. The classrooms are bright, displays lively, there is a well-stocked library, drama space, music rooms, sports hall, theatre, three science labs and three IT suites. Everything you could possible expect in fact, except a swimming pool. The outdoor sports facilities are amazing and the higher fields have a wonderful view over the Northamptonshire countryside.

Senior schools say Spratton children are well-rounded, work hard and are fun. That is quite a big part of every parent's dream.

Stamford Junior School

Linked with Stamford High School, Stamford School

Kettering Road, Stamford, Lincolnshire PE9 2LR

Pupils: 354; 12 boarders • Ages: 2-11 (boarding from 8) • C of E

Fees: Day £8,766 – £11,271; Boarding £16,179 – £20,313 pa

Tel: 01780 484400
Email: admissions@ses.lincs.sch.uk
Website: www.ses.lincs.sch.uk

Head: Since 2012 Emma Smith (early 40s). Convent educated in Berkshire, early years BEd from Kingston University. From a Forces background, husband and sister still serving. Previously worked in the state sector in and around London. Bit of a baptism of fire at previous school. Hired as deputy head and within weeks made acting head due to a suspension. 'I had a very young staff [she was hardly Methuselah herself] with no leadership team. It was an intense experience that I enjoyed, but knew after two years I needed a change. My husband has family in Stamford, so I was delighted to get the job and go back to just teaching for a while.' Starting to get itchy feet when previous incumbent retired and was appointed head. She had some very big shoes to fill but is finding her feet. Nice to see a rather glam head – black fingernails et al.

She's ambitious, with big plans that are coming to fruition. Reception classes have been moved into a newly converted stable block. A new bespoke year 6 block. The school is getting larger, but with smaller class sizes, under her leadership. 'I think emotional intelligence is vital. If you are honest with children they respond well. And never underestimate them. They need to appreciate that they won't get on with everyone in life but need to treat people, particularly their contemporaries, with courtesy and respect. I want the children to bounce through the door in the morning, have an amazing day and then bounce back out again, full of what they've done. My aim is for them to learn to love learning and have a good work ethic.' Because of her ambition, she might not stay long. No plans to leave at the moment, though.

Parents are very supportive. 'She has great vision for the school and is making very positive changes,' said a year 5 parent. 'She ruffled a few feathers at first, but listens to people and has learnt to communicate with parents very effectively. Her handling of a very sad, horrible accident involving one of the pupils has been exemplary. Parents have been kept informed throughout, so avoiding any unnecessary speculation,' said a parent with two children at the school.

Entrance: First come first served into nursery and reception. A few places available higher up the school, via tests from age 7. Quite a large and growing junior school with most children coming from a 20 mile radius. Families attracted by the fact that you can almost certainly stay in the Endowed system until 18.

Exit: Some leave for other schools after nursery, but the majority go into reception. Automatic entry from year 6 into the senior schools means that from year 5 there's a sharp increase in numbers. Vast majority (some 95 per cent) go up to the senior schools, with a handful going to state sector or other independents. A couple each year are warned early that they might not cope with the senior schools. Handled sensitively.

Remarks: Part of Stamford Endowed Schools with its diamond structure. Co-ed in junior and sixth form, single sex 11-16. The junior school is situated just outside the historic town of Stamford. Feels very rural, on a very quiet, leafy, green site in a delightful setting with a very pretty playing field set in a dell. The newly-converted stable block housing reception class adds to this, along with the new nursery building. New year 6 building awash with iPads etc. Lots of outside space, climbing frames and toys obviously well used. The classrooms spill into the outside space down here through large French windows, which were flung wide during our visit. Lots of newly-planted seedlings in the garden. All year 5s do nursery duty at lunch time and go down to help the toddlers. The main building is surrounded by pitches, grass and Astroturf. New learning garden and adventure area by the river. Fresh air seems to be king at this school. Windows are flung wide and the garden is inside with vases of flowers everywhere – all bright and cheerful.

Many parents relocating to Stamford from London, often returning to their roots, choose the school. The town was recently voted by The Sunday Times as the best place in England to live, and we can see why. A lot of pupils are second or third generation. 'We came from a state school in London and I was very worried about fitting in,' said one parent. 'We couldn't have been made more welcome, by the school, or other parents. I think it's a fabulous school. My children have gone from strength to strength and will try anything now, whereas they were very cautious before.'

All children learn musical instruments. Recorder for the early years, strings from year 2 (poor parents) and piano in year 5 and 6. Lots of clubs, ranging from chess to gardening, sewing, sports and orchestra, and there's even a left handed club. New clubs for year 6 include DR, science awards and gardening club, plus Saturday cookery and craft sessions. Artwork all over the place, and it's good. One of the teachers has her work displayed and on sale, great for the pupils to see.

Sport is thriving and open to all. School gymnasts are Under 11 Mixed Floor and Vault National Champions. Rugby, hockey, netball, tennis and swimming teams are doing well. 'The sport is tremendous, but I am disappointed that as a latecomer to the school my son has found it hard to break into some of the A teams, as there are "invitation only" squads for the best players,' said a parent. 'It is hard to improve and catch up if these squads are getting extra coaching. That said, both of my children are very happy and it's my only gripe'.

A lot of learning is through play in the early years. 'We came from overseas where a lot of emphasis was on academic success. I worried at first that the children didn't seem to be pushed hard enough. But I soon accepted that the softly, softly approach works well. My children have been transformed and are so much more relaxed and happy.' 'What I really like about the school is that it feels like a local school and very much part of the community,' another parent told us.

Spanish and French taught from year 3, Italian also available. They have a thumb scanner for the library; we enjoyed that. Every child reads for 15 minutes in class daily. Science week when we visited. Lots of excitement about making false blood for homework – from pupils and parents. ILIC – independent learning and intellectual curiosity – is a big ethos throughout all three schools, and they start them young, instilling a good, enthusiastic work ethic.

Special needs not overlooked. Some 63 have SEN status. SENCo teachers praised by parents. 'My child joined in year 3 and is on the autistic spectrum. The bedding-in period took a while, but the school was very accommodating and listened to professional advice. My child has gone from strength to strength and is thriving'. Another mother said, 'My son is dyslexic and gets lot of support. Extra lessons, spelling groups and assistance are given if needed, but he is not made to feel different.'

Boarding starts in year 3. Most boarders are flexi or weekly, with handful of Forces children full time. Boarding house is a lovely, honey-coloured stone building situated in the dell. Large garden with climbing frames, chickens and rabbits. We were welcomed by two slipper-clad boarders who showed us every inch, chatting all the while. Definitely home from home; they even have jobs to do, with a rota. Nice and bright and airy. No phones upstairs, taken away at night, and no social networking. 'The children need to interact and be sociable, not glued to a phone,' the likeable housemistress told us. Homework supervised and lots of weekend trips: a forthcoming visit to the Natural History Museum involving a sleepover eagerly anticipated. Scruffy the dog is very much part of the boarding family.

There's a very strong parents' association that offers huge support to the school, providing funding for various trips and talks. They're listened to as well. The head is reducing class sizes because of parental pressure – mutual respect is the impression we got.

Parents didn't need to tell us that this is a happy school; we could see it for ourselves. Our delightful guides were proud, chatty and cheerful. Food is good, we were told, particularly the lasagne. Everywhere we went we were greeted with a cheery smile. A joyful place, offering a happy, positive start to education. A very good grounding to take to the increasingly impressive senior schools. Hard to see why you'd go elsewhere locally.

S

Stamford High School

Linked with Stamford Junior School, Stamford School

St Martin's, Stamford, Lincolnshire PE9 2LL

Pupils: 579; 38 full, 21 weekly/flexi boarders • Ages: 11–18 • Sixth form: 196 (joint sixth form) • C of E

Fees: Day £14,265; Boarding £20,022 – £26,427 pa

Tel: 01780 484200
Email: headshs@ses.lincs.sch.uk
Website: www.ses.lincs.sch.uk

Head: Since 2015, Mrs Vicky Buckman, previously deputy head at City of London Freeman's School. Leeds University graduate; spent 15 years as housemistress at Christ's Hospital. She is an ISI inspector, has been involved in sport and D of E, and is a qualified scuba diver.

Principal of all three schools since September 2016 is Will Phelan (40s), previously head of Stamford School. Read medieval and modern history at Royal Holloway, followed by PGCE at Reading and MBA in education management. Formerly deputy head at Warwick, head of sixth form and director of rugby at Abingdon School, and head of year at Royal Grammar School, High Wycombe.

Academic matters: The Stamford Endowed Schools have a diamond structure. Girls and boys are taught together in the junior school, separately from 11 to 16, then come together again for sixth form.

Although the school is increasingly selective as girls go through, entry from the junior school to the senior is virtually automatic, so there is a wider ability range than you might find in some other selective schools. Having said that, the school does reasonably well in external exams. In 2016, 37 per cent of A level grades were A*/A in the joint sixth form, as were 57 per cent of GCSEs at Stamford High School. The joint sixth form allows for a really good range of subjects. There is music technology, design technology, food, politics, drama and theatre studies, textiles and Russian as well as Spanish, French and German. Philosophy and psychology are popular at A level and the school rightly prides itself on being strong all round with no weak departments.

Girls coming up from co-ed junior schools remark approvingly on the calmer class room and single sex atmosphere. A very few are statemented and there is a SENCo across the three schools who has assistants to support those with milder learning difficulties. Much of this support is included in the fees. It is only when long term, intensive intervention is needed that parents are charged extra, and even then it is heavily subsidised. Parents report a high degree of satisfaction with the learning support. They say communication between staff is excellent and the school really does deliver individually tailored programmes.

Lots of additional help is on offer particularly around exam time, when there are voluntary Saturday morning classes and revision sessions during exam leave. Girls report that staff are endlessly willing to give individual help. There is an overarching powerful strategy of 'independent learning and intellectual curiosity' which is embedded in all curriculum areas. Girls are encouraged to enquire 'What questions must I ask to learn more about this?' The aim is that girls will find their own passions to drive them through life. No sitting back and giving up on difficulties allowed here.

Games, options, the arts: Games are strong. The school sends out an impressive number of teams and we sensed that virtually everyone who wants to play for a team gets a chance. When asked what was the best thing about the school, sport figured highly. There are lovely outdoor facilities a short walk from the school on the edge of the town. A few commented that it would be good to have sports fields actually on site, but this would never be possible given the town site, and the walk is very pleasant – at least when we visited on a sunny summer day. There is trampoline, fitness and zumba on offer and the girls play football, row and run with enthusiasm.

The quality of the big public music and drama occasions is very high, drawing on all three schools. Budding thespians are attracted to the school for the drama opportunities, which have gone up a notch with the opening of the new joint performing arts centre.

CCF is popular and strongly supported by the head. One family said they had chosen the school because in their first interview with the head, she was resplendent in her CCF uniform.

The school celebrates girls' out-of-school successes as well as school achievements – we like this and so do parents. There are regular trips, some with the boys' school, including language and sports tours, and adventure activities include D of E and rock climbing. The girls are encouraged to be feisty and physically confident.

Boarding: Boarding is small, in three separate town houses (one for 11-16s and two for sixth formers) very close to school. It is all centre of town, so security is tight but unobtrusively managed. The houses are a delight, with the least institutional feel that we have ever met. The sixth form house feels like a very well-loved student hall of residence with some 'flats' that allow for considerable independence. Co-ed junior boarding house in the grounds of the junior school, with climbing frame, rabbits and chickens in the garden. Boarders come from a range of backgrounds – some Forces families, some local and a smattering of international students. There are weekend trips to London, to local attractions, to the cinema, plus other organised activities.

Background and atmosphere: Set on the High Street, the school seems infused with the calm and dignity of the quintessentially English 18th and 19th century buildings all around, much loved by film producers of costume dramas. It must be one of the most gorgeous English towns in which to educate children. Something of a period feel is continued inside the school, with the girls up to sixth form wearing very long skirts. Sixth formers are allowed knee length school skirts. No-one seemed to mind.

The school is very clear about the advantages of the diamond structure. The high school doesn't feel like a closeted girls' school because there are boys about – going to A level lessons, play or music rehearsals, club meetings or just socialising in the sixth form common room. The single sex years from 11 to 16 are used to build confidence in this can-do community, where girls 'lean in', understanding the importance of high levels of aspiration, determination and ambition. There is a High School spirit of rolling your sleeves up and getting on with it. Girls are not precious princesses. They know life has rocks as well as roses and that you just have to pick yourself up and carry on. There is a breezy wholesomeness about the atmosphere.

Pastoral care, well-being and discipline: Although as a whole the Stamford Endowed Schools educate around 1,600 children, the way they are divided up gives a sense at the High School that you are part of a close community. There is calmness about it and a friendliness recognised by girls and parents.

Pastoral concerns are picked up quickly and the run-of-the-mill late homework is headed off by a quiet word. The preventative approach carries through to actively managing relations with parents. A series of talks – Teenage Challenge – mirrors PHSE sessions with the girls, and topics such as online safety are chosen as a result of parental anxieties. Stretched but not stressed is the strapline that sums up the approach to ensuring girls have a balanced approached to life.

The school structures try to ensure girls mix with everyone. The form groups and form teachers change every year, and those coming in at year 9, 10 or into the sixth form tell us they found it easy to integrate in the absence of any long-established cliques being allowed to form. A few parents who had approached the school about pastoral concerns had felt very well supported – lots of unobtrusive intervention and good advice.

Health problems are very well addressed as are major family problems such as bereavement – again, this seems a result of excellent communication between staff and between staff and families. As you might expect in a school that encourages the girls to take responsibility seriously, externally imposed discipline feels light touch. There is a hugely orderly and purposeful feel about the school. When someone fails to live up to the high expectations, the first response is one of mild surprise and disappointment. That usually works, according to staff. If not, there is the normal range of sanctions. Parents are very supportive of discipline issues. The head senses that they are usually at a loss themselves and only too keen to stand shoulder to shoulder with the school.

The girls say you know where you stand, you know the consequences of misbehaviour but it is not 'scary strict'. They describe their relations with teachers as relaxed. Sixth formers notice the difference in the atmosphere at the boys' school, commenting on the sharp banter that is the male conversational norm.

Pupils and parents: The Stamford Endowed Schools have acted as the local grammar school for a long time and the county scholarship scheme is only just being phased out. The governors are determined to keep the genuine social inclusivity and have a large bursary fund to make this a reality. However, it is not unrealistic to suppose the intake will in the future be a little more well-heeled. But regardless of the financial situation, parents see this as a local school, genuinely embedded in the community.

We met a number of girls whose parents had themselves been to nearby big, traditional boarding schools and who had clearly been delighted to find a school for their daughters with an ethos they recognised that didn't involve boarding, Saturday school and the consequent high fees.

Staff said girls come from hard working families and the girls knew how fortunate they were to be somewhere like Stamford. We found them unpretentious, straightforward and open. Teachers felt they could experiment and take risks in a way not possible in other schools with less engaged students. Stamford itself as well as the school has a safe, middle class enclave feel about it – and parents love it exactly for that.

Parents are sold on the diamond structure. 'It's the best of both worlds,' we heard a number of times, and very few pull girls out after year 11 unless they are really pressed financially, because the sixth form is seen as excitingly different enough to make everyone want to stay on. It must be those knee length skirts. 'My daughter made so many new friends when she went into the sixth form and noticeably matured,' said one delighted mother.

Parents universally told us that they had chosen the school because of the all-round quality and they have not been disappointed.

Entrance: The Endowed Schools have their own entrance exam at 11+. It is the same for the boys and girls and involves maths, English and reasoning. Progression from the junior school is almost automatic. At 13+ by CE. For sixth form entry, generally at least five B grades at GCSE, including in all A level subjects.

Exit: Around 20 per cent leave after GCSEs. Nearly all into higher education, with a sprinkling to Oxbridge (six in 2016), a few medics, some gap years and art foundation courses. There is a careers programme from year 7 to year 13. It's overarching and age appropriate, with careers talks and an annual careers convention for year 10 and above. Much appreciated higher education advice and preparation operates across the two schools.

Money matters: The loss of the county grammar school places will be felt by financially strapped parents in the future, but the school is working hard on its bursary fundraising to compensate in part for the loss. The success of this is going to be important not least because a number of parents spoke about the attractions of the social mix that the free places currently assure. All parents to whom we spoke mentioned value for money. It is of course in a market place with pricey boarding schools, and there is a section of parents who are escapees from London day schools. They can't quite believe just what they are getting for a relatively modest outlay.

Remarks: 'Daughters of the Empire' is a phrase that comes to mind when you meet the girls. They have an uncomplicated, determined outlook on life that makes you feel this England of ours will be safe in their hands. The school encourages them to live life to the full, explore all their talents and put them to the use of others. If you want to temper the self-obsessed, neurotic trends in contemporary teenage culture, this is the place to send your daughter.

Stamford School

Linked with Stamford Stamford Junior School, High School

Southfields House, St Paul's Street, Stamford, Lincolnshire PE9 2BQ

Pupils: 676; 41 full, 46 weekly/flexi boarders • Ages: 11–18 • Sixth form: 217 (joint sixth form) • C of E

Fees: Day £14,265; Boarding £20,022 – £26,427 pa

Tel: 01780 750300
Email: headss@ses.lincs.sch.uk
Website: www.ses.lincs.sch.uk

Head: Since September 2016, Nick Gallop, previously assistant head and head of sixth form at Portsmouth Grammar. Politics degree from Durham; he has also been head of department at Loughborough Grammar, and at Wellington College, where he was later a boarding housemaster. He has coached first XV rugby; married with two young children.

Principal of all three schools since September 2016 is Will Phelan (40s), previously head of school. Read medieval and modern history at Royal Holloway, followed by PGCE at Reading and MBA in education management. Formerly deputy head at Warwick, head of sixth form and director of rugby at Abingdon School, and head of year at Royal Grammar School, High Wycombe. Considered a career as a professional rugby player until injury forced a different direction.

Originally planned to study economics and 'make money' but didn't quite make the grade, so headed to Australia to consider his future. 'Not getting my first choice turned out to be the making of me,' he says. A year as a boarding master in Australia, where he also coached rugby and cricket, made the decision for him. 'I loved being at the school coaching and being with the boys, so decided that I wanted to teach. I've spent 20 years with boys and I know what makes them tick. The boys from Stamford are some of the nicest boys I've met. The school is spread out over a large site, which is perfect, as I don't think boys should be on top of each other, they need room. A Stamford boy is a tryer – he's stretched, but not stressed.'

He is charismatic, very well liked and respected by boys and parents alike (we're sure the mothers love him). Married with three children. A huge man, he towers over the tallest of boys (well, he was going to be a rugby player).

Academic matters: Consistent, solid results. In 2016, 52 per cent A*/A at GCSE, and 37 per cent A*/A at A level (66 per cent A*/B) – results for joint sixth form (Stamford High School and Stamford School). Most boys take 10 GCSEs in a wide range of subjects. French, German, Spanish, Russian and Latin are language options. DT is strong (the workshops and work produced are impressive; two self-propelled vehicles built by the boys caught our eye). Twenty-eight subjects offered in the sixth form that is joined with the High School, most popular being maths and the sciences, with economics and business studies rising fast. Philosophy and ethics rated highly throughout the three schools.

The lessons we observed showed involved, enthusiastic boys. The year 8 Latin scholars were wriggling in their seats, they were so keen – well disciplined, though. Lots of arm raising in the year 11 philosophy and ethics debate and diligent studying in year 9 maths. All boys leapt to their feet when we entered the classrooms. The year 13 lessons had a very different atmosphere. Much less formal but strongly focused pupils. Determined and interested, these boys had their eye on the end game. You could feel expectations of the staff and boys were high.

Learning support is available for boys who need it. Around 80 boys with SEN and 40 or so get learning support. One boy has a statement of special educational needs. Extra support also offered to invited boys on Saturday mornings.

Games, options, the arts: Sport features highly – even the non-sporty boy is encouraged to have a go. A strength of the school is the number of teams in different sports, so even the boy who is 'rubbish' (our words, not theirs) gets to play. But don't be fooled. Stamford's 1st XV was unbeaten last year and are formidable opponents. Eye-catching rugby kit, but one unimpressed mother wanted to know 'why do they make the sixth form play in white shorts? I just can't get them clean'.

Some of these boys are playing at county level, others selected by local premiership sides, and the captain was invited to represent England in the U18 squad, while a previous captain is now playing professionally. The cricket team is largely unbeaten (ex-England international Dean Headley coaches), the squash squad has been unbeaten for three years, and the basketball team (including another national player) too. They're pretty good at hockey and swimming as well. Their first year with a triathlon team resulted in a GB squad selection (and the school had to teach the boy in question to swim).

A parent told us that if a boy was yellow carded in any sport at the weekend he was up in front of the headmaster on Monday morning to explain himself. Excellent. Parents are happy and trust the school. The odd grouse about sporting stars possibly being cut more slack (sour grapes maybe?) but every parent we spoke to was happy and 'hugely impressed.'

The new £6.1 million sports centre dominates the skyline, looking out over the rugby pitches, and offers gym facilities as well as a 25m pool (pity they don't brush the walkways more often) and is well used by all the school.

Music and art are equally strong. SES is the largest independent centre for LAMDA exams in the country and six boys recently opted for music or music tech at university. A visit to the music department revealed a stash of new Macs for composing and music tech as well as the usual instruments.

The combined productions with fellow endowed school, Stamford High School (girls), are very popular (can't imagine why): recent production of Les Misérables involving all three schools was a sell out. Thriving choirs, bands and orchestras, ranging from big band and jazz to full orchestra. House singing and music competitions are hotly contested. New drama and music block.

Artwork is displayed throughout the school. Portraits seemed to be popular, albeit mainly from the upper school, in the more prominent spots. Arty boys are encouraged to spend time in the studio.

CCF section is one of the largest in the country (combined with the girls' school from year 10 up), with opportunities to go flying if you're in the RAF section. The shooting team is good (they have their own range), winning the Bermuda Cup at Bisley and Country Life competitions. Lots of silver in the cabinet.

World Challenge trips to Peru, India, Madagascar, Patagonia and Borneo. D of E popular; 18 boys left recently having already completed their gold award.

Boarding: Although Stamford is predominantly a day school,15 per cent of the pupils board. Most are weekly or three night boarders who live within 100 miles of the school. There are also boys from China, Poland, Holland and Russia. The boarders are divided into two houses – years 7-10 (Byard House) and years 11-13 (Browne). More boys board in the latter years and most have single rooms. Facilities recently updated – new furniture, lots of snooker and table tennis tables, all clean, bright and tidy, with posters on the walls (nothing inappropriate though). The older boarders must be the fittest around as the gym is a regular haunt in the evenings after prep. Co-ed junior boarding house in the grounds of the junior school, with climbing frame, rabbits and chickens in the garden.

We were shown every nook and cranny by the younger boys, who enthusiastically told us about boarders' outings to the cinema, Alton Towers, paintballing, go karting and local Leicester Tigers' matches, as well as table tennis tournaments. All age groups said how like home it is – boys change their own sheets and can bring their own duvet covers – and how much they like the boarding staff. There are televisions, but they don't get used a lot. More time is spent on Xbox and table tennis, after two hours of supervised prep every night. Boarders eat together in the main dining hall and seem happy and relaxed with each other.

Background and atmosphere: Founded in 1532, Stamford School still operates from its original site in the middle of the town (recently voted the best place to live by The Sunday Times). The school chapel, surrounded by its immaculate lawns, is at the heart of the school. Stamford School is part of the Stamford Endowed Schools (includes Stamford Junior School and Stamford High School). Each school is run separately – with its own head but a common principal. Teaching at the Stamford Endowed Schools is via the diamond structure – mixed junior and sixth forms, single sex 11-16 – which seems very successful and strongly supported by the parents. 'Lots of info on drugs, drink, driving and sex, which the boys seem to find easier to take in a single sex environment,' one parent told us. A year 8 parent commented: 'My son is just hitting adolescence and they know exactly how to handle him. The single sex education is a godsend.'

Sixth form teaching is split between the two schools, so there's a 10 minute walk across town if there is a site change in the timetable. This gives the school a collegiate feel and allows the sixth form boys a certain degree of independence. There's a lot of trust involved but it doesn't seem to be abused. Because of this constant walking – great in the summer, not so good in the winter – the boys are highly visible in the town. The local shops can no doubt set their clocks by hordes of hungry boys dashing in for sustenance for the 'long walk' through the beautiful town. (The school food used to be awful, now greatly improved, we're told). No driving is allowed between sites. Woe betide any boy who is caught doing so. We understand keys have been confiscated on occasion. There is also the 'six-inch rule' to be considered. Six inches must be kept between a boy and a girl at all times...

Boys are very involved with the wider community and help out with many of the local charities. The Evergreen Trust in Stamford and Help for Heroes get lots of support. Year 7 boys took part in the Sleep for Shelter Night, spending a night in a cardboard box in the school grounds.

School site is spread over a large area, giving the boys plenty of room. Part of the site features beautiful, honey-coloured stone Georgian and older buildings with beautiful gardens. Perhaps one of the most iconic features of the school (probably to their disappointment) is the incredibly ugly footbridge that connects two parts split by a very busy road. We were told that plans are afoot to improve it.

Pastoral care, well-being and discipline: Discipline is hot and any problems nipped in the bud quickly. School doesn't deny bullying exists, hooray, but it's dealt with promptly, quite often by the boys themselves. Mentoring system means older boys mentor the younger ones (years 7-11) and there is a one-to-one mentoring system between year 10 and year 12 boys. Lots of banter, but lines aren't crossed. The atmosphere is friendly and happy – these boys seem to like each other. Quite how the introvert sitting in the corner fares we're not so sure, but we were assured by a parent that 'the school knows their boys.'

'Support is there if you need it; you just have to ask,' a pupil told us. A younger boy's mother said: 'Parent mail is a fairly new system. We can access the school portal and see what and when homework is due. We are very quickly told if deadlines are missed, so my son knows he is being watched very closely by us all and knuckles down and gets on with it. A great improvement.'

Parents say that 'communication is very strong both ways.' One told us: 'We have needed pastoral help and the school has been very supportive and dealt with matters calmly, effectively and efficiently.'

Pupils and parents: Boys mainly from a 30-mile radius, slightly further afield in the sixth form. Mostly from professional families who value the all-round education of their sons rather than a well-known name. Boys we met were confident, courteous, friendly and grounded. In school's own words, a 'Stamford boy is well rounded and up for anything.' Boys are encouraged to get involved and say that if you get stuck in (and everyone does) 'you fit in.'

Every parent we spoke to gave glowing references: 'Excellent, I would recommend it every time; they turn out grounded, confident boys,' said one. 'My son loved being there so much he says he will send his own son, if he has one,' said another. A third told us: 'They take in boys and send out confident young men, and they guide them through really well.' A few parents felt Stamford was undersold, but they're working on that, and a couple felt communication between the two schools in the sixth form could be improved.

Old boys include General Sir Mike Jackson, former Chief of the General Staff, Nick Anstee, former Lord Mayor of the City of

London, Colin Dexter (Inspector Morse), Iwan Thomas (Olympic athlete), golfer Mark James, conductor Sir Malcolm Sargent and Simon Hodgkinson (England rugby international).

Entrance: Entry is mainly at year 7, based on an entrance exam covering maths, English and verbal reasoning. The main feeder is Stamford Junior School, just under 50 per cent, with an automatic transfer; the remainder come from local primaries and preps. Forces families are well represented, as are farming families.

There's a smaller intake in year 9, based on performance or CE, and in the sixth form five GCSEs at grade B or higher (internal and external) are required.

Exit: A handful leaves after GCSEs – a couple to other sixth forms, usually boarding, a few to the local college for vocational courses. Most boys head to a Russell Group or other top universities. Popular are Durham, Newcastle, Loughborough, Leeds and Sheffield. Engineering, business and sciences slightly favoured but too many choices to judge. One or two into the Forces, the odd boy straight into employment, eg an engineering apprenticeship with Audi, another spending his gap year as a Deloitte scholar.

Money matters: Means-tested bursaries (up to full fees) and academic, sports and music scholarships, all funded by the school. A Stamford School boy could have a parent who is CEO of a multi-national company or be a postman in the town, a huge strength of the school. Many boys are second or even third generation pupils.

Remarks: Stamford is surrounded by some very big hitters – Uppingham, Oundle and Oakham spring to mind – so can be overlooked, as it doesn't seem to have the same kudos. But Stamford more than holds its own, academically and sportswise. It's a hidden gem but we doubt it's going to be hidden for much longer. It shouldn't be. Prosecco rather than champagne, but better value for money and preferred by many.

Stephen Perse Pre-Prep and Junior Schools

Linked with Dame Bradbury's School, Stephen Perse Senior School, Stephen Perse 6th Form College

S

St Eligius Street, Cambridge CB2 1HX

Pupils: 246; co-ed to year 4; girls only years 5 and 6. Fully co-ed from September 2017 • Ages: 3-11

Fees: £11,250 – £14,130 pa

Tel: 01223 346140
Email: admissions@stephenperse.com
Website: www.stephenperse.com

Head of Junior School: Since 2007, Katie Milne BEd (Cantab), education and geography. Originally from Dundee but with very little trace of the accent. Joined the school in 1979 and was acting head twice before appointed head in 2007. Friendly and competent, clearly stands no nonsense but not scary. Revered by all. 'So impressive, she is very on the ball.' And, 'she has great foresight and experience,' from another happy parent. Teaches RS to transition years, 3 and 6. Knows all pupils and parents. Practical with great common sense. Currently overseeing the inclusion of boys up to year 6 and the introduction of the diamond structure.

Acting head of the pre-prep during 2016/17 is Alice Haywood. Maths with education degree and PGCE from Cambridge; taught across the primary age range in local state schools for 11 years; joined Stephen Perse in 2011 as assistant head and year 1 teacher. Maths coordinator, she has since taught years 1-3, supported the pre-prep leadership and written four ibooks on teaching mathematical calculations.

Entrance: Pre-prep is over subscribed and there's a waiting list, particularly now the junior school is co-ed. Each child is assessed informally by the pre-prep head or deputy before being offered a place. Many start part-time at 3+ before building up their hours. More children join in reception, but this number dwindling due to lack of spaces. The occasional one leaves to join siblings at other schools at the end of kindergarten.

Automatic entry from the pre-prep to junior. A few externals join year 3. All assessed in English, maths and non-verbal reasoning with an informal interview. They are looking for bright sparks. More enter in year 5, mainly from the state system, again assessed. Junior school virtually full, waiting list in lower years. Bursaries available, means-tested annually. Children come from a wide area. 'How I wish there was more room to park,' from one disgruntled father. Sadly beyond the school's control, but there is a minibus between the junior school and the Madingley site morning and evening to avoid congestion, a great idea.

Exit: Pre-prep children move on more-or-less automatically to the junior school. Very unusual for a place not to be taken. They make sure that each child is up to standard. One in the last five years not offered a place. Intervention by the inclusion specialist if needed and one-to-one tuition if necessary. The occasional child held back a year in pre-prep, usually late summer babies slow to mature, with parental consent. 'We are always aware of what is coming next in their education and what is expected of our child,' said one happy parent. 'I am often told that my son has more to offer and they always seem to get it out of him.' Uniform cleverly changed slightly for transition to junior school, so despite most not moving buildings there feels to be a big step up.

Virtually all to the senior school with automatic entry. Parents asked to opt out if not wanting a place, unusual. Those unable to cope have usually been kindly weeded out in earlier years, with parents' blessing. Head open to negotiation if suitable characters.

Remarks: The pre-prep (Cambridge city site) still has a fresh, new feel about it. Housed within the same building as the junior school, but very much a separate entity. Despite lack of space the small area is creatively designed, bright and airy. Nice outside space, with room for trikes and bikes. Lots of bright colours throughout, including a teal carpet to match the uniform – teal sweatshirts and plaid.

Junior school on its current site in the centre of Cambridge since the 1960s. Blink and you'd miss it. Plenty of building work since then, and refurbished in 2001. No more space to expand; they've squeezed as much in as they can. Creative use of space though. Bright and airy with all mod cons. Very IT savvy, proud they are a digital school. Fantastic new library, with very friendly librarian. Lots of posters and photos throughout. Impressive split level art and DT rooms. Loved all the hammers hanging up and enjoyed inspecting the jig saw with our guides. Again, note the teal carpet that matches the uniform. Maths is streamed in year 5 when the diamond structure will be introduced.

Boys and girls will be taught separately for core subjects. An inclusion specialist sorts extra help if needed. All parents said the help was there if necessary. Very few SEN pupils; 'we don't offer a place if we cannot meet their needs.' Many children bilingual, some tri. EAL support available. Maximum class size of 24. Older years spend time at the senior school for some lessons.

Children are happy and relaxed and learning without realising, but seeds are being sown for life-long learning. 'They are like sponges at this age,' said the pre-prep head, 'and seem to absorb everything. The learner is at the centre of every decision and each child is treated as an individual.' This was very much backed up by the parents. 'They really know my son and his capabilities and were quick to point out when he was being slightly lazy.' 'I was amazed when I had a look around the school and saw what the pre-prep children were doing. I wanted that for my child.' 'They know the children well and picked up that my child was shortsighted before I did.'

The sister pre-prep site at Madingley is ever present, with the younger children frequently visiting, enjoying the benefits of the forest school. Madingley children often come to the city so that when they all come together in the junior school they know each other well. Both sites taught in parallel.

Bright children, friendly and entertaining and oh so polite – manners are important here (hurrah). Happy to chat as we joined lessons. Independent thinkers with individual approach given to each pupil. 'They are taught to think about things and are not just spoon-fed,' said one parent. 'They are independent learners and get on with their work,' from another. 'My daughter comes home and gets on with her homework with no input expected from me.' 'This school is all about the child as an individual.' Many parents spoke about how progressive the school was and not weighed down by tradition. 'They seem to be able to make every child feel special, which is fantastic,' said one parent and many parents talked about 'how kind the teachers are, it's a caring school.'

Sport vastly improved in recent years with a dynamic teacher mentioned more than once. Good variation for the boys as well as girls. Netball team thriving and lots of other successful teams. Rugby not offered, so budding first XV captains should stay away.

Music plays a large part with most of the children having instrument lessons in school. Percussion and guitar popular, so less grating on the nerves than the recorder, just deafened by the banging of a drum these days. Lots of bands, orchestras and choirs with regular performances; drama too. Plenty of school clubs offering a diverse range including construction and outdoor ed, as well as the usual. Lots of school trips and good use made of what Cambridge has to offer.

Spats dealt with calmly and effectively. 'We trust the school to sort out any problems,' said more than once. 'Any fall-outs are sorted out kindly and efficiently with minimum fuss.' The staff know the children and parents know they care.

A happy, friendly school. 'We noticed the children walking around with their heads up and big smiles. That's why we chose it,' from one. 'I love the ethos of the school and it just jumped out at us,' from another. 'Nowhere is perfect, and in an ideal world there would be more space for pitches and such. But I wouldn't have sent my children anywhere else.'

A good grounding and a love of learning enthusiastically installed at a young age means that this happy mob are more than ready to move around the corner to their impressively academic sister school and have the opportunity to stay within the Stephen Perse Foundation of schools until age 18. 'I love this school and am delighted when my child frequently comes home saying what a great day he's had. What more could I ask for?' 'How I wish I could have gone to a school like this,' from one wistful parent. Quite.

Stephen Perse Senior School

Linked with Dame Bradbury's School, Stephen Perse Pre-Prep and Junior Schools, Stephen Perse 6th Form College

Union Road, Cambridge CB2 1HF

Pupils: 583 • Ages: 11–16

Fees: £16,440 pa

Tel: 01223 454700
Email: office@stephenperse.com
Website: www.stephenperse.com

Head: Since September 2016, Mr David Walker, previously deputy head at Wellington College, where he has also been head of physics and housemaster. Physics and philosophy degree from Bristol; after three years teaching physics at Clifton College, he went off to Cameroon via VSO as head of science at a high school for two years. He returned as a physics teacher at Whitgift before joining Wellington in 2006.

Academic matters: How is it done? Eighty-eight per cent A*/A at GCSE in 2016 with the vast majority taking 11 and some even managing 12. And about a third play an instrument. Answer – very able pupils plus a combination of high quality teaching ('we appreciate just how bright our teachers are'), an examy environment, excellent reporting ('they really know and understand the pupils'), maximum class size of 24, plenty of homework ('we're all geeks – we work so hard') and expectations. The latter is all-pervading – from home ('it's the Cambridge mentality,' mused one pupil), school and, most importantly, the pupils themselves. Arty or sciency pigeonholing is minimal and all areas shine, from single sciences to languages – a goodly clutch including Greek and Latin. Fine facilities; a recently-refurbed 'designer' library where books can be ordered or computers accessed, science labs aplenty – and under development to provice new STEM facilities – and a funky, circular IT suite with two spotlit computer-topped concentric work stations, the 'mother ship', according to our guides. No EFL or SEN unit in the school – only the mildest of learning difficulties are manageable in this environment.

Games, options, the arts: Over the years, netball and hockey teams have enjoyed county successes – but some parental wizzles re games; from the sportier pupils too. It's not a lack of staff, facilities or choice; it's time. For younger ones it's reasonable but, once GCSE courses start, something has to give. Of course, the less sporty are perfectly happy with the 80 minutes a week (minus 10 mins there and 10 mins back from the Astroturfed sports field) – and there is plenty of support for those who want more and can shoehorn a practice or club (dance, basketball, football, badminton, rowing or anything else the girls can initiate) during the lunchbreak or after school. New whizzy sports hall and roof-top pitch under development.

Music flourishes – three orchestras, bands, choirs, chamber groups and concerts abroad. Broad choice of instrumental tuition and plenty of practice rooms. Well-endowed visual arts centre. Tidy general studio with trendy back-lit lettering proclaiming 'ARTS' in 'post-feminist pink', a print room and huge atelier for sixth formers. Not much work on show round the school, but what we saw was carefully considered, with some interesting use of materials in textiles. Annual drama production for every year group plus speech and drama lessons in preparation for LAMDA examinations.

No shortage of extracurricular activities – some before school. Recently reintroduced gold and silver D of E. Long list of foreign visits and collaborative ventures – school has an EU Comenius award in recognition of international activities.

Background and atmosphere: Founded in 1881 as a sister school to the much older Perse Boys. Association now firmly at an end – the Perse Boys has gone co-ed and the Stephen Perse Foundation will be entirely co-ed from 2017. The Stephen Perse Senior School tucks into narrow streets near the centre of Cambridge and is a 10 minute walk from the train station. Understated dark blue front door in a characterless brick wall belies what's beyond – much money spent coupled with bold design statements has made a warm, comfortably stimulating place of learning. Sparkle comes from the brightly lit and imaginatively designed dining-cum-common room, which pleasantly buzzes as pupils happily spend time together, and a courtyard area where there's a large flower power mural created by pupils and a local graffiti artist. A secure, well ordered environment filled with conscientious pupils who have a clear sense of direction – greater freedom in the sixth form produces more of a bustle.

Will welcome boys to the senior school from 2017, teaching most subjects separately from 9-16 years.

Pastoral care, well-being and discipline: Ethos which builds self esteem – 'they're good at making the pupils feel good about themselves,' said a parent. Steady encouragement to be independent and give reasoned opinions – 'they're not "yes women" – but that does make for an interesting time at home.' Pupils speak of positive relationships with staff – for help or advice it's the year head or form tutor. If that doesn't suit there's a choice of school nurses.

School lunch for all except year 11, who are allowed out twice a week. Ample choice with lasagne a firm favourite. Apparently, girls now spend longer in the dining area where the relaxed atmosphere has led to a healthier relationship with food – an unexpected and positive spin-off from the refurbishment.

Biddable, well-behaved lot so no real discipline issues – but just in case, there's a code of conduct which has been drawn up by the student forum. Year 11 take on roles of responsibility and, after the autumn term, are allowed to wear their own clothes – greatly appreciated. Competition between the six 'houses' (house talent contest is highly popular) but form loyalties are the strongest.

Pupils and parents: Pupils mostly local. Articulate and mature. Loyal parent body – quite a few academics who come for a year and a high proportion of working mums. Alumni include author Phillippa Pearce, archaeologist Jacquetta Hawkes, broadcaster Bridget Kendall and Olympic gold medalist Stephanie Cook.

S

Entrance: Exam and interview at 11 (now including boys) – latter is the clincher. About half from the Stephen Perse Junior – entry is more or less automatic. Rest from Dame Bradbury's or local prep and primaries (according to one mum 'a great deal of testing with no let-up with the teaching' can be a shock for those used to a state school regime). A number also join in year 9. 'We like international diversity but not dominance,' so cap of 10-15 per cent on students from abroad. 'We're looking for the brightest and they must have at least an IELTS (International English Language Testing System) score of 6.5 in writing.. 7.5 to 8.5 is typical.' Universities want 7.5 so Stephen Perse is being pretty picky.

Exit: Number staying on for the Stephen Perse 6th Form on the up (approximately half) but Hills Road SFC remains a popular alternative.

Money matters: Wide range of scholarships at KS3 (up to 20 per cent). Means-tested bursaries. Nuffield bursaries awarded annually for science.

Remarks: First-rate selective school with a forward-thinking head who is working hard to make it much more than an academic hothouse.

Stephen Perse 6th Form College

Linked with Dame Bradbury's School, Stephen Perse Pre-Prep and Junior Schools, Stephen Perse Senior School

Fitzwilliam Building, Shaftesbury Road, Cambridge CB2 8AA

Pupils: 155 • Ages: 16-18 • Sixth form: 155 (25 boys)

Fees: £15,975 pa

Tel: 01223 454700
Email: admissions@stephenperse.com
Website: www.sixthform.stephenperse.com/

Head of 6th Form: Since September 2016, Simon Armitage, returning to the role he held from 2007-2013, when he helped to set up the college and was its first head. MA (Oxford, geography), MPhil (Cambridge, environment and development) and PGCE (Cambridge, geography and education). Began his career as an investment valuation surveyor before taking his PGCE and joining Colchester Royal Grammar to teach geography and economics. Has since spent his entire career within the Stephen Perse Foundation, including as director of communications and director of guidance – a role he still holds and which, we understand, is about 'next steps'.

Academic matters: Offers both A levels and IB, 60:40 split, and results are impressive. IB average score was 40 in 2016, achieving the dizzy heights of 42 recently, being the equal top school in the world. At A level in 2016 75 per cent of grades were A*-A, 97 per cent A*-B. A wide choice of subjects, but only academic. No media studies or food tech here. Maths and sciences popular but good to see high uptake of languages and humanities. Lots of artwork and posters throughout the college. 'It's a place for people who like learning,' said one parent. The pressure is on but a lot seems to come from the pupils themselves. 'My daughter was told to stop and relax and give herself a break,' said one mother. 'I was delighted.' High expectations from pupils and teachers with lots of support offered. 'They go that extra mile,' was said more than once and, 'way beyond what you would expect.' Extra help offered if needed. No students currently on SEN register; five currently receive EAL support.

Average class size is small, eight to 10, maximum of 14, usually smaller. 'We are always noticed in lessons and encouraged to speak up,' was a comment from one of our guides. The atmosphere as we wandered around was relaxed and happy. Lots of students working together in independent groups, others actively engaged in lessons. Teachers and pupils friendly and welcoming. Interesting to note that many staff were sitting with their students teaching rather than preaching from on high. Staff know pupils well, even those new to the school. Good use made of the university on their doorstep. Lots of seminars and visits on offer. Very high tech, each student is given their own iPad on arrival with lots of tech support available. Computers everywhere and Apple TVs, all linked to iPads. E-safety very hot.

Games, options, the arts: It's not just about exams here. Every pupil has enrichment studies so compulsory time out from academic toil. Choices change every six weeks, offering chance to dip toes into different waters. zumba popular. Lots of music groups, debating, film clubs and online student newspaper. Quite sporty with mixed football and hockey teams, netball too. Not the place to send your son with aspirations to captain the first XV – only mixed touch rugby on offer. Students represented England in water polo and shooting recently.

Music and drama popular with many shows and concerts each year. Soundproof music room available for practice. Productions in foreign languages to help the linguists. Art room not on site so artists have to return to the senior school, but lots of artwork on display on the walls.

Lots of trips including Cuba, Russia and New York, many cross-curricular.

Background and atmosphere: Part of the Stephen Perse Foundation of schools, it was established in 2008 on a new site separate from the senior school. Attractively housed in two buildings almost next door to each other. Light and airy, making good use of the limited space they have with outside space for al fresco dining. Good quality coffee machines in the social spaces, 'a must', says the head. Co-ed since its inception. Based a short walk from the station so easy to access. Very much a college rather than a school. A good stepping-stone to university. A small establishment so everyone knows each other, and relationships, appear to be very tight, between teachers and pupils also. Very much a sense of the individual here. 'Cosy and homely,' is how one parent described it. Strong links with the senior school, with minibuses running regularly between sites, so easy for the artists to get back and forth and quick for the teachers who teach on both sites.

The number of boys is low, 25, but increasing each year. They seem to fit in well, although there were the odd murmurings of 'the teachers are stricter with the boys than the girls.'

Pastoral care, well-being and discipline: The teachers seem to know the pupils well, and like them. 'We are often asked how we are getting on and how we are,' said one of our guides. Each student has a personal tutor who they see once a week. 'The staff seem to like the students and are incredibly polite to them so get the same treatment back,' said one parent, 'mutual respect all round.' 'Kind and supportive,' from another. Pastoral care reported to be excellent by all parents. 'My daughter had a wobble, which was met with great support and kindness.' No mention of fall outs or bullying and all parents happy that any minor blips are dealt with sensibly and effectively. Counsellors available if required.

Lots of advice about UCAS and university applications. The head is particularly strong at this. 'My son chose the college because of its reputation and slotted in so easily making great friends of both sexes.'

Pupils and parents: Pupils focused, ambitious and bright with high expectations, likewise parents. Most parents professionals, many employed within the universities. Pupils come from a wide area ranging from Norfolk to north London. Many make use of the train and proximity to the station. Parents very supportive of their children and the school. Scholarships available, not just academic – music, art, drama, sport and contribution to school or community.

Entrance: Two-thirds of students come from the Stephen Perse Senior School. The other third mainly from local independents. All external applicants interviewed to include a critical thinking exercise. Students wishing to study further maths A level or high level maths in the IB sit an aptitude test. All students need a minimum of 70 points to be offered a place – A* at GCSE is 10 points – and at least As at GCSE for their chosen subjects. Current school report and reference always required for external candidates.

They have the capacity for 200 students and numbers are growing every year. The senior school will take boys from 2017, so more even numbers expected to trickle through.

Exit: Virtually all to university, 13 to Oxbridge in 2016. Many medics (10 in 2016), but good to see a strong cohort of humanities. Virtually all to Russell Group universities and a handful every year to Europe and beyond (Vienna, Reims and Menton in 2016). Apprenticeships being viewed more favourably in recent times. Between 10 and 20 per cent take a gap year.

Remarks: A small, intimate, very successful college offering a broad education. Attracts bright, focused individuals who are diligent and keen to learn. But they're not dull, far from it. Full of fun, engaging, and well aware that there is much more to life than having your head in a book. Credit must go to the school for this. Voted IB school of the year in 2010 and 2013 by the Sunday Times, a great accolade for its size – it speaks for itself.

Stratford Girls' Grammar School

Shottery Manor, Shottery, Stratford-upon-Avon, Warwickshire CV37 9HA

Pupils: 787 • Ages: 11–18 • Sixth form: 219

Tel: 01789 293759
Email: info@sggs.org.uk
Website: www.sggs.org.uk

Headteacher: Since September 2016, Jacqui Cornell, previously deputy head since 2010.

Academic matters: Everyone is 'pretty bright' here - and exam results bear this out. Thirty-seven per cent A*/A grades at A level in 2016 (75 per cent A*/B). Maths, then sciences the most popular subject choices at A level.

GCSE performance good too, with 83 per cent A*/A grades in 2016. All pupils take three sciences at GCSE. Unlike some schools, languages are flourishing. Everyone does a language at GCSE and around half take a second language too. French from year 7, and German or Spanish on offer from year 8.

School doesn't go in for setting, apart from maths from year 8 (usually two parallel top groups and two parallel second groups). There are very few pupils on the SEND register – with physical, visual or processing needs, or on the autistic spectrum. Parents we spoke to were delighted with the school's results. 'It is very good academically and sets very high standards for the girls,' a mother told us. 'The focus is very much on the girls taking advantage of every opportunity that comes their way and ensuring that they achieve their goals.'

Games, options, the arts: Lots of very keen sportswomen. School is strong on traditional sports – hockey, netball, athletics – but rowing, rugby, badminton and tennis are thriving too. A current pupil is British jump rope champion while another is hopeful for selection to the GB ski team.

Flourishing music department, with practice rooms, classrooms and a recording studio. Orchestras (main orchestra has strong links with Stratford's Orchestra of the Swan), string quartet, choirs and jazz band. More than a third of pupils take instrument lessons in school – wide range of peripatetic teachers visit each week. Drama in performing arts studio (PAS for short), which boasts a wall of fame detailing previous sixth formers' successes. Annual musical and play and senior girls run drama productions for juniors. Art and DT both popular and the school is a great supporter of STEM, with strong links to companies that offer work experience programmes and project management opportunities.

Loads of other activities, including D of E, Young Enterprise, Engineering Education Scheme and community service. Trips galore – Costa Rica scientific research tour and creative writing expedition to Himalayas particularly caught our eye.

Background and atmosphere: School was founded in 1958 by a far-sighted lady mayor. Site is now a mix of old and new buildings but the heart of the school is Shottery Manor, a 15th century manor house steeped in Shakespearean history. The Bard is said to have proposed to Anne Hathaway in the manor's former chapel (now a sixth form study room) and the wooden balcony is thought to have inspired the balcony scene in Romeo and Juliet.

In recent years, an enterprising group of sixth formers, all clad in red, used the balcony to lead the whole school in a dance in support of the One Billion Rising campaign to end violence against women. We reckon Shakespeare would have been enthralled.

The manor is home to the sixth form, and includes the sixth form café, study rooms, meeting areas, common rooms and their own kitchen facilities. Building boasts lots of wood panelling, a priest hole and a beautiful internal stained glass window. There's apparently a ghost – 'but it's a friendly presence,' a member of staff assured us. Pretty sixth-form garden next to the manor (perfect for building a 'snow family' last winter, said a sixth former).

Some of the classrooms look a bit dated but lots of building work going on. New library a hive of activity – the girls read widely and librarian buys 2,000 new fiction titles every year. Everything from Hilary Mantel to Stephenie Meyer. Impressive IT suite, with computers that rise up from the centre of the desk at the flick of a switch. 'All we need is dry ice,' grinned the head of IT, confessing that the school pinched the idea from Coventry University. Girls take IT in years 7 to 9 and are whizzes at designing apps. The school participates in the Apps For Good scheme, and a year 9 group recently won a national competition for their nifty Pitch Pals app (it helps musicians of all abilities tune their instruments), and another group won for their 'I'mOkay' app, for LGBTQ young people with real-life stories about sexuality and gender, simple definitions and the best support services.

S

A new £3.5m building houses the sports hall, fitness suite, drama studio and three classrooms, as well as a refurbished assembly hall and new kitchen and dining facilities.

Pastoral care, well-being and discipline: 'We don't bang the table about school rules, but expectations are very clear,' says the head firmly. Parents agree, although one told us that the school is 'a bit rule-ridden.' No alcohol problems in last five years and no drug problems in last eight (countywide protocol states that drug-taking would result in permanent exclusion). Head reckons that 'any school that says there is no bullying isn't telling the truth' and, like most girls' schools, occasional 'friendship issues' crop up. PSHE sessions and vertical tutor groups (each tutor has between three and five girls from each year in their tutor group and the groups meet once a day) are effective in sorting problems out. 'The tutor groups are like a family,' says the head. 'For the younger girls it's like having big sisters.' Sixth formers can train as peer mentors (they wear blue badges so girls know who they are).

Senior student leadership team of 14 (including head girl, two deputies and four house captains), plus 50 prefects and mentors. Girls write letters of application for posts, then head, senior staff and outgoing team interview them, staff throw in their views and candidates attend hustings assembly in spring term. House system – Cygnus, Orion, Phoenix and Ursa – with house assemblies, concerts, drama and sport.

Year 7 to 11 girls wear black blazers and skirts and pale blue blouses (far more chic than the purple macs and boaters of yesteryear). 'We have quite a few non-uniform days,' says the head, 'but having a uniform equals everything out. The girls don't have to fret about labels or what to wear each day.' Sixth formers wear business suits (any colour). Very jazzy new games kit in purple, navy and yellow – you can certainly spot a Stratford Girls' Grammar pupil at 50 paces.

Sixth-formers can sign out at lunchtime and walk into town. Year 11s granted this privilege on Fridays.

Pupils and parents: Pupils come from a host of state primaries and prep schools, including The Croft, Warwick Prep and The Kingsley School in Leamington Spa. Around 20 per cent live in Stratford-upon-Avon but others travel in by bus from up to an hour and a quarter away – from as far afield as Birmingham and Solihull to the north, Banbury to the south, Evesham to the west and Kenilworth to the east. Around three per cent of girls in years 7 to 11 have EAL requirements.

Entrance: Very competitive indeed, with four or five applicants for every year 7 place - though school hopes to expand to 800 pupils by 2017, which may ease a little of the pressure. Prospective pupils must register by July the previous year and take 11+ entrance test in September (for a place the following year). Priority given to girls living within a 17-mile radius of Stratford-upon-Avon.

Pupils joining sixth form need at least four A grades, two Bs and two Cs at GCSE, including As in the subjects they are taking at A level and at least Bs in English and maths.

Exit: Historically, a few girls leave each year after GCSEs, mainly to go to music or performing arts colleges or to do subjects not offered by the grammar. Virtually all year 13 leavers head to university; one to Oxbrige in 2016 and most to Russell Group. A plethora of subjects, but medicine (two in 2016, plus lots of biomedics and biologists) and law lead the pack, with economics and business degrees following close behind.

Money matters: A handful of girls are eligible for free school meals. School runs a hardship fund so no one misses out on school trips because of financial problems. Parents apply to head in confidence.

Remarks: A friendly, purposeful school that prides itself on educating 'the whole girl.' Unpretentious, sparky and high achieving, these girls will, and do, go far.

Summerhill School

Westward Ho, Leiston, Suffolk IP16 4HY

Pupils: 65; nearly all full boarders • Ages: 5-17

Fees: Day £5,100 – £10,830; Boarding £11,319 – £18,291 pa

Tel: 01728 830540
Email: office@summerhillschool.co.uk
Website: www.summerhillschool.co.uk

Principal: Since 1985, Zoe Readhead (a very youthful late 60s) – proprietor, keeper of the ethos and daughter of school's founder AS Neill. Literally born, bred and educated at Summerhill. Has been a staunch guardian of school's core values when lesser mortals would have wavered. Inspiring, uncompromising, down to earth rather than airy-fairy (is a qualified riding instructor), does not mince words. Married to Tony, a farmer, with four grown-up children all educated at Summerhill. In many ways a traditional family business: son Henry presides over the music studio; son William is deputy head and expected to take over running the school whenever Zoe retires.

Academic matters: Of secondary importance here. Summerhill is a 'free' school (NB in no way related to government-approved 'free' state schools) run on the principle that children have the same rights as adults and should be able to choose their own educational goals unfettered by the interference of anxious parents. Lessons are optional – some children will not attend a single lesson for a number of years, if ever. As the parents' handbook emphasises, 'remember, at Summerhill your kid could theoretically NEVER go to a lesson – they have that right. Staff members are not going to persuade, cajole or bully your child about lessons.' Play is considered as valid a part of a child's development as formal teaching: 'Many kids just need to play until they are ready to learn.'

That said, most pupils end up taking at least a few GCSEs, some take five or more. Results all over the shop from A* to G. 'My daughter might have got better exam marks at a different school,' a parent told us, 'but she got the grades she needed for the next step she was planning to take which is what mattered.' Prime emphasis is put on reading and writing, much of it delivered via one-to-one teaching. We observed a physics lesson which consisted of one seated pupil soberly facing a whiteboard where the teacher was instructing – curiously alternative and traditional all at once. A great environment for independent learners – the school brings this out in many of its pupils – but less ideal for those who thrive on a collegiate buzz and constructive competition from like-minded pupils. Nine full-time, live-in teachers, plus peripatetics, offer normal range of subjects plus environmental management, specialist music lessons, sound recording, drama, catering, psychology, French, German, Chinese and Japanese – staff try to accommodate kids' interests. Pupils are entered for Cambridge International O levels for some subjects rather than GCSEs.

One senses kid gloves in Ofsted's almost comically gushing most recent report (how times have changed from 1999 when it recommended the school be shut down): 'An outstanding feature is the way in which learning is closely tailored to match individual pupil's needs, including those with special educational needs and/or disabilities. A fundamental aspect of the school's curriculum is that learning takes place out of lessons as well as in them.'

'Special needs' not recognised here. Pupils labelled ADHD elsewhere are taken off the Ritalin and dispatched to play in the woods until they feel ready to learn. 'We take a rather old fashioned attitude to things like ADHD,' says Zoe. 'You've got to get on with it. Everyone is treated an individual here and there's so much one-to-one teaching.' However, school does apply for pupils to be given extra time in exams if they're eligible.

Games, options, the arts: Sports not high on the agenda and, despite its rather windswept tennis court, Summerhill is not likely to produce the next Andy Murray. Various games played, including Summerhill's own 'tork'. Swimming for the bold in unheated outdoor pool and for the meek at the Leiston Leisure Centre. Dance is an option and performance of all kinds is valued here. Music important with some excellent teaching and good facilities for music technology and studio recording. Similarly, drama is big among these arty kids and the school has a small theatre. Woodwork taken seriously, operating on same footing as English or maths – except it is probably more popular. Other activities include metalwork (new room joins the woodwork room), Japanese, Chinese, gardening, photography, calligraphy, film-making, crafts, riding, cooking in the café, camping in the grounds, making tree forts etc. But no one is coaxed into any of this: at Summerhill boredom is considered an important ingredient of education. Children become practical, hands on – can light a fire, cook, run a meeting.

Boarding: Not a hippy wilderness – TVs and Xboxes in some of the dorms. Girls' rooms generally nicer than the boys' and fewer girls to a room. Pupils allowed out to Leiston town – a quiet backwater roughly 10 minutes' walk away. No Saturday activities or lessons – 'we just live' – but kids can ask for a lesson if desired.

Background and atmosphere: Founded in 1921 by AS Neill near Dresden, Germany; settled in Leiston in 1927, where it became one of the most famous and controversial schools in the world. The school has been threatened with closure on several occasions, most recently in 1999 after a damning Ofsted report that called the pupils 'foulmouthed' and accused the school of failing the children educationally. Summerhill contested the notice of closure in court and four days into the hearing – in the face of enormous protest from current and former parents and pupils – the government's case collapsed.

Rough and tumble 11-acre setting includes large Victorian house, many single-storey additions, staff accommodation (one basic, hippy-style caravan left, treasured by its occupant – you've got to see it to believe it), wooded grounds. Spectacular beech tree for climbing, rope-swings and general play – a 'Summerhill thing', the pupils told us. Felt less full than on our last visit but school says its numbers wax and wane over the course of the year. Long holidays – five weeks at Christmas, five weeks in the spring and nine weeks each summer, but no half-terms or bank holidays – works well for overseas pupils. Annual festival-style camp for parents and former teachers over a summer term weekend.

Pastoral care, well-being and discipline: Far from being a place where you can do anything you like, Summerhill has more rules than any school we have ever visited. However, there are few fixed rules (other than the laws of the land). Everything is voted on at the Meeting, held twice a week. All children, from age 5 upward, have an equal vote, as do the teachers. No special authority invested in adults, indeed quite the contrary as they are vastly outnumbered. The Meeting is chaired by pupils and will sometimes make outlandish decisions eg to banish bed-times (sooner or later a glassy-eyed pupil will suggest they be reinstated). Misdemeanours are 'brought up' at the Meeting and an appropriate 'fine' is decided upon. Meeting proceedings surprisingly formal, with older pupils chairing on a rotating basis after first attending training sessions – lots of juicy educational stuff going on here. Pupils not afraid to voice complaints about their peers; bullying usually dealt with calmly and swiftly. As a former pupil told us, 'what Summerhill does give you is an ability to communicate with people, and it teaches you to just be nice.'

The school makes much of its claim that it allows kids to be kids. To us, however, at times it felt that it allows kids to be adults. Summerhill's freedom and democracy can extend into unsettling areas. The Meeting decides how to filter internet access and DVD restrictions. Sex is not officially sanctioned, but boys and girls allowed in each others' rooms and there is no effort made to discourage it. The school will assist pupils with contraception 'when it is thought necessary' and parents will not be informed unless the child requests it. Smoking allowed over age 14 but pupils must announce that they are smokers at the Meeting and sit through an anti-smoking information DVD. Smoking rather more prevalent than last time we visited. Drug taking or drinking will get a pupil sent home for four to eight weeks, but a child would only be asked to leave if they consistently made clear they could not fit in eg for extremely disturbed behaviour or consistently failing to follow the community's rules. A young boy we saw walking through the school with an open evil-looking folding knife was chastised by an older pupil.

Everyone up by 8am on weekdays. At lesson times teachers await pupils for 10 minutes, then depart if no-show. Student investigation committee deals with any reported thefts. Food a bit basic, portions smallish, vegetarian option – can be a challenge for hearty or picky eaters, but toast and fruit always available. 'Poc' – weekly pocket money – handed out by age. The school recommends children not bring in extra money (though some do).

Pupils and parents: An international community. The school is well known abroad and around 65 per cent of children come from overseas: Japan, Korea, Holland, China, Germany, France, Poland, Russia.. the nationalities wax and wane over the years. Around half of pupils are receiving some sort of EFL help (if they choose to turn up). Recent drop in Japanese pupils (recession) made up for by upsurge in Chinese. Hodge-podge of languages can be heard as one meanders through the school.

Like home schoolers, parents at Summerhill tend to be ardent advocates of the school, born, no doubt, of having continually to justify their choice of this kind of education. 'A profound place,' said a parent. 'Love creeps up through the floorboards'. Parents here have taken the decision to 'let go' for the benefit of their children; keeping parents at arm's length so that the children can develop free of parental anxiety and interference is a key tenet. There are no school reports and parents will not be informed if their child transgresses. The school's literature says, 'what happens at school is usually considered to be the kid's own business, not necessarily to be shared by parents. Accepting this is part of learning to accept your new independent, free child.' Some children were previously home schooled or attended other alternative schools, though lots come straight from mainstream education. 'Many of us didn't get on in normal schools,' a pupil told us.

Entrance: 'Selection is based on whether we feel the child is suitable for Summerhill and vice-versa – the parents also need to understand and support the ethos of the school.' Takes children on up to age 11 – over 12s rarely enrolled. There are day places, but it is basically a boarding school with children going home twice a term for weekends (although they can ask at the Meeting and usually get away more frequently if they want to). Weekly boarding is an option for the youngest children or as a settling stage for pupils who will become full boarders later. Pupils may enter the school at the start of any term and, as they seldom start with a cohort, it is common for them to take several terms to fully integrate. Interested parents are encouraged to read about the school, and then to visit.

Exit: A few leave at 14 to attend a more traditional GCSE course elsewhere; most leave at 16/17; a small number stay on until 18. Majority go on to some kind of further education. Many proceed to sixth form colleges (and then university) although entering a normal school can be a jolt. Some end up working in skilled craft jobs. Children's writer John Burningham (The Snowman) attended the school, as did several successful actors, musicians, dancers, artists and scientists – others are off making tepees in the Welsh hills.

Money matters: Mega-cheap, but then they do not have the overheads of keeping up historical buildings, state-of-the-art sports centres, interactive whiteboards etc etc. Whole place runs on a shoestring with an air of frugality. Teachers' salaries lowish. Ten per cent fee discount, or more, for children of ex-Summerhillians. Some subjects – like Chinese, riding, dancing and music lessons – charged as extras. School squirreling away funds for the AS Neill Summerhill Trust, which will eventually be able to provide limited bursaries for existing pupils.

Remarks: You know tiger parenting? Well, this is the opposite. A living, breathing St Trinians of a school, and we mean that in the best possible way (indeed, its 1999 battle with Ofsted was made into a CBBC TV series). Other schools seek to incorporate watered-down elements of the Summerhill philosophy, but none provides such an uncompromising, full-on, 'free' education – accepting the good (enlightenment) and the bad (illiteracy) that may result. Thank goodness something like this still exists in 21st century Britain where exams and paper qualifications are almost a religion. Educational philosophies and government initiatives may come and go, but Summerhill glides serenely on.

Thomas Mills High School

Saxtead Road, Framlingham, Woodbridge, Suffolk IP13 9HE

Pupils: 1,099 • Ages: 11–18 • Sixth form: 260

Tel: 01728 723493
Email: inmail@thomasmills.suffolk.sch.uk
Website: www.thomasmills.suffolk.sch.uk

Headteacher: Since 2013, Mr Philip Hurst MA MBA FRSA (very early 40s). Previously deputy/acting head of Philip Morant School, Colchester, where he had taught history earlier in his career; assistant head, Manningtree High School; and head of humanities, Thurstable School, Tiptree. Talent recognised early, as the return to Philip Morant School indicates. Inspired to enter teaching profession by the principal of his own school and believes in long term commitment of heads to their school; unimpressed with practice of heads whizzing around 'troubleshooting'. Is proud of school's reputation and thinks high academic standards reflect the excellence of the teaching and wide programme of extracurricular activities that all staff contribute to. Continues to teach his own subject – 'the biggest buzz of the week' – and is seen around corridors; 'keeps good eye contact with pupils,' we heard. Accepts need for heads to be good managers but believes teaching must remain at the heart of successful leadership in schools. Quiet, relaxed manner, quick on the draw and unstuffy. Plays tennis and is involved at a high level with the St John Ambulance association. A person of inner strength, dedication and far-sightedness; a head to watch.

Academic matters: Glowing exam results at all stages. Able pupils fast tracked and take some GCSEs in year 10, allowing A level teaching to begin in year 11. In 2016, 68 per cent of pupils gained at least five GCSEs at A*-C including English and maths (26 per cent A*/A grades). The school may be a technology, arts and languages academy, but it offers a choice of 26 subjects at GCSE, including Latin and Spanish. A foreign language is compulsory at GCSE and many do two or more. German and French top the poll – over 90 entries for German. Spanish also offered but benefits of learning German with present economic realities are pointed out. Very good results for all technologies – textiles, resistance materials and food. Many take 12 subjects and guides spoke regretfully of not being able to take more. Triple and double science both offered and results are excellent.

Strong science also reflected in high take-up at A level, with chemistry most popular of the 25 subjects offered. Year 7 are class taught with setting thereafter for maths and science – but no streaming. School proud of non-selective sixth form – baseline five GCSEs including maths and English and results indicate relaxed approach succeeds with 50 per cent at A*-B and 17 per cent A*/A in 2016.

Good provision for those that struggle, mostly in class support though department has own area. Pupils and parents loud in praise of staff, 'they make us work', 'excellent teachers who stay long enough to see things through'. Some have taught parents and grandparents; this really is a community school.

Games, options, the arts: Impressive all round. Traditional team sports, including cricket for girls (very popular) played and encouraged by the strong house system retained from grammar school era. Top teams are competing at county level. Recent addition of a multi-use games area (known as the MUGA) and shared with public out of hours. PTA efforts have funded a fitness trail around the grounds and trampolining, riding and dance all available. D of E has high take up, over 100 awards at bronze and silver annually. Language trips exchanges, all year 7s go to Holland for a 'bonding,' week, ski trips and travel as far afield as Africa to work on a community project in Zambia or Peru.

Art extremely popular: half the year take it at GCSE and work is widely exhibited throughout school. New dining hall a backdrop for several spectacular creations. Music superb; hundreds have private instrumental lessons with practice rooms available. Choirs, orchestras, ensembles and bands proliferate; concerts and a major musical involving whole school tackled each year. Drama taught to years 7/8, very popular and taken seriously within school time – 'We spent a whole week rehearsing the play!' – with solid cohort taking GCSE. Large performing arts studio for lessons/rehearsals and staged school hall for big productions.

Background and atmosphere: It is over 300 years since Thomas Mills left a bequest to benefit the people, particularly children, of Framlingham. Two earlier grammars and the 'modern' school pre-date the present high school (now an academy) and this ancestry gives a sense of belonging and permanence. School is proud of its previous incarnations, photographs displayed around corridors and in the library, a relic of former times, a desk with a tip-up lid containing 'ancient' textbooks. Main building dates from post-war era with long corridors and high windows but, the sick room aside (unutterably dreary – possibly deliberately), on the whole well decorated and cheerful. New buildings have sprung up, science, languages, sport, with pleasant courtyards sandwiched between and areas for recreation and lunch time, though new dining room so enticing that even packed lunch eaters join their friends. Good lunches. Placed on the outskirts of Framlingham, the school is calm and quiet, no shouting from pupils (or staff), and we saw more door holding and polite stepping aside than is common. Remarkably tranquil, purposeful atmosphere.

Pastoral care, well-being and discipline: A sense of pride and belonging is fostered by the house system which operates for sport and extracurricular competitions with merits awarded for individual effort towards the house tally (there are six). House shields are displayed in rank order in the main hall and the whole operation is managed by sixth formers. Pupils move through the school with the same tutor and difficulties are dealt with by them. Relatively problem-free intake and pupils largely in tune with purposeful atmosphere.

Pupils and parents: Popularity of the school draws pupils from a wide surrounding area as well as Framlingham itself. Diverse social backgrounds though representative of a prosperous area, and very little ethnic mix. Parents delighted with the school: 'Lucky us, some of my friends have paid fortunes to educate their children'. School well integrated within the life of the town and enjoys good relations with close neighbour, Framlingham College.

Entrance: Around 50 per cent drawn from the six or seven schools within the catchment area, the remainder from outside, though a demographic shift means more places available in this category. Generally oversubscribed and very popular at sixth form with influx of 30 to 40 from other high schools and independent sector.

Exit: Up to half leave after GCSEs. Great majority to higher education with large numbers to top flight universities. Four medics in 2016; wide variety of other subjects studied. A sprinkling join family businesses or enter vocational training.

Remarks: A remarkable school with high academic expectation and achievement, a dazzling array of extracurricular activities and a dedicated staff. Has enjoyed, and is enjoying, outstanding leadership.

Thurston Community College

Norton Road, Thurston, Bury St Edmunds, Suffolk IP31 3PB

Pupils: 1,435 • Ages: 11–18 • Sixth form: 375

Tel: 01359 230885
Email: admin@thurstoncollege.suffolk.sch.uk
Website: www.thurstoncollege.org

Principal: Since 2005, Miss Helen Wilson BSc, MBA, NPQH (40s). Studied applied physics with chemistry at Durham, followed by PGCE at Bristol. Previously assistant principal at Comberton village college and vice-principal at Thurston. Her long experience and tremendous dynamism have enabled the school to make a smooth transition from within a three tiered system to becoming an 11-18 school. Extremely personable, lively and direct, she works hard to ensure staff and pupils feel valued. A team player (her management style is described as

T

'exemplary,' by Ofsted) she is clear that 'appointing the right staff and supporting them' is key to the school's success. Keeps in close touch and believes in regular meetings (also, three whole staff briefings each week) as the means to picking up on possible problems. Has strong support from parents: 'She has a good eye for the right staff' and 'She listens to what parents have to say [through the parents' forum] and takes action.' Her friendliness and ease with pupils is praised: 'She has that way of knowing how to speak to pupils without losing authority.' Continues to teach physics, though as in-class support: 'not enough time to class teach this year because of the merger', and often welcomes pupils to lunches in her office, all part of the system of recognition and award that underpins school life. Her overwhelming energy continues in off-duty sport – 'it is how I let off steam': though competitive hockey was put paid to with a new hip, she now cycles the 10 miles to and from school each day and enjoys skiing and water sports, also good food and drink with family and friends.

Academic matters: Achievement is strongly supported and clear strategies are in place to pick up problems early. Rigorous selection when appointing staff ('we want the outstanding ones') and a regular turnover ensures that standards are constantly appraised and improved. Pupils are referred to as students, rather than pupils, as the principal believes this better reflects the school's ambition to 'inculcate a passion for lifelong independent learning, rather than simply instruct them. They will need to have the skills to manage a life with several career changes.' The acronym SCRIPT is used to express this: self manager, creative thinker, reflective learner, independent participant, team worker. In 2016, 56 per cent passed GCSE in five subjects at grades A*-C including English and maths. Wide choice of subjects on offer including three European languages. Year 7s study French, and 80 per cent of students in year 8 and 9 study a second language (either German or Spanish), and may continue one or more to GCSE. Latin (taught as an 'extra'), separate sciences, child development, dance, horticulture and mechanics also available. Everyone takes religious studies. Academic learning tuition (SEN support) is provided by 21 teaching assistants, mostly operating in the classroom, six qualified higher level teaching assistants and two SENCos. Lots of help available, including catch up classes in numeracy and literacy at break and lunch; there's a breakfast club (porridge served) and homework club each day.

Sixth form students (now on a separate site at Beyton, two miles off) work in surroundings more reminiscent of higher education: lots of private study areas, some supervised, others more relaxed and allowing for quiet discussion. Strong work ethic amongst students and 'it's easy to get help if you need it,' we were told. Good attainment at A level with 18 per cent A*/A, 45 A*-B grades in 2016. Popular subject choices include maths, psychology, all the sciences and English; only a handful study foreign languages.

Games, options, the arts: Despite having only a single, weekly timetabled games lesson (though it lasts 100 minutes), team and other sports flourish through a network of lunchtime and after-school clubs, and friendly inter-house rivalry is encouraged. Football, netball, rugby (girls' as well as boys'), excellent hockey and rounders with teams reaching county and regional stages of competitions and individuals selected for trials at national level. Club tours also organised – Paris this year. Other choices include Thai boxing, table tennis, gymnastics and the supervised fitness suite. Music and drama both timetabled up to year 9 and many pupils have instrumental lessons – practice rooms are available. Drama is a popular GCSE choice and the school stages two major productions each year; 'our daughters have both performed and we were amazed at what they achieved.' Art and textiles/design also have a high take-up at GCSE and students' work is well displayed and promoted. Emphasis in the sixth form is on volunteering projects, D of E, charity fundraising and the national citizenship service scheme.

Background and atmosphere: A large rural comprehensive close to Bury St Edmund's, with a separate sixth form campus in a revamped former middle school at Beyton. Reorganisation of the Suffolk schooling system from three tier to two tier saw it accept pupils from year 7 rather than year 9 in 2014, and the sixth form move to its separate site. With over 1,500 pupils at the main 11 to 16 site at Thurston, it has a, perhaps surprisingly, unflustered air. The entrance, via a car park and reception area, is reminiscent of a Travelodge, though efforts have been made to plant and landscape the approaches. Mostly single storey, inter-connecting buildings of functional appearance, but cheerfully decorated within with carpeted corridors muffling noise, lots of pupils' work displayed, notice boards everywhere covered in information about after-school clubs and goings-on – a definite buzz. Good IT provision, two libraries (one open to the public out of hours) with separate areas for project work and private study. Several halls, of varying sizes, one with raked seating, are used for drama, games lessons and assemblies. Plenty of room to let off steam in surrounding playing fields.

No cloakrooms; pupils each have a locker in their house, close to their tutorial base. Unfussy uniform: pale blue polo shirts and jerseys with school logo, skirts or trousers for girls, though there is a movement to discourage trousers that verge on 'jeggings', not entirely approved of: 'It can be difficult for teenage girls to find sizes that fit well'. Despite large numbers, pupils move calmly around at changes of lesson and settle quickly. No mobiles allowed in class. Food is praised; 'there is lots of choice and we can buy food at break as well as lunch.' The sixth form site has been well converted and decorated, lots of fresh white paint, spanking new facilities including computer terminals, coffee shop, common rooms and libraries overlooking extensive lawns and woodland. More of a college atmosphere, no uniform, a more grown up air altogether; 'most of us are going to university and need to learn to work on our own,' we were told, and certainly saw a lot of independent study going on. The informal, respectful tone set by the principal is carried through and maintained by staff and pupils.

Pastoral care, well-being and discipline: The school is divided up into five houses (named after Suffolk luminaries) and pupils belong to a tutor group within a house for registration and academic and pastoral oversight. These smaller units, of around 300, help to give pupils a sense of identity and belonging. Tutors keep subject staff in the picture if problems arise and they are the first point of contact for parents wishing to discuss their child, although there is also a dedicated advice centre for parents to turn to, particularly with more routine enquiries. Particular nurturing of year 7s; the principal and staff visit all prospective pupils in their primary schools and there is a buddy system in place. A weather eye is kept out for pupils whose behaviour puts them at risk of exclusion, and though this is rare, the principal says, 'I'll do it if I have to.' Houses appoint up to 50 Ambassadors, who help with greeting visitors, acting as sheep dogs at open days and other events. The monthly magazine, Celebrate, records success in every aspect of school life: those winning house stars are published under Ovation, together with news and articles on school life. The school day is divided into 100 minute lessons, 'long enough to get stuck into a subject', spread over a two week timetable. There are longer breaks and lunchtimes than is usual, as pupils mostly travel some distance; 'school must provide plenty of social opportunities.' There is a homework club until 5pm and the school funds extra buses to enable pupils to stay later for sports fixtures and rehearsals.

T

Pupils and parents: The catchment, on the edge of Bury St Edmund's, is largely prosperous, rural and representative of this part of East Anglia; very few from ethnic minorities. A network of school bus routes brings most pupils, some from considerable distance. The school's popularity is endorsed by the number from out of the catchment. Strong approval for the management: 'The principal has a good eye for the right staff and morale seems to be very good.' The uniform, worn up to year 11, is well supported by pupils and parents.

Entrance: The recent expansion as an 11-18 (rather than 13-18) school has resulted in certain year groups higher up the school becoming very large, but there is a firm policy to keep year group sizes below 300 and the principal won't budge on this. Heavily oversubscribed; the catchment rules are stringent and it is important to check the admissions policy of Suffolk County Council. For A levels, at least a grade B in the subject to be studied (or a related subject) is required, with an overall average GCSE points score of 43 or better. Students without a C in maths or English are required to continue studying the subject at after-school sessions, with a view to re-sitting the examination(s).

Exit: Around half stay on after GCSEs, the rest mostly moving on to employment or FE college. At 18 the great majority go on to university, with a wide range of subjects studied eg midwifery, electrical engineering, psychology and neuroscience. Around 40 per cent to Russell group universities; one to Cambridge (philosophy) in 2016.

Remarks: A large, extremely well managed comprehensive where the majority thrive and do well. Led by a dynamic head with a strong vocation and the ideas and determination to take the school to the top.

Town Close House Preparatory School

14 Ipswich Road, Norwich, Norfolk NR2 2LR

Pupils: 509 (two thirds boys) • Ages: 3-13

Fees: £8,097 – £12,399 pa

Tel: 01603 620180
Email: admissions@townclose.com
Website: www.townclose.com

Headmaster: Since 2013, Mr Nicholas Bevington BA PGCE (early 40s). Educated at Portsmouth Grammar, then Keele (read international relations) and Newcastle universities. Began teaching at Elstree School, brisk promotion to head of department, followed by Edgeborough and Abercorn Schools (deputy head) and Bede's Prep, Eastbourne, where he was head.

Tall, youthful looking and charming. His quick wit and energy are going down well with parents. 'We like what we have seen so far,' say most. 'He is really committed, seems very on the ball.' One spoke of feeling, 'slightly overwhelmed. He creates a tremendous buzz.' Definitely not shy and retiring.

Good grasp of local school scene and the place Town Close occupies as a 'stand alone' day prep. Firmly in favour of transfer to senior schools at 13+ and success of pupils at this stage is vindication – lots of awards, many to selective schools, including Eton. He points to fact that pupils also do well in subsequent years – often becoming head boy or head girl. Head knows that these final two years count – 'they have all the fun of leadership as they enter their teens and the extra years give many a chance to mature.'

Proud of school's reputation and feels parents know what they are getting. 'We never try to be something we are not, we don't try to attract children who won't thrive here.' Believes a day prep is ideal for most up to 13 and is not keen on flexi or 'fun' nights to entice children into boarding. 'We have plenty of after-school activities up to 6pm and that suits many of our parents.'

Wife Catherine is a hospital consultant and not involved in day to day matters at the school. They have two small children. He plays the guitar and flute, enjoys tennis and cycling and gardens.

Entrance: Assessment, rather than examination, at all points of entry to the school. Most start in nursery, reception or year 2, though plenty more join higher up as and when places become available. At nursery and reception stage, learning potential is assessed during an hour of class play-based activities, extending to half a day for year 2, including assessment of literacy and non-verbal reasoning, and a full day from year 4 onwards. Informal interview with head for years 2 to 4 (more formally, in the study, for year 5 up). Not, strictly speaking, a hard to get into school, but very popular and generally oversubscribed. 'Quite honestly,' a parent told us, 'I was anxious about the entrance "exam" but all was well. The head got right down to their level, talking to my son, and there was no worry or tears.'

Exit: Given the school's relaxed admission policy, pupils move on to an impressive range of schools, many academically highly selective. The local day independents, Norwich High and Norwich School, are popular at 11 and 13+ (sloping off earlier is discouraged but sometimes happens when parents are anxious about securing places later on).

Sizeable group opt for boarding, mostly to schools nearby – Gresham's, Framlingham and Culford. Some go further afield, to eg Oundle, Uppingham, Oakham or Wycombe Abbey. School gives lots of guidance on choices and scholarships, although head says: 'We can point the way, but in the end it's the parents' choice.'

Remarks: Tucked behind the tree-lined boulevards of south west Norwich, the school grounds are extensive, especially for a city school (school has recently bought its site). An elegant Georgian house, with sweeping lawns, surrounded by various additions – classroom blocks, performance hall for drama and assemblies, sports hall, swimming pool, two playgrounds (junior and senior), woodland walks (school has forest school status), all in excellent condition.

General agreement that dining room needs a makeover. Wide approval for practice of sitting at tables with teachers, passing the salt and waiting until everyone has finished, although the food itself is not raved about. No dreary corridors – carpeted hallways and stunning displays of work throughout. Though warned not to try by his predecessor, the head has even solved the impossible parking and pick-up schedule (timed slots) and tightened security of the grounds into the bargain. Nursery and pre-prep have a separate building with enticing play area.

Pupils extremely polite – door holding and standing up for visitors de rigueur. Our guides maintained extreme discretion throughout – perhaps not the place for free spirits? However, we saw lively pupil/teacher exchanges, including an enthralling discussion of post-mortem research in a history lesson. High levels of expectation – setting from reception in literacy, increasing to full blown setting by ability in years 7 and 8. Reading is seriously encouraged, with excellent library open every lunchtime (we approve) and a jolly nice full-time librarian. Pupils also have timetabled lessons there. School now provides tablets for all year 6-8s. A number of pupils with SEN – mostly dyslexia, a few with language and speech needs. Individual support is given for EAL, but all must be able to follow the curriculum.

Excellent music, with massive take-up of private instrumental lessons and opportunities to play in ensembles and orchestras and sing in choirs. Music, drama and other performing arts are encouraged and showcased as much as sport (pupils have left for the Royal Ballet School). Shakespeare, pantomimes, Last Night of the Proms, it's all happening. 'You enjoy school more if you do stuff,' say pupils.

All team sports played very successfully and several outstanding individuals play at county and even national level. Everyone gets the chance to play in matches but, say pupils, 'it's not always the same Player of the Match.' Parents speak in lip-smacking approval. 'Lovely school,' one told us. 'Ideal for our daughter, who has thrived.' Another, worried about choosing for her son, said: 'We picked absolutely the right one for him. The staff are brilliant and really seem to know the children.' Several spoke of their child's confidence being nurtured and former pupils have nothing but praise. 'I loved my time there and would have stayed if I could,' said one girl. Great majority of pupils are the offspring of successful professionals, notably doctors. Main recruiting channel is the one money can't buy – word of mouth.

Tudor Grange Academy

Dingle Lane, Solihull, West Midlands B91 3PD

Pupils: 1,514 • Ages: 11 – 18 • Sixth form: 275

Tel: 0121 705 5100
Email: office@solihull.tgacademy.org.uk
Website: www.solihull.tgacademy.org.uk

Principal: Since 2014, Mr Darren Turner BA Ed MA Ed, married with four children. Educated at St Luke's College, Exeter, Mr Turner is example of that army of PE teachers who, in the last few years, have marched on to become heads. Most of his energies have been devoted to encouraging and inspiring pupils and teachers, another powerful feature of the PE world. In his time he has led a department to national recognition, winning national DfE awards for contributions to the PE and sport at King's School, Winchester. Meanwhile, he found time to play some good minor counties cricket, some semi-professional football, of which we witnessed evidence later on, and coached rugby for Hampshire and England U17s. He has been a director of sport, and gained his masters in educational leadership from Warwick University in 2010. That was the year he arrived in north Solihull as vice principal of a school which had been closed by the DfE. With the support of a sponsor, the school reopened as a new academy, and in just over two years received outstanding in a full Ofsted inspection. He continues to help other schools through his imagination and inspiration. This, and more, can be found modestly expressed on the website.

T

Mr Turner is not a hearty, muscle-bound PE instructor or bullfrog head barking out orders and communicating by harsh metaphorical blasts on the whistle. He is a lively, entertaining and thoughtful talker whose results are achieved not by the thundering but through keen-eyed perception and emotional intelligence. He seems adept at understanding where gentle, sympathetic encouragement is required or something a little more challenging. One of the staff referred to him as 'the whisperer'; another added that he was fair but jolly tough when necessary. He's certainly no pushover. Several people – parents, staff and cleaning ladies, a very important group of witnesses if you want to know what a school is like – described him as 'a breath of fresh air', commenting on how forthcoming and alertly interested he is and how good a listener.

Phrases like 'breath of fresh air' should not imply criticism of Mr Turner's predecessor, who was responsible for the outstanding Ofsted report and for putting into place the structured foundation upon which the new head is currently building. She did a marvellous job, echoed by Mr Turner, as a thorough planner before leaving for a high-powered government post. What then was required, we were frequently told, was a head who was visible, active, forthcoming and lively. Mr Turner is certainly all those. Wherever we went on our pupil-guided tour the head kept popping up, most memorably pausing to demonstrate some footballing skills with a group of boys in the playground, watched by a group of girls who had stopped to talk with us. 'Oh, off he goes again,' said one. 'Is he always like this or is he trying to impress the visitors?' we asked. 'He's always like this: he's everywhere. Sometimes you wonder if there are twin heads. He's brilliant.'

This is a head who knows most of the pupils by name and cares about them. They, in their turn, recognise that and appreciate it. Above all, he wants them to reach their full potential. Pupils praised his inspirational talks at school assemblies – 'He's a brilliant speaker. He can be a bit cheesy, though I think he knows that and anyway, that always makes it all the more fun.' The word he uses most often is 'empower.' He recognises the school is in good shape, 'but there's always room for improvement, so the situation is ripe with opportunities to improve and to reach full potential. That includes the staff as well: leaders, captains and coaches: parents, pupils, teachers.' Above all, good communications are crucial and that is perhaps the key to this man's success. That and an excellent blend of generous determination with a sprinkling of humour. 'This man doesn't do pomposity.'

Academic matters: Not a grade-chasing school approaching league table results as if they were the Holy Grail. The school's determination to empower both staff and pupils with the confidence to perform to the best of their ability has brought forth some very impressive results. These are prominently displayed in the school's prospectus and other literature as well as on the website. The school is justifiably proud of the results, which are down to good teaching, intervention when necessary and hard-working pupils who have been encouraged to believe in themselves. Some subjects – such as maths – are taught in ability groups. Unlike a distressing number of schools – many in the independent sector – where pupils whose performance suggests they won't achieve good grades are told to leave, there is no suggestion of that here, though there are entry requirements for the sixth form. Instead parents, staff and pupil get together to work out a stratagem for one-to-one help in those subjects requiring extra attention. This is all explained on the school website under the heading Pupil Premium. The result is that in the DfE performance tables the school is in the top 10 of non-selective schools in the country. As one teacher told us, 'We never, never, never give up on our pupils.' The most recent Ofsted report in 2014 graded the school as outstanding in all areas. As an illustration, consider the fact that in the 2016, 88 per cent of pupils achieved five or more A*-C grades, including English and maths with around a third of grades at A*/A and half achieving the EBacc. At A level, 57 per cent of grades in 2016 were A*-B. Ofsted reported that 'students in all subjects make exceptional progress because they are challenged and their personal skills are strongly developed.' The reference to 'personal skills' is very relevant to the principal's mantra.

We saw generous amounts of teaching and witnessed nothing that contradicted Ofsted. We saw lively, clever teaching with lots of encouragement and individual treatment; we saw keen and alert pupils – even those who, despite everything, confessed sadly that they didn't really like the subject but were determined to pass. Underpinning all this is the obvious enthusiasm and happiness of the staff. Attached to the main school is a training school for teachers. Far from going for the posthumous VC, these teachers are bright, enthusiastic and willing to immerse themselves in placements, including Tudor Grange itself. Some, probably the very best, stay on for a year or two, injecting a sense of energy and purpose. The staffroom was friendly, staff happy to talk about the school, serious in purpose and quick to laugh, appearing bright, cheerful and stylish. Pupils wear their uniforms smartly. It all helps.

Games, options, the arts: The school was founded in 1956 and there is a fascinating but unintentional memorial to that – viz an old building looking a little like a WW2 Nissan hut which has narrowly missed a direct hit. It is the old gymnasium, and it just survives beside an area of tarmac where football, basketball, netball and other games are played. A large and unmistakable building dominates. It's the superbly equipped sports hall more than 50 years on. An exercise in architectural history; an example of progress: not beautiful, but functional. We witnessed a tremendously lively girls' cricket session overseen by the captain of England's women's team and met a number of youthful, forthcoming and, yes, very friendly staff. Outside there are plenty of sports pitches which are used in partnership with West Warwickshire Sports Club, and which generate many regional and national sportsmen and women.

In a typical week there are over 60 extracurricular clubs and activities, some very unusual. We saw and admired some wonderful art, photography and creative work involving papier mâché and other materials. One pupil assured us that these activities were open for enjoyment out of class and in spare time; another rolled her eyes as if there was no such thing. We were charmed and startled by a girl asking if we would like to see her heart. It turned out to be the heart of an animal which she had bought from a local butcher and was going to use for a project. It was a lovely example of the open enthusiasm and friendliness that is such an obvious feature of this school.

Plenty of music, both vocal and instrumental, including the increasingly popular ukulele, orchestras and jazz bands. Instrumental lessons are provided by the Solihull Music Services for a minimal fee. We met a delightful and talented pupil who was composing for his entrance exam to music college and heard a lively choir practice. Much exuberance and enjoyment all round.

Background and atmosphere: The school was founded as a grammar school in 1956 for around 650 boys; in 1974 it linked up with the girls' grammar which had always been on the same site. In 1995 it became a technology college, in 2009 it was business and enterprise and two years later an academy for 11-16s; most recently it has extended its age range to include a sixth form and earned almost trumpeting praise from Ofsted. Now it aims at 'world class' education. The atmosphere, especially on the gloriously sunny day when we visited, was delightful. Very few pupils arrived alone and it was noticeable that groups greeted each other with easy warmth. In a natural, relaxed way there seemed to be an underlying sense of interested expectation both socially and academically.

This underlying happiness remained as we walked around meeting groups moving from classroom to classroom. Eye contact and smiles, easy conversation when we stopped to ask questions; wide-ranging topics of conversation, pertinent questions, sometimes amused reactions. Clearly the pupils are used to meeting and talking with alleged adults. Equally friendly was the company in the dining room, and if behaviour in school dining rooms has something to do with the quality of the food, that's not surprising. The food was certainly excellent.

Pastoral care, well-being and discipline: We watched pupils arriving quietly in happy groups, greeting and being greeted by staff; we observed a tutorial group being reminded of special activities in the near future in an atmosphere of relaxed concentration and fun. The tutorial system is rather good and appreciated overall by parents and pupils. Each new pupil is allotted a College, as it's called. These are mixed age groups, with three or four pupils from each year, in which boys and girls remain for their time at school. The leader of the College gets to know them well. Pupils seemed very happy with this arrangement and, of course, they are subliminally learning lessons about responsibility, consideration, age differences, leadership. As far as discipline is concerned, that didn't seem to be much of a problem. Nor did bullying emerge as an issue, though we were told by a few girls of the occasional fights between girls. These were dismissed as trivial and very, very rare. 'In any case,' they said, 'there are pupils and staff who help... Tudor Rangers, that building over there, provides refuge and counselling for children who have been or are being bullied. You can go there if you feel insecure.' The school has a very powerful, clear anti-bullying policy and staff are continually aware of the possibilities. Parents were happy with the lack of bullying.

Pupils and parents: The school has its own allotted catchment area. This has had a significant effect on the local housing market and there are accounts of parents mortgaging themselves up to the hilt because they feel the school is such a valuable asset. We spoke to a number of parents, all of whom reckoned it was a pretty good bargain overall. They are not poor but they are making sacrifices. They particularly like the improved communications and the new regime, though not at the expense of the old. By and large, they all seemed pretty grateful. So, too, did the pupils, in a delightfully unaffected way.

Entrance: Takes 250 into year 7. Preference to looked after children, then those attending the linked primary school, then those living in the catchment area, then siblings.

About 50 per cent of year 11 pupils stay on for the sixth form. Grades required are a minimum of six B grades at GCSEwith at least a C in maths and English. Pupils must achieve a minimum B grade in any subject they wish to take at A level. A large number of external candidates apply for entry into the sixth form; about 20-30 gain places. Pupils already in the school who do not match the entry criteria are signposted to other sixth forms in the local area with whom the school has strong links.

Exit: The school takes considerable trouble to prepare students for courses and universities suitable for their abilities and aspirations. About 80 per cent of sixth formers to university, more than a third to Russell Group unis, two to Oxbridge in 2016, two studying dentistry. There is also much help with apprenticeships and career choices for those leaving after GCSE (46 per cent in 2016). A popular and encouraging feature is the number of pupils who have left for fresh educational adventures and who return to share helpful tales and knowledgeable advice.

Money matters: Trips and excursions incur some cost, but overall the school is excellent value for money, making Solihull a particularly attractive place in which to live.

Remarks: In some ways this extraordinary school embraces the old fashioned virtues, albeit using modern teaching aides. Teaching here is for educating, for broadening horizons, for challenging capabilities, for exciting pupils, for enrichment. It is learning for life and not merely for grades. Parents and pupils feel that targets are personal and individually tailored. We heard very little suggestion of force-feeding driven by anxious staff petrified by Ofsted and grade targets. This is an excellent set-up; some would say worth moving to Solihull for. And we were not bribed by estate agents.

Uppingham Community College

London Road, Uppingham, Rutland LE15 9TJ

Pupils: 890 • Ages: 11–16

Tel: 01572 823631
Email: principal@ucc.rutland.sch.uk
Website: www.uppinghamcollege.org.uk

Principal: Since 2007, Jan Turner (50s). Originally from Lancashire, read theatre studies and English at Liverpool. Both daughters attended UCC before her time and have gone on to great things. 'It was the school I wanted to be head of,' she says, 'as I liked the ethos. It has a very strong sense of community, is very tight knit, and I wanted to part of that.' A very young-looking head whose years belie her. Very well liked and respected by all parents we talked to. 'She has a good view of what she wants to do with the school and is a good leader.' 'There has been a definite uplift since the school has become an academy; she's very ambitious for it.' 'Very switched on and articulate.' 'I like the direction that Mrs Turner is taking the school in.' She still teaches year 11, 'the highlight of my week', as well as year 9s and 10s, one session a week each.

A new free sixth form college in Oakham, Harington School, opened in 2015, offering places to UCC and Catmose students. Mrs Turner is one of the pioneers and is driving it forwards. Exciting times.

She is retiring in July 2017.

Academic matters: In 2016, 23 per cent of GCSE grades were A*/A. Good, solid results for a non-selective school. Most pupils take 10 GCSEs, with many doing a language: French, German and Spanish are on offer. Everyone takes DT (school has specialist technology status). Maths particularly strong here, reflected in the maths block opened in 2014. Streaming in English and maths. Good artwork throughout the school. As it was open evening when we visited, lots of GCSE books were out on display as well – impressive stuff. There is a gifted and talented programme that identifies the top 10 per cent. Bright sparks are identified in year 7 and nurtured. Year 11s supported in post-16 choices.

'Lots of extra help for those that need it or want it,' said one parent. Voluntary and compulsory extra lessons; those that miss homework targets are made to attend lunch time sessions. No slipping through the net here.

'We get an email every week outlining the following week's homework and when it's due, special projects and lessons, so we know exactly what is happening and expected, excellent,' said another parent. No hiding at this school.

Pupils seemed involved in the lessons we observed. Year 8 scientists were conducting experiments, year 11s in small groups having enrichment sessions: this could be extra help with a certain subject, or doing a higher level project which is an extra half GCSE. An IT exam in progress for the year 9s and a very energetic PE session for year 7s. DT session ongoing for year 11s, many working unsupervised, but they knew what they were doing. Every teacher greeted us and there were big smiles all round; they seem to be a happy lot here, staff and pupils alike.

Some 10 per cent of pupils need extra help with learning, and there are 18 with SENs varying from MLD to Asperger's Syndrome. Lots of support available for those who need it.

Games, options, the arts: They're a sporty lot here and take it seriously. Their motto is 'to be better than before.' Successful rugby, netball and football teams, some individuals playing to county standard. There are windsurfing and sailing opportunities – Rutland Water is just outside the town – and a successful newly re-established equestrian team. Lots of cups on display. Each year group has two sports captains, a boy and a girl, who are all part of the sports council. This council can put forward suggestions made by their peers for sports equipment and co-ordinate their year's sports. Nice to see their photos in prominent positions. Relatively new Astroturf and lots of space for playing fields. Many after-school and lunch time practice sessions that seem to be well attended. There is a popular yearly sports exchange with a school in Belgium.

A climbing wall in the gym is well used in extracurricular sessions; they have a very keen teacher. New tennis and netball courts in 2015. The college is currently fundraising for a second sports hall and new performing arts facilities.

Lots of music, with many having individual lessons. Plenty of bands, and orchestra practice after school and at lunch times. Frequent concerts and performances. Drama not mentioned a great deal, but we saw a studio and apparently Bugsy Malone was a great success.

Lots of school trips and exchanges. D of E popular with high take up.

Background and atmosphere: Founded in 1920 in the small market town of Uppingham that's rather dominated by its well-known public school. UCC has been on its present site on the edge of the town since the 1970s, a large, well managed, sprawling site with plenty of outside space and lots of room to grow. Nice to see lots of tables and benches dotted about for dining al fresco.

Smart uniform including blazers and ties introduced a couple of years ago. 'I really like the new uniform,' said one parent. 'It makes them look smart, particularly the girls in their long pleated skirts; no more inappropriate skirt lengths.' One year 11 told us that 'the longer your skirt, the cooler you are.' The girls may wear trousers, but very few were.

School lunches well received. Parents can check what is, or is not, being consumed. Large bright dining hall with a smaller outlet in the new maths block.

'There's lots of opportunities for all pupils, whatever their talents,' said one parent. 'They just need to make use of them.'

Pastoral care, well-being and discipline: Pastoral care very positive. 'It's a very kind, nurturing school,' said a year 11 parent. Pupils stay with the same form teacher throughout their time at the school. 'All my three had excellent form teachers who got to know them really well,' said another year 11 parent. 'They seem to know what makes children tick,' was another comment. Problems apparently nipped in the bud quickly, and relationships between pupils and teachers seem relaxed and open.

'My son had trouble on the school bus and it was quickly sorted out, fairly and logically. I was going to take him off the bus but they made the perpetrators leave instead until the matter was resolved. And they informed the parents, which was excellent, as they needed to know that their year 11 sons were misbehaving,' one parent told us. 'They weren't heavy handed and made sure my son was happy with the outcome.'

Another parent reported that her son wasn't so happy. 'I think the school is excellent but my son, in year 11, is starting to feel disconnected. This is possibly because he is due to leave soon, but who knows.'

Every other parent we talked to was delighted, however. 'They take in little kids and turn out fabulous, lovely adults. I'm going to miss the place when my third child leaves this year.'

A year 7 parent said, 'My daughter came from outside the area, so knew no one when she started. She very quickly found her feet and now loves it. She's very happy there.'

Pupils and parents: Pupils are from Uppingham and the surrounding villages. The catchment area is large and most pupils come from small village schools dotted around Rutland. 'Because most pupils come from small families and attended small village schools, they are used to having opinions and being listened to. They will do anything they are asked, but want to know why. They are far from quietly compliant,' says Mrs Turner. 'The children think about each other, know right from wrong and have a huge sense of responsibility, very much like their parents.'

Parents from a broad spectrum. All we spoke to were very supportive of the school and the vast majority were extremely happy with it. Every one would recommend it. 'The best state school in the area,' said one happy father. Many second generation pupils.

The pupils we met were welcoming, confident and proud of the school. Chatty and friendly. We were scrutinised by some, but not in an unwelcoming way – they were curious and observant.

Old pupils include John Browett, CEO of Monsoon and Accessorize and Ian Carter, President of Hilton International.

Entrance: Preference, after children in care, to those living in the catchment of named primary schools, siblings, children of staff and then by distance.

Exit: The vast majority, 70 per cent, move on to do A levels. Some eight per cent of these go to private sixth forms eg Oakham (many UCC leavers provide Oakham Oxbridge successes), the others mainly to selective state sixth forms out of county, often some distance away. Harington School in Oakham, which opened in 2015, is a new option: it is a free school offering sixth form tuition to the brightest pupils from the two state schools in the county, UCC and Catmose College. Pupils need to attain five Bs at GCSE and A*-C passes in maths and English. Those with less academic inclination to vocational courses or apprenticeships elsewhere.

Remarks: A happy, friendly school that's getting good solid results and turning out pleasant, able young people. And the parents appreciate it. Excellently led by an ambitious head, this school is only heading one way, and that's up.

Uppingham School

81

High Street West, Uppingham, Rutland LE15 9QE

Pupils: 800 • Ages: 13–18 • Sixth form: 355 • C of E

Fees: Day £24,513; Boarding £35,019 pa

Tel: 01572 822216
Email: admissions@uppingham.co.uk
Website: www.uppingham.co.uk

Headmaster: Since September 2016, Dr Richard Maloney MA (theology at St Andrew's) PGCE (Cantab), early 40s, previously head of Bede's Senior School. An alumnus of Latymer Upper School, Dr Maloney began his career in West Yorkshire. In 1997, he became head of RS and, later, head of sixth, at Chigwell School, during which period he completed an MA at King's College, London. In 2006, he was appointed deputy headmaster of Sutton Valence. During his tenure there he became a PhD but left after three years to take up the Bede's headship – whilst still in his 30s. We described him at Bede's as 'A man of palpable energy – physical and intellectual – complemented by equal measures of compassion, dedication, ambition and vision'. He has transformed that school and become hot educational property.

He is married to Tracey, who runs an educational consultancy, and they have two children.

Academic matters: Although the emphasis is on holistic education, academic matters do not suffer. It was obvious from talking to pupils that teachers relish challenging the most able to get as far as they can. All abilities are making excellent progress and exam results are strong, but parents hastened to inform us that Uppingham is no academic hothouse, and compared the approach to education very favourable to what they see as the stressful academic day schools of Cambridge and London. In 2016, 45 per cent of A levels were at A or A* and 76 per cent were at A* to B. At GCSE, 68 per cent A*/A grades in 2016; this stays fairly steadily in the high 60s, low 70s year on year.

The school considers all subjects to be strong, pointing to outstanding results and large numbers taking both science and arts subjects at A level. Pupils enthuse about the history, religious studies and politics, but also approve of the various innovations that the stunning new science block has inspired, including the outdoor science classroom. The new labs are designed with one half for practical work and the other half for the theory – a great improvement to the traditional labs where students make notes between the gas taps and Bunsen burners. With 29 A level subjects on offer, there is a superb range. The post-16 curriculum is under close review but current view is that a combination of A levels, Pre-U, and the Extended Project will offer lots of stimulus for all in the sixth form. Average class size is 16, and nine in the sixth form. There is support for those with mild learning difficulties and those who need help with English language (at extra cost).

Games, options, the arts: You would expect a school that prides itself on its holistic education to provide a rich extracurricular offer and Uppingham doesn't disappoint. Facilities, which are also used by the local community, are outstanding – the biggest stage, the pupils informed us, of any school they had heard of, and drama is supported by fantastic teachers and professional technicians. Endless sports on offer and, pupils assure us, it

U

is for everyone, not just the elite. One year 13 boy spoke with considerable enthusiasm about his engagement with a lowly rugby team. As well as 'major' sports there is a plethora of others – just as well, given that it is compulsory to do something.

Music is outstanding – one parent said that all independent schools say their music is good, but at Uppingham it is really good. Everyone mentions whole school congregational singing in chapel. There are House Shouts in which everyone seems to get involved, and then highly selective choirs and orchestras for the specialists. These groups tour in the UK and overseas as well as having endless performance opportunities in school. Masterclasses given by eminent musicians are regular features. Recording studios, a radio station and music technology encourage those who aspire to find renown in more celebrity spheres, honing their acts along the way in the school Battle of the Bands.

Everyone does CCF, though there is an opt-out for older pupils, who can get involved in community service. Some help in local primary schools, including teaching a Latin programme; others visit elderly people, ride with disabled people or take part in various overseas aid projects.

The art is vibrant and diverse – taking place in the Leonardo Centre, named after the Renaissance Man, the ultimate model for the Uppingham student.

Boarding: All but a tiny handful board. Everyone says it is a school for children who really want the full boarding experience – no flexi approach countenanced here to ease the way for those valuing their own 'me time'. There are separate girls' and boys' boarding houses spread over the small market town. Most are vertical – pupils from every age group – but there is also a sixth form girls' house, as more girls join the school at sixth form level. Some houses are in the centre, having the advantage of being minutes away from teaching areas, others are further out and have the advantage of more space – one boasting its own swimming pool. Prospective families are normally taken to see just a few of the houses, though you can see all 15 if you really want.

Boys' houses have around 50 pupils and girls about 60. Each has a housemaster or mistress living there with their own family. There are resident tutors and a team of non-resident tutors attached to each house. Meals are taken in the house and house staff share the tables with the pupils. There is a rota of other staff circulating around the houses, so the students are very used to visitors.

Background and atmosphere: Uppingham is a boarding school with no half measures. Only a handful of pupils go home for the night – it is a school for those who want people around all the time and masses to do. 'Much too much, really,' said one boy who knew his AS results could have been a bit better if there weren't just such a brilliant amount going on all the time. However, one mother who spoke to us said that the housemasters have a close grip on this sort of problem and can usually sort things out early on.

When we dined at one house, the boys were completely charming – enthusiastic about everything at school and genuinely interested in their visitors. These are young people whose emotional intelligence is being unobtrusively developed on a daily basis. Separate girls' and boys' houses add to the individual flavour of each house. They can come to breakfast in their pyjamas and experience single sex norms as well as the hurly burly of co-ed in the classroom. Parents who had visited a number of houses before the children joined Uppingham said that every houseparent they met had credibility, and had proved to be inspirational.

With all the high quality activity on offer both in regulated and not regulated time, you would have to work very hard at being bored round here. Sixth formers have their own social centre, which is open once a term to other years, but most pupils are dashing from sports fields to drama studios to art rooms to music rehearsals, getting the most out of every minute.

Pastoral care, well-being and discipline: A lot of thought goes into settling in new pupils. They have a mentor in the year above and a sixth form mentor in their house. House staff make sure there is plenty going on at the weekends, so new pupils are quickly immersed in the busy life of the school. We got the sense that the staff all loved communal life, and their enthusiasm is infectious. Pupils all talked about their close friendships – 'My friends are always there for me and probably always will be,' said one year 13, starting to contemplate life beyond Uppingham.

There are school counsellors and a school psychotherapist, and all the pupils we spoke to felt there were plenty of staff to whom they could take any concerns. As part of the curriculum, there is health and social education that supports the usual areas of teenage angst, with self-help techniques as well as information and advice. Sixth formers are trained to support the younger pupils.

There are very firm rules and sanctions about bullying, drugs, smoking and alcohol use. Spirits are taken more seriously than wine. Everyone knows the score, and where a pupil has fallen foul of the sanctions, parents have accepted the firm and clear way the school has dealt with the matter.

Pupils and parents: The large map in the registrar's office with its pins indicating where in the UK families come from shows, not surprisingly, a preponderance from the wealthy parts of the country – largely home counties, but there are plenty from the midlands and the north too. Parents are mostly from the professional and business classes. A steady 12 to 15 per cent of boarders are from overseas. Parents like the real mix of nationalities. They also like the school's approach to the family. 'The school gives you the sense that it is the whole family joining the school; they really want us to get involved too'.

The pupils are fully aware of the preconceptions that others have of them. 'But we are not arrogant,' they assure us. 'The school actively teaches us humility. We are confident, but when you are living with lots of different people and learning how to get on together, it tends to make you confident.' Parents say they are delighted with how Uppingham pupils turn out – they are engaging, personable, gregarious and go out into the world with enthusiasm and interest in other people.

Alumni include John Schlesinger, Stephen Fry, Rick Stein, Jenny Willott, Rowan Atkinson, John Suchet and Tim Melville-Ross.

Entrance: As you would expect, the admissions process is a very well-oiled machine. Many families start the process three years before the actually date of entry. It is all very welcoming and informative. Most join at 13+, but there is also a significant entry at 16+, particularly from girls who have been in a single sex environment. Most of these girls (typically 25-30 a year) are housed in the sixth form girls' house, The Lodge.

There is a pre-testing round at 11 (year 7) with papers in maths and English, an interview and references from current school. Places are then conditional on further tests in year 8, when pupils can sit common entrance (55 per cent average pass mark) or the school's own exam, consisting of maths and English with a further interview.

At sixth form level, there is a six GCSE at B grade minimum requirement for everyone, but virtually all existing pupils get those. For those coming in from outside, there are also sixth form scholarship and non-scholarship exams, plus two interviews – a house one and an academic one.

Exit: Very few leave after GCSEs. In 2016, two to Oxbridge and four to study medicine. Bristol, Newcastle, Oxford Brookes,

Edinburgh, Durham and Exeter also popular. There is a good range of subjects, business, history, sciences, politics and international relations coming out top. The careers advice and particularly support with UCAS applications are highly regarded, with subject staff and house staff all contributing.

Money matters: A serious number of scholarships are awarded at both 13+ and 16+: music, art, DT, sport and all-rounder as well as academic. There is also a new sixth form science scholarship. Typically, in a year group of about 150, there will be 35 scholarships awarded.

There is also some means-tested bursary support available – the registrar says the approach is flexible to respond to the very individual needs of a family.

Remarks: Even though it is big and spreads throughout the small market town of Uppingham, everyone tells us the school has a homely feel. We know just what they mean – though it is probably Home and Gardens homely rather than the average urban semi. It is a rather wonderful bubble, and feels a world away from the relatively close midlands cities. Uppingham is charming English small market town, with its own theatres (owned and run by the school) and its own cafés and shops that the pupils wonder round relatively freely. Parents and pupils love it.

We had some sense that by the time the pupils leave the school, they are hungry for the wider world, but that is a good thing. A sixth former who wanted to party hard might start to find it restricting, but the community feel is energising enough for most. The pupils are aware of how fortunate they are. They are not taking all this for granted, and the ones we spoke to were determined to make the most of all their wonderful opportunities. They were enthusiastic, curious and positive – as one would hope for from a liberal, holistic education. Will they change the world, lead the revolution? Probably not. Will they spread sweetness and light wherever they go? We think probably yes. Will they be responsible citizens of the world? Another yes.

Warwick Preparatory School

Linked with Warwick Junior School, Warwick School

82

Bridge Field, Banbury Road, Warwick CV34 6PL

Pupils: 499: 352 girls, 147 boys • Ages: 3–11 girls; 3–7 boys

Fees: £9,855 – £11,292 pa

Tel: 01926 491545
Email: info@warwickprep.com
Website: www.warwickprep.com

Head: Since September 2016, Mrs Hellen Dodsworth, previously co-head of Coten End Primary School. Studied music and education at Warwick; also has an NPQH. Class teacher and phase leader at Coleshill Heath School before joining Coten End as deputy head. She loves music, theatre and travel, and spends much of her spare time on the touch line, cheering on her two sons.

Entrance: Any time, providing there is room. Most boys and girls enter aged 3 or 4 (now four class reception entry); girls can also join at 7: they are assessed in maths, reading and writing and are invited to bring an object which is special to them and to talk about it. They spend a whole day at the school attending some classes and fooling about in the playground with current pupils. Occasionally pupils are not offered a place on the grounds that 'they would be unlikely to flourish', but this is rare. 'It's all pretty fair,' said a happy parent whose child had been accepted.

Exit: All boys leave at 7, majority to Warwick Junior School. A very few go on to other prep schools to gain boarding experience before moving on again. Girls leave aged 11 with majority going on to King's High, but not all. Others to eg Stratford Grammar, Kingsley School, Bromsgrove School, Cheltenham Ladies.

Remarks: The nursery and prep are the first steps on the great adventure offered by the Warwick Independent Schools Foundation. They share the same campus as Warwick School (boys); the High School (girls) is about a mile away on the outskirts of the town. The prep is more than an adjunct to the other schools on the campus, and though all schools share the same pool of governors, each maintains its autonomy and individuality. Aficionados of architecture might compare the external appearance of the prep buildings with a business park, but they would be compelled to admire the sensitively designed interiors and the thought that has gone into blending practicality with social aesthetics. The overall atmosphere is warm and welcoming, and none more so than the nearby nursery, which is bright and inviting, spacious yet cosy. Real learning through real fun with, as one mum told us, 'lovely staff.' Books and artwork everywhere. Glowing.

The main prep is skilfully designed to complement the stages by which pupils progress through the school; junior, middle and senior are clearly defined but close to each other, minimising transition. Superbly equipped classrooms with all the gadgets, but it is obvious that lively, interactive teaching is what the school is founded on. As part of that theme of creativity, visiting artists inspire and enthuse, adding to the excellent teaching that already goes on. Evidence of this is readily apparent in the many examples of glasswork, pottery, printmaking and painting that adorn walls and corridors everywhere. Running through these activities is a seemingly all-out assault on stereotypical notions of education. We witnessed some wonderful science teaching based on enquiry, experiment and exploration. 'Boys mustn't think they own the magnet,' said one teacher. It was obvious they didn't: girls as well as boys seemed deeply involved, fired with encouraged curiosity. Plenty of excitement and bubble and a sense of igniting interests and inspiring curiosity. Whether it was preparing for scenes from A Midsummer Night's Dream; using, but not relying on, computers for 'specialist thinking'; learning to solder wires and construct the basics of computers themselves; and 'learning to think outside the box', it is fizz, fun and effective. 'I loved the lessons,' a recent leaver told us.

Nor is this joy confined to the classroom. Clubs, before school, lunchtime and after school, offer dancing, singing, science, computing, Spanish, sewing, swimming, football, drama and lots more. Music is popular, about 50 per cent of pupils learn a musical instrument and there is a woodwind section, a brass group, senior and junior choirs, bell-ringing and a harp group. The sporting facilities are good with Astroturf, sports hall and (shared) use of the excellent swimming pool in the senior school. National successes have been scored at netball and locally in equestrian, hockey and swimming events. It seems little short of miraculous that so much is on offer during a five day week. Nor does it end there: hill walking and camping, trips to France, science weeks and editing the new magazine, complete with challenging general knowledge quizzes and interviews.

This is an extremely lively and busy place; it is palpably a very happy and friendly school, challenging and nurturing, hard working, interested and bright children who are also courteous and forthcoming. Good facilities and good leadership. More than a stepping stone to senior schools, it offers sound and broad grounding, inculcating work ethics and consideration for others which should last for life.

Warwick Junior School

Linked with Warwick Preparatory School, Warwick School

83

Myton Road, Warwick CV34 6PP

Pupils: 252 • Ages: 7–11 • C of E

Fees: £9,846 – £11,931 pa

Tel: 01926 776418
Email: j.turner@warwickschool.org
Website: www.warwickschool.org

Headmaster of the Junior School: Since September 2016, Mr Andrew Hymer, previously head of Wolverhampton Grammar Junior School. BA in ancient history and classical archaeology (Sheffield), PGCE (College of Ripon and York St John), DPSE (Birmingham City University), MAEd (Birmingham City University), NPQH. Originally, and briefly, a policeman in South Yorkshire, he has also taught at schools including Ashville College and RGS Worcester, and been deputy head of King's Hawford. Spends most of his free time watching or coaching cricket and rugby.

Entrance: Most boys enter aged 7 but are welcome at any age, providing there is room. Exams in February for entrance the following September for 8+, 9+ and 10+. School can be flexible, so do ask if you are interested in sending your son in the middle of the year. The Warwick schools pride themselves on being academic, but not aggressively so. Thus it is that even 7 year olds are required to takes tests in English, maths, reading and a short story exercise in creative writing. Thereafter the exams require non-verbal reasoning. 'Fair but demanding,' said one parent. Do ask about music scholarships.

Exit: Around half of boys go on to Warwick School (70 in 2016) after sitting the entrance exam (others to KES Grammar Stratford, Princethorpe, Alcester Grammar and Bloxham). In the event of any boy beginning to slip beneath the required standard or perhaps not cutting the mustard, parents and staff will meet and discuss. That is a rare event but it's worth emphasising that the move up is not automatic.

Remarks: The junior school is one part of the whole educational adventure offered by the Warwick Independent Schools Foundation that comprises the prep (boys and girls start together but boys move on aged 7 and girls aged 11), King's High School for girls, and the boys' school (Warwick School) that is divided into junior and senior schools. Each school has its own governing body.

From the moment you approach the entrance past the wonderfully evocative stone bears fashioned in a domestic group, you feel there is something creative and inviting about the set-up. So there is. To arrive during break is to be greeted by a cacophony of joyous noise and delight. Handball courts, cricket stumps, hide and seek, invention, creation, happiness, boys being boys and, 'just messing about,' as one delighted chap told us.

One real advantage of attending any of the Warwick schools lies in being able to use the amazing shared facilities. The boys who showed us round, or joined in with such enthusiasm, were understandably proud and thrilled by these opportunities. Junior school is housed in its own red-brick building on the main senior school site and everything appears to be seamlessly integrated. Junior boys clearly feel very much part of the overall scheme of things and not at all intimidated by the size of the buildings or the senior boys. 'It makes you really look forward to going there,' one boy said before adding hastily, 'but it is very good here.' We have visited the three schools on this campus more than once so have spent a lot of time observing, chatting, listening, being greeted and smiled at, playing the old game of pretending to be lost in order to ask for help and judging the response. Some schools, en masse, can make visitors feel a trifle threatened: 'What are you doing in our space?' Not so Warwick. It's a courteous and happy place and, as the head commented, 'not a tweedy school.'

With such a space in which to thrive offering safety, challenge and opportunity, it is not surprising that the boys at Warwick Junior seem so happy and confident. It's good to visit a place where effort is acknowledged, here it's done by means of the 'Congratulations Board' where anything noteworthy is recorded and celebrated. Pictures are everywhere – art is terrific and flourishing – and photos adorn the passages and staircases. Instead of the familiar and faintly nauseating 'personal' messages saying, 'A warm welcome to all prospective parents today, especially Mr and Mrs Drawley and their young son Aeneas', the screen in the entrance hall celebrates children, childhood, involvement and achievement. 'Will we see your face up on the screen?' we asked a passing boy. He cast an expert eye on the current picture and replied, 'Yes. But you'll have to wait a long time before it comes round.'

Music is taken very seriously at the Warwick schools and here in the junior school about 140 boys learn at least one instrument, contributing to school orchestra, big choir, micro choir, three rock bands, string orchestra, brass monkeys. New boys are loaned stringed instruments to give them the opportunity of learning without parents having to fork out for a Stradivarius. Drama also very popular, there is a hall for such activities in the school but the climax of dramatic activities is a play produced and performed in the professionally run Bridge House Theatre. That same theatre hosts professional concerts, plays and shows and is a wonderful addition to the overall life of the school and surrounding community. There are some interesting clubs and societies including, we noticed, the Japanese Club, whose gastronomic influence spreads as far as a Japanese lunch. Sporting facilities are marvellous, and it comes as no surprise that in the last five years the school has won six national sporting titles in rugby, golf and swimming (the superb pool is clearly a tremendous advantage). Senior boys and girls from the High School visit the younger boys to help out with various activities, partly out of the goodness of their hearts and partly towards their Duke of Edinburgh Awards.

Classrooms are wonderfully bright and inviting and we witnessed some marvellous teaching with bags of enthusiastic responses from the boys and imaginative and lively input from the staff. In one classroom we asked pupils who, we discovered later, had only been at the school a year, what words they would use to describe the school. We received the usual contented answers about food, games, music etc but most revealing, perhaps, was the boy who offered the word 'strict.' 'Is that good or bad?' we asked. 'Good,' he replied. A parent we encountered in the car park used the same word when describing the school. 'It helps the children to know the rules of the game. It's a bit like marking out a tennis court. You can enjoy the game better when you know the rules.'

W

Warwick School

Linked with Warwick Preparatory School, Warwick Junior School

Myton Road, Warwick CV34 6PP

Pupils: 1,266; 56 full boarders • Ages: 11–18 • Sixth form: 284

Fees: Day £12,183; Boarding £24,717 – £26,397 pa

Tel: 01926 776400
Email: enquiries@warwickschool.org
Website: www.warwickschool.org

Head Master: Since 2013, Mr Augustus (Gus) Lock, MA Oxon (late 30s). Educated at Haberdashers' Aske's School, Elstree, he read ancient and modern history at Oxford. First teaching post was at The Manchester Grammar School, thence to Merchant Taylors' School in Northwood, where he became head of middle school and met and married Alison (a French and Italian teacher). Mr Lock then moved to Warwick School, where he served as deputy head before taking on the headship. Gus and Alison have three young children, two of whom attend Warwick Prep School.

Academic matters: It is clear that academic work is a top priority and taken seriously by most of the boys. The pace is vigorous and demanding – for pupils and staff alike – and the overall results are impressive. When we asked if there was any truth in the rumour that Warwick was an exam factory, one boy replied, 'Well, if it is, I haven't noticed it. There is lots of work but you expect that. You just get on with it.' One ex-teacher at Warwick confirmed that the pace was demanding. That word 'pace' crops up a lot – Warwick is a very busy school with lots to offer. It may be a day school but, in the words of another boy, 'it never seems to close. With all the extracurricular activities on offer, a 12 hour day starting at 7.30am is not that unusual.' League table junkies can pore over the statistics, salivating at the various permutations, but here's a quick fix: of the 27 subjects on offer for A level, maths, economics, physics, chemistry, biology and politics account for some 250 entries; English, history, French and Spanish, 50. Just an observation but it does reveal the breadth of subjects on offer and the strengths of scientific subjects in the sixth form. How well they do overall is confirmed by the consistently high percentage of A*-B at A level (85 per cent in 2016, and 57 per cent A*/A). GCSE results from 28 subjects are impressive too: in 2016, 79 per cent of papers were graded A*/A. This is clearly not a school where boys spend time during their first few years 'settling down and making friends' before starting to work seriously.

The facilities for teaching and learning are impressive. Foremost is the new science building of which the school is justifiably proud. Like most of the new buildings at Warwick, it is superbly designed, both aesthetically and functionally. From the moment you enter the large bright foyer, decorated with a fascinating creation stretching up through two floors like a curling spine, you are in a genuinely stimulating building. In this instance it is all about experiment, discovery and excitement. Each of the three floors is allocated to a science, with spacious laboratories designed in consultation with the teachers themselves. All the latest gizmos and terrific teaching to go with them. One huge laboratory is used for extended projects where budding Nobel laureates are joined by the no less budding girls from King's High and students from other local schools. Certainly no sign of science declining in popularity here – many boys go on to university to read science-based subjects. How some of them must pine for the excellence of the facilities at Warwick. But it's not just the scientists who are well served; we hear many reports of excellent teaching in other subjects too. The delightfully designed lecture theatre hosts talks embracing all disciplines from within and beyond the curriculum.

If the heartbeat of real education is a library, Warwick is very healthy. The library is housed in The Masefield Centre, named after an old boy, charmingly described to us by a current pupil as 'some kind of a poet, I believe.' A superb set-up with over 20,000 books, it is an invaluable centre for reference resources and information files as well as CDs, DVDs and now e-books. The school even has e-readers to lend out. The wonderfully enthusiastic librarian told us that the issue of books had recently risen by 30 per cent, and inviting pamphlets, one with an encouraging foreword from the headmaster, explain and exhort. Those pupils we spoke to genuinely appreciated the facility.

Everyone entering the school is screened for dyslexia and those with learning difficulties receive help from the 'very good' learning support team. Curriculum support is also available to those who encounter academic difficulties.

Games, options, the arts: Naturally sport plays an important part. However, this is not a hearty school where prizes and recognition are given only to games players. Colours are awarded for music and drama, for instance, and one boy we spoke to, a confessed non-sportsman, said he didn't feel an outcast in any way. 'There are plenty of opportunities for taking exercise. In fact I'm almost spoilt for choice.' Nevertheless, the ethos that permeates the school – 'if you're going to do something, do it to the best of your ability' – is much in evidence on the games field. In the winter term, for example, over 20 rugby teams could be turning out on a Saturday afternoon. The 1st XV has a very strong fixture list and is renowned for its prowess, but the great thing is that everyone who wants to has a good chance of playing in a team. However, 'it's not all about rugby,' as somebody once said. In addition there is hockey, cricket, swimming, tennis, cross-country, athletics, rowing, canoeing, clay pigeon shooting: you name it. No wonder the boy who didn't like rugby didn't feel left out. Facilities are excellent with a top rate swimming pool (they have been national schools water polo champions more than once), squash courts, tennis courts, a superb sports hall, including an indoor hockey pitch, and games fields that seem to stretch on for ever. A recent cricket tour to Sri Lanka, golf to Spain and rugby to Ireland are just some of the opportunities to play abroad; boys who cannot afford to go are supported financially.

Music is excellent (ask for a copy of their DVD) and generally regarded as cool. Harmony maintained by a charismatic director with a wonderful team of teachers, most of whom are concert players themselves. In a recent and highly successful initiative, new boys were lent an instrument of their choice and given free tuition for a year; the enthusiastic take-up means the music department now has 720 lessons a week to organise. Five orchestras, three wind bands, three jazz bands, rock groups, quartets and much more. Huge programme of concerts and the chapel choir sings every Sunday morning during term; local parents, old boys, friends of the school and boarders attend. The musicians perform all over Europe (as with sports tours, financial support given if necessary) and recently four bands were awarded platinum, two golds and a silver at the National Concert Band Finals – the Little Big Band got a platinum award for the third consecutive year and as a result was presented with a consistent achievement certificate.

Proximity to Stratford may account for the school's high achievements in drama. The superb Bridge House Theatre is kitted out to professional standards with proper lighting and sound equipment, adjustable stage and seating arrangements for 300 people and musicians; it is used by community theatre groups as well as for school productions. A number of boys have taken small parts at the RSC; recently a year 9 pupil played Gershom, first born son of Moses, in Exodus, and a few go on to take theatre studies at A level. One ecstatic mother told us of the huge encouragement given to her young son when he was given a demanding role. 'It boosted his confidence right across the board,' she said. Warwick productions have won awards at the National Student Drama Festival, the only school to have done so. There are large scale drama productions every term as well as pupil led plays, many shared with girls from King's High.

Art and DT very good. All pupils have a double period of art and design a week for their first three years and can then go on to GCSE and beyond.

Astonishing range of clubs and societies to try – debating, scuba diving, robotics (UK champions several years running). Boys can also sign up for D of E, Young Enterprise and CCF. Wonderful opportunities enthusiastically seized. Exam factory, forsooth.

Boarding: Upstairs from chapel in the old building is a little corner of Asia where the 50+ Chinese boys in the sixth form live with the housemaster, a resident tutor and a matron. Boarding is available from year 9. Warwick has been taking Chinese students for many years now and those we chatted to seemed very happy and proud to be there. Activities sensitively arranged to reflect both boys' cultural background and traditional British life – there's Autumn Moon Festival and bonfire night; Christmas and Chinese New Year. Trips, many suggested by boarders' council, include photographers' visit to London and football-themed visit to Manchester, taking in United game.

Background and atmosphere: The gates to the main entrance hint at the tradition of the school. In addition to the Tudor Rose and the school's coat of arms depicting, significantly, the Warwickshire bear without chains, you can read the dates 914, 1545 and 1958. These refer to the traditional dates for the founding of the school by Edward the Confessor, its reinstatement by Henry VIII and the visit of the Queen Mother when the school was once more in the ascendant after a period in the doldrums. From a succession of sites in the town the school moved out to its present position beside the Avon in 1879. The neo-Tudor building with lovely oriel windows is typical of 19th century public school architecture, though to some, apparently, the colour of the brick is reminiscent of a hospital. A fascinating archive room with old photographs of school groups and haunting pictures of teams from 1914, testifies to the pride the school takes in its past. After all, isn't this one of the oldest boys' schools in the country, nay, the world?

The current site is a mixture of old and new buildings, increasingly dominated by the new, close but not jostling. Always an interesting insight into a school is to ask for directions and note the response; those boys we asked were uniformly helpful and charming, courtesy and good manners are the norm here. One new boy told us not to worry; 'Just ask,' he said, 'you can't go far wrong.' He spoke with feeling of the help he had received on arrival. All schools trumpet 'the excellent relationships between pupils and staff'; unobtrusively and naturally, this school demonstrates it. We witnessed a number of conversations between staff and boys and were struck by the obvious mutual respect and friendliness between them.

The school's aims may be serious and pursued with determination but there is an underlying sense of well-being and community which extends to the town; the civilised behaviour of the boys was acknowledged by the residents to whom we spoke. Sixth formers are allowed, with permission, to have lunch in town; so are senior girls from King's High. 'What we almost take for granted,' said one elderly resident, 'is that there is no arrogance about them. No swaggering and showing off. Not like those public school kids.' An interesting observation. Much is done for charity, an excellent way of combining community spirit and awareness of those less fortunate. Along with girls from King's High, teams have twice swum the Channel. According to the records the boys' team was the 50th ever two-way swim; the 13th ever successful swim by any UK team and the first by a boys' school team.

Impressive chapel with college seating where services take place most days of the week, and new 1,000 seater Warwick Hall for assemblies etc.

Pastoral care, well-being and discipline: Typical of the caring efficiency of the school is the trouble it takes to welcome new boys and blend them in. There are unobtrusive but clearly delineated policies to ensure 'there is always someone to pick us up' and the welcome package, is helpful, informative and encouraging. The effortlessly friendly atmosphere that pervades is, perhaps, because boys know where they stand (a phrase oft repeated when we asked). Prefects, selected by peers and staff, regard it as one of their prime functions to ensure boys are happily integrated and that consideration for others is maintained. Rules and guidelines are clear and thorough, even down to expectations of behaviour in the classroom; uniforms are smartly worn. One parent, talking about a boy who had been excluded – a rare event by all accounts – spoke of the trouble the school had gone to ensure the boy was well established in his next school. 'They really do care about the individual, but however friendly, they are strict about implementing the rules.' 'We know what is required of us. Mostly it's common sense,' a senior boy told us. 'Firm but fair.' No-one – boys or staff – claimed that bullying could never happen here, but parents we spoke to said it was quickly and sensitively dealt with. 'Staff are very approachable and understandable,' more than one boy told us.

Pupils and parents: Warwick has a large catchment area, a result not only of its excellent transport links but also the determination of parents and boys to make the effort. By bus, by train, by car, they come; from as far afield as Oxfordshire and Northamptonshire. Just under half the year's intake comes from the junior school and others from local primary schools and nearby prep schools. This is not a toff school; parents come from a broad cross-section of society, mostly professional middle classes, and thanks to the availability of bursaries many who might otherwise not be able to afford it do send their boys. The head and governors plan to raise funds and offer more.

Eclectic is the word that springs to mind when considering notable old boys. Currently there are two MPs, Iain Pears the novelist; Marc Elliott of East Enders; Christian Horner, Red Bull motor racing; Michael Billington, theatre critic; an Italian rugby international, an Australian rugby international, an England Sevens player and, from the ranks of the departed, the poet John Masefield. More evidence of breadth.

Entrance: The school is selective and competition is strong. It's not just the strongest academics who are awarded places; lively, quirky boys who can keep pace and bring with them special talents will be given consideration. Entry points are 11 and 13. Details of the examinations are on the website and follow the usual pattern. For entry to sixth form at least five B grades with A grades needed in some subjects to be studied at AS level.

Exit: Most – about 85 per cent – of boys stay on to do their A levels and nearly all go on to university. As well as purely academic subjects eg maths, classics, English, history, PPE, recent leavers have gone on to read marine vertebrate zoology, management with entrepreneurship, forensic science and architecture. Eight to Oxbridge in 2016 and five medics. Popular destinations include Birmingham, Durham, Leeds, Nottingham, UCL and Loughborough.

Money matters: The school is fortunate in benefiting from a number of ancient charities, some specifically aimed at boys living in the town of Warwick. Scholarships are offered in music and academics but not for sport. About a quarter of boys in the school are assisted financially.

Remarks: This is a winning school and achieves success right across the board. 'I don't know how we do it,' a boy told us in genuine amazement; 'there must be some reason for it.' There are plenty of reasons why this is such an excellent school although, like all good schools, it won't suit everyone. But for those seeking a day school that offers more excellent facilities and opportunities than many boarding schools; for those who are possessed of energy, stamina and self-discipline; above all, for those who can match the pace and plunge in, this might very well be the school. Not a school for drifting in, a school for striking out through the waves. Even across the Channel.

Welbeck, the Defence Sixth Form College

85

Forest Road, Loughborough, Leicestershire LE12 8WD

Pupils: 339 (240 boys, 99 girls); all full boarders • Ages: 16–18

Fees: 0 – £19,000 pa

Tel: 01509 891712
Email: pa@dsfc.ac.uk
Website: www.dsfc.ac.uk/

Principal: Since 2013, Mr Peter Middleton MA. Previously deputy head at Clifton College, Mr Middleton was born in Somerset and educated at Radley before reading chemistry at Oriel College, Oxford. He began his teaching career at Cheltenham College, where he was a deputy housemaster, master in charge of rowing and first VIII coach, and an officer in the army section of the CCF. Not difficult to see the direction he was taking, confirmed by his next move, which was back to Oxford, to St Edward's, where he was a housemaster, re-formed the royal navy section, was master i/c rowing and, by now, an international rowing coach. It wasn't altogether surprising to hear that at Welbeck he likes wearing military uniform occasionally and exchanging the occasional salute. Any whisper of Apthorpe is irrelevant. Married to Clare, an educational psychologist. They have three children.

Clearly he is an ambitious man, and those who know him well speak of his drive, energy and desire to be a head. Not a ruthless man, he struck us as being like a schoolboy with a new train set. He is clearly very excited about running the school, and in his desire to share his excitement we hardly had time to exchange opening civilities before he was gesticulating wildly with something in his hand which, we realised, was being pointed at a screen nearby. The PowerPoint presentation had begun. Very informative it was, and most of what he said as introduction can be found in the prospectus bundle which will arrive when asked for.

In the course of conversations with pupils, staff and parents, it became obvious that his experience as a boarding housemaster has stood him in good stead. We heard how, shortly after his arrival, he had asked pupils to tell him how they thought the overall structure and living arrangements could be improved. As a result he has, we are told, made the boarding houses kinder establishments: they were never foot stamping, command bellowing places, but now housemasters – who, incidentally, seemed a delightful bunch – have more support, so that boys and girls have a wider range of people to whom they can talk, gain wisdom and encouragement, seek advice and just 'chill out together.' Those connected with the boarding came over as enthusiastic and affectionate about the pupils.

Academic matters: The Defence Sixth Form College is unique. It is, as the prospectus states, a fully co-educational sixth form boarding school. Every year 175 young men and women join the college. All are destined for the military and are required to choose one from the Royal Navy, the Army, the Royal Air Force and the DESG (Defence Engineering and Science Group). Papers accompanying the prospectus tell you which grades you must have at GCSE and which subjects you have to take at A level. Always the inevitable emphasis on maths and science – everyone studies maths and the vast majority physics. Fitness tests, interviews and school reports form the basis of acceptance. They are all important. English language and the subjects required are governed by whichever branch of the military you wish to pursue. There are then lists of universities which offer places for what you wish to learn. This is where aspirants must be sure they really want to pursue these routes. Boats could be burned sooner than expected. Under good king Middleton academic aspirations have risen, but there is a limit to the breadth of A levels available. Foreign languages are taught only as enrichment AS options; for instance no Greek or Latin, no art or music A levels. Alongside maths, sciences, technology and computing you can study geography, politics or business studies, but no other humanities. In 2016, 34 per cent A*/A grades, 61 per cent A*-B. Fine for many, but be aware. This school, with all its excellence, is geared towards a specific area: engineering or technical careers in the armed forces or as a civilian within the MOD. Of course a government paid bursary of £4,000pa would be most welcome, but there are stipulations. The school is scrupulously honest and helpful about the various permutations.

Games, options, the arts: One of the most delightful incidents of our tour was witnessing what is locally referred to as the dash for cash. This refers to the possibility of winning a bursary for university, providing your grades reach the requirements and that you are sufficiently fit to be accepted. Hence dash for cash. We watched a boy who was not, on his own admission, a natural athlete driving himself to achieve the required time. The PE staff were cheering him on, shouting encouragement, and some running with him. Passers by paused to cheer him on. It seemed the world had stopped but for those runners. And he did it by about five seconds. So he'll get his bursary. It was, he said, between gasps, 'the happiest day of my life, not so much for the bursary but because I can now go to the university of my choice.' The end of his time at Welbeck is the start of his new life.

As might be imagined there is a wide variety of activities and sport is hugely popular. All pupils are required to join the CCF for varied activities designed to prepare for different challenges and to encourage leadership.

Though we heard talk of art or music, we didn't see or hear any.

Boarding: That the general atmosphere throughout the school seems very happy must owe something to the quality and layout of the boarding accommodation. Everyone boards and the facilities are genuinely homely and in, the words of one of our guides, 'great places to live.' Those in their second and final year live, for the most part, in single ensuite bedsits; those in their first year share three in a room with ensuites. Initially we were a little surprised by having three in a room – two's company etc – but our guides assured us it worked.

Background and atmosphere: Anyone coming across the name Welbeck and thinking it sounds familiar may be thinking of Welbeck Abbey, destroyed by Henry VIII's thugs, and later adapted over the years into a huge house in Nottinghamshire in the midst of vast estates. From 1953, the year of its foundation, the college was housed in the building until 2000 when, despite its ducal associations and grandeur, it was deemed unsuitable and impractical. One snippet of history which might send a frisson of interest through the most dozy readers is that in 1913 Archduke Franz Ferdinand of Austria visited the Duke of Portland at Welbeck Abbey, and was involved in a very serious shooting accident which very nearly caused his death.

The college retains the name of Welbeck, and the specially designed and constructed buildings are excellent. Designed and built by the architectural firm HLM, the buildings are grouped in an enveloping, friendly way which creates a sense of team effort and space, housing very well laid out rooms.

Pastoral care, well-being and discipline: All the pupils we met spoke with appreciative warmth of the staff who were looking after them. They did not seem to possess any of the casual arrogance one sometimes detects in public school pupils. They were open, trusting, forthcoming and friendly. Discipline seemed easy as a result. A good touch is the presence of three serving officers and the college sergeant major, who mingle with pupils and the staff, forging useful links and running the mandatory CCF. One told us how much he was learning by being there, listening and partaking.

Pupils and parents: Pupils and parents come from all over the country and from all walks of life. Most had never boarded before but they were keen to tell us of the benefits they feel they have enjoyed during this two year spell. In amongst the literature sent in reply to parental enquiries there is a pie chart highlighting the types of feeder schools. Most come from other state schools and few from abroad. Not surprising. This is, rightly, perceived as a special school offering specific targets. Not many schools can include in their packet the near certainty of going on to university to read a subject of their choice and with such financial aid. Parents we spoke to were grateful for what the school was doing; some expressed amazed delight.

Entrance: These differ slightly according to which branch of the Forces you are aiming at, but basically include at least an A and a B in maths and physics plus a C in English GCSE. RAF and DESG must have at least 45 GCSE points (including A/A in dual award science) and army and navy at least 40 points from their best seven subjects (at 8 for A*, 7 for A etc). You must also be medically fit and a British, Commonwealth or Irish citizen.

Exit: All those who go to university on the Defence Technical Undergraduate Scheme (DTUS) must go to one of nine universities – Aston, Birmingham, Cambridge, Loughborough, Newcastle, Northumbria, Oxford, Southampton or Strathclyde – to do an approved DTUS course. These are mostly engineering and science based, with a few management degrees. In 2016, three to Oxbridge/Imperial. The majority do go on to join a branch of the armed forces. They almost have to. The prospectus papers contain some delightful articles from pupils who have gone on to work with the military, taking with them the benefits they so readily acknowledge.

Money matters: The school has lots to say about money matters and offers many forms to fill in if, as is the case most of the time, parents require assistance – sponsored fees depend on family income (private self-funded students do not commit to a Forces or MOD career and may go to any university). No-one need be shy. After all, the intention of Welbeck is to help with means-testing when required and to make the seemingly impossible possible. The government, it seems, is poised to help.

Remarks: In view of the Duke of Edinburgh's connexions with Welbeck it is, perhaps, neither too fanciful nor (just) too silly to compare the school with a Battenberg cake. Both the cake and the school have different layers contributing to the whole. A number of parents and friends of the school commented on the difficulty of balancing the various facets of the school. There are the military aspects: going out on exercise, parades, map reading; the academic side: the need to work at the A level subjects in order to get to university and thence to the job; personal fitness to a pretty high standard. No doubt all these activities and the pressure they bring are perceived by many as standard. This school with its serious extras represents a very high standard and many pupils have put all their eggs in one basket. One high-ranking military man we know described Welbeck as the finest preparation not just for the armed forces but for any job in the world. But... it's not for everyone. A commitment to this excellent establishment needs careful thought and dedication.

Winchester House School

44 High Street, Brackley, Northamptonshire NN13 7AZ

Pupils: 301; 90 weekly/flexi boarders • Ages: 3–13 (boarders from year 3)

Fees: Day £10,440 – £18,540; Boarding £23,280 pa

Tel: 01280 702483
Email: registrar@winchester-house.org
Website: www.winchester-house.org

Head: Since 2014, Emma Goldsmith (40s). Born and educated in Durham before reading English at Manchester. Landed first teaching job at Oakham where she threw herself into coaching netball, D of E: 'The last thing in the world I wanted to be was a teacher,' she says, 'but from that point on, I was committed to boarding schools.' Later recruited to help set up sixth form girls' boarding at Rugby and whilst there visited Bloxham School for a sports fixture. She loved it and was recruited to introduce girls and to manage the transition to co-ed, including setting up the first girls' boarding house, rising to deputy head.

Both of her children attended Winchester House, and she was asked to join the board of governors, so approached the headship 'from a unique position.' 'Bowled over by the quality of teaching and level of dedication and commitment of staff.' Focuses on every child leaving with a 'tool kit' for success in their future school. Parents approve, and describe her as the kind of person they would want running their business, as their best friend or their sister: 'She's fantastic,' they say. 'She

Wolverhampton Grammar School

Compton Road, Wolverhampton, West Midlands WV3 9RB

Pupils: 720 • Ages: 7–18 • Sixth form: 171

Fees: £9,822 – £12,939 pa

Tel: 01902 421326
Email: wgs@wgs-sch.net
Website: www.wgs.org.uk

Head: Since 2013, Kathy Crewe-Read. This is her first headship and she is the school's first female head though, thank goodness, most people have stopped talking about that now. It's not that important and besides, there's much more to say about her and the influence she has had on the school since she arrived after her stint as deputy head of the King's School Chester. She read maths at Aberystwyth University and teaches it with energy, challenge and zest. We witnessed a wonderfully lively lesson with younger pupils and, indeed, were roped in. We weren't able to contribute much – for 'much' read 'anything' – but the pupils were patient and friendly, responding enthusiastically to their teacher's energy and zest. Later, one of the pupils told us the head was 'always amazing.'

Potential or current WGS parents should read the blogs the head writes on a regular basis. They provoke thought involving and beyond the school itself. Here is an extract: 'For us at WGS, ISI (the Independent Schools' Inspectorate) is the regulatory body which monitors standards: we have to comply with the mere 400+ regulations that they impose. Each regulation serves a purpose, of course, and they are necessary but, in truth, I confess I also see them as a dead weight that obscures our greater purpose. Not one safety measure is creative or can touch the magic of what lies at the heart of educating your children.'

It's tempting to do an Eng lit crit on that snippet – especially as the head is, in her own words, 'a mathematician who finds blogs very difficult to write.' But by any standards this is an elegant and effective piece of writing which should touch the heart as well as the mind. It is the gentleness which is so powerful and that may be one key to the head's success. 'She is very approachable and listens carefully,' we were told over and over again by the students with whom we spoke. 'She is keen to help if we feel that something is unfair or unreasonable.' 'Don't just grumble,' says the head: 'I can't help unless you come and talk to me about it.' As for the living nightmares of absurd governmental directives driven by a political hunger for grades rather than education, this head is fearless in her condemnation.

Thanks to attending a marvellous jazz concert in the evening, we met lots of parents and past members of the school. They were virtually unanimous in their praise of the head. One young man who, on the day we arrived for the art exhibition was on the gate sporting a cavalier hair style, a welcoming smile and a delightful wit, told us, 'As you can see, she's not fussy about haircuts: she's more interested in what we're doing and what we're thinking about.' One member of staff commented on 'the lightness of her hand upon the tiller. But you always know it's there.' She's excellent company. One governor told us, 'she's just what we were hoping for.' Most parents agree.

Academic matters: We met a parent keen to tell us how it was that her son came to join the school. He is dyslexic but chose the school because he liked the atmosphere. When he arrived he was suffering from a painful physical condition which made his handwriting virtually illegible. Instead of ticking him off for his handwriting, his teachers sought medical advice. With patience and thoughtfulness his handwriting did improve, as did his understanding and written expression. Individual care and attention. A hallmark of this school. Another pupil told us how shortly after she arrived she scored very low marks in a test and was both embarrassed and ashamed. To her relief no one laughed at her.

Neither of these narratives is earth shattering, but the consideration and tact revealed seem at the heart of the school, something staff, pupils and parents comment on. It's clear that this school is not manically driven by league tables. Tucked away in the rather good magazine – the Wulfrunian, for alumni – readers will find the results of GCSEs and A level modestly displayed. But for statistical junkies there is pleasure to be derived from grades: in 2016, 57 per cent A*/A grades at GCSE; and at A level 39 per cent (A*/B 69 per cent). There is also a rather cheeky statistic about other independent schools in Wolverhampton.

Even without those pesky league tables, or partly because of them, it is increasingly clear that education is in danger of being killed off. But not here. The feeling we took away with us was that the relationship between staff and students – both within and without the classroom – was the main reason for the academic success of the school. This is not a hothouse; it's a nurturing and challenging school where, as one parent put it, 'the staff and pupils do have a lot of fun but we are kept closely in the picture and alerted if necessary. Levels of happiness are the clearest indication.' Typical of the creative and imaginative generosity of this school are the videos which are created and recorded, along with written messages, for new students joining the school. They are posted on the school's website, social media channels and sent to new starters.

And what of pupils with academic difficulties? WGS is the home of OpAL (Opportunities through Assisted Learning). It is a dedicated support programme for students with dyslexia and other learning difficulties who need extra support. What is both moving and important is that people with dyslexia are often very bright – Einstein, for instance, was no intellectual sluggard. Here at WGS no one is necessarily expecting an Einstein but the specially trained teaching staff along with individually prepared action plans can boost morale and skills wonderfully. In a sensitive and personal way, pupils' progress is tracked and monitored so that parents are kept in touch. The results are outstanding.

Games, options, the arts: Wonderful sporting facilities. Football, rugby, cricket, tennis, badminton, hockey, netball, etc. On and on goes the list and teams, we hear, play far above their weight. Impressive gymnasium. Courageous students pit their skills and their courage against a very demanding climbing wall in preparation for some of the tremendous expeditions pursued in the holidays. Sports are compulsory for all students up to year 11. Sixth formers can choose to participate in sport as well as community service on a voluntary basis after school. Duke of Edinburgh challenges are not compulsory, which is why the school is so delighted to have 110 students involved. It is also a licensed operator for the D of E award scheme.

Amazingly, the school claims to have over 100 extracurricular activities. These are not compulsory but we were told that out of 154 junior school children, only four chose not to pursue an activity. The facilities are absolutely superb, both inside and out. School buildings – sporting and academic – can be hideous, with no consideration for any overall architectural blending. WGS has an overall effect which pleases the eye and contributes to the atmosphere. In the prospectus there is a beautiful passage describing the overall effect the modern architecture has. 'Progress makes everything a battleground between beauty and utility,' said a poet. WGS contradicts that. The art exhibition we visited confirmed the school's closeness to creativity, experiment, intelligence and spark. Art at WGS is extraordinarily good and it was such a bonus to meet the artists of all ages themselves. Not a hint of Pseuds' Corner: every one talked freely and unpretentiously about what they were aiming to achieve and why; which parts they were pleased with and which parts left them frustrated. Wonderful atmosphere. It wasn't surprising to discover that no one sitting art A level at WGS in the last nine years has failed to achieve either an A* or A grade. That's an astonishing record. The collection of the largest pictures, some almost overpowering, was hung in the 200 seater theatre with powerful lighting. We heard much talk of the recent production there – drama is popular and excellent, we were told by locals who had managed to scrounge tickets. The recent production was Great Expectations and is still being talked about as one of the best performances ever seen at a school which already has a powerful reputation for theatricals.

Saturday mornings are by no means empty of activities, though these are not of the classroom type. There are school fixtures for teams every weekend, and LAMDA for students who want to gain additional qualifications in theatre skills and production. There are often sessions in preparation for D of E.

Another aspect of the creativity that lights up so much of the school is the music. Once again we were able to get our hands on much sought after tickets, for the annual Jazz Spectacular where the jazz was authentic and exciting, the dancing memorable and provocative. We are told that the concert ended with the entire audience dancing a conga all the way round the building. That's the kind of thing that happens when staid old scribblers leave early and pupils, staff and parents, cut loose. This extraordinary school is bursting with creative vitality. The music faculty spreads broadly and competently from choral and solo to orchestral and chamber with much success. Meanwhile, in an area of their own youth, under the watchful eyes of experts, are planning, measuring, filing, carving, sawing and creating some astonishingly imaginative and creatively practical furniture. It must be seen!

Background and atmosphere: Wolverhampton Grammar School was founded by the Merchant Taylors' Company in 1512 and moved to its present position in rather delightful suburbs in 1875. The original buildings are impressive, especially Big School with its huge powerful fireplaces, its impressive ceilings and the gothic-style windows. The Victorian buildings lend an air of dignitas without pomposity. Perhaps it's not too pretentious to suggest that overall there is a feeling of continuity. Certainly the staff and students we met gave off a sense of direction and purpose. But adaptation is a form of creativity as well, and it was not altogether surprising to be told that the excellent arts and drama complex was fashioned from a local car workshop. Everything here is good but unpretentious; the atmosphere we encountered as we walked round with a succession of delightful guides was smilingly friendly. There is a real feeling of happiness.

Pastoral care, well-being and discipline: This feeling of happiness does not come by chance. Once more, that word 'creation' floats to the surface. So many people we asked – and of many ages – said they were happy because they were doing what they liked doing or, if 'liked' is the wrong word, perhaps they were learning constructively without being aware of it. They were, to adapt the Bard, 'Open as day for melting charity.' One older person suggested it had something to do with feeling safe and that had something to do with every pupil having a form tutor able to offer support and advice if required. There seems to be an impressive layer of support and much genuine concern. There's a lot of affection around and that, surely, contributes to that almost tangible feeling of happiness. At the art exhibition we watched the head weaving in and out of groups of pupils, chatting away easily, and spreading good will. As for discipline, the feeling is that common sense prevails, and since everyone knows each other well it's easy to pick up any change in behaviour or to spot unhappy confusion. Parents are always involved. The school is keen on the partnership with parents. 'Most of the time we're aiming for the same results,' one mother told us. 'We trust the staff,' she added,

Pupils and parents: Most pupils come from a radius of 20 miles or less and some we talked to were amusing about the difference between Wolverhampton and Birmingham schools. There seems to be friendly rivalry but none of any snobbish kind. In fact we came across little in the way of arrogance or snobbishness. The parents we spoke to were friendly and unpretentious, happy with the status quo and full of praise for the staff. There were encouraging results from a recent parents' survey, the results of which were published in a recent edition of The Independent, the school magazine. Parents appreciated the chance to air their views and expressed confidence in the school's response. On both occasions we attended where staff and parents were mingling – even dancing – it was good to observe the relaxed and friendly interchange. There were some serious conversations, too.

Entrance: Basically there are three routes into the school: the junior school, ages 7-11; senior school, ages 11-16; sixth form, ages 16-18. There are plenty of opportunities for visiting and absorbing: open days are regarded as fun not only because the school is at its most hospitable but because visitors have the chance to meet other potential first timers and, indeed, parents often make friends with other parents. After all, the parents are joining, too. Very few pupils decide not to go on to the next stage of their time at WGS. Details of all this can be found in the prospectus. Early departures are very rare but the school does think carefully about the suitability of each candidate. The most enthusiastic response about moving up the school we received was when looking round the school we were taken into a class of 11 year olds who, when we asked about the problems of moving up to the senior school,barked out in unison, 'there's a free pass!' Nobody winced visibly.

Exit: Very few leave post-GCSE and nearly everyone who stays goes on to worthwhile courses (three to study medicine and veterinary science in 2016) and universities, including Oxbridge (two in 2016), Birmingham, UCL, St Andrews and others. This is all published in the Wulfrunian and reveals the interesting subjects chosen by successful candidates. Parents and past pupils whom we met spoke of the superb help they had been given with HE and UCAS. It was even said that some pupils joined the sixth form because of this excellent advice.

Money matters: A range of scholarships. Parents feeling the pinch particularly painfully will be especially interested in the scholarship recently set up to honour the school's original purpose, 'educating poor boys.' Nowadays, of course, that means 'poor students'. Parents need not be shy: the bursar looks very friendly – we saw her smiling at the Jazz Concert – and talent is always recognised.

Remarks: This is a remarkable school whose success and history have not in any sense edged it into aloof smugness. It is an establishment which has retained its genuine humanity, unlike so many schools who have felt compelled to bow to league tables and competition, forgetting the magic of learning and education. Competition here seems healthy and invigorating; relations between students and staff are creative and mutually appreciative. Out of such contact and, no doubt, occasional confrontations and subsequent rapprochements, a sense of harmony and learning has emerged. Much of this is due to the lively creativity that fills the school. But perhaps what has permeated throughout is the most generous form of constructive competition. And that is what the aspiring head boy and girl need in order to persuade the interview board of their value. This is a school to celebrate and cherish.

Woodbridge School

Burkitt Road, Woodbridge, Suffolk IP12 4JH

Pupils: 813; 58 full boarders • Ages: 7-18 (boarding from 13) • Sixth form: 197 • C of E

Fees: Day £8,364 – £15,630; Boarding £29,397 pa

Tel: 01394 615041
Email: admissions@woodbridgeschool.org.uk
Website: www.woodbridgeschool.org.uk

Headmaster: Since 2014, Neil Tetley, previously deputy head of Sevenoaks School. History degree and PGCE from Cambridge, then spent a year in Japan before taking up teaching. Ten years at King's College Wimbledon, becoming housemaster and then assistant head, with an interim year at the International School of Brussels. He has a great passion for Russian history, enjoys all things Italian and is an enthusiastic sportsman, particularly enjoying squash and cricket. He is married to Laura, a foreign languages teacher, and they have two young sons.

Head of prep school, The Abbey: Since September 2015, John Brett, previously head of Old Buckenham Hall for five years and, before that, head of St Mary's School, Melrose from 1998 to 2010. He was director of music at Thomas's Battersea between 1993 and 1998 and held the same role at King's Hall School, starting his teaching career in 1985. He and his wife Clare have two children.

Academic matters: Small class sizes, around 20, in The Abbey prep school, gradually moving from class to subject based learning. Specialist teachers from the senior school teach science, languages and art to the higher forms. The Abbey language scheme gives all pupils a taste of four modern languages, Italian, Spanish, Mandarin, French, in consecutive years. Full-time SEN teacher gives support throughout the school. There is setting for maths from year 3 and for English in year 6.

Despite a keen eye for results, the school is not enamoured with league tables believing, as do many, that too much of a focus on the school's overall performance can lead to individual pupil's needs being ignored. Academically the right buttons are being pressed, though disappointing A level results in 2016 with 64 per cent A*-B and 22 per cent A*/A grades; maths, the sciences and performing arts are the stronger suits. At GCSE, 52 per cent A*/A grades in 2016; again maths, sciences and languages performing particularly well. Though less eye-catching, the middle range ability pupils' results reflect their solid achievement and success. Pupils are banded from year 7 and setted in certain subjects eg maths. Classes around 20. Everyone takes French in year 7, adding Latin and Spanish or German in year 8; at least one modern language to GCSE, with Mandarin and Japanese optional extras and Greek and Italian available in the sixth form. Around 60 pupils have mild learning difficulties; several full-time teachers offer support individually and in groups. The emphasis is on keeping pupils fully integrated into the mainstream classes. Strong EAL provision for overseas pupils. This is a school that works for all abilities.

Games, options, the arts: Impressive pitches and courts with the sports hall housed in the Eden project-style Dome, which provides room for several classes at a time. Sport is for all and everyone has the opportunity to play competitively in the school teams, often trouncing the opposition. The sports development programme is devised to encourage the most talented pupils, many of whom catch the selector's eye at county and international levels. Swimming is for the hardy in an outdoor pool. Friday afternoon is time tabled for the Seckford Scheme, an extraordinary range of non-academic activities in which the whole school (staff included) joins. All interests and tastes are encouraged: eg sailing, cookery, chess (school has its own Grand Master), and CCF is a top draw for many. D of E is also popular.

Sport is for all in the prep – the head is very pro everyone playing competitively and everyone has the opportunity to play in a match. Main sports for boys are soccer, rugby, hockey and cricket; for girls, netball, hockey and rounders. Swimming and tennis for all throughout the year, plus athletics in the summer, and cross-country in the Michaelmas and Lent terms: not a place for couch potatoes.

The musical life of the prep school is outstanding. In year 4, all pupils learn a stringed instrument in school, with tuition in small groups, and as a result, a large number continue to play. The Abbey has four choirs, two string orchestras, and a variety of ensemble groups. Concerts and performances are regularly given. Drama and dance also strong. Ballet and tap are taught throughout the school with the emphasis on fun and a chance to perform. The summer play, performed in the Seckford Theatre, is a highlight for the town as well as the school.

Music regarded as mainstream in the senior school – no 'sporty' or 'aesthete' labels and half the school learns one or more instruments. It is 'cool to sing'. School has a close association with Aldeburgh and Snape with masterclasses, courses and recitals taking place regularly. Proliferation of choirs, ensembles, orchestras and bands. Drama also wildly popular with eight plays and shows performed annually in the impressive Seckford Theatre. Dance is increasingly popular. The school's international programme provides visits and exchanges throughout Europe, India, Australia, S Africa, China and Oman. Pupils spend periods of up to 10 weeks at linked schools.

Boarding: Boarders are virtually all from overseas – from a wide range of countries including Spain, Germany, Thailand, China and Hong Kong. Although boarding is available from 13, all boarders are sixth formers. They are fully integrated into the school, and as there are only 58 of them they have a close relationship with the boarding houseparents. They are free to visit the town after school and at weekends; some weekend excursions further afield organised to eg London or Cambridge, plus parties, paintballing etc. Help with language issues available.

Background and atmosphere: Founded in the 17th century, the school is part of the Seckford Foundation and has occupied its present site in the town since the 19th century. It has been fully co-educational for 40 years. School stands on extensive grounds on a hilly plot with the various buildings dotted around, giving a campus atmosphere. The immediate approach to the school passes the slightly unprepossessing boarding house. However, the school buildings are a mix of styles from the Victorian to the contemporary, including the recently-built Seckford Theatre and sixth form centre. Atmosphere in classes, library and areas for independent working is palpably studious. Time-wasting is frowned on and most pupils spin from lessons to sport to activities non stop. One mother commented, 'Pupils can have a crack at everything going – there is a niche for everyone'. Pupils themselves are friendly and polite; teachers, if anything, even more so. Unstuffy relations all round, and the staff give praiseworthy loyal service; most have been there 10 years or more.

The prep school is a short walk away from the senior school. Main building is Tudor, lots of oak panelling, flagged floors, and even rumours of a ghost. Newer buildings for science, art and sport have been added, and the grounds are mature and delightful; 'this is a place for a sunlit childhood'. Pupils about the school are courteous, open doors and smile, but are intent on their own ploys and enjoyment.

Pastoral care, well-being and discipline: Enthusiastic endorsement by parents for vertical tutoring system, which operates from year 10 to 13. Younger pupils have the benefit of knowing older pupils well, and it provides leadership opportunities for sixth formers; 'most pupils know whom they would go to'. Few discipline problems.

Communication with parents is taken very seriously. As well as the usual parents' consultations, staff are available on a day-to-day basis via telephone or email. This care of the children is at the heart of such a happy school.

Pupils and parents: Pupils drawn largely from professional East Anglian families, many with a media background (Aldeburgh, BT close by). A fleet of buses brings pupils from as far afield as Norfolk, Felixstowe and Colchester. The school is very popular in the town and many parents have moved out from London to take advantage. Foreign students, many from the Far East, are encouraged to come for long or short periods, partly to ginger up what would otherwise be a very English school; about two-thirds of sixth form boarders are from the Far East, others from mainland Europe.

Entrance: About half of year 3 is made up from pupils progressing up from the pre-prep department, Queen's House, at 7; others join via test and interview from other local schools. Selective, but with scope for quite a range of ability; 'we are looking for those who can explore all that's on offer'. Places occasionally available in higher forms – always worth asking.

Common entrance or test, together with a report from present school, and interview at 11 or 13. Two-thirds of intake at 11 transfer from The Abbey prep, the rest from local state and private schools. About three-quarters of those tested are accepted. Entry to the sixth form is based on an interview and GCSE predicted grades.

Exit: Vast majority of prep school pupils make the seamless transfer to the senior school. A few go to state schools in the area, or to board elsewhere. The parents of the occasional pupil that might struggle in the senior school will have been given advance warning, and advised to move elsewhere at 11. This is handled sensitively and is rare.

Few leave after GCSEs. Great majority leave sixth form for university; Edinburgh, Newcastle, Oxford Brookes and Reading currently popular, as are sciences, modern languages, English and business/finance courses.

Money matters: Academic scholarships worth up to 50 per cent of fees can be topped-up with means-tested bursaries. Music, sport, all round and art scholarships are also available. Some sibling reductions.

Remarks: A good all-round 'country school in the town'. Lively, and although selective, would suit quite a wide ability range. Exceptional extracurricular provision for what is, largely, a day school.

W

Wymondham College

Golf Links Road, Morley, Wymondham, Norfolk NR18 9SZ

Pupils: 1,100; 640 full/weekly boarders • Ages: 11–18 • Sixth form: 400

Fees: Day free; Boarding £10,044 – £10,710 pa

Tel: 01953 609000
Email: admissions@wymondhamcollege.org
Website: www.wymondhamcollege.org

Principal: Since 2014, Mr Jonathan Taylor, formerly principal at Torch Academy Gateway Trust, Nottinghamshire. Educated at The Leys school, Cambridge, then read theology at Oxford before returning to Cambridge for a PGCE. First teaching post in nearby Cottenham, followed by assistant head at De Aston school, Market Rasen, then deputy head of Toot Hill, Nottinghamshire, before a move to the Torch Academy. A swift progress, leaving outstanding Ofsted reports in his wake. Thoughtful and immensely hard working – breakfast meetings at 7am a regular fixture with key staff- yet he hasn't disappeared in a cloud of management initiatives, preferring lots of contact with pupils and staff and teaching classes of his own. This is going down well – 'It's early days, but he seems to want to know us,' we were told.

In a big school, he is aware of danger of becoming out of touch and sets store by personal example. He greeted every single GCSE pupil outside the exam hall on the day of their first exam this summer to wish them luck and gets occasionally frustrated by the isolated position of his office complex – a new build under the previous principal. He is seen about the campus a lot, often accompanied by his dog, Bertie, who is, needless to say, immensely popular with pupils. Believes there is a special quality about Wymondham College, and 'the common purpose of learning for its own sake'. From personal experience he knows about boarding and understands that there is 'a lot more to a successful state boarding school than tacking a Travelodge onto a comprehensive', as has been suggested in certain quarters. Encourages pupils to contact him directly, email or in person, should they wish to, and some do. Determined to encourage the special qualities of Wymondham College and to raise standards even further – staff have fortnightly personal development sessions and are paired with a senior colleague to help share best practice and provide support.

Lives on the site and is married to Julie, herself a senior education adviser.

Academic matters: Though strictly speaking non-selective, the varied intake (50 per cent boarding) plus provision of music and sports places – and a perception in the area that 'It's for bright children' – means pupils appreciate their good fortune in being there and are motivated to work hard. Parents are a strong support and the school's results reflect all round achievement. In 2016, 89 per cent of pupils got 5+ A*-C GCSEs including English and maths; 32 per cent A*/A grades. Modern languages are compulsory to GCSE level (Spanish most popular). Close to 80 per cent take religious studies at GCSE – interesting for a non-faith school.

Sixth form definitely academic – despite a low bar of three Bs and four Cs required at GCSE for entry, most do well and higher grades are often needed for external applicants. Only four vocational courses offered in the long list of subjects to be studied, with maths taken by over half the cohort. Sciences also have a high take up. Headmaster feels this may reflect current anxieties about the need to take degrees that help lead to good jobs, but 'we are holding the line that subjects should also be studied for their own sake'. In 2016, 31 per cent A*/A grades and nearly 59 per cent A*-B grades at A level.

As the school is regarded as 'being for bright children', there are relatively few pupils, around 12 per cent, requiring learning support, and these are milder cases of dyslexia/dyspraxia/dyscalculia, with only a small number of statemented/EHC plan pupils. Well resourced and a positive attitude about extra support. There are also breakfast and catch-up clubs run by individual departments for those needing an extra boost. All year 7s are tested on entry to the school. There is also a structured programme for teaching EFL. School has a well-established system for identifying the very bright (gifted and talented, in the jargon) early on and they spend an extra two periods a week, plus own time on an extension programme comprising a research project and an extra course chosen from space science, Russian, Latin, literature and ideas and government and politics. The presence of postgraduate fellows in the sixth form and some also resident in the houses help pupils learn good work habits – we saw a light-hearted revision session in action during GCSE study leave – and give sixth formers insider guidance with UCAS and Oxbridge entrance. A programme of visiting speakers and workshops are led by local university staff, notably from UEA and Cambridge.

Games, options, the arts: If sporty, there is plenty on offer. Usual team games – rugby included, and an extensive match schedule for the most competent though fewer games for those lower down the rankings. Games are compulsory up to sixth form, when they become optional.Pupils themselves run the five-a-side football league that operates at lunchtimes. Good facilities including swimming pool, gigantic sports hall which doubles for assemblies/concerts, Astroturf, pitches and courts galore. Keen involvement in D of E (the college runs the county scheme) and CCF also offered, though involvement in this is a voluntary activity and not timetabled.

Music important. The annual Mair cup is an opportunity for all pupils to perform in a competition between houses and is extremely popular. Over 250 have individual instrumental lessons and there are choirs and excellent jazz and concert bands that perform at events locally – including the Royal Norfolk Show. A string group has been recently established.

Flourishing art and textiles, which are taught in the Tech block, a light and airy building designed around a central atrium with good provision for display of finished efforts. Good take-up at GCSE and A level and significant numbers go on to study at degree level.

Boarding: The five boarding houses for the main school are drearily functional, though homelike enough upstairs in the dormitories. Houses are all mixed, though girls and boys have separate floors for sleeping, and day pupils as well as boarders return to houses at break and lunchtimes. Plenty of staff, matrons and resident fellows around, and pupils are cheerful and well-behaved.

A few struggle with homesickness at the beginning. Flexi or part boarding is not on offer and swapping from boarding to day is impossible, so a decision to board, taken at aged 10, has to be considered carefully. 'It's not for everyone and this is why we interview all potential boarders', we were told. Those joining in year 9 generally have fewer problems settling. The houses provide something of a refuge at break and lunchtimes when most return to base, although 'It is annoying if your friends are in another house', said one pupil. House staff around at all key times, and matrons remain on the premises at night. The majority go home at weekends but plenty remain and outings/activities are planned throughout the term. Exeats once each side of half term.

Background and atmosphere: Founded in 1951, the brainchild of Sir Lincoln Ralphs, then chief education officer for Norwich. It is the largest state boarding school in the country. The site is a former US military hospital and, despite the utilitarian nature of the buildings, it is very peaceful and in the middle of nowhere (Wymondham itself is several miles off). Some of the newer buildings – modern languages, for example – are interesting and well designed, but the most interesting of all is the single remaining Nissen hut, now listed and used, rather effectively, as the chapel. The college has a strong Christian ethos, but this is non-denominational. There is great pride in the school's history and traditions, with a memorial garden and key anniversaries celebrated regularly. Striking new sixth form centre, set around a courtyard, with boarding facilities in individual rooms with en-suite bathrooms, a refectory, working and computer areas.

Traditional uniform (including ties for girls) compulsory up to year 11, but it is the cheap and cheerful sort – no Harris tweed or boaters. Pupils don't mind the slightly bleak boarding houses: 'You get used to it so quickly, and anyway, we like the people', we were told by one pupil, with nods and agreement from others. The old system of year 7s being kept in their own separate house has been discontinued and everyone is mixed up from the start. Saturday morning school for all (though not sixth form) accepted readily enough – holidays slightly longer than usual in state schools to compensate. One of the virtues of the site is that there is lots of 'promenade' time out in fresh air between lessons, and this seems to contribute to the calm and disciplined atmosphere of the school.

Pastoral care, well-being and discipline: House-based tutor groups with tutors overseeing academic and extracurricular activities from year 7 to 11. Emphasis is on good relationships. 'Work hard, be kind' is the phrase coined and we heard it quoted by year 11s quite cheerfully, if slightly tongue-in-cheek. The presence of resident fellows in the houses help with friendship and other difficulties and in addition to house staff, the school also has two counsellors and a chaplain, so there is a network of support. Looking out for younger pupils is encouraged and there is very little evidence of bad behaviour or bullying, though school is ever alert and anti-bullying strategies are in place. The parent liaison office helps to smooth communications between home and school, especially for parents of boarders.

Pupils and parents: Pupils come from Norfolk in the main (including boarders), though an increasing number are from further afield thanks, in part, to the improvements to the A11. Over 20 per cent are from overseas, a mixture of Europeans and Chinese mostly, plus those with parents working abroad. Fewer Forces families than formerly; the majority of parents are professional or managerial. 'It's an unpretentious place, not for show-offs, and we like that,' said a parent, and that is the common view. Quite a few have chosen the school because it is a state funded one and without the perceptions of privilege that independent boarding schools may possess. Pupils regard themselves as fortunate and appear straightforward and hard working.

Entrance: Main intake at 11+ but places are available at 13 (boarding only) and again in the sixth form. Day and boarding places are split roughly 50:50. Day places very oversubscribed and awarded according to the LA criteria of looked after children, siblings and distance from school. Once other categories have been dealt with, the distance from the school can be as little as 0.6 mile, though commonly up to two miles. Check carefully – despite the name, the town of Wymondham itself is not in the catchment. Eight musical aptitude and eight sporting aptitude places – four day and four boarding for each. Competition for such places is fierce.

All potential boarders are interviewed by the house heads to check that pupils are prepared for all that boarding entails (a hard call in a 10 minute chat). Places are less competitive, but still oversubscribed. It is perhaps worth adding that although you can apply for both day and boarding places, you must list them in order of preference, and if allocated a boarding place you cannot make a crafty switch to day later on. The number of places in each category is fixed.

Most remain for the sixth form, assuming they meet baseline attainment of four Cs and three Bs at GCSE. Not a high bar, but as numbers applying from outside exceed places available, admission is, effectively, dependant on rank order of results at GCSE for those applying from elsewhere.

Exit: Majority – some 75 per cent – move on to higher education. Wide range of degree subjects studied though a definite bias towards the sciences, maths, computing and business. Almost half to Russell group institutions with seven to Oxbridge in 2016 and 11 medics. The resident Lincoln Fellow in the sixth form is an Oxbridge graduate with a brief to dispel myths about the application process and help pupils with UCAS generally.

Money matters: Tuition is free; fees are payable for boarding provision only. Fees compare favourably with the cost of a local day independent schools. Day boarding and enhanced day boarding, for relatively modest fees, are popular option (they include meals and various after-school activities) but there are no flexible boarding arrangements.

At least one sixth form boarding scholarship a year, worth 100 per cent of fees, for a student with exceptional academic, music or sporting potential.

Remarks: Has a well deserved reputation locally, and increasingly nationally as a leading state boarding school. It is a bargain for parents who want a boarding education for their children, but without the associations of privilege or having to fork out fortunes in school fees. It is a big school and hard-working, socially outgoing types do best.

Wymondham High School

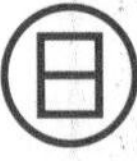

Folly Road, Wymondham, Norfolk NR18 0QT

Pupils: 1,561 • Ages: 11–18 • Sixth form: 324

Tel: 01953 602078
Email: office@wh-at.net
Website: www.wymondhamhigh.co.uk

Principal: Since September 2016 Jonathan Rockey, previously vice principal.

Academic matters: A true community school without hidden filters. At GCSE in 2016 70 per cent gained 5+ A*-C including English and maths; 22 per cent A*/A grades. Short course RE for all. Three sets, known as rivers, for academic subjects and fast track for those who shine in art, music and maths. Average class sizes are 25-26 although they sometimes creep up to 32. Parents speak of fantastically supportive, approachable teachers who go the extra mile – particularly in the maths department where 'they have a good way of getting kids on board.' Governors provide late buses for pupils from outlying villages who want to stay for extended school activities or use after school 'helplines' – all subject areas provide a member of staff to give additional help at least one afternoon a week. Pretty pushy sixth form with strong academic bent – 'outstanding', says Ofsted. Every student is interviewed after the first term in the sixth to see if they've done enough to come off probation. At A level in 2016, 31 of grades were A*/A, 56 per cent A*/B. No wandering off site in between lessons – 'they don't have free periods – they have study periods,' said the jolly but no-nonsense head of sixth. Virtually all stay for the full two years.

Support department for those with special needs and an enthusiastic assistant headteacher who's responsible for inclusion – she's overseeing a pilot scheme to give support through the family. Specialists based in the excellence centre (also caters for the gifted and talented and those who are falling by the wayside), differentiated work and classroom support given by assistants. Laptops and additional time in exams. In year 11, 10 youngsters, the majority of whom are statemented, are given the opportunity to join a two year course – 'pathway two.' This involves spending a day at a local college, a day on work experience and three days in school where they are taught as a discrete group. At time of writing, zero drop-outs – all credit to the school.

Games, options, the arts: Modern sports centre with upgraded gym facility shared with the town and additional activities for the sporty – they've managed to spawn several English schools' athletics and judo champions. Designated a specialist school for the arts – art, drama and music get an extra boost. In 2009, a science specialism was added, with new modern labs being created. Recording facilities, two orchestras, timetabled practice sessions and a small studio theatre which becomes a community arts venue in the evening. Recent rap workshop with an evening performance for parents 'went down a storm,' according to a participant. Productive art and DT departments where kids are happily engaged. After-school activities include Japanese club and African drumming – late buses every day so no one misses out.

Background and atmosphere: School is comfortably nested on the edge of Wymondham, a picturesque country town. Straightforward buildings, the majority of which hail from the 1950s onwards, are well maintained. Clutch of grim mobiles still in use but a recent extension has much improved the library and sixth form study area. Degree of separation between the main school and sixth who don't perform prefectorial duties (that happens in the fifth form) don't have to wear the uniform and are based around a generous quad to one side of the main school. Immaculately mown lawns – the school groundsman used to work at Royal Windsor polo club – and large playing fields provide ample space to spread wings and let off steam.

The 'snack shack' – a centrally plonked brown shed – is a popular way to beat the lunch queue. Serving jacket potatoes and soup, it's been so successful there's another in the pipeline. Sturdy picnic tables – supplied after a request from the school council – are dotted around for outside meets and eats.

Pastoral care, well-being and discipline: Good rapport between staff and kids plus vertical forms affiliated to one of four houses make this very large school a civilised place to be. Pupils settle quickly and support each other. Parents speak of an atmosphere of friendliness and well-being – 'they're good at treating the kids as individuals rather than fitting them into a box.' Well-structured school council gives a voice to all and encourages a sense of partnership. The school is focusing on dress and behaviour with a slightly modified uniform. The

W

Head's Council, made of elected upper sixth students, meets weekly as does the Head's House Captains' Council.

Pupils and parents: Affluent Wymondham and surrounding villages are attractive to those who work in Norwich – easy commuting distance. Wide social mix with a high proportion living in the town – tiny number from ethnic minorities. Sixth formers come from an extensive catchment area including Norwich. Hugely supportive parents with high expectations and chirpy, good humoured pupils who enjoy being at school. Trad uniform until the sixth, who have to wear 'business dress'.

Entrance: Over-subscribed. Stringent catchment rules for yrs 7-11 (Wymondham and satellite villages. Check current precise locations with the LA advice centre – an absolute must). No preference for siblings. For the sixth, seven GCSEs (including English and maths) at C and above with no lower than a B for subjects to be studied at AS.

Exit: After GCSEs, those more suited to practical courses to local sixth form colleges; just under 40 per cent stayed on in 2016. Post A level 80 per cent to university, including seven to Oxbridge and one medic in 2016; visiting speakers from UEA help with preparation. Humanities and creative arts most popular subject areas.

Remarks: Popular, successful community comprehensive with a strong, academic sixth form.

Yarlet School

Yarlet, Stafford, Staffordshire ST18 9SU

Pupils: 161; around 45 flexi-borders • Ages: 2-13 • C of E

Fees: £7,125 – £11,940 pa

Tel: 01785 286568
Email: info@yarletschool.org
Website: www.yarletschool.uk

Headmaster: Since 2009, Mr Ian Raybould BEd ALCM NPQH (late 40s), who studied music and education (4-12 years) at University College, Winchester and London College of Music; taught at King's College, Madrid, where he was head of music and boarding; head of first IAPS prep school in Spain; as an ISI inspector he visited prep, senior and international schools in Europe.

Back here in the UK he conducts the Yarlet school choir and plays the organ for chapel services. He is keen to do more in the area of music and the performing arts. He has expert and enthusiastic backing in those areas and staff speak highly of his involvement and support. He is something of an IT buff – not the booming, bearded kind but the patient and thoughtful kind – and he has greatly improved the learning and administration systems as well as enhancing accessibility for SEN. He is genuinely and personally concerned with helping pupils with SEN – 'particularly tuned in', in his own words – and is chairman of governors at a local special school.

Some male heads, if they insist on showing Good Schools Guide scribblers around themselves, adopt a sort of jaunty, old style naval heartiness, like a captain addressing his crew in a high wind. This provides quite an insight into such a man when he barks out the wrong name to a bewildered pupil. No chance of that happening at Yarlet. This head greets the children easily and warmly like a good father, and they are pleased to see him. It feels like genuine affection, respect and happiness. Being shown round by Mr Raybould is a delight. He is clearly a sincere and thoughtful man and knows his pupils well. They respond fearlessly and confidently, obviously happy. To quote from a mother's email in answer to our questions about the head, 'He seems something of a visionary, and arrived with well-prepared ideas for the future of Yarlet. He intends to sharpen up the academics but not at the expense of the liveliness and pleasure of the classroom. But overall, it's the strong relationships with the children that he seems to enjoy particularly. They like and respect him and want to do well because of him.'

Recently the school was visited by ISI on a routine compliance inspection. After they had looked around, the leader had a final meeting with the head, expressing her pleasure. 'What, in your opinion, is the USP of the school?' asked the head. 'That's easy,' replied the leader; 'it's the warmth and friendliness of the school. It's outstanding.' A number of things contribute to that atmosphere but the most obvious would seem to be the standards and expectations set by the head and staff and the careful way in which the days are planned.

Mr Raybould has two sons, one of whom has moved on from Yarlet with a music scholarship.

Entrance: Not selective, but the school is scrupulously honest about not admitting pupils whose needs cannot be met, so there are boundaries. Mild SEND is accepted and 'there is a dedicated SENCo who ensures that any support is "individualised and targeted"'. At the time of our visit, two pupils had EHC plans for moderate learning difficulties, and 25 per cent of the main school pupils have Individual Education Plans (IEPS), mostly because they have mild learning difficulties, but many of whom are simply below average ability and require individual attention.

Most pupils join the nursery and pre-prep, a magic, sparkling world with well kitted out classrooms and play areas with the sort of toys that make you want to throw away the zero from your age. Delightful, bright-eyed staff whose affection and commitment is obvious. We were told that the head's frequent visits are hugely popular with the younger ones, who are accepted into the school after meeting the head at 2 years old.

Two scholarships, named after the legendary Richard Plant (head 1989-2009), at 11+ for up to 50 per cent fees for those who show academic promise together with all-round ability and enthusiasm. There are sibling discounts in the main school and there is a general bursary fund for parents needing assistance. There is also a combined scholarship for up to two local primary school children from 11, which carries on to senior school (Rugby, Repton and Denstone College are three of the senior schools included in the scheme). Interview at 10, need the ability to pass CE into senior school and a particular strength in at least one arts, music, sports or academic subject. Means-tested. The school is keen to extend the range of primary and public schools involved.

Exit: Most leave at 13 though some at 11. The majority go to a wide spectrum of independent schools with good numbers of academic, music and art scholarships. The head was justifiably pleased to announce on speech day that every pupil had been successful in securing a place to his or her first choice of school, and with the usual wide range of schools: this year eight leavers went to six different schools; the year before there were 13 leavers going on to nine different schools. The breadth of destinations is both encouraging and valuable: a good prep school encourages parents to choose the right school for their offspring. A number of parents spoke highly of the support and guidance the school gives.

Remarks: In his speech on sports day the headmaster took the opportunity to comment on issues beyond academic achievements – which he recognised, of course – to 'those things which make Yarlet special or even unique.' He began, as do we – though not simultaneously – with the exceptional level of art and design. The art teacher is a comparative newcomer to the school and she has had an astonishing effect on the creative side. She is inspirational in her enthusiasm and energy, full of ideas and open minded enough to allow pupils to gain in confidence by going their own way and exploring. The results, as we saw on two occasions – under normal conditions and displayed on sports day – were amazing in their variety, with fearless experimenting and an obvious delight revealed by pupils of all ages. The building was specially designed and built as an art studio: clearly teacher and pupils have responded full-heartedly. What was particularly pleasing to see was work on display by former pupils, one of whom will shortly be displaying her paintings at an art gallery in Birmingham. It's always good to know that lessons at an early age can be absorbed, recalled and relished.

A little further along the compact building there is a useful space for music, including huge concerts occasionally involving 70 people, and very ambitious drama, Shakespeare and popular musicals. We saw some very lively expression of rhythm and dance, and both parents and pupils spoke of music as being a much-loved and exciting part of their lives. There are occasional trips to Stratford.

Thanks to the generosity of parents and, doubtless, others, a brand new specially designed science laboratory has recently taken the place of the ageing science building. There is much excitement about this state-of-the art resource, another example of the overall improvement of facilities – including the library and the creation of a senior pupils' sitting out area, described by one pupil as 'absolutely brilliant.' We met a number of old boys on our second visit, many of whom were amazed by improvements throughout the buildings, the airiness of the dormitories and, as usual on such occasions, the size of the entrance hall. A number of fathers we spoke to had sent their children here or were about to send them because they had such happy memories of their time at Yarlet.

However, one way of life is markedly different. Full time boarding no longer exists, though it is possible to savour the delights of sharing a dormitory with a number of chums. Flexi-boarding takes place on Wednesday and Thursday evenings and averages between 15 and 20 pupils per night. Pupils are supervised by the headmaster and the gap students, who mostly come from Australia. Not only does the head look after these Aussies thoughtfully and generously – after all, they are a long way from home – but he goes through the legal and social aspects of looking after the boarders in great detail. The sleeping arrangements are bright, airy and attractive, and we were told by some excited boys that 'the full English breakfast is delicious.' The head has introduced a number of boarding activities such as camping and pool parties with sensible supervision. Parents can choose how long their children stay of an evening. There is a supervised prep session and tea, and children can go home at 4.30pm, 5.30pm, 6.15pm or 7pm. This flexibility is much appreciated.

Rugby, cricket, football, netball, tennis, swimming: they're all there and played with sporting zest. And with ski trips to Italy, cultural and linguistic visits to France and a well-established exchange programme with a school in Madrid, there are plenty of opportunities for broadening the mind beyond the UK.

A notably strong aspect of the community – a word much used by parents, staff and pupils – is 'moral awareness'. Noticeable, traditional and enjoyable are the daily morning services held in the school's wonderful chapel, services which 'shamelessly but not heavily' consider and celebrate Christian principles. Staff and children seem to enjoy a mutual concern and respect for each other. The ISI inspector was right in her assessment of the warmth and friendliness of the community. We made enquiries about bullying, to pupils, parents and staff, and were not surprised that pupils looked astonished by the question and staff were confident that it was not a feature of the school. Parents were confident that staff and senior pupils were alert to the possibilities, but they felt that if there was any bullying the head and his staff would be very quickly aware. There is a 'worry box' for anyone who is anxious and, yes, worried. Not many notes are written.

Prefects, led by head and deputy head and selected by the staff, are encouraged to keep an eye out for any acts of particular kindness and generosity and to write a brief message about it for the head or senior member of staff. Similarly acts of unkindness. The feeling is that the prefects should not be saddled with the responsibilities of rewards and sanctions. Instead they pass on messages. One young pupil expressed astonishment at being congratulated for an action the head couldn't possibly have seen. The head told us as we wandered around the school that if he were bribed with a million pounds he still would not leave. That might astonish some young pupils, but most of them would understand what prompted that comment.

The publications offered to potential parents are upbeat and good fun. Y Sir? Is a delightful magazine chronicling the fun and games, the visits and the expeditions, the sports results and the concerts, the sheer happiness of the place. It's an honest and appealing document. Other information needed by potential parents is clearly and helpfully laid out.

In its modest, kind and happy way this is a delightful school with a delightful head. Pupils and parents seem universally happy, including those people who require help and encouragement with SEN. That is one of the great strengths of the school. There are many more.

Northern England

Cumbria
Durham
East Riding of Yorkshire
Greater Manchester
Lancashire
Merseyside
North Yorkshire
Northumberland
South Yorkshire
Tyne and Wear
West Yorkshire

Junior Schools
Senior Schools
Junior & Senior Schools
Edinburgh
EAST LOTHIAN
MIDLOTHIAN
Holy Island
ANARKSHIRE
THE SCOTTISH BORDERS
NORTHUMBERLAND
South Shields
Newcastle Upon Tyne
Penshaw
Carlisle
Solway Firth
DURHAM
Hartlepool
Middlesbrough
Darlington
CUMBRIA
NORTH YORKSHIRE
ENGLAND
Morecambe Bay
Harrogate
York
EAST RIDING OF YORKSHIR
LANCASHIRE
Leeds
Bradford
Kingston Upon Hull
Blackpool
Preston
Halifax
Blackburn
Wakefield
Huddersfield
Southport
WEST YORKSHIRE
SOUTH YORKSHIRE
Grims
Bolton
Oldham
Manchester
St. Helens
Liverpool
Birkenhead
Sheffield
Warringto
NOTTINGHAMSHIRE
Lincoln
LINCOLNSHI
FLINTSHIRE
Chester
CHESHIRE
DERBYSHIRE
U.K.)

NORTHERN ENGLAND

A

Abbey Lane Primary School

Abbey Lane, Sheffield, South Yorkshire S8 0BN

Pupils: 577 • Ages: 4–11

Tel: 01142 745054
Email: enquiries@abbeylane.sheffield.sch.uk
Website: www.abbeylaneprimaryschool.co.uk

Headteacher: Since 2012, Mrs Maxine Stafford (40s), previously deputy and acting head. Commended in Ofsted report for maintaining high standards but viewed by parents as unapproachable and lacking in warmth. Ones we spoke to (she refused to meet us) feel she does not listen in a sympathetic way to their concerns, which she sees as criticism, and is immediately on the defensive – 'I dread the day I have to have dealings with her,' said one. 'She always has the deputy head with her – I felt quite intimidated,' said another. While most of the questions in the Ofsted parents' questionnaire had highly positive responses, there is a marked dip when it comes to quality of leadership and management and the school's responses to parental concerns.

Entrance: Apply in the usual way via the local authority, by January 15 of year 6. Waiting list criteria: children in care; living in the catchment area with a sibling at the school; living in the catchment area; having a sibling; others. Distance (straight line measurement) and exceptional social/medical need used for tie breaks. Not generally oversubscribed (entry has risen from 60 to 90) – takes from outside catchment. Full or part time start in September, January or April.

Exit: Vast majority to Meadowhead Comprehensive.

Remarks: Went through an extended period of temporary leadership and staffing upheaval after the retirement of a very popular, long-standing head, but now achieving well at key stage 2 results at the top end, though slight dip over the last year or two. Key stage 1 results stronger, though. Graded good by Ofsted in 2014, in a report which praised teaching and challenge given to the most able (some work at level 6, which is exceptional), but criticism of handwriting and presentation standards. Some use of ability groups for English and maths. Classes within lower years mixed up each year, which not all parents are happy about.

Good support for special needs, but you may have to push to get it. Gifted and talented given special classroom activities.

Situated in a relatively well-off suburb of south west Sheffield; few ethnic minority and well below average proportion of children from poor backgrounds. Younger children housed in traditional, red-brick, original building – light with cheerful displays, but reception classrooms rather cramped; hall can only accommodate one year at a time. Recent large addition provides more spacious, bright classrooms and a small hall used for PE, whilst markedly reducing playground area. Pleasant view of thickly wooded hill behind playground, which is equipped with climbing wall, gazebos and a train-shaped climbing frame. Woodland area just used for teaching at present, there's potential for greater exploitation for forest school purposes.

Friendly, happy atmosphere. Children say bullying very rare and that issues are quickly dealt with; mostly good behaviour. Weekly awards assembly for good work and manners and best class attendance. Golden Time reward system – children choose an activity they enjoy on Friday afternoons. Pupils act as peer mentors, play leaders in breaks and librarians; active school council.

Wide range of after-school activities – main sports, including rugby and cricket, Spanish, zumba (children and parents), choir, drama. Eco, international, arts and healthy schools awards. Takes part in local events such as the Woodseats Festival – the outside cheerfully decorated in red, white and blue bunting when we called in – and raises large sums of money for local and national charities. Mostly local visits; year 6 residential at Derbyshire outdoors centre. Enthusiastic year 2 teacher maintains a blog with lots of photographs of her form's activities on school website.

Attractive uniform – green sweatshirt, green, black and white polo shirts with black or grey trousers and skirts, green and white checked summer dresses. Active PTA (PALS) – does lots of fundraising and organises a picnic in local park for prospective reception children. These have two half-day visits with their parents before they start and staff aim to visit them in their pre-school setting.

A well-regarded and in most respects successful school that needs to work harder on its communication skills.

AKS Lytham

Clifton Drive South, Lytham St Annes, Lancashire FY8 1DT

Pupils: 696 • Ages: 2–18 • Sixth form: 140

Fees: £7,785 – £10,899 pa

Tel: 01253 784100
Email: admissions@arnoldkeqms.com
Website: www.arnoldkeqms.com

Headmaster: Since 2014, Mike Walton BA MA NPQH (50ish). He was state-educated in Folkestone, Kent and then studied geography at Lancaster and stayed there to do his PGCE.

During the '80s and '90s Mr Walton mainly taught in British state schools – apart from sixth months as a volunteer teacher in Northern Sudan. His first headship was at Orchard School in Canterbury – a special school for children with learning and behavioural difficulties. He says that during these years in state education he had a 'missionary zeal' to 'make the world a better place' by teaching the people who needed him the most. In August 2005 he changed direction, moving to Thailand to become principal of Regents International School, Pattaya – a British international boarding school. He was very successful in this role – helping to grow the school and taking on leadership and advisory roles on prestigious boards and bodies both in Asia and beyond. He also led the school in Thailand to develop a curriculum that's taught through partnerships with local voluntary organisations – such as orphanages, street kids' centres or charities working with HIV patients – and encouraged children to engage with big issues such as democracy, international development and environmentalism. He says this showed him how teachers in the independent sector can satisfy that ambition to make the world a better place by 'making good people who go out into the world and do great things.' Mr Walton was a big fish in the world of international schooling. He says the reason he took the job is simple: he came away from the interview at AKS with a strong sense that this was a great school for his three children to attend. He loves the family feel, he says, and the 'holistic vision of education'; and he wanted his kids to experience school in the UK.

He says he values the history of the two schools that came together to form AKS – or ArnoldKEQMS as, we presume, no pupil ever calls it. The school has only existed in its current form on the Lytham St Annes site since September 2013. Blackpool's Arnold School and Lytham-based King Edward VII and Queen Mary School merged in 2012-13 – a year before Mr Walton took office. Mr Walton says he likes the fact that there are traditions to build on but there's also some of the excitement of a start-up; after the turbulence of the merger, the school is ripe for a leader with a vision. (A parent group contested the merger with the Charity Commission and, after failing to win their appeal, some parents moved their children to other schools.) Parents needn't fear any drastic changes to the school, but he admits he's on a mission to improve its marketing and to drive up pupil numbers. Will the internationalist ideals of Regents filter through to his work at AKS? Hopefully yes, he says. Perhaps parents here can expect their children to start talking about global citizenship, or at least getting their hands dirty on local voluntary projects in the not too distant future. It's early days, but Mr Walton says he's inspired by the words of Einstein: 'Try not to become a man of success, but rather try to become a man of value.'

Head of junior school: Since 2014, Miss Katy Wright BA (early 30s). Studied English literature at Lancaster University and then did her PGCE in Bangor. Her first teaching job was at Heathfield School in West Yorkshire (the junior school to Rishworth, an independent co-ed day and boarding school). She was there for five years – arriving as an NQT and leaving as deputy head. She then moved to Arnold School as head of the juniors. The merger with King Edward and Queen Mary School in 2012-13 meant that two junior school heads came to the newly formed AKS and so, in the academic year of 2013-14, Miss Wright took a year out from the headship to take on the role of head of development for the whole school. During this year she also taught DT to years 7-10 and music to years 5-7, and she somehow fitted in the completion of an MSc in psychology at Chester University; but now, following the retirement of the former head of KEQMS, she has returned to the junior school as head teacher of AKS Juniors.

Miss Wright says she always wanted to teach. And she got her first real experience of teaching at the age of 16 when she became an outdoor pursuits instructor in the Lake District. She has a lot of strings to her bow, with specialisms in music, technology, literature and PE. She's practical and businesslike – proud of the school and thrilled with the purpose-built new building, which she and her KEQMS counterpart worked together to help design. We note the tiniest sign of dismay as she stoops to pick up school bags that have fallen from their designated racking outside the classrooms: 'The bags are a bit of a disaster. We've just brought in the shelves and they're not quite working. The kids are so busy – they just rush from one thing to the next and they don't always put their bags back on the shelves properly.' It looked pretty orderly to us...

She's popular with parents. They say she's 'very approachable' and 'listens to what you say'. Parents agree that she always puts the children first, and that's certainly what we saw during our time with her. She knew the name of every child we met during our visit and seemed to be truly in her element when she was interacting with them. She greets pupils with an enthusiastic: 'Hello class!' – in a tone so cheery it would put many a pantomime Buttons to shame.

Academic matters: Academically, the junior school pupils benefit from relatively small class sizes (a maximum of 20 in the infants, 22 in lower juniors and 24 in upper juniors – although in practice these figures are sometimes much lower). There's no setting, although sometimes pupils at the higher or lower range of ability are taken aside in small groups to push forwards or to grapple with a particular challenge.

The junior school employs a full-time learning support assistant who caters for children with dyslexia, ADHD and autism spectrum disorders. They only take children whose needs they can cater for, but if a child's needs are within the specialism of existing staff then they will be supported at no extra cost to the parents. Support is usually provided within lessons. Gifted and talented children are supported both within normal lessons and through links with the senior school. 'We can use the senior school,' says Miss Wright, 'to take them that bit further if that's what they need to reach their ceiling.'

In 2016, 47 per cent of A level entries were awarded an A* or A and that figure was 60 per cent at GCSE. Parents we spoke to were very happy with their children's progress here. One mum was thrilled with her daughter's successful A level results and told us, 'I don't think there's any way she'd have done anything like as well if she hadn't been here – she really benefitted from the small class sizes and the personalised support.' There are never more than 24 pupils in a class; no more than 16 at A level.

The school adds good value – aiming to add at least half a grade to pupils' expected outcomes. All children sit baseline tests in years 7, 10 and 12 to enable close monitoring of potential. Most of the teaching is mixed ability, although there is setting in maths because the brightest pupils can opt to take their GCSE at the end of year 10. Pupils take iGCSEs for English, maths, science and modern languages – as these give the teachers more freedom with the syllabus. The head teacher says that the school is strong across the board academically and he wouldn't want to draw attention to any particular subject area.

The senior school provides support for a broad range of special educational needs and there is usually no extra cost to parents for this (unless a child has a very specific need that would require, for example, an extra member of staff to be employed just to support that one child). Gifted and talented pupils are identified on a register and the school takes steps to stretch them by setting additional work and reading and encouraging them to take part in subject competitions or Olympiads, or to take Open University modules (to name just three provisions of many) but many more of the enrichment activities available to them are also offered to the whole school. There's a real commitment to stretching all of the children, not just the very brightest. The maths and music departments both stand out as offering an excellent range of opportunities for the most able students.

Lots of subject teachers are real specialists. One parent gushed about how inspirational and knowledgeable particular staff members from the art, science and English departments are. Pupils say that the teachers here are really passionate about their subjects and that the small class sizes mean you can't hide if you don't know something. It must be said that the pupils we met – while bright, polite and wholly positive in their attitudes to the school – didn't wow us with their passion for learning; they were distinctly quiet when we asked them to name their favourite authors. But this was a small sample of sixth formers and perhaps rather skewed towards scientists. Apparently the historians 'are always reading'. Perhaps its star pupils are just a little humbler than some of their more precocious and self-assured peers at similar schools. It's clear, though, that the pupils have a positive attitude to education and that there's no sense of any negative learning culture at the school that would push the so-called 'swots' to keep their heads down.

Games, options, the arts: AKS is strong in sport – particularly hockey and rugby, though netball and football are popular too. Pupils raved to us about recent sports tours to Australia and South Africa. Sport also has a significant place in the junior school curriculum. There are games fixtures on Friday and Wednesday afternoons – so pupils playing in a team might leave early on those days, but the timetable is arranged so that they'll only miss a single lesson and then it's double games. The school has recently spent money on improving its sports facilities, which include an international standard artificial all weather sports ground, a brand new sports hall, a gymnasium and extensive playing fields. There's no swimming pool on site but the local pool is just a short walk away. There's a strong ethos of participation for all. Depending on the size of the child (for reasons of safety in contact sports) talented sports players in year 6 may play for year 7 teams. The games department pushes and generously resources girls' sport and, if your child is keen to play competitively, there's a good chance he or she can, as the school tries hard to arrange regular fixtures for B teams as well as A teams. Mr Walton says he wants the benefits of playing in a team to be available to everyone who shows an interest, not just the most able.

If you visit AKS on a Tuesday you'll be surrounded by green uniforms as a large proportion of children take part in the Combined Cadet Force (CCF). D of E is also popular, with 65 pupils going for their gold award at the time of our visit. All the children in year 3 learn the violin, and there's a high level of participation in the junior school's orchestra and choir. Pupils can choose to have peripatetic music lessons in any instrument during the school day. There's a lot of music at the senior school too – various choirs and orchestras – and staff contribute to these as well as pupils. There's a brand new drama studio and many pupils choose to do LAMDA speech and drama exams – as well as taking part in drama clubs and school productions. One mum told us how inclusive the drama is here – anyone showing an interest will be found an opportunity to get involved. The school's art department also lets pupils loose on its excellent facilities in after-school activities such as ceramics club and art club. Extracurricular activities that stand out from the norm include Warhammer club; robotics club; animal club (recent visitors to this include tarantulas, geckos, giant snails, hedgehogs and snakes); and AKS Action – a fundraising and community action group which has pupils volunteering in soup kitchens, making up Christmas boxes for refugees and raising money for local and international good causes.

Background and atmosphere: The feel is anything but claustrophobic. Grand red-brick buildings sprawl outwards towards expansive playing fields. Beyond the school: sand dunes, a beach and the sea. Since the merger of 2012-13 (between Blackpool's Arnold School and Lytham's King Edward VII and Queen Mary School), AKS is now united on one site at Lytham St Annes – previously the home of King Edward VII and Queen Mary School. The site was refurbished at the time of the move so now, as well as adding new sports facilities, they've built a new library, drama studio and science laboratories, and many other facilities have been improved and updated. It's still a period building, though, and it feels busy, comfortable and traditional rather than starkly modern.

The junior school, on the same campus, is in a brand new building and it does seem to function smoothly. It's airy and spacious and – even on the grey day of our visit – very light. There is no IT suite because teaching staff decided that IT should be integrated across the curriculum, so pupils might expect to use laptops in any lesson.

We made our visit to AKS in the knowledge that the year or two preceding the merger had been difficult, to say the least. Some parents from both Arnold and King Edward VII and Queen Mary Schools were vehemently opposed to the amalgamation. They'd formed a campaign group to oppose it and had (unsuccessfully) taken their concerns to the Charity Commission. So we were on the lookout for tensions during our visit and particularly during our discussions with parents. But the truth seems to be that such was the intensity of the bad feeling over the merger – albeit from a relatively small group of parents – that those who objected have removed their children from the school, leaving behind a contented and harmonious community. Parents we spoke to said they were happy that the merger gave both schools a future which had otherwise been looking shaky – following the drop in pupil numbers after the abolition of the assisted places scheme and wider problems with the local and national economy. Parents said they took a lead from their children on this issue: the kids saw the merger as a chance to make new friends and enjoy new opportunities and so parents have followed suit.

Pastoral care, well-being and discipline: Incidents of bullying are logged but they are 'rare' and 'low level'. Mr Walton says they're 'dealt with swiftly' (bullies who offend repeatedly would be expelled). Children do report bullying if they see it. The children we met all said they would tell a teacher and support the victim if they saw it – but none could think of any instances during their time at the school. Certainly the PHSE co-ordinator takes a proactive approach to bullying and the growing threat of cyber-bullying. The PHSE programme is impressively hands-on: everyone learns CPR; there are visitors to talk about drugs, pornography, sex and relationships and LGBT issues; and every year the local fire and ambulance services help to produce a massive reconstruction of a car crash, complete with sixth formers mocked up with dramatic-looking injury make up. We get the sense that the programme really is really about making children safer, happier and emotionally healthier – and not just about ticking boxes. Pupils say, 'it's alright to be gay here,' and 'no-one would mind if you came out'; but they can't think of anyone who actually has come out.. So perhaps not every child of the 450 odd pupils here is fully convinced of its LGBT-friendliness yet. We're told there's 'always someone' for pupils to talk to: sixth form peer mentors, form tutors, year heads and the school matron are all available to offer pastoral support.

On the question of discipline, Mr Walton tries to strike a balance between his instinctual inclination to understand naughty children and offer them 'a chance' and his acknowledgement that in the independent sector parents expect strict discipline. 'All of us can make one mistake,' he says, but he does confirm that a pupil found with one cannabis joint for personal use in his or her school bag would face expulsion. Children might wonder whether he's calling their bluff but we wouldn't test him. In practice, though, there have been no expulsions in recent years – presumably because behaviour is generally good here. The atmosphere on our visit was one of friendly and orderly discipline and industriousness.

Pupils and parents: The fees are at the lower end of the independent schools spectrum and consequently not all the parents are hugely wealthy. There are taxi drivers and shopkeepers in the mix, we're told. Some run local businesses which thrive during the summer months but, as the days darken and the tourists go home, they struggle to meet the fees throughout the winter. But the parents we met appeared to be from comfortably middle class families – some of whom had attended one or other of the schools themselves. The pupils we met were sporty and into science. They didn't conform to the stereotype that the privately educated are arrogant and entitled. They said they enjoyed school; that they knew how lucky they were; and that they wanted to make a contribution to the local community and to society when they left school. Not everyone was ultra-confident talking to us, but they were all polite. They did impress us with their easy and co-operative communication with each other: we sometimes felt as if a committee was answering our questions – but it was an inclusive committee that let everyone speak, so we didn't mind.

Parents are enthusiastic about how much they feel included in the life of the school – although they gripe that arrangements can be made or communicated a little late in the day at times which makes it challenging for parents with busy schedules to turn up to as much as they'd like to. But by and large they say their children feel known and valued. One mum said of her son in the upper juniors: 'They have his measure. He's encouraged and stretched but he's not pushed.'

We didn't find much in the way of household names among the old boys and girls but there are plenty of high achievers. Arnold alumni include the founder of Jaguar Cars, a Nobel Prize-winning chemist, half a dozen England sportsmen (football, cricket, Rugby Union and Rugby League) and a handful of actors, artists and musicians including Jonas Armstrong from the BBC's Robin Hood, Jenna-Louise Coleman from Emmerdale and Doctor Who and Chris Lowe of the Pet Shop Boys. Alumni from KEQMS include comedian Jenny Éclair, a couple of leaders of British industry and a former equerry to the Queen.

Entrance: There are no tests to gain entry to the nursery or infants' school; children wishing to enter the juniors would be expected to come and spend a trial day here. The only real assessments of ability would be for entry into year 6, because children in the junior school gain automatic entry to the senior school, so the junior teachers need to be confident that a year 6 child would be capable of progressing here. The school isn't oversubscribed so there's a very good chance you'll be able to get your child in if you can afford the fees. 'We're not an open door,' says the head teacher, but he's trying to push up numbers. AKS pays great attention to references from children's current schools – we get a sense that selection is as much about behaviour as academic potential. In the January or February of their intended year of entry, applicants to the senior school will be tested in English, maths and non-verbal reasoning. They're looking for 'average ability and above'; and they'll offer places to pupils they feel would cope academically and benefit from what's on offer here. The school encourages families to visit at any time and children can get a better feel for the school by coming for a taster day.

Exit: Almost all juniors move up to the AKS senior school. While external applicants to the seniors have to sit exams, the juniors progress there automatically. 'If we've had a child for seven years,' says Miss Wright, 'then we'll have prepared them for seniors and they'll be fine. Very occasionally we have a child and you think actually their needs are beyond what we can offer, but that conversation would be happening all the way through junior school. It wouldn't be sprung on their parents at the end of year 6. We know our children inside out and back to front.'

About two-thirds of year 11 currently progress to the sixth form. Mr Walton says he'd like that figure to be higher, but there's stiff competition from local state schools and colleges. Not all of year 13 goes to university. 'Sometimes it's a sensible option to go into management training at 17 or 18,' says the head. But most do go on to higher education. In 2016, one to Cambridge and six medics/dentists; Durham and Warwick also popular. Students off to study eg management, criminology, science, song writing.

Money matters: Following the merger and the sale of the old Arnold School site in Blackpool, we're told that AKS is now in good financial health and its future is assured. Parents expect to get great value for money, but the fees are relatively low so the school is careful on how it spends them. Parents should be confident, says Mr Walton, that fees are ploughed fairly into the education of every child at the school, rather than being diverted into specialist sports or academic scholarships to bring in high fliers just to boost the school's sporting or league table success. (Not only does Mr Walton see these type of scholarships as an unfair use of parents' money, but they also go against the inclusive ethos of the school: it's not fair, says the head, if star players are bought in on scholarships with fee-paying parents' money, only for their children to lose their places in sports teams to make way for them.)

Having said this, there are a few assisted places and means-tested bursaries available to pupils in the senior school. Means-tested assisted places offer a maximum reduction of 85 per cent of school fees. They're awarded primarily in year 7 and year 12 and they stay with the child throughout their time here, providing their parents' finances don't change for the better. (The means-testing is reassessed annually.) Some short-term bursaries are also awarded to pupils whose parents are going through 'temporary and unforeseen' financial hardship. Priority for these goes to pupils who have been at the school for at least five years and to pupils in their GCSE and A level years. Some 5-10 per cent of pupils in the senior school receive some level of means-tested financial support. More details are available from the admissions office.

Additionally, a younger child coming to the school qualifies for a 10 per cent sibling discount on their fees while their elder sibling is at the school. This applies to children at any stage in the school – including the nursery or junior school. Clergy bursaries (a discount of two-thirds of school fees for a first child or three-quarters for two or more siblings) are also made available to the children of serving members of the clergy (any Christian denomination). This too applies to children at any stage of the school but, unlike the sibling discount, it is means-tested.

Remarks: This is a happy and positive place to learn. It treats pupils as individuals rather than statistics, encourages them to engage with the wider world and it has a really holistic vision of education. The small class sizes make it a good option for parents who worry their children might be 'invisible' in a large teaching group, and its inclusive ethos means that perhaps children who might be cowed or disheartened by a more competitive or elitist institution find the space and opportunity to flourish here. Parents praise its family feel, the fact that they too feel included and welcome in the community, and an approachable body of teachers who really listen and get to know their children. It's not ostentatious about its success, but it's excellent value compared to the local competition and clearly a great school.

Ampleforth College

Linked with St Martin's Ampleforth

Ampleforth, York, North Yorkshire YO62 4ER

Pupils: 575; 320 boys, 153 girls full boarders • Ages: 13–18 • Sixth form: 238 • RC

Fees: Day £23,223; Boarding £33,390 pa

Tel: 01439 766000
Email: admissions@ampleforth.org.uk
Website: www.ampleforth.org.uk/college

Headmaster: Since December 2016, Fr Wulstan Peterburs OSB BA PhD, who was previously interim head from June 2016. Fr Wulstan first taught in the school in 1994 as a lay teacher of Christian theology and history, entering the monastery in 1998. He was subsequently head of Christian theology and housemaster before being appointed as procurator of Ampleforth Abbey and College in 2010.

Academic matters: Top of the Catholic league but proud of non-elitist intake – from A stream scholars to IQs around 100, who get extra help with English and maths. Ninety per cent of the slowest workers get three A levels, which bears out the college's mission statement – an extract from the Rule of St Benedict: 'the strong should have something to strive for and the weak nothing to run from'. Determined to stress academic rigour and unashamedly and successfully pushing up A and B grades at A level (2016: 45 per cent A*/A, 72 per cent A*-B), 'though these are not laurels on which we are proposing to rest'; still aiming higher and the value-added score increases all the time, especially at A level. GCSE: 63 per cent A*/A.

'They never discard,' says a parent. 'The pupils gain self-respect, the staff have an ability to unlock potential.' School prudently adds that sometimes pupils cannot or will not cope: 'We try to reach an agreement with parents about them leaving'. Overall aim is for everyone to fulfil, and preferably exceed, their academic ability. The most able are challenged by membership of an unashamedly intellectual discussion club.

Core curriculum plus Christian theology throughout, Latin and Greek too, and now computing GCSE. Half GCSE year takes separate sciences, half (of all abilities) double award. English department now doing IGCSE. Humanities traditionally have more takers and the edge at A level, but maths and science continue to strengthen. English very strong (most get A or B); history and Christian theology regularly successful and enormously popular.

Dyslexics taught 'for the most part' in main stream; additional specialist one-to-one teaching available. EAL provision for pupils whose first language isn't English.

Games, options, the arts: Traditionally powerful games school. Strong first XV, respected throughout the North. Hockey exceptionally strong for boys and girls, netball, lacrosse, athletics (own track), squash, golf (own nine-hole course), fly-fishing, renowned independently-owned beagle pack, shooting (brace of pheasants recently spotted hanging on coathanger outside boarding cubicle). Phenomenal 20 rugby sides – 'We want wide participation in school teams', 10 cricket sides, eight tennis teams, and so on. Sports hall, Astroturf, 25-metre pool. Very successful voluntary CCF and it has been known for the girls' platoon to teach the boys a tough lesson by winning the CCF challenge. Flourishing D of E.

Music outstanding – Schola Cantorum choir tours regularly, singing in Catholic and Anglican cathedrals, also impressive girls' Schola Puellarum. Talented chamber music group and the biggest school pipe band south of the border, with own Ampleforth kilts. Enthusiastic singing by whole school in the abbey church, though sometimes, by their own admission, 'more Twickenham than heavenly hosts'.

No longer offers A level, but hugely impressive work on display – a direct result they say of 'an interaction between inspirational teaching and the environment'. New all-singing-and-dancing performing arts theatre (literally – includes sprung floor, wall mirrors and ballet barres) and also smaller studio theatre, popular with pupils, who would like to do even more. Annual pilgrimage for seniors to Lourdes. Own charity, run by students, raised funds to build school in Nepal and to sponsor East European students in school's sixth form. Also several other eye-openingly worthwhile international projects.

The St Laurence Cookery School was opened in 2016 by Old Amplefordian and MasterChef the Professional's star Joey O'Hare. The 12 week Leith's Cookery Toolbox course will now take place twice a year and help students to grasp a range of key cookery skills including time planning, food safety, hygiene, healthy eating and knife skills.

A new staff appointment has strengthened careers advice, including preparation for university and after. It's a work in progress but a deliberate and concerted change – 'it's a meritocratic world and our students need to be prepared'. Long list of extracurricular activities, including some rarer options such as croquet; also the opportunity to strip down and build a Land Rover. And they usually win the regional school shooting range challenge, 'though not quite sure where that fits with the Benedictine philosophy.' Activities are compulsory between 5-7pm and though a small number wriggle and squirm, most are happy to take part because apparently 'being busy makes you happy'. This is definitely a busy school – boarding philosophy through and through and even day pupils do everything (except sleep) here.

Boarding: Houses vary considerably in character, with deliberate spread of ability – seven for boys and three for girls. Charming and articulate boys and girls rub very comfortably alongside each other, the girls raising the bar in a number of areas and the boys raising their game in response. Rolling programme of improvement in boarding houses; 'I have a power shower!' exclaimed one girl proudly. Home from home, clearly, and it matters, especially to the girls. Some girls' houses have nominated 'guardian angels' as peer mentors; varying approach across individual houses, boys tend and befriend as necessary, usually without being asked. A real plus with the boys is that 'this is a place where you don't have to choose between singing in the choir and playing rugby' – it's acceptable, even cool possibly, to do both. Lunch with houseparents each day, central dining room and cafeteria system in use for other meals. Apparently (according to pupils) 'the food is good – for school food', a guarded mix of fierce loyalty and sensitive disclaimer.

Background and atmosphere: Founded 1802. Girls originally in sixth form only but co-education introduced elsewhere in 2010 and now growing throughout school. Magnificent setting in 3,000 acres of stunning countryside, very calming to the soul with the Abbey as its central focus, physically and spiritually. Though fairly remote, 'in fact easy to reach – with some determination – from all parts of the country and world'. Beautiful Victorian gothic main wing plus Giles Gilbert Scott's huge abbey church and school buildings (1930s), with late 1980s and more recent additions.

School keeps in touch with outside world through excellent lecture programme and far-away projects, eg Chile and E Europe. No exeats except for two in winter term, otherwise half-terms. Handy list of local hotels, restaurants and B&Bs sent to parents in very comprehensive booklet, Your Questions Answered. Not unknown for parents to rent a local cottage during their child's time at Ampleforth. Warmth of hospitality legendary, 'Part of the Rule of St Benedict is to welcome guests as Christ welcomed his'.

Pastoral care, well-being and discipline: A key change in recent times is that of the deployment of monastic personnel: there are fewer monks and they no longer perform the role of housemasters. This role has been taken over by families who serve as houseparents – 'very civilising,' was the comment. Monks now act as chaplains to the school houses, 10 chaplains for 10 houses and parents and pupils commend them for being both priests and friends.

Consciences worked on rather than harsh restrictions imposed, all with the aim of turning students into responsible adults. It appears relaxed on the surface; essentially you are 'allowed it until you misuse it'. Fair enough. At the same time, 'this means clear structure and boundaries.'

Tough on bullying – those directly implicated and also bystanders – no one ever implicated in bullying can reach the position of monitor at the top of the school; 'a moment of madness can cost you dear.'

No uniform as such, but dress code in place.

However, recent press articles on the treatment of historic alleged sex offenders (and now a Charity Commission investigation) plus the premature departure of a recently appointed head suggest all may not be well in this part of North Yorks. If/when you visit, it might be worth asking questions because, at the very least, whilst pupils may well remain unaffected, these will almost certainly have proved a distraction internally.

Pupils and parents: Numbers close to full and consistently so. Pupils from all over the UK and beyond, 30 per cent Yorkshire families, 40 per cent elsewhere UK (often with OA connections), remaining 30 per cent from overseas. Five per cent of overseas pupils are expats, rest mainly European mix of French, German, Swiss, Spanish. The recession has gently pushed up overseas numbers and reduced the number from the rest of the UK. 'We're a long way from London and you have to pass a lot of good schools to get here'. That said, many do, the main attractions being the Catholic Benedictine tradition and – bucking the trend here – full boarding provision; 'the school doesn't empty at weekends'. Scions of top and middle Catholic families (80 per cent); the rest mainly Anglican, but special welcome for orthodox.

There's a sense of comfortable ease between parents and school – 'if you want to be involved and constantly in touch, that's possible, If you want to take a more relaxed approach, then that is fine too'. Former pupils include Rupert Everett, Hugo Young, Lord Tugendhat, Lord Nolan, Sir Anthony Bamford (JCB), Michael Ancram, Sir Anthony Gormley, Lawrence Dallaglio, Joe Simpson, Lord Fellowes, James Norton.

Entrance: From a plethora of prep schools, most notably its own – St Martin's Ampleforth. Common entrance (50 per cent), or school test, and interview. Exceptions 'for faith or family', but no one admitted if he or she won't be able to cope with curriculum – even from St Martin's (rare). Sixth form entry: at least five GCSEs at B or above. Non-Catholics expected to take full part in school's religious life.

Exit: Up to 20 per cent leave after GCSEs. In 2016, three to Oxbridge and two medics; Edinburgh and Bristol also popular. Overseas destinations include Stanford University in California, McGill University in Montreal, the University of British Columbia in Vancouver and Trinity College, Dublin.

Money matters: Generous financial help. Academic, music and all-rounder scholarships. Nearly 13 per cent receive means-tested bursary help. In last two years some pupils have attained scholar status after entry.

Remarks: It has been said that people who leave Ampleforth take with them a 'compass for life', a spiritual direction finder, which allows them to hold on to their moral bearings. Three fundamental college aims underpin the thinking and approach here: for parents to call up and say their son/daughter is 'having a whale of a time', to succeed academically and finally, while 'not all super pious', to 'treasure a place in their hearts for the spiritual side of life'. The pupils we met confidently achieved all three.

Parents like and appreciate the 'strong moral feel' of the school 'encompassing faith and learning, as well as 'the welcoming atmosphere'. They describe it as 'surely one of the most beautiful places to go to school', hoping (and praying) that it can 'live up to the challenge and expectations in coming years', that particular challenge being one of 'raising the bar academically with first rate and inspiring teachers'. School is listening and has taken note but NB our comments on recent press reports.

Ashdell Preparatory School

266 Fulwood Road, Sheffield, South Yorkshire S10 3BL

Pupils: 100 • Ages: 3–11 • C of E

Fees: £9,915 – £10,620 pa

Tel: 01142 663835
Email: Office@ashdellprep.co.uk
Website: www.ashdellprep.co.uk

Headteacher: Since 2008, Mrs Anne Camm BEd. School in Ireland, then Trent Park College of Education and Bristol University. Taught at a primary in Ireland; house mistress at Cabin Hill Prep, Belfast, and Edgarley Hall (Millfield prep); head of Birkdale pre-prep. Relaxed, 'very approachable and friendly', 'great' (parents), comfortable, frank and thoughtful, clearly very happy in her job. Reads a story to the younger children each week, enjoys covering classes, knows all the children and parents. Does one ISI inspection a year – a good source of new ideas – but not eager to make radical changes. Her aim is a school where children learn and all, including parents and staff, are happy. Married with two adult daughters. Enjoys reading, travelling, cooking, swimming, gardening and theatre.

Retiring in July 2017, when Ashdell will merge with Sheffield High Infant and Junior School. Nursery to year 2 will be taught on the Ashdell site and retain the name, whilst years 3-6 will move to the Sheffield High Junior site.

Entrance: Pre-prep 1 – short informal assessment with head of department: looking for mature attitude, independence, awareness of colour and number, manual dexterity and curiosity. For other pre-prep classes teachers give school based assessments in literacy and maths during a taster day.

Other classes: NFER age appropriate tests in English and maths at a taster day – wants standard score of 100+. Above average ability overall with a spread. Most children come from the pre-school. Entry at any term.

Means-tested bursaries (up to full fees) mainly for unexpected hardship, only a few on entry; currently 17 per cent have one. Reduction for second children and beyond.

Exit: Mostly to the high achieving Sheffield Girls' High; occasionally to Westbourne, local independent; sometimes two scholarships a year to various schools. Maybe a couple to boarding schools, far fewer now than hitherto, plus small (growing) number to nearby state schools, eg Tapton, Notre Dame.

Remarks: Established 1948; extra building to rehouse prep school 1991. In 2007, Snowdrops, very successful co-ed pre-school for 3 to 5 year olds, opened in association with Birkdale, boys' independent school (biennial joint drama production and other links). Situated in well-heeled suburb of Sheffield, close to a major hospital and university. Pupils mostly from business and professional families, a few from international backgrounds; around 19 per cent ethnic minority.

The school's bright red boards stand out against the weathered sandstone bricks of the houses in the Fulwood Road like colourful lollipops. The prep occupies two adjacent, elegant Victorian houses, with lots of staircases and corridors (staff must be fit, as their room is right at the top), Snowdrops a third, separate one. Classrooms are spacious and light, some with fine mouldings. A vast hall used for assemblies, productions, PE.

Three playgrounds: an enclosed one with small netball court and climbing wall fetchingly decorated with large painted sunflowers; another, enhanced by a fish pond, Wendy house and garden area, also provides parking spaces for drop off and pick up times (this is a difficult area for street parking, so end times are staggered, which has helped a lot). Snowdrops has its own with a bug hotel and charming mini red (the school colour) picnic tables.

Average class size is 13, 18 max, so plenty of individual attention and differentiated learning. Children are stretched, but not in a way that makes them feel stressed, say parents. French and Spanish from reception; cross-curricular topics – National Gallery pictures very productively used; study skills taught, including current events, philosophical thinking, independent research. Sensible amounts of homework; children say lessons are fun; excellent displays throughout. No Sats taken; most recent ISI report judged attainment to be high in relation to children's age and that pupils make good and often excellent progress in relation to those of similar ability.

Plenty of computers and iPads (this not particularly IT adept writer was very taken with the interactive literacy apps used in reception); all have weekly IT lesson by specialist teachers, including coding; 7 year olds learn touch typing. Smallish science lab with resident skeleton a little the worse for wear for having been danced with.

Snowdrops has a very appealing pine play loft occupied by a huge teddy bear and baby bear. Specialist activities, eg PE, music, cooking, accustom the children to moving around the school. Reception is just a door away, another spacious, bright, light room with high ceilings, play loft with role play section beneath and engaging little phonic monkeys sporting a letter, that can be combined with velcro to make words. Much use of local visits to support topics.

Strong additional learning provision appreciated by parents – free individual, small group or in class support. Two/three 40 minute sessions a week; 8am start means older children can avoid missing regular lessons and parents can drop in. Very flexible, dedicated teacher who forms strong bond with 'her' girls and works closely with parents. Has handled severe dyslexia, dyscalculia, auditory processing difficulties; also ESOL and extra support for entrance exams. Physically disabled children would struggle in the main school, though. Screening available for all throughout school as required; recommendations made for further external assessment when needed.

Comprehensive gifted and talented policy plus co-ordinator – class extension work; enrichment through sport, modern language clubs (use made of ESOL children), national competitions, STEM leaders awards, visiting writers' and artists' workshops (hence the framed, original Liz Million cartoons), year 5 and 6 residentials in France. Hosts national quiz competition for local independent schools.

Uses the university's excellent facilities for swimming, games and athletics; teams for usual sports. Strong music – two specialist teachers; choir successful in competitions; full size drum kit for rock club plus African drums. Plenty of drama productions – conventional choices mostly. Art is excellent and central, displayed all over the school – children win awards in national competitions and school has Artsmark gold; some very good photography; own kiln. Cookery and woodwork lessons too. Very wide range of clubs: sports, arts, science; girls produce The Ashdell Buzz (newsletter) and Radio – junior DJs broadcast music for outdoor breaks; chess new and thriving; school and eco councils. Plenty of local trips plus residential at Center Parcs.

Weekly Christian assembly and explores a range of faiths; various festivals celebrated. All year 6s have position of responsibility, eg help with library, head girl, prefects, house captains. Confident, well-behaved, relaxed and happy children, very smart in their grey and cherry red uniforms (every sort of red school and sports bag; the littlies have red and white striped pinnies), who like visiting after they've left. Teachers seen as friendly; family feeling – 'very close-knit,' according to a parent, older girls look after younger ones at lunch and in breaks.

Parents very happy with pastoral care ('really nurturing') and speedy response to difficulties. Confidence box for unhappinesses rarely used; girls feel comfortable enough with head to tell her about minor unkindness. Aims to develop resilience through PSHE classes and older children spend a day at Crucial Crew, run by police to develop streetwise skills and ability to cope with teenage pressures. Trains girls to be well organised in preparation for secondary school.

Very tasty, locally sourced food – we can recommend the home-made tomato soup – from trad sausage and mash with baked beans and chocolate cake to salad bar and veggie sausages. Chef does cooking with girls, so has a hotline to any complaints.

Close links with parents – open door policy re concerns; termly parents' forum; regular newsletters, texts, emails; family breakfast once a week; active PTA. Wrap around care 7.30am-6pm.

Ashdell offers a very sheltered, secure environment that seems in some ways like a throwback to the 1950s, with the grey, felt pudding basin hats (straw ones for the summer) and drawstring shoe bags that took this writer back to her own school days, despite the lavish IT presence. It wouldn't suit parents looking for a thoroughly 21st century prep school, but it successfully meets the need of its niche market (numbers are holding up well), and it is hard not to be charmed by the friendly, happy, enthusiastic children, teachers and head.

Ashville College

Green Lane, Harrogate HG2 9JP

Pupils: 830; 110 boarders • Ages: 4–18 (boarding from year 5) • Sixth form: 168

Fees: Day £7,950- £13,800; Boarding £17,295 – £27,750 pa

Tel: 01423 566358
Email: ashville@ashville.co.uk
Website: www.ashville.co.uk

Headmaster: Since 2010 Mr Mark Lauder MA (mid 40s), educated at Hermitage Academy, Helensburgh, did an MA in English literature and history at the University of Aberdeen, spending his junior honours year at the University of Oregon, Eugene, USA. After graduating he embarked on research at St Edmund Hall, Oxford, where as well as winning a graduate scholarship, he achieved two half blues in rowing. Previously deputy head of Felsted School, Essex, head of history and then housemaster at St Edward's School, Oxford, and before that head of history and master in charge of rowing at Shiplake College, Henley-on-Thames.

Married to peripatetic piano teacher, Caroline, with two sons, both at Ashville College, in junior school. Pupils describe the head as 'having an open door, listening to pupils and making change happen'. Change not so evident to the parents we spoke to – maybe as his approach is 'evolutionary not revolutionary'.

Interests include rowing, rugby, politics and restoring a 17th century Yorkshire parsonage, in between long walks in the Dales and all things Scottish. Believes in whole child development, 'the individual of infinite worth, the social creed of Methodism being the foundation and teacher/pupil relationship the cornerstone'.

Head of junior school: Since September 2014, Simon Bailey (40s), previously deputy head at Taunton Prep. Has also been head of juniors at Colet Court and taught at Dulwich Prep. BA in primary education and PE from Edge Hill College, Lancaster University. He teaches a wide range of subjects, including geography, English, RE, IT, PSHE, PE and games. Proficient triathlete, plays golf and cricket and is an ardent rugby fan. Married to Janine; they have two young children.

Head of pre-prep since 2008, Carol Berrie (50s), formerly deputy for six years after teaching at primary school, Lady Elizabeth Hastings, Thorp Arch near Wetherby. Warm, capable and welcoming, sets high standards for both staff and pupils. Believes in the importance of listening skills in learning. Brimming with enthusiasm, she has great rapport with her pupils. Delightful to see how 'newly graduated' year 3s in the junior school vied for her attention to proudly show their descriptive writing. Has an open door and finds herself increasingly approached by parents for 'wise counselling'. Described by more than one as 'fantastic'.

Academic matters: Curriculum focus on numeracy and literacy in maximum class sizes of 16 in reception and year 1, moving to 18 in year 2. Pupils 'eased' into more formal learning in year 1, building on early years' foundation stage. Rolling three year cross-curricular programme, though discrete science teaching. On the day we visited the school was a hive of activity with the happy buzz of quiet endeavour varying from a 'phonics sound search' in the garden to hands-on Mexican tortilla cooking and sampling in the Make and Bake Room.

Enthusiastic and committed teachers who 'know their pupils well,' say parents. In year 1 pupils screened through verbal and non-verbal reasoning tests to diagnose any learning support needs. One-to-one and small group tuition carried out in designated Quiet Room.

Academic focus continues in numeracy and literacy in the junior school but broad curriculum with specialist teaching in Spanish, French, music, science and ICT. Pupils taught in form groups of maximum 20 children, two per year group in years 3 and 4, increasing to three forms in both year 5 and 6. Setting from year 3 in mathematics and English with gifted and talented programme in mathematics, literacy, music and art having a good impact on results. No complacency here – the competition from local state schools is fierce. Whiteboards in most classrooms, two ICT lessons timetabled per week and netbooks to be introduced in the near future.

Good value-added, especially at GCSE – 43 per cent A*/A in 2016. Science, mathematics, economics and PE all very popular at A level (46 per cent A*/A grades in 2016, 76 per cent A*/B). Not a shining star in the league tables but most pupils exceed predicted potential and very able pupils do particularly well. Good choice of subjects at GCSE; A level offering includes history of art and government and politics.

Average class size 16, max 22, dropping to 10, max 16, in the sixth form. Years 7–9 follow broad curriculum including at least two modern foreign languages (Italian now offered); set for mathematics and languages. For GCSE years, pupils split into ability bands A and B; A are taught Latin and B do extra lessons in English, geography and ICT. Majority take three separate sciences, a few dual award, all at least one modern foreign language.

All year 7 pupils (and year 3 in the junior school) are screened for dyslexia, with further testing and screening as necessary. No pupil has a statement of special educational need/EHC plan, but over 130 pupils receive some additional help for 'mild dyslexic tendencies' – individual support if deemed necessary. Those with dyslexia thrive thanks to the kindly environment and carefully planned programmes of study; indeed in recent years few haven't get the benchmark five A*-Cs at GCSE, and most gain at least a B in English.

Over 60 international students require English as an additional language, mostly taught alongside mainstream English. Target is Cambridge FCE by year 11 and all sixth form sit Cambridge IELTS in year 13.

Games, options, the arts: Facilities – two gyms, 30m swimming pool, fabulous climbing wall, squash courts, fitness room and ample pitches, including a new all weather surface pitch – show importance of sport. Further proof by way of ports centre's £3 million refurbishment, updating changing rooms, gym and adding fitness studios and dedicated BTEC sport classroom. Teams and fixtures galore in traditional team sports. All usual suspects on offer plus American influenced disc golf – something for everyone. Director of activities recently appointed to provide even more challenging outdoor opportunities.

Well-resourced and well-used music centre – a third take individual instrumental or singing lessons. An array of choirs and bands, from chamber to soul and jazz to strings. Talented musicians play in the National Children's and National Youth Orchestras, but plenty of playing and performing opportunities for those just starting out too: Verdi Requiem in Leeds Town Hall, Messiah from Scratch for charity.

Junior school has full use of the senior school music facilities: 50-strong junior orchestra and 65 per cent of the school in the junior choir, winning their category in the recent Harrogate Festival. Performance by senior school and junior school musicians each week in assemblies and all year 4 pupils receive small group violin and cello tuition. Sixty children pay for speech and drama tuition (LAMDA); performance opportunity in annual school play – diverse offerings recently of Pirates of Penzance, Bugsy Malone, A Midsummer Night's Dream and Henry the Tudor Dude.

Dedicated art studios and drama facilities always busy. Unusually for a boarding school, a 4pm finish and no Saturday school, but plenty of choice of after-school activities and clubs and supervised prep until 5.30pm; D of E from year 10. Trip for older students to Malawi ties in with charity fundraising to support the Open Arms Orphanage, which has close links with the school.

Boarding: School viewed as a day school with boarding – under 20 per cent board, and half of these are sixth form; firmly in the head's sights to improve these statistics. Three senior boarding houses, two boys' and one girls', are comfortably furnished with usual facilities: kitchens, common rooms, games areas and computers. Junior boarding in co-ed house, Greenholme, run by year 5 teacher and wife (ex Ashvillian). Small numbers of full, weekly and flexi-boarders, year 5 to year 8, in junior boarding house; consists 70 per cent boys and 30 per cent girls, mainly English expat, Forces families. Seven or eight bedded in 'home from home' environment. Escorted visits to town alternate Saturdays, activities each weekend and some evenings, including geo-caching, extended to day pupils too. Integration further through memberships of local Scouts, football clubs and other groups. Daily tweet to parents keeps them involved and boarder-led newsletter when busy lives allow.

Approximately one-third of senior boarders are from South East Asia – this has reduced in recent years. More emphasis on weekly/flexi boarding and more recruitment from the Forces. Girls and boys encouraged to socialise, with trips regularly organised at weekends and half-termly theme evenings. Plenty of activities on offer after school but all optional. Cultural differences mean not much integration with day pupils after school hours.

Background and atmosphere: Founded in 1877 by the Methodist Church as a senior boys' boarding school, co-ed since 1984. Pleasant, well-maintained site is in a leafy residential area, with a swathe of pitches and playing fields fringed by the trinity of schools (college, junior and pre-prep), sports centre and boarding houses. Evacuated to Windermere during the war as the premises were requisitioned for the war effort and used by Air Ministry.

Plenty of well-kept facilities – atmospheric Memorial Hall is home to lectures, meetings and some concerts, with larger gatherings filling the school hall. Recent, much-needed, extensive refurbishment programme to most classrooms, with the library now excellent. Investment in ICT infrastructure and hardware and more planned. New head of sixth form and review of academic offering, pupil monitoring and facilities in sixth form centre.

Sited between senior school and pre-prep, the junior school presents a cheerful and pleasant environment, though feeling a little cramped with needed expansion planned to accommodate the recent resurgence in numbers and provide specialist teaching areas. Pre-prep is accommodated in a bright, spacious and purpose-built school nestling in a quiet corner of the college's campus, adjacent to the sports facilities and a short distance from the junior school. The school is well resourced with a self-contained hall for assemblies, activities and dining; an open plan library; separate area for technology and baking and a 'quiet room' for individual or group work. Outside, a secure playground and learning environment have recently been enhanced by addition of new play equipment.

Pastoral care, well-being and discipline: Methodist ethos underpins the pastoral care and the school is committed to the development of the full potential of each individual. Parents praise excellent standard of care and say its what they like most about the school. Hot on manners and respect, 'instilling values and standards which are often overlooked in the 21st century'. Strong culture of inter-house competition between four houses, from poetry to public speaking; the prized Rigg Cup for sport. Unusually, continuity of house membership from pre-prep up – adds to house loyalty and vertical bonding. Head believes in picking up problems quickly to 'fix it small' and then 'partnership between school and parents'. This is recognised by parents, who said that the school 'tried very hard to get it right'.

All year 7 are taken to the Lake District for a bonding weekend early in the autumn term; this receives rave reviews not only from the new pupils but also from sixth formers, who work as liaison prefects and, if assigned to year 7, go too.

Fines if caught smoking, with possibility of exclusion for repeated offences. Drugs: out for supplying or intending to – no issues in recent times.

A genuine sense of community that keeps ex-pupils in contact long after they have left the school gates.

Pupils and parents: Mainly from local professional and business families, extending from Ripon to north Leeds and surrounding villages. Quite a few first time buyers; Americans from nearby Menwith Hill military base add an interesting dimension. For about 10 per cent of pupils English is not a first language and overall approximately 14 per cent come from a variety of minority ethnic backgrounds, mainly Chinese, Nigerian and European. Thriving Friends of Ashville runs regular, well-supported activities.

Old boys: Ian Dodds (designer of the Moon Buggy), Commander Ian Grieve (head of anti-terrorism Scotland Yard), Jim Carter (Downton Abbey actor), Simon Theakston (director of Theakston's Brewery and chairman of the Yorkshire Agricultural Show) and Peter McCormick (lawyer to the Football Association).

Entrance: Entry to pre-prep is by informal assessment with head. Entry to junior school is by mathematics and English tests and informal interview with the head of the school, usually as part of a 'taster' day.

For year 7, a day in January with English, mathematics and non-verbal reasoning papers followed by practical activities, plus a report from previous head. Usually a three form entry of 60 pupils, though recent demand has increased this to four forms.

Majority of pupils come from own junior school and nearby preps: Belmont Grosvenor and Brackenfield in Harrogate, Richmond House, Moorlands and Frobelian in Leeds, plus local state primary schools. Six bus routes in operation starting in Leeds, Thorner, Addingham, Ripon and Bramham.

Sixth form entry is via interview and satisfactory reference; five grade Cs with minimum grade Bs in subjects to be studied. Exams, interview and reference are norm for entry at other times.

Exit: All pre-prep usually transfer to junior school. From junior school majority to senior school (90+ per cent) with no entrance exam, some to local state schools, handful to other independent schools.

Around a fifth leave at the end of year 11, most to state sector, further three per cent at end of year 12 – mostly starting afresh, some to foundation courses. Majority of sixth formers go on to higher education, generally a couple to Oxbridge (two in 2016), rest to a wide range of Russell Group/redbrick universities.

Money matters: Academic, music, sports, art and drama scholarships are available in the senior school. Scholarships are awarded on entry into year 7, year 10 and sixth form and are reviewed at key stages. Means-tested bursaries of up to 100 per cent of fees are available either in conjunction with scholarships or on a stand-alone basis. Additional discounts are awarded to the children of Methodist ministers and parents in the Forces.

Remarks: A successful all-round day school with a boarding ethos. Plenty of happy pupils in a caring and supportive environment. Academics and teaching being strengthened. Offers a trinity of schools providing seamless transition through each stage of education, obviously popular with many parents and pupils.

Aysgarth School

Newton-le-Willows, Bedale, North Yorkshire DL8 1TF

Pupils: 202; 89 full, 48 weekly boarders • Ages: 3-13 (boarding from 8)

Fees: Boarding £22,920; Day £7,455- £18,300 pa

Tel: 01677 450240
Email: enquiries@aysgarthschool.co.uk
Website: www.aysgarthschool.com

Headmaster: Since 2015, Rob Morse, previously head of Perrot Hill, with his wife Lottie and their children, Daisy and Harry, and black labrador, Nel. Moved from Somerset, though no newcomer to the north as former deputy head at S Anselm's in Derbyshire. Summary view of parents who have met him is 'that he will serve Aysgarth very well and with his wife will build on the successes of the [previous head and family] Goddards'.

Head of co-ed pre-prep since 2014, Mrs Susie Drake BEd primary education, Liverpool University (early 40s). Has over 20 years', predominantly state school experience, most recently as a primary school adviser for 17 schools in North Yorkshire. Previous roles include early years consultant, deputy headteacher at a Skipton primary school and leading teacher for IT. Interested in educational research, always searching for 'what is right for the children at Aysgarth, rather than being driven purely by the current political agenda'.

Warm, intuitive and wholeheartedly believes in children progressing at their own pace to prevent storing problems for the future and opening the wider school curriculum beyond the classroom door. 'Every moment matters' is her personal mantra and she believes in gently challenging children to be the best they possibly can.

Speaks proudly and in detail of the individual strengths of her teaching team. Feels that she's inherited a happy, steady ship and will build on that. Forging stronger links with local independents and state primaries a focus, mindful of easing the transition to new schools for the girls at 8. Parents very positive about her appointment, one saying that their 'children positively adore her'.

Entrance: Non-selective, but for prep an interview and assessment (no exam) to look for boys with a 'willingness to get stuck in', 'We try not to turn anyone away'. A few scholarships of between 10-25 per cent and some bursary help, which can be up to 100 per cent. Siblings and Forces discounts available.

Exit: Excellent record to public schools: Harrow, Eton, Ampleforth, Uppingham, Radley, Sedbergh, Shrewsbury, Stowe, Fettes and Winchester. Good sprinkling of academic, music and sports scholarships.

Heads and senior staff of senior schools spend one weekend a year at Aysgarth meeting boys and parents after chapel and at social events.

Remarks: Quiet, rural setting with glorious views in 50 acres of parkland, feels remote but only a short distance from the A1. Approached through a sleepy village, purposely anonymous except for landmark of the splendid school tower on the horizon. A grand, purpose-built, 19th century school building, including a gem of a chapel, complemented by modern facilities. As you journey from the entrance your eye is caught by the profusion of discarded balls in the grounds, underlying a parent's description of 'a place where boys can be boys', though girls are welcomed into pre-prep.

Pre-prep established in 1993 in Oak House, a gentle amble from the prep school. Well adapted with well-equipped, secure, outdoor play area running along the front of the attractive building. The curriculum is traditional and broadly based on the national curriculum, though French is introduced in reception.

The weekly early years' newsletter helps parents understand the real learning outcomes from the play-based activity in EYFS, nursery and reception. This becomes more formal in year 1 with specialist teaching beginning to be introduced for French, PE and music. In year 2 concepts are developed through creative topic work. Transition is high on the agenda in year 3, with boys preparing for the prep school and girls for their next step at another school. House captain and other responsibilities allow the children to develop confidence. Golden time in assemblies celebrates rewards for academic achievement and good deeds, focussing on a difference aspect each week.

The rural setting provides the natural habitat for the forest school in 'Mr McGregor's garden' and the woodland areas. All the usual opportunities for music, drama and sport, with fixtures from year 3 and swimming for all. Good range of extracurricular clubs on offer, sport and choir with cookery, forest school and multi-activity acorn club – ballet at an additional charge. Pre- and after-school care is on offer from 8.00am – 6.00pm and there is school transport from Ripon and Asenby, all at extra cost.

In the prep school, small class sizes (max 16) with traditional and demanding curriculum; setting and streaming from year 5. Extraordinary continuity over the years in gaining places at top public schools. Challenge is to keep abreast of 'subtle shifts' in senior schools and 'keep improving in every sense' as the bar gets higher to top schools. SEN provision improving all the time as the school becomes an even more 'broader and kinder place'.

Top notch sports facilities, especially cricket field, swimming pool and newly built sports hall. The Aysgarth game of COW – cricket off the wall – is a love of Aysgarthians old and new, the real challenge being to hit the ball from the playground into the head's garden. Sport is high profile and they play to win, while still managing a well done and a slap on the back for the chap who comes last. Rugby, football, shooting, fishing, sailing, riding, golf and climbing all on offer. Won Rosslyn Park National Sevens Rugby tournament recently.

Art is strong and design technology is popular in well-equipped rooms where the boys can get their hands on serious equipment and tools. Four classrooms which provide light, stimulating spaces for the first year of the prep school. Music is outstanding with over 70 per cent of the pupils singing or playing an instrument. Boys – both the very musical and the less so – can be seen enthusiastically practising their musical instruments in dorms and classrooms at reserved times. They can play anything here, including bagpipes if they so wish, and the choir is 'as cool as being in the first XV' and a joy to hear. Drama lessons and lots of performance opportunities in newly built 200 seat theatre. Good to see boys enjoying reading sessions in the library after lunch.

Many of the boys look as though they are about to take Eton in their stride – happy, confident and courteous, without being arrogant, they are both charming and endearing but clearly relish this boy-friendly atmosphere where you can 'be your own man'.

Staff know the boys well and, although the phrase is often over used, there is really a 'family feel' about this place, thanks chiefly to great enthusiasm and care from the top. Very much focused on full boarding – in fact, north of Oxford, it's the only all boys' boarding prep in England and parents come from both north and south of the border and say, 'It's worth the journey'. Day boys are welcomed, though certainly in the minority, and they follow the boarding routine.

Boarding accommodation on the top three floors of the school, includes serried ranks of sinks, where boys have to be reminded to wash occasionally. Cheerful dorms, a mix of beds and bunks, yet mainly unadorned walls, where caring staff keep a close eye, tidying up after them and providing a homely feel. Delightful to see much-loved soft toys adorning many a bed – in the senior dorms as well.

Common rooms on ground floor showing signs of good wear and tear. Extensive after-hours activities for boarders include both pillow and water fights (though not at the same time) and it's fine to get down and dirty and build dens in the grounds as well as engaging in debating. Full boarding with diverse range of weekend activities and breaks at exeats only.

Food is ample, prepared in-house using fresh ingredients and 'not bad for school food' (though the boys did say they would like a little more salmon and duck on the menu, please), served in a pleasant if slightly old fashioned style dining room, long tables and benches, where good old fashioned courtesy and table manners count.

Clientele mainly solid (upper) middle class from the North and Midlands, with a few Forces families from Catterick. Strong full boarding ethos attracts families from further away, Scotland

B

and Northern Ireland, with 10 per cent international boarders from Europe, Middle East and Russia. Families are a mix of old school and new, many first time into boarding, including some who, interestingly, say they had previously neither considered boarding nor single sex. Initially a little reluctant to let go, these parents place huge value on all that Aysgarth has to offer, both in and out of the classroom, the end result being that their sons are well prepared for the next school, commenting that 'Aysgarth boys are both in demand and popular'.

Governors very active and close to headmaster. There's a lively Old Aysgarthian association. Old boys include Sir Matthew Pinsent and Robert Swan OBE, whose achievements espouse the Aysgarth ethos.

Beech House

Linked with Bolton School Boys' Division, Bolton School Girls' Division

Chorley New Road, Bolton BL1 4PA

Pupils: 201 • Ages: 4-7

Fees: £9,204 pa

Tel: 01204 434759
Email: info@boltonschool.org
Website: www.boltonschool.org/infants

Headteacher: Since 2015, Mrs Tracey Taylor, BEd and NPQH from Edge Hill College, formerly head of Adlington Primary School in Chorley. Mrs Taylor began her teaching career as a reception and year 1 class teacher and has a passion for teaching in the early years.

Entrance: Play-based, one-to-one assessment in the autumn of year prior to reception entry, with places offered in December. 'No formal skills in reading and maths required. We're looking for bright-eyed, curious children who ask questions'. If places become available in years 1 and 2 children are tested in reading, writing and numeracy.

Exit: In recent years virtually all children have gone to Bolton Schools junior departments, Hesketh House for girls and Park Road for boys. 'They're well on their way to being independent learners when they leave us, and we never have to drill them'. Certainly parents enthuse that their children leave exceptionally well prepared for junior school

Remarks: Large, bustling infant school (three forms per year group, with 25 children in each form) housed in a beautiful, modern, architect-designed building. Bright, airy classrooms. Large outdoor spaces with plenty of colourful equipment; 'we have lessons out there in the real fresh air,' a year 2 girl tells us. Lots of computers (all classes have their own blog) and kindles for reading; iPads soon to be available for all. 'Parents are blown away by the facilities when they first come here,' said one parent. French taught from reception right through to year 2 by a native French speaker, and specialist teachers for music and PE also. Budding Beethovens can take piano lessons at extra cost in the school's own piano room. Fully trained SENCo, and school will assess its ability to cope with special needs on an individual basis in consultation with parents. Lift access to all floors.

'My sons are having the time of their lives here,' one parent told us, and this seemed to be the case in the oh, so cute reception ballet class we saw.

This is a smashing school, a welcoming place, where busy children can get on with learning in a happy and secure atmosphere, while having lots of fun to boot.

The Belvedere Academy

17 Belvedere Road, Princes Park, Liverpool L8 3TF

Pupils: 886 • Ages: 11-18 • Sixth form: 248

Tel: 01517 271284
Email: info@belvedereacademy.net
Website: www.belvedereacademy.net

Principal: Since 2006 (one year before the school changed from a selective independent GDST school to a state-funded academy), Mr Peter Kennedy BEd Dip Man Ed (50s). Attended Cardinal Allen Grammar School, Liverpool, Christ College Education, and the then Manchester Polytechnic. Head of English and sixth form in a Knowsley comprehensive, deputy head of two other comprehensives in Knowsley, head Ellen Wilkinson High School (mixed) in Manchester, head of Chorlton High School, Manchester. Married, three grown-up children; outside interests include music, sport, travel.

Approachable, affable, humorous; wants to keep the original school's ethos of hard work and high standard of behaviour, attendance and academic results and adapt it to meet the challenges of a mixed ability cohort from all social strata; enjoys seeing the way the girls gain in confidence and blossom in a secure environment with high expectations. Popular with girls ('I love him!'; 'He's cheerful, has authority but isn't intimidating') and parents (including the original ones): 'He's done amazing things..has had a lot of vision'.

Academic matters: Modern foreign languages and science specialisms; lots of tracking and monitoring. Teaching and learning judged outstanding by Ofsted; teachers seen as friendly, helpful: 'They're amazing – more like friends,' enthused a sixth former. 2016 A levels: 50 per cent A*-B, 19 per cent A*/A. Most take EPQ; general studies in both years. Wide choice includes business, media, drama and theatre studies, economics, government and politics, classical civilisation, psychology, sociology, music, sport and PE – plans to develop links with FE colleges as less academic girls come through rather than increase the number of vocational subjects and advise them accordingly.

2016 GCSE: 47 per cent A*/A grades, 94 per cent got 5+ A*-C grades including English and maths. All do at least one MFL, can do three separate sciences, OCR and GCSE IT; also Latin, business studies, performing arts, health and social care, home economics, media studies, PE; bottom band does Study Plus (extra English and maths). No plans to adjust curriculum to improve English Bacc league table position – prefers to maximise girls' choice. Study skills and revision sessions offered for one week of the Easter holidays for public exam girls, plus 11 Saturday morning sessions over the year (always full). Mentoring programme for all year 11 students

At KS3 all do French and Spanish and three sciences. Five ability bands from entry on basis of admissions tests (movement allowed) – three high (27/8), one middle (20) and one low (12)

which has extra support and a less demanding curriculum, colour coded so not obvious to the younger girls what ability level the colours represent. Setting for maths, English and languages; very good test results, especially maths. Fast track year 9 group starts GCSEs early so could begin AS course in year 11.

Access to network files and lesson materials from home via ICT portal. Top five per cent of gifted and talented identified as well as top 10 – extension classes in enrichment time plus in class extension work and supporting of lower ability girls; sixth formers attend Durham University summer school. Massive investment in well-staffed additional support area – has just been awarded advanced inclusion mark. All girls screened for dyslexia in year 7 (and soon in year 12) by in-house specialist; specialist EAL support. Manager feels school could cope with all difficulties.

Games, options, the arts: Has huge modern sports hall plus multi-purpose gym, mini fitness suite; games take place in public park. The usual sports plus tag rugby (specialist coaching), volleyball, basketball, lacrosse, trampolining, dodgeball, aerobics, unihoc, community sports trust leadership award; city success for netball and badminton teams; national gymnastics gold medallist and taikwondo competitor.

Artsmark Gold: lots of music – ensembles, choir, jazz band, orchestra won a gold medal at the Liverpool Performing Arts Festival; well-equipped music room with space for choir and orchestra rehearsals. Drama studio with flexible seating, annual drama festival – sixth form girls direct younger ones. Spacious dance studio – dance now at KS3, with GCSE to come and eventually A level (performing arts will also become available at A level). Excellent art: mostly painting and drawing with some 3D and print making – current biomedical project has year 12s working with a professional sculptress; art and design plus fine art with art history offered to sixth. Cheerful textiles room – graphic design on the way.

Vast range of activities in lunch hour and enrichment time, at end of lessons three days a week, some organised by sixth – community work, D of E, journalism club (produces school's e-letters), comedy (Liverpool being the home city of Alexis Sayle and Julie Walters, after all), bridge, cartoons, debating, chess, conversational Italian, Mandarin, Fair Trade. Annual languages festival including film festival; year 7 and 8 spelling bee; media studies has lively Oscars night; recent BBC Schools Question Time national champions. Exciting trips – South Africa, China, World Challenge to Vietnam and Cambodia, Shanghai (to promote Liverpool at World Expo).

Background and atmosphere: Until becoming an academy it was The Belvedere School, a selective GDST independent school. In 2001, a seven year pilot funded by Sir Peter Lampl's Sutton Trust opened up all places on the basis of just merit, with parents paying fees on a sliding scale according to income. Thirty per cent attended for free, it obtained its best ever GCSE results, girls from deprived backgrounds won places at top universities. Still part of the GDST. Numbers have grown steadily from just under 400, with 50-60 in each year group (Mr Kennedy does not want to exceed 850).

Located in the Princes Park area of Liverpool, adjoining a now-regenerated Toxteth, it consists of five linked Victorian (1880) villas plus gardens combined with a new purpose-built extension – the government provided £10m for capital development whilst co-sponsors, the GDST and HSBC Global Education Trust, each provided half a million. The pleasing décor is predominantly blue (matching the uniform) throughout. A hallway in the original part, with traditional school photos and book cabinets, has stairs lined with framed old war posters leading to the history area. Some very attractive rooms – music, art, the well-furnished and stocked library plus canteen – have large bay windows and original ceiling mouldings and views of the park and gardens. A huge cooking range from the original scullery in a corridor gives its name – the Range – to a meeting place. Outside the canteen is a playground with picnic tables and outside learning space with trees, shrubs and hut, due to be developed into an eco area with a pond. The sixth form has a common room with several royal blue sofas and chairs, plus a private study area. The new part is all very fresh and has modern ICT suites, MFL rooms and science labs.

The girls look very smart in their royal blue blazers and ties with light blue shirt/blouse and navy skirt. They are even required to have navy blue/black school bags and coats, can wear navy blue hijabs, and waist belt with purse is also part of the uniform – gosh, this GSG writer hasn't seen one of those since she was at her own GDST school! Sixth formers wear a black business suit with plain white shirt or blouse. All this, and much, much more, enumerated in the student handbook – this is a school that pays punctilious attention to detail.

The ethos of 'the Belevedere girl' is promoted from the start, by staff and the older girls from the original school; this encapsulates the GDST values of hard work, respect for teachers, leadership qualities and pride in one's school (reminiscent of the American charter schools). Each form has a head and deputy head girl, who hold office for half the year. It is perfectly acceptable to be clever and industrious; the girls don't feel unduly pressured but encouraged to do their best and aim high – 'They want us to do well – if we do our best, they are happy'. They say the school council's suggestions are taken heed of.

Pastoral care, well-being and discipline: Very good pastoral care and tight on safeguarding. Bullying not seen as a problem by the girls we met – 'Everyone's friendly – you don't have bullies at Belvedere'; 'The teachers are very aware of social problems'. Sixth formers assigned to KS3 forms, may help individuals with reading; NSPCC training for peer mentors ('buddies'). The girls quickly feel secure and comfortable, according to Mr Kennedy. Thorough behaviour management policy – seems to work, as the girls we saw in classrooms and corridors were all focused and well mannered. All teachers, plus dinner ladies, caretakers, support and office staff, have credit books to reward a range of virtues, leading to certificates, badges, gift/book vouchers, awarded in assemblies; also a traditional prize giving ceremony (but apparently they no longer measure how far skirts are above the knee, as they did in this writer's 60s schooldays).

Pupils and parents: A wide range of social backgrounds; almost one quarter ethnic minority – about half with EAL. From 55-60 primary schools from all over Liverpool, Sefton, Warrington, St Helens and Knowsley plus Hamlet (original Belvedere junior). Web based portal allowing parents to access (some) data on their child. Notable old girls: Dame Rose Heilbron (judge), Esther McVey (MP), Linda Grant (author), Baroness Morgan of Huyton (has held various public offices). Access to the 50,000 strong Minerva network of all GDST old girls.

Entrance: Hugely popular – about 500 applicants for 112 places at year 7 (police needed to control the traffic on test day). All take verbal, non-verbal and numerical reasoning tests; the top 10 per cent achievers in the verbal test are accepted for MFL ability promise, the rest are divided into five ability bands (fair banding system) and then reduced by a lottery method. SEN and looked after children criteria also applied.

Sixth form: minimum of five GCSEs at B or above, with at least A/B in prospective A level subjects; takes about 30 external applicants. Plans to build up to 250.

Exit: Roughly 20 per cent after GCSEs to FE colleges for vocational courses. Rest depart post A level to a wide range of universities and subjects. Manchester, Leeds and Liverpool popular; one to Oxford in 2016.

B

Remarks: Now 'the school everyone wants their daughter to go to in Liverpool'. An exciting and inspiring enterprise extending the virtues of independent schools to a much greater social range that might be a trailblazer for future struggling ones. Only reservation is that the emphasis on 'the Belvedere girl' could restrict the development of individuality.

Beverley Grammar School

Queensgate, Beverley, East Riding of Yorkshire HU17 8NF

Pupils: 842 • Ages: 11–18 • Sixth form: 203 (including 97 girls in joint sixth form)

Tel: 01482 881531
Email: office@beverleygrammar.co.uk
Website: www.beverleygrammar.co.uk

Headteacher: Since 2015, Gavin Chappell PGCE (Hull) NPQH, previously head of The Market Weighton School. He joined following a turbulent time which saw Gillian Todd take over as head for a year after previous head Graham Hodson resigned in June 2014, the school having lost its outstanding status – it has now been upgraded from 'requires improvement' to 'good'.

Academic matters: Despite its name, it is non-selective. Previously rated outstanding by Ofsted for many years, but downgraded to 'requires improvement' in April 2013, then reclassified as 'good' in 2015. Specialisms in engineering and cognitive learning.

Joint sixth form with nearby Beverley High School; 29 per cent A*/A and 53 per cent A*/B grades at A level in 2016 – big improvement on disappointing 2015 results. Lessons held at both schools so students divide their time between the two. School says: 'We argue that it's a good half-way house between school where they feel comfortable and what it will be like going to university where everything is new.' At boys' grammar classes held throughout the school, sixth form building now used for mathematics – 'Aspirational value of seeing sixth form throughout school.'

Three pathways to GCSE – in addition to statutory core curriculum with additional GCSEs, diploma or vocational courses in conjunction with local colleges. In 2016, 66 per cent got 5+ A*-C with English and maths, 22 per cent of grades A*/A (GCSE grades still lower than in 2014). Differentiated teaching, only setting in maths and modern foreign languages. Learning mentors to keep year 11s on track.

Impressive SEN provision includes two teachers with specialist qualifications in SEN, dyslexia and the autism spectrum and a number of highly trained teaching assistants. Inclusion is promoted, preparing differentiated learning materials and using support within the classroom or alternatively withdrawing individuals or small groups for specialised tuition. The school makes use of volunteers, including parents and others from the local community. Learning support is an option on the sixth form enrichment programme. Access is not easy on the school site, but adaptations have been made to improve this as far as is possible, given the age and layout of the building – lift and stairlifts to access first floor areas. At least one classroom in subject areas has a sound field system.

Games, options, the arts: Strong on sport ('you name it, we do it') – highlights include annual cross-country race. Also strong on music – about 120 have individual music lessons and ensembles galore from orchestras to choirs to rock group. Showcase of talent has replaced the annual drama production, although examination pieces are performed to an invited audience. 'Drama very strong, a real asset to the school,' said one parent. Extracurricular is – well, take your pick: 'If a boy wants a club to be started, we find a member of staff to start it'. On offer all the healthy options, fitness testing and complete range of ball sports. More wacky, the Warhammer Club and BGS Entertainers; just love the no doubt aptly named Rebels' Reading Club.

Background and atmosphere: Founded in 700 AD, England's oldest state secondary school. Cherishes its traditions but prides itself on moving with the times and achieving new goals – 'like moving an ocean liner, constantly making incremental changes, without which it's difficult to maintain momentum'.

On its present site (the outskirts of Beverley) since 1903 and now a mix of the old (a museum of a hall) and the new (the mathematics building, built as the sixth form block). Sports classroom, showers and changing room annex; library, humanities block and MFL areas all refurbished.

In the main building, look beyond the grubby quarry tiled corridor floor and chewing gum besmirched carpet to the buzz of conversation between lessons, observe the friendly, respectful yet light-hearted exchange between pupil and teacher and note the smile and eye contact from the boy holding the door open – a palpable sense that pupils really enjoy being here.

Pupils now have greater opportunity to contribute to all aspects of school life through student voice, a democratically elected council made up of representatives from each form. Primary purpose to oversee school and community events but consulted on all school decisions from appointment of staff to school improvements. Valued greatly by the boys we spoke to.

Pastoral care, well-being and discipline: A can do philosophy and a 'more carrot, less stick' approach to learning – 'We believe in working hard, but having a lot of fun doing it, so there's a lot of leg pulling goes on in the classrooms. And because we have a relaxed approach to learning, the boys learn because they want to, not because they're being threatened with what will happen if they don't'.

Parents involved at earliest stage over any slips in discipline. School's own social worker may visit child's home to talk over problems. Only one permanent exclusion in three years and exemplary behaviour around school. Creditable reward system of coloured slips/credit cheques which lead to certificates, a monthly cash prize draw and ultimate prizes of badge and special school tie. A mentoring system with a difference to keep learning on track: as well as teachers, mentors can also be volunteers from the community – industrialists, careers advisers, etc – to drum home the value of learning. 'We use counselling, praise and reward to modify behaviour. We are a happy place where everyone achieves.'

The school's ethos of being friendly, open, caring and successful is underpinned by its SPACE programmes that instil respect, tolerance, empathy and responsibility in the boys and pride in their school. Lunchtime 'pop ins', when careers, health, learning and pastoral staff are on hand, also provide a comfort zone for less confident pupils, together with a strong student support system means little evidence of the macho positioning associated with boys' schools. As one pupil put it, 'The occasional outburst of testosterone is dealt with well here.' No formal links with the girls' high school until joint sixth form – opportunity lost?

Five forms per year group, each representative of one of the five houses. Great effort at entry in year 7 to ensure that forms are as homogeneous as possible. House activity dumbed down due to time constraints, limiting opportunity for vertical integration.

Pupils and parents: Very supportive parents, encouraged to be involved with school from the off (volunteer workforce cleared snow from the school playgrounds). Pupils overwhelmingly from white British backgrounds with few eligible for free school meals or whose first language is not English.

Most pupils enter the school with average levels of attainment, though a number are above average and nearly a quarter have learning difficulties and/or disabilities. Parents of year 7 starters invited to sit with their child for half a day of lessons. One mum, fresh from a science lesson, described school as 'absolutely brilliant. There's such an eagerness and keenness here. It's renewed in my son that excitement for learning'.

Famous past pupils in the 20th century include Kenneth Annakin, film director, Paul Robinson, England goalkeeper and John Andrew, Anglican clergyman in New York.

Entrance: Deciding factor is distance from the door. Living in catchment area – Beverley and the surrounding villages of Woodmansey, Walkington and Bishop Burton – is pretty much a must, though falling rolls have opened the doors for those living beyond. Oversubscribed and very appealing (from the large number of disappointed parents).

Exit: Up to two-thirds leave after GCSEs (60 per cent in 2016). Though no Oxbridge in 2016, Cambridge featured in 2015. Other popular destinations Durham, Hull, Lincoln and York St John. In 2016, five budding medics, dentists and vets; 43 per cent of leavers to Russell Group.

Remarks: A heady cocktail – a grown up school that is mature enough to nurture mutual respect, knows its boys, plays to their strengths and delivers, with a dash of good humour thrown in. No wonder boys love it. As one pupil said, 'It's cool to learn.' However, struggling somewhat through unsettled times.

Beverley High School

Norwood, Beverley, East Riding of Yorkshire HU17 9EX

Pupils: 833 • Ages: 11–18 • Sixth form: 203 (including 106 boys in joint sixth form)

Tel: 01482 881658
Email: admindept@beverleyhigh.net
Website: www.beverleyhigh.net

Headteacher: Since 2009, Ms Sharon Japp (early 40s), BA in English and sociology from Leeds, MEd and NPQH. Joined school in 1999 as head of English after teaching posts in West Yorkshire schools. Spell as assistant head and then deputy head from 2004. Previous head served for 22 years – governors certainly believe in continuity here.

Neat, pleasant yet guarded, firm but fair, clearly committed to continuing the strong ethos of the school to 'never rest on its laurels'. Has 'been a good new broom' and built a younger management team who are 'as keen as mustard', according to one parent. Respected by pupils and seems by no means to be remote figurehead. Keen for the girls to have every opportunity to play their part in global and environmental issues, from promoting links with overseas schools to supporting the school's gardening club by using produce from their allotment.

Academic matters: Good choice of subject at GCSE, with one MFL and three sciences standard. Subjects are taught in mixed-ability groups, apart from mathematics and languages at key stage 3 and maths and science at key stage 4. In 2016, 72 per cent of pupils got 5+ A*-C grades including English and maths, 28 per cent A*/A grades. In the joint sixth form with Beverley Grammar, 29 per cent A*/A and 53 per cent A*/B grades at A level in 2016.

Committed teaching staff with an academic tracking and monitoring system that runs like a well-oiled machine. From year 7 to 9, progress leaders track pupil attainment and attitude to learning, using a traffic light system. Managed by an assistant head, a report goes to senior management and strategies are immediately put in place for individual pupils. One parent praised the effectiveness of early intervention for her daughter's mathematics – individual additional twilight sessions for a year transformed her competence and confidence. From year 10, a programme called 'closing the gap' provides significant intervention and support for those who are underperforming.

Pace of work is fast, but hope is to encourage everyone of all abilities. SEN manager uses a team of teaching assistants to give support in the classroom; limited withdrawal, number of pupils with statements in the teens, a provision for visually impaired. Volunteers in years 10–13 give up their free time to help with lunchtime clubs and support in lessons.

Aim is that somewhere around the school, every child's name should be highlighted for some kind of achievement – 'Every girl has a talent and there is a huge expectation and challenge for us all, teacher and pupil alike, to ensure each girl has that opportunity to shine, in whatever domain that might be,' says the head.

Games, options, the arts: Sport very popular – enhanced sports hall shared with community. Good representation at area and county level, particularly in cross-country and athletics. Drama, dance, music and art promoted through the curriculum. One in five has individual music tuition; choirs, orchestras, annual carol service in nearby Minster and summer music concert in St Mary's Church. Currently no joint productions with boys' Grammar School's acclaimed drama department – missed opportunity? Dance in vogue, with first participation in the national dance/drama Rock Challenge. Inter-house competition mainly through sport and dance.

Technology block and art block provide excellent facilities. Good range and number of clubs meet during the week – rock band to award winning Radiowaves. British Council's international school award – Japanese and Sri Lankan partner schools as well as links with Germany and the Netherlands – and Fairtrade schools award. Highlights of school year include more than 60 trips to places at home and abroad. Fundraising for charities chosen by girls.

Background and atmosphere: Uninspiring frontage onto a main road hiding extensive buildings, grass playing fields and wooded grounds – well maintained with nice touches of hanging baskets and container plants around the buildings. Girls value the buildings and their resources and look after them.

Over 100 years old; the first pupils were mainly boarders in adjacent Norwood House. Much has changed but remains true to its original ideals, reported by the first headmistress Miss Rossiter as: 'The school is designed to supply education of the highest class and to give to girls the educational ideals of the great public schools. Great stress will be laid on the formation of character'.

Adept at adopting the best from latest initiatives – became a technology college in the first flush of schools adopting specialist status in technology in 1998. Plenty of computers spread around the buildings, where girls can work unsupervised between lessons; introducing educational use of mobile phones and MP3 players. Holds national healthy school status.

New developments can't come a moment too soon. School is desperately short of large meeting space – in fact the whole school only meets collectively once a year, at the annual carol service in the minster: a real disappointment.

Close links and support from the local authority, particularly with the extended schools team, plus very careful and conservative financial controls, mean that conversion to academy status is not on the agenda at the moment.

A school where teachers give of their best – 'It's all about the children,' says head. 'Teachers are accessible and give an atmosphere of encouragement to the girls,' says one parent, and gave an example of the support her young daughter had been given to take part in a national spelling bee competition – in German. But much is expected of students, too. Classroom noticeboards show details of what pupils need to do to strive always for the next level of attainment – a girl expecting a B grade would never be in any doubt about what was needed to lift herself to an A.

Good staff/pupil relationships result in an atmosphere of maturity and trust. In view of this it is difficult to understand why the uniform skirt length debate, a national phenomenon, was not resolved with pupil cooperation, without the need for parent consultation and public debate. ('Too much emphasis,' said one parent – whose daughters wear the trouser option!). The student leadership team, currently comprising one pupil per year group, works collaboratively on individual projects, from helping to improve lessons to organising and managing charity events.

Although on campus, sixth form (joint with boys' school, Beverley Grammar) is very much a separate entity. Currently, links with Beverley Grammar below sixth form are almost non-existent – little chance to work collaboratively on projects, enterprises, Duke of Edinburgh etc: more missed opportunities here.

Pastoral care, well-being and discipline: The aim is that pupils retain the same form teacher from entry until the end of year 11. Also same progress leader from year 8. Great continuity, but what about personality clashes? 'You try to build a relationship and it provides great life skills,' said one wise pupil. Each form has a captain and deputy, who keep their rôles for a term so that everyone gets a chance at leadership.

Discipline strict but fair and seemingly consistent. Parents are supportive and speak of the good communication they have with teachers – 'We get a mobile phone call if homework is handed in late,' said one. Another talked of her year 7 daughter being mortified by a detention for forgetting to hand in her homework, but agreed with the teacher's stance of 'one rule for all'.

Well-being centre provides a network of support for pupils and their families, incorporating the pastoral team, a nurse, social worker, the SEN manager and the learning mentor.

Pupils and parents: Very supportive local parents encouraged to share school's ambition for their girls. Parents praise communications with the school and feel involved in their daughters' education. Pupils are drawn from local catchment area and take a real pride in their school.

Old girls include Angela Frost CBE, a director at HMRC, a clutch of actresses – Anna Maxwell-Martin and Eleanor Tomlinson – and classical soloist Ildiko Allen. We particularly liked the school noticeboard celebrating latest individual achievements of current and former pupils.

Entrance: Intake of 140 is substantially oversubscribed (two applications per place). Pupils drawn almost exclusively from catchment area – Beverley and the surrounding villages of Tickton, Walkington and Bishop Burton.

Exit: Around 60 per cent leave after GCSEs. Most of year 13 to university (nearly half Russell Group), including three medics and one vet in 2016.

Remarks: Never resting on its laurels, a school that is true to itself and its original purpose – to provide excellent education for girls whilst encouraging, supporting and celebrating each individual success. It believes pupil well-being is fundamental to academic success and this, with an atmosphere of high expectation, committed teaching, close pupil monitoring and early intervention, produces creditable results. Strengthening in-school links with the sixth form and more collaboration with partner school Beverley Grammar, below sixth form, would be the icing on the cake.

Birkdale School

Oakholme Road, Sheffield, South Yorkshire S10 3DH

Pupils: 821 • Ages: 4–18 • Sixth form: 217 (including 69 girls)

Fees: £8,175 – £12,225 pa

Tel: 01142 668409
Email: admissions@birkdaleschool.org.uk
Website: www.birkdaleschool.org.uk

Head Master: Since 2010, Dr Paul Owen MA Phd. Educated Winchester College, then Queen's College, Cambridge. Married to Gail, with one daughter and two sons, all pupils at the school. He came to Birkdale from Wellington School, Somerset, where he served eight years as deputy head, after 18 years teaching mainly physics, and also as a day housemaster.

An unassuming, genial presence and obviously liked by the boys. Parents describe him as 'approachable and very down to earth'. He continues to teach physics and parents commented this keeps him 'firmly in touch' and 'his abilities as a teacher are outstanding'. He is a keen hill walker and trumpet player, and also an active Christian, committed to the strong pastoral ethos of the school.

Head of prep school since 2009, Mr Christopher Burch BA PGCE (40s), previously deputy head of Great Walstead Prep. His wife, Pip, is the school librarian and a pre-prep teaching assistant. They have four sons, two currently in the prep and two now at the senior school. Parents appreciate the whole family involvement. He is a committed and active Christian and fully supports the faith ethos of the school. Friendly and approachable, popular with parents, he patrols the playground every morning to welcome the boys and to catch or be caught by parents, to 'sort out problems when they are pennies before they become pounds'. Parents were keen to emphasise 'nothing is too small to discuss with him.'

Academic matters: Fabulous stand-alone science lab in the prep school. 'Real' science is taught from the beginning, as is French – everything throughout the school is labelled with its French equivalent. Lovely loft art room, full of colour, and a shelf of working wooden catapults a recent exciting project. The substantial school hall is impressively flexible, switching from breakfast club to assembly hall, to gym to refectory to theatre, a military operation several times a day. Specialist teaching from age 4 in French, music, drama, DT and RE. Adding, from year 3, science, history, geography, art and ICT with dedicated classrooms requiring boys to move around the school as necessary, with the right books. Setting in maths, English and science from year 5 with elements for support from year 3. 'The boys are stretched and closely monitored without pressure or stress,' said one parent. All boys are screened for SEN and the help, some in class and some out, is sympathetic and thorough. Parents talk of amazing staff teamwork, and a happy working relationship was apparent when we visited. Discipline well maintained with clear rewards and sanctions and behaviour extremely good, although relaxed. Reward points are collected for the house, posted on a corridor wall and 'are dished out like confetti,' according to a parent.

Results are consistently creditable. In 2016, 51 per cent A*/A and 74 per cent A*/B at A level, and 57 per cent A*/A at GCSE. Maths and sciences popular and successful, however only a small take up for languages at A level. Greek and Mandarin offered as extracurricular clubs. Design technology, comprising graphics, electronics and resistant materials, outstanding with fabulous facilities. Lots of links to local industries and tremendous pride in, and recognition of, Sheffield's enterprising past.

Head is particularly hot on 'learning for its own sake' and has developed several initiatives under the banner 'intellectual curiosity'. Regular random questions appear on screens around the school and pupils are invited to submit a response. An annual competition, open to years 10, 11 and 12, where the six winners have the opportunity to research an idea – imaginative but practical and unrelated to their exam syllabuses – in London's libraries, museums and archives. They then, dauntingly, have to deliver a 20 minute public presentation based on their findings. SEN available for mild cases only and costs extra, however, SENCo has an open door and welcomes any struggling pupil to informal drop-in sessions.

Parents are particularly effusive about the sixth form, one described its head as 'gold dust', and they all had nothing but praise for her tireless individual support steering pupils through the UCAS system. Interview practice for those who need it is thorough and appropriate; two doctors from Sheffield Medical School put potential medics through their paces. Careers advice begins early as part of PHSE, with regular visiting speakers in middle school and trips to the careers library in Sheffield. The school itself also has an excellent careers library, based within the sixth form centre in the Grayson building.

Games, options, the arts: Constraints of being an inner-city school on a Victorian site have forced the playing fields to Castle Dyke, a 10-minute drive away. However, extensive pitches, complete with 10 lane cricket nets and modern pavilion, more than compensate. There is a substantial sports hall with adjoining gym on site and much use made of good local facilities. Rugby is successful, with trips to Australia or New Zealand, likewise cricket, with lots of boys going on to play at county level or beyond. Football ever popular and teams play in the ISFA with an annual tour around Newcastle. Boys can join the clubs but parents would welcome a few more B and C teams for the less gifted. Netball and hockey specifically for girls, and a respectable range of other sporting options are available both during and after school, judo and fencing both very popular.

The prep school outdoor play area is spacious and boys are encouraged into it as often as possible. No on-site games, however the extensive facilities of the senior school at Castle Dyke, 10 minutes away, are fully available. Rugby, cricket and football teams do well in local fixtures and parents of less sporty boys particularly welcome the addition of C teams to give their sons the opportunity to represent their school. Head has worked hard to improve the sport at Birkdale but is keen not to give it 'too high a currency' and encourages the cool games masters to read in public and talk to the boys about the books they are reading.

Impressive art much in evidence throughout the school with a huge and colourful variety of media and styles. Lots of emphasis on fine art and drawing skills, impressive copies of old masters – Vermeer, Rembrandt, even Botticelli. A visiting tutor from the Royal College was working with A level students when we visited. Sixth formers have their own unique studio space, a haven.

Music and drama are thriving with a large, well-equipped studio space and a lovely octagonal concert hall. Loads of opportunities to perform from lunchtime concerts and house plays, to larger public events both in school and the wider community. Rock bands, jazz bands, and a big band, alongside an excellent traditional orchestra, ensembles and various choirs mean there is something for everybody, 'the sort of music kids want,' said a parent. Younger boys are encouraged to join 'tecbox' where they learn how to 'tec' their own assemblies and, as they grow through the school, the musicals and concerts.

Lots of drama in the prep, popular with the boys, and music is high on the agenda with around 100 learning one of a huge variety of instruments. New drama and music rooms. Brass, wind and string groups and guitar ensembles come together in an orchestra and feed into the Sheffield Schools' Training Orchestra, hosted by the school. Parents describe the extracurricular clubs, both after school and at lunchtime, as 'outstanding' both in variety and quality. There's something for everybody from Beat Club to Warhammer, to the increasingly popular Mandarin and a well-attended Christian Union. Plenty of day trips and visits. Longer jaunts begin in year 4 with two nights away in nearby Castleton, culminating in the much anticipated leavers' week in Normandy. Year 5 boys were wildly enthusiastic about their outdoor pursuits trip to the Lake District.

Huge variety of lunchtime activities in the senior school and pupils are encouraged to 'have a go' and fill their diaries. Head firm that 'individual aptitudes can be discovered this way'. The school is incredibly active in its support of charities, with numerous money-raising events led by pupils. Clubs within the enterprise umbrella include over a dozen commercial business start-ups and the monies made here also contribute. Since 2000, the school has supported a village in Nepal by refurbishing the Peace Garden School. Every year a group of pupils, teachers and parents, usually including the odd medic, spend time here, working and teaching. Boys, whether they've been there or not, are full of pride and enthusiasm for the project and parents tell of how life plans have been changed by the experience.

Many other trips across the curriculum include skiing, foreign language and team building expeditions. Younger boys hugely enthusiastic about a drama trip to London and spontaneously demonstrated skills learned from a stage-fighting workshop.

Background and atmosphere: An ambitious school in every way. Founded as a boys' prep in 1904, it created a senior department in 1978, adding a sixth form in 1988. The only all boys independent school in Sheffield, parents say they understand boys extremely well. Girls joined the flourishing sixth form in 1995. The site, which reflects Sheffield's glorious past, has grown as required but haphazardly. Originally based in the large Victorian Oakholme House, it has spread to encompass four neighbouring mansions (Westbury, Endcliffe, Grayson and Johnson), with modern extensions and new builds, creating something of a warren – stairs, steps and steep paths everywhere. 'There isn't a flat surface in Sheffield,' head says. Beautiful original features – cupolas, sanded glass, marble fireplaces – add charm, personality, and maintenance nightmares. 'I have become an expert in Victorian architecture,' says head, somewhat ruefully. Large mature gardens are free for the younger boys to run off steam without over concern for shrubs or lawns. The extensive library is housed in the bay windowed drawing room where the Cole brothers conceived John Lewis. Modern school hall is well used as refectory and theatre, and the twice weekly whole school assemblies. Head dreams of a (much needed) purpose built theatre – watch out, neighbours!

Prep in Clarke House, an extended late Georgian mansion, which was originally owned by master cutler, John Osborn. Houses named after four of the most prestigious master cutlers from Sheffield's history reflect this connection. Some lovely airy classrooms but others are a bit cramped. Pre-prep now housed in style in nearby Belmayne House, giving much needed breathing space back to the prep.

Pastoral care, well-being and discipline: Pastoral care is high on the agenda emanating from the school's strong Christian ethos. It is not heavy-handed but focuses on nurture and mutual respect with the advantage that the school is small enough for everyone to know everyone. First port of call is the form tutor but beyond this staff and prefects are approachable and available. All extremely effective, according to parents: 'It's not just lip service, they really care about and know your child.'

Lots of positive reinforcement; house points are dished out but so are sanctions and younger boys carry dog-eared score-cards stuffed into their blazer pockets. A quirky system called 'drill', where minor miscreants help the dining room staff to scrape plates, apparently nips a lot of problems in the bud. Drugs policy rigorously implemented and there is zero tolerance for bullying. Any incidents are dealt with swiftly but discipline is 'about reformation and the recognition that teenagers can misjudge things,' says head. House loyalty strongly encouraged with masses of opportunities to support with frequent music, drama and enterprise competitions, all with the by-product of raising money for charity. School uniform throughout, but boys are allowed to be comfortably tousled, 'no nitpicking,' according to a parent.

Pupils and parents: Parents represent a healthy cultural mix. Lots of medics and many who make big sacrifices to send their boys. Most fairly local but some travel significant distances, coming from as far as Bakewell and Rotherham. Plenty of social events and parents talk warmly of the strong sense of community within the school. Parking remains a challenge despite best efforts of head to stagger drop-off and pick-up with the extended breakfast and after-school care, and negotiate a first-15-minute-free-parking in the surrounding zones. 'It's the Wild West,' said one parent and all regaled us with their various strategies to combat it. Bus system, shared with the Girls' High school, efficiently covers a wide geographical area. Bursaries ensure a full social spectrum. Old boys include Michael Palin and Rex Harrison plus legal and sporting luminaries.

Entrance: No assessment for entry at 4. From age 6 there is an assessment day, but they rarely don't offer a place if they have availability. Despite strong Christian ethos there are no religious requirements. A number of Hindu, Muslim, and Sikh boys co-exist with church and non-church boys and participate in all assemblies. Head says their parents like the fact the school 'knows where it stands with faith.'

Senior school year group of 72 with 60 per cent from the prep and remainder from a range of other primaries. Entrance is by exam at 11 for all, with interview and school reference given equal importance. Top 20 are invited back for a second day, after which scholarships are allocated. Most boys from the prep go through, with a small handful moving to the state system or boarding. Prep parents are forewarned if the senior school is not considered to be the right place. Girls and boys from many local schools join the sixth form, approximately 40 each year. Requirements are five GCSE passes, with a minimum of four Bs and at least a B for any chosen A level subject.

Exit: Virtually all (some 95 per cent) from the prep to the senior school. Parents given plenty of warning and support if senior school deemed to be wrong for their child. Of those that leave, some go to boarding school, some into the state sector.

In 2016, lost just under a quarter after GCSEs, minimal number at end of year 12. Always a respectable number to Oxbridge – 11 in 2016 – and many to other Russell Group; Newcastle, Birmingham and Nottingham popular, one to Northumbria. Broad range of subjects covered: economics most popular, then engineering and medicine (10 places), with several also off to study law, music, accounting and finance and geography.

Money matters: Variety of scholarships awarded at 11+ and 16+, both academic and music, each with a ceiling of 25 per cent apart from cases of financial need which can be topped up with a bursary. Sixth form have the Arkwright for DT and Ogden Trust for science. Almost a third have some level of financial assistance; bursaries strictly means-tested with some home visits.

Remarks: A lively school, strongly linked to the community and the world beyond with its impressive charitable activities. Pupils are cheerful and enthusiastic, obviously stimulated. Their USP is the ability to focus on individual development within a dynamic and caring community.

Birkenhead School

58 Beresford Road, Oxton, Prenton CH43 2JD

Pupils: 760 (480 boys, 280 girls) • Ages: 11–18 • Sixth form: 106

Fees: £7,650 – £10,740 pa

Tel: 01516 524014
Email: enquire@birkenheadschool.co.uk
Website: www.birkenheadschool.co.uk

Headmaster: Since September 2016, Paul Vicars, previously deputy head of Shrewsbury School. Geography degree from St Andrews; four years at Ernst & Young; then, after a PGCE at Exeter he joined Shrewsbury in 2001, and was a housemaster as well as teaching geography there.

He coaches cricket, hockey and golf and has a passion for music, though now in a supporting role; he is married to Vikki, a history and law teacher, and they have three young children.

Academic matters: Results well ahead of local selective grammars, its main competitors. In 2016, A level: 54 per cent A*/A, 88 per cent A*/B. Majority opt for maths and science (excellent results); largest humanities entries in history, economics and English. GCSE 67 per cent A*/A in 2016. Clearly policy of offering (and staffing) wide option range across only three-form entry pays off in terms of small classes and sets, eg language choice from Latin, Greek, French, German, Spanish. Separate sciences for most to GCSE.

Special needs coordinated by staff member, now helped by three part-time learning support teachers. Parents pay for one-to-one tuition. Not much staff turnover (heads notwithstanding) – very nice place to teach and live. A general impression of fervent commitment to setting high classroom standards – and indeed to life outside the classroom.

Games, options, the arts: Games record amazing for size of school: cricket and rugby have been strong in the recent past. Most of the usual sports, soccer in sixth form. Senior girls' teams in hockey, netball, lacrosse and rounders. Policy of sport for all, through which individuals find their niche and improve fitness: 'We're not simply interested in natural athletes.' Enormous range of outdoor activities: CCF (all three sections), shared with local RC girls' school; D of E (25 taking gold level); 'biggest scout troop in Birkenhead'. Usual tours and expeditions.

Lively music: choral concerts with Liverpool Sinfonia; much instrumental tuition; chapel choir, claimed unique among day schools in holding weekly evensong during term, involving pupils from age 10 to 18. Drama good too.

Background and atmosphere: Founded 1860, became direct grant, then independent in 1976. An unusual campus, hinted at in suburban address. Walking along the four comfortable, tree-lined roads that define the school, you wouldn't guess at the existence of a lively school of 700 lurking behind the screen of large houses and sundry buildings. In fact an agreeable jumble of old and new, including a handsome Victorian chapel and fine cricket field. Years 7 and 8 housed in an elegant mansion, with its own playground and year 8 prefects, helping transition to serious senior school.

At present a handful of girls in the sixth, but they're building up in the prep school and through the school. Co-education originally planned with Birkenhead High School, which has now become an academy, so school is going it alone – to everyone's relief, it seems. Integration of girls has gone smoothly, and should continue; campus is a civilised place, and supervision of all ages discreet but effective. Recent ISI inspection noted 'exemplary' pupils' behaviour.

Liverpool proper may be just across the water, but it feels miles away. The Wirral is a pretty conservative place, and the school is happy with its own traditional elements: little boys wear caps, prefects wear gowns, and the head enters assembly to the head of school's cry of 'School!', whereupon all stand up. Trendy potential parents may not like this.

Recent developments include an extension to sixth form block and improvements to pavilion; a swimming pool is a gleam in the eye. Superb termly newsletter, In Focus, full of pictures, is the brainchild of former head's PA, who continues to run the school's marketing.

Pastoral care, well-being and discipline: Traditional day school system; interlocking staff responsibilities mean it's very hard to fall through the pastoral net – commended in ISI report as outstanding. Report also quotes a boy: 'We don't do bullying here'. One expulsion for drug use in last five years; pupils can be temporarily excluded for rudeness and vandalism – hooray!

Pupils and parents: Pupils mostly from the Wirral and as far as Chester; some walk, some use public transport, many use school bus system shared with Birkenhead High. Pupils seem articulate, confident, happy with work ethos, and yes, a touch conventional. Their alternative sixth form prospectus is worth a read, though hardly very shocking. Parents mostly professional and business, heavily committed to all aspects of school. Flourishing former pupils' society, sharing In Focus with school. Most famous old boy was FE Smith, Lord Birkenhead.

Entrance: Increasingly from own prep – existence of local grammars draws state primary pupils away at 11+. May have been a brief wobble over numbers before the co-education decision, but situation now seems to have steadied, as many parents opt for independent education from the start. Prep pupils not tested at 11+ unless applying for a scholarship – assessed internally, and those not likely to make grade flagged up in good time for parents to find alternative schooling. External candidates tested in English, maths and VR. GCSE hurdle for A levels.

Exit: A few leave at 16+. Vast majority to good universities – most to Russell Group, especially Durham, a handful to Oxbridge most years (one in 2016, and four medics) – to read hard subjects: law, medicine/dentistry, engineering popular.

Money matters: About six academic scholarships a year, a few at sixth form level, some limited-term for music; usually 10 per cent of fees. Birkenhead Foundation Trust bursaries support about eight pupils a year – full remission possible.

Remarks: A confident, humane, non-flashy school in the best grammar school tradition, offering an astonishing array of opportunities for personal development in and out of classroom. Not as driven as some famous ex-grammars in urban areas. It feels nearer Chester than Liverpool, more like Bootham than, say, Bolton. School's claim of an 'open, happy community' rings true, but parents of young thrusters shouldn't be put off.

Bolton School Boys' Division

Linked with Beech House, Bolton School Girls' Division

Chorley New Road, Bolton, Lancashire BL1 4PA

Pupils: 1,017 • Ages: 7–18 • Sixth form: 219

Fees: £9,204 – £11,508 pa

Tel: 01204 840201
Email: seniorboys@boltonschool.org
Website: www.boltonschool.org/seniorboys

Headmaster: Since 2008, Mr Philip Britton, MBE MA MEd FInstP (40s). Was state-educated in the North East then read physics at Oxford, followed by a PGCE from Cambridge and a masters from Leeds. His academic pedigree really is first class: firsts, distinctions, top of the year awards – he's got them all. Passionate both about physics and teaching, he was rather disgruntled that everyone thought he was doing a PGCE because he couldn't think of anything else to do. Before Bolton he was head of physics at The Grammar School in Leeds from the age of 23 and latterly deputy head.

Mr Britton says Bolton is distinguished by the expertise of the subject teachers – boys are taught by real specialists – and his own expertise is second to none. He has an MBE for services to physics, an international award for his contribution to physics education and has worked with the Institute of Physics to improve the physics curriculum and develop better resources.

Staff say he's the cleverest head they've ever had and that he's 'highly supportive' when they're trying to get anything new off the ground. Boys say he's 'kind' but this is a big school and Mr Britton makes no secret of the fact that he doesn't have a huge amount to do with most pupils individually. If there's a problem he encourages parents and boys to approach form tutors, year heads or subject teachers first rather than going straight to the top. He says 'although I could probably pick that boy out of a school photo, the chances are I'll know nothing about the specific issue'. He clearly listens to the community – commissioning regular parents' questionnaires etc – but he comes across as a confident leader rather than a people pleaser. His decision not to see every parent at the drop of a hat 'took a while to bed in' and, he says, 'maybe some parents do find that frustrating but I'm OK with that because I think I'm right'. We didn't meet any dissent from the parents we met, who described him as 'approachable' and 'proactive'.

He gets a parent's eye view of the school because both his own sons attend: 'If my boys come home excited and positive day after day,' he says, 'then I imagine that's hopefully going on at a lot of other kitchen tables too.'

Head of junior school: Since April 2015, Mrs Susan Faulkner, who had been deputy head at the school since 2011. A Durham University graduate, she has also taught at Stonyhurst Junior School and was a deputy head for six years before joining Bolton School.

Academic matters: What the junior school achieves is glaringly obvious when you talk to the kids. We met some in what felt like a large group (but was in fact no more than eight to 10 boys). Our opener was: 'Who likes reading?' We expected a dutiful array of raised hands; what we didn't expect was a loud burst of book-chatter – involving all the children, not just the older ones. There's impassioned debate about favourite authors – ranging from David Walliams, Tom Gates and Roald Dahl to Charles Dickens (Bleak House, if you're wondering – we're guessing an abridged, illustrated children's version but we wouldn't put money on it). One boy confessed – half proud, half guilty – that he just couldn't put his book down last night and was still reading at 11pm. One lad devours poetry books; another goes for non-fiction; they all love the Horrible Histories.

The kids show this kind of zest for everything to do with their learning. One minute they're enthusing about trips to the school's own outdoor pursuits centre in the Lake District, Patterdale Hall; the next they're showing off what they can say in Mandarin. This is the main language studied here, although they also take up French in year 6. It's taught by two specialist linguist teachers: a native speaker from the Confucius Institute in Manchester and the school's own languages teacher, who's learning Mandarin especially. Recognised with Confucius Classroom status making school 'a teaching hub for Chinese learning in the local community'.

It's a selective school and most boys are in the top 25 per cent in terms of ability. In 2016 at A level 51 per cent of entries were awarded an A* or A, nearly 74 per cent A*/B. At GCSE 52 per cent of entries were passed at A* or A. The school serves its bright intake well. Exam results are above average compared to other selective schools. Ongoing monitoring of pupil performance compares the boys not to each other but to their own potential – so a boy near the bottom of his class might still be praised for making great leaps forwards and a boy right at the top of the class can't necessarily relax. 'Maybe Joe or Fred did get 90 per cent in a test,' says Mr Britton, 'but we'll know if actually he should be getting 95 per cent.'

Personalised help is available to pupils at all academic levels. The learning support department arranges one-to-one 'bespoke interventions' for boys who are struggling or who have SEN. These normally happen before school or during breaks to minimise disruption to lessons. Support for children with statements of SEN or who don't speak English at home incurs no extra cost to parents. There are also 'drop in' clinics for any pupil to attend if he needs extra help with a subject or has been absent. Meanwhile high flyers are stretched with AQA Bacc extended projects, Olympiads and competitions and the headmaster runs an invitation-only academic club, the Ainsworth Society, which meets once a term to discuss books and ideas.

In terms of numbers, like many boys' schools, Bolton is strong in maths and science. More than half the sixth form takes maths A level (compared to about 10 per cent taking English). Other popular subjects at A Level include economics, geography and all three sciences. But there's excellence across the board – particularly in languages. Latin, Ancient Greek and Russian are all offered to A level. The award-winning Russian department runs a biennial trip to Russia and takes sixth formers on a week-long residential language course at the University of East Anglia. Average class size is 17 but they're smaller in the sixth form. The curriculum makes room for plenty of physical activity and all boys do some of their learning every year on residential trips to Patterdale Hal, the school's own outdoor pursuits centre in the Lake District. Every pupil has an iPad (at no extra cost, so there's no divide between the haves and the have-nots). They can email homework direct to their teachers as they do it and get comments back the same night.

Boys told us that they felt lucky to have such expert teachers and that they appreciated being stretched. None of the boys we spoke to had experienced peer pressure not to be seen as a swot. One told us: 'I love knowing the answer – lessons are my chance to put my hand up and show off.' Some complained that there was too much homework but parents seemed to think the amount was just right. The boys we met had an impressively mature attitude to learning – taking it on the chin if they thought a comment in a report was unfair: 'I got a two for effort and I thought I deserved a one but it just inspires me to try harder'. All pupils we met felt that they'd know where to go if they needed extra help academically and they'd be well-supported. Most agreed that they were gradually given more and more chances to learn independently as they moved up the school although one sixth former wondered if he'd been rather spoon-fed.

Games, options, the arts: Mr Britton is big on everyone getting involved in extracurricular activities – so much so that boys must do three lunchtime activities a week during their first few years in the seniors. This mildly authoritarian approach to joining in is also reflected in the fact that the outdoor pursuits trip to Patterdale Hall is obligatory and that all sixth formers must do twenty hours of 'compulsory volunteering'. (Yes, really. Look no further if you're an English student searching for an example of an oxymoron.) One sixth form dissenter was scathing: 'Frankly I think it's ridiculous: some kids don't want to do all those clubs or to go to Patterdale and it's completely wasted on them.' But that's very much a minority view. Most parents and pupils see this set-up as a positive reflection of the character of the school. One mum told us that her son recently announced to to her on the way home: 'Do you know what's brilliant? Being busy.'

The pupils start some of the clubs themselves but the school provides help and resources. Yes, you are expected to get involved but if you don't fancy what's on offer you're encouraged to come up with an idea you do like. As you'd expect, the range of sporting, creative, cultural and academic extracurricular activities is superb. You can even buy Bolton School honey produced by the beekeeping club. Pretty much every subject area has a society in which students from different years work together on projects that are often impressively advanced. Whether they're planting electrodes in a cockroach's brain to control its movement remotely; sending a high altitude balloon into space to take photos of the earth from the stratosphere; or working with the school's writer in residence to produce board games, monologues and 'flash fiction' – the boys can access the latest resources with support from experts who know how to use them. On our visit we saw a few clubs that stand out from the norm: at go-karting club the teacher in charge (well we presume he was a teacher but, clad in overalls and engine oil, he didn't look much like one) explained that it's easy enough for kids to pay £20 to drive a go-kart at the weekend so the real opportunity here is for the boys to learn to tinker. Accordingly they split the club's budget to buy three beaten-up chassis for the boys to customise and cannibalise during lunchtimes to make their own mean machine. Sensibly, the actual go-karting is strictly limited to after school when the playground is empty. We also walked in on a buzzing history society University Challenge style quiz – with a team of four teachers competing against four pupils. The young quiz master was clearly relishing his moment of power; the questions were brain-fuddlingly obscure and the raucous crowd rejoiced to see the teachers struggling.

It's a sporty school, with plenty of timetabled physical activity and great facilities including a 25m indoor swimming pool, a climbing wall and a multigym. Football, hockey, rugby, cricket and water polo are all played competitively with great success. But, without girls there to dominate traditionally 'feminine' activities, the school is also very strong in drama (star old boy Sir Ian McKellen is a regular visitor) and in music – with half the boys learning an instrument. Pupils we spoke to didn't feel there was any pressure to go with the crowd. One boy said: 'I like dancing. And I like football. No one minds what I choose to do – why would they?'

Parents loved the range of activities and said they were 'awestruck' by how many hours the teachers put in to school life beyond the curriculum. Many were drawn to the school as much by its ethos and community as by its academic reputation. One mum told us the boys here are 'confident, not cocky. And they'll grow up to be fine young men.'

Background and atmosphere: The campus is spacious and magnificent. It's like an Oxbridge college – a big one. Two grand, mirror image, stone quads house the girls' and boys' divisions. They meet in the middle with a third central quad at the bottom of which is a modern sixth form centre. Here, although boys and girls are still taught separately, some spaces are shared and there's scope for the boys and girls to interact freely. The two divisions share many sports facilities and join for various extracurricular activities – most notably drama productions – so parents say they get the best of both worlds: 'no girls to put them off their work but you don't have a problem of a lad going to university who doesn't know how to talk to any girl except his sister.' There's rather less integration with the two single-sex junior schools on site and with the mixed-sex infant school and nursery. You get the sense that there's a broad sense of community between all the separate sections but that each has a distinct identity and plenty of autonomy. The campus buildings are set in 32 acres of grounds – mainly playing fields.

It's like an old-fashioned grammar school – if a rather grand and smart one. Tradition and family ties are valued here; one pupil explained that he'd been assigned to a particular house because his grandfather had been in it. There's no sense that traditionalism stifles the community – indeed it is thriving in the 21st century – but, on the spectrum between conservative and radical, it seems to us that the leadership doesn't force change on the pupils or teachers for the sake of it.

The school also feels genuinely Boltonian. Only a few miles north of Manchester, the town has a distinctive accent and a proud industrial history. A number of the teachers are local and so are most of the adored support staff, some of whose families have long links with the school. It sees itself as an important institution for the town. It offers its expertise, facilities and the volunteering energies of its pupils to help local state schools and other community groups and this perhaps keeps the school grounded. Its atmosphere is unpretentious, positive and industrious – at times the boys can be both robust and competitive but we felt that this was tempered by kindness and a real respect for difference.

the junior school mums we met appreciate that the school fosters independence in their children right from the start. They feel it's a really warm and nurturing environment. And they all said their children were thriving here. We were most struck by the heights of achievement reached by the pupils. School says this is in part achieved by the decision to use specialists to teach many subjects rather than one class teacher delivering the whole curriculum. We were bowled over by the standards of the pupils' art. This just doesn't look like primary school work. A wall display from a recent picture book illustration project really could have passed for GCSE work, a testament to a 'really remarkable' art teacher. Although we are assured that the diminutive artists aren't completely hand-held – it really is the pupils' own work; they're just magnificently taught. None of this would mean much if it weren't a lovely, friendly community where it's hard to imagine a child being miserable – but it is.

Pastoral care, well-being and discipline: 'So what does school teach you apart from the subjects you study?' we asked the junior boys. 'Be humble'. 'Try to be kind.' 'You must have discipline.' 'It's OK to be different.' Then suddenly we're into a discussion about a Remembrance assembly and what they all think about the fact that war is still going on all over the world. These boys are fascinated by everything. And they adore their school. They say it's 'quite relaxed here really.' 'Yes,' adds another, 'If you've not handed in your homework they just say, "OK but make sure you do it next time."' 'No!' interjects a small, firm voice, 'If you get behind in your work you have to catch up. There's no doubt about it.' The boys agree that behaviour isn't really a problem here: 'They do sort it out if you're naughty.' All say that the teachers would notice if they were upset and that there are adults here they'd confide in. 'And what would you do if you saw someone who was sad?' 'Go over to them and comfort them.' 'Yes, but if they're really sad or they've been bullied I'd definitely tell a teacher too.' A chorus of agreement. So what would they change? Finally silence. One lad says he'd like more freedom but he's shouted down: 'I think most of the rules are really sensible.' 'And remember that we make a lot of the rules ourselves through the school council.' The orderly library buzzes in squeaky hubbub. (The one thing these boys still need to learn is not to talk over each other.) A pause. 'Yeah, I suppose. Yeah, actually there's nothing I'd change.'

We'd describe the atmosphere at the senior school as cheerfully disciplined rather than strict. Exclusions are rare but they do happen. Incidents involving knives or drug-dealing would be non-negotiable out-on-your-ear offences. Mr Britton says he's more concerned about the safety of the silent majority of pupils who behave than he is to show unending compassion to the (hypothetical) boy who endangers others. But the school tries to reform those found guilty of lesser offences. Most pupils are oblivious to this side of school life but the handful who misbehave can expect to face after-school or Saturday morning detentions or even suspension. 'If you've been suspended twice and we still believe in you,' says Mr Britton, 'you'll end up on headmaster's report. At that point we'll tell the boy and his parents that he's the only person who can decide what happens: if he fouls up again, he's out.' Apparently at this point most boys decide they'd rather stay in.

The school is proud of its pastoral system. Form tutors see their group of 22-25 boys twice a day. Mr Britton is confident that pupils can and do feel confident to talk to their form tutors and that they have other people to reach out to if they want – such as year heads or a school nurse. He says they do uncover instances of bullying and deal with them 'swiftly and sensibly'. He's at pains to point out that bullies as well as victims are offered support. Boys told us they feel safe at school and everyone we spoke to agreed that they'd stand up for a victim of bullying and tell a teacher. It's not always gentle here though;

'They don't bitch, but they do banter,' said one mum. Another told us that there was a point when she'd worried about how cruel the boys can be to one another and had even looked around at alternative schools for one son – but her search just showed her 'how good it is here'. Some boys – particularly in the sixth form – feel confident to come out as gay. 'Almost every term we have a "coming out moment",' says Mr Britton, 'and it's no great big drama.' 'The boys are amazing,' said one mum, 'they don't bat an eyelid if someone's gay.'

Pupils and parents: The community of old boys is important to the school and evidently many alumni feel strong emotional ties to the place. On the day of our visit the head was getting ready to travel to an old boys' dinner in Oxford. There's an impressive array of high achieving alumni, providing the school with expertise and inspiration as well as extra cash. As well as Gandalf, notable old boys include actor Ralf Little (from The Royle Family), radio presenter Mark Radcliffe, grand chess master Nigel Short, Nobel prize-winning chemist, Sir Harry Kroto and a long list of notables from the worlds of business, sport, politics, academia and the media.

Half the current intake is from Bolton itself. The school also operates 20 coaches bringing boys in from Preston, Wigan, Warrington, Blackburn and Manchester. The prospectus boasts that because selection is only based on academic ability, 'our intake reflects very closely the mix of population in the north west.' Well, it's true that the school offers bursaries to one in five children – an impressive figure, but it also means that the parents of four in five pupils can dish out – or at least scrape together – close to £11,000 a year per child. But still, there's a real mix of ethnic and religious backgrounds here and, on meeting the boys all sorts of adjectives would probably come to mind – such as bright, courteous, down-to-earth and hard-working – before words like rich or privileged.

Parents we met were engaged with school life and with the education of their sons. Some had never considered state education for their children whereas others had. One parent we spoke to had felt driven to consider an independent school because of the dearth of good state schools near the family home. Another mum had been a pupil at the girls' division here herself whereas another had had a tough time at a state school and wanted something different for her sons. There was a range of accents, backgrounds and approaches in the parents we met: it felt like there's no one type of boy at the school and neither does it suit one particular type of parent.

Entrance: If your child is already at Bolton Infants' School (known as Beech House), they'll automatically be offered a place here at the junior school (since they'll have already gone through academic selection). But any child hoping to transfer to the juniors (known as Park Road) from another primary school in year 3 will have to sit the entrance assessment in the January of the year they'd be joining. They'll be tested in English, maths and verbal reasoning. You can request past papers from the school office.

Pupils also have an interview – 'more of a chat really' – with senior teaching staff. The school's looking for lively, interested children who will thrive both here and in the seniors. School says that the best time to apply is for entry to year 3, when there are usually 10-15 places up for grabs and a bright child has a very good chance of securing one. Too many parents, though, try to get places for entry to years 5 or 6 – perhaps hoping to improve their child's chances of getting into the seniors – and this is a recipe for disappointment as often, no matter how bright the child is, there are no spaces at all for entry to these years; however, school has now opened an extra year 5 class.

Pupils hoping to gain entry to year 7 sit the school's entrance exam in the January of year 6. They'll be set a creative writing essay plus tests in verbal reasoning, non-verbal reasoning and maths. No matter how they did in the tests, all applicants are called for an interview too – held in February. If your son's primary school expects him to achieve level 5 in his key stage 2 Sats he'll be in with a good chance. If you can afford the fees, the competition is roughly two applicants per place. That figure is closer to 3-4 applicants per place if you're after a means-tested bursary – these are only awarded to the eligible boys who scored highest in their tests.

Exit: Almost all juniors progress to the senior school. They have to sit the entrance exam but it's rare for them not to pass. If that did happen it wouldn't be a shock to the parents; they would have known that the child wasn't thriving academically in the junior school and would have been in regular communication with staff to discuss the issues.

Around a quarter leave after GCSEs. Given that almost everyone here is in the top 25 per cent of ability nationally, the spread of universities to which pupils have recently gained entry is solid rather than dazzling. Four to Oxbridge in 2016; other popular destinations include Leeds, Manchester, Newcastle, Sheffield, Durham, Imperial, Edinburgh, Brighton, Loughborough and Warwick. And the school does particularly well with applications to study medicine and dentistry (14 medics in 2016). Pupils told us that they received 'fantastic' support with their university applications.

Money matters: One in five pupils receives a means-tested bursary and half of those have their full fees paid. The school – including the bursary fund – is in robust financial health. Its profit-making arm, Bolton School Services Ltd, generates revenue from venue hire, catering, its coach company and the pre-school nursery.

Remarks: A no-nonsense, busy school where bright boys pick up a great work ethic and a strong community spirit. Excellent teaching, pastoral care and enrichment opportunities and a terrific environment. Difference is celebrated here so there's no typical pupil. It is a big school so a very quiet lad might worry that he'd feel overwhelmed but the school is confident that it has created structures 'to make the big feel small'. We'll give the last words to the mum who told us: 'When we looked round the school Mr Britton said to us: "you'll drop off a young lad at our door and a well-rounded young man will leave." And boy, he did!'

Bolton School Girls' Division

Linked with Beech House, Bolton School Boys' Division

Chorley New Road, Bolton, Lancashire BL1 4PB

Pupils: 947 • Ages: 7–18 • Sixth form: 204

Fees: £9,204 – £11,508 pa

Tel: 01204 840201
Email: seniorgirls@boltonschool.org
Website: www.boltonschool.org

Headmistress: Since 2011, Miss Sue Hincks (40s), a graduate of Magdalen College, Oxford, where she achieved a first in modern languages and history. Previously deputy head at The King's School, Worcester. She enjoys choral singing and walking and is a keen theatre-goer.

This is her first all-girls' environment; she says she is thoroughly enjoying working with such intelligent and feisty girls. Feels that Bolton needs to regain its place alongside the single sex heavyweights in Manchester and wants a school that is very academic but has breadth, and where children leave with fond memories of good times had. Parents tell us she hasn't been afraid to take ownership of the school, and girls sing her praises for attending nearly every school event, including Saturday morning sporting fixtures.

Head of junior school: Since January 2016, Mrs Carol Laverick BSc PGCE, previously headteacher of Westholme Junior School. Local girl (educated Turton High School, followed by maths degree at Edinburgh). First teaching job was as class teacher at St Nicholas' School, Fleet, Hampshire before moving to Bolton School (Girls' Division) initially in similar role and, in final two years, as second mistress of the junior school, before moving to Westholme in September 1999.

Academic matters: The teaching of maths and English is traditional and rigorous in the junior school, but a more creative approach is taken with other subjects. Languages are important here. French is taught right the way through the school, Spanish to years 3, 4 and 5 and Latin to year 6. There are also Italian and German language extracurricular clubs, and the school holds regular international days where the girls are taken off timetable to learn about the cultures of other countries. A member of staff coordinates SEN provision and support is given where required within the classroom, though the school can only cope with limited special needs. Lift access to all floors.

A strongly academic school. In 2016, 71 per cent A*/A at GCSE and 47 per cent at A level (72 per cent A*/B). Maths and science particularly strong, as is DT, with two girls awarded prestigious Arkwright scholarships this year and two full classes running at GCSE.

The sixth form imaginative curriculum enrichment programme aims to broaden and enhance the educational experience and includes sign language, Italian and critical thinking. Alongside the usual, A level options include Greek and theatre studies. Most take four subjects at AS, dropping down to three at A2. Can team up with the Boys' Division to offer subjects where only a few are interested.

Five form entry in year 7 with an average teaching group of 25. This tapers as girls move up the school. Setting in maths from year 7.

Learning support department can't accommodate every SEN as girls must be able to cope with the fast academic pace, but each case is looked at on an individual basis.

Games, options, the arts: Sport is important. Badminton, athletics and dressage all good. School council has been successful in pushing for the introduction of tag rugby and football. Climbing wall and pool shared with Boys' Division, with pool open before school for serious training. Impressive numbers represent town, county and GB in swimming, lacrosse, hockey and cricket.

Drama popular and girls buzzing about frequent productions held in purpose-built theatre. Music also thrives, over 300 girls learn an instrument and the many bands and orchestras combine pupils from the Boys' and Girls' Divisions. Jazz band has performed at the Montreux Jazz Festival. Several girls are members of Manchester's Hallé Choir.

Art is popular with junior school pupils. We were shown a beautiful stained glass window, designed by some of the girls, which has pride of place and of which they are justifiably proud. All children take part in the varied sporting programme which includes netball, athletics, lacrosse and swimming in the senior school's 25m pool, with tag rugby and badminton among the extracurricular activities offered.

Background and atmosphere: History dates back to 1913 when the first Viscount Leverhulme endowed two existing schools to form the Bolton School Foundation, with boys and girls sharing a single site. Grand, grade 2 listed, sandstone building which many pupils described as 'just like Hogwarts'. Located a mile away from Bolton centre in 32 acres of greenery. Strong sense of tradition with an organ played in assemblies and prefects in gowns.

A brand new sixth form centre shared by both the Boys' and Girls' Divisions, though lessons still taught separately. 'The best of both worlds,' states the head. The centre will has Wifi access throughout with pupils able to use 'cloud' data storage. New Girls' dining room and Year 11 common room are latest additions.

Junior school is housed in a modern building where everything the girls could possibly want or need has been catered for (including an iPad for each pupil from 7 to 18). The school boasts its own music rooms, science labs, library, dining hall, ICT suite, sensory garden, art room, netball courts and a playground with amphitheatre seating.

Burgundy uniform liked by girls, but a few parents concerned that the girls looked scruffy. No uniform required in sixth but smart appearance requested. Girls told us that teachers turned a blind eye to the length of skirts and we certainly saw much evidence of this.

Pastoral care, well-being and discipline: Junior school pupils are introduced early on to the 16 habits of mind. These habits, such as finding humour, striving for accuracy and thinking flexibly, are designed to enable the girls think intelligently in all aspects of their lives. The habits are depicted by a gorgeously painted, bright and colourful mural along the main corridor and then constantly reinforced by teachers in lessons, assemblies and classroom displays. 'These habits of mind are terrific,' says one dad. 'My daughter applies them to everything, even the things she does out of school like ballet'.

Peer mentoring by trained members of years 10 and 11 for younger pupils in a specific room on a drop-in basis, with mentors feeding back to staff where necessary. This was much appreciated by pupils we spoke to. Individual circumstances considered when looking at incidents involving drugs and alcohol, but head will expel if needed.

Pupils and parents: Broad socio-economic mix due to the means-tested £2m bursary fund. 'It's no ivory tower,' one parent explained, 'and nor should it be. After all, we want our children prepared for the wider world.' Pupils mainly from Bolton and surrounding areas, many travelling on the bus network shared with Boys' Division. Many pupils from industrious business families, and not unusual for several generations of the same family to come here. One in eight pupils from an Asian background, rising to one in five at sixth form.

Junior school children are well-mannered and purposeful and seemed more than happy to talk to visitors. Year 6 girls excitedly showed us the totem poles they had drawn in art, and a group of year 3 girls eagerly told us how much they loved the new summer dresses the school has introduced.

Old Girls include Monica Ali, author; Dame Janet Smith, former Lady Justice of Appeal; Baroness Morris of Bolton; and Anjali Pathak, brand ambassador for Patak's.

Entrance: Two-form entry to the junior school, Hesketh House, with a maximum of 25 in a class. Most children come from Beech House, Bolton Schools Infant Department, and entry is automatic. External candidates take formal tests in English, maths, verbal and non-verbal reasoning in the January of the year of entry. However, mid-stream enquiries are catered for when places arise.

Around 50 of the year 7 senior school entrants are from the junior school. Others from local preps and state primaries, often tempted to apply here by the many taster days held for year 5s. Very competitive exam at 11 in maths, English, verbal reasoning and non verbal reasoning, followed by interview.

Exit: Almost everyone (99 per cent) from the juniors moves up to the senior school, with a few leaving for local state secondaries or other independent schools. All girls must sit the entrance test and those unlikely to make it are informed in year 5 with guidance and support offered to the girl and her family.

Loses some 10-25 per cent post GCSE (17 per cent in 2016), partially made up by 10 to 15 new arrivals. Small number leave at end of year 12. Girls go on to study a huge range of subjects – business and law to art foundation at mostly good universities across the UK and abroad eg Durham, Leeds, Manchester, Liverpool, Lancaster, Instituto Marangoni, Royal Conservatoire of Scotland, Sofia Medical School, Bulgaria in 2016, together with four to Oxbridge and 12 studying medicine, dentistry or veterinary science.

Money matters: Large bursary fund maintains, as far as possible, the 'principal objectives of the first Lord Leverhulme – that no boy or girl of potential who qualified on academic grounds but whose family were able to offer limited support would be debarred from entry to the school'. School can and will help in unexpected financial crisis. Small, non-means tested academic scholarships now available to pupils entering year 7.

Remarks: A traditional, hard-working, down-to-earth school. Less social stratification here than at some of its counterparts in Cheshire – parents commented on how refreshing this was. One mum got quite choked when she said, 'I watched my daughters walk through that arch as little girls and now they're leaving as educated young women, with strong opinions, ready to face a new era.'

Bootham School

51 Bootham, York, North Yorkshire YO30 7BU

Pupils: 479; 88 full, 14 weekly, 24 flexi boarders (two-thirds boys) • Ages: 3-18 • Sixth form: 175

Fees: Day £6,795 – £17,520; Boarding £19,665 – £30,510 pa

Tel: 01904 623261
Email: admissions@boothamschool.com
Website: www.boothamschool.com

Head: Since September 2016, Christopher Jeffrey BA (50s), previously head of The Grange School, Cheshire. Read history at York. Has also been deputy head at The Perse School, Cambridge. His wife is a nurse; three children. Very involved in the local church, plays the piano and guitar and composes music in his spare time. Fast talking and energetic.

Junior school head: Since 2013, Mrs Helen Todd, previously deputy head at Edge Grove School and before that head of English and drama at Aysgarth School. Married with two young children.

Academic matters: In recent years the school has transformed itself from middle-of-the-road into a Yorkshire leader. Staff aren't exactly sure how this has happened but point to an infectious work ethic ('it's OK to achieve'), backed up by individual attention (Quaker maxim is 'seek that of God in everyone') and powerful sense of community.

National curriculum plus in the junior school: all the basics are soundly covered with extras such as Latin (years 5 and 6), French, German, Spanish (years 2 to 6) and the teaching of thinking skills, all adding to the width and depth. Smartboards in classrooms and extension opportunities for the more able, identified by regular assessment in all areas.

Academic achievement is 'not the be-all and end-all', say parents, but 'results are good nevertheless'. In 2016, 55 per cent A*/A at GCSE, 43 per cent A*/A grades and 76 per cent A*-B at A level. Sees itself as a 'premier science school', and results back this up. English and history popular, excellent art and maths. Class sizes throughout emphatically on the small side. Staff aim to fit A level combinations round pupils' choices, quite a feat in a smallish school. The approach is 'give them room and they'll deliver', which applies equally to staff and pupils. Staff are an engaged and creative bunch. They have room to breathe here and pupils feel the benefit.

Specialist science facilities, new arts centre for music, art and performance, design studios and an IT centre. Wireless network to help laptop users. Excellent John Bright library much used, recent addition of mezzanine floor adding an attractive additional workspace. Teaching lively and interactive; common claim that pupils take responsibility for their own learning and interrogate their teachers carries more weight here than in many schools – an aspect, perhaps, of the Quaker principle of 'speaking truth to authority' (ie don't take it lying down). Has opened its doors by offering masterclasses and summer schools for pupils from other schools, bringing much needed openness across the school community locally and no real surprise that Bootham should drive this. Currently a waiting list for Latin GCSE class for external pupils, all the more impressive as it is run after school.

Wide range of special needs catered for. School goes out of its way to help – ground floor biology lab created to enable pupil with a motor disability to learn alongside her peers.

Games, options, the arts: School encourages sport 'as a healthy part of life that hopefully will be continued'. Sport is played by all for enjoyment, but newish director of sport has brought more training rigour, which had been demanded by some parents. Tennis and football traditionally popular, swimming (own pool), sports hall with climbing wall, no rugby; teams in all sports accommodate everyone, not just the talented. Despite – or because of – this, plenty of creditable achievement all round; basketball team has been district champion, as too were the U18 football team, and individual successes include an international fencer, Olympic swimmer, county netball, hockey and cricket squad members and Leeds academy footballers. Playground cricket is the stuff of legend here and a fiercely guarded tradition – one former pupil went on to become a member of the Hong Kong women's cricket team.

Outstanding design work has received national critical acclaim. Vibrant art department, now housed in new arts centre, with wonderfully creative pupils' work led by practising and exhibiting artists. Music a major strength. Twenty different ensembles and over 60 per cent learn a musical instrument – mainly for enjoyment but many get to grade 8 and beyond, as well as scholarships to London music colleges. Regular buffet concerts held in main hall. Drama also strong; LAMDA on offer.

Expeditions to exotic places like Bolivia, Peru and Iceland and regular exchanges with France and Germany. School has its own well-used observatory (original William Cooke telescope and lovely polished brass fittings) and boasts oldest natural history society in the country.

A school with a conscience, it's no surprise that Bootham is a Fairtrade school and has been named as an Oxfam World Shaper School. It has the highly-regarded Eco-Schools' Ambassador Status Green Flag and can proudly boast that it sends no waste to landfill. BEAST (nickname for Bootham Environment and Sustainability Team) leads the way in reducing the school's carbon footprint, beginning (naturally) in the junior school with mini-BEAST; awarded Eco-Schools Ambassador status – one of only 11 schools in the country – for education leadership in eco matters.

Outdoor learning is taken to another level in the junior school with the forest school in the grounds (racks of wellies in evidence) and yes, they go out in all weathers. All take part in a residential experience (right from reception, which is very rare). It's a gentle start with the youngest children pitching tents in the school hall for an overnight stay, complete with head-torches for a night walk and hot chocolate before bed. Staff and children sleep soundly, anxious parents less so – but the children love it.

Boarding: Good standard of boarding accommodation – possibly better for girls than for boys, but that's not unusual and it bothers the boys less. Flat-sharing for the sixth form (college) girls, which they love and seems sensible in terms of preparation for the future. Good wholesome food, plenty of choice. Day pupils can try boarding in one of many flexible options.

Hard to be bored here – plenty to do, huge range of extracurricular activities after school from bell ringing to water polo; lessons on Saturday morning and fixtures in the afternoon, with evening activities organised by the boarding house teams. Sundays relaxed and informal.

Background and atmosphere: Founded in 1823 on liberal, intellectual, tolerant principles. No need to belong to Society of Friends, or even be Christian, but non-credal umbrella, underlined by regular, silent Meetings, does seem to work a kind of magic, and parents willingly buy into it.

Originally for boys only, became co-ed in 1983. Within shouting distance of the Minster and city walls but the only visible part of the school is the fine Georgian terrace and passers-by would be surprised to learn that the site covers nine acres. From the busy main road, look out for the clearly identifiable Bootham blue-green doors, behind which lie a spacious and tranquil campus, with additional buildings gradually edging alongside. The fact that much of the school is hidden from view adds to an air of mystery about the place, yet the irony is that these buildings house some of the most open-minded people you could ever meet. Original buildings are undergoing a cycle of cosmetic updates and more radical facelifts; new arts centre has greatly boosted arts and music provision and freed up useful space elsewhere.

The junior school is much younger (opened in 1997, on its present site since 2002). Lots of competition locally from good state schools and preps so it's simply a matter of horses for courses. Bootham Junior is smaller than most – only one form entry from nursery up to year 6 – but there is undoubtedly something special about a place for budding young learners run on sound Quaker principles. Staff and children thrive in a warm, calm, happy and purposeful atmosphere – it doesn't leap out at you, it just 'is'.

Junior classrooms are colourful and spacious. Dedicated ICT suite, shared area for art and music and delightful library. Large multi-purpose hall transforms from assembly area to dining room, to PE space and back, throughout the day (plenty of support staff on hand to make it happen). It tells you a lot about a place when you are introduced to the whole team, as we were. Chef was happy to chat about his healthy and child-friendly menu (including delicious homemade bread, cooked daily on the premises). An unprompted and enthusiastic 'really tasty' comment came directly from the children. Picky eaters and allergy sufferers are recognised and cheerfully accommodated. Nobody goes hungry and staff and children happily sit down to eat together.

Lovely outdoor spaces – soft play areas with tricycles, bicycles and toys galore for the youngest children, an adventure playground for the older ones and a vast green field for sport. Tennis and netball courts and the school minibus takes pupils to senior school for a weekly swim from year 2. Raised beds for growing vegetables and quiet sitting areas adjoin the playground, all reassuringly visible from the large plate glass windows of the staff room.

This is a largely non-hierarchical place and not rigidly conformist. Relationships between pupils and staff clearly very good – mutual respect is the order of the day. New pupils surprised and impressed by the fact the 'the head will open a door for you'. Parents comment on friendliness of receptionist, catering and ground staff as well as teaching staff. Younger pupils wear a kind of uniform. A dress code for older ones, though it's not immediately obvious, but an impressive alumni list suggests that perhaps it really doesn't matter as clearly clothes do not necessarily maketh the man. Self-run school council is more than a talking shop and can subject authority to awkward questions about how the school is run. 'Not snobby' say parents, who welcome the fact that pupils are 'encouraged to think about wider social concerns and global issues'.

Slight whinge from some pupils about Saturday morning school, but the upside is that the school is in town and so you can make a quick escape to the shops when lessons are over.

Pastoral care, well-being and discipline: Given the emphasis on a warm, family-type atmosphere, it would be easy to assume a laid-back, rule-less school short on structure and discipline. Not so. Expected standards of behaviour are clear and 'all the usual systems are in place'. No alcohol allowed on premises, suspicion of drug taking renders a pupil liable to random testing, drug peddling leads to expulsion. The key difference is that pupils here are encouraged to consider the effect of their actions on others and that in itself acts as an effective mechanism for self-control, most of the time. In line with the Quaker ethos, pupils say 'school comes down hard on bullying'.

Pupils and parents: Junior school children are bright, chatty and confident, but not obnoxiously so. They also have that rare but essential Quaker ability to maintain thoughtful reflection as necessary. Most are not Quakers (pupils from all backgrounds, all faiths and none), but the ethos pervades and all seem to benefit from this honest, open-minded and peaceful approach to life.

Senior school pupils look like your average floppy-haired teenagers but these are a happy, confident, savvy bunch, probably more comfortable in their own skin than most. A combination of clear yet equitable guidelines and being accepted for what and who you are makes a big difference in these impressionable years. Prospective parents who found themselves being asked a host of questions by their 'delightfully curious' pupil guides signed up immediately – because 'these were the kind of young people we want our children to be'.

No real parent 'type' – more an attitude. Many children of university teachers and medics, plus a raft of curious first time buyers. Once you've had the conversation and removed any preconceived notions, the Quaker reference point makes lots of sense and clearly appeals. Active parents' association holds regular coffee mornings, walks, lectures and a grandparents' day. Weekly recitals – music, poetry-readings and the like – open to all. Regular Saturday morning gatherings with coffee and croissants at no charge – staff often pop in so can be useful for a catch-up. Some even stay for lunch.

Parents say Bootham is 'addictive' and that 'it gets under your skin'. They appreciate the 'open access to teachers via email, enabling parents to discuss any concerns they may have'. Time and time again it's the 'beyond the academic' bit that parents rave about here. Not that there is any lack of academic rigour, there isn't. It's simply that there is something else, not quite tangible and not appearing in league tables, but you can feel it in your bones.

Day pupils mainly from York and up to 25-mile radius of school. Around a quarter of pupils are boarders, nearly 60 per cent from overseas. Of these, 40 per cent are from Hong Kong and 17 per cent from China, with increasing numbers from Nigeria and Russia. They are all English-speaking or near-fluent if not.

Notable former pupils: include AJP Taylor, Brian Rix, Philip Noel Baker (Nobel prizewinner and Olympic medallist), John Bright (parliamentarian), Stuart Rose (former boss of Marks & Spencer), Silvanus Thompson (physicist), plus 16 more fellows of the Royal Society.

Entrance: Into the junior school at any time from nursery to year 6, places permitting. A third of the entry at 11 comes from the junior school, the rest from schools far and wide. Entrants at 11 have an assessment day, at 13 a more traditional exam. For sixth form entry a minimum of seven Cs or six Bs at GCSE required, which must include maths and English. Interview and report from previous school.

Exit: Virtually all junior school pupils move up to the senior school. Some 20 per cent leave post-GCSE, mainly to local sixth form college, either for vocational courses or to avoid Saturday school. Many take gap years. Three to Oxbridge and one medic in 2016; Newcastle popular as well as Durham, Warwick and Exeter. Generally a number to art courses at eg Camberwell, Chelsea & Wimbledon, Leeds College of Art, Manchester School of Art. Psychology a popular course but also engineering and marine biology.

Money matters: Not a rich school: most income generated through fees and fundraising. Some academic scholarships (means-tested), music scholarships (not means-tested) and some special provision for Quaker families.

Remarks: School does well by all and parents say 'differences are celebrated, not shunned or ridiculed'. But don't expect to find a community of meek souls. Far from it. Bootham helps pupils to develop into bright, articulate and considerate individuals. Pupils admit it 'may not suit the highly competitive or the attention-seeker', but having said that, they are quick to add that 'we'd help them to get over themselves..'

Bow Durham School

Linked with Durham School

16

South Road, Durham DH1 3LS

Pupils: 145 • Ages: 3-11 • C of E

Fees: £8,571 – £10,821 pa

Tel: 01913 848233
Email: e.cathrae@durhamschool.co.uk
Website: www.durhamschool.co.uk/prep-school.asp

Head: Since September 2016, Sally Harrod, previously deputy head at Lincoln Minster prep school.

Entrance: Not selective, but low key testing in English, mathematics and verbal reasoning as part of a taster day, plus a reference from current school/nursery. Limited number of means-tested bursaries available at all ages and scholarships from year 3 (maximum £1,000).

Exit: Virtually all to senior school – automatic transfer unless applying for scholarship. Entrance examination only used for assessment purposes.

Remarks: Whilst sitting within the Durham School family, Bow has retained relative independence historically. Founded 1885 as an independent day school for boys 7-13 years, moved to present site in 1888, incorporated into the Durham School Foundation 1976 and formally became the prep for Durham School.

Situated in the heart of leafy suburbs surrounded by academic institutions, the best of the school is not seen on arrival. A rather inauspicious entrance at the back of the original house made us question the satnav, made worse by poor signage to reception. Once we turned the corner (literally), the full extent of the campus was revealed. An eclectic array of buildings, from a toll house 250 years old to red-brick classroom block, sit on an spacious site with cricket square and playgrounds in their midst. A profusion of footballs resonates with the school's roots as a boys' boarding school. Co-ed from 2006, girls make up about a third, but proportion in each class varies, though uniquely boys are completely outnumbered in one prep year group.

Bow has faced strong local competition from good state primary schools and nearby Chorister School, together with an informed and discerning parent body – in Durham education rules ok! Consequently, some years are not at capacity, and pupils are divided into smaller groups for core subjects only.

There is a real drive to raise academic performance throughout both the senior and prep schools. A member of the senior school staff has been seconded to Bow to establish baseline testing and analyse, monitor and review individual pupil progress data. Value-added has always been strong and this emphasis on progress measurement to support individual learning should improve that further.

Prep (7-11 years) mainly sited in the main building (1888), overlooking the cricket square with the cathedral as a backdrop. A red-brick classroom block with later additions and upgrading, though some classrooms are in need of some TLC. Year 3, some year 5 and the science laboratory are located in a block of single storey classrooms a short distance away.

Year 3 is a transition year where children spend 50 per cent of their time with their class teacher studying English, mathematics and humanities. From year 4 it is all specialist teaching and the layout of the buildings means that children need to be organised to ensure they have the right equipment for their lessons and arrive punctually. Good training for senior school life ahead, and it certainly didn't seem to faze those we spoke to.

Small classes divided into two groups for core subjects. Formal French starts in year 3, Latin in year 5; very good key stage 2 results. Wifi now available in most areas, tablets on the way, and networked IT suite, but just two interactive whiteboards (all rooms have a computer and projector). Viewed one put to good use as part of year 5 ancient history topic showing Horrible History Spartans and Athenians.

The children we talked to enjoyed their lessons – 'Lots of fun activities' – and found the teachers helpful. The last ISI inspection recommended 'catering more fully for the able', and there does seem to have been progress in classroom differentiation and opportunities in music, drama and sport, where age is not a barrier to joining a team (subject to the constraints of difference in physical sizes). Strong learning support department led by specialist – close monitoring, in-class support where possible and some outside.

Netball/tennis court, big sports field and shared playing fields with the nearby Chorister School provides good outdoor sports facilities. Multi-purpose sports hall next to pre-prep and shared use of Astro, and indoor swimming pool at senior school, a walk away. Two one hour games sessions a week for years 3 and 4, three for years 5 and 6.

Music and art are housed in The Cottage, 250 years old and listed, originally a toll house on the edge of the campus. Music is strong – well-resourced room and whole class instrumental tuition once a week, starting with fiddlesticks in year 4, moving to ukulele in year 6. Choir, jazz band, Ceilidh band, fiddle group all available. The art room includes facilities for pottery and sculpture as well as drawing and painting. Two plays a year plus speech and drama after school. Wide choice of activities including fencing, judo, gymnastics, table tennis, karate; history visits, trip to Venice and Rome (links with a school there), ski trip to Italy. Excellent outdoor adventure playground in the grounds as well.

Good pastoral care – all new pupils have a guide for the first two weeks. Children feel happy and secure – 'People listen and understand if you've got a problem'. No obvious discipline issues, though we did come across one young girl crying outside a classroom. Staff were aware and ushered her back in on our arrival.

The size of school ensures good links between the year groups and this is enforced with four houses and competitions in sports, swimming and general knowledge. The pupils we met were articulate, open and confident and proud of their school. Praise from the last inspection report – 'well behaved, hard working and polite children'. All year 6s have a turn at being a monitor (prefect). Using the senior school facilities often ensures a smooth transition to senior school.

Lunches were unequivocally declared good, with great choices; milk and apple in dining room at break time for all those that want it.

Pre-prep (5-7 years) housed in a designated building close to the sports hall. Core subjects plus French, history, geography, RE, IT, music and art; good results in key stage 1 tests. Cheerful classrooms with good displays and we saw evidence of good teacher/pupil relationships, though the children's behaviour rapidly declined into noisy activity without their teacher's attention. Use of the sports hall, IT suite and library in Bow; children swim all year round at Durham City Freemans Quay leisure centre or Chester le Street leisure centre. Concerts, nativity play, fundraising for charities, after-school clubs include fencing, judo, percussion, speech and drama. Prepared for transition to prep through attending their assemblies, house competitions, some sport with older pupils and a longer day in summer term.

Early years housed in Quarryheads House, a splendid, 100 year old, former family home (originally assigned to the head of Bow), next to main Bow buildings – white with big bay windows, a red slate roof and white chimney, resembling a children's storybook illustration. This area of the school is led by an experienced and enthusiastic practitioner, passionate and knowledgeable about children's early education, their emotional learning and how to encourage independence – and it shows.

Badger nursery (3-4 years) is on ground floor, and opening the door is like lifting the lid of Pandora's box; a treasure trove of discovery, with stimulation, free flow play and pupil-led learning. We particularly liked the fact that plans for the play corner were changed to a camping out theme in response to requests from the children. The chart of the tree of growing kindness recording small milestones in the journey of socialisation was another lovely idea. Three outdoor areas for soft play, mud play and tranquility. Read Write Inc for those who are ready links into the work that continues in reception.

The nursery works very closely with reception and the transition is very carefully managed. Reception has a terrific, large, open plan space on the first floor with different learning sections and views of trees. Behind it is the Beaver transition area, for older children, a quirkily shaped room with several nooks and crannies, next to the pleasant welcome room for parents. Well equipped – interactive whiteboard, large plasma screen; delightful outdoors play area. Supportive parents: 'Very good attention from the teachers'.

Whilst they feel that their children are happy, parents we spoke to felt that the school could be doing more to build and encourage solid learners. 'Many small improvements could be made to the school,' said one.

Bradford Girls' Grammar School

Linked with Lady Royd Primary

Squire Lane, Bradford, West Yorkshire BD9 6RB

Pupils: 1,051 • Ages: 11–18 • Sixth form: 130

Tel: 01274 545395
Email: headsec@bggs.com
Website: www.bggs.com

Principal: Since 2009, Mrs Kathryn Matthews BSc (40s), educated at Loreto Grammar School in Manchester, then maths and an MA in education at Leeds University. Taught maths at London Oratory; deputy head at Gateways School, Leeds. ISI team inspector and governor at Westbourne Prep in Sheffield. Married with adult children. Enjoys theatre, visiting art galleries, reading and rugby union. Warm and approachable, she is both incisive and refreshingly honest; parents tell us she is absolutely key in retaining their confidence in the school as it evolves. She knows a good teacher when she sees one; valuing staff who can enthuse pupils, she is judicious in her appointments and keen to foster talent at all levels. Having led the school through choppy waters of late, she is determined to maintain the school's high academic standards and enable girls from the local community to succeed: nothing has changed here in that respect.

Academic matters: A non-selective free school since September 2013, it was always strong on value-added and still is. A good way above the national average at both GCSE and A level. Whilst there is an apparent dip in results from previous years, this appears to be as a result of the move to a free school. Put simply, the majority of girls sitting exams here in 2016 hadn't been at the school long so were playing catch up to a certain extent, and therefore the quality of teaching and learning isn't yet reflected in the results – but it will be, no doubt, in time. What the data does show, however, is that the longer the girls are in the school, the better they do.

A level 49 per cent A*-B, 19 per cent A*/A in 2016. Surprisingly wide range of subjects for such a relatively small sixth form, with some subjects run for small numbers; far bigger numbers for maths and sciences than arts and languages; excellent art. At GCSE 30 per cent A*/A in 2016, 65 per cent achieved at least five GCSEs A*/C including English and maths. French, German, Spanish and Latin available for linguists; RE hugely popular and successful right up to A level.

Most girls take nine GCSEs; sciences (all three) are hugely popular and extremely successful. Class sizes up to 28, slightly higher than the 24 ceiling parents had hoped for, so they are watching carefully, but in the school's defence, the increased number is in response to local demand and the need for more secondary school places. Good careers advice and university preparation – girls rave about the quality UCAS advice. The principal takes all girls through their personal statement, useful in giving some of these highly intelligent but utterly modest girls a nudge forward in understanding how to sell themselves when applying for highly competitive university places.

A good number of new staff have joined as a result of the rapid growth of the school, some NQTs, others with a wealth of experience – all seem to be bringing new energy and impetus. No lack of rigour and a strong work ethic – heads down, focused in classrooms and plenty of challenge on offer. 'It's a virtuous circle,' says the principal. 'The girls here are a joy to teach so you can have fun with them and they lap it up' – a revelation for some of the newer teachers who are enjoying the opportunity simply to teach rather than wade through behaviour issues on a daily basis.

SEN department grown from scratch. Now under the watchful eye of Ofsted, there is much more scrutiny all round. School makes good use of LA and national resources and liaises well with parents. Teaching assistants provide support for pupils with a variety of cognitive and sensory difficulties and HTLA support is available for more vulnerable pupils and those who are completely new to English.

Games, options, the arts: Good facilities include an Astroturf, purpose-built sports hall and a swimming pool used by all, right through from the junior school. Good number and range of sports on offer – the girls are not big on contact sport but other choices are wide and varied and the enthusiastic sports staff seem to get everyone moving. Table tennis, cross-country, netball and rounders are especially popular, as is dance, and the girls regularly take part in county, regional and national competitions.

'Music could do better,' admits the school, but recently appointed staff are on the case. Good choir and steel band; peripatetic teachers offer individual tuition in a range of instruments and support the school orchestra as it matures. Drama is popular, currently working on a production of Oliver! Stunning art on display all around the school and some very elaborate textiles greet you on entry. Sixth formers squeeze much into their already-busy schedules with World Challenge, Duke of Edinburgh, National Citizenship Service (NCS), LEAP enterprise, The Community Volunteering Programme (CVP), Sports Leadership Award and Outward Bound programme. Two – carefully selected – girls visit Auschwitz each year. Sports and academic trips to Spain, France, Switzerland, USA and Malawi.

Background and atmosphere: Much remains unchanged – the uniform is the same and the Yorkshire Mouseman furniture is still here, as is the lovely atrium housed in the centre of the original building. The site is attractive, something of a green oasis within the city landscape. The main 1930s building sits alongside a modern purpose-built sixth form building within 17 acres of well-tended games fields, lawns and gardens. Classrooms have had a facelift, there are new lockers, and the place is spotless, with floors so shiny they would impress the neighbouring hospital. The science labs remain in their original 1930s state – nostalgic for some, 'museum pieces' to others, that said, parents describe the science department staff as 'masters [sic] of their craft', so although updated labs are on the wishlist, they are clearly not critical. A number of the senior staff have been here for a good while, 'a good thing,' say parents; they have managed the transition whilst watching the school grow exponentially. As far as structural changes go, the roof's been mended, as has the heating, there's better security all round and, most importantly, the school's future has been secured ad infinitum.

Pastoral care, well-being and discipline: Good pastoral care. Alert to the usual problems coming from girls putting too much pressure on themselves to succeed, but 'nothing that can't be managed by working with parents', according to Mrs Matthews. Sensible, enlightened anti-bullying procedures, sanctions and rewards policies. Younger girls look neat and tidy in their uniform; no uniform for sixth form but there is a dress code of 'business wear' – rather too loosely interpreted by some. Established parents worry that there are now greater demands on the staff and are crossing fingers that standards do not slip as the school reshapes itself. Any concerns are centred on maintaining standards of uniform and behaviour rather than anything academic – it's a watching brief.

Pupils and parents: Parents are a diverse social mix as befits the local area and demographic, but for the most part, what they do share is aspiration. Those girls joining midway through the school – the 'joiners' – are finding their feet, academically and socially, adapting to new policies and procedures, although the transition from local state schools into this former fee-paying grammar was undoubtedly easier for some than others. The 'aspire, succeed, lead' ethos remains and former grammar brigade are reassured by that. It's a complicated landscape in Bradford where, as a designated area of need, a good education is given high status by many and there is no lack of will from most parents for their daughters to succeed. Predominantly Asian families, the ethnic mix is not as wide as it once was, though the school remains non-denominational. Girls are proud to be here and in return they work hard and relish the opportunities – 'D of E take up is brilliant,' say staff, and the amount of voluntary work jammed in alongside studies by the sixth form girls is remarkable. When asked about the increase in class and overall school size, their response is typically candid and clear cut: 'We fall out less because there are more girls to be friends with now, but the lunch queues are longer..' Responsibility is encouraged, there is a school president with deputies, a sixth form committee and elected form prefects – all relics of the school in its previous existence, but still an intrinsic part of the 'new' school and all about recognising and promoting leadership potential.

Strong links with parents and old girls, who include Barbara Castle, Rebecca Sarker (TV actress), Jill McGivering (BBC foreign correspondent), Isobel Hilton (journalist), Pippa Wells (CERN astrophysicist) and Anita Rani (TV presenter and journalist).

Entrance: According to a recent report, this school is now the most oversubscribed in the country pro rata. Over 500 applied for 50 places in 2016 so it's a bit of a lottery, but the admissions process is squeaky clean with much time and attention given to ensuring that it remains so. Non-selective; automatic admission from the junior school (Lady Royd, onsite); five A*/C at GCSE essential for a sixth form place.

Exit: Those leaving post-GCSE do so to move on to further education and/or employment. Big pull post A level to Yorkshire universities – Leeds, Bradford and Huddersfield are very popular. One to Oxford and one to the USA in 2016, smaller numbers to Essex, Nottingham, Sussex and Chester. Majority heading for medicine, dentistry, pharmacy, optometry, radiography, biomedical sciences, maths and engineering – these girls love their sciences. Smaller numbers into law, English, history and psychology, a few take gap years.

Remarks: There was a very long queue to register for places right down the school driveway and beyond when it was announced, in 2013, that this longstanding traditional girls' school was to become a free school. Whilst now hugely oversubscribed, they have managed the transition extremely well, updating where necessary whilst wisely hanging on to the traditions and values that gave this school its good name.

Bradford Grammar School

Keighley Road, Bradford, West Yorkshire BD9 4JP

Pupils: 1,242 • Ages: 6-18 • Sixth form: 249

Fees: £9,645 – £12,321 pa

Tel: 01274 553702
Email: hmsec@bradfordgrammar.com
Website: www.bradfordgrammar.com

Headmaster: Since January 2016, Dr Simon Hinchliffe, previously deputy head. Geography degree from Durham, a masters in education leadership and management from the OU, and a PhD from St Andrews in geography and geoscience. Spent 14 years at Wolverhampton Grammar, where he was head of sixth form. Lives with Heidi, also a teacher, and their two young children.

Acting head: Kerry Howes is holding the fort at the junior school.

Academic matters: Junior school has specialist teaching for art, modern foreign langs (introduction to French, German, Spanish from year 4), music, PE and games; separate sciences start in year 5. Impressive, very well-resourced DT and very advanced computing syllabus for all ages – dynamic curriculum leader. Children stretched and pushed when needed, say parents – individualised approach. Success in national science competition. Strong creative writing – prizes in national and local competitions and plenty of lively pieces in own school magazine, Clockwise.

In 2016, 55 per cent A*/A grades at A level – generally strong over last three years; GCSE: 71 per cent A*/A grades; in top 200 nationally. Strong and popular maths and sciences (with girls too) and successful arts. Particularly wide choice of languages – all do French, German, Latin in years 7-8; year 9 can also do Spanish, Russian and Greek. Ten GCSEs taken (very sane number), including separate sciences and a modern language. Wide A level choice, including electronics, geology, music technology, plus non-examined general studies course or Japanese. Gains honours in national academic and creative writing competitions.

Class sizes range from around 16 in junior school to 24 in senior school to 10 or so in the sixth form. Pupils we met enthusiastic about lessons – 'You learn a lot and have fun', 'You are encouraged to read beyond the exam syllabus and think independently from a young age' (sixth former). Teachers seen as supportive and treating pupils as individuals; classroom atmosphere not neurotically competitive: the main message is 'Do the best you can'; plenty of extra help available at lunch time clubs.

Special needs mainly dyslexia, dyspraxia, Asperger's, mild autism and physical disabilities (not severe behavioural problems). Close links between junior and senior schools. All year 7s screened for dyslexia and reading levels checked in year 9. Extra individual and small group support outside the classroom – students make very good progress. Study skills sessions in years 10 and 11 for all. Plenty of gifted and talented opportunities – flexible approach to specific needs.

Games, options, the arts: All fields on site, plus swimming pool. Major focus on rugby; all the usual sports, except for football, with lots of minor ones, eg water polo, table tennis, golf, rowing, sailing, triathlon and climbing. High powered coaches (junior school as well) for rugby, netball and hockey (fields several teams for each; all juniors represent the school at some point); individual sporting super stars in cycling and water sports, wheelchair basketball, indoor rowing.

Flourishing music in junior school, also with inclusive approach – large orchestra, diversity of groups, including samba, zylophone, guitar. Two choirs – performances with Bradford Cathedral choristers, BBC recordings, prizes at local and regional festivals. Music production every other year and house music competition. Very high standard of music in seniors with huge number of concerts – several orchestras and groups, including electric guitar and the Dixieland Crackerjacks; choirs; music tour in Italy; world champion indoor percussionist, Royal College of Organists associate, members of National Youth Orchestra and Training Choir.

Lots of drama productions by all years in 1980s Hockney Theatre: varied choices, some home grown, musicals every other year – Under Milk Wood, We Will Rock You, Shakespeare Schools Festival, Greek classical plays, Our Country's Good, The Trial – plus lots of theatre-going. Participates in Shakespeare Schools Festival.

Much impressive art on display around the school and in the five art rooms – particularly good oils; all A level students do life drawing class, quite a few progress to art college; work exhibited at Saltaire Arts Trail. DT department has a 3D printer (very upmarket); participation in Formula One in Schools Racing Car Design competition; Arkwright engineering scholars.

Cheerleading club has won UK national championship for past three years. Over 20 junior school clubs including gardening, rock band, thinking skills, philosophy, computer programming, mathletics; digital leaders support pupils, parents and staff. All juniors have chance to be on school council and take on responsibilities (no prefects). Outdoor pursuits residentials for almost all years and French ski trip.

Masses of senior school clubs (one hour 20 minute lunch hour), some run by students, eg Japanese, Chinese, several D of E golds, RAF and army CCF, stitching, philosophy, yoga, Fairtrade, Amnesty International; lower and upper school councils. Sixth formers mentor young carers in conjunction with Barnardo's. Current whole school Wednesday afternoon dedicated to extracurricular activities likely to be modified soon, to create more teaching time, but 'It has to be done in a civilised way,' says deputy head. Trips to Europe, New York, World Challenge in China.

Biennial careers evening, themed business lunches for sixth formers and visiting professionals, work experience at end of years 11 and 12.

Background and atmosphere: Founded in 1548, re-established by Royal Charter as the Free Grammar School of Charles II at Bradford,1662. Present incarnation, in Frizinghall, in lavish 25 acre campus on the outskirts of Bradford, completed 1937 but commandeered by the army during the war (wooden panels hidden by canny bursar to save them from becoming firewood), so only moved from the inner city in 1949, as a direct grant grammar. Became independent in 1975 and fully co-educational

Original building of mellow gritstone supplemented by attractive, coherent modern additions, including spacious bridge linking old and new parts, with view of open country.

B

New £2m library. Grand mock-gothic school hall, rather let down by brown plastic seating, bedecked with trad portraits of past heads, plus a more modest one – by OB David Hockney. The longest serving headmaster, the Rev Keely, 1872-1916, established the modern school as an academic powerhouse and died in 1916, devastated by the large losses of OBs in the war.

Calm atmosphere, even at changeover times, supported by soothing large fish tank in main corridor. Weekly religious assemblies – Christian, Islamic, Sikh and Hindu. Whole school recently inspired by an assembly given by an ex-scholarship boy who made a huge fortune by his mid 20s, realised this didn't make him happy and subsequently built a quarter of a million homes in the Philippines, taking 50,000 out of poverty. Another that made a powerful impact was by a sixth form boy who talked about being homosexual (and had a prominent article about attending the Stonewall Education Conference in the school magazine); online pledge to tackle the use of homophobic language in the process of development. One of the older boys we met spoke of being encouraged to be creative and help others as well as to achieve highly in life, and of the value the school attaches to the arts. Cross-year friendships common through the wealth of activities.

Plenty of well-regarded food choices, all at the same reasonable price and unlimited amounts – hot and salad options, Jamie Oliver flavour of the month, plus sixth form café – pasta, panini and chips. Ordinary cafeteria for the hoi polloi and very fetching eating area for staff and prefects overlooking large, airy sixth form centre/social area – much pine, artificial trees. Minor grumble by younger pupils about overcrowded locker room – plans to rectify this. We do wonder about the new white and burgundy striped shirts: smart, but make the pupils look like incipient City types and set parents back considerably more than the previous plain white ones – wistful murmurings about M&S good value (school is having a re-think about this); the exclusively online ordering system has also proved problematic.

Junior school opened in 1974, in grounds of senior school, on edge of Bradford; co educational since 1999. Attractive modern building – converted stables from original 1930s school – but could do with some more space and all rooms and corridors dependent on artificial light. Very large, versatile hall with original Hockney paintings (sent by iPad). Library well stocked with fiction (reading popular), but situated in senior school. Much use of senior facilities – for science, art, theatre, sports.

Pastoral care, well-being and discipline: The junior school children we met were confident, articulate and thoughtful, appreciative of lively lessons and the varied extracurricular offer. They see the school as friendly, supportive and harmonious, allowing individuality, emphasising respect and trust, and feel bullying is rare and dealt with firmly. Parents given guide to safe internet use and hard-hitting video shown to older children. Well-disciplined classrooms – the little ones looking comically like mini City gents in the new (very expensive) maroon striped shirts.

Usual structures in senior school, plus prefects trained to be mentors to younger pupils. Mixed year sixth form tutor groups enable first years to benefit from support by second years. Two part-time nurses and a part-time counsellor – 'fantastic support for very ill children' (parent); alert to body image problems in boys and girls. Students we met confident bullying rare and dealt with well (endorsed by parent): awareness has been raised (including of cyber-bullying issues), which has led to more kindness – council for bullying with representatives from all forms trained to look out for vulnerable pupils. Thoughtful year 7 transition: activity day in July; induction evening end August; residential at activity centre early in winter term; classes carefully planned to mix children from junior and other schools. Commendations, certificates and colours for academic prowess and contribution to wider school life. Tough on drugs – possession and supplying.

Pupils and parents: Catchment area is West Yorkshire plus small areas of North Yorkshire and Lancashire – majority from Ilkley, Bingley and surrounding areas. Socially and ethnically mixed, reflecting area's demographics. Close to Frizinghall railway station, allowing convenient access by the Hogwarts Express, as the school calls it.

Notable old pupils: David Hockney (takes an active interest); Denis Healey; Sir Ken Morrison (executive chairman of Morrisons); Dan Scarbrough (England rugby player, on staff); Alistair and Jonathan Brownlee (British Olympic triathletes); a head of BBC news, director of the Royal College of Music, ex-Lord Mayor of London and Archbishop of York.

Entrance: Ages 6 to 8, by classroom assessment – a day at school, taking part in class and individual activities, in spring term. At age 9 and 10, exams in English and maths (past papers available). Interview for borderline candidates. At 11, 12 and 13: exams in English and maths (past papers available) in January, plus interview early February. Automatic entry for pupils from the junior school. Taster session at school before acceptance deadline. Candidates for sixth form need minimum 20 GCSE points (A*=4, C=1) with at least A in English and maths and any subject to be taken further; interview and reference from current school.

Exit: Almost all juniors to senior school without sitting 11+. Small number leaves post-GCSE for colleges, music schools and other local state grammars. Sixth formers head for a broad range of universities: Newcastle, Birmingham, Nottingham; Russell Group, London colleges, usually several to Oxbridge – five in 2016. Great diversity of subjects, top share going to medicine/dentistry, engineering, science, economics, business.

Money matters: Very good value – fees at lower end of the scale. Fifteen to 20 per cent have means-tested bursary from school's endowment plus assistance from former pupils, local and national businesses in UK and America (around a million a year allocated to this). Music scholarships cover cost of tuition.

Remarks: Thriving, friendly school with tolerant attitudes and broad values – we hope the curriculum refocusing, designed to promote academic stardom, will preserve these.

Bury Grammar School Girls

Bridge Road, Bury, Lancashire BL9 0HH

Pupils: 765 • Ages: 3–7 (boys), 3–18 (girls) • Sixth form: 93

Fees: £7,758 – £10,440 pa

Tel: 01617 972808
Email: info@bgsg.bury.sch.uk
Website: www.bgsg.bury.sch.uk

Headmistress: Since 2015, Jo Anderson, previously principal of the Girls' Division of the King's School in Macclesfield. Modern languages degree from Leeds, where she also trained as a teacher and completed a masters in education. Has taught at Leeds High, Stockport Grammar, the Queen's School Chester and Manchester Grammar, where she was appointed deputy head of sixth form. She lives in Stockport with her husband and two children, plays the flute and piano, and lists her hobbies as music, politics and swimming.

Head of girls' junior school: Since 2009 Vicki Hall BSc, who added head of the coeducational infant school in 2012 when the previous head retired. Parents approve of this structure, both for the continuity and because Mrs Hall is well liked. She and her two deputies are a dynamic team, and their energy and enthusiasm colour the atmosphere throughout the school.

Academic matters: Children learn in a relaxed atmosphere at the junior school but there is nothing relaxed about the teaching where the emphasis is on thinking skills and independent research, developing the ability to ask good questions in this world of search engines. 'The girls are encouraged to go off on a tangent with subjects they particularly enjoy,' says head. 'We want to move away from spoon feeding.' Sats were abandoned long ago; 'They depress everybody,' says head. 'There are lots of other, more effective ways of assessing and tracking.'

Classes are dynamic and memorable. Lively with lots of movement, desks moved around as necessary; we witnessed laughter and fun but no loss of control. 'We work on mutual respect,' says head and parents concur, all describing behaviour as exemplary. 'It's all about positive reinforcement, and my daughter knows she will be listened to and taken seriously.' Girls are also encouraged to acknowledge kindness and can nominate each other for the 'courtesy cup'.

A new initiative sees French, German and Spanish, previously taught from year 5, introduced from year 3. Classes are mixed ability although maths is set in year 5 and 6, but parents say, 'If your child needs more she gets more, whether to be stretched or supported, without it ever being an issue'.

Monthly book reviews have to include a broad range, novels, poetry and non-fiction. 'It's a great idea although it can become a bit of a whole family thing,' said one parent, but on the whole parents agree homework is not onerous and 'always has a point.'

This is a hard working school with high value-added scores. In 2016, 30 per cent A*/A grades and 73 per cent A*/B at A level, and 59 per cent A*/A at GCSE. No IB; maths IGCSE available for some. Wide range of options available at A level – 25 subjects on offer with some less mainstream subjects jointly taught with Bury Grammar School for Boys. Class sizes are small and extra support is available in lunchtime clubs or one-to-one sessions. 'The school quickly identifies and addresses areas of weakness', according to one parent. The results are strong, especially in maths and science. Psychology, taught by the SENCo, is also successful and popular. Only a handful of mild SENs, no statements and no one requiring extra time despite the thorough support available. School 'doesn't discriminate'.

Although languages are strong at GCSE, only a handful take them at A level, despite smartly refurbished language suites and pictorial evidence of lots of trips and exchanges. Surprisingly few pursue art or music to A level, but perhaps this will change with opening of the new arts centre and improvement of facilities.

ICT suites, and technology in general, have been overhauled. Interactive white boards are everywhere and fully used – even by teachers of a certain age. Apparently some viewed them with reluctance until, as one pupil said, 'they realised what they can do and now they are all really enthusiastic.'

The environment is disciplined but the classes are relaxed and buzzy, with lively discussion encouraged. We witnessed a debate about the Second World War in a history class – much laughter despite differences of opinion. Humour is important in the teaching and some of the staff could give alumna Victoria Wood a run for her money. Parents told us that good relations between staff and pupils get the best out of even the most timid girls.

Ample individual support is given to sixth formers when choosing courses and working through the UCAS process. 'They really care where you go', one pupil said. Old girls come back to do interview practice – a great idea.

Games, options, the arts: Plenty of music in the junior school; 65 per cent have individual music lessons, strings in years 3 and 4, flutes in year 5 and 6. The girls are welcomed into the orchestra 'if you can hold a bow.' Also choirs and recorder groups. We witnessed a lively and impressive rehearsal of the end of year musical, Robin Hood, involving the whole junior section of the school.

Lots of other extracurricular, from puzzles and logic to tag rugby, some during lunchtime, some after school. Plenty of trips, both local and further afield; skiing in Italy, theatre in London and huge enthusiasm for the outdoor pursuits trip to Plas Menai. Eager, confident, articulate girls described their school council duties, which include recycling (the school recently was given a silver eco award) and pooling ideas for improvements from their class suggestion box, with obvious pride when they are realised.

Facilities at the senior school include five new netball courts, on-site games fields and a shared swimming pool. Teams compete locally and across Manchester. Less sporty girls are encouraged to participate and for the younger years, squads are enhanced by clubs. Occasional taster sessions for less mainstream options, including fencing and martial arts. New all-weather pitch to be shared with the boys' grammar.

A variety of music groups, with some of the choirs and orchestras run jointly with the boys' school. The standard is high but there are opportunities for the less gifted to join in. One parent said, 'My daughter's life now revolves around her music but it was the school that recognised and brought out her talent.' Every year the two schools stage an ambitious musical production – 'spectacular', according to a parent.

Impressive choice of over 70 lunchtime activities from D of E to street dancing, Lego robotics, Italian and knitting. CCF, long established at the boys' school, has recently been extended to the girls and is increasingly popular. One pupil assured us that 'you actually cope better with your workload when you're busy'.

Lots of opportunities for foreign travel, with language exchanges, skiing and music trips, all organised well in advance (payments broken down to make them as accessible as possible).

Background and atmosphere: Independent but with a traditional grammar school feel, rooted in the local community with a strong sense of the pragmatic Lancashire character. Parents say school is friendly, welcoming and 'truly genuine'. School was founded in 1884 and amalgamated with the boys' school in 1906. Boys moved to a separate site across the road in 1965. Strong links are maintained, with some combined teaching in the sixth form and a variety of shared activities. The two schools also share kitchens and both dining rooms are in the boys' building. The girls' prep and mixed infants are on the same site and although separate, there is plenty of contact with the younger children.

School doesn't have a grand entrance and the maze-like feel of the buildings, which have been developed and added to over its century of existence, was amplified when we visited by building work. Leading off the beautiful old hall – 'the school's soul' – with war memorials and portraits rooting it in its history, the new arts centre certainly looks to the future. Airy, bright and sharply modern, it offers much-needed accommodation to the art and textiles department and brings the library into the heart of the school. New sixth form centre for boys and girls is impressive and includes classrooms and common rooms.

The 1990s junior school building has airy, modern classrooms, well equipped and full of colourful displays of work. A huge, bright music room doubles for dance and drama and twice weekly junior assemblies. The library, colour-coded for ease of use, is also home to the well used and much appreciated wrap-around care. The spacious, dedicated junior playground has plenty to do, from climbing frames to a bug hotel, and grow bags full of potatoes – dug up and given to the kitchens. Year 6s work a rota to be play leaders for the infants, creating obstacle courses from the shed full of toys – requested through school council and paid for by the PA. Playground rules are taken seriously and, according to the girls, no-one should be left out and there certainly didn't appear to be any lost souls during the play break we witnessed.

Separate infants and nursery building is a lovely dynamic, safe space. Filled with light and colour, the facilities are thoughtful and creative and everything is accessible. The central octagonal hall, airy and bright, is used for twice weekly assemblies for the whole of the prep and for the junior productions. A busy, continuous play area, between the reception classroom and the nursery encourages children to be outside as much as possible, aided also by the rack of colourful wellies on hand.

Public spirit is a fundamental here. Every senior school form gets a charity to support and members are encouraged to work as a team to raise funds. Environmental concerns are taken ultra-seriously, with as much as possible recycled. Salad boxes are salvaged from the kitchens by the school's eco club and given to the gardening club to use as seed trays. Lights are turned off. The healthy eating tuck shop thrives, although someone stuck up 'RIP' when the vending machines were taken away. Not that the school needs a vending machine – they have cake sales galore.

Pastoral care, well-being and discipline: A grounded and sunny junior school with all the nurture afforded by its small size and, thanks to its proximity and links to the senior school, all the facilities and advantages of a large one. Shared major facilities include all sports and the swimming pool, home economics rooms, the dining rooms and the fabulous new arts centre. A shared perspective allows the sense of a caring and stable community to filter throughout. All contributes to the easy passage from juniors to seniors and the strong sense of being part of the whole.

The senior school is proud of its pastoral systems and the general view from parents and pupils is that they are right to be so. Queen bees don't thrive here, whether they are held in check or just don't come. A parent who moved her daughter, previously bullied at another school, told us she was grateful for the subtlety and extent of support given and impressed at how quickly she settled and gained confidence. When we visited it was notable how at ease the girls were with each other. Lots of teamwork, clear codes of conduct and a small environment where all are known as individuals. Unacceptable behaviour is swiftly dealt with and a parent described the school as a 'tight ship where expectations are clear'.

School council is proactive and the girls definitely have a voice and ability to bring change. The school uniform has been redesigned with the girls opting to change their distinctive pale blue jumper for a more ordinary navy version, lighter blazer and 'more flattering' skirt.

Pupils and parents: The largely local junior school parents are full of praise and very involved, and the much valued PA is thriving. Communication is described as excellent and Mrs Hall is readily available to address questions or concerns. 'She is brilliant at diffusing problems, nothing is ever allowed to escalate.' The result is a cheerful, secure and stimulating environment producing well-balanced, confident girls who have had plenty of fun on the way.

Girls do travel in from as far afield as Rochdale and Prestwich. Backgrounds are broad and culturally diverse, but this is not a glossy school, and the fees represent significant outlay for most families. Parents are very involved with an active and thriving PTA.

Entrance: Entrance into the co-ed nursery and pre-school at 3-4 years to become Fledglings or Cygnets (following the swan emblem of Bury Grammar). Children are invited to an assessment half day, 'warm and friendly,' say parents, 'not at all daunting'. Looking for 'children who want to engage with life and learning ... a sparkle in the eye,' says head, but they don't turn many away and if they feel the child is not ready they will suggest a reassessment in six months. An extra class is added to infant school at reception and admission is similar, following a relaxed half day spent with peer group.

Entrance to the juniors at 7 (girls only) is on a mutually convenient day with more formal written assessments within the classroom, a reference from the current school and a brief interview with the head, all very relaxed and enjoyable and the children leave having had fun. The evaluation is of the child's ability and potential and not her previous education.

At 11, exam papers in maths, English with essay and verbal reasoning plus reference from previous school and an interview – all granted equal importance. 'Some of our highest flyers at GCSE were unremarkable in the exam but demonstrated their potential in the more relaxed interview.' Automatic entrance for girls at junior school since beginning of year 5.

Exit: The internal testing at 7+ for girls has recently been stopped and children are only ever asked to leave at this point if there is a major problem, which most likely has already been flagged up. At age 7 the boys move over from the co-educational infants to join the junior section of Bury Grammar School for Boys. Almost all junior girls to the senior school (over 80 per cent in 2016) with only a handful going elsewhere, a couple to other independents and a few to the state sector. The transition is managed well in advance and the year 7s make booklets for the year 6s giving advice and describing their own experiences.

Up to 30 per cent move on after GCSEs. Sixth formers don't head very far to university – Lancaster popular, followed by Edinburgh, Keele and Leeds. Two to Oxbridge in 2016. Head of sixth form believes this is gradually changing, as the school starts to offer more opportunities for gifted students, and more are looking to study further afield. Medicine (11 places in 2016) and science particularly popular, plus degrees targeting professions.

Money matters: Means-tested bursaries available; they operate on a sliding scale and are strictly monitored, always with home visits. Awards are based on a combination of strong academic performance in the entrance exam and financial need. Scholarships awarded in 2016 for the first time for gifted mathematicians, scientists, musicians, sportswomen and students of English.

Remarks: A happy school that really cares. The nurturing family atmosphere gets results and produces girls who are both mature and confident. Down-to-earth, academic girls will do well here.

Canon Slade CofE School

Bradshaw Brow, Bolton, Lancashire BL2 3BP

Pupils: 1,695 • Ages: 11–18 • Sixth form: 350 • C of E

Tel: 01204 333343
Email: contact@canon-slade.bolton.sch.uk
Website: www.canon-slade.bolton.sch.uk

Head Teacher: Since 2014, Mr Alan Mottershead MA (Oxon) PGCE (50s), previously head of Trinity School in Carlisle for 12 years. English degree and PGCE from Oxford. Returning to his roots – his second teaching post was at Canon Slade. This is his third headship. Married to Ann (whom he met at Oxford); they have three grown up children. He's a member of the Soil Association and Woodland Trust, likes fell-walking and river swimming, as well as gardening and orchard planting, and his favourite place is the National Gallery in London.

Academic matters: Intake from the whole ability range and results generally consistently well above average, with an improvement in both GCSE and A level results in 2016 – 27 per cent A*/A grades at GCSE; at A level, 29 per cent A*/A (60 per cent A*-B).

Performing arts particularly strong, reflecting specialist college status; top school nationally for the AVCE vocational performing arts for boys and pupils regularly hit the top five per cent of results nationally at all levels in drama and dance, as well as in modern languages. ICT results were notably disappointing in comparison, but school says they are greatly improving thanks to new head of department, new computer suites and plenty more computers around the school for use in private study. Ambitious gifted and talented programme. Target setting through all years – 'You've got to be prepared to work hard here,' say pupils, 'but they don't leave anyone behind; everyone's encouraged to do their best'. Pupils praise teaching staff, who are 'always on hand at lunch time and after school to give extra help and run extra revision classes before public exams'.

Annual 'walking on water' competition, with physics department giving teams £50 from gifted and talented budget to design and make shoes that'll race across the surface of the swimming pool. History trips to European battlefields and language exchanges with France, Germany and Spain as well as with twin schools in Germany, Spain and Japan. Latin available at both GCSE and A level, even for just one student – 'We'd be loath to give it up'.

Games, options, the arts: Specialist college status for performing arts with extensive opportunities. Drama and dance studios with full length mirrored walls, state-of-the-art sound recording studio with full time technician and school hall with traditional stage for renowned high standard productions. Over 20 per cent of pupils play an instrument and contribute to more than a dozen varied ensembles and Young Musician of the Year competition as part of school arts festival. 'We're sympathetic to those offered contracts with theatre companies or orchestras,' says head, 'as long as their academic life doesn't suffer.' Extensive art rooms are ripe with fruit of pupils' labours – 'You have to knuckle down in here,' they say, 'and we've got our own kiln'. Range of design and tech rooms full of beavering students and from the food tech room a view of the out-of-bounds pond that's protected habitat for an endangered gold-crested newt population.

PE offered at GCSE and A level – 'We've got fantastic sports facilities and loads of opportunities,' say pupils. New changing rooms and a state-of-the art health suite, together with two new classrooms. Half yearly sports assembly for handing out colours – some blazers groan with these. Bright, clean refurbished 17m indoor swimming pool also used by staff three times a week. Pool, floodlit Astroturf, gym and studios all used by local community. Footballer pupils enjoy workshops with Bolton Wanderers FC. National level cross-country success due in part to school's 57 acres which include 'agony hill'; national schools' finals hosted here. Several national athletes including two on Olympic cycling talent programme, a modern pentathlete and a water polo player; senior girls national biathlon champions.

Dozens of extracurricular clubs. 'The car park in early evening is full of parents collecting children from after-school drama, music, sport and other clubs,' says school. Pupils also busy with D of E, Young Enterprise, community service and substantial charity fundraising. Lots of awards including Artsmark Gold, Sportsmark, Investors in People, Leading Edge Status, Excellence in Mentoring among others.

Background and atmosphere: Founded in 1855 by Canon James Slade for 'classical and moral instruction in conformity with the principles of the Church of England'. A life-size oil still oversees the hall and the annual Founder's Day service commemorating his death is much loved by all. A girls' school opened in 1879 and the two joined in 1902. The current buildings grew up decade by decade from the 1950s as a direct grant grammar school and then a C of E voluntary aided comprehensive, with selective entry ending in 1978. Modern, airy chapel. School says significant redecoration and refurbishment – including 'state-of-the-art changing rooms' and 'new, very smart lockers' – has improved the 'grotty bits' the pupils used to complain about. Pupils are proud of their good reputation in the wider community.

Pastoral care, well-being and discipline: Distinctive Christian ethos. Full-time chaplain and team described as being 'at the heart of this community of 2,000, which is his congregation'. Each day a different form group has communion service in the side chapel and all have daily Christian assembly, form prayers or service in main chapel. School motto, Ora et Labora, the imperative forms of the Latin literally translated as 'You must pray and you must work', sets the ethos. 'It's no mistake that the prayer comes before the work,' declares the school, and pupils say, 'Oh, yes, most people are real Christians here but the Christian stuff isn't pressurised'. Ofsted said, 'Pupils' spiritual, moral and cultural development is excellent.' Pupils describe the school as caring with very little bullying. 'We have a low threshold of tolerance for poor behaviour,' says school. 'If we deal with low-level problems like undone top buttons, the rest takes care of itself. We don't tolerate a child being cheeky to a teacher, and if they were to swear at a teacher they'd be excluded.' Detentions and contacting parents are first steps, followed by isolation in school and eventually exclusion. Pupils say, 'Isolation doesn't teach anything – it just causes aggravation,' but parents like the firm hand, saying, 'The children have a healthy respect for the discipline system and the teachers.'

Sixth formers describe their common room as relaxed and friendly. Newish sixth form directorate has given students much greater say on dress codes, management, activities etc via 'student voice' of sixth form council and prefects. Numerous societies and action teams set up.

All carry ID badges which double as pre-paid cashless catering cards for breakfast, break and lunch, which pupils describe as 'very healthy – whoever heard of a tuck shop that only sells fruit?' before admitting they can buy fair trade chocolate as well. Long outdoor queues for the canteen mean that some flout rules by eating packed lunches in playground to delight of scavenging seagulls who rake through the litter – latterly greatly reduced by sixth form eco action group working with school council.

First four years wear green blazers, year 11 graduates to black sweatshirts as transition to smart casual, 'but no denim', of sixth form. New intake, 270 in 10 forms, has outdoor pursuits bonding, lower sixth an induction day of Pennine pursuits.

Pupils and parents: Pupils come from far and wide from seven LAs – Bolton, Manchester, Salford, Bury, Blackburn with Darwen, and as far afield as Lancashire and Yorkshire. Over 1,000 travel on fleets of public and school buses and public trains, some 700 under their own or parental steam. The low percentage of ethnic minorities does not reflect the catchment areas but may, school admits, 'reflect the church-going population. Our pupils have a head start because most of them come from stable homes where their parents want them to do well'. Lower than average percentage eligible for free school meals.

Entrance: Not for those ambivalent about the Christian faith. Children from committed Christian families with a lengthy proven track record of regular church attendance stand the best chance of bagging one of the heavily over-subscribed places. Points given for church attendance as verified by an ordained minister and places offered to the 270 applicants with highest scores through LA co-ordinated system which matches offers with children's given choices. Entrance to sixth form is based on GCSE performance and not on faith criteria. Over 50 per cent of pupils stay on to sixth form taking 90 per cent of places. The rest are also oversubscribed and attract a broader ethnic mix as other faith groups are drawn to overall ethos of school.

Exit: Some 60 per cent leave after GCSEs. Ninety per cent of year 13 to university, respectable number to Russell Group, two to Oxbridge in 2016. Good success for medicine.

Remarks: Fantastic opportunities for performing arts and deserved success from hard work across the board in a caring and unstuffy but distinctly Christian atmosphere.

Casterton, Sedbergh Preparatory School

Linked with Sedbergh School

Kirkby Lonsdale, via Carnforth, Lancashire LA6 2SG

Pupils: 200; 63 boarders • Ages: 6m–13

Fees: Day £7,626 – £15,300; Boarding £17,841 – £22,449 pa

Tel: 01524 279200
Email: ajm@sedberghprep.org
Website: www.sedberghprep.org

Headmaster: Since 2013, Mr Scott Carnochan (40s), previously head of Sedbergh Junior, now head of the newish joint school. Educated at Dollar Academy, BEd from Herriott-Watt Edinburgh, former Scottish U18 rugby cap. Married to Kate, they have two young children; Mrs Carnochan also works in the school, doubling up on the key roles of headmaster's wife and head of marketing. They are a strong, capable and immensely likeable team and parents are huge fans.

Moving on in July 2017 to head Holmewood House.

Entrance: Assessment by head's interview and previous school report for younger children; English, maths and cognitive ability tests for year 4 upwards.

Exit: Nearly all to Sedbergh senior school.

Remarks: Eggs, 'laid with love' (says the sign) from the free range chickens here, plus the goats and the rabbits bring out the 'softer side of a prep school,' says the head. The children, while not quite 'free range' (tiger mothers and helicopter parents need not worry), have an abundance of outdoor space and room to breathe. They mostly ignore the glorious views and the weather that changes almost hourly; they are too busy enjoying their childhood.

Housed in a range of buildings, with plenty to spare; specialist science labs, inspirational art studios, music and superb sports facilities, these prep and pre-prep children are enjoying all the benefits of this former senior school. With reference to the relatively recent merger, parents say, 'it was the best thing that could have happened' – Casterton parents with older girls may disagree somewhat, but undoubtedly the feel-good factor is back and they are bucking the trend in this northern demographic with excellent post-merger recruitment figures and a good solid number of boarders. This is no mean feat in a school tucked away with no passing traffic; you have to seek it out, but advice from parents is 'if you are at all unsure, go and take a look – and take your children with you, that'll do it'. Most of us have at some point seen teary parents and weeping children at school gates at some point – well, here the children were weeping because they'd been for a taster morning and didn't want to leave..

Variously described as a 'broad church' and 'a good all-round education', the facilities are matchless for a prep school, having originally been designed for pupils up to A level. Note the six full size science labs, massive sports hall with cricket nets and a bowling machine, swimming pool, Astroturf, music practice rooms and much more besides, and they make full use of every bit of it. Nothing precious about it; parents say the children 'live in it' rather than 'just exist', and whilst they are quick to add that 'it's the people who really make the place', they also tell us they feel as though they have 'hit the jackpot here'.

You can bring your bike, you can also bring your horse – though not essential if you have a love of riding, as the school has 10 ponies that they happily loan. Work hard and play hard could be the school's motto, though presumably only if translated into Latin; the energy is astounding, before, during and after school. Rugby, hockey, cricket, netball and much more besides mean that there is no lack of fresh air and exercise. For obvious reasons, the location means that boarding makes sense, and it also allows you to join in with activities ranging from a parachute regiment leadership day to abseiling, bouldering, go-karting, clay pigeon shooting, bushcraft and (for the gentler soul) cheese-tasting; essentially, you just 'don't stay in'.

The pupils are a refreshing and captivating blend of childlike naivety and honesty alongside a wisdom that belies their years. Shoe-polishing night for boarders, fastening your top shirt button and a ban on chewing gum are happily tolerated by pupils, but, for them, the deal-breaker would be bullying, 'a real no-no', as is anything which essentially 'makes the atmosphere less friendly'. All meals are prepared in-house from, as far as possible, local produce; adults sit with the children in mixed age groups and apparently the curry is legendary.

Boarding accommodation, in rooms with views to die for, is spacious and homely; there are kitchens for extra toast-making and generally hanging out, plus a sitting room with TV and games for the boys; similar though slightly smaller and prettier accommodation for the girls with the obligatory One Direction posters. It's so quiet here that one boarder told us he falls asleep each night to the sound of the birds singing outside, and then they wake him up again in the morning.

Parents are a mix of medics from Lancaster, local business owners and landed gentry; tweed is somewhat de rigueur – practical and stylish, as befits the place. It's only a 15 minute drive to the senior school from here so parents and staff can and do manage both. Parents say it 'doesn't matter what car you drive, or even if you land your helicopter on the back field, you're made very welcome here'. House staff use Twitter to keep parents of boarders up-to-date, regular photos home of joyful, smiling children.

Clearly the merger and change of status required careful handling, but thanks to good management and huge parental advocacy, they've not only survived but thrived. A portrait of old girl Charlotte Brontë still hangs in the sitting room, and although it's still slightly old school here (and all the better for that – good manners and etiquette still count), she'd hardly recognise the warm and happy place it is today.

Clifton School

Linked with St Olave's School, St Peter's School, York

22

Clifton School, Clifton, York YO30 6AB

Pupils: 217 • Ages: 3–8 • C of E

Fees: £7,470 – £8,655 pa

Tel: 01904 527361
Email: enquiries@cliftonyork.org.uk
Website: www.cliftonyork.org.uk

Head: Since 2011, Mr Phil Hardy BA PGCE (early 30s). Originally from Darlington, studied sports psychology at Northumbria University before spending a brief time in Canada. Married to a management consultant, with a young son, 'who is as laid back as I am'. That said, when it comes to the school, he appears anything but laid back – full of energy and enthusiasm, with big ideas and big plans. Plenty of autonomy as a head but also plenty of support from above. Keen sportsman – golf, football, rugby, cricket and former England hockey player. Displayed a combination of stamina and ambition by beginning his career as a teaching assistant at Yarm Prep and progressing all the way to deputy head, then, latterly, head of its early school (3 to 7) before taking up headship here.

Passionate about how children learn and develop, he has worked hard at building relationships and removing the traditional stand-off between parents and staff. He's introduced staff appraisals and made tangible differences in a very short time. Thankfully, staff appear willing and able to keep up. Communicates regularly with parents via a weekly newsletter, including the ever-popular head's blog, and is also busy on Twitter, with a 'photo of the day' and regular tweets keeping in touch whilst on school trips – parents love it. Charming, smiling, enormously popular, a real find – his predecessor was a hard act to follow, yet parents regard changes he has made 'beneficial', admiring and respecting the way he has made significant changes without 'bulldozing'.

Entrance: 'I would argue with anyone about testing at 3,' says the head. He meets the children and parents and if it 'feels right' and there's a place, you can start. Most popular entry points are nursery and reception. InCAS (assessment in literacy and maths) testing for older children (expected to be above national average). But beyond 4 you'd struggle to get in at all.

Exit: Most pupils have an automatic transfer to St Olave's (98 per cent in 2016). Bootham (competitor across the road) is viewed as a 'softer option' (Bootham may take a different view) for those (very few) unable to cope at St Olave's and St Peter's beyond.

Remarks: Time and a change of head have brought a change of ethos to Clifton School and Nursery, a longstanding school which became part of the St Peter's family in 1994. The move from a quaint and traditional approach to a creative, thematic approach, encouraging independent thinking and a sheer love of learning, has brought new interest and vibrancy. It recently won a best pre-prep in the country award – admittedly Clifton parents' votes were counted in the outcome. That said, it is lovely – bright, colourful and friendly, and the good and great locally are climbing aboard with their children.

Very welcoming, open door approach. The biggest challenge is finding it, as it is tucked away behind other buildings, mainly belonging to St Peter's. New signage helps or, if in doubt, do as we did and get a St Peter's pupil to guide you through the maze of buildings, car parks and walkways. It was also a good way of judging the end product (our guide was excellent). Delightful secretary/receptionist, but she is hidden away. School tells us it has plans to develop a more clearly defined entrance foyer within the year.

Parents take academic rigour as read. P4c (philosophy for children) is not just talked about but happens throughout, with even 3 year olds confidently giving their opinions on books and stories ('You're allowed to dislike it – just tell us why'). Philosophy and thinking skills are writ large into the school day and curriculum – 'Children need to learn to fail and experience failure in order to develop, learn to make mistakes, like James Dyson'. IT is big but intrinsic – 'It should just be an extension of your pencil case'. PE, French and music taught by subject specialists, with French beginning in nursery.

Sport includes swimming, tag rugby, football, cricket, rounders, athletics, netball, hockey and athletics. Plenty of music throughout – busy and enthusiastic choir (consists of every pupil in years 2 and 3).

Two form entry, max class size 20. Unusual for a pre-prep in that it takes children up to the end of year 3. This top end adds strength and you find the oldest pupils here looking and behaving like top juniors, taking part in activities that normally would happen elsewhere in years 5 or 6. Children present at meetings of the governing body (recently related their activities as an eco-school). Bug house and bottle greenhouse in the grounds, forest school environment also under way. Every modern facility and approach, yet still the reassuringly familiar themed play areas and cage of guinea pigs in the reception class.

Superstar awards and assemblies recognise effort and attainment – plenty of praise and encouragement here. Themed days bring parent involvement and whole school activities (recently a cultural Olympiad and French day) and they are still talking about 'the day the space ship landed' and children arrived at school to find an area sealed off with police tape and a police officer standing guard. Fun and hugely creative.

Parents are mostly professionals, 70 per cent of families with both parents working, many commuting, hence the long (8am to 5.30pm) opening hours here. Free before school, small charge after school. Teaching day ends at 3.15pm. Parents told us they value the fact that 'academic challenge is present' but say the school is 'supportive' and full of bright, smiley children. Most said they chose the school on 'gut instinct' – they visited and liked what they saw, having done the rounds of other local schools.

Royal blue uniform, no blazers or ties, kilts for girls, grey trousers or shorts for boys, and polo shirts. All ultra practical.

Dallam School

D

Milnthorpe, Cumbria LA7 7DD

Pupils: 969; 127 boarders, mostly international. • Ages: 11–18 • Sixth form: 212

Fees: Boarding £10,831 – £12,111 pa; Tuition free

Tel: 015395 65165
Email: enquiries@dallam.eu
Website: www.dallam.eu

Headteacher: Since 2013, Mr William Bancroft, 50s, previously head of Settle College. Has a BA in history, though no longer teaches, plus PGCE, postgrad diploma and NPQH; currently chair of the South Lakes Federation of Schools. Warm and welcoming, nothing brash about the man; he's quietly spoken yet at the same time commands both attention and respect, giving the clear impression that he knows what he's doing here. And there is no doubt that he does: he has plenty of headship experience, this is his third to date and both pupil numbers and results are up. He commutes from Lancaster and enjoys walking and skiing when time permits, but acknowledges (without complaint) that school is somewhat all-consuming. Plenty of staff changes since his arrival, which inevitably upsets the apple cart a little, but all appears to be running smoothly now – in fact the place runs like clockwork: prior to our visit they certainly won our prize for speedy and effective communication, which is usually a good sign.

Academic matters: 'Learning for All, Learning for Life' is both the school's motto and its mantra. Excellent track record of outstanding achievement in exams with the full range of GCSEs, BTecs, A levels and International Baccalaureate (IB) on offer. Despite the broad intake, it sits very comfortably alongside selective schools in the area, beating national averages: 76 per cent achieved five or more A* to C at GCSE in 2016, with 19 per cent A*/A grades; 10 per cent A*/A, 50 per cent A*-B at A level. All very creditable, alongside an IB average of 34 points, with one student getting 43 points out of 45 – clearly something here for everyone. As the only IB world state school in Cumbria, it flies the flag for high achievement; of particular note were strong performances in Spanish, English, history and biology where many students achieved maximum marks. Most stay on into sixth form post-16, around 30-40 per cent following the IB route. Also offers the IBCP or IB career-related programme, which includes at least two diploma programme courses plus career-related studies.

The school is proud of its inclusive ethos, so those with special educational needs are well catered for, and proud of its approach to independent learning, teamwork and activity – didactic teaching methods aren't welcome here. There is a bilingual option for year 7 starters, though competitive so not guaranteed. Good primary liaison helps a smooth transition, important with more than 40 feeder schools. Teaching areas are well-equipped and unusually tidy, as are corridors and shared spaces. There are seven science labs and impressive teaching suites for design technology and food technology.

Spanish and French taught throughout, Italian and German on offer for the sixth form. Super-keen linguists can access other languages through the school's community education wing. Class sizes are around 30, apart from sixth form, where they are smaller. In addition to a range of sport and music options, lunchtime and after-school clubs offer curriculum support in science, art, maths ('Help with Homework'), business studies and a curiously-named 'Geek club' – seems good to us that this is somewhere where it's acceptable to be a geek..because whatever it is, we'd like to be part of it.

Attracts a strong pool of teaching staff, the adventure learning programme proving a great added attraction. Add to that the fact that you can train to teach here under the South Cumbria SCITT umbrella, the school widens and deepens the pool in which it can fish for good teachers, embracing energy, enthusiasm and talent from those new to the profession.

Games, options, the arts: Two great sports halls at the Milnthorpe site, fitness suite and Astroturf plus multiple pitches nearby, so the school is well-equipped for year-round sport. Add to that a further sports hall at Heversham (home to the boarders) alongside all-weather tennis courts. They are serious about their sport but don't claim to beat all-comers, perhaps because they don't major in any one sport, preferring to offer a wider range than most; that said, we met a lovely netball player currently playing at national level, so no lack of inspiration or aspiration. The BTec outdoor programme sees students paddling rivers, surfing waves, capsizing canoes and mountain walking, clearly fearless in all weathers. A good range of sport is also on offer as twilight sessions for local primary pupils plus Easter and summer holiday sports camps, offering 'classic adventures'; sounds a bit Swallows and Amazons, but we are in the right part of the country for that and they are open to all and hugely popular.

Dallam was the first in the UK to gain Adventure Learning School status. Taking advantage of proximity to both the Lake District and Yorkshire Dales national parks, students and staff participate in canoeing, hiking, camping and other assorted adventurous pursuits. Year 7 students have a residential experience at Borrowdale and year 8 at Ennerdale, and the principles of outdoor challenge are embedded across the whole curriculum. Typically this will involve different subject departments working together with students on extended studies, often of an investigatory nature, proving learning need not be entirely classroom-based.

Excellent music teaching here with the usual range of instruments available for individual tuition plus various choirs and two bands, including a swing band, and a strong ensemble. Christmas celebrations include a visit to the village church for nine lessons and carols with the music department featuring large. Drama is strong and popular and students tell us that these are the areas where the younger ones have the opportunity to work alongside the sixth form – something they clearly value. High quality drama productions are enjoyed by parents and pupils alike – much talk about the recent production of Oliver!

High quality artwork on display in many areas – pride is clearly evident here. A drama studio, separate dance studio, theatre and large sports hall add to the mix on offer; there's even an outdoor performance area with covered stage that would probably be used much more than it is were it not in Cumbria.

Boarding: For boarders there is even more on offer here. Lots of extra sport plus weekend shopping trips for those needing a retail fix, overnight camping in tepees, paintballing, waterfall and mountain hiking, cinema outings, ice-skating, visits to the theatre and opera, attending pro football and rugby matches, raft-building as well as seasonal activities such as carol singing and bonfire night.

Boarders' home-from-home is the former Heversham Grammar School in the tiny upmarket village of Heversham. It's not far from school but far enough and different enough to feel like home, at least during term time. If you are up in time, you take the minibus shuttle into school each day and back late afternoon or evening. If you're a late riser you'll have to walk and make your excuses when you get there. Parts of the building are Hogwarts-ish: the charmingly named 'big school' is a communal space within the former school hall, with high ceilings, impressive fireplaces and honours boards of former pupils on display.

A plethora of outbuildings and green play space house a music studio, all-weather floodlit tennis courts, sports hall and a wet store housing climbing ropes, wetsuits and kayaks. There is also a fives court much loved by old boys and an allotment and chicken house. Staff are lovely – buckets of warmth and care and very much on their game. Well-behaved sixth formers have individual ensuite rooms, all in very good nick; younger boarders are in rooms of two, three or four – less space, but it's their space and that's important. Updating and improving of facilities is ongoing – this isn't the smartest accommodation but it is more than adequate. Unusually, girls outnumber boys in the boarding stakes, but only slightly, and for peace of mind there is fobbed and timed security into all the main buildings and also between boys' and girls' dorms.

Twenty-one different nationalities make up the boarding set – 'a multi-cultural dimension from which everybody benefits,' says the head. There is some clustering, mostly down to word-of-mouth approval and recommendations from existing and former parents – currently the largest groups of boarders are from Italy (the school is apparently big in Tuscany), Majorca and the Emirates. A small on-site build is part of a plan to expand boarding a little by 2018, with a view to admitting more home-grown boarders as part of a plan to future-proof the facility. The boarders are important on many levels. They add real diversity to the community: 'Some of the most interesting people I've met here are from other countries,' said one pupil; they also, crucially, make the sixth form and IB provision viable in a rural area which really couldn't sustain either of these options without them. Home-cooking, all on-site with menus adapted according to national and international preferences (though the request for sushi hasn't yet been met) and staff keep busy with relentless laundry, all very motherly rather than matronly – there's real warmth and pride in looking after their charges here.

Background and atmosphere: A long and interesting history has created a school with traditional values within a modern setting. The original school was founded in 1613 by Edward Wilson (whose descendants still live locally and continue to work with the school). It all began a mile or so away with the former Heversham Grammar School, now home to the boarders and Dallam community education. The main Dallam School teaching hub is on the site of the former Milnthorpe secondary, all of which has benefited hugely from £12m investment in recent years, creating an attractive, multi-purpose teaching site. Predominantly low level buildings with green paint, the site is very well-maintained with a good car park, plenty of recreational space and residential housing at the perimeter fence. The mountains of the Lake District can be seen in all directions, and whilst on the edge of the large and pleasant village of Milnthorpe, you are a very long way from a Starbucks. The students don't seem to mind this in the least – they describe feeling 'safe' here, a fact which, according to them, allows them more independence, and indeed it does exude a calm yet purposeful atmosphere. The academic challenge is self-evident, but there are also plenty of opportunities for community involvement, public speaking and charity events for those happy to take up the additional challenges on offer – in fact if you don't, 'you'd be missing out,' say parents.

Pastoral care, well-being and discipline: They tuck their shirts in when they see us approaching and girls are nudged into compliance if their skirts are too short – so they know who's in charge. 'We're pretty well-behaved here, it's because we're rural kids,' said one sixth former, summing up the general view. Of course with a mixed intake of teenagers they, like every school in existence, have a few angry young men and scowling girls, but they're definitely in the minority and are carefully monitored and gently prodded into line. Peer pressure being what it is, conformity is the watchword here and parents praise the highly effective Dallam Learner Profile, an achievable and measured reward system of 'soft skills' in years 7,8 and 9 that leads very conveniently into D of E later. Parents tell us that communication is good, 'most staff return calls swiftly, parents are taken seriously, our concerns addressed and we are kept informed of outcomes. Online Parentmail and reliable and useful reporting systems are a bonus'.

Staff are visible in and around the school site, keeping a watching brief, and relationships between staff and pupils manage to appear both friendly and businesslike at the same time. Plenty of responsibility given to pupils, which they like; everyone seems clear on their role in keeping the place ticking smoothly.

Pupils and parents: The parents are mixed and far-flung many with interesting career profiles; liberal-minded university types from Lancaster, plenty of local teachers and headteachers, professionals, farmers and businessfolk from Kendal, Morecambe, Grange and beyond, who are attracted by a school that feels rural yet doesn't suffer the restraints of small rural secondaries elsewhere in the area. It may be sited in a large village, but strong numbers means there are no problems in generating sports teams, maintaining a healthy sixth form and being able to offer good facilities, making it the envy of others.

Pupils are a likeable bunch, at ease with themselves and their surroundings but with no lack of aspiration and ambition. Prefects set an example in all areas; sixth form prefects have walkie-talkies giving them direct access to staff if they feel the need to bring in the heavies whilst on duty and amusingly, even in this digital age when all carry a mobile phone, their walkie-talkies are the envy of younger prefects. They describe their teachers as 'friendly and supportive,' which is always good to hear. They also tell us that the food is good, 'better than it used to be,' apparently, and the bacon buns, if you arrive for breakfast, are 'legendary'. Uniform is smart with a trad blazer badge and lapel badges indicating awards and honours; shirts and ties for all; most are very well turned out and the head will let them know if they don't meet the required standards. For sixth form it's a dress code which appears a little vague in interpretation – no jeans, T shirts or hoodies is clear enough, but there's possibly too much wriggle room in the term 'business wear', certainly for the girls.

Entrance: Over 40 feeder schools, some large, some tiny rural schools, from near and far. No appeals as yet, all wanting a place have one, but that may change in the near future with growing demand. For year 7 day pupil entry, apply via the local authority (unselective). Sixth form applicants need to have at least five A*-Cs at GCSE (or foreign equivalent), including English and maths, to study on the IB or A level programme. IBCP students need to have a minimum of four Cs and two Ds at GCSE. Boarding applicants must have right of residence in the UK and be 'suitable for boarding'.

Exit: Some 50-60 per cent stay post 16, a small number move on to sixth forms elsewhere (mainly because of subject choices), others to apprenticeships. No NEETS here; all have a career plan. At 18 the majority go into higher education, one or two to Oxbridge each year (one to Cambridge in 2016), a good number to Russell Group and with overseas students pushing aspirations, some to university overseas (four in 2016) – the Netherlands is currently popular (and free). Notable former pupils include: Times cartoonist Peter Brooke, opera singer Emma Stannard and BBC journalist and presenter Rob Broomby.

Money matters: Fees for boarding but not for tuition.

Remarks: 'It's ambitious for all its pupils and is small enough to know each one,' a parent told us. Certainly the academic challenge is wider than most and rigorous, too, but there's plenty of room for all-comers, at least for now. Though as a state school with boarding and the IB option to boot, interest in the school is, unsurprisingly, growing from far and wide.

Dame Allan's Schools

Fowberry Crescent, Fenham, Newcastle upon Tyne NE4 9YJ

Pupils: 1,045 • Ages: 3–18 • Sixth form: 202 • C of E

Fees: £7,374 – £11,994 pa

Tel: 01912 750608
Email: enquiries@dameallans.co.uk
Website: www.dameallans.co.uk

Principal: Since 2004, Dr John Hind (50s), PGCE MA (history) from Downing College, Cambridge, MEd (Newcastle), PhD (history) Durham. Previously deputy head of Kingston Grammar and before that at Durham and Exeter. Approachable, speaks enthusiastically of 'our family of schools' and believes in instilling a 'can do' mindset rather than creating an academic hothouse. Approaches each pupil with 'Let's work together and see where we can get to'. Parents commented that 'he runs a tight ship' and though 'a little distant', both parents and pupils have 'warmed to him over time'.

Has made considered, evolutionary changes to remove segregation between the boys' and girls' schools, while retaining their separate identities – most recent, a management restructure to shed traditional boy/girl school delineation.

Married to Ginny, a dentist, with a family of two daughters. Outside school, a keen campanologist and member of the conseil d'administration of the Relais de la Mémoire, an international organisation founded to keep alive WW2 memories in order to promote reconciliation and understanding in Europe and beyond.

Head of junior school: Since 2008 Andrew Edge MA (50s), previously head of years 4-6 here. Studied mediaeval and modern history at St Andrews, then a spell in industry (accountancy and customer service) before a PGCE at Durham. Taught and subsequently appointed deputy head at Ravenscourt Park Prep School in London.

Genial, dapper and approachable; a hands-on head who 'does not like to spend his time behind a desk'. Is keen for school to have its own identity but 'to sit as one within the Dame Allan family'. Wants pupils to think that 'learning is fun', and that they 'want more of that'.

Avid Sunderland football supporter and keen sportsman, playing cricket and golf and coaching pupils' rugby; enjoys travel. Married with one son at alma mater Durham School.

Academic matters: The nursery is bright and well-resourced with two linked reception rooms. French and weekly library sessions from age 3. Home/school diary for each child recording daily life – an example of the quality of care and commitment provided. Numeracy and literacy in the mornings and topic based activity in the afternoons. Specialist PE, dance, drama and French teaching.

Broad curriculum in both KS1 and KS2, specialist French but no Latin, thinking skills recently introduced and learning outdoors, to make best use of the natural environment on their new site. Parents we spoke to said 'staff are fantastic', and that they feel children are being taught in a 'professional, caring, nurturing and safe environment'. Small number of children with SEN – dyslexia – supported in class and one-to-one; even smaller number with EAL requirements, all of whom can access the curriculum. As you might expect in new build, wireless throughout, banks of laptops, even iPads in EYFS.

Full written reports to parents each summer; effort and attainment grades each term; parents' evenings autumn and summer terms. Parents feel informed and appreciate that the school is 'very honest with their views' about the children.

Diamond model: co-ed in junior school, pupils split into single sex schools from age 11 to 16 (co-ed for most extracurricular activities other than sport) before returning to co-ed sixth form, though all are housed in the same buildings. Benefit of single sex teaching adapted to the recognised differences in learning styles of boys and girls, though teachers shared across schools (adaptability tested on recruitment). Subjects are zoned in different parts of the building so integration is inevitable and allowed.

Good subject choice at GCSE with dual award or single sciences, dance and drama; nine subjects as standard. In 2016, girls 77 per cent and boys 58 per cent A*/A grades at GCSE. At A level, choice of 30 subject with enrichment programme, including TEFL and sign language courses. In 2016, combined sixth formers got 43 per cent A*/A grades and 74 per cent A*-B. Personal tutors for sixth form; younger pupils spoke of 'approachable teachers who run out-of-class surgeries and help with time management problems'. Individual learning needs and abilities are identified; reporting system of attainment and effort valued by parents, though some felt could be more 'push and stretch' for the most academically able.

Learning support mainly takes places out of lessons, ideally outside normal curriculum. Currently a charge is levied.

IT is good and investment in infrastructure currently being considered – to BYOD or not to BYOD (bring your own device). Pupils from year 10 told us they found single-sex teaching 'took off pressure in the classroom', but 'plenty of opportunity to get to know each other before sixth form through joint activities, like educational visits and Duke of Edinburgh'.

Games, options, the arts: A wealth of opportunities abound. Music is strong and getting stronger. In year 3 all pupils have vocal/violin coaching on 10 week rota with taster sessions in brass and woodwind in years 5 and 6. New facilities provide opportunity for more choral and dramatic performances. Year 6 production each summer term. Diversity from chamber choir to ceilidh band and just about everything in between. Pupils perform with National Youth Choir and achieve success in national competitions.

Dance is 'right here, right now', as demonstrated in aptly named annual show and impressive, purpose-built dance studio. Not only success for pupils as Youth Dance England finalists, but take-up even extends to the first XV, as part of their training programme. Lots of performance opportunities, from informal lunchtime recitals and studio performances to major school productions; from pupils performing at the Edinburgh Fringe to the choir members singing with the Bach Choir at Newcastle University.

Sport is valued as much for its inclusivity (everyone gets chance to represent school; teams from U9s upwards) as its excellence. For half a century boys have represented their county at rugby, but recent success in squash (girls' success in National Schools competition), swimming (girls recent National Schools champions) and cross-country (representing Northumberland in English Schools competition). Range of sports on offer is dazzling, with weightlifting, archery, tennis, running, taekwondo and netball having all produced internationals. Sport transports away from muddy fields of Tyneside to tours in, for example, South Africa and Italy (rugby), Barbados (cricket), Canada (hockey and netball). Swimming at local pool in Fenham and record of success, particularly in athletics.

Outdoor and leadership education feature strongly, providing increasing challenge for younger pupils and leadership roles as they move up the school. Duke of Edinburgh silver and gold are available from year 10 upwards.

Real adventure is further offered by World Challenge participation – has seen pupils go to Uganda, Kenya, Bolivia, Mongolia, China and the Indian Himalayas. Exchanges flourish to France, Germany etc and in Relais de la Mémoire – joint initiative with French, German and Polish schools to nurture continued learning about and respect for victims of war and holocaust.

Lots of lunchtime and after school activities including the more unusual – clog dancing, eco panel, electronics and fencing. Challenge and success in business-related competition – recent finalists in Bank of England's Target 2.0 and winner of RES Young Economist of the Year. Parents speak of 'individualised opportunities' for each of their children, resulting in 'confident and capable' young adults.

Background and atmosphere: Founded in 1705; girls' school believed to be one of the oldest independent girls' schools in the country. Founded by Dame Eleanor Allan, daughter of a city goldsmith and widow of a wealthy tobacco merchant, to provide a 'proper' education for 40 poor boys and 20 poor girls. Keeps that ethic but has shaken off the pre-1980s segregation of girls at one side, boys at the other.

Current buildings date from mid 1930s, cushioned on all sides by surburban housing and fronted by a green playing field, a snug oasis amidst the mid-war semis. An airy, modern entrance leads to functional ground floor corridors, made interesting by the display areas on the walls. Well resourced and accommodated art, dance, music and sport; library refurbished in recent years to include areas for careers clinics, science and sixth form study. Good sixth form common room and study accommodation, separate enough for independence – with well-placed sixth form staff teaching and office space to allow discreet observation. Lower down school space is at a premium and one girl told us, 'The dream would be a common room for each year'.

Purpose built junior school opened in 2012 on the six acre site of a former Victorian hospital in Spital Tongues, to the north of the city centre. First time ages 3 to 11 have been under one roof. A 24 place nursery, two forms per year to year 4 (maximum 15 per class to year 2, then 20 per class) and then three forms for years 5 and 6.

Attractive two storey, fully accessible building surrounded by three separate play areas, one for EYFS leading directly from their self-contained area, one for KS1 and a third for KS2. Good selection of play apparatus appropriate for each stage of development and KS2 area marked out for netball. Luxury of an all-weather playing surface for other traditional team sports, together with adequate grass pitches.

Ground floor houses nursery and reception with their own separate entrance; KS1 classrooms are designed so that children can work and play together in safe 'breakout areas', moving inside and out. Classrooms are paired and pupils in each 'pair' have their own cloakrooms and toilets. Two multi-purpose halls provide space for assemblies, lunch, parent meetings and gym, dance and indoor games.

Classrooms for the older children are on the upper floor, again with a separate entrance. The library is also on this floor, its red colour and prominent shape (which protrudes through to the building's façade – certainly a conversation piece) an overt statement that learning is at the heart of the school. Shared librarian from senior school takes weekly library lessons for all. Designated art, design and science room has the resources for making short films. Year 6 science club has additional use of senior school laboratories. Great attention to detail has been put into every aspect of this building resulting in an excellent, pupil focused learning environment.

Strong sense of community and family – pupils at ease in a friendly atmosphere. Cherishes church links – historically the cathedral school, and retains links with St Nicholas' Cathedral and Church of SS James and Basil. Places community, charity/fundraising work on a par with academic and sporting achievement.

Separate houses in boys' and girls' schools, though move afoot to 'pair' houses in each school – currently used almost exclusively for sporting competition. Dr Hind feels both schools 'still need a separate identity'.

Pastoral care, well-being and discipline: Excellent pastoral care in junior school where the head knows every child by name. Children seem happy, at ease and confident in their new environment. Assemblies for reception upwards; taking part in the birthday hat celebration and being serenaded by the audience delighted the older children – and a teacher as well. Thought-provoking moral message in the ad hoc adaptation of a well-known children's tale to the extreme climatic events on the day we visited.

Form teachers/tutors perform pastoral role in both senior schools. Trained counsellor to listen to any particular problems, with confidential referrals from school nurse. An effective pupil counselling system called Link, where sixth formers provide a listening ear and guiding hand. Flexible merit system keeps pupils on course. Typically a demerit is a warning sign, two prompts letter home and three invokes detention. Pupils report zero-tolerance of bullying and drugs.

Parents and pupils find any problems dealt with promptly, fairly and effectively. An inclusive school that doesn't give up easily on pupils with behavioural problems.

Pupils and parents: Wide social mix, many parents working hard to afford fees. Catchment is Newcastle and hinterland (Tyne Valley, coast, Durham area, plus wider north east). Pupils mainly from Dame Allan's Junior School (good transition programme for year 6), state primary and middle schools, Newcastle Preparatory School and Chorister School Durham. Most have English as first language, though several speak another language at home.

Old boys/girls include Sir David Lumsden; Ian La Frenais; Elizabeth Fallaize (pro-vice-chancellor of Oxford University) and more recently Ellie Crissell, TV presenter and journalist.

Entrance: Pupils may start in school nursery at age 3 after a taster session; informal assessment for entry to reception at age 4. Standardised tests in reading, mathematics and non-verbal reasoning from year 2 on.

Entry at 11 to senior schools by January assessment in English, maths and verbal reasoning, followed by an interview.

D

Sixth form entry conditional on GCSE results and at least a A, for external candidates, to study a subject at AS level.

Exit: Almost all pupils go on to one of the senior schools. Year 6 prepared for the transition, spending Tuesday afternoons at the Fenham campus with sessions of art and technology, music and using the library. Otherwise mostly to Newcastle independent day schools.

D

Some 80 per cent of seniors stay on for co-ed sixth form. Nearly all go on to university. In 2016, courses and destinations include archaeology and ancient civilisation at Durham, mining engineering at Exeter and meteorology and climate with a year in Oklahoma at Reading. Also foundation art and performance courses at specialist music schools as well as two apprenticeships.

Money matters: Scholarships of up to 50 per cent of fees awarded on entrance examination results. Participating school in Ogden Trust science scholarship scheme. Music scholarships also available. Means-tested bursaries awarded up to 100 per cent of fees if needed. Though not a rich school, eight per cent of pupils currently receive bursaries.

Remarks: A diamond in shape and in character, pupils encouraged to and do take full advantage of many opportunities to learn, travel and develop. No flashy jewels here, pleasant but functional buildings nestled amongst residential housing. Stiff local competition, particularly for girls – Dame Allan's tries harder. Community and family values ingrained and the individual pupils nurtured.

Durham High School for Girls

Farewell Hall, South Road, Durham DH1 3TB

Pupils: 575 • Ages: 3–18 • Sixth form: 67 • C of E

Fees: £8,370 – £12,360 pa

Tel: 01913 843226
Email: headmistress@dhsfg.org.uk
Website: www.dhsfg.org.uk

Headmistress: Since 2012, Mrs Lynne Renwick BEd (50s). Returning to her roots, born in Durham, read history and education and spent a short period working for the National Trust. Moved between independent and state sectors; Tadcaster Grammar; Walton High School for Girls in West Midlands; head of history at GSA British girls' school in Peru; spent time in Japan as part of a British delegation of educators. Head of humanities at Dixon's City Technology College in Bradford, assistant head at All Saints School in York, principal of Our Lady's Abingdon, Oxfordshire. ISI inspector, member of the professional development committee of GSA, former governor of Cranford House School, Oxfordshire.

Says that she 'loved teaching in all girl schools and knew she wanted to be head of one'. Believes that Durham High girls are 'comfortable in their own skins and moulded in a positive way'; they find being in an all girl environment 'just so easy'. Keeps in touch by lunching with groups of girls twice a week.

Married to a freelance illustrator working in advertising and design; no children, but five nieces ranging from teens to 20s. Very interested in conservation of old houses and architecture, loves ice skating – for the past five years has been on the ice between 6.30 and 8.00am every Saturday morning, mastering dancing and keeping fit. Also enjoys reading, hill walking, travelling and interior design.

Head of junior school: Since 2013, Mrs Katherine Anderson (50s), previously acting head. Hasn't strayed far from Durham High: was a pupil here in the 70s and daughter followed in her footsteps; BEd from Neville's Cross Physical Education College in Durham; brief spell teaching PE at a comprehensive school then back to Durham High in 1986 as head of senior school PE. Has been here ever since, in roles including director of marketing and head of junior house. Husband, Richard, is an agricultural engineer.

Academic matters: 'Learning is such fun here' chorused some juniors, citing activities, trips and use of role play to understand characters in reading books. Teaching, children's attitudes to learning and pupil-staff relationships praised in last inspection report. Maximum class size is 15 in key stage 1 and 20 in key stage 2, but most significantly smaller.

Rainbow Hill Nursery, attractive, large, well organised, open plan building, opposite junior classrooms and adjacent to infant school allowing smooth transition to reception. Enclosed soft play area, patio and lovely outside play area and learning environment; lots of hi tech equipment plus traditional resources – the new and the old together. Close links with parents – kept closely informed on children's progress. Average numbers 20; happy, busy, independent little tots looking adorable in tartan pinafores (to match the big girls' uniform).

Topic-led EYFS curriculum in reception continued into termly themes in year 1, though transition to more formalised learning. Setting in maths and some aspects of English from year 2; good provision of extension work for the very bright. Pupils spoke warmly of their teachers and the help they give them.

Qualified SENCo does dyslexia tests (screening of individuals in years 3-4, if needed) and gives one-to-one support outside the classroom (at a cost to parents); also specialist ESOL teacher. All needs could be catered for, apart from severe behavioural difficulties – 'These girls do very well'. Senior school girls help junior ones with reading and basic maths, top juniors with infants in the playground.

Consistently the highest performing school in the county and came out particularly well in the English Bacc league table. A levels: 56 per cent A*/A, 75 per cent A*/B in 2016; usual subjects plus psychology, sociology, Latin, Greek, classical civilisation, sport, theatre studies, art and design – a notable range for such a small sixth form. Impressively, almost half do maths and sciences, EPQ taken – no slacking from these girls.

2016 GCSEs: 60 per cent A*/A. Sciences, fine art, textiles, history, Greek, Latin and music usually strong. French, German, Latin and recently introduced Spanish at key stage 3. Does well in maths, business and Latin and Greek speaking competitions. Astronomy offered extra sessional for high flyers. Very good ICT provision, with area for enrichment and extension activities on school website. Max class sizes: 24 (key stage 3), 20 (key stage 4), 14 (sixth form), but can be a lot smaller. Girls spoke appreciatively of teachers' personal approach and the amount of individual attention they get. Parents speak highly of teachers who 'build relationships with each child individually and get to know what makes them tick'.

Well-resourced library; reading groups for each year; organised annual event of Big Book Bash for year 7s with 10 local schools. Supervised homework club available until 5.30pm. Qualified SENCo can test for dyslexia, works closely with staff, advises on individual needs and liaises with outside agencies. Gives individual support outside the classroom at a cost to parents. Says school could cope with any special needs apart from severe behavioural difficulties and that these girls do very well (endorsed by latest inspection report). EAL specialist support offered at a cost.

Games, options, the arts: The usual range plus cricket, rowing, golf, karate, skiing, rock climbing, basketball, sports coaching awards – encouraging participation as PE compulsory. Sports tours – next destination Sri Lanka. Regional and national success with some individual national high flyers (gymnastics, tumbling, fencing and netball); 1970s sports hall, netball courts and playing field on site – swimming pool, all-weather pitch and fitness suite all accessed off-site. Weekly swimming from year 3 at local pool with annual gala for years 5 and 6.

Durham High's alive with the sound of music. Year 3 all learn the violin, year 4s toot on the recorder (unusual way round), year 5s sound the trumpet and year 6s sing to grade 1. Year 5 singing project with local primary schools, instrumental lessons from nursery, lots of concerts. Over 50 per cent of senior girls take instrumental and singing lessons. Lots of music exams, no competitions or festivals though performance opportunities abound; choirs, orchestra, ensembles, lunchtime concerts, and of course, cathedral connections. Well resourced music technology room – music GCSE popular. Big productions tend to be musicals, but straight plays too, plenty going on in all parts of the school – drama studio fully utilised. The seniors' play is performed at the Gala Theatre in Durham – the school's drama studio stage is, cleverly, the same size, to facilitate the transfer. A year 9 panto toured 25 primary schools; dance performances, too.

Very good art – students' work has been shortlisted for the Royal Academy online exhibition for A level candidates; also textiles, graphics, pottery, photography club. No food tech, though, which girls would like, but after-school cookery club and survival lessons for sixth form. Largest D of E centre in County Durham for the Gold Award, community service, big Amnesty International group, eco activities, school council relaunch. Sixth form enrichment programme covers IT, philosophy, politics, debating, Young Enterprise. Buddying of younger girls by older ones, who help with academic work (eg basic maths and reading), produce their plays and lead their activities (all good personal statement stuff). Healthy competition through house activities, drama, singing and sports; also used for charitable fundraising. Junior clubs include craft, chess, Christian Union, Meccano, ICT problem solving and sport. Karate, ballet, Brownies on offer at a cost. Residentials to Bamburgh and Holy Island and Low Mill activity trip, plus a variety of other local trips; school council.

High quality careers and post-school preparation though focused on university. Task-based enterprise day for years 7 and 8 involves teamwork and workplace scenarios; participates in Durham's future business magnate programme in year 8; Young Enterprise and work experience in year 12.

Background and atmosphere: Opened in 1884 in the centre of the city as a C of E school. Moved to leafy outskirts down the road from university science suite in 1964 – all purpose built. Additions since then – sixth form and art accommodation, science labs, ICT and library building, sports hall and attractive two storey brick buildings, one housing a performing arts studio, music room and classrooms and another the junior school – ring the single storey originals. Lengthy flight of gentle steps leads down to the understated entrance providing a disappointing vista of flat roofs – dispelled once inside by wide corridors, bright and airy classrooms, a veritable Tardis.

A compact site, yet sufficient hard play areas, playing field and well wooded grounds. Nursery and junior girls situated near to the seniors, contributing to the secure, friendly, family feeling. Two ICT suites, a greenhouse for the biology lab, large, well-resourced library (every year has a reading group), pleasant quiet room with modern stained glass windows. Roomy sixth form common room, kitchen (university survival cooking classes on offer) and study areas on edge of campus in building shared with art and design facilities. Infants and year 3 in attractive yellow brick building with bright, light classrooms with plenty of space, great displays and technology in evidence. Older juniors in single storey buildings, a short distance away. Science taught in junior classrooms but gifted scientists and those with an interest in science in years 5 and 6 join others from Durham primary schools each Thursday evening for Science Sparks, held in senior school laboratories.

The sixth form wear dark suits – the rest sport dark green jumpers and blazers, choice of yellow and green tartan kilt or skirt. Wide choice of healthy food in dining room used by all from 3 up. Lunch arrangements and uniform only negative comments from the girls we spoke to – was ever thus.

All girls means just that here, from nursery to sixth form. Social and debating events with local co-ed schools, Oxbridge preparation with co-ed Durham School on offer.

Christian values lie at the heart of the school, embedded in daily school life with regular religious assemblies, a school chaplain, annual whole school communion, baptism and confirmation preparation and Christian Union. Great continuity and commitment post school days; ex-pupil teachers, governors and parents. Parents and daughters agree that 'there is a feeling of belonging, a mindset to want to do well and a shared set of values amongst the pupils.'

Pastoral care, well-being and discipline: Last inspection praised excellent pastoral provision. Childrens' mental health high on teachers' agenda. Without exception, girls spoke of support and encouragement from teachers; being known well; talents spotted; confidence built. Supplemented by trained counsellor plus school chaplain.

Common to girls' schools, we were assured that bullying and discipline is not a problem. 'Our values spread amongst everyone,' said one, accompanied by nodding heads in unison. They are confident that teachers would sort it if anything did occur – 'there is always someone to go to if you are upset'. PHSE advocates being a 'telling school' and anti-bullying; respect shown by staff integral; parents value the updates on contemporary national issues. Head says, 'proposed changes in behaviour policies shared with the girls as part of review process'.

Well thought out transition for year 7s – a welcome ceilidh and preparatory outreach work with feeder schools in science and Latin plus a joint drama production. Buddying system with year 8s, several joint activities through year to cement relationships. Sixth formers act as 'big sisters' to younger ones. Sixth form piloting mixed tutor groups of years 12 and 13 with positive response.

House system in place throughout whole school and 'we get to join the same house as our big sisters,' one junior told us enthusiastically. Weekly celebration assembly in juniors, where pupil with the highest number of house points gets a badge and has photo on a board. De-merits the flip side, although children we spoke to could not think of one misdemeanour worthy of one. Confident, happy and articulate girls, obviously at ease in their environment. A newcomer from a co-ed primary said, 'It's much better without boys, they chatter a lot and are boastful' Parents value the 'very friendly, family environment' where 'the children are very welcoming and happy'; ' there's a feeling of belonging and the children look out for each other'.

Pupils and parents: Pupils from a wide range of backgrounds from Durham and a broad area around the city, from state and independent schools; some EAL. Extensive bus service – to be widened further. Very satisfied, actively supportive parents who are regularly consulted by the school and kept up to date with weekly news bulletins; information booklets and website – in head's marketing radar. Thoughtful, mature, articulate girls. Notable old girls: Wendy Craig (actress), Joanna Burton (opera singer), Wendy Gibson (TV presenter).

Entrance: At 3+, 4+, 7+ and 10+: by age appropriate assessment; nursery: by informal assessment through play. Takes just above average ability. At 11 and 13+: exams in English and maths, interview and school report; takes above average ability. Sixth: five A*-Bs at GCSE including English and maths, with at least B in prospective A level subjects (A grade for some), school report and interview; about 10 join.

Exit: Almost all juniors to senior school – just over 90 per cent in 2016. Up to 40 per cent leave after GCSE for other sixth forms, mainly local high performing state schools. Almost without exception sixth form leavers to university; four to Oxford in 2016, three studying medicine. Leeds popular, as are Northumbria, Newcastle and University of York St John.

Money matters: Scholarships/exhibitions at 11, 12-14 and 16+: academic, sports, music, performing arts; 10 per cent clerical fee remission, a scholarship for daughters of practising Christians of any denomination based on RS test. Means-tested bursaries up to 50 per cent of fees to girls in about the top half of the ability range – gives over 10 per cent of senior school fee income to these. Sixth form: scholarships worth 100 per cent of fees for very able girls whose parents could not otherwise afford the fees; Ogden Trust scholarship (100 per cent of fees); academic scholarships up to 50 per cent on the basis of exams in two chosen subjects; music scholarships and exhibitions; drama, performing arts, art and sports scholarships; clerical bursaries.

Remarks: High performing (academic, theatrical and musical) single sex school. The only all girls day school in Durham and looking to an increasingly wide catchment. Bedrock of Christian values where every girl matters and talents are discovered and nurtured in a close knit community.

Durham School

Linked with Bow Durham School

Quarry Heads Lane, Durham DH1 4SZ

Pupils: 445 (300 boys, 145 girls); 110 boarders • Ages: 11–18 • Sixth form: 165 • C of E

Fees: Day £13,986 – £16,479; Boarding £20,793 – £29,700 pa

Tel: 01913 864783
Email: enquiries@durhamschool.co.uk
Website: www.durhamschool.co.uk

Headmaster: Since 2014, Kieran McLaughlin (early 40s), previously deputy head (academic) at Rugby. Studied natural sciences at Cambridge, specialising in physics and theoretical physics. Has been head of science and technology at Sevenoaks and head of physics at City of London Girls. Attended selective boys' school St Edward's College in Liverpool, having won an assisted place. In the past was the bass player in an obscure Liverpudlian rock band, as well as pursuing the ancient martial art of jiu-jitsu to black belt level. Married with three young children.

Feels that after some change the school needs time to consolidate. He brings experience of a variety of schools (Durham is his sixth): single sex, co-ed, city day, day and boarding, traditional boarding. Although only 15 per cent of pupils are regular boarders (27 per cent when occasional/flexi boarders are included), he says, 'The school feels like a boarding school', and we would agree.

His focus has been on delivering the school's message in the city and beyond. He believes that 'the school is much better than is generally perceived at delivering its core purpose'. Emphasis is on holistic educational experience, evidenced by the value added at A level being in the top 10 per cent of independent schools. Reminders, too, about academic success, and work is in progress to drive standards higher without being 'an academic hothouse'. Durham is a city where education really does matter and word of mouth really does count. One parent we spoke told us that they had researched in depth seven schools before selecting Durham School.

Has a collegiate management style; teaches physics to year 12. Has an easy manner, and when walking around the school it is obvious he is a visible head to his pupils. Very strong vote of confidence from parents, with one summing up the tenor of the parents we spoke to: 'He is an asset to the school and clearly has a firm grasp on the challenges within education and the strategic development needed to stay ahead and maintain standards of excellence'.

Currently not too distracted by the Durham International Schools initiative – a franchising joint venture with Indian company Infinity, looking to clone Durham ethos in the UAE.

Academic matters: A level nearly 37 per cent A*/A, 61 per cent A*-B in 2016. Probably why school is working to develop academic aspects of the sixth form ('more rigour', a study centre, supervised study time, more intellectual societies). Wide choice of subjects includes economics, politics, psychology, philosophy and ethics, government and politics, classical civilisation, photography, theatre and business studies. EPQ now available together with an enrichment programme which includes a lecture series and five societies, supervised by staff but run by students: Academic, Politic, Heretics, Tristam (scientists) and Medsoc (would-be medics). Very good support with university applications and Oxbridge/elite university preparation.

GCSE results 48 per cent A*/A in 2016. Mathematics, two English, separate sciences or dual award and a modern language compulsory. Option choice includes Latin, classical civilisation, ethics and drama, music, PE, DT graphic products and Greek, off timetable. German or Spanish added to French in year 9 (can also do Latin) and language awareness days, with themed meals. Most recent inspection praised pupil-staff relationships, teaching and use of monitoring, but commented on some marking inconsistency, which school is addressing.

Classrooms tend to be traditional, with just one computer plus projector (only a few interactive whiteboards), some darkish, but also some new ones and some modern ICT facilities with a stock of iPads though probably 'bring your own device' the way forward. Wifi connectivity has improved and a VLE to be launched shortly.

Strong learning support department – well qualified, flexible, sensitive; can cope with most needs apart from severe behavioural problems. The spread out nature of the campus could be a problem for anyone with major physical disabilities. Screens all new entrants for dyslexia and ESL, if from overseas (extra charge for ESL – full-time specialist – and learning support sessions); trains other staff. Thorough-going gifted and talented policy – systematic identification and monitoring, early maths GCSE, fourth A level and extra, challenging activities.

Games, options, the arts: Astroturf, functional swimming pool, sports hall, playing fields, very good rowing facilities and access to top flight coaching. Individuals and teams successful at regional, county and national levels with rugby first XV reaching the Natwest Trophy semi finals and the hockey teams getting to the National Schools Regional Finals in 2014.

One of the oldest rowing clubs in the country (dates from 1847) – the whole 1970 crew represented GB and has current international stars. Water polo taking off in a big way, ski team reached finals of English Schools' Championships, a GB fencer; also cross-country, golf, squash, boxing, rifle shooting, wind surfing and climbing. All pupils participate in 4.5 hours of sport and physical activity per week, still partly compulsory in the sixth form. Girls have more chance of being in teams through being in a minority.

Very accomplished choral singing – TV appearances, radio broadcasts, including Radio 4's Sunday Worship and a number of CDs. All Steinway school so plenty of pianists. Orchestras, jazz band, rock group; performance opportunities abound with concerts at The Sage, Gateshead and Durham Cathedral plus foreign tours.

Plenty of opportunity to showcase their dramatic talents in a variety of genres and settings – big musicals like Les Misérables in Durham's Gala Theatre or plays like The Great Gatsby in the school's own performance space, The Luce. Also more informal performances take place in the school's modern studio theatre.

Inter-house competition is rife with the show-stopping annual music competition (staged alternate years in the Sage and the Chapel) top of the bill. Sporting and drama events are staged throughout the year with much-coveted trophies for the winners.

Wide choice of activities from creative writing to computer programming, peer support to the languages film club. D of E and CCF (all three sections). School participates in BBC School Report (writing news bulletins and reports) and the lively and entertaining school newspaper, The Durham Eye, printed in house, has reached the finals of a national schools media competition. Careers education now expanding using network of Old Dunelmians.

Lots of fundraising for charity and foreign trips – staff and pupils seem to have bags of energy and enterprise; Chinese Exchange Visit to Chengdu; World Challenge to Borneo, Africa, Ecuador, Vietnam or India, cricket tour to Antigua, hockey tour to Portugal, rowing camps in Belgium and Norway, winter walking in Scotland, ski trip to the Alps – plenty of opportunities to do good and see the world.

Boarding: With boarding all is possible – full (starts in year 9), weekly and part time. Four of the five houses include day and boarding pupils – three for boys and one for girls. The majority of boarders are from overseas (plus Forces children) – most from Hong Kong, mainland China and Germany – and room allocations mix nationalities. Each house, located along a street outside the main campus, has studies (shared or single), common rooms, kitchen and leisure facilities, and have had some refurbishment. The boarding provision was graded good in the last inspection – a relaxed atmosphere, flexible eating arrangements on Sundays, plenty of activities. Good range of food (we can recommend the home-made veg soup), but boarders we met wanted a more substantial meal later in the evening, after their sports training.

Background and atmosphere: One of oldest schools in the country – goes back to Cardinal Langley's re-founding of Durham Cathedral in 1414; at the end of the last century became more or less independent of the dean and chapter. Originally situated on Palace Green, next to the cathedral; moved to present site on other side of River Wear, 1844, only five minutes' walk from city centre.

The entrance to the school provides an attractive glimpse of the site – though there is no time to enjoy it if arriving at break times. Hordes of pupils stream across the car park on the way to their houses, seemingly oblivious to any car navigating its way to the tightly packed parking bays.

Once stationary, just enjoy the view; mellow sandstone buildings flank grassy lawns leading to the hill that ascends to the chapel. The 98 steps all commemorate old boys who died in the two world wars. On Remembrance Day the whole school lines the stairs at twilight, holding candles, while a wreath is laid on the memorial plaque, which must be very moving. Stunning view of viaduct, cathedral and school from the top. The 1926 traditional chapel has pews etched with the names of all leavers.

Further up is the Astroturf and beyond, up again, are rugby pitches. You need to be pretty fit just to get to them, let alone train and play. The sports hall and sixth form centre can be found in this vicinity after passing the quirky classics building.

There is a real feel of a traditional rural boarding school, with lovely views of sports fields and gardens containing many mature trees. Although the majority of the pupils don't board (day ends at 6pm), each has a house where they have common rooms and their own space to retreat to before and after school and during breaks in the day. Registration is held here each morning with the houseparent and there are strong bonds between fellow house members.

Girls were introduced into the sixth form in 1985 and Durham became fully co-educational in 1998. Girls feel that there has been a move in recent years to fully integrate them in what is now a true co-educational setting. They are outnumbered 2:1 by the boys, but feel 'very comfortable with the balance,' having single sex houses.

There is a strong sense of community and leadership opportunities with house captains and monitors (prefects) who are now selected through written application and interview.

Chapel plays a central role in school life with three assemblies a week. There are also strong links to the cathedral with services and concerts held there. Various school councils and pupils told us that they feel their voices are heard. A parent told us that 'The school finds where the individual can develop and works with it'. Not only discovering academic, sporting or musical latent talent but 'developing confident individuals with great self belief'. Parents like the house system, providing 'ever greater maturity and acceptance of responsibility' to pupils – and the competition too, 'They all get very involved'.

Pastoral care, well-being and discipline: Pastoral care centred on form tutor and house staff, plus chaplain – rated outstanding by inspection, which glowed about relationships in general and moral and social development. Bullying not seen as a problem – pupils we met felt should it occur, it would be dealt with quickly and effectively (school would exclude if necessary), anti-cyber-bullying policy devised by staff and pupils. There is a clear escalation of staff to speak to about any problems, academic or pastoral. Pupils we met told us that they knew who they were and would be happy to talk to a number.

Senior prefects and school and house monitors support younger pupils – 'It's a very caring environment: the house system works very well'. A sixth former who joined in year 12 from a state school spoke of how quickly he had been integrated into friendship groups 'who conducted themselves so differently' from his previous school.

New children have an acquaintance day in the summer term before entry, an induction day just before term starts and a 'buddy' in their house when they arrive. Prep school pupils will also have used the senior school facilities regularly and visited for a day in year 5.

Pupils and parents: At 11, about half from prep school, most of rest from state primaries; at 13 and 16 from a range of state and independent schools. Many of day and weekly boarding pupils from within or close to Durham, others from as far as Sunderland, Newcastle or Darlington. A range of ethnic and financial backgrounds but mostly professional or self-employed.

Plenty of contact with generally satisfied parents – weekly e-letter, website, academic diaries, meetings, a parents' forum. Forthcoming, well-mannered, confident pupils. Proud of their school and appreciative of what they have gained; one boy told us, 'I often wonder what person I would be now if I hadn't been at Durham'. Certainly, new sixth formers joining from local secondaries are bowled over by the collegiality, welcome and attitude to learning.

E

Entrance: At 11+: short tests in English, mathematics and VR; 13+: all have to take tests in English and mathematics plus short interview. Above average ability but a wide range. Sixth form entrants need five GCSEs at B or above with a minimum C in mathematics and English; also by interview and school report.

If overseas applicants can't sit the entrance exam, they can get in with a school reference, but need a good level of English – for sixth form need level 5.5 IELTS. Some stay in sixth for three years – special programme for first year. Has top rated tier 4 boarding sponsors' licence.

Exit: A small number leaves at the end of year 11 for vocational courses or jobs and a few at the end of year 12, after some more maturing. Northern redbrick and 'new' universities favourite, north and south of the border: Newcastle, and Northumbria top choices, Edinburgh, St Andrews, Sheffield, York, Liverpool and Durham popular. A few to Oxbridge – two in 2016 – and US universities sneaking in. Wide range of subjects: civil and chemical engineering popular choices as well, as business, biomedical sciences and psychology, plus a few medics and lawyers.

Money matters: Various academic, music, drama, art and sports awards, at 11+ and 13+, with organ scholarship and Burkitt scholarships and exhibitions added on at 16+. Sibling, Forces and clergy discounts. About 150 pupils have means-tested assistance and 105 non-means-tested admissions scholarships of a maximum of £1,000.

Remarks: A sense of community and history binds the pupils together, underpinned by the strong house system for day and boarding pupils alike. Work in progress on the academic front, but produces well-rounded, confident young people, who have opportunities to develop a wide range of talents to a high level in a supportive, peaceful and very attractive environment.

Ermysted's Grammar School

Gargrave Road, Skipton, North Yorkshire BD23 1PL

Pupils: 814 • Ages: 11–18 • Sixth form: 239

Tel: 01756 792186
Email: admin@ermysteds.n-yorks.sch.uk
Website: www.ermysteds.n-yorks.sch.uk

Head Teacher: Since September 2016, Michael Evans, previously deputy head at St Olave's Grammar School in Kent.

Academic matters: High achievers. At A level in 2016, 67 per cent A*-B with 40 per cent A*/A; most do four along with general studies; AQA Bacc (very good EPQ results); last Ofsted rated teaching outstanding. Non-standard subjects: Latin, classical civilisation, economics (the room presided over by three plaster gnomes sitting on the window sill – the Gnomes of Zurich?), psychology, critical thinking. Also government and politics, drama and theatre studies, PE and French, open to the Girls' High; will run subjects for just one or two students. Strong maths, chemistry, biology, economics, English language and literature, German, history. The very bright have been taking first year Open University courses as well (YASS modules) through science specialism funding – alas, no longer available. Average class size: 18-20. A parent we spoke to felt some of the teaching could be 'more dynamic and contemporary' (others were very happy); this is an area the school is keen to improve.

Deputy head/head of sixth on top of his game: writes brilliant guides – comprehensive and entertaining, to boot – on success at sixth form, choosing universities, writing personal statements and Oxbridge interviews; the latter consists of detailed accounts of past boys' experiences, plus feedback letters about unsuccessful applicants from admissions tutors, and kept us absorbed on our train journey home from Skipton to Sheffield – and very nearly to Doncaster! All students have a mock interview with a professional. Success at national competitions, eg science Olympiads, Maths Team Challenge, Great Shakespeare Debate.

GCSE also fairly strong – 2016: 53 per cent A*-A; sciences (all do three separate ones – science specialist college), PE and RS stand out. Sets can be up to 32 but bottom ones 10-12. High KS3 performance; can take GCSE in astronomy. Lots of science enrichment: links with Leeds University, Salters' Festival, summer camps. Very good value added stats. Plenty of IT – choice of exams – but no wireless networking yet; trialling use of netbooks in English department. Two modern language teachers considered the best in the county by the LA advisor, French and German nationals as assistants.

Focused, well behaved boys in the library and any classes we observed. The ones we spoke to appreciative of teachers: 'Even the busiest teachers can always find time for us', 'They can't do enough for you', 'They tailor the teaching to the individual, not the whole class', 'In the sixth form they let you learn in your own way..they are almost like your friends'.

SENCo able to cover a wide range of special needs but no specialist support available, unless a boy is statemented – differentiation within classroom strategy. Whole school approach to dyslexia – teachers use dyslexia-friendly techniques with everyone; will test if requested, but also piloting initial screening of all year 12s with in house test. English department runs extra sessions of literacy support at KS3.

Games, options, the arts: Sports hall with cricket nets and climbing wall plus mini fitness suite, but limited land, so uses town leisure centre to supplement playing fields and for swimming. New pavilion with sixth form common room in prospect. The usual sports plus cross-country (very strong at county level and current national fell running champs), climbing, orienteering, basketball, badminton, golf, archery. Traditionally a rugger school, though less emphasis on it now; very keen on cricket, played in all weathers (county level success); became Yorkshire hockey champion without its being a school sport – just went in for the competition and won it; sports leader and rugby refereeing qualifications; can do community action instead of games.

Large, well-resourced music room; 'brilliant' big band, managed by 'unbelievably dedicated' teacher – European tour; rock groups, barber shop, plus the usual. Music and drama done with girls from the High (as well as year 10 German exchange) – often musicals, also Shakespeare Schools Festival; several study drama, music or music technology at university and drama schools.

Though art and design exam results are undistinguished, the art we saw was very accomplished and interesting, suggesting the boys are given plenty of freedom to be original; a large, light art room, with a number of connected small rooms used for displays. Modern technology building – manufacturing, resistant materials, electronics, graphics, and now food tech in a new room. Lively school magazine with long, humorous articles.

Work experience in France and Germany, trips to Peru, Iceland and plenty of opportunities for the sixth to boost their personal statements with community work, mentoring junior pupils, helping with sports day at a primary, charity fundraising, teaching at their partner school in Sri Lanka (also cricket and dance tour there), World Challenge.

Background and atmosphere: Preserves a sense of its past as well as being as up to date as funds permit. Voluntary aided – founded 1492 (or possibly 1468) by Pater Toller, Dean of Craven, moved 1875 to present site. 1910 sandstone extension with old wrought iron railings; school bell from original school on display; old boardroom with wooden bookcases housing antiquarian books and portraits of old headmasters. More recent additions all designed sympathetically by the same architect, creating a harmonious effect.

Modern CDT facilities, science labs and classrooms and multi-purpose new refectory with extra-large interactive whiteboard displaying 24 hour news. Good choice of food (healthy school status) which sixth can use as a common room in the afternoons – staff on hand to serve coffee and yummy looking flapjacks. Multi-purpose hall for assemblies and drama performances inter alia, plus small organ; well resourced library with rather fetching maroon and orange decor and separate sixth form learning resource area; amazingly clean and tidy loos (which we don't usually get shown with such pride). Only has one covered play area. Most classrooms are large and light.

Informal motto is 'aiming for excellence', and 'It's OK to work hard – the school runs on the work ethic,' a boy told us. The normal amount of pressure to achieve you would expect in a grammar school, but a spirit of 'friendly competition' and 'You set your own targets'. Not solely focused on academic success and a feeling that 'you are free to be who you are', 'It's a personal school', 'Everyone dumps their bag anywhere and feels it's safe', 'There's a strong community sense'. Keen to get feedback, from boys (on teaching and learning, PSHCE, bullying) and parents before changes are introduced. Sixth formers can go into town at lunchtime and study at home if they have a free half day.

Pastoral care, well-being and discipline: 'The boys' welfare is central,' said a parent. Clear explanation of behaviour expectations and sanctions in boys' planners. Good anti-bullying policy – bullying not seen as an issue by the boys we met: 'It's never mean or malicious', 'The school is very good at managing it – they crack down on it'. Twelve year 10s trained to support lower school boys. Teachers seen as very approachable: 'Your form teacher is always there if you've got a problem', 'There's always someone you can talk to'.

Pupils and parents: Boys come from Skipton and a wide area beyond, from over 50 primary schools. Mostly middle and working class with a small proportion of ethnic minority. The boys we met were delightful – very thoughtful, sensible and unassuming, ranging from sensitive, reformed man (the head boy elect) to a school team member Dr Arnold would have approved of. Active PTA. Maths and science events for parents plus access to evening GCSE astronomy class. Old boys include Iain Macleod (politician) and Simon Beaufoy (scriptwriter of The Full Monty).

Entrance: 11+: VR and non VR tests; takes well above average ability, but quite a broad range for a grammar, extending to the top 30 per cent; much private tutoring by parents. Oversubscribed – uses siblings rule, distance from school; can try exam again for years 8-10 if spaces.

Sixth: up to 15 per cent (20-22) from other secondaries. Need six A*-Cs at GCSE, with B in would be A level subjects (A for maths), but flexible; also interview with head of sixth and tour of school plus meetings with other teachers (all part of selection process) – hugely oversubscribed.

Exit: About 10 per cent leave after GCSE for, eg, apprenticeships, employment, RAF or FE colleges, to do vocational courses or different A levels. Nearly all sixth formers to university; usually several to Oxbridge (six in 2016); other popular destinations Durham, Sheffield, Lancaster, Exeter, Bath, Birmingham and Newcastle.

Remarks: Skipton can be described as a sleepy market town, but this school produces very able boys capable of getting to the top, who may need a bit of pushing to do so. It is getting a great deal right in a wide sense, if the boys we met are typical.

The Froebelian School

Clarence Road, Horsforth, Leeds, West Yorkshire LS18 4LB

Pupils: 185 • Ages: 3–11

Fees: £4,785 – £7,770 pa

Tel: 01132 583047
Email: admissions@froebelian.co.uk
Website: www.froebelian.com

Headteacher: Since 2015, Catherine Dodds BEd PGCE Bretton Hall, University of Leeds Realised her vocation when a teaching assistant at BGGS and first teaching appointment as class teacher and English and drama co-ordinator at Silcoates Junior School. Similar role followed in 2002 at Leeds Girls' High School until 2005 when promoted to deputy head designate, pending the merger with Leeds Grammar. Became one of three junior school deputy heads at the Grammar School at Leeds on the Alwoodley site after the merger in 2008, responsible for operations, assessment and reporting.

A Yorkshire lass, first headship though an experienced practitioner and manager, relishing the autonomy of her role in a stand-alone prep school. Believes in being very visible to pupils and parents alike and is at the school gate morning and afternoon – a presence that also helps to police parent parking infringements in narrow lane next to the school. Teaches ICT and art and, as one might expect in a small school, has quickly got up to speed, knowing the name of every child and their family connections with current pupils and alumni – this is a school that has strong and loyal support through generations.

Took over a very steady ship after 24 years with previous head John Tranmer at the helm. Very aware of the school's reputation for consistent high academic standards and excellent pastoral care, and that any changes are under the spotlight of the small community of extremely loyal governors, parents and alumni. As ever, it's not possible to please everyone all of the time, and parents felt some changes had been rushed and that 'sometimes the old adage "if it ain't broke, don't fix it" comes to mind'.

Building projects lie close to the head's heart, and an internal rationalisation and reconfiguration of accommodation at the school was completed during her first year. This mirrors a personal interest in interior design and property renovation, as well as a love of the outdoors. A keen walker, with the Dales right on the doorstep; gardening another leisure activity, with a recently established veggie patch. A keen luvvie of am dram, her prime outlet now is assemblies. Pupils told us how she led assembly dressed as a pirate. On another occasion parents liked her using shaving foam to illustrate the point that if you say unkind things, you can't just rub them out as you can with foam. They commented that 'these kinds of creative touches really help cement understanding in young children'.

Married with two sons, both at school here.

Entrance: One-form entry mainly at 3+ to lower kindegarten, though a few join at 4+. First to register invited to spend some time in school for informal assessment by staff. A more formal assessment for older children.

First Steps at Froebelian is a nursery a few minutes' drive away for children of 3 months to 5 years. Pre-school room at nursery runs parallel to lower kindergarten in school but a number transfer to the school at 3+ – topped up by a handful of new recruits from elsewhere.

Forward thinking for a prep school, a bursary fund was launched in 2003. Provides means-tested support to a handful of children each year. A fee reduction is given to families with three or more children at the school. No scholarships.

Exit: The majority to fee-paying schools, top choices being co-educational Bradford and Leeds independent grammar schools and Woodhouse Grove (scholarships abound). Harrogate Ladies' College, Ashville and Gateways also feature; occasional entrant to Eton, Wycombe Abbey, Queen Margaret's and other boarding schools further afield. Some schools send admissions staff to Y6 autumn parent meeting.

Well-regarded state schools in Otley, Harrogate and Menston are also contenders, alongside selective Ripon Grammar, with some parents willing to relocate to be in catchment.

The school works closely with parents and pupils to enable entrance to the school of choice – the benefit of being a stand-alone prep.

Remarks: Consistently a high achiever in national KS2 results: 22nd in the national rankings in the last Sunday Times listing. Pupils thrive on good teaching and academic challenge in a warm and nurturing environment. A small but loyal and committed staff, with 40 per cent having been at the school for at least eight years, yet sufficient fresh blood as well. One form entry, classes maximum 26, each with teacher and assistant, with two TAs in kindergarten.

Lower kindergarten housed in the former coach house located across the playground from the main school building. A cosy setting with 26 full time places with additional quiet room for focused activity, smartboard and computers. A structured morning, starting with a number and letter per week, specialist music, sport and IT which continues through to KS1, and play afternoons optional for the 'little acorns' who change into mufti after lunch. Shared learning area just round the corner outside kindergarten (reception) where most children transfer when ready.

Main school building houses KS1 classrooms on the ground floor and pupils move onwards and upwards as they progress to the top class. Classroom settings progress from round tables to serried ranks of desks in the top two classes. Reception teaches EYFS curriculum based on themes changed half termly with direct access to outside learning area. Music, drama and art timetabled with annual nativity and parent assemblies for performance opportunities.

Broad curriculum in KS2 with French, drama, music and DT added to specialist teaching. Progress testing at the end of each topic. Weekly 'directed improvement and reflection time' for pupil self-assessment. Plenty of smartboards and IT hardware around with designated suite for timetabled ICT – classes split and rota of digital literacy and computer science. Top class focus on senior school entrance in autumn term and then five steps challenge (a mini Duke of Edinburgh), and the school production project activities predominate the timetable in spring and summer terms. For seven per cent of pupils English is not their first language but no support is needed. A handful of SEND children have individual education plans, predominantly in-class differentiation. A very few have dedicated one-on-one time with a specialist teacher, at extra charge.

If direct access to facilities for sport is important, this is not the school for you. No changing rooms – boys and girls change in separate classrooms. Playground for PE, the only outdoor on-site space; hall doubles for indoor PE and gym, playing fields a short walk away, Astroturf and swimming pool a bus ride away. Doesn't stop them competing – particularly successful at netball.

Lots of opportunity for drama, including LAMDA classes and thriving weekly drama club. Crowning glory is the Y5 and 6 musical production staged at Yeadon Town Hall after the annual speech day. Y6 pupils work as a production company masterminding every aspect including marketing, staging and participation. Strongly supported by committed teachers, willing and creative parents, and a peri teacher orchestra, the final performance is truly amazing. Music taught in a specialised room. Junior classes split on a rota basis, half recorder and half composition, on an impressive line of keyboards. Every year Y6 composes and performs a leaving song. Visiting peris teach voice, string and wind instruments at extra charge.

Evidence all around school of pupils' artwork with the outcomes of previous annual spring arts weeks. Incorporating expressive and performing arts, woven willow statues in the outdoor learning zone and the 2013 celebratory centenary mural on a playground wall, just some of the evidence of the breadth of this much cherished whole-school project. A DT room for juniors well resourced with equipment including a sublimator for personalising products, kept in pristine condition in keeping with rest of school.

A good range of clubs at lunchtime and after school from Ready Steady Cook to Jabadao. Others including archery and golf at additional cost. Residentials from Y2 upwards increasing in challenge and distance from home. Four houses with sports competitions, fortnightly meetings and weekly merit assemblies where house cup awarded for highest number of merits. Opportunities for responsibility in top year with a different girl and boy school captain each term. Fundraising for chosen charity (changes each year) and Barnardo cottage boxes a standing item.

From humble beginnings in 1913, founded by stationmaster's daughter teacher Mary Hoe and Froebel trained Doris Hunt, with just 10 children. Moved to its current location in 1959 (The Mount, former home to the Thornton family) and became a charity in 1973. With well-documented history, the school retains a distinctive use of class names alongside its ethos built on founding Froebel principles.

The footprint of the compact site has been fully utilised. The original stone house and coach house extended in a complementary style, with creative often multi-functional use of every nook and cranny. A newly refurbished airy space in the coach house is home to science, art, ballet and homework club. No compromise, though, on bright, spacious classrooms, small but well-used library and dazzling displays throughout. Gleamingly clean and well maintained everywhere, palpable evidence of staff that really care.

Tasty grub in the Hub for lunch, seated at fold-away tables and benches as space doubles up for pre-and after-school care 7.30am till 6pm where breakfast and a light tea are served. Outside a lot is packed into the confined playground area that surrounds the school. Edged with tight-packed storage sheds and summerhouses with a greenhouse, eco club planting boxes and – yes – chickens, room is found for adventure climbing equipment (funded by the parents' association), used as a fun playtime activity on a class rota basis. The terraced outdoor learning zone, clinging on to the side of a small cliff, is a creative use of small piece of adjoining land. Steep steps lead from the playground to the naturally landscaped area, a peaceful oasis well designed for natural history and imaginative outdoor learning and activity.

As you might expect no significant behaviour issues here; strong relationships between staff and pupils and positive behaviour policy. New PSHE Jigsaw scheme launched with weekly theme writ large around the entire school, including sessions of 'mindfulness and calm me' and conflict resolution. 'Catch me being good' cards, an accolade for behaviour 'above and beyond', placed in a prize draw half-termly. Froebelian Flyer Superheroes covers eight aspirational attributes needed to collect the complete set of badges and certificates awarded at weekly merit assembly, with additional incentive of juice and choccy biscuit at break. Hundred per cent attendance awards given out half termly – morning late arrival excludes contenders.

A tight knit community, social and family links abound. Parents are generally professionals, high number of medics and over half live in Horsforth or close by in west Leeds. Froebelian's location on the commuter belt from Bradford to Leeds attracts those from further afield. Traditionally mums stayed at home but times are a-changing and lycra clad gym mums lingering in the playground are being replaced by families with two working parents and less time to be involved with the school. Plans are afoot to harness parental support by offering out of hours school facilities for activities such as a choir and running club. Parents say they feel well informed through newsletters, texts and emails. Parent evenings in autumn and spring follow assessment cycle and 'teacher formal notes', with full report at year end.

A small school, parents choose it for the family and 'villagey' feel which helps children 'grow in confidence quickly'. Pupils certainly seem to thrive in this safe and nurturing environment, are well rounded and successfully make their next educational leap. Lack of on-site sports facilities a downside and it's not necessarily on everyone's radar, but definitely one worth a visit.

Fulford School

Fulfordgate, Heslington Lane, Fulford, York YO10 4FY

Pupils: 1,392 • Ages: 11–18 • Sixth form: 294

Tel: 01904 633300
Email: office@fulford.york.sch.uk
Website: www.fulford.york.sch.uk

Headteacher: Since 2013, Ms Lorna Savage (young 50s), came late into teaching following a history degree from Stirling, then working five years in industry before studying for a PGCE via the OU. She has taught here since 1996, and her own children attended the school, so she knows the place inside out, having experienced the full range of teacher and parent roles. With a warm, friendly, Scottish lilt, she gives the impression of being a gentle hand on the tiller whilst also running a tight ship – an effective and impressive combination to manage in a school where expectations are high, on every level. Clear pride in student successes and achievements, plenty of cups and awards in evidence, but it's clear from talking to parents that this is a school with a good heart too and people clearly matter.

Academic matters: There is much to be proud of here – a long-standing reputation for excellent academic results sits alongside a real and genuine commitment to closing the achievement gap between disadvantaged students and others. Opportunities for resilience, independence, team work, creativity and reflection are taken seriously.

Cracking GCSE results: 82 per cent got 5+ A*-C grades with English and maths, 36 per cent A*/A grades; 36 per cent A*/A and 66 per cent A*/B grades at A level in 2016. French from year 7, French and Spanish from year 8 and KS3 now covered in just two years, with GCSE choices made end of year 8 and taught from year 9. Proximity to the university means that, on occasion and where required, the school has brokered additional resources and support in Japanese, Korean and Polish. Plenty of investment in the ICT infrastructure, the VLE is well-used and a valuable additional support for all abilities. Chemistry, physics and biology are all very strong at A level, and BTecs are also available from year 9, which means that all levels of scientific ability (or none) are catered for. Real push for girls in physics and lots of STEM work going on.

Textiles also enormously popular and successful here, and check out the laser printer and cutter and metal casting exhibits. Traditional art much in evidence around school, displayed with pride. Business and economics are popular choices with a designated suite of three classrooms offering up-to-date case studies, visits to companies, outside speakers, role play and internet research to cover a wide range of contemporary topics. AS business students participate in the Nestlé Chocolate Box Challenge, with the winning group competing in the regional final; and a small number of year 13 economics students take part in the Bank of England Target 2.0 Interest Rate competition. A recent visit from the American ambassador gave a real insight into American politics, and such was the success of the Q&A session with students that the school presidents were awarded much-coveted congressional medals during the visit. History film club and World War One battlefield trips add extra colour and realism to the teaching of history, and geographers make much use of the facilities right across Yorkshire before heading off to discover the wonders of plate tectonics and geothermals in Iceland in the sixth form. Good to see plenty of careers advice and guidance in evidence for all abilities; no one left floundering.

No obvious subject weaknesses; academic banding from the start and later setting for core subjects, but reassuringly, there is scope to move across bands, so no feeling unnecessarily stuck or even labelled. The school is also home to an enhanced resource centre with a capacity to offer additional support for 10 students on the autistic spectrum. 'Stretch' activities for the most able involve entry into a number of national and international competitions in a range of academic subjects and extracurricular options.

Games, options, the arts: Muddy boots and trainers around the place suggest sport aplenty before, during and after school. Football, rugby, hockey, netball, athletics, basketball, volleyball, badminton, cricket and more besides all on offer and all played with great skill and enthusiasm, with the school dominating local competitions. Residential activity weekends and trips extend provision and opportunity; highlights include the watersports trip to the South of France each summer and football coaching at the Villarreal club in Spain.

Performing arts are popular, including the drama club, regular theatre trips and the school's links with professional performers and companies; annual whole school productions include such favourites as Bugsy Malone, Joseph, Grease and Little Shop of Horrors. Lots of collaboration with the music department, which is also home to the Fulford Music Academy. Peripatetic staff offer individual music tuition in a range of instruments and there is also a concert band, show band, string ensemble, saxophone group and, for the more technically minded, tuition is given to those interested in becoming a music technician. Jam pods (think instruments not WI) are immensely popular with students, who book spaces at lunchtime to let their creative talents loose.

Extracurricular activities are many and varied and include origami and some high quality and very competitive bridge playing. Interestingly, the whole school recently took part in CPR training – reassuring, should the need ever arise. Posters from the Lord of the Rings, The Hobbit movies and Stonewall ('Some people are gay – get over it') around the walls are reminders of a recent visit from actor Sir Ian McKellan – 'We had 450 students in each assembly join him in a communal You Shall Not Pass, with Sir Ian leading from the front of the hall..which won't be forgotten any time soon,' said a member of staff.

Background and atmosphere: The school opened in 1963 and has been comprehensive since 1970. Little of the original 60s architecture remains; most buildings have been added since then and existing buildings improved, and there is still more to come. The school is situated on the southern outskirts of the city, reasonably close to the racecourse, York marina and, most notably, the university. Given the proximity to key attractions, pretty villages nearby and an excellent school, it's no surprise that house prices around here are somewhat higher than the regional average in this urban/rural catchment mix. Not massively well-funded, though new dining hall, teaching block and sports hall all added, plus improvements to other departments (drama, food technology and photography). However, as a leafy lane school it's at the bottom of the funding pecking order, the tell-tale sign being the fact that the proportion of students eligible for the pupil premium is well below average here, but it's well managed and there is no sense of anything lacking. Tidy landscaping around the grounds makes this place look and feel cared for, and classrooms and corridors are neater and tidier than most. Plenty of playing fields for sport.

Last inspected in 2011, so probably another one looming, but having being judged as 'outstanding' by Ofsted there's probably no tearing hurry. No sense of complacency, though; it's a 'right, what can we do/achieve next?' attitude. The Healthy Achievement Award suggests great food – and apparently it is, because most students, even though given a choice, choose to eat in house. Cashless catering, parents top up a payment card so no need to carry money in school. Charity work is important here, a sense of citizenship and a can-do attitude prevail. The student executive, facing a charity fundraising challenge, put together a very successful Fulford Fest, cleverly picking up on the popular festival notion of selling wristbands to attendees and organising a talent competition for fellow students with an ice cream van in attendance – thereby keeping everyone happy..

Uniform is simple, practical and comfortable – sweatshirts and trousers for most, girls generally preferring trousers to the skirt option. Current drive to tidy it all up a little with a few more restrictions re styling, parents mostly in support of this initiative. No uniform or dress code for sixth form, so casual wear is the norm.

Pastoral care, well-being and discipline: Pastoral system based on four houses, each run by a director of learning, responsible for the progress, personal development and well-being of the students in their care. Students are house captains, allowing plenty of opportunity for developing leadership skills. Strong student support department and high standards of attendance and behaviour, again 'outstanding', according to Ofsted.

Attitudes and expectations are reinforced in displays around school; the core purpose of 'Realising potential, creating the future' as designed by the students themselves, is a mantra that is repeated on every wall in every building, acting as an anchor point for behaviour and thinking. An anti-bullying campaign is well supported by staff and students and led to the setting up of an anonymous email line for anyone with concerns.

Phones are allowed in school, used occasionally in class by sixth formers but under supervision and as part of their studies. Elsewhere they should be on silent and out of sight; if one rings in class, it's confiscated. For those legally old enough, smoking must be off site and is not allowed in school uniform.

Pupils and parents: Parents and their offspring are proud of their school; they demonstrate a sincerity of purpose where yes, academics and industriousness are important (and almost taken as read), but the wider world and concern for others are massively appealing and high on their list of priorities. Parents describe the school's vital magic ingredient as being wrapped around the 'rewarding of positive behaviour' and concern with the students' 'growth as people'. Another major plus is the fact that there appears to be no stigma attached to student support, a view corroborated by a year 7 girl who was keen to tell us that the school is 'hugely inclusive, we learn that people come from different backgrounds and this gives us a balanced view of the world and the different needs of different people' – clearly a future diplomat there.

Parents also value the good home-school communication, telling us 'you never have to wait for a response to an email or letter'. Postcards home are fun – teachers take the time to send these when a student has excelled themselves on a particular day, making everyone's day just that little bit brighter. It demonstrates care, taking the time, simply bothering, and parents notice.

Seen as one of the most diverse schools in a not-very-diverse city, pupils and parents are predominantly from a white, British background, reflecting the local demographic. That said, having an army barracks nearby also means that they have, amongst others, welcomed a small contingent of Nepalese families to the school.

The sixth form is large and students very much in evidence around school. They enjoy a few extra privileges and a new sixth form space, but being so visible means they are, on the whole, excellent role models for younger students, stepping in to support or offer advice if and when required – definitely something brotherly and sisterly about them.

Entrance: Pupils are drawn from villages to the south and east of York as well as the suburbs of Fulford, Fishergate and Heslington. Beyond the primary cluster schools, it also attracts significant numbers of students from other schools in the city and surrounding area to study in its sixth form; minimum five A* to C required for a sixth form place. Much care taken with transition from primary school, helping to bridge the gap, especially with those from tiny village primaries.

Exit: Eighty+ per cent to higher education, around a third to Russell Group; two per cent to Oxbridge and two medics/vets in 2016. Of those not going on to higher education, the progression routes and destinations vary, but increasingly a good number are picking up prestigious and much-sought after places on high value training schemes with companies such as Nestlé and Deloittes. Quite a few leave post-GCSE (38 per cent in 2016) further 15 per cent end of year 12, but zero per cent NEETS; these are not students without a plan.

Remarks: 1066 was the year of the Battle of Fulford, a battle deemed insignificant in what was, as battles go, a very significant year. However it is both significant and ironic that, at least educationally, the fierce battle goes on to gain a place at what has become a popular, well-respected and heavily over-subscribed school here in the leafy suburbs of this grand city.

Gateways School

Harewood, Leeds LS17 9LE

Pupils: 518 • Ages: 2–11 (boys), 2–18 (girls) • Sixth form: 48

Fees: £7,620 – £12,720 pa

Tel: 01132 886345
Email: gateways@gatewayschool.co.uk
Website: www.gatewayschool.co.uk

Headmistress: Since 2012, Dr Tracy Johnson BSc PhD PGCE (mid 40s), read laser physics and optoelectronics at St Andrews. Physics teacher and housemistress at Cheltenham College, then deputy head at Lord Wandsworth College; teaches physics to all year 7 pupils. Married to David, an actuary; two boys, 13 and 14, one at Cundall Manor, one at Ashville College. Enjoys skiing and cycling. Presents papers on, eg, differences between male and female teenage brains and emotional development.

Very focused on improvements in academic achievement, learning support and pastoral care. Also changed catering company very early on – to great effect, as we can testify from our very adventurous salad. Current goals are to encourage more independent thinking at A level and develop a standalone, consistent middle school (years 4 to 9) curriculum, working across the prep and high school sections.

Clearly very much on top of the job and thoroughly enjoying it – 'It's a fantastic first headship,' as the small size of the school means 'everyone knows everyone and everyone knows me'. Practical, firm, lively and open; seen by parents as very approachable, supportive, flexible, commanding 'a tremendous amount of respect without waving a stick' and 'a fantastic role model', as a female academic and scientist'.

Head of prep: Since 2005, Shann Wilcox BEd (late 50s), attended high school in Liverpool, then Leeds University, where she read maths and PE. Taught those subjects at Queensmount School and Wentworth College, Bournemouth, head of juniors at Queen Mary's, Thirsk. Teaches Latin and scholarship class, also a very lively and expert asset for maths. Has introduced specialist teaching from year 3 and developed sports so more matches possible.

Approachable and readily available to parents – 'She knows all the children and the parents', 'She's fantastic..you can go to her with anything' (parents). Impressively on top of the job and very happy in it; firm when necessary. Married to Ian, a quantity surveyor; two adult daughters; enjoys sport and cooking.

Academic matters: Prep teaches national curriculum (but no Sats tests – hooray!) and beyond. French introduced from reception. Unusually, from year 3 has specialist maths, English, science, French, art and DT teaching from high school teachers, plus use of its facilities, which enables fluid transition at 11 years; very small year 4 maths extension group; Latin in year 6. Very systematic checking of achievement and progress; plenty of computers; average class size: 15; 24 max. Half an hour a week enrichment with high school teachers for years 3 to 5. After-school enrichment club available for younger ones with their own teachers. Parents very happy with academic aspects – 'The teachers know the children well and bring them on very well', 'They encourage them and develop their confidence so they achieve more', 'brilliant maths teaching'.

Gifted and talented pupils do extra subjects such as Mandarin, chess and scholarship preparation in class of four to six. In time boys will be prepared for entry and scholarship exams to the Grammar School at Leeds plus other boys' secondaries, where Mrs Wilcox plans to develop relationships.

Strong SEN provision led by dedicated, highly regarded, well qualified and supported SENCo for whole school – mainly for mild learning difficulties; in class support where possible; no extra charge; screening available in year 1; gives guidance to parents as well as teachers.

Non-selective school with a broad ability range and very strong GCSE results: 2016 62 per cent A*/A; English, RS, geography, music, additional maths, separate sciences, Spanish and art stand out. 2015 top performing girls' high school within 25 miles, top school in the UK for value added in maths and science, seventh nationally for overall value added.

Only respectable A level results 2016: 63 per cent A*-B, 31 per cent A*/A, and a marked decline from previous couple of years – head attributes this to a couple of weak cohorts and points out value added levels were maintained. Despite its small size offers 22 A levels – art and design, textiles, photography, media studies, psychology, drama and theatre as well as standard choice. Small sixth form groups, eg five, so lots of individual attention, and will run subjects for just one or two girls – the latter size too pressurised for some but very good preparation for university. Enrichment includes EPQ, certificate of spoken English for higher education, finance, cooking, careers.

Average class size years 7-11: 14; 18 max. Years 7-9 do French, German, Spanish, Latin. Setting in English, maths and science in year 7 (but in general flexible about whether setting is needed). Girls we spoke to feel their lessons are fun and their teachers very helpful and available outside lesson time; parents very happy with progress made. Off school topic days, eg with STEM focus – head and deputy head are both scientists and keen to promote STEM. Experienced, stable staff. Homework club in library till 6pm. Stella programme years 7-13 for able (academically) and talented.

One year pre-GCSE and A level courses offered for Chinese students, who live with local host families and follow a programme that builds up their English skills plus some subject knowledge – gives them a chance to sample A level subjects they might not have otherwise considered. Small group EAL lessons – IELTS taken.

Dedicated, highly regarded, well qualified and supported SENCo: warm, thoughtful, strong on relationships. Assessment available but doesn't screen all year 7s; mainly covers mild learning difficulties. In and outside classroom support at no extra charge; also provides help with individual difficulties as they arise and gives parents guidance; identifies gifted and talented and advises staff.

Games, options, the arts: Prep has good range of music; developing a band. Annual drama production usually a musical. Extracurricular includes horticulture, crafts, orienteering, Spanish, speech and drama exams, karate. Lots of house activity, with officials in each year group from year 3. Has use of senior school sports, dance and drama facilities. Fields teams for trad sports, including tag rugby (with the help of a girl) – inclusive approach; three PE specialists. Large new adventure playground being installed.

Wide range of sports in senior school – trad ones plus basketball, softball, gymnastics, trampolining, badminton;

inclusive approach to teams; successful netball at county level. Fields and modern sports hall with dance studio; ideally would like own Astro but happy with use of local hockey club facilities plus professional coaching; head perfectly sensibly prioritises small classes over having own swimming pool.

Plenty of music: two choirs, orchestra, ensembles when possible; good spread of music styles. Girls organise house music competition; some outstanding singers perform with Opera North or national youth choir.

Speech and drama classes have own space with mini stage – a sixth former has won the Sir Roger Moore award for top mark nationally in grade 8 gold acting medal. Mostly trad plays or musicals plus sixth form panto, produced in modern hexagonal theatre. Interesting art and textiles on display. Lively musical video about school made by sixth form leavers.

Clubs include Amnesty International, business, gardening, debating, young leader award, much D of E. Houses are a big focus – varied competitions. Skiing trip to Italy, netball in South Africa, art in Barcelona, geography in Costa Rica, young leaders' conference in New York.

G

Background and atmosphere: Founded 1941 as girls' prep, developed secondary in 1960s. Rated third best small independent school in the UK by the Telegraph recently. Occupies 22 acre site in rural village of Harewood, between north Leeds and Harrogate. Pleasing mix architecturally of the original building, the Dower House of Harewood House, with wooden panelling and staircases, and attractive, modern buildings in yellow brickwork. Light, bright classrooms; jolly languages area with colourful bunting; quirky cellar space where sixth formers chill out. Fifth formers get the attic – amongst so much niceness and polite behaviour we were reassured to see 'hell yeah dudes' scribbled on a display board exam timetable.

Boys allowed to transfer to prep from mixed early years foundation stage in 2011, in response to parental demand. Only a small number of boys higher up, but year 2 has equal gender balance – keen to recruit more. Spacious, light, bright classrooms in the prep with colourful displays and at least one glass wall. We were particularly taken by the enchanting mini red sofa and armchairs in the library, sited in the atrium. Early years (3 to 5 years): large, attractive, well-resourced areas, in and outside, and access to main school sports, dance and drama facilities, as well as the lavish grounds. Music and PE specialists. Gatehouse Nursery (2 to 3 years): delightful, hexagonal building; bright, colourful space. Lots of outdoor time. Flexible wrap-around care from 7.30am to 6.00pm – children can be booked in at short notice.

School's great charm is the intimate, friendly, family atmosphere, enabling newcomers to settle in quickly, made possible by its small size. Staff know pupils as individuals and are seen as very approachable by girls and parents. For years the senior school had the reputation of being second choice if girls failed to get into the Grammar School at Leeds, but more recently has become the first choice for parents and girls deterred by the size – over 2,000 pupils – and corporate feel of the latter.

Leadership skills fostered – aim is to inject ambition and aspiration, to create future leaders; some success here, going by the impressively poised, mature and well turned out head girl who showed us round. Prefects, house officials in each year group, school council; older girls support younger ones in the high school and prep sections. Girls look very smart in dark tartan skirts with white shirts, red ties, jumpers and blazers. Sixth formers allowed own clothes – office wear.

Well-structured careers programme – networking opportunities with employers and parents, access to mentoring and external qualified careers advisor, years 11 and 12 encouraged to organise own work experience placements after public exams. Most children pleased by the food – lots of variety, with themed days to introduce, eg, Mexican or Indian food – though one termed it 'weird – too adult'. Food council's recommendations are heeded.

Pastoral care, well-being and discipline: Prep school parents we spoke to all praised the quality of communication and relationships with teachers, who respond swiftly to emails and are available at the start and end of the day, enabling problems to get sorted before they can escalate. They value the individual care, secure environment and friendly, family atmosphere.

Senior school strong on support – girls feel they can approach teachers if they have a problem and well prepared for the outside world by their PSHE lessons and form time discussions; counsellor visits regularly. Eating issues, if they occur, dealt with sensitively and flexibly. We were told by our escort that teachers are 'good at knowing when to intervene' and quickly detect if a girl is struggling with a difficulty. Year 9s and 12s mentor year 7s through house system. Plenty of rewards for effort and achievement; punishments and rewards felt to be fair. Parents say the school responds quickly to emails and is open to providing any support that is needed.

Pupils and parents: Pupils mostly from north Leeds and further north, including Wetherby, Harrogate, Ilkley and York (good bus service available); majority from white British, professional and managerial backgrounds.

Open, confident senior school girls, very enthusiastic about the school – appreciative of their small classes enabling so much individual attention, the extracurricular opportunities and trips, and happy to be in a single sex school (though we did not meet many of the older girls, it has to be said).

Famous old girls: Henrietta Hill (youngest female QC); Frances Segelman (sculptor to the royal family).

Entrance: Years 1 to 6: children spend time at the school with their age group and are observed in the classroom. Non-selective, but age-appropriate tests used to identify strengths and weaknesses and check the school is the right fit in a broad sense. Several now arrive for year 6, mainly for scholarship preparation.

Senior school not selective, but external pupils (about one third) sit tests to identify strengths and weaknesses and check school is a good fit. May also have an interview. EAL applicants assessed through interview and reference. Sixth form: minimum of six A*-C GCSEs plus interview; takes average of one fifth external students.

Exit: Pre-reception leavers transfer to state schools, chiefly for financial reasons. In 2016 all girls continued to the senior school (no entry exam), 10 with scholarships: academic (above 11+ standard), sports, music, performing arts, art.

Post-16 around one quarter head mainly for local state sixth forms, for financial reasons, co-education or vocational options. At 18 to various universities, including Russell group (one to Oxford 2016), to study a broad range of subjects.

Money matters: Academic, arts and sports scholarships worth up to 25 per cent of fees for years 7, 9 and 12 (music only up to 15 per cent but includes free tuition for one instrument); exhibition for up to 25 per cent for very good all rounder; foundation award of up to full fees for high academic ability to enable education in an independent school that would otherwise be ruled out. Means-tested bursaries for short term financial difficulties. Reductions for further children (five/10/15 per cent).

Remarks: Its modest size and offer of a well integrated, all-through education, in a secure, very supportive environment, together with high academic standards, are what enable it to flourish at a time when some small independent schools in the north are struggling to survive. Less suitable, though, for girls who would prefer the wider opportunities and challenge of a larger, coed, urban school.

Giggleswick School

    31

Giggleswick, Settle, North Yorkshire BD24 0DE

Pupils: 428; 176 full, 67 flexi boarders • Ages: 3–18 (boarding from 7) • Sixth form: 133 • C of E

Fees: Day £7,518 – £21,321; Boarding £15,456 – £34,800 pa

Tel: 01729 893000
Email: enquiries@giggleswick.org.uk
Website: www.giggleswick.org.uk

Headmaster: Since 2014, Mark Turnbull MA, previously deputy head of Eastbourne College. Studied geography at Liverpool University and did an MA in London; taught geography at Sevenoaks, where he was also head of department, housemaster and head of boarding. An active hockey, cricket and rugby coach, he has led charity and international projects. Married with three children.

Head of junior school: Since 2015, James Mundell LLB PGCE (University of Wales College, Newport), previously acting head.

Academic matters: Mixed age classes years 1/2 and years 3/4. Small class sizes enable personalised learning, and topics are rotated every two years, so no repetition in the curriculum. Parents seem very happy with the outcome, particularly liking 'the way each pupil is treated as an individual and encouraged to develop at their own pace'. Single age classes at years 5 and in the final junior year 6, when all lessons are taught by specialists and home economics is introduced. Parents speak glowingly of the staff, who they say 'are always willing and eager to help/support/listen; nothing is ever too much trouble and most go the extra mile'. Weekly homework in numeracy and literacy. SEN teacher and assistant, working closely with senior school colleagues, provide classroom assistance where need identified – if necessary child withdrawn for one-to-one.

Teaching programmes based on the national curriculum, with languages introduced in reception, but no Latin.

Good reporting to parents, with monthly on-line assessment, tracking effort. Four seasons covered with winter and summer reports, autumn and spring meetings. Also open door welcome for parents, who comment on 'the accessibility and approachability of staff at all levels'.

In 2016, 39 per cent A*/A grades at GCSE and 32 per cent at A level (67 per cent A*/B). Improved academic standards 'spectacular with the same intake', due to personalised learning, with setting in French, maths, science and humanities, focused learning support and 'aspire' programme for gifted and talented. Combined with individual monthly assessment of effort and attainment measured against targets, with tutor sessions to motivate further improvement. All available online to pupil and parents, together with full reports three times a year. Success breeds success and has allowed the school to turn down the odd pupil.

Broad curriculum with separate sciences and a taste of three modern foreign languages and Latin in year 7, reducing to two language subjects by year 9. Choice of 19 GCSE subjects – usually nine or 10 taken. Committed staff, a blend of age and experience who 'provide inspiration to the pupils and are very positive and caring'. 'A pretty impressive bunch' a general view from parents, articulated by one. Small class sizes, less than 20, and significantly smaller groups, down to four pupils, study a selection of the 22 A level courses offered. Sixth form enrichment through the EPQ plus Open University YASS modules – offered alongside A levels for those who require stretch and challenge. Most interests and abilities catered for though those wanting to pursue purely vocational courses are directed elsewhere at 16. No massaging of results here – if you study for a subject you sit the exam. 'Failure not necessarily a bad thing,' says school. 'Sometimes it can provide a much needed wake-up call.'

Special educational needs support tailored to individual need and provided through support in the classroom on the whole. Full time special educational needs co-ordinator and successful buddy system where older children with experience of a learning difficulty mentor younger ones. EFL provided (two to four lessons a week), one-to-one, in study periods, but anyone arriving from abroad must have a basic level of English.

Lots of computers, including some in each boarding house; every pupil has email and a computer link in their study bedroom.

Games, options, the arts: Strong emphasis on sport in the juniors, with sessions five times a week, qualified coaching and excellent facilities. Flourishing music under the baton of own head of music, with the majority of pupils playing an instrument or singing. LAMDA classes for junior 'luvvies' and a chance to shine in annual productions.

Rugby, cricket, cross-country and hockey loom large in the (very full) senior school fixture list. International coaching over the past few years has led to such success that the school has had to drop traditional fixtures in search of more competition. With impressive investment in indoor and outdoor sports facilities almost any and every sporting interest is covered. Seven hard and three grass courts, together with the opportunity to train in Portugal, ensure continued popularity of tennis.

Keen drama started by Russell Harty – several OGs and some pupils active in the profession, but luvvies and their tantrums not tolerated. The Richard Whiteley Theatre, named after the late TV presenter, who was an old boy and governor, provides a suitable and flexible venue for such recent diverse productions as We Will Rock You and Alice in Wonderland.

Art and design taken seriously – a real strength with good facilities across the disciplines, resident artist changing annually, impressively ambitious design work allowing some pupils to skip university foundation courses.

A third of pupils learn an instrument (some play professionally), heavenly chapel choir and lots of bands regularly tour home and abroad. Plenty of opportunity to perform in front of a home crowd with a programme including recitals, concerts and annual rock concert, not to mention the fiercely contested 'themed' inter-house Singing and Speaking competition.

CCF compulsory in year 10, those that carry on can gain silver and gold D of E awards and earn an additional four A/A* GCSEs through the CVQO Public Services BTec scheme, in addition to military qualifications. Making the most of its glorious Dales location, outdoor pursuits activities abound; conservation projects and all the usual opportunities too.

Boarding: Seven houses – four boys', two girls', one junior (years 7 and 8 together with junior school boarders). Different character to each of the boys' houses (not surprising with 500

G

years of history), not so for the girls. All pupils allocated a bed, room mates usually a mix of day and boarding. Small dorms for years 7 and 8, study bedrooms for years 9 and up, shared until year 11 (boys) or sixth form (girls). Senior house staff tutor years 7-10, with pupils choosing their tutors from year 11. Exeats – four a term. Few full junior boarders, though some flexi-boarding in the eight-bedded dorms in the junior boarding house. Full activity programme and a new year 5 boarder spoke glowingly of kindness, good dinners and fun.

The boarding houses we visited were comfortably furnished and in good order though the boys' evidenced more wear and tear. Rooms were reassuringly 'lived in', personalised with posters, photos, soft toys and general clutter. 'Keep calm and carry on' seems to be the universal mantra. Sixth formers play an important role in the smooth running of the house and are rewarded with single rooms. Year 9 prep is done in separate study areas and monitored by sixth formers. Common rooms, displaying fine examples of residents' art, are filled with squashy sofas, board games, puzzles, a Wii, DVDs and music. Strict rules on TV watersheds but Saturday night is film night.

G

Background and atmosphere: Set in the western margins of the magnificent Yorkshire Dales beneath an imposing limestone escarpment, 60 minutes' drive north of Manchester and Leeds (so the brochure says). Founded in 1512, moved to present site in 1869. Attractive buildings overlook Giggleswick village beneath the fabulously restored chapel, complete with landmark copper dome, a fitting reward for the walk up the steep hill.

Immaculate and comfortably sized school campus (big enough to be roomy, small enough to retain a real sense of community) with a calming oasis of lawn in its midst. Happy, relaxed but purposeful atmosphere, knots of pupils engaged in conversation amongst themselves or with staff. Polite and smiling welcome from everyone; a real sense of community.

Promotes a real 'can do' philosophy, encouragement and support for pupils to have a go at anything and everything. Evening prep, activities, clubs, house events, rehearsals and sports practices mean it's a 12 hour school day, with little respite on Saturdays. All the pupils we spoke to seemed to thrive on it, though Sunday evening chapel was popular for the lie in it provided. Not surprisingly, day pupils opt to use their bed in their boarding house on occasions – for a fee.

Recent sympathetic development has included the Richard Whitely theatre, sports halls, all weather pitch, upgrade to classroom facilities and at the heart of the school, the wonderful Sharpe library, where there's always a buzz of activity. IT suite and internet café are popular venues for nightly prep.

All meals eaten in the modern dining hall (cafeteria system, separate sittings, lots of choice and pupil endorsement that the food is good). Boarders can supplement with toast, hot drinks and other snacks they prepare in the house kitchenettes (girls' facilities more extensive than boys' – surprise, surprise).

Sixth form centre with bar on the edge of the main campus– current cohort trying to find ways to make it more 'happening'. Alcohol allowed at weekends but consumption strictly monitored.

Junior school in a green and tranquil setting, discreetly situated on the edge of the campus, in an attractive purpose-built two storey building offering bright modern classrooms with walls covered in dazzling displays of pupil work. A welcoming and happy atmosphere exudes from the spacious early years unit, well accommodated with easy access between indoor and outdoor activity areas. Library, ICT suite, music room, learning support tutorial room and self-contained playground, together with dedicated separate art room and brand new sports hall, provide excellent facilities (particularly considering the small number of pupils).

Pastoral care, well-being and discipline: Lots of 'golds' for good deeds as well as academic achievement in the junior school, building to personal certificates and contributing to house success. Worry box, opened in private weekly, for those who don't feel able to approach friend or teacher. Nice idea – but isn't likely to get much use, we feel. The pupils told us that 'we do fall out but quickly make up with each other.' Parents would agree, as they felt that 'any issues are dealt with swiftly' and that each child's 'strengths, weaknesses, talents and interests are accepted and embraced by staff and pupils alike', so that 'pupils actively congratulate each other on achievements and encourage each other in weaker areas'. The result is happy, self-confident children who show care and concern for those around them.

Senior school parents see pastoral care supported by medical centre, school doctor and chaplain as a major strength. They describe pastoral care as 'fantastic', 'the staff are dedicated and genuinely care about the children'. Correspondingly, there are no significant pupil behaviour problems, though lack of accessibility to temptation in this rural location may help. Chapel is an integral and important part of the school but faith more important than denomination and appreciated by a number of parents who believe 'it adds a special personal spiritual experience'.

Thorough drugs checks (this is no-nonsense Yorkshire) – sniffer dogs brought in termly; compulsory drugs testing used on known and suspected offenders and anyone dealing faces immediate expulsion. Smokers required to attend cessation clinics.

More traffic from boys to girls' houses, visits welcomed but permission must be sought to move away from public areas. Behaviour between sexes 'should not cause embarrassment to anyone'. Staff vigilant for anorexia and similar – system in place to check on pupils suspected of skipping meals, including height/weight monitoring and meal attendance cards.

School engenders a non-bullying culture and staff vigilant for anything that may make a child feel isolated. Sixth formers charged to look out for anyone feeling wobbly. House masters maintain good communication links with parents.

Pupils and parents: Some 55 per cent fully board, the rest are local children from a large catchment area; school transport system. Numbers stable though reduction in boarding. Recession has seen families release property equity by moving to the area – children remain as day pupils; parent commutes to work. Healthy 60:40 ratio boys to girls. School fully co-ed since 1983. Seventeen per cent overseas, 16 per cent expats and Forces – popular with all these. Parents in business and the professions. OGs: James Agate; Richard Whiteley; William Gaunt; Sarah Fox. OG society well established on the internet.

Entrance: Children are welcomed to taster days with no formal entrance examination for junior school, but some assessment, interview with the parent and child and a full report from the previous school. Pupils who are non-native speakers of English may expect to take extra English lessons (EFL) according to need. Children with specific learning difficulties may be accepted provided the school feels able to offer the specialist and general assistance required.

At age 11 Giggleswick entrance exam, at age 13 normally CE together with interview and previous school's report. Entrance into sixth form is by a minimum of five GCSEs at grade B; around 35 new sixth form entrants per year. Giggleswick Junior School, the main feeder for Giggleswick at age 11, shares campus.

Exit: All juniors move up to the senior school. Around 15 per cent leave after GCSEs. Sixth formers to a range of mostly northern universities; one to Oxford and two medics in 2016.

Others to eg Bath, LSE, St Andrews, York, Leeds, Manchester, Newcastle, Durham, Edinburgh, Warwick, Central St Martins.

Money matters: Scholarships and exhibitions for academic, all round achievement, sport and music are awarded at 11+, 13+ and sixth form, with art at 13+ and sixth form and sixth form only design, drama. There are 15-20 awards annually, ranging in value from 10-50 per cent of fees a year, the majority for 20-25 per cent. Means-tested bursaries can increase fee reduction to 75 per cent for scholars who could not otherwise take up an offered place. School has benefited from large gifts from OG Norman Sharpe and more recently Graham Watson (late governor).

Remarks: An 'all round' education with support and encouragement across a spectrum of academic and extracurricular activity, for any willing to take on the challenge. It is a warm and welcoming school with no sign of snobbishness (as you would expect in Yorkshire); secure in its strong moral foundations. As one of our guides said, 'you just have to be prepared to give everything a try, and if you fall out of line there's always someone to help pick you up.'

The Grammar School at Leeds

Alwoodley Gates, Harrogate Road, Leeds LS17 8GS

Pupils: 2,490 • Ages: 3–18 • Sixth form: 420

Fees: £9,630 – £12,906 pa

Tel: 01132 291552
Email: admissions@gsal.org.uk
Website: www.gsal.org.uk

Principal: Since April 2016, Mrs Sue Woodroofe, previously principal of the British School in Brussels (BSB). Trained at Durham as a teacher of English and history and worked in a range of British schools until a family move took her to Belgium and she joined the BSB as deputy head of the secondary school in 2004. She was appointed principal there in 2011.

Head of junior school: Since 2009, Robert Lilley (50s) BA (government and politics from University of Essex) PGCE. Educated at Allerton High, began career in industry, then taught business studies and IT in secondary schools, director of studies at Moorlands (prep), head of junior school at Fulneck, then of Silcoates Schools. Teaches boys' PE and runs chess and Wargaming societies. Relaxed, pleasant, approachable; very popular with pupils and parents – 'Fab...very friendly...honest... conscientious..even-handed...he investigates issues thoroughly and follows up quickly with a solution.' Married to a teacher, three children: one adult, one at university, one at GSL. Enjoys walking and music – plays the guitar and currently learning the trombone to help fill the brass gap in the orchestra.

Arrived one year after the merger of the Girls' and Boys' Grammar Schools – main goal to create identity for new school: wanted to 'keep the grammar school rigour and add the breadth of opportunity of a prep school' by extending extracurricular offer. Also keen to develop partnerships with local primaries via competitions, resource sharing, help with gifted children, activity days.

Since 2015, head of Rose Court nursery and pre-prep is Jo Hall, previously deputy head.

Academic matters: Junior school a Sats-free zone. Some excellent but some average teachers, say parents. The very able provided for by extension work in class, setting in maths, theme days, workshops, mini enterprise group. Won national science and engineering award for week of science activities – specialist science teacher for years 5-6. No significant gender difference in achievement. Children say teachers are helpful, make lessons 'fun, very interactive'. Reasonable amount of homework. Good additional support provided by teaching assistants, subject clinics/clubs too.

One teacher and two assistants for nursery (1:8 ratio), where children are brought on very well – early years foundation stage judged outstanding by Independent Schools Inspectorate. Four reception classes of 15-21, one teacher and one assistant. Also a Sats-free zone filled with busy, happy children enjoying work and play; high achievement levels and plenty of challenge for the very bright, of both genders – parents very happy with progress made. Much use of themed days and weeks, eg science, bushcraft; light amount of homework so parents (often both work) have time to just relax with their children (before and after-school care much used). Strong pastoral care and in house special needs provision, plus visiting speech and language therapist

Good A level results in 2016 (improvement on previous year): 56 per cent A*/A, 88 per cent A*-B; historically strong in sciences, maths, economics (high numbers for these), English lit, French, humanities including RS, government and politics. In 2016 at GCSE: 66 per cent A*/A (slightly down from 2015), with several outstanding individual sets of results. Astronomy and Latin offered; all do RS (many with high grades).

Very impressive successes in national academic competitions for sciences and maths, plus debating, chess, finance/business enterprise (won recent Bank of England interest rate challenge). Also in STEM competitions – awarded three Arkwright Engineering scholarships recently. Uses wide network of links with local businesses and professions to provide other opportunities for gifted and talented students, eg sixth form student able to cook alongside Raymond Blanc.

Classes of 15-22 taught by well established and experienced staff – pupils we met commended them as very helpful and fair and lessons as enjoyable and interactive, going beyond the constraints of exam syllabuses. Parents feel students are pushed to achieve their full potential. Sixth formers deeply appreciative of the 'fantastic' support received for university applications – 'The tutors really care about your applications..They know everyone well..You get sent specific subject bulletins while you are choosing your courses..The careers library is always open' – including preparation for Oxbridge interviews and additional subject tests (separate Oxbridge and UCAS coordinators). Parent: 'They all seem to end up at the right universities.'

Very well qualified and experienced SENCo who works across the whole school, providing valuable continuity, supported by eight assistants, her office discreetly situated at the top of the LRC. Covers wide range of difficulties, including physical – mild rather than severe. Students checked for dyslexia at key points; sixth formers helped to access additional support at university.

Games, options, the arts: All sporting mod cons (parent: 'amazing') including squash courts, leading to impressive success in a wide range of trad sports (national level netball, rugby and hockey) and non trad sports (eg cycling, sailing, badminton, table tennis, golf), from local to international levels. Awarded Independent Sports School of the Year recently. Flourishing girls' football. Opportunities for the less gifted but committed to represent the school too. South African netball tour, golf in Portugal, rugby in Australia.

Masses of music, of all kinds – appearance on Songs of Praise, members of national choirs and orchestras; tour to Czech Republic. Dance and drama studio plus small-scale theatre and open air courtyard performance space produce diverse drama – Fame, Little Shop of Horrors, annual Shakespeare and some less obvious choices. Three students selected for the hugely competitive National Youth Theatre. Vibrant art/technology/ICT quarter supplied with high tech machines; much very good art on display around the school; regular contact with professional artists. Arts festival under way, all students and staff enthusiastically creating gingerbread men in various styles for the driveway.

One afternoon a week dedicated to co-curricular activities in sixth form – lower sixth pioneering an online record of their achievements in this area, to be combined with their academic results to form a GSAL graduation certificate. Clubs and societies galore, many managed by sixth formers, enable all to 'find their niche', eg Model United Nations (now organising a Leeds-wide one), gardening, history of art, poetry slam. CCF (RAF and army sections) collaborates with affiliated state academy; several D of E golds; school council; 20 hours of community service compulsory for lower sixth. Fabulous sum raised for various charities; 27-year partnership with Malawi schools and orphanages. Outdoor activities programme for all pupils in years 7, 9 and 12. Trips to Himalayas, Greece, France, Spain and Germany.

Junior school uses senior school sports facilities to great effect – success in several national competitions in a wide range of sports, standard ones plus table tennis, gymnastics, chess, two high-reaching biathlon stars, a Boccia star (Paralympic sport), a national climber. Parental praise for boys' sports teachers, but some criticism of a lack of support for less talented girls. Wide choice of activities – music, drama, verse speaking, slam poetry, dance, creative writing all thriving. However, getting your child into the more popular (non-sports) ones can be as challenging as 'getting a ticket to the Glastonbury Festival – you have to be very on the ball'; interesting technology topics, eg World War 2 cooking for year 6. Quiz team through to national final. Four houses and school council. Lots of links with senior school – sixth formers help with reading and sports. Transition to senior school organised through art, design and technology workshops; continuity also through shared teachers.

Over 30 different activities per week, including lots of music (very strong – full time specialist teacher) and serious sums (over £4k) raised for national and international charities – well-established link with a school in Malawi plus local nurseries. Pupil Voice (school council).

Background and atmosphere: The largest independent day school in England, formed by a merger of Leeds Girls' High School and Leeds Grammar School in 2008. Girls' school founded in 1876 by Yorkshire Ladies Council for Education, while boys' was founded in 1552 through a bequest from Sir William Sheafield. Occupies a 128 acre site in a well-heeled residential area on the outskirts of the city. Attractive, purpose-built two storey buildings in clean sandstone brick. Big modern hall with organ for year group assemblies. Pleasingly decorated, generous sized, very well stocked library; cheerful modern languages area with colourful bunting consisting of the flags of the main countries leading to the relevant classrooms; spacious sixth form centre with own cafeteria. Vast dining room with wide choice of appetising food (cooked breakfast available) – no complaints here. Tries hard to minimise queuing time, but salad and sandwiches a speedier option than hot, and gets very noisy when full. Smart dark purple uniform – girls wear kilts, sixth formers business-type clothes.

Modern multi-faith chapel with own fine stained glass windows plus original ones from old boys' school. Unusually, students act as faith leaders for the five main faiths (Christian, Jewish, Muslim, Hindu, Sikh), organising lunch time assemblies, celebration of special days and charity fundraising events.

House system (eight houses) central to the rich co-curricular offer – cookery, cycling and triathlon as well as standard competitions, the focus being on having fun trying activities you aren't necessarily brilliant at and making friends across ages and forms. Each house has two captains and four deputies, so plenty of opportunities for leadership, along with the other trad posts. Strong community spirit a testament to the success of the merger – 'There's a lot of camaraderie..friendly competition but not to the point where there's a negative environment,' according to a sixth form girl. More than one of the students we met used the phrase 'friendly competition' when asked if they felt under pressure to always achieve top grades: 'It's OK to do the best you can,' and it's also acceptable not to conform to the norm. Parents say: 'good gender balance...they all get on... not cliquey...a mini university feel.'

Junior school on same site as senior school. Large trad, multi-purpose hall, music room, drama/dance studio, three ICT suites. Very big playground for years 4-6 plus separate quiet playground with picnic tables. Very well stocked, attractive library (over 12,000 books) shows reading really valued. Spacious classrooms – own desk plus large locker. Has increased in size to 100 in a year, so where possible year groups situated together so children feel part of a small unit. Classes of 16-21.

Rose Court nursery/pre-prep on site of ex Leeds Girls' High School – two adapted houses with a modern extension occupied by the nursery. Spacious, light, well-equipped classrooms with very good displays and access to outdoor area; generous sized art, music, ICT, drama/dance rooms.

Pastoral care, well-being and discipline: Confident, articulate junior school children (our tour guide was an extraordinarly self-possessed 10 year old, clearly a CEO in the making), enthusiastic about the quality of their lessons, extracurricular opportunities and friendly atmosphere. Lots of contact with parents, formal and informal, plus staff email addresses in children's planners.

Junior school deputy head just for pastoral care – parents generally happy with this aspect. Bullying can occur, as in any school, said head honestly, but dealt with sensibly. Focus more on reward than punishment – children earn vouchers for the Merit (stationery) shop and can win house points for being kind. Children trained to be well organised in preparation for senior school.

Usual senior school system of form tutors and year heads ('fantastic'), with involvement of heads of houses – tutors know pupils very well; speedy and thoughtful response to problems – pupils say any bullying would be dealt with effectively; a sixth former spoke of 'a vast network if you're struggling.. I always feel I have a teacher to go to'. Alert to eating and other mental health issues. Well planned transition for year 7s, who initially, and understandably, find the school very big, but soon adjust. Firm on smart appearance.

Pupils and parents: Most from north Leeds and surrounding area, eg Ilkley, Harrogate, Tadcaster, Wetherby and Wharfedale. Mainly professional families with two working parents, but a good number with bursaries; wide ethnic mix with many languages spoken. Very engaging junior school children, friendly, lively, confident and enthusiastic, extremely smart in their dark purple and white uniform (kilts for the girls). Two of the parents we spoke to felt this part of the school was more focused on clever, diligent girls than the average child or boys needing more pushing, but others were full of praise ('a lovely school'). About half of seniors from junior school, rest largely from local state schools (entrance tests finely tuned to avoid over-tutored success), plus local preps such as Moorlands, Richmond House and Westville. Confident, articulate, open, natural students. Plenty of contact with parents, whose views are obtained through questionnaires and who are very happy with the school; busy PTA raises serious sums of money.

Many famous, very distinguished old pupils – writers, eg poet Tony Harrison (though his memories of his schooldays are far from genial); Baroness Pauline Neville Jones; Lord Justice Dyson; Marilyn Stowe, family lawyer who played a prominent role in the release of Sally Clark; Sir Gerald Kaufman MP; comedian Barry Cryer, Kaiser Chiefs singer Ricky Wilson; Olympic diver Hannah Starling; golfer Colin Montgomerie.

Entrance: Informal assessments (some reading and number work) for entry into Rose Court; looking for potential and readiness to learn. External candidates for junior school take tests in numeracy, literacy and multiple choice non-verbal reasoning, and spend a day in a class.

Year 7: tests in maths, English, non verbal reasoning, in January (competitive – large numbers apply) plus interview. Years 8-9: similar tests plus interviews in modern foreign languages and sciences and with head of year. Year 10: skills based interviews in core subjects and with head of year. For entry to sixth form at least six Bs at GCSE, with A*/A if choosing maths, sciences or modern foreign languages at A level, reference from current school plus interview; about 20 from outside taken.

Exit: Most move seamlessly from pre-prep to prep. Great majority from prep to senior school (95 per cent in 2016). A lot of help given to parents of any children viewed as unlikely to thrive there.

Very few leave after GCSE. In 2016, 65 per cent to leading Russell Group universities (10 to Oxbridge), to read a full range of academic subjects; 80 per cent of medical, dentistry and veterinary applicants successful (in 2016, 17 places).

Money matters: Over £1 million for means tested bursaries (up to full fees), scholarships, music awards and temporary financial support grants – 200+ pupils benefit.

Remarks: Offers outstanding opportunities, both academic and extracurricular, the latter much valued by students of all ages. Also values kindness, tolerance and giving to others in need, both at home and abroad, thus paying far more than lip service to the cliched educational aim of 'developing the whole person'. Heartfelt accolade from parent: 'The school blows me away. I feel so proud my daughter goes there.'

Greenhead College

Greenhead Road, Huddersfield, West Yorkshire HD1 4ES

Pupils: 2,350 • Ages: 16–19 • Sixth form: 2,350

Tel: 01484 422032
Email: college@greenhead.ac.uk
Website: www.greenhead.ac.uk

Principal: Since September 2016, Simon Lett, previously vice principal at Notre Dame Catholic Sixth Form College in Leeds. Birmingham born, he has taught extensively in FE and sixth form colleges, and was one of the founding members of Longley Park Sixth Form College in Sheffield before joining Notre Dame. He is keen to encourage students to broaden their experiences beyond the classroom. He lives in York with his wife and young twins; he is a keen circuit trainer and a lover of jazz and the arts.

Academic matters: 2016 A levels: 62 per cent A*-B; 34 per cent A*/A (one of the top sixth form colleges nationally); consistent performer. Wide choice: law, government and politics, geology, four modern languages (native speakers for oral practice housed in the wittily named Foreign Embassy, teachers in the Foreign Office), music technology and music; very successful EPQ); four applied subjects. Strong numbers for chemistry (plenty of girls take this and physics), biology, maths, English, law, economics, geography, business studies. Average class sizes 19 for A level; five hours' homework per subject expected; not much gender achievement gap. Success in all three science Olympiads – one British physics finalist, senior maths challenge and national and international business and economics competitions. Nine-strong staff Oxbridge team (interview reports going back 13 years); regional hub for HE extension programme.

In top 10 per cent nationally for value added – ALPS measuring system originates from Greenhead – through specialising in A levels (in a consortium with two other colleges with different curricular offers), so teachers have high levels of expertise; strong enrichment programme that enables students to develop as people, thus gaining confidence and motivation; and expert personal tutors with a generous allocation of time, permitting plenty of individual support. Subject support readily available – study rooms in each area, students often work in staff rooms.

Students (and Ofsted) praise teaching: 'Brilliant...they love their subjects and make them interesting...they're always happy to help and to go beyond the curriculum...lots of extension opportunities..detailed feedback'.

Very dedicated, well-resourced additional support co-ordinator able to assess for exam access arrangements – early screening for learning support needs; can accommodate all kinds of disability and need. These students achieve at least as well as others. Cheerful learning support study area for all comers so no stigma. Second year mathematicians and scientists mentor struggling first year

Games, options, the arts: Has half-size Astro, playing fields, two tennis courts, sports hall and fitness suite, supplemented by very good nearby community facilities. All the standard sports plus eg boxing, judo, golf, squash, archery, fencing, girls' football, yoga. Very successful national level netball and hockey; regional football; a UK level swimmer; climbing and cross-country doing well too. 'Sport maker' employed to encourage take up of all kinds of sporting activity.

Much music including jazz, guitar, advanced theory and music technology; work with Kirklees Music School, Opera North, Halle Orchestra, Huddersfield Contemporary Music Festival and a rock school; Paris tour. Drama less well resourced – no theatre – but busy: annual full-scale production plus original piece taken to local primary; recent promenade play written and produced by students with Chol theatre company.

Really stunning art on display, notably large scale oil paintings – we can understand the end of year exhibition leading to sales, as we saw much looking professional in standard; syllabus permits wide range of art forms. Inspirational department encourages innovation and risk – a number progress to the Slade.

Fab choice of enrichment activities (prize-winning programme) – book-making, Amnesty International, hefty numbers of gold D of E; some geared towards university courses, eg working with a practising engineer on a real company's problem, mock trial comp, medical ethics, Bible studies for Eng Lit; major voluntary service programme. Large sums raised for charities – students organised an economics event involving international experts and money raised for developing world micro investment projects. Trips to Europe, USA, Iceland, Mozambique.

Very strong on careers – interview practice with professionals and academics; employability skills workshops; careers conference; employment/gap fair focused on non HE routes. Annual project and work placement week with work shadowing, eg at Westminster ('My son had an amazing time..he went away a boy and came back a man'), the Bank of England and of the mayor of twin town Besançon – 'brilliant... unbelievable,' say students; media professionals brought into college to manage ambitious projects.

Background and atmosphere: Located close to centre of Huddersfield in a conservation area (which limits scope for expansion). Main building originally 1920s girls' grammar school, became sixth form college 1994; unsightly 1960s science building, 1990s buildings, plus handsome very new maths and physics centre with spacious labs and classrooms; new building with library and computing resources; a vast space used for assemblies, exams and activities; new music and film studies facilities.

H

Some tired areas – dull corridors lined with lockers, a lot of nondescript lino and carpets and walls that need refreshing – but very good displays everywhere, eg book reviews, politics articles, maths art, colour photos of student activities, plus boxes filled with support and extension material. Easy access to staff facilitated by staff timetables and photos up in every area. Rows and rows of silent students, intent on PCs or textbooks, all over the college – the extensive silent study area has no need of staffing. Cheerfully buzzing, but not raucous, relaxation area with bright green chairs, ping pong table, small shop and modern airy extension.

Students respected as individuals – 'We have freedom to thrive'; active LGBT group; two student reps on governing body and student council suggestions acted on; student voice (student feedback) taken seriously.

Pastoral care, well-being and discipline: Twenty-five personal tutors, who mostly teach A level subjects, each support four tutor groups of around 26 – system has national reputation. Learning support team and transition mentor have extensive liaison with partner schools before enrolment; two in-house counsellors. Current focus on developing resilience in preparation for change from modular to linear exams, a foresighted goal other institutions would do well to emulate. Help for students to settle socially on arrival.

Aims to be 'an adult community with no rules', so students learn to take responsibility for own learning and think for themselves, in readiness for university and the world of work, but 'support there if you need it' (parent).

Pupils and parents: A range of ability – 27 per cent from low-performing secondaries – and socio-economic backgrounds; ethnically mixed (15-20 per cent) reflecting the local community. Articulate, confident students, very enthusiastic about the college (they often return to talk to students about their degree courses) and appreciative of all the staff help. Good level of communication with parents.

Distinguished alumni: Mona Siddique (professor, journalist and Radio 4's Thought for the Day contributor); Liz Green, Matthew Roberts and Spencer Stokes (TV and radio presenters); actor Jessica Gunning.

Entrance: Most courses require at least a C grade at GCSE in English and maths; for three A levels, at least three grade Bs; for four A levels, grade A average; for BTec, 5+ grade Cs; higher requirements for specific subjects; all applicants interviewed. Priority to students from 12 11-16 years partner schools in Huddersfield area (70 per cent of places taken up); rest offered on competitive basis irrespective of address, mainly from Kirklees and neighbouring authorities; very oversubscribed.

Exit: Around ninety per cent to university, with some 40 per cent to Russell Group; 14 to Oxbridge in 2015. Durham, Leeds, Manchester, Newcastle, Nottingham, Sheffield and York well represented. Increasing numbers to European universities and a few to American ones. Business, law, English, history, psychology, engineering, maths, medicine (23 medics in 2016) most popular subjects.

Money matters: Bursary fund for students under 19 from low income households or short term extreme need.

Remarks: Well-deserved recipient of recent Sunday Times Parent Power sixth form college of the year award for consistency of academic achievement. Has the right priorities – funds focused on teaching and learning and student support rather than smart offices or decor. Hearteningly enthusiastic and committed students. 'It's been the making of my son – he's really come into his own there,' glowed a parent.

Highfield Prep School (HLC)

Linked with Harrogate Ladies' College

Clarence Drive, Harrogate, North Yorkshire HG1 2QG

Pupils: 310 • Ages: 2–11

Fees: Day £8,850 – £10,095 pa

Tel: 01423 537045
Email: admissions@hlc.org.uk
Website: www.hlc.org.uk/highfield

Head: Since September 2016, James Savile (late 40s) BEd. Studied primary education and French at Southampton, a fellow member of the College of Teaching and a member of the Chartered Institute of Education Assessors, he brings a wealth of experience in independent education. Appointments in the last five years include, most recently, deputy head at Salisbury Cathedral School, headship at Leweston Prep School in Dorset and a year as principal at Dolphin School and Noah's Ark Nurseries in London.

A modern languages specialist and experienced sports coach, with a particular interest in rugby and athletics, he will build on the recent increased focus on PE in the prep school. He says, 'I'm a big believer in sport for all. That means enabling all children to access sport at their own level and developing their individual skills and abilities.'

Passionate about the importance of creativity in schools, he says, 'People talk a lot about literacy but creativity can sometimes get overlooked. I believe creativity encourages freedom of thinking. It allows children to learn about themselves and recognise who they are. This in turn helps build confidence, encourages independent learning and helps children develop a genuine passion for their own education. That perhaps, above all, is what I hope that children will take with them when they leave Highfield.'

Head's ethos is shaped by a passion for getting the best out of each and every child and he believes that 'As teachers it's our responsibility to get to know and understand each individual child the way their parents know and understand them. It's our role to nurture, support and guide them as individuals and to enable their talents to grow.' He firmly believes that the strength of the relationship between parents, staff and pupils plays a key part in achieving this and its evidence in action at Highfield drew him to the school.

Author of a common entrance revision guide in French, his interests also include military history. Married with a son and daughter.

Head of Bankfield nursery since 2014 is Mrs Emily Bayley, a qualified teacher with extensive experience in pre-school and early years education. A lead teacher for North Yorkshire county council promoting best practice and supporting early years teachers across the county and also a qualified forest school leader. A lover of the outdoors, a passion she shares with her dog, Monty (who is a regular visitor to Bankfield), and the children.

Bubbly, enthusiastic and committed, believes that the key to successful early years development lies in working in partnership with parents, and has brought about a cultural shift in welcoming parents into the school at any and all times. Much appreciated by them; as one commented, 'Bankfield was outstanding in its introduction to formal learning for my daughter and I cannot thank Mrs Bayley and her team enough'. Runs EYFS forums for parents on topics such as sleep, nutrition and play. Topically, mathematics is next on the agenda.

Entrance: At 2+ for Bankfield Nursery by visit, registration and welcome session. Into Highfield, all ages though predominantly at 4+ when majority come from Bankfield. Non-selective but external entrants have assessment and interview with invitation to a separate taster day.

Exit: All girls offered places at Harrogate Ladies' College (Highfield senior school); take-up varies and sometimes very small. Some girls and boys to local independents GSAL, St Olave's York, Ashville, Cundall Manor and Bootham. The majority to the outstanding state provision in Harrogate and Ripon or relocation.

Remarks: Pre-prep and nursery is located in Bankfield, a large Victorian house just across the road from the senior school campus and Highfield Prep. Extensive grounds around the house provide direct access to free play on hard playing areas and garden, with plans for a chicken run. The house has converted into a spacious and well-equipped facility yet it retains its home from home atmosphere. Meals are taken in the dining room and much emphasis on nutritious meals and instilling good manners and social etiquette.

Close links with Highfield Prep (head teaches in reception) and shared events to ensure easy transition for pupils to the next stage – important as around 70 per cent of children progress through to Highfield.

Bankfield children are in two groups until Easter (nursery and pre-prep) and then split into three groups for the summer term (two nursery groups and pre-prep) with the luxury of bespoke areas of the house for each group. For pre-school group, specialist teaching in physical education, music, drama, French and forest school starts to ease them into reception. Jolly Phonics scheme introduced and children encouraged to progress at their own pace.

EYFS qualified teaching staff encouraged by the head to share best practice with other schools in North Yorkshire – currently working with a school in Ilkley – and support them in implementing new practice. Children's learning journeys record their progress and achievements and are much prized by pupils and parents alike. No online journals here.

Core hours of 9am-4pm included within fees, extended to 8am-6pm at additional charge. Open term time only though care is available through Easter and summer holidays at a cost.

Highfield Prep is conveniently sited on the main campus, a playground away from the main college building, a mixture of new-build and Victorian conversion. Spacious and airy hall for group activities and assemblies, with no wasted space in circulation areas. Classrooms on three floors with reception on the ground floor, with direct access to a secure, well-resourced outdoor learning area and playground.

Two classes in most year groups, now mostly 60 per cent girls 40 per cent boys throughout, usually in adjacent classrooms though no particular progression through the building. Dazzling impeccable, well ordered displays of pupils' work and information posters in all, well-equipped classrooms and public areas.

School day action packed with classroom-based teaching across the curriculum, no shortage of educational off-site visits and a mind-boggling number of extracurricular clubs and activities (some included in fees); we particularly like imagineering, boyz noyz and mini messy church.

Independent writing strongly encouraged with golden writing sessions every term from reception. Each piece of work is retained in a portfolio, which moves class with the child, thus charting progress. Streaming of English and mathematics from 8+. Pupils not fazed by it: 'we all have to really understand work before we move on but some understand quicker than others,' revealed a group of pupils. Independent working encouraged but help always on hand, in class or with extra tuition. Science follows classroom-based QCA scheme with occasional use of college laboratory for top juniors. SEN catered for in and out of the classroom by dedicated learning support. Generally, in class teacher support free with scale of charges for a more individual programme.

Specialist French and PE, which has increasing focus – three hours a week timetabled, including weekly swimming from reception plus extracurricular clubs. Staff work with Sporting Influence coaches whose mantra is 'improving social skills through sport' – benefits of attitude to work and discipline evident beyond the playing fields. Centred on traditional team sports but including tcoukball, an indoor game where goals are scored by hitting a small trampoline. Increasing inter-house competition and fixtures against other schools, independent and state – with transport provided by school minibus where needed.

Creative arts are now taught in project days, but according to one parent 'a little hit and miss'. Lots of music making; traditional instruments, class recorder lessons in years 3 and 4; taster days to encourage participation – 'being directed to the right instrument makes all the difference'. Orchestra takes part in prep schools' orchestral day at Uppingham School. A 'sing up' gold award school, there are three choirs and smaller ensembles. Highfield's certainly alive with the sound of music. Weekly timetabled specialist drama lessons. Over 50 per cent of pupils have LAMDA lessons; plenty of performance opportunities in school and out in Schools Shakespeare Festival.

IT integrated into the curriculum and used creatively. We saw this in action with a year 5 group activity, where a fable was created, scripted, enacted and filmed using an iPad, edited and then presented to their peers. QR codes part of topic wall displays encouraging pupils to add knowledge through one click online research.

Assessments each half term, open and transparent sharing with pupils with agreed target setting. Full reports and parents' evenings twice yearly. Weekly updates on what children have been learning.

Merit system – usual stickers, house points, merit assemblies. Strong pastoral care, buddy system for new entrants. As one parent put it, pupils are 'aware of each other's feelings – they try to be kind'. The teddy trophy for the tidiest classroom each week is awarded by the cleaning supervisor – a nice touch.

Effective school council, much valued by pupils who see results from their proposals and understand through class discussion the reasons for rejections. Particularly impressive was a scheme where each class democratically chose a range of playground games using an identical sum donated by the parents' association. Ownership also brings the benefits of less loss and damage. Lots of charitable giving; particularly with Ugandan link school. Tens of families sponsor a child and there is a penpal relationship between the pupils. Recently the first trip of seven children, parents and teachers to Bombo took place.

Healthy eating, nutrition and well-being all high on the agenda with input from the school catering manager on top table manner tips, food waste and tasting menus.

Busy and supportive parents' association, parent volunteers in classroom, Prep Post – weekly update on activities and how parents can give curriculum support written by class teachers.

Highfield and Bankfield are co-educational schools that have a growing confidence, distinct identity and give a strong message of 'this is what we offer'. They are parent friendly with a fun to learn ethos, where children are encouraged and have opportunity to participate and succeed in a range of diverse activities.

Harrogate Ladies' College

Linked with Highfield Prep School (HLC)

Clarence Drive, Harrogate HG1 2QG

Pupils: 280; 115 full, some weekly and flexi boarders • Ages: 11–18 • Sixth form: 110

Fees: Day £15,720 – £21,870; Boarding £27,435 – £34,410 pa

Tel: 01423 537045
Email: admissions@hlc.org.uk
Website: www.hlc.org.uk

Principal: Since 2013, Mrs Sylvia Brett BA MA (40s). Read theology at Durham, followed by masters in philosophy and religion at University of London. Worked in alumni relations and as moral tutor at Durham for four years before joining the Royal Masonic School as RS teacher and sixth form housemistress. Then lay chaplain and head of RS at Caldicott followed by head of lower school, RS teacher and year 7 housemistress at Downe House, before being appointed as sole deputy at Roedean.

Head believes in ensuring girls are 'jolly good at lots of different things' when they leave HLC. Breadth of curriculum and extracurricular opportunities vital and girls 'are encouraged to be brave' in extending their comfort zone and trying new activities.

Open, engaging and caring, has a 'passion for deep learning' and getting to know the young people in her care. Declared by sixth formers as 'more personable' than predecessors, impressed with her interest in them and knowledge of special events in their lives. Parents see the head as 'a traditional headmistress who genuinely cares about the school and its pupils' and as 'a strong, reassuring presence, confident and approachable'. More traditional than her predecessor, say girls, who have noted a downturn in emphasis on 'girl power', and parents who, without complaint, felt the drive is 'less towards cutting edge and 21st century'.

Married to Justin, a classics teacher, and has one daughter who is a pupil at the school. When time permits her interests include music (singing and piano), art, swimming, family and friends.

Academic matters: In 2016, a return to previous levels of A*/A grades at A level at 43 per cent, with A*-B at 66 per cent, a great improvement on the previous year's results. 2014 results of 71 per cent A*-B placed HLC as top performing school at A level in Harrogate, but they were just pipped to the post for that position in 2016. Interestingly, in recent years almost half of sixth form pupils, predominantly international boarders, have been new to the school.

Good range of subjects on offer though numbers can restrict options. Historically, strength in mathematics and sciences, a particular bias in the sixth form, but modern languages are fine – normally only the odd D at GCSE, otherwise all A*-C. Only a handful (groups as small as two per language) opt for modern languages at A level, but achieve good results. Over the past four years, a third of girls have pursued a business-related degree course. Launched 2010 in purpose built business suite, the Business School has increased business-related subjects to include accounting, business studies, economics and psychology, which remain popular choices. Wider purpose continues to promote enterprise and entrepreneurship throughout the school. Extended Project Qualification introduced for older pupils; just over 10 per cent uptake so far.

Consistent 52 per cent A*/A at GCSE in 2016, up from 45 per cent in 2013; value added 1+ grade per subject. Strong performance in all three sciences, English literature, modern foreign languages, humanities and drama, all with at least 65 per cent A*/A grades. Broad curriculum and, common with most schools dual award or single sciences recommended after first year of course, one modern foreign language compulsory and a standard range of options. Statistics offered in addition for top set mathematics.

Teaching is generally very good – friendly, good-humoured staff, and girls feel both known and supported on the whole. Generally a willingness to learn and good manners makes teaching a worthwhile experience here. As one parent said, 'Teachers go the extra mile for pupils regularly'. Plenty of new blood though: across the school 95 per cent of staff have less than 10 years of service, with movement in and out of the independent and state sectors.

Practical subjects good too – impressive art throughout the school and girls using a wide range of complex design and technology equipment. Well-equipped food technology room used up to GCSE. Enrichment programme for first year GCSE and sixth form to widen horizons in preparation for higher education. Plenty of IT facilities but an iPad free zone – 'no gimmicks' says the head; 'IT must enhance learning'.

Class size maximum 24, some as low as 12. Parents' evenings and full reports twice yearly, always discussed with head or tutor prior to being sent home. Displays everywhere still a feature – a striking balance of pupil work and thought-provoking material, alongside posters from house captains rallying the troops.

Overseas students encouraged to sit exams in their native language; additional English language tuition available (and certainly encouraged). EAL students used to sit IELTS rather than GCSE English, but pilot study of integration with mainstream English classes in years 10 and 11 has proved highly successful and continues to be the way forward.

Across the whole school over 10 per cent SEN catered for in and out of the classroom by dedicated learning support. Generally, in class teacher support free with scale of charges for a more individual programmes. Needs span support in cognitive and learning, communication and interaction, emotional and mental health, and sensory and physical.

Games, options, the arts: Sport, the life-blood of the school, is keenly pursued by all with lacrosse ('lackie') embedded in the school's culture. Current holders of U13s northern schools' lacrosse title, with good representation at county and regional level. Good range of competitive team sports with recent successes in tennis, district champions in U13 and U15, Harrogate area U14 netball and North Yorkshire Schools Games winners for rounders. Good, much-used, sports facilities include plenty of tennis and badminton courts, multi-gym, 25-metre pool and an enormous indoor general-purpose sports hall which doubles up as a venue for social events, speech day etc.

Dedicated music house accommodates ensembles galore, from samba to string with four choirs. Music is a real strength and majority of girls learn an instrument or two. Musicians regularly run away with prizes at the Harrogate Festival, chapel choir were semi-finalists in a BBC competition, the challenging baroque opera Dido and Aeneas performed, and a wealth of choral performances in cathedral services, at the Royal Hall and on tour, most recently Barcelona.

A level theatre studies on offer, with plays and productions acted out in the suitably-equipped drama studio. The Merchant of Venice staged in Leeds as part of the Shakespeare Schools Festival and annual competitive inter-house drama filled with theatrical thrills and spills. Curriculum supported by regular trips to concerts, theatre and cinema. Many girls take LAMDA lessons (honours and distinctions the norm).

Art, photography and textiles all on offer at A level. Good facilities and the results of talented artists on show around the school. Careers education taken seriously – two weeks' work experience for all followed by presentation and lunch.

An extensive extracurricular menu with over 20 creatively named clubs ranging from Apprentice to Babel Fish and Legobots, with interesting business breakfast club. Golf, sailing and ski trips as well as keen D of E and masses of charity and community work. Burgeoning participation and success in Leeds Young Enterprise. Enterprise days held in the summer term.

Boarding: Four well-presented boarding houses each have attractive study bedrooms, a common room centred on the TV, kitchen and games room, with room for 30 in two houses and 45 in the third. Upper sixth only in Tower with room for 40. Distinction made between 'home' and school by no pupil access to houses during the school day.

Up to four can share a room in lower school, but currently able to spread out a little more. Most sixth formers have their own room with internet access for all in studies and bedrooms. Two taster nights per term offered to day pupils without charge. A growing number of flexi and weekly boarders, but full boarding offers weekends full of trips and activities, off and on site, with over 90 boarders remaining in school most weekends.

Friendly, comfortable feel, no inter-house rivalry: girls mix well with the sense of a supportive sisterhood and good relations with staff. Encouraged to mix across the ages with a buddy system operating for new pupils. A reward system in place for kind deeds, tidiness and helping out. Celebration of international festivals brings an appreciation of different cultures.

Upper sixth housed in Tower – a half way house between school and university where pupils prepare and eat breakfast and a couple of evening meals in house and have greater freedom than lower down the school (team-building exercises at start of upper sixth aid the bonding process). At 16+ girls are allowed out one night a week.

Background and atmosphere: School founded in 1893 on a nearby site and is one of the Allied Schools. Within walking distance of the busy town centre, in the heart of Harrogate's leafy prime real estate, originally part of the Duchy of Lancaster. The pleasant Victorian mock-Tudor buildings with sympathetic additions blend gently with the locality. C of E (own chapel, resounding hymns et al) in small doses for all without exception. New assembly hall officially opened in 2013 to mark school's 120 year anniversary. Separate sixth form centre in main school complete with common rooms, study centre, kitchens, AV room etc with use of business school café. Unique sixth form studies valued by girls as their space and used for personal study until 9.00pm each evening.

'Being the best you can be', the school motto, is at the heart of the ethos here. Resilience, curiosity and confidence are the aims, engendered by an individual knowledge of each girl by their teachers. The school is proud of being in the top one per cent for value added at GCSE, adding 1+ grade per pupil per subject (the top 5 per cent of schools add on average 0.6+ of a grade).

School council meets regularly, though girls would like it to be less of a talking shop and to exert more power. Uniform throughout the school, predominantly navy with tartan skirts, a nod to the traditional colour scheme, perpetuated by the retention of the green cloak for chapel. Dress code for sixth form – business wear – recently more rigorously enforced.

Food is now provided by external catering company, which has seen a marked improvement in the choice and quality of meals available; recently refurbished dining room. Staff and girls dine together in main dining room, self-service with occasional formal dining. All meals here for boarders during the week, only snacks available in houses for L6 boarders and below. Dinner served in the boarding houses for all boarders at the weekend.

Pastoral care, well-being and discipline: Girls we spoke to are happy here. Manners strictly monitored. Clear guidelines for good behaviour that pupils understand and few challenging misdemeanours. Head has introduced a more positive points system, which is seen by girls as less draconian. Occasional links with other schools, but not into creating artificial exposure to boys. Drugs and similar problems uncommon and treated with firmness – head retains discretion, expulsions rare. Health centre, specialist counsellor, tutors and staff all on hand to help if things go wrong.

Pupils and parents: A widening catchment for day, flexi and weekly boarders, from Ilkley to York and beyond. Looking to attract pupils from Borders and Scotland; currently the majority of boarders are from overseas, particularly in the sixth form. There are around 24 nationalities in school though 40 per cent of boarders are from south east Asia. Within the boarding houses there are shared cultural celebrations and activities, but day girls told us that close bonds with their Pacific Rim peers are the exception rather than the rule.

Parents predominantly from the usual professions, many Harrogate notables, also self-employed and some farming families, popular with the Forces. Turns out informed, assured, polite and articulate girls, cooperative rather than competitive. Strong OG network, including Coki Van der Velde, 2015 Barclays Woman of the Year; Julie Mulligan, police and crime commissioner for North Yorkshire; Juliet Bremner, TV news reporter; Laura Winwood, former president of the Oxford Union. Building a network for more recent leavers to stay in touch.

Entrance: Main entry points are 11, 13 and 16 but school flexible. For Y7 entry, taster day in autumn term, school entrance test (mathematics, English, non-verbal reasoning) and interview taken on January assessment day, together with reports from previous school. Highfield Prep is the linked feeder school though recently only a small number have transferred to the college. Both school and parents gave the reasons as competition from excellent local state provision with families cherry-picking stages of independent education.

Minimum five GCSEs at grade C or above required for entry to sixth form, international pupils tested in English and appropriate subjects. Scholarship assessment programme.

Exit: Retention of day pupils at 16 has seen a recent improvement but historically some 15 per cent leave at 16 for local state or independents. An influx of international pupils – currently more than 60 per cent of sixth formers are boarders – results in a sixth form of some 100+ pupils.

Sixth formers leave for a widespread selection of universities, including London colleges, Exeter and Bath, though northern locations preferred, eg Durham, Edinburgh, York and Manchester. No Oxbridge success since four places in 2013, but over 50 per cent to Russell Group. Wide range of courses: economics and business feature strongly but includes international relations and politics, 3D design and architecture, medicine, PPE, engineering, mathematics and law.

Money matters: A range of scholarships of up to 15 per cent of day fees. Fee reductions of 15 per cent for UK armed forces and 10 percent for offspring of former pupils. Means-tested bursaries up to 110 per cent of day fees to include transport, uniform etc.

Remarks: An 'in-town' girls' day/boarding school that shouts 'girl-centred' education, firmly holding onto its roots whilst reaching out to widen opportunity for its pupils to allow them to blossom in their post-school brave new world. Academic results particularly good at GCSE and a dazzling array of out of classroom opportunities means happy girls and supportive parents. Looking at ways to communicate its distinct offering at home and away to combat the pressures from increasingly competitive North Yorkshire schools.

Hymers College

36

Hymers Avenue, Hull HU3 1LW

Pupils: 1,146 • Ages: 8–18 • Sixth form: 198

Fees: £8,658 – £10,600 pa

Tel: 01482 343555
Email: enquiries@hymers.org
Website: www.hymerscollege.co.uk

Headmaster: Since 2006, Mr David Elstone (50s). Read history and geography at University College, Cardiff and has taught at a variety of independent schools (including six years as depute rector at Hutchesons' Grammar School in Glasgow).

Unceremonious and determined, with a good sense of humour and plenty of drive. He was described by one parent as 'immensely caring'. Brought in 'massive changes' and, as one parent told us, he 'kept the high standards but relaxed the whole school down'. Passionate about education and helping young people to become better learners.

Passion extends to Bristol City football club. A former cricket and hockey master, he maintains his interest in cricket and is a member of the MCC. Married with two sons.

Head of junior school: Since 2010, Mr Peter Doyle BSc PGCE (40s). Read economics at Bristol then spent four years in industry. Followed family vocation by doing PGCE at Hull, then taught in primary schools in the home counties before moving to Stamford Bridge Primary as deputy head. He was deputy head at Hymers College Junior for three years before being appointed as head.

Approachable and caring, with an easy manner. He is a constant support at school events and clearly proud of pupils' achievements. He believes in 'building self esteem and confidence in a culture of high expectation' and says school aims to instil in each pupil 'the belief in their ability to succeed'.

A keen squash player, he also enjoys camping and hill walking. Married to Rachel and two of their three children attend the school (younger daughter waiting in the wings at local state primary).

Academic matters: Broad junior school curriculum, with shared senior school teaching in geography and sport. French, German and Spanish taught from year 5. Science taught in junior school science room. As you might expect with a selective entry, most recent ISI report said pupil attainment was 'good in comparison with national age related expectation.'

Teacher observation, dyslexia detector software and assessment are used to pick up learning support needs. SENCo liaises regularly with senior school and school counsellor. Individual learning plans are drawn up, with one-to-one work where appropriate, in agreement with parents. INPP programme of physical exercises for children needing further learning support has 'had a profound impact in the classroom,' says the head. A member of the junior school staff has been trained to deliver the programme.

Parents receive pupil grades three times a year and a full report annually. Main academic subjects are assessed for attainment, progress, attitude and homework. Mark schemes are on show in every classroom and staff are keen to share good practice across school.

Academically selective on intake, 'though not as selective as most grammar schools'. Standards and expectations are high and exam results very commendable. Little, if anything, to match it locally.

In 2016, 49 per cent A*/A grades at A level (74 per cent A*/B) and 66 per cent A*/A at GCSE. Broad curriculum includes Latin. Streaming in maths only until year 10. French, German and Spanish on offer, though linguists in the school would appreciate even more choice. Traditional offering at A level including general studies and the EPQ. At GCSE pupils take a minimum of eight subjects, though more on offer if desired (and able).

The four Rs of educationalist Guy Claxton's Learning Power are fundamental to learning here – resourcefulness, resilience, reflectiveness and reciprocity. The head told us: 'We needed to be more flexible in our teaching methods and personalise the learning experience for our pupils. Teaching has changed dramatically in school. We offer a traditional curriculum but it's not what is taught but how it is taught. We need to help to make our pupils' learning secure'. There has been investment in modern technology, a multi-media language laboratory, whiteboards and iPads for teachers.

Fewer than 40 pupils in the senior school have SEN or a disability. Year 7 pupils are given a screening test in year 7 and individual learning difficulties identified through teacher observation too. Personal learning plans are drawn up via one-to-one work, where pupils are assessed, in agreement with parents. A specialist programme of physical exercises for children needing further learning support has 'had a profound impact in the classroom', says the head. A member of the junior school staff has been trained to deliver the programme. A new learning resource centre opened in 2016.

Programme of careers advice starts in year 7, building up year on year to work experience and careers convention in year 11. Year 12 students use Centigrade programme and there is interview training and a series of sixth form lectures given by experts from a variety of professions, business and industry.

Games, options, the arts: Where talent is recognised (whether in sport, music or the arts) pupils are given support and encouragement but are expected to demonstrate commitment and be prepared to put in extra time and effort after school and on Saturdays. Opting out isn't an option. Games compulsory – rugby and cricket for boys, hockey (notably successful) and netball for girls, tennis (very successful) and athletics for both. Pupils well represented in national competitions. Supervised swim available every morning from 8-8.30am.

Successful and nationally recognised music department, with representation in the National Youth Choir. Nearly 40 per cent of pupils take voice and instrument tuition. Free instrument loan for an indeterminate period. One of the highest number of pupils in the country taking ABRSM exams. New music building with top rate facilities including recording studio. Lots of performances by choirs, ensembles and orchestras – in-house and at venues like Beverley Minster. Junior school was riding high on their 40-strong choir coming second in the BBC's Songs of Praise Choir of the Year competition when we visited. Particularly delighted with judges' comment on how 'happy and relaxed' pupils were. Sixty-five per cent of junior school pupils sing in a choir and choral tour to Paris for year 5s. Lots of opportunities for musical instrument tuition, at additional charge, with free instrument loan for new starters. Percussion, wind and string groups with performances throughout year and annual chamber concert, with performers volunteering for a spot.

Drama is thriving – subject is included in year 7 and 8 curriculum and offered at GCSE and at AS level. Recent productions in 200-seater Judi Dench Theatre include The Magic Flute and Dracula and involved music, art, design, business and electronics departments. Annual productions for each year group. Dance clubs for year 5 and 6 girls and extracurricular programme includes crafty kids (hopefully not aptly named) and photography club. Free after-school supervised homework club for juniors until 5.30pm.

Debating and Young Enterprise very active. D of E scheme regularly attracts over 100 pupils a year. Army Cadet Force (voluntary and after-school) popular with 30 or so members. Sporting and music tours on offer but with a maximum cost to pupils of £1,000 – a nod to the economic downturn. Residential trips feature prominently in junior school; year 5 pupils visit Normandy and the battlefields and year 6s do outdoor pursuits in the Lake District.

Background and atmosphere: Opened in 1893 as a school for boys. School's founder, the Reverend John Hymers, a Cambridge fellow and Rector of Brandesburton, left money in his will for a school to be built 'for the training of intelligence in whatever social rank of life it may be found among the vast and varied population of the town and port of Hull'. The school has remained true to founder's intent, with below average fees and over 120 pupils receiving financial assistance through means-tested bursaries funded by own endowments and The Ogden Trust.

Pleasing approach to the main entrance, which overlooks well-maintained playing fields, all-weather pitches and even a lake for keen ornithologists. Belies first impressions: when stepping inside you are immediately confronted with a view of the traditional assembly hall, lined with doors of carved wooden lockers ajar and adorned with sports bags, spilling items of PE kit, books and papers. It does get better, particularly in the new facilities.

Careful financial management (and some generous benefactors) has enabled extensive recent investment in new theatre, sports hall, sixth form centre, junior school and swimming pool. Attractive and sympathetic to the original buildings, though perhaps at the cost of refurbishing the older ones. Plans afoot to build a new music facility and learning resource centre.

Housed in a bright, modern two-storey building at the edge of the Hymers campus, the junior school accommodation has spacious classrooms, each with their own cloakroom area and designated DT/art and science rooms. School is moving to tables from individual desks (as budgets allow). Pupils consulted on choice and layout of classroom furniture, though some consider the change a mixed benefit – less distraction from slamming desk lids against less storage space, better organisation and heavier school bags. Prominent commendations board in the entrance hall celebrates personal academic achievements awarded at each Friday's assembly. House points are collected for the four houses and are used primarily for sporting competition. Warnings and (forgetting) kit marks recorded in a warning book for each house kept by head of year. Overlooks extensive and well-kept playing fields, with own wildlife pond and good outdoor recreational activities with table tennis tables and play area.

The school manages to attain high levels of academe whilst pupils remain relaxed and happy, seemingly not under pressure. Parents allude to the changes under the current head (comments like 'it's not such an intense school') and praise the dedication of staff and their excellent relationship with the pupils. School's ability to identify talent and encourage pupils to shine, praised by parents, as well as the differentiated teaching. 'All are catered for', said a mother with three very different daughters at the school.

School has cultivated links with the local community. Lots of outreach programmes for pupils while the head sits on a number of local trusts and the court of Hull University. Has helped to raise perception of Hymers in the city.

Pastoral care, well-being and discipline: Junior school says that CARE (stands for care, acceptance, respect and effort) is the core of the pastoral system and the message resounds in every classroom. Pupils say that 'the teachers are all really nice', 'friends are nice and loyal' and 'you're taught to be competitive with yourself.' Parents (40 per cent of whom work in medicine or education) agreed. They told us that children are 'relaxed and happy' here and that 'teachers adapt to the individual child.'

Pastoral care is a real strength of the senior school too. It expects high standards and pupils don't disappoint. All fairly relaxed for much of the time. Parents speak of 'mutual respect and trust between pupils and teachers' and feel well informed. They told us that staff are accessible and problems are dealt with effectively. Pupils are well looked after and look after each other. Buddy system very effective – mentor training for year 12 on active listening and giving advice. Mixed tutor groups in sixth form promote collaboration and cohesion.

Bullying taken seriously – not just for victim but also to change behaviour of bully. School counsellor on hand. Pupils can expect to be expelled for serious misdemeanours, such as bringing drugs into school, but no expulsions for 10 years.

School consistently has equal numbers of boys and girls – in dining room we observed lots of mixed groups across the age range in conversation. According to our sixth form guide there's 'plenty of girl power' here.

Pupils and parents: Large catchment area – Hull, East Yorkshire, North Lincs, buses in all directions. Reflects the lack of ethnic diversity in the area. Wider social spread than most independents, due mainly to generous bursaries and lower than average fees. Many parents are first-time buyers, ranging from professionals (preponderance of medics and educators) to owners of local takeaways.

Pupils are open, bright, positive and enthusiastic. They value the academic support they receive and close friendships they make.

Entrance: Main junior entry points are in years 4 and 5. Entrance exams take place in February for entry the following September and test reasoning ability, comprehension, mathematics and powers of expression. An intake of 72 (three classes of 24) into year 4, topped up to classes of 26 in year 5, though head says that 'if a child has the ability to succeed and be happy at Hymers we will find them a place.' Around five fee remission places per year, all means-tested.

Links with pre-prep Hessle Mount and prep Froebel House mean their pupils are academically tracked and those who meet entry requirements have automatic offer of place. Wide catchment area covers Grimsby, Scunthorpe, Goole, Scarborough and some way into East Riding. There's an extensive school bus network.

For entry at 11+ pupils sit competitive exams in maths, English and verbal and non-verbal reasoning, plus interview. Four-form entry, 108 places in all (about 30 for external pupils, remainder transferring from own junior school). For sixth form, five GCSEs at grade B or above required. About 12 or so enter at 16, replacing the similar number of leavers.

Exit: Almost all juniors progress to senior school after successfully sitting entrance exams. Between 80 and 90 per cent stay post-GCSE – most leavers due to relocation or for wider range of A level options. A good handful to Oxbridge each year – four in 2016; the rest head to a gamut of universities, with northern Russell Group strong favourites. Half study science and mathematics related degrees. Medicine (11 per cent in 2016) and healthcare sought after too, with an equally consistent show of economics, business and social studies.

Money matters: About 15 fee remission places per year – all means-tested bursaries, some full fees.

Remarks: Hymers is an unpretentious place. School has maintained high academic standing yet managed to relax intensity in recent years, though high expectations remain for commitment and ambition. Pupils are confident, well prepared and proud of and valued for their successes across any number of disciplines.

K

Keswick School

Vicarage Hill, Keswick, Cumbria CA12 5QB

Pupils: 1,265; 48 full, 5 weekly boarders • Ages: 11–18 • Sixth form: 288

Fees: Boarding £10,056 pa; Tuition free

Tel: 01768 772605
Email: admin@keswick.cumbria.sch.uk
Website: www.keswick.cumbria.sch.uk

Headmaster: Since 2012, Mr Simon Jackson MA (Oxon) MEd FRSA (30s), previously deputy head, only the eighth head in the last 115 years. Educated at the Royal Latin Grammar School in Buckingham and St Catherine's College, Oxford, where he studied biological sciences. Did his PGCE at Wolfson College, Oxford and MEd at University of Gloucestershire. Married with a young family, he is youthful, well-respected, hugely bright and enthusiastic; 'We plough our own furrow here'. He clearly enjoys the freedoms academy status brings and doubtless wouldn't have it any other way. A scientist and outdoorsy type, he commands respect from all and sundry and you can see why – he has a real presence about the place and wraps enormous charm and an intelligent approach to education around it.

Academic matters: Results at GCSE and A level remarkable across the board in view of non-selective comprehensive entry. At GCSE 75 per cent of pupils got 5+ A*-C grades including English and maths in 2016; 23 per cent A*/A grades; English, maths and science do especially well. Unusually, separate sciences taught by specialists to almost all pupils – school has been awarded science specialist status and was rated outstanding in every respect in a recent science survey inspection. Setting in most subjects from year 8, working towards 10 GCSEs as the expected norm. French or German taught in year 7, two languages (or more) for most after that. In 2016, nearly 29 per cent A*/A grades at A level, 51 per cent A*-B. New buildings opened in 2014 allow an increase in the range of A levels on offer. Leadership and volunteering opportunities are encouraged and welcomed to add breadth. A useful Parents' Guide to Home Learning (aka homework) is on the website. Some provision in small department for SEN – other local schools specialise more in this area.

Teaching styles lean towards the traditional. Staff are an interesting bunch ('inspiring people create aspiration,' says head); an unusually high number have had previous professional lives (a doctor, a lawyer, an engineer and a journalist to name but a few) and came to teaching via a road to Damascus moment. Most stay forever – and not just for the stunning view from the staffroom window. Parents and pupils appreciate staff commitment and teaching quality; school has leading edge status and is a hub for teacher training, attracting interest (and admiration) from far and wide.

Games, options, the arts: Regular successes in sport at county level; all the usual sports on offer, played at a seriously competitive level; 'See you later Sir, we're off to win,' say girls to the head as they set off for a hockey match. Sports fields overlook Derwentwater; large sports hall on site and lots of tennis/netball courts. No swimming pool; the outdoor pool was closed a long time ago due to health and safety legislation, but open water swimming in the lake is surprisingly popular, and for those unafraid of heights, the school even has its own dry ski slope. Professional coaching via links with local sports clubs has enabled talented pupils to excel even further, with former pupils (male and female) now competing successfully at national level.

Music thrives – much instrumental and singing tuition, very successful choir and orchestra and various other ensembles. When we visited school was about to purchase a baby grand piano for the main entrance for passing pupils to enjoy during break. The jazz band is heading for commercial success; you can even hire them for your wedding. Drama popular, school works closely with the Theatre by the Lake and a week-long 'iPerform festival' is a whole school treat each July.

The John Muir award for conservation is undertaken by everyone; beyond that the surrounding mountains and lakes create a whole realm of opportunities to get seriously wet and/or muddy with canoeing, raft-building, orienteering, sailing, rock-climbing, fell-running, horse-riding, mountain biking and skiing all on offer.

Interestingly, many of the extracurricular clubs and activities are organised and run by the pupils themselves – they can suggest, manage and become the budget holder for clubs should they so wish. One boy is already proving himself to be commercially astute, making money from an app business he runs alongside the computer programming club and his school work. The theatre group and astronomy club allow pupils to experience a world far beyond the Lakes, as do numerous overseas trips and an annual German exchange.

Boarding: Even though the boarders are a small percentage of the whole, it adds a sense of all-round care and helps to shape the ethos; Ofsted recently rated boarding school outcomes and boarding provision as outstanding. Boys and girls occupy separate floors in a shared boarding house; rooms are two, three or four bed and equipped with all the basics, there is a shared common room for younger pupils and a separate one for sixth form. Plenty for boarders to do; there is evening prep with tutors in school followed by a raft of optional activities, trips to the cinema and theatre and organised outings every weekend.

Originally intended to accommodate children from remote settlements and the Forces, the boarding list is now made up of UK and EU passport holders from all over the world. More boarding provision would be welcomed by both the school and those on the waiting list for places: they could easily triple the size of the boarding house and then fill it overnight.

Background and atmosphere: As old as Cambridge University, though considerably less well known to all but the locally wise, this school has evolved through the centuries to become one of the top comprehensives in the country. Now, as an academy, it is essentially independent in all but name (and fees); the views alone from this place are worth more than any pupil premium. Originally founded mid 14th century by a local vicar, the boarders still attend the church where it all began. Re-founded in 1898 by Victorian pioneer Cecil Grant, who surprised everyone by creating a coeducational school and also opening a sister school in Harpenden. The Queen has visited three times to date; this is a place that attracts much admiration from interested academics and inspectors alike, and is running out of shelf and wall space for the number of cups and national awards it has won over the years.

On the present site since 1996 on the outskirts of town, it is a mix of buildings, old and new, with more planned and approved for the near future – so the builders are a regular feature here. This is an ambitious place; it has so much, yet wants more. Recent additions include new drama theatre, dance studio, recording studio, expansion to sixth form centre, suite of geography classrooms, media suite and additional science laboratory.

Despite the size and space needed to accommodate 1,120 pupils, the teaching site is compact, the music house and sports fields are just a short walk away. Plenty of IT provision; pupils scan in for registration and use of biometrics allows school to be a cash free zone, with lunch and any equipment extras payable directly with parents able to top up from home. Classrooms are attractive and well-resourced and mostly more attractive in than out; the weather can be bleak here and external decor can and does take a hammering. Impressive art and design on display in circulation areas.

The school motto – 'Levavi Oculus – I Lift My Eyes Up' – is taken very literally in your first year here. Part of the induction for the year 7 intake is to climb Skiddaw, which at 932 metres above sea level and the fourth highest mountain in England, is no mean feat. Surely after that nothing at school will ever feel daunting again, but that's the point, school is proud and defiant in its claim that the pupils here 'are not risk-averse'.

Plenty of civic pride about, big on community spirit and strong sense of identity. Locals benefit from a shared use of (some of) the facilities and this, alongside neighbours in close proximity, keeps the school ever mindful of its public image locally, which is no bad thing.

Pastoral care, well-being and discipline: School majors in its 'sense of community' mantra. Lots of talk of 'partnership'; high expectations are made clear from the outset and pupils play ball. It's a large school yet manages a small school feel – you are known here. School claims pupils are self-disciplined but, realistically, they are teenagers and there is a real sense that someone is always watching. Clearly lots of fun to be had outdoors, but they mean business inside the classroom and pupils get the message early on. Mobile phones are not allowed, unusual but sensible – that said, nobody checks, the need to do so hasn't arisen, yet. The pastoral system is straightforward, clear, and appears to work.

Distinctive and traditional green and maroon uniform for all, including sixth form. Smart crested blazer worn proudly by younger pupils, a few shirts hanging out further up the school but most look smart.

No room for complaints about the food; school boasts the national catering manager of the year and lays claim to the best puddings in the country. They also cater for local primaries as well as running four food outlets on site ('it's a bit like M&S,' said one boy).

Pupils and parents: A whole fleet of school buses, plus excellent local transport (Keswick is a good transport hub and therefore more accessible than you might have thought), helps to attract pupils from a very wide area. This brings an unusually broad social intake from right across the Lake District and out to the industrial belt of west Cumbria and beyond. Although most travel by bus, some parents are prepared to drive many miles a day to get here. 'We had a school just down the road', says one parent, 'but our daughter visited here as a Brownie, remembered it well and knew instantly it was the place for her.. and no regrets, it's well worth the drive'.

Pupils are a busy and breezy bunch – focused academically yet still finding the energy to go above and beyond. They might be surrounded by sheep, but no sheep-like behaviour here – there is a big world out there and they aim to play their part and make the most of it. Some three-quarters of the small boarding contingent are from overseas.

Old Keswickians act as mentors to older pupils, providing advice on university and career pathways and bringing a welcome voice of experience to teenage ambitions and aspirations.

Entrance: No entry tests, though asks for recent report from current school, for information but not selection. Preference given to siblings and prospective boarders – who must have an EU/UK passport; preference to Forces families and others living or travelling abroad frequently. Out of catchment day applicants considered on strict basis of distance from school. Many of the feeder primaries are remote village settings and the school works hard on induction days to make new pupils feel welcome – especially important if you are the only one from your school. Further intake into sixth form, minimum requirement of five A*-C grades, including English and maths, with entry requirement of B grades in maths and sciences.

Exit: About 25 per cent leave after GCSE and a further 10-15 after year 12. Ninety per cent of year 13 leavers go on to university, including a handful each year to Oxbridge (two to Cambridge in 2016); others to eg Durham, Northumbria, Edinburgh, Leeds, Manchester Met, Newcastle and St Andrews.

Money matters: Interestingly, and unusually, scholarships available in biology, geography, music and drama, so do ask.

Remarks: It's an ambitious place – you can take the academics as read, but the adventurous, creative and often entrepreneurial spirit is what gives it the edge. Think of it as Richard Branson meets Bear Grylls with Stephen Hawking thrown in for good luck, and you are some way to finding the heart of the place. And of course, that goes for the female equivalent of those guys too – there's no shortage of female high-flyers, from the girls' rugby team yet to concede a point to a UK champion downhill skier and mountain biker – plenty of impressive girls feature here.

Lady Lumley's School

Swainsea Lane, Pickering, North Yorkshire YO18 8NG

Pupils: 880 • Ages: 11–19 • Sixth form: 176

Tel: 01751 472846
Email: admin@ladylumleys.net
Website: www.ladylumleys.n-yorks.sch.uk

Headteacher: Since 2007, Mr Richard Bramley. Former deputy head at Chelmsford County High School and recently advisory teacher in Islington, North London. Wife also teaches. Daughter and son in sixth forms in Chelmsford. Loves the school and enjoys every minute of his headship. Believes that everyone in the school community can be inspired with a love of learning and, by being so, maximise his or her life chances. Pupils say, 'He's lovely!'

L

Academic matters: Sound GCSE and A level performances; 22 per cent A*/A at GCSE in 2016 and 16 per cent A*/A, 44 per cent A*-B at A level. No prima donna departments here – school claims its strength is quality of teaching across the whole curriculum, especially at key stage 4, and Ofsted largely backs that up. Strongest performances consistently in the basics – English, maths and science. Able linguists given the option of taking GCSE French a year early, with German to follow in year two. Early results impressive.

Also does well by less academic pupils – 15 and 16 year olds can take a double GCSE in engineering, studying partly off-site with engineering firms. Others opt for GCSE health and social care, drawing on links with GPs and hospitals – would-be paramedics, chiropodists etc please note. Vocational path can continue into sixth form with packages including modern apprenticeships. Students encouraged to pick and mix, customising education to boost chances of achieving career goals. Strong, award-winning careers education and guidance, and work experience programmes.

Games, options, the arts: A specialist sports college with extensive sports facilities in a glorious rural setting. New fitness suite and floodlit all-weather pitch used by pupils and local sports clubs with benefits to both. Sports hall, gym, good athletics facilities, all helping to encourage all-round sporting achievements. Drama taught in every year group and those with a musical interest can join the orchestras and choirs. All the usual extracurricular clubs and societies too, but pupils have to risk indigestion to join. One downside of a sprawling catchment area is that buses whisk pupils away at the final bell – makes for busy lunchtimes, with sports practices, science clubs, revision workshops and even dreaded detentions all competing with the sarnies. School is keen on outdoor learning and D of E. Recent expeditions to Ecuador, Tanzania, Morocco and the Himalayas.

Four houses – house events range from Masterchef to Lady Lumley's got Talent to outdoor and adventurous activities.

Background and atmosphere: Set on the edge of the market town of Pickering, a mix of every architectural style over five decades. Built in the 50s, the older buildings are offset by a newish £1m+ administration block, sixth form and community learning centre, with a conference centre for use by school and community. Besides, who couldn't live with a bit of dodgy 50s architecture, when the view is of sweeping school grounds framed by countryside, with even the puff of an old steam railway in the distance? Good disabled access, including lifts.

Biggest surprise? Classroom doors are left open during lessons and all you can hear in the corridors is the teacher's voice. Cloakrooms have been replaced with lockers with a key for pupils, which have been very successful. Even the morning rush into school is orderly. No school-run congestion because of the buses and an uncanny absence of the teenage sillies.

Pastoral care, well-being and discipline: A no-nonsense school which sets high standards and expects pupils to meet them. 'It irons out problems before they escalate,' said one parent, which seems, to use a third metaphor, to hit the nail on the head. Unacceptable behaviour is dealt with quickly and efficiently. Students are given 'cool off' time, which can include that most excruciating of all punishments – writing a letter of apology.

School policy to keep children busy, in and out of lessons, and 'treat them like human beings', giving them the courtesy of decent catering, clean toilets and graffiti-free walls. Strong on caring and community, and rolls up its sleeves to practise what it preaches. School still collects food to make into harvest festival parcels and gets pupils to deliver them to nominated neighbours over many miles – one of a dying breed, we suspect.

Pastoral care boosted considerably by Lady Lumley's Education Foundation, named after its founder, an Elizabethan landowner. Her bequests to the school mean that it can still spend upwards of £20,000 a year on pupil support, from subsidising trips to encouraging pupils' projects. A very nice carrot indeed.

Pupils and parents: A true comprehensive, drawing from an area of affluent professionals and farming communities – lots of the Range Rover set, but also its fair share of children from disadvantaged homes. Good rapport with parents, who receive a report in every term of every year. Pupils' progress tightly monitored with regular tutorials – no hiding place here. Parents talk of a happy school and are pleased with children's achievements.

Entrance: Living in the catchment area is the only way to be sure of a place. A whopping 22 per cent of pupils come from further afield after winning appeals, but if your heart's set on Lady Lumley's, you might have to move house to get in – people do.

Exit: Almost 60 per cent of pupils stay on into the sixth form, expected to increase as vocational courses expand. Around 85 per cent of sixth formers go to university.

Remarks: A solid school which feels part of the community it serves. Recent letter from newly qualified graduate thanks school for giving out-of-class tuition to him and others who needed that extra push: 'It has made all the difference to my future. You made me feel I was somebody and I could achieve my goals,' he writes. Says it all.

Lady Royd Primary

Linked with Bradford Girls' Grammar School

Squire Lane, Bradford, West Yorkshire BD9 6RB

Pupils: 340 • Ages: 4–11

Tel: 01274 545395
Email: registrar@bggs.com
Website: www.bggs.com

Headmistress: Since 2012, Mrs Juliet Rimmer, BSc in human nutrition, PGCE KS2/3 science (Bradford), QTS, currently on sick leave. Deputy Mrs G Coulson is holding the fort and doing a great job, ably assisted by a strong and experienced team of teaching and non-teaching staff.

Entrance: Became a free school in September 2013, with a non-selective entrance policy. There are two classes of around 28 in each year group; the school has tripled in size since becoming a free school. Although there is a nursery on site which is physically joined, be aware that it's legally separate and therefore offers no automatic or direct entry to the school.

Exit: Girls straight through to the senior school, Bradford Girls' Grammar, automatic entry. The boys are not neglected: they are well prepared for any entrance exam or interview requirements to their next school and teachers advise accordingly. They head off to a range of schools within Bradford and beyond, mostly to maintained sector, a few to local independents, especially Bradford Grammar School.

Remarks: A non-selective free school, own identity and buildings but part of Bradford Girls' Grammar. Classrooms are spread across an attractive purpose built modern building (2008) and a section of the main BGGS building with a corridor linking the two. Attractive, bright classrooms with super displays of children's art and writing, the rooms for the oldest children are big enough, but only just. The upward trend in class numbers is a slight concern for parents who hoped it wouldn't shift beyond 24, but the school's popularity has meant a slight creep, probably halted now though by logistics. Younger ones have more space and classrooms adjoin outdoor soft play areas. Larger classes have brought more classroom assistants, so plenty of adults visible and to hand.

Children are smart in navy uniforms, boys in ties, girls in striped blouses, blazers worn by all. Sunrise and Sunset clubs extend the day if required by busy parents and there is a huge range of extracurricular activities taking place at lunchtime and after school. No lack of rigour, expectations are high and results are good; high level of teaching and learning and focused children. Strong results in core subjects at the end of year 6, latest scores are creeping up post-change to free, currently at or slightly above the local and national average at KS2 with excellent value-added measures. French taught by class teachers from year 1, subject specialists on hand for PE, music and science. Plenty of reading – high levels of literacy viewed as a must. Maths is hugely popular; the children tell us they 'love it'. It's traditional teaching plus here – the trad bit being the spelling tests, times tables, handwriting and a daily dose of 'groovy grammar' – whilst also recognising the need for a creative curriculum alongside this, you'll notice the wonderful history/geography/art/design project work on display around the building.

The science lab is a great space and we saw it being used as a scene of crime lab during our visit – children in scene suits, working alongside a visiting forensic scientist dusting for fingerprints – great fun as well as active and real learning in action. A decent range of IT equipment in use and laptops travel the school on a trolley. There are interactive whiteboards in all classrooms and an IT suite is used for whole class teaching. Parents kept up to speed via a learning journal that travels between home and school and a lengthy and detailed end of year report. Expect homework, 'but not too much,' say (some) children; parents like the use of websites making homework 'more fun'. Plenty of rigour throughout, one parent reporting 'a dramatic improvement in our children every year'. Much praise from parents for information evenings at the start of every school year, 'it's great for us, it tells us what to expect,' they say. Well-led SEN department, one-to-one help if needed plus support within and outside the classroom.

Good on pastoral care, evidenced by the pupil anti-bullying ambassadors, who take their role very seriously, a 'worry box' and regular circle times to discuss anything and everything that may arise. Children race to the top of the merit board, huge sense of pride in collecting rewards for good work, the highest possible accolade being a certificate of achievement from the governors. Add to that the house points collected from a range of activities in school and out, including a very popular talent show, there's no shortage of public and private recognition. A celebration assembly takes place each Friday. 'Lunch is good,' say the children, wide choice of options cooked in-house and eaten in the senior school dining room. Tuck shop is a Friday treat and serves 'sort of healthy treats,' they tell us, with a grin.

Wide range of sports on offer, making the very best use of the excellent onsite facilities and energetic and enthusiastic PE staff, no old-school teaching with pumps and whistles here. Drama (LAMDA) and singing are popular; an ever-increasing range of instrumental tuition on offer from peripatetics and the main senior school hall gives them a great space for plays and concerts. Lots of clubs – 'amazing,' say parents: sports – teams do well in competitions (table tennis a strength); music – almost all do individual lessons, various groups (steel pans, guitar, fifes, trumpets), orchestra, choir, concerts; jazz and street dance as well as ballet; debating, poetry reciting, creative writing and handwriting competitions. Trips start locally and then venture further afield with residentials for the older children, north out into the Dales and later on south to London.

The team of teachers and support staff 'make time for you,' say parents, adding that 'the admin team know everything about everything and always reply to your emails'. They see teachers as very approachable and happy to collaborate with them on all kinds of problems. Much eulogising about good communication generally from the school – definitely a bonus and clearly much appreciated.

Friendly, smiling, busy children from the surrounding area. Like the senior school, strong on academics with good relationships and offering a wide range of opportunities. Settling down very nicely now into its new shape, whilst holding on tight to the best of its former construct, sigh of relief all round.

Lancaster Girls' Grammar School

Regent Street, Lancaster LA1 1SF

Pupils: 909 • Ages: 11–18 • Sixth form: 307

Tel: 01524 581661
Email: lggs@lggs.lancs.sch.uk
Website: www.lggs.org.uk

Headteacher: Since 2007, Mrs Jackie Cahalin BA (40s), a historian, three previous years as deputy head at LGGS, only the ninth head in the school's 100+ year history. A friendly, calm yet authoritative presence, she clearly enjoys the company of the girls, and this appears to be reciprocated.

Academic matters: Very sound – one of the top 20 schools nationally, aspirations to be in the top 10. Excellent results at GCSE (69 per cent A*/A grades in 2016). A levels very impressive too (71 per cent A*/B grades and 48 per cent A*/A grades in 2016). Strong languages (French, German, Spanish), has language college status and more recently international school status awarded by the British Council. Latin before school – 'dawn Latin' – is over-subscribed.

Large numbers of girls opt for sciences in the sixth form, skill and interest level being strengthened by studying three separate sciences at GCSE. Maths is the most popular A level subject. Marked technology emphasis (specialist status); sponsorship and collaborative projects including Arkwright scholarships; enviable technology and IT teaching provision. High computer count, interactive whiteboards everywhere ('Lots more than the boys' school,' say the girls). Able staff (about one third men), age profile creeping upwards – they don't want to leave, and you can see why.

Games, options, the arts: By their own admission, not the best sporting facilities, essentially due to lack of space. Sports fields five to 10 minutes away from school. Astroturf pitch and new fitness suite and dance studio. Dance flourishing, with many clubs run by the girls themselves and after-school GCSE dance classes. Sport is important and keenly played, especially hockey and running (representative successes). Much variety beyond these, including rugby, fencing and swimming. Old-fashioned gym brought up to date by the addition of an immensely popular Wii Fit screen. Music strong and multi-form, house music competitions one of the girls' favourite annual events. Joint ventures in music with boys' school; also drama and public speaking. Largest centre in the area for D of E. Strong international links include a link school in India and World Challenge to Madagascar. Plenty of European overseas trips and exchanges and representation at science fairs in South East Asia.

Background and atmosphere: Founded 100 years ago on central site, with more modern additions and surrounded by private houses. Very limited parking and limited outdoor space for play or socialising. However, site restrictions have brought about some inspired and resourceful use of space, as buildings are updated and transformed according to the changing needs of the school. Newer additions include impressive technology, cooking and IT areas, and a brand new sixth form centre with large study area.

Girls appear very academically focused – they have earned their place here and tell us they are 'eager to learn and like the fact that they don't have to wait for others to catch up'. Busy girls, hardly a moment when they are not occupied, thriving on the many challenges and opportunities. Hint of academic snobbery from a few – a little dismissive of 'less academic' subjects at A level; however 'You can be yourself here,' they say, and appear happy in that. The head concurs – 'Girls are braver in lessons in an all girls' school and it's OK to do your homework and to take on leadership roles.' Girls genuinely feel they have a voice on the school council and have been actively involved in uniform updates. Has a healthy eating award and food is 'pretty good', with plenty of choice for all. Was grant maintained, now has academy status, which allows a degree of control over its destiny, including (vitally) academic selection.

Pastoral care, well-being and discipline: Usual form tutor system, backed up by heads of key stages, works well. Relaxed but far from lax – great emphasis on trust, self-discipline and good old-fashioned standards of behaviour; make-up, nail varnish, piercings and hair colour all forbidden – the girls know and, for the most part, respect code.

Pupils and parents: Straightforward girls who are proud to be here and keen to get on and to do their bit for society. They want to do well and make their mark on the world, and it's not hard to believe that they will. Wide range of parental backgrounds, not surprising in middle-sized county town. Parents rightly assume high academic standards but also value the 'what else?' factor – year 7 parent says her daughter settled easily and well, despite friends going elsewhere, thanks to good pastoral care on transition from primary school. Another parent, with three daughters through the school, places huge value on the 'real-life perspective' of the place provided by numerous opportunities to interact with students both from the local boys' school and overseas, via inter-cultural exchanges.

Entrance: Five-form entry and heavily oversubscribed at 11+. Admission is 'according to ability and aptitude' – tests in maths, English and VR. Entrance exam in September and results come fairly speedily to aid the admin selection process. First chance goes to inhabitants of Lancaster and District (map available from school), then residual places to families living outside these. If at first you don't succeed, try again later – up to one third of post-GCSE year group has entered from other schools, with only a minimum qualification of five or more GCSEs at B and above; this is a huge attraction – draws from local maintained schools and the independent sector.

Exit: Very few leave after GCSE, but up to 100 join the sixth form. Almost all go on to higher education – eight to Oxbridge and 11 medics in 2016. History, law and biomedical science also popular courses. Most popular universities are Glasgow, Newcastle, Leeds, Lancaster, Durham, Manchester and Edinburgh.

Remarks: Awarded 'outstanding' in four consecutive inspection reports, a confident, sought-after and successful state grammar school. A place where, despite (because of?) the smallish county town background, girls are encouraged to look outwards as well as inwards, resulting in refreshingly open-minded, ambitious and worldly-wise young women.

L

Lancaster Royal Grammar School

East Road, Lancaster LA1 3EF

Pupils: 1,024; 64 full, 103 weekly boarders • Ages: 11–18 • Sixth form: 310

Fees: Boarding £10,200– £11,250 pa; Day – free

Tel: 01524 580600
Email: theaton@lrgs.org.uk
Website: www.lrgs.org.uk

Headmaster: Since 2012, Dr Christopher Pyle MA (Cantab) PhD (Cantab) NPQH (mid 40s). Previously a deputy head at Perse School, Cambridge and before that head of geography there, particular interest glaciers, hydrology and climate change. Briefly a manager at Anglian Water before taking up teaching. Married to Sally, a mathematics teacher at a local school, with three young sons, two of them pupils at the school. Headed north back to roots in the Lakes and lured to LRGS as 'the nearest thing to an independent school'. Parents and pupils comment positively on the visibility of the head.

He has been churchwarden and PCC member of a large Anglican church. A keen runner, he has also completed the Devizes to Westminster canoe race for charity, and is a fan of the Lakeland fells.

Academic matters: Superb tradition – regularly in top 100 schools nationally at A level; consistently near top of regional table at GCSE; strong value-added results. Perhaps explains why Ofsted data dashboard not a focus for head. Aiming high taken for granted, as is 'getting stuck in' to support it. In 2016, nearly 56 per cent of A level grades A*/A; 63 per cent of GCSE grades A*/A. Very much the traditional grammar school ethos, challenging boys to fulfil their potential in a competitive environment. Mathematics outstanding, stronger classics than a lot of independents.

Wide choice of subjects at A level and Cambridge Pre-U including classics and philosophy – a third do four A levels, a quarter add on EPQ. An expectation to lead and be involved with the wide range of extracurricular; sport top of the league; CCF and D of E, volunteering – home and away with InspirUS (LRGS outreach gifted and talented programme) and the Erasmus programme.

GCSE: exceptional mathematics results and strong science as might be expected. HPQ (stepping stone to EPQ) recently introduced. Narrow ability range, setting in mathematics, English and French up to GCSE; class size averages 28. Ten GCSEs the norm; all do technology up to GCSE – school historically had technology, languages, mathematics and computing specialisms. French, German (with annual exchange) and Spanish timetabled, twilight sessions of Mandarin Chinese on offer. Sciences taught separately up to GCSE and all three are popular sixth form options – seen as a 'sciencey' school, says head. Special needs (eg dyslexia, Asperger's) looked after in-house. The especially gifted are stretched by further enhancement schemes and wide-ranging extracurricular provision.

Librarian works closely with English department to encourage reading – using an accelerated reading programme in years 7 and 8, collecting points per book with results published in a league table. IT infrastructure investment so Wifi throughout school but hardware lacking; some netbooks, but BYO not discouraged.

Games, options, the arts: Team games rather than individual sports dominate though increasing opportunity for minority interests that will last a lifetime. Strong rugby and cricket, taken seriously – they beat most independents. Frequent tours – Hong Kong, Australia, Japan and the 'Windies'. An impressive list of other sports, plenty of outdoor pursuits in nearby Lake District and rowing on the Lune leading to some successful pairs at Henley. Much encouragement to join in – no place for couch potatoes.

Music popular; 10 per cent take individual lessons in school practice rooms in the boarding houses. No need for Gareth Malone – choirs popular and everything instrumental from blues to philharmonic on tap. Annual musical drama production in city theatre (often with Lancaster sister school). Very good art and design results.

An extensive and eclectic range of extracurricular, humorously titled to suit all tastes or none (Texas Hold'em Society?) from Bad Boyz Bakin through Doctor Who Catch Up to PhilThy. These are on top of all the expected sport and fitness, debating, D of E, CCF, expressive and performing arts.

Boarding: Boarding gives the school an edge and identity and attractive facilities have understandably brought a resurgence of interest from 'first generation' boarders, often from the Lakeland valleys. Some 10-12 per cent of boarders in years 7-9, increasing to 20 per cent in year 10; few international boarders. Weekly boarders are the majority but about 60, mainly older boys, are full boarders. Fees for weekly or full boarding are the same so boys have flexibility to stay weekends, often influenced by sports fixtures.

Junior boys have a splendid boarding house with views to die for and a back garden of immaculate cricket pitches with the stunning backdrop of the Ashton Memorial. Dorms are bunk-bedded, cheery, comfortable and well-furnished, with sitting rooms and homely kitchens for tea and toast after school. Seniors have a choice of two houses, School House and Ashton House, each with different character and design. School House is an attractive and well-designed conference centre-style building adjoining a Victorian villa, with some comfortable ensuite single studies alongside relaxed sitting rooms and a modern kitchen, allowing the boys both privacy and companionship as and when required. Ashton House is more traditional, with bigger rooms of up to four beds, but similar recreational spaces and kitchen facilities. The houses exude family atmosphere (with gardens, tree planting and chickens) and the boys speak warmly of collegiality and that this really is 'home from home'.

All the house staff have an academic role and there are now communal study areas in each of the houses for homework, as well as a desk in each of the dorms. Boys are given some freedom (Lancaster is a small city) and there are organised activities most Sundays, whilst Saturdays are taken up with prep and sports fixtures for many.

Catering is considered 'acceptable', no complaints so must be a positive. Dining room has had a recent cosmetic makeover with the addition of rainbow coloured chairs. New Grab and Go café in award nominated new City View building voted a great success by all.

Background and atmosphere: An ancient foundation, in existence by 1235 and endowed in 1472. Moved to its current location in 1852 when Queen Victoria donated £100, hence its 'Royal' tag – and the school still receives the same amount (sadly not index-linked) annually from the Duchy.

An extensive though fragmented site skirting either side of hilly East Road around a busy crossroad – pedestrian and vehicular. Building styles change from gothic to modern from the lower to upper site, and timetabling can mean crossing two roads between lessons, but boys take it in their stride and 20mph speed limits are enforced. Mixture of Victorian houses and purpose-built blocks in traditional style, leading to newer additions (science and business/design centres, new boarding houses). Parking is tricky but most walk or use public transport.

Though there is some resemblance to its independent competitors, lack of funding is evident in some parts of the school. It doesn't necessarily matter, as the school's focus is rightly on excellent teaching and positive learning outcomes, but it does mean the place can look a touch untidy at the edges. Extensive areas of the Old School House have been decommissioned but, at last, it seems priority school funding is coming to the rescue, and the head certainly has grand designs for the building.

Real sense of history and tradition about the place: 'Best of the old and the new' is the head's mantra. Boys bustle purposefully between classrooms that range from tired-looking utilitarian to smartly refurbished. Older parents will be reminded of the grammar school of their youth – 'no-nonsense, no-frills,' said one successful and grateful old boy. An ambitious and exciting 50-year master plan is attracting support from old boys and several years in, there is evidence of some success in the green shoots of improvements.

Pastoral care, well-being and discipline: Boys respond to the no-nonsense direct approach of staff in a school that thoroughly understands them. The school looks to recruit 'schoolmasters' (of either sex) rather than 'teachers'. Thorough care systems for both boarding and day work well – pastoral staff heavily committed to pupils' welfare and relations between boys and teachers admired by parents and inspectors. High personal standards expected. Not much evidence of real wickedness; school suspends for possession and would expel for dealing – and the boys know it.

Thriving mentor scheme where senior boys spend time with junior boys with similar interests and prefects have weekly tutor time with year 7 helping with pastoral and organisational issues. All the pupils (and parents) we spoke to commented on the sense of community and excellent staff/pupil relationships.

Pupils and parents: Lancaster is a city with a small town feel – boys come from every walk of life and are a very genuine mix. Head says the school is not about one size fits all. 'We take quirky characters who are valued in school and can say that there will be clubs for you'. Still 'the school on the hill' to some, yet no wish for this to become a middle class enclave – rather it is open to any boy, from any street, who can cope with living and working alongside a future Oxbridge don. Local day boys given preference; about 40 places go to those further afield. Boarders come from all over but must be a UK subject or have an EEA passport and a UK guardian (some 18 per cent overseas boarders from 10 countries).

Boys and parents very proud of school and its regional standing. As one boy put it, 'LRGS is an awesome place to be'. Parents comment that their sons are thriving academically and relishing life as a boarder. Old boys include Prof T Hugh Pennington, microbiologist; Kevin Roberts CNZM, CEO Worldwide Saatchi and Saatchi (retains the link with six summer internships for U6 boys each year); Jason Queally, Olympic cycling champion; Brigadier Alex Birtwistle, foot and mouth star; Tom Sutcliffe, journalist; and Sir Richard Owen, dinosaur man.

Entrance: By oversubscribed competitive exam at 11 (English/maths/reasoning). Three strands of entry: local day, regional day, boarding. Boarders considered separately but all 'must be of an aptitude and ability suited to an academic curriculum'. All leave at 16 and then reapply for sixth form places: 'Tell us why we should give you a place here' – great practice for university UCAS or even the real world. Regularly increasing intake at 16 and growing interest from independents for sixth form places – grab a boarding place whilst you still can.

Exit: A few – around 15 per cent – leave after GCSE; vast majority to good universities, mainly in the Midlands and North, eg Durham, Edinburgh, Manchester, Newcastle, Warwick and York, though some dipping a toe into southern universities such as Bristol and Bath. In 2016, 14 to Oxbridge and 13 medics.

Remarks: Vibrant, selective grammar school with big reputation in the region; chiefly a day school but also offers excellent boarding provision. Has managed to retain marked degree of independence as an academy, offering a curriculum above and beyond the norm, including classics.

Unashamedly academic but takes all-round education seriously and delivers – recognised by pupils and parents alike. LRGS is a fabulous school which offers a wealth of opportunities to all boys. Besides academic progress, skills and interests are nurtured and developed which adds to the confidence of pupils.

Longridge Towers School

Berwick-upon-Tweed, Northumberland TD15 2XQ

Pupils: 200; 42 boarders • Ages: 3–18 (boarding from 8) • Sixth form: 44

Fees: Day £8,154 – £12,723; Boarding £18,714 – £25,908 pa

Tel: 01289 307584
Email: enquiries@lts.org.uk
Website: www.lts.org.uk

Headmaster: Since September 2016, Jonathan Lee, previously housemaster and maths teacher at Uppingham. Maths degree from St Andrews and is a qualified accountant.

Academic matters: All-through school from 3-18, with French started at 7 and German at 11. Spanish, Italian and Latin as extracurricular but can be taken at GCSE, as can Chinese. Wide range of GCSE subjects with flexible time timetabling based on the needs of each particular year group so that 95 per cent get to take what they want. English, Eng lit and maths for all plus six other options (can include three – or two – separate sciences or science and additional science.) Usual subjects plus ICT, CDT (done in a well-equipped but basic hut in the grounds), sports studies, drama and music. Consistently sound record with a good sprinkling of A and A* in biology and maths and a few in Eng lit and elsewhere. Almost everyone takes drama and IT, both with solid results and no significant weaknesses, though art a bit up and down. In 2016, 37 per cent of GCSEs were A*/A.

At A level, 23 per cent A*/A in 2016. Choice includes the usual subjects plus economics with business studies, sports science and further maths; general studies AS for all now replaced by critical thinking after rather iffy results; while psychology can be taken at AS over two years. Dusting of A*/As across most subjects and a consistently solid 'pass' rate but also quite a smattering of C/D. Inevitably small groups – will put on a mainstream subject for one pupil in sixth form. Anyone with 5+ Cs can take As though B preferred in subject concerned.

SEN support offered mostly by individual withdrawal with personal education plans used to keep teachers aware of needs.

English help for pupils from China etc and efforts to provide extra stimulus for the very bright.

Juniors start from early years foundation stage (tiny classes of five to 10 only) on Oxford Reading Tree, supplemented by lots of Jolly Phonics and Ginn letters and sounds.

Classrooms pretty modern with a few interactive whiteboards and computer projectors, lots of IT including laptop trolleys for use in amazingly antiquated though very adequately equipped labs. The smartest lab is in the junior school building for 7-11s. Called Stobo after a benefactor, the junior school is still clean and new looking with state of art (though cheerfully decorated) classrooms, cloakrooms and hall etc. Early years to junior 3 have humbler but thoroughly refurbished quarters absolutely brimming with colour, imaginative stimulus material and even recorded birdsong. A pleasant fenced outdoor area for tinies and some smashing all weather play equipment, in enthusiastic use.

Games, options, the arts: Sport flourishes with highly successful seven-a-side rugby reaching finals in county tournaments – they struggle to produce a top-level full teams from a small co-ed school but are outstanding in sevens. Recent leaver runs at Scottish, English and Great Britain under 20 championship level, soccer just starting, lots of hockey for girls with several county players, a school champion skier and masses of opportunity for basketball, volleyball, badminton, cricket, tennis, curling (Scottish school finalists) etc. Spacious sports hall (takes a marquee inside for prize days and dances), defunct swimming pool left by previous convent school so minibuses take them to Eyemouth pool but grounds lend themselves to hosting local cross country etc. Pipedream of a new Astroturf hockey pitch is still pretty distant.

Lots of choir, orchestra, jazz groups etc with star pupil in Northern Youth Orchestra but little take up of academic music beyond GCSE. Informal lunchtime concerts much enjoyed by all. Special centre for peripatetic music in a pretty gothic house in the grounds which the previous head rejected as a home. Drama in the round in strange theatre converted from former convent chapel, with jazzy lighting, provided by the enterprising parents' 'school development association'. Recent production is Billy Liar. Art seems a bit marginalised in a building seven minutes walk from main school but is looking to a new art teacher to hot it up next year. Ambition is to reincorporate this in a new sciences and practical subjects building. The school is now full and seemingly growing, so hopes to revamp abandoned plans for new labs into a more inclusive facility.

Boundless activities! Almost all day pupils including juniors stay till 4.40pm for an hour of activity which can include supervised study, tutorials, extra coursework or teaching. Falconry is clearly the latest craze – the juniors couldn't stop talking about it – but also the tip of an impressive iceberg: archery, athletics, lacrosse and other sports, debating, wildlife gardening (with a good muddy pond), Yoga, a new Radio Longridge, science and engineering clubs, cheerleading, war games and lashings of other things. School comments that having rearranged activity times, to suit staff and pupils better, the staff can do what they really like. Bags of trips: German exchange, sport to Canada, South Africa, Iceland etc. Charitable links with Borneo and others. D of E for seniors and Adventure Service challenge for juniors.

Boarding: Boarding on two floors (girls above, boys below) has spacious mostly two-bedded rooms, some with en suite showers. Their height makes them a little stark though inmates are allowed locked doors and a free-ish hand with posters and personal paraphernalia. Pleasant and well-planned recreation room, with spotless kitchenette and generous supplies of luscious fruit.

Background and atmosphere: The extraordinary Victorian Tudor extravaganza built of sandstone ashlar in 1880s for Sir Hubert Jerningham, a liberal MP, on the estate inherited by his wife Annie, Liddell was designed to impress (it does!) by the Buckleys who redid Arundel Castle. It features battlemented stone chimneys, magnificent great hall, now for concerts, with hammer-beams sporting snarling monsters with grotesquely bared teeth, an imperial staircase and an elaborate portico added to shelter the Prince of Wales' carriage (though history is silent over whether he actually arrived to use it) all making Longridge the grandest house in the area. Set in 80 acres of parkland, it became a hotel, then in 1949 an Ursuline Convent school. In 1983 it was restructured as the co-educational Longridge Towers School.

In a fantastic rural setting with imaginative use of the castellated grand areas, the school also has the problem of making stone staircases, high ceilings and a warren corridors of work for 21st century education. The original library had a cunning makeover with a gallery providing working space and banishing the previous nightmare scenario of children on ladders to glass (non-safety) fronted bookcases. There's lots of help on hand and an ambitious programmes of visiting authors etc. 'Service wings' house boarders, dining rooms and kitchens – some tasty dishes (pupils actually like it on the whole) made on site with a few home-grown veg. All obviously well used and well cared for but lots of echoey passages and stairwells, improved by pupil artwork (not always the right way up, though it's hard to tell). Most noticeably some stunning Aboriginal hangings done for a drama performance liven one of the central stairways. Everything clean and mainly litter free, well used and not unnaturally tidy.

Pastoral care, well-being and discipline: Independent Schools Inspectorate really praised pastoral care. Qualified nurse in boarding and system of tutors and year heads (form teachers for juniors) and three school houses which run vertically through juniors to senior school. Pupils respect and value system and genuine interest of staff, so problems are picked up quickly and children tend to monitor and report issues like bullying before they become serious. New junior school council is prized by pupils. Plentiful contact between all ages with seniors helping with reading and games. Unusually friendships across year groups are not uncommon, especially valuable in such a small and variable boarding situation. Strong sense of community enhanced by boarding and also by the school's involvement with its neighbourhood. Activities provided supplement rather than compete with local amenities such as junior golf. Pupils are ready to take responsibility as elected prefects etc within and without school. One sixth former even combines his school duties with being chief coastguard for Lindisfarne.

Pupils and parents: Masses of bus routes bring pupils coming from a scattered area which includes not only Berwick-upon-Tweed, the surrounding border country in both England and Scotland, but also the Holy Island (Lindisfarne) population, whose children need to board on days when the tide cuts off their journey to or from school. Hence boarding has a special wing for them where siblings can be together and the provision has a more temporary feel than the full termly boarding, though they share its amenities and supervision. So boarding at Longridge is more 'flexi' than most and the population fluctuates. Boarding seems to be on the increase with about 32 current maximum and applications going up. A few boarders from abroad, mainly China, otherwise a largely British intake.

Uniform is in a state of flux though everyone looks quite smart. New blue blazers, white shirts, grey trousers and knee straight skirts with prominent kick pleats in blue, white and grey tartan look neat and innocuous, while tinies wear blue and white cotton summer dresses.

Parents run a dynamic programme of events and raise significant amounts for equipment etc. Governors take an active interest in the school and the local worthies, whose families give the names to houses etc, support it with visits and interest.

Entrance: By assessment at all levels but school will take anyone capable of benefiting from what's on offer. Since Longridge pupils come from Scotland and England with different systems involving changes of school at 7, 11, 12, 14 and even different age cut off points, September for England but February for Scotland, need careful induction and class sizes are unpredictable. Now started a class for 3 year olds in response to local demand.

Exit: Some leave from juniors at either 11 and 12 (English and Scottish systems!) mainly to independent, Ampleforth, Merchiston Castle etc, though not usually to local state schools. There is more than a trickle (around 45 per cent) after GCSE to local and Newcastle sixth forms and a few to independent boarding. Those who stay to upper sixth go mostly to uni, a few to blue chip and a surprising quota of sports degrees. Some to academic courses too. Popular destinations include Newcastle, King's College London, Leeds Beckett (vocational courses), York, Edinburgh, Northumbria, Central Lancashire.

Money matters: Not a rich school but awards available for academic (up to 50 per cent), sporting (up to 10 per cent) or musical (free tuition) excellence are offered to those qualifying by exam, achieving county sports honours or by audition. Pupils from Holy Island are sponsored by the local authority, which would otherwise be unable to provide adequate hostel accommodation.

Remarks: Small, with all the advantages of good supervision, care, close-knit community and friendliness a small school can give. Copes very well with the disadvantages of scale, so pupils do not lose out on activities, subjects etc. Berwick-upon-Tweed is jolly lucky to have this alternative at hand.

M

The Manchester Grammar School Junior School

Linked with The Manchester Grammar School

Old Hall Lane, Manchester M13 0XT

Pupils: 240 • Ages: 7–11

Fees: £11,970 pa

Tel: 0161 2247201
Email: admissions@mgs.org
Website: www.mgs.org

Headmistress: Since 2008, Mrs Linda Hamilton BEd. Her roots are local – she was educated at Stretford Grammar School for Girls and then at Manchester University – but she's also worked in Iraq, Qatar and Nigeria (her husband was an engineer in the oil industry). She set up a pre-school in Nigeria but her more recent teaching experience has been in British junior schools. Before coming to MGS she was deputy head at Altrincham Preparatory School.

Mrs Hamilton set up the MGS junior school. She led the development of the curriculum and admissions procedure and was closely involved with the design of the buildings. In 2008 it opened its doors to years 5 and 6 and, since 2011, it's catered for years 3 and 4 as well.

Parents absolutely see her as a good thing. 'She has enormous vision,' said one mum, 'and she's really good at bringing her team with her.' 'She's an incredibly generous leader,' added another, 'she's got no ego; she gives credit to the teachers; she leads a cohesive and happy staff and enjoys their success and the success of the boys.' Everyone seems to find her open and approachable: 'She's always around,' said one parent, 'you can just bump into her and chat.' Parents enthused about her dedication and energy to the school and her warm, mothering commitment to their children. Pupils told us she's 'friendly' and 'really kind'. One lad compared her to Jonny Wilkinson – known by team mates to be first on the pitch and last to leave. She knows everyone's names and seems to have a good idea of what's going on in their lives. They all stand to attention when she walks into a classroom, though – clearly her warmth does nothing to undermine her natural authority.

Mrs Hamilton is also an Independent Schools Inspector and a governor at both a local free school and an academy. She's also closely involved with various local state primary schools. She's a mother of three grown up sons and spends her free time with her family or walking and reading.

Entrance: Selection is by an assessment day. There is no set number of places to fill – it's just about finding the boys who will thrive at MGS. During the day, boys are taught in groups of 8-12. They're taught unfamiliar material – in maths and a topic-based lesson – and then they'll be tested on what they've learnt. They'll also be asked to do some creative writing. None of it is on the national curriculum so boys shouldn't try to prepare in any way. The idea is to spot potential rather than just identifying the best-tutored hopefuls. Boys can apply for entry to years 3, 4, 5 or 6 but, if they're unsuccessful, they have to wait two years before applying again (although a boy who doesn't get into year 6 can still apply to join the senior school in year 7). Mrs Hamilton says she feels a real responsibility when admitting a child to the junior school (because juniors get automatic entry to the seniors so she's having to predict whether a boy with thrive at MGS right up to the sixth form). For this reason she says: 'I never dither. If I'm in two minds I'll always ask him to come back in a couple of years and try again.'

Exit: All junior boys progress to the seniors – without having to do any entrance exams or interviews – a big draw for some parents. Mrs Hamilton keeps a close eye on how boys from the junior school do after they leave – in part to check that her selection procedures are effective. The first cohort of boys who joined the school in year 6 have now done their GCSEs and, she tells us, they 'did very well indeed,' leaving her confident that 'we've got the assessment and curriculum right'.

Remarks: Free from the constraints of the national curriculum, the MGS Junior School goes its own way – teaching pupils way more than just the fundamentals. The curriculum is broad, skills-based and innovative. The school staff created it, specifically for bright boys. 'Particularly with science, we found that what was already available wasn't challenging enough,' says Mrs Hamilton, 'so we developed our own. Once we'd done it for science, we thought why not do it for maths, English and everything else?' The focus on skills is evident in the approach to languages – with boys learning a different language in each year of the junior school: Spanish in year 3, French in year 4, Latin in year 5 and Italian in year 6. 'They're learning how to learn a language,' says Mrs Hamilton.

One afternoon a week is devoted to 'options' – an opportunity for boys to immerse themselves in a subject or activity of their choosing – and a firm favourite with the boys we met. They choose a different subject each term – examples of options include creative art, dance, mini robotics, stitching club and 'top secret' for years 3 and 4, and build a go-cart, debating, amusement park, fantasy stock market, psychology, military strategy or forensics for years 5 and 6.

The pupils we met loved the curriculum; 'we're not just counting frogs,' said one boy, 'we're doing really difficult stuff like designing an eco-friendly house or learning about evolution.' They appreciated the hands-on, project based lessons. One boy remembered fondly a project where you had to choose a religion other than your own and then design and build a place of worship for it out of sticks. Pupils love the 'options' afternoons too. One lad in the seniors credited an options course he'd selected in year 5 as the thing that 'really sparked my interest in military strategy'.

Parents thoroughly approve of the education the school is providing – believing their sons to be challenged and inspired. One mum said, 'They understand my son better than I do in terms of switching his brain on.' Parents say the homework is just right – there's not too much and it differs from other schools because it's genuinely interesting and difficult ('not just lots of boring, pointless tasks like my son was set at his last school'). One mum told us that her son recently announced 'I've got the best homework ever this weekend!' 'My son's come on leaps and bounds since he came here,' said another parent. 'The change is phenomenal.'

The school takes great care of boys with special educational needs and disabilities. Special needs provision is overseen by the well-qualified senior school SENCo and there's a junior school support co-ordinator. Support is offered in and out of classes and boys can be tested for a number of special educational needs. We met the mother of a young boy with severe haemophilia who was effusive in her praise of how well the school deals with her family's special circumstances. She had many examples of ways in which teachers and teaching assistants had found ways to enable her son to take part in physical, potentially risky learning activities in a safe and well-managed way – all done with the full involvement and support of the family: 'They never make us feel like it's too much trouble, and they never make him feel like a special case,' she told us.

A wide range of extracurricular activities are available at lunchtime, after school and a few before school. Most are free and available to all, but a couple have an extra charge or are only available to some boys (eg those learning a particular instrument). There are lots of sporting, physical and outdoorsy activities (less predictable options include TriGolf, Ultimate Frisbee and fencing); and countless options to suit musical, arty and creative tastes (dinosaur sculpture and Spanish art stood out to us from a very long list) as well as clubs for those who want to do extra maths, science, creative writing or languages. Games clubs are also popular, with options including chess, Scrabble and bridge. The curriculum offers activities which seem to bridge the gap between arts and sciences. For example we saw some beautiful – and anatomically correct – giant willow sculptures of dragonflies and other insects hanging from the classroom ceilings – we're not sure if their creation was overseen by an arty science teacher or a biologically-literate art teacher – possibly both. (Subject specialists from the seniors also regularly offer support in junior lessons.) The pupils also have access to the senior school's sports facilities and to its specialist sports teachers and now have new sports hall of their own. Junior pupils have had high level successes in swimming, cricket and football. There are star rugby and football players. Many boys are also highly accomplished musicians. The junior school uses the senior school theatre for its three productions a year.

Often the boys are inspired by a piece of art or literature, but that initial interest takes them to a different area of learning – for example, the children were moved by a novel about a child with a serious facial disfigurement – and from that book, not only did they explore PSHE topics by discussing how that child might like to be treated, but they also had a visit from a plastic surgeon who has helped children with similar conditions – giving them a scientific take on a literary subject and an insider's insight into a real career path.

The junior school buildings – still spanking new from construction in 2008 and 2011 – are built from sustainable wood in the style of Swiss chalets. The original building, Bexwyke (pronounced Bezik) Lodge, now houses years 3 and 4 and Plessyngton Lodge – equally environmentally friendly, built from Scottish pine – houses years 5 and 6. The lodges are spacious, warm and airy. Each has a veranda with pine railings running around it, leading to a large playground. Outside there are benches for boys who want to read and a decking area with wooden tables and stools. The school sits next to a large woodland area with a great variety of wildlife, frequently used in lessons from any number of curriculum areas.

The atmosphere of the junior school is warm and accepting. One boy told us, 'Our teacher was crying when we left year 6 to go up to the seniors – and that shows how much they care about us.' Boys didn't feel unduly pressured to perform academically. 'They have faith in us,' said one lad; 'they want to bring out the best in us but they'll only push us as far as we can go.' Boys told us it doesn't matter if someone is different – 'this school is all about difference,' announced one pupil. In a school that dishes out lapel badges for all manner of achievements, we were heartened to learn that there's a 'great buddy' badge for those who make an extra effort to include people who are getting left out. There seems to be plenty of interaction between other years and even with the seniors. 'My son goes around the village saying hello to much older children,' one mum told us. On our visit we met a large group of boys ranging from year 3 to year 12 and we were very impressed with how gently and indulgently the older boys responded to the juniors. Parents said they were surprised by just how nurturing the school is. One dad said: 'The elite outward reputation is belied by the family atmosphere here.' Another parent told us how well the school helps the boys to empathise with others: 'A boy in my son's class had lost his cat and every boy in that class knew what that would mean to him – they're so concerned about each other.'

There's also a strong outward-looking community spirited feel to the school. Boys get involved in lots of charity fundraising events and Community Action is available as an option. The boys told us proudly how important it is to give back to the community. One lad announced: 'The day MGS pupils forget how lucky we are to be here will be a sad day.'

Boys felt that discipline was fairly gentle: 'If you did some work wrong, they'll try to be encouraging – they'll say "good try, but..."' None of the parents we met had received the dreaded 'call home' about bad behaviour. Mrs Hamilton says they keep the children too busy for them to be naughty. Pastoral care is largely provided by form teachers and teaching assistants (class sizes of no more than 22) but boys also have the option to confide in older pupils if anything is bothering them; senior pupils are involved with the juniors in various capacities as prefects, 'big brothers' and mentors.

Means tested bursaries (up to 100 per cent of fees) are available for boys in the junior school but there aren't so many offered as in the senior school. Judging from the very satisfied parents and boys we met, the money is put to excellent use.

The Manchester Grammar School

Linked with The Manchester Grammar School Junior School

Old Hall Lane, Manchester M13 0XT

Pupils: 1,267 • Ages: 11–18 • Sixth form: 344

Fees: £11,970 pa

Tel: 0161 224 7201
Email: admissions@mgs.org
Website: www.mgs.org

High Master: Since 2013, Dr Martin Boulton (40s). He read engineering at Nottingham University (BEng and PhD) and then worked for mining company De Beers and accountants Arthur Anderson before deciding to retrain as a teacher. After completing his PGCE (at Manchester University) he went to Sherborne School in Dorset – teaching physics, living-in as a boarding house tutor and immersing himself in rugby and mountaineering. In 2001 he moved to Westminster School and was quickly promoted through the ranks until he became under master (deputy head). The move to Manchester was a homecoming for Dr Boulton, who is originally from Manchester and attended MGS himself as a sixth former. He transferred there from a state comprehensive on an assisted place. He says his time there was 'transformational' – raising his aspirations and instilling in him a lifelong love of philosophy and literature – and this personal experience cements his commitment to the school's bursary scheme. He talks with real passion about his hopes for the school to eventually raise enough money to become 'needs-blind' – so that every boy who earns a place at MGS will receive financial assistance if he needs it.

Dr Boulton is warm and approachable. He engages with parents as equals and, as we toured the school with him, we watched him chat with parents, pupils and colleagues with a cheerful and easy manner. He impressed us with his enthusiasm both for the school and for the education it provides and we observed a spontaneous and straightforward approach to the job – a welcome contrast from the PR-conscious caginess we sometimes encounter from heads.

Parents described him as 'very present and approachable'. They like the fact that he still teaches physics and they feel he's got to know their children. One parent was impressed that he'd given up his holiday to step in at the last minute and accompany children on a classics trip to Rome and Naples to cover staff sickness. Pupils were even more effusive in their praise of him. They said he's 'brilliant', a 'real people person' and 'strikes just the right balance between strictness and kindness'. They appreciate the fact that he 'really gets out of his office', playing football, going on trips and running physics revision sessions ('he really knows a lot'). And they were bursting with anecdotes to illustrate his character – from wearing an 'outlandish jumper' to helping up a boy who'd fallen over and making self-deprecating jokes.

Academic matters: In 2016, 88 per cent of A level entries were awarded A*, A or B, with 66 per cent A* or A, and the average score for the International Baccalaureate was 38 out of 45. At GCSE 88 per cent either A* or A, with 64 per cent being A*. It's outperforming all other selective boys' and co-ed schools in the north west and retains its reputation as the outstanding boys' school in the region.

Dr Boulton gave heads of department the freedom to research the most suitable and challenging post-16 courses for their subjects in terms of preparing the boys for university study, so sixth formers now study a combination of A levels, international A levels and Cambridge Pre-U courses. The school aims to go beyond the boundaries of any exam syllabus though so, for example, all sixth formers undertake a two-week off-syllabus research project, which is supervised like an undergraduate dissertation by a member of staff, and then written up as a long essay. The school is no longer offering the International Baccalaureate ('after doing such a great job to sell its benefits to us!' lamented one disappointed dad) because take-up was too low to form decent sized teaching groups.

The most popular subjects studied at A level are (in this order): maths, chemistry, biology, physics, history, economics, geography, politics and modern languages. Comparatively few boys study English, art or drama in the sixth form but those who do choose arty subjects tend to do well in them. Languages are big here. The school wades through red tape to offer a wide range of foreign exchanges and pupils can study three or even four languages right up to A level if they want to. As well as the classics and modern western European languages, pupils can learn Mandarin, Russian or even Czech.

The strength of science at the school, and particularly biology, is reflected in the fact that the top leavers' course is medicine (26 entered medical school in 2016). Other popular university courses are: languages, history, natural sciences, engineering, politics, maths and economics.

Neither parents nor boys we met thought that homework expectations were too onerous. A year 7 pupil is expected to do six hours a week and this rises progressively up to 16 hours for a sixth former. Parents felt that the school is good at selecting boys who will thrive academically without having to work too hard; they have plenty of time for extracurricular activities. Subject teachers are real experts in their fields – many with PhDs and/or publications to their names. The school has a happy workforce and a great reputation among teachers so it recruits and retains excellent staff easily.

The learning support department is also of note – staffed by a highly-trained team of seven, it meets a range of special needs at no extra cost to parents. Many of the boys are 'unusual' – diagnoses of autism spectrum disorders are no rarity – and the school is proud that boys with SEN experience no detectable stigma and speak openly about the support they get. Indeed apparently there's so little stigma to SEN support that boys 'keep referring themselves when there's nothing wrong with them!'

Games, options, the arts: It's a hardy, outdoorsy sort of school. These boys aren't herded inside at the first drop of rain. As you'd expect, school teams and individuals regularly excel – at a county, national and even international level – in a full range of sports, including football, hockey, judo, rowing, rugby, water polo, cricket, badminton and cricket. The school invests in top-level sports coaches and it boasts household names from the world of professional sports such as Mike Atherton and Herbert Toft among its alumni. Sports facilities (including a new sports hall large enough for six badminton courts) aren't slickly photogenic but they do a great job and are well used – both by pupils and the local community.

There are plenty of opportunities to get involved for pupils at all ability levels. The school creates B, C and even D teams when it can and offers alternative options such as golf, softball, martial arts and sports leadership awards. Since everyone on a sports team benefits from free weekend coaching, the school wanted to offer a free healthy activity to those who don't play sport; so every Saturday – whatever the weather – a minibus takes anyone who wants to go on a mountaineering expedition – to the Lake District, the Peak District or north Wales. (MGS

M

is, incidentally, the biggest provider of the Duke of Edinburgh Award in the north of England.)

For one week in the summer all teaching stops and each boy participates in an annual activities week. He can choose from dozens of options: alongside a wide range of sports and outdoorsy activities such as water sports, mountaineering and 'Army Insight', there are creative options (film and photography, play in a week), journalism and research projects (such as Man Utd/Man City and World War II) and the opportunity to cook, camp, volunteer or learn about business or computers.

Music is a big part of school life and, although boys can choose to stop studying music from year 9, many continue to learn and perform instruments or to sing in one of the school's three choirs or participate in one of its 20 different music groups throughout their school careers. There are strong links with the Hallé Orchestra. Its children's choir rehearses at MGS and the MGS choir recently performed alongside the Hallé choir and orchestra at the Bridgewater Hall in a performance of a new choral composition specially commissioned to mark the school's quincentenary. Enthusiastic musicians at MGS enjoy opportunities to perform in grand venues at the highest level – often alongside girls from Manchester High School for Girls and Withington Girls' School – and even on national radio. One boy we met, while generally positive about the quality of musical education at the school, did complain that there aren't enough music practice rooms. Participation in most musical activities is free although, as in most schools, musical instrument tuition is an extra you have to pay for. Music theory lessons up to grade 5 are offered at the school for free though and also, we're told, a gifted musician on a means-tested bursary would be likely to get financial help with music lessons if he needed it.

Even boys who've chosen to pursue science subjects talked to us enthusiastically about drama at the school. There's an annual Shakespeare festival and about six full-scale productions a year (some in collaboration with nearby girls' schools although several boys boasted to us of the dramatic turns they'd played in drag!). Some pupils direct or even write their own productions. A decent number of boys take GCSE drama each year and theatre studies A level is offered. Dramatically-minded MGS old boys have certainly made their mark on the world of performing arts, however. Former National Theatre director Nicholas Hytner, comedian and The Thick of It star Chris Addison, actors Ben Kingsley and Robert Powell, playwright Rory Mullarkey and Kylie Minogue's creative director William Baker are all Manchester Grammar alumni.

The school offers 150 clubs and activities, many of which are led by pupils. We're told that if five boys and a teacher get together with an idea then that's all you need to start a club. One lad set up a Great Minds competition whereby pupils competed to come up with ideas to solve major world problems. Many extracurricular activities are driven by an outward-looking engagement with the needs of local and global communities. Parents assured us that if a major news event happens, the boys will come home talking about it – aware of the issues, inquisitive and at times opinionated. The school expects every pupil to get involved in community service at some point doing their time at MGS and pupils certainly rise to the challenge when it comes to fundraising (one sixth former raised £31,000 through a charity golf project). The school shares its expertise and facilities generously locally, supports two colleges in Uganda and many pupils do outreach work in state schools. With regular trips to far-flung places (Sri Lanka, Morocco, South Africa, China, the USA and Russia to name just a handful) an adventurous boy might well leave school better travelled than his parents. We're assured that financial help is available to ensure that the bursary boys aren't always left languishing in the classroom during such jaunts.

Background and atmosphere: The school was founded by the Bishop of Exeter, Hugh Oldham, in 1515. It was founded with the express intention of giving academically gifted boys the opportunity to study 'the science of [Latin] grammar' regardless of background or wealth. The original site was near Manchester Cathedral but the school moved to its current location in Fallowfield in 1931 – to accommodate a growing student population. It became a direct grant grammar school in 1944 but reverted to independent status in 1976. It was the first in the country to react with a bursary appeal when the assisted places scheme ended in the late 1990s and the only one of five independent schools to pass every section of the Charity Commission's public benefit test unequivocally.

As you drive in you pass playing fields on both sides and then approach a solid, red-brick building with an archway leading to the quad. Inside, some corridors and the grander rooms are lined with dark wooden panels. The imposing Memorial Hall, where assemblies take place, has been recently refurbished. With its ornate ceiling, stained glass windows and plaques to commemorate old boys from the school who were killed in the First World War, we imagine it instils in boys a keen sense of their own place within the school's prestigious history. The school has its own archive room and employs two archivists. A recent exhibition of 'A History of MGS in 50 objects' (an idea unashamedly nicked from Radio 4 and the British Museum) went down well with pupils, parents and old boys. But it's far from stuffy here. Of course the energy comes from the boys themselves and there's no sense that they're cowed by their hallowed surroundings. When the corridors are full in between lessons the atmosphere is buzzing – in fact rather loud – although the boys still managed to hold doors open for a visitor and give directions like the best of young gentlemen.

The school only fundraises for the bursary appeal (and for charities). It has a modest and utilitarian approach to new buildings and facilities. They keep the buildings in good working and decorative order but all the boys and parents we met seemed to support the school's position that improving pupil access is more important than lavish upgrades to the facilities. Educationally, though, the boys enjoy a wealth of benefits: there are two excellent libraries and even a school bookshop (run mainly by pupils) and the school stands in 26 acres, including a woodland area with a diverse population of wildlife.

The boys, like most of the decor, are acceptably neat and tidy but not flashily smart. In years 7-11 they wear blue blazers and grey trousers (almost every blazer we saw was decorated with at least one lapel badge marking some distinction or official role – discipline and aspiration seem to be largely promoted through the distribution of shiny badges.) Sixth formers wear a suit of their choice – and more badges.

Pastoral care, well-being and discipline: We didn't see any rowdiness or bad behaviour during our visit; the boys we spoke to (and not just those hand-picked by the school for us to meet) were impeccably behaved. The school employs two proctors whose responsibility it is to maintain discipline, freeing up pastoral staff to deal with other issues. Saturday morning detentions do happen – usually for offences such as showing disrespect to a teacher or pupil or for persistent failure to hand in homework. Boys would face expulsion for bringing drugs into school but Dr Bolton is realistic that some boys will experiment with drugs and alcohol outside of school. He says that if parents were concerned about their son's drinking or drug use, he'd want them to feel they could come to the school for help and support. 'An extreme zero tolerance position is unhelpful,' he says. The school also has the facility to perform drug testing if necessary. Parents approve of the discipline policies. One dad told us: 'They don't train the boys like dogs, they teach them to think about their behaviour.' He'd been impressed that, when his own son had got into trouble for doing 'something very stupid,' he was held to account for going along with the group rather than for thinking independently. Another parent said he thought discipline policies were successful because the school spots problems early and nips them in the bud.

On his arrival at MGS Dr Boulton altered the pastoral care arrangements so that every teacher in the school has their own tutor group of up to 13 boys. (Even Dr Boulton himself has a tutor group – the boys we met sounded somewhat envious of the lucky dozen whose pastoral needs are met with informal fireside chats in the high master's office.) The new tutorial system was a hit with the parents and pupils we interviewed. One boy told us: 'In a group of just 12 people, your tutor can really get to know you.' MGS does have something of a reputation as a 'tough school' but several parents told us that their own experience contradicts that. A mother of an 'unusual boy,' who 'really stands out from his peers,' was effusive in her praise: 'he's very, very happy here. We're so lucky to have found this school.'

Dr Boulton isn't complacent on the issue of bullying. He says that 'heads who think bullying doesn't go on are kidding themselves'. He says they look for instances of bullying quickly and deal with them proactively. Pupils told us they're encouraged to look out for other boys. One mum told us how impressed she was when the school contacted her to say that a sixth former had noticed some boys being unkind to her son. The school had already been 'proactive' in dealing with the incident and in explaining to the boys concerned the 'serious consequences' of their actions and she felt it was resolved very effectively. A sixth former said to us: 'I had a tough time in year 7 – someone was quite mean to me – but I told the teachers and within two days our parents had come in and it was all sorted out – he and I are really good friends now.'

We saw several anti-bullying posters during our visit and posters that engaged with homophobic bullying in particular. On the question of homophobia, we were told that there were boys in the sixth form who felt able to come out as gay. Boys told us that sexuality was 'not important' to them but boys and staff agreed that lower down the school it might be harder for gay pupils to be open about their sexuality.

M

Pupils and parents: There's a diverse ethnic mix at the school. Many boys are local – from inner city Manchester or from the surrounding suburbs. Others travel in from as far afield as Sheffield, York and North Wales. This certainly isn't just a school for the super rich. Over 220 pupils currently receive means-tested bursaries and the average bursary is for 97 per cent of the fees. But there must be something of a gulf between the affluence of those who receive financial support and many of those who don't. Given that to qualify for a full bursary, parents must have a combined annual income of under £27,000 whereas those who don't get any help come from families who can find nearly £12,000 a year (per child), we imagine that some after-school 'come round for tea' invitations involve a certain amount of seeing how the other half live. But we didn't pick up on any sense of stigma surrounding bursaries – in fact the boys we met were proud of them and wanted there to be more. 'Do we really need a new touchscreen whiteboard just because another school's got one?' asked one boy. 'Of course not, we want to put all the spare money towards improving access.' 'We boast about exam results here, not money,' added another lad proudly. 'It's arrogant to show off about how rich you are.' No-one knows who's in receipt of financial help and the school ensures that trips and extracurricular activities are made available to all.

Parents we met came across as educated and comfortably off. They didn't seem to be super competitive or pushy – and they said they approved of the school's policy of praising individual effort rather than attainment. They agreed that the school generally communicates with families very well.

Notable old Mancunians (beyond the sporting and artistic figures mentioned above) include broadcasters Michael Crick, Martin Sixsmith and Faisal Islam, founder of Pets at Home Anthony Preston, Nobel Prize-winning chemist John Polanyi, historian Michael Wood and concert pianist John Ogden.

Entrance: Pupils hoping to join in year 7 must attend an assessment day. During this they'll be taught three topics in groups of 10 – covering English, maths and a humanities subject. The school deliberately teaches the boys unfamiliar material during the day in order to place everyone on a level playing field. During the assessment days, boys are observed to see how they respond to the school's teaching style and how they interact with one another. In addition to the assessment day, boys must attend the entrance exam day in January when they'll sit two maths and two English tests. Past papers are available on the school's website. Although there is scope to prepare for these exams, Dr Boulton says they're 'not the be all and end all'. They're looking for boys who will benefit from being at MGS – they must be able to keep up in an 'unashamedly academic' school and also to thrive in the wider environment. If a child struggled in one of two of the exams but showed great potential on the assessment day he'd still be in with a chance. Dr Boulton's only steer on what type of child they're looking for – beyond a bright one – is that he should be a 'joiner inner'.

Pupils who want to join the sixth form also attend an assessment day. This includes subject lessons (reflecting the boys' chosen specialisms) and an interview. Conditional offers will be made after the assessment day – a typical offer is for an A grade average across a student's GCSE subjects.

Exit: A few boys (up to 10 per cent) leave at the end of year 11. About half of these choose to leave – for a range of reasons, either because the family is moving, they want to pursue options the school doesn't offer or because they want to move to a co-educational school. A handful leave because they're not offered a place in the sixth form – but the high master is clear that such decisions are based on a pupil's best interests: 'We'll accept them into the sixth form if we think it'll work for them,' he says. Those boys leaving at the end of year 13 almost all go to university – mainly to Russell Group establishments.

In 2016, 22 to Oxbridge; Bristol, Imperial, Nottingham, Birmingham, UCL, Leeds, Durham and Manchester popular too, and there is rising interest in the Ivy League, though only one off to America in 2016.

Money matters: School meals are optional but not included in the fees. Private music lessons and exam resits are also charged as extras. Fees are broadly comparable to similar schools nearby. Sibling discounts are available.

Over 220 boys at MGS receive a means-tested bursary. But currently there aren't enough funds to offer financial support to every boy who needs it and who meets the school's selection criteria, so only the very brightest boys are likely to secure a bursary. If your son is offered a bursary, how much you'll receive depends on your combined family income – awarded on a sliding scale. If you earn under £27,000 you're likely to get 100 per cent of fees paid but if you earn more than £50,250 you'll get nothing. Family incomes are reviewed annually. Additional hardship funds are available for trips and emergency fees support.

HSBC scholarships and other bursaries are also available for state school applicants to the sixth form. These can be combined with a school means-tested bursary to make up the full fees.

Remarks: MGS offers its pupils an outstanding school experience and a first class education. It's an honest, traditional grammar school: outward-looking, high-minded, committed to equality of opportunity and, above all, a wonderful environment for bright boys to thrive in, no matter how quirky or unusual they are. In the words of one sixth former (with no prompting): 'We know we're honoured to be here.'

Manchester High School for Girls

Grangethorpe Road, Manchester M14 6HS

Pupils: 938 • Ages: 4–18 • Sixth form: 182

Fees: £8,133 – £11,253 pa

Tel: 01612 240447
Email: administration@mhsg.manchester.sch.uk
Website: www.manchesterhigh.co.uk

Headmistress: Since 2009, Mrs Claire Hewitt BSc (late 40s). Educated at Wakefield Girls' High School, chemistry degree plus PGCE from Sheffield University. Taught at Harrogate Ladies' College, Fulneck School, Sheffield High becoming deputy head and, in 2005, head of King Edward VI Grammar, Louth. Trim and very crisply turned out, but the air in the head's study has significantly softened. 'We love her so much, she's really friendly,' girls enthuse. Teaches chemistry to all year 7s and passionately committed to single sex education, 'I know where girls do better', but glad the high master of neighbouring Manchester Grammar concurs that collaboration's a great thing. Enthusiastic about Man High's curriculum 'meeting the needs of young women entering the 21st century global workplace' but 'all the time maintaining positivity, having fun'. Proud, therefore, her staff can also let their hair down, for example in a recent Strictly-style 'dance with your teachers' charity talent show. Popular for having brought back jumpers after she saw girls shivering in just blouses and blazers – 'she listens,' girls say; 'a quick win,' she demurs. Married to an MGS old boy, no children but a doting auntie, she's a keen cyclist who loves music.

Head of prep: Since 2015, Emma Nash, previously deputy head of Nottingham Girls' High Junior School. BA in English and drama from Cambridge and MA in school effectiveness and school improvement from London University. She has also taught – mostly English and performing arts – at Haberdashers' Aske's Girls, St Paul's Cathedral School, Warwick School and Lochinver House. Married, a doting auntie and godmother, she owns a grumpy grey cat called Howard Nash.

Academic matters: The prep school facilities mean two forms in some years, one in others, starting with forms of up to 20 in reception with two full-time staff. Infants and juniors have their own halls and libraries, the infants a canopied outdoor play area. Whiteboards and a computer suite. Girls sit yearly NFER tests and parents have welcomed 'a more transparent reporting system using colours for progress – you can really see how she's getting on now'. They also praise the children's self-assessment traffic light scheme where they award their own work a green sticker if they've understood everything, an amber if they're not quite sure and red if they still feel befuddled – 'We don't really get reds,' says school. Lower years use smiley faces. 'The teachers here are really supportive,' stellar girls eloquently enthuse. 'We learn through play and learning objectives and lots of school trips, which are a fun way to bring learning to life.' French taught and compulsory Mandarin in the juniors. Two days a week a SENCo works with a handful of dyslexic and dyspraxic girls.

Outstanding results keep school high in league tables with 94 per cent of A levels scoring A*/B in 2016 and 70 per cent A*/As. At GCSE, 80 per cent A*s and As and at both levels lower grade tails are negligible. Awarded International Baccalaureate IB World School Status in 2010, the average point score was 38 in 2016 and school has been 'working hard to communicate with universities'. Broad choices with Latin and PE to A level. Twenty per cent take Latin GCSE, 10 per cent dance and all take GCSE short course RE. Four form groups each year of some 28 girls, with smaller teaching groups. Great facilities – plenty of ICT provision, two state-of-the-art language labs, new sixth form centre and stunning sports complex. Sparkling modern science labs, just two remain what the girls call 'retro'. Chemistry strong and popular here and a couple of years ago a Man High girl was crowned world no 1 female chemistry student in the International Chemistry Olympiad, going on to study natural sciences at Cambridge. The chem labs have arguably the best views of the neighbouring park through huge windows.

Textiles and art overspill meanwhile dwell in two prefab huts. One parent described the DT here as 'girlie', but school points out that for each of the past five years one student's gone on to study engineering. Girls very proud of their libraries, one studiously silent, the other a burble of information gathering and team work. Well-used subject clinics with girls praising teachers for giving up their time. Some 23 girls receive extra help from a variety of sources including a designated learning support coordinator and heads of year. The especially gifted and talented are well supported; for example one outstanding mathematician's ability warranted one-to-one maths lessons from an early age; she eventually represented the UK in the International Maths Olympiad. 'You've got to be willing to work hard here' and 'we do put pressure on ourselves,' pupils say; 'but girls here are ambitious for their futures and definitely career orientated'.

Games, options, the arts: State-of-the-art sports complex with climbing wall and five star viewing gallery. Bright air-conditioned multi-use dance studio, extensive fitness suite for older girls and staff and top-notch 25m indoor pool. U14 national champions at water polo with six regional and three England squad players; perhaps it's practising with the very successful Manchester Grammar teams? Strong hockey and tennis and a GB runner too. Junior sports awards for community service. Super music house with 13 practice rooms and three class rooms. Over 400 girls take instrument lessons including a clutch of harpists. Comenius choir exchanges. Drama studio has floor to ceiling views of gardens and blackout drapes. Main hall fits all seniors on stacking tiered chairs that can roll back for exam season. School is own D of E awarding authority; large numbers of awards at all levels. Model United Nations, Mock Trial, Young Enterprise, strong community links and a student run paper, Onward. Many joint activities with Manchester Grammar boys higher up school; drama, music, debating and other societies, reciprocal rose delivery on Valentine's day and Man High's sports day held on MGS grounds.

LAMDA speech and drama popular in the prep, and music – 'Somewhat violin heavy,' one parent grimaced; 'we've two harpists,' says school. Much positive feedback with merit badges and golden girls published in the glossy prep newsletter. An agreed pupil behaviour charter sets guidelines and the new house system will bring points. The range of extracurricular clubs includes gardening and an Amnesty International group. Paid after-school care and free pre-school from 8am, 'for if your parents are, say surgeons, and have to get in early'.

Background and atmosphere: From burgeoning jasmine in immaculate flower beds (in summer at least) to elegant lily arrangements in reception, this school is fragrant with the sweet smell of success. The latest ISI inspection speaks of all here 'sharing in a vision of excellence in everything they do'. Girls in a painting class or eating lunch on the benches amongst floribundant rose bowers are becoming accustomed to a very civilised lifestyle. The classrooms are spick and span and even the extensive locker areas neat and tidy. Respectful girls in cream and black open doors and stand for the head and there's no corridor chaos here. The only bottleneck is the lunch queue; lunches compulsory for years 7 and 8 but after that the arrangements are laid back with pay-as-you-go needing £2 or £3 a day or the option to bring your own. The modern architecture (school was rebuilt after extensive WW2 bomb damage) and bright airy accommodation enjoy verdant views of manicured lawns, pretty gardens and an internal quad with a clipped box parterre. The leafy backdrop of Platt Fields Park makes it almost impossible to imagine that Manchester city centre lies just beyond Rusholme's vibrant curry mile. Lots of brothers go to nearby MGS and buses serve both schools, as well as arch rivals Withington Girls. Unashamedly ambitious and without doubt fulfilling its 1874 founding objective 'to provide for Manchester's daughters what has been provided without stint for Manchester's sons'. The termly glossy High Flyer magazine celebrates individual and collective achievements.

Prep school on same site as senior school and enjoying its facilities including the pool, canteen and specialist teachers, yet distinctly separate with its own entrance and playground. The recent ISI inspection describes pretty much everything here as outstanding and says, 'There's a tremendous feeling of friendship'. Polite, respectful, genteel, even, girls in buttoned up yellow gingham wait to see who'll speak first – 'Everyone's really friendly, it's easy to make friends and if we spot someone on their own we'll ask them to join in'. Multi-cultural with a prayer room available.

Pastoral care, well-being and discipline: Peer and staff hierarchy for pastoral care. Head describes school's size as just right, 'any bigger and you lose sight of individuals, any smaller and you compromise on opportunities.' School nurse in four-bed sick bay opposite head's study is often first port of call for worries or problems. Late homework slips, detentions for chewing gum but generally they're an amenable bunch. One parent praised school for working hard with her 'wayward adolescent daughter'. Girls feel they have a voice through school council and because the head stops to talk to them in the corridors. Caretakers live on site and school is approached down its own cul-de-sac drive with car park barriers and security doors with CCTV. No barbed wire visible but it feels very secure. Staff enjoy being looked after by staffroom staff, brownies and a fruit bowl, plus their own work and resource room with computers. Frequent sightings of orderly strings of prep girls in yellow gingham add an aaah factor.

Pupils and parents: Hugely culturally diverse, 20 per cent Muslim, strong Jewish contingent with a third experiencing one of 40 other languages in their home lives. Assemblies also include Christian, Sikh, Hindu, humanist and secular options. From all over Greater Manchester and beyond, mostly from professional families with both girls and staff mentioning the huge proportion of doctors' children here. Much celebration and role modelling of old girls' achievements and careers, with a strong network for contacting those who might be helpful. Significant can-do message constantly reinforced.

Old girls include, famously, Cristabel, Sylvia and Adela Pankhurst; assorted businesswomen such as Clara Freeman OBE, Marks and Spencer's first female executive director; Merlyn Lowther, the Bank of England's first female chief cashier, whose signature was on every bank note; leading lawyers such as Ann Alexander, who acted for the families in the Shipman case; Judy Finnigan, of Richard and Judy fame; Lucy Higginson, editor of Horse and Hound magazine; Labour MP Louise Ellman; and GB fencing star Megan Lomas. Plenty of less daunting role models too in entrance foyer hall of fame, where distinctly non-celeb girls doing great things for charity are also featured.

Entrance: Prep school entry by assessment during a visit for entry to reception and years 1 and 2, and by exams, in January or ad hoc by appointment during the year, in English, maths and reasoning for years 3, 4, 5 and 6, plus previous school report.

Academic selection of clever and very clever girls at 11 initially by exams: maths, essay, comprehension, verbal and non-verbal reasoning. Then interview when girls are asked to bring something of interest to talk about, and primary school report. Whittling down three applicants per place, about half from state primaries. Promotional DVD professionally designed.

Exit: Vast majority of prep girls pass seniors' exam (close to 90 per cent in 2016) and transfer easily to familiar turf. Plenty of support and gentle warning for those who won't.

Impressive and solid leavers' destination lists mostly to first choice of university eg Leeds, Liverpool, Birmingham, Edinburgh and King's College London. A regular handful to Oxbridge (four in 2016, including a medic and a vet). Pupils praise careers service which is integrated into life from year 8, includes aptitude testing and careful individual support for subject choices and future plans; certainly the careers room always seems to be active.

Money matters: Ten per cent, about 12 girls a year, receive some bursary or scholarship help; many very quietly, although some speak positively and publicly of their assistance as part of the new £2 million Pankhurst Bursary Appeal. Twenty per cent discount for third child in school.

Remarks: Beautiful setting for unashamedly ambitious education, high expectations and positive mental attitude; in school's words, 'shaping the next generation of remarkable women'. Girls here expect strong careers but there has been a mellowing and this generation's route to the top seems more likely to come from intelligent hard work than from sharp elbows.

Merchant Taylors' Boys' School

Linked with Merchant Taylors' Girls' School

186 Liverpool Road, Crosby, Liverpool L23 0QP

Pupils: 741: 150 junior, 577 senior • Ages: 7–18 • Sixth form: 160

Fees: Juniors £8,184; Seniors £10,950 pa

Tel: 01519 499333
Email: infomtbs@merchanttaylors.com
Website: www.merchanttaylors.com

Headmaster: Since 2005, Mr David Cook (40s); read history at Birkbeck College, London; taught at Caterham, housemaster and head of history at Giggleswick, deputy head at QEH, Bristol. Held short service commission in Cheshires. Sharp, decisive and energetic, mind clearly spilling over with ideas for school. Good listener, not without gravitas. Son in school and daughter in sister establishment.

Academic matters: Traditional curriculum, including German, Spanish, Latin, Greek; separate sciences. GCSE results 56 per cent A*/A in 2016. Relatively few go on to arts subjects at A level, where science and maths rule. Things may change after current radical curriculum review (head has some interesting ideas about early GCSEs) but few stronger science departments in the north. A level overall 76 per cent at A*/B and 41 per cent A*/A in 2016. Recent innovation is one-to-one clinics for pupils having academic or organisational difficulties. SEN overseen by head of learning support. Teaching staff experienced and effective. Big staff turnover (retirement), over past few years – big opportunity then.

Games, options, the arts: Only room for a few pitches on site, but main fields within walking distance. All the usual sports, taken seriously, plus strong rowing on Southport Marina. Plenty of representation at regional and national levels. Enormous and vigorous CCF (all three services), shared with sister school (250 in all). Plenty of expeditions and trips. Good art and lively drama: several shared productions with girls' school, plus usual in-house plays. About 25 per cent learn an instrument; annual family carol service in Philharmonic Hall raises money for Merseyside charities. Joint debating society with girls is over 100 years old.

Background and atmosphere: Founded in 1620 by London Merchant Taylor, John Harrison, moved to present agreeable site in 1878, in respectable suburb – handsome Victorian main building.The £5.5 million sports centre on site is available for use by all Merchant Taylors' Schools.

Special emphasis on ICT: latest software as teaching tool, and though a day school, every boy has email address and access to many campus computer sites. New school council seems to be more than a talking shop, if pupils' recent victory in matter of toilets is anything to go by.

Atmosphere decidedly northern ex-direct grant grammar school. Academic work a serious priority, more important perhaps than glitzy facilities – some classrooms are on the shabby side but serious refurbishments and new builds in progress.

Pastoral care, well-being and discipline: A small school, so it's claimed every boy is known. Usual day school network of form teacher/ year head/pastoral deputy head means no-one is overlooked. Chaplain also available to talk through problems and independent counsellor drops in once a week for chats in total confidence. Personal health taken seriously. As in all good schools, aim is to develop self-discipline. Drug dealers face the sack.

Pupils and parents: Families from all over Merseyside area. Professional, business, etc, only two to three per cent ethnic minorities, but broad range of social background – 'We are academically, not socially, selective'. Fourteen buses operate daily from as far away as Wigan, South Liverpool, Southport and Warrington; convenient suburban rail link as well. Boys cheery, frank, polite, academically ambitious, a mixture not always understood by southern incomers. Probably a greater community of interest between school and parents than in similar conurbations. Old Boys include Nigel Rees and ex-England rugby international Ben Kay.

Entrance: Academically selective and oversubscribed at 7+ into junior school and 11+ into senior. Junior boys' school makes up 40 per cent of entry to senior; any boy not likely to make it is flagged up well before exam time and discussed with parents. Ten to 15 lost every year to sixth form colleges (some then want to come back), numbers made up by sixth form entry (six Bs required at GCSE).

Exit: About a quarter leave after GCSEs. Sixth form leavers nearly all to Russell Group universities eg Manchester, Liverpool, Leeds, Newcastle, to read traditional subjects (economics, business, history); four medics in 2016 with one pupil going to Madrid to study dentistry.

Money matters: Probably the cheapest HMC day school in the country – a huge selling point. 'Considerable numbers' on sliding scale in own assisted places scheme. Some merit scholarships.

Remarks: Good, solid, dedicated former grammar school in northern mould, where nearly all work hard in and out of classroom. Now in the process of a 21st century update, but not likely to lose its traditional ethos of commitment and emphasis on the daily transaction of the classroom.

Merchant Taylors' Girls' School

Linked with Merchant Taylors' Boys' School

80 Liverpool Road, Crosby, Liverpool L23 5SP

Pupils: 801 • Ages: 4–7 (boys), 4–18 (girls) • Sixth form: 143

Fees: £8,184 – £10,950 pa

Tel: 01519 243140
Email: infomtgs@merchanttaylors.com
Website: www.merchanttaylors.com

Headmistress: Since 2006, Mrs Louise Robinson BA MEd NPQH (50s). Taught ICT and maths at Bolton School Girls' Division, rising to head of ICT and senior mistress; deputy head Manchester High School for Girls; principal Howell's School, Denbigh. Teaches maths and supports ICT – enjoys having contact with the girls, whom she appreciates ('Very engaging and forthcoming', 'We have some very feisty individuals'); accompanied school Ecuador trip. Elegant, astute, with strong opinions, seen as 'a very good manager' by parents but 'very busy' and 'a bit distant' by some. Wants the school to be 'the best at everything', provide 'the best education for life', give opportunities to the 'leaders of the future' to excel and develop all their talents – 'Why wouldn't you?' something of a catch phrase. Husband a retired headteacher; one grown up son; enjoys skiing, gardening and reading.

Primary school head: Since 2007, Miss Julie Yardley BA PGCE (40s). Educated at Birkenhead High, music degree at Liverpool University; worked in sales before primary music training; taught in state schools in the Wirral, Birkenhead High Juniors, head of Bolton Schools Girls' Junior Division; regularly does support teaching at school. Keen to make curriculum more lively with problem solving, active and independent learning approaches and to foster 'give it a go' spirit and perseverance. Energetic, ebullient, enthusiastic. Main hobby music – performing and concerts.

Academic matters: Ability spread in primary school from average to very bright. Class sizes around 15. National curriculum with extras; no key stage tests. Year 5 annual themed activities day; cross-curricular practical work linked with science; we admired a very creative classics project; imaginative events, eg a giant egg appearing in the playground, used to develop investigative skills and newspaper report writing; all teachers plan a weekly gifted and talented activity open to all children. Impressive success in national maths competition.

Learning support mainly for dyslexia and dyspraxia, but if a child has enough ability and school and parents feel this is the right place, would do their best to accommodate all needs; a few EAL children.

In 2016 at A level 76 per cent A*/B (nearly 49 per cent A*/A); especially strong maths, physics, art and design, French, economics, geography and psychology. Also offers business studies, ICT, government and politics, theatre studies, AQA Bacc, home economics; biology, chemistry and English very popular and good numbers for classical civilisation. Almost all subjects very strong at GCSE – 67 per cent A*/A 2016; astronomy possible through club. Some parents would like early entry maths and some more stimulation for top set girls.

Good spread of languages, including Greek, Latin and Mandarin – particularly impressive classics department: we would have liked a go at the interactive Latin course we saw in action. Setting for maths, languages and science. Average class sizes – 20 key stage 3, 14 key stage 4; 10 for sixth form; 24 max; buzzing, focused girls at work; lots of PCs.

Thoroughgoing tracking and monitoring. Success in national/regional science, maths, classics, poetry and politics competitions; STEM subjects and participation in external courses encouraged. Stable staff – 'hugely experienced and talented' (head); girls spoke warmly and appreciatively of their teachers, feeling lessons are fun and varied and they are well taught and supported if having difficulties. Parents very pleased – 'They've brought her out academically...She's really bloomed and exceeded our expectations'.

Well-designed gifted and talented provision for selected members of years 7-10 (the Harrison Group); lectures for sixth form Harrison scholars open to all; lots of support for Oxbridge, law, modern languages and medical school applicants.

Thoughtful and comprehensive provision for special needs in senior school: individual sessions, IEPs with detailed suggestions for teaching strategies, specialist science support teacher; co-ordinator feels she can cover all needs. Grateful praise for the way her daughter's needs have been met from a parent. General initial screening for dyslexia with checks again at end of years 9 and 11; individual EAL support available.

Games, options, the arts: Own courts and use of recently constructed sports centre shared by all four Merchant Taylor senior and junior schools. Usual sports plus badminton, lacrosse, dance (some would like more of this), trampoline, rowing, golf, scuba diving, pilates and step aerobics, so plenty for the less sporty. Local, county, regional and some national level success for hockey, netball, athletics, tennis, cross-country, badminton, swimming; two young national biathlon competitors; runs A and B teams.

Thriving music ('wonderful teachers... one of the greatest strengths of the school' – parent): three orchestras, four choirs, ensembles; choir performs at classy events – Royal Navy, cathedrals, Lord Mayor of London and his High Sheriffs' dinner; film/show music as well as classical; tours to Belgium, Germany, Holland; individuals attend Royal Northern Music College and Chethams' summer school; annual music comp; piano masterclass by Richard Meyrick; Saturday morning co-ed music school, Crescendo!, open to all schools, 7 to 18 year olds.

Lively drama – version of A Midsummer Night's Dream produced by year 6 classes in a week, with input from professional actors and a fashion designer; a girl starred in Matilda the musical – youngest ever winner of an Olivier award. Two joint senior school drama productions annually, one musical, one play, at both schools, eg Calamity Jane, Les Mis, Daisy Pulls It Off, Shakespeare. Drama festival for years 8 and 9 – plays written, directed and organised by sixth formers, who also run drama club; arts award. Lively, well-designed magazine, Calliope; visits from writers.

Truly stunning art – painting, 3D, multi-media; excellent exam results (recent accolade for 'exemplary practice' from AQA); GCSE art looks up to A level standard. Inspiring, vibrant art studio. Year 6 has practical art sessions, eg recycled fashion day, in conjunction with senior school art department. Several fascinating creative partnerships with Liverpool John Moores University School of Art, Aintree and the Royal Liverpool Hospitals, eg a series of works based on treatment of blood disorders. Own art gallery, The Vitreum, hosts exhibitions by leading regional, national and international contemporary artists and designers. Visiting printmakers work with students, thanks to school's own etching press (also has an Albion letterpress, rescued from a barn in France by the dynamic art director) and stone lithography facility.

As well as key stage 3 textiles and home economics, girls take a technology course including mechanisms and computer programming; the STEM club is designing and building a solar powered car – so these girls will have no problem with changing a plug whilst knocking up a soufflé (and translating a Virgil Eclogue to boot, no doubt).

CCF – with the boys' school (all three services) – very big; much D of E; all sixth formers do community service. Debating, Model United Nations comp, European Youth Parliament and business enterprise/investment comps. School council, lots of charity fundraising (run by sixth form committee), fortnightly fair trade stall, Eco schools' Green Flag status – to be featured on Eco Schools' website as case study of good practice. Joint schools' youth club for years 7-9.

Trips to France, Italy (skiing), China, Australia, Greece, Iceland, World Challenge to Equador, culture trip to New York; linked schools in Sierra Leone; year 11 jolly at Alton Tours before GCSE exam leave starts.

Very good careers programme – breakfast events (with boys) for upper sixth give opportunity to meet reps from companies/business people plus joint working lunches and dinners with guest speakers from various fields; work experience in year 11 and through sixth form, in Merseyside and sometimes beyond; Merchants' community network used; annual joint careers fair.

Background and atmosphere: A hotch-potch architecturally – the original house (the Merchant Taylors' Schools were founded in 1620 by John Harrison of the London Merchant Taylors' Livery Company) is juxtaposed with a 1960s concrete monstrosity, 1980s red-brick extensions and modern reception area plus the generous gallery space. Harmonised décor within – lemon walls and blue carpets and chairs. Classrooms look nondescript but attractive displays cover all walls around the school. The sixth form library in the old house is furnished with traditional wooden bookcases, tables and chairs; the ground floor section is enticingly stocked with varied fiction.

Primary school in original 1800s, cream and blue, converted house now supplemented by purpose-built classrooms and specialist teaching rooms, a new dining hall, kitchen, library and fully-equipped medical rooms as well as additional office space and an impressive new glass fronted reception area – the result of a two year £5.5m redevelopment. Adventure playground recently opened.

Much promotion of reading and general knowledge – book lists and shadow competition judging, visits from writers, house quizzes. Lawns (one with benches for alfresco lunches), an eco garden and inspiring modern sculpture of a girl reaching for success.

Much focus on the latter but, we were assured by girls, not in an oppressive way – 'Teachers will help you find out what you're good at', so you 'find your niche'; 'There's something for all aspects of your personality'; 'If you want the best, it's there for you'; 'You can be accepted for what you want to be

– so long as you work for it'. 'Healthy competition', but girls don't feel pressured and support each other, said a parent. 'A unique combination of high expectations in a non-threatening environment,' said another. No opportunities wasted for improvement – including literary extracts on the loo doors. Public speaking encouraged to develop confidence; scholars hone their social skills at a formal dinner with governors.

School council chose names of the four houses – Minerva, Thalia, Gaia, Selene. Smart uniforms – navy blue jackets and skirts, light blue, striped blouses. Food well thought of – plenty of choice; sixth can go out in lunch hour but some choose to stay in. Three full school assemblies/week with religious elements.

Pastoral care, well-being and discipline: Primary school pastoral care centred on class teachers plus strong lunch-time welfare team; year 2 'playground pals' attend to infants' playground; years 5 and 6 help with infants' sports day and read with them – lots of opportunities for responsibility. House points, merit badges, weekly merit assembly. Parents pleased with friendly, accessible teachers.

Very reasonable senior school behaviour policy, elegantly headed 'concordia parvae res crescunt' (small things grow in harmony). Girls' happiness seen as integral to achievement – pupils see the school as very friendly and feel well supported, with plenty of people to turn to if they have problems, which will get sorted out. Sixth form mentors provide a listening service, plus access to two trained counsellors every lunch time. Well planned transition to year 7 including summer holiday scheme – state school children integrate quickly. Focus more on rewards than sanctions – merits for exceptional helpfulness, showing initiative, outstanding effort; honours and prizes.

Pupils and parents: Catchment area from South Liverpool to Bootle and Crosby, north and east beyond Southport, as far as Warrington, Wigan and St Helens. Wide socio economic range – 20-25 per cent have financial support. Ethnically mixed. Open, confident, articulate and thoughtful girls who enjoy all aspects of school life. Good links with parent, who feel involved and that concerns are responded to swiftly and patiently – website, newsletters, handbook.

Famous OGs: Beryl Bainbridge; Jane Garvey and Kelly Dalglish (Woman's Hour/Sky Sports presenters); Professor Janet Finch, vice-chancellor Keele University; Winifred Lambert – distinguished social worker, promoting housing for families and disabled, and lifelong member of the Communist party; Jane Greenwood, Tony award-winning fashion designer; Joy Swift MBE, creator of the original murder mystery weekends.

Entrance: Four to 7-year-olds' assessments usually in spring term but available throughout the year (can join at any age) – observed doing age appropriate activities, looking for readiness to listen and adapt to school life. More places available in year 3 – short tests in English and maths based on key stage 1 curriculum.

Year 7: tests in English, maths, online reasoning plus report from current school, late January/early February (register before December of year 6). Years 8-10: tests in English, maths and reasoning; some spoken and written questions in languages and sciences. Sixth form entry: at least seven GCSEs at grade B or above, A*/A in A level subjects.

Exit: Boys leave the primary school at end of year 2, most for Merchant Taylors' Junior; girls leave at 11, nearly all to senior school. Some 15-20 per cent leave at end of year 11 for local sixth form colleges. Of those who stay most head for Russell Group universities. Manchester, Liverpool John Moores, Durham, Leeds, Liverpool and Newcastle popular (occasional Oxbridge place – one to Oxford to read French and philosophy in 2016). Favoured subjects: psychology, medicine and classical civilisation; otherwise more do various kinds of science than arts.

Money matters: Year 7 entry – discretionary awards varying in amounts (short term, linked to academic merit); scholarships for academic, sporting and musical prowess; five or six school assisted places awarded on academic merit, means-tested, up to full fees (home visits to assess financial need). Sixth form – Harrison scholarships (more kudos than dosh) and some bursaries available. Ten per cent discount for siblings.

Remarks: Very successful, happy mixture of the traditional and 21st century education. High achieving girls who don't feel hothoused. Outstanding art evidence that creativity and individuality are prized too. Excelsior!

The Minster School, York

Deangate, York, North Yorkshire YO1 7JA

Pupils: 157 • Ages: 3–13

Fees: £4,575 – £9,795 pa

Tel: 08449 390000
Email: school@yorkminster.org
Website: www.minsterschoolyork.co.uk

Headmaster: Since 2004, Mr Alex Donaldson MA PGCE Cert ICT (50s). Choral scholar at St John's College, Cambridge; professional singer for five years (counter tenor) with, among others, the Tallis Scholars and the BBC Singers. Still helps out in the Minster. A serious musician, but has a wide perspective on education. Joined school in 1988, promoted head 2004. Warm, relaxed personality; communicates easily with children and popular with parents. Instrumental in introducing more collaborative style of management, though still in many ways the traditional prep school head, who knows his pupils well and what's going on; 'we know each other's foibles,' he smiles. All about 'high expectations – academic, social and musical, and they rise to them.' Wife Jane runs the pre-prep; three children, two at university.

Entrance: Most come up from nursery, but any age considered if room. Non-selective; would-be choristers must audition at age 7, when up to four of each sex are chosen to join prestigious Minster choir. Boys' and girls' choirs of 20 each are separate, take equal part in Minster worship and (unusually) like for like on scholarships (between 60 and 100 per cent including means-testing) – but work hard for it (as do their parents).

Exit: Leaving is apparently tough: 'we will really miss it,' say both parents and children, but feel they are given good guidance for next schools. 'Great advice and they know our children inside out,' said a grateful parent, adding that they are 'well-prepared for senior school and often go on to shine there'. Most to northern independents at 13: St Peter's, Bootham, The Mount (all York city); others recently to Reading School, Radley and Repton. Understandably excellent record in music scholarships. A few to local maintained schools.

Remarks: School famously claims foundation in 627 by Archbishop Paulinus; certainly a 'song school' existed then.

Refounded 1903, specifically at that time to provide choristers for the Minster. Occupies world heritage site slap in the middle of York, bringing the pleasures and pains of operating in the lee of York Minster, which has to be one of the finest buildings in Christendom; 'our school chapel,' smiles the head wryly. Manages to squeeze into a additional space here and there, but expansion is challenging, development a planning nightmare and even returfing the play areas is likely to unearth a Viking or two, bringing the archaeologists flocking and halting any possible progress. Main buildings date from 1832; school also uses string of earlier town houses and handsome Georgian Old Residence for lower school. Despite confined site, it feels remarkably uncluttered, and children seem happily oblivious to the numbers of tourists with cameras slung around their necks peeping through the school gates.

The school's identity and purpose has broadened; prospectus says very firmly, 'Musical ability is not an entrance requirement'; in head's eyes, this is more a school which does music than a music school. The school has been co-educational since 1987, yet that penny is still to drop with local tour guides who still describe it as the 'school for choir boys'. It's now much more than that, though admittedly most prep schools would give teeth to reach even half its standard musically. The Minster still requires – and gets – a top class choir, but it's no longer true that choristers dictate the curriculum or shape of the school day. Even so, over 90 per cent of pupils leave playing one instrument, and about half play two or more. One pupil, while admitting sport was his first love, told us, 'I'm really not musical at all – yet coming here I'm still encouraged to play an instrument for pleasure and I have surprised myself.' Plenty of games, societies, activities and trips; 'they are so busy we can hardly keep up,' enthused one parent. Play areas and cricket nets on site; no gym, pupils have to crocodile to playing fields, Astroturf and swimming nearby at Bootham (admittedly only 10 minutes away). SEN (mostly literacy) catered for (free). Nursery opening in 2017.

Parents choose the school for its 'family atmosphere whilst getting good academic results' – small is king – and 'children of different ages know each other well and staff and the head know children's names'. Children are 'confident, well-mannered and happy to talk easily to anyone,' say parents, and that was certainly our experience here too. Parents mostly professional and business.

Moorfield School

49

Wharfedale Lodge, 11 Ben Rhydding Road, Ilkley, West Yorkshire LS29 8RL

Pupils: 110: 90 girls, 20 boys • Ages: 2.5–11

Fees: £8,880 pa

Tel: 01943 607285
Email: enquiries@moorfieldschool.co.uk
Website: www.moorfieldschool.co.uk

Headmistress: Since 2008, Mrs Jessica Crossley BEd. Originally from South Africa, she studied at Stellenbosch University, specialising in primary teaching and music. Previously a teacher at Moorfield, so knows the school well.

A breath of fresh air, she is warm, hugely enthusiastic and ambitious for her school and pupils. Seems to have won over hearts and minds with her 'I can achieve anything' approach to life and learning. Nurture and academic rigour both sit very comfortably with her. 'It takes a long time to grow a child,' she says. Delightfully unstuffy whilst exuding both intelligence and charm, she walks her talk more convincingly than many and is a real strength of the school.

Married with three grown-up children, she spends her weekends catching up with family and walking her elderly labrador on Ilkley Moor. Lists 'good coffee and singing' as some of life's other pleasures.

Entrance: Twenty children per year group. Most join from nursery and there's a steady dribble into classes most years if space allows. Girl-heavy throughout; no boys as yet in the older classes, but numbers of boys are increasing each year as the youngest work their way through the school.

Children of all abilities accepted, on the premise that the needs of current pupils are not compromised in any way; ability/needs are assessed informally on a taster day. Some year groups are full (numbers are on the up) but space in other years so do check. Annual open day, but school is open to visitors most days by appointment.

Exit: Most popular destinations in 2016 were Harrogate Ladies (one all-rounder scholarship in 2016) and Ilkley Grammar. Other common destinations include Skipton Girls' High and Bradford Grammar. These are all sought-after schools and competition is rife so parents are well advised along the way and children extremely well prepared, helping to ease the transition into their first choice schools.

Remarks: Small, but, in many ways perfectly formed. Housed in Wharfedale Lodge, an imposing Yorkshire stone villa with newer additions, including a purpose-built nursery and hall/ gym. Classrooms are bright, sunny and spacious, with plenty of impressive work on display. The whole place feels loved and cared for, no tatty areas to be seen. Attention to detail is important here – they care, and it shows.

Little passing traffic as the school sits in a prime residential street, nestled in the lea of Ilkley Moor. You have to go out of your way to find it (other schools are more visible and Moorfield wrestles with that). The hillside location means there are limitations – no car park or playing fields on site. However, lose yourself in the mind of a child just for a moment and then weigh that up against spacious grounds fashioned by nature with craggy woods, shady dells, dens and a stream – something other schools attempt to recreate by paying a fortune to landscape gardeners.

The school uses every inch of the available space – safe playground with hard and soft areas, a hard court and new Astro for ball games; forest school happens for real here and the grounds are child heaven, with so much to explore.

Small classes, learning support as required. French from nursery, German from year 3 and a smattering of Russian in year 6; subject specialist teaching at the top of the school. You won't find the school in newspapers' top school lists simply because, like 75 per cent of UK prep schools, they don't do Sats. No lack of rigour though – they take preparation for senior school seriously and will happily talk to you about their assessment criteria.

According to the children, 'the teachers here find really fun ways to drill subjects into your head.' We might struggle a little with the word 'drill' but they are all smiles as they say it and we know what they mean. Parents say the head is good at finding 'young, inspiring teachers' who 'put soul into the place.' Teachers clearly have energy too – they end the day with a seven-minute workout with the head ('don't tell the children, they may want to watch'). Plenty of IT throughout, staff know their way around interactive whiteboards and use them well;

Old school skills such as cooking, masterfully led by the former head of Bettys Cookery School.

Well-stocked library; they are big on reading here, with special rosettes awarded for reading the classics (with or without the help of parents) – and it doesn't count if you just watched the DVD. Specialist music rooms in the refurbished basement. All sing and the majority play an instrument, many more than one.

School makes use of good local facilities for team sports and swimming, as well as running on the moor and around the local tarn. Add to that a spelling bee and a wealth of musical opportunities and there are no excuses for not sleeping well at night. Achieving a rare third green flag as an eco school was much celebrated; there is a vitality here that is both healthy and engaging.

There's a holiday club during the hols – hugely popular with working parents and ladies-who-lunch. 'It's a lifesaver,' say parents, and no complaints from the children, who seem to have a wonderfully busy time. Plenty of 'specials' – climate week, poetry, art, music and drama competitions, fundraising for local charities and more besides. Year 6 pupils end their time at the school with a winter banquet – dress code is 'more dash than cash' so that it doesn't become a fashion show. Otherwise it's a candlelit dinner, with formal invitations (delightfully penned thank you letters follow), the best china and silverware, all at the head's home. It's one of the most eagerly awaited events of the year, and not just for the grand finale that is the chocolate fountain.

Pupils look cheery in practical red and green uniforms, blazers and jumpers for most, sweatshirts for little ones. The time-honoured school hats and caps remain at parents' insistence (admittedly cute around town), but it's more to do with sentimental value than denying the myth that is Ilkley Moor bar t'at (translation available if required). These are busy children. Plenty of sport on and off site, with competitive matches against local schools. 'I expect you to win,' says the head. She's only half-joking, but apparently 'it's still good for your personal development if you lose,' say the pupils. Crikey.

Food is 'great,' say the pupils, notably Mrs Glover's legendary chocolate square, which (they are quick to add) is balanced by a healthy fruit feast on other days. Food is locally sourced and cooked in-house; parents receive menu options on weekly newsletters.

Parents treasure the 'family environment' and appreciate the accommodating flexibility. Not essential to pre-book before and after-school care. Just a phone call needed – invaluable when you are stuck in traffic. Usual to see older girls looking after the little ones at playtime – it's a small school and they know (and will play with) everyone, regardless of age. New pupils are made welcome throughout and parents meet and greet others with coffee and croissant mornings.

The amusingly titled 'boy time' happens on Friday afternoon when the boys (small as they are) head off for rugby or cricket. Plans to add golf too as they grow a little taller. It's early days for co-ed and boys are very much in the minority but they are well catered for and are a happy and much-valued part of the school. Pupils are unfailingly polite and discipline is obvious, without childlike enthusiasm being suppressed. No mobile phones and parents happy with that – 'we want them to be children.'

Ilkley is a small market town with, probably, too many schools as well as an abundance of teashops and antique dealers, yet all are thriving and appear recession-proof. Serious money here and they are a well-heeled bunch, though admittedly the heels are more Hunter (possibly Aigle) than Louboutin. But somehow the locals are all the more likeable for that. The upshot is plenty of choice for your children and a great lifestyle for parents who may well choose to work in Leeds but live here. 'You pays your money (or not) and you takes your choice,' as they say around here, but make sure you don't miss Moorfield when you are doing the rounds.

The Mount School

Dalton Terrace, York, North Yorkshire YO24 4DD

Pupils: 324; 84 boarders • Ages: 2–11 (boys), 2–18 (girls); (boarding from 11) • Sixth form: 80

Fees: Day £7,176 – £17,892; Boarding £19,704 – £29,109 pa

Tel: 01904 667500
Email: registrar@mountschoolyork.co.uk
Website: www.mountschoolyork.co.uk

Principal: Since January 2016, Adrienne Richmond, previously deputy head at Durham High School for Girls. She has also been director of studies at Newcastle Central High. She studied maths at Newcastle and trained as a maths teacher at Manchester. She is an ISI inspector and a D of E award leader, enjoying hill walking and camping.

Head of junior school: Since 2012, Rachel Capper (40s) BEd music (Bretton Hall, University of Leeds). Joined The Mount in 2003 as class teacher after primary and infant teaching in state schools in London and North Wales, with various positions of responsibility in English, SEN, music and IT. Progressed to head of key stage 1 and then deputy head prior to current appointment.

Lives in York with partner, Adrian, who works in IT. Originally from North Wales and enjoys returning to visit friends and family. Personal interests in music, art and theatre and enjoying the outdoors.

Passionate about early years education and pupils being given strong foundations on which to build: 'Freedom to play, explore and learn in a stimulating environment where they learn basic literacy and numeracy skills and develop the ability to take risks and think for themselves. I believe that these principles should continue into the primary phase where it is important that pupils are taught and encouraged to think independently, and to ask questions.'

Academic matters: Skills-based enquiry-led curriculum in junior school with cross-curricular science, humanities and art. Specialist teaching in French, music, dance and swimming from age 3; PE from reception and German from year 3. New life sciences room; year 5 learn science in senior school laboratories and ICT in purpose built suite; no laptops or iPads evident, though.

Girls speak enthusiastically and without prompting of their teachers and the help they give them. Termly assessment weeks produce target cards and are followed up by parents' meetings; annual full written report. Individual progress monitored and if concerns, internal assessment undertaken, in consultation with parents. Support based on individual needs, either by teaching assistant in classroom or individual SEN support out of classroom.

A level results 34 per cent A*/A in 2016, A*/B 70 per cent. Traditional A levels with biggest uptake in maths and sciences (perhaps due to recent recruitment of more international students to sixth form) though class size remains small 'with nowhere to hide,' said one sixth former, smiling ruefully. PE, theatre studies, psychology and business studies on offer too. Ever-expanding enrichment programme with weekly lectures, community and global focus. Strong uptake of EPQ – now extended down to GCSE years.

At GCSE, 44 per cent A*/A in 2016. Good choice of options, 10 subjects standard, MFL either French or German (Spanish GCSE on offer in sixth form). Maths setted in year 7 onwards, English in year 9 onwards. Good IT provision – Wifi and iPads throughout, interactive whiteboards in most classrooms and two modern computer suites plus dedicated department clusters; qualifications including vocational OCR Nationals taken in middle school and sixth form.

Pupils and parents alike comment on the quality and commitment of teachers; girls enjoy lessons. 'They are kind, supportive, encouraging, nurturing as well as being fantastic teachers': one pupil voice spoke for many. A parent told us, 'When she has had a wobble, the teachers have been there supporting her; her form teacher understood and knew my daughter straight away'.

York used for local cross-curricular and thinking skills work via 'Investigating York' in year 7; archaeology is part of history in younger years; links with university. Elements of the Peacejam programme, devised by Nobel Peace Laureates, introduced to the sixth form, form part of a weekly enrichment carousel of activities within the curriculum for whole school.

Selective, though does well with all abilities including EAL – support available. Specialist learning support teaching provided in and out of classroom dependent on need.

Very good careers education, skills-based in year 10, work experience post-GCSE in year 11. Focus in sixth form is university preparation, particularly for medicine and Oxbridge, some jointly with co-educational Quaker school Bootham.

Games, options, the arts: Beautifully kept grounds with grass and hard tennis/netball courts, sports fields for hockey and athletics, an indoor pool and sports hall including a fitness suite. Successful at traditional competitive team sports and offers non-competitive options such as rock climbing, dance and outdoor pursuits. Has players at county and country level in several disciplines.

Very strong and varied musical life, from classical to rock; all abilities participate in Christmas concert; regular concerts with other Quaker schools. Almost half of pupils learn instruments at school. Regular speech and drama successes, regional winners of Poetry by Heart, best delegate at Model United Nations conference and regional team finalists in Rotary Youth Speaks. Annual school production, most recently The Witches; sixth form play produced entirely by pupils. Very impressive artwork throughout the school encompassing ceramics, photography, sculpture, textiles and graphics. Design and technology studied up to A level – no cooking, except for fun; sixth form university preparation.

Huge range of after-school activities, eg jewellery making, photography, ultimate Frisbee – a non-combat, self-refereed game originating in the US; all take part. D of E popular – strong tradition of community involvement. Emphasis on understanding the wider world and global issues is important – Peacejam, Ibba school in Southern Sudan, electronic links to Quaker schools in Palestine and Lebanon.

Junior school plays traditional sports using whole school facilities – regular inter-school competitions. Arts are encouraged here – good take up of individual music lessons from year 1, with school choir and orchestra. LAMDA popular and most recent production Nativity Rock included a cast from pre-school to year 6. Impressive list of after-school activities with some, like judo and fencing, at an extra charge. Annual residential trips from year 2 for outdoor pursuits experience.

Boarding: Sixth form boarding is across the road from the main school building with younger boarding in the upper echelons of the main school building. Accommodation is comfortable and homely, recently refurbished. Three to four to a bedroom still the norm – no single rooms in sixth form.

Whilst 75 per cent of boarders are in school at weekends, the high number of sixth form boarders with right to opt out of activities means smallish numbers and a wide age range. Regular organised off-site activities and freedom for unescorted paired trips to the city centre from year 9.

Background and atmosphere: Origins go back to 18th century; present building, close to the centre of York, has a very fine 1857 façade with modern additions. Approached through iron gate from the car park, it's like entering the Secret Garden, though beautifully maintained, stretching beyond the eye to green fields – an unseen total of 16 acres. The girls make the most of the outdoor space, some practising their tennis strokes, others deep in conversation, and even 12 year olds are not too cool to race to the garden swing at break times.

Classrooms are a mix of old and new, very traditional library, which the girls enjoy, and a spacious and light dining room, serving excellent fare, decorated with posters to inspire the girls to reduce food wastage. Attractive and well-designed new sixth form study centre has revitalised the top end of the school, giving private study areas as well as allowing extra activities such as cookery and social gatherings.

Junior school situated at the end of the main senior school building, in more recent but attractive trinity of buildings. Pre-school offers wrap-around care for 51 weeks of the year for 2 and 3 year olds. The Toddler Room is a cosy island in a secure sea of playground set up for outdoor learning and play. Across the way, early years are on the ground floor of the second building with classrooms for years 1 and 2 above. Bright classrooms with loads of space for the small class sizes; perhaps too small in some. Junior pupils are in classrooms adjacent to the senior school.

What make this site special are the delightful bijou enchanted garden and woodland area close by used for adventurous and investigative outdoor learning led by a specialist teacher. Pupils spoke glowingly of their forest school days. They also have the opportunity to attend the Outdoor Explorers' Club after school. Awarded the Woodland Trust's Green Tree Gold Award for two years' sustained effort by junior school staff and pupils.

Though only a small percentage of staff and girls are Quakers, the ethos is at the heart of the school, manifest in respect for everyone in the community, a high degree of tolerance of differences, caring for others and democratic practices. 'It provides girls with a moral compass,' says the principal. 'They are valued for who they are'. 'Very little herd mentality,' say parents; pupils are demonstrably happy to be themselves. The head girl is appointed by the school, as the 'girls have a strong sense of fairness and justice'; the school council, conducted on Quaker business meeting lines, discusses internal affairs and, unlike most, really does have a voice. Morning Meetings include a period of silent reflection. Widespread involvement rather than bald achievement is regarded highly, and girls view additional activities, such as lectures from visiting speakers, as 'opportunities not to be missed'.

Pastoral care, well-being and discipline: Good work and behaviour in junior school rewarded through individual golden ticket or class golden certificate awarded weekly at one of the assemblies held in the school gym or school hall. Four houses named after York's Quaker chocolatiers provide arena for sporting competition. Principal has worked hard on 'one school strategy' and PeaceJam Juniors (recognised as a school of excellence by the International PeaceJam Foundation), introducing global thinking and strengthening Quaker ethos through meeting silences as in senior school. Girls from senior school doing Duke of Edinburgh Award undertake their community work here too.

Pastoral care onsidered very important – an absolute strength of the school. Girls feel they have an identity, are known and receive a lot of individual attention. Size helps, and activities transcending year groups with good integration of international boarders promote cohesiveness from sixth form down, resulting in the friendly and happy environment. There is a lot of social interaction between year groups, observed in mixed ages, day pupils and boarders all round the same table at lunchtime. Peer mentoring from sixth form for younger pupils.

Non-confrontational approach to discipline, huge amount of trust around the place, which girls appreciate with a typical common sense approach. 'If you mess up, you mess it up for everyone'. Time is given to listen to pupils and they are encouraged to speak and have a voice – in a respectful manner.

Exclusion only for persistent offences or major breach of rules, though the current leadership has not had to deal with incidents involving drugs or alcohol. Even more extraordinary, there is no litter and no evidence of chewing gum. School puts this down to 'pupils having a strong culture of ownership of their school'.

Plenty of contact with parents – school website, weekly newsletter. Termly forum where parent representatives meet the senior leadership team to discuss topics of mutual interest.

Latest ISI report criticised some aspects of staff recruitment checks, though praised the teaching.

Pupils and parents: Not just those with Quaker connection (it's the only all-girls Quaker senior school in England) – large number of local parents, often without an independent school background; not a county set school but local family loyalty over several generations. Wide range of religions or none. Over 60 per cent of senior school board – half are in the sixth form; the majority are full boarders from Pacific Rim, South America, USA and a variety of other countries, though 'not too many from any one language group'. Some European, mainly German Dresden Scholarship pupils plus several MOD funded. Girls wear white shirt, tartan skirt and blue jumper; no uniform for sixth form – 'relaxed' dress code. Famous old girls include Dame Judi Dench, Margaret Drabble, Antonia Byatt, Mary Ure, Kate Bellingham, Laura Sayers.

Entrance: Junior school entrance by observation (looking for potential) as part of relevant year group on a taster day. Now takes boys up to year 5 and will be co-educational to year 6 in 2018.

Assessments for years 7-10 entry in English, maths and verbal reasoning plus interview with principal, who looks for 'spark – interesting girls with wide interests'. School report also important. Average and above average abilities catered for. Six GCSEs A*-C and interview for sixth form.

Exit: Most junior girls (over 80 per cent) move up to The Mount School at the end of year 6. Others move to local independent schools, such as Queen Margaret's, or local state schools such as Fulford School; boys used to move on at 7 to eg The Minster, or local state schools, but can now stay on till year 6.

A very small number leave post-GCSE, most for local sixth form college. Otherwise to a variety of universities, predominantly Russell Group – Exeter, Nottingham and Bath currently popular. One medic in 2016, one to study mechanical engineering at MIT.

Money matters: Year 7 academic and music scholarships; year 9 academic, art and design, sport, music and drama; lower sixth (College) academic, art, sport, drama and music – all give five per cent remission of fees, to which a means-tested bursary of up to 100 per cent can be added. Music and drama scholars get free lessons. Separate bursary fund for Quaker children.

Remarks: True to its Quaker ethos, evident in the school's caring and cohesive community of multi-faith and international students. Girls are highly motivated self-starters, with teachers who prepare them well for life outside the school gates. Articulate, mature, collaborative rather than competitive, but nevertheless driven by a determination to do as well as they can.

Mowden Hall School

Newton, Stocksfield, Northumberland NE43 7TP

Pupils: 140; 37 full, 38 weekly, 26 flexi boarders • Ages: 3–13 years (boarders from year 4) • C of E

Fees: Day £8,970 – £16,500; Boarding £22,890 pa

Tel: 01661 842147
Email: info@mowdenhall.co.uk
Website: www.mowdenhall.co.uk

Headmaster: Since 2014, Mr Neal Bailey BA PGCE (30s), previously directeur of Sauveterre, the French school which hosts the year 7 Mowden children for a term each year. He has also taught at Cothill. Educated at Eton and Newcastle University (international business management), and worked in the City before turning to education. He teaches French and maths and is a talented sportsman, particularly keen on football, running and tennis, plus skiing, surfing, camping and bushcraft.

His wife, Nici, is also a qualified teacher, specialising in individual SEN support, and is head of pastoral care. They have two young sons who have joined the school.

Entrance: Wide ability range – non-selective, informal assessment and interview with head. Vast majority of pre-prep transfer to prep. Pupils come from local or prep schools all over the north of England and southern Scotland – Northumberland, Yorkshire, Cumbria, Dumfries and Galloway, Scottish Borders.

Exit: Oundle, Uppingham, Shrewsbury, Sedbergh, Stowe, Newcastle High and Ampleforth most popular this year, though Eton, Harrow, Radley, Downe House, Rugby, Millfield, Queen Margaret's, Glenalmond, Fettes and Durham feature. Some 40 awards in last five years. Few leave at 11.

Remarks: Splendid setting, on a 50 acre site with fine views, reached via a sweeping drive, dodging wildlife, sleeping policemen and miscreants ignoring the one way system through the estate. Far less isolated and much more accessible (just off the A69 and 10 miles from Newcastle) than its setting would suggest. Though unusual for the times, no mobiles, no iPods or electronic devices allowed. Pupils communicate with their parents by the old fashioned means of weekly letters, email (access after supper) or use of the two payphones. Neither pupils nor parents had any complaints.

Impressive sports fields abound (games every day) and woodland provides a muddy but exciting landscape for den-building competitions and a BMX trail. Also the much anticipated 'gappy games' which involve an energetic 'hare and hounds' pursuit through natural terrain led by the gap students. Indoor heated swimming pool, and a new Astroturf, revolutionising the winter games timetable.

M

The heart of the school is the main house, the Victorian Newton Hall, which houses the head's family, common rooms, library and dining rooms on the ground floor and boarding accommodation on first and second floors. Many additions and conversions, including a gym and theatre. Prep classrooms are housed in estate buildings around the former stable yard. Light bright classrooms with plenty of work on display and heaps of encouragement on hand. Cleverly converted science, art and technology centre in the stable yard (very busy at club time in evenings and over weekends) and super art. Amazingly detailed plaster casts of hands on display after weekend master class run by Oundle head of art. Detailed aboriginal artwork, pottery and portraits on display following recent themes.

Prep children are set for English and mathematics for years 4 and 5, then streamed from year 6. The top class studies Greek and a number will sit scholarships (good track record). Maximum class size 16; French for all from nursery; Latin from year 5. Good and imaginative teaching at all levels. 'Our teachers make learning exciting', said one pupil to a chorus of nodding heads. SENCo with specialist dyslexia qualification provides support throughout the school and EAL qualified teacher works with small number, primarily Spanish children.

Focus on CE kicks off in year 7 after the unique experience of 'entente cordiale', a term spent at Château de Sauveterre near Toulouse, immersed in French and the French way of life. This experience is reinforced on their return through weekly lunches with French speaking staff. Children also spend a week in summer term in year 7 at Tree School in Dorset, a centre for natural sciences. Assisting scientists from the Natural History Museum, children extract DNA from trees and plants for an international project to barcode Britain's plant life.

The next step is a big one and the school has close links with the head and senior staff at a number of senior boarding schools. Choices helped by regular reporting through prep years; effort and attainment grades every three weeks; ranking every quarter; full written report each term. Pupils de-stress after CE with a diverse and challenging three week leavers' programme.

N

The first step can be nursery from the age of 3 and the unstreamed pre-prep, increasingly popular with local families, though small numbers. Accommodated in attractive building with reception to year 3 separated from main house by the netball courts; year 3 providing well-prepared transition to prep school, housed separately in adjoining building. Nursery and reception have direct access to outdoor classrooms and play and all children enjoy the nearby woodland classroom. Own secure playground. Specialist music, French, IT and swimming; drama for all age groups. iPads used as teaching tools along with interactive whiteboards. Good range of clubs and activities; after-school care until 6pm is an extra.

Keenly sporting – particularly successful at rugby, netball and girls' hockey, with soccer, swimming, tennis and cross country also popular. Sport (activities on Tuesdays, ranging from first aid to woodwork) timetabled for an hour each day and all of Wednesday afternoons and Saturday, from year 3. Evening clubs (priority for boarders) offer usuals plus fencing, strength and conditioning sessions, coding, cookery and Scalextrix. Healthy number of musicians; choir and music ensembles from orchestra to rock and blues; music workshop three times a term and as one mum puts it, 'a child who has just started the violin will play a tentative piece on the stage followed by a grade 6 trumpet player, and no one turns a hair'. Big Christmas production; most recent was Joseph, involving cast of over 100. Termly year group drama productions; most recent was a brilliant performance by year 8, Escape from the Wasteland.

Stars and merits for academic work, house points for good behaviour – these far outweigh debits, which require some form of community service and can accumulate to Wednesday afternoon detention. Children are allocated to one of four houses, named after illustrious northerners, and sit with their house chums at lunch. Plenty of healthy, inter-house rivalry.

Relaxed but cheerful, busy and purposeful atmosphere, a family school with a healthy balance of discipline and freedom. Endorsed by parents, who 'love the family atmosphere', and 'believe that if their children are really happy they will flourish'. Pupils encouraged to have a 'broad outlook', be open-minded and prepared to 'have a go', otherwise they may struggle here, at least initially. Good food in agreeable dining room with staff seated at each table, children on rotas to clear plates. Healthy eating is a focus in accordance with the school's enthusiasm for sport, fitness and general well-being; add to that the recently ordained school chaplain and this should ensure that both body and soul remain in good shape.

Boarding numbers are growing. All children (however local) are given the option to board with great flexibility, particularly for their final three years. Response to current market means that flexi-boarding remains an option, although the emphasis is on full boarding. Separate accommodation for girls and boys under the daily operation of popular team. Tidy dorms, though not excessively so; plenty of personalised walls to make them feel homely.

Weekend life is kept busy and full, with Saturday school, lots of expeditions, outdoor pursuits of all kinds (madly popular), plenty of staff on hand. Deputy head ensures that Saturday evenings have a clear focus (themed suppers and termly balls) – and that Sundays are structured. Many boarders opt to stay in for the weekend – four exeats in autumn and two in spring and summer. Children work hard and play hard and when asked what they do at home replied, 'have a rest'.

Parents a mix of long-established Tyne Valley residents, Newcastle professionals, Forces, north Cumbrian and Yorkshire county set, Borders and Scottish landowners and the occasional country squire. Fair percentage of first-time buyers opting for boarding as a lifestyle choice rather than because of any long-standing family traditions. Parents we spoke to see it as a 'go-ahead school on the up'.

Good traditional prep school with lots going on, exuding energy from the top down. Concentrates on developing well-rounded individuals whilst still aiming for those highly competitive top scholarships. Very positive comments from parents.

Newcastle High for Girls – Junior School

Linked with Newcastle High School for Girls

Chapman House, Sandyford Park, Newcastle upon Tyne NE2 1TA

Pupils: 270 • Ages: 3–11

Fees: £7,887 – £9,651 pa

Tel: 01912 016511
Email: j.howe@ncl.gdst.net
Website: www.newcastlehigh.gdst.net

Head of Junior School: Since 2011, Angela Charlton BA Fine Arts from Newcastle (early 50s). Always knew she wanted to teach and in 1997 became deputy head of Fellside Community Primary School. Seconded to Oakfield Infant School as acting head teacher three years later and gained her first headship there in 2000 before moving to Portobello Primary School in Birtley in 2003, where she built an 'outstanding curriculum' (Ofsted) and defied demographics by increasing pupil numbers significantly.

Embedded the creative curriculum into the school's teaching, led the logistical conundrum of operating the school in situ through the massive Chapman House refurbishment programme in 2013, followed by preparation for the merger of Newcastle Church High with Central High, opening as Newcastle High School for Girls in 2014.

Sees the merger of the two schools 'as a wonderful opportunity to create new traditions, moving on whilst taking the best of the past'. A chance to rethink core values – curious, communicative, caring, composed, collaborative, creative, courageous and confident – and refresh the curriculum incorporating more cross-curricular approaches, pertinent for the modern world. Endorsed by parents who say that the head 'has built a very creative environment and the curriculum has been changed to reflect that too. It's not just about mathematics and English (although they are at the core of everything)'.

Engaging, warm and vivacious she rightly sees herself as a 'people person', detecting and nurturing strengths in others, an aspect of her role, which gives her great fulfillment. Very creative, an ideas person she works in close partnership with her mathematician deputy, a dynamic duo.

Has always worked in co-educational settings before current post but has clearly converted to a girls only setting, quoting GDST research into girls' learning styles and advocating convincingly that 'being set up for girls allows them to be more adventurous'.

Openly states that 'she loves the job' and can think of no better occupation than 'developing the minds of young people'. Obviously an evangelist, her daughter is now a teacher and has taken up her first post in the north east.

Art is in her DNA and newly built garden studio at home allows her to relax and unwind – when not in the kitchen cooking up something special.

Entrance: In-class assessment (morning or day long depending on age) and report from current nursery or school. For early years informal group work 'looking for social interaction and readiness'. For older intake, a taster day followed by an in-class assessment day. Most join from nurseries into nursery or reception, some recruitment into juniors from state schools (particularly middle schools) and other independents.

Exit: Virtually all to senior school unless family moves out of area.

Remarks: Follows the national curriculum though augmented by a creative curriculum, forging links between subjects. Built around the school, city and region to embed a love for and pride of their heritage, the girls are hooked into each topic by relevant trips and visits early in the term. This focus on north east commitment chimes with the headmistress whose vision is to educate young women to play their part in the future improvement of prosperity in the area.

Parents are offered flexible nursery sessions in the bright and light accommodation with excellent outdoor play area that is integral to the teaching areas. Each new autumn starter is given a cardboard box to decorate over the summer which provides an insight and conversation piece for the new arrivals.

Child-initiated activity is key; mornings are spent in small group numeracy and literacy, creative work and knowledge and understanding activities. Afternoons are spent outdoors in forest school (whatever the weather), on Spanish, PE, dance, drama and music.

Most progress to reception where maximum class size is 20 but increases to 24 in key stage 2. Extensive outdoor curriculum every day, often linked through the creative curriculum. This is further enhanced through forest school accreditation where experiences range from making habitats for new animals they have created in year 1 to lighting fires and using bow saws and knives in year 6. All juniors have PSHE, philosophy, music, dance and sports lessons.

As part of the sensitive transition to senior school, Y5 and Y6 have a morning's science, PE and Spanish specialist lessons in senior school each week. There is a lot of cross-fertilisation of pedagogy and working across both the junior and senior sites eg the junior head accompanying the senior school classics tour to Greece.

No key stage 2 Sats; instead girls have an externally validated termly assessment that tracks their progression. For the academically more able there are extension groups and mathematics challenge competitions, such as the annual GDST junior mathematics conference. Year 6 takes part in the Virgin £5 Challenge, a format similar to a mini Young Enterprise.

Small percentage of SEN, mainly dyslexic, and an extensive range of recognised interventions are used. Differentiation of curriculum in the classroom for others identified as needing learning support and there is lots of communication and reviews with parents. There are a few EAL and strategies include a spelling and reading group to test understanding, one-to-one phonics, handwriting and reading sessions to ensure understanding and correct pronunciation.

Starts them young with sport, lots of specialist teaching in traditional team sports from year 2, making the most of the two all weather pitches, a real bonus for a junior school. A large hall makes a great space for dance and gym and each year group works on a dance piece to perform in whole school assemblies. Weekly swimming at local pools, including RGS's, a short bus ride away. Lots of GDST competition and local galas, with particular success in netball, hockey and swimming.

Music strong and built into the curriculum for all girls. Large uptake of individual music lessons. Orchestra and active choir with year 6 making it to the final of the GDST Young Choir of the Year competition at Queen Elizabeth Hall, London. Performance opportunities through local music festivals, outreach singing to local elderly residents and Christmas concerts. Instruments introduced in lessons and creative curriculum links music to other topics – one example Djembe drumming skills honed during a study of Kenya.

Lots of drama in class assemblies and year group performances as well as the Shakespeare Schools Festival for year 6, and aspiring thespians were preparing for Macbeth when we were in school. Co-curricular speech and drama and musical theatre classes available at extra charge from external providers; weekly in-house drama club.

As you would expect when head is an artist, the art facilities have two excellent spaces and as one parent told us, 'The girls adore having her for art lessons too. She has really inspired my youngest daughter who showed very little interest in art previously'.

Educational visits abound and usual residentials, culminating in Lancashire PGL adventure centre for year 5 and cultural trip to Edinburgh for year 6.

Girls are looked after from 8.00am – 4.30pm in school, with additional charged after school club until 6pm. A number of holiday clubs including dance, drama and art weeks available for pupils and external attendees alike.

Situated in the affluent suburb of Sandyford, on a leafy and extensive green five acre site, the heart of the school is housed in a grade II listed John Dobson designed mansion originally named Villa Real dating from 1817. A century later it became Nazareth House, a children's home, and extended in 1939 to house over 70 children. It closed in 1996 and reopened in

2000 as Central High Junior School. Underwent extensive, sympathetic and costly renovation and refurbishment in 2013, though with hindsight the décor would have been better not to shout Central's purple everywhere when the merged school has been branded with a rather different hue of blue/green teal.

Accommodation well laid out, plenty of space and light, flexible spaces filled with matching furniture, all curved lines and round tables. Great facilities, as you might expect in a modern, architect-led design – designated art, science, Spanish, library, music class and practice rooms with a simple but beautiful chapel used for all whole school celebrations – and film nights. Wide corridors, with a rather corporate feel as disappointingly lacking wall decoration – though we have since learned that our visit was 'between displays'. Fortunately not the case in classrooms, decorated with examples of the girls' work. A nice touch – each room named after a renowned female role model appropriate to its use.

The lovely and extensive grounds house a dance hall (converted ex-laundry) and dining room. Beyond the free flow EYFS outdoor learning area lies the adventure playground and all weather pitch. The large playground doubles as netball/ tennis courts and there is a greenhouse and raised beds for Go Green and the gardening clubs whose produce is used by the kitchen and enjoyed by the girls who grew them. The crowning glory and an intrinsic part of the curriculum is the forest school, a tree shrouded area with dipping pond, fire pit, ducks and bug hotel.

Strong pastoral system with emphasis on circle time and PSHE programme. Phase leaders work together to ensure that children are and feel safe and 'know that they can come and talk to staff in an open an honest way'. Pivotal to this is the pastoral lead who, when not in her quiet room, is a constant visible presence around the school, particularly at break times. Trusted by girls, she is able to counsel on worries before they become issues.

Parents say, 'Girls being girls squabble at times, but having Mrs Bowman on hand is such a comfort. She can sort anything out and is a wonderful addition to the school'. Even goes as far as buying nut-free treats for a child with a severe allergy so 'that she never feels left out when birthday treats are brought in by parents'. An example of how staff here go above and beyond.

Four houses, led by house captains, democratically elected by their peers, meet up with their senior school counterparts to ensure continuity. House points awarded for good behaviour and work, inter-house competitions. Staff choose school and food forum representatives after consideration of candidates' application letters. Digital leader is a techy post with blog responsibilities, helping to run Code Club with younger pupils and liaising with Y8 senior school pupils on BBC micro:bit.

Girls of Daring leadership programme is an award scheme like a mini Duke of Edinburgh. Years 5 and 6 follow a programme of mindset and reflection in the spring term as part of their PSHE philosophy.

Enthusiastic, articulate girls, willing to challenge and be challenged yet considerate of others' views and perspective. They ooze self-confidence without being arrogant or ill mannered. Overwhelming majority transfer to senior school as parents 'choose school for whole educational journey'. Predominantly middle class intake, professional families and the very wealthy alongside those from more modest backgrounds; lots of siblings and those with a family connection to the two predecessor schools. Brothers go to Royal Grammar, Newcastle Prep or local high achieving state primaries. Extensive transport services by fleet of chaperoned school minibuses shuttle between junior and senior school and to strategically placed hub, filling the gaps in the private bus service and public bus, metro and train links.

Parents feel well informed about their daughters' education. One parent told us that 'the new Twitter account is also a lovely window into the girls' day at school'. Maths and English reports in autumn and spring followed by parents' evenings, though parents say, 'we have normally had lots of contact with the teachers before that'. Full report at end of each academic year. Parents' forum meets each term; very supportive with evidence of their fundraising around the school.

Tucked away from surburban streets in a tranquil oasis, the school offers an excellent education in an environment where girls are nurtured and encouraged to be the best they can. Opportunity has been taken to refresh the curriculum and there is a real feeling of dynamism and energy. A 'joined up' junior school that holds dear the core values that are further developed in the senior school and incorporated in the words of the new school song, written by the first team of prefects in the merged school.

Newcastle High School for Girls

Linked with Newcastle High for Girls – Junior School

Tankerville Terrace, Jesmond, Newcastle upon Tyne NE2 3BA

Pupils: 550 • Ages: 11–18 • Sixth form: 190

Fees: £12,216 pa

Tel: 01912 016511
Email: j.howe@ncl.gdst.net
Website: www.newcastlehigh.gdst.net

Headmistress: Since 2014 Mrs Hilary French MA Oxon MEd PGCE NPQH (early 60s). Head for 10 years of predecessor Central High, which merged with Newcastle upon Tyne Church High in September 2014 to form Newcastle High School for Girls.

A pupil at Sacred Heart Grammar School Newcastle, then a brief sortie south to study history at St Anne's, Oxford, before returning to the north east for teaching qualification and career which began at Thornhill Comprehensive in Sunderland. Switched to independent sector at Dame Allan's School, followed by four years as deputy head at Teesside Prep and High School, then five years as head.

Masterminded the £5m revamp of the junior school, Chapman House, in 2013 and £20m+ new build and refurbishment of the former Church High senior school site. The merged senior school relocated in September 2016 from the old Central High site, close to Royal Grammar School at Eskdale Terrace. A mammoth task.

Welcoming and attentive, she believes that what sets the school apart is that 'they offer a tailored partnership with girls and parents, no set expectation of what each girl can achieve and they are challenged to be the best they can'. When questioned on their strapline 'education like no other,' the head commented, 'Others would say that, but we put it into practice,' and certainly we saw considerable evidence of this.

Sets the gold standard by going to amazing lengths to show personal appreciation to pupils and staff. Sixth form organisers of a fundraising talent event received handwritten accolade and small gift; small groups of budding year 7s from the junior school have the pleasure of lunch with the head in her office and then receive a note from her saying how much she enjoyed their company, referring to their individual interests and talents.

Agrees league table position declined over last three years. Merged school has a broader spectrum of pupils, but is sure that pupils have still achieved their best outcomes, and there remain many successes to celebrate. Has been overwhelmed by the generosity of spirit shown by staff throughout the merger process and embedding the new school.

Believes in building girls' self-confidence but aware of their increasingly pressurised lives, and focus on well-being and mindfulness underpins a sound education built on moral values, respect, courtesy and hard work. Loves the buzz of coming to school and meeting the girls, working with them and their parents. Girls and parents like her and her style of leadership. 'A strong, committed woman, who views the education of girls and their well-being as vitally important. She leads by example and this is reflected through her staff who appear to work as a team,' said a parent.

Firm advocate of GDST, sees it as kitemark for parents and cites benefits from extensive research into girls' learning, network of teaching and learning support and significant investment in the site. A raft of board positions: IoD Women on Board; Schools NE; Centre for Evaluation and Monitoring, which 'helps me keep a finger on the pulse of education'; previous president of the Girls' Schools Association and current chair of GSA/HMC Universities Committee.

Married to Durham University lecturer with one daughter, a teacher, recently relocated to Thomas Walling in Newcastle from a London inner city academy – following mother's footsteps?

Academic matters: 'An academic school, but you can almost take the academic side for granted,' say parents, but there has been a downward trend since the merger. In 2016 34 per cent of A level results A*/A and 65 per cent A*-B (similar to previous Church High results). Headmistress emphasises individual successes: three Oxbridge, seven medics, three dentists and two to prestigious dance school.

Offers huge variety of subjects at A level including classical civilisation, dance and three MFL with biology, chemistry, psychology and mathematics the most popular (half of leavers study STEM courses at university). Excellent extended enrichment programme, which includes the EPQ.

In 2016, consistent with 2015 results, 58 per cent of GCSEs were A*/A, 81 per cent A*-B. Strong classics; outstanding results in the sciences, large numbers take three separate sciences at GCSE though only a handful convert to physics at A level. Philosophy and classics for all in key stage 3 as well as creative use of cross-curricular deep learning enquiry – year 8 worked on designs for headmistress' office and pop up house bases in new build, with presentation to building contractors in Spanish complete with sample materials and mood boards for interior design.

Choice from art history to entrepreneurship in year 10 complementary studies. Three languages on offer with corresponding exchanges to France, Germany and Spain. Uses engineering centre at local boys' school, St Cuthbert's, some projects shared, annual STEM competition design and make a car that can travel the furthest distance. Great excitement: new build has enabled A level and GCSE food nutrition to be on the curriculum – first time for ex-Central girls.

Restructured staff organisation, now in five faculties, review curriculum every year to meet needs of new intake. Pupils are set in year 7 for mathematics and year 8 in English. Spanish is now taught as a core subject from junior school nursery through to year 9, and moving towards most girls taking the GCSE at the end of year 9. Beyond that, no further streaming – important that non-top set girls prevented from feeling a failure.

Spanking new facilities in completely refurbished accommodation or contemporary designed new build. Good library and, as you might expect, computers all over – though girls able to request to use their own mobile technology in class; digital language lab. Girls' leisure facilities have benefitted from improvements to outside grounds. As one parent put it 'I cannot think of any parent who wouldn't want their daughter spending their formative years in such wonderful surroundings'.

SENCo, whose knowledge is 'encyclopedic', carries out baseline assessment on all, though girls with learning difficulties are often picked up by subject teachers who provide most support in the classroom. A small number, mostly dyslexic and the school recently hosted Dyslexia North East Conference. Formal extra support comes at extra cost, less formal support not charged for. Small number of EAL who have personalised provision maps which include subject teacher and digital support, weekly EAL club and buddying by older girls, both as learning coaches and young language leaders.

Providing girls with skills for changing careers in a global market with strong emphasis on contributing to the improvement to north east prosperity is integral to school. NHSG CareerConnect works with girls to set up 3 weeks of work experience after GCSE, and uses a network of OGs, parents and local business to provide talks, internships and opportunities outside the classroom. Building links with big local employers like Siemens and Nissan and headmistress would 'certainly encourage girls to consider higher level apprenticeships rather than university'.

Happy with single sex success, 'Egos are fragile and the girls need the space to have a go, make mistakes without the pressure of living up to stereotypes. When they go on to university they are streets ahead of their co-educational sisters in confidence and ability to tackle the outside world, not timid, shy girls'. Certainly resonates with all the girls we spoke to.

Games, options, the arts: Very strong in sport; ethos of everyone gets a turn, so lots of teams and fixtures, locally, regionally and nationally. Ranked in top 15 of independent schools for sport by Independent School Sport magazine. County success in hockey and national finalists in recent years for biathlon, netball, cross-country, squash, swimming and badminton; some girls represent GB in their sport. Biannual sports tour, most recently to Sri Lanka.

Facilities excellent but dispersed around Jesmond, with superb fitness suite in new building on senior school site, with ex-Central centre incorporating sports hall, music, dance and drama facilities a five minute walk away, all weather surface a little nearer. Girls complain that distance prevents timely trek back to school for next lesson although school does build in walking time into timetable.

Music has good accommodation in the centre, with practice rooms, 'digital den' with computers and keyboards, a fine wigwam-shaped recital hall and recording studios. Two orchestras, folk and jazz bands, choirs and string ensemble on offer, plenty of performance opportunity, high spot Mozart's Requiem at the Northern Chords Festival in Newcastle Cathedral.

Dance now offered throughout the school including at A level and the dance studio is in much demand with clubs, in-house dance events and workshops with visiting professionals. Plenty of competition and performance outside the school gates too.

New drama studio for GCSE and A level work as well as newly established drama club. Drama includes regular full school productions incorporating all the performing arts, played at city centre professional theatre, latterly West Side Story and High School Musical.

Dazzling art curriculum in new light and airy space: ceramics, jewellery making, photography, fine art etc and a lot of fabric work. Girls run their own fashion shows.

D of E very popular, one of the largest participation rates amongst local schools; navy and army CCF with field days and camps. Opportunities for trips to Kenya and Tanzania, the result of links with communities there; USA for politics and arts; Iceland, Berlin, Geneva and even the Galapagos islands among many curriculum and extracurricular opportunities.

School open from 7.00am to 7.00pm for homework and participation in stupefying range of co-curricular activities available before and after school until 6pm and during lunchtimes. Activities range from sports, code club, Shakespeare and Mandarin to colour me happy and learning for learning.

Background and atmosphere: Opened in 2014 from merger of predecessor Central High, founded in 1895, and Church High, founded in 1885, with considerable investment to become northern outpost GDST flagship. Moving from Central High site, senior school now in refurbished converted Victorian Tankerville Terrace villas with attractive new building providing multi-purpose assembly hall, dining room, fitness suite (in much use), science labs with demonstration area and additional classroom spaces. Calm colours, plenty of light, wide corridors with clusters of casual seating, glass walled classrooms providing flexible, airy and very visible spaces.

Landscaped grounds provide a pupil plaza, improved leisure area outside with tennis/netball courts and all weather surface on the horizon. Comfy sixth form common room shared by both years – pretty spick and span compared to others we have seen. Roof terrace fits in with Go Green initiative and designed for gardening club.

Buzz of activity and air of purpose from passing girls in the corridor. Our sixth form guides obviously well known, from acknowledgements received from lower year groups we met. Casual gear sets sixth form apart, a relaxed dress code strongly defended by those we spoke to. Years below smartly turned out in new teal and grey uniform with seahorse school logo. The only display of teenage manners was from girls we passed in the foyer and on the long walk to the sports hall – maybe the haste to avoid the gathering rain clouds.

The many girls we met ranged in age and interests across the gamut of disciplines and were all articulate and socially assured, positive in outlook, reflective, respectful of peer opinions and clearly proud of their school and its facilities; as one parent put it, 'well rounded and strong young females.'

Chaired by head girl, a very active school forum meets every four weeks with deputy head leading associated staff. Representatives from every form cover five strands – charity, e-learning, social and emotional learning, teaching and learning and Go Green. Annual fundraising for Plan UK with Because I am a Girl campaign resulted in £30,000 being distributed to date. Girls also choose their own school charity and run whole host of events in support. Sixth formers volunteer to be part of the SHINE programme, an autumn term outreach to local primary year 5 and 6 pupils, leading and motivating the children who take part in Saturday sessions.

GDST membership offers competitions and collaboration with other member schools across academic, creative and expressive arts, public speaking and debating.

Pastoral care, well-being and discipline: Parents say that one of the really unique things about the school that sets it apart from others is the pastoral care and guidance throughout the school. The girls are nurtured and encouraged by dedicated staff who demonstrate their care – beyond the classroom too, say the girls. The pastoral team keeps an eye on individual ups and downs and specific problems are dealt with sensitively by heads of year, school nurse and counsellor.

Four dynamic new houses named after ships built on the Tyne, celebrating Tyneside's maritime tradition, used for charity fundraising, sporting and performing arts competitions.

Clear anti-bullying policy – but it 'isn't a problem', as girls have respect drummed into them from the off. Merits and demerits promote the good and penalise the bad. Girls educated about the risk of drugs.

Social and emotional learning, well-being and mindfulness fundamental to school's ethos and a real strength. Strong developing PSHE programme in place to help girls know themselves, deal with challenge and failure, organise their time and interact with others. Director of social and emotional learning wants girls to 'have the resilience to push out of their comfort zone'. A dynamic curriculum; pupils provide feedback on whether the content and delivery is relevant and suitable. Parent information meetings held on teenage mental health and well-being.

Pupils and parents: Predominantly middle class intake from throughout region, professional families and the very wealthy alongside those from more modest backgrounds; lots of siblings and those with a family connection to the two predecessor schools. Rich mixture of regional accents and healthy mix of different cultures, a handful of Chinese girls staying with home guardians.

Girls come from near and far, the majority within a 30 mile radius. School well placed for public bus, metro and train links, gaps filled by private bus service and fleet of school minibuses to strategically placed hubs.

Transition from junior to secondary is sensitively handled with weekly senior school lessons from year 5, an 'experience day' and then 'big sister' sixth formers help them settle in.

Communication with parents much improved and they feel that they can phone or email teachers if any concerns, well before termly parents' evening. The new Twitter account much appreciated as a 'lovely window into the girls' day at school', and welcome move to include most things on Firefly, the school's online remote access.

Notable alumnae include Dr Miriam Stoppard, Fiona Sinha, design director at McQ Alexander McQueen and actress Andrea Riseborough.

Entrance: Natural progression from own junior school, with increasing competition for other places – spectacular new facilities an additional enticement. Entrance exam, interview and current school report to get in at year 7. Sixth form entrants need nine GCSEs with at least six at A*/A, with interview and previous school report.

Exit: Under 10 per cent leave post-GCSE. After A level, a few to Oxbridge (three in 2016); Durham and other Russell Group northern and Scottish universities popular, some venture to London, Bristol or the Midlands.

Medicine and dentistry popular career choices, plus other science-based courses, law and business, regular stream to art colleges and drama schools.

Money matters: GDST funds bursaries centrally (all means-tested annually) with over 10 per cent of girls currently benefitting from the bursary scheme.

Remarks: Two Newcastle girls' schools successfully merged, the new GDST north eastern flagship now has facilities that live up to its reputation for excellent academics and pastoral care. The transition to a broader intake has resulted in a dip in examination statistics, but the wide range of subjects and activities and teaching staff with the dedication and ability to draw out each girl's strengths set it apart. A close community where girls feel valued and that their contribution is important – and it shows. A school that really does deliver on its commitment to 'an education like no other'.

N

Newcastle Preparatory School

6 Eslington Road, Jesmond, Newcastle upon Tyne NE2 4RH

Pupils: 305 (roughly two-thirds boys) • Ages: 3-11

Fees: £8,235 – £10,455 pa

Tel: 01912 811769
Email: enquiries@newcastleprepschool.org.uk
Website: www.newcastleprepschool.org.uk

Head Teacher: Since 2002, Mrs Margaret Coates (50s), previously head of infants and juniors at Durham High, before that at RGS Newcastle. Studied English at Westminster College, Oxford. Warm, welcoming, articulate and astute with an obvious love of children. Is well known and knows pupils well; they are comfortable but respectful in her company, though little ones seem to make it 'hug a head day' every day.

Certainly not a helicopter head: believes in giving much responsibility to children for creation of their school world as a counter to potential over-protectiveness – though all within the tenets of the school charter.

Keen to keep teaching up to date, sets a pace for staff, expects all to keep up. 'Stays steadfast when it matters' – an iron fist in velvet glove in the nicest possible way. Parents value her genuinely open door and knowledge of their child, which starts with a personal welcome on day one.

Governor at Durham School (son's alma mater), choral singer, modest pianist, avid reader, keen gardener and novice golfer.

Entrance: Start in school nursery at 3; reception at 4 or year 3 at age 8. No selection, but children spend a morning in school and are informally assessed. Popular choice with Newcastle parents so still receiving post-natal registrations.

Exit: Overwhelming majority to local independent day schools – some to close neighbours, Royal Grammar School and Central Newcastle High for the girls. Boys also to Dame Allan's, Durham, King's Tynemouth and girls to Dame Allan's and Westfield.

Year 6 parents have individual meetings with head who provides guidance on choice of next school for their child. Parents lay great store by this, 'as head really knows our child and what is the right school for them'. 'Senior schools like our pupils,' says the head, 'they have self-esteem, are robust in their learning and have a good work ethic'.

Remarks: Set up in 1885 as a public day school for boys; uniform colours black and gold adopted 120 years ago. Situated in Jesmond, near city centre, opposite one independent senior school and sandwiched between another, in three and a half terraced Victorian houses. Ingenious use of space with linking stairways, classrooms on first and second floors and nursery on ground floor with access to outdoor play area. Top floor extensive science room, well-equipped art and design studio and music facility (in head's sights for refurbishment). Good sport and play facilities; purpose built multi-use sports hall, playing fields and adventure play area, a recent addition, a stone's throw away. All classrooms and walkways crammed with well presented display work – particularly liked the designs of the Queen's Jubilee knickers (apparently have the royal seal of approval).

Traditionally boys have greatly outnumbered girls (spoilt for choice in Newcastle) so consideration for gender differences in learning styles. School working successfully to redress balance, starting with nursery. Pupils gain places (and scholarships) at an impressive list of Newcastle independent schools at 11, from an unselected start. 'A reflection of the traditional, yet broad curriculum, progressive teaching by primary specialists and knowing our children well. A busy, lively school, but not a hothouse,' says the head. All underpinned by ethos – 'happy children do well academically'.

Don't be fooled by recent EYFS inspection: First Steps nursery and two parallel reception classes are more than 'satisfactory'. Well-resourced and staffed, with specialist French, music and PE teachers. First Steps in ground floor, high ceilinged, airy classrooms, small kitchen for baking. Reception on second floor in classes of 20 (maximum). Dedicated outdoor play area, adjacent to nursery, shoehorned between adjacent properties but innovatively designed, to provide a range of early learning experiences.

Few children leave before year 6 but school chooses not to replace, so class average 18 pupils in KS2. No setting or streaming in the two parallel classes in each year, though some 'top set' pupils work together. Specialist art and design from year 3, Spanish, Latin and some German from year 5. Independent cross-curricular learning encouraged through project work. We observed inventive teaching; use of hand actions for year 2s, counting to 100 in fives (brilliant physical counteraction for the boys) and teacher/pupil collaborative interpretation of textbook instructions on Venn diagrams in year 5. Plethora of educational visits enrich classroom experiences. Science link to Dove Marine Laboratory at nearby Cullercoats and impressive annual science week – thanks to parents in medicine, industry, and university.

ICT provision is good with interactive boards in all classrooms and an up-to-date computer suite – netbooks on the horizon? Used to link globally on World Maths Day, an online international mathematics competition. Well-resourced comfortable library is in the centre of school with non-fiction upgrade imminent. Provision for special needs with small group and one-to-one work – included in fees. Assessment at end KS1 though no pupils with statements, but EAL and those with mild learning difficulties. Creative learning team devise gifted and talented activities. Teacher assessment levels on final reports ensures smooth transfer to senior schools.

Many opportunities out of classroom with excellent music (professionally run): choirs, orchestra, jazz band. Drama lessons all way through and classes act out a story and film it. Performance opportunities for everyone each year; main production in summer, most recently Shakespeare for Kids Midsummer Night's Dream; talent assemblies every Friday.

Sport taken very seriously with regular fixtures in traditional team sports and adventure activities during outdoor away weeks. Opportunities for girls' competitive team sports might be restricted due to small numbers in some year groups. Great choice of clubs and societies – includes usual sporting, creative and performing arts, with interesting extras, from early morning fitness, bicycle maintenance (good preparation for annual cycling tour in Holland perhaps), chess (a passion) and girl only 'girl talk', covering all those aspects of growing up you really don't want to discuss in front of boys. After-school activities run to 5pm and summer holiday activity programme available for pupils and their siblings – helpful for working parents.

Clear guidelines to class teachers on how to deal with poor behaviour without embarrassing pupil. Process of escalation through to head for the few persistent offenders. Pupil behaviour is underpinned by the reinforcement of school charter which states that everyone should feel happy and safe, have a right to learn, is important and can succeed. Result is a happy, caring community where children feel valued and value each other. The year 6 'buddy squad' deals with minor incidents each break and lunchtime and ensures no one feels alone. Annual end of year river cruise outing for year 2 and year 6 buddies is a rite of passage.

From nursery up, every child is a member of one of four houses, uniquely named by the children after local Jesmond streets. Up to year 3 house tee shirt and book bags. From year 2 positive merit system for good work and behaviour; year 3 and beyond accumulate to bronze, silver and gold awards and contribute towards house totals.

Head says, 'NPS pupils are independent characters who love life, love learning, have confidence and the strength of conviction to be themselves'. Famous old boy, Cardinal Basil Hume.

Parents, as you would expect in a large city: aspirational, many professionals, particularly from medicine and academia, senior managers from industry and those committed to education and high standards. Mainly hail from northern suburbs, Gateshead; some further afield from Ponteland, Whitley Bay, Tynemouth and Hexham. Head believes that NPS parents are more relaxed about their child's education than at some other schools and 'have faith in what we're doing'. No formal PTA but parents very supportive and help to organise events under auspices of head. Good news – 'no cliques,' say parents and head; bad news – no major contribution to school coffers. No great shakes here, head commented: 'School fees alone should cover all that's needed to educate pupils and provide good facilities and resources'. No scholarships but means tested bursaries of 10-95 per cent of fees.

Prep school and nursery with traditional values and standards and a warm heart. Firmly entrenched as first choice for parents wanting the city's top independent senior schools, and successful with it. Confident, cheerful and courteous children with a busy sense of purpose.

Polam Hall School

Grange Road, Darlington, County Durham DL1 5PA

Pupils: 641; 44 boarders • Ages: 4–19 (boarding from year 7) • Sixth form: 44

P

Fees: Day free; Boarding; £10,425 pa

Tel: 01325 463383
Email: information@polamhall.com
Website: www.polamhall.com

Headmaster: Since 2011, Mr J R Moreland MA (Oxon) PGCE NPQH (50s). Educated at Huddersfield New College (then a grammar school) then went on to read modern history at St Edmund Hall, Oxford. Previously headmaster of Bury Lawn School, Milton Keynes; housemaster, head of history and assistant head Rugby School; taught history at Epsom College; and prior to that history, geography and politics at Watford Boys' Grammar. Played rugby, basketball and athletics at school and university (a double Oxford Blue). Holds Northern Ireland record for the discus and now competes in masters' championships, currently British champion. Teaches history, coaches and huge supporter of school sport. Believes in leading by example – for Sport Relief competed in a relay of pupils running a mile by throwing a combo of discus and wellies the equivalent distance – and won, naturally. His wife, Alison, is also a teacher and they enjoy walking, reading, cinema.

Described by parents as being as different as 'chalk and cheese' from his predecessor, but no criticism intended. Both charming and candid in his approach and looking forward to developing the school further now, after the speed bumps of leading through challenging, but transformative times. In its previous existence as an independent school Polam faced an uncertain future, no doubt about that, and recent changes into a state boarding school have been its saviour. Whilst admitting that the changes mean it has 'lost some of its intimacy', he quickly adds that it has also 'gained vibrancy', because the biggest change is in numbers and that has enhanced the school in so many areas.

Head of junior school: is Catherine Lawton MEd (Man) BA (Sunderland) PGCE (Liverpool) NPQH. Specialist in maths, ICT and music, has taught the whole primary age range.

Head of infant department since January 2014 is Mrs Linzi Mawson. She has a BEd in biological science and PE from the University of Derby. Joined in 1995 as year 2 form teacher and creative curriculum coordinator. A fully qualified swimming instructor, she enjoys teaching her two young sons to swim, walking, Pilates, the theatre and cinema.

Academic matters: It's non-selective on intake – diagnostic tests to assess level of attainment for setting purposes only. Some 20 per cent of pupils on SEN register, attracted by smaller class sizes and attention to detail here. In that context GCSE results are good, displaying excellent value-added, especially in English and maths, with nearly 22 per cent A*/A and 55 per cent A*-B grades in 2016. School says of A level results, from the last cohort who joined when it was an independent school, 'our expectations were modest as they were a very mixed year group, stronger on personality and extracurricular achievements than purely academic.' Results indeed underwhelming: 19 per cent A*-B and nearly 11 per cent A*/A grades.

Pupils expected to work hard, with non-high flyers achieving beyond expectations in all areas; art, music and drama vibrant and popular; physics and chemistry labs fully refurbished; ICT much in evidence. French from junior school and opportunities for German and Spanish from year 8. Sciences taught separately and with specialists from year 9. Mathematics and French set from year 7, science and English from year 10. Small groups at A level, average five per subject; some one-to-one, thus a risk losing group dynamic – 'though equally nowhere to hide,' say sixth-formers. Modest about their SEN provision: 'We strive to support effectively our pupils with special needs, but we do not wish to present ourselves as experts in the field'. Difficulties range from dyslexia, dyspraxia and dysgraphia to Asperger's and autism. Support is provided using a range of educational programmes, one-to-one teaching, assistants to support in class, reduced timetables, focused study support, mentoring, differentiation in class and bringing in outside specialists. Still awaiting its first inspection as a free school.

Games, options, the arts: Rugby, football, hockey, netball, badminton, basketball and gymnastics make up the main part of the sporting curriculum from September to December. Football also popular among the juniors with successful under 9s and under 11s teams (girls' and boys'). Young footballers entering seniors also get chance to compete in Darlington 9-a-side league for year 7s. Annual house swimming gala is a highlight of the spring term. Senior girl netballers compete at a high level, winning many local tournaments in all age groups – ditto boys in basketball. Sports Awards Evening in the summer term is an opportunity to celebrate pupils' sporting success with their families with prizes and trophies including sports colours, various players of the year, and the Polam Hall Sports Personality of the Year voted for by the pupils, staff and parents. Summer fixtures are in athletics, rounders, cricket and tennis with excellent opportunities to perform for the county and in local competitions against other schools, and lunchtime athletics and tennis clubs are popular (some sports clubs are charged for). The cricket team participates in local festivals and competes in friendly hardball fixtures. Trampolining, table tennis and cycling events are growing in popularity. Badminton played year round at the local Dolphin Centre; the KS4 girls have reached the national finals, both KS3 and 4 winning regional finals. You get the slight feeling that the boys are playing catch-up a little in the sport here, purely and simply because it was originally a girls' school – however numbers are now balancing out and stronger teams are emerging as a result. Certainly they take their sport seriously, no doubt under the influence and watchful eye of the sporty head.

Junior school sport is strong too, plenty of fixtures and well-resourced with, the children tell us, 'gappies from Australia' leading games and joining in with the fun. There's a climbing tree in the playground, much loved by the children, marked with red lines as demarcation points beyond which health and safety rules kick in to prevent anyone going too high. Slightly elderly gym, it's a shared space with old-school PE apparatus and also used for assemblies and hymn practice.

The Combined Cadet Force is affiliated to the CCF at Barnard Castle School and offers an army section with activities based around a military setting, though school adds that 'the prime objective is to develop leadership and inner strength'. The weekly meetings, called parades, include map-work, battle drills, section attacks and camp craft; older cadets follow a training course to become instructors. InterACT is the junior branch of the Rotary Club, operating in school as a fully independent club with an elected committee, run entirely by pupils. The club plans and carries out a variety of community work including, for example, a sponsored bag-pack at the local supermarket, a shoebox appeal at Christmas and helping a local food bank. Members also participate in larger events, such as a recent midnight walk to raise money for a local hospice, and in international initiatives including climbing Mount Kilimanjaro and helping to build a school in Africa. On a local level, senior pupils organise and host Christmas and summer parties for OAPs on behalf of Darlington Town Mission. Duke of Edinburgh Award and Young Enterprise schemes operating with sustained success at all levels.

Individual music tuition is popular with a team of 10 peripatetics offering lessons in a range of instruments: examinations from a variety of exam boards including ABRSM, Trinity and Rock School. Seniors can join various ensembles, including senior choir, vocal ensemble, and woodwind ensemble. Busy annual calendar of musical events including scholars' concert in October; Advent and carol services; boarders' carol service, and a Christmas concert in the school theatre. Annual production in the purpose-built and impressive theatre involving juniors and seniors, usually a collaborative event between the drama, music and art departments. Schools tells us that 'during the run-up to any show there is always a creative buzz around school and our pupils are noticeably uplifted by this newfound energy'. Recent productions include Confusions, The Lion the Witch and the Wardrobe and, from the juniors, Hoodwinked. Lunchtime drama club is all the rage and proves a hotbed of dramatic talent and creativity.

Boarding: Some 60 per cent from overseas – the current profile is mainly Hong Kong, China, Thailand, Chile, Spain and Italy, but that is likely to change now that it is a free school, as from this point forwards they will only be allowed to recruit boarders with UK/EEA passports. Accommodation not luxurious but rather homely, clean and comfortable, with three and four bedded rooms the norm and shared rooms even in sixth form. There are shared 'family' kitchens and living rooms and access to TV, games and Wifi as well as quiet rooms for study within each house. House staff are warm and caring, boarders enjoy their company and are often seen relaxing in chatty groups around the attractive grounds after evening prep. Weekly boarding also available and ideal for UK pupils (and their parents) living out in the far-flung Dales and struggling with a long daily commute. Occasional boarding also available if overnight childcare is required.

Boarders have access to a wide programme of evening and weekend activities ranging from educational visits to heritage sites and attractions, through to fun days out at the seaside or theme parks. Less formal activities include bowling, outdoor games played in the school grounds and cinema evenings in the school theatre. Birthdays and other special events are celebrated. Once homework is done, older boarders are allowed to walk into town for shopping or to visit the local gym. There is a strict signing in and out system so no one goes off site without permission. Every boarder for whom English is not their first language is offered regular EAL classes from the outset, if required, helping them to develop proficiency and confidence. Classes usually take place whilst other students are studying a second language but, in addition, boarders also receive individual one-on-one attention, if needed, during their mainstream subjects.

All boarders are involved in electing the boarding council which ensures that everyone's voice is heard. A head boarder, deputies, and heads and deputies of the two competitive boarding houses – the wonderfully named Peace and Harmony – are elected each year and help to organise inter-house competitions and team building events. Much eulogising from parents about the 'mothering' that goes on in boarding, especially from those overseas, who are so very grateful to know that staff take their in loco parenting seriously.

Background and atmosphere: Founded in 1848 by Quakers sisters for young ladies paying 50 guineas a year. In 1854 school moved to Polam Hall, a Georgian mansion set in 19 acres of parkland, close to the town centre, with a history of sharing its grounds with the people of Darlington. Descendants of founding families still represented on governing body and school remains true to its Quaker roots. There is even a museum housed in the main building with artefacts from the school's history, including old uniforms. Still a little tatty in places, no doubt due to a lack of investment in the winding down years of the girls' school here, but it's in hand and awaiting further funding. Own junior school (currently full) on site, so you could be here from 4-19, making it the only all-through mainstream school in Darlington. Junior school shares some of the facilities with the senior school, benefiting from the extra space and provision that allows, including a dining hall, dance studio and science labs. If green is your favourite colour, it's the school, for you – green uniforms, green carpets, green doors, green chairs and green wellies and schoolbags in the cloakrooms.

They've got the builders in as this green, cohesive site – including junior school, senior school and boarding houses – adapts and expands to the growing needs of the school community. Current sixth form centre (Plantation) is much-loved by pupils and described by them as 'shabby chic', but it's rather over-stating things – 'shabby' will suffice. 'Just a bigger version of a teenage messy bedroom,' said one pupil rather sheepishly, but they love the place and it's theirs – and that matters. Moving forward and to attract higher numbers into the sixth form, the school probably needs a new sixth form centre and a sports hall, but prolonged negotiations may need to take place before that happens. Fingers crossed all round. In the meantime, the main focus is on improving and developing teaching facilities, with newer buildings ready for September 2016 and a rolling programme of minor improvements around the site. The car park is too small to cope with the growth in numbers, but school is aware and spends too much time apologising for what is probably an insurmountable problem in this leafy residential area.

The grumbles are minor though, and, to some extent, inevitable given the momentum of change. But, crucially, there is a sense of a shared, warm, caring community throughout with staff and pupils clearly proud of the school they have created here. They have worked hard to maintain the best of the independent school ethos, with the house system still in place, a wide range of extracurricular activities, extended day and very smart and strict uniform policy. One small but significant change was to replace the former school logo and blazer badge depicting buttercups with a tree symbol – audible sigh of relief from boys (and many girls). Settling down now and ticking over very nicely indeed, pupils are clearly happy with their lot and the place is beginning to develop its own persona. A few of the old Polam guard remain on the staff, but fewer by the year and average age decreasing, a natural and predictable development as the school moves forward now. The winds of change have blown hard and constantly over the last 168 years, and yet the school remains in good heart and, in many ways stronger than ever, simply because the future has become clearer. Although state-funded it remains independently run, holding on to much of the autonomy it enjoyed as a private school.

Pastoral care, well-being and discipline: Remaining true to its Quaker roots, there are few formal rules but very clear guidelines as to sanctions; high standards of courtesy and behaviour expected and delivered, based on respect for self and others. 'Approachable and helpful from grass roots up,' is how parents describe the staff here, adding that 'discipline and relationships' are excellent. Strong anti-bullying policy; serious misconduct extremely rare. Peer mentoring enables support and friendships across age groups. Older pupils can volunteer for formal training, where they learn the difference between listening and giving advice and are taught how to ask the right questions to help younger pupils work through issues and come to their own conclusions. Trained pupils wear mentor badges so they can easily be identified. Seniors are given increased responsibility, from leading assemblies to escorting visitors around school and helping with the younger children. Much praise from ISI regarding high quality relationships and support in school. Regular assemblies ('Readings'); it's a Quaker ethos rather than Quaker faith – awareness of the wider world and strong spirit of generosity are important. Read the Made in Polam stories on the website to have a sense of how proud and loyal former pupils value the confidence and skills (as well as the qualifications) gained here. Lots of talk of 'individual attention' from both pupils and staff, and it all seems very genuine – the school bends to the needs and interests of its pupils rather than the other way around. 'Keep busy, have fun, be unique' is a mantra here and they do seem to have the space and support to follow it through.

Q

Pupils and parents: A broad cross-section of abilities, backgrounds and cultures here in a community that welcomes diversity. A changing profile with 25 per cent (and increasing) of pupils from overseas, mainly from year 10 onwards. A number of Forces boarders too. Pupils are friendly, remarkably modest about their achievements and down to earth, reflecting the honest, unpretentious character of this refreshingly wholesome school. 'Hard to have secrets here,' said a sixth form girl; 'we all know each other so very well.' 'Teachers,' they say, 'are friendly; they guide you but don't tell you' – describing the kind of relationships that are not untypical in a smaller school. Parents a genuine mix of urban and rural, first-time buyers, Armed Forces and second and third generation Polamites. Many attracted by the option of being able to move through the school right the way from 4 to 18. Strong Parents' Association organises free events for parent body. Parents' focus group presents views/perspectives to head and are not shy in doing so – 'calling a spade a shovel' is not uncommon in this part of the world. That said, they are also effusive in their praise, grateful for the values that have remained through the years of change, noting with pleasure the continued 'extended Polam experience'. 'Becoming a free school has brought a bigger influx,' say parents, adding that 'they seem to be coping well', apart from the car park, perhaps. Notable alumni include Nadine Bell, NASA scientist and actress Ruth Gemmell.

Entrance: For day children, preference to those with an EHC plan naming the school, then looked after children. Then 20 per cent of places to pupil premium and Forces children. After that, 60 per cent to those living in DL1 or DL3 postcodes, remainder to those living outside these areas. Siblings take priority in each category when there is oversubscription. Boarders need UK/EEA passports.

Exit: Some 50 per cent of day pupils departed post-GCSE recently, though school expects higher retention in the future now that they are a free school. Of those who leave most go on to vocational courses elsewhere and/or feel the pull to larger sixth form colleges. Around 90 per cent of boarders stay on into sixth form. Of 14 sixth form leavers in 2016, all but one got university places – 11 got first or second choice places, two through clearing.

Money matters: Free school, fees only for boarding. One sixth form weekly boarding bursary worth £1,000 per term available for those living 10 miles or more away.

Remarks: A successful school is like a great white shark. In its prime, it chews up the competition, but if it dares to sit still for too long, it dies. Change and progress have been, and will continue to be, important. With class sizes at around 26 and the top three academies in the area very large and over-subscribed, there is much to recommend here. It's likely, of course, that once the word is out and the local grapevine catches up, the school will grow, but the capacity will remain well below 1,000, so take up a place while you still can.

Queen Elizabeth Grammar School (Penrith)

Ullswater Road, Penrith, Cumbria CA11 7EG

Pupils: 890 • Ages: 11–18 • Sixth form: 245

Tel: 01768 864621
Email: secretary@qegs.cumbria.sch.uk
Website: www.qegs.cumbria.sch.uk

Headmaster: Since 2015, Mr Paul Buckland MA, PGCE, NPQH, previously deputy headteacher of North Halifax Grammar School.

A grammar school boy himself (he was educated at Eastbourne Grammar School) Mr. Buckland is married with three children and originally trained as an English and PE teacher before moving into more senior roles first in the English department and then in management.

He enjoys coaching (junior football and athletics), has been a governor of a primary school for a number of years and is also a keen gardener.

Academic matters: Unapologetically academic school, with a traditional grammar school ethos where aiming high is taken for granted. Broad ability at entrance from a huge catchment, broader than most grammars. The annual intake of 120 pupils usually represents over 50 per cent of the applicants, yet still they achieve consistently strong results. In 2016, 61 per cent A*-B at A level and 50 per cent A*/A at GCSE. 'We bat above our average,' head says, 'but this is not a hothouse'. Maths particularly impressive but have relinquished their previous maths and computing specialist status, preferring to spread the focus. Art and geography also extremely successful, but although languages are strong there's not much take-up at A level. Only French and German on offer; however, all do both until year 8 and then at least one to GCSE. No classics. History classes are lively, with the head of history keen to animate learning and recently re-enacted the Battle of Hastings on the school field. Setting in year 8 with regular assessments beyond the end of year exams. All pupils given targets based on their previous personal performance. SEN provision supports pupils as required, beyond those with registered educational needs. SENCo described as outstanding and credited with turning several pupils around.

Careers guidance begins early, particularly to support choices in year 9. Sixth formers are well supported with clear guidance to help steer them through the UCAS minefield, and lots of interview practice for medics and Oxbridge applicants. Parents speak highly of the amazingly committed staff. A good balance of teachers, some with a wealth of experience and understanding of the local community, and some energetic newcomers, attracted to the quality of Cumbrian life, and the happy atmosphere.

Games, options, the arts: Extensive on-site playing fields an advantage of semi-rural location, although Cumbrian weather ensures they do get soggy. Accommodates rugby, important and successful, football, hockey, tennis, netball and basketball, with athletics and cricket in the summer. Also the use of local Astro turf pitches when necessary.

Huge sports hall complete with climbing wall, used every evening by community, and as the northern base of Badminton England. Cross-country is popular thanks to an enthusiastic member of staff whom parents describe as inspirational.

Fabulous art department papered with students' artwork of an impressive standard and variety: it spills into the corridors, and a choice handful is selected for the head's study on a weekly basis. It's remarkably mature, high quality stuff – one outstanding piece spent the summer at the Royal Academy 'One Show' Summer Exhibition.

Plenty of musical opportunities, a variety of choirs including Cambiata, and a swing band and orchestra. Drama is very popular, with great emphasis placed on the annual production, which parents describe as amazing, 'and everybody gets involved'. Costumes are made in craft clubs led by former head of DT, but all bemoan the lack of a theatre or even a hall large enough to accommodate these ambitious performances. 'There are often more people taking part than can be fitted into the remaining audience space,' according to a parent, and the popular shows therefore require a long run.

Wide range of clubs and extra activities, including lunchtime subject clinics, there's something for everybody. Charities are well-supported, instilling a sense of social responsibility. Parents describe their children as 'always busy'. Plenty of trips from field and theatre trips to the hugely successful annual year 8 residential to Derwentwater; an inspirational annual art trip to Venice; ski trips; language trips; and a World Challenge trip for older pupils, recent destinations including Uganda, Peru and Madagascar.

Background and atmosphere: Established in 1564, 2014 brought major celebrations for the 450th anniversary with fêtes, concerts, sporting events and a church service involving pupils and ex-pupils representing every generation. The school takes its role as part of the community seriously and maintains strong links, regularly hosting a variety of local evening activities. It moved to its current site in 1917, adding buildings and extensions over time, none particularly distinguished and something of a warren, but well maintained and fully employed. Further extension work in process, adding two much-needed, state-of-the-art language classrooms. It became an academy in 2011, which seems to have been a mixed blessing, but greatly aided by a strong and active governing body.

A small school for a state grammar, the size is much appreciated by both parents and staff. In a recent survey 99 per cent of parents described the school as very happy. 'Everyone quickly knows everyone,' according to parents, and 'any changes in behaviour are spotted and swiftly dealt with'. Pupils were markedly good-humoured and friendly during our visit, and parents say they are always impressed by behaviour both in school and out.

School uniform compulsory up to year 11, fairly firmly implemented; head keeps spares of everything in his office. The general look is tousled but smart, mirroring the school's relaxed but focused approach. The sixth form centre is apart from the main school, in a nearby converted primary. Sixth formers don't wear uniform, all part of the privileges and responsibilities which prepare them for the task ahead.

Pastoral care, well-being and discipline: Pastoral care is delivered via a form tutor system, but beyond this staff are approachable and available. Parents describe it as extremely effective and any incidents are quickly and efficiently dealt with, before becoming an issue. Parents appreciate the school's straightforward and open lines of communication. Objectives and codes of practice are clear and pragmatically set out in the school's thorough and efficient website. Head says, 'the kids know what is expected of them from the outset and everyone knows where they stand'. Discipline meted out through detentions, from lunchtimes to after school to the dreaded Saturday morning – but head says he 'hasn't given a Saturday detention for years'.

Pupils and parents: Pupils come from all over the sparsely populated, 400 square mile area of Eden. Much of the transport shared with nearby Ullswater comprehensive. Parents represent an incredibly broad social spectrum, from consultants at Carlisle hospital to local farmers to families where neither parent works, but all share a common interest and ambition in the education of their children. Immaterial within the school; head says, 'some of our most challenged are the children of doctors and dentists while a SENCo-supported girl on free school meals is now at Oxford. That's what grammar schools should be about'.

Entrance: Traditional 11+ style exam in September, with papers in maths, verbal and non-verbal reasoning but no essay. They have a good dialogue with their feeder primary schools and always know they are getting the right pupils. The SENCo will visit the school of any prospective pupils already identified with needs, and work with them during the preceding term to ease their transition.

Usually around 20 places available for sixth form. Entry requirements five A*-C GCSEs, A*-B required to pursue most A level study.

Exit: Annually the Russell group is well represented and usually a few make it to Oxbridge (four in 2016). Northern universities are always popular, particularly Leeds, Lancaster and Newcastle, as are several ex-polys, with a few to Northumbria. A wide range of subjects pursued at different levels with lots of pragmatic choices. A few head directly into the world of work, and are as well supported by the school as the academics.

Money matters: Voluntary school fund payment of £15 per year helps buy a few extra luxuries for all pupils to enjoy.

Remarks: A small, cheerful and well-run school, strongly linked to the community. The only selective grammar in Cumbria, it works hard to get the best out of its pupils, taking all-round education seriously, with high levels of achievement in all areas.

Queen Elizabeth Grammar School (Wakefield)

154 Northgate, Wakefield, West Yorkshire WF1 3QX

Pupils: 745 • Ages: 11–18 • Sixth form: 200

Fees: £11,967 pa

Tel: 01924 373943
Email: admissions@qegsss.org.uk
Website: www.wgsf.org.uk

Headmaster: Since 2010, Mr David Craig MA MEd (40s). PGCE at Birmingham University and MEd in educational leadership with the Open University. Previous head of department posts at Edgbaston High, Birmingham and Wolverhampton Grammar School and deputy head at Merchant Taylors' School, Crosby. He aims 'to cement QEGS as one of the best boys' schools in the north of England.' His outside interests include cricket, rugby, choral music and Derby County FC. Married with two children.

However, refuses to meet the Guide or discuss reasons for his shyness.

Academic matters: High standards – 52 per cent of A levels at A*/A in 2016. At GCSE, 65 per cent at A*/A. IGCSE in maths, English and now sciences. 'Boys come here knowing that academic expectation is placed upon them.' Not tempted to push students into different subjects just to help the results tables – 'we have worked hard to improve our academic standards, but some of the results that give me most satisfaction are those achieved by boys who you might not have expected to shine so well at a particular subject'.

Q

A parent told us, 'At QEGS nothing is looked at as impossible. You might not become the best but if you put in the effort, push yourself, you can succeed.' Strong across the board, especially maths, sciences, English and humanities. French and German on offer to all, plus Spanish, business French and Latin. Business studies and some languages, drama, studied with the Girls' High across the road.

Max 24 per class, 10/12 in sixth form. Work clinics available at lunchtime. No streaming. Conscious of rising expectation. Not convinced by International Baccalaureate but embracing A* grade at A level – 'It is getting harder to get into the best universities and we have to be aware of that and prepare our boys accordingly'.

Computers throughout and interactive whiteboards. Good remedial help on hand for mild dyslexia and the like, can 'cope' with mild Asperger's. Children are automatically screened and additional help can be organised, usually at lunch-time, laptops allowed. Recent improvements include new learning resource centre, 240 seat theatre, library, sixth form centre and English department.

Games, options, the arts: Emphasis on sport, music, drama, with Duke of Edinburgh (300 take), chess, bridge and trips/expeditions favoured. Art is very strong, aided by art department in the top of the school with masses of light. Screen printing, photography, etchings. Great music – regular scholarships to the Royal College of Music, finalists in the National Festival of Music; Outstanding Performers at National Festival for Youth Music. Brass section wins prizes, over 300 individual players, swing band (played in front of the Queen during her Jubilee) and junior swing bands (available for hire). Concerts often held in Wakefield Cathedral, where the junior boys provide choristers, joined by girls from the High. Music and drama often joint with High girls, eg Grease, Guys and Dolls. Regularly places students on best drama courses. 'My son had never picked up a musical instrument until he went to QEGS – now his life seems to revolve around music,' said a parent.

Use of over 27 acres of playing fields, pavilion and sports hall with special 'resilient' flooring hired out to locals. Training pool for junior school only, seniors use the pool in town. Proud of its sporting heritage, especially rugby – including old boy Mike Tindall. Produced England U19 cricket captain, England U18 rugby cap etc. Masses of sporting trips to South Africa, Namibia, South America, Australia, Canada, West Indies, plus cultural tours and exchanges to France, Germany, USA and expeditions to Costa Rica, Madagascar and Tanzania.

Background and atmosphere: Founded by Royal Charter in 1591 and moved to present site in 1854. From 1944-76 it was a direct grant school and reverted to fee-paying in 1976. Imposing Victorian gothic façade hides mishmash of good, bad and ugly extensions. Junior school also on site – they play games on the grass in front of the school. Boys all smart in grey uniforms (think boy band in blazers). Modernisation is removing any sense of stuffy grammar school and proud of friendly, all-inclusive atmosphere. Impressive new entrance is very grand. Motto is 'turpe nescire' – 'It is a disgrace to be ignorant': fat chance of that here. Ethos of boys 'doing their best and fulfilling potential'. Inspection speaks of 'dedication and humanity' of staff. Great sixth form centre with popular café. Sixth formers drop uniform in favour of a smart suit (think boy band in suit and tie).

Pastoral care, well-being and discipline: Tutor-led pastoral system with boys encouraged to treat each other with respect. PSE and pastoral care fosters good behaviour by encouraging informed choice by the boys – 'To try to pretend society is not as it is would be wrong. Different challenges face the boys – drugs, sex etc. Through PSE, our pastoral care, assembly and careers education we educate them, give them advice and guidance and help them arrive at their own choices and pathways'. Seems to work – parents report good relationships, camaraderie and 'help each other along' attitude.

Record book incorporates the school rules, inspected by staff and must be signed by parents at preordained levels. Punishments include detentions and suspensions for most serious misdemeanours. Drug possession gets automatic expulsion. Smoking equals detention, three detentions equals suspension. Suspensions and exclusions for bullying, vandalism and aggressive behaviour. Poor academic performance can also find you shown the door.

Pupils and parents: Great motorway and rail links give it a wide catchment area and it is seen as the only acceptable alternative to the state system for miles around. Boys come with strong work ethic and parents and pupils must make a 'positive choice' to come here. Fair assortment from ethnic minorities, 'a broad, UK social mix'. None with EAL requirements. Good breeding ground for bishops – Lincoln and York – plus John Scott, former director of music at St Paul's, latterly at the prestigious Saint Thomas Church NYC, and a tranche of internationalists.

Parents praise links between home and school: 'We have found even the slightest issue or concern we have had is resolved within 48 hours'; 'QEGS gives the boys the tools but also gives them the blueprint and the instructions to follow – other schools just provide the tools'.

Entrance: Most (60 per cent) from QEGS junior, if their results are up to scratch (only two or three a year aren't). Others from Sandal Endowed and Willthorpe feeders. Entrance exam and interview required. Latest inspection said school's induction process was 'excellent'. Always oversubscribed and academic achievement is obligatory – baseline qualifications for entry at sixth form are six GCSEs (but most come with seven or eight) with at least two As in subjects to be taken at AS/A level. Occasional boy comes into the school at other times, subject to academic OK and space.

Exit: A few leave to art courses or employment post-GCSE. Most destined for A levels and heading to good university – a handful to Oxbridge (three in 2016, and eight medics). Sheffield, Sheffield Hallam, Nottingham, Durham and Leeds currently popular, as are law and business.

Money matters: Ogden Trust can get the lucky few a 100 per cent bursary. Must be key stage 2 shiner and parental income of less than £40,000 per annum. Sprinkling of other scholarships and bursaries (which are awarded post exam and reviewed annually) plus music and sixth form schols. Bursaries for choristers in junior school, paid 50/50 by school and cathedral, but only whilst boy is in the choir. Ogden Trust sixth form science scholarships available (worth up to 100 per cent of fees) each year for a student wishing to study maths/science at A level. Parent told us: 'It is a fee-paying school and of course you cannot help but think of the other things you could have used the money for – but it is the best investment a parent could ever make.'

Remarks: Great results and great facilities but not a sweatshop. Very traditional feel and loved for it, but very aware of changing society and ensuring boys are ready for those changes. Downside? Tough to get in – expectations high.

Queen Elizabeth High School

Whetstone Bridge Road, Hexham, Northumberland NE46 3JB

Pupils: 1,266 • Ages: 13–18 • Sixth form: 365

Tel: 01434 610300
Email: admin@queenelizabeth.northumberland.sch.uk
Website: www.qehs.net

Head of School: Since 2012, Andy Byers BA PGCE, late 40s. Deputy head here since 2003, now as head of school he oversees the day-to-day management, responsible for outcomes, pastoral care and behaviour, and is also the main point of contact for most current and prospective parents. His subject is economics, though doesn't currently teach; he commutes daily from his home in Newcastle. A Jarrow man by birth, he has two children and is a season-ticket holder at Newcastle Utd. Interestingly, his family history with the school dates back to the 1940s when his mother was treated here for TB in its previous incarnation as a sanatorium. Plenty of energy, but no showboating; he and his team run a tight ship here and together they have seen the school make huge improvements during the last three years. Disappointed in the latest Ofsted report which coincided with the start of the new inspection framework and appears at odds with the views of the school improvement partners, who had graded it 'outstanding'. The judgement was 'good', but they had expected and hoped for better and they feel it's not reflective of the school. Clearly it hurts a little, because it matters.

Mr Graeme Atkins is executive head of the Queen Elizabeth High School/Hexham Middle School Federation, overseeing strategy and, recently, proposed academy conversion for both schools.

Academic matters: In 2016, 75 per cent of pupils achieved five or more A*-C GCSEs including English and maths; 35 per cent of all entries were A*/As, the real high flying A* subject being maths. At A level, 61 per cent A*/B grades, 29 per cent A*/A. Thirty-two subjects on offer; four languages, four sciences, three art courses and a range of humanities, social sciences and performing arts courses at GCSE and A level; GCSEs include child development and electronics; other vocational courses and some BTecs offered. Good to see Latin, classics, philosophy, psychology, fine art, product design and engineering stretching all the way to A level alongside the more traditional subjects. Language exchanges are plentiful and popular.

Two prize-givings a year celebrating academic success, and ample advice and guidance along the road to improvement in academic performance. 'We make sure that they are on the right path when choosing subject options,' says the head, which, of course is sensible and is a huge part of their success, as confirmed by exam results. Nearly 70 per cent stay on for sixth form each year; the rest go on to local colleges, higher level apprenticeships, a handful to the independent sector. The sixth form area has its own café, coffee machines and study areas, ample space to work and play. Plenty of guidance given to sixth form, 'including advice to study elsewhere if that's most appropriate for them'. Staff are 'endlessly encouraging and supportive,' say parents.

Not selective, and SEND support covers a range of needs. Subject teachers are responsible for providing a differentiated curriculum (supported by the SEND team), using LSAs to support in the classroom as required. SENDCo has an open and flexible approach to intervention knowing that 'students' needs are forever changing, and the SEND department is happy to be as flexible as we can be in order to meet students' day to day needs'. Currently 18 pupils with SEND support and eight pupils with a statement or EHC plan; around a third of SEND support students achieve 5+ A*-C including English and maths, with value-added in line with national averages. Support can feature social skills programmes, including strategies to enhance self-esteem; access to IT resources; programmes to support speech and language; mentoring activities; help with occupational therapy or physiotherapy needs; and strategies to promote emotional well-being (including communication with parents).

Games, options, the arts: Wide choice of extracurricular activities – everything from D of E, music and theatre to popular and active Fair Trade club; worth also seeking out the Brazilian drumming group, rock band workshop and young writers' club. Community education kicks in each evening, lots of zumba. Heaps of social and sporting events and fixtures, internally and externally; the website is loaded with them. Strong links with overseas institutions including a Tibetan monastery and a school in India.

Good range of sports for all abilities – particularly strong on rugby, netball and football. Rugby fixtures are mostly against local independent schools, football, hockey and netball fixtures against everyone else. Sports hall, playing fields, Astroturf, cricket nets, tennis and a fitness room all on site. The rowing club dates back 30 years and enjoys huge success nationally and internationally, producing 13 international athletes and Olympians, male and female, in recent years. Training takes place at weekends and after school; it's a serious business but none of that deters the fearless and determined rowers here and they are, they tell us, 'the best state school in the country for rowing'; a couple of the girls here are in the current GB team. Sport is both 'competitive and for fun here,' say parents.

Superb art on display; there is a whole suite of multi-disciplinary art rooms, and dedicated staff ooze enthusiasm. Inspirational art visits include the Clothes Show, Barcelona, Paris, VARC (Visual Arts in Rural Communities), the Baltic Art Gallery in Newcastle. 'Loads of choirs,' says the head. Music is very strong here, as is drama with a musical theatre performance held annually in the purpose-built theatre. Other events include a BTec music evening, a calendar of solo performances, music concert at Hexham Abbey, GCSE concert evening as well as a spring concert showcasing various musical groups, including the orchestra. Music also features on the creative media production curriculum. The dramatists head to the prestigious Northern Stage, the Theatre Royal in Newcastle and Stratford, and theatre and dance groups drop in to add further colour and buzz.

Background and atmosphere: Once the haunt of marauding Vikings 1,300 years ago, nowadays this Northumberland gem proudly holds the title of England's favourite market town – as voted by Country Life magazine. Hexham Abbey is at the hub of its winding streets, now awash with eclectic independent shops, farmers' markets and tea shops. But this is a rural area and, lovely as it is in the surrounding hills, there is a demographic dip here in the Tyne Valley and funding has fallen year on year. Despite that, QEHS has grown from its charter dating back to 1599 into a specialist performing arts school with a reputation exceeding its catchment area and welcoming applicants from far and wide. The funding deficit shows, the building looks tired in places, in need of a refurb, inside and out, but it's imminent – all part of the plan for 2017/18.

Housed over two sites, it encompasses a late 19th century former hotel – the Hydro Building (it became a TB hospital during the war) – and a more modern (60s with 70s and 80s additions) secondary school building. The Hydro Building is an impressive grade II listed Victorian edifice which once played host to Hollywood greats Douglas Fairbanks Junior and Charles Laughton and leading politicians of the day, including Ramsey McDonald. A Victorian wrought iron lift (no longer in use) is the subject of an urban myth bandied around by feeder schools to intrigue the new starters each year, nicknamed 'the ghost lift': it's a good story, but we await hard evidence. Fine, traditional school hall for assemblies, exams and general gatherings. The wonderful former orangery (the Winter Garden) is an especially attractive part of the school, used by lucky pupils during the day but which at weekends can be hired for parties and wedding receptions. A magical walled garden is manned by green-fingered staff and is mostly frequented by art and SEN pupils, proving a welcome, peaceful and inspiring space. It's also the home to chickens, guinea pigs and rabbits, cared for by a rota of pupils who also hold plant sales for the local community.

Pupils in the Press are celebrated in the school entrance foyer, and there are plenty of them. Also on display are the shirts of former pupils who have gone on to great sporting success (including an Oxford Blue, England women's rugby player and golf pro); real pride is evident. Try to close your ears to the somewhat jarring and strident buzzer that signals the start and finish of break-times and lessons – reminded us of an impatient Italian driver stuck in a traffic jam. Good range of dining options on offer, demarcated according to age and stage, all food prepared in-house and some of it even grown in the garden here.

Lacks a bit of kerb appeal but it is well worth exploring the whole site to appreciate the history of the place and all that is on offer here. Most parents are a loyal bunch; it 'does a great job,' they say.

Pastoral care, well-being and discipline: Co-operative and friendly atmosphere all around the school, parents 'especially impressed by the level of support received by pupils around exam time'. Much praise for the home-school communication system; parents feel well informed and can check at any time on attendance, progress and behaviour should they wish to do so. Year heads and learning mentors are described by parents as 'caring, helpful and approachable' and pupils feel 'known and valued'. Described as 'inclusive' by itself and others, with a 'can-do approach to differently able students,' according to one parent, the school has a good, calm feel about it and genuinely appears to meet all needs. Proactive in problem-solving, high standards are expected and there's no hesitation in taking action if need be, likewise in giving support as necessary – changes in behaviour, mood and progress 'are noted and acted upon,' say parents.

Pupils and parents: A mix of rural, semi-rural and professionals, many of whom work in the hospitals and academia of Newcastle, their advice is to 'support the school and trust the teachers'. It would appear that they do, as 90 per cent attendance at parents' evening is the norm here – remarkable and the envy of many of other schools. Refreshingly, the parent view seems to be less concerned about admin and league tables and more interested in allowing the school to be 'free of political interfering' and 'creative and free-thinking' in its style and approach. That said, it stands extremely well in the league tables and they know it.

This is an attractive town with beautiful scenery close by, adding to the attraction of moving to be in catchment for this school and making a commute to work worthwhile. Some 40 per cent of pupils travel in by bus, from Prudhoe in the east and the border of County Durham to the south. With a year 9 start here, there are no 'littlies' around to bring extra noise and vigour to social areas, enhancing what already feels more like a campus than a playground. There are grassed woodland areas, gardens and hard spaces on which to hang around, and the staff and pupil body moves around between buildings with a civilised fluidity.

A diverse bunch and from a wide range of backgrounds, pupils appear focused and busy. There's a great deal going on here so 'if your child is willing to grasp opportunities then this is a great school for them,' said a parent. Aspirations are high and yet there's no hint of arrogance; neither average nor mundane, they are 'ordinary' in the best possible way. Probably not as streetwise as their urban counterparts; a walk into town, a coffee and a chat, then uphill back to school is about as exciting as it gets for sixth formers at lunchtime.

Entrance: Based on LA catchment criteria. The best and most obvious route in is via one of the three feeder middle schools: its own partner school in Hexham plus St Joseph's and Corbridge. Lots of work done on transition, so pupils coming into year 9 are familiar with the surroundings and settle quickly and easily. Before they start they write a letter to the head to introduce themselves – and yes, he reads them. Parents out of catchment happy to pay their own transport costs and 'feel lucky' to gain a place, adding that the application process 'is simple'. Five A*-Cs at GCSE required for sixth form entry; must include English language. Average point system in place for entry to chosen courses, the highest requirements being for sciences and languages.

Exit: Around 40 per cent leave after GCSEs. Majority of students go on to higher education with a clutch to Oxbridge each year (five in 2016, and four medics). Northern universities top the list of favourites here with Newcastle, Leeds and Northumbria leading the way, Manchester, Durham, York and Lancaster also popular, smaller numbers to London. Others go into higher education, training, apprenticeships or work. Over the past few years many to leading conservatoires and drama schools thanks, in part, to specialist staff.

Remarks: Some schools are all about the window-dressing, this one isn't. In fact window-dressing is something on which it could do better, but that may well be a funding issue and therefore low on the priority list. Crucially, it would appear to be getting all the important things right: results very good and rising, if offers plenty of sport, art, music and other activities all wrapped up with high quality care and teaching – 'exemplary,' in fact, say parents.

Queen Elizabeth's Grammar School

West Park Road, Blackburn, Lancashire BB2 6DF

Pupils: 881 • Ages: 4-18 • Sixth form: 155

Tel: 01254 686300
Email: admissions@qegsblackburn.com
Website: www.qegsblackburn.com

Acting head: Mrs C Y Gammon, previously deputy head, is holding the fort whilst a new head is appointed.

At the junior school, Mrs K L O'Donoghue, is acting head. She was previously deputy head and is standing in whilst the head, Alison Wharmby BEd (Manchester), is on long-term sick leave.

Academic matters: 'All our heads of departments are accountable,' says the school. To this end, marking is closely monitored and there are regular meetings with staff. Science is the school's trump card but other areas such as art also delivering creditable results. Became a free school in September 2014. French taught in dedicated languages room by qualified language teacher through to year 6.

Radical decline in exam results: 44 per cent A*/B grades at A level in 2016 and 16 per cent A*/A; at GCSE, 30 per cent A*/A. Class sizes of around 20-25 in main school and 8-10 for A levels. Students take 10 GCSEs, including English, maths, at least one modern foreign language (French, German or Spanish), a combination of sciences (core plus additional award or separate sciences on offer – IGCSE courses now being taken) and a short course in ethics and philosophy. Latin and Greek available too.

Facilities are good with four networked IT suites, science and language labs plus a dedicated learning support department. Dedicated and enthusiastic staff.

Games, options, the arts: Excellent reputation for games. Three-time Sportsmark Gold award-winners and voted the local Sports School of the Year 2010-11 by Blackburn and Darwen Sports Council. QEGS has also won the Independent Schools FA Cup three times (the first school to win the cup more than once) and has very strong links with local club Blackburn Rovers. Rugby, cricket, swimming, athletics, golf and cross-country are all strong and there's a pool with electronic timing system, open to locals outside school hours.

Good music, all students are required to take part in drama productions (even if it's for one night). Art provision and facility is excellent, with one pupil recently selected for the Royal Academy's A level online exhibition. Art block (opened by former pupil Wayne Hemingway) showcases the extremely impressive talent on offer.

Background and atmosphere: School founded in 1509 by the second Earl of Derby, granted Royal Charter by Queen Elizabeth I in 1567. Moved to present site in leafy Blackburn suburb in 1884. Went direct grant in 1944, returned to private sector in 1976 and back to the state sector again in 2014. Girls have been admitted throughout since 2001 and well integrated, but they are still a tiny minority and the school is keen to change this. Original school building, with stunning stained-glass windows, known as Big School and used as school dining hall. Portraits of previous heads, school silver, team photographs and press cuttings proudly on show.

Large impressive campus boasting five acres (excluding playing fields) and numerous buildings. There are games fields and sports hall 20 minutes away at Lammack, to which the pupils travel by minibus. Light, airy library with panoramic views. The dedicated sixth form common room, Singleton House, has its own café, careers suite and private study room.

Junior school housed in separate building on main QEGS site (formerly known as Horncliffe) but uses many senior school facilities – dining hall, swimming pool etc. Infant school (formally known as early years department) in adjacent building – Lawn Bank – now caters for children aged 4-6.

Conversion to a free school largely precipitated by shortfall in pupils as local families experiencing hard times opt for state schools, there are several popular faith schools in the area and a local girls' school recently turned co-ed.

Pastoral care, well-being and discipline: There's a mentoring system in place to support struggling pupils and a peer mentoring scheme (fourth years looking after first years). The prefect system for both junior and senior school to enable pupils to develop leadership skills, a sense of community and responsibility from a young age. Former pupils' association sees individual former pupils lend their expertise in talks, career advice and work placements.

Long-standing partnership with the Good Samaritan School in Uganda. Biennially, a party of sixth form students travel to the school and help with practical projects to enhance the school (preceding the visit the whole school is involved in fundraising for the project).

Pupils and parents: Pupils come from very mixed backgrounds and around one quarter are of Asian heritage. Catchment is roughly a 20 mile radius of the school. Some pupils are very local and walk to school but there is an extensive bus service covering the whole catchment area. Former pupils include film director Michael Winterbottom; designer Wayne Hemingway; Ivor Bolton, chief conductor of the Mozarteum Orchestra; Sir Netar Mallick, Professor Emeritus of renal medicine in Manchester.

Entrance: Infant school has two classes of 20 for reception (28 from September 2017), year 1 and year 2. Applications via local authority. Main point of entry to senior school is 11+. Fair banding tests. Sixth form entrants need minimum of five Bs at GCSE.

Exit: Virtually all progress from the junior school into the senior school at age 11+. Some 60 per cent leave after GCSEs, mostly for local FE colleges offering subjects like law and media studies that are not available at QEGS. With very few exceptions, all pupils go on to university – Bradford, Lancaster, Manchester, Newcastle, UCLAN popular.

Remarks: The school is efficient, friendly and impressive with a warm atmosphere and respectful students. Students are evidently proud of their school and full of praise for its artistic and sporting endeavours. Now in a new era as a free school.

Queen Ethelburga's College

60

Thorpe Underwood Hall, Ouseburn, York, North Yorkshire YO26 9SS

Pupils: 476; 404 full boarders • Ages: 14–20 (junior boarding from 6) • Sixth form: 210

Fees: Day £14,775 – £15,720; Boarding £34,110 – £35,769; International Boarding £41,799 – £44,118 pa

Tel: 01423 333330
Email: qeoffice@qe.org
Website: www.qe.org

Principal: Since 2006, Mr Steven Jandrell BA (50s), married to Margaret, with a young son at Chapter House. Warm, friendly, genuine and approachable, he understands education and enjoys discussing it. Well-respected and liked by staff and pupils, he's part of the furniture, having been here for many years as head of music and deputy head. Long-standing parents describe him as 'the best head so far'; 'He's a good listener who doesn't bat you away with standard answers'.

Academic matters: Splits into two streams at age 14, the College and the Faculty.

The College is the straightforwardly academic stream, with all students aimed at the EBacc at 16 and A levels (a choice of 24, but no classics) at 18. In 2016, 68 per cent A*/A grades at I/GCSE (overseas students' English accounts for a large percentage of the C or lower grades). College students rarely get less than a B at A level: over 85 A*/A in 2016. Subject choices are dominated by maths, languages (largely Russian and Chinese) and economics – indicative of the strong overseas contingent. UK university destinations are strongly weighted towards business- and science-related subjects at good universities; psychology, maths and law also popular. Used to be a couple a year to Oxbridge, but six in 2016 – all UK students. Five timetable slots in the sixth form, four for A levels and one for 'enrichment' – Faculty has the same pattern.

The Faculty has a much broader remit, with an emphasis on BTecs. There are quite a lot of pupils here who struggle even with English and maths at GCSE – though 32 per cent of grades are A*/A (28 per cent without the Chinese and Russian home languages), 50 per cent are B/C and 20 per cent D and below. A smattering of A levels – mostly maths and home languages, giving the 84 per cent A*/A headlined on the school website – and a strong emphasis on business studies BTec where the results are even better: 50 per cent D*D*D* and none lower than DDD. Vocational rather than academic university destinations, mostly business-related or sport at middle-ranking universities with strong reputations, but an increasing showing in recent years from creative subjects and division 1 universities.

The division, though, is not as simple as that. Some College pupils do a BTec among their A levels; one 2015 Faculty student who went to read engineering at Imperial had four A*s at A level. There's a difference in style – eg self-motivated vs needs mentoring – which affects how pupils are allocated.

Some parents of Faculty pupils clearly feel that they were not sufficiently involved when the choice between Faculty and College was made. QE agree that they tend to insist on their views of which suits each pupil – leading in some cases to unsurprising emotional friction given parental views (which we often encounter) that BTecs are a second-class option with second class outcomes. That's not, though, how the dozen or so Faculty alumni we have communicated with have seen it. They have felt much more in tune with the style and approach built into BTec: more project-based, more continuous assessment, more real. They praise their teaching and the support from their teachers. They formed strong friendships across Faculty and College, and are still in touch with many of them. They chose university courses that worked well for them (careers guidance much praised), and look back with much fondness to their time at QE. Low to mid-range universities are happy to accept BTecs; you'd have to be a truly extraordinary candidate to get to Oxbridge on one (it has been done), other Russell Group vary – business courses at Durham accept openly, equivalent courses at Exeter do too, but not obvious on their website, so do check carefully.

In both Faculty and College pupils as a whole do very much better than you would expect from their earlier results.

Small classes, unashamedly setted, with regular testing for all – pupils say 'it's good for us'. Reports from parents lower down the school are good. Many parental comments on rapid teacher turnover, and the difficulties and disorganisation that this sometimes engendered. The school puts this down to rapid expansion and says 'now that a decision has been taken to remain at around our present number, this problem should no longer be the case; there were only five new appointments for this year out of 180 teaching staff'.

Dyslexia help available. All children tested on arrival in the prep school during the first half term, ed psych's report if necessary, usually individual lessons for free twice a week, if more needed then extra charge. Five specialist teachers of specific learning difficulties. EFL free throughout the school.

Games, options, the arts: Music (for all) very strong, with frequent opportunities for performance. The old refectory (now the Phoenix Centre) contains no fewer than four practice drama and dance studios and a dedicated theatre – most impressive. Art good but not emphasised. Enthusiastic home economics and Leiths food and wine course for sixth formers (no more than two sets of eight per year group), with the smashing kitchen used for grown-up classes in the holidays.

Thirty-four acres of floodlit pitches for hockey, soccer, rugby, high jump, netball, basketball, volleyball etc and six Astroturfs. CCF popular, clubs for IT, archery, fencing, golf. A new swimming pool too. The giant sports centre (sports village, as the school calls it) is an eye-watering, Olympic-level provision; you can look at the main school website and not see a sign of it, but go to www.qesportsvillage.org and prepare to be blown off your feet. This provides a home for the eight 'performance sport' courses (notably rugby and netball) – as one of their five timetable slots, students push their sporting aspirations, with professional coaching, and individual strength and conditioning programmes prepared by staff from Leeds Beckett. A long string of individual and team successes, as you would expect from provision at this level.

D of E with plenty of gold participants. Lots of extracurricular activities – the list is (almost) endless, most free, but a charge is made where there is a strong element of personal tuition (riding, archery, fencing, tennis, golf and kick-boxing).

Boarding: From age 7 (at Chapter House). International students from 66 countries (most notably south east Asia and the various parts of the former USSR) make up about two-thirds of thousand-strong boarding community; most of the other third are Forces children. Modern boarding accommodation consists of smart and well-equipped bedrooms, all now with private bathrooms, all with flat screen TVs (in fact two TVs in some twin rooms – just in case these lucky pupils wish to watch different programmes..) on timers so they do not get in the way of prep or sleep. DVD players, telephones with voicemail, fridges, electric kettles, microwaves, air conditioning, trouser presses and room safes – pretty much everything except a mini-bar, in fact. Great attention to detail and, it would appear, no expense spared – newer boarding houses have fantastic limed oak doors, skirting boards et al. A classy medical centre that resembles a private hospital and oodles of huge common rooms – all with leather sofas, toasters and TVs. Houses for the younger ones surrounded by squidgy playgrounds filled with serious kit. Boys' and girls' accommodation is separate. Day pupil centre for day children plus B&B available if needed. The campus has a strong mobile signal.

Houseparents occasionally express concern that individual facilities are so good that pupils, particularly senior (Chinese) boys, are loath to leave their bed/study rooms and join in communal activities. No Saturday school, but full range of activities on offer during weekends – trips to Whitby, the latest cinema preview. After their first term sixth formers can nip into York or Leeds on a Saturday night, but must meet the pickup by 10pm at the local station (or be in by 10.30pm if they miss the train).

Background and atmosphere: Twenty-five minutes from York and Harrogate and a 10 minute drive from the A1. Run by a collegiate board, chaired by Amy Martin, who lives on site and whose family have been involved with the school since 1991 when she was a student at QE. Has been the driving force behind the school's development over the last few years. Thorpe Underwood dates back to the Domesday Book, where it is described as Chirchie, Usebrana and Useburn, before becoming part of the monastery of Fountains Abbey in 1292. The hall was rebuilt in 1902 in best Edwardian Tudor style and the extensions have been sympathetically carried out with leaded paned windows to match the original. The place is a complex mix of old and new – in style and attitude – and full of surprises.

Impressive newer facilities include a vast dining room (The Undercroft) that doubles as an assembly hall – though the acoustics are pretty grim and mealtimes can be a deafening experience, say some staff. Huge solid oak tables fill the room with comfortable seating on the balcony above, alongside exciting sculptures courtesy of Amy Martin's late uncle. Fruit available at all times with good salad bar, home-cooked food with a veggie option. Self-service queuing system moves around barriers like a busy post office. A lift has been installed for wheelchair users. A popular activity centre has been established on the perimeter of the campus.

The original Hall – previously the home of the Martin family – houses a traditional library, the Phoenix Centre and some notable taxidermy.

Has benefited from millions of pounds' worth of Martin investment. Good, if not lavishly stocked, library, banks of computers, Wifi everywhere. Regular formal dinner parties with silver service and speaker for sixth form 'to give them practice in the real world'. Almost 50/50 boy/girl mix, boarding numbers up, and reasonable fees have brought a considerable flow of day pupils.

All faiths and none are welcome. In fact anyone who can afford it is welcome really – with little academic selection and a determination to meet all needs.

Faculty and College mix well outside the formal school day: activities and boarding are entirely mixed. The Faculty is larger and has more UK students than the College.

Relationship between the genders is good, as are relationships too between nationalities: most Brits make good foreign friends. Has a reputation for turning out well-mannered young people. Much-remarked upon omnipresent CCTV is not now monitored in real time, but still proves useful for 'security, serious disciplinary matters and for lost items of value'.

Pastoral care, well-being and discipline: Parents tell us that the pastoral care here is really good – 'Can't plug it enough'. Tutorial system – tutors change yearly, no more than 20 tutees to each. Has recently introduced THRIVE@QE, an initiative to 'proactively support all pupils' emotional health, well-being and resilience through activities, resources, clubs, workshops, clinics and more.' Charming and encouraging leavers' letter.

Discipline is described as 'sensible' – exclusion for violence and selling drugs, possibly also for taking drugs, 'depending on what it is'. Reserves the right to search boarders' rooms and to test for drugs and alcohol – and does.

There was much comment in the press following a critical report from the Independent Schools Inspectorate on the efficacy of QE's child safeguarding systems. ISI has now given the school, which has made substantial improvements, a clean bill of health.

Further press attention is expected when the former Provost stands trial in July 2017 on allegations of historic sexual offences.

Pupils and parents: Lots of first time buyers, pupils come to board from all over: Scotland, Wales as well as East Anglia and locally on daily basis. Nine buses collect day pupils from all over Yorkshire (not cheap), buses collect from local station. Many overseas students, as above.

Quite a lot of the parents we talked to felt that QE could be better at communicating with them, and at creating a community among parents.

Entrance: Many via Chapter House, but generally aged 14; As and Bs at GCSE for potential A level candidates in the College, broader intake to Faculty. External candidates come from other independents, local state schools or out of the area. Pupils below year 10 accepted at any time during the school year 'if places available'. Promotes itself heavily locally, nationally and internationally – regular pop-outs from Good Housekeeping and the like. Informative DVD which plays in English, Chinese Simplified and Traditional, German, Japanese and Russian. The heaviest prospectus bundle that we have ever encountered, though fear not, it is fairly repetitive. Entry to all schools is based on CAT 4 test, interview and positive school reports. (QE does not want to be specific about levels as 'these change from school to school and are gradually being raised as demand for places rises'.)

Exit: Quite a substantial exit after GCSE – 30 per cent or so, with overseas students typically changing school and UK ones headed for sixth form college. After A levels, most College students off to study law, maths, politics, psychology or medicine recently (three of six Oxbridge places in 2016 for law), a large proportion at Russell Group unis. Business much the most popular course for Faculty students, who virtually all do vocationally-flavoured courses at mid-ranking (recently some division 1) unis: accounting/economics/information management, a wide range of creative subjects (eg fashion design with marketing and music with enterprise) and some science and sport, plus several off to Switzerland to study hospitality. No hoofing out mid-course.

Money matters: The school is well underpinned financially but quite expensive (especially so for overseas pupils) and 'you pay for absolutely everything,' say parents. Countered a little by masses of scholarships, plenty of awards (32 per cent discount for Forces and FCO). Add to that list sports and music scholarships and many, many more. 'You can also pay by Barclaycard or Amex.' Very streetwise management and 'all awards granted will be repayable in full, if the school fees bill is not paid seven days prior to the commencement of each term, and, or, if a pupil does not complete their education with us for any reason, regardless of commencement age, until the completion of the end of year 13...' etc etc. Read the small print very carefully. We have great reservations about these terms.

Remarks: Has come a long way, not just in its facilities but also in its academic provision. Making a success of looking after both the academic and the less academic. If it carries on like this it will end up with a grand reputation.

Queen Margaret's

Escrick Park, Escrick, York, North Yorkshire YO19 6EU

Pupils: 320; 250 full boarders • Ages: 11–18 • Sixth form: 122 • C of E

Fees: Day £19,590 ; Boarding £29,850 pa

Tel: 01904 727600
Email: qm-admissions@queenmargarets.com
Website: www.queenmargarets.com

Head: Since 2015, Mrs Jessica Miles MA PGCE. Prior to this was deputy head of Leweston School in Dorset for seven years. After graduating from Oriel College, Oxford with a degree in modern languages, she worked for short time in public relations and arts administration, then did PGCE at King's College, London. First teaching post was at Dulwich College, where she became head of Spanish, deputy head of upper school and director of rowing. After a move to Dorset and a year teaching Spanish and French at Sherborne School, she moved to Leweston. Married to Paul, with two sons.

Q

Academic matters: Although entry is not particularly selective, academic success matters. Fine GCSE results: 63 per cent A*/A grades in 2016. At A level, mathematics, English, physics, chemistry, geography, art and French popular, but no weaknesses; psychology a new addition. Overall performance fine – 49 per cent A*/A and 78 A*-B grades in 2016. Pupil support department (three full-time) and two teachers for EFL.

Games, options, the arts: Lots of healthy outdoor life – an hour a day of sport for all. Highly successful sports department with games keenly played in glorious surroundings and stunning facilities: lacrosse (long journeys for fixtures), hockey (floodlit all-weather pitch), two swimming pools (one indoor, one outdoor), sports hall, tennis courts, dance studio, new sixth form cardio suite etc – hard to find something they don't have. Riding popular (private riding school on campus); some girls bring ponies, school keeps 15. Good art, but not an 'arty' school. Home economics for all. Strong choral music, and lots of drama in wonderful theatre. Stunning modern chapel, Catholics go to nearby Thicket Priory for mass; half-termly vigil masses in school; annual Anglican and RC confirmations. Extracurricular activities too numerous to mention but include clay pigeon shooting, driving remote control cars and climbing walls. QM diploma for sixth formers.

Boarding: Welcoming, homey boarding house for 11 year olds with a Cath Kidston inspired kitchen for tea, toast and home comforts around the Aga. Girls live in year groups all the way through – 'Prevents them from growing up too fast,' observed one pleased parent. School claims the strong vertical house system, house supper nights on Fridays and an assortment of trips and visits encourage girls of different ages to mix, new social mixing areas encouraging and supporting this. Year 5 has a boarding house named after old girl, Winifred Holtby; lower sixth boarders are housed nearby and enjoy sitting and walking on the Cloisters lawn – they do because they can. Their accommodation recently refurbished with rooms 'designed on American student loft living' – including drawers which are also steps up to their beds. Upper sixth formers have increased independence in attractively converted cottages on site; head girl has the first pick of houses; all have large kitchens, 'great for entertaining', and communal sitting rooms; cottage life has the feel of a college campus.

Background and atmosphere: Founded in Scarborough in 1901, moved to this fine Palladian house (by John Carr), with later 'rustic timber' purpose-built classrooms, in 1949. Glorious sweeping drive, set amongst 60 plus acres of North Yorkshire loveliness, the flag is flying proudly from the rooftop. A school where girls have big hair and even bigger ideas – aspirations and expectations, of self and others, are high. Confident yet not brash, articulate and considered, girls are fiercely loyal, hard working and committed. New social areas where girls of all ages meet together and the use of in-school mentors have brought increased opportunities for greater independence and responsibility. Girls now feel they have a voice and, being girls, they use it. The school earns many approving noises from parents as well as envious glances over the wall from its competitors, with good reason.

It's been top notch academically for quite a while now, but is cultivating a purposeful nurturing side without losing any of its academic rigour. Has a large yet tight and cohesive campus with a number of Victorian additions, clever conversions, award-winning centenary theatre, chapel and indoor swimming pool. Superb library – wood panelling everywhere, open fire, huge windows looking out on to lawns – but not too precious to be used, the range of reference books is impressive; also smaller but well-stocked fiction library with the relaxed feel of a welcoming bookshop.

Circular dining hall (once an indoor lunging school), with somewhat noisy acoustics. Food much improved in recent years, say parents and girls, with school rarities such as a cappuccino machine and balsamic vinegar; younger girls envious of the privilege of pain au chocolat delivered to sixth form houses for breakfast, all very civilised. Breaktime snacks provided, excellent cakes and fruit, girls on school council keep a watchful eye over food provision and choice.

Recent changes include an alteration to prep time; once timetabled and closely monitored – now girls choose where and when they do their prep, and, if need be, learn by getting it wrong. All part of the independence = taking responsibility philosophy. And it's working. However girls are kept 'pretty busy' all the time – new girls are monitored to check they aren't overdoing it and taking on too much in the early days. Uniform is an attractive tartan and charcoal; own clothes worn after tea – don't provide anything that you wouldn't want boil-washed. Smart dress code rather than uniform for sixth form, jackets required.

Pastoral care, well-being and discipline: The pace of life in this rural idyll is anything but slow and a there's a noticeable air of protectiveness towards the girls. 'There are no silly rules,' say parents and girls, but it is by no means light on discipline – 'We are pretty old fashioned about smoking and drinking'. Parents speak with great enthusiasm about the life skills provided by being part of a boarding community, citing 'independence, knowing how to get on with people, young and old, and standing up and being counted' as so very important. All girls have a personal tutor, around eight girls per staff member (including the head), and run on a three year cycle. Add to this a mentor for sixth formers who acts as a guide in their subject of choice to provide extra reading, advice and support university applications.

A café, assortment of TV rooms with games (including Wii), a room for Skyping home (priority given to overseas boarders) and new ICT rooms have really given the place a lift and provided the girls with much-needed places to go. Quiet work rooms for those who need or want it, and other rooms where girls can work or chat, computers arranged in pods and some even blissfully Facebook-free for those serious about working. Sixth formers also have their own socialising area known as the 'cellars' – once used for keeping wine cool, now a cool place for maturing girls to hang out with friends before, during and after school and to bring guests (boys, even) at weekends.

Apart from school, not a great deal to do around here, so a trip to the village shop is an exciting treat – a shock for girls with serious shopping habits. Sixth formers can go into York during free time on Wednesdays and Saturdays; they are usually careful not to abuse this freedom.

Pupils and parents: Friendly pupils, happy to chat and proud of their school, clearly enjoying the many benefits of living and learning in such a lovely environment. No lack of ambition – even younger girls talk about going to university as though it is a self-evident truth: 'You'd be hard-pressed to find someone who is not heading for uni,' they tell us. Parents mainly upper and middle class: landowners, farmers, professionals; boarders – some 20 per cent from overseas – span 13 nations and four continents, many from Scotland ('It's the first real boarding school you hit driving south'), Cumbria, East Anglia, and of course Yorkshire. Essentially the main catchment is the east coast train line. OGs include Winifred Holtby (author), Ann Jellicoe (playwright), Sarah Connolly (opera singer), Dame Justice Eleanor King (High Court judge).

Entrance: Own exam at 11, 12 and 13. Additional intake into sixth form: minimum eight GCSEs, including English, mathematics and a science, with at least two As and three Bs.

Exit: Virtually all sixth formers to higher education nationwide – Bristol, Edinburgh, Oxford Brookes and UCL popular. Courses include law, dentistry, mechanical engineering, forensic anthropology and liberal arts; one medic in 2016. Small trickle post-16 to co-ed sixth form, a few girls becoming restless each year, though many go and look elsewhere before then deciding to stay put.

Money matters: Scholarships at 11, 12, 13 and sixth form; academic, art, choral, dance, drama, music and sport scholarships. Means-tested bursaries.

Remarks: According to one parent, with three daughters at the school, 'Whether your daughter is tall or short, academic or sporty, shy or confident, it works for them all – and that's the beauty of it'.

Queen Mary's School

Baldersby Park, Topcliffe, Thirsk, North Yorkshire YO7 3BZ

Pupils: 250; 24 full, 42 weekly, 38 flexi boarders • Ages: 2–7 (boys), 2–16 (girls); (boarding from 7) • C of E

Fees: Day £7,290 – £17,790; Boarding £19,590 – £23,130 pa

Tel: 01845 575000
Email: admin@queenmarys.org
Website: www.queenmarys.org

Head: Since 2015, Mrs Carole Cameron, previously acting head at Queen Margaret's School in York. Geography degree and MA in education management; she has also been head of Highfield, the Harrogate Ladies' College prep school. She worked in schools in Nottinghamshire, London and Leeds before spending 10 exciting years in international schools in the Caribbean while her family lived in Grenada and the Cayman Islands. She has two grown up daughters.

Academic matters: Play-based learning and participation in junior department productions builds confidence in nursery, with care available until 4.25pm each day and flexibility in the number of sessions. From reception, core learning is in numeracy and literacy – and tinies have computers too. Emphasis is learning through fun, creativity and exploration. Each reception child can take the lead and organise a school trip for their class to enjoy – helps too if parents are farmers. Very small numbers allow interaction with older children at meals, playtimes and in celebrating special events.

Unique to years 1 and 2 are Thrilling Thursdays, when the day is spent out of school in a new experience, or in school with a special visitor. Specialist teaching extended to French and IT, where curriculum has been revamped, as has dance; cross-curricular projects using art and IT.

Girls in prep, years 3 to 6, are accommodated in the main school building and are taught in small, mixed-ability classes for all subjects. Fun, cross-curricular learning such as when an English lesson in invitation writing blossomed into a full-blown tea party for parents. A request to let them make cake – and they did.

Pleasing GCSE results in 2016 with 44 per cent A*/A grades. A very mixed ability school, non-selective intake – all take English, maths, dual sciences, religious studies; nearly all take French as well. Two sets of French in year 7; top set add German and bottom Spanish in year 8. Lots of role-play, telephone conversation and presentation work in lessons. 'Amusing yet educational,' seems to be the general opinion of the pupils. No exchanges but Spanish and French pupils regularly spend one term here. Classics and Latin on timetable and available as GCSE options, bringing GCSE subject choice to 17 – pretty good for a school this size. German and music results consistently good and the humanities well represented.

Introduction of bespoke challenge curriculum, on timetable and led by outdoor adventure instructor, to develop 'collaborative working, leadership, problem solving and resilience alongside presentational skills, ability to research and evaluate'.

Very small tutor groups and tiny classes, setted and streamed. Lunch with form tutor; termly target setting with 'grades, a trigger for conversation'. Saturday morning school followed by drama rehearsals, choir practice and matches. Staff/

pupil relationship exemplary – seems that school never closes and girls can be found wandering around in the Easter holidays having been 'doing extra workshops' with dedicated staff, who never seem to take holidays either. Parents also say staff very good at motivating their daughters without them feeling under pressure.

Good and sensitive SEN, most commonly dyslexia help; either two sessions of one-on-one or shared in a small group. Library used extensively, reading encouraged through wide selection of fiction.

Recent improvements in IT network, high level security where every device in school logged, necessary when lots of own devices; iPads provided in library and dedicated IT suite. Specialist teaching from year 1 with focus on upskilling rather than software package training; programming, network design and logic with project work cross-curricular – though not available as GCSE option.

Prepared for life post-16 through life skills curriculum alongside GCSE – first aid, cooking, managing finances etc. Good careers library, Cambridge profiling, interview training and work experience organised.

Games, options, the arts: Traditional sports, daily, full fixture list with lacrosse, athletics and tennis teams all doing well. Own tennis courts, all-weather pitches and small indoor swimming pool. Outdoor adventure is where the school comes into its own – from adjacent River Swale, popular for canoeing and the occasional swim (hardy girls up north), wild running assault course (aptly named WOLF), and even a 160 feet bungee jump as a special treat. No wonder the girls say, 'You learn to face your fears'. Secret missions, overnight camps and canoe expeditions for juniors – led by outdoor teacher Mr Smith – lay the foundation for what's in store in senior school.

Music is very important and the place hums with junior and senior choirs and delicious concerts open to the general public as well as for inmates – impressive for a school of this size. Chapel choristers wear much-coveted green sweatshirts and give regular performances both home and away. Lots of opportunity for instrumentalists – classical focus though annual battle of the bands competition.

Bright, colourful art in the attics including creative textiles, ceramics; sewing machines in the DT room. Drama good and well supported, musicals popular, though lacking good performance facilities. Cooking timetabled and enjoyed by all.

Superb equestrian facilities; children can and do bring their own ponies and ride daily, girls enjoy mucking in – and out – in the stables at weekends, after lessons and occasionally before breakfast. Outdoor manège of Olympian size, as well as rides across the local landowner's fields, school in constant negotiation with neighbours to increase riders' scope, cross-country course on site. Tadcaster polo club is nearby and looks like becoming the next horsey activity.

Wide range of after-school clubs including the unusual pheasant plucking club, with fruits of their labours enjoyed at a dinner with invited guests. Superb selection of residentials, expeditions for all, plus D of E.

House activity – usual sport and performing arts plus boundary run and Wolf assault course. Fundraising for local and international charities – adopted school in Madagascar, support for child in Sherpa school in Kathmandu.

Boarding: Girls have a sense of ownership of their mansion – no showpiece, consequently shows signs of being well-used, a little shabby in places. Boarding in top echelons; girls 'like sleeping in stately home'. Rash of good-sized dorms, three to five to a room; top bunks for flexi-boarders used only up to year 8. Bathrooms receiving a timely refurbishment; furniture tired in places, some with limited storage, though additional lockers on ground floor. Common rooms small and underwhelming, though totally underutilised, according to head of boarding. 'The girls have such a busy life there's no time for TV,' she said. Dorms on the balcony over the Great Hall are a rite of passage for those in their last year. Girls encouraged to flexi-board from year 4. Often younger sisters of senior girls, their family home usually within 60 mile radius of the school. Some Forces' families, though declining, no international boarders. Very small number of junior boarders stay in school at the weekend; those that do enjoy outdoor activities, local attractions and have 'fun on a shoestring' with their older counterparts.

Very few have never boarded and who can blame them, with pillow fights, mattress surfing down the great hall staircase and abseiling over the banisters as boarder activities. Discos, film nights and socials with Aysgarth boys (strong sibling links) for the younger pupils.

Background and atmosphere: Founded in 1925, moved from Duncombe Park to its present rural setting Baldersby Park in 1983. Said to be the first Palladian mansion built in Britain by Colen Campbell, 1721, and Jacobethanised following a fire in 1902. Impressive approach, long curving driveway bordered by pastures – like stepping into a Gainsborough landscape.

Well-proportioned, former drawing room now a head's study to die for. Glorious main hall used for daily service, with the girls sitting on the carpet, head sitting in front of the stairs, the choir ranged behind in serried ranks. When it is not being used for formal occasions, and even sometimes when it is (aerial performance at Christmas concert by pyjama clad outdoor education teacher to accompanied singing Walking in the Air), girls can be seen walking the trapeze from balcony to balcony high above the main hall, wisely harnessed; not a rite of passage but, as with most things here, girls encouraged to 'have a go'.

Beyond, leading off narrow corridors, a warren of classrooms, a number displaying 'dogs in residence' signs on their door. Home from home applies to staff canine pets as well as pupils. Girls like it and say they find a pooch pat mid lesson beneficial. Classrooms in the main building and converted outhouses; science department boasts a greenhouse and freshwater pond for hands-on experience.

Tucked round the corner from the Palladian mansion is the pastoral setting for the single storey timber classrooms that cosily house early years to year 2. They open out into a secure and spacious play area, and the boys and girls also have use of the main school facilities. Pre-prep is currently a girls' only zone; children receive a lot of individual attention and the department has been awarded the local authority's gold award for quality assurance.

School uniform evolves over the years with girls graduating from beige to green jerseys and royal hunting Stewart tartan kilts. Some rationalisation taken place; senior summer dresses culled.

School food is good quality, wholesome home cooking and girls' earlier wish for 'a visit from Jamie Oliver' to liven things up has almost been granted with appointment of a chef manager who trained in one of his restaurants.

Charming chapel, a peaceful haven for all; school has its own chaplain; school is keen that religion should be 'part of the school routine' but not rammed down the throat. Staff and girls are happy with the relaxed atmosphere – like an extended family (all ages mix) with a mass of sisterly teasing. Younger girls like to play and build dens in the woods, 'benign supervision' allowing a sense of freedom with a nod to health and safety. The early assumption of seniority (at 16 rather than 18) gives girls confidence and maturity – a great balance with the younger girls happily staying young and the older girls demonstrating early maturity and the ability to take on responsibilities.

They love 'the opportunity to try lots of different things' and the 'enduring friendships' they feel they are making, but some feel rural isolation and would welcome more social interface with other schools – work in progress.

Pastoral care, well-being and discipline: Like home. No petty rules and others which are bendable, but an underlying sense of organisation. Definitely carrot not stick, detentions rare; house points with head's awards for a tally of five; woman of the week award – much wider than academic achievement. Badges pepper senior pupils' uniforms – awarded for contribution and achievement across a wide range. Prefects elected by head, staff and year 10 ballot.

Parents' requests granted when reasonable. Not a sophisticated place, no obvious sin, just an occasional ticking off for a girl wearing make-up, but it's few and far between.

Most board – flexi-boarding popular from year 4, building to weekly and termly boarding by year 10. Boarding staff and NZ gappies organise 'fun on a shoestring' weekend activities for around 15 to 25 girls; seniors don't have to join in. Boarding notice boards display weekly winners of 'good egg' and 'make a smile' awards.

Pupils and parents: Local as opposed to county school – combination of first time buyers, local farmers, landowners and professionals – 'not as Tatler and Vogue as some of its competitors'. Relaxed 7.30am drop off time for working parents. Quite a lot of army families though number reducing – Catterick is just up the road – some of whom pop their daughters into the school 'while they are based in Yorkshire' and are so pleased with the place that they leave their daughters there, younger sisters often joining them, when they are posted elsewhere.

Offers six routes on school minibuses – encompassing Aysgarth, Masham, Helmsley, Ripon and Wetherby.

Parents and pupils can use school facilities in the holidays. No real overseas presence, one or two expats, a couple of Spanish and French for a term, but boarding holding up and no wish to change its nature.

Entrance: At any time, middle of term if needed. At all ages. Entry test at senior level – year 7 applicants have an assessment day in January – but, places permitting, only those with special needs beyond the school's capability are liable to be turned away. Senior school feeders local prep schools and primaries.

Exit: At all ages. Some take common entrance at 11, and a small number at 13. Girls have previously mainly gone to Queen Margaret's Eskrick, with one or two to Tudor Hall, Heathfield or co-eds, Uppingham, Millfield, Rugby. Senior girls go on to do A levels at Ampleforth, St Aidan's, Ripon Grammar, Sedbergh, St Peter's, Uppingham etc etc. Good collection of scholarships – music predominates, plus academic and sports.

Money matters: Not a rich school and not endowed, though has benefited recently from generous donations. Scholarships for academics, music, art and sport, plus discount for clergy daughters, sisters and Forces.

Remarks: Girls' – predominantly weekly – boarding school without a sixth form or international pupils. Queen Mary's is a very jolly place, a home from home, with muddy wellies on the doorstep, smiling cheery girls and teachers; a predominance of four-wheeled drives in the car park and very dog-friendly.

It provides a good solid education focusing on creating girls with confidence, a 'have a go' mentality and freedom to grow into their own skin. Fierce competition locally, shows in numbers lower down the school. It's possibly too small for those at the sharp end – but many would thrive here and the girls say they 'wouldn't change a thing'.

Richmond House School

170 Otley Road, Far Headingley, Leeds LS16 5LG

Pupils: 208 • Ages: 3–11

Fees: £8,664 pa

Tel: 01132 752670
Email: enquiries@rhschool.org
Website: www.rhschool.org

Headmistress: Since September 2016, Helen Stiles MA (Cantab) PGCE, previously head of the humanities faculty and RS department at The Grammar School at Leeds.

Entrance: Maximum 30 children enter nursery each September. Nursery and reception classes are housed together in the foundation stage. Two classes of around 18 per year group from reception to year 6. Most children remain in the school from the age of 3, some additional places available later. The entry is not academically selective at the earliest stages. No scholarships available but bursaries are.

Exit: An important factor for many is that the school has a good reputation for supporting children into their next school at 11, plenty with scholarships. This is a wide and ever-changing field in this area with a good number of independent schools and excellent maintained schools available. Many parents have an eye to an expensive future at university and move mountains – or at least address – to creep into the catchment for some of the best state schools around. Independent school favourites are currently Bradford Grammar, Woodhouse Grove, Ashville College and The Grammar School at Leeds, but talk to the school and they will advise without bias and with your child in mind.

Remarks: Opened on present site in 1935, housed in three large Yorkshire stone Victorian villas, typical of the area. It lacks large indoor spaces and kerb appeal, but makes up for that in spades with its spacious and beautifully-maintained 10 acres of sports fields and excellent new car park tucked away to the rear of the buildings – take a look out back and suddenly the place feels very different, with a new adventure playground and a yurt. There's a very attractive sports pavilion and this has to be one of the very few schools with its own crown bowling green, surely a Yorkshire marketing niche? Proximity of Leeds Met University provides access to additional sporting facilities and student coaching expertise plus use of other local squash and badminton courts and swimming pools.

An assortment of Portakabins add little aesthetic appeal to the mix but provide extremely useful, possibly essential, additional space for DT, science and music. Nursery and reception classes are also similarly housed but they have been spruced up and provide delightful, spacious airy classrooms with adjacent play areas for the youngest children. Main buildings house core classrooms, all in good order and well-equipped with plenty of children's work in evidence. Feels small in places to those of us of adult size, lots of narrow stairways in a building that clearly wasn't designed to be a school, but happy smiling children tell us how much they love it and feel at home here. Main hall is multi-purpose – PE/assembly/orchestra. Maths and English streamed from year 5, children 'learning the same things but at a different speed'. Great art on display, much loved and slightly 'wacky' art teacher (say the children), other views are, of course, available. Staff work hard, described as 'driven', which, along with smallish classes, is one reason why the school gives other, more selective, schools a good run for their money.

Probably a broader church than it used to be, with increased focus and balance, but parents still demand (and get) high academic standards while recognising and valuing the care and support the school offers. It feels industrious and busy; success is valued and recognised through a variety of sticker and badge-wearing opportunities. Those with a special gift or ability are championed and the whole school celebrates different cultural and religious events. Sport and music are taken seriously and children compete across the board at a high level; this may be a small school but it aims high and is not afraid to challenge, punching above its weight both locally and nationally in competitions. Specialist teaching in a number of subject areas; French taught from reception, add to that Spanish in years 5 and 6, and you can try your hand at Mandarin and Arabic as club activities.

Parents like and appreciate clear feedback about progress and describe the regular reports home as 'especially motivating'. Reward schemes are part of a proactive approach to pastoral care; problems are dealt with promptly and effectively, say parents. 'Friendship stops', like miniature bus stops, feature prominently in the playground as a safety zone/stop-off point for children short of a friend – it was very gratifying to see children hovering timidly near them at playtime being quickly picked up and drawn into other children's games. Older children look after younger ones, plenty of cross-age friendships and everyone seems to know everyone, staff and children alike.

Food is cooked in-house, a good 'healthy' choice, everyone eats together. A recent request for mangetout proved a challenge, though: hard to keep it al dente when cooking in large quantities. A long lunch break sensibly allows plenty of time and opportunity for extracurricular activities, choir, orchestra, rock band and jazz choir flourishing; around 40 other options from judo to chess to gardening; pupils also form basis of school council and organise charity events.

Parents are medics, lawyers, financiers, business people, university staff. Those working in Leeds find both the location and the out-of-hours school care convenient. More working mothers here than is possibly the norm, though that may be a reflection of changing times. Parents choose the school for variety of reasons, the smaller size and approachability of staff is cited as key for many; you can take the high academic standards as read.

Ripon Grammar School

R

64

Clotherholme Road, Ripon, North Yorkshire HG4 2DG

Pupils: 860; 70 boarders, nearly all weekly • Ages: 11–18 • Sixth form: 289

Fees: Boarding £9,570– £10,575 pa. Day – free

Tel: 01765 602647
Email: admin@ripongrammar.co.uk
Website: www.ripongrammar.co.uk

Headmaster: Since 2004, Mr Martin Pearman (pronounced Pierman) MA (mid 50s). Read chemistry at Oxford, taught previously at Bristol GS, Merchiston Castle, Stamford and Woodhouse Grove, where he was deputy head. Three sons, all attended his school. Staff positive about their head and his method of gradual, thoughtful change. 'It's the atmosphere in this school which sets it apart', he told us. 'The quality of relationships between staff and students is better than in any school I've worked in'. Parents like that the head is very evident in school and approachable – some sixth form chemistry teaching.

A very approachable, unpretentious man, who brings a wide experience of schools and a clear vision of his school's purpose which is 'to serve the local community with a high quality education, increasing the life chances of ordinary boys and girls'. Believes passionately that 'pieces of paper are only part of what makes you' and that time at school is for learning to deal with failure as well as success.

Keen sportsman – cricket, five-a-side and half marathons. Inspired to run London Marathon for a charity that provides outdoor activities for people with disabilities, after a pupil broke her back in a cycling accident. Wife, Fiona, very involved with PTA.

Retiring in July 2017. His successor will be Jonathan Webb, currently deputy head at Durham School. History degree from Cambridge; has also taught at Pocklington School, The Manchester Grammar School and Giggleswick School. He and his wife Helen live near Ripon and they have two sons.

Academic matters: Exam results consistently very good – 70 per cent A*-B at A level in 2016, 36 per cent A*/A grades, with girls just outperforming boys, though boys pipped them with A* grades. STEM subjects unsurprisingly strong – roughly equal numbers of girls and boys take chemistry and mathematics, though physics remains a male stronghold with school working hard to change this.

Some 30 per cent take up of EPQ; good range of enrichment and community activities; pupil-led societies with weekly guest speakers. Well-drilled programme of support and encouragement for Oxbridge candidates. Strong careers and higher education advice with a week's work experience for all in year 12.

Elsewhere some evidence of girl-dominated subjects – for example in art (turning STEM to STEAM), English literature and French, compulsory at GCSE. Latin, classics, psychology, PE also available. German, though declining in many schools, still on offer, and Latin, originally started as a twilight subject, appearing by popular demand at GCSE and A level. Ancient Greek offered as an extracurricular subject at GCSE.

Sixty per cent A*/A at GCSE in 2016; mirroring national trend girls outperformed boys at these top grades and, better still, matched boys in mathematics. Engineering specialism has brought astronomy, statistics and product design into the GCSE curriculum. Complete lab refurbishment in recent years.

Only setting in mathematics and French from year 8. Cross-curricular themed challenge days, off-timetable, set for years 7, 8 and 9 provide opportunities for leadership, teamwork and problem-solving, working with external advisers. Lays the groundwork for later success as regional finalists in Young Enterprise and Prince's Trust competitions.

School does a very fine job over value-added; near the top of the tree nationally. RGS is not as highly selective as some grammar schools in, for instance, Kent and Essex, being unable to draw pupils in great numbers from outside its defined catchment area.

SEN support very good – oversees provision for, eg, visual and hearing impairment and a range of special needs. In addition learning resource manager works with SENCo on intervention strategies. Paired reading with sixth formers in assembly time set up for those identified by on-line literacy assessment.

Games, options, the arts: Compulsory sport: rugby and cricket mainstay for boys, hockey for girls. Football popular for both sexes – girls have been Yorkshire junior champions – also mixed hockey, badminton, rock climbing, dance and swimming in newly refurbished swimming pool. Good representation at area and regional level in range of sports, including national U14 netball finalists. Excellent facilities, new Astroturf and sports hall paid for by independent fundraising campaign, available for local use too. 3G pitch on the way.

Music block plus performing arts facility in the new sixth form centre. Lots of enthusiastic musicians – over 100 receive tuition in school. Big band performs frequently in Ripon Cathedral, even entertained the Queen. Vocalists encouraged to join one of the three choirs. Annual drama production and joint musical production on alternate years.

Superb art on display. Visiting artists augment strong teaching team, most recently famous comic strip illustrator.

Lots of out of the classroom experiences to be had. Duke of Edinburgh, biennial World Challenge, revived music tour in Belgium, Barcelona trip for Spanish speakers, art trips to London and Paris, as well as the more local curriculum enriching visits.

Over 90 different clubs and activities on offer, ranging from the Greenpower electric car, Pageturner bookclub to philosophy – something for even the most reluctant sportsman or woman to get involved in. Pupils encouraged to take the initiative to set up and run activities and clubs. Annual charity week is just one example, sixth form led it encompasses a diverse number of activities raising money for the school's chosen charities.

Boarding: Boys' boarding house, School, is integral and has had a makeover in recent years, met with considerable approval by boarders. Light and spacious rooms, beds not bunks, a relaxed and positive environment for down time and study. Bit of a maze but the character of the building endears itself to its occupants. Johnson, girls' boarding house, recently expanded, with single rooms for some sixth formers – long overdue, by some accounts.

This is a day school with boarding, predominantly weekly boarding; pupils come from North Yorkshire and beyond, a minority from India, Africa, Caribbean and China. Boarders (room for 100 out of 800+) do well academically and the very few in residence over the weekends are well catered for. Good relationships with day pupils extend into informal joint weekend activities and membership of local groups and clubs. Demand for boarding places (14 available a year) outstrips supply, especially post-GCSE, with lots of interest in girls' boarding.

Boarders have a personal tutor and are in mixed age tutor groups. As majority of boarding staff are teachers, 'boarders are very well known as individuals'. Slightly at odds, the head of boarding (also deputy head) does not sleep over, maybe losing an opportunity to feel the vibes from the girls in Johnson.

Background and atmosphere: Long pedigree; there's been a grammar school in Ripon since Anglo Saxon times. School originally housed in city centre and current foundation granted a royal charter by Queen Mary in 1555. Moved to present green and pleasant 23-acre site in 1874, gift from Marquess of Ripon. Original Victorian buildings added to over the years, not always sympathetically, but more recent additions: sports hall, sixth form centre, mathematics and engineering block, state-of-the-art music facilities, observatory and girls' boarding house bring more gravitas to the school façade. The most recent addition, a humanities and modern languages block, opened in 2014.

School has remained true to North Yorkshire LA and eschewed academy status.

There is an air of purposefulness in the school; a quiet hum from classrooms and sensible movement between lessons. High profile house system in the day school involves all pupils and offers leadership opportunities. Competition in sport, rock climbing, debating, Masterchef, University Challenge and house drama competition.

Pastoral care, well-being and discipline: Very good pastoral system in operation; in addition, pupils look after each other, 'very collegiate', as one parent put it. Sixth formers are trained as peer listeners and teams of form tutors ably support heads of school. Newcomers to sixth form are 'buddied' with existing pupils to ease integration.

School says pupils interact well and both poor behaviour and exclusions are rare. At worst, usually sorted by after school detention. Genuinely good relations between staff and students throughout the school; friendly and compassionate house staff create a relaxed boarding environment. Pupils and parents cannot speak highly enough of staff, their commitment and willingness to go 'above and beyond'.

Any bullying 'stamped on' and internet safety policy written by pupils, wired into PCSHE and teaching programmes.

Pupils and parents: Boarders from abroad, Yorkshire Dales and London, some from Forces, day pupils from Ripon and around. Wide range of parental backgrounds and wealth (or lack of it) though only a handful eligible for free school meals, with significant effect on pupil annual grant income. Parents feel well informed on their child's progress with regular reports three times a year and an annual parents' evening. School contact is primarily email and parents like that the termly newsletter and new sports magazine have content provided by the pupils. Very supportive PTA.

Pupils friendly, courteous, articulate and insightful; confident not arrogant, with a real pride in their school. Lots of heads up, eye contact and smiles as you walk around. This is a can do, will do school – pupils talk of friendly rivalry, pushing each to achieve. Strong protestations from both girls and boys on question of true equality: 'not an issue here'. On election of school officers, 'it's the best person for the job every time'.

Former pupils include fashion designer Bruce Oldfield, rugby international Peter Squires, William Hague MP, David Curry MP, Guardian editor Katharine Viner, TV presenter Richard Hammond.

Entrance: Mainly from local primaries but a smattering from prep schools, about 40 schools in total. Heavily oversubscribed at 11+. Selection by verbal and non-verbal reasoning tests administered by local authority; school takes top 28 per cent of cohort.

Sixth form – around 140 external applicants for approximately 30 places for students from other schools. Numbers applying increasing. Sixth form requires minimum six B grades at GCSE but vast majority comfortably exceed this, achieving mainly A*/A grades.

Exit: Around ten per cent leavers at 16+ a few more at end of year 12 (two per cent in 2016). At 18 most progress to university – over half to Russell Group or 1994 Group. Six to Oxbridge in 2016, similar number to study medicine. Science, engineering, art, law and economics also feature. Most popular university destination in 2016 was Durham. Others opt for Newcastle, Manchester, Edinburgh, Sheffield, Durham. A number lured to London, a few overseas. Excellent careers advice has meant leading apprenticeships for students considering alternatives to university.

Money matters: Yorkshire's only state boarding school, free for day pupils, charge for boarding, but still much cheaper than independent alternatives.

Remarks: High achieving without being highly pressurised, with learning and life skill opportunities going beyond exam syllabuses. Aims to provide a blend of tradition – academic rigour and high expectations – with innovation – up-to-date technology and opportunities for the development of the whole person – and does it well. Parents have utter confidence that whatever their child's talents the school will help them to make the best of them. Keen to serve its community and clearly valued by the people of Ripon.

Rossall School

Broadway, Fleetwood, Lancashire FY7 8JW

Pupils: 540; 270 full, 12 weekly board • Ages: 2–18 (boarders from 7) • Sixth form: 96 • C of E

Fees: Day £10,200 – £12,450; Boarding £16,500 – £35,550 pa

Tel: 01253 774201
Email: enquiries@rossall.org.uk
Website: www.rossallschool.org.uk

Head: Since 2013, Ms Elaine Purves BA PGCE (mid-40s). Brought up and state educated in Scotland and then in Nottinghamshire, Studied English and German at Hull University. On graduation she worked briefly for agricultural manufacturer John Deere in Germany before going to Durham to do her PGCE. She nearly returned to East Germany to teach English at Leipzig University, but after the Berlin Wall came down everything became uncertain and she ended up taking her first teaching post in the UK – at Oakham School in Rutland – and she has worked in the independent sector ever since. From Oakham she went to The Royal High School, progressing through the ranks from head of languages eventually to deputy head. After 13 years in Bath, in 2006 she became head of Ipswich High School for Girls, where she stayed for seven years before moving her whole family from Suffolk to Lancashire to take the job at Rossall.

One aspect of Rossall that attracted her was its international intake (50 per cent of pupils come from abroad, and that figure rises to 60-65 per cent by the sixth form). She says: 'Another reason why I wanted to come and work in a school like this was for my children. I wanted them to have that global perspective'. She and her husband have a son and a daughter who are both pupils at Rossall. She says 'they've really thrown themselves into it' here. Her husband was born in Preston, so the family did already have some ties to the north west. The excellent local golf facilities seem to have been a draw for him. And now they live in the head's house on site. She says it's a 'nice thing' to live on site and, although she acknowledges that she pretty much is on call 24-hours a day, she doesn't seem to mind in the slightest.

The first female head at Rossall, Ms Purves still likes to get into the classroom teaching languages and, although she comes across as approachable and softly spoken, we had no doubts that she could command both a class and a workforce. Parents say she's 'fantastic', 'hands-on' and 'approachable'. Several parents said how impressed they were with the way she listens both to parents and to pupils, and they also note approvingly that she turns up to every rugby match.

Head of juniors: Since September 2010, Mrs Katie Lee MA CPP Cert Ed. State educated in Sheffield, she then did teacher training at Lady Mabel College in South Yorkshire. Her original teaching specialism was PE, and she joined Rossall in 1992 as head of girls' games. She went on to spend 10 years as a housemistress in the senior school and to become senior teacher: pastoral. She was appointed head of the junior school in 2010. She has over 30 years' experience teaching students of all ages – from pre-school children right through to adult learners on pre-retirement courses. And she hasn't just taught the privileged; during the miners' strike she was at a state school in a small mining community where 'there'd be families of three, four or five children and one PE kit between them… As a community we looked after those children,' she says, with the air of one who has stories to tell.

Parents adore her. 'She was my own housemistress when I was here,' said one mum, beaming. Other parents describe Mrs Lee as 'a force of nature' and 'hands on'. She's practical, a problem-solver – and someone who shows her face. One parent told how the school changed parking procedures to ease congestion during morning drop-off – 'it was bound to be chaotic but, on the first morning, there she was with her umbrella, waiting for the barrage, ready to sort everyone out.' She gets stuck in for a good cause – she was seen dressed as Cat Woman recently and she's done the Ice Bucket Challenge. But much as she clearly excels at pastoral care, she is also focused on educational excellence. She's proud of how the children thrive following the PYP (the International Baccalaureate's Primary Years Programme) and she keeps a sharp focus on academic standards. When she's not busy holding the reins at Rossall or being a pillar of the local community (in which she has held various voluntary roles), Mrs Lee breeds weimaraner dogs. (This is a doggy school. We met several pooches on campus during our visit.)

Academic matters: The junior school is academically strong and pupils' attainment is high. Classes are small; 20 is an absolute maximum but most are much smaller than this. (There are just 11 in this year's reception.) Everyone in the juniors – even the youngest pre-schoolers – follows the International Baccalaureate's Primary Years Programme (known as the PYP). Some literacy and maths skills are taught separately but everything else is learned through hands-on, pupil-led projects. They study six projects a year, two per term, and at the start of each project the pupils decide what they want to find out and how they will do it. They're encouraged to follow their own interests and respond to their natural curiosity – doing their own research and working at their own rate and level. The PYP encourages pupils to work independently but also to develop strong teamwork and communication skills. Children are bursting with enthusiasm for the PYP: they remember past projects clearly and are proud of their achievements. And they talk enthusiastically about reading, learning the violin, using the IT suite to create PowerPoint presentations… and they give every impression that they love to learn. Parents say they're happy with their children's academic progress too. One mum said of her daughter: 'She doesn't love sport and she's not the best at it but – I don't know what happens – they've brought something out of her. They're giving her confidence and I'm really pleased about that.'

Junior pupils with SEN are supported at no extra cost to parents. Teachers say that the flexibility of the PYP lets them set differentiated work so that the lower ability pupils keep learning at their own rate alongside high achievers with the freedom 'to fly'. Children are assessed at the end of each year and at the end of each PYP unit (ie each project) so their progress is tracked from their entry to the school or nursery right up to year 6. But the focus is on real learning rather than targets. One teacher told us, 'I think it's very sad when children say things like "I'm a level 5"'. There's a fresh approach to learning here – very few schools offer the PYP – and the willingness to do things differently is reflected also in the decision to teach Mandarin to junior pupils instead of a European language.

Rossall provides an all-round education – aiming to meet the needs of every pupil within its broad intake. Usually 18-20 in years 7-11 (an absolute maximum of 22) and a maximum of 18 in the sixth form. The head identifies maths, the sciences, English, technology and art as departments that are doing particularly well. Food studies, Mandarin and drama recently added to curriculum. Parents we met were very happy with their children's attainment. One mother told us how impressed she'd been that the school offered to take her bilingual children, raised until recently in France, out of mainstream French lessons to teach them separately so that they could continue to study French as a first language. But there's a comprehensive and inclusive ethos here. Parents felt that the school was about much more than academia and that it doesn't focus resources and attention on high flyers at the expense of those in the middle or who are struggling. 'They don't single out the star pupils,' said one parent. 'They give praise subtly and they don't make a big song and dance of it.' 'Mine are never made to feel inferior,' said another mum. 'They do their best and they get praise for that.' There's no streaming but there is setting in some subjects. Parents said that sets were constantly under review and so 'you're not stuck in your set'.

Results reflect the broad intake. In 2016, 37 per cent of GCSEs entered were awarded A*-A and at A level that figure was 44 per cent. Roughly a third of sixth formers choose to do the International Baccalaureate rather than A levels and in 2016 they achieved an average of 31 IB points per pupil. The school languishes in the bottom quartile of the independent schools league tables but, unlike the high-flyers in the league tables, Rossall is not a selective school. It's also one of the most international schools in the UK, meaning that a large proportion of the children sitting those GCSE, A level and IB exams (about 60 per cent of them) don't have English as a first language.

International students can enter the main school if their English is already close to fluent. Those whose level of English would hold them back from achieving their potential academically are placed in the International Study Centre. This isn't as separate as it sounds; it's really a stream within the main school where pupils receive intensive English language support. Some pupils only stay in the ISC for a term or two, others stay for a year or more and some complete an intensive one-year IGCSE course there to prepare them for entering the sixth form in the main school.

The school supports pupils with a range of special educational needs. A full-time SEN support teacher has recently joined the school. There may be an additional charge to parents of children with SEN if a very high level of support is required.

Games, options, the arts: This is a very sporty school. Ian Botham sent his son, Liam, here and many alumni have gone on to play rugby, hockey or cricket professionally. More than a dozen pupils – male and female – currently play hockey for Lancashire. And there are countless sports options beyond the more obvious team games: pupils can also play basketball, squash or badminton, or lift weights, climb, dance or shoot. As you'd expect, there is an extensive range of top quality pitches, playing fields, squash courts and the like on campus; almost all sports offered have on-site facilities apart from horse-riding, ice-skating and golf. The 25-metre indoor swimming pool looked particularly inviting – although we didn't jump in – and we weren't surprised to see a large bank of seats on the poolside for crowds of supportive pupils to cheer on their peers. Sport is a unifying force at Rossall: one day the children might be competing fiercely in one of the many inter-house tournaments and the next day they'd be whooping with pride when another pupil scores a winning goal or try against a rival school. Rossall sport is steeped in tradition; 'Ross-Hockey' is a unique game – a hockey-rugby hybrid played only on the beach next to the school; and the school regularly competes in rugby fives tournaments at prestigious public schools as well as hosting its own national 'Rossall Fives' tournament each October.

One pupil we spoke to hinted, diplomatically, that the school could maybe invest a little more in girls' sport – particularly hockey. A couple of mums agreed. One said that the school hadn't traditionally pushed girls' hockey as much as the boys' game, but that she felt things are now improving and that the school has been responsive to criticism. But another mum said there was still some underinvestment in the girls' game. She said that her daughter recently went to training, only four girls turned up and there was no coach. 'It's demoralising,' she said, 'because the ones that do want to play are a bit ignored... and I can see my daughter's face – you know: "Why am I here marking four players on my own?"'

Beyond sport the extracurricular opportunities are seemingly endless – with a particularly wide range of opportunities for arty and musical children and for outdoorsy types. Some more unusual examples include stage set design, costume making, film making, cryptography, psychology, jazz band, knitting, Warhammer and astrophysics (the school boasts a space science centre – complete with a planetarium, Victorian observatory and a telescope – and a resident astronomer). And this is just the tip of the iceberg. Many students are working towards their Duke of Edinburgh Award and pupils from year 9 and above can join the CCF.

Rossall has a diverse tradition in the arts. Choral music is strong here – closely bound in with the life of the historic chapel – but students play different types of music in various performances and concerts throughout the year; and they can learn instruments at school with visiting tutors – for an extra fee. There is also a literary society, which meets regularly to discuss poetry, books and culture. The school puts on two plays a year in one of two well-equipped performance spaces. The drama department also has links with a local theatre school and casting agency, which has enabled some pupils to appear in national radio and television productions. Keen artists are allowed to use the well-stocked workshops and studios every day after school. Each year in the Lent term Rossall devotes a week solely to art, music and drama and parents told us that even the highest performing sports players would never be discouraged to getting involved in the school play or any other creative endeavour.

PE is taken seriously in the juniors too. It starts in the nursery and specialists teach all PE lessons. There is a wide range of popular after-school clubs. Infants are not encouraged to stay late every day as they get tired, although full wraparound care is available, but many juniors choose to stay for extra activities and support with their homework most evenings. The academic day finishes at 4pm for the juniors (as opposed to 3.15pm for the infants) and then from 4-5pm there are clubs (usually three choices per evening) and, says Mrs Lee, 'the children won't go home!' There are science, chess and reading groups; various art, theatre and music activities and a very wide range of sporty clubs including, as well as clubs for most mainstream school sports, Danish Longball Club, 'Urban Workout' and Judo. Many pupils take LAMDA exams in speech and drama and a lot of children are learning a variety of musical instruments, including clarinet, violin, drums, piano and flute. New kitchen for food technology lessons and the Rossall Bake Off where dozens compete for the title of star baker.

Boarding: Pupils can board just five days a week or at weekends too. If day pupils want to flexi-board – which they often do – then they always stay in spare beds within their own house. Flexi-boarding allows day pupils to stay at the school for a night or longer – for pretty much any reason. Parents love it because it gives them a night off (or a weekend in Paris...) but, more importantly, the kids can't get enough of it. They typically flexi-board on a Friday night if they have to be at school early the next morning for a match or on a Saturday night if they want to tag along on the boarding house's Sunday outing.

Although there are no classes on a Saturday, it tends to be a busy day with sports practices and fixtures. Every Sunday boarders can, at no extra cost, go on an outing – examples include bowling or crazy golf activities or trips to Alton Towers or the Manchester Christmas markets. Just over 42 per cent of boarders are international and these will be met at and delivered back to Manchester Airport by a representative of the school at the start and end of term. They don't have an option to stay in school during the holidays, though. If they can't fly home then they'll need to have a UK guardian to look after them.

The boarding houses, including the junior house for 7-13 year olds, are very homely – softer and more cosy than a typical university hall of residence. The boarding houses are a home from home where any pupil can come to relax and socialise during lunchtimes – and consequently there's lots of scope for different age-groups and both local and international pupils to mix. There are some single rooms available and a few are en-suite, but the majority of boarders share with one or two other pupils and share a bathroom on the corridor. Each pupil has a desk in their room and the freedom to put up pictures and customise their living space. Each house has a pair of live-in houseparents – who are either teachers or support staff. The houseparents we met were warm and affectionate – they seemed to love the job and that was reflected in the way the children spoke about them: 'yeah, they're very supportive,' said one sixth former and another added 'they look out for you and you can talk to them about anything'.

Background and atmosphere: An aerial photo in the school's prospectus shows the campus green, soft red and light blue. It is expansive and grassy; the buildings red-brick, grand and turreted; and beyond them stretches a thin strip of pale yellow beach before the misty sea. Even on a grey, murky day the space is picturesque and peaceful. 'Yes, it's a bubble,' one mum said to us, 'but it's a lovely bubble to be in.' This is one of the happiest schools that this reviewer has visited: pupils raved – with no hint of cynicism – about their friends and teachers, the school's traditions and jolly japes in the boarding houses.

The junior school buildings are close to those of the senior school – they're part of a grand, red-brick campus overlooking the sandy coastline. Juniors are in a separate block from the nursery and infants. There's no shortage of technology but the juniors are mainly taught in cosy classrooms in period buildings. There's a strong family feel to the school and this extends to the classroom – because of the small class sizes and the way that the PYP curriculum encourages so much group work, pupils have strong relationships with each other and with their class teachers. Juniors have access to the top quality facilities of the seniors. Beyond the usual extensive sports facilities you'd expect, including new multi-use games area, there is also a 25-metre indoor swimming pool, a nature conservation area, a theatre and a space science and astronomy centre. Children in the nursery have a lovely little garden, including their own woodland area where forest school sessions are held, and a much-loved pet bunny. The grand, historic chapel – which wouldn't look out of place in an Oxbridge quad – is also a significant part of school life, even for the youngest of pupils. It's an Anglican chapel, with a full-time chaplain – but the school population is so mixed, with many international students, that the chaplaincy aims to meet the needs of pupils of all faiths and of none.

The fact that it's a boarding school – and a very international one – is integral to Rossall life. The house system connects boarders with day pupils: all day pupils are assigned to a boarding house and from year 9 onwards they meet there, in cosy common rooms, each morning for registration. Even if they're not staying for a sleepover, this is a school where older pupils in particular just don't want to go home. They can stay late for prep (with teachers on hand to help) and have their tea at school. There's even a licensed bar and café on site, open to sixth formers three nights a week. One dad told us how pleased he was that when his nearly 17-year-old son stays out late, he doesn't need to wonder where he is or what he's up to because he knows he's safe and happy with his friends at school.

Tradition is very big here. Every year during Christmas dinner in the imposing, oak-panelled dining hall, the pupils sing The Twelve Days of Christmas – each house taking a different verse. No-one tells them to do it, the pupils explain, 'it just sort of happens, spontaneously'. It gets quite competitive – each house singing more boisterously than the last. One pupil told me this tradition summed up what's special about Rossall. Might some prospective parents baulk at the hearty traditions, the special public-schooly Rossall sports, the sense that this could be the setting for an undiscovered Enid Blyton saga? Certainly we found no hint of social snobbery – we simply saw young people having a deliciously happy time at school. If grand old traditions make you cringe then Rossall may not be the perfect fit for you as a parent – when it comes to the pupils, though, the school is so warm and good-humoured, and there is such opportunity and encouragement to become the person you want to be, that we felt even if your teenager is something of a non-conformist he or she would still stand a good chance of finding a niche here.

Pastoral care, well-being and discipline: Several parents identified the quality of pastoral care as the single thing they most appreciated about Rossall. They raved about how well their children are known by staff. One dad was full of praise for a teacher who stayed in regular contact with him, by text, to keep him updated on a particularly protracted UCAS application process. 'Teachers always remember what's going on with your child,' said another parent. 'It's just great that there's always that concern... and so I don't worry about my children here at all because I know the staff are really looking out for them.'

The pupils all eat together. Infants sit in their houses – in a mixed age group – and they're served 'like a family' at the table. In the junior school they eat in the senior dining hall and they select their food at the servery. They still sit with teachers who will keep an eye on them to make sure they're actually eating. The staff at the servery let juniors try anything they fancy before committing to having a plateful of it – reducing the risk of children having a hungry afternoon after they didn't like their lunch. Senior pupils enjoy spicy food but there are always plain, sauce-free, traditional options geared towards the tastes of younger children. (Our reviewer found the food to be first class.)

Religion is significant in school life: there's a full-time Church of England school chaplain and the whole school attends chapel every Friday. But, particularly with the diverse, international intake, the school takes care to ensure that worship is inclusive and that other faiths get a look in too.

Pastoral care in the juniors is largely provided by class teachers, with whom pupils are closely bonded. Bullying is dealt with in the first instance by the class teacher and everything is recorded in weekly welfare meetings. All such incidents are communicated to the senior team, including Mrs Lee. Perpetrators can expect a caution initially and potentially a detention with the head. Parents – both of bullies and victims – are always brought in to discuss any serious incident. But bullying and serious disciplinary problems more generally are rare. So, although firm structures and policies are in place, you get the sense that they're very seldom brought into force.

Discipline is firm here in the senior school. Serious breaches of the rules would be dealt with case-by-case but expulsion is a possibility. If you're caught smoking three times, you're out. (Although pupils told us that some of the German boarders are stalwart smokers so, presumably, they're good at not getting caught.) Pupils couldn't think of any instances of bullying in their experience and they spoke with real conviction about how caring an environment this is. They said that pupils wouldn't tolerate bullying – that they would tell a teacher and offer support to the victim. Parents knew of no bullying either. Like most schools, Rossall has a stringent anti-bullying policy. We were impressed that parents told us that they knew of several pupils at the school who had come out as gay – with minimal fuss or drama and complete acceptance from their peers. Parents felt the school was very accepting of difference – perhaps also because of the diversity that the international students bring to the community.

Pupils and parents: The parents are a mixed bunch. A good few are alumni of Rossall but many others were state educated. Some get help with fees from grandparents or from the school's own means-tested bursary scheme. The kids are also diverse. Across the school, 50 per cent are international – coming from a very wide spread of countries and cultures. Further up the school, more than 60 per cent are international. But there are far more British children than those of any other single nationality. The pupils seem inclusive and grounded. And they were positive and polite.

Alumni include Booker-Prize-winning novelist JG Farrell; Father Thomas RD Byles, the Catholic priest who refused to leave the Titanic so that he could help other passengers; eminent figures in the world of sport, music and industry; and a few bastions of the Establishment: a governor of a couple of colonies; a private secretary to Queen Victoria; and the magnificently-named Sir Walton Clopton Wingfield, who patented the game of lawn tennis.

Entrance: There's no formal selection to get into Rossall Juniors. The school will take any child whose needs it can support. To assess this, children go to a taster day and parents come in for a chat, but it's extremely rare for the school to tell parents they can't support their child's needs. The school is not hugely oversubscribed, so almost certainly if you can pay, you're in. The nursery takes children from the age of 2.

There are entrance tests in English, maths and non-verbal reasoning for the senior school but it is rare to say no to a prospective pupil: this would normally only be done if the school couldn't meet his/her needs.

For international students, the admissions procedure is largely a question of assessing their English. The school has a Skype conversation with every student before a place is offered. They must have at least some English: if they can't hold a Skype conversation they can't come here. If their English is already good enough that it won't hold them back academically then they can go straight into the main school. If not, then they may need to first of all come to the International Study Centre (see above in Academic for more information.)

All pupils need to achieve five GCSEs at grade A* to C to enter the sixth form. If they don't they can either repeat the year or leave.

Exit: Almost all juniors progress to the senior school unless they have a particular reason to leave such as family relocation (last year 100 per cent transferred). Junior pupils have a passport to the seniors. Everyone sits the senior school entrance exam but, for children already here in the juniors, it's just used as a baseline assessment and to assess for scholarship, rather than to determine who transfers.Some 35 per cent leave after GCSEs. Most sixth form pupils go on to UK universities with about 10 per cent going to university abroad. Economics and business studies are particularly popular courses but there's a real spread across arts, sciences and humanities. Popular universities are Edinburgh, Lancaster, Manchester, Leeds, London and York; one to Oxbridge in 2016.

Money matters: The school has been in very good financial health for a number of years – the influx of international students has really turned its fortunes around. About six per cent of pupils in the senior school receive significant means-tested bursaries (a 50 per cent reduction of fees or more). There are also some scholarships available for high performers in sport, music, drama or academia.

Remarks: This is a very happy school. Its population is so diverse, there's no one type of child who would fit in better than another. But we did feel the school would particularly appeal to busy parents who perhaps don't have a lot of support locally or who find domestic life to be somewhat relentless – because the school offers a round-the-clock home-from-home programme of activities which could ease the pressure on families at times of stress. It's no academic pressure-cooker and less able pupils will be praised for their efforts just as much as the high flyers but there are excellent teachers, facilities and opportunities that should give the brightest pupils every chance to excel. Overall, Rossall is a warm, inclusive and remarkably happy place to be. Staff and pupils seem to genuinely love it here – and there's not much higher praise you can offer than that.

Royal Grammar School (Newcastle)

Eskdale Terrace, Newcastle upon Tyne NE2 4DX

Pupils: 1,322 • Ages: 7–18 • Sixth form: 349

Fees: £10,251 – £12,168 pa

Tel: 01912 815711
Email: admissions@rgs.newcastle.sch.uk
Website: www.rgs.newcastle.sch.uk

Headmaster: Since 2008, Dr Bernard Trafford MA PhD (50s); former chair of HMC; previously head of Wolverhampton Grammar School. Married to Katherine, two adult daughters. Educated at Downside and St Edmund Hall, Oxford, he is a warm, hugely affable and highly capable man. The ultimate time-shifter and a great role model for all, fitting more into a busy today than many of us manage in a week. Music plays a large part in his life (see his own website for details of his jazz band and compositions); he also writes for various publications, including a weekly comment column in The Journal, where his wise words, immense knowledge and wry humour are valued and enjoyed by readers locally. Famed for his democratic management style, his office is a glass box within the admin section; he's right there in and amongst it all. Somewhat offended by the claim that pupils here 'are all confident, loud, debate and play rugby' – not so, plenty of quiet souls here who also 'find their niche'. 'More, much more, than an exam factory,' says the head, admitting 'working against the zeitgeist by resisting a pre-packaged approach to learning and ensuring that his staff and students go far beyond simply fulfilling exam requirements'.

Retiring in July 2017. His successor will be John Fern, currently deputy head and IB coordinator at King Edward's School, Birmingham. He has also been IB coordinator at Fettes and head of history at Oakham.

Junior school head: Since 1999, Mr Roland Craig BEd (Leeds), youthful, energetic early 60s, formerly at King's Tynemouth where he enjoyed a 'meteoric rise' from teacher to deputy head. Member of the (inappropriately named) Cross Association of representatives from independent schools; also founding chair of the charity Dyslexia North East.

Married with two children, both at RGS, he manages (enjoys even) a very long daily commute from the Cheviot Hills. A

R

charming man who clearly enjoys his job, has an innate understanding of children, loves his sport and finds time out of school for bird-watching, wildlife photography and the odd barn conversion. At the helm of the key senior school feeder, he is 'charged to uphold academic standards' and does so by being highly selective on intake; fewer than half the applicants are offered places each year. He and his team are warm and welcoming and the assessment, though tough, is dealt with fairly and sensitively, in accordance with the ages of the children.

Academic matters: The junior school head and his two deputies are ably assisted by a enthusiastic staff, with specialist senior school staff visiting to teach Spanish, French and music. Classes are around 20 or fewer, working towards 50/50 but slightly boy-heavy in some year groups. Classrooms are bright, modern and very attractive, tables for the younger ones, desks for the older pupils; there's a small hall for drama and music, a larger hall for assemblies, science lab, teaching kitchen, IT suite, library and soft play areas outside. Check out the green screen room – a first for us.

'No cynical old soaks chalking off the days to retirement,' say senior school parents, adding that 'the quality of the teaching staff is outstanding, not just in their subject knowledge and teaching but also their external connections and interests'. No surprise therefore that results are impressive across the board, and consistently so. At A level 62 per cent A*/A in 2016, confirming RGS as one of the leading schools in the country (as measured by academic success). At GCSE, 81 per cent A*/A. Ten subjects the norm at GCSE, though many also take additional maths GCSE; all take three sciences. You don't have to be a medic to come here but.. nearly 40 per cent of their parents are medics (or dentists), and large numbers of offspring follow in their parents' footsteps. Far from a given, though, economics, history and politics also popular and plenty of arts subjects in evidence; superb modern languages suite – French, Spanish, German and Mandarin Chinese all on offer. Add to that classics, design technology and psychology to create a good broad curriculum with more than a few added extras and no obvious weak points. Classes a little on the large side for some parents (25) compared to smaller independent schools in the area, but perhaps that reflects demand – or perhaps the lack of it elsewhere.

Games, options, the arts: Certainly not all work and no play here. Choir, orchestra and bags of sport in the junior school; the girls are north of England hockey champions and the boys field a number of tournament-winning winning football and rugby teams. Records are broken annually at the traditional summer sports day and having a pool on site means that they usually trounce the competition at swimming galas. Chess, drama productions, musical performances, river-dipping, sleepovers, ski trips and jaunts into the Lake District and beyond are all part of school life. Head writes a weekly newsletter to parents, so plenty of useful and interesting information about school life and events available just in case your offspring is less than forthcoming in the 'What did you do at school today?' department. Bags of extracurricular activities and extended school day on offer for busy parents, 7.45am to 6.00pm if you want or need it.

The annual senior sports review boasts a huge number of triumphs with honours at county and national levels. Athletics, climbing, cricket (in which a number of star spin bowlers bamboozled opposing batsmen), fencing, football, gymnastics, hockey, netball, rounders, rugby, running, squash, swimming, water polo and tennis all feature. Plenty of championship competitions, tournaments and galas to add to match fixtures, the sport here is played with a fierce enthusiasm by both boys and girls. Unusual in a school to find both rugby and football so popular and well-supported, but then this is Tyneside..rugby exceptionally strong, beaten by only a handful of other schools ('Sedbergh train running up and down mountains so what can we do?') and regular trips abroad – eg South Africa tour. Probably worth a mention is the female director of sport, ably supported by a vast array of sports teachers (yes, that includes a male head of rugby) and specialist coaches. Superb new sports hall, aerobics room and fitness suite and pool plus all-weather pitch. School buildings are formed around the main rugby pitch, additional outfields rented nearby, much use made of local facilities for minority and individual sports. Fifty-year lease on magnificent Newcastle County Cricket Ground, five minutes' walk from school.

High quality art, of all disciplines, is in evidence around the school, students work with local artists and gallery curators and exhibit their own work in local galleries and at the annual Art Private View for proud parents.

Music does very well, not unexpectedly – £10 million development includes performing arts centre with 300-seat auditorium, recording studio, recital room, drama/dance studio, 10 rehearsal rooms and percussion studio. Masses of orchestras, bands and ensembles.

World Challenge 2014 took two teams of year 10 pupils to charity projects in Ghana. Lots of hard work and challenge, on a number of levels, and it's popular with most, though not all. Some parents find the high financial cost of such long-haul trips prohibitive. Huge variety of clubs – chess meets three times a week and bridge is popular. Outstanding debating – regular prize-winners. Technology club equally successful. CCF for both boys and girls as well as involvement with local community – the inner city partnership, where pupils work with deprived children on a one-to-one basis. Strong charity commitment. D of E flourishing.

Background and atmosphere: Situated in leafy Jesmond, where the great and good of Newcastle live – or aspire to live. Designer clothes and arty coffee shops nearby; the school sits shoulder to shoulder with Newcastle High School for Girls, which may have felt a little too close for comfort when RGS went co-ed back in in 2006. You 'pays your money and you makes your choice' as they say, and increasingly there's clear blue water academically between the two. Girls now make up just over 40 per cent of the cohort and the belief from the top in co-ed is strong, with the school working towards a 50:50 split.

It is crammed into an urban site, yet wraps itself around sports fields so you can see green space from most windows. Junior school is self-contained and purpose-built, with a three form entry. A huge array of silverware – cups and shields galore – displayed in the corridor, so many they have run out of space: clearly big on competition – in everything. They share a dining room with the senior pupils but have their own earlier slot; all food cooked in-house, packed lunches allowed if need be.

The main building has all the solidity of time and history that you would expect from a foundation dating back more than 450 years, and thankfully RGS in particular appears somewhat recession-proof. In fact, put simply, 'premium products don't suffer,' says the head. No arrogance here, merely a straightforward truism. Impressive modern buildings juxtaposed with the Queen Anne frontage, it all works magnificently. Much-loved old hall with war memorial, wood-panelling and pipe organ – a gloriously handsome space right at the heart of the school. Lecture theatre, library, superb performing arts centre, language suite and multiple science labs are more modern additions; no apparent shortage of space and school makes the very best of all that it has. Modern, bright airy, almost corporate, feel to reception, where a warm welcome awaits. Don't try to park nearby, or if you do, allow plenty of extra time and spare cash for parking meters. Far better to use the metro stop less than 100 metres from the front door. Compared to the south, quality of life is very affordable here so the school attracts Geordies wanting to come home or others who stumbled across it whilst attending uni locally.

Sixth formers ('business wear' rather than uniform) abound, assured, confident, articulate beings who wouldn't look out of place in the foyer of Goldman Sachs. The boys fare slightly better with the sixth form dress code than the girls, who tend to interpret the code more loosely, smart suits giving boys the edge. Interesting that staff are more comfortable telling boys to tuck their shirts in than asking a girl to reconsider the length of her skirt – a hangover from the all-boys' era perhaps? For the rest of the school it's a trad uniform that works well all round.

Pastoral care, well-being and discipline: Parents tell us they 'are always welcome to talk to teachers or the head about any issues concerning their child'. Pupils are allocated a personal tutor who stays with them throughout and manages the changing needs of pupils as they grow and develop. Good ethnic mix, plenty of tolerance and respect supported by a vigorous anti-bullying policy. Out for violence and drugs. Smoking not tolerated and no particular problems with drinking or smoking off-site, but staff remain vigilant.

Pupils and parents: Happy, smiling junior school children who are challenged academically and on the sports field, yet thankfully without having the child within knocked out of them. They probably worry less about the transition into senior school than most at the age of 11, simply because they've grown up with it all around them, plenty of familiar faces and facilities.

Senior school parents tell us they have 'learned to value and trust the teachers and their process..in a culture that promotes achievement – starting with the ambition level of the children (and their parents) and is then nurtured by the teachers'. They and their offspring feel supported within the structure, it's proven, it works, they like it and they also reckon it's good value for money too. Huge number of medics and academics from nearby hospitals and university. Plenty of parent participation in the governing body and other parent run bodies, in both the junior and senior schools. All welcome, though no assumption of participation: constraints of time and distance and many here are extremely busy professionals who attend informal events as and when they can: 'we turn up when invited, work our way through the bacon sandwiches, and put a tenner in the collection box'.

Pupils have a real self-belief – 'it won't go wrong' so it doesn't. That said, they work very hard, it's in their bones; 'clever kids who fit a quart into a pint pot,' say staff, 'not hard-nosed but huge aspiration, future leaders abound here'; it's assumed that 100 per cent will go on to university. Good old-fashioned courtesy from most, and staff pick them up if they forget; it's very civilised.

Entrance: Assessment days held in mid January for prospective year 3 and in November for year 5 entrants. It's a whole day procedure, including assembly with the head, followed by testing in maths (including mental arithmetic) and English – spelling, comprehension and creative writing. The day usually ends with an iPad session to check out creativity. There are rumours that pupils are assessed on table manners over lunch but school insists that's not true..Don't over-prepare or hothouse for a place; essentially junior school wants to know 'are they children who will roll up their sleeves and get on with it?' It's a testament to how well it is managed when the children are 'buzzing' at the end of it all – much to the relief of anxious parents.

Tough and competitive senior entry via the school's own entrance exam at 11. About 75 from the junior school, as long as their work is up to scratch. Very healthy entry post-GCSE, far outweighing 16+ leavers – minimum six GCSEs at A*/B required plus report from former school. Entry from over 80 different schools throughout North East.

Exit: Vast majority of juniors move up to the senior school. A dozen or so to Oxbridge as a rule – and indeed 12 in 2016; otherwise to Edinburgh, Bristol, Leeds, Newcastle, Durham, Manchester, Nottingham and London, St Andrew's, mainly to read hard traditional subjects; 19 medics in 2016. Small coterie to art or music colleges, though the latter are more likely to read music at university and then go on to conservatoires, but one to patisserie school in 2016.

Money matters: Much praise from parents for the school's commitment to the bursary scheme; school keen not to be seen as socially divisive. Around 80 pupils helped financially, more than 50 of them at a level of 90 per cent of fees or above. All bursaries means-tested; some sixth form subject-specific awards such as Ogden Trust Bursaries for Physics and Reece Foundation Scholarships for budding engineers.

Remarks: Apparently there is 'aspiration in the water here' or so we are told. Long-standing habits of excellence across the board mean that RGS has long been, and probably always will be, seriously over-subscribed, 'there's comfort in its history,' say parents. The heavy glossy magazine that is the annual review at RGS goes bold this year – En Pointe! – complete with ballet dancers in tutus: a shocker of a headline to those who think this is still an all boys' establishment. Behind it you cannot help but sense a wry, smiling, 'go on, we dare you' attitude that can only come from an establishment that is comfortable in its own skin, happy to take on the world whilst cocking a snook at those who dare to challenge its soul or integrity. Admittedly you don't have to venture far into the magazine to find a rugby player, but that's fair enough..

Ryedale School

Gale Lane, Nawton, York, North Yorkshire YO62 7SL

Pupils: 608 • Ages: 11–16

Tel: 01439 771665
Email: info@ryedale.n-yorks.sch.uk
Website: www.ryedaleschool.org

Headteacher: Since 2014, Mark McCandless, previously deputy and acting head. Educated in NW Ireland and at Leeds Met university, then became a PE teacher. Married with two young daughters; the family has a smallholding where they keep rare breeds of poultry and domestic animals.

Academic matters: High in ranking of North Yorkshire state schools – 65 per cent 5+ A*-C including English and maths at GCSE in 2016; 28 per cent A*/A grades. Specialisms in performing arts and science with maths, leading edge status. Mainly academic subjects at key stage 4 – options include Latin (will run it for three students), particularly successful separate sciences, German (big numbers), art and design, dance, drama, music, PE. Good range of vocational BTecs.

Established partnerships with other local schools for sixth form – now developing own with Malton School: offers history, English lit, theatre studies, music, music technology. Started with 35 students, who attend two days a week – likely to grow; purpose-built common-room attractively decorated and furnished.

Thorough-going tracking and monitoring, stable staff who know pupils very well and set high expectations; developing use

R

of ICT in teaching and learning, eg VLE. Average class size 21 but we saw quite a few smaller ones; high quality, attractive displays in all classrooms. Setting for academic subjects from start of year 7 (flexible approach, smaller groups for lower ability), mixed ability for practical subjects. Very good and improving key stage 3 attainment; year 8s do dance, drama, music, art and food tech (boys too – modern man in the making); ICT GCSE in year 9. We saw lots of well-behaved, focused pupils and lively, pacy teaching; intelligent arguing and independent learning encouraged – pupils feel their views are sought and listened to with respect. Gifted and talented students identified and monitored; senior management team mentor low achieving year 11s, teaching assistants do lower school.

Excellent, warm, very thoughtful SENCo greatly valued by parents ('amazingly wonderful'). Covers broad spectrum of needs – strong on dyslexia awareness and support. Works with external agencies, trains other teachers, who can access subject specialist advice through school's Moodle online learning management system – other schools please emulate. Year 7s with low literacy and numeracy levels supported individually and with paired reading – year 10 and 11 'buddies' do some and mentor them in other ways. Well resourced – 11 teaching assistants and The Cottage, base for more intensive support, providing a refuge for children who find the breaks difficult.

Games, options, the arts: Great range of sports – all the usual ones plus ultimate frisbee and indoor rowing – and sports leadership qual. Smallish sports hall also used for assemblies, good-size fitness suite, netball/tennis courts, several playing fields (Astro on pupils' wish list) and year 11s use Ampleforth College facilities for two hours a week. Impressive success for its size at district, county and national level in various games – some international sportspeople.

Well-resourced performing arts building with drama/dance studio – high standard performances involving large numbers of pupils, eg Guys and Dolls, Dracula, Shakespeare Schools Festival Playhouse; links with Helmsley Arts Centre. High percentage A*/A in drama and music GCSE.

Huge music room with lots of computers, recording studio – various singing and instrumental groups (a quarter of school learn an instrument – very good exam results, singing too), girls' chamber choir, jazz band, rock groups, a few pupils in National Youth Choir/ Orchestra, one in Rotary Young Musician of the Year North of England final, music tour to Paris, visiting choirs from Uganda and New Zealand.

Splendid art room and excellent art much in evidence throughout the school, brightening up what would otherwise be rather drab corridors. Well-equipped DT and (bright green) food tech rooms – has produced a Rotary Club young chef of the year.

Over 80 clubs per week – arts award, chess, Latin, Italian, D of E popular; end of summer term enrichment activities, eg history trip to Berlin, outdoor activities in France; ongoing trip to Camp Kenya. The less academic may do a day a week work experience, rest of key stage 4 have career days.

Background and atmosphere: Built in 1953 in rural location half an hour away from Malton in North Yorkshire – soothing views of fields and trees. Used to have own railway stop till Beecham got busy with his axe – hence all the clubs, as all stay on site during the lunch hour (so no town-school-type mischief). Pleasant, unfussy architecture – yellow brickwork with blue and white paintwork and sloping roofs, much less bleak than some of the '60s concrete we have seen. Very well stocked and laid out library – lots of enticing fiction, modern and classics, good selection of books on art and music, plus factual books geared towards the interests of reluctant boy readers. Light cafeteria with bright orange chairs – fish fingers and chips as well as virtuous choices (has healthy school status), a lively buzz that never felt unruly.

A mixture of the traditional – school motto is the rather Edwardian sounding 'aspire and achieve', prefects, ties groaning with badges for positions and achievements – and what head calls 'cutting edge', eg use of latest technology (science refurbishment planned) and teaching and learning research. House system central – lots of competitions organised by students.

General consensus that school is very friendly, pupils and teachers, with a strong community spirit, closely related to its small size. Active school council that feels its views are regarded – head boy and girl plus deputies attend some governing body meetings regularly.

Pastoral care, well-being and discipline: Parents – really – say no real discipline probs ('They all know where the boundaries are and are very polite,' according to our taxi driver, who turned out to be a very enthusiastic parent-governor – I don't think he was a plant) and no bullying – 'very tight at the first whiff of it,' said another parent. Praise from Ofsted for 'excellent attitudes and relationships' – we found it so quiet in the corridors during our tour we began to wonder if there were any pupils present.

Great care taken with transition starting from end of year 5, when children and parents can attend an open evening at the school. In year 6 teachers give presentations at feeder schools, assisted by year 7s, and children have a taster day during which they are allocated to their houses so they can start to pal up. Older pupils take care of younger ones, a long-standing tradition (as some may come solo from their primary school).

We were told of exceptional efforts made for SEN children by very grateful parents – a day at school just for them and their parents before starting; reorganising the rooming for a pupil with cerebral palsy, to the extent of moving the library to the ground floor ('He was enabled to be equal with all the others'); a child shown around several times before the year began, to alleviate his anxieties about finding his way about, and action plans for any possible future problems created with his parents ('We were blown away by all the care our son was given'); an autistic pupil subject to daily epileptic seizures who has managed to make 'amazing progress' socially and academically – 'They formed a friendship club for her so she would never be on her own during the breaks'.

Pupils and parents: Mainly from Helmsley and Kirkbymoorside, also from village primary schools in a large area of the North Yorks Moors National Park and surrounding countryside. Up to 20 per cent from outside catchment area, such is its reputation. Mainly white middle class – very few ethnic minority, EAL or FSM. The pupils we met were a delight – intelligent, articulate, thoughtful, clearly enjoying their school experience and making the most of their opportunities. We were very impressed on arrival by a conscientious young citizen who diverted from his business to inform our taxi driver in an extremely polite way that his rear number plate was obscured by mud. Notable old pupils: England cricketer Daniel Broadbent and the band, One Night Only.

Active PTA; parents full of praise for school, particularly for SEN, pastoral care, speedy resolution of problems, ease of communication, discipline and mentoring – main wish is for a full range of A levels on site as they feel Ryedale is so much better than the other state schools in the area; only niggle re need for more lockers.

Entrance: Standard admissions process through county authority. Admissions number has now increased to 140.

Exit: Most to further education, eg sixth forms at Ryedale, Malton and Lady Lumley Schools plus Norton College; a few straight into employment.

R

Remarks: A little gem in an appealing rural setting – it was a pleasure to see and talk to happy pupils engrossed in learning and hear the appreciative comments made by parents: 'They go well beyond the call of duty'; 'a fantastic school'. House prices in the area reflect its standing – some parents choose it in preference to a private school.

Sacred Heart Catholic High School

Fenham Hall Drive, Fenham, Newcastle upon Tyne NE4 9YH

Pupils: 1,417 • Ages: 11–19 • Sixth form: 235 • RC

Tel: 01912 747373
Email: enquiries@shhs.org.uk
Website: www.sacredheart-high.org

Headteacher: Since 2013, Anita Bath, who was previously deputy head St Thomas More Catholic School in Blaydon.

Academic matters: For results at GCSE and value added, best state school in Newcastle and one of the best at A level for last six years. Newcastle's centre of excellence for music and the city's 'music hub'. At GCSE in 2016, a third of grades A*/A. At A level, a third A*/A and two-thirds A*-B grades. All from non-selective intake. Science strong at key stage 3, GCSE and A level. Single sex 'avoids stereotypes coming to the fore. So here science and mathematics are more popular than they are in mixed schools because traditionally boys dominate in those subjects,' says head. Eight form entry at year 7, children tested and placed in ability groups in four tiers, two classes in each. Class size up to 32 (average 26) except tier 4 when number drops to 20. Average of 20 at KS4 and 16 in sixth form.

Broad curriculum, including one modern foreign language (possibility of second from year 8) taught at KS3 with flexibility to meet individual girl's needs. English, mathematics, science, technology and religious education are core – science stays right up to 16 'to give the girls a balanced diet'. 'We tailor the curriculum to the gifts of each child. Option blocks follow the child rather than the other way round,' says head.

All-encompassing bespoke progress monitoring and review system for each child, also foundation of teacher performance management, developed in school. DfE suitably impressed, considering rolling it out nationally. Baseline assessment on entry in year 7 predicts GCSE grades and reviews each half term academic targets, behaviour and attendance. As the assistant head data controller put it, 'We build a culture of accountability – there's nowhere to hide!' Individual tailored support provided where needed – highly valued by parents we spoke to. Secure parent platform allows parents online reporting and encourages email contact with teachers. In fact web-based virtual teaching environment provides staff, parents, students, partner schools and organisations with a phalanx of school information – statistics, curriculum, performance, preparation material, email, library system, management information etc.

Desire to see girls achieve excellence in subjects they take rather than push for huge lists of GCSE attempts – 'We give them the time to excel in what they are studying'. Pupils appreciate teachers giving up time to provide extra help: 'They put in a lot of extra effort at lunchtimes and it is great that it is there if you want or need it'.

BTec, City and Guilds and applied A levels on offer in sixth form. Head wants to extend these to provide much greater range: 'We pride ourselves on excellence across the curriculum because students have a right to expect that'. Art and design, dance, drama and ICT available to A2 as might be expected considering school specialisms. Collaboration with Catholic boys' school St Cuthbert's for study there where timetabled subjects clash.

Great store placed on developing and acknowledging staff achievement too: 'I want fresh and energetic teachers'. Sharing of skills/ideas is key. Teachers have visits home and abroad to learn and develop new ideas. School's success is recognised by the National College of School Leadership, which has licensed it to deliver leadership development, one of only 26 providers across the UK.

Games, options, the arts: Full range of sports available from the usual – football, hockey, netball, badminton, trampolining etc – to the unusual – judo, tag rugby and rowing. Something for everyone and willing to add to the list if sufficient support and interest.

Specialist technology and performing arts status – great opportunities for the musically interested and gifted, from rock to string bands and more. Music fund purchases instruments for use by those unable to afford to purchase their own. Drama encouraged (core curriculum in KS3) with lots of performance opportunities and joint productions with St Cuthbert's, most recently Kiss Me Kate. New dance studio – lots of links to Newcastle community dance groups.

Extensive art facilities in spacious, light and airy facilities offering all disciplines from ceramics to sculpture. Separate art room for sixth form. GCSE and A level textile students have the opportunity to strut their stuff in annual fashion show.

Exhaustive extracurricular programme – every faculty has something to offer from mathematics' cipher club to physical education's zumba. Educational visits include theatre, lectures, concerts, museums and holidays/exchanges to France, Germany, ski trips, exchange trips to other Sacred Heart schools. D of E, enterprise days and sports leadership awards.

Girls encouraged to pursue charitable work – each tutor group raises funds for their chosen project. On-going support for visiting, renovating and providing scholarships to Ugandan school – advertising for fundraiser Teachers' Got Talent when we visited.

Background and atmosphere: Sisters of the Society of the Sacred Heart founded a small, private secondary school in Fenham Hall for girls in 1905. From 1920 scholarships were provided, and by 1945 virtually all girls were scholarship students educated at either the grammar or secondary school on the Fenham campus. Became comprehensive in 1977 and academy in 2011. The head sees this as an opportunity as 'Being an academy provides our governors with the freedom and independence which we believe best suits the interests of our school'.

Prior to 2005 on two sites, but £10m spent on the school in past few years: £1.3m on sixth form study centre; £8.7m on new build and remodelling to bring everyone on to one site. New building is in keeping with old. Plans to create vocational studies centre to extend current provision, and enlarge sixth form. Parents told us that 'the school keeps moving forward, offering new opportunities for our children and doing that little bit extra'.

Great pride in being 'a Sacred Heart girl': one sixth former told us, 'At the open day mass you meet people who had been to the school in the past and get the feeling you are part of something special. There is a real sense of community'. Catholic faith and Sacred Heart ethos are important – prayer and worship integral part of school life and each day begins with morning prayer. Group of Sisters lives nearby, one is a governor. Religion not forced upon pupils: 'It is a personal thing and everyone takes from it what they want'. There is a residential retreat at the Youth Village in County Durham each year.

Pastoral care, well-being and discipline: Pastoral care is spearheaded by assistant head, year heads and personal tutors. Each girl will have the same year head and personal tutor from year 7 to year 11 to provide continuity – a real strength. Buddying system teams up trained sixth formers with year 7, 8 and 9 pupils to provide a listening ear. Peer mentoring gives year 10 and 11 pupils regular access to sixth formers for advice. Well-resourced pastoral team with full-time counsellor and parent support adviser, while school chaplain is faith presence in school, providing support to students, staff and parents.

Up to sixth form, rewards system recognises effort and achievement across the spectrum by merits and star awards for specific achievements. These build to bronze, silver and gold awards. Warnings and ample opportunity to correct poor behaviour precede any detention or exclusions. Total exclusions are rare – the last was more than three years ago: 'Exclusion goes against our ethos of welcoming each child and taking them through the ups and downs of school life'.

In a school of this size there is little opportunity for building links between year groups. Assemblies cater for just two year groups together and inter-house competition restricted to sports; clubs and out-of-school activities are seen as ways of bridge-building.

A representative student council has a voice in school whilst leadership opportunities are provided for the two head girls and prefects chosen by their peers and staff. Rules are clear and strictly enforced; unequivocal enforcement of strict uniform code and mobile phones confiscated if seen or heard, released only to a parent on Fridays.

Pupils and parents: A total of 30 different feeder schools but bulk from 13 Catholic schools in north and west of Newcastle. A third come from further afield – Newcastle, Northumberland, Durham. A breadth of social and academic backgrounds with 20 per cent of pupils with English as a second language and 12 SEN statemented children. Former pupils: Newcastle North MP Catherine McKinnell and TV presenter Donna Air.

Entrance: Over-subscribed, at least two applications for each place. Catholic applicants have priority, followed by other faiths. Seventy per cent are baptised Catholics and nearly 20 per cent of Muslim background. No academic selection though 10 per cent of places awarded on aptitude and ability in performing arts.

Exit: Usually 70-80 per cent stay to sixth form. After sixth form, three-quarters to university, rest to foundation courses, employment or gap year. Two to Oxford in 2016, two medics and two lawyers. Excellent at making sure girls make the right choice after sixth form.

S

Remarks: A school that is moving 'onwards and upwards'. Never content to rest on its laurels for its pupils, deserving of its award of outstanding in all categories in the last three Ofsted inspections. Continuity provided by pastoral system is outstanding. Inspired and inspiring teaching observed, stimulating lessons whilst harnessing the latest technology. What really sets the school apart is its development of teaching, and teachers who go that extra mile to set girls on course to make the right choices after Sacred Heart. Every child really does matter here.

Advice to lapsed Catholics: baptise your children, attend Sunday worship and move into the catchment area.

St Aidan's Church of England High School

Oatlands Drive, Harrogate HG2 8JR

Pupils: 1,232 • Ages: 11–18 • Sixth form: 1073 (combined with St John Fisher High) • C of E

Tel: 01423 885814
Email: admin@staidans.co.uk
Website: https://www.staidans.co.uk/

Headteacher: Since 2012, Mr John Wood BA PGCE (early 60s). Educated at Leeds Grammar, where he was a star sportsman – Yorkshire and England U19 cricketer – and Sheffield University, where he read biblical studies. Has been at St Aidan's since 1977, holding a range of posts including pastoral ones, and still teaches religious studies.

Actively involved in the church all his life, often leading acts of worship in family services. Educational advisor on the Bishop's advisory panel for clergy ordination and honorary lay canon at Ripon Cathedral. Wife was a PE teacher and now is a verger at a local church. Two adult children, both educated at St Aidan's. Very interested in all kinds of sport and brass band music.

Very humane, thoughtful, fair-minded and approachable, clearly well liked by the pupils, judging by the friendly greetings he received on our tour, and parents ('lovely..excellent..always around the school..very understanding and quick to respond'), very appreciative of his dedicated staff and collegiate, working closely with his counterpart at St John Fisher RC School as well as with the other schools in the multi academy trust he is keen to develop, along with the new teaching school role, whilst maintaining existing high academic standards.

Academic matters: Five GCSEs A*-C with English and maths usually in the 80s (though was 76 per cent 2016, with 38 per cent of grades A*/A) and excellent value added for all ability levels. Majority take separate sciences; religious studies (compulsory) very strong and and popular; wide range offered, including joint business studies and economics, fine art and graphic communication, French, German and Spanish; ICT and computing. Options for the less academic include the certificate in digital applications, health and social care, core skills, certificate of personal effectiveness. No gender achievement gap – boys can even surpass girls.

Steady A level results overall: 57-60 per cent A*-B, with 28-32 per cent A*/A over last three years (53 per cent A*-B and 28 per cent A*-A in 2016) – good value added. Vast choice, owing to almost 1100 strong combined ecumenical sixth form with St John Fisher RC, includes geology, ancient history, dance, PE, food tech, EPQ, as well as applied business, applied health and social care, music technology, travel and tourism, sport BTec. All do general and religious studies programme. Very strong art – includes photography – maths, English lit, history, sciences, psychology. Big sets, though, up to 27 at start of year 12 for most popular subjects, others up to 22, smaller sets in year 13.

Very good results founded on excellent relationships between teachers (who receive regular, high level professional development) and pupils – the ones we spoke to were very grateful for the generosity of their teachers: 'They're always willing to do 10 times more than they have to'; 'You can always see them in breaks or after school'; as were parents: 'You can email them with a problem and get a quality response that evening..They really deliver on promises'. National competitions to challenge the very gifted; well-resourced library.

Setting for maths from year 7 and from year 8, unusually, also for English, modern langs, science and humanities. This will please parents of the very bright, able to progress at a fast rate, but maybe not those who feel the less bright could be discouraged at an early stage by being placed in a low set (these are smaller, though). Chinese language and culture course for years 7-9 taught by Chinese assistant, who also offers language classes for sixth formers and a club.

Outstanding, profoundly committed head of additional needs, who really does try to meet full range of needs and supports parents, too; around 40 learning assistants, good resources. All year 7s screened and information from parents and primary schools used to identify any difficulties. Two learning support groups of 10, one just for literacy, one for science, French and humanities; flexible curriculum programmes. Support for parents and subject teachers – individual 'provision guides' have hyperlinks to information on appropriate strategies.

Foundation learning programme for group of about 20 key stage 3-4 pupils with severe learning difficulties, in effect a special school within a mainstream school – practical/life/employability skills with literacy, numeracy, speech and language development, leading to Asdan life skills qualification. Two bespoke classrooms in additional learning base. Hut with extensive model railway provides safe space for children who find break times difficult.

Games, options, the arts: Despite limited facilities – one Astro (upgrade on wish list), gym and sports hall, supplemented by local external ones – successful from local to national level in, eg, athletics, football, netball, basketball. Tries to provide matches for as many levels as possible; girls' and boys' football and cricket. Wide choice of sports including equestrianism, handball, golf, climbing as well as all the trad ones. Some very impressive individual achievers; celebrates progress too.

Brilliant, wide ranging music – bands, choirs, orchestras, around 20 ensembles, with input from older students. Annual junior music residential; Evelyn Glennie due to give drumming master class; worship band, Aidan's Flame; much individual prowess on national level – a boy's own choral composition performed at the Royal Albert Hall, conducted by him. Foreign tours in Italy, China, Switzerland.

Plenty of high standard drama – Les Misérables. Fame, Evita, Shakespeare Schools Festival; several get into the National Youth Theatre and top drama schools; lower school annual arts showcase, Spotlight. Lots of dance, at GCSE and A level as well as clubs. Stunning art, on display all over the school – success in prestigious national competitions. Well-equipped technology with wide choice of GCSE options: product design engineering, food and nutrition, textiles and 3D design. Competition plane cockpit construction under way.

Lavish menu of clubs – quantities of D of E golds, public speaking, creative writing, astronomy, Italian, trains, Amnesty International; much charity fundraising, led by sixth formers. Wonderful range of trips: year 9 exchanges with Australia and Sri Lanka, geography in Iceland and Italy, sport in Holland, coast to coast cycling in England, language schools in MFL lands, windsurfing and sailing or work experience in France.

Background and atmosphere: Located near the centre of Harrogate in North Yorkshire; opened 1969, pleasant white main building with some spacious modern classrooms and lots of fresh white corridors. Part of a multi-academy trust with a CE primary. Three outstanding Ofsteds; international school. Despite having around 1600 students on site, atmosphere is calm and orderly. Christian values central, apparent in the concern shown to all pupils as individuals, whether providing after-school help with preparing for an audition or ensuring a severely disabled student can go on a London performing arts trip. From year 7 the pupils absorb the high expectations with regard to behaviour and focus in the classroom, in a community where staff will open doors for them and chat to them while queuing for lunch. The pupils we met said they feel safe and are encouraged to do as well as they can without being compared to others.

School council and sixth form senate (school officers) elected by staff and students after campaigning. Plenty of opportunities for older students to organise, eg fundraising and sixth form ball, or assist with plays, clubs, teaching special needs pupils. 'Amazing food' (student, with enthusiastic endorsement by others), quality-checked by a nutritionist; good choice but eating areas can get crowded. Black/dark grey trousers for all till uniform-free sixth form – we were very taken with the fashionable hoodies for sports.

Unusually, three specialist careers advisors – 'The school is committed to careers,' praised one – who run well-structured, thorough-going programme from year 9 – talks from outside experts; ambitious careers events. We were pleased to see the noticeboard on apprenticeships was the same size as the one for universities.

Pastoral care, well-being and discipline: Usual form tutor and heads of year structure. Mature behaviour promoted through rewards, relationships, working with parents and example set by older students rather than punishment. Bullying in school not seen as a problem by students; cyber bullying dealt with well and swiftly. Aware of mental health needs – discussed in assemblies, some sixth formers had done a well-being course; eating problems dealt with well and discreetly, reported a sixth form girl. School nurse, 'lovely' (female) chaplain and access to professional counselling; sixth formers do peer listening with younger students. Admirable extensive health zone on website with lots of links to useful sites. 'Very nurturing environment.. People always talk about the pastoral care at Aidan's when deciding which Harrogate school to choose,' say parents.

Pupils and parents: Mostly white middle class – Harrogate has a low percentage of ethnic minority. Polite, open students described as 'very biddable and pleasant' by a teacher, 'The kids have a really good moral compass' (parent); all staff with children send them here, which says a lot; ones in all the classes we visited engaged and working well. Associated sixth form also admits students from over 40 other local schools, which 'makes for a very interesting diverse mix – a great experience,' enthused head boy. Parents can access information on schoolwork from website.

Entrance: Heavily oversubscribed. Complicated admissions policy a challenge to get your mind round (but school will help with applications if needed) and known to inspire pre-emptive pew perching: after children in care and those with a sibling already at the school, 80 per cent foundation places for Christians living in the Anglican dioceses of Harrogate and Ripon, with points for church attendance of children and parents (also uses proximity by nearest route); five places for children with demonstrated medical/social need and five for ones of other faiths living in the same deaneries. The rest are community places for children living in the same deaneries, closest to school (up to approximately one mile in practice); then those living outside the deaneries according to amount of church attendance.

Sixth form – tries to accommodate all students, but may prioritise those with sibling already at either school or use proximity. Qualifications required depend on courses to be studied.

Exit: Great majority stay on for sixth form, rest mainly to further education colleges. Very high percentage obtain their choice of university – huge range of higher education institute and subjects, including medicine, dentistry, veterinary science, with large number to top universities: 10 to Oxbridge in 2016.

Remarks: An exceptional school with many of the characteristics of a high-achieving selective one, that also says on its homepage that it is 'proud of the 50 plus students who have a special educational need or educational health care plan and who thrive within the school'.

St John Fisher Catholic High School

Hookstone Drive, Harrogate HG2 8PT

Pupils: 1,427 • Ages: 11–18 • Sixth form: 1,073 (combined with St Aidan's C of E High School); 400 at St John Fisher • RC

Tel: 01423 887254
Email: office@sjfchs.org.uk
Website: www.sjfchs.org.uk

Headteacher: Since 2014, Mr Rob Pritchard. Previously a senior Ofsted inspector, and before that head of St Mary's Catholic High School, Menston, near Leeds, and Holy Family Catholic High School in Carlton. He read chemistry at Sheffield, theology at the University of Wales, Lampeter, and carried out his postgraduate studies at Leeds.

Academic matters: Has humanities and performing arts specialist status, so these subjects are especially carefully monitored and the latter used to develop creativity across the curriculum. Constantly striving to improve its very good results by systematic target setting and use of data. Calm, purposeful atmosphere in classrooms. Lots of computers regularly upgraded; all classes have electronic whiteboards and all teachers laptops. Pupils and parents see the teachers as helpful and generous with their support at exam time. A parent described the teaching as 'dynamic' – 'The children have a lot of fun along with learning'.

The Associated Sixth Form with St Aidan's C of E High School offers an ecumenical environment and each preserves its own identity via separate pastoral systems; over 150 students join from other schools. High praise from the most recent Ofsted report: 'terrific' progress, 'superb' attitudes to learning, 'exceptionally high quality' teaching, 'excellent' relationships. In 2016, 53 per cent A*-B at A level and 28 per cent A*/A. Offers 43 subjects: sciences (very popular), history, ancient history, English lit, German, art, maths, psychology, government and politics, RS, design and technology, drama and theatre studies and performing arts particularly successful. Others include photography, dance, engineering, Spanish, law, geology, sociology, plus vocational courses, eg health and social care, travel and tourism, music technology. All do RE as part of the AS general studies programme then non-examined RE in year 13). AQA baccalaureate is now established – A levels plus extended project and community service. One year intermediate programmes are tailored to meet individual needs and include maths, English and career planning.

Very strong GCSE results – 83 per cent got 5+ A*-C including English and maths in 2016. Art, English, sciences, geography, history, drama and music do particularly well. Wide range of subjects with over 80 per cent students following traditional GCSE courses leading to the English Baccalaureate: all kinds of science – separate, combined or applied for the less able; the biology lab houses two live snakes – which we declined to view. Has a developed citizenship programme leading to GCSE and all students now do a GCSE in applied ICT. Also does very well by the less able/academic or disaffected students, who can take a wide range of practical qualifications more commonly offered by further education colleges, eg BTec business, BTec engineering, digital applications (ICT), health and social care, music technology and performing arts, even if the take up is small. Personalised work-related learning with college courses are available for the small number who require such provision.

School starts GCSE courses in year 9 'to avoid the year 8 dip, offer challenge and enhance the curriculum'. This enables teachers to go beyond the curriculum (hurrah!), has improved behaviour and is popular with teachers, parents and pupils. Strong KS3 results obtained at the end of year 8. English and maths now setted in year 7, then English, French and maths in year 8.

Very enlightened and thorough-going SEN provision: the department has its own IT suite and provides in and outside class support. Weak year 8s are given one-to-one tuition in English and maths, SEN and reluctant learners have individual programmes – they can chose vocational courses at college and/or work experience. Learning mentors and good EAL support. Performing arts used to promote inclusion, eg of less academic KS4 students.

The gifted and talented can do additional GCSEs via independent learning (with an e-tutor), eg the Cambridge school Latin project in years 8-10; separate sciences and additional maths.

Games, options, the arts: Three soccer and one rugby pitches, four tennis/netball courts, an oldish gym and more modern sports hall, plus a big field with lots of trees. Also offers cross-country, cricket, golf at a local course, cheerleading and hoop fusion, self-defence, junior sports leader award, leadership academy. Success in regional, county and national (athletics, football and cross country) competitions; strong tennis. Hopes to have a new all weather pitch plus changing rooms within the next year.

Big focus on the performing arts: has Artsmark Gold and a modern performing arts area; plays tend to be musicals, eg Phantom of the Opera, Sound of Music, Wizard of Oz (seniors) and Mulan, Beauty and the Beast (juniors, with partner primary schools); theatre trips to Leeds and London. Very strong and diverse music includes jazz orchestra, steel pans, strings, Dixie band and a full set of African djembes (drums) shared with the community; the concert ban, jazz band and choir all reached the finals of the National Festival of Music for Youth; students who opt for performing arts GCSE get a free term of music instruction. Also music technology equipment – a recording studio, video editing suite, lots of computers. Dance is a special feature: links with the Ballet Rambert, eg a master class workshop from its artistic director; students belong to the North Yorkshire Dance Company; a twilight dance GCSE class for year 9 gifted and talented boys (urban funk favoured).

Offers a huge range of activities with over 40 clubs and societies including D of E, a winter mountaineering course, fundraising for, eg, CAFOD; aiming for Fairtrade school status. Sixth formers help the staff run activities and with lessons, as well as managing their own facilities via elected committees. York University lecturers and students work with history and politics A level students and debating is strong: the school belongs to a local league and has taken part in an Oxford-based competition. A representative selection of politicians gave talks before the last general election – in the school's mock version, the Lib Dems won by a large majority, with a strong showing by the Greens. International trips to France; Greece and New York (performing arts); Barcelona (art); Germany (history). All year

8 students have an opportunity to do a team-building outdoor activity at the end of the summer term. As an extended school it offers sport and community-based activities in the evenings and at the weekends, including an arts programme.

Background and atmosphere: Voluntary aided; situated on the outskirts of Harrogate – originally a convent school built in 1904, with an attractive 1970s sandstone extension supplemented by seven recent mobiles. The main problem is lack of space – some of the passageways are narrow, which can cause shoving, but students soon adapt, according to a parent; year 7 classrooms, which have largest numbers, seem cramped and some areas need decorating (we would have liked to see more artwork displayed). A small cafeteria for years 7-10 has now been refurbished through a national project initiated by year 8 students – conventional hot food, sandwiches and fruit or a packed lunch for, eg, those who want to eat on the large front lawn; the school has healthy school status. Also a huge plasma screen for menus, school and national news – a number of these in entrance halls. Years 11-13 share a modern, larger and lighter space with a small work area equipped with a few computers; the sixth form common room, painted each year by the students, is rather functional and well worn. Quite a good size library with a wide selection of newspapers and excellent stock of modern teenage fiction, but small adult fiction section.

The traditional chapel plays a central part in the school's spiritual life: one chapel assembly a week for separate year groups, to which various teachers contribute – the one we visited was lively and the students seemed engaged. Each year goes on a retreat, either one day or residential (year 10s visit Lourdes) and year 8s have trips to non-Christian places of worship.

Pupils have a say on school life and learning via the school council and surveys, and participate in lesson observations to identify the best teaching and learning practice. Individuality is allowed: girls wear some of the shortest (plaid) skirts we have ever seen (but school says they have worked on uniform over the last year and skirts are longer) or trousers, with blue shirts, ties and jackets; boys wear blue shirts, now tucked into black trousers – and some of the shortest ties we have ever seen.

Pastoral care, well-being and discipline: Very thoughtful and comprehensive policies, eg the sensible advice issued to pupils on how to cope with bullying, including cyber-bullying. The focus is more on rewards than sanctions. Planners are used by form tutors and parents to get problems resolved quickly and effectively. Year 7s are looked after very well, said a parent: they are encouraged to join clubs, take responsibility and belong to the school community – 'It's a happy, friendly and embracing place that develops confidence'; 'There's an ethos of mutual respect and lots of individual care,' said others.

Electronic system records data – attendance in all lessons, behaviour, academic progress – which teachers, form tutors and parents can access online, and enables tracking and monitoring to identify vulnerable students and children with emotional difficulties. Pupils who need support or time out can visit a reflection area in a secluded part of school with a space for prayer, The Oratory; a quiet room with a snooker table and access to an approachable, young lay chaplain. Year 13s and adults provide mentoring and the learning support centre is open at lunchtimes. The number of exclusions is going down, but zero tolerance of 'inappropriate language to staff' and abuse of illegal substances prevails.

Pupils and parents: The majority are practising Catholics – white, middle class professionals from Harrogate and Wetherby and the surrounding district. However school has greatest ethnic diversity in North Yorkshire, with significant numbers of Polish and Phillipino students. Pupils are lively, outgoing and enthusiastic about the school. Parents are kept well informed via two-weekly e-bulletins, termly newsletters and a parent focus group reviews new systems.

Entrance: Over subscribed: some 335 applicants for 196 places. Has its own complicated admissions system – baptised Catholics get preference. Sixth formers: up to 30 from outside the two main schools; five A*-Cs with at least one B needed. Deadline for applications: mid-March.

Exit: The great majority – around 85 per cent – continue into the Associated Sixth Form. The school is justifiably proud that scarcely any students become NEETS (not in education, employment or training). Most sixth formers proceed to university – a great range, including Newcastle, Sheffield, Northumbria, Leeds; 10 to Oxbridge in 2016. Courses from natural science to business marketing.

Money matters: The Hayra Educational Trust provides a fund for help with extracurricular activities, including gap year projects, for sixth formers.

Remarks: A deeply impressive school in all respects, apart from the limitations of its accommodation – deservedly researched by Ofsted for a report on the features of outstanding state schools.

St Martin's Ampleforth

Linked with Ampleforth College

Gilling Castle, Gilling East, York, North Yorkshire YO62 4HP

Pupils: 150; 30 full boarders, some flexi boarders • Ages: 3–13 • RC

Fees: Day £8,079 – £14,973; Boarding £22,527 pa

Tel: 01439 766600
Email: headmaster@stmartins.ampleforth.org.uk
Website: www.ampleforth.org.uk/stmartins

Headmaster: Since September 2016, Dr David Moses, previously English teacher and housemaster at Ampleforth College. Degree in English and Scottish literature from Edinburgh, followed by doctorate in medieval literature and theology. He is married to Clare and they have two sons.

Entrance: By interview, assessment, and report from current school. All entrants encouraged to come for taster day.

Exit: Nearly all go on to Ampleforth College. A few students return to their home countries for secondary education. Though linked closely with Ampleforth, it is 'a prep school in its own right'.

Remarks: Prep school of Ampleforth, founded in 1929, merged with St Martin's RC prep in 2001. Main building is imposing Gilling Castle – grade 1 listed – glorious but also gloriously expensive to maintain. Unbelievable 16th century Great Chamber, probably the finest Tudor interior in England (don't miss the ceiling and stained glass); the children eat there, though are more interested in checking out the sausages and rarely look up. The castle was the inspiration for Hogwarts in the Harry Potter films, according to JK Rowling's cousin, who went to the college – though site not used for filming. Three miles from the senior school, with all the freedom of its 3,000 acres; tree-climbing, den-building, bike rides through the woods all allowed and indeed encouraged, despite risk assessments, and thankfully deemed infinitely preferable to Playstations, iPods and PSPs. Hazy sunny days of children rolling down grassy banks, making daisy chains, playing on all-weather skateboards, practising in the cricket nets..it's all about space, freedom and spontaneity.

Boarding is important, and growing; quite a few persuade parents to let them convert from day. The integrity of a boarding mix is guarded fiercely here to create a real sense of school community. School day ends at 5.35pm for all; a longish day but includes prep time and plenty of extracurricular activities. Boarders come from all over UK; southern pupils catch a Hogwarts Express at the beginning of term: it is (just) possible to enjoy breakfast in London and lunch in school. Day pupils from Yorkshire; parents a genuine mix of local aristocracy, a few military, professional and non-professional. Open days and school events bring a range of shabby chic Citroens, Land Rovers and Rolls Royces bearing Fortnum and Masons hampers. A good sprinkling from abroad, mainly Europe plus a few South Americans, increasingly popular as education abroad becomes more secular.

Catholics make up 70 per cent; (40 per cent in pre-prep); other denominations are clearly happy to be there, 'being educated in the life of the Christian faith', as the school puts it. Like its Benedictine big brother, it 'asks much from the children's strengths and supports their weaknesses'. Pastoral care very good (chaplain Father John is a friend to all and mainstay of the school); children are confident, courteous and seem happy in their extended school family. Benedictine sense of togetherness and 'anti-me' culture encourages compassion and understanding. Lovely chapel, pretty almost, ideal for this age group, fewer bells and smells than the senior school but full of character nonetheless and the gospel message filters through.

Average class size of 15; standard curriculum up to common entrance, pupils also tested at key stage 1 and 2. Five new classrooms focus on the teaching of languages (and English), French, Latin, Greek all taught; Spanish, Mandarin, German and Italian also on offer as extracurricular activities. Gifted and talented pupils recognised and supported, though children 'not deemed less worthy if less academic or less sporty'. Large well-stocked library is popular. The school is now 40 per cent girls, a sparky and capable bunch; their advent knocked down barriers, opened up the curriculum and raised the game for everyone.

Games predictably important and takes place every afternoon – hence extended teaching day. Rugby and cricket for boys; hockey, netball, rounders for girls. The overseas pupils quickly catch on to the idea of picking up a ball and running with it and the first XV rugby team almost looks like an outing from the UN. Athletics, swimming, cross-country also on offer. School has a floodlit Astroturf pitch. Golf increasingly popular, own golf course, though challenging with much of it on a slope. Plenty of activities, including fishing, riding and shooting; a modern pentathlon team competes nationally.

Music superb, based in fine performing arts block. ISI noted 'high level of musicianship, inspirational teaching'. Schola (choir) sings with senior school, tours across Europe. Over 80 per cent of pupils learn instruments; years 3 and 4 all play the violin, cello, double bass or oboe, with varying degrees of success, but a great opportunity to give it a try.

St Mary's Hall

Linked with Stonyhurst College

Stonyhurst, Lancashire BB7 9PU

Pupils: 258; 43 boarders • Ages: 3–13 (boarders from year 5) • RC

Fees: Day £8,370 – £15,585; Boarding £20,325 – £23,985 pa

Tel: 01254 826242
Email: admissions@stonyhurst.ac.uk
Website: www.stonyhurst.ac.uk

Headmaster: Since 2014, Ian Murphy, previously head of All Hallows prep school in Somerset for nine years. He was educated at Jesuit school Wimbledon College and is married to Rachel, also a teacher. They have two children.

Entrance: Pupils enter all years but most commonly at age 3 and 11; boarding from year 5. Admission to nursery and reception via interview with the head and head of pre-prep; older children admitted following an interview and on receipt of a school report. Ages 10-12 require additional tests in verbal, non-verbal and numerical reasoning. 'Broadly inclusive', looking for 'families who support the school's ethos to develop the whole child'.

Two academic scholarships and one for music awarded for entry at 11 worth between 10-50 per cent of fees. St Francis Xavier awards of 20 per cent of fees are also available to those who 'are most likely to benefit from and contribute to life as full boarders in a Catholic boarding school'. All can be topped up with a means-tested bursary – capped at a maximum of 70 per cent for St Francis Xavier award.

Exit: Straight on to Stonyhurst College. It is rare for a pupil to stray elsewhere, however school will advise appropriately if it feels Stonyhurst would be unsuitable.

Remarks: Set in glorious countryside amongst rolling fields, just a walk through the woods from college. Housed in a Victorian former priests' seminary overlooking verdant grass, junior rugby pitches, and, on a clear day, Pendle Hill. Tucked behind, sits modern yet sympathetic, purpose-built pre-prep Hodder House, with delightful teaching areas, indoors and outside, to facilitate the EYFS multi-sensory approach to learning. The complementary and contrasting nature of the buildings reflect the education here, steeped in Jesuit traditions and beliefs yet forward-thinking with the creative curriculum (gradually making its way up the school), modelled on the International Primary Curriculum, but 'retaining our Ignatian language'.

So be prepared to learn a whole new vocabulary to enter the world of a Jesuit school. For starters, 'lines' are school houses, 'playrooms' are year groups, 'playroom masters' are housemasters and as for the school year groups – Elements, lower and upper, Figures and Rudiments. And then there's the Latin..

Yet the school is forward-thinking enough to pick up on the whims of modern children, issuing a 'credit card' for consistent good work that allows you to jump the lunch queue, MSN offering an active forum for after-school chat and the top year producing its own web page. Whiteboards abound and the ICT centre is open after hours. Traditional in that a scholarship programme is in place to 'push' the brightest; French taught from 3 and Spanish, from 7, Mandarin after-school and Russian on the director of studies' radar. From 11+ common entrance curriculum followed with specialist teaching.Tutor system looks after the development of the 'whole child'.

Project week embraces whole school in early June, from residential trips such as the battlefields for older pupils to celebration of the school's history and famous alumni for the younger. Provides learning opportunities and life skills beyond the confines of the classroom.

Ignatian values and Jesuit traditions underpin all aspects of school life; everyone's contribution is valued and giving of their best an expectation. As one parent commented, 'a heart of faith communicated through everything they do'. 'Everyone helps you out,' said one pupil. 'It's a really good school. Coming here changes your character, pushes you to aspire to make the change, so you can make a difference'. Staff feel that talent is not enough without the confidence to say 'this is what I've got, this is what I can give'. A quiet centre for reflective thought and the beautiful chapel in the heart of the school are open for those that need a peaceful moment.

A music gallery at top of school resounds with chamber choir, brass and strings – lots of uptake, though some pressure applied to join and stay according to parents; with composition on the curriculum at an early age school. Art similarly located up in the 'gods' providing a light and airy environment for some colourful and creative work. Performances are enjoyed in the theatre; one annual school production for leavers (and pre-prep nativity) though plenty of drama and performance opportunity through assemblies before then. After a previous school experience one parent was grateful that curriculum time was not lost 'in constant rehearsals honing a production to perfection'. Sport is popular with excellent coaching and facilities for traditional games (new professional tennis coaches plus 'director of rugby development'), resulting in good representation at area and regional level. Usual carousel of after-school activities, with something to suit all interests.

The prep school pupils live and learn under one roof in the rambling and much-loved Victorian building. First floor classrooms are sandwiched between the age-appropriate, well-equipped ground floor playrooms and dining room on the ground floor and the upper echelons of boys' boarding accommodation on the third floor and girls' on fourth. Strong full or weekly boarding ethos: 'flexible boarding unsettling for all' says director of boarding. Over half from overseas, predominantly Spanish and Mexican, but with a league of nations from Nigeria to Korea. Parents like the diversity of pupils (and staff), a global dimension in this rural retreat. Unlike college, all ages up to 13 board together in comfortable, well-sized rooms shared by four or five, though with far less artwork on the walls usually so conspicuous in boarding houses. Where were all those 'Keep calm and carry on' posters?

Boarding maxim 'tolerance, empathy and independence' emphasises ethos and without doubt, this underpins daily life. Pupils kept busy on a schedule of activity from waking to mid-evening, though daily access to mobile phones allows for regular 'phone homes'. Weekly photo e-newsletter sent to parents by director of boarding very nice touch. Plenty of gappies ensure smooth running operationally and immersed in boarding life providing pastoral support too. Formally addressed by pupils, as 'children get confused with the blur'. Round the clock access to medical professionals, merit system determining amount of weekly tuck, rota of weekend activities, clear rules and systems neatly displayed on central notice boards – it certainly feels like a well-oiled machine.

Pupil voice is heard through the school council and boarding committee and pupils feel engaged with the way their school is run. Charitable giving is important; the school has its own charity and a link with a school near Harare supporting the culture of 'men and women for others'.

Parents are a mixed bag of former pupils and local professionals; 70 per cent Catholic, other denominations accepting the liturgy also welcome. Pupils are hugely loyal, and though well prepared, sad to leave the security of these warm and supportive surroundings.

St Olave's School

Linked with Clifton School, St Peter's School, York

Queen Anne's Road, York, North Yorkshire YO30 7WA

Pupils: 355; 13 full, 12 flexi boarders • Ages: 8–13 • C of E

Fees: Day £11,580 – £14,010; Boarding £21,705 – £24,540 pa

Tel: 01904 527416
Email: enquiries@stolavesyork.org.uk
Website: www.stolavesyork.org.uk

Master: Since 2005, Mr Andy Falconer MBA BA (40s). An ISI inspector, recent chair of IAPS as well as a Walter Hines Page Scholar. Previously deputy head at Chafyn Grove School and before that was head of geography at Craigclowan School. Married to Lesley, a nurse, with three young daughters. Enjoys skiing, grew up near a Scottish ski resort and is a qualified instructor, former travel writer and currently into marathon running, otherwise free time is family time. Kind, charming, with a soft Scottish lilt and a delightful manner. Chats very comfortably with pupils, knows who they are and equally they know him – pupils tuck their shirts in when they see him coming. He misses nothing, touring school with a watchful eye, even turning off lights in empty rooms – 'a Scotsman in Yorkshire,' he grins. Hugely knowledgeable about and committed to the education of children, up to speed on all the latest developments, cherrypicking the best and applying them with skill and understanding to enhance the learning experience. Parents and children trust him implicitly, never doubting that he has the children's best interests at heart. A rock solid practitioner.

Entrance: Automatic from Clifton Pre-Prep (takes ages 3-8), otherwise selective but not massively so, looking for cognitive ability scores of 100+. All entrants are tested in maths, English, reading, spelling, and reasoning. Entrance examinations end of January.

Exit: Almost all to St Peter's School, York. A few to Queen Margaret's, Bootham, Queen Ethelburga's and local state schools.

Remarks: Sited in the former Queen Anne's grammar school buildings – a number of mums are old girls. The buildings have been adapted, extended and improved to create a more welcoming space for children and their parents. It's a very grounded school, not stuffy in any sense. Footbridge to senior school makes it easy to get from one campus to the other, 'distinct and separate, yet linked' (is the official line, and it seems to work).

Good facilities, shares Astroturf and indoor pool with senior school, but has own sports hall with indoor nets; music block; science lab; language rooms; DT; cookery, not as a discrete subject but linked eg to maths, DT, languages (recipes in French); art and ceramic studios; dining hall, Shepherd Hall for assemblies and regular productions, medical room and veg garden.

Parents delight in the school's 'responsiveness', answering questions, dealing with any concerns and, importantly, 'never underestimating children'. Stretch and challenge include sparky discussions on current events in assembly that then continue over supper at home and the ability of staff to 'see qualities in children that others might overlook'. PTA members are busy with social and fundraising events twice a term varying from murder mystery nights to wine-tasting and a denim and diamante evening.

Invariably over-subscribed at 11+, year on year; some leakage of girls at year 6 to girls' schools, but only a handful and they are 'easily replaced,' we are told. Roughly equal numbers of boys/girls, 25 full/flexi boarders. About a fifth of boarders are from overseas, third armed forces, the rest from across the UK or even local – one boarder lives close enough to kick a rugby ball into his own garden. Saturday morning school for everyone 'allows a broader curriculum and more time spent with your mates', says school; 'great fun but requires stamina,' say parents. Parents of day pupils (that's most of them) pass the time having coffee or shopping, almost 50 take to school rowing boats on the river, it's all part of the service. Day pupils travel from as far afield as Scarborough, Harrogate, Selby and Wetherby – short cut to the railway station makes it possible. The train is a good idea because parking is tricky – has to be a quick drop off in the mornings though the playground is opened up so that you can 'park and pick up' after school.

No common entrance or national curriculum testing here yet plenty of rigour. For those heading for public schools beyond York school organises own testing/entrance procedures and supports accordingly. Healthy outlook on education, 'you've got to play the long game,' says the head; 'it's more about learning and thinking and less about testing', quoting that old Chinese proverb about 'not fattening a pig by weighing it'. Doing something right as the library bucks the trend by being packed with boys at breaktime (clever librarian – great choice of 'boy' books) and academic standards, across the board, are high. Average class size 18 with maximum usually 20. Chapel twice a week, traditional C of E service. No issue with bright dyslexics, have strategies to help, specialist tutors, extra lessons and extra time for those who need them.

Staff are encouraged to 'share the learning journey' – the head is learning to play the drums (and gives the children regular updates on his progress in assembly); others offer four week courses to their colleagues (teaching and non-teaching) in a range of subjects, skills and challenges. Years 6 to 8 have all their lessons with subject specialists, younger children gradually work towards this. There is setting throughout for maths and for French and Latin in the top two years. Carousel for French/Spanish/German/Latin in years 4 and 5, pupils choose post year 7.

Music is high profile, a school concert sees two-thirds of pupils taking part. Years 4 and 5 have three class lessons of music each week; add to that the usual choirs, brass groups, sax and clarinet groups, recorder, woodwind and cello groups – plus the school rock band Stereo Flair. Some phenomenal art on display; 'talent is recognised and nurtured,' say parents.

Sport is impressive here, plenty of teams and older pupils competing at national level. Bigger schools such as RGS Newcastle and QEGS Wakefield provide serious challenge; smaller preps may struggle to compete with the first team here. Sporting successes include four times winners of the National Rugby Sevens Tournament; winners of national JET Cup cricket; national finals for hockey, soccer and cricket. Outdoor pursuits, yacht sailing with Ocean Youth Trust and rowing (school has rowing machines as well as river access and own rowing club) plus an Easter ski trip and sports tours (years 5 and 8) keep pupils busy and active all year round.

Lots of extracurricular choice including enterprising young apprentice-type challenges and history model-making club, which essentially means making weapons from wood. Pupils also enjoy charity days and fundraising, pink day for breast cancer, organised by pupils, and green day in support of NSPCC, among recent events. Wide range of after-school clubs and activities, including prep clubs for day children of working parents.

Pupils eat and register in their mixed age houses, helping everyone to 'know the school vertically and horizontally'. Strong house identity (that children describe as 'Harry Potter-esque'), linked to pastoral care. A teacher/mentor follows through with groups of children year on year, a type of wraparound care valued hugely by parent body. Homemade lunches prepared by chef, the legendary Dave.

Smart (ish) navy uniform, different from and more appealing than the brown of the senior school; sports kit is linked across the schools.

St Peter's School, York

Linked with Clifton School, St Olave's School

74

Clifton, York, North Yorkshire YO30 6AB

Pupils: 570; 142 boarders • Ages: 13–18 • Sixth form: 248 • C of E

Fees: Day £16,935; Boarding £28,140 – £28,845 pa

Tel: 01904 527300
Email: g.daniells@stpetersyork.org.uk
Website: www.stpetersyork.org.uk

Head Master: Since 2010, Mr Leo Winkley MA MEd (40s), previously managing head at Bedales. Read theology at Lady Margaret Hall, Oxford. Taught at Ardingly College and The Cheltenham Ladies' College as head of religious studies. Still teaches religious studies and contributes to the global perspectives programme for sixth form: he enjoys teaching – 'it keeps you honest'. A keen runner and follower of sport. Married to medical oncologist Jules; they have three young children. Committed to the breadth and all-round nature of independent education as lessons for life – says 'school should be serious fun', currently encouraging all parties to 'think big'. Pupils tell us he has 'smartened things up a bit and increased pupil involvement', parents say he is a 'fine chap' and has 'got the bit between his teeth'. You get a very warm welcome from this clear-sighted, ambitious strategist; he was born into the world of independent education, son of a headmaster, so knows the perils, pitfalls and joys, though it is different up north and it will be interesting to see how the school develops under his leadership.

Academic matters: Consistent achiever, sets the bar high in a robust local market. Strong work ethos with plenty of stretch and challenge, normal to try hard but fine-tuning from the top is pushing to 'broaden the pupil experience' ie accumulation of exam certificates is great but balance is also important.

Takes the academic rigour for granted; bright pupils will always do well, but hard workers also do well here, hence the very positive value-added. Believes good results are down to having really good teachers as well as selective but not highly selective intake; no weak subject areas; staff know what is expected and are multi-talented and self-driven. 'Learn Something New' is a St Peter's initiative that persuades staff to share interests and learn from each other with a range of activities across the school(s)

S

encouraging staff to try out and learn new skills – 'learning teachers teach better' is the head's strapline.

Class size averages 18 in the middle school (maximum 24) and 12 in the sixth form. The occasional D or E grade creeps in at GCSE, but 76 per cent of passes A*/A in 2016. IGCSEs being taken in maths, science and languages. Equally impressive performance at A level where 55 per cent of grades were A*/A and a very commendable 83 per cent of all entries graded A*-B.

Some support for the handful with mild dyslexia – must be bright and able to cope. Part-time dyslexia specialist. Approximately 10 per cent have an ed psych report; five per cent qualify for extra time in exams. Third modern language replaced by extra English and study skills for some. Gifted and talented programme in place but doesn't target top 10 per cent. 'All the children here are bright; it would be wrong to concentrate on a handful.' Olympiads and similar challenges stretch those with real talent. Global Perspectives an additional course for sixth form with Horizons introduced for middle school. Does not allow students to take any GCSE early and moving towards more challenging IGCSEs.

Careers advice and support flagged up by parents as something to be worked on and improved, especially important for boarders whose parents are not around to have those all-important conversations. They are getting pupils into good and great universities, but what next? Both pupils and parents feel they would like more guidance and direction as life beyond university becomes tougher and more competitive. The school has responded swiftly by bringing in a second careers advisor and opening up careers events, visits, conferences plus 'exploration week' for the lower sixth – 'life after St Peter's' is a drum they will keep on banging.

Games, options, the arts: A surprising amount of outdoor space; you'd never guess it is so close to the city. Nearest to the school is the hallowed ground of the first XV rugby pitch, but there are plenty of others beyond. Sport is compulsory for all. Facilities include two sports centres, one with super climbing wall, multi-surface pitch, fitness centre, indoor swimming pool, extensive well-kept playing fields, boathouse and tennis and squash courts. Rugby popular and strong, rowing crews regularly pick up national honours and awards, boast 20 international rowers in the last eight years. Hockey, rowing and netball are the most popular girls' sports but tennis, athletics, squash, swimming and usual suspects on offer for all. Generally put best coaches with best teams but playing opportunities for all via B teams and house competitions. Competitiveness and fair play are a prominent feature of the school and success is universally applauded at weekly assembly. D of E and CCF flourishing. Plenty of trips including expeditions to Morocco, sports tours to New Zealand and South Africa, language holidays and music tours to the USA, Prague, Italy as well as singing in York Minster.

Very good art facilities, including super gallery. Art department appears in the Guinness Book of Records for a remarkable 100 per cent A*/A grade pass rate achieved four years running, though recent years have seen lower grades creep in – 'we were pleased, it took the pressure off, allowed the pupils to experiment, be more creative rather than formulaic,' said one art master. Many learn a musical instrument or two, 300 individual lessons each week with professional specialist music staff, 160 strong choir and plenty of opportunities to perform; director of music described as 'inspirational'. Each boarding house has a practice room with piano. Over 100 pupils involved with Community Action projects and all participate in charity fundraising.

Boarding: Around a quarter of pupils board, of whom 30 per cent are from overseas. Most are full boarders but a few stay on a flexi/weekly basis. Boarding received an Outstanding rating in last Ofsted inspection. Six day and four boarding houses, the latter well equipped with a selection of common rooms, games rooms and a kitchen for snacks (all eat in school dining hall). Pupils and staff strike a good balance between amity and mutual respect. Houses are headed by husband and wife teams and supported by resident and non-resident assistants. Good pastoral care, 'just wonderful,' say parents. They describe house parents as 'something out of the ordinary', creating boarding houses that are 'home from home' with all the care and support that may be needed and equally 'a kick up the jacksy as required'. Staff vigilant – invariably have one or two they're watching for eating problems etc.

Background and atmosphere: The school was founded in 627 AD by Paulinus, first Archbishop of York, and is one of the world's oldest schools, 'only two older', we are told. In 1844 it was established on its present, impressive, green, grade 2 listed site in Clifton, with 47 acres, river access and all within walking distance of York Minster, the city centre and station.

Beyond the imposing main building, others are a mix of ancient and modern. Some classrooms and corridors are a bit tatty round the edges; we get the sense that it's not a priority – it's a workhorse, not a show pony. Good range of facilities, with all angles covered, though pupils tell us they are pestering the head for a new sports hall; 'it could be so much better'. It's one of the head boy's pet projects, though not on the agenda (yet) – might have to settle for a new boathouse instead. Pupils rave about the new swimming pool, opened by Olympic diver Tom Daley. Other recent additions include four bright biology labs, a sixth form microbiology lab, chemistry lab and design and technology room with Cad Cam technology. Three computer rooms are complemented by clusters of computers throughout the school and houses – virtual learning environment with Wifi throughout the campus.

Pastoral care, well-being and discipline: Advice, help and support may be sought from tutors, house staff, resident health centre staff or the school chaplain. Pupils tell us that the unforgivables are drugs and bullying; if caught smoking it's three strikes and you're out.

Pupils are allowed to visit town twice a week (more in older years) and for younger ones a timetable of supervised events is on offer. All eat in the modern dining hall. Menus offer a wide choice with mixture of typical school meal fare, continental options, salad bar, sandwiches, fruit and healthy eating options. Pupils say food is 'great', with 'boy-sized portions'; Sunday brunch is legendary.

Pupil voice has grown and developed through a pupil symposium. Head's question time is chaired by the head boy or girl – 'direct government-type stuff' – raising all kinds of ideas and questions from the downright silly to the well-considered and serious.

Middle school uniform uninspiring, disliked, yet (bizarrely) defended, by pupils – when push comes to shove there's nothing more conservative or radically opposed to change than your average 15 year old: brown blazer, grey trousers for boys, and brown checked skirt for girls. Apparently the current line is 'brown is good'. Sixth form (boys and girls) wear dark business suits.

Strong Christian ethos; pupils meet thrice weekly for collective act of worship in school chapel – the new chaplain has 'livened things up a bit,' pupils tell us with a grin; assemblies at other times.

Pupils and parents: Day pupils mainly from North Yorkshire, Harrogate, Leeds conurbation, York, and surrounding villages. Majority of boarders live within an hour's drive but others from wide area in the UK. Parents in business and the professions, a popular choice for Forces families, minority from overseas – 'it's a world view we need to develop,' says the head. Mix of Hong Kong, China, Russia, one or two others – about 25 per cent overall.

'Parents,' say school, 'are interested – but not helicopters', ambitious and driven; quite a few first time buyers here but also dynasties with names all over the honours boards.

Old Peterites include Guy Fawkes, Alcuin (eighth century scholar), Greg Wise, John Barry, Laurence Eusden (poet laureate), Harry Gration (journalist, TV presenter), C Northcote Parkinson (inventor of Parkinson's Law) and Clare Wise (director of the British Film Commission).

Entrance: Automatic entry from Clifton Pre-prep to St Olave's (St Peter's junior school) and then from St Olave's to St Peter's. Seventy per cent follow this route, rest by CE and school's own entrance test at any age including 13 or 16 (minimum six GCSE grade B passes). Assessment and filtering does take place in prep and pre-prep to weed out those who won't cope with the demands of St Peter's, but it is rare. Generally entry to St Olave's requires a child to have a reading age at least a year ahead of chronological age (sympathetic to siblings). Will take pupils who pass exam at any time provided a place is available. Other main feeder schools: Terrington Hall, Cundall Manor and Aysgarth, some state schools also.

Exit: Around 10 per cent leave at the end of year 11. Of those leaving after A levels, 95 per cent go directly to university, vast majority selecting Russell Group. Five to Oxbridge in 2016 (though UCL and Imperial often favoured by high fliers). Edinburgh, Newcastle, Birmingham and Sheffield also popular; some 15 per cent applying next year; a few to employment.

Money matters: Not a rich school but has increased bursary funding considerably over the past few years. Means-tested bursaries available at 11, 13 and at sixth form regardless of previous school. Qualification criteria for bursaries on a sliding scale from 10 to 100 per cent based on need, and typically if household income is less than £45,000. Honorary (ie no dosh) subject scholarships are awarded; music awards, including fee remission, available for tuition and instruments.

Remarks: Very much the big brother of the 3-18 triumvirate of St Peter's schools, encompassing Clifton Pre-Prep and St Olave's junior school ('continuity, but difference' is the mantra here) and you get the impression that this is where it all becomes rather serious. If it were a car, we'd probably describe it as a Volvo, albeit a top of the range high performance 4WD version with sporty extras such as a ski rack and maybe a tow bar. It can accommodate the whole family and you can't doubt the quality, reliability and solidity of the product it delivers, pretty much unfailingly, in all areas.

S

St Thomas More Catholic School

Croftdale Road, Blaydon-on-Tyne, Tyne and Wear NE21 4BQ

Pupils: 1,550 • Ages: 11-19 • Sixth form: 300 • RC

Tel: 0191 499 0111
Email: info@stthomasmore.org.uk
Website: www.stthomasmore.org.uk

Head Teacher: Since 2005, Mr Jonathan Parkinson (40s) BSc physics (Leeds University) PGCE. Previously deputy head, assistant head, head of science, head of physics, all at St Thomas More. Previous schools: Carre's Grammar School, Sleaford; All Saints High School, Huddersfield. Positive, energetic and witty with easy but respectful relationship with pupils. Still makes time to teach, last year physics to year 11; this year sixth form psychology. Gets a buzz from 'seeing the lightbulbs go on in little brains, watching children grow and go out into the world as young adults and to know you have had an impact on them.'

Places emphasis on development of staff, looks for innovation and sees 'the teacher in the classroom as absolutely key' to pupil progress and keeping the school moving forward. Not driven by results. 'We do things here for the right reasons – the needs and abilities of the pupils, and our results grow from that', underpinned by 'great emphasis on creating a strong Christian nurturing environment.'

Regular early morning fitness regime in privately operated fitness suite in school; away from school a keen, but slow, runner. Loves Bach; grade 8 flautist but will retake as he 'only scraped through'; runs own ceildh band.

Academic matters: In past awarded technology college status (first in north east); leading edge school (ie encouraged to work in partnership with other schools to raise standards). One of first tranche of teaching schools, joined with Cardinal Hume Catholic School, St Mary's Catholic school and Newcastle University to form Northern Lights Teaching School Alliance with mission to 'Illuminate, Innovate and Inspire'. Full A level and GCSE curriculum, along with GNVQ and BTecs offered and matched to pupil's ability. At A level in 2016, 53 per cent A*-B and 23 per cent A*/A grades; large numbers of students following vocational courses attain distinction and merit grades. At GCSE or equivalent qualifications, 80 per cent 5+ A*-C grades including English and maths, and 16 per cent A*/A grades. Compared with national expectations, pupils leave the school achieving significantly higher grades than their levels of attainment on entry would suggest.

Eight form entry in year 7 offered a broad curriculum and pupils are set by ability in maths and English. Regarded as 'diagnostic year' with scope to alter through year as abilities change. From year 8 setting extended to science, humanities, technology and modern foreign languages. Tests every 10 weeks throughout KS3; reports with grading on attainment and effort, targets set by pupils. A choice of route A, vocational, or route B, academic at KS4 and again in the sixth form. English Bacc recently introduced needing little change to curriculum since approx one-third of students achieve this qualification. Mathematics GCSE started in year 9.

Unusual timetable: two week rota with three lessons of 100 minutes per day.This provides technology and science with required time and is seemingly popular with pupils, though contrary to some contemporary research on effective learning.

Good careers advice and visiting professors from nearby university provide mock interviews for university entrants. Visits to colleges organised for Oxbridge hopefuls.

Games, options, the arts: Growing reputation for music, drama and dance. Abundance of bands, choirs, orchestras stems from compulsory instrument tuition from year 7. Pupils are allocated instruments – can cause some resentment because there's no choice. Team sports abound, with a list of county and national sporting honours. Cricket a strength, led by enthusiastic coach, indoor nets in sports hall which also offers usual range of indoor sports plus climbing wall. Playing fields but all-weather surface on wish list. Wide selection of clubs and societies – from sports to chess, Scrabble and hoola hooping; enjoys exchange/educational visits to French/German-speaking countries and outdoor pursuits weekends. Big school production annually: We Will Rock You and Grease recently. In a school of this size pupils find participation 'a good way to get to know others out of your year'.

Background and atmosphere: Catholic faith is strong in school, evidenced in worship, teaching of mutual respect and in charitable works. Head believes that Christian ethos binds children and staff and encourages all to give of their best. 'This feels like a community; happiness emanates from the classrooms, we have high standards and expectations of everyone, value manners, show respect and expect exemplary discipline'.

Situated in Blaydon, a former industrial area currently undergoing significant housing regeneration. Opened in 1967 as co-educational secondary modern, became comprehensive in 1987 and has doubled in size along the way to current roll. Buildings chart the school's history and growth spanning four decades with uninspiring frontage and narrow corridors of the early build necessitating rigorously enforced traffic movement between lessons. Sport England helped fund the sports hall/fitness room and library. New self-financed humanities and English block is jewel in the crown for both staff and pupils. Airy, light classrooms with interactive whiteboard walls provide good teaching environment and wide corridors link all parts of the school.

Pastoral care, well-being and discipline: Pastoral system is bedrock of school. Pupils allocated to one of four houses in year 7 (following elder siblings) and each year group comprises two forms for each house, developing allegiance and competitive spirit. Competition ranges from sports to chess and the TV classic Countdown. Houses mixed on gender and academic ability. Tutor groups stay the same until year 11 for continuity.

Pastoral system dedicated to ensuring each child feels secure, confident and valued. Programme ensures tutors look after social, emotional and academic needs. 'It is important that children enjoy school and our pastoral system helps ensure they do', says head. Target setting, supported by pastoral mentors, assists development. Strong on discipline and maintaining standards eg inflexible uniform policy, litter-picking duties. Good behaviour, manners and attitude to work are paramount. Merit system based on both academic and social achievement and contribution to the life of their house and the school. Certificates/head's commendation much sought after by pupils. Pupils look up to sixth formers and aspire to be one. Competition for head boy and head girl posts is stiff. Pupils taught respect for others and their school environment.

A school marches on its stomach so it was disappointing to hear that quality, portion size and price of food in the dining room seemed to be a universal disappointment: However, school tells us a new chef has been appointed so no doubt changes are afoot.

Pupils and parents: Bulk of children come from nine Catholic feeder schools, mainly in West Gateshead. Predominantly British white with some from other backgrounds. Comprehensive intake, above average KS2 results. Seventy per cent stay for sixth form. 'Everyone here gets on really well and there are opportunities to get involved in everything, and we are encouraged to do so. I never thought I would say that I love coming to school, but I do.'

Entrance: Oversubscribed. Priority to Roman Catholic children from feeder schools, then those with siblings already at school; other Roman Catholics; other faiths. 'People come here partly because of our results but a lot is down to our reputation for setting high standards of work and behaviour.'

Exit: Majority of A level students go to university. One or two to Oxbridge on occasion.

Remarks: A school true to its Christian foundation; pupils leave well prepared for life outside the school gates and flourish in an environment that promotes mutual respect, high expectation and strong citizenship. Great emphasis on teaching the teachers pays dividends. Consistently good academic results, though these are not the driver here. Pupils work hard, play hard and are clearly very proud of their school. Advice to lapsed Catholics: baptise your children, attend Sunday worship and move into the catchment area.

Sedbergh School

Linked with Casterton, Sedbergh Preparatory School

Malim Lodge, Sedbergh, Cumbria LA10 5HG

Pupils: 512; 500 boarders • Ages: 13–18 • Sixth form: 205 • C of E

Fees: Day £23,400; Boarding £31,770 pa

Tel: 01539 620535
Email: enquiries@sedberghschool.org
Website: www.sedberghschool.org

Head Master: Since 2010, Mr Andrew Fleck MA (late 40s), educated at Marlborough College, read geology at Nottingham and has an MA in education from Sussex. Member of HMC Professional Development Committee, a governor of Westville House Preparatory School and a fellow of the Royal Geographical Society.

Urbane, charming and appears, as one parent put it, 'very comfortable in his own skin'. Committed to the Sedbergh values of a 'properly balanced education', providing pupils with the 'vision, aspirations and leadership skills to succeed in a global labour market' and determined to dispel the public perception that only sports rule here.

Married to Anne, who runs a software development company working primarily in agro-technology and with whom he cycled the deserts of central Iceland and the northern Sahara on a tandem. Interests include sailing, canoeing and cycling – canoed around Ireland, Newfoundland, Japan and Arctic Norway to the Russian border and cycled the east/west European border. Has twin daughters, both at Sedbergh.

Academic matters: In 2016, 56 per cent A*/B grades and nearly 28 per cent A*/A at A level; 42 per cent A*/A grades at GCSE. Not bad for a school with a comprehensive intake, that welcomes all to stay for sixth form and a policy of entering all pupils for exams; very good value-added. Pupils and parents speak of 'caring, dedicated and helpful staff, committed to the children'. Gifted and talented are stretched and learning support (primarily for dyslexia) is provided in the classroom or by individual tuition in a separate building known as The Shack. Head admits more to do in this provision and it is 'work in progress'.

Broad curriculum, French plus German or Spanish on offer for year 9 (overseas visits but no exchange programme). Drama recently introduced at GCSE and jewellery design at GCSE and AS level. Has launched a new BTec subsidiary diploma in agriculture, a joint venture with Newton Rigg College in Penrith and the equivalent of one A level. Also offers EPQ.

Many classrooms, language labs and laboratories have been given a facelift, extensive art facilities and good DT workshops, embracing new IT investment. Well-stocked departmental libraries and shelves of fiction in the boarding houses – does this deter pupils from making the main library a centre of learning and research? Housed in a super conversion of Georgian building on the site of Lupton's original school, the library has been revamped recently, but its primary use seems as a venue for debate, lectures and academic house competitions.

Games, options, the arts: Renowned for its sporting prowess (34 sporting activities on offer) with many pupils winning representative honours, especially in rugby and shooting. Sport is timetabled five times a week, adjusted winter and summer to make best use of daylight. All you would expect in facilities and more (even a heated cricket square) set in idyllic surroundings. Plenty of opportunities to canoe and cave, orienteer and rock climb. Also famous for its Wilson Run – a 10-mile fell race open to ages 16+. All pupils participate in CCF in year 9 but involvement is optional after that, though many continue.

The hills here are certainly alive with the sound of music. Some 350 pupils take individual lessons up to grade 8 and diploma, with representation in national ensembles. Fizzing director has developed choral singing to a crescendo, together with classic chamber groups and orchestra, swing, jazz, rock and CCF bands. Excellent, spacious and recently updated music school with composing and recording facilities, plus the Thornely Studio, a £1 million performance hall with sprung floors.

Lots of performance opportunities for music and drama at home and away with regular trips and tours abroad. Range of clubs and societies available, from mountain biking to debating and specialist lectures in science, medicine and music. Flourishing D of E award scheme. House competitions for everything from singing to chess.

Boarding: The nine boarding houses (six for boys and three for girls) widely dispersed through campus and town, giving pupils plenty of daily exercise as they move through the school day. No wonder a bicycle for transit around campus is a prefect privilege.

Pivotal to the success of the school are the keen house loyalty (quickly assumed by new entrants) and the level of care pupils receive there. Each pupil is assigned to a house where they live, eat all meals, including lunch, collectively, when manners and conversation are nurtured. Excellent food, lots of choice, special diets catered for. Girls' boarding houses are bright, modern and well furnished; all the boys' boarding houses have been refurbished in recent years. One parent commented that her son 'enjoys it so much he never wants to come home'.

Background and atmosphere: Founded in 1525 by Roger Lupton, a provost of Eton. School lies in the centre of a small, picturesque town surrounded by magnificent fells, in the heart of the splendid (if often wet and cold) Yorkshire Dales National Park but only a short drive from the M6. Departments housed in a number of well-spaced, separate buildings.

Girls arrived in 2001 and with the opening of a third girls' boarding house in 2013 they now account for nearly 40 per cent of the school population. They have made their mark as a significant, vibrant and impressive part of the school. Few shrinking violets here, matching the boys for healthy inter-house rivalry, success in extracurricular, whilst helping the academic results along the way. Make sure to check out The Sedberghian, the school magazine, for information on every facet of the place and the pupils who populate it.

Sedburgh merged with Casterton School in 2013. The merged junior school has moved to the Casterton site (and is now known as Casterton, Sedbergh Preparatory School), whilst the merged senior school, named Sedbergh School, remains on this site.

Pastoral care, well-being and discipline: Very effective house system with strong, popular and caring housemasters and mistresses heading up dedicated teams who have good relationships with the pupils. Teachers also attached to houses. Rules recognised by pupils and parents as firm but fair, well thought out and communicated clearly. Structured and well-thought-out sanctions and rewards system. Bullying is rare – the ethos in houses militates against it.

Pupils given freedom around town, a safe bet when you consider you're never far from someone connected to the school. Bar available at weekends to sixth formers; school encourages a sensible attitude to alcohol. Controlled access between boys' and girls' houses but over-familiar relationships between boys and girls discouraged.

Pupils and parents: A complete mix – mostly northern professionals but increasingly from Scotland and the South. Traditionally a school for land-owners, industrialists and farmers' sons (Wordsworth was a parent), but now an eclectic mix including Forces, expats and a few foreigners; around two-thirds boys. Pupils are confident, sparky and generally, though not universally, sporty, very grounded, have a practical approach and are not afraid to get their hands dirty. Willingness to help others, loyalty and compassion are values universally to the fore. A very happy school – lots of laughter in and out of lessons. Still not a place for the timid or loner but anyone else, especially those who appreciate the fantastic surroundings and teamwork, will love it here.

Old boys include Simon Beaufoy (Full Monty); Wills Carling and Greenwood; Lord Bingham (Lord Chief Justice); James Wilby; Sir Jock Slater (First Sea Lord); Sir Christopher Bland (chairman BT); Robert Napier (chief exec of Met Office, ex chief exec WWF and chairman of governors).

Entrance: For most, CE is the normal route, others applying in years 9-11 sit exams in English and maths. A current school report is required. Sixth form requires a minimum of five GCSEs at C or above. Main feeder is Casterton, Sedbergh Preparatory School, but significant proportion come from prep schools across the north of England and beyond.

Exit: Mostly to university – northern popular, a number of Scottish; degree choice spread across science, business and arts. Steady trickle to Oxbridge, one in 2016. Several opt for a gap year having secured their university place. Handful embark on vocational courses or careers at 18, trickle (around 10-15 per cent) leave at 16.

Money matters: A number of scholarships for entry at years 9, 10 and 12: academic, all-round, art, DT, music sport and drama. Awards vary but may be up to half fees. Index-linked major scholarships – in exceptional circumstances. Exhibitions and bursaries also available.

Remarks: Has retained its traditional values and ethos (and market) while responding to the demands of the 21st century. Renowned as a formidable force on the sports field, it seeks to embed that gold standard throughout the school. Pupils, whether sporty, academic, musical or arty, are well catered for and seem to love it, although a love of fresh air and the great outdoors is a distinct advantage. Opportunities are provided in a happy and caring environment to create a 'can do' philosophy in pupils. Numbers suggest that pupils and their parents very much approve. We watch with interest the results of its merger with Casterton School.

Sheffield High School

10 Rutland Park, Sheffield, South Yorkshire S10 2PE

Pupils: 699 • Ages: 4–18 • Sixth form: 182

Fees: £8,571 – £12,090 pa

Tel: 01142 660324
Email: enquiries@she.gdst.net
Website: www.sheffieldhighschool.org.uk

Headmistress: Since 2004, Mrs Valerie Dunsford BA PGCE NPQH (50s), educated at Huddersfield High School and Manchester University (French and Italian). Previously taught at Ryburn Valley High School, Benfield School, Newcastle, and Durham High School for Girls (deputy head). Husband, Stephen, is a teacher; two adult daughters, who both attended Sheffield High. Approachable and unassuming; very committed to developing extensive partnership projects with local primary and secondary maintained schools – the school recently received an Independent Schools Award, for the third time, for the best independent/maintained school collaboration in recognition of years of innovative work; ISI inspector; adept at raising bursary funds from various educational trusts; emotionally astute – 'our girls need educating in how to cope with failure'. Soon gets to know girls individually when they enter the school.

Head of junior school: Since September 2016, Mr Christepher Hald, previously head of juniors at St Mary's School, Cambridge.

The school has announced it will merge with Ashdell Prep, with the year 2s and below moving to the Ashdell site under the Ashdell name, whilst all the years 3-6 will be taught on the Sheffield Junior site under the headship of Mr Hald. The two existing schools are operating in parallel, with their current heads, during 2016/17, fully merging in September 2017.

Academic matters: Junior school achieves high academic standards generally and develops independent learning and thinking skills. Shares staff with the senior school – by years 5-6 mostly specialist teaching. Science is strong, with lots of practical work, and modern languages – French from reception to year 3, Spanish in years 4-5, German in year 6. Two half days a term spent on mixed age, small group, problem-solving work encouraging 'thinking outside the box', plus half termly extended homework tasks. Girls speak appreciatively of their teachers as 'very helpful and clear'; 'They make the lessons fun'.

Good learning support – close liaison with the senior school; specialist dyslexia sessions at an extra charge or free, small group English and maths with a teaching assistant; EAL support too. Can manage mild autism; physical disabilities would be difficult because of the nature of the building, but they would 'try if possible'.

Plenty of computers and electronic white boards – fully integrated IT and an extensive VLE with details of current lessons. Bright, large classrooms with exceptionally good displays – a lot of high quality work; average class size: 19. A very well stocked and attractive library, with a flower-shaped table for laptops and plasma screen – all classes have a weekly session for book-related work/activities. Focused and enthusiastic children.

At A level 69 per cent A*/B, 47 per cent A*/A in 2016. Wide range of options including geology; maths and sciences very popular; especially good results in art and design, sciences, maths, English and geography; will run subjects for just one or two girls. AQA Bacc well established; links with the two Sheffield universities; successful in various academic competitions to national level.

GCSE 69 per cent A*/A in 2016. Languages are a particular feature of the school, which offers Russian (A level only) and Greek and can also provide teaching in Chinese, Persian, Arabic and Italian. At key stage 3 all do three separate sciences, two modern foreign languages (German and Spanish as well as French) and Latin; ethics lessons for year 9.

Very well resourced: has Becta ICT mark and ICT Quality Mark – plenty of well-designed IT suites; extensive VLE, which proved its worth when the school was closed for three days owing to snow. The last ISI report praised the standard of teaching, development of independent learning and positive relationships between girls and between girls and teachers; regular subject clinics for extra informal support; several girls and parents expressed appreciation of how helpful the teachers are; regular subject clinics for extra informal support. A more thorough policy for the gifted and talented now – year 10s onwards have an extension work booklet; classwork has been developed and an option of doing an extended project at the end of year 9.

Very good learning support, under the leadership of the qualified, warm head of pastoral care – all girls are screened for dyslexia in year 7 and again in year 9 (a charge for individual lessons from an outside specialist, but this will become free soon); mild autism, ADHD and other learning difficulties can be managed; they would do their best to accommodate physical disabilities, but much of the school isn't 'wheelchair friendly' – though the sixth form block is fully equipped for the disabled. Girls who would struggle with the standard 10 GCSEs do fewer, allowing time for extra individual or small group support; EAL support also available.

Games, options, the arts: As befits the first girls' school in the country to have its own gym, sports are outstanding, recognised in a recent trophy for outstanding sporting success (having eight teams in national finals for five sports and being national champions in three) and an award for the best independent school in the UK for sport; tours to New Zealand, Fiji, China, Barbados, Dubai; sports leadership award popular. PE Quality Mark with distinction awarded. Busy refurbishing the gym and installing floodlights on the Astroturf.

Has Artsmark Gold. Much music: performances in the community and more trips abroad; joint sixth form choir with a local, mainly boys independent school; a parent thought the standard of the classical music ensembles could be improved (the school demurs) but praised the concert band. Now has its own stage, in a hall, though not a purpose-built theatre – standard choice of plays and musicals but, unusually, year 13s direct and design year 7 and 8 productions; LAMDA exams and dance popular. Some stunning art in a wide range of media – has received a Good Schools Guide award for the top AS results for art and design nationally and enjoyed success in national competitions. Technology has advanced: lots of imaginative key stage 3 work on display; brand new cookery room and cookery and nutrition now on the curriculum for years 7-9 and sixth formers. Interesting creative writing in the school magazine, High Times, with some well-written, unusually long articles on activities.

Over 50 clubs – even knitting; success in business enterprise, debating, film making and poetry competitions; off timetable days for years 7-9 to develop problem-solving, teamwork and leadership skills; D of E popular. Year councils and a school council – seen as an effective vehicle for changes; the Kitchen Cabinet meets with the catering manager. Much eco activity – all forms have an eco representative, various eco awards. Large sums of money raised for charity – a school in Bangladesh is supported and old textiles and computers are given to schools in Kenya. Many other academic and cultural links with schools in Africa, India, China and the USA as well as Europe, and an exotic range of trips including a summer school at a university in China, Peru, the Galapagos Islands, Iceland – recent British Council international school award.

Several opportunities for the sixth to take on responsibilities (all year 12s become prefects) by running clubs for the younger girls; working with staff to improve subject teaching; training as peer educators in sex and relationship issues for years 5 and 8, in conjunction with a local state school and Sheffield University; helping in local state primaries or the school's own junior section; running conversation classes for asylum seekers and refugees in the community. Strong careers education – links with local industry and commerce provide a broad range of work experience opportunities.

Junior school has own gym and access to senior school sports facilities for the older children; netball, badminton and diving success at city and county level. Plenty of music (the music room is a large loft conversion): regular performances, eg at a local retirement village, and an annual musical. The girls have named their ensembles Prawn Cocktails (the wind band), Spaghetti Strings and Angel Delight (the chamber choir) – making a concert a three course meal. Lots of LAMDA and impressive art and design, eg some interesting constructions made from recycled materials, inspired by a visit to a Victorian water wheel.

An extensive range of clubs – jewellery making, sewing, Latin, chess, science, Mandarin Chinese, street dance, yoga, cookery – with input from sixth form girls; fundraising for a school in Kenya; a school council plus participation in the senior school council and whole school Kitchen Cabinet (for suggestions about food); talks from various visitors, including parents, who support multi-cultural topics, such as an Indian wedding and fashion show. A sensory garden area plus adventure playground with stepping stones, netball court, wild area to come; each class has its own lot.

Background and atmosphere: Founded in 1878 by the Girls' Day School Trust, in Broomhill, Sheffield, near to the university. The original Victorian building dates from 1884 – most of the mansions in the road have since been acquired and the modern additions blend in well, apart from the 1960/70s ones. The extremely well-stocked and attractive library also houses an ICT and careers area; art, technology and science areas have recently been extended; clasrooms are being refurbished; and the much-improved sixth form accommodation – small, intimate classrooms looking out onto part of the gardens, lots of modern pine furniture – is a great draw. We were very taken with the two common rooms, decorated according to the girls' specifications in various shades of red, pink and purple, with glamorous large light shades, and the Pink Room, for study/relaxation, with pink and chrome bar stools and tables and cooking facilities (sixth formers can also go out of school for lunch). New year 11 social area too with common room and kitchen facilities.

S

Infants have their own recently acquired house with cheerful, well-resourced classrooms (16 max in reception; 18 max for the rest). We particularly liked the French room's circular blue carpet decorated with green lily pads, numbers and letters; another well-stocked library with an interactive plasma screen for reception (interactive whiteboards in all the other classrooms). A pleasant outdoor area with a mini netball goal and tubs for gardening.

The latest ISI report praises the 'warm, stimulating and happy environment', supported by the girls we spoke to: 'The people are lovely; coming here [for year 12] is the best thing I've ever done – it's like a second home'; 'It's easy to make friends if you're new'; 'There's a strong community spirit'; 'You're free to be yourself'. The uniform is green or navy plaid skirts and blue jumpers – home clothes for the sixth.

School has won the Independent Schools Award three times for the collaboration with maintained schools and for community links.

Pastoral care, well-being and discipline: Good rewards and behaviour policies (the latter reviewed annually by the school council) and pastoral care (parents say problems are dealt with promptly and effectively); smooth transition from the junior to the senior school. Girls are 'given independence within a secure framework, in an empathetic atmosphere,' said a junior parent. Well-behaved children, very smart in their green and blue skirts, green blouses and jumpers, who present as happy, confident, thoughtful and forthcoming. Wide choice of food. Wraparound care 7.45am-5.30pm – a charge for after-school only (includes food).

Bullying not seen as a problem. The school is well aware of the kind of emotional difficulties very able and ambitious girls can suffer from and provides a full-time nurse plus a counsellor, who comes in one day a week, as well as liaising with external support services and holding evenings on teen issues for parents. Also a regular happiness questionnaire with input from the school council, now online, enabling identification of girls with problems. Parents and girls feel concerns are handled promptly and well. Year 7s have most of their lessons in rooms on one corridor, to help them adjust gradually to the school's size; sixth form prefects assist with years 7-8 and the house system allows younger girls to get support from older ones. Sixth form tutor groups formed by combining self-selecting friendship groups.

Pupils and parents: Ethnically (15 per cent EAL, with 40 languages spoken at home), socially and economically diverse – a large number of professional/self-employed. From Sheffield, South Yorkshire, North Nottinghamshire, North Derbyshire; half from the junior school, half from state primary and other prep schools. About 15 join the sixth from outside. Girls present as articulate, confident, grounded, ambitious and appreciative of what the school offers them.

Parents find the staff approachable and accessible and the school responsive to concerns and suggestions – regular contact via newsletters, forums and a very informative website. Girls have lifelong access to the 50,000 strong GDST alumnae network, which helps them with work experience, careers advice and gap year funding.

Old pupils: AS Byatt; Margaret Drabble; Angela Knight (CEO Energy UK); Deborah Ann Barham (comedian).

Entrance: Juniors – informal individual assessment in English and maths at any time (generally above national average ability); reception – informal individual assessment to check for school readiness, at the school or at the child's nursery. Year 7: test in English and maths similar to KS2 Sats, taken by all; year 8-11: age-appropriate tests in maths and English; well above average ability standard needed. Sixth form: seven GCSEs A*-C with at least a B in subjects to be taken at A level.

Exit: Nearly all juniors to senior school. About a third per cent leave post-GCSE for boarding schools, coeducational state or independent schools or Sheffield College for practical courses, and many others join. Sixth form leavers depart for a wide range of universities (five to Oxbridge in 2016) – with Leeds, Manchester, Sheffield and Newcastle popular – and subjects, from chiropractic to civil engineering to criminology. Also nine medics, including one medical physiologist.

Money matters: About 15 – 20 per cent have means-tested bursaries or academic scholarships. Year 7 scholarships awarded on basis of entrance exam; bursaries for girls in the top 50 per cent, up to full fees; HSBC scholarship for children from a state primary. Sixth form scholarships awarded in individual subjects; Ogden Trust scholarship for state school students taking science and maths A levels and physics at university – up to full fees. Four HSBC scholarships awarded annually.

Fifteen per cent discount for third and fourth children at the school; 10 per cent loyalty discount for sixth form girls if they have been at the school for 10 years.

Remarks: The only all-through independent school for girls in Sheffield, offering exceptionally high levels academic and extracurricular opportunities in a very supportive and responsive environment – perhaps not so suitable for the less ambitious and conformist.

Skipton Girls' High School

Gargrave Road, Skipton, North Yorkshire BD23 1QL

Pupils: 795 • Ages: 11–18 • Sixth form: 235

Tel: 01756 707600
Email: sghs@sghs.org.uk
Website: www.sghs.org.uk

Headteacher: Since 2014, Mrs Jenn Plews, previously head of academy since 2013.

Academic matters: In 2016, 43 per cent of A level entries graded A*/A. Classes rarely over 20. Options include engineering, also PE, taken at nearby Ermysted's Grammar School for boys, some of whom take subjects at Skipton Girls' High. 'Boys have a more challenging, risk taking approach, which benefits the girls,' says head. Biology, maths, Eng lit, history, government and politics all strong. Psychology very popular, small numbers for mod langs. All do AS general studies and can choose the A level. Also AS critical thinking.

Very good value added and consistently impressive results at key stage 4 – very high ranking nationally. In 2016, 65 per cent A*/A grades at GCSE. Key stage 4 starts in year 9: girls can take maths in year 9 or 10 and begin AS in year 10/11. All take RE in year 10. Choice of engineering (two groups), systems and control or food tech, also media studies, but only French and German (Spanish also on offer at two-year key stage 3).

Thorough going monitoring and tracking. Lots of differentiation in lessons and choice of learning approaches; teachers seen as very helpful. Several modern ICT suites (two just for sixth form). Netbook lease scheme (paid for over three years) allows complete integration of ICT with learning – girls with netbooks to be seen all over the school. These provide access to the highly developed virtual learning environment (VLE) in and out of class. Sixth form have two year laptop/netbook version with Toshiba, including insurance and on site warranty. This hugely increases the amount and sophistication of work that can be achieved in each lesson.

Another very impressive innovation is a project where girls collaborate with teachers to design course content and approaches, making lessons and homework far more interactive and engaging and developing a deep understanding of learning processes. These girls have a grasp of and fluency in educational terminology that you would expect from recently trained teachers (they are used to presenting the project to outside adults, as well as delivering professional development sessions to their own teachers after school). Consequently lessons may be like tutorials – teachers not seen as 'the sage on the stage,' says deputy head. They can choose their 'individual pathway,' leading to higher motivation and results, with more independence, opportunity to pursue their intellectual curiosity and freedom from the constraints of the national curriculum. The only drawback is that they may start university ready for the second year – we felt quite envious of teachers working in this buzzing environment. An additional outstanding venture is the e-mentoring by sixth formers, who offer help to students at home in the evening via the VLE and by text – with clear bonuses for both parties.

Thoughtful, sensitive special educational needs co-ordinator. Confident she can handle full range of disabilities (no moderate or severe learning ones present, though, owing to the admission tests) and will offer whatever support needed, even if no statement, including one to one in class. She matches her variously qualified assistants, to individual students, to enhance relationships. All screened for dyslexia on entry. School is (deservedly) regional centre for gifted and talented students.

Games, options, the arts: The downside of the site's restricted size is the lack of a decent sports hall (just a small gym, plus well used mini fitness suite and several netball/tennis courts). School uses nearby, very good sports centre. Usual sports, plus football, rugby (competes), gymnastics. Extracurricular zumba, kangoo, non-contact boxing and Thai kick boxing. National achievements in fencing, golf and fell-running, as well as an elite gymnast and ladies' mountain boarding champ – happy to buy in top level coaching.

Music flourishes – a large number learn instruments and professional orchestra in residence, various ensembles, informal teatime and other concerts. Drama (supported by Judi Dench and Celia Imrie – classy) takes place in trad school hall or big Judi Dench Studio, with fetching purple curtains, also used for dance (modern rather than ballet – no barre). Year 11 students can do drama focused EPQ – recent very successful production of Twelfth Night with Ermysted's boys.

Outstanding engineering opportunities – has national reputation for science, technology, engineering and maths (STEM) teaching and works with local schools to promote it. Strong links with industry, eg Bentley, Silver Cross. Girls made winning go-kart out of a 1970s Silver Cross pram for James May's My Sisters' Top Toys TV programme, beating Ermysted's as well as James May, whose entry was purpose-built by the company – yay! Rolls Royce is a sponsor – sixth formers are racing and working on Ford Greenpower electric car, along with RR apprentices, engineers and managers. Two teams working with local companies on real science, engineering and technological problems, including residential at Liverpool University.

Sizeable art room – very good work, especially 3D, displayed around school, though more could be used to brighten up the original building. Annual exhibition of art and engineering projects and products.

Masses of activities – over 80 in a term. Projects with schools in Morocco, Jordan, Germany and trips to places like Iceland, EuroDisney, German exchange. Extended day (7.45am-5.15pm) four days a week – breakfast club, after school support and enrichment.

Excellent sixth form enrichment programme includes counselling, team leading (business management), debating (a strength), new languages (eg Mandarin), engineering education scheme. All do peer mentoring training, some do academic mentoring of younger students or organise activities for them. Work experience/shadowing encouraged – mod lang students can go to Germany or France. Annual higher education day attended by university admissions tutors and university taster courses.

Background and atmosphere: Old building has mostly trad classrooms and science labs, with some drab and poky walls and staircases, but girls like its quirkiness and sense of history and say it's homely. Standard multi-use hall, well stocked library (full of girls during the lunch break). Pleasant, yellow brick modern extension, plus several chocolate coloured Portakabins, euphemistically called 'chalets,' with darkish classrooms (apparently lighter in summer). Brand new £1.8m STEM centre. Small porch and lawn with picnic benches for munching packed lunches. Woods at back of school. Westbank, sixth form centre in Edwardian house, has IT room, bistro and relaxation area with bar stools – girls wear business dress.

Now an academy, school has had two outstanding Ofsteds and is involved in research promoting gender equality in schools and has worked with local universities on the health and welfare of girls. Much scope for influencing decisions and exercising leadership (the girls we met were given this report to check). School council, executive body of students from across year groups involved in three major projects to enhance school, house captain and head girl teams (houses are called Bronte, Curie, Johnson and Franklin). Girls feel they are encouraged to aim high, but not in competition with each other, that their teachers know them well and can judge how much pressure to achieve is appropriate for them individually.

Pastoral care, well-being and discipline: Unusually, has vertical tutor groups of about 22 – two or three from each of years 7-11, plus three or four from years 12-13, whose ability to mentor younger girls frees tutors to concentrate on individuals. This produces a supportive atmosphere ('people get on'), friendships across year groups, easier transition for new year 7s and 12s and improved behaviour. The much valued and used, centrally located student progress centre – 'there's always a friendly face you can talk to if you are feeling down or confused,' according to one of my guides – provides academic and careers advice plus Relate counselling and access to other external health agencies. The school nurse can be accessed by text (very modern). As you would by now expect, discipline is personalised rather than rule bound.

Pupils and parents: Feeder primaries in Skipton and surrounding area – about a quarter from outside catchment area. Skipton is fairly privileged, but pupils come from a range of backgrounds and cultures. Confident, friendly, articulate and enthusiastic girls. Notable old girls include opera singer Elizabeth Harwood and Ruzwana Bashir, who chaired the Oxford Union. Parents are very happy with school ('absolutely fantastic,' one told us), especially with speedy, two-way e-communication via SimplyClick. Key stage 3 parents and daughters meet tutor at mutually convenient time of day to review and set targets rather than conventional parents' evening.

S

Entrance: Governors are responsible for admissions. For entry at 11 girls take tests in maths, English and verbal reasoning in September of year 6 (112 places a year). In-catchment or looked after pupils have priority, then girls with a sister in the school, then distance from home. If spare places are available in years 8 to 11, applicants take school's English, maths and science tests. For entry to sixth form, girls need five GCSEs at C or above including English and maths, usually with a B in A level subjects. Maximum of 20 from outside at this stage, plus replacements for girls who leave – increasing demand.

Exit: Around 20 per cent leave post-GCSE, often to specialise in sport or art at FE colleges or to take up music scholarships at Giggleswick School (though they often ask to return). At 18, vast majority to university, including generally several to Oxbridge. Engineering features, but the most popular subject recently is psychology.

Remarks: The unexceptional exterior is entry to an excitingly futuristic learning world. You sense that these are girls who will not be limited by glass ceilings. Watch out for flying shards!

Stonyhurst College

Linked with St Mary's Hall

Stonyhurst, Clitheroe, Lancashire BB7 9PZ

Pupils: 465; 325 boarders • Ages: 13–18 • Sixth form: 250 • RC

Fees: Day £18,615; Boarding £27,861 – £33,429 pa

Tel: 01254 827073
Email: admissions@stonyhurst.ac.uk
Website: www.stonyhurst.ac.uk

Headmaster: Since September 2016, John Browne, previously head of St Aloysius' College in Glasgow. Music degree from Bristol, postgrad LLB from City and an MBA. He has also been deputy head of Ampleforth, head of Westminster Cathedral Choir and assistant director of music at Berkhamsted and The Latymer. He is married to Marie and they have a son.

Academic matters: Good value-added, especially at GCSE; in 2016, 49 per cent of all passes were A*/A. Sixty-nine per cent of A level passes were graded A*-B, 44 per cent A*/A. Maths consistently popular at A level, achieving good results. Introduced IB in 2013 – 'fits approach to learning in a Jesuit school'; believes success in IB lies in being 'organised, hard-working, academically able but not necessarily super bright'. Second results in 2016 saw a great improvement to an average of 36 points, with one student getting 44 out of 45.

Broad curriculum including French, Spanish and German, together with Greek and Latin. Average class size 18, 10 in the sixth form. Compulsory RE to GCSE, non-examined theology/ethics in sixth form. Four classes set according to ability at entrance. In recent years influx of new teaching staff who 'provide a good balance'; much investment in sharing good practice, training and development.

Pupils are assigned a personal tutor whom they meet weekly to discuss all-round progress. Stays with them through their school career, just one aspect of the Jesuit ethos of individual care. Broad ability intake and thus not the academic powerhouse of city day schools. Genuine desire for each pupil to fulfill their potential – many pupils exceed this and very able pupils do particularly well.

Twenty per cent of pupils have EAL support provided in discrete lessons and within mainstream lessons. Special needs (mainly dyslexic and dyspraxic) similarly provided under supervision of specialist SEN teacher. Learning mentor helps with organisation and study skills.

Plenty of computers around linked up to the school's intranet and all pupils have their own email address. Pupils timetabled IT to year 9, then GCSE option. Laptop internet connections in sixth form study bedrooms; PCs at study work places for younger pupils.

Games, options, the arts: A 'sport for all' policy encompasses both pupils and wealth of activities on offer. Compulsory sport throughout the school, achieving notable success in rugby, golf, hockey and netball. Super indoor swimming pool and all-weather pitch, plus new all weather tennis dome.

Music is highly valued; extensive music department in the basement complete with high tech soundproof pods for practice and lessons. The proud owner of three grand pianos, a Steinway, a Bosendorfer and a Bechstein. College's orchestras, ensembles and choirs thrive – pupils win places with regional orchestras too. Opportunities near and far – most recently the Big Band Belgian Tour.

Good DT department with plenty of scope for those artistically inclined. Strong drama – recent big musical productions emulate West End success in Les Mis, Sweeney Todd and the Sound of Music. Excellent performance space provided by newly upgraded Academy Room. With 'horizontal boarding' pupils divided vertically into four 'lines' for competitions, aka inter-line. More recent emphasis with appointment of a master in charge – now compete across sporting disciplines, and interestingly, share dealing.

Outdoor pursuits in abundance – fishing, canoeing, sailing, fell walking and clay pigeon shooting. Hugely proud of VCs awarded to seven OS; not surprising CCF (compulsory in year 10) thriving. Further afield pupils participate in world challenge trips, pilgrimages to Lourdes, D of E expeditions, to name but a few. IB pupils built a new kitchen garden on the junior site; senior pupils visit once a week.

Service to the community and charity – writ large. Arrupe Programme – sixth form pupils give a period of voluntary service each week in the local community, sixth form holiday week for disabled children and a mentor scheme and swap visits with Catholic primary in Liverpool plus support for partner school in Zimbabwe.

Boarding: Boarding accommodation mostly situated in the upper reaches of the historic buildings. Boys board in playrooms but there is separate accommodation for the girls, in two linked houses, one for sixth form. Each playroom has its own common room and boarding facilities, cared for by a married couple; girls are looked after by a housemistress. On entry it's four or five to a room but this reduces, so by the sixth form single study/bedrooms are the norm. Well-presented, spacious with adequate storage, the standard of facilities is only surpassed by the care each pupil receives, rated outstanding in all respects by a recent Ofsted inspection.

This is essentially a full-time boarding school, 'no mass exodus at weekends', but exeats are readily approved, according to pupils. Long and busy school day, Sunday afternoon appreciated by some as their only free time to do as they please. Much of the weekend is consumed by prep, sports, excursions and church though activities available on a Sunday afternoon should the pupil choose.

Background and atmosphere: Founded by the Jesuits at St Omer, in what is now northern France, for English families forced to pursue a Catholic education abroad. After a succession of moves the school was given refuge at its present site in the Catholic part of Lancashire by Thomas Weld, who later donated the property to the school. The buildings are magnificent, though perhaps don't quite live up to the idyllic photography in the glossy marketing materials. No doubting the majesty of the architecture, and with its own observatory (with a full astronomical telescope and an astronomical society).and nine hole golf course, set in a 2,500-acre estate, most of which is farmed. 'I arrive each morning and cannot believe that this is my school,' commented one pupil.

Much of the school is truly splendid; huge staircases, wood panelling, polished stone, works of art, brimming with history and tradition. Some formerly hidden treasures and the Waterton Collection are now exhibited in the Long Gallery for all to enjoy. The Collections Group, under the auspices of the curator, is allowed access to the treasures in the Square Library. Recent developments include a sympathetically refurbished and equipped library and study centre in the heart of the school. New refectory and sixth form boarding house with en-suite facilities has taken the standard of accommodation up a notch.

Be prepared to learn a whole new vocabulary to enter the world of a Jesuit school. For starters 'lines' are school houses, 'playrooms' are year groups, 'playroom masters' are housemasters and as for the school year groups – Lower Grammar, Grammar, Syntax, Poetry and Rhetoric. Religion is taken seriously but is not oppressive. Co-ed for more than 10 years, feels as if it has always been so. Girls 'have improved communication at all levels'.

A few years ago Stonyhurst hit the tabloids twice but parents we spoke to showed overwhelming support for the way the issues were dealt with. 'Open and honest communication, the school showed compassion while taking a firm line': one parent's words encapsulated the opinion of others.

Pastoral care, well-being and discipline: Spirituality is at the heart of the school, promoting a 'caring, supportive and prayerful community', providing a safe environment that allows 'pupils to feel safe in doing their own thing without fear of ridicule'. Tolerance and respect of each other's differences, collaboration when working together. Demonstrated by the non-sporty keen photographer, whose talents were spotted, and is now the official chronicler for the first XV rugby team, accompanying them on tours and at matches.

Body of prefects called Committee, selected through interview process and votes from staff and lower sixth. Duties include affiliation to a particular playroom. Girl and boy heads of Committee chosen from the group of 13.

Pupils 'are given quite a lot of freedom based on the mutual confidence and trust that exists between pupils and staff,' according to one parent. A Family Handbook sets out clear expectations of conduct and behaviour; rules are few, clear and enforced; 'we expect them to get it right'. A review of sanctions has introduced a more incremental scale of chastisement. Rewards success celebrated through award ceremonies. A 'line' card accumulates debits and credits for academic and social performance which then contribute to the relevant 'line' grand total.

Cases of bullying are rare, dealt with by playroom staff and the pupil-run playroom committees. A few suspensions in the past for soft drug offences, but not a drugs school and no regular random testing. Alcohol restricted to one drink on a Saturday evening under supervision for year 12. Saturday evening access allowed to village pub for year 13 until 10.15pm. Suspension for those bringing alcohol on the premises. Discipline not a big issue here.

Pupils and parents: Diverse – more socially mixed than equivalent schools, with 65 per cent Catholic faith. Southern parents like school's lack of consumerism and social competitiveness. Rich mix of accents – regional and international; 40 per cent of boarders are non-Brits, with small numbers from 28 nations, predominantly Spanish and Mexican, but with a league of nations from Nigeria to Korea. International links are highly valued and there has 'never been a problem with racism'.

Confident, articulate and mature pupils praise the community feel of the school and are rightfully proud of its heritage. Day pupils are encouraged to stay after school for studies and activities – a facility valued by parents – and may feel left out if they choose not to do so.

Alumni include 12 martyrs and seven VCs. Also Arthur Conan Doyle, Charles Laughton, General Walters, Paul Johnson, Peter Moorhouse, Bishop Hollis, Bishop Hines, Charles Sturridge,

Hugh Woolridge, Jonathon Plowright, Bill Cash MP, Bruce Kent, Mark Thompson, Lords Chitnis and Talbot, Kyran Bracken and Robert Brinkley.

Entrance: Day pupils from local Lancashire schools, day and boarding from own prep (St Mary's Hall), boarding from St John's Beaumont and a variety of other schools, both here and abroad. Particularly strong links with Spain. Broad ability intake – 'for some, six GCSEs will be an achievement'. Academic entrance exam but other factors taken into account, particularly family connections with the school. Five GCSE passes at C and above, plus interview, for entry into sixth form though many AS subject choices require a minimum grade B. Those unable to attend for interview eg overseas pupils, write a 500 word essay explaining why they wish to come to Stonyhurst.

Exit: Wide range of English universities, Russell Group and redbrick, London popular, and Edinburgh. Numbers vary to Oxbridge – three places in 2016. Breadth of degree courses from medical (four in 2016) to media arts, engineering to economics with 'ologies' as well. Plenty of international links and scope for travel through the Jesuit community with many students taking a gap year.

Money matters: A variety of scholarships awarded at entry 13+ and sixth form; academic, music and art and design, as well as all-rounder awards, ranging from 10 per cent to a maximum of 50 per cent of fees. St Francis Xavier awards of 20 per cent of fees are also available to those who 'are most likely to benefit from and contribute to life as full boarders in a Catholic boarding school'. All can be topped up with a means-tested bursary.

Remarks: Jesuit values permeate every aspect of this distinguished boarding school, steeped in history and set in beautiful surroundings. A genuine concern for the individual ensures that each pupil is given every opportunity to fulfill the school motto 'Quant Je Pius' – all that I can.

Teesside High School

The Avenue, Eaglescliffe, Stockton-on-Tees TS16 9AT

Pupils: 344 • Ages: 3–18 • Sixth form: 43: 14 boys, 29 girls

Fees: £4,500 – £12,840 pa

Tel: 01642 782095
Email: info@teessidehigh.co.uk
Website: www.teessidehigh.co.uk

Head Teacher: Since 2014, Mr Andrew Wilson MA BMus. Born and educated in Leeds, he gained a first in music at Edinburgh University, followed by masters at Cardiff University, where he studied 18th century English music. Assistant director of music at Ipswich School and RGS Guildford, then director of music at RGS Worcester and Milton Abbey. Prior to joining Teesside High was pastoral deputy at New Hall School, Chelmsford. Mr Wilson is a keen sportsman – played league cricket in his youth and is an avid Yorkshire supporter. Married to Abbey, with three children in the prep and senior school.

Head of prep: Since 2013, Mrs Carolyn Williams. BEd in maths and science from Northumbria, postgrad certificate in leadership and management from Durham. Formerly senior teacher at Yarm, teaches maths; two daughters, one in prep and one in seniors; enjoys country walks with husband, children and dog and is learning to play golf. Parents are impressed by 'changes for the better', firm in their belief that everyone here 'has the children's best interests at heart'.

Academic matters: Little Diamonds nursery takes children from 3; flexible sessions allowed, most moving to full-time as they approach reception age. Wraparound care from 7.45am-6pm suits the needs of busy parents, as do the holiday clubs. French is taught from reception and learning takes places indoors and out, with full use being made of the lovely woodland school in the grounds.

Has just introduced International Primary Curriculum, which teaches a range of different subjects through topics. All mixed ability classes except maths in years 5 and 6; all children have opportunities to use iPads; group music lessons where everyone gets a chance to learn different instruments and play in ensembles.

In 2016, 45 per cent of GCSE grades were A*/A. At A level, a disappointing 43 per cent A*-B and 13 per cent A*/A. Traditional academic curriculum. Option of three separate sciences at GCSE or dual award science course. All key stage 3 pupils study separate sciences, geography, history, RE, music, food and nutrition, art and IT. Most pupils also study three languages, French, German and Latin, but Spanish is also available as an extra.

Free access to IT suite during school hours and each pupil has own email address at school. Staff using iPads to enrich and challenge – homework may occasionally come straight to mobiles via an app. And just to show that they are covering both the ancient and modern here, gifted and talented pupils enjoy ancient Greek in readiness for performing a Greek tragedy in the school grounds.

Small classes (average 15), some very small in sixth form. Experienced staff – over half have 10 or more years' experience with the school. Very low turnover. Pupils are set for most subjects.

Homework ranges from 90 minutes a night for 11-year-olds to three hours a night for sixth form. Pupils get a report of some kind every term, with a full report sent out at end of year. Special needs co-ordinator – support for dyslexia and dyspraxia.

Games, options, the arts: Sport is compulsory for all – several county standard players and a silver equestrian medal for a former pupil at London 2012. Sports include athletics, tennis, football, hockey, rugby, badminton, cricket and canoeing. Superb fitness suite for those less inclined to team sports.

All take part in wide range of activities – including origami, golf, bridge and many more besides. These are sensibly accommodated in an extra long lunchtime break, which allows pupils to eat and enjoy enrichment activities too. All-weather sports pitch and sports hall used throughout the day for teaching and at lunchtime for extra activities. Most year 10 pupils take D of E awards.

Well-equipped music rooms with plenty of keyboards, instruments and computers for budding composers and a new drama and dance studio. Many play a musical instrument and there is a choir, orchestra and jazz band. Large number take speech and drama awards. Art is very popular, paintings and sculpture on show everywhere. House competitions fiercely fought in a wide range of disciplines, including singing, sport, photography and Masterchef.

Background and atmosphere: Teesside High was founded as a girls' school in 1970 when Queen Victoria High School and Cleveland School amalgamated. School is now fully co-educational. Slightly more girls than boys – 60/40 – but no one seems to mind and therefore it doesn't seem to matter. We met plenty of bright, articulate boys able to hold their own and not looking or feeling like a minority. Plenty of success in boys' sports underpins this.

Set in 19 acres bordering the River Tees, with stunning views of the Cleveland Hills and a stone's throw from the delightfully tempting shops and coffee emporiums of picturesque Yarm. School is hidden from sight, tucked away down The Avenue, an approach road bordered by private houses and a retirement home. Main buildings sit neatly in well-kept grounds. Brightly coloured picket fence surrounds the prep school. Lovely grounds, with river frontage, large pond and newly created woodland school used for outdoor teaching in wide range of 'low-risk' activities for pupils of all ages. Recently unearthed air raid bunker in the grounds is being refurbished to bring history lessons to life.

Classrooms and corridors have an air of calm, unusually clean and tidy, lots of good work on display. Food is 'better than good', say pupils. Dining room operates on a cafeteria system, with bright blue tables and murals painted by pupils and choice of hot and cold meals. Halal food on menu and even though this is a day school breakfast and tea are available too. Sixth formers have their own car park and a new sixth form building, which includes teaching rooms, private study areas, common room and conference facilities.

Attractive glass atrium on entry to prep school and lovely work displayed everywhere; this is a busy and productive place. Outside there's a new all-weather playground and pirate ship, Astroturf, space hoppers, Kwik cricket and toys-a-plenty plus separate play area for the youngest. According to the children, 'there's everything you need here to grow up'. Wise heads on young shoulders maybe, yet genuinely proud of their school. Well-equipped music ('we love our singing,' say the children) and ICT rooms; spacious hall used for assemblies and PE for the youngest. Small room for SEN, officially titled Inspirational Learning Zone, but nicknamed The Tardis by the children because apparently, like Dr Who, 'you come out feeling better than when you went in'.

One parent described the teaching staff as Mary Poppins-like: 'an air of authority as necessary but no shouting needed' and new, sometimes shy children are calmly and warmly welcomed into classes. Those classes are small, a factor that has huge appeal and proves the biggest draw for local parents. Now fully co-educational.

Pastoral care, well-being and discipline: The school prides itself on being 'a community in which everyone is treated with respect and understanding and where all talents and gifts are nurtured and valued.' Form tutors play key role in guiding pupils. School is multi-faith and there is a small prayer room.

School sets store by community projects – Christmas parties for OAPs, charity quizzes and visits to local hospice. Dialogue and discussion are strongly encouraged. Head pupil and deputy head pupil run school council – each year group has three reps and recent innovations include chilled water supply and napkins in dining room. Buddy system introduced to encourage older pupils to befriend and help younger pupils. Open forum for parents to raise issues once a term. Behaviour is good – no vandalism, graffiti or discipline problems, says head, just occasional high spirits in corridors. School has introduced extended day to help working parents – now open from 7.45am till 6pm. Also runs popular holiday clubs for 3 to 13-year-olds during school holidays.

Pupils and parents: We met confident, considered, articulate children, happy to chat and excited by their school. They appear sincere and determined in their approach to sport and studies alike, keen to win and do well. Parents equally excited and committed – they've done their homework before choosing the school (plenty of options locally), felt warmly welcomed here and their children settled in quickly.

Parents are mostly medics, accountants, lawyers and local businesspeople. Lots of first-time buyers, though a scattering of alumni offspring too. A small number of overseas pupils live with local families. We spoke to several parents who had moved their children from the maintained sector and were 'delighted' at their children's 'increased levels of interest and achievement'. Parents spoke about the very positive care given to children and the 'individualised' education, enthusing that 'there is so much to offer beyond the curriculum'.

Pupils travel in by bus (organised in-house) from 25-mile radius, from as far afield as south Durham and north Yorkshire. Former pupils include broadcasters Shiulie Ghosh (formerly of ITV News) and Pam Royle (Tyne Tees and Border TV).

Entrance: To prep by taster days, assessment and talk with head. At 11, all pupils (including those from the prep) sit verbal reasoning paper and emotional intelligence questionnaire. Two-thirds entering senior school come from prep, a third from primary schools. Pupils entering sixth form need at least six GCSE passes (preferably grade B and above).

Exit: Sensibly, most prep pupils follow the natural progression into the senior school (100 per cent in 2016) unless the family moves elsewhere. Around half leave after GCSEs. Almost all sixth form leavers go to university; Liverpool, Newcastle, Northumbria, Manchester, Sheffield, St Andrews, Teesside and York St John popular in 2016.

Money matters: School offers means-tested bursaries each year on a first come, first served basis. Scholarships and exhibitions available for academic ability, music (and sport in sixth form and prep).

Remarks: 'Everything is possible' is the school motto and the school certainly feels that way. Staff and pupils at this unpretentious, hardworking school exude a very special charm with a refreshing lack of arrogance.

Wakefield Girls' High School

Wentworth Street, Wakefield, West Yorkshire WF1 2QS

Pupils: 730 • Ages: 11–18 • Sixth form: 170

Fees: £11,967 pa

Tel: 01924 372490
Email: admissions@wghsss.org.uk
Website: www.wgsf.org.uk

Headmistress: Since 2015, Mrs Nina Gunson. A Wakefield old girl herself, Mrs Gunson knows the school's values and ethos well and is committed to single-sex education. She gained a first class degree in molecular and cellular biology from the University of Huddersfield followed by an MSc in multimedia and E-learning.

Mrs Gunson was previously deputy head at Sheffield High School (also all girls) and, before that, assistant head at Buttershaw Business and Enterprise College. She began her teaching career at Bradford Girls' Grammar School.

However, refuses to meet the Guide or discuss reasons for her shyness.

Academic matters: In 2016, 43 per cent A*/A and 76 per cent A*-B at A level. Excellent results in all subjects and a wide range on offer, even if it means groups of only two or three at A level. Most take three A2s plus general studies. Art and design is very popular; the AQA external examiner the day we visited said that the work was the best he had ever seen. It's very well-resourced; girls are allowed a lot of freedom and respond with remarkable creativity, using a variety of media. Biology is popular too, and very strong, as is chemistry; maths, politics, psychology and Spanish also stand out. Boys from QEGS join for a number of subjects, eg theatre studies, ICT and RS. There are no hurdles for existing girls to enter the sixth form but if it's clear a girl will struggle with the pace, she will be encouraged to go down a less academic route elsewhere.

GCSE results are also consistently excellent, 75 per cent A/A* and 99 per cent A*-C in 2016. Large numbers do separate sciences; dual award also offered. Textiles for all in years 7-9 and girls make all the clothes for a fashion show. In design and technology the projects are tailored towards girls' interests and creativity, and product design is offered at GCSE. Lots of PCs and several interactive whiteboards; all girls do the ECDL in year 9 and learn keyboard skills in the junior school. Class sizes are around 24 for years 7-9; 5-25 at GCSE; 2-16 at A level. Setting for maths and French only from Years 8/9.

The well-staffed special needs unit is modern, bright and comfortable, catering for around 150 girls with eg dyslexia, dyscalculia, Asperger's – but not children with statements who, the school considers, would be better served in the state system. Support is given outside lesson time.

Games, options, the arts: Sports facilities are very good and exceptional results are achieved in local and national competitions in the usual range of sports as well as cross-country; netball and hockey are particularly strong, probably because they are started at the age of seven. Nearly half the school takes part in teams. Self-defence and various kinds of gymnastics are also available. Very good drama facilities – a drama studio and access to a purpose-built theatre at QEGS. Lots of productions – mainly conventional choices, apart from the drama comp for years 7-9 where girls write their own plays. Masses of music – a great range of choirs, some enjoying success in local competitions, and music groups for all ages, some in combination with QEGS, plus a wide choice of instrumental lessons (over half the girls learn) including jazz piano and bass guitar, with lots of very good exam results. Concerts, as well as plays, are put on with the boys' school (the Advent Carol Service is held in Wakefield Cathedral) and there is a recording studio funded by the PTA. Girls in years 7-9 create their own dance routines in an inter-form dance competition.

The library is generously resourced and fiction reading actively encouraged at all ages; a major extension is being planned. Plenty of school trips, in England and abroad, eg a swing band tour of north Italy, a hockey and netball tour to Hong Kong, Australia and Singapore, visits to France, Spain, Rome. Year 7 girls have a residential at the start of their first term to help them make friends, which they greatly value. A very wide choice of clubs and societies, including hamster care, fun with food and a gardening club with vegetable garden and wormery. Huge numbers achieve D of E awards.

W

Background and atmosphere: The school belongs to the Wakefield Grammar School Foundation, which offers 3-18 education to both sexes. It occupies a number of buildings in a conservation area near the centre of Wakefield, one-time town houses, the focal point being the original Georgian Wentworth House, with some attractive and thoughtfully-designed modern additions, though some areas are drab and in need of re-decoration. Subjects are located in zones, eg creative arts, embracing music/drama/English/textiles and food tech, with a common, well-equipped computer suite.

There is an immediate buzz as soon as you enter the school. Girls come across as well-mannered, happy, confident and eager to learn. They appreciate the understanding and support they are given by teachers if they have any difficulties, work hard and have fun, too, eg the sixth formers have a fancy dress day in their last week at school, and there is a Christmas review performed by girls with guest appearances by staff. Lots of marvellous artwork and photos of girls' activities on display. Girls' birthdays are highlighted on big TV screens in three locations and all are given a teddy both on entering the junior as well as leaving the senior school – the latter dressed in a school hoodie! There is a strong sense of community, which the girls value; they see the school as friendly and safe.

Huge amounts of money raised for charity, with the girls doing all the organisation, and there are links with a sister school in Tanzania, where girls teach on visits, as well as state school partnership events. The school council's views, eg on food, charities, etc are taken on board; its eco committee is aiming for the 'Green Flag Award'. The sixth form have their own building, an old house (due to be refurbished) with a café, kitchen and common room well supplied with battered sofas – the clutter is all very homely and they are allowed to entertain boys and enjoy a degree of independence there. There are three lovely memorials to old girls who have died young – a stained glass window depicting a rainbow, an indoor fountain and a small garden with wooden animal sculptures – that illustrate the school's humanity and thoughtfulness.

Pastoral care, well-being and discipline: Pastoral care is very good – girls are well known to staff, who soon spot signs of unhappiness. Girls say teachers take any upsets or arguments seriously and that there is no real bullying. The very good bullying policy was re-drafted by girls and there is a very sensible, realistic sixth form handbook. The transition from junior to senior school happens easily, as junior girls are able to use some of the senior school facilities. The girls are given freedom and clear limits (a code of conduct that 'gives guidelines for acceptable behaviour rather than rules') which they rarely breach, allowing a relatively relaxed atmosphere. Very strong line is taken with drugs and smoking.

Pupils and parents: Some wealthy parents but most are professional/middle class. This is not a prosperous area and about a fifth of the girls currently receive assistance with fees – 'No one knows who's on an award; money is not an issue'. The catchment area is extensive: Wakefield, Huddersfield, Barnsley, north Sheffield and south Leeds. Parents organise bus services to fill in any gaps left by public transport. Half of year 7 come from the junior school, the rest from local schools. Ethnically very mixed – one year had a Muslim head girl, 'clearly the best person for the job', so the school decided to adapt the post's duties to accommodate her religious beliefs.

Entrance: Eleven plus by exam in English and maths, with verbal and non-verbal reasoning (110 in verbal reasoning is the cut off point, as 'they must be able to cope with the work – it's an absolutely basic requirement') plus primary school report and reference. The school provides clear, detailed information on what needs to be covered. Almost all junior school girls continue but it's not automatic. Girls can join at other years (preferably not in the middle of exam courses, though). 20-30 leave after GCSE and up to 12 enter at year 12. These need a minimum of 440 points from their nine best GCSEs in a wide range of subjects and A/B in their proposed AS subjects.

Exit: To a wide range of universities – lots of Russell Group. Three to Oxbridge in 2016, seven to study medicine and veterinary science. Newcastle, Nottingham, York, Leeds and London all popular.The most famous old girl is Barbara Hepworth (head's elegant study contains two of her sculptures, as well as an interesting collection of model owls). Other Old Girls are writers Helen Fielding and Joanne Harris, and Katherine Kelly and Priya Kaur Jones from the media world – plus Claire Young, runner up in The Apprentice.

Money matters: Fees are all-inclusive – no extra charge for learning support or exam entries. There is a pot of money for means-tested Foundation Awards, from 25-90 per cent, where parental income is less than £40,000, which funds about 14 bursaries in each year group with additional ones available in the sixth form. Also a 100 per cent fees scholarship awarded at entry in year 7, with possibly another to come. There could be 100 girls on bursaries out of the 730 total. In addition, there is a 100 per cent Ogden award for the sixth form (reserved for state school applicants who want to take science/maths) and 12 other scholarships of 25/50/75 per cent.

Remarks: A very impressive and attractive school, offering a great range of opportunities for girls to develop talents. Affords all the advantages of single sex education combined with plenty of interaction with nearby QEGS. Girls find it almost impossible to think of anything they would like to change – 'You just grow to love the school as it is,' said a year 12 girl. 'You're not judged on your cleverness; you're seen as an individual – everyone's got their own strengths,' said another. Also outstandingly creative – witness the school mag, packed with stunning art and very strong writing.

Westbourne School

60 Westbourne Road, Sheffield, South Yorkshire S10 2QT

Pupils: 384 • Ages: 3–16

Fees: £8,775 – £11,985 pa

Tel: 01142 660374
Email: admin@westbourneschool.co.uk
Website: www.westbourneschool.co.uk

Headmaster: Since 2004, Mr John Hicks MEd (50s). Educated at a grammar school, then Exeter and Kingston Universities; taught at schools in Weybridge, Cobham, London and an international school in Thailand. Teaches maths and sport; thoughtful and said by a parent to be 'very warm, when you get to know him, and parental with the children'. Three adult children; interests include travel, various sports, theatre and playing the guitar.

Head of junior school: Since 2015 is Mrs Lisa Cannell, previously director of professional development at the Tanglin Trust School, a British International School in Singapore, where she was also a teacher of reception to year 6, including gifted and talented pupils.

Academic matters: Overall GCSE results variable: in 2016, 76 per cent got 5+ A*-C grades; 30 per cent A*-A grades. High achievement as one would expect for scholarship set, with 56 per cent A*/A grades, and very good value added, especially with weaker pupils. Course starts in summer term of year 9, all do three separate sciences; options include Spanish, business communication systems, drama, ICT, media studies, sports science, home economics, electronics; after-school French and Spanish classes mainly for children wishing to take a second foreign language, plus (non-examined) Latin. Smaller scholarship set accelerated from year 7, take English language and science six months early and can choose to add an extra two subjects, further maths and astronomy.

Recent ISI inspection's outstanding judgement for teaching and learning endorsed by our very enthusiastic year 6 tour guides: 'Exceptional teaching – they're not like teachers, more like guides. They know you so well they know how to explain things in a way you can understand..They really care about us and find it rewarding to see us develop'. Thorough-going tracking and monitoring.

Classes average 14 but can be smaller for GCSE, eg eight. Setting for core subjects from year 7. Strong on differentiated learning in and out of the classroom – lots of stretch for able mathematicians; science university visits; lively approaches in French, notably a delightful room furnished with bar, bistro-style chairs, tables and stools (très authentique); Spanish room has cheerful yellow and red round table; small physics lab and large, modern biology one. Very good ICT facilities – four suites including Apple Macs, laptops, well developed VLE, much use of interactive whiteboards.

Junior school uses Sats for internal baseline assessment – key stage 2 results well above national average for English and science in particular; very good value-added – small classes: max 16 but could be less. ICT suite, much use of interactive whiteboards, well developed VLE; specialist teachers for French (begun in reception and taught in a lively way, with the assistance of French cartoons and chocolate bars), music, drama and PE. Differentiated work a strength; setting in English and maths in years 5 and 6; after-school maths master class. Philosophy for children throughout and key stage 2 enterprise programme in conjunction with St Luke's hospice, using local business links for support. We saw some exceptionally good year 6 poetry and particularly liked the Roman estate agent's brochures. 'All the teachers have a passion for teaching and for the children,' reported a parent.

Top-notch SENCo keen to promote understanding of learning difficulties throughout the school – assemblies given by pupils and visiting speakers – and to support families: will link up parents. We liked the posters of several well known people with dyslexia, dyspraxia and ADHD on display. Mostly covers dyslexia (all screened on entry, in class support from TAs, individual lessons at extra cost), ADHD, mild autism; would assess other needs at a visit to judge if school could meet them – probably not severe behavioural difficulties. Has regular contact with parents and lots of resources, trains up other staff. Year 6 nurture group receives extra support, kept together in year 7 as long as required. High praise from a mother for the way her child had been supported and brought on, especially for the weekly emails on her progress and the handling of her move to the senior school.

Games, options, the arts: Only has a small Astro and junior school hall but makes use of Sheffield's excellent sports facilities and offers a vast range – the usual ones plus basketball, lacrosse, water sports, girls' football, horse riding and aerobics with zumba, climbing, skiing, golf, tae kwon do, cycling, plus sports leader qual – and high level coaching; two games afternoons a week – no couch potatoes here. Inclusive approach to school teams – fields several. Cross-country strong at city, county and (a girl) national levels, strong netball, hockey, badminton, a Yorkshire squad cricketer, UK reps in swimming, diving, golf, motor racing. Trips to see international matches, annual sports tour to, eg, Lanzarote, Barcelona, Malta.

Music very strong – all in years 3 – 5 learn recorder and ukelele, several learn other instruments; four choirs, orchestra, rock (annual Rockfest), brass and jazz bands, lots of formal (carol service at Sheffield Cathedral) and informal concerts, plays at local festivals, tours to Prague (years 6-11), Belgium, well-supplied with guitars, ukeleles (15, no less) and software; members of the Sheffield Schools' wind band and composition classes. Some take GCSE in year 9.

Big productions – Oliver!, Joseph and His Technicolour Dreamcoat, The Dracula Spectacular – put on in junior school hall or a local theatre; also uses outdoor natural amphitheatre, The Dell. Plays and workshops from visiting professionals, including Dominic West; street dance workshop; older pupils assist with technical aspects of junior school plays. Good, varied art on display around school, some at local exhibitions, success in city and Saatchi Gallery competitions. Food tech in year 6 involves making a healthy two course meal for two for £5.

Wide range of activities – baking (runs open Easter cookery course), chess, bridge, French cinema, eco, geocaching, D of E, business challenge, annual architectural workshop day, science week with parental input. Supports various charities, eg football boots for Africa; community work; pupils come off timetable for a week to study all faiths and cultures (parents contribute). Lots of local educational visits, year 7 residential in North Yorkshire, year 8 week in the Outer Hebrides developing survival skills, expedition to Kilimanjaro, ski trip to Alps. New years 3-6 residential programme. Improved post-16 advice; year 10s do two weeks' work experience at start of year (as better choice of jobs then – very canny), often organising it themselves. Good links with local business community – hosts business breakfast networking event.

Extended day for juniors – breakfast club from 7.45am; creche for reception – year 4 till 5.45pm; years 5-6 can stay to do supervised prep till 4.45 or 5.15pm. Pre-school for 3-4 year olds.

Background and atmosphere: The only all-through to 16 co-ed independent school in Sheffield, which has remarkably few of them. Founded 1885 as a school for 'the education of the children of Sheffield Gentlemen', in a private house; 1888 moved to larger premises in Westbourne Road, 1997 became co-ed, 2001 new co-ed senior school opened, with 2007 extension.

Original building houses years 9-11: undistinguished exterior but attractive, large, light classrooms, mosaics on hall floor and stained glass windows. Surprisingly modest library – pupils consulted about fiction choices and how to spend allocation: trad books versus electronic resources. Gracious, more recently acquired mid-19th century house for years 7-8 (thankfully not modernised by previous occupants, Radio Sheffield) with smaller classrooms and some narrow corridors. Years 7-8 have a playground, years 9-11 enjoy access to a very pleasant garden.

Good size classrooms in junior school with colourful displays; lovely, light reception room with access to outside; large modern science lab, library in a gracious room with bay window, carpet and beanbags – well supplied with enticing fiction, but some bookcases with shelves in need of attention. Computerised system managed very confidently by a year 6; older children consulted about book choices. Covered, open and adventure playgrounds plus lawned area with veg patch for the youngest ones. New food tech area and drama studio shared with senior school.

Comfortable, relaxed atmosphere related to small classes and good humoured, friendly teachers – 'They know the children very well and appreciate them for who they are..The children feel confident about their core selves'; 'They're very motivated, energetic, enthusiastic, compassionate, tuned into children'; 'They're very good at getting the positives out of a child and finding their talents – they don't give up on them,' say parents. Three outstanding ISI early years foundation stage inspections and lots of praise for the other years in recent report. Many parents spoke of the family atmosphere – friendships and activities across years, older children allowed to visit siblings in lunch hour and senior children help out. School council's suggestions are heeded.

Academic achievement respected, not a source of embarrassment. Lots of leadership opportunities – traditional posts plus enterprising charity committee. School council's suggestions regarded. Small dining hall – year 10 and 11s have own café and year 11s allowed out in lunch hour. Food (no packed lunches) divides opinion: school puts thought and care into it and provides a decent choice – hot and veggie option plus salad bar, trad pudding with fresh fruit and yoghurts – but not all children and parents happy (school argues you will never get total satisfaction with this) and some mentioned long queuing times, though attempts made to minimise this. Parking very difficult.

Pastoral care, well-being and discipline: Focus on praise and rewards for a wide range of achievements – central plasma screen displaying weekly commendations; child-friendly prizes and outings. Bullying not seen as a problem but would be dealt with firmly and effectively. Small, bleak sick room.

Trad good manners expected. Well-developed reward systems with child-friendly prizes; lots of badges – some blazers groaning with them. Worry box for problems; year 6 buddy scheme. Excellent year 6 transition programme – taster lessons, shared games afternoons with year 7s, tour by senior school pupils, crossover of year 6 and 7 teachers.

Pupils and parents: Mostly from Sheffield, Rotheram and Derbyshire; mainly professional or business backgrounds, ethnically mixed. Happy, confident, polite, well-behaved children – impeccably focused in all the classes we visited.

Parents very happy too: they like the family atmosphere – 'Everyone knows everyone and the children form friendships across years'; the extra support for the less able and stretch for the very bright; pastoral care; traditional values and a curriculum that combines studying with enjoyable activities every day. Several opportunities to get involved – active PTA, parent and staff choir. Plenty of contact – school magazine, newsletters, email, termly surgery with head.

Old Westbournians: actor Dominic West, various distinguished sports people, eg 2012 Olympics swimmer.

Entrance: Non-selective – taster day with tests; wide ability range – overall above national average. Will take children at various stages, even, unusually, mid year 10 – recently accepted a number of year 11 girls from a local independent school that closed down very suddenly and provided teaching for any GCSE subjects not usually offered.

Exit: Some 80 per cent of juniors move on to the senior school, some with scholarships. Most go on to do A levels at the city's top state comprehensives (mainly Tapton and Notre Dame) or Birkdale (nearby independent school – two scholarships recently); a few to FE college.

Money matters: Six scholarships for internal and external pupils – academic, music, sport, all-rounder – worth 10 per cent of fees; more than five per cent of pupils have bursaries.

Remarks: Mixed ability intake and attention to the individual differentiates Westbourne from the other, selective independent schools in Sheffield. Has a long-standing reputation for developing children who need extra nurturing and is now proving it can achieve very strong results for the most able as well. Close integration between thriving junior and senior schools is an added advantage.

Westville House School

Carter's Lane, Middleton, Ilkley, West Yorkshire LS29 0DQ

Pupils: 111 • Ages: 2–11 • C of E

Fees: £5,430 – £9,405 pa

Tel: 01943 608053
Email: office@westvillehouseschool.co.uk
Website: www.westvilleschool.co.uk

Headmaster: Since 2015, Mr Ian Shuttleworth BEd Sheffield Hallam (early 40s), previously deputy head at Queen Elizabeth Grammar School (QEGS) for six years, and before that held posts at Birkdale Preparatory School and Brontë House. Played rugby union professionally and captained Otley RFC in the English Championship. Also an avid cricketer, having played semi-professionally in the Yorkshire leagues for a number of years. Married with two children, his spare time, unsurprisingly, still involves plenty of sporting options alongside family pursuits. Energetic, sincere and welcoming, he's popular with parents and children and is clearly relishing the role, bringing new impetus and drive. 'Under Mr Shuttleworth's guidance, we feel the school is going from strength to strength,' say parents.

Entrance: Most start around the age of 2 – there's an excellent opportunity to try the place out first with Tiny Tots, free (yes, really) fun-filled Thursday afternoon sessions led by the onsite team. Non-selective throughout, older children seeking a place are invited for a taster day but no gruelling tests. One form entry throughout so places are limited by space; small number of bursaries available so worth enquiring.

Exit: Usually to first choice schools eg The Grammar School at Leeds, Bradford Grammar School, Ermysted's Grammar in Skipton, Skipton Girls' High School, Ilkley Grammar School, Giggleswick School, occasionally Harrogate Ladies' College and Woodhouse Grove becoming increasingly popular. Considering the school is non-selective on entry, they do very well with a number of scholarships each year to fee-paying senior schools – great value-added.

Remarks: Founded in Ilkley in 1960, moving to its present site in 1992. The ceremonial flagpole is a nice touch – they are proud of their school. The views alone make this place very special – right across the valley to the Cow and Calf Rocks, yes it's blowy up here and you can experience all four seasons in one day, but the warm and friendly welcome alone makes it worth a visit. A little off the beaten track so there's no passing traffic, which makes it lovely and safe for children but not great for marketing purposes. Yet you're really only five minutes' drive from Ilkley town centre, and the rolling hills and natural woodlands up here make this an ideal environment for adding in a forest school curriculum. Fresh air and exercise – 'multi-sensory learning in crystal clear air,' they tell us in the literature; think Switzerland without the cowbells.

No lack of academic rigour, regular testing so they know where they are but 'not glued to their desks' either, plenty of talk of breadth and balance across a traditional prep curriculum with added outdoor benefits. Classes are small, nowhere to hide. Parental expectations are high; this school is viewed as a stepping stone to the many good schools in the area, both state and fee-paying and, to date, it delivers. Awards and scholarships to other schools are a source of much pride. Staff know the children extremely well and much praise in a recent inspection report for high quality teaching and learning across the board, including excellent marking, which was flagged as a weakness in a previous inspection.

The newish head with experience in other good schools has 'rebooted the academics', bringing closer attention to detail and more accountability for teachers, who are to be heard casually dropping phrases like 'learning intentions' into their teaching, even with the youngest children. There is also a new reading scheme throughout, an updated ICT infrastructure and tablet computers are on order. French taught from the start, Spanish added for the older children. Relationships are warm and fairly relaxed – there is a feelgood factor here – children (and staff) know what's expected and rarely challenge the status quo. Parents talk of 'a palpable fresh and positive feel with all the staff pulling together to deliver the best they can to the pupils'.

Learning support is available; numbers receiving support are low; small charge for one-to-one but small group support is free as and when necessary. The more able are flagged and challenged. No wheelchair access for the main building and partially sighted children would struggle on this site. Class sizes vary, as do gender ratios; one form entry throughout and whilst there is undoubtedly room for more at present, places may be snapped up more quickly in coming months and years following the opening of the new and impressive early years facility.

Form teachers teach most subjects, including science; specialists for art, sport and music. Enthusiastic new director of music is keen for all to 'have a go' – aspiring musicians not restricted by age; if you want to try and your fingers are long enough, then 'go for it!' Classrooms are bright and cheery with plenty of light and interactive whiteboards. Lovely displays of high quality art in corridors and stairwells. Recent programme of redecoration from the ground floor up and most teaching rooms are delightful, 'it's a little like the Forth Bridge' says the Head and some specialist rooms at the top of the original building are a little tired and awaiting updates at the time of writing – but they are on the case. The exterior is looking very smart following a full paint job, white with blue trimmings; it's a former nurses' home that has been described as looking a little like a 'seaside hotel', but it's around the back that it's full of surprises. What the nurses certainly didn't have is a full-sized sports hall and playing fields. They probably also didn't have a mud kitchen (messy but enormous fun and pots and pans 'to clang and bang'..), areas dedicated to bushcraft and soft play areas and lawns with climbing frames, trikes and tractors. The woodland area has a pond and there's the rustic Holloway Hut for outdoor play and learning.

Communication with parents is excellent; they describe it as 'first class'. Look at the website for the latest edition of Buzz: it's described by staff as the 'essence of WHS' and tells you everything you need to know about recent events and the day-to-day life of the school. The only gripe we could find from parents is the need for a larger car park – clearly it's a frustration for many but one they can live with, all things considered.

Rascals is the before and after-school care programme; school is open from 7.45am to 6.00pm. No packed lunches here, it's home-cooked food served in the dining hall, with staff sitting alongside the children in 'family groups'. Assemblies most days and whilst the school is technically non-denominational, there is a faith assembly on a Monday and Father Philip from the local church is a regular visitor and good friend of the school. The school can and will provide a prayer room on request.

Plenty of opportunities for leadership at the top of the school – house captains, head boy and head girl, each with a deputy, and children are well represented on the school council. Three school houses, named after wild birds; plenty of healthy competition between them. Clubs and activities include rugby coaching, cricket, netball, running, French cinema, drama, dance, music, young voices, forest school and yhatze, amongst others.

Always a sporty school, the current head has raised the game and, for a small school, the range of sport on offer is very impressive. Most takes place on site and the school minibus shuttles children to the town pool for swimming and local rugby and cricket clubs for tournaments. The sports hall is huge and multi-purpose, great for sport; it's a beast of a building, swallowing up these small children who just love the space it provides, especially in the long winters up here. Pull-down audience seating for concerts and plays all year round, acoustics not great, but drama and music are strong despite that. Netball courts and large playing fields are tucked away behind the school.

Keen eco led by children – Green Flag award, grow own vegetables in large garden. Charity fundraising – links with school in Africa. Plenty of local and regional trips – year 6, unusually, have three residentials (science and geography; sports tour; outdoor pursuits). Thursday afternoon is clubs time – mixed ages and broad range, following staff interests, eg chess, juggling, arts and crafts, ocarina, bridge, outdoor pursuits. It's also the afternoon for the Tots Club which is widening its range of activities all the time: still to come is Rugby Tots, Alphabet Tots and most lately Ninja Tots.

The newly built facility for reception/admin and early years teaching is fabulous and has freed up useful extra teaching space in the main building, allowing a dedicated area for design technology and a larger library for the older children. This attractive and well-planned new build is a tangible investment in the future of the school and they are hoping it will prove a huge draw for local parents.

Tartan pinafore dresses and/or culottes are the winter uniform for girls, dresses in summer. For boys it's white shirts and ties-on-elastic with a choice of long trousers or shorts. Blazers for all and hats are also set to make a return following popular demand, though they might need to hang on to them on windy days.

Goodwill and loyalty in spades from a convivial staff, both teaching and non-teaching, who greet you with genuine northern warmth and geniality. Most parents have done the rounds before signing up and the warm welcome here is mentioned over and over again. Parents also praise the school's expectation that pupils will be 'polite, considerate and respectful towards staff and each other'. Behaviour is good; the children here know what's expected and behave accordingly, no arrogance but bags of confidence and happy to chat.

A four-wheel drive vehicle might be a must come winter; these are no-nonsense hardy folk for whom Barbours and wellies are de rigueur for a few months each year. Very wide catchment area, from Gargrave to Otley, High Skyreholme in Dales to Baildon plus Ilkley day nurseries. Parents are a mix of professionals, often working in Leeds or Manchester, and local business owners. High number of working mums too, more new money than old; they reflect the local demographic, and are happy to pay the added house price premium here in Ilkley and manage the commute. Rumour has it it's worth it for the green open spaces, the stylish independent shops, Bettys (other tea shops are available), an array of fine-dining options and a choice of good senior schools within reach. 'It's an exciting time to be at Westville' parents tell us.

Windermere School

Browhead, Patterdale Road, Windermere, Cumbria LA23 1NW

Pupils: 331; roughly half boarders • Ages: 3–18 (boarders from 8) • Sixth form: 74 • C of E

Fees: Day £7,455 – £16,920; Boarding £23,640 – £29,970 pa

Tel: 01539 446164
Email: admissions@windermereschool.co.uk
Website: www.windermereschool.co.uk

Headmaster: Since 2009, Mr Ian Lavender MA (Oxon) NPQH. Has a strong background in independent secondary school education, boarding and the Round Square ethos, having been a housemaster at Gordonstoun School for 11 years and before that a chemistry teacher at Cranleigh School and Eton College. He also has broad experience that extends well beyond teaching, including an early career in management consulting and service with the Territorial Army. His wife is a GP and they have three children. A quietly spoken, measured and thoughtful man, parents say 'he cares deeply about the students...and is an impressive headmaster'. Now in his sixth year at the school, he is beginning to 'see things more clearly'; there is no lack of ambition: his vision is that Windermere becomes 'the best small school in the country'.

Head of the preparatory school: Since September 2016 is Mrs Rachael Thomas.

Academic matters: They simply ask that 'you bring along effort, commitment, determination, a sense of humour, an open mind, enthusiasm, energy and a pencil case'. Though you should probably add to that wellies and wet weather gear – Lake District essentials, pretty much all year round. It would be a crime to be right here in glorious countryside, with lakes and mountains on your doorstep, and not make the most of it – so they do. The prep school's Adventure! (sic) strand runs right through all that they do and the intention is that 'children are interacting, engaged and thrilled, whether climbing a rock face or in the classroom'. So, if you are learning about forces in science, you paddle your canoe on the lake and see and feel them for real; you then replay that in the classroom and (probably) remember it forever. The children who read, wrote about and painted dragons, and then sailed across to an island in the middle of the lake only to find a dragon's nest and plenty of other 'evidence' of dragon life, were undoubtedly 'engaged and thrilled'.

If that all sounds a little too Swallows and Amazons for you then fear not; no lack of academic rigour in the classroom and even good old-fashioned handwriting practice is seeing something of a revival here in the prep. A sensible cross-curricular approach to the teaching of humanities which means that the dots are joined up between and across subjects, leading to real learning connections being made and, vitally, transference of knowledge. The mornings are essentially for maths and English; science is big here and at the centre of the planning for all subjects. French taught by a specialist from the senior campus; drama and music also important, there are peripatetics for individual music tuition in addition to class music. Classes are small, some very small, one form entry throughout. Words and phrases like 'resilience', 'critical thinking', 'empathy' 'collaboration' and 'problem-solving' are part of the children's own vocabulary here, and from an early age. Personalised pathways are 'a reality not just an aspiration'; tracking happens in form time, measuring skills such as team work and leadership alongside academic success. Soon parents will also be able to access this information via a parent login on the school's VLE system.

Windermere senior school pupils might not be dancing right at the top of the league tables but they appear hard-working and happy. Due in part to the broad intake, the results at GCSE, whilst undoubtedly solid (51 per cent A*/A in 2016), can't compete with bigger, more selective schools so it focuses on its considerable international appeal. Crucially, however, it is the highest performing independent school in Cumbria post 16, not least because there is no A level on offer here; it's the rigour of IB or a small choice of BTecs, and that's it. Exams and the choice of exams are a natural sieving process and the school's choice of the IB route means the game is raised considerably in sixth form; average IB point score 33 in 2016, with eight students getting 40+ points. Now accredited to teach the IB carers' programme alongside the diploma. With small classes (around 12), teaching is up close and personal, there's nowhere to hide, and pupil-teacher relationships appear warm and relaxed. Personal academic tutors guide and, if necessary, hand-hold, helping students in their choice of subjects and mentoring them along the way. Parents tell us 'there are many inspirational teachers here', with a number of them prepared to offer extra tutorials on request at lunchtime or after school.

French, German, Italian and Spanish are all taught in this language-rich environment, with Latin and Greek being offered off-timetable as extras, classes running every Thursday evening. Outside of class, eager young linguists who keep their ears open can experience over 20 languages being spoken around school. Students are given the opportunity to participate in worldwide exchanges by spending up to a term in another Round Square school. There are also annual language trips to France and Spain and Germany.

Full-time head of learning support, dyslexia specialist and two part-time assistants; it's a strong department. Parents are charged for the support according to whether it's in-class or on an individual basis.

Games, options, the arts: Sport at the prep goes way beyond the usual team sports and track events; sailing and kayaking have taken off enormously, with senior staff and coaches supporting some activities. They have their own tennis court and playing fields and use the Astroturf and sports hall at the senior campus for additional space. The school's own backdrop is its own dream playing space – here children camp, build dens, walk the fells, climb mountains (and read their own poetry when they get to the top), and so much more besides. The school even has a member of staff with the wonderful title Head of Adventure – a first for us.

Built on a slope; the site brings its own challenges and there aren't acres of pitches here in the senior campus; the biggest area of flat ground is the lake, so that's where most activities take place. Better suited to small team sports, and there are probably more expeditions than fixtures, but they do have an Astroturf and a sports hall for year-round play. Whilst they can't compete with the big boys at team sports, they take it seriously and offer the full range of usual school sports and others besides, including equestrianism, sailing and kayaking. Hodge Howe, the school's own watersports centre and the only school centre in the country to hold RYA champion club status, has two boathouses, a private beach and a pavilion with a classroom (also available for wedding receptions..) and a fleet of sailing boats and kayaks. Other outdoor activities include camping trips, fell walking, ghyll scrambling, orienteering, caving and climbing, so if you are the adventurous type and not joined at the hip to your hair straighteners or worried by a patchy mobile phone signal, there's plenty here for you. All students in years 7, 8 and 9 complete the Windermere Adventure Award. They also spend one morning a fortnight outside school doing anything from mountain biking to conservation and environmental work.

Newly refurbished prep school art and design centre is a haven for art-lovers, fantastic inspirational work on display led by a studio artist from Kendal who spends three days in school each week. The vaulted cellars look and feel as though they should house expensive wines but in fact are changing rooms and DT teaching areas; every bit of the building is used. Good library/media centre; learning support on hand if required. Heaps of extracurricular activity; summer activity camps started in 2016. Soft play areas around school buildings for little ones and a greenhouse provides the school kitchen with vegetables and a space for science lessons and the thriving gardening club.

Senior school art takes place in the old stables; super natural light and plenty of Apple Macs for those with a penchant for design and design technology, and kilns for keen potters; it's an appropriately messy yet inspirational space. Drama is popular; it's a small school so very inclusive, and everyone who wants to take part can do, whether centre stage or behind the scenes.

Lots of individual tuition in music and the Holst Room, a space designed for its acoustics, is a valuable teaching and performance space. It's not the strongest subject, here according to parents, so a particularly musical child may not be able to shine, but there is undoubtedly a 'have a go' attitude to the subject, as with everything else.

The school supports community projects in South Africa; each year students help out with resources and provide physical help to a project with Tiger Kloof School – in fact just mentioning the name of the school brings a warm smile and glow of pride to the faces of the older students, who view it as an extension of their school life at Windermere.

A highly rated international summer school is proving increasingly popular and has effectively added a fourth term to the school year.

Boarding: Despite the national park location, it's only 90 minutes to either Manchester or Liverpool airports (outside London considered a safer option by some nervous parents), three hours to London by train and the school has a fleet of shuttle buses catering for students' many and varied travel needs.

Word of mouth is the biggest factor in attracting parents, both locally and overseas. There are a few expat Forces parents who love the leadership challenges here, and whilst more than half of the students are from within the UK, the rest represent around 24 different countries far and wide, including China, Germany, Hong Kong, Lithuania, Poland, Romania, Ukraine, Spain and Russia.

Customary dorms in single sex houses on site for boarders aged 8-16 (only a handful of junior boarders); there are a few single rooms but not many choose them, most preferring to share. Plenty of messy individualisation of space with One Direction posters, soft toys and family photos. Each house has a staff house 'family', comfortable shared common rooms with views across the lake for socialising, karaoake and TV watching, and well-equipped kitchens for snacking. In the girls' house at least, baking seems popular with Mary Berry cake recipes much in evidence. Food cooked in-house, good quality and plentiful, just as well with all that fresh air.

Well-behaved sixth formers earn the right to have more space and freedom in self-contained flats in a co-educational house on site, still supervised, of course, but a step along the road to preparation for life beyond school. A sixth form bar allows (with parental permission) two drinks with dinner on a Saturday night; younger pupils love the occasional takeaway, shared with friends in the boarding house. If that sounds a little tame, there's not much else you can get up to here (a definite plus for many parents), but cinema visits and occasional weekend trips to the Trafford Centre in Manchester or Alton Towers keep restless adolescents happy. They are also very busy after school, so much so that a parent of a day boy told us they relocated to be on the school's doorstep simply because their son was 'reluctant to go home after school – way too much going on'.

Background and atmosphere: On this site since 1924 and co-ed since 1999, there is a good mix of boys and girls here. Extensive additional building took place in the '70s and '80s, but the national park setting places real limitations on new building – essentially it's all about how the place looks from the lake. Some attractive newer and recently refurbed buildings are scattered around the grounds of the Victorian mansion of the original Browhead estate, some boarding facilities, others classrooms and labs. Highlights are the Jenkins Centre for music, performing arts, languages and a superb dining room and Crampton Hall – a spacious auditorium for theatrical and musical productions.

The prep has a small hall for lunch, drama, dance and assemblies; classrooms are colourful, spacious, bright and airy with views to die for. Some classrooms in the main building – a towered Victorian Lakeland slate building – with other newer add-ons. The main reception area is lovely, with an impressive staircase, other areas need a coat of paint but there is a constant and continual programme of decorating and updating – bit like the Forth Bridge. Eco-pod classrooms provide vital extra space – strange-looking buildings (think Marmite – love them or hate them) but you can't fault their eco-credentials of recycled materials and sheep's wool in their construction. Traditional wooden desks in most classrooms, they are smart and new and much-loved by the children and parents. Staff are young and enthusiastic and the coffee table in the prep visitor waiting area has copies of the Beano rather than the usual Horse and Hound or Tatler, which speaks volumes about this child-centred school. Smiling children in attractive striped blazers (note matching upholstery in reception hall) who are happy to chat, that's if you can get them to stand still for a moment.. they are busy, on a mission almost, but clearly having great fun, creating the sort of childhood memories here that others can only dream of.

Round Square is a worldwide association of schools that is all about the whole person – the Kurt Hahn view that says students can only understand life by experiencing it in exciting and challenging ways. Opportunities for travel and exchanges to other Round Square schools bring extra opportunities, and they welcome international students who wish to experience British culture whilst bringing with them their own perspective and world view. There is a real sense that, although surrounded by mountains here, their hearts and heads go way beyond the valley and into the wider world beyond. The core of the IB diploma programme encompasses many of the Round Square principles, making the curriculum ideal here. Daily reflection is an important start to the day and something valued hugely by the students themselves. 'It lifts you up,' they tell us; 'you're in school, lessons haven't started yet but you're saying hello to everyone'; 'it's a nice place to be' and it is often, apparently, like a mini TED talk to start your day, food for thought and a valued and laudable touchstone. Outside speakers are welcomed as regular visitors and students also attend conferences and exchanges worldwide.

Pastoral care, well-being and discipline: Many parents are attracted by the fact that the school isn't especially selective – telling us they didn't want their offspring to be a 'public school product' but rather they 'wanted their individuality to be valued'. They appreciate the weekly online newsletter and feel that they 'could walk into the school at any time if they had any concerns at all'. Also of great value to parents is the way in which 'teachers respond very promptly to even the smallest queries... pastoral care is excellent,' they say. Overseas parents enjoy a 'close relationship' with the staff and love the fact that their offspring often enjoy tea or dinner with the head and his wife.

Staff do, of course, keep a careful watching brief, but essentially Windermere pupils are encouraged to be self-disciplined. Problems are rare, as older and younger students jog along happily in the knowledge that they want for nothing (except perhaps a Starbucks) in this sprawling, healthy and supportive environment. Strong views from the sixth formers themselves on smoking – 'why would you?' It seems there's a degree of self-policing going on.

Students appear comfortable and relaxed but with an uncommon sense of responsibility too; they recently 'simply couldn't stand back and do nothing' following the recent earthquakes in Nepal, and within hours were actively fundraising within the local community in support of the victims. Charity fundraising such as this, alongside work in a soup kitchen and orphanage, affords them a 'very different reality,' say parents – 'one which puts their very privileged life into sharp focus'.

Pupils and parents: Any passing traffic is likely to be either hikers or tourists, so recruitment is a challenge, though undoubtedly helped in the overseas market by the Beatrix Potter and Peter Rabbit connection. It's a lifestyle choice living here in the Lake District, and some parents have huge commutes to city offices, whilst others are simply escaping the city altogether. Fewer landed gentry than in days of old, more hardworking hotel and restaurant owners or young semi-retired professionals who have made their money in the City and moved here for a breath of fresh air.

High on the list of attractions for many is the extensive programme of adventurous outdoor activities – something the pupils coming through from the school's own prep department have already enjoyed in abundance. It seems to result not only in hardy pupils but also in a 'can do' attitude, parents buying in to the opportunities for growth and independence in a safe environment. The words 'warmth' and 'friendliness' are oft repeated by parents when talking about the staff; they are aware that this is more typical of a small school and for them, it's a valid and valuable trade off for bigger and better facilities.

Entrance: Non-selective at prep level but children are observed in class for entry at EYFS, KS1 and KS2. All pupils and parents meet the head. Nearly all move up to the senior school, making up the majority of the 11+ entry. The school likes to look for 'potential' rather than performance and 'well-rounded students with a genuine interest in education in the broadest sense of the word,' say staff. Candidates for entry (below 16+) sit papers in English, mathematics and non-verbal reasoning. Year 12 places conditional on a minimum of five GCSEs at grade C or above.

Exit: Some 40 per cent leave after GCSEs. Most sixth form leavers continue in higher education at home or overseas, some via gap years. In 2016, high scorers to UCL, Durham, Edinburgh and St Andrews, plus a couple off to the US and Canada. A handful have gone on to key musical success. Notable former pupils include dressage Olympian Emma Hindle and internationally respected soprano Claire Booth.

Money matters: Non means-tested scholarships are available in performing arts, visual arts, general academic subjects and sport. There are some means-tested bursaries available.

Remarks: The photograph on the cover of the school's prospectus looks like an oil painting – and yes, that really is the view from the school. A glorious backdrop in which to learn and grow, and the school makes full use of it. It's not the ideal destination for the child without a cagoule or for whom manicured lawns and extensive sporting facilities are key, but you do have all the amenities of the Lake District at your disposal, so give even those indoor types a month or so and they'll be away from their Playstations and kayaking with the best of them.

On a sunny day you can see for miles. On other days you can't see your hand in front of your face. The weather can change in an instant, but no one allows that fact to get in the way of an existence where hard work, good friends, rosy cheeks and fresh air in your lungs are all part of the package. The introduction of the International Baccalaureate has upped the game academically at the top end and also encouraged a more diverse intake, with pupils introduced to a wider range of subjects with exceptional extracurricular enhancements.

Withington Girls' Junior School

Linked with Withington Girls' School

Wellington Road, Fallowfield, Manchester M14 6BL

Pupils: 131 • Ages: 7–11

Fees: £8,685 pa

Tel: 01612 241077
Email: office@wgs.org.uk
Website: www.wgs.org

Head: Since 2004, Mrs Kathryn Burrows (50s). She has a geography degree from St Andrews University and a PGCE from Bristol. She trained as a senior school teacher, specialising in geography and PE, but she only did a couple of years teaching, in Northern Ireland, before spending a good 10 years outside the system. During this time she was an army wife – moving from posting to posting, taking up opportunities when they came along (she taught tennis in Cyprus at one point) and raising four children along the way. Since returning to live a more settled life in the UK, she returned to her old primary school – Lady Barn House – as head of games and later moved to Withington as head of the junior school. She went to Withington herself – as did her two sisters and later her daughter. She says, 'It's changed beyond recognition – it was very strict then... but I was quite schooly so I loved it'. She says that coming to a mainstream teaching career later in life has meant that she still has buckets of energy and enthusiasm. She's very attentive to the welfare of the children. There's a 'chatterbox' outside her office where girls can leave her notes. She talks about making 'pre-emptive strikes' to prevent small problems turning into big ones. Parents speak about her with a real warmth and positivity. 'She's fabulous,' says one mum. Everyone seems to have a story about Mrs Burrows dealing with whatever tiny crises feel enormous to a little girl with speed and sensitivity.

Entrance: The school takes up to 20 girls into the 'transition' class (year 3) from the age of 7. They try to stop the selection experience feeling intimidating – with year 6 helpers on hand to show the girls around – but still it's a test. There's a one-hour paper in English and another in maths. There's also a short reading assessment and the girls will be informally observed during a morning of play and activities. Mrs Burrows says they enjoy themselves, though: 'Sometimes they go away with a pocketful of telephone numbers of girls they've made friends with ... and they want to come again the next week'. They're looking for girls with the potential to go on to succeed in the senior school entrance exams so standards are high. As a rough guide, you'd need your child to be at or near the top of her class already. A few more places in year 4, and expands to two forms in year 5, with up to 24 new places, plus a few more in year 6.

Exit: Nearly all the junior school pupils pass the exams to the seniors and stay on at Withington Girls throughout their school careers. Mrs Burrows teaches the year 6 students herself and personally prepares them for the entrance exams to the senior school. It does occasionally happen that a girl doesn't make it through, but this would never be a shock to her or her family – as performance is closely monitored and communicated to families.

Remarks: Academic standards are, as you'd expect, very high. Almost all children attain a standard equivalent to at least national curriculum level 5 across every subject by the end of year 6. But parents say their children aren't put under pressure. One mother said that she felt the school was significantly less academically pressured than the state primary her daughter had previously attended – perhaps because juniors sit no external assessments.

As well as the bread and butter of literacy, maths, science, languages, humanities and art and technology, the children do PE every day, music twice a week and drama once a week. They also have 'thinking and learning' lessons where they're encouraged to engage with abstract concepts, think critically and ask difficult questions.

There's very little separation between the junior and senior sections of Withington Girls School so do have a look at our review of the senior school as well as this one. New junior school building and central Hub recently opened, but the juniors also regularly make use of the equipment, classrooms and specialist teachers from the senior school. They're very well connected with the older girls: sixth formers provide affectionate peer support and many of the senior school's extracurricular activities are on offer to the whole school. Some junior girls took part in the recent production of The Sound of Music, for example, and the science department houses the 'Little Critters Pets Corner' – a rodent-heavy pet care club which allows juniors and year 7s to mix, chat and cuddle small furries during their lunch breaks. As with the senior school, there are just too many clubs, societies, days out and visiting speakers to list, but pupils told us that the recently formed Eco Warriors club was a particular favourite among juniors. This perhaps builds on the WGS tradition of developing the social conscience of the community-spirited young women in its care – or maybe it's just a chance to get muddy growing strawberries and then eat them with cream.

The school comes across as warm and cosy. Parents love how well their children are known. One mum was touched by her daughter's report after her first term at the school because finally, after many years at another primary where reports had repeatedly contained the same few cursory lines badgering her to 'speak up in class more', she felt that the teacher at WGS had got to know her child individually and to appreciate the contributions she was making in her own way.

Some parents might not want to take their daughters to a single sex environment so young. Others may feel that such a selective and high-achieving environment is just too much too soon for their little ones. The junior school is essentially a feeder for the senior school, so if you're not sure that WGS is what you want for your daughter at age 11, then there could be some upset when all of her classmates progress to the seniors without her – but then again, she won't be accepted to the juniors unless the school is confident there's a future here for her. This is a gentle school with a real focus on fun and imagination. Children here aren't pushed to achieve or to go in any particular direction, but they see all around them examples of how learning can change their lives. If your daughter does come here, you can expect her to aim high.

Withington Girls' School

Linked with Withington Girls' Junior School

Wellington Road, Fallowfield, Manchester M14 6BL

Pupils: 529 • Ages: 11–18 • Sixth form: 151

Fees: £11,685 pa

Tel: 01612 241077
Email: office@wgs.org.uk
Website: www.wgs.org

Headmistress: Since September 2016, Mrs Sarah Haslam, previously deputy head. Undergrad degree from Lancaster and postgrad teaching qualification from Sheffield; began her career teaching English in 1990 at a co-ed Manchester school and joined Withington Girls' School in 1995. As well as teaching English, she has had roles including head of years 10 and 11 and, since her appointment as deputy head in 2007, lead responsibility for pastoral care and safeguarding. She is also an Independent Schools Inspector, an Independent Schools Teacher Induction Panel lead trainer and has been a governor of another independent school. She has a keen interest in the arts and also loves the outdoors, particularly hill walking and sailing.

Academic matters: By any standard, Withington Girls' School is exceptionally successful academically. In 2016, 96 per cent of all GCSE entries were graded A* or A, as were 82 per cent of A levels. Quite a few sixth formers complete Open University modules in the holidays – you know, just for a bit of fun. Pupils are regularly successful, often outstandingly so, in maths, science and linguistic Olympiads and Oxbridge essay competitions. We could keep listing the accolades but it's notable that the school doesn't.

Exam results are almost buried on the school website; they're item number 16 on a menu that isn't even visible from the front page. It may be a cliché for heads to gush about 'educating the whole person' but there's evidence that Withington does take that ambition seriously. Many of the parents we spoke to had initially worried the school might be a hothouse – but all agreed that their fears were unfounded. Sixth formers told us that the only pressure pupils may experience is what they put on themselves – and that the teachers can be relied upon to calm them down; reminding them that a B may be below average here but nationally it's a great result. One parent said she wished termly reports would rank the children in their class so that she knew how her daughter compared to her peers, but we suspect the school very deliberately withholds such information because it's not interested in ranking children against each other.

W

It's extremely rare for a child to leave the school because she's struggling academically, although it does happen. Usually problems are nipped in the bud with close monitoring and one-to-one support. Whereas many similar schools maintain their place in the league tables by setting exacting GCSE targets for entry to the sixth form, Withington doesn't exclude existing pupils from A level study on the grounds of relatively disappointing GCSE results. So long as a girl is happy at the school, they say they will honour their commitment to educate her to the age of 18.

All the parents we spoke to said they were very happy with their daughters' achievement and nobody thought their child was overwhelmed with homework. One mother suggested that perhaps girls achieve so much in the lessons that the school doesn't feel the need to set reams of homework. There's a sense that the girls are such smart and focussed learners they know how to stay on top of their studies efficiently so that there's plenty of time left for living. That's certainly what the school wants. The selection policy is all about finding pupils who won't just 'cope' with the pace and challenge of the curriculum; 'they must flourish'. Adamant that they wouldn't offer a place to a girl who would only get through the academic hurdles with hard slog and extra tutoring because they want everyone to have time to take part in whatever's on offer.

The school is particularly strong in maths and science. Nearly half the pupils do maths A level. But a good range of other subjects is offered at A level, including psychology, philosophy and drama. Across the board – in the arts, humanities, languages and sciences – there's no subject where the number of A and A* grades awarded isn't vastly above the national average.

A recent ISI inspection found that pupils with special educational needs and those with English as an additional language are well integrated into classes and that 'they make excellent progress, in line with their peers'. Pupils with SEN or a learning disability or difficulty have full access to the curriculum, and benefit from the full range of extracurricular activities. All pupils are taught with skilful differentiation within mainstream classes. Additional one-to-one support and extra spelling and language support groups are organised (at no extra charge) by the learning support department.

Games, options, the arts: Each edition of the school Bulletin – published four times a year – details student participation in more extracurricular events, of every description, than you would imagine could be crammed into a school year, let alone three months. Girls aren't steered in a particular direction so much as encouraged to try whatever they fancy. One pupil told us she'd worried that the school wouldn't be sporty enough for her but, since joining, she says she's had excellent opportunities to develop and she plays in several school teams as well as at county level. The school offers weekly zumba classes and sixth formers also have access to a gym and a personal trainer. One year 13 student enthused about playing in the WGS orchestra and the Stage Band – her only gripe was that she couldn't be in two places at once so had had to sacrifice her place in a sports team to commit to her music. Compulsory enrichment programme for sixth formers includes – alongside eg professional skills and finance – courses ranging from painting for pleasure to voices of dissent. Teams from the school have had outstanding success in national debating competitions, an international business challenge and the Model United Nations. The drama department is lively and inclusive – most recently collaborating with the music department to stage a lavish whole school production of The Sound of Music. Many students leave Withington having already completed their gold Duke of Edinburgh Award. And all this really is just a taster.

If there's one element of the extracurricular life of the school that really stands out, it's what might loosely be termed service to the community. There are annual volunteering trips to the Gambia and to Uganda. Pupils from every year put huge efforts into charity fundraising. The sums they raise perhaps tell us most about the wealth and generosity of the school's circle of adult benefactors, but the hard work and enthusiasm come from the children themselves. They really do care about their local community. They know they're privileged and they think that brings responsibilities. Almost all sixth formers do community service locally. 'Do you have to?' we asked. A pause. 'No but... well, everyone wants to.' Recently a local state primary lost its playing fields. The WGS year 9 came up with a solution: they hosted and organised a sports day for them on their own playing fields. A sixth former spoke earnestly about how moved she was by a talk from a former substance abuser on her path back to sobriety, and the same girl said she will never forget the privilege of having met a holocaust survivor on a recent trip. You get the feeling that this is one aspect of a Withington education that lasts a lifetime.

Background and atmosphere: We parked outside on Wellington Road – and wondered briefly if that was a good idea. This isn't really Withington. It's Fallowfield. It's not a rich area. The street is peaceful enough, but far from what you'd expect as the home of a centre of academic excellence. The school buildings are smart and welcoming, though. It feels secure but it's no fortress. The entrance lobby, with its huge glass sliding doors, would feel like the reception area of a medium-sized business if it weren't populated by busy-looking young women popping to and from reception with forms to hand in and messages to deliver. We're guided to a sofa to wait for the sixth formers who will show us round the school. On a coffee table are today's Guardian and Independent and a folder of press cuttings about the school. We're struck that every girl who passes us, whether she's 7 or 17, makes eye contact and offers a spontaneous, friendly smile.

The environment – inside and out – is neat, light and pleasant. It doesn't feel luxurious, but the space is generous and fit for purpose. As you'd expect, impressive displays of student work line the corridors and classroom walls. The sports, science and drama facilities are all tip top. The sixth form centre is quietly buzzing. A few students are studying at tables, many more lounge on sofas chatting – it could be about work...

The sixth formers have their own exclusive café, the Bistro. It serves hot drinks, tempting snacks and light lunches and is host to the breakfast club for the whole school. School dinners for everyone are provided in the main servery. Money has been spent on improving the catering over recent years. There are plenty of options and the menus look tempting and healthy. But still there are a few complaints. One mum told us her younger child loves the food but the elder one won't eat it. Although she thought her daughter was being picky, she wished the school would let her bring in a packed lunch because 'she's flagging by the afternoon'.

The founders stipulated that the school should be kept small, and nearly every parent we spoke to was attracted by the school's size. One mum said of her daughter, 'she was almost invisible at her old school but here she's like a different child.' The junior school is fully integrated with the seniors – there's no separate block so older girls pass young children in the corridors all the time. Parents suggest this softens the behaviour of teenagers who might otherwise become a little self-absorbed. The atmosphere is gentle and warm. It's on the quiet side, but individually the pupils are lively, confident and forthcoming. Maybe it's quieter than other schools because they know how to listen. It's also a very diverse community. Two in five pupils are non-white and there are lively faith groups from the major world faiths. Because of the bursaries, it's far from a preserve of the rich. One mum said, 'my daughter's got friends from Hale and from Moss Side and I love that'. Another said, 'I don't believe a child could come out of that school in any way racially prejudiced'. What seems to bring the girls together is their genuine pleasure in being there. They know they've got a lovely school so it's in their interests to keep it like that.

Pastoral care, well-being and discipline: Parents say they feel their daughters are known personally and that teachers are proactively looking out for their well-being. A sixth former told us she was pleasantly surprised when a teacher casually mentioned that she'd noticed she'd made some new friends – it made her feel that they were keeping an eye on everyone and would notice if anything wasn't right. When we asked the girls about friendship problems, they struggled to think of instances. One pupil said she felt as they got older she'd noticed a gradual shift towards more inclusive and less competitive behaviour. She said there was a notable change in how girls viewed a charity dance show they were involved in both in year 8 and then in year 10. 'In year 8 it was a bit of a competition but two years later we'd kind of worked out ourselves that it didn't need to be like that'. She said that in the sixth form 'everyone's friends with everyone – it's not as cliquey as lower down in the school'. The girls say that if ever anyone sees a pupil being excluded or treated unkindly they would all step in to put a stop to it. Staff agree: 'We've had sixth formers come to us and say "We're worried about X," and normally we already know because we're worried about X too, but it's nice that they come to us'. A couple of the mothers we interviewed had seen their daughters bullied in previous schools but none had faced any such problem here. Staff aren't complacent, though, acknowledging that it's much harder to detect serious bullying these days as it so often takes place online. Childnet regularly presents to the juniors and to year 7; the school offers internet safety training to parents and the girls know all the different lines of communication and support open to them if they're unhappy for any reason.

The pupils behave beautifully, apparently without being told to. External discipline is barely there, but self-discipline is everywhere. There are very few rules. Pupils are drilled in the 'Three Rs of respect for self, respect for others and responsibility for personal actions'. One parent said she'd never heard of anyone having a detention. We couldn't find a parent who'd received the dreaded 'letter home'. School says that no indiscretion is 'beyond redemption' and, in the event of a major transgression, would aim to be proportionate and to understand the context. But there are clear policies about drugs, bullying and suchlike and the school wouldn't rule out expulsion as a last resort. It's all a bit hypothetical, though. 'Oh, they can be terribly naughty sometimes,' said one mum cheerfully, but we suspect it's more Mallory Towers than Grange Hill.

Pupils and parents: Most of the mums we spoke to weren't in receipt of bursaries. These were well-to-do families for whom private schooling was always going to be an option. More than half of them were first attracted by the size and ethos of the school – several of them looking for a cosy community for a shy child – but their second consideration was its academic reputation.

Your child won't be happy at Withington unless she's very bright. Beyond intelligence, it would help if she's willing to work (although perhaps a previously lazy child would be spurred into action by the other children). There's no 'Withington type'. The school appreciates individuality. 'They can be quirky here,' said one mum. Outgoing children will have countless opportunities to enjoy the limelight but there's certainly a common thread that painfully shy and quiet children, who were unhappy in other schools, have blossomed here. Some have found a new confidence and others remain quiet – but contentedly so. WGS's reputation in STEM subjects must surely attract parents who know their daughter is gifted in maths and science, but for every old girl who's a particle physicist or an engineer there's another who's an opera singer or a fashion designer.

Entrance: If your daughter is applying to join the school at 11, she'll sit tests in English, maths and verbal reasoning. After the tests girls may be invited to interview – 'an informal chat'. They're looking for flair. Sometimes that shows itself particularly in one area – but she won't get a place unless they're confident she'll be able to keep up in all areas of the curriculum. They're interested not just in the answers your child gives but also in how she gets to them. Lessons at Withington cover a lot of ground at quite a pace so children who are lively and quick to catch on will fare best. School 'saddened' by the 'arms race' to tutor for entrance exams. The WGS tests do their damnedest to delve beneath the instructions of private tutors and canny prep schools to discover real potential. The interviewer won't be impressed if your daughter goes quiet when she's asked, 'What do you do when you're not studying?' Sample papers are available from the school office but girls are advised just to look through them so they seem familiar rather than to practise.

Exit: Most girls stay on to join the sixth form although a few leave for financial reasons or because they want to board. Everyone leaving year 13 goes to university – although some take a gap year first (for which there are small travel grants available). Most students choose traditional academic subjects but a few take more practical or vocational courses, in the arts, for example, or with a business or management component to them. Medicine is consistently popular with Withington girls (13 medics and two dentists in 2016). So is Oxbridge (eight places in 2016). In terms of leavers' destinations, it's one of the most successful schools in the country, with over 90 per cent of pupils going to one of the 30 most selective UK universities eg Durham, Birmingham, Exeter, Nottingham.

Money matters: A 2012 Financial Times report named Withington the best value independent day school in the UK. Given that this is the only school in the north of England to be in the FT's top 20 'best schools' list, the fees compare well with those of its local competitors. They're still way out of reach for most Manchester families, though. But about 90 girls in the senior school – that's one in six – receives a means-tested bursary, some of 100 per cent. The bursary fund is protected by a trust and the current level of provision is secure in perpetuity – but fundraising continues to extend the scheme further.

Remarks: This is an excellent school if you've got a clever daughter. It's serious rather than showy. There's no swimming pool or equestrian centre. It's a cosy but energetic community, particularly good for instilling confidence in girls who've been overwhelmed by larger or less protective schools. It prizes hard work, learning for its own sake and concern for others. Whether she's sporty, artistic, timid or fearless, if your daughter can get through the exams easily, she's likely to love it here.

Yarm School

87

The Friarage, Yarm, Stockton on Tees TS15 9EJ

Pupils: 1,109 • Ages: 3–18 • Sixth form: 215

Fees: £7,281 – £12,288 pa

Tel: 01642 786023
Email: dmd@yarmschool.org
Website: www.yarmschool.org

Headmaster: Since 1999, Mr David M Dunn BA PGCE (50s). Previously deputy head at Stewart's Melville College in Edinburgh; head of year 11 at Bolton School. Immensely cheerful, welcoming, energetic and forward-thinking, he is clearly and rightly proud of achievements here. Described by parents as 'courageous' and having done 'a fantastic job' in bringing hopes, dreams and new buildings to fruition. Only the second head in the school's history. Big on pastoral care – 'happy children have better self-esteem, learn better and have a go at anything. Treat every child as an individual and celebrate all their achievements.' Two daughters in school and wife is PE teacher with pastoral responsibility for the sixth form.

Prep school head: Since Sept 2013, Mr Bill Sawyer, formerly primary head of Braeburn Mombasa International School. He has worked elsewhere in Kenya and in a London state primary, and he is a very keen sportsman whose particular passion is cricket, together with rugby, hockey, football, tennis and squash. He also boxes as part of his fitness training and enjoys kitesurfing. His wife, Sarah, is a primary teacher and they have two young children.

Academic matters: Specialist teachers for PE, French and music from the age of 3. Play-based curriculum moves swiftly into early literacy/numeracy and pupils are down to work by the end of reception, ready to tackle KS1 in year 1 through a national curriculum enriched with geography, history, music and PE. All classes, reception to year 2, get weekly ICT lesson in the ICT suite at the prep school. Strong creative element in the teaching, lots of investigative work, indoors and out.

Prep follows national curriculum but cherry-picks other subjects from art, design technology, PE and sport. 'The focus is on active teaching,' says the school. InCAS is used to track and monitor pupil progress from year 1. Modern languages and ICT all taught by subject specialists. Gifted and talented pupils are identified and challenged through a range of stimulating extra activities and those with special needs are offered specialist support as required. National finalists in recent general knowledge competition, multiple awards in national junior maths challenge and regular winners at local arts festival.

Pupils normally take 10 GCSE subjects but some more. Teaching begins straight away in the morning with assembly, less academic subjects (sports etc) kept for afternoons. 'It's great to get a crisp start in the mornings when we all learn at our best' affirms head.

Up with the very best, 61 per cent of GCSE entries graded A*/A in 2016. IGCSE in maths, English, physics, chemistry, biology and business studies. At A level in 2016, 81 per cent A*-B, 57 per cent A*/A. Top Teesside school. The recipe is simple: take cream of the local catchment area, add superb facilities and great, committed teachers and the results speak for themselves. Strong right across the curriculum and no lack of academic rigour, traditional academic curriculum, no vocational, though willingness to tailor courses to suit the individual. Pupils are in forms for first, second and third year but in ability sets for maths and modern languages from first year. More setting is introduced in the third year and by fourth year forms vanish.

Games, options, the arts: Yarm seems to excel at everything, from sport to music; the trophy cabinet is heaving. Next to River Tees so rowing is big – former pupils have competed in Olympics, including 2012 gold medallist Katherine Copeland. Great results too in rugby, hockey (boys and girls), netball and tennis. Very inclusive and runs teams for all ages/skill levels to foster team spirit. Regularly provides sportsmen and women for county and country.

Lots of top grades in art, eye-catching DT and textiles, engineering ('let's build a car.') and fine arts. Check out the hugely impressive design awards. Music teaching includes violin or cello for everyone in year 3 (no opting out, but no extra cost for this either) and the have-a-go approach extends to brass in year 4 alongside endless peripatetic teachers for individual tuition. Choral society and school choir sings evensong in Durham and Ripon Cathedrals. Orchestra, jazz and funk

Y

band, concert band and various ensembles ensure widespread participation. Drama also a major strength across all ages and genres from classical Greek to Shakespeare and contemporary; very popular duologues competition also.

Breathtaking breadth of extracurricular activities – with every member of staff offering at least one. All the usual on offer such as debating and technology club but add to that rock-climbing, horse-riding, golf, strictly ballroom, circuit training, ancient Greek, political journalism, stockbroker challenge, meditation and ultimate frisbee and you're still not a quarter of the way through the list; you can even try your hand at silversmithing – a must-do for those aspiring to dentistry. Clubs and activities happen at lunchtime and after school and D of E is also thriving here. For two lessons a week prep school children can choose what they want to do, and they select anything from horse riding to Italian – a great opportunity to try lots of different subjects and sports.

Residential trips start in year 3 with Whitby, York in year 4, London in year 5, while year 6s head for France and the remote Scottish island of Rua Fiola. Good opportunities for foreign travel in the senior school too: previous years have seen a summer trek through the mountains of north eastern India and a winter trip to Cambodia. There are plenty of trips to Yarm's partner school in Werther, Germany each year, also long-standing annual exchanges to France and Spain. Typically trips to places like Holland (hockey), Northern Ireland (rugby), Cambodia (cultural), Berlin (languages), Austria (skiing), France (history and French), Barcelona (business studies), Italy (skiing) and Belgium (battlefields tour). Closer to home there is plenty of opportunity for outdoor pursuits/adventure trips (two full-time outdoor education teachers); this is a school that understands just how much can be learned outside the classroom.

Top London acousticians and Birmingham architects were employed to design the auditorium for performing arts and there isn't time or space here to eulogise enough about the 800 seat theatre with its 80 person orchestra pit, retractable seating, two (naturally) grand pianos, bespoke organ, touch-of-a-switch window blackouts, all stunningly housed in natural materials including Norwegian oak and Lake District slate. Has to be seen to be appreciated – you will forget you are in a school.

Background and atmosphere: Badge features a phoenix and the school has risen from nothing. Lacking a 'proper' grammar school for some years, executives at nearby ICI wanted a good school for their boys – so they started their own. They bought the old Yarm Grammar School building and started a new school with 50 boys in 1978. School bought the nearby Friarage (18th century stone-built mansion) in 1980, and by 1996 the whole of the senior school was based there, allowing prep school (opened in 1991) use of the old grammar school building. School has grown rapidly since. Girls joined in 2001, there is now a 50:50 boy/girl mix and the school has 'grown up'. Major £20 million redevelopment of facilities has taken place, including stunning classrooms with interactive whiteboards, widescreen 3D teaching televisions and state-of-the-art sound system; refurbished science labs; double-height dance studio; well-equipped gym and all-weather, floodlit netball and cricket facility.

Well-equipped nursery (term time only) offers a blend of play and teaching on a one adult to eight children ratio. Boasts role-play areas, quiet rest room, maths room, literacy room, dining room, conservatory, landscaped gardens and delightful outside play area. Pre-prep is housed in an attractive new building; classrooms are bright, spacious, colourful, with their own verandas. All well-equipped – a great deal of thought given to 'the little things that matter,' like canvas webbing on door hinges to prevent little fingers being trapped. Plenty of indoor/outdoor play facilities and a woodland yurt on a hill overlooking the senior school. Pre-prep takes 4 to 7-year-olds in seven classes (two for reception, two for year 1, three for year 2).

From medieval buildings to modern sandstone developments, from the Friarage dovecote – 'probably the oldest building for miles around' – to the sixth form centre housed in the old stable block, the whole environment feels cared for and respected. Outdoor lockers, zoned in year group pods, ensure no tatty dark corridors inside school, which instead are proudly festooned with striking art and design technology work.

Parents say the school has 'character' – and they don't just mean the buildings, comparing to bigger purpose-built schools that are as 'soulless as Stevenage..' Here parents feel they know people, you can talk to them if there is a problem: 'They stamp on everything and do it well. Some of the boys might have their shirts hanging out but they get the important things right'. Good relationships with staff mean parents are happy to support school activities. Staff turnover here is low and although parents become slightly twitchy at any staff departures it would appear to be an unnecessary concern – 'a good one leaves but another equally good one comes along'.

Real sense of a working community, huge staff – '260 on the payroll'; teaching and non-teaching staff all play their part, 'it's like a village, there's nothing we can't do ourselves,' confirms the head. Chefs ('not dinner ladies here'), and an in-house team of electricians, joiners, painters, gardeners and general workers all kept busy taking good care of the place – evident sense of pride and belonging. Teaching staff are well-supported and valued with every department having its own well-equipped workbase. Intelligent management philosophy – 'set the bar high and people join in'. School recognises the needs of working parents and opens from 8.00am to 5.00pm with children old and young kept busy and supervised on campus.

Pastoral care, well-being and discipline: Prep school parents rave about the quality of care and support, as well as the fact that the children are 'kept busy at all times.' Lots of little ones have big brothers and sisters at the senior school and they are welcomed on to the senior school site after hours to wait for older siblings. Ice creams on offer whilst waiting in the school's own coffee shop. These are happy, bright, confident children who are given lots of opportunities for taking responsibility and accept them with genuine enthusiasm and pride.

Senior school majors in pastoral care. Each student is allocated a tutor who is key to their happiness and success at school. Programme of personal, social and health education is led by tutor and he/she is first point of contact with parents. Heads of year and head of sixth form co-ordinate work of tutors and monitor academic progress. Home-school links are strong, helped by regular reports, parents' evenings and a weekly newsletter. Tutor groups belong to one of four houses – Aidan, Bede, Cuthbert and Oswald – which promotes mixing of age groups for social, sporting and fundraising events. Also peer support mentoring and sixth formers take a lead on some house activities to assist younger pupils.

Pupils and parents: You only have to spend half an hour window-shopping in Yarm High Street to realise that there is serious money in this town. Not everyone is local, however, and 12 private coaches bring children in from a wide catchment area beyond the town: Sunderland in the north, Thirsk in the south, Catterick in the west, Saltburn in the east. 90 per cent from white, middle to upper professional/management family background, remainder split Asian, American, African, preponderance of medics. Ten per cent helped by school bursary. Also Ogden Sixth Form Science Scholarships. Just one per cent have EAL requirement and eight per cent SEN – mostly mild dyslexia. Maximum class size in senior school is 22, sixth form just 16 (average is nine). Teacher/pupil ratio of one to 10.

Pupils are very comfortable to be around, and while they are aware of great opportunities offered here, they are careful not to abuse them. Parents closely involved and Yarm School Association well supported for social activities. Regular personal contact with parents allied to weekly newsletters, photo books, IT link-ups etc.

Entrance: Main points of entry to the prep are nursery, reception and year 3. A scattering at other ages; school tells us they look for average or above ability. For senior school, entrance exams in maths and English held January before September entry. Good school reports and interview also needed. Scholarships available and also possibility of a bursary.

Exit: Nearly all prep school pupils move up to the senior school. Sixth formers mostly head off to university, with about 10 per cent a year to Oxbridge (12 in 2016). Medicine/dentistry/veterinary science all popular: 21 places in 2016. For the rest, northern universities – Durham, York, Leeds, Teesside, Newcastle, Northumbria – seem favourites, mostly to study traditional degree courses. Twenty per cent leave post-GCSE.

Money matters: Reliant on fee income. Invests mainly in staff, books, IT and recently, major school redevelopment.

Remarks: Pupils and staff are refreshingly unpretentious and hard working: no 'old school' complacency here, which can only be a good thing and adds to the charm. Very strong academically, excellent sporting achievements and more design awards than any other school in the country. The picture-perfect riverside classroom development is seriously high spec – and green too – heated by deep ground-source heat pumps and solar panels providing hot water. Add to that the views over the River Tees to farmland beyond, the riverside decking and Costa coffee bar franchise where teachers sit marking work in between lessons and pupils converse over a skinny latte..it's a wonder anyone ever goes home.

Scotland

City of Aberdeen
Angus
Argyll
Ayrshire
Bute
Clackmannanshire
Dunbartonshire
City of Dundee
East Lothian
City of Edinburgh
Fife
City of Glasgow
Invernessshire
Lanarkshire
Moray
Perthshire
Renfrewshire
Roxburghshire
Stirlingshire

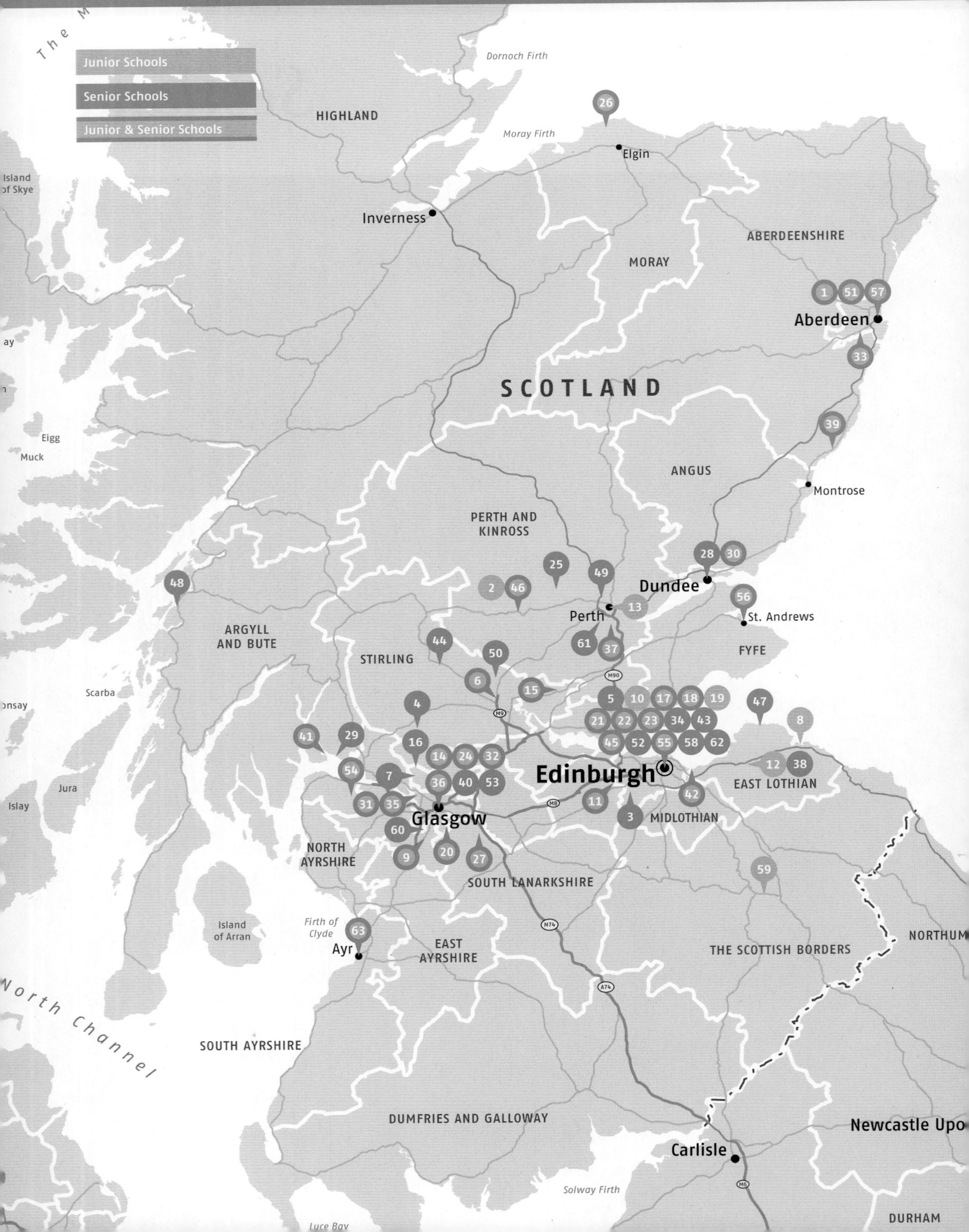
Junior Schools
Senior Schools
Junior & Senior Schools
The M
Dornoch Firth
HIGHLAND
Moray Firth
Elgin
Island of Skye
Inverness
ABERDEENSHIRE
MORAY
Aberdeen
SCOTLAND
Eigg
Muck
ANGUS
Montrose
PERTH AND KINROSS
Dundee
Perth
St. Andrews
ARGYLL AND BUTE
STIRLING
FYFE
Scarba
Edinburgh
EAST LOTHIAN
Jura
Islay
Glasgow
MIDLOTHIAN
NORTH AYRSHIRE
SOUTH LANARKSHIRE
Island of Arran
Firth of Clyde
Ayr
EAST AYRSHIRE
THE SCOTTISH BORDERS
NORTHUM
North Channel
SOUTH AYRSHIRE
DUMFRIES AND GALLOWAY
Newcastle Upo
Carlisle
Solway Firth
Luce Bay
DURHAM
M90
M9
M8
M74
A74
M6
1 2 3 4 5 6 7 8 9 10 11 12 13 14 15 16 17 18 19 20 21 22 23 24 25 26 27 28 29 30 31 32 33 34 35 36 37 38 39 40 41 42 43 44 45 46 47 48 49 50 51 52 53 54 55 56 57 58 59 60 61 62 63

SCOTLAND

A

Albyn School

17–23 Queens Road, Aberdeen AB15 4PB

Pupils: 670; 2 full time boarders • Ages: 2–18 • Sixth form: 60

Fees: £8,060 – £12,730 pa

Tel: 01224 322408
Email: admissions@albynschool.co.uk
Website: www.albynschool.co.uk

Headmaster: Since 2008, Dr Ian Long BA AKC BA MA PhD FRGS FRSA (50s), educated at King's College School, Wimbledon, read geography at King's London and, after a brief spell with Shell (always good to get the outside perspective) worked in a variety of schools – all girls, co-ed, that sort of thing – before becoming head of sixth form at Brentwood, followed by eight years as (academic) deputy head of City of London Freemen's School, during which time he also did his doctorate (in rural council housing). Ridiculously over-qualified.

A lapsed rower and a clever clogs who came to a school on the cusp; the previous head had worked miracles: some a tad expensive. Long has tightened up the finance side. No more babies (staffing ratio hideous) and huge increase in both nursery and chaps throughout the school. 'Always wanted to work abroad' but hadn't quite expected to find Scotland, and possibly Aberdeen in particular, quite so different from previous experiences. (After all, it nearly was abroad).

Fair amount of movement in the governing body. Long runs the school with bursar, two deputy heads, brace of assistant heads and head of lower (junior) school; who is a self-effacing star but see below. Moves afoot to add HR, marketing and admissions into top team.

An engaging and entertaining head with a sparkling sense of humour, he is also dead efficient and our request for detailed exam results by subject over the previous three years arrived before we left the place (previously it hit our computer before we did). His wife, Gwyneth, was deputy head at Channing School in Highgate, having started her teaching career at St Leonard's School down the coast in Fife as a Latin teacher and assistant housemistress. She teaches classics in the school.

Fairly brutal time over the past year, and not just the downturn in oil: head reckons that some 60 per cent of parents are either directly involved in black gold or in allied professions: IT and the like. But numbers are more or less steady: 'lost a couple, gained a couple'.

Head of lower school: Since April 2015, Paul Bertolotto (late 30s but looks just out of uni) BEd MEd ChT CREDL (another ridiculously over-qualified headmaster). Educated at St Augustine's in Edinburgh, followed by Edinburgh uni, he thought 'long and hard' about accepting the job in Aberdeen. Oil was in free-fall, and Aberdeen well supplied with independent schools (four at last count). But the upshot of it all is that he and his wife bought the house of their dreams for considerably less than they first thought of. Bertolotto previously spent 11 years at Edinburgh Academy junior school and is ecstatic about the Aberdeen young: 'bright, bouncy and engaged'. When this ed muttered about the rabbit-warren nature of the classrooms, he pointed out that the lower school worked well, and indeed it does: clustered round individual cloakrooms with bright sunny classrooms.

A spot of background: Hamilton School, a ducky little prep/pre-prep/nursery school a couple of hundred yards down the road, closed abruptly (Care Inspectorate and Education Scotland were stunned: we weren't, looked at it once, and took it out of The Guide as not being fit for purpose). Complex social, financial and fiscal chaos hit the fan, with Care Inspectorate and Education Scotland getting serious egg on their faces and, as a result, upping their visits to the independent sector and becoming increasingly aggressive, particularly with Albyn, which has re-invented itself over the last 10 years (going from Dame school with girlies, to co-ed throughout) and a beacon of success with both educational and social plaudits all round: an obvious target. And it has an English headmaster to boot. Parochial twits.

Academic matters: Lower school follows (somewhat expensive) International Primary Curriculum (IPC), which seems sensible when you realise it was designed by Shell, taught globally and Albyn is an international oily school. IPC is thematic based, with rather natty books to be filled in when 'I understand'. Terrific exposure to all manner of cultures: this is exciting stuff. Jolly Phonics in nursery, handwriting important.

Roughly divided until P7 when extra influx of pupils means year now split into three. Specialist teacher for PE and music in P1, ditto French and Spanish P3: in P4 (8/9 year olds) all get specialist games coaching, and take Mandarin in P6 (having been able to join the Chinese Club in P3). Spanish club kicks in at P7, and of course, music and singing for all.

Scottish system: school presented a hotch potch of examinees: with massive numbers and successes in both disciplines with chemistry, physics, biology, maths, English and selection of mod langs. All must take one lang at Nat 5 and choose two, having done a 'taster course' in German, French, Spanish and Mandarin, for min two years at S1; currently Mandarin the most popular. Geography needs a kick: classics working its way up; classical civilisation and mythology (wowser) growing, from S1/2 (and we loved our culture lesson). Greek possible: but no takers to date. Dumb clucks!

Computing science has poked its head above the parapet; but won't set the world alight yet. Nary a presentation at Advanced Higher level. Business management and modern studies make a showing, with the former probably better overall. Product design and information systems new kids on the block, and stunning. German not currently the flavour of the month. Drama with higher level PE on offer. Spanish (from the upper fifth), Mandarin and engineering science (with its own centre) are the latest additions to the curriculum. Certain amount of almost individual teaching; the results are impressive (if hardly cost-effective). Strong showing in maths challenge and problem-solving. Graphic communication (now replaced by engineering science) increasingly popular with successes at National 5 level, ditto art and design. In 2016, 59 per cent As at Higher level and 41 per cent at Advanced Higher.

All expected to take eight subjects at S4 (National 5s), but IGCES preferred for classical civilisation, history and music, with A levels preferred for classical civilisation, history, music and economics, with five Highers and three Advanced Highers the norm. Timetabling must be a nightmare.

School offers candidates in no less than three disciplines; we know from experience that music at A level is preferred by (almost) all schools – broader course, that sort of thing (often even quite conservative state schools offer both A level art and music). Some blue sky thinking could be useful; the current mish-mash isn't even all things to all people. We briefly discussed (and dismissed) moving to the IB; 'school not yet ready for it'. Can't help feeling that subject choices themselves are in a state of flux.

Class size is low 20s, with low teens for practical subjects (school says 20, but in practice this is much smaller; most classes are 10/15). Comprehensive computer system, class-taught as well as in suites, laptops abound. All pupils have their own email and can email homework and queries to staff. European computer driving licence available, keyboarding taught early in the school; interactive whiteboards in most rooms. iPads now being distributed throughout – school supplied, 'so we can control the content'. But also school insured and upgraded. No mobiles during school hours.

All assessed on entry, two learning support teachers cover the whole school, and a pupil's IEP follows throughout their time. No problems with dyslexia, dyspraxia and mild Asperger's, and in the past did well for a pupil who was profoundly deaf. 'Some timetabled EFL support now available – mostly for clever Chinese – plus lots of support in the classroom', SEN teacher takes individual groups and double teaches a bit – she is very 'willing' – and was off to help out in a German lesson after we had talked. Scribing, readers and all the rest. No extra charge for SEN help. Digital exams being mooted by SQA, school is investigating voice recognition programmes.

Parents of pupils who underperformed at National 5s were stunned to discover that their young did not automatically go forward into sixth form: retakes possible, but school is keen to build on its academic successes. Vociferous (mainly local) parents are less than amused.

Games, options, the arts: Main games field at Milltimber, five miles away – pupils are bused, fabulous athletics track. Albyn uses Aberdeen's state-of-the-art sports village for a number of sports: athletics, hockey, football, netball. Positive netball and hockey with regional representation and masses of individual sports: national representation in several. Snowboarding and skiing popular plus golf. With boys throughout the upper school, serious thought was given to what sport the boys would play: 'Both rugby and football have fervent adherents among parents of the boys, but the latter may be more realistic if we are not to be beaten 80–0 for the next five years'; school recently trounced Glenalmond at footie (head of sport former Aberdeen player). 'Rowing may be the answer.' And so it is. Boys and girls are already competing successfully up to Nat Schools level: boating out of Robert Gordon's University boathouse (pairs, quads) but, as yet no eights.

Stunning art department, with a number of pupils going on to higher things in the art world, though not art school per se recently. Very jolly papier mâché, acrylic and silk screen work, fabric design which alas looked sad when made up (tacky finishing and no attention to detail). Hot on costume design and much use made of local museums. Exciting stained glass – bendy stained glass if you follow. Always a joy to come here. Strong art and architectural stream. Impressive computer graphics mostly on CD covers,

Fantastic music – 'most play a musical instrument' – and loads of participation in either choir or instrumental ensembles. New head of music and snazzy professional standard recording studio. Good representation in the National Youth Orchestra plus jazz, ceilidh bands. Blues band. Keen drama and dance (Dancercise important). No CCF or pipe band, though one or two pipers. Clarsach.

Enthusiastic Young Enterprise (soap box collaborative – whatever that is) and highly competitive D of E with oodles of golds. Strong club culture – quizzes, chess, gardening – but alas no more Scottish country dancing. Keen on public speaking and debating. Head has encouraged trips: Borneo, Barbados, Morocco and Zambia and cultural tours to Italy and south of France. (Some – mainly indigenous – parents, are not entirely convinced of their necessity: this is Aberdeen, after all).

We found the D of E squad preparing for parents' evening during our tour: boots, cagoules, tents, mattresses et al were all on show. 'And', said the master in charge, 'if the parents haven't got the kit, or balk at the price, most of us can find something in our garages'. Now that's the kind of school we like.

Boarding: A boarding house was opened in August 2016 for eight boarders. The three-story building is a five minute walk from school and includes individual bedrooms all with ensuite facilities.

Background and atmosphere: Founded in 1867 by Harriet Warrack, who started teaching girls at home, advertising locally for pupils. Albyn Place (just down the road) became the school's home in 1881, hence the name, and Albyn School for Girls moved to Queen's Road in 1925. The son of one of the gardeners at Duff House, Alexander Mackie was an early moving light, writing books on English (he was a university examiner) and made the school an Aberdeen institution, with emancipated Albyn girls on Aberdeen University student council by 1907. Boys started in the junior department in 2005 and have worked their way up, roughly 55/45 per cent girls/ boys at the moment. The head was pleased to find his original desk in a passage and it now graces his office (the roll-top concealing all manner of educational detritus).

School based in four attached Victorian merchants' houses, with fantastic ceilings, well-used library and predictable garden expansion. Harriet House houses the toddlers, aged 2 to 3 years, while the juniors have new-build, with classrooms clustered round a splendid hall (with windows on the first floor) giving both extra light and affording entertainment; tiny people were practising hurdling and stretching when we visited: hurdles just too far apart for the smallest. Lifts in junior school make disabled access available almost everywhere. Kitchen and dining area dramatically revamped. Junior school order meals in advance; seniors pay-as-you-go. Lockers being rebuilt: currently not big enough for games kit.

Last two years has seen an amalgamation of the nurseries, new science labs, and classroom block with 10 teaching rooms. The existing school has a strong family feel, but logistically it is a complicated complex of corridors and levels between the houses. Fire doors everywhere. The new-build was part cantilevered over the existing playground to protect play space from Aberdonian weather.

Most recent build in autumn 2014 includes sixth form study area with hideous purple and plum high backed chairs (pupils' choice of colours) and surprisingly comfortable plastic chairs at work stations. No plugs. Laptops arrive by trolley load. Junior library (filled with the same young whom we met in the gym) all agreed, when asked, that 'yes, it was a good school'. Lecture theatre/performance space and fitness suite overlooking gym and containing rather a desirable throne.

Impressive music department above hall/gym. The latter, which can accommodate the whole school, has undergone a mega makeover. Weekly assemblies. Broadly Christian in outlook, but more esoteric religions are covered: and, with our guides, we spent some time sleuthing Patricia, who runs the God squad, to no avail.

Latest development is a couple of portakabins (one of the biggest we have ever seen cantilevered over t'other) which act as temporary base for engineering department. New department expected to be up and running by May 2016 (or 'heads will roll'); planning consent obtained.

Pastoral care, well-being and discipline: School divided into four quite competitive clans (clan chiefs), Douglas, Stuart, Forbes and Gordon, for games originally but now principal pastoral unit of school. No tutors; pupils can, and do, relate to form teachers and guidance staff when in difficulty. Wickedness equals yellow card, followed by red card, usual punishment is an essay. Sense of community – school aims to boost the confidence of the shyest child. Policy of zero tolerance for drink 'n' drugs 'n' rock 'n' roll, so expect to be out for persistent bullying or drugs. Cigarettes and alcohol on school premises = detention followed by exclusion followed by out. 'Bullying

A

is usually changing friendship groups' seems about right, but actual bullying is regarded as a no-no. Cyber-bullying has become increasingly problematic. Confidential 'electronic reporting system' under trial. If there is real cause for concern, then parents are summonsed for a 'discussion'.

Queen's Cross church used for Easter (Scotland's first gay minister – which used to upset some of the parent base) and Christmas at St Mark's, which can hold the whole school. First school we have visited to have an LGBT counsellor; we asked if there was much interest, to which answer came there 'only one 15 year old girl came to ask whether she could be bisexual, but she also had a boyfriend.'

Pupils and parents: Mixture of professionals – around 60 per cent oil and gas, the occasional farmer or marine engineer in the parent body. The former often have to either move or install their young at short notice. Huge ethnic mix. Fair number of first-time buyers; parents can drop off early (from 8am, breakfast available) and pick up late (6pm, having done their homework) for pupils in the lower school but this comes with cost. Recent Nigerian influx through local church, and quite a number of Chinese pupils of late.

International bias, but lots of home-grown ones too; strong middle class ethos with girls neat in check dresses or kilts (any tartan, but proper kilts, not skirts – though we didn't see the full eight yards), compulsory for girls from October to April. Some wear them all year round. Boys are allowed to wear kilts but few do: mostly on special occasions. Thrift shop now on line: first time buyers prefer first time uniform.

Comprehensive parent-organised bus system, min age 5/6: tinies, unless with older sibling, not encouraged.

Entrance: Entry from lower to upper is automatic. Pupils can and do join at any time – throughout the year (assuming space available). Growing number, but 'still only a handful' join school for Highers/Advanced Highers at S5/6.

Exit: Around a third leave post Highers in S5, mostly to Scottish unis or for financial constraints. Most to university, odd gap year. Oxbridge trickle, ditto LSE, otherwise mainly to the (freebie) Scottish unis. Edinburgh most popular for a range of subjects from artificial intelligence to medical and biological chemistry. Three medics in 2016.

Money matters: Incredibly strict scale of rules for payment but (Aberdeen, remember) parents can get a two per cent discount if they pay the whole annual whack within a fortnight of the beginning of the autumn term. Discounts of five per cent for second child from pre-school nursery up, and 50 per cent rebate for third and subsequent children. School 'will do what it can to help parents in difficult times, as long as they are open and talk to us'. Can, and will do, 100 per cent bursary if need be, including uniform and help with trips; (apply December, entry test Jan: school carries out stringent financial checks). Be aware, too, the SQA charges exam fees, and there is extra cost for materials used in art and design.

Remarks: Co-ed throughout, this is a school on a roll, small enough for every child to be known as an individual and big enough to offer the best in modern teaching methods. Not a scary school, and some first time buyers do find the independent sector intimidating: welcoming, nurturing and ticking all the boxes. Go for it.

Ardvreck School

Gwydyr Road, Crieff, Perthshire PH7 4EX

Pupils: 128; 44 boarders • Ages: 3–13 (boarding from 7)

Fees: Day £13,965; Boarding £16,655 – £20,991 pa

Tel: 01764 653112
Email: admissions@ardvreck.org.uk
Website: www.ardvreckschool.co.uk

Headmaster: Since 2015, Dan Davey, previously head of Bramcote Junior School in Yorkshire. An experienced head – this is his third headship – he is married to Nichola, who teaches modern languages and helps on the pastoral side. They have three sons.

Entrance: Via pre-prep but most come at 8. Boarding in the last year no longer compulsory but great majority do. Prospective pupils visit school, meet head and get a pupil tour, then spend a taster day in school (or overnight if boarding) wearing school uniform 'so they don't stick out'. Each child is issued with a 'school brother or sister'. They arrive at 10.30am and leave after lunch the following day. Head reports back to parents after feedback from staff.

Exit: Over the past five years senior school destinations have included Ampleforth, Bryanston, Eton, Fettes, Glenalmond, Gordonstoun, Harrow, Marlborough, Merchiston, Millfield, Oundle, Radley, Rugby, Sherborne, Stowe, St Mary's Calne, Strathallan and Uppingham.

Remarks: Jolly popular. School founded in 1883 by former housemaster from nearby Glenalmond. Purpose-built with swimming pool (rather grand but in a polythene tent nonetheless) and a fairly ad hoc collection of classrooms (some a lot better than others) perched on 42 hilly acres (woods etc) – we had 75 acres previously, wonder what happened to them? Littlest Ardvreckers all together at one end of the hog's back – rows of green wellies. Currently slightly boy heavy, not many in nursery (Morrisons down the road slightly cheaper), down in boarding numbers.

Younger boarders live in main house (boys and girls on different floors) in a motley collection of cosy rooms; top two years live in his'n'hers chalets 'to prepare them for public school'. Common rooms tarted up after our previous comments, selected television only, no Wiis for the younger boarders, whose mobiles are handed out when needed. Skype on offer. Older girls can do their own washing, stay abed late on Sundays – boys apparently watch Match of the Day at 8am. Dorms filled with climbing boots and rucksacks, school does three mini Barvicks (expeditions) each summer term. Fixed exeat every third weekend, Friday noon to 10.15am on Mondays now in summer term only, otherwise back to base by 6pm Sundays (but school 'not inflexible' to requests). Parents particularly pleased that this is a proper boarding school and not a day school with weekly sleepovers, consequently popular with the army and diplomatic corps as well as traditional parents. Day pupils stay till 6pm and usually try to board eventually (their choice). NB: School won Tatler Award for Best School Food a few years back (signature dish home made chicken pie).

Impressive weekend programme (parents and pupils confirm 'no time to get bored'); bonfire building practice the Sunday before our previous visit, which coincided with grandparent day (a tough, fairly toffish lot, some of whom fill in for expat parents). We spent 20 rainy minutes in mid-March hearing notices, observing the flag being raised and listening to the junior pipe band (senior boys on a rugby toot to Oundle) play Highland Cathedral followed by croissants, choccy spread and coffee. Pupils were in (their family) kilts and green jerseys. Not really a first-time buyer school, popular with quite grand Scots, many of whom aim to send their young South. Parents 'a close-knit group of families', with pupils 'tending to remain friends well into middle age' and beyond.

A splendid child-orientated school, though becoming 'seriously academic'. Class sizes 15/16, no streaming, but maths taught in sets. Two parallel CE classes in sixth, plus scholarship class. Lots of scholarships and awards, but no honours board ('The only honours board we have is our war memorial'). Percentage-wise, Ardvreck topped the Scottish League Table (not that we think there is such a thing) in scholarships recently with a whopping 18 to schools all over, in almost every discipline (three academic).

Head of learning support plus three pick up both the bright and those with dyslexia et al, three student teachers help in class. One hour at one-to-one, plus one hour group sessions are free, thereafter £20 per hour. All assessed on arrival for maths, English and spelling age. Handwriting important, and lousy writers (like this editor) referred to handwriting clinic. Keyboarding skills important, computers much used for teaching maths and English as well as more trad stuff; French from 4, lyrical art room (buzzy new art teacher). Two retirements shortly in the modern lang dept, replacements being actively sought; policy change in the offing: possibly more Spanish and a smattering of German. Watch this space. Revamp on the cards for the IT department.

'School has begun an enrichment programme in which leading educationalists are invited to the school in order to engage with the children about interesting topics' is how the school puts it, we say fantastic selection of really interesting speakers, with talks open both to day parents and local state children. Think International Relations, Young Engineers' Science Workshop, Expeditions in the Arctic or the History of the Plague (bubonic, pneumonic and septicemic) with pupils given envelopes containing their possible immortality. Magic. If not Faustian.

New expressive arts centre opened by Turner shortlisted Scottish artist Nathan Coley. Fab orchestra – 40 play at assembly each Friday – with trips both for the choir and the orchestras in the offing. Singing and drama outstanding – school regularly features in the ribbons at the Perth Festival, orchestra plays on Thursday assembly. Popular pipe band played at St Giles Cathedral for Prince William's inauguration as a Knight of the Thistle, at The Old Course, St Andrews, and St Ninian's Cathedral in Perth and on telly... trips too, to Edinburgh, the zoo, the botanic garden and Glasgow for the Burrell, as well as toots to Normandy, and Berlin (with pipes and drums).

Outstanding on the games front – all sports, all comers, though parents from other schools have been heard to mutter about trying too hard (still). Trips all over the shop, both sports and subject based. New sports inclusion policy introduced and going down well – 'School continues to thrive on games field but not at the expense of sports for all'. Games pitches fairly well scattered on the flatter areas. New combo-hall, with carpentry below, all singing and dancing above, cunningly perched on really quite a steep slope. Four tennis courts, three netball courts, hockey pitch, Astroturf and shooting range. Serious rugby coaching camp during summer hols with top Scots and English players (Lewis Moody et al).

Balerno Community High School

3

B

5 Bridge Road, Balerno EH14 7AQ

Pupils: 694 • Ages: 11–18 • Sixth form: S5 113, S6 90

Tel: 01314 777788
Email: admin@balernochs.edin.sch.uk
Website: www.balernochs.edin.sch.uk

Headteacher: Since August 2016 Neil McCallum, previously depute head teacher at James Gillespie's. BEd in PE from Greenock Academy; taught PE at Forrester High, and was head of PE at James Gillespie's before promotion to depute head.

Academic matters: An inclusive school with a broad intake. Despite its leafy image, Balerno embraces a socially disparate catchment. Support for learning is run by a team of two specialists plus some really dedicated learning assistants, and school is looking to integrate it with the guidance system. There are three support for pupils leaders, alongside the support for learning leader. Scribing, individual sessions and withdrawal from class all available, plus comprehensive tutorial support, use of ICT (laptops available) and extra time in exams. Extra help from dedicated staff for the relatively few non-native English speakers. All teaching areas with Smartboards and Ivona Text to Speech software. Teaching is stimulating, if the lesson we took part in is anything to go by. Lots of well-informed S2 students, demonstrating verbal and personal assurance as well as an aptitude for scientific and historical research, acting as well-informed prosecution and defence in a mock trial. Courses on offer to suit all needs – with bags of helpful advice on new Scottish curriculum on the parents' website. SQA results opaque. ASDAN, vocational courses, business courses etc on offer as well as plenty of homework clubs, exam technique help etc. Mr Sives is developing access to as wide a range of courses as possible to suit all aptitudes and would like to develop this aspect of the already strong links Balerno has with the local community. A huge range of activities includes access to Malleny Gardens (Scottish National Trust) for some work experience.

Games, options, the arts: Benefiting from a 3G pitch, Balerno has an impressive sporting record. PE is one of the top depts in the city. Participation levels are high with elite level performance in rugby, football,hockey, swimming, netball and golf.

Terrific drama – with exam courses at all levels. Lashings of music with instruments of all types resulting in a plethora of groups and choirs – some impressive – plus current megastar Nina Nesbitt learned her craft here as well as shooting videos in the surrounding woods. The school's creativity drive has seen them work with the Royal Lyceum Theatre over three years and have the highest level of accredited Teachers of creativity in the country.

Imaginatively international outlook for a Scottish suburban school, with masses of exchanges including Copenhagen, Stuttgart, and Budapest, under the Comenius initiative. Senior students participate in numerous international conferences run by Model United Nations.

There is a huge array of extracurricular stuff from all sorts of sport and the range of outdoor education, Duke of Edinburgh etc you might expect from an independent schools as well as things like debating (at a pretty high level), journalism, Young Enterprise and Stock Market Challenge, trips for most subjects and a fantastic range of productions (West Side Story, Bugsy Malone and Chicago recently; Les Mis in 2015) and concerts. The

B

school even has its own credit union, the Pentland Savers, run entirely by students. As an 'Eco School level 1' – whatever that may mean – and 'Healthy School level 2', Balerno is not letting the grass grow under its feet.

Won the Lothian finals for Young Enterprise 3 years in a row against tough private sector competition. Work experience for all at S4 and work shadowing in sixth. Parents and school find the positions – a joint effort. Popular clubs post-school, at lunchtime and in the evening: Spanish, web development, electronics and publishing as well as extracurricular dance, snowboarding (Hillend and the real thing), hockey and athletics. Keen charity input.

Background and atmosphere: Has historic antecedents – the charming logbook kept by the principal teacher of St Mungo's Episcopal School in Balerno during the 19th century is a joy: 'Wet and windy all week. One child was blown into the Water of Leith but was fortunately rescued. One child was bit by a dog.. '. The present school was opened on a glorious greenfield site on the banks of the Water of Leith, after several years of 'swithering' in 1983. Somehow in the process the futuristic vision of a community school turned into something resembling a 60s nuclear power station. It's nearly as difficult to get in since the entrance is un-signposted and in an apparently dead-end corner. (The welcome, however, is warm.) Huge long passages, bare concrete staircases with scaffolding poles as banisters and narrow staircases. Much money has disappeared attempting to install ceilings where they were never meant to be and school has sensibly given up the attempt and is spending whatever it can get on facilities. The plus factor is a long spacious indoor area which feels like a shopping mall and is wonderful for community events like craft fairs. It also forms a wet weather concourse with access to everything.

The community affiliation provides the school with all sorts of ancillary activities including a serious 20-metre swimming pool as well as some outstanding public areas. Balerno people definitely see it as their school and are proud of its achievements and its role in community education and enterprise.

Pastoral care, well-being and discipline: Strong anti-bullying strategies in conjunction with S6. All pupils join one of three houses called after local areas, siblings in same house; heads of houses are in charge of pastoral care and guidance. Tutorial system for all, same tutor throughout the school, good contact for parents on academic matters. Head Start for 'vulnerable' pupils before they begin at Balerno, when the new S1, sixth form and staff spend a week confidence building. S1 pupils also spend a bonding week with their guidance and pastoral staff at one of three residential centres during their first term (Monday to Friday) where they gain their Gold Junior Duke of Edinburgh award. Regular year group and house assemblies. Head boy and girl play a strong leadership role. Mentors and buddies provided by the senior house teams along with literacy and numeracy champions and paired reading initiatives. School uniform definitely for all, with high standards of presentation demanded. Very low exclusion rates and instances of indiscipline rare.

Pupils and parents: Balerno is right on the edge of the countryside so it attracts every strata of the farming population as well as both comfortably suburban and distinctly urban areas of Edinburgh. About 10 per cent ethnic minorities. Exceptionally well-organised parent council and a PTA raising significant funds.

Entrance: From three dedicated primaries: Dean Park, Ratho and Kirknewton, plus at least 20 others whose pupils request placements every year. Pupils from outwith the area may have problems with the regular school bus but parents' council helps to provide extra buses.

Exit: A few leave to try their hand in the workplace after S4 (low employment rate), or go on to tertiary education elsewhere. Most stay on for two more years. Two-thirds of students go on to further or higher education; strong links with the local high-tariff universities: Edinburgh, Heriot Watt for science, Aberdeen and Glasgow, plus a tiny trickle to Oxbridge or southern unis.

Remarks: A community school which is learning to use its local roots for the benefit of community and pupils alike.

Balfron High School

Roman Road, Balfron G63 0PW

Pupils: 900 • Ages: 11–18 • Sixth form: 300

Tel: 01360 440469
Email: balfronhs@stirling.gov.uk
Website: www.balfronhigh.org.uk

Head Teacher: Since 2013, Ms Elaine Bannatyne, previously at Bearsden Academy for over 10 years, both as depute head and previously as principal teacher of guidance. Before that she worked as a PE teacher at Greenock High School.

Academic matters: School has taken to the curriculum for excellence with a vengeance. The three existing houses act as mothership for three school-lets (known as schools, following the American model) with a ninth of each year in each school. The form teacher for each year stays with that class throughout their time in school. Class teachers are responsible for the pastoral care of their children and may well teach their form for some seven hours a week, so all pupils know there is someone out there batting for them. Max class size 20 in the first year, in practical subjects and in maths and English in S3, with extra maths and Eng in S3 if needed. Slightly complicated system of mix-and-match with hist and geog (social subjects course) – 'a standard rota used by schools and not complicated', says school; specialist staff from S2. Fiercely academic – 'Not so', says school, 'we do far more here than concentrate on academic subjects' – and high uptake in all Advanced Higher subjects. Strong science school with marvellous labs (but marvellous everything, see below); biology lab has a greenhouse incorporated into its roof. Labs are an astonishing, carpeted, 90 metres square.

Few up-to-date results as school requests its removal from GSG website (we know that 40 per cent of S5 pupils got 5+ Highers, with 19 getting straight As, and that one pupil got 100 per cent in his National 5 French and maths exams in 2016). Flexible learning not a problem and sixth formers and local adults (evenings) can log on to do distance learning courses; sociology the current flavour of the month. Strong links with Forth Valley College and Skillforce for less academic. Computers abound, three pupils per machine, and emails for all. Whiteboards in every classroom. Problems picked up early, and reported immediately, so that any child finding difficulty should be 'sorted out' quickly – via house meeting, which will include deputy head plus support-for-learning teacher and other appropriate staff, and remedial strategies discussed: professional support, ed psychs pulled in if needed. Qualified head of support for learning plus three others and four assistants in school. This is an inclusive school, capable of dealing with physical disabilities. Terrific library overlooking the atrium, with views out over the games pitches to The Campsies.

Games, options, the arts: School incorporates a fabulous leisure complex with pool, sports hall and weights much used by the local community and open from 7am to 10pm, 365 days a year. Excellent swimming (25-metre pool), Astroturf, pitches and athletics track. Masses of games after school, Stirling Council (and the lottery) provide a sports co-ordinator; rugby good – both national and international players in the school, and list of names of all national players of any sport in reception. Art is state of, with every possible medium catered for and finished products creeping onto the walls and a rather chic patio. Computer-linked CDT mass of machines. First year must do home economics, thereafter optional between third and sixth – flash new kitchens with microwaves. Terrific theatre and drama, the theatre available to the community, and masses of music, with local involvement. String, wind and jazz plus Teudan Teth fiddle band, myriad choirs and boy groups plus countless talent shows and clubs at lunch time. Work experience for all at 14. Masses of trips and exchanges, for culture and education (ie skiing is out). Strong links with school in Malawi and a huge amount of exchange – staff as well as pupils. School will underwrite those who can't afford it. Huge amount of charity work and much local involvement, including a guide dog puppy called Faith.

Background and atmosphere: Opened in May 2002 by Helen Liddle, who celebrated the partnership between Stirling Council and Jarvis by sticking the first leaf on the 'school tree of learning', which climbs up the corner of the atrium adjacent to the dining room, where pupils either bring their own or use swipecards (which conceals the free school meals problem – about four per cent). Graduands (to continue the American theme) have their name embossed on a leaving leaf, which is firmly fixed to the 30 foot high tree by the intrepid janitor.

A magnet school. State-of-the-art in every dimension – each subject has a pod of rooms off the main core, terrific views, marvellous outside area (the sun does occasionally shine north of the Highland Line). Magical food with mass of choice. All the rooms are networked for sound (as well as inter/intra netted) and at 10.45am loudspeaker announcements about sin on the school bus, praise for work well done and extra music lessons boom over the speakers. Electronic noticeboard advertising weekend jobs at the local pub. School became a community school proper in 2003 but the old boards still reassuringly in place. School uniform for all: trainers out and shirt and tie back due to pupil demand, atop some of the shortest skirts we have seen this year; smart blue blazers with green trim loaned annually to sixth formers, who must have them cleaned before they are returned.

Pastoral care, well-being and discipline: System of pupil support, good PSHE and anti-bullying strategies in place. 'Balfriending' is a buddy system between first and sixth years which really works. Masses of contact, sixth pick up problems early; incidents are logged, the victim supported and the bully sanctioned – sanctions range from verbal warnings through 'the imposition of a written exercise' (restorative exercise' = reflections) to temporary or even permanent exclusions and ed psychs etc. Head maintains that most bullying is really just 'a breakdown in relationships'.

Pupils and parents: Huge catchment area: 800 children bused in each day. Good middle class ethos prevails – 'we are a comprehensive school' – combo of real country plus incomers, friendly and welcoming children; few from ethnic minority backgrounds. Enthusiastic parents' council which seems to spend time worrying about 'incidents' behind the (unused) bike shed and why special praise seems to be singled out for athletes. School stresses that they raise money for the school, help with careers advice and interviews, and work with school to manage road traffic problems.

Entrance: From local primaries, capped at 180, usually 30 or so placing requests.

Exit: Few leave after National grades, around 90 per cent stay for Higher of whom 70 per cent will stay till S6. Most to Scottish universities – Ed and Glasgow top of the pops with the odd one or two to St Andrews, and occasional trickle to Oxbridge.

Remarks: Stunning school, happy staff, good work ethos, some of the best views in Scotland. Worth moving to the Trossachs for.

Basil Paterson Middle School & Tutorial College

65 & 66 Queen Street, Edinburgh EH2 4NA

Pupils: 35 • Ages: 14–19 (but currently some in their 20s) • Sixth form: 20

Fees: £12,000 pa

Tel: 01312 225 6070
Email: info@basilpatersonschool.co.uk
Website: www.basilpatersonschool.co.uk/

Head: Claire Samuel.

Academic matters: Edinburgh's oldest and most famous tutorial college, founded in 1929 to offer 'bespoke education for all', comes under the umbrella of the Oxford Intensive School of English (OISE) empire. The answer to many a parent's prayer. Huge number of subjects on offer: Scottish Highers, Advanced Highers and National 5s; plus GCSE and A levels with all three English exam boards. College is an accredited exam centre for SQA, Edexcel, OCR and AQA, plus Cambridge Specialist exams.

Edinburgh is rich in tutors, and a team of part-timers cover almost every subject under the sun. Maximum class size six, many individual lessons. Flexi-tuition popular, college is open till 6.30pm, students top up existing grades, study subjects incompatible with the customary five column choices. Most follow the well-worn path to further education. Not an SEN refuge per se, but often the perfect solution for the dyslexic, students who have struggled in their learning careers to date or who have been absent for a period of time, or those previously educated abroad who find a tutorial college more appealing than a conventional sixth form.

Well-equipped science lab, art students now opt for trad art colleges. Three hours' tuition per subject for GCSE per week, four or six for Highers and Advanced Highers/full A levels. Impressive success rate from tiny numbers – most GCSEs A*-C grades. Some courses require continuous course work assessment (evaluation and review) and the odd learner may be advised to either change course or level of study. SEN assistance on hand (specialist staff), the SQA now need physical evidence of the need for scribes or extra time, an ed psych report is no longer sufficient. The full-time course includes supervised study as well as a social programme in conjunction with the larger English language wing, not much take up in the

B

latter. Popular revision sessions during the Easter holidays are regularly oversubscribed.

Middle school for 14-16 year olds opened in August 2012 (SQA National 4s and 5s only).

Games, options, the arts: Queen Street is home to the Edinburgh New Town Cooking School which seemed to us to be a useful add-on, but most prefer the gym at nearby Bannantynes; learners have a key to Queen Street gardens, but use Meadowbank sports centre for circuit training, swimming, tennis and the like.

Boarding: College can offer non-local students accommodation through their international EFL host family set-up, not a lot of take-up. Most students are home grown, living with family/ies or in flats in and around Edinburgh.

Background and atmosphere: Two splendid Georgian houses strategically joined together at ground and basement in Edinburgh's posh Queen Street. Some original ceilings still visible, with 12 classrooms of random size, some with spectacular views to the north over the Firth of Forth, state-of-the-art computers (email access for all), student common room and study centre. A dedicated wireless area encourages the use of personal laptops. Place currently needs a spot of TLC round the edges.

Pastoral care, well-being and discipline: Learners are expected to take a certain amount of responsibility for their studies. Each student and parent/guardian must sign a student support agreement to agree to abide by the school rules. Strong anti-drug bias. Equally hot on time-keeping, regular phone calls both to parents and to students: habitual offenders may be expelled. Homework must be handed in on time, with the threat of remaining on the premises till finished. Regular reports to parents, couple of parents' evenings during the year to 'meet the tutors', compulsory for tutors – on our last visit they were still throwing out the empties – apparently not really a bonding experience for parents.

Pupils and parents: Currently 10 per cent from abroad plus first-time candidates (visa requirements apply for non-Brits); retakes and those hopeful of upping grades. Numbers have a habit of more than doubling during the autumn term as pupils decide to change tack. Most learners fall into the 16-19 age bracket, but the college has students of all ages – up to 70+.

Entrance: Enrolment form must be completed and £300 deposit paid before starting classes. Students are encouraged to meet with the head before starting to discuss subject choices, suitability etc.

Exit: Most go on to universities across the UK. Past students have gone on to study at (among others) Glasgow, Edinburgh, St Andrew's, Aberdeen, Leeds, Newcastle, Strathclyde, Heriot-Watt, University of Manchester, Napier, and Goldsmith's.

Money matters: Fees are per subject per year and are invoiced termly or by other arrangement.

Remarks: Up and running. An Edinburgh legend still delivering the goods. Numbers usually double between September and December.

Beaconhurst

52 Kenilworth Road, Bridge of Allan, Stirling FK9 4RR

Pupils: 323 (including 44 in nursery) • Ages: 3–18

Fees: £8,847 – £12,042 pa

Tel: 01786 832146
Email: secretary@beaconhurst.com
Website: www.beaconhurst.com

Headteacher: Since 2015, Sandra Bannerman (50s), previously deputy head. A product herself of Scottish education, she has a degree in English from Glasgow University and a postgrad from Edinburgh. Taught English for many years in the British School in Brussels; she continues to teach Advanced Highers. Her two daughters are both also English graduates.

The sudden departure of the preceding head, John Owen, caused nervousness amongst parents; however, Mrs Bannerman has worked hard to quell anxieties. Parents felt the transition was not well handled but consensus is she is incredibly capable and has already done much to be celebrated. A big personality, staff welcome her more collegiate approach to management and parents welcome her accessibility.

Academic matters: Beaconhurst is a broad church but still gets some good results. In 2016, 57 per cent A/B in Highers and 42 per cent A, with 63 per cent A/B and 28 per cent A in Advanced Highers. Maths, English and science are streamed from S1, with flexible movement both ways. Classes are small, smaller still for the lower streams, enabling lots of individual attention. School does well in the annual maths/science national challenges and very well with Young Enterprise. Pupils encouraged to take eight subjects in S4 including a compulsory MFL, with occasional bespoke adjustments, usually for dyslexic pupils or talented sportspeople, to accommodate extra training.

Languages are important with lots of early input, German introduced, gently, in J1, and French added in J5. Dyslexic pupils offered touch-typing instead of second language if appropriate. Spanish and Italian also on offer, but no classics. By the time choices are made in S2, all-through pupils are making an informed decision, also facilitated by the first foray into exploring careers. Timetables are built to accommodate pupils' choices and it is not unusual to find a single pupil in an Advanced Higher class. Specialist teachers in the junior school from the start; even the nursery pupils trot into the science labs for 'experiential play', an advantage of an all-through school. A small but busy learning support department offers excellent targeted support to the handful of pupils with dyslexia and other learning difficulties, and also enrichment for high achievers. Juniors are assessed from the start. Laptops, tablets and targeted software, scribes, readers etc., pupils get what they need. Parents are impressed with the school's readiness to keep up with latest research.

Catch-up classes are available after school and often at lunchtime, particularly for the sporty undertaking extra training or time out to attend events (triathlon particularly time-intensive), but also for any stumbling pupil who just needs a bit extra. Parents praise the staff for being 'so generous with their time'. One parent said, 'They are vocational teachers to a man [sic]. They understand their job is to make sure children learn and don't just stand up and spout.' Pupils are equally aware of the extra mile given to them and acknowledge it motivates them to achieve. Effort and enthusiasm is rewarded and although there is a culture of high expectations, as much value is placed on being a brilliant mountain biker as excelling in maths.

Games, options, the arts: Beaconhurst has an established relationship with Stirling University sports centre and every pupil, including the youngest infant, has a full annual membership to their fabulous facilities. The relationship goes beyond facilities use and there is a mutual benefit, with university students bringing their know-how and support to the school, while gaining work experience, particularly but not just in sport. Recent student research monitored daily physical activity in the nursery, where pupils demonstrated the value of a Fundamental Movement Programme for cognitive development, particularly amongst girls, and the school has adopted the findings into its daily programme.

Hockey is the main team sport and the first team do well, but it is fully inclusive and everyone gets a chance to compete. No rugby, a decision taken due to the size of the school. Tennis, golf and triathlon popular, with high level specialist coaching, including some support from Tennis Scotland. School particularly keen to develop lifelong passion, and these are all sports easily continued beyond. They compete on the national stage for tennis, and currently have three pupils in international competition, but it's not just about the gifted, although these are well supported. Training not in year groups; older pupils inspire and support the younger, and cross-year friendships established.

The large school gym is well used for gymnastics, dance (especially Scottish) and trampolining, one member of staff a sports acrobat. Upper school pupils can opt to gain an industry accredited qualification as a gym instructor. Outdoor education high on the agenda, with its own, recently established, stand alone department. D of E compulsory to silver, gold optional. Compulsory outdoor education week for all senior school and transition pupils. Kayaking from J4 onwards in local rivers and beyond – one pupil enthusiastic about a recent lake-to-lake trip, 40 miles of kayaking and camping. Head of outdoor education alarmingly nicknamed Dangerous Dave, whose approach to health and safety is about teaching all, even the very youngest, how to behave safely and healthily, and how to take responsibility for oneself, all risk-assessed. Juniors learn bushcraft with him, including woodcutting and firebuilding. And most pupils could take their cycling proficiency and swim confidently by the time they are 6.

Drama is taught to Advanced Higher but expressive arts is compulsory for all from S4-S6, and Friday afternoons are dedicated to a large scale, annual, pupil-driven musical production. Pupils choose which department to join – performance, media or backstage, including all technical, set production, costumes – designing and making (boys boning corsets for their recent Les Mis). Anyone who wants to be in the cast can, and every year they discover a pupil who didn't know they could sing. Newly appointed head of expressive arts focusing on expanding productions throughout the school and developing the school's enhanced relationship with Stirling University's Macrobert Arts Centre, with the first joint initiative currently underway. Plenty of musical options, choir for all, with an impressive variety for a small school. New head of music has turned the small school numbers into an advantage and has expanded the existing orchestra into a 'community' orchestra, involving pupils of all ages and any musical parents, teachers and support staff. Their first performance at a recent concert was, from all accounts, a triumph. An assortment of clubs, all the usual and more, with junior and senior debating and thriving eco clubs. Eco awareness hugely important to the school; Beaconhurst is the only school in Scotland to date to have a Soil Association silver award, and an eco committee, with representatives from each year, ensures this is kept on track.

Lots of trips including annual ski trip to New Hampshire; cross-country skiing in Norway; history trip to France; several others abroad and closer to home. Regular trips to sit in on lectures, recently one on metaphor at Glasgow Uni and another to Forth Valley to witness a DNA experiment. International trips also offered through the school's Round Square membership, most recently to Transylvania. Exchanges also available within the programme: one pupil to Canada recently and school welcomed pupils from Australia and Malaysia.

Background and atmosphere: Beaconhurst School came into being in 1976 with the merger of Beacon School for girls with Stirling's Hurst Grange for boys, moving into the girls' Bridge of Allan site, ultimately becoming an all-through day school in the early 90s. Centred around the original Victorian house on the crest of the hill, classroom blocks have been gradually added, somewhat haphazardly filling the site. Steps and steep paths everywhere, with a level of fitness required to get from chemistry to maths, or lunch to German. The expansive view from the glass-sided dining hall is, however, beautiful, and lunch outside on its terrace in the warmer months a treat indeed. Every inch of the grounds is used, with tree ropes, tennis courts, an eco garden, a dedicated nursery area complete with a willow den, a climbing wall, and a mountain bike trail imaginatively tucked in. Crossing the playground can be precarious, navigating between improbably tiny children impressively cycling on two wheels.

The position of the junior school and nursery in the centre of the campus physically demonstrates its integration within the whole school. The award-winning nursery is celebrated by all, and deservedly so. Senior pupils are able to take on responsibilities within school and work with younger pupils. The atmosphere throughout is traditional yet progressive; pupils have formal relationships with staff, good manners notable, but parents describe strong bonds between them and particularly appreciate the calm, friendly atmosphere this seems to generate.

Round Square membership engages the school with an international network and emphasises the importance placed on their shared educational philosophy promoting internationalism, democracy, environment, adventure, leadership and service.

Pastoral care, well-being and discipline: The school is a close community and everyone knows each other; even the most shy develops a level of confidence. All pupils allocated a tutor when in transition, for their entire school career. Tutor groups are formed within a vertical system, with a maximum of 14 within each, and one-to-one personal reviews at the end of each term. Siblings are placed in the same group, so tutors get to know families very well and pupils forge strong relationships beyond their year group.

Progression from one stage of the school to the next is carefully handled with pupil well-being at the forefront. Nursery children moving up to juniors have a J5 buddy, especially to help them negotiate the playground, and transition pupils are teamed with an S4 mentor, with the expectation the friendship can continue. The four house system is central to the school structure; pupils are placed in a house from nursery. Termly house assemblies are organised by the S6 house captains, bringing the whole house together with formal presentations. House points are allocated for achievement, and withdrawn, the juniors get stickers, and there are regular inter-house competitions. For seniors, discipline is meted out by their head of house, usually a detention and never taken lightly. Junior parents praise swift action by staff to deal with issues which can occur in small classes. Parents also welcome the recently created Parents' Forum, which meets termly and establishes an open line of communication between parents and the heads.

PHSE taught throughout school but integrated into everything. Dinner ladies promote healthy eating and will sit with the younger pupils to help. They get to know all the woes and are key members of the pastoral team. Prefects also support the pastoral team and work hard. It's not a popularity contest and they are each awarded a role with specific duties complete with a job description. Positions are applied for and allocated after interviews. All part of the school's keen eye for leadership development.

Pupils and parents: The parents describe a huge mix, some working hard to send their kids, some super wealthy, several first time independent. Many pupils travel some distance, a fleet of school mini buses scoop them up or shuttle them from the nearby train station. The reach largely covers a 30 mile radius with a handful from beyond even that, Perth and even Edinburgh, attracted mostly by the standard of tennis coaching and triathlon.

A fair few live locally, walking distance for smart Bridge of Allan, families content not to be drawn by the bigger brands of Dollar or Morrison's. Watch out for tiny children cycling like a line of ducklings behind parents on the school run, deserving the school's cycle-friendly school award.

Entrance: Two taster trial days attending all classes with a 'buddy'. On the second day, tests for literacy and numeracy. Junior level applicants are assessed informally through observation.

Exit: Some juniors head to Dollar or Morrison's for a bigger pool. Most seniors to further ed, lots to Scottish universities, especially Edinburgh, Glasgow and St Andrews, and usually a couple of medics and vets. Sports, drama and IT related careers also popular. Range of destinations with much support given to all.

Money matters: Some bursaries, closely means-tested and annually reviewed. Usually able to support a change of circumstance.

Remarks: A small, happy school, encouraging and hard working, with strong international links and a real focus on supporting individual achievement and development. The importance of outdoor education adds a healthy glow to all.

Bearsden Academy

Stockiemuir Road, Bearsden G61 3SF

Pupils: 1,185 • Ages: 11–18 • Sixth form: 350

Tel: 01419 552344
Email: office@bearsdenacademy.e-dunbarton.sch.uk
Website: www.bearsdenacademy.e-dunbarton.sch.uk

Headteacher: Since 2008, Mr George F Cooper (40s), who neither wants to talk to us, nor to 'give any more details': he comes from Ayr Academy, where he was depute head and was previously head of English. He was – to quote our informant – 'at Ayr for many many years' and came to Bearsden Academy in the footsteps of the legendary Mike Doig, who turned the school around, following a period of some unsettlement. Cooper faced a serious challenge a few years ago when the school moved to a new site on the perimeter of St Andrews Primary, on the old college site, a term later than planned.

Academic matters: School takes National 5s, Highers and Advanced Highers. German and French but no Spanish, and three separate sciences; maths and English results 'consistently strong'. Pupils are setted in their second year for English, maths, French and sciences. Not a vast choice of subjects but totally adequate with the non-academic well represented. Most pupils take eight subjects at National grade. No details of exam results as 'we do not wish to be featured in your publication'.

Pupils are allocated a guidance teacher during their last year at primary, who acts as tutor throughout their time in secondary. Smashing library which also includes a careers office and much-used sixth form study centre. Six fully-equipped computing/business rooms – the library has a well-equipped computer room – fabulous dedicated space (books being added to all the time). Work ethos is important here, ditto homework, and homework diary must be signed by parent or guardian but pupils can complain 'to their Guidance teacher if they feel that they are unable to cope with homework'.

Support for learning throughout, with learning support staff visiting the linked primary schools to ensure a smooth transition. Four support for learning assistants, who work with children both on an individual basis and in class, scribing if need be; can deal with normal (mild) Asperger's et al, no currently diagnosed ADHD. New-build wheelchair friendly, no (real) problems with profoundly deaf or visually handicapped pupils. EAL on hand, over 22 different nationalities in the school, many of whom do not speak English as their first language.

Games, options, the arts: Stunning games hall and, as a community school, this is much used by locals too. Good spread of games pitches; school does remarkably well at rugby, football, with athletics well-represented. Outstanding success in football and basketball. No tennis courts or swimming pool but skiing, snowboarding are popular options, regular trips abroad – the Alps as well as Aviemore. Ex-pupil Olympic rower Katherine Grainger won silver at Rio to add to gold in London and silvers in Sydney, Athens and Beijing. Superb home economics facility, with pupils learning how to wash and iron, as well as cook and operate electronic sewing machines.

Cultural trips to Paris and Florence and large successful art department, fabric design as well as pure art. Music fantastic, choirs and orchestras of all descriptions, rock band seems to be on the wane. Drama extracurricular but a popular club – pantomime and Shakespeare in alternating years. Long-standing Young Enterprise. Work experience in fourth year, with loads of private placements. Clubs highly popular, and the board game club specialises in esoteric conundrums that make the mind boggle; enthusiastic web club. Massive charity input from seniors in particular, with five-figure sums raised every year. World Challenge Expeditions to Thailand, Mongolia, Tanzania et al.

Background and atmosphere: Now on swish new site. Prefectorial duties include keeping a weather eye on behaviour around school premises. Pupils all neat and tidy in school uniform which is mandatory, with a very strict dress code – no advertising, track suit tops, denim, baseball caps or trainers outwith PE and particularly no football colours or any item of clothing which could potentially cause friction.

Pastoral care, well-being and discipline: Exemplary. School has a very positive attitude to bullying – 'Friends against Bullying', senior pupils volunteer to work with the first year group, visit them first thing each day and wear badges indicating that anyone who feels they are being bullied can come to them to discuss the problem. There are also 'supervised' lunch time clubs that youngsters can come to, as well as study-buddies. Chaplaincy team of five – Church of Scotland, Baptist, all take a year each – Church of Rome declines to allow Catholic priests to join this ecumenical team which is a bit odd considering one of the local primary schools (St Andrews) is Catholic and 90 per cent of their pupils come on. Room set aside during Ramadan for prayer.

Strong discipline code, range of punishments, from Behaviour Card which must be signed by all staff, with the ultimate sanction being exclusion. Pupils who persist in being disruptive or who are late are sent to the Behaviour Support Base for the rest of the lesson which they have disrupted and often for the next lesson in that subject; they also have detention at lunch time. Previous head would exclude but only temporarily; drugs not previously a problem and they were patted on the back by drugs supremo Maxi Richards, who has an input in the senior PSHE programme.

Pupils and parents: Four per cent on free school meals; a good middle class bunch from Milngavie, Bearsden, Canniesburn as well as Drumchapel, north west Glasgow. 'Somewhat' oversubscribed, school has a good reputation and is handy for buses and trains. Priority to siblings, followed by East Dunbartonshire location (distance from front door to front door). Large number of ethnic backgrounds, over 100+ youngsters from non-English speaking families – most Asians and Chinese but Africans, Middle Eastern and east Europeans are well represented. Absolutely no problems with the mix, the school is a 'seriously harmonious group'. Good PTA with parents getting quite deeply involved with the school programme of speakers and interview skills as well as the trad charity role.

Entrance: Automatic from local primaries; then by formula. New arrivals can get immediate entry if space available.

Exit: Only 10 per cent leave post-National to do further education elsewhere or go into employment. A few leave post-Highers with university entrance qualifications but most stay for sixth form, notably those going to uni down south. Majority of leavers go to central Scottish universities – no particular bias – industry, dentistry and medicine popular. Regular two or three to Oxbridge annually. Some to study music, some to art school. Youngsters tend to go straight to uni, but an increasing gap year take up.

Money matters: State, with help on hand to supplement low-income families to go on school trips. Two forms of financial help available to those who stay at school after the age of 16. Footwear and clothing grant for those whose family or guardians qualify as low-income; and the other, the Scottish Executive Education Maintenance Allowance Scheme (EMA), for any pupils living in the area and going to school in East Dunbartonshire.

Remarks: A positive school, firmly setting its sights on the 21st century. Exciting times on newish site; we will watch this space with interest.

Belhaven Hill School

Dunbar, East Lothian EH42 1NN

Pupils: 125; 70 boarders • Ages: 7–13

Fees: Day £10,740– £15,450; Boarding £22,077 pa

Tel: 01368 862785
Email: headmaster@belhavenhill.com
Website: www.belhavenhill.com

Head: Since September 2016, Henry Knight, previously head of Woodcote House. BA in classical civilization (Royal Holloway), PGCE, MEd (40s). WH is the only school he has worked in previously. Joined as an English teacher there in 2003, a complete career change after running corporate hospitality for Berry Bros. 'As part of that I set up a wine school and found I enjoyed imparting information and became sure education was what I wanted to do,' he says. He saw an ad for a junior English teacher and house master at WH and the rest is history. Paid his dues as head of department, then joined the senior management team and took on several greater responsibilities before eventually becoming head. Married to Susannah, who will play an active role at the school. They have three children and want their family to be at the centre of school life at Belhaven.

Entrance: No test, but register as soon as possible. Children spend a day at Belhaven the term before they come. Informal test when they come in but no official screening until age 9 – 'when we don't often find any surprises'.

Exit: Oundle, Rugby, Glenalmond, Queen Margaret's, Fettes, Radley, Ampleforth, Eton and Harrow, Wycombe Abbey, St Mary's Calne, plus all the big Scottish schools. Thereafter, anywhere.

Remarks: Numbers still high; full for the next few years: number of day children, many of whom convert to boarding. Brilliant house staff, matrons (and talkative cooking squad – but no requirement for kosher or halal; ditto cleaners – all natty in blue tabliers). Brace of learning support staff. Ed psych comes in to meet head of LS. The learning support base, aka The Hut, has been revamped (to the envy of some non-learning support pupils). Withdrawn from class, one-to-one, small groups, dual teaching – all disciplines covered, at no extra cost; though if a child has severe and particular difficulties school is relaxed about parents employing additional help.

Still perceived as Scotland's school for the occasional toff which specialises in sending the little darlings to public school in the south, but now with a much broader base. School went co-ed in 1995, and thereafter welcomed the day squad. Boys based in late 18th century sandstone house with tower and imaginative additions: fairly pedestrian rumpus room; rules for backgammon laid out on the table but apparently no board. Dorms recently revamped with carpets and pin boards, alas bunks now a thing of the past (and round the world ditto): collection of tartan curtains, desks rather than bedside cabinets for older pupils. The snazzy girls' house has a spit new circular Rosy room, with plasma television and brightly coloured beanbags, though we doubt whether 32 young ladies could all watch telly together.

No books or newspapers spotted in either the boys' or the girls' common rooms; head assured us there were books and papers aplenty in the reconfigured library just steps away. We are delighted that there are books and magazines in the library but this ed wants to see them everywhere on tables/chairs any place that children might find themselves waiting. Daily papers visible in girls' house kitchen (The Times and Scotsman, since you ask); we were told that pupils could 'come and get them at bedtime'; heck, daily papers should be on every coffee table and flat surface, ditto magazines: Reader's Digest was perfect, but New Scientist will do just as well for interesting titbits. Bored children are good at instant literary grazing. But perhaps it was too early in the term.

Eight new classrooms, most grouped cloister-like round the lily pond – Jeremy Fisher, where art thou? – fab double and a half decker music school, but still a bit of a rabbit warren. All pupils online, two computer rooms. Own laptops not a problem. Pupils set in core subjects – maths, English, science and languages – throughout, but lots of to-ing and fro-ing. Science from age 8 and dedicated science, as in physics, chemistry and biology, from age 10. No setting for music, art and PE (friendships important). Tutors for top two years, otherwise classroom based, with form teachers and class sizes to 10/14. No scholarship stream as such, but more a case 'of children extended through setting and provided with opportunities for further support in activities and prep' (quite, scholarship stream in all but name). Clinic (aka drop in centre on Fridays) where lesser performers can seek help, and high flyers challenge. Vast choice of extracurricular activities; bright creatures steered towards the more intellectually challenging.

Latin, as you might expect, and Greek on offer (but on rather an ad hoc basis post CE, that sort of thing). Drama and dance increasingly popular, and wow, the costumes. Inspired art, ceramics and design, with climbing wall on the outside of this converted squash court – sand below, not high, hats not de rigueur. Slightly tired, if functional, sports hall which adapts for school plays, has ping pong tables aloft and new cricket nets. Secured open swimming pool.

Piping much encouraged with FPs core of pipe bands in English public schools and in demand at weddings and funerals; or getting their tuppence worth on the corner of Princes Street to garner for gap years. Manicured grounds including two cricket pitches, six tennis courts, masses of Astroturf, a putting course and an 18-hole golf course 'over the wall'. Bracing sea air. Streams of unbeaten teams in almost every discipline. Regular trips to Hillend artificial ski slope. Young encouraged to have their own chunk of the head's walled garden in which they take great pride: fierce competition for annual trophies. One member of staff, along with the children, uses all the apples from the orchard to make one big brew of apple juice for the children and staff to drink but expect home-made apple pies, dumplings and crumbles. Grub for all in the dining room – benches and tables – with quartered oranges on offer during our visit.

Happy children when we visited, racing round lily pond – 'how many more times?'; relaxed uniform, ties and grown up stuff (long trousers, white shirts) only in last two years. Social parents and children, with masses of input from locals – tranches of farmers/Charlotte Rangers from East Lothian, plus the usual quota of quite grand children from the north and an increasing gang from south of the border, usually with Scottish connections. Girls fully absorbed. Grandparents and parents ('wish I'd been there,' said one prosperous Edinburgh property developer, who was educated within the city limits) have nothing but praise. Daily assembly, but don't expect surprises, charming little prayer book just printed for newbies ('put their name in it, it has to last three years'); God important, ditto values, bullying or aggravated teasing kept firmly under control, 'girls worse than boys'.

The school is flourishing. Can't fault it.

Belmont House School

Sandringham Avenue, Newton Mearns, Glasgow G77 5DU

Pupils: 250 • Ages: 3–18 • Sixth form: 25

Fees: £6,435 – £12,180 pa

Tel: 01416 392922
Email: admin@belmontschool.co.uk
Website: www.belmontschool.co.uk

Principal: Since 2006, Mr Melvyn D Shanks (early 50s) BSc DipEd MInstP CPhys SQH, who was educated at The High School of Glasgow, read physics and maths at Glasgow University (a 'lapsed physicist', he still teaches maths 'a little bit') followed by Strathclyde – ridiculously overqualified. Spent five years at his alma mater before coming to Belmont as head of physics in 1990, then deputy head in 1997, and says that 'the most difficult thing was to move from being in the common room to becoming deputy head'. 'Really, really excited', though it was slightly daunting 'becoming CEO'. When asked if ever he felt 'it was the time to move on', another opportunity opened at Belmont and 'it was irresistible'. Loves his pupils: each of our questions was answered with a story. Willie this, Ahmed that. Bright, bubbly and bouncy. Always a joy to interview someone so in tune with his life.

Very much on the ball, he has a deprecating sense of humour and showed us round the school with pride (this time pointing out the re-furbed cupula – safety glass now). Married, with one son a qualified teacher and another in the school. Keen on staff development and people management, he runs the school with senior vice principal, head of junior school, vice principal and financial manager. No obvious problems in getting staff.

Academic matters: Extremely coy about exam results with no sign on them on the website.

Max class size 20 with core subjects, English and maths in the mid-teens, and most other subjects only nine or 10 per class. Setted throughout in English and maths, (all compulsory to National 5s) with French (from age 3), Spanish from age 9 and computing. German no longer offered. 'Fluid groups' within each class for literacy, numeracy and spelling. Three sciences, from Transitus (ie 10,11 year olds), history, geography and modern studies as per norm, plus art and PE. No classics. Business and IT throughout school and compulsory at National 5s. Pupils can do admin post National 5s. Eight National 5s overall. Most stay on for Advanced Highers and can add the odd free-standing modules in sixth form. No particular bias – strong on the science front, IT and languages.

Whiteboards, digital, overhead projectors – the lot: 'looking at virtual learning'. Umm. Keyboarding for all in Transitus (should be compulsory in every school). Classroom layout varies according to whim, with juniors either grouped round their teachers or working in standard classrooms. Vast array of cups for academic and personal excellence. Good range of computers throughout school and not just in suites; two trolleys of laptops motor round classes. The introduction of tablets and iPads under discussion. Post-school tutorials in all subjects 'given by all staff, including the principal', from October through May – free (aka drop-in centres for all). Senior pupils help younger ones with reading, IT skills etc. Very much a family school: even if they aint all siblings.

Learning support: all tested on arrival (cognitive ability) – broad intake, and siblings give the school an even broader base. High functioning children with Asperger's, dyslexia, dyspraxia et al are fine, two qualified support for learning staff who follow pupils throughout. Free unless ed psych needed. Pupils withdrawn from class, double taught in class if need be and can use the after-school/lunchtime tutorial system in all subjects if they feel the need. Dyslexics needing serious help currently use lap tops, scribes/readers or – and a welcome innovation this – e-readers – ie earphones, so pupils do not stick out in class. Magic.

Main school (1840 mansion) not that wheelchair friendly (but only six classrooms not accessible, and new build has a lift). Stunning recent inspection – school could have written it themselves.

Mixed age common room – some of the staff looked as though they were on the wrong side of the desk, but all truly dedicated. 'Granny' was coming in to tell a class of 7 year olds what it was like when she was growing up (we met her – well, we didn't meet her this time, but huge parental and grandparental input – veterinarian parents give deeply popular talks. We could have said lectures, but this is not the bias of the school).

Games, options, the arts: For a small school they do 'not too badly' at rugby; footie, three girls' netball teams, all play volleyball and basketball. Playing fields some half a mile away – bussed. Keen on tennis and golf, regulars in the British ski championships. Lots of inter-house athletics. Not really a school that does brilliantly in team games against other schools. Cricket poking its head above the parapet. Mass of individual sports and local club participation.

Jolly art room, variety of different disciplines, fabric strong and fun fashion on display (amazing: superb waistcoats: would have taken one home had it been offered), kiln. CAD part of the syllabus. Music important – all learn glockenspiel, guitar or drums in six week chunks or they sing. Terrific and popular choir (though head admits that music has 'dropped a tad'. Orchestra (and junior orchestra – based on ability not age) – good charity concert output. But nary a pipe band, though individual pipers. Extracurricular drama – and super pics on display. D of E well supported. Strong on public speaking and takes part (a little bit) in local competitions, debating club. Oodles of various clubs, Lego popular; eco-monitors. Eco-school and club both junior and senior. Cycling proficiency tests for juniors.

Trips and tripettes for all both cultural and sporty, school will underwrite where necessary – but not by much.

Background and atmosphere: Originally a trad boys' prep (founded in 1929) moved to handsome white stucco building on the Broom estate in 1930. Decided to go all the way in mid 70s, and co-ed in 2000; and, by a happy co-incidence, at the same time as Laurel Bank and Park School (aka Laurel Park) hit pay dirt. Original thoughts of girls gradually working their way up the school went out of the window.

Magical and somewhat ridiculous plans for relocation nearby (overlooking the M77) turned down on planning. School reinvented itself, and now boasts a raft of classrooms atop a (slightly sunken) games hall – volley ball stuck in the roof (needs a scaffold for rescue operation) – which is adjacent to the kitchen and doubles for dining (two sittings, takes 10 minutes to fold up and stow the tables); junior school pupils pre-order their lunch for the week and pay with cheque on Mondays, seniors pay as they go. (Weekly menu available in advance: looked good, smelt better, picnic lunchers welcome). Windows overlook hall on first floor, along with four science labs, plus two IT rooms and a music suite, as well as drama and general purpose classrooms. Splendidly light and airy. This is now old hat, but still a bit of the old rabbit-warren at the back where juniors are ensconced in highly decorated opening-up classrooms.

Nursery around 24 post-3 year olds 'all hopefully dry' in partnership with East Renfrewshire in large modern building in the centre of the campus. School has undergone a mega revamp, outside painted, inside painted, carpets all over, new electrics; we would have insisted that the conduits be concealed, but approve of conduits in historic buildings (NB conduits are those boring pipes that carry electric cables).

A nice touch: school colour is purple; chairs dotted around the building are upholstered in matching purple, kitchen staff wear purple hats and tabliers. Head sported a purple striped shirt and purple tie, and half the staff seemed to be wearing purple in some form or another.

After-school club for up to Transitus (homework too) 3.20-6pm, £5 per session. Extensive new outdoor learning space.

First-ever female school captain appointed recently. Good supportive governors.

Pastoral care, well-being and discipline: HMI reports, 'The behaviour of children and young people is outstanding.' Not really a naughty school – standard disciplines apply, detentions the favoured punishment. Bullying stamped on, graffiti instantly removed. Buddy system for younger pupils. Pupils have tutors (a promoted position), with each tutor having 20 tutees – possible to change tutors if a personality clash. Staggered breaks by age. Strong 'old-fashioned' discipline with children lining up in the playground in twos at the end of break: charming. Older pupils open doors and stand aside to let us past. Twice weekly ecumenical assemblies: all faiths represented and holy days celebrated.

Pupils and parents: Huge ethnic mix. Good middle-class collection; around 60 per cent first time buyers with 10 per cent from the Glasgow Asian population, most of whom have 'strong traditional family businesses'; some from Indian sub-continent stay with rellies and come daily with their cousins. (This appears to be a growing trend, particularly in Glasgow). Smaller core of Jewish pupils than previously. Smattering of Chinese, broad multi-cultural community. Pupils come from as far afield as Ayr, Kilmarnock, East Kilbride, Paisley, as well as nearby Pollokshields, plus one or two from 'north of the river'. There was 'no call' for hand-me-down uniform shop: first time buyers you see: hence 'discrete' secondhand clothes shop – buy the trusty blazer online.

Currently 60/40 boy girl split, but this is liable to change at the drop of the proverbial.

Entrance: 'Low-key informal assessment' for nursery, automatic transfer to junior and senior schools, separate test for children from age 7 upwards based on CAT school reports and interview if necessary. Can join mid-term if space available ('We accelerate the entrance process').

Exit: Almost all stay on, either for Highers or Advanced Highers. Some (around 10 per cent) may leave earlier to follow vocational training, and head is eager to advise – another story here – others to join the family business. Mostly to Scottish universities – Glasgow popular, Aberdeen, Dundee, Strathclyde, Edinburgh, St Andrews; occasional one or two to Oxbridge but none recently. Tranches of medics, lawyers, vets, accountants, engineers and architects. The odd gap year. Very occasionally parents use Belmont as trad prep school, moving to posh elsewhere, but most leavers logistical.

Money matters: Not a rich school, but will do their darndest to hang onto pupils to next public exam if parents who fall on hard times are upfront about it.

Remarks: Super – the perfect local school, works well, not scary, but nurturing and trad enough to tick all the boxes. Can't fault it. Tiny classes, over a third girls. Dedicated staff. Definitely worth considering.

Cargilfield School

45 Gamekeeper's Road, Edinburgh EH4 6HU

Pupils: 305; 24 weekly, 34 flexi boarders • Ages: 3-13; (boarding from 8)

Fees: Day £9,810 – £15,120; Boarding £18,555 pa

Tel: 0131 3362207
Email: registrar@cargilfield.com
Website: www.cargilfield.com

Headmaster: Since 2014, Rob Taylor, previously registrar at Harrow School. He has also been head of Ashdown Prep School

C

in Sussex. He is married to Sarah, and they have three children. Took over from acting head following the abrupt departure in October 2013 of previous head and his wife.

Entrance: Nursery and pre-prep popular; upper school numbers have grown enormously; places pretty well guaranteed through pre-prep but tests if learning difficulties suspected. Wannabes assessed: occasional places may occur throughout the school – logistics.

Exit: Fettes, Oundle, Eton, Uppingham, Rugby and St Margaret's York most popular recently. A few to Loretto, Gordonstoun, Merchiston and Kilgraston

Remarks: Cargilfield had a bad case of wobbles with rapid head turn-over. We arrived to find the school covered in scaffolding and wondered about a new, new-build, but no, just roof repairs. (The £1.2 million games changing rooms are up and running.) This former parent of the pre-prep (still brill) regrets the reduction of play area (previously 23 acres now 15: posho pads equal new builds); the sports hall (a 21st century prerequisite) impinges on the games pitch, alongside a couple of cedar-clad (rather grand inside) huts, which blend well, but look like early huts for battery hens (or photographs of Bletchley Park), and provide a new teaching centre plus a 10-room (soundproof) music school with a mini-concert rehearsal room, used for drama too. A stonking 80 per cent take extra music. Strong choir, which tours 'down south', and terrific strings ensemble: 'our top area and they have won major awards at the Edinburgh Music Festival'; pop group. Pipe band is second to none, taster sessions for all in pre-prep, they were practising on the games pitch as we left, certain amount of interesting baton chucking.

Impressive two-storey classroom block for English, ICT and history, with colonnades, cloisters and walkways. Certain amount of internal restructuring, with dorms becoming classrooms (and vice versa).

Pupils setted and streamed, maths from age 8. Most year groups divided into three: scholarship stream (currently boasting some 14 pupils) for the last three or four years plus two mixed-ability classes. French from nursery, Latin from 9 or 10; ancient Greek at 11, classical civilisation, Spanish for the last two years. (German and Mandarin clubs). Fantastic learning support (known as learning development) all assessed on entry; head of learning support plus two and a half staff. One of the best departments in Scotland, combining individual and co-teaching: max 5.5 hours per week. Currently has a parent-underwritten (ie they pay school fees and for a dedicated teacher) unit for two pupils who have very special needs, (previous) head hesitated for a moment, but agreed this was still in place, 'an unusual arrangement'. But isn't this what the independent sector is about? School can no longer accommodate many of the weaker brethren, unless they are, in fact, brethren. Jolly Phonics and any 'other combination that works' on the reading front.

Founded in 1873, the school moved to its purpose-built site in 1890. Girls' boarding house is full, difficult to find space for flexis. Jolly sitting-rooms on ground floor (along with showers etc) and some of the prettiest dorms we have seen in a long time. Odd space in boys' dorms: trad old school dorms, huge, with sofas and games tucked into corners – given the choice, chaps preferred more mates to smaller bedrooms. Chaps in bunks, girls have drawers below beds, total replacement of furniture and fittings factored in every three years. Two-weekly boarding for all (max 74 boarders at any one time, 35 weekly, 15 full time). Day pupils regularly join boarders for a huge variety of weekend activities (though all must stay for three nights and can't just pick and choose). Mega weekend activities, no Saturday school ('children more relaxed and less tired on Mondays'). Nine year olds camping in the Highlands, 12/13 year olds at Hadrian's Wall.

Deep complaints from parents whose young played Cargilfield girls' netball squad at the recent Belhaven tournament. Cargilfield wore sponsored hoodies, with Cargilfield First Netball Team on the back, and 'Imagine having Strutt & Parker on your bosom,' said one irate papa.

Kayaking, shooting, international coaching in fishing, fencing, judo, hockey, skiing both at Hillend and the real thing. Two small Astroturfs. Eighty clubs on offer – chess champions with boards set up all over the place (and visiting chess master). Trips all over, both at weekends and longer ones abroad to Rome and France. Much use made of resources in grand Scots cities. New website.

Discounts for MoD children (handy for Scottish Command). Hundred per cent bursaries on offer: means-tested – five or six pupils on this kind of bursary (but not necessarily every year), graduated sibling discount. Mixed bunch of parents, grander than previously, FWAGS now thinner on the ground, one or two proper foreigners, tiny ethnic mix. Boarders from Yorkshire, the Borders, West Coast, Aberdeenshire, Angus and Perthshire. Bus on Sundays from Angus, and daily from Saxe Coburg Place in Edinburgh and Fife but, as children often stay until after 8pm, parents must collect them themselves.

Pre-prep and nursery based in stunning £3.5m building with cherished (quite small) Astroturf and enclosed play area, share big school facilities. School not keen on folk using the nursery as a spring-board for a couple of years and then heading off elsewhere (like this editor!).

Clifton Hall School

Clifton Road, Newbridge, Edinburgh EH28 8LQ

Pupils: 355 • Ages: 3–18 • Sixth form: 20

Fees: £8,970 – £11,280 pa

Tel: 01313 331359
Email: headmaster@cliftonhall.org.uk
Website: www.cliftonhall.org.uk

Headmaster: Since 2005 Mr Rod Grant BA PGDPSE (new qualification last year) (early 40s). Came from Hutcheson's where he was principal teacher of English, responsible for literacy. His original brief at Clifton Hall stretched through primary to S1. School had already started an all through policy, but had anticipated adding pupils year on year. Grant admitted to being a tad 'unsettled' but has no thoughts of leaving, nor of expanding beyond 400. During our discussion it was difficult to keep his eyes straying from assorted young playing random hockey in the walled garden outside his office window.

From Prestwick in Ayrshire (where he has a second career as a 'property developer' – he lets out his flats there), educated at Merchiston, read English at Edinburgh, but abandoned this to join his brother in a wine bar venture. Returning to academia, he completed his degree at the Open University (having, in the interim, been housemaster at Drumley House School – deceased – in Ayrshire; his blog is highly entertaining), doing his PGCE at Paisley and cutting his teeth at a state primary in nearby Broxburn.

Less than three months into his headship, Grant was faced with a fire sale when approached by the governors of the tiny failing St Serf's school (94 pupils aged 5-18, lousy prep inspectors' report, mediocre senior report) suggesting a merger – and, after much gubernatorial activity, the schools amalgamated in September 2008. Huge amounts of dosh were spent converting previous dorms into classrooms – for 20 – but they look a bit squashed with 16 or 17, installing fire doors and the like, and awaiting an invasion. Which hasn't stopped. The school roll has increased by 184 per cent, 'the highest', Grant said proudly, 'in Scotland'. Double wowser. Pupil pin map shows a huge spread, from Galashiels in the borders to Falkirk, East Lothian and north of the Forth, numbers from Edinburgh. School picked up 19 from the demise of St Margaret's; buses from there, buses all over.

Certain amount of new build, some good, some bad, and some just plain ugly. Most resemble farm buildings, but then we are in (very basic) farming country. Mega £4m+ scheme in pipeline to cover the games pitches to the right of the drive with a combo 400 seater theatre, full basketball pitch and collection of classrooms. This editor suggested sinking the basketball pitch and the theatre (neither need daylight) and revamping the workshop and classrooms. The games pitch, charming club house and happy young playing hockey enhance the drive to the castle; though the less said about the monstrous carbuncle of a theatre workshop in the north west corner the better. Does what it says on the tin – but more suited to a building site than in plain view of the [Grimms] fairy tale 1857 Bryce Castle. Cladding is easy on the eye.

Rumours rife about the £1.7 million the merger realised – Grant is not so upfront, 'We spent what we got'. New kitchen adjacent to games hall, which doubles as dining room. Very fancy pants sports pavilion, all singing and dancing – the games facilities are let occasionally.

Popular weekly coffee mornings for parents, good catch up time, and a boon for the lonely or just plain concerned. Grant's common sense view on bullying – and now cyber bullying since our last visit – and some of the wilder health and safety regulations ought to be circulated round the head's grapevine. His wife, Helen, teaches in the junior school; they live on site.

Academic matters: Grant doesn't publish results so you will have to take a view on the reason for this. Nor does he do bells. Same form taker throughout for all in senior school. Set for maths from S2 (stops the boredom factor), otherwise parallel classes, no streaming. We found a brace of S4 classes studying John Steinbeck's Of Mice and Men. Simultaneously. Good pupil interaction, inspired relaxed teachers. French from 3, Spanish and German from 8, keyboarding skills in primary for all. Non-selective, good basic grounding, building blocks, combo of Jolly Phonics/blends/word recognition and synthetics on the reading front. Serious experiments with liquids – will a penny float? Graduating to humanities, via computers, art and PE, dedicated staff. Very hands on, the early years seem like learning through play, though we came across a fearsomely proactive class of 9/10 year olds in the computer room – touch-typing.

All the usual suspects in senior school plus admin, geology, philosophy and media studies in S5 and S6. Free choice for Highers et al, Eng and maths essential, otherwise list preferred subjects in choice order. Grant promises to run a course if only one taker. Two computer suites (one Apple, one PC) used by all for timetabled lessons as well as IT – networked, intranetted, wireless. Labs designed by science staff, complete with prep room and adjacent scientific classroom. School follows Scottish system. No problem with absorbing the new National qualifications.

Nursery recently expanded, bung full of all the things you would love to have but don't feel you can afford, sandpits, water-play. Technically open till 3.00pm (from 8am) but after-school club (£6 per session) picks up the slack. Stories (floor covering looked rather hard but we were assured the young didn't mind; we were pleased to see a random collection of cushions). Imaginative play area outside: looked slightly cramped for 40,

Two dedicated SENCos:one in junior and t'other in senior school, plus an assistant. Pupils either withdrawn from class individually, in groups or offered dual teaching. Can cope with minor physical handicap – senior classrooms are upstairs – and Asperger's (mild).

Games, options, the arts: Team games on every available speck of green greeted our arrival. Cunning junior rugby/football goal makes Heath Robinson look like Einstein. But what fun.

Enthusiastic music; two were studying Advanced Higher music in the former chapel during our visit, whilst a hotch-potch of students were writing, directing, producing a piece on Marilyn Monroe. We suggested blow heaters. Peripatetic staff. Exciting art – intricate dress design. Strong focus on preparing the young for the real world; and pushing creativity, practical nuts and bolts as well as the academic. Eco committee – school recently gained Green Flag status. Charity involvement via houses – children choose their own projects. Pupil council, with reps from every class and Eco council, with reps who suss out what the school can do to improve the environment. At our last visit we were sceptical about proposed outdoor classroom under pupil construction (in Scotland?). But they did it, with a combo of straw bales on larch and lime rendered (pupils wore rubber gloves). Wow.

Gym (with bars and benches) doubles as dining room, three sittings, takes two and a half hours (external caterer). Charming swimming pool, timetabled lessons for all (local primaries use it, scuba club one night a week and disabled group at weekends). Parents were watching a group of 5/6 year olds' swimming lesson during our visit. Senior school a bit dodgy on team games, though lots of clubs (judo, ballet, fencing, swimming) – no tennis courts seen. Sports facilities can be hired out by locals. Nine hole par three golf course on horizon but no all-weather pitch as yet.

Background and atmosphere: Clifton Hall is a magical Bryce house, complete with impressive oil paintings and the odd bit of antique furniture, in 54 acres of child-inspiring grounds off the Newbridge roundabout – the junction of A8, M8 and M9. A boon for parents to the west of Edinburgh, who can either take advantage of the school buses, which leave Bathgate, Livingstone, Newington and the West End of Edinburgh daily at 8am (departs at 5pm each evening) or drop off their poppets on the way to work, school open 8am to 6pm. The lodge at the entrance, previously let for not much more than a peppercorn, is now a humming café (post Nat 5s only) generating £1000 plus a week.

Happy young sunning themselves outside when we visited, unaware that Euphame Macalzean, heiress of Clifton Hall, burnt alive in 1691 for witchcraft, has regularly been seen visiting her old nurse near the lodge.

Founded as a boarding boys' (only) prep school in 1930, school became a limited company in 1964, thence weekly boarding, thence day, followed by girls, pre-prep and nursery. Clifton Hall had already started taking senior pupils before the amalgamation with St Serfs; ideally placed, it has all the vibes of a grand public/prep schools, games pitches, busy swimming pool on site, surrounded by (climbable) trees, contained, secure and with none of the health and safety issue of boarders.

First thing you see, even before you enter the school proper, is a showcase of last year's trophies: an Olympic torch, carried by one of their youngsters and nestling cosily beside a Scotland under 16s rugby cap, and a fiddle score. The hall (good Victorian panelling) is decorated in French; and while the somewhat hotch-potch configuration of class rooms is in good heart, we noticed the parquet flooring in the music room, labelled Library, former chapel (and quite obviously originally a billiard room) was ready for a spot of TLC.

Senior, junior and nursery all have their own dedicated play space, the head can watch from his study – has been known to invite concerned parents to watch their darlings at play. Weekly menus handed out to all, so parents don't cook the 'same for their tea'. Lots of parent participation.

Previously painted in rather jolly primary colours, particularly in the basement, school has opted for uniform blue, and, despite our previous comments, the whole place looks bandbox fresh. The gorgeous doo'cot was about to have serious input from Historic Scotland. It didn't.

C

Pastoral care, well-being and discipline: Head has common sense attitude. Small enough school to care – tinies walk down school paths hand in hand. Matron sign still visible on first floor door. Children devised own set of Golden Rules (representatives from each class on pupil council) – each pupil must have both a request and a thank you.

Pupils and parents: Huge catchment area. Eighty-five per cent plus first-time buyers, ditto two working parents. A complete mix. The occasional parent follows the trad route, prep at 8 and senior school at 13, but most stay the course. FPs (aka CHOPS) include Rory Bremner, Jim Clark and Jamie Bruce Jones of Caledonia play, designer of the splendid wooden castle in the nursery garden.

Entrance: Mainly through the (non-selective entry) nursery – a proper nursery school (member of the Edinburgh City Partnership Scheme) with many of the children wearing uniform, and junior school. Otherwise first come, first served, assessment to pick up glitches. Overbooked for nursery and first few years of primary. Space sometimes available in the senior school. Will accept pupils at any time; gentle school, a number from maintained sector who have been bullied (cyber bullying the new head on the block: trolling). Grant reckons to have a good 'conversion' rate of potential parents, emailing them within three days of interest being shown, and keen on first names. Regular parents' evenings. Two or three per cent ethnic mix.

Exit: Most to some form of further education; most stay in Scotland. Aberdeen, Heriot Watt, St Andrews, Edinburgh, Glasgow, Robert Gordons, Oxford. The odd gapper.

Money matters: Fees include almost all extras; trust fund on hand to pick up financial hiccups 'for a year or two' – 'safety net' rather than 'safety blanket'.

Remarks: Wowser. 'School is going places and it is growing,' was what we said last time. Governors very bullish, and so they should be. Head has maintained and increased momentum.

The Compass School

West Road, Haddington, East Lothian EH41 3RD

Pupils: 121 • Ages: 4–12

Fees: £8,235 – £9,540 pa

Tel: 01620 822642
Email: office@thecompassschool.co.uk
Website: www.thecompassschool.co.uk

Headmaster: Since 1997, Mr Mark Becher (pronounced Becker) MA PGCE (40s), educated Queen Margaret's Academy Ayr, Dundee University, (modern history) and PGCE at Craigie College of Education in Ayr (aka the University of the West of Scotland). Previously head of sport and primary teacher at The Mary Erskine and Stewart's Melville Junior School, and primary teacher at Edinburgh Academy. A 'keen distance runner', he teaches sport, Latin and history and runs school with a deputy (associate assessor of HMI, whom we did not meet; she was out on assignment) management team and part-time bursar.

Entrance: Children can (and do) join at any time – after an informal assessment – and begin at any stage of the school year. Not selective.

Can apply for 'financially assisted places' at any entry stage; specific bursaries for forms 6, 7 and 8 plus sibling discounts (third off for the youngest of three siblings in school at the same time) and parents can ask for help if struck by financial meltdown. Bursarial help for trips too, so that no child feels disadvantaged.

Vouchers (as for qualifying pupils in nursery) can either be used to offset nursery fees: go towards early bird or Compass Care, or towards clubs based on site (ie not skiing or golf). Two per cent off if pay early and four per cent above base if pay late. Extra costs for milk, lunch and recorder lessons.

Exit: Most leave at 12 for Edinburgh independents, usually day (but those heading for Merchiston usually board age 13 when they hit senior school) or local state school. Destinations vary year by year but include George Heriots School, The Edinburgh Academy, Fettes, Loretto, George Heriots, George Watsons College, Stewarts Melville, Mary Erskine, North Berwick High School and Knox Academy. 'Everyone gets where they want.' Loretto featured highly in wish list (it is, after all the closest) but pupils and parents are spoilt for choice in the Edinburgh independent sector. Few now leave at 8 for trad prep schools, but a steady trickle nonetheless.

Remarks: Founded in 1963 by Mrs Alny Younger, to cater for local children between ages 4 and 8 (before the little darlings went off to 'proper' prep schools), The Compass has expanded beyond recognition, and is now a beacon independent primary and junior school (actually we can't think of any other independent in this particular category) with sparkling million quid new build and regular stream of both national and international visitors.

West Road, Haddington's poshest street, boasts elegant Edwardian villas, many of which have an inalienable planning veto over the field in front of The Compass, which has fab views to the south (geography and botany on the hoof, so to speak). Planning for the new extension must have been nightmare, so it is not surprising that the natty hall (too small even for short tennis, but brill for cricket and judo) is much used by locals outwith school hours. New classrooms for senior pupils have been shoehorned into an expanded attic with books, DVDs and tablets crammed into every available corner. Actually, books, DVDs and tablets crammed into almost any corner.

Grand galleried staircase leads from trad hall up to original classrooms (and head's office), gas-fired guarded coal-look-alike stove in the corner in strong contrast to the new build. Family is important here: houses are known as families, with houseparents rather than captains; but, just to complicate matters, there are captains and vice captains too. School council with representatives from each class.

New kitchen adjacent to dining room (formerly the billiard room with magnificent cupula and original panelling) and well placed to cater for functions in the hall. Slight whiff of to-day's broccoli (before 10am?) – though fresh fruit and raw veggies aplenty at meal times. Pre-school and after-school care based in dining room and linked classroom. Bit complicated, but see below.

Every vertical surface is covered either in children's artwork (framed under direction of Ricky de Marco, Lothian's secret art treasure) or team photographs/composite snapshots of trips (Paris/London) and tripettes (Netherurd, the Cairngorms: climb first Munro) – all dependent on age with overnight stays for some of the quite young.

The dedicated nursery runs in partnership with East Lothian Council: max pupils 20 (discount if pupils live in East Lothian). Previously, The Compass offered a composite class for 8-12 year olds, but now school leads seamlessly through eight year groups up to age 11/12. School roll more or less static around 130 boys and girls. Head takes pride in running a successful Scottish primary – based on the philosophy of the Scottish Curriculum for Excellence but with specialist teaching – 'ideal preparation' – allowing pupils to feed the Edinburgh private sector well ahead of the field. 'Four years ahead in French,' one school complained; 'No apologies for letting children work to their capabilities,' says Becher.

Reading by way of Jolly Phonics; school adds: 'with a strong emphasis on developing early literacy' (which we presume means reading books). French from nursery; Spanish from ages 9-12 with Latin and a nod to classics age 10. School small enough to pick up problems before they overwhelm. Impressive support for learning, full time teacher – who was handling a mixed class of perhaps 5 or 6 year olds with gentleness and humour. Small groups plus one-to-one (no extra cost). Help for those on whatever spectrum never far away; though perhaps some may need more specialist support. Assessments whenever. School-provided iPads being rolled out – from age 8, which pupils handled with skill. Interactive whiteboards (so last year now) being replaced by interactive tellies: 65 grand's worth last year alone.

Pupils compete in a variety pack of sports from age 9 – rugby, cricket and hockey matches and swimming galas, all with impressive wins 'against bigger schools'. Same goes for music – a huge range of activities packed into a 9am to 3.30pm day with after-school supervision (paid for) and activities (nominal cost only). All sing in the choir (won The Edinburgh Festival Primary Schools' Choir trophy twice) and sing at Murrayfield, The Queen's Hall, wherever. New build has allowed for dedicated art/science rooms (views to the south) and dedicated music room: clarsach, flute, recorder, singing. School big on drama: pupils star in school plays, made to feel important and have a certain amount of responsibility, which gives each the confidence to move happily into larger schools at secondary level.

No dedicated games field as such; school uses Haddington Astroturf (they share it with Knox academy,) Haddington rugby club grass pitches, Haddington golf club, swims in the local Aubigny sports centre, performs in Loretto theatre, and borrows local churches. The atmosphere has a 'good prep school buzz' but feels more fun than frenetic.

Daily assembly, broadly Christian, but other religions appreciated. Hymn practice, outside speakers – often obliquely giving career advice, but that too. Emphasis on encouraging expectations and instilling a sense of right and wrong.

When we last visited The Compass an enthusiastic band of parents (ill-advised parents at that) had converted the splendid, not very big child-friendly garden – Astro/hopscotch/climbing frames – into a 'global experience' with ducky little paths and 'regional' flowerbeds. We were thrilled to see that the garden is back to being Chase me Charlie country, complete with outdoor classroom and one of the most exciting climbing frame/walls ever designed.

School uniform is sold in house (superior secondhand shop too) and in Edinburgh.

Early bird from 7.45am (after breakfast) and Compass Care up to 6pm. Extra cost. Extra cost too for pupils wanting a 'light tea'. Opportunity for older pupils to do homework, though without supervision. 'Compass Care will not be responsible for the completion or standard of the homework'.

Good proportion of first time independent buyers with catchment from east Edinburgh along the coast to Berwick on Tweed and south to the Lammermuirs. No buses as yet, but lots of shared school runs. Fairly narrow ethnic mix, but that's East Lothian for you. School would be pleased to field a broader diaspora. First-rate, and friendly. Local parents raised £250,000 in last few years and treat school as a social hub, but recent incomers from the South have been heard to mutter about 'academic standards'. Still worth moving to Haddington for.

Craigclowan School

Edinburgh Road, Perth PH2 8PS

Pupils: 243 • Ages: 3–13

Fees: £11,820 pa

Tel: 01738 626310
Email: head@craigclowan-school.co.uk
Website: www.craigclowan-school.co.uk

Head: Since January 2016, John Gilmour, previously deputy head and head of RE at Castle Court School in Dorset.

He joined the Royal Navy after leaving school, trained as an officer at Britannia Royal Naval College in Dartmouth and then studied geography at Liverpool. Having spent time on nuclear submarines, he moved into education and taught geography and RE at several prep schools, becoming head of geography and of pastoral care at Dumpton Prep before joining Castle Court.

He moved to Craigclowan along with his wife Liz, who has returned to her Scottish roots, and their two daughters, Eve and Charlotte.

Entrance: Children from all over the northern central belt, usually within 40 minutes' travel/30 mile radius; aspirational, numbers of first time buyers, middle-class professionals, the occasional toff, some of whom have been known to use the pre-prep before hitting trad preps elsewhere.

Exit: To Strathallan, Glenalmond, Dollar Academy, Fettes College, Merchiston Castle School, Morrison's Academy, Kilgraston School, Ampleforth College and a number of other independent senior schools in England each year. 'Orses for courses.

Remarks: Craigclowan, the only day prep in Perthshire, is perched on 13 undulating acres above the M90 on the southern fringe of Perth; pedestrian classroom blocks now surround this poor man's Greek Thompson Victorian villa, and the child-inspired brightly coloured class superseded by light airy modern boxes with purposeful young efficiently going about their business. Pupil art all over. Tarmac, still covered in crazy games – snakes and ladders, floral trails, chess – has recently been joined by cow of many colours. The eight foot tall Menhir was moved here some 100 odd years before.

Certain amount of tarting up recently; senior classrooms revamped (smelt strongly of paint). Pictures of whole class on every door; books everywhere. Proper lab with ancillary prep room; now totally Wifi with white boards all over; banks of laptops promised for the future. Art room: early in the term, but buzzing, good ceramics and fabric. Plans afoot to enlarge the basement library (currently in one of the old brightly coloured classrooms) with a 'dedicated learning resource centre' and knock a door out into the quad. We always approve of easier access to books and the house ain't listed.

Astroturf for tennis and hockey. Tiny artificial ski slope: some time ago it was rumoured to have been 'ealth and safety-ed but now almost suffering from overuse; fathers run lessons Saturday mornings and much of the school decamps to Glen Shee on spring term Saturdays. The downstairs passage was chocker with skis of the smallest sizes, ditto helmets (think nursery slopes on Meribel); 'that's what we are about.'

Wish list includes levelling the front games field to make two rugby pitches, re-laying the cricket square and building a new sports pavilion (referred to as a cricket pavilion in handout; is there a difference?). Not that easy to find prep school teachers with the right amount of energy and enthusiasm who can not only teach but also 'do the extra bit' – like running weekend courses; hockey, cricket, camping.

Popular walled garden, developed in conjunction with 'a school-established local gardening club': pupils grow own grub, (lettuces popular) and starred in Beechgrove Garden.

Nursery a joy, tinies work in cheerful subdivided classrooms not quite attached to the well-used, multi-purpose sports hall (particularly popular during wet breaks), and adjacent to dining room: staff and pupils eat together, hot, cold and veggie option.

Spare waterproof ponchos and a welly cupboard for forest school: essential these days for the (sub)urban child. Paddling pool, outdoor classroom. Masses of mite-sized equipment, including real carpentry tools and wood to use them on (the Care Commission saw and approved). Partnership with Perth, vouchers, website shows actual reductions (a first). Plans ahead for revamping a couple of nursery class rooms and for a new 'light and bright foyer area' for the pre-school – sounds like a cinema!

Virtually all stick with school from nursery. Reading via Jolly Phonics, or jolly anything come to that, 'anything that works': all children to age 10 are heard reading every day: form takers, assistants, gappers. SENCo on hand, glitches spotted early, problem discussed with parents, ed psychs if need be, ditto IEPs. Assistance too with maths. Learning support for 'any child who needs help for any reason, either for a long or a short term, and for the very able'. Two teachers for every year, plus trained support staff – with many getting one-to-one attention in little work stations all over.

Rewards equals house points for juniors (houses important here and sibling led), smiley stickers (because they like them best) and 'golden time' (activities of their choice). Plaudits for stuff both in and out of school. Sanctions: detention.

Four and 5 year olds divided alphabetically, with those whose birthdays fall in the spring or summer joining proper school the summer term before their 5th birthdays. Two classes throughout, roughly 13 in each, some streaming further up; scholarship class at top – usually eight – impressive selection of scholarships to all over.

Aged 8, young are set for maths and English, they also start French; this is late, we usually find French exposure in nursery. Latin introduced age 10/11, but Latin club from 8 and 'zinging' Latin teacher. Bullying dealt with quickly and firmly, with parents involved if need be. The young whom we met/know are bubbly and fun: and staff fell over themselves to be helpful during our visit.

Small pipe band, chanter for all, 60/70 per cent learn some sort of instrument, odd ensembles, orchestras. Music room in main house surrounded by soundproof practice rooms, and staff practising for a 'Craigclowan's got talent' evening. Well furnished with instruments, snazzy keyboards and mirrors galore. Much involvement with the Perth Festival. Carol service at St Ninians; school supplies choristers throughout the year.

Lots of foreign contact as well as regular tours abroad – part of the Comenius project. Eco school with a couple of green flags. 'This is a vibrant, seven-day-a-week, co-ed day school, with classes on five days and a mass of extracurricular activity'. Recent rearrangement of the day means a less rushed lunch, and slightly longer day. Parents can (and do) leave their young at 8am and collect them again at 6pm. Late stayers, unless otherwise occupied with after skool activities often finish prep before home time. After-school 'prep supervision' costs £4.50 per hour (nice little earner). Pre-prep all get a homework book for parents to admire.

Huge range of clubs/activities, 60+, including archery, street dance, judo, sailing, fly-fishing and golf plus additional junior school stuff. Craigclowan hosted senior schools fair last year; 16 assorted schools touted their wares. A success to be repeated.

PTA, 'a good bunch, supportive, like the ethos of the place', run a lift-share, and a monthly second-hand uniform and sports equipment shop. All singing and dancing; 'weekly Scottish dancing for juniors and Ceilidhs for all pupils'. School seemed to think parents welcomed the new sports kit (twice in five years), pinafore dresses and summer dresses: 'I had to find an extra 200 quid and that was just for the sports kit,' was one disgruntled reaction.

Craigholme School for Girls

72 St Andrews Drive, Pollokshields, Glasgow G41 4HS

Pupils: 277 • Ages: 3–18 • Sixth form: 25

Fees: £8,550 – £11,320 pa

Tel: 01414 270375
Email: admissions@craigholme.co.uk
Website: www.craigholme.co.uk

Principal: Since August 2016, June Gilliland, formerly deputy principal for nine years. Has also been head of business studies at the High School of Glasgow and deputy principal at Ayr Academy.

Head of junior school: Since Sept 2016 is Pamela Mitchell.

Academic matters: Small classes in junior school; specialist French from age 4, IT, music and PE from nursery on. Top year takes selected subjects – science, music, art, home economics – in senior school. 'Determinedly academic'. Books and novels feature strongly in learning as 'preferable to the sort of snippets you get in reading books': children start off with (Jolly) Phonics, leavened with other methods as appropriate. French now from nursery and German in J6. J7s get specialist teaching in both sciences and art in preparation for their move to 'big school'. Not that there is much of a physical move: the three Victorian villas are cunningly linked (though a map for a visiting ed could be useful).

National 5s 'not a problem', with some thunderingly good results: English and maths, as you might expect; fair returns in French and German (still the least popular lang), good nod at Spanish – though no recent presentation of langs at Advanced Highers. Italian ab initio in sixth form. Less than magical results in the sciences: human biology the most impressive ('particularly well suited to pupils interested in the biomedical sciences and professions allied to medicine'). Chemistry includes forensic chemistry module in S6. Mass of examinees in all three disciplines: surprisingly few doing physics at advanced level – this currently seems to be the subject of choice with girls (but not here) though department runs a supporting engineering club. New teacher may well change this. Nary a classic. Two parallel-ish classes throughout. 'Easy selection', streamed for maths and English. Drop in centres/clinics in all subjects, both at lunch time and after school.

Drama and art and design returns pleasing, and stunning results in cake craft (cake craft??) – home ec has smashing new facilities which have tempted year 6 back to do a cake-icing module – supposedly great training in manual dexterity: for dentists – with hospitality much to the fore.

Mixed bunch of results at both Higher and Advanced Higher level: business management strong at Higher level, and new geography teacher will probably up the number of candidates: but with such recent departmental shake ups, we are not surprised by the less than stunning results in either humanities or the sciences. And will watch the next few years' results with interest. We are never really happy to discover that history is taught 'by rotation' with modern studies in S1 and 2. In 2016, 84 per cent of Highers A/B.

Drama, art and design and fashion and textile technology put forward in penny numbers with success. Seventeen subjects offered at Advanced level. Small classes (12-16). French from aged 4 for all, with German from S2 and Spanish from S1. Specialist science and art use senior facilities from J7.

Smashing light-filled study library tucked under the eaves manned and open until 5pm. New ICT kit in pipeline and fundraising on-going, though neither ICT nor computer studies feature at any level in public exams. Key boarding for all. Classrooms more or less zoned by subject, crass lighting spoils otherwise elegant ceilings.

Screening for 'identified pupils' dyslexia et al, with trained help and support, both help in class and/or withdrawn for extra tuition; independent word talk much appreciated. One-to-one devices available. ESOL on the cards, but hardly needed. iPads for all under discussion.

Games, options, the arts: Impressive state of the art sports centre, with timetabled local use ('you just missed': think it was Paralympic wheelchair footie). Much used in Commonwealth Games for netball: sprung floored, seven badminton court size, indoor tennis, hockey, volleyball and archery – double curtains to deflect arrows. Climbing wall, dance studio, fitness suite, Astro pitch, blaize, plus grass track. Two dedicated teachers. Athletics high on the agenda, ditto canoeing. Rowing new kid on the block, both on the Clyde and at Strathclyde Country Park. School talks of 'spear-heading holiday sport camps, sport for Asian women'.

'Riding the crest of a wave', the junior choir and the training choir had just won their respective Glasgow music festival prizes, and the cross-country teams came first among the Glasgow schools just before our previous visit. Oodles of choirs, orchestras off to Salzburg in May, New York and Great Wall of China recently. Pupils can 'have a go' at any instrument: penny whistles, ukuleles and bongo drums featured in the music room – peris pulled in if necessary. Seventeen electronic pianos: clubs in all disciplines travel to every corner of the globe. Ambitious stuff for what was once a Glasgow barely grown up dame school. Drama, musicals, high achievers' concert: Eastwood theatre is venue of choice. Emphasis on debating and public speaking.

Exciting art: felt-making (seems to be the new fad) plus all the usual suspects, jewellery, silk painting, screening. Stunning home economics – aka hospitality suite (on former stage) with state of the art cooking facilities, sewing machines and natch cooking lessons – though we weren't quite sure they cut tomatoes correctly. Health and food technology, fashion and textiles, place was buzzing. Girls make own ball gowns.

Strong charity input: cupcakes – looked amazing – for McMillan coffee morning. D of E, YE and event management: no stone left unturned.

Background and atmosphere: Three Victorian merchant's houses cunningly joined by purpose-built stone and glass halls to form a nearly harmonious whole. Large reception rooms and linking social spaces, including a multipurpose assembly hall, much used, assemblies on three days a week: sixth form girls – by request – sit on raised dais behind head who 'isn't sure he likes talking to people behind his back' (Farrelly adds: 'Throwaway comment; I am very comfortable with the girls there'). The three houses are linked by the Dungeon, a rightly named basement passage, despite cream paint and gaudy lockers, boasts common room and acres of cloakrooms, cheerfully crowded with girls in unusually tidy scarlet blazers and Craigholme tartan kilts.

Senior and junior school exist hugga mugga, with, to this eye, no discernible geographic zone, with principal in overall charge. The nursery, which takes boys, has a separate site on St Andrews Drive.

Former gym hall now a self-service canteen, and accessible from both inside and out. Salad and fruit in abundance, not so sure about the pizza. Food all 'cooked on site'. Up to S4 café attendance is compulsory, packed lunches okay. It was gloriously sunny during our visit and we found groups happily lunching outside – the early birds got the sun.

Jolly attic conversion for sixth form common room. When asked what they wanted to do next, one young lady said she thought she might become an accountant. 'Thought you were going to become a lawyer,' said her peers. To which she replied, 'but that was last week'.

None could see any disadvantage at being all-girls school: 'no curtailment to social life in a city environment'. Seeming very much at home, they take responsibility for granted – not really surprising since some had been at Craigholme for 14/15 years. Almost every inch of wall space crammed with evidence of activity.

Building freshly painted over all, one or two window sills outside need some TLC and we found a ropy roof where the slates resembled a mouth of 60s teeth. Needs a person on a ladder.

Pastoral care, well-being and discipline: Houses – Scottish islands – run vertically from start of junior school. Form teachers are first point of contact for parents. 'Bullying prevented by careful placing and management of vulnerable pupils rather than by sanction. A minimum of major problems thanks to monitoring, small tutorials and good PSE.' Talk to parents if problems persist.

Successes, even small ones, build confidence, so all junior children have a personal 'magic moment file' recording their achievements. This may include the experience of risk-taking and not always being equal to challenges – 'They have to explore their strengths and weaknesses in order to make informed decisions'.

'Few sinful girls, wee chat with me usually sorts it out'; detention a deterrent. School believes pupil voice important, currently two elected from every year, junior school represented too. Leadership weekends for sixth formers. School council being revamped.

Variety pack of assemblies, 'celebrate all religions' with priests, rabbis, chaplains, imams all getting their shout. Parents pulled on too: usually for question and answer sessions plus local MSP.

Pupils and parents: Largely affluent middle-class catchment spread over south side of Glasgow, with three school buses and a good train service bringing girls from as far as Cumbernauld to Ayrshire, including some areas north of the Clyde. Number of first-time buyers and ethnic minorities (around 20 per cent of the latter: head scarves ok). School open from 7am – 7 pm. Supportive parents raise funds for the foundation (to raise the

ICT bar) giving 'their time and expertise to extend the pupils' life skills': big ball, fun run.

FPs include scientist Rosalynne Watt (won the Siemens prize at Cambridge while doing PhD and the Institute of Physics Young Researcher in Combustion runner-up), paediatric emergency physician Joanne Stirling, artist Sally Carlaw, crime novelist Louise Hughes, ex-editor Scottish Field, Claire Grant and TV journalists, Victoria Lee and Carla Romana and British skiing champ Nicole Ritchie (most recently on artificial snow).

D

Entrance: Assessment for all, even the nursery. Main entry points J1, J7/6 and S1, though a few join S5/6. Despite the exam, will take girls 'who have abilities in other areas'. Sample papers not available, as 'potential rather than achievement' is the key. Numbers steady during recession, though the entry pattern has changed, with parents nervous of committing from the start of J1. This pattern is changing as smaller state primaries re-group and amalgamate. Will take pupils at any time (mid week/term fine if space available) and at any age.

Exit: The majority of girls from juniors form a core of about half of S1. About 60 per cent stay on to S6, most of those leaving opt for FE or early uni. (Cash counts.) Scottish unis tops (cash counts again) with Glasgow most popular, also Strathclyde and West of Scotland; but trickle down South, no apparent Oxbridge presence; anywhere from Aberdeen to Bristol. Economics most popular degree subject; occasional gap year, some to drama, art colleges and not necessarily in the UK.

Money matters: Not a rich school but will support parents in financial crisis. Approachable attitude encourages early consultation about potential problems. All assistance is means-tested rigorously (including capital/investment income). Bursaries, awarded annually throughout, though primarily for S1 entrants and those whose circumstances change. Nursery is run in partnership with Glasgow city council, and qualifying families receive a refund on the fees.

Good secondhand clothes shop: Pre-loved, school picky and place popular.

Remarks: Refreshing. Such a change from our last visit. Still a nice school with nice girls in a nice part of Glasgow, but goodnes, the difference: last time we came away with a slight feeling of overall repression – 'can't do this because of the recession' sort of thing. Keep pushing the boat: this is sterling stuff. Impressive staff and up-to-date, open-to-change teaching and leadership.

Dollar Academy

Dollar, Clackmannanshire FK14 7DU

Pupils: 1,596; 84 boarders • Ages: 5–18 • Sixth form: 134

Fees: Day £9,054 – £12,105; Boarding £23,427– £28,008 pa

Tel: 01259 742511
Email: rector@dollaracademy.org.uk
Website: www.dollaracademy.org.uk/

Rector: Since 2010, Mr David Knapman BA (maths) MPhil (40s), previously deputy head of Hampton School in London, where he still has a foot on the property ladder. At Hampton he established a no-nonsense reputation but was also notable for his work with charities and the local community. Educated at Morrisons, 'doon the road', followed by Sheffield and Exeter. Married to Brigitte with two sons (younger one attended the school). His mother lives in Dunblane and 'is my fiercest critic; she keeps her ear to the ground'. Plays tennis regularly and enjoys 'playing the piano badly'. Wife also a teacher, came from a country background and is 'pleased to be in Scotland', they like walking the hills and are planning to tackle Ben Lomond this summer (Munro bashing very popular around here).

They live in a stunning Georgian street which houses a collection of school buildings – much in demand by film crews no doubt – we yomped to the burn to see Mylne Bridge (built and named for the local minister and first rector, who opened the school in 1818, to give him a short cut to the kirk) and were told that if it 'weren't for that pine tree, we could see Castle Campbell' (we googled it – it is pretty impressive).

Has a dry sense of humour; hugely enthusiastic and 'very popular – going down well' and 'doing just fine,' say our spies. Sits in on classes, walks round every day and never misses a match, concert or play. Boarding numbers going up and examination results at a record high last year.

He was mentored by Dr Ken Greig, rector of Hutchesons Grammar in Glasgow (we hadn't realised that heads had mentors too) who seems to have grown a beard in solidarity. A mixture of young and old teachers, housing not cheap in the Dollar area but it is the perfect place for families.

Assistant rector and head of prep and junior school since 2010, after four years in big school, Mrs Alison Morrison, BSc (Cantab) PGDE (40s). Economics graduate, following spells in the City, advertising and television changed course (professional graduate diploma of education) at the University of Edinburgh, and has one of the most stunning collection of reviews on Rate my Teacher we have ever seen.

Academic matters: There is no formal setting in the prep and junior school with pupils receiving differentiated teaching and learning within each class. Efficient support for learning in place, with rector getting progress reports. One-to-one, small groups and supported learning in class. Variety of reading methods used, but Jolly – or unjolly come to that – Phonics in the main.

Not quite all singing and dancing new computer system, touch-typing for all, strong on techy subjects. We found a lovely gang of 8 year olds happily making intricate ribbon pictures (for calendars?) in the fabric/home economics room. Some of the chaps were enormously imaginative. Our attempts were rubbish.

Aged 10 (J1), pupils move to junior school, certain amount of specialist teaching in specialist rooms: hist, geog, science plus art, PE and music, by senior school staff. French, German and Spanish (the former two more popular – contrary to the apparent national trend) from J1. Three parallel classes J1, moving to four parallel classes in J2. Junior school is seen as a transition between prep and senior school.

Strong academic tradition in seniors, particularly science with a compressed science option on offer for 14-16 year olds and large numbers for medical school; English and mod langs good (housed in new Westwater Building, which won a couple of design awards); German and French more popular than Spanish; Mandarin available; Latin, Greek and classical studies (heroes for zeros) all on offer and four dedicated classics teachers. All three langs from junior school plus some Japanese, Russian, Italian, philosophy, car mechanics and other jolly options. Broad streaming for English (with EFL if needed), tight setting for maths and mixed ability in most subjects, plus. Large business department offering economics, business management, finance and accountancy.

Rector and/or senior staff have a 20 minute meeting with every pupil (and their parents, who usually keep stumm during the interview) to discuss their personal subject choice. Pupils choose the subjects they want to study and classes are worked round them, rather than the trad system of block choice. There is a distinct emphasis on the academic rather than the vocational.

School follows a mixed bag of courses: National 5 (plus National 4 in maths), Intermediate I and II; Highers, Advanced Highers and the Scottish baccalaureate – which doesn't seem to have many followers outside Dollar. In 2016, 59 per cent of Highers and 57 per cent of Advanced Highers were A grade; 32 pupils got five a grades at Higher.

Classes of 6-24. Efficient support for learning in place; one-to-one, small groups and support learning in class all on offer. School has a positive approach to those with ADHD: pupils can drop into the dyslexia centre at any time. Serious homework, carefully spelt out in a smart little green book full of info for parents which interestingly persists in referring to the school as the Academy. 'Whatever else, we expect that all pupils in the Academy should have enough work to occupy their evenings and any child who indicates otherwise misunderstands.' Not quite all singing and dancing new computer system (school report says 'could do better'), touch-typing for all, strong on techy subjects – most to Advanced Higher level.

Games, options, the arts: No sport is compulsory. That said, boasts a first XV rugby team unbeaten for the first seven years of this century.Shooting 'phenomenal'; always a strong showing at Bisley. Hockey hot stuff. Regular tours to Europe and further afield: Canada, Japan, Italy, Argentina et al. Numerous individual county reps in major and minor sports – golf, skiing and badminton, as well as more esoteric activities such as shotput, curling, table tennis, equestrian vaulting (gymnastics on horseback) and triathlon (NB Clackmannanshire ain't that big), plus national and international team members eg Scottish rugby U18 squad. Mass of games fields, 63 acres of school grounds, much-used hall and swimming pool. Amazing circular Maguire Building – sports, arts, drama – million pound bequest from FP Brian Maguire; formidable school art on display and used for external exhibitions too – even the Scottish Examinations Authority asked for a painting for their new premises. Second bequest from the Price family resulted in a new 5.3 metre inflatable for the navy section. All weather surface was opened by Linda Clement, Scottish Ladies' hockey captain. Presumably by bullying off.

Strong volunteer CCF – good following, not just because of the trips to Canada. Three pipe bands, who all sport the Campbell tartan; the B band was third in the national CCF championships this year. Two orchestras, jazz bands, oodles of choirs; the annual Christmas concert in the Usher Hall was a sell-out with almost 2,000 in the auditorium. Drama timetabled with masses of productions – the rector believes that 'pupils gain confidence through performance'; lots of smaller concerts – 'six performers, 30 in the audience'; that sort of thing. Hot on debating, all sorts of trophies as well as representation in the winning Scotland team at recent world champs in South Africa – a tour de force. Ballroom dancing on Fridays; participants learn Latin American and rock 'n' roll, Japanese dancing the latest wheeze but no medals for this nor for Scottish country dancing. Prize winners sport their bronze, silver, gold or Scottish Awards proudly on their blazers thereafter.

Munro bashing, D of E, exchange and trips, work experience at home and abroad, go-kart racing at Knockhill, skiing, motor mechanics, surfing, falconry. Clubs for everything, usually post school, late buses nightly. Fabric technology timetabled. Over 70 options in total; terrific facilities; powerful charities committee (15 mile sponsored walk raised over £50,000, staff, parents and doggies all included).

Boarding: Boarders from age 9 (though not a lot of them). Two individual (Victorian villas) houses for girls, recently revamped – and dead posh they are too. The boarding houses are small, two with up to 24 girls in each, one for boys that takes up to 49; all three have had recent million pound facelifts, stunning. Usual range of after-school and weekend activities – cooking to sub aqua.

Background and atmosphere: Captain John McNabb, a former herd boy who rose to become a ship's captain and, latterly, a ship husband – literally looking after ships in port – died in 1802, leaving half his fortune, £55,000, to found a school to educate children of 'the parish wheir I was born'. Rumours abound whether the monies came from slavery or piracy but they were certainly augmented by bribes from ship owners eager to be first past the post. After much shilly shallying, the Rev Andrew Mylne, a trustee, commissioned Playfair to build a 'hospital' which finally opened in 1818. The first co-ed in Scotland. McNabb's corpse was rediscovered in the 1930s and proudly brought back to Scotland, and cremated. Gruesome or what. His ashes are entombed in the wall above the main Bronze Doors; this has to be the only school in the land where pupils pass under the founder every day. By 1830, the grounds at Dollar had become an Oeconomical and Botanical garden, boasting some of the rarest trees in the country – certainly the most northerly tulip tree, as well as a Corsican pine, and specimen sequoias. Pupils originally had their own plot of garden, though we are not sure whether this was for ornamental purposes or whether they were expected to augment the school kitchen. The interior of Playfair's original building was gutted by fire in 1961, which allowed a certain amount of internal rearrangement. Zinging concert hall (the Gibson Building), improved science block. Current wish-list includes a new technology, engineering science and earth science building – to be built out of 'funds'. The grounds are open to the public daily. And the library is no longer lollipop pink.

Formerly a direct grant school, Dollar became independent in 1974 – a day school, with a boarding element, around 50 per cent of boarders international. Easily accessible from most of Scotland and just a short hop from the Forth Road Bridge and Edinburgh Airport. Wet weather a feature of the place and masses of matches are rained (or snowed) off (school says very rarely due to new all-weather Astroturf courts and pitches). NB The school uniform includes beanies (first time ever for us on a clothes' list) and macs with fleecy linings. Rector says he doesn't mind what they wear on their heads, as long as they are warm.

Dollar Academy is unusual – though not unique – in dividing the pre-teens into different teaching blocks. Pupils aged 5 to 9 are taught in a splendid airy building (though they use the main school facilities, dining, games, swimming, music, art) under the aegis of deputy head of the prep and junior school. Two parallel classes in prep; max class size 26 (16-26 with classes expanding slightly each year as pupils grow older).

Pastoral care, well-being and discipline: Automatic out for drugs. Lousy work equals detentions post-school or early morning – dead unpopular with parents, plus out if 'The pupil is not deriving benefit from being at the school or indicates by his/her conduct that he/she does not accept the rules of the Academy.' Pupils not particularly streetwise – but modern studies popular and strong politics and international relations society.

Victorian values, with clear rules; many of the petty restrictions have been done away with.

Pupils and parents: The vast majority comes from within a 30 mile radius – impressive number of buses, plus Forces children and a contingent from the Scottish diaspora worldwide. Dollar itself has the reputation of having the highest percentage of graduates of any town in the country. School has a long tradition of looking after the children of tea-planters, missionaries and engineers – still. Perhaps a tad parochial and 'mercifully' free of Sloanes. Exceptionally strong and active FP network, including Sir Frank Swettenham, the first Governor of Malaysia, Sir James Dewar, the inventor of the vacuum flask, and the sculptor, George Paulin. The governing body is mostly FPs, which ensures that the place has freedom to develop but an awareness of its history shapes the thinking – no bad thing.

Entrance: To junior dept at 5 or 10, the latter by fairly stiff exam. To senior usually at 11 or 12, by examination, which is quite selective. Generally oversubscribed for entry at fifth and sixth forms; each case individually considered; good GCSE or National/Intermediate grades required plus good refs and an ability to put something into the school. Open day in September, but parents and prospective pupils are welcome to visit at any point of the year, which gives the opportunity to see the school in action.

Exit: Virtually all juniors go on to senior school, though the occasional one may peel off for trad schools ('very very rare for someone to leave,' says the rector).

A handful to Oxbridge each year (one to Cambridge in 2016 – history). Otherwise most students head for the Scottish universities: Edinburgh, St Andrews, Glasgow, Aberdeen, with under a quarter going south or abroad. Six medics in 2016. Low gap year take up: either a reflection of the recession or the 'get on with it' mentality. The chairman of governors and his wife have set up a trust with more than £1 million to encourage the youngsters to take up challenges involving travel. If that doesn't persuade entrepreneurs overseas.

Money matters: Collection of means tested-academic bursaries at 11 and 12, plus ESU, Forces and boarding bursaries (usually means-tested, with tuition not covered). Fees very reasonable; governors tough on non-payers.

Remarks: Very sound – this large, solid, co-ed school provides education in the best Scottish 'get on with it' tradition, facing the 21st century with the expectations and values of an earlier age, mercifully free of most of the excesses of the 60s. 'Robust teaching and meritocracy' are important here. Up there with the best of the merchant schools.

Douglas Academy

Craigton Road, Milngavie G62 7HL

Pupils: 993 • Ages: 11–18 • Sixth form: S5: 190; S6: 125

Tel: 01419 552365
Email: office@douglas.e-dunbarton.sch.uk
Website: www.douglas.e-dunbarton.sch.uk

Head: Since 2008, Mr Seamus Black MA (50s), educated at St Xavier School, Coatbridge (a local-ish lad, then), read Italian and French at Glasgow University and came to the old Douglas Academy for a year – 'to get to know the traditions', having been previously deputy head of Shawlands Academy. He still teaches when he can and is often 'out and about' – a wandering head, he keeps a beady eye and is incredibly proud both of the new school and of the 'high quality' of his staff and 'pupil attainments'. Keen on parent involvement, he runs the school with a management team of seven, including the head of music. He also talks incredibly quickly and is very on the ball. Married, his family lives in Dunbarton.

Acting Headteacher: Barry Smedley is holding the fort whilst Seamus Black is on leave.

Academic matters: A strong school – results consistently high and the HMI report is peppered with 'very goods'. Three sciences on offer, many take two, pupils do well in science and maths challenges. French and Italian, Spanish option at sixth form, plus Mandarin. Fair amount of autonomy in employing staff, 'But if there are teachers free within the authority, then we have to take them' (an iniquitous system that caused much grief to England – high time it was abandoned here too); otherwise school advertises and can make its own appointments.

Regular success across the board at National grades, music specialists take both National and Higher music without fuss and, 'effortless'. Specialists take 'specially tailored courses', but see below. Most pupils get a 'variety pack' of eight subjects at National grade, including core subjects; most stay on for Highers, and a 'goodly proportion' stay for Advanced Higher – school responds to 'the needs of the pupil': a certain amount of mix and match with Intermediate grades. Asterisked (ie outstanding) performance noted in history, modern languages, art and English. In 2016, 45 per cent of S5 got 5+ Highers and 39 per cent of S6 got 1+ Advanced Highers.

Staff visit local primaries and meet new pupils the term before they hit big school. Children are setted for maths in October of their first term, and for some other subjects in their second year. Classrooms equipped with IT, interactive white boards and learning wall, as you might expect with a top notch new build: teachers happy and au fait with the most modern of facilities and the results speak for themselves.

Extensive support for learning, with a strong team which offers both guidance and support in class, offering help for the brightest as well as for those with learning difficulties, and with an acknowledged expertise in Asperger's.

Games, options, the arts: Does well at rugby, hockey and athletics – 'strong competitive edge'. Not for layabouts – a doing school. State of the art, all-weather rugby, football and hockey pitches, huge games hall plus two gyms, fitness suite, much used by the community, who also do evening and keep-fit classes here. Tennis, cross-country course. Mass of charity involvement (beat the High School of Glasgow) and national award winners.

Became a centre of excellence for music in 1979 and boasts a first orchestra of 'almost professional standard', plus an outstanding chamber orchestra, senior wind band and second orchestra – very full (60+), which often has first year pupils playing, as well as non-music specialists. Chamber choir, junior choir, senior choir, who swept the board at the most recent Glasgow Music Festival, with the former beating the adult section to boot. On a par with St Mary's Music School in Edinburgh. Music lessons carry a nominal charge for non-music specialists, and local concerts are always a sell-out, particularly the annual Christmas concert at St Paul's in Milngavie. Almost equal numbers of boy and girl choristers: serious senior choir, the junior one is merely 'good' but, by any other school's standards, it would be outstanding. Most of the music staff have top jobs in Scotland's orchestras and choirs. Adjectives tend to fail when dealing with centres of excellence, but take it as read that any superlative would be inadequate.

Pupils follow the normal curriculum, but 20 per cent of their time is spent on music. Music specialists come from all over Scotland, Ullapool to Newton Stewart, and their chosen instrument can be in any discipline from fiddle to piano. No quotas for entry, around about eight or 10 annually, currently 49 dedicated music scholars, places free and open to all (help given with transport), with pupils from further away boarding at Dalrymple House (about 75 per cent), opposite the Botanic Gardens in Glasgow's west end (they share with pupils from the centre of excellence for dance at nearby Knightswood). Two homework tutors.

Background and atmosphere: Superlative new build in old school grounds with magical views of the Campsies to the north. Transition was more or less 'seamless'. School dress equals blazer (S6 pupils), white shirt/blouse, school ties, trousers or skirts and no trainers – 'Parents and pupils have high expectations'.

Pastoral care, well-being and discipline: Team of ministers from local churches involved with school. 'Drugs not an issue' and good (state) guidance system in place ('highly effective'), plus link tutors who have informal relationships with the pupils, offering both emotional and social support. Clearly defined rules about bullying and loads of staff backup – 'good extended team'.

Pupils and parents: No 'significant number' from ethnic minorities and no problems with religious festivals – 'praying (as in five times a day) never an issue'. Parents 'feel welcome', and good fundraising and pastoral parents' association in place.

Entrance: Four associated primary schools, one of which is tiny and rural. Pupils from (the Catholic) St Joseph's may come here, and almost all do, or they may prefer to be bused the 30 minutes or so there and back to the local secondary Catholic school in Kirkintilloch. Excellent child-orientated joining handbook.

Exit: Around 65 per cent to university, most to Scottish universities.

Remarks: Stunning state school for musicians, which moved to a split, new, fantastic, state of the art campus in 2009 – worth moving house for if you are not in the catchment area, even if you aren't a musician. Exam results impressive and getting even more so. Outstanding recent HMI report. Strength through knowledge, the school motto, very much a byword.

The Edinburgh Academy

42 Henderson Row, Edinburgh EH3 5BL

Pupils: 561 • Ages: 2–18 • Sixth form: 150

Fees: £7,908 – £13,248 pa

Tel: 01315 564603
Email: admissions@edinburghacademy.org.uk
Website: www.edinburghacademy.org.uk

Rector: Since 2008, Mr Marco Longmore MA PGCE, schooled at Milburn Academy in Inverness, thence history at Edinburgh (and medieval history at that) followed by PGCE at Moray House. Splendidly dry sense of humour.

Has done the rounds of the Edinburgh schools: after seven years both at Heriot's and Watson's (head of history and mod studies) he came to The Academy (as it is known in Edinburgh society) from Alleyn's School in Dulwich (bit of a change there) where he was senior deputy head. Runs school – two sites – with head of junior school and a clutch of senior deputies and deputy rectors thrown in. Geits (11 year olds) are based in a 'dedicated area' in senior school campus and not at junior school on Arboretum Road as might be expected. Junior school is some hefty 15 minutes' walk away: plumb opposite the games pitches. Longmore lives in posh pad on the Arboretum campus, with his wife Karen and their young, now up and flying.

Rector has overseen/is overseeing an apocalyptic sea change in this, once the Edinbourgousie's school of choice (sons of lawyers, accountants et al strived to get into THE Academy whilst their sisters reckoned that if they were accepted into St George's School for Girls, they were set up for life – geddit?) Schools shared the same parents, half terms and holidays. Perfection. Not so long ago, term dates no longer matched. Baptism of fire: rector and girlies arrived together (though there had been girls in sixth form for some time). Edinburgh Academy went co-ed. (Didn't do St George's much good – numbers still down – don't believe the hype). The founding fathers would be turning in their graves, but both sexes at ease with each other: no obvious cliques, raucous mixed melée was loading cricket nets/kayaks onto the roof of one of a fleet of school buses and departing in obvious glee at the end of a school day during our visit.

Bit between the teeth: Longmore has plans afoot for restructuring some of the older (and sadder) buildings, sweeping away 60s disasters, and forming six new classrooms with additional open spaces. No plans to expand numbers (max 600 senior school: 380 junior school, current roll 550 senior). We must confess to be a little bamboozled about the whole scheme of things, but as planning has not yet been applied for, we wait with bated breath.

Head of junior school: Since 2011, Mr Gavin Calder MA PGCE SQA (40s), a borderer. He came to EA Junior School having taught his way round the independent junior school sector: Robert Gordon's, Loretto, and, most recently, head of Lomond (junior school, we presume) in Helensburgh. Having worked with SCIS on a number of junior initiatives, he happily endorses Curriculum for Excellence (which has been greeted – rather like National 5s – with less than overwhelming enthusiasm across the board).

Academic matters: Sixty pupils in P1 (three forms: age 5) and iPads for all to Geits (11/12 – who are based in Henderson Row at senior school in dedicated space), certain amount of Milly Molly Mandy waffle in prospectus about 'each stage providing a firm basis for learning at the next level'. Listening part of the programme, which includes Big Writing and Muckle Reading. (Many a mickle makes a muckle... but what on earth has that to do with reading: and do the stout citizens of Edinburgh really want their young taught Lallans?) French from nursery. Set for maths, which includes money, measurements and relates to everyday life: easy moves up and down. Basic humanities, ICT and lessons on computers – have invested in iPad learning – keyboarding for all. Computers nanny-netted and linked: all pupils have school email address.

Forget the la-la land speak. This is a thunderingly good school, combining the best of 21st century thinking with well tried and tested methods. All children arriving in P1 are assessed (baseline assessment) as are those at nursery before starting junior school proper. Mixed ability classes. Regular assessments for both the gifted and the challenged, with, in the latter case, ed psychs called in where appropriate. Co-teaching as required, with special computer access.

Senior school is divided into 'transition' (11/13), middle years (14/16) and sixth form (17/18). Ed Academy previously followed the well-worn (and parent-appreciated) path of GCSEs for all, followed by either As or Highers. Those destined for English unis were encouraged to follow the A level route and vice versa. 2016 results indicate that 43 per cent of GCSEs were A*/A; 67 per cent of A levels were A*/A; Highers 54 per cent A and Advanced Highers 53 per cent A. First year sixth regularly collect enough

E

Highers for university entrance and promptly leave; not sure that following the Scottish route only might not lead to a very light second year sixth. School has now discontinued GCSEs and A levels except for art and music ('Broader syllabus,' admits the rector), offering just Highers and Advanced Highers.

The advantage of no longer offering dual sixth form disciplines should be both a logistical and financial improvement. Mandarin from age 10, plus French ('nuff said), German and Spanish on offer. Solo performances in Japanese and Portuguese: presumably native speakers. School will pull in dedicated tutors for native speakers to push 'em through the exam path.

'No problem getting staff'. Good mixture of old and young, rector keen not to encourage the Mr Chips effect and prefers a fluid changeover. Parents have expressed frustration that neither Russian, law, nor psychology are on the table, but with the new syllabus perhaps there will be room to introduce more esoteric subjects.

Broad academic range of pupils. The tradition of 'dux', the brightest boy or girl in the school (Magnus Magnusson was dux in his day), is extended to include wider group of high achievers, the Dux Club. (School adds, 'This is based on single sitting achievement of five or more As at Higher, or predicted three A at Advanced Higher.)

Max class size 20, and less both for practical and in sixth form: school adopts a 'block' approach to classes, with ability setting where possible. Surprisingly, we can find no reference to any form of SEN (or ESOL) in the official school prospectus; we at The Good Schools Guide, consider SEN provision to be fundamental to each and every school. We expect co-teaching at the youngest level, and we presume that every child will be assessed (regularly if need be) with ed psychs pulled in where necessary. Brushing it onto page 13 of the senior school handbook is not an option, though refreshingly the application form does make mention of IEPs. That having been said, school offers individual learning programmes of 'one or two 40 minute lessons a week'. 'Multi-sensory teaching methods are used', which is a new one to this ed (the mind boggles). Exam allowances organised and co-teaching in English, mod langs and maths – whew. Scribing currently under debate. Rector comments: 'I will take your point on the chin but I would highlight that in fact we have very extensive SEN support at the school from primary to senior school with five FT staff and two intern supports, plus additional specialist subject discipline input from other staff. This is in class, group extraction and one to one.'

Non-native English speakers seem to follow a rather gentler academic regime.

PE and music attract few followers, ditto drama; though fair number studied business studies/modern studies.

Games, options, the arts: Unlike other senior schools (who go the hockey/footie route in the spring term), EA plays rugby during both the autumn and spring term, hence tradition for providing a mini squad for the Scottish rugby side (over 100 international caps to date), with usual rash of caps, would-be caps in the wings. No change here.

Main games field beside the junior school with its fantastic (community) sports hall including climbing wall, shared with local residents (planning condition) and much in demand for children's parties. Serious new revamp, with both main pavilion and hockey pavilion having a makeover. No pool (yet); specialist weights and gym, and two all-weather hockey pitches. Girls field 10 hockey teams as well as netball and athletics. Plus individual sports badminton, fives, skiing, squash, golf, tennis, yoga and soft ball.

Outstanding art department, brilliant ceramics; well attended evening life class. Artist in residence, jewellery making popular: number of leavers go on to art and foundation courses.

Music all-singing and dancing. Superlatives abound. Trips and tours of course, pipe band. Any pupil learning an instrument can play in concerts 'even if it is only three notes and child has been learning the trombone for three weeks'. Concerts outstandingly professional (the odd radio concert). Prize-winning choirs and – earlier comments notwithstanding – a good showing at Higher level, ditto A. Recent choral trip to Italy, chamber choir Barnado's national choir of the year last year, and previously BBC Songs of Praise choir of the year. School also runs an amateur choir for stout citizens of Edinburgh on Wednesday evenings during term time (Edinburgh Academy Choral Society) under direction of current director of music, no singing test: open to all. Cough sweets and cherry brandy pervade.

Drama important; sympathetic conversion of physics building to a state-of-the-art performing arts centre, the Magnusson Centre for Performing Arts (£2.5m): green room littered with costumes for current production: theatre and dance studio with girls' and boys' showers and changing for every imaginable activity below. Inside is breathtaking, though original features have not been vandalised: outside some additional curious tiled 'ears' provide ventilation for the new activities.

CCF popular (everyone has to join, including girls) – flurry of battledress and air force blue on Remembrance Day; piping particularly strong, with successes in both quartet and trios. Keen D of E; lots of hobbies – and good charity input – the charity committee does a massive amount of fundraising: over £100,000 in last eight years. P6 (11 year olds or thereabouts) join the Junior Award Scheme Scotland (akin to the D of E) working towards bronze, silver and gold awards – the latter two in the senior school.

Background and atmosphere: Lord Cockburn (Cocky) and Sir Walter Scott (amongst others) founded school in 1824. Built in trad Edinburgh sandstone in true Athenian style, the Greek motto on the main portico reads 'Education is the mother of both wisdom and virtue'. Buildings in main school a mixed bunch, some designer-inspired additions, including a fabulous oval assembly hall, plus a mass of add-ons as well as classrooms and impressive new labs around bleak tarmac courtyards; new seating and planting across the school helps to soften the traditional yards. Administrative area, which includes rector's office, has elegant garden – and electric gates – which look awesome, but open like Sesame as you approach... same for mega courtyard where railings have recently been replaced (and you thought they were always there).

Generous Edinburghoisie-sponsored libraries; successful FPs remember their font of learning with pride. School sold five abandoned tennis courts for development several years ago which caused press comment, and built the James Clerk Maxwell (known as Dafty when at school) science building. Redundant boarding houses provided funds for future developments. New reception area for visitors and admissions in senior school not yet fully functional. School dissed the field centre in Angus and put the dosh towards supporting outdoor education for all. 'Just opened an indoor climbing centre with race reviews from experienced climbers'.

Junior school based at Arboretum Road. Much improved from the time this ed's son was there (think gulag): jolly classrooms, with dedicated space for P1-P3 and nursery (Denholm Green).

Boys wear bright blue blazers; girls, a tailored version, new skirt in the pipeline, we could see nothing wrong with the current model. Place no longer either looks or feels like a boys' school: 50/50 in nursery and roughly 55/45 throughout the rest of the school.

Oval hall much used for lettings – and this ed has reeled here. School makes much of its free central Edinburgh parking. Impressive dining room with juice, cordials (surprise surprise), halal, salads and veggie option. All cooked on site. Good Wifi: not only in library, complete with purple chairs and turquoise stools (full time librarian) but over the entire campus to support one-to-one iPads that are being 'rolled out to pupils'.

Pastoral care, well-being and discipline: Junior school parents are expected and 'allowed' to help with homework, but parents (and pupils) must 'inform staff if they do not understand a particular piece of work'. Young expected to complete projects in their own time. Certificates awarded when pupils have collected sufficient number of merits. Tally system for perpetual wickedness (or even just for the odd bit of wickedness) means detention (time out) during lunch break. Strong mix of trad and enlightened younger staff. Fairly hefty anti-bullying procedure in place.

Senior school pupils divided into four 'divisions' (houses, and if your father was there – or your grandfather – then you are in the same house), pastoral care via depute rector (pastoral and personnel), heads of year plus form takers (class teachers); good PSHE. Head ephor (prefect) is a key link with rector and school. School 'not complacent that drugs are confined to an area south of Princes Street', or 'stop at the railings – incidents do occur'. No automatic exclusion unless dealing is involved. 'If at all possible we give the pupils a second chance'; parents are involved. 'Pupil may forfeit the right to remain in the school (for a varying length of time).' Will test 'on suspicion'. City temptations are close. One or two teeny reports of bullying still around, but really just aggravated teasing and no more than any nit-picker might expect. No change here. Mobiles forbidden during school day.

Pupils and parents: All sorts, with a large traditional intake of professional classes. Small tranche from abroad, mainly Europe. 'Broad ethnic spread,' says the rector who, along with head of junior school, is keen on playing down traditional middle-class image of the school – hence extended and very popular nursery hours and 8.00am breakfast for seniors. Pupils are pleasantly self-confident and polite – occasional touch of arrogance or uncouth youth but not more than teenage adolescence. Robert Louis Stevenson and Archbishop Tait of Canterbury are FPs, plus colourist Francis Cadell, Magnus Magnusson and Eric Stevenson, who, both during his lifetime, and on his death, gave many millions of pounds to athletics, and bursarial funds: school still benefits from the Eric H Stevenson Trust. Plus (of course) partners in many of Edinburgh's institutions.

Entrance: Primary 1 assessments held in early January. Primary 2-6 assessments can be arranged at times to suit parents – also one main assessment afternoon in late November. (Waiting lists operate where demand exceeds supply.) Almost automatic through nursery.

Maths and English from junior school to Geits age 11 (though more or less automatic); Geits to S1: maths, English and mod lang. Ditto entry to S2; 'arrangements can be made to sit assessments for entry at other times of the session.' 'Arrangements can be made for overseas applicants to sit our entrance tests abroad'. Sixth form entry on assessment, interview, school reference and report plus predicted grades (though prospectus seems to prefer the word 'predicated' which is charmingly quaint). Five passes at GCSE at C for entry to sixth form: hardly a high bar. Apply at any time, and if space available...

Traditionally patronised by the great and the good of Edinburgh and does well by them, plus an increasing number of first-time buyers (around 40 per cent). Entry handbook makes ages and stages for entry very clear. Girls' advent has, as expected, increased the application rate (for both sexes) but not changed the system.

Excellent bus handbook with pick up times and costings, East, Mid, West Lothian all covered plus a couple of handy inner routes. Buses drop off at both junior and senior school: school opens 8am (one pupil came daily by train from Newcastle, and could be seen dashing along George Street as the train was invariably late). Pick up time 5pm, though pupils can stay till 6pm (at cost).

Exit: Nearly all juniors (95 per cent in 2016) move on to the senior school aged 10/11, to 'Geits' (the equivalent of Primary 7 in the Scottish system), though there may be one or two that fall by the wayside: either to trad public schools or fail to make the grade, or because of relocation.

Hardly any post-16 drop out. 'Around 90 per cent' to various universities, roughly 70 per cent to Scottish (now, of course, free to Scots residents) the rest elsewhere; fewer take a gap year. Four to Oxbridge in 2016 and two medics; Aberdeen, Bristol, Durham, Edinburgh; Glasgow, Napier, Northumbria, RGU, St Andrews, Strathclyde all popular; as ever, sciences and engineering feature strongly, with creative and social subjects on the increase. Art something of a speciality, though five off to art college in 2016. Enlightened careers department (rector again: 'Very very good'). Quantities of embryo lawyers, doctors and merchant bankers, plus engineering, physics, technology, English, modern languages, sports studies, history, international relations. 'What they do thereafter may be different – but they are not cloned down the three routes which you mention. Some into the professions, progressively more into art, drama, interior design, the media and administration.' School can manage SATS (for American universities). Unconditional offers from Scottish universities based on Scottish Highers taken in (lower) sixth year do not always make for academic concentration in seventh (upper sixth), but we have said that already.

Money matters: Wowser £670,000 dosh available for means-tested bursaries. Good crop of scholarships for musicians and academics; school may support parents in financial difficulties until the next practical exit point: but not paying fees is not an option. 'Parents must be realistic and up front'. 'No endowments per se – majority of scholarships and other bursaries come out of fee income.' Pace Eric Stevenson. Familial discounts for third child (and more). Bursaries are means-tested up to 100 per cent fees in line with OSCR demands.

Remarks: School looks good (and will look even better when planned developments come to fruition). Feels like a well-established co-ed. But, and it is a big but: we are concerned that without the A level/GCSE cachet this, the smallest of the Edinburgh independent co-ed day schools, might find parents drifting to the more academic Heriot's, or the former Merchant schools; all of which, though larger, are considerably cheaper. And money talks.

Edinburgh Steiner School

60 Spylaw Road, Edinburgh EH10 5BR

Pupils: 250 • Ages: 3–18 • Sixth form: 12

Fees: £3,240 – £10,326 pa

Tel: 01313 373410
Email: admissions@edinburghsteinerschool.org.uk
Website: www.edinburghsteinerschool.org.uk

Chair of the College of Teachers: No head as such – role of chair is rotated, elected from management group of the college (roughly 10 per cent of staff) who meet weekly on Thursdays (Wed afternoons involve the whole staff), but even if chosen to be chair, the position is voluntary and offer can be refused. Current chair, Nick Brett, is on his second term: a two or three year stint.

'Major educational decisions are taken by the College of Teachers and executed by the school's management team in conjunction with teachers'. Steiner is egalitarian. Bursar, board of trustees and College of Teachers are responsible for finance, admin and building development. Forget trad hierarchy – teachers in the Steiner Waldorf world 'share responsibility and authority for the daily running of the school and the educational programme'. Upper school, years 9 to 12, each have a class guardian chosen from among the staff.

E

Academic matters: Pupils start each day with a 'wake-up call': daily choir /or morning verse (orchestra once a week) followed by the main lesson, a one and a half hour slot (previously two hours in the lower school) when 'topic blocks' are covered in four-week chunks: astronomy, philosophy, history of architecture: whatever. These are not necessarily exam fodder, but the Open College Network (OCN) recommended that the 'narrative's' main lesson be 'accepted without amendment and accredited' – OCN levels 1 and 2 are equivalent to A or B/C at GCSE.

Proper French and German from age 9 with grammar and stuff, only stories and singing for littler ones. German fairly unpopular currently (as in most schools we have visited lately), but with Steiner regime at the core and six to eight week German/French exchange with other Steiner schools there is no option; exchanges themselves funded by pupils: jumble sales, pizza cook ins and the like. (Plus global exchanges with other Rudolf Steiner schools). Spanish on wish list. Physics, chemistry and biology from age 11 (apparently increased numbers of science lessons for 14-16 year olds), with religion represented either by stories of the saints, the legend of King Arthur and 'biographies showing the strength and compassion of the human spirit in challenge and adversity'. History includes fairy tales, legends of saints (again?) and a variety pack of mythology; not much more than lip service to geography that we could find mentioned in the exhaustive timetable we were given.

Spanking new computer room which incorporates careers and guidance (though access is blighted by an uncompromising cupboard which makes the fiction library little more than a passage with book shelves and – rather hard – bean bags). 'Real care is taken to ensure that every pupil who leaves has a plan in place for when they leave school. All the traditional options are open to them, but also support is given for a huge range of onward destinations.' And school will help out, when students have left, if they want a career change (as indeed do most schools).

Computers still thin on the ground; most classrooms equipped with computer-generated projectors and computers not encouraged (nor telly) till age 14, either at home or at school. Computer lessons include deconstructing and reconstructing old PCs as well as designing websites (school one impressive). More pianos than computers in classrooms: and pretty sad upright ones at that. No universal iPads.

Lower School follows European system whereby no formal learning is undertaken until young have lost their baby teeth – otherwise 'attachment to womb is too great'. Young need some form of independence, though they will have learnt colours and shapes in kindergarten, they are not expected to attempt either to write or to read (and they start by reading what they have written) until firmly settled into lower school. When asked about whether the school taught reading by 'phonics' the answer came 'that yes, in the Steiner way, by association with art form and letters'.

Class teachers stay with each class throughout lower school (roughly 15 per class and 25 max per year group) until they move on to upper school, taking the main lesson each day after morning verse and eurythmy. Basic reading and writing, plus simple maths age 6 (though we were surprised to find 10 year olds being given a lesson in division by 10: 'if I divide this basket into 10 pieces...')

Classes of about 20 in upper school, though we did find 28 doing mechanics which is too many for any 'caring' fee paying school. Average year group 25. Brighter pupils can leapfrog, and vice versa; EAL for older foreign nationals (charged): younger ones pick it up as they go along. 'Huge learning support' – regular testing for all for dyslexia et al in lower school and again on entry to senior school at 14; some pupils have IEPs. Dyslexics 'fully integrated; double teaching, with lap tops in upper school. Extra time in exams and scribes abound. Can 'cope' with 'mild autism'; but 'got to keep the balance'. (Check the Steiner web site for theories on dyslexia et al).

Buildings rotten for physically handicapped, though previously did quite well with a profoundly deaf pupil: 'not keen on ADHD'. School follows a multi-sensory approach to learning difficulties with the emphasis on co-ordination and 'curative' specialists. Qualified special needs staff in both lower and upper school, plus one 'floater'. General dyslexic (dyspraxic etc) help is covered within the fee structure, but if parents request extra, it costs.

Offers GCSEs, National 5s, Highers and Advanced Highers. The normal two-year GCSE syllabus is studied over one year, with maths, English, German and French GCSE taken aged 16, followed by humanities, the sciences and art at 17, and Highers at 18. Got it? (The natty results we were sent only gave particulars of Highers A-C rate in 2016 – 88 per cent – plus all seven Advanced Higher grades were A) but not a squeak about GCSE: perhaps they have fallen off the system.)

Though no academic selection, results are good in general, some seriously good. Strong German and French. Nice scattering of As in English over past three years (in each year only nine were presented). Maths, not the top of the pops, and last year not a soul took French, though in previous years French has done well – new head of French on cards perhaps? German has been consistently in the ribbons (apart from being the least popular subject) over the last few years. Sciences and lots of practical science with hands-on lessons in somewhat antiquated lab – everything taught 'experientially and children learn by doing' – pretty good. 'By teaching science, art and religion in this integrated way, we hope to implant in our young people a holistic view of life, so that they may regard the world with understanding and serve it with respect.' But see below, new(ish) lab with only one chap in Higher physics class: girls currently physics crazy (though recent results won't set the world on fire) with engineering the new black. Philosophy the new kid on the block.

Steiner teachers are trained in-house – this is one of four training centres. Prospective disciples come from all walks of life: some are former pupils, some former parents and some come from trad teaching backgrounds (sometimes they stay with Steiner and sometimes go back to mainstream). The part-time course is spread over three years and includes an introduction to Rudolf Steiner and Anthroposophy: the esoteric science, Goethean science and artistic practice (and this is in the first year), plus Parsifal: biographical questions with reference to the Grail legend, eurythmy, creative speech, painting drawing etc. During the second and third year all must do teaching practice.

School doctor is a 'fully qualified medical practitioner who is also a specialist in Anthroposophical medicine..The doctor visits the school several times a year..The appointments are helpful for pupils, parents and teachers..Because appointments are infrequent they cannot undertake to treat acute illnesses which need ongoing supervision'. We spent some time investigating Anthroposophical medicine online; both on their dedicated site, and via the Steiner website. We are not happy with what we found on either site, but school upbraided us and told us that 'they did not follow any of these principles' – which include karmic theories and a whole lot of weird disciplines. Check them out yourselves.

Games, options, the arts: Small (puddled during our visit) basketball court, cricket and hockey; seven-a-side rugby at Meggetland Stadium 'dead popular'. School also uses Harrison Park and Craiglockhart Sports Centre and Gym: a 10 minute hike away. Timetabled PE and gym, acrobatics a recent addition – pupils wear Steiner tee shirts and tracksuit bottoms. D of E popular (though no mention of YE, which normally comes in the same breath).

Hall used for gym, theatre etc. Options and the arts integrated into syllabus – art exam results consistently good; we were impressed by the standard of architectural drawing, one of the staff (who was French) spoke so quickly that this ed was no more informed than she was before she asked the question. Comprehensive art, including specialist drawing and painting. Lessons in hand operated sewing machines and pattern making (electric sewing machines come later), knitting a – presumably – beanie, plus embroidery and those dreaded socks again. Buttons? Pottery, sculpting (and all must do a head in their final year); some terrific work around, plus needle felting, metal and copper work, fabric design, weaving, knitting (and turning a heel: which seems an outdated skill) from age 6: for both boys and girls. Extra charge for craft materials. Specialist teachers pulled in when necessary: book binding was mentioned. Music and drama ditto and inclusive, charge for cancelled music lessons and for recorders (recorder group). Debating popular.

When we visited previously we experienced the daily eurythmy session, now curtailed to one period a week for upper school; still a right of passage for lower school after morning verse.

Background and atmosphere: Three trad Edinburgh Victorian villas, set 'twixt George Watson's extensive campus and various parts of Napier University. Somewhat bizarre carving up of rooms: one or two fab ceilings (carved again) most rooms have fire places, motley collection of mantelpieces. Stairs need edging for visually challenged. Dangerous. Stonking new library/interview room is a joy.

Exciting Swiss/Mother Hubbardish chalet for kindergarten (3+-6) with classrooms painted standard Steiner colours: class 1 peach, class 2 pink (four young were baking in a corner during our visit) and class 3 green. This ed is not convinced by the use of pastel colours, but as school uniform, or lack of it, stipulates no bright colours be worn, this gentling must pay dividends. Three acres of shoehorned campus, children playing anywhere and everywhere within white lines neatly segregated by picket fence for early years. Proper pupil gardens: gardening is part of the syllabus. 'We eat what we grow'. This ed wondered about the riot of foxgloves. Charming, loads of outdoor play area, with water a new feature, and trees to climb: 'Ealth & Safety apparently not bothered'. The young were outside during our visit, happily pouring water, climbing trees and chasing each other. Looked dead normal to this ed. Jolly dedicated space, fenced off from the rest of the school.

New 'woodland' area with tiny designated hut under construction. Every bit of space is used, some tatty areas, nothing precious – place still smacks of a lack of funds, though the paths are better maintained than previously, and classrooms were clean and businesslike – except for one which was less than adequate; young had to peer round the corner to see the blackboard where a somewhat matronly teacher was giving 8/9 year olds a lesson.

Christian school, celebrates all seven important events (starting with Michaelmas) other faiths' holy days factored in. 'But religion is basically right and wrong,' said our guide.

Steiner schools do not follow the (now largely historical) orthodox attitude to education, but 'treat each child as a blank canvas to be filled with interlinking academic, artistic and practical information, delivered in such a way as to incite curiosity, encourage creativity and an awareness of others'. Has long been regarded as a 'school offering alternative education to somewhat scruffy children in hippy clothes, who took no exams and pretty well ran riot'; however, since the Scottish government introduced their much reviled Curriculum for Excellence, Edinburgh Steiner has become an educational flagship, albeit an holistic one. To quote The Scotsman: 'All schools strive for innovation but one that does more than strive is Edinburgh's Rudolf Steiner. It lives and breathes innovation'. The educational philosophy that Rudolf Steiner put into practice in 1919 for the children of the employees of the Waldorf-Astoria cigarette factory has finally come home to roost. Recently described by The Times as following 'the philosophy of taking into account the academic, physical, emotional and spiritual needs of a child.'

School lunches: 90 per cent organic (following the principles of Steiner's biodynamic organic movement) and locally sourced. Daily menus suggested and prepared by all in upper school, who cook and serve lunch for their peers under supervision. Surplus funds from lunch money put towards upper school end of term trip.

Cooking lessons for all, baking in kindergarten during our visit. Organic pizzas once a week baked in pupil-constructed outside pizza oven. Serious allergies appreciated and quite strict guide lines for those bringing in food.

Holds an open day one Friday each month and visitors (usually prospective parents) are welcome and allowed into classrooms while lessons are in progress.

Pastoral care, well-being and discipline: Beautifully illustrated handbook: Edinburgh Steiner School reads like the 60s guide to a leftish hippy wonderland: but surprisingly full of (deeply non-hippy) rules and regs. Guardians are point of contact for parental angst in upper school.

Standard formula parent/guardian-teacher meetings summer and winter terms; kindergarten staff visit children at home during the Easter term: 'you will be encouraged to minimise your children's exposure to television and computers.. you will also be expected to make space in your life to think about child development and how to best support it. You will be encouraged to establish rhythm in your home, with family meals and structured bedtime routines. Choosing outdoor activities and nutritious food will also optimise the beneficial effect of our pedagogy'.

Move over big brother, this ain't a school for the kinder of high flyers who may have to jet off to Zurich at short notice. Come back 1984, all is forgiven.

Bullying an interesting one. If you believe Mumsnet it is rife: Edinburgh Steiner has an anonymous 'Eyes and Ears' box to cope with local hiccups and our guide was quite relaxed about the problem: 'doesn't happen much, but we are on top of it'.

No mobiles, all messages via school office, and, during our visit to the English class, one young man, who arrived late was asked if he had a late note. He replied 'it was with the school office'; confession time: we didn't check.

Pupils and parents: In addition to Steiner aficionados, parents are a disparate bunch of mainly middle class enthusiasts who are fed up with, or whose children do not get along in, other local schools. Plus some 'out-boarders', pupils from further afield, who stay with local families, plus some exchange students from Rudolf Steiner schools elsewhere, as well as those from non-Steiner schools. Certain number of refuseniks, be they from the independent or the state sector. Not that great an obvious ethnic mix.

This is a hands-on school and parents are expected to contribute during the term, as well as 'helping with redecorating etc during 'work week' at the end of the summer term, which may not fit with the planned family holiday in Sotto Grande or Benidorm. Relaxed dress code – no uniform;

a (very) general policy states that pupils should be clean and tidy – no garish colours, logos, football strips, ripped jeans, hair colour or excessive jewellery; fairly impressive standard of make-up on some of the older girls; no hijabs (by choice). Pupils are comfortable in the company of visitors, happy to chat and share their work, interests and aspirations and quite honest about how they were bullied at their last school.

Our guide told us that he was sad that 'the original Steiner philosophy' that the school should be available to the lesser well off was no longer the case. He had expected to teach the offspring of social and care workers and was surprised to be teaching the young of professional classes. This ed pointed out that over 50 years ago her husband's cousin, whose father, a brigadier, member of the Upper House and head engineer of a major construction firm, had sent his daughter there. So what was new?

Well, actually, parking: certain number of places within campus, otherwise masses of meters on road outside.

Entrance: Suck it and see: visit school, take child to interview, with a second and longer visit if need be. Pupils come throughout the year, at any time, either through kindergarten or, often, age 12, when they have either discovered problems with their current school or need to have their self-confidence boosted.

Pupils who have previously been in the independent sector are asked for a financial reference from that school. Pupils are interviewed by kindergarten teacher, class teacher in lower school or appropriate guardian. A 'second teacher will attend all interviews'. Two or three day trial possible, but only after they have signed up and paid the mandatory fee.

Staff are caring bunch. One child asked to leave in 'living memory'; otherwise does its best to bring out the best in each and every one, 'instilling life-long learning'. We were surprised to see one pupil eating a banana in class.

Exit: Ninety-five per cent of pupils leaving at the upper end of the school go on to some sort of further education; most to Scottish unis, especially Glasgow and Edinburgh and arti colleges: rash of academic and vocational courses, from marine science to the British Racing School in Newmarket, maths, psychology, politics, fine art, history of art, textiles, drama, and, of course, engineering, odd lawyer, medic, nary an accountant recently. Oxbridge 'not out of the frame', but doesn't figure lately. Gap years popular, furthering the Steiner philosophy wherein journeying is an important part of life.

Money matters: Staff pay in 'low £20,000s' but 80 per cent discount for children in school. Five per cent of previous year's fee income available each year for bursarial help: strict guidelines, and particular help available where parents may be 'considering leaving the school for financial reasons'. When we asked whether 'bursarial help' extended to contributing towards school trips, we were assured that 'other parents/ school rally round'. The Corbyn effect obviously got here early.

Not as cheap as you might first think, huge amount of extra, and not that hidden, charges.

Steiner aficionados are currently working with the Scottish Government and Edinburgh LA to secure state funding. All awards are means-tested max: 40 per cent of fees. (But NB no mention of extras.)

Remarks: Founded 1939, the Edinburgh Rudolf Steiner offers cradle-to-grave, alternative education, with some brilliant teaching and perfect for the child who finds the trad schooling system difficult. We are disturbed by what our researches into the cult of Anthroposophy threw up: the staff whom we met seemed charming and rational, but if we are to believe what we read then perhaps we should delve deeper into the school's philosophy before giving it a high five. And, to be honest, we would prefer to see pupils learning to sew on a button rather than turning a heel. (Apparently they now 'sew buttons on their recorder cases in year 3, and make 'machine sewn garments in class 7/8 – boys too, we presume.)

All singing and dancing – on the surface – and, if you can face the slings and arrows of Anthroposophy – then go for it. But, do you/would you prevent your young from watching the daily news or Dr Who on telly and allow a (thoroughly well qualified) teacher to dictate when, what and how you eat? And remember, you, the parent, is expected to actively participate both during term time and during the holidays.

ESMS Junior School

Linked with The Mary Erskine School / Stewart's Melville College

11 Queensferry Road, Edinburgh EH4 3EQ

Pupils: 1,254 • Ages: 3–11

Fees: Day £7,638 – £9,102; Boarding £18,999 – £19,545 pa

Tel: 01313 111111
Email: admissions@esms.org.uk
Website: www.esms.org.uk

Headmaster: Since September 2016, Mike Kane, prevously head of upper school at Stewart's Melville College.

Entrance: Automatic from nursery (where you should register at birth), otherwise by assessment. Oversubscribed: hugely so age 4/5; not quite so blistering further up; waiting lists throughout. Priority to siblings – as always – but occasional places available at every level. And, unlike some other independent schools, waiting lists have not disappeared during the economic turndown. Roll is currently the highest in history. From age 6 up, assessment for all, plus reports from previous school. Main entry point after Primary 1 is at Primary 6 – very few places available at Primary 7.

Exit: Almost all to senior school; occasional toff may have skived off at 8 or 9 to trad prep school, but this ain't really a toffs' school even if it is on the edge of Edinburgh's New Town. Minimal trickle leave to go elsewhere, and occasional to-ing and fro-ing with other independents.

Remarks: Enormous. over 1250 girls and boys in total, around 10 children means-tested and on some form of financial support. Lower junior school (nursery to age 8) is based at Ravelston and upper junior school is at the Stewart's Melville College site on Queensferry Road. They remain in the junior school until the age of 11 or 12 (P7) before moving up to Stewart's Melville College for boys or The Mary Erskine School for girls.

Spread over both sites, little people don't feel quite so overwhelmed, the nursery and first three years of proper school are tucked into a corner of the Ravelston (MES) campus in stunning new purpose-built classrooms with secure dedicated playgrounds for each age group, surrounded by grass (well, mostly games pitches) and mature trees. Ravelston House (described by Colin McWilliam as a swish villa in the Adam-esque manner, Alexander Keith 1790) is mainly offices and senior girls' class rooms.

Nursery: (vouchers and dry please), from age 3, based at New Ravelston. Forty 3 year olds (Snowdrops) in own rooms; joined by 80 more in four splendidly decorated rooms (well, it was nearly Hallowe'en) bung full of the kind of kit no child can resist. Specially trained teachers, nursery nurses; the result of lot of dosh, discussion and planning: wizard outcome including sensory quiet room – moving lights, swimming fish projected over the ceiling, soft music and seating. Parents encouraged to get involved. But 30 is still quite a big pond for little fishes to play in.

Serious wrap around care from 7.45am-6pm. E-Plus operates throughout the year, on offer to all the junior school, and includes parent workshops. Forest school for all (and forest school trained leaders) 'where they discover for themselves the magic of (the not really very wild) outdoors'.

School proper age 4/5; reading, writing, 'rithmetic: reading taught which ever way works best, phonics, sound recognition: glitches picked up early (if not already flagged). Every boy and girl screened and assessed annually, support either in class, small groups, workshops, or one-to-one. This is a busy academic school and for some the going may prove too tough: and, after much consultation with the parents ('we hate doing it') the odd child may be advised to go elsewhere, either to a special or a smaller school. Head of learning support and four other qualified LS teachers work across whole school. School not afraid of any of the dys-strata, and discipline rigorous enough to cope with ADHD et al. Drop in lunch-time support; Listening Team of teachers available on rota during playtime and lunchtime to listen to children who want to chat about worries or problems. Lots of input from sixth form pupils, who help with reading and classroom support (boys are as much a part of this programme as girls). Reading time set aside for each child, each day. Spelling Bees – Scottish champions and UK runners up in 2012 but sadly The Times decided not to run the competition since then; head still runs a very popular lunchtime Spelling Bee club – the children challenge teachers in all three schools each year, usually successfully, as well as senior pupils.

Age 6, all move to Wester Ravelston for a couple years (extra class added for 7 year olds) where they now enjoy new play facilities. Five parallel classes for 5 and 6 year olds, six for 7 to 9 year olds and eight thereafter, with by which time the young will have moved to the Stewart's Melville campus with full use of all the big school facilities (except that they have their own dedicated spaces). Certain amount of setting (fluid ability groups) for maths and language with specialist teaching for the sciences and art. School majors on academics. Strong emphasis on basics: spelling, presentation; Lewis insists on fountain pens as a 'commitment to presentation skills, matching commitment to basic good manners'. Maximum class size 25, 20 for practical subjects: home economics, science, ICT. The subject-based curriculum at the top of the junior school eases the transition to senior school.

Computers all over, interactive white boards, new ICT room; excellent libraries: well-used open-plan library more-or-less surrounds the head's office. We have grown accustomed to iPads/tablets being an essential learning tool for all pupils; ESMS have issued them to all staff (steepish learning curve for some). Brilliant when linked up to whiteboards, embarrassing if staff get it wrong and display their pathetic attempts at Scrabble or worse by mistake (we have been thus amused elsewhere).

Sport fantastic, as you would expect in the junior department of a truly great school: swimming pool, super gyms, massive games options – rugby, football (Scottish champions again, ditto cross-country champions, tours all over), cricket, hockey etc, with at least 10 teams in action every Saturday, plus inspired expeditions and the like, Italy, Greece, London, skiing, annual exchange of 10 year olds with Colorado Academy. Trips cost, but funds on hand to help the less financially able, for curriculum enhancing, sport, art, rather than for jollies.

Music and drama outstanding. As ever. Stunning Tom Fleming Centre (FP, actor, broadcaster) carved out of old – rather grand, but past its sell by date – Victorian assembly room. Brilliant scheme: the architects dug down into the cellars. Original entrance to the great outside is now a delightful Romeo and Juliet balcony, floor level in the old hall, now half way up the wall. Variable seating for 800 pops up and down. Myriads of clever uses. Green room (not exactly bustling during our visit, but the detritus was there). Zillions of loos (this said with pride) and banisters of stairs down replicated exactly the existing. Wowser.

Call from London producer: crisis in London: adults needed for Evita (internal management foul up): round robin to parents produced the necessary quorum. (Not the same parents every night, you understand, but enough to man the chorus). Next producer call: adults and parents please. Back to London's West End again. And again in January, with junior children in three professional operas in March (which will take total appearances by junior school children in professional musicals and operas to almost 820 since 1994, recently in Joseph yet again and Jesus Christ Superstar). Plus, of course, the odd play in the festival, at Christmas. And, since 2013, the junior school became the choir of the Edinburgh Tattoo (a welcome respite from previous songsters). Each year boys and girls sing their hearts out – and join the throng of professionals marching off (and waving) to the massed bands at the end. Five choirs, four orchestras, a hefty 300 learn an instrument. Fabulous art, with a great millennium staircase decorated by all the pupils.

Parents mostly first time buyers, huge amount of charity work both for and outwith the school; they have terrific contact with Malawi and have built a girls' secondary school there – it is called The Edinburgh Girls' High School and the pupils wear Mary Erskine uniform. Over £50,000 raised in the junior school alone for its other charities last year eg all 200 Primary 7 children walking for up to 12 hours in the hills to raise £20,000+ to support a local OE centre and two others walking for 40 miles across the width of Scotland over two days to raise another £13,000 for children's sports charities. Walking even further this year along the West Highland Way and the John Muir Way – again the emphasis on challenge.

New build started in July 2015: the current somewhat basic range of junior classrooms is being demolished, with the top end of junior school moving in sequence, two years at a time, into the almost adjacent Queensway House (the white modern block on the corner of the roundabout). Architects wanted to build a 28 classroom gulag: school was horrified, with such a mass of young, they try to keep 'em in 'villages'. This is an anticipated 10/15 year operation. ESMS bought Queensway House (themselves) but as they still nominally come under the aegis of the Merchant Company Education Board, the rebuild will not entirely be self-financed.

Coaches to and from school, from all over, but only after age 8: from Dunbar, Dunfermline, Melrose and Falkirk as well as all round Edinburgh. Coach at beginning and end of school day between the two campuses, otherwise it's shanks' pony or one of the many school fleet buses. Parking now deeply restricted on school campus, each member of staff has a coloured sticker on the car which indicates which day they may not park on school grounds. We had to park in the street: but were ferried to and fro by school contracted taxi. Boarding from age 11 upwards, either full time or weekly, flexi on offer with bed and breakfast ok if space available, just under 50 quid a night, couple of segregated houses quite close to school, each house capable of holding max 30 at any one time: married couple at the helm in both. Boarding costs about nine grand a year per child more than straight school.

Strong anti-bullying programme. Every child made to feel loved. Central to the ethos and now rolled out over the whole school, but started in the junior school is a nine point set of values: written everywhere: illustrated everywhere: each boy and girl must show appreciation, commitment, confidence, enthusiasm, grace, integrity, kindness, respect and responsibility. They are expected to thank everyone for everything, open doors, allow others to pass. 'Boys' behaviour has improved enormously.' Etiquette is important.

The unannounced HMI report a few years back couldn't fault the place. We rather agree.

Fernhill School

F

Fernbrae Avenue, Rutherglen, Glasgow G73 4SG

Pupils: 200 • Ages: 2–18 • Sixth form: 10 • RC

Fees: Primary £7,360 – £9,950; Secondary £10,470 – £10,770 pa

Tel: 0141 634 2674
Email: info@fernhillschool.co.uk
Website: www.fernhillschool.co.uk

Head Teacher: Since 2014, Dr Laura Murphy BSc PhD PGDE (all in chemistry from Glasgow University), previously depute head, who took over from Theresa Hayburn, who had been in the post less than two years. Dr Murphy (whom we have not met) spent 22 years in chemical industry with ICI before becoming a teacher. Non-executive appointments include Scottish Enterprise Forth Valley Board, Street Child Africa (including a field trip to Ghana to observe projects) and Chemical Sciences Scotland (interested in helping to define government strategy for Scottish science education). A practising Catholic with a sense of social justice.

Academic matters: 'Does very, very well', firmly rooted in the Scottish exam system, with National 5, Higher and Advanced Higher courses firmly on stream. This is an academic school, which offers a full curriculum, results are pretty impressive – good pass rate at all levels (Highers 65 per cent A, Advanced Highers 78 per cent A in 2016). 'A wonderful spirit of team work' pervades and pupils 'work well together'. Teachers can give real personal attention to pupils of all abilities. Five Highers the norm, though perhaps staff pupil ratio might be a tad OTT.

Huge investment in IT over the past five years, keyboarding for all, flat screens, local area network, and 40 stand-alone machines. Computing is offered as an exam subject up to Advanced Higher level. Staff all dual qualified and can book computer suites for lessons. Interactive whiteboards on site. Humanities well taught and good SEN provision. Pupil support taken seriously and – from evidence of results gained from a mixed ability intake – very effective.

Games, options, the arts: Amazing range of sports on offer – mixed hockey starts from lower primary and continues through the school, plus all the usual activities: netball, volleyball, football; house matches as well as inter-schools friendlies. Size means team sport tends to be participative as well as competitive; for primary athletics had a clean sweep at the South Lanarkshire track events. Parents are enthusiastically involved in annual sports days, keen swimming at a local swimming pool nearby (absolutely stunning after another refurbishment) and successful cross-country team. Saturday sports for teams. 'Staff are brilliant at encouraging star quality athletes,' though high fliers tend to go to local clubs for high-level training etc.

Some clubs post-school and a wide variety during lunch. Chess popular, debating and public speaking important, poetry a successful addition. Masses of woodwind and violins, the occasional trumpeter and pianist and, at last, an orchestra, going from strength to strength. Lots of group playing and house competitions – music is fun here. Regular visits to the Royal Concert Hall in Glasgow and regular choir trips to Europe. Drama is introduced in the school with a number of productions allowing good cross-school participation. Airy all-purpose art department including fabric and fashion design, 'band-box smart into the bargain'; pupils design the fabric and follow all the way through to the finished item – impressive.

Background and atmosphere: Perched beside a golf course close to the Cathkin Braes, the central Victorian family home, overlooking the city of Glasgow, nestles in nine 'nook and cranny' acres. Private and very secure with locked gates. It was founded in 1972 as a primary school and pushed the leaving age up – demand and supply. Classrooms added when necessary, though the main quad is splendidly uniform. Two more recent teaching blocks are smart and practical, while the collection of cabins and smaller classrooms was brightened with boxes and baskets of flowers on a summer visit.

Runs on Catholic ethos – pupils deliciously polite, tons of praise for all and oodles of cups, awards and prizes for a various activities. Immaculate – strap shoes, caps for boys and round felt hats for girls, even with their summer dresses and long white socks. Strong links formed between senior and primary pupils, with buddies at break time. Packed lunches, hot lunches Wed/Thurs, most pupils eat lunch in the hall but senior pupils have a bit more privacy in their own common room.

Financial problems brought the school to the brink of closure in summer 2014, but parents and board members pledged a six-figure sum which enabled a refinancing of the business.

Pastoral care, well-being and discipline: Founded on respect for other people and 'treat them properly' ethos reinforced by anti-bullying assemblies and workshops in first and second year secondary. Of course pupils sometimes fall out, but no real bullying. Strong PSE and MRE (social and religious education in old speak) programmes, four houses and tutor system in place. Drugs, smoking and alcohol awareness days. Drugs simply don't happen – a very particular ethos and catchment which means that on the whole children stay children and enjoy their childhood.

Own chaplain and strong links with the local community. All practising RC pupils are prepared for the sacraments of first communion and confirmation within the school. Primary school staff are all practising Catholics, but not essential for teachers in the senior school. Welcomes all: Hindu, Muslim etc – no religious or sectarian bigotry. Feast days of other religions are recognised and the school acknowledges other faiths with understanding and respect.

Pupils and parents: From all over – some travel quite a long distance: North Lanarkshire, Ayrshire, buses. An oasis of middle-class respectability. Can leave pupils from 8.30am, which is handy for commuting parents. A number of after-school clubs and a late stay facility assists parents until 5.30pm.

Entrance: Entrance assessment and interview for all pupils – looking above all for potential.

Exit: Now takes boys as well as girls into the senior school, and will gradually become co-ed throughout. Most pupils leave after sixth form, with some leaving directly after Highers in S5. Gap years for some post-Higher; 95 per cent go on to university, usually in Scotland, though a few head down south. More now staying on for S6 and Advanced Highers. Selection of degree courses including law, medicine, dentistry, plus some traditional academics and business – impressive for a small school.

Money matters: Financial assistance is available and always means-tested. Chair and deputy chair of the board of governors review bursary provision.

Remarks: Still a school serving a very specific Catholic heartland population, but will accept pupils of all faiths – strong moral values. Ideal, of course, for a wide range of children needing small, loving and caring environment with the benefit of a strong religious backbone, but this is an academic and adventurous school with 'some pretty lively pupils and a fantastically committed staff'. Difficult to find – one of Glasgow's well-kept secrets. To which this editor can only add the recession has not been kind..

Fettes College

Carrington Road, Edinburgh EH4 1QX

Pupils: 763; 475 full boarders • Ages: 7–18 • Sixth form: 248

Fees: Day £14,970 – £25,545; Boarding £23,385 – £32,340 pa

Tel: 01313 116744
Email: admissions@fettes.com
Website: www.fettes.com

Headmaster: Since 1998, Mr Michael C B Spens MA (60s), educated at Marlborough and Selwyn College Cambridge, where he read natural sciences. Came to Fettes after five years as head of Caldicott, having previously spent 20 years at Radley, where he was housemaster and taught geology, after a short spell in business. The transition between junior and senior schools is always an interesting one, but Mr Spens has weathered his double change with charm and élan – one might say nonchalance, but that would be harsh, and misleading; quarter is not easily found here: there is a tightly-wound spring beneath the cultivated appearance of charm and relaxation. Expect zero tolerance on the drugs front, 'The students don't want it around', and the Fettesian druggy alcy image no longer makes headlines in the Scottish press. Fettes is challenging all-comers as Scotland's school of choice, surprisingly, even on the day front, 'And we're more expensive than the others,' says the head – but then we are talking Edinburgh (think mink and nae knickers). Married to Debbie, they have three young children (one at Fettes, one on a gap year and one at university) and a much-loved labrador ('Kiwi, because she's all black'). Charismatic, vibrant, fun. Fettes and Mr Spens are zinging. Currently forefront of the campaign to keep Scottish independent schools' charitable status and all over the Sunday papers.

Leaving in July 2017. His successor will be Geoffrey Stanford, currently deputy head at Sevenoaks. Classics degree from Oxford, captain in the Grenadier Guards and worked in the City before joining Millfield to teach economics, business studies and Latin. Has also been boarding housemaster and head of department at Pangbourne. He has rowed for Eton, Sandhurst and the British Army at Henley, completed the Marathon des Sables and Devizes to Westminster canoe race, and taken part in a succession of expeditions to the Himalayas, including leading an international team to the summit of Mount Everest. He also enjoys playing the French horn. He is married to Susanna and they have two young sons.

Head of prep school: Since 2003, Mr A A Edwards BA London (mid-40s). Formerly a housemaster at Gresham's School, Norfolk. Married to Jill; three sons and one young daughter. A history graduate and a talented sportsman.

Academic matters: Prep school has tiny classes, excellent remedial, super facilities and plumb in the centre of Edinburgh. Latin early, computers everywhere.

Almost all senior school heads of departments have changed during the past few years – 'new young staff', 'very good', 'strong', 'Edinburgh is a strong draw'; and, having played the Scottish versus the English system along with all the other big players, added the IB in 2006. Pupils can choose whether they want to specialise, therefore do A levels (2016: 74 per cent A*-B, 46 per cent A*/A), or take the broader IB syllabus: excellent results – average score 37. At GCSE, 73 per cent A*/A grades.

Three sciences on offer throughout, plus trad French, German and Spanish, as well as Mandarin (available for beginners as well as for native speakers). No particular bias – physics, chemistry, history and geography outstanding at GCSE level, maths and English almost equally strong; results in all disciplines equally impressive at A level. Art results outstanding throughout the school. Tranche of outstanding French GCSEs taken early. Strong tradition of classics; government and politics and history of art available at A level. Broad range of subjects, but not the biggest take up at A level in langs, classics or further maths.

Foreign pupils with minimal English are no longer accepted willy-nilly, unless they happen to be particularly bright or have siblings in the school. EFL is on hand, but pupils who don't have 'a pretty good working knowledge of English' are encouraged to do an English lang course before they arrive (Edinburgh School of English is popular).

Good staff:pupil ratio. 'Computers zooming ahead' – wireless networked throughout, with all senior school students having their own laptop.

Games, options, the arts: Wide range of opportunity for games. 'Rugby is strong, though no longer a religion' (73 blues to date). Needle matches with Glenalmond and Merchiston on the rugby field and Strathallan in hockey. Lacrosse impressive, girls play hockey and netball as well; sixth form not forced to play team games at all – 20+ other sports including swimming and aerobics also available. Big sports centre and swimming pool providing a wide range of other sports, old pool now an exam hall/ceilidh and disco area.

Music 'a huge strength' with loads of bands, orchestras, three choirs and a string quartet etc etc, two popular concerts in spring and autumn plus carol service all in aid of charity. Keen drama with imaginative productions, pupils often perform at the Edinburgh Festival (and win awards). Frankenstein the most recent production with over 100 pupils involved. New art centre in pipeline (still) and 'very inspirational head of art' (another one, if you follow) recently appointed. Pipe band popular. CCF, community service, D of E etc. Masses of trips, everywhere, for everything.

Boarding: Two prep school and eight senior school houses, all single sex, for day and boarding pupils, with tutors attached. New posho boarding house – Craigleith, dead modern – to accommodate the expanded sixth form, which is due to increase by 25 per cent. The sixth form centre houses 125 upper sixth pupils in two identical wings (surely this should be 126 or 124?) each with their own individual room and provides a transition between the disciplines of school and uni with pupils being able to cook their own meals if they want to.

Background and atmosphere: William Fettes (later Sir William), the son of an Edinburgh grocer, made his fortune during the Napoleonic Wars when 'he became Scotland's leading contractor for provisions for the army'; his only son died in 1815, and William in 1836. Whilst he had originally intended to found a hospital, he later 'decided to create a school for orphans and the needy'; and – after prudent investment – the trustees decided that with £166,000 in the kitty, there were enough funds to acquire land, and both build and endow a school: Fettes opened in 1870 with 200 boys.

Vast Grimms' fairy tale of a building, turreted and with acres of wood panelling and shiny black floors (are they granite or stone flag underneath the tarry surface?) purpose-built in 1870 by Bryce. Part of the main building still has the original steam-driven heating which starts up twice a day with alarming groans and wheezes – ripe for the engineering museum, methinks.

Various Victorian edifices scattered about the school's wonderful 90 acre grounds plonk in the middle of Edinburgh. 'School uses Edinburgh much more now,' says the head. Spectacular development after school sold 'redundant' acres to build Fettes Village, a collection of neat little boxes which splits the games field and provided the cash for much-needed expansion. The collection of new and converted buildings that house the prep department are much bigger than they look from the outside, an example of space well used, and about to be extended. Currently in process of building Fettes North – new block that will house 25 classrooms plus music school, art school, history of art building and sixth form studio and workshop.

The school has gradually metamorphosed from famous trad boys' school to genuinely co-ed. The flavour has changed from home-grown Scots to more exotic (school says '75 per cent UK, 15 per cent British expats, 10 per cent foreign nationals with over 40 countries represented in this').

Pastoral care, well-being and discipline: Despite colourful stories in the Edinburgh press in past years – drugs, booze, etc, grossly overstated, says the head – there is a clear framework of discipline that is well understood by all. This is a school with a zero tolerance policy on drugs. Edinburgh is the drugs capital of the north and running a school in the middle of it is no joke. Under-age drinking is an acknowledged problem. Three tier system on the discipline side: housemaster/deputy head/head = rustication/formal warning and suspension or expulsion. Ditto smoking. Very clear house-visiting rules – no overt demonstrations of affection; bonking equals out. And yes, they do lose the occasional pupil for all these misdemeanours, ditto bullying. Strong anti-bullying ethos. Prefects very responsible – imaginative anti-bullying code involves culprits writing down what they must or must not do and signing it. Expulsion is always an option.

Pupils and parents: School topped up with many non-Brits in the old days, now the mix is veering more towards the British norm but still collections of internationals – Russians, Chinese, Japanese, Americans, Ukrainians, but fewer Bulgarians than previously. Increasing numbers of locals and Scots from all over. 'Pupils from 40 different countries, East European connection sadly dropping off.' Very strong old Fettesian stream, plus loads of first-time buyers, intellectuals etc etc. Good vibrant mix. Old Fettesians include John de Chastelaine, Ian McLeod, James Bond, Tilda Swinton, Lord Woolf and Tony Blair – remembered fondly for 'his acting ability'.

Entrance: To prep by assessment test and interview.

CE or school's own exam to senior school for those not coming from UK preps. Approx 40 students a year join the sixth form after GCSE elsewhere, currently much sought after as pupils pile in from other, mainly Scottish, schools.

Exit: Virtually all juniors to senior school – internally set exam for entry. Hardly any leave post-GCSE. Most to university – Aberdeen, Durham, Edinburgh, Exeter, Glasgow, King's College London, Manchester, Newcastle, St Andrews, Warwick to study eg engineering, English, maths or law. Five to Oxbridge in 2016, plus three medics and two vets.

Money matters: Well-endowed with scholarships including academic, music, sports, all-rounder, piping, art, up to 10 per cent of fees. Also means-tested bursaries: 'The level of these awards depend upon parents' financial means and can cover up to the full value of the fees'.

Special (Todd) bursaries for Old Fettesians, 12.5 per cent discount for Forces (not so many of these around). However risks being stripped of charitable status by the Scottish Charity Regulator if it does not make fees more affordable for lower income families.

Remarks: Undoubtedly the strongest school in Edinburgh – possibly riding too high? To quote one governor, 'It is better to have a challenge, otherwise we become complacent'. Head adds, 'No danger of becoming complacent; the most dangerous thing in a school is to stand still.' Exciting cosmopolitan mix in an exciting city.

George Heriot's School

Lauriston Place, Edinburgh EH3 9EQ

Pupils: 1,645 • Ages: 4–18 • Sixth form: 370

Fees: £7,737 – £11,604 pa

Tel: 01312 297263
Email: admissions@george-heriots.com
Website: www.george-heriots.com

Principal: Since 2014, Cameron Wyllie (50s) MA PGCE, Dip Ed. Wyllie joined Heriot's from Daniel Stewart's and Melville College in 1991, as head of English, and was head of senior school from 2002: a shoo-in, he was here as a boy and we couldn't be more pleased. We hate to use the expression 'a safe pair of hands'; but this is precisely what he is. Though, that having been said, the abrupt half term disappearance of previous head seemed to have had no impact on the school (silly appointment in the first place; governors should be shot: possibly too ill-informed and unwieldy a gang). ('Was there a crisis?' 'Didn't notice', said our charming guides). Principal runs Heriot's with a raft of deputies et al; including head of senior school Robert Dickson and Mrs Lesley Franklin, head of junior school, which is further subdivided into Early Years, Middle Primary and Upper Primary. Acknowledged as a serious debating coach: our interview with the principal was more him quizzing me than vice versa, which is unusual for this ed.

He is retiring in December 2017. Junior school head Lesley Franklin, who has worked at the school for over 20 years, will succeed him as principal. German degree from St Andrews and teaching qualification from Reading. Experienced hockey coach. She is married to Angus and they have two daughters, both at the school.

Academic matters: Junior school in three sections: early years encompasses 3-5 years, middle primary 5-8 years and upper primary 8-11.

School follows the Scottish system of National 5s and Highers etc: these still a tad difficult to quantify: recent press hysteria over second maths exam has scared both pupils and parents rotten. Given the broad intake (from nursery up) and the number of subjects on offer, you can't fault the place. Vague about results: 97 per cent A-C at Highers and 96 per cent at Advanced Highers in 2016 but no more details. Maximum class size 26, 'but usually much fewer'. Classes streamed early, set for maths age 9; and English from 11. Steeped in 'Euro-awareness', a sort of Euro-starter course at 8, with either French, German or Spanish at 10. A second language can be taken at 13.

Finely-tuned support for learning, but limited in the amount of help they can give – will not take children with statement of needs except in 'exceptional circumstances', but any child with a suspected problem is seen by the support for learning department, which then swings into action. Both withdrawn and team teaching on hand, either individual or in small groups. School will bear the cost of extra lessons and may, in certain circumstances, cover the cost of an outside educational psychologist – they have their own, who is free. Can cope with ADD/ADHD up to a certain degree – 'We would consult with parents to see how their children might be best served'. Remedial help throughout: seamless across the departments/junior/senior school. EFL lessons available. Computers all over the shop, loads of new suites.

Occasional education speak jargon – 'learning enhancement' – but basically trad tried teaching methods absorbing all mods and cons. Books and paper rather than online for all. Each pupil has a dedicated tutor who usually stays with them throughout the school, plus rolling guidance system.

Games, options, the arts: This is a games school; some 32 different sports offered. Rugby: school boasts many caps. Girls' hockey, football (girls and boys), riding, orienteering and tennis very powerful; basketball and athletics increasingly good; games played at Goldenacre, along with all the other Edinburgh schools mafia; FPs use the pitches too. Pupils bussed across Edinburgh, cross-country running and rowing are favourite alternative sports – the school has a boathouse on the canal. Badminton in the frame, plus fencing and very good swimming (though not their own pool). New sports complex (Energy Zone), deep down in the Grassmarket itself, knocks spots of most we have seen. Brilliant conversion in the bowels of the former art school: must have cost a bomb and been hell to get through Edinburgh planning boys (locals have access) but wowser. Gym with every bell and whistle – permission needed before using, and seriously lofty sports hall, with automatic ventilation, connected but not linked – if you follow – into a dance studio where a group was practising The Gay Gordons, described by our guides as Ceilidh Dancing which is a new one to this Scottish country dance fiend. Sports hall and dance studio snug against the wall of Greyfriars Kirk (home of the faithful Bobby).

Drama now timetabled and taken at both national and higher levels. Head of music has done wonders for this department – choirs as well as a variety of chamber and other orchestras. Electronic music a recent addition. Pipe band. CCF optional.

Art streaking ahead – stunning and diverse department: A level art (broader course and much cherished) offered post Highers, and photography now to Higher level. Is there nothing this school doesn't do? Triple art period on the go during our visit, supposed to be photography, but certain amount of impressive felting etc and fabric design, plastic design, in fact design in general out of this world.

Sixth year does voluntary service, working in the nursery, helping with lower primary pupils and outside placements, eg the outpatients at the Astley Ainslie – dementia/stroke patients, that kind of thing.

Massive school mag, so heavy that it burst out of the envelope it was sent in, and arrived chez this ed in a GPO poly bag.

Background and atmosphere: George Heriot, jeweller to King James the VI (and I), who had started business life in a booth by St Giles, left the princely sum of £23,625 'for the building of a hospital' (ie a charity school) on a 'site at the foot of Gray's Close', for boys whose fathers had died. Fabulous ogee curved-roofed towers; the place was first inhabited by Cromwell in 1650 and, whilst principally designed by William Wallace, this magical inner-city school can boast of almost every important 17th century Scottish architect – finishing with the court favourite, Robert Mylne (and the inspiration for Hogwarts). Claims to be the longest-inhabited school building in Scotland. Magnificent Pugin chapel revamped by James Gillespie Graham in 1837; pupils still sit on backless benches. A rather snazzy library in the lower half of a hall has been disastrously (school rejects this epithet – not surprisingly) split in two to provide a concert hall above. While all schools are perennially short on space, this is the most blatant piece of architectural sacrilege we have come across.

Alas, Founder's Day no longer celebrated with 'buskins' (garlands) round the founder's statue on June Day: 'Ealth and Safety intervened and the ceremony in main courtyard has now been kicked outside, though placements (the 180 registration marks) are still visible in the quadrangle.

The foundation was feudal superior of great tracts of Edinburgh, and had close links with Donaldson's hospital for the deaf – now moved to Linlithgow. Certain amount of confusion about the future of the former Donaldson's site, which has lain dormant for many years. Heriot's after-school club was held there daily, now known as wrap-around care; it is based on main campus.

The hospital became a school in 1886, changed its name and the 180 foundationers were joined by paying pupils. Boarding was phased out in 1902 and girls admitted in 1979; became fully independent in 1985. FPs are known as Herioters.

Inner city school, manicured lawns, this year celebrating the bravery of those Herioters who were killed in the First World War: 20 on the same day in Gallipoli.

Fantastic views of Edinburgh Castle; future plans for the site include expansion of the music facilities. Terrific new build ahead (couple of terrapins/temporary buildings still around, for P6 and art – pupils love them because 'they are warm'). Uniform for all, different ties for prefects and sixth. Trips all over the shop in every discipline.

The sixth form café, which abuts the tiered auditorium (Powerpoint higher chemistry presentation in action given by dishy head of chem), uses Starbucks-type mugs, and there were a fair quantity perched on unoccupied benches.

The junior school is spread throughout the campus and the mixing of senior and junior pupils is a real strength. Early years in dedicated nursery and Greyfriars Buildings with rows of tiny wellies. Their dedicated play area has bungy tarmac surface, 'ealth and safety' again, but badly prone to puddling. Middle primary, with whom we played a complicated game of stone, paper, scissors and ended up by giving a seminar on the correct way to pass scissors, is mainly based in the north east corner of the campus.

Pastoral care, well-being and discipline: Code of conduct equals school's rules, which parents and pupils have to sign, based on 'personal safety, safety for others and respect for others, property and the environment'. Ladder of sanctions. Good guidance team who are proactive in reducing tension; both sides must face up to an issue. Persistent misbehaviour, and not responding, equals out; detentions and discussions with parents more normal. Occasional suspensions, no real problems with drugs, alcohol and cigarettes. Concern if school work suffers, no random drugs tests. Church of Scotland chaplain; school uses Greyfriars Kirk (of Bobby fame) for services.

School opens from 8am, with late model Range Rovers fouling up the traffic as they drop their little darlings at Potter Row. Bike racks for cycling pupils. Only early years' parents can drop of within school campus.

Pupils and parents: Sturdy middle class lot, 25 per cent based in Edinburgh-average ethic (school says, 'we cover a social range far greater than the average private school', but not that Brideshead). Thriving parents' association. Recent (rather grand) parent who was moved job-wise to Edinburgh, couldn't praise the place enough. Son was struggling with maths in his previous school and tipped up after one term as head of class determined to make maths his career. They were over the moon.

G

Entrance: Nursery is first come first served; juniors by group and individual assessment. English,maths and reasoning tests for entry to primary 6 and 7.Tests (English, maths, VRQ, NVRQ) plus interview at primary and senior level, including from own junior school; though not from JS to SS; predicted grades for pupils joining post-National 5s.

Exit: Nearly all juniors move up to senior school. Four to Oxbridge in 2016, otherwise about three-quarters to Scottish universities plus eg Exeter, York and Newcastle. Lawyers, medics (six in 2016), engineers, techies etc.

Money matters: Felt the loss of assisted places keenly but is pretty well back up to speed. Foundation still provides 100 per cent bursary for 'children of primary or secondary school age, who are resident in Edinburgh or the Lothians, whose father has died and whose mother might not otherwise afford the cost of private education'. Raft of other bursaries and scholarships, will keep children in place during financial crisis.

Remarks: Thunderingly good inner-city school in a spectacular position, doing what it does do well.

George Watson's College

67–71 Colinton Road, Edinburgh EH10 5EG

Pupils: 2,281 • Ages: 3–18 • Sixth form: 235

Fees: £7,461 – £11,577 pa

Tel: 01314 466000
Email: admissions@gwc.org.uk
Website: www.gwc.org.uk

Principal: Since 2014, Mr Melvyn Roffe BA FRSA (mid 40s). Read English at York, studied education at Durham, came from Wymondham College in Norfolk; previously worked in both maintained and independent sector, married with a son and daughter.

Head of senior school: Since September 2016, Gordon Boyd, previously assistant director, education at Norfolk County Council. Edinburgh born and bred, he studied English at Aberdeen and did his teacher training at Cambridge before going to Zambia with VSO. Experience in a variety of schools culminated in a headship at City of Norwich School. He is married to Helen and they have three children. He enjoys swimming, skiing and running half marathons, among other interests.

Head of junior school: Since December 2016, Mr George Salmond. Well known to the Watson's Family, George is a graduate of the Northern College of Education in Dundee. He joined the school in 1995 as a Primary 5 class teacher and has developed his career through a variety of teaching and leadership roles at Watson's.

Less known to some would be that George won 146 caps playing cricket for Scotland – 104 as captain – and until this year was a Grade One Referee officiating at over 50 Premier League matches and a cup final at Hampden Park.

Academic matters: The nursery is charming. It is also enormous. Three parallel classes with over 30 children in each. But jolly none the less, with all the bells and whistles you expect from toddler teaching. Play areas, sand pits, water, tiny tables and dedicated play area outside. Learning begins through play in nursery. Pre-school year only, partnership scheme. Wrap around care (Nursery Plus at new Myreside House) available drop off 7.45am collect 6.00pm (same as junior school). Nursery Plus open throughout the year, except for two weeks at Christmas. In view of previous head's embargo this ed visited the junior school during a recent open morning, and was met by a raft of charming and caring nursery staff: had we been accompanied we would have been allowed to try out various games and had great fun.

Five parallel mixed ability classes of 25/30 in the junior school, based in colour coded suites of rooms: purple, beige, yellow, green and blue for the first three years. Each interlinking room has its own suite, friendly and not the least bit intimidating (though possibly a bit confusing to start with). French from age 7 with native speakers. Pupils remain in these groups, with the occasional odd one or two added if space available and that ain't often the case. Jolly Phonics, look 'n' say, dual teaching in class where necessary, Watsons is the school for SEN hiccups. Special catch-up classes run for any latecomers. ICT skills taught and used widely to support other subjects. Back up for maths too. Dedicated library, where the librarian seemed totally fazed by our questions. We had a charming young guide who seemed as pleased as punch to revisit her former classrooms.

Age 9 (P4) all move to upper primary, a barracks of a child education building. Rows of bleak corridors with classrooms on either side and more staircases up and down than one could imagine. Dedicated science lab with explosive experiments with Alkaseltzer and a plastic screw top container ongoing in the passage outside. Safety glasses and a fair risk of failure seemed the order of the day. Mixed-ability groups with setting only for maths at the top end of the school. Extensive library, plus audio books with a raft of headphones so all can listen at the same time, a respite from the non-stimulation – okay, odd bits of art – of the corridors. Tame librarian. Our guide thought class sizes were 25/30 and 'two classes were divided into three' for practical subjects. Good dyslexia support throughout – anxious to get away from any image of having 'a school with a unit'. SEN drop in centres abound, and plethora of assistants and trainee teachers. Sixth formers help with reading too.

Academically, a highly successful senior school and also groundbreaking in that it offers the IB, as well as Scottish Highers and Advanced Highers, with the odd A level (music and art) thrown in. The only Scottish school offering this particular combination. At S3/4 Watson's is still offering Intermediate 2, having rejected the new Curriculum For Excellence's National Level structure on the basis that it does not give a sufficiently strong foundation for further study, sacrificing depth to breadth.

School points out that Watson's curriculum for S1 and 2 is certainly broad and gives access to further study in two languages and three sciences. French, German or Spanish or Chinese from S1, plus Latin for all in S2. Sciences are studied in rotation with chemistry and technology in S1 and biology and physics in S2. As well as the usual suspects, economics, business studies, religion and philosophy, health and food tech, plus PE and games, are all fitted in by means of a cunning seven-day cycle – forget the day of the week, just remember today's number! Setting in maths and English for S1 and languages from S2 but otherwise largish classes of 25, with 20 for practical subjects. All pupils study maths, English and a language as exam courses, with a wide choice for the further eight they can take.

The IB students have to commit from the beginning of S5, as it is a two-year course – six subjects, three at each of two levels roughly equivalent to Higher and Advanced Higher, plus a big theory of knowledge course with an extended essay and time allocated to creative things and service. School says it attracts the polymaths, and not necessarily all the brightest. At IB the average point score was 34 in 2016. At Advanced Highers, 79 per cent A/B grades, at Highers, S5s got 73 per cent A/B grades and S6 got 60 per cent. Pupils certainly feel they do well and offers were pouring in from up-market universities at the time of our visit. Our two prospective medic guides were waiting anxiously as medic offers usually come in last.

Strong maths department with masses of Higher and Advanced Higher takers. Max class size 25 but 20 (as ever) for practical subjects. Fantastic technology centre devoted almost entirely to electronics. Phalanx of up-to-date labs for all three sciences (taken seriously to the extent that there is only straight biology, no human or social options). Provision of every sort of educational IT goes without saying. Trad langs: French, German, Spanish and Italian, plus huge Mandarin following, Russian if required (but no automatic 'catering' for ethnic langs). Lashings of exchanges and native speaking assistants. Help available ESOL for non-native English speakers.

George Watson's has been instrumental in the development of SEN in Scotland and retains its excellent reputation. It is 'not selective' by ethos and prides itself on identifying potential problems (has its own educational psychologist). Drop-in centre caters for the brightest as well as those who need oodles of help, or just a short sharp explanation with some bothersome subject. Heads of special needs in both junior and senior schools, plus assistants in class (usually in junior school) and either one-to-one or group sessions. No charge. One of a few schools to teach study skills throughout the school; literacy skills on offer when needed. Sixth formers with good Higher passes help out and also scribe. Help too, from scores of parent volunteers who – amongst other activities – record text onto tapes.

Careers advice starts from 15 upwards, beginning with the usual Morrisby testing used by independent schools (pupils thought it was quite helpful) to help make informed choices when deciding on five or six subjects from the choice of 26. Extension modules and additional subjects available for the last year. Classics and classical civilisation, media studies a sixth form option. Frequent professional development training for all staff throughout the school.

Games, options, the arts: Rightly famed as a rugby school, this is an ambitiously sporting place. The pool (complete with redundant but historic chimney) and one sports hall have recently reopened after a lengthy renewal programme and there are copious further facilities. Watson's runs the Galleon sports club, open to other organisations as well as the school and local community, complete with dining and accoutrements at the Myreside pavilion as well as every kind of sporting venue. A plethora of sports clubs of just about everything you could think up, for both primary and secondary, with list of successes at all levels for the standard school sports, football, hockey etc and a swathe of other activities. Rowing, for instance, achieved European medal status. The Galleon offers extensive and exciting holiday clubs and activities, supplementing all year round and after-school care.

Both senior and junior World Pipe and Drum Champions recently with pipe teams touring Japan. Unrivalled choice from about 80 clubs and societies: 20 sports clubs, four orchestras, three bands, musical ensembles and several choirs, plus organised games, strong drama and no lack of engineering etc, with teams building and racing their own Formula cars. Something for absolutely everyone. Impressive and extensive art department. School trips abound at home and abroad. Popular third year 12 day project which, our guides said, had been a seminal experience and terrific bonding with contemporaries. This backpacking marathon, which tests staff and parents as well as pupils, is currently celebrating 50 years of expeditions by attempting to bag all 283 Scottish Munros – only 24 left to go at time of writing.

In yer face drama and music in junior school – four choirs, two recorder groups, chamber orchestra, ensembles and pipes. Oodles of extra activities and clubs. Primary pupils have full use of all senior facilities with hockey for girls, rugby for boys (only) and swimming for all.

Background and atmosphere: George Watson, merchant and financier, left a legacy of 12 grand in 1723 to provide 'post-primary boarding education' to the 'children and grandchildren of decayed Merchants of Edinburgh and of the Ministers of the Old Church thereof,' with a preference for those with the surname Davidson or Watson. School opened in 1741, operating under the aegis of the Merchant Company until the mid 1980s, having moved to current site in 1932 (after a period in the wilderness) and amalgamating with George Watson's Ladies College in 1974.

A splendid and impressive façade, so extensive that the Pentagon or Hermitage spring to mind, charmingly softened by trees and sweeping lawns/games fields. H-shaped listed building, unashamedly institutional with acres of shiny floors, wide corridors and polished oak. The enormous school hall forms the link between the long two-storied runs of classrooms etc at front and back. Breaktime confronts visitors with battalions of teenagers, all remarkably welcoming and relaxed. The easy rapport between staff and pupils is noticeable, despite the impossibility of knowing everyone with such large numbers.

Vast 50-acre campus includes variety of pitches, plus art, junior and nursery schools in a somewhat random selection of architecture. Huge dining hall operates a swipe card system for pupils from P4 up. Parents can top these up on-line via their credit cards; school provides packed lunches or hot/cold menu which is published on their website, though only for pupils and parents. Like Watson's itself, the website is of such a scale that it isn't always easy to find what you want.

Pastoral care, well-being and discipline: Oddly, pastoral care does not feature at all on the school website, nor can one find the policy statements that most schools put out. What is there and is evidently effective and respected is a seven-point school charter devised by pupils.

The ethos of respect for others means, in practice, our guides explained, that fighting is not tolerated and seldom happens, ditto bullying. A tried and tested system manages this huge school, with two year heads per year group following pupils all the way through the school. First year pupils keep the same form teacher for two years; the next three years follow suit and pupils then choose their tutor.

Sixth formers are actively involved throughout the school. Strong anti-bullying policy, parents immediately informed and

G

consulted if child is involved, and are apparently impressed by the help given in difficult situations. Detentions plentiful, but expulsion rare. Regular training for specialist guidance staff who help with listening and advising.

Pupils and parents: Popular (in the trad sense of the word) Edinbourgeoisie, wannabes and incomers taking for granted that it is Edinburgh's top school. Pupils certainly appear motivated and purposeful. Very much a local school, though some travel quite a distance – buses from East, Mid and West Lothian. Boarding now defunct. Strong PA with bags of fundraising functions etc.

Former pupils include Sir David Steel (The Right Hon Lord Steel of Aikwood), Sir Malcolm Rifkind, Sir Chris Hoy, former Scottish rugby internationals Gavin and Scott Hastings, broadcasters Sheena McDonald and Martha Kearney and eco-sculptor Angela Palmer. Older generations may be more impressed by Sir Basil Spence, Rebecca West, Martin Bell and Sir Eric Anderson, previously provost of Eton.

G

Entrance: Nursery from age 3. Early entries up to primary 3 by interview, takes about an hour. From primary 4 upwards entry is by written test and interview. Interviews in December: lang, maths and verbal reason, plus a spot of writing. Main entry to college is P7 (age 12) when four classes become five and pupils hoping to go on to the senior school get a useful boost. Around three-quarters of senior entrants have come from junior school. Assessment before entry at all levels; where places are in short supply, academic achievement and presence of siblings already in school both count. Entry at 12 and upwards is by selection where vacancies arise, taking maths, English and verbal reasoning papers along with interview. Waiting lists at some stages. Fresh blood post Standard grades (more come than leave). The introduction of the IB means there are a few more places available for S5 as these courses are not quite full.

Exit: No guarantee of advancement from nursery to main primary school but, once in, virtually all go on to senior school, unless family circumstances dictate otherwise. Around 98 per cent stay on after Highers for further studies, choosing either the SQA or IB routes. Well over 90 per cent go on to higher education. Over 80 per cent go on to Scottish universities, with Glasgow, Aberdeen, Edinburgh, Heriot-Watt, Dundee and Strathclyde popular in 2016.

Money matters: George Watson's Family Foundation: primarily for 10/11 year olds, though awards available in junior school and current pupils 'may apply for short-term help at any stage.' Means-tested. Will keep a pupil to the next public exam in extenuating circs, plus extra help for those with a 'recognised learning disability.' A range of up to 11 academic and two music scholarships each year: 25 per cent. Sports bursaries, Enablement Fund and the school is part of the Ogden Trust Science Scholarship Scheme. Numerous short-term or long-term bursaries for those in need; with assistance for more than 120 pupils. In 1997 the school's own foundation was established to further the original Watson credo and has recently funded the new music school extension, the GWC Centre for Sport and a lift for disabled students. Fees can be paid monthly by direct debit.

Remarks: Something of a Leviathan and definitely all things to all pupils and parents, with a distinguished and deserved reputation. Communication with parents and pupils said to be effective and every pupil treated as an individual. Big is beautiful in that very few schools can offer quite such a diversity of experience and opportunity in and out of the classroom. Size has also meant that it is groundbreaking in educational areas such as SEN and the IB.

The Glasgow Academy

Colebrooke Street, Glasgow G12 8HE

Pupils: 1,250 • Ages: 3–18 • Sixth form: 105

Fees: £3,876 – £11,787 pa

Tel: 01413 425494
Email: exrel@tga.org.uk
Website: www.theglasgowacademy.org.uk

Rector: Since 2005, Mr Peter Brodie MA (Oxon), PGCE (50s). Educated at Abingdon, with a masters in English from St John's, Oxford, followed by a PGCE at Oxford and a (later) masters in education management (part-time) at Canterbury Christ Church University College. 'A good intellectual training exercise,' he told us. He came from King's Canterbury. 'Let's not talk about me, let's talk about the school. I haven't changed.' But boy, the school has 'improved and moved forward.' An inspired appointment, he runs the school with a senior management team (OK, yawn, yawn) but Brodie spreads his net wide. The new deputy rector comes from Buenos Aires and the next is coming from Oakham, neither of which is next door.

Efficient chain of command, with a can do, will do approach. 'Peter comes up with ideas, and leaves us to get on with it,' say staff. Mass of new staff, but one or two older ones still in situ so 'good mix in staff room.' Encourages staff to do further training. Our chauffeur to the Milngavie site was doing a school-sponsored masters in education.

He is also dead efficient. As we said last time, he is the only head who, when faced with a barrage of questions to which he did not instantly know the answer, left detailed info for us to collect with the rest of the bumf from his office. This time he pre-empted us, and we left with a couple of trees' worth of facts and spread sheets, including all the exam data and a jolly CD plus an earlier GSG print out neatly annotated in green biro. Chalk is in the blood – his father was a headmaster and his mother taught PE.

Bubbly, enthusiastic and fun. Keen on teaching with the 'wow' factor and passionate about 'encouraging children to make the most of the opportunities school can provide.' Brodie believes strongly that 'a culture of high expectations combined with good pastoral care helps children grow in confidence and achievement.' Quite. Sees every pupil each year with 'three bits of work, selected by themselves,' and whilst he finds himself bamboozled by the computer programmes with which he is presented by S1 and S2, he adores the mini-films they make. But then, in a previous life, he was the arts festival manager, and produced numerous plays.

Still potty about postcards, the rector had 2,000-odd printed from the best artwork on his arrival. Several reprints later, he delights in sending pupils cards to congratulate them on any success – a good bit of art, an interesting essay, debating victories (national champs for last two years), sporting achievements, you name it. He has done much to reinforce the house system, appointing oodles of new members of staff, plus eight new heads of houses ('stunning appointments,' he told us).

Head of prep: Since 2007, Mr Anthony (Tony) M Brooke BEd, (50s). Educated at Eastbourne College, followed by University of Southampton. Previously head of Sutton Valence prep, and before that was at Yardley Court (now part of the Somerhill group). Controls this prep conglomerate with the lightest of touches. Leaving in July 2017.

Assistant head, responsible for Milngavie, is Miss Jean McMorran DCE PGDip in leadership and management Dip TEFL, who also rolls out the combined prep money education programme and is a whizzo in the maths world.

Academic matters: All three preps follow roughly the same programme. Romans when we visited, birds the following week. Enthusiastic reading programme. Older children are encouraged to read to younger ones. The school is involved with the Sydney Film School in making a programme about their accelerated reading (Jolly Phonics and Jolly Grammar). French from 7 for all; Milngavie alone does Mandarin. All pupils at Colebrooke and Kelvinbridge use senior school facilities – labs, dining room etc.

Senior school follows Scottish system. Computer suites all over and hot on programming. School is wireless and pupils can email queries and prep to staff. Science labs and lots of add-ons (next step is creation of a dedicated science block with an egg-shaped auditorium, which will hold an entire year or house, and loads of glass-fronted labs and chill out areas). Expansion of numbers (50 more on the books for next year), ditto classrooms means average of 17 in senior school (S1 – S3) with fewer for practical subjects. Minimum class size – one. Sciences, computing studies, and geography strong at National grade, huge numbers doing biology and maths (Intermediate 1 and 2) as well as Highers and Advanced Highers. Maths set in P7/S1. Further maths taken at GCSE – one candidate in 2016, who got A*. English and humanities impressive, with a gratifying take-up in French. Spanish on offer, but not much take up to date; two took Arabic GCSE in 2016 and both got Bs. A number of French/Spanish come for a two-year stint (parents on secondment to Iberdrola, down the road). Native speakers (any language) encouraged to take Highers in their mother tongue. Product design on offer, with variable uptake. Highers: 37 per cent A grades in 2016; Advanced Highers 37 per cent A grades.

Links with both Glasgow and Strathclyde Universities – Italian at the former and lab work at both. A vast and complex sixth form guide details both academic and ancillary courses available. Rector keen to 'raise the academic bar.'

Childcare qualification for sixth formers, who can take the early education and childcare SQA intermediate 2, which includes the REHIS certificate in food hygiene (essential qualification for work in restaurants or commercial kitchens). Trenchant mentoring involving sixth formers, who also help out with the tinies. Home economics popular at sixth form level – part of the life skills course.

Good SEN pickup. Psychological and spatial memory and reasoning for all from P1, and other year groups assessed on a rolling basis. Remedial help on hand, laptops in evidence and extra help in exams. No problems with children with ADHD. Support for learning much in evidence – learning support based in purpose-designed refurbished accommodation, with trained support staff in both senior and prep. Support is mainly lesson-based with teaching assistants, though child will be withdrawn either for one-to-one or small groups if necessary. Drop-in clinics manned by different people each day. No shame in popping in for a quick explanation. Good buddy system, with senior pupils helping out where necessary (slightly more girl mentors as far as the three Rs are concerned). Good dissemination of information. All staff aware of individual teaching strategies for those on the help register. No extra charge for remedial lessons. No problems for the visually challenged – extra large print.

Games, options, the arts: School mag lists a myriad of sporting successes. Sixteen sports, 18 internationalists, Olympian reps, that sort of thing. Individual sports too – badminton, rowing (pairs champions). Rugby school (more than 100 former pupils have won Scotland caps). Four playing field areas with Astroturf, floodlights, some hundreds of metres apart from each other at Anniesland (the home of many Glasgow independent schools' playing fields). Plus an all-weather pitch in the middle of the campus. Recently acquired extra ground from Jordanhill – bought a bit and share a bit. Hockey, cricket, footie, athletics, as well as tennis. Games are important here – zillions of inter-house competitions as well as inter-school matches. Rugby and hockey tours.

Masses of inter-house activities at lunchtime – '10 ways to win points for your house.' Outstanding pipe band, with lots of exposure – duty band at Murrayfield for a Scotland vs England match, Kelvinhall etc. CCF non-compulsory but still popular. D of E – trillions of golds. Trips almost everywhere, in every dimension (art as well as skiing). New dedicated expedition leader organises outdoor activities, weekend expos: rock climbing on the Costa Blanca, mountaineering in the windy north of Scotland (scary photograph in mag). Language trips all over. The rector feels a real need to get the Glasgow young out of their cosy environment and see the big bad world outside.

Music is strong, with choirs for all, orchestra, string, wind band and various ensemble. Concerts back on form and dynamic head of music is spearheading musical resurgence. More than 500 individual music lessons a week, from harp to clarsach. Twenty-three visiting music staff. Recorder for all aged 8 and 9, plus keyboard at 10 and 11 (plus drums, guitar and base guitar). Unusually, school prefers the Scottish music exam syllabi. Over 80 musicians to New York recently.

Drama timetabled for past few years (pleasing results). Fiddler on the Roof and Hot Mikado the most recent productions, with West Side Story in the wings.

Spectacular art and stunning art room at the top of Colebrooke Terrace. Pottery, fabric and every conceivable discipline. Strong follow-through to art schools all over. Some of the most imaginative school art we have seen – walls lined with this year's art and not just a conglomerate of previous years' goodies. Again, unusually, school prefers the English exam system for art – 35 per cent A*/As at GCSE in 2016, and one candidate took A level art. Huge number of girls doing design technology, though this may have something to do with the dishy member of staff in charge (still).

Background and atmosphere: School founded as a limited company in 1845 (the oldest fully independent school in Scotland). Reconstituted as a memorial to the 327 staff and pupils killed in the First World War. Merged with Westbourne School for Girls in 1991. Based on the banks of the River Kelvin. The Glasgow underground system is but 100 yards away, and the western end of the M8 a busy quarter of a mile distant. The handsome Glasgow sandstone main building is surrounded by music, humanities and science blocks, with random play areas scattered about. The two-storey computer linked library (The Well) is hub of the school. Pupils study here during their free periods, and can ask for any book or any DVD to be ordered.

The school has extending its campus into Colebrooke Street, where Sanders Centre, with 15 labs, auditorium, food tech dept and much more was recently opened by Lord Strathclyde. To the north, the £6 million prep school curves round the banks of the River Kelvin. It has awesome classrooms and canvas-covered roof top (theatrical/social) space and stunning chrome- studded glass walls over the precipitous drop.

Fifty-minute lunch break is filled with inter-house and club activities and only S6 pupils permitted to leave school grounds. Good assembly (Cargill Hall) and dining hall complex, with vending machines (carefully controlled) and good buffet catering. Pupils have eating cards so parents can check up exactly what their little darlings have been eating. All pupils wear uniform – the senior girls natty in kilts incorporating the Westbourne colours. Five Higher successes entitle pupils to decorate their blazers with a blue ribbon (quite a lot around). Sixth form have a duplex chill-out area on two floors in the old 'writing room.' Serious debating at the Gavel Club. Terrific booklet of information for parents includes info on how to pack/carry your back pack (no more than 15 per cent of your bodyweight), an incredibly detailed clothes list and a code of conduct at sports fixtures for pupils, parents and staff.

All three prep sites operate a terrific nursery school. Toddlers sport tracksuits, with waterproof trackies for wet weather. Heavily-staffed. Milngavie and Dairsie provide local pre-prep facilities both north and south of the river Clyde, with all youngsters moving to Kelvinbridge aged 9 and joining up with those already there. Terrific child-care facilities. Drop off at Kelvinbridge and Milngavie and Dairsie from 8am, Mini Cool Kids' Club from 3.10pm to 3.50pm at all three sites, plus after-school care from 3.50pm to 6pm (depends on age of pupil, homework supervision if necessary). Strict rules for collection at the end of the day, including passwords and fines.

Pastoral care, well-being and discipline: Senior pupils are allocated one of four houses, through which much of the extracurricular activity is channelled. Each house has a male and female head, plus PSE and anti-bullying procedure in place. Popular house points system, including debating and music. All pupils advised on Facebook strategy – rector concerned that online grooming is a real threat. Strong chain of command – heads of year and tutors for all (who stay with the pupil throughout their time at school). Each tutor has 11 or 12 tutees whom they see for 'at least' 10 minutes every morning. Good pastoral structure in place and it works. The occasional theft – 'Yes, we're into sin,' said the rector, but no recent problems. Suggestion box – mainly used by first two years of senior school, and dealt with by the depute rector. Positive behaviour committee. School council. School into Fairtrade and very eco-aware. Sixth form gets wide range of lectures from a variety of speakers, including forensic scientists, MSPs, reps from Department for International Development, uni professors and fire brigade. God equals total exposure from a raft of faiths – pupils actively encouraged to contribute to themes for the week. RE is not an exam subject. Hot on charity fundraising. Links with school in New Delhi.

Pupils and parents: The usual Glasgow mafia. Excellent links with the west and M8 conurbations. Good PTA, basically sound middle class. Loads of former pupils' children, plus first time buyers. Buses from further afield. Old pupils include Sir Angus Grossart, Niall Ferguson, Sir Jeremy Isaacs, Lord Vallance, Sir James Barrie, Donald Dewar, Sir John Cargill Flashman creator George MacDonald Fraser and singer Darius Campbell.

Entrance: Many up through nursery via kindergarten. Largely automatic from junior schools – school's own test. Some incomers at sixth form level. They need grade 1 at National level for courses to be studied at Higher level, plus interview with rector or his deputy and department heads. Newbies can arrive at any time assuming space available. Occasional waiting lists.

Exit: Some 'local' parents may simply use the toddler groups and go into the state system, but most go on to junior, followed by senior school. Very occasional pupil may leave at 8 to go to trad prep schools and some may go to junior depts of trad senior schools at 11.

Trickle post Higher, ie at S5, otherwise most stay till S6, either for Advanced Highers or adding to their existing portfolio. Most to university, vast majority Scottish. Oodles of medics. Law popular, ditto business and engineering.

Money matters: The school has worked hard to get comprehensive bursary scheme in place – the hope is that 'financial need should never prevent anyone.' Emergency fund may be available to help with trips. Will certainly keep pupils to next available exam stage.

Remarks: A good solid school, with an exciting and dynamic head moving seamlessly through the 21st century. Well thought out, incredibly useful. Impressive set-up, cradle to grave, can't fault it. Should not be overlooked under any circumstances.

Glenalmond College

Glenalmond, Perth PH1 3RY

Pupils: 380; 330 boarders • Ages: 12–18 • Sixth form: 162

Fees: Day:£16,470 – £21,954; Boarding: £24,147 – £33,840 pa

Tel: 01738 842000
Email: registrar@glenalmondcollege.co.uk
Website: www.glenalmondcollege.co.uk

Warden: Since 2015, Ms Elaine Logan, previously deputy head at Loretto. Born in Perth; read English at Edinburgh; spent 14 years at Dollar Academy before moving to Loretto, where taught English, drama and PSHCE, was a housemistress and recently child protection officer and acting head. A trained singer with a wide range of musical interests and experiences including solo singing in jazz and dance bands, she has three children.

Academic matters: Follows the English system. Only. An astonishing 24 subjects on offer at A level, including ancient history, DT and PE. No current Greek scholars; but Latin-ists, Russian and Dutch candidates and now offers Mandarin. A few of musicians, and, as ever, one taking music technology ('one of the relatively few schools to offer this as an examined subject'). Several presentations in French. Pleasing number of candidates in the usual suspects – maths, English, history, and geography the strongest both in candidates and success, though the odd D creeps in. Economics popular, government and politics available. Computer science at GCSE and A level. Science strong – science and maths block is awkwardly placed on the slope to the north of the main complex and connected at various levels, the traditional build-it-by-numbers confection we see so often, with tubular rails and bog standard three-level classrooms. Some excellent science results, but school still leans towards the arts; religious studies A level equals philosophy and ethics. DT rather the poor relation. Suspect the syllabus may be in a state of change – it can't make sense to present so few candidates in so many subjects in not a very large school, which is what we said last time too. In 2016, 26 per cent A*/A grades at A level and 48 per cent at GCSE.

Setting in the third year – core subjects still set individually, four sets. Loads of class related trips. Recent timetable revision resulted in longer lessons and a fortnightly rotation.

New heads of art, chemistry, English, lang, maths, geography, biology, history of art and learning support; collection of buzzy young staff around, though still one or two who reckon that teaching at Glenalmond is 'a way of life'. Contractually, staff must live on site (now allowed to live off site for three years before retiring), which makes it more difficult to get part-timers.

Two computer suites tick the boxes; internet access in houses (nannynet, intranet, wireless), 10-fold increase in broadband speed. Fibre optics, JANET, two networks throughout school, Apple and PCs, computers in classrooms. Laptops all over the place. Software used to detect fraud with pupils downloading coursework from elsewhere (does it work, we wonder?).

All screened on entry. Dyslexia support represented at meetings of heads of departments. Certified ed psych's report needed for extra time in exams; SENCo and three fully trained dyslexia staff, plus classroom assistant – 'strategies for life as well as time management'; can deal with most of the dys-strata – 'loads of one-to-one lessons', dedicated learning support room. Prep club more or less acts as a drop-in centre for instant help, from prefects as well as contactable tutors ('we can knock on most doors at any time' said one sixth former.)

Originally dubbed the scholars' club, exclusively for scholars and exhibitioners, the William Bright Society (WBS) runs both a lecture series (open to all including parents) and a thinking series – variety of erudite texts: this year by Hobbes, Locke, JJ Rousseau, Paine, Declaration of Independence etc: read, digest, discuss. WBS now attracts a wider base, with nominees from form takers/housemasters (this editor was flattered to be asked but wasn't quite sure she was up for 'induction and pseudoscience'). Additional programmes include long term academic planning, Oxbridge prep, and research programmes with local unis.

Most of the male chauvinists are now a thing of the past (we hope).

Games, options, the arts: Half term letter summer a few years back announced that because of 'ealth and safety considerations, needle rugby matches with Strath and the like were to be abandoned (well, school had lost comprehensively that year 79-0 to Strath, 52-7 to Loretto, and 67-0 to George Watsons). We understood, from a prep source, that the aforementioned schools had been known to 'educate' hefty chaps from the southern hemisphere during the rugby months in the northern hemisphere and vice versa; and that the Strath team weighed more than the Scottish one. Watch this space.

Boys' hockey coming up fast, girls' hockey and lacrosse strong, ditto tennis and netball. Sports are a key part of life here and daily participation is compulsory (the constitutionally disinclined can get by with a spot of umpiring), regular interruption by vile weather. Rich in all-weather, spectacularly floodlit pitches including whizzy new Astro. School majors in outdoor pursuits activities and uses its site to good advantage – all sorts of activities: conservation projects, Munro Club, full-bore shooting as well as clays, indoor and outdoor.22 range, Scottish Islands Peaks Race, skiing with regular trips to freezing Glenshee (a number of past and current members of Scottish ski teams – own artificial ski slope was 'ealth and safety-ed), curling a not too surprising newcomer, own nine hole golf course at Cairnies (golf scholarship), sailing. Several gold D of E assessors on staff – hugely popular option, with trips to Norway and the more rugged parts of the USA. Fishing (on the River Almond).

Terrific CCF (Coll has strong army links) – fifth form CCF (both sexes) now an option but compulsory in fourth form, regular camps throughout term popular ('important to be serious about it,' said our 15 year old guide; 'looks good on your CV, and helps with your D of E'). Oy? We think skool should be fun. Strong emphasis on leadership training: more cadets for officer training from Glenalmond than any other school in Scotland. Granny bashing, or community service, for non-militant sixths. Mass of add-ons: chainsaw course, first aid at work; food hygiene course (essential if you want to work in food industry in the hols). Masses of charitable fundraising: 100 mile sponsored walks. That sort of thing.

Newish head of art has two splendid pics of his own on the wall. OK, early in the year, but we were less than convinced by either the layout of the department, nor the pupil work. Some ceramics to die for. Computer links with the outside world. Life class. Imaginative drama with musicals top of the pops. Recent refurbishment and remodelling of the theatre. Costa coffee shop in theatre foyer (and jolly good it was too).

Strong music assisted by new chapel organ: we just missed choir practice. Resident vicar looks strangely '70s and could do with a haircut. Two pipe bands, which hotshot on the charity front: played at Lords for England/Australia International.

Boarding: This proper boys' boarding school took girls at sixth form in 1990 (last ditch saloon), went 'all the way' in 1995; admissions now running 50/50. Currently five boys' boarding houses and three for girls (45 per cent girls).

New boys' boarding house, Skrines (old one has been converted into learning support centre), one of the smartest houses we have seen in a long time – 'the largest single investment in the school's history' – providing bedroom and communal accommodation that the school claims is 'comparable with the best in Britain'. Decent-sized single rooms and huge four bedrooms for the youngest with good wide corridors – still blighted by the site of the garage.

Architect obviously took his eye off the ball – the showers – nasty plastic sort of triangular things – are rapidly showing signs of wear (well, boys will swing from the shower rails). Ditto the silly islands in the Brew rooms – most now gone. The lighting in the Brew rooms is sensor controlled, which makes television viewing and film nights a health and safety hazard. (Ladders required to baffle the sensors – geddit? Ladder climbing not allowed.)

Fifth form girls (ie GCSE year) move to a previous boys' house, Cairnies (now upgraded), quite distant from the main campus, adjacent to the golf course – same architect. The aforementioned showers, whilst in better heart, are too small for girls to wash their hair in (think about it); they much prefer to use the old fashioned (which school thought had been abandoned) five bath, power shower room in the basement instead.

The double bedrooms are smaller than cabins in steerage on a not very good shipping line – not enough space for a rabbit to work, far less girls studying for their GCSEs, though, in mitigation, it has one of the best common rooms we have seen. We await developments with interest. This had to be the worst million pounds spent anywhere. School maintained 'this is an unreasonable remark, as the overwhelming reaction from girls and their parents to the accommodation in Cairnies' (no bedrooms on the ground floor, bars on ground floor windows, deserted at night! Scary stuff) 'has been wholly positive.' Not from my contacts it ain't, and if it is so powerfully appreciated, why are there plans to turn it vertical?

Boys and girls mix socially during the day and after prep in school, but not in each others' houses, although moves are afoot for each house to have a co-ed common room for limited access. Sixth form bar on Saturdays; Scotland is unique in that sixth formers are allowed access to booze plus grub under 'well monitored circumstances'.

Glenalmond is remote – (school sez 'only an hour from the centre of Edinburgh': this ex-racing driver-trained ed has never done it in that time) and rather set apart from the world – you can't just wander round at will. Shopping bus to Perth twice a week, in house tuck shops, with variable hours. Fixed exeats on either side of half term – 'Parents have free and welcome access to their children at any time and can take them out on Saturdays and Sundays (after chapel)'.

We toured Goodacre's. Pupils graduate from individual tables in prep room – overseen by prefect – to desks in their dorms, and one lucky fourth form dorm had four beds, two showers, two basins and a loo – how's that for ensuite? At age 14? Pupils can use the clothes washing machines when matron doesn't need them (sock bags). Good games/telly room, book case in corner bung full of books, DVDs, games. Housemaster, previously in the real world with Price Waterhouse, has written the seminal IB text book on business and economics, professional tutor with the uni of Buckingham, laments the little uptake he has from pupils who want to study economics and business studies. This is a waste of opportunity and yet school/GSG website indicates that many current students are indeed going down that line.

Background and atmosphere: Known to the pupils as Coll. Founded in 1847 by Prime Minister Gladstone, Scotland's oldest, most elegant school. Spectacular self-contained quad with cloisters, centred on the chapel (with its surprising spiral staircase) set in immaculate 300 acre estate surrounded by some of the smartest grouse shooting in Scotland. Several modern additions stuck round the back, including Basil Spence music block, science and maths block. Gorgeous library (chapel of learning, 'natch), well stocked (real old collection as well as lots of modern stuff) inviting armchairs; media area downstairs. Jemma Pearson bronze of Gladstone. The mixed sixth form common room was crowded, noisy and relaxed.

Informative school prospectus (an earlier prospectus could have been a VisitScotland guide to Perthshire, not at all the sort of thing to impress grannies, who might well end up footing the bill); jolly handy supplement goes into enormous detail. Weekends said to be more organised. Boy and girl joint heads of college, which scares the pants off OGs.

Magical dining room with good buffet hot/cold – we had a delightful chicken tikka. Interestingly, there is a hospital-type antiseptic hand wipe machine at the exit to the dining room; most used it, but shouldn't it have been at the entrance? Apparently there are 'also three at the entrance to the dining hall'; we must have missed them.

Pastoral care, well-being and discipline: Previous high jinks some time ago have resulted in a massively impressive, tightly worded code of behaviour which covers everything from cycling without a helmet to public displays of affection between pupils, as well as extensive drugs etc document – 'Smoking is a major social gateway to the smoking of illegal drugs. The College may regard persistent tobacco smoking as a reason for asking parents and pupils to agree to future drug testing'. These documents are unique in our experience and we are slightly concerned that sometimes alleged offences may be judged in black and white – the HMI boarding report was rather fazed by it too. Pupils and parents 'receive a copy of the Code of Behaviour Expectations, Encouragement and Sanctions'. We didn't.

Basically: random drugs testing on suspicion, out if positive; smoking equals house gating, warden's gating and letters home, followed by suspension. Smoking in a building equals suspension even for the first time. Drinking to excess in permitted zones equals warden's gating, followed by bans and possible suspension, no spirits allowed in the (local) recognized pubs and watering holes. No bringing alcohol back to school under any circumstances. Local keepers still complain about empties and other detritus on the neighbouring grouse moor. (We like a tad of spirit!)

No reported bullying – head of boarding both neutral and approachable. Anorexia said to be less of a problem – couple of girls under watchful eye, but nothing serious. Jury still out on how to deal with cyberbullying (trolling).

Pupils and parents: Scotland's school for toffs – 'Jolly nice parents,' says the school. Traditionally, Scottish upper middle and middle class, army, Highland families. About 20 per cent locals and 21 per cent foreigners from all over, plus seven per cent expats. All real foreigners must have guardians, via parents or contacts, or school will fix 'em up with guardianship agencies 'with whom we have worked successfully in the past'. EAL in place. Number of first time buyers, though trad parents are coming back in handfuls. Girls float daily in tweed jackets and black skirts, and long tartan kiltettes for best; chaps have moved from grey shirts to white, and look a tad like refugees from the local state school with their often outgrown grey bags and blazers. Tweed coats for sixth form only. Full kilt with short tweed jacket for best. Second hand shop.

This is seven day a week boarding; the 50 or so day boys and girls stay to 6pm most nights and 9pm on Wednesdays, Saturday morning school with match play if required in the afternoons; odd bed available. More ecumenical than an Episcopalian foundation might imply – 20 per cent Catholic, who are prepared for confirmation, plus Church of Scotland.

FPs (known as OGs) a generous bunch, include Sandy Gall, Robbie Coltrane, Miles Kington, Allan Massie, David Sole and Andrew MacDonald (Trainspotting fame), Adair Turner (former chairman of FSA) Charlie (Lord) Falconer, erstwhile flatmate of Tony Blair – who was at arch-rival school: Fettes.

Entrance: Own entrance exam at 12, most at 13+ via CE, oodles from Belhaven, Ardvreck, Craigclowan, St Mary's Melrose, Malsis and Aysgarth, with a clutch from Cargilfield, Mowden etc, as well as state primaries or overseas. Entrance not a difficult hurdle at the moment ('academic threshold 50 per cent'). Department heads visit primaries/preps and do 'fun experiments' pour encourager.

Sixth form intake need six passes at national five or GCSE or entrance test and previous school's recommendation; a number from Germany.

Exit: Hardly any leave post GCSEs. Majority to university or some form of higher education – Glasgow, Edinburgh, St Andrews, Bristol, Newcastle popular, ditto Forces. Two to Oxbridge in 2016 and two vets.

Money matters: Discounts for siblings of 25 per cent, a whopping 50 per cent for fourth child, 10 per cent for children whose parents are in the Forces and Fil Cler bursaries for offspring of the clergy. Otherwise myriads of bursaries, means-tested, from five to 100 per cent. Music (including piping), art, sport, plus all round scholarships. Latest wheeze is for individuals to sponsor deserving but needy pupils by direct giving (anonymously).

Remarks: This editor christened Glenalmond 'the Eton of the North' in our first edition: serious glitch caused downturn in numbers, girls were introduced and Glenalmond started regaining momentum. Girls now more confident (complete with rash of pearl earrings and sophisticated make-up) and altogether more girl-like – rather than honorary boys as previously. School says: 'In last HMI inspection, we were rated as excellent for improvements in performance.' Well it would, wouldn't it? We wonder why it took 10 years to turn Glenalmond back into the sort of place non-first time buyers are prepared to boast about.

Gordonstoun

Elgin, Moray IV30 5RF

Pupils: 531; 458 full boarders • Ages: 7–18 • Sixth form: 220

Fees: Day £24,189 – £26,607; Boarding £32,361 – £35,922 pa

Tel: 01343 837837
Email: admissions@gordonstoun.org.uk
Website: www.gordonstoun.org.uk

Principal: Since 2011, Mr Simon Reid BA (50s), a South African who read English at the University of Witwatersrand. Came to Britain in 1985 because he 'wanted to teach English literature in the country where it was written'. Comes from Worksop College where he was deputy head, having started his UK teaching career at Brentwood School, thence Stowe, and Christ's Hospital (housemaster for six years, and whence he will be returning in 2017). His wife, Michele, is French, the family bilingual. Two grown up young.

Enthusiastic about the Round Square ethos, Reid upbraided us when we spouted our usual mantra: please could we have results by subject by number of pupils by results... with a sharp, 'for some pupils a B or a C in any subject is a triumph in itself.' We know, we know academia is not what Gordonstoun is about, but we like to trace trends. By the time they leave, 'Gordonstoun pupils should know about service, face up to challenge, be capable of leading, globally aware, resilient not arrogant', which is fine and dandy as far as it goes. Focus is useful. Perhaps it should be adopted as the sixth Gordonstoun commandment?

Off in July 2017 to head Christ's Hospital. His successor will be Lisa Kerr, currently a strategy and PR consultant to a range of businesses. Music degree from York; has worked as a radio producer and director and ran a group of local radio stations before going on to represent the sector, latterly as director of strategy at RadioCentre, the industry body for UK commercial radio. Set up her own PR agency. She has been a governor at Gordonstoun 2006, and will be its first female principal, as well as, unusually, coming from a business rather than education background.

Titus Edge, currently head of senior school, will become headmaster.

Head of junior school: Mr Robert McVean, BSc (40s), taught science at the junior school from 2000, became its head in 2003. Educated at Hurstpierpoint College, he read environmental biology at Swansea, thence five years in the state sector, followed by Edinburgh Academy. Married to Laura (bubbly and fun; she helps with SEN), two children in the school ('all been huge fun, wouldn't have changed a thing').

Academic matters: 'Students are here for the whole broad experience'; 'The balance is important'. Huge range of ability, from those 'at the lower end of the academic scale', to all A* candidates. 'School getting more academic', says the head. In 2016, 30 per cent A*/A grades at GCSE, 47 per cent A*-B and 26 per cent A*/A at A level. 'What is worth noticing this year is that the highest number of students achieving above their predictions, whether that is at A* level or below. This is far more important than detailed examination results and highlights the distinctiveness of our broad curriculum and ethos'. Native speakers can do A levels in their own langs. Classes setted for maths and English from 13. Networked computers throughout, wireless connection in all boarding houses. Bespoke international citizenship course new kid on the block, Reid takes it at top end: not PSHE or RS but 'examining real problems against a global background'. Good remedial support – all pupils screened on arrival. Will scribe for exams. EAL available at all levels.

Games, options, the arts: Community service is important at Gordonstoun. All do service training aged 16 and choose which discipline to follow: the fire brigade (the most popular), mountain rescue, coastguards, canoe life guards, ski patrol, first aid, technical, marine training and rescue, conservation, pool life guards. Number of exchanges with other Round Square schools – Canada, Germany, Australia. Local projects and joint international expeditions to India, Sinai, Thailand, Kenya, Honduras to work on conservation/ecological schemes. The latter are expensive – students are encouraged to fundraise to meet own costs. Outdoor pursuits expeditions, sleeping in snow holes, add a whole new dimension.

School has its own 80 foot sail-training yacht, Ocean Spirit of Moray, timetabled sailing weeks (when the weather can be 'pretty wild', according to the skippers, ditto the crew). Tall Ships' race a regular feature; school has a new 28 foot training cutter and a rash of new Lasers (which could make for interesting sailing).

Mainstream games on course but long distances to other schools for matches cause problems. Reid says 'school plays locals and rugby league'. New sports hall opened in 2013 by Olympians Heather Stanning and Zara Tindall. Those over 16 can be in charge of swimming pool and do lifeguard training. Outstanding Ogston theatre, new extension, performing arts studio with sprung dance floor. Newest drama studios look stunning. We were shown the previous green room, now a storage area of monumental proportions, in detail; how anyone finds anything in the place goodness only knows. Par hazard, our guide was the daughter of a long time friend; our other guide was a most charming clever-clogs about to hit global mathematical hotspots (from Norfolk, full blown scholarship). A level pupils lead dance workshops in local primaries. Each year group has 'headmaster's reels' of a Saturday, with a caller. Head not yet been known to wear the kilt.

Trips all over – Europe, Australasia, points west. Magnificent art, lots of disciplines, graphic design impressive. Particularly strong DT with pupils learning not only to make lights but also cost them effectively.

Boarding: Houses spread all over, some quite a hike from the main school (you would never guess they were originally army huts). Recent HMI/Care Commission inspection awarded 'excellent' for two out of the five categories and 'very good' in the remaining three. Minimal exeats – distances are huge (even more so for 30 per cent overseas boarders), but pupils often do not want to go home, regular socials (by block on Saturdays), films and formal dinners. This is a school that has to make its own entertainment. Flexi and weekly boarding recently introduced for junior school pupils; an average of 35 or so juniors in each weekend, which is jam-packed with activities. Shopping bus to Elgin on Friday, but only the upper sixth can visit on Saturdays and can 'have meals out in the evening'.

Certain amount of re-jigging houses: head has masterminding a £10.5 million (apparently no problem getting dosh) refurbishment of the Round Square boarding house and making the old building above accessible to all 'by creating a curriculum centre for international and spiritual citizenship'. Girls' houses bung full, but some boys' houses (sixth form particularly) could be busier, but junior boarding a run-away success. The lease on Duffus House at the entrance to the school will be given up within the next five years. Prospectus lists nearby hotels, B&Bs (with prices) and ways of getting to school (a good four hours from Edinburgh but less than that flying from London). Non-stop social life which swings right through the holidays – caveat for Southerners.

Background and atmosphere: Founded in 1934 by the German educationalist, Kurt Hahn, Jewish refugee, founder of Salem School in Baden-Württemberg and believer in educating and developing all aspects of children, not just the academic. Grounds and setting lovely – half a mile from the Moray Firth with cliffs and beaches nearby, and not as cold as one might think (Gulf Stream). Gordonstoun House is a former residence of Gordon-Cumming of card-cheating fame. Beautiful circular stable block (hence Round Square) houses the library and boys' house. Cunning music rooms round exotic chapel (shaped like an open book – magnificent, but repairs to the pews are sadly botched).

Rather jolly and purpose-built junior school in the grounds of senior school with self-contained classrooms and dorms all in the same building, the dorms, strategically placed on the second floor, with glorious views.

Pastoral care, well-being and discipline: Occasional problems with drugs, smoking and alcohol (not to mention the P word) – 'not totally whiter than white'. No automatic expulsions; pupils get alcohol or smoking points, and head negotiates with the parents. 'Not accurate, head manages according to Gordonstoun code of conduct', according to Reid. 'The Code of Conduct is not on our website but is posted to every parent before their child joins the school and is re-sent if there are any changes', in other words, the goal posts have changed. Drugs: straight to the head, usually straight out. Will take pupils who have had to leave other schools: contract in place. Head tough on perpetual offenders, particularly bullies – 'Children have eventually had to leave the school as a result', said the previous head. Commendably clear rules. Girls and boys can visit each others' houses but only allowed in the opposite sex's 'mixed common room' (sounds a blast) and nowhere else. Each pupil has an academic tutor, boarders have houseparents and assistant houseparents in every house. God worshipped in a Christian fashion, more than lip-service to other faiths. Local minister can prepare for confirmation.

Pupils and parents: A third English, a third Scottish and a third from the rest of the world – wide diversity of students, some deeply rich, some less so, with the less so benefiting from serious scholarships. Numbers of first time buyers. Parents dropping off their young have been known to stay 'for a few days'. FPs include royals; William Boyd; Eddie Shah; the composer of The Flower of Scotland – Roy Williamson; Martin Shea; Alan Shiach; Lara Croft; Sophie Morgan, who commentated for Channel 4 for the Paralympics; 2012 Olympian gold medal winner, rower Heather Stanning. Numbers currently (Reid changed this to 'marginally') down, particularly boarding boys and day pupils (60 in senior school).

Entrance: Juniors enter by assessment and interview plus report from previous school. Dedicated scholarships for juniors, who will lose them if they don't keep up to snuff. Many senior pupils have come up through the junior school (usually automatically, at 13), with others from Ardvreck, Cargilfield, Belhaven (under the new management) and prep schools south of the border. Assessment for those joining at year 10 (about 10 each year) and influx to sixth form. Pupils are assessed both academically and for personality. Odd places sometimes available for pupils, 'at any level of the school for short periods – although not normally less than one term'. Keen to keep up its intake from outside Scotland – may pay travel/hotel bills for prospective parents. Gordonstoun challenge – usually in June – invites UK prep schools to send teams of four or five, all expenses paid for a three day jamboree at Gordonstoun. The idea, of course, being that the little darlings will be so impressed, that whatever school they had previously considered will be cast aside.

Exit: Nearly all juniors move up to the senior school and hardly any post-16 leavers. To universities all over eg Edinburgh, Bath, St Andrews, Newcastle, Leeds, Nottingham. Courses range from aeronautical engineering, Japanese studies and agriculture to law. Two outstanding musicians to the Royal Academy of Music and the Royal Conservatoire of Scotland in 2016.

Money matters: Set fee; parents can 'opt above', and some do, 'notably so'. Scholarships and bursaries awarded after means-testing. Hardship fund. Success of flourishing international summer school helps with dosh. Fundraising doesn't seem that difficult. Stunning new bursaries for children of fisherfolk. Second hand clothes shop. Picked up the tab when Aberlour House was closed in 2004 (it was losing money); the buildings were sold and funds realised more or less paid for the stunning new build, Aberlour, in the grounds.

Remarks: Children and parents appear happy. Fashionable, co-ed outdoor pursuit-ish boarding school with vast range of pupil backgrounds, not overtly academic, though current head vows it is getting more so. Increasingly popular junior school in the grounds has been an enormous addition. Budget airline flights to nearest airports popular with southern-based families as well as those further afield. Regular direct links from Inverness to Amsterdam: Aberdeen to Frankfurt, and thence to points global. It is still a long drive from Edinburgh and Glasgow.

Hamilton College

Bothwell Road, Hamilton ML3 0AY

Pupils: 580 • Ages: 3–18 • Sixth form: 52

Fees: £7,425 – £9,855 pa

Tel: 01698 282700
Email: principal@hamiltoncollege.co.uk
Website: www.hamiltoncollege.co.uk

Principal: Since September 2016, Tom McPhail, appointed when previous head John Taylor left for 'personal reasons' after only one year.

Academic matters: The school 'has high academic expectations' and, using the Scottish exam system, offers Nationals at S4, generally five Highers at S5 and a combination of Highers and Advanced Highers at S6. French, from J5, German and Latin, from SI, on offer. All three sciences taught from S1.

Results are solid with high spots in history and chemistry. RMPS for all has an excellent pass rate. Most take English and maths Higher and the school 'usually manages to meet subject requests at Higher and Ad H'. Some non-core subjects such as business management, PE, technical studies etc on offer. School says take up of Ad Highers is growing. Classes fairly small; year groups of 70ish split into four and setted for maths, English, French etc. Loads of competitive triumphs too: with impressive victories in maths challenge and the Gilbert Murray Classical Essay competition amongst others. In 2016, 55 per cent of Highers and 47 per cent of Advanced Highers grade A.

Learning support team with qualified helpers gives both in-class and separate help to dyslexics etc, the team working closely with teaching and pupil support (guidance) staff and with parents. Staff relate personally to small groups so 'no one should slip through the net'. Lots of internet help with 'Moodle', an online course management service via the school website.

Games, options, the arts: Impressive record of art school entry (lots to Glasgow) and some distinguished past pupils. Walls zing with really exciting work, often killing two birds with one stone by using a theme from literature or even chemistry. The art room has a fantastic outlook and is jam-packed full of pupils' sculptures, photography etc. The slightly self-effacing modesty of the art teacher does not conceal the fact some outstanding work happens under his skilful care.

Music up to Ad Higher with a good wide range of instrumental teaching and bags of opportunities to perform in orchestras, choirs, groups, musicals and foreign trips. Choirs and orchestra tour the Black Forest with a mixed programme, as well as concerts and drama in school in local churches etc. Drama especially active with entries to Glasgow Shakespeare festival (Hamlet). No exam courses, but Victoria College, London Certificate of Speech and Drama.

Football (girls and boys, but not together), rugby, hockey (girls just had their first trip ever – to Ireland), netball etc – with lots of after-school practices and matches. Bullish athletics with juniors winning locally and a Scottish national long jumper, ditto swimming. Scarcely surprising with a really good indoor pool and games hall and two gyms to practise in. School teams are battling in national competitions but lots of opportunities for tip top players in local clubs, as well as some inspiring input via the school: playing with Glasgow Warriors, inviting Hamilton Academical player to visit etc etc.

Most extracurricular clubs, sport and some orchestras after school for juniors and seniors. The extracurricular booklet, complete with timetable to be downloaded from the extremely efficient website, includes 40 plus activities like chess (hosted regional championship), book club, stocks and shares group, Young Enterprise (for older pupils) and entrepreneurs (for younger ones), ski club (trip to Austria), press review and Scripture Union..

Loads of curriculum based visits locally and abroad – Auschwitz recently via Holocaust Memorial Trust. D of E started recently, with lots of bronze and silver hopefuls looking to gold soon and a fair share of outdoor activities/trips. Debating and public speaking just getting going again.

Background and atmosphere: Probably the starkest school building in the Scottish independent sector – a pale blue shoebox with bright red signage rising oddly behind some spectacular ornate railings (a relic of the former Hamilton Palace) but with stunning views and masses of space overlooking Hamilton Park race course. The pitches are actually in the middle of the track, reached by a tunnel. In spite of its appearance the school, a Christian foundation, originally one of a group of three started in the Manchester area, was jolly lucky to get a redundant '60s teacher training college complete with terrific (then – and still pretty good now) games facilities, lovely indoor pool, stunning hall and purpose-built large light classrooms. The central assembly hall holds the entire school and its banks of 'in the round' eating and magnificent pyramidal wooden roof make it a really good auditorium space, well equipped and much used by the school and external lets.

Inside is purposeful with busy pupils. The central space and upper floors belong to the seniors, with the juniors and nursery on the ground floor of each 'wing', separated from the central space by the hall on one side. On the other is a spacious courtyard with an ecological greenhouse made from recycled plastic bottles and lots of garden equipment – takes ecology seriously. It also prides itself on its health promotion and has a gold award from Lanarkshire. The purpose-built library and dining area run along the back of the building next to the racecourse, both huge with masses of glass. The rather bare dining room is 'heaving at lunch times' and the library is open to students at intervals and after school, as well as in constant use by classes during the day after school. A spectacular glass box, perched on a vast expanse of flat roof, is the staffroom, which must reach equatorial temperatures when the sun shines – but fortunately this is Scotland.

The junior school and nursery, however, are crammed with colour and activity, using every spare inch of wall and floor space. The senior school, with its wide corridors and huge entrance hall, complete with LCD display showing lunch menus ('which pass the Gold HPS standard with ease') and other bits of vital school info, is well maintained, despite a few dark stair corners. It all feels a bit institutional and functional, but clearly does function very well as an institution. The overtly Christian ethos encourages lots of charity fundraising and a very impressive 'Transform' project with a school in Burkina Faso, involving annual visits by groups of sixth formers and reciprocal trips for teachers. Part of this initiative, providing internet facilities for the school, has was featured on BBC World News.

Pupils wear burgundy blazers, with blue braiding for prefects and pale blue shirts, black trousers for boys and Lindsay tartan for girls. Ties for all – striped for boys and plain for girls – plus tracksuits and cagoules in house colours for games: quite a pricey item and uniform policy is strict.

Pastoral care, well-being and discipline: A new house system with three houses, Lewis, Harris and Skye, delivers most of the pastoral care, plus each child is allocated an individual guidance teacher. Inspectors recently commended this. Form teachers also help. The prefect team are appointed and have to apply and be interviewed. Head prefects 'do a lot', including representing the school at outside functions. Staff think discipline is good and few sanctions are needed – 'Bunking off school just does not happen'. Smoking – couldn't remember catching anyone in school, but zero tolerance, and if pupils are seen smoking outside school or in town, parents are contacted. Drugs 'not a problem', but would result in permanent exclusion. Stringent mobile phone policy, available, like most other Hamilton info, on the website, says phones will be confiscated for the day – 'We're just trying to get them to use them sensibly'. Bullying not a big problem, 'But, as everywhere, it happens,' so a raft of measures – sanctions (see policy on website), counselling, life skills programme, meetings with parents.

Pupils and parents: Huge catchment area taking in most of the south side of Glasgow and Lanarkshire, with extensive bus routes to Lanark, Biggar Kilsyth, Cumbernauld and East Kilbride. Intake multi-ethnic. Friends of Hamilton College, a very go-ahead body, fundraises for school equipment and does charity stuff too. It has recently donated a (second hand) cardiovascular fitness suite (huge) much used by pupils, staff and parents.

Lots of famous arty former pupils including Katie Leung (acted Cho Chang in Harry Potter); Lorna Ritchie, set and costume designer (worked for Jonathan Miller); and Blair Thompson, Scottish artist and winner of numerous awards (in The Herald's top 20 Scottish artists) – all of whom started their careers in Hamilton's art room.

Entrance: Mainly to nursery, J1 and S1 but will accept at any stage. Entry assessments for all.

Exit: Most juniors move up, but an increasingly rare number drop out after National grade (S4) and again after Highers (S5), though the past few years have seen more staying on to S6. The majority to university, mainly Scottish (as there are no fees), though the very occasional to Oxbridge or other English ones. Quite a few to further ed and apprenticeships or work in family businesses.

Money matters: Not a rich school but well managed. Bursary scheme up to 100 per cent strictly means-tested and awarded by committee of governors etc. Will try to help a family in sudden financial trouble. Discounts of 10 per cent for second, 20 per cent for third and 40 per cent for fourth child and 25 per cent+ sibling discount for 'full time Christian workers'.

Remarks: Not to be ignored! A good solid school, perhaps a little old fashioned until recently pulled by its bootstraps into the 21st century – 'It's now at the leading edge in Scotland for its use of ICT in learning teaching and admin'. Sound, good value for money, and certainly worth a look if you live in the area or in oversubscribed East Renfrewshire. 'Exceptionally positive' recent inspection. It may not be beautiful, but it is certainly useful and might even be exciting.

Harris Academy

Perth Road, Dundee DD2 1NL

Pupils: 1,308 • Ages: 11–18 • Sixth form: 152

Tel: 01382 435700
Email: harris@dundeecity.gov.uk
Website: www.harrisacademy.ea.dundeecity.sch.uk

Head Teacher: Since January 2016, Mr Barry Millar, previously head teacher at Perth Grammar School.

Academic matters: Well above average: no particular bias, but with around 50 per cent of all pupils leaving after National grades (most go to Dundee College) it is a little difficult to give an accurate picture. Smashing results for those who do stay on to sixth form – way above national average (though with 38 per cent with three Highers – or better – it's not that hard a target to beat). Masses of computers etc, all heavily used, with waiting systems in place if need be. Impressive library with yet more machines, class teaching on computers as well as IT. Pupils do keyboarding and basic ICT skills and use the skills in presentations: powerpoint, sound, film-making, animated flow charts. Max class size (legal limit) 33, but down to 20 for practical subjects.

First couple of years all study English, maths, science, history, geography, modern studies, home economics (magic), technology (great) plus one modern language: French, German or Spanish. Latin on hand, but no Greek. Streaming after first year when a fast track for English, maths and modern languages comes into force. Teaching disciplines are a combination of individual, small group, whole class teaching and discussion. Strong learning support.

School attracts a number of ethnic minorities whose parents are billeted to the local university, hospital or area, 14 currently in the school. Russian, Bengali, Urdu and Cantonese the most frequently spoken at home – native speakers can take these at standard grade. EAL is taught by the special educational needs team, and the HMI thought they were a bit stretched. Pupil support staff co-teach where necessary in class, but 'such support may result in a revised elaborated or alternative curriculum and include individual or small group tuition'. Supported study includes homework clubs, and a teacher is available early on Tuesday mornings or Thursday evenings to help pupils with problems. Good encouragement, too, for the more gifted. Terrific use of external facilities. HMI also a bit dissy about homework – the amount, the marking et al, but that was some time ago, and the results of the recommendations are not yet available. The HMI other comment which concerns us is that brighter pupils 'do not appear to be sufficiently stretched'.

Eight National grades for all as far as possible. Languages, humanities and modern studies above average and good showing in the Scottish and UK Maths Challenges; ditto the Dundee Enterprising Maths competition. Inspiring programme of lectures from outside speakers. Serious advice for all pupils on which road to take. Good choice post National with Highers and Advanced Highers in a raft of subjects, plus tourism and hospitality at National grades. Regular assessments and good parental feedback.

School is an important cog in the education of children in the autistic spectrum and takes 10 pupils (never fewer) by request and allocation from the west of Dundee and the city itself (Morgan Academy takes those who live East of Dundee). These pupils are scattered across the age range, and school only accepts the next pupil when space becomes available. 'Lovely laddies' (mainly boys, but that's the nature of autism) all have individual educational programmes which are regularly monitored and amended. Some are totally supported individually and educated in the base (only one currently); others attend mainstream lessons but may be entirely supported in class, or allowed to attend certain classes for a short period – eg physics: in mainstream for six weeks, and then back to the unit. Most take National grade maths and all have speech and oral communication. School OK for physical handicaps – 'Only one lift, but there are ways of moving round the school'. The base is popular with 'normal kids' who choose to join those in the autistic spectrum at lunchtime – a reverse integration. Many of these pupils will go on to Elmwood College in Fife, where the school has close links.

Games, options, the arts: Games fields half a mile away, gyms on site plus swimming pool. Large sports complex off-site. PE timetabled and impressive line up of games (extracurricular) including the very popular rugby, hockey, football for boys and girls, athletics, basketball (enthusiastic coach), water polo etc.

Art, as you might imagine, deeply computer-linked: ceramics, painting, ICT, no CAD as such but the facility to use computer-based design. Computer suite in art room, home economics, metalwork area, all computer based and hands on. Mass of instrumentalists, music strong and popular with ceilidhs and rock concerts (including FPs) – huge charitable input, 'everything and anything'. Choirs, bands, orchestras. Popular theatre club, though not available as an exam subject, despite pupils' requests. Outstanding debating, thrashing all comers; vibrant YE and truly popular D of E, with a whacking list of gold, silver and bronze successes. Not the longest list of clubs we have ever seen, but thoroughly active, mass of trips abroad: humanities with proper exchanges popular.

Background and atmosphere: Founded in 1885 and 'the oldest public school in Dundee', moved to the handsome granite building in 1931, school then added on a hotchpotch of flat-roofed excrescences in the '60s. Complete £32m rebuild on same site finished in 2016.

Free school meals (but the cafeteria is cashless). Help with school uniform (school provides the basics ex-stock) and trips. Grants available. If pupils stay for fifth year the odds are they will stay on to sixth: five Highers the norm.

Pastoral care, well-being and discipline: Sixth formers buddy first formers – 'very protective and good anti-bullying strategy'. Strong PSE reinforced by RME. Pupils are divided into four houses, and the pupil support strategy is handled by house representatives, each house having two guidance and two support-for-learning teachers. Terrific inter-house competition, both in the academic and the sporting field, with marks being allocated for each and house championship fiercely fought over.

Defined sanction system: if pupils disobey one of five clearly defined rules, then they 'may be excluded for up to three days' for continuous disobedience, and head will meet with the parents. School 'is not prepared for disruptive children or anti-social behaviour' to permeate and would much rather produce 'decent sensible sensitive citizens' who are a lot 'more use than an anti-social chemist'. To this end (and this is a first for us) has installed a splendid reward system (Pavlov eat your heart out). Each pupil (who has the school code drilled into them during their first week, 'so they can't say they don't know what is expected of them') is given a personal plan which must be stamped at the end of each lesson. Pupils earning 250 marks are awarded a certificate, can skip an afternoon's school and see a film of their choice – and get a Mars bar. Five hundred stamps qualify for a silver certificate and a free ticket for Megabowl;

gold equals a trip to Alton Towers, with a certain amount of parent input, and platinum a three day trip to London. Platinum winners have to have their cards stamped after almost every lesson to qualify. Links with top year of feeder primaries – guidance staff and teacher visit regularly (HMI reckoned the school 'could try harder') and first year pupils all decamp with their teachers to Falkland Youth Centre for bonding and team-building stuff.

Pupils and parents: A mixed bunch, some here briefly, charming and well-mannered. Good parental support and school booklet encourages this. Farmers, businesspeople, as well as the university and hospitals. FPs include Donald Findlay QC, Bruce Milan, James Crabb (accordion player), the footballer Christian Daily and the much beloved George Galloway – who does not even receive a mention in the FP online site under 'government'. (Should we have checked 'media/television personalities'?)

Entrance: Always full. Pupils come from five main feeders with a couple of dozen placement requests annually. Certain amount of logistical movement. Standard rules about addresses and siblings.

Exit: Either post National grade, or (usually) post sixth form. Some 70 odd per cent to universities, mostly to Scotland but the occasional trickle to Oxbridge. Inspired careers advice.

Remarks: Inspirational – and now in a brand new school building.

Hermitage Academy

Cardross Road, Colgrain, Helensburgh G84 7LA

Pupils: 1,400 • Ages: 12–18 • Sixth form: 170

Tel: 01436 672145
Email: enquirieshermitageacademy@argyll-bute.gov.uk
Website: www.hermitageacademy.argyll-bute.sch.uk

Head: Since 2007, Mr Geoff T Urie (40s), who was educated at Paisley Grammar and read geography at Glasgow University. He first came to the school as depute head before spending a couple of years at Ardrossan Academy – 'I had to come back to move to the new campus'. He runs this conglomerate with a depute and staff of over 100: no apparent difficulty with getting new teachers. He is proud and welcoming and was pleased to spend some time with this editor, who dropped in out of the blue.

Academic matters: Scottish system. All do National grade English and maths (for which they are setted) plus personal and social development, PE and RE. Three sciences throughout. Courses on offer vary between foundation, general and credit levels – huge choice from graphic communication, hairdressing, home economics, motor vehicle engineering (City and Guilds), woodworking, as well as uniformed and emergency services (popular), terrific fashion and textile, design, health and food, plus product design, baby sitting and accounting, and all the usual subjects. Maximum class size 30, but in reality much lower – with half below 20. French, German and Spanish offered to exam level, Spanish and Italian lunch time clubs as well. Exam results show a pleasing number getting good grades.

IT everywhere, whiteboards and overhead projectors. Student planner and fairly strict homework expectations, can email queries to staff, much use is made of GLOW and HABIT revision programmes. Help on hand for weaker students – two dedicated teachers plus the support team (this is an inclusive school, with some pupils getting a mega amount of help) led by 'a DHT pupils' support and 11 principal teachers, as well as 10 principal teachers of guidance and a principal teacher of support for learning'. Learning support either short sharp bursts out of class ('the kick-up' room), or assistance during lesson time. IEPs where necessary and good links with Get It Right For Every Child, the local partnership agency which oversees what happens next.

Games, options, the arts: Splendid sports hall with electronic scoring, two proper gyms with ropes and strong gymnastic following; terrific dance studio, weights room – 'busy all the time'. No pool (uses local one, but currently under refurbishment), two football pitches plus Astroturf, tennis courts. A couple of football players spent some time training with AC Milan – which has to be a senior mega moment. Sports activities are, in the main, extracurricular – massive amount nonetheless (funded through the Active Schools programme), with senior pupils helping official coaches and enthusiastic (and successful) involvement in football, swimming, athletics and golf. Three Peaks race, Young Enterprise (rather jolly tartan recently accepted and registered with the Scottish Tartan Authority, scarf currently on sale, but watch this space). Activity days and rash of clubs.

Big school, big bands: symphony, wind, brass, swing with samba on the cards. Choirs, and hefty trad Scottish in/output with fiddlers, Gaelic choir and pipe band. The best fabric ever, ditto fashion design. Drama – latest offering Casualty Jane. Amazing record of charitable activity. Has strong links with Comenius and different European schools – Germany, the Czech Republic, with loads of trips in every discipline.

Background and atmosphere: Drop dead gorgeous modern building in stark black and white opened a few years ago – built to hold 1,700 and not currently full. Overlooks the Clyde – all singing and dancing. Long wide passages, two huge spaces (architects of new school builds always seemed to economise here) with a splendid ground floor dining hall: holds 1,000 and, when we visited just as lunch was finishing, it was quiet, orderly and remarkably tidy – the cleaners had perhaps one small waste paper basket full of detritus; stage at one end with ancillary green rooms and storage, professional lighting and rather posh red plush curtains. Pupils operate a swipe card system which disguises any free school meal stigma. Glorious assembly hall above (seats 1,300, soundproofed and used for exams as well), stunning views with amazing decorative mega pipes at roof level – probably nothing more mundane than the central heating system but it looks 22nd century stuff.

Terrific library with cunning circular window roof lights (head always coming in and turning lights off in the interests of economy, forgetting that those furthest from the windows are then studying in the dark). Library pupil-led – everything state of the art, can't fault it. Vast car parking area, see-through bike sheds hold 80 bikes (but you can't smoke behind them). Head had rather hoped that the local fuzz would turn up to 'keep an eye' at admission time, and is not quite sure whether he is pleased or disappointed that they refused: not enough naughtiness apparently. Traditionalists are happy that the old HS (Hermitage School) shield has made the transition, as has the wheel of the Lucy Ashton, which for so many years greeted pupils at the previous academy.

Pastoral care, well-being and discipline: Managed by group of depute head teacher and heads of every year, plus dedicated

H

guidance teachers. Strong PSE; pro-active anti-bullying strategy in place with all newbies being given an anti-bullying card, 'It's OK to talk'. Sixth year pupils active in Friends Against Bullying – their photographs are displayed on notice boards, and oodles of anti-bullying programmes in place. The odd exclusion. School uniform for all – prefects wear red ties.

Pupils and parents: Everything from farmers to local business folk, to Forces personnel based at nearby Faslane – inclusive in every possible way. Strong parent-teacher body.

Entrance: Some placement requests, otherwise school has 10 linked primaries from as far as Arrochar, Cardross and Kilgreggan; also has 'close links' with Parklands School in Helensburgh, which is Catholic – pupils might well be expected to attend an RC secondary RC, but 'find it more convenient' to come here. Operates a 'hooked on Hermitage' programme – masses of to-ing and fro-ing by learning support and subject teachers; all P6/7 pupils spend two days at Hermitage in June to meet their guidance teacher and S6 buddy, plus two pupil/parent evenings throughout the year. Serious input into changeover – works well.

H

Exit: Impressive careers advice which extends beyond a pupil's time at school. Currently some 170 pupils in sixth year – about 85/90 per cent stay on after National grades, of whom a further 90 per cent stay on thereafter. Latest statistics show that some 60 per cent either went into further or higher education.

Money matters: Funding available for essential (or non essential, come to that) trips for those who couldn't otherwise afford it.

Remarks: Impressive new build, inclusive school – appears to work exceeding well.

High School of Dundee

Euclid Crescent, Dundee DD1 1HU

Pupils: 997 • Ages: 3–18 • Sixth form: 215

Fees: £8,499 – £12,063 pa

Tel: 01382 202921
Email: admissions@highschoolofdundee.org.uk
Website: www.highschoolofdundee.org.uk

Rector: Since 2008, Dr John Halliday BA PhD (Cantab) (60) (no thoughts of retiring). Educated at Abingdon and previously head of Albyn School in Aberdeen, following the demise of Rannoch (after a short spell at Dollar). Having shaken Albyn (which we fully expected to fail) by the scruff of the neck, introduced chaps and baby nursery, he laid the foundations of the stonking Albyn school of today.

In Dundee, the upper school was rattling, lower school resembled the Marie Celeste and place was more of a mausoleum than a vibrant hub of education. Halliday was a shoo-in to wake up this slumbering giant; a process made more daunting by having an almost entirely new senior management team (he had a hand in the selection process). We asked if all was happiness still in the upper echelons: 'Your team, you run with them' was the answer, which doesn't quite imply unqualified success. School roll highest ever.

Still plays the viola in the school orchestra. Married with three children, now up and flying.

During our first visit to Dundee High, Halliday confessed to missing the buzz of the classroom, so took up chalk again, and taught 'the odd spot of German'. However, recent acquisition (2013) of the Dundee head post office, a splendid French Renaissance affair, just metres from the main school, makes further forays unlikely. Plans afoot to 'create a centre of excellence for performing and visual arts'; 'this is a once in a century opportunity'.

School humming with happy pupils and, judging from instructions given to reception whilst we were waiting (rector's secretary had double booked), some less happy children, too: 'Ring these five parents, Dr Halliday wants to see them at 15 minute intervals this afternoon; hopefully their children should have warned them'. Sounded ominous.

Heads usually divide automatically into building/developing heads and academic heads. Halliday is unusual in that he straddles both disciplines. We spent some time studying plans and came away with a natty blue and gold campaign fundraising book (though we had to go online to find the cost of the proposed conversion – £16m). The appeal, due to last five years, was launched with fireworks, pipe band, red carpet and a cast of thousands. Rector maintains that 'if every member of our current school community gives up just one cup of coffee per day for the campaign period we'll raise nearly £10m.' Presumably Starbucks rather than Haag. This is high priority stuff; certain amount of demolition required for nasty 60s add-on, but space available for a variety of concert/chamber orchestra (300 seater) auditoria, plus theatre space and refectory (three million quid) linked to (catering) kitchens and health and food technology; plus drama, art and design. Current dining hall a bleak (often wet and windy 200 metres or so away). Public use a given, conferences and the like anticipated. (Black box, white box: et al).

Mrs Julie Rose BEd is in charge of junior years and nursery.

Academic matters: A Scottish school through and through, with high expectations. French from P4, with a P7 trip to Paris eagerly anticipated by pupils. P6 and 7 get lots of lessons in the senior school: computers, art, drama etc. Classes in early years strictly capped at 20 for L1 rising to 22 for L3, but school will make an extra class when the demand, though space is tight. Good support for stragglers plus a thinking skills course for every year group – one group was busily doing Sudoku. Littlest start with Oxford Reading Tree plus lots of phonics and multiple reading methods. The class we visited was having a ball – expressively reading aloud. Children happily busy in every corner, though an older group caught in a lull had time to talk maturely about the imminent French trip and their huge array of hobbies.

National 5s absorbed seamlessly, all expected to take seven or eight: solid range of subjects. Results pretty good overall, and spectacular in modern languages, chemistry, history. Most teaching in mixed form groups but English, maths and languages are set. English department had a couple of finalists in the Pushkin Prize for short stories. Increased take-up in French, Spanish and German. Rota for langs: Latin, German, Spanish, French, Mandarin then choose. Strong history, which gets its fair whack of the S1/2 curriculum, not being reduced to a share of rota system as in many schools. English and maths taken by most at both Higher and Advanced Higher level. Not much take up for Latin and minimal for Greek (on offer, plus Russian, in S6); range of marginal subjects – sociology, technical studies, PE, managing environmental resources, plus philosophy, economics; respectable numbers taking all sorts of maths specialisms: stats, mechanics etc. Class sizes from three or four to mid-20s. Masses of techno equipment – PCs, internet link via Abertay University etc and trolleyed laptops for class use in the junior school. S6 can do enhancement courses at Dundee University. iPads for all from P6, parent bought and insured.

In 2016, 65 per cent As at National 5, 63 per cent As at Highers for S5 and 55 per cent for S6, with 55 per cent As at Advanced Highers.

Learning skills centre with five dedicated staff provides support and specialist teaching in junior and senior schools for 'mild to moderate specific learning difficulties' (dyslexia, dyspraxia, ADHD, mild Asperger's). Early intervention encouraged. Support also for the super bright. Few need ESOL which tends to be given in class at primary and rarely needed at secondary. Much-used library, with areas for different ages and activities and full time librarians on hand who also arrange multifarious library talks and activities.

Games, options, the arts: Pupils bused to games in the multi-million Mayfield sports centre, complete with a brace of international-class hockey Astropitches (water-based/sand-dressed), plus academy of sport and health/well-being which includes diet and physical development, involving 'internationalists up to the highest level.' Swimming in Dundee University pool. Strong rugby, girls' hockey, netball and athletics, tennis, cricket. D of E flourishing – oodles of golds. CCF, pipe band – with girls as well as boys; riding and skiing teams are the tip of an iceberg of physical activities from line skating to golf.

Current art department chilly with garret view of Dundee roofscape: multi-purpose: textile, scarf making, jewellery (boys and girls) involves chemistry to help with 'decorative fusing'. Music strong with concerts in the town and a musical production biennially – currently The Good Person of Szechwan and Joseph in the junior school. Numerous orchestras, groups and choirs. We spoke at length to head of music, whom we have known since he was in (very) short trousers. He is ecstatic, both about the school itself and about the future development.

Drama timetabled with productions at all levels. Art, music and drama all available as exam subjects up to Advanced Higher with impressive results. Formidable debating in true Scottish school tradition.

Masses of choice for juniors including earlybird and lunchtime IT and a gardening club (currently providing a wintry courtyard with paper flowers).

Background and atmosphere: School founded in 1239, though royal charter from Queen Victoria didn't arrive until 1859; a city 'treasure' with an enlightened governing body drawn from the great and good (the 'Guildry' and 'Nine Trades'), elected from parents, past pupils or co-opted for their skills. Certain amount of trad: prize-giving in Caird Hall, end of term services at St Andrew's church.

The neo-classic (slightly grubby), Doric porticoed façade (so beloved by Scottish school architects) is protected by railed playground, fiercely patrolled by janitors, but open to visiting editors and parents collecting their offspring at the end of school day. Flanked on one side by the 1890s Margaret Harris Building, once the girls' school, which houses the juniors, and, on the other the (ex) Trinity Church, which provides a hall (not big enough for the whole school), ground floor library and attic drama space. The McManus Gallery, much used by the art department, is more-or-less opposite. The magnificent, late Victorian French Renaissance style former head post office building (adjacent to DC Thompson) is perhaps 50 metres from the school gates. A triumph to have bought it (DC Thompson is on the move as well, but we doubt school could either afford, or need, an extra humungous building).

Departments are cunningly grouped in a collection of buildings, some quite grand, gradually accumulated along Bell Street and curiously interspersed with courtyards, one of which sports tall, thin climbing wall. Roomy and light teaching rooms, plenty of space, though not much greenery. Pupils mill about, open, friendly, and happy to talk about their work. Some corners/staircases a bit dark and 'schooly', but most bright and clean, though neither corridors nor pupils are unnaturally tidy. Boys wear navy blue, while girls wear 'softer' grey blazers with a grey Dundee High tartan skirt. The tartan looks best as pinnies for tinies. Parents' thrift shop well used.

New nursery for 3-4 year olds on Mayfield campus. The purpose-built £1m facility is open 50 weeks of the year from 7.30am to 6pm.

Pastoral care, well-being and discipline: Four vertical houses, with familial continuity from juniors to seniors, run by guidance staff, have two forms in each year group, with guidance teacher being first point of contact for pupils and parents. Despite freedom to go into town at lunch breaks, rector reports far more phone calls from citizens complimenting the helpfulness of pupils than complaints: certain number of hiccups lately.

Guidelines are clear: suspension for first offence – smoking and the like, pupils with drugs can expect to be expelled.

Pupils and parents: Some 50 per cent from Dundee, 50 per cent from Fife, Angus and Perthshire: five different (school organised and subsidised) bus routes. Mix of farmers, professionals and people working for universities/hospitals. Fair ethnic mix and fair number of first time buyers: school has come back into its own. Pupils can bring own cars but not drive others. Former pupils include William Wallace, AL Kennedy, Lord Cullen and Lord Ross, and more recently Andy Nichol, Mark Beaumont, Frank Hadden, Joanna Vanderham and KT Tunstall. BBC's Andrew Marr had a short spell in the juniors.

Natty trifold info sheet for parents lists every conceivable way of contacting school. With apps and downloads. Should be mandatory.

Entrance: By assessment at all stages, including cognitive ability, with two-thirds coming into seniors from juniors. Demand and waiting list not much hit by recession, though bursary applications are up. Main entrance points F1, F5 and F6; occasional gaps throughout the school, and offered, if pupil up to academic scratch, when demand exceeds supply, on a sibling basis. Mid-term arrivals not out of the frame. Reports from previous school required for those arriving from elsewhere, plus proof of ability to meet 'financial obligations'.

Exit: Virtually all juniors move up to seniors. Few leave post S4 and S5. Almost all to university, generally Scottish with a smattering to eg Durham or Oxbridge; 'high interest in science and medicine', biotech and life sciences, plus business and law degrees. Mock interviews for all.

Money matters: The first school inspected and passed by OSCR (Scottish charity regulator); school gives about £800,000 in bursaries every year (approximately 13-14 per cent of its annual turnover). Bursaries, all means-tested, are normally awarded to form 1, and, more recently P6/7; but applications from current parents in financial trouble will be considered. Stringent means-testing for all. Number of independent trusts also give financial support to individuals in the school. No specialist scholarships for academic, art, music sport etc.

Certain number of not too obvious extras eg music lessons. Pupils in upper school provide their own text books and stationery, lunch costs based on age (cheaper by the term: buy a book of vouchers); ditto bus – return is cheaper than one way; and – which is somewhat surprising – home economics enthusiasts pay for lessons. This is a new one to us (though we are now getting accustomed to exam fees being notified and charged).

Remarks: Impressive: Halliday has transformed the place. The fine tradition of Scottish education is alive, well and living (independently and at a price) in Dundee. New developments eagerly awaited. 'Like Dundee,' says the rector, 'the school is modest about its achievements'.

The High School of Glasgow

637 Crow Road, Glasgow G13 1PL

Pupils: 1,022 • Ages: 3–18 • Sixth form: 93

Fees: £8,910 – £11,919 pa

Tel: 01419 549628
Email: rector@hsog.co.uk
Website: www.glasgowhigh.com

H

Rector: Since 2015, John O'Neill, previously senior deputy rector. A graduate of Glasgow University, he joined the school in 2004 from Merchiston Castle School, where he was housemaster and head of sixth form.

Head of junior school: Since August 2016, Heather Fuller BEd, previously deputy head. Degree in primary education from Strathclyde. Taught for 13 years at Hamilton College; two years as development officer for assessment at Education Scotland; joined the High School in 2015.

Academic matters: A thunderingly good school on all fronts. Two parallel classes for each year group in the junior school, with 'group teaching where appropriate'. Sixth formers at senior school act as buddies when pupils move up to senior school. Class size 28 and down, French from the age of 8, IT from the start – IT Works, spread sheets, word processing, data bases, dedicated computer lab: the works.

Eight National grades the norm: geography, modern studies, biology, classics and modern langs particularly strong, though perhaps chemistry hasn't been returning quite so many As as, say, physics or human biology – but a thumpingly good department nonetheless. Strong and successful following in French, German, Spanish and Latin. Pleasing lack of 'studies', drama called drama (up to Advanced Higher) and not theatre studies, ditto classics (which of course may not be the same thing as classical civilisation) with varying numbers doing modern studies, business management, information systems and economics with equally varying results. Good to see fashion and textiles to Advanced level, though tiny trickle, as with home economics, but tranches doing art and design with pleasing number of A grades. Occasional glitch but nothing to worry about. Geography and history notably high on the wow factor but impressive results in all disciplines, and not apparently too many problems with silk purses and sows' ears. In 2016, 85 per cent A grades at National 5, 72 per cent at Higher (S5) and nearly 57 per cent at Advanced Higher (S6).

Streamed in maths throughout and English from S2, then banded for langs, bright pupils extended, five maths sets, Latin for all first two years, French and German throughout, Spanish offered at third year and as a crash course in the sixth year. Business management popular. Serious and successful representations as ever in maths Olympiads. Fewer girls than boys doing Higher physics, though still a few. Stunning new lab conversion (all those flat roofs – though everything has to be well checked as school built – not on green field – but close to previous coal workings) with old labs amalgamated to provide both working and practical areas, Greenhouse re-attached to new biology lab on second floor; school offers human biology as well as the 'normal' option, and pupils can take this as a crash subject in their final year at school – useful for those entering the medical profession (Glasgow University is popular for medics). Dedicated sixth form labs where pupils can leave their experiments up and running (under supervision if required). Approx 30 per cent follow science-related courses. One of the best sixth form handbooks we have come across, complete with university entrance requirements and advice – other schools would do well to copy. Huge variety of subjects and options – sewing for all – fluffy toys and embroidered lined denim bags in the lunch hour. Max class size 26, with 20 for practical subjects.

Excellent and organised learning support throughout, with masses of liaison from junior school, and good follow-on in all disciplines. Head of learning support is also SQA special arrangements co-ordinator (extra time in exams et al), with mass of experience, she comes from the state sector, plus part-time colleague, double teaching, some drop in help, scribing, good record of tracking children with problems and following up. Dyslexic pupils from junior school teamed up with senior pupils for the first two years, to encourage and help them with any organisational difficulties and with homework etc. Impressive library, computers everywhere; dedicated for the fifth and sixth form only, during their study time, but all pupils can and do use them during their lunch break.

Games, options, the arts: Junior school shares senior school facilities, bussed to Anniesland for rugby and hockey, swimming at the Allander centre, not a huge amount of playground on site (a couple of converted tennis courts), but each age group has its own. Small gym (ie not a sports hall), and impressive convertible hall/theatre. Excellent and imaginative drama. Superb music, three choirs, orchestra, wind, guitar, chamber, chanter – you name it. Specialist art teacher, the entire complex (building is too simple a word) is covered in child-paintings and models.

Senior school surrounded by 23 acres of games fields (new water based hockey pitch) and car parks; masses of district, county, country players (Olympic representation) and tranches of representatives in almost every discipline. Regular rugby/hockey trips to Canada. Huge range of activities, including sailing, skiing (trips to the States popular) as well as D of E. Cultural trip to China and to Cuba recently. Visits to elderly and strong links with local group of autistic children. Lots of charity projects, often house-based. Masses of popular clubs, lunchtime and post school. Our lunchtime trip round the school found a host of impromptu debaters, charity organisers and proper choir practices.

Impressive debating skills – silver mementos of previous glory all over the shop: The Observer Mace, the Cambridge Union, the Oxford Union and ESU. Regular finalists including ESU finalists last year. D of E enthusiasts and much encouragement.

Massive and exciting drama and music, trips all over the place. The former in super new purpose-built studio – always interesting to have the theatre on the first floor (drama very much a whole school thing, with the home economics dept doing costume and the art dept the scenery). Full-time teacher of drama. Mass of sponsoring – the Fraser of Allander lecture room, Wolfson Foundation in Science and such-like. Regular spectacular productions. 'Really exciting music department', which has won chamber music awards in recent years. Smart new music practice rooms with mirrored walls. Choirs and orchestras abound, trips abroad, travelling for competitions and the like. Fauré Requiem in Paisley Abbey and orchestral/choral concerts in Glasgow University Chapel highly acclaimed. Lord (Norman) Macfarlane, who is deeply involved both with the school (at both levels) and with the Kelvingrove Art Gallery reincarnation has involved each with the other. Sparky art department with a gallery, but not much take up at Higher levels – work is a serious matter in the west. School challenges this, saying 'an encouraging take up at Higher levels with pupils regularly going on to art colleges'. 'Art on the up'. Study skills for all plus time management, politics and interview skills in sixth form.

Background and atmosphere: Founded as The Choir School of Glasgow Cathedral in 1124, gained grammar school status during the 15th century and became a high school in 1834. Despite its high academic standing, school was closed by Glasgow Corporation in 1976. An appeal launched by the High School Former Pupils' Club funded the new purpose-built senior school on the sports ground at Anniesland Cross, already owned by the FPs, and the new school opened the day after the old school closed – a triumph. The High School merged with the former PNEU dame school, Drewsteignton, in Bearsden, three miles away, now the junior school.

The flat-roofed building at Anniesland has expanded considerably; with new additions sprouting all over the place (usually on the roof), though fortunately without any obvious loss of playing fields. Square split level assembly hall, artificial floodlit pitch, new stand complex which incorporates an impressive and well-used club house plus school dining room ('with caterer from heaven'). Sixth form area houses coffee shop and loud music as well as dedicated computers and work areas. School uniform for all, with girls in tartan skirts. The old house system remains, with each house having its own particular area in the school.

The junior school is Glasgow prep they all – with good reason – fight to get into. Still holds true. Numbers a tad down this year, but huge number of pupils shoehorned with enormous skill into tiniest site imaginable. But think Victorian villa, think stained glass windows, think very steep site, think 360 odd children, think the impossible. Massive new build a few years back, positively Swiss engineering to construct a magical new basement, fantastic kindergarten (with its own entrance); masses of light – this is imaginative architecture at its most productive.

Pastoral care, well-being and discipline: Junior has same ethos as senior school – positive relationships and anti-bullying plans. Elected junior school council – who have a serious input and recently quizzed the catering manager about the lunch supplied.

Highly defined house system with colours but not names carrying on from junior to senior school, siblings follow siblings into the same house. PSHE largely house-based with house staff playing a major role in extracurricular and social activities. Transitus (11/12 year old) pupils are lovingly tended with lots of back-up from junior school, particularly with learning support.

No recent drugs cases, though a couple have been asked to leave in the past for going OTT, but certainly would expel if drugs were brought into the school. 'Staff beady eyed'. Suspensions for 'major offences'. Otherwise punishments range through sanctions, lunchtime detentions, clearing up litter (black bags) to school detention after school on Fridays.

Excellent blue booklet on promoting positive relationships – good PSE step guide, practised from the junior school. Jazzy new format school mag.

Pupils and parents: Ambitious, strong work ethos, almost half come from the affluent Bearsden/Milngavie complex and the remainder from different parts of Glasgow and outlying towns and villages, plus Helensburgh. Good trains from Coatbridge drop pupils at Anniesland. Bus system – junior ones link up with senior school runs; some pupils from Ayrshire, the Trossachs (aka the edges of Argyll). Popular amongst the middle classes. Pupils can and do drive to school, large pupil car park. The geographic jump from the centre of Glasgow to the West End has changed the bias of the school, which now has fewer Asian and Jewish pupils (no synagogue in the West End), though a significant number from the South Side. Still large element of first time buyers plus one or two recently arrived Europeans.

Previous pupils include Bonar Law, Sir John Moore of Corunna, Campbell Bannerman, Lord Macfarlane of Bearsden, Sir Teddy Taylor, Lady Cosgrove and Lesley Riddoch.

Entrance: Takes around 50 into kindergarten. But get in early – school remains in great demand for entrance thereafter. Parents have coffee and cakes and the children are taken to the kindergarten and assessed individually. Social interaction and 'emotional readiness' rather than crammed academics the yardstick, so children with a reading age of 6 will not necessarily come up trumps. Interviews are held annually – if you don't get a place the first time round, you may be kept 'on hold' and could be accepted, so don't give up. Recently 30 applications for five places between primaries 1 and 6. Priorities to siblings, FPs' children and the rest of the field.

To senior school at 10 and 11. Automatic from junior school, otherwise three times oversubscribed – 50-60 applicants for approximately 32 places at Transitus and 30-40 for first year. 'Healthy uptake'. Odd vacancies in most years, own entrance exam, small number after National grades, 'not many, really'. Fifth year candidates should have grade 1 passes in virtually all their National grade exams, or As at GCSE if they have come from England. Sixth year entrance based on exam results and school reports.

H

Exit: Automatic transfer from junior to senior school. P7 (Transitus – ie 11/12 year olds) are accommodated at Anniesland.

Virtually all to degree courses all over, with a fairly high percentage to Scottish universities; a regular few to Oxbridge (two in 2016, plus nine medics). Mostly popular Edinburgh, Glasgow, St Andrews and Aberdeen. Rising numbers take a gap years. Work experience popular and all sixth year encouraged to undertake community service. No particular bias in career – medics, engineers, accountants, IT course, lawyers, possibly less enthusiasm for the humanities.

Money matters: School sympathetic to genuine problems, no academic scholarships but 50-60 bursaries awarded on a financial need basis (and rector is pleased when he can help pupils of a suitably high calibre in financial need). Ongoing bursary fund.

Remarks: School on a roll, going from strength to strength. A remarkable success story – and, as we said before, a high school truly worthy of its name.

Hutchesons' Grammar School

21 Beaton Road, Glasgow G41 4NW

Pupils: 1,294 • Ages: 4–18 • Sixth form: 161

Fees: £9,098– £11,574 pa

Tel: 01414 232933
Email: admissions@hutchesons.org
Website: www.hutchesons.org

Rector: Since August 2016, Colin Gambles, previously deputy head of S4/S5 at Robert Gordon's College. A biology and psychology teacher, he has also worked at George Watson's College, West Buckland School and Newcastle-under-Lyme School.

Primary school head: Since 2014, Miss Fiona MacPhail.

Academic matters: Exciting new primary school lang course, Global Education, sounds incredibly dreary but stars a wandering 'super teddy bear' (how about the Paddington chronicles?) and exposes pupils to both the language and customs of various countries on a weekly basis: Latin (with staff presumably in togas), French, German, Spanish, Italian, Russian and Gaelic. Parents deeply enthusiastic – bring in fur hats, sombreros and whole school participates with gusto.

Terrific school, three then four parallel classes, most come at 5 and almost all go on to senior school. Good dyslexia help on hand, screening for all, gentle test and assessment – twice a year for tinies, who must have 'passed their 4th birthday' the February before they join. Jolly Phonics (but actually a mixture of reading schemes).

Formidable senior results; regular strings of As in Highers (69 per cent in 2016) with pupils regularly getting six or more in S5 (ie fifth year) and many staying on to study a broad range of Advanced Highers or top up extra Highers in sixth year, despite the fact that they will already have university entrance qualifications in the bag. In 2016, 59 pupils gained five or more As and 18 six As.

Special interest courses in sixth year – Italian, Portuguese and survival cookery (plus own cook book). Results per pupil make other schools quake with envy and broad enough pupil base to offer a moving feast of ancillary subjects. Classical Greek comes and goes, head of classics may just make Greek a serious Higher contender. Vast classics department – Latin compulsory till third year. This is senior stuff. School is open early and late, staff will hold individual drop-in sessions if needed. Biology no longer top of the pops (pupils do human biology too) – maths, English and chemistry head of the pack; pupils encouraged to take as wide a spread as possible – and they do. Only French, German and Spanish on the language front. Native speakers can take Highers in their own tongue. Language labs, satellite TV.

Double-decker library at the forefront of technology uses finger print recognition and is stacked with as many DVDs (Shakespeare on film) as books, and computers everywhere intranetted and internetted. No EFL, 'they've got to have good English to access the syllabus', and no setting for first year – 'Got to find their feet first, this is a big step' – though set for everything thereafter. All pupils screened at 11 and any problems with reading and writing picked up by SENCo, who will 'work within the context of the class', no withdrawn lessons, but fierce academia means that those whose dyslexia holds them back academically may be either screened out or given the tools to succeed – Hutcheson's primary department particularly hot on this. Class sizes of 20/25 at bottom end of the senior school, reducing in number as specialist subjects kick in.

Games, options, the arts: Sports stadium opened a few years ago on old playing fields at secondary school which now incorporates impressive Astroturf hockey pitch and international training standard Tartan athletics track. Astroturf hockey pitches at Clydesdale ground adjacent to the school, plus international standard cricket ground. Pupils are bussed to Auldhouse for rugby. No swimming pool on site (problems with old coal minings underneath); huge sports hall with fitness centre and gym (certain amount of public access required – as ever – by over-vigilant planning Hitlers, but school has succeeded in restricting this to evenings only). All the usual games – rugby almost a religion, county and country representatives abound. Hockey (couple of staff in the UK Olympic squad) etc, plus rowing (rector was a rower, but 'not enough hours in the day') and '25 sporting options'. Curling growing in popularity – Olympic win did wonders for the sport. Trophies in every discipline.

Good and busy drama – consistent finalists in the Scottish drama and music festivals. Three big productions each year. Expect even more emphasis on drama when new building gets into its stride – all three classrooms were in use during our visit including five senior students watching a somewhat raunchy version of As You Like It upstairs.

Terrific music, school does A level music, deeply unhappy – as are the majority of music departments in Scotland – about the National and Higher music syllabi ('Scottish music exams not that hot'); several orchestras, pipe band, jazz. No CCF; granny bashing and masses of charity work popular; recent links with local state schools – the Mark Scott Leadership for Life Award was set up 'after the tragic sectarian murder of Mark Scott' in 1995, school works in partnership with the RC Holyrood school (NB Glasgow can be as sectarian as Northern Ireland in places).

Art fantastic, with kiln, fabric design plus home economics – though no huge number doing the latter. Raft of other options: pupils can do advanced driving (fairly strict rules in place about driving other pupils), archaeology, first aid, Italian and Portuguese. Lots of trips abroad and pupil exchanges. D of E et al. Photo montage on website of trips to Paris, Italy, Switzerland, Australia and Spain – mostly subject based, sports tours, but just the occasional jolly.

Background and atmosphere: Both Hutcheson's Hospital and School were founded in Ingram Street in 1641 by the brothers Thomas and George Hutcheson (the latter was Glasgow's first banker). In 1841 the school moved to the 'quietness of the situation, good air, roomy and open site' of Crown Street in Glasgow's Gorbals, before moving to leafy Pollokshields in 1960, five minutes from the M8 and a doddle from either side of the river. Good local buses, ditto train service. Amalgamated with the girls' school in 1976 (the primary then moved into the girls' school at Kingarth Street, but see below) and went independent in 1985; the board of governors is full of the great and the good of Glasgow: the Merchants House, Hutchesons' Hospital, the Trades House plus the Church of Scotland Presbytery, some ex-officio, some co-opted, 'who have got their act together' – could one say at last? Ex-officio boards can be very elephant in the room-ish.

Large, wide open corridors, huge blocks of classrooms. Super chunks of new-build on what is basically a 60s flat roof horror; masses of photographs, good pupil-inspired art. Subjects are grouped either horizontally or vertically, superb – if dated in places – facilities. New labs. Dining area extended, still pretty busy at all times.

Hutchies acquired the adjacent United Reformed church at the turn of the century. Active during our last visit, the dwindling congregation has now joined up with the church down the road, and the school has full use of this brilliantly converted space, complete with internal stained glass window, red Glasgow sandstone walls (one of them new) and comfy red purple and grey chairs (originally for the congregation). The church hall has transformed into an auditorium with collapsible seating – school not sure now how they ever managed without it – which is home to weekly sixth year lectures, Talking Points, held on Friday mornings and ranging from Mindpower: Fact, Fiction and Fakery via The Genetics of Engineering to Eating Disorders. The series is open to all by ticket – mega wows. This is architecture at its best, creating an entire music centre with practice rooms in the crypt and all manner of exciting performance space, plus a computing centre – for computing lessons rather than for use as an alternative teaching area: 36 networked computers. Would that all schools could be so imaginative. It is also a popular fundraiser, let out for weddings, barmitzvahs, conferences.

Weekly assemblies are divided by year group – the rector delivers four assemblies a week, two to each group. Individual year groups hold separate assemblies on alternate days elsewhere. 'The trouble with such a large school is there is nowhere large enough to take the whole school at the same time.' School operates on swipe cards – the original cashless economy: pupils top up their cards and use them to buy lunch (very good, lots of veggies and salads), breakfast or whatever. Pioneered no fizzy drinks from vending machines. School uniform in regulation black and white – no obvious anomalies that we saw.

Delicious trad 1912 primary school building (which sported electric light) was girls only until 1975 when school went co-ed and Hutchie's primary was born. Stunning library (glass front, zillions of books) carved out of a couple of classrooms in the front passage, opened 2010.

Pastoral care, well-being and discipline: Senior school divided into four fairly loose houses for games, competitions and the like. Seniors 'buddy' littles when they join senior school. Tutors for all over a two-year period. School admits to 'a bit of bullying', but strictures in place to combat it. Miscreants' parents 'would be invited to withdraw their children'. NB Hutchie pupils are expected to maintain the same high standard of discipline when they are beyond school premises. Not overtly Protestant, the pupils have many gods.

School runs a Seasons for Growth Loss and Grief education programme, understanding the effects of change. There is a qualified counsellor who is also one of the matrons, who gives individual emotional support.

Pupils and parents: A mixed bag – 'social, ethnic and economic A-Z'. Cosmopolitan collection of parents, about a third bus their children daily – over 20 miles – from Paisley, Renfrewshire, Lanarkshire, north of the river, Ayr and Falkirk, courtesy of good road links and school bus service. Occasional 'real' foreigner. Long tradition of having a significant number of Jews – separate assemblies on Thursdays; perhaps 10 per cent from Asian backgrounds. Muslims may go to the mosque at lunch time on Friday, have separate lessons for gym and no problem with scarves (though girls eschew dancing). Recent assembly had a Muslim, a Jew and a Protestant all discussing charitable giving.

Number of FPs' children. FPs include John Brown of the shipyard, plus John Buchan, Russell Hillhouse, Carol Smillie, Ross Harper, James Maxton, Richard Emanuel, Lord McColl, Ken Bruce, Lord Irvine, Olivia Giles, RD Laing, Lord Adair.

Entrance: All primary school applicants assessed; up to 120 apply for 60 places.

One hundred a year more or less automatic up from the primary school to the senior school, plus 100 extra (all pupils then get mixed up) mostly from state primaries, by written test. Admission for all usually in August but, if space available, can join at any term.

Exit: Nearly all move from primary up to senior school. Ninety-five plus per cent to university. No real enthusiasm for gap, education is a serious business in Scotland – particularly as many parents, often first time buyers find the current economic climate difficult. Most to Scottish universities, but 50 per cent fewer applicants now to unis south of the border – the tuition fees, you understand.

Money matters: Currently discounts for siblings, around 40 full-fee bursaries and some prizes for sixth formers. More funds being actively sought. All bursaries are means-tested. But 'there should be no bar to a really able pupil profiting from a Hutchies education' – full bursaries are not unusual. Certain amount of concern recently when Hutchies failed the OSCr test, but this is now a thing of the past. For info: Hutchie's income was over 14 million quid last year AND you only get a four per cent discount if you pay five years in advance (with a five per cent per annum projected increase built in). Remember that founder George H was a banker.

Remarks: Awesome. Fiercely academic but pupils achieve their impressive grades from a fairly unselective background. Traditional teaching with enormous breadth, at its very best and using the most up to date tools available. As a previous rector said, 'It's cool to succeed here' – no change in that. Cradle to grave stuff this.

International School of Aberdeen

Pitfodels House, North Deeside Road, Aberdeen AB15 9PN

Pupils: 355 • Ages: 3–18 • Sixth form: 44

Fees: £10,550 – £10,935 + £2,100 capital fee pa

Tel: 01224 730300
Email: admin@isa.aberdeen.sch.uk
Website: www.isa.aberdeen.sch.uk

Director: Since January 2017, Sarah Bruce, previously middle and high school principal. Qualifications in kinesiology and education, with an MEd from the University of Toronto; taught PE for two years at the Canadian Academy in Kobe, Japan (as did her predecessor), before joining Havergal College in Toronto, progressing from health and PE teacher to head of upper school. Moved to Aberdeen in 2013, initially as upper school learning support and middle school science teacher.

Academic matters: School nominally follows the IB, but they also cover High School diplomas. Most pupils do the IB diploma; average point score 34 in 2016. Pupils get Advanced credit for having taken the IB, but it is by no means suitable or even needed by all. Fair mish-mash. Massive amount of to-ing and fro-ing; over 35 nationalities are represented in the student population, 32 different languages spoken, most pupils come for two or three years, some only for one, and 'odd one beyond five'. Pupils go on the roll of honour (spelled, of course, 'honor') society if they have done well in the realms of academe, leadership and service. All very American and fairly in your face, with a strong emphasis on service.

School is divided into three distinct parts: elementary – pre-school to grade 5 (ie 10 year olds), middle school (grades 6-8) and high school (grades 9-12). Each department has its own distinct area in the school, with tinies having a splendid enclosed play area on squidgy tarmac.

Sixty per cent of all staff are British 'local' hire, with spouses in oil, or 'just living here', and 40 per cent have a mixture of backgrounds, from English-speaking countries in the main, though native speakers employed for Spanish and French (the two languages offered for IB) plus Dutch mother tongue (think Shell). School appears to run as a commune with no heads of departments, plus two counsellors. Whilst senior pupils seek advice from staff, younger pupils are ambivalent about whether they go to a teacher or an older pupil ('natural helpers') for assistance. EAL where necessary – three dedicated teachers. Roughly 30 pupils in each year group, 13/20 per class. Choices accelerated, and learning support available – two dedicated members of staff. School is brutally honest – if pupils need more than 20 per cent support per week, then they will have to go elsewhere, ie local mainstream.

Games, options, the arts: Stunning sports wing housing a double gymnasium, huge games hall, fitness centre, multi-purpose spaces, 25 metre six lane swimming pool, much used by locals – as are the gym/games facilities, fitness suite and multi-gym. Terrific outdoor sports area: two all-weather basketball courts (teams play internationally), tennis courts, facilities for football and golf (which they also play internationally and in the Scottish League) plus volleyball. Teams visit London, Stavanger, Spain and Portugal as well as running their own internal league. Cabinets of shining silver in previous school not yet up, but dedicated space available in canteen/rec area.

Terrific music space, with recording studios et al. No orchestras but number of instruments taught, ditto choirs – pupils make music outside school. Rather clever computer programme which goes red when you hit the wrong note – deeply popular. Serious theatre which replicates the one they lost – magical acoustics – plus black room, an infinite space used for theatre or odd parents' meetings; history of lavish drama. Impressive art all over and whizzo new art rooms with outside area for really mucky stuff; external kiln. This is all things for all people – quadruple wows all round.

High charity presence: sleepovers for the homeless, shoe-box appeal and the 8 year olds visit local 'rest' homes and read and perform to them. American boy scouts, cub scouts, girl guides and Brownies, but no D of E.

Background and atmosphere: School founded in 1972 by Mr McCormick and bought by the oil companies in 1980. The latter own the buildings and oversaw the negotiations with Aberdeen town council, which had to approve each and every bit of the new build, but the oil consortium underwrote the school (and undertake all the improvements – wish lists et al), leasing the buildings to the school for a peppercorn. The school is run by a charitable trust, with the members of the board being appointed in proportion to the number of employees' children in the school at one particular moment. A local solicitor sees fair play. School owns 16 acres of land, with nine acres of games fields off site.

The (unsigned) reception area is through the much revamped late Victorian (1881) Pitfodels House, which boasts double glazed curved windows (a first for this editor, who is quite into houses) and beautifully replicated mouldings (wood) leading to the street (see below). Two wings on either side of the library, one for the games area and one for the classroom block. Very light and airy, with hidden lights wherever from south facing windows – in the roof, on the staircases – which seem to float with exciting banisters; 40 huge magically filled classrooms – the junior ones interlinked so that classes can combine if need be; wide passages with a mass of gossip areas, comfy seats – gosh! Pupil pics abound, so not that soulless. The landscaped gardens contain a mass of car park area and sport a splendid if somewhat surprising three storey granite tower, thought to date from the mid 17th century.

New build is based on a village street, with the library as the hub – a glorious double decker library with a random collection of computers – plus, of course, dedicated computer rooms elsewhere. The canteen, at the end of the street, boasts both bog standard school seating and high level tables and chairs, plus cafeteria style seating. Pupils revel in the ability to be both grown up and silly at the same time. The newish chef has turned school catering around – now making a healthy profit. Children have an account but can buy outwith. (NB Peanut butter not allowed – epi-pens and de-fib machines on hand.) At the end of the street an eight metre climbing wall and, when the cafeteria peripherals are pushed to one side (all the side boards are on wheels), school has a huge entertainment space for exhibitions and the like – cunning.

Pupil lockers (high enough off the ground for them to put bags under) line their respective teaching areas and are still decorated in rather uninspired wrapping paper on their birthdays. Lots of happy birthday singing at lunch. Much talk of how super Scotland is, and a certain amount of Celtic indulgence. Trips all over the shop.

Pastoral care, well-being and discipline: School anxious to dispel the myth of spoilt little rich kids; keen PSE and strong RME. Guidance by clans or houses. Staff are trained in different cultures and dealing with people in a different fashion (how things are done at home) – 'Kids are kids'; 'Knock on wood – no overt bullying, but quite a lot of teasing'. No bullying because of habits, more 'teasing because of personality traits' (his words not ours). Drug presentation evenings, and head has – 'Oh yeah, on occasion' – disciplined and suspended (never expelled) miscreants for a day or two: details of all suspendable offences in handbooks, complete with list of drug test cut-off levels. School keen on independent study and motivation, and no gum may be chewed in class.

Pupils and parents: No school uniform, but of course everyone conforms – we were, though, slightly surprised to see a 7(?) year old in mini skirt with high heels and sparkly tights.

Most students arrive via school bus. Good parent contact with weekly newsletters. Recent influx of locals, who pay a lesser fee. With the new build, which is a couple of miles closer to the centre of Aberdeen, school is actively canvassing for more locals; current downturn in pupil numbers due to declining gas and oil industries.

Entrance: Whenever. Undersubscribed; could hold 600.

Exit: Most to universities in Britain, with several off to the US and a few heading to study elsewhere eg France, Spain and the Caribbean; one medic in 2016.

Money matters: Fees paid by oil companies, otherwise one or two non-oil American expats, bursaries and financial aid available so that school more reflects the cost of a 'normal' British school. IB academic scholarships available for final two years.

Remarks: We previously said, 'Smashing school – an eye-opener,' but never expected that our next visit would indeed be the result of smashing the school. It had, in 2006, been 10 days into building their new gym, which would have released their old gym to become a theatre, when Aberdeen County Council announced the route of the new ring road – straight through the old school. But now? We are (un)reliably informed that the new build (which is fantastic) cost £51 million – and it looks it! Wow! Wow! Wow!

Totally logical, of course, to follow an international programme but, with such an influx of non-native teachers, it might be possible for a family to be billeted in Scotland for a year or so and experience no native culture at all. Thank you for sharing.

James Gillespie's High School

Lauderdale Street, Edinburgh EH9 1DD

Pupils: 1,211 • Ages: 11–18 • Sixth form: 330

Tel: 01314 471900
Email: admin@jamesgillespies.edin.sch.uk
Website: www.jamesgillespies.edin.sch.uk

Headteacher: Since 2012, Mr Donald J Macdonald BSc MBASQH Dip Ed (50s), previously head of Liberton High (school's exceptional progress under his watch resulted in an invitation to 10 Downing Street). Has taught science, physics and maths at a range of Scottish schools including Knox Academy and Portobello High. Married, with two daughters; lists golf, fishing and Scottish malt whisky amongst his many interests.

Academic matters: Class size 30 (20 for practical subjects), setted early for maths in the September of their first year, second year setted for English. Three separate sciences for all from the third year onwards. No classics, but French, German, Spanish and Urdu, a growing number also learn Gaelic (a feeder school where pupils do all subjects in Gaelic). All languages are taught up to Advanced Higher level. Newly introduced psychology popular. School does mix of Nationals, Higher, Advanced Highers and A levels for physics, art (in order to form a portfolio), Urdu and geography – an interesting diversification for a state school. Excellent support for learning, dyslexia, dyspraxia, and help with exams, both withdrawn from class and team teaching in class. ADHD is OK – 'Most very well-behaved'. All staff trained to support pupils with a variety of talents. Pupils come from 40+ different countries – 'the most diverse population in Scotland': EFL available (free) for all who need it. CDT is 50/50 craft and design and all computer-based – 350 computers in the school. Recent BECTA award for best website. In 2016, 41 per cent of S5 got 5+ Highers, as did 61 per cent of S6, with 57 per cent getting 1+ Advanced Higher (all the highest results on record). This included two students who got 100 per cent in Advanced Higher maths (very popular at this level).

Games, options, the arts: PE, swimming and extensive after-school activities all now on site. School is now a recognised Sports Hub with links to 15 or more local adult clubs. Girls' football, tennis, swimming, cricket and netball are particularly popular. Massive music uptake, with carol service normally held in the Usher Hall, over 500 regularly on the stage. Senior orchestra, junior orchestra, lessons free. Strong, spectacular art, photography, impressive fabric design. Huge dance area, media popular with lights and editing studios, three drama studios. Wizard home economics department – better than most homes we know. Trips all over the place, in many disciplines – skiing, Paris for art, historians to the trenches, geographers to do glacial research in the French Alps. Exchanges with several countries including: France, Spain, Germany, South Africa, China, Finland, Holland and Switzerland.

Background and atmosphere: Founded in 1803 as a result of a legacy from James Gillespie, 'a wealthy Edinburgh manufacturer of snuff and tobacco', who was born in Roslin. Started with 65 students and one master and led a peripatetic existence. At one point the prep school for the Merchant Company's secondary schools. By 1908 had a roll of over 1000, including girls, and offered secondary education under the aegis of the Edinburgh school board, moving to Bruntsfield House, just off The Meadows, in 1966 and going fully co-ed in 1978. The earliest building on this site dates from 1300, and the current building, Bruntsfield House, was built in 1605, with later additions and improvements. Sir George Warrender, whose family was to be awarded the title Bruntsfield, bought the house from the original owners and was intrigued to find that if you hung a sheet from every window you could access from the inside, still sheetless windows outside. A secret room was discovered, with blood-stained floor, ashes in the grate and a skeleton under the wainscot. The Green Lady haunts the top storeys to this day.

School entirely rebuilt across the whole campus, including the construction of the Malala building, the main teaching block, and the refurbishment of the grade A listed Bruntsfield House, with an official opening in October 2016. Whole exercise jointly funded by City of Edinburgh Council and the Scottish Government.

Pastoral care, well-being and discipline: Follows the state guidelines – good PSHE, good anti-bullying strategy in place: 'We get the youngsters to talk it through.. We bring them together and get the bully to accept their behaviour is wrong'. 'No current problems' with cigarettes, alcohol or drugs, but will exclude on either a temporary or permanent basis if necessary. Last head only ever made two drugs-related temporary exclusions, but it would be permanent if any hint of dealing. Also out permanently for a violent attack, though temporary exclusion for 'physical violence'. Homework books which must be signed by parent or guardian. No uniform, which is going slightly against the current Edinburgh trend – 'If it ain't broke, don't fix it'.

Pupils and parents: Free intake, so diverse: 47 languages spoken. Large number of professional families (Marchmont is a popular area for the university) plus 'a significant group of working class, with relatively poor backgrounds'. Huge ethnic mix, with some girls wearing the chador – they may well do PE and swim wearing full leggings and long-sleeved T-shirts (though parents can ask to withdraw their daughters from these lessons, few do). Lifts installed for wheelchair-bound pupil, minor physical handicaps OK. Strong parent/teacher involvement.

Entrance: First year capped at 220; catchment area redrawn but some places still available by request – very popular, with pupils from as far away as Penicuik and Musselburgh. Obliged to take children on a first come first served basis, waiting lists. Certain number of pupils who have obtained university entrance elsewhere in the independent sector join in sixth form for Higher Still (and a better chance at Oxbridge).

Exit: Number leaves before Higher grades, either to further education or work; good proportion to universities, mainly Scots, studying medicine, science, art college, followed by social subject and music in that order. Annual trickle to Oxbridge (generally between six and 10).

Remarks: Can't fault it.

Jordanhill School

45 Chamberlain Road, Jordanhill, Glasgow G13 1SP

Pupils: 1,062 • Ages: 5–18 • Sixth form: 180

Tel: 01415 762500
Email: info@jordanhill.glasgow.sch.uk
Website: www.jordanhill.glasgow.sch.uk

Rector: Since 1997, Dr Paul Thomson BSc PhD Dip Ed (50s), educated at Dollar Academy, thence to Glasgow uni for a combined honours in maths and physics plus (later) a PhD, having done his Dip Ed at Jordanhill, once next door, but now consigned to the John Anderson campus. Thomson's meteoric career path found him appointed as one of the youngest heads in Scotland; that apart, he has a fearsome intellect and spouted facts and figures faster than most heads we have met, adding all the while that 'it is available on the web page'. A member of the board of the SQA, chair of the Advisory Council (2013-17) and now chair of the Qualifications Committee. Keen to 'improve the educational environment', he has masterminded a mega building programme extending the refectory, constructing an all weather pitch (much in use during our rather damp visit) and building (and we suspect doing more than a little designing) a stunning new classroom block – the South building (replacing what was once a gloomy collection of classrooms). He has also transformed the hall, entrance and public spaces of the original building – but see below. Unlike many heads, Thomson regards these developments as 'a pupil necessity and therefore worth spending time and thought on', rather than as an end in itself to glorify Jordanhill and his own cleverness in getting the funding.

Jordanhill is the only direct grant-aided non-special school in Scotland, and runs its own budget, as does each department. A block grant comes from the Scottish Government to whom the school is answerable. Thomson regards himself quite rightly as a CEO, working 'with the staff' and running the place with a budget of £5,600 per child per annum (used to be more in real terms, but what with recent cuts...). He obviously misses teaching; his entire demeanour changed during our tour round the school: whenever we found a child to be talked to – about anything – gone was the efficient question-answering model and in its place appeared an interested smiley friend. (He also does all the 'early' UCAS references.) But youngsters apart, we suspect he does not tolerate fools with ease (he thinks he has 'mellowed a little' recently). He also picks up emotional flack, and, after our whistle-stop tour of the new developments we coffee-ed in the staff room (young, vibrant, get the picture?) where a teacher related how much help he had been given when he had 'found it all too much': still at the school, he now has a different role.

Head of primary: Since August 2014 is Mr Richard Buchan, previously head teacher at Garrowhill Primary in Glasgow for nine years.

Academic matters: The school is inclusive: the most successful state school (albeit grant-aided) in Scotland. Four classes of 25 (rather than the trad legal limit of 33) with practical classes of 15 (max 20). Some setting in maths. French from primary 1, Spanish on offer from age 14 to Advanced Higher level. Langs taught via a star system; when the whole class fills the chart they get French breakfast (croissants perhaps?) A Swire Chinese Language Centre opened in August 2016, which combined with the Confucius Classroom awarded to the school in late 2015 offers Mandarin from Primary 5 onwards to Higher and Advanced Higher to pupils at Jordanhill and neighbouring schools.

Arrangements on hand for non native-speakers to have help with extra English (ESOL) and take exams in their native langs, through Shawlands Academy, the Punjabi and Urdu centres etc. Gaidhlig and Gaelic are both listed, though not taught at Jordanhill; pupils studying Cantonese, Greek, Italian, Latin, Mandarin, Russian or Urdu may well be able to include them in their programme. Special needs well catered for – 'If they can cope then we will take them, unless their needs are such that the school cannot accommodate them'; some pupils have records of needs. SEN students have open access to networks; three dedicated staff work across primary and secondary schools, plus five pupil support assistants, scribing where necessary. Paired reading with sixth formers wherever; support sessions during lunch, after school, in the evening, this is tailored formally structured study support. Standard testing for all aged 8-13: English, maths, spelling, VR; anomalies picked up early and the school's ed psych advises if necessary.

Public exam results across the board streaks ahead of other Scottish (and Glasgow) schools in particular, and an astonishing 90 per cent of pupils stay on for second year sixth. In 2016, 55 per cent A grades at Higher and 45 per cent at Advanced Higher. Masses of external activity, much to-ing and fro-ing with local unis and colleges: higher psychology in partnership with Anniesland College, in the evenings. School is well used. Regular successes in quizzes and competitions both nationally and abroad.

Overhead projectors; whiteboards as standard, school both hard wired and wireless: computers (400+ of them) in every discipline, in the art rooms, wherever. Trolleys of notebooks motor round classrooms. Rector adds, 'School has ICT mark and previously won ICT leadership reward'.

Homework clubs and online learning via O365. Ditto supported study. Several groups of pupils doing research projects have direct links with staff. Powerpoint demos by all, from P7; P6 and rest of junior school observe before a general discussion on the quality of the presentation with either the rector or other members of staff. (Rector's face lit up like a beacon when he described this). Debating and public speaking timetabled for 11-13 year olds. Loads of interaction. Evening support classes for exam years, labs are open at lunchtime and post-school. Good modern library, more computers and even more in the careers department. Lifts and ramps all over the shop.

Games, options, the arts: Impressive number of playing fields, or use of them. Certain amount of mixing and matching amongst the Anniesland educational fraternity, with Jordanhill having bought the Laurel Park games hall whilst Glasgow Academy owns the Laurel Park games pitch. With me so far? School owns one rugby pitch, uses one from the uni, and has a couple of footie pitches on a 75 year lease from Strathclyde uni. Not bad for a non-independent school on an inner city site. The impressive all-weather pitch is home to the Hillhead Hockey Club, who train and play here. Two gyms on main campus.

Fantastic games and oodles of caps – capped pupils wear green ties; colours gold collars, half colours gold stripe etc, and can be awarded for team, individual, musical success or any international representation. Pupils also wear date badges and can end up looking a little like a Christmas Tree. Trad games: rugby, hockey, football, cross-country running and athletics.

Stunning north-facing art department in the South building, lots of art on display, magical fabrics, jewellery and photography. Kiln and silk screen machine in place. Sculpture and good CDT.

Drama strong, top two years do a show for the whole school, and drama timetabled P6 – S2. Higher drama link up with Knightswood Secondary. Inspiring music, with specialist staff from P6 up. 'The best music department in the country,' says the rector; 300 plus pupils play an instrument, 26 different ensembles, serious orchestras. All swinging, and particularly keen on composing. Concerts popular with parents. Outstanding music results.

Clubs for everything, chess particularly popular. Hot on debating, and citizenship. Health and Fashion Technology offers diverse provision, more post-National grades, when students also study international cuisine (head's face lit up again). 'Healthy take-up, both home economics rooms refurbished'. Deep envy from this editor.

Ambitious outdoor education programme with pupils spending afternoons or weeks away depending on year group; costs, but funds available for those who otherwise couldn't afford to go (less than two per cent free school meals in the senior school as opposed to almost 30 per cent for the rest of Glasgow). Senior pupils have a biannual trip to the developing world, part project part tourism. World Challenge. Oodles of trips abroad: Euroscola at the European Parliament in Strasbourg, Paris, Berlin and China. Massive charity involvement – both fundraising and community work in the locality. Jolly school mag written by pupils, staff and FPs, clearly laid out with brilliant editing, comes out twice a year, easy to read, with none of the trendy under shadowing that doting grannies find so irritating (not to mention GSG editors).

Background and atmosphere: Founded in 1920 as a demo school for Jordanhill College of Education, became direct grant in 1987, having narrowly escaped closure in 1969. Handsome classical grade B listed building. Rector has stunning panelled offices (think Eltham Palace); huge classrooms with high ceilings and wide pupil-proof corridors have had a makeover. The hall has been brilliantly elongated – parquet flooring matches, the wall bars have gone, lighting in place and retractable seating. Blackout blinds. Acid etched glass panelled doors to die for, actually, most of school has natty oak doors to die for. The entrance and foyer have been redeveloped to match and the staffroom likewise. Fantastic redevelopment of the site of a somewhat miserable building previously owned by Strathclyde uni, bought by Jordanhill and transformed into one of the most exciting class/art/spaces we have seen. This bright 15 room classroom block, with north facing art room and huge atrium on the ground floor, has been neatly dovetailed in. We were confidently told the atrium had a popular foodie kiosk in the corner; with our luck, it was unmanned during our visit. Much used as a drop-out zone; each pupil has a lockable locker and there are cunning (quite light) moveable circular seats. Good informal performing space; the balcony above overlooks. The next development was a £150,000 revamp of the adjacent science building with support from the Wolfson Foundation (£40,000).

Primary based on the first two floors of the handsome classical grade B listed building, with a couple of dedicated play areas, one with lyrical views of the playing fields, and David Stow building designed by David Barclay 1914-22, the former Jordanhill College. Tinies have use of all the main school facilities; we arrived to find them milling around the super new enclosed Astroturf in front of the main school building, and skipped past various crocodiles when we retraced our steps back to the main school with the rector. Dig that fort!

School surrounded by (some) games pitches. The high fence which divided the school from the college is now a thing of the past, as, indeed is Jordanhill College. Now amalgamated with Strathclyde uni, it moved (lock, stock and barrel) in 2012 to the John Anderson Campus under the westering of Glasgow Cathedral. Following demolition of the random collection of 'temporary' classrooms, the magnificent David Stow building is now exposed to the west in all its glory. Housing development will commence shortly. Of course the games pitch is inalienably zoned educational. The total potential development land would appear to be 16.6 hectares (out of 21) at 16 houses per hectare, and the ongoing discussion is as much tree and flora protection as infrastructure. There is talk of the games pitches being administered by The Charitable Trust of Jordanhill school. Chicken and egg: school may have to grow to accommodate new potential pupils.

Strong links with local Jordanhill parish church. Strong links too with Glasgow state schools – joint improvement meetings for staff and pupils, whilst the latter have a joint pre-vocational programme, plus Your Turn project involving pupils across the city. Pupils from other schools can come to Jordanhill to pick up Highers or Advanced Highers not catered for in their own schools.

Pupils are neat in brown uniforms, but decorated as above. Tinies wear charming green pinnies. Efficient and fairly unforgiving uniform guidelines in the prospectus supplement. Headscarves not a problem. Sixth year have a dedicated study room. JOSS operates an after-school club for tinies in the nearby church hall.

Pastoral care, well-being and discipline: Four houses – the heads of houses are guidance staff with combined office and interview rooms. Pupils meet with their tutors for 10 minutes each day; the latter are responsible for PSE. School policy is to clamp down hard on any form of bullying. Neither the rector nor his predecessor have permanently excluded; a clearly defined code of sanctions, including letters home, litter duty (brill) and detention. Regular links between sixth form and littles – combined reading and the BFG club. Minister from Jordanhill parish church takes assemblies, but this is an ecumenical school, with all religions' festivals observed – rector is keener that pupils learn 'to conduct themselves properly in church' and understand other faiths (by, eg, visiting local synagogues, mosques and temples) rather than pay lip service to any particular religion.

Pupils and parents: Serves a predominantly owner-occupier area – professionals, who form an enthusiastic parent-teacher association, with parent volunteers in primary department and loads of fundraising. Nine per cent ethnic minorities. Cashless buffet (looked good); young may not buy food for others. Only pupils S4 and above allowed off campus for lunch. Fairly sensible set of rules: and equally clear list of sanctions, most requiring parental signature.

Entrance: Inclusive, by address; oversubscribed, waiting lists. Traditionally, 33 pupils are added to those who come up from primary to senior, thus four classes of roughly 25. Inclusive, by address, over-subscribed, waiting lists. Siblings get priority. Some places may become available in odd years, ditto (never advertised) available post National grades. First come, first served, and, in the case of advanced Highers (or SBacc) if the subjects you want to take are already full, then you must try elsewhere. Worth moving/killing for.

Exit: Virtually all move from primary to senior school. Some 75 per cent to university. Trickle to Oxbridge, a few to universities down south – Imperial for engineering, Liverpool, Manchester, the odd musician to the Royal Academy of Music, and tranches to art school, with or without a foundation course. But most stay in the west of Scotland. Dentistry, medicine and veterinary school all popular.

Remarks: Outstanding, with an inspirational, slightly left of centre rector (though mebbe – perish the thought, he might have mellowed just a tad). Better resourced than many schools in the independent sector – and it's free. A beacon – Glasgow independent sector eat your heart out: Jordanhill should be compulsory viewing for the lot of you.

Kelvinside Academy

33 Kirklee Road, Glasgow G12 0SW

Pupils: 375 • Ages: 3–18 • Sixth form: S5 60 pupils, S6 46 pupils

Fees: £7,500 – £11,880 pa

Tel: 01413 573376
Email: admissions@kelvinsideacademy.org.uk
Website: www.kelvinsideacademy.org.uk

Rector: Since April 2016, Mr Ian H Munro (30s), previously deputy head at Shiplake College and apparently the youngest rector of an HMC school in the world. Teaching qualification from Edinburgh and MEd from Cambridge. Has also taught at Heriot's and Gordonstoun. He and his wife Catherine, also a teacher, have a great love for the outdoors, and particularly enjoy sailing off the west coast of Scotland. Ian is a keen follower of rugby, football and cricket and has coached the Great Britain U16 and Scottish junior rowing teams.

Head of junior school: Since 2008, Mr Andrew Dickenson MA (50s). A historian, he was educated at the City of London Freemen's school, and came to Glasgow after nine years at Edinburgh Academy, moving from director of studies to deputy head of junior school. We found him comfortable, relaxed and confident. Avuncular, though some of his Facebook entries would appear to disagree (seemed a bit chippy to us). He still teaches.

K

Academic matters: Follows the Scottish system, with National 4s and 5s; 'happy with it and working our way through'; 'not much point in making a fuss', writing some of the papers (National 4s only). No intention of following the IB route. In 2015, 57 per cent A grades at Higher level in S4 and 39 per cent at Advanced Higher.

Small class sizes, four parallel classes, upper school setted for English, maths and modern languages: French from age 5, German and Spanish from P7. No classics. Native speakers can take exams (Highers etc) in their own lang, school will pull in tutors, though those needing EFL can get help in school (dedicated EFL teacher). Business/enterprise, business management popular with 12/13 year olds who follow through with some spectacular success with Young Enterprise: best wheeze was Kelvinside teddy bears.

School is rejigging the IT infrastructure, moving to on-line marking and getting rid of paper. New head of digital learning, school moving to wireless, with netbooks and tablets surrounded by a virtual learning environment in both junior and upper school. Super computer complex which includes a multimedia lab 'that anyone can use'

New head of learning support too, every child assessed on entry, glitches firmly knocked on the head: one-to-one sessions, if necessary, otherwise small groups, from juniors up; trained teachers in each faculty. Free. Drop-in sessions, parents can drop in too, drop-ins for homework. School will 'bend over backwards' to help individual pupils'. Good work-shadowing arrangements for 14/15 year olds.

Pupils from the state Cleveden Academy a bare half mile away join the odd science and English lesson, use games fields at Balgray: works to both schools' advantage.

Games, options, the arts: Small school, so everyone who wants to, gets a chance to shine. Loads of music – masses of tinies carrying instruments bigger than themselves were struggling off to junior orchestra when we visited, a lovely sight. 'Huge numbers, string, wind, full and junior orchestra, jazz group, one or two (four to be exact) pipers; Sibelius in music tech dept. Award winning string orchestra, good showing in Glasgow Music Festival. Expressive arts important: drama timetabled and impressive in the Gilchrist Hall. Thoroughly Modern Millie, Jekyll and Hyde (for which 80 young auditioned). Heaps of extras. Liberal studies include a wide range of classes – philosophy et al. Psychology, cooking long since abandoned (shame about the latter). Photography plus all the usual suspects in the art dept. Fabric, fashion, textiles. Life drawing in the Botanic Gardens (could be chilly). CAD.

Balgray playing fields, less than a mile away, opposite the boating pond: Rugby and cricket powerful, girls play hockey. PE is mixed and can be taken by staff of either sex ('no issues'). Rowing (pace Katherine Grainger) has tremendous support, academicals in the Glasgow Schools boat, and currently doing heads of the river (Clyde). Two serious gyms, fitness suite. Cleveden Academy uses games pitch, which now has a posh Miller Drummond pavilion: about to celebrate its first fundraising breakfast as we write. School expects happy fundraising from enthusiastic parents – and gets it.

Trips all over, both for sport and fun; rugby tour to Paris, Holland for hockey. CCF compulsory for all for one year, thereafter voluntary, all three services. Popular shooting range in the attic, and country reps. Skiing both at home and abroad, country reps again. D of E and camping at Rannoch costed into fees, dedicated specialist out-door member of staff.

Background and atmosphere: Kelvinside Academy started life in 1879 in the elegant Grade A building by James Sellars, now much expanded, but still with wide passages, high ceilings, ornate assembly halls. The school was re-named The Kelvinside Academy War Memorial Trust, after the Great War; and war memorials for FPs who died in both wars line the main school stairs. Glasgow was awash with the building of splendid temples to learning during the 1870s/80s; many have dropped by the wayside, some have changed hands, but Kelvinside remains a beacon to an earlier age. Numbers have increased; school, co-ed since 1998, includes junior and nursery. The state of the art nursery is based at the leafy Balgray playing fields and the school now has a dedicated sixth form centre.

Parents can drop off early/collect late (late waiting till 6pm), brekky from 8am. Rather a fine double-decker library. Outside caterer, pupils have to opt in, meal times staggered (halal not a problem); sandwiches eaten in the Mall, kiosk with salads, rolls, fruit on sale.

Proper charity work undertaken by school which raises funds for conventional charities but also help out at the pointy end with the Glasgow soup kitchen (hands on: most indigents aged between 30-60; often ex-cons, drug addicts, with health problems). This is community out-reach at its best: one staff for every two pupils. Juniors clear up the river Kelvin (Friends of the River Kelvin) and spend time gardening for the elderly.

Pastoral care, well-being and discipline: House system strong, house tutors remain with their charges throughout pupils' time in school. PSE important. Regular assemblies, often taken by prefects; year group assemblies, school ecumenical, but carol service, Easter celebrated, as well as Remembrance day, Jewish, Muslim high days and holidays acknowledged. Will take pupils thrown out from other schools, who must agree not to take drugs during their time at Kelvinside. Cheating, stealing 'can lead to suspension; bullying can lead to good-bye'. School boasts 'a strong partnership with parents'. Robust bullying policy overhauled: cyber bullying a 'real worry'; that, and grooming. Holiday club to help with baby-sitting problems.

Pupils and parents: Middle class, professional, a significant number of first-time buyers, lots of travelling. From Gairlochead, the Trossachs, to Dunlop in Ayrshire. Bus from Newton Mearns/Southside (Clyde tunnel useful). Selection of ethnic minorities, but then Glasgow is a city of growth. Parental poll: most seem pleased with current incumbent, but 'after John Broadfoot was here for so long', and then to have 'two changes in less than in four terms'. Unusual to find fence-sitters in the education world. Particularly in Glasgow.

Good fundraisers, from posh balls to burgers on the games pitch. 'Very welcoming,' says school. Secondhand shop run by parents. And one of the best websites we have come across, not a fancy pants word amongst them. The joy.

Pupils can drive themselves to school with permission, usual caveats about pupil only and no friends. FPs include Sir Tom Risk, erstwhile governor of The Bank of Scotland, Sir Hugh Frazer of the eponymous department store, Lord Rodger, high court judge, Harry Rottenburg and rugby player Ritchie Grey.

Entrance: Through the nursery, or wherever; traditionally at 5, 11, 12 or sixth form level. Academically selective – by interview and assessment, previous school report, five Nationals plus As for subjects to be taken at Higher level.

Exit: Over 80 per cent to university – usually Scotland; also to Stanford and UCL in 2015. Off to study natural sciences, engineering, veterinary medicine, economics, music, history of art etc.

Money matters: Usual discounts for siblings, collection of bursaries and more wished for. Bursaries are rigorously means tested, private detectives, wardens, the lot. Rotten Foundation (as in Harry Rottenburg, 1875, who invented – amongst other things – the original starting block, first used in the 1948 Olympics) unfailingly generous. Scholarships = hefty book tokens not cash.

Will help 'wherever possible' if financial difficulties occur; 'not a problem', 80 per cent pay by direct debit, and discount if parents pay up front for the year.

Remarks: Strong traditional school, takes tinies through to upper sixth, seamless, co-ed, back under firm hand after a little wander in the wilderness (Rate my Teachers tells all). School became co-ed 1998 (the last of the Glasgow schools to combine). Numbers (as fairly prevalent in independent sector at this moment) a tad down. Smaller gentler school, 'not the sausage machine of the ones on either side'.

Kilgraston School

Bridge Of Earn, Perthshire PH2 9BQ

Pupils: 310; 126 full boarders. • Ages: 2–18 (boarding from 8) • Sixth form: 69 • RC

Fees: Day £10,155 – £16,470; Boarding £21,495 – £28,140 pa

Tel: 01738 812257
Email: headoffice@kilgraston.com
Website: www.kilgraston.com

Principal: Since April 2015, Mrs Dorothy MacGinty, previously head of St Francis' College in Hertfordshire, where she has also been head of biology, head of games, boarding housemistress and deputy head. She is married to Frank and they have three children; the youngest has joined Kilgraston.

Head of junior school: Since April 2016, Andrew Stewart, who has taught at the school for several years and was previously an outdoor education teacher.

Academic matters: Latin and sciences from 10. Tiny classes, 10/12, max 18 in prep, all assessed for glitches, 'qualified' expert on hand, 'if staff diagnose cause for concern, they have an instant referral sheet'. Jolly phonics or 'anything else that works'. Three maths clinics a week, but more or less set for maths ('differentiated maths classes') from early. Lots of support.

Eighteen month year groups; individual classes can accommodate all sorts and sizes. Pupils say science on the up with new head of physics, stunning recently completed science block, complete with shower and disabled loo. In 2016, 46 per cent A grades at Higher level and 65 per cent at Advanced Higher.

Efficient remedial unit (CReSTeD WS); specialist teachers for dyslexia and dyspraxia – one-to-one teaching, small groups. School has completed our SEN questionnaire, but would not expand on exactly how inclusive Kilgraston was. Well nigh impossible for the physically challenged, stairs all over the place.

Lang labs popular, EFL offered. Many exchanges, French, German and Spanish (both pupils and staff), via Sacred Heart network.

Games, options, the arts: Impressive 25m swimming pool complex, sports hall (fitness suite and climbing wall) faced in sandstone, with niches echoing those in the stable building (well-converted into prep school with attached nursery) – historic Scotland at its best. Wide choice of sports. Eight floodlit tennis courts, international-sized, all-weather, floodlit hockey pitch and specialist academy coaching (costs extra). Some golf. Touch rugby. Netball popular, girls play local Bridge of Earn club, good for community spirit. Dedicated director of weekend and outdoor activities encourages all sorts of co-curricular options such as whitewater rafting, canoeing, sailing. Oodles of clubs.

The only school in Scotland with equestrian facilities on campus – 60m x 40m (double size dressage arena, how does that work, we wonder?) floodlit manège and livery. Coaching by Olympians and internationalists. The horse mad can graduate with an SVQII in basic horse care (worming and the like), which, as far as we can work out is the equivalent of Pony Club B or the lowest qualification to start on a BHS certification course. Seems potty not to offer the BHSAI. That having been said, one or two equestriennes have done commendably well in local competitions with Kilgraston sponsoring a show at Gleneagles Hotel.

The art department overlooks the Rotunda and boasts an enormous computer-linked loom. Exciting ceramics, regular master classes. D of E, debating, leadership courses. Strong drama. Music centre in the attics, with keyboards and 14 individual sound-proofed study rooms; guitars and stringed instruments everywhere (and hanging from the walls); sound recording studio, music lessons (cost extra). Writers' group. Debating. Cooking: tantalising smells in the kitchens. Girls no longer make their own ball gowns for the annual Merchiston hoolie, just fabric design, some of which was to die for but ain't quite so good for the pocket. Sewing machine time is spent altering their purchases to fit.

Boarding: Boarding for girls only, from age 8, rather jolly loose boxes on the top floor, each girl has her own space, but no

K

doors, so night time confidences easy peasy. Bedsits from third year, tinies' dorms divided into individual cabins. Moderated Wifi access and single rooms with washing facilities for girls from age 12.

School stops at 4.10pm on Fridays for day and weekly boarders, but masses of alternative activities for those who stay. Computers, games hall/tennis courts, art, music and sewing rooms open throughout the weekend. Charming and well-used chapel: God important here – most attend assembly and mass on Sundays, feast days still special. Lady Day a blast.

Background and atmosphere: Founded in 1920 – one of 200 networked schools and colleges of the Society of the Sacred Heart. Moved to the handsome red Adamesque sandstone house in 1930, set in 54 acres of parkland (though to be brutally honest it does look a bit like a grand pony club camp when you go down the drive); masses of extensions including Barat wing: huge wide passages filled with pupil art. Splendid new science block. Library off the rotunda has had a face lift.

New sixth form centre carved out of former labs give every girl 'a private study space': presumably for the 35/40 day pupils in the sixth. Boarders have their own bedrooms and work stations. Bit sheep and goats-ish?

No books or newspapers to be seen in existing sixth form centre; we were told that 'books were in the careers centre' (a hop skip and a jump away) and so they were, but we do like to see something/anything to read whenever the young are in limbo/waiting for a chum.

K

Prep based in the brilliantly converted stables, historic Scotland at its best; central courtyard has a sprung floor – for dances, assemblies and the like with nursery opening off one side and the prep off the other, intimate classrooms up narrow stairs, books everywhere. Delightful. Central courtyard bustling with small people during our visit (it was tipping down) though a happy hand-holding crocodile appeared from the dedicated outdoor playground.

Pastoral care, well-being and discipline: Sacred Heart ethos prevails – staff enormously caring, 'will go the extra mile'. Pastoral conferences every week, independent counsellor on tap, bullying handled by BFG. 'Educate on cyber-bullying' from early. We think the dangers of trolling are not yet fully expounded. Disciplinary committee, gatings, suspensions, fatigues round school for smoking. Drinkers are suspended and a not-so-recent problem was 'nipped in the bud'. Will test areas, not girls, if drugs suspected. Charming little handbook for new pupils full of helpful advice. Problems like anorexia not discussed as openly as in some schools.

Girls not as streetwise as they think they are – tendency to cover woolly pullies and blazers with badges: bosoms and badges are strange bedfellows. New blue jacket for lower sixth changes to tweed jacket for upper sixth (quelle expense). All covered in badges. Could have been the 50s (though oddly enuff, make up quite common).

Pupils and parents: Trad boarders from all over Scotland and beyond (London and overseas – about 20 per cent of boarders). Day children from Fife, Dundee and Perthshire Stirling. Buses. Tranches of first time buyers: 'useful little school, just south of Perth.' RC but plenty of non-Catholics, including Muslims.

Entrance: Head meets with prospective prep school parents; fair number of first time buyers; gentle assessment, otherwise by interview and school report. Automatic (£500 carrot) from nursery. Taster days are welcomed.

Senior entry not that difficult, numbers down, though not consistently throughout. Space available both for day and boarders. Scholarship exams in February. Junior school entrants do CE. Otherwise 11+ from primary schools and 12+ from prep schools. Pupils can come whenever, half term/next week if space available. Sixth form entry: school report and exams to date; pupils from overseas or local state schools and are steered to 'appropriate' levels of study.

Exit: Juniors all prepared for CE elsewhere but most (95 per cent) stay the course.One or two leave before sixth form. Most to uni, most choose Scotland, huge variety: from Chinese studies to fashion and accountancy. One to Oxbridge in 2016; creatives to Glasgow School of Art and Conservatoire of Wales; a couple to London. The odd gapper.

Money matters: Up to 10 academic, art and music scholarships. Also riding, tennis and sporting scholarships. Almost one-third receive assistance of some sort. School is 'good at finding trust funding' for those who have fallen on hard times.

Remarks: The only all-girls' boarding school in Scotland. Small, not overtly Catholic, splendid facilities. A gentling school which majors on horse activities and superb sports; that having been said, leavers' destinations are wide and far reaching in every possible discipline. Numbers steady, confident about next academic year.

Knox Academy

Pencaitland Road, Haddington, East Lothian EH41 4DT

Pupils: 760 • Ages: 11–18 • Sixth form: 230

Tel: 01620 823387
Email: knoxacademy@knox.elcschool.org.uk
Website: www.ka-net.org.uk

Head Teacher: Since 2012, Mrs Sarah Ingham BD PGCE (40s, but looks like 30s). Joined Knox Academy in 2001, previously depute head. Educated at Bolton School Girls Division and St Andrews (BD), Herriot-Watt (PGCE), Glasgow Caledonian (postgrad counselling and supervision diploma) and Edinburgh (postgrad educational leadership and management certificate – the headship qualification). Cor. She taught religious and moral education at Kirkcudbright Academy and Currie Community High School, where her husband Charles still works. A star – bubbly and fun, with splendid auburn locks and trendy eBay shoes. 'I love it, the best job in the world,' she says of her role. She took this editor with enormous pride to see her pièce de résistance, Tots and Teens, a proper nursery where embryo nursery nurses – not to mention a whole raft of other teenagers – help to look after local youngsters (from 3 up: nappies not a problem) for £1 per session. Mothers meet in the food court for coffee at collection time – a boon for stay at home mums.

A great believer in giving service back to the community, the head runs the school with a £3 million budget. A new housing estate is in the offing at Leatham Mains, so pupils are capped at 800. New-build is at the planning stage, five new classrooms to be added to this already expanded school (need a compass to negotiate). Can choose own staff – 'interview, choose and watch them teach: no good spending half a million on someone who can't perform.' Oodles applied for a PE post last year, 15 or 16 for geography, but not always that big a choice. The 'good young female physics teacher' is a real bonus. This is devolved management at its best.

Academic matters: Keen on curriculum for excellence, the school is inclusive. Thirty pupils per class, 20 for practical stuff, and streaming in maths. (Busy maths club, popular with high flyers). Does well – strategies in place throughout.

S3 pupils have the choice of including literacy, numeracy or The Prince's Trust (which covers both, but includes life skills, independence and team work) as part of their personal curriculum at National 4 level. Massive choice at S4, including practical woodworking and hospitality (practical cookery). Oddly enough, not a lot of take up in computer games design. Otherwise, expect the usual subjects, with alternatives of enterprise and employability, personal development and volunteering – to be chosen with advice from tutor. Refreshing to find a school where academic attainment is not the be all and end all. That said, the school punches well above its weight both in national and East Lothian exam results. Spectacularly.

Eighteen per cent got 5+ Highers and 10 per cent 1+ Advanced Higher in 2016.

Three dedicated guidance staff, plus two learning support; help in class if needed. Pupils with mild(ish) SEN are catered for. SEN and guidance staff work together and share a bright passage of individual rooms; pupils with special needs 'do not necessarily attend all classes,' special computers with huge type available for the visually challenged and laptops to help the dyslexic. Mixture of 'learnings' on hand, with support either on an individual basis or in class. Youth worker provides pupils support to deal with 'any difficulties' and 'help and support transition into the real world'. Inclusion and integration is the name of the game. Deaf, registered blind (striped pillars) and wheelchair friendly.

No particular bias academically. French and Latin only (the very occasional trip to Rome) in the language department, occasional odd lang clubs – depends on staff interest. English and maths essential for all at all grades. School has been working towards the new curriculum for five or six years and – unlike smaller establishments – embraces National 4 and 5 with enthusiasm.

Impressive list of Highers, including administration, business management, music and religious, moral and philosophical studies. Also available at Advanced Higher level, along with a host of other options. This is a school that caters well for the academic and the ordinary mortal. Pupils list five out of 23 subjects offered in order of preference, with a couple of reserves: a timetabling nightmare, but how sensible. Optional Easter holiday revision weeks at all levels.

Raft of computers – 40 in the computer department, a further 60 in the business education department, more in the jolly library, which has rather noisy air conditioning and also houses the careers department, plus a couple of laptop trollies. The careers officer comes once a week and pupils can either just pop in or make an appointment for one-to-one consultation.

Games, options, the arts: PE timetabled and on offer to higher level – huge following. Games fields on site, all the usual suspects – rugby popular, volleyball, basketball, hockey, netball, girls' and boys' footie teams and golf (one chap currently on the East Lothian fast track and more than 100 volunteered to pick rubbish at the Open at Muirfield). Badminton courts, climbing wall, fives court. School currently swims in the local Aubigny centre and does remarkably well in competitions – good support from the East Lothian sports development officers. Physical activities coordinator based in the school manages the huge (and we mean huge) outdoor education department. Outstanding athletes on the sports leadership skills work programme get time off to train.

Sixth formers have a team building weekend early in the year, and pupils not on exam leave have an activities week: from extreme sports to visits to Paris, the Alps, Italy and London, day trips to Edinburgh, the Dynamic Earth, spooky Mary King's Close or the Science Museum in Glasgow. Italy, Prague, Amsterdam on the cards, with seniors heading to New York in a couple of years and 30 off to China for a month. Home-based options include hospitality and fishing; digital films have rather fallen by the wayside. Myriads of trips abroad; Young Explorers' Trust et al, D of E and sixth year do an hour's community service each week.

Superb music in the old building. Musicians give two concerts annually, oodles of orchestras, choirs, and bands. Popular pipe band. Drama, panto at Christmas and well-used dance studio. Stunning art department – good selection of paintings in view. Magical and inspirational fabric and hatting department, plus ceramics and all the rest. Home economics equally buzzing – the smell of newly-baked bread was mouthwatering. School seriously into Europe – representatives went to the first Youth Eco-Parliament in Berlin. The Alice Burnett twinning scholarship is popular and school encourages languages via a language week (the whole school goes French, Italian or Latin for the week). Good links with France, Italy, Finland, Sweden and now Rwanda. School recently gained its second British Council International School Award, the first Scottish school so to do.

Citizenship course is 'part and parcel of the curriculum.' School council has a training day for all, with proper speakers and a grown up agenda. All do work experience at S4 (the school has a core list of placements if pupils can't find their own). Pupils have to write letters of application and go through the whole gamut – excellent practice (though Knox will step in if all else fails – and will even supply steel-capped boots, if that is what it needs). No charge, unlike some schools south of the border.

A few years back, the school won the BBC Schools' Question Time and pupils were involved in producing a televised programme. Good YE extends as far as 13-year-olds, who have moved on from decorating flowerpots to board games. Always tried out on the head first. Profits go to charity – school is keen on 'the big traditional charities' like UNICEF and locally they support the sick kids' hospital.

Background and atmosphere: The most recent in a line of education establishments in Haddington, dating back to 1379. The previous school, dedicated to John Knox at the end of the 19th century, still boasts a statue of him in the grounds and has been converted into sheltered housing for the elderly, some of whom may have come here in their youth. School moved to its present site in the 1930s – loads of additions since. The assembly hall, bigger before the recent additions, is currently 'ealth and safety-ed' at 500.

Blue new-build looks spectacular (cleverly organised so that the gym and sports hall will be available to locals), with access to the dining hall. Food here is good – healthy eating a priority (eat your heart out, Jamie Oliver), though to be honest, the cooked menu was a little drear; salad bar and sandwiches. Regular exposure to different cultures. Thai food for all, Dim Sum for a day.

Dress code for all – white shirts, school ties and black trousers or skirts, black jeans now an acceptable alternative. School blazers mandatory for S5 and S6, gold braiding for prefects.

Pastoral care, well-being and discipline: Twelve minutes each morning for all with their tutor, short messages and encouragement. Head is keen on mantra of wisdom, engagement, respect. Tutors emphasise responsibility and attainment – pupils should try to 'punch above their weight.' Strong on service, volunteering. Equally strong on discipline, with letters home to parents and detention the ultimate deterrent.

Pupil points system where pupils can gain or lose points and receive certificates once a certain level has been reached. Proactive anti-bullying strategy – zero tolerance. Zero tolerance too on the drugs front (not so sleepy Haddington has a fairly hefty problem). Sixth formers do a buddying routine with first year pupils, and keep a watchful eye for the dreaded b...y word.

Pupils and parents: Eclectic, though predominantly white middle class, like its catchment. A mixture of East Lothian farmers (usually well founded), the butcher, the baker, the candlestick maker, plus a home-grown cache of third generation unemployed and a recent influx of Eastern Europeans. Certain number of recent refugees from the independent sector.

School conceals a 'long demographic' – real deprivation in some areas (school has funds to assist with emergency clothing, allowing those who absolutely can't afford it to join in activities week, with help from John Watson's Trust). Surprising nine per cent on free dinners. Around 80 to 90 in S5 and S6 qualify for the weekly £30 EMRA payment (means-tested and quite complicated).

Supportive parent-school partnership and KASG (Knox Academy Support Group), an excellent and effective fundraising initiative. Parents' evening once a year for each year group.

Entrance: Automatic from King's Meadow Primary, St Mary's Roman Catholic Primary in Haddington, ditto Yester Primary in Gifford. The rest by placement requests (a lot of those).

Youngsters come for a couple of taster days the term before they are due to start. Head wishes there was some way of keeping cusp birthday children in primary for another year to help them develop with their peers.

Exit: Good follow through from S4 to S5 (around 90 per cent) and from S5 to S6 (about 80 per cent). Up to half go to university – mostly Scottish.

Remarks: Excellent. No adverse comments from any of our contacts. So go for it, but make sure you are in the catchment area first, and watch it, the catchment area shrinketh.

L

Lathallan School

Brotherton Castle, Johnshaven, Angus DD10 0HN

Pupils: 227; 11 full, 10 weekly, 11 flexi boarders • Ages: 6m–18 (boarding from 10) • Sixth form: 33

Fees: Day £10,230 – £17,670; Boarding £21,207 – £24,225 pa

Tel: 01561 362220
Email: admissions@lathallan.org.uk
Website: www.lathallan.org.uk

Headmaster: Since 2009, Mr Richard Toley BA MPhil PGCE (40s) who joined Lathallan in 2006 as director of co-curriculum from nearby High School of Dundee. Educated at The Merchant Taylor's School, Liverpool, followed by St David's Lampeter MPhil at St Andrews and PGCE at Strathclyde. He and his wife live on site, with their young now in school.

Six years down the road (Toley was catapulted into headship after an 18 month apprenticeship) he is comfortably confident in his role. (We usually pop in for a quick check on our way down from Aberdeen, though alas this time we were both caught in traffic and had to do some crisis management, so missed our meet). School moved from being 'just' a prep school with a hugely popular and often over-subscribed nursery in 2006, to building up a senior base year by year.

A historian, charming and relaxed, Toley teaches classics (as in classical studies) and history 12 periods a week in the senior school, and runs school with senior school head, Mr Duncan Lyall BSc PGCE (40s), an Edinburgh lad, and Mr James Ferrier BA (Cantab) PGCE (50s), head of junior school since 2011, having first come to school in 2001 from Moor Park in Shropshire. Lyall, who read mechanical engineering at Edinburgh, is married with a brace of young, and came to Lathallan from Peebles High, having previously taught in both the borders and Aberdeen.

Ferrier lives on campus with his wife, was educated at Hardyes School, Dorset, read humanities of Christ Church, followed by PGCE at the University of Kent, and runs his part of the Lathallan empire with gentle humour.

Impressive collection of uber-powerful governors plus parent governors, 'tremendous backing'.

Academic matters: Scottish curriculum: 17+ subject options at all levels. Recent results encouraging, good scattering of As across the board in 2015 in both Highers (40 per cent) and Advanced Highers (69 per cent) As ever, we ask for individual results per subject, with number of candidates in each subject and results (as in 12 did English Higher, two got A, four B, five C – that sort of thing). Whilst school 'does hold such results, it does not divulge them'. So now you know. Interesting results we did get: of the 17 candidates presenting for Nat 5s (118 exams) a mere 57 scored A, with four candidates being D(oomed) and 10 unplaced. S5s do a combo of Nat 5s and Highers, which is unusual. Several unplaced in both disciplines, but 40 per cent A pass rate over all (though we have no idea in which subjects) and 69 per cent A at Higher level is encouraging, though number of presentees unplaced; school is non-selective and for some a C or a D may be a real achievement. The staff whom we have met over the years have been bubbly and enthusiastic.

Variety pack of langs on offer – Mandarin – whenever (number of native speakers in school) plus French (from P1) and Spanish (S1) (native speakers). Not a lot of take-up in the former, though occasional outstanding results at all levels. Pupils study both French and Spanish throughout S2 before opting for one or t'other for Nat 5s.

Latin from aged 11 (classical studies at Higher and Advanced Higher), crash course in Italian (ab initio) – offered at Higher level, but no take-up – plus the usual suspects: maths, English, three sciences, history, geography (pleasing and popular), business and classical studies, art, PE and drama, and managing environmental resources (MER). This is penny number stuff, occasional glitch.

Civilianship the latest addition – ie how to open doors, ladies first, that sort of thing; school is talking to exam boards as to how they could make this an examinable subject. Think finishing schools, think nanny, think how clever.

All assessed for dyslexia et al on arrival. Two dedicated learning support staff, one-to-one, clusters, or co-teaching, throughout school. Costs the same as a piano lesson. Back-up for the bored and the brightest. Class sizes around 13 (max 16), pupils streamed for maths and English both taught in refurb'ed classrooms in the castle, interactive whiteboards all over.

IT impressive – Dell computers plus Apple Macs in senior school. iPads for all seems to be the current flavour of the month (last time we did a round up it was the 'virtual learning experience'). Only for those in the dyslexia stream at Lathallan. We were told that Toley 'was not convinced' by rolling 'em out across the board.

Science still in a hotch-potch of temporary buildings beside the nursery complex: but zinging new science centre more than a couple of metres off the ground (as ever, near the nursery complex). We have a natty brochure with pics, showing three dedicated science labs plus one for environmental study and junior science lab. Plus accessible loos, shower – got to have 'em now and pupil inspired 'treehouse' (to enhance outdoor learning experiences). Natty brochure has fundraising options, so we hope there is enough dosh to complete the project. Impressive sounding new head of science Ian Smith comes from Cults Academy where he was head principal teacher of chemistry.

Staff whom we have met are young, enthusiastic and fun. Twenty-six on the books and six part-timers. Peris pulled in for the more esoteric subjects (or instruments). No apparent problem in attracting staff, particularly in the current financial climate, when property prices have in some quarters reached basement level. The Aberdeen catchment area was pricey.

Games, options, the arts: Music everywhere – bagpipe boxes all over the porch and hall, both girls and boys in pipe bands much in demand for charities and have entertained Princess Anne of late, played in the Angus show, the Glamis gathering, the Scottish parliament etc. Pipes and drums played at the battlefields in Belgium during the Great War memorial year and compete in the Royal Pipe Band competitions with success. Scottish country dancing no longer has parental input; marvellous photographs in the porch of a junior Scottish country dancing lesson – note the kilt loops and the ecstasy on the faces of the young. Strong drama: new head of music previously with Aberdeen Youth Theatre; no orchestra per se (yet) but wind and ceilidh bands.

Toley has introduced a new formal school-wide traditional PE programme, which 'through age-appropriate indoor exercises aims to improve co-ordination and mental agility both in and outside the academic classroom' (sounds a tad Steiner-ish). School thinks this sounds harsh. 'We have a real focus on sports/ PE and outdoor education but this sounds almost military'. 'We realise the importance of exercise.' 'We want our pupils to be well-rounded by participating in PE/sports and outdoor ed.'

Thrashing all comers in under-16 rugby 7s, new games pavilion (board member head of SRU); 7s rugby team toot to Dubai on the cards, but 'mainly it is regional' with all points south of Gordonstoun. All 7+ year olds play sport daily, tennis courts double up for netball (Astroturf), 10 acres of playing field overlooking the North Sea and own beach (bracing), plus refurbished gym. Lots of jolly rugby trips and netball tours. Sea at the bottom of the garden, but no sea sports – too rough. Impressive games area adjacent to junior/baby school. Astro: tennis: you name it; plus dedicated gym (though hall in main school building equally adaptable).

Head of outdoor education is Monro-potty, 'probably climbed them all three times,' says Toley. D of E timetabled and huge numbers – school claims 'highest percentage of participation in the D of E scheme in all of the country (Scotland)'.

First two years of senior school spend six days in the mountains, mountain rescue, navigation (shades of Round Square). Skiing, both at home and abroad for all. Huge emphasis on outdoor education, self-resilience, and leadership training. New 50 foot long zip wire in the wood (100 foot drop). Scary. Six pupils and guides did an unsupported, exploratory exped to Eastern Greenland last August. (Scary again). Recent trip to Iceland has even more scary photos. SCIS sponsored Outdoor Education Conference planned for 2016.

ISCO (careers guidance) enrollment (as ever) and ongoing advice as to 'what happens next'.

Boarding: Influx of foreign boarders since full boarding reopened: 30 boarders housed in separate wings of the castle (previous staff quarters), co-ed boarding tidily arranged, mainly oil-y children, from Thailand, China, Spain, Nigeria, Russia. Scottish Guardian Overseas Association oversees them (and individual guardians have to pick up the flack if their charges are sent 'home', ie gated). Some locals, bed and breakfasting available. ESOL on hand to help with language glitches. Interesting to see whether boarding numbers hold up during current oil turn-down.

Background and atmosphere: Founded in the imposing Victorian Brotherton Castle (1867) in the early 1930s. Originally trad boys' boarding prep school, set in 62 acres of woodland which catered for 'the folk over the hill'; now a thriving nursery (handful of real babes being pushed out in three prams when we visited; good North Sea air) through to Advanced Highers co-ed offering full, weekly or flexi-boarding (from age 10).

Regular exchange programmes with 'smallish' schools in Canada, Switzerland and Australia; the latter were enjoying their six weeks in Angus during a previous visit. More than 25 clubs; 'we rotate them,' says Toley.

William Bruce house-lets (which pre-date the castle) guard corners of the long abandoned formal garden which makes a splendid play area. Library and resource centre in main building with classrooms and nursery in bright converted stable block with massive additions (and home to new science build but see above). Some lessons in temporary classrooms. Irritating steps both too shallow and too wide link the two sites. Nursery/ junior wing surrounded by play/games areas, stunning nursery playground. Collection of toddler sized loos and mini basins: one wonders how they cope at home.

Newly refurb'ed common room for senior school pupils. School uniform provided in house, with jolly fleecy waterproof jackets which staff wear too. Staff all have to take the minibus test.

Pastoral care, well-being and discipline: School small enough for every child to be known (cherished is a word that comes to mind if it didn't sound so soppy), strong anti-bullying policy. Occasional gatings for wickedness, no child yet asked to leave. School is 'bespoke, focused'.

Pupils and parents: Increasing number of first time buyers. FPs supportive, strong parental input, parents will drive many miles out of their way to drop off their tinies in the nursery. Return buses for older children from Stonehaven, Edzell and Aberdeen with coaches from Brechin, Forfar and Montrose.

Aberdeen business community plus local farmers, commuters, usually from within 90 minute radius (which takes you to Dundee). Rob Wainwright an old boy (and does the odd spot of coaching), ditto Ian Lang (Lord Lang of Monkton).

Niche school: perfect for the occasional non-performing refugee from bigger trad schools: Fettes, Merchiston, Robert Gordons. Children thrive in the smaller environment. 'We care'. (Those parents to whom we spoke fell into the latter category. Their relief was palpable.)

Entrance: Lathallan Nursery: from six weeks, 80 tinies registered but no more than 49 at any one time. Entrance to junior school seamless from nursery test-ette for problems and 'nearly all go' (95 per cent). Juniors are checked 'carefully' and if problems obvious, they get a 'proper test'.

Entry to senior school at any time to any year group if places available, many come via junior school. Otherwise form 5 (P7: 11, 12 year olds). Taster day. Informal tests in English, maths and verbal reasoning, but not a selective school. Numbers up from prep school, 10/12 a year. Currently full first three years of senior school (and nursery and pre-junior school ie ages 5 and 6).

Exit: Tiny trickle leave for trad independents age 13, occasional departure age 8, otherwise the odd relocation. Sixth formers head in the main to the Scottish unis: St Andrews, Edinburgh, Aberdeen, Heriot Watt, Stirling and Glasgow.

Money matters: Money matters 'under control', up to 100 per cent bursaries (and extra help if necessary): huge raft: academic, sports, rugby 7s, netball, music and pipes and drums. Sibling discount. Secondhand clothes shop. Will keep child if parents fall on hard times with the usual caveat of being up front about the problem.

Lathallan Nursery in partnership with Aberdeen County council (discounts). Hours roughly 7.30am to 6pm but check fee structure, deeply expensive if child not collected by designated time (emergency cover and charged by the quarter hour). This is a 50 week nursery with two weeks off for Christmas.

Remarks: This is the tail that wagged the dog. We have visited Lathallan over the past 20 odd years: six headmasters. This was a school which had – quite frankly – been toiling. Sometimes it had a nursery which took babes from 2 months, sometimes from 3 years. In any case it was a boys' boarding prep school with an increasingly dismal roll call (even after they took girls and day pupils) and a glorious view. Two (or was it three?) heads ago, the brave decision (we thought nuts) was made to expand, on a year by year basis, to become a fully fledged school, with Highers and Advanced Highers and all. We were wrong. Very wrong (and we won't rehearse further the various decisions down the line). Remarkable success story which keeps on growing.

Lenzie Academy

Myrtle Avenue, Kirkintilloch, Lenzie, East Dunbartonshire G66 4HR

Pupils: 1,240 • Ages: 11–18 • Sixth form: 370

Tel: 01419 552379
Email: office@lenzieacademy.e-dunbarton.sch.uk
Website: www.lenzieacademy.e-dunbarton.sch.uk

Head Teacher: Since 2011, Mr Brian Paterson BA PGCE (late 40s), previously head of Abronhill High. Educated at Paisley Uni, his PGCE was in modern studies and economics at Jordanhill. He taught in Glasgow and Lanarkshire before doing eight years as principal teacher, firstly in Harris Academy, Dundee and then in Boclair Academy, East Dunbartonshire, where he also spent seven years as depute head teacher. He has been a marker and setter for SQA, an educational consultant for the BBC and a writer of educational materials.

From a Glasgow background where pupils left school at 16 and university was not an option, he was grateful to the teachers who encouraged him and wants to give something back, feeling it is his civic duty. Not attracted to a more lucrative career though he once 'wobbled for 10 minutes'. Life is now pretty full on at school – recently included being the murder victim in an ASDAN project – so down time is spent mainly as a taxi driver for his children, one still in primary and one in sixth form, both in East Renfrewshire plus a daughter at Strathclyde. He likes to play football twice weekly in the staff seven-a-side club but getting away for some hill-walking at weekends is a bit of a pipe dream. Having run an academic school at Abronhill he sees himself as having taken on the challenge of making a school with a pretty distinguished record into something of real excellence. His go-ahead SMT of six deputes are unlikely to allow many bottoms to get stuck on laurels. Very clear on priorities, he will not waste energy on problems that are likely to resolve themselves or are not resolvable.

The immediate plan is a £650,000 facelift – a complete paint job (not before time); school is also being comprehensively re-roofed and getting new doors for all entrances and the tired looking football/hockey pitch outside the school is getting new all-weather surface. He is strengthening the house system, giving pupils more responsibilities and making things more competitive in the academic sense, not just in sport. Tracking and monitoring are being sharpened up so he can quickly spot weak areas or potential failings. Longer term he wants to build up drama and has his eye on how to make more studio space, if funds permit. Grass will certainly have no chance under his purposeful feet.

Academic matters: Classes currently at 30, with eight forms per year group (capped at 240). Uses the Scottish SQA system – in 2016, 72 per cent of S4s got 5+ at National 5, and 35 per cent of S5s got 5+ Highers. Advanced Higher results impressive too, with significant increase in performance – 39 per cent of S6 got 1+ Advanced Higher in 2016. Impressive range of subjects on offer, even in comparison with the best of the independent sector. Most teaching areas a bit trad to look at but some top notch equipment everywhere. Nice to see similar numbers of boys and girls in Higher design and engineering, however battered the benches. They clearly know their own minds.

Plenty of pupils do three sciences at S grade, while the bulk do two and no one is allowed to get away without one. All do one modern foreign lang to S4, currently French or German, with Spanish just starting up, though no Latin, Italian or eg Mandarin, even in clubs. The advantage of size is that there are over 30 subjects on offer for S5/6 many of them at four different levels: Advanced Higher, Higher, National 4 and 5. This range is further increased by distance learning, so there isn't much limit to what you can do, especially as flexibility includes letting pupils take subjects at other local schools if the timetable won't fit. Plugged into Strathclyde and Heriot Watt's SCHOLAR learning programmes and into the local consortium.

A magnet school – pupils from other (state) schools come to Lenzie to study Highers and Advanced Highers not available in their own. Stunning computer studies results at all levels and the school has a record of jolly good results over a number of years in maths, all three sciences, art and design and health and food technology. Interactive whiteboards much used. Results, already pretty spot on, have generally improved in response to tighter monitoring and academic mentoring programmes.

SEN well staffed – monitoring is good and still improving. A supportive culture in school includes a scribes' and readers' club. Provisions vary from year to year as children with severe difficulties, either physical or intellectual, attract appropriate help. This is a totally inclusive school by ethos.

Over 100 pupils do not have English as their first language (speaking 31 different languages) and extra help and EAL are available. Homework club at lunch time and super supported study scheme post-school – 200 pupils regularly stay on – when pupils can access the ICT suites.

Games, options, the arts: Apart from a huge – though not as huge as originally planned – games hall and two pitches on site (currently getting the new Astroturf), provision looks a bit limited but the school uses local club pitches five minutes away to impressive effect and offers all the usual sports, with some enthusiastic players including a national athletics champion. Bidding to be a full School of Rugby (has 'lite' accreditation); new dance studio. Lots of way out stuff too: outdoor education, a successful sailing club and even collie racing. Huge numbers of extracurricular activities.

Art department is very go ahead with Higher photography course, portraiture with a real artist, and masses of work going on with colour. Vibrant displays in the art rooms and some smashing mosaic murals all over the school to brighten it up. Vocational courses in tourism, textiles, hospitality and so on, there's even one in cake decoration; all put on as serious opportunities in Scotland's current economic climate.

Music is big too with plenty of classical and quite a few groups on the performance side and academic on offer up to Advanced Higher. No pipe band but plenty of electronics just coming in despite the expense. Huge production every year with Guys and Dolls the most recent.

Background and atmosphere: Unremarkable 1960s buildings, now looking distinctly retro, date from when the school moved to a roomier site from a square set, stone building in Lenzie, which is now the primary school. Pleasant brick court in one wing with a sadly run down garden (but grass won't grow there, we were assured); inside corridors are wide and classrooms really light and spacious. The other wing has such narrow passages that that a one-way system is essential but it's brightened by the work and info put up by various academic departments. Lenzie hasn't had the benefit of the funds lavished on its snazzy neighbours in Bearsden and Kirkintilloch, but there's lots of ground around the school for development and already an inviting patio for sitting out, when the Scottish weather allows.

Nice smart new dining hall with gallery for social use and carrels for study, plus every possible device to make it a multifunctional centre. No pre- or post-school cafeteria, though the area is open to early comers from 8.15am and school is open til 6pm or so when community use starts.

Main hall is desparately dingy but brightened up on our visit by a comprehensive 'Hopes for the Future' inter-disciplinary learning display from an S2 project. Terrific programme of renovation is ongoing but the formerly plentiful 'glory holes' have been eradicated and there are endless lockers everywhere.

Pastoral care, well-being and discipline: Guidance is done in forms and a teacher stays with the class as it goes up the school. The six deputes are year heads and meet with the guidance teacher once a month to discuss every member of each class thoroughly. Not much need to use the bullying code but it's there and the occasional fight calls for extreme sanctions – mainly expulsion for a day or so. Behaviour guidelines classify bad behaviour in three levels; the third gets a 'demerit' reported to parents and if Mr Paterson gets his way this will also go into competitive house records.

Mr Paterson is tightening up uniform and there's a smart new (remarkably inexpensive) navy blazer with green braid and new school badge (the old one was all wrong and blazers were baggy). We saw a few coloured hairdos and nose rings and some very short skirts. Everyone seems to wear just about anything for games.

Pupils and parents: The pupils we met were polite and quiet and staff friendly and concerned. There are pupil councils for each year group consisting of two pupils from each class and this is being co-ordinated with house councils which will help socialising to be through all age groups.

Quite a large proportion come from ethnic minorities, since local universities attract staff from abroad. Majority of parents from the locality and 'leafy Lenzie' is fairly upmarket. Parents are supportive and run a Friends of Lenzie Academy (FOLA 125) which does a great job raising funds for the school. The Parent Council is supportive of the school's activities and developments.

Entrance: Entry is capped at 240, of which usually 130 or so are locals. Some apply from outside the area which now includes part of a huge newly built estate, most of which is outside the actual catchment area but so close that those applying are likely to get priority.

Exit: Most pupil stay on until S6, with a few leaving at the end of S4 and S5 (most of the latter early entry university candidates). About 80 per cent to HE/FE, mostly Scottish unis; three to Oxbridge and five medics in 2016.

Remarks: A whacking great school with a dynamic head and tremendous possibilities, already doing a grand job for 'leafy Lenzie'.

Lomond School

10 Stafford Street, Helensburgh, Argyll and Bute G84 9JX

Pupils: 361; 52 boarders • Ages: 3–18 • Sixth form: 39

Fees: Day £7,980 – £11,100; Boarding £25,230 pa

Tel: 01436 672476
Email: admissions@lomondschool.com
Website: www.lomondschool.com

Head: Since 2014, Mrs Johanna Urquhart, previously depute head (academic) at George Watson's College. She has a degree in maths and statistics and a masters in education, specialising in leadership and management. She has also been depute head at Breadalbane Academy.

Academic matters: Setted in English, French and maths at the age of 12, French taught from age five, German from 11. Huge range of subjects on offer, including such esoteric ones as graphic communication, modern studies and business management, as well as French, German and Spanish. Three sciences. Latin GCSE taught by video conference link and distance learning. In 2016, 42 per cent A grades in Advanced Highers, 43 per cent A grades in Highers and 61 per cent A grades in National 5.

Maximum class size 20. Sixth form were working supervised (which is unheard of at that age) in the library when we visited. Homework very important – children keep a diary and expect to do at least two and a half hours each night in their National grade year. Has strong links with private schools in China, Germany and US. Computers everywhere, networked, and all have access to the internet; keyboarding skills for all, electronic interactive whiteboard presentations for all by all. Tutors for all. Good learning support (and provision for those with dyslexia, ADD or ADHD). English as a second language on hand.

Games, options, the arts: Huge playing field just along the (tree-lined) road. Full-sized floodlit Astroturf hockey pitch. Rugby and hockey the two main winter games, with tennis, cricket and athletics in the summer and oodles of add-ons. Swimming in the local pool, option of squash, riding and badminton. Inter-house matches popular. Mass of lunch time clubs, D of E popular and, of course, sailing, The Scottish Islands Peaks Race, Lomond Challenge (a beastly tough triathlon) – not a school for sissies. New games hall, adjacent to the Astroturf, includes badminton courts, climbing wall, dance studio, fitness suite and indoor cricket lanes. Further development to include another smaller Astroturf.

Traditional Scottish music important – clarsach players, fiddlers, pipers and singers are in regular demand. Strong music, based in the old stables – one wall entirely covered with guitars, not just for decoration, judging by the enthusiasm the guitar teacher generated. Recording facilities in place. Big bands and chamber orchestras, over 20 instruments on curriculum with some 150 individual lessons. Sparkling art department, with old school desks press-ganged into use. Huge variety of disciplines – photography with spit-new kit, magical screen printing, jewellery making, as well as the more prosaic (which it wasn't) sculpture, painting and etching. Tremendous enthusiasm here – enchanting flower costume, complete with design, basque and wings, made for last summer's play, on show. Strong drama.

Boarding: Burnbrae now the most modern boarding house in Scotland – boys and girls (boarders from age 10) share the same building but are separated by a state-of-the-art security system using biometric readers.

Background and atmosphere: Based on the northern edge of the posh, sleepy, seaside town of Helensburgh, originally housed in a series of Victorian villas. Present school is an amalgam of Larchfield, founded in 1845, and the girls' school, St Bride's, founded in 1895. The schools combined in 1977; later a stunning rebuild. The resulting school is a curious combination of old and new, with three floors replacing the original two and subject rooms being grouped in series. Most impressive – massive amount of glass, super new dining hall, good gym and terrific entrance hall with glorious views out over the Clyde. All pupils wear uniform (kilts for females) – neat and tidy with ties and a thoroughly purposeful air.

Pastoral care, well-being and discipline: Strong anti-bullying procedure in place – the 'no blame' circle appears to be the most effective. Confidential suggestion boxes all over the school are really part of the anti-bullying programme. Good PSD programme. CCTV cameras throughout. Children not 'given a lot of rope', eg any substance abuse leads to suspension, 'pending a discussion of their school future'. Dealing equals straight out. Smoking is apparently 'not happening just now', but smoking in uniform is 'not on'.

Pupils and parents: An upmarket lot – solid middle class, from the surrounding area (they organise the buses), some from as far away as Glasgow. Number of Forces families (Faslane naval base next door) and some from further 'round the bay' send their children here (the local state school thought to be too state). A few mainland Chinese usually come for most of their secondary schooling, plus connection with Germany, whence the occasional pupil comes for a year or a term – not much take-up of Scots going to Germany in exchange.

Bonar Law was educated at Larchfield, as well as John Logie Baird – his school report, displayed in the dining room, apart from showing that he was 14th out of 14 in maths, expresses the hope that he will eventually 'go on and do something with his life'!

Entrance: Either up via nursery or from local state primaries.

Exit: Usual dribble away after National grades and could fill up the resulting places several times over, trickle leaves after Highers; some, eg those going south to university, tend to stay and do their Advanced Highers. Most will end up at university – destinations include St Andrews, Edinburgh, Glasgow, Aberdeen, Stirling, Strathclyde, Swansea.

Money matters: Not a rich school. Will support pupils in financial difficulties; an increasing number of means-tested bursaries (up to 100 per cent) available at the age of 10 and 11 and post-National grades.

Remarks: A jolly, busy school, perfect for those who want to keep their children at home without the hassle of going daily to Glasgow.

L

Loretto School

1–7 Linkfield Road, Musselburgh, East Lothian EH21 7RE

Pupils: 591; 179 full, 37 flexi boarders • Ages: 3–18 (boarding from 11) • Sixth form: 190

Fees: Day £8,550 – £21,750; Boarding £17,700 – £31,950 pa

Tel: 01316 534444
Email: admissions@loretto.com
Website: www.loretto.com

Headmaster: Since 2014, Dr Graham Hawley BSc PhD PGCE, previously head of Kelly College, Tavistock; has also taught at Ardingly and Warwick School. Educated at Mill Hill School, followed by Durham and Exeter. Not a pinstripe suited, hands on lapels, sound bite delivering headmaster of the bullfrog sort – a modest and gently amusing conversationalist who listens sensitively. Dr Hawley's first class hons in natural sciences and his doctorate have taken him to solitary places: the west coast of Scotland, Devon, Cornwall, India, Bangladesh and Sumatra. Do not think Gussie Fink-Nottle – think someone who is highly intelligent and articulate, with a close eye for detail and the willing ability to notice and pay attention to everyone. Married to Rachel; two children.

Head of junior school: Since 2009, Mr Philip Meadows MA(Cantab), Cert Ed. Head of chemistry at Loretto 1987-96, then housemaster at Sedbergh School and head of Mowden Hall School, Northumberland, and Tettenhall College Junior School (a day school in Wolverhampton). Married to Sylvia, three teenage children, two of whom are still at Loretto. Comfortingly larger than life, Meadows came over brilliantly on school's video. Still teaches chemistry. Confidential manner and utterly reassuring, a wow with nervous parents.

Academic matters: Junior school generously staffed. All assessed aged 9, extra help tailored to child. French from early, two French specialists. Science lab and computer room linked via cable to the communications and resource centre in senior school.

Monthly senior school tutorial assessments are 'minuted and followed through' with pupils and parents, but watch this space. School follows the English system – GCSEs and A levels for all. In 2016, 30 per cent A*/A grades at A level and 43 per cent at GCSE. No (current) thoughts of moving to the IB, but goodness knows what is going to happen in the world of academe over the next few years. Classics back on stream but not – currently – offered at A level. Goodly selection of top end passes; maths, physics strong as ever, but Eng lit and art in the ribbons; v strong German – native speakers perhaps? Music a tad sad exam-wise in the last few years, and not many sporting heroes...

Traditionally strong on science and engineering, humanities, government and politics (number in both cabinets recently); business studies creeping up the ladder, plus economics, French and Spanish. Boy/girl ratio pretty even across the field, Russian and Mandarin available at all levels, native speakers encouraged to sit for qualifications in their own langs, tutors can be pulled on if necessary. Three sciences standard at GCSE, though one can be dropped for art.

Setting in English, maths and languages, most subjects from third form. School recently became an Associate school of the Royal Society, which sounds pretty grand but only lasts two years. Apparently girls no longer set the academic bar, 'it depends on the year group'. The staff we met were all bright, bubbly and enthusiastic. ESL (extra cost) and learning support available throughout. Drop in centres, 'staff very helpful' said head boy. Special societies for clever clogs. Smartboards in classrooms and networked computers everywhere, including study-bedrooms. Impressive visiting lecturer programme, usually one per week, members of upper sixth regularly give lectures too; interview practice for all.

Games, options, the arts: Juniors share main school facilities such as the Astroturf (which, to be honest, is quite a long hike for smaller legs) and theatre. Lots of extracurricular activities: judo, skiing, juniors join senior pipe band. Parent-inspired knitting club deeply popular.

Singing as ever good and keen: the whole school sings in the war memorial chapel choir and performs at the Schools Proms at the Royal Albert Hall. Music improving in leaps and bounds, with orchestra and jazz band, most of the second form (ie 12 year olds) study one or more instruments. The pipe band performed with Sir Paul McCartney in Liverpool recently. Wow! Claims to have been the first all-Steinway independent school in Europe – Steinways throughout campus. Drama on the up – theatre studies taken at all exam levels (sprinking of As at A), school is a registered LAMDA centre. Art scholars do life classes, screen printing and textiles. Campus and online Loretto radio station as well as all singing and dancing recording studio.

PE is an examinable subject, strong sport – girls' athletics and lacrosse do well; the appointment of a head of girls' games has given it a real impetus. Impressive string of wins on the rugby pitch over the last few years has put 1st XV firmly back in the top league. Fine all-weather court, new Olympic blue Astroturf at Pinkie (pretty garish), and acres of playing fields. Canoeing in the Musselburgh lagoons, but not a lot of use made of the sea itself (enthusiasts sail in North Berwick).

The golf academy is flourishing, currently number one in Europe (school has a long tradition of senior golfing FPs), and golf is professionally coached throughout the school, with all pupils using top class practice facilities on campus, including a nine-hole Huxley all-weather putting green. Rounds are played at the local Craigielaw, and Archerfield down the firth. Rash of success over the years, older pupils' lessons re-jigged to accommodate coaching; three golf scholarships to leading American universities to date; wins in many county championships. Summer residential golf camps are run to encourage new golfers to apply (ie as pupils at the school). Variety of trips and exchanges, for pupils, and for staff.

Boarding: New Eleanora Almond girls' house – arranged by apartments – was due to open on the High Street the day after our visit (it had been ready for months, but the Care Commission had been a little tardy in inspections). Holm House (with lift for disabled access) and Balcarres, for girls, are adjacent to the (small) sports centre, junior girls' house and girls' sixth form house. Study bedrooms in sixth form house. Senior common rooms for sixth form with a certain amount of male access; barbecues are popular at the girls' houses and attended by all. Girls' boarding bung full, certain availability for chaps (but not dead empty you understand). The Yard (under staff supervision) is the new social centre for sixth form weekend shenanigans.

Full boarding, weekly boarding, flexi-boarding plus day pupils, the latter particularly well integrated. Sixth form boarders can get permission to go into Edinburgh on any night of the week 'providing that their work is in order'. They can go to a film, the theatre, concerts (rock or otherwise), and the upper sixth can go racing in Musselburgh, all of 10 yards from main school entrance. The young told this editor that they take taxis home after partying in Edinburgh and charge it to their parents' bill, this has been kyboshed by the school and buses are gaining in popularity. Younger boarders take the school bus of a weekend to Kinaird Park, which houses a collection of utterly desirable shops – a great improvement on Musselburgh. This is a chilly corner of East Lothian and the east wind whistling across the racecourse from the North Sea is an almost permanent feature (school is not so sure, and boasts of the Musselburgh micro-climate).

Background and atmosphere: Founded in 1827 in the 'honest toun' (which is why Pinkie House had the first electronic gates in Scotland), and bought by Hely Hutchison Almond in 1862 (a distinguished scholar of unconventional convictions – Scotland's answer to Dr Arnold). Loretto went fully co-ed in 1995. The traditional East Lothian ochre-coloured buildings straddle the A1; on occasion, the tunnel below is used for sailing boats...don't ask, it needs to be flooded first. Slightly disjointed campus with various outbuildings, including The Nippers and a wodge of playing fields north of the river Esk. Rolling plan of refurbishing houses and a certain amount of tinkering location-wise. School House has become the day centre. Pinkie House, with its important painted ceiling in the gallery under the roof, has a particularly gruesome extension and is home to some of the sixth form boys who have obviously driven out the ghost of the first Lady Seaton, Green Jean, wife of Alexander, who jumped from the gallery (there is a most unflattering portrait of her on the main staircase). The gallery itself, dissed by Historic Scotland as a dorm (too much sweating) is now a function room (roof repaired, £45k worth of fire alarms and sprinklers, bank of loos), licensed for 120, temporary kitchen available – that sort of thing. Lesser rooms converted into rather grand exam centre and extra lecture rooms. Linkfield, previously a pupil-led bar (ah, those were the days), now houses the CCF and outdoor centre etc. CCF for all, navy and army only.

Kilts on Sundays – some remnants of the traditional uniform remain. Red jackets the norm for all, with navy collars distinguishing sixth form: 'just get it sewn on, no need for new blazer'. Still no ties for daily dress. An absolute ban on any form of platform heels – no more 'tottering on the asphalt'. Second hand shop.

'The CRC (communication and resource centre) now houses a modern sixth form centre – designated areas for independent academic study, university admissions, individual tutoring and socializing'. Quite. This was formerly a disaster area with unusable polychrome covered computers on the first floor, it's now a jolly library with all sorts of nooks and crannies in the midst of the main school campus, useful when time is too short to get back to study bedrooms, and a good resource centre. Must have had more money thrown at it than you would believe, and finally, it works! 'The aim is to create an ambience more like a university's and provide good opportunities to develop leadership skills'. Yah.

Pastoral care, well-being and discipline: Zero tolerance for drugs no longer the norm – pupils are not automatically out for being caught actively using any drug; though they are for dealing. 'Each case treated on its merits'. No random testing unless pupil has been suspended and is back on probation. The GSG wonders about 'legal spikes'. School is tough on persistent bullying ('We spend hours on it – please don't use the word "tough" '), cyber bullying the next kid on the block. Recognised ladder for punishments, no longer entirely in the houseparents' domain: breathalyser, gatings, rustications and out for alcohol; gatings and letters home for smoking. NB pupils can be expelled both for their own misdemeanours or if their parents have 'treated the school or members of its staff unreasonably.'

Pupils and parents: Usual Scottish collection. Not a lot of foreigners; representatives from 21 countries currently

L

(penny numbers); large number of OLs' sons, daughters and grandchildren, some of whom join for the sixth form only. Numbers of first time buyers, particularly amongst the day crew, who see Musselburgh as a viable alternative to going all the way into town. Buses from all over: East Lothian, central Edinburgh, the Borders and more in the pipeline. School operates a six morning, three afternoon schedule; day pupils can and do go home during the week at 4.30pm if they have no further activities (otherwise it is 6.30/8.30pm).

Not really a Sloane/Charlotte Ranger school. OLs include a gang of MPs, Lord Lamont, Lord (Hector) Laing, Andrew Marr and Alastair Darling.

Entrance: Junior school bulging with 190 pupils. Small numbers come in at age of 3 from nursery and are joined by throngs at age 12 when pupils prepare for big school proper. Entry at all stages throughout the junior school. Five year olds take an 'informal' test. Scholarship awards (academic and all-rounder) may be offered to external candidates at 11 and 12 years old; these last for their entire time at Loretto. Some academic exhibitions for current pupils aged 10.

Snnior school has own entrance exam or CE from Scottish and northern prep schools; 20 per cent of pupils come up from The Nippers en masse. Special exam and interview for those from the state sector or from overseas. Around 50 per cent now day, outstanding 20 per cent increase in boarders during the last few years, with more boys coming in sixth. Six GCSEs at C and above for entry into sixth form, with As in subjects to be taken at A level. Scholarships and bursaries are available.

Exit: Almost all of the Nipper pupils move up to the senior school at 12, occasional logistical drop out. Vast majority (85 per cent or so) stay on to sixth form. Edinburgh and Edinburgh Napier universities popular as well as Lancaster and Newcastle. Sporadic Oxbridge trickle (two in 2016) and a few to study overseas eg Arkansas State and Amhurst College as well as eg Harper Adams.

Money matters: Scholarships for academics, musicians, drama, art, sport, golf, plus scholarships for those from the state sector and for those coming up from The Nippers etc etc. Bursaries rigorously means tested (private detectives, that sort of thing) but the fiercely academic Almond Scholarship, worth 100 per cent plus is income blind. Sixth form scholarships and bursaries awarded to those 'who have deserved well of Loretto'.

Remarks: Famous Scottish co-ed public school that has embraced day pupils to combine the best of both worlds: trad boarding with robust day option. Small enough to gentle those in need of nurturing and big enough to compete with the rest of the Scottish pack. And with an almost unbeaten XV...

The Mary Erskine School / Stewart's Melville College

Linked with ESMS Junior School

Ravelston, Edinburgh EH4 3NT

Pupils: 734; 17 full, 3 weekly/flexi boarders (ME); 778; 20 full, 1 flexi boarders (SM) • Ages: 12–18 • Sixth form: 246 (joint sixth form)

Fees: Day £10,917; Boarding £21,357 – £21,903 pa

Tel: 0131 3475700
Email: admissions@esms.org.uk
Website: www.esms.org.uk

Principal: Since 2000, Mr David Gray BA PGCE (50s), who was educated at Fettes, read English at Bristol, where he did his PGCE. Taught English in a Bristol comprehensive, before moving to a language school in Greece, then taught English and modern Greek at Dulwich and was head of English at Leeds Grammar, before heading Pocklington School in East Yorkshire for eight years. Since the Erskine Stewart's Melville vast conglomerate forms the largest independent school in Europe, it is not surprising he feels he is in a position here 'to give something back to Scotland having been away for almost a quarter of a century'. Brought up in Inverness, he is proud of his Scottish roots and sees himself and Stewart's Melville/ Mary Erskine as at the 'most exciting cutting-edge of Scottish education' and stresses that he's the first overall principal who is actually Scottish. Mr Gray spends part of the week in each school. We visited him at his base in Mary Erskine, where he was busily involved in compiling a history of the school for his teaching contact with the girls.

Very much a hands-on head, the principal reckons to keep sane (and fit) by swimming and jogging at 7am each morning, and is a familiar sight as he cycles between the two campuses. He also 'works the room' quite beautifully, 'we all think we know him well and that he knows our children almost as well as we do,' said one father (a gift no doubt inherited from his politician father?). Keen on promoting self-confidence in his pupils, he sees himself as an 'educator', and teaches English and coaches cricket at Stewart's Melville. After 15 years he feels pleased that the school has 'become a gentler place' and that the 'children are wedded to our ethos of reasonable, sensible behaviour'. No need for draconian action on the discipline side recently and, when there is silliness, 'the student body can be very conservative on behaviour,' while parents 'don't want to be ashamed of the school.'

Mr Gray runs the twin senior schools with two deputy heads, and the head of the co-ed junior school. Mrs Linda Moule is vice principal of the schools as well as deputy head, since 2009, of The Mary Erskine School; she was previously vice principal of New Hall School in Chelmsford. Mr Neal Clark, deputy head of Stewart's Melville for the last 15 years describes himself as a 'grammar school boy, in tune with Scottish social culture.' Regular upgrades of facilities and a new block of classrooms is currently being built at Mary Erskine.

Academic matters: The principal and three heads have agonised together over the pros and cons of single-sex v co-ed. All four speak with the same passion – and often the same phrasing –

of their 'best of both worlds' system. Boys and girls educated together at junior school, separately from age 12-17 – gains for girls (being able to get on with learning) and boys (feeling free to talk about poetry etc) – then the social etc plus factors of co-ed for sixth year and all activities. 'Not a highly selective school,' however, described by an educationalist as a 'grade one academic machine.' Classes of up to 25 (20 for practical classes) setted, with groups subdivided to extend the most able.

School has embraced the new Advanced Higher in depth – greater analysis, independent study, projects and dissertation. Mr Clark – glad that so many students do three Advanced Highers with considerable success – notes that, in recent years, as admission to Scottish universities has become very competitive, there remains a strong desire to undertake further Highers. Recent results show a pleasing number of As and Bs across the board. At Stewart's Melville College 77 per cent of Advanced Highers graded A/B in 2016; girls at Mary Erskine achieved 87 per cent. Higher results also impressive (Mary Erskine achieved 87 per cent A/B in 2016), particularly at MES 'on the languages front' and for SMC in history, English and science. French, German, Spanish and Latin on offer to Advanced Higher Grade.

Very good links (still) with the Merchant Company which does masses of business breakfasts and links with professional firms around Edinburgh. Single IT network across all three schools with 'massive schools' intranet', interactive whiteboards galore and close on 1000 computers. Biology dept links with the horticultural dept of the world-famous Edinburgh Botanic Gardens. Impressive careers structure across both schools and excellent library facilities. Pupils can sign in for private study.

Schools combine for sixth form, most extras, and pastoral structure. In the interests of integration sixth formers have to take academic courses from both schools – a feat resulting in limitless (almost) variety of course permutations, miraculous timetabling and a quite a few bus journeys. Outstanding back-up for those with learning difficulties; school has own counsellor; 'will never abandon anyone.'

Games, options, the arts: Big is beautiful; providing a list of over 90 different clubs for all – from goldsmithing to Greek, costume design to curling and cross-country – lunch time and post school. Popular. Major sports have separate clubs for ages/stages and 27 rugby teams. Good at football too. Girls prefer hockey and basketball, still better at shooting than boys and both sexes join the voluntary CCF (trillions of girls, over 400 members in all). A second super new floodlit Astroturf at MES, 'so everyone gets a chance,' dramatic wavy roofed swimming pool (at Stewart's Melville) with co-ed sixth form slump-out room adjacent, new gym (at MES), cricket pavilion (MES again). FPs and current pupils share sporting facilities at MES; extra games pitches at Inverleith. Needle matches in almost all disciplines, with FPs representing both county and country across the board.

Smart dining room complex serves all juniors and 80 per cent seniors opt in. Sixth form coffee bars with stunning overview of school and pitches.

Incredibly strong drama – regular performances at the Edinburgh Festival and throughout the year at the Playhouse etc. Masses of every sort of orchestras. Pupils can learn to fly, ski (Hillend and the real thing, the Alps, Canada); brilliant debating team (regularly the Scottish Debating Champions, European Youth Parliament finalists) and SMC has represented Great Britain abroad all over the shop. Good home economics. Arts spectacular. Dramatic art room atop MES (with adjoining pottery and greenhouse). Multi million pound performing arts centre's opening splash was Snowman composer, Howard Blake and Scottish Chamber Orchestra. Centre took 12 years in the planning – seats 800 with a retractable stage and dividing walls, replacing the old assembly hall – which was huge and impressive – and jolly nice in its way.

Boarding: Two boarding houses, Dean Park House and Erskine House, furnished like large (and very well-equipped) family houses and based on the edge of the Stewart's Melville campus. Tremendous family feel, boarders are encouraged to invite friends home, caring house parents and only 60 boarding places (each house can accommodate 30 pupils.) Boarders organise most of their own out-of-school activities eg quiz nights, weekend outings, summer barbecues.

Background and atmosphere: Stewart's Melville campus is based round the magnificent David Rhind-designed Daniel Stewart's Hospital which opened in 1885 and merged with Melville College in 1972. Fairy-tale Victorian gothic with a cluster of necessary modern additions surrounded by ever-decreasing games pitches and car parks. The old chapel is now a library complete with organ and stained glass windows. Stewart's Melville is also home to the senior department of the junior school – see separate entry.

Mary Erskine was founded in 1694, as the Merchant Maiden Hospital, moved to Ravelston in 1966, changing its name to The Mary Erskine School, and amalgamated with the boys' school in 1978. (Girls wear charming Mary Erskine tartan kilts.) MES clusters in decidedly 1960s architecture with, now, quite a lot of more modern extensions, round the pretty but sadly overwhelmed Ravelston House (1791): swimming pool, tennis courts, games pitches, Astroturfs etc. The last much used by FPs. The nursery department and the youngest classes of the junior school are also based here.

Regular buses from East and West Lothian and Fife service both schools, which operate as one, under the auspices of Erskine Stewart's Melville Governing Council. Each school, though, is fiercely proud of its individual heritage.

Pastoral care, well-being and discipline: Both schools have a tutorial system for the first year, followed by house system in upper schools. Houses are common to both schools and house competitions have mixed sex teams. Good links with parents. Brief is that 'all children have a right to be happy here.' Code of conduct established by consulting pupils so 'they know exactly where they stand.' Excellent anti-bullying policy: wary pastoral staff and peer-support group 'with professional training' stop 'children slipping through the net.' Sophisticated PSE programme right up the school, including study skills. Buddy system for those coming up from junior schools. Automatic expulsion, 'zero-tolerance,' for those bringing in illicit substances – 'those on the periphery of the same incident will not necessarily be excluded but can come back in as long as they agree to random testing'. Fags 'unacceptable and pupils suspended'. Booze 'not an issue in school'.

Pupils and parents: Edinburgh hotch-potch of New Town and suburbs, with many first-time buyers and lots up from England. Siblings and FPs' children. Taking over a third of Edinburgh's independent secondary pupils, it's less elitist and perhaps less dusty than some city schools. Children living far out can spend the night when doing evening activities. Parent-teacher group ('the red socks brigade') slightly better organised into a Friends of the School group, fundraising, ceilidhs, 'good cash cow.'

Entrance: At 11,12, 13 or fifth and sixth form. Automatic from junior school. Entrance assessments held in January but can be arranged at any time. Waiting lists for some stages but just go on trying. Entrance to upper school is by interview, plus school report plus GCSEs/National grades (five credit passes for S5 entry.) Numbers up overall.

Exit: Minimal leakage pre-Highers, most sixth year go on to university (gap years growing in popularity, especially for girls), most opt for Scottish universities – Aberdeen, Edinburgh, Dundee, Glasgow, St Andrews and Strathclyde popular – but a number apply to English universities (London, Bristol etc). In 2016, three to Oxbridge, and six medics (Stewart's Melville); six to Oxbridge, and eight medics (Mary Erskine). SATs (for American colleges) not a problem; some students also go to European universities. Art college, music/drama are popular alternatives.

Money matters: Scholarships/bursaries available, some linked to the Merchant Company, others sibling directed. 'No child will be left wanting in a (financial) crisis.'

Remarks: A glance at the school mags, Merchant Maiden and The Collegian, sums it up: multiple hockey, rugby and cricket teams, Oxbridge places, fabulous art, photos and writing, plus fascinating glimpses from boys and girls reporting on the same activities with subtly different views.

An outstanding school: happy pupils, happy staff – focused on self-development with impressive results.

McLaren High School

Mollands Road, Callander FK17 8JH

Pupils: 590 • Ages: 11–18 • Sixth form: 167 in S5/6

Tel: 01877 330156
Email: mclarenhs@stirling.gov.uk
Website: www.mclarenhigh.co.uk

M

Rector: Since 2013, Marc Fleming (40s) BA (applied consumer studies), SQH, previously depute head of Dalziel High. Taught home economics at Galashields Academy and The Community School of Auchterarder. Keen promotor of Scotland and outdoor education; likes travelling round the Scottish mainland and islands. Owner of black labrador Hugo and sponsor of guide dog Gizmo.

Academic matters: Follows Scottish system with all mainstream subjects and a fair selection of practical courses (rural skills etc, though design technology is still at development stage). Could not provide subject specific exam results, but overall figures compare well with Scottish and Stirling figures and have moved pretty steadily upwards over the last few years: in 2016, 30 per cent of S5 and 37 per cent of S6 pupils got 5+ Highers. Outstanding history, spurred on by lots of enthusiastic but rigorous teaching. Tellingly, demand for places on the battlefields trip exceeds demand for the Disneyland Paris trip.

Careful setting, max class size 30, with no more than 20 for practical subjects. French at all levels, some Spanish, business management up to Higher, also admin. Pupils work in flexible ability groups – 'individual timetables' and varying amounts of work experience where necessary. They are encouraged 'to aim for the best', 'take as many (exams) as you can'. Support, both academic and pastoral, is for everyone, the gifted as well as pupils with additional needs – good rooms available for individual counselling etc.

Labs, classrooms etc are all spanking new and up to date and lots of practical work (we met two pale girls retreating from dissection of a kidney – the rest clearly revelling in it). IT well equipped, interactive whiteboards in most classes. Lower school pupils clearly engaged in lessons while exam candidates had special revision classes available. Pupils trapped at home over snowy winter increasingly have access to course information via the internet. McLaren has embraced the spirit of the Scottish Curriculum for Excellence. S1 and 2 have a weekly Ace Challenge, which brings in outside experts and allows pupils and teachers to gain from methods of, for instance, professional artists. Mr Martin's conviction that outdoor experience is paramount is underlined by the large section on the website on role of outdoor experience in all subjects.

Special needs coordinated via the pupil support system, which assigns a teacher to each year group so as to have an overview of pupils' needs as they progress through their school career. Lots of individual help, from within school and Stirling specialist departments, and comprehensive learning resource centre (library in everyday speak) with help on hand and supervision for extra study or homework etc. All achievement (academic or other) recognised.

Games, options, the arts: Given the time restrictions of a huge catchment requiring multiple coach runs, McLaren manages to pack in a lot: clubs and activities in the lunch hour and after school. Choirs, jazz, swing, guitar ensembles, string groups, lots of Scottish trad (pupils shine at the Mod). Stirling provides plentiful musical tuition in spite of other cutbacks, and even the most remote families manage to stay for after-school practices etc, thanks to supportive parents. Stirling's largest school orchestra in its smallest high school. In-school music festival with outside adjudicators – over 100 pupils compete, with the non-musical pupils as supportive audiences. Impressive stage with professional-looking lighting for the annual musical – no one seemed quite sure whether it was really was Guys & Dolls but everyone enthused.

The reinstated Dux Ludorum, ie the head of games, dating from 1904, is now awarded as a medal to the top boy and girl athletes. The on-site McLaren leisure centre is used for PE and fitness sessions, but gym and smashing dance areas in school. Rugby, for all levels and both sexes, tennis, cross-country etc supplemented by all sorts of other activities – canoeing, skiing, dance etc etc. Lots of chances to take part in outdoor pursuits including Duke of Edinburgh. Lots of excursions – skiing popular, with regular trips to France and Austria. Boundless trips and visits, from theatres, authors and artist field days et al – in line with the 'outdoor learning' ethos.

Background and atmosphere: McLaren High, established in 1892, grew from Free Church School in Callander, endowed in 1849 by Donald McLaren, a banker from the Strathearn area, who provided a 'salary of sufficient amount to induce men of superior talents and acquirements to become and continue to be teachers in the said school'. 'His daughter, Mary McLaren, ensured that the McLaren educational trust endowments were used for the benefit of the children throughout West Perthshire, including Balqhuidder, without distinction of income or class.' The Clan McLaren's interest in the school is reciprocated, and past pupils' networks are particularly strong. One member even attends annual reunions from New Zealand and several staff are past pupils. Pupils and parents see the school as a key element in the Trossachs community, with lots of links between local drama, jazz and traditional music, shared sports facilities and a section of the school available for community education. Pupil representatives are involved on local civic panel and are members of Stirling Council's student forum and of the School Improvement Planning Team.

Stunning site, on the edge of the river just south of Callander, with breathtaking views of Ben Ledi. A comprehensive refurbishment has provided a handsome, modern-looking school fit for the 21st century – 'like getting a new school but better because it keeps some of the character'. Central part of the school imaginatively retains the old school hall with flexible, Japanese-style, pale wood partitions cunningly placed to make a variety of spaces, including a modern cafeteria, much coveted for dances and ceilidhs. Buildings have been reorientated into a clean calm school, surprisingly bare, with restful eau de nil downstairs, but masses of pupil work in classroom area. Sculpted grass banks create an outside theatre space (in Scotland?) and pretty round columns with circular seats make a pleasant gathering space from a junction between old and new buildings.

The canteen is attractive and popular, with high take up meals prepared under the new 'Hungry for Success' healthy eating campaign. Cashless canteen system in operation, but could not cope with 100 per cent take up, thus no worries about the 'healthy eaters' who choose the brisk walk into Callandar. Pupils drifting back for afternoon lessons, largely coatless in the Scottish drizzle, were informal but friendly.

Visits from the local Presbyterian, Church of Scotland, Roman Catholic and the Episcopalian Church in Scotland, but other communities are not forgotten by religious and moral education classes, which recently enacted a seriously researched Muslim wedding ceremony, despite the almost entirely Scottish UK ethnic profile of the school.

Pastoral care, well-being and discipline: Powerful team of three deputes runs a well-organised pastoral structure in which any disciplinary action required is delivered with 'warmth and, when necessary, with steeliness'. It certainly seems to work because the school is immaculate, bar a couple of flaky paint patches in stairways – almost no litter and certainly no graffiti.

'ORCA' (order, respect, care, achievement) makes an easy mantra which pupils really do seem to remember and value, prompted by various pictures of a whale placed in strategic places. Time-keeping is emphasized; good community policing. Very high profile prefects with gold edged blazers (basic uniform is minimal black trousers/skirts, jerseys and white shirts, deliberately kept as cheap as possible). Sinners get letters to parents and 'withdrawal of privileges'. The head of each year group is tutor to it throughout, managing general pastoral care as well as pupil support.

Masses of student involvement: student forum includes the top team of the head boy and girl, plus deputies. Active pupil council of all ages meets regularly to discuss specific concerns. First year pupils have a 'buddying system' (the McMentor system) to ease their transition into the senior school.

Pupils and parents: Very strong PTA – recently successfully fundraised for a new Astroturf. All sorts, from a 600 square mile catchment area – tourism, farming, home-workers, Stirling University.

Entrance: By registration: automatic, places for all. Top year juniors have an induction day sampling things they can do when they get to McLaren. Innovative transition project, in which feeder primaries send their top year for a day out with McLaren's first year, with lots of resulting creative work and accolades from Learning Teaching Scotland, was a great success.

Exit: Nearly all go through to sixth form; of those, some 40 per cent to university, mostly Scottish ones.

Money matters: Original McLaren foundation (tiny as far as income goes) but school is well supported by local businesses, which can and will provide extra funds for excursions etc.

Remarks: Comprehensive indeed and a much-admired school. In its idyllic situation, a close-knit community in the heart of romantic landscape, the 'very positive ethos of the school based on its core values and high quality relationships between staff and pupils' (HMI) seems hardly surprising. It is, however, a tough, well-organised and self-critical school, as well as warm-hearted, doing a sound job for a very diverse population.

Merchiston Castle School

45

294 Colinton Road, Edinburgh EH13 0PU

Pupils: 585; 297 full boarders. • Ages: 7–18 • Sixth form: 151

Fees: Day £14,100 – £22,710; Boarding £19,650 – £30,600 pa

Tel: 01313 122200
Email: admissions@merchiston.co.uk
Website: www.merchiston.co.uk

Headmaster: Since 1998, Mr Andrew Hunter BA PGCE, educated at Aldenham and Manchester University, where he read combined studies: English, theology and biblical studies. Came to Merchiston after eight years at Bradfield, where he ended as housemaster of Army House and, before that, eight years at Worksop, housemaster of Pelham House. Trails of glory on games fields: ex-county hockey, squash and tennis player (school has tennis academy in partnership with Tennis Scotland). An expat, he was brought up on a Kenyan coffee farm and started school at Kenton College, Nairobi. Married to the glamorous Barbara, who teaches art and design. Three grown up children. Keen on the arts, theatre, wine tasting.

He goes from strength to strength – spot of tinkering with the syllabus, trawling all over the UK, Europe, and the world on behalf of school, plus a dabble into building. A purpose-built sixth form house opened after an £8 million fundraiser. Excellent Hunter-inspired 45 page information booklet that is undoubtedly the best guide to any school we have ever seen, plus a really comprehensive leaflet on exam results, including a rather complicated value-added section – other schools please note.

Head of junior school: Since 2012, Mrs Niamh Waldron (40s); came to the school in 2005 and was previously head of The Pringle Centre.

Academic matters: Junior school has its own director of studies, tinies taught in the starkly modern Pringle Centre classrooms – we enjoyed a treatise on tropical fish from the youngest year group; computers in every classroom and a bank of laptops for class use. Langs from the start. Specialist teachers for science, maths, the arts. Learning support teacher dedicated to the juniors, who heads a team of one full-timer and roughly three part-timers. No pupil accepted who can't 'access mainstream education' (min 100 IQ). All pupils assessed on entry on a whole year group basis for reading, writing and 'rithmetic. Support is individually tailored to each pupil's profile. Plus cluster groups for foreign languages and Latin (age 11): as much to get boys up to speed as for actual diagnosable problems. In-class support too, plus 'concentrated units' for spelling, reading and individual subjects. Maths on the whole catered for by the maths department, whilst the SEN specialists provide support lower down the school – sometimes withdrawn and sometimes in class.

Chaps take lessons in main school aged 10, are set aged 11, and follow three individual sciences aged 12, moving seamlessly up to senior school (without common entrance) at the age of 13 or thereabouts.

School continues to ply the mainly English system, though a few sit a combination of As and Scottish Highers over two years. In 2016, 43 per cent A*/A grades at A level; 58 per cent A*/A grades at GCSE. Tiny numbers doing Advanced Highers (three Mandarin, one music in 2016) and small numbers HIghers (26 per cent A-B grades in 2016). All boys must do two separate sciences at GCSE and a large proportion go on to study science at A level. Maths, English and science results very good; humanities good, too, and increasingly popular. A level critical thinking, economics and classical civilisation and junior school Mandarin added recently. Excellent showing in out-of-school activities, maths, physics and chemistry Olympiads and the like.

Recent investments include Mount Olympus – a suite of classrooms for classics, economics and geography, and the Masterchef kitchen, in which senior pupils complete a practical course and gain knowledge of nutrition, food hygiene and healthy eating. The Balfour Paul science laboratory was opened by Air Marshall Sir John Baird, Merchistonian (1951-55), primarily for use by junior pupils. The labs have all been refurbished – interesting design, repeated throughout the school: a mixture of trad tables and octagonal plinths. Interactive whiteboards and projectors in many classrooms – increasing use of computers as teaching tools; pupils from age 12 upwards are required to have their own laptop. Also a good IT suite plus more computers in the magical, double-decker Spawforth Library, but prep is not necessarily done online. Pupils must score 100 in IQ assessments to follow main curriculum and do the standard eight or nine GCSEs.

All pupils are assessed on entry on a whole year group basis for their reading, writing and maths. Support is specially geared for each pupil – all have individually tailored profiles. Timetabled support varies from year to year, with small groups for foreign languages and Latin, as much to get boys up to speed as for actual diagnosable problems. In-class support too, plus 'concentrated units' for spelling, reading and individual subjects. Maths on the whole catered for by the maths department, whilst the SEN specialists provide support lower down the school – sometimes via withdrawal, sometimes in class. Support for the gifted too. SENCo appears to be a one woman, 24 hour, referral unit – boys can and do come at all times. Complex problems need more info and background than she feels the SEN department can give.

All the dys-stream catered for, plus two or three currently with 'mild Asperger's' diagnosed in-school; ADHD not a problem, physical disability not 'a real problem': classes are relocated if access complicated; profoundly deaf boy recently went through the school with a (free) monitor paid for by West Lothian authority – wow! Can scribe in exams and pupils get extra time both in school and public exams. Really quite a large number of boys 'in the system'. Laptops not provided by the school, but masses in the special needs department, all on the school network, and parents often buy their own.

Games, options, the arts: Rugby popular, cricket, athletics, curling back in favour, hockey growing, skiing, sailing. Well-used sports hall, very well-used swimming pool, weights room replaced by fitness centre, new Astro. Merchiston Golf Academy based at nearby Kings Acre golf club. Tennis academy run jointly with St George's and Tennis Scotland – serious ambitions.

Wide variety of activities and successes in many areas. Popular CCF – community service and work in special schools a viable alternative, rifle range built into school wall. The head and the dean of sixth form extremely keen on outreach, so the latest initiative is a group of lower sixth formers mentoring in several Edinburgh primary schools. Masses of trips all over the place in every discipline.

Fantastic pipe band, sounding good during our visit, with some of the smallest pipers looking like embryo masons, lugging their oblong bagpipe cases with grave determination. Strong choral tradition, including close harmony group, and a number of orchestras and bands. Super art department, with terrific paintings both in the department and displayed all over the school. DT uses Cad Cam – good juxtaposition with computer suite and music hall, open till late.

Boarding: Traditionally a boarding school, both Pringle (Merchiston Juniors) and Merchiston itself now boast a fair number of day boys, many of whom sleep over on occasion, often boarding full time by their last year in Pringle. Known to the rest of us as flexi-boarding, Merchiston prefers the term 'step-up' (softly softly catchee monkey). Pringle House can sleep max 46 boys at any one time. Enclosed in its own private (secret) garden; boys can climb the one tree as far as the white mark and do all the things that little boys like doing without being made to feel silly. Book-inspired day room, plus obligatory television and rather complicated game of Diplomacy up on the wall.

Boys work in their dorm space and day boys have desks in the same area – superb posters. Sixth formers are billeted to each house for the year to act as monitors and have attractive kitchens to make their tasks less onerous. Cooking the flavour of the month – stunning pupil-inspired kitchens. 'Steaks would be good,' said our guide and housemaster. Impressive sixth form boarding house, Laidlaw House – 126 ensuite bedrooms, modern kitchens, a café area, multi-gym and open plan social spaces with stunning views of Edinburgh.

Just under a quarter of boarders are overseas. Flexi-boarding from age 7, also an option for senior boys though at the housemaster's discretion and dependent on availability, without charge if they are about official business – 'debates, plays and the like', or for £45 a night if for 'parental convenience'.

Background and atmosphere: Founded in 1833 by scientist Charles Chalmers, moved from Merchiston Castle (now owned by Napier University) to the rather gaunt, purpose-built Colinton House in 1930 (ruins of Colinton Castle in grounds). Set in 100 acres of park-like playing fields, with stunning views to the north.

Merchiston Juniors, aka Pringle, is tucked tidily into the south west corner of the school grounds, though pupils have access to, and use of, the entire campus eg swimming pool, gym, games fields.

School in good heart, well used, nothing flash here but no signs of real distress either. Huge amount of cash recently spent on revamping loos and individual showers and refurbishing various boarding houses.

Sick bay with visiting sports physiotherapists, own ultrasound machine and a delightful bubblegum pink isolation room (which would put any self-respecting boy off thoughts of malingering). Dining hall with servery and buffet service. Food very good – soup, meat and veg, acres of bread and rice pudding when we visited, impressive salad bar for a boys' school too. Boys praise the new arrangement: 'The food is still good at the end of term' – when the budget is low.

First floor Memorial Hall doubles as a chapel (service inter-denominational) and dance hall and boasts Cameron tartan cushions on removable pews, with an impressive tartan stair carpet up to the entrance. Girls are regularly corralled in from (primarily) St George's, but also Kilgraston and St Margaret's, for reel parties, with lots of practice before the real thing – Merchiston boys are regularly voted the best dancing partners in Scotland. Visiting girls 'not a problem' – they come and go at weekends and can join the boys in the sixth form club. Vast number of trips and options for boarders – day pupils can join if space available.

Pastoral care, well-being and discipline: Good rapport between pupils and staff. The horizontal house system is said to have made bullying practically 'non-existent' and 'Anyway, physical bullying has been superseded by text bullying from mobile phones'. Head will and has asked pupils to leave. Believes in tough love, though a couple of prefects to whom we spoke obviously hadn't needed to hear the phrase before. Mr Hunter is keen on parent/pupil/school partnership; will take in boys who have been excluded elsewhere – both boy and parent sign a contract and the boy will be subject to very stringent and regular drugs testing routine. Expect to be drugs tested if either caught or suspected of dealing or dabbling, followed by (but nothing in black and white) temporary or permanent exclusion.

Ordinary misdemeanours (alcohol, smoking etc) are treated on their own demerits. No longer cool to smoke. Discipline seminars. Jolly school policies booklet, reprinted every year, of which head is justifiably proud, lists all the dos and don'ts of the place. Purchase of cigarettes or alcohol on or off the campus and dealings with betting shops are no-go areas. Betting is a new one to the GSG, but perhaps other schools aren't as clear-cut in their expectations.

Low grade rumours persist about charges of historic abuse: the school 'has been made aware of allegations concerning a former member of staff. We have passed this information to the police and we understand they are currently making enquiries' (latest update – no case to answer – no complaint has been made). 'We have also notified the Care Inspectorate, Education Scotland, the Registrar of Independent Schools and the General Teaching Council for Scotland'. Recent Care Inspectorate reports have been fairly sniffy about 'the quality of child protection practice': a couple of former teachers were charged previously, with an even earlier incident resulting in suicide. As the current case involves a female member of staff having 'inappropriate relationships' with pupils at this all boys' school, the outcome should be intriguing.

Pupils and parents: 'A down to earth school, rooted in values,' says the head. The only all-boys boarding school in Scotland. Strong middle class ethos, good values – no change here. Record number of pupils in the school. Around five per cent are expats. Real foreigners come from all over – Japan, Hong Kong and mainland China as well as the States, Mexico, plus a number from Europe, usually for the sixth form. Germany popular at present. Head keen not to lose the boarding ethos and littlies at Pringle are encouraged to flexi-board. Day officially ends at 4.10pm, but pupils can stay till after supper if they want to – must be the cheapest babysitting service in the country. Boys open, friendly and well-mannered.

Entrance: Most join juniors at 7, via maths and English tests, informal interview and report from current school.

At 13 and 16, always via exams – own entrance exam, scholarship exam or CE – 55 per cent pass mark; boys come from junior school and from prep schools all over Scotland and the north of England. Entry to sixth form automatic from inside school, others need a satisfactory report from previous school. Range of scholarships and means-tested bursaries.

Exit: Unless intellectual impairment intervenes, or logistics apply, all juniors move on to senior school (around 40 a year).

Refer again to the useful little booklet for details of the favoured universities – two to Oxbridge in 2016, others to eg Aberdeen, Bath, Dundee, Glasgow, Leeds, Manchester. Science, engineering, economics, management/business and languages/classics/English the favoured subjects. Pupils go on to be fully paid up members of the Edinburgh mafia – law lords etc.

Money matters: Myriads of scholarships and bursaries for almost everything but all are now means-tested – scholarships awarded for the honour alone. Sibling discounts with Kilgraston, Casterton and Queen Margaret's York. New Laidlaw scholarships donated by Merchistonian to pay full fees for several boys each year – targeting 'talented individuals whose financial circumstances would not otherwise allow them to attend Merchiston'.

Remarks: No change. Still the top boys' school in Scotland (indeed, the only boys-only boarding school north of the home counties, which extraordinary position achieved through defection to co-education by the rest) and on the way up anyway. Charismatic head; boys are encouraged to 'try their hardest, make the most of their talents and look after each other'. 'No thoughts of going co-ed,' say head, staff and boys – the latter positively shuddered at the idea.

Morrison's Academy

Ferntower Road, Crieff, Perthshire PH7 3AN

Pupils: 340 • Ages: 3–18 • Sixth form: 62

Fees: £8,337 – £12,630 pa

Tel: 01764 653885
Email: principal@morrisonsacademy.org
Website: www.morrisonsacademy.org

Rector and Principal: Since 2015, Gareth Warren, previously depute rector at George Watson's College. Degree in pharmacology and PGCE; taught chemistry at several UK schools and was head of science at an independent school in Bermuda for three years.

M

Academic matters: School follows Scottish curriculum: good take-up for Advanced Highers and remarkably good results all round (48 per cent A grades in 2016). Outstanding results in Highers across the board (56 per cent A grades in 2016). The traditional bias towards science is slightly fading in favour of arts-based courses. Intermediate 2 more or less across the board, with photography for media at sixth form only on offer. Sciences perform consistently well, also maths; National 5s (68 per cent As in 2016) ditto accountancy, goodish art and design, not really much language take up, humanities OK. No obvious terminal cases; human biology popular at Higher level and results indicate that it is obviously either better taught or more interesting than its bog standard twin. Inspirational English department produces plays 'every other year' as part of the syllabus (alternate years = musicals).

Fantastic flat screen computers all over the place – pupils can take their European Computer Driving Licence, though no-one was quite sure whether the head of the computer department still built his own. Can cope with special needs and programmes much used. Dyslexia, dyspraxia and mild Asperger's not a problem – no extra charge. (Junior school has 1.6 remedial teachers and this continues all the way up.)

Games, options, the arts: Masses of pitches (including new all-weather) at Dallerie, a 10 minute walk from the main buildings, and school plays all the standard games. Good rugby. Swimming pool on site, still labelled Baths (bless). Stronger pipe band than ever, with Scots reclaiming it as their own; parents seem to think that this eruption of interest in piping and drumming is a direct consequence of closing the boarding houses, as the pipe band was previously once almost run as a private fiefdom with Chinese (who made up the majority of boarders) students playing a mega part – made for interesting photographs. Band plays at Murrayfield rugby internationals as part of massed bands. Huge CCF, D of E strong (straight to silver if part of the CCF) – almost all get bronze, lots of silver and gold. Forty-five extracurricular activities in total.

Enthusiastic art department in inspired converted attics – terrific fabrics, which were exhibited at The Scottish Parliament, but still no CAD. Music and drama strong (and based in what was once the girls' loos – check out the plumbing in the store cupboard); not totally soundproof practice rooms: 'We can hear what they are working at,' said the head of music. Stunning girls' chamber choir which plays regularly to local acclaim.

Background and atmosphere: Built in 1859, this Scottish baronial-styled building with its crow-stepped gables was described thus at the time: 'Its healthful locality and commanding view of extensive and beautifully romantic scenery cannot be surpassed, if at all equalled, by any such public building in Scotland'. The gift of Thomas Mor(r)ison, who lived in the neighbouring village of Muthill and made his fortune as a master builder in Edinburgh (constructed its new town). He instructed his trustees to erect an institution carrying his name 'to promote the interests of mankind, having a particular regard to the education of youth and the diffusion of useful knowledge'.

Always independent, at one stage did have grant-aided pupils, but this finished in the late 1970s. Fabulous buildings revamped following the sale of underused outlying houses. The impressive original school building, with its large open corridors, works well today, though some of the more recent constructions are less inspiring. The glorious first floor hall, much used for theatricals and the like, doubles for daily assemblies and socials, boasts a new organ and a 'recently restored' floor. Recording studios on the wish list. Redevelopment of the library, the installation of an artificial hockey pitch and increased ICT in classrooms are all planned for the coming year. A magnificent newer build for maths and jolly attic transformation into a vast art complex. Dining refectory off campus – rector lunches with heads of houses on Tuesdays, food said to be 'OK', though our guide and most of her peers preferred to eat at The Tuckie across the (not very busy) road.

New purpose-built nursery recently opened on campus.

Pastoral care, well-being and discipline: Excellent pastoral care. School quite tough on sin, though pupils on the whole 'quite docile' – 'Tobacco could get you suspended', regular boozing could ultimately result in expulsion and use of drugs means that 'you should expect to be expelled'. Not really a streetwise school.

Pupils and parents: Pupils from all over the middle belt – Falkirk, Stirling, Dunblane, Comrie, Perth (masses), Auchterarder – are bused to school (no trains since Beeching). Catchment area extends to south of Stirling and north: past the House of Bruar and Crianlarich. Not really a toffs' school.

Entrance: Children can and do arrive at any time – during the term and at the start of any term. Interview and testing for nursery and junior school and more or less automatic entrance into senior school from the junior. Some join the senior school at 11 from the state sector or from local prep schools such as Ardvreck or Craigclowan – interview and exam. Sixth form entrants are assessed on their potential, taking into account their grades at National grade or GCSE.

Exit: Three or four off to (usually) Scottish independent schools at either 11 or 13. Otherwise a dribble occasionally to Oxbridge; regular mini stream usually to engineering or allied science at Imperial or Manchester, Newcastle, Leeds. Most stay in Scotland with law, computing, business and sciences prevailing, though sports science and sports medicine in the ribbons.

Money matters: Discounts for siblings, one or two means-tested bursaries, scholarships for the final year.

Remarks: A good proud school which does well by its pupils.

North Berwick High School

Grange Road, North Berwick, East Lothian EH39 4QS

Pupils: 880 • Ages: 11–18 • Sixth form: 121

Tel: 01620 894661
Email: northberwick.hs@northberwickhigh.elcschool.org.uk
Website: www.northberwickhigh.net

Head Teacher: Since 2013, Mrs Lauren Rodger MA PGCE. A former pupil of North Berwick High, she studied English at Aberdeen University, then did PGCE at Manchester. Head of English at St Margaret's School in Edinburgh for eight years and was chair of the SCIS English professional development group. Achieved the Scottish Qualification for Headship in 2006 and was depute head teacher at North Berwick High for seven years. Occasionally teaches English and regularly takes a leadership class for senior pupils. Runs the school with three depute head teachers and a business manager. Her three children were educated at the school.

Academic matters: North Berwick High follows the Scottish system: National qualifications followed by Intermediates and Highers and then Advanced Highers. Six parallel classes at S1 and S2, with pupils set for maths in S1 and S2. Thereafter, six parallel classes, taking into account option choices, when specialist subject teaching kicks in – deliberately made broad to ensure that pupils' needs and interests are met within the national framework. Maximum class size 25 (a few exceptions), 18/20 for practical subjects.

Consistently turns in best results in East Lothian – always in what Scottish figures describe as the first decile (top 10th) overall in Scotland for S4 results and better than that for Highers. HMIe calls exam performance 'outstanding'. At S4 level, all three sciences, English and maths, history, modern studies, and PE stand out as really solid and taken by a majority of pupils, while achievement and take-up in French is notable. Spanish has become an increasingly popular choice, with pupils sitting up to Higher level.

Higher level sciences, English and maths, geography (among best in Scotland), modern studies and PE are very strong and this trend continues on the whole to Advanced Higher with physics and history outstanding. The adventurous range of Higher subjects includes graphic communications, philosophy, psychology, technological studies, product design and information systems.

Good remedial back-up means children with records of needs are not a problem, nor those with ADHD; double teaching in class, laptops as needed, plus extra time in exams and for those with learning needs which cannot be tackled in the classroom, workshops on basic processes, individual educational programmes and individual tutorials. Reading Recovery programme, plus educational psychologists, outreach

N

teachers et al. Support for learning for the most able as well. The school takes and is well-equipped for the quite severely disabled and works successfully to integrate all into mainstream lessons. Vocationally orientated courses on offer from Prince's Trust, hospitality at Intermediate level, and lots of enterprising opportunities. The hairdressing salon, offering Intermediate qualifications, is open to local people (a really good community service). The school aims to meet the needs of all pupils, not just the top section, and recent emphasis has been on enhancing this 'but not taking the eye off the academic ball'.

The integrated pupil support faculty includes a pupil support base in which the most vulnerable pupils have a 'sanctuary' with additional needs met in various ways: in class by teachers, auxiliaries and S6 pupil helpers. Some are extracted to work on particular areas in the support base, or on a well-established programme of paired reading. Alphasmart and laptop computers in use where required. Individual education programmes in place.

All classrooms have interactive whiteboards and multimedia systems, allowing interactive learning and teaching in all areas, plus dozens of wireless laptops.

Games, options, the arts: Has an enviable collection of games pitches with the local sports centre and swimming pool next door – they have partnership with local users. Astroturf, two gyms in school, plus dance studio with mirrors, of course. Strong rugby and getting stronger with some real successes and girls' basketball under 14 and boys under 14 and under 18 teams reaching Scottish Cup finals. Huge hockey fixture list for girls, plus volleyball, football, cross-country, and clubs for badminton, netball, sailing, swimming. Local authority development officers on hand for coaching. D of E very popular. Trillions of clubs for everything including the latest success story, bee-keeping, and lots of things for the non-sporty. More than 40 different choices, many on offer to several different age groups. Drama, D of E, debating etc as expected plus science and language clubs, eco (with coveted Green Flag award) and fair trade groups, chess newspaper, scripture union etc. Sports activities coordinator, an ex-pupil, has got even more involved. Plenty of serious fun fundraising for carefully planned range of charities with almost everything linking with the efforts of the local community, which has school at its heart.

Music exceptional, though no pipe band of their own – pupils (of both sexes) play with the town band. Bands, orchestras, masses of instrumental: wind, jazz, brass, piano etc. Senior and junior choirs (some really outstanding singers) and a popular staff/seniors choir – carols sung outside the church for charity at Christmas. Musicians have played with the Scottish National Orchestra in the Usher Hall. Scottish country dancing popular, as are regular ceilidhs. A group even taught highland dancing to a school in Malawi on their trip there.

Recording studio; huge assembly hall used for school drama (very good) and by the locals – for partying as well as plays. Deaf loop in operation. Rows of keyboards, computers and highly decorative guitars stored on walls in music room are all in regular use. Oodles of practice rooms. Creative chaos reigns in the art department, crammed with fabulous work: ceramics, amazing sandblasted glass, block printed fabrics to die for, fantastic costume design with beautiful embroidery and even architectural layouts. Swathes of young artists go on to art schools all over the country. Huge art library and darkroom are supplemented by CAD, Macs and computer links to art department. DT is impressive though mainly in wood. Home economics (cookery) now refurbished with good take up from both sexes and fashion now attracts a few boys. Impressive computer suites and everything technological imaginable can be taken for granted.

Lots of trips, Italy, Belgium, Washington, China, Ardeche, London and to crown it all, visits to partner school in Malawi.

Background and atmosphere: Founded in 1893 with 13 pupils. Originally North Berwick boasted a Parish School (which started in 1661) and the Burgh School; these amalgamated in 1868 and joined forces with the High School in 1931. The current buildings date from 1940s, and very impressive they are too. Refurbishments in 1990s and more recently an interior revamp have created a school which still looks and feels like a real Scottish Academy but is absolutely up to date in every detail. The intriguing café space has been brilliantly constructed surrounding the old central courtyard so that it forms a circular 'high street' right round a charming herb garden, mercifully sheltered from the fierce coastal winds. It is the venue for the Christmas fair, which is a highlight of town life in North Berwick and makes healthy sums for charity.

Light and airy classrooms, which must have some of the best views in Britain, cheek by jowl with the pyramidal Berwick Law on one side and in sight of the Bass Rock and spectacular coastline on the other. Strong links with the spectacular Scottish Seabird Centre, which is used for regular study, as well as providing summer and weekend jobs for impoverished pupils. Loads of participation in town life, concerts for the elderly, tree planting, riding for the disabled. Pupils have contributed entertainment, singing, dance and the like further afield, including Edinburgh.

The huge library is subdivided into little seminar areas and crannies for private study. A tidy school, and pretty well maintained, with lots of eau de nil paint (a favourite with Scottish schools) giving a clean calm feel, though the unwise choice of white painted breezeblock does not respond well to regular wiping down. Walls full of pupil work on display everywhere.

Pastoral care, well-being and discipline: Good PSE and strong anti-bullying programmes backed up by a restorative positive behaviour policy and behaviour codes. Pastoral care is delivered via the four houses each managed by a member of the guidance team. Pastoral staff co-ordinate with the deputes, who function as year heads, and an extensive support and counselling team. Working with parents is a key factor. Embedded in a geographically self-sufficient community, the school has taken on a role in community welfare and co-operates with initiatives such as the Youth Project to help keep young people safe and well-balanced out of school as well as in.

Pupils take real responsibility in school, as heads of school, and of houses, as prefects, as mentors for younger pupils and as representatives to the community. Head boy/girl elected annually by pretty stringent process. An onerous task – they have to do the Burns' Night supper at the local Marine Hotel, which brushes up their public speaking. The head boy and girl are principal speakers for S1/2/3 prize-giving at the traditional time in June, and then for the senior prize giving in mid-September, which is followed by soft drinks, wine for the adults and nibbles in the dining hall; very popular.

Four chaplains visit, three Church of Scotland and one Episcopalian, who help to tackle moral issues and teach pupils to listen and be open to the views of others.

Pupils and parents: North Berwick has its share of Edinburgh commuters, bankers and businesspeople from England etc but also an indigenous farming and services community, so intake is pretty mixed. Not quite exclusively Scottish middle class, though only a minuscule element of ethnic diversity. Incredibly supportive parents – usually over 95 per cent turn up for parents' evenings and a very strong PTA, wizards at fundraising. Parent-led parent council drawn from parents, staff and a couple of members of the local community.

Uniform is kept as simple as possible: white shirts with black and red ties and sweatshirt plus blazers for top years. Pupils encouraged to stay in school at lunchtime. Cafeteria is well used for informal relaxation and they can bring packed lunch or eat in the sports centre. Closes at lunchtime on Fridays for staff training, which may not be over-convenient for working parents. School buses for all outlying districts.

Entrance: Effective programme of visits to feeder primaries, mainly Law Primary (700) which shares the site but also drawing in the scattered small schools in Aberlady, Athelstaneford, Dirleton, Gullane and Law. Head meets parents, and children have a two-day induction programme followed by another parent meeting. Entry automatic if family lives in catchment.

Exit: Two departure dates a year, one at Christmas, the other at the conventional end of school year. Over 90 per cent stay on for fifth year and only few go before sixth. Some leave to go into further education, some work, 60 per cent to university – quite a mix: medics, law, business administration, economics, English, maths, education. Primarily to Scottish universities but a regular and quite impressive trickle to Oxbridge annually.

Money matters: No child disadvantaged – good back up from the local LA, as well as parent-inspired foundation.

Remarks: A real thriving local school, doing well by everybody. About as good as it gets.

Oban High School

Soroba Road, Oban, Argyll PA34 4JB

Pupils: 1,005; 50 boarders • Ages: 11–18 • Sixth form: 140

Tel: 01631 564231
Email: enquiriesobanhigh@argyll-bute.sch.uk
Website: www.obanhigh.argyll-bute.sch.uk

Head Teacher: Since 2008, Mr Peter Bain MA MSc PGCE, who was educated at Musselburgh Grammar and read history at Edinburgh University, where he did his masters in the science of historical research, followed by PGCE at Jordanhill plus courses on headship and leadership. Started life in the civil service, which gives him the strategies to deal with the vagaries of Argyll and Bute Council education service. Six schools under his belt, from the depths of Fife to quite grand Trinity in Edinburgh: he comes from Eyemouth High School, Berwickshire, where he was depute head, and runs Oban High with four deputes.

Bouncy, caring and fun, he is married, with two children currently in the next door primary, and potty about surfing and snowboarding (neither of which spring to mind as usual Oban activities), waxes lyrical about drama. Runs a complex and complicated ship with children ranging from bright middle class, some with a fairly lively hippy ancestry, to offspring of local farmers and fisherfolk, and, following the closure of Drumore Special Unit, has a dedicated unit for autistic children with severe and complex needs (some of whom need two carers). We high-fived one young man several times during our tour. A fulfilling and challenging job, and one he relishes.

'My vision for the future of Oban High School is to work in partnership with pupils, parents and the local community to ensure that every single pupil becomes a successful learner by developing their knowledge and their talents to the best of their ability. We will endeavour to provide an enriched and broad experience beyond the academic, thus ensuring that they become confident individuals and effective contributors within society.' This is what he said, and he seems to be getting there (and how). Recently he commissioned a professional assessment from Investors in People which came out with flying colours.

Academic matters: Full range of subjects offered at National, Highers and Advanced Highers, including Gaelic (both for native Gaelic speakers and for learners – amongst whom the head counts himself, as do many of his staff) plus politics and sociology. Business studies popular and good success here. Results significantly above average for Scottish state schools in most subjects. Good emphasis on the academic. Advanced Higher mathematicians have mind-blowing residential weekends, maths challenge popular. Scientists work alongside the Scottish Association for Marine Science. Exciting new laser cutter (£10k) in design and tech department. ICT is taught in five well-equipped rooms but other departments have good access to the school's many computer facilities.

Effective learning support operates for those with specific learning difficulties. Class sizes generally smaller than in most state schools – average 23 for academic and 20 for practical subjects. SQA certificate an option. Home economics superb, master classes from chef of the Isle of Eriska Hotel (five star, two rosette restaurant – that sort of thing) and prize winners in national competitions. Subject choices (choose one subject from each column) include the Prince's Trust and skills for work, plus uniformed emergency services (fire brigade), land management, make up, hairdressing and hospitality. Pathways – a structured 24 week timetabled semi-secondment – allows pupils in S4 to try out various (more or less) service activities: the fire brigade were recruiting during our visit and the police expected to come on board shortly. Work experience too with the Northern Lighthouse Board – 12 would-be engineers learn how to make buoys. About 90 per cent stay on post National grades and a further 70 per cent for Advanced Highers.

No real problem getting staff – head has strategies to uncover Argyllshire wannabes, and is contemptuous of applicants who haven't done their homework before interview. School has silver award from Inverstors in People (the only one in Scotland). 'Very good' HMIe reports.

Games, options, the arts: The school now operates three specialist schools within the campus: School of Rugby, School of Traditional Music and School of Dance.

Large games/assembly hall, well-equipped dance/fitness studio, two gyms; wide range of sports available including sailing, climbing, basketball, rugby (uses Oban Rugby club as well as their own; currently a Scottish Rugby Union School of Rugby where those seeking to play for their country can get an early start), grass pitch with flood-lighting, footie (girls very strong) and badminton plus shinty (akin to hockey), basketball, sailing, boxing, dance and cheerleading. Cross-country running, athletics, hill-walking, climbing, canoeing and gorge-walking are timetabled in PE curriculum from S3 upwards, as is D of E. Number of golds. Serious and successful swimming (off campus).

Impressive wind band, strings section, plus 75 strong prize-winning pipe band (world champions last year), samba band, choir and Gaelic choir (which competes successfully in the Royal National Mod). School of Traditional Music offers specialist programmes in pipes, clarsach, accordion, voice, piano, guitar and fiddle for those aiming at conservatoire level. Music and drama have merged and all S1 and S2 learn keyboards. School of Dance, in conjunction with Taynult based Balletwest (who also use the hall for their outreach classes), is amazing – we could have been watching any professional troupe, anywhere. Scottish country dancing (hall – splendidly sprung – also used by locals). Fantastic art and really inspiring fabric and design, school took part in Homecoming '09. Air-training corps, Scout troop, sea cadets. Plenty of other extracurricular activities on offer – difficulties because of long distances and buses are generally overcome. Variety of trips in most disciplines, free for those on free school meals – no one is excluded.

Boarding: Hostel for islanders and those who live afar, recently beset with problems, but with a new manager at the helm it is up to scratch. Spare space available for the new S1s to stay and spend a couple of days in the school before their arrival in August.

Background and atmosphere: Smart-looking façade conceals a mass of serious rebuild, but the old school is still there. War memorials and jolly photographs. Dining hall is cashless and parents' handbook publishes list of food available with prices. S1 not allowed to leave school grounds during their first half term. Loads of displays throughout the school including an imaginative art gallery exhibiting students' creations.

Uniform is largely adhered to, with individual styling by some and a constant battle with girls and ties.

Currently building a brand new school for 1300 pupils with specialist performing arts, sports and vocational facilities.

Pastoral care, well-being and discipline: All year groups are divided into tutor groups of 20 pupils or fewer. Each has its own tutor and sixth year prefect buddies. Year groups are managed by a head of year and school depute. School boasts an attendance officer, health worker and social worker. 'Good discipline prevails with effective sanctions for those who don't conform' – often involving local social workers. All staff trained in assertive discipline. Successful Truancy Watch scheme operates in conjunction with the local community. Lots of certificates and awards. Local ministries (all 10 of them) support a chaplaincy centre H20, which in turn supports an array of local services via The Well and two and a half workers who – along with pupils – organise activities for pensioners and the disadvantaged. Huge charity input.

Pupils and parents: The lot, including incomers, but not many ethnic minorities. Majority Scottish, many travelling long distances from North Argyll and the Islands. Famous Old Boys/Girls: Iain Crichton-Smith (writer), Kirsten Campbell (BBC political correspondent) and Maureen Scanlon (MSP), Shona and Mairi Crawford (British ladies' ski team) and Lorne McIntyre (author and journalist).

Entrance: Catchment area plus placing requests. Twenty plus feeder primary schools – some are tiny, with perhaps eight or nine pupils in total. Six are on the islands – this involves 'hopping on a plane or a ferry to visit those who will transfer to Oban that year; takes a whole day, rather than popping round the corner for a couple of hours'. Enormous care taken to ensure S1s are not swamped on arrival. Head visits all primary schools, as do the support for learning staff (if necessary) plus new form teachers; pupils and their parents visit the school.

Exit: Automatic jobs for all at the end of the summer term: Oban is a popular tourist destination. Come September/October, some may have gone off to university (mostly Scottish, very occasional Oxbridge), some to further education, training schemes or family firms (fishing, farming) and some may sneak back to school for a bash at further qualifications.

Remarks: Wow. Has to be one of the most challenging and inclusive schools in the United Kingdom. Brilliant – really holds the community together.

Perth Grammar School

Gowans Terrace, Perth PH1 5AZ

Pupils: 1,030 • Ages: 12–18 • Sixth form: S5 153, S6 123

Tel: 01738 472800
Email: perthgrammar@pkc.gov.uk
Website: www.perthgrammar.pkc.sch.uk

Head Teacher: Since February 2016, Ms Fiona Robertson, previously deputy head at Mackie Academy, Aberdeenshire.

Academic matters: Since the catchment area covers both inner city areas of Perth and part of county Perthshire, courses provide for academic high fliers and direct entry to employment. Initially all classes are mixed ability, but some subjects are set for ability during the course of S1 and S2: maths and French from S1, English, Spanish and German from S3. All do National grades or vocational courses – hairdressing, construction, horticulture (new poly-tunnel), engineering, childcare, sport and recreation (all joint with Perth College etc) – and technical – technical studies, graphic communications, home ec, admin, craft/design etc, as well as a solid set of academic possibilities.

S5/6 offers fullish range of academic Highers and Ad Highers, kept under review according to the needs of each year group. Results and take up both improving steadily. Courses in hairdressing (a non-examined level 6 Higher equivalent) and beauty (with Perth College, which has massage beds etc), Professional Development Award in General Insurance (now Aviva is a major Perth employer) etc are tailored to fit up-and-coming employment opportunities.

Learning support department of 22 (teachers and support staff) led by Bill Colley, who used to be head of New Butterstone. Children who came in as non-copers are now making out in mainstream. Lots of initiatives: C 20 group with a pre-level A life-skills programme – 'Super Soups' enterprise group making profits for charity, equalities programme. School now a magnet school for special needs. New 'assertive tutoring' guidance programme gives one-to-one support to keep up motivation and work output when necessary.

Games, options, the arts: Sports stadium with a proper grandstand and a good running track. This is used by Perth clubs for evening training and school's team of Scottish national level coaches can make after school practices join up with evening club times. This facility is shared by the St John's RC School, recently opened on other side of the site. Perth Grammar is a step ahead, already offering sports training to its feeder primaries. Usual range of soccer, netball, hockey, athletics etc. Forty-five per cent of year 1 took up sports clubs last year, 75 per cent this year. The Sustrans sport health initiative has provided oodles of bike lockers, which are dotted colourfully all over the grounds, and a flash of inspiration provided girls arriving dishevelled from their bike helmets with free access to the hairdressing department for half an hour before school.

Lots of outdoor activities, climbing wall at planning stage and plentiful trips, sporting and other, abroad: ski trip, Rome, Boston and New York, China and Barcelona. Music and drama now getting a turn with a summer musical production in the recently equipped hall. A few competitive activities are adding to the feel-good factor: a team won the under 15 Girls' Final of the SSFA; gardening (Perth in Bloom trophy); science (Perth and Kinross Schools science quiz); architecture (a team designing school leisure space won the Dundee College Creative Space competition). Lots of effective fundraising: over £22,000 for Rachel House children's hospice and other projects, such as a very active link with a school in Bangladesh and more planned with Poland and Spain. All these are beginning to open the doors to the world beyond both downtown Perth and rural Perthshire

Background and atmosphere: Perhaps the most unpromising school buildings ever devised. Gaining admission via an unanswered buzzer, and finding the school office, curiously located on the upper floor some way from the entrance, were only possible because both staff and pupils were so friendly and helpful. Narrow corridors, pretty clean considering, though all still in garish colours, inevitably noisy and battered with the regular passage of 1100 children. Maintenance budget prioritises classrooms and equipment, often stretching it by buying secondhand, with impressive results such as the home ec room, enthusiastically in use by boys and girls alike.

The extensive suite of art rooms is filled with masses of creative squalor and pupils working with enthusiasm. Sad to see the old tennis courts now used as car parks. The school suffers from its setting, sandwiched between two council housing estates in a semi-industrial part of Perth, though this may improve with the extensive, though not universally attractive, new-build round about. The school hall, once the library, is far too small, but has been opened up and given a large screen wall for wet day amusement etc, while school rents empty industrial space locally as exam halls away from school noise, thus freeing the school from a month of break times spent whispering in corridors. A school canteen serving sensible fare using 'cashless catering', the card system Scottish schools use to avoid having cash in school, but it also supplies a perky kiosk, The House of Munch, by the hairdressing portacabin, with baguettes, hot drinks etc, in an effort to tempt pupil customers from the rather too local McDonald's.

However the shortcomings of buildings and general ambiance are more than made up more by the friendly, welcoming and extremely smart staff, which to a certain extent seems to have brushed off on the pupils, who look on the whole happy and purposeful. No mean achievement in that part of Perth.

Pastoral care, well-being and discipline: Two-pronged approach: first, code of 'pride, respect and ambition', implemented by the second, a team of deputes, three heading the houses, Almond, Earn and Lomond, and the fourth dedicated to support for staff and pupils, with the aim of further raising standards. A full time member of staff heads the attendance project. Parents are involved at every stage, communicated through Group Call, which texts parents both with general school information and, if necessary, about problems, parents' evenings reminders, homework, absence etc. Formal reports covering progress and social issues are only once a year, but the school stresses that parents can make contact at any time, not just at parents' meetings. Social education is managed by the guidance department and includes programmes on bullying etc. Any instance of bullying is dealt with quickly and rules (on website) are simple and practical, including those on mobile phones and Mp3 players. Sanctions are mainly detention and withdrawal from class (into supervised alternative), though exclusion is the last resort. Tutor system based on houses is well enough staffed to allow individual monitoring/support where needed.

Pupils and parents: The catchment includes the least salubrious parts of Perth and a chunk of 'county' Perthshire, spreading north to Dunkeld and east almost to Crieff. Previously this meant that Breadalbane Academy creamed off the rural bits, but this trend has now reversed, which must make for a dynamic mixture. The Perth sector features alarmingly in Scotland's deprivation stats. Dress code (more PC than uniform) is black blazers, skirts/trousers, school tie, white shirt, and the usual means-tested uniform allowance is available. Perth LA does not give breakdowns on ethnic mix – but then Perth is pretty Scottish, anyway.

Entrance: To year 1 from designated primaries, with a few moving into the area.

Exit: Two-thirds stay on for S5 and about half to S6. Approximately 30 per cent to university and a good chunk to all sorts of vocational course, with an increasing swing to apprenticeship type employment. Very few unplaced.

Remarks: Certainly not the Eton of the north, but a school in which every single statistic that should be climbing is doing so, some slowly (academic averages), but all surely, and some exponentially – minor successes, teams and competitions. A long way to go, but everyone and everything seem to be growing on the journey. Nice to see the leafy glens knowing a good bit of Scottish education when they see it.

Queen Victoria School

Dunblane, Perthshire FK15 0JY

Pupils: 265; all full boarders from Forces families • Ages: 10–18 • Sixth form: 30

Fees: Boarding: Funded by the MOD but a parental contribution is expected for some expenses.

Tel: 01786 822288
Email: enquiries@qvs.org.uk
Website: www.qvs.org.uk

Head: Since 2016, Mr Donald Shaw, previously senior academic and deputy head.

Academic matters: A very firmly Scottish school using only the Scottish curriculum. Forces children often find themselves moving from school to school – the known record is 11 and the average four or five – so P7 (approximately half way between top primary and first year secondary in English terms) is used to assess and consolidate. The very occasional pupil may have to repeat a year at this stage. After the entry year spent consolidating in three streams (red, green and blue) carefully not labelled by ability, pupils are setted (by ability) for maths, English and sciences. Curriculum is trad but flexible, classes not more than 20. Down to earth labs (new ones on the way as part of a complete classroom rebuild planned by the MoD for the middle term future) and lots of computers in class and available in houses at night, including impressive Macs for the enterprising art department (better for photography and image manipulation).

Learning support flexible and pupils say 'really supportive', with in-class help, withdrawal, extra tuition in groups or one-to-one etc as appropriate. Good rapport between SEN and teachers. School prides itself on 'holistic' education but results hard to obtain. Though wholly MoD funded, QV competes and compares with independent rather than state schools in style (both academic and pastoral).

Games, options, the arts: Games staff assert proudly that as a small school QV 'punches above its weight' in both girls' and boys' sports. Football, rugby, hockey, netball and athletics strong, tennis less so. Spacious terraced pitches, huge multi-purpose sports hall with free access to smashing fitness training for older pupils and ancient but serviceable swimming pool often on loan to neighbouring primaries.

Military music is king of the activities curriculum. The pipe band has played for every home rugby international since 1922, until recent ban on health and safety grounds. QV pipes, drums and dancers (PDD) are renowned throughout Scotland and perform in the Edinburgh military tattoo and all over the world. Every pupil must learn one PDD skill. Marching is also compulsory and during our visit pupils joining after S2 (year 10) were doing daily catch up marching practice. The head girl reckoned that her brother's role of drum major was as iconic as her own. Pupils said that almost everyone enjoyed and felt a sense of pride in the military identity the school gives them. Masses of tours abroad, mainly with band but also recently to Malawi on a school building project.

Pupils choose own charities and recently raised £1,700 for Help for Heroes, as well as doing a sponsored walk to help themselves (the school development fund). About 80 clubs in all, ranging from skiing to jewellery making and some participation is compulsory. CCF plays a strong part with units for all three forces – myriad activities extending into holiday time and D of E is much in evidence. The friendly dogginess of school is highlighted by girls doing D of E service at a stray dogs' home and completed by Molly, the IT department dog.

Boarding: Full boarding, seven days a week for all, though weekend leave is allowed, except for parade days. The more recent boarding accommodation is well thought out and comfortable. Two houses for boys and one for girls, plus one co-ed junior house (Trenchard). A particularly telling touch there – the common room with clocks showing the time in Afghanistan and Iraq. Older pupils volunteer to spend a term or so in Trenchard to act as mentors for new arrivals. Sixteen and over can visit cinemas etc in relatively sleepy Dunblane.

Background and atmosphere: With a mission 'to provide stable and uninterrupted education for the children of Scottish service personnel', has to balance an imposing site steeped in military history with the need for a 'home from home' environment for children with parents on inaccessible active service. Founded by public subscription as a memorial to Scots who fell in the South African wars, has been co-ed since 1996. The magnificent chapel is dedicated to Queen Victoria and its splendour, enhanced by modern audiovisual equipment and comfy seats, typifies emphasis placed on service to queen and country. Pupils confirmed that this gives most of them a sense of purpose and identity. The school chaplain cares for all denominations though children can go to Dunblane for mass etc.

The granite cliff of a main building, opened by Edward VII in 1908, is maintained, like everything else on site, by the MoD – hence the brilliantly polished but battered floors, doors etc. Public gifts from, for example the MacRobert Trust, have provided a smashing and recently refurbished, up to date and very fully used library, plus (much earlier) pool and sports hall. The accretion of buildings, each in the style of the current MoD (War Office), has made a hotchpotch of buildings over the years.

The development fund has taken over from the centenary appeal. Its planned new theatre/auditorium had to be abandoned because MoD requirements were escalating the expense. Priority is now a major upgrade of the existing theatre, still hidden under wraps/tin hats.

The san, shiny with new pastel paint and a 'chill out area' complete with relaxation tapes, candles and every kind of health information leaflet, retains its 'hospital ward' since QV, unlike other boarding schools, cannot ship pupils home at the first sign of an epidemic. Efficient looking bedsteads sport teddies and pretty bedspreads. Someone was in for a bit of space and motherly care on the day we visited.

One of the few schools where pupils really do look smart and seem to enjoy it. Formal dress is real military red, high collared jackets, with hunting Stewart kilts and Lovat tweed for everyday, plus some fantastic ceremonial gear – nylon bearskins and the like. MoD supplies, so cost not a problem.

Food looks good; no one complained though not all were entirely complimentary.

Pastoral care, well-being and discipline: Not many real problems bar the occasional smoker and, 'surprisingly', no drugs. Very structured disciplinary system including categories of offences, a behaviour management group and punishments such as litter picking days or clearing tables. Strong PSE and careful discussion of problems – medical services much involved here. Observable loving attention to the real underlying needs of children away from home underpins pastoral care – impressive. Pupils claimed to like the training of a military style discipline ('teaches you how to manage your things') but evidently also enjoyed a bit of teenage squalor in their bedrooms without undue interference.

Pupils and parents: By definition, parents are serving members of Scottish Forces or are/have been stationed in Scotland (eg Ghurkas in Glasgow). Founded for NCOs, but officers' children are eligible, so a real mixed bag. Oddly the MoD don't fund a past pupils' database but voluntary help is starting this – with a huge reservoir of Scottish history to tap. Strong parent network and generations of same families. Liaison group welcomes new families and supports children. No guardian system needed because most have relatives or close colleagues ready to help.

Entrance: Applications deadline 15 January and admissions board sits in Feb/March. School is full but tries to keep a few places for emergency postings/compassionate need etc. Purpose is to take orphans and needy (in that order) and parents meet the high powered, but 'not too scary', admissions panel, while children are assessed for academic and emotional suitability.

Exit: Increasing percentage to university (now about 50 per cent) though still low in view of its academic record. A few go straight into the Forces. Others to local colleges or nursing. Most have a gap year. No notice required since MoD posts are instantaneous.

Money matters: Places are funded by the MOD if you meet the eligibility criteria, but a 'parental contribution' is expected (to cover cost of travel, activities etc). Details of the parental contribution are available from the admissions secretary.

Remarks: Thriving – an amazing opportunity for those who qualify.

Robert Gordon's College

Schoolhill, Aberdeen AB10 1FE

Pupils: 1,612 • Ages: 4–18 • Sixth form: 170

Fees: £8,990 – £12,305 pa

Tel: 01224 646346
Email: enquiries@rgc.aberdeen.sch.uk
Website: www.rgc.aberdeen.sch.uk

Head of College: Since 2014, Simon Mills, previously head of Lomond School, Helensburg. A Cambridge geographer, he worked in the oil industry before taking up teaching. Has been boarding housemaster at Stamford School and Blundell's, and senior deputy head at Portsmouth Grammar. Grew up in St Andrews and educated in Perthshire. Passions include skiing, windsurfing, sailing, golf and all things outdoor. Married to Ruth, a primary teacher; they have three children.

Academic matters: Unashamedly academic – 'Top passes per pupil, top passes per candidate'. Follows the Scottish system, hot on maths and sciences, 'Science strong – exceptionally large number of excellent results – and consistently good on languages,' which more-or-less echoes the majority of parental careers (oil, business). School thrilled to have pupils achieving top marks in Scotland in Advanced Higher science subjects over past few years (we said this last time too). Now home to the Wood Foundation Centre for Science and Technology – the largest school teaching centre for science education in Britain. Five Highers the norm in fifth year (lower sixth). Huge choice of subjects – 30 on offer and masses of add-ons: philosophy, psychology, cooking, plus pre-med courses, Scots law course, university skills, Chinese (Japanese no longer). Business management and economics come as a Pre-U, which counts as a Higher. In 2016, Highers 61 per cent A grades.

Good ICT – internet connection sourced through the university (ie free), computers throughout, from nursery up. Email for all. Computer-based projectors in every room, interactive whiteboards throughout – though often backed up with the old fashioned sort; some teachers prefer 'em.

Eight or 10 parallel classes throughout, max 22, two classes of 'mixed ability' (from an indisputably high base) in each of the four houses, French for all, Latin for all, Greek for the bright (up to Advanced Higher), Mandarin Chinese for the ambitious. Some setting for maths in P4, otherwise not till S1, S2: English and maths 'continuous assessment' thereafter. German popular, ditto Italian and Spanish – the latter to Advanced Higher level. Tuition to advanced level in 'many pupils' native tongues'.

Support for learning department straddles junior and senior school and is linked into guidance. Actual hands-on assistance plus dual teaching in class, mainly from specialists. School doesn't really do dyslexia per se; 'a few of the most able have support to overcome ADD, dyslexia'. One or two on the Aspergal spectrum. Any pupil who hits 'either a temporary or a permanent barrier' will be given as 'much help as is necessary'. 'Learning and support for learning definitely comes into that'. But no drop-in centre, though we were assured by our guides that the 'staff are fantastic and will give you all the help you need. Whenever you need it.'

Games, options, the arts: Art school at the top of one of the wings – variety of disciplines, keen on photography; graphic communication now on stream. Architecture taught both in the art and the ICT department, ditto design. Drama timetabled throughout junior and senior to higher level, good and thriving, with three new staff and ditto studios. Theatre set design has a good following.

Music department recently refurbished (we said this last time, but they've gone and done it again) and flourishing, new practice rooms – masses of instruments on offer, trips all over the place: Barcelona, Italy, the recent trip to USA was a tour de force. Enormous (brass) oompah band, pipe band part of the CCF (army and RAF sections only). Hugely popular D of E – 'biggest in Scotland' – with oodles of bronze, plus silver and golds galore. Zillions of clubs and societies. Craig Centre for Performing Arts is a new performance and digital recording venue.

Magnificent 45-acre sports ground at Countesswells with artificial pitches for tennis/hockey et al is bisected by mega pylons ('you don't notice them after a while'); an amazing water-based hockey pitch – remember Cyril Lawn? (gets hosed down at half-time to keep it super smooth) – is used by the international squad. (The grounds at Countesswells are commandeered during the hols both for junior sports camps and international hockey practice.) Historically, school has fielded strong rugby, but also hockey, cricket and golf. Internationalists in all disciplines and trips abroad for fun as well as for rugby (Canada, Italy, Australia), hockey (Prague, Ireland), skiing (USA). Powerful swimming team 'narrowly beaten for Bath Cup in last two years and regularly among the best in Britain'. Well-used swimming pool due for a revamp (water polo, canoeing) on site. Two gyms; new games hall.

Expeditions in every discipline: Malaysia (scuba diving aka biology) Iceland (geography), Australia (sports).

Background and atmosphere: 'Robert Gordon was born in Aberdeen in 1668; he spent most of his life as a merchant in the Baltic ports, building a significant fortune in the process. He always had the idea of building a Hospital for maintenance, aliment, entertainment and education of young boys and, when he died in 1731, that was his legacy.' Magnificent 'Old Hoose' by William Adam in the centre of Aberdeen; the Governor's Room is splendidly evocative: complete with models of early pupils in uniform.

Originally occupied by Hanoverian troops under the Duke of Cumberland on their way to Culloden; the first 14 boys did not take up residence until 1750. The Hospital changed its name to Robert Gordon's College in 1881, went co-ed in 1989 and added a nursery unit in 1993 (popular after-school club for nursery and junior pupils until 5.30pm each day, where they can either play or do supervised homework).

Until recently, the school only occupied the northern side of the extended quadrangle, having gifted the lion's share to The Robert Gordon University in 1909 ('for the enhancement of adult education'). But the university is amalgamating its entire campus down by the riverside at Garthdee and RG governors agreed to buy it back for £10.4 million (out of 'housekeeping' – no special fund needed – we understand that the dosh was paid up front, and skool gets back buildings piecemeal as uni abandons them). The Blackfriars Building and former engineering workshop are now a stonking modern junior school with glass walls and specialist rooms for anything you can imagine, from art and music to languages and video conferencing, plus various 'relocated and refurbished departments', including English, maths, technology and drama, from the senior school. The move has reduced class sizes, adding an extra class in each junior school year group as well as extra sets in the senior school. Though to be honest, our guides found the new lay-out a tad confusing: 'How do we get to the lecture theatre?' (We suggested a Hansel and Gretel approach....)

R

Enchanting nursery department with cunning horse-shoe shaped desks (junior school has them too, but with longer legs) in a 360 degree configuration.

The final tranche fell in (technology building and total control of the quad) in 2015, with the school able to spread back into its wings, demolish the excessively nasty 'temporary' buildings which were going up in the playground during our last visit and equip itself for the 21st century including new science and technology centre with 35 new labs and workshops. This is exciting stuff – few inner city schools get such an opportunity. School has no thought of expanding its actual roll.

Sixth formers who help with school meals are spared paying for lunch, though from 14 onwards they can (and most do) go into the town for food. The (upmarket) Olive Garden is stowed out at lunch time (Scots vernacular for crowded). The weekly menu for breakfast and lunch is published online (so the poor darlings don't get macaroni cheese twice in one day). Girls wear rather jolly Dress Gordon kilted skirts. The whole school processes behind the pipe band down the streets of Aberdeen to St Nicholas Church on Founder's Day. The head boy and girl carry the standards behind a somewhat futuristic school mace, which is borne ('very proudly') by the head janitor (and we were presented with a paper knife more or less in the same mould – we love being bribed).

Pastoral care, well-being and discipline: House system recently reinforced, with class captains at all levels plus sixth form assistants at 11 to help those newly arrived in the senior school feel more at home. Guidance system in operation – tutors – as well as good PSHE. Fairly sin-free school – pupils allowed out for lunch and 'no bad reports'. No smoking on the premises (campus too small), one expelled for drugs over past few years. Strong anti-bullying programme, would be suspended for booze, which is a bit obvious out of school; ditto smoking. Heads of school hot on discipline and when, during our wander, we came across some rather boisterous junior chaps practising drop shots (with the nursery dept balls) they were summoned to order by the head boy with the word 'Gents'...

Pupils and parents: This is the school in Aberdeen. Lots of university parents (easy to drop off), oodles of professional and oil-related ditto, plus farmers etc. Day starts early at 8.30am and children often come from as far away as Montrose, ie 35/40 miles. Parking at drop-off and collection times hideous. Vast and increasing number of first time buyers consistent with the vagaries of the oil industry, and strong global ethnic mix. Good Quadrangle newsletter bi-monthly and parental involvement. Parents love the school so much that often, having spent years in the oily wilderness, they buy a proper house and, at the next placement, Maw and the wains stay behind, leaving Paw to travel the world alone.

Entrance: Interview for nursery and 5-year-olds entering junior school; test for those over 9 and exam for senior school. Fewer leave pre-Highers than arrive: usual strictures for entry plus test. Pupils either come up from primary school or from local state schools, hugely oversubscribed – particularly for the junior school and S1, but Aberdeen has a fluid population and it is worth applying at any time: school can cope with a short period of 'overlap' if they know a family is about to be relocated. Rather jolly in-house instruction manual for S1s (ie first year senior school). Official open day second Saturday in November.

Exit: Coming and going with relocation, otherwise 95 per cent to universities all over, the odd gap year. 'Few don't go to university.' Still fairly conservative in choice – vast majority to Edinburgh or Robert Gordon in 2016. Around 10 per cent south of the border to eg Durham or London; two to Oxbridge in 2016 (philosophy and theology and medicine). A few to eg Canada or Australia. Medics (seven in all in 2016), lawyers (18) and would-be scientists, engineers and economists top the wish-list, almost all getting into their first choice.

Money matters: Unusually, monies are paid 40 per cent autumn term, 35 per cent spring term and 25 per cent summer term; two per cent extra if parents pay either by 10 monthly direct debits or credit cards. Sibling discount now reduced to zero for second child in the school, and 30 per cent thereafter – though pre-existing (more generous) arrangements stand until child leaves.

Huge number of endowments – Robert Gordon's expectation being that 'those who came to the Hospital and did well in later life would plough back some of their gains'. In 1816, 'A generous bequest by Alexander Simpson of Collyhill made it possible to extend the accommodation', and Gordonians and FPs have continued to do so ever since.

Some 185 children on some form of bursary, with 100 per cent help available to those in real need with bright children. The Aberdeen Educational Endowment provides extra bursaries. Around 20 means-tested free places in S1 each year. A mega appeal for more dosh (as ever) and an appeal to help convert the newly reacquired bits of quad running concurrently as we write.

Remarks: Strong co-ed day school. If you want to keep the little darlings at home, and live near enough, you couldn't do better. Not a school for social climbers and probably rather intimidating for gentle souls. In reality, each age group is fairly tightly timetabled and logistically compartmentalised, so there's not really a lot of overlap on any space. Crocodiles of tablier-ed tinies line up for the dining room as pre-teens kick around a ball (which was rapidly confiscated).

The Royal High School (Edinburgh)

East Barnton Avenue, Edinburgh EH4 6JP

Pupils: 1,250 • Ages: 11–18 • Sixth form: 140

Tel: 01313 362261
Email: admin@royalhigh.edin.sch.uk
Website: www.royalhigh.edin.sch.uk

R

Rector: Since 2014, Mrs Pauline Walker BSc PGCE (40s), educated in the maintained sector, followed by Heriot Watt; previously head of Gracemount High School. Studied maths and computing (a 'computing geek' married to a computing engineer); buzzy, fun and good at reading upside down. At ease, both with the school and herself – well, if you come from Gracemount.. SEN – systems in place; physical handicap – systems in place; bullying.. this is proper CEO stuff and parents to whom we spoke were/are delighted with the 'new rector'.

Certain amount of revamping the curriculum, tinkering with the timings; new outdoor classroom ('fairy glen' – you can't spot it from outside); forest school on wish list. School day now starts 8.32am (first lesson 8.40; teaching day now extended to seven 50 minute blocks Monday to Thursday, and four 50 minute blocks on Friday, when day stops at 12.30 'to allow staff and pupils [to attend] city wide events which tend to begin at 1.30pm'.

Academic matters: Max class size 30, going down to 20 for practical subjects and much less in higher years. Regular turnover of staff, with younger and more numerous common room. Usual suspects: maths, English and modern languages set in S1/S2 (four blocks per week per subject), other subjects set in S3 where necessary ('broad band setting'). German, Spanish, French on offer plus taster Mandarin from S1. Classical studies to Advanced Higher level ('strong, engaging teacher').

Strong on humanities; modern studies popular. Least hot on geography (still); sciences holding up well (currently oversubscribed). Hopefully detailed marks by subject for national exams will come zinging their way through the ether; and whilst we did indeed get a copy of school's standards and quality report, it is fairly difficult to evaluate overall successes. Though we can tell you that 34 per cent got 5+ Highers by the end of S5, and 63 per cent by the end of S6, whilst 48 per cent got 1+ Advanced Higher. Academic Dux each year – Advanced Higher langs down a tad; apparently it costs a lot to prepare pupils for Advanced Highers – 'no Advanced Higher funding'. Drama and history still raising bar, oversubscribed library lunch time history club (time clubs generally oversubscribed anyway). Clubs for almost everything, often curriculum related: maths, chess, whatever. Pupils wanting to follow more esoteric subjects can often be accommodated in other Edinburgh schools ('we go by taxi'). 'Additional vocational courses and opportunities will also be on offer'. (We would so like to see these given the same weighting as academic qualifications). Good take up in national competitions, with gratifying numbers in ribbons: in every discipline. Debating strong, regularly head to head with High School of Glasgow

Computers everywhere. Number of pupils with 'record of needs': IEPs and variety of strategies available: one-to-one, plus support teaching and a family support group on Raising Teens with Confidence. Head of learning support, plus two trained staff plus seven assistants on hand; strategies in place, too, for the brighter pupil. Drop in centre for the challenged and the bored. Curricular support for the staff. Sixth form involved in mass of extracurricular activity ranging from paired reading for younger members, plus befriending and 'helping in subject departments across the school' (slavery perhaps?). Recognised fast track for primary pupils, who may combine studies in both places. French and German, plus optional Spanish, with Urdu on the side. Masses of trips abroad in every discipline. Year tutor stays with that class for their time at school. Classrooms and facilities used by adults and locals out of hours – this is a community school in all but name. No crèche.

Games, options, the arts: House system (nations) in place for pastoral care, inter-house competitions and assemblies, as well as games. Terrific new games set up with games hall, fitness room, swimming pool and gym, much used, and former pupils (who have a rather posh sports pavilion on campus) use all the sporting facilities (car parking a bit tight). Myriad of rugby/football pitches, including bright green Astroturf; the school does well on the games front with masses of individual and team activities; athletics, badminton, cross-country, fencing and curling, sailing and water sports. Rugby (SRU-sponsored) and football for both boys and girls, plus basketball. 'Something for everyone'. Number both in national and international squads. Couple of nearby golf clubs; 'pupils can play for next to nothing during the week'.

Exotic trips abroad: skiing in the States, rugby to South Africa to name a couple, and participants run a daily blog home to keep parents and class mates in touch; the battlefields of Belgium proved popular (school has funds to cover cost of those pupils who can't afford any essential trip, though not that number of free school meals).

Music strong: full-blooded orchestra ('only full school orchestra in Edinburgh'). Pipe band – pay to join. Choir 'in high demand' fundraises for a variety of charities. Dance in all its disciplines. Drama on the up, strong links with the Edinburgh Festival fringe and regular performers. Art dept perched on top floor: imaginative stuff, flat plus ceramics, but gosh, it must be tough to be creative in a blue box. Home economics popular; fabric plus design technology (computer linked with state-of-the-art engineering software).

Computers all over and parent 'involved in Virtual Learning Curve' – watch this space.

Grounds home to OSCARS after-school and summer camp, 5-14 year olds.

Background and atmosphere: Unique history: dates from 1128; the school 'provided education for 60 boys'; the site most people associate with the school is on Calton Hill, a site much loved by telly news cameras (think overnight vigils, think home rule for Scotland), stunning Hamilton portico currently threatened with 'Mickey Mouse' ears: and a wildly unpopular hotel scheme.

Girls admitted in 1974. Established on the current site in 1968 (were it not for the name, we could have been looking at Davidson Mains or Cramond High), PPP involvement means school buildings are superbly maintained, 'windows cleaned', that sort of thing. Three storeys of fairly uninspired blue boxes (aka classrooms with prep rooms for science labs); fitness suite in basement (previously sixth form study area) Not nearly enuff public space, break was a logistical nightmare; rector says this is improved. One constant, however, is the memorial door, out of which each graduating student steps, to be greeted on the other side by the president of the FPs' club. The huge marble door is a memorial to those who died in the First World War and the west-facing stained-glass windows to FPs who fell in the second. 'Significant prize-giving.' Highly vaunted end-of-school leavers' dance, held in assorted Edinburgh hotels. Strong charity commitment.

Uniform worn by all, natty information leaflet detailing what is and what is not acceptable. Hijabs should be black or white. Pupils can be sent home for inappropriate dress. Pupils looked more uniform (hah) and tidier than previously. Variety of sports and club ties. Footwear and clothing grants available for those on child tax credits, income support.

'Bonding' week during the first year, when the whole class plus class teachers takes off for a week's jolly at an outdoor pursuits centre each May.

Range of grub provided by Amey on a three week cycle, available from dining room; school has its nutrition group, SNAG; but local shops in Davidson's Mains do well from school lunchers eschewing school provided fare.

Pastoral care, well-being and discipline: Regular assemblies, good, strong PSE programme, school has to follow City of Edinburgh 'guidelines', so difficult to exclude, but will do so in the case of bullying, physical or otherwise, and abuse. Bullying strategy handbook for all. Very few 'refusers'; consistent 95 per cent plus attendance'. 'Civilised guidance strategies in place'. Regular school assemblies. Pupils who misbehave in class are sent out of the room; we found two or three all looking fairly sheepish. Counsellors on site in almost every discipline including GLB.

Pupils and parents: Strong PSA and parent council organisation basically 'affluent middle class, but a very wide intake – with a whole range of social and ethnic backgrounds'; the catchment area covers Davidsons Mains, Clermiston, Blackhall and Cramond. The school is capped at a 220 pupil intake and there is always a waiting list but in actual fact pupil base comes from all over Edinburgh.

Entrance: Automatic from various feeder primaries if live in catchment address, but see above. Some join the school from other state schools post-national grades (steady stream from Stu Mel down the road), otherwise, penny numbers arrive on a relocation basis.

Exit: Odd logistical departure. Over 90 per cent of all pupils generally stay for fifth year (ie Highers) and some 75 per cent for sixth year. Around half to university. Trickle to Oxbridge, masses to the Scottish universities or tertiary education. Bias towards engineering, architecture, creativity of design courses. FPs include Sir Walter Scott, Alexander Graham Bell, Lord Cockburn, Ronnie Corbett, Sarah Boyack (MSP).

Money matters: Building maintained by PPP. Regular PSA fundraising including raffles and fairs, tranche of endowments (including Mary, Queen of Scots) provide tiny scholarships ('through awards') for pupils who have done well at the school; not a lot, 'just a nice wee extra'. Below average number of free school meals: social profile of school diverse.

Remarks: This is a high school in the old-fashioned sense – strong discipline and work code, good results, masses of extracurricular activities – which also doubles as a local centre with adult learning classes and much use of the sports facilities. You can't get much better for nowt.

St Aloysius' College

45 Hill Street, Garnethill, Glasgow G3 6RJ

Pupils: 830 • Ages: 11–18 • Sixth form: S5 and S6: 250 • RC

Fees: £10,818 – £11,214 pa

Tel: 0141 332 3190
Email: admissions@staloysius.org
Website: www.staloysius.org

Head Master: Since August 2016, Matthew Bartlett, previously head of Dover Grammar School for Girls. He spent his early teaching career at Manchester Grammar, before leading the history department at Nottingham High, and then spent eight years as deputy head at St Bede's College.

Academic matters: The Jesuit approach to education is summed up as 'improvement in living and learning to the greater glory of God and the common good'. In practice this means educational rigour. Breadth in S1 and 2 includes French and Latin for all as well as three separate sciences fitted in by having a term of each. S3 and 4 offer Intermediate 2 in core subjects with everyone taking a language and a science (no general science but biology most popular by a small margin and a reasonable take up of more than the minimum of one). Italian and Spanish, no German but product design, economics. Music, PE, econ and business studies all available at Higher and Advanced Higher as well as the usual suspects. French and art shine at Higher and chemistry and biology most popular at Advanced Higher. In 2016, 69 per cent A grades at Higher level at S5 and 53 per cent at S6; 46 per cent at Advanced Higher. In National 5s, 65 per cent A grades.

State-of-the-art labs with lofty urban views in the award-winning but controversial Clavius building, which also has extensive IT suites. Despite their streamlined design they look lived in, and staff are enthusiastic and friendly. Clavius, named after a 15th century Jesuit astronomer, typifies St Aloysius' approach: up-to-date technology and teaching imbued with an aura of history and the sacred. Staff report an increased interest in science and maths courses at uni. Economics and business studies are also popular, and a sixth former reported attending a conference of Jesuit sixth formers on Catholic social teaching had been useful for both subjects.

SEN is taken very seriously for an essentially academic school with a team of four specialist teachers and several classroom assistants. Lots of expertise and knowledgeable innovation is lavished in this area using Glasgow's pool of experience, as well as technology and personal mentoring.

Games, options, the arts: A rugby school though, like any team, it has its ups and downs, at best being up among the top schools. Girls enthusiastic about hockey and cross-country. Large multi-purpose gym in former convent building with serious-looking fitness equipment used for training teams. Not much space on site though three playgrounds are jigsawed in among the streets and buildings which cling to the top of a fearsome hill. Extensive rugby pitches are a longish bus ride away in the direction of Stirling, hockey pitches have been added and Astroturf is on its way.

Exceptionally good art department in the old Mount building – particularly striking was a very sophisticated architecture project for a hospital physio department with rib-like supports based on the 'simple and effective' human framework. Plenty of Macs – a whole room of them for design work. Oodles of boys (few girls) working at product design in their lunch hour, which is used for a plentiful choice of activities: chess, debating etc together with the usual field for a school with academic ambition, but also a few oddballs such as Manga cartoon creation (on computers) and heraldry. Lots of sport after school and matches at weekends. Skiing trips evidently very popular but equally a full range of exchanges, cultural trips etc. D of E and outdoor education in plenty with John Muir activities (mini D of E) for younger children

Music shares the Mount with art and drama. Choirs and orchestra expect 90 per cent attendance and are flourishing. Instrumental teaching rooms sport a huge range of music computers for seniors as well as music teaching centre for the junior school.

As might be expected the school is very charity conscious, with pupils helping on Lourdes pilgrimages for the sick and handicapped, working with disabled children and supporting local initiatives. During our visit a scrumptious-looking cake sale in aid of Salt and Light, a Glasgow non-conformist charity, was in enthusiastic progress. The school's ethos encourages helping with Jesuit and other initiatives abroad, both as gap years and in later life.

Background and atmosphere: From 1859-2004 the school was run and mainly staffed by the Jesuits, who still live next door and are visibly around in school. A gradual transition to lay staff was completed by the appointment of the first lay head in 2004, but all the key posts in school are still held by practising Catholics. The adjoining St Ignatius church is used for full school masses, though there is a smaller chapel with daily mass before school, attended by a few pupils normally and quite full in Lent. Crucifixes in every classroom, frequent reminders in form of saintly statues or portraits in almost every stair turn and corner, plus the requirement to write AMDG (Latin initials 'for the greater glory of God') on every piece of work presented, means pupils are constantly reminded of their faith.

The main building in Garnethill, a once particularly insalubrious sector of Glasgow, was the original Jesuit house. A handsome stone mansion perched on a precipitous hill. Inside it is opulent but institutional, with a wide square stairwell under a lofty atrium surrounded by black and while paved landings.

Solid oak doors lead to the series of small libraries, the head's office and sixth form workrooms, which once accommodated the brothers. In the neighbouring teaching space, polished red lino and dark wood reinforces the institutional feel, which pervades most of the more modern, well-equipped but definitely functional teaching spaces. It's pretty spick and span, despite acres of book-strewn bright blue lockers everywhere. The rear half of the newest Clavius building has a multi-purpose hall for extra dining space, lectures and the occasional class mass. Open at one side to an outdoor seating area, this is several stories high but not quite big enough to make the building feel spacious. It seems a curious use of space, as the two stairways are so narrow that a one way up, the other down, system operates. The startling Clavius and the slightly older junior school building are still seen as 'sore thumbs' in an area graced by a Rennie McIntosh Art School and other gracious piles.

Strict uniform rules are adhered to – not a tie sagging or shirt untucked. Very dark green blazers and grey trousers or below the knee box-pleated grey skirts, 'pretty comfortable', for the girls. S6s are distinguished by smart ribbon trim and special jerseys while games colours etc are edgings on the embroidered pockets.

Pastoral care, well-being and discipline: The change from a house pastoral system to year heads and form tutors has not been uniformly popular, though our S6 guide thought it worked. Discipline is strict. Expulsion has been used, though 'only as last resort'. No in-school problems with drugs, and out of school, 'it's the parents' responsibility, though we try to give every possible support'. Mobiles taken for granted as necessary and not a problem in school, though dangers of Facebook bullying etc are to the fore in the social programme provided. The school community 'forms a safe haven in which pupils take their teachers' concern for granted and know their mistakes mean trouble but not rejection'. Huge emphasis on weighing the evidence before making moral or other decisions, supplemented by plentiful talks on current issues – devolution, gay marriage etc – always presenting all points of view. Questioned on the sensitive issue of child abuse in Catholic institutions, school was certain that there had been no instance in recent memory.

Pupils say the canteen food is good and S6, who are allowed out into the city, prefer cheaper school food and a chat in the common room. They can come into school from crack of dawn and the canteen is open, though not after-school when clubs, extra tuition and homework clubs run until 6pm.

Pupils and parents: Some 95 per cent are Catholic, the highest in any UK independent school, and the remainder, Greek or Russian orthodox, Episcopalian or Muslim, the only proviso being that they accept the school pattern of Catholic activities. Being dead centre in the city gives better access to Catholics from all round (Glaswegians don't cross the city) and also to some who come from Edinburgh on the train to Queen's Street, a quick walk or taxi ride away.

Lots of loyal alumni keeping in touch. Parents exceptionally supportive of school ethos.

Entrance: School claims 'to admit pupils in the top half of the general population. Seventy-five per cent of our pupils come from the top quarter of the population' – we are talking academically here. Priority given to practising Catholics and those who 'share the aims and values of Jesuit education'. More-or-less automatic transfer from the junior school. Active sibling policy. Assessment by tests but previous school reports, school reference (and preferably one from the parish priest) are all taken into account. If pupils transfer from another independent school, St Aloysius checks that there are no outstanding fees as well as getting a reference!

Exit: Fewer now leave after Highers (S5) as uni entry on Highers alone is getting tougher – though 25 per cent still go straight on to uni from S5. The vast majority to Scottish unis with Newcastle and Oxbridge – a few each year – being the only real alternatives.

Lots do work experience and good works abroad in gap years.

Money matters: The school receives no state funding – not even, apparently, for classroom assistants for those with a record of needs, which is odd. The original Jesuit concept was that their role was to educate free of charge and the school has a certain amount of funding available. Parents are asked whether they need bursarial help at the time of application, almost automatic for families on income support, plus family discounts, but no named or dedicated bursaries. School does what it can to help. Will also try and help out if family hits financial crisis but with the usual strictures – parents must be upfront about the extent of their problems.

Remarks: A quintessentially Catholic school, with a strong academic tradition still closely attached to its Jesuit roots. St Aloysius is not afraid to combine modern thinking and technology with the best of old fashioned Catholic values. It's out on a limb from the rest of Scottish education, but dedicated to giving a rigorous academic, personal and spiritual grounding to its pupils.

St Columba's School

Duchal Road, Kilmacolm, Inverclyde PA13 4AU

Pupils: 700 • Ages: 3–18 • Sixth form: 56

Fees: £8,220 – £11,245 pa

Tel: 01505 872238
Email: secretary@st-columbas.org
Website: www.st-columbas.org

Rector: Since 2002, Mr David Girdwood DL BSc PGCE MEd SQH (50s); educated at Alva Academy followed by St Andrews, Jordanhill, Stirling and Edinburgh universities; previously 'taught chemistry for 15 years' at Stewarts Melville, now a governor. His solicitor wife works in Glasgow, two daughters at university (one doing a PhD). The rector first visited St Columba's as part of an HMI team and was 'enchanted that pupils gathered for assembly should be so numerous that Transitus sat on the stage in front of the rector'. Not so the boss of the HMI team and, as we reported previously, the Transitus 11-12 year old class is now banished (apart from forays to the, science, art and music blocks) to the (admittedly all singing and dancing) junior dept (but the new new build – planning permission notwithstanding – aims to bring them back into the senior fold).

School recently bought a couple of Victorian villas adjoining school on Gryffe Road, with the intention of building a mega new class room block in what was, basically three adjoining plots (much needed – particularly in the science departments). Alas, the planners were agin it, as were the neighbours; a gentler scheme is now in place, and, with luck, the proposed one story extensions with grassed over roofs may yet come to completion. The neighbours appear to have been – more or less – won over. Basically a political hiccup; Kilmacolm has

S

been arbitrarily transferred out of quiescent Renfrewshire into educationally militant Inverclyde.

Several staff were surprised at the rector's modus vivendi in his first couple of years. Staff appraisal weekends, committees to develop anti-bullying policy, child-protection, and health and safety guide lines were unknown to the stalwarts of St Columba's academe. Twelve years on, Girdwood, still keen to include governors, management and staff in decision making, announced that 'there is yet another (very important) questionnaire doing the parental rounds', to ascertain parents' and pupils' views. Trad vocal local parents, who felt that participation at various seminars seemed (often inconveniently) mandatory, were somewhat underwhelmed at the prospect of yet another school gathering or three, whilst first time buyers were enchanted at another opportunity to network. Gossip is a wicked medium!

Also a 'proper' questionnaire, to help children find their chosen career, designed by an outside company, Futurewise, and sponsored by ISCO. Pupils age 14, 15 and 16 complete a combo aptitude/ability test and interest questionnaire with follow up discussion evenings at school (a strategy this editor never found particularly useful where her own brood were concerned: just expensive, though in this case included in fees).

Leaving in summer 2017. His successor will be Andrea Angus, currently head of senior school at Robert Gordon's College. Maths degree from Edinburgh and PGCE from the University of Wales in Cardiff. Spent 12 years at the Mary Erskine School, where she was also educated, in roles including head of maths and director of studies.

Head of junior school: Since 2011 is Mrs Alison Duncan MA PGDE, SQH, (30s) previously depute head at St Columba's for a year and head of year at Stewart's Melville junior school; a Fifer, educated at St Columba's RC in Dunfermline, she read Russian and German at St Andrews and briefly taught German in Fife. Tidy minded, warm, bubbly and friendly: believes children should be resilient and self confident. Husband an engineer.

Academic matters: Early years youngsters roughly divided into two groups. During our visit, one lot were tucking into chopped up banana, sliced strawberries and hummus (interesting mixture), plain yogurt and water (followed by a lesson in teeth-brushing); some were drawing their dreams – two drawers to a large piece of paper; one or two were playing with magic sand. Jolly and vibrant. Regular classes 8.30am-12.30pm, but increased demand recently; the recession has done wonders for nursery numbers. Traditionally, Kilmacolm mothers didn't work: coffee mornings, charity and the like ok, but none of this pen-pushing nonsense, you understand. Come the recession, enter the working mum.

Two forms a year in junior school with max 25 in each. Reading, writing, 'rithmatic intensive for the first couple of years, glitches picked up early and learning support in place, with ed psychs and IEPs if and when needed, after consultation with parents. Music, drama and French (native speakers) from 4.

Scottish curriculum on offer – highly structured learning with masses of parental encouragement. The new Scottish kids on the block, National 4s and 5s, replace Standard grades. Most schools, as here, seem to be 'doing' National 5s over a two year period; St Columba's has joined the pack.

French, Spanish and German on offer; all three available at Higher level 'but not simultaneously' – head of lang dept writes text books. German 'holding its own remarkably well' – some native speakers. Latin for all, currently 12 enthusiastic Latinists, no Greek scholars and minimal take-up for the former at sixth form.

At Higher grade in 2016, over 65 per cent A grades, some of the best in the school's history. At Advanced Higher grade, 49 per cent A grades.

Support for learning important with two dedicated staff (including the head of guidance) covering both the senior and junior schools; help on hand for dyslexics (15-20 pupils have IEPs) and for those who find some subjects particularly difficult (one-to-one if necessary – costs extra). 'Can cope' with ADHD and Ritalin. No problem with pupils with disabilities (but no lifts in the classroom block). Comprehensive measures to check that St C's is doing well by its pupils, including testing which picks up problems as well as monitoring progress. ICT strong with pupils 'taught on computers rather than taught computing'; trolleyloads of laptops rolled round each floor of the labs (also liftless).

Class size 20, three classes per year, and pupils setted from 12 (SI) for English, French, and maths; larger numbers have allowed a fourth set which is often a small group that helps strugglers. New science block with six modern labs; old library now a business study centre. Pupils can work in the library in their free time.

Staff common room younger after 'lots of retirements' with recent head of department posts in maths and physics 'attracting high calibre from good schools', though, according to the rector, 'it rather depends on timing: ads in September are not good, March is magic'. Interestingly, there was a knitting lesson in the staff room when we visited. Stunning new head of humanities.

Games, options, the arts: School is sportier than it looks. Good and enthusiastic rugby team reached the final of the Scottish rugby plate twice in the recent past; hockey team has won the South West Cup (again!) Regular rugby and hockey tours to Canada, Barcelona, Italy etc. Astroturf pitch near senior school for hockey and tennis, though most rugby games are played on local park opposite the junior school, which has a vast games hall, tactfully curtained off for little ones so they're not overwhelmed, and a fearsome-looking fitness room. Loos and showers in new primary building are next to the sports hall and the boys' showers have the controls outside, which could – but doesn't – cause hours of entertainment. Tennis is at the Kilmacolm tennis club adjoining Shallot (as the junior school, previously the girls' boarding house, is known), but on an individual basis, rather than available to the whole school. Why? Variety of pupils compete at national or UK level in seven or so different sports. D of E hugely popular. Extra tennis courts and smallish Astroturf on t'other side of the not very busy Gryffe Road.

Impressive art and music (fabric design to die for) in the Cargill Centre, opened by the Princess Royal in 1998 and now a tad jaded. No pottery or sculpture noticed. Rather unexpected Victorian chaise longue on the top floor. Mass of soundproof practice rooms, huge number of instruments on offer and equally large number of peripatic staff. Music and pipe band popular (terrific trip to New York recently), for girls as well as boys, as is choir (lots of travel), NYC tartan week last year, jazz band, art, photography. Biennial exhibitions with real artists as well as pupils, parents and local art club.

The self-contained ground floor houses a technology department with serious equipment but fun teaching and some rather strange offerings. Home economics for 11s, 12s and the usual pre-uni stuff for sixth form; head girl busy sifting flour during our visit.

Exchanges going out of fashion (inhibited by health and safety); recent links with St Petersburg and a one-way Russian exchange. Debating a real wow with victories in Scottish and international competitions – school has had its first ever member of the Scottish debating team (rector's daughter!) The

10/11 year olds have three day away stays in the Lakes (baby outdoor pursuits sort of stuff).

Regular revision classes, weekends, evenings, and classes for all locals, from 7 to 70-year olds, everything from computers, to languages, to bridge. Very popular and good for the community, classes run from September to May, now back on form, for a couple of years no one came.

Background and atmosphere: Originally part of the Girls' School Company, the school, founded in 1897, abandoned boarding in 1970; the junior school went co-ed in 1978 (in the face of falling numbers) and re-sited at Knockbuckle Road; senior school went co-ed in 1981. The two villas on Bridge of Weir Road, which used to house the nursery, were sold with junior department getting the lion's share: splendid hall (full of role play during our visit) plus proper assembly room with stage; a grown up gym and weights room tucked at the northern end (regularly let out to local enthusiasts). As a result of various new builds and subsequent shuffling round of classes, Transitus, the youngest class in the senior school, is based down here. Healthy amount of walking (a long half mile) as older juniors visit senior school for music, art, IT, home economics and the sciences, but junior school is otherwise self-contained.

Fair amount of tinkering with senior school fabric under the previous (impressive) incarnation, but whilst the original red-brick building is still 'just' recognisable, it seems to have a lot of space dedicated to cloakrooms and passages; the dining hall doubles as assembly, with fold up stool/tables that stack in a cupboard.

Recent building work added 13 classrooms and a new library. The senior school campus is pretty cramped, with little play space, mostly rather dreary tarmac. Junior school surrounded by proper lawns and gardens.

Pastoral care, well-being and discipline: Four houses (sibling and FP tradition) and inter-house everything. Zero tolerance – drugs/theft means out. 'No significant problems with bullying,' said the rector; small school so probably not. Juniors address potential bullying via a week of stories and activities in assembly, six 'golden rules', all 'dos' not 'don'ts'.

Pupils and parents: Pupils come from a 30km radius, very much a Renfrewshire school, with about 70 per cent from within 8km, regular bus comes from north Ayrshire, and a small nucleus from Dunoon 'across the watter'. Pupils catch the 7.30am boat and join up with the Greenock/Port Glasgow bus. Juniors and seniors can stay in school until 6pm. Kilmacolm, a popular sprawling suburban village, once served by the railway, is booming: first time buyers, a tiny wide ethnic base as well as the traditional Kilmacomics (sic). FPs Lord (Ian) Lang, and Eleanor Laing MP. Don't get it wrong, this is not a toffs' school by any means, just good and sensible; pupils 'are not terribly streetwise'.

S

Entrance: Own test and interview to Transitus and senior school. 'People fail it,' rector says, though not perhaps, now, as rigorously as previously, ditto siblings/FPs' children, but automatic entry from junior school. Certain amount of sixth form entry. No waiting lists at the moment.

Exit: Small trickle (very small trickle) leave to go to trad prep schools at 8 or public schools at 13. One or two leave after they have got university entrance qualifications – ie first year sixth transfer (latest wheeze is to opt for the local state school and apply to Oxbridge – or Bristol – from there) or even for a final year toughening up in a boarding school. Otherwise approx 97 per cent to university, usually in Scotland: Edinburgh, Aberdeen, Heriot Watt, Aberdeen and Strathclyde most popular. Four medics and one off to Canada in 2016. Engineering, business, law and economics also favoured courses.

Money matters: Means-tested bursaries, more now than previously: OSCR threatens and school is madly doing homework and risks losing charitable status if it can't make its fees more accessible for lower income families. The school can be hit hard when one of the local companies goes down (and suffered badly on the demise of the local sugar company). Fees remarkably reasonable, but all parents must cough up £350 for a debenture when their child is accepted; this is returned at the end of the child's time at school (without interest or increase in value). There is a 50 per cent penalty if a place is accepted and not taken up. Discount of 25 per cent for the third and subsequent children. Blazers and summer/winter uniforms for all girls. Juniors have waterproof jackets; little ones wear fetching green overalls for lunch.

Remarks: Thoroughly sound, rather than setting the world alight. 'Still a local school' with local middle class and aspiring attitudes. Tiny ethnic mix. Victorian values, popular, the reason that houses in boring Kilmacolm (and this editor once lived there) change hands at a premium, and, to quote an incredulous local landowner (who has done quite well out of the school), 'they actually move into the village because of the school'.

St George's School (Edinburgh)

Garscube Terrace, Murrayfield, Edinburgh EH12 6BG

Pupils: 804; 48 full/flexi boarders • Ages: 2–18 • Sixth form: 177

Fees: Day £7,980 – £12,960; Boarding £24,435 – £27,090 pa

Tel: 01313 118000
Email: admissions@stge.org.uk
Website: www.stge.org.uk

Head: Since January 2017, Alex Hems, previously deputy head of Wycombe Abbey. English degree from Oxford; has also been head of sixth form at North London Collegiate, head of senior school at St Paul's Girls and deputy head at Francis Holland. She is married to William and they have two daughters.

Academic matters: School no longer narrowly academic; girls follow English or Scottish system as best fits the bill. League tables are meaningless in this school, given that two systems are followed. Current exam boards' status on either side of the border is nothing short of chaotic, St G's timetabling both systems must be a nightmare. 'Absolutely no thought of moving to the IB'. Some impressive results in both disciplines, though rather more glitches than we have seen previously, and quite a number of soft subjects with tiny numbers: early education and childcare, media studies, travel and tourism, all at Higher level. We have no difficulty with penny numbers doing langs, but to have one each taking graphic communication, information systems and computing, and two doing modern studies cannot make economic sense. Results include those from the Royal Environmental Health Institute of Scotland: number of pupils have achieved introductory (two hour course) or elementary certificates in food hygiene (six hour course) though we couldn't find any hospitality exams higher than Intermediate 2.

Possibly more followers of the Scottish system, physics and geography strong (oil?). As ever the English system popular for art and design, religious moral and philosophical studies, hefty showing in Highers. 'Lots of flexibility' in course selection (this editor reckons too much; but no doubt horses for courses). School employs VLE – Virtual Learning Environment; students can access/collect coursework, or refer to staff notes online. Claims to be the 'top school in Scotland for A levels and Advanced Highers'. As do many others, though perhaps not both at the same time. In 2016, 60 per cent A grades at Higher level and 66 per cent at Advanced Higher; 61 per cent A*/A at A level. At GCSE, 41 per cent A*/A grades. No particular bias: English, maths, langs; French, German, Spanish, Latin and classical Greek. Latin for all in L4 (top end of the junior school), thereafter girls must choose from a 'revolving carousel' of double period tasters in Spanish, German, Mandarin. The latter popular with both pupils and parents in the school's Chinese centre. Thirty-six native speakers in school, many pupils host sessions in their native languages: Russian, Chinese, Gaelic; and can study for individual A levels (or whatever) in those langs. School will arrange specialist tutors. Rate my teachers makes interesting reading, the head does not feature. Four or five parallel classes in the upper school, max class size 21 and down.

Latin from age 10. Certain amount of tinkering about with what age is taught where, sounded immensely complicated, but the gist of the argument is that by moving girls around and splitting the junior school into two, the tedium of being in a single sex school for up to 15 years might not appear so drear. P5-P6 (11/12 year olds) are taught in the main campus, before they move to lower school proper for a couple of years before they move back to main school. Got it?

Much to-ing and fro-ing with local unis, pupils and staff combine on various projects, 'and take part in an impressive outreach programme which encompasses both the academic and the appreciation of the wider world'. 'Joint seminars in a plethora of subjects with an eclectic collection of schools, the state sector as well as other independents (in all disciplines: sport and music as well as academia)', according to the school. Good general studies, curriculum choice support and careers advice (careers breakfasts), 500 options in careers dept.

Comprehensive learning support, pick up early, can deal with most of the dys-strata and ADHD; laptops encouraged. SENCo on site, four specialist teachers plus rash of assistants. Small ESOL department to help non-nationals (charge). Drop-in centre for instant problem solving, 'weekly support sessions in every subject, plus subject clinics at lunch time, in break, before school or by email in the evening' (so presumably pupils have access to staff emails). This is what we like to hear. Buddy system: older girls help tinies with reading and much else besides. All girls in junior schools (combined) are assessed for learning hiccups; as with senior school, pupils are withdrawn from class: one-to-one, small clusters, or helped by assistants in class.

School split into three distinct departments – junior, which encompasses the nursery, lower and upper (senior in GSG speak). Head has offices in both lower and upper. School not totally wheelchair friendly but will make allowances and change classrooms if necessary (lift in junior school new build), chairlift in the main building; no problem with boarding houses. Hearing loops.

Games, options, the arts: Fabulous centenary sports hall with viewing area over hall and squash courts; much-used lacrosse pitches, floodlit all-weather pitch. Trad games played with a vengeance: lacrosse tours, hockey tours, swimming, judo, cycling. Local sports clubs use facilities: Grange Junior Hockey Club et al. Robertson Music Centre houses untold numbers of choirs, ensembles, three orchestras, over 600 musicians (can be hired for functions, popular with Alex McCall Smith's Really Terrible Orchestra, as well as National Youth Choir of Scotland, Edinburgh Youth Orchestra and Waddell School of Music). Impressive collection of music results. Vibrant art department, pottery, textiles, sculpture et al. Drama and theatre good, timetabled, not much pursued at higher level. All juniors use senior school facilities, gym, music, drama, games pitches.

Oodles of D of E, dozens of bronze but tails off somewhat as girls grow older. CCF, Outreach outdoor education from age 10. Sixth formers join forces with Merchiston for dances, sport, art, music, drama etc. Zillions of after-school clubs that offer everything from keyboarding to extra IT. Hot on exchanges: girls as young as 12 whizz off to spend a month or so in Canada, Hong Kong, Australasia, Chile, wherever.

Boarding: Boarders, from 11, 50 per cent overseas, live in a couple of converted Edwardian villas behind the tennis courts in an uninspiring road full of equally dreary (if upwardly mobile) villas. Hardly swinging Edinburgh. Purpose-built bungalow for sixth formers, singles or twins, all very jolly, lots of extra activities, but perhaps not very stimulating. Serious revamp recently; re-wired, new heating. Mixture of real foreigners and long distance Scots who can have friends to stay (charge). Flexi and weekly boarding option.

Background and atmosphere: St George's High School for Girls, a member of the Girls' School Association, founded in 1886 as a training school for women teachers, transmogrified into St G's in 1888. The purpose-built, colonial neo-Georgian 1914 complex by A F Balfour-Paul is pure Jean Brodie, and sits uneasily with inspiring new additions. Lower school in converted former boarding house (plus ugly add-on); magical extension for junior school, complete with dance studio (that hall again) and dedicated nursery area has a cantilevered first floor over a bungee surface popular with senior pupils as well as a strategic undercover play area for tinies. Stunning dining hall (exit bridge known as Bridget), entertainment area below has released valuable space for extra libraries and study. Parents can (and do) use the dining centre as a coffee shop.

New uniform compulsory for all within the year, certain leeway in upper sixth. Kilts for all from lower sixth down, in St G's ancient red millennium tartan, with optional trimmed fitted jackets, 'kilts not more than six cm above the knee' (most appeared much longer). Otherwise pretty standard, check dresses, blue gym tunics, navy tights, red or blue wellies. No problems with headscarves (number of Muslims in the school), presumably like the hair bands they will need to be in school colours. Sibling-led house system.

Long-running romance with the Edinburgh Academy fractured by EA's decision to go co-ed, though they still share the same bus routes. St Gs tells us that links with Merchiston Castle are very much alive; the Edinburgh rumour mill, not to mention the local education rumour mill, assured this editor that St Gs had made an approach to Merchiston to link up on a more formal footing some time ago. Everest dissed this as a canard, but numbers are less buoyant than previously, particularly lower down the school (despite St Margaret's untimely demise).

Student council includes both juniors and seniors, terrific charity input/output; latest wheeze was to approach posh Edinburgh restaurants for their chef's fav recipes, publish them in a book and charge the restaurants to advertise. Help with City Mission. YPI with the (oily Sir Ian) Wood Foundation gives girls practice in marshalling arguments and persuading fund to dosh out for good causes. God followed broadly via Christian principles, regular assemblies, PSE cross year on Fridays, business on Mondays, year groups Thursdays and Fridays. Local minister for high days and holidays. Loads of staff jollies: keep fit, choir, and dedicated welfare programme.

IT (mostly wireless) and for tinies and in the boarding houses. School website dominated by downmarket woman's magazine type romantic fuzzy pic of Balfour-Paul's garden side. Website should be a window into the school; St G's is full of head's previous speeches but pretty low on content: collection of badly written (and often incomprehensible) mission statements but no staff list with email addresses, list of governors, senior management team – info that could be useful. For an academic school to live or die by something out of People's Friend is incomprehensible.

Pastoral care, well-being and discipline: Miscreants are given heavy hints that they should 'move elsewhere' (and sometimes they do). 'No need to break out; this is a liberal environment.' 'No sniff of drugs.' Good PSE, positive behaviour policy which incorporates 'the best of human rights legislation'.

Pupils and parents: The Edinbourgeousie: middle class Scots, professionals, incomers, wannabes and first time buyers. Boarders from the Highlands and Islands, the Borders and the Scottish diaspora abroad (alma mater stuff). Handful of real foreigners. Skype useful. Global links and exchanges. Trad. Lots of parent/pupil forums on every subject under the sun; Friends of St George's for social events. Quick poll round parents (in address book) produced no surprises: non-stimulated girls were bored at the top end, parents were fed up at having to buy a new uniform for such a short time (not in secondhand shop yet), sixth formers seemed to be working (and playing) hard. Particularly the latter. School shouldn't be so petty about make up. Not really a sophisticated bunch, and probably not yummy mummys' school of choice.

Entrance: Entry via nursery or interview aged 4/5. 'Unashamedly academic in outlook' was how we previously described this school, indeed there was a time when wannabe parents coached their 5 year olds pre school interview. School maintains, 'not so strict an entrance test; important that we can meet a child's needs'. At 11, will welcome a girl who is able to keep up with the pace of academic life but who seems set for Bs and Cs rather than A*s. Assessment, school report and interview. Entry to sixth form is more or less automatic for home-grown pupils; external pupils by interview and school report. Demands for sixth form places heavy. 'Skype handy for interviewing girls from abroad'.

Exit: Nearly all juniors move up to the senior school. Some leave after GCSE/Standard grade to go co-ed; otherwise gap, uni, and higher education of all sorts – Scots law popular, as are the sciences, medicine (18 medics in 2016) and business management. Around 60 per cent opt for Scottish universities, eg Aberdeen, St Andrew's, Edinburgh and Glasgow. Bristol, Durham, York and London unis also popular; odd bods to US, Ireland, France, Hong Kong, Thailand.

Money matters: Means-tested bursary scheme now replaces assisted places; 'mustn't let the really bright down'. Full bursaries available, plus help with school uniform. Will keep child if parents fall on hard times, as long as bursar is kept in the loop. Sibling discounts. Joint discount with Merchiston Castle School. After being told to provide more help for pupils from low income families, school passed the charity test in 2013 and has maintained its charitable status.

Remarks: The top girls' school in Scotland (pace chaps in nursery); more liberal than previously. Tatler calls it the 'St Paul's of the north', but with only four girls' schools in Scotland (two of which are overgrown dame schools and one of which takes boarders and ponies) there's not much competition.

At regular intervals this editor is asked for advice by parents who have had their little darlings at St George's since they were in nappies and are looking for a change of scene in sixth form (teenagers being what they are and Edinburgh being what it is). We have to say that, in all honesty, if it is a challenge they need then they must go South, for there is nowhere in Scotland that can hold a candle to St George's, be it in the realm of academe or of global awareness.

St Leonards School

South Street, St Andrews, Fife KY16 9QJ

Pupils: 502; 127 full boarders • Ages: 4–19 (boarding from year 7) • Sixth form: 135

Fees: Day £9,624 – £13,137; Boarding £29,688 – £32,040 pa

Tel: 01334 472126
Email: info@stleonards-fife.org
Website: www.stleonards-fife.org

Headmaster: Since 2008, Dr Michael (Mike) Carslaw BSc MBA PhD (early 50s), educated at Merchiston, read zoology at Newcastle, spent three years doing VSO in Ghana ('discovered I loved teaching') followed by PGCE at Exeter ('where I met my wife'); comes to St Leonards via City of London Freemen's and Ardingly (responsible for more heads than you can shake a stick at). A Scot and a weedgie (as is this editor: work it out) he is a shoo-in and won The Tatler public school head of the year a couple of years back (he would have won ours too, but we don't do that sort of thing). St Leonards now has a head with vision, common sense and ambition, this is real CEO stuff; school is back on track, after suffering a variety of slings and arrows from a previous collection of headless chickens.

Once Scotland's girls' academic (boarding) school of choice, St Leonards has weathered the storm caused by so-called brother schools opening their doors to the fairer sex to counteract (their) falling numbers (NB: fairer sex originally chosen on looks, rather than academic ability – how's that for daft?). School more or less went into free fall. Day girls were welcomed. Chaps were encouraged into the sixth form (for free – all two of them). A sixth form stand-alone college was trialled. Junior school (aka St Kats, St Katharine's) dissed boarders. Certain amount of family silver was sold.

The breakthrough came when junior school absorbed local co-ed prep, New Park, in 2005: chunk of New Park Educational Trust kicks in (took a wee while: rest of this moderately rich trust is devoted to 'providing equipment, project costs and bursaries', 'primarily in North East Fife – occasional individual bursary': so now you have chapter and verse). Boys and girls work their way up the school in true co-ed fashion: roughly 50/50.

In 2006, St Leonards adopted the two year IB as standard for all in sixth form. Brave stuff: going IB all the way is expensive; staff need to be trained, with mandatory follow-up courses both in and out of house. Fees need to be paid, by staff and pupil alike.

Carslaw an IB enthusiast, 'better to have scientists who can write essays'; the IB is popular with international pupils, of whom, as we write, there are over 30 different nationalities; and is 'still delighted to be part of such a vibrant school community

S

with so much going on.' Obvious good rapport with both staff and pupil: fun; our canter round the school was a delight.

Having moulded the three parts of the school into a cohesive unit, with sixth formers having more-or-less university privileges – tickets to the uni-library, can use uni gym and go 'by arrangement to lectures of interest', relaxed trips to approved cafés – that sort of thing; Carslaw now has a double-edged mission. The university town of St Andrews is a great draw, as is (whisper it soft) the golf; but school could still do with more punters. Both Carslaw and his marketing manager make global trips to far flung places pour encourager international students to both enjoy the St Leonards and the St Andrews experience. They also employ agents. Dividends are paying off. Numbers are up: particularly on the boarding side, where the elegant Edwardian houses no longer quite resemble the Marie Celeste.

An ongoing rolling programme of upgrading starts soon (where £2.5 million is a sum regularly bandied about). The external fabric is in need of serious help (sea breezes are hell on paintwork): windows and sills are flaking, though much has been done within the neglected exteriors. A full time painter has been employed – think Forth Road Bridge and multiply him by 10 and they would still be toiling.

Academic matters: School prides itself on 'high quality education right from the preparatory school through to the senior school.' Scotland's only all-IB sixth form – focuses 100 per cent on the IB (average 34 points in 2016, with six students getting 40+ points). 'We haven't taken any half measures with the qualification by offering alternative post-16 options, we have dedicated ourselves to it and we believe that's to the great benefit of our students.' New IB subjects include business management, computer science, psychology and sports science. Sixth formers help out in junior school as part of the charitable leg of the IB (CAS) with up to 50 hours' assistance 'reading, 'riting, 'rithmetic sort of thing.

Most pupils take GCSES/IGCSES in the normal way (33 per cent A*/A grades in 2016), before seamlessly switching disciplines. A one year pre-IB course ticks all the boxes for those joining school age 15 (often refugees from state systems) as well as international students who sit fewer IGCSE/GCSEs, and, if needed, get up to speed in English (about a fifth of non-native English speakers need some EAL help, and must pass a written proficiency test – ESOL). St Andrews Uni fields a raft of international speakers, St Leonards boasts help in 'a wide range of native langs in all year groups'...'be aware that some of this tuition may be subject to an additional charge', 'dependent on number of students and lang'.

When we visited (the week before summer half term) those taking the diploma were done and dusted: exams over, pupils were now home (think pay for six terms, school for five and a half: though, to be honest, 'yearly fees are divided, for the convenience of parents into three equal instalments'.. 'students can, and do, remain in school after their IB exams if that is easier for them, until prize-giving and leavers' ball'). Pupils know their results by first week in July.

Head says, 'The IB is probably the least tinkered about with qualification in the world – its basic philosophy of keeping a breadth of subjects going into the sixth form but also studying three to a level comparable to Advanced Higher or A level has remained.' 'Native lang' for IB may be English, Russian, German, French, Mandarin (currently on offer) or whatever, while Latin qualifies as a foreign language, as well as French, Spanish, German, Italian (ab initio). UCAS gives points for individual subjects studied under the IB system which means that non-linguists/mathematicians, previously disadvantaged in the overall IB grading, now get full credit for their strong subjects.

Most study two or three langs, with all doing French from year 1 and Spanish and/or German/Latin from 10/11. Max class size 20, smaller for practical or specialist subjects.

School appoints a St Leonards Associate Researcher or two, often a PhD student at St Andrews, to liaise with pupils and point them at the joys of research – or, as we said previously, 'helping them to develop an appreciation and knowledge of research'. Quite. Senior pupils have access to the university library and regularly attend lectures. (Lots of profs' children and consequently no dearth of academic governors or visiting speakers.)

Dyslexia/dyspraxia support – 'no statemented pupils accepted' – mostly provided for 'a small proportion of pupils' in mainstream teaching, but a good programme both withdrawal, group sessions and one-to-one if necessary (stunning, said one thrilled parent – 'saved our lives') at extra cost. School tests if they reckon extra help needed; specialist staff of four straddle both senior and junior schools.

Games, options, the arts: Proper matches for chaps as well as chapesses. Think Edinburgh Schools, Robert Gordon's... Full range of sporting options – rugby, lacrosse, hockey against Glenalmond, Strath and Dundee High: the hallowed main school site (birth of lacrosse in the UK) now boasts rugby matches et al (roll over Dame Louisa). Girls' sports still strong, with usual mass of international lax players. Practice matches held on beach if games pitches frozen.

Loads of individual sports and international coaches – needle chaps' tennis match in progress during our canter: judo, trampoline, skiing, badminton, swimming – university uses pool for water polo; snowboarding and surfing; rock-climbing as well as expeditions to the Alps. Annual skiing trips both at home and abroad; sailing now thoroughly embraced, ditto windsurfing and all 'local water sports activities' – and about time too. Local (and not so local) race-horse trainers use beach for exercise, as does the Scots Guards polo team, now based at Leuchars and St Andrews uni polo team. It being St Andrews, golf reigns supreme with about a third of the school playing; all lucky boarders can and do become youth members of the St Andrews Links Trust (as residents in St Andrews) so they can play the Old Course.

Nearby well-equipped BHS riding centre (moderately expensive, but not over the top) with a hot horse shower (wow!) offers a variety of options, from bringing your own nag to renting one of theirs. 'Weekly lessons available for keen able riders'.

Great new all-weather pitch, despite prolonged problems with Historic Scotland about floodlights, 'which would damage the fabric of the city wall': v expensive telescopic solution finally arrived at. Currently fundraising for new sports hall development.

Outstanding art department, attracting pupils outside normal lessons as well as curricular – huge range of alternative media, dark rooms, textiles etc. Current craze is for zig-zag (as in card zig-zagging) art work. Fun, but difficult to live with, perhaps.

Head of art was hanging fiendish model birds from the ceiling during our visit – complete with two elderly black labs – preparatory to the next biannual art show – open to the public. Artists in residence. Regularly in the ribbons for local photography prize – the Kodak Cup – 10 times since 2002.

Music strong in fabulous Bob Steedman (husband of four heads ago, who, alas, died recently) designed centre. St Leonards Junior School pupils sang in front of the cameras at the televised St Andrews Royal Wedding Breakfast celebrations. Rash of bands/orchestras, 'choir for every day of the week', ambitious singing programmes. Pipe band; we were treated to a brilliant rendition by an 11 year old, who warned us that his favourite piece was 14 minutes long. We heard about four (though it seemed to take him longer to find his pipes).

Drama on the up; school performs twice a year in the revamped nearby Byre theatre in St Andrews (popular with both school and public) students must study history of theatre as well as pounding boards. Drama types take shows to Ed Festival and go on mega drama-fest to Broadway every other year. Trips (one per subject per year) planned on a two-year cycle. D of E of course. Youth Enterprise with goodies often sold in aid of local school-adopted fav charity TICCL.

Boarding: Weekly and termly boarding from year 7: emphasis is on day. Fairly harem scarum boarding houses, passages littered with rather grand bookcases and rows of servant's bells – relics of a former age. Day pupils in the sixth form included in house system with 'day rooms' in boarding houses. Couple of small dorms, mostly single rooms, usual teenage tip sort of thing, but they were in the midst of revising. Stunning shower: (and this was in a house about to be done up!). £3 million refurb of all three boarding houses started recently – first revamped one opened recently: 'Aspects of the interior patterns have been created using a sketch by a current student (and art scholar) – a Bishopshall Toile has been created of signature St Leonards scenes, and appears on all the curtains as well as cushions in the boarding house'.

No Saturday lessons. We were concerned at possible lack of organised activities for boarders at weekend, but were assured, several times, 'that they were too busy with their various IB projects'. Various jaunts to Edinburgh and Dundee were mooted but we are still a tad concerned. Head adds 'Boarders generally are taken up with sport on Saturdays, there is a boarders' outing every Sunday, the last few have been Elie (sic) (Ely?) Watersports, beach kite buggies on west sands, go karting, bubble football etc etc.'

Off duty gear as you might expect. School praised for high standard of pastoral care for boarders by the Care Inspectors.

Background and atmosphere: Founded by dons and wives of St Andrews's profs for their daughters in 1877 in what was once a medieval priory, backing on to the sea wall, the sprawling hotch-potch collection of impressive-looking granite has neither form nor symmetry: think Topsy. Dame Louisa Lumsden was first head (Dame Frances Dove, who succeeded her many years later, founded Wycombe Abbey in 1896).

Curious combo of gracious living: elegant house drawing rooms reminiscent of Country Life plus lawned courts nestling among old stone building in dreaming spires style, combined with faintly scruffy corridors, classrooms, common rooms. (Bursar/cabinet maker needs to be shot: steel screws: Georgian half moon inlaid card table – pschaw.)

St Leonards inhabits a notoriously windswept corner of Fife, on the sea, bracing air, bone-chilling easterly gales, tracksuits popular for games. Nay, essential.

Golf, riding and the beach all great draws, as well as trips up town and forays to the surrounding countryside. Castle and cathedral a couple of minutes away. Mega library and selection of 'Maryana' in Queen Mary's House (oddly flanked by a boys' loo). Library much in use by those in sixth form, but available to all. Mary Queen of Scots and King Charles II reputed to have stayed at Queen Mary's Library when it was a private house, but not, of course, at the same time.

Splendid menu posted online: lunch we had was sumptuous and imaginative. All food scourced 'locally' (ie within 100 miles). International students can and do cook their own dishes. Veggie option, naturally, and fresh fruit available whenever. Central dining room recently given an internal overhaul: outside still pretty rank.

Comprehensive buses for day pupils: Dundee, Kirkcaldy, (Auchter)muchty, Perth, the East Neuk, and presumably special pick up at Leuchars following deployment of Scots Guards. Juniors can be dropped off early (8am) and collected late (5.30pm). (This represents a reduced school day but incorporates time for activities, which has 'settled down well and parents appreciate it'). Otherwise return journey leaves 5.40pm.

Sixth formers wear suits (or a fair approximation thereof) during the working day. Boys rather tidier than some we have seen at that age; girls less so: sixth formers adopt a theme (or two) in black – quite short shorts and thick tights apparently ok (skool says quite short skirts...). Machine washable blazers and blue tartan kilts for girls, grey breeks for chaps are senior/junior school uniform with blue woolly pullies. Ah but we hanker for the cloaks of yesteryear. Second hand shop run by the 'bullish' PA which also organises family fun tennis etc.

School is proud of its Scottish heritage and tradition – Burns Day celebrated though Scottish Country Dancing is apparently only taught in the junior school.

Pastoral care, well-being and discipline: School rules feature punctuality, security and civilised behaviour; the student handbook has a rash of rules, most of which are sheer common sense: L-drivers may not drive other pupils and the like. But members of the sixth form have a mass of privileges – can visit some (some definitely out of bounds) local pubs if aged 18 and over, smoke off-campus – je m'en doute in these days of stalag Scotland ('but not if I feel they are bringing the school into disrepute and are identifiable as St Leonards pupils,' says head) and are generally expected to behave like grown-ups. No smoking on campus, no under-age drinking and absolute zero tolerance of drugs. Parents like the drugs policy – random drugs testing and testing on suspicion, out for pushing, forfeit right to remain in school for using – depends on individual and other factors and for how long, and pupils may be allowed back under fairly arduous conditions. Suspension for continued failure to observe the booze rules. Police are called for theft. No chaplain but team of local ministers who regularly preach. Plenty of fundraising for good causes.

Pupils and parents: No boarding in junior school, hence strong Scots contingent in senior school; small number of UK boarders but most from abroad, particularly at sixth form level, when incomers swell the ranks to follow the IB course – a boon. Those pupils whom we met (either IB or newbies) were a more sophisticated bunch – particularly the former – than we would normally expect in a school which is so geographically challenged...with sea on three sides.

Eclectic mix of international and first time buyers: Fifers see school as a viable option. Think butcher, baker, candlestick maker, farmer, landed estate owner and very senior CEOs. Think oligarchs, think wannabe Donald Trumps. No longer does this ed hear from mates that 'we put Amelia/Georgina/Freddie into St Leonards, but really it didn't take'. Parents, both past, and present are now positive about the place.

St Leonards has a strong old girls' network and many at the school are offspring or grand offspring of Seniors; Seniors must now be referred to as FPs. Some concern previously from Seniors about school's new direction though others welcomed its new impetus. Famous Seniors include Betty Harvey Anderson, Dame Kathleen Ollerenshaw (previous president of St Leonards) past head Mary James, Gillian Glover of the Scotsman (who didn't last the course), Stella Tennant (ditto), Baroness Byford and Anji Hunter.

Entrance: At any time. Mid-term ok. Accepts CE, but usually own (written) entrance assessment (English and maths) or scholarship exam. Seamless transition from juniors to seniors. Six GCSEs or equivalent for sixth with As and Bs in subjects to be studied at higher level in the IB. 'We usually pick up 15/20 at sixth from entry' for IB. School prefers to meet with international applicants but, if pushed, will Skype.

Exit: 'Minimum' drop out at transition from juniors to seniors and some (20 per cent or so) depart post-GCSE (only accept good English speakers to sixth form). Around 90 per cent to universities – mostly Scottish and northern English destinations eg Durham, Newcastle, Warwick, around a third abroad (including Munch and Moscow in 2016). Subjects range from law to medicine to aviation management to music. Many do a gap year, armed with addresses of welcoming Seniors throughout the world (a boon for worried parents).

Money matters: A means-tested, assisted places scheme in operation from year 5; open to application from existing parents in financial difficulties: sibling discount. Raft of scholarships: though only of nominal monetary value, and usually only lasting a couple of years – ranging from academic through music, drama and sport – golf scholarships very popular (as you might imagine).

Remarks: The IB is a winner. Dr Carslaw has the world in his hands: St Leonards runs seamlessly from age five to 18.. the IB niche gives it an academic edge with an international flavour. All he needs is more punters, though currently boarding is full, with waiting lists in some years.

St Margaret's School for Girls (Aberdeen)

17 Albyn Place, Aberdeen AB10 1RU

Pupils: 368 • Ages: 3–18 • Sixth form: 35

Fees: £7,685 – £12,174 pa

Tel: 01224 584466
Email: info@st-margaret.aberdeen.sch.uk
Website: www.st-margaret.aberdeen.sch.uk

Head: Since 2014, Miss Anna Tomlinson MTheol PGCE (late 30s). Studied theology at University of St Andrews. Also has PGCE from St Martin's College, Lancaster and Scottish Qualification for Headship from University of Edinburgh. Formerly deputy head at St George's School for Girls, Edinburgh, where she led the development of an extensive international education programme and school's boarding provision.

Her outside interests include choral music, travel and cooking.

Academic matters: Academically strong across the board. The lovely exam website to which we were directed by the school only gives percentages and our request for results by subject by grade hiccupped, with the head saying that she 'can't disclose this information due to our exam results being small and the risk of pupils being identified'. Nevertheless, 59 per cent A grades at Advanced Higher, 64 per cent A at Higher level and 76 per cent A at National 5 in 2016. Stonking 17 subjects offered at Higher level. Previous head tweaked the curriculum, dropping admin and adding economics and PE in sixth form, together with crash courses in Italian and higher philosophy. Sixth formers can do modules from the Open University: astronomy, molecules, medicine and nutrition. All setted for maths, English for first two years, but classes fluid, lots of movement.

French (from 5), Latin, compulsory for one year from age 11, German and Spanish option age 13. NB before the school trip to China last year trippers were given Mandarin lessons: the girls had a happy time communicating, but the accompanying staff 'remained stumm'. Head keen that girls should have the advantage of 'learning independently' and enjoy their lessons (not quite sure how the living independently lessons fit in). Three ICT suites, all intranetted, plus personal laptops/ipads.

Programmed support for learning throughout the school with help for the gifted as well as the underperformer. Dyslexia, dyspraxia, ADHD and mild Asperger's: individual, clusters, plus support in class if needed. No automatic testing on entrance for additional needs but 'everyone has a spelling assessment which is a good indicator.' Departments keep detailed notes of problems that might be 'just around the corner.' Support available from form teachers, and dedicated head of guidance, and they can go 'to anyone if in difficulties', though not, apparently, instantaneously, 'make an appointment with the maths base,' says school, 'or come to me'. Paired reading initiative, senior girls 'trained in specific reading techniques' work with younger pupils in their free time. Apart from 'fostering community spirit', senior readers get brownie points through 'certification from the Institute of Management'; ie it looks good on the UCAS personal statement.

Games, options, the arts: Impressive netball and tennis teams. School keen on team games, especially hockey (reams of Scotland reps) but loads of individual sports too; swimming important (current county reps); all juniors have regular dips in local pool. Trad athletics, tennis, rounders; snow boarding/skiing by Garth Dee on dry slope, and the real thing, both in Scotland and abroad. Huge take up. Skool competes regionally. Curling is the new kid on the block, 10 year olds up ('well we had to do something during the last two awful winters'), curling rink about five miles north of school. Individual representative in the Olympic dressage. Impressive, but not really a feather in the school's personal cap.

Art and design department is 'fantastic', with a stunning panorama of urban Aberdeenshire providing part of the flexible natural lighting. Art dept recently produced a mural 'to brighten a dingy corner of the playground'; used to provide scenery for school plays, but these are now performed in the local art centre, and sadly the art dept has lost a potential stimulator for those – possibly non-academic girls – who might want to follow a career in scenery design. Shame. Trad disciplines plus ceramics, printmaking, metal jewellery-making (sold via YE, masses on show outside head's office), sculpture ('small sculpture because there is no room for storage'). Bookbinding on the cards (but probably as a club). St M's keen not to have a 'precious' image, so food technology only up to second year, but it reappears as preparation for living in sixth.

Art and music taken to Advanced Higher level. Lively drama, Sound of Music recent performance, three major musical productions regularly, it's hardly surprising that there is a 'resurgence of drama as an academic subject'. Music vibrant. Collection of orchestras: string, chamber, jazz plus outstanding 'travelling' choir with regular trips (Prague next, but no Harleys?). Number of current pupils and FPs in the National Youth Orchestra, and the (proper as opposed to pop) proms. St Margaret's schools worldwide band together for choir tours, heads chit-chat electronically. 'Gives the school a global dimension,' (though didn't stop the one in Edinburgh going belly up).

Masses of activities: 20+ clubs and classes include ballet, highland dancing, eco, wildlife, film, choi kwang do, tennis, French, dance, chess and very strong debating/public speaking. St M's ain't that brave and usually competes in the North East region of Scotland, though a starring 15 year old did well representing Scotland at the Euro-Parliament competition at Brussels, not so long ago.

Prioritising arts/music/games a problem of huge take-up overall in a small school. Staff need to be flexible and not squabble over musical games players. ('Can be a problem', said

S

the head.) Strong D of E, regular golds. YE 'made fudge last year, not good for diets'. Masses of charity input, particularly with the YPI (Youth Philanthropy Institute) and (oily Sir Ian) Wood Family Foundation where 16 year olds find and adopt a charity, do detailed research and then give a presentation to trustees. Reward: £3,000 per charity. Good global awareness from international pupil mix; school has achieved its first Green Flag award (loads of oily children, this must be either a wake up call, or a feather in the collective cap). Comprehensive careers department. Week's work experience for all age 15 (we wonder whether – as in the South, parents have to ante up?).

Background and atmosphere: Founded in 1846, St Margaret's is the only all girls' school in the north of Scotland. Based in a hotchpotch conversion of Victorian merchants' houses (Albyn Place and the adjacent Queens Road in Aberdeen are home to some six or seven various schools). The gardens at the back are filled with fairly uninspiring new-builds, recently refurbished art studio and resources centre. But alas, though the flat roofed new classroom block looks ripe for development, the architects have been rather economical with concrete. Expansion can only be achieved by demolition and rebuild, which may in fact be a cheaper option: currently new builds are exempt from VAT. Plans in pipe dream for new hall with classrooms above. But perhaps not quite yet.

Charming well-equipped library. Corridors everywhere: walls drip with bright artwork, photos of pupils, productions, school trips, expeditions, press cuttings etc – friendly and buzzing. Wizard adventure playground on refurbished lawn, slightly squiffy globe on tarmac, with detailed maps fixed to nearby tables. Couple of trees removed ('ealth and safety) have been recycled as table and chair, to a design by pupil for her higher art work

Cooked lunch available, with girls ordering main dishes in advance, in a pretty cramped room in the basement which doubles as after-school club for tinies, adjacent to the revamped dead posh loos. Girls eat by class, own sandwiches. School not wheelchair friendly (no classrooms on ground floor). Early drop off from 8am, pupils can stay till 5.30pm, clubs etc after school. Senior blazers (expensive) are worn only on the way to/from school. Grey kilts or straight skirts. Special braid on blazers for sixth form, more braid for prefects, some of whom end up looking like Christmas trees. Good secondhand shop (well, this is Aberdeen) run by parents and one enterprising parent has found a cheaper supplier and started a shop within the school to sell uniform for about two-thirds of regular shop price (there are provisions for really cheap kit for those on 100 per cent bursaries).

Pastoral care, well-being and discipline: Strong moral background with joint PSE and RME syllabus. Some Muslims in the school, headscarves and longer skirts OK; pupils made to feel inclusive with Ramadan respected, special prayer room available. Ecumenical assemblies. All join in the Easter service and Christmas concert and the whole school troops off to the cathedral for St Margaret's Day when the smallest have to be restrained from trying to find St Margaret's shield on the roof and falling over in the process.

Worry boxes for juniors; dedicated junior guidance counsellor and buddy system. Strong anti-bullying programme. Head of guidance an experienced 'resolver', each case 'resolved on merit'. 'Both the bullied and the bullyer need support'. Detention for the few and far between 'naughty girls' replaced by a PC 'extra learning opportunity to brush up their skills' (sometimes after school). Whole school assembly most Fridays, pupil council and charity reps meetings include juniors and seniors. With 30 school prefects plus form prefects, sport and activity captains etc, most pupils get a chance to lead. Social life is active with PTA dances and discos and a friendly eye kept that 'someone's brother will arrange partners.'

A change of emphasis in sixth form; newish sixth form head, and realistically tidy sixth form flat. The sixth formers prepare for the world beyond Aberdeen with their own out-of-school conference: annual theme this year (as last, and the one before) 'Being the Best You Can Be', led by past pupils and specialists: speakers include FPs who have become CEOs in their fields of expertise.

Pupils and parents: Large number of first time buyers, large number of non-Brits, strong parent association. And very strong FP links. Charming. Polite and well-mannered. Tessa Jowell is an old girl. Girls come from surrounding areas and the city itself. Dedicated buses.

Entrance: Assessments for all, mini test for tinies where they play in groups and are surreptitiously assessed by experts. Siblings not usually turned away. Young coming up through the nursery/junior school will have been quietly assessed throughout their time, and if wobbles are detected, the school will have a 'discreet word' with the parents. No surprises then. Girls can (and do) come at any time if space available. Currently waiting list for year 1.

Exit: Most others to Scots unis after sixth form, though just occasionally some opt for Scottish universities immediately after Highers. Inevitable before a four-year degree. Occasional Oxbridge place – two off to Cambridge to study law in 2016; one or two others across the border to Derby and Sheffield. Around 60 per cent off to study STEM subjects; others to eg music, geography and international relations.

Money matters: Means-tested bursaries up to 100 per cent, plus help with books and uniform. School has sinking fund to cover impoverished lead soprano singing in Vienna, but does not cover jollies. Will keep a child to next public exam if parents have problems but with the usual caveat about parents being upfront and realistic.

Remarks: Jolly nice, old-fashioned school with proper values and the best of modern teaching methods. School seems merrier under present regime. Numbers a tad down but financial climate not helpful. Certain amount of recent fabric titivation and exciting wish list for the future. If single sex education is what you want, St Margaret's is a school which does its girls exceeding well.

St Mary's Music School

Coates Hall, 25 Grosvenor Crescent, Edinburgh EH12 5EL

Pupils: 80; 32 boarders • Ages: 9–19 • Sixth form: 14

Fees: individually assessed

Tel: 0131 538 7766
Email: info@st-marys-music-school.co.uk
Website: www.st-marys-music-school.co.uk

Head: Since 2013, Dr Kenneth Taylor BSc PhD PGCE PG Dip (50s); scholarship to Dulwich College, read chemistry at Edinburgh university and spent three years as a research chemist (we do like heads to have done something in the real world) and came to St Mary's from Biggar High where he was depute head, having skipped around the maintained sector in the borders.

A sportsman and musician (hill-running a passion – latest feat The Pentland Skyline Race: 16 miles, 6,200 foot climb), he played the piano and violin when younger and still sings (a bit) and plays the viola. Lives in Edinburgh with three young and regularly cycles to school (across Edinburgh). Delightful and outgoing, he enjoys encouraging the young in all manner of disciplines and has a deprecating sense of humour.

We previously dropped the school from the Guide because of a couple of cases of (historic) sexual abuse and Taylor mentions this to the whole school about once a term, systems now in place, but he advises any pupil who feels uneasy about any member of staff (or indeed anything) to talk to head of guidance, any (other perhaps) teacher or tell their parents. At The Good Schools Guide, we do not dwell on past problems unless they are still causing angst: St Mary's has moved on, and the somewhat shambolic 'luvvie' environment replaced by a rather more efficient regime. Taylor is unhappy about our mentioning this now historic abuse, but as there are screeds on the internet, we would look foolish if we ignored it.

Academic matters: Complicated. In the junior school, pupils from P5/7 often form a composite class: follow standard subjects with IT tabled throughout. Splendid triple class room with interactive telly: iPads being introduced. Delicious old-fashioned desks – alas without the Bakelite inkwells. Tiny classes (as you might expect with annual intake of only 10 per year); German and French from early: essential for singing. Latin mandatory S1/2 – and available at both Advanced Higher and SQA.

From P5-S6 school moves seamlessly through to Nat 5s to Highers and Advanced Highers. Highers are successfully crammed (well, smaller classes) into three and a half hours a week rather than the usual five to eight. Results impressive across the board. School really too small to supply individual subject results. Maths (strong), English, Higher music at S3/4 and Higher English S5. Moving from OCR A level music to Cambridge Pre-U for music in 2017 – harmony, counterpoint, composition.

Arrangements in place for pupils who need extra support; those with personal statements have one-to-one sessions, otherwise withdrawn from class and IEPs. Dyslexia and dysgraphia the main culprits.

The junior school is composed of choristers and instrumentalists, more of the former (both boys and girls – the latter introduced in 1976, though young instrumentalists since 1972). Choristers, both boys and girls, leave school at 14 (broken voices, sexual discrimination, that sort of thing – can't chuck out 14 year old boys unless girlies go at same age). Some may re-audition and return as instrumentalists.

Games, options, the arts: Small art room more or less adjacent to head's office stuffed with tables and art work on shelves. Both flat and 3D stuff on display.

Catch-all rather sad-looking all-weather surface area (school rather grandly calls it a sports court) serves its purpose. No gym (so mandatory one hour PE per week must be achieved by other means); boarders are members of Drumsheugh baths, a stout half mile distant, and the local running club. Didn't see too many fatties on our wander round, so something seems to be working.

All pupils, both junior and senior, spend roughly 50 per cent of their time doing some form of music, be it practice or individual lessons: we came across a variety pack. 'Coaching sessions with an accompanist' ('gets them used to it'), says Taylor and we found one young piano-accompanied flautist sharing her lesson not only with a splendid Steinway but also with a somewhat overpowering organ.

Hideously complicated timetable, but sung evensong most evenings at 5.30pm in the cathedral and regular rehearsals either in Song School or cathedral itself (latter has 'soft' acoustics: 'ideal for singing but not practical for orchestral practice').

Music, of course is what the school is all about, with an emphasis on chamber music: regular concerts at venues all over Edinburgh. School itself has nowhere big enough for both orchestra and audience – former chapel too long and thin (Taylor says 'small'), dining room (beastly 60s excrescence) too low and cramped.

Any and every instrument played with peris pulled in for the more esoteric. (Currently an ad online for a clarsach teacher for Sat mornings). 'No problems in getting staff', school handy for Haymarket (and Glasgow): tries to arrange a full day's teaching for visiting (musical) peris; odd orchestral player, 12 full-time staff.

Director of music takes instrumentalists to the odd concert (28 last year), and usually manages to get reduced rate – 'one or two quid sort of thing' – to boost ranks of punters – though full whack for some events (we originally wrote popular – as in the Latin – but Taylor preferred 'some'). Regular masterclasses: annual Nigel Murray masterclass – school sources suitable spaces for numbers: 130 violinist and their teachers last time; 60 cellists, that sort of thing; always oversubscribed. Occasional foray into performing at the Edinburgh International Festival (gives concerts three Sundays on the trot at St Mary's Cathedral). Pupils regularly do their own thing, performing both a Schubert string quartet and 'a specially commissioned piece' plus jazz in Dumfries and Galloway. Friday evening concerts and strong input on the charity front: this ed has been entertained by St Mary's young at a variety of fundraisers (and private homes).

Highly acclaimed and popular Saturday morning classes for up to a 150 youngsters aged 4-13; serious stuff and not just an airy fairy introduction to music. 'These classes are an enjoyable introduction to music,' says the head. Quite: those whom we know who take part say they are enormous fun: which is perhaps a better accolade than an 'enjoyable introduction'.

Boarding: Two floors of accommodation for boarders in Coates Hall; mainly twins with a few triple rooms, all en suite. Free time mostly spent practising.

Background and atmosphere: Tucked away in an enchanting corner off Grosvenor Crescent some 300 metres from the Cathedral. St Mary's was founded in 1880 as song (choir) school for The (Episcopal) Cathedral Church of St Mary the Virgin (funded by spinster heiress sisters Barbara and Mary Walker and built to a design by George Gilbert Scott in 1879). Based in Old Coates Hall and the Song School, the latter still used for daily practice (magical Phoebe Traquair murals) within the cathedral precinct until 1995, St Mary's (name changed 1971) bought Coates Hall, which had closed in 1994. Neophyte Anglican priests had rather fallen off the radar; the 18th century Old Coates Hall (part of the original bequest) is now the Edinburgh Theological Institute, providing accommodation, teaching and meeting rooms for both ordained and Anglican seminarians, albeit on a smaller scale.

Coates Hall, built in 'baronial style' by David Bryce in 1850, and bought by the Edinburgh Theological College in 1891, when Sydney Mitchell (better known for banks and psychiatric hospitals) added the splendid gothic chapel to the right of the main door – is too small for concerts. However, it but boasts a fine-looking but non-functioning organ and an amazing turquoise decorated grand piano, which looks as though it is covered in potato cuts: paint job is apparently worth more than the piano itself. Bryce also designed the gatehouse. Extensive-ish grounds (for the middle of Edinburgh) filled with trees, badly parked cars (as ever in danger of small children with balls), and a couple of ugly modern teaching blocks. Plus the inevitable catch-all 'sports surface'.

Considering the expense of maintaining a highly complicated Victorian roof, the building is in remarkably good if complex heart, though we weep at the carving of rooms into offices. Head's study is in a former garage.

The main building is rabbit warreny in the extreme, with staircases going off in random directions – five steps here sort of thing – leading to a hotch-potch of bedrooms (seminarians had great views), now almost all en suite, twins and singles (school is let in hols to boost funds – which is why one of the practice rooms boasts a basin). Wiggly Ikea mirrors grouped in pairs throughout, and myriads of photographs – often with tinies overwhelmed by the size of their instrument.

However, however, however, and all Edinburgh is abuzz. There are plans afoot. The important neo-classical Old Royal High School (Thomas Hamilton 1829) perched high on Calton Hill and abandoned by Royal High School in 1968 – though home to odds and sods thereafter – it had been mooted as home for the Scottish Parliament until the late (not that lamented) Enrico Miralles' fiasco of a new parliament building arrived on the scene (currently requiring squillions to maintain) comes under the aegis of Edinburgh council, who, in their wisdom, granted a 125 year lease to a poncy hotel company in 2010 (though info did not leak out until Jan 2015). The lease is dependent on planning permission. The plans shown to date have the good burghers of Edinburgh (and not just the Edinbourgoisie) up in arms. Every historic buildings organisation is objecting. World Heritage is objecting. Mutterings of Micky Mouse ears, and, say it soft, mutterings of brown envelopes are whizzing about ('school distances itself from this sort of comment'; but not the vocal Edinburgher). A trust has been formed (and here, let it be said that this ed will be first in line should bulldozers move in) to save the Old Royal High School. Long term Edinburgh resident and American philanthropist, Carol Colburn Grigor (Chair of the Colburn Music School in Los Angeles) has offered to underwrite the cost of both repairing the building and transforming it into a new home for St Mary's Music School. An offer has been made for the building as it stands: £1.5 million – which would take Edinburgh council out of the equation. The (new) Royal High School in Barnton is thrilled at the prospect, they have cupboards full of 'artefacts' that came from the old building, pictures too valuable to hang on the walls and odd bits of memorabilia, including a stuffed kangaroo that they would love to hand back. ('Occupying valuable cupboard space').

St Mary's is upbeat about the proposal. Their architect has drawn up complicated plans (which include a foyer for master classes and the like underneath the debating chamber with a semi-sunk two storey extension to the east for study bedrooms and further practice rooms. 'Exciting' says Taylor 'raise the profile of the school'.

S

Pastoral care, well-being and discipline: All choristers are day pupils. No reported disciplinary hiccups; pupils are more likely to be found discussing some obscure German 15th century composer than indulging in verbal point scoring. During our visit (break time) four really quite small people came out to the playground, one fell and was immediately surrounded (not sure about tears) by her own peer group and some elder children who were close by, who picked her up and escorted her back inside. Now that is what we like to see in a school.

School uniform for all, and worn with pride.

Pupils and parents: Pupils come from all over. No obvious social grouping, many pupils from musical families. Terrific parental support. Youngsters from abroad need local guardians.

Entrance: Audition in either discipline, at any stage, half way through term if space available: though most join at the start of the academic year. 'Looking for musical ability and potential'. School 'mushrooms' towards the top.

Exit: All choristers age 14 (though may come back as instrumentalists); rest usually after Advanced Highers to some form of tertiary education. Possibly 95 per cent may go to a conservatoire or into music college, but this is by no means written in stone and one of the most promising recent musicians is currently studying engineering. Regular careers talks from FPs who emphasise how difficult it is to make a proper living out of playing in an orchestra and how few openings there are for soloists.

Money matters: Oodles of bursaries. Taylor told us to check online for fee info: two hours later we were still in the dark. Would appear to be in line with current fees elsewhere. Cathedral covers 50 per cent of all choristers (who get a couple of quid or so for weekly performances and rather more for weddings and funerals), Scottish government contributes a chunk (aided places) and music school doles out bursaries – rigorously – with financial background of applicants tooth-combed. Fair to say that no musical prodigy from any background would be left wanting.

Remarks: Exciting times. St Mary's worthy of a new home. Watch this space.

St Mary's School (Melrose)

Abbey Park, High Street, Melrose TD6 9LN

Pupils: 180; up to 30 flexi boarders • Ages: 2–13 (boarders from 7)

Fees: Day £12,279 – £15,129; Boarding £17,091 pa

Tel: 01896 822517
Email: office@stmarysmelrose.org.uk
Website: www.stmarysmelrose.org.uk

Headmaster: Since 2010, Mr William (Liam) Harvey BEd (40s). The son of a local doc, and an FP, he went on to George Watson's followed by a BEd in PE at Liverpool John Moores University. Taught PE to A level in the state secondary sector before moving to Belhaven as housemaster and head of history and PE.

We met Harvey's Canadian wife, Marnia, efficiently organising the mysteries of the gap student's computer. Their daughters are in the school.

Entrance: All things to all men. The only independent school in the borders; children come from within a 50 mile radius, can come mid-term at any time if space available, otherwise automatically up from kindergarten. The odd state child has been known simply to come for an '18-month blast' before going back into the maintained sector, but this is rarer and rarer and none this year. Some come at 11 to do CE.

Exit: 'Most but not all' stay on until they go to their senior school at 11, 12, or 13 (the occasional toff pops off to Belhaven, Aysgarth, but none so far under the new regime), preferred secondary schools used to be Glenalmond, Fettes, Merchiston, Loretto, St George's in Edinburgh or Longridge Towers in Berwick, Queen Margaret's York and whilst these did indeed feature in our random poll, increasingly numbers are more likely to be turning south, Sedburgh gaining in popularity, Ampleforth and even Harrow. Winchester, Eton next?

Remarks: Wow. Didn't recognise the place. Totally transformed since our last visit and some of the most exciting (and cleverly sited to act as a windbreak) skool buildings we have ever seen. The Hamilton building opened in 2010 was funded by a gift from 'an anonymous benefactor'. Guestimate cost? A million near as dammit. Named after John Hamilton who founded the school in 1895 (good, if somewhat belated, way to celebrate a centenary).

Two non-parallel buildings with terrific reception area, full of photographs – though a tad Nuffield in aspect (think neutral carpets and comfy seating). Only thing missing is the coffee machine, although we were topped up with copious amounts – the head had his own insulated mug. Reception area littered with prospectuses of senior schools – not, as previously, concentrating on the Scottish mafia, but Shrewsbury, Uppingham, Cheltenham and Harrow. Quite a change, though those whom we asked mainly seemed to be heading North. Wide corridors – one outside the art dept was recently turned into a drawing 'road' where parents and pupils depicted the best aspects of their childhood (and jolly good some of them were too – we particularly liked the footballer). Photographs everywhere in main building, the art building – with yet more light, airy, and huge classrooms has walls filled with pupil offerings and classrooms for younger pupils.

We previously described St Mary's as a 'Jolly useful little school, incredibly flexible, with flexi, weekly and day pupils; one or two toffs, but mostly farmers and local professionals who stay to the bitter end, plus 'masses of' first time buyers.' But gosh. Still tiny classes, max 18 but usually much less, only one stream, scholars will be 'hived off' and set at 10 if necessary and 'provided with evening tutorials with subject teachers'. Latin from 8, languages from 5, taster term of French, then specialists in French for common entrance. Fantastic and envy-making French trips when the entire form decamp to a monastery for a week. Science taught separately for the last four years, and pupils move round the staff (from age 9 – a transition class).

'Strong' dyslexia department, all singing and dancing and recently reorganised, oversees regular testing, and support for the very bright. Withdrawn help and support staff (masses of 'em, chaps as well as chapesses) go into class too – 'pretty flexible' (might be the school motto). Keen on handwriting. Interactive whiteboards abound, all classrooms are computered to the hilt, state of the art. Loads of staff changes since head's arrival (but see below), certain number of redundancies, and terrific young buzzy staff abound (think policemen). School now boasts 'a strong academic team'.

Drama strong and timetabled, the school has links with local borders youth theatre. Good music, rehearsals and lessons in functional school hall, whilst pre-prep has own gym, with Noah and his ark drawn by the young. The somewhat surprising cloistered classroom corridor (the 'veranda classrooms') have been relegated to music, a theatre store room, boarders' activity room, music and a thrift shop.

Day children can stay from 7.30am (and breakfast in school) right through to 7.30pm, by which time they will have done their prep and had supper, kindergarten can stay till 4pm. Tinies wear delightful green and white check tabliers and girls evolve from gym slips to proper kilts; we checked, most were eight pleats thick. Dining room with weekly menu, over-high benches for littlies to sit at table. Brown bread only and lots of sugar-free puds, mainly organic as far as possible. Robert the chef comes complete with starched chef's hat and sparkling white uniform. Cor. He also makes scrumptious millionaire's shortbread for the head's guests – not sugar-free at all, and has lost a mega amount of weight since we last saw him... now deeply into marathons. One is always told to beware the skinny chef, but he is still triumphant, and gives the boarders special cooking lessons (it was Burns night/lunch during our visit, and the haggis was piped in with aplomb). Pheasant (plucking lessons and all) on the menu next.

The Harveys live in the main school house, with dorms above, separate corridors for boys and for girls – room for up to 30 flexi boarders. The girls live in somewhat cramped conditions in a conversion of what used to be the main drawing room – fantastic ceiling, but divided into three – with what must be one of the grandest ceiling-ed bathrooms ever. Jolly dorms upstairs, all brightly painted with splendid stripy duvet covers. Very homey; bunks, the odd poster, random teddy bears – and currently being upgraded. B&B charged per night.

Squads and teams triumph all over the place. Swimming off-site in Gala(shiels) and main games pitches just across some National Trust land. Smashing little school.

St Ninian's High School

Eastwood Park, Rouken Glen Road, Giffnock, East Renfrewshire G46 6UG

Pupils: 1,800 • Ages: 12–18 • Sixth form: S5/6 600 • RC

Tel: 01415 772000
Email: headteacher@st-ninians.e-renfrew.sch.uk
Website: www.ea.e-renfrew.sch.uk/stninians

Headteacher: Since 2005, John Docherty (60s), studied geography at University of Glasgow followed by a one-year teacher training course. Previously assistant head at St Ninian's and before that headteacher at St Andrew's, Clydebank. Started out as a geography teacher and worked in Glasgow's East End, the area where he grew up and lived until he got married and which is home to some of Scotland's 'poorest communities'. From there it must have been an interesting leap to St Ninian's which could be described as serving some of Scotland's wealthiest. Talking of his early experience, he says: 'It was highly enjoyable and very fulfilling. The pupils were hard working and the school worked very hard to support them and their families. In comparison, both schools [have the] same high standards, vision and expectations. The differences were income and life experiences due to being wealthier.' It is evident he has a strong belief that no matter the circumstances one must always 'Let Youth Flourish' (the motto of the school – Floreat Iuventus), whether academically, in sport or the arts.

Mr Docherty is witty, confident and supportive, described as 'always having an open door.' Innovative in curriculum change (even perhaps a rebel), he doesn't bow down to Holyrood's Curriculum for Excellence and wasn't slow to criticise its failings: 'good teachers should be allowed to teach.'

St Ninian's has been transformed academically under his leadership. He states modestly that he is 'very proud of the pupils and staff for what they do every day to provide an excellent school. The achievements are the result of the bigger team, I'm only one part of the great success of the school.'

Discipline is a priority too and no child escapes in the morning without 'straightening their tie' or 'tucking their shirts in.' A 'bugbear' for one parent (and we imagine many children), but the pupils do look impressively smart and stand out in the community.

Mr Docherty is married with one daughter. His wife is also a teacher (French and Spanish). He describes himself as a 'family man' and enjoys reading and playing tennis. He also devotes some quiet time to reflecting in prayer. His faith is evidently very important to him and he say that it 'influences all I do, through the desire to offer my service to others.'

Academic matters: St Ninian's consistently ranks as one of Scotland's top three state schools and the number of pupils achieving five Highers at the end of S5 has increased by 100 per cent in the last decade. In 2016, 57 per cent of pupils achieved five Highers by S5 and 77 per cent left with five or more Highers. By S6, 53 per cent had achieved one Advanced Higher.

Language teaching is a particular strength: 90 per cent study French at National Five and just under a third are studying a language in S5 and S6. First school in Scotland to have been awarded World Confucius Hub of Mandarin, establishing the teaching of Mandarin in East Renfrewshire. This successful programme has been expanded and over the past four years three students have been awarded scholarships to study the language in Tianjin, China

Children study the standard core curriculum in S1 and then, unusually, narrow down their subject choices for the start of S2. On our tour one pupil pointed out that he hadn't been in the 'art department since S1.' For this reason some parents have 'mixed feelings' about it and feel choosing subjects comes 'a bit too early.' However, a parent added, 'the kids enjoy having fewer subjects and studying what they like.' Mr Docherty says it was 'a successful decision to have implemented' and allows 'a progression of subjects, straight from S1 to S6.' And there is no denying the exam results.

Popular annual careers evenings with 100 plus exhibitors, and with over 1,200 visitors, are targeted at all careers. Talks from local business people and university professors take place in the school lecture theatre throughout the year.

Head keen to allay parental concerns that East Renfrewshire's top schools are 'exam factories' and only suited to academic children. He points out that leavers' attainment for the 'lowest 20' and 'middle 60' per cent were the highest in Scotland. Reassuringly, pupils and parents consistently used one word when talking about the school: 'supported'; as one parent put it: 'I think the commitment from the teachers is outstanding. They offer excellent support and communication to parents, including fabulous workshops ... to help us support our kids.'

Dedicated SEN department with specialist teaching and non-teaching support. Children with complex needs are 'well integrated into the school and highly successful.'

Games, options, the arts: In keeping with west coast of Scotland tradition, football is perhaps the most popular sport – the boys were keen to point out the new 4G turf all-weather pitches. School team reached Scottish Schools FA Shield final and trophies are proudly displayed in cabinets. One S5 pupil picked for U17 Scottish team and played in 2016 European Championship Qualifiers in Portugal. Other events include school golf championships, 'Hutchie 5' hockey championships at private school Hutchesons' Grammar and the Whitecraig's Rugby Club festival for selected pupils. A fledging American football club has also been welcomed, particularly among the boys. All sports are open to girls, who are highly successful at netball, football, athletics, hockey, skiing and other minority sports. Talented athlete programme is in place 'to support all young people who are involved in national teams.'

Over 80 clubs (all on-site, except equestrian and skiing) include young engineers, Mandarin, business and charity clubs (exploring subjects such as the trafficking of women and children), as well as the Young Philanthropy Initiative, an active citizenship programme for teams of S2 pupils to raise money for local charities. Off-site clubs have tuition costs and transport is partly subsidised by the school.

Some activities run at lunch time and we saw labs busy with keen science club students, a few pupils dancing in one of the gym halls and a lone student on a spin bike in the fitness suite – although quite rightly the majority of students were enjoying their food. One pupil said the after-school spin class where staff and pupils do spin together was very popular: 'It's good fun and funny seeing the teachers giving it their best.'

Thriving, newly refurbished music department complete with grand piano, and sound-proofed practice rooms for different instruments. Massive uptake of music and myriad bands including the ceilidh band, soul band, chamber choir, symphony and string orchestras. The most talented go on to perform in Celtic Connections and Scotland's National Orchestra. Popular drama department, with fun school drama club for S1 pupils, which is run by S6 Advanced Higher drama students. Previous shows include Oliver! and My Fair Lady, and Wizard of Oz is scheduled for 2017. Plenty of trips made to Glasgow theatres and many of the children in amateur dramatic clubs, which sometimes perform at Eastwood Theatre, adjacent to the school.

Off-beat art department with music playing, described by a pupil as the most 'laid-back place in the school.' Every available space covered with impressive artwork, the best of which included somewhat frightening modern portraits as well as Day of the Dead masks. Fashion shows and art exhibitions celebrate the creative work of the young people.

Sporting, creative and cultural school trips 'can be expensive' so run every second year to allow parents to pay in instalments. Recent destinations include the French Alps (skiing), Iceland (geography), Berlin (art) and, perhaps less exotic, the Scottish Parliament (modern studies) to meet the First Minister, Nicola Sturgeon. Children also travelled to Ghana as part of an S6 building project, and local artwork that they brought back is displayed on school walls.

Background and atmosphere: St Ninian's was founded in 1984 to serve a small Catholic population. Given that at the time 'some people wondered where the children would come from', it's ironic that this is now the biggest school in East Renfrewshire and highly desirable. 'Demand for places outstrips supply' and measures are being introduced to curtail admissions.

The modern, low-rise building with separate sports hall and playing fields is situated in a pleasant, leafy civic area that houses the council buildings and Eastwood Leisure Centre and theatre. Inside the wide corridors serve as a gallery for the children's work and achievements. Recent extensions have provided new science, geography and modern language classrooms, and certainly these parts do feel much fresher, though all areas are clean and tidy.

At first glance the school seems traditional, values such as discipline, working hard, kindness and community involvement are important and there is a strong Catholic ethos (although intake includes children from other faiths or none). At the same time, perhaps surprisingly, it is quite modern. There are no strict hierarchies distancing pupils from teachers and senior staff; teachers mingle with the students and would pride themselves on being approachable. The centre of school activity is the forum, an octagonal space which is light and airy and gives access to the glass-fronted library and an art room featuring stained glass created by the pupils.

Pupils are easily identified in Giffnock by their maroon woollen blazers and visitors might be forgiven for thinking this was a private school. Parents are 'very supportive' of the strict uniform policy.

Pastoral care, well-being and discipline: Dedicated pastoral teachers 'who are your point of contact as a parent' meet with children once a week and can be found 'out and about with young people every day.' One pupil said they felt 'so lucky to be surrounded by such excellent people.' Pupils talked of how they 'felt listened to' and that 'teachers take suggestions on-board.' Parents are kept involved: unrushed parents' evenings, regular meetings, home phone calls. One parent of a new S1 pupil said: 'Within a few weeks of ... starting, the pastoral teacher called to see how I thought she was settling, and also to let me know they thought she was fine. A nice touch.'

One parent felt that perhaps too much help was given and that 'sometimes the kids struggle when they get to university and have to do it on their own'. However, the S6 children enthused about how much they appreciated the advice given with their UCAS applications 'without being hand-held'.

High standards are expected: having discipline, being organised and believing in yourself is deemed important to achieve success. Overwhelming majority are model pupils, but on extremely rare occasions over the years a child might just need 'a day out'.

Workshops are given to children in S1–S4 to help manage workload and develop study techniques. 'Early stage problems are dealt with quickly' and a youth counselling service is also available.

Pupils and parents: No secret that many move to the area for the schools and are prepared to pay increasing house prices. Stylish mums dropping off immaculate children from shiny Range Rovers can be seen, but there's also a big chunk of lower middle class families 'working to pay their mortgage' and giving their kids the best possible education they can. Parents are hands-on, and if unhappy are quick to say so. Around 16 per cent of school population is from ethnic minorities but this figure could drop as changes in admission criteria prioritise baptised Catholics. Free coach service to and from school for those who live more than three miles away. Others walk, cycle or use public transport.

Pupils we saw were the usual bunch of happy teenagers, noisily going about their business at lunchtime, some chatting and eating pizza from polystyrene cartons on the go. One told us it was considered 'cool to be clever' and 'cool to be hard working.' S6 pupils were particularly articulate and well-mannered and incredibly proud to be part of a 'welcoming school community that works together to achieve the best we can.' However, 'no school is perfect', and a couple of rule-breakers were frowned upon by senior pupils for having a peek at their mobile phones on the stairwell.

Former pupils include actors James McCardle (Star Wars: The Force Awakens) and Daniel Cameron (BAFTA Scotland New Talent awards 2016) plus footballers Aiden McGeady and Andy Robertson.

Entrance: Catchment area has tightened over the years but currently includes parts of Thornliebank, Giffnock, Clarkston, Busby, Waterfoot and Newton Mearns. Pupils come from primary schools including Our Lady of the Missions in Giffnock, St Joseph's in Busby and St Cadoc's in Newton Mearns.

Controversially, baptised Catholics within the Eastwood side of East Renfrewshire now given priority, although placing requests will still be available. This will affect children of non-Catholic faith already in catchment Catholic primary schools in two years' time.

Exit: Around two-thirds go on to higher education with the remainder heading for FE colleges, apprenticeships or employment. Good numbers accepted for medicine, veterinary science and dentistry courses (18 in 2016). One to Oxbridge in 2016, but understandably most prefer not to pay and stick with Scottish universities such as Caledonian, Strathclyde, Glasgow, Edinburgh, Aberdeen and St Andrews (and why not if it's good enough for Will and Kate?). Three former pupils achieved first-class honours in 2016.

Remarks: One of the top academic state schools in Scotland, St Ninian's has a strong Catholic ethos coupled with a modern approach that ensures children are well-nurtured and supported. Success is celebrated, as is 'working hard', one of the school's key values. Whether academically, on the sports field, musically or in the arts, it seems that the fortunate young people who attend St Ninian's do indeed flourish.

Strathallan School

Forgandenny, Perth, Perthshire PH2 9EG

Pupils: 540; 331 full boarders • Ages: 9–18 • Sixth form: 220

Fees: Day £13,848 – £21,114 pa; Boarding £22,191 – £31,116 pa

Tel: 01738 812546
Email: admissions@strathallan.co.uk
Website: www.strathallan.co.uk

Headmaster: Since 2000, Mr Bruce Thompson MA (Oxon) (mid 50s), educated at Newcastle High, thence New College where he read literae humaniores (classics to the rest of us) and came to Strathallan via Cheltenham College, where he was head of classics, and Dollar Academy – he wanted to 'try the Scottish system'. 'Loves Scotland, and loves Strathallan,' as does his wife, Fabienne (French: teaches at local prep school, worked in travel and tourism, expert skier – coaches it and most likely to be found whizzing round the campus on her bike). Two daughters, now up and running.

Leaving in July 2017.

Housemistress of Riley (Junior House) is Mrs Emma Lalani.

Academic matters: Not tremendously academic (school says 'strong academic record' – umm: 2016 A level results showed 39 per cent A*/As; GCSEs 40 per cent A*/As). Splendid mega million quid (expandable) computer suite, where 'the young are given screwdrivers to dismantle the things and sixth formers then expected to fix 'em', to quote the charming hands on head of computing. 'Problem solving skills' more important than rote. Three network engineers on site. Intranet access all over. Mandatory keyboarding in first form, then 'can catch up online'.

Strath not following blindly (as have so many others) into the Virtual Learning Experience where pupils are expected to work exclusively online (with teachers correcting and parents informed – online). We were enchanted to find a history teacher carefully hand marking (slightly scruffy) handwritten exam papers. Trips to battlefields, and re-enactments the norm.

Strong on langs – particularly Chinese (Chinese counsellor on staff), Spanish and German – native speakers perhaps? – French a poor relation. On our delightful trip round the school in blazing sunshine (groups of ad hoc revision classes squatted on the grass: tieless teachers and pupils – this was shirtsleeve order stuff) we met the head of foreign langs, who was introduced as 'teaching Russian'. Confusion reigned: Russian is not an offered option, though native Russian speakers may get tuition to get them up to speed for A levels ('can do public exams'). Ditto any native speaker. Classical civilisation (aka Heroes for Zeros – head doesn't like that sobriquet). Latin still in the frame.

Class size around 20: usual thing, smaller for practical stuff and as pupil specialisation kicks in. GCSE for all, 'no Scottish qualifications below age 16,' said the head. Nine or 10 GCSEs the norm; all do each science, although around a third take the dual award.

Twenty assorted A levels on offer: school plays the system, both Scottish and English. Seventy-five per cent follow the A level route; others opt for Highers over two years. School tries to please parents but the choice between A levels and Highers is always contentious. Highers are particularly popular for wannabe medics as school is one of the few to offer human biology. In 2016, 72 per cent A-C grades.

Mixed age common room: discrimination 'even to raise the subject of age.' Staff live on campus with their families, a boon for younger staff who might otherwise be reluctant to commit to somewhere with no nearby university for PhDs or MBAs (think Open University). Finding a new head of physics proved a (finally solvable) nightmare. Head of academics, a recent appointment, comes from Dean Close: good to get fresh and experienced blood in the place.

School has always had a welcome reputation for supporting weaker brethren (siblings in particular) and has a small but effective learning support system which had a smashing HMI report with talk of 'systematic identification', 'sensitive support', 'informative advice' (yawn yawn). All pupils screened on entry with ed psychs brought in where necessary. One-to-one, small groups, plus after-school clinics in various disciplines which act as drop-in centres. Two full-time trained staff, plus ancillaries, cover entire age range. Extra time for exams. Regular assessment orders for all. 'Rarely costs extra.' School can cope with mild Asperger's/autism and the dys-stream: if SEN is on your radar, check out its comprehensive 'can-do' list below: physical infirmity not a problem, most classrooms on ground floor and lifts whizz you up to top floor of all new builds complete with disabled bathrooms in head of house. Massive EFL input for those who do not have English as their mother tongue: 'normally no extra charge for this.'

Tutors per year group, meet weekly, max 10 per tutor. Strong features of support for learning include: systematic identification of pupils with specific learning difficulties and sensitive support for individual pupils; well-planned arrangements for pupils requiring special assistance with examinations; informative advice to teachers on the learning needs of pupils requiring support; an appropriate range of programmes for pupils for whom English was an additional language; effective use of the expertise of external specialists such as educational psychologists; and after-school 'clinics' run by a number of subject departments. The priority is to provide long term support for individuals and groups of pupils and to respond positively to the needs of pupils referred from individual departments. Teachers have been provided with briefings on issues such as dyslexia and the focus in the last year has been on helping departments adapt approaches and materials to pupils' different needs. The department consists of two full-time members of staff with the help of three other teachers.

S

Games, options, the arts: Plaudits fail. We are gob-smacked. School has county, national, international, Commonwealth and Olympic presence across the board and at all ages: from rugby, footie, tennis, hockey, netball; fantastic swimming (speedos, goggles and shaven chests); silver at recent Commonwealth Games. Team and individual. Shooting: clay and small bore (plus popular CCF – boys and girls, voluntary) fencing, own golf course, sailing.

School mag and termly news catch up bung full of smiling prize winners/competitors (mebbe this ed is blind/stupid, but couldn't find an essay, poem, trip description anywhere). Head says, 10 pages of art and DT work in centre of skool mag: this ed was hoping for an essay or a poem.

Think Millfield of the North. Rugby squad thrashes all comers, beat Glenalmond 79-4. Coll now refuses to play them, abandoned rugby and gave out that Strath were importing South Africans and Kiwis to boost their front line. Fact: only one South African (son of a Strathallian) has played for the XV, his little bro comes shortly. South African exchange students come in the hockey term. Tennis academy triumphed in all three of the UK senior finals recently. Serious and successful skiing. County/national/international coaches in most disciplines. The list of sporting achievements is endless and impressive.

To celebrate its centenary, school has given itself a fitness/weight-training centre (open at night), dance and drama practice area and possibly the most enormous covered sports area this ed has ever seen to complement the 70s sports hall (complete with climbing wall) and utterly delicious 20s gym. Think snow. Think footie, think tennis, think space age.

State-of-the art school over three floors with marvellous light and inspired work (we said that last time but it is still top of the pops) – current conundrum is how to retrieve two ginormous feet which were finalists in the Saatchi Schools competition. Enthusiastic head of art opens art rooms whenever: 'can always work on my own projects'; always open three nights a week. Unusual screen printing/photography combination involving rough-hewn branches and strange frame: eye-catching and imaginative (but one rather wonders.). Darkroom, pottery, kiln, very much in use, fabric design and inspired corsets on display (for outside rather than inside wear, you understand) some slightly uninspired work in progress.

Art/history combined field trips to Venice, Prague and the like.

Good music. Stop here. Stupendous music. Enormous diversification. Pipe major plays with Red Hot Chilli Pipers (as do many of his pupils). Seventy-strong boys' choirs for house music competition blow the roof off, choristers at St Ninians in Perth get paid a less than living wage – choral scholarships on offer, church music popular 'and fun,' said our guide. Headmaster's Music (freebie) in Perth Concert Hall (which holds 1,000 and is always full) has musicians (often the same musician) swapping seamlessly from complicated classical concertos to self-composed electronic dance music and rock. Several of the young have professional contracts under their belts. This is exciting stuff.

Loads of drama: small theatre, previously the dining hall, insides scooped out (which doubles as exam hall); new dance and drama studio.

Mass of charity work: mega Kenyan input. Help in charity shop. D of E. (Granny bashing apparently a thing of the past: pupils used to give them computer lessons... times change).

Break time when we visited, fresh fruit, milk, buns and fairy cakes with sports coaches huddled on sunny wooden benches working out next matches, plus Parker – said to be the most ferocious guard dog.

Boarding: Houses new and newish, boys and girls have own study bedrooms for their last four years, lots of kitchens and common room areas on each floor. New girls' house completed with an increase in girls. Heads of girls' houses have disabled type loos (lifts): an interesting juxtaposition.

Random books (which is what we like to see) in common rooms, plus mandatory CDs. And tuck shop – seemed to be over-full of cereal packs.

Much general to-ing and fro-ing, but co-ed works well here; girls' houses out of bounds to boys on Sunday mornings so that girls 'can laze around in their dressing gowns if they want.' PR whizzo disputed this: silly PR guru: our guide confirmed it as 'brilliant' (school says 'still not the case').

Chapel every other Sunday, new chaplain in the wings (ex RAF, natch). School facilities much used by groups during holiday period. New girls' house the furthest away, but otherwise houses fairly cloistered.

Background and atmosphere: School founded in 1913 by Harry Riley, based in 19th century red sandstone country house with masses of sympathetic additions, set in 153 beautifully manicured acres. Couple of double-deck libraries, one with the carpet reflecting the plaster work in the ceiling; adjacent media rooms – cosy and useful. Fairly utilitarian chapel (children quite rude about it) and refurbished dining room, million quid – ceiling dropped, new floor – though not sure it is that good for dancing. Main classrooms 150 yards away beyond the old stable building which has been transformed into junior house, Riley, boasting an atrium plus library and music practice rooms etc. Just across the valley from senior school (a splendid and accessible wooded dell) where youngest boarders and day children have dedicated sports and play area. Drop in centre for both day and boarders, tellies, prep tables (older pupils come and give the occasional hand) and computers for Skyping and the like. Games room.

All eat in dining room, with younger pupils getting a head start – think that means they eat first – rather than pigging all the grapes.

Classroom blocks clustered and cloistered on t'other side of the valley now refurbed, latest improvements include three state-of-the-art chemistry labs, 'nother new lab this summer. Not an overwhelming school, beautifully landscaped, though some of the signs – to car park et al – are out of kilter. School council operates under aegis of head girl and boy. House council meetings plus international council.

Reel parties by year group and Scottish country dancing an essential. Raft of hobbies: beekeeping current craze (head disputed this: but apiarist on staff, and senior girls love it: suspect they may get some honey). Trippettes to Perth and Edinburgh at weekend, riding nearby (sleek collection of bays in neighbouring field). Girls have a dressmaking enthusiast on tap and one of 'em made her own ball gown last year – to the amazement of her peers. (Leavers' Ball a wow).

Pastoral care, well-being and discipline: Seven houses in senior school, four for boys and three for girls. Houseparents live on site with two staff on duty in each house every night. B&B in senior school only. Academic tutor attached to each pupil and tutorial team in every house. Tutors often using the time available for informal chats.

Thompson 'aware that things happen' and talks of rustication and drugs testing 'in case of suspicion'. Automatically suspends for drugs and contact police. Tiny glitch recently, all aware of legal highs 'always a concern'. Random tests on suspicion.

Head works hard on bullying awareness, lots of briefing – expectations, ownership, relationships, 'be reasonable'. 'Like running a huge great family,' with a 'good cross age group.' Boy/girl relationship 'works well'. Punishment system for misdemeanours of 'fatigues' – jobs around the buildings and grounds – 'no shortage of them'.

Assemblies on Fridays. Loads of medals and congratulations all round. Oodles of trips, both fun and cultural – skiing much enjoyed. Prague, Vienna, battlefields of France and concentration camps in Germany ('eerie,' said our guide).

Food said to be 'excellent'; 'fresh bread and milk every day'. Fruit everywhere.

Pupils and parents: A quarter of the pupils from overseas, mostly expats, plus 80-odd foreign pupils from Spain, Russia, Africa, China, Eastern Europe, Hong Kong, Germany, currently 23 different nationalities. No exeats, guardians needed for half terms (our guide seemed to think that there 'was always a house available for those who prefer to stay in school'; 'not so', said the school). Popular with Scots (regional accents of all kinds), well-placed, an hour from both Edinburgh and Glasgow, plus a small contingent from south of the border. (School claims it is 'two hours from London Heathrow': three from Heathrow or Gatwick more like.)

Day pupils allocated to one of the houses; daily buses to and from Perth, Kinross, Auchterarder, Stirling, Crieff and Dundee. About a third or more come daily, with younger day children converting to boarders on going to senior school age 13.

FPs Dominic Diamond (computer games whizzo), Colin Montgomerie (golfer), Sir Jack Shaw, (Bank of Scotland), John Gray (former chairman of the Hong Kong and Shanghai Bank). Not a toffs' school, despite brief showing in the fashion stakes when David Pighills took the school co-ed. 'Very good relationship with parents,' says the head. Grandparents, whom we met couple of days ago were over the moon: granddaughter just left, 'loved it to bits' (and thought head a star): grandson ('deeply difficult') 'doing well at uni'. Couldn't praise the place high enough.

We only saw pupils in shirt sleeves or sports kit. Girls wear elegant (washable) tartan skirts which make the most of the strangest of shapes, long kilts on Wednesdays – seems a funny way to predict a cold spell.

Entrance: At 9, 10, 11 or 12 for the junior house (entry day and aptitude report/tests) then automatic entry, otherwise by CE. Not a high bar. Later entry by report and interview if space available.

All pupils screened for learning difficulties on entry and IEPs plus ed psychs rolled on if necessary but see above.

Excellent route map for parents unfamiliar with public school entry procedures.

Exit: More than 95 per cent to range of universities – two-thirds Scottish, nearly all the rest English; one to Oxbridge in 2016. Forces popular. Odd gap year.

Money matters: School financially strong. Mega centenary appeal 'helped the most recent developments'.

Junior scholarships, open scholarships and sixth form scholarship plus academic, all-rounder, sport, music, cathedral and art scholarships. Parents can apply for means-tested help with fees – 'moving towards bursaries' for all.

Many parents in oil industry: school had downturn last time oil went belly up but appears to be weathering this current hiccup: industry covers school fees when parents based abroad, but not when either in Europe or the UK.

Remarks: Outstanding head – tops in Scotland. The school is in fantastic heart and at ease in the local community. Not for the would be Brideshead contingent. Can't fault it.

Wallace College

12 George IV Bridge, Edinburgh EH1 1EE

Pupils: 20 • Ages: 15–19

Fees: Varies according to course.

Tel: 0131 220 3634
Email: info@wallacecollege.co.uk
Website: www.wallacecollege.co.uk

Director of Studies: Since 1993, Lily Crawford MA (60s – you could knock 10 years off and still guess wrong); a Glasgow lass, who read English literature at Edinburgh and previously taught in the state system in Edinburgh and Falkirk. Slow speaking, deep thinking, she is point of contact for new students, passionate about keeping costs down and directing studies to be fit both for uni matriculation and future employment. Previously an examiner for AQA, SQA and the BAC, she has all the necessary know-how. Crawford leads students through the UCAS maze, helps with personal statements, engineers extra time (scribes if need be – but SQA must have proof positive of need). Very much hands on and, quite obviously, the glove fits.

Academic matters: Exam centre for AQA, Edexcel, OCR, CIE: GCE, A2, GCSE and IGCSE; SQA: National 5, Highers, Advanced Highers. One year three term courses start in September. Wallace prides itself on 'accelerated study programmes': super motivated can take a conventional two year course within the year; mega boost, too, in October and February with daily three hour concentrated blocks of lessons: five subjects each week. A two term IGCSE syllabus runs from January. Raft of options on offer; all tutors (of all ages: easy to find in Edinburgh) come with honours degrees, college will pull on extra lang tutors (usually native speaking) or just tutors for more esoteric requirements. Technical subjects cost more than a tad more – hiring lab time is expensive, though Wallace can often rustle up kit for physics experiments. All the usual suspects, plus philosophy, economics, accounting, computing and mod studies. Engineering not really feasible.

The flexi-study programme is geared to help 'students who wish to combine independent study with support from qualified tutors'; many of these are home schooled and just need pointers to keep them up to speed: 'read this chapter, forget that, this is really important' sort of thing. Usual course is two hours per subject a week for 10 weeks, but variations possible. No more than five independent learners per class, which may be timetabled to suit individual students: lessons in the afternoons to accommodate a morning job, five days' work reorganised into three for those who live further away. Back to the Crawford mantra – keep the cost down.

Max students at any one time 35, classes tiny, usually six or less, often one-to-one and never more than eight. Students come for regular sixth form studies, to improve GCSE/National grades, As, Highers or Advanced Highers, or to expand their portfolio. No hard and fast rules. Emphasis on essay writing, good SEN help available. Three hours per subject per week, plus an hour's test with regular feedback, and detailed end of term report.

The acclaimed holiday revision courses, usually oversubscribed, are a haven for those still at school and overseas students, often in the independent sector, who find some of our educational lingo, particularly in exams, a tad quirky: 'It takes a man with a wheelbarrow 10 hours to move 1000 kilos of sand one kilometre, how long would it take three men with wheelbarrows?' And just what is a wheelbarrow? In a maths exam?

Games, options, the arts: No affiliations with sports clubs and the like, but director of studies can 'point in the right direction'. Theatre trips arranged if useful for course work (extra).

Boarding: Accommodation can be arranged, either through the EFL wing myriad of approved host families, or in university halls, assuming space available.

Background and atmosphere: Privately owned college, founded in 1972, incorporating English language school, variety of tutorial options, and a popular revision course (all disciplines except the BAC) during half terms and holidays. Tucked neatly away behind a (Georgian) red door above an unprepossessing row of shops on George IV Bridge, not quite within the sight of Edinburgh Castle, spectacular views from the west (castle et al). Very much into the 21st century, twitters away: 'GCSE results come out on August 22nd', happy tweets from students.

Pastoral care, well-being and discipline: Strong anti-drugs policy.

No parents' evenings as such; parents 'welcome to pop in and see Crawford or individual tutors', otherwise most communication is by email.

Pupils and parents: All sorts: aged 15+ to 19. Pupils come from all backgrounds for all reasons, including those who find that conventional school does not cater for their particular selection of subjects, those who have lived outside the trad school atmosphere, those who have been educated abroad, and those who have parted either willingly or unwillingly from their previous school.

Entrance: By interview with the director of studies.

Exit: College takes enormous trouble to launch students on the next step of their careers; matriculation the norm. Edinburgh uni popular, as with all the (free) Scottish universities.

Remarks: Good alternative for those who don't get on with traditional schools.

Wellington School

Carleton Turrets, Craigweil Road, Ayr KA7 2XH

Pupils: 441 • Ages: 3–18 • Sixth form: 33

Fees: £6,150 – £12,060 pa

Tel: 01292 269321
Email: info@wellingtonschool.org
Website: www.wellingtonschool.org

Headmaster: Since 2015, Simon Johnson MA (Cantab) PGCE, previously assistant rector at Dollar Academy. Maths degree from Cambridge and PGCE from Moray House College in Edinburgh. Has taught at Fettes and Mary Erskine as well as Dollar. An experienced outdoor educator, he enjoys hill walking, climbing and skiing as well as running and golf. He is also an accomplished pianist with a passion for Bach and Brahms.

Academic matters: Max 18 per class in primary, with slight expansion in size at age 10 and 11; two parallel classes throughout the prep and pre-prep; set from senior school with max class size of 20 (three or four classes per year group). Numbers capped 'naturally' – by building and room size. School working on 'sixth year experience'; though most stay on after Highers anyway. (Plans afoot and dosh apparently at the ready for new ICT and sixth form centre but... probably not enuff brown envelopes.) We saw nothing but Dell flat screens and interactive whiteboards in every classroom.

Languages particularly strong, with Prestwick just down the road it's a natural; long-term exchanges with Germany and France; deeply involved with Comenius and regular exchanges with Europe including Slovenia and Hungary. New links with Jaipur. All do French from primary and can elect to do German at senior level but results not all singing and dancing at any level and minimal take-up at Advanced Higher level. Slightly wider spread and success rate in Highers, with geography and English popular, ditto maths and biology. In 2016 63 per cent A grades at Higher level and 66 per cent at Advanced Higher, 70 per cent at National 5.

Few classicists, no Greek. Applied maths now offered at Advanced Higher level, but few takers, 18 assorted Highers subjects on offer, but penny numbers really, very few Germanists.

Humanities strong, ditto sciences with well-equipped labs; few results of less than C (which in GSG parlance = fail). Media studies dropped recently in favour of proper academia. We hate league tables, preferring to see subject results, which we think more informative, but despite having a non-selective intake, Wellington has been consistently up there with the big boys. Native speakers can expect tutorial help to coach them through Highers etc, in their native tongue; Hungarian, Serbian, Croatian whatever. EFL on tap to help newcomers get up to speed.

New phonics reading programme should go some way to improving literacy; SENCo and a team of dedicated staff. Pupils assessed in primary, and individual lessons where necessary, will pull in ed psychs as needed. Drop in centres to hit problems on the head asap, auxiliary (ie dual teaching) in primary school, with perhaps 20 pupils receiving 'serious help' throughout the school.

Games, options, the arts: Twenty acre sports ground (a long) five mins away at Doonside in Alloway has pavilion, changing and reception facilities, Astroturf and floodlighting; parents use it for fundraising events, as well as coaching and refereeing courses, barbeques (bouncy castles, good car parking) and the like. Locals use it too. Parlour, a sports guru, is sad that rugby, though strong, still doesn't have the numbers to thrash all comers. Terrific hockey, with hockey sticks kept in wheelie bins. Fair showing of Scottish caps; semi-finalists in the U14 tennis tournament working with the Prestwick tennis academy – both short and conventional. Swimming in the nearby Citadel pool in Ayr, school keen to use the sea more – it is, after all, quite literally on the doorstep. So expect kayaking, canoeing, (sailing?) – 'it takes time', but links on the horizon with local clubs. Skating, riding, golf growing in popularity, oodles of clubs in junior dept – (karate popular). Cycling plus lots of individual sports and head keen to build on the outdoor aspect; expect miracles shortly. New resurfaced tarmac playground, and local (flat) beach much used for every conceivable activity. Alas some of the LA cutbacks have affected local partnerships, D of E and leadership expeditions (many of the specialist tutors also worked in the state sector) and Parlour doesn't reckon that Wellington can afford specialists on their own.

Spectacular music but space limited simply because of the number of simultaneous activities. Orchestra was practising in the dining room while the choir was in the music room when we visited. Mass of choirs, orchestras and school shows – down to P1. New music recording suite a couple of years back, loads of music technology. Jazz band. Can't fault it.

New head of art is into jewellery and art rooms a-buzz with pupils post-school. Fabric design and stunning silkscreen printing, as well as conventional flat art and three dimensional stuff. Art & design results healthy but surprisingly few takers for music even at National grade. Vast array of post-school clubs, with science on Wednesdays when the 'whole school hums'.

Background and atmosphere: Originally founded in Wellington Square in 1836 by the wife of an Ayr teacher for 12 young ladies (think dame school), the school moved to Carleton Turrets on the leafy outskirts of Ayr in 1923, dropping boarders and moving to co-ed some 15 years ago. More or less 50/50 these days, though perhaps not enuff chaps to form proper teams. After a certain amount of logistical reorganisation, the senior school now occupies the Carleton Turrets, with the more recently acquired Craigweil House home to the music school, the lang dept and the dining room – the latter operates on a fairly tight timetable.

The primary and nursery school are accommodated in Drumley, just across the road (they have their own dining facilities). A number bring packed lunches and it is a removable privilege to eat these in classrooms. Since our last visit school has combined the nursery and junior years under one head: 'better accountability, much easier'. The nursery now has a popular outdoor wing when a dozen or so youngsters spend the entire day in the fresh air at Doonside, jolly pavilion and packed lunch: plus foxes, woods and adventure playground (come hell or high water, they wear specially designed drysuits).

The three turreted Victorian grade B buildings (splendid stained glass windows) on the sea front have obvious limitations on expansion. The gym at Carleton Turrets doubles as assembly hall (new windows looking onto the playground) and a proper weights room is strategically placed to one side, but this editor was sad that offices still seemed to occupy so much space. New Alcatraz entry system to front/side door, not sure whether it is to keep the ungodly out or...

School looked in jolly good heart, though it still feels a bit dameish. Books in every classroom as well as on all the landings – with a shelf labelled 'for oversized books'. New, state of the art library, most of the classrooms on the top floors have whizzo views over to Arran and Goatfell, which must make concentration difficult. Fairly restricted play areas round the actual buildings but expansive (flat) links and beach opposite for informal footie and the like at break times.

Enthusiastic parental input, particularly at weekends. Ayr is proud of the school. Parents run secondhand clothes shop.

Pastoral care, well-being and discipline: School works closely with parents. Efficient tutorial system throughout senior school, reports twice a term followed by parents' meeting to discuss the report. Strong inter-house competitions, siblings in same houses. Not a lot of sin, orange indiscipline slips for minor sin, three slips equals letter home, red slips for more serious sin, automatic letter home. All slips count against the pupil's house Conduct Shield. Weekly detention at lunchtime for repeated offenders or referral to behavioural timetable if pupil consistently sinful. Ultimate deterrent is expulsion. PSHE and anti-bullying strategies (anti-bullying email and strategically placed anti-bullying boxes), plus seminars on healthy eating et al. 'Occasional physical transgression', school keen on anti-bullying parent focus groups.

Detailed clothes list (down to hair clasps) and handy parental book of rules; actually handy books – both paper and online – on almost every subject. Newly reformed pupil-led school council. Recent HMI report thought more God would be good – 'I would hope our assemblies are meaningful,' 'huge moral dimension'. No change here. Increasing number of pupil-led assemblies. Visiting chaplain. Active and helpful board of governors.

Pupils and parents: Not a Sloane school. Strongly middle class, parents (and grandparents) who may have gone to more trad schools elsewhere hold The Wellie in high regard; number of first time buyers, professionals, builders, company directors, refugees from 'London and Manchester'. Nice well-behaved pupils, not obviously that street-wise. Parent organised buses locally.

Entrance: Via nursery; P1-P7 children spend a morning in school, thereafter school's own test in English and maths. Usual entry stage to senior school S1 but pupils accepted at any time if space available. Currently heavily oversubscribed for nursery, P1 and S1. Occasional entry for Highers or Advanced Highers.

Exit: Around 15 per cent leave after GCSEs. Most stay the course; few leave after Highers, some may go to state system post-primary. Mainly to Scottish universities, vets, medics, biologists, mathematicians.

Money matters: Sibling discounts and bursaries available, both for external and internal candidates.

Remarks: Smashing useful local school for Ayrshire, if limited in facilities by its site – sports/dining/assembly hall needed, a redundant church would be nice. No feel that it is still a girls' school with boys tacked on – it is properly co-ed throughout. Ticks all the boxes.

Schools for special educational needs

Junior Schools
Senior Schools
Junior & Senior Schools
SCOTLAND
Edinburgh
Glasgow
20
Newcastle Upon Tyne
Belfast
Keswick
5
Ripon
Leeds
Bradford
Kingston Upon Hull
Liverpool
Sheffield
Dublin
ENGLAND
Stoke-on-trent
Nottingham
15
Leicester
Norwich
Birmingham
Coventry
Cambridge
25
6
2
7
WALES
12
Colchester
Oxford
1
17
13
London
8
26
10
21
Bristol
11
Cardiff
4
16
Bath
3
19
24
14
22
18
Warminster
23
9
Southampton
Brighton
Exeter

SCHOOLS FOR SPECIAL EDUCATIONAL NEEDS

A

Abingdon House School

Broadley Terrace, London NW1 6LG

Pupils: 57 • Ages: 4-14

Fees: £29,850 pa

Tel: 0845 2300426
Email: ahs@abingdonhouseschool.co.uk
Website: www.abingdonhouseschool.co.uk

Headteacher: Since 2014, Mr Roy English MA PGCE Adv Dip SEN (early 50s). Stepped up to the post after six years as deputy, following a stint as senior teacher and head of maths at Fairley House School. Has spent a career in SEN teaching, persuaded to try it by a charismatic Welsh head in a SEN school during first year of teaching. He was only two weeks into the post when we met him, and was neat, modest and quietly spoken about his role. No doubt he will grow in strength as his vision to increase numbers and expand the school's music and arts is fulfilled.

Popular with parents. 'He knows how the school runs' and is 'more than just a safe pair of hands,' they say. He recognises the importance of forging good relations with the students and accompanies them to the park regularly. 'Consistency is very important for parents,' he remarks. Has two grown up daughters and three grandchildren. Hobbies include a passion for outdoor pursuits, marathon runs and triathlons, which he shares with the older children in their regular cross-country forays along Regent's Park canal.

Entrance: All children have learning difficulties, often with a diagnosis: ASD, Asperger's, dyspraxia, dyslexia, ADD, speech and language or social communication problems. Many arrive with poor self-esteem and social anxiety from mainstream schools. Children are taken after a two-day multi disciplinary assessment with teachers and therapists, which includes a try-out within the classroom. 'Paperwork isn't everything,' the head warns. 'We take our admissions on the individual, not on any particular difficulty.' As a consequence the classes are both mixed ability and mixed socially. Many children are privately funded and some by LA, from both north and south of the river; 25 per cent from overseas. The school supports parents with tribunal applications.

Exit: 'We don't see it as a through school,' remarks the head. 'The majority we plan to get back to other schools.' He estimated a school career at Abingdon House for most children of between one and three years. Some go on to nurturing independents like The Moat, Portland Place, Wetherby and St Augustine's Priory while others go to mainstream state secondaries.

One of the parents voiced their worries about leaving – 'most parents are sweating on the top line about where their kids go to when they leave,' she said. She mentioned there was some help with transition to further schools but felt more could be done to build formal bridges to other schools.

Remarks: Classes are named after endangered species such as rockhoppers, sea turtles and panthers and are kept small (max eight in younger years and 12 in older years). Age groups are mixed and the emphasis is on flexibility across classes to meet a child's changing needs. As one mum put it: 'They group them according to emotional ability and how they fit in.' Smaller groups and pairs are formed for maths and literacy as well as therapy sessions.

Teachers are supported in class by therapists (speech and language; music; play) as well as frequent input from physio and OT. The school's enlightened understanding of the importance of speech and language support in building a child's confidence is palpable; parents can opt for extra one-to-one after school too. Physio and OT (known as 'Cosmo') is invisibly woven into lessons two or three times a week, perhaps as beanbags or climbing the apparatus. Lessons are peppered with sensory breaks, disguised as fun. Parents praised the inclusion of the learning support, not only for saving them the trouble and expense of outside tutors, but for genuine inclusiveness, 'she didn't feel excluded or singled out'.

The national curriculum is adapted to a thematic approach so that children who attend nurture groups or extra therapy sessions don't miss out on vital stages. We witnessed a group of the youngest children unaware it was a numeracy lesson, as they sang and jumped to 20. Elsewhere, sensory supports were used, some children with adapted chairs while others had a screen to minimise distractions. ICT is the head's passion so laptops and iPads are available for each child as well as a designated ICT room with a cluster of desktops. A giant model of a dissected frog leaps at you in the modest science lab, which doubles as the library. Another classroom houses a venerable pet turtle.

Sports specialist teacher oversees taekwondo, yoga and games and the children get to visit a neighbouring playground and swim at a local leisure centre. Basketball, cricket and football are played on a nearby all-weather pitch, although one parent remarked: 'I don't think games once a week is enough – they are a bit fair weather.' School strenuously denies it. Nonetheless, what the school lacks in hearty outdoor facilities, it makes up for in culture. On the top floor, music, DT, art and drama are synthesised in a whitewashed garret known affectionately as 'creative central.' An inspiring music teacher was showing how to make rhythmic patterns from homespun instruments, conjuring a tiny steel band from catering-size food cans from the kitchen. DT students construct their own cajon (Latin American drum) from scratch. Rainbow rugs on the floor and table football make this a cool place to hang out at break, too. The children are encouraged to try out the instruments on show: ukulele, guitar, keyboard, trumpet, as well as lots of percussion. The first term's one-to-one tuition is free, then the child can opt to take up the instrument as an extra and many have progressed with great success (music exams to grades 4 and 5). Others had formed a funky five piece band to entertain the parents at the termly school show.

Round the school the children's artworks testify to the popularity of the subject. A magnificent big game trophy sculpted in paper sits outside the art room, still life drawings and textiles adorn the walls; toy theatre shows make the most of the limited space in-house, while the end of term concert takes over the neighbouring church hall. The school won the Independent Schools Association 3D figures category with some witty papier mâché Olympians. A visit from the ASD artist, David Downes, provided an inspiring role model for these children.

Established in 2004 and originally occupying two terraced houses in Kensington, Abingdon House moved to Lisson Grove in 2010 – to the site of a former theatre school (Amy Winehouse's graffiti still exists behind a wall on the upper floor). Hidden behind Marylebone station, the traditional Victorian schoolhouse stands sandwiched between church buildings and a Turkish hammam. It is a densely urban area, buses and Boris bikes mixing with office workers and their sandwich bags. Nevertheless, the buildings are beautifully maintained, making the most of the original structure to create a clean and practical space. Fun touches include blue and yellow handrails, to avoid collision on the stairs. An economy-sized dining room delivers 'fabulous food' according to one mum, and is presided over by a popular caterer with a can-do attitude to fussy children and parents. There is a compact hall which morphs into an indoor play area with colourful wall-mounted climbing frame. Alternatively, children can choose one of the play courts at street level to bounce on a trampoline or play with giant Lego and outdoor games. There is no disguising the compromised outdoor space, but these are city children and one parent assured me they get to experience the best that the metropolis can offer by stepping out in their high-vis vests to Regent's Park and London Zoo. Westminster is cultivating a local wildlife park, which offers pond-dipping and vegetable-growing opportunities, but as one parent put it, 'if you have a boy who needs to play rugby, it's not necessarily for him'.

The children arrive each day by private transport or school bus from up to 10 miles away, in neat royal blue blazer with gold trim and sporting a traditional school cap. Boys outnumber girls six to one. Early starters eat at a breakfast club and there's homework club after school for children who find it difficult to get down to it at home. One mum happily paid the extra cost for her daughter – 'homework club works beautifully for her, she doesn't want to do it with me.' It includes 10 minutes reading a day, and is supplemented by spelling and other subjects as the children get older. Art club, sports, Lego, computer and swimming club are also popular, dance club ranges from flamenco to street dance and many of the activities come free of charge. Being in the heart of the city gives the teachers plenty of choice when it comes to day trips: Kensington museums, Imperial War Museum, London Aquarium and Kew Gardens. One mum was disappointed that there were no residential school trips – 'I think they could because they have a great staff ratio there.'

Parents knew to contact their child's teacher through the home/school book and were confident that they were being kept informed – 'communication is kept open,' we were assured, by email and phone. Discipline does not appear to be a problem. 'They are a good group of kids, it has a very nice vibe to it,' remarked one mum, and the head confirmed behaviour is managed consistently by staff. A rainmaker is used in class rather than a raised voice, which might stress an anxious child. There is a traffic light system to give warnings. Stickers and a merit chart contribute towards 'golden time,' which comes in the form of a fun activity or outing to the park. Parents confirmed it worked – 'the school stops any bullying developing...it's a very big preoccupation for SEN parents.'

For a London child with specific learning difficulties, this is a thoughtful and nurturing find. As one mum put it: 'Abingdon House ticks a lot of boxes.' Self-esteem thrives with the seamless inclusion of therapies within the curriculum and generous ratio of expert staff. Shame about the lack of playground space, but nevertheless, the charming, Victorian setting is brought to life by chattering youngsters, particularly in the vibrant art and music studio – a specialist oasis in the heart of the city.

The school is extending into key stage 4 and now includes a year 9 class, year 10 and 11 will follow in 2017 and 2018 respectively.

Alderman Knight School

Ashchurch Road, Tewkesbury, Gloucestershire GL20 8JJ

Pupils: 119 • Ages: 4–16

Tel: 01684 295 639
Email: admin@aldermanknight.gloucs.sch.uk
Website: www.aldermanknight.gloucs.sch.uk

Head teacher: Since 2006, Clare Steel. 'Personable, warm and professional,' is how one mother described her. It is a good description. Steel has established a strong rapport with pupils and parents. She started her teaching career as a chemistry teacher at Stroud High School for Girls before joining Alderman Knight School – first time around – from 1992 to 1995. She worked at the Whitminster Pupil Referral Centre, Cam House Special School in Cheltenham, and Kingsmead Secondary School before becoming the SEN adviser for Gloucestershire and an Ofsted inspector. She was then a school improvement adviser before returning to Alderman Knight.

Academic matters: Alderman Knight is often described as a halfway house between a mainstream and what many people perceive a special school to be.

'Expectations are really high here,' says Steel. Ofsted praised the fact that children come in with lower than average levels of attainment but make rapid progress and have rated it as outstanding on two occasions. It is a leading school for communication excellence.

The school provides a safe environment with small groups and individual attention. The curriculum is tailored to individual needs, encompassing academic subjects, vocational and life skills.

Steel's next challenge is to develop a sixth form. This will meet the needs of a relatively small number of pupils who are not able to manage in local provider colleges. 'The more able young people would be able to cope with the academic demands of an FE college but have high anxiety so cannot access mainstream.' The school is to have a new building and will take post-16 pupils from across the county who need 'the halfway house'. Key to this new development is the collaborative working with Tewkesbury School.

The secondary department runs a similar model to a mainstream with pupils following a secondary curriculum delivered by specialist teachers in specialist teaching rooms. Pupils are grouped according to need as well as age.

Some of the children go over to Tewkesbury School for certain subjects where they have a particular talent to help support their learning and develop their social interaction skills within a mainstream setting. Recently, one pupil achieved a GCSE in maths at Tewkesbury School following successful integration. Steel liaises with local schools and her staff are able to provide advice and training for staff in mainstream – both primary and secondary – who are require additional support in working with children with anxiety disorders.

They take exam success seriously but have realistic expectations. Due to additional needs, some of their children will not fare well with written formal examinations but can excel at coursework and practical work so they choose the qualifications carefully. They use 33 different types of accreditation, with a whole range for each subject. They do GCSEs, BTecs, entry level qualifications, ASDAN. Many pupils follow the BTec home cooking and OCR Cambridge National for photography.

They have a good range of technology for students but it is carefully controlled. There are interactive whiteboards in the classroom, laptops, a computer suite where children learn coding and programming. While they have class sets of iPads, the school prefers to use LearnPads where the teacher can see on a machine exactly what each child is doing and lock them out of apps or sites which are irrelevant or distracting.

Children were keen to show teachers what they had been doing in the morning and a group of children were talking excitedly about Pompeii and volcanoes: 'I wonder what it would feel like to know your home was going to be destroyed,' said one girl.

Games, options, the arts: Alderman Knight School is an Artsmark Gold school with designated art teaching spaces. There is an emphasis on design and creativity. There are good links with the Rose Theatre in Tewksbury. Their staff come in and run sessions with pupils. The school has put on musicals: Bugsy Malone, Grease and Oliver! were ones that the children mentioned. In alternate years they hold an Alderman Knight's Got Talent at the Rose Theatre. They also have links with the National Star College, which has very good facilities for music and art. They often have samples of the work at the Cirencester Brewery Arts Exhibitions.

Children are encouraged to develop a wide range of musical skills, so one boy was arranging to borrow a guitar from school to practise at home, and a collection by customers at a local fish and chip shop provided funds for some new musical instruments from triangles to ukuleles.

There is a sensory room in the school, but also an empty room opposite, so children can take in beanbags and have a time out with no stimulation if that is what they need. They have a forest school in one corner of the grounds where children had recently worked with volunteers from a local insurance company and an artist to do some willow weaving. They also use a local farm for camps, countryside skills and making fires.

There is lots of cooking. A former food technologist from industry who retrained as a teacher is in charge of this, so it ranges from life skills, where they go and buy food from local supermarket, cook it and eat it, through to a pop-up restaurant where they invite six guests, devise a menu, cook, serve and clean up. Every Thursday groups of pupils run the tea room at Tewkesbury Abbey, doing the tills, serving customers, loading the dishwasher.

Background and atmosphere: The building has a Wow factor. It is light, bright and modern with a colourful horse sculpture in the courtyard and a peacock mural in reception, celebrating the efforts of parents and the local community to fight threats of closure and keep the school open. There is also an electronic display featuring Children's News, interesting facts and animal stories and the week's question: 'What is the most important discovery in history?'

The staff are open and friendly, from the person who answers the phone to the teachers and dinner ladies. It is a calm school, full of natural light, and every class has its own safe outdoor space straight out of the classroom in case children need to break away. Many of the rooms feature individual desks which can be grouped together but give the option of children working individually in their own space.

About half the children have a cooked dinner, the rest bring packed lunches. Lunch might be curry and rice with sweetcorn and peppers, or a baked potato with choice of fillings. The pudding might be, for example, carrot cake or fresh fruit. One of the boys told us: 'They can accommodate allergies or food needs. I am wheat intolerant.' Children sit six to a table and one serves the rest. They all help to clear and wipe the table, and teaching staff, including the head teacher, are always in the dining room, keeping an eye on behaviour and offering praise for good social skills. After lunch children have free time for playing outdoors or going to one of the clubs on offer. As some children come to school in taxis and others live long way away, it is not sensible to offer all clubs after school. The structured activities at lunchtime are important not only to support the development of communication and interaction skills but also to limit the opportunities for anti-social behaviour and bullying.

Pastoral care, well-being and discipline: There are a number of children with complex emotional difficulties and high levels of anxiety. Pastoral care is a real strength in the school. There is a high staff to pupil ratio (some 55 staff for 119 children) so they know one another well. They work with tutors for seven hours a fortnight on personal and social development, communication and emotions.

The children wear a school uniform: red sweatshirts for primary, blue for secondary. The school encourages children to do homework but liaises with parents to see if homework is feasible or if it will cause extra stress and overload.

An inclusive summer school runs for two weeks with the usual range of activities: cooking, Minecraft, zumba, loom bands, swimming at Tewkesbury School. It hosts 70+ children from 30+ schools. Siblings can come along as can children with additional needs from other Gloucestershire schools.

There is a craft club on alternate Saturday afternoons where students make things for local craft fairs. Children can bring their brothers and sisters to this. On a Saturday morning there is a football club. Friends of Alderman Knight School organises events which give families a chance to socialise. They recently hired Malvern Splash for a Saturday night family swim: 'It takes a lot of stress off families to know that they are with people who have had the same experiences. It doesn't matter if your child has a meltdown.' They do family cooking evenings when parents and children cook with staff support and then they eat together.

Therapy and staffing: A learning mentor supports pupils with their emotional and social needs. They do work with external providers, especially on mental health issues, and buy in support when they need it. They use different strategies and approaches so, for example, only some of the toilets have hand dryers, so children who are overwhelmed by those noises can have them gradually introduced. 'It is a balancing act,' says Steel. 'Our overriding aim is to help them to be happy, responsible members of the wider community and make successful transitions to adulthood.

Staff tend to stay for a long time. Many have come from mainstream and have enjoyed the change. Some teaching assistants have degrees, some have qualifications in special education when they come, but there is intensive programme of professional development for all the staff.

Classes have a teacher and a TA who is attached to the class, not to a curriculum subject, and rarely to an individual child.

Some children who come from mainstream are surprised that they do not have their own TA. Everything is done in small groups, carefully differentiated, and only the children with the most extreme forms of learning difficulties and behavioural problems work one-to-one with a TA. Even then this may be an interim measure. 'They surprise themselves with what they can do independently,' says Steel.

Hannah Silverman is in charge of social personal development, community links and behaviour. 'We work on the skills that parents want us to incorporate. This might range from learning to tie a shoelace to going out to a park to overcome a phobia of dogs gradually.'

Staff brainstormed the top 30 things they wanted children to have experienced by the time they left school. These included going for a ride on the bus and going to the seaside.

Accessing respite is a real problem for families, so the school has started using its life skills flat for respite care. Two children stay in the flat on a Friday night with staff to give the parents a night off. They might go bowling, cook a meal together or watch DVDs.

Pupils and parents: Pupils have moderate learning difficulties, complex needs, and many have autistic spectrum disorders. They come from all over Gloucestershire; a small number come in from neighbouring authorities. The majority have been to local pre-school in their local community before joining the school. There are twice as many boys as girls.

Pupils appreciate the small classes and the attention they receive. 'I like it here. They treat pupils respectfully and we look after each other.' They enjoy the extramural activities and many spoke about their experience of taking part in musicals and going horse riding, which is organised through Riding for the Disabled. Some of the children seemed to be aware that the school helped to reduce the impact of their autism on the family: 'My mum is not so stressed now I'm here.'

The parents are pleased with the changes they have seen in their children. One parent said: 'My son was unhappy. I knew it would be disruptive to change school, but he had lost his confidence and had low self-esteem. He's found himself here.' A father appreciated the range of activities in and out of school hours offered: 'My kids have little social life. I live in the sticks and they have real problems keeping friends. They remember and talk about what they have done at school, the bones in the body, layers of the earth. In the last school they did everything on iPads, including music. Now there's much more to focus on experiences and discussion. They made doorbells in DT and brought them home. It broke my heart, but I had to drill holes in the bedroom door to put up their bells!'

Entrance: Children can join the school at any time. They do not need a specific diagnosis as the school meets a wide range of needs, but must have an EHCP or statement, and are referred by local authorities.

Exit: Leavers go to FE colleges, a company called Plant Hire, or a learning scheme for people with special needs at Brambles Country College. Some do horticulture and small animal work. Others work in supermarkets, driving jobs, farm work, computing.

Remarks: This is a special school that models provision on the best of mainstream with smaller groups. The atmosphere is calm and purposeful and children are encouraged to develop their talents and to garner as many qualifications as possible with a view to moving on to college, employment or local training schemes. There's a strong family atmosphere, and an emphasis on good manners and social skills.

Children will not necessarily have the help of a teaching assistant, and will be pushed to be as independent as possible. This may not suit some parents, but children seem to thrive. 'The curriculum is so exciting!' said one boy. 'I never want a day off.'

Appleford School

Elston Lane, Shrewton, Nr Salisbury, Wiltshire SP3 4HL

Pupils: 131 (87 boys, 44 girls); 77 boarders • Ages: 7–18 • Sixth form: 13 (10 boys, 3 girls)

Fees: Day £17,439; Boarding £26,766 pa

Tel: 01980 621020
Email: secretary@appleford.wilts.sch.uk
Website: www.appleford.wilts.sch.uk

Headmaster: Since 2012, Mr David King BEd (40s). Previously head at Bishop Dustan School in Newton Abbot and before that at 24/7 College near Honiton, Devon, both special schools catering for children with emotional and behavioural difficulties. Married to Shelagh, a learning needs specialist, with grown up children and much-loved home in Devon (the reason why, like some of his pupils, he's a part time boarder with digs in the village, returning home at weekends).

Thrives on risk. Before entering teaching, he contemplated a career as a professional climber (we're talking Mont Blanc without the safety gear) until a serious fall coupled with parental pressure to 'make something of yourself, David' compelled him to choose a career.

Security and long holidays originally lured him into primary school teaching in assorted Somerset primaries in 1989. Becoming special needs coordinator (and maths specialist) followed by the realisation that he had an affinity with underachieving children were what kept him there.

After securing pioneering dyslexia friendly status while at Wembdon St George's Primary School, Bridgwater, disenchantment set in with the growing pressure of Sats force-feeding. While dyslexic pupils 'might fleetingly have achieved level 4 in the test, they certainly weren't working to it.' In 2000, left to set up a family-run outdoor activity centre on Exmoor, gaining the management expertise and – thanks to an advantageous sale – financial freedom to pick and choose senior leadership posts, this time in the independent sector. While his two previous posts saw him transform underperforming schools into slickly run operations to a tight timescale, he decided he wanted a 'forever' school to keep him going until retirement. Saw Appleford and was hooked.

Wiry and immaculately dressed, he's a fizzing ball of energy barely contained (does 'occasional' triathlon – a necessity, you'd have thought, to avoid overload). Personal best for pupil annual review meetings is 23 minutes – 'don't do fripperies' – though he's a benevolent force. During our interview, several children erupted through his door, clearly confident of (and receiving) a sympathetic reception as long as they observed the basic courtesies (he's big on manners).

Clear on how he wants school to be seen. Not special (despite label) but 'just a school that teaches children in a specialist way'. His philosophy is 'you're dyslexic; get over it,' (pace Nelson Rockefeller) and by way of proof, he cites host of inspirational, high-achieving success stories (Zoe Wanamaker has recently become school patron).

Almost his first act as head was to extend the leaving age from 14 to 16. Wants a sixth form too, and has approval for it – 'it's logical' – with woodland site earmarked for new building, planning permission permitting, though 100–120 would be maximum school size. 'We don't want to be a production line.'

One parent wondered if pace was a bit too fast and furious, but most are smitten, as are staff. 'I'm massively impressed,' was a typical comment. 'I'm blown away, he's amazing,' said one parent (echoed ad nauseam and unprompted). Pupils are impressed too. 'The candidates were taken round the school and he was the children's favourite,' a mother told us. 'When I said, "you have a new head ... and it's David King," my son punched the air.'

You can't help wondering what will happen if his super-fast, risk-embracing management style finds him twiddling his fingers in four years or so when he's got the school where he wants it and is no longer living on the edge but a good bus ride from it. Officially, however, he's here for the duration.

Academic matters: Underlying aim is to create a relaxed environment where children who arrive with their confidence in tatters can start to learn again. 'You want them to have lost that fear factor and that's what Appleford does,' says a parent.

It's achieved with sense and sensibility: small classes in reassuringly compact and well-equipped rooms, including decent science lab and art room with kiln and delightful solar powered planes, taken by exceptional, humorous teachers (puns a speciality). IEPs (individual education plans) that are formulaic elsewhere here are (almost) living breathing things, constantly referred to and updated.

Subjects are carefully thought through, with maths and English dominating the morning timetable. Humanities block-booked so pupils have eight weeks of geography or history rather than disorienting chopping and changing, and modern languages banished, allowing more focus on drama (one senior pupil, convincingly in character as a nervous flyer, was being convincingly, but gently manhandled on to a plane by energetic peers).

However long it takes, the approach that yields the light-bulb moment will be found, without recourse to punitive and pointless fact repetition. 'There's no point saying the same thing over and over again,' says an English teacher.

Very occasionally a child will be removed by a parent desperate for signs of progress and disappointed by the deliberately gentle pace. 'You get the odd failure but they are much more to do with the parent than the child,' says a father. Head is aware of need for better expectations management. 'The reality is that you are always going to be dyslexic and there's the possibility that your academic progress will always lag behind,' he says. He is adamant, though, that dyslexia must never be used as an excuse. Whatever pupils are capable of achieving, from a decent bag of GCSEs to vocational awards, 'they are jolly well going to do it,' and with the certificates to prove it, too. He wants as many subjects as possible to lead to a tangible, confidence-boosting qualification, pre-GCSE entry level English for year 9s, for example, together with maths, science and ICT.

For pupils, the school's approach is a revelation. 'Teachers here never say "It's time to move on," when you're still trying to write something down from the board,' says a clearly relieved 11 year old. Good things tend to come to those who wait, agree old hands. 'The reading is coming on,' one mother told us. 'It's not brilliant but much, much improved. We've sort of got our little boy back again.' First cohort took GCSEs in 2015, everyone achieving at least one pass (G or above) but an A* in there as well. Courses for sixth form include BTecs and life skills qualifications (AQA and Asdan) as well as GCSE retakes.

Games, options, the arts: Sport is helped along by high-powered sports team (world class Iron Man among them) and good facilities including two grass pitches and all-weather tennis courts. Though ostensible wow factor is provided by super new climbing wall in flash but hot sports hall (wonky surface 'bobbles if underfloor heating isn't on,' says one teacher), the ubiquitous presence of Mr King at matches ('he always watches' say pupils) osmosing energy from the sidelines, may well prove the greatest galvaniser of the lot.

'We used to lose all our matches,' a year 9 pupil told us, but embryonic winning streak has seen recent U13 rugby and hockey teams (both mixed, as is football, with star girl players) triumph over local mainstream schools. 'You'd have thought they were the special school, not us,' says the head, of one notable victory. Champions do emerge, such as a 2016 Olympic equestrian hopeful. School could do more to trumpet successes, feels head, pointing, by way of proof, to photograph of two England and Ireland rugby captains (both former pupils) relegated to shady spot under sports hall light switch.

While there's no pool, pupils all swim and boarders can also join local scouts and guides. With an ever-increasing sporting menu, most pupils find something they tolerate and are encouraged to come up with their own ideas. Pupil 'crushed when first arrived, didn't want to interact' had researched plan for birdwatching club and proudly showed off new badge.

Lots of outings, cultural and sporting – they range from visits to Hampton Court and National Army Museum to a team-building canoeing trip. Set to increase, as all year 9s will now work towards compulsory D of E bronze awards.

Chances to shine are many and various, with music and drama specialists working wonders. With recent production of Oliver coming in for lots of praise and 40 per cent of pupils learning instruments, emphasis is on encouraging even the most reluctant to try something new. New music and drama room should help with this.

Boarding: Homely feel is helped by cosy boarding houses, recently expanded to four as age range has increased and completed (hurrah!) by that increasing rarity, the house dog (poodle in girls' boarding house, chows in the boys' house, all allergy friendly as they don't shed and very popular). Lots of boarding treats including trips to museums, parks and ice rinks. Back at school there are Christmas craft sessions and sewing, while the fifty per cent or so who stay on at weekends have exclusive access to the bath (it's a daily shower in the week) – and Sunday roast.

Background and atmosphere: Set in a compact and easy to navigate site in rural Wiltshire (Stonehenge a mere monolith's throw away). The school (Victorian gothic main building, ringed by additions of assorted styles and ages) exudes longevity (though actually founded only in the 1980s), together with an indefinable 'something' that frequently has potential parents hooked before they've even parked.

Head, hugely influenced by his Merseyside upbringing, saw his grammar school as an 'enclave of tradition in the sprawl of comprehensives and misery' and is a firm believer in the traditions that make schools work – honour boards, houses, prefects and juniors. Wants families to feel as proud of being here as they would 'at Eton or anywhere else,' staff too.

Head has overseen widespread sprucing up of buildings. Some, like new year 9 boys' quarters, done by pupils themselves as part of life skills programme ('no dungeons,' otherwise free choice of colourways).

Reception in original house is now very smart, staff and pupils, ditto. Former have been now kitted out in academic robes for speech day (qualifications are 'excellent,' says the head, 'so why not shout about them?'); latter in revamped uniforms: ties, blazers (head boy/girl has exclusive red-trimmed version) and trousers for boys (fiddly fastenings and dearth of larger sizes made them hard work for some) while girls have attractive pleated (and machine washable) kilts, handmade in Scotland. Three weeks into term, they weren't popular with all. ('It's horrible,' says one, quizzed by head.)

Boarding and teaching block includes home economics room for upper school, there's a DT room and a new boarding house in the village for girls. Recent improvements include two new science labs. But star of the show is undoubtedly the new dining hall masterminded by the bursar, who has Grand Design tendencies and, in a shock departure from the norm, 'loves spending money,' says head. Instead of the high, echo-ridden ceilings that bedevil many a sensitive child attempting to avoid sensory overload, its noise-cancelling panels make pupil voices round oval tables (shape is most conducive to conversation, apparently) a pleasure to hear.

Food is good, too, despite recent and much lamented departure of national prize-winning chef. Pupils choose between green and red apple menus in advance. They sit at correspondingly decorated tables, take turns to serve each other and also clear up and wipe tables. Grace is said and manners are a big thing. 'You could take any of our children to a top restaurant and they'd know exactly how to behave,' says head.

Pastoral care, well-being and discipline: Huge amounts of positive reinforcement and bullying 'instantly jumped on,' says mother, whose child suffered some name calling. One parent said that the morale-boosting good behaviour certificates, previously doled out en masse for small achievements like helpfulness, were now harder to come by. However there is a celebration assembly every week. Particularly liked by one parent was post-match praise, where, regardless of the result, 'everybody in the team stood up in assembly and said something positive about another player.'

Head is especially proud that one child, asked who he could go to if he had a problem by inspectors said 'everybody' and that teamwork, that much over-used word, is much in evidence. In the run up to speech day, teachers shared out admin and catering tasks so support staff could be part of it rather than beavering away in the background. They're also kept in the loop about children's needs and it shows: one pupil, who had mistakenly ticked wrong lunch choice and was miserably regarding disliked meal, was speedily offered alternative without comment or fuss.

Head has also cast his beady eye over behaviour and, predictably, revamped school policy. His predecessor, though lovely, was 'perhaps over-empathetic,' thinks an insider. Now, consequences for unacceptable behaviour are clear, with recently introduced four-colour traffic lights system. Sanctions range from warnings or break time detentions for minor infringements (bad manners or not doing as asked) to code red for leaving the school grounds without permission. Latter would will result in a fixed term exclusion (permanent if repeated in the same academic year). There had been an (unsuccessful) dash for freedom the week before our visit. Pupils were still rather vague about detail. 'Is swearing a yellow or amber light?' mused one.

There's also a 'black book' that lives in the staffroom and records, like St Peter, every detail of pupil goings-on (positive and negative). Purpose is less punitive than to provide hour-by-hour update on burgeoning pupil issues and tailor approach accordingly.

Therapy and staffing: Therapists, who radiate enthusiasm, provide flexible support. Multi-sensory approaches abound, with a big emphasis on hands-on activity. We saw senior pupils, wielding enormous maps and rulers, tracking down six-figure grid references in geography while even 7 and 8 year olds use Bunsen burners and sometimes even make their own bonfire night fireworks. An equine therapy centre opposite the school, run by local GP and featuring five ponies from Balmoral donated by the Queen, can work wonders for pupils with complex needs.

Pupils and parents: School has many more boys than girls. Big geographical range, with some coming from as far afield as Hong Kong, others from assorted southern counties, often some distance away. Flexi boarding eases pain of gruelling daily long distance round trip, though upping sticks to be closer isn't unheard of. As one father told us: 'I've had experience with all our children of state, private and now, I suppose, a special needs environment. It's without a shadow of a doubt the best school I've been to.'

Few non-white pupils. Relatively wide range of backgrounds from Forces to professions. Small minority (eight or nine) funded by local authorities, many families somehow scraping together money for the fees. Having found the school, articulate, friendly parents will do almost anything to keep their child here. Though geographic spread makes get-togethers tricky, parents work mini-miracles when it comes to fundraising.

Entrance: Parents meet head and provide ed psych report. Pupils are then assessed during two-day visit (and nights, if planning to board) before final decision is made.

Families apply from all over, with long-distance commutes common. Once they find the school, they will do anything, including moving home, to lick the logistics into shape (flexi-boarding can ease the pain). Statemented pupils (currently 18) face the customary battle with local authorities, though once admitted, head mounts a formidable defence to ensure they stay.

Pressing need to keep pupil numbers up and finances ticking over meant school slightly lost its way, unofficially broadening admissions criteria to include those with a primary diagnosis of ADHD. No longer, says head. Dyslexia must be the key issue, though 'if pupils have additional needs, as long as it doesn't impact on their learning or the learning of others, then that's fine.'

MOD funding possible for Forces families. School also offers eight bursaries worth up to 25 per cent. Sibling discounts range from five per cent for second child to ten per cent for fourth.

Exit: Up till 2012, pupils had to leave at 14, many miserably returning to mainstream education but can now stay on until 18. Head would like leavers' destinations to be accurate reflection of underlying ability, so range is likely to cover everything from academic mainstream schools to more vocational further education colleges.

Blossom House School

Station Road, Motspur Park, New Malden KT3 6JJ

Pupils: 210 • Ages: 3–19 • Sixth form: 26

Fees: £27,300 – £37,500 pa

Tel: 020 8946 7348
Email: admin@blossomhouseschool.co.uk
Website: www.blossomhouseschool.co.uk

Principal: Since its founding in 1983, Mrs Joanna (Joey) Burgess (60s) DipCST MRCSLT Dip RSA SpLD PGCE. Educated at St Paul's Girls' School and Oldry Fleming School of Speech and Language Therapy. Well known, liked and very much respected locally; married to Paddy, they have four daughters (one teaching at the school) and four grandchildren. Likes to spend her leisure time with her family or playing tennis or golf and socialising. Enchanting, with a wicked sense of humour, the diminutive Mrs B is described by parents as elegant, petite, beautiful and kind, with a steely will. 'Joey doesn't just light up the room – she lights up lives,' said one grateful parent. Another added, 'She runs a great school, is open, approachable and willing to take on suggestions.'

Blossom may be very much Joey's babe, child, teen.. but it is clear that everything is child-centred. 'Many are fragile; an unhappy, anxious child is not in a good place when it comes to learning so we have to unpick that'. Pupils are appreciative, saying, 'She speaks clearly, doesn't confuse us and gives really good assemblies.' Her vision, energy, business brain, passion and total commitment steer the ship, but it's no solo voyage – an abundance of willing, first-rate help from the well-oiled engine room. True, we detected a hint that Joey likes control, finds it difficult to let go, 'She isn't perfect, but we wouldn't want her to be – she does what is important, and in her book that includes looking after us too,' say staff. Looking every inch like a lady who lunches, her Friday feasts, laid on for her hardworking team, are legendary. 'We have the most wonderful dos – it is a very sociable school. Joey wouldn't have it any other way – she loves a party'.

Academic matters: Classes are small, typically eight or fewer, with groups of three or four for literacy, numeracy and speech and language therapy. All have an Individual Education Programme (IEP) based on personal learning styles, combined with visual communication aids, such as timetables of the day. There's structure (which children love), but the aim is to make youngsters adaptable and flexible.

Teaching is multi-sensory, with 'over-teaching', and is linked to an innovative sensory integration programme which helps children regulate and focus: 'It is possibly the most important thing we have introduced'. Every lesson has a learning break, where children head outside for a couple of minutes to exercise and recharge. 'It has made such a difference to their level of concentration'; formats vary according to age but are universally appreciated.

All follow the national curriculum, adapted as necessary. Touch typing from age 7. Pupils grade lesson activities on a scale of 1-3 to indicate the degree of difficulty they experience, giving staff instant feedback and enabling them to adjust their teaching accordingly. Popular projects include 'we are writers', which saw a gamut of poems and prose in print.

Senior pupils make guided exam choices – 'It's a bit like speed dating,' said one enlightened youngster. 'You spend five minutes with staff talking about their subject, then move to the next.' All work towards GCSEs and/or entry level exams, vocational qualifications and practical courses in a range of subjects including art and design, science, maths, English, DT (food or graphic products), media and ICT. Children say they'd like to see GCSE history, German and Polish offered, otherwise diddly-squat on their wish lists. At GCSE, single science and art are among the most successful subjects.

While most achieve many things parents were told (pre-Blossom) they never would, we uncovered the odd parental grumble that older children are not academically stretched. If we are being picky, we suspect some in the senior school might benefit from academic extension and challenge – for example, we saw a maths lesson where teens collectively and impressively identified pentadecagons, icosagons et al, but felt disappointed when they were not then given the opportunity to see basic reflection through to a correct conclusion. However, pushing for academic success has to be balanced against fragile esteems and anxieties – 'What good is a pile of GCSEs if a child is too scared to set foot outside the door?' Indeed.

Games, options, the arts: All youngsters have group music and art lessons – teachers aim to develop creativity, build self-esteem and encourage interaction and communication. Visits to art galleries and plays and sessions in school with artists are popular, but not as frequent as some parents would like. Variety of sports on offer and older pupils are encouraged to work towards Duke of Edinburgh and sports leader awards. Tends to play inter-house sport rather than inter-school, as early outings resulted in crushing defeats and squashed esteems. Not a uniformly popular move. 'My child is sporty and would love the chance to compete against other schools. It's sad, but I guess you have to consider others,' rued one parent.

Background and atmosphere: Started life in 'the pink house' (originally Joey's grandmother's residence). Four pupils then have mushroomed 50-fold now, and the school moved in 2015 to nearby Motspur Park. The new building, formerly offices, has been undergone extensive refurbishment and is now a light and airy, fabulously-equipped modern school. There is good outdoor space (playground being developed) with a multi-purpose park down the road. 'Joey planned every inch, indoor and out – she knew what was needed: it's fab.' It has all the facilities you could hope for: sports hall, dance studio, art and DT rooms, science lab, well-equipped food tech room, music room etc.

Pastoral care, well-being and discipline: Parents praise the care lavished on their offspring: 'My child loves going to school, the structure, the space, socialising with his friends and the kind teachers'. Many older children arrive feeling angry, let down, stupid and unworthy, so staff unapologetically focus on the individual and work to reduce anxiety and stress. 'We do what is needed – if that is a Theraband on a chair or bluetac to squash, that's fine,' said one therapist, adding, 'Tinies arrive surrounded by chaos and mess. It is our job to untangle. We help them make the links, so they understand their significance to themselves and others.'

All bring own healthy lunches. Eating together, from nursery to 19, is encouraged, with food tasting and exploration very much part of Blossom life. We witnessed the youngest children happily sampling foods of different colours and textures – all the more remarkable when only weeks prior, many had had rigid diets and were reluctant to eat with others. 'It makes family life easier – simple things like trips to the shops, outings, holidays etc are now possible, as well as treats such as trips to restaurants,' say parents.

While children undoubtedly have their moments, we witnessed an abundance of courtesy and encouragement. Being kind to each other is important, as are good behaviour and achievement. Positive steps, however small, are rewarded via a highly-regarded token system. Pupils are controlled but not contained. School rules are simple and clear, 'consequences' rather than punishments for inappropriate behaviour. Three entries in the inappropriate book equals a trip to Joey – 'She doesn't shout, but she does try to help you get it right'. We saw this in action at the start of our visit, when we encountered two male miscreants who moaned animatedly that 'the school was sexist and teachers didn't listen' – yet when we spied them later they were happy, relaxed and smiling. Naturally we tried hard to uncover the alleged sexism, but the best we could muster was a girls' club with no equivalent for the boys.

Therapy and staffing: Offers a relatively rare, educational-health-emotional package of teaching, speech and language therapy, occupational and physiotherapy, art, music and drama therapy. Young, energetic staff, some of whom come as part of their initial teacher training and return to hone their skills, plus a good sprinkling of the more mature and experienced.

Pupils and parents: From a wide area of London, Surrey and Kent. Fees reflect the high level of support, but 90 per cent are funded by their local authority. We were particularly impressed by just how articulate some of the older youngsters are, but recognise that talking about and understanding emotions and anxieties are different skill sets.

The active FOBH (Friends of Blossom House) organises an assortment of events including sibling days. School runs numerous parental events including termly curriculum and feedback meetings plus self awareness, and drug awareness sessions: 'It's important we take the blinkers off'. Despite the plethora of events, we received mixed messages from parents – some feel very much part of the school, others less so, possibly because of distance and personal circumstances.

Almost all have nothing but praise for the school. 'We don't just move house, but heaven and earth to be here. We are defensive – we've been through the mill'. Every parent has a story, feels the system is money-orientated, not child-centred – 'Tribunal is expensive, unfair. It is about how good your solicitor is and how many other children the LA have funded ahead of yours. The individual child and their right to an education are missing from that equation'.

Entrance: At 3+ into the nursery; term of their fifth birthday to the junior school; 11+ to the senior school, 16+ to sixth form. Admission at any time, subject to a place, suitability and funding. Progression through the school(s) depends on: progress, what's right for the child and funding. A primary diagnosis of speech, language and communication impairments is required.

Most have additional needs including ASD, dyspraxia, sensory integration difficulties (can cater for the 'fizzy, whizzy' child but not the aggressive or violent), dyslexia (school is CReSTeD registered) and ADHD, occasional selective mute. It is not unusual for youngsters to exhibit a deal of frustration and anxiety as a result of their language disorders, but the school would not suit those whose primary needs are either ASD or behavioural.

Entry is via a detailed four-day assessment followed, for some, by a trial six week period to ensure the child will benefit from a Blossom education. On entry, approximately one third of the nursery children have very limited speech, but thanks to timely, expertly delivered interventions, this reduces significantly as youngsters progress through the school. Many come from mainstream. 'Some cope there initially – they don't look any different to their peers – but as they get older, their difficulties become apparent and frustrations are compounded. It takes a deal of time and devotion for us to get them back on track'.

School says no tablet of stone dictating what child will suit Blossom – it is not only about the profile of the child but also the cohort and group at the time: 'Sometimes we can take children who are a little less able because there may be a peer group who have come through from the nursery with similar needs'.

Exit: Majority stay at 11+, a few to specialist schools: More House (Farnham), Moor House (Oxted), The Moat, St Dominic's Godalming, mainstream Sibford or St Catherine's, or occasionally to (supported) mainstream state schools: Wimbledon College, Ursuline Convent etc. Post-16 provision now well established.

Money matters: More than 90 per cent are LA funded. Hopes to offer some bursaries in the future. Fledgling tribunal fund.

Remarks: Blossom by name, blossom by nature. Regrettably all too many have to tread through manure to get here, but once they do, children flourish and families thrive. 'Without Blossom House I don't think we would have survived as a family – they gave us back our child, our lives'. For the right child with speech, language and communication issues few rosier places to develop, mature and bloom.

Breckenbrough School

Sand Hutton, Thirsk, North Yorkshire YO7 4EN

Pupils: 49 • Ages: 9–19

Tel: 01845 587238
Email: office@breckenbrough.org.uk
Website: www.breckenbrough.org.uk

Head: Since 2008, Mr Geoff Brookes, previously at The Mount School in York, before that deputy head at Easingwold School; has two grown-up children. A real enthusiast, he is warm, friendly and welcoming and more than happy to share his views on education and working with young people in general. Very hands-on, closely involved with pupils and parents, communication is his thing and he's a great advocate for the Quaker ethos of 'seeing the good in everyone'. Very relaxed with the ruling here on the use of first names between pupils and staff; it's vital, he says 'to respect the person not the title' – can't argue with that. Out of school this apparently gentle man plays in a rock duo around the pubs of York and is a bit of a Francophile too, escaping across the Channel for the holidays. Probably this relaxation and ability to escape is what enables this calm, sound and reasoned approach to the day job.

Academic matters: Working in small teaching groups, the boys follow personalised programmes of learning with additional support as necessary. A primary trained teacher works with the younger boys and most go on to take at least eight GCSEs; academic success equates well within the national average, despite boys often having low Sats levels on entry. Teaching groups often organised according to social and academic compatibility and there are opportunities for accelerated learning for those with exceptional ability in a particular subject. Weaker students complete entry level portfolios, with the intention that all achieve a basic level qualification or better.

Plenty of art and CDT in evidence as well as the usual humanities and languages, all underpinned by an extensive outdoor education programme. The lack of ambiguity and logical methods make maths an especially popular subject here, science and IT are equally strong; our very bright and super-impressive sixth form guide had aspirations to become 'an ethical hacker' on completion of a university degree and explained, in some detail, the huge value in that for the nation. Working in partnership with other providers such as York College, school offers additional NCFE courses and a solid range of A levels, accommodating the needs and wishes of individual students wherever possible. Additional enrichment comes in the form of music and drama, and the life skills programme and work experience are also key curriculum components here. Plenty of detail of schemes of work subject by subject on the school's website.

Teachers are subject specialists, ably assisted by support assistants with key workers alongside. Classrooms are spacious and well-resourced with interactive whiteboards; there is also a science lab and food tech room, an art room with views of the extensive gardens and more besides, both in the main building and in various adjacent outbuildings. The vast majority of boys go on to full-time further education, training and work.

Pupils appear focussed and busy, staff ever watchful, yet balancing that with allowing pupils to work and learn independently as far as possible.

Games, options, the arts: They are big on personal challenge, much of which comes from the outdoor pursuits programme, with ample opportunities for developing skills in leadership and problem-solving. In addition to the usual range of sports on offer, climbing, mountain-biking, kayaking and even flying are there to stretch and challenge, and increasingly students here are gaining qualifications in outdoor education. If motorcycle maintenance is your thing you'll have plenty of opportunities to strip down the odd engine and get your hands seriously greasy here, and the annual ski trip is popular with those daring enough to hit the slopes beyond Yorkshire. Follow your interests, yes, but no backing away from new challenges either – moving forward is the order of the day.

Art is strong, with fine arts, photography, textiles and graphics all on offer, and pupils are producing work at a very high level at both GCSE and A level. Outside you'll find an all-weather sports pitch, playing fields, a pond, trampoline, climbing frames and swings. Football is very popular; there are many ways to let off steam here, with physical activities taking place before, during and after school.

Music is popular; there are plenty of instruments around and they encourage potential. At the time of our visit one boy was just heading off to study music at university, having found and developed his passion here.

Boarding: Weekly boarding available on 38 week placements. Accommodation is primarily in the main building, with two separate blocks for sixth formers. Plenty of respect for space and privacy; everyone has their own bedroom, which they are encouraged to make 'homely' and, as teenagers, they certainly do that. Some are obsessively, compulsively tidy, as befits the profile, others less so, but either way it's theirs, which is what matters to them. Areas for relaxing, cooking, washing (laundry and yourself) are good and well-resourced; there is plenty of space in these large rooms with high ceilings. Boys can go back to their rooms before and after lessons – the need for a bit of respite and time out is recognised. Lots to do in the evenings and at weekends, some activities educational, others social, varying from outdoors and messy to indoors and IT-based; swimming and cinema trips are especially popular.

Bed-times are staggered according to age and they are up at 7.45am for a cooked breakfast, served, like all other meals, in the school's dining room. Late-risers who do not make it for the cooked breakfast can grab tea and toast in the boarders' kitchens if need be.

Background and atmosphere: Situated in the Vale of York between the Yorkshire moors and the Dales National Park, Breckenbrough is a non-profit making residential special needs school, established in 1934 and on its present site since 1958. It is a Quaker Foundation school, the only one of its kind in the UK, and accordingly has an ethos of 'bringing out the best in everyone' alongside conflict resolution. This has proved to be highly successful and, as such, Breckenbrough has gained a reputation for its approach to working with its pupils – where every child matters. The academic provision is constantly evolving, changing and developing alongside the needs and aspirations of its pupils, yet the culture is a well-established entity, guarded, protected and valued by all. 'It's who we are,' they say, and they know exactly what they mean by that.

Assembly takes place each Friday in the very grand-sounding Great Hall complete with imposing staircase and wood-panelling. Formerly a grand private home, the main building is impressive, additional outbuildings and add-ons less so, but the space is well-used and the boys amble around from building to building, sometimes dodging the rain, but happily and safely. Friendships cross age ranges, probably much more than in mainstream schools, and there is plenty of wit, charm and intellect in evidence here, all of which is welcomed and valued.

Pastoral care, well-being and discipline: It's a nurturing environment, and 'trust, time, space and listening' is the mantra. Plenty of structure in place to reduce the likelihood of difficulties and conflicts, with school rules applied flexibly and sensitively. Punishment is rare; constructive resolutions are the way forward here – it takes more time but is infinitely preferable and the benefits are obvious. Not a soft option, but looking beyond the behaviour brings acceptance and allows the pupils to 'be', and a culture of honesty, transparency and trust enable staff and pupils to work through a situation and move towards restorative justice. It's a formula that works. Learning to become self-regulating and autonomous, recognising the importance of personal safety are useful tools here in moving forward. Parents talk about their children being 'fundamentally the same, yet profoundly changed' by their experiences at the school. 'Thank you for getting my son back for me,' said one parent.

Staff work hard to identify the causes and triggers of pupils' anxieties. Once the triggers are identified they support pupils to control and reduce their fears, and be more confident in increasingly wider social scenarios. Home/school communication is both good and regular, and essential to providing the wider support so that pupils move between the two as easily and comfortably as possible. It's all about building on the good whilst celebrating individuality and allowing the boys to enjoy whatever they are good at, growing into confident individuals who understand themselves and the world around them.

Therapy and staffing: Full-time registered psychologist on site and access to speech and language, occupational, music and creative arts therapists as necessary.

Pupils and parents: Ordinary people are eager to tell you their extraordinary stories; this is a school that touches hearts and minds and stays with students long after they have moved on. Many bring the baggage of false starts in mainstream education, and parents and pupils alike are often nervous and disillusioned on arrival. Specialised knowledge and understanding of autism – invariably limited in even the most well-intentioned of mainstream schools – makes all the difference to the lives of the boys and their families lucky enough to stumble upon this North Yorkshire outpost.

Essentially, the school is looking for a boy who is willing and able to 'buy-in and work with them' and who has, not far below the surface, 'a genuine desire to be successful and make a happier life for himself'.

Pupils are interested and interesting – they sweep away the cobwebs of social convention, happily asking you who you are, and why you are there, none of which of course is unreasonable; it's their school. After often poor and worrying experiences elsewhere, it is with a sense of relief all round that they settle in so well and relatively quickly and easily, finally able to drop the guard that they didn't even know they been carrying. The sense of reciprocity, reason and compromise that underpins relationships here is vital to its success in helping pupils find what they need to make the leap socially and academically.

Of course sometimes things do go awry; just when they think they have worked out all the complexities and contradictions, a small change or something unfamiliar can send them spinning back into unfair air space. But it's talked through, calmly, reasonably, for as long as it takes, with staff retaining a reassuring, dignified presence by their side.

Parents and pupils talk about 'Breck', as it is affectionately known, with such fondness and pride. One mother talked to us about her son being 'lost' before arriving here – 'I will be forever grateful, long may it flourish,' she added.

Entrance: All referred by their LA because mainstream couldn't or wouldn't cope. Inevitably, given current systems in place, it involves hurdling a long line-up of bureaucratic walls. It's not easy and isn't a question of paying fees – no parent does that – but 'you do have to work hard and stick to your guns with cash-strapped local authorities,' said the voice of experience.

Pupils span the range of autistic spectrum disorders, Asperger's, behavioural, emotional and social difficulties, specific and multiple learning difficulties, ADD, pathological demand avoidance, attachment disorders, conduct disorders and more besides.

Exit: On leaving, the pupils progress on to university, further education or work, and the support goes on with 'Beyond Breckenbrough' tracking and supporting pupils until the age of 25, and an 'Aftercare' charity available to all for as long as they need it. Transitional planning is excellent. It can be tough to leave Breck and the level of support it provides, but the school ensures that pupils are ready and able to take the next step, wherever that may be, a number later going on to have successful careers of their own choosing.

Money matters: Each boy's EHC plan shows what support he needs. Fees are paid by LEAs.

Remarks: 'More than a school' is the tag line of this school where 80 years of wisdom and radical experiment continue to change the lives of boys on a daily basis. In the words of a visiting Guardian journalist: 'A trail bike putters into life on a raw North Yorkshire morning, then the engine roars and a teenager wobbles off down a mud track, manages a corner and settles in to control. "There's a lad who started off this morning with attention deficit hyperactivity disorder," says a member of staff who formerly raced in the Isle of Man TT, "but he hasn't got it now, and he won't have for the next 20 minutes.." '

'Breckenbrough is an amazing place,' say parents. 'On our first visit we knew it was the right place for our son'. Staff support both parents and pupils, which is, they say, 'a life-saver', and they mean it. Transformational stories abound here – 'our son has been transformed into a very humorous and handsome young man, who has grown in confidence, is engaged in learning and willing to try new ideas, new foods, visit new places, take on new experiences and actually have fun and start living. It is', they say, 'truly the most special place in Yorkshire'.

Bredon School

Pull Court, Bushley, Tewkesbury, Gloucestershire GL20 6AH

Pupils: 249 (185 boys, 64 girls; 97 boarders) • Ages: 7–18 (boarding from 9) • Sixth form: 80

Fees: Day £9,657 – £18,435; Boarding £19,896 – £28,890 pa

Tel: 01684 293156
Email: enquiries@bredonschool.co.uk
Website: www.bredonschool.org

Principal: Since 2013, David Ward. Previous headships at St Felix School in Suffolk and Skegness Grammar. Wanted to be a head from the age of 13, and here has found his perfect posting. He talks with feeling about the child who struggles with the concept of a sentence, and plotting out an essay; who cannot scribble down the homework as the bell rings, so 'unless you're pretty good at remembering you're stuffed'. He's been there, because he is dyslexic.

His headship has brought a very welcome return to the school's original purpose – prior to his arrival it had moved to a more academic intake. 'I wanted to go back, to the pupil who is slightly below CE, the square peg, and make a hole that peg would fit. I want Bredon to stand out,' principal says.

Has he got it right? Well the school has grown under his watch from 178 to 250 pupils, with boarding numbers up to 100. 'It will probably stay at that,' Ward says.

He's a former rugby international, a qualified canoeing coach, and weekends see him cycling with his equally sporty wife (a physiotherapist) and two daughters when they are home from university.

A warm relationship with pupils is evident – lots of cheerful 'hello sir's called out as we tour the school. Stood his place in the queue and cleared the table behind us when we had (a very decent) school lunch.

Academic matters: Bredon stands out for its support for children who need additional learning help, and so it attracts above average numbers of pupils with special educational needs. However it also caters for mainstream pupils, and more than half of the pupils take some, and up to eight, GCSEs. The more able children are often siblings of children who have been placed here for the additional support, or from families eschewing the exam factories in favour of a more rounded and outdoorsy education.

Children can be admitted with IQs in the lower average range (80+, where 100 is average), and one-third will take only vocational or Asdan (life skills and work skills) courses. The school provides specialist help for difficulties such as dyslexia, dyspraxia, dyscalculia, speech and language difficulties, and milder (high functioning) autism.

In 2016, nearly 60 per cent of students taking GCSE qualifications achieved grades A*-C in five subjects or more.

Sixth formers can choose from 29 A level courses (art and photography are popular), BTecs (including business studies, catering and engineering options), vocational options, and they can do an AS level over two years. There is also an on site Cisco Academy. Run in partnership with technology giant Cisco Systems, this offers students who enjoy programming and taking apart computers the training for technical jobs, and qualifications for higher education courses in engineering and computer science. Pupils can compete for an annual 20 places on a Cisco apprenticeship – one ex-pupil won a place, and is now working in Japan. In a classroom which will have teenage techies salivating, the pupils were studying cabling and safety issues around static electricity. A batch of computer cases stood ready for pupils to learn to build their own computer. Pupils can opt to do IT Essentials level 2 in year 9 and 10, while year 12 and 13 do a Cisco Certified Network Association course.

Sixth formers can do day release courses at college, and all except the A level students do some work experience. Failing GCSE English or maths is not a barrier to sixth form. 'Some may be repeating GCSE English and maths two or three times; it doesn't stop them going into the sixth form and retaking them while doing something else as well,' says the principal.

Throughout the school Bredon's ethos is 'making the glove fit the hand,' as Ward describes it. Self-esteem has often taken a battering before children arrive here, but is buffed up by the school's policy of finding the subjects that will enable them to shine. 'We see SEN as a gift not a hindrance, dyslexics are very creative, often gifted in 3D, and in communication,' Ward says. Much work goes into selecting the right courses at the right level – the school aims to ensure that children are only entered for exams which they will pass, and students who find exams in themselves overwhelmingly stressful will be steered towards courses graded by continual assessment instead. 'The curriculum is very cleverly altered to take account of the children's challenges, and the whole school celebrates difference and encourages the children to play to their strengths,' one parent said.

The school is gradually closing down the pre-prep department. September 2017 will see the last year 3 intake, and from September 2018 it will be entry from year 4 only. Currently the senior school starts in year 7, but from September 2017 years 7 and 8 will form part of the lower school.

The junior school is currently small, with just under 40 pupils. It is set in cosy wooden huts, with a jumble of scooters and pedal cars parked outside. Junior pupils spend two hours per week in the forest school, learning to build shelters, making hot chocolate over camp fires, weaving, and studying natural habitats.

There is no homework before year 9, which has some parents hanging out the flags. The main language is Spanish, but others such as German, Italian and Dutch are offered through personal tuition (often to overseas students where these are their native tongue).

Ward likes to employ teachers who have been in industry, and we met ex-industry professionals running catering, engineering and photography.

Pupils in a catering lesson were perfecting stir fries for a BTec assessment, spurred on by a recent demo from a Malaysian chef who cooked for the British Olympic team. Pheasant casseroles were bubbling in the oven, which a previous group had prepared to tie-in with their English studies of the book Danny

B

the Champion of the World. Boarders come to the kitchens for evening sessions in basic cookery and dinner party menus.

DT begins from year 4 in a dedicated engineering building – younger pupils were making wooden trains and tealight holders, while year 9s were hotforming and spray painting. Pupils can take a BTec level 2 option which is equivalent to a GCSE in key stage 4.

Key stage 4 pupils are also offered agricultural options including animal and crop husbandry, horticulture, livestock production and animal welfare, and workshop-based skills such as welding, and vehicle and machinery maintenance. Pupils prepare the animals to show at major agricultural events.

Games, options, the arts: Great for the animal lover – the school is set on a full working farm, with livestock including Black Face and Badger Face sheep, Saddleback pigs (including three tiny piglets on our visit), 20 turkeys (seasonal!), rabbits called Lady Gaga, Caramel and Snuggles, and three cats. Pupils up to year 9 have timetabled sessions where they muck out and feed the animals, undertake maintenance tasks, and plant and weed produce.

The school has a purpose-built shooting ground, and its clay pigeon team has won the Schools Challenge competition three years in succession. One former pupil is now an Olympic competitor in the sport.

There's also air rifle shooting, marathon canoeing, yoga clubs, dancing clubs, a climbing wall and all the usual team sports. It's not compulsory to do team games, which will be music to some dyspraxic ears, but we saw enthusiastic football games going on during lunch break. One parent warned that sport is less competitive and structured than the norm in other schools, which can be frustrating for very sporty children.

There's lots of mucky outdoor fun in the 85 acre grounds: 'the main uniform requirement is an overall and wellies,' principal says. After-school activities include swimming, cookery, computing, chess and film club.

Boarding: Children can board from 9 years up, and there's a choice of full, weekly and flexi-boarding. Boarders can stay for exeat weekends, but the school closes completely for end of half-term breaks.

Junior boarding is on two landings in Pull Court. Younger children share a room with 4-6 beds, while years 8 and 9 have two-bedded rooms. In a historic house, they are limited by how much modernising they can do, but the house's grand proportions make for spacious rooms.

The older children are in separate boarding houses, and have been the first to benefit from a £150,000 refurbishment of boarding facilities. Sixth formers have single rooms with shared bathrooms, and after further refurbishment is completed, all pupils from year 10 upwards will have single rooms.

Evening activities include Minecraft, Warhammer, rugby, horse riding, badminton and archery. Weekends bring a range of optional trips to the cinema, ice skating, paintballing, and so on.

Background and atmosphere: The school was founded in 1962 by Lt Col Tony Sharp OBE, whose motto 'The journey is as important as the destination' is embraced by the current principal.

It's not unusual for parents to first consider it for a child who is experiencing difficulties, but then decide its style will suit all of their children. One parent said: 'For three active boys we loved the outdoor opportunities and hands-on learning. Bredon is a school that children want to go to, they come home tired, muddy and happy. This way of teaching opens a child's mind, it encourages them to think for themselves and problem solve.'

Another commented: 'I think prospective parents shouldn't just see Bredon as a school for children with additional needs. The benefits of an active education suit so many children. Many parents choose a school by results, often overlooking where each individual child has come from. At Bredon every success is celebrated. A grade D for one child is as incredible as an A* for another. The standard of education is excellent and there for all levels of ability.'

Arrival is impressive – it takes several minutes to drive through the grounds, past grazing sheep, to reach the main school building, the glorious Pull Court 16th century mansion in Cotswold Stone. Inside there's wood panelling and grand fireplaces aplenty. Outside, ha-has and fountains, giant chessboards, and a lit walkway, where each lamp bears a plaque in remembrance of people who once worked in the great house and died in action in the Second World War.

It's not all grandeur – the walls remain of the old walled garden, but it now encompasses a pitch for hockey and basketball. Some of the teaching blocks are in Portakabins. But even inside Pull Court it's warm and relaxed, the kind of atmosphere to make you want to curl up on a sofa with a book.

There's a huge cabinet of silverware in the entrance hall, but true to form, the trophies recognise all kind of talents, including farmer of the year, and gardener of the year. There's an old boys association, and former pupils are invited back to 'fleece their knowledge' and inspire the children. Fridays bring Wainwright lectures – where a programme of speakers come in to tell the children what it is like to be a lawyer or farm machinist, how to run a bank account or sort out your tax affairs.

The school has recently changed ownership to the Cavendish Group, which the principal says has put it on a firm financial footing, and brought investment into the boarding facilities and departments.

We heard some grumbles about communication with the school – 'haphazard' and 'sporadic', some parents felt.

Pastoral care, well-being and discipline: 'It's all about pastoral care. If you get that right, the child feels engaged and valued, will focus on the things they are good at, and will try harder with support,' Ward says emphatically.

'My youngest son left his first school saying that dyslexia ruined his life, now he hardly ever need notice it, he tells me about all of the great dyslexics and how he will one day be great and probably a millionaire,' confirmed one parent.

As soon as children join the school, staff produce a profile and a passport for them, so each member of the teaching staff knows exactly what support they need. Children who struggle with sensory overload are given a card which they can show if they feel they are going to explode – this allows them to leave a lesson for a 10 minute breather. The school has a mindfulness officer, who takes assemblies of silent reflection.

One parent, who moved her son here after he was bullied at another school, said: 'My son is like a changed child – he is happy, relaxed, engaged; beginning to make friends and is now making progress in lessons. Bredon School has completely transformed my child.'

There's much encouragement to communicate with each other. Pupils hand in mobiles on arrival and don't get them back until they leave at the end of the day. Ward changed tables in the dining room to round ones, 'so children have to look everyone in the eye'. Lots of pupil committees – on food, on boarding, a prefects' group – where children can voice opinions and air any disgruntlement.

Around 80 students have speech and language therapy, mainly around the social use of language. Sessions are held in a cosy cabin in the grounds, like a Santa's grotto in winter, and there is a balcony out the front with tables and chairs for summer sessions. The therapy can be quite inventive. One boy wouldn't speak, so the school brought in a magician to teach him tricks. The boy now communicates as he performs his tricks.

The speech and language provision is 'incredible,' according to one parent, who reported that therapy is integrated into all lessons. Another said: 'They are a very professional, committed part of the school team working largely on improving communication and relationship skills, but also providing a calm influence and environment that can be accessed during break times and lunch hours if required by the students.'

We also heard good reports about counselling offered – 'very effective', said one parent.

Out-of-class learning support is delivered in the Access Centre either individually or in small groups. All staff in the school have British Dyslexia Association qualifications, and all teach in the SEN framework. 'They are the first teachers in the eight years he has been at school who really understand him; they know what causes him distress and distracts his learning,' one parent said.

Pupils and parents: Girls are outnumbered around two-to-one, and we saw some classes with only the odd girl in them. However there is much more mixing between age groups than in many schools, so it may not be a big issue if your daughter likes to hang out with other girls.

Children travel quite some distance for the unique provision here – a fleet of 13 minibuses fan out to bring day children from cities including Birmingham, Bristol and Bromsgrove. UK boarders from further afield are chaperoned on the train home. A number of children are from Forces families. International pupils make up around seven per cent of the school population, and come from China and Europe (Italy, Holland and Belgium). The school is 45 minutes from Birmingham airport. Principal travels out to China every 18 months to see Chinese parents in their own home, and protects them from some unscrupulous agents by insisting he will only accept children when the agent comes to see him in person.

Around two-thirds of the pupils have an EHC (Education, Health and Care) plan and are funded by a total of 29 local authorities. These children typically have conditions such as specific learning difficulties, slow processing, and mild autism, and fall in a wide IQ range of 80-120 (100 is average).

Entrance: There is no entry exam – the first step is to send in your child's school reports and professional assessments (if applicable). If the school feels it is suitable for your child, you will be invited for an interview, followed by a guest stay of three days for a day pupil, or a week for a boarder. During this time the school will undertake its own assessments, and monitor how well the child is interacting with the other children.

Children will only be turned away when it is felt they will have difficulty in accessing the curriculum, or have behaviours which are outside the school's expertise.

Children are able to join all through the year, and at any stage of the school – there tends to be a swell in numbers at the point when it is established that CE will not be the best route for a child.

There are open days every month, attended by current parents who you can quiz.

Exit: The majority of pupils go on to further education colleges, to take courses such as engineering, catering and farming, or into work. Around 15 per cent go to university, with destinations including Loughborough, Westminster, Southampton, Bournemouth and Plymouth.

Money matters: Fees range from £9,657 for key stage 2 day places, to £28,890 for upper school boarding. Withdrawal lessons, therapy, dedicated TA support, and EAL courses are charged as extras. Discounts for siblings and Forces families. Children with an EHCP can seek local authority funding for a place.

Remarks: We reckon you could fill a Bredon in every county with those children who don't sit easily in mainstream or special schools. And that means not just the children with learning difficulties; but also the bullied, the timid, the anxious; and the hale and hearty who learn better with tools in hand and mud on feet.

Unfortunately it's a real one-off, which might mean a house move or considering boarding (but although scarily remote on the map, there are buses to big towns). Parents rave about the support but its all-ability welcome means you should also expect quirkiness among the classmates. And the non-competitive, stress-reducing atmosphere means it ain't the place if rugby matches against big name school A teams is top of your list. Not everyone's cup of tea, but it has a deliriously happy following.

Bruern Abbey School

Chesterton House, Chesterton, Bicester, Oxfordshire OX26 1UY

Pupils: 138; 90 full, 20 flexi boarders • Ages: 7–13

Fees: Day £22,962; Boarding £27,672 pa

Tel: 01869 242448
Email: secretary@bruernabbey.org
Website: www.bruernabbey.org

Headmaster: Since 2011, Mr John Floyd MA PGCE (30s). Born in London, grew up in The Ivory Coast, Holland and New York. Eucated at Cothill and Radley, read geography at Edinburgh University. Previously deputy head of Westminster Cathedral Choir School; prior to that, as a graduate of the Teach First programme, he spent an illuminating three years at Crown Woods – an inner London comp. Married to Henrietta, they have two young sons. He enjoys fly-fishing and food – especially 'proper cooking' which he learned during a gap year in the South of France. Still occasionally runs 'silly distances', the length of Hadrian's Wall just one of many.

A large, ultra-ordered, exceptionally tidy desk dominates one corner of his study, a touch of the OCDs we mused but the reality is a dyslexic head who practises many of the coping strategies he advocates to his charges. A quick glance at the ceiling reveals not the anticipated intricate, ornate plasterwork but a coffee-coloured, water-marked, paint-peeling to-do list – courtesy of a burst pipe. As fits with the school philosophy of boys' needs first, they have sparkly new facilities for ablutions while the head makes do. Young, smartly dressed, well-spoken with a distinctive crop of ginger hair, Mr Floyd has injected a new sense of purpose and order to Bruern. All speak of his warmth, light touch and finely tuned sense of humour. He has the knack of the one-liner – wit, rather than sarcasm and jokes. Staff praise his wonderful organisational skills, ambitious ideas, distinct strategy and purpose. They speak of the seamless transition from old head to new. Head says, 'It was meant to be a year but after a term of Cameron-Clegg co-habiting and polite "after-yous" I was trusted to steer a new course'. Admits it has been more manoeuvring by degrees than wholesale changes but that's very much a nod to the prized work of his 'amazing' mentor. Parents impressed, 'He's sensible, good fun; he gets it, he gets them.'

Entrance: Though intake starts at 7, most join at 9 or 10 after being let down by educational system elsewhere. Majority weekly board, some flexi, handful of day boys. All have specific learning difficulties, dyslexia, dyscalculia and/or dyspraxia, a sprinkling also have additional needs eg Asperger's and ADHD (medicine okay). Parents must provide recent educational psychologist's report. Typically looking for IQ of 110+, but flexes with talent in music, art and sport welcomed. Young hopefuls invited to spend a day and a night at school for informal interview and assessment

Exit: All pass common entrance to their guided first choice senior schools. Charterhouse and St Edward's most popular destinations in 2016, then Stowe, Bloxham, Marlborough and Milton Abbey. Three scholarships and one music award in 2016. 'We measure success by the outcome of their first senior year – are they settled and happy?' Parents speak of the CE zone, 'They achieve exponentially. It's really impressive. The children stay at weekends and eat, sleep, breathe CE – revision, past-papers, exam conditions – so they are wholly in the zone.'

Remarks: Many youngsters here have typically suffered a terrible crisis of confidence and most are unable to access or assimilate a conventionally delivered curriculum. Almost half the timetable is dedicated to English and maths, French a must (except in very exceptional circumstances). Withdrawal is limited to the essential but class sizes are kept at 10 or under, with individual attention as a given. 'Boys don't come here to have learning support but to be in a class with others and a teacher who understands their difficulties,' says head. All juniors have one group lesson per week with the wonderfully experienced SENCo. The session determines strengths and foibles; what makes the children tick and what causes them to kick: 'When I write their reports or speak to the ed psych, I truly understand each child.' Not that staff wait to put in place whatever is required: 'My child has needs beyond his dyslexia and they quickly implemented what he needed; no waiting, no protracted multi-agency discussions'.

Subjects, including Latin, are taught separately but classroom thinking is joined-up, with cross-curricular themes whenever opportunity affords. In an RE lesson children studied a timeline, estimating when the Old Testament was written by examining evidence and reaching supported conclusions. We dropped in on a French dictation where, in an attempt to understand and improve along the way, words were analysed and sounds explained as the pupils worked. It's a long day and expectations are high but lessons are fun and much is done to build confidence and success. 'My son comes home animatedly recounting the funny things, bits of naughtiness, and hilarity of the day. He enjoys every lesson but they do work hard.' Most boys are quirky, go off-piste, do the unexpected. 'My child has started writing a book. His spelling is atrocious but his imagination unbounded, thanks to inspirational teaching and an emphasis on giving the boys an interest in learning rather than just unquestionably absorbing it.' Computers everywhere. All learn to touch-type, the laptop a lifeline, voice recognition technology and dyslexia friendly software all in evidence.

A number of teachers are dyslexic and so get what the boys don't get. 'Teachers genuinely really, really care about us and make learning fun and enjoyable,' say boys. Each has an individual learning plan tailored to his specific strengths and weaknesses with speech, language and occupational therapists on hand when needed. Parents gush with enthusiasm: 'Staff help the boys understand their difficulties, develop coping mechanisms, haul them through CE. Their approach is extraordinary; it is a shame all my (non-dyslexic) children couldn't go there.' Another added, 'We keep waiting for the bubble to burst but it gets better. We missed the boat for our first son, discovered Bruern for our second and the instant our third showed signs of struggling we catapulted him in.' Former parents include a rock star, ex-cabinet minister and best-selling novelist; current crop includes actresses and directors. But plenty of 'ordinary' boys too. Parents say, 'It's a hard-core community, no embarrassment, no shame. Typically others have experienced the same or worse so if they find a way to do something they will share that with you, so you don't undergo the same agony.'

Invariably parents stumble into Bruern, battle-weary and beleaguered. 'My child was in a trench, he crawled into Bruern. They didn't just pull him out, they winched him up and propelled him to heights we never thought possible.' Most tell of at least a few wobbles along the way. Years of embedded frustration won't disappear overnight but there are plenty of safety nets and, for most, it doesn't take long for the Bruern panacea to work its magic. One or two parental grumbles about overzealous boys but equally, many are shy or reserved. Said one parent, 'Some have serious learning difficulties, some can be disruptive but so can children everywhere. My child is measured but it's good for him to see different colours of intelligence and temperament. The mix reflects society, it helps them develop tolerance, understanding and awareness of others and their strengths and difficulties and makes them realise you can't just write someone off.'

There's a huge, collective sense of responsibility for pastoral care. Immediacy is the name of the game so, as well as end of term reports, expect frequent calls or emails. Parents speak of excellent and frank home-school communication. 'Staff are wonderfully blunt, if your child needs a projectile near his derrière they'll make that pellucid,' said one, another added, 'When boys are naughty, mucking around, they get punished – detentions usually but it's not a big deal in grand scheme of things.' Children are continually praised and rewarded for their efforts, though the head put a stop to the constant dishing out of sweet treats, 'very Pavlov's dogs,' and is now trialling different reward systems.

Bruern is steeped in faded grandeur – peeling, lived in, respected. It may be full of scuffs and scruffs but it smells good and exudes a generous warmth of spirit and a quirky, homely feel. That said, a lick of paint here and there would do wonders. Takes its name from a Cistercian monastery, the current yellow stone building dates from the late 19th century with recent sympathetic additions. This grand house set in 23 acres of grounds and woodland tranquillity may look like a traditional country prep but its dual mission of helping boys overcome learning problems and prepare them for CE to major English and Scottish public schools, makes the place unique. Dorms are large, airy, clean and tidy but need smartening – frayed carpet regrettably draws the eye (though we're told smartening is imminent). Bathrooms newly kitted out, but even we couldn't feign enthusiasm for shiny urinals.

Being relatively young by English school standards Bruern is not blessed with a huge endowment fund, but does benefit from loyal parents who work hard to fundraise, not for fripperies but for fixtures as well as fittings. It's not so much about thrift but spending wisely and keeping fees affordable. Most school cash is ploughed into teaching and learning needs; however, thanks in part to parents, there are signs of considered investment. We spied a good-sized pool with retractable roof and chanced on the wonderful new DT log-cabin where boys beavered, smoothing away the last imperfections of their creations, on multi-purpose work-benches. Art, now in own dedicated studio, provokes mixed responses – some parents enamoured, others give it a 'could do better'. Our investigations suggest art has been something of a Cinderella subject but recent success in local art competition is set to change that. Majority of boys play at least one instrument and many sing in the chapel choir. Sport is important and abundant with regular fixtures – cricket, football, rugby – for all (recent sports tour to India). No indoor gym or Astroturf so they make full use of local countryside with riding, shooting, polo, archery, golf (nearby course) and cross-country. Twenty boys did a 300km charity bike ride to France. Food is a major part of school life (all faiths, intolerances and allergies catered for). Al-fresco dining on dry days plus weekly, revered, formal candlelit suppers to which parents are invited. The Thursday session begins with a spell in chapel followed by mirth, mayhem and manners as eloquent boys host their appreciative guests.

Uniform of yellow polo top and pale brown shorts decorated with generous helpings of mud and pud is not the most fetching we've seen but it does mean these giant buttercups can be spotted hiding in the woods, climbing trees, jumping the stream. The colour, chosen for its calming cheerfulness, flatters few, yet somehow suits its atypical charges and their boys' own world. Bruern is wholesome, hearty, heartening, but could be tricky for the risk-averse or precious (parent or child). 'We do risk assessments, boys climb trees, we stress they shouldn't climb beyond a certain height but they do. They take risks, sometimes they fall out but that's life.' Parents add, 'Children don't need nannying, they need to fuel their imagination, feed their spirit of adventure, take risks, know it's okay to get things wrong, learn from their mistakes. They need space, to run about, ride bikes and to play; they get to do all of that and more too, but they also get unfaltering support.'

The typical Bruern boy is well-spoken, polite, articulate, amusing and enthusiastic. Said one parent, 'My child cried on his first day but has smiled ever since.' A truly unique school; youngsters devour copious helpings of carefully prepared academia, served with generous dustings of laughter, a sprinkle of boyish boisterousness and the odd dash of naughtiness. Presents boys with an exceptional opportunity to understand and tackle their difficulties and make prodigious progress.

Calder House School

8

Thickwood Lane, Colerne, Chippenham, Wiltshire SN14 8BN

Pupils: 44 (31 boys, 13 girls) • Ages: 5–12

Fees: £16,725 pa

Tel: 01225 743566
Email: enquiries@calderhouseschool.co.uk
Website: www.calderhouseschool.co.uk

Headmistress: Since September 2015, Mrs Karen Parsons, previously deputy head of the Royal High Junior School, Bath, where she was also head of maths. She was educated at Devonport High School for Girls and Oxford, where she read maths with computing, and pursued her passion for amateur dramatics and all things musical. These days she relaxes by singing with the Wiltshire Wailers and enjoys her book club, playing the piano, swimming, walking in the stunning Somerset countryside where she lives, and watercolour painting. She is married to Chris, a former captain in the Royal Navy. They have three grown-up sons.

Entrance: A day-long assessment which includes cognitive and learning tests, as well as maths and literacy, carried out by director of studies and specialist teaching staff; 'We will only take children we can make a difference to'. The day also involves the child shadowing another, as a taster of what's to come. Takes up to 48 children with specific learning difficulties: dyslexia, dyspraxia, dyscalculia and speech and language disorder; some have statements/EHC plans. The aim is to be a temporary, remedial measure, for an average of two years, before the child can join mainstream education. Parents pay for the assessment, but this is deducted from the fees, if a place is offered (refunded, if not). Children arrive from a 25 mile radius, encompassing Gloucestershire, Swindon, Wiltshire and Bath; most are privately funded, some fully or partly LA funded.

Exit: Almost all children move back into mainstream education and the head cultivates links with local schools: Warminster, Sheldon, Our Lady's Abingdon, Clayesmore, Hayesfield, Beechen Cliff, King Edward's Bath, Monkton, Prior Park and Hardenhuish are popular choices. Many leave after year 6, though a year 7 curriculum is possible. One parent said of her son, 'I don't feel he could be any better prepared as he takes his next steps into secondary education'; another wished the school would extend to secondary level.

Remarks: Set deep in Wodehouse country, in the charming village of Colerne (you half expect there to be livestock on the village green), the school is a converted coach house with paddock for playground. The head's study is a wooden framed outhouse, while the library retains the original ironwork from the horse boxes and stable boy's quarters. Happy children skip in and out of the stable doors to the classrooms and play in a huge tithe barn, complete with fort and ping pong table. The surrounding fields are homes to badgers' sets and herons.

Founded in 1995 by Sandra and Colin Agombar, after success setting up the sister school in Battersea (The Dominie). Their experience as parents of Edward, who had specific learning difficulties as a child, inspired them (Edward now works at the school as a learning assistant). The family still live on the estate and are hands-on at the school; loved by the children, 'Mrs Ag is the best thing', almost as much as their dog, 'Freddie comes in the school photo and once a year we get cake on his birthday'. Calder House has built on its success, but doesn't plan to expand in numbers, 'I don't want to turn it into another failing prep school,' and the intimacy was repeatedly praised by parents. 'The whole ethos and size of the school meets my daughter's needs very well'; 'The day is designed round each individual child, that's what makes it so special'.

There's no mistaking the emphasis of the school, to promote the core skills: numeracy, literacy and spelling. Classes are small (maximum eight) with an SEN qualified teacher and assistant to each class. The groups shrink to smaller numbers still (two or three) for sub-skills. These are the identified target skills for each individual, including speech and language, visual and auditory memory development, gross and fine motor and co-ordination skills. Each child has a bespoke timetable fitted to his or her needs, colour coded to match the flooring of the different classrooms. Therapies (SLT, OT and physio) are inclusive, even one-to-one sessions, so no hidden costs, and these take place in intimate classrooms. Core skills tap into the individual learning style for each child, whether kinaesthetic or through auditory or visual channels. A poster in the dyslexia suite asks, 'Do you speak Monster?' and addresses non-word repetition skills; fine motor difficulties are tackled with the Teodorescu handwriting course; a favourite English teacher with, according to one boy, 'a balance of talking and doing things', was passing round a pot of basil to emphasise the multi-sensory approach to working. Elsewhere, in a numeracy lesson, we witnessed interactive software for visual memory difficulties. Teaching doesn't come more specialist than this.

Books, not gadgets, are the cool accessory for these children and no chance is missed to promote a love of reading. 'Reading is the most important thing for our kids.' The bursar, a published children's author, judges a book review competition each month. The library stocks material in paper and electronic forms for Kindles (a great way for a self-conscious child to disguise reading level from peers) and visits from the local mobile library deliver topic-based texts. A lonely hearts club pin board in the corner of the library lets children post suggested titles for friends or teachers, and a 'book in a bag' scheme enables a child to pass on a recommendation for a friend. Even the display cupboard for cups and trophies features a set of precious books, Roald Dahl stories given by his widow. And it works like magic. The school council we observed, saw 10 children of varying ages spontaneously break into a lively book group discussion.

Other subjects are addressed after lunch, in a thematic way, and in mixed ability groups. When we visited, art and English were combined in some attractive 3D models of Michael Morpurgo's book Kensuke's Kingdom. There's less time for these subjects than at a mainstream school, so geography, science, history, sports and Latin are given fleeting slots in the busy timetable. There are no science or DT labs and a smallish IT suite. Art and music were less visible than at many other schools; 'they try to sneak it in with the other disciplines,' said a mum (in fact, the children had to alert us to being in the art room). 'We can't have peripatetic (music) as the timetable is so tight,' laments school. However, with a view to confidence boosting, English Speaking Board exams are taken with great success. '(My daughter) arrived a very troubled, under-confident girl and left a strong young woman sure of her talents', said one dad. Parents described the teaching as outstanding – 'The teachers are so patient, they will take the time to explain' – and it obviously bears fruit: 'My daughter has done two academic year's worth of work in one,' bragged one mum.

On sports day, traditional sack races and spacehopper tag mix with team sports. There is both a field and hard court for five-a-side football; tag rugby; cricket, rounders and pop (mixed) lacrosse. The 30 acre grassy estate is heaven for cross-country runners and an ex-world champion offers kayaking on the Avon at nearby Chippenham. A swimming class five or six times a term makes use of the local army pool. Competitive sports matches are played both between houses and against neighbouring schools, though, a mum confided, it is not always the A team that visits. 'Every child gets to represent Calder House. The football kids feel 10 feet tall when they put the vest on'. One child regretted that one hour of sport a week was not enough. Nonetheless, there is no doubting that this is an outdoorsy paradise for these youngsters. For the budding farmer there are vegetable beds with radishes, potatoes and a herb plot, while in the founders' garden a hen coop allows the children a chance to watch eggs hatching in the spring. It is no wonder that the school has won gold in the eco-schools awards. Drama and music were less visible; there is an annual Christmas and summer production, which gives each child a speaking role, and the Wooster drama cup to aim for. A 'Celebration' assembly each week practises speaking and listening, as well as a termly assembly for each class to perform to parents and grandparents. As a parent of one boy boasted, 'His confidence has improved; it's essential; it affects your whole life. They've empowered him to have a go at things'.

Lunchtime activities include Lego, knitting, art, drumming, sports and gardening. There are no after-school clubs, 'but it is such an intensive day, he wouldn't be up to it,' sighed one parent. Lunch is eaten in the barn, on warm days, round a huge picnic table, listening to instalments of a chapter book. No hot lunch facilities – sadly missed by one child and a few parents. Imaginative school trips to local farms and National Trust sites or to the panto in Bath, and further afield to the Imperial War and Science Museums in London.

Children in their royal blue, white and grey uniforms (no school tie to avoid singling out dyspraxics) are chatty and curious, bursting to answer questions in lessons, yet with traditional hands-up and separate desks. The balance of enthusiasm and discipline is exemplary, maintained by the promise of Golden Time. There are merit points for academic success, and house points for other achievements, culminating in a hard-won house cup. 'They can really respond to it,' said a mum, 'because they know where they are'. Parents reported no signs of bullying, and rule-breaking is dealt with fairly: 'They are very quiet, very firm and once it's over and been dealt with, then they move on'. Parents were happy with communication with teaching staff via homework diary or email to office staff; 'They respond straight away'. All the teachers are available at termly parents' evenings, and most of them informally in the car park at the end of the day. The school obviously makes a big effort to foster good relations with staff and children. 'They are very good at learning how the children interact,' said one mum, and it succeeds; 'Going home is the worst thing,' moaned one boy. 'I wish it was a boarding school'. Parents didn't mind the lack of PTA and were described as supportive and 'very proactive', independently holding monthly coffee mornings, car sharing and meeting up in the holidays. 'It's a real community. Waiting to pick up your children, you all know you are there because they need help. You don't feel your child is a bit different'. Previous pupils include an ice-hockey champion and a parliamentary candidate for Bath.

The school uses the emblem of a rescued starfish to stress the preciousness of each individual. With high quality teaching, attention to detail in tailor-made timetables and careful social mixing, the school makes stars out of underachievers. The rate of progress in the core skills is remarkable; only niggles were the lack of time for a wider curriculum. As one parent put it, Calder House is 'The perfect blueprint; every LA should have one'.

Cambian Wing College

126 Richmond Park Road, Bournemouth BH8 8TH

Pupils: 45 (36 boys, 9 girls); 29 boarders • Ages: 16–25

Fees: Usually funded by local authorities

Tel: 01202 635630
Website: www.cambiangroup.com

Principal: Since 2015 Kim Welsh, who was previously deputy head for five years. Was originally in banking, but transferred to teaching to be more compatible with family life. Prior to joining Wing she worked as a SENCo at a local school, and as a programme leader at the mainstream Bournemouth and Poole College.

Her finance background puts her at ease in the business side of running a college; and when she couldn't find a suitable nursery place for her daughter, a wheelchair user, she simply started a chain of SEN nurseries. Her own experience of going to appeal to get her daughter into a mainstream school, and challenging situations where her designated classroom was on the first floor with no lift access, gives her great sympathy with the challenges the students and their parents face.

Her children are now grown up, and downtime revolves around 'trekking, hiking, dogs and horses'.

Leaving in July 2017.

Academic matters: The college's specialism is in Asperger's and high functioning autism, but a lot of the students have an additional diagnosis, typically learning difficulties such as dyslexia and dyspraxia.

Pupils work at entry level 2 upwards (entry level 1 not a barrier in the case of a spiky profile) through to A levels.

Learners follow one of three pathways: Empower, to develop independence and living skills, studying vocational qualifications at level 1/E3; Inspire, to develop employability skills through vocational courses at level 2; and Achieve, to prepare for higher or further education – these students study A levels or vocational qualifications at level 3. All study English, maths and ICT to levels between E3 and A level, and a variety of enrichment activities, work experience, and independent living skills.

Currently they offer maths, English, and psychology A levels on site. Psychology is a popular course: 'Often they are aware something is not right, and they do a fair bit of research on their own, so psychology is interesting for them, it puts their experience into context, without the emphasis on them as an individual,' says Welsh. ICT is also popular, with students taking a variety of qualifications in programming, digital skills, animation, Photoshop and so on, and a number working towards careers in cyber security.

If pupils wish to do other subjects the college can bring in external tutors (this year there is only one candidate for history and computer science), or pupils may be supported to take subjects such as photography and motor vehicle maintenance at mainstream colleges.

Given the nature of the students' difficulties, gaining qualifications is only half the story. They also follow a tutorial programme designed to give them skills for adulthood, such as how to go around town safely, and protect themselves. 'They are vulnerable in the community, because they don't have an obvious disability. If they have strong opinions and voice them in the community it might not go down well; they have to be taught what they can and can't say, and to consider what others think,' says Welsh. Students receive travel training, and work through a programme of escorted and shadow trips, to learn to get around safely by themselves.

All students do work experience on Fridays, either externally or working in the college's own enterprises, which include furniture restoration; a digital studio which creates websites and calendars; baking goods for local cafés; working in the allotment and producing vegetable boxes; and creative work such as making cards and candles. Much work goes into helping students to understand the mindset necessary for work. One young man with the ability to do an engineering apprenticeship needs to understand that he can't choose not to go in if he feels tired, or refuse if he is asked to make the tea. The real life work experience throws up the issues such as these which students need to learn to manage. 'They often need to debrief on strategies to use when outside the protective bubble of the college,' says Welsh.

One of Welsh's favourite success stories is the pupil who 'was in the top 10 of tricky students' but has now applied for a teaching assistant post at the college. 'He had significant challenging behaviour, he was annoyed at having his diagnosis. He gets where the children are coming from,' says Welsh.

Another who was an education refuser, who spent his days locked in his bedroom and took six months to get beyond the car park of the college, is now attending and doing well. And there are the ex-students now at university, who haven't rid themselves of their difficulties, but have learned strategies to manage them.

And as any parent considering this college will know, a giant step can be made over something seemingly minor. 'If we can get them to start looking after their personal hygiene that will make a huge difference to their future,' says Welsh.

Games, options, the arts: Students all do some form of sport as part of their programme, and the choices include athletics, football, mountain biking, swimming, orienteering and badminton.

Thursday afternoons are given over to enrichment activities on and off campus. These include dog walking for the elderly, fundraising and working in charity shops. On site we saw pupils watching and reviewing films, doing artwork, and making pizzas and carrot cake in the food tech room.

Boarding: 'Exceptional quality room, food, support and environment. Could not ask for better,' said one parent.

There are two 52-week and two 38-week houses, ranging in size from five to nine bedded. These are all big Edwardian houses, dotted around the town – students travel to college in a fleet of people-carriers, 'so that it doesn't look like special needs transport'. Thanks to the Edwardian architecture, all bedrooms are double bedroom sized, and all single occupancy. Most are ensuite.

Houses are mixed sex based on group dynamics, and mixed ages – the older pupils tasked as role models to demonstrate the expectations of the house. Students won't necessarily spend all three years in the same house, if they can be better prepared for transition by moving. There are waking night staff. A 'bully box' in the hallway enables pupils to raise concerns if they don't want to talk directly to staff.

There's a laundry room – students expected to do their own – and a cosy lounge area with a comprehensive DVD and games library. Students can either have the house meal – menus decided by weekly meetings – or cook for themselves. There's a barbecue outside for summer nights.

Evenings and weekends are filled with gaming, swimming, bowling, laser quest, trips to the New Forest, hiking in the Purbecks, fishing, and snowboarding. The house group decides what they want to do, and pupils are free to join the group activity or do something on their own with their personal tutor.

Background and atmosphere: The college is set in the student area of Bournemouth. It was converted in 2007 from a former language college, so it is new and purpose-built looking. It's all clean and modern, and smells nice.

The differences between this and a mainstream college are subtle. There's a students' common room decked in bright blue and orange, with a service counter for drinks and snacks. But inside the classrooms individual work spaces predominate for pupils who don't instinctively like working in groups. All of the classrooms are locked to keep the students focused as they move around between lessons, 'otherwise they will go into a room with a computer, and it will be difficult to get them off. You have to ensure balance, otherwise their obsessions can override,' says Welsh.

On the top floor there's a therapy room, and a chill room which can be blacked out and has a range of sensory equipment and music for pupils who need to take time out.

Pastoral care, well-being and discipline: According to parents, it's on the emotional side that this college makes a real difference. Often students have foundered in previous settings which have exacerbated their anxiety or autism. The understanding they find here enables them, perhaps for the first time, to work to their full potential.

'Our son was very anxious and internalised his frustrations,' said a parent. 'He presented as very well-behaved, articulate and bright, which is why his difficulties were not understood or picked up in mainstream school. His confidence and his mood improved here. He had been severally depressed in the years before attending The Wing College.'

A new parent reported that the changes have been rapid. 'Our daughter was in a very bad way when she arrived, very anxious and very dependent. The changes in a few weeks are amazing,' she said.

The college works to develop self-management strategies in the pupils who often struggle with sensory issues – the noise, lighting, or smell, for example.

Parents also praise the work done in raising self-confidence and self-esteem. A parent of a child who has been through many failed placements said: 'I think she is starting to believe in herself more, and feels wanted at this placement. This never happened before: she would be waiting for them to say she had to leave. I know this won't happen at the Wing. They try to understand the child and adapt to their needs. I have never felt happy with her placements until now. It's been a long and tough road.'

One thing parents may find difficult to accept is that once the pupil reaches the age of 18, they can choose not to share information with parents. Prior to this there is a weekly home link, but if the student wants to put an end to this at 18 the college 'has a diplomatic conversation with the parents'. It's important that the learner feels listened to, says Welsh. A few pupils ask that reports are not sent home, but might consent to staff filling in their parents verbally.

Therapy and staffing: There are dedicated TAs just for the education side, but care support workers can also work in education if they have a particular relationship with a learner and are the best person to do so. TAs and care staff all have level 3 qualifications. Parents note the staff turnover endemic to this sector, but Welsh feels that the career progression opportunities provided by the college being part of the Cambian Group result in more stable staffing than the industry norm. Agency staffing is limited to the odd night shift.

'A big selling point is clinical services here,' says Welsh. There are two assistant psychologists, a clinical psychologist, and a psychiatrist. The therapy team includes a speech and language therapist, two occupational therapists, and two holistic therapists (massage and fitness).

Therapy is often delivered 'on the floor' by a roving team, at the point of need and in context. Sometimes the pupil will be more amenable to working with a support worker, and they will deliver therapy under the therapist's direction. Speech and language therapy run social communication groups.

Pupils and parents: The college only went co-ed in 2015, hence the boys heavily outnumber girls, but the number of girls is expected to climb rapidly based on new referrals.

Entrance: An autism diagnosis is not essential, but only two or three pupils don't have this. Pupils join at 16 from specialist independent schools, low secure hospitals, pupil referral units, and 'a lot from placement breakdowns in mainstream'.

Behavioural aspects are looked at on individual basis. 'A lot of behaviour is because they are not in the right environment. Some students have challenging behaviour but it reduces fairly swiftly, so we don't give a blanket no straight away, we look at what is causing that behaviour. Some pupils admitted with a two-to-one staff ratio are now not even on one-to-one,' says Welsh.

Pupils can be admitted with mental health issues if these are stable and managed, and where these may be down to them not being in the right provision – typical cases might be those in a low secure unit because their diagnosis has not been addressed, or in one case where the pupil was thought to be hearing voices but it was in fact his own internal monologue. The college will not take students who are still on section, or where the primary need is mental health, and says it cannot support eating disorders.

Other reasons for refusal of a place would be around behaviour, or where the college doesn't feel it is appropriate, for example if a student needs a lot of outdoor space. But the first stage of assessment is designed to sift from the paperwork the students who may be suited, and for whom there is an appropriate peer group. Students come in for an informal visit, and staff will assess them in their current setting. After that they will be invited to spend at least a day and often an overnight too at the college.

A few students have to go to tribunal to obtain funding, and the college will offer support and guidance to the family and attend the tribunal.

Exit: One-quarter go into further education, 40 per cent into supported employment, 10-15 per cent into each of independent employment and apprenticeships. College and university destinations include Oxford Brooks, Portsmouth, Winchester, Southampton Solent, Cardiff, Exeter, Westminster and Bournemouth.

Money matters: Open to self-funding.

Remarks: Doing a good job for those pupils who fall in the gap between mainstream and special colleges. Students learn that their condition means they will always find the onslaught of sensory challenges and anxiety-inducing events in the outside world difficult, but they can learn successful strategies to cope with this, and make a successful move to work or higher education.

Good option for those who are resistant to their diagnosis or the idea of being educated alongside 'weird kids'. College looks every bit like a mainstream, and great thought is given to this – like transport by people-carriers instead of a bus plastered with special needs livery.

Centre Academy

92 St John's Hill, London SW11 1SH

Pupils: 50 • Ages: 8–19

Fees: £27,600 – £40,100 pa

Tel: 020 7738 2344
Email: info@centreacademy.net
Website: www.centreacademy.net

Head of School: Since 2013, Natalia Ambridge BA PGCE MA (40s) Started in publishing, trained as a teacher and worked for six years at Bedford Prep. Since 2013 has been head at Centre Academy and on the governing board for both Centre Academy schools. Original degree in philosophy and theology which she taught as an option last year at school and is currently studying for a doctorate in education. Cool, calm, executive style with an elegance appreciated by students ('you look smart, Miss') She has brought about some changes to staffing and is keen to broaden the curriculum as much as possible whilst looking for programmes leading to qualifications suited to the broad range of abilities at the school – she has brought in ASDAN, which allows each pupil to leave with a skills-based qualification even if they are not doing the American High School Diploma. She introduced monthly assemblies and is working to coordinate assessment results for better tracking of pupil progress.

Principal, Dr Duncan Rollo, BA MA PhD (60s) previously head for six years now principal and administrative director, remains both passionate about special needs education in general and both Centre Academy schools. He is responsible for financial matters, building projects and maintenance, and curriculum development. Much of his time is taken with admissions and the highly successful placing of students into further education when they leave. He spends two days at Centre Academy London and three days at Centre Academy East Anglia.

Academic matters: Very small classes, especially in lower years – several parents we spoke to said that is one of the main reasons they chose the school – allows for tailoring teaching very individually to students without either the 'stigma of a learning support assistant,' according to one parent whose child came from a local primary where this had happened, 'nor the dependence this created'. Rather than being given a TA or taken out for one-to-one lessons, they are in inclusive, appropriate ability classes with high levels of support and encouragement.

The school has a preponderance of students over 14 years, at which stage teaching is geared towards GCSEs or Functional Skills levels 1 and 2. English a clear strength of the school with inspiring teaching. We spoke with students eager to explain themes they had discovered in crime and punishment and to show us a school magazine where students had published their stories as well as having performed them during assemblies. New maths and ICT teachers following departure of previous maths teacher and deputy head. Humanities is a combined course – history, geography and citizenship. A small science lab for combined science courses – again as interactive and practical as possible. We saw an individual foreign language lesson (Spanish) – such is the level of personalised study programme. ICT popular with some of the students. Homework is given and is partly completed during the 'show my homework' prep session at the end of school when teachers are available to make sure students know what they are expected to do and give help. Pupils then have up to an hour and a half of homework to do at home.

Almost all students stay on post-16, at which point there are two pathways – Foundation and the American High School Diploma. The diploma uses continuous assessment which takes much of the stress out of learning. Clear expectations and structure allow students to work well and achieve 'beyond our expectations,' according to parents who say teachers are 'extremely aware of children's problems'. There is a narrow and focused curriculum of primarily academic courses. 'We can supplement for sports and drama and there is time later for vocational skills,' according to one parent, 'but they need their language and academic work happening at school. It is what this school does best'.

In such a small school there is clearly not going to be a wide breadth of courses, but there is a 'good range of ability' and pupils taught in groups according to ability level. High expectations and 'no mollycoddling – academically the school will get them as far as they can get,' according to one parent.

Games, options, the arts: Weekly sports lessons on Wednesday afternoon when pupils use the gym in sports centre nearby. Swimming classes in the local pool for the younger years. Occupational therapist goes with sports teacher to assist. Balls and a basketball hoop for breaktime very much in use when we visited. Less active pupils occupied with Lego and construction games during break. A small but very well used and organised art room with evidence of sculpture, papier mâché, mask making and painting around the school as well as filling students' art portfolios. Music is a whole school activity on Fridays – notation as well as singing. There is a student council offering further opportunities to speak and be heard. Debating is considered an important skill and much encouraged at every opportunity – in all classes as well as during tutorial groups, current affairs discussions, oral English presentations. EAL given where needed. Other clubs include chess club, film club, board games and creative writing.

Background and atmosphere: Charming brick Victorian school with small interconnected rooms and high windows and a very small playground – larger older students dwarfed the space. No kitchen or dining room so pupils bring in packed lunch and there are microwaves in common room. Clearly crying out for new classrooms – including space for more practical subjects and science labs and a better equipped playground for which planning projects in the pipeline. A reasonably stocked and well-used library. There is something cosy and safe about the school, which is clean and freshly painted. We were impressed by good manners and the orderly way pupils moved between lessons, while still having plenty of energy to use during break time. Great respect between pupils reflects way they are treated by teachers.

Pastoral care, well-being and discipline: Mentors see groups of students three times a day to check that they are prepared for lessons, to check diaries and deal with issues of well-being. Diaries and mentor system ensure good communication with parents, who say 'email response time is excellent', with mentors informing other teachers of particular issues during daily staff meeting. Pupils say school 'encourages you to explore what you like to do' and to 'live up to your potential'. Several said they were now 'less shy' and 'more confident around people'. All pupils we spoke to agreed that it was better here than their last schools – and this is from pupils who, on the whole, dislike change. Pupils know what it is like to be seen as different and as a result are particularly kind and respectful of each other. None of the parents or pupils we spoke to felt there were problems of discipline, but mature behaviour very much encouraged, with going out rights allowing older pupils to leave school at lunchtime a few days a week. There is some outside contact between pupils at birthday parties and at holidays, but with such a small cohort it is limited: this might suit a child who is not too concerned about a big social circle and is happier in a small group. Parents of more sociable students slightly regretted the small numbers of pupils but decided it was a small price to pay for what was otherwise described by one parent as finding 'heaven on earth, where 'they are encouraged to be a small family' and where they 'take children who have been rejected socially and academically and turn them into beautiful creations'.

Therapy and staffing: Staff taken from a range of experiences – both mainstream and special needs. Very high teacher to student ratio – one-to-three in three classes the day we visited, and not much more higher up the school. Full time speech and language therapist has devised a spelling scheme and uses this for individual lessons as well as running weekly group social skills classes. She communicates frequently with parents, who praised the ease of contact and her care. The wider emphasis on speaking and listening provides opportunities which encourage speech, language and communication, and they have found that students who did not necessarily speak to teachers did chat within the safety of their otherwise non-verbal groups. Occupational therapist has dedicated room in playground and sees pupils in accordance with individual statement requirements as well as supporting PE.

Pupils and parents: Pupils come from 22 different boroughs – primarily in London but also many from Surrey. Almost all have statement/EHC plan. Around 80 per cent funded by local authority. Others paid for by grateful parents from abroad, companies relocating staff and parents who work in town and are pleased to find a special needs school so near to central London. Few physical disabilities (the old building is simply not suitable in many cases), but suitable for students with reasonably good cognitive ability and high functioning autism, or with Asperger's syndrome, dyspraxia, dyslexia, ADD or processing difficulties.

Entrance: Admissions from 8 years, but since most pupils local authority funded and EHC plans take time, school also has an entrance at 13/14 years. All admissions involve speaking to Dr Rollo first, then if considered there might be a good fit, application papers sent out, review of reports and interviews with the family. If he feels school can provide for the needs of primarily high functioning pupils with learning difficulties including dyslexia/ADD/dyspraxia and mild autistic spectrum disorder, they are invited for assessment days at the school to see how they fit. They take pupils with good cognitive level or the 'potential to do well' and to work towards Foundation level or above. Even then, it may take some time for a reply – so allow time for any admission application. But clearly not all parents are put off as many push education tribunals for funding to get their child there, and at least one parent we spoke to had moved nearby especially to be near so his child could attend. Small school space means that students with behavioural issues are not admitted unless these are simply an articulation of the frustration being felt and where poor behaviour may by resolved within the calm structure of this school. Limitations within the building make wheelchair access well nigh impossible.

Exit: A few leave for sixth form college but most stay on to 18 years. A real strength of the school is the advocate they have in Dr Rollo, who prepares references and helps with personal statements and an explanation of the USA High School Diploma to back up applications to further education colleges and universities. Places found for students where possible – two pupils moved to help live/work at the school's sister school in East Anglia for a post High School Diploma year, for example, one on a child management course. Otherwise to further education such as Derwen College, Regent's University, Richmond University, Carshalton College, Westminster College.

Money matters: This is not a cheap option if there is no local authority funding. It is a totally private school run by the M&M Murphy Partnership (which owns both this school and the East Anglia Centre Academy). There are two independent governors on the board of governors, together with one parent governor and three staff members – accountability, and critical yet supportive governance, may be hard with staff governors making up a half of the board. One parent said that if she were rich she would leave a legacy to the school to be able to continue its wonderful work – high praise indeed, and an indication of the relief and gratitude felt by many despondent parents for the presence of this little London school.

Remarks: A serious school that not only gives students every help to progress during their school years but prepares them for independent life and learning after school. A safe environment with teaching at a range of ability levels, allowing pupils to develop both academically and in self-esteem. Good focus on moving pupils on to further education, for which they have been given the study skills and independence to succeed. Suits pupils who need individual care and small classes to achieve their potential.

The Dominie

55 Warriner Gardens, London SW11 4DX

Pupils: 32 • Ages: 6–12

Fees: £26,100 pa

Tel: 020 7720 8783
Email: info@thedominie.co.uk
Website: www.thedominie.co.uk

Principal: Since 2007, the hugely experienced Anne O'Doherty BA Dip SpLD Dip Montessori (50+). Previously co-ran Kensington Dyslexia Centre, also taught at The Dominie since 2001. A potent combination of charisma, expertise, approachability and good sense: you can see why she is called 'inspirational'. Loves theatre, music, dance and reading. Parents can make an appointment to see her at any time to discuss their child, plus termly parent teacher meetings and reports. Organises annual drinks party for parents and staff, enthusiastically described as 'the best parent party in London'.

Secret weapon is Maisie the cairn terrier, who multi-tasks as school dog/school mascot/alternative school counsellor and sometimes sits on parents' knees at their first meeting. Much in evidence during our visit until picked up by her dog walker.

Deservedly something of a legend in the dyslexia world, it is Miss O'D's understanding of what children coming to The Dominie need that sets her apart. She cultivates excellent communication and mutual trust with London day school feeders. Firmly on the side of her pupils, understanding that most have had a rough time. 'Anne really likes the children; she really does look after each individual. She likes all of them in their different ways,' said happy parent report. Parents united about her genuine passion for rebuilding self-esteem in order to learn, and focus on turning around previously negative school experiences. 'My child is a different person, in all the right ways' is a not uncommon theme.

Entrance: Clearly for children with specific learning difficulties: dyslexia, dyspraxia, dyscalculia, dysgraphia, speech, language and communication and associated learning difficulties. This small school was created specifically for these particular children. Miss O'D takes children who will fit in with The Dominie way of working because they are the children for whom the school can make the most difference. Our instincts were confirmed that this is definitely not a school for children with more serious difficulties who need more help than it can provide.

Entry process starts with phone call followed by initial meeting with Miss O'D. Parental expectations managed with assertive charm born of years of experience. Potential pupils undergo three day assessment and observation by teachers and therapists. Children seem to enjoy them and school is looking for potential and not worried about spellings at this stage. More interested in children's learning methods, approach to school work and crucial compatibility with existing peer group. If no place offered, and she understands that parents find this hard, Miss O'D explains her reasons and guides towards a more suitable school, providing some integrity for often traumatised parents.

Exit: Majority to mainstream schools like More House in Knightsbridge, Broomwood Hall, Bethany School and Thames

Christian College, with learning support structure and good pastoral care in place. Some to more specialist environments to meet particular needs. Leavers are grateful for the difference that Dominie made and for believing in them and giving them the skills to move on.

Remarks: Classwork and homework are individualised and teacher/therapist to pupil ratio is high, but no culture of ongoing one-to-one support.

Maximum 32 pupils, who tend to stay three or four years, and class sizes about eight. Children are engaged, and some very outgoing and chatty, especially the girls we met. There seemed to be more girls than boys, but this changes year on year.

On arrival, children's levels are rich and varied. The aim is to raise each child to age-appropriate levels in spite of their spiky profiles common to SpLd. Innovative learning includes a much talked about specialist philosophy teacher and school Question Time for 9-11 year olds three times a week, with support of speech and language therapy, to develop public speaking and comprehension skills.

All teachers are fully qualified and have additional dyslexia qualifications, with high quality teaching assistants who are generally graduates, supported by team of SLTs and very experienced physio Sally Wright, who works across classes on handwriting, posture for learning etc. You get the impression that they really know the individual strengths and weaknesses of each of the children.

Parents report that even by half term of the first term the difference in their child's learning, confidence and progress can be 'unbelievable, as the first thing they do is to work on the main cause of the child's learning anxiety'. There is no pretence that children will outgrow their learning difficulties, but focus is on teaching strategies, resilience and confidence. Children are taught tricks for learning times tables which are 'really functional and help them understand multiplication once and for all'. Teachers react fast to lack of confidence/enthusiasm observed or reported by parents. Home-school communication is very good, and during parents' evenings they 'actually explain how our children learn'.

Therapy input works alongside class teaching without being intrusive. Most work is small group or whole class, with occasional one-to-one work. Clear acknowledgement that learning is hard for the children within the context of high but realistic expectations. It feels purposeful and organised. Lessons capture learning opportunities and develop working memory and processing speeds. One class was loving playing a game jumping on word meanings with their speech and language therapist (SLT). Children are given learning strategies to encourage them to progress as independently as possible.

Based in a converted shoe-polish factory in an affluent residential street near Battersea Park. Clever use of indoor space, but packed lunches have to be eaten in classrooms. Interior is bright and cheerful with regulation pupils' artwork liberally applied.

School has been kept small, which parents and pupils appreciate. Flip side of this is no lunch hall or outdoor space, so possibly not suitable for very physical, energetic children. Daily play time and weekly sports afternoon in Battersea Park (three minute walk) dependent on weather conditions, but Latchmere Leisure Centre is the indoor alternative. Options include two cooking clubs, guitar club, drama club, and not one but two homework clubs for the older children to build up their stamina for working independently. Surely a dream for parents exhausted by the battle ground of homework. Much anticipated Christmas play written by the drama teacher where every child has a real part. Children were rehearsing with gusto. Limited space in the school hall make this the hottest ticket in south west London.

Miss O'D is in charge of pastoral care and knows her pupils well. She and Maisie have a kindly, no nonsense approach. Effort and motivation wildly celebrated alongside progress and achievement. Praise is highly valued. Everyone has difficulties so no one is different. As it is a specialist school, children come from wide geographical areas, and play-dates are more likely at weekends. Parents have to make more of an effort to connect their children. Often extra staff training days are good opportunities for play-dates, but complicated for working parents.

The benefits of being a very small school generally outweigh any social and geographical disadvantages for the children. To be graded outstanding by Ofsted is increasingly difficult, but it's no surprise that The Dominie has achieved it. It is expensive at £8,500 per term, and many parents self fund. This is a self-confident school that knows its market. Parents are very supportive: 'Being able to go to The Dominie was like coming home for my child'. Many children achieve beyond what they, and previous schools, believed was possible. Many even learn to love reading, which says it all, really.

E

Egerton-Rothesay School

Durrants Lane, Berkhamsted, Hertfordshire HP4 3UJ

Pupils: 156 (108 boys, 48 girls) • Ages: 6–19 • Sixth form: 17 (13 boys, 4 girls)

Fees: £15,255 – £ 21,711 pa

Tel: 01442 865275
Email: admin.dl@eger-roth.co.uk
Website: www.eger-roth.co.uk

Headteacher: Since 2013, Mr Colin Parker BSc DipEd PGCE CMath (50s); was senior officer in the Cunard Line and taught maths and computing at Bishop Fox's School in Taunton before joining Egerton-Rothesay in 2003. Has been head of maths and business studies, head of house and head of upper senior school. Interested in broadcast media – he was a freelance sports journalist of the BBC in the 80s – and supports Watford FC. Married to Chisa, a translator; with one daughter. Reserved and precise, he thoughtfully balances the children's academic and pastoral needs; 'We are not a special school, we have a mainstream curriculum...our vision is to help those students who do not survive in a mainstream environment without support'. He is conscious that what makes the school special is the attention to the individual: 'We don't want to expand so we can't help the pupils here now. We think this is an ideal number'. Encourages the students to look beyond their difficulties, '...if you want to have a go, why not have a go? We build the timetable to give everyone a chance'. Respected by the parents, 'approachable, lovely, caring head, but firm' and popular with the children. As one mum said, 'he definitely knows how to be on their level...he has a sense of humour'.

Academic matters: Mainstream curriculum for a population with additional needs, including speech and language, interaction difficulties, dyslexia, dyspraxia, ADHD and Aspergers, as well as complex communication needs. School divided into learning bases named after trees (Poplar, Rowan, Oak, Beech) denoting year groupings. The considered base-names capture the school's focus on inclusion: 'We don't want children sitting alone under trees. We needed an area somewhere they could return to and meet friends or work quietly during break times'.

The youngest children (years 2-6) have their own building, where four classes, with sets for numeracy and literacy, are supported by a class teacher, who follows the national curriculum in a topic based approach. Class sizes are tiny, no more than 10, but usually fewer; 'What makes the school attractive to the parents is the fact that it's small,' remarked the head. Staff to pupil ratio is high, with some teaching assistants in constant attendance on one child, while others move round the group, as required. Interwoven in the children's day are therapy sessions and individual support from specialist teachers, and the whole class enjoys snack and movement breaks. With over 100 children with EHC plans, teaching is differentiated both at group and individual level. In the new, timber-clad building we saw the youngest children chatting at group tables, while others chose to sit apart, some on therapeutic bouncy chairs. In a neighbouring room, a small maths set was seated at tables in a horseshoe.

The senior school has a more formal feel with specialist subject teachers, and students moving between classrooms, clasping files. Years 7, 8 and 9 may take a range of core subjects, including a foreign language (Spanish), with different teaching methods to suit the child; 'We will do whatever it takes to help a child access the curriculum,' one teacher told us. We saw Shakespeare plays in comic book format, photocopies in buff for dyslexic learners, a scribe for a slow writer and several dyslexic children using laptops and Claroread software. One teacher described how she moves the desks for group discussion for one English set, but has to shift them back for the next so as not to discompose the children who have high-level autism. From year 10, the child chooses exam subjects: GCSE, BTec, DiDA, Foundation or Entry level, whatever is appropriate and achievable. 'Everyone who comes here can access nearly all the subjects from a comprehensive school,' asserted the head. GCSEs in art, maths, drama, ICT and DT were popular. He bemoaned the recent changes in GCSE English as a hurdle for a language-impaired child. 'The whole exam system has gone against us... now they have taken out speaking and listening, so to get a grade C (English) is a hard task'. However, double or triple science is on offer, as well as a host of vocational qualifications, including business administration and land based studies, to name a few. Cookery is popular, following Jamie Oliver's BTec home cooking skills course. One boy's verdict on the teaching: 'Even lessons like RE, the teacher makes it really interesting'.

The small, recently-added sixth form gives slow learners a chance to retake or increase number of subjects, and offers independent workers the opportunity to take advanced courses, such as art. There is a conscious emphasis on confidence-boosting and social skills before further education. As the head points out, re-entering a mainstream college at 16 'is a massive change for our pupils'. Head has no plans to offer A levels: 'If we offer A levels, which are very resource-intensive, that stretches staff and takes away from children lower down who need support'. One parent was concerned the amount of homework was not enough; another remarked, 'it's appropriate'.

Games, options, the arts: With a timetable bursting with academic and therapeutic options, it is surprising there is time for sports, but a few periods a week are devoted to PE or team sports (rugby, football, cricket, netball, tennis, rounders). Some KS2 and all KS3 pupils swim locally, and a nearby sports centre provides a climbing wall and cricket nets. Small numbers mean team sports and inter-schools matches are restricted; nevertheless, 'they have a way of involving every child,' said one mum, whose son had arrived at the school with sportsphobia. 'He hated the ball coming anywhere near him...now it's one of his favourite subjects'. Another mum mentioned how the sports teaching helped her son's co-ordination difficulties: 'He didn't know which leg to kick with...now he plays in the local league'. Sports GCSE and BTec are popular, and we heard of a boy on work experience at a local primary school, with a view to training as a sports coach.

Friday afternoon is timetabled with a choice of activities, as after-school clubs clash with the long bus journeys. Choices include climbing or skiing at Hemel Hempstead, golf, motocross, martial arts, ice skating (all payable extra). Others, eg yoga, cookery and building a bog garden, come free.

'When it comes to creative output,' said one mum, 'they have all sorts of ways to let your child express themselves'. A separate drama studio is used for GCSE drama and there's a drama tech activity for non-performing children. The more extrovert choose to audition for the summer shows; recent productions include Bugsy Malone, My Fair Lady and Madness' Our House. One mum remarked, 'I'd like them to have a theatre as opposed to performing in the gym'. Music GCSE is taught, as well as whole class music lessons in KS3. A wealth of private instrument tuition is available, including music tech and theory. One parent said she had opted for instrument teaching out of school, as her son's timetable was already bulging with therapy sessions, and she did not want him missing vital work. A small DT room, including 3D printer and specialist art studio, with potter's wheel, provides the materials for the imaginative child.

Background and atmosphere: Lying just outside Berkhamsted in Hertfordshire, a town steeped in history since the doomsday book, the school's 1980s suburban architecture and leafy façade suggest little of the area's heritage. Founded after the merger of two private prep schools in 1988, Egerton Rothesay has developed the original low-level buildings with a couple of attractive new additions. The youngest classes, Poplar base, occupy one of these, a semi open-plan construction, with small classrooms off a pleasant main hall, used for daily assemblies as well as individual therapy space. Boxes of sticklebricks and puppets are neatly stacked away for indoor play, while outdoors there's a small separate playground with cabin, climbing frame and tyres to swing from. Children in the literacy class were busy typesetting their autumnal acrostic poems for poetry day when we visited, while the neighbouring room was the scene of excited chatter about the Great Fire of London.

Across the way, past carefully tended borders and neat tubs of begonias, the older years were found in small groups, studying discrete subjects. A history teacher was providing visual support in the form of a time-line on the whiteboard. These kinaesthetic learners had built their own history park in the grounds, with a timeline of pebbles, alongside a wattle and daub wall. A neat science lab and two ICT rooms were found along quiet corridors; while two small libraries, one for the juniors, held several classic titles in graphic novel form, no e-readers yet, but these were under discussion. The sixth form room, with a row of wellies for land-based studies, opens directly onto the grounds. Outside a polytunnel grows fruit and vegetables, available for sale to staff (who had been offered first refusal of a fine beetroot that morning). Lunches are prepared and cooked on site and eaten in a dining room, annexed from the old school hall. We were pleased to see that the Christian school still observed fishy Friday, with more exotic foods such as pork escalope in sticky plum sauce or Halloumi Saganaki on other days. A vegetarian option and deli counter added to the choice.

In a sleek new building, with an arrangement of exposed timber roof-beams like a giant geometric puzzle, we found maths being taught in bright, dual aspect classrooms. Rowan base, for children with complex learning conditions, shares the ground floor with a large dance studio, also used for PE and assemblies. Therapies and social communication specialists were tucked away in their own wing with cosy, sensory room, while in the grounds were netball rings, two tennis courts and a pitch for ball games.

Pastoral care, well-being and discipline: A Christian ethos underpins the school, with a supervision team headed by the school chaplain. A system of 'listening ears' is available to students, which includes class teacher, base leader and an independent youth worker. Assemblies take place daily, in addition to regular services at a local church.

Four houses, named Plantagenet, Tudor, Stuart and Hanover, provide 'an ideal way to get all the years working together,' said the head. When quizzed about behaviour management, the head's response was, 'we treat them with respect' with a drive to build confidence rather than knock it. One mum said, 'Not every day, but every week, my son gets positively rewarded'. A merit and a de-merit system helps, culminating in a house cup for the younger ones and iTunes vouchers for the older ones. There are internal suspensions for the most severe transgressions, but a comfy, cooling-off room in the social communication suite prevents many of these. `Bullying is very, very rare' commented the head, but he conceded that keeping control of social media was a full time job for school and parents. No phones allowed in school until the sixth Form.

Parents were fully aware how to contact the staff by phone or email, in case of a problem, and received a list of contact details at the start of term. 'They are quite keen on us saying things straight away,' said one mum. A home/school linkbook records a daily query, and termly parents' evenings enabled frank face-to-face chats. The social communication specialist added, 'I can see them at the drop of a hat'. The school goes that extra mile to keep parents in the loop, with bulk texts, bulk emails, twitter updates, a weekly newsletter and a phone-friendly website.

Therapy and staffing: With a large number of statutory requirements and a population of children with additional needs, the capable head of SEN and therapy has a prominent place at the school, 'worth her weight in gold,' said a parent. OTs and SLTs take individual sessions and/or groups in a separate annexe. In Poplar base, we saw a sensory timetable for the younger children's attention needs, in the form of calming and alerting activities, while Makaton signing was used by teachers in class to support communication. The SLT also helps out within the class, where necessary. In a senior maths class, we saw children drawing colour-coded smilies on their work, red, amber and green, to indicate how well they had understood the lesson. 'It saves putting hands up and singling out the child,' explained the teacher. Students with social difficulties can chill on the beanbags in the sanctuary room. Interaction specialists, trained in counselling and psychotherapy, run individualised sessions – the calming sessions with cute 'breathing puppy' are particularly engaging. Dyslexia and dyscalculia teachers give tailor-made tuition, and a physio visits the more complex children, as required. There is a distinct parents' evening to meet the therapists once a term. All staff are trained in first aid, including epilepsy care.

Pupils and parents: Although sympathetic and caring, this is not a school that is too informal; the children are dressed in uniform, a sensible navy sweatshirt and navy skirt, grey trousers for boys (year 10s have swapped the white polo for shirt and tie). We met children who greeted us naturally, though respectfully ('Mr..' or 'Miss...') with lots to say, and confidence to say it. They arrive from a 35 mile radius in the schools' buses. Parking, we hear, is a difficult subject, but more is currently planned. Bus routes are individualised to suit the families and the rides are popular, even with the youngest children, though a wrench for the mums; 'I was crying on the first day,' said one. When questioned about after-school friendships, one mum said, 'The biggest problem is that we live so far away from each other... but we manage it'. Parents are brought together via the Friends of Egerton PTA for coffee mornings, quiz night and the winter fair.

Entrance: All children have additional needs (mostly speech and language, interaction, dyspraxia, dyslexia, dyscalculia). Not suitable for emotional and behavioural issues as primary diagnosis. The application process takes time and is individually tailored. Before meeting the parents, the head of SEN reads through paperwork, a three-day assessment follows, in which the child joins a group and meets necessary support staff, before a place is offered. The registrar offers weekly tours of the school to prospective parents. Open days each term, when the children volunteer as guides; 'It's good for them to take a bit of responsibility and talk about their school,' laughed the head, adding nervously, 'We don't know what they are going to say to you'. Applications for all years (except year 11) are considered.

Exit: Those who don't stay on for sixth form take up courses at local FE colleges: West Herts and Amersham and Wycombe are popular. The school stages interview technique sessions in preparation. Leavers' courses include university degrees in maths/physics, forensics, vocational training in travel/leisure, animal care, hair and beauty, sports. Some join the army or take ICT training.

Money matters: A percentage funded by LA via EHC plans; some self-funded. Several parents have had to brave tribunals for a place. 'I've done tribunal twice, that's how good ERS is'.

Remarks: A school that achieves a solid, mainstream education with a thoughtful, caring approach and an abundance of individual attention. Not showy or over-resourced in hardware, forget foreign trips or swimming pools, but rich in specialist teachers to boost confidence and surmount learning differences. Cheerful children are encouraged to think big at ERS. As one mum told us of her son who had become disaffected with education, 'within a week he was the child we remembered'.

Fairley House School

30 Causton Street, London SW1P 4AU

Pupils: 195 • Ages: 5–16

Fees: £30,300 pa

Tel: 020 7976 5456
Email: office@fairleyhouse.org.uk
Website: www.fairleyhouse.org.uk

Headmaster: Since 2013, Mr Michael Taylor BA PGCE FRGS (40s). A geographer, he came here from four years as deputy head at More House near Farnham, another good specialist school. He clearly gets on well with both parents and children. Parents say 'boyish', 'deals with problems well', 'has a laugh with the pupils but keeps their respect', 'hands shaken, greeted by name, knows if they have been away.'

Previous principal, Jackie Murray, is now school's principal educational psychologist. Still a force in the land.

Academic matters: Regularly inspected and accredited by CReSTeD, the register for specialist schools with provision for dyslexia and SpLDs. Pupils are split into a junior department – 5 to 9 years – and a senior department – now 10 to 16 years, class size usually 8-12 pupils. The main emphasis being on numeracy and literacy, everyone is put into a small group to match their ability and skills for maths and English and rejoins their class for other subjects. Children are taught to understand their own learning styles and shown strategies to overcome barriers to learning to achieve their targets. The aim is to return children to mainstream schools as soon as they are able, which school has great success in doing. Test results such as Sats are very respectable, especially from children who can have quite pronounced difficulties.

Every child has an IEP which is regularly reviewed by the trans-disciplinary team to monitor progress and ensure that individual needs are being catered for. Mornings start with exercises; depending on the individual, this could be physical, orthoptic or attention focused. All the classrooms, including the science lab, are buzzing with activities, visual reminders and clues, anything that is memorable: models made by the children, word banks for a current history topic or colour-coded parts of speech. Every teacher has specialist qualifications which ensure that all classes are fully accessible and multisensory. 'Having teachers who are nice to you and understand has changed my life,' said a 10-year-old. The learning support is an integral part of the whole school approach to teaching. The transdisciplinary approach is used across the curriculum, helpfully allowing therapy delivery to be linked to specific subjects and development. Homework is colour-coded to help with the organisation, and deadlines must be met to prepare the children for returning to mainstream school. Help and advice is on hand for those who get stuck.

Parents thrilled to have found the place. A typical story: 'His previous school [a well-known London prep] had given up on him: "He will never learn his times tables". He had shut down completely. On his first day here he learned his nine times table. He has made huge progress, so much more confident, maths is no longer an issue.' Or: 'It was like letting a different child into my house. Cool and collected where he had been crying and angry.'

Games, options, the arts: Wonderfully imaginative art displays line the corridors and even the ceilings are decorated in many areas of the building. Pupils make their own ceramic tiles depicting various scenes from history and also design and execute murals. The most recent addition is the newly-built art studio and kiln room. The children enjoy a great variety of artistic activities including textiles, fashion, design and technology, sewing and puppet-making.

A range of sports – all the traditional ones, alongside canoeing, fencing and yoga. Although doesn't have its own playing fields, they make good use of local facilities at Battersea Park and the Queen Mother sports centre. Music and drama are taught as separate subjects and integrated into other curriculum areas to help children develop good communication skills. Everyone is encouraged to learn a musical instrument and the school runs its own acting awards and music medals scheme. Parents pack into the termly dramatic and musical productions.

Extracurricular activities include museum and theatre trips along with a wide choice of lunchtime and after-school clubs. Club options change regularly depending on the clientele and demand.

Background and atmosphere: Founded in 1975 by a speech therapist, Daphne Hamilton Fairley, as a charitable trust in memory of her oncologist husband, killed by an IRA bomb. The upper school site, originally a church, has been cleverly converted into a four-storey building. The junior school pupils are housed in a Victorian infants' school in the shadows of Lambeth Palace, backing on to Archbishop's Park, complete with sports facilities and an adventure playground for the children's use. Both buildings are well decorated, with a lot of space dedicated to the children's achievements, visual timetables and fantastic works of art. The atmosphere is purposeful, peaceful and well organised, encouraging pupils to be themselves. Lots of smiling and cheerful faces – nobody should feel the odd one out here.

Pastoral care, well-being and discipline: Structured mentoring system involving 18 members of staff to whom children can refer themselves. Aim is to work in a strong partnership with parents to help ensure things do not go wrong for pupils due to simple misunderstandings. Seems to be working, as parents feel pastoral care has improved over the last few years. 'Not too strict. Jokey,' said a parent, but at the end of the day kids waiting for the bus are orderly, and board quietly.

Therapy and staffing: Depending on the individual needs of the pupil, speech therapy and occupational therapy are incorporated into classroom learning, art, drama and sports. Younger children will be making 'ch' out of chocolate buttons whilst older ones are baking round pies to help understand and remember the mathematical sign pi. Children are taught to touch-type once they have achieved a reading age of approximately 8 years. In-house speech and occupational therapists run their own sensory integration programmes and motor coordination classes. The therapy staff organising the motor coordination classes have been specially trained in America and continue to attend training in the USA to keep up to date.

Pupils and parents: Scattered all over London, and a few from the edges of the home counties – requires an effort to get to know other families. Everybody and anybody affected by neuro-diversity. By all accounts, lots of very supportive and enthusiastic parents who are keen to get involved with school activities. Most recently the parent group has fundraised to update and restock the school library. Weekly newsletters, back-up information on the website and parents can use a communication book or email teachers. Comprehensive, well-designed website, but not 'read friendly' as yet.

Entrance: Children are invited to spend two days here, where they will have a transdisciplinary all-round assessment to ensure that the school will be able to meet their needs. After the assessment, parents are provided with reports from an educational psychologist, speech therapist and occupational therapist and then invited for a conference to discuss how the school can help and support their child. Assessments cost £290–£890. In the event of the school not being able to offer a place they will suggest other options to parents.

Most pupils have a diagnosis of specific learning differences, usually dyslexia and/or dyspraxia and the related conditions ADD, ADHD and Asperger's. Also able to accommodate some pupils who have non-conventional learning styles and find mainstream schools inaccessible.

Exit: The average stay for pupils at Fairley House is approximately two/three years. Depending on when a child arrives at the school, there is a tendency for the Fairley programme to end at odd ages (from an entrance point of view) like 12 or 14, which some potential next schools get stuffy about. Some parents clearly feel that the school could have been more helpful in the search for where to go to next. Top destinations are Bedales (senior and junior), DLD College, Hall School (Wimbledon), Kingham Hill, Millfield (senior and junior), Milton Abbey, Portland Place, Bedes (senior and junior), St Christopher and Windlesham House – but there are a wide range of others who welcome Fairley pupils.

Money matters: A few bursaries are available for trainee teachers. As yet, unable to offer bursaries to pupils, but will assist parents with tribunals and the statementing procedure. Approximately 26 per cent of pupils have a statement of special educational needs/EHC plan and are funded by their local authorities.

Remarks: Certainly good value for money, but the fees are terrifying and beyond the reach of many without local authority funding. A remarkable school for its holistic, multi-sensory and transdisciplinary approach. A beacon for children with learning and processing differences and parents who have been tearing their hair out trying to cope in other situations.

Frewen College

14

Rye Road, Northiam, Rye, East Sussex TN31 6NL

Pupils: 110 (about a third boarders) • Ages: 7–18 • Sixth form: 26

Fees: Day £15,285 – £24,345; Boarding £22,899 – £33,795 pa

Tel: 01797 252494
Email: office@frewencollege.co.uk
Website: www.frewencollege.co.uk

Principal: Since 2014, Nick Goodman. The former art teacher has worked his way through senior roles at the international CATS College Canterbury, mainstream comprehensive Mascalls School in Kent, and as head of arts faculty at Munich International School. He was drawn to the new challenge of a specialist school, 'where pupils need specialist help, and where it is possible to make a real difference and improve their chances', as well as a feeling we understood as he showed us round the magnificent grounds, of 'who wouldn't want to work here?'

He took a fine art degree, and like many an art student, coupled his interest with playing guitar and performing in bands. Pity the neighbours as he still loves experimental music – 'swinging radios round on ropes, dragging cans through underpasses, and putting those sounds into musical pieces,' as he explains it. Last seen at a Sparks gig, he's a big fan of Eno and Bowie – he marked the latter's death with a 20 minute off-the-cuff assembly. 'Everyone should know who Bowie was,' he says. He also stress-busts through a major renovation of his house, and making cider from its orchard.

His watch has brought a modernising touch to the school – bringing it up to date with 21st century methods in scrutinising pupil progress. He has also cast the graphic designer's wand over the school's prospectus and bus livery, and created a notably clear and informative website. 'I want people to think "Wow that's a really nice school, it looks like any other independent school," which means not using a comic sans font and a rainbow,' he says.

Parents praise the fact that he involves them in decision making through the 'Principal's forum' which has resulted in revised approaches to homework and additional after-school clubs.

Academic matters: Pupils all have a specific learning difficulty or speech and language disorder, and often arrive in a battered state. 'They have usually been struggling for years, in a school which doesn't understand that they have been trying twice as hard as the other pupils. They have often taken big knocks to their self-confidence and self-esteem, and sometimes come to the conclusion that they must be stupid,' says the head.

Hence there's a big focus on building confidence – often through music and drama productions – and on creating a calm, low pressure environment. 'It's about not putting too much pressure on them because that is counter-productive, instead we put the pressure on ourselves to get the results out of them,' says Goodman.

Dyslexia/dyspraxia aids are an everyday matter here – classroom cupboards are stocked with writing slopes, pencil grips, wobble cushions, and coloured paper for those who have a problem with the contrast between black and white. Touch-typing, predictive text and voice-recognition technologies are all employed.

Most students take five or more GCSEs – in 2016, 85 per cent of grades were A*-E and 50 per cent A*-C. Pupils can sit eight GCSEs, or entry level qualifications, or a combination of both.

There are no languages, which will be a relief to some dyslexic ears, however Goodman hopes to introduce beginners' courses as an extracurricular activity. 'Pupils want it to be as much like every other school as it can,' he says. 'For example they redesigned the uniform to include a blazer and tie; they want to look as smart as their counterparts.'

Year 7 is designed as a transition year to ease the jump between all subjects taught by a class teacher and a dozen subject teachers. So in the first senior year pupils have the same teacher for English, history, geography, PSHE and sometimes maths, moving to specialists for art, music, drama, DT and science. During this year they work on topic-based learning, with a new one for each term.

Students take the double science award (instead of three individual GCSEs) and the labs are pretty basic for a secondary school. But there was enthusiastic experimenting going on during our visit. One boy told us they were mixing acid with a base and heating it up. And what were they expecting to happen? 'It is going to evaporate from a liquid to a gas and you are going to see salts,' suggested one. 'I'm hoping it's going to turn green,' said another, of perhaps a more creative bent.

For ICT they take the Creative-I Media curriculum, which includes elements such as web design and graphic design, and is less about coding and programming – many achieve a distinction, which is equivalent to an A at GCSE.

Art is one of the most popular options as you might expect among a dyslexic cohort. The art rooms are suitably stationed up in the eaves, and turn out highly respectable results at GCSE, with some pupils going on to art colleges.

When it comes to sixth form, officially pupils need at least five A*-Cs at GCSE to do A level and BTec level 3 courses, but a wide range of vocational courses are also offered. The majority of courses are taken at Bexhill College, but there are other options such as practical horticulture at Plumpton College. The school's sixth form is designed to be a halfway house, so that pupils spend part of their time at college, and part at school where they continue to work on English, maths, and personal and social development, as well as GCSE resits where required, and receive support with assignments from the teaching assistants. They can also work on Duke of Edinburgh awards and undertake work experience.

The prep school is situated across the road. Class sizes across the school average at six (maximum eight) but there are just four pupils in the combined year 3/4 class. The prep is so teeny (18 pupils) that its assembly hall is a cosy room. A year 6 class was experimenting with a set of seeds which had been sent to space – they were potting them alongside regular seeds for comparison.

Games, options, the arts: With small pupil numbers and a sizeable dyspraxic contingent who struggle with co-ordination you'd imagine it would be difficult to field a competitive team, but Goodman insists the football team is very successful against other independent schools in the region. But those who have suffered the jeers for their lack of sporting prowess will find blissful relief here. 'Often the person who comes last at sports day gets the biggest round of applause, and kids will run alongside them to support them,' says Goodwin.

'The way in which the children learn to support each other is exceptional,' says one parent. 'And Mr Fitzy with his outdoors programme achieves fantastic things with children whom most PE teachers would leave back in the changing room.' 'Mr Fitzsimmons and his team are brilliant in making sports fun and achievable for all,' agreed another parent. 'He also does camps in the school grounds which are excellent and very character building,' she said.

The one-time lily pond is now an outdoor pool, used for kayak practice in winter and possibly bracing (unheated) swimming in summer. There's also a cricket field, rugby pitches, running track and tennis courts, and the 60 acres are regularly put to use for cross-country. Other sports offered include cricket, rugby, basketball, horseriding and archery.

The school has run its first overseas trip, with a ski trip to the south of France. More are on the agenda, says Goodman.

Music boasts a big uptake, with more than half of the children learning an instrument.

Boarding: Around one-third of the 110 pupils board. Exeats have been made non-compulsory – so no need for overseas students to find somewhere to go every third weekend. All the international pupils, and some UK ones, stay at weekends, while parents who wish to take their child home are asked to do so on the designated exeat weekends.

Boys' dorms are in the main house, girls' are in the modern former headteacher's house in the grounds. Most rooms are two or three bedded, with the odd single for sixth formers. All have a compact ensuite with loo and shower cubicle, and a there's a washbasin in the bedroom. Lovely views as standard.

Common rooms offer an array of video games, PlayStations and a football table, and there's a kitchen with microwave for snack attacks.

Background and atmosphere: Certainly has the wow factor. You are greeted at the top of the drive by the stunning main house and its early 17th century black and white Jacobean façade. Inside it's all original leaded lights and rare Italian plasterwork ceilings. The house was in the Frewen family for 300 years and the walls groan with their gigantic portraits in oil. In the drawing room, used for meetings and music, sits the sedan chair used by Lady Frewen, who perished in a house fire in 1752. Pupils say they've seen her ghost, and even the head admits to catching something out of the corner of his eye, and hearing knocking on his study door long after everyone has gone home.

The grounds are like something out of The Draughtsman's Contract. There's a giant chessboard in topiary, a walled garden, Elizabethan bowling alley, formal yewery, and arboretum of redwoods and oaks. The English block in Portakabins contrasts sharply with the grandeur, but if Goodman has his way these will be bulldozed and replaced with a new multi-purpose block. In all there are 60 acres of school land, and a further 100 acres of woodland which belongs to the Frewen family but which the school is able to use for school camps and the like.

The glorious surroundings and feeling of space are sure to ease the anxiety-ridden child, but it's setting in the middle of nowhere could make for a challenging school run – luckily school buses fan out to the big towns, and the school can make arrangements to get boarders to London and airports.

School houses are named after famous dyslexics – Jamie Oliver, Steven Redgrave, Keira Knightley and Ann Bancroft.

Pastoral care, well-being and discipline: 'Our pupils have struggled themselves or been bullied, so they tend to be really supportive of others coming in and make them very welcome,' says the head.

Stress and anxiety are par for the course in this cohort where, head says, pretty much every child has been through feeling a failure and being unable to understand why they can't do it when they are trying very hard. Every child has a mentor, and the school runs mindfulness and counselling sessions, and will buy in psychotherapy for those with severe anxiety.

The environment helps them to destress and calm, Goodwin says, and there's a policy of involving pupils a lot in decisions to help them feel empowered. One example is the homework policy – students said they felt it was important but there was too much of it. They proposed one subject per night, of 20 minutes duration, and a week in which to complete it – a policy that was adopted for the senior school up to the GCSE years.

'Frewen is above all a very happy school – any issues are dealt with quickly and all children know and understand that they have a right to be happy,' said a parent.

One who needed convincing to move her child out of mainstream added: 'On a personal level he has developed enormously. He is a confident, happy, well balanced boy and he enjoys interacting with his peers and staff members and has formed good friendships. We really do not think he would be the same child had we kept him in mainstream school as he would have been teased and bullied as being different.'

Therapy and staffing: All staff have level 3 dyslexia training – any teaching assistant arriving without qualifications will be put through training within their first year. This means, Goodwin says, that where children in other schools are taken out for a couple of hours' specialist teaching per week, here they are not taken out at all as all staff have the relevant expertise.

'Everything is delivered correctly by high calibre specialist teachers and therapists,' confirmed a parent.

The school also has in-house speech and language and occupational therapists, and therapy is described as 'excellent' by one parent. 'You are kept informed as to what is going on in therapy which is helpful so you can back the therapists up by continuing their good work at home,' she said.

Pupils and parents: Wide range socially. Boys outnumber girls, although Goodman expects the current ratio of one-third girls to creep nearer to 50:50 over the next couple of years. The school hosts around a dozen international students, hailing from North and South America, India, Malaysia, Singapore, Tunisia, Egypt and Europe. Overseas pupils must have English as their first, or strong second, language.

Minibuses ply the routes to Tunbridge Wells, Ashford and Hastings. Arrangements can be made for pupils from London to be accompanied on the train for weekends in the Capital by gap year students, and the school will organise taxis to the airport for overseas students.

The school caters for a wide ability so that some pupils will gain seven GCSEs and go on to do A levels, while others have below average cognitive ability (but would not fall into a moderate learning difficulty category).

Some transfer out to mainstream, but not as often as you would think, according to Goodman. 'For parents it's important to know that is a possibility, but more often parents realise we cater for the full range of ability and they choose to stay here.'

Entrance: The entry profile has been tightened up in the last couple of years. The school is now concentrating firmly on the SpLDs – so children will have a diagnosis of dyslexia, dyspraxia, dyscalculia or speech and language difficulties as their primary need. A few will have an autism spectrum disorder as a secondary need and where this is mild; but Goodman says this is not the school for those with a primary need of autism, since they need a different style of teaching. The school caters for pupils with a wide range of ability. Some children have a below average cognitive profile, but the curriculum would be beyond the reach of those with moderate learning difficulties.

Numbers at different stages in the school reflect the fact that it becomes easier to get specialist funding as a child gets older and it becomes more apparent that mainstream cannot work for them, although Goodman wishes it was otherwise. 'Early intervention is really important; the sooner they get to a specialist school the more impact we can have: if they don't arrive until year 10 by then a lot of damage has been done,' he says. However, he reckons only a minority of parents have to resort to tribunal.

Children can enter at any point in the school year. If a child appears to fit from the paperwork, they will be invited for a two or three day assessment to include overnights if they plan to board.

Exit: At the end of year 11, around half go into the sixth form, created in 2014, and the rest go to further education colleges, sometimes in their home town when they have been boarders. The first cohort to leave the sixth form in 2016 were off to colleges including Wandsworth, Harrow, West Kent, Hastings South Coast, Plumpton, West Suffolk, and Bexhill. Two students in the lower sixth are expected to go to university.

Money matters: Around one-third of pupils are privately funded, the rest gain funding from their local authority 'but have to be quite severely dyslexic' in order to manage this. 'Parents have to demonstrate to the local authority that the child can't manage with the provision in mainstream school,' says Goodman. This means there is a greater weight of self-funded children in the prep, where parents have realised there is an issue early on, while local authorities tend to insist on trying mainstream adjustments first.

Remarks: There was one constant theme in our interviews with parents, and that was the transformation they witnessed in their child's self-confidence after being placed here. 'Miraculous,' said one; 'She didn't want to curl up and die any more,' said another.

And although many worried about taking their child out of mainstream, they hadn't looked back. One parent said: 'We were extremely worried about taking [him] out of a mainstream environment, worrying that going to a school for children with special educational needs would label him. But the day we looked around the school, we knew that it would be the perfect place for [him] – I was almost in tears seeing somewhere where he could belong and wouldn't feel different or out of place.'

The campus is like something out of Alice in Wonderland, and if you're lucky your child might sip on the magic potion that Frewen has to offer and transform before your eyes.

Maple Hayes Hall School

Abnalls Lane, Lichfield, Staffordshire WS13 8BL

Pupils: 103 • Ages: 7–17

Fees: Funded by local authorities

Tel: 01543 264387
Email: office@dyslexia.gb.com
Website: www.dyslexia.gb.com/

Principal: Since 1982, Dr Neville Brown (80s). Smartly dressed in a navy blazer and neatly polished shoes. Reformed truant and a bit of a rebel, but more about that later. Academic to the core, he has an impressive list of degrees and qualifications in teaching and educational psychology. Former ITV Central teacher of the year. British Dyslexia Association award for lifetime contribution to the field of dyslexia. Times/Sternberg Award for those who have done the most for society and good causes at an older age.

It's a family business. Mrs Brown is the bursar and their son, Dr Daryl Brown, is the head. Language and literacy are both the vocation and hobby of the Browns – father and son are writing a dyslexia-friendly dictionary. Words with the same core will be grouped together on the same page, making it easier to grasp the meanings behind parts of words.

Dr Neville gets what it's like to be an intelligent child in an education system that doesn't support children with dyslexia. 'From my own history, I was dispatched to three infant schools successively and I played truant from all three. Nobody knows how I learnt to read.'

At junior school, he avoided the cane by turning up. He made rapid progress, becoming an avid reader. 'I read comics and horror stories and Dickens and all sorts of things'. A further change of schools led to more truanting, until he started grammar school, where the emphasis on learning to write had a knock on effect with reading. 'If you're teaching people only to read and not to write, they don't read very well,' he says.

Academic matters: Independent day school for pupils aged 7 to 17 with dyslexia and comorbid conditions. National curriculum followed, except that modern foreign languages not usually taught, seen as an added pressure. At key stage 4, pupils can study for GCSEs in English, maths, dual science, geography, history, art. Those who excel at maths can take their exam early and go on to study GCSE statistics. BTecs in design and technology and ICT. Music and RE are taken up to year 9 and beyond if wished. The school produces good GCSE results year in, year out. Recent results show that every school leaver got at least five GCSEs, between 15-43 per cent at A*-C. Dr Neville is adamant that the curriculum should be academically challenging. 'Every child should have a broad education. We're not sacrificing that, we refuse to do it.' No options – Dr Neville says that continual improvement in literacy means that GCSE grades are difficult to predict, which may mean that students drop a subject that they might do well in two years later at GCSE.

What sets this school apart is its unique morphological approach to teaching literacy, developed 30 years ago by Dr Neville. Firmly opposed to the use of phonics for teaching literacy to children with dyslexia. 'They don't benefit from it,' he says. Here, staff use cards with icons to depict the meanings of words or parts of words, bypassing the need to sound words out. He is also not a fan of the multisensory approach – students practise their writing using a unisensory technique with a blindfold, retrieving their morphemes directly from kinæsthetic memory and joining them up to make complex words.

When new words are introduced, pupils write them down with their meanings to reinforce the learning, then they are tested. Teachers use this integrative process to embed knowledge in other subjects throughout the curriculum. For example, a digitally-produced pie chart might be used in geography to reinforce IT as well as numeracy.

Scribes or other forms of recording aren't used. The thinking behind this is that the use of these methods leads to dependency on support and avoids dealing with the problem. So ICT is not used as an alternative to acquiring reading, writing and presentation skills. Right from the start, children are taught fully cursive script.

If your child finds routine comforting, they will like the regular pattern to the days and weeks. Eight half-hour periods a week are dedicated to literacy, which is also incorporated into the teaching of all other subjects within the curriculum. Each class has a tutor responsible for literacy development who liaises with the educational psychologist and a head who is also a psychologist. Many of texts in the well-equipped library are written and printed for the school and some of the classrooms have their own mini libraries.

Year 9 pupils have the opportunity to develop communication and journalistic skills by participating in the BBC News School Report project. One year they covered the thorny issue of potholes in the country road leading to the school. They interviewed road users, including a cyclist, to find out their views. A number of students appeared on camera reading out their findings and Staffordshire County Council's response.

No more than 12 children to one teacher. Many classes are smaller, in the main between four and 10. Big enough to feel like a mainstream class, yet small enough for children to get sufficient attention. Longish school day, starting at 9am, through to 4.40pm Monday to Friday and 9-11am on Saturdays, followed by voluntary extra GCSE courses. Terms are shorter than usual to compensate. One parent said when his daughter started here, she coped well with the increased hours, adapting 'like a fish to water.'

Many of the pupils struggle to concentrate for long spells, so single lessons mainly kept to half-hour periods. When the bell goes, they move to a different classroom which has the effect of resetting their attention span. Double or triple lessons are broken up into two or three distinct activities. Tasks are set in small bites, to keep within the short attention span of many of the pupils. One parent said, 'The structure helps, and the short lessons.'

After school there is a 40 minute prep time, supervised by a teacher who is available for support, as and when. It breaks pupils in to being responsible for their homework without feeling overwhelmed.

'We don't consciously split them into primary and secondary phase,' says Dr Neville. This makes for an easy transition. One parent said, 'When my son went from one phase to the next it was a walk up the stairs. Not a big deal'.

Children are encouraged to look ahead and consider what they want from their working lives. Careers guidance and education provided throughout key stages 3 and 4. The library has a careers section, as well as computer access for resources. Work experience is arranged by parents and takes place in the holidays. Employers are asked for reports which are kept with school records.

General consensus among parents seems to be that the system works and that pupils are achieving much better grades than anyone ever felt possible before they started at Maple Hayes. 'If you want your child to succeed in life, they've got to be able to read and write, they've got to be independent. This school promotes independence,' said one. Others say, 'Dr Brown's like Merlin. All of a sudden these children can read and write' and 'My daughter was never taught to write until she came to this school. It turned her life around.'

Games, options, the arts: Clubs mainly run at lunchtime, because of potential transport issues at the end of the day. Wide range of activities on offer means that students can chose a hobby or sport that plays to their strengths. Activities include soccer, five-a-side football, cricket, gymnastics, bird-watching, mask-making, board games and recycling. Accredited courses in first aid and alcohol awareness also on offer. Even though it's a small school, the pupils compete in the independent schools regional championships for swimming, cross-country running and athletics.

Good use is made of the school's rural setting and extensive grounds, with riding being a popular activity. Horses are carefully selected for their gentle temperaments. Riding improves balance which has a positive knock-on effect in other areas, such as cycling. Year 8 students can go on an outdoor pursuits course and in year 9 they can go on a residential geography field trip.

The school doesn't compromise on aiming for high standards in academic subjects at the expense of encouraging creativity and soft skills. Dr Neville is a keen musician himself, playing piano, keyboard and the organ. Teachers use the lively group music lessons to encourage communication and interaction. One mum whose daughter is artistic appreciates that this aspect is challenged and developed. 'The school offers the opportunity to excel at art,' she said.

Drama is brought to life by making sure that the pupils get the chance to see theatre in action. An annual treat is an outdoor performance by the Shakespeare in the Park theatre group in the school's Italian garden. It's a laid back affair, with families picnicking on the lawns.

At lunchtime and breaks, the children have the chance to mix and play. 'A lot of these young ones, when they come here, it's the first time they've been really socially engaged and play engaged. We don't provide massive artefacts for their play, we let them play imaginatively,' says Dr Neville.

Background and atmosphere: School founded in 1982, when Dr and Mrs Brown sold everything they had to raise money to buy the 18th century manor house and turn it into a school for underachieving and dyslexic children. Approach to the school is along a quiet leafy lane, admittedly with a few potholes. Lovely, spacious grounds, incorporating 200 acres of farmland, set deep in the heart of gymkhana country. Deer graze on grassy banks not far from the main school building, a mellow red-brick Georgian house. Delicate white-flowering shrubs occupy flower beds either side of the pillared central porch. Inside the building, it is clean, bright and tastefully decorated. Many original features have been retained, such as the intricate fireplace surrounds. The family have worked hard, often doing physical labour themselves to restore and develop the building. Dr Daryl Brown remembers digging the foundations of one of the buildings with a digger on the back of a tractor. There's a homely atmosphere – cheerful artwork adorns the walls and there's a buzz of chatter as pupils spill out into the hall before heading off for lunch.

Pastoral care, well-being and discipline: Staff are keen to show pupils that dyslexia is not a bar to being successful. High-profile, positive role models who have dyslexia often visit the school, including actor Henry Winkler, aka the Fonz, and Princess Beatrice.

Discipline at Maple Hayes is traditional — all about setting clear boundaries, with the expectation of good manners and self-discipline. Praise and reward with merits when things go right, possibility of demerits, escalating to Saturday morning detentions when things go wrong. Fixed term and permanent exclusions for serious misbehaviour. Parents say, 'It's disciplined here. They know the rules. Proper discipline. Ties done up, buttons done up.' And, 'it's about traditional values.' But it's not unreasonably strict, 'They are treated fairly,' said another parent.

Uniform includes sensible shoes, smart shirts and black trousers or skirts. Briefcases, rather than shoulder bags or backpacks. Mobile phones not allowed in school, although parents may request that their child has one travelling to or from school, which must be handed in on arrival. No chewing gum or fizzy drinks. School dinners are varied and well received. Parents say, 'There's chilli, curry, puddings, biscuits, cakes. All prepared freshly on site by the school chef,' and, 'Proper cooked meal, three courses,' and, 'She ate like never before when on trial week'.

Children are encouraged to take care of themselves and help others, and it seems to have sunk in. One student overheard fretting to another that they had forgotten their shoes for PE. Their friend reassured them, 'Don't worry. It will be fine, I'm always forgetting mine.' One mum was pleased to notice her son helping an elderly lady with her shopping. She puts it down to the ethos of the school sinking in. 'That's what this school is all about, respect for yourself, respect for elders'.

The school forum allows pupils to contribute to the decision-making processes. Issues raised at the forum include giving their views on 'confidence at school'. Pupil representatives discussed effective ways in which teachers build their confidence and mulled over how they might improve. They also talked about what confidence means to them as individuals.

Parents we spoke to are happy that their children are well cared for and that their emotional needs are met. Students are keen to come to school and stress-related health issues improve. One mum said, 'Our daughter used to self-harm when she was at her last school; there's none of that when here. Felt like a family all the way.' Others said, 'Our son came for trial week. In only a week, he was a different child, no tummyache, no tears, no headache.' And 'If he hadn't got a place here, by the age of 13 or 14 he would no longer have been in school.'

Staff are kind and practical in their approach to teaching. One parent, whose child has dyspraxia, said, 'My daughter can't run around. Her teacher showed her how to run, rather than just telling her to run.' Parents also say that their children find the staff approachable and prepared to talk problems over. 'Positive and consistent from the top, to the chef, minibus driver. Genuinely care for the kids.'

Dr Neville says that success is the key to happiness at school. 'With very rare exceptions, emotional difficulties are dependent on failure, so you give them success. You teach them so that they know how to do their weekly tests on literacy.'

Therapy and staffing: 'Every teacher here has their own tutor group for literacy and they are appointed for their subject prowess, plus their willingness to undergo training,' says Dr Neville. Staff turnover is low. One 70-year-old teacher retired recently after 25 years. Most teacher training is in-house – they all have completed courses in SEN and been taught the school's literacy method. School is a research centre, hence all the internal training. Staff are also encouraged to do CPD elsewhere. No teaching assistants, just teachers and small classes. No therapists, avoiding disruptive withdrawal from classes.

Pupils and parents: Pupils come from a wide area, including Nottinghamshire, Cheshire, Leicestershire, and Shropshire. Children aged between 7 and 17, 110 currently on roll. About a third of parents are on benefits. Virtually all the pupils are statemented or have an Education, Health and Care plan. As well as dyslexia, many have additional special needs such as dysgraphia (about 40 per cent), dyscalculia, dyspraxia or Asperger's syndrome. As with all the students, those with Asperger's must have a diagnosis of dyslexia. Those with extremely mild autism might be accepted, but they must not have behavioural difficulties that could affect the other students.

Home-school communication consists of termly reports and annual parents' evenings, and more general information is in the newsletter. 'If parents have got a concern, then they pop in and somebody deals with it; we're small enough to do that,' says Dr Neville.

Entrance: Prospective pupils must be assessed by an educational psychologist, which can be arranged by the school. Children whose test results suggest specific learning difficulties will be offered an interview to determine whether or not the school and child are a good match. If so, they will be offered a free, week-long trial. All being well, they will be offered a placement for a minimum of three years.

Pupils are placed in classes with others at a similar literacy and curriculum level. This may mean that children will take their GCSEs a year early. Others who have joined the school after the age of 12 with low literacy levels may need an extra year to reach GCSE.

Exit: Shame there's no sixth form here, but the school puts a lot of effort into supporting pupils onto the next step. Careers advisors attend parents' evenings for year 9 upwards. Dr Neville remembers two brothers who went straight into the family farming business after school, but apart from that, students all go on to attend FE colleges or sixth forms. Many go to university – further educational achievements include a masters in electronic engineering and doctorates in physics and English. Former pupils include a teacher, psychologist, restaurant manager and small business owner. One parent said, 'When my son was in year 10 we could look at college courses with optimism. Five years ago we never thought we'd be able to do that.'

Money matters: Almost 100 per cent of students have their fees and transport paid for by their local authorities. Dr Brown senior is extremely supportive of parents in their efforts to get funding from their local authorities. He has attended countless tribunals and seen them through to successful conclusions in most cases.

Remarks: Only school in the country to use Dr Neville Brown's morphological approach to literacy teaching. Excellent academic results speak for themselves. Both Drs Neville and Daryl Brown are qualified educational psychologists with many years of experience, giving them a unique insight into the obstacles faced by these children.

Plenty of happy parents testify to the success of the methods, saying that the school has given their children 'confidence', 'a future', 'prospects' and 'a life'. So if your child is lucky enough to be offered a place here, grab it with both hands.

M

Mark College

Blackford Road, Mark, Highbridge, Somerset TA9 4NP

Pupils: 75; 40 full/weekly boarders • Ages: 10–19 • Sixth form: 20

Fees: £23,000 – £75,000 full boarding depending on needs

Tel: 01278 641632
Email: markcollege@priorygroup.com
Website: www.priorychildrensservices.co.uk/find-a-location/mark-college-somerset/

Principal: Since 2014, Chris Sweeney, ably supported by his chocolate labrador Poppy. Was all set to follow the family path to university, do the done thing and become a lawyer, when his astute father recommended instead that he follow his passion, which was working with children. So he started as a classroom assistant at Freemantles, a special school in Surrey, and studied for a degree in psychology part-time. It was the start of a track which weaved through the various roles in schools, and enables him to understand operations from every perspective. He followed Freemantles with teaching roles in a variety of SEBD and complex ASD schools – Westfield in Bucks, Little Down in Slough, Holyport Manor in Maidenhead and Priory in Taunton. He has also been a consultant training others in behaviour management, and has taken a series of interim headships at schools in difficulty.

'Has a lot of interaction with the pupils for a headmaster, my son mentions him a lot,' said a parent.

Weekends find him talking shop with his wife who is also a teacher, and enjoying activities revolving around dogs, horses, running and swimming with kids of 9 and 12.

Also running the engine room are vice principal Polly Adams, who takes care of the business side of things and is the main point of contact for parents from referral through to providing a much praised shoulder through the child's school life; and Graham Scott, appointed to the headteacher role in January 2016, who has the dual benefit of the gleam in his eye as a new appointee, coupled with a decade teaching in the school which means he knows it inside out. They are a comfortable team, clearly all doing what they are best at.

Academic matters: Lots of scope for children of mainstream ability but who just need that extra support – around 50 per cent of the children will take seven or eight GCSEs. One leaver last summer achieved three As at A level.

But there are also options for those for whom formal exams and traditional qualifications are a barrier – such as BTecs, Asdan courses, vocational courses and COPE (Certificate of Personal Effectiveness) courses. Bespoke is the word, so for some that might mean taking a GCSE in maths, but an entry level course in English.

Sixth formers spend varying amounts of their time at Mark working on maths, literacy, and social skills, and the rest at FE colleges where they will be subtly supported by key workers, who can also help them with coursework back at the house. Mark works with local colleges including Strode, Western, Wyvern and Bridgwater, and students can usually do any course they fancy these institutions, from construction to photography. A levels offered on site are art, maths and DT – for others the students go out to college.

Intake currently starts at age 10, but there are plans afoot to extend to take children from the start of key stage 2.

Class sizes are a maximum 10, and are arranged by year group with students then given differentiated work. We saw this at work in a year 7 literacy class, where students were reading books which ranged from comic style to Harry Potter size tomes. Progress from one to the other can be rapid with the right teaching, we're told – one mother saw her son's reading age increase by 10 years in two years.

Classrooms are all mainstream-looking. There's a food tech room, a woodwork room with all the kit and the DT teacher's dog Wilf watching the goings-on from behind a child gate; and a chemistry lab for practicals, where students ably explained the work under way to make reagents to test for water.

Games, options, the arts: Unusually for a school in the specialist sector it manages lots of inter-school sports competitions, from football to cross-country. The school's diminutive size may mean they are fielding a team of varying ages and abilities, but a good relationship with local schools means their opponents will rustle up a team to match and provide a good game for all.

There's a huge sports hall, which boarders can also use in the evenings for football and basketball; also pitches for rugby, cricket and football, and an athletics track.

Boarding: Children can board from the outset at age 10. There are three boarding houses on the school site: one for boys under 16; boys over 16; and one house for the girls (only four girls currently board). The school is searching for additional boarding accommodation off site, for the more independent sixth formers. The remote location of the college means it's not the easiest place for teenagers to develop independence skills and a social life; the idea would be for this group to live off site, and the sixth formers needing more support could stay on campus.

All bedrooms are single; sixth formers have ensuite bathrooms, the younger children share. They are simply furnished with a bed, wardrobe, and desk, and the brown door-lined corridors look a little institutional. There are three lounge areas providing for different preferences – one for the gamers, one for TV, and one for those who want a quiet life. There's a kitchen where they can prepare snacks, although all meals are taken in the school dining hall. Washing is done by the school laundry, but the kitchen has washer/dryer which is used for independence training in year 11, when pupils learn to launder and iron clothes.

The benefits of boarding are immense, said one parent. 'It's made him. His communication and confidence has grown immensely, and he can now do things for himself that he never used to.' Another reported that her son at 14 is now capable of doing all his own laundry and cooking a full meal.

Placements are for 36 weeks only. Termly boarders have an exeat in the middle of each half term, and some local B&Bs provide guardianship and exeat arrangements for international students. Some children returning to London for weekends get taxis to meet coaches to the capital. There is also the possibility of weekly boarding, or flexi boarding – some pupils might do one night per week to focus on life skills, independence training, or social skills.

Evening activities include on site clubs in sports, movies, chess, animation, drama and cooking; students also go out to a local youth drama group, air cadets and scouts. Parents say the school goes out of its way to cater for individual interests – such as taking a minibus with one boy who likes to attend a local rugby club.

Weekends involve shopping trips, bowling, cinema, and swimming. Sign-up sheets on the noticeboards were offering trips to laser quest and the Wetlands Centre.

Background and atmosphere: A Georgian house sits at the centre of the 24 acre grounds, from which a series of buildings spread. All very rural and pastoral, with wooden doors and exposed bricks aplenty, the scruffy edges giving it a cosy, farmhouse feel. The uneven floors and classrooms crammed into sloping eaves mean it is not a suitable campus for anyone with mobility difficulties. A red phone box stands in the grounds, once the means for students to communicate with home, now 'an art piece,' says the principal.

It's a noticeably happy and serene environment; children smiled at us as they walked past in the corridors, and waved cheerily to the head through his window.

Pastoral care, well-being and discipline: 'If you get the education right you don't have behaviours,' says Sweeney. The proof? One student who had to be educated on his own at his previous school owing to his behaviour, now a calm member of the class.

Sweeney believes certainty and consistency are crucial when it comes to behaviour. When an issue arises a child is given a chance to apologise, and if he does, it's over. If it is not resolved, staff will issue an amber slip which means there will be a consequence – five minutes with the teacher at breaktime, perhaps; it progresses through to senior management if the breach continues.

'How can we avoid issues arising is the biggie for me,' Sweeney says. 'Ninety per cent of the behaviour we see comes from a social communication issue, a misunderstanding, or the environment has become too much, and the child uses it as a coping strategy. So we work on alternative strategies for them to manage that scenario next time.' It's highly effective, reports one parent, who says her child is now unrecognisable from the one who joined with serious behavioural problems.

There are lots of measures in place for children who find a school environment overwhelming. One pupil takes all of her lessons in the boarding house. Several pupils wear ear defenders.

And there's a space known as Room X, a room where children can come either for timetabled individual work, or when they are struggling or anxious and need to leave a classroom.

This understanding extends throughout the school – one student will only eat roast dinners, so the kitchen makes him one every single day.

There is currently no formal respite in the holidays, but therapy often continues with children coming in during school holidays, and anxious children who need to keep in contact with school can come in to potter around, have lunch at school, and do a bit of therapy.

Therapy and staffing: Therapy is all provided in-house, by a team including one full-time and one part-time speech and language therapist, an occupational therapist, and a psychotherapist. Some students will receive direct therapy with the qualified therapist, others will have a programme devised by the therapist but delivered by support staff. There are also social communication groups – one for a sixth form group took them to the pub to show them how to manage that situation.

There are 14 TAs, known as the vulnerable learners' team. They work as one-to-ones in class with particular children, or may provide support to children who need it around social times. They all have internal training and complete external courses. Bank staff may be used around exam time to provide readers and scribes, but otherwise staff absences are managed using cover supervisors to maintain consistency for the children.

Care staff are all required to have a NVQ3 qualification, and there is no use of temporary staff in the boarding side – instead one of the TAs or teaching staff would step in. Parents rave about the care staff, one relating how a member of staff went shopping in her own time and brought back five pairs of shoes for a pupil to try on, so he could avoid a meltdown in a shoe shop.

Pupils and parents: The pupil body here looks like those at any mainstream school, and they are all verbal. Girls are heavily outnumbered, at only around one in eight pupils.

Mark is well geared up for international students, who represent about 20 per cent of the school body, and currently hail from Nigeria, Saudi Arabia, Italy, Turkey, Oman and Pakistan.

Communication with parents comes in the form of emails, phone calls, termly reports and parent days, with Polly Adams reportedly providing 'outstanding' support to parents.

The college is currently putting in place non-statement annual reviews – these yearly meetings between parents and all staff involved with the child are a required feature where local authorities foot the bill, but the college realised that self-funding parents miss out on this, so is now introducing them for this group.

Entrance: It's designated as a SpLD school, but that is interpreted in its widest sense – pupils might have dyslexia, dyscalculia, ASD, ADHD, speech and language difficulties, difficulties around social communication, or a history of anxiety or bullying which may mean a student has been out of school for a long spell, and needs the calm, quiet environment Mark can provide.

Children tend to be of average or above average ability. 'The classic student is the one for whom mainstream doesn't provide enough, but a local authority special school wouldn't fit their profile. We're like a mini-mainstream,' says Sweeney.

Pupils unlikely to gain a place are those with serious learning or cognitive difficulties, or where behaviour problems are a primary need (although some have issues with behaviour owing to frustration).

The assessment process involves reviews of papers, a visit for the child and parents, a trial of one or two days and nights, and sometimes assessments. For overseas students staff will often do Skype assessments. The assessment decision rests on 'can we meet the child's needs, and what is the impact on the rest of the school going to be?'

Exit: Most students stay into the sixth form, with the odd exceptions who want to do courses not available locally. At 18, last year three from a year group of 10 went to university, one went into work, and the rest to some form of further education – at this point often back to colleges in their home area.

Money matters: Around 60 per cent of pupils are local authority funded, the others are self-funding. Fees can range from £23,000 to £75,000, depending on the amount of therapy and support required. Around 60 per cent of the pupils who are funded by a local authority have to resort to tribunal first – the school staff will support to the extent of appearing at the hearing to outline the difference they can make for the child, but they aim to avoid getting into adversarial situations with local authorities.

Remarks: Unless you happen to live in the West Country, the biggest downside is going to be the location; a difficult journey to anywhere else. However some parents say the calming influence of the deep rural situation is a bonus, and for others any transport difficulties are overridden by what the school can provide. It's that very rare provision for children who fall through the gap between mainstream and special schools, and it looks and acts to all intents like a mainstream school. And children arriving here who've had a rough ride previously at school will feel like they've been wrapped in lavender-scented cotton wool.

The Moat School

Bishops Avenue, London SW6 6EG

Pupils: 70 • Ages: 9–16

Fees: £24,000 – £28,800 pa

Tel: 020 7610 9018
Email: office@moatschool.org.uk
Website: www.moatschool.org.uk

Headteacher: Since 2013, Miss Clare King (30s). Has only taught at The Moat, where she started as an NQT and received accelerated promotion. Previously director of studies and deputy head.

Academic matters: Small classes (approx 10) and a learning support assistant ensure each child is given attention, especially during the first three years of secondary school. Education is broad – pupils taught lots of communication and study skills alongside literacy and maths. They are weaned off the extra help during the two year GCSE syllabus but by then class sizes get even smaller. Each pupil is issued with a laptop and helped to manage this responsibility by having convenient lockers to store them in between lessons (an example of the practical solutions to problems of organisation for dyslexics).

'A good range of subjects,' according to pupils, who all aim to leave with at least five GCSEs, though no language or classics teaching. All sit maths, English and science (many sitting additional science), but creativity high on school's and pupils' agenda since popular subjects are business communication, design technology, drama and media studies. The year groups and classes are small and so results vary each year, but in 2016, 61.7 per cent of GCSE grades were A*-C. Considering almost every child ends up with access arrangements that often include a scribe or a reader, this is no mean feat, but clearly The Moat is not a school for those primarily seeking academic results. BTecs and V certificates offered alongside GCSEs.

Everything taught as kinaesthetically as possible – we saw a paper ball being thrown from teacher to pupil and back while being questioned – to help keep focus, keep energy levels high and pupils on their toes. Media studies and business studies are popular GCSE subjects – partly because they are ideal for visual learners with plenty of ICT input, but also because of 'brilliant' teachers. Teachers clearly working together – staff meetings, socialising, eating together, extra training – all evidence of a good staff team. Specialist subject teachers are trained in specific learning difficulties and share good practice via cross-curricular learning. For example, vocabulary is extended with a 'word of the week' programme that is used in all lessons. Concentration problems associated with learning difficulties eased by having regular break times rather than endless and confusing lesson changes. With many practical solutions to pupils' learning difficulties, stress is removed from the equation allowing for calm, purposeful teaching. Therapeutic provision now improved with embedded initiatives including whole-school paired reading, sensory diets and Brain Gym.

Because most pupils have specific learning difficulties and all teachers are trained in special needs, individual pupils are not withdrawn from lessons for extra literacy but instead an integrated Skills for Learning programme takes the form of small, cross-age range groups, who are mentored in literacy skills three times a week throughout their school life, working on specific areas of weakness.

Games, options, the arts: Practical subjects predictably popular – science, media studies, music, art, PE. Drama a large part of the school curriculum with all children taking part in productions in one form or another. School achievements include productions in West End theatres as part of competitions (including Shakespeare for Schools). Sport encouraged but it is definitely not a competitive school and sport is 'more about keeping fit than winning'. Usual range of sport takes place in the playground – no large playing fields, though some rowing and yoga too, and tennis courts across the road. Music for GCSE but also plenty of individual music lessons – drums, saxophone, guitar, piano etc – and music therapy. Facilities for composition as part of music technology in GSCE. Gorgeous art all over the school includes collaborative and fine art (and lots of visits to galleries) but also wider design technology and resistant materials, and even film making. On our visit we saw very practical wood turning and food technology lessons – skill-based practical activities that suit pupils who have lots to offer, allowing for achievement outside the strictly academic spheres. Extracurricular activities are not an after-school option but each day ends with an hour of a chosen extension activity such as quilting, drama, cricket, debate, sport. D of E and residential school trips each year, as well as much-loved day trips related to school studies (theatre, galleries, museums etc).

Background and atmosphere: Food is cooked on the premises and staff join students for lunch with vegetarian option and salad bar (only used by teachers according to one pupil), though predictable complaints by pupils about food – not enough, not enough choice, too many vegetables. Pupils and staff may eat together but the fact that no first names are used for teachers is indicative of clear boundaries and rules which include zero tolerance of bad behaviour. This helps keep the school calm and stress free, critical for many academically fragile pupils. Many choose to stay inside and read magazines at break rather than play football. Not really enough 'chilling' space, according to pupils, and especially for the girls who are in the minority anyway and who want to be outside but not standing around avoiding footballs.

The building is practical but dull, some areas clearly in need of a refit. This fits with the ethos of the school somehow – practical solutions and purpose more important than image. Even the terminology used is unambiguous – each morning starts with a 'gathering', Friday's gathering is for giving merits to pupils and sharing successes. The year book is called The Keep, as pupils hold on to these at the end as a memory of their school life. Pupils say they are 'respected for who we are, not how we look'; 'it is what's inside that counts'; and what is inside the school is respected and respectful pupils and staff, working together to achieve.

Pastoral care, well-being and discipline: Behaviour and control are evidently an important part of what is taught and learned at Moat House. Clear boundaries and sanctions intended to assist with the teenage problem of organisation and lost property that is exacerbated by dyslexia and dyspraxia. Friday litter detention for loss or carelessness with laptops. After three warnings for misbehaviour students are sent to the Referral Room, a reflection sheet is completed together with staff following the misdemeanour to work out what happened, why and whether an apology or other action needed. A serious offence (physical violence, swearing) or three referrals leads to consequences that range from weekend detention to temporary exclusion. Pupils need to be 'persuaded to behave appropriately', but if not, then it is not the right school for them. Pupils we spoke to found sanctions fair, but explained that 'it didn't happen much'. Understanding their own thinking and learning styles and self-reflection are encouraged and a school counsellor is available for children who are referred or who ask for time to talk.

Therapy and staffing: Occupational therapist available and two speech therapists work with individual children but also teach language and communication skills throughout year 7. Speech therapists run 'Talk About' sessions in small groups to discuss how to speak in public, how to present oneself, how we make other people feel; these culminate in an outing to practise skills in public. Pupils particularly appreciated 'the chance to go out' and the female students especially liked their separate sessions and 'having time to talk about girl things'.

Pupils and parents: Pupils come from far and near, making socialising outside school tricky. Eighty per cent have statements/EHC plans and are paid for by local authorities from all over London. They are all likely to be dyslexic but come from a wide range of backgrounds and there's no one type – sporty, academic, shy, drama queens – all sorts sharing a common tolerance. They need to be bright enough to manage the expectation that they attempt GCSEs but academic achievement is not the only goal. Parents say there is plenty of communication and regular reviews, with open access to teachers – many of whom assist parents by emailing homework or notes directly if pupils can't organise their homework alone. All parents we spoke to raved about the teachers. Concerns by parents over lack of consistency in homework being dealt with by a review of the entire homework policy and strategy – showing some openness to criticism – and parents felt that their suggestions were acted upon. The school council is active and pupils use this as a conduit for change. Students say, 'Teachers come to you if they see you are struggling and don't wait for you to ask or put your hand up'. Many famous patrons act as role models of achievement, including Richard Rogers, Jeremy Irons, Ruby Wax.

Entrance: Entrance by way of careful review of a pupil's reports. The head will also take a view when the child comes in for an 'acquaint' day, and if the school feels they can support the child they will take them in even if reports are poor. Primarily a school for a child with dyslexia or dyspraxia, many also have expressive language difficulties, however intake is broadening to include those who are vulnerable or need extra nurturing, and are not thriving in competitive preps. Many more interviewed than taken on because a good match needed in such small classes. Most from mainstream primary schools, but also we met several from Blossom House and some from Fairley House in year 9, though late entry to the school a real disadvantage since the preparatory learning that takes place from year 7 all builds towards good learning skills for GCSE.

New year 5 and 6 class in 2016.

Exit: The school ends at GCSE; some parents and pupils expressed the desire for the school to continue to sixth form, but at present 75 per cent of pupils go into mainstream sixth form colleges or schools rather than supported placements and so the need is not there for this provision. It's a credit to the school that staff are able to wean the pupils off special support. No data re where every child goes after sixth form but school suggests that about a third go on to higher education.

Money matters: Fee structure changing to price bands to reflect a broader intake. Those without SpLDs and therapy needs will pay at the lowest price band, and those requiring higher levels of therapy and support will pay at the top end.

The Constable Educational Trust set up the school in 1997 and continues to run it (one remaining founder governor). They have opened two new primary free schools which, while not for dyslexic children specifically, work towards early identification of learning difficulties. This is evidently not a wealthy school; it relies on charitable donations and fundraising efforts. Money used for education rather than capital projects – no stinting on school trips and outings or staff:pupil ratios. All credit to a school that spends money on pupils rather than buildings – though the buildings are ready for some input too.

Remarks: This special school is remarkably conventional in many ways – discipline, high behavioural expectations, solid learning leading to GCSEs in usual range of subjects. What is unusual is such innovative and integrated teaching. This reviewer found it a joy to see alternative ways of learning and teaching employed to such good effect.

Moon Hall School

Pasturewood Road, Holmbury St Mary, Dorking, Surrey RH5 6LQ

Pupils: 40; 3 full, 15 flexi boarders • Ages: 7–12 • C of E

Fees: Day: £18,795 – £19,545; Boarding: £20,800 – £21,550 pa

Tel: 01306 731464
Email: enquiries@moonhallschool.co.uk
Website: www.moonhallschool.co.uk

Headteacher: Since September 2016, Emma Fraser SENCo BA QTS EYPS Dip SpLD, previously SENCo at Rosemead Prep, where she had been the SEN teacher since 1998.

Entrance: Moon Hall caters for children with a diagnosis of dyslexia, dyspraxia or dyscalculia. Parents are asked to provide a report from an educational psychologist. If the child's profile looks suitable, they spend a day at the school, being carefully (but gently) scrutinised and assessed 'to see if the school is appropriate'.

School doesn't accept children with emotional or behavioural problems and is unable to help those with severe speech and language difficulties. Children are 'taught from where they are at' – so no problem with mid-year entry.

Exit: To ease the transition at the end of year 6, the head gives advice to parents on the appropriate next school for their child. Some (around 30 per cent) go on to Moon Hall College (run by Moon Hall's founder, Berry Baker) or Belmont Prep. Others to eg Seaford College, Manor House, Prior's Field, Worth, Duke of Kent, Box Hill, St Edmunds, The Royal.

Remarks: This is a CReSTeD category DSP school. Founded in 1985 by Mrs Berry Baker in her home, Moon Hall at Ewhurst, the school is now located on a 65-acre site, amid the tranquility and beauty of the Surrey hills.

Well-resourced and purpose built, Moon Hall is in the grounds of Belmont Preparatory School. The site, uniform, meals, sport, productions and many non-teaching facilities (including weekly and flexi-boarding) are shared, but the schools are separate and have different governing bodies. The relationship works well, with Moon Hall children taking part in Belmont productions and playing a full part in sports and teams. Pupils can transfer to Belmont after Moon Hall.

Teachers are dyslexia specialists, turnover is low and professional development is encouraged. Therapy, including speech and language therapy and occupational therapy, available for those who need it. Full national curriculum is taught but humanities are slimmed to allow for intensive work in literacy and maths. Art, music, science and DT (no MFL, no classics) are delivered by subject specialists. IT programmes, such as Mindview and Read Write Gold, and use of laptops support curriculum delivery.

Meticulously planned multi-sensory lessons are delivered in small, flexible groups – even one-to-one if need arises. Pupils we saw were engaged and responsive in lessons and we noted a variety of techniques, including games, being used to support concepts. The aim is for pupils to access the curriculum at year 7 with confidence, and they do. Work is marked swiftly and feedback prompt. Sensibly, homework is done at school, though parents are expected to hear the children read every evening and ensure touch typing is practised. Holiday homework is set to ensure learning remains on track. Home-school communication is very good and cooperative in spirit.

Most of the pupils take Sats at the end of key stage 2. Recently, of those entered, 79 per cent achieved level 4 or 5 in reading and 50 per cent in writing, while in maths 91 per cent achieved these levels. Not all make top-notch progress all of the time, though school expects all to achieve over time and standardised reading tests indicate reading age can increase by up to two years in a six month period. It isn't just the scores that matter. 'My son has made very good progress... he can read and he is picking up books', one parent told us. Others spoke of lives being transformed. 'There is pixie dust around the school', said another parent. In reality there is no magic wand. It's a matter of hard work coupled with an understanding of how children learn and excellent, timely delivery.

Pupils are lively, well-mannered children who clearly delight in their school. We heard comments like 'it really helps you – they move you up step by step' and 'it's like a giant family'. But it isn't just the work that excites. Children animatedly recounted tales of woodland adventures, exploration and den building.

Problems are dealt with swiftly and, conscious that bullying can be an issue, children are taught via PSHE 'to be kind to one another'. Pastoral support garners unanimous and whole-hearted praise from parents, pupils and alumni and school's in-boxes bulge with life-changing testimonials. 'Moon Hall gave me the best possible start on my academic journey', said one child, while a parent commented, 'If you have a child who is moderately to severely dyslexic and is lacking in confidence, look no further'. The only regret seemed to be that transition at the end of year 6 is 'too early'.

Parents describe Moon Hall as friendly and welcoming and are delighted with the opportunities afforded by sport. As one said: 'It's brilliant. The girls are given the opportunity to shine'. Odd niggle, though, that Belmont PE staff are not always sensitive to the needs of Moon Hall children. Parents, some of whom have been through the mill, appreciate the support of others in the same boat, plus the coffee mornings and social events organised by the active parents' committee.

More House School (Farnham)

Moons Hill, Frensham, Farnham, Surrey GU10 3AP

Pupils: 470; 120 full/weekly boarders • Ages: 8–18 (boarders from year 6) • Sixth form: 55 • RC

Fees: Day £12,540 – £17,580; Boarding £19,548 – £27,360 pa

Tel: 01252 792303
Email: schooloffice@morehouseschool.co.uk
Website: www.morehouseschool.co.uk

M

Headmaster: Since September 2015, Jonathan Hetherington BA MSc (30s) previously deputy head in charge of boarding. An English graduate who quit PGCE training first time round as 'wasn't ready', was persuaded into the school by head of music (a Southampton Uni contemporary) initially to help with productions, then into English department, finally qualifying as a teacher through work-based graduate training programme and becoming head of boarding in 2011.

Wife, Lizzie teaches music at the school – eyes met across sweet music-making of uni orchestra (Mr H is a lapsed 'cellist, Mrs H professional standard French horn and piano) and they're a very personable pair. Now have two young children with all the attendant hoop-jumping and guilt trips that come with trying to be there for them, each other – and the school.

Feels 'fiercely protective' of the school – increasingly so the longer he spends there – as do other staff. Knocked external candidates into cocked hat in headship interviews, scoring 80 per cent satisfaction rating with pupils who were involved in the process. Parents don't know him so well, but previous head Mr Huggett's endorsement good enough for most. 'Too brilliant to give [headship] to someone he didn't implicitly trust. Subsequently, I trust him,' says one.

Academic matters: Children arrive as significant underachievers. 'Though previous school had special provision, they were just biding their time. Here they want them to come out with the grades they can achieve rather than floating along,' said parent.

Individual learning – 'almost a bespoke education,' says parent (a view seconded by inspectors) – starts with confidence boosting. One erratic speller, in bottom English set at previous school, was promptly promoted to top group on arrival, school's attitude, says Mr Hetherington, that 'doesn't matter if you can't spell as long as you can read it.' Parents see school's celebration of differences 'rather than dwelling on the difficulties,' key to rapid progress, helped by school-wide support. 'You'll have child struggling over words in assembly, the boy next to him will look over his shoulder and prompt him. There's no embarrassment, they feel good about themselves and it doesn't matter,' says staff member.

Though results can fluctuate wildly, 2016 was good year, with over half of pupils achieving five GCSEs including English and maths, and 24 per cent of grades at A*/A. Sixth form also successful (21 per cent of A levels/Btecs with A*-A grades in 2016 and 71 per cent A*/C). School warns against dwelling over much on any one batch, good or bad, as cohorts can zig zag from feast to famine. Parents realistic about goals. 'We're hoping my son will achieve C grades – but that would be fantastic, that's like an A* star grade.'

Some, though not all, will take eight or nine GSCEs, one subject at least dropped if necessary in favour of additional support. 'Means they're doing the right amount of GCSEs with extra help, rather than doing too much,' thinks parent.

Does wonders for children failed, often gruesomely, elsewhere – routine humiliation and lack of understanding all frequent flyers in parent outpourings (we heard of one child so terrified by meeting with teachers in former school that hid in grounds). School has heard it all before. Idiosyncrasies no surprise either, including pupils who need to remove shoes in lessons. And why not? 'Helps them feel grounded,' says school.

On arrival teachers take it gently so pupils lower barricades. 'That's when they show their true selves and you can work with them properly,' says Mr Hetherington. Parents praise on-line tracking system with at-a-glance information on grades and homework. There's also weekly challenge, linked to overall targets, reviewed at weekly meeting between pupil and staff mentor. Designed to be achievable, so if only 50 per cent of the way, means 'we have set the wrong challenge,' says school and will be broken down into smaller, more manageable chunks.

Pupils can be 'a little bit fizzy,' thought parent, frustration very occasionally spilling over into classroom outbursts but swiftly contained by calm, enthusiastic staff, who either love atmosphere and stay for years, or don't and swiftly move on. 'Working here is exciting and fun,' says one long-timer.

Low stress environment, with years 4 to 6 largely form room based, year 7 pupils, though still counting as juniors, getting more independence. Class sizes average 10 pupils, with teacher to pupil ratio of around one to six, lessons extremely orderly though clearly fun (year 8 boy explaining how to convey healthy eating message so young people understand 'difference between a bag of crisps and spinach' in lively English lesson). Some enthralling lessons – were told of history lesson stretching into extra time when pupils, utterly immersed in debate, didn't want to leave.

Truly inclusive – unobtrusive sign 'Some people are gay, get over it,' above classroom said it all. One parent extolled absence of corporate 'me, me, me' factor. Rather than blasting messages from rooftops, school quietly gets on with it. 'Not done in false way – don't shout about being inclusive and going all out to prove it,' thought mother.

Exam process similarly well handled. 'At other school had to get own independent assessment for son to be allowed extra 25 per cent time to get through GCSEs but here it's sheep-shearing – school takes care of it,' said mother, extolling fact that parents, previously anxious micromanagers of very last detail of son's education, may not even be aware that it's happening. 'Don't remember doing a single thing – they manage those boys through GCSE.'

Until recently, operated carousel system in year 9 with taster half term in all 18 GCSE options. Brilliant but organisational Spaghetti Junction, now replaced by less hair-tearing system where boys select favourite three or four non-core subjects and have until Easter to change.

Big focus on practical skills and subjects – engineering and DT high profile subjects with GCSE numbers rising to around 20 and more qualifications, vocational and academic, added with new building opened by Lord Richard Rogers, wielding chain cutters rather than scissors. Lots of goodies inside including 3D printer, but highlight is building design software, used by just 30 UK schools, a dream home generator that calculates everything from brick numbers to energy consumption and changes dimensions or shape at touch of a button (could generate revenue by renting out to parents planning home extensions).

Emerging confidence bubbles up in wry humour, school magazine featuring pupil art – lizard-like creature emerging with shy smile from container labelled 'trick or treat' and equally nifty way with wordplay; admirable take on Gilbert and Sullivan's Modern Major General one of many examples.

Plenty of the very bright (some with diagnosis of high functioning ASD) 'who know everything there is to know about black holes – there's a range – and it is a full range,' says parent. Top achievers end up at university, quirky often finding niche among like-minded souls.

Games, options, the arts: Pupils burst out of shells and take audiences by storm, en masse (three choirs, jazz, sax, brass, ukulele and steel bands) and as individual twinkling lights (film makers, composers and a table tennis champion) among them. Events range in scale and ambition; Vaudeville evening – boys 'incredibly brave' to perform to 100-strong audience, says school – is biggest all-comers show.

Musicians, around 10 at GCSE, A*-C grades for all the norm (less popular at A level), 'doing just fine and boys with dyspraxia and dyslexia can excel,' says longstanding department head. All brilliant – unless you happen to be in the library, unwisely sited above main performance space. 'Not a good match,' says Mr H – and it's sensibly relocating to quiet zone elsewhere.

High calibre sportsmen might also struggle slightly with bountiful pupil enthusiasm not always translated into performance. 'Some have two left feet and fall over,' says parent. Super keen encouraged to set up new teams, though, and with well-equipped fitness suite (rows of bikes), zip wire above sports field (huge fun, we're told), plenty to enjoy. Patient teachers, with therapist input as needed, make inclusion an effortless affair. Even teachers turn out en masse for spinning sessions and, watching 11 boys making way over and under stretchy ropes forming scaled up version of cat's cradle with evident enjoyment, easy to understand why.

Trips also character forming, from organisational challenge of D of E awards (one boy had to call home to locate jacket in his rucksack) to intellectual response to concerts. 'When I left, I felt like cartoon character with his face charred from a bomb explosion,' reports sixth former in school mag after hearing works by Brahms and Mendelssohn.

While parents' group raises funds for school, pupils operate further afield – have supported training of doctor through primary school in Tanzania, also provide equipment for Bells Piece, nearby home for adults with learning disabilities.

Boarding: Large numbers board (around 120, most flexi, around 20 per cent full), with years 6 to 8 housed in upper floor of main school – very youngest in eight-bed dorms, others in rooming in twos and threes, older pupils in St Anthony's House with some single rooms for sixth formers. Third boarding house now gives middle years a place of their own, though there's much mixing and matching of year groups at the weekend, says school.

Houses are conspicuously clean, tidy and odour-free (not even a hint of après trainer) and currently being smartened up. Parents welcome moves to create more homely feel with upgraded bathrooms and bedrooms. Curtains in particular 'can be a bit tired,' thought parent.

A couple of mothers we spoke would like to see more overt cosiness beyond the cuddly toys well tucked into younger boarders' beds, though agreed that school has work cut out creating home from home with boarders who aren't universally enthusiastic about the experience, some still mastering cut and thrust of social interaction. '[My son] doesn't want to put pictures up on the wall, just get on with it,' said mother. 'He'd rather be at home.' Same day response to parent emails also on one wish list, though school at pains to stress importance of good communications – and parents welcome to visit at any time.

Overall, process generally well managed, with boarders having bad days 'cajoled into better frame of mind,' said mother and efficiency the norm, school's own survey of boarding parents yielding 93 per cent satisfaction rate.

Plenty of opportunities to get out and about at the weekend, from shopping in Guildford and Farnham to excursions to theme parks, local cinemas and professional sports fixtures. Can get active with ten-pin bowling, indoor and outdoor water parks, mountain bike trailing and rock-climbing as well as Laser-quest and nearby high ropes centre.

School's own facilities include the swimming pool, sports hall, gym, sports fields and high ropes course. Can also indulge in model making or a spot of Scalextric – or cook (boarders have 'at least' six kitchens).

Though there's big focus on learning to live independently, school doesn't stint on the essentials, with three cooked meals and clothes washed and pressed daily. 'Even iron socks,' says housemistress, though boys collect and distribute finished results to banish any notions of house elves.

Background and atmosphere: Founded as Catholic school in 1940 by 'mad monk who also ran circus and trained boys to perform in it,' says school, some way off today's more evolved aim of recognising each other as 'God's special creation and treat[ing] everyone with love and respect.' While religious affiliation remains, 'we're not a card-carrying Catholic school,' says school and though there's a brand new chapel, opened in 2015, it's used by all.

Plan to add a building a year without borrowing (school makes small surplus every year) – has resulted in controlled tumble of purposeful buildings down steep hill and appointment of (almost) builders-in-residence (arrived a decade ago and still here – busily at work on day of visit).

Light wood and lots of it is the favoured look, original building (1970s re-build of 19th century original following fire) somewhat lost in the mêlée. Plenty of homely touches include wheelback chairs and refectory tables in dining room (legacy of furniture-collecting previous owner).

Pastoral care, well-being and discipline: Terrific teachers adept at ensuring mountains scaled back to molehills. 'Can I have a word?' isn't signal for out and out panic, say parents. APP (additional pastoral provision) team on hand to step in with extra support if normal system of pupil mentoring isn't enough.

While parents all agree that school won't stand for any nonsense, form tutors 'have a twinkle in their eye' – it's about sensible information sharing and proportionate response. Just one pupil asked to leave in recent memory, for persistent disruption and only after second chances exhausted.

Similarly good at mugging up on background to problems before acting; nicknames no longer enjoyed a case in point, sensitive teacher explanations helping to de-esclate potential crisis. 'In every school will be some incidents, some nasty, some unintentional, goes with the territory,' thought parent. 'School keeps a close watch on it.'

Undiluted praise for real time teacher-to-teacher communications. 'If a child is going from one classroom to the next and there's an incident, the teacher will know about it by the time they arrive,' said one mother.

Clearly worded school policies – plain English, no jargon, easily understood by all. Parents can call dedicated number if have concerns about bullying. Six stages before official warnings to cease offending, from detention to being given no go areas on school premises before reach permanent exclusion – there's lots of help for bullies as well as their targets and acknowledgement that 'some children set themselves up as victims,' says school.

Therapy and staffing: Support, usually in groups of three to four, is carefully matched to needs (includes social skills) and timetabled – so nobody misses favourite subjects (a common gripe in mainstream schools) or feels different from peers, with one floor of junior building wall-to-wall with therapists – 10 speech and language, five OTs (attend junior PE lessons), eight tutors (seven literacy, one numeracy). Intensity slightly reduced in sixth form but pupils still have dedicated SALT 'star'.

Pupils and parents: Development of boarding and extension of age range makes this a school worth moving for and plenty of families do, local education authorities paying fees for around 50 per cent, others self-funding, sometimes selling up and downsizing.

School's reputation goes beyond immediate area with pupils from Hampshire, Berkshire and Oxfordshire as well as SW London and Surrey. Friends' organisation circulates whole school contacts list, invaluable for arranging lift shares.

Entrance: Regularly tops parents' wish but rightly choosy about who it takes, with focus on very closely defined learning difficulties the key to success. Two key questions are 'can we meet his needs?' and 'would his arrival cause concern?'.

Specific learning difficulties is school's raison d'être, though around 20 per cent also have high functioning Asperger's. It's a non-negotiable 'no' to behavioural difficulties, however, boys with ADHD/ADD considered only if a secondary diagnosis and demonstrably under control, usually with medication.

Though informal meetings with hopeful families possible, won't get far unless paperwork aligns with desired profile so before visiting and losing heart to school, advisable to send through all reports (school, ed psych and other specialists) for vetting. If satisfactory, will be followed by 'sensitive' assessment to assess academic and social strengths, with overnight stay for would-be boarders. Some families will be advised to wait a year or so, then re-apply. No EAL pupils, though – would be too much for child to cope with on top of learning needs.

Prefer not to backclass though will countenance if essential – misery at previous school not conducive to flourishing grade levels. School, however, adept at reading between lines to find submerged educational potential, even if current achievement levels very low, and ensure it's successfully raised to the surface.

Exit: Most stay till at least GCSE, a few moving elsewhere post 16, many staying into sixth form, around half to some form of further or higher education, remainder into employment or training (including apiary). In 2015, two off to the London College of Communication (art and design), three to Surrey (physics, history and American studies), one to Bath (mathematics), one to Essex (business management), plus a wide range elsewhere. End up successfully pursuing range of careers – one old boy is budding soap star, another training as a farrier. School's own 'Where are they now?' research, following up 200 recent leavers, found just two unemployed, remainder involved in everything from acting to finance, sales, teaching and apprenticeships.

Money matters: Sensible fee structure avoids surprise extras with pupils banded according to level of support required. No big endowments. If school could admit on need only, it would and there's plenty of sympathy for sacrifices often required. Parents hoping for LEA funding told firmly to have money in place for DIY route, just in case.

Remarks: One set of parents, used to stopping for stiff drink on way home after parent-teacher meetings at previous school, switched to champagne celebration after coming here. Others, struggling to meet fees, don't begrudge a single penny. School has got back the boy nobody else could reach. 'They've literally turned his life round and ours as well.'

Nunnykirk Centre for Dyslexia

20

Netherwitton, Morpeth, Northumberland NE61 4PB

Pupils: 25; 8 weekly boarders • Ages: 9–18 • Sixth form: 8

Fees: Please apply to school

Tel: 01670 772685
Email: secretary@nunnykirk.co.uk
Website: www.nunnykirk.co.uk

Head Teacher: Since 2015, Barry Clarke, previously senior lecturer and course leader at Bishop Grosseteste University in Lincolnshire. He has previously worked for Lincolnshire County Council in a number of roles, including teacher in charge of a pupil referral unit and the local authority's school improvement consultant concentrating on behaviour, inclusion and SEN.

Barry's key subjects are science and ICT and he has also taught maths and PE. He is a keen sportsman, including running, cycling, football and a variety of racquet sports. He and his wife Erica, also a teacher, have been regular visitors to Northumberland on holiday

Academic matters: This is a CreSTeD SP school specialising in dyslexia and all the associated info-processing quirks that huddle under that umbrella term. With the right intervention, children improve quickly here. Ofsted inspectors were uncharacteristically charmed by what they saw but couldn't put their finger on how they did it. Cast aside all objective criteria, stop ticking boxes and switch to subjective mode – a good school is an affair of the heart. It's the individual focus, the being known and liked, that enables these children to achieve so far beyond expectation, above and beyond the application of any modish methodology. Two former pupils recently received first class honours degrees at a good university and have both been asked by the university to stay on to study for a PhD. The school wants pupils to feel comfortable in telling people they are dyslexic and that requires confidence. No lack of academic rigour, plenty of challenge and achievements are both recognised and celebrated. Tiny classes, most four to five, max eight, one-to-one as necessary. Results put this school in the top five per cent of the value added tables – says it all.

National curriculum, all go for GCSEs, most tackle five to eight, and entry levels for those who need longer. English and maths, good IT, and options spanning history and geography through photography to rural science. No modern languages – 'They can do them later if they want'. Vocational subjects also popular. Big hands-on element in all things. Sixth form options vary from year to year – the school works with the pupils' choices and tries to accommodate all, including a range of academic and vocational qualifications. AS and A2 photography and art available. Classrooms are basic but certainly adequate;

a science lab (home to corn snakes), art room, library and various multi-use spaces for music, drama, assemblies and group teaching. The cellars no longer store wine but provide an atmospheric gallery space to display high quality artwork.

Games, options, the arts: The extracurricular programme is an essential element of the rescue remedy, not only because achievements in other areas cross-fertilise performance in the classroom, but also because parts of the academic curriculum are embedded within it. Much of what they do is vigorous. Sport, given the numbers, is not competitive at school level, but they play the customary ball games and athletics; plenty of playing fields and outdoor areas for sitting, thinking and playing. Floodlit courts for tennis, basketball and five-a-side. The gym, with weights, punchbag and array of exercise machines, is popular. Swimming and the use of the sports hall in Alnwick, and sailing (RYA quals) at Amble. Annual endurance race for all, summer sports day with bbq, former pupils often returning to join in.

Plenty of art, well done – photography especially good. Music brave and enthusiastic, if not symphonic. Lots of plays. D of E, of course, and scouts, karting, mountain biking, canoeing, bird watching, cross-stitching, egg painting – all tastes catered for. Rural studies is the big thing – a number of pupils go on to qualify and earn their living in the field, literally.

Boarding: Weekly boarders come from as far south as Birmingham and as far north as Edinburgh. No more than two to a room in the warren upstairs. It may look well worn, but they don't mind this a bit – it's fun. Supervision levels are high, older ones guide the younger ones with a warm welcome for new arrivals. So much goes on in the evening, no time for telly, and it's not missed. Day pupils welcome to stay on for activities. Plenty of computer use, but Facebook not allowed – 'They can do that at home'. Former pupils have set up their own Nunnykirk website for networking.

Background and atmosphere: Founded in 1977 with just two boys and one girl, essentially for children not at home in the hurly-burly of bigger schools. Studies of pigs show that, though they like toys and nice buildings, they'd much rather have a good relationship with humans – children are no different. It's a tiny staff and all are encouraged to develop their own approaches and run hobbies: 'This is no place for anyone wanting to work 9-4'. Informal and shirt-sleeves-y. Stability and routine are the foundations of this notably calm, notably busy school. Most teaching is done in the manor house, though a couple of wooden outbuildings provide much-needed additional space. The gardens are very attractive, with a river running by, perfect for fishing, rafting and dam-building – it's the only school we've visited with a dedicated wellie shed. Fruit and veg grown in the walled garden – 'We eat what we produce' – and a menagerie of pigs, ducks, geese and turkeys (on the menu at Christmas – it might be remote but they don't run away from the real world here) all in the care of pupils. Bothy in the grounds, home to go-carts – hands-on mechanics all part of the learning curve: 'If you drive it and you break it, then you fix it' – fair enough.

You know you're remote when a sign on the school drive asks you to 'slow down for red squirrels'. And if you see a teenager reaching out of a window, standing on one leg with an arm in the air, it's only because they are trying to get a mobile phone signal. Set in the midst of Northumbrian loveliness, a few miles from Morpeth, this Greek revival John Dobson manor house is home to a hugely impressive hive of activity. Admittedly it could do with an injection of funds (where is Richard Branson when they need him?) but you cannot fault the quality of educational provision. These children enjoy a wealth of all that is good in education: highly committed and knowledgeable teachers, a curriculum that works for and with them rather than against them, and all the individual care and support they need. Staff here not only teach but also mentor and support in an old-fashioned but much-missed approach as role models, showing how to work and live alongside each other in a civilised society. A climate of mutual respect where independence and taking responsibility are not only encouraged but expected.

Pastoral care, well-being and discipline: Well looked after children greet visitors with unfussed naturalness, and these do – no reservations on that score: they are happy to chat and to talk about their work. Standards are high – important for those rougher diamonds when they first arrive. Manners are excellent, discipline not an issue, and they all know exactly where the line is. Smoking? Not a blind eye in the house. It's a big deal – parents instantly informed. Drugs? Out.

Food is good, the pupils reckon – high praise. They're not mad, all of them, including parents, about the gluten-free diet, and some pounce on the toaster when they get home. Additives are out, sugar rare, fish oils in, fruit abounds. The school is certain this makes a difference, keeps them calmer and more focused. A written record is kept of what each child eats. Healthy living tuck shop.

Student council and an anonymous pupil voice box, though most happy just to chat with the head about any concerns. Efforts are made to mix with the local community despite location – excellent work experience for years 10 and 11 with local businesses. Trips to the cinema and theatre and overseas visits for sixth formers.

Therapy and staffing: SENCo leads team of therapists. As classes so small, much of support happens here with use of tried and tested techniques (eg finger counting for maths) but additional one-to-one help provided if necessary. Laptops available in every lesson.

Pupils and parents: Pupils a mixed bunch socio-economically, spanning the 50 per cent funded by their LA to the scions of stately homes. More girls needed. Because this is the only school of its type between Oxford and John O'Groats, a big geographic mix (they offer weekly boarding). For many parents this is not at all what they wanted, so the school goes to great lengths to allay fears and thereafter keep in touch – parents united in grateful applause. Day children from 45-minute radius.

Big expectations made of parents – 'If work is sent home, we expect it to be done – and we expect parents to help' – though many parents are grateful for the offer of teacher-supported prep in school. It's all about partnership, which means 'parents have got to make an effort, too'. One parent described it as 'feeling part of a large happy family', crediting not just the teaching staff but also cooks, cleaners, gardeners, matron – everybody – for their work in creating such a special atmosphere. Another parent told us that she had 'gone from constantly worrying about her child's future to being confident in his development,' since moving him here from a mainstream school where his learning difficulties were 'neither identified nor managed'. A training day for parents where you can find out what they do, how they do it, how you can help. If your child thrives remarkably, they won't hang on – but many opt to stay nevertheless – they reckon they'll do even better. Informative website.

Entrance: Careful selection process. All the usual reports, but the (long) interview's the thing. Boys and girls here are refugees from mainstream schools with, most of them, anything from an antipathy to a horror of being educated, plus a history of being teased or bullied. Repairs to damaged self-esteem are all part of the package, but no entrenched EBDs of any sort – they're outside their specialism: 'If we feel we can't help there's no point'. IQs reckoned from 95 up. Formal acceptance after a trial half term when, if a child has settled, an IEP is drawn up.

Entrance to sixth form is not automatic. Year 11 students follow an interview process and their best interests are discussed with parents and staff.

Exit: Careful advice precedes post-16 decision making, finding the right course at the right college. It's a huge leap, obviously, reliant on the self belief they've acquired. They go on to the full rainbow – degree courses to clock making. Decided bias in favour of hands on, fresh air careers.

Money matters: Some bursaries for private feepayers. For parents seeking to persuade their LA to apply the statement, the news is that, sadly, although the needs haven't changed, the funding has, and it's getting harder.

Remarks: Parents describe it as 'a little dyslexic oasis'.

Riverston School

63–69 Eltham Road, Lee Green, London SE12 8UF

Pupils: 213 • Ages: 1–19 • Sixth form: 12

Fees: £8,700 – £13,800 pa

Tel: 020 8318 4327
Email: office@riverstonschool.co.uk
Website: www.riverstonschool.co.uk

Head: Since 2001, Mrs Sarah Salathiel (50s), who started as a PE teacher at Riverston 37 years ago shortly after graduating from Dartford College London, and has worked her way from the girls' PE teacher via various roles to become head. She still teaches PE and is a force to be reckoned with as she races round the school teaching, handing out awards and running assemblies, meeting with parents and now working on the 'Riverston Group', since the owners of Riverston School have acquired a second school in the North of England. Her husband, Phillip, is now the deputy head and SENCc. Her personal drive and determination must be a large part of the growing success of the school, of which she is fiercely protective – there are even plans afoot to develop another school abroad. 'We were most impressed by the head – she sold the school to us,' according to the parent of a young boy on the autism spectrum.

Academic matters: The nursery is well equipped with enthusiastic nursery nurses and assistants. The space is clean and cheerful and children roll around happily to music with evidence of creative work on the walls. This is oversubscribed, since parents like the longer hours available in the pre-school and the fact that they will not have to move on to a different junior school. In the junior school the children move from an amalgamated class to separate year groups with some separate subject teachers (music, PE and French) and there are very small classes, which attract parents who want their children to have more individual teaching. There is evidence of purposeful teaching and real learning in all the junior school. We watched a class involved in role play and a freer style of learning than may be possible in larger classes. The junior school also makes much use of the outside space (perhaps having an ex-PE teacher as a head encourages this enjoyment of the external space and physical activity?) and there is an active forest school with its own wood hut for exploratory learning from nature. There is an influx of (mostly special needs) pupils at year 5 who move then to avoid having the stress of the year 6 exam entry into a secondary school. This lower entry point is also due to the fact that children are getting earlier diagnoses and assessments allowing parents to choose private special schools over mainstream primary schools.

The senior school feels more serious than the junior school, as completely appropriate. There is no non-contact time – much appreciated by the parents we spoke to – and a much-needed full timetable for students, many of whom are not good at organising their own learning. There are several ability groups within each small year group, so students are taught at their own level. High expectations are evident from the fact that all the students have qualifications when they leave. There is a choice of some 12 BTec subjects, as well as a reasonable range of GCSEs (including entry level where needed) – maths, English, science (new science teacher very keen to promote a move to separate sciences eventually for those who are keen), French, Greek, ICT, business studies, computer science. In 2015 nine students took GCSEs and 78 per cent of results were A*-C – a cause of great pride to the school and the pupils.

In the sixth form the 12 or so students (half girls) see this a good stepping stone to prepare for further education or the outside world. Students are not expected to do private studying but are building their study skills and confidence. As well as A levels with almost one-to-one tuition, students get careers guidance, work experience (including in the school's own nursery), interview practice and life skills teaching such as transport and travel planning, cooking and money. Students also continue with additional literacy and numeracy. The school is looking for a designated head of sixth form (position currently held by a very experienced and longstanding English teacher: 'I can't be doing everything and the older kids have very particular needs') as the sixth form grows. Many pupils staying on from senior school, who see it as a continuation of their schooling – including one boy who is staying on for a year 13+, something the school thinks will grow as the students may still not be ready to leave school at 18.

Games, options, the arts: A reasonably large tarmac playground with some playground activities. Separate areas for the early years and younger junior school pupils with colourful playground equipment and wooden tables. A fairly new gym building for internal sports and assemblies. Physical activity is promoted in the school and all the pupils partake in sports – football, netball, rounders, hockey, cross-country and athletics, with extracurricular rugby, karate, trampoline and dance. Competitive sports encouraged. Forest school takes place in a grass area at the front of the school or at the local park. Swimming at public pool for those in the junior school, with swimming club once a week for those who want to continue to pursue this activity. Sports leadership qualification is encouraged as an ideal practical course to help sportspeople to build towards a career.

Background and atmosphere: Riverston was started by Elizabeth Lewis, and continued by her son Michael Lewis and his wife who are the current owners and governors. There is a sense of history and continuity and tradition despite the fact that it has changed from a mainstream school to having a student body that is now largely (80 per cent of senior school) special needs. The building is made up of three large Victorian townhouses joined through in a slightly maze-like manner. Classrooms in this part of the building are small and inevitably feel like being in a bedroom or sitting room – cosy for the junior school students. There are more modern extensions and additional buildings perched on the side for senior school classrooms –

R

science labs, libraries, a modern kitchen. Teenagers in uniform slouch in common rooms, jumping to open the door politely for visitors. When you move round the school, it does not feel like a special needs school – routines very much like in any school with students waiting outside classrooms to be let in for lessons, moving around the school chatting and laughing. Only the very small numbers in the classes and the differentiated groups give a hint of the fact that education is very much tailored to the students.

Pastoral care, well-being and discipline: This is the selling point of the school – it has always had a reputation for good pastoral care and this has led to the school filling a niche market for those pupils who need more support than most. There are also regular multi-disciplinary meetings which give space for communication about individual children. Each child has a tutor and they are the point of contact first thing in the morning and after lunch. They check on homework and personal issues and are the first point of call for parents. There are subject teachers who attend the multi-disciplinary meetings together with therapists. This is the heritage of a small school when communication would have taken place in the staff room and is gradually changing with new systems for more formal systems of communicating as the school grows. One parent we spoke to felt that the head did not delegate to teachers and that all decisions had to go through her – it can not be easy working for a husband and wife leadership team, with a husband and wife ownership team, but it does mean that the school has a strong sense of direction.

Therapy and staffing: There is a full time speech therapist for the large numbers of pupils with language difficulties. There are many pupils with autism spectrum disorder, but all are verbal. She sees pupils according to their statements or EHC plans, though privately paying pupils also have access to the speech therapist. We spoke to one parent who was concerned that once a week was not nearly enough for their son with speech and language difficulties – this may need to change as the school takes on more pupils with autism spectrum disorder. The speech therapist feeds back to teachers on work that is being done and tries to ensure that goals are supported in other lessons during the week. There is a part-time occupational therapist with her own well-equipped space. Most interesting is the fact that there is a counsellor three days a week with a dedicated office for seeing pupils and parents and teachers. A rare thing in a school, but something that is very appreciated by teachers, parents and pupils we spoke to – and clearly popular as she was fully booked. School caters for dyslexia, there are several learning support teachers who work with dyslexic pupils and to support writing, reading and spelling. Their work is carried through into the classrooms, partly through extensive continuous professional development (much of it in-house) and partly with the help of the several learning support assistants who help in classrooms.

Staff recruitment always difficult in core subjects. Most teachers arrive with some SEN background, but high amounts of training for those with little SEN experience. Specialist teaching starts in junior school (French, music, PE, drama) and by sixth form teaching is almost one-to-one tutoring. Part of the stability of the school comes from a low staff turnover, but staff recruited ideally have special needs experience, and there is very regular staff training. This might be an inset on positive handling or restraint, dyscalculia or speech therapy skills. There is also weekly optional training for staff to learn and share good practice. Twenty-five staff are currently working towards a masters in childhood communication impairments as one of the governors is an accredited tutor, as well as a speech therapist, and she gives the training to staff.

Pupils and parents: The school has over 200 pupils, of which two-thirds are boys. There are some 60 in the early years foundation stage, which has a very mixed intake of local pupils whose parents choose this independent school over their local primary – partly perhaps because they have a nursery and extended hours are possible. Quite a few pupils are not native English speaking (20 EAL pupils) and from a refreshing mix of ethnic and social backgrounds. The junior school has some 50 pupils, while the upper school has increasing numbers of special needs pupils (currently 75 with statements/EHC plans – about 50 per cent of the whole school, and 80 per cent of the senior school) paid for by local authorities after parents have finally managed to get funding and named this school as their school of choice.

Around 50 per cent of pupils are on the autism spectrum. Pupils are mixed also in terms of ability – and there is a range of pathways for different needs. School also caters for pupils with epilepsy. One parent we spoke to said that the school has given her daughter space to be herself – an individual with her own individual manner. The new sixth form is still very small, but with its own space and growing need, this is beginning to attract pupils who do not want to go to larger sixth form colleges and appreciate the very individual care and support they get. 'Most of the kids are very nice' was the comment we got from pupils.

Entrance: Very flexible – the school says it welcomes visits and is aware that the experience needs to be kept comfortable for both parents and pupils. In our experience, it is necessary to speak directly to the head if you want to arrange a visit. If the school feels it can provide, the child given a three day trial assessment – or up to a whole week if necessary. In particular, school looks for behaviour it will not be able to manage in order to protect the existing cohort. Staff work hard to explain and justify to parents (and, as required, by local authorities) exactly why they cannot take any child, and will make suggestions of other schools that might be a better fit.

Exit: Pupils leave from the junior school to local secondary schools, and some leave the senior school to go to local mainstream schools (Kent grammar schools or local state schools). On the whole the pupils with special needs stay on as long as possible – hence the sixth form which even has a year 13+. The last years of senior school are preparation for further education or employment. In the main pupils go on to further education – eg Eltham College, Greenwich College – or on to apprenticeships. Employment helped by sixth form careers guidance and two weeks' work experience. Work links with local nurseries, the Co-op or with Greenwich Council.

Money matters: The school says that money is stable now that so many students are paid for by local authorities, with regular income and the steady growth in student numbers. But this is a private school and accounts are kept private too. There is a dedicated financial director as well as a director who is responsible for appraisal. The head is on the board of governors too, so this is a close knit arrangement. That may be to the school's strength and has clearly allowed for 90 years of continuous growth.

Remarks: This would be a good school for a child who wants to be in a cohort of understanding children with learning differences. The school has high expectations – very full timetable, all take qualifications, wide range of subjects taught – but they make it achievable by ensure that each child gets a 'bespoke' education. Very small classes at all sorts of levels of ability, a good amount of therapy and extra support, counselling, drama and pastoral care. Large enough to have the feel of a mainstream school – assemblies, mentoring between years, prefects etc – but small enough to give each child the support they need. A real ethnically, socially and ability mixed London school for the child who needs a little more attention.

Shapwick School

Shapwick Manor, Shapwick, Bridgwater, Somerset TA7 9NJ

Pupils: 90; 60 full boarders • Ages: 8–19 • Sixth form: 26: (19 boys, 7 girls)

Fees: Day £18,519 – £19,386; Boarding £24,258 – £27,858 pa

Tel: 01458 210384
Email: office@shapwickschool.com
Website: www.shapwickschool.com

Headmaster: Since 2014, Mr Adrian Wylie BA BEd NPQH (late 40s), born in Northern Ireland but educated in England: at Bath University for his first degree in business admin, at the now defunct King Alfred's College (subsumed by the university of Winchester) for his BEd in maths, and at Birmingham for his postgrad diploma in autism.

His early career comprised management experience at Benetton and his own landscape gardening business; he combined this latter stage with some part-time work as a teaching assistant – in the days when ordinary mortals working in non-related fields could do such things. 'I found kids then who couldn't do stuff, and particularly maths. I wanted to find ways to switch them on again – hence the BEd in maths'. Since then, his determination 'to remove barriers to learning' has led to a subsequent career entirely in specialist schools, state and independent, as part of the Priory group. His last post, before being invited to join Shapwick when its previous head went off on long term sick leave, was as head of the Forum School in Dorset, a specialist school for autistic children.

Mr Wylie showed refreshing frankness when outlining to us Shapwick's recent fall from Ofsted's grace (an honesty greatly appreciated by parents, many of whom wrote lengthy letters of protest at its findings). Happily, the school has now addressed all criticism and is back in Ofsted's satisfactory, if not good, books. 'It's the sort of place which gets under your skin; it's done a wonderful job in its own bubble – good pastorally, caring and inclusive teaching – but there was work to be done here'. His experience of the gamut of special needs means he is sure that 'no-one gets a good deal' if the mix of needs in a particular school is too diverse, so he is resolved to bring his school back to where its specialism lies, namely dyslexia, dyspraxia and dyscalculia. Parents reckon he is forward-thinking and proactive, with a great team around him. 'A fresh pair of eyes who has shaken things up a little,' as one mother summed him up.

Outside school, gardening remains a keen interest: 'I'm devoted to the lawn and keep it very green and very stripy,' and a self-confessed shoe enthusiast, but no lizard skin Italian winkle-pickers adorned the headmasterly feet, sadly. Mr Wylie has two sons, both working in London, one in film, the other in publishing.

Academic matters: Well, they certainly do matter, but barriers to learning matter as much, and are addressed first at Shapwick. The national curriculum is broadly followed (tweaked where necessary), leading to GCSEs in up to eight subjects including maths, English and science, some taken early where appropriate. Most end up with two science GCSEs, one taken in year 10 and a second additional one in year 11, although all three disciplines are taught separately; weaker scientists are offered a non-examined entry level certificate in science. Options include the usual creative subjects, which those who struggle with too much written work might find more appealing, and 'the school bent over backwards to accommodate my son's GCSE choices, which clashed,' reported one mother. BTec science and PE also available.

We loved the art department and the evident love of the subject shown us by a GCSE candidate and her accomplished portfolio. All teaching is multi-sensory and class sizes number no more than about eight. Literacy support lessons are given to all students, set according to ability; some get individual support, others attend reading clinic at the start of each day. From year 9, study skills are offered, which include social competency and fine motor skills, as is Englishtype, a course designed to improve keyboard skills. Well-resourced IT and broadband throughout. Liaison between teachers and with parents is close, and follow-up swift and generally effective. School has had CReSTeD category 'SP' for many years.

In 2016, 42 per cent of students got at least five GCSEs from A*-C including English and maths, not bad at all considering the high number of children with SpLD statements, and in line with, or exceeding in many cases, individual targets. More pupils have achieved A*/C in maths than English, largely attributable to the fact that 'the students' struggles with literacy have so great an impact on their ability to tackle the GCSE', as the school puts it; many take functional skills instead. In 2016, 72 per cent of students gained A*-E in maths – and 100 per cent in English. School has put both subjects under the spotlight for improvement in the coming year(s). Recent changes to reduce or eliminate coursework may not serve these students well. Stand-out subjects are film studies, art and photography and engineering. Criticisms of tracking, lesson planning and differentiation raised by Ofsted have been tackled head on, and all standards have now been met.

We saw a group of students gathered under a tree for a PHSCE lesson, discussing an occasion on which they had behaved in a way that made them less then proud, with hindsight. All eyes lit upon the head as we walked past: he could not escape the teacher's questioning, revealing an incident from his youth which we are too discreet to repeat here. It was rather more than a lesson, also an exercise in speaking skills, self-knowledge and reflection.

At sixth form, students attend Bridgwater College for their academic or vocational courses, yet still have the specialist support and expertise provided by Shapwick two days a week. Two boys we spoke to felt well enough equipped to enrol at colleges nearer their homes without support.

Games, options, the arts: The usual suspects on offer on one dedicated afternoon per week. School facilities include Astro and tennis courts; swimming is offered as a course in the spring term for younger students at nearby Burnham. The emphasis is on sport for all, rather than winning at all costs, so that everyone gets a game, and is likely to represent the school at some point. Small numbers of girls mean inevitably that the school fields fewer teams against its opponents, but younger ones get the opportunity to play in mixed teams for football and rounders. The fixture list bravely includes national but neighbouring titan Millfield, alongside less egregiously sporting institutions. Players and athletes get out and about to regional events, but also make use of the fabulous countryside on the school's doorstep, Quantock, Mendip and the Somerset levels for D of E, Ten Tors practice and outdoor education, laid on as an activity in years 10 and 11. Climbing, caving and dry ski-ing all in close proximity. ATC is available for those with military aspirations. Art and DT are popular, and both departments busy and vibrant; students' paintings adorn the walls. Music taught as individual lessons rather than a class subject; players and singers come together at least once a year at a Christmas concert in a local church, and the school band, Sunburnt Fury, (wonderfully) includes players of all instruments taught in

S

school. The school's somewhat sketchy website could usefully provide more detail here. Trips include Berlin for historians, London for actors and the dales for geographers, plus places of interest nearer home, such as Bath.

Boarding: About two-thirds board – and it's full boarding including Saturday morning school, with two exeats per term. That said, boarders are free to go home or to friends after Saturday commitments, with appropriate permissions. Boarding houses are scattered through surrounding villages anything up to five miles from the main school; school minibuses run a busy shuttle service at the beginning and end of each day. Boarding provision has been the subject of recent criticism by Ofsted, but the school has taken strenuous steps to implement its recommendations, which have now been met. Whilst no-one could describe the boarding as luxurious, it seemed perfectly adequate to us, with enough space in dorms and homely communal areas plus clean bathrooms to satisfy most mothers. Praise is lavished on the care given by the staff to the students, however.

Background and atmosphere: Shapwick's origins go back to Glastonbury, and Millfield's then head, who set up a school for dyslexic children in the 1970s, but it takes its name from the sleepy village on the Somerset levels where the beautiful Tudor manor house which forms its centrepiece is to be found. Both house and school have been through several changes in ownership, but Shapwick is now part of Kedleston Schools, a company owning 10 specialist schools in the UK (and its only SpLD member), and owns several other buildings in the village, as well as outlying boarding houses. Plenty of schools occupy pretty English villages, but what marks this one out is the air of relief and sanctuary from mainstream education, by which the students here have not been well served. Everyone we spoke to expressed their thankfulness at having found Shapwick: one boy summed it up when he simply said 'Mum, they get me'. Other students spoke eloquently about the lack of stigma – 'everyone's in the same boat' – and the way lessons were tailored to the way they learn. The small classes, high student:teacher ratio and family feel of boarding means everyone knows each other; the catering staff turning out traditional and delicious school nosh (yummy cottage pie when we visited) in cramped conditions know every child and every food foible. Despite the far from equal numbers of boys and girls (about three times as many boys as girls), relations between them seemed perfectly entirely respectful. The extreme rurality of the setting does not appear to bother them one whit, nor the conventional uniform with collar, tie and blazer for all. A bubble? Possibly, but one where kids incompatible with mainstream education can get on and learn things their way.

Prep school now integrated into the main school and its site, though it retains its own dedicated area and identity. Any fears of younger children being overwhelmed are likely to be allayed by small total numbers (fewer than 100 students), tiny classes, high student:teacher ratio and exceptional attention paid to each individual.

Was due to close in July 2016 due to falling numbers, but we understand has been bought by a parent and will stay open, with money going into refurbishment of school buildings.

Pastoral care, well-being and discipline: The boundaries between academic and pastoral support are blurred here, as so much of the academic support builds a sense of self-worth through enhancing capability in the classroom and exam hall. High expectations of behaviour are set, modelled by staff and generally met; sanctions are couched in language which encourages students to reflect on how changing their response or behaviour could have resulted in a better outcome. Parents appreciate the way in which their children are urged to look out for each other; 'an all-round education,' remarked one mother. Rewards tend not to have material value, but concentrate on public recognition and intrinsic worth; the school strives to ensure that all students get a regular pat on the back. Disciplinary sanctions might include less free time at break or before bed, or a loss of privileges, but restorative action is used where appropriate. Separation between school and 'home' – ie between the classroom and boarding house – is absolute in the application of disciplinary measures.

Therapy and staffing: Each student has an IEP devised for his/her own particularities, and a team of speech, language and occupational therapists run sessions during and outside the school day, on individual and group level, depending on need.

Pupils and parents: Grateful, grateful, grateful to be there and determined that their children can access the same educational opportunities as everyone else – unifying factors in an otherwise diverse group of people. Time and time again, we heard heart-rending tales from both parents and students of appalling degrees of incomprehension and lack of resources or expertise in mainstream education before Shapwick. 'My daughter arrived traumatised from a local prep school two years ago, and is now reading, writing, is confident and happy with a hectic social life,' one father, whose family life has been transformed, told us. Such experiences have produced fierce loyalty to the school, and a unifying uprising of protest against what were perceived to be recent harsh judgements by Ofsted, which were felt to miss the point about the place. One mother has recently set up the Friends of Shapwick to raise funds for 'our extremely empty fundraising pot,' which she would not have done had she not felt so passionate about it. We found the students to be as thoughtful, polite and chatty as any we have met; perhaps less social poise, but given the obstacles they had overcome, perhaps not surprisingly. Owing to its SpLD status, its geographical spread is wide, including a few from abroad, though all are native English speakers.

Entrance: Entry is at any point from the age of 8, and school is firm in its policy to admit only those with SpLD in dyslexia, dyspraxia and dyscalculia with an up-to-date report from an educational psychologist confirming that any potential student has at least average potential. During the taster which forms part of the selection process (one day for day students, a week for boarders), further tests may also be run. Previous heads must attest to the satisfactory behaviour of all hopefuls. No open days: visits and applications done individually.

Exit: The vast majority to further education or apprenticeships in areas such as childcare, horticulture and media; others to foundation degree courses in the arts, one recently to a joint honours course at Keele. Very few gap years, but not unknown

Money matters: Cheaper than almost all boarding schools but reflects its facilities, if not its generous staff:student ratio. Fees cover usual expenses; speech language and occupational therapy charged as extras. Some fees are paid by local authorities after, in most cases, a bruising encounter with an educational tribunal.

Remarks: Sticking to its guns as a SpLD school, and emerging from a period of instability and damaging judgments from Ofsted, now under the new regime of an experienced head. Held in huge affection and respect by all we met: if it can just deliver on vital GCSE maths and English, as well as the undoubted and marvellous work it does on its students' sense of self-worth, then its future should have been assured.

Slindon College

Slindon, Arundel, West Sussex BN18 0RH

Pupils: 80; 26 boarders • Ages: 8–18 • Sixth form: 19

Fees: Day £20,940; Boarding £30,420 pa

Tel: 01243 814320
Email: registrar@slindoncollege.co.uk
Website: www.slindoncollege.co.uk

Headmaster: Since 2014, Mr David Quick BSc PGCE PGC SEN NPQH, previously vice principal (student support) across the federated schools of St John's and King Richard Schools in Cyprus. Has also been assistant headteacher at Windsor School (an MoD boarding school in Germany). Started his career in finance, but having a father who was a college lecturer and a mother who was a deputy headteacher, it wasn't long before he saw the light and qualified as a teacher at Swansea University.

Has been a member of the BECTa science working group, and an assistant examiner in GCSE physics and A level chemistry. He's a D of E expedition assessor and a rugby coach, loves cooking and baking, orienteering, skiing and travelling. Married to Michaela; their three children are at university.

Academic matters: Small classes – none bigger than 12 – allow for lots of differentiated teaching and plenty of one-to-one where needed. Most aim for GCSEs and BTecs and school is inventive and imaginative at finding out who can do what and tailoring the curriculum to suit. Everyone is pushed to achieve their potential, whatever it might be, so all take core subjects of English lang and lit, maths, science (single or double) and IT. Then most take four from an excellent list of options which includes DT, graphics, art, history and geography and a BTec in food skills. Two outstanding areas are photography – to professional standards – and the BTec in horticulture, pioneered here with the sensible and sane aim of equipping boys for employment in eg garden centres. French, German and Spanish all available though mostly taken by native speakers. In 2016, 50 per cent achieved five or more A*-C grades at GCSE. 'Farm tech' latest innovation. Supervised prep is done each morning – another clever move as no-one feels much like it after classes when there are donkeys to visit and vegetables to tend, to say nothing of the superb work being done in the graphics/photography studios.

S

'Primary' takes from year 4. Lowest form has room for nine boys and two who come for taster days – lots of these. Excellent room: highly structured yet welcoming – big sofa, reading area, PCs, 'small animal' nook and plenty of stimulating equipment. Each day begins with a work-out – motor skills and hand-eye coordination stuff. 'Enrichment' classes for years 10 and 11 to plug gaps and provide one-to-one; staff good at buttonholing those who would benefit. School has own assessment system which takes in more than the academic – all testament to the terrific value-added embedded here.

Sixth form offers various options including a one-year course to prepare leavers for college, BTecs in eg food tech and animal care – school houses two donkeys, Loopy and Norman, a red-bearded dragon, a Mongolian gerbil and a corn snake. In 2016, 100 per cent of A levels at A*-C.

Games, options, the arts: Photography, graphics and arts impress – new iMacs, four professional quality printers and a policy of constantly being ahead of the game. This dept is at the heart of the school. 'We have a very good budget – what we want we get. We build the self-confidence in here that feeds other subjects; we have a huge impact on confidence.' Textiles are witty and fun – we enjoyed the imaginative ties with their fish, Mondrian, guitar and cupcake motifs. Lively tie-dye T-shirts, cushion covers on a graffiti theme. Fabulous extravagant costumes. No concessions here to 'special needs', 'we push the boundaries'. DT is strong – clever, practical chairs made from simple designs and painted in primary colours. Long tradition of building 'green power' electric cars. Drama and music potter along – lots of enthusiasm and musicians take grade exams and achieve well.

Huge, super fields on which football and rugby are played, a floodlit court, purpose-built squash courts, archery, golf, taekwondo, basketball, tennis, mountain biking, cross-country, skateboarding etc dependent upon interest. Outdoor heated pool is open from Easter to late October. No shortage of things to do even though there is, as yet, no sports hall. Some worthy achievements here – especially in cross-country. Excellent bunch of extracurricular activities – something for all. Stage lighting, cookery, shooting, chess and masses more – especially outdoorsy stuff, including D of E. Boarders have range of trips at weekends – matches, theme parks, museums, bowling, films, shopping.

Boarding: All boarders can opt in or out of weekend boarding on a weekly basis. However, about 10 per cent are full boarders (34 weeks) as they stay in every weekend by choice.

Joint heads of boarding (from year 6) have nearly 20 years' experience between them. Bernie used to run a residential home for Met police cadets and Daniel is a PE teacher. Bernie is also a counsellor and anger management expert – very confidence-inspiring. Together, a laudable mix of tough and tender – seen as mentors and vital recourse in wobbly moments – 'once they're in the boarding house they're home', says Bernie. 'It's highly disciplined,' a parent said, 'without going over the top. My son takes responsibility for himself because they empower him to do so.'

Much refurbing in process, especially in older boys' study bedrooms with desks, comfy chairs and proper carpet. Strip lighting and tired lino depress the adult visitor somewhat but the boys don't care. Most rooms, including dorms, are a good size and have stunning views. Boarders in rooms of four at lower end to singles and doubles at the top. Inviting 'family room' for everyone – staff and boys – in the evenings, with sofas, TV, board games and someone's dog. Here the residents learn about social interaction, taking turns, winning and losing and coping with either. Games room has table football, snooker etc – cash prizes funded by tuck shop takings.

Weekend activities are many and varied: a typical weekend would involve a late rise on a Saturday and Sunday with a full English breakfast. This would be followed by a trip out to go shopping/paintballing/visiting a theme park or adventure centre etc. There is always a Saturday evening trip out too, which would involve the cinema or bowling or perhaps a meal out in the local Chinese/Indian restaurant. For those too tired to go out again, there is an opportunity to watch a latest release film in the boarding house with the film and popcorn evening. Sunday morning is spent at leisure and there is a trip out after traditional Sunday lunch to involve a fun element, perhaps the beach in the summer.

Background and atmosphere: The site and buildings are owned by the National Trust. The impressive main school house is a sturdy and robust three-storey pile in Sussex flint on top of a superb site overlooking the south Sussex landscape. On a clear day you can see over to the sea and the Isle of Wight. Internally – and it must be a nightmare to keep up – it could do with patching and painting here and there. Nice Hogwarty features like a lodge with real crenellations and little gothic porches and leaded lights must make a pretty enticing first impression on unsure potential pupils and their parents.

Pastoral care, well-being and discipline: Hands-on – in all senses: no politically correct squeamishness about grabbing a lad to haul him off for extra support or an arm round the shoulders if he's upset. Sensitivities are understood – in a small school all the compulsions and obsessions are OK – 'we have lots of places to go to if you need to get away.' Catering staff know the boys and their dietary needs and 'everyone knows what to do if somebody freaks,' we were assured. 'Everyone's allowed to be the person they want to be as long as they're not upsetting others.' Parents enthuse: 'We were dreading private school but it was like a home from home, loving and so warm. It changed our lives.'

Day boys allowed to board eg for a birthday sleepover or to give parents a break. Sensible system of 'boxes' in all classrooms so that pupils can keep relevant books and materials where they will need them rather than tote them around and forget them. This way they always have sanctions, yes, but success of system depends on rewards – 'lots of carrots and very little stick.' If you breathe', we were told, 'you get a trophy – perhaps just for being Mr Nice Guy!' Everything here is designed to be real and realistic – 'We're not going to allow our boys to be set up for failure – it's a hard world out there and they're going to have to deal with it.' 'My son feels respected,' one mother told us.

Parents are warmly appreciative, 'It turned my son around,' one mother told us, 'they've listened and given him time. They work at his pace, push him at the subjects he's good at and support him where he needs it.' Another told us, 'Nothing seems to be too much trouble for them.' Another said, 'If my son is anxious the head always calls me himself.'

Therapy and staffing: Accreditation by the National Autistic Society in process at time of our visit arising from the increased numbers of boys on the ASD spectrum now being admitted. All the usual aids are employed – Pecs, Teacch, Makaton – but those are seen as less important than the smaller classes and individual attention in which the school specialises. Kinaesthetic learning, lots of structuring, scaffolding and other support to motivate, encourage and support. Speech and language therapy threaded through the entire curriculum – body language, social interaction, communication skills seen as core to all. OT similar. School has invested in more LSAs in recent years. Lifeskills and PSHE loom large on the timetable. Brain Train works to activate a larger percentage of the brain and much emphasis on 'visual learning' for those who benefit. New sensory room. Good library – books are colour coded to guide readers to their own levels.

Pupils and parents: ADHD/ASD spectrum. Serious behavioural problems not accommodated here. Around 15 boys' families are from overseas so very sensible policy of taking them out 'to stop them getting institutionalised'. Most locals come from Hants and Sussex; boarders from everywhere. Few with EAL needs.

Entrance: Now takes from year 4. Immense care taken over entry – can take up to a week to assess. Ed psych reports, statements, interview, trial period etc etc. Sensible, direct and straightforward approach.

Exit: About two-thirds leave after year 11; more now stay on for expanding sixth form. All leavers go on to some kind of further education. School has own horticultural apprenticeship scheme to enable the boys and their parents to set up little businesses to give them a future. They bring in driving instructors and do all they can to prepare for The Big Out There.

Money matters: Virtually all additional therapeutic input covered by fees. Few means-tested bursaries. Ten per cent reduction for siblings and for the children of HM Forces personnel.

Remarks: A sixth former told us what he felt: 'What I like is the opportunities and that they're keeping it a small school. The facilities are great and the food is excellent – I always look forward to my croissant on Thursdays and we have barbeques in the summer. I think Slindon has moved me on as a person and I've matured here. If there's a problem, there's always someone there.'

Sunnydown School

Portley House, 152 Whyteleafe Road, Caterham, Surrey CR3 5ED

Pupils: 83; 44 flexi-boarders • Ages: 11–16

Fees: Funded by local authorities

Tel: 01883 342281
Email: office@sunnydown.surrey.sch.uk
Website: www.sunnydown.surrey.sch.uk

Head Teacher: Since 2014, Paul Jensen. He's dapper, in a blue suit, patterned socks, shoes with contrasting laces – a Paul Smith/Ted Baker sartorial style which doesn't often grace a head's office. But parents, boys, and Ofsted alike all appreciate his modern approach. The previous incumbent was head for 33 years, and Ofsted has heralded the team under Jensen's leadership with successfully turning around a decline in standards which had been 'masked by a lack of transparency'. It's an approach defined by a whirligig of acronyms – he rattles out RICE and REST and SMSC, of which more later.

He was previously deputy head at Clarendon, a school for learning difficulties, and at Melrose (for social, emotional and mental health difficulties). But he began his career in mainstream, teaching science and maths in his native Australia.

He brings some of the Aussie outback to the school too (grew up in a community with fewer people than this school, he says). He takes the boys fishing, they 'catch their own trout and kill it with a priest,' he told us. You might be picturing, as we did, a dog-collared chap administering the last rites, however, we learned that a priest in angler lingo is a ceramic instrument. Boys love his company when they go fishing, we're told. 'Got lots of energy, and I think it's good for these boys having a relatively young, and a male, headmaster,' is one parent's view.

You always want a head who 'gets' your child – and here you can expect an additional layer of understanding: Jensen's own son has Asperger's. His wife teaches English in the school.

'Firm but fair, extremely patient, understanding and supportive of the boys and parents. I really like the positive vibe he brings and how far he has moved the school along in the short time he has been head. He understands the boys and really seems to know how to deal with each individual,' said another parent.

His interview with GSG is held up by an animated conversation with one boy around feeding the school snake. And then dealing with a spot of bullying over a lunchbox. Just as it should be.

Academic matters: Sunnydown is a Surrey county school for communication and interaction needs (COIN). 'It's for the

S

academically able, emotionally vulnerable,' Jensen summarises. 'There's lots of conflict resolution, and behaviours associated with autistic tendencies. These are not naughty children. If someone swears, you need to know, what the context is behind that.'

Pupils all have some form of communication and interaction need, and 90 per cent have an autism diagnosis. They need to have mainstream academic ability, as they typically study up to eight GCSEs. Results see a smattering of B and C grades, but most achieve grades at the lower end.

Pupils follow one of two pathways in KS4, linked to their emotional resilience. 'If they can do four English exams and cope with the work, then they will take pathway 2. If they are going to struggle because the pressure is too great then they will do fewer GCSEs in pathway 1. That way they can get a D for one GCSE instead of two Fs,' Jensen says.

The resilience issue is one of the school's key approaches. All boys are measured on entry for scores in a group of attributes known as RICE – resilience, independence and co-operation; and they aim for them to be 'engaged, encouraged, and empowered' throughout their time at Sunnydown. Their IEP targets will then focus on developing any of these areas that are lacking. So a low resilience score, for example, will lead to additional interventions such as time allocated to spend with a learning mentor. Friday afternoons have timetabled sessions of mindfulness and PHSE with their form tutor. 'A big focus in key stage 3 is developing the emotional resilience for GCSEs – the boys find exams anxiety-inducing, so we work on breathing techniques, and their responses to these circumstances,' says Jensen.

All of the pupils also do a BTec in home cooking skills. Boys were engrossed in cake making on our visit. Many also do cookery as an extracurricular club, and they recently held a Mexican night where they cooked for their parents. The kitchens are well-equipped, even having a camera on the teacher's desk so boys can watch demos in close-up. The DT room too has all the serious looking equipment you could wish for.

They don't take a language, although there is an extracurricular Spanish club.

Many of the boys have difficulty with processing speed 'which leads to frustration then the behaviours creep in,' head says. Various measures are used to help them get down what they want on paper, such as software which records and types speech, and which can read text to them. We saw lessons that were interactive and highly verbal – an RE class revising what they knew about Christianity in the form of a quiz with one boy in the hot seat; and an English lesson on Dickens' Christmas Carol where pupils examined the ghost's character in the style of the '20 Questions' game.

Parents had one complaint about the academic provision, and that was the lack of a sixth form.

S

Games, options, the arts: No shortage of trips – a bi-annual ski trip, performing arts theatre visits and residentials, geography trips to Lulworth Cove, and a Spanish trip in the offing. There are sporting events with mainstream and special schools, with golf tournaments a particular highlight. There's a BMX track in the neighbouring forest, and a bike workshop where boys learn to service and repair their bikes.

An annual feel-good week focuses on SMSC education – social, moral, spiritual and cultural. This comprises days out, to Chessington, Thorpe Park, and the movies; charity work – this year they did a 20 mile bike ride to raise funds for Cardiac Risk in the Young, in memory of an ex-pupil's brother; and a whole school walk, where they go out rambling for a day, play games, and have a picnic lunch.

Boarding: About half of the pupils board for at least part of the week – some stay a couple up nights, and the maximum is four nights, Monday to Thursday. There are 33 beds in total, with dorms of two to five beds split by age. Rooms have the grand proportions of the Victorian house, with large windows overlooking the grounds.

'The boarding facility is second to none. I have absolutely no doubts about the care that is provided for my son, to the point I sometimes think they know him better than I do,' said one parent.

'They have amazing experiences that are not only there to keep the boys entertained but also to help them in getting ready for life after Sunnydown. They help to develop their life skills such as cooking, money management, e-safety and road safety which the boys at Sunnydown are generally lacking. The AQA awards they have started doing are just adding more experience and skills that will help my son be safer and more independent; bike maintenance, fishing, laundry, travelling, cleaning and organisation are just some of them,' said another.

Background and atmosphere: The school is based in the former Victorian family home of a London wine merchant. As such it's pretty attractive among state special schools, with decent outdoor space, tarmaced tennis/basketball court area and a forest trail. It sits down a road of large detached houses, in a cluster with two primaries and a mainstream secondary.

The school is 60 years old, but its nature has changed, most recently moving from a dyslexia provision to catering for students with Communication and Interaction Needs (CoIN) in the last decade. A large proportion of students have an ASD diagnosis.

Pastoral care, well-being and discipline: If your child is autistic, when choosing a school (especially for the teenage years) you need to have the question of how they will deal with anxiety right at the top of the agenda, because you can forget any academic progress if that is not well managed. So we were pleased to find here the head telling us that reducing anxieties was central to the school's ethos, and parents reporting on how effectively this is done.

'My son has become much happier, more confident and more positive about himself. His anxieties have reduced considerably and he is starting to understand his feelings, ways of controlling them and how to respond appropriately to different situations. He still has a way to go but the change in him within the first two years was incredible,' said one parent.

Another reported a 'dramatic increase in confidence', and said: 'Sunnydown has quite literally changed his quality of life, he is happy and not constantly put down from bullying or misunderstanding events. He is beginning to speak up if there is a problem and therefore seek assistance, resolving issues rather than bottling them up. I think it is a combination of the teaching style and level of support available that has made the difference.'

Most of the pupils here would previously have had meltdowns in mainstream, but Jensen says it is an incredibly calm school. They use MAPA (Managing Actual and Potential Aggression) methods to provide an early warning system of a pupil becoming distressed, and much work goes on to teach pupils themselves to recognise the signs – they can then extract themselves from the classroom, and perhaps go to the outdoor gym to take a breather.

Of course among a pupil body who all struggle with interaction and recognising others' feelings, issues will flare up, but 'are swiftly dealt with', parents said. One said that her son had been bullied when he first joined, and the school's response had been 'marvellous'. 'Some of these kids have always been bullied in mainstream; they come into this safe environment and they are trying to find their feet,' she explains. 'They had a meeting with everyone concerned, and part of it was about getting my son to recognise why it was happening, because the other child had always been bullied, and to come to terms with what he could do to make this boy feel less anxious. We were able to talk about it afterwards and relate it to a rescue dog we knew who always growled at people, because all he had ever known was bad treatment.'

Therapy and staffing: As a state school the therapy provision is minimal – a speech therapist and assistant work in the school one day a week each, with groups of boys, and alongside the TAs and teachers. With a caseload of 85 boys, you get the picture.

There are 15 teaching assistants, and six full-time care staff – there is some crossover between the two, with care staff sometimes doing tutorial work, and the TA team supporting the care staff. All care staff take a level 3 diploma in health and social care within six months of joining. Four TAs have undertaken additional training and are known as learning mentors.

'The experience and passion that the staff have is evident when you see them engage with the boys,' one parent said.

Pupils and parents: Pupils here are at the milder end of the spectrum, so the outward signs of autism are minimal (an odd bit of hand flapping seen), and we were struck by how confidently and adeptly the boys chatted to us and answered our questions. All are verbal, but some 'are selective with whom they are going to speak to', head says. Some may prefer their own company, but others are sociable – one parent was delighted to see 'a real camaraderie among the boys', and for her son, the chance to have a social group uncomplicated by his difficulties. 'Towards the end of primary school we suddenly started to see a huge gap in development between him and his neurotypical friends. But here it is great because all his chums at school are quirky like him,' she said.

Another parent wanted to warn prospective parents that this could be double-edged. 'Entering a special school environment does carry its own difficulties which we did not foresee. As all the children have needs, behaviours can be learnt or copied. No autistic child is alike; they won't automatically get along and share the same interests; it is not a completely smooth journey, that's for sure.'

But for others, the difference in support compared to a previous mainstream placement made all the difference. 'The first annual review we had was the best ever. No battles to ask for more support, the school had identified extra areas of need and already addressed the support level accordingly,' said one.

The parent body seems to be a real strength of this school. This is always difficult in special schools, when parents are exhausted and time-strapped by dealing with their child's needs, and there's little school gate interaction when children are taxied in from long distances. But here we're told it's a 'very active and involved parent body'. The school holds three 'working weekends' per year, when parent volunteers come in to help with tasks such as clearing a forest area, and each time somewhere between 50 and 80 people will turn up. 'Being a parent of an autistic child can make you feel very isolated, and the school really helps and encourages parents to network and get to know each other,' said one mother.

Entrance: The majority of pupils join from mainstream primaries, and it is essential to have an EHC plan or statement.

Applications for the next year 7 were stacked practically floor to ceiling when we visited. Pupils unlikely to be suitable are those with behavioural difficulties stemming from social and emotional needs, rather than an autism-related lack of ability to communicate; those with complex learning difficulties (but it is common for pupils to have slow processing and language difficulties); and those who the head feels could be accommodated in mainstream.

As a county school, admissions and final decisions remain the responsibility of the local authority.

Exit: Some 95 per cent go on to a mainstream college which has an autistic base or with some support – including Reigate, Redhill, Nescott, and Brooklands. Boys generally do level 2 courses in areas such as computing, sports coaching, horticulture and animal husbandry. Those who are too vulnerable for mainstream colleges occasionally go to specialist sixth form provision.

Money matters: Places are local authority funded.

Remarks: With the big push to inclusion this is a rare beast, which caters for pupils at the milder end of the autism spectrum in terms of behaviours, and at the more academic end. Parents considering it will be sitting on the cusp and agonising over the decision, because their sons will have the academic ability for a mainstream school: would they do better there? We have to say most probably not, because there they will not get this understanding and smart management of autistic anxieties and behaviours, the same opportunity to develop the life skills which will not come naturally to them, and the advantages of a more tolerant friendship group. If you have a local authority prepared to fund a place here, our advice is grab it.

Swalcliffe Park School Trust

Swalcliffe, Banbury, Oxfordshire OX15 5EP

Pupils: 46 • Ages: 11–19 • Sixth form: 15

Fees: Funded by local authorities

Tel: 01295 780302
Email: admin@swalcliffepark.co.uk
Website: www.swalcliffepark-oxon.frogos.net/app/os

Principal: Since 2011, Kiran Hingorani BSc PGCE MEd (50s). Hails from Tyneside and read biological sciences at Newcastle University before training as a teacher. Whilst a schoolboy at Stonyhurst College ('Not the happiest years of my life, I must admit'), engaged in a school project organising holidays for disadvantaged children, which inspired him to a career in SEN. A brief period in mainstream, followed by seven years at Percy Hedley School in Newcastle for children with cerebral palsy and communication difficulties, prior to joining Alderwasley Hall School Derbyshire in 1995, later promoted to principal. Before arriving at Swalcliffe Park, travelled the world as a volunteer in community development projects, then as education advisor for CISV International, working with peace education and development projects. Now firmly rooted in the Cotswolds, 'my last staging post', and using his business acumen to negotiate with 20 different local authorities.

He presents as dapper, well-laundered, and surprisingly cool on the hottest day of the year, as he expounds on his leadership model. Despite a lot of stuff that obviously comes from business management, casual references to the nuclear industry or Apple, his understanding of the children's and parents' needs is real. Neatly packaged in a logo of colour-coded shapes, which appear throughout the school, right down to the soft furnishings, he describes 'The Four Whys' – Communication, Independence, Self-Management, Achievement – the model by which the school turns troubled ASD boys into confident achievers. 'It's about giving them strategies for decision making...a bunch of GCSE results are useless for anyone who can't leave their bedroom,' he declares. 'Loads will go wrong, life's about making mistakes, we're about how you deal with it'.

Parents' views ranged from 'really inspirational...a clear vision for moving the school forward', to 'I haven't come across him too often'. A Newcastle United fan, who also enjoys travelling and has scaled the Himalayas and Mont Blanc (though we noticed he balked at our suggestion of biking to school) and cruising the canals by narrowboat. Next, he intends to navigate the stormy waters of educational research, collaborating with universities on 'quality of life' projects. Already in development is technology for communicating with parents and software monitoring sleep patterns.

Academic matters: A school for boys with high-functioning ASD, Swalcliffe Park follows the national curriculum during the school day with a separate 'independence curriculum' after hours. The teaching prepares the students for public exams, 'the expectation is that the boys will get GCSEs', reported our guide, with a range of core subjects found on a mainstream school's timetable (maths, science, art, English etc) but few foreign languages (can be taken as an optional activity). Tiny class sizes, maximum six, determined by age, personality and social functioning; the younger classes (KS3) enjoy continuity of teacher and a desk, like in primary school, to foster a sense of security. KS4 sees the boys moving to designated teaching rooms for science, ICT, art and DT, with specialist staff. Vocational courses offered in some subjects (eg catering and hospitality); BTec qualification in ICT is popular as well as non-exam courses in food, art and horticulture. Staff ratio is high, with 90 employees, including therapists and non-teaching staff; all boys have a keyworker as well as a class teacher. One mum described how the many female staff and therapists have allowed her son to develop relationships with women, despite the single sex population of the school, 'he shakes hands and high fives with ladies and men alike'. In-house sixth form has increased four-fold in recent years, partly as a result of some self-regulation and social communication difficulties for the boys in attending external courses off site. Increasing number of A level subjects are being offered, in addition to a wide choice of vocational courses at local colleges.

Teachers adapt to the Asperger's spiked learning profile, as many students, despite some with a high IQ (some Mensa members on roll), have had poor experience of previous schools or spent time out of education altogether. Parents praised the teachers' ability to restart their child's learning; 'It's the first time I've seen my son engage in learning,' said one. 'They look at what topics boys are interested in'. Some parents reported boys retaking a year, or spreading public exams over two years. We noticed children head-down, quietly engaged in study at a computer screen. Several members of staff are long-standing but there was no suggestion of complacency; 'You can see passion behind the teaching' said a mum.

Games, options, the arts: For a population who finds team sports a challenge, ('we've a school of 46 individuals,' said the head of care), we were impressed to see volleyball and football in play. Add to that the possibility of basketball, tennis, athletics, hockey and an indoor bouldering wall, and the school begins to rival the top independents for choice. The football team, coached by a popular PE master, an ex-professional player, plays fixtures against local schools. When quizzed about ASD boys coping with losing a match, the head commented, 'We are learning to.' With 22 acres of grounds, there is no shortage of space for games, and the many fish in the lake have grown blasé about being caught and returned regularly. Boys choose from horseriding or mountain biking in the Cotswolds to kayaking. For thespians, there is a pantomime at Christmas, featuring staff and boys, and a Britain's Got Talent show for any who fancy singing, dancing or writing a poem. 'You see boys who struggle to hold a conversation belting out songs on stage,' boasts the principal, and there is a new creative arts building. No music therapist, but individual instrument teachers offer drumming, guitar or clarinet lessons and recitals are adapted for shy performers who prefer not to face the audience. Not much evidence of boys' artwork on the newly painted walls, but one parent assured me the ceramics were wonderful and results in art GCSE are strong. Professional prints, provided by Art For People with Autism, adorn the corridors.

Excess adolescent energy is engaged in the extracurricular clubs, including D of E and Cadet Corps. Green Power club, sponsored by Siemens, takes advantage of the area's F1 flavour and gives the boys the opportunity to build an eco car (looked rather like an electric go-kart to us) and to test drive it until the battery fades; other popular options include Warhammer club, slack-lining or, as one mum put it, 'just hanging around in the grounds'. The school encourages participation in local groups, like scouts and the cycling club, to build up social skills.

Swalcliffe may be rural but the school makes a good effort to get about, with school trips ranging from the Imperial War Museum to Lord's Cricket Ground and Wembley Stadium. An ambitious residential outdoor pursuits trip took the whole school to Snowdonia for a week.

Boarding: Separate from the school is the boarding life, which begins around 4pm, with free time, dinner then organised activities, such as Monopoly or movie night. Six houses, named variously after trees, buildings and ex-masters (eg Willow, Coachhouse and Maurice) provide the settings for self-help skills: boys learn to plan, shop and cook meals for the whole 'family', so developing independence and social skills by the back door. The house families are selected vertically, ie across the year groups, with an eye to blending personalities and encouraging older boys to be role models for younger ones. Movement between houses is encouraged if the boys want to join friends in other houses. Perhaps a hangover from the principal's own boarding experience, 'I hated boarding...so I am very concerned to make sure the residential experience is a success'. The houses mirror a family group, a parent tells us: 'One lays the table, someone loads the dishwasher...all have to help out'. Day boys are attached to a house and can stay late or for the odd night. Boarding options cover the whole range: weekly, fortnightly, flexi, 52 weeks and holiday respite. As the head remarks, 'We can't solve problems when they crop up in families, but there are times when we can help out '.

To enter the boarding house, boys use their discreet hotel style key-card, which allows egress at appropriate times of day. 'To get your own key card makes you feel quite grown up,' remarked one mum. It also deals with the privacy and anxiety issues around possessions, common to boarding schools. The six houses follow a similar pattern in layout and style – standard furnishings, we were told, give boys stability (and reduce arguments, perhaps?). A spacious kitchen, where the boys cook and eat together; a smartly furnished sitting room with communal screen for family viewing, while the individual bedrooms have single bed, desk and a personal TV for private downtime. We noticed all the boys have an en suite shower room, for their plentiful supplies of Lynx, with a (rarely used) communal bathroom down the corridor. Personal touches, such as duvets from home, are encouraged, and one boy's pet gecko had pride of place in the sitting room. The house manager and non-teaching staff are known by first names (more formal address for school staff) and there is always someone on duty overnight. Food is produced centrally but arrives in house for reheating and garnish, with a three weekly rotating menu, full of lads' favourites such as steak, curry or a meatball sub.

Students may opt to cook their own supper, so developing independence. One mum commented, 'I'm quite surprised at the things on the menu. It's not plain food they give them'. The menu and activity timetable is pinned up on the house notice board, along with the ubiquitous 'Four Whys', but otherwise there are little in the way of house regulations to suggest an institution. 'There are plenty of rules', laughed the head of care, 'but we pick things up that are important to have rules about'.

Back at the house, boys change out of the blue polo shirts, navy jumpers and dark trousers. There is an optional white T shirt and the school is conscious that even these soft fabrics can be a problem for ASD boys with sensory processing difficulties. 'They understand if some people need to wear something underneath the uniform,' explained one mum.

Background and atmosphere: The water lilies were blooming and dragonflies hovered across the lake the day we visited Swalcliffe Park School. Though first impressions were more suggestive of a Georgian country house than a special school for high functioning ASD boys, in the distance a couple of boys lounged on the lawns and the shouts of a football game could be heard on a hidden Astroturf. The tranquillity was therapeutic. 'It has a calming influence on everyone,' said one mum. 'The setting is very calming for the boys,' said another, 'though not good for one's mobile signal'. Hidden away in Swalcliffe village, famous for a huge medieval tithe barn, a school was founded in the manor house in 1969 but now houses a select group of students, mostly boarders (3:1 boarders/day) and a few looked after children, for whom it is home. The elegant stone manor house has been cunningly converted to residential accommodation, while the more functional schoolrooms are in renovated stable blocks across a courtyard. The classrooms are intimate, but science, food tech and DT suites enjoy larger spaces with an array of equipment. There's an ICT suite with it's own network and a separate studio for OT. Beyond the buildings is an independent living house for post-16s as well as acres of grounds, some given to woodland, ideal for moments of solitude, or 'to whack some trees with a stick,' as the principal suggested. The lake is well stocked with fish as well as a good many footballs and frisbees. One mum described how 'catching 50 fish' was one of her son's (easily achieved) targets, and there are quaint corners for rural pastimes, like tending bird boxes and chickens.

Pastoral care, well-being and discipline: Self-management is one of the Four Whys, so managing unsocial behaviour can be on a boy's progress targets. The emphasis is on self-regulation, and developing strategies for difficult situations. 'The big wide world out there has rules,' said one mum; 'they've got to find a way to cope with that', and the approach has to work beyond the school gates. 'I make them ask themselves, what are you going to do if this happens in Tesco?' says the principal. Retaining the same keyworker from year to year is encouraged, to build a trusting relationship between student, family and school, and the clinical psychologist is available, if necessary, for cognitive behavioural therapy.

The students are rewarded with pocket money for achieving targets via a points system. Warnings for misconduct, missing a house treat or an early bedtime is the worst we heard about for poor behaviour, and parents are given a weekly account of points won or lost. There is no problem with alcohol, the principal tells me, but they have had Facebook issues, common to adolescents. 'They are autistic, but they are also teenage boys'.

Each boy's timetable includes three meetings a day with their tutor to prepare for the session ahead. There's an up to the minute system of electronic record keeping and a handover meeting at the beginning and end of each day with residential staff to ensure information is never lost. One mum felt there was a mismatch between the awareness of school staff and residential: 'The house staff needs to have a better grasp of children's difficulties'. Although another felt, 'It's just a relief to be somewhere where your child's needs are understood without question'. Parents are kept in the loop by a weekly email from the keyworker, and were generally happy with the lines of communication; one parent commented she had all email addresses from the principal down. Another claimed her queries had always been listened to, and that issues were 'all very transparent; no hiding'.

Therapy and staffing: In-house therapists, three for speech and language, an occupational therapist, counsellor and a massage therapist manage the specific learning needs, either with individual sessions or 'by stealth', through games and house activities in the evenings. Movement breaks are timetabled for antsy learners, while deep pressure massage helps towards behaviour. Speech and language tasks examine complex understanding, inference and the language of exam questions. Two clinical psychologists visit, part-time. Individual learning targets are set for the boys according to the four principles, Independence, Communication, Self-Management, Achievement, one target for each principle per term. Although it appears highly systemised at times ('we're quite evangelical about our Four Whys') the head reminds us, 'boys come here because they struggle with their understanding of life'. There was some parental criticism about the length of time the therapy assessments took, but delight at the accuracy of the findings and detail in the final reports.

Pupils and parents: All students have a diagnosis of high level ASD, some have added difficulties of ADHD, Tourette's, dyspraxia or dyslexia. The school does not take boys with emotional/behavioural difficulties and there are no international students. A statement or EHC plan is in place, on entry to the school. Parents felt united by the trials of having a child with SEN, and many have fought hard to get their son a place at the school – it can take up to two years from first applying. Parents said, 'We don't meet that often', beyond the termly school function: the pantomime, parents' evening or sports day, however, one parent ran a virtual forum for parents of Asperger's children. There was warm praise from several parents for the family liaison officer, 'it was a relief to talk to someone who gets it', but sadness that she was about to leave. Managing transitions when someone is replaced was an area of mild concern; 'It is essential that everyone knows how to tell the boys someone is leaving,' commented one mum. The principal acknowledged the difficulty. 'We are very aware of transitions and changes to daily routines – an unexpected visitor can unsettle them'. Boarders come from as far afield as Suffolk and Bristol.

Entrance: Joining throughout the year, the new recruits have undertaken a rigorous assessment process. Observations can last three days, and the student sees teachers, therapists and residential staff, as well as having a trial sleepover, to ensure the student and school are suited. 'They are really scrupulous about that,' remarked one mum. Even so, many take a while to settle, staggering the overnight stays until they are comfortable with boarding. 'It can take six months from enrolment to staying here,' said our guide. The school supports the parents with advice and reports during a tribunal process.

Exit: Leavers' destinations are innumerable, and include university studies in astrophysics, art and ICT courses at college, animal care, car mechanics and catering training. One good-looking lad went into modelling.

Money matters: All students are funded by their local authority.

Remarks: Swalcliffe Park is a remote but rare find: a school which builds boys' self-esteem with consistently high teaching standards and thoughtful pastoral care. Despite a lack of mobile phone signal, the school has found these boys' wavelength and the hand-picked students thrive in such a tranquil setting, amid the honey-coloured stone buildings and soaring copper beech trees. No wonder they hide it away.

The Unicorn School (Abingdon)

20 Marcham Road, Abingdon, Oxfordshire OX14 1AA

Pupils: 69: 16 girls, 53 boys • Ages: 6–16

Fees: £18,960 pa

Tel: 01235 530222
Email: info@unicornoxford.co.uk
Website: www.unicornoxford.co.uk

Head Teacher: Since 2015, Mr Andrew Day BEd (40s), educated at Ysgol Gyfun Ystalyfera (Welsh speaking comprehensive in West Glamorgan), then University of Wales Institute, Cardiff. Began career at Bristol Grammar Lower School (maths, ICT plus lots of games coaching), then director of studies at Hornsby House, followed by Wycliffe Prep then Cheltenham College Junior prior to headship at Calder House School, specialist SEN prep in Wiltshire. Headhunted and persuaded by the governors of The Unicorn School to take up the challenge of extending the specialist dyslexia teaching to year 11. Passionate about helping special needs children; 'school phobics need to find an area they can excel at'. After six days in the post, the school was visited and downgraded by Ofsted, but, fleet of foot, Day has risen to the challenge of updating policies and practices, and has now opened an adjoining stable cottage for the increasing numbers. Although the population has a primary diagnosis of dyslexia, with some social communication difficulties, he has introduced software for working memory and given due prominence to dyscalculia; 'maths is my main subject and what I am really interested in...It is exciting to take the school to GCSE,' he intones in his modest Welsh voice. 'It came from the parents. They had seen the progress their children had made here'.

Academic matters: Teaches adapted national curriculum including: humanities, science, DT, drama, French and ICT. 'We skill them up; they touch-type, learn to spell-check, word-process and have a large dollop of numeracy and literacy – not only in formal morning sessions but across all their learning. We give them strategies to help them cope in mainstream, at university and in the work-place and beyond.' Mornings focus on numeracy and literacy, 'My son couldn't do his letter sounds; six months later we're seeing real progress not just in his reading but in blending sounds and spelling too. Importantly his confidence is stratospheric – he wants to read everything, even menus and road signs!' Nightly homework is within reach, fingertip stuff, appropriate to the individual child. 'School is skilled at adjusting parental expectations, the focus is very much on the individual, and measuring them against themselves,' say parents. For some schools, concentrating on individual achievement and expectations may be sub-text for 'not much progress', but here there's nowhere to hide, they track everything. It isn't unusual to find children advancing three plus years in under 12 months.

Staff know every trick in the book. The ruses and wiles youngsters may have adopted elsewhere are instantly spotted here, 'If my son tries to hide they're on him like a rash.' Frequently adopt a cross-curricula themed approach, tailored to specific needs, which children love, 'When we did Rise Of The Robots all our subjects were linked to it, so we could understand it better, it was such fun.' Teaching throughout takes account of individual learning styles, 'They see how my son learns and work with that; they adapt to him'. Timetable currently structured around maths, 'We identified this as an area we wanted to develop and improve'. Learning is practical and accessible; expect to find forensics, finger-printing and fun, 'When we looked at cells we did so by considering illness and what systems and organs are affected; it helped it make sense.' Focusing on strengths equally important as plugging weaknesses, 'My child has severe difficulty with hand-writing but they discovered, and encouraged, a talent for creative writing and now he is voluntarily writing a comic book in his free time.'

Now offers GCSEs.

Games, options, the arts: Incredibly proactive at getting children off campus and away from the Unicorn bubble: sports at Radley College, swimming in a number of locations, delicious lunch at nearby Abingdon School (Unicorn youngsters not remotely fazed by presence of burly sixth-formers). Daily sports sessions include football, hockey, netball (play in small schools league), plus sailing, swimming, judo etc. Mornings begin with 'shake-up and wake-up', a brain gym derivative which gets mind and body working in tandem. Movement and dance sessions are geared to the youngsters. 'My child is dyspraxic but he loves the sessions; he has become body and space aware. They teach them in a fun way, get them to be dragons or monsters..'

Plethora of after-school clubs: shooting, cookery, eco – 'kids are very green, well-informed and have good general knowledge' – sports etc peppered with trips to Warwick Castle, theatre, France. Technology and gadgets feature in abundance: visiting shows, such as Bionic Ear plus trips to RM real room and Lego robotic sessions, always popular. Strong community focus – active link with Mwalimu School, Africa (do look at the delightful project book in reception). Plenty for parents, including coffee mornings and socials. Many openly relieved to have found Unicorn: 'Our lives are so different, I was suffering stress-related illnesses, that's all gone. Unicorn has improved all of our lives, not just my child's.'

Background and atmosphere: Founded in 1991, now housed in a converted Edwardian house near the centre of town, with a new building next door for KS3. Akin to a small-independent day school with gym, DT and art room plus smart, bright classrooms, it's kitted out with practical teaching aids, computers (all learn to touch-type), interactive whiteboards et al. Outside space is adequate with two carefully designed, compact playgrounds – one with Astro for footie or netball, the other with climbing frame constructed with the dsypraxic child in mind. Year 10 opened in 2016 and year 11 will open in 2017.

Pastoral care, well-being and discipline: Children have their say too; there's an active school council which decided recent uniform changes, including minutiae such as modifications to the crest. A friendly, polite bunch with limitless curiosity, we were enamoured by their interest in others, 'There's continual movement so they are always welcoming, accepting and tolerant of newbies.' Virtually all simply existed in education prior to Unicorn so foremost aim is to boost confidence and self-belief then plug gaps, before moving to independent learning. 'My child was nervous for all of two days, after that the euphoria set-in; he made friends and hasn't ever looked back.' Children are incredibly articulate, with damming stories to tell: 'I wasn't

U

getting an education at my old school', 'I thought I was stupid', 'I was shy and angry', 'My old school didn't get why I didn't get it',' I used to panic and go blank when the teacher asked me a question', 'I was told my writing was babyish.' We listened to heart-rending tales of merciless bullying, 'At my old school one boy made up a song about my dyslexia and taunted me with it'. No such tales at Unicorn, 'Here you can be who you want to be', 'They give you time to think and to learn.' Understandable then that the most prolific comment, even from recent arrivals, was a simple, 'I love it.' The only down-side for some being the journey time – can be lengthy.

Therapy and staffing: On-site speech and language therapists, art therapist and sensory integration trained, highly-praised occupational therapist. Said one parent, 'My son loves his OT sessions. Sometimes he works alone, others with his friend. He thinks he is just playing but the progress he is making is incredible.' Staff an eclectic bunch – parents say, 'There isn't a staff mould, they're all very individual, yet they make a great team'. Teachers are all qualified dyslexia specialists (or training to be), with one involved in successful outreach programmes to local state and independent schools (would like to do more). Classes are small (typically 8 or 10 students) and all children have at least one, one-to-one session daily, 'Because every child has one-to-one there is no stigma, it is part and parcel of school life but importantly it is completely centred on the needs of the individual child.'

Pupils and parents: A haven for both the child with specific learning difficulties and their parents, 'We were like Jack Russells – wouldn't let go; constantly battling with school, the LA, specialists, each other. Now we have found Unicorn we can relax. We no longer have to scream to be heard or battle for our child to be understood.'

Entrance: All pupils should have a report from an educational psychologist identifying either moderate to severe dyslexia as their primary need or dyspraxia, dyscalculia or speech and language difficulties (ICAN registration hoped for). Approximately 40 per cent have speech and language difficulties. Will take those with mild ASD if primary need is SpLD. Entry on first come first served basis; assessed over two-days. Some funded by home LA, though not Oxfordshire who operate an inclusion policy.

Exit: Pupils stay between one and three years, typically two. Aim is to give support, coping strategies and return to mainstream education. 'They let you know when they are cooked and ready to move on.' Places sought at known supportive schools, popular choices include Larkmead (Abingdon), d'Overbroecks in Oxford and Kingham Hill (Oxon); parents given plenty of help to find the right one. Some preps, eg Moulsford and Dragon, send pupils for a couple of years of timely intervention then take them back when appropriate. Now offers GCSEs.

Remarks: Not only does Unicorn provide much needed cover from the bullets and bullies, but the joy of learning is tangible. The school restores faith, builds confidence; it enables children to look forward, to take charge of their learning, cope with whatever they meet, to progress and thrive. Should you need a specialist school with a big heart, a will of steel and an outstanding track record, look no further.

School index